2024
Directory of
California
WholeSalers and Service Companies

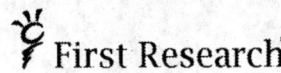

Published January 2024 next update January 2025

WARNING: Purchasers and users of this directory may not use this directory to compile mailing lists, other marketing aids and other types of data, which are sold or otherwise provided to third parties. Such use is wrongful, illegal and a violation of the federal copyright laws.

CAUTION: Because of the many thousands of establishment listings contained in this directory and the possibilities of both human and mechanical error in processing this information, Mergent Inc. cannot assume liability for the correctness of the listings or information on which they are based. Hence, no information contained in this work should be relied upon in any instance where there is a possibility of any loss or damage as a consequence of any error or omission in this volume.

Publisher

Mergent Inc.
444 Madison Ave
New York, NY 10022

©Mergent Inc All Rights Reserved
2024 Mergent Business Press
ISSN 1080-2614
ISBN 979-8-89251-061-5

TABLE OF CONTENTS

Summary of Contents & Explanatory Notes 4
User's Guide to Listings 6

Products & Services Section
SIC Numerical Index 9
SIC Alphabetical Index 13
Firms Listed by SIC 17

Alphabetic Section
Firms listed alphabetically by company name 1007

Geographic Section
County/City Cross-Reference Index 1385
Firms Listed by Location City 1389

SUMMARY OF CONTENTS

Number of Companies 20,949
Number of Decision Makers 34,560
Minimum Number of Employees 60

EXPLANATORY NOTES

How to Cross-Reference in This Directory

Sequential Entry Numbers. Each establishment in the Products & Services Section is numbered sequentially (P-00000). The number assigned to each establishment is referred to as its Entry Number. To make cross-referencing easier, each listing in the Products & Services, Alphabetic and Geographic Sections includes the establishment's entry number. To facilitate locating an entry in the Products & Services Section, the entry numbers for the first listing on the left page and the last listing on the right page are printed at the top of the page next to the Standard Industrial Classification (S.I.C) description.

Source Suggestions Welcome

Although all known sources were used to compile this directory, it is possible that companies were inadvertently omitted. Your assistance in calling attention to such omissions would be greatly appreciated. A special form on the facing page will help you in the reporting process.

Analysis

Every effort has been made to contact all firms to verify their information. The one exception to this rule is the annual sales figure, which is considered by many companies to be confidential information. Therefore, estimated sales have been calculated by multiplying the nationwide average sales per employee for the firm's major SIC/NAICS code by the firm's number of employees. Nationwide averages for sales per employee by SIC/NAICS codes are provided by the U.S. Department of Commerce and are updated annually. All sales—sales (est)—have been estimated by this method. The exceptions are parent companies (PA), division headquarters (DH) and headquarter locations (HQ) which may include an actual corporate sales figure—sales (corporate-wide) if available.

Types of Companies

Descriptive and statistical data are included for companies in the entire state. These comprise manufacturers, machine shops, fabricators, assemblers and printers. Also identified are corporate offices in the state.

Employment Data

This directory contains companies with 60 or more employees. The employment figure shown in the Products & Services Section includes male and female employees and embraces all levels of the company: administrative, clerical, sales and maintenance. This figure is for the facility listed and does not include other plants or offices. It should be recognized that these figures represent an approximate year-round average. These employment figures are broken into codes A through E and used in the Alphabetic and Geographic Sections to further help you in qualifying a company. Be sure to check the footnotes at the bottom of the page for the code breakdowns.

Standard Industrial Classification (SIC)

The Standard Industrial Classification (SIC) system used in this directory was developed by the federal government for use in classifying establishments by the type of activity they are engaged in. The SIC classifications used in this directory are from the 1987 edition published by the U.S. Government's Office of Management and Budget. The SIC system separates all activities into broad industrial divisions (e.g., manufacturing, mining, retail trade). It further subdivides each division. The range of manufacturing industry classes extends from two-digit codes (major industry group) to four-digit codes (product).

For example:

Industry Breakdown	Code	Industry, Product, etc.
*Major industry group	20	Food and kindred products
Industry group	203	Canned and frozen foods
*Industry	2033	Fruits and vegetables, etc.

*Classifications used in this directory

Only two-digit and four-digit codes are used in this directory.

Arrangement

1. The **Product & Services Section** contains complete in-depth corporate data. This section lists companies under their primary SIC. SIC codes are in numerical order with companies listed alphabetically under each code. A numerical and alphabetical index precedes this section.

> IMPORTANT NOTICE: It is a violation of both federal and state law to transmit an unsolicited advertisement to a facsimile machine. Any user of this product that violates such laws may be subject to civil and criminal penalties, which may exceed $500 for each transmission of an unsolicited facsimile. Mergent Inc. provides fax numbers for lawful purposes only and expressly forbids the use of these numbers in any unlawful manner.

2. The **Alphabetic Section** lists all companies with their full physical or mailing addresses and telephone number.

3. The **Geographic Section** is sorted by cities listed in alphabetic order and companies listed alphabetically within each city.

USER'S GUIDE TO LISTINGS

PRODUCT & SERVICES SECTION

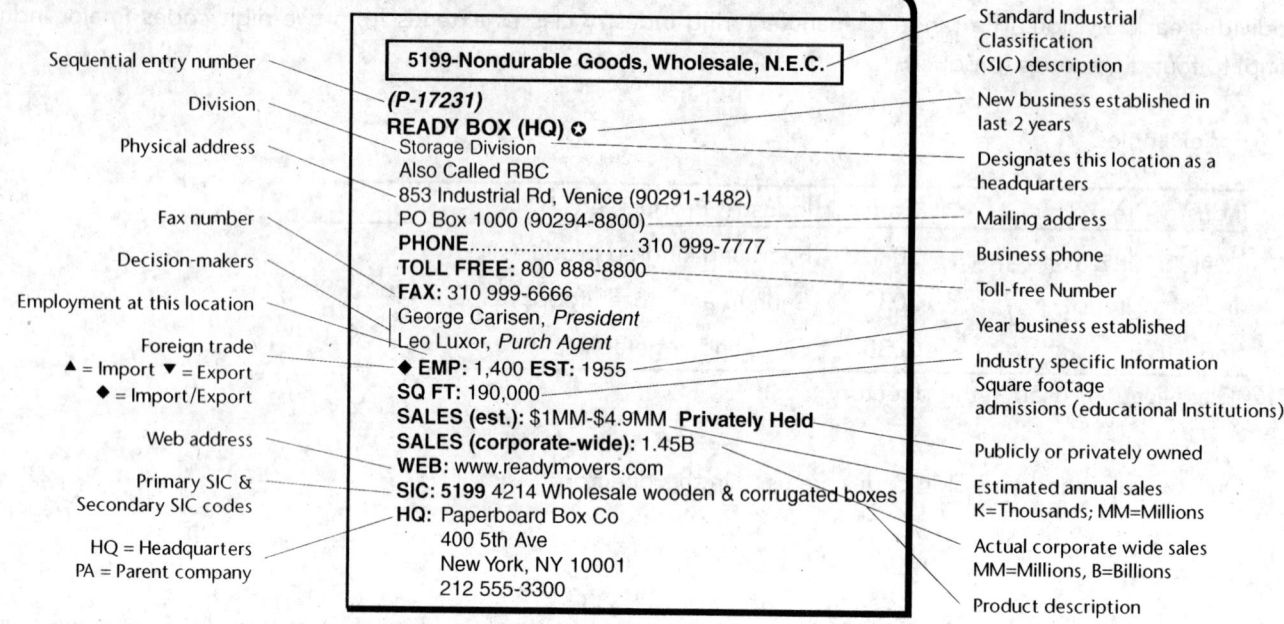

ALPHABETIC SECTION

GEOGRAPHIC SECTION

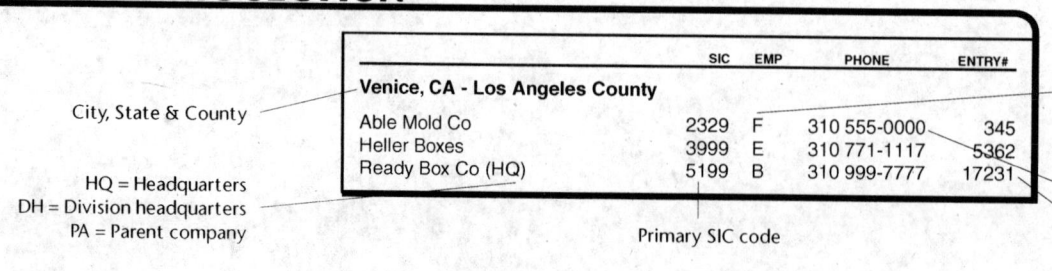

NUMERICAL INDEX of SIC DESCRIPTIONS
ALPHABETICAL INDEX of SIC DESCRIPTIONS

PRODUCTS & SERVICES SECTION
Companies listed alphabetically under their primary SIC
In-depth company data listed

ALPHABETIC SECTION
Company listings in alphabetical order

GEOGRAPHIC INDEX
Companies sorted by city in alphabetical order

SIC INDEX

Standard Industrial Classification Numerical Index

SIC NO   PRODUCT

01 agricultural production - crops
0111 Wheat
0131 Cotton
0134 Irish potatoes
0139 Field crops, except cash grain
0161 Vegetables and melons
0171 Berry crops
0172 Grapes
0173 Tree nuts
0174 Citrus fruits
0175 Deciduous tree fruits
0179 Fruits and tree nuts, nec
0181 Ornamental nursery products
0182 Food crops grown under cover
0191 General farms, primarily crop

02 agricultural production - livestock and animal specialties
0211 Beef cattle feedlots
0212 Beef cattle, except feedlots
0213 Hogs
0241 Dairy farms
0252 Chicken eggs
0253 Turkeys and turkey eggs
0254 Poultry hatcheries
0259 Poultry and eggs, nec
0279 Animal specialties, nec
0291 General farms, primarily animals

07 agricultural services
0711 Soil preparation services
0721 Crop planting and protection
0722 Crop harvesting
0723 Crop preparation services for market
0742 Veterinary services, specialties
0751 Livestock services, except veterinary
0752 Animal specialty services
0761 Farm labor contractors
0762 Farm management services
0781 Landscape counseling and planning
0782 Lawn and garden services
0783 Ornamental shrub and tree services

08 forestry
0811 Timber tracts
0831 Forest products
0851 Forestry services

10 metal mining
1041 Gold ores

12 coal mining
1221 Bituminous coal and lignite-surface mining
1241 Coal mining services

13 oil and gas extraction
1311 Crude petroleum and natural gas
1321 Natural gas liquids
1381 Drilling oil and gas wells
1382 Oil and gas exploration services
1389 Oil and gas field services, nec

14 mining and quarrying of nonmetallic minerals, except fuels
1422 Crushed and broken limestone
1429 Crushed and broken stone, nec
1442 Construction sand and gravel
1481 Nonmetallic mineral services
1499 Miscellaneous nonmetallic mining

15 construction - general contractors & operative builders
1521 Single-family housing construction
1522 Residential construction, nec
1531 Operative builders

SIC NO   PRODUCT

1541 Industrial buildings and warehouses
1542 Nonresidential construction, nec

16 heavy construction, except building construction, contractor
1611 Highway and street construction
1622 Bridge, tunnel, and elevated highway
1623 Water, sewer, and utility lines
1629 Heavy construction, nec

17 construction - special trade contractors
1711 Plumbing, heating, air-conditioning
1721 Painting and paper hanging
1731 Electrical work
1741 Masonry and other stonework
1742 Plastering, drywall, and insulation
1743 Terrazzo, tile, marble, mosaic work
1751 Carpentry work
1752 Floor laying and floor work, nec
1761 Roofing, siding, and sheetmetal work
1771 Concrete work
1781 Water well drilling
1791 Structural steel erection
1793 Glass and glazing work
1794 Excavation work
1795 Wrecking and demolition work
1796 Installing building equipment
1799 Special trade contractors, nec

20 food and kindred products
2011 Meat packing plants
2013 Sausages and other prepared meats
2015 Poultry slaughtering and processing
2022 Cheese; natural and processed
2023 Dry, condensed, evaporated products
2024 Ice cream and frozen deserts
2026 Fluid milk
2033 Canned fruits and specialties
2034 Dehydrated fruits, vegetables, soups
2035 Pickles, sauces, and salad dressings
2038 Frozen specialties, nec
2041 Flour and other grain mill products
2043 Cereal breakfast foods
2044 Rice milling
2048 Prepared feeds, nec
2051 Bread, cake, and related products
2052 Cookies and crackers
2064 Candy and other confectionery products
2068 Salted and roasted nuts and seeds
2079 Edible fats and oils
2084 Wines, brandy, and brandy spirits
2086 Bottled and canned soft drinks
2087 Flavoring extracts and syrups, nec
2091 Canned and cured fish and seafoods
2092 Fresh or frozen packaged fish
2095 Roasted coffee
2098 Macaroni and spaghetti
2099 Food preparations, nec

22 textile mill products
2211 Broadwoven fabric mills, cotton
2253 Knit outerwear mills
2259 Knitting mills, nec
2295 Coated fabrics, not rubberized
2299 Textile goods, nec

23 apparel, finished products from fabrics & similar materials
2311 Men's and boy's suits and coats
2321 Men's and boy's furnishings
2326 Men's and boy's work clothing
2329 Men's and boy's clothing, nec
2331 Women's and misses' blouses and shirts
2339 Women's and misses' outerwear, nec
2341 Women's and children's underwear

SIC NO   PRODUCT

2361 Girl's and children's dresses, blouses
2369 Girl's and children's outerwear, nec
2384 Robes and dressing gowns
2386 Leather and sheep-lined clothing
2389 Apparel and accessories, nec
2392 Household furnishings, nec
2399 Fabricated textile products, nec

24 lumber and wood products, except furniture
2411 Logging
2421 Sawmills and planing mills, general
2431 Millwork
2434 Wood kitchen cabinets
2435 Hardwood veneer and plywood
2441 Nailed wood boxes and shook
2448 Wood pallets and skids
2452 Prefabricated wood buildings
2499 Wood products, nec

25 furniture and fixtures
2511 Wood household furniture
2512 Upholstered household furniture
2514 Metal household furniture
2515 Mattresses and bedsprings
2519 Household furniture, nec
2521 Wood office furniture
2531 Public building and related furniture
2541 Wood partitions and fixtures
2542 Partitions and fixtures, except wood
2591 Drapery hardware and blinds and shades
2599 Furniture and fixtures, nec

26 paper and allied products
2621 Paper mills
2653 Corrugated and solid fiber boxes
2671 Paper; coated and laminated packaging
2672 Paper; coated and laminated, nec
2673 Bags: plastic, laminated, and coated
2674 Bags: uncoated paper and multiwall
2679 Converted paper products, nec

27 printing, publishing and allied industries
2711 Newspapers
2721 Periodicals
2731 Book publishing
2741 Miscellaneous publishing
2752 Commercial printing, lithographic
2759 Commercial printing, nec

28 chemicals and allied products
2813 Industrial gases
2819 Industrial inorganic chemicals, nec
2821 Plastics materials and resins
2833 Medicinals and botanicals
2834 Pharmaceutical preparations
2835 Diagnostic substances
2836 Biological products, except diagnostic
2842 Polishes and sanitation goods
2844 Toilet preparations
2851 Paints and allied products
2869 Industrial organic chemicals, nec
2873 Nitrogenous fertilizers
2875 Fertilizers, mixing only
2879 Agricultural chemicals, nec
2891 Adhesives and sealants
2899 Chemical preparations, nec

29 petroleum refining and related industries
2911 Petroleum refining
2951 Asphalt paving mixtures and blocks
2952 Asphalt felts and coatings
2992 Lubricating oils and greases

30 rubber and miscellaneous plastic products
3011 Tires and inner tubes

SIC INDEX

3053 Gaskets; packing and sealing devices
3069 Fabricated rubber products, nec
3081 Unsupported plastics film and sheet
3083 Laminated plastics plate and sheet
3085 Plastics bottles
3086 Plastics foam products
3088 Plastics plumbing fixtures
3089 Plastics products, nec

31 leather and leather products

3143 Men's footwear, except athletic
3149 Footwear, except rubber, nec
3172 Personal leather goods, nec
3199 Leather goods, nec

32 stone, clay, glass, and concrete products

3211 Flat glass
3229 Pressed and blown glass, nec
3231 Products of purchased glass
3241 Cement, hydraulic
3253 Ceramic wall and floor tile
3269 Pottery products, nec
3271 Concrete block and brick
3272 Concrete products, nec
3273 Ready-mixed concrete
3275 Gypsum products
3281 Cut stone and stone products
3295 Minerals, ground or treated

33 primary metal industries

3312 Blast furnaces and steel mills
3315 Steel wire and related products
3341 Secondary nonferrous metals
3355 Aluminum rolling and drawing, nec
3357 Nonferrous wiredrawing and insulating
3398 Metal heat treating

34 fabricated metal products

3429 Hardware, nec
3431 Metal sanitary ware
3432 Plumbing fixture fittings and trim
3433 Heating equipment, except electric
3441 Fabricated structural metal
3442 Metal doors, sash, and trim
3443 Fabricated plate work (boiler shop)
3444 Sheet metalwork
3448 Prefabricated metal buildings
3452 Bolts, nuts, rivets, and washers
3469 Metal stampings, nec
3471 Plating and polishing
3479 Metal coating and allied services
3491 Industrial valves
3499 Fabricated metal products, nec

35 industrial and commercial machinery and computer equipment

3519 Internal combustion engines, nec
3523 Farm machinery and equipment
3533 Oil and gas field machinery
3535 Conveyors and conveying equipment
3537 Industrial trucks and tractors
3541 Machine tools, metal cutting type
3545 Machine tool accessories
3549 Metalworking machinery, nec
3553 Woodworking machinery
3556 Food products machinery
3559 Special industry machinery, nec
3561 Pumps and pumping equipment
3562 Ball and roller bearings
3564 Blowers and fans
3565 Packaging machinery
3569 General industrial machinery,
3571 Electronic computers
3572 Computer storage devices
3577 Computer peripheral equipment, nec
3578 Calculating and accounting equipment
3585 Refrigeration and heating equipment
3589 Service industry machinery, nec
3599 Industrial machinery, nec

36 electronic & other electrical equipment & components

3612 Transformers, except electric
3613 Switchgear and switchboard apparatus
3621 Motors and generators
3625 Relays and industrial controls
3629 Electrical industrial apparatus
3631 Household cooking equipment
3645 Residential lighting fixtures
3646 Commercial lighting fixtures
3648 Lighting equipment, nec
3651 Household audio and video equipment
3661 Telephone and telegraph apparatus
3663 Radio and t.v. communications equipment
3669 Communications equipment, nec
3672 Printed circuit boards
3674 Semiconductors and related devices
3675 Electronic capacitors
3678 Electronic connectors
3679 Electronic components, nec
3691 Storage batteries
3694 Engine electrical equipment
3695 Magnetic and optical recording media
3699 Electrical equipment and supplies, nec

37 transportation equipment

3711 Motor vehicles and car bodies
3713 Truck and bus bodies
3714 Motor vehicle parts and accessories
3715 Truck trailers
3721 Aircraft
3724 Aircraft engines and engine parts
3728 Aircraft parts and equipment, nec
3731 Shipbuilding and repairing
3751 Motorcycles, bicycles, and parts
3761 Guided missiles and space vehicles
3799 Transportation equipment, nec

38 measuring, photographic, medical, & optical goods, & clocks

3812 Search and navigation equipment
3821 Laboratory apparatus and furniture
3822 Environmental controls
3823 Process control instruments
3824 Fluid meters and counting devices
3825 Instruments to measure electricity
3826 Analytical instruments
3827 Optical instruments and lenses
3829 Measuring and controlling devices, nec
3841 Surgical and medical instruments
3842 Surgical appliances and supplies
3843 Dental equipment and supplies
3844 X-ray apparatus and tubes
3845 Electromedical equipment
3851 Ophthalmic goods
3861 Photographic equipment and supplies

39 miscellaneous manufacturing industries

3911 Jewelry, precious metal
3931 Musical instruments
3942 Dolls and stuffed toys
3944 Games, toys, and children's vehicles
3949 Sporting and athletic goods, nec
3955 Carbon paper and inked ribbons
3993 Signs and advertising specialties
3996 Hard surface floor coverings, nec
3999 Manufacturing industries, nec

40 railroad transportation

4011 Railroads, line-haul operating

41 local & suburban transit & interurban highway transportation

4111 Local and suburban transit
4119 Local passenger transportation, nec
4121 Taxicabs
4131 Intercity and rural bus transportation
4141 Local bus charter service
4142 Bus charter service, except local
4151 School buses
4173 Bus terminal and service facilities

42 motor freight transportation

4212 Local trucking, without storage
4213 Trucking, except local
4214 Local trucking with storage
4215 Courier services, except by air
4221 Farm product warehousing and storage
4222 Refrigerated warehousing and storage
4225 General warehousing and storage
4226 Special warehousing and storage, nec

44 water transportation

4412 Deep sea foreign transportation of freight
4424 Deep sea domestic transportation of freight
4449 Water transportation of freight
4481 Deep sea passenger transportation, except ferry
4489 Water passenger transportation
4491 Marine cargo handling
4492 Towing and tugboat service
4493 Marinas
4499 Water transportation services, nec

45 transportation by air

4512 Air transportation, scheduled
4513 Air courier services
4522 Air transportation, nonscheduled
4581 Airports, flying fields, and services

46 pipelines, except natural gas

4613 Refined petroleum pipelines

47 transportation services

4724 Travel agencies
4725 Tour operators
4729 Passenger transportation arrangement
4731 Freight transportation arrangement
4783 Packing and crating
4785 Inspection and fixed facilities
4789 Transportation services, nec

48 communications

4812 Radiotelephone communication
4813 Telephone communication, except radio
4822 Telegraph and other communications
4832 Radio broadcasting stations
4833 Television broadcasting stations
4841 Cable and other pay television services
4899 Communication services, nec

49 electric, gas and sanitary services

4911 Electric services
4922 Natural gas transmission
4924 Natural gas distribution
4931 Electric and other services combined
4932 Gas and other services combined
4939 Combination utilities, nec
4941 Water supply
4952 Sewerage systems
4953 Refuse systems
4959 Sanitary services, nec
4961 Steam and air-conditioning supply
4971 Irrigation systems

50 wholesale trade - durable goods

5012 Automobiles and other motor vehicles
5013 Motor vehicle supplies and new parts
5014 Tires and tubes
5021 Furniture
5023 Homefurnishings
5031 Lumber, plywood, and millwork
5032 Brick, stone, and related material
5033 Roofing, siding, and insulation
5039 Construction materials, nec
5043 Photographic equipment and supplies
5044 Office equipment
5045 Computers, peripherals, and software
5046 Commercial equipment, nec
5047 Medical and hospital equipment
5048 Ophthalmic goods
5049 Professional equipment, nec
5051 Metals service centers and offices
5063 Electrical apparatus and equipment
5064 Electrical appliances, television and radio
5065 Electronic parts and equipment, nec
5072 Hardware
5074 Plumbing and hydronic heating supplies

SIC INDEX

5075 Warm air heating and air conditioning
5078 Refrigeration equipment and supplies
5082 Construction and mining machinery
5083 Farm and garden machinery
5084 Industrial machinery and equipment
5085 Industrial supplies
5087 Service establishment equipment
5088 Transportation equipment and supplies
5091 Sporting and recreation goods
5092 Toys and hobby goods and supplies
5093 Scrap and waste materials
5094 Jewelry and precious stones
5099 Durable goods, nec

51 wholesale trade - nondurable goods

5111 Printing and writing paper
5112 Stationery and office supplies
5113 Industrial and personal service paper
5122 Drugs, proprietaries, and sundries
5131 Piece goods and notions
5136 Men's and boy's clothing
5137 Women's and children's clothing
5139 Footwear
5141 Groceries, general line
5142 Packaged frozen goods
5143 Dairy products, except dried or canned
5144 Poultry and poultry products
5145 Confectionery
5146 Fish and seafoods
5147 Meats and meat products
5148 Fresh fruits and vegetables
5149 Groceries and related products, nec
5153 Grain and field beans
5159 Farm-product raw materials, nec
5162 Plastics materials and basic shapes
5169 Chemicals and allied products, nec
5171 Petroleum bulk stations and terminals
5172 Petroleum products, nec
5181 Beer and ale
5182 Wine and distilled beverages
5191 Farm supplies
5192 Books, periodicals, and newspapers
5193 Flowers and florists supplies
5194 Tobacco and tobacco products
5198 Paints, varnishes, and supplies
5199 Nondurable goods, nec

52 building materials, hardware, garden supplies & mobile homes

5211 Lumber and other building materials
5231 Paint, glass, and wallpaper stores
5251 Hardware stores
5261 Retail nurseries and garden stores
5271 Mobile home dealers

53 general merchandise stores

5311 Department stores
5331 Variety stores
5399 Miscellaneous general merchandise

54 food stores

5411 Grocery stores
5431 Fruit and vegetable markets
5441 Candy, nut, and confectionery stores
5461 Retail bakeries
5499 Miscellaneous food stores

55 automotive dealers and gasoline service stations

5511 New and used car dealers
5521 Used car dealers
5531 Auto and home supply stores
5541 Gasoline service stations
5551 Boat dealers
5561 Recreational vehicle dealers
5571 Motorcycle dealers
5599 Automotive dealers, nec

56 apparel and accessory stores

5611 Men's and boys' clothing stores
5621 Women's clothing stores
5632 Women's accessory and specialty stores
5651 Family clothing stores
5661 Shoe stores
5699 Miscellaneous apparel and accessories

57 home furniture, furnishings and equipment stores

5712 Furniture stores
5713 Floor covering stores
5719 Miscellaneous homefurnishings
5722 Household appliance stores
5734 Computer and software stores

58 eating and drinking places

5812 Eating places
5813 Drinking places

59 miscellaneous retail

5912 Drug stores and proprietary stores
5921 Liquor stores
5932 Used merchandise stores
5941 Sporting goods and bicycle shops
5942 Book stores
5944 Jewelry stores
5946 Camera and photographic supply stores
5947 Gift, novelty, and souvenir shop
5949 Sewing, needlework, and piece goods
5961 Catalog and mail-order houses
5963 Direct selling establishments
5992 Florists
5994 News dealers and newsstands
5995 Optical goods stores
5999 Miscellaneous retail stores, nec

60 depository institutions

6011 Federal reserve banks
6021 National commercial banks
6022 State commercial banks
6029 Commercial banks, nec
6035 Federal savings institutions
6036 Savings institutions, except federal
6061 Federal credit unions
6062 State credit unions
6081 Foreign bank and branches and agencies
6082 Foreign trade and international banks
6091 Nondeposit trust facilities
6099 Functions related to depository banking

61 nondepository credit institutions

6111 Federal and federally sponsored credit
6141 Personal credit institutions
6153 Short-term business credit
6159 Miscellaneous business credit
6162 Mortgage bankers and correspondents
6163 Loan brokers

62 security & commodity brokers, dealers, exchanges & services

6211 Security brokers and dealers
6221 Commodity contracts brokers, dealers
6231 Security and commodity exchanges
6282 Investment advice
6289 Security and commodity service

63 insurance carriers

6311 Life insurance
6321 Accident and health insurance
6324 Hospital and medical service plans
6331 Fire, marine, and casualty insurance
6351 Surety insurance
6361 Title insurance
6371 Pension, health, and welfare funds
6399 Insurance carriers, nec

64 insurance agents, brokers and service

6411 Insurance agents, brokers, and service

65 real estate

6512 Nonresidential building operators
6513 Apartment building operators
6514 Dwelling operators, except apartments
6515 Mobile home site operators
6519 Real property lessors, nec
6531 Real estate agents and managers
6541 Title abstract offices
6552 Subdividers and developers, nec
6553 Cemetery subdividers and developers

67 holding and other investment offices

6712 Bank holding companies
6719 Holding companies, nec
6722 Management investment, open-ended
6726 Investment offices, nec
6732 Trusts: educational, religious, etc.
6733 Trusts, nec
6794 Patent owners and lessors
6798 Real estate investment trusts
6799 Investors, nec

70 hotels, rooming houses, camps, and other lodging places

7011 Hotels and motels
7021 Rooming and boarding houses
7032 Sporting and recreational camps
7033 Trailer parks and campsites
7041 Membership-basis organization hotels

72 personal services

7211 Power laundries, family and commercial
7213 Linen supply
7215 Coin-operated laundries and cleaning
7216 Drycleaning plants, except rugs
7217 Carpet and upholstery cleaning
7218 Industrial launderers
7219 Laundry and garment services, nec
7221 Photographic studios, portrait
7231 Beauty shops
7241 Barber shops
7261 Funeral service and crematories
7291 Tax return preparation services
7299 Miscellaneous personal services

73 business services

7311 Advertising agencies
7312 Outdoor advertising services
7313 Radio, television, publisher representatives
7319 Advertising, nec
7322 Adjustment and collection services
7323 Credit reporting services
7331 Direct mail advertising services
7334 Photocopying and duplicating services
7335 Commercial photography
7336 Commercial art and graphic design
7338 Secretarial and court reporting
7342 Disinfecting and pest control services
7349 Building maintenance services, nec
7352 Medical equipment rental
7353 Heavy construction equipment rental
7359 Equipment rental and leasing, nec
7361 Employment agencies
7363 Help supply services
7371 Custom computer programming services
7372 Prepackaged software
7373 Computer integrated systems design
7374 Data processing and preparation
7375 Information retrieval services
7376 Computer facilities management
7377 Computer rental and leasing
7378 Computer maintenance and repair
7379 Computer related services, nec
7381 Detective and armored car services
7382 Security systems services
7383 News syndicates
7384 Photofinish laboratories
7389 Business services, nec

75 automotive repair, services and parking

7513 Truck rental and leasing, without drivers
7514 Passenger car rental
7515 Passenger car leasing
7519 Utility trailer rental
7521 Automobile parking
7532 Top and body repair and paint shops
7537 Automotive transmission repair shops
7538 General automotive repair shops
7539 Automotive repair shops, nec
7542 Carwashes

SIC INDEX

7549 Automotive services, nec

76 miscellaneous repair services
7623 Refrigeration service and repair
7629 Electrical repair shops
7631 Watch, clock, and jewelry repair
7692 Welding repair
7694 Armature rewinding shops
7699 Repair services, nec

78 motion pictures
7812 Motion picture and video production
7819 Services allied to motion pictures
7822 Motion picture and tape distribution
7829 Motion picture distribution services
7832 Motion picture theaters, except drive-in
7833 Drive-in motion picture theaters
7841 Video tape rental

79 amusement and recreation services
7922 Theatrical producers and services
7929 Entertainers and entertainment groups
7933 Bowling centers
7941 Sports clubs, managers, and promoters
7948 Racing, including track operation
7991 Physical fitness facilities
7992 Public golf courses
7993 Coin-operated amusement devices
7996 Amusement parks
7997 Membership sports and recreation clubs
7999 Amusement and recreation, nec

80 health services
8011 Offices and clinics of medical doctors
8021 Offices and clinics of dentists
8031 Offices and clinics of osteopathic physicians
8041 Offices and clinics of chiropractors
8042 Offices and clinics of optometrists
8049 Offices of health practitioner
8051 Skilled nursing care facilities
8052 Intermediate care facilities
8059 Nursing and personal care, nec
8062 General medical and surgical hospitals

8063 Psychiatric hospitals
8069 Specialty hospitals, except psychiatric
8071 Medical laboratories
8072 Dental laboratories
8082 Home health care services
8092 Kidney dialysis centers
8093 Specialty outpatient clinics, nec
8099 Health and allied services, nec

81 legal services
8111 Legal services

82 educational services
8211 Elementary and secondary schools
8221 Colleges and universities
8222 Junior colleges
8231 Libraries
8243 Data processing schools
8249 Vocational schools, nec
8299 Schools and educational services

83 social services
8322 Individual and family services
8331 Job training and related services
8351 Child day care services
8361 Residential care
8399 Social services, nec

84 museums, art galleries and botanical and zoological gardens
8412 Museums and art galleries
8422 Botanical and zoological gardens

86 membership organizations
8611 Business associations
8621 Professional organizations
8631 Labor organizations
8641 Civic and social associations
8651 Political organizations
8661 Religious organizations
8699 Membership organizations, nec

87 engineering, accounting, research, and management services
8711 Engineering services
8712 Architectural services
8713 Surveying services
8721 Accounting, auditing, and bookkeeping
8731 Commercial physical research
8732 Commercial nonphysical research
8733 Noncommercial research organizations
8734 Testing laboratories
8741 Management services
8742 Management consulting services
8743 Public relations services
8744 Facilities support services
8748 Business consulting, nec

89 services, not elsewhere classified
8999 Services, nec

91 executive, legislative & general government, except finance
9111 Executive offices
9131 Executive and legislative combined
9199 General government, nec

92 justice, public order and safety
9221 Police protection
9222 Legal counsel and prosecution
9224 Fire protection

94 administration of human resource programs
9431 Administration of public health programs
9441 Administration of social and manpower programs

95 administration of environmental quality and housing programs
9512 Land, mineral, and wildlife conservation
9532 Urban and community development

96 administration of economic programs
9621 Regulation, administration of transportation
9641 Regulation of agricultural marketing

SIC INDEX

Standard Industrial Classification Alphabetical Index

SIC NO	PRODUCT

A

6321 Accident and health insurance
8721 Accounting, auditing, and bookkeeping
2891 Adhesives and sealants
7322 Adjustment and collection services
9431 Administration of public health programs
9441 Administration of social and manpower programs
7311 Advertising agencies
7319 Advertising, nec
2879 Agricultural chemicals, nec
4513 Air courier services
4522 Air transportation, nonscheduled
4512 Air transportation, scheduled
3721 Aircraft
3724 Aircraft engines and engine parts
3728 Aircraft parts and equipment, nec
4581 Airports, flying fields, and services
3355 Aluminum rolling and drawing, nec
7999 Amusement and recreation, nec
7996 Amusement parks
3826 Analytical instruments
0279 Animal specialties, nec
0752 Animal specialty services
6513 Apartment building operators
2389 Apparel and accessories, nec
8712 Architectural services
7694 Armature rewinding shops
2952 Asphalt felts and coatings
2951 Asphalt paving mixtures and blocks
5531 Auto and home supply stores
7521 Automobile parking
5012 Automobiles and other motor vehicles
5599 Automotive dealers, nec
7539 Automotive repair shops, nec
7549 Automotive services, nec
7537 Automotive transmission repair shops

B

2673 Bags: plastic, laminated, and coated
2674 Bags: uncoated paper and multiwall
3562 Ball and roller bearings
6712 Bank holding companies
7241 Barber shops
7231 Beauty shops
0211 Beef cattle feedlots
0212 Beef cattle, except feedlots
5181 Beer and ale
0171 Berry crops
2836 Biological products, except diagnostic
1221 Bituminous coal and lignite-surface mining
3312 Blast furnaces and steel mills
3564 Blowers and fans
5551 Boat dealers
3452 Bolts, nuts, rivets, and washers
2731 Book publishing
5942 Book stores
5192 Books, periodicals, and newspapers
8422 Botanical and zoological gardens
2086 Bottled and canned soft drinks
7933 Bowling centers
2051 Bread, cake, and related products
5032 Brick, stone, and related material
1622 Bridge, tunnel, and elevated highway
2211 Broadwoven fabric mills, cotton
7349 Building maintenance services, nec
4142 Bus charter service, except local
4173 Bus terminal and service facilities
8611 Business associations
8748 Business consulting, nec
7389 Business services, nec

C

4841 Cable and other pay television services
3578 Calculating and accounting equipment
5946 Camera and photographic supply stores
2064 Candy and other confectionery products
5441 Candy, nut, and confectionery stores
2091 Canned and cured fish and seafoods
2033 Canned fruits and specialties
3955 Carbon paper and inked ribbons
1751 Carpentry work
7217 Carpet and upholstery cleaning
7542 Carwashes
5961 Catalog and mail-order houses
3241 Cement, hydraulic
6553 Cemetery subdividers and developers
3253 Ceramic wall and floor tile
2043 Cereal breakfast foods
2022 Cheese; natural and processed
2899 Chemical preparations, nec
5169 Chemicals and allied products, nec
0252 Chicken eggs
8351 Child day care services
0174 Citrus fruits
8641 Civic and social associations
1241 Coal mining services
2295 Coated fabrics, not rubberized
7993 Coin-operated amusement devices
7215 Coin-operated laundries and cleaning
8221 Colleges and universities
4939 Combination utilities, nec
7336 Commercial art and graphic design
6029 Commercial banks, nec
5046 Commercial equipment, nec
3646 Commercial lighting fixtures
8732 Commercial nonphysical research
7335 Commercial photography
8731 Commercial physical research
2752 Commercial printing, lithographic
2759 Commercial printing, nec
6221 Commodity contracts brokers, dealers
4899 Communication services, nec
3669 Communications equipment, nec
5734 Computer and software stores
7376 Computer facilities management
7373 Computer integrated systems design
7378 Computer maintenance and repair
3577 Computer peripheral equipment, nec
7379 Computer related services, nec
7377 Computer rental and leasing
3572 Computer storage devices
5045 Computers, peripherals, and software
3271 Concrete block and brick
3272 Concrete products, nec
1771 Concrete work
5145 Confectionery
5082 Construction and mining machinery
5039 Construction materials, nec
1442 Construction sand and gravel
2679 Converted paper products, nec
3535 Conveyors and conveying equipment
2052 Cookies and crackers
2653 Corrugated and solid fiber boxes
0131 Cotton
4215 Courier services, except by air
7323 Credit reporting services
0722 Crop harvesting
0721 Crop planting and protection
0723 Crop preparation services for market
1311 Crude petroleum and natural gas
1422 Crushed and broken limestone
1429 Crushed and broken stone, nec
7371 Custom computer programming services
3281 Cut stone and stone products

D

0241 Dairy farms
5143 Dairy products, except dried or canned
7374 Data processing and preparation
8243 Data processing schools
0175 Deciduous tree fruits
4424 Deep sea domestic transportation of freight
4412 Deep sea foreign transportation of freight
4481 Deep sea passenger transportation, except ferry
2034 Dehydrated fruits, vegetables, soups
3843 Dental equipment and supplies
8072 Dental laboratories
5311 Department stores
7381 Detective and armored car services
2835 Diagnostic substances
7331 Direct mail advertising services
5963 Direct selling establishments
7342 Disinfecting and pest control services
3942 Dolls and stuffed toys
2591 Drapery hardware and blinds and shades
1381 Drilling oil and gas wells
5813 Drinking places
7833 Drive-in motion picture theaters
5912 Drug stores and proprietary stores
5122 Drugs, proprietaries, and sundries
2023 Dry, condensed, evaporated products
7216 Drycleaning plants, except rugs
5099 Durable goods, nec
6514 Dwelling operators, except apartments

E

5812 Eating places
2079 Edible fats and oils
4931 Electric and other services combined
4911 Electric services
5063 Electrical apparatus and equipment
5064 Electrical appliances, television and radio
3699 Electrical equipment and supplies, nec
3629 Electrical industrial apparatus
7629 Electrical repair shops
1731 Electrical work
3845 Electromedical equipment
3675 Electronic capacitors
3679 Electronic components, nec
3571 Electronic computers
3678 Electronic connectors
5065 Electronic parts and equipment, nec
8211 Elementary and secondary schools
7361 Employment agencies
3694 Engine electrical equipment
8711 Engineering services
7929 Entertainers and entertainment groups
3822 Environmental controls
7359 Equipment rental and leasing, nec
1794 Excavation work
9131 Executive and legislative combined
9111 Executive offices

F

3499 Fabricated metal products, nec
3443 Fabricated plate work (boiler shop)
3069 Fabricated rubber products, nec
3441 Fabricated structural metal
2399 Fabricated textile products, nec
8744 Facilities support services
5651 Family clothing stores
5083 Farm and garden machinery
0761 Farm labor contractors
3523 Farm machinery and equipment
0762 Farm management services
4221 Farm product warehousing and storage
5191 Farm supplies
5159 Farm-product raw materials, nec
6111 Federal and federally sponsored credit
6061 Federal credit unions
6011 Federal reserve banks
6035 Federal savings institutions
2875 Fertilizers, mixing only
0139 Field crops, except cash grain
9224 Fire protection
6331 Fire, marine, and casualty insurance
5146 Fish and seafoods
3211 Flat glass

SIC INDEX

2087 Flavoring extracts and syrups, nec
5713 Floor covering stores
1752 Floor laying and floor work, nec
5992 Florists
2041 Flour and other grain mill products
5193 Flowers and florists supplies
3824 Fluid meters and counting devices
2026 Fluid milk
0182 Food crops grown under cover
2099 Food preparations, nec
3556 Food products machinery
5139 Footwear
3149 Footwear, except rubber, nec
6081 Foreign bank and branches and agencies
6082 Foreign trade and international banks
0831 Forest products
0851 Forestry services
4731 Freight transportation arrangement
5148 Fresh fruits and vegetables
2092 Fresh or frozen packaged fish
2038 Frozen specialties, nec
5431 Fruit and vegetable markets
0179 Fruits and tree nuts, nec
6099 Functions related to depository banking
7261 Funeral service and crematories
5021 Furniture
2599 Furniture and fixtures, nec
5712 Furniture stores

G

3944 Games, toys, and children's vehicles
4932 Gas and other services combined
3053 Gaskets; packing and sealing devices
5541 Gasoline service stations
7538 General automotive repair shops
0291 General farms, primarily animals
0191 General farms, primarily crop
9199 General government, nec
3569 General industrial machinery,
8062 General medical and surgical hospitals
4225 General warehousing and storage
5947 Gift, novelty, and souvenir shop
2361 Girl's and children's dresses, blouses
2369 Girl's and children's outerwear, nec
1793 Glass and glazing work
1041 Gold ores
5153 Grain and field beans
0172 Grapes
5149 Groceries and related products, nec
5141 Groceries, general line
5411 Grocery stores
3761 Guided missiles and space vehicles
3275 Gypsum products

H

3996 Hard surface floor coverings, nec
5072 Hardware
5251 Hardware stores
3429 Hardware, nec
2435 Hardwood veneer and plywood
8099 Health and allied services, nec
3433 Heating equipment, except electric
7353 Heavy construction equipment rental
1629 Heavy construction, nec
7363 Help supply services
1611 Highway and street construction
0213 Hogs
6719 Holding companies, nec
8082 Home health care services
5023 Homefurnishings
6324 Hospital and medical service plans
7011 Hotels and motels
5722 Household appliance stores
3651 Household audio and video equipment
3631 Household cooking equipment
2392 Household furnishings, nec
2519 Household furniture, nec

I

2024 Ice cream and frozen deserts
8322 Individual and family services
5113 Industrial and personal service paper

1541 Industrial buildings and warehouses
2813 Industrial gases
2819 Industrial inorganic chemicals, nec
7218 Industrial launderers
5084 Industrial machinery and equipment
3599 Industrial machinery, nec
2869 Industrial organic chemicals, nec
5085 Industrial supplies
3537 Industrial trucks and tractors
3491 Industrial valves
7375 Information retrieval services
4785 Inspection and fixed facilities
1796 Installing building equipment
3825 Instruments to measure electricity
6411 Insurance agents, brokers, and service
6399 Insurance carriers, nec
4131 Intercity and rural bus transportation
8052 Intermediate care facilities
3519 Internal combustion engines, nec
6282 Investment advice
6726 Investment offices, nec
6799 Investors, nec
0134 Irish potatoes
4971 Irrigation systems

J

5094 Jewelry and precious stones
5944 Jewelry stores
3911 Jewelry, precious metal
8331 Job training and related services
8222 Junior colleges

K

8092 Kidney dialysis centers
2253 Knit outerwear mills
2259 Knitting mills, nec

L

8631 Labor organizations
3821 Laboratory apparatus and furniture
3083 Laminated plastics plate and sheet
9512 Land, mineral, and wildlife conservation
0781 Landscape counseling and planning
7219 Laundry and garment services, nec
0782 Lawn and garden services
2386 Leather and sheep-lined clothing
3199 Leather goods, nec
9222 Legal counsel and prosecution
8111 Legal services
8231 Libraries
6311 Life insurance
3648 Lighting equipment, nec
7213 Linen supply
5921 Liquor stores
0751 Livestock services, except veterinary
6163 Loan brokers
4111 Local and suburban transit
4141 Local bus charter service
4119 Local passenger transportation, nec
4214 Local trucking with storage
4212 Local trucking, without storage
2411 Logging
2992 Lubricating oils and greases
5211 Lumber and other building materials
5031 Lumber, plywood, and millwork

M

2098 Macaroni and spaghetti
3545 Machine tool accessories
3541 Machine tools, metal cutting type
3695 Magnetic and optical recording media
8742 Management consulting services
6722 Management investment, open-ended
8741 Management services
3999 Manufacturing industries, nec
4493 Marinas
4491 Marine cargo handling
1741 Masonry and other stonework
2515 Mattresses and bedsprings
3829 Measuring and controlling devices, nec
2011 Meat packing plants
5147 Meats and meat products

5047 Medical and hospital equipment
7352 Medical equipment rental
8071 Medical laboratories
2833 Medicinals and botanicals
8699 Membership organizations, nec
7997 Membership sports and recreation clubs
7041 Membership-basis organization hotels
5136 Men's and boy's clothing
2329 Men's and boy's clothing, nec
2321 Men's and boy's furnishings
2311 Men's and boy's suits and coats
2326 Men's and boy's work clothing
5611 Men's and boys' clothing stores
3143 Men's footwear, except athletic
3479 Metal coating and allied services
3442 Metal doors, sash, and trim
3398 Metal heat treating
2514 Metal household furniture
3431 Metal sanitary ware
3469 Metal stampings, nec
5051 Metals service centers and offices
3549 Metalworking machinery, nec
2431 Millwork
3295 Minerals, ground or treated
5699 Miscellaneous apparel and accessories
6159 Miscellaneous business credit
5499 Miscellaneous food stores
5399 Miscellaneous general merchandise
5719 Miscellaneous homefurnishings
1499 Miscellaneous nonmetallic mining
7299 Miscellaneous personal services
2741 Miscellaneous publishing
5999 Miscellaneous retail stores, nec
5271 Mobile home dealers
6515 Mobile home site operators
6162 Mortgage bankers and correspondents
7822 Motion picture and tape distribution
7812 Motion picture and video production
7829 Motion picture distribution services
7832 Motion picture theaters, except drive-in
3714 Motor vehicle parts and accessories
5013 Motor vehicle supplies and new parts
3711 Motor vehicles and car bodies
5571 Motorcycle dealers
3751 Motorcycles, bicycles, and parts
3621 Motors and generators
8412 Museums and art galleries
3931 Musical instruments

N

2441 Nailed wood boxes and shook
6021 National commercial banks
4924 Natural gas distribution
1321 Natural gas liquids
4922 Natural gas transmission
5511 New and used car dealers
5994 News dealers and newsstands
7383 News syndicates
2711 Newspapers
2873 Nitrogenous fertilizers
8733 Noncommercial research organizations
6091 Nondeposit trust facilities
5199 Nondurable goods, nec
3357 Nonferrous wiredrawing and insulating
1481 Nonmetallic mineral services
6512 Nonresidential building operators
1542 Nonresidential construction, nec
8059 Nursing and personal care, nec

O

5044 Office equipment
8041 Offices and clinics of chiropractors
8021 Offices and clinics of dentists
8011 Offices and clinics of medical doctors
8042 Offices and clinics of optometrists
8031 Offices and clinics of osteopathic physicians
8049 Offices of health practitioner
1382 Oil and gas exploration services
3533 Oil and gas field machinery
1389 Oil and gas field services, nec
1531 Operative builders
3851 Ophthalmic goods

SIC INDEX

5048 Ophthalmic goods
5995 Optical goods stores
3827 Optical instruments and lenses
0181 Ornamental nursery products
0783 Ornamental shrub and tree services
7312 Outdoor advertising services

P

5142 Packaged frozen goods
3565 Packaging machinery
4783 Packing and crating
5231 Paint, glass, and wallpaper stores
1721 Painting and paper hanging
2851 Paints and allied products
5198 Paints, varnishes, and supplies
2621 Paper mills
2671 Paper; coated and laminated packaging
2672 Paper; coated and laminated, nec
2542 Partitions and fixtures, except wood
7515 Passenger car leasing
7514 Passenger car rental
4729 Passenger transportation arrangement
6794 Patent owners and lessors
6371 Pension, health, and welfare funds
2721 Periodicals
6141 Personal credit institutions
3172 Personal leather goods, nec
5171 Petroleum bulk stations and terminals
5172 Petroleum products, nec
2911 Petroleum refining
2834 Pharmaceutical preparations
7334 Photocopying and duplicating services
7384 Photofinish laboratories
3861 Photographic equipment and supplies
5043 Photographic equipment and supplies
7221 Photographic studios, portrait
7991 Physical fitness facilities
2035 Pickles, sauces, and salad dressings
5131 Piece goods and notions
1742 Plastering, drywall, and insulation
3085 Plastics bottles
3086 Plastics foam products
5162 Plastics materials and basic shapes
2821 Plastics materials and resins
3088 Plastics plumbing fixtures
3089 Plastics products, nec
3471 Plating and polishing
5074 Plumbing and hydronic heating supplies
3432 Plumbing fixture fittings and trim
1711 Plumbing, heating, air-conditioning
9221 Police protection
2842 Polishes and sanitation goods
8651 Political organizations
3269 Pottery products, nec
0259 Poultry and eggs, nec
5144 Poultry and poultry products
0254 Poultry hatcheries
2015 Poultry slaughtering and processing
7211 Power laundries, family and commercial
3448 Prefabricated metal buildings
2452 Prefabricated wood buildings
7372 Prepackaged software
2048 Prepared feeds, nec
3229 Pressed and blown glass, nec
3672 Printed circuit boards
5111 Printing and writing paper
3823 Process control instruments
3231 Products of purchased glass
5049 Professional equipment, nec
8621 Professional organizations
8063 Psychiatric hospitals
2531 Public building and related furniture
7992 Public golf courses
8743 Public relations services
3561 Pumps and pumping equipment

R

7948 Racing, including track operation
3663 Radio and t.v. communications equipment
4832 Radio broadcasting stations
7313 Radio, television, publisher representatives
4812 Radiotelephone communication

4011 Railroads, line-haul operating
3273 Ready-mixed concrete
6531 Real estate agents and managers
6798 Real estate investment trusts
6519 Real property lessors, nec
5561 Recreational vehicle dealers
4613 Refined petroleum pipelines
4222 Refrigerated warehousing and storage
3585 Refrigeration and heating equipment
5078 Refrigeration equipment and supplies
7623 Refrigeration service and repair
4953 Refuse systems
9641 Regulation of agricultural marketing
9621 Regulation, administration of transportation
3625 Relays and industrial controls
8661 Religious organizations
7699 Repair services, nec
8361 Residential care
1522 Residential construction, nec
3645 Residential lighting fixtures
5461 Retail bakeries
5261 Retail nurseries and garden stores
2044 Rice milling
2095 Roasted coffee
2384 Robes and dressing gowns
5033 Roofing, siding, and insulation
1761 Roofing, siding, and sheetmetal work
7021 Rooming and boarding houses

S

2068 Salted and roasted nuts and seeds
4959 Sanitary services, nec
2013 Sausages and other prepared meats
6036 Savings institutions, except federal
2421 Sawmills and planing mills, general
4151 School buses
8299 Schools and educational services
5093 Scrap and waste materials
3812 Search and navigation equipment
3341 Secondary nonferrous metals
7338 Secretarial and court reporting
6231 Security and commodity exchanges
6289 Security and commodity service
6211 Security brokers and dealers
7382 Security systems services
3674 Semiconductors and related devices
5087 Service establishment equipment
3589 Service industry machinery, nec
7819 Services allied to motion pictures
8999 Services, nec
4952 Sewerage systems
5949 Sewing, needlework, and piece goods
3444 Sheet metalwork
3731 Shipbuilding and repairing
5661 Shoe stores
6153 Short-term business credit
3993 Signs and advertising specialties
1521 Single-family housing construction
8051 Skilled nursing care facilities
8399 Social services, nec
0711 Soil preparation services
3559 Special industry machinery, nec
1799 Special trade contractors, nec
4226 Special warehousing and storage, nec
8069 Specialty hospitals, except psychiatric
8093 Specialty outpatient clinics, nec
3949 Sporting and athletic goods, nec
5091 Sporting and recreation goods
7032 Sporting and recreational camps
5941 Sporting goods and bicycle shops
7941 Sports clubs, managers, and promoters
6022 State commercial banks
6062 State credit unions
5112 Stationery and office supplies
4961 Steam and air-conditioning supply
3315 Steel wire and related products
3691 Storage batteries
1791 Structural steel erection
6552 Subdividers and developers, nec
6351 Surety insurance
3841 Surgical and medical instruments
3842 Surgical appliances and supplies

8713 Surveying services
3613 Switchgear and switchboard apparatus

T

7291 Tax return preparation services
4121 Taxicabs
4822 Telegraph and other communications
3661 Telephone and telegraph apparatus
4813 Telephone communication, except radio
4833 Television broadcasting stations
1743 Terrazzo, tile, marble, mosaic work
8734 Testing laboratories
2299 Textile goods, nec
7922 Theatrical producers and services
0811 Timber tracts
3011 Tires and inner tubes
5014 Tires and tubes
6541 Title abstract offices
6361 Title insurance
5194 Tobacco and tobacco products
2844 Toilet preparations
7532 Top and body repair and paint shops
4725 Tour operators
4492 Towing and tugboat service
5092 Toys and hobby goods and supplies
7033 Trailer parks and campsites
3612 Transformers, except electric
5088 Transportation equipment and supplies
3799 Transportation equipment, nec
4789 Transportation services, nec
4724 Travel agencies
0173 Tree nuts
3713 Truck and bus bodies
7513 Truck rental and leasing, without drivers
3715 Truck trailers
4213 Trucking, except local
6733 Trusts, nec
6732 Trusts: educational, religious, etc.
0253 Turkeys and turkey eggs

U

3081 Unsupported plastics film and sheet
2512 Upholstered household furniture
9532 Urban and community development
5521 Used car dealers
5932 Used merchandise stores
7519 Utility trailer rental

V

5331 Variety stores
0161 Vegetables and melons
0742 Veterinary services, specialties
7841 Video tape rental
8249 Vocational schools, nec

W

5075 Warm air heating and air conditioning
7631 Watch, clock, and jewelry repair
4489 Water passenger transportation
4941 Water supply
4449 Water transportation of freight
4499 Water transportation services, nec
1781 Water well drilling
1623 Water, sewer, and utility lines
7692 Welding repair
0111 Wheat
5182 Wine and distilled beverages
2084 Wines, brandy, and brandy spirits
5632 Women's accessory and specialty stores
5137 Women's and children's clothing
2341 Women's and children's underwear
2331 Women's and misses' blouses and shirts
2339 Women's and misses' outerwear, nec
5621 Women's clothing stores
2511 Wood household furniture
2434 Wood kitchen cabinets
2521 Wood office furniture
2448 Wood pallets and skids
2541 Wood partitions and fixtures
2499 Wood products, nec
3553 Woodworking machinery
1795 Wrecking and demolition work

SIC INDEX

X

3844 X-ray apparatus and tubes

PRODUCTS & SERVICES SECTION

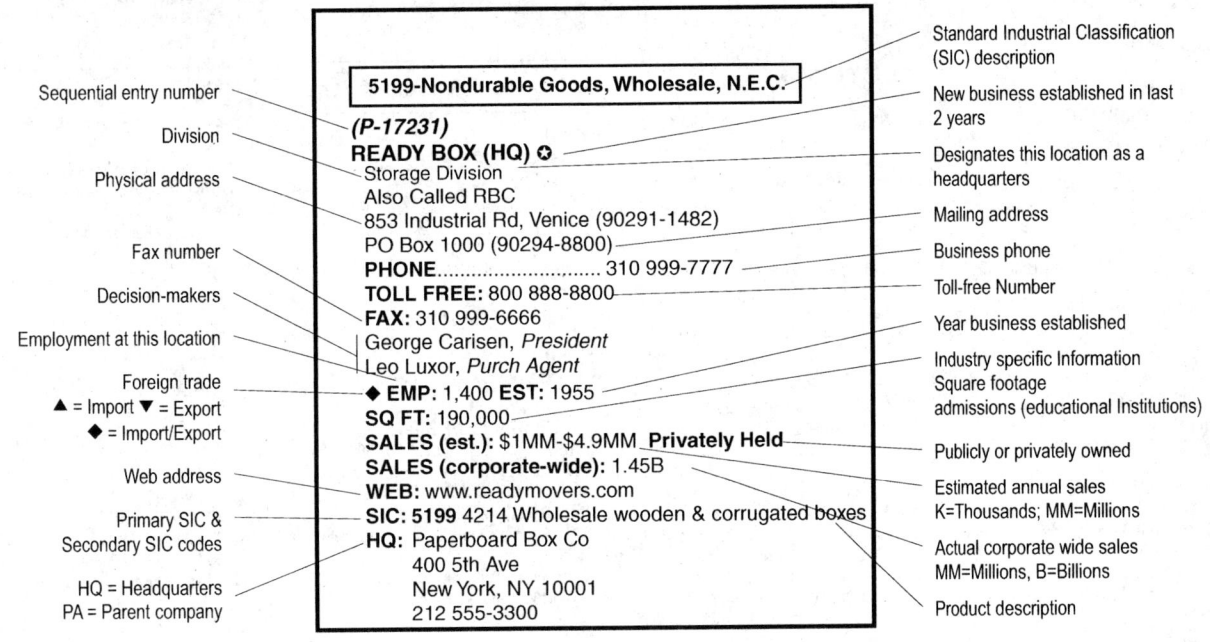

- Companies in this section are listed numerically under their primary SIC Companies are in alphabetical order under each code.
- A numerical and alphabetical index precedes this section.
- **Sequential Entry Numbers.** Each establishment in this section is numbered sequentially. The number assigned to each establishment's Entry Number. To make cross-referencing easier, each listing in the Product's & Services, Alphabetic and Geographical Section includes the establishment's entry number. To facilitate locating an entry in this section, the entry numbers for the first listing on the left page and the last listing on the right page are printed at the top of the page next to the Standard Industrial Classification (SIC) description.
- Further information can be found in the Explanatory Notes starting on page 5.
- See the footnotes for symbols and abbreviations.

IMPORTANT NOTICE: It is a violation of both federal and state law to transmit an unsolicited advertisement to a facsimile machine. Any user of this product that violates such laws may be subject to civil and criminal penalties which may exceed $500 for each transmission of an unsolicited facsimile. Harris InfoSource provides fax numbers for lawful purposes only and expressly forbids the use of these numbers in any unlawful manner.

0111 Wheat

(P-1)
MULLER RANCH LLC
15810 County Road 95 (95695-9222)
PHONE................................530 662-0105
Frank Muller, *Pt*
Thomas Muller, *Pt*
EMP: 85 **EST:** 1978
SALES (est): 9.62MM **Privately Held**
SIC: 0111 0115 0161 Wheat; Corn; Tomato farm

(P-2)
T & P FARMS
1241 Putnam Way (95912-0738)
P.O. Box 83 (95912-0083)
PHONE................................530 476-3038
Perry Charter, *Pt*
Tom Charter, *Pt*
EMP: 84 **EST:** 1976
SALES (est): 2.35MM **Privately Held**

SIC: 0111 0112 0181 0161 Wheat; Rice; Seeds, vegetable: growing of; Tomato farm

0131 Cotton

(P-3)
J G BOSWELL COMPANY
21101 Bear Mountain Blvd (93311-9412)
P.O. Box 9759 (93389-9759)
PHONE................................661 327-7721
Dave Cosyns, *Mgr*
EMP: 403
SALES (corp-wide): 370.2MM **Privately Held**
Web: www.eastlakeco.com
SIC: 0131 0111 0724 Cotton; Wheat; Cotton ginning
PA: J. G. Boswell Company
101 W Walnut St
Pasadena CA
626 583-3000

(P-4)
J G BOSWELL COMPANY
Also Called: Ranching Shop
28001 S Dairy Ave (93212)
P.O. Box 877 (93212-0877)
PHONE................................559 992-5141
Paul Athorp, *Bmch Mgr*
EMP: 71
SALES (corp-wide): 370.2MM **Privately Held**
Web: www.eastlakeco.com
SIC: 0131 0724 0182 Cotton; Cotton ginning ; Food crops grown under cover
PA: J. G. Boswell Company
101 W Walnut St
Pasadena CA
626 583-3000

(P-5)
STONE LAND COMPANY (PA)
Also Called: Stone Ranch
28521 Nevada Ave (93266)
P.O. Box 146 (93266-0146)
PHONE................................559 947-3185
Jack G Stone, *Pr*
William Stone, *
Sally Moreno, *
▲ **EMP:** 100 **EST:** 1948
SQ FT: 2,000
SALES (est): 15.61MM
SALES (corp-wide): 15.61MM **Privately Held**
Web: www.stoneland.co.in
SIC: 0131 0191 0111 Cotton; General farms, primarily crop; Wheat

(P-6)
TEIXEIRA AND SONS LLC
Also Called: Teixeira and Sons
22759 S Mercey Springs Rd (93635-9539)
PHONE................................209 827-9800
Tom Teixeira, *Bmch Mgr*
EMP: 111
SALES (corp-wide): 3.56MM **Privately Held**

0131 - Cotton (P-7)

SIC: 0131 Cottonseed farm
PA: Teixeira And Sons, Llc
22759 S Mercey Springs Rd
Los Banos CA
209 827-9800

(P-7)
VIGNOLO FARMS INC
33342 Dresser Ave (93308-9634)
P.O. Box 1270 (93263-1270)
PHONE..................................661 746-2148
Robert J Vignolo, Pr
EMP: 150 EST: 1938
SQ FT: 2,500
SALES (est): 4.86MM Privately Held
Web: www.topbrassmarketing.com
SIC: 0131 0172 0134 Cotton; Grapes; Irish potatoes

(P-8)
WOLFSEN INCORPORATED
Sjr Farming
1269 W I St (93635-3930)
PHONE..................................209 827-7700
Albert Laguna, Mgr
EMP: 157
SALES (corp-wide): 9.9MM Privately Held
Web: www.wolfseninc.com
SIC: 0131 Cotton
PA: Wolfsen Incorporated
1269 W I St
Los Banos CA
209 827-7700

0134 Irish Potatoes

(P-9)
TASTEFUL SELECTIONS LLC
13003 Di Giorgio Rd (93203-9529)
PHONE..................................661 854-3998
EMP: 160 EST: 2010
SALES (est): 37.91MM Privately Held
Web: www.tastefulselections.com
SIC: 0134 5148 0723 Irish potatoes; Potatoes, fresh; Crop preparation services for market

0139 Field Crops, Except Cash Grain

(P-10)
AMERICAN FARMS LLC
1107 Harkins Rd (93901-4435)
P.O. Box 599 (93902-0599)
PHONE..................................831 424-1815
Steven Gill, *
EMP: 100 EST: 1985
SQ FT: 3,000
SALES (est): 8.81MM
SALES (corp-wide): 9.4MM Privately Held
Web: www.americanfarms.net
SIC: 0139 0161 Feeder crops; Lettuce farm
PA: Mesa Packing, Llc
510 Broadway St
King City CA
831 385-9173

(P-11)
CHRISTOPHER RANCH LLC (PA)
305 Bloomfield Ave (95020-9516)
PHONE..................................408 847-1100
William Christopher, Managing Member
Donald Christopher, Managing Member
▲ EMP: 170 EST: 1953
SQ FT: 220,000
SALES (est): 45.36MM
SALES (corp-wide): 45.36MM Privately Held
Web: www.christopherranch.com
SIC: 0139 0175 Herb or spice farm; Cherry orchard

(P-12)
GARLIC COMPANY
18602 Zerker Rd (93263-9101)
PHONE..................................661 393-4212
John Layous, Mng Pt
Joe Lane, *
◆ EMP: 125 EST: 1980
SQ FT: 150,000
SALES (est): 36.52MM Privately Held
Web: www.thegarliccompany.com
SIC: 0139 2099 0191 Herb or spice farm; Food preparations, nec; General farms, primarily crop

(P-13)
HAYDAY FARMS INC
15500 S Commercial St (92225-2750)
P.O. Box 1226 (92226-1226)
PHONE..................................760 922-4713
Atsuya Ichida, Pr
Dale Tyson, *
◆ EMP: 75 EST: 1986
SQ FT: 2,160
SALES (est): 4.9MM Privately Held
Web: www.haydayfarms.com
SIC: 0139 0722 0723 Hay farm; Hay, machine harvesting services; Field crops, except cash grains, market preparation services

(P-14)
MEDTERRA CBD LLC
18500 Von Karman Ave (92612-0518)
PHONE..................................800 971-1288
John Hartenbach, CEO
John Preston Larsen, *
EMP: 89 EST: 2017
SALES (est): 12.09MM Privately Held
Web: www.medterracbd.com
SIC: 0139 Herb or spice farm

(P-15)
NATURA HOLDINGS LLC
Also Called: Natura Lifescience
8280 Elder Creek Rd (95828-1704)
PHONE..................................916 209-0038
EMP: 63 EST: 2019
SALES (est): 6.9MM Privately Held
Web: www.natura.io
SIC: 0139

(P-16)
PAX LABS INC
660 Alabama St Ste 2 (94110-2190)
PHONE..................................415 829-2336
Michael Murphy, Pr
EMP: 67 EST: 2017
SALES (est): 12.45MM Privately Held
Web: www.pax.com
SIC: 0139 3999

(P-17)
QUAIL H FARMS LLC
5301 Robin Ave (95334-9317)
P.O. Box 247 (95334-0247)
PHONE..................................209 394-8001
J Michael Hennigan, Managing Member
Jackie E Smith, *
▼ EMP: 80 EST: 2005
SALES (est): 6.67MM Privately Held
SIC: 0139 Sweet potato farm

(P-18)
RICHARD IEST DAIRY INC
13507 Road 17 (93637-9040)
PHONE..................................559 673-2635
EMP: 99 EST: 2011
SALES (est): 9.88MM Privately Held
SIC: 0139 Field crops, except cash grain

0161 Vegetables And Melons

(P-19)
AMAZING COACHELLA INC
Also Called: Peter Rabbit Farms
85810 Peter Rabbit Ln (92236-1897)
PHONE..................................760 398-0151
EMP: 100 EST: 1950
SALES (est): 16.04MM Privately Held
Web: www.peterrabbitfarms.com
SIC: 0161 Vegetables and melons

(P-20)
BALLETTO RANCH INC (PA)
5700 Occidental Rd (95401-5533)
P.O. Box 2579 (95473-2579)
PHONE..................................707 568-2455
John Balletto, Pr
▲ EMP: 111 EST: 1977
SALES (est): 12.26MM
SALES (corp-wide): 12.26MM Privately Held
Web: www.ballettoranch.com
SIC: 0161 Lettuce farm

(P-21)
BALOIAN PACKING CO INC (PA)
Also Called: Baloian Farm
446 N Blythe Ave (93706-1003)
P.O. Box 11337 (93772-1337)
PHONE..................................559 485-9200
Edward Baloian, Ch Bd
Timothy Baloian, *
Emily Baloian, *
▲ EMP: 70 EST: 1985
SQ FT: 35,000
SALES (est): 25.98MM
SALES (corp-wide): 25.98MM Privately Held
Web: www.baloianfarms.com
SIC: 0161 0723 Broccoli farm; Vegetable packing services

(P-22)
BALOIAN PACKING CO INC
Also Called: Baloian Farms
3138 W Whites Bridge Ave A (93706-1125)
PHONE..................................559 441-7043
EMP: 80
SALES (corp-wide): 25.98MM Privately Held
Web: www.baloianfarms.com
SIC: 0161 0723 Broccoli farm; Vegetable packing services
PA: Baloian Packing Co., Inc.
446 N Blythe Ave
Fresno CA
559 485-9200

(P-23)
BOLTHOUSE FARMS
3200 E Brundage Ln (93304)
PHONE..................................661 366-7205
William Bolthouse, Owner
◆ EMP: 2300 EST: 1915
SALES (est): 39.11MM
SALES (corp-wide): 1.33B Privately Held
Web: www.bolthouse.com
SIC: 0161 Carrot farm
HQ: Wm. Bolthouse Farms, Inc.
7200 E Brundage Ln
Bakersfield CA
661 366-7209

(P-24)
BOSKOVICH FARMS INC
4224 Pleasant Valley Rd (93012-8533)
P.O. Box 1352 (93032-1352)
PHONE..................................805 987-1443
Ken Mumford, Mgr
EMP: 110
SALES (corp-wide): 93.16MM Privately Held
Web: www.boskovichfarms.com
SIC: 0161 0115 Vegetables and melons; Corn
PA: Boskovich Farms, Inc.
711 Diaz Ave
Oxnard CA
805 487-2299

(P-25)
C & G FARMS INC
Also Called: Amaral Ranches
25453 Iverson Rd (93925-9605)
P.O. Box 2216 (93926-2216)
PHONE..................................831 679-2978
Carlos Amaral, Pr
George Amaral, *
▼ EMP: 200 EST: 1997
SQ FT: 2,000
SALES (est): 14.67MM Privately Held
SIC: 0161 Lettuce and leaf vegetable farms

(P-26)
CALIFORNIA WATERCRESS INC (PA)
550 E Telegraph Rd (93015-9667)
P.O. Box 874 (93016-0874)
PHONE..................................805 524-4808
Alfred C Beserra, Pr
Teresa Beserra, *
EMP: 65 EST: 1966
SQ FT: 1,000
SALES (est): 1.91MM
SALES (corp-wide): 1.91MM Privately Held
Web: www.californiawatercress.com
SIC: 0161 Vegetables and melons

(P-27)
DAN AVILA & SONS FARMS INC
2718 Roberts Rd (95307-9627)
PHONE..................................209 495-3899
Daniel Avila, Owner
EMP: 60 EST: 2001
SALES (est): 2.68MM Privately Held
SIC: 0161 0139 Watermelon farm; Sweet potato farm

(P-28)
DARRIGO BROS CO CALIFORNIA
20911 Harris Rd (93962)
P.O. Box 850 (93902-0850)
PHONE..................................831 455-2913
John Ryan, Brnch Mgr
EMP: 260
SALES (corp-wide): 231.95MM Privately Held
Web: www.andyboy.com
SIC: 0161 Broccoli farm
PA: D'arrigo Bros. Co., Of California
21777 Harris Rd
Salinas CA
831 455-4500

(P-29)
DIMARE ENTERPRISES INC (PA)
Also Called: Dimare Company
1406 N St (95360-1309)
P.O. Box 517 (95360-0517)
PHONE..................................209 827-2900

PRODUCTS & SERVICES SECTION

0171 - Berry Crops (P-51)

Thomas F Dimare, *Pr*
Jeff Dolan, *
Paul J Dimare, *
EMP: 250 **EST:** 1975
SQ FT: 20,000
SALES (est): 23.48MM
SALES (corp-wide): 23.48MM **Privately Held**
Web: www.dimarefresh.com
SIC: 0161 0174 Vegetables and melons; Citrus fruits

(P-30)
FRESH LEAF FARMS LLC
25867 Esperanza Rd (93907)
PHONE.................................831 796-3760
EMP: 149
SIC: 0161 Vegetables and melons
HQ: Fresh Leaf Farms, Llc
  1250 Hansen St
  Salinas CA
  831 422-7405

(P-31)
FRESH VENTURE FARMS LLC
1181 S Wolff Rd (93003-2105)
PHONE.................................805 754-4449
EMP: 80 **EST:** 2012
SQ FT: 4,000
SALES (est): 2.15MM **Privately Held**
SIC: 0161 0191 Vegetables and melons; General farms, primarily crop

(P-32)
GENERIS HOLDINGS LP (PA)
7200 E Brundage Ln (93307-3016)
PHONE.................................661 366-7209
Jeffrey Dunn, *CEO*
EMP: 262 **EST:** 2019
SALES (est): 1.33B
SALES (corp-wide): 1.33B **Privately Held**
Web: www.bolthouse.com
SIC: 0161 2037 2033 2099 Carrot farm; Fruit juices; Vegetable juices: packaged in cans, jars, etc.; Sauce, gravy, dressing, and dip mixes

(P-33)
GEORGE CHIALA FARMS INC
Also Called: Chiala, George Packing
15500 Hill Rd (95037-9516)
PHONE.................................408 778-0562
George Chiala Senior, *Pr*
George Chiala Junior, *Marketing*
Alice Chiala, *
▲ **EMP:** 120 **EST:** 1972
SQ FT: 14,000
SALES (est): 41.03MM **Privately Held**
Web: www.gcfarmsinc.com
SIC: 0161 0723 4783 Vegetables and melons; Vegetable crops market preparation services; Containerization of goods for shipping

(P-34)
HENRY HIBINO FARMS LLC
106 Rico St (93907-2101)
PHONE.................................831 757-3081
Henry Hibino, *Owner*
EMP: 75 **EST:** 1950
SQ FT: 20,000
SALES (est): 4.87MM **Privately Held**
SIC: 0161 Vegetables and melons

(P-35)
IWAMOTO & GEAN FARM
Also Called: Harry's Berries
2064 Olga St (93036-2715)
PHONE.................................805 659-4568
Kaz Iwamoto, *Genl Pt*
Richard Gean, *Pt*
Mariko Gean, *Pt*
Yoshiko Iwamoto, *Pt*
EMP: 70 **EST:** 1977
SALES (est): 2.18MM **Privately Held**
SIC: 0161 0171 Vegetables and melons; Strawberry farm

(P-36)
LUCKY FARMS INC
1194 E Brier Dr (92408-2838)
P.O. Box 985 (92354-0985)
PHONE.................................909 799-6688
Wen S Liaou, *Pr*
Gary Liaou, *
▲ **EMP:** 60 **EST:** 1982
SQ FT: 28,000
SALES (est): 4.64MM **Privately Held**
Web: www.luckyfarms.com
SIC: 0161 Corn farm, sweet

(P-37)
OCEAN MIST FARMING COMPANY (PA)
Also Called: Ocean Mist Farms
10855 Ocean Mist Pkwy (95012-3235)
PHONE.................................831 633-2144
C Edward Boutonnet, *CEO*
Ed Bouponnet, *
Joseph Micheli, *
Don Bracco, *
Chris Drew, *
EMP: 150 **EST:** 1973
SQ FT: 2,000
SALES (est): 76.03MM
SALES (corp-wide): 76.03MM **Privately Held**
Web: www.oceanmist.com
SIC: 0161 Lettuce and leaf vegetable farms

(P-38)
SALINAS LAND COMPANY (PA)
44557 Teague Ave (93927)
P.O. Box 25010 (93002-2250)
PHONE.................................805 648-3363
Rick Lagomarsino, *Pr*
John A Lagomarsino, *
Greg Smith, *
EMP: 180 **EST:** 1917
SQ FT: 3,000
SALES (est): 4.01MM
SALES (corp-wide): 4.01MM **Privately Held**
SIC: 0161 Vegetables and melons

(P-39)
SAN MIGUEL PRODUCE INC
Also Called: Cut N Clean Greens
600 E Hueneme Rd (93033-8298)
PHONE.................................805 488-0981
Roy I Nishimori, *CEO*
Jan Berk, *
▲ **EMP:** 500 **EST:** 1979
SALES (est): 34.38MM **Privately Held**
Web: www.sanmiguelproduce.com
SIC: 0161 0723 4212 Vegetables and melons; Vegetable packing services; Farm to market haulage, local

(P-40)
SANTA BARBARA FARMS LLC (PA)
1200 Union Sugar Ave (93436-9740)
PHONE.................................805 736-9776
Robert M Witt, *CEO*
R C Gerber, *CFO*
Charles Witt, *
▲ **EMP:** 60 **EST:** 1980
SQ FT: 2,800
SALES (est): 30.6MM
SALES (corp-wide): 30.6MM **Privately Held**
SIC: 0161 0181 Vegetables and melons; Florists' greens and flowers

(P-41)
SANTA BARBARA FARMS LLC
1105 Union Sugar Ave (93436-9737)
PHONE.................................805 736-5608
John Donati, *Pr*
EMP: 190
SALES (corp-wide): 30.6MM **Privately Held**
SIC: 0161 0181 Vegetables and melons; Florists' greens and flowers
PA: Santa Barbara Farms, Llc
  1200 Union Sugar Ave
  Lompoc CA
  805 736-9776

(P-42)
SEASHOLTZ JOHN
Also Called: SEASHOLTZ, JOHN
1355 M St (93622-2338)
PHONE.................................559 659-3805
EMP: 196
SALES (corp-wide): 3.87MM **Privately Held**
Web: www.redroostertm.com
SIC: 0161 Vegetables and melons
PA: Seasholtz Co., Llc
  4965 N Crystal Ave Ste A
  Fresno CA
  559 229-0453

(P-43)
SILVA FARMS LLC (PA)
111 Alpine Dr (93926)
PHONE.................................831 675-2327
▼ **EMP:** 80 **EST:** 1980
SQ FT: 30,000
SALES (est): 9.11MM **Privately Held**
SIC: 0161 Broccoli farm

(P-44)
TANIMURA ANTLE FRESH FOODS INC (PA)
Also Called: Tanimura & Antle
1 Harris Rd (93908-8608)
P.O. Box 4070 (93912-4070)
PHONE.................................831 455-2950
Rick Antle, *Pr*
Mike Antle, *
Robert Nielsen, *
Steve Bassi, *FARM PRODUCTION**
Carmen Ponce, *Land Vice President**
◆ **EMP:** 100 **EST:** 1982
SQ FT: 135,000
SALES (est): 321.47MM
SALES (corp-wide): 321.47MM **Privately Held**
Web: www.taproduce.com
SIC: 0161 0182 0723 2099 Lettuce farm; Food crops grown under cover; Vegetable packing services; Food preparations, nec

(P-45)
TEIXEIRA FARMS DESERT INC
2600 Bonita Lateral Rd (93458-9798)
PHONE.................................805 928-3801
Allan Teixeira, *Pr*
Marvin Teixeira, *
Dean Teixeira, *
Glenn Teixeira, *
EMP: 76 **EST:** 1950
SALES (est): 9.58MM **Privately Held**
SIC: 0161 Broccoli farm

(P-46)
TRIPLE E PRODUCE LP
8690 W Linne Rd (95304-9109)
P.O. Box 239 (95378-0239)
PHONE.................................209 835-5123
EMP: 200
SIC: 0161 Tomato farm

(P-47)
UESUGI FARMS INCORPORATED
1020 State Highway 25 (95020-8074)
EMP: 162
Web: www.uesugifarms.com
SIC: 0161 Vegetables and melons

(P-48)
VANN BROTHERS
365 Ruggieri Way (95987-5155)
PHONE.................................530 473-2607
William B Vann, *Pt*
Garnett Vann Junior, *Pt*
EMP: 110 **EST:** 1973
SQ FT: 4,500
SALES (est): 19.23MM **Privately Held**
Web: www.vannfamilyorchards.com
SIC: 0161 0721 0131 0111 Tomato farm; Orchard tree and vine services; Cotton; Wheat

(P-49)
WM BOLTHOUSE FARMS INC (HQ)
Also Called: Bolthouse Farms
7200 E Brundage Ln (93307-3016)
PHONE.................................661 366-7209
Jeffrey Dunn, *CEO*
Mike Rosenthal, *
◆ **EMP:** 1000 **EST:** 1970
SQ FT: 700,000
SALES (est): 618.7MM
SALES (corp-wide): 1.33B **Privately Held**
Web: www.bolthouse.com
SIC: 0161 2037 2033 2099 Carrot farm; Fruit juices; Vegetable juices: packaged in cans, jars, etc.; Sauce, gravy, dressing, and dip mixes
PA: Generis Holdings, Lp
  7200 E Brundage Ln
  Bakersfield CA
  661 366-7209

0171 Berry Crops

(P-50)
DARENSBERRIES LLC
Also Called: D B Specialty Farms
714 S Blosser Rd (93458-4914)
P.O. Box 549 (93456-0549)
PHONE.................................805 937-8000
EMP: 250 **EST:** 1994
SQ FT: 1,500
SALES (est): 9.63MM **Privately Held**
Web: www.darensberries.com
SIC: 0171 Strawberry farm

(P-51)
ECLIPSE BERRY FARMS LLC
11812 San Vicente Blvd Ste 250 (90049-6632)
PHONE.................................310 207-7879
Norman Gilfenbain, *Managing Member*
Robert Wiviott, *Managing Member*
Rudy Garza, *Managing Member**
Ventura Strawberry, *
▼ **EMP:** 100 **EST:** 1999
SQ FT: 2,500
SALES (est): 8.84MM **Privately Held**

0171 - Berry Crops (P-52)

SIC: 0171 5148 Berry crops; Fresh fruits and vegetables

(P-52)
ETCHANDY FARMS LLC
4324 Vineyard Ave (93036-1056)
P.O. Box 5770 (93031-5770)
PHONE.....................805 983-4700
EMP: 99 EST: 2014
SQ FT: 400
SALES (est): 2.39MM **Privately Held**
SIC: 0171 Strawberry farm

(P-53)
FARMHILL LLC
1800 San Juan Rd (95004-9027)
P.O. Box 1119 (96067-1119)
PHONE.....................831 726-1986
FAX: 831 726-2650
EMP: 100
SALES (est): 2.05MM **Privately Held**
SIC: 0171 Strawberry farm

(P-54)
FRESHWAY FARMS LLC
2165 W Main St (93458-9739)
P.O. Box 5369 (93456-5369)
PHONE.....................805 349-7170
Paul M Allen, *Managing Member*
EMP: 150 EST: 2014
SALES (est): 8.85MM **Privately Held**
Web: www.mainstreetproduce.com
SIC: 0171 0161 Strawberry farm; Broccoli farm

(P-55)
J&G BERRY FARMS LLC
720 Rosemary Rd (93454-8007)
PHONE.....................831 750-9408
Jose Luis Rocha, *Managing Member*
Guadalupe Rocha, *
EMP: 220 EST: 2016
SALES (est): 2.89MM **Privately Held**
SIC: 0171 7389 Strawberry farm; Business Activities at Non-Commercial Site

(P-56)
LAS POSAS BERRY FARMS LLC
730 S A St (93030-7138)
PHONE.....................805 483-1000
Manuel Magdaleno, *CEO*
EMP: 100 EST: 2013
SALES (est): 1.87MM **Privately Held**
SIC: 0171 Berry crops

(P-57)
NORCAL HARVESTING LLC (PA)
Also Called: Bayview Farms
27 Quail Run Cir (93907-2345)
P.O. Box 3372 (93912-3372)
PHONE.....................831 443-4999
▲ EMP: 65 EST: 1996
SALES (est): 15.93MM **Privately Held**
Web: www.norcalharvesting.com
SIC: 0171 Strawberry farm

(P-58)
ORANGE COUNTY PRODUCE LLC
210 W Walnut Ave (92832-2347)
PHONE.....................949 451-0880
Matthew K Kawamura, *Managing Member*
EMP: 100 EST: 1998
SALES (est): 9.85MM **Privately Held**
Web: www.ocproduce.com
SIC: 0171 Strawberry farm

(P-59)
RED BLOSSOM FARMS INC
1389 W Main St (93458-4903)
PHONE.....................805 686-4747
David Lawrence, *Pr*
EMP: 99 EST: 2021
SALES (est): 544.07K **Privately Held**
SIC: 0171 Berry crops

(P-60)
RED BLOSSOM SALES INC
865 Black Rd (93458-9701)
PHONE.....................805 349-9404
Ruben Trevino, *Mgr*
EMP: 572
Web: www.redblossom.com
SIC: 0171 Strawberry farm
PA: Red Blossom Sales, Inc.
400 W Ventura Blvd # 140
Camarillo CA

(P-61)
REITER AFFL COMPANIES LLC
124 Carmen Ln Ste A (93458-7768)
PHONE.....................805 925-8577
Mario Pena, *Mgr*
EMP: 108
SALES (corp-wide): 43.32MM **Privately Held**
Web: www.berry.net
SIC: 0171 Berry crops
PA: Reiter Affiliated Companies, Llc
730 S A St
Oxnard CA
805 483-1000

(P-62)
REITER AFFL COMPANIES LLC
Also Called: Reiter Berry Watsonville
140 Westridge Dr (95076-6602)
PHONE.....................831 786-4244
EMP: 108
SALES (corp-wide): 43.32MM **Privately Held**
Web: www.berry.net
SIC: 0171 Raspberry farm
PA: Reiter Affiliated Companies, Llc
730 S A St
Oxnard CA
805 483-1000

(P-63)
REITER AFFL COMPANIES LLC
411 Walker St (95076-4225)
PHONE.....................831 761-1424
EMP: 108
SALES (corp-wide): 43.32MM **Privately Held**
Web: www.berry.net
SIC: 0171 Raspberry farm
PA: Reiter Affiliated Companies, Llc
730 S A St
Oxnard CA
805 483-1000

(P-64)
RINCON PACIFIC LLC
1312 Del Norte Rd (93010-8502)
PHONE.....................805 986-8806
EMP: 100 EST: 2001
SALES (est): 4.44MM **Privately Held**
SIC: 0171 Strawberry farm

(P-65)
SANTA ROSA BERRY FARMS LLC
3500 Camino Ave Ste 250 (93030-7999)
PHONE.....................805 981-3060
EMP: 300 EST: 2010
SQ FT: 3,500
SALES (est): 8.84MM **Privately Held**
Web: www.srbfarms.com
SIC: 0171 Berry crops

(P-66)
SUPERIOR FRUIT LLC
4324 E Vineyard Ave (93036-1056)
PHONE.....................805 485-2519
Richard Jones, *
EMP: 200 EST: 2017
SQ FT: 6,000
SALES (est): 3.21MM **Privately Held**
SIC: 0171 Strawberry farm

0172 Grapes

(P-67)
7TH STANDARD RANCH COMPANY
Also Called: Sun Pacific Farming
33374 Lerdo Hwy (93308-9782)
PHONE.....................661 399-0416
Berne Evans, *Pt*
Robert Reniers, *Pt*
EMP: 500 EST: 1986
SQ FT: 140,000
SALES (est): 20.8MM **Privately Held**
Web: www.sunpacific.com
SIC: 0172 4222 Grapes; Refrigerated warehousing and storage

(P-68)
ANTHONY VINEYARDS INC
52301 Enterprise Way (92236)
PHONE.....................760 391-5488
Roberto Bianco, *Mgr*
EMP: 100
SALES (corp-wide): 12.58MM **Privately Held**
Web: www.anthonyvineyards.com
SIC: 0172 0174 Grapes; Grapefruit grove
PA: Anthony Vineyards, Inc.
5512 Valpredo Ave
Bakersfield CA
661 858-6211

(P-69)
BALLETTO RANCH INC
Also Called: Balletto Ranch Shop
3800 Guerneville Rd (95401-3956)
P.O. Box 2579 (95473-2579)
PHONE.....................707 568-2455
Garth Harding, *Prin*
EMP: 110
SALES (corp-wide): 12.26MM **Privately Held**
Web: www.ballettoranch.com
SIC: 0172 Grapes
PA: Balletto Ranch, Inc.
5700 Occidental Rd
Santa Rosa CA
707 568-2455

(P-70)
CEDERLIND FARMS LP
2514 Kenney Ave (95388-9745)
PHONE.....................209 606-8586
Jeff Cederlind, *Pt*
EMP: 99 EST: 1998
SALES (est): 2.27MM **Privately Held**
SIC: 0172 Grapes

(P-71)
DELU VINEYARDS INC
15175 N Devries Rd (95242-9217)
PHONE.....................209 334-6660
Alexander Delu, *Pr*
EMP: 80 EST: 1958
SALES (est): 1.04MM **Privately Held**
SIC: 0172 0722 Grapes; Grapes, machine harvesting services

(P-72)
DOMAINE CARNEROS LTD
1240 Duhig Rd (94559-9713)
P.O. Box 5420 (94581-0420)
PHONE.....................707 257-0101
Eileen Crane, *Prin*
Robert Aldridge, *Prin*
◆ EMP: 80 EST: 1986
SQ FT: 50,000
SALES (est): 19.77MM **Privately Held**
Web: www.domainecarneros.com
SIC: 0172 2084 Grapes; Wines

(P-73)
GIUMARRA VINEYARDS CORPORATION
Giumarra Winery
11220 Edison Hwy (93307-8431)
P.O. Box 1969 (93303-1969)
PHONE.....................661 395-7071
Barry Douglas, *Mgr*
EMP: 133
SALES (corp-wide): 134.67MM **Privately Held**
Web: www.giumarravineyards.com
SIC: 0172 Grapes
PA: Giumarra Vineyards Corporation
11220 Edison Hwy
Edison CA
661 395-7000

(P-74)
GIUMARRA VINEYARDS CORPORATION (PA)
11220 Edison Hwy (93220)
P.O. Box 1969 (93303-1969)
PHONE.....................661 395-7000
Wayne Childress, *CEO*
Mimi Corsaro-dorsey, *Sec*
Jeffrey Giumarra, *
◆ EMP: 500 EST: 1946
SQ FT: 10,000
SALES (est): 134.67MM
SALES (corp-wide): 134.67MM **Privately Held**
Web: www.giumarravineyards.com
SIC: 0172 2084 2086 Grapes; Wines; Fruit drinks (less than 100% juice): packaged in cans, etc.

(P-75)
J & L VINEYARDS
1850 Ramada Dr Ste 3 (93446-3932)
PHONE.....................559 268-1627
Donald Laub, *Pt*
Raymond Jacobson, *Pt*
EMP: 100 EST: 1980
SALES (est): 2.46MM **Privately Held**
SIC: 0172 Grapes

(P-76)
JACK NEAL & SON INC
360 Lafata St (94574-1410)
PHONE.....................707 963-7303
Mark J Neal, *Pr*
Tina Galambos, *
EMP: 200 EST: 1968
SQ FT: 20,000
SALES (est): 10.58MM **Privately Held**
Web: www.jacknealandson.com
SIC: 0172 Grapes

(P-77)
JAKOV DULCICH AND SONS LLC

PRODUCTS & SERVICES SECTION

0174 - Citrus Fruits (P-98)

31956 Peterson Rd (93250-9606)
PHONE..................................661 792-6360
Jakov Dulcich, *Prin*
▲ **EMP:** 250 **EST:** 1963
SALES (est): 14.69MM **Privately Held**
Web: www.dulcich.com
SIC: 0172 Grapes

(P-78)
KAUTZ VINEYARDS INC (PA)
Also Called: Kautz Ironstone Vineyards
1894 6 Mile Rd (95247-9543)
PHONE..................................209 728-1251
John K Kautz, *CEO*
Stephen Kautz, *
Gail Kautz, *
Kurt Kautz, *
◆ **EMP:** 100 **EST:** 1989
SQ FT: 75,000
SALES (est): 10.07MM **Privately Held**
Web: www.ironstonevineyards.com
SIC: 0172 5812 Grapes; Eating places

(P-79)
KLEIN FOODS INC
Also Called: Rodney Strong Vineyards
11455 Old Redwood Hwy (95448-9523)
P.O. Box 6010 (95448-6010)
PHONE..................................707 431-1533
Thomas B Klein, *Pr*
Tobin Ginter, *
◆ **EMP:** 100 **EST:** 1988
SQ FT: 20,000
SALES (est): 25MM **Privately Held**
Web: www.rodneystrong.com
SIC: 0172 2084 5182 Grapes; Wines; Wine and distilled beverages

(P-80)
M CARATAN DISC INC
Also Called: Caliente Farms
33787 Cecil Ave (93215-9597)
PHONE..................................661 725-2566
Martin Caratin, *CEO*
▼ **EMP:** 150 **EST:** 1946
SQ FT: 6,000
SALES (est): 13.53MM **Privately Held**
Web: www.mcaratan.com
SIC: 0172 0174 0723 Grapes; Orange grove ; Almond hulling and shelling services

(P-81)
ONEILL BEVERAGES CO LLC
Also Called: O'Neill Vintners & Distillers
8418 S Lac Jac Ave (93648-9708)
PHONE..................................559 638-3544
EMP: 200
SALES (corp-wide): 113.24MM **Privately Held**
Web: www.oneillwine.com
SIC: 0172 2084 Grapes; Wines
PA: O'neill Beverages Co. Llc
  101 Larkspur Landing Cir
  Larkspur CA
  559 638-3544

(P-82)
ONEILL BEVERAGES CO LLC (PA)
Also Called: O'Neill Vintners & Distillers
101 Larkspur Landing Cir Ste 350 (94939-1746)
PHONE..................................559 638-3544
Jeffrey B O'neill, *CEO*
Donald Heer, *
Matthew Towers, *
◆ **EMP:** 63 **EST:** 2004
SQ FT: 5,000
SALES (est): 113.24MM
SALES (corp-wide): 113.24MM **Privately Held**

Web: www.oneillwine.com
SIC: 0172 2084 Grapes; Wines

(P-83)
RICHARD BAGDASARIAN INC
65500 Lincoln St (92254-6500)
P.O. Box 698 (92254-0698)
PHONE..................................760 396-2168
Nicholas L Bozick, *CEO*
Michael Bozick, *
Bobbie Bozick, *
Darrell Billings, *
▲ **EMP:** 60 **EST:** 1951
SQ FT: 40,000
SALES (est): 9.48MM **Privately Held**
Web: www.bagdasarianinc.com
SIC: 0172 0174 Grapes; Citrus fruits

(P-84)
SAN BERNABE VINEYARDS
53001 Oasis Rd (93930-9667)
PHONE..................................831 385-4897
Claude Hoover, *Pr*
Dorothy Indelicato, *
Frank Indelicato, *
EMP: 85 **EST:** 1988
SQ FT: 15,000
SALES (est): 4.96MM
SALES (corp-wide): 549.38MM **Privately Held**
SIC: 0172 2084 Grapes; Wines, brandy, and brandy spirits
PA: Delicato Vineyards, Llc
  12001 S Highway 99
  Manteca CA
  209 824-3500

(P-85)
SCHEID VINEYARDS INC
1972 Hobson Ave (93927-9605)
PHONE..................................831 386-5022
EMP: 103
SALES (corp-wide): 54.23MM **Publicly Held**
Web: www.scheidvineyards.com
SIC: 0172 Grapes
PA: Scheid Vineyards Inc.
  305 Hilltown Rd
  Salinas CA
  831 455-9990

(P-86)
SCHEID VINEYARDS INC (PA)
Also Called: Scheid Family Wines
305 Hilltown Rd (93908-8902)
PHONE..................................831 455-9990
Scott D Scheid, *Pr*
Alfred G Scheid, *
Heidi M Scheid, *
Kurt J Gollnick, *
Michael S Thomsen, *
EMP: 97 **EST:** 1997
SQ FT: 6,700
SALES: 54.23MM
SALES (corp-wide): 54.23MM **Publicly Held**
Web: www.scheidvineyards.com
SIC: 0172 2084 Grapes; Wines

(P-87)
SIMONIAN BROTHERS INC
Also Called: Simonian Farming Co
3580 S Newcomb Ave (93640-9743)
PHONE..................................559 655-4722
Jim Simonian, *Brnch Mgr*
EMP: 66
SALES (corp-wide): 9.48MM **Privately Held**
Web: www.simonianfruit.com
SIC: 0172 Grapes

PA: Simonian Brothers Inc.
  511 N 7th St
  Fowler CA
  559 834-5921

(P-88)
VINCENT B ZANINOVICH SONS INC
Also Called: V B Z
20715 Ave 8 (93261)
P.O. Box 1000 (93261-1000)
PHONE..................................661 720-9031
John V Zaninovich, *CEO*
Vincent Zaninovich, *
Andrew Zaninovich, *
◆ **EMP:** 1000 **EST:** 1930
SQ FT: 15,450
SALES (est): 24.68MM **Privately Held**
SIC: 0172 Grapes

0173 Tree Nuts

(P-89)
BATTH FARMS INC
Also Called: Batth Farms
5434 W Kamm Ave (93609-9400)
PHONE..................................559 864-9421
Charanjit Singh Batth, *CEO*
EMP: 90 **EST:** 1969
SQ FT: 1,200
SALES (est): 9.76MM **Privately Held**
Web: www.batthfarms.com
SIC: 0173 0175 0172 2034 Almond grove; Prune orchard; Grapes; Raisins

(P-90)
CAMPOS BROS FARMS
Also Called: Campos Bros. Farms
15516 S Walnut Ave (93609-9648)
PHONE..................................559 864-9488
◆ **EMP:** 300
SIC: 0173 0191 Almond grove; General farms, primarily crop

(P-91)
CHICO NUT COMPANY
2020 Esplanade (95926-2222)
P.O. Box 5365 (95927-5365)
PHONE..................................530 894-5441
◆ **EMP:** 80 **EST:** 1987
SALES (est): 4.6MM **Privately Held**
Web: www.chiconut.com
SIC: 0173 Almond grove

(P-92)
J G BOSWELL COMPANY
36889 Hwy 58 (93206-9616)
PHONE..................................661 764-9000
EMP: 308
SALES (corp-wide): 370.2MM **Privately Held**
Web: www.eastlakeco.com
SIC: 0173 0161 0131 Pistachio grove; Tomato farm; Cotton
PA: J. G. Boswell Company
  101 W Walnut St
  Pasadena CA
  626 583-3000

(P-93)
KEENAN FARMS INC
31510 Plymouth Ave (93239-9721)
P.O. Box 99 (93204-0099)
PHONE..................................559 945-1400
Robert M Keenan, *CEO*
Charles J Keenan Iii, *VP*
◆ **EMP:** 100 **EST:** 1972
SALES (est): 23.28MM **Privately Held**
Web: www.keenanfarms.com

SIC: 0173 2068 Pistachio grove; Nuts: dried, dehydrated, salted or roasted

(P-94)
SUPREME ALMONDS CALIFORNIA INC
16897 Highway 43 (93280-9611)
PHONE..................................661 746-6475
Randy Loemhof, *Pr*
◆ **EMP:** 100 **EST:** 2008
SALES (est): 4.46MM **Privately Held**
Web: www.supremealmonds.com
SIC: 0173 Almond grove

(P-95)
WONDERFUL ORCHARDS LLC (HQ)
6801 E Lerdo Hwy (93263-9610)
PHONE..................................661 399-4456
◆ **EMP:** 150 **EST:** 1998
SQ FT: 10,000
SALES (est): 157.67MM
SALES (corp-wide): 2.04B **Privately Held**
Web: www.wonderfulorchards.com
SIC: 0173 0179 Almond grove; Olive grove
PA: The Wonderful Company Llc
  11444 W Olympic Blvd # 210
  Los Angeles CA
  310 966-5700

(P-96)
WONDERFUL ORCHARDS LLC
Also Called: Wonderfulpistachiosandalmonds
13646 Highway 33 (93249-9719)
P.O. Box 400 (93249-0400)
PHONE..................................661 797-6400
Dennis Elam, *Brnch Mgr*
EMP: 262
SALES (corp-wide): 2.04B **Privately Held**
Web: www.wonderfulorchards.com
SIC: 0173 0191 Almond grove; General farms, primarily crop
HQ: Wonderful Orchards Llc
  6801 E Lerdo Hwy
  Shafter CA
  661 399-4456

(P-97)
WONDERFUL ORCHARDS LLC
21707 Lerdo Hwy (93251-9758)
PHONE..................................661 797-2509
Robert Baker, *Mgr*
EMP: 98
SALES (corp-wide): 2.04B **Privately Held**
Web: www.wonderfulorchards.com
SIC: 0173 0191 Almond grove; General farms, primarily crop
HQ: Wonderful Orchards Llc
  6801 E Lerdo Hwy
  Shafter CA
  661 399-4456

0174 Citrus Fruits

(P-98)
EXETER PACKERS INC
Also Called: Sun Pacific Shippers
1095 E Green St (91106-2503)
PHONE..................................626 993-6245
Bob Reniers, *Genl Mgr*
EMP: 119
SALES (corp-wide): 41.55MM **Privately Held**
Web: www.sunpacific.com
SIC: 0174 0172 0161 0723 Orange grove; Grapes; Tomato farm; Fruit (fresh) packing services
PA: Exeter Packers, Inc.
  1250 E Myer Ave

0174 - Citrus Fruits (P-99)

Exeter CA
559 592-5168

(P-99)
HRONIS INC A CALIFORNIA CORP (PA)
10443 Hronis Rd (93215-9556)
PHONE..................661 725-2503
Kosta Hronis, *Pr*
Pete Hronis, *
▼ EMP: 145 EST: 1945
SQ FT: 150,000
SALES (est): 30.34MM
SALES (corp-wide): 30.34MM **Privately Held**
Web: www.hronis.net
SIC: **0174** 0172 Citrus fruits; Grapes

(P-100)
JOHNSTON FARMS FMLY LTD PARTNR
13031 E Packinghouse Rd (93220)
PHONE..................661 366-3201
Tari Johnston, *Prin*
Gerald Johnston, *Prin*
Dennis B Johnston, *Prin*
Kevin Johnston, *Prin*
Terry Henderson, *Prin*
◆ EMP: 65 EST: 1953
SQ FT: 100,000
SALES (est): 9.3MM **Privately Held**
Web: www.johnstonfarms.com
SIC: **0174** 0134 0161 Orange grove; Irish potatoes; Pepper farm, sweet and hot (vegetables)

(P-101)
SATICOY LEMON ASSOCIATION
Also Called: Saticoy Fruit Exchange
7560 Bristol Rd (93003-7027)
P.O. Box 46 (93061-0046)
PHONE..................805 654-6500
John Elliott, *Brnch Mgr*
EMP: 99
SALES (corp-wide): 26.61MM **Privately Held**
Web: www.saticoylemon.com
SIC: **0174** Lemon grove
PA: Saticoy Lemon Association
103 N Peck Rd
Santa Paula CA
805 654-6500

(P-102)
WONDERFUL CITRUS LLC (HQ)
1701 S Lexington St (93215-9200)
PHONE..................661 720-2400
Craig B Cooper, *Managing Member*
EMP: 63 EST: 2011
SALES (est): 81.95MM
SALES (corp-wide): 2.04B **Privately Held**
Web: www.wonderfulcitrus.com
SIC: **0174** Citrus fruits
PA: The Wonderful Company Llc
11444 W Olympic Blvd # 210
Los Angeles CA
310 966-5700

(P-103)
WONDERFUL COMPANY LLC
Also Called: Paramount Citrus
1901 S Lexington St (93215-9207)
PHONE..................661 720-2400
Freddie Hernandez, *Mgr*
EMP: 273
SALES (corp-wide): 2.04B **Privately Held**
Web: www.wonderful.com
SIC: **0174** 3911 Citrus fruits; Jewelry, precious metal
PA: The Wonderful Company Llc
11444 W Olympic Blvd # 210
Los Angeles CA
310 966-5700

0175 Deciduous Tree Fruits

(P-104)
CIRCLE K RANCH LP (PA)
8640 E Manning Ave (93662-9763)
PHONE..................559 834-1571
Melvin Kazarian, *Genl Pt*
Ronald Kazarian, *Pt*
EMP: 68 EST: 1946
SQ FT: 25,000
SALES (est): 2.31MM
SALES (corp-wide): 2.31MM **Privately Held**
Web: www.circlekranch.com
SIC: **0175** Nectarine orchard

(P-105)
FARMINGTON FRESH SALES LLC
Also Called: Farmington Fresh
7735 S Highway 99 (95215-9623)
P.O. Box 951 (95201-0951)
PHONE..................209 983-9700
EMP: 250
SIC: **0175** 4731 Apple orchard; Agents, shipping

(P-106)
GERAWAN FARMING LLC
1467 E Dinuba Ave (93654-3586)
PHONE..................559 638-9281
Dan Gerawan, *Brnch Mgr*
EMP: 197
SALES (corp-wide): 498.13MM **Privately Held**
Web: www.prima.com
SIC: **0175** 0723 Apple orchard; Fruit (fresh) packing services
HQ: Gerawan Farming Llc
7700 N Palm Ave Ste 206
Fresno CA

(P-107)
GERAWAN RANCHES
10045 W Lincoln Ave (93706-9342)
PHONE..................559 787-8780
EMP: 230
SALES (corp-wide): 4.32MM **Privately Held**
SIC: **0175** 0172 Peach orchard; Grapes
PA: Gerawan Ranches
7108 N Fresno St Ste 450
Fresno CA
559 787-8780

(P-108)
KAP LP
10363 Davis Ave (93631-9539)
P.O. Box 456 (93631-0456)
PHONE..................559 897-5132
Mike Jackson, *Pt*
Colleen Jackson, *Ltd Pt*
Brent Jackson, *Mng Pt*
Susan Jackson Diepersloot, *Ltd Pt*
▼ EMP: 77 EST: 1981
SQ FT: 140,000
SALES (est): 6.48MM **Privately Held**
Web: www.kingsburgorchards.com
SIC: **0175** Apple orchard

(P-109)
MIKE JENSEN FARMS LLC
13138 S Bethel Ave (93631-9216)
PHONE..................559 897-4192
EMP: 200 EST: 1984
SQ FT: 14,000
SALES (est): 9.76MM **Privately Held**
Web: www.hmcfarms.com
SIC: **0175** 2033 2099 Apricot orchard; Fruits: packaged in cans, jars, etc.; Food preparations, nec

(P-110)
NISSHO OF CALIFORNIA INC
89055 64th Ave (92274-9607)
PHONE..................760 727-9719
Abel Bustamante, *Mgr*
EMP: 309
SALES (corp-wide): 23.11MM **Privately Held**
Web: www.nisshoca.com
SIC: **0175** Deciduous tree fruits
PA: Nissho Of California, Inc.
1902 S Santa Fe Ave
Vista CA
760 727-9719

(P-111)
PACIFIC FARMS AND ORCHARDS INC
Also Called: Pacific Farms
22880 Gerber Rd (96035-9728)
P.O. Box 955 (96035-0955)
PHONE..................530 385-1475
Sam Mudd, *Pr*
Brendon Flynn, *Sec*
▲ EMP: 67 EST: 1971
SQ FT: 4,000
SALES (est): 1.65MM **Privately Held**
Web: www.pacificfarms.com
SIC: **0175** 0173 0119 0111 Prune orchard; Walnut grove; Barley farm; Wheat

(P-112)
PETERSON FAMILY INC
38694 Road 16 (93631-9106)
PHONE..................559 897-5064
Vernon E Peterson, *Prin*
EMP: 100 EST: 1975
SALES (est): 4.84MM **Privately Held**
SIC: **0175** 0174 Apple orchard; Citrus fruits

(P-113)
RICH HARVEST INC
Also Called: Courtesy Moving and Storage
3515 N Sabre Dr (93727-7817)
PHONE..................559 252-8000
Gerald Peters, *Pr*
EMP: 100 EST: 1998
SALES (est): 2.46MM **Privately Held**
Web: www.richharvestfarms.com
SIC: **0175** 4783 4221 Deciduous tree fruits; Packing and crating; Farm product warehousing and storage

(P-114)
VANN FAMILY LLC
Also Called: Vann Family Orchard
6141 Abel Rd (95987-5816)
PHONE..................530 473-3317
EMP: 104
SALES (corp-wide): 734.03K **Privately Held**
SIC: **0175** Deciduous tree fruits
PA: Vann Family, Llc
365 Ruggieri Way
Williams CA
530 473-2607

0179 Fruits And Tree Nuts, Nec

(P-115)
DOLE HOLDING COMPANY LLC
1 Dole Dr (91362-7300)
PHONE..................818 879-6600
David H Murdock, *Ch Bd*
EMP: 74999 EST: 2004
SALES (est): 452.35K **Privately Held**
SIC: **0179** 0174 0175 0161 Pineapple farm; Citrus fruits; Deciduous tree fruits; Lettuce farm
PA: Dhm Holding Company, Inc.
1 Dole Dr
Westlake Village CA

(P-116)
HADLEY DATE GARDENS INC
47382 Madison St (92201-6630)
PHONE..................760 347-3044
EMP: 79
SALES (corp-wide): 3.43MM **Privately Held**
Web: www.hadleys.com
SIC: **0179** Date orchard
PA: Hadley Date Gardens, Inc.
79220 Corp Ctr Dr Ste 102
La Quinta CA
760 399-5191

(P-117)
HENRY AVOCADO CORPORATION (HQ)
Also Called: Customripe Avocado Company
2208 Harmony Grove Rd (92029-2054)
P.O. Box 300867 (92030-0867)
PHONE..................760 745-6632
Philip Henry, *Pr*
◆ EMP: 70 EST: 1924
SQ FT: 35,000
SALES (est): 20.04MM
SALES (corp-wide): 1.05B **Publicly Held**
Web: www.henryavocado.com
SIC: **0179** 4213 Avocado orchard; Trucking, except local
PA: Mission Produce, Inc.
2710 Camino Del Sol
Oxnard CA
805 981-3650

(P-118)
MUNGER BROS LLC
Also Called: Munger Farm
786 Road 188 (93215-9508)
PHONE..................661 721-0390
Kewel K Munger, *
▲ EMP: 600 EST: 1998
SQ FT: 50,000
SALES (est): 24.34MM **Privately Held**
SIC: **0179** 2033 Avocado orchard; Canned fruits and specialties

0181 Ornamental Nursery Products

(P-119)
A-G SOD FARMS INC
Also Called: Addink Turf
2900 Adams St Ste C120 (92504-8317)
PHONE..................951 687-7581
Sonya Dawe, *Mgr*
EMP: 78
SALES (corp-wide): 16.87MM **Privately Held**
Web: www.agsod.com
SIC: **0181** Sod farms

0181 - Ornamental Nursery Products (P-142)

PA: A-G Sod Farms, Inc.
2900 Adams St Ste C120
Riverside CA
951 687-7581

(P-120)
COLOR SPOT HOLDINGS INC (PA)
Also Called: Color Spot Nurseries
3742 Blue Bird Canyon Rd (92084-7432)
PHONE..................760 695-1430
Rodney Omps, *Sec*
Jerry Halamuda, *CEO*
Oscar Truyol, *COO*
Chip Mello, *COO*
EMP: 1498 EST: 2007
SALES (est): 229.55MM
SALES (corp-wide): 229.55MM **Privately Held**
SIC: 0181 Bedding plants, growing of

(P-121)
CSN WINDDOWN INC
420 Espinosa Rd (93907-8894)
PHONE..................831 444-0523
Michael F Vukelich, *Mgr*
EMP: 72
SALES (corp-wide): 229.55MM **Privately Held**
SIC: 0181 Plants, potted: growing of
HQ: Csn Winddown, Inc.
27368 Via Industria # 20
Temecula CA

(P-122)
CSN WINDDOWN INC
Also Called: Color Spot Lodi
5400 E Harney Ln (95240-6903)
PHONE..................209 369-3018
David Barrett, *Pr*
EMP: 73
SALES (corp-wide): 229.55MM **Privately Held**
SIC: 0181 5193 Plants, potted: growing of; Flowers and florists supplies
HQ: Csn Winddown, Inc.
27368 Via Industria # 20
Temecula CA

(P-123)
DEVIL MOUNTAIN WHL NURS LLC
29001 Ortega Hwy (92675)
PHONE..................949 496-9356
EMP: 93
Web: www.devilmountainnursery.com
SIC: 0181 Nursery stock, growing of
PA: Devil Mountain Wholesale Nursery, Llc
9885 Alcosta Blvd
San Ramon CA

(P-124)
DRAMM AND ECHTER INC
Also Called: D&E Propogators
1150 Quail Gardens Dr (92024-2365)
PHONE..................760 436-0188
◆ EMP: 85 EST: 1972
SALES (est): 9.49MM **Privately Held**
Web: www.drammechter.com
SIC: 0181 5193 Flowers: grown under cover (e.g., greenhouse production); Flowers and nursery stock

(P-125)
DUARTE NURSERY INC
23456 E Flood Rd (95236-9429)
PHONE..................209 887-3409
EMP: 350
SQ FT: 1,558
SALES (corp-wide): 49.31MM **Privately Held**
Web: www.duartenursery.com
SIC: 0181 Nursery stock, growing of
PA: Duarte Nursery, Inc.
1555 Baldwin Rd
Hughson CA
209 531-0351

(P-126)
DUARTE NURSERY INC
Also Called: Duarte Properties
1555 Baldwin Rd (95326-9522)
PHONE..................209 531-0351
John Duarte, *Pr*
Jeff Duarte, *
Anita Duarte, *
EMP: 400 EST: 1989
SALES (est): 24.82MM **Privately Held**
Web: www.duartenursery.com
SIC: 0181 Nursery stock, growing of

(P-127)
EUROAMERICAN PROPAGATORS LLC
32149 Aquaduct Rd (92003-4807)
PHONE..................760 731-6029
▲ EMP: 375
Web: www.euroamericanpropagators.com
SIC: 0181 Ornamental nursery products

(P-128)
GLAD-A-WAY GARDENS INC
2669 E Clark Ave (93455-5815)
P.O. Box 2550 (93457-2550)
PHONE..................805 938-0569
Brian Caird, *Pr*
Erin Caird, *
Lance Runels, *
▲ EMP: 172 EST: 1964
SQ FT: 15,000
SALES (est): 9.93MM **Privately Held**
Web: www.gladaway.com
SIC: 0181 Flowers: grown under cover (e.g., greenhouse production)

(P-129)
GOLDEN STATE BULB GROWERS INC
3060 Hilltop Rd (95039-9692)
PHONE..................831 728-0500
▼ EMP: 175
Web: www.goldenstatebulb.com
SIC: 0181 Bulbs, growing of

(P-130)
HINES GROWERS INC
Also Called: Cshg Holdings
27368 Via Industria Ste 201 (92590-4855)
PHONE..................800 554-4065
▲ EMP: 942 EST: 2012
SALES (est): 434.05K
SALES (corp-wide): 229.55MM **Privately Held**
SIC: 0181 5261 Ornamental nursery products; Retail nurseries and garden stores
HQ: Csn Winddown, Inc.
27368 Via Industria # 20
Temecula CA

(P-131)
HINES HORTICULTURE INC (PA)
Also Called: Hines Nurseries
12621 Jeffery Rd (92620)
PHONE..................949 559-4444
▲ EMP: 500 EST: 1920
SALES (est): 446.34MM **Privately Held**
SIC: 0181 5261 Ornamental nursery products; Retail nurseries and garden stores

(P-132)
HMCLAUSE INC (DH)
260 Cousteau Pl Ste 210 (95618-5490)
PHONE..................800 320-4672
Remi Bastien, *CEO*
Matthew M Johnston, *
Andre Cariou, *
◆ EMP: 133 EST: 1856
SQ FT: 200,000
SALES (est): 108MM
SALES (corp-wide): 229.38MM **Privately Held**
Web: www.hmclause.com
SIC: 0181 3999 Seeds, vegetable: growing of; Seeds, coated or treated, from purchased seeds
HQ: Groupe Limagrain Holding
Biopole Clermont Limagne
St Beauzire
473634000

(P-133)
JIMENEZ NURSERY INC
Also Called: Jimenez Nursery and Landscapes
3800 Via Real (93013-3051)
P.O. Box 2460 (93120-2460)
PHONE..................805 684-7955
Manuel Jimenez, *CEO*
Alicia Jimenez, *Sec*
EMP: 100 EST: 1996
SALES (est): 6.8MM **Privately Held**
Web: www.jimeneznursery.com
SIC: 0181 Nursery stock, growing of

(P-134)
KAWAHARA NURSERY INC
698 Burnett Ave (95037-9022)
P.O. Box 1358 (95038-1358)
PHONE..................408 779-2400
David Kawahara, *Pr*
John Kawahara, *
▲ EMP: 240 EST: 1947
SALES (est): 28.2MM **Privately Held**
Web: www.kawaharanursery.com
SIC: 0181 5193 Nursery stock, growing of; Flowers and florists supplies

(P-135)
L E COOKE CO
26333 Road 140 (93292-9452)
PHONE..................559 732-9146
David Henry Cox, *CEO*
Ron Ludekens, *
Phillip Cox, *
▲ EMP: 200 EST: 1944
SQ FT: 6,000
SALES (est): 4.91MM **Privately Held**
Web: www.lecooke.com
SIC: 0181 Nursery stock, growing of

(P-136)
LA VERNE NURSERY INC
3653 Center St (93040-8051)
PHONE..................805 521-0111
EMP: 90
Web: www.everde.com
SIC: 0181 Nursery stock, growing of
PA: La Verne Nursery, Inc.
1025 N Todd Ave
Azusa CA

(P-137)
MARATHON LAND INC
2599 E Hueneme Rd (93033-8112)
P.O. Box 579 (93044-0579)
PHONE..................805 488-3585
TOLL FREE: 800
Jurgen Gramckow, *Pr*
EMP: 130 EST: 1977
SQ FT: 3,000
SALES (est): 3.45MM **Privately Held**
Web: www.sod.com
SIC: 0181 Sod farms

(P-138)
MATSUDAS BY GREEN ACRES LLC
Also Called: Green Acres Nursery and Supply
10600 Florin Rd (95830-9404)
P.O. Box 6750 (95763-6750)
PHONE..................916 673-9290
Mark B Gill, *Managing Member*
Mark Gill, *Managing Member**
Ashley Gill, *Managing Member**
EMP: 180 EST: 2013
SALES (est): 23.46MM **Privately Held**
Web: www.matsudasnursery.com
SIC: 0181 Nursery stock, growing of

(P-139)
MATSUI NURSERY INC (PA)
1645 Old Stage Rd (93908-9737)
PHONE..................831 422-6433
Toshikiyo Andy Matsui, *Pr*
▲ EMP: 81 EST: 1967
SQ FT: 3,000,000
SALES (est): 21.84MM
SALES (corp-wide): 21.84MM **Privately Held**
Web: www.matsuinursery.com
SIC: 0181 Nursery stock, growing of

(P-140)
MONROVIA NURSERY COMPANY (PA)
Also Called: Monrovia Growes
817 E Monrovia Pl (91702-6297)
P.O. Box 1385 (91702-1385)
PHONE..................626 334-9321
Miles R Rosedale, *CEO*
Richard Van Landingham, *Pr*
William B Usrey, *Pr*
Dennis Conner, *General Vice President*
▲ EMP: 567 EST: 1926
SQ FT: 50,000
SALES (est): 436.68MM
SALES (corp-wide): 436.68MM **Privately Held**
Web: www.monrovia.com
SIC: 0181 5193 5261 Nursery stock, growing of; Flowers and florists supplies; Retail nurseries and garden stores

(P-141)
MULROSES USA INC
741 S San Pedro St (90014-2417)
PHONE..................213 489-1761
Patricio Nasser, *Mgr*
EMP: 100 EST: 2010
SALES (est): 1.55MM **Privately Held**
SIC: 0181 Roses, growing of

(P-142)
NORMANS NURSERY INC
Also Called: Norman's Nursery
5770 Casitas Pass Rd (93013-3061)
PHONE..................805 684-1411
Martin Manzo, *Mgr*
EMP: 142
SALES (corp-wide): 95.85MM **Privately Held**
Web: www.nngrower.com
SIC: 0181 Nursery stock, growing of
PA: Norman's Nursery, Inc.
8665 Duarte Rd
San Gabriel CA
626 285-9795

0181 - Ornamental Nursery Products (P-143)

(P-143)
OCEAN BREEZE INTERNATIONAL
Also Called: Mobis Wholesale
3910 Via Real (93013-1266)
PHONE..................805 684-1747
Rene Van Wingerden, Pr
June Van Wingerden, VP
▲ EMP: 60 EST: 1974
SQ FT: 900,000
SALES (est): 9.11MM Privately Held
SIC: 0181 Flowers: grown under cover (e.g., greenhouse production)

(P-144)
OLIVE HILL GREENHOUSES INC
3508 Olive Hill Rd (92028-8296)
P.O. Box 1510 (92088-1510)
PHONE..................760 728-4596
George A Godfrey, Owner
▲ EMP: 100 EST: 1974
SQ FT: 2,000
SALES (est): 5.28MM Privately Held
Web: www.olivehill.net
SIC: 0181 Nursery stock, growing of

(P-145)
PACIFIC ERTH RSRCES LTD A CAL (PA)
Also Called: Pacific Sd/Pcfic Arbor Nrsries
305 Hueneme Rd (93012-8522)
P.O. Box 240 (93011-0240)
PHONE..................805 986-8277
Richard Rogers, Mng Pt
Elizabeth Rogers, Pt
EMP: 80 EST: 1958
SQ FT: 8,000
SALES (est): 8.63MM
SALES (corp-wide): 8.63MM Privately Held
SIC: 0181 Sod farms

(P-146)
PACIFIC ERTH RSRCES LTD A CAL
Also Called: Pacific Sod
315 Hueneme Rd (93012-8522)
P.O. Box 240 (93011-0240)
PHONE..................209 892-3000
Raymond Freitas, Mgr
EMP: 90
SALES (corp-wide): 8.63MM Privately Held
SIC: 0181 Sod farms
PA: Pacific Earth Resources, Ltd., A California Limited Partnership
305 Hueneme Rd
Camarillo CA
805 986-8277

(P-147)
PLANTEL NURSERIES INC
3990 Foxen Canyon Rd (93454-9666)
PHONE..................805 934-4300
Gerald Tonascia, Mgr
EMP: 270
SALES (corp-wide): 19.39MM Privately Held
Web: www.plantelnurseries.com
SIC: 0181 5193 Seeds, vegetable: growing of ; Nursery stock
PA: Plantel Nurseries, Inc.
2775 E Clark Ave
Santa Maria CA
805 349-8952

(P-148)
PLUG CONNECTION INC
2627 Ramona Dr (92084-1634)
PHONE..................760 631-0992
Tim Wada, Pr
Bradley Rhoads, *
▲ EMP: 80 EST: 1987
SQ FT: 350,000
SALES (est): 17.28MM Privately Held
Web: www.plugconnection.com
SIC: 0181 Nursery stock, growing of

(P-149)
PYRAMID FLOWERS INC
3813 Doris Ave (93030-4706)
PHONE..................805 382-8070
Fred Van Wingerden, Pr
Edith Van Wingerden, *
▲ EMP: 120 EST: 1991
SQ FT: 900,000
SALES (est): 16.07MM Privately Held
Web: www.pyramidflowers.com
SIC: 0181 Flowers, grown in field nurseries

(P-150)
RECOLOGY BLSSOM VLY ORGNICS -
6224 Stoddard Rd (95356-9198)
PHONE..................209 545-4401
Mark Grover, Pr
Lorraine Grover, *
EMP: 100 EST: 1970
SQ FT: 10,850
SALES (est): 16.5MM Privately Held
Web: www.groverlandscapeservices.com
SIC: 0181 0782 0783 0781 Ornamental nursery products; Landscape contractors; Tree trimming services for public utility lines ; Landscape planning services

(P-151)
RICHARD WILSON WELLINGTON
Also Called: Colorama Wholesale Nursery
1025 N Todd Ave (91702-1602)
P.O. Box 1328 (91740-1328)
PHONE..................626 812-7881
Richard Wilson, Owner
▲ EMP: 100 EST: 1984
SQ FT: 70,000
SALES (est): 3.09MM Privately Held
Web: www.coloramanursery.com
SIC: 0181 5193 Nursery stock, growing of; Nursery stock

(P-152)
RIVER RIDGE FARMS INC
3135 Los Angeles Ave (93036-1010)
PHONE..................805 647-6880
Rieuwert Jan Vis, Pr
▲ EMP: 95 EST: 1992
SQ FT: 440
SALES (est): 2.42MM Privately Held
Web: www.riverridgefarms.net
SIC: 0181 5193 Flowers, grown in field nurseries; Plants, potted

(P-153)
SIERRA GOLD NURSERIES INC
5320 Garden Hwy (95991-9499)
PHONE..................530 674-1145
Jack Poukish, CEO
Brian Berg, *
Ellen Berg, *
▲ EMP: 86 EST: 1952
SQ FT: 2,500
SALES (est): 10.92MM Privately Held
Web: www.sierragoldtrees.com
SIC: 0181 Nursery stock, growing of

(P-154)
SIERRA-CASCADE NURSERY INC (PA)
472-715 Johnson Rd (96130-8727)
PHONE..................530 254-6867
Steve Fortin, Pr
Randy Jertberg, *
Robert Murie, *
Robert Akeson, *
▼ EMP: 400 EST: 1975
SQ FT: 2,600
SALES (est): 34.42MM
SALES (corp-wide): 34.42MM Privately Held
Web: www.sierracascadenursery.com
SIC: 0181 Nursery stock, growing of

(P-155)
SILVER TERRACE NURSERIES INC
501 North St (94060)
PHONE..................650 879-2110
Richard Ruggeri, Pr
Robert Ruggeri, *
EMP: 70 EST: 1934
SQ FT: 5,000
SALES (est): 2.16MM Privately Held
SIC: 0181 Florists' greens and flowers

(P-156)
SPEEDLING INCORPORATED
2640 San Juan Hwy (95045-9783)
PHONE..................813 645-3221
EMP: 79
Web: www.speedling.com
SIC: 0181 Bulbs and seeds
HQ: Speedling, Incorporated
4447 Old Us 41 S
Ruskin FL
813 645-3221

(P-157)
SUN VALLEY GROUP INC (PA)
3160 Upper Bay Rd (95521-9690)
PHONE..................707 822-2885
Leendert De Vries, Pr
◆ EMP: 350 EST: 1991
SQ FT: 8,700
SALES (est): 47.47MM Privately Held
Web: www.tsvg.com
SIC: 0181 Flowers: grown under cover (e.g., greenhouse production)

(P-158)
SUPERIOR SOD I LP
17821 17th St Ste 165 (92780-2172)
P.O. Box 1911 (93581-5911)
PHONE..................909 923-5068
Michael Considine, Pt
Richard H Considine, Pt
Peter Moore, Pt
Trudy Considine, Pt
EMP: 125 EST: 1988
SQ FT: 1,400
SALES (est): 4.5MM Privately Held
Web: www.superiorsod.com
SIC: 0181 0782 Sod farms; Lawn and garden services

(P-159)
WESTERLAY ORCHIDS LP
Also Called: Westerlay Orchids
3504 Via Real (93013-3048)
PHONE..................805 684-5411
Antoine Overgaag, Pr
▲ EMP: 117 EST: 2003
SALES (est): 9.94MM Privately Held
Web: www.westerlay.com
SIC: 0181 Flowers: grown under cover (e.g., greenhouse production)

0182 Food Crops Grown Under Cover

(P-160)
CHANNEL ISLNDS VGTBLE FRMS INC (PA)
595 Victoria Ave (93030-4710)
PHONE..................805 984-1910
Steve Nishimori, Pr
Karen Nishimori, *
EMP: 60 EST: 1994
SQ FT: 2,000
SALES (est): 2.48MM
SALES (corp-wide): 2.48MM Privately Held
SIC: 0182 Vegetable crops, grown under cover

(P-161)
GROWERS TRANSPLANTING INC (HQ)
360 Espinosa Rd (93907-8895)
P.O. Box 3756 (93912-3756)
PHONE..................831 449-3440
Charles I Kosmont, CEO
Bill Rover, VP
Kevin Doyle, *
Leslie Surber, CFO
▲ EMP: 83 EST: 1981
SQ FT: 4,000,000
SALES (est): 53.46MM Privately Held
Web: www.growerstrans.com
SIC: 0182 Vegetable crops, grown under cover
PA: Monterey Peninsula Horticulture, Inc.
360 Espinosa Rd
Salinas CA

(P-162)
HOKTO KINOKO COMPANY
130 S Myers St (90033-3212)
PHONE..................323 526-1155
EMP: 94
Web: www.hokto-kinoko.com
SIC: 0182 Mushrooms, grown under cover
HQ: Hokto Kinoko Company
2033 Marilyn Ln
San Marcos CA

(P-163)
HOUWELINGS CAMARILLO INC
645 Laguna Rd (93012-8523)
PHONE..................805 250-1600
Cornelius Houweling, CEO
EMP: 338 EST: 2021
SQ FT: 3,000,000
SALES (est): 520MM Privately Held
Web: www.houwelings.com
SIC: 0182 Food crops grown under cover

(P-164)
MOUNTAIN MEADOW MUSHROOMS INC
26948 N Broadway (92026-8315)
PHONE..................760 749-1201
Bob Crouch, Pr
Elizabeth Crouch, *
Manuel Zuniga, *
Roberto Ramirez, *
EMP: 72 EST: 1982
SQ FT: 110,000
SALES (est): 4.28MM Privately Held
Web: www.mmmushroom.com
SIC: 0182 Mushrooms, grown under cover

PRODUCTS & SERVICES SECTION

0191 - General Farms, Primarily Crop (P-188)

(P-165)
PREMIER MUSHROOMS LP
2847 Niagara Ave (95932)
PHONE..............................530 458-2700
Jose Flores, *Manager*
EMP: 102
Web: www.premiermushrooms.com
SIC: **0182** Mushrooms, grown under cover
PA: Premier Mushrooms, L.P.
2880 Niagara Ave
Colusa CA

0191 General Farms, Primarily Crop

(P-166)
ARNAUDO BROS TRANSPORT INC (PA)
Also Called: Arnaudo Bros Trucking
16505 S Tracy Blvd (95304-9436)
PHONE..............................209 835-0406
Steve Arnaudo, *Pr*
Leo Arnaudo, *
Ed Arnaudo, *
EMP: 65 EST: 1947
SQ FT: 1,200
SALES (est): 5.33MM
SALES (corp-wide): 5.33MM **Privately Held**
SIC: **0191** **4212** General farms, primarily crop ; Local trucking, without storage

(P-167)
AV FENIX LLC
6464 Wood Rd (93041)
P.O. Box 1478 (93011-1478)
PHONE..............................805 279-3457
Alfonso Lopez, *Managing Member*
EMP: 60 EST: 2015
SALES (est): 1.18MM **Privately Held**
SIC: **0191** General farms, primarily crop

(P-168)
BLACKJACK FRMS DE LA CSTA CNTL
Also Called: Black Jack Farms
2385 A St (93455-1073)
PHONE..............................805 347-1333
Jose Garcia, *CEO*
EMP: 140 EST: 2017
SALES (est): 2.31MM **Privately Held**
SIC: **0191** General farms, primarily crop

(P-169)
BRAGA FRESH FAMILY FARMS INC (PA)
33750 Moranda Rd (93960)
P.O. Box 425 (93960-0425)
PHONE..............................831 675-2154
Rodney Braga, *Pr*
EMP: 95 EST: 2013
SQ FT: 10,000
SALES (est): 150MM
SALES (corp-wide): 150MM **Privately Held**
Web: www.bragafresh.com
SIC: **0191** General farms, primarily crop

(P-170)
BRAGA FRESH FAMILY FARMS INC
Also Called: Braga Fresh Imperial
817 W Hackleman Rd (92243-9508)
PHONE..............................760 353-1155
Asa Braga, *Owner*
EMP: 180
SALES (corp-wide): 150MM **Privately Held**
Web: www.bragafresh.com
SIC: **0191** General farms, primarily crop
PA: Braga Fresh Family Farms, Inc.
33750 Moranda Rd
Soledad CA
831 675-2154

(P-171)
CALIFRNIA ARTCHOKE VGTBLE GRWE
Also Called: Ocean Mist Farms
10855 Ocean Mist Pkwy (95012-3235)
PHONE..............................831 633-2144
Edward Boutonnet, *Pr*
Leslie Tottino, *
George Boutonnet, *
Don Reasons, *
Albert Pieri, *
EMP: 60 EST: 1924
SALES (est): 9.63MM **Privately Held**
Web: www.oceanmist.com
SIC: **0191** General farms, primarily crop

(P-172)
CAMPOS FAMILY FARMS LLC
4726 W Jacquelyn Ave (93722-6406)
PHONE..............................559 275-3000
EMP: 60 EST: 2011
SALES (est): 4.82MM **Privately Held**
SIC: **0191** General farms, primarily crop

(P-173)
CRYSTAL ORGANIC FARMS LLC
10000 Stockdale Hwy Ste 200 (93311-3601)
PHONE..............................661 845-5200
Jeff Meger, *Pr*
EMP: 799 EST: 2003
SALES (est): 1.67MM
SALES (corp-wide): 1.86B **Privately Held**
SIC: **0191** General farms, primarily crop
PA: Grimmway Enterprises, Inc.
14141 Di Giorgio Rd
Arvin CA
800 301-3101

(P-174)
DAN R COSTA INCORPORATED
17239 Louise Ave (95320-8732)
PHONE..............................209 234-2004
Dan R Costa, *Pr*
Shirley Costa, *
EMP: 250 EST: 1983
SALES (est): 4.64MM **Privately Held**
Web: dfd.dannysfalldecor.com
SIC: **0191** **0115** **0723** General farms, primarily crop; Corn; Vegetable packing services

(P-175)
DICK ANDERSON & SONS FARMING
Also Called: Vasto Valle Farms
15900 W Dorris Ave (93234)
P.O. Box 10 (93234-0010)
PHONE..............................559 945-2511
Richard Anderson, *Pr*
Craig Anderson, *
Robert Anderson, *
EMP: 135 EST: 1968
SQ FT: 1,000
SALES (est): 4.98MM **Privately Held**
SIC: **0191** General farms, primarily crop

(P-176)
DV CUSTOM FARMING LLC
2101 Mettler Frontage Rd E (93307-9649)
PHONE..............................661 858-2888
EMP: 80 EST: 2004
SALES (est): 2.49MM **Privately Held**
SIC: **0191** General farms, primarily crop

(P-177)
EMPRESAS DEL BOSQUE INC
51481 W Shields Ave (93622-9579)
P.O. Box 2455 (93635-2455)
PHONE..............................209 364-6428
Joe L Del Bosque Junior, *Pr*
EMP: 325 EST: 2005
SQ FT: 1,600
SALES (est): 4.47MM **Privately Held**
Web: www.delbosquefarms.com
SIC: **0191** General farms, primarily crop

(P-178)
FARM FRESH TO YOU LLC (PA)
Also Called: Capay Organic
3880 Seaport Blvd (95691-3449)
P.O. Box 980610 (95798-0610)
PHONE..............................916 303-7145
Freeman Barsotti, *CEO*
EMP: 180 EST: 1976
SALES (est): 49.04MM
SALES (corp-wide): 49.04MM **Privately Held**
Web: www.farmfreshtoyou.com
SIC: **0191** General farms, primarily crop

(P-179)
GREENHEART FARMS INC
Also Called: Greenheart
902 Zenon Way (93420-5807)
PHONE..............................805 481-2234
Hoy Buell, *CEO*
Henry Katzenstein, *
Leo Wolf, *
▲ EMP: 350 EST: 1979
SQ FT: 225,000
SALES (est): 18.19MM **Privately Held**
Web: www.greenheartfarms.com
SIC: **0191** General farms, primarily crop

(P-180)
GRIMMWAY ENTERPRISES INC
Also Called: Premiere Packing
6301 Zerker Rd (93263-9628)
P.O. Box 81498 (93380-1498)
PHONE..............................661 399-0844
EMP: 89
SALES (corp-wide): 1.86B **Privately Held**
Web: www.grimmway.com
SIC: **0191** **0174** General farms, primarily crop ; Citrus fruits
PA: Grimmway Enterprises, Inc.
14141 Di Giorgio Rd
Arvin CA
800 301-3101

(P-181)
HANSEN RANCHES LLC
7124 Whitley Ave (93212-9669)
P.O. Box 398 (93212-0398)
PHONE..............................559 992-3111
James Hansen, *Pt*
EMP: 60 EST: 1987
SQ FT: 4,000
SALES (est): 5.11MM **Privately Held**
Web: www.hansenranches.com
SIC: **0191** General farms, primarily crop

(P-182)
HARRIS FARMS INC
Harris Ranch Inn & Restaurant
24505 W Dorris Ave (93210-9667)
PHONE..............................559 935-0717
Jonathan Farrington, *Genl Mgr*
EMP: 340
SALES (corp-wide): 46.02MM **Privately Held**
Web: www.harrisranch.com
SIC: **0191** **7011** **5813** **5812** General farms, primarily crop; Hotels and motels; Drinking places; Eating places
PA: Harris Farms, Inc.
29475 Fresno Coalinga Rd
Coalinga CA
559 884-2435

(P-183)
HARRIS FARMS INC (PA)
Also Called: Harris Ranch Beef Co
29475 Fresno Coalinga Rd (93210-9699)
Rural Route 1 Box 400 (93210)
PHONE..............................559 884-2435
EMP: 200 EST: 1938
SALES (est): 46.02MM
SALES (corp-wide): 46.02MM **Privately Held**
Web: www.harrisfarms.com
SIC: **0191** **0211** **2011** **7011** General farms, primarily crop; Beef cattle feedlots; Meat packing plants; Hotels

(P-184)
J MARCHINI & SON INC
12000 Le Grand Rd (95333-9708)
PHONE..............................559 665-2944
EMP: 185
Web: www.jmarchinifarms.com
SIC: **0191** General farms, primarily crop
PA: J. Marchini & Son, Inc.
8736 Minturn Rd
Le Grand CA

(P-185)
JACOBS FARM/DEL CABO INC
Also Called: Jacob's Farm
1751 Coast Rd (95060-5602)
PHONE..............................831 421-9171
Larry Jacobs, *Brnch Mgr*
EMP: 91
SALES (corp-wide): 68.22MM **Privately Held**
Web: www.jacobsfarmdelcabo.com
SIC: **0191** General farms, primarily crop
PA: Jacobs Farm/Del Cabo, Inc.
2450 Stage Rd
Pescadero CA
650 879-0580

(P-186)
JACOBS FARM/DEL CABO INC
390 Swift Ave Ste 8 (94080-6221)
PHONE..............................650 827-1133
Ted Witt, *Mgr*
EMP: 91
SALES (corp-wide): 68.22MM **Privately Held**
Web: www.jacobsfarmdelcabo.com
SIC: **0191** General farms, primarily crop
PA: Jacobs Farm/Del Cabo, Inc.
2450 Stage Rd
Pescadero CA
650 879-0580

(P-187)
JOE HEGER FARMS LLC
1625 Drew Rd (92243-9584)
PHONE..............................760 353-5111
EMP: 150 EST: 1999
SALES (est): 4.85MM **Privately Held**
SIC: **0191** General farms, primarily crop

(P-188)
KIRSCHENMAN ENTERPRISES INC
10100 Digiorgio Rd (93307)
PHONE..............................661 366-5736
Wayne Kirschenman, *CEO*

0191 - General Farms, Primarily Crop (P-189)

▼ EMP: 60 EST: 1963
SQ FT: 25,000
SALES (est): 10.26MM Privately Held
Web: www.kirschenman.com
SIC: 0191 General farms, primarily crop

(P-189)
LAKESIDE ORGANIC GARDENS LLC (PA)
25 Sakata Ln (95076-5132)
PHONE..................831 722-6266
Richard Peixoto, Managing Member
EMP: 335 EST: 2000
SALES (est): 37.24MM
SALES (corp-wide): 37.24MM Privately Held
Web: www.lakesideorganic.com
SIC: 0191 General farms, primarily crop

(P-190)
LION RAISINS INC
Also Called: Lion Brothers Farms-Newstone
12555 Road 9 (93637-9089)
P.O. Box 1350 (93662-1350)
PHONE..................559 662-8686
Jeff Bergeron, Mgr
EMP: 180
SALES (corp-wide): 52.72MM Privately Held
Web: www.lionraisins.com
SIC: 0191 General farms, primarily crop
PA: Lion Raisins, Inc.
    9500 S De Wolf Ave
    Selma CA
    559 834-6677

(P-191)
MURANAKA FARM
11018 W Los Angeles Ave (93021-9744)
P.O. Box 189 (93020-0189)
PHONE..................805 529-0201
EMP: 237
SALES (corp-wide): 26.4MM Privately Held
Web: www.muranakafarm.com
SIC: 0191 General farms, primarily crop
PA: Muranaka Farm
    11018 E Los Angeles Ave
    Moorpark CA
    805 529-0201

(P-192)
OLAM FARMING INC
205 E River Park Cir Ste 310 (93720)
PHONE..................559 446-6446
Leon Anthony, Prin
◆ EMP: 449 EST: 2009
SALES (est): 4.32MM
SALES (corp-wide): 463.76MM Privately Held
SIC: 0191 General farms, primarily crop
HQ: Olam Americas, Llc
    205 E River Park Cir # 310
    Fresno CA
    559 447-1390

(P-193)
PAPPAS & CO INC
181 Naples St (93640-2030)
P.O. Box 477 (93640-0477)
PHONE..................559 233-1203
EMP: 120
SIC: 0191 0723 7359 General farms, primarily crop; Fruit (fresh) packing services; Equipment rental and leasing, nec

(P-194)
PLENTY UNLIMITED INC (PA)
570 Eccles Ave (94080-1905)
PHONE..................650 735-3737
Matt Barnard, CEO
Nate Storey, CSO
Nick Kalajian, Sr VP
Mike Gupta, CFO
Kurt Kelty, COO
EMP: 73 EST: 2014
SQ FT: 200,000
SALES (est): 47.63MM
SALES (corp-wide): 47.63MM Privately Held
Web: www.plenty.ag
SIC: 0191 2099 General farms, primarily crop; Salads, fresh or refrigerated

(P-195)
RANCHO LAGUNA FARMS LLC
2410 W Main St (93458-9712)
P.O. Box 6617 (93456-6617)
PHONE..................805 925-7805
Larry Ferini, Managing Member
Tracy Ferini, *
EMP: 100 EST: 1996
SALES (est): 9.82MM Privately Held
Web: www.lagunaproduce.com
SIC: 0191 General farms, primarily crop

(P-196)
RED BLOSSOM SALES INC
Also Called: Red Blossom Farms
9 Harris Pl (93901-4563)
PHONE..................831 751-9169
Michelle Huber, Mgr
EMP: 429
Web: www.redblossom.com
SIC: 0191 General farms, primarily crop
PA: Red Blossom Sales, Inc.
    400 W Ventura Blvd # 140
    Camarillo CA

(P-197)
SAN DIEGO FARMS LLC
Also Called: Fresh Origins
570 Quarry Rd (92069-9744)
PHONE..................760 736-4072
Norma St Amant, CEO
Carlos Pancardo, *
EMP: 177 EST: 1996
SALES (est): 17.43MM Privately Held
Web: www.freshorigins.com
SIC: 0191 General farms, primarily crop

(P-198)
SCALIA FARMS
1001 N Demaree St (93291)
PHONE..................559 651-2711
EMP: 79
SALES (corp-wide): 908.39K Privately Held
SIC: 0191 General farms, primarily crop
PA: Scalia Farms
    1440 N Shirk Rd
    Visalia CA
    559 651-2711

(P-199)
SCARBOROUGH FARMS INC
731 Pacific Ave (93030-7322)
P.O. Box 1267 (93032-1267)
PHONE..................805 483-9113
Ann Stein, Pr
Wayne G Jansen, *
Ann Stein, VP
EMP: 150 EST: 1986
SALES (est): 9.21MM Privately Held
Web: www.scarboroughfarms.com
SIC: 0191 General farms, primarily crop

(P-200)
TELLES RANCH INC
44328 W Nees Ave (93622-9647)
P.O. Box 35 (93622-0035)
PHONE..................209 364-6262
Frank R Telles, Pr
Richard C Telles, *
Mona Jo Telles, Dir
EMP: 150 EST: 1930
SQ FT: 5,000
SALES (est): 3.6MM Privately Held
SIC: 0191 General farms, primarily crop

(P-201)
TOOR FARMING LLC
27725 Road 92 (93277-9481)
PHONE..................559 500-1331
Santokh Toor, Managing Member
Arpinder Toor, *
Bitta Toor, *
▲ EMP: 70 EST: 2001
SALES (est): 6.07MM Privately Held
SIC: 0191 General farms, primarily crop

(P-202)
TRAVIS JAMES WATTS
646 Willowgreen Cir (95632-3314)
PHONE..................209 810-6159
Travis James Watts, Owner
EMP: 200 EST: 2013
SALES (est): 2.94MM Privately Held
SIC: 0191 General farms, primarily crop

(P-203)
TREESAP FARMS LLC
Also Called: Everde Growers
2500 Rainbow Valley Blvd (92028-9778)
PHONE..................760 990-7770
Jonathan Saperstein, Brnch Mgr
EMP: 166
SALES (corp-wide): 121.71MM Privately Held
Web: www.everde.com
SIC: 0191 General farms, primarily crop
PA: Treesap Farms, Llc
    5151 Mitchelldale St B2
    Houston TX
    713 613-5600

(P-204)
UNILEVER UNITED STATES INC
1400 Waterloo Rd (95205-3743)
PHONE..................209 466-9580
EMP: 489
SALES (corp-wide): 62.39B Privately Held
Web: www.unileverusa.com
SIC: 0191 General farms, primarily crop
HQ: Unilever United States, Inc.
    800 Sylvan Ave
    Englewood Cliffs NJ
    201 735-9661

(P-205)
VAN GRONINGEN & SONS INC (PA)
15100 Jack Tone Rd (95336-9729)
PHONE..................209 982-5248
Robert Van Groningen, Pr
Dan Vangroningen, *
Monica Kuil, *
▼ EMP: 359 EST: 1971
SQ FT: 3,000
SALES (est): 48.94MM
SALES (corp-wide): 48.94MM Privately Held
Web: www.vgandsons.com
SIC: 0191 0762 General farms, primarily crop; Farm management services

(P-206)
VAQUERO FARMS INC
43405 W Panoche Rd (93622-9720)
PHONE..................559 659-2790
Havier Rodriguez, Mgr
EMP: 60
SQ FT: 150
SALES (corp-wide): 5.57MM Privately Held
SIC: 0191 General farms, primarily crop
PA: Vaquero Farms, Inc.
    24591 Silver Cloud Ct # 100
    Monterey CA
    209 476-0002

(P-207)
VINO FARMS INC
51375 S Netherlands Rd (95612-5019)
PHONE..................916 775-4095
John Ledbetter, Owner
EMP: 122
SALES (corp-wide): 46.59MM Privately Held
Web: www.vinofarms.com
SIC: 0191 General farms, primarily crop
PA: Vino Farms, Inc.
    1377 E Lodi Ave
    Lodi CA
    209 334-6975

(P-208)
WOOLF FARMING CO CAL INC
Also Called: Lansing Farming Co
7041 N Van Ness Blvd (93711-7169)
P.O. Box 219 (93234-0219)
PHONE..................559 945-9292
Stuart P Woolf, Pr
John L Woolf Iii, Ch
Bernice Woolf, *
Anne A Delaware, *
Michael T Woolf, *
EMP: 624 EST: 1974
SQ FT: 4,500
SALES (est): 21.67MM Privately Held
Web: www.woolffarming.com
SIC: 0191 General farms, primarily crop

0211 Beef Cattle Feedlots

(P-209)
COALINGA FEED YARD INC
35244 Oil City Rd (93210-9221)
P.O. Box 835 (93210-0835)
PHONE..................559 935-0836
James Anderson, Pr
Leland Haun, Sec
Christine Fisher, Stockholder
EMP: 60 EST: 1960
SQ FT: 1,000
SALES (est): 1.83MM Privately Held
SIC: 0211 Beef cattle feedlots

0212 Beef Cattle, Except Feedlots

(P-210)
CALFTECH CORPORATION
13939 Rd L52 (93272)
PHONE..................559 752-2302
▲ EMP: 85 EST: 1985
SALES (est): 2.48MM Privately Held
SIC: 0212 Beef cattle, except feedlots

(P-211)
J G BOSWELL COMPANY
26073 Santa Fe Ave (93212)
P.O. Box 877 (93212-0877)
PHONE..................559 992-5011
Mark Grewal, VP
EMP: 427
SALES (corp-wide): 370.2MM Privately Held

Web: www.eastlakeco.com
SIC: 0212 Beef cattle, except feedlots
PA: J. G. Boswell Company
101 W Walnut St
Pasadena CA
626 583-3000

0213 Hogs

(P-212)
LINDA TERRA FARMS (PA)
5494 W Mount Whitney Ave (93656-9329)
P.O. Box 758 (93656-0758)
PHONE..................559 867-3473
John Coelho, CEO
EMP: 170 EST: 1974
SQ FT: 1,014
SALES (est): 21.5MM
SALES (corp-wide): 21.5MM Privately Held
Web: www.pickapig.com
SIC: 0213 0182 0172 Hogs; Fruits, grown under cover; Grapes

0241 Dairy Farms

(P-213)
ALTA-DENA CERTIFIED DAIRY LLC (DH)
17637 E Valley Blvd (91744-5731)
PHONE..................626 964-6401
Jack Tewers, *
Steve Schaffer, *
Bob Pettigrew, *
EMP: 370 EST: 1945
SQ FT: 100,000
SALES (est): 49.72MM Privately Held
SIC: 0241 Dairy farms
HQ: Dean West Ii, Llc
2515 Mckinney Ave # 1100
Dallas TX

(P-214)
BOSMAN DAIRY LLC
6802 Avenue 120 # A (93272-9525)
PHONE..................559 752-7018
Clarence Bosman, Pt
Frank Bosman, Pt
EMP: 130 EST: 1959
SALES (est): 4.91MM Privately Held
SIC: 0241 Dairy farms

(P-215)
DOUBLE DIAMOND DAIRY & RANCH
729 E Jefferson Rd (95317-9707)
PHONE..................209 722-8505
Wendy Vander Dussen, Pt
Michael Vander Dussen, Pt
EMP: 90 EST: 1999
SALES (est): 3.38MM Privately Held
SIC: 0241 Dairy farms

(P-216)
HIGH PLAINS RANCH LLC (PA)
2911 Hanford Armona Rd (93230-9379)
PHONE..................559 583-1277
Bernard Te Velde, Managing Member
EMP: 120 EST: 2014
SQ FT: 2,000
SALES (est): 9.33MM
SALES (corp-wide): 9.33MM Privately Held
SIC: 0241 Dairy farms

(P-217)
HOLLANDIA DAIRY INC (PA)
622 E Mission Rd (92069-1999)
PHONE..................760 744-3222
TOLL FREE: 800
Peter De Jong, CEO
Patrick Schallberger, *
Arie H Dejong, *
EMP: 185 EST: 1950
SQ FT: 20,000
SALES (est): 44.68MM
SALES (corp-wide): 44.68MM Privately Held
Web: www.hollandiadairy.com
SIC: 0241 Milk production

(P-218)
IEST FAMILY FARMS
Also Called: Richard Iest Dairy
14576 Avenue 14 (93637-8922)
PHONE..................559 674-9417
Richard Iest, Pt
Gerrlyn Iest, *
Danny Iest, *
EMP: 70 EST: 1978
SALES (est): 9.07MM Privately Held
SIC: 0241 Dairy farms

(P-219)
MADDOX DAIRY LLC
12863 W Kamm Ave Spc 2 (93656-9761)
PHONE..................559 866-5308
Stephen Maddox, Managing Member
Stephen Maddox, Managing Member
Julia Maddox Chow, *
EMP: 65 EST: 2015
SALES (est): 4.39MM Privately Held
Web: www.ruanngenetics.com
SIC: 0241 Milk production

(P-220)
MADDOX DAIRY A LTD PARTNERSHIP (PA)
12863 W Kamm Ave Spc 2 (93656-9761)
PHONE..................559 867-3545
Steven Maddox, Pt
Douglas Maddox, Pt
Patrick Maddox, Pt
EMP: 60 EST: 1981
SALES (est): 1.85MM
SALES (corp-wide): 1.85MM Privately Held
SIC: 0241 Milk production

(P-221)
MAPLE DAIRY LP
Also Called: Maple Dairy
15857 Bear Mountain Blvd (93311-9413)
PHONE..................661 396-9600
John Bos, Pt
A J Bos, Pt
EMP: 75 EST: 1998
SALES (est): 15.59MM Privately Held
Web: www.makinmilk.com
SIC: 0241 Dairy farms

(P-222)
VALLEY MILK LLC
400 N Washington Rd (95380-9550)
PHONE..................209 410-6701
Donald A Machado, Managing Member
▼ EMP: 65 EST: 2016
SALES (est): 5.55MM Privately Held
Web: www.valleymilkca.com
SIC: 0241 2026 Milk production; Fluid milk

(P-223)
WITHROW CATTLE
Also Called: Withrow Dairy
5301 Pleasant Grove Rd (95668-9752)
PHONE..................916 780-0364
Shane Johnson, Mgr
EMP: 65
SALES (corp-wide): 2.35MM Privately Held
SIC: 0241 Dairy farms
PA: Withrow Cattle
5301 Pleasant Grove Rd
Pleasant Grove CA
916 780-0364

0252 Chicken Eggs

(P-224)
DEMLER BROTHERS LLC
25818 Highway 78 (92065-6309)
PHONE..................760 789-2457
EMP: 99 EST: 2016
SALES (est): 2.56MM Privately Held
SIC: 0252 Chicken eggs

(P-225)
FOSTER FARMS LLC (HQ)
1000 Davis St (95334-1526)
P.O. Box 457 (95334-0457)
PHONE..................209 394-7901
EMP: 90 EST: 2000
SALES (est): 488.82MM
SALES (corp-wide): 8.23B Privately Held
Web: www.fosterfarms.com
SIC: 0252 2015 Chicken eggs; Poultry slaughtering and processing
PA: Atlas Holdings, Llc
100 Northfield St
Greenwich CT
203 622-9138

(P-226)
GEMPERLE ENTERPRISES
Also Called: Gemperle Farms
10218 Lander Ave (95380-9627)
PHONE..................209 667-2651
Steve Gemperle, Managing Member
◆ EMP: 90 EST: 1952
SQ FT: 8,000
SALES (est): 16.21MM Privately Held
Web: www.gemperle.com
SIC: 0252 5144 2015 Chicken eggs; Eggs; Egg processing

0253 Turkeys And Turkey Eggs

(P-227)
DIESTEL TURKEY RANCH (PA)
Also Called: Distel Family Ranch
22200 Lyons Bald Mountain Rd (95370-8772)
P.O. Box 4314 (95370-1314)
PHONE..................209 532-4950
Timothy Diestel, CEO
Joan Diestel, *
David Harmer, *
Jason Diestel, *
Heidi Diestel, *
EMP: 125 EST: 1949
SQ FT: 5,000
SALES (est): 23.58MM
SALES (corp-wide): 23.58MM Privately Held
Web: www.diestelturkey.com
SIC: 0253 Turkey farm

(P-228)
FOSTER TURKEY PRODUCTS
1000 Davis St (95334-1526)
P.O. Box 457 (95334-0457)
PHONE..................209 394-7901
Ron Foster, Pr
Thomas Foster, *
George Foster, *
Norma Foster Madig, *
EMP: 409 EST: 1982
SALES (est): 823.97K
SALES (corp-wide): 1.25B Privately Held
SIC: 0253 Turkeys and turkey eggs
PA: Foster Poultry Farms, Llc
1000 Davis St
Livingston CA
209 394-7901

0254 Poultry Hatcheries

(P-229)
FOSTER POULTRY FARMS LLC
834 Davis St (95334)
P.O. Box 457 (95334-0457)
PHONE..................209 394-7901
Chris Carter, Brnch Mgr
EMP: 322
SALES (corp-wide): 1.25B Privately Held
Web: www.fosters.com
SIC: 0254 2015 Poultry hatcheries; Poultry, processed, nsk
PA: Foster Poultry Farms, Llc
1000 Davis St
Livingston CA
209 394-7901

0259 Poultry And Eggs, Nec

(P-230)
REICHARDT DUCK FARM INC
3770 Middle Two Rock Rd (94952-4625)
PHONE..................707 762-6314
John T Reichardt, Pr
Kathy Shaw, *
▼ EMP: 95 EST: 1901
SQ FT: 1,296
SALES (est): 1.94MM Privately Held
Web: www.reichardtduckfarm.com
SIC: 0259 Duck farm

0279 Animal Specialties, Nec

(P-231)
OLIVAREZ HONEY BEES INC
6398 County Road 20 (95963-9475)
P.O. Box 847 (95963-0847)
PHONE..................530 865-0298
Ray A Olivarez Junior, CEO
EMP: 97 EST: 2002
SALES (est): 9.09MM Privately Held
Web: www.ohbees.com
SIC: 0279 2099 Apiary (bee and honey farm); Almond pastes

0291 General Farms, Primarily Animals

(P-232)
BAJA FRESH SUPERMARKET
Also Called: Monrovia Ranch Market
14827 Seventh St (92395-4023)
P.O. Box 661912 (91066-1912)
PHONE..................760 843-7730
EMP: 330
SIC: 0291 General farms, primarily animals
PA: E & T Foods, Inc.
328 W Huntington Dr
Monrovia CA

0291 - General Farms, Primarily Animals (P-233)

(P-233)
BARTON RANCH INC
Also Called: R.P. Barton Ranch
22398 Mcbride Rd (95320-9637)
PHONE....................209 838-8930
Gerald L Barton, *Pr*
Gary Barton, *
Brent Barton, *
Donald Barton, *
EMP: 100 **EST:** 1979
SQ FT: 1,800
SALES (est): 2.34MM **Privately Held**
Web: www.goldriverorchards.com
SIC: 0291 General farms, primarily animals

(P-234)
BOOTH RANCHES LLC
440 Anchor Ave (93646-2200)
PHONE....................559 626-4472
Otis Booth Junior, *Brnch Mgr*
EMP: 79
SALES (corp-wide): 26.17MM **Privately Held**
Web: www.boothranches.com
SIC: 0291 General farms, primarily animals
PA: Booth Ranches Llc
12201 Avenue 480
Orange Cove CA
559 626-4732

(P-235)
HAMMONDS RANCH INC
47375 W Dakota Ave (93622-9516)
PHONE....................209 364-6185
James M Hammonds, *Pr*
William E Hammond, *
Mary Hicks, *
EMP: 100 **EST:** 1929
SQ FT: 3,500
SALES (est): 8.91MM **Privately Held**
SIC: 0291 General farms, primarily animals

(P-236)
NORCO RANCH INC (DH)
720 S Stockton Ave (95366-2790)
P.O. Box 910 (92860-0917)
PHONE....................951 737-6735
Ric Sundal, *CEO*
EMP: 350 **EST:** 1951
SALES (est): 21.89MM
SALES (corp-wide): 2.89B **Privately Held**
SIC: 0291 General farms, primarily animals
HQ: Moark, Llc
28 Under The Mountain Rd
North Franklin CT
951 332-3300

(P-237)
R RANCH MARKET
1112 Walnut Ave (92780-5607)
PHONE....................714 573-1182
Jubira Martinez, *Owner*
EMP: 148 **EST:** 2011
SALES: 500.65K
SALES (corp-wide): 56.64MM **Privately Held**
Web: www.rranchmarkets.com
SIC: 0291 General farms, primarily animals
PA: R-Ranch Market, Incorporated
13985 Live Oak Ave
Irwindale CA
626 814-2900

(P-238)
SCHOOLSFIRST FEDERAL CREDIT UN
10910 Foothill Blvd Ste 100 (91730)
PHONE....................800 462-8328
EMP: 64
SALES (corp-wide): 335.16MM **Privately Held**
Web: www.schoolsfirstfcu.org
SIC: 0291 General farms, primarily animals
PA: Schoolsfirst Federal Credit Union
2115 N Broadway
Santa Ana CA
714 258-4000

(P-239)
SHARP HEALTHCARE
Also Called: Sharp Rees-Stealy Med Group
1400 E Palomar St (91913-1800)
PHONE....................619 397-3088
Donna Mills, *CEO*
EMP: 76
SALES (corp-wide): 2.37B **Privately Held**
Web: www.sharp.com
SIC: 0291 General farms, primarily animals
PA: Sharp Healthcare
8695 Spectrum Center Blvd
San Diego CA
858 499-4000

0711 Soil Preparation Services

(P-240)
AC IRRIGATION HOLDCO LLC
10000 Stockdale Hwy # 100 (93311-3602)
PHONE....................661 368-3550
Derek Yurosek, *Managing Member*
Jonathan Thomas, *CEO*
EMP: 163 **EST:** 2018
SALES (est): 2.95MM **Privately Held**
SIC: 0711 Soil preparation services

0721 Crop Planting And Protection

(P-241)
CALIFORNIA VALLEY LAND CO INC (PA)
Also Called: Woolf Enterprises
18036 Gale (93234)
P.O. Box 219 (93234-0219)
PHONE....................559 945-9292
Stuart P Woolf, *Pr*
John L Woolf, *
Michael T Woolf, *
EMP: 93 **EST:** 1960
SQ FT: 4,500
SALES (est): 18.84MM
SALES (corp-wide): 18.84MM **Privately Held**
SIC: 0721 Planting services

(P-242)
OAKRIDGE LANDSCAPE INC (PA)
28042 Avenue Stanford Unit E (91355-1105)
PHONE....................661 295-7228
Jeffrey E Myers, *CEO*
EMP: 63 **EST:** 2001
SALES: 29.39MM
SALES (corp-wide): 29.39MM **Privately Held**
Web: www.oakridgelandscape.net
SIC: 0721 0781 Irrigation system operation, not providing water; Landscape services

(P-243)
S & S RANCH INC
Also Called: Stamoules Produce Company
904 S Lyon Ave (93640-9735)
PHONE....................559 655-3491
Pagona Stefanopoulos, *CEO*
Athanasios Stefanopoulos, *
▼ **EMP:** 85 **EST:** 1925
SQ FT: 500
SALES (est): 8.12MM **Privately Held**
Web: www.stamoules.com
SIC: 0721 Planting services

(P-244)
SEAMAN NURSERIES INC
336 Robertson Blvd Ste A (93610-2867)
PHONE....................559 665-1860
William Seaman, *Pr*
EMP: 70 **EST:** 1980
SALES (est): 3.94MM **Privately Held**
SIC: 0721 0762 5261 Orchard tree and vine services; Farm management services; Retail nurseries

(P-245)
SUNRIDGE NURSERIES INC
441 Vineland Rd (93307-9556)
PHONE....................661 363-8463
Craig Stoller, *CEO*
Glen Stoller, *
Terrie Stoller, *
EMP: 70 **EST:** 1977
SQ FT: 60,000
SALES (est): 13.44MM **Privately Held**
Web: www.sunridgenurseries.com
SIC: 0721 Vines, cultivation of

0722 Crop Harvesting

(P-246)
BOSQUE JOE L DEL JR
51481 W Shields Ave (93622-9579)
P.O. Box 2455 (93635-2455)
PHONE....................209 364-6428
Joe D Bosque Junior, *Owner*
EMP: 325 **EST:** 1985
SALES (est): 3.31MM **Privately Held**
Web: www.delbosquefarms.com
SIC: 0722 Crop harvesting

(P-247)
BOSWELL PROPERTIES INC
101 W Walnut St (91103-3636)
PHONE....................626 583-3000
Curt Rowe, *Pr*
Melvin L Eltiste, *
Joseph A Morris, *
Sherm Railsback, *
EMP: 427 **EST:** 1982
SALES: 478.81K
SALES (corp-wide): 370.2MM **Privately Held**
Web: www.tulago.com
SIC: 0722 6552 Cotton, machine harvesting services; Subdividers and developers, nec
PA: J. G. Boswell Company
101 W Walnut St
Pasadena CA
626 583-3000

(P-248)
DANELL BROS INC
Also Called: Hanford Truck Repair & Parts
8265 Hanford Armona Rd (93230-9344)
PHONE....................559 582-1251
Danny Danell, *Pr*
Mike Danell, *
Marigail Danell, *
▲ **EMP:** 80 **EST:** 1970
SQ FT: 3,000
SALES (est): 4.51MM **Privately Held**
Web: www.danellcustomharvesting.com
SIC: 0722 0241 Crop harvesting; Dairy heifer replacement farm

(P-249)
DANELL CUSTOM HARVESTING LLC
8265 Hanford Armona Rd (93230-9344)
PHONE....................559 582-1251
EMP: 150 **EST:** 2010
SALES (est): 4.45MM **Privately Held**
Web: www.danellcustomharvesting.com
SIC: 0722 Crop harvesting

(P-250)
I S A CONTRACTING SVCS INC
958 O St (93622-2221)
PHONE....................559 659-1080
Ileana Arvizu, *Pr*
EMP: 600 **EST:** 2006
SQ FT: 5,000
SALES (est): 8.54MM **Privately Held**
SIC: 0722 Crop harvesting

(P-251)
NEW HOPE HARVESTING LLC
918 Nita Ct (93454-3122)
PHONE....................805 478-4469
Guadalupe Gaspar, *Prin*
Eugenia Martinez, *
EMP: 60 **EST:** 2015
SALES (est): 4MM **Privately Held**
SIC: 0722 Crop harvesting

(P-252)
NOBLESSE OBLIGE INC
Also Called: Eight Star Equipment
2015 Silsbee Rd (92243-9671)
PHONE....................760 353-3336
Alex Abatti Junior, *Pr*
David Wells, *
Sid Swarthout, *
EMP: 250 **EST:** 1985
SALES (est): 1.79MM **Privately Held**
Web: www.abatti.com
SIC: 0722 Combining services

0723 Crop Preparation Services For Market

(P-253)
ALLIED AVOCADOS & CITRUS INC
1203 S Sespe St (93015-9767)
PHONE....................805 625-7155
Brayen Guzman, *Pr*
Lupe Guzman, *
EMP: 60 **EST:** 2015
SALES (est): 28MM **Privately Held**
Web: www.alliedfruits.com
SIC: 0723 Fruit (farm-dried) packing services

(P-254)
ANDERSEN & SONS SHELLING INC
Also Called: Andersen
4530 Rowles Rd (96092)
P.O. Box 100 (96092-0100)
PHONE....................530 839-2236
Patrick Knudt Andersen, *Pr*
Michael Andersen, *
Franklin Andersen, *
◆ **EMP:** 100 **EST:** 2003
SALES (est): 25.19MM **Privately Held**
Web: www.andersenshelling.com
SIC: 0723 0762 Walnut hulling and shelling services; Farm management services

(P-255)
APEEL TECHNOLOGY INC (PA)
Also Called: Apeel Sciences

PRODUCTS & SERVICES SECTION

0723 - Crop Preparation Services For Market (P-276)

71 S Los Carneros Rd (93117-5506)
PHONE...............................805 203-0146
James Rogers, *CEO*
William Strong, *CFO*
EMP: 283 **EST:** 2012
SALES (est): 48.97MM
SALES (corp-wide): 48.97MM **Privately Held**
Web: www.apeel.com
SIC: 0723 2099 Crop preparation services for market; Almond pastes

(P-256)
BEE SWEET CITRUS INC
Also Called: Cvp Southern Properties
416 E South Ave (93625-2813)
PHONE...............................559 834-5345
◆ **EMP:** 250 **EST:** 1988
SALES (est): 29.02MM **Privately Held**
Web: www.beesweetcitrus.com
SIC: 0723 4731 Fruit (fresh) packing services ; Brokers, shipping

(P-257)
BLUE DIAMOND GROWERS
10840 E Mckinley Ave (93657-9480)
PHONE...............................559 251-4044
EMP: 92
SALES (corp-wide): 652.87MM **Privately Held**
Web: www.bluediamond.com
SIC: 0723 Crop preparation services for market
PA: Diamond Blue Growers
    1802 C St
    Sacramento CA
    800 987-2329

(P-258)
BLUE DIAMOND GROWERS
4800 Sisk Rd (95356-8730)
PHONE...............................209 545-6221
Bruce Mickelson, *Mgr*
EMP: 200
SALES (corp-wide): 652.87MM **Privately Held**
Web: www.bluediamondstore.com
SIC: 0723 2068 Almond hulling and shelling services; Nuts: dried, dehydrated, salted or roasted
PA: Diamond Blue Growers
    1802 C St
    Sacramento CA
    800 987-2329

(P-259)
BOSKOVICH FARMS INC (PA)
711 Diaz Ave (93030-7247)
P.O. Box 1352 (93032-1352)
PHONE...............................805 487-2299
George S Boskovich Junior, *CEO*
Philip J Boskovich Junior, *Pr*
▲ **EMP:** 205 **EST:** 1915
SQ FT: 7,000
SALES (est): 93.16MM
SALES (corp-wide): 93.16MM **Privately Held**
Web: www.boskovichfarms.com
SIC: 0723 5812 0161 Crop preparation services for market; Eating places; Rooted vegetable farms

(P-260)
CAL TREEHOUSE ALMONDS LLC
2115 Road 144 (93215-9524)
P.O. Box 286 (93216-0286)
PHONE...............................661 725-6334
Robert Houston, *Pr*
EMP: 122

SQ FT: 68,803
SALES (corp-wide): 18.64MM **Privately Held**
Web: www.treehousealmonds.com
SIC: 0723 Crop preparation services for market
PA: Treehouse California Almonds Llc
    6914 Road 160
    Earlimart CA
    559 757-5020

(P-261)
CENTRAL VALLEY AG TRNSPT LLC
Also Called: Central Valley AG Trnspt Inc
5509 Langworth Rd (95361-7909)
PHONE...............................209 544-9246
Michael Barry, *Pr*
Paul Konzen, *
Ryan Hogan, *
EMP: 93 **EST:** 2007
SALES (est): 4.5MM
SALES (corp-wide): 20.98MM **Privately Held**
Web: www.cv-ag.com
SIC: 0723 1629 Field crops, except cash grains, market preparation services; Railroad and railway roadbed construction
PA: Central Valley Ag Grinding, Llc
    5509 Langworth Rd
    Oakdale CA
    209 869-1721

(P-262)
CORONA - CLLEGE HTS ORNGE LMON
8000 Lincoln Ave (92504-4343)
PHONE...............................951 359-6451
John Demshki, *Pr*
▼ **EMP:** 300 **EST:** 1905
SQ FT: 180,000
SALES (est): 20.93MM **Privately Held**
Web: www.cchcitrus.com
SIC: 0723 Fruit (fresh) packing services

(P-263)
EARTHBOUND FARM LLC (PA)
Also Called: Taylor Farms
1721 San Juan Hwy (95045-9780)
PHONE...............................831 623-7880
◆ **EMP:** 995 **EST:** 1988
SQ FT: 15,000
SALES (est): 44.81MM **Privately Held**
Web: www.earthboundfarm.com
SIC: 0723 2037 2099 Vegetable packing services; Frozen fruits and vegetables; Food preparations, nec

(P-264)
EXETER ENGINEERING INC
Also Called: TTI Technologies
109 W Pine St (93221-1612)
P.O. Box 457 (93221-0457)
PHONE...............................559 592-3161
Jeffrey Batchman, *CEO*
▲ **EMP:** 70 **EST:** 1978
SQ FT: 20,000
SALES (est): 11.68MM **Privately Held**
Web: www.exeterengineering.com
SIC: 0723 Vegetable sorting services

(P-265)
EXETER PACKERS INC (PA)
Also Called: Sun Pacific Packers
1250 E Myer Ave (93221-9345)
P.O. Box 217 (93221-0217)
PHONE...............................559 592-5168
Berne Evans Iii, *CEO*
Robert Reniers, *
Ernie Larsen, *

◆ **EMP:** 230 **EST:** 1975
SQ FT: 70,000
SALES (est): 41.55MM
SALES (corp-wide): 41.55MM **Privately Held**
Web: www.sunpacific.com
SIC: 0723 Fruit (fresh) packing services

(P-266)
EXETER PACKERS INC
Also Called: Euclid Parking
23744 Avenue 181 (93257-9579)
PHONE...............................559 784-8820
EMP: 118
SALES (corp-wide): 41.55MM **Privately Held**
Web: www.sunpacific.com
SIC: 0723 Fruit (fresh) packing services
PA: Exeter Packers, Inc.
    1250 E Myer Ave
    Exeter CA
    559 592-5168

(P-267)
EXETER-IVANHOE CITRUS ASSN
Also Called: Ivanhoe
901 Rocky Hill Dr (93221-1322)
PHONE...............................559 592-3141
Kevin Riddle, *Pr*
Terry Orr, *Genl Mgr*
EMP: 75 **EST:** 1925
SQ FT: 30,000
SALES (est): 4.9MM **Privately Held**
Web: www.exetercitrus.com
SIC: 0723 Fruit (fresh) packing services

(P-268)
FISHER RANCH LLC
10610 Ice Plant Rd (92225-2757)
PHONE...............................760 922-4151
EMP: 99 **EST:** 1998
SALES (est): 4.32MM **Privately Held**
Web: www.fisherranch.com
SIC: 0723 Field crops, except cash grains, market preparation services

(P-269)
FOWLER PACKING COMPANY INC (PA)
Also Called: Fowler Packing
8570 S Cedar Ave (93725-8905)
PHONE...............................559 834-5911
Dennis Parnagian, *CEO*
Kenneth Parnagian, *
Randy Parnagian, *
Philip Parnagian, *
◆ **EMP:** 125 **EST:** 1946
SQ FT: 6,300
SALES (est): 59.72MM
SALES (corp-wide): 59.72MM **Privately Held**
Web: www.fowlerpacking.com
SIC: 0723 4783 5148 Fruit (fresh) packing services; Packing and crating; Fresh fruits and vegetables

(P-270)
FRUIT PATCH INC
38773 Road 48 (93618-9718)
PHONE...............................559 591-6140
◆ **EMP:** 500
SIC: 0723 0175 Fruit (fresh) packing services ; Peach orchard

(P-271)
GILLETTE CITRUS INC
10175 S Anchor Ave (93618-9204)
PHONE...............................559 626-4236
Jay Gillette, *Pt*
Dean Gillette, *

Mark Gillette, *
EMP: 60 **EST:** 1983
SQ FT: 14,000
SALES (est): 2.01MM **Privately Held**
Web: www.gillettecitrus.com
SIC: 0723 Fruit (fresh) packing services

(P-272)
GRIMMWAY ENTERPRISES INC
6101 Zerker Rd (93263-9611)
P.O. Box 81498 (93380-1498)
PHONE...............................661 393-3320
Bob Grimm, *Prin*
EMP: 355
SALES (corp-wide): 1.86B **Privately Held**
Web: www.grimmway.com
SIC: 0723 Vegetable packing services
PA: Grimmway Enterprises, Inc.
    14141 Di Giorgio Rd
    Arvin CA
    800 301-3101

(P-273)
GRIMMWAY ENTERPRISES INC
Also Called: Grimmway Frozen Foods
830 Sycamore Rd (93203-2132)
P.O. Box 81498 (93380-1498)
PHONE...............................661 854-6250
Brandon Grimm, *Mgr*
EMP: 355
SALES (corp-wide): 1.86B **Privately Held**
Web: www.grimmway.com
SIC: 0723 Vegetable packing services
PA: Grimmway Enterprises, Inc.
    14141 Di Giorgio Rd
    Arvin CA
    800 301-3101

(P-274)
GRIMMWAY ENTERPRISES INC
Also Called: Grimmway Farms
11412 Malaga Rd (93203-9641)
P.O. Box 81498 (93380-1498)
PHONE...............................661 854-6200
EMP: 1020
SALES (corp-wide): 1.86B **Privately Held**
Web: www.grimmway.com
SIC: 0723 4783 Vegetable packing services; Containerization of goods for shipping
PA: Grimmway Enterprises, Inc.
    14141 Di Giorgio Rd
    Arvin CA
    800 301-3101

(P-275)
GRIMMWAY ENTERPRISES INC
Also Called: Grimmway Farms
6900 Mountain View Rd (93307-9627)
P.O. Box 81498 (93380-1498)
PHONE...............................661 845-5200
Bob Grimm, *Owner*
EMP: 200
SALES (corp-wide): 1.86B **Privately Held**
Web: www.grimmway.com
SIC: 0723 Vegetable packing services
PA: Grimmway Enterprises, Inc.
    14141 Di Giorgio Rd
    Arvin CA
    800 301-3101

(P-276)
GUADALUPE COOLING COMPANY INC
2040 Guadalupe Rd (93434)
PHONE...............................805 343-2331
TOLL FREE: 800
Dan Vincent, *Mgr*
EMP: 73
SALES (corp-wide): 14.03MM **Privately Held**

0723 - Crop Preparation Services For Market (P-277)

Web: www.westernprecooling.com
SIC: 0723 Vacuum cooling
PA: Guadalupe Cooling Company Inc
2040 Guadalupe Rd
Nipomo CA
805 249-3110

(P-277)
HARRIS WOOLF CAL ALMONDS LLC
26060 Colusa Ave (93210-9245)
P.O. Box 49 (95303-0049)
PHONE.................................559 884-2147
Joel Perkins, Managing Member
◆ EMP: 150 EST: 2014
SQ FT: 110,000
SALES (est): 39.46MM Privately Held
Web: www.harriswoolfalmonds.com
SIC: 0723 Tree nut crops market preparation services

(P-278)
HILLTOP RANCH INC
Also Called: Hilltop Trading
13890 Looney Rd (95303-9710)
PHONE.................................209 874-1875
David Harrison Long, CEO
Dave Long Junior, VP
Dexter Long, *
Christine Long, *
Brad Filbrun, *
◆ EMP: 175 EST: 1980
SQ FT: 134,800
SALES (est): 23.98MM Privately Held
Web: www.hilltopranch.com
SIC: 0723 5441 Almond hulling and shelling services; Candy, nut, and confectionery stores

(P-279)
HILLTOWN PACKING CO INC
9 Harris Pl Ste A (93901-4563)
PHONE.................................831 784-1931
Chris Huntington, Pr
Louis Huntington Junior, Sec
Louis Huntington Senior, Stockholder
▼ EMP: 300 EST: 1987
SALES (est): 8.92MM Privately Held
SIC: 0723 Vegetable packing services

(P-280)
ITO PACKING CO INC
1592 11th St Ste H (93654-2939)
P.O. Box 707 (93654-0707)
PHONE.................................559 638-2531
▲ EMP: 200
Web: www.itopack.com
SIC: 0723 Fruit (fresh) packing services

(P-281)
J G BOSWELL COMPANY
Also Called: Processing Office
710 Bainum Ave (93212-9603)
P.O. Box 457 (93212-0457)
PHONE.................................559 992-2141
EMP: 100
SALES (corp-wide): 370.2MM Privately Held
Web: www.eastlakeco.com
SIC: 0723 Crop preparation services for market
PA: J. G. Boswell Company
101 W Walnut St
Pasadena CA
626 583-3000

(P-282)
JLG HARVESTING INC
27 Zabala Rd (93908-7702)
P.O. Box 5205 (85366-2461)
PHONE.................................831 422-7871
Jose Luis Garcia, Pr
EMP: 300
SIC: 0723 Crop preparation services for market
PA: Jlg Harvesting, Inc.
1450 S Atlantic Ave
Yuma AZ

(P-283)
KERN RIDGE GROWERS LLC
25429 Barbara St (93203-9748)
P.O. Box 455 (93203-0455)
PHONE.................................661 854-3141
▼ EMP: 500 EST: 1973
SQ FT: 53,000
SALES (est): 48.27MM Privately Held
Web: www.kernridge.com
SIC: 0723 5148 Vegetable packing services; Vegetables, fresh

(P-284)
KLINK CITRUS ASSOCIATION
Also Called: Klink Citrus Exchange
32921 Road 159 (93235-1455)
P.O. Box 188 (93235-0188)
PHONE.................................559 798-1881
Eric Meling, CEO
EMP: 170 EST: 1917
SQ FT: 50,000
SALES (est): 4.17MM Privately Held
SIC: 0723 Fruit (fresh) packing services

(P-285)
LOBUE BROS INC (PA)
Also Called: Lobue Citrus
201 S Sweetbriar Ave (93247-2422)
PHONE.................................559 562-2548
◆ EMP: 100 EST: 1934
SALES (est): 8.08MM
SALES (corp-wide): 8.08MM Privately Held
Web: www.lobuecitrus.com
SIC: 0723 Fruit (fresh) packing services

(P-286)
MANN PACKING CO INC (DH)
49 Katherine St (93926)
P.O. Box 3006 (93926-3006)
PHONE.................................831 422-5341
Lorri Koster, CEO
Michael Jarrod, *
William Beaton, *
Richard Ramsey, *
EMP: 450 EST: 1939
SQ FT: 90,000
SALES (est): 214.71MM Privately Held
Web: www.veggiesmadeeasy.com
SIC: 0723 4783 0722 Vegetable packing services; Packing and crating; Crop harvesting
HQ: Del Monte Fresh Produce N.A., Inc.
241 Sevilla Ave
Coral Gables FL
305 520-8400

(P-287)
MARIANI PACKING CO INC (PA)
500 Crocker Dr (95688-8706)
PHONE.................................707 452-2800
Mark A Mariani, CEO
George Sousa Junior, Pr
Marian Ciabattari, *
George Sousa Senior, VP
Paul Mariani, *
◆ EMP: 275 EST: 1982
SALES (est): 114.7MM
SALES (corp-wide): 114.7MM Privately Held
Web: www.mariani.com

SIC: 0723 2034 5148 Fruit (farm-dried) packing services; Dried and dehydrated fruits; Fresh fruits and vegetables

(P-288)
MEYER LLC
Also Called: Meyer Tomatoes
102 Broadway St (93930-2833)
P.O. Box 606 (93930-0606)
PHONE.................................831 385-4047
EMP: 134
SIC: 0723 Vegetable packing services

(P-289)
MISSION PRODUCE INC (PA)
Also Called: MISSION
2710 Camino Del Sol (93030-7967)
P.O. Box 5267 (93031-5267)
PHONE.................................805 981-3650
◆ EMP: 244 EST: 1983
SALES (est): 1.05B
SALES (corp-wide): 1.05B Publicly Held
Web: www.missionproduce.com
SIC: 0723 0179 5431 Fruit (fresh) packing services; Avocado orchard; Fruit stands or markets

(P-290)
MONARCH NUT COMPANY LLC
Also Called: Munger Farms
786 Road 188 (93215-9508)
PHONE.................................661 725-6458
Kamie Munger, Managing Member
David Munger, *
◆ EMP: 250 EST: 1986
SQ FT: 20,000
SALES (est): 19.2MM Privately Held
SIC: 0723 7389 Tree nuts (general) hulling and shelling services; Packaging and labeling services

(P-291)
NATIONAL CUSTOM PACKING INC
13526 Blackie Rd (95012-3212)
PHONE.................................831 724-2026
Jonathon Thornton, Pr
Fred J Haas, *
Ron Marker, *
Louise Mcnary, Sec
EMP: 294 EST: 1984
SQ FT: 12,000
SALES (est): 3.93MM Privately Held
Web: www.nationalcustompacking.com
SIC: 0723 Fruit (fresh) packing services
PA: The Vps Companies Inc
310 Walker St
Watsonville CA

(P-292)
NEWSTAR FRESH FOODS LLC
126 Sun St (93901-3751)
PHONE.................................831 758-7800
Brian Mclaughlin, Contrlr
EMP: 1278
Web: www.newstarfresh.com
SIC: 0723 Vegetable crops market preparation services
PA: Newstar Fresh Foods, Llc
850 Work St Ste 101
Salinas CA

(P-293)
OLAM AMERICAS LLC (DH)
Also Called: Olam Edible Nuts
205 E River Park Cir Ste 310 (93720-1571)
PHONE.................................559 447-1390
Gregory C Estep, CEO
◆ EMP: 1000 EST: 2006
SALES (est): 505.22MM

SALES (corp-wide): 463.76MM Privately Held
Web: www.olamgroup.com
SIC: 0723 Crop preparation services for market
HQ: Olam Us Holdings Inc
2077 Cnvntion Ctr Cncrse
College Park GA
404 209-2676

(P-294)
OLAM AMERICAS INC
Also Called: OLAM AMERICAS INC
1350 Pacheco Pass Hwy (95020-9559)
P.O. Box 990 (93930-0990)
PHONE.................................408 846-3200
Randall Stewey, Brnch Mgr
EMP: 318
SALES (corp-wide): 463.76MM Privately Held
Web: www.olamgroup.com
SIC: 0723 Crop preparation services for market
HQ: Olam Americas, Llc
205 E River Park Cir # 310
Fresno CA
559 447-1390

(P-295)
OLAM SPICES & VEGETABLES INC
47641 W Nees Ave (93622-9539)
PHONE.................................209 364-2132
EMP: 220
SALES (corp-wide): 10.81MM Privately Held
Web: www.actii.com
SIC: 0723 Crop preparation services for market
PA: Olam Spices & Vegetables Inc
1350 Pacheco Pass Hwy
Gilroy CA
408 846-3200

(P-296)
OLAM WEST COAST INC
Also Called: Olam Spices & Vegetables
47641 W Nees Ave (93622-9539)
PHONE.................................209 364-6164
EMP: 121
SALES (corp-wide): 463.76MM Privately Held
SIC: 0723 Crop preparation services for market
HQ: Olam West Coast, Inc.
205 E Rver Pk Cir Ste 310
Fresno CA
559 256-6224

(P-297)
OLAM WEST COAST INC
1350 Pacheco Pass Hwy (95020-9559)
PHONE.................................559 447-1390
Jennifer Kinzer, Prin
EMP: 121
SALES (corp-wide): 463.76MM Privately Held
SIC: 0723 Crop preparation services for market
HQ: Olam West Coast, Inc.
205 E Rver Pk Cir Ste 310
Fresno CA
559 256-6224

(P-298)
OLAM WEST COAST INC
6401 Automall Pkwy (95020-7132)
PHONE.................................559 447-1390
Jennifer Kinzer, Prin
EMP: 121

PRODUCTS & SERVICES SECTION
0723 - Crop Preparation Services For Market (P-318)

SALES (corp-wide): 463.76MM **Privately Held**
SIC: **0723** Crop preparation services for market
HQ: Olam West Coast, Inc.
205 E Rver Pk Cir Ste 310
Fresno CA
559 256-6224

(P-299)
PEARL CROP INC (PA)
Also Called: Linden Nut
1550 Industrial Dr (95206-3929)
PHONE.................................209 808-7575
Ulash Turkhan, *CEO*
Halil Ulas Turkhan, *
Hulya Dayac, *Stockholder*
◆ EMP: 60 EST: 2007
SQ FT: 126,000
SALES (est): 90MM
SALES (corp-wide): 90MM **Privately Held**
Web: www.pearlcrop.com
SIC: **0723** Crop preparation services for market

(P-300)
RAMCO ENTERPRISES LP
Also Called: Ramco Employment Services
520 E 3rd St Ste B (93030-0182)
PHONE.................................805 486-9328
EMP: 372
SALES (corp-wide): 125.53MM **Privately Held**
Web: www.ramcoenterpriseslp.com
SIC: **0723** Crop preparation services for market
PA: Ramco Enterprises, L.P.
710 La Guardia St
Salinas CA
831 758-5272

(P-301)
S STAMOULES INC
Also Called: Stamoules Produce Co
904 S Lyon Ave (93640-9735)
PHONE.................................559 655-9777
Peggy Stefanopoulos, *Pr*
Danny Stefanopoulos, *
Tom Stefanopoulos, *
Chrisopher S Stefanopoulos, *
Elena Stefanopoulos, *
▼ EMP: 1000 EST: 1925
SQ FT: 40,000
SALES (est): 49.88MM **Privately Held**
Web: www.stamoules.com
SIC: **0723** Fruit (fresh) packing services

(P-302)
SATICOY LEMON ASSOCIATION (PA)
Also Called: Saticoy Fruit Exchange
103 N Peck Rd (93060-3013)
P.O. Box 46 (93061-0046)
PHONE.................................805 654-6500
Glenn A Miller, *Pr*
Jerry Pogorzelski, *
Jima Garrett, *
▲ EMP: 100 EST: 1933
SALES (est): 26.61MM
SALES (corp-wide): 26.61MM **Privately Held**
Web: www.saticoylemon.com
SIC: **0723** Fruit (fresh) packing services

(P-303)
SIMONIAN BROTHERS INC (PA)
Also Called: Simonian Fruit
511 N 7th St (93625-2331)
P.O. Box 340 (93625-0340)
PHONE.................................559 834-5921
David Simonian, *Ch Bd*
Harold J Simonian, *
James P Simonian, *
Jeffery Simoninan, *
▼ EMP: 68 EST: 1960
SQ FT: 70,000
SALES (est): 9.48MM
SALES (corp-wide): 9.48MM **Privately Held**
Web: www.simonianfruit.com
SIC: **0723** 7389 Fruit (fresh) packing services ; Packaging and labeling services

(P-304)
SIMONIAN BROTHERS INC
Also Called: Simonian Fruit Company
350 N 7th St (93625-2328)
PHONE.................................559 834-5921
EMP: 66
SALES (corp-wide): 9.48MM **Privately Held**
Web: www.simonianfruit.com
SIC: **0723** Fruit (fresh) packing services
PA: Simonian Brothers Inc.
511 N 7th St
Fowler CA
559 834-5921

(P-305)
SUN WORLD INC
5544 California Ave Ste 280 (93309-1616)
PHONE.................................805 833-6460
Howard P Margulaes, *Ch Bd*
David O Margulaes, *VP Mktg*
John P Brincko, *Pr*
Paul W Knupp, *Sec*
◆ EMP: 1500 EST: 1977
SQ FT: 17,441
SALES (est): 10.67MM **Privately Held**
Web: www.sun-world.com
SIC: **0723** Crop preparation services for market

(P-306)
SUN WORLD INTERNATIONAL INC (PA)
16351 Driver Rd (93308-9733)
P.O. Box 80298 (93380-0298)
PHONE.................................661 392-5000
◆ EMP: 1500 EST: 1976
SQ FT: 160,000
SALES (est): 44.92MM **Privately Held**
Web: www.sun-world.com
SIC: **0723** 0172 0174 0175 Vegetable crops market preparation services; Grapes; Citrus fruits; Deciduous tree fruits

(P-307)
SUNSHINE RAISIN CORPORATION (PA)
Also Called: National Raisin Company
626 S 5th St (93625-9745)
P.O. Box 219 (93625-0219)
PHONE.................................559 834-5981
Lindakay Abdulian, *Pr*
May Firkus, *
Paul David Bedrosian, *
◆ EMP: 249 EST: 1968
SQ FT: 400,000
SALES (est): 126.16MM
SALES (corp-wide): 126.16MM **Privately Held**
Web: www.nationalraisin.com
SIC: **0723** Crop preparation services for market

(P-308)
TALLEY FARMS
2900 Lopez Dr (93420-4999)
P.O. Box 360 (93421-0360)
PHONE.................................805 489-2508
Brian Talley, *Pr*
Rayn Talley, *
Todd Talley, *
Rosemary Talley, *
▲ EMP: 175 EST: 1954
SQ FT: 2,000
SALES (est): 21.28MM **Privately Held**
Web: www.talleyfarmsfreshharvest.com
SIC: **0723** 0161 Vegetable packing services; Vegetables and melons

(P-309)
TANIMURA ANTLE FRESH FOODS INC
Also Called: Salad Time Farms
4401 Foxdale St (91706-2161)
P.O. Box 4070 (93912-4070)
PHONE.................................831 424-6100
Randy Sipled, *Mgr*
EMP: 125
SALES (corp-wide): 321.47MM **Privately Held**
Web: www.taproduce.com
SIC: **0723** Vegetable packing services
PA: Tanimura & Antle Fresh Foods, Inc.
1 Harris Rd
Salinas CA
831 455-2950

(P-310)
TAYLOR FRESH FOODS INC (PA)
150 Main St Ste 400 (93901-3442)
P.O. Box 1649 (93902-1649)
PHONE.................................831 676-9023
Bruce Taylor, *CEO*
◆ EMP: 150 EST: 1995
SQ FT: 2,500
SALES (est): 1.86B **Privately Held**
Web: www.taylorfarms.com
SIC: **0723** Vegetable crops market preparation services

(P-311)
TELESIS ONION CO
Also Called: TELESIS ONION CO.
21484 S Colusa (93624)
P.O. Box 690 (93624-0690)
PHONE.................................559 884-2441
Dan Garcia, *Mgr*
EMP: 115
SALES (corp-wide): 4.28MM **Privately Held**
SIC: **0723** Vegetable packing services
PA: Telesis Onion Co., Inc.
3265 W Figarden Dr
Fresno CA
559 884-2441

(P-312)
THE WONDERFUL COMPANY LLC (PA)
Also Called: Teleflora
11444 W Olympic Blvd Ste 210 (90064-1507)
P.O. Box 30119 (90030-0119)
PHONE.................................310 966-5700
◆ EMP: 250 EST: 2010
SALES (est): 2.04B
SALES (corp-wide): 2.04B **Privately Held**
Web: www.wonderful.com
SIC: **0723** 2084 Fruit crops market preparation services; Wines

(P-313)
WALTER L JONES FAMILY LTD
Also Called: Sun Valley Packing
7381 Avenue 432 (93654-9016)
P.O. Box 351 (93654-0351)
PHONE.................................559 591-1515
EMP: 70 EST: 1962
SALES (est): 6.78MM **Privately Held**
SIC: **0723** 0175 0172 Fruit (fresh) packing services; Peach orchard; Grapes

(P-314)
WEST PAK AVOCADO INC (PA)
Also Called: Avocado Packer & Shipper
38655 Sky Canyon Dr (92563-2536)
PHONE.................................951 296-5757
▲ EMP: 110 EST: 1982
SALES (est): 86.69MM
SALES (corp-wide): 86.69MM **Privately Held**
Web: www.westpakavocado.com
SIC: **0723** Crop preparation services for market

(P-315)
WILBUR PACKING COMPANY INC
1500 Eager Rd (95953)
P.O. Box 3730 (95992-3730)
PHONE.................................530 671-4911
Richard G Wilbur, *Pr*
Randy Baucom, *
Emily L Friend, *CAO*
Richard R Wilbur, *
◆ EMP: 100 EST: 1944
SQ FT: 60,650
SALES (est): 9.45MM **Privately Held**
Web: www.wilburpacking.com
SIC: **0723** 2034 Crop preparation services for market; Dried and dehydrated fruits, vegetables and soup mixes

(P-316)
WONDERFUL CITRUS PACKING LLC (HQ)
Also Called: Paramount Citrus Packing Co
1901 S Lexington St (93215-9207)
PHONE.................................661 720-2400
Craig B Cooper, *Managing Member*
◆ EMP: 273 EST: 1950
SQ FT: 400,000
SALES (est): 280.36MM
SALES (corp-wide): 2.04B **Privately Held**
Web: www.wonderfulcitrus.com
SIC: **0723** 0174 2033 Fruit (fresh) packing services; Orange grove; Fruit juices: fresh
PA: The Wonderful Company Llc
11444 W Olympic Blvd # 210
Los Angeles CA
310 966-5700

(P-317)
WONDERFUL COMPANY LLC
5001 California Ave (93309-1671)
PHONE.................................559 781-7438
EMP: 921
SALES (corp-wide): 2.04B **Privately Held**
Web: www.wonderful.com
SIC: **0723** Fruit crops market preparation services
PA: The Wonderful Company Llc
11444 W Olympic Blvd # 210
Los Angeles CA
310 966-5700

(P-318)
WONDERFUL COMPANY LLC
6801 E Lerdo Hwy (93263-9610)
PHONE.................................661 399-4456
EMP: 1793
SALES (corp-wide): 2.04B **Privately Held**
Web: www.wonderful.com
SIC: **0723** Fruit crops market preparation services
PA: The Wonderful Company Llc
11444 W Olympic Blvd # 210

0723 - Crop Preparation Services For Market (P-319)

Los Angeles CA
310 966-5700

(P-319)
WONDERFUL COMPANY LLC
11444 W Olympic Blvd Ste 210 (90064-1559)
PHONE..................................661 720-2609
Craig B Cooper, *Mgr*
EMP: 291
SALES (corp-wide): 2.04B **Privately Held**
Web: www.wonderful.com
SIC: 0723 Fruit (fresh) packing services
PA: The Wonderful Company Llc
11444 W Olympic Blvd # 210
Los Angeles CA
310 966-5700

(P-320)
YOUNGSTOWN GRAPE DISTRS INC
1625 G St (93654-3435)
P.O. Box 271 (93654-0271)
PHONE..................................559 638-2271
Michael J Forrest, *CEO*
▲ **EMP:** 206 **EST:** 1983
SQ FT: 100,000
SALES (est): 24.87MM **Privately Held**
Web: www.youngstownd.com
SIC: 0723 5148 Crop preparation services for market; Fruits

0742 Veterinary Services, Specialties

(P-321)
ACCESS SPCLTY ANIMAL HOSPITALS
9599 Jefferson Blvd (90232-2917)
PHONE..................................310 558-6100
Amy Gram, *Admn*
EMP: 73 **EST:** 2011
SALES (est): 4.78MM **Privately Held**
Web: www.accessanimalhospitals.com
SIC: 0742 Animal hospital services, pets and other animal specialties

(P-322)
ADOBE ANIMAL HOSPITAL
4470 El Camino Real (94022-1003)
PHONE..................................650 948-9661
Dave M Ross, *Pr*
Jerry Berg, *
EMP: 100 **EST:** 1964
SQ FT: 6,577
SALES (est): 9.65MM **Privately Held**
Web: www.adobe-animal.com
SIC: 0742 Animal hospital services, pets and other animal specialties

(P-323)
ADOBE ANIMAL HOSPITAL
15965 Los Gatos Blvd Ste 100 (95032-3414)
PHONE..................................408 357-8000
Anne Harrell, *Prin*
EMP: 100 **EST:** 2015
SALES (est): 2.32MM **Privately Held**
Web: www.adobe-animal.com
SIC: 0742 Animal hospital services, pets and other animal specialties

(P-324)
ADVANCED CRTCAL CARE EMRGNCY S
9599 Jefferson Blvd (90232-2917)
PHONE..................................310 558-6111
Richard Mills, *CEO*
Amy Grant, *Pr*
EMP: 126 **EST:** 2004
SALES (est): 9.48MM **Privately Held**
Web: www.accessanimalhospitals.com
SIC: 0742 Animal hospital services, pets and other animal specialties

(P-325)
ANIMAL RESCUE SQUAD INTL II
5122 Hamel St (95618-4425)
PHONE..................................530 761-6008
Hsuan-hui Yang, *CEO*
EMP: 800 **EST:** 2021
SALES (est): 9.25MM **Privately Held**
SIC: 0742 Veterinary services, specialties

(P-326)
ANIMAL SPECIALTY GROUP
Also Called: Kortz Gregg Dvm Dplomate Acvim
4641 Colorado Blvd (90039-1105)
PHONE..................................818 244-7977
Kirk Wendelburg D.v.m., *Owner*
EMP: 60 **EST:** 1990
SALES (est): 10.34MM **Privately Held**
Web: www.asgvets.com
SIC: 0742 Veterinarian, animal specialties

(P-327)
ANIMUS INC
Also Called: Alpine Animal Hospital
2460 W El Camino Real (94040-1421)
PHONE..................................650 969-8555
R L Collinson, *Owner*
EMP: 143
SALES (corp-wide): 10.41MM **Privately Held**
Web: www.alpinevetonline.com
SIC: 0742 Animal hospital services, pets and other animal specialties
PA: Animus, Inc.
34501 7th St
Union City CA
800 306-7910

(P-328)
ASSOCTED VTRNARY PRACTICES INC
Also Called: Brentwood Veterinary Hospital
4519 Ohara Ave (94513-2206)
PHONE..................................925 634-1177
Duane Schnittker D.v.m., *Prin*
EMP: 124 **EST:** 1979
SQ FT: 1,500
SALES (est): 4.74MM
SALES (corp-wide): 860.07MM **Privately Held**
Web: www.brentwoodvet.net
SIC: 0742 Animal hospital services, pets and other animal specialties
HQ: National Veterinary Associates, Inc.
1 Baxter Way Ste 200
Westlake Village CA
805 777-7722

(P-329)
BEST FRIENDS ANIMAL HOSPITAL
Also Called: Habib, Sindy Dvm
4925 Longridge Ave (91423-2118)
PHONE..................................818 766-2140
Sindy Habib, *Pt*
Jaqueline Gray, *Pt*
EMP: 77 **EST:** 2000
SQ FT: 4,474
SALES (est): 771.15K **Privately Held**
Web: www.bestfriendsanimalhospital.com
SIC: 0742 Animal hospital services, pets and other animal specialties

(P-330)
BISHOP RANCH VETERINARY CENTER
2000 Bishop Dr (94583-2344)
PHONE..................................925 743-9300
James Delano, *Pt*
Frank Utchen, *Pt*
Jay Kerr, *Pt*
James Pogrel, *Pt*
EMP: 85 **EST:** 2006
SALES (est): 10.4MM **Privately Held**
Web: www.webvets.com
SIC: 0742 Animal hospital services, pets and other animal specialties

(P-331)
COUNTY OF LOS ANGELES
Also Called: Animal Care & Control
216 W Victoria St (90248-3525)
PHONE..................................310 523-9566
Marvin Stitts, *Prin*
EMP: 62
SALES (corp-wide): 31.7B **Privately Held**
Web: animalcare.lacounty.gov
SIC: 0742 9199 Veterinary services, specialties; General government administration
PA: County Of Los Angeles
500 W Temple St Ste 437
Los Angeles CA
213 974-1101

(P-332)
COUNTY OF LOS ANGELES
Also Called: Animal Care & Control
4275 Elton St (91706-3423)
PHONE..................................626 962-3577
Janin Berry, *Mgr*
EMP: 63
SALES (corp-wide): 31.7B **Privately Held**
Web: animalcare.lacounty.gov
SIC: 0742 9199 Veterinary services, specialties; General government administration
PA: County Of Los Angeles
500 W Temple St Ste 437
Los Angeles CA
213 974-1101

(P-333)
COUNTY OF YUBA
Also Called: Animal Care Services
5245 Feather River Blvd (95901)
PHONE..................................530 741-6478
Steve Durfor, *Mgr*
EMP: 77
SALES (corp-wide): 233.12MM **Privately Held**
Web: www.yuba.org
SIC: 0742 9111 Veterinary services, specialties; County supervisors' and executives' office
PA: County Of Yuba
915 8th St Ste 109
Marysville CA
530 749-7575

(P-334)
DELPHIC ENTERPRISES INC
Also Called: Pinnacle Veterinary Center
23026 Soledad Canyon Rd (91350-2634)
PHONE..................................661 254-2000
Nirip Shokar, *Pr*
EMP: 72 **EST:** 2016
SALES (est): 2.36MM
SALES (corp-wide): 75.43MM **Privately Held**
Web: www.vetsantaclarita.com
SIC: 0742 Animal hospital services, pets and other animal specialties
HQ: People, Pets And Vets, Llc
6541 Sexton Dr Nw Ste G
Olympia WA
360 866-7331

(P-335)
LM VETERINARY ENTERPRISES INC
8725 Santa Monica Blvd (90069-4507)
PHONE..................................310 659-5287
EMP: 71
SALES (corp-wide): 282.61K **Privately Held**
SIC: 0742 Veterinary services, specialties
PA: Lm Veterinary Enterprises, Inc.
1412 Huntington Dr
South Pasadena CA

(P-336)
MERCY FOR ANIMALS INC
8033 W Sunset Blvd Ste 864 (90046-2401)
PHONE..................................347 839-6464
Nathan Runkle, *CEO*
EMP: 117 **EST:** 2015
SALES (est): 18.22MM **Privately Held**
Web: www.mercyforanimals.org
SIC: 0742 Veterinary services, specialties

(P-337)
MOULTON ANIMAL HOSPITAL INC
27261 La Paz Rd Ste I (92677-3604)
PHONE..................................949 831-7297
Stanley Creighton D.v.m., *Pr*
EMP: 78 **EST:** 1989
SALES (est): 865.27K
SALES (corp-wide): 860.07MM **Privately Held**
SIC: 0742 Animal hospital services, pets and other animal specialties
HQ: National Veterinary Associates, Inc.
1 Baxter Way Ste 200
Westlake Village CA
805 777-7722

(P-338)
NADCO INC
360 S Elm Dr Apt 3 (90212-4628)
PHONE..................................310 623-7776
Nissan Mosapor, *Brnch Mgr*
EMP: 71
SALES (corp-wide): 5.22MM **Privately Held**
Web: www.mash.vet
SIC: 0742 Animal hospital services, pets and other animal specialties
PA: Nadco, Inc.
6565 Santa Monica Blvd
Los Angeles CA
855 350-7387

(P-339)
NATIONAL VETERINARY ASSOC INC (HQ)
1 Baxter Way (91362-3851)
PHONE..................................805 777-7722
Greg Hartmann, *CEO*
Thomas Sawicki, *
R James Woloshyn, *
Cheryl Desantis, *
EMP: 67 **EST:** 1996
SALES (est): 860.07MM
SALES (corp-wide): 860.07MM **Privately Held**
Web: www.nva.com
SIC: 0742 Animal hospital services, pets and other animal specialties
PA: Veterinary Specialists Of North America Llc

PRODUCTS & SERVICES SECTION

0752 - Animal Specialty Services (P-359)

106 Apple St Ste 102
Tinton Falls NJ
732 704-9222

(P-340)
PEOPLE PETS AND VETS LLC
Also Called: Prestige Animal Hospital South
10986 Sierra Ave Ste 400 (92337-7673)
PHONE..................909 453-4213
Sudeep Wahla, *Brnch Mgr*
EMP: 223
SALES (corp-wide): 75.43MM **Privately Held**
Web: www.prestigeanimalhospital.com
SIC: 0742 Animal hospital services, pets and other animal specialties
HQ: People, Pets And Vets, Llc
6541 Sexton Dr Nw Ste G
Olympia WA
360 866-7331

(P-341)
PEOPLE PETS AND VETS LLC
Also Called: Prestige Animal Hospital North
16055 Sierra Lakes Pkwy Ste 100 (92336)
PHONE..................909 329-2860
Sudeep S Wahla, *Brnch Mgr*
EMP: 246
SALES (corp-wide): 75.43MM **Privately Held**
Web: www.prestigeanimalhospital.com
SIC: 0742 Animal hospital services, pets and other animal specialties
HQ: People, Pets And Vets, Llc
6541 Sexton Dr Nw Ste G
Olympia WA
360 866-7331

(P-342)
SAGE VETERINARY CENTERS LP
1410 Monument Blvd (94520-4368)
PHONE..................925 288-4856
Gina Del Vecchio, *Mng Pt*
EMP: 461 **EST:** 1992
SALES (est): 46.99MM
SALES (corp-wide): 860.07MM **Privately Held**
Web: www.sagecenters.com
SIC: 0742 Animal hospital services, pets and other animal specialties
HQ: National Veterinary Associates, Inc.
1 Baxter Way Ste 200
Westlake Village CA
805 777-7722

(P-343)
TONY LRSSAS ANMAL RSCUE FNDTIO
2890 Mitchell Dr (94598-1635)
PHONE..................925 256-1273
Elena Bicker, *Ex Dir*
EMP: 70 **EST:** 1991
SQ FT: 37,000
SALES (est): 13.75MM **Privately Held**
Web: www.arflife.org
SIC: 0742 8699 Veterinary services, specialties; Animal humane society

(P-344)
V C A CENTRAL ANIMAL HOSPITAL
281 N Central Ave (91786-4215)
PHONE..................909 981-2855
Doctor Ronald L Beeley, *Pr*
Leanne Palm, *
Richard T Johnson, *
Theresa Dieringer, *
Marjorie Fong, *

EMP: 84 **EST:** 1973
SALES (est): 4.86MM
SALES (corp-wide): 42.84B **Privately Held**
Web: www.vcahospitals.com
SIC: 0742 Animal hospital services, pets and other animal specialties
HQ: Vca Inc.
12401 W Olympic Blvd
Los Angeles CA
310 571-6500

(P-345)
VALLEY ANIMAL MEDICAL CENTER
46920 Jefferson St (92201-7920)
PHONE..................760 342-4711
Gary Homec, *Pr*
EMP: 799 **EST:** 1979
SQ FT: 12,000
SALES (est): 2.3MM **Privately Held**
Web: www.animalmedicalvets.com
SIC: 0742 Animal hospital services, pets and other animal specialties
PA: Pet Drx Veterinary Group, Inc.
560 S Winchester Blvd
San Jose CA

(P-346)
VCA ANIMAL HOSPITALS INC
Also Called: VCA Vtrnary Specialists of Vly
22123 Ventura Blvd (91364-1649)
P.O. Box 848 (91365-0848)
PHONE..................818 883-8387
EMP: 65
SALES (corp-wide): 42.84B **Privately Held**
Web: www.vcaspecialtyvets.com
SIC: 0742 Animal hospital services, pets and other animal specialties
HQ: Vca Animal Hospitals, Inc.
12401 W Olympic Blvd
Los Angeles CA

(P-347)
VCA ANIMAL HOSPITALS INC
Also Called: Animal Specialty Group
5610 Kearny Mesa Rd Ste B (92111-1313)
PHONE..................858 560-8006
EMP: 62
SALES (corp-wide): 42.84B **Privately Held**
Web: www.vcahospitals.com
SIC: 0742 Animal hospital services, pets and other animal specialties
HQ: Vca Animal Hospitals, Inc.
12401 W Olympic Blvd
Los Angeles CA

(P-348)
VCA ANIMAL HOSPITALS INC
Also Called: VCA West Los Angles Anmal Hosp
1900 S Sepulveda Blvd (90025-5620)
PHONE..................310 473-2951
David Bruyette, *Brnch Mgr*
EMP: 88
SALES (corp-wide): 42.84B **Privately Held**
Web: www.vcahospitals.com
SIC: 0742 Animal hospital services, pets and other animal specialties
HQ: Vca Animal Hospitals, Inc.
12401 W Olympic Blvd
Los Angeles CA

(P-349)
VCA PRFESSIONAL ANIMAL LAB INC
12401 W Olympic Blvd (90064-1022)
PHONE..................310 571-6500
Robert L Antin, *Pr*
EMP: 66 **EST:** 1986
SALES (est): 2.1MM

SALES (corp-wide): 42.84B **Privately Held**
SIC: 0742 Animal hospital services, pets and other animal specialties
HQ: Vca Inc.
12401 W Olympic Blvd
Los Angeles CA
310 571-6500

(P-350)
VETERINARY PRACTICE ASSOC INC
Also Called: Veterinary Specialty Hospital
10435 Sorrento Valley Rd (92121-1607)
PHONE..................949 833-9020
Keith P Richter, *CEO*
EMP: 150 **EST:** 2004
SQ FT: 26,280
SALES (est): 21.06MM **Privately Held**
Web: www.ethosvet.com
SIC: 0742 Animal hospital services, pets and other animal specialties

(P-351)
VETERINARY SPECIALTY HOSP
Also Called: Veterinary Specialty Hospital
10435 Sorrento Valley Rd (92121-1607)
PHONE..................858 875-7500
James Robert Dennis, *Pt*
EMP: 149 **EST:** 2007
SALES (est): 12.66MM **Privately Held**
Web: vshsd.ethosvet.com
SIC: 0742 Animal hospital services, pets and other animal specialties

(P-352)
VETERINARY SRGCAL SPCLSTS A VTR
Also Called: Veterinary Surgical Specialists
2965 Edinger Ave (92780-7256)
PHONE..................949 936-0055
Diane Craig, *Pr*
Richard Pankowski, *
EMP: 64 **EST:** 1998
SQ FT: 13,000
SALES (est): 6.32MM
SALES (corp-wide): 30.75MM **Privately Held**
Web: www.vssoc.com
SIC: 0742 Animal hospital services, pets and other animal specialties
PA: Vvp Ca And Co, Lp
1 Pine St
Tinton Falls NJ
848 205-2080

(P-353)
VH 10 VH LP ✪
Also Called: Spca
2343 Fillmore St (94115-1812)
PHONE..................415 554-3000
Evan Hendrickson, *Dir*
EMP: 60 **EST:** 2022
SALES (est): 2.09MM **Privately Held**
Web: www.sfspca.org
SIC: 0742 Animal hospital services, pets and other animal specialties

(P-354)
VICAR OPERATING INC (DH)
Also Called: Veterinary Centers America VCA
12401 W Olympic Blvd (90064-1022)
PHONE..................310 571-6500
Robert Antin, *Pr*
EMP: 91 **EST:** 1985
SALES (est): 97.06MM
SALES (corp-wide): 42.84B **Privately Held**
Web: www.vcaantech.com
SIC: 0742 Animal hospital services, pets and other animal specialties
HQ: Vca Inc.

12401 W Olympic Blvd
Los Angeles CA
310 571-6500

0751 Livestock Services, Except Veterinary

(P-355)
AMERICAN BEEF PACKERS INC
13677 Yorba Ave (91710-5059)
PHONE..................909 628-4888
Lawrence Miller, *Pr*
EMP: 250 **EST:** 2008
SALES (est): 20.7MM **Privately Held**
SIC: 0751 2011 5147 Slaughtering: custom livestock services; Beef products, from beef slaughtered on site; Meats and meat products

(P-356)
STANDARD CATTLE LLC
8105a S Lassen Ave (93660-9728)
PHONE..................559 693-1977
Michael Vanderdussen, *Managing Member*
▲ **EMP:** 75 **EST:** 2005
SALES (est): 4.97MM **Privately Held**
Web: www.standardcattlellc.com
SIC: 0751 Cattle services

0752 Animal Specialty Services

(P-357)
BCFS HEALTH AND HUMAN SERVICES
2301 Pennsylvania Ave (94533-1966)
PHONE..................707 422-8802
Kevin C Dinnin, *Pr*
EMP: 274
SALES (corp-wide): 88.4MM **Privately Held**
Web: www.discoverbcfs.net
SIC: 0752 Shelters, animal
HQ: Bcfs Health And Human Services
4346 Nw Loop 410
San Antonio TX
210 733-7932

(P-358)
CAMP BOW WOW FRANCHISING INC
Also Called: Camp Bow Wow
12401 W Olympic Blvd (90064-1022)
PHONE..................310 571-6500
Robert Antin, *Pr*
EMP: 162 **EST:** 2014
SALES (est): 1.98MM
SALES (corp-wide): 42.84B **Privately Held**
Web: www.campbowwow.com
SIC: 0752 Grooming services, pet and animal specialties
HQ: Vicar Operating, Inc.
12401 W Olympic Blvd
Los Angeles CA
310 571-6500

(P-359)
CANINE CMPNONS FOR INDPENDENCE (PA)
2965 Dutton Ave (95407-7734)
P.O. Box 446 (95402-0446)
PHONE..................707 577-1700
Paul Mundell, *CEO*
Alan Feinne, *
Paul Mundell, *Sec*
John D Miller, *
EMP: 71 **EST:** 1975

0752 - Animal Specialty Services (P-360)

PRODUCTS & SERVICES SECTION

SQ FT: 40,000
SALES (est): 33.53MM
SALES (corp-wide): 33.53MM **Privately Held**
Web: www.canine.org
SIC: 0752 Training services, pet and animal specialties (not horses)

(P-360)
COUNTY OF LOS ANGELES
Also Called: Department Animal Care & Ctrl
11258 Garfield Ave (90242-4007)
PHONE..............................562 658-2085
John Emberry, *Brnch Mgr*
EMP: 63
SALES (corp-wide): 31.7B **Privately Held**
Web: www.lacounty.gov
SIC: 0752 Shelters, animal
PA: County Of Los Angeles
500 W Temple St Ste 437
Los Angeles CA
213 974-1101

(P-361)
COUNTY OF LOS ANGELES
Also Called: Animal Care & Control
31044 Charlie Canyon Rd (91384-3904)
PHONE..............................661 257-3191
Rosendo Perez, *Mgr*
EMP: 63
SALES (corp-wide): 31.7B **Privately Held**
Web: animalcare.lacounty.gov
SIC: 0752 Shelters, animal
PA: County Of Los Angeles
500 W Temple St Ste 437
Los Angeles CA
213 974-1101

(P-362)
GUIDE DOGS FOR BLIND INC (PA)
Also Called: G D B
350 Los Ranchitos Rd (94903-3606)
P.O. Box 151200 (94915-1200)
PHONE..............................415 499-4000
Chris Benninger, *CEO*
Kenneth Stupi, *
Brad Hibbard, *
Brent Ruppel, *
John Cavalcanti, *
EMP: 170 EST: 1942
SALES (est): 86.16MM
SALES (corp-wide): 86.16MM **Privately Held**
Web: www.guidedogs.com
SIC: 0752 8299 Animal training services; Educational service, nondegree granting: continuing educ.

0761 Farm Labor Contractors

(P-363)
ALESIA VITICULTURE SVCS LLC
7620 Alpine Rd (94020-9741)
PHONE..............................650 333-5490
Joaquin Casanueva, *Managing Member*
EMP: 75 EST: 2015
SALES (est): 3.1MM **Privately Held**
Web: www.alesiavs.com
SIC: 0761 7389 Farm labor contractors; Business Activities at Non-Commercial Site

(P-364)
EL CAMINO LABOR LLC
1082 Monterey St (93960-3048)
PHONE..............................831 809-9537
EMP: 60 EST: 2018
SALES (est): 2.43MM **Privately Held**

SIC: 0761 Farm labor contractors

(P-365)
HARO & HARO ENTERPRISES INC
115 W Walnut St Ste 4 (95240-3541)
PHONE..............................209 334-2035
FAX: 209 334-2173
EMP: 1000
SALES (est): 12.66MM **Privately Held**
Web: www.haroandharo.com
SIC: 0761 Farm labor contractors

(P-366)
KREGER INC
3520 W Howard Ave (93277-4058)
PHONE..............................559 884-2585
EMP: 700
SALES (est): 6.37MM **Privately Held**
Web: www.kreger.com
SIC: 0761 7361 Farm labor contractors; Labor contractors (employment agency)

(P-367)
PALO ALTO VINEYARD MGT LLC
50 Adobe Canyon Rd (95452-9044)
P.O. Box 1399 (95452-1399)
PHONE..............................707 996-7725
EMP: 90 EST: 1997
SQ FT: 1,000
SALES (est): 4.63MM **Privately Held**
SIC: 0761 Farm labor contractors

(P-368)
R AND R LABOR INC
710 Kirkpatric Ct Ste A (95023-2808)
PHONE..............................831 638-0290
Ramiro Rodriguez Junior, *Pr*
Jose Rodriguez, *
EMP: 300 EST: 1980
SALES (est): 4.82MM **Privately Held**
SIC: 0761 Farm labor contractors

(P-369)
RODGZ FARM LABOR CONTG LLC
4422 College Way (95961-4622)
PHONE..............................530 329-8403
EMP: 80 EST: 2017
SALES (est): 534.82K **Privately Held**
SIC: 0761 Crew leaders, farm labor: contracting services

(P-370)
VALLEY PRIDE INC (PA)
10855 Ocean Mist Pkwy D (95012-3232)
PHONE..............................831 633-5883
Joseph T Pezzini, *Pr*
Troy Boutonnet, *
EMP: 399 EST: 1987
SQ FT: 1,500
SALES (est): 9.31MM
SALES (corp-wide): 9.31MM **Privately Held**
SIC: 0761 Crew leaders, farm labor: contracting services

0762 Farm Management Services

(P-371)
AG-WISE ENTERPRISES INC (PA)
5100 California Ave Ste 209 (93309-0716)
P.O. Box 9729 (93389-9729)
PHONE..............................661 325-1567
Bruce Berreta, *Pr*

Ed Ray, *
EMP: 150 EST: 1983
SQ FT: 4,400
SALES (est): 17.05MM **Privately Held**
Web: www.ag-wiseinc.com
SIC: 0762 Farm management services

(P-372)
BIANCHI AG SERVICES INC
Also Called: BIANCHI AG. SERVICES, INC.
3056 Colusa Hwy (95993-8931)
PHONE..............................530 923-7675
Jim Bianchi, *Brnch Mgr*
EMP: 87
SALES (corp-wide): 17.47MM **Privately Held**
SIC: 0762 Farm management services
PA: Bianchi Ag Services, Inc.
1210 Richvale Hwy
Richvale CA
530 882-4575

(P-373)
EASTSIDE MANAGEMENT CO INC
1131 12th St Ste C (95354-0813)
PHONE..............................209 578-9852
Steven Zeff, *Pr*
EMP: 140
SIC: 0762 Farm management services
PA: Eastside Management Company, Inc.
1518 K St
Modesto CA

(P-374)
ESPARZA ENTERPRISES INC
251 W Main St Ste G&F (92227-2201)
PHONE..............................760 344-2031
Luis Esparza, *Brnch Mgr*
EMP: 792
SALES (corp-wide): 135MM **Privately Held**
Web: www.esparzainc.com
SIC: 0762 Farm management services
PA: Esparza Enterprises, Inc.
3851 Fruitvale Ave
Bakersfield CA
661 831-0002

(P-375)
ILLUME AGRICULTURE LLC
9100 Ming Ave Ste 200 (93311-1382)
P.O. Box 22020 (93390-2020)
PHONE..............................661 587-5198
Jeffrey Fabbri, *Managing Member*
Dan Fabbri, *
EMP: 120 EST: 1939
SALES (est): 15.14MM **Privately Held**
Web: www.illumeag.com
SIC: 0762 5963 Farm management services; Food services, direct sales

(P-376)
KENDALL-JACKSON WINE CENTER
5007 Fulton Rd (95439)
P.O. Box 296 (95439-0296)
PHONE..............................707 571-7500
EMP: 168 EST: 1984
SALES (est): 13.68MM **Privately Held**
Web: www.kj.com
SIC: 0762 5182 Vineyard management and maintenance services; Wine and distilled beverages

(P-377)
LARRY JACINTO FARMING INC
9555 N Wabash Ave (92374-2714)
P.O. Box 275 (92359-0275)

PHONE..............................909 794-2276
EMP: 100 EST: 1992
SQ FT: 3,000
SALES (est): 2.05MM **Privately Held**
Web: www.jacintofarms.com
SIC: 0762 Farm management services

(P-378)
MESA VINEYARD MANAGEMENT INC (PA)
110 Gibson Rd (93465-9510)
P.O. Box 789 (93465-0789)
PHONE..............................805 434-4100
Dana Merrill, *Pr*
Matt Andrus, *
EMP: 75 EST: 1988
SQ FT: 3,200
SALES (est): 15.63MM **Privately Held**
Web: www.mesavineyard.com
SIC: 0762 Vineyard management and maintenance services

(P-379)
REDWOOD EMPIRE VINYRD MGT INC
22000 Geyserville Ave (95441)
P.O. Box 729 (95441-0729)
PHONE..............................707 857-3401
Kevin W Barr, *Pr*
Nancy Barr, *
Linda Barr, *
EMP: 100 EST: 1985
SALES (est): 9.39MM **Privately Held**
Web: www.revm.net
SIC: 0762 0172 Vineyard management and maintenance services; Grapes

(P-380)
SIERRA PACIFIC FARMS INC (PA)
Also Called: Somis Pacific AG Management
43406 Business Park Dr (92590-5526)
P.O. Box 1537 (92593-1537)
PHONE..............................951 699-9980
Scott A Mcintyre, *CEO*
Debbie Mcintyre, *CFO*
EMP: 68 EST: 1988
SQ FT: 3,000
SALES (est): 16.34MM
SALES (corp-wide): 16.34MM **Privately Held**
Web: www.spfarminc.com
SIC: 0762 Farm management services

(P-381)
SUN PACIFIC FARMING COOP INC (PA)
Also Called: Allied Farming Company
1250 E Myer Ave (93221-9345)
P.O. Box 1125 (93221-7125)
PHONE..............................559 592-7121
Berne H Evans Iii, *CEO*
Bob Reniers, *
EMP: 500 EST: 1973
SQ FT: 70,000
SALES (est): 73.7MM
SALES (corp-wide): 73.7MM **Privately Held**
Web: www.sunpacific.com
SIC: 0762 Citrus grove management and maintenance services

(P-382)
SUN PACIFIC FARMING COOP INC
Also Called: Sun Pacific Farms
33374 Lerdo Hwy (93308-9782)
PHONE..............................661 399-0376
Ernie Larson, *Mgr*

PRODUCTS & SERVICES SECTION **0781 - Landscape Counseling And Planning (P-403)**

EMP: 96
SALES (corp-wide): 49.23MM **Privately Held**
Web: www.sunpacific.com
SIC: **0762** 5148 0174 Citrus grove management and maintenance services; Fresh fruits and vegetables; Citrus fruits
PA: Sun Pacific Farming Cooperative, Inc.
1250 E Myer Ave
Exeter CA
559 592-7121

(P-383)
VIMARK INC
Also Called: Vimark Vineyards
19500 Geyserville Ave (95441-9310)
P.O. Box 576 (95441-0576)
PHONE.................707 857-3588
EMP: 85
SALES (corp-wide): 6.62MM **Privately Held**
Web: www.vimarkvineyards.com
SIC: **0762** Vineyard management and maintenance services
PA: Vimark, Inc.
101 D St Fl 2nd
Santa Rosa CA
707 542-3134

(P-384)
VINO FARMS INC
10651 Eastside Rd (95448-9490)
PHONE.................707 433-8241
Roy Davis, *Mgr*
EMP: 171
SALES (corp-wide): 46.59MM **Privately Held**
Web: www.vinofarms.com
SIC: **0762** Vineyard management and maintenance services
PA: Vino Farms, Inc.
1377 E Lodi Ave
Lodi CA
209 334-6975

(P-385)
WC AG SERVICES INC
800 E Keyes Rd (95307-7539)
P.O. Box 488 (95307-0488)
PHONE.................209 538-3131
Fred Franzia, *Pr*
John Franzia, *VP*
Joseph Franzia, *Sec*
EMP: 2500 EST: 1987
SQ FT: 2,093
SALES (est): 22.97MM **Privately Held**
Web: www.broncowine.com
SIC: **0762** Farm management services

0781 Landscape Counseling And Planning

(P-386)
AMERICAN LANDSCAPE INC
Also Called: American Golf Construction
7013 Owensmouth Ave (91303-2006)
PHONE.................818 999-2041
Gary Peterson, *Pr*
Jamie Tsui, *
▲ EMP: 250 EST: 1973
SQ FT: 14,000
SALES (est): 28.48MM **Privately Held**
Web: www.americanlandscape.com
SIC: **0781** Landscape services

(P-387)
AMERICAN LANDSCAPE MGT INC (PA)
Also Called: Custom Lawn Services
7013 Owensmouth Ave (91303-2006)
PHONE.................818 999-2041
Mickey Strauss, *Pr*
Gary Peterson, *
EMP: 125 EST: 1975
SQ FT: 14,000
SALES (est): 21.82MM **Privately Held**
Web: www.americanlandscape.com
SIC: **0781** Landscape services

(P-388)
AZTECA LANDSCAPE
4073 Mennes Ave (92509-6722)
PHONE.................951 369-9210
EMP: 85
SIC: **0781** Landscape services
PA: Azteca Landscape
1180 Olympic Dr Ste 207
Corona CA

(P-389)
BAYSCAPE MANAGEMENT INC
Also Called: Coast Landscape Management
1350 Pacific Ave (95002)
P.O. Box 880 (95002-0880)
PHONE.................408 288-2940
Thomas Ellington, *Pr*
EMP: 100 EST: 2005
SALES (est): 9.45MM **Privately Held**
Web: www.bayscape.net
SIC: **0781** Landscape services

(P-390)
BENCHMARK LANDSCAPE SVCS INC
12575 Stowe Dr (92064-6805)
PHONE.................858 513-7190
John A Mohns, *Pr*
Sharon R Mohns, *
EMP: 220 EST: 1984
SQ FT: 18,000
SALES (est): 20.23MM **Privately Held**
Web: www.benchmarklandscape.com
SIC: **0781** Landscape services

(P-391)
BENNETT ENTPS A CAL LDSCP CNTG
Also Called: Bennett Landscape
25889 Belle Porte Ave (90710-3393)
PHONE.................310 534-3543
Sean Bennett, *Pr*
EMP: 90 EST: 1977
SQ FT: 10,500
SALES (est): 9.48MM **Privately Held**
Web: www.bennett-landscape.com
SIC: **0781** Landscape services

(P-392)
BILL & DAVES LDSCP MAINT INC
1401 E Edinger Ave (92705-4814)
PHONE.................714 850-0213
EMP: 101
SALES (corp-wide): 2.13MM **Privately Held**
Web: www.billanddaves.com
SIC: **0781** Landscape services
PA: Bill & Dave's Landscape Maintenance, Inc.
32750 Keller Rd
Winchester CA
951 943-6455

(P-393)
BRIGHTVIEW GOLF MAINT INC
405 Glen Annie Rd (93117-1427)
PHONE.................805 968-6400
Richard Hasah, *Mgr*
EMP: 101
SALES (corp-wide): 2.77B **Publicly Held**
SIC: **0781** Landscape services
HQ: Brightview Golf Maintenance, Inc.
27001 Agoura Rd Ste 350
Agoura Hills CA
818 223-8500

(P-394)
BRIGHTVIEW GOLF MAINT INC (DH)
27001 Agoura Rd Ste 350 (91301-5112)
PHONE.................818 223-8500
Burton Sperber, *Ch Bd*
Richard A Sperber, *
Michael L Dingman, *
Gregory Pieschala, *
Anthony Garruto, *
EMP: 100 EST: 1965
SALES (est): 44.34MM
SALES (corp-wide): 2.77B **Publicly Held**
SIC: **0781** Landscape services
HQ: Brightview Companies, Llc
27001 Agoura Rd Ste 350
Calabasas CA
818 223-8500

(P-395)
BRIGHTVIEW LANDSCAPE DEV INC
8450 Miramar Pl (92121-2528)
PHONE.................858 458-9900
Vince Germann, *Mgr*
EMP: 300
SQ FT: 16,050
SALES (corp-wide): 2.77B **Publicly Held**
Web: www.brightview.com
SIC: **0781** Landscape services
HQ: Brightview Landscape Development, Inc.
27001 Agoura Rd Ste 350
Calabasas CA
818 223-8500

(P-396)
BRIGHTVIEW LANDSCAPE DEV INC
7039 Commerce Cir Ste A (94588-8006)
PHONE.................925 463-0700
Jeffrey A Colton, *Brnch Mgr*
EMP: 141
SQ FT: 8,400
SALES (corp-wide): 2.77B **Publicly Held**
Web: www.brightview.com
SIC: **0781** Landscape services
HQ: Brightview Landscape Development, Inc.
27001 Agoura Rd Ste 350
Calabasas CA
818 223-8500

(P-397)
BRIGHTVIEW LANDSCAPE DEV INC
20 Business Park Way Ste 200 (95828)
PHONE.................916 386-4875
Dan Harper, *Brnch Mgr*
EMP: 120
SALES (corp-wide): 2.77B **Publicly Held**
Web: www.brightview.com
SIC: **0781** Landscape services
HQ: Brightview Landscape Development, Inc.
27001 Agoura Rd Ste 350
Calabasas CA
818 223-8500

(P-398)
BRIGHTVIEW LANDSCAPE SVCS INC
20551b Corsair Blvd (94545-1005)
PHONE.................510 487-4826
Tom Stoutt, *Brnch Mgr*
EMP: 85
SALES (corp-wide): 2.77B **Publicly Held**
Web: www.brightview.com
SIC: **0781** Landscape services
HQ: Brightview Landscape Services, Inc.
27001 Agoura Rd Ste 350
Agoura Hills CA
818 223-8500

(P-399)
BRIGHTVIEW LANDSCAPE SVCS INC
715 W La Cadena Dr (92501-1338)
PHONE.................951 684-2730
EMP: 71
SALES (corp-wide): 2.77B **Publicly Held**
Web: www.brightview.com
SIC: **0781** Landscape services
HQ: Brightview Landscape Services, Inc.
27001 Agoura Rd Ste 350
Agoura Hills CA
818 223-8500

(P-400)
BRIGHTVIEW LANDSCAPE SVCS INC
1900 S Lewis St (92805-6718)
PHONE.................714 215-7423
EMP: 71
SALES (corp-wide): 2.77B **Publicly Held**
Web: www.brightview.com
SIC: **0781** Landscape services
HQ: Brightview Landscape Services, Inc.
27001 Agoura Rd Ste 350
Agoura Hills CA
818 223-8500

(P-401)
BRIGHTVIEW LANDSCAPE SVCS INC
32202 Paseo Adelanto (92675-3601)
PHONE.................714 546-7843
EMP: 99
SALES (corp-wide): 2.77B **Publicly Held**
Web: www.brightview.com
SIC: **0781** Landscape services
HQ: Brightview Landscape Services, Inc.
27001 Agoura Rd Ste 350
Agoura Hills CA
818 223-8500

(P-402)
BRIGHTVIEW LANDSCAPE SVCS INC
8726 Calabash Ave (92335-3040)
PHONE.................909 946-3196
Leon Vitort, *Brnch Mgr*
EMP: 99
SALES (corp-wide): 2.77B **Publicly Held**
Web: www.brightview.com
SIC: **0781** Landscape services
HQ: Brightview Landscape Services, Inc.
27001 Agoura Rd Ste 350
Agoura Hills CA
818 223-8500

(P-403)
BRIGHTVIEW LANDSCAPE SVCS INC
4030 Alvis Ct (95677-4011)
PHONE.................916 415-1004
EMP: 99
SALES (corp-wide): 2.77B **Publicly Held**
Web: www.brightview.com
SIC: **0781** Landscape services
HQ: Brightview Landscape Services, Inc.

0781 - Landscape Counseling And Planning (P-404)

27001 Agoura Rd Ste 350
Agoura Hills CA
818 223-8500

(P-404)
BRIGHTVIEW LANDSCAPE SVCS INC
8500 Miramar Pl (92121-2530)
PHONE..................858 458-1900
Patrick Ceatter, *Mgr*
EMP: 114
SALES (corp-wide): 2.77B **Publicly Held**
Web: www.brightview.com
SIC: 0781 Landscape services
HQ: Brightview Landscape Services, Inc.
27001 Agoura Rd Ste 350
Agoura Hills CA
818 223-8500

(P-405)
BRIGHTVIEW LANDSCAPE SVCS INC
4677 Pacheco Blvd (94553-3625)
PHONE..................925 957-8831
Martin Becker, *Mgr*
EMP: 114
SALES (corp-wide): 2.77B **Publicly Held**
Web: www.brightview.com
SIC: 0781 Landscape services
HQ: Brightview Landscape Services, Inc.
27001 Agoura Rd Ste 350
Agoura Hills CA
818 223-8500

(P-406)
BRIGHTVIEW LANDSCAPE SVCS INC
415 W 30th St (91950-7207)
PHONE..................619 474-4478
Curtis Brook, *Pr*
EMP: 85
SALES (corp-wide): 2.77B **Publicly Held**
Web: www.brightview.com
SIC: 0781 Landscape services
HQ: Brightview Landscape Services, Inc.
27001 Agoura Rd Ste 350
Agoura Hills CA
818 223-8500

(P-407)
BRIGHTVIEW LANDSCAPE SVCS INC
1960 S Yale St (92704-3929)
PHONE..................714 546-7843
Dave Hanson, *Mgr*
EMP: 284
SALES (corp-wide): 2.77B **Publicly Held**
Web: www.brightview.com
SIC: 0781 0782 Landscape services; Lawn and garden services
HQ: Brightview Landscape Services, Inc.
27001 Agoura Rd Ste 350
Agoura Hills CA
818 223-8500

(P-408)
BRIGHTVIEW LANDSCAPE SVCS INC
825 Mahler Rd (94010-1603)
PHONE..................650 289-9324
Kyle G Sager, *Brnch Mgr*
EMP: 99
SALES (corp-wide): 2.77B **Publicly Held**
Web: www.brightview.com
SIC: 0781 Landscape services
HQ: Brightview Landscape Services, Inc.
27001 Agoura Rd Ste 350
Agoura Hills CA
818 223-8500

(P-409)
BRIGHTVIEW LANDSCAPE SVCS INC
17846 Van Buren Blvd (92508-9195)
PHONE..................714 939-6600
EMP: 71
SALES (corp-wide): 2.77B **Publicly Held**
Web: www.brightview.com
SIC: 0781 Landscape services
HQ: Brightview Landscape Services, Inc.
27001 Agoura Rd Ste 350
Agoura Hills CA
818 223-8500

(P-410)
BRIGHTVIEW LANDSCAPE SVCS INC
5779 Preston Ave (94551-9521)
PHONE..................925 243-0288
EMP: 71
SALES (corp-wide): 2.77B **Publicly Held**
Web: www.brightview.com
SIC: 0781 Landscape services
HQ: Brightview Landscape Services, Inc.
27001 Agoura Rd Ste 350
Agoura Hills CA
818 223-8500

(P-411)
BRIGHTVIEW LANDSCAPE SVCS INC
825 Mabury Rd (95133-1024)
PHONE..................408 453-5904
Nada Duna, *Mgr*
EMP: 199
SALES (corp-wide): 2.77B **Publicly Held**
Web: www.brightview.com
SIC: 0781 0782 Landscape services; Lawn and garden services
HQ: Brightview Landscape Services, Inc.
27001 Agoura Rd Ste 350
Agoura Hills CA
818 223-8500

(P-412)
BRIGHTVIEW LANDSCAPE SVCS INC
5745 Alder Ave (95828-1107)
PHONE..................916 381-2800
John Bianco, *Mgr*
EMP: 227
SALES (corp-wide): 2.77B **Publicly Held**
Web: www.brightview.com
SIC: 0781 Landscape services
HQ: Brightview Landscape Services, Inc.
27001 Agoura Rd Ste 350
Agoura Hills CA
818 223-8500

(P-413)
BRIGHTVIEW LANDSCAPE SVCS INC
2064 Eastman Ave Ste 104 (93003-7787)
PHONE..................805 642-9300
Frank Annino, *Mgr*
EMP: 114
SALES (corp-wide): 2.77B **Publicly Held**
Web: www.brightview.com
SIC: 0781 Landscape services
HQ: Brightview Landscape Services, Inc.
27001 Agoura Rd Ste 350
Agoura Hills CA
818 223-8500

(P-414)
BRIGHTVIEW LANDSCAPE SVCS INC
1 University Dr (92656-8081)
PHONE..................949 480-4187
EMP: 71
SALES (corp-wide): 2.77B **Publicly Held**
Web: www.brightview.com
SIC: 0781 Landscape services
HQ: Brightview Landscape Services, Inc.
27001 Agoura Rd Ste 350
Agoura Hills CA
818 223-8500

(P-415)
BRIGHTVIEW LANDSCAPE SVCS INC
7039 Commerce Cir Ste B (94588-8006)
PHONE..................925 924-8900
Doug Lape, *Mgr*
EMP: 114
SALES (corp-wide): 2.77B **Publicly Held**
Web: www.brightview.com
SIC: 0781 0782 Landscape services; Lawn and garden services
HQ: Brightview Landscape Services, Inc.
27001 Agoura Rd Ste 350
Agoura Hills CA
818 223-8500

(P-416)
BRIGHTVIEW LANDSCAPE SVCS INC
17813 S Main St Ste 105 (90248-3542)
PHONE..................310 327-8700
Andrea Musick, *Mgr*
EMP: 242
SQ FT: 1,530
SALES (corp-wide): 2.77B **Publicly Held**
Web: www.brightview.com
SIC: 0781 0782 Landscape services; Landscape contractors
HQ: Brightview Landscape Services, Inc.
27001 Agoura Rd Ste 350
Agoura Hills CA
818 223-8500

(P-417)
BRIGHTVIEW LANDSCAPE SVCS INC
47 Plateau (92656-8027)
PHONE..................310 829-4707
Brett Park, *Pr*
EMP: 71
SALES (corp-wide): 2.77B **Publicly Held**
Web: www.brightview.com
SIC: 0781 Landscape architects
HQ: Brightview Landscape Services, Inc.
27001 Agoura Rd Ste 350
Agoura Hills CA
818 223-8500

(P-418)
BRIGHTVIEW TREE CARE SVCS INC
715 W La Cadena Dr (92501-1338)
PHONE..................951 684-2730
Todd Huffman, *Pr*
Steven Guarneri, *
EMP: 99 **EST:** 2005
SALES (est): 7.33MM
SALES (corp-wide): 2.77B **Publicly Held**
SIC: 0781 Landscape services
PA: Brightview Holdings, Inc.
980 Jolly Rd Ste 300
Blue Bell PA
484 567-7204

(P-419)
BRIGHTVIEW TREE COMPANY
P.O. Box 1611 (92307-0031)
PHONE..................760 955-2560
EMP: 86
SIC: 0781 Landscape services
HQ: Brightview Tree Company
24151 Ventura Blvd # 100
Calabasas CA
818 223-8500

(P-420)
BRIGHTVIEW TREE COMPANY
28915 E Funck Rd (95230-9567)
PHONE..................209 886-5511
Gina Mortenson, *Mgr*
EMP: 86
SQ FT: 784
Web: www.brightview.com
SIC: 0781 Landscape services
HQ: Brightview Tree Company
24151 Ventura Blvd # 100
Calabasas CA
818 223-8500

(P-421)
CALIFORNIA SKATEPARKS
285 N Benson Ave (91786-5614)
PHONE..................909 949-1601
Joseph M Ciaglia Junior, *CEO*
Joseph M Ciaglia Junior, *Pr*
EMP: 150 **EST:** 1977
SALES (est): 12.75MM **Privately Held**
Web: www.californiaskateparks.com
SIC: 0781 Landscape services

(P-422)
CLEARKIN INC
4115 Blackhawk Plaza Cir Ste 100 (94506-4828)
P.O. Box B (94526)
PHONE..................925 838-2551
Martin Cleary, *Mgr*
EMP: 155
Web: www.brightview.com
SIC: 0781 0782 Landscape services; Lawn and garden services
PA: Clearkin, Inc.
4931 Pacheco Blvd
Martinez CA

(P-423)
COAST LM INC
7400 Folsom Blvd (95826-2605)
PHONE..................800 578-8810
Kelly Solomon, *Prin*
EMP: 155
Web: www.brightview.com
SIC: 0781 Landscape services
PA: Coast Lm, Inc.
4100 Paoli Loop Rd
American Canyon CA

(P-424)
COMET BUILDING MAINTENANCE INC
21 Commercial Blvd Ste 12 (94949-6109)
P.O. Box 2163 (94912-2163)
PHONE..................415 382-1150
Richard J Brasile, *CEO*
EMP: 70 **EST:** 1983
SQ FT: 1,800
SALES (est): 4.72MM **Privately Held**
Web: www.cometps.com
SIC: 0781 7349 Landscape services; Janitorial service, contract basis

(P-425)
CRESTVIEW LANDSCAPE INC
13915 Saticoy St (91402-6521)
PHONE..................818 962-7771
Harold Young, *CEO*
Augustine Bucio, *
EMP: 100 **EST:** 2020
SALES (est): 2.53MM **Privately Held**

PRODUCTS & SERVICES SECTION　　　　　　0781 - Landscape Counseling And Planning (P-448)

Web: www.crestviewlandscape.com
SIC: 0781 Landscape services

(P-426)
DAVID L GATES & ASSOCIATES INC
Also Called: Gates, David L & Associates
1655 N Main St Ste 365 (94596-4641)
PHONE..................925 736-8176
David L Gates, *Pr*
Linda Gates, *VP*
EMP: 64 EST: 1976
SALES (est): 8.51MM **Privately Held**
Web: www.dgates.com
SIC: 0781 8712 0782 Landscape architects; Architectural services; Lawn and garden services

(P-427)
DEL CONTES LANDSCAPING INC
41900 Boscell Rd (94538-3196)
PHONE..................510 353-6030
Tom Del Conte, *CEO*
EMP: 100 EST: 1972
SQ FT: 960
SALES (est): 12.24MM **Privately Held**
Web: www.dclandscaping.com
SIC: 0781 Landscape services

(P-428)
DL LONG LANDSCAPING INC
5475 G St (91710-5233)
PHONE..................909 628-5531
David L Long, *Pr*
EMP: 100 EST: 1974
SQ FT: 1,550
SALES (est): 4.61MM **Privately Held**
SIC: 0781 Landscape architects

(P-429)
ELS INVESTMENTS
Also Called: Environmental Ldscp Solutions
2701 Citrus Rd (95742-6314)
PHONE..................916 388-0308
Darryl Alan Thompson Junior, *Pr*
Shawna Thompson, *
EMP: 110 EST: 2008
SALES (est): 16.08MM **Privately Held**
Web: www.els-green.com
SIC: 0781 1771 Landscape services; Concrete work

(P-430)
EXECUTIVE LANDSCAPE INC
2131 Huffstatler St (92028-8861)
P.O. Box 1075 (92088-1075)
PHONE..................760 731-9036
Edwin Earle, *CEO*
Kathleen D Earle, *
Walter Earle, *
EMP: 230 EST: 1993
SQ FT: 1,800
SALES (est): 9.54MM **Privately Held**
Web: www.executivelandscapeinc.com
SIC: 0781 Landscape services

(P-431)
FRANK CARSON LDSCP & MAINT INC
Also Called: Carson Landscape Industries
9530 Elder Creek Rd (95829-9306)
PHONE..................916 856-5400
Frank M Carson, *CEO*
Kathy Pipis, *
EMP: 200 EST: 1975
SQ FT: 36,000
SALES (est): 15.94MM **Privately Held**
Web: www.carson1975.com

(P-432)
FS COMMERCIAL LANDSCAPE INC (PA)
5151 Pedley Rd (92509-3937)
PHONE..................951 360-7070
G John Wood, *Pr*
EMP: 75 EST: 1993
SQ FT: 1,500
SALES (est): 11.5MM **Privately Held**
Web: www.fscommerciallandscape.com
SIC: 0781 Landscape services

(P-433)
GACHINA LANDSCAPE MGT INC
1130 Obrien Dr (94025-1411)
PHONE..................650 853-0400
Harumi Jacl Gachina, *CEO*
EMP: 269 EST: 1988
SQ FT: 12,000
SALES (est): 23.87MM **Privately Held**
Web: www.gachina.com
SIC: 0781 Landscape services

(P-434)
GOTHIC LANDSCAPING INC
Also Called: Gothic Grounds Mgmt
27413 Tourney Rd Ste 200 (91355-5606)
PHONE..................661 257-5085
Ron Georgio, *Pr*
EMP: 99
SALES (corp-wide): 119.26MM **Privately Held**
Web: www.gothiclandscape.com
SIC: 0781 0782 Landscape services; Lawn and garden services
PA: Gothic Landscaping, Inc.
27413 Tourney Rd
Santa Clarita CA
661 678-1400

(P-435)
HART HOWERTON LTD (PA)
1 Union St Fl 3 (94111-1223)
PHONE..................415 439-2200
EMP: 90 EST: 1982
SQ FT: 20,000
SALES (est): 13.2MM **Privately Held**
Web: www.harthowerton.com
SIC: 0781 8712 Landscape architects; Architectural services

(P-436)
HARVEST LANDSCAPE ENTPS INC (PA)
Also Called: Harvest Landscape Maintenance
8030 E Crystal Dr (92807-2524)
P.O. Box 3877 (92857-0877)
PHONE..................714 693-8100
Stephen G Schinhofen, *CEO*
Robert Gavela, *CPO*
EMP: 156 EST: 2003
SALES (est): 28.03MM
SALES (corp-wide): 28.03MM **Privately Held**
Web: www.hlei.us
SIC: 0781 Landscape services

(P-437)
HEAVENLY CONSTRUCTION INC
Also Called: Heavenly Greens
370 Umbarger Rd Ste A (95111-2070)
PHONE..................408 723-4954
Daniel Theis, *Pr*
EMP: 73 EST: 2003
SQ FT: 75,000
SALES (est): 8.68MM **Privately Held**
Web: www.heavenlygreens.com

SIC: 0781 Landscape services

(P-438)
HEMINGTON LANDSCAPE SVCS INC
4170 Business Dr (95682-7230)
P.O. Box 1999 (95682-1999)
PHONE..................530 677-9290
Mark E Hemington, *Pr*
Jill Hemington, *
EMP: 100 EST: 1983
SALES (est): 8.98MM **Privately Held**
Web: www.hemington.com
SIC: 0781 Landscape services

(P-439)
HYDRO-DIG INC
700 E Sycamore St (92805-2831)
PHONE..................714 772-9947
Martin C Rippens, *Pr*
Gary Tavan, *
EMP: 70 EST: 1964
SQ FT: 5,000
SALES (est): 964.93K **Privately Held**
SIC: 0781 Landscape architects

(P-440)
I PWLC INC
408 Olive Ave (92083-3438)
P.O. Box 3557 (92085-3557)
PHONE..................760 630-0231
Richard Ruiz, *CEO*
EMP: 90 EST: 2004
SQ FT: 1,000
SALES (est): 4.69MM **Privately Held**
Web: www.pacwestlandcare.com
SIC: 0781 Landscape services

(P-441)
LTC CONSTRUCTION INC (HQ)
Also Called: Landscape & Tree Company, Inc.
93540 Viking Pl (95747)
PHONE..................916 246-9987
Chris Huppe, *Pr*
Gina Huppe, *
EMP: 68 EST: 1990
SQ FT: 215,000
SALES (est): 23.46MM
SALES (corp-wide): 42.63MM **Privately Held**
Web: www.landscapetreeco.com
SIC: 0781 0782 Horticulture services; Lawn and garden services
PA: Jensen Corporate Holdings, Inc.
1250 Ames Ave
Milpitas CA
408 446-1118

(P-442)
MARINA MAINTENANCE GROUP INC
Also Called: Marina Landscape Maint Inc
1900 S Lewis St (92805-6718)
PHONE..................714 939-6600
Robert B Cowan, *CEO*
EMP: 450 EST: 2014
SALES (est): 21.31MM
SALES (corp-wide): 2.77B **Publicly Held**
Web: www.marinaco.com
SIC: 0781 Landscape services
HQ: Brightview Landscapes, Llc
980 Jolly Rd Ste 300
Blue Bell PA
484 567-7204

(P-443)
MEDALLION LANDSCAPE MGT INC (PA)
10 San Bruno Ave (95037-9214)

P.O. Box 1768 (95038-1768)
PHONE..................408 782-7500
John Gates, *CEO*
Joyce Dawson, *
Ildefonso Fonsie Bettencourt, *
EMP: 65 EST: 1995
SALES (est): 23.92MM **Privately Held**
Web: www.mlmi.com
SIC: 0781 Landscape counseling services

(P-444)
MERCHANTS LANDSCAPE SERVICES
8748 Industrial Ln # 1 (91730-4526)
PHONE..................909 981-1022
Freddy Martinez, *Mgr*
EMP: 96
SALES (corp-wide): 90.51MM **Privately Held**
Web: www.merchantslandscape.com
SIC: 0781 Landscape planning services
HQ: Merchants Landscape Services, Inc
1639 E Edinger Ave Ste C
Santa Ana CA
714 972-8200

(P-445)
MISSION LDSCP COMPANIES INC
536 E Dyer Rd (92707-3737)
P.O. Box 16069 (92623-6069)
PHONE..................714 545-9962
David Dubois, *CEO*
Beth Du Boise, *
Cindy Clark, *
EMP: 200 EST: 1973
SQ FT: 11,000
SALES (est): 20.31MM **Privately Held**
Web: www.missionlandscape.com
SIC: 0781 Landscape services

(P-446)
MISSION LDSCP COMPANIES INC
16672 Millikan Ave (92606-5008)
P.O. Box 16069 (92623-6069)
PHONE..................800 545-9963
David Dubois, *CEO*
EMP: 90 EST: 1977
SALES (est): 33.29MM **Privately Held**
Web: www.missionlandscape.com
SIC: 0781 Landscape counseling services

(P-447)
MONARCH LDSCP COMPANIES LLC
550 S Hope St Ste 1675 (90071-2692)
PHONE..................213 797-5934
Brian Helgoe, *CEO*
EMP: 79 EST: 2017
SALES (est): 1.9MM **Privately Held**
SIC: 0781 Landscape services

(P-448)
MONUMENT CONSTRUCTION INC
Also Called: Techcon
18450 Technology Dr Ste E1 (95037)
PHONE..................408 778-1350
Paul Maxwell Swing, *Pr*
Diane Swing, *
EMP: 90 EST: 2000
SALES (est): 10.62MM **Privately Held**
Web: www.techconcorp.com
SIC: 0781 Landscape services

0781 - Landscape Counseling And Planning (P-449)

(P-449)
NATURES IMAGE INC
20361 Hermana Cir (92630-8701)
PHONE.................................949 680-4400
EMP: 95 EST: 1996
SQ FT: 13,800
SALES (est): 9.8MM **Privately Held**
Web: www.naturesimage.net
SIC: **0781** 0782 Landscape services; Landscape contractors

(P-450)
NEW PATH LANDSCAPE SVCS INC
Also Called: Allied Landscape Services
16170 Vineyard Blvd Ste 180 (95037-5498)
PHONE.................................408 310-8476
Filiberto Fonseca, *Pr*
Gino Borello, *
Yelena Slutskaya, *Accounting*
EMP: 65 EST: 2005
SALES (est): 8.88MM **Privately Held**
SIC: **0781** Landscape services

(P-451)
NIEVES LANDSCAPE INC
1629 E Edinger Ave (92705-5001)
PHONE.................................714 835-7332
Gregorio Nieves, *Pr*
Patricia White, *
EMP: 150 EST: 1985
SALES (est): 8.34MM **Privately Held**
Web: www.nieveslandscape.com
SIC: **0781** Landscape services

(P-452)
NISSHO OF CALIFORNIA INC (PA)
1902 S Santa Fe Ave (92083-7721)
PHONE.................................760 727-9719
Nobu J Kato, *CEO*
Ed Trotter, *
EMP: 111 EST: 1989
SQ FT: 10,000
SALES (est): 23.11MM
SALES (corp-wide): 23.11MM **Privately Held**
Web: www.nisshoca.com
SIC: **0781** 0782 Landscape services; Turf installation services, except artificial

(P-453)
PAC WEST LAND CARE INC
Also Called: Pacific West Tree Service
408 Olive Ave (92083-3438)
P.O. Box 99 (92085-0099)
PHONE.................................760 630-0231
Barry Blue, *Pr*
EMP: 130 EST: 1979
SQ FT: 3,000
SALES (est): 1.86MM **Privately Held**
Web: www.pacwestlandcare.com
SIC: **0781** Landscape services

(P-454)
PACIFIC COAST LDSCP MGT INC
3960 Holway Dr (94514-1001)
P.O. Box 757 (94514-0757)
PHONE.................................925 513-2310
Alvaro Beltran, *Pr*
Robin Rowley, *
EMP: 60 EST: 1997
SALES (est): 4.79MM **Privately Held**
Web: www.pacificcoastlandscape.net
SIC: **0781** 0782 Landscape services; Lawn and garden services

(P-455)
PACIFIC GREEN LANDSCAPE INC (PA)
8834 Winter Gardens Blvd (92040-5419)
PHONE.................................619 390-1546
Michael C Regan, *Pr*
EMP: 109 EST: 1979
SQ FT: 1,450
SALES (est): 10.85MM
SALES (corp-wide): 10.85MM **Privately Held**
Web: www.pacificgreenlandscape.com
SIC: **0781** Landscape services

(P-456)
PETALON LANDSCAPE MGT INC
1766 Rogers Ave (95112-1109)
PHONE.................................408 453-3998
Rudy Sotelo, *CEO*
John Linn, *
EMP: 65 EST: 2001
SQ FT: 5,000
SALES (est): 6.21MM **Privately Held**
Web: www.petalon.com
SIC: **0781** Landscape services

(P-457)
PIERRE LANDSCAPE INC
5455 2nd St (91706-2072)
PHONE.................................626 587-2121
Harold Young, *CEO*
Joseph Lowden, *
Monty Khouri, *
EMP: 200 EST: 1980
SQ FT: 9,425
SALES (est): 48.36MM **Privately Held**
Web: www.pierrelandscape.com
SIC: **0781** Landscape architects

(P-458)
PLATINUM LANDSCAPE INC
42575 Melanie Pl Ste C (92211-5162)
PHONE.................................760 200-3673
Christopher Johnson, *Pr*
Cherie Johnson, *
EMP: 150 EST: 2002
SQ FT: 3,000
SALES (est): 21.52MM **Privately Held**
Web: www.platinumlandscapeinc.com
SIC: **0781** Landscape services

(P-459)
RANCHO DEL ORO LDSCP MAINT INC
4167 Avenida De La Plata Ste 109 (92056)
P.O. Box 4608 (92052-4608)
PHONE.................................760 726-0215
Uriel Espinoza, *Pr*
Richard Kirk, *
Albertano Cardenas, *
EMP: 73 EST: 2001
SQ FT: 1,400
SALES (est): 4.53MM **Privately Held**
Web: www.rdolandscape.com
SIC: **0781** Landscape services

(P-460)
SAN VAL CORP (PA)
Also Called: San Val Alarm System
72203 Adelaid St (92276-2321)
P.O. Box 12860 (92255-2860)
PHONE.................................760 346-3999
Robert L Sandifer, *Pr*
Sharon L Sandifer, *
EMP: 425 EST: 1975
SALES (est): 17.31MM
SALES (corp-wide): 17.31MM **Privately Held**
Web: www.sunshinelandscapecv.com
SIC: **0781** 7381 Landscape services; Burglary protection service

(P-461)
SEQUOIA ENVIRONMENTAL SVCS INC
1 University Dr (92656-8081)
PHONE.................................949 480-4742
Danny Mcnamara, *CEO*
Malcolm Thomas, *
Scott Collins, *
EMP: 64 EST: 2015
SALES (est): 2.33MM **Privately Held**
Web: www.sequoiaes.com
SIC: **0781** 7349 Landscape services; Janitorial service, contract basis

(P-462)
SHASTA LANDSCAPING INC
1340 Descanso Ave (92069-1306)
PHONE.................................760 744-6551
Leonard R Hogan, *CEO*
Leonard R Hogan, *CEO*
Daniel Hogan, *
Debara Prescott, *
Susan Hogan, *
EMP: 75 EST: 1979
SQ FT: 6,000
SALES (est): 4.86MM **Privately Held**
Web: www.shastalandscaping.com
SIC: **0781** Landscape services

(P-463)
SHORELINE LAND CARE INC (PA)
Also Called: Landcare Logic
4925 Market St (92102-4731)
P.O. Box 23125 (92193-3125)
PHONE.................................858 560-8555
Craig Gerber, *CEO*
EMP: 64 EST: 2003
SALES (est): 2.46MM
SALES (corp-wide): 2.46MM **Privately Held**
Web: www.landcarelogic.com
SIC: **0781** Landscape services

(P-464)
SITEWORKS LANDSCAPE INC
5327 Jacuzzi St Ste 1b (94804-5810)
PHONE.................................510 843-0409
Thomas Brumfield, *Brnch Mgr*
EMP: 84
Web: www.siteworkslandscape.com
SIC: **0781** Landscape services
PA: Siteworks Landscape, Inc.
2319 4th St
Berkeley CA

(P-465)
SOUTHWEST LANDSCAPE INC
2205 S Standard Ave (92707-3036)
P.O. Box 15611 (92735-0611)
PHONE.................................714 545-1084
Dan Hansen, *Pr*
Robert Hansen, *
EMP: 80 EST: 1982
SQ FT: 7,800
SALES (est): 2.39MM **Privately Held**
Web: www.southwestlandscape.org
SIC: **0781** Landscape services

(P-466)
SPECIALIZED LDSCP MGT SVCS INC
Also Called: SLM Services
4212 Peast Los Angeles Ave # 4211 (93063)
PHONE.................................805 520-7590
Rene Emeterio, *Pr*
Wendy Emeterio, *
EMP: 77 EST: 2006
SALES (est): 2.35MM **Privately Held**
Web: www.slmlandscape.net
SIC: **0781** Landscape services

(P-467)
SPERBER LDSCP COMPANIES LLC (PA)
30700 Russell Ranch Rd Ste 120 (91362-9503)
PHONE.................................818 437-1029
Richard A Sperber, *CEO*
EMP: 240 EST: 2018
SALES (est): 103.65MM
SALES (corp-wide): 103.65MM **Privately Held**
SIC: **0781** Landscape services

(P-468)
SWA GROUP (PA)
2200 Bridgeway (94965-1750)
P.O. Box 5904 (94966-5904)
PHONE.................................415 332-5100
Gerdo Aquino, *CEO*
Kevin Shanley, *
Rene Bihan, *Prin*
John Wong, *Prin*
EMP: 60 EST: 1957
SQ FT: 12,000
SALES (est): 34.1MM
SALES (corp-wide): 34.1MM **Privately Held**
Web: www.swagroup.com
SIC: **0781** Landscape architects

(P-469)
TERRA PACIFIC LANDSCAPE (HQ)
12891 Nelson St (92840-5018)
PHONE.................................714 567-0177
Rich Wingard, *Pr*
EMP: 89 EST: 1988
SALES (est): 17.78MM
SALES (corp-wide): 119.26MM **Privately Held**
Web: www.terrapac.com
SIC: **0781** Landscape services
PA: Gothic Landscaping, Inc.
27413 Tourney Rd
Santa Clarita CA
661 678-1400

(P-470)
TREEBEARD LANDSCAPE INC
9917 Campo Rd (91977-1609)
P.O. Box 2777 (91979-2777)
PHONE.................................619 697-8302
Tim Hillman, *Pr*
Craig Des Lauriers, *
EMP: 100 EST: 1974
SQ FT: 2,500
SALES (est): 4.66MM **Privately Held**
Web: www.treebeardlandscape.com
SIC: **0781** Landscape services

(P-471)
YARDZEN CO
480 Gate 5 Rd (94965-1461)
PHONE.................................415 729-0115
EMP: 71 EST: 2019
SALES (est): 1.1MM **Privately Held**
Web: www.yardzen.com
SIC: **0781** Landscape services

PRODUCTS & SERVICES SECTION

0782 - Lawn And Garden Services (P-494)

0782 Lawn And Garden Services

(P-472)
AK LANDSCAPING MAINT INC
42929 Madio St (92201-1978)
PHONE.................................760 347-9747
Deann Arehia, *Off Mgr*
EMP: 77
SIC: 0782 Landscape contractors
PA: A.K. Landscaping Maintenance, Inc.
82233 Lemon Grove Ave
Indio CA

(P-473)
AMERICAN LANDSCAPE MGT INC
Also Called: Custom Lawn Services
1607 Los Angeles Ave Ste I (93004-3237)
PHONE.................................805 647-5077
Armondo Bello, *Mgr*
EMP: 75
Web: www.americanlandscape.com
SIC: 0782 0783 0781 Landscape contractors; Ornamental shrub and tree services; Landscape planning services
PA: American Landscape Management, Inc.
7013 Owensmouth Ave
Canoga Park CA

(P-474)
ARAGON COMMERCIAL LDSCPG INC
2305 S Vasco Rd (94550-9681)
PHONE.................................408 998-0600
Scott Tabler, *Pr*
EMP: 135 **EST:** 1974
SQ FT: 7,000
SALES (est): 4.58MM **Privately Held**
Web: www.aragonlandscaping.com
SIC: 0782 0781 Landscape contractors; Landscape services

(P-475)
AZTEC LANDSCAPING INC (PA)
7980 Lemon Grove Way (91945-1820)
PHONE.................................619 464-3303
Genaro Garcia, *Pr*
Ramon Aguilar, *
Rafael Aguilar, *
EMP: 180 **EST:** 1981
SQ FT: 30,000
SALES (est): 23.16MM
SALES (corp-wide): 23.16MM **Privately Held**
Web: www.azteclandscaping.com
SIC: 0782 0783 7349 Landscape contractors; Ornamental shrub and tree services; Janitorial service, contract basis

(P-476)
BLOSSOM VALLEY CNSTR INC
1125 Mabury Rd (95133-1029)
P.O. Box 611537 (95161-1537)
PHONE.................................408 993-0766
Mark Collishaw, *Pr*
Robert Jimenez, *
EMP: 60 **EST:** 1984
SQ FT: 5,000
SALES (est): 8.84MM **Privately Held**
SIC: 0782 Landscape contractors

(P-477)
BRIGHTVIEW COMPANIES LLC
11555 Coley River Cir (92708-4224)
PHONE.................................714 437-1586
EMP: 220
Web: www.brightview.com
SIC: 0782 Landscape contractors
PA: Brightview Companies, Llc
2275 Research Blvd
Rockville MD

(P-478)
CAGWIN & DORWARD LLC
887 Howe Rd Ste A (94553-3468)
PHONE.................................415 892-7710
Steve Glenin, *Mgr*
EMP: 70
SALES (corp-wide): 53.15MM **Privately Held**
Web: www.cagwin.com
SIC: 0782 Landscape contractors
PA: Cagwin & Dorward, Llc
1422 Technology Ln
Petaluma CA
415 892-7710

(P-479)
CAL-WEST NURSERIES INC
138 North Dr (92860-1637)
PHONE.................................951 270-0667
Michael Whiting, *Pr*
EMP: 150 **EST:** 1968
SQ FT: 1,700
SALES (est): 4.55MM **Privately Held**
Web: www.calwestlandscape.com
SIC: 0782 0181 Landscape contractors; Nursery stock, growing of

(P-480)
CALIFORNIA LDSCP & DESIGN INC
Also Called: CA Landscape and Design
273 N Benson Ave (91786-5614)
PHONE.................................909 949-1601
Joseph Ciaglia Junior, *CEO*
Margaret Mingura, *
EMP: 120 **EST:** 1988
SQ FT: 1,500
SALES (est): 9.95MM **Privately Held**
Web: www.calandscape.com
SIC: 0782 Landscape contractors

(P-481)
CENTRESCAPES INC
165 Gentry St (91767-2184)
PHONE.................................909 392-3303
Mark Marcus, *Pr*
Grace Loya, *
EMP: 88 **EST:** 1992
SQ FT: 7,000
SALES (est): 4.77MM **Privately Held**
Web: www.centrescapes.com
SIC: 0782 Landscape contractors

(P-482)
CHAMPAGNE LANDSCAPE NURS INC
3233 N Cornelia Ave (93722-4606)
P.O. Box 9755 (93794-9755)
PHONE.................................559 277-8188
Robert Champagne, *Pr*
Gail Champagne, *
Robert N Champagne, *
Courtney Woody, *
EMP: 87 **EST:** 1971
SALES (est): 2.37MM **Privately Held**
Web: www.champagnelandscapenursery.com
SIC: 0782 0781 Garden maintenance services; Landscape architects

(P-483)
DECKER LANDSCAPING INC
13265 Bill Francis Dr (95603-9022)
PHONE.................................916 652-1780
EMP: 75 **EST:** 1993
SQ FT: 2,500
SALES (est): 4.28MM **Privately Held**
Web: www.deckerlandscaping.com
SIC: 0782 0781 Landscape contractors; Landscape architects

(P-484)
DESERT HAVEN ENTERPRISES
43437 Copeland Cir (93535-4672)
P.O. Box 2110 (93539-2110)
PHONE.................................661 948-8402
Jenni C Moran, *CEO*
Roberta Terry, *
EMP: 543 **EST:** 1954
SQ FT: 15,000
SALES (est): 10.94MM **Privately Held**
Web: www.deserthaven.org
SIC: 0782 8331 Lawn and garden services; Work experience center

(P-485)
DIVERSCAPE INC
Also Called: Diversified Landscape Co
21730 Bundy Canyon Rd (92595-8780)
PHONE.................................951 245-1686
Vicki Moralez, *Pr*
Paul Moralez, *
EMP: 90 **EST:** 1989
SQ FT: 4,000
SALES (est): 10.03MM **Privately Held**
Web: www.diversifiedlandscape.com
SIC: 0782 1611 Garden maintenance services; General contractor, highway and street construction

(P-486)
DOMINGUEZ LANDSCAPE SVCS INC
7945 14th Ave (95826-4303)
P.O. Box 292727 (95829-2727)
PHONE.................................916 381-8855
Robert Dominguez, *Pr*
Bonnie J Dominguez, *
EMP: 78 **EST:** 1980
SALES (est): 4.75MM **Privately Held**
SIC: 0782 Landscape contractors

(P-487)
DOOSE LANDSCAPE INCORPORATED
785 E Mission Rd (92069-1903)
PHONE.................................760 591-4500
Robert J Doose, *Pr*
Tom Doose, *
Susan Daugherty, *
Shelley Nolet, *
EMP: 85 **EST:** 1967
SQ FT: 11,300
SALES (est): 4.71MM **Privately Held**
Web: www.doose.com
SIC: 0782 Landscape contractors

(P-488)
EMERALD LANDSCAPE SERVICES INC
26415 Summit Cir (91350-2991)
PHONE.................................714 844-2200
John C Croul, *Pr*
EMP: 70 **EST:** 1986
SALES (est): 5.07MM
SALES (corp-wide): 28.3MM **Privately Held**
Web: www.emeraldlandscapeservices.com
SIC: 0782 0781 Landscape contractors; Landscape planning services
PA: Stay Green Inc.
26415 Summit Cir
Santa Clarita CA
661 291-2800

(P-489)
EXCEL LANDSCAPE INC
710 Rimpau Ave Ste 108 (92879-5724)
P.O. Box 77995 (92877-0133)
PHONE.................................951 735-9650
Jose Alfaro, *Pr*
▲ **EMP:** 120 **EST:** 1975
SQ FT: 1,200
SALES (est): 5.9MM **Privately Held**
Web: www.excellandscape.com
SIC: 0782 Lawn care services

(P-490)
FENDERSCAPE INCORPORATED
Also Called: Proscape Landscape
1446 E Hill St (90755-3527)
PHONE.................................562 988-2228
David Fender, *Pr*
Linda Fender, *
EMP: 127 **EST:** 1984
SQ FT: 1,893
SALES (est): 4.48MM **Privately Held**
Web: www.proscapelandscaping.com
SIC: 0782 Landscape contractors

(P-491)
GARDENERS GUILD INC
2780 Goodrick Ave (94801-1110)
PHONE.................................415 457-0400
Kevin Davis, *Pr*
Mike Davidson, *
Paul Swanson, *
Ginny Kuhel, *
EMP: 140 **EST:** 1972
SQ FT: 25,000
SALES (est): 13.56MM **Privately Held**
Web: www.gardenersguild.com
SIC: 0782 Landscape contractors

(P-492)
GATEWAY LANDSCAPE CNSTR INC
6735 Sierra Ct Ste A (94568-2656)
PHONE.................................925 875-0000
Corey Pontrelli, *Pr*
David J Garcia, *
EMP: 75 **EST:** 1984
SQ FT: 3,000
SALES (est): 4.41MM **Privately Held**
Web: www.gatewaylci.com
SIC: 0782 1711 Landscape contractors; Irrigation sprinkler system installation

(P-493)
GOTHIC LANDSCAPING INC (PA)
Also Called: Gothic Ground Management
27413 Tourney Rd (91355-5602)
PHONE.................................661 678-1400
Jon S Georgio, *Pr*
Mike Georgio, *Prin*
Roger Zino, *Vice Chairman*
Ronald Georgio, *VP*
EMP: 200 **EST:** 1984
SQ FT: 5,000
SALES (est): 119.26MM
SALES (corp-wide): 119.26MM **Privately Held**
Web: www.gothiclandscape.com
SIC: 0782 Landscape contractors

(P-494)
GS BROTHERS INC (PA)
20331 Main St (90745-1033)
PHONE.................................310 833-1369
Alan M Gaudenti, *Pr*

0782 - Lawn And Garden Services (P-495)

Robert M Gaudenti, *
EMP: 190 **EST:** 1963
SALES (est): 7.17MM **Privately Held**
Web: www.gsbrothers.com
SIC: 0782 Landscape contractors

(P-495)
HABITAT RSTRATION SCIENCES INC (PA)
1217 Distribution Way (92081-8817)
PHONE....................760 479-4210
Mark Girard, Pr
June Collins, *
EMP: 65 **EST:** 2004
SALES (est): 11.29MM
SALES (corp-wide): 11.29MM **Privately Held**
Web: www.hrsrestoration.com
SIC: 0782 Landscape contractors

(P-496)
HEAVILAND ENTERPRISES INC
8710 Miramar Pl (92121-2551)
PHONE....................858 412-1576
EMP: 115
SALES (corp-wide): 12.13MM **Privately Held**
SIC: 0782 Landscape contractors
PA: Heaviland Enterprises, Inc.
2180 La Mirada Dr
Vista CA
760 598-7065

(P-497)
HEAVILAND ENTERPRISES INC (PA)
2180 La Mirada Dr (92081-8815)
PHONE....................760 598-7065
TOLL FREE: 800
Thomas J Heaviland, CEO
EMP: 75 **EST:** 1978
SQ FT: 2,500
SALES (est): 12.13MM
SALES (corp-wide): 12.13MM **Privately Held**
Web: www.brightview.com
SIC: 0782 1542 Landscape contractors; Commercial and office buildings, renovation and repair

(P-498)
IKES LANDSCAPE INC
2700 Tiber Ave (95616-2958)
PHONE....................530 758-1698
Eric Aichwalder, Pr
Don Kearney, *
Aletha Aichwalder, *
EMP: 80 **EST:** 1974
SQ FT: 2,000
SALES (est): 4.89MM **Privately Held**
SIC: 0782 5992 Landscape contractors; Plants, potted

(P-499)
IRRISCAPE CONSTRUCTION INC
20182 Carancho Rd (92590-4348)
PHONE....................951 694-6936
Robert Smith, Pr
EMP: 100 **EST:** 1983
SQ FT: 1,500
SALES (est): 4.8MM **Privately Held**
Web: www.irriscapeconstruction.com
SIC: 0782 Landscape contractors

(P-500)
JAMES H COWAN & ASSOCIATES INC
5126 Clareton Dr Ste 200 (91301-4529)
PHONE....................310 457-2574
Clark J Cowan, Pr
Kendall Whitney, *
EMP: 95 **EST:** 1952
SQ FT: 3,500
SALES (est): 4.26MM **Privately Held**
SIC: 0782 Landscape contractors

(P-501)
JENSEN CORP LANDSCAPE CONTR
1983 Concourse Dr (95131-1708)
PHONE....................408 446-4881
John Vlay, CEO
Shamina Edwards, *
EMP: 150 **EST:** 2008
SALES (est): 5.93MM **Privately Held**
SIC: 0782 1521 Landscape contractors; Single-family housing construction

(P-502)
JENSEN CORPORATE HOLDINGS INC
960 Lakeville St (94952-3330)
PHONE....................707 527-6187
EMP: 183
SALES (corp-wide): 42.63MM **Privately Held**
SIC: 0782 Landscape contractors
PA: Jensen Corporate Holdings, Inc.
1250 Ames Ave
Milpitas CA
408 446-1118

(P-503)
JENSEN CORPORATE HOLDINGS INC (PA)
1250 Ames Ave (95035-6364)
PHONE....................408 446-1118
John Vlay, CEO
Quang Trinh, *
Donald Defever, *
Rodney W Morimoto, Vice President Business*
Kirk Brown, Estimator*
EMP: 117 **EST:** 1969
SQ FT: 13,000
SALES (est): 42.63MM
SALES (corp-wide): 42.63MM **Privately Held**
SIC: 0782 Landscape contractors

(P-504)
JPA LANDSCAPE & CNSTR INC
256 Boeing Ct (94551-9258)
P.O. Box 1292 (94566-0129)
PHONE....................925 960-9602
Ed Morrissey, Pr
Jody Morrissey, *
EMP: 75 **EST:** 1995
SQ FT: 9,000
SALES (est): 8.42MM **Privately Held**
Web: www.jpalandscape.com
SIC: 0782 Landscape contractors

(P-505)
KDK PACIFIC COAST ENTPS LLC
Also Called: Foreverlawn Pacific Coast
18650 Collier Ave Ste B (92530-2724)
PHONE....................330 715-3143
EMP: 62 **EST:** 2015
SALES (est): 1.24MM **Privately Held**
SIC: 0782 Turf installation services, except artificial

(P-506)
KITSON LANDSCAPE MGT INC
5787 Thornwood Dr (93117-3801)
PHONE....................805 681-9460
Sarah Kitson, Pr
Brent Kitson, *
Sally Kitson, *
David Fudurich, *
EMP: 80 **EST:** 1969
SQ FT: 52,272
SALES (est): 5.46MM **Privately Held**
Web: www.kitsonlandscape.com
SIC: 0782 Landscape contractors

(P-507)
LANDCARE USA LLC
Also Called: Trugreen
216 N Clara St (92703-3518)
PHONE....................949 559-7771
Kenny Stites, Brnch Mgr
EMP: 91
SALES (corp-wide): 124.7MM **Privately Held**
Web: www.trugreen.com
SIC: 0782 Lawn care services
PA: Landcare Usa L.L.C.
5295 Westview Dr Ste 100
Frederick MD
301 874-3300

(P-508)
LANDCARE USA LLC
Also Called: Trugreen
770 Metcalf St (92025-1667)
PHONE....................760 747-1174
Brett Horan, Brnch Mgr
EMP: 65
SALES (corp-wide): 124.7MM **Privately Held**
Web: www.trugreen.com
SIC: 0782 Lawn care services
PA: Landcare Usa L.L.C.
5295 Westview Dr Ste 100
Frederick MD
301 874-3300

(P-509)
LANDCARE USA LLC
Also Called: Trugreen
3213 Fitzgerald Rd (95742-6813)
PHONE....................916 635-0936
Kevin Arnett, Brnch Mgr
EMP: 91
SALES (corp-wide): 124.7MM **Privately Held**
Web: www.trugreen.com
SIC: 0782 Lawn care services
PA: Landcare Usa L.L.C.
5295 Westview Dr Ste 100
Frederick MD
301 874-3300

(P-510)
LANDCARE USA LLC
Also Called: Trugreen
5248 Governor Dr (92122-2800)
PHONE....................858 453-1755
Craig Gerber, Mgr
EMP: 182
SALES (corp-wide): 124.7MM **Privately Held**
Web: www.trugreen.com
SIC: 0782 Lawn care services
PA: Landcare Usa L.L.C.
5295 Westview Dr Ste 100
Frederick MD
301 874-3300

(P-511)
LANDCARE USA LLC
Also Called: Trugreen
7755 Deering Ave (91304-5653)
PHONE....................818 346-7552
Raul Sanchez, Brnch Mgr
EMP: 78
SALES (corp-wide): 124.7MM **Privately Held**
Web: www.landcare.com
SIC: 0782 Lawn care services
PA: Landcare Usa L.L.C.
5295 Westview Dr Ste 100
Frederick MD
301 874-3300

(P-512)
LANDCARE USA LLC
1064 Serpentine Ln Ste A (94566-4810)
PHONE....................925 462-2193
Jeff Ahrens, Brnch Mgr
EMP: 143
SALES (corp-wide): 124.7MM **Privately Held**
Web: www.landcare.com
SIC: 0782 Lawn care services
PA: Landcare Usa L.L.C.
5295 Westview Dr Ste 100
Frederick MD
301 874-3300

(P-513)
LANDCARE USA LLC
Also Called: Trugreen
85 Old Tully Rd (95111-1910)
PHONE....................408 727-4099
EMP: 78
SALES (corp-wide): 124.7MM **Privately Held**
Web: www.trugreen.com
SIC: 0782 Lawn care services
PA: Landcare Usa L.L.C.
5295 Westview Dr Ste 100
Frederick MD
301 874-3300

(P-514)
LANDESIGN CNSTR & MAINT INC
Also Called: Landesign Construction & Maint
1328 Airport Blvd (95403-1009)
P.O. Box 2326 (95405-0326)
PHONE....................707 578-2657
EMP: 90 **EST:** 1990
SQ FT: 1,000
SALES (est): 8.8MM **Privately Held**
Web: www.landesign-inc.com
SIC: 0782 Landscape contractors

(P-515)
LANDSCAPE DEVELOPMENT INC
1290 Carbide Dr (92881-7268)
PHONE....................951 371-9370
Tom Mcdaniel, Pr
EMP: 148
SALES (corp-wide): 89.85MM **Privately Held**
Web: www.landscapedevelopment.com
SIC: 0782 Landscape contractors
PA: Landscape Development, Inc.
28447 Witherspoon Pkwy
Valencia CA
661 295-1970

(P-516)
LANDSCAPE DEVELOPMENT INC (PA)
28447 Witherspoon Pkwy (91355-4174)
PHONE....................661 295-1970
Mark J Crutcher, CEO
Gary Horton, *
Casper Correll, *
Tim Myers, *
Jenny Lunde, *

0782 - Lawn And Garden Services (P-539)

▲ EMP: 350 EST: 1983
SALES (est): 89.85MM
SALES (corp-wide): 89.85MM Privately Held
Web: www.landscapedevelopment.com
SIC: 0782 5039 Landscape contractors; Soil erosion control fabrics

(P-517)
LIBERTY LANDSCAPING INC (PA)
5212 El Rivino Rd (92509-1807)
PHONE.................................951 683-2999
Alejandro Casillas, Pr
EMP: 200 EST: 1997
SQ FT: 43,560
SALES (est): 11.55MM
SALES (corp-wide): 11.55MM Privately Held
Web: www.libertylandscaping.com
SIC: 0782 0783 Landscape contractors; Tree trimming services for public utility lines

(P-518)
MARINA LANDSCAPE INC
Also Called: Marina
3707 W Garden Grove Blvd (92868-4803)
PHONE.................................714 939-6600
EMP: 430 EST: 1982
SALES (est): 52.81MM Privately Held
Web: www.marinaco.com
SIC: 0782 Landscape contractors

(P-519)
MARIPOSA LANDSCAPES INC (PA)
Also Called: Mariposa Horticultural Entps
6232 Santos Diaz St (91702-3267)
PHONE.................................626 960-0196
Terry Noriega, Pr
Antonio Valenzuela, *
EMP: 98 EST: 1977
SQ FT: 2,000
SALES (est): 26.19MM
SALES (corp-wide): 26.19MM Privately Held
Web: www.mariposa-ca.com
SIC: 0782 Garden maintenance services

(P-520)
MARTINA LANDSCAPE INC
811 Camden Ave (95008-4103)
PHONE.................................408 871-8800
Joe Martina, Pr
EMP: 80 EST: 1947
SQ FT: 2,000
SALES (est): 2.35MM Privately Held
Web: www.martinalandscape.com
SIC: 0782 Landscape contractors

(P-521)
MERCHANTS LANDSCAPE SERVICES
2865 Main St Ste A (91911-4848)
PHONE.................................619 778-6239
Eric Anderson, Mgr
EMP: 97
SALES (corp-wide): 90.51MM Privately Held
Web: www.merchantslandscape.com
SIC: 0782 Landscape contractors
HQ: Merchants Landscape Services, Inc
  1639 E Edinger Ave Ste C
  Santa Ana CA
  714 972-8200

(P-522)
MIKE MCCALL LANDSCAPE INC
4749 Clayton Rd (94521-2936)
PHONE.................................925 363-8100
Mike Mccall, Pr
Mark Tate, *
EMP: 140 EST: 1977
SQ FT: 1,000
SALES (est): 14.88MM Privately Held
Web: www.mmlinc.net
SIC: 0782 Landscape contractors

(P-523)
MPL ENTERPRISES INC
Also Called: Mike Parker Landscape
2302 S Susan St (92704-4421)
PHONE.................................714 545-1717
Michael Parker, Pr
EMP: 90 EST: 1976
SQ FT: 2,000
SALES (est): 2.11MM Privately Held
Web: www.mikeparkerlandscape.com
SIC: 0782 Landscape contractors

(P-524)
NAMVARS INC
11815 Sorrento Valley Rd Ste A (92121-1046)
P.O. Box 400 (92003-0400)
PHONE.................................858 792-5461
Ali A Namvar, Prin
EMP: 80 EST: 1988
SALES (est): 2.19MM Privately Held
Web: www.roya.com
SIC: 0782 Landscape contractors

(P-525)
NEW WAY LANDSCAPE & TREE SVCS
7485 Ronson Rd (92111-1507)
PHONE.................................858 505-8300
Randy Newhard, CEO
Kathryn Dejong, *
Dan Suhovecky, *
Debra Newhard, *
EMP: 175 EST: 1980
SQ FT: 6,400
SALES (est): 20.37MM Privately Held
Web: www.newwaypro.com
SIC: 0782 Landscape contractors

(P-526)
OCONNELL LANDSCAPE MAINT INC
Also Called: O'Connell Landscape Maint
860 E Watson Center Rd (90745-4120)
PHONE.................................800 339-1106
Jack Rush, Brnch Mgr
EMP: 557
SALES (corp-wide): 50.47MM Privately Held
Web: www.oclm.com
SIC: 0782 Landscape contractors
PA: O'connell Landscape Maintenance Inc.
  23091 Arroyo Vis
  Rcho Sta Marg CA
  949 589-2007

(P-527)
PARK WEST LANDSCAPE INC
13105 Crenshaw Blvd (90250-5513)
PHONE.................................310 363-4100
Rose Vargas, Brnch Mgr
EMP: 95
SALES (corp-wide): 99.29MM Privately Held
Web: www.parkwestinc.com
SIC: 0782 Landscape contractors
HQ: Park West Landscape, Inc.
  22421 Gilberto Ste A
  Rcho Sta Marg CA

(P-528)
PARK WEST LANDSCAPE MAINT INC (PA)
Also Called: Park Landscape Maint 1-2-3-4
22421 Gilberto Ste A (92688-2104)
PHONE.................................949 546-8300
Robert Morrison, Pr
Mike Tracy, *
Tom Tracy, Stockholder*
Tom England, *
EMP: 300 EST: 1986
SQ FT: 10,000
SALES (est): 4.3MM
SALES (corp-wide): 4.3MM Privately Held
SIC: 0782 Lawn care services

(P-529)
PARKWOOD LANDSCAPE MAINT INC
16443 Hart St (91406-4608)
PHONE.................................818 988-9677
David Melito, Pr
EMP: 95 EST: 1988
SQ FT: 1,500
SALES (est): 8.86MM Privately Held
Web: www.parkwoodlandscape.com
SIC: 0782 Landscape contractors

(P-530)
PENNEY LAWN SERVICE INC
Also Called: Penny Lawn Service
4000 Allen Rd (93314-9091)
PHONE.................................661 587-4788
Dan Penny, Owner
Sandy Penny, *
EMP: 100 EST: 1989
SQ FT: 1,275
SALES (est): 4.53MM Privately Held
Web: www.penneylawnservice.com
SIC: 0782 Landscape contractors

(P-531)
PROCIDA LANDSCAPE INC
8465 Specialty Cir (95828-2523)
PHONE.................................916 387-5296
John Procida Junior, Pr
EMP: 160 EST: 1980
SQ FT: 15,000
SALES (est): 9.78MM Privately Held
Web: www.procidalandscape.com
SIC: 0782 Lawn care services

(P-532)
RENTOKIL NORTH AMERICA INC
Also Called: Ambius
165 Vallecitos De Oro (92069-1436)
PHONE.................................858 689-9161
Sandy Hammond, Brnch Mgr
EMP: 79
SALES (corp-wide): 4.47B Privately Held
SIC: 0782 Lawn and garden services
HQ: Rentokil North America, Inc.
  1125 Berkshire Blvd # 15
  Wyomissing PA
  470 643-3300

(P-533)
RESIDENT GROUP SERVICES INC (PA)
Also Called: Rgs Services
1156 N Grove St (92806-2109)
PHONE.................................714 630-5300
TOLL FREE: 800
James M Gilly, Pr
Michael K Hayde, *
EMP: 149 EST: 1983
SQ FT: 15,000
SALES (est): 19.85MM
SALES (corp-wide): 19.85MM Privately Held
Web: www.rgsls.com
SIC: 0782 Landscape contractors

(P-534)
RICHMOND ENGINEERING CO INC
Also Called: Lewis Lifetime Tools
15472 Markar Rd (92064-2313)
PHONE.................................800 589-7058
Daniel Wright, Pr
◆ EMP: 120 EST: 1954
SQ FT: 120,000
SALES (est): 8.88MM Privately Held
Web: www.yardbutler.com
SIC: 0782 Lawn and garden services

(P-535)
RMA LAND CONSTRUCTION INC
2707 Saturn St (92821-6705)
PHONE.................................714 985-2888
EMP: 79
Web: www.rmaland.com
SIC: 0782 1542 Landscape contractors; Commercial and office building, new construction

(P-536)
SANSEI GARDENS INC
3250 Darby Cmn (94539-5601)
PHONE.................................510 226-9191
Brian Takehara, Pr
EMP: 110 EST: 1973
SQ FT: 3,000
SALES (est): 10.52MM Privately Held
Web: www.sanseigardens.com
SIC: 0782 Landscape contractors

(P-537)
SOTO COMPANY INC
34275 Camino Capistrano Ste A (92624-1917)
PHONE.................................949 493-9403
Joe Soto, Pr
Carol Soto, *
EMP: 75 EST: 1975
SQ FT: 4,000
SALES (est): 2.42MM Privately Held
Web: www.sotocompany.com
SIC: 0782 Landscape contractors

(P-538)
SUNGARDEN COMPANY INC
4 Wayne Ct Ste 3 (95829-1305)
PHONE.................................916 379-9088
Bruno Sandoval, Pr
Anne Sandoval, *
EMP: 100 EST: 1987
SQ FT: 10,000
SALES (est): 9.99MM Privately Held
Web: www.thegrowingcompany.com
SIC: 0782 Landscape contractors

(P-539)
SUNSET LANDSCAPE MAINTENANCE
27201 Burbank (92610-2500)
P.O. Box 1333 (91702-1333)
PHONE.................................949 455-4636
James Roughan, Pr
Claudia Roughan, *
EMP: 100 EST: 1976
SQ FT: 6,300
SALES (est): 4.52MM Privately Held
Web: www.andrelandscape.com
SIC: 0782 Landscape contractors

0782 - Lawn And Garden Services (P-540)

(P-540)
TRACY RYDER LANDSCAPE INC
Also Called: Tracy Ryder Landscape Cnstr
22421 Gilberto Ste A (92688-2104)
PHONE.....................949 858-7017
Michael S Tracy, *Mgr*
EMP: 70
SALES (corp-wide): 99.29MM **Privately Held**
SIC: **0782** Lawn and garden services
HQ: Tracy Ryder Landscape, Inc.
5375 Cameron St Ste G
Las Vegas NV
702 248-6336

(P-541)
TREE SCULPTURE GROUP
Also Called: Tarra Landscape
642 Mccormick St (94577-1110)
PHONE.....................510 562-4000
Craig Lundin, *CEO*
Craig Lundin, *Pr*
EMP: 60 EST: 1968
SALES (est): 4.68MM **Privately Held**
Web: www.terralandscape.com
SIC: **0782** Landscape contractors

(P-542)
TROPICAL PLAZA NURSERY INC
9642 Santiago Blvd (92867-2521)
PHONE.....................714 998-4100
Leslie T Fields, *Pr*
Mike Feilds, *
EMP: 100 EST: 1950
SQ FT: 5,000
SALES (est): 8.25MM **Privately Held**
Web: www.tropicalplaza.com
SIC: **0782** Landscape contractors

(P-543)
ULTIMATE LANDSCAPING MGT
700 E Sycamore St (92805-2831)
PHONE.....................714 502-9711
James Berne, *Pr*
EMP: 80 EST: 1984
SALES (est): 2.38MM **Privately Held**
SIC: **0782** Landscape contractors

(P-544)
VALLEY LANDSCAPING & MAINT INC
12900 N Lower Sacramento Rd (95242)
PHONE.....................209 334-3659
Don Oliver, *Pr*
Jed Phelps, *
Lori Peck, *
EMP: 120 EST: 1975
SQ FT: 5,000
SALES (est): 6.61MM **Privately Held**
Web: www.valleylandscaping.net
SIC: **0782** Landscape contractors

(P-545)
VENCO WESTERN INC
2400 Eastman Ave (93030-5187)
PHONE.....................805 981-2400
TOLL FREE: 800
Linda Del Nagro Burr, *Pr*
William Burr Stcklder, *Prin*
EMP: 200 EST: 1977
SQ FT: 15,000
SALES (est): 12.51MM **Privately Held**
Web: www.vencowestern.com
SIC: **0782** Landscape contractors

(P-546)
VINTAGE ASSOCIATES INC
Also Called: Vintage Nursery
78755 Darby Rd (92203-9621)
P.O. Box 5250 (92248-5250)
PHONE.....................760 772-3673
Gregory Gritters, *Pr*
EMP: 160 EST: 1989
SQ FT: 1,000
SALES (est): 12.83MM **Privately Held**
Web: www.thevintageco.com
SIC: **0782** 5193 5261 Landscape contractors; Nursery stock; Retail nurseries

(P-547)
W B STARR INC
20602 Canada Rd (92630-8100)
PHONE.....................949 770-8835
William B Starr, *Pr*
Martha L Starr, *
EMP: 65 EST: 1975
SQ FT: 10,000
SALES (est): 4.77MM **Privately Held**
Web: www.wbstarr.com
SIC: **0782** Garden maintenance services

(P-548)
WEST COAST ARBORISTS INC
3625 Stevenson Ave (95205-2409)
PHONE.....................408 855-8660
EMP: 117
SALES (corp-wide): 53.7MM **Privately Held**
Web: www.wcainc.com
SIC: **0782** Landscape contractors
PA: West Coast Arborists, Inc.
2200 E Via Burton
Anaheim CA
714 991-1900

(P-549)
WEST COAST ARBORISTS INC (PA)
2200 E Via Burton (92806-1221)
PHONE.....................714 991-1900
EMP: 100 EST: 1972
SALES (est): 53.7MM
SALES (corp-wide): 53.7MM **Privately Held**
Web: www.wcainc.com
SIC: **0782** Landscape contractors

0783 Ornamental Shrub And Tree Services

(P-550)
A & E ARBORISTS TREE CARE INC
225 Butte Ave (95993-9367)
PHONE.....................530 790-5312
Andrew C Boger, *Pr*
EMP: 268 EST: 2018
SALES (est): 61.28MM **Privately Held**
Web: www.aearborists.com
SIC: **0783** Planting, pruning, and trimming services

(P-551)
A PLUS TREE LLC
985 Walnut Ave (94592-1021)
P.O. Box 7156 (85338-0636)
PHONE.....................707 644-1672
Jeremy Tibbets, *Prin*
EMP: 180 EST: 2008
SALES (est): 20.85MM **Privately Held**
Web: www.aplustree.com
SIC: **0783** Planting, pruning, and trimming services

(P-552)
ARBORWELL INC (PA)
2337 American Ave (94545-1807)
PHONE.....................510 881-4260
Alvin Foye Sortwell, *Pr*
Ann B Sortwell, *
Dennis Shanagher, *
Brad Carson, *
Kris Yamaguchi, *
▲ EMP: 131 EST: 1997
SQ FT: 5,000
SALES (est): 18.36MM
SALES (corp-wide): 18.36MM **Privately Held**
Web: www.arborwell.com
SIC: **0783** Planting, pruning, and trimming services

(P-553)
CLS LANDSCAPE MANAGEMENT INC
Also Called: Cls Landscape Management
4329 State St Ste B (91763-6082)
PHONE.....................909 628-3005
Kevin L Davis, *Pr*
Kimberly Davis, *
EMP: 325 EST: 1983
SQ FT: 2,500
SALES (est): 21.09MM **Privately Held**
Web: www.clslandscape.com
SIC: **0783** 0782 Ornamental shrub and tree services; Lawn and garden services

(P-554)
COASTAL MOUNTAIN TIMBER INC
Also Called: Cmt
3737 Carson Rd Unit A (95709-9593)
P.O. Box 941 (95709-0941)
PHONE.....................530 303-3378
Todd Alter, *CEO*
Robin Lee, *
EMP: 60 EST: 2018
SQ FT: 1,800
SALES (est): 4.95MM **Privately Held**
SIC: **0783** Ornamental shrub and tree services

(P-555)
DAVEY TREE SURGERY COMPANY (HQ)
2617 S Vasco Rd (94550-8322)
P.O. Box 5015 (94551-5015)
PHONE.....................925 443-1723
Karl J Warnke, *CEO*
R Douglas Cowan, *
Howard Bowles, *
Rick Edson, *
David Adante, *
EMP: 873 EST: 1928
SQ FT: 5,000
SALES (est): 51MM
SALES (corp-wide): 1.51B **Privately Held**
Web: www.davey.com
SIC: **0783** Tree trimming services for public utility lines
PA: The Davey Tree Expert Company
1500 N Mantua St
Kent OH
330 673-9511

(P-556)
LEONARD CHAIDEZ INC
Also Called: Leonard Chaidez Tree Service
2298 N Batavia St (92865-3106)
P.O. Box 29 (92815-0029)
PHONE.....................714 279-8173
Leonard Chaidez, *Pr*
Deborah Foushee, *
EMP: 60 EST: 1977
SQ FT: 2,000
SALES (est): 2.46MM **Privately Held**
SIC: **0783** 0781 8748 0782 Planting, pruning, and trimming services; Landscape services; Environmental consultant; Lawn and garden services

(P-557)
MAXIMUS TREE WORKS LLC
Also Called: Tree Services
1410 Beltline Rd Ste 1 (96003-1410)
PHONE.....................480 822-8050
Johnnie Morales, *Managing Member*
Jessica Dean, *Managing Member*
EMP: 83 EST: 2019
SALES (est): 2.51MM **Privately Held**
SIC: **0783** Tree trimming services for public utility lines

(P-558)
ORIGINAL MOWBRAYS TREE SVC INC (PA)
686 E Mill St (92408-1610)
PHONE.....................909 383-7009
Dwight Anderson, *Prin*
EMP: 105 EST: 1972
SQ FT: 1,000
SALES (est): 48.73MM **Privately Held**
Web: www.mowbrays.com
SIC: **0783** Tree trimming services for public utility lines

(P-559)
ORIGINAL MOWBRAYS TREE SVC INC
17332 Millwood Dr (93292-9577)
PHONE.....................559 798-0530
Gloria Mowbray, *Brnch Mgr*
EMP: 95
Web: www.mowbrays.com
SIC: **0783** Tree trimming services for public utility lines
PA: The Original Mowbray's Tree Service Inc
686 E Mill St
San Bernardino CA

(P-560)
PACIFIC COAST TREE EXPERTS
21525 Strathern St (91304-4137)
PHONE.....................805 506-1211
Nicolas Pinedo, *Prin*
Armando Valdez, *
Antonio Ramirez Bonilla, *
Nicolas Pinedo, *Pr*
EMP: 150 EST: 2010
SALES (est): 8.34MM **Privately Held**
Web: www.pacificcoasttreeexperts.com
SIC: **0783** Planting, pruning, and trimming services

(P-561)
WEST COAST ARBORISTS INC
11405 Nardo St (93004-3201)
PHONE.....................805 671-5092
Lorenzo Perez, *Owner*
EMP: 116
SALES (corp-wide): 53.7MM **Privately Held**
Web: www.westcoastarborists.com
SIC: **0783** Planting, pruning, and trimming services
PA: West Coast Arborists, Inc.
2200 E Via Burton
Anaheim CA
714 991-1900

PRODUCTS & SERVICES SECTION   1311 - Crude Petroleum And Natural Gas (P-580)

(P-562)
WEST COAST ARBORISTS INC
21718 Walnut Ave (92313-4437)
PHONE..................................909 783-6544
Patrick Mahoney, *Pr*
EMP: 117
SALES (corp-wide): 53.7MM **Privately Held**
Web: www.westcoastarborists.com
SIC: **0783** Planting, pruning, and trimming services
PA: West Coast Arborists, Inc.
    2200 E Via Burton
    Anaheim CA
    714 991-1900

(P-563)
WEST COAST ARBORISTS INC
5424 N Barcus Ave (93722-5067)
PHONE..................................559 275-2086
Patrick Mahoney, *Brnch Mgr*
EMP: 117
SALES (corp-wide): 53.7MM **Privately Held**
Web: www.westcoastarborists.com
SIC: **0783** Tree trimming services for public utility lines
PA: West Coast Arborists, Inc.
    2200 E Via Burton
    Anaheim CA
    714 991-1900

0811 Timber Tracts

(P-564)
BOETHING TREELAND FARMS INC (PA)
Also Called: Treeland Farms
23475 Long Valley Rd (91367-6006)
PHONE..................................818 883-1222
Bruce Edgar Pherson, *CEO*
Haydi Boething Danielson, *
Marji Boething, *
Marjorie Boething Arnold, *Stockholder**
Cathy Boething Pherson, *Stockholder**
EMP: 60 EST: 1953
SQ FT: 1,500
SALES (est): 29.8MM
SALES (corp-wide): 29.8MM **Privately Held**
Web: www.boethingtreeland.com
SIC: **0811** 5261 Tree farm; Retail nurseries

(P-565)
BOETHING TREELAND FARMS INC
Also Called: Boething Treeland Nursery
20601 E Kettleman Ln (95240-9756)
PHONE..................................209 727-3741
Seilpe Gomez, *Brnch Mgr*
EMP: 72
SALES (corp-wide): 29.8MM **Privately Held**
Web: www.boethingtreeland.com
SIC: **0811** Tree farm
PA: Boething Treeland Farms, Inc.
    23475 Long Valley Rd
    Woodland Hills CA
    818 883-1222

(P-566)
BRIGHTVIEW TREE COMPANY
Also Called: Specimen Contracting
9500 Foothill Blvd (91040-1857)
PHONE..................................818 951-5500
Tadd Russikoff, *Mgr*
EMP: 86
Web: www.brightview.com
SIC: **0811** Tree farm

HQ: Brightview Tree Company
    24151 Ventura Blvd # 100
    Calabasas CA
    818 223-8500

(P-567)
BRIGHTVIEW TREE COMPANY
Also Called: Environmental Industries
3200 W Telegraph Rd (93015-9623)
PHONE..................................714 546-7975
Susan Flores, *Brnch Mgr*
EMP: 86
Web: www.brightview.com
SIC: **0811** 0782 Tree farm; Lawn services
HQ: Brightview Tree Company
    24151 Ventura Blvd # 100
    Calabasas CA
    818 223-8500

(P-568)
BRIGHTVIEW TREE COMPANY
8501 Calaveras Rd (94586-9434)
P.O. Box 289 (95230-0289)
PHONE..................................925 862-2485
John Serviss, *Brnch Mgr*
EMP: 86
SIC: **0811** Tree farm
HQ: Brightview Tree Company
    24151 Ventura Blvd # 100
    Calabasas CA
    818 223-8500

(P-569)
HOLIDAY TREE FARMS INC
329 Van Norman Rd (90640-5314)
P.O. Box 1688 (91793-1688)
PHONE..................................323 276-1900
Greg Rondeau, *Prin*
EMP: 126
SALES (corp-wide): 40.29MM **Privately Held**
Web: www.holidaytreefarm.com
SIC: **0811** Tree farm
PA: Holiday Tree Farms, Inc.
    800 Nw Cornell Ave
    Corvallis OR
    541 753-3236

(P-570)
PINERY LLC
13701 Highland Valley Rd (92025-2300)
P.O. Box 2484 (91729-2484)
PHONE..................................858 675-3575
Cheryl Guardia, *
▲ EMP: 60 EST: 2009
SQ FT: 2,800
SALES (est): 9.83MM **Privately Held**
Web: www.pinerytree.com
SIC: **0811** Christmas tree farm

0831 Forest Products

(P-571)
SIERRA FREST PDTS HOLDINGS INC ✪
9000 Road 234 (93270-9560)
P.O. Box 10060 (93270-0060)
PHONE..................................559 535-4893
Dave Thomas, *CEO*
Seth Hokit, *
Greg Mitchell, *
EMP: 110 EST: 2023
SALES (est): 2.31MM **Privately Held**
SIC: **0831** Forest products

0851 Forestry Services

(P-572)
REDDING TREE GROWERS CORP
18985 Avenue 256 Apt A (93221-9558)
P.O. Box 845 (93221-0845)
PHONE..................................559 594-9299
Francisco Acevedo, *Pr*
Amelia Acevedo, *
EMP: 100 EST: 1990
SALES (est): 6.43MM **Privately Held**
Web: redding-tree-growers-corp.sbcontract.com
SIC: **0851** Reforestation services

1041 Gold Ores

(P-573)
GOLDEN QUEEN MINING CO LLC
2818 Silver Queen Rd (93501-7021)
P.O. Box 1030 (93502-1030)
PHONE..................................661 824-4300
Thomas Clay, *Ch Bd*
Robert Walish, *
Andree St-germain, *CFO*
EMP: 180 EST: 2014
SQ FT: 2,500
SALES (est): 92.48MM
SALES (corp-wide): 57.04MM **Privately Held**
SIC: **1041** Gold ores mining
PA: Golden Queen Mining Co. Ltd
    580 Hornby St Suite 880
    Vancouver BC
    604 417-7952

(P-574)
MERIDIAN GOLD INC
Also Called: Royal Mountain King
4461 Rock Creek Rd (95228-7059)
PHONE..................................209 785-3222
Edgar Smith, *Brnch Mgr*
EMP: 474
SALES (corp-wide): 1.63B **Privately Held**
SIC: **1041** Gold ores
HQ: Meridian Gold Inc.
    4635 Longley Ln Ste 110
    Reno NV

1221 Bituminous Coal And Lignite-surface Mining

(P-575)
CHEVRON MINING INC
Moly
67750 Bailey Rd (92366)
PHONE..................................760 856-7625
EMP: 245
SALES (corp-wide): 162.47B **Publicly Held**
SIC: **1221** Surface mining, bituminous, nec
HQ: Chevron Mining Inc.
    116 Invrneco Dr E Ste 207
    Englewood CO
    303 930-3600

1241 Coal Mining Services

(P-576)
COLOMBIA ENERGY RESOURCES INC
Also Called: (AN EXPLORATION STAGE COMPANY)

1 Embarcadero Ctr Ste 500 (94111-3610)
EMP: 133
SIC: **1241** 1221 1222 Coal mining exploration and test boring; Bituminous coal and lignite-surface mining; Bituminous coal-underground mining

(P-577)
RIO TINTO MINERALS INC
Also Called: Reno Tenco
14486 Borax Rd (93516-2017)
PHONE..................................760 762-7121
Xiaoling Liu, *CEO*
Hugo Bague, *
Preston Chiaro, *
◆ EMP: 150 EST: 2006
SALES (est): 100.81MM
SALES (corp-wide): 55.55B **Privately Held**
Web: www.borax.com
SIC: **1241** Coal mining services
HQ: U.S. Borax Inc.
    200 E Randolph St # 7100
    Chicago IL
    773 270-6500

(P-578)
TAFT PRODUCTION COMPANY
950 Petroleum Club Rd (93268-9748)
P.O. Box 1277 (93268-1277)
PHONE..................................661 765-7194
Daniel S Jaffee, *Pr*
EMP: 95 EST: 2002
SALES (est): 28.51MM
SALES (corp-wide): 413.02MM **Publicly Held**
Web: www.oildri.com
SIC: **1241** 1081 Coal mining services; Metal mining services
PA: Oil-Dri Corporation Of America
    410 N Michigan Ave Fl 4
    Chicago IL
    312 321-1515

1311 Crude Petroleum And Natural Gas

(P-579)
AERA ENERGY LLC
10000 Ming Ave (93311-1301)
P.O. Box 11164 (93389-1164)
PHONE..................................661 665-5000
Erik Bartsch, *Pr*
Ted Witt, *COO*
Sergio De Castro, *CFO*
Lynne Carrithers, *Legal*
Sara Oneill-bouton Senior, *External Affairs Vice President*
EMP: 918 EST: 1994
SALES (est): 5.32MM **Privately Held**
SIC: **1311** Crude petroleum production

(P-580)
AERA ENERGY LLC
Also Called: Kernridge Division
19590 7th Standard Rd (93251-9709)
PHONE..................................661 334-3100
Marie Crosby, *Prin*
EMP: 96
SALES (corp-wide): 381.31B **Privately Held**
Web: www.aeraenergy.com
SIC: **1311** Natural gas production
HQ: Aera Energy Services Company
    10000 Ming Ave
    Bakersfield CA
    661 665-5000

1311 - Crude Petroleum And Natural Gas (P-581)

(P-581)
BREITBURN ENERGY PARTNERS LP
707 Wilshire Blvd Ste 4600 (90017-3612)
PHONE................213 225-5900
EMP: 671
SIC: **1311** Crude petroleum production

(P-582)
CALIFORNIA RESOURCES CORP (PA)
Also Called: CRC
1 World Trade Ctr Ste 1500 (90831-0002)
PHONE................888 848-4754
Francisco J Leon, *Pr*
Tiffany Thom Cepak, *
Manuela Molina, *Ex VP*
Shawn M Kerns, *Ex VP*
Michael L Preston, *Chief Strategy Officer*
EMP: 69 EST: 2014
SALES (est): 2.71B
SALES (corp-wide): 2.71B **Publicly Held**
Web: www.crc.com
SIC: **1311** Crude petroleum and natural gas

(P-583)
CALIFORNIA RESOURCES PROD CORP (HQ)
Also Called: Vintage Production California
27200 Tourney Rd Ste 200 (91355-4910)
PHONE................661 869-8000
EMP: 125 EST: 2005
SALES (est): 84.76MM
SALES (corp-wide): 2.71B **Publicly Held**
SIC: **1311 1382** Crude petroleum production; Oil and gas exploration services
PA: California Resources Corporation
 1 World Trade Ctr Ste 150
 Long Beach CA
 888 848-4754

(P-584)
OCCIDENTAL PETROLEUM CORPORATION OF CALIFORNIA
Also Called: OXY
10889 Wilshire Blvd Fl 10 (90024-4213)
EMP: 3600
SIC: **1311** Crude petroleum production

(P-585)
THE STRAND ENERGY COMPANY
515 S Flower St Ste 4800 (90071-2241)
PHONE................213 225-5900
EMP: 380
SIC: **1311** Crude petroleum and natural gas production

(P-586)
THUMS LONG BEACH COMPANY
111 W Ocean Blvd Ste 800 (90802-7930)
PHONE................562 624-3400
EMP: 205
SIC: **1311** Crude petroleum production

(P-587)
WORLD OIL CORP
9302 Garfield Ave (90280-3896)
P.O. Box 1 (90280-0001)
PHONE................562 928-0100
EMP: 140 EST: 1973
SALES (est): 134.75MM **Privately Held**
Web: www.worldoilcorp.com
SIC: **1311** Crude petroleum and natural gas

1321 Natural Gas Liquids

(P-588)
HEXAGON AGILITY INC
3335 Susan St Ste 100 (92626-1647)
PHONE................949 236-5520
Hans Peter Havdal, *CEO*
Seung Baik, *Pr*
EMP: 99 EST: 2016
SALES (est): 63.23MM **Privately Held**
Web: www.hexagonagility.com
SIC: **1321** Natural gas liquids production
PA: Hexagon Composites Asa
 Korsegata 4b
 Alesund

1381 Drilling Oil And Gas Wells

(P-589)
AERA ENERGY SERVICES COMPANY (HQ)
10000 Ming Ave (93311-1301)
P.O. Box 11164 (93389-1164)
PHONE................661 665-5000
Erik Bartsch, *Pr*
EMP: 800 EST: 1994
SALES (est): 1.73B
SALES (corp-wide): 381.31B **Privately Held**
Web: www.aeraenergy.com
SIC: **1381** Directional drilling oil and gas wells
PA: Shell Plc
 Shell Centre
 London
 800 731-8888

(P-590)
AERA ENERGY SERVICES COMPANY
Also Called: Security Front Desk
59231 Main Camp Rd (93251-9740)
PHONE................661 665-4400
Mike Brown, *Prin*
EMP: 128
SALES (corp-wide): 381.31B **Privately Held**
Web: www.aeraenergy.com
SIC: **1381** Directional drilling oil and gas wells
HQ: Aera Energy Services Company
 10000 Ming Ave
 Bakersfield CA
 661 665-5000

(P-591)
AERA ENERGY SERVICES COMPANY
Also Called: Aera Energy South Midway
29235 Highway 33 (93252-9793)
PHONE................661 665-3200
Andy Anderson, *Mgr*
EMP: 122
SALES (corp-wide): 381.31B **Privately Held**
Web: www.aeraenergy.com
SIC: **1381** Directional drilling oil and gas wells
HQ: Aera Energy Services Company
 10000 Ming Ave
 Bakersfield CA
 661 665-5000

(P-592)
ELYSIUM JENNINGS LLC
1600 Norris Rd (93308-2234)
PHONE................661 679-1700
EMP: 145 EST: 2003
SALES (est): 4.12MM **Privately Held**
SIC: **1381** Drilling oil and gas wells
PA: E & B Natural Resources Management Corporation
 1608 Norris Rd
 Bakersfield CA

(P-593)
EXCALIBUR WELL SERVICES CORP
22034 Rosedale Hwy (93314-9704)
PHONE................661 589-5338
Stephen Layton, *Pr*
Stephen Layton, *CEO*
Frachsco Galesi, *
Gordon Isbel, *
EMP: 120 EST: 2006
SALES (est): 20.11MM **Privately Held**
Web: www.excaliburwellservices.com
SIC: **1381 1389** Drilling oil and gas wells; Fishing for tools, oil and gas field

(P-594)
GOLDEN STATE DRILLING INC
3500 Fruitvale Ave (93308-5106)
PHONE................661 589-0730
Philip F Phelps, *Pr*
Velma Phelps, *
James Phelps, *
EMP: 75 EST: 1977
SALES (est): 11.47MM **Privately Held**
Web: www.gsdrilling.com
SIC: **1381** Directional drilling oil and gas wells

(P-595)
PAUL GRAHAM DRILLING & SVC CO
Also Called: Paul Graham Drilling
2500 Airport Rd (94571-1034)
P.O. Box 669 (94571-0669)
PHONE................707 374-5123
Kevin P Graham, *Pr*
Clarence Santos, *
Jill Graham, *
EMP: 170 EST: 1968
SQ FT: 30,000
SALES (est): 24.14MM **Privately Held**
Web: www.paulgrahamdrilling.com
SIC: **1381 7389 7359** Drilling oil and gas wells; Crane and aerial lift service; Industrial truck rental

1382 Oil And Gas Exploration Services

(P-596)
CALIFRNIA RSRCES ELK HILLS LLC
27200 Tourney Rd Ste 200 (91355-4910)
PHONE................661 412-0000
Michael L Preston, *
Marshall D Smith, *
EMP: 400 EST: 1997
SALES (est): 92.42MM
SALES (corp-wide): 2.71B **Publicly Held**
SIC: **1382** Oil and gas exploration services
PA: California Resources Corporation
 1 World Trade Ctr Ste 150
 Long Beach CA
 888 848-4754

(P-597)
CALIFRNIA RSURCES LONG BCH INC
27200 Tourney Rd Ste 200 (91355-4910)
PHONE................888 848-4754
EMP: 92 EST: 1989
SALES (est): 8.28MM
SALES (corp-wide): 2.71B **Publicly Held**
SIC: **1382** Oil and gas exploration services
PA: California Resources Corporation
 1 World Trade Ctr Ste 150
 Long Beach CA
 888 848-4754

(P-598)
DCOR LLC (PA)
Also Called: Dcor
1000 Town Center Dr Fl 6 (93036-1132)
P.O. Box 3401 (93006-3401)
PHONE................805 535-2000
Andrew Prestridge, *
Alan C Templeton, *
Jeff Warren, *
Bob Garcia, *
EMP: 193 EST: 2001
SALES (est): 89.01MM
SALES (corp-wide): 89.01MM **Privately Held**
Web: www.dcorllc.com
SIC: **1382** Oil and gas exploration services

(P-599)
DRILLMEC INC
8140 Rosecrans Ave (90723-2754)
PHONE................281 885-0777
Paulo Brando Ballerini, *Pr*
Massimo Tartagni, *
◆ EMP: 74 EST: 1998
SALES (est): 24.66MM
SALES (corp-wide): 578.09MM **Privately Held**
SIC: **1382** Oil and gas exploration services
HQ: Soilmec Spa
 Via Dismano 5819
 Cesena FC
 054 731-8548

(P-600)
E & B NTRAL RESOURCES MGT CORP (PA)
1608 Norris Rd (93308-2234)
PHONE................661 679-1714
Steve Layton, *Pr*
Jeff Blesener, *
Jeff Jones, *
Steven K Porter, *
Frank J Ronkese, *
EMP: 65 EST: 1972
SALES (est): 169.42MM **Privately Held**
Web: www.ebresources.com
SIC: **1382** Oil and gas exploration services

(P-601)
LINNCO LLC
5201 Truxtun Ave (93309-0421)
PHONE................661 616-3900
EMP: 888
SALES (corp-wide): 127.72MM **Privately Held**
SIC: **1382** Oil and gas exploration services
PA: Linnco, Llc
 600 Travis St Ste 5100
 Houston TX
 281 840-4000

(P-602)
OCCIDENTAL PETROLEUM INVESTMENT CO INC
10889 Wilshire Blvd Fl 10 (90024-4213)
PHONE................310 208-8800
EMP: 4000
SIC: **1382 8744** Oil and gas exploration services; Facilities support services

1389 - Oil And Gas Field Services, Nec (P-625)

(P-603)
QRE OPERATING LLC
707 Wilshire Blvd Ste 4600 (90017-3501)
PHONE..................213 225-5900
EMP: 82 **EST:** 2010
SALES (est): 921.8K **Privately Held**
SIC: 1382 Oil and gas exploration services
PA: Qr Energy, Lp
707 Wilshire Blvd # 4600
Los Angeles CA

(P-604)
SAMEDAN OIL CORPORATION
Also Called: Noble Energy
1360 Landing Ave (90740-6525)
PHONE..................661 319-5038
EMP: 447
SALES (corp-wide): 80.5MM **Privately Held**
SIC: 1382 Oil and gas exploration services
PA: Samedan Oil Corporation
1001 Noble Energy Way
Houston TX
580 223-4110

(P-605)
SENTINEL PEAK RSOURCES CAL LLC
1200 Discovery Dr Ste 100 (93309-7343)
PHONE..................661 395-5214
EMP: 79
SALES (corp-wide): 89.69MM **Privately Held**
Web: www.sentinelpeakresources.com
SIC: 1382 Oil and gas exploration services
HQ: Sentinel Peak Resources California Llc
6501 E Belleview Ave # 400
Englewood CO
720 749-1105

(P-606)
SENTINEL PEAK RSOURCES CAL LLC
5640 S Fairfax Ave (90056-1266)
PHONE..................323 298-2200
EMP: 79
SALES (corp-wide): 89.69MM **Privately Held**
Web: www.sentinelpeakresources.com
SIC: 1382 Oil and gas exploration services
HQ: Sentinel Peak Resources California Llc
6501 E Belleview Ave # 400
Englewood CO
720 749-1105

(P-607)
WARREN E&P INC
Also Called: Warren E & P
400 Oceangate Ste 200 (90802-4306)
PHONE..................214 393-9688
James A Watt, *CEO*
Romy Massey, *Contact Person**
EMP: 67 **EST:** 1973
SQ FT: 7,000
SALES (est): 18.42K **Privately Held**
SIC: 1382 Oil and gas exploration services
PA: Warren Resources, Inc.
14131 Midway Rd Ste 500
Addison TX

1389 Oil And Gas Field Services, Nec

(P-608)
C&J WELL SERVICES LLC
3752 Allen Rd (93314-9242)
PHONE..................661 589-5220
Joana Lerma, *Managing Member*
Danielle Hunter, *
EMP: 900 **EST:** 2021
SALES (est): 45.15MM **Privately Held**
Web: www.cjwellservices.com
SIC: 1389 Servicing oil and gas wells

(P-609)
CAPSULE MANUFACTURING INC
Also Called: Capsule Mfg
1399 N Miller St (92806-1412)
PHONE..................949 245-4151
Chad Bowker, *Pr*
EMP: 68 **EST:** 2015
SALES (est): 4.3MM **Privately Held**
Web: www.capsulemfg.com
SIC: 1389 Construction, repair, and dismantling services

(P-610)
CJ BERRY WELL SERVICES MGT LLC
3752 Allen Rd (93314-9242)
PHONE..................661 589-5220
Joana Lerma, *Prin*
Danielle Hunter, *
Stacy Urbina, *
EMP: 900 **EST:** 2021
SALES (est): 34.51MM **Privately Held**
SIC: 1389 Servicing oil and gas wells

(P-611)
CL KNOX INC
Also Called: Advanced Industrial Services
34933 Imperial Ave (93308-9579)
PHONE..................661 837-0477
Leslie Knox, *Pr*
Chris Knox, *
EMP: 80 **EST:** 1992
SALES (est): 10MM **Privately Held**
Web: www.aisleaders.com
SIC: 1389 8742 Oil field services, nec; Industrial consultant

(P-612)
CUMMINGS VACUUM SERVICE INC
Also Called: Cummings Transportation
19605 Broken Ct (93263-9583)
PHONE..................661 746-1786
Pam Cummings, *Pr*
Ted Cummings, *
EMP: 60 **EST:** 1980
SQ FT: 3,000
SALES (est): 8.4MM **Privately Held**
Web: www.cummings2.com
SIC: 1389 Oil field services, nec

(P-613)
HILLS WLDG & ENGRG CONTR INC
Also Called: Hwe Mechanical
22038 Stockdale Hwy (93314-8889)
PHONE..................661 746-5400
Debora M Hill, *VP*
Robert Hill, *Stockholder**
EMP: 92 **EST:** 1999
SALES (est): 9.58MM **Privately Held**
Web: www.hillswelding.com
SIC: 1389 Testing, measuring, surveying, and analysis services

(P-614)
JERRY MELTON & SONS CNSTR INC
Also Called: Jerry Melton & Sons Cnstr
100 Jamison Ln (93268-4329)
PHONE..................661 765-5546
Jerry W Melton, *Pr*
Judy Melton, *
Steven Melton, *
Karen Melton, *
EMP: 85 **EST:** 1971
SALES (est): 9.3MM **Privately Held**
SIC: 1389 Oil and gas wells: building, repairing and dismantling

(P-615)
MDM SOLUTIONS LLC
575 Anton Blvd Ste 300 (92626-7169)
PHONE..................800 669-6361
Michael Flower, *Managing Member*
Michael Bryant, *
Cynthia Williams, *
Doug Sipe, *
EMP: 310 **EST:** 2015
SALES (est): 16.56MM **Privately Held**
Web: www.mdmcorp.com
SIC: 1389 Oil and gas wells: building, repairing and dismantling

(P-616)
MMI SERVICES INC
4042 Patton Way (93308-5030)
PHONE..................661 589-9366
Steve Mcgowan, *CEO*
Steve Mcgowan, *Pr*
Mel Mcgowan, *CEO*
Eric Olson, *
EMP: 250 **EST:** 1985
SQ FT: 4,500
SALES (est): 39.65MM **Privately Held**
Web: www.mmi-services.com
SIC: 1389 Oil field services, nec

(P-617)
NABORS WELL SERVICES CO
2567 N Ventura Ave # C (93001-1201)
PHONE..................805 648-2731
Paul Smith, *Mgr*
EMP: 92
Web: www.nabors.com
SIC: 1389 Oil field services, nec
HQ: Nabors Well Services Co.
515 W Greens Rd Ste 1000
Houston TX
281 874-0035

(P-618)
NABORS WELL SERVICES CO
1025 Earthmover Ct (93314-9529)
PHONE..................661 588-6140
Tom Jaquez, *Mgr*
EMP: 162
Web: www.nabors.com
SIC: 1389 Oil field services, nec
HQ: Nabors Well Services Co.
515 W Greens Rd Ste 1000
Houston TX
281 874-0035

(P-619)
NABORS WELL SERVICES CO
19431 S Santa Fe Ave (90221-5912)
PHONE..................310 639-7074
EMP: 85
Web: www.nabors.com
SIC: 1389 Oil field services, nec
HQ: Nabors Well Services Co.
515 W Greens Rd Ste 1000
Houston TX
281 874-0035

(P-620)
NABORS WELL SERVICES CO
1954 James Rd (93308-9749)
PHONE..................661 392-7668
Dave Warner, *Dist Mgr*
EMP: 204
Web: www.nabors.com
SIC: 1389 Oil field services, nec
HQ: Nabors Well Services Co.
515 W Greens Rd Ste 1000
Houston TX
281 874-0035

(P-621)
NABORS WELL SERVICES CO
7515 Rosedale Hwy (93308-5727)
PHONE..................661 589-3970
Alan Pounds, *Mgr*
EMP: 275
Web: www.nabors.com
SIC: 1389 1382 Servicing oil and gas wells; Oil and gas exploration services
HQ: Nabors Well Services Co.
515 W Greens Rd Ste 1000
Houston TX
281 874-0035

(P-622)
OIL WELL SERVICE COMPANY
10255 Enos Ln (93263-9572)
PHONE..................661 746-4809
Rick Hobbs, *Off Mgr*
EMP: 60
SALES (corp-wide): 35.06MM **Privately Held**
Web: www.ows1.com
SIC: 1389 Swabbing wells
PA: Oil Well Service Company
1241 E Burnett St
Signal Hill CA
562 612-0600

(P-623)
OIL WELL SERVICE COMPANY (PA)
1241 E Burnett St (90755-3594)
PHONE..................562 612-0600
Jack Frost, *Pr*
Matt Hensley, *
Connie Laws, *
Richard Laws, *
EMP: 105 **EST:** 1940
SALES (est): 35.06MM
SALES (corp-wide): 35.06MM **Privately Held**
Web: www.ows1.com
SIC: 1389 Oil field services, nec

(P-624)
OIL WELL SERVICE COMPANY
Also Called: Oil Well Service
1015 Mission Rock Rd (93060-9730)
PHONE..................805 525-2103
Harvey Himinell, *Mgr*
EMP: 60
SALES (corp-wide): 35.06MM **Privately Held**
Web: www.ows1.com
SIC: 1389 Oil field services, nec
PA: Oil Well Service Company
1241 E Burnett St
Signal Hill CA
562 612-0600

(P-625)
PACIFIC PETROLEUM CALIFORNIA INC
Also Called: Oil Field Services
1615 E Betteravia Rd Ste A (93454-9000)
P.O. Box 2646 (93457-2646)
PHONE..................805 925-1947
EMP: 285 **EST:** 2005
SALES (est): 46.86MM **Privately Held**
Web: www.pacpetrol.com
SIC: 1389 7353 Lease tanks, oil field: erecting, cleaning, and repairing; Oil field equipment, rental or leasing

1389 - Oil And Gas Field Services, Nec (P-626)

(P-626)
PACIFIC PROCESS SYSTEMS INC (PA)
7401 Rosedale Hwy (93308-5736)
PHONE..................661 321-9681
Jerry Wise, *CEO*
Alan George, *
Robert Peterson, *
▼ **EMP:** 90 **EST:** 1995
SQ FT: 7,000
SALES (est): 35.14MM **Privately Held**
Web: www.pps-equipment.com
SIC: 1389 7353 5082 Testing, measuring, surveying, and analysis services; Oil field equipment, rental or leasing; Oil field equipment

(P-627)
PSC INDUSTRIAL OUTSOURCING LP
Also Called: Hydrochempsc
200 Old Yard Dr (93307-4268)
PHONE..................661 833-9991
EMP: 61
SALES (corp-wide): 5.17B **Publicly Held**
Web: www.hpc-industrial.com
SIC: 1389 Oil field services, nec
HQ: Psc Industrial Outsourcing, Lp
900 Georgia Ave
Deer Park TX
713 393-5600

(P-628)
SCHLUMBERGER TECHNOLOGY CORP
Also Called: Dowell Schlumberger
6120 Snow Rd (93308-9531)
P.O. Box 81437 (93380-1437)
PHONE..................661 864-4721
FAX: 661 393-6525
EMP: 100
SIC: 1389 1382 Oil field services, nec; Oil and gas exploration services
HQ: Schlumberger Technology Corp
100 Gillingham Ln
Sugar Land TX
281 285-8500

(P-629)
TITAN OILFIELD SERVICES INC
Also Called: Titan Oilfield Services
21535 Kratzmeyer Rd (93314-9482)
PHONE..................661 861-1630
Terry Hibbitts, *CEO*
Terry Hibbitts, *Pr*
Tim Barman, *
Tony Palacpac, *
EMP: 68 **EST:** 2011
SALES (est): 9.95MM **Privately Held**
Web: www.vinemarketing.com
SIC: 1389 Oil field services, nec

(P-630)
TRUITT OILFIELD MAINT CORP
1051 James Rd (93308-9753)
P.O. Box 5066 (93388-5066)
PHONE..................661 871-4099
Kimberly Sue New, *Pr*
Steve New, *
EMP: 300 **EST:** 1978
SQ FT: 3,000
SALES (est): 23.72MM **Privately Held**
Web: www.truittcorp.com
SIC: 1389 Oil field services, nec

(P-631)
TRYAD SERVICE CORPORATION
5900 E Lerdo Hwy (93263-4023)
PHONE..................661 391-1524
James Varner, *Pr*
Danny Seely, *
▲ **EMP:** 90 **EST:** 1933
SALES (est): 9.18MM **Privately Held**
Web: www.jdrush.com
SIC: 1389 Oil and gas wells: building, repairing and dismantling

(P-632)
U S WEATHERFORD L P
2815 Fruitvale Ave (93308-5907)
PHONE..................661 589-9483
Rick Benton, *Brnch Mgr*
EMP: 227
Web: www.weatherford.com
SIC: 1389 Oil field services, nec
HQ: U S Weatherford L P
179 Weatherford Dr
Schriever LA
985 493-6100

(P-633)
VANDERRA RESOURCES LLC
1801 Century Park E Ste 2400 (90067-2326)
PHONE..................817 439-2220
EMP: 500
SIC: 1389 Oil field services, nec

1422 Crushed And Broken Limestone

(P-634)
CALMAT CO
16101 Hwy 156 (93252)
P.O. Box 22800 (93390-2800)
PHONE..................661 858-2673
Angela Bailey, *Mgr*
EMP: 129
Web: www.vulcanmaterials.com
SIC: 1422 Crushed and broken limestone
HQ: Calmat Co.
500 N Brand Blvd Ste 500 # 500
Glendale CA
818 553-8821

1429 Crushed And Broken Stone, Nec

(P-635)
SAN RAFAEL ROCK QUARRY INC (HQ)
Also Called: Dutra Materials
2350 Kerner Blvd Ste 200 (94901-5595)
PHONE..................415 459-7740
EMP: 70 **EST:** 1994
SALES (est): 54.09MM
SALES (corp-wide): 191.66MM **Privately Held**
Web: www.sanrafaelrockquarry.com
SIC: 1429 1629 Basalt, crushed and broken-quarrying; Marine construction
PA: The Dutra Group
2350 Kerner Blvd Ste 200
San Rafael CA
415 258-6876

(P-636)
TRIANGLE ROCK PRODUCTS LLC
500 N Brand Blvd Ste 500 (91203-3319)
PHONE..................818 553-8820
Stanley G Bass, *Pr*
EMP: 308 **EST:** 1978
SQ FT: 20,000
SALES (est): 4.63MM **Publicly Held**
SIC: 1429 1442 2951 3273 Igneous rock, crushed and broken-quarrying; Construction sand and gravel; Asphalt paving mixtures and blocks; Ready-mixed concrete
HQ: Calmat Co.
500 N Brand Blvd Ste 500 # 500
Glendale CA
818 553-8821

1442 Construction Sand And Gravel

(P-637)
GRANITE ROCK CO (PA)
350 Technology Dr (95076-2488)
P.O. Box 50001 (95077-5001)
PHONE..................831 768-2000
Peter Lemon, *Pr*
Mary E Woolpert, *
Bruce G Woolpert, *Vice Chairman*
Rita Alves, *
EMP: 100 **EST:** 1900
SQ FT: 10,000
SALES (est): 521.49MM
SALES (corp-wide): 521.49MM **Privately Held**
Web: www.graniterock.com
SIC: 1442 3273 5032 2951 Gravel mining; Ready-mixed concrete; Sand, construction; Asphalt and asphaltic paving mixtures (not from refineries)

(P-638)
HANSEN BROS ENTERPRISES (PA)
Also Called: Hbe Rental
11727 La Barr Meadows Rd (95949-7722)
P.O. Box 1599 (95945-1599)
PHONE..................530 273-3100
Orson Hansen, *Pr*
Sue Peterson, *
Frank Bennallack, *
EMP: 70 **EST:** 1953
SQ FT: 20,000
SALES (est): 26.42MM
SALES (corp-wide): 26.42MM **Privately Held**
Web: www.gohbe.com
SIC: 1442 3273 1794 7359 Gravel mining; Ready-mixed concrete; Excavation work; Equipment rental and leasing, nec

(P-639)
TEICHERT INC
Also Called: Teichert Aggregates
13879 Butterfield Dr (96161-3331)
P.O. Box 447 (96160-0447)
PHONE..................530 587-3811
Ed Herrnberger, *Manager*
EMP: 86
SALES (corp-wide): 844.71MM **Privately Held**
Web: www.teichert.com
SIC: 1442 Construction sand and gravel
HQ: A. Teichert & Son, Inc.
3500 American River Dr
Sacramento CA

(P-640)
TEICHERT INC
Also Called: Teichert Aggregates
36314 S Bird Rd (95304-8678)
PHONE..................209 832-4150
Jerry Hansen, *Manager*
EMP: 72
SALES (corp-wide): 844.71MM **Privately Held**
Web: www.teichert.com
SIC: 1442 Construction sand and gravel
HQ: A. Teichert & Son, Inc.
3500 American River Dr
Sacramento CA

(P-641)
TEICHERT INC
Also Called: Teichert Aggregates
2601 State Highway 49 (95614-9528)
P.O. Box 280 (95614-0280)
PHONE..................530 885-4244
Ed Herrnberger, *Manager*
EMP: 124
SALES (corp-wide): 844.71MM **Privately Held**
Web: www.teichert.com
SIC: 1442 Construction sand and gravel
HQ: A. Teichert & Son, Inc.
3500 American River Dr
Sacramento CA

(P-642)
TEICHERT INC
Also Called: Teichert Aggregates
3331 Walnut Ave (95901-9421)
PHONE..................530 749-1230
Brandon Stauffer, *Manager*
EMP: 95
SALES (corp-wide): 844.71MM **Privately Held**
Web: www.teichert.com
SIC: 1442 Construction sand and gravel
HQ: A. Teichert & Son, Inc.
3500 American River Dr
Sacramento CA

(P-643)
TEICHERT INC
Also Called: Teichert Aggregates
4249 Hammonton Smartville Rd (95901)
PHONE..................530 743-6111
Brandon Stauffer, *Manager*
EMP: 119
SALES (corp-wide): 844.71MM **Privately Held**
Web: www.teichert.com
SIC: 1442 Construction sand and gravel
HQ: A. Teichert & Son, Inc.
3500 American River Dr
Sacramento CA

(P-644)
TEICHERT INC
Also Called: Teichert Aggregates
3417 Grant Line Rd (95742-7000)
P.O. Box 981 (95763-0981)
PHONE..................916 351-0123
Mike Cunnigham, *Manager*
EMP: 93
SALES (corp-wide): 844.71MM **Privately Held**
Web: www.teichert.com
SIC: 1442 Construction sand and gravel
HQ: A. Teichert & Son, Inc.
3500 American River Dr
Sacramento CA

(P-645)
TEICHERT INC
Also Called: Teichert Aggregates
8760 Kiefer Blvd (95826-3917)
P.O. Box 15002 (95851-0002)
PHONE..................916 386-6900
Mike Cunnigham, *Manager*
EMP: 103
SALES (corp-wide): 844.71MM **Privately Held**
Web: www.teichert.com
SIC: 1442 Construction sand and gravel
HQ: A. Teichert & Son, Inc.

PRODUCTS & SERVICES SECTION

1521 - Single-family Housing Construction (P-665)

3500 American River Dr
Sacramento CA

1481 Nonmetallic Mineral Services

(P-646)
MP MINE OPERATIONS LLC
67750 Bailey Rd (92366)
PHONE..................702 277-0848
James H Litinsky, *CEO*
Michael Rosethal, *
EMP: 108 **EST:** 2017
SALES (est): 47.09MM
SALES (corp-wide): 527.51MM **Publicly Held**
SIC: 1481 1099 Mine exploration, nonmetallic minerals; Rare-earth ores mining
PA: Mp Materials Corp.
1700 S Pavilion Center Dr # 800
Las Vegas NV
702 844-6111

1499 Miscellaneous Nonmetallic Mining

(P-647)
DICAPERL CORPORATION (DH)
Also Called: Grefco Dicaperl
23705 Crenshaw Blvd # 10 (90505-5236)
PHONE..................610 667-6640
Ray Perelman, *CEO*
Glenn Jones, *
Mike Cull, *
Barry Katz, *
▼ **EMP:** 90 **EST:** 1992
SQ FT: 5,000
SALES (est): 20.49MM **Privately Held**
Web: www.dicalite.com
SIC: 1499 3677 Perlite mining; Filtration devices, electronic
HQ: Grefco Minerals Inc.
1 Bala Ave Ste 310
Bala Cynwyd PA
610 660-8820

(P-648)
IMERYS MINERALS CALIFORNIA INC (HQ)
2500 San Miguelito Rd (93436-9743)
P.O. Box 519 (93438-0519)
PHONE..................805 736-1221
Douglas A Smith, *Pr*
John Oskam, *
John Leichty, *
◆ **EMP:** 67 **EST:** 1991
SQ FT: 11,600
SALES (est): 276.98MM
SALES (corp-wide): 276.98MM **Privately Held**
Web: www.imerys.com
SIC: 1499 3295 Diatomaceous earth mining; Minerals, ground or treated
PA: Imerys Filtration Minerals, Inc.
2500 San Miguelito Rd
Lompoc CA
805 736-1221

1521 Single-family Housing Construction

(P-649)
A CLARK/MCCARTHY JOINT VENTURE
18201 Von Karman Ave # 800 (92612-1000)
PHONE..................714 429-9779
EMP: 1125
SIC: 1521 Single-family housing construction

(P-650)
A M ORTEGA CONSTRUCTION INC
58 Kellogg St (93001-1732)
PHONE..................951 360-1352
Archie Maurice Ortega, *Brnch Mgr*
EMP: 65
SALES (corp-wide): 55.54MM **Privately Held**
Web: www.amortega.com
SIC: 1521 Single-family housing construction
PA: A. M. Ortega Construction, Inc.
10125 Channel Rd
Lakeside CA
619 390-1988

(P-651)
ACE INDUSTRIAL SUPPLY INC (PA)
7535 N San Fernando Rd (91505-1044)
PHONE..................818 252-1981
Tim Stearns, *Prin*
Richard Benton, *Prin*
◆ **EMP:** 65 **EST:** 1983
SQ FT: 25,000
SALES (est): 48.24MM **Privately Held**
Web: www.acetools.com
SIC: 1521 Single-family housing construction

(P-652)
ALBERT D SEENO CNSTR CO INC
3240 Stone Valley Rd W Ste 2 (94507-1555)
PHONE..................925 671-7711
Albert D Seeno Junior, *CEO*
Richard B Seeno, *
Thomas A Seeno, *
EMP: 80 **EST:** 1959
SQ FT: 30,000
SALES (est): 23.88MM **Privately Held**
Web: www.seenohomes.com
SIC: 1521 New construction, single-family houses

(P-653)
ALTEN CONSTRUCTION INC
1141 Marina Way S (94804-3742)
PHONE..................510 234-4200
EMP: 80 **EST:** 1995
SQ FT: 14,000
SALES (est): 25.95MM **Privately Held**
Web: www.altenconstruction.com
SIC: 1521 Single-family housing construction

(P-654)
ANDREW CHEKENE ENTERPRISES INC
Also Called: AC Enterprises
21965 Meekland Ave (94541-3862)
PHONE..................650 588-1001
Andrew Chekene, *Pr*
Rafael Munoz, *
EMP: 215 **EST:** 2007
SQ FT: 3,000
SALES (est): 47.63MM **Privately Held**
Web: www.constructionbyace.com
SIC: 1521 Single-family housing construction

(P-655)
APTIM FEDERAL SERVICES LLC
4005 Port Chicago Hwy (94520-1180)
PHONE..................925 288-9898
Frank Hackett, *Brnch Mgr*
EMP: 287
SALES (corp-wide): 2.39B **Privately Held**
Web: www.aptim.com
SIC: 1521 Single-family housing construction
HQ: Aptim Federal Services, Llc
1200 Brickyard Ln Ste 202
Baton Rouge LA
225 932-2500

(P-656)
APTIM FEDERAL SERVICES LLC
1230 Columbia St Ste 1200 (92101-8517)
PHONE..................619 239-1690
Eric Malcolm, *Brnch Mgr*
EMP: 538
SALES (corp-wide): 2.39B **Privately Held**
Web: www.aptim.com
SIC: 1521 Single-family housing construction
HQ: Aptim Federal Services, Llc
1200 Brickyard Ln Ste 202
Baton Rouge LA
225 932-2500

(P-657)
AWT CONSTRUCTION GROUP INC
4740 E 2nd St Ste 22 (94510-1012)
PHONE..................707 746-7500
James Kint, *Pr*
Gregory W Smith, *
Monique Kint, *
EMP: 65 **EST:** 2007
SQ FT: 3,000
SALES (est): 16.53MM **Privately Held**
Web: www.awtconstructioninc.com
SIC: 1521 1542 Single-family housing construction; Commercial and office building contractors

(P-658)
AZ CONSTRUCTION INC (PA)
Also Called: Ace Fence Company
727 Glendora Ave (91744-4014)
PHONE..................626 333-0727
Amy Tsui, *Pr*
America Tang, *VP*
EMP: 114 **EST:** 2013
SALES (est): 11.65MM
SALES (corp-wide): 11.65MM **Privately Held**
Web: www.acefencecompany.com
SIC: 1521 Single-family housing construction

(P-659)
BCCI CONSTRUCTION LLC
150 E Dana St (94041-1508)
PHONE..................650 543-8900
James Tunkey, *Brnch Mgr*
EMP: 139
SALES (corp-wide): 4.31B **Privately Held**
Web: www.bcciconst.com
SIC: 1521 New construction, single-family houses
HQ: Bcci Construction Llc
1160 Battery St Ste 250
San Francisco CA
415 817-5100

(P-660)
BILL BROWN CONSTRUCTION CO
242 Phelan Ave (95112-6109)
PHONE..................408 297-3738
William E Brown, *Pr*
EMP: 76 **EST:** 1978
SQ FT: 1,650
SALES (est): 10.69MM **Privately Held**
Web: www.bbrownconstruction.com
SIC: 1521 1794 1791 Single-family housing construction; Excavation work; Structural steel erection

(P-661)
BREHM COMMUNITIES (PA)
1935 Camino Vida Roble Ste 200 (92008-5568)
PHONE..................760 448-2420
Forrest W Brehm, *Pr*
EMP: 64 **EST:** 1963
SQ FT: 5,984
SALES (est): 6.51MM
SALES (corp-wide): 6.51MM **Privately Held**
SIC: 1521 New construction, single-family houses

(P-662)
BROOKFELD STHLAND HOLDINGS LLC
Also Called: Brookfield Residential
3200 Park Center Dr Ste 1000 (92626-7163)
PHONE..................714 427-6868
EMP: 160 **EST:** 1996
SALES (est): 43.89MM
SALES (corp-wide): 69.06B **Privately Held**
SIC: 1521 Single-family housing construction
HQ: Brookfield Homes (Us) Llc
3201 Jermantown Rd
Fairfax VA
703 270-1400

(P-663)
BROWNCO CONSTRUCTION CO INC
Also Called: Brownco Construction
1000 E Katella Ave (92805-6617)
PHONE..................714 935-9600
Scot Alan Brown, *Pr*
Jeff Radtke, *
EMP: 87 **EST:** 1999
SQ FT: 15,000
SALES (est): 24.04MM **Privately Held**
Web: www.browncoinc.com
SIC: 1521 Single-family housing construction

(P-664)
BUENA VISTA CNSTR GROUP INC
14958 Venado Dr (95683-9322)
PHONE..................916 354-9832
Michael Barsam Cody, *Admn*
EMP: 62 **EST:** 2012
SALES (est): 2.01MM **Privately Held**
Web: www.buenavistaconstructioncompany.com
SIC: 1521 New construction, single-family houses

(P-665)
CASA ACQUISITION CORP
99 Almaden Blvd Ste 400 (95113-1604)
PHONE..................400 207-9499
EMP: 187
SALES (corp-wide): 994.44MM **Publicly Held**

1521 - Single-family Housing Construction (P-666)

SIC: 1521 1531 6552 Single-family housing construction; Operative builders; Land subdividers and developers, residential
HQ: Casa Acquisition Corp.
8390 E Crescent Pkwy # 650
Greenwood Village CO
303 770-8300

(P-666)
CHAMPION HOME BUILDERS INC
299 N Smith Ave (92878-3241)
PHONE.................951 256-4617
EMP: 78
SALES (corp-wide): 2.61B **Publicly Held**
Web: www.championhomes.com
SIC: 1521 2451 New construction, single-family houses; Mobile homes, except recreational
HQ: Champion Home Builders, Inc.
755 W Big Beavr Rd # 1000
Troy MI
248 614-8200

(P-667)
COASTLINE CNSTR & AWNG CO INC
5742 Research Dr (92649-1617)
PHONE.................714 891-9798
John W Almquist, *Pr*
EMP: 100 **EST:** 1980
SQ FT: 1,600
SALES (est): 4.88MM **Privately Held**
Web: www.coastlineconawn.com
SIC: 1521 Mobile home repair, on site

(P-668)
COUNTY OF RIVERSIDE
Facilities Mgmt
3450 14th St (92501-3812)
PHONE.................951 955-4800
Michael Sylvester, *Dir*
EMP: 100
SALES (corp-wide): 4.58B **Privately Held**
Web: www.countyofriverside.us
SIC: 1521 9532 7349 Single-family housing construction; Urban and community development; Building maintenance services, nec
PA: County Of Riverside
4080 Lemon St Fl 11
Riverside CA
951 955-1110

(P-669)
CVC CONSTRUCTION CORP
1544 N Maple Ave (93703-4404)
PHONE.................559 276-6050
Dave Carrick, *Pr*
EMP: 384
Web: www.cvcconstruction.com
SIC: 1521 Single-family housing construction
HQ: Cvc Construction Corp
530 Bercut Dr Ste G
Sacramento CA

(P-670)
DALINGHAUS CONSTRUCTION INC
445 Birch St (92530-2798)
PHONE.................877 360-9227
Bradley Allan Dalinghaus, *CEO*
Brian Dalinghaus, *
EMP: 60 **EST:** 2013
SALES (est): 9.71MM **Privately Held**
Web: www.dalinghausconstruction.com
SIC: 1521 New construction, single-family houses

(P-671)
DE MATTEI CONSTRUCTION INC
1794 The Alameda (95126-1729)
PHONE.................408 295-7516
Mark De Mattei, *Pr*
John Hinton, *
▲ **EMP:** 60 **EST:** 1985
SQ FT: 5,000
SALES (est): 23.28MM **Privately Held**
Web: www.demattei.com
SIC: 1521 1542 New construction, single-family houses; Commercial and office building contractors

(P-672)
DENNIS ALLEN ASSOCIATES (PA)
Also Called: Allen Associates
201 N Milpas St (93103-3201)
PHONE.................805 884-8777
Dennis W Allen, *Pr*
Ian Cronshaw, *
Jennifer Cushnie, *
EMP: 95 **EST:** 1983
SALES (est): 40.76MM **Privately Held**
Web: www.buildallen.com
SIC: 1521 1542 General remodeling, single-family houses; Commercial and office buildings, renovation and repair

(P-673)
DISASTER RSTRTION PRFSSNALS IN
Also Called: Service Master By ARS
1517 W 130th St (90249-2103)
PHONE.................310 301-8030
Ahmad Elzarou, *CEO*
EMP: 80 **EST:** 2003
SALES (est): 8.91MM **Privately Held**
SIC: 1521 7299 1542 Repairing fire damage, single-family houses; Home improvement and renovation contractor agency; Commercial and office building contractors

(P-674)
EBC INC (PA)
Also Called: Ellis Building Contractors
219 Manhattan Beach Blvd Ste 3 (90266-5324)
PHONE.................310 753-6407
Brad Ellis, *Pr*
Patricia Ellis, *
EMP: 95 **EST:** 1980
SALES (est): 4.89MM
SALES (corp-wide): 4.89MM **Privately Held**
SIC: 1521 1542 New construction, single-family houses; Commercial and office building, new construction

(P-675)
ELEVEN WESTERN BUILDERS INC (PA)
2862 Executive Pl (92029-1524)
PHONE.................760 796-6346
Rick W Backus, *CEO*
Richard Huey, *
EMP: 82 **EST:** 1983
SQ FT: 20,000
SALES (est): 49.34MM
SALES (corp-wide): 49.34MM **Privately Held**
Web: www.ewbinc.com
SIC: 1521 New construction, single-family houses

(P-676)
EXCEL CONTRACTORS INC
Also Called: Progression Drywall
348 E Avenue K8 Ste B (93535-4514)
PHONE.................661 942-6944
John Rockey, *Pr*
Rose Rockey, *
EMP: 100 **EST:** 1987
SALES (est): 18.65MM **Privately Held**
SIC: 1521 1742 1542 Single-family home remodeling, additions, and repairs; Drywall; Commercial and office building, new construction

(P-677)
FORT HILL CONSTRUCTION (PA)
12711 Ventura Blvd Ste 390 (91604-2431)
PHONE.................323 656-7425
George Peper, *Pr*
Mike Mc Grail, *
Gordon Foote, *
Joseph Goldfarb, *
James Kweskin, *
▲ **EMP:** 70 **EST:** 1971
SQ FT: 4,000
SALES (est): 10.22MM
SALES (corp-wide): 10.22MM **Privately Held**
Web: www.forthill.com
SIC: 1521 New construction, single-family houses

(P-678)
GENERATION CONSTRUCTION INC
15650 El Prado Rd (91710-9108)
P.O. Box 991 (91708-0991)
PHONE.................909 923-2077
Antwan De Paul, *Pr*
EMP: 150 **EST:** 1986
SALES (est): 24.43MM **Privately Held**
Web: www.gconstruction.com
SIC: 1521 Single-family housing construction

(P-679)
GOLDEN COAST CNSTR RESTORATION
4811 Chippendale Dr Ste 301 (95841-2555)
PHONE.................916 955-7461
Alex Kotyakov, *Pr*
EMP: 68 **EST:** 2004
SALES (est): 9.38MM **Privately Held**
Web: www.goldencoastco.com
SIC: 1521 1542 1522 New construction, single-family houses; Commercial and office buildings, renovation and repair; Residential construction, nec

(P-680)
GOOD LIFE CONSTRUCTION INC
7748 Firestone Way (95843-4698)
PHONE.................916 833-1379
Dimitri Tupikov, *CEO*
Aleksandr Tupikov, *CFO*
Andrey Tupikov, *Sec*
EMP: 85 **EST:** 2011
SALES (est): 21MM **Privately Held**
Web: www.goodlifeconstruction.com
SIC: 1521 Single-family housing construction

(P-681)
GRANVILLE HOMES INC
Also Called: Gv Visual
1306 W Herndon Ave Ste 101 (93711-7183)
PHONE.................559 268-2000
Darius Assemi, *CEO*
Farid Assemi, *
EMP: 60 **EST:** 1980
SALES (est): 48.93MM **Privately Held**
Web: www.gvhomes.com
SIC: 1521 New construction, single-family houses

(P-682)
JAMES ALLISON ESTATES & HOMES
1902 Wright Pl (92008-6583)
PHONE.................866 463-5780
EMP: 175 **EST:** 2008
SALES (est): 8.27MM **Privately Held**
SIC: 1521 New construction, single-family houses

(P-683)
JF SHEA CONSTRUCTION INC
17400 Clear Creek Rd (96001-5113)
P.O. Box 494519 (96049-4519)
PHONE.................530 246-4292
Ed Kernaghan, *VP*
EMP: 60
SALES (corp-wide): 2.1B **Privately Held**
Web: www.jfsheaconstruction.com
SIC: 1521 New construction, single-family houses
HQ: J.F. Shea Construction, Inc.
655 Brea Canyon Rd
Walnut CA
909 594-9500

(P-684)
JF SHEA CONSTRUCTION INC
Also Called: Shea Homes
2580 Shea Center Dr (94551-7547)
PHONE.................925 245-3660
Layne Marceau, *Pr*
EMP: 68
SALES (corp-wide): 2.1B **Privately Held**
Web: www.sheahomes.com
SIC: 1521 New construction, single-family houses
HQ: J.F. Shea Construction, Inc.
655 Brea Canyon Rd
Walnut CA
909 594-9500

(P-685)
JF SHEA CONSTRUCTION INC (HQ)
Also Called: Shea Homes For Active Adults
655 Brea Canyon Rd (91789-3078)
P.O. Box 489 (91788-0489)
PHONE.................909 594-9500
▲ **EMP:** 200 **EST:** 1958
SALES (est): 471.87MM
SALES (corp-wide): 2.1B **Privately Held**
Web: www.jfshea.com
SIC: 1521 1622 6512 New construction, single-family houses; Tunnel construction; Commercial and industrial building operation
PA: J. F. Shea Co., Inc.
655 Brea Canyon Rd
Walnut CA
909 594-9500

(P-686)
JMH ENGINEERING AND CNSTR
2457 Brayton Ave (90755-3508)
PHONE.................562 317-1700
EMP: 80
SALES (corp-wide): 10.47MM **Privately Held**
Web: www.jmheandc.com
SIC: 1521 Single-family housing construction
PA: Jmh Engineering And Construction
3291 Wendy Way
Los Alamitos CA
562 547-8270

(P-687)
JR CONSTRUCTION INC
8123 Engineer Rd (92111-1907)

PRODUCTS & SERVICES SECTION

1521 - Single-family Housing Construction (P-711)

PHONE..................858 505-4760
Ramon B Camacho, *Pr*
EMP: 70 **EST:** 1992
SALES (est): 9.18MM **Privately Held**
SIC: 1521 Single-family housing construction

(P-688)
K A R CONSTRUCTION INC
1306 Brooks St (91762-3611)
PHONE..................909 988-5054
Kurt Alan Rothweiler, *Prin*
EMP: 70 **EST:** 2010
SALES (est): 12.06MM **Privately Held**
Web: www.karconstruction.com
SIC: 1521 Single-family housing construction

(P-689)
K HOVNNIAN CLFRNIA OPRTONS IN (HQ)
Also Called: K. Hovnanian Companies Cal Inc
400 Exchange Ste 200 (92602-1340)
PHONE..................714 368-4500
Nicholas Pappas, *Pr*
EMP: 65 **EST:** 1994
SALES (est): 234.91MM
SALES (corp-wide): 2.92B **Publicly Held**
SIC: 1521 New construction, single-family houses
PA: Hovnanian Enterprises, Inc.
90 Matawan Rd Ste 105
Matawan NJ
732 747-7800

(P-690)
KATERRA
1950 W Corporate Way (92801-5373)
PHONE..................720 449-3909
EMP: 91 **EST:** 2019
SALES (est): 1.21MM **Privately Held**
SIC: 1521 Single-family housing construction

(P-691)
KATERRA CONSTRUCTION LLC
1950 W Corporate Way (92801-5373)
PHONE..................720 449-3909
EMP: 728
SALES (corp-wide): 1.13B **Privately Held**
Web: www.katerra.com
SIC: 1521 Single-family housing construction
HQ: Katerra Construction Llc
2494 Sand Hill Rd Ste 100
Menlo Park CA
650 422-3572

(P-692)
KB HOME GRATER LOS ANGELES INC (HQ)
10990 Wilshire Blvd # 700 (90024-3913)
PHONE..................310 231-4000
Bruce Karatz, *CEO*
EMP: 90 **EST:** 1957
SQ FT: 40,000
SALES (est): 64.08MM
SALES (corp-wide): 6.9B **Publicly Held**
Web: www.kbhome.com
SIC: 1521 1522 Single-family home remodeling, additions, and repairs; Multi-family dwelling construction, nec
PA: Kb Home
10990 Wilshire Blvd Fl 7
Los Angeles CA
310 231-4000

(P-693)
KB HOME GRATER LOS ANGELES INC
36310 Inland Valley Dr (92595-7595)
PHONE..................951 691-5300
George Brenner, *Mgr*
EMP: 164
SALES (corp-wide): 6.9B **Publicly Held**
SIC: 1521 1522 Single-family home remodeling, additions, and repairs; Multi-family dwelling construction, nec
HQ: Kb Home Greater Los Angeles Inc.
10990 Wilshire Blvd # 700
Los Angeles CA
310 231-4000

(P-694)
KOTA CONSTRUCTION LLC
1200 Lawrence Dr Ste 180 (91320-1316)
PHONE..................855 800-5682
EMP: 98 **EST:** 2020
SALES (est): 1.25MM **Privately Held**
SIC: 1521 Single-family housing construction

(P-695)
LARGO CONCRETE INC
591 Camino De La Reina Ste 620 (92108)
PHONE..................619 356-2142
EMP: 190
Web: www.largoconcrete.com
SIC: 1521 Single-family housing construction
PA: Largo Concrete, Inc.
2741 Walnut Ave Ste 110
Tustin CA

(P-696)
LENNAR HOMES CALIFORNIA INC (DH)
Also Called: Lennar Builders
1 California St Fl 27 (94111-5401)
PHONE..................949 349-8000
EMP: 124 **EST:** 1996
SALES (est): 91.05MM
SALES (corp-wide): 33.67B **Publicly Held**
SIC: 1521 6552 New construction, single-family houses; Subdividers and developers, nec
HQ: Lennar Homes, Inc.
5505 Blue Lagoon Dr
Miami FL
305 559-4000

(P-697)
LONGO CONSTRUCTION
209 W Ascot Ave (95673-4701)
PHONE..................916 397-5869
Matthew Longo, *Prin*
EMP: 76 **EST:** 2010
SALES (est): 792.81K **Privately Held**
SIC: 1521 Single-family housing construction

(P-698)
MACARTHUR TRNST CMNTY PRTNERS
345 Spear St Ste 700 (94105-6136)
P.O. Box 190220 (94119-0220)
PHONE..................415 989-1111
Susan Johnson, *VP*
EMP: 78 **EST:** 2004
SALES (est): 312.05K **Privately Held**
SIC: 1521 Single-family housing construction
PA: Bridge Economic Development Corporation
345 Spear St Ste 700
San Francisco CA

(P-699)
MAI CONSTRUCTION INC
50 Bonaventura Dr (95134-2104)
PHONE..................408 434-9880
Roger Mairose, *Ch Bd*
Mike Mairose, *
Barry Paxton, *
Debbie Squires, *
Wendy Mairose, *
EMP: 87 **EST:** 1973
SQ FT: 38,036
SALES (est): 23.3MM **Privately Held**
Web: www.maiconst.com
SIC: 1521 Single-family housing construction

(P-700)
MCCLONE CONSTRUCTION COMPANY
4340 Product Dr (95682-8492)
P.O. Box 939 (95682-0939)
PHONE..................559 431-9411
Scott Mcclone, *Brnch Mgr*
EMP: 191
Web: www.mcclone.net
SIC: 1521 Single-family housing construction
PA: Mcclone Construction Company
5170 Hillsdale Cir Ste B
El Dorado Hills CA

(P-701)
MGB CONSTRUCTION INC
91 Commercial Ave (92507-1111)
PHONE..................951 342-0303
Emily Beach, *Pr*
Emilly Beach, *
EMP: 150 **EST:** 2001
SALES (est): 18.96MM **Privately Held**
Web: www.mgbconstruction.net
SIC: 1521 Single-family housing construction

(P-702)
MIDSTATE CONSTRUCTION CORP
1180 Holm Rd Ste A (94954-7120)
PHONE..................707 762-3200
Roger Nelson, *Pr*
Patrick Draeger, *
Wesley Barry Ii, *VP*
Richard Oberdorfer, *
Jim Debolt, *
EMP: 80 **EST:** 1987
SQ FT: 18,928
SALES (est): 33.64MM **Privately Held**
Web: www.midstateconstruction.com
SIC: 1521 1541 1542 New construction, single-family houses; Industrial buildings, new construction, nec; Commercial and office building, new construction

(P-703)
MIKE ROVNER CONSTRUCTION INC
1758 Junction Ave Ste C (95112-1022)
PHONE..................408 453-6070
Mike Rovner, *Pr*
EMP: 142
Web: www.rovnerconstruction.com
SIC: 1521 New construction, single-family houses
PA: Mike Rovner Construction, Inc.
5400 Tech Cir
Moorpark CA

(P-704)
NHS WESTERN DIVISION INC
Also Called: Fixd Construction Co.
115 S Palm Ave (91762-3847)
PHONE..................909 947-9931
Damien Melle, *CEO*
Mia Melle, *
EMP: 89 **EST:** 2012
SALES (est): 4.91MM **Privately Held**
SIC: 1521 Single-family housing construction

(P-705)
NORTH WIND CNSTR SVCS LLC
730 Howe Ave Ste 700 (95825-4641)
PHONE..................916 333-3015
EMP: 69 **EST:** 2011
SALES (est): 5.56MM **Privately Held**
Web: www.northwindgrp.com
SIC: 1521 Single-family housing construction

(P-706)
PAPICH CONSTRUCTION CO INC (PA)
Also Called: Sierra Pacific Materials
398 Sunrise Ter (93420-4419)
P.O. Box 2210 (93448-2210)
PHONE..................805 473-3016
Jason William Papich, *Pr*
April Papich, *
EMP: 61 **EST:** 1997
SQ FT: 6,000
SALES (est): 126.74MM
SALES (corp-wide): 126.74MM **Privately Held**
Web: www.papichco.com
SIC: 1521 Single-family housing construction

(P-707)
PAUL RYAN ASSOCIATES
Also Called: Ryan Associates
200 Gate 5 Rd Ste 113 (94965-1456)
PHONE..................415 861-3085
▲ **EMP:** 66 **EST:** 1981
SALES (est): 19.11MM **Privately Held**
Web: www.ryanassociates.com
SIC: 1521 New construction, single-family houses

(P-708)
PENINSULA CUSTOM HOMES INC
1401 Old County Rd (94070-5202)
PHONE..................650 574-0241
Richard L Breaux, *CEO*
Bryan Murphy, *
EMP: 60 **EST:** 1979
SALES (est): 9.25MM **Privately Held**
Web: www.pchi.com
SIC: 1521 New construction, single-family houses

(P-709)
PETE MOFFAT CONSTRUCTION
250 Lowell Ave (94301-3723)
PHONE..................650 656-9720
Pete Moffat, *Pr*
EMP: 60 **EST:** 2018
SALES (est): 1.64MM **Privately Held**
Web: www.petemoffat.com
SIC: 1521 Single-family housing construction

(P-710)
QUALITY GROUP HOMES INC
Also Called: Consortium For Community Svcs
4928 E Clinton Way Ste 108 (93727-1526)
PHONE..................559 252-6844
Sarah Thomas, *Dir*
EMP: 184
Web: www.qualitygrouphomes.org
SIC: 1521 New construction, single-family houses
PA: Quality Group Homes, Inc.
4928 E Clinton Way # 108
Fresno CA

(P-711)
REYNEN & BARDIS CNSTR LLC (PA)
10630 Mather Blvd (95655-4125)
PHONE..................916 366-3665
Chris Bardis, *Pr*
John Reynen, *
EMP: 120 **EST:** 1999
SALES (est): 22.92MM

1521 - Single-family Housing Construction (P-712)

SALES (corp-wide): 22.92MM **Privately Held**
Web: www.bardishomes.com
SIC: 1521 6552 New construction, single-family houses; Land subdividers and developers, residential

(P-712)
ROMERO GENERAL CNSTR CORP
8320 Nelson Way (92026-5211)
PHONE...............................760 715-0154
Jerusha Finster, *Brnch Mgr*
EMP: 102
Web: www.romerogc.com
SIC: 1521 Single-family housing construction
PA: Romero General Construction Corp.
2150 N Cntre Cy Pkwy Ste
Escondido CA

(P-713)
SC BUILDERS INC
190 5th St (94103-2917)
PHONE...............................415 757-0405
Samuel B Abbey, *Brnch Mgr*
EMP: 61
SALES (corp-wide): 61.85MM **Privately Held**
Web: www.scbuildersinc.com
SIC: 1521 New construction, single-family houses
PA: Sc Builders, Inc.
910 Thompson Pl
Sunnyvale CA
408 328-0688

(P-714)
SCENARIO COCKRAM USA INC
605 8th St (91340-1400)
PHONE...............................407 613-2949
EMP: 207
Web: www.cockramscenario.com
SIC: 1521 Single-family housing construction
HQ: Scenario Cockram Usa Inc.
7600 Kingspointe Pkwy # 101
Orlando FL
818 650-0999

(P-715)
SEARS HOME IMPRV PDTS INC
Also Called: Sears
730 S Orange Ave (91790-2613)
PHONE...............................626 671-1892
EMP: 119
SALES (corp-wide): 4.18B **Privately Held**
Web: www.searshomeservices.com
SIC: 1521 General remodeling, single-family houses
HQ: Sears Home Improvement Products, Inc.
1024 Florida Central Pkwy
Longwood FL
407 767-0990

(P-716)
SEARS HOME IMPRV PDTS INC
Also Called: Sears
1155 Veterans Blvd (94063-2036)
PHONE...............................650 645-9974
EMP: 119
SALES (corp-wide): 4.18B **Privately Held**
Web: www.searshomeservices.com
SIC: 1521 General remodeling, single-family houses
HQ: Sears Home Improvement Products, Inc.
1024 Florida Central Pkwy
Longwood FL
407 767-0990

(P-717)
SEARS HOME IMPRV PDTS INC
Also Called: Sears
491 Tres Pinos Rd (95023-5592)
PHONE...............................831 245-0062
EMP: 119
SALES (corp-wide): 4.18B **Privately Held**
Web: www.searshomeservices.com
SIC: 1521 General remodeling, single-family houses
HQ: Sears Home Improvement Products, Inc.
1024 Florida Central Pkwy
Longwood FL
407 767-0990

(P-718)
SEARS HOME IMPRV PDTS INC
Also Called: Sears
2900 N Bellflower Blvd (90815-1149)
PHONE...............................562 485-4904
EMP: 119
SALES (corp-wide): 4.18B **Privately Held**
Web: www.searshomeservices.com
SIC: 1521 General remodeling, single-family houses
HQ: Sears Home Improvement Products, Inc.
1024 Florida Central Pkwy
Longwood FL
407 767-0990

(P-719)
SEARS HOME IMPRV PDTS INC
Also Called: Sears
5665 Rosemead Blvd (91780-1804)
PHONE...............................626 988-9134
EMP: 119
SALES (corp-wide): 4.18B **Privately Held**
Web: www.searshomeservices.com
SIC: 1521 General remodeling, single-family houses
HQ: Sears Home Improvement Products, Inc.
1024 Florida Central Pkwy
Longwood FL
407 767-0990

(P-720)
SEATTLE TNNEL PRTNERS A JINT V
555 Anton Blvd Ste 1000 (92626-7019)
PHONE...............................206 971-8701
▲ **EMP:** 300 **EST:** 2010
SALES (est): 15.47MM **Privately Held**
SIC: 1521 Single-family home remodeling, additions, and repairs

(P-721)
SHEA HOMES AT MONTAGE LLC
655 Brea Canyon Rd (91789-3078)
PHONE...............................909 594-9500
John C Morrissey, *Prin*
EMP: 143 **EST:** 2013
SALES (est): 1.67MM
SALES (corp-wide): 2.1B **Privately Held**
SIC: 1521 Single-family housing construction
HQ: Shea Homes Limited Partnership, A California Limited Partnership
655 Brea Canyon Rd
Walnut CA

(P-722)
SHEAR BUILDERS INC
Also Called: Sbi Landscape Materials
1000 River Rd (95439-8824)
PHONE...............................707 284-8989
Ron Matteri, *Brnch Mgr*
EMP: 63
Web: www.sbimaterials.com
SIC: 1521 New construction, single-family houses
HQ: Shear Builders, Inc.
10540 Old Redwood Hwy
Windsor CA
707 431-1617

(P-723)
SHIMMICK CONSTRUCTION CO INC
16481 Scientific Bldg 2 (92618-4394)
PHONE...............................510 777-5000
Trina Clay, *Prin*
EMP: 161
SALES (corp-wide): 13.15B **Publicly Held**
Web: www.shimmick.com
SIC: 1521 Single-family housing construction
HQ: Shimmick Construction Company Incorporated
530 Technology Dr Ste 300
Irvine CA

(P-724)
SIGNATURE HOMES INC
4670 Willow Rd Ste 200 (94588-8588)
PHONE...............................925 463-1122
EMP: 73 **EST:** 1987
SALES (est): 24.33MM **Privately Held**
Web: www.sighomes.com
SIC: 1521 New construction, single-family houses

(P-725)
SILVERADO FRAMING & CNSTR
Also Called: Residential Framer
3091 E La Cadena Dr (92507-2630)
P.O. Box 2941 (92516-2941)
PHONE...............................951 352-1100
Ed Solis, *Pr*
EMP: 100 **EST:** 2011
SQ FT: 2,500
SALES (est): 9.68MM **Privately Held**
Web: www.silveradoframing.com
SIC: 1521 Single-family housing construction

(P-726)
SUFFOLK CONSTRUCTION CO INC
525 Market St Ste 2850 (94105-2772)
PHONE...............................415 848-0500
Jason Cardamone, *Mgr*
EMP: 265
SALES (corp-wide): 845.82MM **Privately Held**
Web: www.suffolk.com
SIC: 1521 Single-family housing construction
PA: Suffolk Construction Company, Inc.
65 Allerton St
Boston MA
617 445-3500

(P-727)
SUPERIOR CONSTRUCTION INC
265 N Joy St (92879-0600)
P.O. Box 1148 (92878-1148)
PHONE...............................951 808-8780
Kenneth Day, *Pr*
EMP: 100 **EST:** 1976
SQ FT: 3,000
SALES (est): 9.05MM **Privately Held**
Web: www.superiorconstruction.com
SIC: 1521 1542 New construction, single-family houses; Commercial and office building, new construction

(P-728)
TNHC REALTY AND CNSTR INC
1990 N California Blvd Ste 650 (94596-3701)
PHONE...............................925 244-0700
Lawrence Webb, *CEO*
EMP: 185
SALES (corp-wide): 6.91MM **Privately Held**
Web: www.newhomeco.com
SIC: 1521 New construction, single-family houses
PA: Tnhc Realty And Construction Inc.
15231 Laguna Canyon Rd # 25
Irvine CA
949 382-7800

(P-729)
TRICON AMERICAN HOMES LLC
15771 Red Hill Ave (92780-7303)
P.O. Box 15086 (92735-0086)
PHONE...............................844 874-2661
Kevin Baldridge, *Managing Member*
EMP: 155 **EST:** 2012
SALES (est): 35.69MM
SALES (corp-wide): 645.59MM **Privately Held**
Web: www.triconresidential.com
SIC: 1521 Single-family home remodeling, additions, and repairs
PA: Tricon Residential Inc
7 St Thomas St Suite 801
Toronto ON
416 925-7228

(P-730)
TRILOGY AT RIO VISTA MSTR ASSN
1200 Clubhouse Dr (94571-9801)
PHONE...............................707 374-6871
Steven Tindle, *Mgr*
EMP: 89 **EST:** 1999
SALES (est): 1.98MM
SALES (corp-wide): 2.1B **Privately Held**
SIC: 1521 General remodeling, single-family houses
HQ: J.F. Shea Construction, Inc.
655 Brea Canyon Rd
Walnut CA
909 594-9500

(P-731)
TUPAZ HOMES LLC
2038 Biarritz Pl (95138-2259)
PHONE...............................408 377-1622
Rosario Tupaz, *Managing Member*
Beebe Tupaz, *
EMP: 100 **EST:** 1997
SALES (est): 8.69MM **Privately Held**
SIC: 1521 Single-family housing construction

(P-732)
UCP INC
Also Called: Ucp
99 Almaden Blvd Ste 400 (95113-1604)
PHONE...............................408 207-9499
EMP: 187
SIC: 1521 1531 6552 Single-family housing construction; Operative builders; Land subdividers and developers, residential

(P-733)
ULTIMATE BUILDERS INC
Also Called: ULTIMATE BUILDERS INC
23679 Calabasas Rd (91302-1502)
PHONE...............................818 481-2627
EMP: 85
SALES (corp-wide): 11.43MM **Privately Held**
Web: www.repipe1.com

SIC: **1521** New construction, single-family houses
PA: Ultimate Builders, Inc.
19326 Ventura Blvd # 201
Tarzana CA
818 342-2568

(P-734)
ULTIMATE REMOVAL INC
Also Called: Ultimate Demo
2168 Pomona Blvd (91768-3332)
P.O. Box 1220 (91769-1220)
PHONE..............................909 524-0800
EMP: 124 EST: 1995
SQ FT: 9,900
SALES (est): 9.8MM **Privately Held**
Web: www.ultimateremoval.com
SIC: **1521** Single-family housing construction

(P-735)
UNTITLED LABS INC
Also Called: Made Renovation
One Market Spear Tower 36th Fl (94105)
PHONE..............................415 858-7078
Roger Dickey, *CEO*
EMP: 83 EST: 2018
SALES (est): 7.21MM **Privately Held**
Web: www.untitled-labs.com
SIC: **1521** General remodeling, single-family houses

(P-736)
US BEST REPAIR SERVICE INC
Also Called: US Best Repairs
1652 Edinger Ave Ste E (92780-6530)
PHONE..............................888 750-2378
Mark Zaverl, *CEO*
EMP: 101 EST: 2008
SALES (est): 20.15MM **Privately Held**
Web: www.usbestrepairs.com
SIC: **1521 1522 1542** Single-family home remodeling, additions, and repairs; Remodeling, multi-family dwellings; Commercial and office buildings, renovation and repair

(P-737)
VAN ACKER CNSTR ASSOC INC
Also Called: Van Acker Construction
1060 Redwood Hwy Frontage Rd (94941-1613)
PHONE..............................415 383-5589
Gary Van Acker, *Pr*
▲ EMP: 134 EST: 1976
SQ FT: 15,000
SALES (est): 27.3MM **Privately Held**
Web: www.vanacker.com
SIC: **1521** New construction, single-family houses

(P-738)
VASONA MANAGEMENT INC
Also Called: Vasonic Construction
37390 Central Mont Place (94536-6549)
PHONE..............................510 413-0091
Dan Scharnow, *VP*
EMP: 174
SALES (corp-wide): 22.22MM **Privately Held**
Web: www.vasonamanagement.com
SIC: **1521** New construction, single-family houses
PA: Vasona Management, Inc.
1500 E Hamilton Ave # 210
Campbell CA
408 354-4200

(P-739)
WARMINGTON RESIDENTIAL CAL INC
3090 Pullman St (92626-5901)
PHONE..............................714 557-5511
James Warmington Junior, *Pr*
Matt Tingler, *
Mike Riddlesberger, *
EMP: 150 EST: 2003
SALES (est): 22.87MM **Privately Held**
Web: www.homesbywarmington.com
SIC: **1521** New construction, single-family houses

(P-740)
WEST COAST ARBORISTS INC
8163 Commercial St (91942-2928)
PHONE..............................858 566-4204
EMP: 116
SALES (corp-wide): 53.7MM **Privately Held**
Web: www.westcoastarborists.com
SIC: **1521 0783** Single-family home remodeling, additions, and repairs; Ornamental shrub and tree services
PA: West Coast Arborists, Inc.
2200 E Via Burton
Anaheim CA
714 991-1900

(P-741)
WESTCOR CONSTRUCTION OF CAL
2351 W Lugonia Ave Ste D (92374-5014)
PHONE..............................909 796-8900
Michael A Coronado, *Pr*
Kevin R Booth, *
James D Hammer, *
EMP: 72 EST: 2000
SQ FT: 4,600
SALES (est): 1.15MM **Privately Held**
SIC: **1521** New construction, single-family houses
PA: Westcor Construction
5620 Stephanie St
Las Vegas NV

(P-742)
WL BUTLER INC
5666 La Ribera St Ste A (94550-2501)
PHONE..............................650 361-1270
Frank York, *Pr*
EMP: 69 EST: 2017
SALES (est): 4.69MM **Privately Held**
Web: www.wlbutler.com
SIC: **1521** Single-family housing construction
PA: W. L. Butler Construction, Inc.
1629 Main St
Redwood City CA

(P-743)
XL CONSTRUCTION CORPORATION
1810 13th St Ste 110 (95811-7149)
PHONE..............................916 282-2900
Eric Raff, *Brnch Mgr*
EMP: 75
Web: www.xlconstruction.com
SIC: **1521** Single-family housing construction
PA: XI Construction Corporation
851 Buckeye Ct
Milpitas CA

1522 Residential Construction, Nec

(P-744)
716 MANAGEMENT INC
Also Called: Brentwood Builders
3900 W Alameda Ave # 120 (91505-4316)
PHONE..............................818 471-4956
EMP: 70 EST: 2016
SALES (est): 5.1MM **Privately Held**
Web: www.brentwood.builders
SIC: **1522 1542 1531 1521** Residential construction, nec; Restaurant construction; Single-family home remodeling, additions, and repairs

(P-745)
ADVANCE CONSTRUCTION TECH INC
48995 Milmont Dr (94538-7315)
P.O. Box 36221 (95158-6221)
PHONE..............................510 876-8403
Robert Rosenberg, *CEO*
EMP: 80 EST: 2009
SALES (est): 8.85MM **Privately Held**
Web: www.actconstruction.net
SIC: **1522** Residential construction, nec

(P-746)
AXIS SERVICES INC
Also Called: Axis Construction
2544 Barrington Ct (94545-1133)
PHONE..............................510 732-6111
Bizhan Mahallati, *CEO*
Parisa Mahallati, *
EMP: 110 EST: 1991
SALES (est): 34.65MM **Privately Held**
Web: www.axisconstruction.com
SIC: **1522** Residential construction, nec

(P-747)
BERNARDS BUILDERS INC
555 1st St (91340-3051)
PHONE..............................818 898-1521
Doug Bernards, *Ch*
Jeffrey G Bernards, *
Greg Simons, *
Ken Menager, *
John Kramer, *
EMP: 330 EST: 2013
SALES (est): 64.61MM
SALES (corp-wide): 98.91MM **Privately Held**
SIC: **1522** Residential construction, nec
PA: Bernards Bros. Inc.
555 1st St
San Fernando CA
818 898-1521

(P-748)
BLH CONSTRUCTION COMPANY
20750 Ventura Blvd Ste 155 (91364-2338)
PHONE..............................818 905-3837
Charles Brumbaugh, *CEO*
Brian Holland, *
EMP: 150 EST: 2001
SALES (est): 45.91MM **Privately Held**
SIC: **1522** Apartment building construction

(P-749)
COBALT CONSTRUCTION COMPANY
Also Called: Cobalt Southwest Company
2259 Ward Ave Ste 200 (93065-1880)
P.O. Box 802018 (91380-2018)
PHONE..............................805 577-6222
Darin Kruse, *CEO*
▲ EMP: 70 EST: 1978
SQ FT: 43,000
SALES (est): 24.63MM **Privately Held**
Web: www.cobaltcc.com
SIC: **1522 8711 1542** Multi-family dwellings, new construction; Construction and civil engineering; Commercial and office building, new construction

(P-750)
CONDON-JOHNSON & ASSOC INC
3434 Grove St (91945-1812)
PHONE..............................858 530-9165
George Burr, *Genl Mgr*
EMP: 100
SALES (corp-wide): 88.55MM **Privately Held**
Web: www.condon-johnson.com
SIC: **1522** Residential construction, nec
PA: Condon-Johnson & Associates, Inc.
480 Roland Way Ste 200
Oakland CA
510 636-2100

(P-751)
COUNTRY BUILDERS INC
Also Called: Country Builders Construction
5915 Graham Ct (94550-9710)
PHONE..............................925 373-1020
Weldon Offill, *Pr*
EMP: 150 EST: 1979
SQ FT: 5,000
SALES (est): 8.84MM **Privately Held**
Web: www.countrybuilders.com
SIC: **1522** Apartment building construction

(P-752)
CP EMPLOYER INC (PA)
1000 Sansome St Fl 1 (94111-1342)
PHONE..............................415 273-2900
Ron Zeff, *CEO*
Brian Smith, *CCO*
Dan Garibaldi, *Development CONS*
Phillip Owens, *
EMP: 120 EST: 1995
SALES (est): 69.08MM
SALES (corp-wide): 69.08MM **Privately Held**
SIC: **1522 6531 6519** Multi-family dwellings, new construction; Real estate agents and managers; Real property lessors, nec

(P-753)
CP MULTIFAMILY CNSTR CAL INC
1000 Sansome St Fl 1 (94111-1342)
PHONE..............................415 273-2900
Ron Zeff, *CEO*
EMP: 250 EST: 2016
SALES (est): 10.34MM **Privately Held**
SIC: **1522** Multi-family dwellings, new construction

(P-754)
DANCO BUILDERS
5251 Ericson Way Ste A (95521-9274)
PHONE..............................707 822-9000
Daniel J Johnson, *Pr*
Kirk Heberly, *
Kendra Johnson, *Stockholder*
EMP: 100 EST: 1985
SQ FT: 15,000
SALES (est): 64.84MM **Privately Held**
Web: www.danco-group.com
SIC: **1522 1542** Apartment building construction; Nonresidential construction, nec

(P-755)
EDEN HOUSING INC (PA)
22645 Grand St (94541-5031)
PHONE..............................510 582-1460
Linda Mandolini, *Pr*
John Gaffney, *
Tatiana Bank, *
Shola Olatoye, *
EMP: 78 EST: 1968

1522 - Residential Construction, Nec (P-756)

SQ FT: 10,000
SALES (est): 90.99MM
SALES (corp-wide): 90.99MM **Privately Held**
Web: www.edenhousing.org
SIC: **1522** Multi-family dwellings, new construction

(P-756)
FAIRFIELD DEVELOPMENT INC (PA)
Also Called: Ffd Ii
5355 Mira Sorrento Pl Ste 100 (92121-3812)
PHONE.................858 457-2123
Christopher E Hashioka, *Prin*
James L Bosler, *
Ted Bradford, *
Jay Walker, *
Alan G Bear, *
▲ EMP: 225 EST: 1985
SALES (est): 332.75MM
SALES (corp-wide): 332.75MM **Privately Held**
SIC: **1522** Multi-family dwelling construction, nec

(P-757)
G B GROUP INC (PA)
780 Jarvis Dr (95037-2885)
PHONE.................408 848-8118
Gregory D Brown, *CEO*
Mark Greening, *
Jeffery Dame, *
Regan L Brown, *
Pat Falconio, *
EMP: 79 EST: 1992
SALES (est): 45.07MM **Privately Held**
Web: www.gbgroupinc.com
SIC: **1522** 1542 8322 1541 Hotel/motel and multi-family home renovation and remodeling; Nonresidential construction, nec; Rehabilitation services; Renovation, remodeling and repairs: industrial buildings

(P-758)
GILBANE BUILDING COMPANY
2033 Gateway Pl Ste 450 (95110-3726)
PHONE.................858 658-6700
John Keefer, *Mgr*
EMP: 75
SALES (corp-wide): 5.6B **Privately Held**
Web: www.gilbaneco.com
SIC: **1522** Residential construction, nec
HQ: Gilbane Building Company
7 Jackson Walkway Ste 2
Providence RI
401 456-5800

(P-759)
HURLEY CONSTRUCTION INC
1801 I St Ste 200 (95811-3000)
PHONE.................916 446-7599
EMP: 80 EST: 1995
SQ FT: 2,500
SALES (est): 11.18MM **Privately Held**
Web: www.antoncap.com
SIC: **1522** Multi-family dwellings, new construction

(P-760)
INTERNATIONAL BUILDING INV INC
6117 Grant Ave (95608-3331)
P.O. Box 2022 (95662-2022)
PHONE.................916 716-9565
Roderick Brian Edwards, *CEO*
EMP: 75 EST: 1987
SALES (est): 15.39MM **Privately Held**
Web: www.ibi-ca.com

SIC: **1522** 7389 Remodeling, multi-family dwellings; Business Activities at Non-Commercial Site

(P-761)
JAMES E ROBERTS-OBAYASHI CORP
20 Oak Ct (94526-4006)
PHONE.................925 820-0600
Larry R Smith, *CEO*
EMP: 110 EST: 1978
SQ FT: 4,000
SALES (est): 48.96MM **Privately Held**
Web: www.jerocorp.com
SIC: **1522** 1542 Multi-family dwellings, new construction; Commercial and office building, new construction

(P-762)
JUDSON ENTERPRISES INC (PA)
Also Called: K-Designers
2440 Gold River Rd Ste 100 (95670-6390)
PHONE.................916 596-6721
Larry D Judson, *Pr*
Michael Burgess, *
Brian Vidlock, *
Tony Tobia, *
▲ EMP: 265 EST: 1978
SQ FT: 28,000
SALES (est): 76.02MM
SALES (corp-wide): 76.02MM **Privately Held**
Web: www.k-designers.com
SIC: **1522** Residential construction, nec

(P-763)
KB HOME SOUTH BAY INC
5000 Executive Pkwy Ste 125 (94583-4210)
PHONE.................925 983-2500
Chris Apostolopoulos, *CEO*
Robert Freed, *
Joe Gregorich, *
Andrew Kusnick, *
EMP: 140 EST: 1985
SQ FT: 5,500
SALES (est): 20.16MM
SALES (corp-wide): 6.9B **Publicly Held**
Web: www.kbhome.com
SIC: **1522** 1521 Residential construction, nec ; Single-family housing construction
HQ: Kb Home Greater Los Angeles Inc.
10990 Wilshire Blvd # 700
Los Angeles CA
310 231-4000

(P-764)
KENNARD DEVELOPMENT GROUP
Also Called: Kdg Construction Consulting
1025 N Brand Blvd Ste 300 (91202-3633)
PHONE.................818 241-0800
Lydia Kennard, *CEO*
Jeffrey Lilly, *
EMP: 98 EST: 1980
SQ FT: 2,500
SALES (est): 15.65MM **Privately Held**
Web: www.kdgaviation.com
SIC: **1522** 1541 1623 1611 Residential construction, nec; Industrial buildings and warehouses; Water, sewer, and utility lines; Highway and street construction

(P-765)
MARK SCOTT CONSTRUCTION INC
2250 Boynton Ave (94533-4320)
PHONE.................707 864-8880

Dave Bergmini, *Mgr*
EMP: 100
Web: www.msconstruction.com
SIC: **1522** Residential construction, nec
PA: Mark Scott Construction, Inc.
2835 Contra Costa Blvd A
Pleasant Hill CA

(P-766)
NIBBI BROS ASSOCIATES INC
Also Called: Nibbi Bros Concrete
1000 Brannan St Ste 102 (94103-4824)
PHONE.................415 863-1820
Robert L Nibbi, *Pr*
Mike Nibbi, *
Richard Fedick, *
John Kugler, *Chief Estimator*
Larry Nibbi, *
EMP: 150 EST: 1998
SALES (est): 49.44MM **Privately Held**
Web: www.nibbi.com
SIC: **1522** 1542 Residential construction, nec ; Custom builders, non-residential

(P-767)
OLEN RESIDENTIAL REALTY CORP (HQ)
Also Called: Olen Companies, The
7 Corporate Plaza Dr (92660-7904)
PHONE.................949 644-6536
Igor M Olenicoff, *Pr*
EMP: 70 EST: 1992
SALES (est): 47.52MM **Privately Held**
SIC: **1522** Multi-family dwellings, new construction
PA: Olen Properties Corp.
7 Corporate Plaza Dr
Newport Beach CA

(P-768)
PARKHURST TERRACE
100 Parkhurst Cir (95003-9657)
PHONE.................831 685-0800
Cheryl Digrazia, *Prin*
EMP: 91 EST: 2011
SALES (est): 441.7K **Privately Held**
SIC: **1522** Apartment building construction
HQ: Midpen Property Management Corporation
303 Vintage Park Dr # 250
Foster City CA
650 356-2900

(P-769)
PROJECT FROG INC
114 Sansome St Ste 1320 (94104-3800)
PHONE.................415 814-8500
Ann Hand, *CEO*
Mark Miller, *
▲ EMP: 86 EST: 2006
SALES (est): 27.59MM **Privately Held**
Web: www.projectfrog.com
SIC: **1522** Residential construction, nec

(P-770)
RDR BUILDERS LP
Also Called: Rdr Production Builders
1333 E Kettleman Ln (95240-9765)
PHONE.................209 368-7561
EMP: 85 EST: 1977
SALES (est): 17.98MM **Privately Held**
Web: www.rdrbuilders.com
SIC: **1522** 1542 Multi-family dwellings, new construction; Commercial and office building, new construction

(P-771)
REBCO COMMUNITIES INC
Also Called: Warmington Homes California
3090 Pullman St (92626-5901)

P.O. Box 2946 (92628-2946)
PHONE.................714 557-5511
EMP: 310
SIC: **1522** Residential construction, nec

(P-772)
REGIS CONTRACTORS LP
18825 Bardeen Ave (92612-1520)
PHONE.................949 253-0455
EMP: 294 EST: 1995
SQ FT: 18,000
SALES (est): 1.97MM
SALES (corp-wide): 98.06MM **Privately Held**
SIC: **1522** Apartment building construction
PA: Sares Regis Group Operating, Inc.
18802 Bardeen Ave
Irvine CA
949 756-5959

(P-773)
SAARMAN CONSTRUCTION LTD
1900 N Loop Rd (94502-8014)
PHONE.................415 749-2700
Chih-cheng Tsai, *Pr*
Jeffrey M Saarman, *
Steven P Saarman, *
Irma Saarman, *
EMP: 250 EST: 1977
SQ FT: 4,500
SALES (est): 50.97MM **Privately Held**
Web: www.saarman.com
SIC: **1522** 1521 Condominium construction; General remodeling, single-family houses

(P-774)
SBCI INC (PA)
Also Called: South Bay Construction Company
1711 Dell Ave (95008-6904)
PHONE.................408 379-5500
Peach Cameron, *Pr*
Jb Cahoon, *Pt*
Cameron Peach, *Pt*
Dusty Furtado, *Pt*
EMP: 108 EST: 1993
SQ FT: 10,100
SALES (est): 48.79MM **Privately Held**
Web: www.sbci.com
SIC: **1522** Apartment building construction

(P-775)
SBHIS
740 Bay Blvd (91910-5254)
PHONE.................619 427-2689
EMP: 87 EST: 2014
SALES (est): 2.27MM **Privately Held**
Web: www.sbhis.net
SIC: **1522** Residential construction, nec

(P-776)
SHEA HOMES VANTIS LLC
Also Called: Shea Homes
655 Brea Canyon Rd (91789-3078)
PHONE.................909 594-9500
EMP: 95 EST: 2011
SALES (est): 1.39MM
SALES (corp-wide): 2.1B **Privately Held**
Web: www.jfshea.com
SIC: **1522** Apartment building construction
HQ: Shea Homes Limited Partnership, A California Limited Partnership
655 Brea Canyon Rd
Walnut CA

(P-777)
SILICONSAGE CONSTRUCTION INC
560 S Mathilda Ave (94086-7607)
PHONE.................408 916-3205

PRODUCTS & SERVICES SECTION

1531 - Operative Builders (P-798)

Sanjeev Acharya, *CEO*
EMP: 200 **EST:** 2014
SALES (est): 14.54MM **Privately Held**
SIC: 1522 Multi-family dwellings, new construction

(P-778)
THOMPSON BUILDERS CORPORATION
Also Called: Thompson Builders
5400 Hanna Ranch Rd (94945-5066)
PHONE..................................415 456-8972
Paul Thompson, *Pr*
F Joseph Hass, *
▲ **EMP:** 170 **EST:** 1988
SQ FT: 6,000
SALES (est): 80.07MM **Privately Held**
Web: www.tbcorp.com
SIC: 1522 1542 8711 7389 Multi-family dwelling construction, nec; Commercial and office building, new construction; Construction and civil engineering; Design services

(P-779)
TRI POINTE HOMES INC
57 Furlong (92602-1812)
PHONE..................................714 389-5933
Paul Faubion, *Brnch Mgr*
EMP: 135
SALES (corp-wide): 4.35B **Publicly Held**
Web: www.tripointehomes.com
SIC: 1522 Residential construction, nec
HQ: Tri Pointe Homes, Inc.
3161 Michelson Dr # 1500
Irvine CA

(P-780)
TRI POINTE HOMES INC
2700 Camino Ramon Ste 130 (94583-5004)
PHONE..................................925 804-2220
Jeffrey Frankel, *Pr*
EMP: 135
SALES (corp-wide): 4.35B **Publicly Held**
Web: investors.tripointehomes.com
SIC: 1522 Residential construction, nec
HQ: Tri Pointe Homes, Inc.
3161 Michelson Dr # 1500
Irvine CA

(P-781)
TRI POINTE HOMES INC (HQ)
Also Called: Tri Pointe
3161 Michelson Dr Ste 1500 (92612-4400)
P.O. Box 57088 (92619-7088)
PHONE..................................949 438-1400
Douglas Bauer, *CEO*
Barry S Sternlicht, *
Douglas F Bauer, *
Thomas J Mitchell, *Pr*
Michael D Grubbs, *CFO*
EMP: 100 **EST:** 2009
SALES (est): 1.38B
SALES (corp-wide): 4.35B **Publicly Held**
Web: www.tripointehomes.com
SIC: 1522 Residential construction, nec
PA: Tri Pointe Homes, Inc.
940 Suthwood Blvd Ste 200
Incline Village NV
775 413-1030

(P-782)
VAN DAELE HOMES INC
2900 Adams St Ste C25 (92504-8312)
PHONE..................................951 354-2121
Michael B Van Daele, *CEO*
EMP: 62 **EST:** 2013
SALES (est): 1.61MM **Privately Held**
Web: www.vandaele.com

SIC: 1522 Residential construction, nec

(P-783)
WALTON CONSTRUCTION INC
Also Called: Walton Construction Services
358 E Foothill Blvd Ste 100 (91773-1204)
PHONE..................................909 267-7777
Blake Jackson, *Pr*
E Lee Jackson, *
Rick Walker, *
David Jackson, *
EMP: 80 **EST:** 2004
SQ FT: 8,000
SALES (est): 23.54MM **Privately Held**
Web: www.waltonci.com
SIC: 1522 1542 Apartment building construction; Commercial and office building contractors

(P-784)
WERMERS MULTI-FAMILY CORP
Also Called: Wermers
5120 Shoreham Pl Ste 150 (92122-5936)
PHONE..................................858 535-1475
Thomas W Wermers, *Pr*
Jeff Bunker, *
Barry Weber, *
Richard Wood, *
Tom Wermers, *
EMP: 130 **EST:** 1997
SQ FT: 7,000
SALES (est): 37.93MM **Privately Held**
Web: www.wermerscompanies.com
SIC: 1522 Hotel/motel and multi-family home construction

(P-785)
WESTERN NATIONAL PRPTS LLC (PA)
Also Called: Arkebauer Properties
8 Executive Cir (92614-6746)
P.O. Box 19528 (92623-9528)
PHONE..................................949 862-6200
David Stone, *Ch Bd*
Michael K Hayde, *
Rex Delong, *
Debra Meute, *
Jeffrey R Scott, *
▲ **EMP:** 129 **EST:** 1981
SQ FT: 37,000
SALES (est): 60.61MM
SALES (corp-wide): 60.61MM **Privately Held**
Web: www.wng.com
SIC: 1522 6513 6512 6531 Apartment building construction; Apartment building operators; Nonresidential building operators; Real estate agents and managers

(P-786)
ZASTROW CONSTRUCTION INC
Also Called: Reliance Company
3267 Verdugo Rd (90065-2035)
PHONE..................................323 478-1956
Mark Zastrow, *Pr*
Kai Wilson, *
Patti Eldridge, *
EMP: 100 **EST:** 1976
SQ FT: 2,000
SALES (est): 13.01MM **Privately Held**
Web: www.leisdstudent.ws
SIC: 1522 Multi-family dwelling construction, nec

1531 Operative Builders

(P-787)
BEAZER MORTGAGE CORPORATION

Also Called: Beazer
1800 E Imperial Hwy Ste 200 (92821-6062)
PHONE..................................714 480-1635
John Short, *Mgr*
EMP: 100
SALES (corp-wide): 2.32B **Publicly Held**
Web: www.beazer.com
SIC: 1531 Speculative builder, single-family houses
HQ: Beazer Mortgage Corporation
2002 Summit Blvd
Brookhaven GA

(P-788)
BRADDOCK LOGAN VENTR GROUP LP (PA)
Also Called: Diablo Lodge Partnership
4155 Blackhawk Plaza Cir (94506-4903)
P.O. Box 5300 (94526-1076)
PHONE..................................925 736-4000
Joseph Raphel, *Mng Pt*
EMP: 105 **EST:** 1947
SQ FT: 10,000
SALES (est): 22.95MM
SALES (corp-wide): 22.95MM **Privately Held**
SIC: 1531 Speculative builder, single-family houses

(P-789)
DR HORTON INC
2280 Wardlow Cir Ste 100 (92878-9079)
PHONE..................................951 272-9000
Steve Fitzpatrick, *Brnch Mgr*
EMP: 64
SALES (corp-wide): 33.48B **Publicly Held**
Web: www.drhorton.com
SIC: 1531 Speculative builder, single-family houses
PA: D.R. Horton, Inc.
1341 Horton Cir
Arlington TX
817 390-8200

(P-790)
FIELDSTONE COMMUNITIES INC (PA)
16 Technology Dr Ste 125 (92618-2325)
PHONE..................................949 790-5400
William H Mcfarland, *CEO*
Frank Foster, *
Peter Ochs, *
David Langlois, *
Alan Arthur, *
EMP: 130 **EST:** 1986
SQ FT: 15,000
SALES (est): 22.74MM **Privately Held**
SIC: 1531 Speculative builder, single-family houses

(P-791)
GREENBRIAR HOMES COMMUNITIES
4340 Stevens Creek Blvd Ste 240 (95129-1102)
PHONE..................................510 497-8200
Carol M Meyer, *Ch Bd*
Gilbert M Meyer, *
EMP: 100 **EST:** 1978
SQ FT: 12,000
SALES (est): 8.36MM **Privately Held**
SIC: 1531 Operative builders

(P-792)
HOOPA MODULAR BUILDING ENTP
151 Cal Pac Rd (95546)
PHONE..................................530 625-4551
Len Mayor, *CEO*

EMP: 115 **EST:** 2000
SQ FT: 20,000
SALES (est): 9.19MM **Privately Held**
SIC: 1531 Operative builders

(P-793)
KB HOME (PA)
10990 Wilshire Blvd Fl 7 (90024-3907)
PHONE..................................310 231-4000
Jeffrey T Mezger, *Ch Bd*
Matthew W Mandino, *Ex VP*
Jeff J Kaminski, *Ex VP*
Brian J Woram, *Ex VP*
Albert Z Praw, *Executive Real Estate Vice President*
EMP: 100 **EST:** 1957
SALES (est): 6.9B
SALES (corp-wide): 6.9B **Publicly Held**
Web: www.kbhome.com
SIC: 1531 Operative builders

(P-794)
LENNAR CORPORATION
15131 Alton Pkwy Ste 190 (92618-2384)
PHONE..................................949 349-8000
Jonathan Jaffe, *COO*
EMP: 100
SALES (corp-wide): 33.67B **Publicly Held**
Web: www.lennar.com
SIC: 1531 Speculative builder, single-family houses
PA: Lennar Corporation
5505 Blue Lagoon Dr
Miami FL
305 559-4000

(P-795)
LENNAR MLTFMILY CMMUNITIES LLC
Also Called: LENNAR MULTIFAMILY COMMUNITIES, LLC
492 9th St Ste 300 (94607-4055)
PHONE..................................415 975-4980
EMP: 261
SALES (corp-wide): 33.67B **Publicly Held**
SIC: 1531 Cooperative apartment developers
HQ: Quarterra Multifamily Communities, Llc
500 E Morehead St Ste 300
Charlotte NC
704 998-0363

(P-796)
LEWIS COMPANIES (PA)
1156 N Mountain Ave (91786-3633)
PHONE..................................909 985-0971
Richard A Lewis, *Pr*
Goldy S Lewis, *
Robert E Lewis, *
Roger G Lewis, *
Randall W Lewis, *
EMP: 200 **EST:** 1973
SALES (est): 40.14MM
SALES (corp-wide): 40.14MM **Privately Held**
Web: www.lewisgroupofcompanies.com
SIC: 1531 Operative builders

(P-797)
THE RYLAND GROUP INC
3011 Townsgate Rd Ste 200 (91361-5878)
PHONE..................................805 367-3800
▼ **EMP:** 1502
SIC: 1531 1521 6162 Operative builders; Single-family housing construction; Mortgage bankers and loan correspondents

(P-798)
TRI POINTE HOMES INC
5 Peters Canyon Rd Ste 100 (92606-1791)
PHONE..................................949 478-8600

1531 - Operative Builders (P-799)

Sarah Shahin, *Off Mgr*
EMP: 135
SALES (corp-wide): 4.35B **Publicly Held**
Web: www.tripointehomes.com
SIC: 1531 Speculative builder, single-family houses
HQ: Tri Pointe Homes, Inc.
3161 Michelson Dr # 1500
Irvine CA

(P-799)
VAN DAELE DEVELOPMENT CORP
Also Called: Van Daele Homes
2900 Adams St Ste C25 (92504-4334)
PHONE....................951 354-6800
Michael B Van Daele, *CEO*
Jeff Hack, *
Michael Van Daele, *Prin*
EMP: 110 **EST:** 1987
SQ FT: 6,000
SALES (est): 40.23MM **Privately Held**
Web: www.vandaele.com
SIC: 1531 Speculative builder, single-family houses

(P-800)
WARMINGTON HOMES (PA)
3090 Pullman St (92626-7936)
PHONE....................714 434-4435
Timothy P Hogan, *Pr*
James P Warmington, *Ch Bd*
Michael Riddlesperger, *CFO*
▲ **EMP:** 120 **EST:** 1972
SQ FT: 40,000
SALES (est): 49.31MM
SALES (corp-wide): 49.31MM **Privately Held**
Web: www.homesbywarmington.com
SIC: 1531 Speculative builder, single-family houses

(P-801)
WARMINGTON HOMES
15615 Alton Pkwy Ste 150 (92618-7302)
PHONE....................949 679-3100
EMP: 127
SALES (corp-wide): 49.31MM **Privately Held**
Web: www.homesbywarmington.com
SIC: 1531 Speculative builder, single-family houses
PA: Warmington Homes
3090 Pullman St
Costa Mesa CA
714 434-4435

(P-802)
WARMINGTON HOMES
Also Called: Warmington Residential
4160 Dublin Blvd Ste 130 (94568-7734)
PHONE....................925 866-6700
Larry Riggs, *Ex VP*
EMP: 128
SALES (corp-wide): 49.31MM **Privately Held**
Web: www.homesbywarmington.com
SIC: 1531 Speculative builder, single-family houses
PA: Warmington Homes
3090 Pullman St
Costa Mesa CA
714 434-4435

1541 Industrial Buildings And Warehouses

(P-803)
AMAYA CURIEL CORPORATION
Also Called: Amaya Curiel Y CIA S.A.
9775 Marconi Dr Ste G (92154-7267)
PHONE....................619 661-1230
Roberto Curiel, *Prin*
EMP: 900 **EST:** 1972
SALES (est): 30.26MM **Privately Held**
SIC: 1541 Warehouse construction

(P-804)
AMERICAN DE ROSA LAMPARTS LLC
Also Called: Luminance
10650 4th St (91730-5918)
PHONE....................800 777-4440
EMP: 95
SALES (corp-wide): 31.1MM **Privately Held**
Web: luminance.us.com
SIC: 1541 Industrial buildings and warehouses
HQ: American De Rosa Lamparts, Llc
370 Falls Commerce Pkwy
Cuyahoga Falls OH

(P-805)
BAKELL LLC
Also Called: Jdi Distribution
24723 Redlands Blvd Ste F (92354-4021)
PHONE....................800 292-2137
Private Information, *Managing Member*
Justin Jordan, *
Deborah Blevins, *
EMP: 65 **EST:** 2015
SALES (est): 11.9MM **Privately Held**
Web: www.bakell.com
SIC: 1541 5149 2051 3299 Food products manufacturing or packing plant construction; Baking supplies; Bakery; wholesale or wholesale/retail combined; Mica products

(P-806)
BCM CONSTRUCTION COMPANY INC
2990 State Highway 32 Ste 100 (95973-8649)
PHONE....................530 342-1722
Kurtis Carman, *Pr*
Matt Bowman, *
Nancy Chinn, *
Scott January, *
EMP: 60 **EST:** 1997
SQ FT: 1,700
SALES (est): 26.01MM **Privately Held**
Web: www.bcmconstruction.com
SIC: 1541 Industrial buildings, new construction, nec

(P-807)
BETHLEHEM CONSTRUCTION INC
425 J St (93280-2335)
PHONE....................661 758-1001
Michael J Addleman, *Brnch Mgr*
EMP: 86
SALES (corp-wide): 48.14MM **Privately Held**
Web: www.bethlehemconstruction.com
SIC: 1541 1542 Warehouse construction; Commercial and office building, new construction
PA: Bethlehem Construction Incorporated
5505 Titchenal Way
Cashmere WA
509 782-1001

(P-808)
BLACH CONSTRUCTION COMPANY (PA)
Also Called: Blach
2244 Blach Pl Ste 100 (95131-1899)
PHONE....................408 244-7100
Mike Blach, *Pr*
Gaye Landau, *
Margaret Blach, *
Daniel Rogers, *
Juan Barroso, *
EMP: 80 **EST:** 1973
SQ FT: 24,000
SALES (est): 64.68MM
SALES (corp-wide): 64.68MM **Privately Held**
Web: www.blach.com
SIC: 1541 1542 Industrial buildings and warehouses; Commercial and office building, new construction

(P-809)
CALIFORNIA SHTMTL WORKS INC
Also Called: California Sheet Metal
1020 N Marshall Ave (92020-1829)
PHONE....................619 562-7010
Robin Hoffos, *Pr*
Joe Isom, *
▲ **EMP:** 90 **EST:** 1913
SQ FT: 15,000
SALES (est): 46.02MM **Privately Held**
Web: www.califsheetmetal.com
SIC: 1541 3444 Renovation, remodeling and repairs: industrial buildings; Sheet metalwork

(P-810)
CLARK CNSTR GROUP - CAL INC
18201 Von Karman Ave Ste 800 (92612-1092)
PHONE....................714 754-0764
Richard M Heim, *Pr*
EMP: 450 **EST:** 2012
SALES (est): 143.48MM
SALES (corp-wide): 1.66B **Privately Held**
SIC: 1541 1542 Industrial buildings and warehouses; Nonresidential construction, nec
HQ: Clark Construction Group, Llc
7500 Old Georgetown Rd # 600
Bethesda MD
301 272-8100

(P-811)
CMC REBAR WEST
10840 Norwalk Blvd (90670-3826)
PHONE....................714 692-7082
Lee Albright, *Brnch Mgr*
EMP: 89
SIC: 1541 Industrial buildings and warehouses
HQ: Cmc Rebar West
3880 Murphy Canyon Rd # 100
San Diego CA

(P-812)
CMC REBAR WEST
1060 Kaiser Rd (94558-6235)
PHONE....................707 863-3933
Howard Bennion, *Brnch Mgr*
EMP: 101
Web: www.cmc.com
SIC: 1541 Steel building construction
HQ: Cmc Rebar West
3880 Murphy Canyon Rd # 100
San Diego CA

(P-813)
CMC REBAR WEST
7326 Mission Gorge Rd (92120-1224)
PHONE....................858 737-7700
EMP: 126
SIC: 1541 Steel building construction
HQ: Cmc Rebar West
3880 Murphy Canyon Rd # 100
San Diego CA

(P-814)
CRAIN WALNUT SHELLING LP
10695 Decker Ave (96055-9628)
PHONE....................530 529-1585
Charles R Crain Junior, *Pt*
EMP: 369 **EST:** 2019
SALES (est): 45.74MM **Privately Held**
SIC: 1541 Food products manufacturing or packing plant construction

(P-815)
D-LINE CONSTRUCTORS INC
Also Called: D Line Constructors
498 Embarcadero W Ste 8 (94607-3706)
PHONE....................510 251-6400
Josue Antonio Prada, *CEO*
EMP: 80 **EST:** 2010
SALES (est): 20.07MM **Privately Held**
Web: www.dlineconstructors.com
SIC: 1541 1622 1771 1623 Industrial buildings and warehouses; Bridge, tunnel, and elevated highway construction; Concrete work; Water, sewer, and utility lines

(P-816)
DENVER D DARLING INC
Also Called: Darco Construction
8402 Katella Ave (90680-3215)
PHONE....................714 761-8299
Denver D Darling, *Pr*
Wayne Darling, *
EMP: 75 **EST:** 1978
SQ FT: 10,000
SALES (est): 8.2MM **Privately Held**
Web: www.darcoconstruction.com
SIC: 1541 1771 Industrial buildings, new construction, nec; Concrete work

(P-817)
EDNA H PAGEL INC
Also Called: Sweetener Products
2050 E 38th St (90058-1615)
P.O. Box 58426 (90058-0426)
PHONE....................323 234-2200
EMP: 96
SIC: 1541 5153 4213 Food products manufacturing or packing plant construction; Soybeans; Trucking, except local

(P-818)
FRIZE CORPORATION
16605 Gale Ave (91745-1802)
PHONE....................800 834-2127
James N Frize, *Pr*
EMP: 80 **EST:** 1981
SQ FT: 25,000
SALES (est): 36.61MM **Privately Held**
Web: www.frizecorp.com
SIC: 1541 1542 Industrial buildings and warehouses; Commercial and office building contractors

(P-819)
FULLMER CONSTRUCTION
1725 S Grove Ave (91761-4530)
PHONE....................909 947-9467
Robert A Fullmer, *Pr*
Gary Fullmer, *
Brad Anderson, *
James Fullmer, *
Gered Yetter, *
◆ **EMP:** 120 **EST:** 1946
SQ FT: 20,000
SALES (est): 63.17MM **Privately Held**

1541 - Industrial Buildings And Warehouses (P-840)

Web: www.fullmerco.com
SIC: **1541** Industrial buildings, new construction, nec

(P-820)
GRAY WEST CONSTRUCTION INC
Also Called: Gray Wc
421 E Cerritos Ave (92805-6320)
PHONE.................................714 491-1317
Brian Silver, *CEO*
EMP: 175 EST: 1999
SALES (est): 11.03MM **Privately Held**
SIC: **1541** Renovation, remodeling and repairs: industrial buildings

(P-821)
GRIMMWAY ENTERPRISES INC
Grimmway Farm
12020 Malaga Rd (93203-9527)
PHONE.................................661 854-6240
EMP: 178
SALES (corp-wide): 1.86B **Privately Held**
Web: www.grimmway.com
SIC: **1541** 1542 Industrial buildings and warehouses; Nonresidential construction, nec
PA: Grimmway Enterprises, Inc.
14141 Di Giorgio Rd
Arvin CA
800 301-3101

(P-822)
H C OLSEN CNSTR CO INC
710 Los Angeles Ave (91016-4250)
PHONE.................................626 359-8900
Linda Jacqueline Pearson, *CEO*
Karl Pearson, *
EMP: 75 EST: 1946
SQ FT: 12,800
SALES (est): 37.27MM **Privately Held**
Web: www.hcolsen.com
SIC: **1541** Industrial buildings, new construction, nec

(P-823)
HAL HAYS CONSTRUCTION INC (PA)
4181 Latham St (92501-1729)
PHONE.................................951 788-0703
Hal Hays, *Ex Dir*
EMP: 113 EST: 1990
SQ FT: 28,400
SALES (est): 56.37MM **Privately Held**
Web: www.halhays.com
SIC: **1541** 1542 1623 1629 Industrial buildings and warehouses; Commercial and office buildings, renovation and repair; Water, sewer, and utility lines; Dams, waterways, docks, and other marine construction

(P-824)
HEIL CONSTRUCTION INC
701 S Myrtle Ave (91016-3422)
PHONE.................................626 303-7141
EMP: 70
SIC: **1541** 1542 8741 Industrial buildings and warehouses; Commercial and office building contractors; Business management

(P-825)
HERRERO BUILDERS INCORPORATED (PA)
2100 Oakdale Ave (94124-1516)
PHONE.................................415 824-7675
Mark D Herrero, *Ch Bd*
Rick Herrero, *
▲ EMP: 128 EST: 1955

SQ FT: 10,000
SALES (est): 130.12MM
SALES (corp-wide): 130.12MM **Privately Held**
Web: www.herrero.com
SIC: **1541** Industrial buildings, new construction, nec

(P-826)
ISEC INCORPORATED
10105 Carroll Canyon Rd (92131-1109)
PHONE.................................858 279-9085
Louis L Anderson, *Pr*
EMP: 132
SALES (corp-wide): 317.22MM **Privately Held**
Web: www.isecinc.com
SIC: **1541** Industrial buildings, new construction, nec
PA: Isec, Incorporated
6000 Greenwood Plaza Blvd # 200
Greenwood Village CO
303 790-1444

(P-827)
KCS WEST INC
250 E 1st St Ste 700 (90012-3813)
PHONE.................................323 269-0020
Elmond Wan, *Pr*
EMP: 68 EST: 2007
SALES (est): 28.86MM **Privately Held**
Web: www.kcswest.com
SIC: **1541** Industrial buildings and warehouses
HQ: Kajima International Inc.
3550 Lenox Rd Ne Ste 1850
Atlanta GA
440 544-2600

(P-828)
KERNEN CONSTRUCTION
2350 Glendale Dr (95519-9205)
P.O. Box 1340 (95525-1340)
PHONE.................................707 826-8686
Kurt Kernen, *Prin*
Scott Farley, *
EMP: 60 EST: 1983
SQ FT: 120
SALES (est): 21.19MM **Privately Held**
Web: www.kernenconstruction.com
SIC: **1541** 1542 Industrial buildings, new construction, nec; Commercial and office building, new construction

(P-829)
KEVCON INC
10679 Westview Pkwy (92126-2961)
PHONE.................................760 432-0307
Kevin Kutina, *Pr*
EMP: 84 EST: 1988
SQ FT: 600
SALES (est): 5.26MM **Privately Held**
Web: www.kevcon.us
SIC: **1541** 1542 8741 Industrial buildings and warehouses; Commercial and office building contractors; Management services

(P-830)
LA TERRA FINA USA LLC
1300 Atlantic St (94587-2004)
PHONE.................................510 404-5888
Peter Molloy, *Pr*
Scott Byrnes, *
EMP: 200 EST: 1994
SQ FT: 24,000
SALES (est): 127.76MM **Privately Held**
Web: www.laterrafina.com
SIC: **1541** Food products manufacturing or packing plant construction

(P-831)
LEDCOR CMI INC
6405 Mira Mesa Blvd Ste 100 (92121-4147)
PHONE.................................602 595-3017
David W Lede, *Ch*
Cliff Lede, *Vice Chairman*
EMP: 82 EST: 2003
SALES (est): 12.29MM **Privately Held**
Web: www.ledcor.com
SIC: **1541** 1611 1629 1623 Industrial buildings and warehouses; Highway and street construction; Mine loading and discharging station construction; Pipeline construction, nsk

(P-832)
MA STEINER CONSTRUCTION INC
8854 Greenback Ln Ste 1 (95662-4084)
PHONE.................................916 988-6300
EMP: 64 EST: 2011
SALES (est): 12.47MM **Privately Held**
Web: www.masteinerconst.com
SIC: **1541** 1794 1542 1611 Industrial buildings, new construction, nec; Excavation and grading, building construction; Commercial and office building, new construction; Highway and street construction

(P-833)
MILLIE AND SEVERSON INC
3601 Serpentine Dr (90720-2440)
PHONE.................................562 493-3611
Scott Feest, *Pr*
Brian Cresap, *Prin*
Robert E Wissmann, *
John Grossman, *
Mark Huber, *
EMP: 75 EST: 1945
SQ FT: 15,000
SALES (est): 47.48MM **Privately Held**
Web: www.mandsinc.com
SIC: **1541** Industrial buildings, new construction, nec
PA: Severson Group Incorporated
3601 Serpentine Dr
Los Alamitos CA

(P-834)
MINSHEW BROTHERS STL CNSTR INC
12578 Vigilante Rd (92040-1112)
P.O. Box 1000 (92040-0902)
EMP: 105 EST: 1992
SQ FT: 22,000
SALES (est): 34.93MM **Privately Held**
SIC: **1541** 1791 Steel building construction; Structural steel erection

(P-835)
MORLEY BUILDERS INC (PA)
Also Called: Benchmark Contractors
3330 Ocean Park Blvd (90405-3202)
PHONE.................................310 399-1600
EMP: 140 EST: 1984
SALES (est): 92.7MM
SALES (corp-wide): 92.7MM **Privately Held**
Web: www.morleybuilders.com
SIC: **1541** 1522 1542 1771 Industrial buildings and warehouses; Multi-family dwelling construction, nec; Commercial and office building contractors; Concrete work

(P-836)
OLTMANS CONSTRUCTION CO
270 Conejo Ridge Ave Ste 210 (91361-4957)

PHONE.................................805 495-9553
Robert Larson, *Mgr*
EMP: 438
SQ FT: 2,600
SALES (corp-wide): 153.33K **Privately Held**
Web: www.oltmans.com
SIC: **1541** 1542 Industrial buildings and warehouses; Nonresidential construction, nec
PA: The Oltmans Construction Co
10005 Mission Mill Rd
Whittier CA
562 948-4242

(P-837)
OLTMANS CONSTRUCTION CO (PA)
10005 Mission Mill Rd (90601-1739)
P.O. Box 985 (90608-0985)
PHONE.................................562 948-4242
Joseph O Oltmans Ii, *Ch Bd*
John Gormly, *
Charles Roy, *SERV*
Jim Woodside, *
Gerald Singh, *
▼ EMP: 85 EST: 1932
SQ FT: 33,000
SALES (est): 153.33K
SALES (corp-wide): 153.33K **Privately Held**
Web: www.oltmans.com
SIC: **1541** 1542 Industrial buildings, new construction, nec; Commercial and office building, new construction

(P-838)
PACIFIC MFG & DESIGN LLC (PA)
13860 Stowe Dr (92064-8800)
PHONE.................................813 784-9958
Cheryl Landon, *Admn*
Ben Landon, *Managing Member*
EMP: 60 EST: 2018
SALES (est): 6.98MM
SALES (corp-wide): 6.98MM **Privately Held**
Web: www.pmad.com
SIC: **1541** Food products manufacturing or packing plant construction

(P-839)
PERFORMANCE MECHANICAL INC (HQ)
Also Called: P M I
701 Willow Pass Rd Ste 2 (94565-1803)
P.O. Box 1516 (94565-0151)
PHONE.................................925 432-4080
EMP: 580 EST: 1985
SALES (est): 83.04MM
SALES (corp-wide): 11.08B **Publicly Held**
Web: www.perfmech.com
SIC: **1541** 1711 8711 Industrial buildings and warehouses; Mechanical contractor; Engineering services
PA: Emcor Group, Inc.
301 Merritt 7 Fl 6
Norwalk CT
203 849-7800

(P-840)
RQ CONSTRUCTION LLC
1620 Faraday Ave (92008-7313)
PHONE.................................760 631-7707
EMP: 170 EST: 1996
SALES (est): 218.46MM **Privately Held**
Web: www.rqconstruction.com
SIC: **1541** Industrial buildings, new construction, nec

1541 - Industrial Buildings And Warehouses (P-841)

(P-841)
RUSSELL HOBBS INC
2301 W San Bernardino Ave (92374-5007)
PHONE.................909 792-8257
Russell Hobbs, *Brnch Mgr*
EMP: 61
SALES (corp-wide): 558.24MM **Privately Held**
SIC: **1541** Industrial buildings and warehouses
HQ: Russell Hobbs, Inc.
3633 S Flamingo Rd
Miramar FL
954 883-1000

(P-842)
SHIMS BARGAIN INC
Also Called: JC Sales
7030 E Slauson Ave (90040-3621)
PHONE.................323 726-8800
Andy Kim, *Mgr*
EMP: 115
Web: www.jcsalesweb.com
SIC: **1541** Industrial buildings and warehouses
PA: Shims Bargain, Inc.
2600 S Soto St
Vernon CA

(P-843)
SMITH MCHNCL-LCTRICAL-PLUMBING
Also Called: Smith Electric Service
1340 W Betteravia Rd (93455-1030)
PHONE.................805 621-5000
Michael Brannon, *Pr*
Larry Brannon, *
EMP: 150 EST: 1980
SQ FT: 10,000
SALES (est): 56.64MM **Privately Held**
Web: www.smith-electric.com
SIC: **1541** 1711 1731 1542 Industrial buildings, new construction, nec; Plumbing, heating, air-conditioning; Fire detection and burglar alarm systems specialization; Nonresidential construction, nec

(P-844)
SPECTRUM CNSTR GROUP INC
514 Via De La Valle Ste 210 (92075-2459)
PHONE.................949 299-1400
Bisher Aljazzar, *CEO*
EMP: 99 EST: 2016
SALES (est): 23.55MM **Privately Held**
Web: www.spectrumcgi.com
SIC: **1541** 1622 1542 1611 Steel building construction; Bridge, tunnel, and elevated highway construction; Commercial and office building, new construction; Highway and street construction

(P-845)
SQUARE H BRANDS INC
3615 E Vernon Ave (90058-1815)
PHONE.................323 267-4600
Bobby Codilla, *Prin*
EMP: 100
SALES (corp-wide): 39.02MM **Privately Held**
Web: www.hoffybrand.com
SIC: **1541** Food products manufacturing or packing plant construction
PA: Square H Brands, Inc.
2731 S Soto St
Vernon CA
323 267-4600

(P-846)
STANTRU RESOURCES INC
Also Called: Stantru Reinforcing Steel
11175 Redwood Ave (92337-7137)
P.O. Box 310189 (92331-0189)
PHONE.................909 587-1441
Ida Ichen, *Pr*
William M Klorman, *
EMP: 83 EST: 1991
SALES (est): 8.31MM **Privately Held**
Web: www.stantru.com
SIC: **1541** 1542 Industrial buildings, new construction, nec; Commercial and office building, new construction

(P-847)
SWINERTON BUILDERS (HQ)
Also Called: Swinerton MGT & Consulting
2001 Clayton Rd Ste 700 (94520-2401)
PHONE.................925 602-6400
Eric Foster, *CEO*
Gary J Rafferty, *Pr*
Frank Foellmer, *Ex VP*
Linda G Schowalter, *Sr VP*
John T Capener, *CAO*
▲ EMP: 63 EST: 1908
SQ FT: 300,353
SALES (est): 194.96MM **Privately Held**
Web: www.swinerton.com
SIC: **1541** 1542 1522 8742 Industrial buildings, new construction, nec; Commercial and office building, new construction; Hotel/motel, new construction; Management consulting services
PA: Swinerton Incorporated
2001 Clayton Rd Fl 7 Flr 7
San Francisco CA

(P-848)
T B PENICK & SONS INC
15435 Innovation Dr Ste 200 (92128-3443)
PHONE.................858 558-1800
Marc E Penick, *CEO*
Timothy Penick, *Pr*
John T Boyd, *CFO*
Keely Prochaska Ctrl, *Prin*
EMP: 150 EST: 1905
SQ FT: 30,000
SALES (est): 115.43MM **Privately Held**
Web: www.tbpenick.com
SIC: **1541** 1542 Industrial buildings and warehouses; Nonresidential construction, nec

(P-849)
TAISEI CONSTRUCTION CORPORATION
970 W 190th St Ste 920 (90502-1063)
PHONE.................714 886-1530
▲ EMP: 120
SIC: **1541** 1542 Industrial buildings and warehouses; Nonresidential construction, nec

(P-850)
TAWA SUPERMARKET INC
6363 Regio Ave (90620-1025)
PHONE.................714 521-8899
EMP: 88
SALES (corp-wide): 490.41MM **Privately Held**
Web: www.168markets.com
SIC: **1541** Industrial buildings and warehouses
PA: Tawa Supermarket, Inc.
6281 Regio Ave
Buena Park CA
714 521-8899

(P-851)
TRI-TECH RESTORATION CO INC
3301 N San Fernando Blvd (91504-2531)
PHONE.................818 565-3900
EMP: 70 EST: 1995
SQ FT: 35,000
SALES (est): 16.31MM **Privately Held**
Web: www.tritechrestoration.com
SIC: **1541** Industrial buildings and warehouses

(P-852)
UNIVERSAL DUST CLLCTR MFG SUP (PA)
Also Called: UDC
1041 N Kraemer Pl (92806-2611)
PHONE.................714 630-8588
Theresa A Shaffer, *CEO*
Curt Schendel, *
George G Shaffer, *
Deborah Huerta, *
EMP: 89 EST: 1984
SQ FT: 30,000
SALES (est): 36.57MM
SALES (corp-wide): 36.57MM **Privately Held**
Web: www.udccorporation.com
SIC: **1541** Industrial buildings, new construction, nec

(P-853)
UPRITE CONSTRUCTION CORP
Also Called: General Contractor
2211 Michelson Dr Ste 500 (92612-1391)
PHONE.................949 877-8877
Robert Dellaringa, *CEO*
Joe Martino, *
Phil Tanghal, *
Jay Olson, *
Tracy Zalke, *
EMP: 73 EST: 1991
SQ FT: 3,500
SALES (est): 34.58MM **Privately Held**
Web: www.upriteco.com
SIC: **1541** 5082 Warehouse construction; General construction machinery and equipment

(P-854)
VANCE BROWN INC (PA)
Also Called: Vance Brown Builders
2585 E Bayshore Rd (94303-3210)
PHONE.................650 849-9900
EMP: 96 EST: 1932
SALES (est): 35MM
SALES (corp-wide): 35MM **Privately Held**
Web: www.vancebrown.com
SIC: **1541** 1542 Industrial buildings and warehouses; Commercial and office building, new construction

(P-855)
VISIONARY NUTRITION LLC
9957 Medford Ave Ste 4 (94603-2360)
PHONE.................510 567-1200
EMP: 180 EST: 2020
SALES (est): 20.72MM **Privately Held**
Web: www.visionarynutrition.net
SIC: **1541** Food products manufacturing or packing plant construction

(P-856)
W N G CONSTRUCTION JV INC (PA)
4175 E La Palma Ave Ste 125 (92807-1842)
PHONE.................714 524-7100
Wafik Bishai, *Pr*
George Toro, *VP*
Tommie Brozick, *CFO*
EMP: 74 EST: 2013
SQ FT: 1,200
SALES (est): 11.85MM
SALES (corp-wide): 11.85MM **Privately Held**
SIC: **1541** 1542 Industrial buildings and warehouses; Commercial and office building contractors

(P-857)
WEST COAST DISTRIBUTION INC
4440 E 26th St (90058-4318)
PHONE.................323 588-6508
EMP: 82
SALES (corp-wide): 9.4MM **Privately Held**
Web: www.montagefulfillment.com
SIC: **1541** 4789 Industrial buildings and warehouses; Pipeline terminal facilities, independently operated
PA: West Coast Distribution, Inc.
2602 E 37th St
Vernon CA
323 588-6508

1542 Nonresidential Construction, Nec

(P-858)
2H CONSTRUCTION INC
2653 Walnut Ave (90755-1830)
PHONE.................562 424-5567
Sean Hitchcock, *Pr*
Ronald Compton, *
Ericka Hitchcock, *
EMP: 70 EST: 1997
SQ FT: 8,000
SALES (est): 32.56MM **Privately Held**
Web: www.2hconstruction.com
SIC: **1542** Commercial and office building, new construction

(P-859)
ABHE & SVOBODA INC
880 Tavern Rd (91901-3810)
PHONE.................619 659-1320
David Grant, *Mgr*
EMP: 81
SALES (corp-wide): 1.96MM **Privately Held**
Web: www.abheonline.com
SIC: **1542** Commercial and office building, new construction
PA: Abhe & Svoboda, Inc.
18100 Dairy Ln
Jordan MN
952 447-6025

(P-860)
ADVANCED RESTORATION INC
8880 Cal Center Dr (95826-3222)
PHONE.................916 888-9816
Jose Regalado, *CEO*
EMP: 120 EST: 2011
SALES (est): 6.37MM **Privately Held**
Web: www.advancedrestorations.com
SIC: **1542** Greenhouse construction

(P-861)
AIS CONSTRUCTION COMPANY
7015 Vista Del Rincon Dr (93001)
P.O. Box 4209 (93403-4209)
PHONE.................805 928-9467
Andy Sheaffer, *Pr*
EMP: 85 EST: 1996
SQ FT: 4,000
SALES (est): 12.4MM **Privately Held**

PRODUCTS & SERVICES SECTION
1542 - Nonresidential Construction, Nec (P-881)

Web: www.aisconstruction.com
SIC: **1542** Commercial and office building contractors

(P-862)
AK CONSTRUCTORS INC
Also Called: AK Electrical Services
1751 Jenks Dr (92878-5016)
PHONE..................951 280-0269
Kenneth G Dougher, *Pr*
Micheal Harrington, *
Kurt Meyers, *
Robert Griffin, *
EMP: 65 **EST:** 2003
SALES (est): 25.48MM **Privately Held**
Web: www.akconstructors.com
SIC: **1542** Commercial and office building, new construction

(P-863)
ALSTON CONSTRUCTION CO INC (PA)
400 Capitol Mall (95814-4436)
PHONE..................916 340-2400
Paul Little, *CEO*
Paul David Little, *
Evan Hamilton, *
Adam Nickerson, *
EMP: 100 **EST:** 1998
SALES (est): 1.27B
SALES (corp-wide): 1.27B **Privately Held**
Web: www.alstonco.com
SIC: **1542 1541** Commercial and office building, new construction; Industrial buildings and warehouses

(P-864)
AMERICAN INCORPORATED (PA)
Also Called: American Air
1345 N American St (93291-9334)
PHONE..................559 651-1776
Corwyn Oldfield, *CEO*
Frank Saucedo, *
Lois Oldfield, *
EMP: 232 **EST:** 1973
SQ FT: 115,000
SALES (est): 187.48MM
SALES (corp-wide): 187.48MM **Privately Held**
Web: www.aminc.com
SIC: **1542 1541 1731 1711** Commercial and office building contractors; Industrial buildings and warehouses; Electrical work; Plumbing contractors

(P-865)
ANDERSON BURTON CNSTR INC (PA)
121 Nevada St (93420-2609)
PHONE..................805 481-5096
Joann Anderson, *Pr*
EMP: 99 **EST:** 1999
SQ FT: 5,000
SALES (est): 47.58MM **Privately Held**
Web: www.andersonburton.com
SIC: **1542 1522** Commercial and office building, new construction; Residential construction, nec

(P-866)
ANDREW L YOUNGQUIST CNSTR INC
3187 Red Hill Ave Ste 200 (92626-3454)
PHONE..................949 862-5611
EMP: 90 **EST:** 1996
SQ FT: 10,319
SALES (est): 13.25MM **Privately Held**

SIC: **1542 1522 8741** Commercial and office building contractors; Residential construction, nec; Construction management

(P-867)
AUSTIN COMMERCIAL LP
402 W Broadway Ste 400 (92101-3554)
PHONE..................619 446-5637
James Cole, *Off Mgr*
EMP: 130
SALES (corp-wide): 2.22B **Privately Held**
Web: www.austin-ind.com
SIC: **1542** Commercial and office building, new construction
HQ: Austin Commercial, Lp
3535 Travis St Ste 300
Dallas TX
214 443-5500

(P-868)
AUSTIN COMMERCIAL LP
5901 W Century Blvd Ste 600 (90045-5442)
PHONE..................310 421-0269
Clive Buchan, *Brnch Mgr*
EMP: 160
SALES (corp-wide): 2.22B **Privately Held**
Web: www.austin-ind.com
SIC: **1542** Commercial and office building, new construction
HQ: Austin Commercial, Lp
3535 Travis St Ste 300
Dallas TX
214 443-5500

(P-869)
BALFOUR BEATTY CNSTR LLC
13520 Evening Creek Dr N Ste 270 (92128-8105)
PHONE..................858 635-7400
EMP: 100
SALES (corp-wide): 9.19B **Privately Held**
Web: www.balfourbeattyus.com
SIC: **1542** Commercial and office building, new construction
HQ: Balfour Beatty Construction, Llc
3100 Mckinnon St Fl 3
Dallas TX
214 451-1000

(P-870)
BARNHART INC
10620 Treena St Ste 300 (92131-1141)
P.O. Box 270399 (92198-2399)
PHONE..................858 635-7400
◆ **EMP:** 291
SIC: **1542** 8741 Commercial and office building, new construction; Construction management

(P-871)
BAYSIDE INSULATION & CNSTR INC
Also Called: Bayside Insulation
1635 Challenge Dr (94520-5206)
PHONE..................925 288-8960
Shahram Ameli, *CEO*
Al Badakhshan, *
EMP: 62 **EST:** 2001
SQ FT: 10,000
SALES (est): 20.06MM **Privately Held**
Web: www.baysideinsulation.com
SIC: **1542** Commercial and office building, new construction

(P-872)
BERGMAN KPRS LLC (PA)
2850 Saturn St Ste 100 (92821-1701)
PHONE..................714 924-7000

Mark C Bergman, *Prin*
Joel H Stensby, *
Lev Rabinovich, *
Paul Kristedja, *
EMP: 125 **EST:** 1982
SQ FT: 7,500
SALES (est): 62.4MM
SALES (corp-wide): 62.4MM **Privately Held**
Web: www.bergmankprs.com
SIC: **1542** Restaurant construction

(P-873)
BJORK CONSTRUCTION COMPANY INC (PA)
4420 Enterprise Pl (94538-6344)
PHONE..................510 656-4688
Jean Bjork, *Pr*
Jean Bjork, *Pr*
Don Bjork, *Field Operations Vice President*
Jesica Bjork, *OK Vice President*
Janet Maiden, *
EMP: 118 **EST:** 1988
SQ FT: 6,500
SALES (est): 27.58MM
SALES (corp-wide): 27.58MM **Privately Held**
Web: www.bjorkconstruction.com
SIC: **1542 1522 1623** Nonresidential construction, nec; Multi-family dwelling construction, nec; Water, sewer, and utility lines

(P-874)
BOLDT COMPANY
375 Beale St Ste 500 (94105-2177)
PHONE..................415 762-8300
EMP: 88
SALES (corp-wide): 1.05B **Privately Held**
Web: www.boldt.com
SIC: **1542** Specialized public building contractors
HQ: The Boldt Company
2121 E Capitol Dr
Appleton WI
920 739-6321

(P-875)
BOMEL CONSTRUCTION CO INC
701 Palomar Airport Rd Ste 270 (92011-1047)
PHONE..................760 431-6360
Mike Lucio, *Brnch Mgr*
EMP: 68
SALES (corp-wide): 102.23MM **Privately Held**
Web: www.bomelconstruction.com
SIC: **1542** Commercial and office building, new construction
PA: Bomel Construction Co., Inc.
96 Corporate Park Ste 100
Irvine CA
714 921-1660

(P-876)
BOMEL CONSTRUCTION CO INC
939 E Francis St (91761-5631)
PHONE..................909 923-3319
Richard Laughlin, *Mgr*
EMP: 91
SALES (corp-wide): 102.23MM **Privately Held**
Web: www.bomelconstruction.com
SIC: **1542** Commercial and office building, new construction
PA: Bomel Construction Co., Inc.
96 Corporate Park Ste 100
Irvine CA
714 921-1660

(P-877)
BR BUILDING RESOURCES CO
2247 Lindsay Way (91740-5398)
P.O. Box 2090 (91740-2090)
PHONE..................626 963-4880
Gary Pellant, *Pr*
Juan Banos, *
Jose Banos, *
Vanessa Banos, *
Ramon Banos, *
EMP: 120 **EST:** 2009
SQ FT: 9,000
SALES (est): 28MM **Privately Held**
Web: www.brco.com
SIC: **1542** Commercial and office buildings, renovation and repair

(P-878)
BRADDOCK & LOGAN SERVICES INC
4155 Blackhawk Plaza Cir Ste 201 (94506-4613)
P.O. Box 5300 (94526-1076)
PHONE..................925 736-4000
Joseph E Raphel, *CEO*
EMP: 200 **EST:** 1947
SALES (est): 22.5MM **Privately Held**
SIC: **1542 1522** Nonresidential construction, nec; Residential construction, nec

(P-879)
BROWARD BUILDERS INC
1200 E Kentucky Ave (95776-5906)
PHONE..................530 666-5635
Dennis Broward, *Pr*
Randy Cantrell, *
EMP: 100 **EST:** 1990
SQ FT: 7,000
SALES (est): 60.05MM **Privately Held**
Web: www.browardbuilders.com
SIC: **1542 1531** School building construction; Cooperative apartment developers

(P-880)
BROWN CONSTRUCTION INC
Also Called: Brown Construction Inc A Cal
1465 Enterprise Blvd Ste 100 (95691)
P.O. Box 980700 (95798-0700)
PHONE..................916 374-8616
Ron Brown, *Pr*
Matt Defazio, *
Liz Mccapes, *VP*
Kathryn Mc Guire, *
Ken Brown, *
EMP: 71 **EST:** 1968
SQ FT: 11,000
SALES (est): 210.15MM **Privately Held**
Web: www.brown-construction.com
SIC: **1542 1522** Commercial and office building, new construction; Apartment building construction

(P-881)
BUILD GROUP INC (PA)
160 S Van Ness Ave (94103-2519)
PHONE..................415 367-9399
Ross Edwards, *Pr*
Eric Horn, *
Ron Marano, *
Scott Brauninger, *
▲ **EMP:** 100 **EST:** 2006
SQ FT: 8,000
SALES (est): 696.63MM
SALES (corp-wide): 696.63MM **Privately Held**
Web: www.buildgc.com
SIC: **1542** Commercial and office building, new construction

1542 - Nonresidential Construction, Nec (P-882)

(P-882)
BUILD GROUP INC
Also Called: Build Sjc
1210 Coleman Ave (95050-4338)
PHONE....................408 986-8711
EMP: 65
SALES (corp-wide): 696.63MM **Privately Held**
Web: www.buildgc.com
SIC: 1542 Commercial and office building, new construction
PA: Build Group, Inc.
160 S Van Ness Ave
San Francisco CA
415 367-9399

(P-883)
BUILD GROUP INC
2121 N California Blvd Ste 301 (94596-7392)
PHONE....................415 367-9399
EMP: 95
SALES (corp-wide): 696.63MM **Privately Held**
SIC: 1542 Commercial and office building, new construction
PA: Build Group, Inc.
160 S Van Ness Ave
San Francisco CA
415 367-9399

(P-884)
BYCOR GENERAL CONTRACTORS INC
Also Called: Bycor General Contractors
6490 Marindustry Dr (92121-5297)
PHONE....................858 587-1901
Scott Kaats, *CEO*
Richard A Byer, *
EMP: 90 **EST:** 1975
SQ FT: 10,041
SALES (est): 118.05MM **Privately Held**
Web: www.bycor.com
SIC: 1542 Commercial and office building, new construction

(P-885)
C OVERAA & CO (PA)
Also Called: Overaa Construction
200 Parr Blvd (94801-1120)
PHONE....................510 234-0926
Jerry Overaa, *CEO*
Christopher Manning, *
EMP: 186 **EST:** 1907
SQ FT: 20,000
SALES (est): 413.53MM
SALES (corp-wide): 413.53MM **Privately Held**
Web: www.overaa.com
SIC: 1542 Commercial and office building, new construction

(P-886)
C W DRIVER INCORPORATED
Also Called: C. W. DRIVER, INCORPORATED
7588 Metropolitan Dr (92108-4401)
PHONE....................619 696-5100
Joe Grosshart, *Dir*
EMP: 106
SALES (corp-wide): 186.96MM **Privately Held**
Web: www.cwdriver.com
SIC: 1542 Commercial and office building, new construction
PA: C. W. Driver, Llc
468 N Rosemead Blvd
Pasadena CA
626 351-8800

(P-887)
C W DRIVER LLC (PA)
468 N Rosemead Blvd (91107-3010)
PHONE....................626 351-8800
Dana Roberts, *CEO*
Dana Roberts, *Pr*
Bessie Kouvara, *CFO*
John Janacek, *Mine Operations Vice President*
John Thornton, *Mine Operations Vice President*
EMP: 60 **EST:** 1919
SQ FT: 14,000
SALES (est): 186.96MM
SALES (corp-wide): 186.96MM **Privately Held**
Web: www.cwdriver.com
SIC: 1542 Commercial and office building, new construction

(P-888)
CAHILL CONTRACTORS INC (PA)
425 California St Ste 2200 (94104-2101)
PHONE....................415 986-0600
John E Cahill Junior, *CEO*
Chuck Palley, *
Darrell Diamond, *
Gerald K Cahill, *
William R Cahill, *
▲ **EMP:** 99 **EST:** 1974
SALES (est): 93.38MM
SALES (corp-wide): 93.38MM **Privately Held**
Web: www.cahill-sf.com
SIC: 1542 Commercial and office building, new construction

(P-889)
CAHILL CONTRACTORS LLC
425 California St Ste 2200 # 2200 (94104-2207)
PHONE....................415 986-0600
Michael Grant, *CFO*
Trilce Farrugia, *
EMP: 99 **EST:** 2016
SALES (est): 8.61MM **Privately Held**
Web: www.cahill-sf.com
SIC: 1542 1522 Commercial and office building, new construction; Residential construction, nec

(P-890)
CALIFORNIA STRL CONCPTS INC
28358 Constellation Rd Ste 660 (91355-5010)
PHONE....................661 257-6903
Jeffrey Horne, *CEO*
Penny Horne, *
EMP: 85 **EST:** 2006
SALES (est): 10.67MM **Privately Held**
Web: www.cscbuilding.net
SIC: 1542 Commercial and office building, new construction

(P-891)
CASTLE & COOKE INVESTMENTS INC
1 Dole Dr (91362-7300)
PHONE....................310 208-3636
EMP: 200 **EST:** 2008
SALES (est): 32.02MM **Privately Held**
SIC: 1542 7011 7359 1522 Commercial and office building, new construction; Resort hotel; Equipment rental and leasing, nec; Hotel/motel, new construction

(P-892)
CHARLES E THOMAS COMPANY INC (PA)
Also Called: C E T
13701 Alma Ave (90249-2513)
PHONE....................310 323-6730
Jerry Thomas, *Pr*
Brian Hurley, *
Greg Thomas, *
Ann Thomas, *
▼ **EMP:** 60 **EST:** 1949
SQ FT: 15,000
SALES (est): 58.1MM
SALES (corp-wide): 58.1MM **Privately Held**
Web: www.cethomas.net
SIC: 1542 7699 Design and erection, combined: non-residential; Service station equipment repair

(P-893)
CHARLES PNKOW BLDRS LTD A CAL
1111 Broadway Ste 200 (94607-4171)
PHONE....................510 893-5170
EMP: 450
SALES (corp-wide): 94.75MM **Privately Held**
Web: www.pankow.com
SIC: 1542 Commercial and office building, new construction
PA: Charles Pankow Builders, Ltd., A California Limited Partnership
199 S Los Robles Ave # 3
Pasadena CA
626 304-1190

(P-894)
CIRKS CONSTRUCTION INC
Also Called: Kdc Construction
3300 Industrial Blvd (95691-5028)
PHONE....................916 362-5460
Ryan Ferris, *Brnch Mgr*
EMP: 93
SALES (corp-wide): 191.38MM **Privately Held**
Web: www.kdcconstruction.com
SIC: 1542 Commercial and office building, new construction
PA: Cirks Construction Inc.
1927 N Glassell St
Orange CA
714 632-6717

(P-895)
CLARK & SULLIVAN BUILDERS INC
1340 Blue Oaks Blvd Ste 150 (95678-7039)
P.O. Box 7100 (89510-7100)
PHONE....................916 338-7707
Theodore Foor, *Pr*
B J Sullivan, *
Kevin Stroupe, *
EMP: 150 **EST:** 2001
SALES (est): 23.64MM
SALES (corp-wide): 85.59MM **Privately Held**
SIC: 1542 1541 Commercial and office building, new construction; Industrial buildings, new construction, nec
PA: C. S. General, Inc.
905 Industrial Way
Sparks NV
775 355-8500

(P-896)
CLARK & SULLIVAN CONSTRS INC
2024 Opportunity Dr Ste 150 (95678-3026)
PHONE....................916 338-7707
Ted Foor, *Brnch Mgr*
EMP: 120
SALES (corp-wide): 85.59MM **Privately Held**
Web: www.clarksullivan.com
SIC: 1542 Commercial and office building, new construction
HQ: Clark & Sullivan Constructors, Inc.
905 Industrial Way
Sparks NV
775 355-8500

(P-897)
CLARK CNSTR GROUP - CAL LP
18201 Von Karman Ave # 800 (92612-1092)
PHONE....................714 429-9779
Richard M Heim, *CEO*
EMP: 393 **EST:** 2004
SQ FT: 5,000
SALES (est): 144.65MM
SALES (corp-wide): 1.66B **Privately Held**
SIC: 1542 Commercial and office building, new construction
HQ: Clark Construction Group, Llc
7500 Old Georgetown Rd # 600
Bethesda MD
301 272-8100

(P-898)
CLUNE CONSTRUCTION COMPANY LP
1 Post St Ste 300 (94104-5249)
PHONE....................415 395-7245
Bob Dahlstrom, *Pr*
Emmett Glynn, *CFO*
Steve Wallenfang, *Pt*
EMP: 211 **EST:** 2014
SALES (est): 7.91MM
SALES (corp-wide): 138.28MM **Privately Held**
Web: www.clunegc.com
SIC: 1542 Commercial and office building, new construction
PA: Clune Construction Company, L.P.
10 S Riverside Plz # 2200
Chicago IL
312 609-3635

(P-899)
COLOMBO CONSTRUCTION CO INC
3211 Rio Mirada Dr (93308-4945)
PHONE....................661 316-0100
EMP: 75 **EST:** 1946
SALES (est): 20.02MM **Privately Held**
Web: www.colomboconstruction.com
SIC: 1542 1541 Commercial and office building, new construction; Industrial buildings, new construction, nec

(P-900)
CONSOLIDATED CONTG SVCS INC
181 Avenida La Pata Ste 200 (92673)
PHONE....................949 498-7500
Jose A Elias-calles, *CEO*
Joseph A Troya, *
Scott B Eaton, *
EMP: 65 **EST:** 1983
SQ FT: 14,500
SALES (est): 87.12MM **Privately Held**
Web: www.consolidatedcontracting.com
SIC: 1542 1541 8361 Commercial and office building, new construction; Industrial buildings and warehouses; Aged home

PRODUCTS & SERVICES SECTION   **1542 - Nonresidential Construction, Nec (P-921)**

(P-901)
CREW BUILDERS INC
8130 Commercial St (91942-2926)
P.O. Box 6205 (92166-0205)
PHONE..............................619 587-2033
Jeff D Salewsky, *CEO*
Jon Archer, *
EMP: 120 **EST:** 2006
SALES (est): 27.16MM Privately Held
Web: www.crewbuilders.com
SIC: 1542 Commercial and office building, new construction

(P-902)
DEVCON CONSTRUCTION INC (PA)
690 Gibraltar Dr (95035-6317)
PHONE..............................408 942-8200
TOLL FREE: 800
Gary Filizetti, *Pr*
Justine Pereira, *
Brett Sisney, *
EMP: 450 **EST:** 1976
SQ FT: 45,000
SALES (est): 497.26MM
SALES (corp-wide): 497.26MM Privately Held
Web: www.devcon-const.com
SIC: 1542 Commercial and office building, new construction

(P-903)
DIEDE CONSTRUCTION INC
12393 N Highway 99 (95240-7269)
P.O. Box 1007 (95258-1007)
PHONE..............................209 369-8255
Steven L Diede, *Pr*
Wayne J Diede, *
Bruce J Diede, *
Lillian Diede, *
EMP: 100 **EST:** 1978
SQ FT: 23,000
SALES (est): 47.96MM Privately Held
Web: www.diedeconstruction.com
SIC: 1542 1771 1761 Commercial and office buildings, renovation and repair; Foundation and footing contractor; Roof repair

(P-904)
DMC CONSTRUCTION INCORPORATED
2110 Del Monte Ave (93940-3712)
PHONE..............................831 656-1600
Dan Mcaweeney, *Pr*
Dan Mc Aweeney, *
EMP: 80 **EST:** 1976
SQ FT: 3,500
SALES (est): 7.43MM Privately Held
Web: www.dmcmp.com
SIC: 1542 1541 School building construction; Renovation, remodeling and repairs: industrial buildings

(P-905)
DOME CONSTRUCTION CORPORATION (PA)
393 E Grand Ave (94080-6233)
PHONE..............................650 416-5600
EMP: 174 **EST:** 1969
SALES (est): 556.31MM
SALES (corp-wide): 556.31MM Privately Held
Web: www.domebuilds.com
SIC: 1542 1541 Commercial and office buildings, renovation and repair; Renovation, remodeling and repairs: industrial buildings

(P-906)
DPR CONSTRUCTION INC (PA)
1450 Veterans Blvd (94063-2617)
PHONE..............................650 474-1450
George Pfeffer, *Pr*
Eric Lamb, *
Peter Salvati, *
James Dolen, *
Michael Ford, *
▲ **EMP:** 1200 **EST:** 1990
SQ FT: 36,300
SALES (est): 7.07B Privately Held
Web: www.dpr.com
SIC: 1542 Commercial and office building contractors

(P-907)
DPR CONSTRUCTION A GEN PARTNR
1510 S Winchester Blvd (95128-4334)
PHONE..............................408 370-2322
Jim Carter, *Mgr*
EMP: 154
Web: www.dpr.com
SIC: 1542 Commercial and office building, new construction
HQ: Dpr Construction, A General Partnership
1450 Veterans Blvd
Redwood City CA

(P-908)
DPR CONSTRUCTION A GEN PARTNR
1801 J St (95811-3009)
PHONE..............................916 568-3434
Trish Timothy, *Mgr*
EMP: 180
Web: www.dpr.com
SIC: 1542 Commercial and office building, new construction
HQ: Dpr Construction, A General Partnership
1450 Veterans Blvd
Redwood City CA

(P-909)
DPR CONSTRUCTION A GEN PARTNR
88 W Colorado Blvd Ste 301 (91105)
PHONE..............................626 463-1265
Dal Swain, *Brnch Mgr*
EMP: 101
Web: www.dpr.com
SIC: 1542 Commercial and office building, new construction
HQ: Dpr Construction, A General Partnership
1450 Veterans Blvd
Redwood City CA

(P-910)
DPR CONSTRUCTION A GEN PARTNR
5010 Shoreham Pl Ste 100 (92122-6900)
PHONE..............................858 646-0757
Peter Salvati, *Dir*
EMP: 239
Web: www.dpr.com
SIC: 1542 Commercial and office building, new construction
HQ: Dpr Construction, A General Partnership
1450 Veterans Blvd
Redwood City CA

(P-911)
DPR CONSTRUCTION A GEN PARTNR (HQ)
Also Called: Dpr Construction
1450 Veterans Blvd (94063-2617)
PHONE..............................650 474-1450
EMP: 2632 **EST:** 1990
SQ FT: 36,300
SALES (est): 2.37B Privately Held
Web: www.dpr.com
SIC: 1542 Commercial and office building, new construction
PA: Dpr Construction, Inc.
1450 Veterans Blvd
Redwood City CA

(P-912)
DRAEGER CONSTRUCTION INC
605 Commercial St (95112-1430)
EMP: 600
Web: www.draegerconstruction.com
SIC: 1542 1521 1522 Commercial and office buildings, renovation and repair; Repairing fire damage, single-family houses; Residential construction, nec

(P-913)
ENGEL HOLDINGS INC
Also Called: Cabrillo Hoist
14754 Ceres Ave (92335-4205)
P.O. Box 3179 (91729-3179)
PHONE..............................866 950-9862
Conal Molloy, *Pr*
▲ **EMP:** 103 **EST:** 1977
SQ FT: 2,000
SALES (est): 36.31MM
SALES (corp-wide): 2.16B Privately Held
Web: www.safwayatlantic.com
SIC: 1542 Commercial and office building contractors
HQ: Safway Atlantic, Llc
700 Commercial Ave
Carlstadt NJ
201 636-5500

(P-914)
ENVIRONMENTAL CONSTRUCTION INC
21550 Oxnard St Ste 1060 (91367-7123)
PHONE..............................818 449-8920
Farid Soroudi, *CEO*
Zia Abhari, *
EMP: 90 **EST:** 2004
SQ FT: 2,500
SALES (est): 26.52MM Privately Held
Web: www.environmentalconstructioninc.com
SIC: 1542 Commercial and office building contractors

(P-915)
ERIC F ANDERSON INCORPORATED
Also Called: Eric F. Anderson
1066 Beecher St (94577-1250)
P.O. Box 2076 (94577-0207)
PHONE..............................510 430-8404
EMP: 65 **EST:** 1945
SALES (est): 18.34MM Privately Held
Web: www.efainc.com
SIC: 1542 1531 1751 Shopping center construction; Cabinet and finish carpentry

(P-916)
ERICKSON-HALL CONSTRUCTION CO (PA)
500 Corporate Dr (92029-1517)
PHONE..............................760 796-7700
Dave Erickson, *CEO*
Mike Hall, *
Mike Conroy, *
Mat Gates, *
EMP: 86 **EST:** 1998
SALES (est): 52.91MM
SALES (corp-wide): 52.91MM Privately Held
Web: www.ericksonhall.com
SIC: 1542 Commercial and office building, new construction

(P-917)
F & H CONSTRUCTION (PA)
1115 E Lockeford St (95240-0878)
P.O. Box 2329 (95241-2329)
PHONE..............................209 931-3738
Charles Allen Ferrell, *Pr*
Harold Erwin Jones, *
Stephen Seibly, *
Darren Schulz, *
Dan Blackburn, *
EMP: 75 **EST:** 1972
SQ FT: 8,000
SALES (est): 35.06MM
SALES (corp-wide): 35.06MM Privately Held
Web: www.f-hconst.com
SIC: 1542 1541 Commercial and office building, new construction; Industrial buildings, new construction, nec

(P-918)
FJ WILLERT CONTRACTING CO
1869 Nirvana Ave (91911-6117)
PHONE..............................619 421-1980
Fred M Willert, *Pr*
EMP: 110 **EST:** 1972
SQ FT: 11,748
SALES (est): 49.84MM Privately Held
Web: www.fjwillert.com
SIC: 1542 Commercial and office building, new construction

(P-919)
FLINT BUILDERS INC
Also Called: Flint Builders
401 Derek Pl (95678-7153)
PHONE..............................916 757-1000
John Stump, *Pr*
Cathy Robb, *
Robert Downey, *
Jared Wright, *
Kevin Mosher, *
EMP: 89 **EST:** 2013
SALES (est): 150MM Privately Held
Web: www.flintbuilders.com
SIC: 1542 Commercial and office building, new construction

(P-920)
GALKOS CONSTRUCTION INC
15262 Pipeline Ln (92649-1136)
PHONE..............................714 373-8545
Lonnie Gialketsis, *VP*
EMP: 95
SALES (corp-wide): 18.05MM Privately Held
Web: www.galkos.com
SIC: 1542 Nonresidential construction, nec
PA: Galkos Construction, Inc.
15262 Pipeline Ln
Huntington Beach CA
714 373-8545

(P-921)
GGG DEMOLITION INC (PA)
1130 W Trenton Ave (92867-3536)
PHONE..............................714 699-9350
Gregg Miller, *Sec*
EMP: 97 **EST:** 2012

1542 - Nonresidential Construction, Nec (P-922)

SALES (est): 16.47MM
SALES (corp-wide): 16.47MM **Privately Held**
Web: www.gggdemo.com
SIC: **1542** Specialized public building contractors

(P-922)
GORDON PRILL INC
310 E Caribbean Dr (94089-1148)
PHONE..............408 745-7164
Gopal K Aggarwal, *CEO*
EMP: 64 EST: 1989
SQ FT: 24,000
SALES (est): 29.22MM **Privately Held**
Web: www.gordonprill.com
SIC: **1542** 8741 8712 8711 Commercial and office building contractors; Construction management; Architectural services; Engineering services

(P-923)
GRANI INSTALLATION INC (PA)
5411 Commercial Dr (92649-1231)
PHONE..............714 898-0441
Gregory A Grani, *CEO*
EMP: 100 EST: 1973
SQ FT: 6,000
SALES (est): 23.05MM
SALES (corp-wide): 23.05MM **Privately Held**
Web: www.grani.biz
SIC: **1542** 1742 Commercial and office buildings, renovation and repair; Acoustical and ceiling work

(P-924)
GREEN VALLEY CORPORATION
Also Called: Barry Swenson Builders
740 Front St Ste 315 (95060-4560)
PHONE..............831 475-7100
Jennifer Cosby, *Mgr*
EMP: 70
SALES (corp-wide): 98.09MM **Privately Held**
Web: www.swensonbuilders.com
SIC: **1542** Commercial and office building, new construction
PA: Green Valley Corporation
777 N 1st St Fl 5
San Jose CA
408 287-0246

(P-925)
GROUNDLVEL - OVRAA JOINT VENTR
5013 Forni Dr Ste C (94520-8524)
PHONE..............925 446-6084
Mark Rogelstad, *Prin*
Bryan Lee, *Prin*
EMP: 99 EST: 2018
SALES (est): 4.08MM **Privately Held**
SIC: **1542** Commercial and office building, new construction

(P-926)
HALSTEAD PARTNERSHIP
Also Called: Sundt Construction
2850 Gateway Oaks Dr Ste 450 (95833-4347)
PHONE..............916 830-8000
John Wald, *Mng Pt*
EMP: 60 EST: 1994
SALES (est): 23.86MM **Privately Held**
SIC: **1542** Commercial and office building, new construction

(P-927)
HAMANN CONSTRUCTION
1000 Pioneer Way (92020-1923)
PHONE..............619 440-7424
Jeffrey C Hamann, *CEO*
Jeffrey C Hamann, *Pr*
Gregg Hamann, *
EMP: 75 EST: 1954
SQ FT: 15,000
SALES (est): 42.19MM **Privately Held**
Web: www.hamannco.com
SIC: **1542** Commercial and office building, new construction

(P-928)
HAR-BRO LLC (HQ)
2750 Signal Pkwy (90755-2207)
PHONE..............562 528-8000
EMP: 80 EST: 1956
SALES (est): 49.46MM
SALES (corp-wide): 161.86MM **Privately Held**
Web: www.goblusky.com
SIC: **1542** 1521 1522 Commercial and office building, new construction; New construction, single-family houses; Apartment building construction
PA: Blusky Restoration Contractors, Llc
9110 E Nichols Ave # 180
Centennial CO
303 789-4258

(P-929)
HARRIS CONSTRUCTION CO INC
Also Called: Harris Construction
5286 E Home Ave (93727-2103)
PHONE..............559 251-0301
Mike Spencer, *Pr*
Richard F Spencer, *
Timothy Thornton, *
▲ EMP: 150 EST: 1914
SQ FT: 6,000
SALES (est): 86.36MM **Privately Held**
Web: www.harrisconstruction.com
SIC: **1542** 1541 Hospital construction; Food products manufacturing or packing plant construction

(P-930)
HARVEY INC
Also Called: Harvey General Contracting
9455 Ridgehaven Ct Ste 200 (92123-1632)
PHONE..............858 769-4000
EMP: 125 EST: 2005
SALES (est): 31.33MM **Privately Held**
Web: www.harveyusa.com
SIC: **1542** Commercial and office building, new construction

(P-931)
HATHAWAY DINWIDDIE CNSTR CO
565 Laurelwood Rd (95054-2419)
PHONE..............415 986-2718
Greg Cosko, *Pr*
David A Lee, *
EMP: 100 EST: 1946
SQ FT: 7,000
SALES (est): 37.35MM **Privately Held**
Web: www.hathawaydinwiddie.com
SIC: **1542** Commercial and office building, new construction

(P-932)
HATHAWAY DINWIDDIE CNSTR CO
Also Called: Hathaway Dinwiddie
275 Battery St Ste 300 (94111-3378)
PHONE..............415 986-2718
▲ EMP: 400 EST: 1996
SQ FT: 21,000
SALES (est): 158.53MM **Privately Held**
Web: www.hathawaydinwiddie.com
SIC: **1542** Commercial and office building, new construction
PA: Hathaway Dinwiddie Construction Group
275 Battery St Ste 300
San Francisco CA

(P-933)
HATHAWAY DINWIDDIE CNSTR GROUP (PA)
275 Battery St Ste 300 (94111-3378)
PHONE..............415 986-2718
EMP: 60 EST: 1996
SQ FT: 18,000
SALES (est): 158.53MM **Privately Held**
Web: www.hathawaydinwiddie.com
SIC: **1542** Commercial and office building, new construction

(P-934)
HEALTHCARE DESIGN & CNSTR LLC
Also Called: Hdc
18302 Irvine Blvd Ste 120 (92780-3436)
PHONE..............714 245-0144
Scot Berlinski, *Pr*
EMP: 73 EST: 2013
SALES (est): 67MM **Privately Held**
Web: www.hdcbuilders.com
SIC: **1542** Hospital construction

(P-935)
HENSEL PHELPS CONSTRUCTION CO
4750 Willow Rd Ste 100 (94588-2963)
PHONE..............408 452-1800
Jon W Ball, *VP*
EMP: 200
SALES (corp-wide): 5.33B **Privately Held**
Web: www.henselphelps.com
SIC: **1542** 1541 Commercial and office building, new construction; Industrial buildings and warehouses
PA: Hensel Phelps Construction Co.
420 6th Ave
Greeley CO
970 352-6565

(P-936)
HILBERS INC
Also Called: Hilbers Contractors & Engrg
770 N Walton Ave Ste 100 (95993-9469)
PHONE..............530 673-2947
Kurt G Hilbers, *CEO*
Kurt G Hilbers, *Pr*
Larry E Hilbers, *
Tom Jones, *
Mary Hilbers, *
EMP: 75 EST: 1988
SQ FT: 6,790
SALES (est): 41.97MM **Privately Held**
Web: www.hilbersinc.com
SIC: **1542** 1541 Commercial and office building, new construction; Industrial buildings, new construction, nec

(P-937)
HITT CONTRACTING INC
3733 Motor Ave Ste 200 (90034-6403)
PHONE..............424 326-1042
EMP: 307
SALES (corp-wide): 1.22B **Privately Held**
Web: www.hitt.com
SIC: **1542** 1531 Nonresidential construction, nec; Operative builders
PA: Hitt Contracting, Inc.
2900 Fairview Park Dr
Falls Church VA
703 846-9000

(P-938)
HOLBROOK CONSTRUCTION INC
9814 Norwalk Blvd Ste 200 (90670-2992)
PHONE..............714 523-1150
Laurence A Holbrook, *Pr*
EMP: 75 EST: 1985
SQ FT: 3,000
SALES (est): 9.1MM **Privately Held**
Web: www.holbrookconstruction.net
SIC: **1542** Commercial and office building, new construction

(P-939)
HOUALLA ENTERPRISES LTD
Also Called: Metro Bldrs & Engineers Group
2610 Avon St (92663-4706)
PHONE..............949 515-4350
Fouad Houalla, *Pr*
▲ EMP: 85 EST: 1987
SQ FT: 1,200
SALES (est): 22.44MM **Privately Held**
Web: www.metrobuilders.com
SIC: **1542** Commercial and office building, new construction

(P-940)
ICON WEST INC
520 S La Fayette Park Pl Ste 503 (90057-5422)
PHONE..............213 385-0027
Bernard F Ashkar, *CEO*
Michael Halaoui, *
EMP: 60 EST: 1997
SALES (est): 86MM **Privately Held**
Web: www.icon-west.com
SIC: **1542** 1522 Commercial and office building, new construction; Hotel/motel and multi-family home construction

(P-941)
INTERIOR LGIC GROUP HLDNGS IV (PA)
10 Bunsen (92618-4210)
PHONE..............800 959-8333
Alan K Davenport, *Pr*
Jason Peel, *CFO*
Bob Hess, *CAO*
Anne Liu, *CAO*
Chris Filandro, *CIO*
EMP: 87 EST: 2018
SALES (est): 97.93MM
SALES (corp-wide): 97.93MM **Privately Held**
Web: www.interiorlogicgroup.com
SIC: **1542** Commercial and office building contractors

(P-942)
J D DIFFENBAUGH INC
6865 Airport Dr (92504-1903)
P.O. Box 4457 (92514-4457)
PHONE..............951 351-6865
Jack Hawkins Junior, *CEO*
Marvin J Hawkins Junior, *Pr*
EMP: 60 EST: 1959
SQ FT: 15,000
SALES (est): 24.15MM **Privately Held**
Web: www.diffenbaugh.com
SIC: **1542** 1541 Commercial and office building, new construction; Industrial buildings, new construction, nec

1542 - Nonresidential Construction, Nec (P-964)

(P-943)
J GROTHE ENTERPRISES INC
Also Called: J G Construction
15632 El Prado Rd (91710-9108)
PHONE...............................909 993-9393
John P Grothe, *CEO*
EMP: 76 EST: 1979
SQ FT: 15,400
SALES (est): 8.95MM Privately Held
Web: www.jg-companies.com
SIC: 1542 Shopping center construction

(P-944)
J R ROBERTS CORP (HQ)
7745 Greenback Ln Ste 300 (95610-5866)
PHONE...............................916 729-5600
Robert Olsen, *CEO*
Robert C Hall Junior, *Pr*
Mike Vinks, *
EMP: 100 EST: 1979
SQ FT: 9,000
SALES (est): 25.3MM
SALES (corp-wide): 162.92MM Privately Held
Web: www.jrroberts.com
SIC: 1542 Commercial and office building, new construction
PA: Deacon Construction, Llc
   901 Ne Glisan St Ste 100
   Portland OR
   503 297-8791

(P-945)
J R ROBERTS ENTERPRISES INC
7745 Greenback Ln Ste 300 (95610-5866)
PHONE...............................916 729-5600
Robert F Olsen, *Ch Bd*
Robert C Hall Junior, *Pr*
James F Reilly, *
EMP: 110 EST: 1984
SALES (est): 10.47MM Privately Held
SIC: 1542 1522 Commercial and office building contractors; Multi-family dwellings, new construction

(P-946)
JM STITT CONSTRUCTION INC
3165 Palisades Dr (92878-9432)
PHONE...............................951 271-3440
Julia Stitt, *Pr*
John Stitt, *
Julia Stitt, *CFO*
Justin Stitt, *
Katie Stitt, *
EMP: 60 EST: 1985
SALES (est): 25.38MM Privately Held
Web: www.jmstittconstruction.com
SIC: 1542 Commercial and office building, new construction

(P-947)
JMB CONSTRUCTION INC
Also Called: JMB
132 S Maple Ave (94080-6302)
PHONE...............................650 267-5300
Margaret P Burke, *Pr*
▲ EMP: 100 EST: 1976
SALES (est): 50.06MM Privately Held
Web: www.jmbconstruction.com
SIC: 1542 Commercial and office building, new construction

(P-948)
JOHN F OTTO INC
Also Called: Otto Construction
1717 2nd St (95811-6214)
PHONE...............................916 441-6870
Carl Barrett, *Pr*
Carol Otto, *
Allison Otto, *
John W Otto, *
Preston Hatch, *
EMP: 140 EST: 1958
SQ FT: 10,000
SALES (est): 181.46MM Privately Held
Web: www.ottoconstruction.com
SIC: 1542 1541 Commercial and office building, new construction; Industrial buildings, new construction, nec

(P-949)
JOHN M FRANK CONSTRUCTION INC
Also Called: John M Frank Service Group
913 E 4th St (92701-4748)
PHONE...............................714 210-3600
John M Frank, *CEO*
Laurie Dawson, *
EMP: 80 EST: 1984
SALES (est): 31.92MM Privately Held
Web: www.johnmfrankconstruction.com
SIC: 1542 5411 5812 Commercial and office building, new construction; Supermarkets; Family restaurants

(P-950)
KARSYN CONSTRUCTION INC
4697 W Jacquelyn Ave (93722-6413)
PHONE...............................559 271-2900
EMP: 60 EST: 1995
SALES (est): 10.99MM Privately Held
Web: www.karsyn.com
SIC: 1542 Commercial and office building, new construction

(P-951)
KIEWIT CORPORATION
Also Called: Measure of Excellence Cabinets
12700 Stowe Dr Ste 180 (92064-8883)
PHONE...............................858 208-4425
EMP: 80
SALES (corp-wide): 17.08B Privately Held
SIC: 1542 Commercial and office building contractors
HQ: Kiewit Corporation
    3555 Farnam St Ste 1000
    Omaha NE
    402 342-2052

(P-952)
KITCHELL CORPORATION
2450 Venture Oaks Way Ste 500 (95833-4226)
PHONE...............................916 648-9700
Naveed Saboonchi, *Brnch Mgr*
EMP: 120
SALES (corp-wide): 643.69MM Privately Held
Web: www.kitchell.com
SIC: 1542 Commercial and office building, new construction
PA: Kitchell Corporation
    1707 E Highland Ave # 100
    Phoenix AZ
    602 264-4411

(P-953)
KOLL CONSTRUCTION LP
4343 Von Karman Ave Ste 150 (92660-1200)
PHONE...............................949 833-3030
Donald M Koll, *Managing Member*
EMP: 100 EST: 1996
SALES (est): 19.8MM Privately Held
SIC: 1542 Nonresidential construction, nec

(P-954)
KPRS CONSTRUCTION SERVICES INC (PA)
Also Called: Kprs
2850 Saturn St Ste 110 (92821-1701)
PHONE...............................714 672-0800
Joel H Stensby, *Pr*
Paul Kristedja, *
Lev Rabinovich, *
EMP: 91 EST: 1995
SQ FT: 31,000
SALES (est): 80.12MM
SALES (corp-wide): 80.12MM Privately Held
Web: www.kprsinc.com
SIC: 1542 8711 Commercial and office building, new construction; Building construction consultant

(P-955)
KRAMER RGM INC
3230 Monument Way (94518-2406)
PHONE...............................925 671-7717
EMP: 65 EST: 2019
SALES (est): 1.87MM Privately Held
Web: www.rgmkramer.com
SIC: 1542 Commercial and office building, new construction

(P-956)
L & S HALLMARK CONSTRUCTION INC
Also Called: Hallmark Construction
3360 De La Cruz Blvd (95054-2606)
PHONE...............................408 727-4422
EMP: 137
Web: www.hallmarkconstruction.com
SIC: 1542 Commercial and office buildings, renovation and repair

(P-957)
LATHROP CONSTRUCTION ASSOC INC (PA)
4001 Park Rd (94510-1172)
P.O. Box 2005 (94510-0819)
PHONE...............................707 746-8000
Roy Van Pelt, *Ch*
Ricky J Martellaro, *
C Gary Kalian, *
Olav Lyssand, *
EMP: 68 EST: 1981
SQ FT: 14,000
SALES (est): 31.15MM
SALES (corp-wide): 31.15MM Privately Held
Web: www.lathropconstruction.com
SIC: 1542 School building construction

(P-958)
LEDESMA & MEYER CNSTR CO INC
9441 Haven Ave (91730-5845)
PHONE...............................909 297-1100
Kris Meyer, *Pr*
Joseph M Ledesma, *
EMP: 68 EST: 1997
SALES (est): 7.62MM Privately Held
Web: www.lmcci.com
SIC: 1542 School building construction

(P-959)
LEVEL 10 CONSTRUCTION LP (PA)
1050 Enterprise Way Ste 250 (94089)
PHONE...............................408 747-5000
Dennis Giles, *Pr*
Jim Evans, *CFO*
EMP: 220 EST: 2011
SQ FT: 12,000
SALES (est): 144.68MM
SALES (corp-wide): 144.68MM Privately Held
Web: www.level10gc.com
SIC: 1542 Commercial and office buildings, renovation and repair

(P-960)
LEVEL-IT INSTLLTIONS GROUP INC
3700 Yale Way (94538-6183)
PHONE...............................604 942-2022
EMP: 60 EST: 2019
SALES (est): 20MM Privately Held
Web: www.levelitgroup.com
SIC: 1542 Nonresidential construction, nec

(P-961)
LMC HOLLYWOOD HIGHLAND
Also Called: Lennar Multi Family Community
95 Enterprise Ste 200 (92656-2611)
PHONE...............................949 448-1600
Todd Farrell, *CEO*
EMP: 500 EST: 2013
SALES (est): 43.15MM Privately Held
SIC: 1542 Commercial and office building contractors

(P-962)
LUSARDI CONSTRUCTION CO
6376 Clark Ave (94568-3036)
PHONE...............................925 829-1114
Kurt Evans, *Mgr*
EMP: 135
SALES (corp-wide): 84.75MM Privately Held
Web: www.lusardi.com
SIC: 1542 Commercial and office building, new construction
PA: Lusardi Construction Co.
    1570 Linda Vista Dr
    San Marcos CA
    760 744-3133

(P-963)
MCCARTHY BLDG COMPANIES INC
Also Called: San Jose Office
3975 Freedom Cir Ste 950 (95054-1455)
PHONE...............................408 908-7005
EMP: 388
SALES (corp-wide): 5.39B Privately Held
Web: www.mccarthy.com
SIC: 1542 Commercial and office building, new construction
HQ: Mccarthy Building Companies, Inc.
    12851 Manchester Rd
    Saint Louis MO
    314 968-3300

(P-964)
MCCARTHY BLDG COMPANIES INC
Southern California Division
20401 Sw Birch St Ste 300 (92660-1726)
PHONE...............................949 851-8383
Randy Highland, *Brnch Mgr*
EMP: 75
SALES (corp-wide): 5.39B Privately Held
Web: www.mccarthy.com
SIC: 1542 Commercial and office building, new construction
HQ: Mccarthy Building Companies, Inc.
    12851 Manchester Rd
    Saint Louis MO
    314 968-3300

1542 - Nonresidential Construction, Nec (P-965)

(P-965)
MCCARTHY BLDG COMPANIES INC
1113 Bush (92868-4222)
PHONE..................949 851-8383
Pat Peterson, *Brnch Mgr*
EMP: 97
SALES (corp-wide): 5.39B Privately Held
Web: www.mccarthy.com
SIC: 1542 Commercial and office building, new construction
HQ: Mccarthy Building Companies, Inc.
   12851 Manchester Rd
   Saint Louis MO
   314 968-3300

(P-966)
MCCARTHY BLDG COMPANIES INC
6363 Regent St (90255-3545)
PHONE..................949 851-8383
EMP: 81
SALES (corp-wide): 5.39B Privately Held
Web: www.mccarthy.com
SIC: 1542 Commercial and office building, new construction
HQ: Mccarthy Building Companies, Inc.
   12851 Manchester Rd
   Saint Louis MO
   314 968-3300

(P-967)
MCCARTHY BLDG COMPANIES INC
18943 Airport Way (92707-5211)
PHONE..................949 851-8383
EMP: 81
SALES (corp-wide): 5.39B Privately Held
Web: www.mccarthy.com
SIC: 1542 Commercial and office building, new construction
HQ: Mccarthy Building Companies, Inc.
   12851 Manchester Rd
   Saint Louis MO
   314 968-3300

(P-968)
MCCARTHY BLDG COMPANIES INC
20401 Sw Birch St Ste 200 (92660-1796)
PHONE..................949 851-8383
EMP: 347
SALES (corp-wide): 5.39B Privately Held
Web: www.mccarthy.com
SIC: 1542 1541 Institutional building construction; Industrial buildings, nec
HQ: Mccarthy Building Companies, Inc.
   12851 Manchester Rd
   Saint Louis MO
   314 968-3300

(P-969)
MCCARTHY BLDG COMPANIES INC
1460 Churchill Downs Ave (95776-6113)
PHONE..................530 665-4774
EMP: 744
SALES (corp-wide): 5.39B Privately Held
Web: www.mccarthybuildingcompanies.com
SIC: 1542 1541 Institutional building construction; Industrial buildings, new construction, nec
HQ: Mccarthy Building Companies, Inc.
   12851 Manchester Rd
   Saint Louis MO
   314 968-3300

(P-970)
MERUELO ENTERPRISES INC (PA)
9550 Firestone Blvd Ste 105 (90241-5560)
PHONE..................562 745-2300
Alex Meruelo, *CEO*
Al Stoller, *
Joe Marchica, *
EMP: 501 EST: 1986
SALES (est): 528.99MM
SALES (corp-wide): 528.99MM Privately Held
Web: www.meruelopenterprises.com
SIC: 1542 Nonresidential construction, nec

(P-971)
MISSION CONSTRUCTORS INC
195 Bay Shore Blvd (94124-1321)
PHONE..................415 282-8453
Jaime Maciel Gonzalez, *CEO*
Isabelle Concio, *
EMP: 85 EST: 2012
SQ FT: 5,000
SALES (est): 22.4MM Privately Held
SIC: 1542 Specialized public building contractors

(P-972)
MOOREFIELD CONSTRUCTION INC (PA)
600 N Tustin Ave Ste 210 (92705-3781)
PHONE..................714 972-0700
Mike Moorefield, *Pr*
Larry Moorefield, *
Hal Moorefield, *
EMP: 60 EST: 1957
SQ FT: 8,490
SALES (est): 166.48MM
SALES (corp-wide): 166.48MM Privately Held
Web: www.moorefieldconstruction.com
SIC: 1542 Shopping center construction

(P-973)
MURPHY-TRUE INC
Also Called: Jim Murphy & Associates
464 Kenwood Ct Ste B (95407-5709)
PHONE..................707 576-7337
Jim M Murphy, *CEO*
Leighton J True Iii, *VP*
EMP: 60 EST: 1968
SQ FT: 5,000
SALES (est): 38.24MM Privately Held
Web: www.j-m-a.com
SIC: 1542 1521 Commercial and office building, new construction; New construction, single-family houses

(P-974)
NEFF CONSTRUCTION INC
1701 S Bon View Ave Unit 104 (91761-4412)
P.O. Box 1488 (91762-0488)
PHONE..................909 947-3768
EMP: 60 EST: 2000
SALES (est): 21.25MM Privately Held
Web: www.neffcon.com
SIC: 1542 Commercial and office building contractors

(P-975)
NEVELL GROUP INC
179 Mason Cir (94520-1213)
PHONE..................714 579-7501
Michael Nevell, *CEO*
EMP: 387
SALES (corp-wide): 120.36MM Privately Held
Web: www.nevellgroup.com
SIC: 1542 Commercial and office building, new construction
PA: The Nevell Group Inc
   3001 Enterprise St # 200
   Brea CA
   714 579-7501

(P-976)
NEVELL GROUP INC (PA)
Also Called: N G I
3001 Enterprise St Ste 200 (92821-6210)
PHONE..................714 579-7501
Michael J Nevell, *Pr*
Bruce Pasqua, *
Bryan Bodine, *
Chris Taylor, *
EMP: 125 EST: 2002
SQ FT: 35,000
SALES (est): 120.36MM
SALES (corp-wide): 120.36MM Privately Held
Web: www.nevellgroup.com
SIC: 1542 Commercial and office building, new construction

(P-977)
NEVELL GROUP INC
Also Called: Nevell Group Inc San Diego
3284 Grey Hawk Ct (92010-6651)
PHONE..................760 598-3501
Greg Thomas, *Brnch Mgr*
EMP: 388
SALES (corp-wide): 120.36MM Privately Held
Web: www.nevellgroup.com
SIC: 1542 Commercial and office building, new construction
PA: The Nevell Group Inc
   3001 Enterprise St # 200
   Brea CA
   714 579-7501

(P-978)
NIBBI BROS INC
1000 Brannan St Ste 102 (94103-4824)
PHONE..................415 863-1820
Sergio J Nibbi, *Ch Bd*
Larry Nibbi, *CEO*
Robert L Nibbi, *Pr*
Michael Nibbi, *VP*
EMP: 165 EST: 1952
SQ FT: 5,000
SALES (est): 49.51MM Privately Held
Web: www.nibbi.com
SIC: 1542 1541 Commercial and office building, new construction; Industrial buildings and warehouses

(P-979)
NOVO CONSTRUCTION INC (PA)
1460 Obrien Dr (94025-1432)
PHONE..................650 701-1500
James C Fowler, *CEO*
Jim Fowler, *
Robert Williamson, *
EMP: 85 EST: 2000
SQ FT: 10,000
SALES (est): 872.51MM
SALES (corp-wide): 872.51MM Privately Held
Web: www.novoconstruction.com
SIC: 1542 Commercial and office building, new construction

(P-980)
OLIVER & COMPANY INC
1300 S 51st St (94804-4628)
PHONE..................510 412-9090
Steven Henri Oliver, *CEO*
Josh Oliver, *
Jeff Shields, *
▲ EMP: 90 EST: 1971
SQ FT: 6,302
SALES (est): 41.67MM Privately Held
Web: www.oliverandco.net
SIC: 1542 Commercial and office building, new construction

(P-981)
PAAT & KIMMEL DEVELOPMENT INC
600 N Mountain Ave (91786-4331)
PHONE..................909 315-8074
Victor Paat, *CEO*
EMP: 60 EST: 2014
SALES (est): 9.98MM Privately Held
SIC: 1542 Commercial and office building, new construction

(P-982)
PACIFIC BUILDING GROUP (PA)
9752 Aspen Creek Ct Ste 100 (92126-1082)
PHONE..................858 552-0600
Gregory A Rogers, *CEO*
Jim Roherty, *
Ron Maize, *
Lisa Hitt, *
William Hansen, *
▲ EMP: 96 EST: 1984
SQ FT: 17,880
SALES (est): 59.16MM
SALES (corp-wide): 59.16MM Privately Held
Web: www.pacificbuildinggroup.com
SIC: 1542 Commercial and office building, new construction

(P-983)
PARKCO BUILDING COMPANY
24795 State Highway 74 (92570-8759)
PHONE..................714 444-1441
W Adrian Hoyle, *Pr*
EMP: 99 EST: 2013
SALES (est): 9.51MM Privately Held
Web: www.parkcobuilding.com
SIC: 1542 1771 1799 Commercial and office building, new construction; Foundation and footing contractor; Erection and dismantling of forms for poured concrete

(P-984)
PCL CONSTRUCTION SERVICES INC
655 N Central Ave Ste 1600 (91203-1438)
PHONE..................818 246-3481
Dale Kain, *Mgr*
EMP: 191
SQ FT: 17,619
SALES (corp-wide): 5.99B Privately Held
SIC: 1542 Commercial and office building, new construction
HQ: Pcl Construction Services, Inc.
   2000 S Colo Blvd Ste 2-50
   Denver CO
   303 365-6500

(P-985)
PCL CONSTRUCTION SERVICES INC
100 Universal City Plz (91608-1002)
PHONE..................818 509-7816
EMP: 99
SALES (corp-wide): 5.99B Privately Held
SIC: 1542 Commercial and office building, new construction
HQ: Pcl Construction Services, Inc.
   2000 S Colo Blvd Ste 2-50
   Denver CO
   303 365-6500

PRODUCTS & SERVICES SECTION
1542 - Nonresidential Construction, Nec (P-1009)

(P-986)
PCL CONSTRUCTION SERVICES INC
4690 Executive Dr Ste 100 (92121-3073)
PHONE..........................858 657-3400
EMP: 121
SALES (corp-wide): 5.99B **Privately Held**
SIC: 1542 Commercial and office building, new construction
HQ: Pcl Construction Services, Inc.
2000 S Colo Blvd Ste 2-50
Denver CO
303 365-6500

(P-987)
PCL INDUSTRIAL SERVICES INC
1500 S Union Ave (93307-4144)
PHONE..........................661 832-3995
Joe W Carrieri, *CEO*
Gary L Basher, *
EMP: 300 **EST:** 2002
SALES (est): 128.25MM **Privately Held**
SIC: 1542 Commercial and office building, new construction

(P-988)
PENWAL INDUSTRIES INC
10611 Acacia St (91730-5410)
PHONE..........................909 466-1555
Chris A Pennington, *Prin*
▲ **EMP:** 100 **EST:** 1981
SQ FT: 65,000
SALES (est): 26.16MM **Privately Held**
Web: www.penwal.com
SIC: 1542 3999 8742 3993 Shopping center construction; Advertising display products; Management consulting services; Signs and advertising specialties

(P-989)
PERENNIAL CONSTRUCTION CORP
1682 Langley Ave (92614-5620)
PHONE..........................212 727-1807
Aaron Strom, *Pr*
EMP: 60 **EST:** 2018
SALES (est): 9.49MM **Privately Held**
Web: www.perennialcs.com
SIC: 1542 1521 Commercial and office buildings, renovation and repair; General remodeling, single-family houses

(P-990)
PERRY COAST CONSTRUCTION INC
Also Called: West Coast Construction
3811 Wacker Dr (91752-1142)
PHONE..........................951 774-0677
Robert Perry, *Pr*
Erin Perry, *
Britney Perry, *
EMP: 105 **EST:** 2012
SALES (est): 21.35MM **Privately Held**
Web: www.wcconcrete.com
SIC: 1542 Restaurant construction

(P-991)
PHILMONT MANAGEMENT INC
3450 Wilshire Blvd Ste 850 (90010-2211)
PHONE..........................213 380-0159
Monica Nam, *Pr*
EMP: 99 **EST:** 1997
SQ FT: 6,000
SALES (est): 10.77MM **Privately Held**
Web: www.philmontinc.com
SIC: 1542 Commercial and office building, new construction

(P-992)
PLANT CONSTRUCTION COMPANY LP
300 Newhall St (94124-1498)
PHONE..........................415 285-0500
▲ **EMP:** 300 **EST:** 1990
SALES (est): 64.98MM **Privately Held**
Web: www.plantconstruction.com
SIC: 1542 Commercial and office buildings, renovation and repair

(P-993)
PLATINUM CONSTRUCTION INC
865 S East St (92805-5356)
PHONE..........................714 527-0700
Darrin W Streilein, *Pr*
EMP: 100 **EST:** 2005
SALES (est): 20.62MM **Privately Held**
SIC: 1542 1541 1742 Commercial and office building contractors; Steel building construction; Plastering, drywall, and insulation

(P-994)
PNG BUILDERS
Also Called: General Contractor
2392 S Bateman Ave (91010-3312)
PHONE..........................626 256-9539
Steven Mathison, *CEO*
Louie Garcia, *
Michelle Mcneal, *Prin*
Gina Bockhold, *
EMP: 70 **EST:** 1959
SQ FT: 33,000
SALES (est): 151.56MM **Privately Held**
Web: www.pacific-inc.com
SIC: 1542 1522 Commercial and office building contractors; Residential construction, nec

(P-995)
PR CONSTRUCTION INC
1995 N Batavia St (92865-4107)
PHONE..........................714 637-7848
Sean Brennan, *CEO*
Sean Brennan, *Pr*
Chris Harris, *
EMP: 72 **EST:** 1990
SQ FT: 11,500
SALES (est): 35.45MM **Privately Held**
Web: www.prconstruction.net
SIC: 1542 1531 Nonresidential construction, nec

(P-996)
QUIRING CORPORATION
5118 E Clinton Way Ste 201 (93727-2014)
PHONE..........................559 432-2800
Paul K Quiring, *Pr*
Greg Quiring, *
Jim Kennedy, *
Jack Torres, *
Sue Kliewer, *
EMP: 62 **EST:** 1947
SQ FT: 4,000
SALES (est): 26.91MM **Privately Held**
Web: www.quiring.com
SIC: 1542 Commercial and office building, new construction

(P-997)
QUIRING GENERAL LLC
Also Called: Construction
5118 E Clinton Way Ste 201 (93727-2014)
PHONE..........................559 432-2800
Greg A Quiring, *Managing Member*
John Wood, *CFO*
Paul Quiring, *CEO*
EMP: 80 **EST:** 2011
SQ FT: 6,200

SALES (est): 46.09MM **Privately Held**
Web: www.quiring.com
SIC: 1542 Commercial and office building, new construction

(P-998)
R & L BROSAMER INC
2916 W Main St (93291-5731)
P.O. Box 238 (94507-0238)
PHONE..........................559 739-8215
Larry Roeder, *Off Mgr*
EMP: 360
SALES (corp-wide): 3.62B **Privately Held**
Web: www.brosamer.com
SIC: 1542 Commercial and office building, new construction
HQ: R & L Brosamer, Inc.
1390 Willow Pass Rd # 95
Concord CA

(P-999)
R J LANTHIER COMPANY INC
485 Corporate Dr (92029-1507)
PHONE..........................760 738-9798
EMP: 80
SIC: 1542 1711 Nonresidential construction, nec; Warm air heating and air conditioning contractor

(P-1000)
R Q CONSTRUCTION INC
1620 Faraday Ave (92008-7313)
PHONE..........................760 631-7707
EMP: 140 **EST:** 1996
SALES (est): 37.99MM **Privately Held**
Web: www.rqconstruction.com
SIC: 1542 Commercial and office building, new construction

(P-1001)
RANCHO SANTA FE TECHNOLOGY INC (PA)
5961 Kearny Villa Rd (92123-1004)
PHONE..........................858 565-7224
EMP: 60 **EST:** 1990
SALES (est): 10.58MM **Privately Held**
Web: www.rsft.com
SIC: 1542 Commercial and office building, new construction

(P-1002)
RANCHWOOD CONTRACTORS INC
923 E Pacheco Blvd (93635-4327)
PHONE..........................209 826-6200
Greg Hostetler, *Pr*
Catherine Hostetler, *
EMP: 92 **EST:** 1984
SQ FT: 3,500
SALES (est): 13.87MM **Privately Held**
Web: www.ranchwood.com
SIC: 1542 1521 Commercial and office building, new construction; New construction, single-family houses

(P-1003)
RBA BUILDERS INC
16490 Harbor Blvd Ste A (92708-1392)
PHONE..........................714 895-9000
Robert Anderson, *CEO*
EMP: 82 **EST:** 2007
SALES (est): 49.78MM **Privately Held**
Web: www.rbabuildersinc.com
SIC: 1542 Commercial and office building, new construction

(P-1004)
RD OLSON CONSTRUCTION INC
400 Spectrum Center Dr Ste 1200 (92618-5022)
PHONE..........................949 474-2001
EMP: 125 **EST:** 1979
SALES (est): 41.12MM
SALES (corp-wide): 41.12MM **Privately Held**
Web: www.rdolson.com
SIC: 1542 1522 Commercial and office buildings, renovation and repair; Hotel/motel and multi-family home construction
PA: The Robert D Olson Corporation
400 Spectrum Center Dr # 12
Irvine CA
949 474-2001

(P-1005)
REDHORSE CONSTRUCTORS INC
36 Professional Center Pkwy (94903-2703)
PHONE..........................415 492-2020
David J Warner, *Pr*
▲ **EMP:** 75 **EST:** 1981
SQ FT: 3,500
SALES (est): 19.99MM **Privately Held**
Web: www.redhorseconstructors.com
SIC: 1542 Commercial and office building, new construction

(P-1006)
REEVE-KNIGHT CONSTRUCTION INC
128 Ascot Dr (95661-3422)
PHONE..........................916 786-5112
Robert H Reeve, *CEO*
Joe E Knight, *
M Kathy Reeve, *
Cynthia Knight, *
EMP: 75 **EST:** 1991
SQ FT: 9,200
SALES (est): 34MM **Privately Held**
Web: www.reeve-knight.com
SIC: 1542 Commercial and office building, new construction

(P-1007)
RESOURCE ENVIRONMENTAL INC
13100 Alondra Blvd Ste 108 (90703-2262)
PHONE..........................562 468-7000
Richard Miller, *CEO*
Jared Sloan Cooper, *
EMP: 75 **EST:** 2005
SALES (est): 29.37MM **Privately Held**
Web: www.resourceenvironmental.com
SIC: 1542 Nonresidential construction, nec

(P-1008)
RMR CONSTRUCTION COMPANY
2424 Oakdale Ave (94124-1581)
PHONE..........................415 647-0884
Ray Reinertson Junior, *Pr*
Robert Reinertson, *
Marie Reinertson, *
EMP: 140 **EST:** 1979
SQ FT: 12,000
SALES (est): 21.93MM **Privately Held**
SIC: 1542 Commercial and office buildings, renovation and repair

(P-1009)
ROBERT CLAPPER CNSTR SVCS INC
Also Called: RC Construction Services
700 New York St (92374-2921)
PHONE..........................909 829-3688
Robert W Clapper, *Prin*
Rebecca Clapper, *
EMP: 100 **EST:** 1994
SALES (est): 25.57MM **Privately Held**
Web: www.rcconstruction.com

1542 - Nonresidential Construction, Nec (P-1010)

(P-1010)
ROEBBELEN CONSTRUCTION INC
1241 Hawks Flight Ct (95762-9648)
PHONE..........................916 939-4000
Hans J Roebbelen, *CEO*
Kenneth Roebbelen, *
David Thuleen, *
Kenneth Debruhl, *
Alma Roebbelen, *
EMP: 80 **EST:** 1989
SQ FT: 25,000
SALES (est): 25.84MM **Privately Held**
Web: www.roebbelen.com
SIC: 1542 1541 Commercial and office building, new construction; Industrial buildings and warehouses

(P-1011)
ROEBBELEN CONTRACTING INC
1241 Hawks Flight Ct (95762-9648)
PHONE..........................916 939-4000
Kenneth Wenham, *Pr*
Robert Kjome, *Chief Business Development Officer*
Frank Lindsay, *
Robert Mclean, *COO*
Joe Debiasio, *
EMP: 275 **EST:** 1959
SQ FT: 28,000
SALES (est): 224.13MM **Privately Held**
Web: www.roebbelen.com
SIC: 1542 1541 8741 Commercial and office building, new construction; Industrial buildings and warehouses; Construction management

(P-1012)
RUDOLPH AND SLETTEN INC (HQ)
120 Constitution Dr (94025-1107)
PHONE..........................650 216-3600
Jonathan Foad, *Pr*
Michael P Mohrman, *
EMP: 100 **EST:** 1960
SQ FT: 27,000
SALES (est): 497.3MM
SALES (corp-wide): 3.79B **Publicly Held**
Web: www.rsconstruction.com
SIC: 1542 1541 Commercial and office building, new construction; Industrial buildings and warehouses
PA: Tutor Perini Corporation
   15901 Olden St
   Rancho Cascades CA
   818 362-8391

(P-1013)
RUDOLPH AND SLETTEN INC
3614 Zephyr Ct (95206-4207)
PHONE..........................209 941-1040
Gene Huffman, *Owner*
EMP: 101
SALES (corp-wide): 3.79B **Publicly Held**
Web: www.rsconstruction.com
SIC: 1542 Commercial and office building, new construction
HQ: Rudolph And Sletten, Inc.
   120 Constitution Dr
   Menlo Park CA
   650 216-3600

(P-1014)
RUDOLPH AND SLETTEN INC
1504 Eureka Rd Ste 200 (95661-3058)
PHONE..........................916 781-8001
Dan Dolinar, *Brnch Mgr*
EMP: 105
SALES (corp-wide): 3.79B **Publicly Held**
Web: www.rsconstruction.com
SIC: 1542 1541 Commercial and office building, new construction; Industrial buildings and warehouses
HQ: Rudolph And Sletten, Inc.
   120 Constitution Dr
   Menlo Park CA
   650 216-3600

(P-1015)
RUDOLPH AND SLETTEN INC
2855 Michelle Ste 350 (92606-1013)
PHONE..........................949 252-1919
Eric Lascurain, *Dir*
EMP: 144
SALES (corp-wide): 3.79B **Publicly Held**
Web: www.rsconstruction.com
SIC: 1542 1541 Commercial and office building, new construction; Industrial buildings and warehouses
HQ: Rudolph And Sletten, Inc.
   120 Constitution Dr
   Menlo Park CA
   650 216-3600

(P-1016)
S J AMOROSO CNSTR CO LLC (PA)
390 Bridge Pkwy (94065-1061)
PHONE..........................650 654-1900
Dana Mcmanus, *Ch Bd*
EMP: 330 **EST:** 1939
SQ FT: 22,500
SALES (est): 104.81MM
SALES (corp-wide): 104.81MM **Privately Held**
Web: www.sjamoroso.com
SIC: 1542 Commercial and office building, new construction

(P-1017)
S J AMOROSO CNSTR CO LLC
275 Baker St Ste B (92626-4504)
PHONE..........................650 654-1900
Richard Armsworthy, *Brnch Mgr*
EMP: 64
SALES (corp-wide): 104.81MM **Privately Held**
Web: www.sjamoroso.com
SIC: 1542 Commercial and office building, new construction
PA: S. J. Amoroso Construction Co., Llc
   390 Bridge Pkwy
   Redwood City CA
   650 654-1900

(P-1018)
SAN JOSE CONSTRUCTION CO INC
1210 Coleman Ave (95050-4397)
PHONE..........................408 986-8711
EMP: 65
Web: www.sanjoseconstruction.com
SIC: 1542 Commercial and office building, new construction

(P-1019)
SAN-MAR CONSTRUCTION CO INC
4875 E La Palma Ave Ste 602 (92807-1955)
PHONE..........................714 693-5400
Sandra Drew, *CEO*
EMP: 200 **EST:** 1993
SQ FT: 3,000
SALES (est): 32.3MM **Privately Held**
Web: www.san-mar.com
SIC: 1542 Commercial and office building, new construction

(P-1020)
SANDER LANGSTON LP
Also Called: Snyder Langston
17962 Cowan (92614-6026)
PHONE..........................949 863-9200
TOLL FREE: 800
Stephen Jones Senior, *Ch*
John Rochford, *
Jason Rich, *
Gary Campanaro, *
EMP: 175 **EST:** 1986
SQ FT: 16,000
SALES (est): 413MM **Privately Held**
Web: www.snyderlangston.com
SIC: 1542 8742 1522 Commercial and office building, new construction; Real estate consultant; Residential construction, nec

(P-1021)
SANDERS CONTRACTING INC
P.O. Box 492 (94514-0492)
PHONE..........................925 308-7305
Kevin Garcia, *Pr*
Kari Garcia, *
EMP: 60 **EST:** 2018
SALES (est): 7MM **Privately Held**
Web: www.sanderscontracting.net
SIC: 1542 Commercial and office building contractors

(P-1022)
SD DEACON CORP CALIFORNIA
7745 Greenback Ln Ste 250 (95610-5865)
PHONE..........................916 969-0900
EMP: 70 **EST:** 1999
SALES (est): 24.17MM
SALES (corp-wide): 162.92MM **Privately Held**
SIC: 1542 Commercial and office building, new construction
PA: Deacon Construction, Llc
   901 Ne Glisan St Ste 100
   Portland OR
   503 297-8791

(P-1023)
SEVERSON GROUP INCORPORATED (PA)
3601 Serpentine Dr (90720-2440)
PHONE..........................562 493-3611
Jonathan Edward Severson, *Pr*
Robert Severson, *
Brian Cresap, *
Scott Feest, *
EMP: 60 **EST:** 1990
SQ FT: 15,000
SALES (est): 47.78MM **Privately Held**
Web: www.theseversongroup.com
SIC: 1542 1541 Commercial and office building, new construction; Industrial buildings, new construction, nec

(P-1024)
SHAWMUT WOODWORKING & SUP INC
Also Called: Shawmut Design and Cnstr
11390 W Olympic Blvd Fl 2 (90064-1607)
PHONE..........................323 602-1000
Leonard Porzio, *Prin*
EMP: 145
SALES (corp-wide): 278.72MM **Privately Held**
Web: www.shawmut.com
SIC: 1542 Commercial and office building, new construction
PA: Shawmut Woodworking & Supply, Inc.
   560 Harrison Ave Ste 200
   Boston MA
   617 622-7000

(P-1025)
SHIMMICK NICHOLSON CNSTR JV
8201 Edgewater Dr Ste 202 (94621-2023)
PHONE..........................510 777-5000
Mark Rawlinson, *VP*
EMP: 1774 **EST:** 2020
SALES (est): 2.53MM
SALES (corp-wide): 13.15B **Publicly Held**
SIC: 1542 Nonresidential construction, nec
HQ: Shimmick Construction Company Incorporated
   530 Technology Dr Ste 300
   Irvine CA

(P-1026)
SIERRA PACIFIC CONSTRS INC
Also Called: Sierra Pacific Constructors
22212 Ventura Blvd Ste 300 (91364-1517)
PHONE..........................747 888-5000
Cary Gerhardt, *Prin*
Cary Gerhardt, *CEO*
Ken Laspada, *
EMP: 99 **EST:** 1983
SQ FT: 13,500
SALES (est): 46.03MM **Privately Held**
Web: www.spcinc.com
SIC: 1542 Commercial and office buildings, renovation and repair

(P-1027)
SILMAN VENTURE CORPORATION (PA)
Also Called: Silman Construction
1600 Factor Ave (94577-5618)
PHONE..........................510 347-4800
Tom Mangin, *CEO*
Rick Silva, *
Bill Daniel, *Prin*
Brendan East, *Prin*
Brian Mccarver, *Prin*
EMP: 125 **EST:** 2007
SQ FT: 17,000
SALES (est): 77.3MM
SALES (corp-wide): 77.3MM **Privately Held**
Web: www.silmanindustries.com
SIC: 1542 Commercial and office building, new construction

(P-1028)
SILVER CREEK INDUSTRIES LLC
2830 Barrett Ave (92571-3258)
PHONE..........................951 943-5393
Brett D Bashaw, *CEO*
Micheal Rhodes, *
EMP: 175 **EST:** 2005
SQ FT: 25,000
SALES (est): 91.07MM **Privately Held**
Web: www.silvercreekmodular.com
SIC: 1542 2452 Commercial and office building contractors; Prefabricated wood buildings

(P-1029)
SINANIAN DEVELOPMENT INC
Also Called: Sinanian
18980 Ventura Blvd Ste 200 (91356-3228)
PHONE..........................818 996-9666
Antranik Sinanian, *CEO*
Andy Sinanian, *
Sinan Sinanian, *
Harry Sinanian, *Stockholder*

1542 - Nonresidential Construction, Nec (P-1048)

EMP: 70 EST: 1981
SQ FT: 4,000
SALES (est): 33.76MM Privately Held
Web: www.sinanian.com
SIC: 1542 1522 6552 Commercial and office building, new construction; Residential construction, nec; Subdividers and developers, nec

(P-1030)
SOLPAC INC
Also Called: Soltek Pacific
2424 Congress St (92110-2819)
PHONE...............................619 296-6247
Stephen W Thompson, CEO
Dave Carlin, *
John Myers, *
Kevin Cammall, *
EMP: 245 EST: 1994
SQ FT: 7,386
SALES (est): 42.71MM Privately Held
Web: www.soltekpacific.com
SIC: 1542 Commercial and office building, new construction

(P-1031)
SOUTH COAST PIERING INC
Also Called: Saber
7301 Madison St (90723-4029)
PHONE...............................800 922-2488
Franz M Froehlich, CEO
EMP: 70 EST: 2003
SALES (est): 8.5MM Privately Held
SIC: 1542 Commercial and office buildings, renovation and repair

(P-1032)
SPAN CONSTRUCTION & ENGRG INC (PA)
Also Called: Span Construction
3353 Yeager Rd (93637-8740)
PHONE...............................559 661-1111
King F Husein, CEO
Firoz Mohamed Husein, *
George Goddard, *
Douglas M Standing, *
▼ EMP: 85 EST: 1979
SALES (est): 50.3MM
SALES (corp-wide): 50.3MM Privately Held
Web: www.spanconstruction.com
SIC: 1542 1541 1791 Commercial and office buildings, prefabricated erection; Industrial buildings, new construction, nec; Structural steel erection

(P-1033)
STREAMLINE FINISHES INC
26429 Rancho Pkwy S Ste 140 (92630-8330)
PHONE...............................949 600-8964
William Seidel, Pr
EMP: 80 EST: 2004
SQ FT: 6,000
SALES (est): 22.76MM Privately Held
Web: www.streamlinefinishes.com
SIC: 1542 Commercial and office building contractors

(P-1034)
SUMMER SYSTEMS INC
28942 Hancock Pkwy (91355-1069)
PHONE...............................661 257-4419
Don London, Pr
Connie London, *
EMP: 80 EST: 1988
SQ FT: 20,000
SALES (est): 25.94MM Privately Held
Web: www.summersystems.net

SIC: 1542 Nonresidential construction, nec

(P-1035)
SWINERTON BUILDERS
Swinerton Renewable Energy
16798 W Bernardo Dr (92128-2850)
PHONE...............................858 622-4040
Don Adair, Mgr
EMP: 65
Web: www.swinerton.com
SIC: 1542 Commercial and office building, new construction
HQ: Swinerton Builders
2001 Clayton Rd Ste 700
Concord CA
925 602-6400

(P-1036)
SWINERTON BUILDERS HC
Also Called: Hmh Builders
15 Business Park Way Ste 101 (95828-0958)
PHONE...............................916 383-4825
Gary J Rafferty, Ch Bd
Eric M Foster, *
Alan G Wolf, *
Curtis F Johnson, *
Leonard J Bischel, *
EMP: 150 EST: 1957
SQ FT: 25,000
SALES (est): 33.08MM Privately Held
Web: www.swinerton.com
SIC: 1542 Commercial and office building, new construction
PA: Swinerton Incorporated
2001 Clayton Rd Fl 7 Flr 7
San Francisco CA

(P-1037)
SWINERTON INCORPORATED (PA)
2001 Clayton Rd Fl 7 (94107)
PHONE...............................415 421-2980
Eric Foster, CEO
Eric M Foster, *
Gary J Rafferty, *
Frank Foellmer, *
Linda G Showalter, *
▲ EMP: 200 EST: 1888
SQ FT: 66,943
SALES (est): 1.16B Privately Held
Web: www.swinerton.com
SIC: 1542 1541 6531 1522 Commercial and office building, new construction; Industrial buildings and warehouses; Real estate managers; Residential construction, nec

(P-1038)
TASLIMI CONSTRUCTION CO INC
1805 Colorado Ave (90404-3411)
PHONE...............................310 447-3000
Shidan Taslimi, Prin
Mehran Taslimi, *
Susanne Taslimi, *
EMP: 66 EST: 1985
SQ FT: 8,500
SALES (est): 21.87MM Privately Held
Web: www.taslimi.com
SIC: 1542 Commercial and office building, new construction

(P-1039)
TECHNO COATINGS INC
785 E Debra Ln (92805-6334)
PHONE...............................714 774-4671
EMP: 75
SALES (corp-wide): 41.05MM Privately Held
Web: www.technocoatings.com

SIC: 1542 Commercial and office buildings, renovation and repair
PA: Techno Coatings, Inc.
1391 S Allec St
Anaheim CA
714 635-1130

(P-1040)
TECHNO COATINGS INC
795 E Debra Ln (92805)
PHONE...............................714 774-4671
EMP: 75
SALES (corp-wide): 41.05MM Privately Held
Web: www.technocoatings.com
SIC: 1542 1629 1721 1799 Commercial and office buildings, renovation and repair; Blasting contractor, except building demolition; Painting and paper hanging; Coating of concrete structures with plastic
PA: Techno Coatings, Inc.
1391 S Allec St
Anaheim CA
714 635-1130

(P-1041)
TECHNO COATINGS INC (PA)
Also Called: Techno West
1391 S Allec St (92805-6304)
PHONE...............................714 635-1130
EMP: 200 EST: 1974
SALES (est): 41.05MM
SALES (corp-wide): 41.05MM Privately Held
Web: www.technocoatings.com
SIC: 1542 1629 1721 1799 Commercial and office buildings, renovation and repair; Blasting contractor, except building demolition; Painting and paper hanging; Coating of concrete structures with plastic

(P-1042)
TEMALPAKH INC
Also Called: Works Floor & Wall, The
73750 Spyder Cir (92211-6023)
PHONE...............................760 770-5778
Gerald A Flowers, CEO
Michael Collins, *
Rusty Harling, *
EMP: 65 EST: 1998
SQ FT: 13,000
SALES (est): 15.04MM Privately Held
SIC: 1542 5713 5211 Commercial and office buildings, renovation and repair; Floor covering stores; Tile, ceramic

(P-1043)
TILLER CONSTRUCTORS PARTNR INC
Also Called: Tiller Constructors
306 W Katella Ave Ste A (92867-4755)
PHONE...............................714 771-5600
Lin Lindstedt, Pr
Kerry Evert, *
EMP: 64 EST: 1988
SQ FT: 4,000
SALES (est): 18.37MM Privately Held
Web: www.tillerconstructors.com
SIC: 1542 Institutional building construction

(P-1044)
TRITON STRUCTURAL CONCRETE INC
15435 Innovation Dr Ste 225 (92128-3442)
PHONE...............................858 866-2450
Tim Penick, CEO
John Boyd, *
EMP: 250 EST: 2007
SALES (est): 35.13MM Privately Held
Web: www.tritonstructural.com

SIC: 1542 Commercial and office building, new construction

(P-1045)
TURNER CONSTRUCTION COMPANY
1900 S State College Blvd Ste 200 (92806-6197)
PHONE...............................714 940-9000
Bernie Morrissey, VP
EMP: 300
Web: www.turnerconstruction.com
SIC: 1542 Commercial and office building, new construction
HQ: Turner Construction Company Inc
66 Hudson Blvd E Fl 36
New York NY
212 229-6000

(P-1046)
TURNER CONSTRUCTION COMPANY
2500 Venture Oaks Way Ste 200 (95833-4222)
PHONE...............................916 444-4421
Donna Afflerdach, Brnch Mgr
EMP: 75
Web: www.turnerconstruction.com
SIC: 1542 Commercial and office building, new construction
HQ: Turner Construction Company Inc
66 Hudson Blvd E Fl 36
New York NY
212 229-6000

(P-1047)
TUTOR PERINI CORPORATION (PA)
Also Called: Tutor Perini
15901 Olden St (91342-1051)
PHONE...............................818 362-8391
Ronald N Tutor, Ch Bd
Michael R Klein, *
Gary G Smalley, Ex VP
Ghassan M Ariqat, Ex VP
Michael F Smithson, Ex VP
▲ EMP: 160 EST: 1894
SALES (est): 3.79B
SALES (corp-wide): 3.79B Publicly Held
Web: www.tutorperini.com
SIC: 1542 8741 1611 1791 Commercial and office building contractors; Construction management; Concrete construction: roads, highways, sidewalks, etc.; Structural steel erection

(P-1048)
TUTOR-SALIBA CORPORATION (HQ)
15901 Olden St (91342-1051)
PHONE...............................818 362-8391
Ronald N Tutor, CEO
David L Randall, *
William B Sparks, *
Jack Frost, *
John D Barrett, *
▲ EMP: 100 EST: 2003
SQ FT: 20,000
SALES (est): 242.56MM
SALES (corp-wide): 3.79B Publicly Held
Web: www.tutorperini.com
SIC: 1542 1629 7353 1799 Commercial and office building; Subway construction; Cranes and aerial lift equipment, rental or leasing; Rigging and scaffolding
PA: Tutor Perini Corporation
15901 Olden St
Rancho Cascades CA
818 362-8391

1542 - Nonresidential Construction, Nec

(P-1049)
TUTOR-SALIBA PERINI
15901 Olden St (91342-1051)
PHONE.................818 362-8391
EMP: 7733
SIC: 1542 1611 1622 Specialized public building contractors; Highway and street construction; Bridge, tunnel, and elevated highway construction

(P-1050)
UNGER CONSTRUCTION CO
910 X St (95818-2128)
P.O. Box 188589 (95818-8589)
PHONE.................916 325-5500
EMP: 103 EST: 1927
SALES (est): 26.08MM Privately Held
Web: www.ungerconstruction.com
SIC: 1542 1541 Commercial and office building, new construction; Warehouse construction

(P-1051)
USS CAL BUILDERS INC
8031 Main St (90680-2452)
PHONE.................714 828-4882
Allen Othman, CEO
Jennifer Hotrum, *
Eric Othman, *
EMP: 135 EST: 1992
SALES (est): 49.41MM Privately Held
Web: www.usscalbuilders.com
SIC: 1542 Specialized public building contractors

(P-1052)
VILA CONSTRUCTION CO
Also Called: Richard H Vila
5371 Heavenly Ridge Ln (94803-2626)
PHONE.................510 236-9111
Richard H Vila, Pr
Maria Elena Vila, Sec
EMP: 75 EST: 1946
SALES (est): 23.12MM Privately Held
Web: www.vilacc.com
SIC: 1542 1751 1541 Commercial and office buildings, renovation and repair; Carpentry work; Industrial buildings and warehouses

(P-1053)
WE ONEIL CONSTRUCTION CO CAL
Also Called: W E O'Neil Construction
9485 Haven Ave Ste 101 (91730-5877)
PHONE.................909 466-5300
John Finn, Brnch Mgr
EMP: 161
SALES (corp-wide): 233.95MM Privately Held
Web: www.weoneil.com
SIC: 1542 1541 1522 1521 Commercial and office building, new construction; Industrial buildings and warehouses; Residential construction, nec; New construction, single-family houses
HQ: W.E. O'neil Construction Co Of California
909 N Pcf Cast Hwy Ste 40
El Segundo CA
310 643-7900

(P-1054)
WEBCOR CONSTRUCTION LP
1 Almaden Blvd Ste 460 (95113-2246)
PHONE.................408 277-0311
EMP: 131
Web: www.webcor.com
SIC: 1542 Nonresidential construction, nec
HQ: Webcor Construction L.P.
207 King St Ste 300
San Francisco CA

(P-1055)
WEBCOR CONSTRUCTION LP
Also Called: Webcor Builders
2150 W Washington St Ste 308 (92110-2044)
PHONE.................619 798-3891
Matt Rosie, CEO
EMP: 131
SIC: 1542 Nonresidential construction, nec
HQ: Webcor Construction L.P.
207 King St Ste 300
San Francisco CA

(P-1056)
WEBCOR CONSTRUCTION LP
Also Called: Webcor Builders
7801 Capwell Dr (94621-2103)
PHONE.................510 748-7950
Matt Rosie, CEO
EMP: 131
SIC: 1542 Nonresidential construction, nec
HQ: Webcor Construction L.P.
207 King St Ste 300
San Francisco CA

(P-1057)
WEBCOR CONSTRUCTION LP
Also Called: Webcor Builders
333 S Grand Ave Ste 4400 (90071-1548)
PHONE.................213 239-2800
Leo Bandini, Mgr
EMP: 131
Web: www.webcor.com
SIC: 1542 Commercial and office building, new construction
HQ: Webcor Construction L.P.
207 King St Ste 300
San Francisco CA

(P-1058)
WEBCOR CONSTRUCTION LP
Also Called: Webcor Builders
2320 Blanding Ave Ste 200 (94501-1403)
PHONE.................510 748-1900
EMP: 131
Web: www.webcor.com
SIC: 1542 Commercial and office building, new construction
HQ: Webcor Construction L.P.
207 King St Ste 300
San Francisco CA

(P-1059)
WEBCOR CONSTRUCTION LP (DH)
Also Called: Webcor Builders
207 King St Ste 300 (94107-5499)
PHONE.................415 978-1000
Jes Pedersen, CEO
Matt Rossie, COO
Matt Reece, CFO
EMP: 71 EST: 2007
SALES (est): 2.23B Privately Held
Web: www.webcor.com
SIC: 1542 Commercial and office building, new construction
HQ: Obayashi Usa, Llc
950 Tower Ln Ste 800
Foster City CA
650 952-4910

(P-1060)
WEST PACIFIC SERVICES INC
4445 Eastgate Mall Ste 200 (92121)
PHONE.................888 401-0188
Joshua L Prado, CEO
EMP: 138 EST: 2009
SALES (est): 11.84MM Privately Held
SIC: 1542 Nonresidential construction, nec

(P-1061)
WESTGATE CNSTR & MAINT INC
5045 Fulton Dr Ste D (94534-1635)
PHONE.................707 208-5763
Hilton Ham, Pr
EMP: 86 EST: 2001
SALES (est): 6.1MM Privately Held
SIC: 1542 Commercial and office building, new construction

(P-1062)
WHITING-TURNER CONTRACTING CO
250 Commerce Ste 150 (92602-1345)
PHONE.................949 863-0800
Len Cannatelli Junior, Ex VP
EMP: 412
SALES (corp-wide): 8.62B Privately Held
Web: www.whiting-turner.com
SIC: 1542 1541 Commercial and office building, new construction; Industrial buildings and warehouses
PA: The Whiting-Turner Contracting Company
300 E Joppa Rd Ste 800
Baltimore MD
410 821-1100

(P-1063)
WHITING-TURNER CONTRACTING CO
800 R St (95811-6411)
PHONE.................916 355-1355
Jack Stackalis, VP
EMP: 176
SALES (corp-wide): 8.62B Privately Held
Web: www.whiting-turner.com
SIC: 1542 Commercial and office building, new construction
PA: The Whiting-Turner Contracting Company
300 E Joppa Rd Ste 800
Baltimore MD
410 821-1100

(P-1064)
WL BUTLER INC
1629 Main St (94063-2121)
PHONE.................650 361-1270
William Butler, CEO
Frank York, *
Gina Tankersley, *
David A Nevens Junior, COO
Gina Henson, *
EMP: 250 EST: 1974
SALES (est): 51.33MM Privately Held
Web: www.wlbutler.com
SIC: 1542 Commercial and office building, new construction

(P-1065)
WM KLORMAN CONSTRUCTION CORP
23047 Ventura Blvd Fl 2 (91364-1146)
PHONE.................818 591-5969
William M Klorman, Pr
Doug Fowler, *
EMP: 65 EST: 1981
SQ FT: 4,000
SALES (est): 23.64MM Privately Held
Web: www.klorman.com
SIC: 1542 1521 Commercial and office building, new construction; New construction, single-family houses

(P-1066)
WRIGHT CONTRACTING LLC
Also Called: Wright Contracting EPA
3020 Dutton Ave (95407-7886)
P.O. Box 1270 (95402-1270)
PHONE.................707 528-1172
Mark Davis, Pr
Bryan Wright, *
Stephen M Wright, *
EMP: 60 EST: 2016
SALES (est): 11.05MM Privately Held
Web: www.wrightcontracting.com
SIC: 1542 Nonresidential construction, nec

(P-1067)
XL CONSTRUCTION CORPORATION (PA)
851 Buckeye Ct (95035-7408)
PHONE.................408 240-6000
Richard Walker, CEO
Marcus Staniford, *
Eric Raff, *
John Boneso, *
Tom Humbert, *
EMP: 360 EST: 1992
SALES (est): 171.33MM Privately Held
Web: www.xlconstruction.com
SIC: 1542 Commercial and office building, new construction

(P-1068)
ZUMWALT CONSTRUCTION INC
5520 E Lamona Ave (93727-2276)
PHONE.................559 252-1000
Kurt E Zumwalt, Pr
Teri Zumwalt, *
EMP: 100 EST: 1995
SQ FT: 2,000
SALES (est): 54.96MM Privately Held
Web: www.zumwaltconstruction.com
SIC: 1542 1522 Commercial and office building, new construction; Residential construction, nec

1611 Highway And Street Construction

(P-1069)
A-1 ADVANTAGE ASPHALT INC
Also Called: Advantage Asphalt
10308 Placer Ln Ste 100 (95827-2511)
PHONE.................916 388-2020
Melissa Mallo, Pr
Greg Mallo, *
Melissa Mallo, Sec
EMP: 60 EST: 1999
SQ FT: 6,000
SALES (est): 10.88MM Privately Held
Web: www.advantageasphalt.com
SIC: 1611 Surfacing and paving

(P-1070)
ADOPT-A-HIGHWAY MAINTENANCE
Also Called: Adopt-A-Beach
3158 Red Hill Ave Ste 200 (92626-3416)
PHONE.................800 200-0003
Peter Morin, CEO
Patricia Nelson, *
Dennis Day, *
Dan Day, *
EMP: 104 EST: 1990
SQ FT: 6,000
SALES (est): 29.52MM Privately Held
Web: www.adoptahighway.com
SIC: 1611 4959 Highway and street maintenance; Sanitary services, nec

1611 - Highway And Street Construction (P-1091)

(P-1071)
ALL AMERICAN ASPHALT (PA)
Also Called: All American Agrigate
400 E 6th St (92879-1521)
P.O. Box 2229 (92878-2229)
PHONE..................................951 736-7600
Mark Albert Luer, Pr
EMP: 60 EST: 1969
SALES (est): 142.17MM
SALES (corp-wide): 142.17MM Privately Held
Web: www.allamericanasphalt.com
SIC: 1611 5032 Highway and street paving contractor; Brick, stone, and related material

(P-1072)
ALL AMERICAN ASPHALT
All American Service and Sup
1776 All American Way (92879-2070)
P.O. Box 2229 (92878-2229)
PHONE..................................951 736-7617
Kim Mcguire Managing, Brnch Mgr
EMP: 179
SALES (corp-wide): 142.17MM Privately Held
Web: www.allamericanasphalt.com
SIC: 1611 Highway and street paving contractor
PA: All American Asphalt
400 E 6th St
Corona CA
951 736-7600

(P-1073)
ALL AMERICAN ASPHALT
Camco Construction Supply
1776 All American Way (92879-2070)
PHONE..................................951 736-7617
Kim Mcguire, Brnch Mgr
EMP: 60
SALES (corp-wide): 142.17MM Privately Held
Web: www.allamericanasphalt.com
SIC: 1611 Highway and street paving contractor
PA: All American Asphalt
400 E 6th St
Corona CA
951 736-7600

(P-1074)
AMERICAN ASP REPR RSRFCING INC (PA)
Also Called: American Asphalt
24200 Clawiter Rd (94545-2216)
P.O. Box 3367 (94540-3367)
PHONE..................................510 723-0280
Allan A Henderson, CEO
Kim Henschel, *
Steve Aguirre, *
EMP: 99 EST: 1983
SALES (est): 29.33MM
SALES (corp-wide): 29.33MM Privately Held
Web: www.americanasphalt.com
SIC: 1611 Surfacing and paving

(P-1075)
AMERICAN CVIL CNSTRS W CAST LL
Also Called: ACC West Coast
2990 Bay Vista Ct Ste D (94510-1195)
PHONE..................................707 746-8028
Jeffrey Foerste, Pr
Clifford Barber, *
David Wilkerson, *
EMP: 75 EST: 1987
SQ FT: 19,000
SALES (est): 21.66MM
SALES (corp-wide): 9.78B Publicly Held

SIC: 1611 1622 Surfacing and paving; Bridge construction
HQ: Infrastructure And Energy Alternatives, Inc.
6325 Digital Way Ste 460
Indianapolis IN
765 828-2580

(P-1076)
AMG CONSTRUCTION GROUP
1103 W Gardena Blvd Unit 201 (90248-5239)
PHONE..................................800 310-2609
Calvin Jackson, CEO
EMP: 69 EST: 2016
SQ FT: 1,600
SALES (est): 4.77MM Privately Held
SIC: 1611 General contractor, highway and street construction

(P-1077)
ANVIL BUILDERS INC
1550 Park Ave (94608-3502)
PHONE..................................415 285-5000
EMP: 125 EST: 2010
SALES (est): 47.23MM Privately Held
Web: www.anvilbuilders.com
SIC: 1611 1623 General contractor, highway and street construction; Water, sewer, and utility lines

(P-1078)
APCO PAVING COMPANY
1790 Farm Bureau Rd (94519-2442)
PHONE..................................925 827-9850
Jesse Avila, Pr
EMP: 91
Web: www.apcopavingco.com
SIC: 1611 Surfacing and paving
PA: Apco Paving Company
2545 Monument Blvd
Concord CA

(P-1079)
ATKINSON CONSTRUCTION INC
18201 Von Karman Ave Ste 800 (92612-1092)
PHONE..................................303 410-2540
John O'keefe, Pr
EMP: 450 EST: 2004
SALES (est): 122.5MM
SALES (corp-wide): 1.66B Privately Held
Web: www.clarkconstruction.com
SIC: 1611 1622 Highway and street construction; Bridge, tunnel, and elevated highway construction
HQ: Clark Construction Group, Llc
7500 Old Georgetown Rd # 600
Bethesda MD
301 272-8100

(P-1080)
BEADOR CONSTRUCTION CO INC
2900 Bristol St (92626-5941)
PHONE..................................951 674-7350
EMP: 80 EST: 1996
SALES (est): 23.45MM Privately Held
SIC: 1611 General contractor, highway and street construction

(P-1081)
BECHO INC
15901 Olden St (91342-1051)
PHONE..................................818 362-8391
TOLL FREE: 800
Tim Smith, Pr
William B Sparks, *
Steve Pavoggi, *
Louis Lucido, *
Jim Tripp, *
▲ EMP: 60 EST: 1979
SQ FT: 8,000
SALES (est): 24.79MM
SALES (corp-wide): 3.79B Publicly Held
Web: www.bechoinc.com
SIC: 1611 1622 1799 Highway and street paving contractor; Bridge construction; Shoring and underpinning work
PA: Tutor Perini Corporation
15901 Olden St
Rancho Cascades CA
818 362-8391

(P-1082)
BENS ASPHALT & MAINT CO INC
Also Called: Medina Construction
2537 Rubidoux Blvd (92509-2142)
PHONE..................................951 248-1103
EMP: 90
Web: www.bensasphalt.com
SIC: 1611 Surfacing and paving
PA: Ben's Asphalt & Maintenance Company, Inc.
2200 S Yale St Ste A
Santa Ana CA

(P-1083)
BRUTOCO ENGINEERING & CONSTRUCTION INC
Also Called: Brutoco Engineering
1272 Center Court Dr Ste 101 (91724-3667)
EMP: 200 EST: 1967
SALES (est): 20.21MM Privately Held
Web: www.brutoco.net
SIC: 1611 1629 1622 General contractor, highway and street construction; Dams, waterways, docks, and other marine construction; Bridge construction

(P-1084)
CALIFORNIA DEPARTMENT TRNSP
Also Called: Caltrans
2019 W Texas St (94533-4461)
P.O. Box 8 (94533-0084)
PHONE..................................707 428-2031
E L Poplin, Brnch Mgr
EMP: 126
SALES (corp-wide): 534.4MM Privately Held
Web: dot.ca.gov
SIC: 1611 9621 Highway and street maintenance; Regulation, administration of transportation
HQ: California, Department Of Transportation
1120 N St
Sacramento CA

(P-1085)
CALIFORNIA DEPARTMENT TRNSP
Also Called: Caltrans Eastern Reg Rd Maint
1940 Workman Mill Rd (90601-1414)
PHONE..................................562 692-0823
Edward Toledo, Mgr
EMP: 63
SALES (corp-wide): 534.4MM Privately Held
Web: dot.ca.gov
SIC: 1611 9621 Highway and street maintenance; Regulation, administration of transportation
HQ: California, Department Of Transportation
1120 N St
Sacramento CA

(P-1086)
CALIFORNIA DEPARTMENT TRNSP
1607 Adams Ave (92243-1903)
PHONE..................................760 352-1129
Sal Gonzalez, Mgr
EMP: 63
SALES (corp-wide): 534.4MM Privately Held
Web: dot.ca.gov
SIC: 1611 9621 Highway and street maintenance; Regulation, administration of transportation
HQ: California, Department Of Transportation
1120 N St
Sacramento CA

(P-1087)
CENTRAL STRIPING SERVICE INC
3489 Luyung Dr (95742-6861)
PHONE..................................916 635-5175
James Lesniewski, Pr
Geri Lesniewski, *
EMP: 68 EST: 1967
SQ FT: 12,000
SALES (est): 10.84MM Privately Held
Web: www.centralstripingservice.com
SIC: 1611 1799 Highway and street maintenance; Parking lot maintenance

(P-1088)
CHRISP COMPANY (PA)
43650 Osgood Rd (94539-5631)
P.O. Box 1368 (94538-0136)
PHONE..................................510 656-2840
Robert P Chrisp, CEO
David Morris, *
Roger Weisbrod, *
EMP: 93 EST: 1979
SQ FT: 8,000
SALES (est): 47.05MM
SALES (corp-wide): 47.05MM Privately Held
Web: www.chrispco.com
SIC: 1611 Highway signs and guardrails

(P-1089)
CITY OF PASO ROBLES
747 Spring St Ste B (93446-2898)
PHONE..................................805 237-3999
EMP: 80 EST: 1989
SALES (est): 5.54MM Privately Held
Web: www.prcity.org
SIC: 1611 Highway and street construction

(P-1090)
CITY OF SAN DIEGO
2781 Caminito Chollas (92105-5039)
PHONE..................................619 527-7482
EMP: 187
SALES (corp-wide): 2.67B Privately Held
Web: www.sandiego.gov
SIC: 1611 9199 Highway and street maintenance; General government administration
PA: City Of San Diego
202 C St
San Diego CA
619 236-6330

(P-1091)
COUNTY OF ALAMEDA
Also Called: Public Works Dept
399 Elmhurst St (94544-1307)
PHONE..................................510 670-5455
Daniel Woldesenbet, Dir
EMP: 123

1611 - Highway And Street Construction (P-1092)

Web: www.acgov.org
SIC: **1611** 9199 Highway and street paving contractor; General government administration
PA: County Of Alameda
1221 Oak St Ste 555
Oakland CA
510 272-6691

(P-1092)
COUNTY OF LOS ANGELES
Also Called: Public Works, Dept of
1525 Alcazar St Bldg 1 (90033-1001)
PHONE..................626 458-1700
Robert Scharf, *Dir*
EMP: 73
SALES (corp-wide): 31.7B **Privately Held**
Web: www.lacounty.org
SIC: **1611** 9511 Highway and street maintenance; Sanitary engineering agency, government
PA: County Of Los Angeles
500 W Temple St Ste 437
Los Angeles CA
213 974-1101

(P-1093)
D A MCCOSKER CONSTRUCTION CO
Also Called: Independent Construction Co
3911 Laura Alice Way (94520-8544)
PHONE..................925 686-1780
Brian Clay Mccosker, *Pr*
David A Mccosker, *Ch Bd*
Brian Cartmell, *CTRL* *
EMP: 200 EST: 1910
SALES (est): 39.99MM **Privately Held**
Web: www.indycc.com
SIC: **1611** Surfacing and paving

(P-1094)
DENNIS M MCCOY & SONS INC
32107 Lindero Canyon Rd Ste 212 (91361-4255)
PHONE..................818 874-3872
Dennis Mccoy, *CEO*
Morgan Mccoy, *Pr*
EMP: 75 EST: 1994
SQ FT: 3,000
SALES (est): 12.16MM **Privately Held**
Web: www.mccoyandsons.com
SIC: **1611** Grading

(P-1095)
DESILVA GATES CONSTRUCTION LP (PA)
Also Called: Desilva Gates Construction
11555 Dublin Blvd (94568-2854)
P.O. Box 2909 (94568-0909)
PHONE..................925 361-1380
EMP: 100 EST: 1932
SALES (est): 115.47MM **Privately Held**
Web: www.desilvagates.com
SIC: **1611** 1794 1542 General contractor, highway and street construction; Excavation and grading, building construction; Nonresidential construction, nec

(P-1096)
DISNEY CONSTRUCTION INC
Also Called: Disney Construction
533 Airport Blvd Ste 120 (94010-2007)
PHONE..................650 689-5149
Richard L Disney, *Pr*
EMP: 60 EST: 2005
SALES (est): 20.05MM **Privately Held**
Web: www.disneyconstruction.com
SIC: **1611** Highway and street construction

(P-1097)
DOUG VEERKAMP GENERAL ENGINEERING INC (PA)
2585 Cold Springs Rd (95667-3211)
PHONE..................530 626-0825
EMP: 171 EST: 1983
SALES (est): 27.7MM
SALES (corp-wide): 27.7MM **Privately Held**
Web: www.dougveerkamp.com
SIC: **1611** 1711 Grading; Septic system construction

(P-1098)
DRAGADOS USA INC
3200 Park Center Dr Ste 600 (92626-7163)
PHONE..................657 229-7800
John Edward Mcgrath, *Brnch Mgr*
EMP: 93
Web: www.dragados-usa.com
SIC: **1611** General contractor, highway and street construction
HQ: Dragados Usa, Inc.
810 7th Ave Fl 9
New York NY

(P-1099)
DRAGADOS USA INC
Also Called: Dragados USA
5050 Laguna Blvd Ste 112 (95758-4151)
PHONE..................916 738-9927
EMP: 102
Web: www.dragados-usa.com
SIC: **1611** General contractor, highway and street construction
HQ: Dragados Usa, Inc.
810 7th Ave Fl 9
New York NY

(P-1100)
DRYCO CONSTRUCTION INC (PA)
42745 Boscell Rd (94538-3106)
PHONE..................510 438-6500
Daren R Young, *Pr*
Rafael Torres, *
Kevin Mitchell, *
William Mccrea, *VP*
Sandra Young, *
EMP: 179 EST: 1978
SQ FT: 3,700
SALES (est): 117.04MM
SALES (corp-wide): 117.04MM **Privately Held**
Web: www.dryco.com
SIC: **1611** 1721 5211 Highway and street paving contractor; Pavement marking contractor; Lumber and other building materials

(P-1101)
EAGLE PAVING COMPANY INC
13915 Danielson St Ste 201 (92064-8884)
PHONE..................858 486-6400
Joel Batule, *CEO*
Joel Batule, *Pr*
James B Bostick, *
EMP: 75 EST: 2006
SQ FT: 3,920
SALES (est): 54.65MM **Privately Held**
Web: www.eaglepaving.us
SIC: **1611** Surfacing and paving

(P-1102)
EBS GENERAL ENGINEERING INC
1345 Quarry St Ste 101 (92879-1734)
PHONE..................951 279-6869
Joseph Nanci, *Pr*
EMP: 90 EST: 1994
SQ FT: 4,000
SALES (est): 11.67MM **Privately Held**
Web: www.ebs-inc.us
SIC: **1611** Highway and street construction

(P-1103)
EMERALD ACQUISITION LLC
Also Called: Emerald Paving Company
6381 Industry Way (92683-3693)
PHONE..................714 891-8752
Derek M Davis, *CEO*
Derek M Davis, *Pr*
Mike Clarke, *Ex VP*
Erinn Steingold, *CFO*
EMP: 132 EST: 2006
SQ FT: 20,000
SALES (est): 12.7MM **Privately Held**
Web: www.empave.com
SIC: **1611** Surfacing and paving
PA: M A C Contracting Corp.
6301 W Sunrise Blvd
Plantation FL

(P-1104)
FEC FTURE CONTRS ENGINEERS INC
184 Technology Dr Ste 205 (92618-2435)
PHONE..................949 328-9758
Sam Katbi, *CEO*
EMP: 60 EST: 2010
SALES (est): 8.56MM **Privately Held**
SIC: **1611** 1531 1542 1522 General contractor, highway and street construction; Commercial and office building, new construction; Residential construction, nec

(P-1105)
FOOTHILL / ESTRN TRNSP CRRDOR
Also Called: Transportation Corridor Agency
125 Pacifica Ste 100 (92618-3324)
PHONE..................949 754-3400
Michael Kraman, *CEO*
Amy Potter, *
EMP: 70 EST: 1986
SQ FT: 10,000
SALES (est): 209.38MM **Privately Held**
SIC: **1611** General contractor, highway and street construction

(P-1106)
GHILOTTI CONSTRUCTION CO INC
600 S Napa Junction Rd (94503-1277)
PHONE..................707 556-9145
Mark Bower, *Brnch Mgr*
EMP: 138
Web: www.ghilotti.com
SIC: **1611** 1623 General contractor, highway and street construction; Underground utilities contractor
PA: Ghilotti Construction Company, Inc.
246 Ghilotti Ave
Santa Rosa CA

(P-1107)
GOODFELLOW BROS CALIFORNIA LLC
50 Contractors St (94551-4863)
PHONE..................925 245-2111
Frank Williams, *
EMP: 500 EST: 1927
SALES (est): 64.03MM
SALES (corp-wide): 600MM **Privately Held**
Web: www.goodfellowbros.com
SIC: **1611** General contractor, highway and street construction

PA: Gbi Holding Co.
1407 Walla Walla Ave
Wenatchee WA
509 662-7111

(P-1108)
GRANITE CNSTR NORTHEAST INC
585 W Beach St (95076-5123)
PHONE..................831 724-1011
Michael F Donnino, *Sr VP*
EMP: 372
Web: www.graniteconstruction.com
SIC: **1611** General contractor, highway and street construction
HQ: Granite Construction Northeast, Inc.
1302 N 19th St Ste 300
Tampa FL

(P-1109)
GRANITE CONSTRUCTION COMPANY (HQ)
585 W Beach St (95076-5123)
P.O. Box 50085 (95077-5085)
PHONE..................831 724-1011
Laurel Krzeminski, *Ex VP*
Christopher S Miller, *Ex VP*
Richard A Watts, *Sr VP*
▼ EMP: 200 EST: 1922
SQ FT: 39,000
SALES (est): 696.77MM **Publicly Held**
Web: www.graniteconstruction.com
SIC: **1611** 1622 Highway and street construction; Bridge construction
PA: Granite Construction Incorporated
585 W Beach St
Watsonville CA

(P-1110)
GRANITE CONSTRUCTION COMPANY
Also Called: Southern California Regional
38000 Monroe St (92203-9500)
PHONE..................760 775-7500
Jay Mcquillen, *Mgr*
EMP: 393
Web: www.graniteconstruction.com
SIC: **1611** 1771 General contractor, highway and street construction; Concrete work
HQ: Granite Construction Company
585 W Beach St
Watsonville CA
831 724-1011

(P-1111)
GRANITE CONSTRUCTION COMPANY
Also Called: Stockton
10500 S Harlan Rd (95231-9603)
P.O. Box 151 (95201-0151)
PHONE..................209 982-4750
James Hopp Essick, *Brnch Mgr*
EMP: 200
Web: www.graniteconstruction.com
SIC: **1611** General contractor, highway and street construction
HQ: Granite Construction Company
585 W Beach St
Watsonville CA
831 724-1011

(P-1112)
GRANITE CONSTRUCTION COMPANY
5335 Debbie Rd (93111-2001)
P.O. Box 6744 (93160-6744)
PHONE..................805 964-9951
Bruce Mcgowan, *Mgr*
EMP: 169

1611 - Highway And Street Construction (P-1133)

PRODUCTS & SERVICES SECTION

SQ FT: 65,396
Web: www.graniteconstruction.com
SIC: **1611** General contractor, highway and street construction
HQ: Granite Construction Company
585 W Beach St
Watsonville CA
831 724-1011

(P-1113)
GRANITE CONSTRUCTION INC
213 Columbia Way (93535-5335)
PHONE................805 667-8210
EMP: 95
Web: www.graniteconstruction.com
SIC: **1611** General contractor, highway and street construction
PA: Granite Construction Incorporated
585 W Beach St
Watsonville CA

(P-1114)
GRANITE ROCK CO
Also Called: Pavex Construction Company
355 Blomquist St (94063-2701)
PHONE................650 869-3370
John Franich, *Mgr*
EMP: 72
SALES (corp-wide): 521.49MM Privately Held
Web: www.graniterock.com
SIC: **1611** Highway and street paving contractor
PA: Granite Rock Co.
350 Technology Dr
Watsonville CA
831 768-2000

(P-1115)
GRIFFITH COMPANY (PA)
Also Called: Tahoe Stag
3050 E Birch St (92821-6248)
PHONE................714 984-5500
Jamie Angus, *Pr*
Jim Waltze, *
Thomas L Foss, *
Ryan Aukerman, *
Steve Ruelas, *
EMP: 187 EST: 1922
SQ FT: 100,000
SALES (est): 350MM
SALES (corp-wide): 350MM Privately Held
Web: www.griffithcompany.net
SIC: **1611** General contractor, highway and street construction

(P-1116)
GRIFFITH COMPANY
1128 Carrier Parkway Ave (93308-9666)
P.O. Box 70157 (93387-0157)
PHONE................661 392-6640
Rus Grigg, *Mgr*
EMP: 341
SALES (corp-wide): 350MM Privately Held
Web: www.griffithcompany.net
SIC: **1611** General contractor, highway and street construction
PA: Griffith Company
3050 E Birch St
Brea CA
714 984-5500

(P-1117)
GRIFFITH COMPANY
12200 Bloomfield Ave (90670-3742)
PHONE................562 929-1128
Dan Magrew, *Mgr*
EMP: 60

SQ FT: 4,036
SALES (corp-wide): 350MM Privately Held
Web: www.griffithcompany.net
SIC: **1611 1622** General contractor, highway and street construction; Bridge construction
PA: Griffith Company
3050 E Birch St
Brea CA
714 984-5500

(P-1118)
HARPER FEDERAL CNSTR LLC
14130 Biscayne Pl (92064-6640)
PHONE................619 543-1296
Jeffrey A Harper, *Managing Member**
Ronald D Harper, *
EMP: 80 EST: 2007
SALES (est): 21.98MM Privately Held
SIC: **1611 1711 1751 1742** Grading; Plumbing, heating, air-conditioning; Carpentry work; Plastering, drywall, and insulation

(P-1119)
HILLCREST CONTRACTING INC
1467 Circle City Dr (92879-1668)
P.O. Box 1898 (92878-1898)
PHONE................951 273-9600
Glenn J Salsbury, *Pr*
E G Lindholm, *
EMP: 75 EST: 1984
SQ FT: 11,600
SALES (est): 20.52MM Privately Held
Web: www.hillcrestcontracting.com
SIC: **1611** General contractor, highway and street construction

(P-1120)
IES COMMERCIAL INC
Also Called: Ies
6885 Flanders Dr Ste A (92121-2933)
PHONE................858 210-4900
Brad Sandman, *Prin*
EMP: 154
Web: www.ielectric.com
SIC: **1611 7812 1623 7382** General contractor, highway and street construction; Audio-visual program production; Cable laying construction; Security systems services
HQ: Ies Commercial, Inc.
2801 S Fair Ln Ste 101
Tempe AZ
480 379-6200

(P-1121)
INTERNATIONAL PAVING SVCS INC
Also Called: I P S
1199 Opal Ave (92359-1284)
P.O. Box 10458 (92423-0458)
PHONE................909 794-2101
Brent Rieger, *Pr*
EMP: 80 EST: 2007
SALES (est): 18.92MM Privately Held
Web: www.ipspaving.com
SIC: **1611** Surfacing and paving

(P-1122)
JACOBSSON ENGRG CNSTR INC
72310 Varner Rd (92276-3362)
P.O. Box 14430 (92255-4430)
PHONE................760 345-8700
Dan Jacobsson, *Pr*
Ingeborg Jacobsson, *
EMP: 75 EST: 1991
SQ FT: 9,000
SALES (est): 9.77MM Privately Held

Web: www.jacobssoninc.com
SIC: **1611** Highway and street construction

(P-1123)
JB BOSTICK COMPANY INC (PA)
2870 E La Cresta Ave (92806-1816)
PHONE................714 238-2121
James B Bostick, *Pr*
Jerry Hamlin, *
EMP: 75 EST: 1964
SQ FT: 2,870
SALES (est): 24.7MM
SALES (corp-wide): 24.7MM Privately Held
Web: www.jbbostick.com
SIC: **1611 1771** Grading; Concrete work

(P-1124)
JJ FISHER CONSTRUCTION INC
261 W Dana St Ste 100 (93444-9151)
P.O. Box 2219 (93444-2219)
PHONE................805 723-5220
EMP: 65 EST: 2010
SALES (est): 10.27MM Privately Held
SIC: **1611 1771 1794 1761** Gravel or dirt road construction; Concrete work; Excavation work; Gutter and downspout contractor

(P-1125)
KEC ENGINEERING
26320 Lester Cir (92883-6399)
P.O. Box 909 (92878-0909)
PHONE................951 734-3010
James Elfring, *Pr*
Les Card, *
Scott Pfeiffer, *Ex VP*
EMP: 110 EST: 1953
SALES (est): 21.7MM Privately Held
Web: www.kecengineering.com
SIC: **1611** General contractor, highway and street construction

(P-1126)
KIEWIT CORPORATION
Also Called: Keiwit Infrastructure West Co
4650 Business Center Dr (94534-6890)
PHONE................707 439-7300
Jeff Petersen, *Brnch Mgr*
EMP: 63
SALES (corp-wide): 10.41B Privately Held
Web: www.kiewit.com
SIC: **1611** General contractor, highway and street construction
HQ: Kiewit Corporation
1550 Mike Fahey St
Omaha NE
402 342-2052

(P-1127)
KIEWIT INFRASTRUCTURE WEST CO
10704 Shoemaker Ave (90670-4040)
PHONE................562 946-1816
Ken Riley, *Mgr*
EMP: 125
SQ FT: 12,514
SALES (corp-wide): 10.41B Privately Held
Web: www.kiewit.com
SIC: **1611 1542 1541** General contractor, highway and street construction; Nonresidential construction, nec; Industrial buildings and warehouses
HQ: Kiewit Infrastructure West Co.
2200 Columbia House Blvd
Vancouver WA
402 342-2052

(P-1128)
LAIRD CONSTRUCTION CO INC
9460 Lucas Ranch Rd (91730-5743)
PHONE................909 989-5595
James R Laird, *Pr*
Jerold B Laird, *
Ralph J Laird, *
Sarah B Laird, *
EMP: 65 EST: 1946
SQ FT: 5,000
SALES (est): 5.85MM Privately Held
Web: www.lairdconstruction.com
SIC: **1611 1794** Highway and street paving contractor; Excavation work

(P-1129)
LARRY JACINTO CONSTRUCTION INC
9555 N Wabash Ave (92374-2714)
P.O. Box 615 (92359-0615)
PHONE................909 794-2151
Larry Frankland Jacinto, *CEO*
EMP: 80 EST: 1971
SQ FT: 8,500
SALES (est): 22.22MM Privately Held
Web: www.larryjacintoconstruction.com
SIC: **1611** Grading

(P-1130)
LB3 ENTERPRISES INC
12485 Highway 67 # 3 (92040)
P.O. Box 130 (92022-0130)
PHONE................619 579-6161
Lawrence Lee Brown, *Pr*
Debra Brown, *
EMP: 90 EST: 2004
SALES (est): 25.37MM Privately Held
Web: www.lb3enterprises.com
SIC: **1611 1623 7389** Grading; Water, sewer, and utility lines; Business services, nec

(P-1131)
MACRO-Z-TECHNOLOGY COMPANY (PA)
Also Called: M Z T
841 E Washington Ave (92701-3878)
PHONE................714 564-1130
Bryan J Zatica, *CEO*
EMP: 97 EST: 1989
SQ FT: 3,000
SALES (est): 30.96MM Privately Held
Web: www.mztco.com
SIC: **1611 1542 8711** Concrete construction: roads, highways, sidewalks, etc.; Commercial and office building contractors; Engineering services

(P-1132)
MAMCO INC (PA)
Also Called: Alabbasi
764 Ramona Expy Ste C (92571-9716)
PHONE................951 776-9300
Marwan Alabbasi, *CEO*
Elizabeth Alabbasi, *
Rumzi Alabbasi, *
EMP: 116 EST: 2002
SQ FT: 2,200
SALES (est): 33.61MM Privately Held
Web: www.alabbasi.biz
SIC: **1611** General contractor, highway and street construction

(P-1133)
MANERI TRAFFIC CONTROL INC
Also Called: M T C
4949 2nd St (92028-9790)
PHONE................951 695-5104
Maria Maneri, *CEO*
Johnny Maneri, *

1611 - Highway And Street Construction (P-1134)

EMP: 70 **EST:** 2007
SQ FT: 900
SALES (est): 9.35MM **Privately Held**
SIC: 1611 7389 Highway and street sign installation; Flagging service (traffic control)

(P-1134)
MARATHON GENERAL INC
1728 Mission Rd (92029-1111)
PHONE..............................760 738-9714
Mark Miller, *Pr*
Steven Gallant, *
Donald Tolen, *
EMP: 80 **EST:** 1988
SQ FT: 3,000
SALES (est): 32.51MM **Privately Held**
Web: www.mgipaving.com
SIC: 1611 General contractor, highway and street construction

(P-1135)
MARTIN BROTHERS CNSTR LLC (PA)
8801 Folsom Blvd Ste 260 (95826-3250)
PHONE..............................916 386-1600
Felipe Martin, *CEO*
EMP: 60 **EST:** 1996
SQ FT: 9,300
SALES (est): 36MM
SALES (corp-wide): 36MM **Privately Held**
Web: www.martinbrothers.net
SIC: 1611 1794 1541 1795 General contractor, highway and street construction; Excavation work; Industrial buildings, new construction, nec; Demolition, buildings and other structures

(P-1136)
MATICH CORPORATION (PA)
1596 E Harry Shepard Blvd (92408-0197)
P.O. Box 10 (92346-1010)
PHONE..............................909 382-7400
Stephen A Matich, *CEO*
Martin A Matich, *
Randall Valadez, *
Robert M Matich, *
Patrick A Matich, *
EMP: 60 **EST:** 1918
SQ FT: 10,000
SALES (est): 47.71MM
SALES (corp-wide): 47.71MM **Privately Held**
Web: www.matichcorp.com
SIC: 1611 2951 General contractor, highway and street construction; Asphalt paving mixtures and blocks

(P-1137)
MCE CORPORATION (PA)
4000 Industrial Way (94520-1289)
P.O. Box 508 (94522-0508)
PHONE..............................925 803-4111
Jeff Core, *Pr*
Dan Furtado, *
Steve Loweree, *
EMP: 65 **EST:** 1983
SQ FT: 12,000
SALES (est): 51.85MM
SALES (corp-wide): 51.85MM **Privately Held**
Web: www.mce-corp.com
SIC: 1611 0782 General contractor, highway and street construction; Lawn and garden services

(P-1138)
MESA CONTRACTING CORPORATION
22845 Savi Ranch Pkwy Ste D (92887-4628)

EMP: 120 **EST:** 1978
SALES (est): 10.46MM **Privately Held**
Web: www.mesacontracting.com
SIC: 1611 Grading

(P-1139)
MIDSTATE BARRIER INC
Also Called: MBI
3291 S Highway 99 (95215-8032)
P.O. Box 30550 (95213-0550)
PHONE..............................209 944-9565
Dale Breen, *CEO*
Clark Ebinger, *
EMP: 75 **EST:** 1987
SQ FT: 20,000
SALES (est): 22.25MM **Privately Held**
Web: www.midstatebarrier.com
SIC: 1611 Highway signs and guardrails

(P-1140)
MONTEREY PENINSULA ENGINEERING
192 Healy Ave (93933-2203)
P.O. Box 2317 (93942-2317)
PHONE..............................831 384-4081
EMP: 150 **EST:** 1980
SALES (est): 23.96MM **Privately Held**
Web: www.mpe2000.info
SIC: 1611 1623 Grading; Water and sewer line construction

(P-1141)
MOUNTAIN G ENTERPRISES INC
Also Called: Mountain G Engineering
950 Iron Point Rd Ste 190 (95630-8304)
P.O. Box 1040 (95651-1040)
PHONE..............................866 464-6351
Marcos Gomez, *CEO*
Juan Gomez, *
EMP: 250 **EST:** 2016
SQ FT: 3,000
SALES (est): 42.02MM **Privately Held**
Web: www.mgeinc.com
SIC: 1611 8711 8748 Grading; Civil engineering; Environmental consultant

(P-1142)
MUSE CONCRETE CONTRACTORS INC
8599 Commercial Way (96002-3902)
PHONE..............................530 226-5151
Boyce Muse, *Pr*
Joan Muse, *
Garrett Brown, *
EMP: 94 **EST:** 1982
SALES (est): 21.23MM **Privately Held**
Web: www.museconcrete.com
SIC: 1611 1771 Concrete construction: roads, highways, sidewalks, etc.; Concrete work

(P-1143)
MYERS & SONS CONSTRUCTION LP
5777 W Century Blvd Ste 600 (90045-5636)
PHONE..............................424 227-3285
EMP: 141
Web: www.myers-sons.com
SIC: 1611 Highway and street construction
HQ: Myers & Sons Construction, L.P.
45 Morrison Ave
Sacramento CA

(P-1144)
MYERS & SONS CONSTRUCTION LP (HQ)
45 Morrison Ave (95838-3201)
PHONE..............................916 283-9950

EMP: 109 **EST:** 2010
SALES (est): 181.59MM **Publicly Held**
Web: www.myers-sons.com
SIC: 1611 Highway and street construction
PA: Sterling Infrastructure, Inc.
1800 Hughes Landing Blvd
The Woodlands TX

(P-1145)
NATIONAL PAVING COMPANY INC
4361 Fort Dr (92509-6784)
P.O. Box 3649 (92519-3649)
PHONE..............................951 369-1332
Richard J Lindholm, *Pr*
Lawrence Spicher, *
EMP: 78 **EST:** 1986
SQ FT: 4,000
SALES (est): 22.14MM **Privately Held**
Web: www.nationalpaving.com
SIC: 1611 Highway and street paving contractor

(P-1146)
NORTH BAY CONSTRUCTION INC
431 Payran St (94952-5908)
P.O. Box 751389 (94975-1389)
PHONE..............................707 283-0093
John E Barella, *Pr*
Steve Geney, *
EMP: 80 **EST:** 1977
SQ FT: 7,000
SALES (est): 9.71MM **Privately Held**
SIC: 1611 1623 Highway and street paving contractor; Sewer line construction

(P-1147)
O C JONES & SONS INC (PA)
1520 4th St (94710-1748)
PHONE..............................510 526-3424
Kelly Kolander, *Pr*
Robert Pelascini, *
Rob Layne, *
Barbara Jones, *
Beth Yoshida, *
EMP: 150 **EST:** 1924
SQ FT: 80,000
SALES (est): 99.77MM
SALES (corp-wide): 99.77MM **Privately Held**
Web: www.ocjones.com
SIC: 1611 Grading

(P-1148)
OGRADY PAVING INC
2513 Wyandotte St (94043-2314)
PHONE..............................650 966-1926
Thomas M O'grady Junior, *Pr*
Craig Young, *
Celine Duran, *
EMP: 110 **EST:** 1956
SQ FT: 3,200
SALES (est): 22.22MM **Privately Held**
Web: www.ogradypavinginc.com
SIC: 1611 Highway and street paving contractor

(P-1149)
OTAY RIVER CONSTRUCTORS LLC
860 Harold Pl (91914-3550)
P.O. Box 600 (92346-0600)
PHONE..............................619 397-7500
Rich Linford, *Pr*
▲ **EMP:** 130 **EST:** 2002
SQ FT: 17,000
SALES (est): 21.73MM **Privately Held**

SIC: 1611 Highway and street construction

(P-1150)
OUTBACK CONTRACTORS INC
13670 State Highway 36 E (96080-7849)
P.O. Box 1035 (96080-1035)
PHONE..............................530 528-2225
Mattie Bunting, *CEO*
EMP: 221 **EST:** 2008
SQ FT: 625
SALES (est): 50.5MM **Privately Held**
Web: www.outback-inc.com
SIC: 1611 Concrete construction: roads, highways, sidewalks, etc.

(P-1151)
PALP INC
Also Called: Excel Paving Co
2230 Lemon Ave (90806-5124)
P.O. Box 16405 (90806-0995)
PHONE..............................562 599-5841
Curtis P Brown, *CEO*
George Mcrae, *Sr VP*
Bruce Flatt, *
Michelle Drakulich, *
EMP: 225 **EST:** 1976
SQ FT: 11,000
SALES (est): 49.18MM **Privately Held**
Web: www.excelpavingcompany.com
SIC: 1611 8711 Highway and street paving contractor; Engineering services

(P-1152)
PETERSON-CHASE GENERAL ENGINEERING CONSTRUCTION INC
16351 Construction Cir W (92606-4414)
PHONE..............................949 252-0441
EMP: 60 **EST:** 1985
SALES (est): 9.59MM **Privately Held**
Web: www.petersonchase.com
SIC: 1611 General contractor, highway and street construction

(P-1153)
POWERTEC COMPANY INC (PA)
1151 W Vermont Ave (92802-1825)
P.O. Box 7296 (92513-7296)
PHONE..............................951 332-1198
Jesus M Adame, *CEO*
Jesus Murguia Adame, *Pr*
Michael Castillo, *VP*
Camerino Lauriano, *Sec*
Hector Hernandez, *CFO*
EMP: 65 **EST:** 2017
SALES (est): 12MM
SALES (corp-wide): 12MM **Privately Held**
SIC: 1611 8748 8741 General contractor, highway and street construction; Telecommunications consultant; Office management

(P-1154)
RGW CONSTRUCTION INC
550 Greenville Rd (94550-9297)
PHONE..............................925 606-2400
EMP: 200 **EST:** 1990
SALES (est): 25.98MM **Privately Held**
Web: www.rgwconstruction.com
SIC: 1611 Highway and street construction

(P-1155)
RICK HAMM CONSTRUCTION INC
201 W Carleton Ave (92867-3607)
PHONE..............................714 532-0815
Rick Hamm, *Pr*
Llana Hamm, *
EMP: 90 **EST:** 1977

PRODUCTS & SERVICES SECTION

1611 - Highway And Street Construction (P-1174)

SQ FT: 25,000
SALES (est): 19.49MM **Privately Held**
Web: www.rickhamm.com
SIC: **1611** 1771 1791 1741 General contractor, highway and street construction; Patio construction, concrete; Precast concrete structural framing or panels, placing of; Masonry and other stonework

(P-1156)
RIVERSIDE CONSTRUCTION COMPANY INC
4225 Garner Rd (92501-1057)
P.O. Box 1146 (92502-1146)
PHONE..................................951 682-8308
EMP: 150 EST: 1966
SALES (est): 22.61MM **Privately Held**
Web: www.rivconstruct.com
SIC: **1611** General contractor, highway and street construction

(P-1157)
RJ NOBLE COMPANY (PA)
15505 E Lincoln Ave (92865-1015)
P.O. Box 620 (92856-9020)
PHONE..................................714 637-1550
Michael J Carver, *Pr*
Craig Porter, *
James N Ducote, *
EMP: 144 EST: 1950
SQ FT: 5,500
SALES (est): 60.76MM
SALES (corp-wide): 60.76MM **Privately Held**
Web: www.rjnoblecompany.com
SIC: **1611** Highway and street paving contractor

(P-1158)
ROMERO GENERAL CNSTR CORP (PA)
Also Called: Romero Construction
2150 N Centre City Pkwy Ste I (92026)
PHONE..................................760 489-8412
Keith Reilly, *Pr*
EMP: 73 EST: 1992
SQ FT: 3,500
SALES (est): 33.7MM **Privately Held**
Web: www.romerogc.com
SIC: **1611** Highway and street paving contractor

(P-1159)
RSVC COMPANY
Also Called: Reliable Service Company
3051 Myers St Ste B (92503-5525)
P.O. Box 7189 (92513-7189)
PHONE..................................951 684-6578
Mark David Aldaco, *Pr*
Mark David Aldaco, *CEO*
Keith Gruber, *
EMP: 188 EST: 2004
SALES (est): 48.53MM **Privately Held**
Web: www.rsvc.com
SIC: **1611** 8741 8712 General contractor, highway and street construction; Management services; Architectural services

(P-1160)
SECURITY PAVING COMPANY INC (PA)
Also Called: Valley Base Materials
3075 Townsgate Rd Ste 210 # 200 (91361-3027)
PHONE..................................818 362-9200
Mike Mattivi, *CEO*
Mike Mattivi, *Prin*
Albert Mattivi, *

Thomas J Mattivi, *
EMP: 99 EST: 1947
SALES (est): 74.25MM
SALES (corp-wide): 74.25MM **Privately Held**
Web: www.securitypaving.com
SIC: **1611** Highway and street paving contractor

(P-1161)
SEMA CONSTRUCTION INC
320 Goddard Ste 150 (92618-4630)
PHONE..................................949 470-0500
Steve Mills, *Mgr*
EMP: 100
Web: www.sema.inc
SIC: **1611** 1771 Highway and street construction; Concrete work
PA: Sema Construction, Inc.
    7353 S Eagle St
    Centennial CO

(P-1162)
SIALIC CONTRACTORS CORPORATION
Also Called: Shawnan
12240 Woodruff Ave (90241-5608)
PHONE..................................562 803-9977
Shawn Smith, *Pr*
John Smith, *
EMP: 68 EST: 1993
SQ FT: 24,000
SALES (est): 7.42MM **Privately Held**
SIC: **1611** General contractor, highway and street construction

(P-1163)
SIERRA TRAFFIC MARKINGS INC
9725 Del Rd Ste B (95747-9759)
PHONE..................................916 784-0430
Ron Johnson, *CEO*
Kathleen Johnson, *
EMP: 70 EST: 2010
SALES (est): 20.1MM **Privately Held**
Web: www.sierratrafficmarkings.com
SIC: **1611** Surfacing and paving

(P-1164)
SKANSKA USA CVIL W CAL DST INC (DH)
1995 Agua Mansa Rd (92509-2405)
PHONE..................................951 684-5360
Richard Cavallero, *CEO*
Michael Aparicio, *
Todd Sutton, *
Joseph Nogues, *
Michael Cobelli, *
EMP: 700 EST: 1919
SQ FT: 15,000
SALES (est): 475.28MM
SALES (corp-wide): 15.55B **Privately Held**
Web: usa.skanska.com
SIC: **1611** 1622 1629 8711 General contractor, highway and street construction; Bridge construction; Dam construction; Engineering services
HQ: Skanska Usa Civil Inc.
    7520 Astoria Blvd Ste 200
    East Elmhurst NY
    718 340-0777

(P-1165)
STEVENS CREEK QUARRY INC (PA)
Also Called: Scq Construction
21771 Stevens Creek Blvd Ste 100 (95014-1164)
PHONE..................................408 253-2512

Richard A Voss, *Pr*
Bob Romano, *
Richard Voss, *
Diana Voss, *
EMP: 60 EST: 1954
SALES (est): 20.92MM
SALES (corp-wide): 20.92MM **Privately Held**
Web: www.scqinc.com
SIC: **1611** 7353 1442 General contractor, highway and street construction; Heavy construction equipment rental; Construction sand mining

(P-1166)
SULLY-MILLER CONTRACTING CO (DH)
Also Called: Blue Diamond Materials
135 S State College Blvd Ste 400 (92821-5819)
PHONE..................................714 578-9600
John Harrington, *Pr*
William Boyd, *
Scott Bottomley, *
Christian Ransinangue, *
EMP: 64 EST: 1997
SALES (est): 210.35MM
SALES (corp-wide): 114.31MM **Privately Held**
Web: www.sully-miller.com
SIC: **1611** Highway and street paving contractor
HQ: Colas Inc.
    73 Hedqrters Plz N Towe 1
    Morristown NJ

(P-1167)
SULLY-MILLER HOLDING CORP
135 S State College Blvd Ste 400 (92821-5819)
PHONE..................................714 578-9600
George W Sully, *Pr*
EMP: 125
SALES (est): 2.04MM
SALES (corp-wide): 114.31MM **Privately Held**
Web: www.sully-miller.com
SIC: **1611** Highway and street paving contractor
HQ: Colas Inc.
    73 Hedqrters Plz N Towe 1
    Morristown NJ

(P-1168)
SUPERIOR PAVING COMPANY INC
Also Called: United Paving Company
1880 N Delilah St (92879-1892)
PHONE..................................951 739-9200
Sabas Trujillo, *CEO*
EMP: 85 EST: 2008
SQ FT: 3,000
SALES (est): 25.33MM **Privately Held**
Web: www.united-paving.com
SIC: **1611** Highway and street paving contractor

(P-1169)
SYSTEMS PAVING INC (PA)
1570 Brookhollow Dr (92705-5438)
PHONE..................................949 263-8301
Larry Green, *Ch*
Douglas Lueck, *
Steven Leuck, *
Syed Zaidi, *
EMP: 61 EST: 1992
SQ FT: 13,000
SALES (est): 47.89MM **Privately Held**
Web: www.systempavers.com

SIC: **1611** Surfacing and paving

(P-1170)
TEICHERT INC
Also Called: Teichert Construction
265 Val Dervin Pkwy (95206-4001)
P.O. Box 1118 (95201-1118)
PHONE..................................209 983-2300
Mark Nilsen, *Dist Mgr*
EMP: 61
SALES (corp-wide): 844.71MM **Privately Held**
Web: www.teichert.com
SIC: **1611** 5032 Highway and street construction; Brick, stone, and related material
HQ: A. Teichert & Son, Inc.
    3500 American River Dr
    Sacramento CA

(P-1171)
TEICHERT INC
Also Called: Teichert Construction
24207 County Road 100a (95616-9410)
P.O. Box 1890 (95617-1890)
PHONE..................................530 406-4200
Mark Stacy, *Dist Mgr*
EMP: 113
SALES (corp-wide): 844.71MM **Privately Held**
Web: www.teichert.com
SIC: **1611** Highway and street construction
HQ: A. Teichert & Son, Inc.
    3500 American River Dr
    Sacramento CA

(P-1172)
TEICHERT INC
Also Called: Teichert Construction
4401 Duluth Ave (95678-5999)
PHONE..................................916 645-4800
Dave Swartz, *Dist Mgr*
EMP: 83
SALES (corp-wide): 844.71MM **Privately Held**
Web: www.teichert.com
SIC: **1611** 5032 Highway and street construction; Brick, stone, and related material
HQ: A. Teichert & Son, Inc.
    3500 American River Dr
    Sacramento CA

(P-1173)
TEICHERT INC
Also Called: Teichert Construction
5771 Toyota Pl (93725)
P.O. Box 520 (93625-0520)
PHONE..................................559 813-3100
Gordon Stout, *Prin*
EMP: 120
SALES (corp-wide): 844.71MM **Privately Held**
Web: www.teichert.com
SIC: **1611** 5032 Highway and street construction; Brick, stone, and related material
HQ: A. Teichert & Son, Inc.
    3500 American River Dr
    Sacramento CA

(P-1174)
TORO ENTERPRISES INC
2101 Ventura Blvd (93036-8951)
P.O. Box 6285 (93031-6285)
PHONE..................................805 483-4515
EMP: 67 EST: 1994
SALES (est): 53.95MM **Privately Held**
Web: www.toroenterprises.com

1611 Concrete construction: roads, highways, sidewalks, etc.

SIC: 1611 Concrete construction: roads, highways, sidewalks, etc.

(P-1175)
UNITED ROCK PRODUCTS CORP
Also Called: Sully Miller Contracting
135 S State College Blvd Ste 400 (92821-5819)
PHONE..............................714 578-9600
John Harrington, *Pr*
▲ **EMP:** 104 **EST:** 1988
SQ FT: 2,000
SALES (est): 10.43MM
SALES (corp-wide): 114.31MM **Privately Held**
Web: www.sully-miller.com
SIC: 1611 Highway and street paving contractor
HQ: Sully-Miller Contracting Company Inc
135 S State College Blvd # 400
Brea CA
714 578-9600

(P-1176)
VSS INTERNATIONAL INC (HQ)
Also Called: V S S
3785 Channel Dr (95691-3421)
P.O. Box 981330 (95798-1330)
PHONE..............................916 373-1500
Jeffrey Reed, *Pr*
Alan Berger, *
Diane Minor, *Corporate Secretary**
John Shoden, *
Ron Bolles, *
▲ **EMP:** 62 **EST:** 1974
SQ FT: 5,000
SALES (est): 55.84MM
SALES (corp-wide): 163.99MM **Privately Held**
Web: www.slurry.com
SIC: 1611 3531 2951 Highway and street paving contractor; Construction machinery; Asphalt paving mixtures and blocks
PA: Basic Resources, Inc.
928 12th St Ste 700
Modesto CA
209 521-9771

(P-1177)
WESTERN ENGINEERING CONTRACTORS INC
3171 Rippey Rd (95650-9504)
P.O. Box 1387 (95650-1387)
PHONE..............................916 652-3990
EMP: 120 **EST:** 1982
SALES (est): 34.52MM **Privately Held**
Web: www.westeng.com
SIC: 1611 1623 Highway and street paving contractor; Underground utilities contractor

1622 Bridge, Tunnel, And Elevated Highway

(P-1178)
AMERICAN BRIDGE/FLUOR ENTERPRISES INC
1390 Willow Pass Rd # 33 (94520-5200)
PHONE..............................510 808-4623
▲ **EMP:** 80
SIC: 1622 Bridge construction

(P-1179)
C C MYERS INC
3286 Fitzgerald Rd (95742-6811)
P.O. Box 2948 (95741-2948)
PHONE..............................916 635-9370
EMP: 225
Web: www.ccmyers.com
SIC: 1622 Bridge construction

(P-1180)
FLATIRON WEST INC
1200 Concord Ave (94520-4959)
PHONE..............................707 742-6000
Richard Tradinski, *Mgr*
EMP: 150
Web: www.flatironi-15.com
SIC: 1622 1629 Bridge construction; Industrial plant construction
HQ: Flatiron West, Inc.
12121 Scripps Summit Dr # 400
San Diego CA

(P-1181)
FLATIRON WEST INC
16341 Chino Corona Rd (91708-9233)
PHONE..............................909 597-8413
Thomas J Rademacher, *CEO*
EMP: 160
Web: www.flatironi-15.com
SIC: 1622 1611 Bridge construction; Highway and street construction
HQ: Flatiron West, Inc.
12121 Scripps Summit Dr # 400
San Diego CA

(P-1182)
FLUOR DANIEL CONSTRUCTION CO (DH)
Also Called: Fluor Daniel Construction
3 Polaris Way (92656-5338)
PHONE..............................949 349-2000
Paul Buckham, *Pr*
EMP: 500 **EST:** 1953
SALES (est): 102.17MM
SALES (corp-wide): 13.74B **Publicly Held**
SIC: 1622 Bridge, tunnel, and elevated highway construction
HQ: Fluor Enterprises, Inc.
6700 Las Colinas Blvd
Irving TX
469 398-7000

(P-1183)
GRANITE CONSTRUCTION INC (PA)
Also Called: Granite
585 W Beach St (95076-5123)
P.O. Box 50085 (95077-5085)
PHONE..............................831 724-1011
Kyle T Larkin, *Pr*
Michael F Mcnally, *Ch Bd*
Elizabeth L Curtis, *Ex VP*
James A Radich, *Ex VP*
Jigisha Desai, *CSO*
EMP: 268 **EST:** 1922
SALES (est): 3.3B **Publicly Held**
Web: www.graniteconstruction.com
SIC: 1622 1629 1442 1611 Bridge construction; Dam construction; Construction sand and gravel; General contractor, highway and street construction

(P-1184)
HAZARD CONSTRUCTION COMPANY
Also Called: Hazard Construction
10529 Vine St Ste 1 (92040-2447)
P.O. Box 229000 (92192-9000)
PHONE..............................858 587-3600
Jason Mordhorst, *Pr*
Klaus Guttau, *VP*
EMP: 100 **EST:** 1926
SALES (est): 99.35MM **Privately Held**
Web: www.hazardconstruction.com
SIC: 1622 1611 Bridge construction; Highway and street construction

(P-1185)
MCM CONSTRUCTION INC (PA)
6413 32nd St (95660-3001)
P.O. Box 620 (95660-0620)
PHONE..............................916 334-1221
Richard Mccall, *Pr*
Harry D Mcgovern, *VP*
EMP: 70 **EST:** 1973
SQ FT: 5,000
SALES (est): 75.66MM
SALES (corp-wide): 75.66MM **Privately Held**
Web: www.mcmconstructioninc.com
SIC: 1622 Bridge construction

(P-1186)
MCM CONSTRUCTION INC
19010 Slover Ave (92316-2459)
PHONE..............................909 875-0533
Nella Flores, *Brnch Mgr*
EMP: 77
SALES (corp-wide): 75.66MM **Privately Held**
Web: www.mcmconstructioninc.com
SIC: 1622 Bridge construction
PA: M.C.M. Construction, Inc.
6413 32nd St
North Highlands CA
916 334-1221

(P-1187)
OC 405 PARTNERS JOINT VENTURE
3100 W Lake Center Dr Ste 200 (92704-6917)
PHONE..............................858 251-2200
Ashok Patel, *Ofcr*
Tony Bagheri, *Ofcr*
Luigi Realini, *Ofcr*
Loris Paravano, *Ofcr*
EMP: 75 **EST:** 2016
SQ FT: 69,000
SALES (est): 16.39MM **Privately Held**
Web: www.oc405partners.com
SIC: 1622 Bridge construction
HQ: Ohla Usa, Inc.
2615 Ulmer St
Flushing NY

(P-1188)
R M HARRIS COMPANY INC
1000 Howe Rd Ste 200 (94553-3446)
PHONE..............................925 335-3000
David R Harris, *CEO*
Mark Snapp, *
EMP: 100 **EST:** 1976
SQ FT: 4,500
SALES (est): 16.1MM **Privately Held**
Web: www.rmhci.com
SIC: 1622 1611 Bridge, tunnel, and elevated highway construction; Highway and street construction

(P-1189)
RCI GENERAL ENGINEERING
5015 Feather River Blvd (95965-9606)
P.O. Box 2531 (95965-2531)
PHONE..............................530 533-3918
Jake Richter, *Pr*
EMP: 70 **EST:** 2016
SALES (est): 9.85MM **Privately Held**
Web: www.rcige.com
SIC: 1622 Bridge, tunnel, and elevated highway construction

(P-1190)
STEVE P RADOS INC
1638 Pioneer Way (92020-1636)
PHONE..............................619 328-1360
Steve Rados, *Mgr*
EMP: 110
SALES (corp-wide): 68.32MM **Privately Held**
Web: www.rados.com
SIC: 1622 Highway construction, elevated
HQ: Steve P Rados Inc
2002 E Mcfadden Ave # 200
Santa Ana CA
714 835-4612

1623 Water, Sewer, And Utility Lines

(P-1191)
A & H COMMUNICATIONS INC
15 Chrysler (92618-2009)
PHONE..............................949 250-4555
Brian Elliott, *Pr*
Brett Howard, *
EMP: 250 **EST:** 2000
SALES (est): 24.09MM **Privately Held**
Web: www.aandh.com
SIC: 1623 Cable laying construction

(P-1192)
ARB INC (HQ)
Also Called: California Arb, Inc.
26000 Commercentre Dr (92630-8816)
PHONE..............................949 598-9242
Tom Mccormick, *CEO*
Scott Summers, *
Timothy Healy, *
John P Schauerman, *
John M Perisich, *Corporate Secretary**
▲ **EMP:** 140 **EST:** 1960
SALES (est): 526.23MM **Publicly Held**
Web: www.prim.com
SIC: 1623 1629 Oil and gas line and compressor station construction; Industrial plant construction
PA: Primoris Services Corporation
2300 N Field St Ste 1900
Dallas TX

(P-1193)
ARGONAUT CONSTRUCTORS INC
360 Sutton Pl (95407-8121)
P.O. Box 639 (95402-0639)
PHONE..............................707 542-4862
Michael Smith, *CEO*
Michael D Smith, *
Michael A Smith Stockhldr Juni or, *VP*
EMP: 175 **EST:** 1957
SQ FT: 10,000
SALES (est): 42.89MM **Privately Held**
Web: www.argonautconstructors.com
SIC: 1623 1611 Oil and gas pipeline construction; Highway and street paving contractor

(P-1194)
ARIZONA PIPELINE COMPANY (PA)
17372 Lilac St (92345-5162)
P.O. Box 401865 (92340-1865)
PHONE..............................760 244-8212
Lowell Duane Moyers, *Ch*
Nina Moyers, *CEO*
Phyliss Moyers, *Dir*
Tom Seals, *Sec*
EMP: 400 **EST:** 1979
SQ FT: 5,000

PRODUCTS & SERVICES SECTION

1623 - Water, Sewer, And Utility Lines (P-1215)

SALES (est): 214.75MM
SALES (corp-wide): 214.75MM **Privately Held**
Web: www.arizonapipeline.com
SIC: **1623** Pipeline construction, nsk

(P-1195)
ARIZONA PIPELINE COMPANY
1745 Sampson Ave (92879-1864)
PHONE..............................951 270-3100
John Guzlow, *Div Mgr*
EMP: 200
SALES (corp-wide): 214.75MM **Privately Held**
Web: www.arizonapipeline.com
SIC: **1623** 8711 Underground utilities contractor; Engineering services
PA: Arizona Pipeline Company
 17372 Lilac St
 Hesperia CA
 760 244-8212

(P-1196)
BALI CONSTRUCTION INC
9852 Joe Vargas Way (91733-3108)
PHONE..............................626 442-8003
Ted Polich Iii, *Pr*
Michael E Brooks, *
EMP: 100 EST: 1987
SQ FT: 7,000
SALES (est): 58.08MM **Privately Held**
Web: www.baliconstruction.com
SIC: **1623** Underground utilities contractor

(P-1197)
BLOIS CONSTRUCTION INC
3201 Sturgis Rd (93030-8931)
P.O. Box 672 (93032-0672)
PHONE..............................805 485-0011
James B Blois, *Pr*
Steve Woodworth, *
Dan Schultz, *
EMP: 150 EST: 1965
SQ FT: 10,000
SALES (est): 44.91MM **Privately Held**
Web: www.bloisconstruction.com
SIC: **1623** Underground utilities contractor

(P-1198)
BOUDREAU PIPELINE CORPORATION
Also Called: A & B Equipment
463 N Smith Ave (92878-4305)
PHONE..............................951 493-6780
EMP: 300 EST: 2000
SQ FT: 14,000
SALES (est): 66.84MM **Privately Held**
Web: www.boudreaupipeline.com
SIC: **1623** Pipeline construction, nsk

(P-1199)
BURTECH PIPELINE INCORPORATED
Also Called: Burtech Plumbing
1325 Pipeline Dr (92081-8835)
PHONE..............................760 634-2822
Dominic J Burtech, *Pr*
Julie Burtech, *
EMP: 70 EST: 1994
SALES (est): 27.46MM **Privately Held**
Web: www.burtechpipeline.com
SIC: **1623** Water main construction

(P-1200)
CA STATION MANAGEMENT INC
3200 E Guasti Rd Ste 100 (91761-8661)
PHONE..............................909 245-6351
Taqi Chaudry, *CEO*
EMP: 250 EST: 2016

SALES (est): 23.62MM **Privately Held**
SIC: **1623** 7389 8082 Underground utilities contractor; Telephone answering service; Home health care services

(P-1201)
CAMERON INTRSTATE PIPELINE LLC
488 8th Ave (92101-7123)
PHONE..............................619 696-3110
Ryan O'neal, *VP*
EMP: 200 EST: 2005
SALES (est): 28.44MM **Privately Held**
Web: www.sempra.com
SIC: **1623** Oil and gas pipeline construction

(P-1202)
CASS CONSTRUCTION INC (PA)
Also Called: Cass
1100 Wagner Dr (92020-3047)
P.O. Box 309 (92022-0309)
PHONE..............................619 590-0929
Jimmie Nelson, *Ch Bd*
Kyle P Nelson, *
Laura Nelson, *
EMP: 345 EST: 1974
SQ FT: 5,700
SALES (est): 43.87MM
SALES (corp-wide): 43.87MM **Privately Held**
Web: www.cassarrieta.com
SIC: **1623** 1611 Underground utilities contractor; Grading

(P-1203)
CEDAR CREEK CORPORATION
15875 Jellys Ferry Rd (96080-7964)
PHONE..............................530 364-2143
Katie Gove, *CEO*
Katie Marie Gove, *
Gary Gove, *
Nicholas Vona, *
John Kalapaca, *
EMP: 120 EST: 2016
SALES (est): 18.04MM **Privately Held**
Web: www.cedarcreekcorp.com
SIC: **1623** Electric power line construction

(P-1204)
CITY OF UKIAH
300 Plant Rd (95482-6974)
PHONE..............................707 467-2818
Jerry Gall, *Mgr*
EMP: 145
SALES (corp-wide): 33.78MM **Privately Held**
Web: www.cityofukiah.com
SIC: **1623** 9111 Water, sewer, and utility lines ; Mayors' office
PA: City Of Ukiah
 300 Seminary Ave
 Ukiah CA
 707 463-6203

(P-1205)
DIVERSIFIED UTILITY SVCS INC
3105 Unicorn Ave (93308-6858)
P.O. Box 80417 (93380-0417)
PHONE..............................661 325-3212
Leigh Ann Anderson, *CEO*
Steven S Anderson, *
William Mitchell, *Stockholder*
Cody Anderson, *Stockholder*
EMP: 272 EST: 1997
SALES (est): 48.45MM **Privately Held**
Web: www.diversifiedutilityservices.com
SIC: **1623** Underground utilities contractor

(P-1206)
DOTY BROS EQUIPMENT CO (HQ)
11232 Firestone Blvd (90650-2201)
PHONE..............................562 864-6566
EMP: 100 EST: 1931
SALES (est): 55.5MM
SALES (corp-wide): 528.99MM **Privately Held**
Web: www.dotybros.com
SIC: **1623** Pipeline construction, nsk
PA: Meruelo Enterprises, Inc.
 9550 Firestone Blvd # 105
 Downey CA
 562 745-2300

(P-1207)
DRESSER/AREIA CONSTRUCTION
3940 Valley Ave (94566-4865)
PHONE..............................800 392-9891
Jody Areia, *Pr*
Dan Dresser, *
EMP: 188 EST: 1989
SQ FT: 4,000
SALES (est): 1.81MM
SALES (corp-wide): 9.78B **Publicly Held**
SIC: **1623** Underground utilities contractor
HQ: Mastec North America, Inc.
 800 S Douglas Rd Ste 1200
 Coral Gables FL
 305 599-1800

(P-1208)
ELECTRIC TECH CONSTRUCTION INC
Also Called: Electric Tech
1910 Mark Ct Ste 130 (94520-1280)
PHONE..............................925 849-5324
Tim Pessin, *Prin*
Dean Balough, *
Kathryn Balough, *
Tim Pessin, *VP*
EMP: 80 EST: 2007
SQ FT: 5,000
SALES (est): 25.55MM **Privately Held**
Web: www.etech-inc.net
SIC: **1623** 1731 Telephone and communication line construction; Electrical work

(P-1209)
FLOYD JOHNSTON CNSTR CO INC
2301 Herndon Ave (93611-8911)
PHONE..............................559 299-7373
Evelyn Johnston, *VP*
EMP: 75 EST: 1969
SQ FT: 6,000
SALES (est): 15.89MM **Privately Held**
SIC: **1623** Water main construction

(P-1210)
GD NIELSON CONSTRUCTION INC
147 Camino Oruga (94558-6215)
PHONE..............................707 253-8774
Diann Nielson, *Pr*
George S Nielson, *
EMP: 60 EST: 1978
SALES (est): 14.89MM **Privately Held**
Web: www.nielsoninc.com
SIC: **1623** 1629 1799 Sewer line construction ; Drainage system construction; Boring for building construction

(P-1211)
GENERAL PRODUCTION SVC CAL INC
Also Called: G P S
1333 Kern St (93268-9700)
P.O. Box 344 (93268-0344)
PHONE..............................661 765-5330
Charles Beard, *CEO*
Oreste Risi, *
EMP: 180 EST: 1967
SALES (est): 49.99MM **Privately Held**
Web: www.genprod.com
SIC: **1623** Oil and gas pipeline construction

(P-1212)
GSE CONSTRUCTION COMPANY INC (PA)
7633 Southfront Rd Ste 160 (94551)
PHONE..............................925 447-0292
Dennis Gutierrez, *CEO*
Sue Gutierrez, *
EMP: 138 EST: 1980
SQ FT: 23,400
SALES (est): 516.7K
SALES (corp-wide): 516.7K **Privately Held**
Web: www.gseconstruction.com
SIC: **1623** 1542 Water and sewer line construction; Nonresidential construction, nec

(P-1213)
HCI LLC (HQ)
Also Called: H C I
6830 Airport Dr (92504-1904)
P.O. Box 5389 (92860-8097)
PHONE..............................951 520-4200
Steven G Silagi, *Pr*
◆ EMP: 300 EST: 1981
SALES (est): 105.09MM
SALES (corp-wide): 182.13MM **Privately Held**
Web: www.hci-inc.com
SIC: **1623** Telephone and communication line construction
PA: Lombardy Holdings, Inc.
 151 Kalmus Dr Ste F6
 Costa Mesa CA
 951 808-4550

(P-1214)
HENKELS & MCCOY INC
2840 Ficus St (91766-6501)
PHONE..............................909 517-3011
Michael Giarratano, *Sr VP*
EMP: 300
SALES (corp-wide): 9.78B **Publicly Held**
Web: www.henkels.com
SIC: **1623** Electric power line construction
HQ: Henkels & Mccoy, Inc
 985 Jolly Rd
 Blue Bell PA
 215 283-7600

(P-1215)
HERMAN WEISSKER INC (HQ)
1645 Brown Ave (92509-1859)
PHONE..............................951 826-8800
Luis Alberto Armona, *CEO*
Ron Politte, *
Marty Mayeda, *
EMP: 176 EST: 1959
SQ FT: 12,000
SALES (est): 107.21MM
SALES (corp-wide): 528.99MM **Privately Held**
Web: www.hermanweissker.com
SIC: **1623** 1731 Underground utilities contractor; Electrical work
PA: Meruelo Enterprises, Inc.
 9550 Firestone Blvd # 105

Downey CA
562 745-2300

(P-1216)
HP COMMUNICATIONS INC (PA)
13341 Temescal Canyon Rd (92883-4980)
PHONE..................................951 572-1200
Nicholas Goldman, *Pr*
Ahmad Olomi, *Ex VP*
Chris Price, *VP*
EMP: 82 **EST:** 1998
SQ FT: 130,680
SALES (est): 101.53MM
SALES (corp-wide): 101.53MM **Privately Held**
Web: www.hpcomminc.com
SIC: 1623 Communication line and transmission tower construction

(P-1217)
HP COMMUNICATIONS INC
15453 Olde Highway 80 (92021-2409)
PHONE..................................951 579-8339
Dustin Walters, *Rgnl Mgr*
EMP: 79
SALES (corp-wide): 101.53MM **Privately Held**
Web: www.hpcomminc.com
SIC: 1623 Communication line and transmission tower construction
PA: Hp Communications, Inc.
13341 Temescal Canyon Rd
Corona CA
951 572-1200

(P-1218)
HP COMMUNICATIONS INC
1931 Mateo St (90021-2832)
PHONE..................................951 457-0133
Ralph Ochoa, *Rgnl Mgr*
EMP: 79
SALES (corp-wide): 101.53MM **Privately Held**
Web: www.hpcomminc.com
SIC: 1623 Communication line and transmission tower construction
PA: Hp Communications, Inc.
13341 Temescal Canyon Rd
Corona CA
951 572-1200

(P-1219)
IRISH COMMUNICATION COMPANY (DH)
2649 Stingle Ave (91770-3326)
P.O. Box 457 (91770-0457)
PHONE..................................626 288-6170
Gregory C Warde, *CEO*
Dan Mitchell, *
Pat D Furnare, *
Larry Manke Rcdd, *VP*
Dennis Brackney, *
EMP: 100 **EST:** 1985
SQ FT: 9,000
SALES (est): 48.45MM
SALES (corp-wide): 64.03MM **Privately Held**
Web: www.irishteam.com
SIC: 1623 8748 1731 Telephone and communication line construction; Telecommunications consultant; Communications specialization
HQ: Irish Construction
2641 River Ave
Rosemead CA
626 288-8530

(P-1220)
IRISH COMMUNICATION COMPANY
Also Called: Irish Construction Company
8449 Specialty Cir (95828-2523)
PHONE..................................916 383-9000
EMP: 150
SALES (corp-wide): 64.03MM **Privately Held**
Web: www.irishteam.com
SIC: 1623 Telephone and communication line construction
HQ: Irish Communication Company Inc
2649 Stingle Ave
Rosemead CA
626 288-6170

(P-1221)
IRISH CONSTRUCTION (HQ)
2641 River Ave (91770-3392)
P.O. Box 579 (91770-0579)
PHONE..................................626 288-8530
Gregory C Warde, *Ch Bd*
William E Wilbanks, *
Randall W Dale, *
Jerry L Olmscheid, *
Ken West, *
EMP: 150 **EST:** 1947
SQ FT: 15,000
SALES (est): 64.03MM
SALES (corp-wide): 64.03MM **Privately Held**
Web: www.irishteam.com
SIC: 1623 Telephone and communication line construction
PA: Manhattan Capital Corporation
2641 River Ave
Rosemead CA
626 288-8530

(P-1222)
JR FILANC CNSTR CO INC (PA)
740 N Andreasen Dr (92029-1414)
PHONE..................................760 941-7130
Mark E Filanc, *CEO*
Vincent L Diaz, *
Linda Stangel, *
EMP: 100 **EST:** 1952
SQ FT: 13,200
SALES (est): 89.94MM
SALES (corp-wide): 89.94MM **Privately Held**
Web: www.filanc.com
SIC: 1623 1629 Pumping station construction; Waste water and sewage treatment plant construction

(P-1223)
K S FABRICATION & MACHINE INC
Also Called: KS Fabrication & Machine
6205 District Blvd (93313-2141)
P.O. Box 41630 (93384-1630)
PHONE..................................661 617-1700
Kevin S Small, *CEO*
Becky Scott, *
EMP: 150 **EST:** 1999
SALES (est): 24.06MM **Privately Held**
Web: www.ksilp.com
SIC: 1623 Water, sewer, and utility lines

(P-1224)
K T A CONSTRUCTION INC
1920 Cordell Ct Ste 105 (92020-0900)
PHONE..................................619 562-9464
Paul Michael Henderson, *CEO*
Mike Henderson, *
Marilyn L Henderson, *
EMP: 62 **EST:** 1979
SQ FT: 5,200
SALES (est): 13.44MM **Privately Held**
Web: www.ktaconstruction.com
SIC: 1623 Sewer line construction

(P-1225)
K W EMERSON INC
413 W Saint Charles St (95249-9618)
P.O. Box 549 (95249-0549)
PHONE..................................209 754-3839
Rusti Emerson, *Pr*
E Jean Emerson, *
Dan Emerson, *
Alison Engell, *
Rusti Emerson, *Ofcr*
EMP: 63 **EST:** 1961
SQ FT: 2,550
SALES (est): 38.98MM **Privately Held**
Web: www.kwemerson.com
SIC: 1623 1794 Underground utilities contractor; Excavation and grading, building construction

(P-1226)
KANA PIPELINE INC
12620 Magnolia Ave (92503-4636)
PHONE..................................714 986-1400
Dan Locke, *Pr*
EMP: 100 **EST:** 1984
SQ FT: 55,000
SALES (est): 31.69MM **Privately Held**
Web: www.kanapipeline.com
SIC: 1623 1629 Water main construction; Drainage system construction

(P-1227)
KEN SMALL CONSTRUCTION INC
6205 District Blvd (93313-2141)
PHONE..................................661 617-1700
EMP: 67 **EST:** 1968
SALES (est): 9.7MM **Privately Held**
SIC: 1623 Pipeline construction, nsk

(P-1228)
KS INDUSTRIES LP (PA)
Also Called: K S I
6205 District Blvd (93313-2141)
P.O. Box 41630 (93384-1630)
PHONE..................................661 617-1700
Kevin Small, *Pt*
EMP: 2000 **EST:** 1979
SQ FT: 20,000
SALES (est): 490.64MM
SALES (corp-wide): 490.64MM **Privately Held**
Web: www.ksilp.com
SIC: 1623 Water, sewer, and utility lines

(P-1229)
LADWP METRO WATER YARD
Also Called: Engineering Department
433 E Temple St (90012-4035)
PHONE..................................213 367-6665
Malad Tagave, *Manager*
EMP: 68
SALES (est): 3.24MM **Privately Held**
SIC: 1623 Water main construction
PA: L.A.D.W.P. Metro Water Yard
433 E Temple St
Los Angeles CA
213 367-6665

(P-1230)
LEWIS AND TIBBITTS INC
1470 Industrial Ave (95112-2714)
PHONE..................................408 925-0220
EMP: 104 **EST:** 1973
SALES (est): 40.19MM **Privately Held**
Web: www.diglt.com
SIC: 1623 Pipeline construction, nsk

(P-1231)
LINKUS ENTERPRISES LLC
Also Called: Honeywell Authorized Dealer
5595 W San Madele Ave (93722-5068)
PHONE..................................559 256-6600
Horacio Guzman, *CEO*
EMP: 301
Web: www.linkuscorp.com
SIC: 1623 Telephone and communication line construction
PA: Linkus Enterprises, Llc
18631 Lloyd Ln
Anderson CA

(P-1232)
LOMBARDY HOLDINGS INC (PA)
151 Kalmus Dr Ste F6 (92626-5965)
P.O. Box 6019 (92860-8034)
PHONE..................................951 808-4550
Marc Laulhere, *CEO*
Pam Laulhere, *
EMP: 200 **EST:** 1940
SQ FT: 80,000
SALES (est): 182.13MM
SALES (corp-wide): 182.13MM **Privately Held**
SIC: 1623 5211 Telephone and communication line construction; Electrical construction materials

(P-1233)
M C C EQUIPMENT RENTALS INC
Also Called: McC Pipeline
32389 Dunlap Blvd (92399-1724)
P.O. Box 1730 (92399-1439)
PHONE..................................909 795-9300
Kenneth Paul Munoz, *Pr*
EMP: 61 **EST:** 2003
SQ FT: 1,300
SALES (est): 9.6MM **Privately Held**
Web: www.mccpipeline.com
SIC: 1623 Pipeline construction, nsk

(P-1234)
MANUEL BROS INC
Also Called: Renaissance Construction
908 Taylorville Rd Ste 104 (95949-9632)
P.O. Box 995 (95945-0995)
PHONE..................................530 272-4213
Gary Smith, *Pr*
Robert Moen, *
EMP: 94 **EST:** 1974
SQ FT: 3,000
SALES (est): 5.93MM
SALES (corp-wide): 17.07B **Publicly Held**
SIC: 1623 Telephone and communication line construction
PA: Quanta Services, Inc.
2727 North Loop W Ste 100
Houston TX
713 629-7600

(P-1235)
MCGUIRE AND HESTER (PA)
2810 Harbor Bay Pkwy (94502-3040)
PHONE..................................510 632-7676
Michael R Hester, *Pr*
Brock N Grunt, *
Bruce Daseking, *
Kevin Hester, *
Jeff Hoebel, *
EMP: 298 **EST:** 1926
SQ FT: 22,000
SALES (est): 66.01K
SALES (corp-wide): 66.01K **Privately Held**
Web: www.mcguireandhester.com

PRODUCTS & SERVICES SECTION
1623 - Water, Sewer, And Utility Lines (P-1257)

SIC: **1623** 7353 1611 0782 Underground utilities contractor; Heavy construction equipment rental; General contractor, highway and street construction; Garden planting services

(P-1236)
METRICOM NETWORKS
290 W Orange Show Rd Ste 101 (92408-3345)
PHONE..................................480 522-0700
Brandon Milloy, *CEO*
Brandon Milloy, *Pr*
EMP: 62 **EST:** 2019
SALES (est): 7.34MM **Privately Held**
Web: www.metricomnetworks.com
SIC: 1623 Transmitting tower (telecommunication) construction

(P-1237)
MICHELS PACIFIC ENERGY INC
2200 Laurelwood Rd (95054-1515)
PHONE..................................920 924-8725
Robert Gitter, *Contrlr*
EMP: 100 **EST:** 2019
SALES (est): 8.32MM **Privately Held**
Web: www.michels.us
SIC: 1623 Pipeline construction, nsk

(P-1238)
MLADEN BUNTICH CNSTR CO INC
1500 W 9th St (91786-5636)
PHONE..................................909 920-9977
Mladen Buntich Junior, *Ch Bd*
Lee Roesner, *
Scott Peterson, *
▲ **EMP:** 60 **EST:** 1975
SQ FT: 4,000
SALES (est): 23.16MM **Privately Held**
Web: www.buntich.com
SIC: 1623 8711 8322 Sewer line construction; Engineering services; Individual and family services

(P-1239)
MP NEXLEVEL CALIFORNIA INC
266 Industrial Rd Ste B (94070-6236)
PHONE..................................650 486-1359
Robbi Pribyl, *Pr*
EMP: 445 **EST:** 2007
SALES (est): 4.58MM
SALES (corp-wide): 6.56B **Publicly Held**
Web: www.mpnexlevel.com
SIC: 1623 Gas main construction
HQ: Mp Nexlevel, Llc
  500 County Road 37
  Maple Lake MN
  320 963-2400

(P-1240)
MURRIETA DEVELOPMENT COMPANY INC
42540 Rio Nedo (92590-3727)
PHONE..................................951 719-1680
EMP: 126 **EST:** 1981
SALES (est): 24.35MM **Privately Held**
Web: www.murrietadevelopment.com
SIC: 1623 Water, sewer, and utility lines

(P-1241)
MYERS & SONS CONSTRUCTION LLC
45 Morrison Ave (95838-3201)
PHONE..................................916 283-9950
Clinton C Myers, *Prin*
Marlena Stockton, *
EMP: 149 **EST:** 2017
SALES (est): 154.7MM **Publicly Held**
Web: www.myers-sons.com
SIC: 1623 1622 Water, sewer, and utility lines ; Bridge, tunnel, and elevated highway construction
PA: Sterling Infrastructure, Inc.
  1800 Hughes Landing Blvd
  The Woodlands TX

(P-1242)
NOR-CAL PIPELINE SERVICES
983 Reserve Dr (95678-1340)
PHONE..................................916 442-5400
EMP: 70 **EST:** 2009
SALES (est): 21.19MM **Privately Held**
Web: www.norcalpipe.com
SIC: 1623 Pipeline construction, nsk

(P-1243)
NOVA GROUP INC (HQ)
185 Devlin Rd (94558-6255)
P.O. Box 4050 (94558-0450)
PHONE..................................707 265-1100
Ronald M Fedrick, *Ch Bd*
Scott R Victor, *
Carole Bionda, *
Chris Mathies, *
Walter Birdsall, *Finance*
◆ **EMP:** 88 **EST:** 1957
SQ FT: 15,000
SALES (est): 103.67MM
SALES (corp-wide): 17.07B **Publicly Held**
Web: www.novagrp.com
SIC: 1623 Underground utilities contractor
PA: Quanta Services, Inc.
  2727 North Loop W Ste 100
  Houston TX
  713 629-7600

(P-1244)
NOVA/TIC GVRNMENT PRJCTS A JIN
185 Devlin Rd (94558-6255)
P.O. Box 4050 (94558-0450)
PHONE..................................707 257-3200
Ronald M Fedrick, *Pr*
Scott R Victor, *Pr*
Chris Mathies, *VP*
Carole L Bionda, *VP*
Walter M Birdsall, *VP*
◆ **EMP:** 150 **EST:** 1999
SQ FT: 15,000
SALES (est): 15.24MM **Privately Held**
Web: www.novagrp.com
SIC: 1623 Water, sewer, and utility lines

(P-1245)
NRCI TELECOM
265 Applegate School Rd (95703-9768)
PHONE..................................530 878-3970
EMP: 96
SALES (corp-wide): 3.46MM **Privately Held**
Web: www.nrcitelecom.com
SIC: 1623 Water, sewer, and utility lines
PA: Nrci Telecom
  18960 Moonlight Ct
  Meadow Vista CA
  530 878-3970

(P-1246)
NTS INC
Also Called: Newberry Technical Services
8200 Stockdale Hwy Ste M10306 (93311-1029)
PHONE..................................661 588-8514
EMP: 425
Web: www.ntsinc.com
SIC: 1623 1541 1771 Pipeline construction, nsk; Industrial buildings, new construction, nec; Concrete work

(P-1247)
ORION CONSTRUCTION CORPORATION
2185 La Mirada Dr (92081-8830)
PHONE..................................760 597-9660
Richard Dowsing, *CEO*
Mark Dowsing, *
EMP: 80 **EST:** 1987
SQ FT: 7,000
SALES (est): 29.24MM **Privately Held**
Web: www.orionconstruction.com
SIC: 1623 1629 1542 Water, sewer, and utility lines; Industrial plant construction; Nonresidential construction, nec

(P-1248)
PACIFIC W SPACE CMMNCTIONS INC
Also Called: P W C
900 W Gladstone St (91773-1734)
P.O. Box 1857 (91740-1857)
PHONE..................................909 592-4321
Sheryl F Patton, *CEO*
Rich Patton, *
Betty Fonteno, *
Joanna Patton, *
EMP: 69 **EST:** 1981
SQ FT: 2,000
SALES (est): 19.95MM **Privately Held**
Web: www.pwcinc.com
SIC: 1623 Communication line and transmission tower construction

(P-1249)
PAULUS ENGINEERING INC
2871 E Coronado St (92806-2504)
PHONE..................................714 632-3322
Ronald Paulus, *Pr*
Jason Paulus, *
EMP: 60 **EST:** 1996
SQ FT: 40,000
SALES (est): 11.57MM **Privately Held**
Web: www.paulusengineering.com
SIC: 1623 Sewer line construction

(P-1250)
PRECISION PIPELINE LLC
10400 Trademark St (91730-5826)
PHONE..................................909 229-6858
EMP: 441
SALES (corp-wide): 9.78B **Publicly Held**
Web: www.precisionpipelinellc.com
SIC: 1623 Pipeline construction, nsk
HQ: Precision Pipeline Llc
  3314 56th St
  Eau Claire WI
  715 874-4510

(P-1251)
PRESTON PIPELINES INC (PA)
Also Called: Preston Pipelines
133 Botehlo Ave (95035-5325)
PHONE..................................408 262-1418
Michael D Preston, *Pr*
Dave Heslop, *
Gary Menges, *
Rich Lewis, *
Ron Bianchini, *
EMP: 150 **EST:** 1970
SQ FT: 12,000
SALES (est): 96.16MM
SALES (corp-wide): 96.16MM **Privately Held**
Web: www.prestonco.com
SIC: 1623 Pipeline construction, nsk

(P-1252)
PRIMORIS SERVICES CORPORATION
26000 Commercentre Dr (92630-8816)
PHONE..................................949 598-9242
Peter J Moerbeek, *Prin*
EMP: 123
Web: www.primoriscorp.com
SIC: 1623 Pipeline construction, nsk
PA: Primoris Services Corporation
  2300 N Field St Ste 1900
  Dallas TX

(P-1253)
QUAGGA CORPORATION
90 Blue Ravine Rd 200a (95630-4715)
PHONE..................................916 357-5129
EMP: 75
SIC: 1623 5065 Communication line and transmission tower construction; Communication equipment

(P-1254)
QUALITY TELECOM CONS INC (PA)
Also Called: Quality Techniques Engrg Cnstr
3740 Cincinnati Ave (95765-1204)
P.O. Box 807 (95650-0807)
PHONE..................................916 315-0500
Scott Duncan, *Pr*
Jacob Duncan, *
Candice Northam, *
Osh Duncan, *
EMP: 89 **EST:** 2001
SALES (est): 29.77MM
SALES (corp-wide): 29.77MM **Privately Held**
Web: www.qtcinc.com
SIC: 1623 1731 4899 8748 Communication line and transmission tower construction; Communications specialization; Communications signal enhancement network services; Telecommunications consultant

(P-1255)
RANGER PIPELINES INCORPORATED
1790 Yosemite Ave (94124-2622)
P.O. Box 24109 (94124-0109)
PHONE..................................415 822-3700
Thomas Hunt, *Pr*
Peter Cuddihy, *
Mary Shea-hunt, *Sec*
EMP: 101 **EST:** 1982
SQ FT: 20,000
SALES (est): 35.88MM **Privately Held**
Web: www.rangerpipelines.com
SIC: 1623 Pipeline construction, nsk

(P-1256)
S C VALLEY ENGINEERING INC
656 Front St (92020-4232)
PHONE..................................619 444-2366
Samuel H Wathen, *Pr*
EMP: 60 **EST:** 1982
SALES (est): 14.04MM **Privately Held**
Web: www.scvalleyinc.com
SIC: 1623 7359 Underground utilities contractor; Equipment rental and leasing, nec

(P-1257)
S E C C CORPORATION (PA)
502 N Sheridan St (92878-4022)
PHONE..................................909 393-5419
Michael C Aranda, *Pr*
Mary Aranda, *
EMP: 75 **EST:** 1995
SALES (est): 42.57MM **Privately Held**
Web: www.secc-corp.com
SIC: 1623 Telephone and communication line construction

1623 - Water, Sewer, And Utility Lines (P-1258)

PRODUCTS & SERVICES SECTION

(P-1258)
S E PIPE LINE CONSTRUCTION CO
11832 Bloomfield Ave (90670-4610)
PHONE.....................562 868-9771
Charles Rikel, *Pr*
James Doulames, *VP*
Thomas Tustin, *Sec*
EMP: 100 **EST:** 1946
SQ FT: 5,000
SALES (est): 23.83MM **Privately Held**
Web: www.sepipeline.com
SIC: 1623 Gas main construction

(P-1259)
SCHILLING PARADISE CORP
697 Greenfield Dr (92021-2983)
PHONE.....................619 449-4141
EMP: 175 **EST:** 2009
SALES (est): 28.19MM **Privately Held**
Web: www.schillingcorp.com
SIC: 1623 1731 Underground utilities contractor; General electrical contractor

(P-1260)
SCW CONTRACTING CORPORATION
2525 Old Highway 395 (92028-8794)
PHONE.....................760 728-1308
Jeffrey Dean Scrape, *CEO*
Susanne Scrape, *
EMP: 70 **EST:** 1980
SQ FT: 3,000
SALES (est): 15.39MM **Privately Held**
Web: www.scwcompanies.com
SIC: 1623 1791 3449 Underground utilities contractor; Structural steel erection; Miscellaneous metalwork

(P-1261)
SEMPRA LNG INTERNATIONAL LLC
488 8th Ave (92101-7123)
PHONE.....................661 399-2077
Lisa Glatch, *Pr*
EMP: 82 **EST:** 2015
SALES (est): 4.49MM **Privately Held**
Web: www.sempra.com
SIC: 1623 4922 Natural gas compressor station construction; Pipelines, natural gas

(P-1262)
SHOFFEITT PIPELINE INC
15801 Rockfield Blvd Ste L (92618-2869)
PHONE.....................949 581-1600
Kathy Shoffeitt, *Pr*
John Shoffeitt, *
John Shoffeitt Junior, *Sec*
EMP: 80 **EST:** 2013
SQ FT: 3,200
SALES (est): 9.58MM **Privately Held**
Web: www.shoffeittpipeline.com
SIC: 1623 Underground utilities contractor

(P-1263)
SOLCOM INC
Also Called: Solcom Communications Inc
24801 Huntwood Ave (94544-1813)
PHONE.....................510 940-2490
Tony Mcmenamin, *Pr*
EMP: 500 **EST:** 2002
SALES (est): 21.97MM **Privately Held**
Web: www.solcom.us
SIC: 1623 Telephone and communication line construction

(P-1264)
SOLCOM GROUP INC
28835 Mack St (94545-1215)
PHONE.....................510 940-2490
▲ **EMP:** 60
SIC: 1623 Telephone and communication line construction

(P-1265)
SOLEX CONTRACTING INC
42146 Remington Ave (92590-2547)
PHONE.....................951 308-1706
Jerry Allen, *Pr*
EMP: 110 **EST:** 2004
SQ FT: 12,000
SALES (est): 40.3MM **Privately Held**
Web: www.solexcontracting.com
SIC: 1623 1542 1541 Communication line and transmission tower construction; Commercial and office building, new construction; Renovation, remodeling and repairs; industrial buildings

(P-1266)
SPIESS CONSTRUCTION CO INC
Also Called: Scci
201 S Broadway St Ste 140 (93455-4611)
P.O. Box 2849 (93457-2849)
PHONE.....................805 937-5859
Scott A Coleman, *Pr*
Barry L Matchett, *
Frank L Forthun, *
EMP: 60 **EST:** 1977
SALES (est): 26.11MM **Privately Held**
Web: www.weldedsteeltanks.com
SIC: 1623 Sewer line construction

(P-1267)
SPINIELLO COMPANIES
2650 Pomona Blvd (91768-3220)
PHONE.....................909 629-1000
Priscilla Moyer, *Mgr*
EMP: 152
SALES (corp-wide): 92.17MM **Privately Held**
Web: www.spiniello.com
SIC: 1623 Underground utilities contractor
PA: Spiniello Companies
354 Eisenhower Pkwy # 1200
Livingston NJ
973 808-8383

(P-1268)
SRD ENGINEERING INC
5300 Highland Ct (92886-4000)
P.O. Box 517 (59061-0517)
PHONE.....................714 630-2480
Deborah Denton, *CEO*
EMP: 65 **EST:** 1991
SALES (est): 9.41MM **Privately Held**
SIC: 1623 Water and sewer line construction

(P-1269)
SUKUT CONSTRUCTION LLC
4010 W Chandler Ave (92704-5202)
PHONE.....................714 540-5351
Michael Crawford, *Prin*
Paul Kuliev, *
EMP: 99 **EST:** 2014
SALES (est): 20.61MM **Privately Held**
Web: www.sukut.com
SIC: 1623 1629 1611 Water, sewer, and utility lines; Earthmoving contractor; Grading

(P-1270)
T C CONSTRUCTION COMPANY INC
Also Called: Tc Construction Company
10540 Prospect Ave (92071-4529)
PHONE.....................619 448-4560
Terry W Cameron, *CEO*
Austin Cameron, *
Derek Franken, *
Jack Gieffels, *
Darren Tharp, *
EMP: 230 **EST:** 1976
SQ FT: 16,000
SALES (est): 62.22MM **Privately Held**
Web: www.tcincsd.com
SIC: 1623 1611 Underground utilities contractor; Highway and street paving contractor

(P-1271)
THE ORTIZ CORPORATION
2000 Mckinley Ave (91950-5427)
PHONE.....................619 434-7925
EMP: 88 **EST:** 2021
SALES (est): 13.24MM **Privately Held**
Web: www.ortizcorporation.com
SIC: 1623 Underground utilities contractor

(P-1272)
TURN AROUND COMMUNICATIONS INC
100 N Barranca St Ste 260 (91791-1637)
P.O. Box 6121 (91734-2121)
PHONE.....................626 443-2400
Sayeid Kouhkan, *Pr*
EMP: 170 **EST:** 2002
SALES (est): 25.77MM **Privately Held**
Web: www.turnaroundcommunications.net
SIC: 1623 Telephone and communication line construction

(P-1273)
UTILITY PARTNERS AMERICA LLC
508 Enos Ln (93314-9536)
PHONE.....................864 269-2302
David Alsbrookks, *Mgr*
EMP: 62
Web: www.utilitypartners.com
SIC: 1623 Pipe laying construction
PA: Utility Partners Of America, Llc
7600 Pelham Rd Ste B
Greenville SC

(P-1274)
VADNAIS TRENCHLESS SVCS INC
11858 Bernardo Plaza Ct Ste 100 (92128-2440)
PHONE.....................858 550-1460
Paul Vadnais, *CEO*
Jeff Anderson, *
Jesse Mangan, *
▲ **EMP:** 100 **EST:** 1964
SALES (est): 9.26MM **Privately Held**
Web: www.vadnaiscorp.com
SIC: 1623 Sewer line construction

(P-1275)
VALVERDE CONSTRUCTION INC
10936 Shoemaker Ave (90670-4533)
P.O. Box 3223 (90670-0223)
PHONE.....................562 906-1826
Joe A Valverde, *Pr*
Joe A Valverde, *Pr*
Edward Valverde, *
Rose Valverde, *
Christopher Valverde, *
EMP: 135 **EST:** 1972
SQ FT: 9,000
SALES (est): 25.68MM **Privately Held**
Web: valverde.webflow.io

SIC: 1623 Water main construction

(P-1276)
VCI CONSTRUCTION LLC (HQ)
1921 W 11th St Ste A (91786-3508)
PHONE.....................909 946-0905
John Xanthos, *Pr*
Logan Teal, *
Vic Marovish, *
EMP: 100 **EST:** 1998
SQ FT: 29,500
SALES (est): 95.76MM
SALES (corp-wide): 3.81B **Publicly Held**
Web: www.vcicom.com
SIC: 1623 Underground utilities contractor
PA: Dycom Industries, Inc.
11780 Us Highway 1 # 600
Palm Beach Gardens FL
561 627-7171

(P-1277)
W A RASIC CNSTR CO INC (PA)
4150 Long Beach Blvd (90807-2650)
PHONE.....................562 928-6111
Peter L Rasic, *CEO*
EMP: 147 **EST:** 1978
SQ FT: 8,500
SALES (est): 121.56MM
SALES (corp-wide): 121.56MM **Privately Held**
Web: www.warasic.com
SIC: 1623 Sewer line construction

(P-1278)
W M LYLES CO
42142 Roick Dr (92590-3695)
PHONE.....................951 296-2354
EMP: 113
SALES (corp-wide): 17.85MM **Privately Held**
Web: www.wmlyesco.com
SIC: 1623 Water, sewer, and utility lines
HQ: W. M. Lyles Co.
525 W Alluvial Ave
Fresno CA
559 441-1900

(P-1279)
W M LYLES CO
3925 Progress Dr (95765-1330)
P.O. Box 4378 (93744-4378)
PHONE.....................916 375-1833
John Lunsford, *Mgr*
EMP: 113
SALES (corp-wide): 17.85MM **Privately Held**
Web: www.wmlyesco.com
SIC: 1623 Pipeline construction, nsk
HQ: W. M. Lyles Co.
525 W Alluvial Ave
Fresno CA
559 441-1900

(P-1280)
WATKINS CONSTRUCTION CO INC
Also Called: Johnston Vacuum Tank Service
112 E Cedar St (93268-9708)
P.O. Box 243 (93268-0243)
PHONE.....................661 763-5395
Eddie Watkins, *Pr*
Eddie Watkins Senior, *Pr*
Eddie Watkins Junior, *Pr*
EMP: 60 **EST:** 1967
SQ FT: 4,800
SALES (est): 9.28MM **Privately Held**
Web: www.wci-jvt.com
SIC: 1623 Oil and gas pipeline construction

PRODUCTS & SERVICES SECTION

1629 - Heavy Construction, Nec (P-1302)

(P-1281)
WEST TECH CONTRACTING INC
568 N Tulip St (92025-2533)
PHONE......................760 233-2570
EMP: 70 EST: 1991
SALES (est): 15.13MM **Privately Held**
Web: www.west-techcontracting.com
SIC: **1623** Oil and gas pipeline construction

(P-1282)
WEST VALLEY CNSTR CO INC (PA)
Also Called: West Valley Construction
603 Campbell Technology Pkwy (95008-5086)
PHONE......................408 371-5510
Kevin Kelly, *CEO*
Jeff Azevedo, *
Jeff Boss, *
Jimm Vosburgh, *
David Barnes, *
EMP: 150 EST: 1958
SQ FT: 9,000
SALES (est): 106.92MM
SALES (corp-wide): 106.92MM **Privately Held**
Web: www.westvalleyconstruction.com
SIC: **1623** Water main construction

(P-1283)
ZIM INDUSTRIES INC (PA)
Also Called: Bakersfield Well & Pump Co
4532 E Jefferson Ave (93725-9807)
PHONE......................559 834-1551
EMP: 70 EST: 1979
SALES (est): 40.49MM
SALES (corp-wide): 40.49MM **Privately Held**
Web: www.zimindustries.com
SIC: **1623** 5084 1781 1611 Water and sewer line construction; Pumps and pumping equipment, nec; Water well drilling; Concrete construction: roads, highways, sidewalks, etc.

1629 Heavy Construction, Nec

(P-1284)
AMERICAN CIVIL CONSTRS LLC
3701 Mallard Dr (94510-1246)
PHONE......................707 746-8028
Pete Wells, *Mgr*
EMP: 60
SALES (corp-wide): 9.78B **Publicly Held**
SIC: **1629** 0783 0181 Land preparation construction; Spraying services, ornamental bush; Sod farms
HQ: American Civil Constructors Llc
4901 S Windermere St
Littleton CO
303 795-2582

(P-1285)
ANDERSON PCF ENGRG CNSTR INC
1370 Norman Ave (95054-2056)
PHONE......................408 970-9900
Peter E Anderson, *CEO*
Matthew Mirenda, *
Ann Anderson, *
EMP: 100 EST: 1966
SQ FT: 3,000
SALES (est): 39.82MM **Privately Held**
Web: www.andpac.com
SIC: **1629** 1623 Dams, waterways, docks, and other marine construction; Pumping station construction

(P-1286)
AUBURN CONSTRUCTORS LLC
730 W Stadium Ln (95834-1130)
PHONE......................916 924-0344
Dean Bailey, *Pr*
Bill Franceschini, *
Kevin Couper, *
EMP: 80 EST: 1990
SQ FT: 5,500
SALES (est): 24.58MM **Privately Held**
Web: www.auburnconstructors.com
SIC: **1629** Industrial plant construction

(P-1287)
BARNARD BESSAC JOINT VENTURE
395 Shoreway Rd (94065-1601)
PHONE......................650 212-8957
EMP: 100 EST: 2018
SALES (est): 5.29MM **Privately Held**
SIC: **1629** Industrial plant construction

(P-1288)
BELECTRIC INC
951 Mariners Island Blvd Ste 300 (94404-1560)
PHONE......................510 896-3940
◆ EMP: 64
Web: www.belectric.com
SIC: **1629** Power plant construction

(P-1289)
BEMUS LANDSCAPE INC
951 Calle Negocio Ste D (92673-6202)
P.O. Box 74268 (92673-0143)
PHONE......................714 557-7910
William Howard Bemus, *Pr*
Jonathon Parry, *
Martine Bemus, *
EMP: 300 EST: 1973
SQ FT: 7,000
SALES (est): 47.49MM **Privately Held**
Web: www.bemus.com
SIC: **1629** 0782 Drainage system construction; Landscape contractors

(P-1290)
BRIGHTVIEW COMPANIES LLC (DH)
27001 Agoura Rd Ste 350 (91301-5112)
PHONE......................818 223-8500
John Feenan, *CEO*
Jeff Herold, *
Thomas C Donnelly, *
◆ EMP: 175 EST: 2006
SALES (est): 2.2B
SALES (corp-wide): 2.77B **Publicly Held**
Web: www.brightview.com
SIC: **1629** 0782 0781 Golf course construction; Lawn and garden services; Landscape services
HQ: Brightview Landscapes, Llc
980 Jolly Rd Ste 300
Blue Bell PA
484 567-7204

(P-1291)
CAL WEST UNDERGROUND INC
951 6th St (92860-1442)
PHONE......................951 371-6775
Jeffrey M Abernathy, *Pr*
EMP: 63 EST: 1999
SQ FT: 1,200
SALES (est): 14.86MM **Privately Held**
SIC: **1629** Trenching contractor

(P-1292)
CATTRAC CONSTRUCTION INC
Also Called: Cattrac
15030 Slover Ave (92337-7237)
PHONE......................909 355-1146
Stephanie A Dineen Jacinto, *CEO*
Greg Dineen, *
EMP: 60 EST: 1971
SQ FT: 5,000
SALES (est): 19.98MM **Privately Held**
Web: www.cattrac.com
SIC: **1629** 7353 4213 Earthmoving contractor; Earth moving equipment, rental or leasing; Trucking, except local

(P-1293)
CLARK BROS INC
745 Broadway St (93721-2807)
PHONE......................209 392-6144
Lawrence A Clark, *CEO*
Sarah Woolf, *
Adrew Clark, *Stockholder* *
Allan W Clark, *
EMP: 100 EST: 1949
SQ FT: 5,000
SALES (est): 50.06MM **Privately Held**
Web: www.clarkbrosinc.com
SIC: **1629** 3589 Trenching contractor; Water treatment equipment, industrial

(P-1294)
CURTIN MARITIME CORP
725 Pier T Ave (90802-6234)
P.O. Box 2531 (90801-2531)
PHONE......................562 983-7257
Martin Jeremiah Curtin Junior, *CEO*
Kelly Curtin, *
EMP: 326 EST: 1997
SQ FT: 65,340
SALES (est): 91.59MM **Privately Held**
Web: www.curtinmaritime.com
SIC: **1629** 4492 Marine construction; Tugboat service

(P-1295)
DILLINGHAM CONSTRUCTION NA
1020 Serpentine Ln Ste 110 (94566-4758)
P.O. Box 1089 (94566-1089)
PHONE......................925 249-8850
John Capener, *Pr*
EMP: 1677 EST: 1987
SQ FT: 70,000
SALES (est): 38MM **Privately Held**
SIC: **1629** 1622 1542 1522 Waste water and sewage treatment plant construction; Tunnel construction; Commercial and office building, new construction; Hotel/motel, new construction

(P-1296)
DRILL TECH DRILLING & SHORING INC (PA)
2200 Wymore Way (94509-8548)
PHONE......................925 978-2060
▲ EMP: 85 EST: 1994
SALES (est): 113.65MM **Privately Held**
Web: www.drilltechdrilling.com
SIC: **1629** Earthmoving contractor

(P-1297)
DUTRA DREDGING COMPANY (HQ)
2350 Kerner Blvd Ste 200 (94901-5595)
PHONE......................415 721-2131
EMP: 60 EST: 1904
SQ FT: 2,000
SALES (est): 20.33MM
SALES (corp-wide): 191.66MM **Privately Held**
Web: www.dutragroup.com
SIC: **1629** Marine construction
PA: The Dutra Group
2350 Kerner Blvd Ste 200
San Rafael CA
415 258-6876

(P-1298)
DUTRA GROUP (PA)
Also Called: Dutra Group, The
2350 Kerner Blvd Ste 200 (94901-5595)
PHONE......................415 258-6876
Harry K Stewart, *CEO*
Bill T Dutra, *
James Hagood, *
▲ EMP: 100 EST: 1973
SQ FT: 22,000
SALES (est): 191.66MM
SALES (corp-wide): 191.66MM **Privately Held**
Web: www.dutragroup.com
SIC: **1629** 8711 1429 Marine construction; Civil engineering; Igneus rock, crushed and broken-quarrying

(P-1299)
ENVIROGENICS SYSTEMS COMPANY
9255 Telstar Ave (91731-2845)
PHONE......................818 573-9220
Doctor Fadi Abbash, *Pr*
R Kadaj, *
EMP: 100 EST: 1967
SQ FT: 91,000
SALES (est): 6.48MM **Privately Held**
SIC: **1629** Industrial plant construction

(P-1300)
FORD CONSTRUCTION COMPANY INC
300 W Pine St (95240-2022)
PHONE......................209 333-1116
Richard Piombo, *Sec*
Nicholas B Jones, *
EMP: 100 EST: 1979
SQ FT: 8,500
SALES (est): 26.77MM **Privately Held**
Web: www.ford-construction.com
SIC: **1629** 1623 Dam construction; Water and sewer line construction

(P-1301)
FOUNDATION CONSTRUCTORS INC (PA)
81 Big Break Rd (94561-3081)
P.O. Box 97 (94561-0097)
PHONE......................925 754-6633
TOLL FREE: 800
Dermot Fallon, *CEO*
Pete Brandl, *
Gary Prlichek, *
Earl Robbins, *
Don Hilton, *
▲ EMP: 100 EST: 1971
SQ FT: 6,000
SALES (est): 49.44MM
SALES (corp-wide): 49.44MM **Privately Held**
Web: www.foundationpiledriving.com
SIC: **1629** Marine construction

(P-1302)
FOUNDATION PILE INC
8375 Almeria Ave (92335-3283)
P.O. Box 97 (94561-0097)
PHONE......................909 350-1584
Derek Halecky, *CEO*
Peter Brandl, *
Dermot Fallon, *
Earl Robbins, *

1629 - Heavy Construction, Nec (P-1303)

Nikki Sjoblom, *
EMP: 97 **EST:** 1978
SALES (est): 15.7MM
SALES (corp-wide): 49.44MM **Privately Held**
Web: www.foundationpiledriving.com
SIC: 1629 1794 Pile driving contractor; Excavation and grading, building construction
PA: Foundation Constructors, Inc.
81 Big Break Rd
Oakley CA
925 754-6633

(P-1303)
FRONTIER-KEMPER CONSTRUCTORS INC (HQ)
Also Called: Fkc-Lake Shore
15900 Olden St (91342-1051)
P.O. Box 6690 (47719-0690)
PHONE.................................818 362-2062
▲ **EMP:** 70 **EST:** 1972
SALES (est): 107.51MM
SALES (corp-wide): 3.79B **Publicly Held**
Web: www.frontierkemper.com
SIC: 1629 Earthmoving contractor
PA: Tutor Perini Corporation
15901 Olden St
Rancho Cascades CA
818 362-8391

(P-1304)
GHILOTTI CONSTRUCTION CO INC (PA)
Also Called: Gcc
246 Ghillotti Ave (95407-8152)
PHONE.................................707 585-1221
Richard W Ghilotti, *CEO*
EMP: 132 **EST:** 1992
SQ FT: 9,000
SALES (est): 95.5MM **Privately Held**
Web: www.ghilotti.com
SIC: 1629 Land preparation construction

(P-1305)
HELLAS CONSTRUCTION INC
5135 Avenida Encinas Ste A (92008-4341)
PHONE.................................760 891-8090
James Towsley, *Owner*
EMP: 387
Web: www.hellasconstruction.com
SIC: 1629 Athletic and recreation facilities construction
HQ: Hellas Construction, Inc.
12000 W Parmer Ln
Cedar Park TX
512 250-2910

(P-1306)
HERZOG CONTRACTING CORP
3760 Kilroy Airport Way Ste 120 (90806-2455)
P.O. Box 1089 (64502-1089)
PHONE.................................562 595-7414
EMP: 88
SALES (corp-wide): 490.1MM **Privately Held**
Web: www.herzog.com
SIC: 1629 1611 4953 Railroad and railway roadbed construction; Highway and street paving contractor; Sanitary landfill operation
HQ: Herzog Contracting Corp.
600 S Riverside Rd
Saint Joseph MO
816 233-9001

(P-1307)
IRWIN INDUSTRIES INC
2301 Rosecrans Ave Ste 3185
(90245-4918)
P.O. Box 8678 (25303-0678)
PHONE.................................704 457-5117
EMP: 710
SIC: 1629 1731 1796 7353 Power plant construction; Electric power systems contractors; Power generating equipment installation; Heavy construction equipment rental

(P-1308)
JILK HEAVY CONSTRUCTION INC
500 S Kraemer Blvd Ste 380 (92821-6779)
PHONE.................................310 830-6323
EMP: 60 **EST:** 1995
SALES (est): 21.91MM **Privately Held**
Web: www.jilkhc.com
SIC: 1629 Marine construction

(P-1309)
MANSON CONSTRUCTION CO
340 Golden Shore Ste 310 (90802-4229)
PHONE.................................562 983-2340
Tim Henson, *Brnch Mgr*
EMP: 70
SALES (corp-wide): 487.77MM **Privately Held**
Web: www.mansonconstruction.com
SIC: 1629 Marine construction
HQ: Manson Construction Co.
5209 E Marginal Way S
Seattle WA
206 762-0850

(P-1310)
MANSON CONSTRUCTION CO
1401 Marina Way S # F (94804-3723)
PHONE.................................510 232-6319
Charlie Gibson, *VP*
EMP: 70
SQ FT: 1,500
SALES (corp-wide): 487.77MM **Privately Held**
Web: www.mansonconstruction.com
SIC: 1629 Marine construction
HQ: Manson Construction Co.
5209 E Marginal Way S
Seattle WA
206 762-0850

(P-1311)
MARATHON CONSTRUCTION CORP
10108 Riverford Rd (92040-2740)
PHONE.................................619 276-4401
Michael V Furby, *Pr*
R B Zinser, *
Robert A Wheelington, *
Charles Cunningham, *
◆ **EMP:** 60 **EST:** 1981
SQ FT: 2,500
SALES (est): 11.88MM **Privately Held**
Web: www.marathonsd.com
SIC: 1629 Marine construction

(P-1312)
NORDIC INDUSTRIES INC
1437 Furneaux Rd (95961-7404)
PHONE.................................530 742-7124
Jens Karlshoej, *Pr*
Inge Karlshoej, *
Poul Karlshoej, *
Brian Bushnell, *
Francisco Martins, *
EMP: 74 **EST:** 1990
SQ FT: 5,000
SALES (est): 19.05MM **Privately Held**
Web: www.nordicind.com

(P-1313)
PATRICKS CONSTRUCTION CLEAN-UP
7851 14th Ave (95826-4301)
PHONE.................................916 452-5495
Patricio Mercado, *Owner*
EMP: 100 **EST:** 2000
SALES (est): 9.69MM **Privately Held**
Web: www.pccuinc.com
SIC: 1629 Land clearing contractor

(P-1314)
POWER ENGINEERING CONSTRUCTION COMPANY
1501 Viking St Ste 200 (94501-6968)
PHONE.................................510 337-3800
EMP: 70 **EST:** 1986
SALES (est): 23.13MM **Privately Held**
Web: www.powerengconstruction.com
SIC: 1629 Industrial plant construction

(P-1315)
RE LA MESA LLC
300 California St Fl 8 (94104-1416)
PHONE.................................415 675-1500
EMP: 100
SALES (est): 2.75MM **Privately Held**
SIC: 1629 Land leveling

(P-1316)
SCHWAGER DAVIS INC
198 Hillsdale Ave (95136-1398)
PHONE.................................408 281-9300
Guido A Schwager, *Pr*
▲ **EMP:** 82 **EST:** 1986
SQ FT: 12,000
SALES (est): 27.74MM **Privately Held**
Web: www.schwagerdavis.com
SIC: 1629 1622 Railroad and railway roadbed construction; Bridge construction

(P-1317)
SHIMMICK CONSTRUCTION CO INC
1 Harbor Ctr (94585-2427)
PHONE.................................707 419-5434
EMP: 161
SALES (corp-wide): 13.15B **Publicly Held**
Web: www.shimmick.com
SIC: 1629 1521 Earthmoving contractor; Single-family housing construction
HQ: Shimmick Construction Company Incorporated
530 Technology Dr Ste 300
Irvine CA

(P-1318)
SHIMMICK CONSTRUCTION CO INC (HQ)
Also Called: Transprttion Oprtons MGT Slton
530 Technology Dr Ste 300 (92618-1350)
PHONE.................................949 591-5922
Steve Richards, *Pr*
Greg Dukellis, *
Andrew Sloane, *
John White, *
Devin Nordhagen, *
EMP: 119 **EST:** 1990
SQ FT: 30,000
SALES (est): 575.38MM
SALES (corp-wide): 13.15B **Publicly Held**
Web: www.shimmick.com
SIC: 1629 1623 Earthmoving contractor; Sewer line construction
PA: Aecom

13355 Noel Rd Ste 400
Dallas TX
972 788-1000

(P-1319)
SKANSKA USA CVIL W RCKY MTN DS (DH)
Also Called: Skanska Rocky Mountain Dst
1995 Agua Mansa Rd (92509-2405)
PHONE.................................970 565-8000
Curtis Broughton, *Sr VP*
Curtis Broughton, *Sr VP*
David Sitton, *
Chris Eastin, *
Emeric Ondeck, *
EMP: 70 **EST:** 1950
SQ FT: 22,500
SALES (est): 139.41K
SALES (corp-wide): 15.55B **Privately Held**
SIC: 1629 1611 1711 Dam construction; General contractor, highway and street construction; Mechanical contractor
HQ: Skanska Usa Civil Inc.
7520 Astoria Blvd Ste 200
East Elmhurst NY
718 340-0777

(P-1320)
SLATER INC
11045 Rose Ave (92337-7051)
P.O. Box 759 (92334-0759)
PHONE.................................909 822-6800
Phillip S Slater, *CEO*
Steve David, *VP*
Edward Johnson, *CFO*
EMP: 97 **EST:** 1981
SQ FT: 6,000
SALES (est): 20.59MM **Privately Held**
Web: www.slaterinc.com
SIC: 1629 8711 Drainage system construction; Engineering services

(P-1321)
TIMEC ACQUISITIONS INC (DH)
155 Corporate Pl (94590-6968)
PHONE.................................707 642-2222
Pat Mcmahon, *Pr*
Gary Green, *
Dennis Turnipseed, *
EMP: 850 **EST:** 1998
SQ FT: 25,000
SALES (est): 152.83MM **Privately Held**
Web: www.timec.com
SIC: 1629 Industrial plant construction
HQ: Broadspectrum Pty Ltd
L 8 80 Pacific Hwy
North Sydney NSW

(P-1322)
TIMEC COMPANIES INC (DH)
Also Called: Timec
473 E Channel Rd (94510-1137)
PHONE.................................707 642-2222
Denis Turnipseed, *Pr*
EMP: 350 **EST:** 1971
SALES (est): 142.26MM **Privately Held**
Web: www.timec.com
SIC: 1629 1799 Industrial plant construction; Welding on site
HQ: Timec Acquisitions Inc
155 Corporate Pl
Vallejo CA
707 642-2222

(P-1323)
TIMEC COMPANIES INC
Also Called: Timec
2997 E Maria St (90221-5801)
PHONE.................................310 885-4710
Craig Crowder, *CEO*

EMP: 238
Web: www.timec.com
SIC: 1629 Industrial plant construction
HQ: Timec Companies Inc
  473 E Channel Rd
  Benicia CA
  707 642-2222

(P-1324)
UCI CONSTRUCTION INC (PA)
167 Grobric Ct (94534-1673)
P.O. Box 5547 (94524-0547)
  PHONE.................................925 370-9808
  EMP: 60 **EST:** 1981
  SALES (est): 46.43MM
  SALES (corp-wide): 46.43MM **Privately Held**
  Web: www.uciconstruction.com
  SIC: 1629 Chemical plant and refinery construction

(P-1325)
WOOD BROS INC
14147 18th Ave (93245-9741)
P.O. Box 216 (93245-0216)
  PHONE.................................559 924-7715
  William S Wood, *CEO*
  Donald T Wood, *
  EMP: 100 **EST:** 1984
  SQ FT: 30,000
  SALES (est): 28.76MM **Privately Held**
  Web: www.woodbrosinc.com
  SIC: 1629 Dredging contractor

1711 Plumbing, Heating, Air-conditioning

(P-1326)
10X HVAC OF CA LLC ✪
Also Called: General AC & Plbg
31170 Reserve Dr (92276-6653)
  PHONE.................................760 343-7488
  Patrick Somers, *Pr*
  EMP: 75 **EST:** 2022
  SALES (est): 2.75MM **Privately Held**
  SIC: 1711 Plumbing, heating, air-conditioning

(P-1327)
20/20 PLUMBING & HEATING INC (PA)
Also Called: Honeywell Authorized Dealer
7343 Orangewood Dr Ste B (92504-1027)
  PHONE.................................951 396-2020
  Thomas Lew Baker, *CEO*
  EMP: 97 **EST:** 2014
  SALES (est): 46.55MM
  SALES (corp-wide): 46.55MM **Privately Held**
  Web: www.2020ph.com
  SIC: 1711 Plumbing contractors

(P-1328)
20/20 PLUMBING & HEATING INC
674 Rancheros Dr (92069-3005)
  PHONE.................................760 535-3101
  EMP: 103
  SALES (corp-wide): 46.55MM **Privately Held**
  Web: www.2020ph.com
  SIC: 1711 Plumbing contractors
  PA: 20/20 Plumbing & Heating, Inc.
    7343 Orangewood Dr Ste B
    Riverside CA
    951 396-2020

(P-1329)
8MINUTENERGY US SOLAR LLC
4370 Town Center Blvd Ste 110 (95762-7140)
  PHONE.................................916 608-9060
  Thomas Buttgenbach, *Pr*
  Rahul Mathur, *
  Stephanie Perry, *
  Michael Healy, *CCO*
  Deborah Builder Senior, *OK Vice President*
  EMP: 150 **EST:** 2018
  SALES (est): 4.26MM **Privately Held**
  Web: www.8minute.com
  SIC: 1711 Solar energy contractor

(P-1330)
A & D FIRE PROTECTION INC
7130 Convoy Ct (92111-1019)
  PHONE.................................619 258-7697
  Andrew R Otero, *Pr*
  EMP: 80 **EST:** 1988
  SQ FT: 10,000
  SALES (est): 11.2MM **Privately Held**
  Web: www.adfiresprinklers.com
  SIC: 1711 1542 Fire sprinkler system installation; Nonresidential construction, nec

(P-1331)
A O REED & CO LLC
4777 Ruffner St (92111-1578)
P.O. Box 85226 (92186-5226)
  PHONE.................................858 565-4131
  Steve Andrade, *Ch Bd*
  David Clarkin, *
  Craig Koehler, *
  EMP: 500 **EST:** 1914
  SQ FT: 55,000
  SALES (est): 148.26MM **Privately Held**
  Web: www.aoreed.com
  SIC: 1711 Mechanical contractor

(P-1332)
ACCO ENGINEERED SYSTEMS INC
Also Called: Geo. H. Wilson
250 Harvey West Blvd (95060-2127)
  PHONE.................................831 423-9522
  EMP: 115
  SALES (corp-wide): 1.51B **Privately Held**
  Web: www.accoes.com
  SIC: 1711 7623 Process piping contractor; Air conditioning repair
  PA: Acco Engineered Systems, Inc.
    888 E Walnut St
    Pasadena CA
    818 244-6571

(P-1333)
ACCO ENGINEERED SYSTEMS INC
1133 Aladdin Ave (94577-4311)
  PHONE.................................510 346-4300
  Gregg Holbrook, *Brnch Mgr*
  EMP: 200
  SALES (corp-wide): 1.51B **Privately Held**
  Web: www.accoes.com
  SIC: 1711 7623 Process piping contractor; Air conditioning repair
  PA: Acco Engineered Systems, Inc.
    888 E Walnut St
    Pasadena CA
    818 244-6571

(P-1334)
ACCO ENGINEERED SYSTEMS INC (PA)
Also Called: Acco
888 E Walnut St (91101-1895)
  PHONE.................................818 244-6571
  EMP: 900 **EST:** 1934
  SALES (est): 1.51B
  SALES (corp-wide): 1.51B **Privately Held**
  Web: www.accoes.com
  SIC: 1711 7623 3448 Process piping contractor; Air conditioning repair; Buildings, portable: prefabricated metal

(P-1335)
ACH MECHANICAL CONTRACTORS INC
411 Business Center Ct (92373-8084)
  PHONE.................................909 307-2850
  Hector Vargas, *
  EMP: 80 **EST:** 2000
  SQ FT: 14,450
  SALES (est): 20.46MM **Privately Held**
  Web: www.achmechanical.com
  SIC: 1711 Mechanical contractor

(P-1336)
AD RECEIVABLES CORP (PA)
5457 Crenshaw Blvd (90043-2407)
P.O. Box 431490 (90043-9490)
  PHONE.................................323 296-8787
  Jack Stephan Senior, *Pr*
  Jack Stephan Junior, *VP*
  Russell Stephan, *
  EMP: 64 **EST:** 1946
  SQ FT: 18,000
  SALES (est): 4.93MM
  SALES (corp-wide): 4.93MM **Privately Held**
  Web: www.adeedo.com
  SIC: 1711 Plumbing contractors

(P-1337)
ADMIRAL REFRIGERATION INC
20867 Alaminos Dr (91350-1806)
  PHONE.................................661 505-7913
  Dale T Nichols, *CEO*
  EMP: 77
  SALES (corp-wide): 551.55K **Privately Held**
  Web: www.admiralrefrigeration.com
  SIC: 1711 Refrigeration contractor
  PA: Admiral Refrigeration Inc.
    28310 Avenue Crocker C
    Valencia CA
    661 505-7913

(P-1338)
AEGIS FIRE SYSTEMS LLC
Also Called: Aegis Fire Systems
500 Boulder Ct Ste A (94566-8311)
  PHONE.................................925 417-5550
  Matt Hammon, *CEO*
  EMP: 100 **EST:** 2012
  SALES (est): 26.13MM
  SALES (corp-wide): 416.15MM **Privately Held**
  Web: www.aegisfire.com
  SIC: 1711 Fire sprinkler system installation
  HQ: Rapid Fire Protection, Inc.
    1530 Samco Rd
    Rapid City SD

(P-1339)
AGC INC
745 Camden Ave Ste B (95008-4101)
  PHONE.................................408 369-6305
  Jon Mohs, *Pr*
  Randy Attaway, *
  Beth Guinnane, *
  ▼ **EMP:** 65 **EST:** 2000
  SQ FT: 2,200
  SALES (est): 32.86MM **Privately Held**
  Web: www.agcinc.com
  SIC: 1711 Mechanical contractor

(P-1340)
AIR SYSTEMS INC
Also Called: Emcor Services
940 Remillard Ct Frnt (95122-2684)
  PHONE.................................408 280-1666
  John W Davis, *Pr*
  Arthur Williams, *
  Don Billups, *
  Eric Ensenal, *Comm Vice President*
  Jon Gundersen, *Strategy Vice President*
  EMP: 500 **EST:** 2003
  SALES (est): 158.53MM
  SALES (corp-wide): 11.08B **Publicly Held**
  Web: www.airsystemsinc.com
  SIC: 1711 7623 Plumbing contractors; Refrigeration service and repair
  PA: Emcor Group, Inc.
    301 Merritt 7 Fl 6
    Norwalk CT
    203 849-7800

(P-1341)
AIR SYSTEMS SVC & CNSTR LLC
10381 Old Placerville Rd Ste 100 (95827-2510)
  PHONE.................................916 368-0336
  EMP: 130 **EST:** 1996
  SQ FT: 10,000
  SALES (est): 46.67MM **Privately Held**
  Web: www.airsystems1.com
  SIC: 1711 7623 Mechanical contractor; Refrigeration service and repair

(P-1342)
AIR-TRO INCORPORATED
Also Called: Air-Tro Air Conditioning & Htg
1630 S Myrtle Ave (91016-4634)
  PHONE.................................626 357-3535
  EMP: 70 **EST:** 1969
  SALES (est): 16.13MM **Privately Held**
  Web: www.airtro.com
  SIC: 1711 Warm air heating and air conditioning contractor

(P-1343)
AIRCO MECHANICAL INC (PA)
Also Called: AMI Manufacturing
8210 Demetre Ave (95828-0919)
  PHONE.................................916 381-4523
  Wyatt Jones, *CEO*
  Joann Hillendrand, *
  EMP: 244 **EST:** 1974
  SQ FT: 105,000
  SALES (est): 40MM
  SALES (corp-wide): 40MM **Privately Held**
  Web: www.aircomech.com
  SIC: 1711 8711 Mechanical contractor; Engineering services

(P-1344)
AIRE-RITE AC & RFRGN LLC
Also Called: Imperial Rfrgn & Ice Mchs
15122 Bolsa Chica St (92649-1025)
P.O. Box 3419 (92605-3419)
  PHONE.................................714 895-2338
  Donald Langston, *CEO*
  David Langston, *
  Carol Langston, *
  EMP: 97 **EST:** 1972
  SQ FT: 22,000
  SALES (est): 21.5MM
  SALES (corp-wide): 627.87MM **Privately Held**
  Web: www.airerite.com
  SIC: 1711 Plumbing, heating, air-conditioning
  PA: Ares Holdings, Llc
    1045 S John Rodes Blvd
    Melbourne FL
    321 727-2865

1711 - Plumbing, Heating, Air-conditioning (P-1345)

(P-1345)
ALDOC INC
910 E Orangefair Ln (92801-1103)
PHONE...................714 836-8477
P S Meckley, *Pr*
Philip Shurman Meckley, *
EMP: 60 EST: 2005
SALES (est): 4.34MM **Privately Held**
SIC: 1711 Plumbing contractors

(P-1346)
ALL TMPERATURES CONTROLLED INC
Also Called: Honeywell Authorized Dealer
9720 Topanga Canyon Pl (91311-4134)
PHONE...................818 882-1478
George Mego, *Pr*
EMP: 72 EST: 1978
SQ FT: 13,481
SALES (est): 11.67MM **Privately Held**
Web: www.alltemperaturescontrolled.com
SIC: 1711 Warm air heating and air conditioning contractor

(P-1347)
ALLIED FIRE PROTECTION
555 High St (94601-3905)
PHONE...................510 533-5516
Ted Vinther, *Pr*
EMP: 150 EST: 1965
SQ FT: 29,000
SALES (est): 22.34MM **Privately Held**
Web: www.alliedfire.com
SIC: 1711 Fire sprinkler system installation

(P-1348)
ALLIED HEATING & AIR CONDITIONING CO INC
Also Called: Allied Mechanical
12 De Luca Pl (94901-3909)
PHONE...................415 459-5232
EMP: 104 EST: 1984
SALES (est): 19.02MM **Privately Held**
Web: www.alliedhvac.com
SIC: 1711 7623 1761 Warm air heating and air conditioning contractor; Air conditioning repair; Sheet metal work, nec

(P-1349)
ALPHA MECHANICAL INC
4990 Greencraig Ln Ste A (92123-1673)
PHONE...................858 278-3500
Boris Barshak, *Brnch Mgr*
EMP: 115
Web: www.alphamechanical.com
SIC: 1711 Fire sprinkler system installation
PA: Alpha Mechanical, Inc.
    1866 Friendship Dr
    El Cajon CA

(P-1350)
ALPHA MECHANICAL INC (PA)
1866 Friendship Dr (92020-1171)
PHONE...................858 278-3500
Boris Barshak, *Prin*
Renee Larzalere, *Prin*
Cort Clifford, *Prin*
EMP: 70 EST: 2004
SALES (est): 49.16MM **Privately Held**
Web: www.alphamechanical.com
SIC: 1711 Fire sprinkler system installation

(P-1351)
ALPHA MECHANICAL HEATING & AIR CONDITIONING INC
4885 Greencraig Ln (92123-1664)
PHONE...................858 279-1300
EMP: 250
SIC: 1711 Sprinkler contractors

(P-1352)
ALTERNATIVE ENERGY SYSTEMS INC
Also Called: AES
13620 State Highway 99 N (95973-9481)
PHONE...................530 345-6980
Lance Mcclung, *Pr*
Tim Hamor, *
EMP: 70 EST: 2004
SALES (est): 10.84MM **Privately Held**
Web: www.savingenergyforlife.com
SIC: 1711 Solar energy contractor

(P-1353)
AMERICAN CONTRACTORS INC
Also Called: American Plumbing Contractors
404 W Blueridge Ave (92865-4204)
PHONE...................714 282-5700
Gilbert L Wiggam, *CEO*
Christopher Wiggam, *
EMP: 65 EST: 1974
SQ FT: 11,000
SALES (est): 21.48MM **Privately Held**
Web: www.aciplumbing.com
SIC: 1711 1623 Plumbing contractors; Sewer line construction

(P-1354)
AMERICAN RSDNTIAL SVCS IND INC
Also Called: Rescue Rooter Bay East
24800 Industrial Blvd (94545-2224)
PHONE...................650 409-1986
Chris Peterson, *Genl Mgr*
EMP: 324
SALES (corp-wide): 1.52B **Privately Held**
SIC: 1711 Plumbing contractors
HQ: American Residential Services Of Indiana, Inc.
    10403 Baur Blvd Ste E
    Saint Louis MO

(P-1355)
AMPAM PARKS MECHANICAL INC
17036 Avalon Blvd (90746-1206)
PHONE...................310 835-1532
Charles E Parks Iii, *CEO*
John D Parks, *
James C Wright, *
Chris Kennedy, *
▲ EMP: 800 EST: 1997
SQ FT: 16,000
SALES (est): 156.98MM **Privately Held**
Web: www.ampam.com
SIC: 1711 Plumbing contractors

(P-1356)
AMS AMERICAN MECH SVCS MD INC
2116 E Walnut Ave (92831-4845)
PHONE...................714 888-6820
Charles S Knight, *Genl Mgr*
EMP: 170
SALES (corp-wide): 1.52B **Privately Held**
Web: www.amsofusa.com
SIC: 1711 Mechanical contractor
HQ: Ams American Mechanical Services Of Maryland, Inc.
    13300 Mid Atlantic Blvd
    Laurel MD
    301 206-5070

(P-1357)
ANDERSEN COMMERCIAL PLBG INC
1608 Yeager Ave (91750-5853)
PHONE...................909 599-5950
Paul Andersen, *CEO*
Duane Kerr, *
EMP: 101 EST: 1993
SQ FT: 2,000
SALES (est): 11.64MM **Privately Held**
Web: www.andersenplumbing.com
SIC: 1711 Plumbing contractors

(P-1358)
ANDERSON ROWE & BUCKLEY INC
2833 3rd St (94107-3501)
PHONE...................415 282-1625
Robert E Buckley Iii, *Pr*
Robert E Buckley Iii, *
Richard I Buckley Junior, *VP*
Rosy Zucchiatti, *Sec*
EMP: 170 EST: 1921
SQ FT: 40,000
SALES (est): 27.15MM **Privately Held**
Web: www.arbmechanical.com
SIC: 1711 Mechanical contractor

(P-1359)
ANDERSON AIR CONDITIONING LP
2100 E Walnut Ave (92831-4845)
PHONE...................714 998-6850
Edward Dunn, *Genl Pt*
Mitchell J Haynam, *Ltd Pt*
EMP: 60 EST: 1969
SALES (est): 10.38MM **Privately Held**
Web: www.aac-ams.com
SIC: 1711 Warm air heating and air conditioning contractor
PA: American Mechanical Services Of Maryland, L.L.C.
    13300 Mid Atlantic Blvd
    Laurel MD

(P-1360)
ANDERSON SYSTEMS INC
5958 Corta St (93117-3916)
PHONE...................805 683-6133
EMP: 60 EST: 1984
SALES (est): 14.41MM **Privately Held**
Web: www.andersys.com
SIC: 1711 Plumbing contractors

(P-1361)
APEX MECHANICAL SYSTEMS INC
7440 Trade St Ste A (92121-3412)
PHONE...................858 536-8700
Randall E Melhouse, *CEO*
Kathy Draper, *
David R Draper, *
Blaine Stratton, *Stockholder**
Edward Draper, *Stockholder**
EMP: 79 EST: 2003
SALES (est): 14.9MM **Privately Held**
Web: www.apexmech.com
SIC: 1711 Mechanical contractor

(P-1362)
AQUALINE PIPING INC
Also Called: Residential Plumbing
2108 Bering Dr Ste C (95131-2013)
PHONE...................408 745-7100
Joshua B Moores, *CEO*
Chrystal L Steele, *
EMP: 75 EST: 2011
SALES (est): 15.16MM **Privately Held**
Web: www.aqualinepiping.com
SIC: 1711 7389 Plumbing contractors; Business Activities at Non-Commercial Site

(P-1363)
ARROWHEAD BRASS & PLUMBING LLC
5147 Alhambra Ave (90032-3413)
PHONE...................800 332-4267
Fred Schneider, *CEO*
▲ EMP: 80 EST: 1936
SQ FT: 35,000
SALES (est): 9.87MM **Privately Held**
Web: www.arrowheadbrass.com
SIC: 1711 Plumbing contractors

(P-1364)
ASI HASTINGS INC
Also Called: Asi Heating, Air and Solar
4870 Viewridge Ave Ste 200 (92123)
PHONE...................619 590-9300
TOLL FREE: 800
Philip Justo, *Pr*
Kenneth Justo, *
EMP: 120 EST: 1952
SQ FT: 2,000
SALES (est): 23.86MM
SALES (corp-wide): 91.05MM **Privately Held**
Web: www.asiheatingandair.com
SIC: 1711 Heating systems repair and maintenance
PA: Service Champions, Llc
    3150 E Birch St
    Brea CA
    714 777-7777

(P-1365)
ASSOCIATE MECH CONTRS INC
622 S Vinewood St (92029-1925)
PHONE...................760 294-3517
Richard Reinholz, *Pr*
Laura Reinholz, *Corporate Secretary**
Christina Payne, *
EMP: 150 EST: 2011
SALES (est): 47.38MM **Privately Held**
Web: www.amechinc.com
SIC: 1711 Mechanical contractor

(P-1366)
ASTRO MECHANICAL CONTRACTORS INC
603 S Marshall Ave (92020-4214)
PHONE...................619 442-9686
EMP: 85 EST: 1960
SALES (est): 15.88MM **Privately Held**
Web: www.astro-mech.com
SIC: 1711 1542 Plumbing contractors; Nonresidential construction, nec

(P-1367)
ATLAS MECHANICAL INC (PA)
Also Called: Honeywell Authorized Dealer
8260 Camino Santa Fe Ste B (92121)
PHONE...................858 554-0700
EMP: 74 EST: 1991
SALES (est): 57.7MM **Privately Held**
Web: www.atlasmechanical.com
SIC: 1711 3531 Ventilation and duct work contractor; Construction machinery

(P-1368)
AWHAP ACQUISITION CORP
28358 Constellation Rd Ste 698 (91355-5010)
PHONE...................888 611-4328
Alex Stuckey, *CEO*
EMP: 152 EST: 2020
SALES (est): 7.79MM **Privately Held**
SIC: 1711 Plumbing, heating, air-conditioning

PRODUCTS & SERVICES SECTION 1711 - Plumbing, Heating, Air-conditioning (P-1391)

(P-1369)
AXIS MECHANICAL INC
908 Bern Ct (95112-1236)
PHONE.................................408 573-7400
Mike Herrera, *Pr*
Jonathan Diaz, *
Tom Best, *
EMP: 65 **EST:** 2012
SALES (est): 18.97MM **Privately Held**
Web: www.axismechanicalinc.com
SIC: 1711 Plumbing, heating, air-conditioning

(P-1370)
AYOOB & PEERY PLUMBING CO INC
975 Indiana St (94107-3007)
PHONE.................................415 550-0975
Peter Vincent Mchugh, *CEO*
EMP: 80 **EST:** 1979
SQ FT: 20,000
SALES (est): 16.06MM **Privately Held**
Web: www.ayoobpeery.com
SIC: 1711 Mechanical contractor

(P-1371)
BARR ENGINEERING INC
19 Castano (92688-1662)
PHONE.................................562 944-1722
Peter Buongiorno, *Pr*
Pamela Price-recchia, *Sec*
Mike Buongiorno, *
EMP: 82 **EST:** 1958
SALES (est): 21.69MM **Privately Held**
Web: www.barrengineering.com
SIC: 1711 Warm air heating and air conditioning contractor

(P-1372)
BAY CITY MECHANICAL INC (PA)
870 Harbour Way S (94804-3613)
PHONE.................................510 233-7000
Helge Theiss-nyland, *Pr*
Bobbie Amos, *
Joe Percia, *
John Swahn, *
EMP: 250 **EST:** 1992
SQ FT: 85,000
SALES (est): 112.16MM **Privately Held**
Web: www.baycitymech.com
SIC: 1711 Mechanical contractor

(P-1373)
BAYVIEW ENGRG & CNSTR CO INC
5040 Robert J Mathews Pkwy (95762-5702)
PHONE.................................916 939-8986
Robert Ellery, *CEO*
Bart Wood, *
Pete Ellery, *
EMP: 80 **EST:** 2009
SQ FT: 6,000
SALES (est): 8.66MM **Privately Held**
Web: www.bayviewecci.com
SIC: 1711 8711 Boiler setting contractor; Engineering services

(P-1374)
BCM CUSTOMER SERVICE
12155 Kirkham Rd (92064-6870)
PHONE.................................858 679-5757
Brian R Cox, *CEO*
EMP: 90 **EST:** 1996
SQ FT: 30,000
SALES (est): 4.66MM **Privately Held**
SIC: 1711 1796 Plumbing, heating, air-conditioning; Installing building equipment

(P-1375)
BELL PRODUCTS INC
722 Soscol Ave (94559-3014)
P.O. Box 396 (94559-0396)
PHONE.................................707 255-1811
Paul D Irwin, *Pr*
Stan Foltz, *
EMP: 74 **EST:** 1945
SQ FT: 24,400
SALES (est): 21.35MM **Privately Held**
Web: www.bellproducts.com
SIC: 1711 Ventilation and duct work contractor

(P-1376)
BERNEL INC
Also Called: Vfs Fire Protection Services
501 W Southern Ave (92865-3217)
PHONE.................................714 778-6070
Randy Roland Nelson, *CEO*
Kevin Berthoud, *
Mario Lopez, *
EMP: 140 **EST:** 1994
SQ FT: 7,800
SALES (est): 29.35MM **Privately Held**
Web: www.vfsfire.com
SIC: 1711 7382 Fire sprinkler system installation; Security systems services

(P-1377)
BFP FIRE PROTECTION INC
17 Janis Way (95066-3537)
PHONE.................................831 461-1100
Chris Amos, *Pr*
EMP: 60 **EST:** 1989
SQ FT: 6,400
SALES (est): 5.56MM **Privately Held**
Web: www.bfpfireprotection.com
SIC: 1711 8711 Fire sprinkler system installation; Engineering services

(P-1378)
BILL HOWE PLUMBING INC
Also Called: Am-PM Sewer & Drain Cleaning
9210 Sky Park Ct (92123-4478)
PHONE.................................800 245-5469
William Howe, *Pr*
Tina Howe, *
EMP: 85 **EST:** 1982
SALES (est): 27.09MM **Privately Held**
Web: www.billhowe.com
SIC: 1711 Plumbing contractors

(P-1379)
BLAND A/C & HEATING INC (PA)
Also Called: Bland Solar & Air
4303 E Brundage Ln (93307-2305)
PHONE.................................661 836-3800
▲ **EMP:** 68 **EST:** 1984
SALES (est): 20MM **Privately Held**
Web: www.blandcompany.com
SIC: 1711 Plumbing, heating, air-conditioning

(P-1380)
BLOCKA CONSTRUCTION INC
445 Boulder Ct (94566-8308)
PHONE.................................510 657-3686
Robert Blocka, *Pr*
Bob Blocka, *
Jean Blocka, *
EMP: 70 **EST:** 1993
SQ FT: 7,300
SALES (est): 42MM **Privately Held**
Web: blockainc.wordpress.com
SIC: 1711 1731 Mechanical contractor; General electrical contractor

(P-1381)
BLUE MOUNTAIN CNSTR SVCS INC
Also Called: Blue Mountain Air
707 Aldridge Rd Ste B (95688-9564)
PHONE.................................800 889-2085
Gregory S Owen, *Pr*
▲ **EMP:** 200 **EST:** 2001
SQ FT: 37,000
SALES (est): 95.76MM **Privately Held**
Web: www.bluemountainair.net
SIC: 1711 Heating and air conditioning contractors

(P-1382)
BLUE OAK ENERGY LLC
Also Called: Blue Oak Energy
3947 Lennane Dr Ste 130 (95834-1971)
PHONE.................................530 747-2026
Tobin Booth, *CEO*
Danny Lee, *
EMP: 65 **EST:** 2003
SALES (est): 6.45MM
SALES (corp-wide): 482.42MM **Privately Held**
Web: www.blueoakenergy.com
SIC: 1711 8711 Solar energy contractor; Engineering services
PA: Trc Companies, Inc.
21 Griffin Rd N
Windsor CT
860 298-9692

(P-1383)
BONESO BROTHERS CNSTR INC
2758 Concrete Ct (93446-5936)
PHONE.................................805 227-4450
Steve Boneso, *Pr*
Rob Boneso, *
EMP: 80 **EST:** 1999
SQ FT: 4,000
SALES (est): 40MM **Privately Held**
Web: www.bonesobrothersconstruction.com
SIC: 1711 1542 Mechanical contractor; Nonresidential construction, nec

(P-1384)
BRIGHTVIEW LANDSCAPE DEV INC
13691 Vaughn St (91340-3072)
PHONE.................................818 838-4700
Greg Motschenbacher, *Brnch Mgr*
EMP: 77
SALES (corp-wide): 2.77B **Publicly Held**
Web: www.brightview.com
SIC: 1711 0781 Irrigation sprinkler system installation; Landscape services
HQ: Brightview Landscape Development, Inc.
27001 Agoura Rd Ste 350
Calabasas CA
818 223-8500

(P-1385)
BRIGHTVIEW LANDSCAPE DEV INC
8 Hughes Ste 125 (92618-2079)
PHONE.................................714 546-7975
Gins Garmann, *Mgr*
EMP: 164
SALES (corp-wide): 2.77B **Publicly Held**
Web: www.brightview.com
SIC: 1711 0781 Irrigation sprinkler system installation; Landscape services
HQ: Brightview Landscape Development, Inc.
27001 Agoura Rd Ste 350
Calabasas CA
818 223-8500

(P-1386)
BROADWAY MECH - CONTRS INC
873 81st Ave (94621-2509)
PHONE.................................510 746-4000
Fred Nurisso, *Pr*
Kenneth Nurisso, *
EMP: 150 **EST:** 1971
SALES (est): 48.49MM **Privately Held**
Web: www.broadwaymechanical.com
SIC: 1711 Mechanical contractor

(P-1387)
BROMIC HEATING PTY LIMITED
7595 Irvine Center Dr Ste 100 (92618-2958)
PHONE.................................855 552-7432
EMP: 100 **EST:** 2017
SALES (est): 4.49MM **Privately Held**
Web: www.bromic.com
SIC: 1711 Mechanical contractor

(P-1388)
BRYMAX CONSTRUCTION SVCS INC
7436 Lorge Cir (92647-3619)
PHONE.................................949 200-9619
Brooke Willems, *CEO*
Michael Willems, *
Steve Sylvester, *
Tony Teriitehau, *
EMP: 79 **EST:** 2015
SALES (est): 25.32MM **Privately Held**
Web: www.brymaxservices.com
SIC: 1711 5075 5065 4225 Plumbing, heating, air-conditioning; Warm air heating and air conditioning; Electronic parts and equipment, nec; General warehousing and storage

(P-1389)
C & L REFRIGERATION CORP
Also Called: HONEYWELL AUTHORIZED DEALER
4111 N Palm St (92835-1025)
P.O. Box 2319 (92822-2319)
PHONE.................................800 901-4822
Ronald J Cassell, *CEO*
Ronald J Cassell Junior, *CEO*
Denise Lowe, *CFO*
Larry Jaslove, *
EMP: 150 **EST:** 1978
SQ FT: 18,000
SALES (est): 50.97MM **Privately Held**
Web: www.clrefrigeration.com
SIC: 1711 Refrigeration contractor

(P-1390)
CALIFORNIA COML SOLAR INC
Also Called: Calcom Energy
9479 N Fort Washington Rd Ste 105 (93730-0660)
PHONE.................................559 667-9200
Fred Ketcho, *CEO*
Rob Burkholder, *
Alison Baird, *
EMP: 108 **EST:** 2012
SALES (est): 26.79MM **Privately Held**
Web: www.calcomenergy.com
SIC: 1711 Solar energy contractor

(P-1391)
CALIFORNIA UNITED MECH INC (PA)
Also Called: United Mechanical
2185 Oakland Rd (95131-1574)
PHONE.................................408 232-9000
Tom Sosine, *CEO*
Jon Gundersen, *

1711 - Plumbing, Heating, Air-conditioning (P-1392)

Blaine Flickner, *
EMP: 330 **EST:** 2003
SQ FT: 40,000
SALES (est): 91.33MM
SALES (corp-wide): 91.33MM **Privately Held**
Web: www.umi1.com
SIC: 1711 Mechanical contractor

(P-1392)
CALVIN DUBOIS
Also Called: Sun Energy Construction
9057 Arrow Rte (91730-4452)
PHONE.................909 222-6662
Dennis Jay, *CEO*
Calvin Dubois, *
EMP: 73 **EST:** 2018
SALES (est): 10.96MM **Privately Held**
Web: www.sunenergyco.com
SIC: 1711 Solar energy contractor

(P-1393)
CAN-AM PLUMBING INC
151 Wyoming St (94566-6277)
PHONE.................925 846-1833
Ronald Capilla, *Pr*
Michael Capilla, *
Martin Ogara, *
EMP: 250 **EST:** 1972
SQ FT: 16,000
SALES (est): 23.96MM **Privately Held**
Web: www.canamplumbing.com
SIC: 1711 Plumbing contractors

(P-1394)
CASPIAN COMMERCIAL PLBG INC
711 Ivy St (91204-1003)
PHONE.................818 649-2500
Anahit Alexandrian, *Pr*
EMP: 65 **EST:** 2011
SALES (est): 9.31MM **Privately Held**
Web: www.ftpccp.com
SIC: 1711 Plumbing contractors

(P-1395)
CFP FIRE PROTECTION INC
153 Technology Dr Ste 200 (92618-2461)
PHONE.................949 727-3277
EMP: 100 **EST:** 2002
SQ FT: 21,960
SALES (est): 13.22MM **Privately Held**
Web: www.cfpfire.com
SIC: 1711 Fire sprinkler system installation
PA: Mx Holdings Us, Inc.
153 Technology Dr Ste 200
Irvine CA

(P-1396)
CHRISTIAN BROTHERS MECHANICAL SERVICES INC
Also Called: CB Controls
11140 Thurston Ln (91752-1426)
PHONE.................951 361-2247
EMP: 110 **EST:** 1985
SALES (est): 18.35MM **Privately Held**
Web: www.cbhvac.com
SIC: 1711 Warm air heating and air conditioning contractor

(P-1397)
CIRCULATING AIR INC (PA)
Also Called: Honeywell Authorized Dealer
7337 Varna Ave (91605-4009)
PHONE.................818 764-0530
TOLL FREE: 800
Joseph Gallagher, *Ex VP*
Susan Gallagher, *
Marcy Ahlstrom, *
EMP: 100 **EST:** 1965
SQ FT: 13,000
SALES (est): 24.86MM
SALES (corp-wide): 24.86MM **Privately Held**
Web: www.circulatingair.com
SIC: 1711 Mechanical contractor

(P-1398)
CIRCULATING AIR INC
1109 W Columbia Way (93534-8146)
PHONE.................661 942-2048
Joe Galleger, *Mgr*
EMP: 71
SALES (corp-wide): 24.86MM **Privately Held**
Web: www.circulatingair.com
SIC: 1711 Warm air heating and air conditioning contractor
PA: Circulating Air, Inc.
7337 Varna Ave
North Hollywood CA
818 764-0530

(P-1399)
CLARKE & RUSH MECHANICAL INC
Also Called: Honeywell Authorized Dealer
4411 Auburn Blvd (95841-4108)
PHONE.................916 306-5835
EMP: 85 **EST:** 1962
SALES (est): 18.64MM **Privately Held**
Web: www.clarke-rush.com
SIC: 1711 8748 Warm air heating and air conditioning contractor; Energy conservation consultant

(P-1400)
CLAY DUNN ENTERPRISES INC
Also Called: Air-TEC
1606 E Carson St (90745-2504)
P.O. Box 5444 (90749-5444)
PHONE.................310 549-1698
Clayton N Dunn, *Pr*
Hayley Amberg, *
EMP: 138 **EST:** 1969
SQ FT: 18,000
SALES (est): 45.04MM **Privately Held**
Web: www.airtecperforms.com
SIC: 1711 Warm air heating and air conditioning contractor

(P-1401)
CLIMATE PROS LLC
3550 Arden Rd (94545-3921)
PHONE.................510 784-8990
EMP: 148
Web: www.climatepros.com
SIC: 1711 Refrigeration contractor
PA: Climate Pros, Llc
55 N Brandon Dr
Glendale Heights IL

(P-1402)
COMFORT AIR INC
1607 French Camp Tpke (95206-1960)
P.O. Box 1969 (95201-1969)
PHONE.................209 466-4601
Steven J Evans, *Pr*
Gregory A Gaut, *
Paulette Gaut, *
EMP: 75 **EST:** 1946
SQ FT: 7,000
SALES (est): 18.76MM **Privately Held**
Web: www.comfortairstocktonca.com
SIC: 1711 Warm air heating and air conditioning contractor

(P-1403)
CONTROL AIR CONDITIONING CORPORATION
Also Called: Honeywell Authorized Dealer
5200 E La Palma Ave (92807-2019)
PHONE.................714 777-8600
EMP: 360
SIC: 1711 3444 Warm air heating and air conditioning contractor; Ducts, sheet metal

(P-1404)
CONTROL AIR ENTERPRISES LLC
30655 San Clemente St (94544-7133)
PHONE.................510 441-1800
Mike Eepn, *Brnch Mgr*
EMP: 475
SALES (corp-wide): 277.7MM **Privately Held**
Web: www.controlac.com
SIC: 1711 Warm air heating and air conditioning contractor
PA: Control Air Enterprises Llc
5200 E La Palma Ave
Anaheim CA
714 777-8600

(P-1405)
CONTROL AIR NORTH INC
30655 San Clemente St (94544-7133)
PHONE.................510 441-1800
Greg Ellis, *Pr*
Mike Pence, *
Ken Ellis, *
Stan Ellis, *
Darrell Griffith, *
EMP: 100 **EST:** 1995
SALES (est): 46.91MM **Privately Held**
Web: www.controlac.com
SIC: 1711 Warm air heating and air conditioning contractor

(P-1406)
COOLAND INC
16830 S Main St (90248-3122)
PHONE.................424 329-3550
Sungill Park, *Brnch Mgr*
EMP: 72
SALES (corp-wide): 426.88K **Privately Held**
Web: www.coolandinc.com
SIC: 1711 Heating and air conditioning contractors
PA: Cooland, Inc.
20950 Normandie Ave
Torrance CA
310 320-3660

(P-1407)
COOLSYS COML INDUS SLTIONS INC (DH)
145 S State College Blvd Ste 200 (92821-5818)
PHONE.................714 510-9609
EMP: 155 **EST:** 1995
SALES (est): 480.58MM
SALES (corp-wide): 3.06B **Publicly Held**
Web: www.sourcerefrigeration.com
SIC: 1711 Refrigeration contractor
HQ: Coolsys, Inc.
145 S State College Blvd
Brea CA
714 510-9577

(P-1408)
COSCO FIRE PROTECTION INC
4223 W Sierra Madre Ave Ste 108 (93722-3933)
PHONE.................559 275-3795
Lisa Dean, *Brnch Mgr*
EMP: 103
Web: www.coscofire.com
SIC: 1711 Fire sprinkler system installation
HQ: Cosco Fire Protection, Inc.
29222 Rancho Viejo Rd # 205
San Juan Capistrano CA

(P-1409)
COSCO FIRE PROTECTION INC
Also Called: 76
4990 Greencraig Ln (92123-1673)
PHONE.................858 444-2000
Alexander Hernandez, *Mgr*
EMP: 78
Web: www.coscofire.com
SIC: 1711 Fire sprinkler system installation
HQ: Cosco Fire Protection, Inc.
29222 Rancho Viejo Rd # 205
San Juan Capistrano CA

(P-1410)
COUNTYWIDE MECH SYSTEMS LLC
1400 N Johnson Ave Ste 104-115 (92020-1650)
PHONE.................619 449-9900
Paul Duke, *Pr*
David Cimpl, *Treas*
EMP: 230 **EST:** 2011
SQ FT: 5,000
SALES (est): 93.71MM **Privately Held**
Web: www.countywidems.com
SIC: 1711 Mechanical contractor
PA: Mmc Corp
7801 W 110th St
Overland Park KS

(P-1411)
COUTS HEATING & COOLING INC
1693 Rimpau Ave (92881-3202)
PHONE.................951 278-5560
EMP: 160 **EST:** 1978
SALES (est): 27.77MM **Privately Held**
Web: www.couts.com
SIC: 1711 Warm air heating and air conditioning contractor

(P-1412)
CRITCHFIELD MECH INC STHERN CAL
15391 Springdale St (92649-1100)
PHONE.................949 390-2900
Mike Pearlman, *CEO*
EMP: 100 **EST:** 2004
SALES (est): 4.17MM **Privately Held**
Web: www.cmihvac.com
SIC: 1711 Warm air heating and air conditioning contractor

(P-1413)
CRITCHFIELD MECHANICAL INC
4085 Campbell Ave (94025-1939)
PHONE.................650 321-7801
Joe Critchfield, *Ch*
EMP: 394
SALES (corp-wide): 162.27MM **Privately Held**
Web: www.cmihvac.com
SIC: 1711 Mechanical contractor
PA: Critchfield Mechanical, Inc.
1901 Junction Ave
San Jose CA
408 437-7000

(P-1414)
CRITCHFIELD MECHANICAL INC (PA)

Also Called: CMI
1901 Junction Ave (95131-2103)
PHONE..............................408 437-7000
▲ EMP: 100 EST: 1977
SALES (est): 162.27MM
SALES (corp-wide): 162.27MM Privately Held
Web: www.cmihvac.com
SIC: 1711 Mechanical contractor

(P-1415)
D W NICHOLSON CORPORATION (PA)
24747 Clawiter Rd (94545-2225)
P.O. Box 4197 (94540-4197)
PHONE..............................510 887-0900
John L Nicholson, Prin
Thomas S Reed, Prin
Clifford A Schuch, Prin
EMP: 247 EST: 1935
SQ FT: 12,000
SALES (est): 23.2MM
SALES (corp-wide): 23.2MM Privately Held
Web: www.dwnicholson.com
SIC: 1711 1731 8711 1796 Mechanical contractor; General electrical contractor; Engineering services; Millwright

(P-1416)
DAGGETT SOLAR POWER 3 LLC
100 California St Ste 400 (94111-4509)
PHONE..............................415 627-1600
Jonathan Bram, Managing Member
EMP: 154 EST: 2016
SALES (est): 17.01MM
SALES (corp-wide): 472.67MM Privately Held
SIC: 1711 Solar energy contractor
PA: Clearway Energy Group Llc
100 California St Ste 400
San Francisco CA
415 627-1600

(P-1417)
DAVE WILLIAMS PLBG & ELEC INC
75140 Saint Charles Pl Ste C (92211-9044)
PHONE..............................760 296-1397
Daniel Williams, Pr
Dave Williams, *
EMP: 110 EST: 2008
SALES (est): 4.83MM Privately Held
Web: www.dwpeinc.com
SIC: 1711 Plumbing contractors

(P-1418)
DAVIS CONSTRUCTION PLBG INC
32120 Mountain Shadow Rd (93510-1933)
P.O. Box 215 (93510-0215)
PHONE..............................661 269-4325
Jeff Davis, Pr
Cindy Davis, *
Brooke Messerly, *
EMP: 60 EST: 1983
SQ FT: 1,000
SALES (est): 5.86MM Privately Held
Web: www.davisconstructionplumbing.com
SIC: 1711 Plumbing contractors

(P-1419)
DC SOLAR SOLUTIONS INC
4901 Park Rd (94510-1190)
PHONE..............................925 203-1088
EMP: 61
SIC: 1711 Solar energy contractor

(P-1420)
DELTA COREY INC
4931 Park Rd (94510-1190)
P.O. Box 637 (94510-0637)
PHONE..............................707 747-7500
EMP: 125
Web: www.coreydelta.com
SIC: 1711 Mechanical contractor

(P-1421)
DESERT MECHANICAL INC
Also Called: Dmi
15870 Olden St (91342-1241)
PHONE..............................702 873-7333
Casey M Condron, Pr
Alex L Hodson, *
Andre Burnthon, *
Joseph Guglielmo, *
Dan Naylor, *
EMP: 1100 EST: 1977
SQ FT: 25,000
SALES (est): 97.67MM
SALES (corp-wide): 3.79B Publicly Held
Web: www.lvdmi.com
SIC: 1711 Plumbing contractors
PA: Tutor Perini Corporation
15901 Olden St
Rancho Cascades CA
818 362-8391

(P-1422)
DLIGHT DESIGN INC
2100 Geng Rd Ste 210 (94303-3307)
PHONE..............................415 872-6136
Ned Tozun, CEO
Sam Goldman, *
Ronald Pfende, *
▲ EMP: 800 EST: 2007
SALES (est): 35.87MM Privately Held
Web: www.dlight.com
SIC: 1711 5074 Solar energy contractor; Heating equipment and panels, solar

(P-1423)
DYNAMIC PLUMBING SYSTEMS INC
5920 Winterhaven Ave (92504-1048)
PHONE..............................951 343-1200
EMP: 306
SIC: 1711 Plumbing contractors

(P-1424)
EAGLE SYSTEMS INTL INC
Also Called: Synergy Companies
28436 Satellite St (94545-4863)
PHONE..............................510 259-1700
Steven R Shallenberger, Pr
Russell Jacobsen, *
EMP: 375 EST: 2002
SQ FT: 6,962
SALES (est): 21.59MM Privately Held
Web: www.synergycompanies.com
SIC: 1711 1731 1742 1793 Warm air heating and air conditioning contractor; General electrical contractor; Plastering, drywall, and insulation; Glass and glazing work

(P-1425)
ECB CORP (PA)
Also Called: Omniduct
6400 Artesia Blvd (90620-1006)
PHONE..............................714 385-8900
Robert Brumleu, Pr
▲ EMP: 100 EST: 1980
SQ FT: 56,000
SALES (est): 57.91MM
SALES (corp-wide): 57.91MM Privately Held
Web: www.omniduct.com
SIC: 1711 3444 Ventilation and duct work contractor; Ducts, sheet metal

(P-1426)
ECOTECH RFRGN & HVAC INC
630 S Sunkist St Ste R (92806-4529)
PHONE..............................888 833-8100
Erich Christopher Munzner, CEO
EMP: 60 EST: 2014
SALES (est): 2.42MM Privately Held
Web: www.ecotech-hvacr.com
SIC: 1711 Refrigeration contractor

(P-1427)
ELECTRIC ON TARGET INC
17691 Mitchell N Ste B (92614-6827)
PHONE..............................949 247-3842
Rubio Rubio, CEO
Aaron Egdahl Pric, Prin
Brian Watts, *
EMP: 67 EST: 2008
SALES (est): 11.65MM Privately Held
Web: www.ontargetelectric.com
SIC: 1711 Solar energy contractor

(P-1428)
ENERGY CONCEPTS ENTPS INC
1835 N Fine Ave Ste 106 (93727-1671)
PHONE..............................559 485-2504
James R Pugh, CEO
EMP: 65 EST: 2014
SALES (est): 2.89MM Privately Held
Web: www.energyconceptsfresno.com
SIC: 1711 7389 Solar energy contractor; Design services

(P-1429)
ENERGY ENTERPRISES USA INC (PA)
Also Called: Canopy Energy
6842 Van Nuys Blvd Ste 800 (91405-4625)
PHONE..............................424 339-0005
Lior Agam, CEO
EMP: 100 EST: 2011
SQ FT: 11,000
SALES (est): 16.07MM
SALES (corp-wide): 16.07MM Privately Held
Web: www.canopyenergy.com
SIC: 1711 Solar energy contractor

(P-1430)
ENVIRNMNTAL HTG A SLUTIONS INC
8417 Washington Blvd Ste 170 (95678-6235)
PHONE..............................916 990-2952
Matthew Evans, CEO
Matthew Evans, Prin
EMP: 60 EST: 2011
SALES (est): 5.65MM Privately Held
Web: www.ehasolutions.com
SIC: 1711 Warm air heating and air conditioning contractor

(P-1431)
ENVIRNMNTAL SYSTEMS INC NTHRN (PA)
Also Called: Honeywell Authorized Dealer
3353 De La Cruz Blvd (95054-2633)
PHONE..............................408 980-1711
V C Enfantino, Pr
Eugene L Enfantino, *
EMP: 83 EST: 1975
SQ FT: 13,800
SALES (est): 22.56MM
SALES (corp-wide): 22.56MM Privately Held
Web: www.esite.net
SIC: 1711 7623 3444 Mechanical contractor; Refrigeration service and repair; Sheet metalwork

(P-1432)
ENVISE (HQ)
Also Called: Envise
12131 Western Ave (92841-2914)
PHONE..............................800 613-6240
Chris Lofaso, CEO
EMP: 113 EST: 2015
SALES (est): 88.86MM
SALES (corp-wide): 1.42B Privately Held
Web: www.southlandind.com
SIC: 1711 Plumbing, heating, air-conditioning
PA: Southland Industries
12131 Western Ave
Garden Grove CA
800 613-6240

(P-1433)
ENVISE
12131 Western Ave (92841-2914)
PHONE..............................714 901-5800
Travis Feltcher, Brnch Mgr
EMP: 63
SALES (corp-wide): 1.42B Privately Held
Web: www.southlandind.com
SIC: 1711 Plumbing, heating, air-conditioning
HQ: Envise
12131 Western Ave
Garden Grove CA
800 613-6240

(P-1434)
ESS LLC
Also Called: Evergreen Solar Services
5227 Dantes View Dr (91301-2313)
PHONE..............................888 303-6424
Jacob Stephens, Pr
Eliahu Arbib, Prin
Shaul Arbiv, Prin
EMP: 100 EST: 2011
SALES (est): 3.04MM Privately Held
SIC: 1711 Solar energy contractor

(P-1435)
FAMAND INC
1604 Airport Blvd (95403-8204)
PHONE..............................707 255-9295
Charlie Butts, Brnch Mgr
EMP: 96
SALES (corp-wide): 39.72MM Privately Held
Web: www.ies-hvac.com
SIC: 1711 Plumbing, heating, air-conditioning
PA: Famand, Inc.
1512 Silica Ave
Sacramento CA
916 988-8808

(P-1436)
FERREIRA SERVICE INC (PA)
1811 Tortuga St (93510-1898)
P.O. Box 3142 (94583-8142)
PHONE..............................925 831-9330
Susan Ferreira, CEO
Albert Ferreira, *
EMP: 65 EST: 1978
SQ FT: 10,000
SALES (est): 6.25MM
SALES (corp-wide): 6.25MM Privately Held
Web: www.ferreira.com
SIC: 1711 Mechanical contractor

(P-1437)
FIDELITY HOME ENERGY INC
2235 Polvorosa Ave Ste 230 (94577-2200)
P.O. Box 3287 (94583-8287)

1711 - Plumbing, Heating, Air-conditioning (P-1438)

PHONE..............................858 220-7784
EMP: 197
Web: www.fidelityhome.net
SIC: 1711 1522 Solar energy contractor; Remodeling, multi-family dwellings

(P-1438)
FIRE SAFE SYSTEMS INC
1312 Kingsdale Ave (90278-3926)
PHONE..............................310 542-0585
EMP: 60 EST: 1993
SQ FT: 3,000
SALES (est): 8.57MM Privately Held
Web: www.firesafesystems.com
SIC: 1711 Fire sprinkler system installation

(P-1439)
FOREFRONT POWER LLC
100 Montgomery St Ste 725 (94104-4377)
PHONE..............................415 800-1604
Michael D Smith, *CEO*
Yohei Kishi, *
EMP: 92 EST: 2016
SALES (est): 15.36MM Privately Held
Web: www.forefrontpower.com
SIC: 1711 Solar energy contractor
PA: Mitsui&Co., Ltd.
    1-2-1, Otemachi
    Chiyoda-Ku TKY

(P-1440)
FRANK M BOOTH INC
5900 Hollis St Ste C (94608-2008)
PHONE..............................530 742-7134
EMP: 77
SALES (corp-wide): 110MM Privately Held
Web: www.frankbooth.com
SIC: 1711 Mechanical contractor
PA: Frank M. Booth, Inc.
    222 3rd St
    Marysville CA
    530 742-7134

(P-1441)
FRANK M BOOTH INC
Also Called: Valley Sheet Metal
251 Michelle Ct (94080-6202)
PHONE..............................650 871-8292
F Martin Booth, *CEO*
EMP: 77
SQ FT: 70,000
SALES (corp-wide): 110MM Privately Held
Web: www.frankbooth.com
SIC: 1711 8712 3444 1761 Mechanical contractor; Architectural services; Sheet metalwork; Sheet metal work, nec
PA: Frank M. Booth, Inc.
    222 3rd St
    Marysville CA
    530 742-7134

(P-1442)
FRED WILL AND BILL INC
Also Called: Brisbane Mechanical
211 S Hill Dr Fl 2 (94005-1263)
EMP: 200 EST: 1903
SQ FT: 140,000
SALES (est): 22.9MM Privately Held
Web: www.fwspencersoninc.com
SIC: 1711 Plumbing contractors

(P-1443)
FREEDOM FOREVER LLC (PA)
43445 Business Park Dr Ste 104 (92590-3670)
PHONE..............................888 557-6431
EMP: 89 EST: 2016
SALES (est): 227.62MM

SALES (corp-wide): 227.62MM Privately Held
Web: www.freedomforever.com
SIC: 1711 Solar energy contractor

(P-1444)
FREEDOM FOREVER LLC
3322 Garfield Ave (90040-3102)
PHONE..............................714 955-8735
EMP: 1904
SALES (corp-wide): 227.62MM Privately Held
Web: www.freedomforever.com
SIC: 1711 Solar energy contractor
PA: Freedom Forever Llc
    43445 Bus Pk Dr Ste 104
    Temecula CA
    888 557-6431

(P-1445)
FREEDOM SOLAR SERVICES
Also Called: Freedom Forever
43445 Business Park Dr Ste 110 (92590-3671)
PHONE..............................888 557-6431
Brett Leon Bouchy, *CEO*
EMP: 150 EST: 2012
SALES (est): 13.15MM Privately Held
Web: www.freedomforever.com
SIC: 1711 Solar energy contractor

(P-1446)
FRESNO PLUMBING & HEATING INC (PA)
Also Called: Ace Hardware
2585 N Larkin Ave (93727-1357)
PHONE..............................559 294-0200
Larry Kumpe, *CEO*
Dean Kumpe, *
EMP: 180 EST: 1981
SQ FT: 20,000
SALES (est): 27MM
SALES (corp-wide): 27MM Privately Held
Web: www.fresnoplumbinginc.com
SIC: 1711 5251 Plumbing contractors; Hardware stores

(P-1447)
FRONTIER MECHANICAL INC
Also Called: Frontier Plumbing
6309 Seven Seas Ave (93308-5133)
PHONE..............................661 589-6203
Rick Palmer, *Pr*
Brenda Palmer, *Stockholder**
EMP: 93 EST: 1987
SQ FT: 120,000
SALES (est): 9.12MM Privately Held
Web: www.frontier-plumbing.com
SIC: 1711 1521 Plumbing contractors; New construction, single-family houses

(P-1448)
GAF ENERGY LLC
125 Mitchell Blvd (94903-2051)
PHONE..............................510 330-6870
EMP: 80
SALES (corp-wide): 6.27B Privately Held
Web: www.gaf.energy
SIC: 1711 Solar energy contractor
HQ: Gaf Energy Llc
    5981 Optical Ct
    San Jose CA
    973 628-3038

(P-1449)
GENERAL ENGINEERING WSTN INC (PA)
Also Called: Thermal Air
1140 N Red Gum St (92806-2516)

PHONE..............................714 630-3200
Stephen Weiss, *CEO*
Joseph Urban, *
EMP: 60 EST: 1973
SQ FT: 10,000
SALES (est): 28.33MM
SALES (corp-wide): 28.33MM Privately Held
Web: www.thermalair.com
SIC: 1711 Mechanical contractor

(P-1450)
GENERAL UNDERGROUND
701 W Grove Ave (92865-3213)
P.O. Box 29830 (92809-0194)
PHONE..............................714 632-8646
Robert Anderson, *CEO*
Terry Householder, *
Karla Distrola, *
EMP: 110 EST: 1985
SQ FT: 8,000
SALES (est): 23.69MM Privately Held
Web: www.gufpinc.com
SIC: 1711 Fire sprinkler system installation

(P-1451)
GEO H WILSON INC
250 Harvey West Blvd (95060-2127)
P.O. Box 1140 (95061-1140)
PHONE..............................831 423-9522
EMP: 85
SIC: 1711 Heating and air conditioning contractors

(P-1452)
GREATER SAN DIEGO AC CO INC
Also Called: Honeywell Authorized Dealer
3883 Ruffin Rd Ste C (92123-4813)
PHONE..............................619 469-7818
Randy Baillargeon, *Pr*
Ryan Baillargeon, *
EMP: 115 EST: 1993
SQ FT: 8,500
SALES (est): 21.8MM Privately Held
Web: www.gsdac.com
SIC: 1711 Warm air heating and air conditioning contractor

(P-1453)
GRID ALTERNATIVE
1171 Ocean Ave Ste 200 (94608-1147)
PHONE..............................510 731-1310
Tim Sears, *Prin*
Erica Mackie, *Prin*
EMP: 300 EST: 2009
SALES (est): 5.76MM Privately Held
Web: www.gridalternatives.org
SIC: 1711 Solar energy contractor

(P-1454)
H L MOE CO INC (PA)
Also Called: Keefe Plumbing Services
526 Commercial St (91203-1510)
PHONE..............................818 572-2100
Martha Tennyson, *CEO*
Michael C Davis, *
Bernice Davis, *
Richard Herrea, *
Robert Francis, *
EMP: 130 EST: 1927
SALES (est): 21.94MM
SALES (corp-wide): 21.94MM Privately Held
Web: www.moeplumbing.com
SIC: 1711 Plumbing contractors

(P-1455)
HARRISON ENTERPRISES INC
Also Called: General Air Conditioning & Htg
31170 Reserve Dr (92276-6653)
PHONE..............................760 343-7488
Patrick Somers, *Pr*
Frank Harrison, *
EMP: 68 EST: 1993
SQ FT: 3,500
SALES (est): 6.38MM Privately Held
Web: www.callthegeneral.com
SIC: 1711 1731 Plumbing contractors; Electrical work

(P-1456)
HELIX MECHANICAL INC
1100 N Magnolia Ave Ste L (92020-1953)
PHONE..............................619 440-1518
Stephen Baker, *CEO*
Michael Hurley, *
Patrick Harrelson, *
EMP: 109 EST: 2003
SALES (est): 15.84MM Privately Held
Web: www.helixmechanical.com
SIC: 1711 1751 Mechanical contractor; Carpentry work

(P-1457)
HOMEENERGY INC
2930 Domingo Ave (94705-2454)
PHONE..............................707 200-3758
Thomas Enzendorfer, *CEO*
Jordan Peters, *
EMP: 80 EST: 2018
SALES (est): 3.77MM Privately Held
SIC: 1711 Solar energy contractor

(P-1458)
HPS MECHANICAL INC (PA)
3100 E Belle Ter (93307-6830)
PHONE..............................661 397-2121
Les Denherder, *Pr*
Scott Denherder, *
EMP: 127 EST: 1959
SALES (est): 47.31MM
SALES (corp-wide): 47.31MM Privately Held
Web: www.hpsmechanical.com
SIC: 1711 Plumbing contractors

(P-1459)
HUMPHREY PLUMBING INC
880 S Kilroy Rd (95380-9570)
PHONE..............................209 634-4626
Justin Humphrey, *Pr*
Robin Humphrey, *
EMP: 75 EST: 1985
SQ FT: 7,500
SALES (est): 4.94MM Privately Held
Web: humphreyplumbing.business.site
SIC: 1711 Plumbing contractors

(P-1460)
ICOM MECHANICAL INC
Also Called: Icom
477 Burke St (95112-4101)
P.O. Box 975 (95108-0975)
PHONE..............................408 292-4968
TOLL FREE: 800
Donald George Isaacson, *CEO*
Dane Littleton, *
Alan Glace, *
Tom Radich, *
Elizabeth Wozniak, *
EMP: 225 EST: 1981
SQ FT: 24,000
SALES (est): 39.94MM Privately Held
Web: www.icominc.com
SIC: 1711 Mechanical contractor

PRODUCTS & SERVICES SECTION

1711 - Plumbing, Heating, Air-conditioning (P-1483)

(P-1461)
INCOM MECHANICAL INC
975 Transport Way Ste 5 (94954-6860)
PHONE.................707 586-0511
Charles J Lacoti, *Pr*
Gabrielle Candrian, *
Phil Lacoti, *
Jeff Lacoti, *
EMP: 65 **EST:** 1987
SQ FT: 7,000
SALES (est): 9.74MM **Privately Held**
Web: www.incommechanical.com
SIC: 1711 Plumbing contractors

(P-1462)
INDUSTRIAL COML SYSTEMS INC
Also Called: San Marcos Mechanical
1165 Joshua Way (92081-7840)
PHONE.................760 300-4094
Robin Sides, *Pr*
Matt Harbin, *
Cindy Sides, *
EMP: 160 **EST:** 1982
SQ FT: 15,000
SALES (est): 35.44MM **Privately Held**
Web: www.1ics.net
SIC: 1711 Ventilation and duct work contractor

(P-1463)
INFINITY ENERGY CNSTR INC
3825 Atherton Rd Ste 101 (95765-3704)
PHONE.................888 839-2937
Bryson Solomon, *CEO*
EMP: 74 **EST:** 2020
SALES (est): 952.88K
SALES (corp-wide): 66.42MM **Privately Held**
SIC: 1711 Solar energy contractor
PA: Infinity Energy Inc.
3825 Atherton Rd Ste 101
Rocklin CA
916 474-4723

(P-1464)
INFINITY PLUMBING DESIGNS INC
9182 Stellar Ct (92883-4923)
PHONE.................951 737-4436
Andrew D Carlson, *Pr*
EMP: 300 **EST:** 2006
SQ FT: 5,925
SALES (est): 27.1MM **Privately Held**
Web: www.infinityplumbingdesigns.com
SIC: 1711 Plumbing contractors

(P-1465)
INNOVATIVE MAINTENANCE SOLUTIONS INC
Also Called: IMS
725 Del Paso Rd (95834-1106)
PHONE.................916 568-1400
EMP: 115
Web: www.ims.gs
SIC: 1711 0781 1731 7349 Heating and air conditioning contractors; Landscape services; Lighting contractor; Janitorial service, contract basis

(P-1466)
INTECH MECHANICAL COMPANY INC
7501 Galilee Rd (95678-6992)
PHONE.................916 797-4900
Richard B Chowdry, *Pr*
Julie Chowdry, *
EMP: 100 **EST:** 1996
SQ FT: 7,000
SALES (est): 6.36MM **Privately Held**
Web: www.intech-mech.com
SIC: 1711 Plumbing contractors

(P-1467)
INTECH MECHANICAL COMPANY LLC
7501 Galilee Rd (95678-6992)
PHONE.................916 797-4900
Michael Friesen, *
Gary Myers, *
Julie Chowdry, *
EMP: 150 **EST:** 2014
SQ FT: 39,775
SALES (est): 35.55MM **Privately Held**
Web: www.intech-mech.com
SIC: 1711 8711 Plumbing contractors; Heating and ventilation engineering

(P-1468)
INTEGRATED ENERGY GROUP LLC ✪
3929 E Guasti Rd Ste F (91761-1546)
PHONE.................605 381-7859
Shane Scaletti, *
EMP: 155 **EST:** 2023
SALES (est): 60MM **Privately Held**
SIC: 1711 Solar energy contractor

(P-1469)
IRON MECHANICAL INC (PA)
721 N B St Ste 100 (95811-0301)
PHONE.................916 341-3530
Terrance Risse, *Pr*
EMP: 95 **EST:** 2009
SQ FT: 3,000
SALES (est): 24.99MM
SALES (corp-wide): 24.99MM **Privately Held**
Web: www.ironmechanical.com
SIC: 1711 Mechanical contractor

(P-1470)
J & J AIR CONDITIONING INC
Also Called: Honeywell Authorized Dealer
1086 N 11th St (95112-2927)
PHONE.................408 920-0662
Jerry Hurwitz, *Owner*
Susan Borkin, *
EMP: 60 **EST:** 1978
SQ FT: 10,000
SALES (est): 20.7MM **Privately Held**
Web: www.jjair.com
SIC: 1711 Warm air heating and air conditioning contractor

(P-1471)
J M CARDEN SPRINKLER CO INC
2909 Fletcher Dr (90065-1406)
PHONE.................323 258-8300
Michael Carden, *Pr*
Richard Wallace, *
Carroll B Carden, *
EMP: 60 **EST:** 1953
SQ FT: 48,000
SALES (est): 9.43MM **Privately Held**
Web: www.jmcfire.com
SIC: 1711 Fire sprinkler system installation

(P-1472)
JACKSON & BLANC
7929 Arjons Dr (92126-4301)
PHONE.................858 831-7900
Kirk Jackson, *CEO*
John Fusca, *
▲ **EMP:** 110 **EST:** 1931
SQ FT: 36,000
SALES (est): 65.48MM **Privately Held**
Web: www.jacksonandblanc.com
SIC: 1711 Mechanical contractor

(P-1473)
JPI DEVELOPMENT GROUP INC
41205 Golden Gate Cir (92562-6991)
PHONE.................951 973-7680
Brad Janikowski, *Pr*
Dan Janikowski, *
EMP: 60 **EST:** 2000
SQ FT: 6,000
SALES (est): 21.93MM **Privately Held**
Web: www.jpidevelopmentgroup.com
SIC: 1711 Plumbing contractors

(P-1474)
JR PERCE PLBG INC SACRAMENTO
3610 Cincinnati Ave (95765-1203)
PHONE.................916 434-9554
Dennis Pierce, *Pr*
EMP: 150 **EST:** 1927
SQ FT: 11,000
SALES (est): 37.81MM **Privately Held**
Web: www.onlinejrp.com
SIC: 1711 Plumbing contractors

(P-1475)
K & S AIR CONDITIONING INC
Also Called: K&S
143 E Meats Ave (92865-3309)
PHONE.................714 685-0077
Steven Patz, *Pr*
Renee Patz, *
EMP: 140 **EST:** 1952
SQ FT: 18,000
SALES (est): 26.8MM **Privately Held**
Web: www.kandsair.com
SIC: 1711 Warm air heating and air conditioning contractor

(P-1476)
KEN STARR INC
Also Called: Home Comfort USA
1120 N Tustin Ave (92807-1712)
PHONE.................714 632-8789
Ken Starr, *Pr*
Paul Buono, *
EMP: 80 **EST:** 2011
SQ FT: 9,000
SALES (est): 19.68MM **Privately Held**
Web: www.homecomfortusa.com
SIC: 1711 Warm air heating and air conditioning contractor

(P-1477)
KEY AIR CNDITIONING CONTRS INC
10905 Laurel Ave (90670-4513)
PHONE.................562 941-2233
Richard Rivera, *Pr*
Larry Stikeleather, *
Robert Donat, *
EMP: 64 **EST:** 1993
SQ FT: 35,000
SALES (est): 26.54MM **Privately Held**
Web: www.keyairconditioning.net
SIC: 1711 Warm air heating and air conditioning contractor

(P-1478)
KINCAID INDUSTRIES INC
31065 Plantation Dr (92276-6623)
PHONE.................760 343-5457
EMP: 79 **EST:** 1995
SQ FT: 7,000
SALES (est): 21.87MM **Privately Held**
Web: www.kincaidindustries.com

(P-1479)
KINETICS MECHANICAL SVC INC
6336 Patterson Pass Rd Ste H (94550-9577)
PHONE.................925 245-6200
Ralph E Dorotinsky, *Pr*
Craig Kirk, *
EMP: 100 **EST:** 1997
SQ FT: 10,000
SALES (est): 14.38MM **Privately Held**
Web: www.kms-inc.com
SIC: 1711 Mechanical contractor

(P-1480)
L J KRUSE CO
Also Called: Honeywell Authorized Dealer
920 Pardee St (94710-2626)
P.O. Box 2900 (94702-0900)
PHONE.................510 644-0260
David J Kruse, *Pr*
Andrew S Kruse, *
Janell Yates, *
Karen Lown, *
EMP: 60 **EST:** 1916
SQ FT: 14,000
SALES (est): 12.52MM **Privately Held**
Web: www.ljkruse.com
SIC: 1711 Plumbing contractors

(P-1481)
LA SOLAR GROUP INC
Also Called: LA SOLAR GROUP
560 Library St (91340-2524)
PHONE.................818 373-0077
Ara Petrosyan, *CEO*
EMP: 91 **EST:** 2012
SALES (est): 55.41MM **Privately Held**
Web: www.la-solargroup.com
SIC: 1711 Solar energy contractor

(P-1482)
LAWSON MECHANICAL CONTRACTORS (PA)
6090 S Watt Ave (95829-1301)
P.O. Box 15224 (95851-0224)
PHONE.................916 381-5000
Rodney Lawson, *Pr*
Rod Barbour, *
David Lawson, *
EMP: 97 **EST:** 1947
SQ FT: 31,000
SALES (est): 38.9MM
SALES (corp-wide): 38.9MM **Privately Held**
Web: www.lawsonmechanical.com
SIC: 1711 Plumbing contractors

(P-1483)
LDI MECHANICAL INC (PA)
Also Called: Honeywell Authorized Dealer
1587 E Bentley Dr (92879-1740)
PHONE.................951 340-9685
Lloyd Smith, *Pr*
Mike Smith, *
Robert Smith, *
Steve Buren, *
Jeff Minarik, *
EMP: 155 **EST:** 1985
SQ FT: 38,000
SALES (est): 94.22MM
SALES (corp-wide): 94.22MM **Privately Held**
Web: www.ldimechanical.com
SIC: 1711 Mechanical contractor

1711 - Plumbing, Heating, Air-conditioning (P-1484)

(P-1484)
LEFCO INC
Also Called: Lefco
1650 Las Plumas Ave (95133-1657)
PHONE................................408 729-4800
EMP: 70 EST: 1974
SALES (est): 7.46MM **Privately Held**
SIC: **1711** Warm air heating and air conditioning contractor

(P-1485)
LEGACY MECH & ENRGY SVCS INC
Also Called: Legacy Mechanical
3130 Crow Canyon Pl Ste 410 (94583-1346)
PHONE................................925 820-6938
Bill Longbotham, *VP*
Jack Larkin, *
Chip Eskildsen Pe, *VP*
EMP: 100 EST: 2002
SQ FT: 4,000
SALES (est): 31.85MM **Privately Held**
Web: www.legacymechanical.com
SIC: **1711** Mechanical contractor

(P-1486)
LESCURE COMPANY INC
2301 Arnold Industrial Way Ste C (94520-5360)
P.O. Box 968 (94549-0968)
PHONE................................925 283-2528
Michael Lescure, *Pr*
Allen Lescure, *
EMP: 70 EST: 1947
SQ FT: 10,000
SALES (est): 9.45MM **Privately Held**
Web: www.lescurecompany.com
SIC: **1711** Plumbing contractors

(P-1487)
LITE SOLAR CORP
Also Called: Lite Solar
3553 Atlantic Ave (90807-4515)
PHONE................................562 256-1249
EMP: 150
Web: www.litesolar.com
SIC: **1711** Solar energy contractor

(P-1488)
LIVE ACTION GENERAL ENGRG INC
2972 Larkin Ave (93612-3916)
PHONE................................559 292-2900
Bobby Tracy, *Pr*
EMP: 130 EST: 2014
SALES (est): 60MM **Privately Held**
Web: www.eliteteamoffices.com
SIC: **1711** 1771 1611 3531 Solar energy contractor; Concrete work; Surfacing and paving; Plows: construction, excavating, and grading

(P-1489)
LOVAZZANO MECHANICAL INC
189 Constitution Dr (94025-1106)
PHONE................................650 367-6216
Bruce Lovazzano Senior, *CEO*
EMP: 70 EST: 1991
SQ FT: 3,100
SALES (est): 9.26MM **Privately Held**
Web: www.lovazzano.com
SIC: **1711** Plumbing contractors

(P-1490)
LOZANO PLUMBING SERVICES INC
Also Called: Plumbing Master
3615 Presley Ave (92507-4448)
P.O. Box 53137 (92517-4137)
PHONE................................951 683-4840
Andrew Lozano, *Pr*
Felipe Lozano, *
Andrew Lozano, *Sec*
EMP: 130 EST: 2004
SALES (est): 13.56MM **Privately Held**
Web: www.plumbingmaster.com
SIC: **1711** Plumbing contractors

(P-1491)
LPSH HOLDINGS INC (PA)
Also Called: Horizon Solar Power
7100 W Florida Ave (92545-3410)
PHONE................................855 647-5061
Frank Kneller, *CEO*
Leroy Polvoorde, *
Gail Polvoorde, *
EMP: 96 EST: 2013
SALES (est): 50.62MM
SALES (corp-wide): 50.62MM **Privately Held**
SIC: **1711** Solar energy contractor

(P-1492)
LPSH HOLDINGS INC
Also Called: Horizon Solar Power
3570 W Florida Ave Ste 168 (92545-3518)
PHONE................................951 926-1176
Zachary Allman, *Acctg Mgr*
EMP: 429
SALES (corp-wide): 50.62MM **Privately Held**
SIC: **1711** Solar energy contractor
PA: Lpsh Holdings, Inc.
7100 W Florida Ave
Hemet CA
855 647-5061

(P-1493)
LUPPEN AND HAWLEY INC
6330 N Point Way (95831-1067)
PHONE................................916 456-7831
EMP: 110
Web: www.luppenandhawleyinc.com
SIC: **1711** 1731 Plumbing contractors; Electrical work

(P-1494)
M & M PLUMBING INC
6782 Columbus St (92504-1118)
PHONE................................951 354-5388
Robert Malcom, *Pr*
Glenn Malcolm, *
EMP: 80 EST: 2002
SALES (est): 4.7MM **Privately Held**
Web: www.mmplumbing.net
SIC: **1711** Plumbing contractors

(P-1495)
MAINSTREAM ENERGY CORPORATION
Also Called: Rec Solar
775 Fiero Ln Ste 200 (93401-7904)
PHONE................................805 528-9705
EMP: 493
Web: www.mainstreamenergy.com
SIC: **1711** 5049 Solar energy contractor; Scientific and engineering equipment and supplies

(P-1496)
MARELICH MECHANICAL CO INC (HQ)
24041 Amador St (94544-1201)
PHONE................................510 785-5500
Keith R Atteberry, *Pr*
Terry J Kvochak, *
Andrew Ostrowski, *
John Powell, *
Chad Johnston, *
EMP: 65 EST: 1946
SQ FT: 40,000
SALES (est): 47.6MM
SALES (corp-wide): 11.08B **Publicly Held**
Web: www.marelich.com
SIC: **1711** 1623 3822 Mechanical contractor; Pipeline construction, nsk; Environmental controls
PA: Emcor Group, Inc.
301 Merritt 7 Fl 6
Norwalk CT
203 849-7800

(P-1497)
MATRIX HG INC
115 Mason Cir Ste B (94520-8530)
PHONE................................925 459-9200
EMP: 186 EST: 2002
SALES (est): 79.62MM **Privately Held**
Web: www.matrixhginc.com
SIC: **1711** Plumbing, heating, air-conditioning

(P-1498)
MDDR INC
Also Called: Econo Air
1921 Petra Ln (92870-6749)
PHONE................................714 792-1993
Michael Richards, *Pr*
Rhonda Richards, *
EMP: 110 EST: 1991
SALES (est): 23.89MM **Privately Held**
Web: www.myeconoair.com
SIC: **1711** 1731 Warm air heating and air conditioning contractor; Electrical work

(P-1499)
MEMEGED TEVUOT SHEMESH (PA)
Also Called: Titan Solar
5550 Topanga Canyon Blvd Ste 280 (91367-6478)
PHONE................................866 575-1211
Ofir Haimoff, *Pr*
EMP: 152 EST: 2011
SQ FT: 20,000
SALES (est): 7.72MM
SALES (corp-wide): 7.72MM **Privately Held**
SIC: **1711** 5074 Solar energy contractor; Heating equipment and panels, solar

(P-1500)
MESA ENERGY SYSTEMS INC (HQ)
Also Called: Emcor Services Mesa Energy
2 Cromwell (92618-1816)
PHONE................................949 460-0460
Robert A Lake, *Pr*
Charles G Fletcher Junior, *VP*
Michael Ecshner, *
Kip Bagley, *
Steve Hunt, *
EMP: 210 EST: 1984
SQ FT: 55,000
SALES (est): 114.02MM
SALES (corp-wide): 11.08B **Publicly Held**
Web: www.mesaenergy.com
SIC: **1711** 7623 Warm air heating and air conditioning contractor; Refrigeration service and repair
PA: Emcor Group, Inc.
301 Merritt 7 Fl 6
Norwalk CT
203 849-7800

(P-1501)
MODERN AIR MECHANICAL
2200 Cooper Ave (95348-4306)
P.O. Box 3017 (95344-1017)
PHONE................................209 722-1815
EMP: 80 EST: 1983
SALES (est): 34.74MM **Privately Held**
Web: www.modernair.biz
SIC: **1711** Warm air heating and air conditioning contractor

(P-1502)
MONSTER MEP INC
1521 Terminal Ave (95112-4316)
P.O. Box 6 (95031-0006)
PHONE................................408 727-8362
Jeffery Miller, *Pr*
EMP: 60 EST: 1997
SQ FT: 10,000
SALES (est): 7.86MM **Privately Held**
Web: www.monstermechanical.com
SIC: **1711** Plumbing contractors

(P-1503)
MUIR-CHASE PLUMBING CO INC
Also Called: M C
4530 Brazil St Ste 1 (90039-1002)
PHONE................................818 500-1940
Don Chase, *Pr*
Jay Chase, *
James M Muir, *
Grant Muir, *
Gail Comstock, *
EMP: 90 EST: 1975
SQ FT: 5,000
SALES (est): 23.76MM **Privately Held**
Web: www.muirchase.com
SIC: **1711** 7699 Plumbing contractors; Sewer cleaning and rodding

(P-1504)
MULTI MECHANICAL INC
Also Called: Honeywell Authorized Dealer
469 Blaine St (92879-1304)
PHONE................................714 632-7404
Brandon Abblitt, *CEO*
EMP: 75 EST: 2003
SALES (est): 23.6MM **Privately Held**
Web: www.honeywell.com
SIC: **1711** Mechanical contractor

(P-1505)
MURRAY PLUMBING AND HTG CORP (PA)
Also Called: Murray Company
18414 S Santa Fe Ave (90221-5612)
PHONE................................310 637-1500
Kevan Steffey, *Ch*
James De Flavio, *
EMP: 326 EST: 1913
SQ FT: 26,000
SALES (est): 354.84MM
SALES (corp-wide): 354.84MM **Privately Held**
Web: www.murraycompany.com
SIC: **1711** Plumbing contractors

(P-1506)
N V HEATHORN INC
Also Called: N V H
1980 Olivera Rd Ste C (94520-5454)
PHONE................................510 569-9100
Edward W Heathorn, *Pr*
Norman T R Heathorn, *
David A Heathorn, *
Wendy C Heathorn, *
EMP: 63 EST: 1932
SALES (est): 12.87MM **Privately Held**

PRODUCTS & SERVICES SECTION **1711 - Plumbing, Heating, Air-conditioning (P-1527)**

Web: www.nvheathorn.com
SIC: 1711 1629 Warm air heating and air conditioning contractor; Waste water and sewage treatment plant construction

(P-1507)
NATIONAL AIR INC
Also Called: National Air and Energy
2053 Kurtz St (92110-2014)
PHONE.............................619 299-2500
Jared M Wells, CEO
EMP: 110 EST: 1995
SQ FT: 10,500
SALES (est): 24.49MM **Privately Held**
Web: www.natlair.com
SIC: 1711 Mechanical contractor

(P-1508)
NEW ENGLAND SHTMTL & MECH CO
2731 S Cherry Ave (93706-5423)
P.O. Box 27409 (93729-7409)
PHONE.............................559 268-7375
John Sloan, CEO
Joshua Wilkinson, *
EMP: 220 EST: 2008
SALES (est): 53.38MM
SALES (corp-wide): 17.85MM **Privately Held**
Web: www.nesm.com
SIC: 1711 Mechanical contractor
PA: Lyles Diversified, Inc.
525 W Alluvial Ave
Fresno CA
559 441-1900

(P-1509)
NEW POWER INC
887 Marlborough Ave (92507-2133)
PHONE.............................800 980-9825
Thomas Shaffer, Pr
Matt Collins, *
EMP: 83 EST: 2009
SALES (est): 7.73MM **Privately Held**
Web: www.newpower.company
SIC: 1711 Solar energy contractor

(P-1510)
NEXGEN AC & HTG LLC
Also Called: Nexgen Air Conditioning & Plbg
700 N Valley St Ste K (92801-3824)
PHONE.............................760 616-5870
Ismael Valdez, CEO
Yanela Valdez, *
EMP: 84 EST: 2015
SALES (est): 11.92MM
SALES (corp-wide): 215.03MM **Privately Held**
SIC: 1711 Warm air heating and air conditioning contractor
PA: Wrench Group Llc
1787 Williams Dr
Marietta GA
678 784-2260

(P-1511)
NEXGEN AIR LOS ANGELES
Also Called: Nexgen Air Heating and Plbg
19205 Parthenia St (91324-3643)
PHONE.............................818 900-2525
EMP: 110
SALES (corp-wide): 8.63MM **Privately Held**
Web: www.nexgenairandplumbing.com
SIC: 1711 Warm air heating and air conditioning contractor
PA: Nexgen Air Los Angeles
5472 E La Palma Ave
Anaheim CA
714 331-9633

(P-1512)
NP MECHANICAL INC
9129 Stellar Ct (92883-4924)
P.O. Box 309 (92878-0309)
PHONE.............................951 667-4220
Cecil J Hallinan, CEO
Richard Hallinan, *
EMP: 400 EST: 2005
SALES (est): 60.32MM **Privately Held**
Web: www.npmechanicalinc.net
SIC: 1711 Mechanical contractor

(P-1513)
O & M INDUSTRIES (PA)
Also Called: O & M South
5901 Ericson Way (95521-9239)
PHONE.............................707 822-8800
EMP: 80 EST: 1946
SALES (est): 24.35MM
SALES (corp-wide): 24.35MM **Privately Held**
Web: www.omindustries.com
SIC: 1711 1761 1791 Warm air heating and air conditioning contractor; Sheet metal work, nec; Structural steel erection

(P-1514)
O C MCDONALD CO INC
1150 W San Carlos St (95126-3440)
P.O. Box 26560 (95159-6560)
PHONE.............................408 295-2182
James Mc Donald, Pr
EMP: 150 EST: 1906
SQ FT: 10,500
SALES (est): 46.18MM **Privately Held**
Web: www.ocmcdonald.com
SIC: 1711 3585 3541 3444 Mechanical contractor; Refrigeration and heating equipment; Machine tools, metal cutting type; Sheet metalwork

(P-1515)
OHAGINS INC
210 Classic Ct Ste 100 (94928-1660)
PHONE.............................707 303-3660
Carolina O'hagin, CEO
Greg Daniels, *
Mark Marquez, *
▲ EMP: 60 EST: 1969
SQ FT: 57,000
SALES (est): 4.84MM **Privately Held**
Web: www.ohagin.com
SIC: 1711 Ventilation and duct work contractor

(P-1516)
ON-TIME AC & HTG LLC
Also Called: Service Champions
261 Arthur Rd (94553-2207)
PHONE.............................925 566-2422
EMP: 62
SALES (corp-wide): 215.03MM **Privately Held**
Web: www.servicechampions.net
SIC: 1711 Septic system construction
HQ: On-Time Air Conditioning & Heating, Llc
7020 Commerce Dr
Pleasanton CA
925 598-1911

(P-1517)
ON-TIME AC & HTG LLC
Also Called: Service Champions
96 Rickenbacker Cir (94551-7211)
PHONE.............................925 800-5804
EMP: 71
SALES (corp-wide): 215.03MM **Privately Held**
Web: www.servicechampions.net
SIC: 1711 Warm air heating and air conditioning contractor
HQ: On-Time Air Conditioning & Heating, Llc
7020 Commerce Dr
Pleasanton CA
925 598-1911

(P-1518)
ON-TIME AC & HTG LLC (HQ)
Also Called: Service Champions
7020 Commerce Dr (94588-8021)
PHONE.............................925 598-1911
Keviin J Comerford, CEO
EMP: 88 EST: 2002
SALES (est): 59.33MM
SALES (corp-wide): 215.03MM **Privately Held**
Web: www.servicechampions.net
SIC: 1711 Warm air heating and air conditioning contractor
PA: Wrench Group Llc
1787 Williams Dr
Marietta GA
678 784-2260

(P-1519)
ONE CALL PLUMBER SANTA BARBARA
1016 Cliff Dr Apt 309 (93109-1784)
PHONE.............................805 364-6337
EMP: 100 EST: 2017
SALES (est): 2.49MM **Privately Held**
SIC: 1711 Plumbing contractors

(P-1520)
ORANGE COUNTY SERVICES INC
Also Called: George Brazil Plbg Htg & AC
3022 N Hesperian St (92706-1151)
PHONE.............................714 541-9753
Mike Jones, Genl Mgr
EMP: 94
SIC: 1711 1731 Plumbing contractors; Electrical work
PA: Orange County Services, Inc.
3801 Lenawee Ave
Culver City CA

(P-1521)
ORIGINAL SID BLACKMAN PLBG INC
1160 S 2nd St (92243-3446)
P.O. Box 3487 (92244-3487)
PHONE.............................760 352-3632
Thomas Blackman, Pr
Michael Wickline, *
EMP: 68 EST: 1992
SALES (est): 4.97MM **Privately Held**
Web: www.blackmanplumbing.net
SIC: 1711 Plumbing contractors

(P-1522)
PACIFIC RIM MECH CONTRS INC
1701 E Edinger Ave Ste F2 (92705-5028)
PHONE.............................714 285-2600
John Heusner, Mgr
EMP: 250
SALES (corp-wide): 227.5MM **Privately Held**
Web: www.prmech.com
SIC: 1711 Mechanical contractor
PA: Pacific Rim Mechanical Contractors, Inc.
9125 Rehco Rd
San Diego CA
858 974-6500

(P-1523)
PACIFIC RIM MECH CONTRS INC (PA)
Also Called: Honeywell Authorized Dealer
9125 Rehco Rd (92121-2270)
PHONE.............................858 974-6500
Joseph Mucher, CEO
Eric Bader, *
Theodore J Keenan, *
Brian Turner, *
Colin Cook, *
EMP: 400 EST: 2002
SQ FT: 50,000
SALES (est): 227.5MM
SALES (corp-wide): 227.5MM **Privately Held**
Web: www.prmech.com
SIC: 1711 Mechanical contractor

(P-1524)
PAN-PACIFIC MECHANICAL LLC (PA)
Also Called: Pan-Pacific Mechanical
18250 Euclid St (92708-6112)
PHONE.............................949 474-9170
Reed Mcmackin, CEO
Cindy Lanette Mcmackin, Pr
Rex Mcmackin, VP
Joe Koh, *
Jon Houchin, *
▲ EMP: 150 EST: 1947
SQ FT: 60,000
SALES (est): 405.33MM
SALES (corp-wide): 405.33MM **Privately Held**
Web: www.ppmechanical.com
SIC: 1711 Plumbing contractors

(P-1525)
PAN-PACIFIC MECHANICAL LLC
48363 Fremont Blvd (94538-6580)
PHONE.............................650 561-8810
Tom Sakurai, Mgr
EMP: 424
SALES (corp-wide): 405.33MM **Privately Held**
Web: www.ppmechanical.com
SIC: 1711 Plumbing contractors
PA: Pan-Pacific Mechanical Llc
18250 Euclid St
Fountain Valley CA
949 474-9170

(P-1526)
PAN-PACIFIC MECHANICAL LLC
Also Called: Pan-Pacific Plumbing & Mech
11622 El Camino Real Ste 100 (92130-2049)
PHONE.............................858 764-2464
EMP: 425
SALES (corp-wide): 405.33MM **Privately Held**
Web: www.ppmechanical.com
SIC: 1711 Mechanical contractor
PA: Pan-Pacific Mechanical Llc
18250 Euclid St
Fountain Valley CA
949 474-9170

(P-1527)
PARAGON MECHANICAL INC
16160 Caputo Dr (95037-5539)
P.O. Box 58 (95052-0058)
PHONE.............................408 727-7303
EMP: 115 EST: 1986
SALES (est): 19.33MM **Privately Held**
Web: www.paragonmechanical.com
SIC: 1711 Warm air heating and air conditioning contractor

(PA)=Parent Co (HQ)=Headquarters
✪ = New Business established in last 2 years

1711 - Plumbing, Heating, Air-conditioning (P-1528)

(P-1528)
PETERSON MECHANICAL INC
21819 8th St E (95476-9797)
P.O. Box 450 (95476-0450)
PHONE..................707 938-8481
EMP: 90 EST: 1915
SALES (est): 20.4MM Privately Held
Web: www.petersonmechanical.com
SIC: 1711 Mechanical contractor

(P-1529)
PLUMBING PIPING & CNSTR INC
5950 Lakeshore Dr (90630-3371)
PHONE..................714 821-0490
Bruce Cook Junior, Pr
EMP: 100 EST: 1960
SQ FT: 12,600
SALES (est): 27.37MM Privately Held
Web: www.1ppc.com
SIC: 1711 Plumbing, heating, air-conditioning

(P-1530)
PLUMBING SOLUTION SPECIALIST
28202 Cabot Rd Ste 300 (92677-1249)
P.O. Box 17022 (92817-7022)
PHONE..................714 326-1064
Marcos Uriarte, Owner
EMP: 75 EST: 2010
SALES (est): 2.72MM Privately Held
Web: www.plumbingsolutionsspecialist.com
SIC: 1711 Plumbing contractors

(P-1531)
PLUMBING SYSTEMS WEST INC
31491 Outer Highway 10 (92373-7568)
PHONE..................909 794-3823
Bob Grable, Pr
EMP: 68 EST: 2013
SALES (est): 3.36MM Privately Held
Web: www.plumbingsystems.net
SIC: 1711 Plumbing contractors

(P-1532)
PPC ENTERPRISES INC
Also Called: Premier Plumbing Company
5920 Rickenbacker Ave (92504-1042)
PHONE..................951 354-5402
Jeffrey Geiger, Pr
Dawn Geiger, *
EMP: 125 EST: 1982
SQ FT: 10,000
SALES (est): 12.16MM Privately Held
Web: www.premierplumbingcompany.com
SIC: 1711 Plumbing contractors

(P-1533)
PRECISE AIR SYSTEMS INC
Also Called: Hvac Installation and Repair
5467 W San Fernando Rd (90039-1014)
P.O. Box 39609 (90039-0609)
PHONE..................818 646-9757
TOLL FREE: 877
Fred Khachekian, Pr
EMP: 91 EST: 1975
SQ FT: 3,200
SALES (est): 18.5MM Privately Held
Web: www.preciseairsystems.com
SIC: 1711 Warm air heating and air conditioning contractor

(P-1534)
PRO TRAFFIC SERVICES INC
321 Hunter St (92065-3005)
PHONE..................760 906-6961
Janet Andrews, Pr
Neil Treffers, *
Greg Wakeman, *
EMP: 99 EST: 2018
SALES (est): 3.56MM Privately Held
Web: www.ptats.com
SIC: 1711 Plumbing, heating, air-conditioning

(P-1535)
PRO-CRAFT CONSTRUCTION INC
500 Iowa St Ste 100 (92373-8068)
PHONE..................909 790-5222
Timothy Mcfayden, Pr
Susan Mc Fayden, *
EMP: 142 EST: 2006
SALES (est): 27.03MM Privately Held
Web: www.procraftci.com
SIC: 1711 Plumbing contractors

(P-1536)
PRO-TECH FIRE PRTCTION SYSTEMS
8880 Cal Center Dr Ste 400 (95826-3222)
PHONE..................916 388-0255
Michael Walsh, Prin
EMP: 100
Web: www.pro-techfire.com
SIC: 1711 Fire sprinkler system installation
HQ: Pro-Tech Fire Protection Systems Corp.
8540 Younger Creek Dr # 2
Sacramento CA

(P-1537)
PROCESS COOLING INTL INC (PA)
Also Called: Applied Process Cooling
4812 Enterprise Way (95356-8718)
PHONE..................209 578-1000
Gary Dunn, Pr
Paul Saubolle, *
▲ EMP: 100 EST: 1982
SQ FT: 4,500
SALES (est): 62.53MM
SALES (corp-wide): 62.53MM Privately Held
Web: www.apcco.net
SIC: 1711 8711 Refrigeration contractor; Engineering services

(P-1538)
R & R MECHANICAL CONTRACTORS INC
1400 N Johnson Ave # 114 (92020-1616)
PHONE..................619 449-9900
EMP: 100 EST: 1998
SALES (est): 8.97MM Privately Held
SIC: 1711 Mechanical contractor

(P-1539)
RAM MECHANICAL INC
3506 Moore Rd (95307-9402)
PHONE..................209 531-9155
Neil Hodgson, Pr
Neil Hodgson, Prin
James A Frias, Prin
EMP: 60 EST: 2004
SQ FT: 22,500
SALES (est): 25.17MM Privately Held
Web: www.ram-mechanical.com
SIC: 1711 8711 3599 3535 Mechanical contractor; Engineering services; Custom machinery; Conveyors and conveying equipment

(P-1540)
RAM PLUMBING
14745 Addison St (91403-1635)
PHONE..................800 487-5812
EMP: 88
SALES (corp-wide): 835.47K Privately Held
Web: www.ramplumbing.com
SIC: 1711 Plumbing contractors
PA: Ram Plumbing
14431 Ventura Blvd
Sherman Oaks CA
818 907-5812

(P-1541)
RAWLINGS MECHANICAL CORP (PA)
11615 Pendleton St (91352-2502)
P.O. Box 703 (91353-0703)
PHONE..................323 875-2040
Robert S Bratton, Pr
Rex Horney, *
Patricia Wood, *
EMP: 74 EST: 1953
SQ FT: 22,000
SALES (est): 21.12MM
SALES (corp-wide): 21.12MM Privately Held
Web: www.rawlingsmechanical.com
SIC: 1711 Mechanical contractor

(P-1542)
RAY L HELLWIG MECHANICAL CO INC
1309 Laurelwood Rd (95054-2759)
PHONE..................408 727-5080
EMP: 100 EST: 1991
SALES (est): 9.78MM Privately Held
Web: www.hellwigmechanical.com
SIC: 1711 Heating and air conditioning contractors

(P-1543)
RAY L HELLWIG PLUMBING & HEATING INC
1301 Laurelwood Rd (95054-2743)
PHONE..................408 727-5612
EMP: 290
SIC: 1711 Plumbing contractors

(P-1544)
RC MAINTENANCE HOLDINGS INC
569 Bateman Cir (92878-4012)
PHONE..................951 903-6303
Richard Collins Junior, Pr
Christine Meva, Acctg Mgr
EMP: 130 EST: 2020
SALES (est): 22.14MM Privately Held
Web: www.rcstoremaintenance.com
SIC: 1711 Plumbing, heating, air-conditioning

(P-1545)
REC SOLAR COMMERCIAL CORP
Also Called: Rec Solar
3450 Broad St Ste 105 (93401-7214)
PHONE..................844 732-7652
Matt Walz, CEO
Gary Morris, *
EMP: 200 EST: 2013
SQ FT: 15,000
SALES (est): 87.92MM
SALES (corp-wide): 28.77B Publicly Held
Web: www.northern-pine.com
SIC: 1711 Solar energy contractor
PA: Duke Energy Corporation
526 S Church St
Charlotte NC
704 382-3853

(P-1546)
REFRIGERATION SOLUTIONS LLC
Also Called: RSI
1166 National Dr Ste 10 (95834-1938)
PHONE..................916 281-2000
Thomas A Ryan, Managing Member
EMP: 77 EST: 2016
SALES (est): 11.63MM
SALES (corp-wide): 3.06B Publicly Held
Web: www.rsiclimate.com
SIC: 1711 Refrigeration contractor
HQ: Coolsys Commercial & Industrial Solutions, Inc.
145 S State College Blvd
Brea CA

(P-1547)
RELIABLE ENERGY MANAGEMENT INC
Also Called: Honeywell Authorized Dealer
6829 Walthall Way (90723-2028)
PHONE..................562 984-5511
EMP: 80 EST: 1995
SALES (est): 18.92MM Privately Held
Web: www.relenergy.com
SIC: 1711 Warm air heating and air conditioning contractor

(P-1548)
RESIDENTIAL FIRE SYSTEMS INC
8085 E Crystal Dr (92807-2523)
PHONE..................714 666-8450
Ty Maley, Pr
Cesar Anchondo, *
Jack Maley, *
Ruben Hernandez, *
EMP: 75 EST: 2000
SQ FT: 6,200
SALES (est): 19.62MM Privately Held
Web: www.resfire.com
SIC: 1711 5063 Fire sprinkler system installation; Signaling equipment, electrical

(P-1549)
RLH FIRE PROTECTION INC (PA)
4300 Stine Rd Ste 800 (93313-2354)
P.O. Box 42470 (93384-2470)
PHONE..................661 322-9344
Michael Norton, CEO
Jason Norton, *
Gary Stites, *
Geoff Kallenberger, *
Gregg Fulton, *
EMP: 75 EST: 1984
SQ FT: 8,000
SALES (est): 42.31MM
SALES (corp-wide): 42.31MM Privately Held
Web: www.rlhfp.com
SIC: 1711 1542 Fire sprinkler system installation; Nonresidential construction, nec

(P-1550)
ROUNTREE PLUMBING AND HTG INC
1624 Santa Clara Dr Ste 130 (95661-3522)
PHONE..................650 298-0300
Stephen Singewald, Pr
Pat Singewald, *
EMP: 60 EST: 1961
SQ FT: 10,000
SALES (est): 9.84MM Privately Held
Web: www.rountreeinc.com
SIC: 1711 Plumbing contractors

PRODUCTS & SERVICES SECTION

1711 - Plumbing, Heating, Air-conditioning (P-1574)

(P-1551)
RUSSELL MECHANICAL INC
3251 Monier Cir Ste A (95742-6812)
PHONE..................................916 635-2522
Danny L Russell, *Pr*
Steve Russell, *
Karen Russell, *
EMP: 90 **EST:** 1982
SQ FT: 22,000
SALES (est): 18.95MM **Privately Held**
Web: www.russellmechanical.com
SIC: 1711 1799 7389 3441 Mechanical contractor; Welding on site; Design services; Fabricated structural metal

(P-1552)
S S W MECHANICAL CNSTR INC
Also Called: Ssw
670 S Oleander Rd (92264-1502)
P.O. Box 3160 (92263-3160)
PHONE..................................760 327-1481
Sean Wood, *Pr*
W T Hayes, *
EMP: 140 **EST:** 1996
SQ FT: 7,000
SALES (est): 23.51MM **Privately Held**
Web: www.sswmechanical.com
SIC: 1711 Plumbing contractors

(P-1553)
SAHARGUN PLUMBING INC
Also Called: Sahargun Mechanical
2216 Stewart St (95205-3232)
PHONE..................................209 474-2611
EMP: 70
Web: www.sahargun.com
SIC: 1711 Mechanical contractor

(P-1554)
SAN BENITO HTG & SHTMTL INC
Also Called: Honeywell Authorized Dealer
1771 San Felipe Rd (95023-2543)
P.O. Box 321 (95024-0321)
PHONE..................................831 637-1112
Robert Rodriguez, *Pr*
Araceli Rodriguez, *
Enrique T Rodriguez, *
Priscilla Rodriguez, *
EMP: 85 **EST:** 1985
SQ FT: 12,000
SALES (est): 4.61MM **Privately Held**
Web: www.sanbenitoheating.com
SIC: 1711 1761 Warm air heating and air conditioning contractor; Sheet metal work, nec

(P-1555)
SCHMIDT FIRE PROTECTION CO INC
4760 Murphy Canyon Rd Ste 100 (92123-4334)
PHONE..................................858 279-6122
John J Durso, *Pr*
Greg Konold, *
John J Durso, *VP*
EMP: 72 **EST:** 1969
SQ FT: 13,800
SALES (est): 11.29MM **Privately Held**
Web: www.schmidtfireprotection.com
SIC: 1711 Fire sprinkler system installation

(P-1556)
SDG ENTERPRISES
Also Called: Century West Plumbing
822 Hampshire Rd Ste H (91361-2850)
PHONE..................................805 777-7978
Nick Simili, *Pr*
Robert Garcia, *
Vincent Simili, *
Vincent Dipinto, *
EMP: 100 **EST:** 1999
SQ FT: 3,000
SALES (est): 9.65MM **Privately Held**
SIC: 1711 Plumbing contractors

(P-1557)
SEAI ELK GROVE LLC
1170 N Gilbert St (92801-1401)
PHONE..................................949 281-7897
David Yoo, *CFO*
▲ **EMP:** 62 **EST:** 2011
SQ FT: 2,000
SALES (est): 4.34MM **Privately Held**
SIC: 1711 Solar energy contractor
HQ: S-Energy America, Inc.
1170 N Gilbert St
Anaheim CA
949 281-7897

(P-1558)
SERVICE GENIUS LOS ANGELES INC
8925 Fullbright Ave (91311-6124)
PHONE..................................818 200-3379
William Monk, *Pr*
EMP: 100 **EST:** 2018
SALES (est): 10MM **Privately Held**
Web: www.servicegenius.com
SIC: 1711 Warm air heating and air conditioning contractor

(P-1559)
SHELDON MECHANICAL CORPORATION
26015 Avenue Hall (91355-1241)
PHONE..................................661 286-1361
Dan Boute, *Pr*
Stanley Nisenson, *
Beverly Nisenson, *
Chrystal Bout'e, *
EMP: 80 **EST:** 1984
SQ FT: 45,000
SALES (est): 24.01MM **Privately Held**
Web: www.sheldonmech.com
SIC: 1711 Mechanical contractor

(P-1560)
SHERWOOD MECHANICAL INC
6630 Top Gun St (92121-4112)
PHONE..................................858 679-3000
Mitch Roberts, *Pr*
James Robert, *
Bill Smyth, *
EMP: 100 **EST:** 2003
SALES (est): 22.29MM **Privately Held**
Web: www.sherwoodmechanical.com
SIC: 1711 Mechanical contractor

(P-1561)
SILICON VALLEY MECHANICAL INC
2115 Ringwood Ave (95131-1725)
P.O. Box 10415 (28461-0415)
PHONE..................................408 943-0380
Blaine Flickner, *CEO*
EMP: 218 **EST:** 2014
SALES (est): 52.01MM **Privately Held**
Web: www.svminc.com
SIC: 1711 Mechanical contractor

(P-1562)
SIMPLY SOLAR
Also Called: Contractor
1740 Corporate Cir (94954-6924)
PHONE..................................707 285-7037
Jake Hassid, *CEO*
EMP: 62 **EST:** 2021
SALES (est): 9.88MM **Privately Held**
Web: www.simplysolar.com
SIC: 1711 1761 Solar energy contractor; Roofing contractor

(P-1563)
SKYPOWER HOLDINGS LLC
4700 Wilshire Blvd (90010-3831)
PHONE..................................323 860-4900
Kerry Adler, *CEO*
Avi Shemesh, *Pr*
EMP: 101 **EST:** 2010
SALES (est): 8.55MM **Privately Held**
Web: www.cimgroup.com
SIC: 1711 Solar energy contractor

(P-1564)
SMA SOLAR TECHNOLOGY AMER LLC
Also Called: SMA America
3925 Atherton Rd (95765-3720)
PHONE..................................916 625-0870
◆ **EMP:** 200 **EST:** 2009
SALES (est): 247.26MM
SALES (corp-wide): 1.11B **Privately Held**
Web: www.sma-america.com
SIC: 1711 Solar energy contractor
PA: Sma Solar Technology Ag
Sonnenallee 1
Niestetal HE
56195220

(P-1565)
SMART ENERGY SOLAR INC
Also Called: Smart Energy USA
1641 Comm St (92880)
PHONE..................................800 405-1978
Leo Joaquin Bautista, *Prin*
EMP: 120 **EST:** 2013
SALES (est): 20.03MM **Privately Held**
Web: www.smartenergyusa.com
SIC: 1711 Solar energy contractor

(P-1566)
SOLAR COMPANY INC
20861 Wilbeam Ave Ste 1 (94546-5832)
PHONE..................................510 888-9488
Mark Danenhower, *Pr*
Duane Redman, *
EMP: 90 **EST:** 2009
SQ FT: 4,000
SALES (est): 9.92MM **Privately Held**
Web: www.ilovemysolar.com
SIC: 1711 Solar energy contractor

(P-1567)
SOLAR SPECTRUM LLC
Also Called: Sungevity
27368 Via Industria Ste 101 (92590-4855)
PHONE..................................844 777-6527
Patrick Mcgivern, *CEO*
William Nettles, *
David White, *
EMP: 266 **EST:** 2017
SALES (est): 51.19MM **Privately Held**
SIC: 1711 8713 Solar energy contractor; Surveying services

(P-1568)
SOLCIUS LLC
Also Called: SOLCIUS LLC
12155 Magnolia Ave Ste 12b/C (92503-4967)
PHONE..................................951 772-0030
Bryan Jackson, *Brnch Mgr*
EMP: 227
SALES (corp-wide): 69.13MM **Privately Held**
Web: www.solcius.com
SIC: 1711 Solar energy contractor
PA: Solcius, Llc
1555 N Freedom Blvd
Provo UT
800 960-4150

(P-1569)
SOLECON INDUSTRIAL CONTRS INC
1401 Mcwilliams Way (95351-1125)
PHONE..................................209 572-7390
Jeffrey Grover, *Pr*
Elaine Grover, *
Will Grover, *
Dave Hedrick, *
Robert Stamy, *
EMP: 70 **EST:** 1981
SQ FT: 15,000
SALES (est): 16.34MM **Privately Held**
Web: www.soleconindustrial.com
SIC: 1711 Plumbing contractors

(P-1570)
SOUTH COAST MECHANICAL INC
800 E Orangethorpe Ave (92801-1123)
PHONE..................................714 738-6644
James Reynolds, *CEO*
Zoltan Bulgozdi, *
EMP: 75 **EST:** 2004
SALES (est): 21.97MM **Privately Held**
Web: www.scfacilityservices.com
SIC: 1711 7699 Mechanical contractor; Industrial machinery and equipment repair

(P-1571)
STERLING PLUMBING INC
3111 W Central Ave (92704-5302)
PHONE..................................714 641-5480
Rodney Robbins, *Pr*
Leslie Schaefer, *
EMP: 100 **EST:** 2003
SALES (est): 13.16MM **Privately Held**
Web: www.sterlingplumbinginc.com
SIC: 1711 Plumbing contractors

(P-1572)
STRATEGIC MECHANICAL INC
4661 E Commerce Ave (93725-2204)
PHONE..................................559 291-1952
Lonnie F Petty, *Pr*
Donn Petty, *
Chad Petty, *
EMP: 120 **EST:** 2004
SQ FT: 60,000
SALES (est): 30.43MM **Privately Held**
Web: www.strategicmechanical.com
SIC: 1711 3444 3441 Mechanical contractor; Awnings and canopies; Fabricated structural metal

(P-1573)
SUNBELT CONTROLS INC
735 N Todd Ave (91702-2244)
PHONE..................................626 610-2340
Jim Boyd, *Brnch Mgr*
EMP: 74
SALES (corp-wide): 1.51B **Privately Held**
Web: www.sunbeltcontrols.com
SIC: 1711 Mechanical contractor
HQ: Sunbelt Controls, Inc.
4511 Willow Rd Ste 4
Pleasanton CA

(P-1574)
SUNCO LIQUIDATION INC
Also Called: Sungevity
66 Franklin St Ste 310 (94607-3732)
PHONE..................................510 496-5500
EMP: 266
SIC: 1711 8713 Solar energy contractor; Surveying services

(PA)=Parent Co (HQ)=Headquarters
✪ = New Business established in last 2 years

2024 Directory of California WholeSalers and Service Companies

1711 - Plumbing, Heating, Air-conditioning (P-1575)

(P-1575)
SUNPOWER CORPORATION SYSTEMS
23900 Mc Combs Rd (93280-9215)
PHONE.................................661 758-2501
EMP: 62
SALES (corp-wide): 788.22K Publicly Held
Web: prod.aws-prod.sunpower.com
SIC: 1711 Solar energy contractor
HQ: Sunpower Corporation, Systems
1414 Hrbour Way S Ste 190
Richmond CA

(P-1576)
SUNPOWER CORPORATION SYSTEMS (DH)
Also Called: Powerlight
1414 Harbour Way S Ste 1901 (94804)
PHONE.................................510 260-8200
Peter Faricy, CEO
Peter Aschenbrenner, *
Lisa Bodensteiner, *
Charles D Boynton, *
Eric Branderiz, *
◆ EMP: 100 EST: 2007
SQ FT: 5,000
SALES (est): 128.1MM
SALES (corp-wide): 788.22K Publicly Held
Web: www.sunpowercorp.com
SIC: 1711 Solar energy contractor
HQ: Sunpower Corporation
1414 Hrbour Way S Ste 190
Richmond CA
408 240-5500

(P-1577)
SUNPRO SOLAR INC
34859 Frederick St Ste 101 (92595-7007)
PHONE.................................951 678-7733
Adam Evans, Pr
Adam Joshua Evans, *
EMP: 64 EST: 2008
SQ FT: 2,300
SALES (est): 9.57MM Privately Held
Web: www.adtsolar.com
SIC: 1711 Solar energy contractor

(P-1578)
SUNRUN DELPHI MANAGER 2016 LLC
595 Market St (94105-2802)
PHONE.................................415 536-6704
EMP: 97 EST: 2017
SALES (est): 2.27MM Publicly Held
SIC: 1711 Solar energy contractor
PA: Sunrun Inc.
225 Bush St Ste 1400
San Francisco CA

(P-1579)
SUPERIOR AUTOMATIC SPRNKLR CO
4378 Enterprise St (94538-6305)
PHONE.................................408 946-7272
Bob Lawson, Pr
Marci Kearney, *
Peter Hulin, *
EMP: 100 EST: 1973
SQ FT: 15,000
SALES (est): 18.93MM Privately Held
Web: www.superior-fire.com
SIC: 1711 Fire sprinkler system installation

(P-1580)
SUTTLES PLUMBING & MECH CORP
2267 Agate Ct (93065-1843)
PHONE.................................818 718-9779
Stephanie Aguilar, Pr
Bryan Suttles, *
Stephen Suttles, *
Sheralyn Suttles, *
EMP: 75 EST: 1970
SQ FT: 6,000
SALES (est): 18.39MM Privately Held
Web: www.suttlesplumbing.com
SIC: 1711 Plumbing contractors

(P-1581)
SYSERCO INC
1425 N Mcdowell Blvd Ste 115 (94954-6500)
PHONE.................................707 664-8443
Derek Eggers, CEO
EMP: 69
SALES (corp-wide): 28.98MM Privately Held
Web: www.syserco.com
SIC: 1711 Warm air heating and air conditioning contractor
PA: Syserco, Inc.
215 Fourier Ave Ste 100
Fremont CA
510 498-1171

(P-1582)
SYSERCO INC (PA)
215 Fourier Ave (94539-7837)
PHONE.................................510 498-1171
EMP: 96 EST: 1972
SALES (est): 28.98MM
SALES (corp-wide): 28.98MM Privately Held
Web: www.syserco.com
SIC: 1711 Warm air heating and air conditioning contractor

(P-1583)
TESLA ENERGY OPERATIONS INC (HQ)
3055 Clearview Way (94402-3709)
PHONE.................................888 765-2489
Elon Musk, Ch Bd
▲ EMP: 616 EST: 2006
SQ FT: 68,025
SALES (est): 1.42B
SALES (corp-wide): 81.46B Publicly Held
Web: www.solarcity.com
SIC: 1711 Solar energy contractor
PA: Tesla, Inc.
1 Tesla Rd
Austin TX
512 516-8177

(P-1584)
THERMAL MECHANICAL
425 Aldo Ave (95054-2322)
P.O. Box 4730 (95056-4730)
PHONE.................................408 988-8744
Richard Rood, CEO
David Rood, *
EMP: 77 EST: 1969
SQ FT: 30,000
SALES (est): 24.36MM Privately Held
Web: www.thermalmech.com
SIC: 1711 Mechanical contractor

(P-1585)
THERMALAIR INC (HQ)
1140 N Red Gum St (92806-2516)
PHONE.................................714 630-3200
Stephen C Weiss, CEO
William Reece, *
Rich Perez, *
EMP: 67 EST: 1948
SQ FT: 8,500
SALES (est): 28.33MM
SALES (corp-wide): 28.33MM Privately Held
Web: www.thermalair.com
SIC: 1711 Mechanical contractor
PA: General Engineering Western, Inc.
1140 N Red Gum St
Anaheim CA
714 630-3200

(P-1586)
THORPE DESIGN INC
410 Beatrice Ct Ste A (94513)
P.O. Box 1149 (94513-3149)
PHONE.................................925 634-0787
James Thorpe, Pr
Renee Thorpe, *
Kim Jones, *
EMP: 60 EST: 1986
SQ FT: 500
SALES (est): 12.02MM Privately Held
Web: www.thorpedesign.com
SIC: 1711 Fire sprinkler system installation

(P-1587)
TRILOGY PLUMBING INC
1525 S Sinclair St (92806-5934)
PHONE.................................714 441-2952
Dennis Burk, Pr
Linda Burk, *
EMP: 250 EST: 2003
SQ FT: 18,000
SALES (est): 35.79MM Privately Held
Web: www.trilogyplumbing.com
SIC: 1711 Septic system construction

(P-1588)
TRUE AIR MECHANICAL INC
Also Called: True Home Heating and AC
4 Faraday (92618-2714)
PHONE.................................888 316-0642
Scott Flora, CEO
EMP: 180 EST: 2010
SALES (est): 41.02MM Privately Held
Web: www.trueairinc.com
SIC: 1711 Warm air heating and air conditioning contractor

(P-1589)
UNIVERSITY MARELICH MECH INC
1000 N Kraemer Pl (92806-2610)
PHONE.................................714 632-2600
Scott Baker, Sr VP
Walter S Baker, *
John R Wycoff, *
John Ellis, *
EMP: 87 EST: 2005
SQ FT: 24,384
SALES (est): 5.2MM
SALES (corp-wide): 11.08B Publicly Held
SIC: 1711 Mechanical contractor
PA: Emcor Group, Inc.
301 Merritt 7 Fl 6
Norwalk CT
203 849-7800

(P-1590)
VALS PLUMBING AND HEATING INC
413 Front St (93901-3690)
PHONE.................................831 424-1633
Ray Spears, Pr
Valerio L Roberti, *
Laura Roberti, *
EMP: 60 EST: 1954
SQ FT: 12,500
SALES (est): 9.12MM Privately Held
Web: www.valsplumbing.com

SIC: 1711 5999 Warm air heating and air conditioning contractor; Plumbing and heating supplies

(P-1591)
VILLARA CORPORATION (PA)
Also Called: Walk Through Video
4700 Lang Ave (95652-2005)
PHONE.................................916 646-2700
Calvin Rick Wylie, Prin
Gary Beutler, *
Tom Beutler, *
▲ EMP: 482 EST: 1947
SALES (est): 147.27MM
SALES (corp-wide): 147.27MM Privately Held
Web: www.villara.com
SIC: 1711 Warm air heating and air conditioning contractor

(P-1592)
VIVINT SOLAR DEVELOPER LLC
Also Called: Vivint Solar Developer
614 Wilshire Ave Ste A (95203-1933)
PHONE.................................209 942-2040
EMP: 75
SIC: 1711 Solar energy contractor
HQ: Vivint Solar Developer, Llc
1800 W Ashton Blvd
Lehi UT
801 377-9111

(P-1593)
W L HICKEY SONS INC
1960 Hartog Dr Ste 10 (95131-2212)
P.O. Box 61209 (94088-1209)
PHONE.................................408 736-4938
Adam Hickey, Pr
Edward Hickey, *
EMP: 150 EST: 1904
SQ FT: 10,000
SALES (est): 22.42MM Privately Held
Web: www.wlhs.com
SIC: 1711 Plumbing contractors

(P-1594)
WALTER ANDERSON PLUMBING INC
Also Called: Anderson Plbg Htg A Condition
1830 John Towers Ave (92020-1134)
PHONE.................................619 449-7646
Mary Jean Anderson, CEO
Kyle Anderson, *
EMP: 125 EST: 1978
SQ FT: 10,000
SALES (est): 26.15MM
SALES (corp-wide): 559.73MM Privately Held
Web: www.andersonplumbingheatingandair.com
SIC: 1711 Plumbing contractors
PA: Essential Services Intermediate Holding Corporation
3416 Robards Ct
Louisville KY
502 657-1903

(P-1595)
WENCON DEVELOPMENT INC
Also Called: Quick Mount Pv
2700 Mitchell Dr Ste 2 (94598-1602)
PHONE.................................925 478-8269
Claudia Wentworth, Pr
Sam Cast, *
Stuart H Wentworth, *
▲ EMP: 88 EST: 1993
SQ FT: 1,700
SALES (est): 27.27MM Privately Held
Web: www.wencon.com

PRODUCTS & SERVICES SECTION   **1721 - Painting And Paper Hanging (P-1617)**

SIC: **1711** Solar energy contractor
HQ: Esdec, Inc.
    976 Brady Ave Nw Ste 100
    Atlanta GA
    404 512-0716

(P-1596)
WEST COAST AC CO INC
1155 Pioneer Way Ste 101 (92020-1964)
PHONE..................................619 561-8000
David Dudley, *CEO*
Colin Fisher, *
James Clower, *
EMP: 150 EST: 1960
SQ FT: 24,000
SALES (est): 24.58MM **Privately Held**
Web: www.wcac.com
SIC: **1711** Warm air heating and air conditioning contractor

(P-1597)
WESTATES MECHANICAL CORP INC
2566 Barrington Ct (94545-1133)
PHONE..................................510 635-9830
Nigel Cowan, *CEO*
Daniel Loeffler, *
William Bird, *
EMP: 60 EST: 2003
SALES (est): 9.78MM **Privately Held**
Web: www.westatesmechanical.com
SIC: **1711** Mechanical contractor

(P-1598)
WESTERN FIRE PROTECTION INC (PA)
13630 Danielson St (92064-6830)
PHONE..................................858 513-4949
EMP: 91 EST: 1989
SALES (est): 19.88MM **Privately Held**
Web: www.westernfireprotection.com
SIC: **1711** Fire sprinkler system installation

(P-1599)
XCEL MECHANICAL SYSTEMS INC
1710 W 130th St (90249-2004)
PHONE..................................310 660-0090
Kevin Michel, *Pr*
EMP: 175 EST: 1996
SQ FT: 10,000
SALES (est): 74.62MM **Privately Held**
Web: www.xcelmech.com
SIC: **1711** Mechanical contractor

(P-1600)
ZERO ENERGY CONTRACTING INC
13850 Cerritos Corporate Dr Ste D (90703-2467)
PHONE..................................626 701-3180
Michael Murphy, *Ch Bd*
Paul Hanson, *
Jerry Suk, *
Joseph Power Cbd, *Prin*
EMP: 125 EST: 2010
SQ FT: 8,000
SALES (est): 6.73MM **Privately Held**
SIC: **1711** Solar energy contractor

(P-1601)
ZERO ENERGY CONTRACTING LLC
13850 Cerritos Corporate Dr Ste D (90703-2467)
PHONE..................................626 701-3180
EMP: 93 EST: 2009
SALES (est): 9.9MM **Privately Held**

SIC: **1711** Solar energy contractor

1721 Painting And Paper Hanging

(P-1602)
ADVANCED INDUSTRIAL SVCS INC
Also Called: Advanced Industrial Svcs Cal
7831 Alondra Blvd (90723-5005)
PHONE..................................562 940-8305
Rex Johnston Junior, *Pr*
EMP: 85 EST: 2007
SALES (est): 9.85MM **Privately Held**
Web: www.adinservices.com
SIC: **1721** Industrial painting

(P-1603)
ADVANTAGE PNTG SOLUTIONS INC
14734 Yorba Ct (91710-9210)
PHONE..................................951 739-9204
Anthony Trujillo, *CEO*
Shevon Gonzales, *
EMP: 60 EST: 2014
SALES (est): 4.57MM **Privately Held**
Web: www.advantagepaintingsolutions.com
SIC: **1721** Residential painting

(P-1604)
ARENA PAINTING CONTRACTORS INC
525 E Alondra Blvd (90248-2903)
PHONE..................................310 316-2446
Wilson Grant, *CEO*
Guy Grant Ii, *Pr*
EMP: 100 EST: 1982
SQ FT: 10,000
SALES (est): 11.5MM **Privately Held**
Web: www.arenapainting.biz
SIC: **1721** Commercial painting

(P-1605)
ARMSTRONG INSTLLTION SVC A CAL
Also Called: Armstrong Construction Company
4575 San Pablo Ave (94608-3325)
PHONE..................................408 777-1234
Mitchell Fine, *CEO*
Arthur Levine, *
EMP: 130 EST: 1966
SQ FT: 8,000
SALES (est): 8.87MM **Privately Held**
Web: www.armstrong1234.com
SIC: **1721 1761 1793** Exterior residential painting contractor; Roofing, siding, and sheetmetal work; Glass and glazing work

(P-1606)
BORBON INCORPORATED
2560 W Woodland Dr (92801-2636)
PHONE..................................714 994-0170
David Morales, *Pr*
EMP: 120 EST: 1974
SALES (est): 11.43MM **Privately Held**
Web: www.borbon.net
SIC: **1721** Exterior residential painting contractor

(P-1607)
CAL/PAC PNTNGS CTNGS ACQSTION
608 N Eckhoff St (92868-1004)
PHONE..................................714 628-1514
Dave Bedillion, *Pr*

Mike Stevenson, *
EMP: 60 EST: 2001
SQ FT: 2,000
SALES (est): 3.01MM **Privately Held**
SIC: **1721** Residential painting

(P-1608)
CAMPBELL PAINTING INC
Also Called: Campbell Construction
14175 Telephone Ave Ste M (91710-5761)
PHONE..................................919 591-4300
Gerry Campbell, *CEO*
EMP: 60 EST: 2005
SALES (est): 4.62MM **Privately Held**
Web: www.campbellpaintingca.com
SIC: **1721** Painting and paper hanging

(P-1609)
CERTIFIED COATINGS COMPANY
2320 Cordelia Rd (94534-1600)
PHONE..................................707 639-4414
David Joseph Brockman, *CEO*
Pamela Langan, *
EMP: 100 EST: 2006
SQ FT: 8,000
SALES (est): 23.88MM
SALES (corp-wide): 299.4MM **Privately Held**
Web: www.certifiedcoatings.com
SIC: **1721** Industrial painting
PA: Muehlhan Ag
    Schlinckstr. 3
    Hamburg HH
    40752710

(P-1610)
CWPNC INC
Also Called: College Works Painting
1682 Langley Ave (92614-5620)
PHONE..................................714 564-7904
Matthew K Stewart, *Pr*
Jason Reid, *
Jeff Gunhus, *
Tracy Meneses, *
Spencer Pepe, *
EMP: 61 EST: 1998
SQ FT: 3,000
SALES (est): 3.73MM **Privately Held**
SIC: **1721** Residential painting
PA: National Services Group, Inc.
    1682 Langley Ave
    Irvine CA

(P-1611)
D C VIENT INC (PA)
1556 Cummins Dr (95358-6412)
P.O. Box D (95352-3668)
PHONE..................................209 578-1224
Darlene Vient, *Pr*
Douglas C Vient, *
Douglas J Vient Junior, *Sec*
Danielle Bell, *Stockholder*
EMP: 100 EST: 1954
SQ FT: 12,000
SALES (est): 14.69MM
SALES (corp-wide): 14.69MM **Privately Held**
Web: www.dcvient.com
SIC: **1721** Residential painting

(P-1612)
D P S INC
Also Called: Empire Community Painting
1682 Langley Ave (92614-5620)
PHONE..................................888 278-8200
Jason Reid, *Pr*
Jeff Gunhus, *VP*
Tracy Meneses, *CFO*
Matt Stewart, *VP*

Spencer Pepe, *Sec*
EMP: 84 EST: 1993
SQ FT: 1,000
SALES (est): 2.54MM **Privately Held**
SIC: **1721** Painting and paper hanging
PA: National Services Group, Inc.
    1682 Langley Ave
    Irvine CA

(P-1613)
DUGGAN & ASSOCIATES INC
1442 W 135th St (90249-2218)
PHONE..................................323 965-1502
Chris M Duggan, *Pr*
◆ EMP: 65 EST: 1989
SQ FT: 10,000
SALES (est): 8.3MM **Privately Held**
Web: www.dugganla.com
SIC: **1721** Residential painting

(P-1614)
EMPCC INC
Also Called: Empire Community Painting
1682 Langley Ave Fl 2 (92614-5620)
PHONE..................................888 278-8200
Jason Reid, *Pr*
Jeff Gunhus, *
Matt Stewart, *
Spencer Pepe, *
Tracy Meneses, *
EMP: 284 EST: 2003
SQ FT: 1,000
SALES (est): 1.1MM **Privately Held**
SIC: **1721** Painting and paper hanging
PA: Mjp Empire, Inc.
    1682 Langley Ave Fl 2
    Irvine CA

(P-1615)
GENERAL COATINGS CORPORATION
9349 Feron Blvd (91730-4516)
PHONE..................................909 204-4150
Craig Kinsman, *Owner*
EMP: 84
SALES (corp-wide): 35.9MM **Privately Held**
Web: www.gencoat.com
SIC: **1721** Painting and paper hanging
PA: General Coatings Corporation
    6711 Nancy Ridge Dr
    San Diego CA
    858 587-1277

(P-1616)
GENERAL COATINGS CORPORATION
600 W Freedom Ave (92865-2537)
PHONE..................................858 587-1277
Craig Kinsman, *Brnch Mgr*
EMP: 83
SQ FT: 7,047
SALES (corp-wide): 35.9MM **Privately Held**
Web: www.gencoat.com
SIC: **1721** Painting and paper hanging
PA: General Coatings Corporation
    6711 Nancy Ridge Dr
    San Diego CA
    858 587-1277

(P-1617)
GENERAL COATINGS CORPORATION (PA)
6711 Nancy Ridge Dr (92121-2231)
PHONE..................................858 587-1277
Craig A Kinsman, *CEO*
Andrew Fluken, *
EMP: 250 EST: 1987

1721 - Painting And Paper Hanging (P-1618)

SQ FT: 14,000
SALES (est): 35.9MM
SALES (corp-wide): 35.9MM **Privately Held**
Web: www.gencoat.com
SIC: **1721** 1799 Painting and paper hanging; Waterproofing

(P-1618)
GENERAL COATINGS CORPORATION
1220 E North Ave (93725-1930)
PHONE.................................559 495-4004
Lee Morrison, *Prin*
EMP: 83
SALES (corp-wide): 35.9MM **Privately Held**
Web: www.gencoat.com
SIC: **1721** 1799 Painting and paper hanging; Coating of concrete structures with plastic
PA: General Coatings Corporation
6711 Nancy Ridge Dr
San Diego CA
858 587-1277

(P-1619)
GEORGE E MASKER INC
Also Called: Masker Painting
7699 Edgewater Dr (94621-3028)
PHONE.................................510 568-1206
Alan Bjerke, *Pr*
EMP: 100 EST: 1963
SQ FT: 18,000
SALES (est): 22.66MM **Privately Held**
Web: www.maskerpainting.com
SIC: **1721** Exterior commercial painting contractor

(P-1620)
GIAMPOLINI & CO
Also Called: Giampolini/Courtney
1482 67th St (94608-1016)
PHONE.................................415 673-1236
Greg Quilici, *Pr*
Tom Quilici, *
Patrick Roland, *
James Patrick Roland, *
EMP: 225 EST: 1912
SQ FT: 9,720
SALES (est): 33.76MM **Privately Held**
Web: www.giampolini.com
SIC: **1721** 1542 1742 Exterior commercial painting contractor; Commercial and office buildings, renovation and repair; Plastering, drywall, and insulation

(P-1621)
GPS PAINTING WALLCOVERING INC
1307 E Saint Gertrude Pl Ste C (92705-5228)
PHONE.................................714 730-8904
Eliot Schneider, *Pr*
EMP: 110 EST: 2001
SALES (est): 18.85MM **Privately Held**
Web: www.gpspaintingandwallcovering.com
SIC: **1721** Painting and paper hanging

(P-1622)
HARRIS & RUTH PAINTING CONTG (PA)
28408 Lorna Ave (91790)
PHONE.................................626 960-4004
Terry Cairy, *Pr*
Mark Heydorff, *
Bruce Boyer, *
EMP: 70 EST: 1970
SQ FT: 1,000
SALES (est): 8.79MM
SALES (corp-wide): 8.79MM **Privately Held**
Web: www.harrisruthpainting.com
SIC: **1721** Exterior commercial painting contractor

(P-1623)
J M V B INC
Also Called: Spc Building Services
12118 Severn Way (92503-4804)
P.O. Box 614 (92856-6614)
PHONE.................................714 288-9797
Benjamin J Rodriguez, *Pr*
EMP: 80 EST: 1993
SALES (est): 2.42MM **Privately Held**
Web: www.spcbs.com
SIC: **1721** Painting and paper hanging

(P-1624)
JEFFCO PAINTING & COATING INC
1260 Railroad Ave (94592-1012)
P.O. Box 1888 (94590-0655)
PHONE.................................707 562-1900
Steve Jeffress, *Pr*
Gene Glockner, *
EMP: 100 EST: 1978
SALES (est): 12.67MM **Privately Held**
Web: www.jeffcoptg.com
SIC: **1721** 3471 Industrial painting; Sand blasting of metal parts

(P-1625)
JERRY THOMPSON & SONS PNTG INC
Also Called: Jerry Thtompson & Sons Pntg
3 Simms St (94901-5414)
PHONE.................................415 454-1500
Stephen G Thompson, *Pr*
Dennis J Thompson, *
EMP: 140 EST: 1993
SALES (est): 14.78MM **Privately Held**
Web: www.jtspainting.com
SIC: **1721** Residential painting

(P-1626)
JFP PAINTING
2078 2nd St (92860-2804)
PHONE.................................951 736-6037
Anna Floris, *Prin*
EMP: 60 EST: 1996
SALES (est): 2.64MM **Privately Held**
SIC: **1721** Painting and paper hanging

(P-1627)
LEADING EDGE AVIATION SVCS INC
5251 California Ave # 170 (92617-3077)
PHONE.................................714 556-0576
EMP: 800
SIC: **1721** 4581 3721 Aircraft painting; Aircraft maintenance and repair services; Motorized aircraft

(P-1628)
LIVING COLORS INC
16034 Rayen St (91343-4814)
PHONE.................................818 893-5068
Raymond Sponsler, *Pr*
Paula Sponsler, *
EMP: 60 EST: 1973
SALES (est): 2.42MM **Privately Held**
Web: www.lcipaint.com
SIC: **1721** Residential painting

(P-1629)
MOLINAS PNTG WALLCOVERING INC
4285 Pacheco Blvd (94553-2227)
PHONE.................................925 228-7487
Oscar Molina, *CEO*
Oscar M Molina, *CFO*
Vanessa Molina, *Sec*
Marissa Molina, *Bookpr*
EMP: 75 EST: 2003
SQ FT: 3,750
SALES (est): 4.8MM **Privately Held**
SIC: **1721** Wallcovering contractors

(P-1630)
PBC PAVERS INC
Also Called: Peterson Bros Construction
2929 E White Star Ave (92806-2628)
PHONE.................................714 278-0488
Robert Peterson, *Pr*
Eldin Peterson, *
▲ EMP: 80 EST: 1995
SALES (est): 10.06MM **Privately Held**
Web: www.pbccompanies.com
SIC: **1721** Pavement marking contractor

(P-1631)
PETERSON PAINTING INC
5750 La Ribera St (94550-9204)
PHONE.................................925 455-5864
Raymond Peterson, *Pr*
John Peterson, *
EMP: 350 EST: 1970
SQ FT: 10,000
SALES (est): 8.14MM **Privately Held**
SIC: **1721** Residential painting

(P-1632)
POWER MAINTENANCE SERVICES INC
Also Called: Pilot Painting & Construction
5555 Corporate Ave (90630-4708)
P.O. Box 6377 (92816-0377)
PHONE.................................714 229-5900
Steve Gilkey, *Pr*
EMP: 60 EST: 2017
SQ FT: 7,856
SALES (est): 4.53MM **Privately Held**
SIC: **1721** Residential painting

(P-1633)
PRIMECO
220 Oceanside Blvd (92054-4903)
PHONE.................................760 967-8278
EMP: 90 EST: 1992
SQ FT: 2,100
SALES (est): 12.62MM **Privately Held**
Web: www.primeco.com
SIC: **1721** 1542 Residential painting; Commercial and office building contractors

(P-1634)
PS2 (PA)
Also Called: Ps2
17903 S Hobart Blvd (90248-3613)
PHONE.................................310 243-2980
Peter Schmit, *Pr*
Peter Short, *
EMP: 68 EST: 1997
SQ FT: 2,000
SALES (est): 10.36MM
SALES (corp-wide): 10.36MM **Privately Held**
Web: www.ps2-inc.com
SIC: **1721** Residential painting

(P-1635)
R & A PAINTING INC
11730 Sheldon Lake Dr (95624-9649)
P.O. Box 292730 (95829-2730)
PHONE.................................916 688-3955
Antonio Rodrigues, *Pr*
Cidalia Rodrigues, *
EMP: 60 EST: 1990
SALES (est): 1.99MM **Privately Held**
Web: www.rapainting.com
SIC: **1721** Commercial painting

(P-1636)
RANDALL - MCANANY COMPANY
1528 W 178th St (90248-3204)
PHONE.................................310 822-3344
Timothy Mc Anany, *Pr*
Nancy Mc Anany, *
EMP: 60 EST: 1978
SALES (est): 4.51MM **Privately Held**
Web: www.rmcompany.com
SIC: **1721** Commercial painting

(P-1637)
RC WENDT PAINTING INC
21612 Surveyor Cir (92646-7068)
PHONE.................................714 960-2700
Robert C Wendt, *Pr*
Scott Wendt, *
Jeri Wendt, *
EMP: 110 EST: 1980
SALES (est): 4.02MM **Privately Held**
Web: www.wendtcompanies.com
SIC: **1721** Residential painting

(P-1638)
REDWOOD PAINTING CO INC
620 W 10th St (94565-1806)
P.O. Box 4663 (97501-0188)
PHONE.................................925 432-4500
Charles Del Monte, *CEO*
Charles Duke Del Monte, *
George Del Monte, *
EMP: 110 EST: 1947
SQ FT: 19,000
SALES (est): 24.75MM
SALES (corp-wide): 2.72B **Privately Held**
Web: www.redwoodptg.com
SIC: **1721** Commercial painting
HQ: F. D. Thomas, Inc.
217 Bateman Dr
Central Point OR
541 664-3010

(P-1639)
RTE ENTERPRISES INC
Also Called: Color Concepts
21530 Roscoe Blvd (91304-4144)
PHONE.................................818 999-5300
EMP: 100 EST: 1987
SQ FT: 2,000
SALES (est): 4.95MM **Privately Held**
Web: www.ceocolorcon1.com
SIC: **1721** 1742 Painting and paper hanging; Plastering, drywall, and insulation

(P-1640)
SANDERS & WOHRMAN CORPORATION
709 N Poplar St (92868-1013)
PHONE.................................714 919-0446
John Thomas Wohrman, *Prin*
Todd Wohrman, *
EMP: 150 EST: 1979
SQ FT: 12,000
SALES (est): 23.36MM **Privately Held**
Web: www.swcoatings.com
SIC: **1721** Residential painting

(P-1641)
SCHAPER CONSTRUCTION INC (PA)
Also Called: Schaper Co
1177 N 15th St (95112-1422)
PHONE.................................408 437-0337

PRODUCTS & SERVICES SECTION

1731 - Electrical Work (P-1662)

Leon Schaper, *CEO*
EMP: 90 **EST:** 1985
SQ FT: 8,400
SALES (est): 25.32MM
SALES (corp-wide): 25.32MM **Privately Held**
Web: www.schaperco.com
SIC: 1721 1611 1542 Exterior residential painting contractor; General contractor, highway and street construction; Nonresidential construction, nec

(P-1642)
SIPCO SURFACE PROTECTION INC (DH)
Also Called: Muehlhan Marine
2320 Cordelia Rd (94534-1600)
PHONE.................707 639-4414
William C Legrande, *Pr*
Paul Oatman, *CFO*
Pamela Langan, *Treas*
◆ **EMP:** 68 **EST:** 1994
SQ FT: 13,000
SALES (est): 4.1MM
SALES (corp-wide): 299.4MM **Privately Held**
Web: www.muehlhan.com
SIC: 1721 Industrial painting
HQ: Muehlhan Surface Protection Inc.
2320 Cordelia Rd
Fairfield CA
707 639-4421

(P-1643)
URBAN PAINTING INC
630 Las Gallinas Ave (94903-3657)
PHONE.................415 485-1130
Michael James Urban, *Pr*
James De Martini, *
Chris Urban, *
Robert S Urban, *Stockholder*
EMP: 60 **EST:** 1983
SALES (est): 4.39MM **Privately Held**
Web: www.urbanco.com
SIC: 1721 Commercial painting

(P-1644)
VERTEX COATINGS INC
1291 W State St (91762-4015)
PHONE.................909 923-5795
EMP: 74 **EST:** 1990
SQ FT: 11,000
SALES (est): 8.86MM **Privately Held**
Web: www.vertexcoatings.com
SIC: 1721 Commercial painting

(P-1645)
WEST COAST INTERIORS INC
Also Called: West Coast Painting
1610 W Linden St (92507-6810)
PHONE.................951 778-3592
Mark Herbert, *CEO*
Dan Slavin, *Marketing*
Santos Garcia, *
Colleen Butler, *
Keith Caneva, *Corporate Controller*
EMP: 600 **EST:** 1968
SQ FT: 8,000
SALES (est): 44.28MM **Privately Held**
Web: www.wcdp.com
SIC: 1721 Wallcovering contractors

(P-1646)
WILSON & HAMPTON PNTG CONTRS
1524 W Mable St (92802-1022)
P.O. Box 9949 (92812-7949)
PHONE.................714 772-5091
TOLL FREE: 800
Doug Hampton, *Pr*
Douglas J Hampton, *
Robert D Hampton Iii, *Sec*
Clifford C Hampton, *
Cliff Hampton, *COO*
EMP: 60 **EST:** 1923
SQ FT: 44,000
SALES (est): 4.31MM **Privately Held**
Web: www.wilsonhampton.com
SIC: 1721 7641 Residential painting; Furniture repair and maintenance

(P-1647)
WM B SALEH CO
1364 N Jackson Ave (93703-4624)
PHONE.................559 255-2046
Mark Saleh, *Pr*
William B Saleh, *
Katherine Brusellas, *
EMP: 75 **EST:** 1959
SQ FT: 6,800
SALES (est): 8.21MM **Privately Held**
Web: www.salehcompany.com
SIC: 1721 Residential painting

1731 Electrical Work

(P-1648)
4LIBERTY INC
7675 Dagget St Ste 200 (92111-2256)
PHONE.................619 400-1000
EMP: 85 **EST:** 2010
SALES (est): 5.33MM **Privately Held**
Web: www.4liberty.com
SIC: 1731 Telephone and telephone equipment installation

(P-1649)
A M ORTEGA CONSTRUCTION INC (PA)
Also Called: Western Rim Pipeline
10125 Channel Rd (92040-1703)
PHONE.................619 390-1988
Archie Maurice Ortega, *Pr*
Linda Ortega, *
EMP: 110 **EST:** 1974
SQ FT: 10,000
SALES (est): 55.54MM
SALES (corp-wide): 55.54MM **Privately Held**
Web: www.amortega.com
SIC: 1731 Electrical work

(P-1650)
A-C ELECTRIC COMPANY
A-C Electric, Co Div F
2560 S East Ave (93706-5103)
P.O. Box 81977 (93380-1977)
PHONE.................559 233-2208
Jim Mcgurk, *Mgr*
EMP: 76
SQ FT: 5,096
SALES (corp-wide): 96.92MM **Privately Held**
Web: www.a-csolar.com
SIC: 1731 8711 General electrical contractor ; Electrical or electronic engineering
PA: A-C Electric Company
2921 Hanger Way
Bakersfield CA
661 410-0000

(P-1651)
AA/ACME LOCKSMITHS INC
Also Called: Aa
1660 Factor Ave (94577-5618)
PHONE.................510 483-6584
Timothy J Whall, *CEO*
Jim Devries, *Pr*
Jeff Likosar, *CFO*
Dan Bresingham, *CAO*
P Gray Finney, *Sec*
EMP: 95 **EST:** 1974
SQ FT: 20,000
SALES (est): 23.43MM
SALES (corp-wide): 6.4B **Publicly Held**
SIC: 1731 5999 Fire detection and burglar alarm systems specialization; Alarm signal systems
PA: Adt Inc.
1501 W Yamato Rd
Boca Raton FL
561 988-3600

(P-1652)
AAA ELCTRCAL CMMUNICATIONS INC (PA)
Also Called: AAA Facility Services
25007 Anza Dr (91355-3414)
PHONE.................800 892-4784
Joann Katinos, *CEO*
Brian Higgins, *Pr*
EMP: 133 **EST:** 1995
SQ FT: 6,000
SALES (est): 34.13MM **Privately Held**
Web: www.aaafacilityservices.com
SIC: 1731 1711 7349 1721 General electrical contractor; Plumbing, heating, air-conditioning; Building maintenance services, nec; Commercial painting

(P-1653)
AAA NETWORK SOLUTIONS INC
8401 Page St (90621-3821)
PHONE.................714 484-2711
John A Mckenna Junior, *CEO*
Jeffrey E Nachbor, *
EMP: 60 **EST:** 2009
SALES (est): 24.39MM
SALES (corp-wide): 1.81B **Privately Held**
Web: www.convergeone.com
SIC: 1731 General electrical contractor
HQ: Convergeone, Inc.
10900 Nesbitt Ave S
Minneapolis MN

(P-1654)
ABS
79 E Daily Dr (93010-5807)
PHONE.................805 453-9359
EMP: 75 **EST:** 2018
SALES (est): 373.65K **Privately Held**
SIC: 1731 Electrical work

(P-1655)
AC SQUARE INC
371 Foster City Blvd (94404-1104)
P.O. Box 8179 (94404-8179)
PHONE.................650 293-2730
EMP: 300
Web: www.acsquare.com
SIC: 1731 Fiber optic cable installation

(P-1656)
ACS COMMUNICATIONS INC
Also Called: Fiber Optic Technologies
680 Knox St Ste 150 (90502-1325)
PHONE.................310 767-2145
Robby Sawyer, *Pr*
EMP: 94
SIC: 1731 Communications specialization
HQ: Acs Communications, Inc.
2535 Brockton Dr Ste 400
Austin TX
512 837-4400

(P-1657)
AJ KIRKWOOD & ASSOCIATES INC
4300 N Harbor Blvd (92835-1091)
PHONE.................714 505-1977
Arch Kirkwood, *Ch*
James Klassen, *
Michael Hewson, *
Aidan Culligan, *
Sam Sandoval, *
EMP: 500 **EST:** 1996
SALES (est): 144.08MM **Privately Held**
Web: www.ajk-a.com
SIC: 1731 8748 7389 General electrical contractor; Communications consulting; Design services

(P-1658)
ALBD ELECTRIC AND CABLE
Also Called: A Lighting By Design
1031 S Leslie St (90631-6843)
PHONE.................949 440-1216
Chad Lambert, *CEO*
James Black, *
EMP: 100 **EST:** 2002
SALES (est): 22.67MM **Privately Held**
Web: www.albdinc.com
SIC: 1731 3651 General electrical contractor ; Household audio and video equipment

(P-1659)
ALESSANDRO ELECTRIC INC
11335 Sunrise Gold Cir (95742-6512)
PHONE.................916 283-6966
Clint Alessandro, *Pr*
Clinton Lee Alessandro, *
EMP: 75 **EST:** 2005
SALES (est): 17.22MM **Privately Held**
Web: www.alessandroelectric.com
SIC: 1731 7389 General electrical contractor ; Business services, nec

(P-1660)
ALL GUARD ALARM SYSTEMS INC (PA)
Also Called: GRAND CENTRAL STATION
1306 Stealth St (94551-9356)
PHONE.................800 255-4273
Denis Cooke, *Ch Bd*
Patricia Cooke, *
Michael Cooke, *
EMP: 66 **EST:** 1980
SQ FT: 12,600
SALES (est): 11.03MM
SALES (corp-wide): 11.03MM **Privately Held**
Web: www.allguardsystems.com
SIC: 1731 7382 Fire detection and burglar alarm systems specialization; Burglar alarm maintenance and monitoring

(P-1661)
ALLIED UNIVERSAL
9320 Hazard Way Ste A1 (92123-1227)
PHONE.................619 444-0219
Amy Davis, *Prin*
EMP: 154 **EST:** 2018
SALES (est): 4.98MM **Privately Held**
Web: www.aus.com
SIC: 1731 Safety and security specialization

(P-1662)
ALVAH CONTRACTORS INC
263 S Maple Ave (94080-6305)
PHONE.................650 741-6785
Cameron Hale, *Pr*
Dennis Mueller, *
EMP: 350 **EST:** 2008
SALES (est): 24.64MM **Privately Held**
Web: www.alvahgroup.com
SIC: 1731 General electrical contractor

1731 - Electrical Work (P-1663)

(P-1663)
AMERICAN ENGRG CONTRS INC
Also Called: Budget Electric
25445 S Schulte Rd (95377-9709)
PHONE..................................209 229-1591
Larry Walling, *Pr*
Patricia Walling, *
EMP: 180 **EST:** 1979
SQ FT: 4,000
SALES (est): 9.3MM **Privately Held**
Web: www.budgete.com
SIC: 1731 General electrical contractor

(P-1664)
AMERICAN SOLAR DIRECT INC
11766 Wilshire Blvd Ste 500 (90025-6551)
PHONE..................................424 214-6700
EMP: 107
SIC: 1731 Electrical work

(P-1665)
AMS ELECTRIC INC
Also Called: Prime Electric
6905 Sierra Ct Ste A (94568-2708)
PHONE..................................925 961-1600
William Breyton, *Prin*
John Modica, *
Craig Ayers, *Prin*
Michael Stellato, *Prin*
EMP: 75 **EST:** 2003
SQ FT: 25,000
SALES (est): 9.93MM **Privately Held**
Web: www.ams-electric.com
SIC: 1731 General electrical contractor

(P-1666)
ANDERSON & HOWARD ELECTRIC INC
Also Called: Anderson Howard
15 Chrysler (92618-2009)
PHONE..................................949 250-4555
Greg Elliott, *Pr*
Brian E Elliott, *
Tom Howard, *
Charles B Howard, *
EMP: 210 **EST:** 1967
SALES (est): 53.32MM **Privately Held**
Web: www.aandh.com
SIC: 1731 General electrical contractor

(P-1667)
APOLLO ELECTRIC
330 N Basse Ln (92821-3906)
PHONE..................................714 256-8414
Leroy H Holt, *CEO*
Gregg L Holt, *
EMP: 60 **EST:** 1966
SQ FT: 18,000
SALES (est): 24.51MM **Privately Held**
Web: www.apolloelect.com
SIC: 1731 General electrical contractor

(P-1668)
ARDENT COMPANIES INC
4842 Airport Dr (93308-9786)
PHONE..................................661 633-1465
Glenn Dubuc, *Dist Mgr*
EMP: 75
SALES (corp-wide): 11.08B **Publicly Held**
Web: www.ardent.us
SIC: 1731 General electrical contractor
HQ: Ardent Companies, Inc.
4824 Rosedale Ln
Bakersfield CA
661 633-1465

(P-1669)
ASSI SECURITY (PA)
1370 Reynolds Ave Ste 201 (92614-5529)
PHONE..................................949 955-0244
William Dominic Vuono, *Pr*
Michael Willey, *
EMP: 67 **EST:** 1993
SQ FT: 10,000
SALES (est): 15.66MM
SALES (corp-wide): 15.66MM **Privately Held**
Web: www.assisecurity.com
SIC: 1731 7382 Voice, data, and video wiring contractor; Security systems services

(P-1670)
ATMC INCORPORATED (PA)
Also Called: Atm Consultants
725 W Baseline Rd (91711-1615)
PHONE..................................909 390-0470
Toshio Hashioka, *Pr*
EMP: 60 **EST:** 1982
SQ FT: 12,000
SALES (est): 7.22MM
SALES (corp-wide): 7.22MM **Privately Held**
Web: www.focusbroadband.com
SIC: 1731 5044 Banking machine installation and service; Bank automatic teller machines

(P-1671)
BAKER ELECTRIC & RENEWABLES LLC
1298 Pacific Oaks Pl (92029-2900)
PHONE..................................760 745-2001
EMP: 586 **EST:** 1938
SALES (est): 127.8MM **Privately Held**
Web: www.baker-electric.com
SIC: 1731 8711 General electrical contractor; Engineering services

(P-1672)
BANISTER ELECTRICAL INC
2532 Verne Roberts Cir (94509-7904)
PHONE..................................925 778-7801
Daniel T Pauline, *Pr*
EMP: 70 **EST:** 2006
SALES (est): 4.74MM **Privately Held**
SIC: 1731 General electrical contractor

(P-1673)
BARNUM & CELILLO ELECTRIC INC (PA)
135 Main Ave (95838-2089)
PHONE..................................916 646-4661
Fred Troy Barnum, *CEO*
Paul Celillo, *
EMP: 148 **EST:** 1990
SQ FT: 3,000
SALES (est): 57.97MM **Privately Held**
Web: www.barnumcelillo.com
SIC: 1731 General electrical contractor

(P-1674)
BAY ALARM COMPANY (PA)
Also Called: S A S
5130 Commercial Cir (94520-8522)
P.O. Box 8140 (94596-8140)
PHONE..................................925 935-1100
Bruce A Westphal, *Ch Bd*
Roger L Westphal, *CEO*
Stacy M Russell, *Ex Sec*
◆ **EMP:** 70 **EST:** 1946
SQ FT: 12,000
SALES (est): 137.09MM
SALES (corp-wide): 137.09MM **Privately Held**
Web: www.bayalarm.com
SIC: 1731 7382 5063 Fire detection and burglar alarm systems specialization; Burglar alarm maintenance and monitoring; Electrical apparatus and equipment

(P-1675)
BERGELECTRIC CORP (PA)
3182 Lionshead Ave (92010-4701)
PHONE..................................760 638-2374
Edward Billig, *Pr*
Ron Wood, *
Steve Buhr, *
William Wingerning, *
Alan Mashburn, *
▲ **EMP:** 100 **EST:** 1946
SALES (est): 705.05MM
SALES (corp-wide): 705.05MM **Privately Held**
Web: www.bergelectric.com
SIC: 1731 General electrical contractor

(P-1676)
BERGELECTRIC CORP
3182 Lionshead Ave (92010-4701)
PHONE..................................760 746-1003
Tom Anderson, *Brnch Mgr*
EMP: 760
SALES (corp-wide): 705.05MM **Privately Held**
Web: www.bergelectric.com
SIC: 1731 General electrical contractor
PA: Bergelectric Corp.
3182 Lionshead Ave
Carlsbad CA
760 638-2374

(P-1677)
BERGELECTRIC CORP
2210 Meyers Ave (92029-1003)
PHONE..................................760 746-1003
Thomas R Anderson, *Ch Bd*
EMP: 93
SALES (corp-wide): 705.05MM **Privately Held**
Web: www.bergelectric.com
SIC: 1731 General electrical contractor
PA: Bergelectric Corp.
3182 Lionshead Ave
Carlsbad CA
760 638-2374

(P-1678)
BERGELECTRIC CORP
955 Borra Pl (92029-2011)
PHONE..................................760 291-8100
Thomas R Anderson, *Ch Bd*
EMP: 80
SALES (corp-wide): 705.05MM **Privately Held**
Web: www.bergelectric.com
SIC: 1731 General electrical contractor
PA: Bergelectric Corp.
3182 Lionshead Ave
Carlsbad CA
760 638-2374

(P-1679)
BERGELECTRIC CORP
750 W Pinedale Ave (93711-5744)
PHONE..................................559 860-2590
Thomas R Anderson, *Ch Bd*
EMP: 74
SALES (corp-wide): 705.05MM **Privately Held**
Web: www.bergelectric.com
SIC: 1731 General electrical contractor
PA: Bergelectric Corp.
3182 Lionshead Ave
Carlsbad CA
760 638-2374

(P-1680)
BERGELECTRIC CORP
46740 Lakeview Blvd (94538-6529)
PHONE..................................510 314-8590
Thomas R Anderson, *Ch Bd*
EMP: 74
SALES (corp-wide): 705.05MM **Privately Held**
Web: www.bergelectric.com
SIC: 1731 General electrical contractor
PA: Bergelectric Corp.
3182 Lionshead Ave
Carlsbad CA
760 638-2374

(P-1681)
BERGELECTRIC CORP
11333 Sunrise Park Dr (95742-6532)
PHONE..................................916 636-1880
Pete Casazza, *Rgnl VP*
EMP: 157
SALES (corp-wide): 705.05MM **Privately Held**
Web: www.bergelectric.com
SIC: 1731 General electrical contractor
PA: Bergelectric Corp.
3182 Lionshead Ave
Carlsbad CA
760 638-2374

(P-1682)
BERGELECTRIC CORP
15776 Gateway Cir (92780-6469)
PHONE..................................949 250-7005
Mark Bauer, *Mgr*
EMP: 189
SALES (corp-wide): 705.05MM **Privately Held**
Web: www.bergelectric.com
SIC: 1731 General electrical contractor
PA: Bergelectric Corp.
3182 Lionshead Ave
Carlsbad CA
760 638-2374

(P-1683)
BILL SHARP ELECTRICAL CONTR
5136 Caterpillar Rd (96003-2048)
P.O. Box 2187 (96093-2187)
PHONE..................................530 338-1735
EMP: 66
Web: www.sharpelectric.us
SIC: 1731 General electrical contractor
PA: Bill Sharp Electrical Contractor
1101 Oregon St
Weaverville CA

(P-1684)
BLACK DIAMOND ELECTRIC INC
1300 Verne Roberts Cir (94509-7903)
PHONE..................................925 777-3440
Jason C Pauline, *CEO*
EMP: 100 **EST:** 1996
SALES (est): 31.86MM **Privately Held**
Web: www.blackdiamondelectric.com
SIC: 1731 General electrical contractor

(P-1685)
BOCKMON & WOODY ELC CO INC
1528 El Pinal Dr (95205-2643)
P.O. Box 1018 (95201-1018)
PHONE..................................209 464-4878
Gary E Woody, *Pr*
Jeff Bockmon, *
Gary M Woody, *
Nick Woody, *
EMP: 190 **EST:** 1990
SQ FT: 36,000
SALES (est): 40MM **Privately Held**
Web: www.bockmonwoody.com
SIC: 1731 General electrical contractor

PRODUCTS & SERVICES SECTION

1731 - Electrical Work (P-1708)

(P-1686)
BRAYER ELECTRIC COMPANY (PA)
15095 Wicks Blvd (94577-6621)
PHONE....................800 581-2544
EMP: 90 EST: 1928
SALES (est): 20.19MM
SALES (corp-wide): 20.19MM **Privately Held**
Web: www.brayerelectric.com
SIC: **1731** Electrical work

(P-1687)
BRIGGS ELECTRIC INC (PA)
14381 Franklin Ave (92780-7010)
PHONE....................714 544-2500
Jeff Perry, *
Thomas J Perry, *
Todd Perry, *
▲ EMP: 100 EST: 1946
SQ FT: 5,500
SALES (est): 51.07MM
SALES (corp-wide): 51.07MM **Privately Held**
Web: www.briggselectric.com
SIC: **1731** General electrical contractor

(P-1688)
BUTTERFIELD ELECTRIC INC
2101 Freeway Dr Ste A (95776-9510)
P.O. Box 25 (95776-0025)
PHONE....................530 666-2116
Rick Butterfield, *Pr*
Rorie Butterfield, *
EMP: 165 EST: 1985
SQ FT: 14,000
SALES (est): 37.94MM **Privately Held**
Web: www.butterfieldelectric.com
SIC: **1731** General electrical contractor

(P-1689)
C H REYNOLDS ELECTRIC INC (PA)
Also Called: Ch Reynolds
1281 Wayne Ave (95131-3599)
PHONE....................408 436-9280
Charles Reynolds, *Pr*
Paul J Derania, *CFO*
Jason Bright, *COO*
John Anderson, *Senior Vice President Ret Division*
Will Pres Electrical Division Swick Senior V, *Prin*
EMP: 400 EST: 1983
SQ FT: 25,000
SALES (est): 86.33MM
SALES (corp-wide): 86.33MM **Privately Held**
Web: www.chreynolds.com
SIC: **1731** General electrical contractor

(P-1690)
C T AND F INC
7228 Scout Ave (90201-4902)
PHONE....................562 927-2339
EMP: 80
Web: www.ctandf.net
SIC: **1731** General electrical contractor

(P-1691)
CALENERGY LLC
7030 Gentry Rd (92233-9720)
PHONE....................402 231-1527
Bill Fehrman, *Pr*
EMP: 350 EST: 2013
SALES (est): 46.4MM **Privately Held**
SIC: **1731** Electric power systems contractors

(P-1692)
CAROL ELECTRIC COMPANY INC
3822 Cerritos Ave (90720-2420)
PHONE....................562 431-1870
John R Fuqua, *Ch Bd*
Allen Moffitt, *
Brian Moffitt, *
EMP: 90 EST: 1979
SQ FT: 10,000
SALES (est): 17.4MM **Privately Held**
Web: www.carolelectric.com
SIC: **1731** General electrical contractor

(P-1693)
CBF INC
Also Called: Cbf Electric & Data
735 Battery St Fl 2 (94111-1536)
PHONE....................415 495-3085
John M Walsh, *Pr*
John M Walsh, *Pr*
Leanne Goff, *
Novelynn Tejada, *
EMP: 110 EST: 1951
SQ FT: 6,300
SALES (est): 119.83MM **Privately Held**
Web: www.cbfelectric.com
SIC: **1731** General electrical contractor

(P-1694)
CBR ELECTRIC INC
22 Rancho Cir (92630-8325)
PHONE....................949 455-0331
Cary Raffety, *Pr*
EMP: 150 EST: 1989
SQ FT: 4,000
SALES (est): 9.76MM **Privately Held**
Web: www.cbrelectric.com
SIC: **1731** General electrical contractor

(P-1695)
CHAMPION ELECTRIC INC
3950 Garner Rd (92501-1005)
PHONE....................951 276-9619
Glenn Rowden, *Pr*
Cynthia D Rowden, *
Tom Rowden, *
EMP: 65 EST: 1991
SQ FT: 12,000
SALES (est): 10.84MM **Privately Held**
Web: www.championelec.com
SIC: **1731** General electrical contractor

(P-1696)
CHICO ELECTRIC INC
36 W Eaton Rd (95973-0160)
PHONE....................530 891-1933
Norman Nielsen, *CEO*
EMP: 60 EST: 1960
SQ FT: 8,500
SALES (est): 12.06MM **Privately Held**
Web: www.chicoelectric.com
SIC: **1731** General electrical contractor

(P-1697)
CHULA VISTA ELECTRIC CO
9344 Wheatlands Rd Ste A (92071-5643)
PHONE....................619 420-4500
EMP: 65 EST: 1931
SALES (est): 19.69MM **Privately Held**
Web: www.c-v-e.com
SIC: **1731** General electrical contractor

(P-1698)
CITY-WIDE ELECTRONIC SYSTEMS INC
440 Highland Ave (92020-5209)
P.O. Box 2069 (92021-0069)
PHONE....................619 444-0219
EMP: 100
SIC: **1731** General electrical contractor

(P-1699)
CLIMATEC LLC
13715 Stowe Dr (92064-6836)
PHONE....................858 391-7000
Eince Scalise, *Brnch Mgr*
EMP: 64
SALES (corp-wide): 230.19MM **Privately Held**
Web: www.climatec.com
SIC: **1731** Environmental system control installation
HQ: Climatec, Llc
2851 W Kathleen Rd
Phoenix AZ
602 944-3330

(P-1700)
CLIMATEC LLC
16735 Saticoy St Ste 111 (91406-2700)
PHONE....................818 855-8528
EMP: 70
SALES (corp-wide): 230.19MM **Privately Held**
Web: www.climatec.com
SIC: **1731** 7373 Environmental system control installation; Office computer automation systems integration
HQ: Climatec, Llc
2851 W Kathleen Rd
Phoenix AZ
602 944-3330

(P-1701)
COLLINS ELECTRICAL COMPANY INC (PA)
3412 Metro Dr (95215-9440)
PHONE....................209 466-3691
Eugene C Gini, *Pr*
Dianne R Gini, *
Kevin Gini, *
Brian Gini, *
Craig Gini, *
EMP: 200 EST: 1928
SQ FT: 80,000
SALES (est): 94.22MM
SALES (corp-wide): 94.22MM **Privately Held**
Web: www.collinselectric.com
SIC: **1731** General electrical contractor

(P-1702)
COMET ELECTRIC INC
21625 Prairie St (91311-5833)
PHONE....................818 340-0965
Adam Saitman, *CEO*
Steve Goad, *VP*
Keith Berson, *Ex VP*
Jason Pennington, *CFO*
EMP: 150 EST: 1993
SQ FT: 12,000
SALES (est): 43.92MM
SALES (corp-wide): 68.83MM **Privately Held**
Web: www.cometelectric.com
SIC: **1731** General electrical contractor
PA: Valley Electric Co. Of Mt. Vernon, Inc.,
1100 Merrill Creek Pkwy
Everett WA
425 407-0832

(P-1703)
COMMUNCTION WIRG SPCALISTS INC
Also Called: C W S
8909 Complex Dr Ste F (92123-1418)
PHONE....................858 278-4545
Eric Templin, *Pr*
Richard Templin, *
Donna Templin, *Stockholder*
EMP: 80 EST: 1991
SQ FT: 5,500
SALES (est): 8.93MM **Privately Held**
Web: www.cwssandiego.com
SIC: **1731** Telephone and telephone equipment installation

(P-1704)
COMMUNICATION TECH SVCS LLC
1590 S Milliken Ave Ste H (91761-2326)
PHONE....................508 382-2700
Chris Ungson, *Brnch Mgr*
EMP: 266
Web: www.cts1.com
SIC: **1731** 8748 Voice, data, and video wiring contractor; Communications consulting
PA: Communication Technology Services, Llc
33 Locke Dr Ste 201
Marlborough MA

(P-1705)
COMTEL SYSTEMS TECHNOLOGY INC
1292 Hammerwood Ave (94089-2232)
PHONE....................408 543-5600
Richard Nielsen, *Pr*
Andrea Nielsen, *
EMP: 70 EST: 1972
SQ FT: 10,760
SALES (est): 19.7MM **Privately Held**
Web: www.comtelsys.com
SIC: **1731** Communications specialization

(P-1706)
CON J FRANKE ELECTRIC INC
317 N Grant St (95202-2633)
PHONE....................209 462-0717
Barry Frain, *Pr*
Lewis Frain, *
Diana Frain, *
EMP: 100 EST: 1925
SQ FT: 7,000
SALES (est): 53.64MM **Privately Held**
Web: www.cjfranke.com
SIC: **1731** General electrical contractor

(P-1707)
CONTRA COSTA ELECTRIC INC (DH)
825 Howe Rd (94553-3441)
P.O. Box 2523 (94553-0317)
PHONE....................925 229-4250
Michael Dias, *Pr*
Tom Tatro, *VP*
Dave Galli, *CFO*
Charlie Hadsell, *VP*
Joey Ramirez, *VP*
EMP: 300 EST: 1946
SALES (est): 148.79MM
SALES (corp-wide): 11.08B **Publicly Held**
Web: www.ccelectric.com
SIC: **1731** General electrical contractor
HQ: Dyn Specialty Contracting, Inc.
1420 Spring Hill Rd # 500
Mc Lean VA

(P-1708)
CONTRA COSTA ELECTRIC INC
3208 Landco Dr (93308-6156)
PHONE....................661 322-4036
EMP: 104
SALES (corp-wide): 11.08B **Publicly Held**
Web: www.ccelectric.com

1731 - Electrical Work (P-1709)

SIC: 1731 General electrical contractor
HQ: Contra Costa Electric, Inc.
825 Howe Rd
Martinez CA
925 229-4250

(P-1709)
COOPER LIGHTING LLC
285 Rood Rd Ste 101 (92231-9535)
PHONE.................................760 357-4760
EMP: 113
Web: www.cooperlighting.com
SIC: 1731 Lighting contractor
HQ: Cooper Lighting, Llc
1121 Highway 74 S
Peachtree City GA
770 486-4800

(P-1710)
COSCO FIRE PROTECTION INC
7455 Longard Rd (94551-8238)
PHONE.................................925 455-2751
Phil Raya, Mgr
EMP: 69
Web: www.coscofire.com
SIC: 1731 3494 8711 7382 General electrical contractor; Sprinkler systems, field; Engineering services; Security systems services
HQ: Cosco Fire Protection, Inc.
29222 Rancho Viejo Rd # 205
San Juan Capistrano CA

(P-1711)
COVE ELECTRIC INC
77971 Wildcat Dr Ste F (92211-4133)
PHONE.................................760 568-9924
Charles Bojkovsky, Pr
Jeannie Stewart, *
Michele Bojkovsky, Stockholder*
Steve Tavares, *
EMP: 70 EST: 1976
SQ FT: 4,500
SALES (est): 10.61MM Privately Held
Web: www.coveelectric.com
SIC: 1731 General electrical contractor

(P-1712)
CROSSTOWN ELEC & DATA INC
5454 Diaz St (91706-2026)
PHONE.................................626 813-6693
Dave Heermance, CEO
EMP: 100 EST: 1998
SQ FT: 2,500
SALES (est): 28.7MM Privately Held
Web: www.crosstowndata.com
SIC: 1731 General electrical contractor

(P-1713)
CSI ELECTRICAL CONTRACTORS INC
41769 11th St W Ste B (93551-1418)
PHONE.................................661 723-0869
Roland Tamayo, Brnch Mgr
EMP: 448
SALES (corp-wide): 3.01B Publicly Held
Web: www.csielectric.com
SIC: 1731 General electrical contractor
HQ: Csi Electrical Contractors, Inc.
10623 Fulton Wells Ave
Santa Fe Springs CA

(P-1714)
CSI ELECTRICAL CONTRACTORS INC
310 Via Vera Cruz Ste 106 (92078-2631)
PHONE.................................760 227-0577
Steve Watts, Brnch Mgr
EMP: 449

SALES (corp-wide): 3.01B Publicly Held
Web: www.csielectric.com
SIC: 1731 General electrical contractor
HQ: Csi Electrical Contractors, Inc.
10623 Fulton Wells Ave
Santa Fe Springs CA

(P-1715)
CSI ELECTRICAL CONTRACTORS INC (HQ)
Also Called: C S I
10623 Fulton Wells Ave (90670-3741)
P.O. Box 2887 (90670-0887)
PHONE.................................562 946-0700
Steven M Watts, CEO
Paul Pica, *
Rick Yauney, *
EMP: 150 EST: 1990
SQ FT: 49,044
SALES (est): 146.31MM
SALES (corp-wide): 3.01B Publicly Held
Web: www.csielectric.com
SIC: 1731 General electrical contractor
PA: Myr Group Inc.
12150 E 112th Ave
Henderson CO
303 286-8000

(P-1716)
CUPERTINO ELECTRIC INC
Also Called: Cupertino Electric
350 Lenore Way (95018-8973)
P.O. Box 1517 (95018-1517)
PHONE.................................408 808-8260
EMP: 598
SALES (corp-wide): 505.35MM Privately Held
Web: www.cei.com
SIC: 1731 General electrical contractor
PA: Cupertino Electric, Inc.
1132 N 7th St
San Jose CA
408 808-8000

(P-1717)
CUPERTINO ELECTRIC INC (PA)
Also Called: Cei
1132 N 7th St (95112-4438)
PHONE.................................408 808-8000
Tom Schott, Pr
Bill Slakey, *
Debra Olson, *
Brett Boncher, *
Estrella Parker, *
▲ EMP: 400 EST: 1954
SQ FT: 90,000
SALES (est): 505.35MM
SALES (corp-wide): 505.35MM Privately Held
Web: www.cei.com
SIC: 1731 General electrical contractor

(P-1718)
CUPERTINO ELECTRIC INC
1740 Cesar Chavez Fl 2 (94124-1134)
PHONE.................................415 970-3400
Adam Spillane, Brnch Mgr
EMP: 897
SALES (corp-wide): 505.35MM Privately Held
Web: www.cei.com
SIC: 1731 General electrical contractor
PA: Cupertino Electric, Inc.
1132 N 7th St
San Jose CA
408 808-8000

(P-1719)
DAN FREITAS ELECTRIC INC
983 E Levin Ave (93274-6525)

PHONE.................................559 686-9572
Daniel Freitas, Pr
Jeanette Freitas, *
EMP: 60 EST: 1984
SQ FT: 14,460
SALES (est): 9.15MM Privately Held
Web: www.danfreitaselectric.com
SIC: 1731 General electrical contractor

(P-1720)
DECKER ELECTRIC CO INC ELECTRICAL CONTRACTORS (PA)
1282 Folsom St (94103-3817)
PHONE.................................415 552-1622
▲ EMP: 85 EST: 1896
SALES (est): 112.32MM
SALES (corp-wide): 112.32MM Privately Held
Web: www.deckerelectric.com
SIC: 1731 General electrical contractor

(P-1721)
DILIGENCE SECURITY GROUP
66 Franklin St Ste 300 (94607-3734)
PHONE.................................510 710-5806
Joy Baucom, CEO
Kenton Barnes, *
EMP: 200 EST: 2020
SALES (est): 13.67MM Privately Held
Web: www.diligencesecuritygroup.com
SIC: 1731 7389 Safety and security specialization; Business Activities at Non-Commercial Site

(P-1722)
DYNALECTRIC COMPANY
1111 Pioneer Way (92020-1964)
PHONE.................................619 328-4007
Daivd Rispolrch, Mgr
EMP: 300
SALES (corp-wide): 11.08B Publicly Held
Web: www.dynalectric-dc.com
SIC: 1731 General electrical contractor
HQ: Dynalectric Company
22930 Shaw Rd Ste 100
Dulles VA
703 288-2866

(P-1723)
EDWARDS TECHNOLOGIES INC
139 Maryland St (90245-4116)
PHONE.................................310 536-7070
Brian Edwards, Pr
Roberta Perry, Prin
▲ EMP: 64 EST: 1984
SQ FT: 10,000
SALES (est): 24.4MM Privately Held
Web: www.edwardstechnologies.com
SIC: 1731 Sound equipment specialization

(P-1724)
ELCOR ELECTRIC INC
3310 Bassett St (95054-2702)
PHONE.................................408 986-1320
George Woodley, Genl Mgr
Clint Woodley, *
EMP: 120 EST: 1989
SQ FT: 5,000
SALES (est): 24.72MM Privately Held
Web: www.elcorelectric.com
SIC: 1731 General electrical contractor

(P-1725)
ELEC-TECH ENTERPRISES INC
3508 Stanbridge Ave (90808-2652)
PHONE.................................562 602-1015
Gary Urke, Pr
Gary Urke, Pr

Ron Inlow, VP
EMP: 62 EST: 1989
SALES (est): 4.88MM Privately Held
Web: www.electechca.com
SIC: 1731 General electrical contractor

(P-1726)
ELECTRICAL & INSTRUMENTATION UNLIMITED OF CALIFORNIA INC
Also Called: Eiu of California
6950 District Blvd (93313-2072)
P.O. Box 40878 (93384-0878)
EMP: 200
SIC: 1731 General electrical contractor

(P-1727)
ELECTRONIC CONTROL SYSTEMS LLC
Also Called: Albireo Energy
12575 Kirkham Ct Ste 1 (92064-8844)
PHONE.................................858 513-1911
EMP: 145 EST: 1996
SQ FT: 17,000
SALES (est): 58.27MM
SALES (corp-wide): 141.53MM Privately Held
SIC: 1731 7382 Energy management controls; Security systems services
PA: Albireo Energy, Llc
3 Ethel Rd Ste 300
Edison NJ
732 512-9100

(P-1728)
ELITE ELECTRIC
9415 Bellegrave Ave (92509-2741)
PHONE.................................951 681-5811
Carl Eric Dawson, Pr
EMP: 80 EST: 1978
SQ FT: 1,720
SALES (est): 10.05MM Privately Held
Web: www.elite-electricinc.com
SIC: 1731 General electrical contractor

(P-1729)
ENERGY WATCH
3555 Landco Dr (93308-6169)
PHONE.................................661 324-0930
Stefanie Doubert, Mgr
EMP: 90 EST: 2005
SALES (est): 1.69MM Privately Held
Web: www.kernenergywatch.com
SIC: 1731 General electrical contractor

(P-1730)
ENERPATH SERVICES INC
1758 Orange Tree Ln (92374-2856)
PHONE.................................909 335-1699
Stephen Guthrie, Pr
Janina Guthrie, Treas
Jonathan Baty, Sec
EMP: 86 EST: 1989
SQ FT: 4,500
SALES (est): 3.24MM Privately Held
SIC: 1731 8748 Lighting contractor; Lighting consultant

(P-1731)
ENSIGN US DRLG CAL INC
3701 Fruitvale Ave (93308-5109)
PHONE.................................661 387-8400
Brian Watts, Prin
EMP: 247
SALES (corp-wide): 778.27MM Privately Held
Web: www.ensignusd.com
SIC: 1731 Energy management controls
HQ: Ensign United States Drilling (California) Inc.

PRODUCTS & SERVICES SECTION

1731 - Electrical Work (P-1755)

7001 Charity Ave
Bakersfield CA

(P-1732)
ESYS ENERGY CONTROL COMPANY
4520 Stine Rd Ste 7 (93313-2372)
PHONE.................................661 833-1902
Fabio Russoniello, *Pr*
EMP: 60 **EST:** 1985
SQ FT: 12,000
SALES (est): 12.59MM **Privately Held**
Web: www.esys.us
SIC: 1731 5084 Electronic controls installation; Controlling instruments and accessories

(P-1733)
FAITH ELECTRIC LLC
1980 Orange Tree Ln Ste 106 (92374-2803)
PHONE.................................909 767-2682
Elijah Adams, *Managing Member*
EMP: 200 **EST:** 2014
SQ FT: 5,000
SALES (est): 80MM **Privately Held**
Web: www.faithelectricllc.com
SIC: 1731 General electrical contractor

(P-1734)
FIRST FIRE SYSTEMS INC (PA)
Also Called: Fire Systems
5947 Burchard Ave (90034-1701)
PHONE.................................310 559-0900
Juda Roshanzamir, *Pr*
Robbie Kashani, *
EMP: 99 **EST:** 1980
SQ FT: 9,400
SALES (est): 11.88MM
SALES (corp-wide): 11.88MM **Privately Held**
Web: www.ffstech.com
SIC: 1731 Fire detection and burglar alarm systems specialization

(P-1735)
FISHEL COMPANY
5878 Autoport Mall (92121-2514)
PHONE.................................858 658-0830
Sal Padula, *Brnch Mgr*
EMP: 119
SALES (corp-wide): 758.31MM **Privately Held**
Web: www.teamfishel.com
SIC: 1731 1623 Telephone and telephone equipment installation; Water main construction
PA: The Fishel Company
1366 Dublin Rd
Columbus OH
614 274-8100

(P-1736)
FISK ELECTRIC COMPANY
15870 Olden St (91342-1241)
PHONE.................................818 884-1166
Orvil Anthony, *Sr VP*
EMP: 165
SALES (corp-wide): 3.79B **Publicly Held**
Web: www.fiskcorp.com
SIC: 1731 General electrical contractor
HQ: Fisk Electric Company
10855 Westview Dr
Houston TX
713 868-6111

(P-1737)
FOSHAY ELECTRIC CO INC
950 Industrial Blvd (91911-1608)
PHONE.................................858 277-7676
Theresa M Faucher, *Pr*
Mark Faucher, *
Michael Beringhaus, *
EMP: 100 **EST:** 1947
SALES (est): 9.92MM **Privately Held**
Web: www.foshayelectric.com
SIC: 1731 General electrical contractor

(P-1738)
GOULD ELECTRIC INC
12975 Brookprinter Pl Ste 280 (92064-8895)
P.O. Box 504377 (92150-4377)
PHONE.................................858 486-1727
EMP: 125
Web: www.gouldelect.com
SIC: 1731 General electrical contractor

(P-1739)
GREGG ELECTRIC INC
608 W Emporia St (91762-3709)
PHONE.................................909 983-1794
Randall F Fehlman, *Pr*
James Fehlman, *
Victoria Mensen, *
EMP: 150 **EST:** 1961
SQ FT: 15,000
SALES (est): 23.39MM **Privately Held**
Web: www.greggelectric.com
SIC: 1731 General electrical contractor

(P-1740)
GUARDIAN INTEGRATED SEC INC (PA)
21828 Lassen St Ste A (91311-3603)
PHONE.................................800 400-3167
Abraham Ramzan, *CEO*
EMP: 120 **EST:** 2014
SALES (est): 12.56MM
SALES (corp-wide): 12.56MM **Privately Held**
Web: www.guardianintegratedsecurity.com
SIC: 1731 Safety and security specialization

(P-1741)
H & D ELECTRIC
5237 Walnut Ave Ste 100 (95841-2694)
P.O. Box 41360 (95841-0360)
PHONE.................................916 332-0794
Mark E Cooper, *Pr*
EMP: 360 **EST:** 1957
SQ FT: 14,400
SALES (est): 47.14MM **Privately Held**
Web: www.hdelectric.com
SIC: 1731 General electrical contractor

(P-1742)
H A BOWEN ELECTRIC INC
2055 Williams St (94577-2305)
P.O. Box 2153 (94577-0329)
PHONE.................................510 483-0500
Herbert A Bowen, *Pr*
EMP: 60 **EST:** 1979
SQ FT: 9,000
SALES (est): 17.12MM **Privately Held**
Web: www.bowenelectric.com
SIC: 1731 General electrical contractor

(P-1743)
HAMILTON AND DILLON ELC INC
1128 Reno Ave (95351-1128)
P.O. Box 581890 (95358-0033)
PHONE.................................209 529-6292
Bobby Hamilton, *Pr*
John Dillon, *
EMP: 60 **EST:** 1998
SQ FT: 5,000
SALES (est): 4.28MM **Privately Held**
Web: www.hamdill.com

SIC: 1731 General electrical contractor

(P-1744)
HAMMER HEAD SECURITY INC
4551 S B St (95206-3956)
PHONE.................................209 227-6566
Lakhvir Singh, *CEO*
Sarbjit Kaur, *COO*
EMP: 170 **EST:** 2016
SALES (est): 9.3MM **Privately Held**
Web: www.hammerheadprotection.com
SIC: 1731 Safety and security specialization

(P-1745)
HELIX ELECTRIC INC
13100 Alondra Blvd Ste 108 (90703-2262)
P.O. Box 85298 (92186-5298)
PHONE.................................562 941-7200
Acey Long, *VP*
EMP: 876
SALES (corp-wide): 408.8MM **Privately Held**
Web: www.helixelectric.com
SIC: 1731 General electrical contractor
PA: Helix Electric, Inc.
6795 Flanders Dr
San Diego CA
858 535-0505

(P-1746)
HELIX ELECTRIC INC (PA)
Also Called: Helix Renewables
6795 Flanders Dr (92123-2903)
P.O. Box 85298 (92186-5298)
PHONE.................................858 535-0505
EMP: 220 **EST:** 1985
SALES (est): 408.8MM
SALES (corp-wide): 408.8MM **Privately Held**
Web: www.helixelectric.com
SIC: 1731 General electrical contractor

(P-1747)
HHS COMMUNICATIONS INC
2042 S Grove Ave (91761-5617)
PHONE.................................909 230-5170
Royce S Jaime, *Pr*
EMP: 60 **EST:** 2007
SALES (est): 6.63MM
SALES (corp-wide): 350.16MM **Privately Held**
Web: www.congruex.com
SIC: 1731 Fiber optic cable installation
PA: Congruex Llc
2615 13th St
Boulder CO
720 749-2318

(P-1748)
HIGH-LIGHT ELECTRIC INC
1460 E Cooley Dr Ste 100 (92324-3933)
P.O. Box 1248 (92324-0822)
PHONE.................................951 352-9646
Erwin Mendoza, *Pr*
EMP: 60 **EST:** 1996
SALES (est): 17.61MM **Privately Held**
Web: www.hleincusa.com
SIC: 1731 General electrical contractor

(P-1749)
HMT ELECTRIC INC
2340 Meyers Ave (92029-1008)
PHONE.................................858 458-9771
Brian Hudak, *CEO*
EMP: 85 **EST:** 2007
SQ FT: 2,000
SALES (est): 25.2MM **Privately Held**
Web: www.hmtelectric.com
SIC: 1731 General electrical contractor

(P-1750)
HOT LINE CONSTRUCTION INC
9020 Brentwood Blvd Ste H (94513-4049)
PHONE.................................925 634-9333
Kelly Kutchera, *CEO*
Carol G Bade, *
Troy D Myers, *
EMP: 640 **EST:** 1986
SQ FT: 4,000
SALES (est): 264.55MM **Privately Held**
Web: www.hotlineconstructioninc.com
SIC: 1731 1799 Electric power systems contractors; Cable splicing service

(P-1751)
HOWE ELECTRIC INC
4682 E Olive Ave (93702-1689)
PHONE.................................559 255-8992
Clinton Howe, *Brnch Mgr*
EMP: 145
SQ FT: 12,502
SALES (corp-wide): 30.48MM **Privately Held**
Web: www.howe-electric.com
SIC: 1731 General electrical contractor
PA: Howe Electric, Inc.
4690 E Olive Ave
Fresno CA
559 255-8992

(P-1752)
HOWE ELECTRIC CONSTRUCTION INC
Also Called: H E C I
4682 E Olive Ave (93702-1689)
PHONE.................................559 255-8992
Todd Howe, *Pr*
Ty Howe, *
Monica Teare, *
Marjorie Montes, *
EMP: 140 **EST:** 2007
SALES (est): 18.68MM **Privately Held**
Web: www.howe-electric.com
SIC: 1731 General electrical contractor

(P-1753)
ICS INTEGRATED COMM SYSTEMS
6680 Via Del Oro (95119-1392)
PHONE.................................408 491-6000
Aaron Colton, *CEO*
▲ **EMP:** 65 **EST:** 2002
SQ FT: 18,000
SALES (est): 25.38MM **Privately Held**
Web: www.ics-integration.com
SIC: 1731 Fire detection and burglar alarm systems specialization

(P-1754)
IDEX GLOBAL SERVICES INC
2301 Kerner Blvd Ste D (94901-5554)
PHONE.................................415 482-4242
Dominic Dimare, *Mgr*
EMP: 135
Web: www.idexgs.com
SIC: 1731 Communications specialization
HQ: Idex Global Services, Inc.
851 Van Ness Ave Fl 2
San Francisco CA
415 249-3400

(P-1755)
IES COMMERCIAL INC
1633 Maria St (91504-3420)
PHONE.................................713 860-1500
Steve Tucker, *Owner*
EMP: 61
Web: www.ielectric.com

1731 - Electrical Work (P-1756)

PRODUCTS & SERVICES SECTION

SIC: **1731** General electrical contractor
HQ: les Commercial, Inc.
2801 S Fair Ln Ste 101
Tempe AZ
480 379-6200

(P-1756)
INTERIOR ELECTRIC INCORPORATED
747 N Main St (92868-1105)
PHONE.............................714 771-9098
Mark Beverly, *Pr*
Mark Maskevich, *
Chad Stewart, *
Gus Baquerizo, *
Glen Nielsen, *
EMP: 75 **EST:** 1987
SQ FT: 10,000
SALES (est): 13.23MM **Privately Held**
Web: static-errorpic.s3-eu-west-1.amazonaws.com
SIC: 1731 General electrical contractor

(P-1757)
IPITEK INC
Also Called: Ipitek
2461 Impala Dr (92010-7227)
P.O. Box 130878 (92013-0878)
PHONE.............................760 438-1010
Michael M Salour, *Ch Bd*
EMP: 170 **EST:** 1982
SQ FT: 40,000
SALES (est): 21.12MM **Privately Held**
SIC: 1731 Fiber optic cable installation

(P-1758)
JEEVA CORPORATION
Also Called: Satellite Pros
750 E E St Unit B (91764-3821)
PHONE.............................909 238-4073
Orlando Uranga, *CEO*
Rita Uranga, *
EMP: 70 **EST:** 2011
SQ FT: 1,800
SALES (est): 2.26MM **Privately Held**
SIC: 1731 Cable television installation

(P-1759)
JMG SECURITY SYSTEMS INC
17150 Newhope St Ste 109 (92708-4273)
PHONE.............................714 545-8882
TOLL FREE: 800
Ken Jacobs, *CEO*
Michael Christensen, *
Gil Ledesma, *
Sue Tjelmeland, *
Gary Beale, *
EMP: 70 **EST:** 1987
SQ FT: 14,000
SALES (est): 19.64MM **Privately Held**
Web: www.jmgsecurity.com
SIC: 1731 5063 Safety and security specialization; Burglar alarm systems

(P-1760)
JOHNSON-PELTIER
Also Called: Johnson-Peltier
12021 Shoemaker Ave (90670-4718)
PHONE.............................562 944-3408
EMP: 75 **EST:** 1957
SALES (est): 13.93MM **Privately Held**
Web: www.johnson-peltier.com
SIC: 1731 General electrical contractor

(P-1761)
KDC INC (HQ)
Also Called: Kdc Systems
4462 Corporate Center Dr (90720-2539)
PHONE.............................714 828-7000
Earnest Lee Brown, *Pr*
Ben Martin, *
Dusty Lord, *
EMP: 207 **EST:** 1976
SQ FT: 57,000
SALES (est): 99.86MM
SALES (corp-wide): 11.08B **Publicly Held**
Web: www.kdc-systems.com
SIC: 1731 1611 3823 General electrical contractor; General contractor, highway and street construction; Process control instruments
PA: Emcor Group, Inc.
301 Merritt 7 Fl 6
Norwalk CT
203 849-7800

(P-1762)
KITE ELECTRIC INCORPORATED
Also Called: K E
2 Thomas (92618-2512)
PHONE.............................949 380-7471
Tracy Adams, *Pr*
EMP: 120 **EST:** 2000
SALES (est): 9.35MM **Privately Held**
Web: www.kiteelectric.com
SIC: 1731 Electrical work

(P-1763)
KOSITCH ENTERPRISES INC
Also Called: Mission Electric Company
5700 Boscell Common (94538-5111)
PHONE.............................510 657-4460
Jeffrey Kositch, *CEO*
EMP: 80 **EST:** 1978
SQ FT: 9,000
SALES (est): 25.54MM **Privately Held**
Web: www.mission-elec.com
SIC: 1731 General electrical contractor

(P-1764)
L TECH NETWORK SERVICES INC
3424 Garfield Ave # A (90040-3104)
PHONE.............................562 222-1121
Douglas Mchose, *CEO*
Robert O Lopez, *
EMP: 65 **EST:** 1996
SALES (est): 4.79MM **Privately Held**
Web: www.ltechnet.com
SIC: 1731 1623 7382 7349 Communications specialization; Cable laying construction; Security systems services; Building and office cleaning services

(P-1765)
LASER ELECTRIC INC
650 Opper St (92029-1020)
PHONE.............................760 658-6626
Denise Hartnett, *CEO*
Kevin Hartnett, *
EMP: 120 **EST:** 1987
SQ FT: 11,000
SALES (est): 36.15MM **Privately Held**
Web: www.laserelectric.com
SIC: 1731 General electrical contractor

(P-1766)
LEED ELECTRIC INC
13138 Arctic Cir (90670-5508)
PHONE.............................562 270-9500
Seth Jamali Dinan, *Pr*
EMP: 135 **EST:** 1979
SQ FT: 8,480
SALES (est): 21.38MM **Privately Held**
Web: www.leedelectric.com
SIC: 1731 General electrical contractor

(P-1767)
LMS ELECTRIC
Also Called: LMS Electric
2735 Honolulu Ave (91020-1756)
PHONE.............................818 248-1165
Louis M Sever Iii, *Pr*
EMP: 65 **EST:** 2009
SQ FT: 6,500
SALES (est): 10MM **Privately Held**
Web: www.lmselectric.com
SIC: 1731 General electrical contractor

(P-1768)
M & R JOINT VENTURE ELECTRICAL
231 Benton Ct (91789-5213)
PHONE.............................909 598-7700
Robert E Meadows, *VP*
EMP: 60 **EST:** 1994
SALES (est): 13.46MM **Privately Held**
Web: www.morrow-meadows.com
SIC: 1731 General electrical contractor

(P-1769)
MARK III CONSTRUCTION INC (PA)
Also Called: Mark III Dvlpers Dsgn/Builders
5101 Florin Perkins Rd (95826-4817)
PHONE.............................916 381-8080
Daniel Carlton, *CEO*
Jennifer O'brien Cooley, *Pr*
Mark O'brien, *Dir*
Tim O'brien, *Dir*
Michael O'brien, *Treas*
EMP: 72 **EST:** 1975
SQ FT: 11,000
SALES (est): 77.65MM
SALES (corp-wide): 77.65MM **Privately Held**
Web: www.mark-three.com
SIC: 1731 1542 1711 8711 General electrical contractor; Commercial and office building, new construction; Plumbing contractors; Professional engineer

(P-1770)
MARK LAND ELECTRIC INC
7876 Deering Ave (91304-5005)
PHONE.............................818 883-5110
Lloyd Saitman, *CEO*
Stewart Franklin, *
John Bennet, *
EMP: 141 **EST:** 1981
SQ FT: 10,000
SALES (est): 26.38MM **Privately Held**
Web: www.lmela.com
SIC: 1731 General electrical contractor

(P-1771)
MAY-HAN ELECTRIC INC
Also Called: M & M Electric
1600 Auburn Blvd (95815-1906)
PHONE.............................916 929-0150
Cecilia J Hanson, *CEO*
Audrey Daugherty, *
Connie Gisler, *
EMP: 65 **EST:** 1964
SQ FT: 16,000
SALES (est): 13.66MM **Privately Held**
SIC: 1731 Lighting contractor

(P-1772)
MB HERZOG ELECTRIC INC
15709 Illinois Ave (90723-4112)
PHONE.............................562 531-2002
Ryan M Herzog, *CEO*
Kevin Ryan, *
EMP: 200 **EST:** 1974
SQ FT: 6,200
SALES (est): 35.18MM **Privately Held**
Web: www.herzogelectric.com
SIC: 1731 General electrical contractor

(P-1773)
MCH ELECTRIC INC (PA)
7693 Longard Rd (94551-8208)
PHONE.............................925 453-5041
James Humphrey, *Pr*
Christine Morris, *
EMP: 74 **EST:** 1999
SQ FT: 2,600
SALES (est): 40.73MM
SALES (corp-wide): 40.73MM **Privately Held**
Web: www.mchelectric.com
SIC: 1731 General electrical contractor

(P-1774)
MCKEE AND COMPANY ELECTRIC
594 Monterey Blvd (94127-2416)
PHONE.............................415 724-2738
Steven Mckee, *CEO*
EMP: 73 **EST:** 2017
SALES (est): 9.7MM **Privately Held**
Web: www.mckeeselectric.com
SIC: 1731 General electrical contractor

(P-1775)
MCMILLAN ELECTRIC
1480 Folsom St (94103-3702)
PHONE.............................415 826-5100
William Musgrave, *Pr*
David Auch, *
Ryan Mahoney, *
Michael Mcalister, *VP*
Russell Schmittou, *
EMP: 280 **EST:** 1965
SALES (est): 97.03MM **Privately Held**
Web: www.mcmillanco.com
SIC: 1731 General electrical contractor

(P-1776)
MEDLEY COMMUNICATIONS INC (PA)
43015 Black Deer Loop Ste 203 (92590-3567)
PHONE.............................951 245-5200
Darrin Medley, *Pr*
EMP: 175 **EST:** 1985
SALES (est): 10.2MM **Privately Held**
Web: www.medleycom.net
SIC: 1731 8748 Cable television installation; Communications consulting

(P-1777)
METROPOLITAN ELEC CNSTR INC
2400 3rd St (94107-3111)
PHONE.............................415 642-3000
Nick Dutto, *Prin*
Mark Friedeberg, *
EMP: 210 **EST:** 1981
SQ FT: 23,000
SALES (est): 69.93MM **Privately Held**
Web: www.metroelectric.com
SIC: 1731 General electrical contractor

(P-1778)
MIKE BROWN ELECTRIC CO
561a Mercantile Dr (94931-3040)
PHONE.............................707 792-8100
James Brown, *Pr*
James G Brown, *
Tiffany Howe, *
EMP: 120 **EST:** 1979
SQ FT: 14,000
SALES (est): 53.88MM **Privately Held**

PRODUCTS & SERVICES SECTION

1731 - Electrical Work (P-1801)

Web: www.mbelectric.com
SIC: **1731** General electrical contractor

(P-1779)
MOBIZ IT INC
Also Called: Mobiz
1175 Idaho St Ste 103 (92374-4591)
PHONE.................................909 453-6700
Hamad Riaz, *CEO*
EMP: 100 **EST:** 2017
SALES (est): 30MM Privately Held
SIC: **1731** 8742 7373 7371 Electrical work; Management consulting services; Systems integration services; Computer software systems analysis and design, custom

(P-1780)
MODESTO INDUSTRIAL ELEC CO INC
Also Called: Industrial Electrical Co
2516 N Sunnyside Ave (93727-1371)
PHONE.................................559 292-4714
Ron Forthun, *Mgr*
EMP: 91
SALES (corp-wide): 26MM Privately Held
Web: www.industrialelectricalco.com
SIC: **1731** 5063 7694 General electrical contractor; Motors, electric; Electric motor repair
PA: Modesto Industrial Electrical Co., Inc.
1417 Coldwell Ave
Modesto CA
209 527-2800

(P-1781)
MODESTO INDUSTRIAL ELECTRICAL CO INC (PA)
Also Called: Industrial Electrical Company
1417 Coldwell Ave (95350-5703)
PHONE.................................209 527-2800
EMP: 89 **EST:** 1935
SALES (est): 26MM
SALES (corp-wide): 26MM Privately Held
Web: www.industrialelectricalco.com
SIC: **1731** 5063 7694 7699 General electrical contractor; Motors, electric; Electric motor repair; Industrial machinery and equipment repair

(P-1782)
MORROW-MEADOWS CORPORATION (PA)
Also Called: Cherry City Electric
231 Benton Ct (91789-5213)
PHONE.................................858 974-3650
Robert E Meadows, *VP*
EMP: 850 **EST:** 1964
SQ FT: 55,000
SALES (est): 302.64MM
SALES (corp-wide): 302.64MM Privately Held
Web: www.morrow-meadows.com
SIC: **1731** General electrical contractor

(P-1783)
MORROW-MEADOWS CORPORATION
13000 Kirkham Way Ste 101 (92064-7148)
PHONE.................................858 974-3650
Gary Dadmon, *Mgr*
EMP: 384
SALES (corp-wide): 302.64MM Privately Held
Web: www.morrow-meadows.com
SIC: **1731** General electrical contractor
PA: Morrow-Meadows Corporation
231 Benton Ct
City Of Industry CA
858 974-3650

(P-1784)
MSL ELECTRIC INC
2918 E La Jolla St (92806-1305)
PHONE.................................714 693-4837
Warren L Moore, *Pr*
Sally Moore, *
EMP: 60 **EST:** 2002
SALES (est): 12.18MM Privately Held
Web: www.mslelectric.com
SIC: **1731** General electrical contractor

(P-1785)
NAZZARENO ELECTRIC CO INC
1250 E Gene Autry Way (92805-6716)
PHONE.................................714 712-4744
Paul Rick Nazzareno, *Pr*
EMP: 75 **EST:** 1993
SQ FT: 10,000
SALES (est): 4.2MM Privately Held
Web: www.nazzareno.com
SIC: **1731** General electrical contractor

(P-1786)
NB BAKER ELECTRIC INC
2120 Harmony Grove Rd (92029-2053)
PHONE.................................760 546-6030
Theodore N Baker, *Prin*
EMP: 64 **EST:** 2019
SALES (est): 4.33MM Privately Held
Web: www.bakerhomeenergy.com
SIC: **1731** General electrical contractor

(P-1787)
NEAL ELECTRIC CORP (HQ)
2790 Business Park Dr (92081-7860)
P.O. Box 1655 (92074-1655)
PHONE.................................858 513-2525
Daniel Zupp, *Pr*
Luis Armona, *
Casimier Wesolowski, *
Harry Schirer, *
Alex Meruelo, *
EMP: 75 **EST:** 2008
SQ FT: 30,000
SALES (est): 54.46MM
SALES (corp-wide): 528.99MM Privately Held
Web: www.nealelectric.com
SIC: **1731** General electrical contractor
PA: Meruelo Enterprises, Inc.
9550 Firestone Blvd # 105
Downey CA
562 745-2300

(P-1788)
NETRONIX INTEGRATION INC (HQ)
2365 Paragon Dr Ste D (95131-1335)
PHONE.................................800 600-3939
Craig E Jarrett, *Pr*
Kimberly Jarrett, *
Kevin Thompson, *
EMP: 92 **EST:** 2007
SQ FT: 13,500
SALES (est): 41.9MM
SALES (corp-wide): 686.58MM Privately Held
Web: www.netronixint.com
SIC: **1731** 3699 General electrical contractor; Security control equipment and systems
PA: Pavion Corp.
4151 Lafayette Center Dr # 70
Chantilly VA
703 631-3377

(P-1789)
NEW AGE ELECTRIC INC
1085 N 11th St (95112-2928)
PHONE.................................408 279-8787
Kurt Rocklage, *Pr*
EMP: 60 **EST:** 1989
SQ FT: 8,500
SALES (est): 22.45MM Privately Held
Web: www.newageelectric.com
SIC: **1731** General electrical contractor

(P-1790)
NORTH STATE ELEC CONTRS INC
11101 White Rock Rd Ste 100 (95670-6996)
PHONE.................................916 572-0571
Rodney Bingaman, *Pr*
EMP: 80 **EST:** 2007
SQ FT: 24,000
SALES (est): 26.89MM Privately Held
Web: www.northstate-eci.com
SIC: **1731** General electrical contractor

(P-1791)
NWEC NEVADA INC
Also Called: New Wave Electric
2612 Temple Heights Dr (92056-3512)
PHONE.................................760 757-0187
EMP: 75 **EST:** 2011
SALES (est): 10.55MM Privately Held
SIC: **1731** General electrical contractor

(P-1792)
OBRYANT ELECTRIC INC (PA)
9314 Eton Ave (91311-5809)
PHONE.................................818 407-1986
Cathy O'bryant, *Pr*
Steve O'bryant, *Sec*
EMP: 120 **EST:** 1978
SQ FT: 25,000
SALES (est): 46.42MM
SALES (corp-wide): 46.42MM Privately Held
Web: www.obryantelectric.com
SIC: **1731** General electrical contractor

(P-1793)
OBSIDIAN SECURITY INC
500 Arguello St Fl 2 (94063-1566)
PHONE.................................949 520-2866
Glenn Chisholm, *CEO*
EMP: 66
SALES (corp-wide): 5.39MM Privately Held
Web: www.obsidiansecurity.com
SIC: **1731** Safety and security specialization
PA: Obsidian Security, Inc.
680 Nwport Ctr Dr Ste 200
Newport Beach CA
949 520-2866

(P-1794)
OEG INC
41458 Christy St (94538-5105)
PHONE.................................408 909-9399
EMP: 77
SALES (corp-wide): 6.97B Publicly Held
Web: www.oeg.us.com
SIC: **1731** General electrical contractor
HQ: Oeg, Inc.
3200 Nw Yeon Ave
Portland OR
503 234-9900

(P-1795)
OILFIELD ELECTRIC COMPANY
Also Called: Oilfield Electric & Motor
1801 N Ventura Ave (93001-1503)
PHONE.................................805 648-3131
Alan Dale Fletcher, *CEO*
Jana Fletcher, *
EMP: 60 **EST:** 1941
SQ FT: 10,000
SALES (est): 11.95MM Privately Held
Web: www.oilfld.com
SIC: **1731** 7629 General electrical contractor; Electrical repair shops

(P-1796)
PACIFIC INTL ELC CO INC
Also Called: Pacific Industrial Electric
230 N Orange Ave (92821-4072)
P.O. Box 9788 (92822-9788)
PHONE.................................714 990-9280
Roxanne Medina, *CEO*
Frederick Lewis Pradels, *
Garry White, *
EMP: 63 **EST:** 1971
SQ FT: 14,500
SALES (est): 26.28MM Privately Held
Web: wordpress.pacificindustrialelectric.com
SIC: **1731** 8711 General electrical contractor; Electrical or electronic engineering

(P-1797)
PACIFIC METRO ELECTRIC INC
3150 E Fremont St (95205-3918)
P.O. Box 127 (95201-0127)
PHONE.................................209 939-3222
Glen Rigsbee, *Pr*
EMP: 60 **EST:** 1995
SALES (est): 8.79MM Privately Held
Web: www.pacificmetroelectric.com
SIC: **1731** General electrical contractor

(P-1798)
PACIFIC UTLITY INSTLLATION INC
510 Malloy Ct (92878-4045)
PHONE.................................714 970-6430
▲ **EMP:** 65 **EST:** 1997
SALES (est): 13.39MM Privately Held
Web: www.pacificutility.com
SIC: **1731** 1623 General electrical contractor; Water, sewer, and utility lines

(P-1799)
PAGANINI ELECTRIC CORPORATION
Also Called: Paganini Companies
190 Hubbell St Ste 200 (94107-2219)
PHONE.................................415 575-3900
Kenneth A Paganini, *CEO*
Michael K Paganini, *
EMP: 115 **EST:** 1948
SQ FT: 20,000
SALES (est): 28.43MM Privately Held
Web: www.pagcos.com
SIC: **1731** General electrical contractor

(P-1800)
PARADISE ELECTRIC INC
697 Greenfield Dr (92021-2983)
PHONE.................................619 449-4141
Mike Manos, *Pr*
Jeff Platt, *
EMP: 389 **EST:** 1988
SQ FT: 7,000
SALES (est): 2.82MM
SALES (corp-wide): 81.49MM Privately Held
Web: www.schillingcorp.com
SIC: **1731** General electrical contractor
HQ: Builders Tradesource Corp
697 Greenfield Dr
El Cajon CA

(P-1801)
PATRIC COMMUNICATIONS INC (PA)
Also Called: Advanced Electronic Solutions
15215 Alton Pkwy Ste 200 (92618-2613)

1731 - Electrical Work (P-1802)

PHONE.................................619 579-2898
Sean P Mcdermott, *Pr*
Richard P Apgar, *
Kathy Alford, *
EMP: 70 **EST:** 1981
SALES (est): 10MM **Privately Held**
SIC: 1731 1751 3699 Fire detection and burglar alarm systems specialization; Carpentry work; Security devices

(P-1802)
PAVLETICH ELC CMMNICATIONS INC (PA)
Also Called: Pavletich Electric
6308 Seven Seas Ave (93308-5132)
PHONE.................................661 589-9473
EMP: 89 **EST:** 1994
SQ FT: 15,000
SALES (est): 15.14MM **Privately Held**
Web: www.pavelectric.com
SIC: 1731 General electrical contractor

(P-1803)
PETRELLI ELECTRIC INC
11615 Davenport Rd (91390-4690)
P.O. Box 801148 (91380-1148)
PHONE.................................661 268-7312
Cindy Petrelli, *CEO*
Salvatore Petrelli, *
EMP: 66 **EST:** 1983
SALES (est): 13.05MM **Privately Held**
Web: petrellielectr.wpengine.com
SIC: 1731 7629 General electrical contractor; Electrical equipment repair, high voltage

(P-1804)
PHASE 3 COMMUNICATIONS INC (PA)
Also Called: Phase 3 Communications
1355 Felipe Ave (95122-2602)
PHONE.................................408 946-9011
EMP: 97 **EST:** 1994
SALES (est): 18.73MM **Privately Held**
Web: www.p3com.net
SIC: 1731 1799 Fiber optic cable installation; Cable splicing service

(P-1805)
PINNACLE NETWORKING SVCS INC
Also Called: PINNACLE COMMUNICATION SERVICE
730 Fairmont Ave (91203-1078)
PHONE.................................818 241-6009
Avo Amirian, *CEO*
Joe Licursi, *
EMP: 130 **EST:** 1994
SQ FT: 10,000
SALES (est): 19.9MM **Privately Held**
Web: www.pinnacleinc.com
SIC: 1731 8748 Communications specialization; Telecommunications consultant

(P-1806)
PIVOT INTERIORS INC
Pivot Interiors-Receiving Only
3200 Park Center Dr Ste 100 (92626-7104)
PHONE.................................949 988-5400
Ken Baugh, *CEO*
EMP: 93
SALES (corp-wide): 91.38MM **Privately Held**
Web: www.pivotinteriors.com
SIC: 1731 Electrical work
PA: Pivot Interiors, Inc.
3355 Scott Blvd Ste 110
Santa Clara CA
408 432-5600

(P-1807)
PMN DESIGN ELECTRIC INC
Also Called: Design Electric
39 Wyoming St (94566-6277)
PHONE.................................925 846-0650
Peter Nowak, *Pr*
EMP: 80 **EST:** 1976
SQ FT: 4,430
SALES (est): 27.94MM **Privately Held**
Web: www.designelectriccompany.com
SIC: 1731 General electrical contractor

(P-1808)
POINT ONE ELEC SYSTEMS INC
6751 Southfront Rd (94551-8218)
PHONE.................................925 667-2935
Michael G Curran, *Pr*
Thomas F Curran, *
Ken Miller, *
EMP: 60 **EST:** 1998
SQ FT: 30,000
SALES (est): 8.28MM **Privately Held**
Web: www.point1.com
SIC: 1731 General electrical contractor

(P-1809)
PONDEROSA ELECTRIC INC
3911 E La Palma Ave Ste D (92807-1719)
PHONE.................................949 253-3100
Dale Arnold, *Pr*
EMP: 60 **EST:** 1986
SALES (est): 4.89MM **Privately Held**
Web: www.ponderosaelectric.com
SIC: 1731 General electrical contractor

(P-1810)
PORTERMATT ELECTRIC INC
5431 Production Dr (92649-1524)
PHONE.................................714 596-8788
Tim Matthews, *Pr*
John F Porter Iii, *VP*
EMP: 90 **EST:** 1998
SQ FT: 5,300
SALES (est): 19.31MM **Privately Held**
Web: www.portermatt.com
SIC: 1731 1799 General electrical contractor; Athletic and recreation facilities construction

(P-1811)
PRIME ELECTRIC INC
Also Called: Prime Electric, Inc.
1941 Ringwood Ave (95131-1721)
PHONE.................................925 961-1600
EMP: 905
SALES (corp-wide): 149.63MM **Privately Held**
Web: www.primee.com
SIC: 1731 General electrical contractor
PA: Prime Electric Llc
3460 161st Ave Se
Bellevue WA
425 747-5200

(P-1812)
PROFESSNL ELEC CNSTR SVCS INC
Also Called: Pecs
9112 Santa Anita Ave (91730-6143)
PHONE.................................909 373-4100
EMP: 102 **EST:** 2007
SQ FT: 15,000
SALES (est): 21.52MM **Privately Held**
Web: www.pecs.biz
SIC: 1731 8711 1542 General electrical contractor; Engineering services; Nonresidential construction, nec

(P-1813)
PYRO-COMM SYSTEMS INC (PA)
Also Called: Pyro
15215 Alton Pkwy (92618-2359)
PHONE.................................714 902-8000
Michael Donahue, *Pr*
Nanci Donahue, *
EMP: 150 **EST:** 1980
SALES (est): 38.45MM
SALES (corp-wide): 38.45MM **Privately Held**
Web: www.pyrocomm.com
SIC: 1731 5063 Fire detection and burglar alarm systems specialization; Fire alarm systems

(P-1814)
RED TOP ELECTRIC CO-EMERYVILLE INC
Also Called: Red Top Electric
6751 Southfront Rd (94551-8218)
PHONE.................................925 667-2900
EMP: 100 **EST:** 1946
SALES (est): 28MM **Privately Held**
Web: www.teamredtop.com
SIC: 1731 General electrical contractor

(P-1815)
REDWOOD ELECTRIC GROUP INC (PA)
2775 Northwestern Pkwy (95051-0947)
PHONE.................................707 451-7348
Victor Castello, *Pr*
Jeff Tarzwell, *
Gordon Armstrong, *
Bruce Kelly, *
EMP: 680 **EST:** 1974
SQ FT: 35,000
SALES (est): 124.81MM
SALES (corp-wide): 124.81MM **Privately Held**
Web: www.redwoodeg.com
SIC: 1731 General electrical contractor

(P-1816)
REPUBLIC ELECTRIC INC
3820 Happy Ln (95827-9721)
PHONE.................................916 294-0140
Eric Stafford, *Mgr*
EMP: 115
Web: www.republicelectricwest.com
SIC: 1731 General electrical contractor
PA: Republic Electric, Inc.
3985 N Pecos Rd
Las Vegas NV

(P-1817)
REPUBLIC ELECTRIC WEST INC
3820 Happy Ln (95827-9721)
PHONE.................................916 294-0140
Eric J Stafford, *Pr*
Gerald Stafford, *
Jerry Stafford, *
EMP: 70 **EST:** 1999
SALES (est): 10.35MM **Privately Held**
Web: www.republicelectricwest.com
SIC: 1731 General electrical contractor

(P-1818)
REX MOORE GROUP INC
Also Called: Rex Moore
6001 Outfall Cir (95828-1066)
PHONE.................................916 372-1300
David Rex Moore, *Pr*
Doug Cuthbert, *
William C Hubbard, *
John Anderson, *
J Brock Littlejohn, *
EMP: 450 **EST:** 2001
SQ FT: 36,000
SALES (est): 96.85MM **Privately Held**
Web: www.rexmoore.com
SIC: 1731 8711 General electrical contractor; Engineering services

(P-1819)
REX MORE ELEC CNTRS ENGNERS IN (PA)
6001 Outfall Cir (95828-1066)
PHONE.................................916 372-1300
David R Moore, *CEO*
William C Hubbard, *
James B Littlejohn, *
Steven R Moore, *
EMP: 350 **EST:** 1922
SQ FT: 36,000
SALES (est): 87.06MM
SALES (corp-wide): 87.06MM **Privately Held**
Web: www.rexmoore.com
SIC: 1731 General electrical contractor

(P-1820)
REX MORE ELEC CNTRS ENGNERS IN
5803 E Harvard Ave (93727-1366)
P.O. Box 7677 (93747-7677)
PHONE.................................559 294-1300
John Abele, *Mgr*
EMP: 200
SALES (corp-wide): 87.06MM **Privately Held**
Web: www.rexmoore.com
SIC: 1731 General electrical contractor
PA: Rex Moore Electrical Contractors & Engineers, Inc.
6001 Outfall Cir
Sacramento CA
916 372-1300

(P-1821)
RGA ELECTRIC INC
Also Called: Anthony Electric
10207 Freeman Ave (90670-3409)
PHONE.................................562 941-6380
Dorothy M Pantleo, *Pr*
Geno J Pantleo, *
EMP: 62 **EST:** 1959
SQ FT: 23,000
SALES (est): 15MM **Privately Held**
Web: www.anthonyelectric.com
SIC: 1731 General electrical contractor

(P-1822)
RK ELECTRIC INC
49211 Milmont Dr (94538-7349)
PHONE.................................510 772-4125
Lonnie Robinson, *Pr*
Raul Real, *
Dan Yeggy, *
Dale Swanson, *
EMP: 130 **EST:** 1985
SQ FT: 11,500
SALES (est): 23.9MM **Privately Held**
Web: www.rkelectric.com
SIC: 1731 General electrical contractor

(P-1823)
ROADWAY ENGINEERING WORKS INC
3442 6th St (95307-3751)
P.O. Box 285 (95426-0285)
PHONE.................................209 541-0920
EMP: 65
Web: www.roadwayeng.com
SIC: 1731 Electrical work

PRODUCTS & SERVICES SECTION
1731 - Electrical Work (P-1846)

(P-1824)
RODDA ELECTRIC INC (PA)
380 Carrol Ct Ste L (94513-7353)
PHONE..................925 240-6024
Raymond Rodda, CEO
EMP: 109 EST: 1998
SQ FT: 21,000
SALES (est): 45.18MM
SALES (corp-wide): 45.18MM Privately Held
Web: www.roddaelectric.com
SIC: 1731 General electrical contractor

(P-1825)
ROSENDIN ELECTRIC INC (PA)
Also Called: Rosendin Electric
880 Mabury Rd (95133-1021)
P.O. Box 49070 (95161-9070)
PHONE..................408 286-2800
Mike Greenawalt, CEO
Tom Sorley, *
Paolo Degrassi, *
Sam Lamonica, CIO*
Lorne Rundquist, *
EMP: 3000 EST: 1919
SQ FT: 45,000
SALES (est): 2.06B
SALES (corp-wide): 2.06B Privately Held
Web: www.rosendin.com
SIC: 1731 General electrical contractor

(P-1826)
ROSENDIN ELECTRIC INC
1730 S Anaheim Way (92805-6537)
PHONE..................714 739-1334
Cliff Thompson, Brnch Mgr
EMP: 668
SALES (corp-wide): 2.06B Privately Held
Web: www.rosendin.com
SIC: 1731 General electrical contractor
PA: Rosendin Electric, Inc.
    880 Mabury Rd
    San Jose CA
    408 286-2800

(P-1827)
ROSENDIN ELECTRIC INC
2777 Orchard Pkwy (95134-2008)
PHONE..................408 321-2200
Mary Marshall, Prin
EMP: 668
SALES (corp-wide): 2.06B Privately Held
Web: www.rosendin.com
SIC: 1731 General electrical contractor
PA: Rosendin Electric, Inc.
    880 Mabury Rd
    San Jose CA
    408 286-2800

(P-1828)
ROWAN INCORPORATED
Also Called: Rowan Electric
2778 Loker Ave W (92010-6611)
PHONE..................760 692-0700
Paul J Rowan, CEO
Mark B Rowan, *
EMP: 67 EST: 1998
SQ FT: 6,000
SALES (est): 50.69MM Privately Held
Web: www.rowanelectric.com
SIC: 1731 General electrical contractor

(P-1829)
RYE ELECTRIC INC
28202 Cabot Rd Ste 300 (92677-1249)
PHONE..................949 441-0345
Christopher Golden, Pr
EMP: 75 EST: 2018
SALES (est): 13.25MM Privately Held
Web: www.ryecompany.com

SIC: 1731 Electrical work

(P-1830)
SASCO ELECTRIC INC
Also Called: Sasco Valley Electric
598 Gibraltar Dr (95035-6315)
PHONE..................408 970-8300
Tim Bott, Brnch Mgr
EMP: 327
SALES (corp-wide): 483.56MM Privately Held
Web: www.sasco.com
SIC: 1731 7373 General electrical contractor; Computer integrated systems design
HQ: Sasco Electric Inc.
    2750 Moore Ave
    Fullerton CA
    714 870-0217

(P-1831)
SBE ELECTRICAL CONTRACTING INC
2817 Mcgaw Ave (92614-5835)
PHONE..................714 544-5066
Jeffery S Wilson, CEO
EMP: 105 EST: 2016
SALES (est): 9.4MM Privately Held
Web: www.sbeoc.com
SIC: 1731 General electrical contractor

(P-1832)
SCHETTER ELECTRIC INC (PA)
471 Bannon St (95811-0203)
P.O. Box 1377 (95812-1377)
PHONE..................916 446-2521
Frank E Schetter, Pr
Vince Bernacchi, *
Linda Schetter, Stockholder*
EMP: 90 EST: 1959
SQ FT: 7,800
SALES (est): 42.23MM
SALES (corp-wide): 42.23MM Privately Held
Web: www.schetter.com
SIC: 1731 General electrical contractor

(P-1833)
SCHETTER ELECTRIC INC
737 Arnold Dr Ste D (94553-6859)
PHONE..................925 228-2424
Tom Stucker, Brnch Mgr
EMP: 120
SALES (corp-wide): 42.23MM Privately Held
Web: www.schetter.com
SIC: 1731 General electrical contractor
PA: Schetter Electric, Inc.
    471 Bannon St
    Sacramento CA
    916 446-2521

(P-1834)
SCHETTER ELECTRIC LLC
471 Bannon St (95811-0296)
P.O. Box 1377 (95812-1377)
PHONE..................916 446-2521
Frank Schetter, CEO
Vince Bernacchi, *
Marlin Cole, *
Brett Nogleberg, ESTIMATING*
EMP: 90 EST: 2018
SALES (est): 21.22MM
SALES (corp-wide): 42.23MM Privately Held
Web: www.schetter.com
SIC: 1731 General electrical contractor
PA: Schetter Electric, Inc.
    471 Bannon St
    Sacramento CA
    916 446-2521

(P-1835)
SEAL ELECTRIC INC
1162 Greenfield Dr (92021-3314)
PHONE..................619 449-7323
EMP: 145 EST: 1996
SQ FT: 5,000
SALES (est): 23.53MM Privately Held
Web: www.sealelectric.com
SIC: 1731 General electrical contractor

(P-1836)
SECURECOM INC
4822 Golden Foothill Pkwy Unit 4 (95762-9829)
PHONE..................916 638-2855
Kevin Mcelwee, Pr
EMP: 61
Web: www.securecom.net
SIC: 1731 Fire detection and burglar alarm systems specialization
PA: Securecom, Inc.
    3398 Main St A
    Springfield OR

(P-1837)
SERRANO ELECTRIC INC
15920 Concord Cir (95037-5451)
PHONE..................408 986-1570
Daniel Serrano, Pr
Daniel Serrano, Pr
Harry Serrano, *
Leslie Nakamura, *
EMP: 85 EST: 1986
SQ FT: 8,000
SALES (est): 15.39MM Privately Held
Web: www.serranoelectric.com
SIC: 1731 General electrical contractor

(P-1838)
SFADIA INC
Also Called: Green Energy Innovations
8485 Artesia Blvd Ste A (90621-4194)
PHONE..................323 622-1930
Pilje Park, Pr
Pil Soon Um, *
▲ EMP: 86 EST: 2010
SALES (est): 12.26MM Privately Held
Web: www.geinnovationsinc.com
SIC: 1731 Energy management controls

(P-1839)
SKYWALKER SOUND
1110 Gorgas Ave (94129-1406)
P.O. Box 3000 (94912-3000)
PHONE..................415 662-1000
Rollin Feld, Prin
EMP: 107 EST: 2008
SALES (est): 9.68MM Privately Held
Web: www.skysound.com
SIC: 1731 8299 Sound equipment specialization; Music school

(P-1840)
SOL NOVA ELECTRIC LLC
330 Rancheros Dr Ste 116 (92069-2939)
PHONE..................833 765-6682
EMP: 110 EST: 2017
SALES (est): 28.52MM Privately Held
Web: www.gosolnova.com
SIC: 1731 Electrical work

(P-1841)
SOUND INPATIENT PHYSICIANS INC
Also Called: Sound Physicians
702 Marshall St (94063-1829)
PHONE..................650 257-3470
EMP: 72
SALES (corp-wide): 504.63MM Privately Held

Web: www.soundphysicians.com
SIC: 1731 Sound equipment specialization
PA: Sound Inpatient Physicians, Inc.
    1498 Pacific Ave Ste 400
    Tacoma WA
    253 682-1710

(P-1842)
SOUND RIVER CORPORATION
Also Called: Atk Audiotek
28238 Avenue Crocker (91355-1248)
PHONE..................661 705-3700
Michael M Macdonald, Pr
James Harmala, *
John M Stewart, *
EMP: 85 EST: 1983
SQ FT: 25,000
SALES (est): 24.1MM Privately Held
Web: www.atkaudiotek.com
SIC: 1731 7359 Voice, data, and video wiring contractor; Sound and lighting equipment rental

(P-1843)
SOUTHERN CONTRACTING COMPANY
559 N Twin Oaks Valley Rd (92069-1710)
P.O. Box 445 (92079-0445)
PHONE..................760 744-0760
Timothy R Mcbride, CEO
Richard W Mc Bride, *
Tim Mc Bride, *
▲ EMP: 125 EST: 1963
SQ FT: 8,400
SALES (est): 36.56MM Privately Held
Web: www.southerncontracting.com
SIC: 1731 General electrical contractor

(P-1844)
SPANIO INC
679 Bryant St (94107-1612)
PHONE..................415 598-8578
Archan Padmanabhan Rao, CEO
EMP: 120 EST: 2018
SALES (est): 14.35MM Privately Held
Web: www.span.io
SIC: 1731 Energy management controls

(P-1845)
SPECIALTY CONSTRUCTION INC
645 Clarion Ct (93401-8177)
PHONE..................805 543-1706
Rudolph Bachmann, Pr
Jeffrey Martin, *
Chris Teaford, *
Doug Clay, *
Steve Haymaker, *
EMP: 80 EST: 1992
SQ FT: 8,000
SALES (est): 27.35MM Privately Held
Web: www.specialtyconstruction.com
SIC: 1731 Telephone and telephone equipment installation

(P-1846)
SPECTRA INDUSTRIAL SVCS INC
Also Called: Spectra Industrial Electric
21818 S Wilmington Ave Ste 402 (90810-1642)
PHONE..................310 835-0808
Michael J Merrill, Pr
Richard Mangan, *
EMP: 70 EST: 1989
SQ FT: 20,000
SALES (est): 9.9MM Privately Held
Web: www.spectrainc.com

1731 - Electrical Work (P-1847)

PRODUCTS & SERVICES SECTION

SIC: **1731** Access control systems specialization

(P-1847)
SPG SOLAR INC
1039 N Mcdowell Blvd Ste B (94954-1173)
PHONE.............................707 781-1000
◆ EMP: 100
Web: www.spgsolar.com
SIC: **1731** Electrical work

(P-1848)
SPRIG ELECTRIC CO (HQ)
Also Called: Archkey Technologies
1860 S 10th St (95112-4108)
PHONE.............................408 298-3134
Pepper Snyder, *CEO*
Mark Mandarelli, *CIO**
Clint Ramsey, *
Laura Lacomble, *
Hossein Tofangsazan, *
EMP: 225 EST: 1970
SQ FT: 24,100
SALES (est): 105MM
SALES (corp-wide): 1.03B **Privately Held**
Web: www.archkey.com
SIC: **1731** General electrical contractor
PA: Archkey Solutions Llc
   1572 Larkin Williams Rd
   Fenton MO
   636 492-7500

(P-1849)
SRBRAY LLC
Also Called: Power Plus
229 N Sherman Ave (92882-1844)
PHONE.............................951 898-3850
EMP: 83
Web: www.powerplus.com
SIC: **1731** 7359 Standby or emergency power specialization; Equipment rental and leasing, nec
PA: S.R.Bray Llc
   5500 E La Palma Ave
   Anaheim CA

(P-1850)
ST FRANCIS ELECTRIC INC
975 Carden St (94577-1102)
P.O. Box 2057 (94577-0317)
PHONE.............................510 639-0639
Robert Spinardi, *Pr*
Guy Smith, *
Joseph Medeiros, *
EMP: 250 EST: 1947
SQ FT: 32,500
SALES (est): 47.63MM **Privately Held**
Web: www.stfranciselectric.com
SIC: **1731** General electrical contractor

(P-1851)
ST FRANCIS ELECTRIC LLC
975 Carden St (94577-1102)
P.O. Box 2057 (94577-0317)
PHONE.............................510 639-0639
Guy Smith, *CEO*
EMP: 250 EST: 2014
SALES (est): 70MM **Privately Held**
Web: www.stfranciselectric.com
SIC: **1731** General electrical contractor

(P-1852)
STC NETCOM INC (PA)
11611 Industry Ave (92337-6931)
PHONE.............................951 685-8181
Giuseppe Floro, *Pr*
Jeffry Kinne, *
Shawnda Letourneau, *
EMP: 70 EST: 1990
SQ FT: 6,000
SALES (est): 13.5MM **Privately Held**
Web: www.stcnetcom.com
SIC: **1731** Fiber optic cable installation

(P-1853)
STEINY AND COMPANY INC
27 Sheridan St (94590-6911)
P.O. Box 3008 (94590-0673)
PHONE.............................707 552-6900
FAX: 707 552-7705
EMP: 110
SALES (corp-wide): 89.21MM **Privately Held**
SIC: **1731** 8711 General electrical contractor; Engineering services
PA: Steiny And Company, Inc.
   221 N Ardmore Ave
   Los Angeles CA
   626 962-1055

(P-1854)
STEINY AND COMPANY INC
221 N Ardmore Ave (90004-4503)
PHONE.............................213 382-2331
EMP: 300
Web: www.steinyco.com
SIC: **1731** General electrical contractor

(P-1855)
SUN ELECTRIC LP
2101 S Yale St Ste B (92704-4424)
PHONE.............................714 210-3744
Jeffery J Ber Bernardino, *Ltd Pt*
EMP: 100 EST: 2003
SALES (est): 7.33MM **Privately Held**
SIC: **1731** General electrical contractor

(P-1856)
SUNSHINE COMMUNICATIONS SE INC
350 Cypress Ln Ste D (92020-1664)
P.O. Box 3509 (33572-1005)
PHONE.............................619 448-7600
Robert Straub, *CEO*
EMP: 235 EST: 1998
SALES (est): 22.95MM **Privately Held**
Web: www.sunshinecom.com
SIC: **1731** Cable television installation

(P-1857)
SUNWEST ELECTRIC INC
3064 E Mariloma (92806-1810)
PHONE.............................714 630-8700
Brien Pariseau, *Pr*
Doug Lyvers, *
EMP: 175 EST: 1985
SQ FT: 20,000
SALES (est): 24.14MM **Privately Held**
Web: www.sunwestelectric.net
SIC: **1731** Electrical work

(P-1858)
SUPERIOR ELEC MECH & PLBG INC
8613 Helms Ave (91730-4521)
PHONE.............................909 357-9400
David A Stone Junior, *CEO*
Walt Schobel, *
Pam Metzer, *
EMP: 291 EST: 2001
SQ FT: 50,000
SALES (est): 40.09MM **Privately Held**
Web: www.superioremp.com
SIC: **1731** 1711 General electrical contractor; Mechanical contractor

(P-1859)
SYNCHRONOSS TECHNOLOGIES INC
60 S Market St Ste 700 (95113-2370)
PHONE.............................800 575-7606
EMP: 316
Web: www.synchronoss.com
SIC: **1731** 7379 7371 Computerized controls installation; Online services technology consultants; Computer software development and applications
PA: Synchronoss Technologies, Inc.
   200 Crossing Blvd Fl 8
   Bridgewater NJ

(P-1860)
T MCGEE ELECTRIC INC
2390 S Reservoir St (91766-6410)
P.O. Box 1111 (91708-1111)
PHONE.............................909 591-6461
Trent L Mc Gee, *Pr*
EMP: 100 EST: 1986
SALES (est): 7.71MM **Privately Held**
Web: www.tmcgeeelectric.com
SIC: **1731** General electrical contractor

(P-1861)
TAFT ELECTRIC COMPANY (PA)
1694 Eastman Ave (93003-5782)
P.O. Box 3416 (93006-3416)
PHONE.............................805 642-0121
James Marsh, *Pr*
Carol A Smith, *
Jeff Wofford, *
EMP: 209 EST: 1942
SQ FT: 40,000
SALES (est): 99.9MM
SALES (corp-wide): 99.9MM **Privately Held**
Web: www.taftelectric.com
SIC: **1731** 1629 General electrical contractor; Waste water and sewage treatment plant construction

(P-1862)
TERMINAL SEC SOLUTIONS INC
3806 Worsham Ave (90808-1896)
PHONE.............................877 858-3855
EMP: 63 EST: 2018
SALES (est): 2.11MM **Privately Held**
Web: www.termsec.com
SIC: **1731** Safety and security specialization

(P-1863)
THERMA HOLDINGS LLC (PA)
Also Called: Therma
1601 Las Plumas Ave (95133-1613)
PHONE.............................408 347-3400
Jeffrey Sprau, *CEO*
Phillip Le Bris, *CFO*
EMP: 117 EST: 2017
SALES (est): 590.14MM
SALES (corp-wide): 590.14MM **Privately Held**
Web: www.therma.com
SIC: **1731** General electrical contractor

(P-1864)
TRI-SIGNAL INTEGRATION INC (PA)
Also Called: Honeywell Authorized Dealer
28110 Avenue Stanford Unit D
(91355-1119)
PHONE.............................818 566-8558
Robert Mckibben, *Pr*
Rett Hicks, *
Michael Swisher, *
Dennis Furden, *
EMP: 100 EST: 1998
SQ FT: 16,000
SALES (est): 44.75MM
SALES (corp-wide): 44.75MM **Privately Held**
Web: www.tri-signal.com
SIC: **1731** Fire detection and burglar alarm systems specialization

(P-1865)
TRI-SIGNAL INTEGRATION INC
5007 Windplay Dr Ste 1 (95762-9359)
PHONE.............................916 933-3155
Robert Brady, *Mgr*
EMP: 114
SALES (corp-wide): 44.75MM **Privately Held**
Web: www.tri-signal.com
SIC: **1731** Fire detection and burglar alarm systems specialization
PA: Tri-Signal Integration Inc.
   28110 Avenue Stanford D
   Santa Clarita CA
   818 566-8558

(P-1866)
TRL SYSTEMS INCORPORATED
Also Called: T R L
9531 Milliken Ave (91730-6006)
PHONE.............................909 390-8392
Lynn Purdy, *Ch*
Mark L Purdy, *
EMP: 100 EST: 1980
SQ FT: 14,000
SALES (est): 50.75MM **Privately Held**
Web: www.trlsystems.com
SIC: **1731** General electrical contractor

(P-1867)
VALLEY COMMUNICATIONS INC (PA)
6921 Roseville Rd (95842-1660)
PHONE.............................916 349-7300
Ken Hurst, *Pr*
Kate Dewitt, *
Jeff Frydenlund, *
EMP: 60 EST: 1983
SQ FT: 12,000
SALES (est): 22.67MM
SALES (corp-wide): 22.67MM **Privately Held**
Web: www.valley-com.com
SIC: **1731** 3699 Voice, data, and video wiring contractor; Security control equipment and systems

(P-1868)
VALLEY UNIQUE ELECTRIC INC
75 Park Creek Dr Ste 101 (93611-4432)
PHONE.............................559 237-4795
Mark Worthington, *Dir*
Walt Worthington, *
Hogi Selling Iii, *CFO*
EMP: 100 EST: 1979
SALES (est): 10:4MM **Privately Held**
Web: www.valleyunique.com
SIC: **1731** 5719 5063 General electrical contractor; Lighting fixtures; Lighting fixtures, residential

(P-1869)
VASKO ELECTRIC INC
4300 Astoria St (95838-3004)
PHONE.............................916 568-7700
Darryl A Vasko, *Pr*
Ron Gracik, *
John Nichol, *
EMP: 80 EST: 1982
SQ FT: 8,500
SALES (est): 23.57MM **Privately Held**
Web: www.vasko.com
SIC: **1731** General electrical contractor

1741 - Masonry And Other Stonework (P-1893)

(P-1870)
VECTOR RESOURCES INC (PA)
Also Called: Vectorusa
20917 Higgins Ct (90501-1723)
PHONE.....................310 436-1000
TOLL FREE: 800
David Zukerman, *Pr*
Robert Messinger, *
John Schuman, *Dist Vice President**
Jeffrey Zukerman, *
EMP: 169 **EST:** 1988
SALES (est): 89.14MM
SALES (corp-wide): 89.14MM **Privately Held**
Web: www.vectorusa.com
SIC: 1731 3651 7373 Communications specialization; Clock radio and telephone combinations; Systems engineering, computer related

(P-1871)
VELLUTINI CORPORATION
Also Called: Royal Electric Co
8481 Carbide Ct (95828-5609)
PHONE.....................916 226-2100
EMP: 150 **EST:** 1971
SALES (est): 51.88MM **Privately Held**
Web: www.royalelect.com
SIC: 1731 General electrical contractor

(P-1872)
VERY GOOD SECURITY INC
548 Market St (94104-5401)
PHONE.....................844 847-0232
Chuck Yu, *CEO*
Paul Machle, *CFO*
EMP: 102 **EST:** 2015
SALES (est): 5.89MM **Privately Held**
Web: www.verygoodsecurity.com
SIC: 1731 Safety and security specialization

(P-1873)
WB ELECTRIC INC
6790 Monterey Rd (95020-6643)
P.O. Box 894 (95021-0894)
PHONE.....................408 842-7911
Randy Walker, *CEO*
Susan Walker, *
EMP: 60 **EST:** 1987
SALES (est): 9.48MM **Privately Held**
Web: www.wbelectric.com
SIC: 1731 General electrical contractor

(P-1874)
WEST COAST LTG & ENRGY INC
18550 Minthorn St (92530-2784)
PHONE.....................951 296-0580
Johnny Odell Leach, *Pr*
Johnny Odell Leach, *Pr*
Tammy Leach, *
EMP: 90 **EST:** 1994
SQ FT: 2,646
SALES (est): 13.39MM **Privately Held**
Web: www.wcleinc.com
SIC: 1731 General electrical contractor

(P-1875)
WESTECH SYSTEMS INC
827 Jefferson Ave (93612-2260)
PHONE.....................559 455-1720
Helder Domingos, *Pr*
Larry Troglin, *
Helder Domingos, *VP*
Jeri Swenson, *
EMP: 60 **EST:** 1997
SQ FT: 10,000
SALES (est): 41.34MM **Privately Held**
Web: www.westechsys.com
SIC: 1731 1711 Electrical work; Solar energy contractor

(P-1876)
WORLD WIND ELECTRICAL SVCS INC
Also Called: World Wind & Solar
228 W Tehachapi Blvd (93561-1634)
PHONE.....................661 822-4877
Edward Cummings, *Pr*
EMP: 396 **EST:** 2009
SALES (est): 3.76MM
SALES (corp-wide): 581.19MM **Privately Held**
SIC: 1731 3621 8742 Electrical work; Windmills, electric generating; Maintenance management consultant
HQ: Pearce Services, Llc
1222 Vine St Ste 301
Paso Robles CA
805 467-2528

(P-1877)
WORLDWIND SERVICES LLC
Also Called: World Wind & Solar
1222 Vine St Ste 301 (93446-2333)
PHONE.....................661 822-4877
Mark Mclanahan, *CEO*
Kristin Osborn, *
Matthew Gillette, *
EMP: 700 **EST:** 2007
SALES (est): 85.19MM
SALES (corp-wide): 581.19MM **Privately Held**
Web: www.worldwindsolar.com
SIC: 1731 1389 8742 Electrical work; Construction, repair, and dismantling services; Maintenance management consultant
HQ: Pearce Services, Llc
1222 Vine St Ste 301
Paso Robles CA
805 467-2528

(P-1878)
X3 MANAGEMENT SERVICES INC
700 La Terraza Blvd Ste 110 (92025)
P.O. Box 460669 (92046-0669)
PHONE.....................760 597-9336
David G Cranford, *CEO*
Arlette Zuniga, *
EMP: 85 **EST:** 2005
SALES (est): 22.84MM **Privately Held**
Web: www.x3corp.net
SIC: 1731 1531 1541 1711 Electrical work; Operative builders; Industrial buildings and warehouses; Solar energy contractor

(P-1879)
YOUNG ELECTRIC CO
Also Called: Young Communications
195 Erie St (94103-2416)
PHONE.....................415 648-3355
James P Young, *Pr*
Richard Green, *
Wayne Huie, *
EMP: 120 **EST:** 1977
SQ FT: 5,000
SALES (est): 28.44MM **Privately Held**
Web: www.youngelec.com
SIC: 1731 General electrical contractor

1741 Masonry And Other Stonework

(P-1880)
BRATTON MASONRY INC (PA)
2763 N Argyle Ave (93727-1379)
PHONE.....................559 291-9423
EMP: 90 **EST:** 1972
SALES (est): 8.15MM
SALES (corp-wide): 8.15MM **Privately Held**
SIC: 1741 Masonry and other stonework

(P-1881)
DESIGN MASONRY INC
20703 Santa Clara St (91351-2424)
PHONE.....................661 252-2784
EMP: 70 **EST:** 2009
SALES (est): 12.03MM **Privately Held**
Web: www.designmasonry.com
SIC: 1741 Stone masonry

(P-1882)
FRANK S SMITH MASONRY INC
2830 Pomona Blvd (91768-3224)
PHONE.....................909 468-0525
Frank E Smith, *Pr*
Brian E Smith, *
Kevin J Smith, *
EMP: 100 **EST:** 1938
SQ FT: 54,000
SALES (est): 9.63MM **Privately Held**
Web: www.franksmithmasonry.com
SIC: 1741 Bricklaying

(P-1883)
GBC CONCRETE MASNRY CNSTR INC
561 Birch St (92530-2732)
PHONE.....................951 245-2355
Tom Daniel, *Pr*
EMP: 170 **EST:** 1985
SQ FT: 8,000
SALES (est): 27.64MM **Privately Held**
Web: www.gbcconstruction.com
SIC: 1741 1771 Foundation building; Concrete work

(P-1884)
HBA INCORPORATED
512 E Vermont Ave (92805-5603)
P.O. Box 25861 (92825-5861)
PHONE.....................714 635-8602
Gerald G Pyle, *Pr*
Joe Alessandrini, *
EMP: 100 **EST:** 2006
SALES (est): 11.03MM **Privately Held**
Web: www.hbabuild.com
SIC: 1741 Masonry and other stonework

(P-1885)
J GINGER MASONRY LP (PA)
8188 Lincoln Ave Ste 100 (92504-4329)
PHONE.....................951 688-5050
John L Ginger, *Ltd Pt*
EMP: 265 **EST:** 1978
SALES (est): 48.92MM **Privately Held**
Web: www.jgingermasonry.com
SIC: 1741 Masonry and other stonework

(P-1886)
JOHN JACKSON MASONRY
5691 Power Inn Rd Ste B (95824-2313)
PHONE.....................916 381-8021
Tom Sneed, *Pr*
Matt Carlson, *
Robert Prater, *
EMP: 60 **EST:** 1963
SQ FT: 6,200
SALES (est): 19MM **Privately Held**
Web: www.johnjacksonmasonry.com
SIC: 1741 Bricklaying

(P-1887)
KLEARY MASONRY INC
4612 Auburn Blvd Ste 2 (95841-4275)
PHONE.....................916 869-6835
Nick Kleary, *Pr*
EMP: 230 **EST:** 1960
SQ FT: 700
SALES (est): 21.55MM
SALES (corp-wide): 5.58B **Privately Held**
SIC: 1741 Masonry and other stonework
HQ: Cornerstone Building Brands, Inc.
5020 Weston Pkwy Ste 400
Cary NC
866 419-0042

(P-1888)
MASON GROUP
638 Lindero Canyon Rd (91377-5457)
PHONE.....................818 707-8989
Jerome J Mazzeo, *CEO*
EMP: 62 **EST:** 2017
SALES (est): 1.97MM **Privately Held**
Web: www.masongroup.net
SIC: 1741 Masonry and other stonework

(P-1889)
MASONRY CONCEPTS INC
15408 Cornet St (90670-5534)
PHONE.....................562 802-3700
Dana Kemp, *Pr*
Ronald O Udall, *
Peter Sturdivant, *
Russell Knight, *
EMP: 100 **EST:** 1983
SQ FT: 10,000
SALES (est): 17.18MM **Privately Held**
Web: www.masonry-concepts.com
SIC: 1741 Masonry and other stonework

(P-1890)
MASONRY GROUP NEVADA INC
8188 Lincoln Ave Ste 99 (92504-4329)
PHONE.....................951 509-5300
EMP: 99
SALES (est): 1.15MM **Privately Held**
SIC: 1741 Masonry and other stonework

(P-1891)
NIBBELINK MASONRY CNSTR CORP
Also Called: Nibbelink Masonry
1120 W Avenue L8 (93534-7028)
PHONE.....................661 948-7859
Troy Nibbelink, *Pr*
Gerald J Nibbelink, *
EMP: 60 **EST:** 1976
SQ FT: 2,000
SALES (est): 19.04MM **Privately Held**
Web: www.nibbelinkmasonryconst.
SIC: 1741 1771 Masonry and other stonework; Exterior concrete stucco contractor

(P-1892)
PRO STRUCTURAL INC
29190 Riverside Dr (92530-2610)
PHONE.....................951 526-2010
Robert A Yowell, *Pr*
Russell T Frazier, *VP*
Holly Yowell, *CFO*
EMP: 60 **EST:** 2015
SALES (est): 4.58MM **Privately Held**
Web: www.prostructuralinc.com
SIC: 1741 Masonry and other stonework

(P-1893)
SPECTRA COMPANY
2510 Supply St (91767-2113)
PHONE.....................909 599-0760
Ray Adamyk, *CEO*
Ann Dresselhaus, *
▲ **EMP:** 125 **EST:** 1985
SQ FT: 7,000
SALES (est): 16.09MM **Privately Held**

1741 - Masonry And Other Stonework (P-1894)

PRODUCTS & SERVICES SECTION

Web: www.spectracompany.com
SIC: **1741** 1771 1743 1721 Masonry and other stonework; Concrete work; Terrazzo, tile, marble and mosaic work; Painting and paper hanging

(P-1894)
SUPERIOR MASONRY WALLS LTD
300 W Olive St Ste A (92324-1765)
PHONE.................................909 370-1800
EMP: 75 **EST:** 2011
SALES (est): 4.65MM **Privately Held**
Web: www.superiormasonrywalls.com
SIC: **1741** Masonry and other stonework

(P-1895)
VARIATIONS IN STONE INC
360 La Perle Pl (92627-3758)
PHONE.................................949 438-8377
Joseph Dorando, *CFO*
James Joseph Dorando, *
EMP: 75 **EST:** 2015
SALES (est): 2.09MM **Privately Held**
SIC: **1741** Masonry and other stonework

(P-1896)
VINCENT CONTRACTORS INC
Also Called: Vincent Scaffolding
4501 E La Palma Ave Ste 200 (92807-1904)
PHONE.................................714 660-0165
Justin Erdtsieck, *Pr*
Kenny Vo, *
EMP: 430 **EST:** 2016
SQ FT: 5,538
SALES (est): 23.86MM **Privately Held**
SIC: **1741** 1742 Masonry and other stonework; Plastering, drywall, and insulation

(P-1897)
WIRTZ QUALITY INSTALLATIONS
7932 Armour St (92111-3718)
PHONE.................................858 569-3816
Victor Fox, *Pr*
Ida Wirtz, *
John Wirtz, *
Ryan Wilson, *
EMP: 85 **EST:** 2009
SALES (est): 3.6MM **Privately Held**
Web: www.wirtzquality.com
SIC: **1741** 1752 1743 1799 Masonry and other stonework; Floor laying and floor work, nec; Terrazzo, tile, marble and mosaic work; Cleaning building exteriors, nec

1742 Plastering, Drywall, And Insulation

(P-1898)
A A GONZALEZ INC
13264 Ralston Ave (91342-7607)
P.O. Box 408 (91341-0408)
PHONE.................................818 367-2242
EMP: 100 **EST:** 1992
SALES (est): 4.87MM **Privately Held**
Web: www.aagonz.com
SIC: **1742** Plastering, drywall, and insulation

(P-1899)
ALAN SMITH POOL PLASTERING INC
Also Called: H2o Leak Pros
227 W Carleton Ave (92867-3607)
PHONE.................................714 628-9494
Stephen Scherer, *Pr*
Teresa Smith, *
Alan Smith, *
▲ **EMP:** 78 **EST:** 1981
SQ FT: 5,000
SALES (est): 24.79MM **Privately Held**
Web: www.alansmithpools.com
SIC: **1742** Plastering, plain or ornamental

(P-1900)
ALCAL SPECIALTY CONTG INC
Arcade Insulation
946 N Market Blvd (95834-1268)
PHONE.................................916 929-3100
Jason Wallace, *Mgr*
EMP: 94
SALES (corp-wide): 1.19B **Privately Held**
Web: www.alcalarcade.com
SIC: **1742** Insulation, buildings
HQ: Alcal Specialty Contracting, Inc.
946 N Market Blvd Ste B
Sacramento CA
916 929-3100

(P-1901)
ALCAL SPECIALTY CONTG INC
42950 Osgood Rd (94539-5627)
PHONE.................................510 477-9380
Jesse Corona, *Mgr*
EMP: 82
SALES (corp-wide): 1.19B **Privately Held**
Web: www.alcalhome.com
SIC: **1742** Insulation, buildings
HQ: Alcal Specialty Contracting, Inc.
946 N Market Blvd Ste B
Sacramento CA
916 929-3100

(P-1902)
ALERT INSULATION COMPANY INC
15913 Old Valley Blvd Ste A (91744-5439)
PHONE.................................626 961-9113
Donald W Kent, *Pr*
Charles Klinakis, *
EMP: 66 **EST:** 1989
SQ FT: 4,500
SALES (est): 9.56MM
SALES (corp-wide): 2.67B **Publicly Held**
Web: www.alertinsulation.com
SIC: **1742** Insulation, buildings
PA: Installed Building Products, Inc.
495 S High St Ste 50
Columbus OH
614 221-3399

(P-1903)
ALL WALL INC
46150 Commerce St Ste 102 (92201-3418)
PHONE.................................760 600-5108
Saul M Gonzalez, *Pr*
Yvette Ambriz, *
Saul Miranda, *
EMP: 89 **EST:** 2012
SALES (est): 4.38MM **Privately Held**
Web: www.allwalldi.com
SIC: **1742** 1721 7389 Drywall; Exterior residential painting contractor; Business services, nec

(P-1904)
ALLEN DRYWALL & ASSOCIATES
380 Lang Rd (94010-2003)
PHONE.................................650 579-0664
Richard Allen, *Pr*
Julie Allen, *
EMP: 60 **EST:** 1989
SALES (est): 4.98MM **Privately Held**
Web: www.allendrywall.com
SIC: **1742** Drywall

(P-1905)
ANCCA CORPORATION
Also Called: N-U Enterprise
7 Goddard (92618-4600)
PHONE.................................949 553-0084
Nicole Hunt, *Sec*
EMP: 99 **EST:** 2008
SALES (est): 3.99MM **Privately Held**
SIC: **1742** Plastering, drywall, and insulation

(P-1906)
ANNING-JOHNSON COMPANY
22955 Kidder St (94545-1670)
PHONE.................................510 670-0100
R Todd Fearon, *VP*
EMP: 140
SQ FT: 16,000
SALES (corp-wide): 461.98MM **Privately Held**
Web: www.anningjohnson.com
SIC: **1742** Drywall
HQ: Anning-Johnson Company
1959 Anson Dr
Melrose Park IL
708 681-1300

(P-1907)
BAYSIDE INTERIORS INC (PA)
3220 Darby Cmn (94539-5601)
PHONE.................................510 438-9171
Steven A Rivera, *CEO*
Burke Nicholson, *
Michael Nicholson, *
Norma Nicholson, *
Jon Braden, *
▲ **EMP:** 95 **EST:** 1984
SQ FT: 20,000
SALES (est): 24.23MM
SALES (corp-wide): 24.23MM **Privately Held**
Web: www.baysideinteriors.com
SIC: **1742** Drywall

(P-1908)
BERGER BROS INC
154 N Aspan Ave (91702-4224)
PHONE.................................626 334-2699
EMP: 350
Web: www.bergerbro.com
SIC: **1742** Plastering, plain or ornamental

(P-1909)
BEST INTERIORS INC
4395 Murphy Canyon Rd (92123-4337)
PHONE.................................858 715-3760
EMP: 80
SALES (corp-wide): 39.63MM **Privately Held**
Web: www.bestinteriors.net
SIC: **1742** Drywall
PA: Best Interiors, Inc.
2100 E Via Burton
Anaheim CA
714 490-7999

(P-1910)
BEST INTERIORS INC (PA)
2100 E Via Burton (92806-1219)
PHONE.................................714 490-7999
Dennis Ayres, *Pr*
Michael Herrig, *
EMP: 150 **EST:** 1986
SQ FT: 20,000
SALES (est): 39.63MM
SALES (corp-wide): 39.63MM **Privately Held**
Web: www.bestinteriors.net
SIC: **1742** Drywall

(P-1911)
BOYETT CONSTRUCTION INC (PA)
Also Called: Boyett
2404 Tripaldi Way (94545-5017)
PHONE.................................510 264-9100
Vernon H Boyett, *Pr*
James Roberts, *Sec*
EMP: 78 **EST:** 1988
SQ FT: 2,600
SALES (est): 21.73MM **Privately Held**
Web: www.boyettconstruction.com
SIC: **1742** 1751 Drywall; Window and door installation and erection

(P-1912)
BRADY COMPANY/SAN DIEGO INC
8100 Center St (91942-2925)
P.O. Box 968 (91944-0968)
PHONE.................................619 462-2600
Scott Brady, *CEO*
EMP: 300 **EST:** 1946
SQ FT: 4,000
SALES (est): 23.48MM **Privately Held**
Web: www.brady.com
SIC: **1742** 1542 Plastering, plain or ornamental; Commercial and office buildings, renovation and repair

(P-1913)
BRADY SOCAL INCORPORATED
8100 Center St (91942-2925)
PHONE.................................619 462-2600
Ricky Marshall, *Pr*
Scott Brady, *
EMP: 99 **EST:** 2009
SALES (est): 18.81MM **Privately Held**
Web: www.brady.com
SIC: **1742** 1751 Drywall; Window and door installation and erection

(P-1914)
C R S DRYWALL INC
Also Called: Cr Drywall
135 San Jose Ave (95125-1018)
PHONE.................................408 998-4360
EMP: 80 **EST:** 1996
SQ FT: 4,000
SALES (est): 4.99MM **Privately Held**
Web: www.crdrywall.com
SIC: **1742** Drywall

(P-1915)
CALDERON DRYWALL CONTRS INC
1931 E Meats Ave Trlr 127 (92865-4002)
PHONE.................................714 696-2977
EMP: 84
SALES (corp-wide): 7.61MM **Privately Held**
SIC: **1742** Drywall
PA: Calderon Drywall Contractors Inc.
2085 N Nordic St
Orange CA
714 900-1863

(P-1916)
CALIFORNIA DRYWALL CO (PA)
2290 S 10th St (95112-4114)
PHONE.................................408 292-7500
Greg Eckstrom, *VP*
Kent Bowles, *
Stephen Eckstrom, *
David Garrett, *
EMP: 249 **EST:** 1946
SQ FT: 15,000
SALES (est): 64.09MM
SALES (corp-wide): 64.09MM **Privately Held**

PRODUCTS & SERVICES SECTION
1742 - Plastering, Drywall, And Insulation (P-1941)

Web: www.caldrywall.com
SIC: 1742 Drywall

(P-1917)
CAPITAL CITY DRYWALL INC
6525 32nd St Ste B1 (95660-3028)
PHONE..................916 331-9200
John Beers, *Pr*
Andrew Sellers, *
EMP: 100 EST: 2000
SQ FT: 2,500
SALES (est): 8.7MM **Privately Held**
Web: www.capitalcitydrywall.com
SIC: **1742** Drywall

(P-1918)
CAPITAL DRYWALL LP
333 S Grand Ave Ste 4070 (90071-1544)
PHONE..................909 599-6818
Frank Scardino, *Pr*
Art Toscano, *
Angela Gates, *
EMP: 249 EST: 1980
SQ FT: 8,000
SALES (est): 2.45MM **Privately Held**
SIC: **1742** Drywall
PA: U.S. Builder Services, Llc
    272 E Deerpath Ste 308
    Lake Forest IL

(P-1919)
CASTON INC
354 S Allen St (92408-1508)
PHONE..................909 381-1619
James I Malachowski Junior, *Pr*
EMP: 100 EST: 2010
SALES (est): 18.13MM **Privately Held**
Web: www.castoninc.com
SIC: **1742** Drywall

(P-1920)
CEN CAL PLASTERING INC
15300 East Wyman Rd (95330)
PHONE..................209 981-5265
EMP: 398
SALES (corp-wide): 40.9MM **Privately Held**
Web: www.cencalplastering.com
SIC: **1742** Plastering, plain or ornamental
PA: Cen Cal Plastering, Inc.
    1256 W Lathrop Rd
    Manteca CA
    209 858-1045

(P-1921)
CHURCH & LARSEN INC
16103 Avenida Padilla (91702-3223)
PHONE..................626 303-8741
Raymond W Larsen, *Pr*
Kenneth R Larsen, *
Kenneth P Larsen, *
EMP: 250 EST: 1980
SQ FT: 10,800
SALES (est): 9.54MM **Privately Held**
Web: www.churchandlarsen.com
SIC: **1742** Drywall

(P-1922)
CUSTOM DRYWALL INC
1570 Gladding Ct (95035-6814)
PHONE..................408 263-1616
Gene Cox, *Pr*
EMP: 90 EST: 1961
SQ FT: 10,000
SALES (est): 4.94MM **Privately Held**
Web: www.custom-drywall-inc.com
SIC: **1742** Drywall

(P-1923)
DALEYS DRYWALL AND TAPING INC
960 Camden Ave (95008-4104)
PHONE..................408 378-9500
Craig Spencer Daley, *Pr*
Chris Daley, *
Brittni Daley, *
EMP: 381 EST: 1963
SQ FT: 20,000
SALES (est): 45.39MM **Privately Held**
Web: www.daleysdrywall.com
SIC: **1742** Drywall

(P-1924)
DH SMITH COMPANY INC
6000 Hellyer Ave Ste 150 (95138-1031)
P.O. Box 730189 (95173-0189)
PHONE..................408 532-7617
EMP: 85 EST: 1996
SQ FT: 20,000
SALES (est): 6.89MM **Privately Held**
SIC: **1742** Plastering, plain or ornamental

(P-1925)
DIAZ PLASTERING INC
6013 Nathaniel Way (93313-2968)
P.O. Box 11014 (93389-1014)
PHONE..................661 244-8228
Jovani Diaz, *Pr*
EMP: 60 EST: 2010
SALES (est): 4.22MM **Privately Held**
Web: www.diazplastering.com
SIC: **1742** Plastering, plain or ornamental

(P-1926)
ELLJAY ACOUSTICS INC
511 Cameron St (92870-6425)
PHONE..................714 961-1173
Ronald B Bishop, *Pr*
EMP: 70 EST: 1966
SQ FT: 6,900
SALES (est): 9.12MM **Privately Held**
Web: www.elljay.com
SIC: **1742** Acoustical and ceiling work

(P-1927)
ERIC STARK INTERIORS INC
2284 Paragon Dr (95131-1306)
PHONE..................408 441-6136
Eric Stark, *Pr*
EMP: 100 EST: 1992
SQ FT: 10,000
SALES (est): 8.53MM **Privately Held**
SIC: **1742** Drywall

(P-1928)
FARWEST INSULATION CONTRACTING
Also Called: Pacific Insulation
2741 Yates Ave (90040-2623)
PHONE..................310 634-2800
Linda Chadarria, *Mgr*
EMP: 88
SALES (corp-wide): 26.97MM **Privately Held**
Web: www.farwestinsulation.com
SIC: **1742** Insulation, buildings
PA: Farwest Insulation Contracting, Inc
    1220 S Sherman St
    Anaheim CA
    714 520-5600

(P-1929)
FIVE STAR PLASTERING INC
23022 La Cadena Dr Ste 200 (92653-1362)
PHONE..................949 683-5091
EMP: 100 EST: 2010
SALES (est): 3.86MM **Privately Held**

Web: www.fivestarplastering.com
SIC: **1742** Drywall

(P-1930)
FRYE CONSTRUCTION INC
18807 Highway 65 (93308-9794)
P.O. Box 21568 (93390-1568)
PHONE..................661 588-8870
EMP: 60
Web: www.fryeconstructioninc.com
SIC: **1742** Drywall

(P-1931)
FUTURE ENERGY CORPORATION
4120 Avenida De La Plata (92056-6001)
PHONE..................760 477-9700
Jeffrey Adkins, *Brnch Mgr*
EMP: 70
SALES (corp-wide): 24.18MM **Privately Held**
Web: www.futureenergysavers.com
SIC: **1742** 1521 Acoustical and insulation work; Single-family home remodeling, additions, and repairs
PA: Future Energy Corporation
    8980 Grant Line Rd
    Elk Grove CA
    800 985-0733

(P-1932)
FUTURE ENERGY CORPORATION (PA)
Also Called: Future Energy Savers
8980 Grant Line Rd (95624-1415)
P.O. Box 87 (95693-0087)
PHONE..................800 985-0733
TOLL FREE: 800
Jeffrey Adkins, *CEO*
EMP: 80 EST: 1982
SQ FT: 6,800
SALES (est): 24.18MM
SALES (corp-wide): 24.18MM **Privately Held**
Web: www.futureenergysavers.com
SIC: **1742** Insulation, buildings

(P-1933)
HANSON DRYWALL INC
Also Called: Hanson Drywall
635 W San Martin Ave (95046-9414)
PHONE..................831 297-4581
Joshua K Hanson, *Prin*
EMP: 80 EST: 2017
SALES (est): 4.74MM **Privately Held**
SIC: **1742** Drywall

(P-1934)
HI-TEMP INSULATION INC
4700 Calle Alto (93012-8537)
PHONE..................805 484-2774
Sieg Borck, *CEO*
Fecialita Allen, *
▲ EMP: 410 EST: 1964
SQ FT: 100,000
SALES (est): 48.41MM **Privately Held**
Web: www.hi-tempinsulation.com
SIC: **1742** Insulation, buildings

(P-1935)
INFINITY DRYWALL CONTG INC
225 S Loara St (92802-1019)
PHONE..................714 634-2255
Dennis Lafreniere, *Pr*
Liza Lafreniere, *
James Darling, *
EMP: 60 EST: 2006
SALES (est): 8.01MM **Privately Held**
Web: www.infinitydw.com

SIC: **1742** 1751 Drywall; Framing contractor

(P-1936)
INTERIOR EXPERTS GEN BLDRS INC
4534 Carter Ct (91710-5060)
PHONE..................909 203-4922
Adam Lopez, *Pr*
EMP: 80 EST: 1992
SQ FT: 9,000
SALES (est): 11.08MM **Privately Held**
Web: www.interiorexperts.com
SIC: **1742** Drywall

(P-1937)
J & J ACOUSTICS INC
2260 De La Cruz Blvd (95050-3008)
PHONE..................408 275-9255
James Jean, *Pr*
Joseph Jean, *
Marge Meide, *
EMP: 140 EST: 1975
SALES (est): 18.58MM **Privately Held**
Web: www.jjacoustics.com
SIC: **1742** Drywall

(P-1938)
JADE INC
11126 Sepulveda Blvd Ste B (91345-1130)
PHONE..................818 365-7137
Steven Arteaga, *CEO*
Jay Arteaga, *
Michelle Vojtech, *
Cheryl Taylor, *
Gail De Ande, *
EMP: 75 EST: 1974
SQ FT: 5,000
SALES (est): 4.97MM **Privately Held**
Web: www.jadedrywall.com
SIC: **1742** Drywall

(P-1939)
JOHN JORY CORPORATION (PA)
2180 N Glassell St (92865-3308)
P.O. Box 6050 (92863-6050)
PHONE..................714 279-7901
Kenneth Johnson, *CEO*
Jack Jory, *
EMP: 385 EST: 1965
SALES (est): 28.26MM
SALES (corp-wide): 28.26MM **Privately Held**
Web: www.johnjorycorp.com
SIC: **1742** Drywall

(P-1940)
KEENAN HPKINS SDER STWELL CNTR (PA)
Also Called: Khs & S Contractors
5109 E La Palma Ave Ste A (92807-2066)
PHONE..................714 695-3670
David Suder, *Pr*
John Platon, *
Dennis Norman, *
Philip Cherne, *
Cindy Runge, *
▲ EMP: 65 EST: 1996
SALES (est): 107.22MM
SALES (corp-wide): 107.22MM **Privately Held**
Web: www.khss.com
SIC: **1742** 1751 1743 1741 Plastering, plain or ornamental; Carpentry work; Terrazzo, tile, marble and mosaic work; Masonry and other stonework

(P-1941)
KENYON CONSTRUCTION INC
Also Called: Kenyon Plastering

1742 - Plastering, Drywall, And Insulation (P-1942)

1286 N Broadway Ave (95205-3039)
PHONE..............................209 462-4060
Don Bee, Genl Mgr
EMP: 61
SALES (corp-wide): 80.09MM **Privately Held**
Web: www.kenyonweb.com
SIC: **1742** Plastering, plain or ornamental
PA: Kenyon Construction, Inc.
4001 W Indian School Rd
Phoenix AZ
602 484-0080

(P-1942)
LANCASTER BURNS CNSTR INC
Also Called: L B Construction
8655 Washington Blvd (95678-5945)
PHONE..............................916 624-8404
EMP: 150 EST: 1992
SQ FT: 43,000
SALES (est): 36.1MM **Privately Held**
Web: www.lbconstructioninc.com
SIC: **1742** 1751 1791 3449 Drywall; Framing contractor; Building front installation, metal; Bars, concrete reinforcing; fabricated steel

(P-1943)
LEVEL 5 DRYWALL INC
Also Called: Specialty Construction
70 Glenn Way Ste 4 (94070-6220)
PHONE..............................650 486-1657
Alan Amirteymour, CEO
EMP: 80 EST: 2015
SALES (est): 4.68MM **Privately Held**
Web: www.levelfivedrywall.com
SIC: **1742** 1751 Drywall; Lightweight steel framing (metal stud) installation

(P-1944)
MAGNUM DRYWALL INC
2030 Fortune Dr Ste 200 (95131-1835)
PHONE..............................510 979-0420
Gary Robinson, CEO
EMP: 72 EST: 1991
SALES (est): 24.81MM **Privately Held**
Web: www.magnumdrywall.com
SIC: **1742** 1721 1751 Plastering, drywall, and insulation; Painting and paper hanging; Carpentry work

(P-1945)
MARTIN BROS/MARCOWALL INC (PA)
17104 S Figueroa St (90248-3021)
P.O. Box 2089 (90247-0089)
PHONE..............................310 532-5335
Mohammad Chahine, CEO
EMP: 110 EST: 1966
SQ FT: 6,000
SALES (est): 45.05MM
SALES (corp-wide): 45.05MM **Privately Held**
Web: www.martinbros.net
SIC: **1742** Drywall

(P-1946)
MGM DRYWALL INC
1050 Commercial St Ste 102 (95112)
PHONE..............................408 292-4085
Miguel Guillen, Pr
Martina Guillen, *
EMP: 100 EST: 2000
SALES (est): 18.91MM **Privately Held**
Web: www.mgmdrywall.com
SIC: **1742** 1721 3446 Drywall; Residential painting; Acoustical suspension systems, metal

(P-1947)
MOWERY THOMASON INC
1225 N Red Gum St (92806-1821)
PHONE..............................714 666-1717
Robert J Heimerl, Pr
Todd Heimerl, *
Toni Heimerl, *
EMP: 175 EST: 1957
SQ FT: 8,000
SALES (est): 20.21MM **Privately Held**
Web: www.mowerythomason.com
SIC: **1742** Drywall

(P-1948)
NEW WEST PARTITIONS
2550 Sutterville Rd (95820-1020)
PHONE..............................916 456-8365
Kem P Modellas, CEO
Mark Modellas, *
EMP: 120 EST: 1994
SQ FT: 3,000
SALES (est): 28.95MM **Privately Held**
Web: www.newwestpartitions.com
SIC: **1742** Drywall

(P-1949)
NOROGACHI CONSTRUCTION INC/CA
600 Industrial Dr Ste 100 (95632-8164)
PHONE..............................916 236-4201
Anival Guerrero, CEO
Laura Guerrero, *
Gerardo Guerrero, *
EMP: 100 EST: 2005
SALES (est): 8.88MM **Privately Held**
Web: www.norogachiconstruction.com
SIC: **1742** 1542 Drywall; Institutional building construction

(P-1950)
OJ INSULATION LP (PA)
Also Called: Abco Insulation
600 S Vincent Ave (91702-5145)
PHONE..............................800 707-9278
Pamela A Henson, Pt
EMP: 148 EST: 2006
SQ FT: 12,000
SALES (est): 22.6MM
SALES (corp-wide): 22.6MM **Privately Held**
Web: www.ojinc.com
SIC: **1742** 1751 1741 Insulation, buildings; Carpentry work; Masonry and other stonework

(P-1951)
ORANGE COUNTY PLST CO INC
3191 Airport Loop Dr Ste B1 (92626)
PHONE..............................714 957-1971
EMP: 128 EST: 1995
SALES (est): 7.92MM **Privately Held**
SIC: **1742** Plastering, plain or ornamental

(P-1952)
PACIFIC BUILDING GROUP
13541 Stoney Creek Rd (92129-2050)
PHONE..............................858 552-0600
Jim Roherty, Brnch Mgr
EMP: 94
SALES (corp-wide): 59.16MM **Privately Held**
Web: www.pacificbuildinggroup.com
SIC: **1742** Acoustical and ceiling work
PA: Pacific Building Group
9752 Aspen Creek Ct # 100
San Diego CA
858 552-0600

(P-1953)
PACIFIC SYSTEMS INTERIORS INC
190 E Arrow Hwy Ste D (91773-3314)
PHONE..............................310 436-6820
Michelle Orr Mcneal, Dir
EMP: 150 EST: 1987
SQ FT: 30,000
SALES (est): 39.51MM **Privately Held**
Web: www.psi.builders
SIC: **1742** 1542 Drywall; Nonresidential construction, nec

(P-1954)
PADILLA CONSTRUCTION COMPANY
Also Called: Garris Plastering
1620 N Brian St (92867-3422)
PHONE..............................714 685-8500
Ralph Padilla, Prin
EMP: 250 EST: 1963
SALES (est): 23.42MM **Privately Held**
Web: www.padillaconstruction.com
SIC: **1742** Plastering, drywall, and insulation

(P-1955)
PETRO-CHEM INDUSTRIES INC
Also Called: Petro-Chem Insulation
2300 Clayton Rd (94520-2100)
PHONE..............................707 644-7455
EMP: 96 EST: 1989
SALES (est): 12.6MM **Privately Held**
Web: www.petrocheminc.com
SIC: **1742** Insulation, buildings

(P-1956)
PETROCHEM INSULATION INC
Also Called: Petrochem
3117 E South St (90805-3742)
PHONE..............................310 638-6663
Erich Freudenthaler, Mgr
EMP: 93
SALES (corp-wide): 2.72B **Privately Held**
Web: www.petrocheminc.com
SIC: **1742** 3531 Insulation, buildings; Construction machinery
HQ: Petrochem Insulation, Inc.
1501 W Fthnead Pkwy # 550
Tempe AZ
707 644-7455

(P-1957)
PROWALL LATH AND PLASTER
360 S Spruce St (92025-4052)
P.O. Box 3058 (92033-3058)
PHONE..............................760 480-9001
Mary Kathawa, Pr
EMP: 99 EST: 2009
SALES (est): 2.68MM **Privately Held**
Web: www.prowalllathandplaster.net
SIC: **1742** Plastering, plain or ornamental

(P-1958)
QUALITY PRODUCTION SVCS INC
18711 S Broadwick St (90220-6427)
PHONE..............................310 406-3350
Arshak George Kotoyantz, Pr
EMP: 100 EST: 1995
SALES (est): 11.61MM **Privately Held**
Web: www.qpscompany.com
SIC: **1742** Drywall

(P-1959)
RFJ CORPORATION
Also Called: Rfj Meiswinkel
930 Innes Ave (94124-2905)
PHONE..............................415 824-6890
Joseph Meiswinkel, Pr
EMP: 60 EST: 1983
SQ FT: 15,000
SALES (est): 8.99MM **Privately Held**
Web: www.rfjmeiswinkel.com
SIC: **1742** Plastering, plain or ornamental

(P-1960)
ROYAL WEST DRYWALL INC
2008 2nd St (92860-2804)
PHONE..............................951 271-4600
Paul Diguiseppe, CEO
EMP: 100 EST: 1988
SQ FT: 20,473
SALES (est): 9.3MM **Privately Held**
Web: www.royalwestdrywall.com
SIC: **1742** Drywall

(P-1961)
RUTHERFORD CO INC (PA)
2107 Crystal St (90039-2901)
PHONE..............................323 666-5284
Paul Rutherford, Pr
Sheila Rutherford, *
Brad Rutherford, *
James Rutherford, *
EMP: 100 EST: 1970
SQ FT: 15,000
SALES (est): 9.17MM
SALES (corp-wide): 9.17MM **Privately Held**
Web: www.rutherfordco.net
SIC: **1742** Plastering, plain or ornamental

(P-1962)
S & S DRYWALL INC (PA)
202 N 27th St (95116-1120)
PHONE..............................408 294-4393
Gabriel Silveira, Pr
Maria Silveira, Sec
EMP: 199 EST: 1987
SALES (est): 9.36MM
SALES (corp-wide): 9.36MM **Privately Held**
Web: www.ssdrywall.net
SIC: **1742** Drywall

(P-1963)
SIERRA LATHING COMPANY INC
1189 Leiske Dr (92376-8633)
PHONE..............................909 421-0211
Gary K Waldron, CEO
Connie Waldron, *
EMP: 200 EST: 1958
SQ FT: 10,000
SALES (est): 8.55MM **Privately Held**
SIC: **1742** 1751 Drywall; Framing contractor

(P-1964)
SPECIALTY TEAM PLASTERING INC
4652 Vintage Ranch Ln (93110-2079)
PHONE..............................805 966-3858
Jaime Melgosa, Pr
Robin Melgosa, *
EMP: 130 EST: 1993
SQ FT: 1,000
SALES (est): 9.28MM **Privately Held**
Web: www.specialtyteamplastering.com
SIC: **1742** Plastering, plain or ornamental

(P-1965)
STANDARD DRYWALL INC (HQ)
Also Called: S D I
9831 Channel Rd (92040-3173)
PHONE..............................619 443-7034
Robert E Caya, CEO
Blaine Caya, *
EMP: 300 EST: 1956
SALES (est): 118.19MM **Privately Held**

PRODUCTS & SERVICES SECTION

1751 - Carpentry Work (P-1989)

Web: www.standarddrywall.com
SIC: **1742** Drywall
PA: E M P Interiors Inc
  9831 Channel Rd
  Lakeside CA

(P-1966)
SUNSHINE METAL CLAD INC
7201 Edison Hwy (93307-9011)
PHONE..................................661 366-0575
James R Eudy, *Pr*
Linda Payne, *
▲ **EMP:** 100 **EST:** 1979
SQ FT: 50,000
SALES (est): 9.89MM **Privately Held**
Web: www.smcinsulation.com
SIC: **1742** Insulation, buildings

(P-1967)
SUPERIOR WALL SYSTEMS INC
Also Called: Sws
1232 E Orangethorpe Ave (92831-5224)
PHONE..................................714 278-0000
Ronald Lee Hudson, *CEO*
Greg Smith, *
EMP: 500 **EST:** 1979
SQ FT: 40,000
SALES (est): 48MM **Privately Held**
Web: www.superiorwallsystems.com
SIC: **1742** Drywall

(P-1968)
TEMECULA VALLEY DRYWALL INC
Also Called: Timberlake Painting
41228 Raintree Ct (92562-7089)
PHONE..................................951 600-1742
Doug A Misemer, *CEO*
Lorry Hales, *
Sandy Villella, *
EMP: 75 **EST:** 1990
SQ FT: 8,000
SALES (est): 11.05MM **Privately Held**
Web: www.tvdrywall.com
SIC: **1742** 1721 Drywall; Painting and paper hanging

(P-1969)
TOMMY GUN PLASTERING INC
944 4th St (92320-1205)
PHONE..................................909 795-9966
Tommy Lucero, *CEO*
EMP: 60 **EST:** 2002
SQ FT: 1,800
SALES (est): 3.16MM **Privately Held**
Web: www.tommygunplastering.com
SIC: **1742** Drywall

(P-1970)
TOWNE DRYWALL INC
10612 Prospect Ave Ste 105 (92071-8500)
PHONE..................................619 334-3750
Marc Towne, *Pr*
EMP: 68 **EST:** 2016
SALES (est): 4.76MM **Privately Held**
SIC: **1742** Drywall

(P-1971)
VEZINA INDUSTRIES INC
Also Called: Window Instlltion Insul Instll
33543 Avenue 9 (93636-7950)
PHONE..................................559 479-8287
Michael Vezina, *Pr*
Irene Vezina, *
EMP: 75 **EST:** 2018
SQ FT: 9,000
SALES (est): 10.01MM **Privately Held**
Web: www.vezinaindustries.com

SIC: **1742** 1522 1521 Insulation, buildings; Residential construction, nec; General remodeling, single-family houses

(P-1972)
WEST COAST DRYWALL & CO INC
Also Called: West Coast Drywall & Paint
1610 W Linden St (92507-6810)
PHONE..................................951 778-3592
Mark Herbert, *CEO*
Dan Slavin, *
Santos Garcia, *
Colleen Butler, *
Keith Caneva, *Corporate Controller*
EMP: 400 **EST:** 2002
SQ FT: 18,962
SALES (est): 36.86MM **Privately Held**
Web: www.wcdp.com
SIC: **1742** Drywall

(P-1973)
WESTERN DRYWALL INC
4971 Salida Blvd (95368-9420)
P.O. Box 11130 (95361-1025)
PHONE..................................209 543-9361
Cecil Shatswell, *Pr*
John Shatswell, *
Kevin Shatswell, *
EMP: 70 **EST:** 1977
SALES (est): 7.31MM **Privately Held**
Web: www.westerndrywall.com
SIC: **1742** Drywall

1743 Terrazzo, Tile, Marble, Mosaic Work

(P-1974)
ARRIAGA USA INC (PA)
Also Called: Stoneland
12000 Sherman Way (91605-3727)
PHONE..................................818 982-9559
Shalom Rubin, *Pr*
◆ **EMP:** 60 **EST:** 2002
SALES (est): 9.24MM
SALES (corp-wide): 9.24MM **Privately Held**
Web: www.stonelandusa.com
SIC: **1743** Tile installation, ceramic

(P-1975)
CAL CUSTOM TILE
Also Called: Rick Berry
1300 Commerce Way (93657-8731)
PHONE..................................559 875-1460
Rick Berry, *Pr*
Michele Berry, *
EMP: 95 **EST:** 1981
SQ FT: 10,000
SALES (est): 10.29MM **Privately Held**
Web: www.calcustomtile.com
SIC: **1743** Tile installation, ceramic

(P-1976)
CERAMIC TILE ART INC
11601 Pendleton St (91352-2502)
PHONE..................................818 767-9088
Itamar Levy, *Pr*
▲ **EMP:** 75 **EST:** 1993
SALES (est): 2.44MM **Privately Held**
Web: www.ceramictileart.us
SIC: **1743** Tile installation, ceramic

(P-1977)
COASTAL TILE INC
Also Called: Coastal The
13226 Moorpark St Apt 104 (91423-5177)
PHONE..................................818 988-6134

Ronig Yemini, *Pr*
Eyal Reguev, *
▲ **EMP:** 100 **EST:** 1993
SALES (est): 3.91MM **Privately Held**
SIC: **1743** Tile installation, ceramic

(P-1978)
D & J TILE COMPANY INC
1045 Terminal Way (94070-3226)
PHONE..................................650 632-4000
David Newman, *Prin*
John Reich, *
◆ **EMP:** 100 **EST:** 1990
SALES (est): 12.66MM **Privately Held**
Web: www.djtile.com
SIC: **1743** Tile installation, ceramic

(P-1979)
DELLA MAGGIORE TILE INC
87 N 30th St (95116-1124)
PHONE..................................408 286-3991
Nick D Maggiore, *Pr*
Julie D Maggiore, *
▲ **EMP:** 80 **EST:** 1977
SQ FT: 20,000
SALES (est): 5.61MM **Privately Held**
Web: www.dellamaggiore.com
SIC: **1743** Tile installation, ceramic

(P-1980)
ELEGANZA TILES INC (PA)
3125 E Coronado St (92806-1915)
PHONE..................................714 224-1700
Mike Darmawan, *CEO*
Vonny Purnama, *VP*
◆ **EMP:** 70 **EST:** 2002
SALES (est): 23.84MM
SALES (corp-wide): 23.84MM **Privately Held**
Web: www.eleganzatiles.com
SIC: **1743** Tile installation, ceramic

(P-1981)
EMSER TILE LLC
5300 Shea Center Dr (91761-7883)
PHONE..................................909 974-1600
Gabriel Castro, *Brnch Mgr*
EMP: 60
SALES (corp-wide): 273.97MM **Privately Held**
Web: www.emser.com
SIC: **1743** Tile installation, ceramic
PA: Emser Tile, Llc
  8431 Santa Monica Blvd
  Los Angeles CA
  323 650-2000

(P-1982)
FISCHER TILE AND MARBLE INC
1800 23rd St (95816-7112)
PHONE..................................916 452-1426
Jay H Fischer, *Pr*
▲ **EMP:** 150 **EST:** 1906
SQ FT: 22,000
SALES (est): 9.13MM **Privately Held**
Web: www.fischertile.com
SIC: **1743** Tile installation, ceramic

(P-1983)
GINO RINALDI INC
Also Called: Rinaldi Tile & Marble
51 Fremont St (95076-5213)
PHONE..................................831 761-0195
Gino Rinaldi Senior, *Pr*
Yvonne Rinaldi, *
▲ **EMP:** 80 **EST:** 1973
SQ FT: 10,000
SALES (est): 11.28MM **Privately Held**
Web: www.rinalditileandmarble.com

SIC: **1743** Tile installation, ceramic

(P-1984)
JEFFREY COURT INC
Also Called: Jeffrey Court
620 Parkridge Ave (92860-3124)
PHONE..................................951 340-3383
▲ **EMP:** 77 **EST:** 1991
SALES (est): 11.02MM **Privately Held**
Web: www.jeffreycourt.com
SIC: **1743** Tile installation, ceramic

(P-1985)
MATRIX SURFACES INC
5449 E La Palma Ave (92807-2022)
PHONE..................................714 696-5449
Jerry Eugene Jones, *CEO*
Laura J Jones, *
▲ **EMP:** 60 **EST:** 2001
SQ FT: 5,000
SALES (est): 9.98MM **Privately Held**
Web: www.matrixsurfaces.com
SIC: **1743** Tile installation, ceramic

(P-1986)
NATIONAL CRMIC TILE STONE CORP
Also Called: Constrction - Tile Instllation
9980 Horn Rd Ste 100 (95827-1905)
PHONE..................................916 776-8715
Jim Cline, *Pr*
Eric Witcher, *
Roger Leasure, *
EMP: 80 **EST:** 2009
SALES (est): 14.85MM **Privately Held**
SIC: **1743** Tile installation, ceramic

(P-1987)
SHERMN-LEHR CSTM TILE WRKS INC
5691 Power Inn Rd Ste A (95824-2361)
PHONE..................................916 386-0417
James P Loehr, *Pr*
Eber T Sherman, *
Joyce Loehr, *
Jane Sherman, *
EMP: 100 **EST:** 1979
SQ FT: 3,400
SALES (est): 9.86MM **Privately Held**
Web: www.shermanloehr.com
SIC: **1743** Tile installation, ceramic

(P-1988)
TRM CORPORATION (PA)
Also Called: Superior Tile Co
2378 Polvorosa Ave (94577-2218)
P.O. Box 2106 (94621-0006)
PHONE..................................510 895-2700
Tommy Conner, *CEO*
Robert Herman, *
Patty Moore, *
Jerry T Sue, *
▲ **EMP:** 65 **EST:** 1975
SQ FT: 12,000
SALES (est): 29.31MM
SALES (corp-wide): 29.31MM **Privately Held**
Web: www.superiortilestone.com
SIC: **1743** Tile installation, ceramic

1751 Carpentry Work

(P-1989)
ACOSTA AND SONS INC
736 Wakefield Ct (95361-7761)
P.O. Box 546 (95361-0546)
PHONE..................................209 322-3181
Clifford Acosta, *CEO*

1751 - Carpentry Work (P-1990)

Clifford Acosta, *Pr*
Gary Acosta Senior, *CEO*
Gary Acosta Junior, *Dir*
Joel Acosta, *
EMP: 60 **EST:** 1962
SQ FT: 12,000
SALES (est): 4.62MM **Privately Held**
SIC: 1751 5712 Window and door installation and erection; Cabinet work, custom

(P-1990)
ALLIED FRAMERS INC
4990 Allison Pkwy (95688-9346)
PHONE..................707 452-7050
EMP: 130 **EST:** 1995
SQ FT: 6,000
SALES (est): 12.37MM **Privately Held**
Web: www.alliedframers.com
SIC: 1751 Framing contractor

(P-1991)
CAPITOL BUILDERS HARDWARE INC (HQ)
Also Called: Capitol Door Service
4699 24th St (95822-1412)
PHONE..................916 451-2821
David Karacozoff, *CEO*
Kirk Karacozoff, *
Chris Matheny, *
EMP: 68 **EST:** 1957
SQ FT: 25,000
SALES (est): 20.93MM
SALES (corp-wide): 11.51B **Privately Held**
Web: www.capitolbh.com
SIC: 1751 5031 5072 Finish and trim carpentry; Metal doors, sash and trim; Builders' hardware, nec
PA: Assa Abloy Ab
  Klarabergsviadukten 90
  Stockholm
  850648500

(P-1992)
CLEAR VIEW WINDOWS & DOORS INC
28106 Avenue Crocker (91355-1207)
P.O. Box 802242 (91380-2242)
PHONE..................661 257-5050
EMP: 70
SIC: 1751 5031 Window and door (prefabricated) installation; Metal doors, sash and trim

(P-1993)
CLOSET WORLD INC
14438 Don Julian Rd (91746-3101)
PHONE..................626 855-0846
EMP: 90
Web: www.closetworld.com
SIC: 1751 5211 Cabinet building and installation; Closets, interiors and accessories
PA: Closet World, Inc.
  3860 Capitol Ave
  City Of Industry CA

(P-1994)
COMMERCIAL DOOR COMPANY INC
1374 E 9th St (91766-3831)
PHONE..................714 529-2179
TOLL FREE: 800
David O Holmes, *CEO*
Carol Holmes, *
EMP: 60 **EST:** 1949
SQ FT: 10,000
SALES (est): 9MM **Privately Held**
Web: www.commercialdoorcompany.com
SIC: 1751 Garage door, installation or erection

(P-1995)
COMMERCIAL WOOD PRODUCTS COMPANY
Also Called: Cwp
10019 Yucca Rd (92301-2242)
PHONE..................760 246-4530
EMP: 115
Web: www.commercialwood.com
SIC: 1751 Cabinet building and installation

(P-1996)
CRAFTSMAN LATH AND PLASTER INC
8325 63rd St (92509-6004)
PHONE..................951 685-9922
Kevin Tunstill, *Pr*
EMP: 350 **EST:** 2015
SALES (est): 9.68MM **Privately Held**
Web: www.craftsmanlp.com
SIC: 1751 Carpentry work

(P-1997)
CWP CABINETS INC
15447 Anacapa Rd Ste 102 (92392-2481)
PHONE..................760 246-4530
Michael Rodriguez, *CEO*
EMP: 115 **EST:** 2011
SALES (est): 9.81MM **Privately Held**
SIC: 1751 2434 2541 5712 Cabinet building and installation; Wood kitchen cabinets; Wood partitions and fixtures; Cabinet work, custom

(P-1998)
FENNEL INC
Also Called: Thompson Cnstr Sup Door Frame
1169 Sherborn St (92879-5005)
P.O. Box 78300 (92877-0143)
PHONE..................951 284-2020
Kenneth R Thompson, *CEO*
Robert Leos, *
EMP: 65 **EST:** 2012
SALES (est): 2.66MM **Privately Held**
SIC: 1751 5251 5999 Garage door, installation or erection; Door locks and lock sets; Art, picture frames, and decorations

(P-1999)
GRANT CONSTRUCTION INC
7702 Meany Ave Ste 103 (93308-5199)
PHONE..................661 588-4586
Grant Fraysier, *Pr*
EMP: 93 **EST:** 1994
SQ FT: 1,000
SALES (est): 43.04MM **Privately Held**
Web: www.grant-construction.com
SIC: 1751 1771 Framing contractor; Concrete work

(P-2000)
HAKES SASH & DOOR INC
31945 Corydon St (92530-8524)
PHONE..................951 674-2414
Allen J Hakes, *Pr*
EMP: 190 **EST:** 2005
SQ FT: 2,000
SALES (est): 24.49MM **Privately Held**
Web: www.hakesdoor.net
SIC: 1751 3442 5211 Window and door installation and erection; Window and door frames; Sash, wood or metal

(P-2001)
HERITAGE INTERESTS LLC (PA)
4300 Jetway Ct (95660-5702)
P.O. Box 214609 (95821-0609)
PHONE..................916 481-5030
Edward Zuckerman, *Pr*
Charlie Gardemeyer, *
Dennis Gardemeyer, *
EMP: 90 **EST:** 2011
SQ FT: 80,000
SALES (est): 36.03MM
SALES (corp-wide): 36.03MM **Privately Held**
Web: www.heritageinterests.com
SIC: 1751 5031 2431 Cabinet and finish carpentry; Lumber, plywood, and millwork; Windows and window parts and trim, wood

(P-2002)
HOME ORGANIZERS INC
Also Called: Closet World, The
3860 Capitol Ave (90601-1733)
PHONE..................562 699-9945
Frank Melkonian, *Pr*
EMP: 660 **EST:** 2001
SALES (est): 41.37MM **Privately Held**
Web: www.closetworld.com
SIC: 1751 2541 Cabinet building and installation; Cabinets, lockers, and shelving

(P-2003)
ISEC INCORPORATED
2363 Teller Rd Ste 106 (91320-6058)
PHONE..................805 375-6957
Kevin Zimmerman, *Brnch Mgr*
EMP: 72
SALES (corp-wide): 317.22MM **Privately Held**
Web: www.isecinc.com
SIC: 1751 Cabinet and finish carpentry
PA: Isec, Incorporated
  6000 Greenwood Plaza Blvd # 200
  Greenwood Village CO
  303 790-1444

(P-2004)
ISEC INCORPORATED
1855 N 1st St Unit D (95620-9758)
P.O. Box 6849 (80155-6849)
PHONE..................707 693-6555
Ed Miller, *Brnch Mgr*
EMP: 101
SALES (corp-wide): 317.22MM **Privately Held**
Web: www.isecinc.com
SIC: 1751 Cabinet and finish carpentry
PA: Isec, Incorporated
  6000 Greenwood Plaza Blvd # 200
  Greenwood Village CO
  303 790-1444

(P-2005)
ISEC INCORPORATED
Also Called: Intermountain Specialty Eqp
20 Centerpointe Dr Ste 140 (90623-2563)
PHONE..................714 761-5151
Greg Timmerman, *VP*
EMP: 130
SQ FT: 5,000
SALES (corp-wide): 317.22MM **Privately Held**
Web: www.isecinc.com
SIC: 1751 Cabinet and finish carpentry
PA: Isec, Incorporated
  6000 Greenwood Plaza Blvd # 200
  Greenwood Village CO
  303 790-1444

(P-2006)
LAURENCE-HOVENIER INC
179 N Maple St (92878-3260)
PHONE..................951 736-2990
Ronald Laurence, *Pr*
Fred Hovenier, *
EMP: 190 **EST:** 1979
SQ FT: 6,000
SALES (est): 24.69MM **Privately Held**
SIC: 1751 Framing contractor

(P-2007)
LOZANO CASEWORKS INC
242 W Hanna St (92324-2772)
PHONE..................909 783-7530
EMP: 70
SIC: 1751 2522 Cabinet building and installation; Cabinets, office: except wood

(P-2008)
MISSION BELL MFG CO INC ◆
16100 Jacqueline Ct (95037-5526)
PHONE..................408 778-2036
Bret Sisney, *Pr*
Nicolette Faultner, *
EMP: 280 **EST:** 2022
SALES (est): 24.94MM **Privately Held**
SIC: 1751 2421 2541 1799 Cabinet and finish carpentry; Building and structural materials, wood; Cabinets, lockers, and shelving; Building site preparation

(P-2009)
NORCAL INC
Also Called: Seeley Brothers
1400 Moonstone (92821-2801)
PHONE..................714 224-3949
Michael Seeley, *Pt*
Phil Norys, *
Joe Calvillo, *
EMP: 175 **EST:** 1987
SQ FT: 62,000
SALES (est): 48.78MM **Privately Held**
Web: www.seeleybros.com
SIC: 1751 Finish and trim carpentry

(P-2010)
NORTHWEST EXTERIORS INC
4404 N Knoll Ave (93722-7825)
PHONE..................559 456-1632
Jimmy Brown, *Brnch Mgr*
EMP: 64
Web: www.northwestexteriors.com
SIC: 1751 5211 5031 Window and door (prefabricated) installation; Cabinets, kitchen; Metal doors, sash and trim
PA: Northwest Exteriors, Inc.
  11200 Sun Center Dr
  Rancho Cordova CA

(P-2011)
PRIME TECH CABINETS INC
2215 S Standard Ave (92707-3036)
PHONE..................949 757-4900
Hassan Farjamrad, *Pr*
Zora Farjamrad, *
EMP: 110 **EST:** 1988
SALES (est): 9.36MM **Privately Held**
Web: www.ptcabinets.com
SIC: 1751 Cabinet building and installation

(P-2012)
PRODUCTION FRAMING SYSTEMS INC (PA)
2000 Opportunity Dr Ste 140 (95678-3020)
PHONE..................916 978-2888
Steve J Benjamin, *Pr*
Kerry Palmer, *
EMP: 150 **EST:** 1993

PRODUCTS & SERVICES SECTION   **1752 - Floor Laying And Floor Work, Nec (P-2035)**

(P-2013)
RANCH HOUSE DOORS INC
Also Called: R H D
1527 Pomona Rd (92878-4359)
PHONE..................................951 278-2884
Michael James Neal, *CEO*
Cristian Neal, *
Sandra Neal, *
EMP: 70 **EST:** 1997
SQ FT: 33,000
SALES (est): 11.06MM **Privately Held**
Web: www.ranchhousedoors.com
SIC: 1751 Garage door, installation or erection

(P-2014)
RJP FRAMING INC
1139 Sibley St Ste 100 (95630-3572)
P.O. Box 5057 (95762-0001)
PHONE..................................916 941-3934
Laurie Payne, *Pr*
Robert Payne, *
EMP: 180 **EST:** 2004
SALES (est): 24.42MM **Privately Held**
Web: www.rjpframing.com
SIC: 1751 Framing contractor

(P-2015)
ROCKY COAST BUILDERS INC
135 Market Pl (92029-1353)
PHONE..................................760 489-7770
Douglas J Ladderbush, *CEO*
Cris Madsen, *
Amanda Kerins, *
EMP: 60 **EST:** 1979
SQ FT: 6,200
SALES (est): 13.17MM **Privately Held**
Web: www.rockycoastbuilders.com
SIC: 1751 Framing contractor

(P-2016)
ROY E WHITEHEAD INC
Also Called: Rew
2245 Via Cerro (92509-2412)
PHONE..................................951 682-1490
David Whitehead, *CEO*
Chris Bagley, *
Dan Gilley, *
Byron Mitchell, *
Dennis Whitehead, *
EMP: 75 **EST:** 1955
SQ FT: 36,000
SALES (est): 11.88MM **Privately Held**
Web: www.royewhitehead.com
SIC: 1751 Cabinet building and installation

(P-2017)
SHOOK & WALLER CNSTR INC
7677 Bell Rd Ste 101 (95492-7432)
PHONE..................................707 578-3933
Eddie Waller, *Pr*
Steven Shook, *
Shawn Dolan, *
EMP: 64 **EST:** 1980
SQ FT: 8,000
SALES (est): 10.95MM **Privately Held**
Web: www.shookandwaller.com
SIC: 1751 1521 1542 Framing contractor; New construction, single-family houses; Nonresidential construction, nec

(P-2018)
SR FREEMAN INC
2380 S Bascom Ave Ste 200 (95008-4389)
PHONE..................................408 364-2200
Shone Freeman, *Pr*
Josie Freeman, *
EMP: 60 **EST:** 1992
SALES (est): 17.79MM **Privately Held**
Web: www.srfreemaninc.com
SIC: 1751 Framing contractor

(P-2019)
STOCKHAM CONSTRUCTION INC
475 Portal St (94931-3006)
PHONE..................................707 664-0945
EMP: 450 **EST:** 1991
SQ FT: 15,301
SALES (est): 117.47MM **Privately Held**
Web: www.stockhamconstruction.com
SIC: 1751 1742 Lightweight steel framing (metal stud) installation; Drywall

(P-2020)
SURECRAFT SUPPLY INC
2875 Executive Pl (92029-1524)
EMP: 131
Web: www.surecraft.com
SIC: 1751 Carpentry work

(P-2021)
TAYLOR TRIM & SUPPLY INC
Also Called: Finish Carpentry
2342 Meyers Ave (92029-1008)
PHONE..................................760 740-2000
Timothy P Taylor, *CEO*
Sarah Garcia, *
Marlene Taylor, *
▲ **EMP:** 75 **EST:** 1990
SQ FT: 13,200
SALES (est): 15.75MM **Privately Held**
Web: www.taylortrim.com
SIC: 1751 Finish and trim carpentry

(P-2022)
TRIMCO FINISH INC
3130 W Harvard St (92704-3937)
PHONE..................................714 708-0300
EMP: 160
Web: www.trimcofinish.com
SIC: 1751 Finish and trim carpentry

(P-2023)
TWR ENTERPRISES INC
1661 Railroad St (92878-5003)
PHONE..................................951 279-2000
Thomas W Rhodes, *Pr*
EMP: 200 **EST:** 1985
SQ FT: 20,000
SALES (est): 19.94MM **Privately Held**
Web: www.twrframing.com
SIC: 1751 Framing contractor

(P-2024)
UNITED MARKETING GROUP INC
Also Called: Elite Gates
5957 S St Andrews Pl (90047-1308)
PHONE..................................323 778-4283
EMP: 95
SALES (corp-wide): 2.16MM **Privately Held**
SIC: 1751 Garage door, installation or erection
PA: United Marketing Group, Inc.
3226 Escollera Ave
Santa Rosa Valley CA
310 842-7453

(P-2025)
WALTERS & WOLF INTERIORS (PA)
41450 Boscell Rd (94538-3103)
PHONE..................................415 243-9400
Randall Alan Wolf, *CEO*
Michael Wolf, *
Jeff Belzer, *
▲ **EMP:** 80 **EST:** 1980
SQ FT: 30,000
SALES (est): 10.57MM
SALES (corp-wide): 10.57MM **Privately Held**
Web: interiors.waltersandwolf.com
SIC: 1751 Carpentry work

(P-2026)
WESLAR INC
28310 Constellation Rd (91355-5078)
PHONE..................................661 702-1362
Larry Kern, *Pr*
Wes Toy, *
EMP: 100 **EST:** 1981
SQ FT: 5,500
SALES (est): 4.11MM **Privately Held**
SIC: 1751 Framing contractor

(P-2027)
WIN-DOR INC (PA)
450 Delta Ave (92821-2935)
PHONE..................................714 576-2030
TOLL FREE: 800
Gary Templin, *CEO*
Wolfgang Wirthgen, *
EMP: 170 **EST:** 1994
SQ FT: 73,000
SALES (est): 46.75MM **Privately Held**
Web: www.windorsystems.com
SIC: 1751 3446 Window and door (prefabricated) installation; Guards, made from pipe

(P-2028)
X-ACT FINISH & TRIM INC
248 Glider Cir (92878-5033)
PHONE..................................951 582-9229
Jessie A Moreno, *Pr*
EMP: 60 **EST:** 2003
SALES (est): 10.28MM **Privately Held**
Web: www.xactfinish.com
SIC: 1751 Finish and trim carpentry

1752 Floor Laying And Floor Work, Nec

(P-2029)
B T MANCINI CO INC (PA)
Also Called: B.T. Mancini Company
876 S Milpitas Blvd (95035-6311)
P.O. Box 361930 (95036-1930)
PHONE..................................408 942-7900
Brooks T Mancini Junior, *Pr*
Brooks T Mancini Junior, *Pr*
Brooks T Mancini Senior, *VP*
David B Roddick, *
Tom Mcgovern, *VP*
▲ **EMP:** 100 **EST:** 1964
SQ FT: 36,000
SALES (est): 51.63MM
SALES (corp-wide): 51.63MM **Privately Held**
Web: www.btmancini.com
SIC: 1752 1761 Wood floor installation and refinishing; Roofing, siding, and sheetmetal work

(P-2030)
CREATIVE DESIGN INTERIORS INC (PA)
Also Called: C D I
737 Del Paso Rd (95834-1106)
PHONE..................................916 641-1121
Ronald Lapp, *Pr*
Kathy Lapp, *
EMP: 100 **EST:** 1991
SQ FT: 10,000
SALES (est): 22.8MM **Privately Held**
SIC: 1752 Ceramic floor tile installation

(P-2031)
DFS FLOORING INC (PA)
15651 Saticoy St (91406-3234)
PHONE..................................818 374-5200
Richard Friedman, *CEO*
Greg Keyes, *
EMP: 65 **EST:** 1986
SQ FT: 19,865
SALES (est): 26.6MM
SALES (corp-wide): 26.6MM **Privately Held**
Web: www.dfsflooring.com
SIC: 1752 Wood floor installation and refinishing

(P-2032)
H V WELKER CO INC
Also Called: Welker Bros
970 S Milpitas Blvd (95035-6323)
PHONE..................................408 263-4400
Stuart Welker, *Pr*
Stuart H Welker, *
Vincent A Grana, *
Timothy C Reynolds, *
Jack Sanguinitti, *
EMP: 65 **EST:** 1954
SQ FT: 18,375
SALES (est): 22.85MM **Privately Held**
Web: www.welkers.com
SIC: 1752 Floor laying and floor work, nec

(P-2033)
HOEM & ASSOCIATES INC
951 Linden Ave (94080-1753)
PHONE..................................650 871-5194
Russell William Hoem, *CEO*
Sean Hogan, *
Mike Valerio, *
EMP: 115 **EST:** 1937
SQ FT: 24,000
SALES (est): 54MM **Privately Held**
Web: www.hoemassociates.com
SIC: 1752 Carpet laying

(P-2034)
HOME CARPET INVESTMENT INC (PA)
Also Called: Americas Finest Carpet Company
730 Design Ct Ste 401 (91911-6160)
PHONE..................................619 262-8040
Carlos Ledesma, *CEO*
EMP: 81 **EST:** 1998
SQ FT: 2,500
SALES (est): 22.39MM **Privately Held**
Web: www.americasfinestcarpet.com
SIC: 1752 7217 Carpet laying; Carpet and upholstery cleaning

(P-2035)
HY-TECH TILE INC
1130 Palmyrita Ave Ste 350 (92507-1706)
P.O. Box 5577 (92517-5577)
PHONE..................................951 788-0550
Brian Lyman, *Pr*
Tom Shoemaker, *
Cristina Olteanu, *
Narcis Postolache, *
EMP: 110 **EST:** 1994
SQ FT: 12,000
SALES (est): 16.37MM **Privately Held**
Web: www.hytechtile.com

(PA)=Parent Co (HQ)=Headquarters
✪ = New Business established in last 2 years

1752 - Floor Laying And Floor Work, Nec (P-2036)

SIC: 1752 1743 Ceramic floor tile installation ; Terrazzo, tile, marble and mosaic work

(P-2036)
INTERIOR SPECIALISTS INC
Also Called: Interior Logic Group HM Rmdlg
18565 Jamboree Rd Ste 125 (92612-2543)
PHONE.................................800 959-8333
EMP: 274
SALES (corp-wide): 499.75MM **Privately Held**
Web: www.interiorlogicgroup.com
SIC: 1752 Carpet laying
HQ: Interior Specialists, Inc.
  1630 Faraday Ave
  Carlsbad CA
  760 929-6700

(P-2037)
INTERIOR SPECIALISTS INC (HQ)
1630 Faraday Ave (92008-7463)
P.O. Box 61929 (92602-6064)
PHONE.................................760 929-6700
Alan Davenport, *Pr*
Robert Hess, *CFO*
Dennis Crowley, *VP Opers*
Pat Crowley, *NAT'L SLS*
Randy Bafus, *VP Sls*
▲ **EMP:** 75 **EST:** 1985
SALES (est): 499.75MM
SALES (corp-wide): 499.75MM **Privately Held**
Web: www.interiorlogicgroup.com
SIC: 1752 1799 Carpet laying; Drapery track installation
PA: Faraday Holdings, Llc
  1630 Faraday Ave
  Carlsbad CA
  760 929-6700

(P-2038)
J W FLOOR COVERING INC (PA)
Also Called: J. W. Floor Covering
9881 Carroll Centre Rd (92126-4554)
PHONE.................................858 536-8565
John Wallace, *Owner*
John S Wallace, *
Gary Grado, *
EMP: 140 **EST:** 1983
SQ FT: 20,500
SALES (est): 48.9MM
SALES (corp-wide): 48.9MM **Privately Held**
Web: www.jwfloors.com
SIC: 1752 Floor laying and floor work, nec

(P-2039)
SIMAS FLOOR CO INC (PA)
Also Called: Simas Floor Co Design Center
3550 Power Inn Rd (95826-3892)
PHONE.................................916 452-4933
Ken Simas, *Pr*
David G Simas, *
John U Simas, *
EMP: 180 **EST:** 1951
SQ FT: 10,000
SALES (est): 23.3MM
SALES (corp-wide): 23.3MM **Privately Held**
Web: www.simasfloooranddesign.com
SIC: 1752 5713 Floor laying and floor work, nec; Floor covering stores

(P-2040)
VINTAGE DESIGN LLC (HQ)
25200 Commercentre Dr (92630-8810)
PHONE.................................949 900-5400
Timothy Patrick Buckley, *CEO*
EMP: 60 **EST:** 1986
SQ FT: 16,000
SALES (est): 53.89MM
SALES (corp-wide): 321MM **Privately Held**
Web: www.vintagedesigninc.com
SIC: 1752 Carpet laying
PA: Artisan Design Group, Llc
  3401 Olympus Blvd Ste 450
  Coppell TX
  682 324-9402

1761 Roofing, Siding, And Sheetmetal Work

(P-2041)
A PREMAN ROOFING INC
Also Called: A Preman Roofing
875 34th St (92102-3331)
PHONE.................................619 276-1700
Aaron Preman, *CEO*
EMP: 75 **EST:** 2003
SALES (est): 22.58MM **Privately Held**
Web: www.premanroofing.com
SIC: 1761 1711 Roofing contractor; Solar energy contractor

(P-2042)
AEP SPAN INC
2110 Enterprise Blvd (95691-3428)
PHONE.................................916 372-0933
Al Price, *Mgr*
EMP: 80 **EST:** 2001
SQ FT: 16,000
SALES (est): 1.11MM **Privately Held**
Web: www.ascprofiles.com
SIC: 1761 3448 3444 3443 Roofing contractor; Prefabricated metal buildings and components; Sheet metalwork; Fabricated plate work (boiler shop)
HQ: Asc Profiles Llc
  2110 Enterprise Blvd
  West Sacramento CA
  916 376-2800

(P-2043)
ALL FAB PRCSION SHEETMETAL INC
1980 Senter Rd (95112-2603)
PHONE.................................408 279-1099
Son P Ho, *CEO*
Kelly T Ho, *
▲ **EMP:** 100 **EST:** 2000
SALES (est): 26.98MM **Privately Held**
Web: www.allfabprecision.com
SIC: 1761 3444 Sheet metal work, nec; Sheet metalwork

(P-2044)
BEST CONTRACTING SERVICES INC
4301 Bettencourt Way (94587-1519)
PHONE.................................510 886-7240
Mohmmad Beigi, *Brnch Mgr*
EMP: 100
SALES (corp-wide): 120.29MM **Privately Held**
Web: www.bestcontracting.com
SIC: 1761 Roofing contractor
PA: Best Contracting Services, Inc.
  19027 S Hamilton Ave
  Gardena CA
  310 328-9176

(P-2045)
BEST CONTRACTING SERVICES INC (PA)
Also Called: Construction
19027 S Hamilton Ave (90248-4408)
PHONE.................................310 328-9176
Sean Tabazadeh, *CEO*
Modjtaba Tabazadeh, *
Fatemeh Tabazadeh, *
▲ **EMP:** 400 **EST:** 1982
SQ FT: 57,000
SALES (est): 120.29MM
SALES (corp-wide): 120.29MM **Privately Held**
Web: www.bestcontracting.com
SIC: 1761 Roofing contractor

(P-2046)
BIGHAM TAYLOR ROOFING CORP
22721 Alice St (94541-6401)
PHONE.................................510 886-0197
Stephen E Bigham, *CEO*
Don Taylor, *
Laura Jo Bigham, *
▲ **EMP:** 70 **EST:** 1977
SQ FT: 10,000
SALES (est): 22.2MM **Privately Held**
Web: www.btroof.com
SIC: 1761 Roofing contractor

(P-2047)
BLIGH ROOF CO
Also Called: Bligh Pacific
11043 Forest Pl (90670-3905)
P.O. Box 3083 (90670-0083)
PHONE.................................562 944-9753
EMP: 75 **EST:** 1976
SALES (est): 8.05MM **Privately Held**
Web: www.bligh.
SIC: 1761 Roofing contractor

(P-2048)
BLUES ROOFING CO
182 Topaz St (95035-5429)
PHONE.................................408 240-0680
EMP: 70 **EST:** 1973
SALES (est): 10.1MM **Privately Held**
Web: www.bluesroofing.com
SIC: 1761 Roofing contractor

(P-2049)
BYERS ENTERPRISES INC
Also Called: Byers Leafguard Gutter Systems
11773 Slow Poke Ln (95945-8417)
PHONE.................................530 272-7777
Raymond W Byers Senior, *CEO*
EMP: 69 **EST:** 1988
SQ FT: 2,400
SALES (est): 18.94MM **Privately Held**
Web: www.thatsbyers.com
SIC: 1761 Gutter and downspout contractor

(P-2050)
CHALLENGER SHEET METAL INC
9353 Abraham Way Ste A (92071-5641)
PHONE.................................619 596-8040
Joel Quinonez, *CEO*
Robert Basso, *
▲ **EMP:** 80 **EST:** 1987
SQ FT: 18,000
SALES (est): 18.62MM **Privately Held**
Web: www.challengersm.com
SIC: 1761 Sheet metal work, nec

(P-2051)
CLAUD TOWNSLEY INC
Also Called: Central Roofing Company
555 W 182nd St (90248-3400)
PHONE.................................310 527-6770
William E Knapp, *Pr*
Jonathan Townsley, *
Janet Townsley, *
EMP: 60 **EST:** 1992
SQ FT: 12,000
SALES (est): 10.31MM **Privately Held**
Web: www.centralroof.com
SIC: 1761 Roofing contractor

(P-2052)
CMF INC
Also Called: Custom Metal Fabricators
1317 W Grove Ave (92865-4137)
PHONE.................................714 637-2409
David Duclett, *CEO*
Mark Allen, *
Darren Sagert, *
EMP: 100 **EST:** 1956
SQ FT: 11,000
SALES (est): 31.58MM **Privately Held**
Web: www.cmfinc.com
SIC: 1761 Sheet metal work, nec

(P-2053)
COMMERCIAL INDUS ROOFG CO INC
Also Called: C & I
9239 Olive Dr (91977-2306)
PHONE.................................619 465-3737
TOLL FREE: 800
Barry Turnour, *Pr*
EMP: 60 **EST:** 1986
SQ FT: 4,500
SALES (est): 13.48MM **Privately Held**
Web: www.ciroofing.com
SIC: 1761 Roofing contractor

(P-2054)
COOL ROOFING SYSTEMS INC
1286 Dupont Ct (95336-6003)
PHONE.................................209 825-0818
EMP: 77
Web: www.cool-roofing.com
SIC: 1761 Roofing contractor

(P-2055)
D7 ROOFING SERVICES INC
Also Called: D7 Roofing Services
2851 Gold Tailings Ct (95670-6189)
PHONE.................................916 447-2175
Jeffrey Lyn Williamson, *CEO*
James J English Junior, *VP*
EMP: 70 **EST:** 1997
SQ FT: 15,000
SALES (est): 10.29MM **Privately Held**
Web: www.d7roofing.com
SIC: 1761 Roofing contractor

(P-2056)
DANNY LETNER INC
Also Called: Letner Roofing Company
1490 N Glassell St (92867-3612)
PHONE.................................714 633-0030
EMP: 230 **EST:** 1957
SALES (est): 62.43MM **Privately Held**
Web: www.letner.com
SIC: 1761 Roofing contractor

(P-2057)
DRI COMMERCIAL CORPORATION
Also Called: D R I
2081 Business Center Dr Ste 195 (92612)
PHONE.................................949 266-1900
EMP: 159
Web: www.dricommercial.com
SIC: 1761 Roofing contractor

(P-2058)
DRI COMPANIES
2081 Business Center Dr Ste 195 (92612)
PHONE.................................949 266-1900

PRODUCTS & SERVICES SECTION
1761 - Roofing, Siding, And Sheetmetal Work (P-2082)

EMP: 264
Web: www.dricompanies.com
SIC: 1761 Roofing contractor

(P-2059)
DUKE PACIFIC INC
13950 Monte Vista Ave (91710-5535)
P.O. Box 1800 (91708-1800)
PHONE..................................909 591-0191
Gregory C Severson, Pr
Judith E Braaten, *
EMP: 100 EST: 1958
SQ FT: 10,000
SALES (est): 16.33MM Privately Held
Web: www.dukepacific.com
SIC: 1761 Roofing contractor

(P-2060)
DWAYNE NASH INDUSTRIES INC
Also Called: Kodiak Roofing & Waterproofing
8825 Washington Blvd Ste 100 (95678-6213)
PHONE..................................916 253-1900
Dwayne Nash, CEO
David Pope, *
▲ EMP: 250 EST: 1992
SQ FT: 23,617
SALES (est): 95.05MM Privately Held
Web: www.kodiakroofing.com
SIC: 1761 Roofing contractor

(P-2061)
EBERHARD
15220 Raymer St (91405-1016)
PHONE..................................818 782-4604
Brian Lee Mowatt, CEO
Dave Stefko, Sr VP
EMP: 150 EST: 1976
SALES (est): 23.61MM Privately Held
Web: www.eberhardco.com
SIC: 1761 1799 Roofing contractor; Waterproofing

(P-2062)
EDJE-ENTERPRISES
18500 Pasadena St Ste B (92530-2775)
PHONE..................................951 245-7070
Edward Joseph Jennen, CEO
Maryjane Jennen, *
EMP: 82 EST: 2006
SALES (est): 7.9MM Privately Held
Web: www.edje-enterprises.com
SIC: 1761 Architectural sheet metal work

(P-2063)
ENTERPRISE ROOFING SERVICE INC
2400 Bates Ave (94520-1217)
P.O. Box 5130 (94524-0130)
PHONE..................................925 689-8100
Lawrence T Reardon, Pr
Aubrey Shehorn, *
Lynda She Horn, *
Steven L Reardon, *
EMP: 80 EST: 1960
SQ FT: 1,200
SALES (est): 15.35MM Privately Held
Web: www.enterpriseroofing.com
SIC: 1761 Roofing contractor

(P-2064)
FLAHERTY BROTHERS CNSTR INC
3470 Fostoria Way Ste D (94526-5572)
PHONE..................................650 268-9779
David Flaherty, Pr
David Flaherty, CEO
EMP: 60 EST: 2010

SALES (est): 4.87MM Privately Held
Web: www.flahertybc.com
SIC: 1761 1542 Roofing contractor; Commercial and office building contractors

(P-2065)
FOUR CS SERVICE INC
1560 H St (93721-1616)
PHONE..................................559 237-3990
Preston Cross, CEO
Graydon Cross, *
EMP: 70 EST: 1974
SQ FT: 22,500
SALES (est): 7.74MM Privately Held
Web: www.fourcsmetal.com
SIC: 1761 Sheet metal work, nec

(P-2066)
FRESNO ROOFING CO INC
5950 E Olive Ave (93727-2710)
P.O. Box 7676 (93747-7676)
PHONE..................................559 255-8377
Scott Logan Raypholtz, CEO
Michael Raypholtz, *
EMP: 60 EST: 1953
SQ FT: 23,746
SALES (est): 6.12MM Privately Held
Web: www.fresnoroofingco.net
SIC: 1761 Roofing contractor

(P-2067)
HARBERT ROOFING INC
19799 Hirsch Ct (96007-4945)
PHONE..................................530 223-3251
Harbert W Harbert, Pr
EMP: 64 EST: 1980
SQ FT: 20,000
SALES (est): 10MM Privately Held
Web: www.harbertroofing.com
SIC: 1761 Roofing contractor

(P-2068)
HERBERT MALARKEY ROOFING CO
9301 Garfield Ave (90280-3804)
PHONE..................................562 806-8000
John Stromme, Mgr
EMP: 72
Web: www.malarkeyroofing.com
SIC: 1761 Roofing contractor
HQ: Herbert Malarkey Roofing Company
3131 N Columbia Blvd
Portland OR
503 283-1191

(P-2069)
HOWARD ROOFING COMPANY INC
245 N Mountain View Ave (91767-5629)
PHONE..................................909 622-5598
Larry K Malekow, Pr
Ron A Malekow, *
Mitch T Caldwell, *
EMP: 70 EST: 1977
SQ FT: 27,000
SALES (est): 7.4MM Privately Held
Web: www.howardroofing.com
SIC: 1761 Roofing contractor

(P-2070)
JM ROOFING COMPANY INC
Also Called: Action Roofing
534 E Ortega St (93103-3016)
PHONE..................................805 966-3696
John J Martin Junior, Pr
Peggy Martin, *
Steve Martin, *
Sharon Fritz, *
EMP: 70 EST: 1985

SQ FT: 5,000
SALES (est): 10.57MM Privately Held
Web: www.aroofing.com
SIC: 1761 Roofing contractor

(P-2071)
LA ROCQUE BETTER ROOFS INC
9077 Arrow Rte Ste 100 (91730-4430)
PHONE..................................909 476-2699
Guy D Larocque, Pr
Linda Robinson, *
EMP: 75 EST: 1984
SALES (est): 4.33MM Privately Held
Web: www.larocquebetterroofs.com
SIC: 1761 Roofing contractor

(P-2072)
LAWSON ROOFING CO INC
1495 Tennessee St (94107-3420)
PHONE..................................415 285-1661
Frank E Lawson Senior, Ch Bd
Frank E Lawson Junior, Pr
Richard J Lawson, *
EMP: 70 EST: 1907
SQ FT: 10,000
SALES (est): 11.35MM Privately Held
Web: www.lawsonroofing.com
SIC: 1761 1799 Roofing contractor; Waterproofing

(P-2073)
LEONARD ROOFING INC
43280 Business Park Dr Ste 107 (92590-3676)
PHONE..................................951 506-3811
Bruce S Leonard, Pr
▲ EMP: 98 EST: 2004
SALES (est): 15.82MM Privately Held
SIC: 1761 Roofing contractor

(P-2074)
MASS PRECISION INC
2070 Oakland Rd (95131-1608)
PHONE..................................408 786-0378
EMP: 95
SALES (corp-wide): 88.61MM Privately Held
Web: www.massprecision.com
SIC: 1761 Sheet metal work, nec
PA: Mass Precision, Inc.
2110 Oakland Rd
San Jose CA
408 954-0200

(P-2075)
PACIFIC STRUCFRAME LLC
1600 Chicago Ave Ste R11 (92507-2040)
PHONE..................................951 405-8536
John B Hanna, Pr
EMP: 91 EST: 2017
SQ FT: 2,000
SALES (est): 4.73MM Privately Held
Web: www.pacificstrucframe.com
SIC: 1761 Roofing, siding, and sheetmetal work

(P-2076)
PERFORMANCE SHEETS LLC
440 Baldwin Park Blvd (91746-1407)
PHONE..................................626 333-0195
Mike Crosson, Pr
Michael Feterik, Managing Member*
Greg Hall, Managing Member*
Forest Felvey, *
▲ EMP: 125 EST: 2006
SALES (est): 24.56MM Privately Held
Web: www.performancesheets.net

SIC: 1761 Sheet metal work, nec
HQ: Smurfit Kappa North America Llc
125 E John Carpenter Fwy
Irving TX
800 306-8326

(P-2077)
PETERSEN-DEAN COMMERCIAL INC
Also Called: Petersendean
1705 Enterprise Dr (94533-5801)
PHONE..................................707 469-7470
James Petersen, Pr
David V Beek, *
EMP: 127 EST: 2003
SALES (est): 1.67MM Privately Held
SIC: 1761 1711 Roofing contractor; Solar energy contractor
PA: Petersen-Dean, Inc.
6950 Preston Ave
Livermore CA

(P-2078)
PLATINUM ROOFING INC
11500 W Olympic Blvd Ste 530 (90064-1509)
PHONE..................................408 280-5028
Bill Shevlin, CEO
Sean Marzola, *
EMP: 80 EST: 2000
SALES (est): 13.56MM Privately Held
Web: www.platinumroofinginc.com
SIC: 1761 Roofing contractor

(P-2079)
R2G ENTERPRISES INC
Also Called: Advanced Fabrication Tech
31154 San Benito St (94544-7912)
PHONE..................................510 489-6218
Stephen Green, Pr
EMP: 65 EST: 2004
SALES (est): 4.15MM Privately Held
SIC: 1761 Sheet metal work, nec

(P-2080)
RED POINTE ROOFING LP (PA)
1814 N Neville St (92865-4216)
PHONE..................................714 685-0010
Aaron Martin, Pt
John Patterson, Pt
Sean Brophy, Pt
EMP: 83 EST: 2013
SALES (est): 24.96MM
SALES (corp-wide): 24.96MM Privately Held
Web: www.redpointeroofing.com
SIC: 1761 Roofing contractor

(P-2081)
REGAN ROOFING INC
Also Called: Commercial Rsdntial Rofg Contr
2420 Industry St Ste B (92054-4878)
PHONE..................................855 652-4050
Patrick Regan, Pr
Kelly Regan, *
EMP: 60 EST: 2012
SALES (est): 10.33MM Privately Held
Web: www.regan-roofing.com
SIC: 1761 Roofing contractor

(P-2082)
ROOFING CONSTRUCTORS INC
Also Called: Western Roofing Service
15002 Wicks Blvd (94577-6600)
PHONE..................................415 648-6472
Mark F Santacrose, Prin
Dave Reginelli, Prin
John Nolan, *
Robert Ferrando, *
George O'neill, Sr VP

1761 - Roofing, Siding, And Sheetmetal Work (P-2083)

▼ EMP: 150 EST: 1951
SQ FT: 3,000
SALES (est): 26.5MM
SALES (corp-wide): 823.93MM Privately Held
Web: www.tectaamerica.com
SIC: 1761 Roofing contractor
PA: Tecta America Corp.
  9450 Bryn Mawr Ave
  Rosemont IL
  847 581-3888

(P-2083)
ROYAL WESTLAKE ROOFING LLC
Also Called: Boral Industries
3093 Industry St Ste A (92054-4895)
PHONE..................760 967-0827
Jose Davila, Mgr
EMP: 122
SIC: 1761 Roofing contractor
HQ: Royal Westlake Roofing Llc
  2700 Post Oak Blvd # 1900
  Houston TX
  949 756-1605

(P-2084)
SBB ROOFING INC (PA)
Also Called: Bilt-Well Roofing & Mtl Co
3310 Verdugo Rd (90065-2845)
P.O. Box 65827 (90065-0827)
PHONE..................323 254-2888
Bruce Radenbaugh, Pr
Steven Radenbaugh, *
EMP: 180 EST: 1984
SQ FT: 5,000
SALES (est): 8.87MM
SALES (corp-wide): 8.87MM Privately Held
Web: www.biltwellroofing.com
SIC: 1761 Roofing contractor

(P-2085)
SONORAN ROOFING INC
4161 Citrus Ave (95677-4008)
PHONE..................916 624-1080
John Daly, CEO
Jim Pelton, *
EMP: 160 EST: 1991
SQ FT: 5,000
SALES (est): 7.57MM Privately Held
Web: www.sonoranroofing.com
SIC: 1761 Roofing contractor

(P-2086)
STATE ROOFING SYSTEMS INC
15444 Hesperian Blvd (94578-3959)
PHONE..................510 317-1477
Keith Symons, Pr
Jack White, *
EMP: 100 EST: 1981
SQ FT: 6,000
SALES (est): 21.07MM Privately Held
Web: www.stateroofingsystems.com
SIC: 1761 Roofing contractor

(P-2087)
T&C ROOFING INC
Also Called: Town & Country Roofing
2155 Elkins Way Ste H (94513-7365)
PHONE..................925 513-8463
Jeff Tamayo, Pr
Sara Tamayo, *
EMP: 75 EST: 1981
SQ FT: 5,000
SALES (est): 11.53MM Privately Held
Web: www.tcroof.com
SIC: 1761 Roofing contractor

(P-2088)
TECTA AMERICA SOUTHERN CAL INC
1217 E Wakeham Ave (92705-4145)
PHONE..................714 973-6233
Daniel L Klein, CEO
EMP: 60 EST: 2002
SALES (est): 9.73MM
SALES (corp-wide): 823.93MM Privately Held
Web: www.tectaamerica.com
SIC: 1761 Roofing contractor
PA: Tecta America Corp.
  9450 Bryn Mawr Ave
  Rosemont IL
  847 581-3888

(P-2089)
TINCO SHEET METAL INC
958 N Eastern Ave (90063-1308)
PHONE..................323 263-0511
Brian Powell, Pr
Michael Nevarez, *
Laura Nevarez, *
Jim Stock, *
▲ EMP: 250 EST: 2003
SQ FT: 18,000
SALES (est): 38MM Privately Held
Web: www.tincosheetmetal.com
SIC: 1761 Roofing contractor

(P-2090)
WATERPROOFING ASSOCIATES INC
Also Called: WATERPROOFING ASSOCIATES
1295 Norman Ave (95054-2027)
PHONE..................650 937-1299
EMP: 86 EST: 1991
SALES (est): 51.21MM Privately Held
Web: www.roofwa.com
SIC: 1761 1799 Roofing contractor; Waterproofing

(P-2091)
WESTERN PACIFIC ROOFING CORP
3462 E La Campana Way (92262-5416)
PHONE..................661 273-1336
EMP: 110
SALES (corp-wide): 11.21MM Privately Held
Web: www.westpacroof.com
SIC: 1761 1799 Roofing contractor; Waterproofing
PA: Western Pacific Roofing Corp.
  2229 E Avenue Q
  Palmdale CA
  661 273-1336

(P-2092)
WICKS SOLAR INC
2170 Hutton Rd Bldg A (93444-9717)
PHONE..................805 546-9056
Jared Bobb, CEO
Ryan Rae, *
Justin Wickersham, *
EMP: 68 EST: 2019
SALES (est): 3.59MM Privately Held
Web: www.wicksroofing.com
SIC: 1761 Roofing contractor

(P-2093)
ZIMMERMAN ROOFING INC
3675 R St (95816-6624)
P.O. Box 19056 (95819-0056)
PHONE..................916 454-3667
David Zimmerman, Pr
EMP: 65 EST: 1980

SQ FT: 5,500
SALES (est): 4.32MM Privately Held
Web: www.zimroof.com
SIC: 1761 Roofing contractor

1771 Concrete Work

(P-2094)
AMERICAN CONCRETE WASHOUTS INC
8620 Antelope North Rd (95843-3973)
PHONE..................916 496-2798
Michael Liston, Brnch Mgr
EMP: 69
SALES (corp-wide): 1.02MM Privately Held
Web: www.americanconcretewashouts.com
SIC: 1771 Concrete work
PA: American Concrete Washouts, Inc.
  7013 Folsom Auburn Rd
  Folsom CA
  916 990-0842

(P-2095)
ARCIERO BROTHERS INC
5614 E La Palma Ave (92807-2110)
PHONE..................714 238-6600
EMP: 130
SIC: 1771 Concrete repair

(P-2096)
B & M CONTRACTORS INC
4473 Cochran St (93063-3065)
PHONE..................805 581-5480
Dave Moore, Pr
Randall Bilsland, *
EMP: 70 EST: 2000
SALES (est): 4.51MM Privately Held
Web: www.bamconcrete.com
SIC: 1771 Concrete work

(P-2097)
BAYMARR CONSTRUCTORS INC
6950 Mcdivitt Dr (93313-2046)
P.O. Box 22074 (93390-2074)
PHONE..................661 395-1676
Eric Recktenwald, CEO
Jack Whitney, *
Pat Howes, *
EMP: 111 EST: 1988
SQ FT: 10,000
SALES (est): 18.24MM Privately Held
Web: www.baymarr.com
SIC: 1771 Concrete work

(P-2098)
BEDROCK COMPANY
2970 Myers St (92503-5524)
PHONE..................951 273-1931
Glenn E Jackson Junior, CEO
Carlene Jackson, Corporate Secretary*
EMP: 70 EST: 1993
SQ FT: 5,000
SALES (est): 18.26MM Privately Held
Web: www.thebedrockco.com
SIC: 1771 Concrete work

(P-2099)
BEN F SMITH INC
Also Called: Concrete Construction
8655 Miramar Pl Ste B (92121-2567)
PHONE..................858 271-4320
Stuart Shelton, Mgr
EMP: 180
SALES (corp-wide): 19.75MM Privately Held

Web: www.benfsmithinc.com
SIC: 1771 Concrete work
PA: Ben F. Smith, Inc.
  4420 Baldwin Ave
  El Monte CA
  626 444-2543

(P-2100)
BERKEL & COMPANY CONTRS INC
81 Langton St Unit 15 (94103-3960)
P.O. Box 335 (66012-0335)
PHONE..................415 495-3627
Brian Zuckerman, Mgr
EMP: 96
SALES (corp-wide): 150.13MM Privately Held
Web: www.berkelandcompany.com
SIC: 1771 Foundation and footing contractor
PA: Berkel & Company Contractors, Inc.
  2649 S 142nd St
  Bonner Springs KS
  913 422-5125

(P-2101)
BERKELEY CEMENT INC
1200 6th St (94710-1402)
PHONE..................510 525-8175
Ron Fadelli, CEO
Andy A Fadelli, *
Ronald M Fadelli, *
Scott Fadelli, *
EMP: 140 EST: 1947
SQ FT: 10,000
SALES (est): 85.24MM Privately Held
Web: www.bciconcrete.com
SIC: 1771 Concrete pumping

(P-2102)
BLAZONA CONCRETE CNSTR INC
525 Harbor Blvd Ste 10 (95691-2246)
PHONE..................916 375-8337
J Dennis Blazona, CEO
Karen Blazona, *
EMP: 102 EST: 1980
SALES (est): 42.22MM Privately Held
Web: www.blazona.biz
SIC: 1771 Concrete work

(P-2103)
CAL-WEST CONCRETE CUTTING INC
1153 Vanderbilt Cir (95337-6120)
P.O. Box 4460 (95337-0008)
PHONE..................209 823-2236
Rick Cissell, Mgr
EMP: 218
SALES (corp-wide): 23.85MM Privately Held
Web: www.calwestconcretecutting.com
SIC: 1771 Concrete work
PA: Cal-West Concrete Cutting, Inc.
  3000 Tara Ct
  Union City CA
  510 656-0253

(P-2104)
CASEY-FOGLI CON CONTRS INC (PA)
1970 National Ave (94545-1710)
PHONE..................510 887-0837
Vincent Ippolito, CEO
EMP: 99 EST: 1968
SQ FT: 4,000
SALES (est): 12.79MM
SALES (corp-wide): 12.79MM Privately Held
Web: www.caseyfogli.com

PRODUCTS & SERVICES SECTION

1771 - Concrete Work (P-2128)

SIC: **1771** Concrete work

(P-2105)
CASPER COMPANY
3825 Bancroft Dr (91977-2122)
PHONE..................................619 589-6001
Roger Casper, *CEO*
William R Haithcock, *
Ken S Ringer, *
Greg T Casper, *
Steven Casper, *
EMP: 143 EST: 1984
SQ FT: 6,000
SALES (est): 48.02MM **Privately Held**
Web: www.caspercompany.com
SIC: **1771** Concrete work

(P-2106)
CELL-CRETE CORPORATION (PA)
Also Called: Cell-Crete
135 Railroad Ave (91016-4652)
PHONE..................................626 357-3500
EMP: 80 EST: 1965
SALES (est): 92.86MM
SALES (corp-wide): 92.86MM **Privately Held**
Web: www.cell-crete.com
SIC: **1771** Flooring contractor

(P-2107)
CEMENT CUTTING INC
3610 Hancock St Frnt (92110-4335)
PHONE..................................619 296-9592
Harold O Grafton, *CEO*
John Gregory Becker, *
Steven Morgan, *
Steve Quinn, *
EMP: 80 EST: 1977
SQ FT: 7,000
SALES (est): 15.85MM **Privately Held**
Web: www.cementcutting.com
SIC: **1771** Concrete work

(P-2108)
CENTURY WEST CONCRETE INC
9782 Indiana Ave (92503-5563)
PHONE..................................951 712-4065
Esteban Damian C Diaz, *CEO*
EMP: 310 EST: 2014
SALES (est): 7.85MM **Privately Held**
Web: www.centurywestconcrete.com
SIC: **1771** Concrete work

(P-2109)
COFFMAN SPECIALTIES INC (PA)
9685 Via Excelencia Ste 200 (92126-7500)
PHONE..................................858 536-3100
Colleen Coffman, *Pr*
Kevin Coffman, *
EMP: 247 EST: 1990
SQ FT: 6,000
SALES (est): 125.39MM **Privately Held**
Web: www.coffmanspecialties.com
SIC: **1771** Concrete work

(P-2110)
CONCO COMPANIES
5141 Commercial Cir (94520-8523)
PHONE..................................303 996-9841
Matt Gonsalves, *Prin*
EMP: 96 EST: 2012
SALES (est): 5.26MM **Privately Held**
Web: www.conconow.com
SIC: **1771** Concrete work

(P-2111)
CONCRETE NORTH INC
10274 Iron Rock Way (95624-1355)
PHONE..................................209 745-7400
James Grimes, *CEO*
Kim Grimes, *
EMP: 75 EST: 2010
SALES (est): 28.94MM **Privately Held**
Web: www.concretenorth.net
SIC: **1771** Foundation and footing contractor

(P-2112)
CORNERSTONE CONCRETE INC
255 Benjamin Dr (92879-6509)
PHONE..................................951 279-2221
Matthew R Valente, *Prin*
EMP: 87 EST: 2011
SALES (est): 2.63MM **Privately Held**
Web: www.contractorsincollaboration.com
SIC: **1771** Concrete work

(P-2113)
D AND D CONCRETE CNSTR INC
Also Called: Construction
13795 Blaisdell Pl Ste 201 (92064-8896)
PHONE..................................858 748-5011
Dereck Leffler, *Pr*
Dereck Leffler, *Pr*
Diane Leffler, *
EMP: 60 EST: 1989
SQ FT: 2,500
SALES (est): 9.59MM **Privately Held**
SIC: **1771** Foundation and footing contractor

(P-2114)
DEMCON CONCRETE CONTRS INC
Also Called: Demcon Concrete Contractor
13795 Blaisdell Pl Ste 202 (92064-8896)
PHONE..................................858 748-5090
Derek Leffler, *Pr*
Edwin Stougton, *
Mike Wildley, *
Diane Leffler, *
EMP: 75 EST: 2000
SALES (est): 16.24MM **Privately Held**
Web: www.demcon.us
SIC: **1771** Concrete work

(P-2115)
DOLAN CONCRETE CONSTRUCTION
3045 Alfred St (95054-3303)
PHONE..................................408 869-3250
Leo A Gutierrez, *Pr*
Benjamin C Newsom, *
Robert F Dumesnil Junior, *VP*
Dolores E Dolan, *Stockholder*
EMP: 90 EST: 1954
SQ FT: 8,500
SALES (est): 23.45MM **Privately Held**
Web: www.dolanconcrete.com
SIC: **1771** Curb construction

(P-2116)
EKEDAL CONCRETE INC
19600 Fairchild Ste 123 (92612-2509)
PHONE..................................949 729-8082
Dave Ekedal, *Pr*
Ryan Ekedal, *
EMP: 100 EST: 1974
SALES (est): 8.28MM **Privately Held**
Web: www.ekedalconcrete.com
SIC: **1771** Concrete work

(P-2117)
ESAU CONCRETE INC
Also Called: Pcs Concrete & Masonry
101 Business Park Way (95301-9483)
PHONE..................................209 357-7601
Veryl Esau, *Pr*
Michael Seay, *
EMP: 100 EST: 1979
SALES (est): 16.67MM **Privately Held**
Web: www.pcsconcrete.net
SIC: **1771 1791 1531 1541** Concrete work; Concrete reinforcement, placing of; Warehouse construction

(P-2118)
FBD VANGUARD CONSTRUCTION INC
550 Greenville Rd (94550-9203)
PHONE..................................925 245-1300
Billie Sposeto, *Pr*
EMP: 120 EST: 2002
SALES (est): 26.31MM **Privately Held**
Web: www.vc-inc.net
SIC: **1771** Concrete work

(P-2119)
GENERAL PAVEMENT MANAGEMENT INC
Also Called: GPM
850 Lawrence Dr Ste 100 (91320-1508)
PHONE..................................805 933-0909
EMP: 85 EST: 1957
SALES (est): 23.13MM **Privately Held**
Web: www.gpmpavement.com
SIC: **1771 1721 1611** Blacktop (asphalt) work ; Pavement marking contractor; Surfacing and paving

(P-2120)
GINO/GIUSEPPE INC
Also Called: G & G Construction Co
700 Enterprise Ct (95301-9505)
PHONE..................................209 358-0556
Giusppe Castiglione, *CEO*
Giuseppe Castiglione, *
Gino Graziano, *
EMP: 250 EST: 1983
SQ FT: 7,600
SALES (est): 21.36MM **Privately Held**
SIC: **1771** Foundation and footing contractor

(P-2121)
GONSALVES & SANTUCCI INC
Also Called: Conco Cement Co
13052 Dahlia St (92337-6926)
PHONE..................................909 350-0474
Steve Gonzales, *Pr*
EMP: 475
SALES (corp-wide): 164.76MM **Privately Held**
Web: www.conconow.com
SIC: **1771** Concrete pumping
PA: Gonsalves & Santucci, Inc.
  5141 Commercial Cir
  Concord CA
  925 685-6799

(P-2122)
GRAHAM CONCRETE CNSTR INC
Also Called: Gcc
1323 Dayton Ave Ste 103 (93612-5869)
PHONE..................................559 292-6571
James Graham, *Pr*
Jason Graham, *
EMP: 75 EST: 1979
SQ FT: 10,000
SALES (est): 4.32MM **Privately Held**
Web: www.grahamconcrete.com
SIC: **1771** Concrete work

(P-2123)
GROUNDWORKS INC
2145 Elkins Way Ste C (94513-7363)
PHONE..................................925 513-0300
Bryan Lucay, *Pr*
Lalo Sanchez, *
EMP: 80 EST: 2002
SQ FT: 2,500
SALES (est): 3.59MM **Privately Held**
Web: www.gworksinc.com
SIC: **1771 1611 1629** Concrete work; Grading; Drainage system construction

(P-2124)
GUY YOCOM CONSTRUCTION INC
10712 E Mariposa Rd (95215-9595)
PHONE..................................951 284-3456
EMP: 194
SALES (corp-wide): 128.83MM **Privately Held**
Web: www.yocominc.com
SIC: **1771** Concrete work
PA: Guy Yocom Construction, Inc.
  3299 Horseless Carriage R
  Norco CA
  951 284-3456

(P-2125)
GUY YOCOM CONSTRUCTION INC (PA)
3299 Horseless Carriage Rd Ste H (92860-3604)
PHONE..................................951 284-3456
Guy W Yocom, *Prin*
Richard Majestic, *
Dave Kent, *
Greg Wilson, *
Shirley Kowalke, *
EMP: 212 EST: 1978
SQ FT: 41,000
SALES (est): 128.83MM
SALES (corp-wide): 128.83MM **Privately Held**
Web: www.yocominc.com
SIC: **1771** Concrete work

(P-2126)
HB PARKCO CONSTRUCTION INC (PA)
24795 State Highway 74 (92570-8759)
PHONE..................................714 567-4752
Brett D Behrns, *VP*
W Adrian Hoyle, *
Micheal Barry, *
EMP: 394 EST: 2002
SALES (est): 2.56K
SALES (corp-wide): 2.56K **Privately Held**
Web: www.hbparkco.com
SIC: **1771** Parking lot construction

(P-2127)
HEIDI CORPORATION
Also Called: Donald J Schefflers Cnstr
727 N Vernon Ave (91702-2232)
PHONE..................................626 333-6317
Donald J Scheffler, *Pr*
▲ **EMP: 75 EST: 1990**
SQ FT: 15,000
SALES (est): 10.39MM **Privately Held**
Web: www.donaldschefflerconstruction.com
SIC: **1771** Concrete work

(P-2128)
INLAND CC INC
Also Called: ICC
7010 Wyndham Hill Dr (92506-7506)
PHONE..................................909 355-1318

1771 - Concrete Work (P-2129)

Marvin Hawkins, CEO
Karen Hawkins, *
EMP: 150 **EST:** 1995
SALES (est): 22.78MM **Privately Held**
Web: www.inlandconcrete.net
SIC: 1771 Foundation and footing contractor

(P-2129)
JEZOWSKI & MARKEL CONTRS INC
749 N Poplar St (92868-1013)
PHONE 714 978-2222
Leonard Michael Barth, *Prin*
Joseph Dean, *
Dorothy Destefano, *
EMP: 145 **EST:** 1953
SQ FT: 4,500
SALES (est): 24.5MM **Privately Held**
Web: www.jmcontractors.com
SIC: 1771 Foundation and footing contractor

(P-2130)
JOHNSON WESTERN GUNITE COMPANY
940 Doolittle Dr (94577-1021)
PHONE 510 568-8112
EMP: 100
SIC: 1771 Gunite contractor

(P-2131)
JOSEPH J ALBANESE INC
851 Martin Ave (95050-2903)
P.O. Box 667 (95052-0667)
PHONE 408 727-5700
Phillip Albanese, *CEO*
EMP: 700 **EST:** 1955
SALES (est): 143MM **Privately Held**
Web: www.jjalbanese.com
SIC: 1771 Foundation and footing contractor

(P-2132)
JT WIMSATT CONTG CO INC (PA)
28064 Avenue Stanford Unit B (91355-1159)
PHONE 661 775-8090
John Ewing Wimsatt, *CEO*
John E Wimsatt Iii, *Pr*
Tricia Wimsatt, *
EMP: 270 **EST:** 1992
SALES (est): 63.72MM **Privately Held**
Web: www.jtwimsatt.com
SIC: 1771 Concrete work

(P-2133)
LARGO CONCRETE INC
1690 W Foothill Blvd Ste B (91786-8433)
PHONE 909 981-7844
Paul Burkel, *Prin*
EMP: 285
Web: www.largoconcrete.com
SIC: 1771 Concrete work
PA: Largo Concrete, Inc.
2741 Walnut Ave Ste 110
Tustin CA

(P-2134)
LARGO CONCRETE INC
891 W Hamilton Ave (95008-0402)
PHONE 408 874-2500
Ken Long, *Mgr*
EMP: 570
Web: www.largoconcrete.com
SIC: 1771 Concrete work
PA: Largo Concrete, Inc.
2741 Walnut Ave Ste 110
Tustin CA

(P-2135)
LARGO CONCRETE INC (PA)
2741 Walnut Ave Ste 110 (92780-7040)
PHONE 714 731-3600
EMP: 70 **EST:** 1989
SALES (est): 150.81MM **Privately Held**
Web: www.largoconcrete.com
SIC: 1771 Concrete work

(P-2136)
M F MAHER INC
Also Called: Maher M F Concrete Cnstr
490 Ryder St (94590-7217)
PHONE 707 552-2774
Malcolm F Maher, *Pr*
Ronald Maher, *
Janice K Maher, *
EMP: 70 **EST:** 1970
SQ FT: 4,000
SALES (est): 8.97MM **Privately Held**
Web: www.mfmaher.com
SIC: 1771 Concrete work

(P-2137)
MCCLONE CONSTRUCTION COMPANY
3880 El Dorado Hills Blvd (95762-4566)
PHONE 916 358-5495
William R Patterson, *Brnch Mgr*
EMP: 172
Web: www.mcclone.net
SIC: 1771 Concrete work
PA: Mcclone Construction Company
5170 Hillsdale Cir Ste B
El Dorado Hills CA

(P-2138)
MORLEY CONSTRUCTION COMPANY (HQ)
3330 Ocean Park Blvd (90405-3202)
PHONE 310 399-1600
Mark Benjamin, *Pr*
Mark Benjamin, *Ch Bd*
Bert Lewitt, *
Reginald Jackson, *
Tod Paris, *
▲ **EMP:** 80 **EST:** 1947
SQ FT: 20,000
SALES (est): 30.27MM
SALES (corp-wide): 92.7MM **Privately Held**
Web: www.morleyconcrete.com
SIC: 1771 1522 1542 Concrete work; Condominium construction; Commercial and office building, new construction
PA: Morley Builders, Inc.
3330 Ocean Park Blvd
Santa Monica CA
310 399-1600

(P-2139)
NED L WEBSTER CONCRETE CNSTR
8800 Grimes Canyon Rd (93021-9768)
PHONE 805 529-4900
Ned Webster, *Prin*
EMP: 75 **EST:** 2000
SALES (est): 4.49MM **Privately Held**
SIC: 1771 Concrete work

(P-2140)
NOAH CONCRETE CORPORATION
Also Called: Noah Concrete
5900 Rossi Ln (95020-7013)
PHONE 408 842-7211
Don Alvarez, *CEO*
▲ **EMP:** 60 **EST:** 1996
SALES (est): 10.71MM **Privately Held**
Web: www.noahconcretecorporation.com
SIC: 1771 Concrete work

(P-2141)
ODYSSEY LANDSCAPING CO INC
Also Called: Odyssey Environmental Services
5400 W Highway 12 (95242-9170)
PHONE 209 369-6197
Martin Gates, *Pr*
EMP: 80 **EST:** 1982
SQ FT: 2,400
SALES (est): 12.74MM **Privately Held**
Web: www.odysseylandscape.com
SIC: 1771 0781 Concrete work; Landscape architects

(P-2142)
PACIFIC PAVINGSTONE INC
Also Called: Pacific Outdoor Living
8309 Tujunga Ave Unit 201 (91352-3215)
PHONE 818 244-4000
Terry Morrill, *Pr*
Trent Morrill, *
Chad Morrill, *
EMP: 115 **EST:** 1999
SALES (est): 13.09MM **Privately Held**
Web: www.pacificpavingstone.com
SIC: 1771 Driveway contractor

(P-2143)
PACIFIC STHWEST STRUCTURES INC
7845 Lemon Grove Way Ste A (91945-1880)
PHONE 619 469-2323
Daniel Fitzgerald, *Pr*
EMP: 150 **EST:** 1995
SQ FT: 7,500
SALES (est): 14.6MM **Privately Held**
Web: www.pssiconcrete.com
SIC: 1771 Concrete work

(P-2144)
PACIFIC STRUCTURES SC INC (PA)
Also Called: Pacific Structures
1212 Abbot Kinney Blvd Apt A (90291-3366)
PHONE 415 970-5434
Ross Edwards, *Ch Bd*
David E Williams, *Pr*
Ron Marano, *CFO*
Eric Horn, *Treas*
Scott Brauninger, *Dir*
EMP: 249 **EST:** 2008
SALES (est): 50.65MM
SALES (corp-wide): 50.65MM **Privately Held**
Web: www.pacific-structures.com
SIC: 1771 Concrete work

(P-2145)
PECK & HILLER COMPANY
870 Napa Valley Corporate Way Ste A (94558)
PHONE 707 258-8000
Russell B Peck, *Prin*
Tom H O'connor, *VP*
Ben Kerr, *
EMP: 100 **EST:** 1949
SQ FT: 8,680
SALES (est): 19.07MM **Privately Held**
Web: www.peckandhiller.com
SIC: 1771 Foundation and footing contractor

(P-2146)
PENHALL COMPANY
Also Called: Penhall San Leandro 153
13750 Catalina St (94577-5502)
PHONE 510 357-8810
Scott Hustad, *Mgr*
EMP: 61
Web: www.penhall.com
SIC: 1771 Concrete work
HQ: Penhall Company
7501 Esters Blvd Ste 150
Irving TX

(P-2147)
PENHALL HOLDING COMPANY
1801 W Penhall Way (92801-6700)
PHONE 714 772-6450
Kathy Wall, *Sec*
EMP: 111 **EST:** 2010
SALES (est): 10.42MM **Privately Held**
Web: www.penhall.com
SIC: 1771 Concrete work

(P-2148)
PETERSON BROTHERS CNSTR INC
Also Called: Pbc Companies
2929 E White Star Ave (92806-2628)
PHONE 714 278-0488
Elden Peterson, *CEO*
Robert K Peterson, *
Patrick Burns, *
Mike Hoefnagels, *
Jack Saldate, *
▲ **EMP:** 600 **EST:** 1983
SALES (est): 66.72MM **Privately Held**
Web: www.pbccompanies.com
SIC: 1771 3531 1741 Concrete work; Pavers ; Concrete block masonry laying

(P-2149)
PRECISION EMPRISE INC
335 Beach Rd (94010-2005)
P.O. Box 8013 (94404-8013)
PHONE 650 867-8657
Victor S Nunnemaker, *Pr*
Joseph Fouret, *CEO*
EMP: 63 **EST:** 2005
SALES (est): 680.1K **Privately Held**
Web: www.pccnorcal.com
SIC: 1771 Curb and sidewalk contractors

(P-2150)
R E MAHER INC
4545 Hess Rd (94503-9727)
PHONE 707 642-3907
Rod E Maher, *CEO*
EMP: 95 **EST:** 1997
SQ FT: 1,000
SALES (est): 9.79MM **Privately Held**
Web: www.remaherinc.com
SIC: 1771 Foundation and footing contractor

(P-2151)
RESCUE CONCRETE INC
9275 Beatty Dr (95826-9702)
P.O. Box 276812 (95827-6812)
PHONE 916 852-2400
David Winn, *Pr*
EMP: 60 **EST:** 1995
SALES (est): 2.37MM **Privately Held**
Web: www.rescueconcrete.com
SIC: 1771 Concrete work

(P-2152)
RJS & ASSOCIATES INC
1675 Sabre St (94545-1013)
PHONE 510 670-9111
Travis Simmons, *CEO*

PRODUCTS & SERVICES SECTION

1781 - Water Well Drilling (P-2175)

Maxwell Simmons, *
EMP: 225 **EST:** 1994
SQ FT: 10,000
SALES (est): 49.99MM **Privately Held**
Web: www.rjsdesignbuild.com
SIC: 1771 1521 Foundation and footing contractor; Single-family housing construction

(P-2153)
ROBERT A BOTHMAN INC (PA)
Also Called: B & B Concrete
2690 Scott Blvd (95050-2511)
PHONE.................408 279-2277
Robert A Bothman, *CEO*
Robert A Bothman, *Prin*
James Moore, *
Brian Bothman, *
Andy Bothman, *
EMP: 95 **EST:** 1978
SQ FT: 20,000
SALES (est): 51.58MM
SALES (corp-wide): 51.58MM **Privately Held**
Web: www.devbothman.com
SIC: 1771 0782 Concrete work; Landscape contractors

(P-2154)
RON NURSS INC
Also Called: Blueline Construction
11290 Sunrise Park Dr Ste B (95742-6895)
PHONE.................916 631-9761
Ron Nurss, *Pr*
Darcy Nurss, *
EMP: 65 **EST:** 1985
SQ FT: 6,400
SALES (est): 4.15MM **Privately Held**
Web: www.blueline-construction.com
SIC: 1771 Concrete work

(P-2155)
SANTA ANA CREEK DEVELOPMENT COMPANY
Also Called: Mark Company
2288 N Batavia St (92865-3106)
PHONE.................714 685-3462
EMP: 100 **EST:** 1964
SALES (est): 16.91MM **Privately Held**
Web: www.themarkco.com
SIC: 1771 1611 1623 Concrete work; Grading; Pipeline construction, nsk

(P-2156)
SCI INC
Also Called: SCI
18501 Collier Ave Ste B106 (92530-2764)
PHONE.................951 245-7511
Mark A Dix, *
EMP: 65 **EST:** 1999
SQ FT: 3,000
SALES (est): 13MM **Privately Held**
Web: www.tiltupsbysci.com
SIC: 1771 Concrete work

(P-2157)
SERVICON SYSTEMS INC
3329 Jack Northrop Ave (90250-4426)
PHONE.................310 970-0700
Julio E Ramirez, *Brnch Mgr*
EMP: 1472
SALES (corp-wide): 83.82MM **Privately Held**
Web: www.servicon.com
SIC: 1771 Flooring contractor
PA: Servicon Systems, Inc.
3965 Landmark St
Culver City CA
310 204-5040

(P-2158)
SINCLAIR CONCRETE
7205 Church St (95663-9411)
PHONE.................916 663-0303
Keith Sinclair, *Sec*
Keith Sinclair, *Pr*
Karin Sinclair, *
EMP: 85 **EST:** 1982
SALES (est): 10.59MM **Privately Held**
Web: www.sinclairconcrete.com
SIC: 1771 Foundation and footing contractor

(P-2159)
SOUTHLAND PAVING INC
361 N Hale Ave (92029-1716)
PHONE.................760 747-6895
Richard Fleck, *CEO*
Daniel Devlin, *
Robert Kennedy, *
Anne Fleck, *
EMP: 75 **EST:** 1983
SQ FT: 35,000
SALES (est): 25.3MM **Privately Held**
Web: www.southlandpaving.com
SIC: 1771 2951 Blacktop (asphalt) work; Asphalt paving mixtures and blocks

(P-2160)
SOUTHWEST CONSTRUCTION CO INC
2909 Rainbow Valley Blvd (92028-8859)
PHONE.................760 728-4460
David Simon, *Pr*
Lorie Simon, *
Paul Simon, *
EMP: 60 **EST:** 1980
SQ FT: 5,000
SALES (est): 5.15MM **Privately Held**
Web: www.southwestconstructioncoinc.com
SIC: 1771 Concrete work

(P-2161)
STEFAN MERLI PLASTERING CO INC (PA)
Also Called: Merli Concrete Pumping
1230 W 130th St (90247-1502)
PHONE.................310 323-0404
Stefan R Merli, *Pr*
Gunther Merli, *
Adele Merli, *
EMP: 63 **EST:** 1958
SQ FT: 5,000
SALES (est): 18.23MM
SALES (corp-wide): 18.23MM **Privately Held**
SIC: 1771 Concrete pumping

(P-2162)
STRUCTRAL PRSRVTION SYSTEMS LL
11800 Monarch St (92841-2113)
PHONE.................714 891-9080
Mike Szoke, *Mgr*
EMP: 350
Web: www.structural.net
SIC: 1771 Concrete repair
HQ: Structural Preservation Systems, Llc
10150 Old Columbia Rd
Columbia MD

(P-2163)
SUPERIOR GUNITE (HQ)
12306 Van Nuys Blvd (91342-6049)
PHONE.................818 896-9199
Anthony L Federico, *Pr*
David Bowers, *
Steve Crawford, *
EMP: 145 **EST:** 1964
SQ FT: 5,000
SALES (est): 46.72MM
SALES (corp-wide): 3.79B **Publicly Held**
Web: www.shotcrete.com
SIC: 1771 Gunite contractor
PA: Tutor Perini Corporation
15901 Olden St
Rancho Cascades CA
818 362-8391

(P-2164)
TEAM C CONSTRUCTION
1272 Greenfield Dr (92021-3316)
PHONE.................619 579-6572
David Clarke, *Pr*
EMP: 70 **EST:** 1995
SQ FT: 2,000
SALES (est): 9.43MM **Privately Held**
Web: www.teamcconstruction.com
SIC: 1771 Concrete work

(P-2165)
TEAM FINISH INC
155 Arovista Cir Ste A (92821-3842)
PHONE.................714 671-9190
Thomas M Stangl, *Pr*
Mary Stangl, *
EMP: 80 **EST:** 1996
SQ FT: 1,200
SALES (est): 4.99MM **Privately Held**
SIC: 1771 Concrete work

(P-2166)
TERRY TUELL CONCRETE INC
287 W Fallbrook Ave Ste 105 (93711)
P.O. Box 3933 (93650-3933)
PHONE.................559 431-0812
Terry Tuell, *Pr*
Matthew Tuell, *
EMP: 90 **EST:** 1974
SQ FT: 3,000
SALES (est): 9.34MM **Privately Held**
Web: www.terrytuell.com
SIC: 1771 Concrete work

(P-2167)
UNITED BROTHERS CONCRETE INC
41905 Boardwalk Ste K (92211-9091)
PHONE.................760 346-1013
Lauro Barcenas, *Pr*
Luis Barcenas, *
Oscar Barcenas, *
EMP: 150 **EST:** 1999
SQ FT: 2,000
SALES (est): 24.2MM **Privately Held**
SIC: 1771 Concrete work

(P-2168)
URATA & SONS CONCRETE INC
3430 Luyung Dr (95742-6871)
PHONE.................916 638-5364
Charles Urata, *Pr*
Kelly Urata, *
John Bell, *
EMP: 125 **EST:** 1972
SQ FT: 10,000
SALES (est): 43.94MM **Privately Held**
Web: www.urataconcrete.com
SIC: 1771 Foundation and footing contractor

(P-2169)
URATA & SONS CONCRETE LLC
3430 Luyung Dr (95742-6871)
PHONE.................916 638-5364
Charles A Urata, *Managing Member*
EMP: 99 **EST:** 2018
SALES (est): 7.82MM **Privately Held**
Web: www.urataconcrete.com
SIC: 1771 Concrete work

(P-2170)
WAYNE E SWISHER CEM CONTR INC
2620 E 18th St (94509-7229)
PHONE.................925 757-3660
Wayne Swisher, *Pr*
Elma Swisher, *
EMP: 75 **EST:** 1970
SQ FT: 4,000
SALES (est): 12.62MM **Privately Held**
Web: www.swishercement.com
SIC: 1771 Foundation and footing contractor

(P-2171)
Z-BEST CONCRETE INC
2575 Main St (92501-2238)
PHONE.................951 774-1870
Roger Crott, *Pr*
Jerry Faust, *
EMP: 80 **EST:** 1989
SQ FT: 2,400
SALES (est): 12.41MM **Privately Held**
SIC: 1771 1741 Concrete work; Masonry and other stonework

1781 Water Well Drilling

(P-2172)
GREGG DRILLING LLC
2726 Walnut Ave (90755-1832)
PHONE.................562 427-6899
John Gregg, *Pr*
Patrick Keating, *
Chris Christensen, *
Sonja De Keyser-meurs, *Sec*
EMP: 160 **EST:** 2018
SQ FT: 17,000
SALES (est): 8MM **Privately Held**
Web: www.greggdrilling.com
SIC: 1781 Water well drilling

(P-2173)
KENAI DRILLING LIMITED
2651 Patton Way (93308-5745)
PHONE.................661 587-0117
Gene Kramer, *Brnch Mgr*
EMP: 131
Web: www.kenaidrilling.com
SIC: 1781 Servicing, water wells
PA: Kenai Drilling Limited
6430 Cat Canyon Rd
Santa Maria CA

(P-2174)
YELLOW JACKET DRLG SVCS LLC
9460 Lucas Ranch Rd (91730-5743)
PHONE.................909 989-8563
EMP: 126
SALES (corp-wide): 21.45MM **Privately Held**
Web: www.yellowjacketdrilling.com
SIC: 1781 Water well drilling
PA: Yellow Jacket Drilling Services, Llc
3922 E University Dr # 1
Phoenix AZ
602 453-3252

(P-2175)
ZIM INDUSTRIES INC
Bakersfield Well & Pump Co
7212 Fruitvale Ave (93308-9529)
PHONE.................661 393-9661
John Zimmerer, *Mgr*
EMP: 140
SALES (corp-wide): 40.49MM **Privately Held**
Web: www.zimindustries.com

SIC: 1781 7699 Servicing, water wells; Pumps and pumping equipment repair
PA: Zim Industries, Inc.
4532 E Jefferson Ave
Fresno CA
559 834-1551

1791 Structural Steel Erection

(P-2176)
ALLIED STEEL CO INC
1027 Palmyrita Ave (92507-1701)
PHONE..................951 241-7000
Brian P Chapman, *Pr*
Perry K Chapman, *
Nicky Chapman, *
Jeanette Chapman, *
EMP: 60 **EST:** 1944
SQ FT: 48,000
SALES (est): 11.13MM **Privately Held**
Web: www.alliedsteelco.com
SIC: 1791 3441 Structural steel erection; Fabricated structural metal

(P-2177)
ANVIL STEEL CORPORATION
Also Called: Anvil Iron
134 W 168th St (90248-2729)
PHONE..................310 329-5811
Gerry Bustrum, *CEO*
Paul Schifino, *
Mike Norton, *
▲ **EMP:** 90 **EST:** 1973
SQ FT: 4,000
SALES (est): 24.92MM **Privately Held**
Web: www.anvilsteel.com
SIC: 1791 Iron work, structural

(P-2178)
ARTIMEX IRON INC
315 Cypress Ln (92020-1695)
PHONE..................619 444-3155
EMP: 116 **EST:** 1973
SALES (est): 9.4MM **Privately Held**
Web: www.artimexiron.com
SIC: 1791 Iron work, structural

(P-2179)
BAJA CONSTRUCTION CO INC (PA)
223 Foster St (94553-1029)
P.O. Box 3080 (94553-8080)
PHONE..................925 229-0732
TOLL FREE: 800
Robert Hayworth, *Ch*
Robert J Hayworth, *
Brandon Morford, *
Laura Daum, *
Luis Fabian, *
EMP: 90 **EST:** 1981
SQ FT: 7,200
SALES (est): 26.82MM
SALES (corp-wide): 26.82MM **Privately Held**
Web: www.bajacarports.com
SIC: 1791 Structural steel erection

(P-2180)
BAPKO METAL INC
721 S Parker St Ste 300 (92868-4732)
PHONE..................714 639-9380
Fred Bagatourian, *Pr*
Heather Wiliams, *
Clint Rieber, *
EMP: 80 **EST:** 1978
SALES (est): 25.64MM **Privately Held**
Web: www.bapko.com
SIC: 1791 3441 Structural steel erection; Fabricated structural metal

(P-2181)
CAL-STATE STEEL CORPORATION
1397 Lynnmere Dr (91360-1946)
PHONE..................310 632-2772
Salvador Valenzuelam, *CEO*
Les Furdek, *
David Olson, *
▲ **EMP:** 150 **EST:** 1963
SQ FT: 10,000
SALES (est): 4.68MM **Privately Held**
Web: www.calstatesteel.com
SIC: 1791 Iron work, structural

(P-2182)
CALIFRNIA ERCTORS BAY AREA INC
4500 California Ct (94510-1021)
PHONE..................707 746-1990
David W Mceuen, *CEO*
Dennis Mc Euen, *
EMP: 61 **EST:** 1964
SQ FT: 16,000
SALES (est): 9.38MM **Privately Held**
Web: www.calerectors.com
SIC: 1791 Iron work, structural

(P-2183)
INTEGRITY REBAR PLACERS
1345 Nandina Ave (92571-9402)
PHONE..................951 696-6843
Kenneth Negrete, *Pr*
Richard Rabay, *
Mario Duran, *Prin*
▲ **EMP:** 200 **EST:** 2005
SALES (est): 21.23MM **Privately Held**
Web: www.integrityrebarplacers.com
SIC: 1791 Structural steel erection

(P-2184)
KCB TOWERS INC
27260 Meines St (92346-4223)
P.O. Box 100 (92346-0100)
PHONE..................909 862-0322
S Lynn Bogh, *CEO*
Miles Bogh, *
Sharon Bogh, *
EMP: 100 **EST:** 1982
SQ FT: 12,000
SALES (est): 18.1MM **Privately Held**
Web: www.kcbtowers.com
SIC: 1791 3441 Concrete reinforcement, placing of; Fabricated structural metal

(P-2185)
KWAN WO IRONWORKS INC
31628 Hayman St (94544-7122)
PHONE..................415 822-9628
Florence Kong, *Pr*
▲ **EMP:** 120 **EST:** 1992
SQ FT: 32,000
SALES (est): 24.92MM **Privately Held**
Web: www.kwanwo.com
SIC: 1791 5051 Iron work, structural; Metals service centers and offices

(P-2186)
LEGACY REINFORCING STEEL LLC
1057 Tierra Del Rey Ste F (91910-7882)
PHONE..................619 646-0205
Brian Briggs, *Pr*
EMP: 75 **EST:** 2019
SALES (est): 2.65MM **Privately Held**
SIC: 1791 3449 Structural steel erection; Bars, concrete reinforcing: fabricated steel

(P-2187)
M BAR C CONSTRUCTION INC
1770 La Costa Meadows Dr (92078-5106)
PHONE..................760 744-4131
Michael Jason Ianni, *CEO*
EMP: 85 **EST:** 2005
SALES (est): 41.41MM **Privately Held**
Web: www.mbarconline.com
SIC: 1791 1623 Structural steel erection; Electric power line construction

(P-2188)
MARTINEZ STEEL CORPORATION
1500 S Haven Ave Ste 150 (91761-2971)
PHONE..................909 946-0686
Harry Williams, *CEO*
Debbie Martinez, *
Joe Martinez, *
EMP: 200 **EST:** 1994
SALES (est): 22.13MM **Privately Held**
Web: www.martinezsteel.com
SIC: 1791 Structural steel erection

(P-2189)
MARTINEZ STEEL INC
8920 Vernon Ave Ste 128 (91763-1663)
PHONE..................909 946-0686
EMP: 60 **EST:** 1994
SQ FT: 852
SALES (est): 2.54MM **Privately Held**
Web: www.martinezsteel.com
SIC: 1791 Concrete reinforcement, placing of

(P-2190)
MID STATE STEEL ERECTION (PA)
1916 Cherokee Rd (95205-2721)
PHONE..................209 464-9497
Jerry Shipman, *Pr*
Patty Shipman, *
EMP: 70 **EST:** 1978
SALES (est): 9.57MM
SALES (corp-wide): 9.57MM **Privately Held**
Web: www.midstatesteel.net
SIC: 1791 Structural steel erection

(P-2191)
MILLENNIUM REINFORCING INC
1046 Calle Recodo (92673-6261)
P.O. Box 73698 (92673-0124)
PHONE..................949 361-9730
Matthew Taylor, *CEO*
EMP: 265 **EST:** 2009
SALES (est): 8.58MM **Privately Held**
Web: www.millenniumreinforcing.com
SIC: 1791 Structural steel erection

(P-2192)
NEHEMIAH REBAR SERVICES INC
4110 Business Dr Ste B (95682-7268)
P.O. Box 2149 (95682-2149)
PHONE..................530 676-6310
Kevin W Rhodes, *Pr*
Kevin W Rhodes, *CEO*
EMP: 150 **EST:** 2004
SALES (est): 30.35MM **Privately Held**
Web: www.nehemiahrebar.com
SIC: 1791 Structural steel erection

(P-2193)
PJS LUMBER INC
Also Called: P.J.'s Rebar
250 D St (95380-5431)
PHONE..................209 850-9444
Shane Mcmillan, *Prin*

EMP: 60 **EST:** 2017
SALES (est): 2.18MM **Privately Held**
SIC: 1791 Structural steel erection

(P-2194)
QUALITY ERECTORS CNSTR CO INC
Also Called: Quality Erectors & Cnstr Co
3130 Bayshore Rd (94510-1232)
PHONE..................707 746-1233
Jesse Esquivel, *Pr*
Jesse Esquivel, *
Karen Anne Esquivel, *
EMP: 60 **EST:** 1980
SALES (est): 17.25MM **Privately Held**
Web: www.qec-inc.com
SIC: 1791 1761 Structural steel erection; Sheet metal work, nec

(P-2195)
QUALITY REINFORCING INC
13275 Gregg St (92064-7120)
PHONE..................858 748-8400
Bryan Miller, *Pr*
▲ **EMP:** 85 **EST:** 1987
SQ FT: 5,000
SALES (est): 9.85MM **Privately Held**
Web: www.qualityreinforcing.com
SIC: 1791 Concrete reinforcement, placing of

(P-2196)
R & B REINFORCING STEEL CORP
13581 5th St (91710-5166)
PHONE..................909 591-1726
David Mcdaniel, *CEO*
Robert Bessette, *
Nancy Bessette, *
EMP: 80 **EST:** 1983
SQ FT: 30,000
SALES (est): 9.24MM **Privately Held**
Web: www.rbsteel.net
SIC: 1791 Iron work, structural

(P-2197)
REBAR ENGINEERING INC
10706 Painter Ave (90670-4581)
P.O. Box 3986 (90670-1986)
PHONE..................562 946-2461
Charles L Krebs, *Pr*
Jack Garroutte, *
EMP: 250 **EST:** 1963
SQ FT: 6,500
SALES (est): 34.55MM **Privately Held**
Web: www.rebarengineering.com
SIC: 1791 Concrete reinforcement, placing of

(P-2198)
RIKA CORPORATION
Also Called: Diversified Metal Works
332 W Brenna Ln (92867-5637)
PHONE..................949 830-9050
John E Ferguson, *CEO*
Justin Ferguson, *
▲ **EMP:** 100 **EST:** 1977
SQ FT: 8,000
SALES (est): 5.64MM **Privately Held**
Web: www.dmwk.com
SIC: 1791 Structural steel erection

(P-2199)
ROMAK IRON WORKS
380 Industrial Ct (94510-1138)
PHONE..................707 751-2420
EMP: 65 **EST:** 1911
SALES (est): 11.74MM **Privately Held**
Web: www.romak.com
SIC: 1791 1799 Structural steel erection; Ornamental metal work

PRODUCTS & SERVICES SECTION

1794 - Excavation Work (P-2222)

(P-2200)
RP CONSTRUCTION SERVICES LLC
305 Dela Vina Ave (93940-3701)
PHONE..............................855 428-3000
Eben Russell, CEO
EMP: 160 EST: 2014
SALES (est): 35.29MM
SALES (corp-wide): 17.07B **Publicly Held**
Web: www.rpcs.com
SIC: 1791 Iron work, structural
PA: Quanta Services, Inc.
2727 North Loop W Ste 100
Houston TX
713 629-7600

(P-2201)
STROCAL INC
4651 Quail Lakes Dr (95207-5258)
P.O. Box 77937 (95267-1237)
PHONE..............................209 948-4646
▲ EMP: 336
Web: www.strocal.com
SIC: 1791 3441 Structural steel erection; Fabricated structural metal

1793 Glass And Glazing Work

(P-2202)
GIROUX GLASS INC (PA)
Also Called: Giroux
850 W Washington Blvd Ste 200 (90015-3359)
PHONE..............................213 747-7406
Nataline Lomedico, CEO
Anne-merelie Murrell, Ch Bd
Stephanie Lamb, *
Robert Bob Burkhammer, Ex VP
Bob Linford, *
▲ EMP: 120 EST: 1946
SALES (est): 49.64MM
SALES (corp-wide): 49.64MM **Privately Held**
Web: www.girouxglass.com
SIC: 1793 Glass and glazing work

(P-2203)
PROGRESS GLASS CO INC (PA)
25 Patterson St (94124-1328)
PHONE..............................415 824-7040
Tom Burkard, CEO
Chuck Burkard, *
Thomas C Burkard Junior, Prin
Thomas C Burkard Iii, Pr
Jim Holmberg, *
▲ EMP: 105 EST: 1956
SQ FT: 16,250
SALES (est): 17.94MM
SALES (corp-wide): 17.94MM **Privately Held**
Web: www.progressglass.com
SIC: 1793 Glass and glazing work

(P-2204)
ROYAL GLASS COMPANY INC
3200 De La Cruz Blvd (95054-2602)
PHONE..............................408 969-0444
John Maggiore, CEO
James Maggiore, *
▲ EMP: 80 EST: 1988
SALES (est): 31.63MM **Privately Held**
Web: www.royalglasscoinc.com
SIC: 1793 Glass and glazing work

(P-2205)
RYNOCLAD TECHNOLOGIES INC
780 E Francis St Ste M (91761-5553)
PHONE..............................951 264-3441
EMP: 200 EST: 2011
SALES (est): 25MM **Privately Held**
Web: www.rynoclad.com
SIC: 1793 Glass and glazing work

(P-2206)
SAFECO DOOR & HARDWARE INC
Also Called: Safeco Glass
31054 San Antonio St (94544-7904)
PHONE..............................510 429-4768
Mahboubeh Ahmadi, Pr
Ali Missaghi Akoub, *
Milagors Missaghi, *
Hamid Ahmadi, *
EMP: 65 EST: 2001
SQ FT: 13,000
SALES (est): 3.32MM **Privately Held**
SIC: 1793 Glass and glazing work

(P-2207)
TOWER GLASS INC
9570 Pathway St Ste A (92071-4100)
PHONE..............................619 596-6199
Evelyn Dee Swaim, CEO
Barry Swaim, *
EMP: 100 EST: 1989
SQ FT: 15,000
SALES (est): 22.44MM **Privately Held**
Web: www.towerglass.com
SIC: 1793 Glass and glazing work

(P-2208)
WALTERS & WOLF GLASS COMPANY (PA)
Also Called: Walter & Wolf
41450 Boscell Rd (94538-3103)
PHONE..............................510 490-1115
Randall A Wolf, Pr
Nick Kocelj, *
Jeff Belzer, *
▲ EMP: 135 EST: 1977
SALES (est): 86.87MM
SALES (corp-wide): 86.87MM **Privately Held**
Web: www.waltersandwolf.com
SIC: 1793 Glass and glazing work

(P-2209)
WALTERS & WOLF GLASS COMPANY
1975 Puddingstone Dr (91750-5818)
PHONE..............................909 392-1961
Tom Lackey, Brnch Mgr
EMP: 76
SALES (corp-wide): 86.87MM **Privately Held**
Web: www.waltersandwolf.com
SIC: 1793 Glass and glazing work
PA: Walters & Wolf Glass Company
41450 Boscell Rd
Fremont CA
510 490-1115

(P-2210)
WOODBRIDGE GLASS INC
14321 Myford Rd (92780-7022)
PHONE..............................714 838-4444
Virginia Siciliani, Pr
John Siciliani, *
Jim Siciliani, *
▲ EMP: 205 EST: 1981
SQ FT: 8,500
SALES (est): 47.51MM **Privately Held**
Web: www.woodbridgeglass.com
SIC: 1793 5231 Glass and glazing work; Glass, leaded or stained

1794 Excavation Work

(P-2211)
A J EXCAVATION INC
Also Called: American Fencing
514 N Brawley Ave (93706-1014)
PHONE..............................559 408-5908
EMP: 150 EST: 2009
SALES (est): 9.82MM **Privately Held**
Web: www.movendirt.com
SIC: 1794 Excavation work

(P-2212)
ANDREW M JORDAN INC
Also Called: A & B Construction
225 3rd St (94607-4309)
PHONE..............................510 999-6000
Andrew M Jordan, Pr
EMP: 90 EST: 1991
SALES (est): 25.89MM **Privately Held**
Web: www.a-bconstruction.net
SIC: 1794 Excavation and grading, building construction

(P-2213)
BAY CITIES PAV & GRADING INC
1450 Civic Ct Bldg B (94520-7950)
PHONE..............................925 687-6666
Ben L Rodriguez, CEO
Marlo Manqueros, *
Kim Rodriguez, *
EMP: 250 EST: 1947
SQ FT: 4,000
SALES (est): 61.7MM **Privately Held**
Web: www.baycities.us
SIC: 1794 1611 7353 Excavation work; Highway and street construction; Earth moving equipment, rental or leasing

(P-2214)
CALEX ENGINEERING INC
Also Called: Calex Engineering Co.
23651 Pine St (91321-3106)
PHONE..............................661 254-1866
Ryan Seitz, Pr
Mike Neilson, *
EMP: 70 EST: 1975
SQ FT: 1,800
SALES (est): 33.69MM **Privately Held**
Web: www.calex.net
SIC: 1794 Excavation work

(P-2215)
CARONE & COMPANY INC
Also Called: Diablo Valley Rock
5009 Forni Dr Ste A (94520-8525)
PHONE..............................925 602-8800
Richard Lloyd Carone, Pr
EMP: 60 EST: 1998
SQ FT: 48,000
SALES (est): 13.12MM **Privately Held**
Web: www.caroneandcompany.com
SIC: 1794 Excavation work

(P-2216)
CREW INC
19618 S Susana Rd (90221-5716)
PHONE..............................310 608-6860
David M Lalonde, Pr
Darrin Lalonde, *
EMP: 60 EST: 1994
SQ FT: 5,000
SALES (est): 15.41MM **Privately Held**
Web: www.crewgrading.com
SIC: 1794 Excavation and grading, building construction

(P-2217)
GHILOTTI BROS INC
Also Called: Concrete Craft
525 Jacoby St (94901-5305)
PHONE..............................415 454-7011
Michael Ghilotti, CEO
Dante W Ghilotti, *
Michael M Ghilotti, *
Thomas G Barr, *
Daniel Y Chin, *
▲ EMP: 290 EST: 1914
SQ FT: 86,249
SALES (est): 67.95MM **Privately Held**
Web: www.gbi1914.com
SIC: 1794 1623 1771 1611 Excavation work; Water, sewer, and utility lines; Concrete work; Highway and street construction

(P-2218)
GUINN CORPORATION
6533 Rosedale Hwy (93308-5903)
P.O. Box 1339 (93302-1339)
PHONE..............................661 325-6109
Gary Guinn, CEO
Tim Guinn, *
Jeff Affonso, *
EMP: 75 EST: 1952
SQ FT: 3,600
SALES (est): 25.57MM **Privately Held**
Web: www.guinnconstruction.com
SIC: 1794 Excavation and grading, building construction

(P-2219)
JEFF CARPENTER INC
1380 W Oleander Ave (92571-7863)
PHONE..............................951 657-5115
Jeff Carpenter, Pr
EMP: 15 EST: 1985
SQ FT: 1,300
SALES (est): 4.67MM **Privately Held**
Web: www.jeffcarpenterinc.com
SIC: 1794 Excavation work

(P-2220)
LOVCO CONSTRUCTION INC
Also Called: Lovco Construction
1300 E Burnett St (90755-3512)
P.O. Box 90335 (90809-0335)
PHONE..............................562 595-1601
Terry C Lovingier, Pr
Steve Barnett, *
Katie Lovingier, *
Matt Lovinger, *
Mike Mcgougan, VP
EMP: 125 EST: 1988
SQ FT: 2,500
SALES (est): 22.19MM **Privately Held**
Web: www.lovcoconstruction.com
SIC: 1794 1771 1611 Excavation and grading, building construction; Concrete work; Highway and street construction

(P-2221)
LUPTON EXCAVATION INC
8467 Florin Rd (95828-2512)
PHONE..............................916 387-1104
Kenneth Lupton Junior, Pr
EMP: 75 EST: 1987
SQ FT: 4,000
SALES (est): 9.7MM **Privately Held**
Web: www.luptonexcavation.com
SIC: 1794 Excavation and grading, building construction

(P-2222)
MAGGIORA AND GHILOTTI INC
555 Du Bois St (94901-3965)
PHONE..............................415 459-8640
EMP: 100 EST: 1964

SALES (est): 15.93MM **Privately Held**
Web: www.maggiora-ghilotti.com
SIC: 1794 Excavation work

(P-2223)
MGE UNDERGROUND INC
2501 Golden Hill Rd (93446-6391)
P.O. Box 4189 (93447-4189)
PHONE..................805 238-3510
Michael Joe Goldstein, *Pr*
Summer Golstein, *
EMP: 372 **EST:** 1997
SALES (est): 110.99MM **Privately Held**
Web: www.mgeunderground.com
SIC: 1794 Excavation work

(P-2224)
REED THOMAS COMPANY INC
1025 Santiago St (92701-3800)
PHONE..................714 558-7691
Harvey T Biegle, *Pr*
EMP: 90 **EST:** 1981
SQ FT: 8,800
SALES (est): 11.05MM **Privately Held**
Web: www.reedthomas.com
SIC: 1794 Excavation and grading, building construction

(P-2225)
STURGEON SON GRADING & PAV INC (PA)
3511 Gilmore Ave (93308-6205)
P.O. Box 2840 (93303-2840)
PHONE..................661 322-4408
John E Powell, *CEO*
Oliver Sturgeon, *
Paul Sturgeon, *
EMP: 180 **EST:** 1927
SQ FT: 3,500
SALES (est): 47.93MM
SALES (corp-wide): 47.93MM **Privately Held**
SIC: 1794 8711 Excavation work; Engineering services

(P-2226)
SUKUT CONSTRUCTION INC
4010 W Chandler Ave (92704-5202)
PHONE..................714 540-5351
Michael Crawford, *Pr*
Myron Sukut, *
Paul Kuliev, *
▲ **EMP:** 200 **EST:** 1968
SQ FT: 12,000
SALES (est): 137.75MM **Privately Held**
Web: www.sukut.com
SIC: 1794 1611 1623 1629 Excavation and grading, building construction; General contractor, highway and street construction; Water and sewer line construction; Dams, waterways, docks, and other marine construction

(P-2227)
TIDWELL EXCAV ACQUISITION INC
Also Called: Tidwell Excavating
1691 Los Angeles Ave (93004-3213)
PHONE..................805 647-4707
Alex Miruello, *Pr*
Timothy Wayne Goodwin, *
Louis Armona, *
EMP: 90 **EST:** 1956
SALES (est): 9.78MM
SALES (corp-wide): 528.99MM **Privately Held**
Web: www.tidwell-inc.com
SIC: 1794 Excavation and grading, building construction
PA: Meruelo Enterprises, Inc.

9550 Firestone Blvd # 105
Downey CA
562 745-2300

1795 Wrecking And Demolition Work

(P-2228)
ALARCON BOHM CORP
5301 Adeline St (94608-3107)
P.O. Box 24301 (94623-1301)
PHONE..................510 893-4405
Kevin J Bohm, *Pr*
EMP: 60 **EST:** 1993
SQ FT: 15,000
SALES (est): 4.06MM **Privately Held**
Web: www.bohmgroup.com
SIC: 1795 Wrecking and demolition work

(P-2229)
AMERICAN WRECKING INC
2459 Lee Ave (91733-1407)
PHONE..................626 350-8303
Jose Luis Galaviz, *Pr*
Robert Hall, *
Warne Galaviz, *
Jay Gonzalez, *
EMP: 100 **EST:** 1989
SQ FT: 1,000
SALES (est): 35.43MM **Privately Held**
Web: www.americanwreckinginc.com
SIC: 1795 Demolition, buildings and other structures

(P-2230)
BLUEWATER ENVMTL SVCS INC
2075 Williams St (94577-2305)
PHONE..................510 346-8800
TOLL FREE: 800
Chris J Kirschenheuter, *CEO*
Todd Kirschenheuter, *
EMP: 100 **EST:** 1991
SQ FT: 15,000
SALES (est): 16.72MM **Privately Held**
Web: www.bayviewservices.com
SIC: 1795 Demolition, buildings and other structures

(P-2231)
CLAUSS CONSTRUCTION
9911 Maine Ave (92040-3107)
PHONE..................619 390-4940
Joshua Clauss, *CEO*
Patrick Michael Clauss, *
EMP: 80 **EST:** 1991
SALES (est): 17.18MM **Privately Held**
Web: www.claussconstruction.com
SIC: 1795 1629 4959 Wrecking and demolition work; Earthmoving contractor; Toxic or hazardous waste cleanup

(P-2232)
CLEVELAND WRECKING COMPANY
1580 Chabot Ct (94545-2423)
PHONE..................510 674-2600
EMP: 1858
SALES (corp-wide): 13.15B **Publicly Held**
SIC: 1795 Demolition, buildings and other structures
HQ: Cleveland Wrecking Company
999 W Town And Country Rd
Orange CA
626 967-4287

(P-2233)
DANNY RYAN PRECISION CONTG INC

Also Called: Precision Contracting
16782 Millikan Ave (92606-5010)
PHONE..................949 642-6664
Danny Ryan, *Pr*
EMP: 90 **EST:** 1991
SALES (est): 13.04MM **Privately Held**
Web: www.adepprecision.com
SIC: 1795 1799 Demolition, buildings and other structures; Asbestos removal and encapsulation

(P-2234)
EMPIRE DEMOLITION INC
137 N Joy St (92879-1321)
PHONE..................909 393-8300
Kris Huff, *CEO*
Collin Cumbee, *
EMP: 100 **EST:** 1997
SALES (est): 11.13MM **Privately Held**
Web: www.empiredemolition.com
SIC: 1795 Demolition, buildings and other structures

(P-2235)
FERMA CORPORATION
6655 Smith Ave Ste A (94560-4219)
PHONE..................510 794-0414
Rob Verga, *Mgr*
EMP: 180
SALES (corp-wide): 49.97MM **Privately Held**
Web: www.fermacorp.com
SIC: 1795 Demolition, buildings and other structures
PA: Ferma Corporation
6639 Smith Ave
Newark CA
650 961-2742

(P-2236)
GD HEIL INC
1031 Segovia Cir (92870-7137)
PHONE..................714 687-9100
James A Langford, *CEO*
James A Langford, *CEO*
Gary Heil, *
Steve Mc Clain, *
Laura Heil, *
EMP: 160 **EST:** 1992
SQ FT: 20,770
SALES (est): 23.24MM **Privately Held**
Web: www.gdheil.com
SIC: 1795 Demolition, buildings and other structures

(P-2237)
INTERIOR RMOVAL SPECIALIST INC
8990 Atlantic Ave (90280-3505)
PHONE..................323 357-6900
Carlos Herrera, *CEO*
Isabel Herrera, *
EMP: 150 **EST:** 1994
SALES (est): 225 **Privately Held**
Web: www.irsdemo.com
SIC: 1795 Demolition, buildings and other structures

(P-2238)
J&G INDUSTRIES INC
7545 Irvine Center Dr Ste 200 (92618-2932)
PHONE..................949 207-3505
EMP: 61
SALES (corp-wide): 2.26MM **Privately Held**
Web: www.j-gindustries.com
SIC: 1795 Demolition, buildings and other structures
PA: J&G Industries, Inc.

7511 Suzi Ln
Westminster CA
714 903-2002

(P-2239)
KROEKER INC
4627 S Chestnut Ave (93725-9238)
PHONE..................559 237-3764
Joyce Kroeker, *Pr*
Ed Kroeker, *
Jeff Kroeker, *
Rodney Ainsworth, *
John Ramirez, *
EMP: 120 **EST:** 1991
SQ FT: 9,000
SALES (est): 21.36MM **Privately Held**
Web: www.kroekerinc.com
SIC: 1795 1629 4953 Demolition, buildings and other structures; Land reclamation; Recycling, waste materials

(P-2240)
MILLER ENVIRONMENTAL INC
1130 W Trenton Ave (92867-3536)
PHONE..................714 385-0099
Gregg Miller, *Pr*
Rob Schaefer, *
Mindy Peek, *General*
EMP: 150 **EST:** 1999
SQ FT: 3,000
SALES (est): 32.31MM **Privately Held**
Web: www.miller-env.com
SIC: 1795 4953 Demolition, buildings and other structures; Hazardous waste collection and disposal

(P-2241)
NORTHSTAR CONTG GROUP INC
13320 Cambridge St (90670-4904)
PHONE..................714 639-7600
John Leonard, *VP*
EMP: 60
SALES (corp-wide): 776.44MM **Privately Held**
SIC: 1795 1799 Wrecking and demolition work; Asbestos removal and encapsulation
HQ: Northstar Contracting Group, Inc.
2614-20 Barrington Ct
Hayward CA

(P-2242)
NORTHSTAR DEM & REMEDIATION LP (DH)
404 N Berry St (92821-3104)
PHONE..................714 672-3500
Jose Alonso, *VP*
Gregory G Dicarlo, *
Jeffrey P Adix, *
Gary Thibodeaux, *
Kamal Sookram, *
EMP: 174 **EST:** 2007
SQ FT: 19,000
SALES (est): 92.89MM
SALES (corp-wide): 776.44MM **Privately Held**
SIC: 1795 1799 8744 Demolition, buildings and other structures; Decontamination services; Environmental remediation
HQ: Northstar Group Services, Inc.
370 7th Ave Ste 1803
New York NY
212 951-3660

(P-2243)
STOMPER COMPANY INC
3135 Diablo Ave (94545-2701)
PHONE..................510 574-0570
Donna R Rehrmann, *Pr*
George Rehrmann, *

1799 - Special Trade Contractors, Nec (P-2264)

PRODUCTS & SERVICES SECTION

EMP: 60 EST: 1968
SQ FT: 15,000
SALES (est): 9.96MM **Privately Held**
Web: www.stompercompany.com
SIC: **1795** Demolition, buildings and other structures

(P-2244)
SVG CONTRACTORS INC
Also Called: Sv Group
155 E Main Ave Ste 110 (95037-7519)
PHONE..................................408 218-0993
Scott Helf, *CEO*
Scott Joseph Helf, *
EMP: 75 EST: 2013
SQ FT: 4,000
SALES (est): 9.07MM **Privately Held**
SIC: **1795 1799** Demolition, buildings and other structures; Asbestos removal and encapsulation

1796 Installing Building Equipment

(P-2245)
AMERICAN SCAFFOLD INC (PA)
3210 Commercial St (92113-1514)
P.O. Box 2364 (36526-2364)
PHONE..................................619 231-4898
Alvin Jr Mcdonald Ruis, *CEO*
▲ EMP: 74 EST: 2002
SQ FT: 3,000
SALES (est): 14.96MM
SALES (corp-wide): 14.96MM **Privately Held**
Web: www.americanscaffold.com
SIC: **1796** Installing building equipment

(P-2246)
BIGGE CRANE AND RIGGING CO (PA)
10700 Bigge St (94577-1032)
P.O. Box 1657 (94577-0393)
PHONE..................................510 638-8100
TOLL FREE: 888
◆ EMP: 175 EST: 1916
SALES (est): 50.21MM
SALES (corp-wide): 50.21MM **Privately Held**
Web: www.bigge.com
SIC: **1796** Machine moving and rigging

(P-2247)
CLASSIC INSTALLS INC
41755 Elm St (92562-1408)
PHONE..................................951 678-9906
Dirk Steffen, *CEO*
EMP: 70 EST: 2007
SALES (est): 11.04MM **Privately Held**
Web: www.classicinstalls.com
SIC: **1796** Installing building equipment

(P-2248)
HMI INDUSTRIAL CONTRACTORS INC
Also Called: Hmi Industrial Contractors
3899 Security Park Dr (95742-6920)
PHONE..................................916 386-2586
Ruth Gilman, *CEO*
Don Gilman, *VP*
EMP: 62 EST: 1992
SQ FT: 37,000
SALES (est): 15MM **Privately Held**
Web: www.hmiindustrial.com
SIC: **1796** Millwright

(P-2249)
PERFORMANCE CONTRACTING INC
4955 E Landon Dr (92807-1972)
PHONE..................................913 310-7120
William Massey, *Mgr*
EMP: 99
SALES (corp-wide): 1.11B **Privately Held**
Web: www.performancecontracting.com
SIC: **1796** Installing building equipment
HQ: Performance Contracting, Inc.
    16220 Rdmond Wdnvlle Rd N
    Woodinville WA
    913 888-8600

(P-2250)
TK ELEVATOR CORPORATION
940 Riverside Pkwy Ste 20 (95605-1513)
PHONE..................................916 376-8700
TOLL FREE: 800
Guy Buckman, *Brnch Mgr*
EMP: 77
SALES (corp-wide): 2.67MM **Privately Held**
Web: www.tkelevator.com
SIC: **1796 7699** Elevator installation and conversion; Elevators: inspection, service, and repair
HQ: Tk Elevator Corporation
    788 Cir 75 Pkwy Se # 500
    Atlanta GA
    678 319-3240

(P-2251)
UNITED RIGGERS & ERECTORS INC (PA)
4188 Valley Blvd (91789-1446)
P.O. Box 728 (91788-0728)
PHONE..................................909 978-0400
Brian D Kelley, *CEO*
Thomas J Kruss, *
EMP: 100 EST: 1966
SQ FT: 58,000
SALES (est): 20.54MM
SALES (corp-wide): 20.54MM **Privately Held**
Web: www.ure-inc.com
SIC: **1796** Machinery installation

(P-2252)
WEST COAST IRON INC
Also Called: Westcoast Iron
9302 Jamacha Rd (91977-4203)
PHONE..................................619 464-8456
EMP: 75 EST: 1988
SALES (est): 18.68MM **Privately Held**
Web: www.westcoastiron.com
SIC: **1796 1541 3441** Installing building equipment; Steel building construction; Building components, structural steel

1799 Special Trade Contractors, Nec

(P-2253)
AETNA INTERNATIONAL INC (DH)
Also Called: Aetna
1616 16th St Ste 200 (94103-5171)
PHONE..................................415 575-0912
EMP: 63 EST: 1995
SALES (est): 3.73MM
SALES (corp-wide): 322.47B **Publicly Held**
SIC: **1799 1761** Waterproofing; Roofing contractor
HQ: Aetna Inc.
    151 Farmington Ave
    Hartford CT

(P-2254)
ALCORN FENCE COMPANY (PA)
1088 Hamilton Rd (91010-2742)
P.O. Box 1249 (91010)
PHONE..................................818 983-0650
Thomas Joseph Stack, *CEO*
Greg Erickson, *
Oscar Mancialla, *
EMP: 60 EST: 1942
SQ FT: 18,000
SALES (est): 21.04MM
SALES (corp-wide): 21.04MM **Privately Held**
Web: www.alcorn-fence.com
SIC: **1799** Fence construction

(P-2255)
ANTIS ROOFG WATERPROOFING LLC
Also Called: Antis Roofing
2649 Campus Dr (92612-1601)
PHONE..................................949 461-9222
EMP: 85 EST: 1988
SALES (est): 18.8MM **Privately Held**
Web: www.antisroofing.com
SIC: **1799 1761** Waterproofing; Roofing contractor

(P-2256)
ARTISAN GLASS AND DESIGN INC
Also Called: Glazier
2665 W Woodland Dr (92801-2629)
PHONE..................................714 542-0507
Robert King, *CEO*
EMP: 67 EST: 2007
SALES (est): 3.12MM **Privately Held**
Web: www.artisanglassdesign.com
SIC: **1799 1793** Glass tinting, architectural or automotive; Glass and glazing work

(P-2257)
ASBESTOS INSTANT RESPONSE INC
3517 W Washington Blvd (90018-1122)
PHONE..................................323 733-0508
Eric Chevasson, *Pr*
Steven Liederman, *
EMP: 65 EST: 2000
SQ FT: 1,500
SALES (est): 7.85MM **Privately Held**
Web: www.airinc.ws
SIC: **1799** Asbestos removal and encapsulation

(P-2258)
ATI RESTORATION LLC
Also Called: American Restoration Services
25000 Industrial Blvd (94545-2349)
PHONE..................................510 429-5000
TOLL FREE: 888
Kyle Picket, *Mgr*
EMP: 60
Web: www.atirestoration.com
SIC: **1799** Antenna installation
PA: Ati Restoration, Llc
    3360 E La Palma Ave
    Anaheim CA

(P-2259)
ATI RESTORATION LLC (PA)
Also Called: ATI
3360 E La Palma Ave (92806-2814)
PHONE..................................714 283-9990
Gary Moore, *CEO*
Ryan Moore, *
Jeff Moore, *
Scott Moore, *OF OPRS & ENVIRONMENTAL HEALTH SERVICES*
Yun Kim, *
▲ EMP: 128 EST: 1989
SQ FT: 57,000
SALES (est): 287.11MM **Privately Held**
Web: www.atirestoration.com
SIC: **1799 1541 1742 1731** Antenna installation; Industrial buildings and warehouses; Plastering, drywall, and insulation; Electrical work

(P-2260)
BAYVIEW ENVIRONMENTAL SVCS INC
6925 San Leandro St (94621-3320)
PHONE..................................510 562-6181
Marvin Henderson, *CEO*
EMP: 225 EST: 1993
SQ FT: 12,000
SALES (est): 38.1MM **Privately Held**
Web: www.bayviewservices.com
SIC: **1799 4212 4959** Asbestos removal and encapsulation; Hazardous waste transport; Toxic or hazardous waste cleanup
PA: Bayview Services, Inc.
    6925 San Leandro St
    Oakland CA

(P-2261)
BURDICK PAINTING
705 Nuttman St (95054-2623)
PHONE..................................408 567-1330
John C Cintas, *CEO*
EMP: 67 EST: 1967
SQ FT: 8,000
SALES (est): 9.01MM **Privately Held**
Web: www.burdickpainting.com
SIC: **1799 1721** Paint and wallpaper stripping; Commercial painting

(P-2262)
C E TOLAND & SON
5300 Industrial Way (94510-1025)
PHONE..................................707 747-1000
Clyde E Toland Junior, *Ch Bd*
Blake Toland, *
▲ EMP: 120 EST: 1942
SQ FT: 90,000
SALES (est): 22.49MM **Privately Held**
Web: www.cetoland.com
SIC: **1799** Ornamental metal work

(P-2263)
CALIFORNIA CLOSET COMPANY INC
Also Called: California Closet Co
5921 Skylab Rd (92647-2062)
PHONE..................................714 899-4905
Mike Cassidy, *Genl Mgr*
EMP: 115
SALES (corp-wide): 3.75B **Privately Held**
Web: www.californiaclosets.com
SIC: **1799** Closet organizers, installation and design
HQ: California Closet Company, Inc.
    2001 W Phelps Rd Ste 1
    Phoenix AZ
    510 763-2033

(P-2264)
CALIFRNIAS GNITE POOL PLST INC
510 Greenville Rd (94550-9297)
PHONE..................................925 960-9500
Manuel Rodriguez, *Pr*
Jose Arellano, *
Monroe Rodriguez, *
Alvaro Lando, *

(PA)=Parent Co (HQ)=Headquarters
✿ = New Business established in last 2 years

1799 - Special Trade Contractors, Nec (P-2265)

EMP: 60 EST: 1992
SQ FT: 15,625
SALES (est): 4.61MM Privately Held
Web: www.californiasgunite.com
SIC: 1799 Swimming pool construction

(P-2265)
CHAMPION SCAFFOLD SERVICES INC
Also Called: Champion Scaffold
112 Railroad Ave (94801-3924)
PHONE.....................510 788-4731
Art Cruz, Pr
Jessica Smith, *
EMP: 60 EST: 2009
SALES (est): 4.72MM Privately Held
Web: www.championscaffold.com
SIC: 1799 Scaffolding

(P-2266)
CLOSET FACTORY INC (PA)
12800 S Bdwy (90061-1116)
PHONE.....................310 516-7000
John La Barbera, CEO
Greg Stein, *
Kathryn La Barbera, *
EMP: 99 EST: 1983
SQ FT: 40,000
SALES (est): 61.86MM
SALES (corp-wide): 61.86MM Privately Held
Web: www.closetfactory.com
SIC: 1799 Closet organizers, installation and design

(P-2267)
CLOSET WORLD INC
320 S 6th Ave (91746-3126)
PHONE.....................800 576-7717
EMP: 60
Web: www.closetworld.com
SIC: 1799 Closet organizers, installation and design
PA: Closet World, Inc.
3860 Capitol Ave
City Of Industry CA

(P-2268)
COURTNEY INC (PA)
16781 Millikan Ave (92606-5009)
PHONE.....................949 222-2050
George Courtney, CEO
Mildred Courtney, *
EMP: 80 EST: 1994
SALES (est): 34.89MM Privately Held
Web: www.courtneyinc.com
SIC: 1799 Waterproofing

(P-2269)
CROWN FENCE CO
12070 Telegraph Rd Ste 340 (90670)
PHONE.....................562 864-5177
TOLL FREE: 800
Eric Fiedler, Prin
Chris E Nickelatti, Prin
Lief Nicolaisen, Prin
Eric W Fiedler, Prin
Doug Eustace, Prin
▲ EMP: 96 EST: 1923
SALES (est): 20.38MM Privately Held
Web: www.crownfence.com
SIC: 1799 5039 Fence construction; Wire fence, gates, and accessories

(P-2270)
CSRW INC
Also Called: Allied Construction Services
7602 National Dr (94550-8809)
PHONE.....................925 724-2324
Jason B Rittenbach, Pr

Donovan Rittenbach, *
EMP: 84 EST: 2002
SQ FT: 4,500
SALES (est): 18.14MM Privately Held
Web: www.alliedsvcs.com
SIC: 1799 1542 Waterproofing; Commercial and office building, new construction

(P-2271)
D&A ENDEAVORS INC
Also Called: SERVPRO of Beverly Hills
8484 Wilshire Blvd Ste 605 (90211-3227)
PHONE.....................310 390-7540
Arezo Jeffries, CEO
Daniel Jeffries, *
EMP: 80 EST: 2014
SALES (est): 5.31MM Privately Held
Web: www.servprobeverlyhillswestwood.com
SIC: 1799 8744 7349 1741 Construction site cleanup; Environmental remediation; Building maintenance services, nec; Tuckpointing or restoration

(P-2272)
DAVE GROSS ENTERPRISES INC
Also Called: Adams Pool Specialties
7 Wayne Ct (95829-1300)
PHONE.....................916 388-2000
David William Gross, CEO
Michel Mcdonnell, VP
Barbara Hall Ctrl, Prin
EMP: 65 EST: 1998
SQ FT: 25,000
SALES (est): 3.83MM Privately Held
Web: www.adamspoolsac.com
SIC: 1799 Swimming pool construction

(P-2273)
EXCEL MDULAR SCAFFOLD LSG CORP
2555 Birch St (92081-8433)
PHONE.....................760 598-0050
Benjamin Bartlett, Brnch Mgr
EMP: 1197
Web: www.excelscaffold.com
SIC: 1799 Rigging and scaffolding
PA: Excel Modular Scaffold And Leasing Corporation
720 Washington St Unit 5
Hanover MA

(P-2274)
FARWEST CORROSION CONTROL CO (PA)
12029 Regentview Ave (90241-5517)
PHONE.....................310 532-9524
Troy Gordon Rankin Junior, CEO
Roy Rankin Junior, Pr
Steve Sosa, *
Marian Rankin, *
◆ EMP: 65 EST: 1956
SQ FT: 42,000
SALES (est): 47.89MM
SALES (corp-wide): 47.89MM Privately Held
Web: www.farwestcorrosion.com
SIC: 1799 Corrosion control installation

(P-2275)
FENCECORP INC
3045 Industry St (92054-4834)
PHONE.....................760 721-2101
Gary Hansen, Prin
EMP: 85
SALES (corp-wide): 69.2MM Privately Held
Web: www.fencecorp.us

SIC: 1799 Fence construction
HQ: Fencecorp, Inc.
18440 Van Buren Blvd
Riverside CA

(P-2276)
FENCECORP INC
6837 Power Inn Rd (95828-2401)
PHONE.....................916 388-0887
EMP: 85
SALES (corp-wide): 69.2MM Privately Held
Web: www.fencecorp.us
SIC: 1799 Fence construction
HQ: Fencecorp, Inc.
18440 Van Buren Blvd
Riverside CA

(P-2277)
FENCECORP INC (HQ)
18440 Van Buren Blvd (92508-9258)
PHONE.....................951 686-3170
T Perrry Massie, CEO
Dale Marriott, *
Floyd Nixon, *
Gary Hansen, *
EMP: 170 EST: 2006
SQ FT: 5,000
SALES (est): 23.93MM
SALES (corp-wide): 69.2MM Privately Held
Web: www.fencecorp.us
SIC: 1799 Fence construction
PA: Fenceworks, Inc.
870 Main St
Riverside CA
951 788-5620

(P-2278)
FENCEWORKS INC (PA)
Also Called: Golden State Fence Co.
870 Main St (92501-1016)
PHONE.....................951 788-5620
Jason Ostrander, CEO
Mel Kay, *
▲ EMP: 250 EST: 1998
SQ FT: 20,000
SALES (est): 69.2MM
SALES (corp-wide): 69.2MM Privately Held
Web: www.fenceworks.us
SIC: 1799 Fence construction

(P-2279)
FRESH AIR ENVMTL SVCS INC
Also Called: Fresh Air
10675 Rush St (91733-3439)
PHONE.....................323 913-1965
Kevan Stark, Pr
EMP: 60 EST: 1993
SQ FT: 7,000
SALES (est): 4.72MM Privately Held
Web: www.4freshair.biz
SIC: 1799 Asbestos removal and encapsulation

(P-2280)
G W SURFACES (PA)
Also Called: Showershapes
2432 Palma Dr (93003-5732)
PHONE.....................805 642-5004
James A Garver, Pr
Georgann Garver, *
Tidus Gutierrez, *
EMP: 100 EST: 1976
SQ FT: 30,000
SALES (est): 18.65MM
SALES (corp-wide): 18.65MM Privately Held
Web: www.gwsurfaces.com

SIC: 1799 Counter top installation

(P-2281)
GETTLER-RYAN INC (PA)
6805 Sierra Ct Ste G (94568-2615)
PHONE.....................925 551-7555
Jeffrey M Ryan, CEO
Dave Byron, *
Janice Grant, *
EMP: 65 EST: 1963
SQ FT: 20,000
SALES (est): 24.12MM
SALES (corp-wide): 24.12MM Privately Held
Web: www.grinc.com
SIC: 1799 Petroleum storage tanks, pumping and draining

(P-2282)
GREGG DRILLING & TESTING INC (PA)
2726 Walnut Ave (90755-1832)
PHONE.....................562 427-6899
John M Gregg, Pr
Patrick Keating, *
Chris Christensen, *
▲ EMP: 71 EST: 1985
SQ FT: 17,000
SALES (est): 24.77MM
SALES (corp-wide): 24.77MM Privately Held
Web: www.greggdrilling.com
SIC: 1799 1781 Core drilling and cutting; Water well drilling

(P-2283)
HERZOG CONTRACTING CORP
2155 Hancock St (92110-2012)
PHONE.....................619 849-6990
EMP: 87
SALES (corp-wide): 490.1MM Privately Held
Web: www.herzog.com
SIC: 1799 Antenna installation
HQ: Herzog Contracting Corp.
600 S Riverside Rd
Saint Joseph MO
816 233-9001

(P-2284)
HIGH END DEVELOPMENT INC
665 Stone Rd (94510-1141)
PHONE.....................925 687-2540
James Metzger, Pr
Larry V Harmen, *
Anthony Froyd, *
EMP: 143 EST: 2006
SALES (est): 22.66MM Privately Held
Web: www.highenddevelopment.com
SIC: 1799 Waterproofing

(P-2285)
HUB PARKING TECHNOLOGY USA INC
1631 Neptune Dr (94577-3162)
PHONE.....................510 483-7275
EMP: 99
SALES (corp-wide): 12.25MM Privately Held
Web: www.hubparking.com
SIC: 1799 Parking facility equipment and maintenance
PA: Hub Parking Technology Usa Inc.
761 Commonwealth Dr # 204
Warrendale PA
724 776-7275

1799 - Special Trade Contractors, Nec (P-2307)

(P-2286)
J&M KEYSTONE INC
2709 Via Orange Way Ste A (91978-1745)
PHONE..................................619 466-9876
David Carpenter, *CEO*
Kevin Casenhiser, *
Gary Moore, *
Ryan Moore, *
Jeffrey Moore, *
EMP: 117 **EST:** 1991
SQ FT: 9,100
SALES (est): 17.4MM **Privately Held**
Web: www.jmkeystone.com
SIC: 1799 1542 8744 7349 Steam cleaning of building exteriors; Commercial and office buildings, renovation and repair; Environmental remediation; Air duct cleaning
PA: Ati Restoration, Llc
3360 E La Palma Ave
Anaheim CA

(P-2287)
JANUS CORPORATION (PA)
1081 Shary Cir (94518-2407)
PHONE..................................925 969-9200
Mike Ely, *CEO*
Sean Tavernier, *
Craig M Uhle, *
Barb Eaves, *
EMP: 69 **EST:** 1989
SQ FT: 15,000
SALES (est): 23.44MM **Privately Held**
Web: www.januscorp.com
SIC: 1799 Asbestos removal and encapsulation

(P-2288)
JEFFRIES GLOBAL INC
Also Called: SERVPRO Jeffries Global
8484 Wilshire Blvd Ste 605 (90211-3227)
PHONE..................................888 255-3488
Daniel Jeffries, *Prin*
EMP: 85 **EST:** 2020
SALES (est): 5.69MM **Privately Held**
SIC: 1799 Asbestos removal and encapsulation

(P-2289)
JONES/COVEY GROUP INCORPORATED
Also Called: Jones Covey Group
9595 Lucas Ranch Rd Ste 100 (91730-5725)
PHONE..................................888 972-7581
Bret Christopher Covey, *CEO*
Robert Christie, *
EMP: 63 **EST:** 2001
SQ FT: 2,400
SALES (est): 43.57MM **Privately Held**
Web: www.jonescovey.com
SIC: 1799 Service station equipment

(P-2290)
KARCHER ENVIRONMENTAL INC
Also Called: Karcher Environmental
1718 Fairway Dr (94577-5628)
PHONE..................................510 297-0180
EMP: 70
SALES (corp-wide): 9.81MM **Privately Held**
Web: www.karcherenv.com
SIC: 1799 Asbestos removal and encapsulation
PA: Karcher Environmental, Inc.
2300 E Orangewood Ave
Anaheim CA
714 385-1490

(P-2291)
KELLER NORTH AMERICA INC
1780 E Lemonwood Dr (93060-9510)
PHONE..................................805 933-1331
Alan Ringen, *Brnch Mgr*
EMP: 95
Web: www.keller-na.com
SIC: 1799 Building site preparation
HQ: Keller North America, Inc.
7550 Teague Rd Ste 300
Hanover MD
410 551-8200

(P-2292)
KING SUPPLY COMPANY LLC
6340 Valley View St (90620-1032)
PHONE..................................714 670-8980
Michelle Mccloud, *Brnch Mgr*
EMP: 73
Web: www.kingmetals.com
SIC: 1799 Ornamental metal work
PA: King Supply Company, Llc
9611 E R L Thornton Fwy
Dallas TX

(P-2293)
LAYFIELD USA CORPORATION (DH)
10038 Marathon Pkwy (92040-2771)
PHONE..................................619 562-1200
Thomas Rose, *CEO*
Rob Rempel, *
Steve Palubiski, *
▲ **EMP:** 100 **EST:** 2004
SALES (est): 48.68MM
SALES (corp-wide): 3.77MM **Privately Held**
Web: www.layfieldgroup.com
SIC: 1799 Building board-up contractor
HQ: Layfield Group Limited
11120 Silversmith Pl
Richmond BC
604 275-5588

(P-2294)
M GAW INC
Also Called: Jet Sets
6910 Farmdale Ave (91605-6210)
PHONE..................................818 503-7997
Michael Gaw, *Pr*
EMP: 90 **EST:** 1991
SQ FT: 15,000
SALES (est): 9.24MM **Privately Held**
Web: www.jetsets.com
SIC: 1799 Prop, set or scenery construction, theatrical

(P-2295)
MALCOLM DRILLING COMPANY INC (PA)
92 Natoma St Ste 400 (94105-2620)
PHONE..................................415 901-4400
John M Malcolm, *CEO*
Terry Tucker, *Pr*
Heinrich Majewski, *VP*
John Roe, *VP*
▲ **EMP:** 70 **EST:** 1968
SQ FT: 7,500
SALES (est): 653.29MM
SALES (corp-wide): 653.29MM **Privately Held**
Web: www.malcolmdrilling.com
SIC: 1799 Building site preparation

(P-2296)
MATRIX ENVIRONMENTAL INC
2330 E Cherry Industrial Cir (90805-4417)
PHONE..................................562 236-2704
Jason Mckeever, *Pr*
EMP: 60 **EST:** 2003
SQ FT: 9,000
SALES (est): 21.97MM **Privately Held**
Web: www.matrixla.net
SIC: 1799 Athletic and recreation facilities construction

(P-2297)
MISSION POOLS OF ESCONDIDO
Also Called: Mission Pools of Lake Forest
22600 Lambert St Ste 1104 (92630-1627)
PHONE..................................949 588-0100
Don Ogden, *Mgr*
EMP: 105
SALES (corp-wide): 24.07MM **Privately Held**
Web: www.missionpools.com
SIC: 1799 Swimming pool construction
PA: Mission Pools Of Escondido
755 W Grand Ave
Escondido CA
760 743-2605

(P-2298)
MP AERO LLC
7701 Woodley Ave (91406-1721)
PHONE..................................818 901-9828
EMP: 85 **EST:** 2013
SQ FT: 15,000
SALES (est): 10.62MM **Privately Held**
Web: www.mpaero.com
SIC: 1799 3721 Renovation of aircraft interiors; Research and development on aircraft by the manufacturer

(P-2299)
MY OFFICE INC
8333 Arjons Dr Ste D (92126-6320)
PHONE..................................858 549-6700
Ronald D Harrell, *CEO*
▲ **EMP:** 65 **EST:** 1990
SALES (est): 15.18MM **Privately Held**
Web: www.4myoffice.com
SIC: 1799 Office furniture installation

(P-2300)
NAVAL COATING INC
2080 Cambridge Ave (92007-1708)
PHONE..................................619 234-8366
Alan Lerchbacker, *Pr*
EMP: 149 **EST:** 1969
SALES (est): 24.79MM **Privately Held**
Web: www.navalcoating.us
SIC: 1799 1721 2851 Sandblasting of building exteriors; Industrial painting; Paints and allied products

(P-2301)
NMI INDUSTRIAL HOLDINGS INC
Also Called: Nmi Industrial
8503 Weyand Ave (95828-2610)
PHONE..................................916 635-7030
EMP: 90 **EST:** 2010
SALES (est): 23.97MM **Privately Held**
Web: www.nmiindustrial.com
SIC: 1799 8711 Building site preparation; Construction and civil engineering

(P-2302)
NORTHSTAR CONTG GROUP INC
2616 Barrington Ct (94545-1100)
PHONE..................................510 491-1330
Trip Turner, *Pr*
EMP: 97
SALES (corp-wide): 776.44MM **Privately Held**
SIC: 1799 Asbestos removal and encapsulation
HQ: Northstar Contracting Group, Inc.
2614-20 Barrington Ct
Hayward CA

(P-2303)
PACIFIC AQUASCAPE INC
17520 Newhope St Ste 120 (92708-8203)
PHONE..................................714 843-5734
Johan Perslow, *Ch*
Cory M Severson, *
Bob Lobo, *
Kevin Curran, *
EMP: 75 **EST:** 1994
SQ FT: 21,000
SALES (est): 16.75MM **Privately Held**
Web: www.pacificaquascape.com
SIC: 1799 Swimming pool construction

(P-2304)
PARC SPECIALTY CONTRACTORS
1400 Vinci Ave (95838-1716)
PHONE..................................916 992-5405
Greg Johnson, *Pr*
Mike Kidd, *
John Kimmel, *
Paul Lane, *
EMP: 85 **EST:** 1997
SQ FT: 10,000
SALES (est): 9.72MM **Privately Held**
Web: www.parcspecialty.com
SIC: 1799 Asbestos removal and encapsulation

(P-2305)
PARKING NETWORK INC
1625 W Olympic Blvd (90015-3853)
PHONE..................................213 613-1500
Frank Zelaya, *CEO*
Rose Zelaya, *
EMP: 120 **EST:** 2001
SALES (est): 9.84MM **Privately Held**
SIC: 1799 8748 Parking lot maintenance; Business consulting, nec

(P-2306)
PREMIER POOLS AND SPAS LP (PA)
Also Called: Premier Pool Service
11250 Pyrites Way (95670-4481)
PHONE..................................916 852-0223
Keith H Harbeck, *Genl Pt*
Paul Porter, *
Keith H Harbeck, *Pt*
EMP: 90 **EST:** 1988
SQ FT: 3,500
SALES (est): 24.32MM **Privately Held**
Web: www.premierpoolsandspas.com
SIC: 1799 7389 6794 Spa or hot tub installation or construction; Swimming pool and hot tub service and maintenance; Franchises, selling or licensing

(P-2307)
PROFORM INTERIOR CNSTR INC
663 33rd St Ste C (92102-3300)
PHONE..................................619 881-0041
James Pettit, *Pr*
Reid Schneider, *
EMP: 73 **EST:** 2014
SQ FT: 5,000
SALES (est): 4.64MM **Privately Held**
Web: www.proforminteriors.com
SIC: 1799 Home/office interiors finishing, furnishing and remodeling

1799 - Special Trade Contractors, Nec (P-2308)

(P-2308)
PSG FENCING CORPORATION
330 Main St (92501-1028)
PHONE..................................951 275-9252
EMP: 83
Web: www.psgfencinginc.com
SIC: 1799 Fence construction
PA: P.S.G. Fencing Corporation
1218 D St
Los Banos CA

(P-2309)
QUALITY SYSTEMS INSTLLTONS LTD
Also Called: Q S I
105 Associated Rd (94080-6013)
PHONE..................................650 875-9000
Jon Chase, Pr
Robert W Lindstrom, *
Daniel Castillo, *
EMP: 60 EST: 1986
SALES (est): 4.83MM Privately Held
Web: www.qsiltd.com
SIC: 1799 Office furniture installation

(P-2310)
R4K3 LLC
Also Called: Kitchen Plus
1961 Taylor St (95993-9705)
PHONE..................................425 462-0375
EMP: 70 EST: 1993
SALES (est): 9.85MM Privately Held
Web: www.aredalecabinetry.com
SIC: 1799 Kitchen and bathroom remodeling

(P-2311)
RAINBOW WTRPROFING RESTORATION
600 Treat Ave (94110-2016)
PHONE..................................415 641-1578
Christopher Abel, Pr
Rob Browne, *
EMP: 124 EST: 1927
SALES (est): 21.34MM Privately Held
Web: www.rainbow415.com
SIC: 1799 Waterproofing

(P-2312)
RESTEC CONTRACTORS INC
22955 Kidder St (94545-1670)
PHONE..................................510 670-0100
John Andrzejewski, Pr
Freeman Boyett, *
R Todd Fearon, *
David Brueggen, *
EMP: 100 EST: 1985
SALES (est): 12.31MM
SALES (corp-wide): 461.98MM Privately Held
Web: www.resteccontractors.com
SIC: 1799 Asbestos removal and encapsulation
HQ: Vertecs Corporation
14700 Ne 95th St Ste 201
Redmond WA
425 885-1990

(P-2313)
REY-CREST ROOFG WATERPROOFING
Also Called: Rey-Crest Roofg Waterproofing
3065 Verdugo Rd (90065-2014)
PHONE..................................323 257-9329
George Reyes, Pr
Georgia Reyes, *
EMP: 80 EST: 1969
SQ FT: 10,000
SALES (est): 8.84MM Privately Held
Web: www.rey-crestroofing.com
SIC: 1799 1761 Waterproofing; Roofing contractor

(P-2314)
SELEX INC
930 Shiloh Rd (95492-9659)
PHONE..................................707 836-8836
Dave Boettger, Brnch Mgr
EMP: 61
SALES (corp-wide): 9.95MM Privately Held
SIC: 1799 Fence construction
PA: Selex, Inc.
442 Longfellow St
Livermore CA
707 836-8836

(P-2315)
SHORING ENGINEERS
Also Called: Shoring & Excavating
12645 Clark St (90670-3951)
PHONE..................................562 944-9331
George A Woodley Senior, VP
George A Woodleysr, *
George A Woodley Junior, VP
Jason E Weinstein, *
Ren Contreras, *
▲ EMP: 60 EST: 1966
SALES (est): 19.73MM Privately Held
Web: www.shoringengineers.com
SIC: 1799 8711 Shore cleaning and maintenance; Engineering services

(P-2316)
SKYLINE SCAFFOLD INC
3131 52nd Ave (95823-1022)
PHONE..................................916 391-8929
Amy Johnson, CEO
David Johnson, *
EMP: 98
SALES (est): 18.67MM Privately Held
Web: www.skylinescaffold.com
SIC: 1799 Scaffolding

(P-2317)
SUNLAND SCAFFOLD
24885 Whitewood Rd # 106 (92563-2004)
P.O. Box 2587 (92593-2587)
PHONE..................................951 595-9402
Arnulfo Wiedensohler, Pr
EMP: 60 EST: 2019
SALES (est): 1.45MM Privately Held
SIC: 1799 Scaffolding

(P-2318)
TAILORED LIVING CHOICES LLC
Also Called: Tailored Living
1957 Sierra Ave (94558-2840)
PHONE..................................707 259-0526
Vicki Robinson, Managing Member
EMP: 112 EST: 2006
SALES (est): 8.99MM Privately Held
Web: www.tailoredlivingchoices.com
SIC: 1799 Home/office interiors finishing, furnishing and remodeling

(P-2319)
TEAM WEST CONTRACTING CORP
2733 S Vista Ave (92316-3269)
PHONE..................................951 340-3426
Dawn Lilly, Prin
Jerry R Pacheco, *
Stephen Knehans, *
EMP: 92 EST: 2009
SQ FT: 7,200
SALES (est): 8.54MM Privately Held
Web: www.twc-corp.com

(P-2320)
TESERRA (PA)
Also Called: California Pools
86100 Avenue 54 (92236-3813)
P.O. Box 1280 (92236-1280)
PHONE..................................760 340-9000
Bob Smith, Pr
James Harebottle, *
EMP: 399 EST: 1985
SQ FT: 10,000
SALES (est): 42.96MM
SALES (corp-wide): 42.96MM Privately Held
Web: www.teserraoutdoors.com
SIC: 1799 Swimming pool construction

(P-2321)
THE TEECOR GROUP INC
Also Called: Key Environmental Services
1450 S Burlington Ave (90006-5409)
PHONE..................................213 632-2350
Kalani K C Childs, Pr
Eric Youssef, *
EMP: 60 EST: 1999
SQ FT: 5,000
SALES (est): 4.15MM Privately Held
Web: www.teecor.com
SIC: 1799 Asbestos removal and encapsulation

(P-2322)
TOPBUILD SERVICES GROUP CORP
Also Called: Masco
1341 Oakland Rd (95112-1317)
PHONE..................................408 882-0411
Bob Colla, Brnch Mgr
EMP: 2527
SALES (corp-wide): 5.01B Publicly Held
Web: www.topbuild.com
SIC: 1799 Prefabricated fireplace installation
HQ: Topbuild Services Group Corp.
475 N Williamson Blvd
Daytona Beach FL
386 304-2200

(P-2323)
TURN KEY SCAFFOLD LLC
410 W 30th St (91950-7269)
P.O. Box 120340 (91912-3440)
PHONE..................................619 642-0880
Alvin Ruis Iii, Pr
EMP: 106 EST: 2017
SALES (est): 7.36MM Privately Held
Web: www.tksscaffold.com
SIC: 1799 Scaffolding

(P-2324)
UNIQUE SCAFFOLD
2501 Annalisa Dr (94520-1220)
PHONE..................................925 457-3379
John Soto, CEO
Joe Garcia, *
EMP: 70 EST: 2011
SALES (est): 4.54MM Privately Held
Web: www.uniquescaffold.us
SIC: 1799 Scaffolding

(P-2325)
UNITED MARBLE & GRANITE INC
2163 Martin Ave (95050-2701)
PHONE..................................408 347-3300
Manuel De Oliveira, Pr
▲ EMP: 80 EST: 1998
SALES (est): 6.91MM Privately Held
Web: www.unitedmarbleusa.com

(P-2326)
US SOLID SURFACES
23481 Connecticut St (94545-5305)
PHONE..................................510 300-8980
Donovan Joseph Nimmo, Pr
EMP: 60 EST: 2015
SALES (est): 3.09MM Privately Held
SIC: 1799 Counter top installation

(P-2327)
VALLEY WATERPROOFING INC
825 Civic Center Dr Ste 6 (95050-3960)
P.O. Box 20003 (95160-0003)
PHONE..................................408 985-7701
Donna O'brien, Pr
Michael O'brien, VP
EMP: 80 EST: 1981
SQ FT: 1,000
SALES (est): 5MM Privately Held
Web: www.valleywaterproofing.com
SIC: 1799 Waterproofing

(P-2328)
WALTON ENGINEERING INC
3900 Commerce Dr (95691-2157)
P.O. Box 1025 (95691-1025)
PHONE..................................916 372-1888
Michael Walton, Pr
Richard Walton, *
EMP: 65 EST: 1988
SQ FT: 13,000
SALES (est): 9.66MM Privately Held
Web: www.waltonengineering.com
SIC: 1799 1542 7389 Service station equipment installation, maint., and repair; Service station construction; Drafting service, except temporary help

(P-2329)
WASHINGTON ORNA IR WORKS INC (PA)
Also Called: Washington Iron Works
17926 S Broadway (90248-3540)
P.O. Box 460 (90247-0846)
PHONE..................................310 327-8660
Daniel Welsh, CEO
Tom Pederson, *
Luke Welsh, *
Chris Powell, *
EMP: 117 EST: 1966
SQ FT: 141,240
SALES (est): 25.62MM
SALES (corp-wide): 25.62MM Privately Held
SIC: 1799 3446 Ornamental metal work; Architectural metalwork

(P-2330)
WATERPRFING ROFG SOLUTIONS INC
11041 Santa Monica Blvd Ste 306 (90025-3523)
PHONE..................................310 571-0892
Homayoun Kazemi, CEO
Mauricio Barahona, *
EMP: 72 EST: 2001
SALES (est): 11MM Privately Held
Web: www.wandrsolutions.com
SIC: 1799 Waterproofing

(P-2331)
WAYNE PERRY INC (PA)
8281 Commonwealth Ave (90621-2537)
PHONE..................................714 826-0352
Wayne Perry, Pr
Adam Leiter, *
Ron Perry, *

PRODUCTS & SERVICES SECTION   2024 - Ice Cream And Frozen Deserts (P-2350)

Greg Nicholson, *
Daniel Mcgill, VP
EMP: 185 EST: 1969
SQ FT: 4,000
SALES (est): 33.36MM
SALES (corp-wide): 33.36MM Privately Held
Web: www.wpinc.com
SIC: 1799 8711 Decontamination services; Engineering services

(P-2332)
WEST COAST COUNTERTOPS INC
1200 Marlborough Ave Ste B (92507-2158)
PHONE.....................951 719-3670
▲ EMP: 90 EST: 1990
SALES (est): 9.04MM Privately Held
SIC: 1799 5211 Counter top installation; Counter tops

(P-2333)
WEST COAST FIRESTOPPING INC
1130 W Trenton Ave (92867-3536)
PHONE.....................714 935-1104
Karl Stoll, Pr
EMP: 80 EST: 2007
SALES (est): 9.79MM Privately Held
Web: www.westcoastfirestop.com
SIC: 1799 Fireproofing buildings

(P-2334)
WLMD
Also Called: Wellmade Products
1715 Kibby Rd (95341-9301)
PHONE.....................209 723-9120
Mark R Riley, CEO
Doug Bartman, *
Jerry Yon, *
▲ EMP: 130 EST: 1992
SQ FT: 120,000
SALES (est): 15.83MM Privately Held
Web: www.wlmd.com
SIC: 1799 1761 Lightning conductor erection; Roofing, siding, and sheetmetal work

(P-2335)
WOODS MAINTENANCE SERVICES INC
Also Called: Hydro-Pressure Systems
7250 Coldwater Canyon Ave (91605-4203)
PHONE.....................818 764-2515
Barry Woods, Pr
Barry Woods, Pr
Diane Woods, *
Jeff Woods, *
Josh Woods, *
EMP: 135 EST: 1975
SALES (est): 9.36MM Privately Held
Web: www.graffiticontrol.com
SIC: 1799 Cleaning building exteriors, nec

(P-2336)
YYK ENTERPRISES OPERATIONS LLC (PA)
3475 E St (92102-3335)
PHONE.....................619 474-6229
Ted Kines, CEO
Steve Johnstone, *
EMP: 190 EST: 1981
SQ FT: 4,000
SALES (est): 24.02MM
SALES (corp-wide): 24.02MM Privately Held
Web: www.yykenterprises.com
SIC: 1799 1721 3731 Sandblasting of building exteriors; Ship painting; Shipbuilding and repairing

(P-2337)
ZODIAC POOL SYSTEMS LLC
2611 Commerce Way Ste B (92081-8455)
PHONE.....................760 599-9600
Oscar Guerrero, Managing Member
EMP: 73
SALES (corp-wide): 517.04MM Privately Held
Web: www.fluidrausa.com
SIC: 1799 7389 Swimming pool construction; Swimming pool and hot tub service and maintenance
HQ: Zodiac Pool Systems Llc
    2882 Whiptail Loop Ste 1
    Carlsbad CA
    760 599-9600

2011 Meat Packing Plants

(P-2338)
COLUMBUS FOODS LLC
30977 San Antonio St (94544-7109)
PHONE.....................510 921-3400
Ralph Denisco, CEO
John Piccetti, *
Adam Ferrif, *
▲ EMP: 345 EST: 1917
SALES (est): 19.92MM Privately Held
SIC: 2011 5143 5147 Luncheon meat, from meat slaughtered on site; Cheese; Meats and meat products

(P-2339)
FIRSTCLASS FOODS - TROJAN INC
Also Called: First Class Foods
12500 Inglewood Ave (90250-4217)
P.O. Box 2397 (90251-2397)
PHONE.....................310 676-2500
Salomon Benzimra, Pr
Felix Benzimra, VP Sls
Albert Benzimra, Sec
Lucy Benzimra, CFO
EMP: 135 EST: 1963
SQ FT: 45,000
SALES (est): 20.89MM Publicly Held
SIC: 2011 5147 Meat packing plants; Meats and meat products
HQ: Us Foods, Inc.
    9399 W Higgins Rd # 100
    Rosemont IL

(P-2340)
RICHWOOD MEAT COMPANY INC
2751 N Santa Fe Ave (95348-4109)
P.O. Box 2599 (95344-0599)
PHONE.....................209 722-8171
Michael J Wood, Pr
Hellen Diane Inks-fragie, CFO
Carol J Wood, Stockholder*
Steven J Wood, *
EMP: 100 EST: 1964
SQ FT: 43,000
SALES (est): 57.73MM Privately Held
Web: www.richwoodmeat.com
SIC: 2011 5147 5421 Meat packing plants; Meats, fresh; Meat and fish markets

2013 Sausages And Other Prepared Meats

(P-2341)
AIDELLS SAUSAGE COMPANY INC
Also Called: Aidells Sausage
2411 Baumann Ave (94580-1801)
PHONE.....................510 614-5450
TOLL FREE: 800
Ernie Gabiati, Pr
EMP: 900 EST: 2007
SQ FT: 15,000
SALES (est): 77.99MM
SALES (corp-wide): 53.28B Publicly Held
Web: www.aidells.com
SIC: 2013 5147 Sausages, from purchased meat; Meats and meat products
HQ: The Hillshire Brands Company
    400 S Jefferson St Ste 1n
    Chicago IL
    312 614-6000

(P-2342)
DEREK AND CONSTANCE LEE CORP (PA)
Also Called: Great River Food
19355 San Jose Ave (91748-1420)
PHONE.....................909 595-8831
Derek E Lee, Pr
▲ EMP: 95 EST: 1985
SQ FT: 50,000
SALES (est): 8.85MM
SALES (corp-wide): 8.85MM Privately Held
Web: www.greatriverfood.com
SIC: 2013 1541 Sausages and other prepared meats; Food products manufacturing or packing plant construction

2015 Poultry Slaughtering And Processing

(P-2343)
COMMODITY SALES CO
517 S Clarence St (90033-4225)
PHONE.....................323 980-5463
William T Zant, Pr
EMP: 120 EST: 1967
SQ FT: 14,522
SALES (est): 5.21MM Privately Held
SIC: 2015 5144 5142 Poultry slaughtering and processing; Poultry and poultry products; Packaged frozen goods

(P-2344)
FOSTER POULTRY FARMS
Also Called: FOSTER POULTRY FARMS
900 W Belgravia Ave (93706-3909)
PHONE.....................559 265-2000
Jessi Amezcua, Brnch Mgr
EMP: 303
SALES (corp-wide): 1.25B Privately Held
Web: www.fosterfarms.com
SIC: 2015 5812 0173 5191 Chicken slaughtering and processing; Chicken restaurant; Almond grove; Animal feeds
PA: Foster Poultry Farms, Llc
    1000 Davis St
    Livingston CA
    209 394-7901

(P-2345)
OLIVERA EGG RANCH LLC
Also Called: Olivera Foods
3315 Sierra Rd (95132-3099)
P.O. Box 32126 (95152-2126)
PHONE.....................408 258-8074
▲ EMP: 60 EST: 1949
SQ FT: 35,000
SALES (est): 8.85MM Privately Held
SIC: 2015 5143 5142 5144 Egg processing; Cheese; Packaged frozen goods; Eggs

2022 Cheese; Natural And Processed

(P-2346)
RIZO LOPEZ FOODS INC
Also Called: Don Francisco Cheese
201 S Mcclure Rd (95357-0519)
P.O. Box 1689 (95319-1689)
PHONE.....................800 626-5587
Edwin Rizo, Pr
Ivan Rizo, *
▲ EMP: 313 EST: 1990
SQ FT: 3,800
SALES (est): 94.46MM Privately Held
Web: www.tiofranciscocheese.com
SIC: 2022 5143 2023 5141 Natural cheese; Dairy products, except dried or canned; Dry, condensed and evaporated dairy products; Groceries, general line

(P-2347)
SAPUTO CHEESE USA INC
5611 Imperial Hwy (90280-7419)
PHONE.....................562 862-7686
Rick Mckenney, Brnch Mgr
EMP: 412
SALES (corp-wide): 3.79B Privately Held
Web: www.saputo.com
SIC: 2022 5143 Natural cheese; Cheese
HQ: Saputo Cheese Usa Inc.
    10700 W Res Dr Ste 400
    Milwaukee WI

2023 Dry, Condensed, Evaporated Products

(P-2348)
NATURALIFE ECO VITE LABS
Also Called: Paragon Laboratories
20433 Earl St (90503-2414)
PHONE.....................310 370-1563
Jay Kaufman, CEO
Richard Kaufman, *
Claire Kaufman, *
Steven Billis, *
▲ EMP: 100 EST: 1971
SQ FT: 25,000
SALES (est): 22.91MM Privately Held
Web: www.paragonlabsusa.com
SIC: 2023 2844 2834 5122 Dietary supplements, dairy and non-dairy based; Toilet preparations; Suppositories; Vitamins and minerals

2024 Ice Cream And Frozen Deserts

(P-2349)
EDYS GRAND ICE CREAM
Also Called: Windy City Express
5929 College Ave (94618-1325)
PHONE.....................510 652-8187
▼ EMP: 3700
SIC: 2024 5143 Ice cream and ice milk; Ice cream and ices

(P-2350)
SUPER STORE INDUSTRIES
Also Called: Mid Valley Dairy
2600 Spengler Way (95380-8591)
PHONE.....................209 668-2100
Joe Mc Gill, Mgr
EMP: 100
Web: www.ssica.com
SIC: 2024 5143 Ice cream and frozen deserts; Ice cream and ices

2026 Fluid Milk

(P-2351)
BERKELEY FARMS LLC
Also Called: Buds Ice Cream San Francisco
17637 E Valley Blvd (91744-5731)
P.O. Box 4616 (94540-4616)
PHONE.................................510 265-8600
▲ **EMP:** 400
SIC: 2026 0241 5143 Fluid milk; Dairy farms; Butter
PA: Super Store Industries
16888 Mckinley Ave
Lathrop CA

2033 Canned Fruits And Specialties

(P-2352)
COBBLESTONE FRUIT ✪
730 N Oliver Ave (93657-8918)
PHONE.................................559 524-1005
Robert Hives, CEO
EMP: 150 **EST:** 2022
SALES (est): 15.04MM **Privately Held**
SIC: 2033 7389 Fruits and fruit products, in cans, jars, etc.; Business Activities at Non-Commercial Site

(P-2353)
STAPLETON - SPENCE PACKING CO (PA)
Also Called: Stapleton
1900 State Highway 99 (95948-9401)
P.O. Box 948 (95948-0948)
PHONE.................................408 297-8815
Martin Bradley Stapleton, Pr
Gavin Heitman, *
◆ **EMP:** 79 **EST:** 1951
SQ FT: 105,000
SALES (est): 18.06MM
SALES (corp-wide): 18.06MM **Privately Held**
Web: www.stapleton-spence.com
SIC: 2033 5085 Fruits and fruit products, in cans, jars, etc.; Cans for fruits and vegetables

2034 Dehydrated Fruits, Vegetables, Soups

(P-2354)
CARUTHERS RAISIN PKG CO INC (PA)
12797 S Elm Ave (93609-9711)
PHONE.................................559 864-9448
Donald Kizirian, Pr
Don Kizirian, *
Dennis Housepian, *
Gina Elsea, *
◆ **EMP:** 68 **EST:** 1985
SQ FT: 4,000
SALES (est): 12.3MM
SALES (corp-wide): 12.3MM **Privately Held**
Web: www.caruthersraisinpacking.com
SIC: 2034 5084 4513 Dried and dehydrated fruits, vegetables and soup mixes; Processing and packaging equipment; Air courier services

2035 Pickles, Sauces, And Salad Dressings

(P-2355)
PACIFICA FOODS LLC
Also Called: Stir Foods
1851 N Delilah St (92879-1800)
PHONE.................................951 371-3123
Ming Milton Liu, *
EMP: 140 **EST:** 2000
SALES (est): 60MM
SALES (corp-wide): 240.72MM **Privately Held**
Web: www.stirfoods.com
SIC: 2035 5149 2033 Seasonings and sauces, except tomato and dry; Sauces; Tomato products, packaged in cans, jars, etc.
PA: Corona-Orange Foods Intermediate Holdings Llc
1581 N Main St
Orange CA
714 637-6050

2038 Frozen Specialties, Nec

(P-2356)
AJINOMOTO FOODS NORTH AMER INC
Also Called: Windsor Foods
4200 Concours Ste 100 (91764-4982)
PHONE.................................909 477-4700
Steve Charles, Mgr
EMP: 244
Web: www.ajinomotofoods.com
SIC: 2038 5142 Frozen specialties, nec; Packaged frozen goods
HQ: Ajinomoto Foods North America, Inc.
4200 Concours Ste 100
Ontario CA

(P-2357)
HARVEST FARMS INC
45000 Yucca Ave (93534-2526)
PHONE.................................661 945-3636
Craig Shugert, CEO
Eric Shiring, *
▲ **EMP:** 100 **EST:** 1947
SQ FT: 18,000
SALES (est): 24.09MM
SALES (corp-wide): 519.54MM **Privately Held**
Web: www.harvestfarms.com
SIC: 2038 5144 Lunches, frozen and packaged; Poultry and poultry products
HQ: Good Source Solutions, Inc.
3115 Melrose Dr Ste 160
Carlsbad CA
858 455-4800

(P-2358)
SPECIALTY BRANDS INCORPORATED
4200 Concours Ste 100 (91764-4982)
P.O. Box 51467 (91761-1057)
PHONE.................................909 477-4851
EMP: 1900
SIC: 2038 5142 Frozen specialties, nec; Packaged frozen goods

2041 Flour And Other Grain Mill Products

(P-2359)
SUNOPTA GRAINS AND FOODS INC
12128 Center St (90280-8046)
PHONE.................................323 774-6000
EMP: 62
SALES (corp-wide): 934.66MM **Publicly Held**
Web: www.sunopta.com
SIC: 2041 5153 Flour and other grain mill products; Grains
HQ: Sunopta Grains And Foods Inc.
7078 Shady Oak Rd
Eden Prairie MN

(P-2360)
THE SWEET LIFE ENTERPRISES INC
Also Called: Aryzta Sweet Life
2350 Pullman St (92705-5507)
PHONE.................................949 261-7400
EMP: 115
Web: www.sweetlifeinc.com
SIC: 2041 5149 Doughs and batters; Crackers, cookies, and bakery products

2043 Cereal Breakfast Foods

(P-2361)
EAST WEST TEA COMPANY LLC
Also Called: Golden Temple
1616 Preuss Rd (90035-4212)
PHONE.................................310 275-9891
EMP: 226
SALES (corp-wide): 97.82MM **Privately Held**
Web: www.yogiproducts.com
SIC: 2043 2099 2064 8721 Cereal breakfast foods; Tea blending; Candy and other confectionery products; Billing and bookkeeping service
PA: East West Tea Company, Llc
1325 Westec Dr
Eugene OR
541 461-2160

2044 Rice Milling

(P-2362)
CALIFORNIA FAMILY FOODS LLC
6550 Struckmeyer Rd (95912)
PHONE.................................530 476-3326
David Myers, Pr
Bruce Meyers, Managing Member*
Tom Charter, Managing Member*
Perry Charter, *
▼ **EMP:** 75 **EST:** 1995
SQ FT: 75,000
SALES (est): 20.07MM **Privately Held**
Web: www.californiafamilyfoods.com
SIC: 2044 0723 Rice milling; Rice drying services

(P-2363)
WEHAH-LUNDBERG INC
Also Called: Lundberg Family Farms
5311 Midway (95974)
P.O. Box 369 (95974-0369)
PHONE.................................530 882-4551
▼ **EMP:** 220
SIC: 2044 0723 4221 Rice milling; Rice drying services; Farm product warehousing and storage

2048 Prepared Feeds, Nec

(P-2364)
NATURAL BALANCE PET FOODS LLC (PA)
2358 University Ave Ste 2280 (92104-2720)
P.O. Box 397 (91785-0397)
PHONE.................................800 829-4493
Brian Connolly, CEO
▲ **EMP:** 64 **EST:** 1989
SQ FT: 55,000
SALES (est): 29.94MM **Privately Held**
SIC: 2048 5199 Prepared feeds, nec; Pet supplies

(P-2365)
NUTRA-BLEND LLC
Also Called: Thomas Products
2140 W Industrial Ave (93637-5210)
PHONE.................................559 661-6161
Mike Osborne, Brnch Mgr
EMP: 408
SALES (corp-wide): 2.89B **Privately Held**
Web: www.nutrablend.com
SIC: 2048 5191 Pulverized oats, prepared as animal feed; Animal feeds
HQ: Nutra-Blend, L.L.C.
3200 2nd St
Neosho MO
417 451-6111

2051 Bread, Cake, And Related Products

(P-2366)
COOLISH HOLDINGS LLC
Also Called: Wildflour Bakery
21160 Califa St (91367-5002)
PHONE.................................818 575-7280
Marty Weissberg, Admn
EMP: 62 **EST:** 2012
SQ FT: 30,000
SALES (est): 12.26MM **Privately Held**
Web: www.kananbaking.com
SIC: 2051 5812 5142 5149 Breads, rolls, and buns; Restaurant, family: independent; Bakery products, frozen; Bakery products

(P-2367)
COTTAGE BAKERY INC
Also Called: Frozen Bakery
1831 S Stockton St (95240-6302)
P.O. Box 1720 (95241-1720)
PHONE.................................209 334-3616
◆ **EMP:** 400 **EST:** 1972
SALES (est): 138.16MM
SALES (corp-wide): 3.45B **Publicly Held**
SIC: 2051 2053 5149 Bread, cake, and related products; Frozen bakery products, except bread; Bakery products
PA: Treehouse Foods, Inc.
2021 Spring Rd Ste 600
Oak Brook IL
708 483-1300

(P-2368)
LITTLE BROTHERS BAKERY LLC
Also Called: Little Brothers Bakery
320 W Alondra Blvd (90248-2423)
PHONE.................................310 225-3790
Paul C Giuliano, Managing Member
Anthony S Giuliano, *
Joann Giuliano, *

PRODUCTS & SERVICES SECTION
2084 - Wines, Brandy, And Brandy Spirits (P-2386)

▲ EMP: 65 EST: 1999
SQ FT: 15,000
SALES (est): 9.86MM Privately Held
Web: www.littlebrothersbakery.com
SIC: 2051 5149 Bakery: wholesale or wholesale/retail combined; Bakery products

(P-2369)
OAKHURST INDUSTRIES INC (PA)
Also Called: Freund Baking
2050 S Tubeway Ave (90040-1624)
P.O. Box 911457 (90091-1238)
PHONE..............................323 724-3000
James Freund, Pr
Ronald Martin, *
Jonathan Freund, *
Linda F Freund, *
EMP: 140 EST: 1981
SQ FT: 81,000
SALES (est): 51.88MM Privately Held
Web: www.oakhurstmetals.com
SIC: 2051 5149 Buns, bread type: fresh or frozen; Groceries and related products, nec

2052 Cookies And Crackers

(P-2370)
CHARLIES SPECIALTIES INC
501 Airpark Dr (92833-2501)
PHONE..............................724 346-2350
Jay Thier, Pr
Edward G Byrnes Junior, Ch
Thomas C Byrnes, *
EMP: 117 EST: 1967
SALES (est): 1.53MM
SALES (corp-wide): 38.32MM Privately Held
SIC: 2052 5149 5142 2045 Cookies; Groceries and related products, nec; Packaged frozen goods; Prepared flour mixes and doughs
PA: Byrnes And Kiefer Company
   131 Kline Ave
   Callery PA
   724 538-5200

(P-2371)
J & J SNACK FOODS CORP CAL (HQ)
5353 S Downey Rd (90058-3725)
PHONE..............................323 581-0171
Dennis Moore, VP
▲ EMP: 112 EST: 1978
SQ FT: 132,000
SALES (est): 103.41MM
SALES (corp-wide): 1.38B Publicly Held
Web: www.jjsnack.com
SIC: 2052 5149 Pretzels; Cookies
PA: J & J Snack Foods Corp.
   350 Fellowship Rd
   Mount Laurel NJ
   856 665-9533

(P-2372)
UTBBB INC
10711 Bloomfield St (90720-2503)
PHONE..............................562 594-4411
Gary Marks, CEO
William R Ross, *
Gene Kester, *
◆ EMP: 92 EST: 1985
SQ FT: 1,000
SALES (est): 3.94MM
SALES (corp-wide): 3.45B Publicly Held
SIC: 2052 5141 Cookies and crackers; Food brokers
HQ: Treehouse Private Brands, Inc.
   2021 Spring Rd Ste 600
   Oak Brook IL

2064 Candy And Other Confectionery Products

(P-2373)
CLIF BAR & COMPANY LLC (HQ)
1451 66th St (94608-1004)
PHONE..............................510 596-6300
Sally Grimes, CEO
Hari Avula, *
Kevin Cleary, *
▲ EMP: 253 EST: 1986
SQ FT: 120,000
SALES (est): 550.92MM Publicly Held
Web: www.clifbar.com
SIC: 2064 5149 Candy bars, including chocolate covered bars; Specialty food items
PA: Mondelez International, Inc.
   905 W Fulton Market # 200
   Chicago IL

(P-2374)
GENESIS FOODS CORPORATION
Also Called: Garvey Nut & Candy
8825 Mercury Ln (90660-6707)
PHONE..............................323 890-5890
TOLL FREE: 800
▲ EMP: 60
Web: www.garveycandy.com
SIC: 2064 5149 Candy and other confectionery products; Cookies

(P-2375)
HIRA PARIS INC
Also Called: Andy Anand Chocolates
3811 Schaefer Ave Ste B (91710-5400)
PHONE..............................909 634-3900
Thaminder Singh Anand, Pr
Sing Datu, VP
EMP: 200 EST: 2020
SALES (est): 10.57MM Privately Held
SIC: 2064 5149 Candy bars, including chocolate covered bars; Chocolate

2068 Salted And Roasted Nuts And Seeds

(P-2376)
STEWART & JASPER MARKETING INC (PA)
Also Called: Stewart & Jasper Orchards
3500 Shiells Rd (95360-9798)
PHONE..............................209 862-9600
Jim Jasper, Pr
Susan Dompe, *
Jason Jasper, *
◆ EMP: 175 EST: 1993
SQ FT: 225,000
SALES (est): 49.66MM
SALES (corp-wide): 49.66MM Privately Held
Web: www.stewartandjasper.com
SIC: 2068 0723 0173 5148 Nuts: dried, dehydrated, salted or roasted; Crop preparation services for market; Tree nuts; Fresh fruits and vegetables

2079 Edible Fats And Oils

(P-2377)
WILSEY FOODS INC
40 Pointe Dr (92821-3652)
PHONE..............................714 257-3700
Takashi Fukunaga, CEO
Steve Takagi, Pr
Hiro Matsumura, VP
◆ EMP: 1000 EST: 1919
SQ FT: 103,378
SALES (est): 52.94MM Privately Held
Web: www.venturafoods.com
SIC: 2079 5149 Cooking oils, except corn: vegetable refined; Shortening, vegetable
HQ: Mbk Usa Holdings, Inc.
   200 Park Ave Fl 36
   New York NY
   212 878-6773

2084 Wines, Brandy, And Brandy Spirits

(P-2378)
C MONDAVI & FAMILY (PA)
Also Called: Charles Krug Winery
2800 Main St (94574-9502)
P.O. Box 191 (94574-0191)
PHONE..............................707 967-2200
John Lennon, Pr
Mark Mondavi, *
Peter Mondavi Junior, Treas
Mike Spiegel, *
▲ EMP: 85 EST: 1866
SQ FT: 175,000
SALES (est): 34.78MM
SALES (corp-wide): 34.78MM Privately Held
Web: www.charleskrug.com
SIC: 2084 0172 Wine cellars, bonded: engaged in blending wines; Grapes

(P-2379)
DOMAINE CHANDON INC (DH)
1 California Dr (94599-1426)
PHONE..............................707 944-8844
Matthew Wood, CEO
◆ EMP: 100 EST: 1973
SQ FT: 240,000
SALES (est): 63.36MM
SALES (corp-wide): 503.87MM Privately Held
Web: www.chandon.com
SIC: 2084 5812 0762 5813 Wines; Eating places; Vineyard management and maintenance services; Drinking places
HQ: Moet Hennessy Usa, Inc.
   7 World Trade Ctr At250
   New York NY
   212 251-8200

(P-2380)
E & J GALLO WINERY (PA)
Also Called: New Amsterdam Spirits
600 Yosemite Blvd (95354-2760)
P.O. Box 1130 (95353-1130)
PHONE..............................209 341-3111
Joseph E Gallo, CEO
◆ EMP: 2500 EST: 1942
SALES (est): 2.11B
SALES (corp-wide): 2.11B Privately Held
Web: www.gallo.com
SIC: 2084 0172 Wines; Grapes

(P-2381)
E & J GALLO WINERY
5610 E Olive Ave (93727-2707)
P.O. Box 1081 (93714-1081)
PHONE..............................559 458-0807
Joe Rossi, Brnch Mgr
EMP: 107
SALES (corp-wide): 2.11B Privately Held
Web: www.gallo.com
SIC: 2084 0172 Wines; Grapes
PA: E. & J. Gallo Winery
   600 Yosemite Blvd
   Modesto CA
   209 341-3111

(P-2382)
E & J GALLO WINERY
Also Called: Lerexa Winery
18000 River Rd (95334-9514)
PHONE..............................209 394-6200
Kent Mann, Mgr
EMP: 93
SALES (corp-wide): 2.11B Privately Held
Web: www.gallo.com
SIC: 2084 0172 Wines; Grapes
PA: E. & J. Gallo Winery
   600 Yosemite Blvd
   Modesto CA
   209 341-3111

(P-2383)
F KORBEL & BROS (PA)
Also Called: Korbel Champagne Cellars
13250 River Rd (95446-9593)
PHONE..............................707 824-7000
Gary B Heck, Pr
Danny Baker, Ex VP
Matthew Healey, VP Fin
Harold Duncan, VP Opers
David Faris, Treas
◆ EMP: 200 EST: 1882
SQ FT: 66,000
SALES (est): 96.1MM
SALES (corp-wide): 96.1MM Privately Held
Web: www.korbel.com
SIC: 2084 0172 Wines; Grapes

(P-2384)
FALKNER WINERY INC
40620 Calle Contento (92591-5041)
PHONE..............................951 676-6741
EMP: 65 EST: 1993
SALES (est): 9.11MM Privately Held
Web: www.falknerwinery.com
SIC: 2084 7299 Wines; Banquet hall facilities

(P-2385)
FERRAR-CRANO VNYRDS WINERY LLC (PA)
Also Called: Ferrari-Carano
8761 Dry Creek Rd (95448-9133)
P.O. Box 1549 (95448-1549)
PHONE..............................707 433-6700
Rhonda Carano, CEO
▲ EMP: 114 EST: 1981
SQ FT: 46,000
SALES (est): 19.35MM
SALES (corp-wide): 19.35MM Privately Held
Web: www.ferrari-carano.com
SIC: 2084 0172 Wines; Grapes

(P-2386)
FIRESTONE VINEYARD LP
Also Called: Curtis Winery
5000 Zaca Station Rd (93441-4566)
P.O. Box 244 (93441-0244)
PHONE..............................805 688-3940
Michael L Gravelle, Pt
Adam Firestone, Pt
▲ EMP: 85 EST: 1976
SQ FT: 45,000
SALES (est): 8.65MM
SALES (corp-wide): 69.09MM Privately Held
Web: www.firestonewine.com
SIC: 2084 0172 Wines; Grapes
HQ: Foley Family Wines, Inc.
   200 Concourse Blvd
   Santa Rosa CA

2084 - Wines, Brandy, And Brandy Spirits (P-2387)

PRODUCTS & SERVICES SECTION

(P-2387)
JACKSON FAMILY WINES INC (PA)
Also Called: Vineyards of Monterey
425 Aviation Blvd (95403-1069)
PHONE.................707 544-4000
Barbara Banke, *Dir*
Charles Shea, *Product Vice President**
Viviann Stapp, *
▲ EMP: 100 EST: 1987
SQ FT: 25,000
SALES (est): 280.96MM Privately Held
Web: www.jacksonfamilywines.com
SIC: **2084** 0172 5813 Wines; Grapes; Wine bar

(P-2388)
JVW CORPORATION
Also Called: Jordan Vineyard & Winery
1474 Alexander Valley Rd (95448-9003)
P.O. Box 878 (95448-0878)
PHONE.................707 431-5250
John Jordan, *CEO*
Thomas N Jordan Junior, *Pr*
◆ EMP: 75 EST: 1972
SQ FT: 50,000
SALES (est): 19.48MM Privately Held
Web: www.jordanwinery.com
SIC: **2084** 0172 Wines; Grapes

(P-2389)
MILDARA BLASS INC
Also Called: Windsor Vineyards
205 Concourse Blvd (95403-8258)
P.O. Box 368 (95492-0368)
PHONE.................707 836-5000
Kate Langford, *Pr*
▲ EMP: 280 EST: 1996
SALES (est): 14.69MM
SALES (corp-wide): 283.23MM Publicly Held
SIC: **2084** 5182 Wines; Brandy and brandy spirits
HQ: Vintage Wine Estates, Inc.
   205 Concourse Blvd
   Santa Rosa CA

(P-2390)
PERNOD RICARD USA LLC
Also Called: Kenwood Vineyards
9592 Sonoma Hwy (95452-8028)
P.O. Box 669 (95452-0669)
PHONE.................707 833-5891
EMP: 75
SQ FT: 1,414
SALES (corp-wide): 384.98MM Privately Held
Web: www.kenwoodvineyards.com
SIC: **2084** 0172 Wines; Grapes
HQ: Pernod Ricard Usa, Llc
   250 Park Ave Fl 17
   New York NY
   212 372-5400

(P-2391)
PETALUMAIDENCE OPCO LLC
Also Called: Vineyard Post Acute
101 Monroe St (94954-2328)
PHONE.................707 763-4109
Jason Murray, *Prin*
Mark Hancock, *
EMP: 124 EST: 2016
SALES (est): 12.32MM
SALES (corp-wide): 1.53B Privately Held
Web: www.vineyardpostacute.com
SIC: **2084** 8051 Wines; Skilled nursing care facilities
HQ: Providence Group Wine Country, Llc
   262 N University Ave
   Farmington UT
   801 447-9829

(P-2392)
SAN ANTONIO WINERY INC (PA)
Also Called: San Antonio Gift Shop
737 Lamar St (90031-2514)
PHONE.................323 223-1401
Santo Riboli, *CEO*
Maddelena Riboli, *
Cathey Riboli, *
◆ EMP: 101 EST: 1917
SQ FT: 310,000
SALES (est): 50.72MM
SALES (corp-wide): 50.72MM Privately Held
Web: www.sanantoniowinery.com
SIC: **2084** 5182 5812 Wines; Wine; Eating places

(P-2393)
SIERRA SUNRISE VINEYARD INC
Also Called: Montevina Winery
20680 Shenandoah School Rd (95669-9511)
P.O. Box 248 (94574-0248)
PHONE.................209 245-6942
Louis Trinchero, *Ch Bd*
Roger Trinchero, *CEO*
Robery Tortelson, *Pr*
Vera Trinchero Torres, *Sec*
Jeff Meyers, *VP*
EMP: 63 EST: 1970
SQ FT: 52,000
SALES (est): 2.18MM
SALES (corp-wide): 188.11MM Privately Held
Web: www.tfewines.com
SIC: **2084** 0172 Wines; Grapes
PA: Sutter Home Winery, Inc.
   100 Saint Helena Hwy S
   Saint Helena CA
   707 963-3104

(P-2394)
STERLING VINEYARDS INC
Also Called: STERLING VINEYARDS, INC.
1105 Oak Knoll Ave (94558-1304)
P.O. Box 365 (94515-0365)
PHONE.................707 252-7410
Vincent Vinnodo, *Mgr*
EMP: 103
SALES (corp-wide): 8.88MM Privately Held
Web: www.sterlingvineyards.com
SIC: **2084** 0172 Wines; Grapes
PA: Sterling Vineyards
   1111 Dunaweal Ln
   Calistoga CA
   707 942-3300

(P-2395)
SUTTER HOME WINERY INC (PA)
Also Called: Trinchero Family Estates
100 St Helena Hwy (Hwy. 29) S (94574-2204)
P.O. Box 248 (94574-0248)
PHONE.................707 963-3104
Bob Torkelson, *Pr*
◆ EMP: 200 EST: 1946
SQ FT: 17,000
SALES (est): 188.11MM
SALES (corp-wide): 188.11MM Privately Held
Web: www.sutterhome.com
SIC: **2084** 0172 Wines; Grapes

(P-2396)
TREASURY CHATEAU & ESTATES
Also Called: Chalone Vineyard
10300 Chalk Hill Rd (95448-9558)
P.O. Box 518 (93960-0518)
PHONE.................707 299-2600
▲ EMP: 170
Web: www.chalonevineyard.com
SIC: **2084** 5182 Wines; Wine

(P-2397)
WILSON CREEK WNERY VNYARDS INC
Also Called: Wilson Creek Winery
35960 Rancho California Rd (92591-5088)
PHONE.................951 699-9463
William J Wilson, *CEO*
Michael Wilson, *
Craig Johns, *
EMP: 110 EST: 2000
SQ FT: 6,000
SALES (est): 24.19MM Privately Held
Web: www.wilsoncreekwinery.com
SIC: **2084** 8999 Wines; Personal services

2086 Bottled And Canned Soft Drinks

(P-2398)
AMERICAN BOTTLING COMPANY
Also Called: Dr Pepper Snapple Group
1188 Mt Vernon Ave (92507-1829)
PHONE.................951 341-7500
Vince Spurgeon, *Mgr*
EMP: 76
Web: www.drpepper.com
SIC: **2086** 5149 Soft drinks: packaged in cans, bottles, etc.; Soft drinks
HQ: The American Bottling Company
   6425 Hall Of Fame Ln
   Frisco TX

(P-2399)
AMERICAN BOTTLING COMPANY
230 E 18th St (93305-5609)
PHONE.................661 323-7921
Brian Sutton, *Mgr*
EMP: 76
Web: www.keurigdrpepper.com
SIC: **2086** 5149 Soft drinks: packaged in cans, bottles, etc.; Soft drinks
HQ: The American Bottling Company
   6425 Hall Of Fame Ln
   Frisco TX

(P-2400)
AMERICAN BOTTLING COMPANY
1166 Arroyo St (91340-1824)
PHONE.................818 898-1471
Ed Nemecek, *Brnch Mgr*
EMP: 76
Web: www.keurigdrpepper.com
SIC: **2086** 5149 Soft drinks: packaged in cans, bottles, etc.; Soft drinks
HQ: The American Bottling Company
   6425 Hall Of Fame Ln
   Frisco TX

(P-2401)
AMERICAN BOTTLING COMPANY
1166 Arroyo St (92865)
PHONE.................714 974-8560
Mark Jones, *Mgr*
EMP: 185
Web: www.keurigdrpepper.com
SIC: **2086** 5149 Soft drinks: packaged in cans, bottles, etc.; Soft drinks
HQ: The American Bottling Company
   6425 Hall Of Fame Ln
   Frisco TX

(P-2402)
AMERICAN BOTTLING COMPANY
Also Called: 7 Up / R C Bottling Co
3220 E 26th St (90058-8008)
PHONE.................323 268-7779
Russ Wolfe, *Contrlr*
EMP: 113
Web: www.keurigdrpepper.com
SIC: **2086** 5149 Soft drinks: packaged in cans, bottles, etc.; Groceries and related products, nec
HQ: The American Bottling Company
   6425 Hall Of Fame Ln
   Frisco TX

(P-2403)
BEVERAGES & MORE INC
Also Called: Bevmo
28011 Greenfield Dr (92677-4428)
PHONE.................949 643-3020
Christoph Killin, *Brnch Mgr*
EMP: 135
SALES (corp-wide): 1.61B Privately Held
Web: www.bevmo.com
SIC: **2086** 5149 5921 Bottled and canned soft drinks; Beverages, except coffee and tea; Beer (packaged)
HQ: Beverages & More, Inc.
   1401 Willow Pass Rd # 90
   Concord CA

(P-2404)
CHAMELEON BEVERAGE COMPANY INC (PA)
6444 E 26th St (90040-3214)
PHONE.................323 724-8223
◆ EMP: 68 EST: 1995
SQ FT: 100,000
SALES (est): 12.42MM Privately Held
Web: www.chameleonbeverage.com
SIC: **2086** 5149 Water, natural: packaged in cans, bottles, etc.; Soft drinks

(P-2405)
CRYSTAL GEYSER WATER COMPANY
1233 E California Ave (93307-1205)
PHONE.................661 323-6296
Gerhard Gaugel, *Brnch Mgr*
EMP: 66
Web: www.crystalgeyser.com
SIC: **2086** 5141 2099 2033 Mineral water, carbonated: packaged in cans, bottles, etc.; Groceries, general line; Food preparations, nec; Canned fruits and specialties
HQ: Crystal Geyser Water Company
   501 Washington St
   Calistoga CA
   707 265-3900

(P-2406)
PEPSI-COLA METRO BTLG CO INC
Also Called: Pepsi-Cola
6261 Caballero Blvd (90620-1191)
PHONE.................714 522-9635
Margaret Gramann, *Mgr*
EMP: 247
SALES (corp-wide): 86.39B Publicly Held
Web: www.pepsico.com
SIC: **2086** 5149 Carbonated soft drinks, bottled and canned; Soft drinks
HQ: Pepsi-Cola Metropolitan Bottling Company, Inc.
   700 Anderson Hill Rd

PRODUCTS & SERVICES SECTION

2092 - Fresh Or Frozen Packaged Fish (P-2424)

Purchase NY
914 767-6000

(P-2407)
PEPSI-COLA METRO BTLG CO INC
Also Called: Pepsi-Cola
19700 Figueroa St (90745-1098)
PHONE..............................310 327-4222
Stefan Freeman, *Mgr*
EMP: 259
SALES (corp-wide): 86.39B **Publicly Held**
Web: www.pepsico.com
SIC: 2086 5149 Carbonated soft drinks, bottled and canned; Soft drinks
HQ: Pepsi-Cola Metropolitan Bottling Company, Inc.
700 Anderson Hill Rd
Purchase NY
914 767-6000

(P-2408)
REYES COCA-COLA BOTTLING LLC
Also Called: Coca-Cola
8729 Cleta St (90241-5202)
PHONE..............................562 803-8100
Kim Curtis, *Mgr*
EMP: 90
SQ FT: 76,395
SALES (corp-wide): 850.14MM **Privately Held**
Web: us.coca-cola.com
SIC: 2086 5149 Bottled and canned soft drinks; Groceries and related products, nec
PA: Reyes Coca-Cola Bottling, L.L.C.
3 Park Plz Ste 600
Irvine CA
213 744-8616

(P-2409)
REYES COCA-COLA BOTTLING LLC
Also Called: Coca-Cola
10670 6th St (91730-5912)
PHONE..............................909 980-3121
Sid Campa, *Mgr*
EMP: 318
SALES (corp-wide): 850.14MM **Privately Held**
Web: www.reyescocacola.com
SIC: 2086 5149 Bottled and canned soft drinks; Groceries and related products, nec
PA: Reyes Coca-Cola Bottling, L.L.C.
3 Park Plz Ste 600
Irvine CA
213 744-8616

(P-2410)
REYES COCA-COLA BOTTLING LLC
Also Called: Coca-Cola
5255 Federal Blvd (92105-5710)
PHONE..............................619 266-3300
Randy Cleveland, *Mgr*
EMP: 366
SALES (corp-wide): 850.14MM **Privately Held**
Web: www.reyescocacola.com
SIC: 2086 5149 Bottled and canned soft drinks; Groceries and related products, nec
PA: Reyes Coca-Cola Bottling, L.L.C.
3 Park Plz Ste 600
Irvine CA
213 744-8616

(P-2411)
SEVEN UP BTLG CO SAN FRANCISCO (HQ)
Also Called: Seven-Up Bottling
2875 Prune Ave (94539-6731)
PHONE..............................925 938-8777
Roger Easley, *Ch Bd*
Linda Orsi, *
EMP: 175 **EST:** 1935
SALES (est): 61.48MM **Publicly Held**
Web: www.7up.com
SIC: 2086 5149 4225 Soft drinks: packaged in cans, bottles, etc.; Groceries and related products, nec; General warehousing and storage
PA: Keurig Dr Pepper Inc.
53 South Ave
Burlington MA

(P-2412)
SEVEN UP BTLG CO SAN FRANCISCO
Also Called: Seven-Up Bottling
2670 Land Ave (95815-2380)
P.O. Box 15820 (95852-0820)
PHONE..............................916 929-7777
Tom Tontes, *Mgr*
EMP: 164
Web: www.drpepper.com
SIC: 2086 5078 Soft drinks: packaged in cans, bottles, etc.; Refrigerated beverage dispensers
HQ: Seven Up Bottling Company Of San Francisco
2875 Prune Ave
Fremont CA
925 938-8777

(P-2413)
SHASTA BEVERAGES INC
14405 Artesia Blvd (90638-5886)
PHONE..............................714 523-2280
Bruce Mcdowell, *Mgr*
EMP: 71
SALES (corp-wide): 1.17B **Publicly Held**
Web: www.shastapop.com
SIC: 2086 5149 Soft drinks: packaged in cans, bottles, etc.; Soft drinks
HQ: Shasta Beverages, Inc.
26901 Indl Blvd
Hayward CA
954 581-0922

(P-2414)
WISER FOODS INC
5405 E Village Rd Unit 8219 (90808-7030)
P.O. Box 8219 (90808-0219)
PHONE..............................310 895-0888
Jeri Powers, *CEO*
Jeri Diane Powers, *
EMP: 100 **EST:** 2017
SALES (est): 6.94MM **Privately Held**
Web: www.wiserfoods.global
SIC: 2086 5169 1541 8742 Bottled and canned soft drinks; Alcohols; Food products manufacturing or packing plant construction ; Administrative services consultant

2087 Flavoring Extracts And Syrups, Nec

(P-2415)
BI NUTRACEUTICALS INC
2384 E Pacifica Pl (90220-6214)
PHONE..............................310 669-2100
◆ **EMP:** 120
SIC: 2087 2833 5122 5149 Flavoring extracts and syrups, nec; Medicinals and botanicals; Vitamins and minerals; Seasonings, sauces, and extracts

(P-2416)
WEIDER HEALTH AND FITNESS
21100 Erwin St (91367-3772)
PHONE..............................818 884-6800
Eric Weider, *Pr*
George Lengvari, *
Bernard J Cartoon, *
Lian Katz, *
Tonja Fuller, *
EMP: 466 **EST:** 1940
SQ FT: 6,000
SALES (est): 24.35MM **Privately Held**
SIC: 2087 7991 7999 Beverage bases, concentrates, syrups, powders and mixes; Physical fitness facilities; Physical fitness instruction

2091 Canned And Cured Fish And Seafoods

(P-2417)
PACIFIC AMERICAN FISH CO INC (PA)
Also Called: Pafco
5525 S Santa Fe Ave (90058-3523)
PHONE..............................323 319-1551
Peter Huh, *CEO*
Paul Huh, *
◆ **EMP:** 150 **EST:** 1977
SQ FT: 100,000
SALES (est): 45.22MM
SALES (corp-wide): 45.22MM **Privately Held**
Web: www.pafco.net
SIC: 2091 5146 Fish, filleted (boneless); Fish, fresh

2092 Fresh Or Frozen Packaged Fish

(P-2418)
AZUMA FOODS INTL INC USA (HQ)
Also Called: Azuma Foods Intl Inc USA
20201 Mack St (94545-1224)
PHONE..............................510 782-1112
Takahiro Tamura, *CEO*
Toshinobu Azuma, *
Takahiro Tamura, *Pr*
Toshie Azuma, *
◆ **EMP:** 74 **EST:** 1990
SQ FT: 70,000
SALES (est): 21.27MM **Privately Held**
Web: www.azumafoods.com
SIC: 2092 5146 Fresh or frozen packaged fish; Seafoods
PA: Azuma Foods Co., Ltd.
3095-45, Nagai, Komonocho
Mie-Gun MIE

(P-2419)
CFWF INC
842 Flint Ave (90744-3739)
PHONE..............................310 221-6280
▲ **EMP:** 102
SIC: 2092 5146 Fresh or frozen packaged fish; Fish and seafoods

(P-2420)
ETHOS SEAFOOD GROUP LLC
18531 S Broadwick St (90220-6440)
PHONE..............................312 858-3474
EMP: 62 **EST:** 2012
SALES (est): 1.04MM
SALES (corp-wide): 91.81MM **Privately Held**
Web: www.smseafoodcr.com

SIC: 2092 5146 Fresh or frozen packaged fish; Fish and seafoods
PA: Santa Monica Seafood Company
18531 S Broadwick St
Rancho Dominguez CA
310 886-7900

(P-2421)
FISH HOUSE FOODS INC
1263 Linda Vista Dr (92078-3827)
PHONE..............................760 597-1270
Ron Butler, *Pr*
Ronald J Butler, *
Rex Butler, *
Karen Butler, *
EMP: 273 **EST:** 1985
SQ FT: 52,000
SALES (est): 4.28MM
SALES (corp-wide): 18.65MM **Privately Held**
Web: www.fishhousefoods.com
SIC: 2092 5149 Seafoods, fresh: prepared; Groceries and related products, nec
PA: The Fish House Vera Cruz Inc
3585 Main St Ste 212
Riverside CA
760 744-8000

(P-2422)
OCEAN DIRECT LLC (HQ)
Also Called: Boardwalk Solutions
13771 Gramercy Pl (90249-2470)
PHONE..............................424 266-9300
▼ **EMP:** 184 **EST:** 2003
SQ FT: 20,000
SALES (est): 54.9MM
SALES (corp-wide): 105.26MM **Privately Held**
Web: www.oceandirect.com
SIC: 2092 2022 2037 2033 Fresh or frozen fish or seafood chowders, soups, and stews ; Natural cheese; Frozen fruits and vegetables; Vegetables and vegetable products, in cans, jars, etc.
PA: Richmond Wholesale Meat, Llc
2920 Regatta Blvd
Richmond CA
510 233-5111

(P-2423)
SANTA MONICA SEAFOOD COMPANY (PA)
Also Called: Santa Monica Seafood
18531 S Broadwick St (90220-6440)
PHONE..............................310 886-7900
TOLL FREE: 888
Roger O'brien, *CEO*
Michael Cigliano Ii, *VP*
▲ **EMP:** 100 **EST:** 1939
SQ FT: 65,000
SALES (est): 91.81MM
SALES (corp-wide): 91.81MM **Privately Held**
Web: www.santamonicaseafood.com
SIC: 2092 5149 Seafoods, frozen: prepared; Seafoods

(P-2424)
STATE FISH CO INC
624 W 9th St Ste 100 (90731-7288)
PHONE..............................310 547-9530
◆ **EMP:** 230
Web: www.statefish.com
SIC: 2092 5146 Fresh or frozen packaged fish; Fish, frozen, unpackaged

2095 Roasted Coffee

(P-2425)
APFFELS COFFEE INC
Also Called: Apffels Coffee
12115 Pacific St (90670-2989)
P.O. Box 2506 (90670-0506)
PHONE..................562 309-0400
Darryl Blunk, *CEO*
Alvin Apffel, *
Edward Apffel, *
Mike Rogers, *
◆ EMP: 67 EST: 1914
SQ FT: 100,000
SALES (est): 9.82MM **Privately Held**
Web: www.apffels.com
SIC: **2095** 5149 Coffee roasting (except by wholesale grocers); Coffee, green or roasted

(P-2426)
CAFFE DAMORE INC
1916 S Tubeway Ave (90040-1612)
▲ EMP: 105
Web: www.kerryfoodservice.com
SIC: **2095** 5046 Instant coffee; Coffee brewing equipment and supplies

(P-2427)
GROUNDWORK COFFEE ROASTERS LLC
Also Called: Groundwork Coffee
5457 Cleon Ave (91601-2834)
PHONE..................818 506-6020
EMP: 160 EST: 2011
SQ FT: 4,650
SALES (est): 16.69MM **Privately Held**
Web: www.groundworkcoffee.com
SIC: **2095** 5812 5149 Roasted coffee; Contract food services; Coffee, green or roasted

(P-2428)
PEERLESS COFFEE COMPANY INC
Also Called: Peerles Coffee and Tea
260 Oak St (94607-4512)
PHONE..................510 763-1763
TOLL FREE: 800
George J Vukasin Junior, *CEO*
Kristina V Brouhard, *
John Ziglar, *
EMP: 85 EST: 1924
SQ FT: 65,000
SALES (est): 22.58MM **Privately Held**
Web: www.peerlesscoffee.com
SIC: **2095** 5149 Coffee roasting (except by wholesale grocers); Tea

2098 Macaroni And Spaghetti

(P-2429)
MARUCHAN INC
1902 Deere Ave (92606-4819)
PHONE..................949 789-2300
Shino Saki, *Mgr*
EMP: 242
Web: www.maruchan.com
SIC: **2098** 5146 Noodles (e.g. egg, plain, and water), dry; Fish, cured
HQ: Maruchan, Inc.
  15800 Laguna Canyon Rd
  Irvine CA
  949 789-2300

2099 Food Preparations, Nec

(P-2430)
ASIANA CUISINE ENTERPRISES INC
Also Called: Ace Sushi
22771 S Western Ave Ste 100 (90501)
PHONE..................310 327-2223
Harlan Chin, *Pr*
Gary Chin, *
▲ EMP: 560 EST: 1990
SQ FT: 6,000
SALES (est): 25.43MM **Privately Held**
Web: www.acesushi.com
SIC: **2099** 5812 8741 Ready-to-eat meals, salads, and sandwiches; Fast food restaurants and stands; Management services

(P-2431)
CALAVO GROWERS INC (PA)
Also Called: Calavo
1141 Cummings Rd Ste A (93060-9118)
PHONE..................805 525-1245
Lecil Cole, *Pr*
Steven Hollister, *
Shawn Munsell, *CFO*
Mark Lodge, *COO*
Ronald A Araiza, *FOODS & RFG SLS*
EMP: 91 EST: 1924
SALES (est): 1.19B
SALES (corp-wide): 1.19B **Publicly Held**
Web: www.calavo.com
SIC: **2099** 5148 Salads, fresh or refrigerated; Fruits

(P-2432)
CALIFORNIA NATURAL PRODUCTS
Also Called: Power Automation Systems
1250 Lathrop Rd (95330-9709)
P.O. Box 1219 (95330-1219)
PHONE..................209 858-2525
Craig Lemieux, *CEO*
Timothy Preuninger, *
David Stott, *
◆ EMP: 375 EST: 1976
SQ FT: 220,000
SALES (est): 91.67MM
SALES (corp-wide): 176.71MM **Privately Held**
Web: www.gehlfoodandbeverage.com
SIC: **2099** 7389 Food preparations, nec; Packaging and labeling services
PA: Gehl Foods, Llc
  W185n11300 Whitney Dr
  Germantown WI
  262 251-8570

(P-2433)
CURATION FOODS INC (HQ)
2811 Airpark Dr (93455-1417)
P.O. Box 727 (93434-0727)
PHONE..................800 454-1355
James G Hall, *Pr*
◆ EMP: 80 EST: 1979
SQ FT: 200,000
SALES (est): 161.79MM
SALES (corp-wide): 185.79MM **Publicly Held**
Web: www.apioinc.com
SIC: **2099** 0723 Food preparations, nec; Vegetable packing services
PA: Lifecore Biomedical, Inc.
  3515 Lyman Blvd
  Chaska MN
  952 368-4300

(P-2434)
DOLE FRESH VEGETABLES INC (HQ)
Also Called: Dole
2959 Salinas Hwy (93940-6400)
P.O. Box 2018 (93942-2018)
PHONE..................831 422-8871
Howard Roeder, *CEO*
Timothy Escamilla, *
Ray Riggi, *
David H Murdock, *
Roger Billingsly, *
◆ EMP: 150 EST: 1983
SQ FT: 15,000
SALES (est): 131.69MM
SALES (corp-wide): 3.38B **Privately Held**
SIC: **2099** 0723 Food preparations, nec; Fruit (fresh) packing services
PA: Chiquita Holdings Limited
  3rd Floor, 25 Park Lane
  London

(P-2435)
GPDE SLVA SPCES INCRPORATION (PA)
Also Called: Peterson's Spices
8531 Loch Lomond Dr (90660-2509)
PHONE..................562 407-2643
Ravi De Silva, *Pr*
Rupa De Silva, *
Binuka De Silva, *
Nalin Kulasooriya, *
◆ EMP: 80 EST: 2008
SQ FT: 60,000
SALES (est): 13.27MM **Privately Held**
Web: www.cinnamononline.com
SIC: **2099** 5149 Chili pepper or powder; Spices and seasonings

(P-2436)
HESPERIA UNIFIED SCHOOL DST
Also Called: Hesperia Usd Food Service
11176 G Ave (92345-8315)
PHONE..................760 948-1051
EMP: 63
SALES (corp-wide): 116.14MM **Privately Held**
Web: www.hesperiausd.org
SIC: **2099** 8322 8299 Box lunches, for sale off premises; Geriatric social service; Arts and crafts schools
PA: Hesperia Unified School District
  15576 Main St
  Hesperia CA
  760 244-4411

(P-2437)
JSL FOODS INC (PA)
3550 Pasadena Ave (90031-1946)
PHONE..................323 223-2484
Teiji Kawana, *Pr*
Koji Kawana, *
◆ EMP: 71 EST: 1990
SALES (est): 91.01MM **Privately Held**
Web: www.jslfoods.com
SIC: **2099** 5142 2052 Pasta, uncooked: packaged with other ingredients; Packaged frozen goods; Cookies

(P-2438)
NATREN INC
3105 Willow Ln (91361-4919)
PHONE..................805 371-4737
Yordan Trenev, *CEO*
Natasha Trenev, *
Odessa Braza, *
EMP: 60 EST: 1983
SQ FT: 22,000
SALES (est): 11.65MM **Privately Held**
Web: www.natren.com
SIC: **2099** 8011 Food preparations, nec; Offices and clinics of medical doctors

(P-2439)
ORGANICGIRL LLC
900 Work St (93901-4386)
P.O. Box 5999 (93915-5999)
PHONE..................831 758-7800
Steve Taylor, *
EMP: 650 EST: 2007
SQ FT: 125,000
SALES (est): 74.55MM **Privately Held**
Web: www.iloveorganicgirl.com
SIC: **2099** 5148 Ready-to-eat meals, salads, and sandwiches; Fresh fruits and vegetables

(P-2440)
PACIFIC SPICE COMPANY INC
Also Called: Pacific Natural Spices
6430 E Slauson Ave (90040-3108)
PHONE..................323 726-9190
Gershon Schlussel, *CEO*
Gershon D Schlussel, *
Akiba E Schlussel, *
Sharon Schlussel, *
◆ EMP: 130 EST: 1966
SQ FT: 150,000
SALES (est): 25.25MM **Privately Held**
Web: www.pacificspice.com
SIC: **2099** 5149 Spices, including grinding; Spices and seasonings

(P-2441)
QUOC VIET FOODS INC
Also Called: Cafvina Coffee & Tea
12221 Monarch St (92841-2906)
PHONE..................714 283-3663
Tuan Nguyen, *Pr*
Theresa Nguyen, *
Kim Vu, *Stockholder*
Khanh Nguyen, *Stockholder*
Alan Khoa Nguyen, *Stockholder*
▲ EMP: 80 EST: 2002
SQ FT: 2,000
SALES (est): 18.03MM **Privately Held**
Web: www.quocviet.com
SIC: **2099** 2095 5149 2034 Seasonings and spices; Coffee roasting (except by wholesale grocers); Coffee and tea; Soup mixes

(P-2442)
READY PAC FOODS INC (HQ)
4401 Foxdale St (91706-2161)
PHONE..................626 856-8686
Mary Thompson, *CEO*
Tim Clark, *Chief*
Jay Ellis, *SO*
Dan Redfern, *CFO*
Scott Mcguire, *SCO*
◆ EMP: 2000 EST: 2000
SQ FT: 135,000
SALES (est): 973.11MM
SALES (corp-wide): 2.67MM **Privately Held**
Web: www.readypac.com
SIC: **2099** 5148 Salads, fresh or refrigerated; Vegetables, fresh
PA: Bonduelle
  Rue De La Woestyne
  Renescure
  328426060

(P-2443)
SUPHERB FARMS
Also Called: Supherb Farms
300 Dianne Dr (95380-9523)

PRODUCTS & SERVICES SECTION
2339 - Women's And Misses' Outerwear, Nec (P-2461)

P.O. Box 610 (95381-0610)
PHONE..................209 633-3600
Frederic Jaubert, *Mgr*
Michael Finete, *
Sally Smedal, *
Don Douglas, *
Maurice Barrera, *
◆ **EMP:** 220 **EST:** 1992
SQ FT: 65,190
SALES (est): 53.15MM **Privately Held**
Web: www.supherbfarms.com
SIC: 2099 5149 2037 2034 Seasonings and spices; Sauces; Vegetables, quick frozen & cold pack, excl. potato products; Vegetables, freeze-dried

2211 Broadwoven Fabric Mills, Cotton

(P-2444)
AVITEX INC (PA)
Also Called: Veratex
20362 Plummer St (91311-5371)
PHONE..................818 994-6487
Avi Cohen, *CEO*
▲ **EMP:** 250 **EST:** 1992
SQ FT: 15,000
SALES (est): 18.88MM **Privately Held**
Web: www.veratex.com
SIC: 2211 5131 Sheets, bedding and table cloths: cotton; Linen piece goods, woven

2253 Knit Outerwear Mills

(P-2445)
ISIQALO LLC
Also Called: Spectra USA
5610 Daniels St (91710-9024)
PHONE..................714 683-2820
Nick Agakanian, *
▼ **EMP:** 350 **EST:** 2012
SALES (est): 22.72MM **Privately Held**
Web: www.spectrausa.net
SIC: 2253 5136 5137 2321 T-shirts and tops, knit; Men's and boy's clothing; Women's and children's clothing; Sport shirts, men's and boys': from purchased materials

2259 Knitting Mills, Nec

(P-2446)
SAS TEXTILES INC
3100 E 44th St (90058-2406)
PHONE..................323 277-5555
Sohrab Sassounian, *Pr*
Soheil Sassounian, *
Albert Sassounian, *
▲ **EMP:** 70 **EST:** 1991
SQ FT: 40,000
SALES (est): 9.5MM **Privately Held**
Web: www.sastextile.com
SIC: 2259 2257 7389 Convertors, knit goods ; Weft knit fabric mills; Textile and apparel services

2295 Coated Fabrics, Not Rubberized

(P-2447)
AOC LLC
Also Called: AOC California Plant
19991 Seaton Ave (92570-8724)
PHONE..................951 657-5161
John Mulrine, *Mgr*
EMP: 100
Web: www.aocresins.com
SIC: 2295 2821 5169 Resin or plastic coated fabrics; Plastics materials and resins; Synthetic resins, rubber, and plastic materials
HQ: Aoc, Llc
955 Highway 57
Piperton TN

2299 Textile Goods, Nec

(P-2448)
AMERICAN DAWN INC (PA)
Also Called: ADI
401 W Artesia Blvd (90220-5518)
PHONE..................800 821-2221
Adnan Rawjee, *Pr*
Mahmud G Rawjee, *
◆ **EMP:** 60 **EST:** 1980
SQ FT: 212,000
SALES (est): 25.02MM
SALES (corp-wide): 25.02MM **Privately Held**
Web: www.americandawn.com
SIC: 2299 5023 5131 2393 Linen fabrics; Linens and towels; Textiles, woven, nec; Cushions, except spring and carpet: purchased materials

2311 Men's And Boy's Suits And Coats

(P-2449)
NEW CHEF FASHION INC
3223 E 46th St (90058-2407)
PHONE..................323 581-0300
Guy Lucien Salama, *Pr*
Chantal Salama, *
▲ **EMP:** 70 **EST:** 1989
SALES (est): 11.21MM **Privately Held**
Web: www.newchef.com
SIC: 2311 2339 2326 5137 Men's and boys' uniforms; Women's and misses' outerwear, nec; Men's and boy's work clothing; Uniforms, women's and children's

2321 Men's And Boy's Furnishings

(P-2450)
CREATIVE DESIGN INDUSTRIES
2587 Otay Center Dr (92154-7612)
PHONE..................619 710-2525
▲ **EMP:** 125 **EST:** 1982
SALES (est): 10.57MM **Privately Held**
SIC: 2321 5137 Men's and boy's furnishings; Sportswear, women's and children's

2326 Men's And Boy's Work Clothing

(P-2451)
PPD HOLDING LLC (PA)
10119 Jefferson Blvd (90232-3519)
PHONE..................310 733-2100
Paige Adams-geller, *Chief Design Officer*
EMP: 63 **EST:** 2012
SALES (est): 49.17MM
SALES (corp-wide): 49.17MM **Privately Held**
SIC: 2326 2331 6719 Men's and boy's work clothing; Women's and misses' blouses and shirts; Investment holding companies, except banks

(P-2452)
STRATEGIC DISTRIBUTION L P
Also Called: Cherokee Uniforms
9800 De Soto Ave (91311-4411)
PHONE..................818 671-2100
▲ **EMP:** 240 **EST:** 2003
SALES (est): 51.44MM **Privately Held**
Web: www.careismatic.com
SIC: 2326 2337 3143 3144 Work uniforms; Uniforms, except athletic: women's, misses', and juniors'; Men's footwear, except athletic; Women's footwear, except athletic
PA: Careismatic Brands, Inc.
9800 De Soto Ave
Chatsworth CA

2329 Men's And Boy's Clothing, Nec

(P-2453)
ANDARI FASHION INC
Also Called: Andari
9626 Telstar Ave (91731-3004)
PHONE..................626 575-2759
Wei Chen Wang, *Pr*
Lillian Wang, *
Charles Chang, *
◆ **EMP:** 120 **EST:** 1991
SQ FT: 50,000
SALES (est): 12.54MM **Privately Held**
Web: www.andari.com
SIC: 2329 2339 2253 5199 Sweaters and sweater jackets, men's and boys'; Women's and misses' accessories; Sweaters and sweater coats, knit; Art goods and supplies

(P-2454)
BOARDRIDERS INC (HQ)
Also Called: Billabong
5600 Argosy Ave Ste 100 (92649-1063)
PHONE..................714 889-5404
Arne Arens, *CEO*
Greg Healy, *Pr*
Thomas Chambolle, *INTERIM PRESIDENT EMEA*
Stephen Coulombe, *CRO*
Carol Scherman, *Ex VP*
▼ **EMP:** 599 **EST:** 1986
SALES (est): 494.99MM **Privately Held**
Web: www.boardriders.com
SIC: 2329 2339 3949 5136 Men's and boys' sportswear and athletic clothing; Women's and misses' athletic clothing and sportswear ; Sporting and athletic goods, nec; Sportswear, men's and boys'
PA: Authentic Brands Group Llc
1411 Broadway Fl 4
New York NY

(P-2455)
HURLEY INTERNATIONAL LLC (PA)
Also Called: Hurley
3080 Bristol St (92626-3093)
PHONE..................949 548-9375
Adrian L Bell, *
Ann M Miller, *
◆ **EMP:** 200 **EST:** 2001
SALES (est): 99.67MM
SALES (corp-wide): 99.67MM **Privately Held**
Web: www.hurley.com
SIC: 2329 5137 Knickers, dress (separate): men's and boys'; Women's and children's clothing

(P-2456)
STREAMLINE DSIGN SLKSCREEN INC (PA)
Also Called: Old Guys Rule
1299 S Wells Rd (93004-1901)
PHONE..................805 884-1025
Thom Hill, *CEO*
▲ **EMP:** 60 **EST:** 1995
SQ FT: 33,000
SALES (est): 9.86MM **Privately Held**
Web: www.oldguysrule.com
SIC: 2329 5136 5611 Men's and boys' sportswear and athletic clothing; Men's and boy's clothing; Men's and boys' clothing stores

2331 Women's And Misses' Blouses And Shirts

(P-2457)
STONY APPAREL CORP (PA)
Also Called: Eyeshadow
1201 S Grand Ave (90015-2105)
PHONE..................323 981-9080
▲ **EMP:** 175 **EST:** 1996
SALES (est): 44.25MM **Privately Held**
Web: www.stonyapparel.com
SIC: 2331 2335 7389 Women's and misses' blouses and shirts; Women's, junior's, and misses' dresses; Apparel designers, commercial

2339 Women's And Misses' Outerwear, Nec

(P-2458)
AMBIANCE USA INC (PA)
Also Called: Ambiance Apparel
2415 E 15th St (90021-2936)
PHONE..................323 587-0007
Sang Noh, *CEO*
In Y Noh, *
◆ **EMP:** 100 **EST:** 1999
SALES (est): 18.45MM
SALES (corp-wide): 18.45MM **Privately Held**
Web: www.ambianceapparel.com
SIC: 2339 5137 Women's and misses' outerwear, nec; Women's and children's clothing

(P-2459)
L&L MANUFACTURING CO INC
Also Called: L & L Distributors
12400 Wilshire Blvd # 360 (90025-1059)
EMP: 270
SIC: 2339 2329 2369 8741 Sportswear, women's; Men's and boys' sportswear and athletic clothing; Girl's and children's outerwear, nec; Management services

(P-2460)
MARIKA LLC
5553 Bandini Blvd B (90201)
PHONE..................323 888-7755
▲ **EMP:** 100 **EST:** 1982
SQ FT: 160,000
SALES (est): 10.02MM **Privately Held**
Web: www.marika.com
SIC: 2339 5137 Athletic clothing: women's, misses', and juniors'; Women's and children's outerwear

(P-2461)
TREIVUSH INDUSTRIES INC
Also Called: B B Blu
940 W Washington Blvd (90015-3312)

2341 - Women's And Children's Underwear (P-2462)

PHONE..................213 745-7774
Menachem Treivush, Pr
EMP: 100 EST: 1983
SQ FT: 125,000
SALES (est): 9.15MM Privately Held
Web: www.treivush.com
SIC: 2339 5137 Sportswear, women's; Sportswear, women's and children's

2341 Women's And Children's Underwear

(P-2462)
AFR APPAREL INTERNATIONAL INC
Also Called: Parisa Lingerie & Swim Wear
25365 Prado De La Felicidad (91302-3652)
PHONE..................818 773-5000
Amir Moghadam, Pr
Brenda J Moghadam, *
▲ EMP: 60 EST: 1992
SALES (est): 25MM Privately Held
Web: www.parisausa.com
SIC: 2341 2342 2369 5137 Women's and children's nightwear; Bras, girdles, and allied garments; Bathing suits and swimwear: girls', children's, and infants'; Lingerie

(P-2463)
GUESS INC (PA)
Also Called: Guess
1444 S Alameda St (90021-2433)
PHONE..................213 765-3100
Carlos Alberini, CEO
Alex Yemenidjian, Non-Executive Chairman of the Board*
Paul Marciano, CCO*
Markus Neubrand, CFO
Dennis Secor, Ex VP
◆ EMP: 700 EST: 1981
SQ FT: 341,700
SALES (est): 2.69B
SALES (corp-wide): 2.69B Publicly Held
Web: www.guess.com
SIC: 2341 2325 2369 6794 Women's and children's underwear; Men's and boy's trousers and slacks; Girl's and children's outerwear, nec; Copyright buying and licensing

(P-2464)
NATIONAL CORSET SUPPLY HOUSE (PA)
Also Called: Louden Madelon
3240 E 26th St (90058-8008)
PHONE..................323 261-0265
Roy Schlobohm, CEO
◆ EMP: 65 EST: 1948
SQ FT: 25,000
SALES (est): 9.74MM
SALES (corp-wide): 9.74MM Privately Held
Web: www.shirleyofhollywood.com
SIC: 2341 5137 Women's and children's undergarments; Corsets

2361 Girl's And Children's Dresses, Blouses

(P-2465)
LEIGH JERRY CALIFORNIA INC (PA)
Also Called: Jerry Leigh Entertainment AP
7860 Nelson Rd (91402-6044)
PHONE..................818 909-6200
Andrew Leigh, CEO
Barbara Leigh, *
◆ EMP: 251 EST: 1977
SQ FT: 40,000
SALES (est): 95.93MM
SALES (corp-wide): 95.93MM Privately Held
Web: www.jerryleigh.com
SIC: 2361 5137 Girl's and children's dresses, blouses; Sportswear, women's and children's

2369 Girl's And Children's Outerwear, Nec

(P-2466)
GRACING BRAND MANAGEMENT INC
Also Called: Gbm
1108 W Valley Blvd Ste 660 (91803)
PHONE..................626 297-2472
Sabrina Yam, CEO
Vico Yam, *
EMP: 492 EST: 2017
SALES (est): 20.17MM Privately Held
SIC: 2369 5137 5131 2211 Bathing suits and swimwear: girls', children's, and infants'; Swimsuits: women's, children's, and infants'; Trimmings, apparel; Apparel and outerwear fabrics, cotton

2384 Robes And Dressing Gowns

(P-2467)
TERRY TOWN CORPORATION
8851 Kerns St Ste 100 (92154-6298)
PHONE..................619 421-5354
Saip Ereren, CEO
◆ EMP: 100 EST: 1988
SALES (est): 33.19MM Privately Held
Web: www.terrytown.com
SIC: 2384 5023 5719 Bathrobes, men's and women's: made from purchased materials; Linens and towels; Bedding (sheets, blankets, spreads, and pillows

2386 Leather And Sheep-lined Clothing

(P-2468)
SCULLY SPORTSWEAR INC (PA)
Also Called: Scully Leather Wear
1701 Pacific Ave (93033-1879)
PHONE..................805 483-6339
Daniel Scully Iii, CEO
Robert Swink, *
▲ EMP: 60 EST: 1906
SQ FT: 80,000
SALES (est): 13.2MM
SALES (corp-wide): 13.2MM Privately Held
Web: www.scullyleather.com
SIC: 2386 5099 Coats and jackets, leather and sheep-lined; Luggage

2389 Apparel And Accessories, Nec

(P-2469)
ML KISHIGO MFG CO LLC
11250 Slater Ave (92708-5421)
PHONE..................949 852-1963
Loren H Wall, CEO
Karen Wall, *
▲ EMP: 86 EST: 1971
SALES (est): 14.09MM
SALES (corp-wide): 14.5B Privately Held
Web: www.kishigo.com
SIC: 2389 5099 Men's miscellaneous accessories; Safety equipment and supplies
PA: Bunzl Public Limited Company
York House
London
207 725-5000

2392 Household Furnishings, Nec

(P-2470)
JOMAR TABLE LINENS INC
Also Called: Linen Lovers
4000 E Airport Dr Ste A (91761-1566)
PHONE..................909 390-1444
EMP: 80 EST: 1982
SALES (est): 4.14MM Privately Held
SIC: 2392 7336 Tablecloths: made from purchased materials; Silk screen design

(P-2471)
PACIFIC URETHANES LLC
Also Called: Pacific Urethanes
1671 Champagne Ave Ste A (91761-3660)
PHONE..................909 390-8400
▲ EMP: 200 EST: 2010
SQ FT: 250,000
SALES (est): 44.62MM
SALES (corp-wide): 5.15B Publicly Held
SIC: 2392 5021 Blankets, comforters and beddings; Beds and bedding
PA: Leggett & Platt, Incorporated
1 Leggett Rd
Carthage MO
417 358-8131

2399 Fabricated Textile Products, Nec

(P-2472)
NORTH BAY RHBLITATION SVCS INC (PA)
Also Called: NORTH BAY INDUSTRIES
649 Martin Ave (94928-2050)
PHONE..................707 585-1991
Robert Hutt, CEO
William Stewart, *
EMP: 229 EST: 1968
SQ FT: 18,000
SALES (est): 14.66MM
SALES (corp-wide): 14.66MM Privately Held
Web: www.nbrs.org
SIC: 2399 0782 8331 Banners, pennants, and flags; Lawn services; Community service employment training program

2411 Logging

(P-2473)
ANDERSON LOGGING INC
1296 N Main St (95437-8407)
P.O. Box 1266 (95437-1266)
PHONE..................707 964-2770
Michael Anderson, Pr
Joseph Anderson, *
Maribelle Anderson, *
EMP: 100 EST: 1977
SQ FT: 3,000
SALES (est): 8.02MM Privately Held
Web: www.andersonlogging.com
SIC: 2411 4212 Logging camps and contractors; Lumber (log) trucking, local

(P-2474)
JOHN WHEELER LOGGING INC
13570 State Highway 36 E (96080-8878)
P.O. Box 339 (96080-0339)
PHONE..................530 527-2993
Dave Holder, Pr
Vern Mc Coshum, *
EMP: 105 EST: 1966
SQ FT: 3,500
SALES (est): 9.93MM Privately Held
SIC: 2411 4212 Logging camps and contractors; Local trucking, without storage

(P-2475)
ROBINSON ENTERPRISES INVESTMENT CO INC
Also Called: Robinson Timber
293 Lower Grass Valley Rd Ste 201 (95959-3120)
PHONE..................530 265-5844
EMP: 75 EST: 1971
SALES (est): 7.2MM Privately Held
Web: www.robinsonenterprises.com
SIC: 2411 5171 7353 Logging camps and contractors; Petroleum bulk stations; Heavy construction equipment rental

2421 Sawmills And Planing Mills, General

(P-2476)
SIERRA PACIFIC INDUSTRIES
Also Called: SIERRA PACIFIC INDUSTRIES
1538 Lee Rd (95971-9687)
PHONE..................530 283-2820
Randy Lilburn, Brnch Mgr
EMP: 225
SQ FT: 216
SALES (corp-wide): 1.29B Privately Held
Web: www.spi-ind.com
SIC: 2421 4939 Sawmills and planing mills, general; Combination utilities, nec
PA: Sierra Pacific Industries Inc.
19794 Riverside Ave
Anderson CA
530 378-8000

2431 Millwork

(P-2477)
DANMER INC
Also Called: Danmer Custom Shutters
8000 Woodley Ave (91406-1226)
PHONE..................516 670-5125
▲ EMP: 250
Web: www.danmer.com
SIC: 2431 5023 Window shutters, wood; Window covering parts and accessories

(P-2478)
MTD KITCHEN INC
13213 Sherman Way (91605-4649)
PHONE..................818 764-2254
Gil Alkoby, CEO
EMP: 85 EST: 2012
SALES (est): 7.24MM Privately Held
Web: www.mtdkitchen.com
SIC: 2431 2441 1799 2434 Millwork; Cases, wood; Kitchen cabinet installation; Vanities, bathroom: wood

2434 Wood Kitchen Cabinets

(P-2479)
B YOUNG ENTERPRISES INC
Also Called: Mission Vly Cab / Counter Tech

12254 Iavelli Way (92064-6818)
PHONE.....................858 748-0935
EMP: 75
SIC: 2434 2521 5031 5211 Wood kitchen cabinets; Cabinets, office: wood; Kitchen cabinets; Cabinets, kitchen

(P-2480)
CABINETS 2000 LLC
11100 Firestone Blvd (90650-2269)
PHONE.....................562 868-0909
Frank Hamadani, *Ch*
Nematollah Abdollahi, *
Sherwood Prusso, *
Azam Abdollahi, *
Sue Abdollahi, *
EMP: 180 EST: 1988
SQ FT: 103,000
SALES (est): 26.4MM
SALES (corp-wide): 2.54B **Privately Held**
Web: www.cabinets2000.com
SIC: 2434 1751 Wood kitchen cabinets; Cabinet and finish carpentry
PA: Cabinetworks Group, Inc.
  20000 Victor Pkwy Ste 100
  Livonia MI
  734 205-4600

2435 Hardwood Veneer And Plywood

(P-2481)
SWANER HARDWOOD CO INC (PA)
5 W Magnolia Blvd (91502-1719)
PHONE.....................818 953-5350
Gary Swaner, *Pr*
Keith M Swaner, *
Beverly Swaner, *
Stephen Haag, *
▲ EMP: 70 EST: 1967
SQ FT: 4,500
SALES (est): 36.61MM
SALES (corp-wide): 36.61MM **Privately Held**
Web: www.swanerhardwood.com
SIC: 2435 5031 Hardwood veneer and plywood; Lumber: rough, dressed, and finished

2441 Nailed Wood Boxes And Shook

(P-2482)
NEFAB PACKAGING INC
8477 Central Ave (94560-3431)
PHONE.....................408 678-2500
Ana Gonzales, *Brnch Mgr*
EMP: 98
SALES (corp-wide): 903.19MM **Privately Held**
Web: www.nefab.com
SIC: 2441 5113 5199 Shipping cases, wood: nailed or lock corner; Cardboard and products; Packaging materials
HQ: Nefab Packaging, Inc.
  204 Airline Dr Ste 100
  Coppell TX
  469 444-5268

2448 Wood Pallets And Skids

(P-2483)
COMMERCIAL LBR & PALLET CO INC (PA)
135 Long Ln (91746-2633)
PHONE.....................626 968-0631
Raymond Gutierrez, *Pr*
EMP: 150 EST: 1941
SQ FT: 10,000
SALES (est): 30.43MM
SALES (corp-wide): 30.43MM **Privately Held**
Web: www.clcpallets.com
SIC: 2448 5031 Pallets, wood; Lumber: rough, dressed, and finished

(P-2484)
UNITED PALLET SERVICES INC
4043 Crows Landing Rd (95358-9404)
PHONE.....................209 538-5844
Wayne Randall, *Pr*
Darrel Roberson, *VP*
Amber Mcmahon, *Sec*
EMP: 150 EST: 1976
SQ FT: 46,884
SALES (est): 22.67MM **Privately Held**
Web: www.unitedpalletservices.com
SIC: 2448 7699 Pallets, wood; Pallet repair

2452 Prefabricated Wood Buildings

(P-2485)
AMERICAN MODULAR SYSTEMS INC
Also Called: AMS
787 Spreckels Ave (95336-6002)
PHONE.....................209 825-1921
Daniel Sarich, *Pr*
Tony Sarich, *
EMP: 100 EST: 1982
SQ FT: 85,000
SALES (est): 33.01MM **Privately Held**
Web: www.americanmodular.com
SIC: 2452 1542 Modular homes, prefabricated, wood; Nonresidential construction, nec

2499 Wood Products, Nec

(P-2486)
QUALITY FIRST WOODWORKS INC
1264 N Lakeview Ave (92807-1831)
PHONE.....................714 632-0480
Mark Nappy, *Pr*
Chad Nappy, *
EMP: 115 EST: 1989
SQ FT: 30,000
SALES (est): 9.11MM **Privately Held**
Web: www.qfwinc.com
SIC: 2499 1751 Decorative wood and woodwork; Cabinet building and installation

2511 Wood Household Furniture

(P-2487)
DOUG MOCKETT & COMPANY INC
1915 Abalone Ave (90501-3706)
P.O. Box 3333 (90266-1333)
PHONE.....................310 318-2491
Tyra Cunningham, *Pr*
Susan Darby Gordon, *
Sonia Marie H Mockett, *
◆ EMP: 65 EST: 1984
SALES (est): 11.53MM **Privately Held**
Web: www.mockett.com
SIC: 2511 5072 Unassembled or unfinished furniture, household: wood; Furniture hardware, nec

2512 Upholstered Household Furniture

(P-2488)
A RUDIN INC (PA)
Also Called: A Rudin Designs
6062 Alcoa Ave (90058-3902)
PHONE.....................323 589-5547
Arnold Rudin, *Pr*
Ralph Rudin, *
◆ EMP: 92 EST: 1918
SQ FT: 117,000
SALES (est): 8.06MM
SALES (corp-wide): 8.06MM **Privately Held**
Web: www.arudin.com
SIC: 2512 5021 Upholstered household furniture; Household furniture

(P-2489)
R C FURNITURE INC
1111 Jellick Ave (91748-1212)
PHONE.....................626 964-4100
Rene Cazares, *Pr*
▲ EMP: 81 EST: 1986
SQ FT: 25,000
SALES (est): 17.02MM **Privately Held**
Web: www.renecazares.com
SIC: 2512 5021 Upholstered household furniture; Furniture

2514 Metal Household Furniture

(P-2490)
EARTHLITE LLC (DH)
Also Called: Earthlite
990 Joshua Way (92081-7855)
P.O. Box 51245 (90051-5545)
PHONE.....................760 599-1112
James Chenevey, *CEO*
Philippe Barret, *
Tara Grodjesk, *WELLNESS**
◆ EMP: 95 EST: 1987
SQ FT: 68,000
SALES (est): 42.65MM
SALES (corp-wide): 98.64MM **Privately Held**
Web: www.earthlite.com
SIC: 2514 5091 2531 Tables, household: metal; Spa equipment and supplies; Chairs, portable folding
HQ: Earthlite Holdings, Llc
  150 E 58th St Fl 37
  New York NY
  212 317-2004

(P-2491)
MURRAYS IRON WORKS INC (PA)
7355 E Slauson Ave (90040-3626)
PHONE.....................323 521-1100
▲ EMP: 165 EST: 1966
SALES (est): 9.07MM
SALES (corp-wide): 9.07MM **Privately Held**
Web: www.murraysiw.com
SIC: 2514 3446 5021 5961 Metal household furniture; Fences or posts, ornamental iron or steel; Furniture; Furniture and furnishings, mail order

(P-2492)
RSI HOME PRODUCTS INC
RSI HOME PRODUCTS, INC.
620 Newport Center Dr Ste 1030 (92660)
PHONE.....................949 720-1116
Terri Stevens, *Brnch Mgr*
EMP: 83
SALES (corp-wide): 2.07B **Publicly Held**
Web: www.americanwoodmark.com
SIC: 2514 2541 1751 Metal household furniture; Wood partitions and fixtures; Cabinet and finish carpentry
HQ: Rsi Home Products Llc
  400 E Orangethorpe Ave
  Anaheim CA
  714 449-2200

2515 Mattresses And Bedsprings

(P-2493)
BRENTWOOD HOME LLC (PA)
Also Called: Silverrest
701 Burning Tree Rd Ste A (92833-1447)
PHONE.....................562 949-3759
Vy Nguyen, *CEO*
EMP: 128 EST: 2015
SQ FT: 80,000
SALES (est): 24.13MM
SALES (corp-wide): 24.13MM **Privately Held**
Web: www.brentwoodhome.com
SIC: 2515 5021 5712 Mattresses, containing felt, foam rubber, urethane, etc.; Mattresses ; Mattresses

(P-2494)
WIDLY INC
Also Called: American Furniture Alliance
785 E Harrison St Ste 100 (92879-1350)
PHONE.....................951 279-0900
▲ EMP: 130
SIC: 2515 5021 Mattresses and bedsprings; Furniture

2519 Household Furniture, Nec

(P-2495)
CROWN PAINTING INC
641 Galaxy Way (95356-9606)
P.O. Box 1845 (95361-1845)
PHONE.....................209 322-3275
Gretchen Arbini, *Pr*
Ronald G Anderson, *
EMP: 80 EST: 2012
SALES (est): 6.66MM **Privately Held**
Web: www.crownpaintinginc.com
SIC: 2519 1721 Furniture, household: glass, fiberglass, and plastic; Painting and paper hanging

2521 Wood Office Furniture

(P-2496)
MONTBLEAU & ASSOCIATES INC (PA)
555 Raven St (92102-4523)
PHONE.....................619 263-5550
Ron P Montbleau, *Pr*
Marti Montbleau, *
David Zammit, *
Barton Ward, *
EMP: 87 EST: 1980
SQ FT: 32,000
SALES (est): 18.62MM
SALES (corp-wide): 18.62MM **Privately Held**
Web: www.montbleau.com
SIC: 2521 1751 2434 Wood office furniture; Cabinet building and installation; Wood kitchen cabinets

2531 Public Building And Related Furniture

(P-2497)
JOHNSON CONTROLS INC
Also Called: Johnson Controls
5770 Warland Dr Ste A (90630-5047)
PHONE.....................562 594-3200
Dough Beebe, *Mgr*
EMP: 150
Web: www.johnsoncontrols.com
SIC: 2531 1711 5075 5065 Seats, automobile ; Heating systems repair and maintenance; Warm air heating and air conditioning; Electronic parts and equipment, nec
HQ: Johnson Controls, Inc.
    5757 N Green Bay Ave
    Milwaukee WI
    920 245-6409

(P-2498)
MORTECH MANUFACTURING
411 N Aerojet Dr (91702-3253)
PHONE.....................626 334-1471
Gino Joseph, *Pr*
Gino Joseph, *CEO*
Paul Joseph, *
Christy Haines, *
◆ **EMP:** 82 **EST:** 1986
SQ FT: 43,000
SALES (est): 11.64MM **Privately Held**
Web: www.mortechmfg.com
SIC: 2531 5087 Altars and pulpits; Funeral director's equipment and supplies

2541 Wood Partitions And Fixtures

(P-2499)
AMTREND CORPORATION
1458 Manhattan Ave (92831-5222)
PHONE.....................714 630-2070
Hamid A Malik, *Pr*
Javeeda Malik, *
EMP: 85 **EST:** 1980
SQ FT: 45,000
SALES (est): 16.52MM **Privately Held**
Web: www.amtrend.com
SIC: 2541 2521 7641 2512 Wood partitions and fixtures; Wood office furniture; Upholstery work; Upholstered household furniture

(P-2500)
ARCHITECTURAL WOODWORKING CO
582 Monterey Pass Rd (91754-2417)
PHONE.....................626 570-4125
John K Jack Heydorff, *Pr*
John F Heydorff, *Stockholder**
Richard A Schaub, *
Edward Illig, *
Thomas C Heydorff, *
EMP: 100 **EST:** 1963
SQ FT: 60,000
SALES (est): 9.58MM **Privately Held**
Web: www.awcla.com
SIC: 2541 1751 Office fixtures, wood; Carpentry work

(P-2501)
CCM ENTERPRISES (PA)
10848 Wheatlands Ave (92071-2855)
PHONE.....................619 562-2605
Cody L Nosko, *CEO*
Duane Nosco, *
Virginia Jaggi, *
EMP: 60 **EST:** 1995
SQ FT: 67,543
SALES (est): 5MM **Privately Held**
Web: www.ccmmfg.com
SIC: 2541 1799 Counter and sink tops; Kitchen and bathroom remodeling

(P-2502)
COLUMBIA SHOWCASE & CAB CO INC
11034 Sherman Way Ste A (91352-4927)
PHONE.....................818 765-9710
Samuel M Patterson Junior, *CEO*
▲ **EMP:** 125 **EST:** 1950
SQ FT: 170,000
SALES (est): 14.56MM **Privately Held**
SIC: 2541 1542 Cabinets, except refrigerated: show, display, etc.: wood; Commercial and office building contractors

(P-2503)
EUROPEAN WHOLESALE COUNTER
10051 Prospect Ave (92071-4321)
PHONE.....................619 562-0565
Pete Sciarrino, *CEO*
EMP: 150 **EST:** 2008
SQ FT: 40,000
SALES (est): 14.66MM **Privately Held**
Web: www.europeancompany.com
SIC: 2541 1799 Counter and sink tops; Counter top installation

(P-2504)
LEONARDS CARPET SERVICE INC (PA)
Also Called: Xgrass Turf Direct
1121 N Red Gum St (92806-2582)
PHONE.....................714 630-1930
Leonard Nagel, *Pr*
Joel Nagel, *
▲ **EMP:** 75 **EST:** 1970
SQ FT: 52,000
SALES (est): 23.06MM
SALES (corp-wide): 23.06MM **Privately Held**
Web: www.leonardscarpetservice.com
SIC: 2541 1771 1799 Table or counter tops, plastic laminated; Flooring contractor; Artificial turf installation

2542 Partitions And Fixtures, Except Wood

(P-2505)
CUTTING EDGE CREATIVE LLC
9944 Flower St (90706-5411)
PHONE.....................562 907-7007
Jennifer Franklin, *Managing Member*
Ward Lookabaugh, *
▲ **EMP:** 75 **EST:** 1996
SALES (est): 9.45MM **Privately Held**
SIC: 2542 3496 7319 Racks, merchandise display or storage: except wood; Miscellaneous fabricated wire products; Display advertising service

(P-2506)
EVOLV SURFACES INC
Also Called: Fox Marble & Granite
825 Potter St (94710-2745)
PHONE.....................415 767-4600
Charles Mclaughlin, *Pr*
▲ **EMP:** 122 **EST:** 1986
SALES (est): 19.65MM **Privately Held**
Web: www.evolvsurfaces.com
SIC: 2542 5032 Counters or counter display cases, except wood; Marble building stone

(P-2507)
STEVES PLATING CORPORATION
3111 N San Fernando Blvd (91504-2527)
PHONE.....................818 842-2184
Terry Knezevich, *CEO*
Roger C Knezevich, *
EMP: 140 **EST:** 1956
SQ FT: 80,000
SALES (est): 15.18MM **Privately Held**
Web: www.stevesplating.com
SIC: 2542 3446 3471 7692 Fixtures, store: except wood; Ladders, for permanent installation: metal; Plating of metals or formed products; Welding repair

2591 Drapery Hardware And Blinds And Shades

(P-2508)
CENTURY BLINDS INC
300 S Promenade Ave (92879-1754)
P.O. Box 77940 (92877-0131)
PHONE.....................951 734-3762
Mitch Shapiro, *CEO*
▲ **EMP:** 100 **EST:** 1992
SALES (est): 23.71MM **Privately Held**
Web: www.altawindowfashions.com
SIC: 2591 3429 5719 5023 Blinds vertical; Hardware, nec; Vertical blinds; Vertical blinds
HQ: Hunter Douglas Scandinavia Ab
    Kristineholmsvagen 14a
    AlingsAs
    32277500

2599 Furniture And Fixtures, Nec

(P-2509)
JBI LLC (PA)
Also Called: Jbi Interiors
2650 E El Presidio St (90810-1115)
PHONE.....................310 886-8034
Pete Jensen, *Music Manager*
Bonnie Holt, *
Michael Buchbinder, *
Gregg Buchbinder, *
◆ **EMP:** 200 **EST:** 1968
SQ FT: 270,000
SALES (est): 63.16MM
SALES (corp-wide): 63.16MM **Privately Held**
Web: www.jbi-interiors.com
SIC: 2599 5046 Restaurant furniture, wood or metal; Restaurant equipment and supplies, nec

2621 Paper Mills

(P-2510)
LD PRODUCTS INC
Also Called: 4inkjets
3700 Cover St (90808-1782)
PHONE.....................888 321-2552
Aaron Leon, *CEO*
Patrick Devane, *Sr VP*
◆ **EMP:** 193 **EST:** 1999
SQ FT: 25,000
SALES (est): 51.65MM **Privately Held**
Web: www.ldproducts.com
SIC: 2621 5045 Stationary, envelope and tablet papers; Printers, computer

(P-2511)
SAN DIEGO DAILY TRANSCRIPT
Also Called: Daily Transcript
34 Emerald Gln (92677-9379)
P.O. Box 85469 (92186-5469)
PHONE.....................619 232-4381
Ed Frederickson, *Pr*
EMP: 63 **EST:** 1886
SQ FT: 30,000
SALES (est): 10.95MM
SALES (corp-wide): 13.77MM **Privately Held**
SIC: 2621 4813 Printing paper; Online service providers
PA: Calcomco, Inc.
    5544 S Red Pine Cir
    Kalamazoo MI
    313 885-9228

2653 Corrugated And Solid Fiber Boxes

(P-2512)
BAY CITIES CONTAINER CORP (PA)
Also Called: Bay Cities Logistics
5138 Industry Ave (90660-2503)
PHONE.....................562 948-3751
Greg A Tucker, *CEO*
Patrick Donohoe, *
Michael Musgrave, *
▲ **EMP:** 94 **EST:** 1956
SALES (est): 150.82MM
SALES (corp-wide): 150.82MM **Privately Held**
Web: www.bay-cities.com
SIC: 2653 3993 5113 Boxes, corrugated: made from purchased materials; Signs and advertising specialties; Corrugated and solid fiber boxes

(P-2513)
GEORGIA-PACIFIC LLC
Georgia-Pacific
24600 Avenue 13 (93637-9019)
P.O. Box 1327 (93639-1327)
PHONE.....................559 674-4685
Steve Mindt, *Genl Mgr*
EMP: 98
SALES (corp-wide): 36.93B **Privately Held**
Web: www.gp.com
SIC: 2653 5113 Boxes, corrugated: made from purchased materials; Corrugated and solid fiber boxes
HQ: Georgia-Pacific Llc
    133 Peachtree St Nw
    Atlanta GA
    404 652-4000

(P-2514)
HERITAGE CONTAINER INC
4777 Felspar St (92509-3040)
P.O. Box 605 (91752-0605)
PHONE.....................951 360-1900
Richard Gabriel, *CEO*
Thomas Gabriel, *
Nancy Zuniga, *
EMP: 100 **EST:** 1988
SQ FT: 95,000
SALES (est): 16.5MM **Privately Held**
Web: www.heritagecontainer.com
SIC: 2653 5199 Boxes, corrugated: made from purchased materials; Packaging materials

(P-2515)
HERITAGE PAPER CO (HQ)
2400 S Grand Ave (92705-5211)
PHONE.....................714 540-9737

PRODUCTS & SERVICES SECTION
2679 - Converted Paper Products, Nec (P-2534)

Ron Scagliotti, *CEO*
Lenet Derksen, *
▲ **EMP:** 75 **EST:** 1976
SQ FT: 150,000
SALES (est): 28.99MM
SALES (corp-wide): 50.82MM **Privately Held**
Web: www.heritagepaper.net
SIC: 2653 5199 Boxes, corrugated: made from purchased materials; Packaging materials
PA: Pioneer Packing, Inc.
   2430 S Grand Ave
   Santa Ana CA
   714 540-9751

(P-2516)
HERITAGE PAPER LLC (PA)
Also Called: Heritage Paper Co
6850 Brisa St (94550-2566)
P.O. Box 44441 (94144-0001)
PHONE..........................925 449-1148
John Tatum, *CEO*
Richard Heinz, *
▲ **EMP:** 130 **EST:** 1986
SQ FT: 129,000
SALES (est): 22.83MM
SALES (corp-wide): 22.83MM **Privately Held**
Web: www.goldenwestpackaging.com
SIC: 2653 5113 Boxes, corrugated: made from purchased materials; Corrugated and solid fiber boxes

(P-2517)
HOOVER CONTAINERS INC
19570 San Jose Ave (91748-1404)
P.O. Box 10366 (92838-6366)
PHONE..........................909 444-9454
▲ **EMP:** 60
SIC: 2653 5113 Boxes, corrugated: made from purchased materials; Corrugated and solid fiber boxes

(P-2518)
HPI LIQUIDATIONS INC
13100 Danielson St (92064-6840)
PHONE..........................858 391-7302
EMP: 245
SIC: 2653 5199 Boxes, corrugated: made from purchased materials; Packaging materials

(P-2519)
LIBERTY DIVERSIFIED INTL INC
Also Called: Harbor Packaging
13100 Danielson St (92064-6840)
PHONE..........................858 391-7302
EMP: 245
SALES (corp-wide): 1.02B **Privately Held**
Web: www.libertydiversified.com
SIC: 2653 5199 Boxes, corrugated: made from purchased materials; Packaging materials
PA: Liberty Diversified International, Inc.
   5600 Highway 169 N
   New Hope MN
   763 536-6600

(P-2520)
MARFRED INDUSTRIES
Also Called: Amatix
12708 Branford St (91353)
▲ **EMP:** 300
SIC: 2653 5113 Boxes, solid fiber: made from purchased materials; Shipping supplies

(P-2521)
MCDONALD PACKAGING INC
Also Called: Rightpaq

2601 S Garnsey St (92707-3338)
EMP: 150 **EST:** 1972
SALES (est): 19.56MM **Privately Held**
SIC: 2653 5199 Boxes, corrugated: made from purchased materials; Packaging materials

(P-2522)
PK1 INC (HQ)
Also Called: American River Packaging
401 S Granada Dr (93637-5054)
PHONE..........................559 662-1910
Thomas Kandris, *CEO*
Ronald Frederick, *
▲ **EMP:** 100 **EST:** 1980
SQ FT: 240,000
SALES (est): 21.73MM
SALES (corp-wide): 317.12MM **Privately Held**
Web: www.goldenwestpackaging.com
SIC: 2653 5113 4783 Boxes, corrugated: made from purchased materials; Industrial and personal service paper; Packing goods for shipping
PA: Golden West Packaging Group Llc
   15400 Don Julian Rd
   City Of Industry CA
   888 501-5893

(P-2523)
RELIABLE CONTAINER CORPORATION
9206 Santa Fe Springs Rd (90670-2618)
PHONE..........................562 861-6226
EMP: 275
SIC: 2653 5113 Boxes, corrugated: made from purchased materials; Corrugated and solid fiber boxes

(P-2524)
RM ESOP INC
340 El Cmino Real S Ste 3 (93901)
PHONE..........................831 789-8300
◆ **EMP:** 175
SIC: 2653 5113 Boxes, solid fiber: made from purchased materials; Corrugated and solid fiber boxes

(P-2525)
SCOPE PACKAGING INC
Also Called: Sp
13400 Nelson Ave (91746-2331)
PHONE..........................714 998-4411
TOLL FREE: 800
Mike E Flinn, *CEO*
Cindy Baker, *
▲ **EMP:** 75 **EST:** 1966
SQ FT: 70,000
SALES (est): 1.98MM **Privately Held**
SIC: 2653 7389 Boxes, corrugated: made from purchased materials; Packaging and labeling services

(P-2526)
SOUTHLAND BOX COMPANY
4201 Fruitland Ave (90058-3118)
P.O. Box 512214 (90051-0214)
PHONE..........................323 583-2231
▲ **EMP:** 170 **EST:** 1945
SALES (est): 69.74MM **Privately Held**
Web: www.southlandbox.com
SIC: 2653 5113 Corrugated boxes, partitions, display items, sheets, and pad; Corrugated and solid fiber boxes
PA: Tomoku Co., Ltd.
   2-2-2, Marunouchi
   Chiyoda-Ku TKY

2671 Paper; Coated And Laminated Packaging

(P-2527)
VINYL TECHNOLOGY INC (PA)
200 Railroad Ave (91016-4643)
PHONE..........................626 443-5257
Carlos A Mollura, *Ch Bd*
Daniel Mollura, *
Carlos Mollura Junior, *VP*
Rodney Mollura, *
Haydee Mollura, *
◆ **EMP:** 199 **EST:** 1981
SQ FT: 68,000
SALES (est): 46.38MM
SALES (corp-wide): 46.38MM **Privately Held**
Web: www.vinyltechnology.com
SIC: 2671 7389 Plastic film, coated or laminated for packaging; Sewing contractor

2672 Paper; Coated And Laminated, Nec

(P-2528)
PRECISION DYNAMICS CORPORATION (HQ)
Also Called: Pdc-Identicard
25124 Springfield Ct Ste 200 (91355)
PHONE..........................818 897-1111
J Michael Nauman, *CEO*
Robin Barber, *
Robert Case, *
John Park, *
◆ **EMP:** 161 **EST:** 1956
SQ FT: 75,000
SALES (est): 74.12MM
SALES (corp-wide): 1.33B **Publicly Held**
Web: www.pdcorp.com
SIC: 2672 2754 5047 3069 Adhesive papers, labels, or tapes: from purchased material; Labels: gravure printing; Instruments, surgical and medical; Tape, pressure sensitive: rubber
PA: Brady Corporation
   6555 W Good Hope Rd
   Milwaukee WI
   414 358-6600

(P-2529)
SEAL METHODS INC (PA)
11915 Shoemaker Ave (90670-4717)
P.O. Box 2604 (90670-0604)
PHONE..........................562 944-0291
Eugene Welter, *Prin*
Geri Welter, *
◆ **EMP:** 90 **EST:** 1974
SQ FT: 75,000
SALES (est): 24.2MM
SALES (corp-wide): 24.2MM **Privately Held**
Web: www.sealmethodsinc.com
SIC: 2672 3053 5085 Masking tape: made from purchased materials; Gaskets, all materials; Gaskets

2673 Bags: Plastic, Laminated, And Coated

(P-2530)
ROPLAST INDUSTRIES INC
3155 S 5th Ave (95965-5858)
PHONE..........................530 532-9500
Robert Berman, *Ch*
Robert Bateman, *
◆ **EMP:** 164 **EST:** 1989

SQ FT: 160,000
SALES (est): 12.1MM
SALES (corp-wide): 3.49B **Privately Held**
Web: www.prezero.us
SIC: 2673 5199 Plastic bags: made from purchased materials; Packaging materials
HQ: Prezero Us, Inc.
   4388 Serrano Dr
   Jurupa Valley CA
   858 677-0884

(P-2531)
TRANS WESTERN POLYMERS INC
7539 Las Positas Rd (94551-8202)
P.O. Box 2399 (54912-2399)
PHONE..........................925 449-7800
◆ **EMP:** 400
Web: www.twpoly.com
SIC: 2673 5023 3089 Plastic bags: made from purchased materials; Kitchen tools and utensils, nec; Tableware, plastics

2674 Bags: Uncoated Paper And Multiwall

(P-2532)
ENDPAK PACKAGING INC
9101 Perkins St (90660-4512)
PHONE..........................562 801-0281
Edgar A Garcia, *CEO*
Carlos Garcia, *
EMP: 90 **EST:** 1992
SQ FT: 45,600
SALES (est): 16.71MM **Privately Held**
Web: www.endpak.com
SIC: 2674 5199 Paper bags: made from purchased materials; Packaging materials

2679 Converted Paper Products, Nec

(P-2533)
CALPACO PAPERS INC (PA)
3155 Universe Dr (91752-3252)
PHONE..........................323 767-2800
Paul Maier, *Pr*
Francis A Maier, *
▲ **EMP:** 136 **EST:** 1968
SQ FT: 606,000
SALES (est): 13.76MM
SALES (corp-wide): 13.76MM **Privately Held**
Web: www.actfulfillment.com
SIC: 2679 5111 Paper products, converted, nec; Printing and writing paper

(P-2534)
WORLD CENTRIC
Also Called: World Centric
1500 Valley House Dr Ste 210 (94928-4938)
PHONE..........................707 241-9190
Aseem Das, *CEO*
◆ **EMP:** 65 **EST:** 2004
SALES (est): 18.92MM **Privately Held**
Web: www.worldcentric.com
SIC: 2679 2675 5113 Plates, pressed and molded pulp: from purchased material; Die-cut paper and board; Industrial and personal service paper

2711 Newspapers

(P-2535)
2100 FREEDOM INC (HQ)
625 N Grand Ave (92701-4347)
PHONE..............................714 796-7000
Richard E Mirman, *CEO*
Aaron Kushner, *
EMP: 100 **EST:** 2012
SALES (est): 1.04B
SALES (corp-wide): 1.04B **Privately Held**
SIC: 2711 2721 7313 2741 Newspapers, publishing and printing; Periodicals; Newspaper advertising representative; Miscellaneous publishing
PA: 2100 Trust, Llc
   625 N Grand Ave
   Santa Ana CA
   877 469-7344

(P-2536)
DAILY JOURNAL CORPORATION (PA)
915 E 1st St (90012-4042)
PHONE..............................213 229-5300
Steven Myhill-jones, *Interim Chief Executive Officer*
Tu To, *CFO*
EMP: 66 **EST:** 1888
SQ FT: 34,000
SALES (est): 54.01MM
SALES (corp-wide): 54.01MM **Publicly Held**
Web: www.dailyjournal.com
SIC: 2711 2721 7313 7372 Newspapers, publishing and printing; Magazines: publishing and printing; Newspaper advertising representative; Prepackaged software

(P-2537)
FREEDOM COMMUNICATIONS INC
Also Called: Freedom Newspapers
625 N Grand Ave (92701-4347)
P.O. Box 11450 (92711-1450)
PHONE..............................714 796-7000
▲ **EMP:** 7542
SIC: 2711 2721 7313 2741 Newspapers, publishing and printing; Periodicals; Newspaper advertising representative; Miscellaneous publishing

(P-2538)
INDEPNDENT BRKLEY STDNT PUBG I
Also Called: DAILY CALIFORNIAN
2483 Hearst Ave (94709-1320)
P.O. Box 1949 (94701-1949)
PHONE..............................510 548-8300
Karim Doumar, *Pr*
EMP: 247 **EST:** 1871
SQ FT: 4,100
SALES (est): 237.64K **Privately Held**
Web: www.dailycal.org
SIC: 2711 7372 Newspapers, publishing only, not printed on site; Application computer software

(P-2539)
MCCLATCHY NEWSPAPERS INC (DH)
Also Called: Sacramento Bee
1601 Alhambra Blvd Ste 100 (95816-7051)
P.O. Box 15779 (95852-0779)
PHONE..............................916 321-1855
Tony W Hunter, *CEO*
Jeffrey Dorsey, *

◆ **EMP:** 2500 **EST:** 1857
SALES (est): 709.52MM
SALES (corp-wide): 709.52MM **Privately Held**
Web: www.mcclatchy.com
SIC: 2711 2759 7375 Newspapers, publishing and printing; Commercial printing, nec; On-line data base information retrieval
HQ: Jck Legacy Company
   1601 Alhambra Blvd # 100
   Sacramento CA
   916 321-1844

(P-2540)
MORRIS NEWSPAPER CORP CAL (HQ)
Also Called: Manteca Bulletin
531 E Yosemite Ave (95336-5806)
P.O. Box 1958 (95336-1156)
PHONE..............................209 249-3500
Jennifer Merrick, *Dir*
Dennis Wyatt, *
EMP: 65 **EST:** 1972
SQ FT: 8,000
SALES (est): 5.54MM
SALES (corp-wide): 285.74MM **Privately Held**
Web: www.mantecabulletin.com
SIC: 2711 6531 Newspapers, publishing and printing; Real estate agents and managers
PA: Morris Multimedia, Inc.
   27 Abercorn St
   Savannah GA
   912 233-1281

(P-2541)
PASADENA NEWSPAPERS INC (PA)
Also Called: Pasadena Star-News
605 E Huntington Dr Ste 100 (91016-6352)
PHONE..............................626 578-6300
Dean Singleton, *Pr*
▲ **EMP:** 190 **EST:** 1884
SALES (est): 10.49MM **Privately Held**
Web: www.pasadenastarnews.com
SIC: 2711 7313 Commercial printing and newspaper publishing combined; Newspaper advertising representative

(P-2542)
SAN DIEGO UNION-TRIBUNE LLC (PA)
Also Called: San Diego Union Tribune, The
600 B St Ste 1201 (92101-4505)
P.O. Box 120191 (92112-0191)
PHONE..............................619 299-3131
Jeff Light, *Pr*
EMP: 600 **EST:** 2009
SALES (est): 136.6MM **Privately Held**
Web: www.sandiegouniontribune.com
SIC: 2711 7313 7383 Newspapers: publishing only, not printed on site; Newspaper advertising representative; News reporting services for newspapers and periodicals

2721 Periodicals

(P-2543)
ADVANSTAR COMMUNICATIONS INC
2525 Main St Ste 300 (92614-6680)
PHONE..............................714 513-8400
FAX: 714 513-8403
EMP: 80
SALES (corp-wide): 1.06B **Privately Held**

SIC: 2721 7389 Magazines: publishing only, not printed on site; Trade show arrangement
HQ: Advanstar Communications Inc.
   2501 Colorado Ave Ste 280
   Santa Monica CA
   310 857-7500

(P-2544)
BBM FAIRWAY INC (PA)
3520 Challenger St (90503-1640)
P.O. Box 2703 (90509-2703)
EMP: 120 **EST:** 1961
SALES (est): 10.07MM
SALES (corp-wide): 10.07MM **Privately Held**
Web: www.bobit.com
SIC: 2721 7319 8742 Magazines: publishing only, not printed on site; Media buying service; Marketing consulting services

(P-2545)
INFOWORLD MEDIA GROUP INC (DH)
Also Called: Infoworld
501 2nd St Ste 500 (94107-4133)
PHONE..............................415 243-4344
Robert Ostrow, *CEO*
Patrick J Mc Govern, *
William P Murphy, *
Derek Butcher, *
Miles Dennison, *Associate Publisher*
▲ **EMP:** 75 **EST:** 1979
SQ FT: 50,000
SALES (est): 28.57MM
SALES (corp-wide): 1.84B **Privately Held**
SIC: 2721 2741 7389 Magazines: publishing only, not printed on site; Newsletter publishing; Trade show arrangement
HQ: Idg Communications, Inc.
   140 Kendrick St Ste A110
   Needham MA
   508 872-8200

(P-2546)
VIZ MEDIA LLC
Also Called: Viz Media Music
1355 Market St Ste 200 (94103-1307)
P.O. Box 77010 (94107-0010)
PHONE..............................415 546-7073
Brad Woods, *
▲ **EMP:** 200 **EST:** 1986
SALES (est): 109.91MM **Privately Held**
Web: www.viz.com
SIC: 2721 2731 7819 6794 Comic books: publishing only, not printed on site; Books, publishing only; Video tape or disk reproduction; Copyright buying and licensing
PA: Shogakukan Inc.
   2-3-1, Hitotsubashi
   Chiyoda-Ku TKY

(P-2547)
WIRED VENTURES INC
Also Called: Wired
520 3rd St Ste 305 (94107-6805)
PHONE..............................415 276-8400
Louis Rossetto, *Ch Bd*
Jane Metcalfe, *Prin*
EMP: 175 **EST:** 1992
SALES (est): 23.41MM **Privately Held**
Web: www.wired.com
SIC: 2721 6719 Magazines: publishing only, not printed on site; Investment holding companies, except banks

2731 Book Publishing

(P-2548)
AMAZING FACTS INC
Also Called: Amazing Facts Ministries
1203 W Sunset Blvd (95765-1305)
P.O. Box 1058 (95678-8058)
PHONE..............................916 434-3880
Doug Batchelor, *Pr*
Steve Keiser, *
Allen Hrenyk, *
EMP: 70 **EST:** 1966
SQ FT: 28,000
SALES (est): 4.32MM **Privately Held**
Web: www.amazingfacts.org
SIC: 2731 4832 4833 Pamphlets: publishing and printing; Religious; Television broadcasting stations

(P-2549)
NOLO
6801 Koll Center Pkwy Ste 300 (94566-7047)
PHONE..............................510 549-1976
Bob Dubow, *CEO*
Annika Rogers, *
Jackie Thompson, *Bridge Division Vice President*
John Plessas, *Lawyer*
Laurence Nathanson, *Business Division Vice President*
EMP: 120 **EST:** 1981
SALES (est): 10.32MM
SALES (corp-wide): 188.19MM **Privately Held**
Web: www.nolo.com
SIC: 2731 8111 8742 Books, publishing only; Legal services; Marketing consulting services
PA: Autodata Solutions Group, Llc
   909 N Pacific Coast Hwy # 11
   El Segundo CA
   310 280-4000

(P-2550)
TOKYOPOP INC (PA)
4136 Del Rey Ave (90292-5604)
PHONE..............................323 920-5967
Stuart J Levy, *Pr*
John Parker, *
Victor Chin, *
◆ **EMP:** 90 **EST:** 1997
SALES (est): 7.69MM
SALES (corp-wide): 7.69MM **Privately Held**
Web: www.tokyopop.com
SIC: 2731 3652 7812 7371 Books, publishing only; Compact laser discs, prerecorded; Video tape production; Custom computer programming services

(P-2551)
WEST PUBLISHING CORPORATION
Also Called: The Rutter Group
5161 Lankershim Blvd (91601-4962)
PHONE..............................800 747-3161
William Rutter, *Brnch Mgr*
EMP: 382
SALES (corp-wide): 10.66B **Publicly Held**
Web: home.westacademic.com
SIC: 2731 8111 Book publishing; General practice attorney, lawyer
HQ: West Publishing Corporation
   610 Opperman Dr
   Eagan MN
   651 687-7000

PRODUCTS & SERVICES SECTION

2759 - Commercial Printing, Nec (P-2570)

2741 Miscellaneous Publishing

(P-2552)
AIO ACQUISITION INC (HQ)
Also Called: Personnel Concepts
3200 E Guasti Rd Ste 300 (91761-8661)
P.O. Box 3353 9003 (91761)
PHONE.................................800 333-3795
▲ **EMP:** 92 **EST:** 1989
SALES (est): 28.25MM
SALES (corp-wide): 1.33B **Publicly Held**
Web: www.personnelconcepts.com
SIC: 2741 7319 Posters: publishing and printing; Circular and handbill distribution
PA: Brady Corporation
6555 W Good Hope Rd
Milwaukee WI
414 358-6600

(P-2553)
ASSOCIATED DESERT SHOPPERS INC (DH)
Also Called: The White Sheet
73400 Highway 111 (92260-3908)
PHONE.................................760 346-1729
Harold Paradis, *Pr*
Esperanza Barrett, *
Rey Verdugo Senior, *Dir Opers*
EMP: 75 **EST:** 1987
SQ FT: 4,000
SALES (est): 11.47MM
SALES (corp-wide): 3.68B **Publicly Held**
SIC: 2741 7313 Shopping news: publishing and printing; Newspaper advertising representative
HQ: Schurz Communications, Inc.
1301 E Douglas Rd Ste 200
Mishawaka IN
574 247-7237

(P-2554)
CHINESE OVERSEAS MKTG SVC CORP (PA)
Also Called: Chinese Consumer Yellow Pages
3940 Rosemead Blvd (91770-1952)
PHONE.................................626 280-8588
Alan Kao, *Pr*
Gorden Kao, *Dir*
▲ **EMP:** 60 **EST:** 1982
SQ FT: 9,298
SALES (est): 8.06MM
SALES (corp-wide): 8.06MM **Privately Held**
Web: www.ccyp.com
SIC: 2741 7389 8742 Directories, telephone: publishing only, not printed on site; Trade show arrangement; Marketing consulting services

(P-2555)
GRAPHIQ LLC
101a Innovation Pl (93108-2268)
P.O. Box 1259 (93067-1259)
PHONE.................................805 335-2433
Kevin Oconnor, *Pr*
Scott Leonard, *
EMP: 120 **EST:** 2009
SALES (est): 18.63MM **Publicly Held**
Web: www.graphiq.com
SIC: 2741 4813 Internet publishing and broadcasting; Web search portals
PA: Amazon.Com, Inc.
410 Terry Ave N
Seattle WA

(P-2556)
LOG(N) LLC
5651 Dreyer Pl (94619-3109)
PHONE.................................323 839-4538
Jinal Jhaveri, *Managing Member*
Forum Desai, *COO*
EMP: 68 **EST:** 2010
SALES (est): 1.06MM **Privately Held**
Web: www.mismo.team
SIC: 2741 7379 Internet publishing and broadcasting; Computer related consulting services

(P-2557)
SUPERMEDIA LLC
Also Called: Verizon
3131 Katella Ave (90720-2335)
P.O. Box 3770 (90720-0377)
PHONE.................................562 594-5101
Del Humenik, *Mgr*
EMP: 79
SQ FT: 150,078
SALES (corp-wide): 1.2B **Publicly Held**
SIC: 2741 7372 2791 Directories, telephone: publishing only, not printed on site; Prepackaged software; Typesetting
HQ: Supermedia Llc
2200 W Airfield Dr
Dfw Airport TX
972 453-7000

(P-2558)
TELLME NETWORKS INC
1065 La Avenida St (94043-1421)
PHONE.................................650 693-1009
John Lamacchia, *Ch*
Robert Komin, *
▲ **EMP:** 330 **EST:** 1999
SALES (est): 24.76MM
SALES (corp-wide): 211.91B **Publicly Held**
Web: www.247.ai
SIC: 2741 4812 Telephone and other directory publishing; Radiotelephone communication
PA: Microsoft Corporation
1 Microsoft Way
Redmond WA
425 882-8080

2752 Commercial Printing, Lithographic

(P-2559)
COLOUR CONCEPTS INC
Also Called: Partner Printing
1225 Los Angeles St (91204-2403)
EMP: 150 **EST:** 1989
SQ FT: 36,000
SALES (est): 22.86MM **Privately Held**
Web: www.partnerprinting.com
SIC: 2752 7371 Offset printing; Computer software development

(P-2560)
IMPRESS COMMUNICATIONS INC
9320 Lurline Ave (91311-6041)
PHONE.................................818 701-8800
Paul Marino, *CEO*
▲ **EMP:** 92 **EST:** 1974
SQ FT: 50,000
SALES (est): 16.5MM **Privately Held**
Web: www.impress1.com
SIC: 2752 7336 7319 Offset printing; Commercial art and graphic design; Display advertising service

(P-2561)
KP LLC (PA)
13951 Washington Ave (94578-3220)
PHONE.................................510 346-0729
Brett Olszewski, *CEO*
▲ **EMP:** 80 **EST:** 1929
SQ FT: 12,000
SALES (est): 100.08MM
SALES (corp-wide): 100.08MM **Privately Held**
Web: www.kpcorp.com
SIC: 2752 7334 7331 7374 Offset printing; Photocopying and duplicating services; Direct mail advertising services; Computer graphics service

(P-2562)
MADISN/GRHAM CLOR GRAPHICS INC
Also Called: Colorgraphics
150 N Myers St (90033-2109)
PHONE.................................323 261-7171
Cappy Childs, *CEO*
Arthur Bell, *
Chris Madison, *
Terry Bell, *
▲ **EMP:** 380 **EST:** 1953
SQ FT: 96,000
SALES (est): 21.39MM **Privately Held**
Web: www.colorgraphics.com
SIC: 2752 7336 2796 Offset printing; Graphic arts and related design; Platemaking services

(P-2563)
MAIL HANDLING GROUP INC
Also Called: Mail Handling Services
2840 Madonna Dr (92835-1830)
PHONE.................................952 975-5000
Brian Ostenso, *President COOC*
Michael Murphy, *
EMP: 120 **EST:** 1977
SALES (est): 9.98MM **Privately Held**
SIC: 2752 7331 7374 Offset printing; Mailing service; Data processing service

(P-2564)
MIDNIGHT OIL AGENCY LLC
Also Called: Midnight Oil Agency, Inc.
3800 W Vanowen St Ste 101 (91505-1173)
PHONE.................................818 295-6100
EMP: 285 **EST:** 1989
SALES (est): 39.54MM
SALES (corp-wide): 430.34MM **Privately Held**
Web: www.moagency.com
SIC: 2752 8742 Commercial printing, lithographic; Marketing consulting services
PA: The Imagine Group Llc
1000 Valley Park Dr
Shakopee MN
800 942-7088

(P-2565)
PHOENIX MARKETING SERVICES INC
651 Wharton Dr (91711-4819)
PHONE.................................909 399-4000
▲ **EMP:** 95
Web: www.phoenixmarketing.net
SIC: 2752 5199 Offset printing; Advertising specialties

(P-2566)
TULLY-WIHR COMPANY
148 Whitcomb Ave (95713-9036)
PHONE.................................530 346-2649
EMP: 119
Web: www.tullywihr.com

SIC: 2752 8742 7371 Forms, business: lithographed; Management consulting services; Custom computer programming services

(P-2567)
VOMELA SPECIALTY COMPANY
Also Called: Vomela
9810 Bell Ranch Dr (90670-2952)
PHONE.................................562 944-3853
Loren Maxwell, *Brnch Mgr*
EMP: 123
SALES (corp-wide): 258.06MM **Privately Held**
Web: www.vomela.com
SIC: 2752 7336 Poster and decal printing, lithographic; Commercial art and graphic design
PA: Vomela Specialty Company
845 Minnehaha Ave E
Saint Paul MN
651 228-2200

2759 Commercial Printing, Nec

(P-2568)
DIGITAL ROOM HOLDINGS INC (HQ)
Also Called: New Printing
8000 Haskell Ave (91406-1321)
PHONE.................................310 575-4440
Michael Turner, *CEO*
Brett Zane, *CFO*
▲ **EMP:** 63 **EST:** 2016
SALES (est): 188.44MM **Publicly Held**
Web: www.digitalroominc.com
SIC: 2759 7336 Commercial printing, nec; Graphic arts and related design
PA: Sycamore Partners Management, L.P.
9 W 57th St Ste 3100
New York NY

(P-2569)
INFOIMAGE OF CALIFORNIA INC (PA)
Also Called: Infoimage
175 S Hill Dr (94005-1203)
PHONE.................................650 473-6388
Howard Lee, *Pr*
Rose Lee, *
Calvin Fong, *
Eddie Yuen, *
Lilly Fong, *
EMP: 74 **EST:** 1984
SALES (est): 23.48MM
SALES (corp-wide): 23.48MM **Privately Held**
Web: www.infoimageinc.com
SIC: 2759 7331 7374 Laser printing; Mailing service; Data processing service

(P-2570)
SUPERIOR PRINTING INC
Also Called: Superior Press
9440 Norwalk Blvd (90670-2928)
PHONE.................................888 590-7998
Robert Traut, *Pr*
Kevin Traut, *
Jason Traut, *
EMP: 95 **EST:** 1953
SQ FT: 32,000
SALES (est): 20.15MM **Privately Held**
Web: www.superiorpress.com
SIC: 2759 5112 Commercial printing, nec; Business forms

2813 Industrial Gases

(P-2571)
AIR LIQUIDE ELECTRONICS US LP
1502 W Anaheim St (90744-2303)
PHONE..............................310 549-7079
EMP: 4366
SALES (corp-wide): 109.44MM **Privately Held**
Web: www.airliquide.com
SIC: **2813** 3564 8631 2819 Industrial gases; Blowers and fans; Labor organizations; Industrial inorganic chemicals, nec
HQ: Air Liquide Electronics U.S. Lp
9101 Lyndon B Johnson Fwy # 800
Dallas TX
972 301-5200

(P-2572)
AMERICAN AIR LIQUIDE INC (DH)
46409 Landing Pkwy (94538-6496)
PHONE..............................510 624-4000
Benoit Potier, *Ch*
Gregory Alexander, *
Pierre Dufour, *
Jean-pierre Duprieu, *Ex VP*
Scott Krapf, *
◆ EMP: 90 EST: 1940
SQ FT: 40,000
SALES (est): 314.84MM
SALES (corp-wide): 109.44MM **Privately Held**
SIC: **2813** 5084 3533 4931 Industrial gases; Welding machinery and equipment; Oil and gas drilling rigs and equipment; Electric and other services combined
HQ: Air Liquide International
75 Quai D Orsay
Paris
140625555

2819 Industrial Inorganic Chemicals, Nec

(P-2573)
CODEXIS INC (PA)
Also Called: CODEXIS
200 Penobscot Dr (94063-4718)
PHONE..............................650 421-8100
John J Nicols, *Pr*
Bernard J Kelley, *
Ross Taylor, *
EMP: 89 EST: 2002
SQ FT: 77,300
SALES (est): 138.59MM
SALES (corp-wide): 138.59MM **Publicly Held**
Web: www.codexis.com
SIC: **2819** 2869 8731 Catalysts, chemical; Industrial organic chemicals, nec; Commercial research laboratory

(P-2574)
OMYA CALIFORNIA INC
Also Called: O M Y A
7299 Crystal Creek Rd (92356-8646)
PHONE..............................760 248-7306
▲ EMP: 100
SIC: **2819** 8741 3281 Calcium compounds and salts, inorganic, nec; Management services; Cut stone and stone products

(P-2575)
OMYA INC
7299 Crystal Creek Rd (92356-8646)
PHONE..............................760 248-5200
Rainer Seidler, *CEO*
EMP: 100
Web: www.omya.com
SIC: **2819** 8741 3281 Calcium compounds and salts, inorganic, nec; Management services; Cut stone and stone products
HQ: Omya, Inc.
9987 Carver Rd Ste 300
Blue Ash OH
513 387-4600

2821 Plastics Materials And Resins

(P-2576)
J-M MANUFACTURING COMPANY INC
10990 Hemlock Ave (92337-7250)
PHONE..............................909 822-3009
Stephen Yang, *Mgr*
EMP: 94
SQ FT: 72,000
SALES (corp-wide): 998.24MM **Privately Held**
Web: www.jmeagle.com
SIC: **2821** 3084 5051 3085 Polyvinyl chloride resins, PVC; Plastics pipe; Pipe and tubing, steel; Plastics bottles
PA: J-M Manufacturing Company, Inc.
5200 W Century Blvd
Los Angeles CA
310 693-8200

2833 Medicinals And Botanicals

(P-2577)
S&B PHARMA INC
Also Called: Norac Pharma
405 S Motor Ave (91702-3232)
PHONE..............................626 334-2908
Doctor Daniel Levin, *Pr*
▲ EMP: 66 EST: 2012
SALES (est): 10.36MM **Privately Held**
Web: www.noracpharma.com
SIC: **2833** 8731 2834 Medicinals and botanicals; Commercial physical research; Pharmaceutical preparations
PA: Alkem Laboratories Limited
Devashish Building, Alkem House,
Mumbai MH

2834 Pharmaceutical Preparations

(P-2578)
ADIANA INC
1240 Elko Dr (94089-2212)
PHONE..............................650 421-2900
Paul Goeld, *CEO*
EMP: 370 EST: 1997
SQ FT: 12,000
SALES (est): 1.02MM
SALES (corp-wide): 3.91B **Publicly Held**
SIC: **2834** 8731 Pharmaceutical preparations; Commercial physical research
HQ: Cytyc Corporation
250 Campus Dr
Marlborough MA

(P-2579)
AKCEA THERAPEUTICS INC (HQ)
Also Called: Akcea Therapeutics
2850 Gazelle Ct (92010)
PHONE..............................617 207-0202
Brett Monia, *Pr*
Elizabeth Hougen, *Treas*
Melissa Yoon, *Sec*
Michael Pollock, *Chief Commercial Officer*
Tracy Berns, *Chief Compliance Officer*
EMP: 76 EST: 2017
SALES (est): 488.54MM
SALES (corp-wide): 587.37MM **Publicly Held**
Web: www.ionispharma.com
SIC: **2834** 8731 Pharmaceutical preparations; Biological research
PA: Ionis Pharmaceuticals, Inc.
2855 Gazelle Ct
Carlsbad CA
760 931-9200

(P-2580)
BEIGENE USA INC
1840 Gateway Dr Fl 3 (94404-4027)
PHONE..............................877 828-5568
EMP: 317
Web: www.beigene.com
SIC: **2834** 5122 8731 Pharmaceutical preparations; Pharmaceuticals; Commercial research laboratory
HQ: Beigene Usa, Inc.
55 Cambrdge Pkwy Ste 700w
Cambridge MA
781 801-1887

(P-2581)
BIOVAIL TECHNOLOGIES LTD
1 Enterprise (92656-2606)
PHONE..............................703 995-2400
David Tierney, *Pr*
EMP: 61 EST: 1988
SQ FT: 55,000
SALES (est): 3.74MM
SALES (corp-wide): 8.12B **Privately Held**
SIC: **2834** 8731 3841 2087 Pharmaceutical preparations; Commercial physical research; Surgical and medical instruments; Flavoring extracts and syrups, nec
PA: Bausch Health Companies Inc
2150 Boul Saint-Elzear O
Laval QC
514 744-6792

(P-2582)
BRIDGEBIO PHARMA INC (PA)
Also Called: BRIDGEBIO
3160 Porter Dr Ste 250 (94304-1222)
PHONE..............................650 391-9740
Neil Kumar, *Pr*
Brian C Stephenson, *CFO*
EMP: 248 EST: 2015
SQ FT: 3,900
SALES (est): 77.65MM
SALES (corp-wide): 77.65MM **Publicly Held**
Web: www.bridgebio.com
SIC: **2834** 8731 Pharmaceutical preparations; Biotechnical research, commercial

(P-2583)
CONTINENTAL VITAMIN CO INC
Also Called: Cvc Specialties
4510 S Boyle Ave (90058-2418)
PHONE..............................323 581-0176
Ron Beckenfeld, *Pr*
Lillian Beckenfeld, *
EMP: 60 EST: 1969
SQ FT: 80,000
SALES (est): 9.54MM **Privately Held**
Web: www.cvc4health.com
SIC: **2834** 5122 Vitamin preparations; Vitamins and minerals

(P-2584)
CYTOKINETICS INCORPORATED (PA)
Also Called: CYTOKINETICS
350 Oyster Point Blvd (94080-1912)
PHONE..............................650 624-3000
Robert I Blum, *Pr*
John T Henderson, *
Andrew M Callos, *CCO*
Fady I Malik, *Ex VP*
Ching W Jaw, *Sr VP*
EMP: 250 EST: 1997
SQ FT: 234,892
SALES (est): 94.59MM
SALES (corp-wide): 94.59MM **Publicly Held**
Web: www.cytokinetics.com
SIC: **2834** 8731 Pharmaceutical preparations; Biotechnical research, commercial

(P-2585)
ELITRA PHARMACEUTICALS
3510 Dunhill St Ste A (92121-1201)
PHONE..............................858 410-3030
Paul R Hamelin, *CEO*
Harry Hixson Junior, *Ch Bd*
J Gordon Foulkes, *Senior Vice President Research & Development*
EMP: 65 EST: 1997
SQ FT: 35,735
SALES (est): 4.81MM **Privately Held**
Web: www.elitra.net
SIC: **2834** 8731 Pharmaceutical preparations; Commercial physical research

(P-2586)
FIVE PRIME THERAPEUTICS INC
Also Called: Five Prime
111 Oyster Point Blvd (94080-2038)
PHONE..............................415 365-5600
Thomas Civik, *Pr*
William Ringo, *Interim Chief Executive Officer*
David V Smith, *CAO*
Francis W Sarena, *CSO*
Helen Collins, *CMO*
EMP: 87 EST: 2001
SQ FT: 115,466
SALES (est): 13.18MM
SALES (corp-wide): 26.32B **Publicly Held**
Web: www.amgen.com
SIC: **2834** 8733 Pharmaceutical preparations; Biotechnical research, noncommercial
PA: Amgen Inc.
1 Amgen Center Dr
Thousand Oaks CA
805 447-1000

(P-2587)
GLOBAL BLOOD THERAPEUTICS INC
Also Called: Gbt
181 Oyster Point Blvd (94080-2044)
PHONE..............................650 741-7700
Ted W Love, *Pr*
Jeffrey Farrow, *CFO*
Eric Fink, *Chief Human Resources Officer*
David L Johnson, *CCO*
EMP: 352 EST: 2012
SQ FT: 164,150
SALES (est): 194.75MM
SALES (corp-wide): 100.33B **Publicly Held**
Web: www.pfizer.com
SIC: **2834** 8731 Pharmaceutical preparations; Biological research
PA: Pfizer Inc.
66 Hudson Blvd E Fl 20
New York NY
212 733-2323

PRODUCTS & SERVICES SECTION
2834 - Pharmaceutical Preparations (P-2606)

(P-2588)
GRAIL LLC (HQ)
1525a Obrien Dr (94025-1463)
PHONE.................................833 694-2553
Bob Ragusa, *CEO*
Matthew Young, *
Marissa Song, *Corporate Secretary**
Joshua Ofman, *CMO**
Gautam Kollu, *Chief Commercial Officer**
EMP: 61 **EST:** 2011
SALES (est): 210.91MM
SALES (corp-wide): 4.58B **Publicly Held**
Web: www.grail.com
SIC: 2834 8731 Pharmaceutical preparations
; Biotechnical research, commercial
PA: Illumina, Inc.
5200 Illumina Way
San Diego CA
858 202-4500

(P-2589)
IGM BIOSCIENCES INC
325 E Middlefield Rd (94043-4003)
PHONE.................................650 965-7873
Fred Schwarzer, *Pr*
Lisa L Decker, *Chief Business Officer*
George A Gauthier, *CCO*
Bruce Keyt, *CSO*
Misbah Tahir, *CFO*
EMP: 258 **EST:** 1993
SQ FT: 68,100
SALES (est): 1.07MM **Privately Held**
Web: www.igmbio.com
SIC: 2834 8731 Pharmaceutical preparations
; Biotechnical research, commercial

(P-2590)
INTERMUNE INC (DH)
1 Dna Way (94080-4918)
PHONE.................................415 466-4383
Daniel G Welch, *Pr*
John C Hodgman, *
Jonathan A Leff, *Executive Research & Development Vice President**
Sean P Nolan, *Chief Business Officer**
Andrew Powell, *CORP SE**
EMP: 215 **EST:** 1998
SQ FT: 56,000
SALES (est): 52.42MM **Privately Held**
Web: www.gene.com
SIC: 2834 8731 Pharmaceutical preparations
; Medical research, commercial
HQ: Roche Holdings, Inc.
1 Dna Way
South San Francisco CA
650 225-1000

(P-2591)
INTERNATIONAL VITAMIN CORPORAT (PA)
Also Called: I V C
1 Park Plz Ste 800 (92614-5998)
PHONE.................................949 664-5500
▲ **EMP:** 72 **EST:** 2009
SQ FT: 166,000
SALES (est): 619.44MM **Privately Held**
Web: www.ivcinc.com
SIC: 2834 5149 8099 Vitamin preparations;
Organic and diet food; Nutrition services

(P-2592)
IONIS PHARMACEUTICALS INC (PA)
Also Called: Ionis
2855 Gazelle Ct (92010-6670)
PHONE.................................760 931-9200
Brett P Monia, *CEO*
Joseph Loscalzo, *
Elizabeth L Hougen, *Ex VP*
Joseph T Baroldi, *Chief Business Officer*
C Frank Bennett, *CSO*
▲ **EMP:** 340 **EST:** 1989
SALES (est): 587.37MM
SALES (corp-wide): 587.37MM **Publicly Held**
Web: www.ionispharma.com
SIC: 2834 8731 3845 Pharmaceutical preparations; Medical research, commercial
; Electromedical equipment

(P-2593)
KEZAR LIFE SCIENCES INC (PA)
4000 Shoreline Ct Ste 300 (94080-2005)
PHONE.................................650 822-5600
John Fowler, *CEO*
Graham Cooper, *Ch Bd*
Marc L Belsky, *CFO*
Niti Goel, *CMO*
Nick Mordwinkin, *Chief Business Officer*
EMP: 75 **EST:** 2015
SQ FT: 24,357
Web: www.kezarlifesciences.com
SIC: 2834 8731 Pharmaceutical preparations
; Biotechnical research, commercial

(P-2594)
KINNATE BIOPHARMA INC (PA)
103 Montgomery St Ste 150 (94129-1716)
PHONE.................................858 299-4699
Mark Meltz, *Admn*
Nima Farzan, *Pr*
Dean Mitchell, *Ch Bd*
Mark Meltz, *COO*
Eric Murphy, *CSO*
EMP: 60 **EST:** 2018
SQ FT: 3,676
Web: www.kinnate.com
SIC: 2834 8731 Pharmaceutical preparations
; Biological research

(P-2595)
KODIAK SCIENCES INC (PA)
Also Called: KODIAK
1200 Page Mill Rd (94304-1122)
PHONE.................................650 281-0850
Victor Perlroth, *Ch Bd*
John A Borgeson, *Ex VP*
EMP: 88 **EST:** 2009
SQ FT: 155,000
Web: www.kodiak.com
SIC: 2834 2836 8731 Pharmaceutical preparations; Biological products, except diagnostic; Biotechnical research, commercial

(P-2596)
KOSAN BIOSCIENCES INCORPORATED
3832 Bay Center Pl (94545-3619)
P.O. Box 4000 (08543-4000)
PHONE.................................650 995-7356
Helen S Kim, *Pr*
Peter Davis Ph.d., *Ch Bd*
Gary S Titus, *Sr VP*
Peter J Licari Ph.d., *Operations*
Jonathan K Wright, *Sr VP*
EMP: 90 **EST:** 1996
SALES (est): 9.98MM
SALES (corp-wide): 46.16B **Publicly Held**
SIC: 2834 8731 Pharmaceutical preparations
; Commercial research laboratory
PA: Bristol-Myers Squibb Company
430 E 29th St Fl 14
New York NY
212 546-4000

(P-2597)
LEINER HEALTH PRODUCTS INC (DH)
Also Called: Leiner Health Products
901 E 233rd St (90745-6204)
PHONE.................................631 200-2000
Jeffrey A Nagel, *CEO*
Michael Collins, *
Harvey Kamil, *
◆ **EMP:** 200 **EST:** 1952
SQ FT: 488,000
SALES (est): 208.09MM **Privately Held**
Web: www.leiner.com
SIC: 2834 5122 Vitamin, nutrient, and hematinic preparations for human use;
Vitamins and minerals
HQ: Nhs U.S., Llc
121 River St Ste 9
Hoboken NJ
631 200-2000

(P-2598)
MIRATI THERAPEUTICS INC (PA)
Also Called: Mirati
3545 Cray Ct (92121-1169)
PHONE.................................858 332-3410
Charles M Baum, *Interim Chief Executive Officer*
Faheem Hasnain, *Ch Bd*
Alan Sandler, *CMO*
Laurie Stelzer, *CFO*
James Christensen, *CSO*
EMP: 574 **EST:** 1995
SQ FT: 118,000
SALES (est): 12.44MM
SALES (corp-wide): 12.44MM **Publicly Held**
Web: www.mirati.com
SIC: 2834 8731 Pharmaceutical preparations
; Biotechnical research, commercial

(P-2599)
MURAD LLC (HQ)
2121 Park Pl Fl 1 (90245-4843)
PHONE.................................310 726-0600
Elizabeth Ashmun, *
▲ **EMP:** 160 **EST:** 1990
SQ FT: 8,000
SALES (est): 94.06MM
SALES (corp-wide): 62.39B **Privately Held**
Web: www.murad.com
SIC: 2834 5122 Vitamin, nutrient, and hematinic preparations for human use;
Pharmaceuticals
PA: Unilever Plc
Unilever House
London
207 572-1202

(P-2600)
ONYX PHARMACEUTICALS INC
1 Amgen Center Dr (91320-1730)
PHONE.................................650 266-0000
Pablo Cagnoni, *Pr*
Bob Goeltz, *Ex Dir*
Matthew K Fust, *Ex VP*
Suzanne M Shema, *Ex VP*
Helen Torley, *Ex VP*
EMP: 741 **EST:** 2013
SQ FT: 297,111
SALES (est): 106.32MM
SALES (corp-wide): 26.32B **Publicly Held**
SIC: 2834 8049 Drugs affecting parasitic and infective diseases; Occupational therapist
PA: Amgen Inc.
1 Amgen Center Dr
Thousand Oaks CA
805 447-1000

(P-2601)
ORPHAN MEDICAL INC
3180 Porter Dr (94304-1287)
PHONE.................................650 496-3777
Matthew Fust, *CFO*
EMP: 80 **EST:** 1994
SQ FT: 15,000
SALES (est): 24.06MM **Privately Held**
Web: www.jazzpharma.com
SIC: 2834 8731 Pharmaceutical preparations
; Commercial physical research
HQ: Jazz Pharmaceuticals, Inc.
3170 Porter Dr
Palo Alto CA
650 496-3777

(P-2602)
POLYPEPTIDE LABS SAN DIEGO LLC
9395 Cabot Dr (92126-4310)
PHONE.................................858 408-0808
EMP: 72 **EST:** 1986
SQ FT: 43,000
SALES (est): 42.06MM **Privately Held**
Web: www.polypeptide.com
SIC: 2834 2833 8731 Pharmaceutical preparations; Medicinals and botanicals;
Biotechnical research, commercial
HQ: Polypeptide Laboratories Inc.
365 Maple Ave
Torrance CA

(P-2603)
PROMETHEUS LABORATORIES INC
9410 Carroll Park Dr (92121-5201)
PHONE.................................858 824-0895
EMP: 405 **EST:** 1996
SQ FT: 99,000
SALES (est): 105.96MM **Privately Held**
Web: www.prometheuslabs.com
SIC: 2834 8011 Pharmaceutical preparations
; Offices and clinics of medical doctors

(P-2604)
PROTAGONIST THERAPEUTICS INC (PA)
Also Called: Protagonist Therapeutics
7707 Gateway Blvd Ste 140 (94560-1160)
PHONE.................................510 474-0170
Dinesh V Patel, *Pr*
Harold E Selick, *Ch Bd*
Donald Kalkofen, *CFO*
David Y Liu, *CSO*
Samuel Saks, *CMO*
EMP: 68 **EST:** 2006
SQ FT: 57,900
SALES (est): 26.58MM **Publicly Held**
Web: www.protagonist-inc.com
SIC: 2834 8731 Pharmaceutical preparations
; Commercial physical research

(P-2605)
RAPT THERAPEUTICS INC
Also Called: RAPT THERAPEUTICS
561 Eccles Ave (94080-1906)
PHONE.................................650 489-9000
Brian Wong, *Pr*
William Rieflin, *
William Ho, *CMO*
Dirk Brockstedt, *CSO*
Eric Hall, *Interim Chief Financial Officer*
EMP: 62 **EST:** 2015
SQ FT: 36,754
SALES (est): 1.53MM **Privately Held**
Web: www.rapt.com
SIC: 2834 8731 Pharmaceutical preparations
; Biotechnical research, commercial

(P-2606)
RAYZEBIO INC
5505 Morehouse Dr Ste 300 (92121-1720)
PHONE.................................619 937-2754
Ken Song, *Pr*
Richard Heyman, *Non-Executive Chairman of the Board**

2834 - Pharmaceutical Preparations (P-2607)

Arvind Kush, *CFO*
Susan Moran, *CMO*
EMP: 88 **EST:** 2020
SQ FT: 28,000
Web: www.rayzebio.com
SIC: 2834 8731 Pharmaceutical preparations ; Medical research, commercial

(P-2607)
RIGEL PHARMACEUTICALS INC (PA)
611 Gateway Blvd Ste 900 (94080-7029)
PHONE.....................650 624-1100
EMP: 159 **EST:** 1996
SALES (est): 120.24MM **Publicly Held**
Web: www.rigel.com
SIC: 2834 8733 Pharmaceutical preparations ; Medical research

(P-2608)
ROBINSON PHARMA INC
3701 W Warner Ave (92704-5218)
PHONE.....................714 241-0235
Tam H Nguyen, *CEO*
EMP: 121
Web: www.robinsonpharma.com
SIC: 2834 7389 Pharmaceutical preparations ; Packaging and labeling services
PA: Robinson Pharma, Inc.
3330 S Harbor Blvd
Santa Ana CA

(P-2609)
SICOR INC (HQ)
19 Hughes (92618-1902)
PHONE.....................949 455-4700
Carlo Salvi, *Vice Chairman*
▲ **EMP:** 800 **EST:** 1986
SQ FT: 170,000
SALES (est): 139.6MM **Privately Held**
Web: www.tevausa.com
SIC: 2834 8731 Drugs acting on the cardiovascular system, except diagnostic; Medical research, commercial
PA: Teva Pharmaceutical Industries Limited
5 Bazel
Petah Tikva

(P-2610)
TRAVERE THERAPEUTICS INC (PA)
Also Called: TRAVERE
3611 Valley Centre Dr Ste 300 (92130)
PHONE.....................888 969-7879
EMP: 248 **EST:** 2008
SQ FT: 149,123
SALES (est): 212.02MM **Publicly Held**
Web: www.travere.com
SIC: 2834 8731 Pharmaceutical preparations ; Biotechnical research, commercial

2835 Diagnostic Substances

(P-2611)
BIOCARE MEDICAL LLC (PA)
60 Berry Dr (94553-5601)
PHONE.....................925 603-8000
Luis De Luzuriaga, *CEO*
Jamie Conroy, *CFO*
▼ **EMP:** 130 **EST:** 1997
SQ FT: 51,000
SALES (est): 49.89MM **Privately Held**
Web: www.biocare.net
SIC: 2835 3841 5047 Diagnostic substances; Diagnostic apparatus, medical; Diagnostic equipment, medical

(P-2612)
DANISCO US INC (HQ)
Also Called: Genencor International
925 Page Mill Rd (94304-1013)
PHONE.....................650 846-7500
James C Collins, *CEO*
Mark A Goldsmith, *
◆ **EMP:** 200 **EST:** 1989
SQ FT: 128,000
SALES (est): 532.49MM
SALES (corp-wide): 12.44B **Publicly Held**
SIC: 2835 8731 2899 2869 Diagnostic substances; Commercial physical research; Chemical preparations, nec; Industrial organic chemicals, nec
PA: International Flavors & Fragrances Inc.
521 W 57th St
New York NY
212 765-5500

(P-2613)
DIASORIN MOLECULAR LLC
11331 Valley View St (90630-5300)
PHONE.....................562 240-6500
Carlo Rosa, *CEO*
EMP: 200 **EST:** 2016
SALES (est): 90MM **Privately Held**
Web: molecular.diasorin.com
SIC: 2835 5047 In vitro diagnostics; Diagnostic equipment, medical
HQ: Diasorin Inc.
1951 Northwestern Ave S
Stillwater MN
651 439-9710

(P-2614)
SYNTRON BIORESEARCH INC
2774 Loker Ave W (92010-6610)
PHONE.....................760 930-2200
Charles Yu, *Pr*
▲ **EMP:** 278 **EST:** 1986
SALES (est): 32.73MM **Privately Held**
Web: www.syntron.net
SIC: 2835 5122 Diagnostic substances; Biologicals and allied products

(P-2615)
TECO DIAGNOSTICS
1268 N Lakeview Ave (92807-1831)
PHONE.....................714 693-7788
K C Chen, *Pr*
◆ **EMP:** 70 **EST:** 1985
SQ FT: 40,000
SALES (est): 17.09MM **Privately Held**
Web: www.tecodiagnostics.com
SIC: 2835 5049 Diagnostic substances; Laboratory equipment, except medical or dental

2836 Biological Products, Except Diagnostic

(P-2616)
ADVERUM BIOTECHNOLOGIES INC (PA)
Also Called: Adverum
100 Cardinal Way (94063-4755)
PHONE.....................650 656-9323
Laurent Fischer, *Pr*
Patrick Machado, *Ch Bd*
Paul B Cleveland, *Ch Bd*
Mehdi Gasmi, *SCIENCE*
Jennifer Cheng, *VP*
EMP: 186 **EST:** 2006
SQ FT: 36,000
Web: www.adverum.com
SIC: 2836 8731 Biological products, except diagnostic; Biotechnical research, commercial

(P-2617)
ALLOGENE THERAPEUTICS INC (PA)
Also Called: ALLOGENE THERAPEUTICS
210 E Grand Ave (94080-4811)
PHONE.....................650 457-2700
David Chang, *Pr*
Arie Belldegrun, *Ex Ch Bd*
Eric Schmidt, *CFO*
EMP: 191 **EST:** 2017
SQ FT: 68,072
SALES (est): 243K
SALES (corp-wide): 243K **Publicly Held**
Web: www.allogene.com
SIC: 2836 8731 Biological products, except diagnostic; Biological research

(P-2618)
AMERICAN PEPTIDE COMPANY INC
1271 Avenida Chelsea (92081-8315)
PHONE.....................408 733-7604
▲ **EMP:** 86
SIC: 2836 5169 Biological products, except diagnostic; Chemicals and allied products, nec

(P-2619)
ATARA BIOTHERAPEUTICS INC (PA)
Also Called: Atara Bio
2380 Conejo Spectrum St Ste 200 (91320-1444)
PHONE.....................650 278-8930
Pascal Touchon, *Pr*
Ronald C Renaud, *
Jakob Dupont, *Ex VP*
Utpal Koppikar, *Sr VP*
Amar Murugan, *Sr VP*
EMP: 568 **EST:** 2012
SQ FT: 13,670
SALES (est): 63.57MM
SALES (corp-wide): 63.57MM **Publicly Held**
Web: www.atarabio.com
SIC: 2836 8731 Biological products, except diagnostic; Biotechnical research, commercial

(P-2620)
CIDARA THERAPEUTICS INC (PA)
Also Called: Cidara
6310 Nancy Ridge Dr Ste 101 (92121)
PHONE.....................858 752-6170
Jeffrey L Stein, *Pr*
Daniel D Burgess, *Ch Bd*
Preetam Shah, *Chief Business Officer*
Paul Daruwala, *COO*
Taylor Sandison, *CMO*
EMP: 71 **EST:** 2012
SQ FT: 29,638
SALES (est): 64.29MM
SALES (corp-wide): 64.29MM **Publicly Held**
Web: www.cidara.com
SIC: 2836 8731 Biological products, except diagnostic; Biotechnical research, commercial

(P-2621)
DYNAVAX TECHNOLOGIES CORP (PA)
2100 Powell St 7th Fl (94608-1873)
PHONE.....................510 848-5100
EMP: 82 **EST:** 1996
SQ FT: 23,976
SALES (est): 722.68MM **Publicly Held**
Web: www.dynavax.com

SIC: 2836 8731 Biological products, except diagnostic; Biological research

(P-2622)
SENTI BIOSCIENCES INC (PA)
2 Corporate Dr Fl 1 (94080-7047)
PHONE.....................650 382-3281
Timothy Lu, *Pr*
Omid Farokhzad, *Ex Ch Bd*
Curt Herberts Iii, *COO*
Deborah Knobelman, *CFO*
EMP: 68 **EST:** 2016
SQ FT: 40,000
SALES (est): 4.29MM
SALES (corp-wide): 4.29MM **Publicly Held**
Web: www.sentibio.com
SIC: 2836 8731 Biological products, except diagnostic; Biotechnical research, commercial

2842 Polishes And Sanitation Goods

(P-2623)
CLOROX SERVICES COMPANY (HQ)
Also Called: Clorox
1221 Broadway (94612-1837)
PHONE.....................510 271-7000
EMP: 100 **EST:** 1996
SALES (est): 663.89MM
SALES (corp-wide): 7.39B **Publicly Held**
Web: www.thecloroxcompany.com
SIC: 2842 5169 Polishes and sanitation goods; Specialty cleaning and sanitation preparations
PA: The Clorox Company
1221 Broadway Ste 1300
Oakland CA
510 271-7000

(P-2624)
GENLABS (PA)
5568 Schaefer Ave (91710-9041)
P.O. Box 1697 (91708-1697)
PHONE.....................909 591-8451
EMP: 135 **EST:** 1968
SALES (est): 33.66MM
SALES (corp-wide): 33.66MM **Privately Held**
Web: www.genlabscorp.com
SIC: 2842 2841 5169 7389 Polishes and sanitation goods; Soap and other detergents ; Chemicals and allied products, nec; Packaging and labeling services

(P-2625)
MAINTEX INC (PA)
13300 Nelson Ave (91746-1516)
P.O. Box 7110 (91744-7110)
PHONE.....................800 446-1888
TOLL FREE: 800
▲ **EMP:** 140 **EST:** 1960
SALES (est): 35.04MM
SALES (corp-wide): 35.04MM **Privately Held**
Web: www.maintex.com
SIC: 2842 5087 Cleaning or polishing preparations, nec; Janitors' supplies

2844 Toilet Preparations

(P-2626)
COBE CHEMICAL CO INC
Also Called: Cobe Laboratories
1016 S Vail Ave (90640-6020)
PHONE.....................877 691-3590

PRODUCTS & SERVICES SECTION

2899 - Chemical Preparations, Nec (P-2645)

▲ EMP: 75
Web: www.cobechem.com
SIC: 2844 5999 5122 Perfumes, cosmetics and other toilet preparations; Cosmetics; Cosmetics, perfumes, and hair products

(P-2627)
DR SQUATCH LLC
4065 Glencoe Ave Apt 300b (90292-6079)
PHONE.............................631 229-7068
Josh Friedman, Pr
Daniel Larson, CFO
EMP: 250 EST: 2013
SALES (est): 72.08MM Privately Held
Web: www.drsquatch.com
SIC: 2844 7389 Perfumes, cosmetics and other toilet preparations; Business services, nec

(P-2628)
H2O PLUS LLC (PA)
111 Sutter St Fl 22 (94104-4540)
PHONE.............................800 242-2284
Joy Chen, Pr
Robert Seidl, VP
◆ EMP: 90 EST: 1993
SQ FT: 82,000
SALES (est): 14.99MM Privately Held
SIC: 2844 5999 5122 Perfumes, cosmetics and other toilet preparations; Cosmetics; Cosmetics

(P-2629)
NYX LOS ANGELES INC
Also Called: Nyx Cosmetics
588 Crenshaw Blvd (90503-1705)
PHONE.............................323 869-9420
◆ EMP: 140
SIC: 2844 5122 Perfumes, cosmetics and other toilet preparations; Cosmetics

(P-2630)
PACIFIC WORLD CORPORATION (PA)
100 Technology Dr Ste 200 (92618-2466)
PHONE.............................949 598-2400
William George, CEO
Stuart Noyes, *
Bart Dibie, *
Justin Martini, *
Bob Nabholz, *
◆ EMP: 99 EST: 1947
SALES (est): 21.42MM
SALES (corp-wide): 21.42MM Privately Held
Web: www.pacificworldcorp.com
SIC: 2844 3421 3999 5199 Cosmetic preparations; Clippers, fingernail and toenail ; Fingernails, artificial; General merchandise, non-durable

(P-2631)
PLZ CORP
2321 3rd St (92507-3306)
PHONE.............................951 683-2912
Ian Sishman, Mgr
EMP: 69
SALES (corp-wide): 766.3MM Privately Held
Web: www.plzcorp.com
SIC: 2844 5122 5087 Cosmetic preparations ; Cosmetics, perfumes, and hair products; Beauty parlor equipment and supplies
PA: Plz Corp.
2651 Wrrnvlle Rd Stre 300 300 Stre
Downers Grove IL
630 628-3000

(P-2632)
SUN DEEP INC (PA)
Also Called: Sun Deep Cosmetics
31285 San Clemente St (94544-7814)
P.O. Box 2814 (94526-7814)
PHONE.............................510 441-2525
Sundeep Gill, Ex Dir
Jay Gill, CEO
Prabhleen S Gill, Pr
Ravi Gill, Sec
Sundeep Gill, VP
◆ EMP: 82 EST: 1987
SQ FT: 40,000
SALES (est): 19.68MM
SALES (corp-wide): 19.68MM Privately Held
Web: www.sundeepinc.com
SIC: 2844 5122 Cosmetic preparations; Cosmetics, perfumes, and hair products

(P-2633)
UNIVERSAL PACKG SYSTEMS INC (PA)
Also Called: Paklab
14570 Monte Vista Ave (91710-5743)
PHONE.............................909 517-2442
Jeffery Morlando, CEO
Alan Kristel, COO
William Wachtel, Sec
◆ EMP: 750 EST: 1987
SALES (est): 379.38MM
SALES (corp-wide): 379.38MM Privately Held
Web: www.paklab.com
SIC: 2844 7389 3565 2671 Cosmetic preparations; Packaging and labeling services; Bottling machinery: filling, capping, labeling; Plastic film, coated or laminated for packaging

(P-2634)
VEGE - KURL INC
Also Called: Vege-Tech Company
412 W Cypress St (91204-2402)
PHONE.............................818 956-5582
Eric W Huffman, Pr
Helen Huffman, *
EMP: 60 EST: 1959
SALES (est): 9.8MM Privately Held
Web: www.vegelabs.com
SIC: 2844 2833 5122 Shampoos, rinses, conditioners: hair; Medicinals and botanicals ; Cosmetics, perfumes, and hair products

2851 Paints And Allied Products

(P-2635)
FRAZEE INDUSTRIES INC
Also Called: Frazee Paint & Wallcovering
6625 Miramar Rd (92121-2508)
PHONE.............................858 626-3600
EMP: 900
Web: www.sherwin-williams.com
SIC: 2851 5198 5231 Paints, waterproof; Paints; Paint

2869 Industrial Organic Chemicals, Nec

(P-2636)
WACKER CHEMICAL CORPORATION
Also Called: Precision Silicones
13910 Oaks Ave (91710-7010)
PHONE.............................909 590-8822
Sudipta Das, Brnch Mgr
EMP: 63
SALES (corp-wide): 7.03B Privately Held
Web: www.wacker.com
SIC: 2869 5169 Silicones; Industrial chemicals
HQ: Wacker Chemical Corporation
4950 S State Rd
Ann Arbor MI
517 264-8500

2873 Nitrogenous Fertilizers

(P-2637)
KELLOGG SUPPLY INC
Also Called: Kellogg Garden Product
12686 Locke Rd (95237-9701)
PHONE.............................209 727-3130
EMP: 103
SALES (corp-wide): 36.89MM Privately Held
Web: www.kellogggarden.com
SIC: 2873 5191 2875 Nitrogenous fertilizers; Fertilizer and fertilizer materials; Fertilizers, mixing only
PA: Kellogg Supply, Inc.
350 W Sepulveda Blvd
Carson CA
310 830-2200

2875 Fertilizers, Mixing Only

(P-2638)
BRANDT CONSOLIDATED INC
3654 S Willow Ave (93725-9036)
PHONE.............................559 499-2100
EMP: 64
SALES (corp-wide): 793.12MM Privately Held
Web: www.brandt.co
SIC: 2875 5191 Fertilizers, mixing only; Farm supplies
HQ: Brandt Consolidated, Inc.
2935 S Koke Mill Rd
Springfield IL
217 547-5800

(P-2639)
GENERAL HYDROPONICS INC
Also Called: General Hydroponics
3789 Vine Hill Rd (95472-2348)
P.O. Box 1576 (95473-1576)
PHONE.............................707 824-9376
▲ EMP: 72
Web: www.generalhydroponics.com
SIC: 2875 3999 8748 Fertilizers, mixing only; Hydroponic equipment; Business consulting, nec

2879 Agricultural Chemicals, Nec

(P-2640)
CIBUS INC
6455 Nancy Ridge Dr (92121-2249)
PHONE.............................858 450-0008
Rory Riggs, Ch Bd
Peter Beetham, *
Wade King, CFO
Greg Gocal, CSO
EMP: 237 EST: 2010
SQ FT: 53,423
SALES (est): 157K Privately Held
Web: www.calyxt.com
SIC: 2879 8731 0721 Agricultural chemicals, nec; Agricultural research; Crop planting and protection

(P-2641)
YASHENG GROUP
251 Ginko Ter (94086-6564)
PHONE.............................650 363-8345
▲ EMP: 10000
Web: www.yashenggroup.com
SIC: 2879 0111 0115 0116 Agricultural chemicals, nec; Wheat; Corn; Soybeans

2891 Adhesives And Sealants

(P-2642)
CUSTOM BUILDING PRODUCTS LLC
6511 Salt Lake Ave (90201-2126)
PHONE.............................323 582-0846
Tom Milan, Manager
EMP: 141
Web: www.custombuildingproducts.com
SIC: 2891 3273 2899 5032 Adhesives and sealants; Ready-mixed concrete; Chemical preparations, nec; Ceramic wall and floor tile, nec
HQ: Custom Building Products Llc
7711 Center Ave Ste 500
Huntington Beach CA
800 272-8786

(P-2643)
MITSUBISHI CHEMICAL CRBN FBR
Also Called: Mitsubishi Chemical Carbon Fiber and Composites, Inc.
1822 Reynolds Ave (92614-5714)
PHONE.............................800 929-5471
Takashi Sasaki, VP
EMP: 110
Web: www.mccfc.com
SIC: 2891 5169 Adhesives; Chemical additives
HQ: Mitsubishi Chemical Carbon Fiber And Composites, Inc
5900 88th St
Sacramento CA

2899 Chemical Preparations, Nec

(P-2644)
KIK POOL ADDITIVES INC
5160 E Airport Dr (91761-7824)
PHONE.............................909 390-9912
John A Christensen, Pr
David M Christensen, VP
Debra Schonk, VP
Brian Patterson, CFO
Chet Yoakum, VP
▲ EMP: 140 EST: 1958
SALES (est): 16.87MM Privately Held
Web: www.kem-tek.com
SIC: 2899 3089 7389 5169 Chemical preparations, nec; Plastics hardware and building products; Packaging and labeling services; Swimming pool and spa chemicals

(P-2645)
MOC PRODUCTS COMPANY INC (PA)
Also Called: Auto Edge Solutions
12306 Montague St (91331-2279)
PHONE.............................818 794-3500
Mark Waco, CEO
Dave Waco, *
◆ EMP: 75 EST: 1954
SQ FT: 100,000
SALES (est): 73.97MM
SALES (corp-wide): 73.97MM Privately Held

2911 - Petroleum Refining (P-2646)

PRODUCTS & SERVICES SECTION

Web: www.mocproducts.com
SIC: **2899** 7549 5169 Corrosion preventive lubricant; Automotive maintenance services; Chemicals and allied products, nec

2911 Petroleum Refining

(P-2646)
CHEVRON CORPORATION (PA)
Also Called: Chevron
6001 Bollinger Canyon Rd (94583-5737)
PHONE..............................925 326-2189
Michael K Wirth, *Ch Bd*
Joseph C Geagea, *Ex VP*
Pierre R Breber, *VP*
Rhonda J Morris, *Chief Human Resource Officer*
R Hewitt Pate, *VP*
EMP: 1658 EST: 1926
SALES (est): 246.25B
SALES (corp-wide): 246.25B **Publicly Held**
Web: www.chevron.com
SIC: **2911** 1311 1382 1321 Petroleum refining; Crude petroleum production; Oil and gas exploration services; Natural gas liquids

(P-2647)
CHEVRON GLOBAL ENERGY INC (HQ)
Also Called: Chevron Global Lubricants
6001 Bollinger Canyon Rd (94583-5737)
P.O. Box 6046 (94583-0746)
PHONE..............................925 842-1000
Jock D Mckenzie, *Ch Bd*
Larry Bennison, *Operations*
Barry A Chafitz, *General*
Malcolm J Mcauley, *Sr VP*
Richard J Guiltinan, *VP*
EMP: 100 EST: 1936
SQ FT: 200,000
SALES (est): 625.85MM
SALES (corp-wide): 246.25B **Publicly Held**
Web: www.chevron.com
SIC: **2911** 4731 5172 Petroleum refining; Freight transportation arrangement; Petroleum products, nec
PA: Chevron Corporation
6001 Bollinger Canyon Rd
San Ramon CA
925 326-2189

2951 Asphalt Paving Mixtures And Blocks

(P-2648)
CALMAT CO (DH)
Also Called: Vulcan Materials
500 N Brand Blvd Ste 500 (91203-1904)
PHONE..............................818 553-8821
Tom Hill, *CEO*
James W Smack, *
Daniel F Sansone, *
Danny R Shepherd, *
EMP: 150 EST: 1891
SQ FT: 40,000
SALES (est): 976.92MM **Publicly Held**
Web: www.vulcanmaterials.com
SIC: **2951** 1442 1429 3273 Asphalt and asphaltic paving mixtures (not from refineries); Construction sand and gravel; Igneus rock, crushed and broken-quarrying; Ready-mixed concrete
HQ: Legacy Vulcan, Llc
1200 Urban Center Dr
Vestavia AL
205 298-3000

(P-2649)
GRANITE ROCK CO
365 Blomquist St (94063-2701)
PHONE..............................650 482-3800
Rich Sacher, *Mgr*
EMP: 61
SQ FT: 2,500
SALES (corp-wide): 521.49MM **Privately Held**
Web: www.graniterock.com
SIC: **2951** 2992 5032 Asphalt and asphaltic paving mixtures (not from refineries); Lubricating oils and greases; Brick, stone, and related material
PA: Granite Rock Co.
350 Technology Dr
Watsonville CA
831 768-2000

(P-2650)
PAVEMENT RECYCLING SYSTEMS INC
Also Called: West Coast Milling
48028 90th St W (93536-9366)
PHONE..............................661 948-5599
Steve Ward, *Mgr*
EMP: 60
Web: www.pavementrecycling.com
SIC: **2951** 1611 Asphalt paving mixtures and blocks; Surfacing and paving
PA: Pavement Recycling Systems, Inc.
10240 San Sevaine Way
Jurupa Valley CA

2952 Asphalt Felts And Coatings

(P-2651)
OWENS CORNING SALES LLC
Also Called: Owens Corning
1501 N Tamarind Ave (90222-4130)
P.O. Box 5665 (90224-5665)
PHONE..............................310 631-1062
David Randalph, *Brnch Mgr*
EMP: 162
Web: www.owenscorning.com
SIC: **2952** 2951 1761 Roofing felts, cements, or coatings, nec; Asphalt paving mixtures and blocks; Roofing, siding, and sheetmetal work
HQ: Owens Corning Sales, Llc
1 Owens Corning Pkwy
Toledo OH
419 248-8000

2992 Lubricating Oils And Greases

(P-2652)
CHEMTOOL INCORPORATED
1300 Goodrick Dr (93561-1508)
PHONE..............................661 823-7190
Bill Hart, *Mgr*
EMP: 125
SALES (corp-wide): 302.09B **Publicly Held**
Web: www.lubrizol.com
SIC: **2992** 2899 5172 Oils and greases, blending and compounding; Chemical preparations, nec; Lubricating oils and greases
HQ: Chemtool Incorporated
801 W Rockton Rd
Rockton IL
815 957-4140

3011 Tires And Inner Tubes

(P-2653)
YOKOHAMA CORP NORTH AMERICA (HQ)
Also Called: Yokohama Tire
1 Macarthur Pl (92707-5927)
PHONE..............................540 389-5426
Yasuo Tominaga, *CEO*
Takaharu Fushimi, *
◆ EMP: 250 EST: 1917
SALES (est): 792.7MM **Privately Held**
Web: www.yokohamatire.com
SIC: **3011** 5014 Tires and inner tubes; Tires and tubes
PA: Yokohama Rubber Company, Limited, The
2-1, Oiwake
Hiratsuka KNG

3053 Gaskets; Packing And Sealing Devices

(P-2654)
INERTECH SUPPLY INC
Also Called: Inertech
641 Monterey Pass Rd (91754-2418)
PHONE..............................626 282-2000
James Huang, *Pr*
Charlie C Miskell, *
Bruce Wang, *
Walter Lee, *
▲ EMP: 75 EST: 1991
SQ FT: 14,000
SALES (est): 5.07MM **Privately Held**
Web: www.inertech.com
SIC: **3053** 5085 2891 Gasket materials; Gaskets; Adhesives and sealants

(P-2655)
SEWING COLLECTION INC
3113 E 26th St (90058-8006)
PHONE..............................323 264-2223
Touraj Tour, *Pr*
Houshang Tour, *
◆ EMP: 100 EST: 1991
SQ FT: 135,000
SALES (est): 24.36MM **Privately Held**
Web: www.sewingcollection.com
SIC: **3053** 5199 4953 Packing materials; Packaging materials; Recycling, waste materials

(P-2656)
WEST COAST GASKET CO
300 Ranger Ave (92821-6217)
PHONE..............................714 869-0123
Louis Russell, *Prin*
Jean Grey, *
EMP: 75 EST: 1979
SQ FT: 50,000
SALES (est): 16.07MM **Privately Held**
Web: www.westcoastgasket.com
SIC: **3053** 3061 3469 5085 Gaskets, all materials; Mechanical rubber goods; Metal stampings, nec; Industrial supplies

3069 Fabricated Rubber Products, Nec

(P-2657)
INNOCOR WEST LLC
300 S Tippecanoe Ave 310 (92408)
PHONE..............................909 307-3737
Carol S Eicher, *CEO*
Doug Vaughan, *CFO*
▲ EMP: 373 EST: 2003
SQ FT: 150,000
SALES (est): 2.08MM **Privately Held**
SIC: **3069** 5021 Pillows, sponge rubber; Mattresses
HQ: Innocor, Inc.
200 Schulz Dr Ste 2
Red Bank NJ

(P-2658)
ONEILL WETSUITS LLC (PA)
Also Called: O'Neill Wetsuits
1071 41st Ave (95062-4400)
P.O. Box 6300 (95063-6300)
PHONE..............................831 475-7500
Pat O'neill, *Managing Member*
◆ EMP: 70 EST: 1952
SQ FT: 14,000
SALES (est): 24.04MM **Privately Held**
Web: us.oneill.com
SIC: **3069** 5091 Wet suits, rubber; Watersports equipment and supplies

(P-2659)
PROMOTONAL DESIGN CONCEPTS INC
Also Called: Creative Inflatables
9872 Rush St (91733-2635)
PHONE..............................626 579-4454
Adam Melendez, *CEO*
◆ EMP: 71 EST: 1984
SALES (est): 7.87MM **Privately Held**
Web: www.promotionaldesigngroup.com
SIC: **3069** 7389 5092 2394 Balloons, advertising and toy: rubber; Balloons, novelty and toy; Toy novelties and amusements; Canvas and related products

3081 Unsupported Plastics Film And Sheet

(P-2660)
COMPASS INNOVATIONS INC
Also Called: Careray USA
2352 Walsh Ave (95051-1301)
PHONE..............................408 418-3985
Jianqiang Liu, *CEO*
EMP: 120 EST: 2017
SALES (est): 22.86MM
SALES (corp-wide): 28.37MM **Privately Held**
Web: www.careray.com
SIC: **3081** 5047 Photographic and X-ray film and sheet; X-ray film and supplies
PA: Jiangsu Kangzhong Numeral Medical Equipment Co., Ltd.
Room 501, Floor ,B3, Floor A2, Shengwu Nami Park, No.218, Xinghu Suzhou JS
51286860288

(P-2661)
SAINT-GOBAIN SOLAR GARD LLC (DH)
Also Called: Saint-Gobain Performance Plas
4540 Viewridge Ave (92123-1637)
P.O. Box 2864 (52733-2864)
PHONE..............................866 300-2674
M Shawn Puccio, *
◆ EMP: 88 EST: 2001
SQ FT: 65,000
SALES (est): 82.56MM
SALES (corp-wide): 397.78MM **Privately Held**
Web: www.solargard.com
SIC: **3081** 5162 3479 Plastics film and sheet; Plastics film; Coating of metals and formed products
HQ: Saint-Gobain Performance Plastics Corporation

20 Moores Rd
Malvern PA
440 836-6900

3083 Laminated Plastics Plate And Sheet

(P-2662)
JOHNSON LAMINATING COATING INC
20631 Annalee Ave (90746-3502)
PHONE..............................310 635-4929
Scott Davidson, *Pr*
▲ **EMP:** 75 **EST:** 1960
SQ FT: 50,000
SALES (est): 22.67MM **Privately Held**
Web: www.johnsonlaminating.com
SIC: 3083 3081 2891 1541 Laminated plastics sheets; Unsupported plastics film and sheet; Adhesives and sealants; Food products manufacturing or packing plant construction

3085 Plastics Bottles

(P-2663)
CLASSIC CONTAINERS INC
1700 S Hellman Ave (91761-7638)
PHONE..............................909 930-3610
Manny G Hernandez Senior, *CEO*
Ernie Hernandez, *
Maria Hernandez, *
Manny Hernandez Junior, *Treas*
EMP: 280 **EST:** 1988
SQ FT: 60,000
SALES (est): 24.1MM **Privately Held**
Web: www.classiccontainers.com
SIC: 3085 3089 5085 Plastics bottles; Plastics containers, except foam; Industrial supplies

3086 Plastics Foam Products

(P-2664)
HUHTAMAKI INC
4209 Noakes St (90023-4024)
PHONE..............................323 269-0151
Mark Pettigrew, *Brnch Mgr*
EMP: 119
SALES (corp-wide): 4.65B **Privately Held**
Web: www.huhtamaki.com
SIC: 3086 3089 2657 2656 Cups and plates, foamed plastics; Plastics containers, except foam; Folding paperboard boxes; Sanitary food containers
HQ: Huhtamaki, Inc.
   9201 Packaging Dr
   De Soto KS
   913 583-3025

(P-2665)
PMC LEADERS IN CHEMICALS INC (HQ)
12243 Branford St (91352-1010)
PHONE..............................818 896-1101
Gary Kamins, *Pr*
EMP: 200 **EST:** 1992
SQ FT: 180,000
SALES (est): 224.15MM
SALES (corp-wide): 1.71B **Privately Held**
Web: www.pmcglobalinc.com
SIC: 3086 5169 Plastics foam products; Chemicals and allied products, nec
PA: Pmc Global, Inc.
   12243 Branford St
   Sun Valley CA
   818 896-1101

3088 Plastics Plumbing Fixtures

(P-2666)
AQUATIC CO
Lasco Bathware
8101 E Kaiser Blvd Ste 200 (92808-2287)
PHONE..............................714 993-1220
Scott Hartman, *Mgr*
EMP: 110
SQ FT: 5,000
SALES (corp-wide): 535.81MM **Privately Held**
Web: www.aquaticbath.com
SIC: 3088 1711 5211 Shower stalls, fiberglass and plastics; Plumbing, heating, air-conditioning; Bathroom fixtures, equipment and supplies
HQ: Aquatic Co.
   665 Industrial Rd
   Savannah TN

(P-2667)
JACUZZI PRODUCTS CO
14525 Monte Vista Ave (91710-5721)
PHONE..............................909 548-7732
Jim Barry, *Mgr*
EMP: 340
SALES (corp-wide): 411.72K **Privately Held**
Web: www.jacuzzi.com
SIC: 3088 5091 Tubs (bath, shower, and laundry), plastics; Fitness equipment and supplies
HQ: Jacuzzi Products Co.
   13925 City Center Dr # 200
   Chino Hills CA
   909 606-1416

(P-2668)
KING BROS ENTERPRISES LLC
29101 The Old Rd (91355-1014)
P.O. Box 9203 (91392-9203)
PHONE..............................661 257-3262
▲ **EMP:** 125
SIC: 3088 5169 Plastics plumbing fixtures; Synthetic resins, rubber, and plastic materials

(P-2669)
PEGGY S LANE INC
Also Called: C M P
2701 Merced St (94577-5601)
PHONE..............................510 483-1202
TOLL FREE: 800
Matt Clementz, *Pr*
EMP: 100 **EST:** 1979
SQ FT: 35,000
SALES (est): 9.03MM **Privately Held**
Web: www.marbleproducts.com
SIC: 3088 3281 1752 1743 Tubs (bath, shower, and laundry), plastics; Cut stone and stone products; Floor laying and floor work, nec; Terrazzo, tile, marble and mosaic work

3089 Plastics Products, Nec

(P-2670)
ASSOCIATED MATERIALS INC
1 Maritime Plz 12th Fl (94111-3404)
PHONE..............................415 788-5111
EMP: 3000 **EST:** 2010
SALES (est): 392.4MM **Privately Held**
Web: www.associatedmaterials.com
SIC: 3089 5033 5031 3442 Plastics hardware and building products; Roofing and siding materials; Windows; Metal doors, sash, and trim
PA: Associated Materials Group, Inc.
   3773 State Rd
   Cuyahoga Falls OH

(P-2671)
DESIGN WEST TECHNOLOGIES INC
2701 Dow Ave (92780-7209)
PHONE..............................714 731-0201
Ryan Hur, *Pr*
▲ **EMP:** 65 **EST:** 1994
SQ FT: 60,000
SALES (est): 16.26MM **Privately Held**
Web: www.dwtusa.com
SIC: 3089 8711 Injection molded finished plastics products, nec; Electrical or electronic engineering

(P-2672)
FLUIDMASTER INC (PA)
30800 Rancho Viejo Rd (92675-1564)
PHONE..............................949 728-2000
Robert Andersonschoepe, *CEO*
Michael Draves, *
Robert Connell, *
Terry Bland, *
◆ **EMP:** 127 **EST:** 1957
SALES (est): 135.53MM
SALES (corp-wide): 135.53MM **Privately Held**
Web: www.fluidmaster.com
SIC: 3089 3432 1711 Injection molding of plastics; Plumbing fixture fittings and trim; Plumbing contractors

(P-2673)
MERGER SUB GOTHAM 2 LLC
6261 Katella Ave Ste 250 (90630-5200)
PHONE..............................714 462-4603
Nicholas Kovacevich, *CEO*
EMP: 109 **EST:** 2021
SALES (est): 11.2MM
SALES (corp-wide): 137.09MM **Publicly Held**
SIC: 3089 5085 Plastics containers, except foam; Industrial supplies
PA: Greenlane Holdings, Inc.
   1095 Broken Sound Pkwy Nw # 100
   Boca Raton FL
   877 292-7660

(P-2674)
MI TECHNOLOGIES INC
Also Called: Lutema
2215 Paseo De Las Americas Ste 30 (92154-7908)
PHONE..............................619 710-2637
Amir Tafreshi, *CEO*
Ali Irani-tehrani, *Prin*
John Celms, *
▲ **EMP:** 700 **EST:** 2004
SQ FT: 8,000
SALES (est): 71.57MM **Privately Held**
Web: www.discount-merchant.com
SIC: 3089 3672 5731 3999 Injection molding of plastics; Printed circuit boards; Consumer electronic equipment, nec; Barber and beauty shop equipment

(P-2675)
MILGARD MANUFACTURING LLC
Also Called: Milgard Windows
26879 Diaz Rd (92590-3470)
PHONE..............................480 763-6000
Cory Hall, *Brnch Mgr*
EMP: 339
SALES (corp-wide): 822.1MM **Privately Held**
Web: www.milgard.com
SIC: 3089 3442 5211 3231 Windows, plastics ; Sash, door or window: metal; Door and window products; Products of purchased glass
HQ: Milgard Manufacturing Llc
   1010 54th Ave E
   Tacoma WA
   253 922-4343

(P-2676)
NISHIBA INDUSTRIES CORPORATION
2360 Marconi Ct (92154-7241)
PHONE..............................619 661-8866
Yoshiaki Nishiba, *Pr*
▲ **EMP:** 72 **EST:** 1987
SQ FT: 2,500
SALES (est): 9.23MM **Privately Held**
Web: www.anaglb.com
SIC: 3089 3544 5162 Plastics hardware and building products; Special dies, tools, jigs, and fixtures; Plastics materials and basic shapes
PA: Nishiba Industry Co., Ltd.
   5-1350, Hirosawacho
   Kiryu GNM

(P-2677)
PC VAUGHAN MFG CORP
Also Called: Rostar Filters
1278 Mercantile St (93030-7522)
PHONE..............................805 278-2555
Jeff Starin, *CEO*
Jeff Starin, *Pr*
EMP: 65 **EST:** 1979
SQ FT: 40,000
SALES (est): 7.67MM **Privately Held**
Web: www.rostarfilters.com
SIC: 3089 3569 3714 5085 Automotive parts, plastic; Filters: oil, fuel, and air, motor vehicle; Filters, industrial

(P-2678)
POLYMER LOGISTICS INC
1725 Sierra Ridge Dr (92507-7133)
PHONE..............................951 567-2900
Albert Terrazas, *Brnch Mgr*
EMP: 60
SALES (corp-wide): 217.91MM **Privately Held**
Web: www.toscaltd.com
SIC: 3089 5085 5162 Pallets, plastics; Boxes, crates, etc., other than paper; Plastics materials and basic shapes
HQ: Polymer Logistics, Inc.
   1175 Peachtree St Ne # 1900
   Atlanta GA

(P-2679)
PRETIUM PACKAGING LLC
Also Called: Pretium Packaging
13980 Mountain Ave (91710-9018)
PHONE..............................714 777-9580
Lisa Engert, *Mgr*
EMP: 150
SALES (corp-wide): 868.81MM **Privately Held**
Web: www.pretiumpkg.com
SIC: 3089 3544 3085 5113 Blow molded finished plastics products, nec; Industrial molds; Plastics bottles; Bags, paper and disposable plastic
PA: Pretium Packaging, L.L.C.
   1555 Page Industrial Blvd
   Saint Louis MO
   314 727-8200

3089 - Plastics Products, Nec (P-2680)

(P-2680)
STAR SHIELD SOLUTIONS LLC
4315 Santa Ana St (91761-7872)
PHONE..................866 662-4477
Gil Stanfill, *Managing Member*
EMP: 60 **EST:** 2007
SALES (est): 5.88MM **Privately Held**
Web: www.starshieldsolutions.com
SIC: 3089 7389 Automotive parts, plastic; Financial services

(P-2681)
TALCO PLASTICS INC
3270 E 70th St (90805-1821)
PHONE..................562 630-1224
EMP: 64
SALES (corp-wide): 22.23MM **Privately Held**
Web: www.talcoplastics.com
SIC: 3089 4953 Extruded finished plastics products, nec; Recycling, waste materials
PA: Talco Plastics, Inc.
  1000 W Rincon St
  Corona CA
  951 531-2000

(P-2682)
TOTEX MANUFACTURING INC
3050 Lomita Blvd (90505-5103)
PHONE..................310 326-2028
Tommy Tong, *Pr*
▲ **EMP:** 70 **EST:** 1998
SALES (est): 11.17MM **Privately Held**
Web: www.totexmfg.com
SIC: 3089 5063 Battery cases, plastics or plastics combination; Batteries, dry cell

(P-2683)
VANTAGE ASSOCIATES INC
12333 Los Nietos Rd (90670-2911)
PHONE..................562 968-1400
Paul Roy, *CEO*
EMP: 65
SQ FT: 20,000
SALES (corp-wide): 21.95MM **Privately Held**
Web: www.vantageassoc.com
SIC: 3089 2499 5085 3621 Plastics processing; Spools, reels, and pulleys: wood; Industrial supplies; Motors and generators
PA: Vantage Associates Inc.
  12333 Los Nietos Rd
  Santa Fe Springs CA
  619 477-6940

3143 Men's Footwear, Except Athletic

(P-2684)
CAREISMATIC BRANDS INC (PA)
Also Called: Cherokee Uniform
9800 De Soto Ave (91311-4411)
PHONE..................818 671-2100
Girisha Chandraraj, *CEO*
Robert Pierpoint, *CFO*
Sidharth Lakhani, *COO*
◆ **EMP:** 203 **EST:** 1995
SQ FT: 140,000
SALES (est): 189.35MM **Privately Held**
Web: www.careismatic.com
SIC: 3143 3144 5139 2339 Men's footwear, except athletic; Women's footwear, except athletic; Shoes; Women's and misses' outerwear, nec

---

3149 Footwear, Except Rubber, Nec

(P-2685)
SOLE TECHNOLOGY INC (PA)
Also Called: Etnies
26921 Fuerte Dr (92630-8149)
PHONE..................949 460-2020
Pierre Senizergues, *Pr*
Paul Migaki, *
◆ **EMP:** 124 **EST:** 1996
SALES (est): 57.31MM **Privately Held**
Web: www.soletechnology.com
SIC: 3149 5139 Athletic shoes, except rubber or plastic; Footwear

---

3172 Personal Leather Goods, Nec

(P-2686)
MALIBU LEATHER INC
510 W 6th St Ste 1002 (90014-1311)
PHONE..................310 985-0707
Allen Cinoglu, *Pr*
EMP: 125 **EST:** 2009
SQ FT: 12,000
SALES (est): 6.8MM **Privately Held**
SIC: 3172 5199 5948 Personal leather goods, nec; Leather, leather goods, and furs ; Luggage and leather goods stores

---

3199 Leather Goods, Nec

(P-2687)
ARIAT INTERNATIONAL INC (PA)
1500 Alvarado St Ste 100 (94577-2635)
PHONE..................510 477-7000
Elizabeth Cross, *CEO*
Pankaj Gupta, *CFO*
◆ **EMP:** 922 **EST:** 1991
SALES (est): 479.85MM **Privately Held**
Web: www.ariat.com
SIC: 3199 5139 5137 5136 Equestrian related leather articles; Footwear; Women's and children's clothing; Men's and boy's clothing

---

3211 Flat Glass

(P-2688)
CARDINAL GLASS INDUSTRIES INC
Also Called: Cardinal C G
24100 Cardinal Ave (92551-9545)
PHONE..................951 485-9007
Scott Paisley, *Brnch Mgr*
EMP: 141
SALES (corp-wide): 1B **Privately Held**
Web: www.cardinalcorp.com
SIC: 3211 5039 3229 Flat glass; Glass construction materials; Pressed and blown glass, nec
PA: Cardinal Glass Industries Inc
  775 Pririe Ctr Dr Ste 200
  Eden Prairie MN
  952 229-2600

3229 Pressed And Blown Glass, Nec

(P-2689)
WEST COAST QUARTZ CORPORATION (HQ)
Also Called: W C Q
1000 Corporate Way (94539-6105)
PHONE..................510 249-2160
Johng Bae, *CEO*
Dave Lopes, *
Howard Cho, *
Jun Hyung Kim, *
▲ **EMP:** 97 **EST:** 1981
SQ FT: 60,000
SALES (est): 23.31MM **Privately Held**
Web: www.wcq.com
SIC: 3229 3679 3674 5065 Glassware, industrial; Quartz crystals, for electronic application; Semiconductors and related devices; Semiconductor devices
PA: Worldex Industry & Trading Co.,Ltd
  53-77 4gongdan-Ro 7-Gil
  Gumi

(P-2690)
ZEONS INC
291 S La Cienega Blvd Ste 102 (90211)
PHONE..................323 302-8299
Naved Jafry, *Pr*
EMP: 312 **EST:** 2014
SQ FT: 3,500
SALES (est): 7.94MM **Privately Held**
SIC: 3229 1629 6211 Insulators, electrical: glass; Power plant construction; Investment certificate sales

---

3231 Products Of Purchased Glass

(P-2691)
ANTHONY INC
Also Called: Anthony International
12812 Arroyo St (91342-5301)
PHONE..................818 365-9451
Jeff Clark, *Brnch Mgr*
EMP: 119
SALES (corp-wide): 8.51B **Publicly Held**
Web: www.anthonyintl.com
SIC: 3231 5078 3585 Doors, glass: made from purchased glass; Display cases, refrigerated; Evaporative condensers, heat transfer equipment
HQ: Anthony, Inc.
  12391 Montero Ave
  Sylmar CA

(P-2692)
AVALON GLASS & MIRROR COMPANY
Also Called: Avalon Glass & Mirror
642 Alondra Blvd (90746-1049)
PHONE..................323 321-8806
Salvador G Gomez, *Pr*
Randy Seeinberg, *
Ed Rosengrant, *
Ruben Huerta, *
▲ **EMP:** 66 **EST:** 1950
SQ FT: 100,000
SALES (est): 4.37MM **Privately Held**
Web: www.avalonmirrorglass.com
SIC: 3231 5023 5231 3211 Mirrored glass; Glassware; Glass; Flat glass
PA: Gwla Acquisition Corp.
  8600 Rheem Ave
  South Gate CA

(P-2693)
CHAM-CAL ENGINEERING CO
12722 Western Ave (92841-4017)
PHONE..................714 898-9721
▲ **EMP:** 85 **EST:** 1970
SALES (est): 9.17MM **Privately Held**
Web: www.chamcal.com
SIC: 3231 8711 Mirrors, truck and automobile: made from purchased glass; Engineering services

(P-2694)
LARRY MTHVIN INSTALLATIONS INC (HQ)
Also Called: L M I
501 Kettering Dr (91761-8150)
PHONE..................909 563-1700
Larry Methvin, *CEO*
▲ **EMP:** 200 **EST:** 1975
SQ FT: 28,000
SALES (est): 48.45MM
SALES (corp-wide): 4.88B **Publicly Held**
Web: www.larrymethvin.com
SIC: 3231 3431 1751 Doors, glass: made from purchased glass; Shower stalls, metal; Carpentry work
PA: Patrick Industries, Inc.
  107 W Franklin St
  Elkhart IN
  574 294-7511

3241 Cement, Hydraulic

(P-2695)
CALPORTLAND COMPANY
Also Called: California Portland Cement
9350 Oak Creek Rd (93501-7738)
PHONE..................661 824-2401
Bruce Shaffer, *Brnch Mgr*
EMP: 130
Web: www.calportland.com
SIC: 3241 5032 5211 Masonry cement; Brick, stone, and related material; Cement
HQ: Calportland Company
  2025 E Financial Way
  Glendora CA

(P-2696)
CALPORTLAND COMPANY (DH)
Also Called: Arizona Portland Cement
2025 E Financial Way (91741-4692)
P.O. Box 5025 (91740-0885)
PHONE..................626 852-6200
Michio Kimura, *Ch Bd*
Allen Hamblen, *
James A Repman, *
James A Wendoll, *
John Renninger, *
▲ **EMP:** 77 **EST:** 1891
SQ FT: 28,000
SALES (est): 864.13MM **Privately Held**
Web: www.calportland.com
SIC: 3241 3273 5032 Portland cement; Ready-mixed concrete; Brick, stone, and related material
HQ: Taiheiyo Cement U.S.A., Inc.
  2025 E Fincl Way Ste 200
  Glendora CA
  626 852-6200

(P-2697)
RMC PACIFIC MATERIALS LLC (PA)
Also Called: Cemex
6601 Koll Center Pkwy Ste 300 (94566-3163)
P.O. Box 5252 (94566-0252)
◆ **EMP:** 200 **EST:** 1998
SQ FT: 30,000

PRODUCTS & SERVICES SECTION

3273 - Ready-mixed Concrete (P-2714)

SALES (est): 49.11MM
SALES (corp-wide): 49.11MM Privately Held
SIC: 3241 3273 3531 1442 Cement, hydraulic; Ready-mixed concrete; Asphalt plant, including gravel-mix type; Sand mining

3253 Ceramic Wall And Floor Tile

(P-2698)
OCEANSIDE GLASSTILE COMPANY (PA)
Also Called: Mandala
5858 Edison Pl (92008-6519)
PHONE.................................760 929-4000
Sean M Gildea, *CEO*
Jim Jensen, *VP*
John Marckx, *Ex VP*
Rick Blacklock, *VP*
Jeff Nibler, *VP*
◆ EMP: 375 EST: 1992
SQ FT: 48,000
SALES (est): 76.08MM Privately Held
Web: www.glasstile.com
SIC: 3253 5032 Mosaic tile, glazed and unglazed; ceramic; Tile, clay or other ceramic, excluding refractory

3269 Pottery Products, Nec

(P-2699)
HAGEN-RENAKER INC (PA)
914 W Cienega Ave (91773-2415)
P.O. Box 41324 (90853-1324)
PHONE.................................909 599-2341
Susan Renaker Nikas, *Pr*
Mary Lou Salas, *
EMP: 80 EST: 1946
SQ FT: 88,064
SALES (est): 5.32MM
SALES (corp-wide): 5.32MM Privately Held
Web: www.hagenrenaker.com
SIC: 3269 0181 Figures: pottery, china, earthenware, and stoneware; Nursery stock, growing of

3271 Concrete Block And Brick

(P-2700)
WESTERN STATES WHOLESALE INC (PA)
Also Called: C-Cure
1420 S Bon View Ave (91761-4405)
P.O. Box 3340 (91761-0934)
PHONE.................................909 947-0028
Randall Humphreys, *CEO*
Robert Humphreys, *
Donna Humphreys, *
▲ EMP: 70 EST: 1995
SQ FT: 60,000
SALES (est): 23.04MM Privately Held
Web: www.wswcorp.com
SIC: 3271 5072 5032 5211 Concrete block and brick; Bolts; Drywall materials; Lumber products

3272 Concrete Products, Nec

(P-2701)
AVILAS GARDEN ART (PA)
14608 Merrill Ave (92335-4219)
PHONE.................................909 350-4546
Ralph G Avila, *Owner*
EMP: 60 EST: 1981
SQ FT: 7,000
SALES (est): 8.64MM
SALES (corp-wide): 8.64MM Privately Held
Web: www.avilasgardenart.com
SIC: 3272 5261 5211 5199 Precast terrazzo or concrete products; Lawn ornaments; Masonry materials and supplies; Statuary

(P-2702)
BOND MANUFACTURING CO INC (PA)
2516 Verne Roberts Cir Ste H3 (94509-7904)
PHONE.................................866 771-2663
Daryl Merritt, *CEO*
Ronald Merritt, *
Cameron Jenkins, *
◆ EMP: 97 EST: 1946
SQ FT: 250,000
SALES (est): 22.21MM
SALES (corp-wide): 22.21MM Privately Held
Web: www.bondmfg.com
SIC: 3272 5083 Fireplaces, concrete; Lawn and garden machinery and equipment

(P-2703)
DCC GENERAL ENGRG CONTRS INC
2180 Meyers Ave (92029-1001)
PHONE.................................760 480-7400
Frank D'agostini, *Pr*
Scott Woods, *
EMP: 75 EST: 1982
SQ FT: 2,100
SALES (est): 9.89MM Privately Held
Web: www.dccengineering.com
SIC: 3272 1771 3531 Concrete products, nec; Curb and sidewalk contractors; Asphalt plant, including gravel-mix type

(P-2704)
GOLDEN EMPIRE CON PDTS INC
Also Called: Structurecast
8261 Mccutchen Rd (93311-9407)
PHONE.................................661 833-4490
Brent Dezember, *Pr*
Ann Dzember, *
EMP: 65 EST: 1997
SQ FT: 10,000
SALES (est): 10.04MM Privately Held
Web: www.structurecast.com
SIC: 3272 1791 Precast terrazzo or concrete products; Precast concrete structural framing or panels, placing of

(P-2705)
JENSEN ENTERPRISES INC
Also Called: Jensen Precast
14221 San Bernardino Ave (92335-5232)
PHONE.................................909 357-7264
TOLL FREE: 800
Carol Kohanle, *Mgr*
EMP: 300
SALES (corp-wide): 237.25MM Privately Held
Web: www.jensenprecast.com
SIC: 3272 7699 5211 5039 Concrete products, precast, nec; Waste cleaning services; Masonry materials and supplies; Septic tanks
PA: Jensen Enterprises, Inc.
    9895 Double R Blvd
    Reno NV
    775 352-2700

(P-2706)
SAN BENITO SUPPLY (PA)
1060 Nash Rd (95023-5303)
PHONE.................................831 637-5526
Mark Schipper, *Pr*
Ted Schipper, *
EMP: 129 EST: 1978
SQ FT: 1,870
SALES (est): 19.59MM
SALES (corp-wide): 19.59MM Privately Held
Web: www.sbs-cas.com
SIC: 3272 5032 Concrete products, nec; Brick, stone, and related material

(P-2707)
SIERRA PRECAST INC
Also Called: U.S. Concrete Precast Group
1 Live Oak Ave (95037-9245)
PHONE.................................408 779-1000
Eric Scholz, *Pr*
EMP: 74 EST: 1974
SQ FT: 4,000
SALES (est): 2.24MM Publicly Held
SIC: 3272 1771 Panels and sections, prefabricated concrete; Concrete work
HQ: U.S. Concrete, Inc.
    331 N Main St
    Euless TX
    817 835-4105

(P-2708)
SOUTHWEST CONCRETE PRODUCTS
519 S Benson Ave (91762-4002)
PHONE.................................909 983-9789
Bob Dzajkich, *Pr*
Eileen Dzajkich, *
Natalie Dzajkich, *
▲ EMP: 160 EST: 1966
SQ FT: 25,000
SALES (est): 10.5MM Privately Held
SIC: 3272 5032 Manhole covers or frames, concrete; Brick, stone, and related material
PA: Taiheyo Kenkou Center Co.,Ltd.
    164-2, Rokuchome, Yotsukuramachi
    Iwaki FSM

(P-2709)
WILLIS CONSTRUCTION CO INC
2261 San Juan Hwy (95045-9565)
PHONE.................................831 623-2900
Lawrence M Willis, *CEO*
Mark Hildebrand, *
Tom Yezek, *
Roger Ely, *
◆ EMP: 120 EST: 1976
SQ FT: 4,000
SALES (est): 24.07MM Privately Held
Web: www.willisconstruction.com
SIC: 3272 1791 Concrete products, precast, nec; Precast concrete structural framing or panels, placing of

3273 Ready-mixed Concrete

(P-2710)
HOLLIDAY TRUCKING INC (PA)
1401 N Benson Ave (91786-2166)
PHONE.................................909 982-1553
Frederick N Holliday, *Pr*
Penny Holliday, *
John Holliday, *
Ronald Chambers, *
EMP: 60 EST: 1964
SQ FT: 2,000
SALES (est): 5.03MM
SALES (corp-wide): 5.03MM Privately Held
Web: www.hollidayrock.com
SIC: 3273 4212 Ready-mixed concrete; Local trucking, without storage

(P-2711)
ROBAR ENTERPRISES INC (PA)
17671 Bear Valley Rd (92345-4902)
PHONE.................................760 244-5456
Jonathan D Hove, *CEO*
Robert E Hove, *
Al Calvanico, *
EMP: 150 EST: 1981
SQ FT: 26,000
SALES (est): 63.93MM
SALES (corp-wide): 63.93MM Privately Held
Web: www.robar.com
SIC: 3273 5051 3441 Ready-mixed concrete; Steel; Building components, structural steel

(P-2712)
ROBERTSONS RDYMX LTD A CAL LTD (HQ)
Also Called: Robertson's
200 S Main St Ste 200 (92882-2212)
P.O. Box 3600 (92878-3600)
PHONE.................................951 493-6500
TOLL FREE: 800
Jon Troesh, *Pt*
Greg Edwards, *
▲ EMP: 85 EST: 1991
SQ FT: 22,008
SALES (est): 511.78MM Privately Held
Web: www.rrmca.com
SIC: 3273 3531 5032 2951 Ready-mixed concrete; Bituminous, cement and concrete related products and equip.; Asphalt mixture; Asphalt paving mixtures and blocks
PA: Mitsubishi Materials Corporation
    3-2-3, Marunouchi
    Chiyoda-Ku TKY

(P-2713)
SUPERIOR READY MIX CONCRETE LP
Also Called: American Ready Mix
1564 Mission Rd (92029-1194)
PHONE.................................760 728-1128
Greg Sage, *Mgr*
EMP: 71
SALES (corp-wide): 205.26MM Privately Held
SIC: 3273 1442 Ready-mixed concrete; Construction sand and gravel
PA: Superior Ready Mix Concrete L.P.
    1564 Mission Rd
    Escondido CA
    760 745-0556

(P-2714)
TEICHERT INC (PA)
5200 Franklin Dr Ste 115 (94588-3326)
P.O. Box 15002 (95851-0002)
PHONE.................................916 484-3011
Judson T Riggs, *Pr*
Louis V Riggs, *
Narendra M Pathipati, *
Anne S Haslam, *
▲ EMP: 161 EST: 1887
SALES (est): 844.71MM
SALES (corp-wide): 844.71MM Privately Held
Web: www.teichert.com
SIC: 3273 5032 1611 1442 Ready-mixed concrete; Brick, stone, and related material; Highway and street construction; Construction sand and gravel

3275 Gypsum Products

(P-2715)
PACIFIC COAST BUILDING PRODUCTS INC (PA)
10600 White Rock Rd Ste 100 (95670-6294)
P.O. Box 419074 (95741-9074)
PHONE..............................916 631-6500
◆ EMP: 120 EST: 1953
SALES (est): 1.19B
SALES (corp-wide): 1.19B Privately Held
Web: www.paccoast.com
SIC: 3275 3271 5031 1761 Wallboard, gypsum; Concrete block and brick; Lumber, plywood, and millwork; Roofing contractor

3281 Cut Stone And Stone Products

(P-2716)
HALABI INC (PA)
Also Called: Duracite
4447 Green Valley Rd (94534-1365)
PHONE..............................707 402-1600
TOLL FREE: 800
Fadi M Halabi, CEO
George Marino, *
EMP: 137 EST: 1995
SALES (est): 23.63MM
SALES (corp-wide): 23.63MM Privately Held
SIC: 3281 1799 Cut stone and stone products; Counter top installation

(P-2717)
RUGGERI MARBLE AND GRANITE INC
25028 Vermont Ave (90710-3116)
PHONE..............................310 513-2155
Andre Ruggeri, Pr
Robert Ruggeri, *
◆ EMP: 80 EST: 1991
SALES (est): 3.94MM Privately Held
Web: www.ruggerimarble.com
SIC: 3281 5032 Marble, building: cut and shaped; Ceramic wall and floor tile, nec

3295 Minerals, Ground Or Treated

(P-2718)
IMERYS TALC AMERICA INC (DH)
1732 N 1st St Ste 450 (95112-4579)
◆ EMP: 277 EST: 1992
SALES (est): 87.78MM
SALES (corp-wide): 3.28MM Privately Held
SIC: 3295 1499 Talc, ground or otherwise treated; Talc mining
HQ: Imerys
43 Quai De Grenelle
Paris
142229512

(P-2719)
JON BROOKS INC (PA)
Also Called: Laguna Clay Company
14400 Lomitas Ave (91746-3018)
PHONE..............................626 330-0631
Jon Brooks, Pr
Laurie Brooks, *
◆ EMP: 100 EST: 1981
SQ FT: 117,000
SALES (est): 20.91MM
SALES (corp-wide): 20.91MM Privately Held
Web: www.lagunaclay.com
SIC: 3295 5085 Clay, ground or otherwise treated; Refractory material

3312 Blast Furnaces And Steel Mills

(P-2720)
PRICE INDUSTRIES INC
Also Called: International Iron Products
10883 Thornmint Rd (92127-2403)
PHONE..............................858 673-4451
Kenneth Alan Price, Pr
Barbara Price, *
EMP: 75 EST: 1968
SQ FT: 4,000
SALES (est): 8.73MM Privately Held
Web: www.priceindustries.com
SIC: 3312 3441 1791 5072 Structural and rail mill products; Fabricated structural metal; Structural steel erection; Bolts, nuts, and screws

3315 Steel Wire And Related Products

(P-2721)
NATIONAL WIRE AND CABLE CORPORATION
Also Called: National Wire and Cable
136 N San Fernando Rd (90031-1780)
P.O. Box 31307 (90031-0307)
PHONE..............................323 225-5611
EMP: 170 EST: 1952
SALES (est): 22.05MM Privately Held
Web: www.nationalwire.com
SIC: 3315 5031 Cable, steel: insulated or armored; Molding, all materials

3341 Secondary Nonferrous Metals

(P-2722)
TST INC (PA)
Also Called: Alpase
13428 Benson Ave (91710-5258)
PHONE..............................951 685-2155
Andrew G Stein, CEO
Robert A Stein, *
Greg Levine, *
James Davidson, *
◆ EMP: 260 EST: 1961
SQ FT: 123,000
SALES (est): 45.96MM
SALES (corp-wide): 45.96MM Privately Held
Web: www.tst-inc.com
SIC: 3341 5093 Aluminum smelting and refining (secondary); Metal scrap and waste materials

3355 Aluminum Rolling And Drawing, Nec

(P-2723)
METALS USA BUILDING PDTS LP (DH)
Also Called: Metals USA
955 Columbia St (92821-2923)
PHONE..............................713 946-9000
Charles Canning, Pt
Robert Mcpherson, Pt
▲ EMP: 700 EST: 1960
SQ FT: 60,000
SALES (est): 270.44MM
SALES (corp-wide): 17.02B Publicly Held
Web: www.metalsusa.com
SIC: 3355 5031 1542 Structural shapes, rolled, aluminum; Building materials, exterior; Commercial and office buildings, renovation and repair
HQ: Metals Usa, Inc.
800 W Cypress Creed Rd St
Fort Lauderdale FL
215 673-3595

3357 Nonferrous Wiredrawing And Insulating

(P-2724)
CENTURY WIRE & CABLE INC
7400 E Slauson Ave (90040-3300)
PHONE..............................800 999-5566
David Lifschitz, CEO
Carl Tom, *
Rowdy Oxford, *
William Suddarth, *
EMP: 100 EST: 1982
SALES (est): 25.27MM
SALES (corp-wide): 123.67MM Privately Held
Web: www.centurywire.com
SIC: 3357 5063 Nonferrous wiredrawing and insulating; Electrical apparatus and equipment
HQ: Gehr Industries, Inc.
7400 E Slauson Ave
Commerce CA
323 728-5558

(P-2725)
GEHR INDUSTRIES INC (HQ)
Also Called: Gehr Group
7400 E Slauson Ave (90040-3300)
PHONE..............................323 728-5558
David Lifschitz, CEO
Carlton Tom, VP
Mark Goldman, COO
William Suddarth, VP
▲ EMP: 140 EST: 1966
SQ FT: 260,000
SALES (est): 57.64MM
SALES (corp-wide): 123.67MM Privately Held
Web: www.gehrindustries.com
SIC: 3357 5063 5072 5085 Nonferrous wiredrawing and insulating; Electrical apparatus and equipment; Hardware; Industrial supplies
PA: The Gehr Group Inc
7400 E Slauson Ave
Commerce CA
323 728-5558

(P-2726)
WINCHSTER INTRCNNECT CM CA INC
Also Called: C B S
1873 Diamond St (92078-5128)
PHONE..............................800 848-4257
Lewis Brian Falk, CEO
Donald Falk, *
Shannon Baroni, *
▲ EMP: 175 EST: 1965
SQ FT: 40,000
SALES (est): 46.8MM
SALES (corp-wide): 17.49B Privately Held
Web: www.falmat.com
SIC: 3357 5063 Nonferrous wiredrawing and insulating; Wire and cable
HQ: Aptiv Corporation
5820 Innovation Dr
Troy MI

3398 Metal Heat Treating

(P-2727)
ADB INDUSTRIES
Also Called: Subsidy of Be Aerospace
1400 Manhattan Ave (92831-5222)
PHONE..............................310 679-9193
Brian Dietz, Pr
EMP: 256 EST: 1961
SQ FT: 50,000
SALES (est): 4.75MM
SALES (corp-wide): 67.07B Publicly Held
SIC: 3398 8711 7692 3444 Brazing (hardening) of metal; Engineering services; Welding repair; Sheet metalwork
HQ: Tsi Group, Inc.
94 Tide Mill Rd
Hampton NH

(P-2728)
NEWTON HEAT TREATING CO INC
19235 E Walnut Dr N (91748-1494)
P.O. Box 8010 (91748-0010)
PHONE..............................626 964-6528
Greg Newton, Pr
Linda Malcor, *
EMP: 71 EST: 1968
SQ FT: 1,900
SALES (est): 12.13MM Privately Held
Web: www.newtonheattreating.com
SIC: 3398 8734 3444 Metal heat treating; X-ray inspection service, industrial; Sheet metalwork

3429 Hardware, Nec

(P-2729)
DOVAL INDUSTRIES INC
Also Called: Doval Industries Co
3961 N Mission Rd (90031-2931)
PHONE..............................323 226-0335
Cruz Sandoval, CEO
▲ EMP: 65 EST: 1985
SALES (est): 4.68MM Privately Held
Web: www.doval.com
SIC: 3429 5072 2759 Keys, locks, and related hardware; Hardware; Screen printing

(P-2730)
MCMAHON STEEL COMPANY INC
1880 Nirvana Ave (91911-6118)
PHONE..............................619 671-9700
Derek J Mcmahon, Pr
Kevin Mcmahon, VP
EMP: 120 EST: 1970
SQ FT: 14,300
SALES (est): 23.18MM Privately Held
Web: www.mcmahonsteel.com
SIC: 3429 1791 3441 Hardware, nec; Structural steel erection; Fabricated structural metal

(P-2731)
SATURN FASTENERS INC
425 S Varney St (91502-2193)
PHONE..............................818 973-1807
Raymond David Barker Junior, C
Laura Elaine Barker, *
Raymond D Barker Junior, Pr
▲ EMP: 112 EST: 1989
SQ FT: 38,000
SALES (est): 16.83MM Privately Held
Web: www.saturnfasteners.com
SIC: 3429 5085 5072 3452 Metal fasteners; Industrial supplies; Bolts, nuts, and screws; Bolts, nuts, rivets, and washers

PRODUCTS & SERVICES SECTION

3452 - Bolts, Nuts, Rivets, And Washers (P-2749)

HQ: Acument Global Technologies, Inc.
6125 18 Mile Rd
Sterling Heights MI
586 254-3900

(P-2732)
SPEP ACQUISITION CORP (PA)
Also Called: Sierra Pacific Engrg & Pdts
4041 Via Oro Ave (90810-1458)
P.O. Box 5246 (90749-5246)
PHONE.................................310 608-0693
Barry Stein, *Pr*
Larry Mirick, *
◆ **EMP:** 70 **EST:** 1986
SQ FT: 48,300
SALES (est): 20.69MM
SALES (corp-wide): 20.69MM Privately Held
Web: www.spep.com
SIC: 3429 8711 5072 Hardware, nec; Engineering services; Hardware

3431 Metal Sanitary Ware

(P-2733)
SEACHROME CORPORATION
Also Called: Seachrome
1906 E Dominguez St (90810-1002)
PHONE.................................310 427-8010
Sam C Longo Junior, *CEO*
▲ **EMP:** 112 **EST:** 1983
SQ FT: 50,000
SALES (est): 22.1MM Privately Held
Web: www.seachrome.com
SIC: 3431 5072 3842 3429 Bathroom fixtures, including sinks; Builders' hardware, nec; Surgical appliances and supplies; Hardware, nec

3432 Plumbing Fixture Fittings And Trim

(P-2734)
GMS LANDSCAPES INC
207 Camino Leon (93012-8635)
PHONE.................................805 402-3925
Sarah Corbin, *Pr*
EMP: 85 **EST:** 2017
SALES (est): 3.75MM Privately Held
SIC: 3432 0781 Plumbing fixture fittings and trim; Landscape services

3433 Heating Equipment, Except Electric

(P-2735)
BMI INC
Also Called: Honeywell Authorized Dealer
4060 Alvis Ct (95677-4012)
PHONE.................................530 749-0808
Jeff Brower, *Pr*
Duane Knickerbocker, *
EMP: 75 **EST:** 1980
SQ FT: 5,000
SALES (est): 22.92MM Privately Held
Web: www.browermechanical.com
SIC: 3433 7629 Heating equipment, except electric; Electrical household appliance repair

3441 Fabricated Structural Metal

(P-2736)
MADISON INC OF OKLAHOMA
18000 Studebaker Rd (90703-2679)
PHONE.................................918 224-6990
John Samuel Frey, *Pr*
Robert E Hansen, *
Barbara Cruncleton, *
EMP: 67 **EST:** 1946
SALES (est): 22.77MM
SALES (corp-wide): 90.88MM Privately Held
SIC: 3441 1541 3448 3444 Fabricated structural metal; Prefabricated building erection, industrial; Prefabricated metal buildings and components; Sheet metalwork
PA: John S. Frey Enterprises
1900 E 64th St
Los Angeles CA
323 583-4061

(P-2737)
MCWHIRTER STEEL INC
42211 7th St E (93535-5400)
PHONE.................................661 951-8998
David Mcwhirter, *Pr*
Angela Mcwhirter, *CFO*
Nathan Mcwhirter, *Dir*
EMP: 95 **EST:** 1992
SQ FT: 21,000
SALES (est): 14.14MM Privately Held
Web: www.mcwhirtersteel.com
SIC: 3441 1791 Fabricated structural metal; Structural steel erection

(P-2738)
METAL SUPPLY LLC
11810 Center St (90280-7832)
PHONE.................................562 634-9940
TOLL FREE: 800
Dion Genchi, *Pr*
Bruce E Hubert, *
▼ **EMP:** 63 **EST:** 1961
SQ FT: 50,000
SALES (est): 9.38MM Privately Held
Web: www.metalsupply.com
SIC: 3441 5051 Fabricated structural metal; Iron and steel (ferrous) products

(P-2739)
SPARTAN INC
3030 M St (93301-2137)
PHONE.................................661 327-1205
John Wood, *Pr*
Louis Stern, *
John D Clemmey, *
Teresa Wood, *
▼ **EMP:** 65 **EST:** 2002
SQ FT: 125,000
SALES (est): 10.96MM Privately Held
Web: www.spartaninc.net
SIC: 3441 8711 Fabricated structural metal; Engineering services

(P-2740)
TRUSSWORKS INTERNATIONAL INC
1275 E Franklin Ave (91766-5450)
PHONE.................................714 630-2772
Michael Farrell, *Pr*
Ali Shantyaei, *
EMP: 60 **EST:** 2007
SALES (est): 9.21MM Privately Held
Web: www.twifab.com
SIC: 3441 3446 1791 Fabricated structural metal; Architectural metalwork; Building front installation, metal

3442 Metal Doors, Sash, And Trim

(P-2741)
R LANG COMPANY
Also Called: Truframe
8240 W Doe Ave (93291-9263)
P.O. Box 7960 (93290-7960)
PHONE.................................559 651-0701
Richard A Lang, *Pr*
Judith D Lang, *
▼ **EMP:** 75 **EST:** 1967
SALES (est): 12.8MM Privately Held
Web: www.rollaway.com
SIC: 3442 3444 3211 5031 Screen doors, metal; Skylights, sheet metal; Flat glass; Windows

3443 Fabricated Plate Work (boiler Shop)

(P-2742)
CONSOLIDATED FABRICATORS CORP (PA)
Also Called: Confab
14620 Arminta St (91402-5902)
PHONE.................................800 635-8335
Michael J Melideo, *CEO*
Jeff Lombardi, *
▲ **EMP:** 110 **EST:** 1974
SQ FT: 150,000
SALES (est): 39.04MM
SALES (corp-wide): 39.04MM Privately Held
Web: www.con-fab.com
SIC: 3443 5051 3444 Dumpsters, garbage; Steel; Studs and joists, sheet metal

3444 Sheet Metalwork

(P-2743)
AERO BENDING COMPANY
560 Auto Center Dr Ste A (93551-4485)
PHONE.................................661 948-2363
Robert Burns, *Pr*
EMP: 80 **EST:** 1944
SQ FT: 26,000
SALES (est): 10.8MM Privately Held
Web: www.aerobendingco.com
SIC: 3444 5088 Sheet metalwork; Aircraft engines and engine parts

(P-2744)
MAC CAL COMPANY
Also Called: Mac Cal Manufacturing
2520 Zanker Rd (95131-1127)
PHONE.................................408 441-1435
Michael Hall, *Pr*
Renee Hall, *
Cathy Mcdonald, *CFO*
EMP: 80 **EST:** 1960
SALES (est): 24.64MM Privately Held
Web: www.maccal.com
SIC: 3444 3479 7336 Sheet metal specialties, not stamped; Name plates: engraved, etched, etc.; Silk screen design

(P-2745)
SHADE STRUCTURES INC
Also Called: Fabritec Structures
115 E 2nd St Ste 101 (92780-3684)
PHONE.................................714 427-6980
Cathy Wanamaker, *Brnch Mgr*
EMP: 71
Web: www.usa-shade.com
SIC: 3444 1799 2394 Sheet metalwork; Welding on site; Canvas and related products
HQ: Shade Structures, Inc.
2580 Esters Blvd 100
Dfw Airport TX
214 905-9500

3448 Prefabricated Metal Buildings

(P-2746)
ALLIED CONTAINER SYSTEMS INC
Also Called: ACS
511 Wilbur Ave Ste B4 (94509-7563)
PHONE.................................925 944-7600
Brian Horsfall, *Ch Bd*
Susan Horsfall, *
◆ **EMP:** 140 **EST:** 1992
SQ FT: 20,000
SALES (est): 19.65MM Privately Held
SIC: 3448 8748 3559 Prefabricated metal buildings and components; Environmental consultant; Chemical machinery and equipment

(P-2747)
FCP INC (PA)
23100 Wildomar Trl (92595-9699)
P.O. Box 1555 (92595-1555)
PHONE.................................951 678-4571
Russell J Greer, *CEO*
Barret Hilzer, *
EMP: 84 **EST:** 1982
SQ FT: 200,000
SALES (est): 12.24MM
SALES (corp-wide): 12.24MM Privately Held
Web: www.fcpbarns.com
SIC: 3448 1541 Prefabricated metal components; Steel building construction

(P-2748)
MOBILE MODULAR MANAGEMENT CORP
Also Called: Trs Rentelco
11450 Mission Blvd (91752-1015)
PHONE.................................800 819-1084
Thomas Sanders, *Mgr*
EMP: 175
SALES (corp-wide): 733.82MM Publicly Held
Web: www.mgrc.com
SIC: 3448 7519 Prefabricated metal buildings and components; Trailer rental
HQ: Mobile Modular Management Corporation
5700 Las Positas Rd
Livermore CA
925 443-8052

3452 Bolts, Nuts, Rivets, And Washers

(P-2749)
DOUBLECO INCORPORATED
Also Called: R & D Fasteners
9444 9th St (91730-4509)
P.O. Box 250 (91785-0250)
PHONE.................................909 481-0799
Craig Scheu, *Pr*
EMP: 100 **EST:** 1986
SQ FT: 30,000
SALES (est): 23.62MM Privately Held
Web: www.rdfast.com

3452 - Bolts, Nuts, Rivets, And Washers (P-2750)

SIC: **3452** 5072 Bolts, metal; Bolts

(P-2750)
KING HOLDING CORPORATION
360 N Crescent Dr (90210-4874)
PHONE.................................586 254-3900
EMP: 7970
SIC: 3452 3465 3469 3089 Bolts, nuts, rivets, and washers; Automotive stampings; Metal stampings, nec; Injection molded finished plastics products, nec

3469 Metal Stampings, Nec

(P-2751)
GLOBAL PCCI (GPC) (PA)
Also Called: Gpc
2465 Campus Dr Ste 100 (92612-1502)
PHONE.................................757 637-9000
Sherri Bovino, *Pt*
EMP: 120 **EST:** 1989
SQ FT: 10,000
SALES (est): 17.65MM **Privately Held**
SIC: 3469 4499 Metal stampings, nec; Salvaging, distressed vessels and cargoes

(P-2752)
MEYER CORPORATION US (HQ)
Also Called: Meyer Wines
1 Meyer Plz (94590-5925)
PHONE.................................707 551-2800
Stanley Kin Sui Cheng, *CEO*
Ed Blackman, *
Christopher Banning, *
◆ **EMP:** 80 **EST:** 1980
SQ FT: 180,000
SALES (est): 89.59MM **Privately Held**
Web: www.hestan.com
SIC: 3469 3631 5023 Cooking ware, except porcelain enameled; Household cooking equipment; Kitchenware
PA: Meyer International Holdings Limited
   C/O Vistra (Bvi) Limited
   Road Town

(P-2753)
PACIFIC PRECISION METALS INC
Also Called: Tubing Seal Cap Co
1100 E Orangethorpe Ave Ste 253 (92801-1164)
P.O. Box 51481 (91761-0081)
PHONE.................................951 226-1500
Ajay N Thakkar, *Pr*
EMP: 130 **EST:** 1987
SQ FT: 2,063
SALES (est): 23.77MM **Privately Held**
SIC: 3469 3429 2599 8711 Stamping metal for the trade; Door locks, bolts, and checks; Cabinets, factory; Machine tool design
PA: Triyar Sv, Llc
   10850 Wilshire Blvd
   Los Angeles CA

(P-2754)
SPOTTER GLOBAL INC
8620 Thornton Ave (94560-3330)
PHONE.................................515 817-3726
Luke Zhao, *CEO*
EMP: 140 **EST:** 2021
SALES (est): 10.96MM **Privately Held**
SIC: 3469 5064 Household cooking and kitchen utensils, metal; Electric household appliances, nec

(P-2755)
STEICO INDUSTRIES INC
Also Called: Steico
1814 Ord Way (92056-1502)
PHONE.................................760 438-8015
Troy Steiner, *CEO*
▲ **EMP:** 230 **EST:** 2001
SQ FT: 52,000
SALES (est): 51.17MM
SALES (corp-wide): 1.02B **Privately Held**
Web: www.steicoindustries.com
SIC: 3469 5051 Metal stampings, nec; Metals service centers and offices
HQ: Senior Operations Llc
   300 E Devon Ave
   Bartlett IL
   630 372-3500

3471 Plating And Polishing

(P-2756)
AAA PLATING & INSPECTION INC
424 E Dixon St (90222-1420)
PHONE.................................323 979-8930
Gerald Wahlin, *CEO*
Charles Schwan, *
EMP: 95 **EST:** 1958
SQ FT: 50,000
SALES (est): 11.64MM **Privately Held**
Web: www.aaaplating.com
SIC: 3471 8734 Anodizing (plating) of metals or formed products; Metallurgical testing laboratory

(P-2757)
ALL METALS PROCESSING OF SAN DIEGO INC
Also Called: AMC
8401 Standustrial St (90680-2619)
PHONE.................................714 828-8238
EMP: 120
Web: www.allmetalsprocessing.com
SIC: 3471 3479 8734 Electroplating of metals or formed products; Enameling, including porcelain, of metal products; X-ray inspection service, industrial

(P-2758)
ALL MTALS PROC ORANGE CNTY LLC
8401 Standustrial St (90680-2619)
PHONE.................................714 828-8238
Scott Christman, *CFO*
Bob Wolfsberger, *
Rose Blikian, *
Michael Coburn, *
Derek Watson, *
EMP: 125 **EST:** 2015
SALES (est): 19.36MM **Privately Held**
Web: www.allmetalsprocessing.com
SIC: 3471 3479 8734 Electroplating of metals or formed products; Enameling, including porcelain, of metal products; X-ray inspection service, industrial

(P-2759)
CONTINUOUS COATING CORP (PA)
Also Called: Clinch-On Cornerbead Company
500 W Grove Ave (92865-3210)
PHONE.................................714 637-4642
Ralph M Scott, *Pr*
Kenneth N Harel, *
EMP: 72 **EST:** 1956
SALES (est): 14.04MM
SALES (corp-wide): 14.04MM **Privately Held**
Web: www.continuouscoating.com
SIC: 3471 3444 7389 Electroplating of metals or formed products; Sheet metal specialties, not stamped; Metal slitting and shearing

(P-2760)
ELITE METAL FINISHING LLC (PA)
Also Called: Metal Finishing Pntg Lab Tstg
540 Spectrum Cir (93030-8988)
PHONE.................................805 983-4320
Joel Clemons, *Pt*
Joe Hansen, *
George Hansen, *
EMP: 109 **EST:** 2001
SQ FT: 55,000
SALES (est): 20.1MM
SALES (corp-wide): 20.1MM **Privately Held**
Web: www.elitemetalfinishing.com
SIC: 3471 8734 Plating of metals or formed products; Testing laboratories

(P-2761)
THERMIONICS LABORATORY INC
Thermionics Metal Proc Inc
3118 Depot Rd (94545-2708)
PHONE.................................510 786-0680
Al Nielsen, *Mgr*
EMP: 75
SQ FT: 1,300
SALES (corp-wide): 36.51MM **Privately Held**
Web: www.thermionics.com
SIC: 3471 8711 7342 Cleaning and descaling metal products; Engineering services; Disinfecting and pest control services
HQ: Thermionics Laboratory, Inc.
   3118 Depot Rd
   Hayward CA
   510 538-3304

(P-2762)
ULTRAMET
12173 Montague St (91331-2210)
PHONE.................................818 899-0236
Andrew Duffy, *CEO*
Walter Abrams, *
Richard B Kaplan, *Stockholder*
James Kaplan, *Stockholder*
▲ **EMP:** 79 **EST:** 1970
SQ FT: 43,000
SALES (est): 16.07MM **Privately Held**
Web: www.ultrametcpt.com
SIC: 3471 8731 Electroplating and plating; Commercial physical research

3479 Metal Coating And Allied Services

(P-2763)
INNOVATIVE COATINGS TECHNOLOGY CORPORATION
Also Called: Incotec
1347 Poole St 106 (93501-1658)
PHONE.................................661 824-8101
EMP: 127 **EST:** 1992
SALES (est): 22.04MM **Privately Held**
Web: www.incoteccorp.com
SIC: 3479 8732 Coating of metals with plastic or resins; Research services, except laboratory

3491 Industrial Valves

(P-2764)
CIRCOR AEROSPACE INC (HQ)
2301 Wardlow Cir (92878-5101)
P.O. Box 2824 (29304-2824)
PHONE.................................951 270-6200
Carl Nasca, *Pr*
Christopher Celtruda, *VP*
Kathy Fazio, *Ex Sec*
Michael Dill, *VP*
Renuka Ayer, *VP*
◆ **EMP:** 245 **EST:** 1947
SQ FT: 100,000
SALES (est): 61.87MM
SALES (corp-wide): 786.92MM **Privately Held**
Web: www.circoraerospace.com
SIC: 3491 3494 3769 5085 Pressure valves and regulators, industrial; Plumbing and heating valves; Space vehicle equipment, nec; Seals, industrial
PA: Circor International, Inc.
   30 Corporate Dr Ste 200
   Burlington MA
   781 270-1200

3499 Fabricated Metal Products, Nec

(P-2765)
AMERICAN SECURITY PRODUCTS CO
Also Called: Amsec
11925 Pacific Ave (92337-8231)
P.O. Box 317001 (92331-7001)
PHONE.................................951 685-9680
Drew Meng, *Pr*
Thomas Cassutt, *CFO*
Robert Sallee, *VP*
◆ **EMP:** 237 **EST:** 1946
SQ FT: 150,000
SALES (est): 44.62MM **Privately Held**
Web: www.americansecuritysafes.com
SIC: 3499 1731 Safes and vaults, metal; Safety and security specialization

(P-2766)
EVANS INDUSTRIES INC
Darnell-Rose Div
17915 Railroad St (91748-1113)
PHONE.................................626 912-1688
Bob Batistic, *Mgr*
EMP: 73
SALES (corp-wide): 39.4MM **Privately Held**
Web: www.mmgmfg.com
SIC: 3499 5072 Wheels: wheelbarrow, stroller, etc.: disc, stamped metal; Casters and glides
HQ: Evans Industries, Inc.
   3150 Livernois Rd Ste 170
   Troy MI
   313 259-2266

3519 Internal Combustion Engines, Nec

(P-2767)
CUMMINS PACIFIC LLC (HQ)
Also Called: Cummins
1939 Deere Ave (92606-4818)
PHONE.................................949 253-6000
TOLL FREE: 800
Mark Yragui, *Pr*
▲ **EMP:** 85 **EST:** 2002
SALES (est): 87.89MM
SALES (corp-wide): 28.07B **Publicly Held**
Web: www.cummins.com
SIC: 3519 5063 7538 Internal combustion engines, nec; Generators; General automotive repair shops
PA: Cummins Inc.
   500 Jackson St
   Columbus IN
   812 377-3842

PRODUCTS & SERVICES SECTION

3549 - Metalworking Machinery, Nec (P-2784)

(P-2768)
TRACY INDUSTRIES INC
Also Called: Genuine Parts Distributors
3200 E Guasti Rd Ste 100 (91761-8661)
P.O. Box 1260 (91762-0260)
PHONE..................................562 692-9034
Timothy Engvall, *CEO*
David Rosenberger, *
Erma Jean Tracy, *
Timothy Engvall, *Treas*
▲ **EMP:** 216 **EST:** 1946
SALES (est): 18.84MM **Privately Held**
SIC: 3519 7538 Internal combustion engines, nec; Engine rebuilding: automotive

3523 Farm Machinery And Equipment

(P-2769)
FLORY INDUSTRIES (PA)
4737 Toomes Rd (95368)
P.O. Box 908 (95368-0908)
PHONE..................................209 545-1167
Jason Flory, *Ch*
Mike Eger, *
EMP: 80 **EST:** 1904
SQ FT: 12,000
SALES (est): 107.12MM
SALES (corp-wide): 107.12MM **Privately Held**
Web: www.goflory.com
SIC: 3523 5083 3441 0173 Harvesters, fruit, vegetable, tobacco, etc.; Farm equipment parts and supplies; Fabricated structural metal; Tree nuts

(P-2770)
MINERAL EARTH SCIENCES LLC
100 Mayfield Ave (94043-4122)
PHONE..................................650 532-9590
Elliott Grant, *CEO*
EMP: 80
SALES (est): 5.04MM **Privately Held**
SIC: 3523 7371 Farm machinery and equipment; Computer software development and applications

(P-2771)
STORM INDUSTRIES INC (PA)
Also Called: Storm
23223 Normandie Ave (90501-5050)
PHONE..................................310 534-5232
Dale R Philippi, *CEO*
Guy E Marge, *
Georgia Claessens, *
▲ **EMP:** 100 **EST:** 1977
SALES (est): 77.26MM
SALES (corp-wide): 77.26MM **Privately Held**
Web: www.stormind.com
SIC: 3523 6552 Irrigation equipment, self-propelled; Subdividers and developers, nec

(P-2772)
VALLEY FABRICATION INC
1056 Pellet Ave (93901-4539)
P.O. Box 3618 (93912-3618)
PHONE..................................831 757-5151
George Glen Heffington, *CEO*
Peter De Groot, *
▲ **EMP:** 60 **EST:** 1988
SQ FT: 86,000
SALES (est): 10.68MM **Privately Held**
Web: www.valleyfabrication.com
SIC: 3523 7699 5013 Farm machinery and equipment; Farm machinery repair; Truck parts and accessories

(P-2773)
VALMETAL TULARE INC
2955 S K St (93274-7164)
PHONE..................................559 685-0340
▲ **EMP:** 75 **EST:** 1979
SALES (est): 9.94MM **Privately Held**
Web: www.usfarmsystems.com
SIC: 3523 7699 Dairy equipment (farm), nec; Agricultural equipment repair services

3533 Oil And Gas Field Machinery

(P-2774)
AERA ENERGY SERVICES COMPANY
29010 Shell Rd (93210-9235)
PHONE..................................559 935-7418
EMP: 160
SALES (corp-wide): 381.31B **Privately Held**
Web: www.aeraenergy.com
SIC: 3533 1311 Oil and gas drilling rigs and equipment; Crude petroleum and natural gas production
HQ: Aera Energy Services Company
10000 Ming Ave
Bakersfield CA
661 665-5000

3535 Conveyors And Conveying Equipment

(P-2775)
OMRON ROBOTICS SAFETY TECH INC (HQ)
4225 Hacienda Dr (94588-2720)
PHONE..................................925 245-3400
Rob Cain, *Pr*
Seth Halio, *
Deron Jackson, *
▲ **EMP:** 157 **EST:** 2005
SQ FT: 57,000
SALES (est): 90.02MM **Privately Held**
Web: www.adept.com
SIC: 3535 7372 Robotic conveyors; Prepackaged software
PA: Omron Corporation
801,
Horikawahigashiiruminamifudodocho,
Shiokojidoori, Shimogyo-
Kyoto KYO

(P-2776)
SDI INDUSTRIES INC (DH)
Also Called: Autostore Integrator
24307 Magic Mountain Pkwy # 443 (91355-3402)
PHONE..................................818 890-6002
Krish Nathan, *CEO*
Mark Conrad, *
▲ **EMP:** 150 **EST:** 1978
SALES (est): 51.1MM
SALES (corp-wide): 2.67MM **Privately Held**
Web: www.sdi.systems
SIC: 3535 3537 8748 8711 Conveyors and conveying equipment; Industrial trucks and tractors; Business consulting, nec; Engineering services
HQ: Element Logic As
Dyrskuevegen 26
Klofta

(P-2777)
TERRA NOVA TECHNOLOGIES INC
10770 Rockville St Ste A (92071)
PHONE..................................619 596-7400
Ronald Kelly, *Pr*
EMP: 80 **EST:** 2019
SQ FT: 8,366
SALES (est): 12.41MM **Privately Held**
Web: www.tntinc.com
SIC: 3535 8742 Conveyors and conveying equipment; Management consulting services
HQ: Cementation Usa Inc.
10150 S Centennial Pkwy # 400
Sandy UT

3537 Industrial Trucks And Tractors

(P-2778)
J&S GOODWIN INC (HQ)
5753 E Santa Ana Canyon Rd Ste G-355 (92807-3230)
PHONE..................................714 956-4040
Arthur J Goodwin, *CEO*
Sharon Goodwin, *
Mark Mcgregor, *CFO*
Scott Currie, *
Dan Broschak, *
◆ **EMP:** 65 **EST:** 1989
SQ FT: 3,000
SALES (est): 40.94MM
SALES (corp-wide): 8.59B **Publicly Held**
SIC: 3537 5088 5084 Trucks, tractors, loaders, carriers, and similar equipment; Golf carts; Materials handling machinery
PA: Polaris Inc.
2100 Highway 55
Medina MN
763 542-0500

(P-2779)
PAPE MATERIAL HANDLING INC
2600 Peck Rd (90601-1620)
P.O. Box 60007 (91716-0007)
PHONE..................................562 692-9311
Steve Smith, *Mgr*
EMP: 100
Web: www.papemh.com
SIC: 3537 5084 Forklift trucks; Industrial machinery and equipment
HQ: Pape' Material Handling, Inc.
355 Goodpasture Island Rd
Eugene OR

3541 Machine Tools, Metal Cutting Type

(P-2780)
CREMACH TECH INC (PA)
Also Called: Creative Machine Technology
369 Meyer Cir (92879-1078)
PHONE..................................951 735-3194
Mike Mcneeley, *CEO*
Mike Mcneeley, *Prin*
Jae Wan Choi, *
EMP: 66 **EST:** 1994
SQ FT: 34,000
SALES (est): 19.34MM **Privately Held**
Web: www.cmtus.com
SIC: 3541 8711 Machine tools, metal cutting type; Designing: ship, boat, machine, and product

(P-2781)
R H STRASBAUGH (PA)
Also Called: Strasbaugh
825 Buckley Rd (93401-8192)
PHONE..................................805 541-6424
Alan Strasbaugh, *CF*

Brad Diaz, *VP*
Eric Jacobson, *CUST SERV*
Michael Kirkpatrick, *S&M/Dir*
EMP: 72 **EST:** 1964
SQ FT: 135,000
SALES (est): 16.96MM
SALES (corp-wide): 16.96MM **Privately Held**
Web: www.gainliftoff.com
SIC: 3541 3559 5065 Grinding, polishing, buffing, lapping, and honing machines; Semiconductor manufacturing machinery; Electronic parts and equipment, nec

3545 Machine Tool Accessories

(P-2782)
RAFCO-BRICKFORM LLC (PA)
Also Called: Rafco Products Brickform
11061 Jersey Blvd (91730-5135)
PHONE..................................909 484-3399
Robert Freis, *Managing Member*
Matt Bissantti, *Managing Member*
▲ **EMP:** 72 **EST:** 1973
SQ FT: 79,000
SALES (est): 17.78MM
SALES (corp-wide): 17.78MM **Privately Held**
SIC: 3545 5169 Machine tool accessories; Adhesives, chemical

(P-2783)
WETMORE TOOL AND ENGRG CO
Also Called: Wetmore Cutting Tools
5091 G St (91710-5141)
PHONE..................................909 364-1000
Jerome David, *CEO*
Phil Kurtz, *Pr*
Mike Gallegos, *CFO*
Keith Rowland, *Ex VP*
▲ **EMP:** 75 **EST:** 1999
SQ FT: 32,000
SALES (est): 7.09MM
SALES (corp-wide): 11.77B **Privately Held**
Web: www.dormerpramet.com
SIC: 3545 5084 3544 3541 Cutting tools for machine tools; Industrial machinery and equipment; Special dies, tools, jigs, and fixtures; Machine tools, metal cutting type
HQ: Dormer Pramet Ab
Tre Hjartans Vag 2
Halmstad
35165200

3549 Metalworking Machinery, Nec

(P-2784)
GOLDEN STATE ENGINEERING INC
15338 Garfield Ave (90723-4092)
PHONE..................................562 634-3125
Alexandra Rostovski, *CEO*
Mary Saguini, *
Eugenio Rostovski, *
Tom Scroggin, *
EMP: 120 **EST:** 1968
SQ FT: 65,000
SALES (est): 20.59MM **Privately Held**
Web: www.goldenstateeng.com
SIC: 3549 3541 3451 8711 Metalworking machinery, nec; Grinding, polishing, buffing, lapping, and honing machines; Screw machine products; Engineering services

3549 - Metalworking Machinery, Nec (P-2785)

(P-2785)
LTI BOYD
600 S Mcclure Rd (95357-0520)
PHONE..............................800 554-0200
▲ **EMP:** 680 **EST:** 2011
SALES (est): 5.86MM **Privately Held**
Web: www.boydcorp.com
SIC: 3549 3053 8711 Metalworking machinery, nec; Gaskets; packing and sealing devices; Industrial engineers
PA: Sentinel Capital Partners Llc
  51 E 42nd St Fl 53
  New York NY

3553 Woodworking Machinery

(P-2786)
KVAL INC
Also Called: Kval Machinery Co
825 Petaluma Blvd S (94952-5134)
PHONE..............................707 762-4363
Gerald Kvalheim, *CEO*
Gerald Kvalheim, *Pr*
Dave Kvalheim, *
Mark Kvalheim, *
Andrew M Kvalheim, *
▲ **EMP:** 125 **EST:** 1950
SALES (est): 39.8MM **Privately Held**
Web: www.kvalinc.com
SIC: 3553 5084 Woodworking machinery; Industrial machinery and equipment

3556 Food Products Machinery

(P-2787)
HEAT AND CONTROL INC (PA)
21121 Cabot Blvd (94545-1132)
PHONE..............................510 259-0500
◆ **EMP:** 175 **EST:** 1950
SALES (est): 347.43MM
SALES (corp-wide): 347.43MM **Privately Held**
Web: www.heatandcontrol.com
SIC: 3556 7699 Food products machinery; Machinery cleaning

3559 Special Industry Machinery, Nec

(P-2788)
AMERICAN INDUSTRIAL PARTNERS LP
1 Maritime Plz Ste 1925 (94111-3530)
PHONE..............................415 788-7354
EMP: 1428
SIC: 3559 7371 Foundry machinery and equipment; Custom computer programming services

(P-2789)
GOLDEN BY-PRODUCTS INC
Also Called: Scrap Tire Company
13000 Newport Rd (95303)
P.O. Box 1 (95303-0001)
PHONE..............................209 668-4855
EMP: 70
Web: www.goldenscraptire.com
SIC: 3559 0173 Tire grooving machines; Almond grove

(P-2790)
MERITEK ELECTRONICS CORP (PA)
5160 Rivergrade Rd (91706-1406)
PHONE..............................626 373-1728
Pa-shih Oliver Su, *CEO*
◆ **EMP:** 65 **EST:** 1993
SQ FT: 60,000
SALES (est): 20.99MM **Privately Held**
Web: www.meritekusa.com
SIC: 3559 5065 Electronic component making machinery; Electronic parts

(P-2791)
STARCO ENTERPRISES INC (PA)
Also Called: Four Star Chemical
3137 E 26th St (90058-8006)
PHONE..............................323 266-7111
George D Stroesenreuther, *CEO*
Ross Sklar, *
▲ **EMP:** 74 **EST:** 1973
SQ FT: 25,000
SALES (est): 16.32MM
SALES (corp-wide): 16.32MM **Privately Held**
Web: www.thestarcogroup.com
SIC: 3559 5169 5191 Degreasing machines, automotive and industrial; Specialty cleaning and sanitation preparations; Farm supplies

3561 Pumps And Pumping Equipment

(P-2792)
CIRCOR NAVAL SOLUTIONS LLC (HQ)
656 Marsat Ct Ste A (91911-4683)
P.O. Box 5020 (28111-5020)
PHONE..............................413 436-7711
Tony Najjar, *CEO*
Kelly J Ruscoe, *
Joshua Powell, *
◆ **EMP:** 86 **EST:** 1985
SQ FT: 200,000
SALES (est): 85MM
SALES (corp-wide): 786.92MM **Privately Held**
Web: www.warrenpumps.com
SIC: 3561 5084 Pumps and pumping equipment; Industrial machinery and equipment
PA: Circor International, Inc.
  30 Corporate Dr Ste 200
  Burlington MA
  781 270-1200

(P-2793)
HASKEL INTERNATIONAL LLC (HQ)
100 E Graham Pl (91502-2027)
PHONE..............................818 843-4000
Chris Krieps, *CEO*
Dave Alan Barta, *
Elmer Lee Doty, *
Maria Blase, *
▲ **EMP:** 125 **EST:** 1986
SQ FT: 78,000
SALES (est): 51MM
SALES (corp-wide): 5.92B **Publicly Held**
SIC: 3561 3594 5084 5085 Pumps and pumping equipment; Fluid power pumps; Hydraulic systems equipment and supplies; Hose, belting, and packing
PA: Ingersoll Rand Inc.
  525 Harbour Place Dr # 600
  Davidson NC
  704 896-4000

3562 Ball And Roller Bearings

(P-2794)
INDUSTRIAL TCTNICS BRINGS CORP (DH)
18301 S Santa Fe Ave (90221-5519)
PHONE..............................310 537-3750
Michael J Hartnett, *CEO*
EMP: 149 **EST:** 1990
SQ FT: 70,000
SALES (est): 51.59MM
SALES (corp-wide): 1.47B **Publicly Held**
Web: www.rbcbearings.com
SIC: 3562 5085 Roller bearings and parts; Bearings
HQ: Roller Bearing Company Of America, Inc.
  102 Willenbrock Rd
  Oxford CT
  203 267-7001

3564 Blowers And Fans

(P-2795)
ATLAS COPCO MAFI-TRENCH CO LLC (DH)
Also Called: Atlas Copco
3037 Industrial Pkwy (93455-1807)
PHONE..............................805 928-5757
◆ **EMP:** 208 **EST:** 2007
SQ FT: 90,000
SALES (est): 101.25MM
SALES (corp-wide): 13.47B **Privately Held**
SIC: 3564 3533 8744 Turbo-blowers, industrial; Oil and gas field machinery; Facilities support services
HQ: Atlas Copco North America Llc
  6 Century Dr Ste 310
  Parsippany NJ

(P-2796)
TERRA UNIVERSAL INC
800 S Raymond Ave (92831-5234)
PHONE..............................714 526-0100
G H Sadaghiani, *CEO*
▲ **EMP:** 195 **EST:** 1975
SQ FT: 88,000
SALES (est): 41.62MM **Privately Held**
Web: www.terrauniversal.com
SIC: 3564 3567 3569 3572 Purification and dust collection equipment; Heating units and devices, industrial: electric; Filters; Computer storage devices

(P-2797)
WEMS INC (PA)
Also Called: Wems Electronics
4650 W Rosecrans Ave (90250-6841)
P.O. Box 528 (90251-0528)
PHONE..............................310 644-0251
Ronald Hood, *CEO*
Nancy Howe, *Information Technology*
Carroll Whitney, *
Charles Wilson, *
EMP: 84 **EST:** 1960
SQ FT: 78,000
SALES (est): 20.45MM
SALES (corp-wide): 20.45MM **Privately Held**
Web: www.wems.com
SIC: 3564 3612 6513 Blowers and fans; Transformers, except electric; Apartment building operators

3565 Packaging Machinery

(P-2798)
MAF INDUSTRIES INC (HQ)
36470 Highway 99 (93673-7120)
P.O. Box 218 (93673-0218)
PHONE..............................559 897-2905
Thomas Blanc, *Pr*
Philippe Blanc, *
Raul Mejia, *
▲ **EMP:** 80 **EST:** 1989
SQ FT: 30,000
SALES (est): 25.85MM **Privately Held**
Web: www.maf-roda.com
SIC: 3565 5084 Packing and wrapping machinery; Food industry machinery
PA: Maf
  Cbi
  Anglet

3569 General Industrial Machinery,

(P-2799)
DELTA TAU DATA SYSTEMS INC CAL (HQ)
Also Called: Omron Delta Tau
21314 Lassen St (91311-4254)
PHONE..............................818 998-2095
Yasuto Ikuta, *Pr*
Tamara Dimitri, *
James Fornear, *
▲ **EMP:** 129 **EST:** 1976
SALES (est): 46.56MM **Privately Held**
Web: automation.omron.com
SIC: 3569 7372 3625 3577 Robots, assembly line: industrial and commercial; Prepackaged software; Relays and industrial controls; Computer peripheral equipment, nec
PA: Omron Corporation
  801,
  Horikawahigashiiruminamifudodocho,
  Shiokojidoori, Shimogyo-
  Kyoto KYO

(P-2800)
NORCO INDUSTRIES INC (PA)
Also Called: Flo Dynamics
365 W Victoria St (90220-6062)
PHONE..............................310 639-4000
◆ **EMP:** 137 **EST:** 1964
SALES (est): 82.94MM
SALES (corp-wide): 82.94MM **Privately Held**
Web: www.norcoind.com
SIC: 3569 2531 5085 3537 Jacks, hydraulic; Seats, automobile; Industrial supplies; Industrial trucks and tractors

(P-2801)
PACIFIC CONSOLIDATED INDS LLC
Also Called: PCI
12201 Magnolia Ave (92503-4820)
PHONE..............................951 479-0860
Bob Eng, *Managing Member*
Paul Stevens, *
Robert Eng, *
Alicia Fernandez, *
John Horton, *
◆ **EMP:** 77 **EST:** 2003
SQ FT: 85,000
SALES (est): 47.21MM
SALES (corp-wide): 47.21MM **Privately Held**
Web: www.pcigases.com

PRODUCTS & SERVICES SECTION

3572 - Computer Storage Devices (P-2818)

SIC: **3569** 1382 Gas separators (machinery); Oil and gas exploration services
PA: Pci Holding Company, Inc.
12201 Magnolia Ave
Riverside CA
951 479-0860

(P-2802)
WASSER FILTRATION INC (PA)
Also Called: Pacific Press
1215 N Fee Ana St (92807-1804)
PHONE.................................714 696-6450
Sean Duby, *Pr*
▲ **EMP:** 70 **EST:** 1987
SQ FT: 20,000
SALES (est): 9.49MM
SALES (corp-wide): 9.49MM **Privately Held**
Web: www.pacpress.com
SIC: **3569** 5084 Filters, general line: industrial; Industrial machinery and equipment

3571 Electronic Computers

(P-2803)
CONTINUOUS COMPUTING CORP
Also Called: Ccpu
10431 Wateridge Cir Ste 110 (92121)
PHONE.................................858 882-8800
Mike Dagenais, *CEO*
Ron Pyles, *
Erez Barnavon, *
Robert Telles, *
Michael Coward, *
EMP: 132 **EST:** 1998
SQ FT: 48,000
SALES (est): 25.78MM **Privately Held**
SIC: **3571** 3661 4812 5045 Computers, digital, analog or hybrid; Telephone and telegraph apparatus; Radiotelephone communication; Computers, peripherals, and software
HQ: Radisys Corporation
8900 Ne Walker Rd Ste 130
Hillsboro OR
503 615-1100

(P-2804)
GATEWAY US RETAIL INC
7565 Irvine Center Dr (92618-4918)
PHONE.................................949 471-7000
Wayne R Inouye, *Pr*
Brian Firestone, *Executive Strategy Vice President*
▲ **EMP:** 182 **EST:** 1998
SQ FT: 147,000
SALES (est): 9.97MM **Privately Held**
SIC: **3571** 3577 5045 Electronic computers; Computer peripheral equipment, nec; Computers, peripherals, and software
HQ: Gateway, Inc.
7565 Irvine Center Dr # 150
Irvine CA
949 471-7000

(P-2805)
GENERAL DYNMICS MSSION SYSTEMS
General Dynmics Advnced Info S
100 Ferguson Dr (94043-5239)
P.O. Box 7188 (94039)
PHONE.................................650 966-2000
John Stewart, *Brnch Mgr*
EMP: 71
SALES (corp-wide): 39.41B **Publicly Held**
Web: www.gdmissionsystems.com

SIC: **3571** 8731 Electronic computers; Commercial physical research
HQ: General Dynamics Mission Systems, Inc.
12450 Fair Lakes Cir
Fairfax VA
877 449-0600

(P-2806)
HP INC (PA)
Also Called: HP
1501 Page Mill Rd (94304-1126)
P.O. Box 10301 (94303-0890)
PHONE.................................650 857-1501
Enrique J Lores, *Pr*
Charles V Bergh, *
Marie Myers, *CFO*
Julie Jacobs, *CLO*
Jon Faust, *Global Controller*
EMP: 2500 **EST:** 1939
SALES (est): 62.98B
SALES (corp-wide): 62.98B **Publicly Held**
Web: www.hp.com
SIC: **3571** 7372 3861 3577 Personal computers (microcomputers); Prepackaged software; Cameras, still and motion picture (all types); Printers, computer

(P-2807)
INDIGO AMERICA INC
1501 Page Mill Rd (94304-1126)
PHONE.................................650 857-1501
Catherine A Lesjak, *Brnch Mgr*
EMP: 86
SALES (corp-wide): 62.98B **Publicly Held**
SIC: **3571** 7372 Personal computers (microcomputers); Prepackaged software
HQ: Indigo America Inc
165 Dascomb Rd Ste 1
Andover MA

(P-2808)
KONTRON AMERICA INCORPORATED
9477 Waples St Ste 150 (92121-2937)
PHONE.................................800 822-7522
John Goode Junior, *Pr*
Ken Lowe, *
Thomas Sparrvik, *
▲ **EMP:** 75 **EST:** 1999
SQ FT: 40,000
SALES (est): 10.6MM **Privately Held**
Web: www.kontron.com
SIC: **3571** 7373 Electronic computers; Computer integrated systems design

(P-2809)
ORACLE AMERICA INC (HQ)
Also Called: Sun Microsystems
500 Oracle Pkwy (94065-1677)
PHONE.................................650 506-7000
Jeffrey O Henley, *Ch*
Safra A Catz, *
Dorian Daley, *
Cindy Reese, *
Steve Au Yeung, *
▲ **EMP:** 3500 **EST:** 1986
SALES (est): 2.72B
SALES (corp-wide): 49.95B **Publicly Held**
Web: www.oracle.com
SIC: **3571** 7379 7373 7372 Minicomputers; Computer related consulting services; Systems integration services; Operating systems computer software
PA: Oracle Corporation
2300 Oracle Way
Austin TX
737 867-1000

(P-2810)
PREMIO INC (PA)
918 Radecki Ct (91748-1132)
PHONE.................................626 839-3100
Crystal Tsao, *CEO*
Tom Tsao, *
Ken Szeto, *
Eliza Leung, *
▲ **EMP:** 120 **EST:** 1989
SQ FT: 140,000
SALES (est): 41.5MM **Privately Held**
Web: www.premioinc.com
SIC: **3571** 7373 7378 Personal computers (microcomputers); Computer integrated systems design; Computer maintenance and repair

(P-2811)
ROSEWILL INC
17560 Rowland St (91748-1114)
PHONE.................................800 575-9885
EMP: 715
SALES (corp-wide): 2.38B **Publicly Held**
Web: www.rosewill.com
SIC: **3571** 5045 Electronic computers; Computers, peripherals, and software
HQ: Rosewill, Inc.
17708 Rowland St
City Of Industry CA

(P-2812)
RUGGED SYSTEMS INC
Also Called: Core Systems
13000 Danielson St Ste Q (92064-6827)
PHONE.................................858 391-1006
Chris O Brien, *CEO*
Chris Alan Schaffner, *
EMP: 156 **EST:** 2006
SQ FT: 63,000
SALES (est): 21.82MM **Privately Held**
Web: www.ruggedcomputersystems.com
SIC: **3571** 7373 Electronic computers; Computer integrated systems design

(P-2813)
SUPER MICRO COMPUTER INC (PA)
Also Called: Supermicro
980 Rock Ave (95131-1615)
PHONE.................................408 503-8000
Charles Liang, *Ch Bd*
David Weigand, *CCO*
Sara Liu, *
Don Clegg, *Senior Vice President Worldwide Sales*
George Kao, *VP Opers*
▲ **EMP:** 2222 **EST:** 1993
SQ FT: 2,273,000
SALES (est): 7.12B **Publicly Held**
Web: www.supermicro.com
SIC: **3571** 3572 7372 Electronic computers; Computer storage devices; Prepackaged software

(P-2814)
TERADATA OPERATIONS INC (HQ)
17095 Via Del Campo (92127-1711)
PHONE.................................937 242-4030
Oliver Ratzesberger, *COO*
Stephen Brobst, *
Mark Culhane, *
Laura Nyquist, *
EMP: 100 **EST:** 2007
SALES (est): 877MM **Publicly Held**
Web: www.teradata.com
SIC: **3571** 7379 Electronic computers; Computer related consulting services
PA: Teradata Corporation
17095 Via Del Campo

San Diego CA

3572 Computer Storage Devices

(P-2815)
ADD-ON CMPT PERIPHERALS LLC
Also Called: Addon Networks
15775 Gateway Cir (92780-6470)
PHONE.................................949 546-8200
Matt Mccormick, *CEO*
Scott Krzywicki, *
Katie Patton Ctrl, *Prin*
▲ **EMP:** 73 **EST:** 1999
SALES (est): 19.59MM
SALES (corp-wide): 12.62B **Publicly Held**
Web: www.addonnetworks.com
SIC: **3572** 3577 5045 Computer storage devices; Computer peripheral equipment, nec; Computers and accessories, personal and home entertainment
PA: Amphenol Corporation
358 Hall Ave
Wallingford CT
203 265-8900

(P-2816)
CENTON ELECTRONICS INC (PA)
Also Called: Centon
27412 Aliso Viejo Pkwy (92656-3371)
PHONE.................................949 855-9111
Jennifer Miscione, *CEO*
Gene Miscione, *
Laura Miscione, *
◆ **EMP:** 60 **EST:** 1978
SQ FT: 20,000
SALES (est): 15.18MM
SALES (corp-wide): 15.18MM **Privately Held**
Web: www.centon.com
SIC: **3572** 5734 7379 Computer storage devices; Computer software and accessories; Computer related consulting services

(P-2817)
NETAPP INC (PA)
Also Called: Netapp
3060 Olsen Dr (95128-2155)
PHONE.................................408 822-6000
George Kurian, *CEO*
T Michael Nevens, *
Cesar Cernuda, *Pr*
Michael J Berry, *Ex VP*
Harvinder S Bhela, *CPO*
▲ **EMP:** 1600 **EST:** 1992
SQ FT: 300,000
SALES (est): 6.36B **Publicly Held**
Web: www.netapp.com
SIC: **3572** 7373 7372 Computer storage devices; Computer integrated systems design; Prepackaged software

(P-2818)
OVERLAND STORAGE INC (HQ)
Also Called: Overland-Tandberg
2633 Camino Ramon Ste 325 (94583-9149)
PHONE.................................408 283-4700
Eric L Kelly, *Ch*
Peter Tassiopoulos, *Vice Chairman*
Kurt L Kalbfleisch, *CFO*
◆ **EMP:** 433 **EST:** 1980
SALES (est): 90.3MM
SALES (corp-wide): 96.42MM **Privately Held**
Web: www.overlandtandberg.com

3572 - Computer Storage Devices (P-2819)

SIC: **3572** 7372 Computer storage devices; Prepackaged software
PA: Silicon Valley Technology Partners, Inc.
12645 Cambridge Dr
Saratoga CA
408 255-0580

(P-2819)
SHAXON INDUSTRIES INC
337 W Freedom Ave (92865-2647)
PHONE..................................714 779-1140
Ahmet Erdogan, *CEO*
Yuksel Acik, *
Bahadir Tulunay, *
Bekir Aydinoglu, *
Christina Rodriguez, *
▲ **EMP:** 85 **EST:** 1978
SALES (est): 15.45MM **Privately Held**
Web: www.shaxon.com
SIC: **3572** 5045 3678 3661 Computer storage devices; Computers and accessories, personal and home entertainment; Electronic connectors; Telephone and telegraph apparatus

(P-2820)
VIOLIN MEMORY INC (PA)
4555 Great America Pkwy Ste 150 (95054-1243)
PHONE..................................650 396-1500
EMP: 129 **EST:** 2005
SALES (est): 35.32MM **Privately Held**
Web: www.chip.ca
SIC: **3572** 8731 Computer storage devices; Computer (hardware) development

3577 Computer Peripheral Equipment, Nec

(P-2821)
3DCONNEXION INC
6505 Kaiser Dr (94555-3614)
PHONE..................................510 713-6000
Rory Dooley, *Pr*
James V Mccanna, *CFO*
Lew Epstein, *
Niraj Swarup, *
EMP: 75 **EST:** 2001
SALES (est): 24.73MM **Privately Held**
Web: www.3dconnexion.com
SIC: **3577** 5045 Computer peripheral equipment, nec; Computers and accessories, personal and home entertainment
HQ: Logitech Inc.
3930 N 1st St
San Jose CA
510 795-8500

(P-2822)
ADD-ON CMPT PERIPHERALS INC
15775 Gateway Cir (92780-6470)
PHONE..................................949 546-8200
James Patton, *CEO*
Matthew Mccormick, *VP*
Brent Loomis, *
Thomas Virden, *
▲ **EMP:** 130 **EST:** 2000
SQ FT: 11,000
SALES (est): 25.99MM **Privately Held**
Web: www.addonnetworks.com
SIC: **3577** 5045 Computer peripheral equipment, nec; Computers, peripherals, and software

(P-2823)
ARISTA NETWORKS INC (PA)
Also Called: Arista
5453 Great America Pkwy (95054-3645)
PHONE..................................408 547-5500
EMP: 271 **EST:** 2004
SALES (est): 4.38B **Publicly Held**
Web: www.arista.com
SIC: **3577** 4813 7372 Computer peripheral equipment, nec; Online service providers; Prepackaged software

(P-2824)
ARUBA NETWORKS INC (HQ)
Also Called: Aruba Networks Cafe
6280 America Center Dr (95002-2563)
P.O. Box 2000 (95002-2000)
PHONE..................................408 941-4300
Keerti Melkote, *Pr*
Jon Faust, *
Partha Narasimhan, *
Vishal Lall, *
EMP: 270 **EST:** 2002
SALES (est): 497.78MM
SALES (corp-wide): 28.5B **Publicly Held**
Web: www.hpe.com
SIC: **3577** 3663 7371 Computer peripheral equipment, nec; Mobile communication equipment; Computer software development
PA: Hewlett Packard Enterprise Company
1701 E Mossy Oaks Rd
Spring TX
678 259-9860

(P-2825)
BELKIN INTERNATIONAL INC (DH)
Also Called: Belkin Components
555 S Aviation Blvd Ste 180 (90245)
PHONE..................................310 751-5100
Steven Malony, *CEO*
Chester Pipkin, *
Jasjit Jay Singh, *
◆ **EMP:** 450 **EST:** 1983
SQ FT: 218,000
SALES (est): 473.4MM **Privately Held**
Web: www.belkin.com
SIC: **3577** 5045 5065 Computer peripheral equipment, nec; Computers and accessories, personal and home entertainment; Intercommunication equipment, electronic
HQ: Foxconn Interconnect Technology Limited
C/O Conyers Trust Company (Cayman) Limited
George Town GR CAYMAN

(P-2826)
BROCADE CMMNCTIONS SYSTEMS LLC (DH)
1320 Ridder Park Dr (95131-2313)
PHONE..................................408 333-8000
Hock E Tan, *Pr*
Thomas H Krause Junior, *CFO*
Jean Samuel Furter, *
EMP: 800 **EST:** 1995
SQ FT: 562,000
SALES (est): 646.06MM
SALES (corp-wide): 33.2B **Publicly Held**
Web: www.broadcom.com
SIC: **3577** 4813 Computer peripheral equipment, nec; Proprietary online service networks
HQ: Lsi Corporation
1320 Ridder Park Dr
San Jose CA
408 433-8000

(P-2827)
C ENTERPRISES INC
Also Called: C Enterprises
16868 Via Del Campo Ct (92127-1771)
PHONE..................................760 599-5111
Brian Tauber, *Pr*
Steven Yamasaki, *COO*
EMP: 64 **EST:** 1984
SALES (est): 15.15MM
SALES (corp-wide): 85.25MM **Publicly Held**
Web: www.centerprises.com
SIC: **3577** 5045 3357 3229 Computer peripheral equipment, nec; Computers and accessories, personal and home entertainment; Nonferrous wiredrawing and insulating; Pressed and blown glass, nec
PA: Rf Industries, Ltd.
16868 Via Del Campo Ct
San Diego CA
858 549-6340

(P-2828)
CISCO SYSTEMS INC (PA)
Also Called: Cisco Systems
170 W Tasman Dr (95134-1706)
PHONE..................................408 526-4000
Charles H Robbins, *Ch Bd*
R Scott Herren, *Ex VP*
Maria Martinez, *Ex VP*
Deborah L Stahlkopf, *CLO*
Jeff Sharritts, *CUSTOMER*
EMP: 700 **EST:** 1984
SALES (est): 57B
SALES (corp-wide): 57B **Publicly Held**
Web: www.cisco.com
SIC: **3577** 7379 Data conversion equipment, media-to-media: computer; Online services technology consultants

(P-2829)
FUJITSU MANAGEMENT SERVICES OF AMERICA INC
Also Called: Fujitsu Software
1250 E Arques Ave (94085-5401)
PHONE..................................408 746-6000
◆ **EMP:** 115
SIC: **3577** 8721 Computer peripheral equipment, nec; Accounting, auditing, and bookkeeping

(P-2830)
GIGAMON INC (HQ)
3300 Olcott St (95054-3005)
PHONE..................................408 831-4000
Paul Hooper, *CEO*
Shane Buckley, *Pr*
Christel Ventura, *CPO*
▲ **EMP:** 163 **EST:** 2009
SQ FT: 105,600
SALES (est): 310.86MM **Privately Held**
Web: www.gigamon.com
SIC: **3577** 7372 Computer peripheral equipment, nec; Prepackaged software
PA: Elliott Management Corporation
40 W 57th St
New York NY

(P-2831)
HANAPS ENTERPRISES
Also Called: Digital Storm
8100 Camino Arroyo (95020-7304)
PHONE..................................669 235-3810
Paramjit Chana, *CEO*
Surnderjit Chana, *
▲ **EMP:** 70 **EST:** 2003
SALES (est): 19.38MM **Privately Held**
Web: www.digitalstorm.com

SIC: **3577** 7379 Computer peripheral equipment, nec; Computer related maintenance services

(P-2832)
JUNIPER NETWORKS INC (PA)
Also Called: JUNIPER NETWORKS
1133 Innovation Way (94089-1228)
PHONE..................................408 745-2000
EMP: 300 **EST:** 1996
SALES (est): 5.3B **Publicly Held**
Web: www.juniper.net
SIC: **3577** 7372 Computer peripheral equipment, nec; Prepackaged software

(P-2833)
MITEK SYSTEMS INC (PA)
Also Called: Mitek
600 B St Ste 100 (92101-4505)
PHONE..................................619 269-6800
Scipio Carnecchia, *CEO*
Scott Carter, *Ex Ch Bd*
Fuad Ahmad, *Interim Chief Financial Officer*
Jason L Gray, *CLO CCO*
Michael E Diamond, *Sr VP*
EMP: 113 **EST:** 1986
SQ FT: 29,000
SALES (est): 143.94MM
SALES (corp-wide): 143.94MM **Publicly Held**
Web: www.miteksystems.com
SIC: **3577** 7372 Computer peripheral equipment, nec; Business oriented computer software

(P-2834)
MOTION ENGINEERING INC (DH)
Also Called: M E I
33 S La Patera Ln (93117-3214)
PHONE..................................805 696-1200
EMP: 60 **EST:** 1987
SQ FT: 21,000
SALES (est): 27.8MM
SALES (corp-wide): 5.22B **Publicly Held**
Web: www.motioneng.com
SIC: **3577** 8711 3823 Computer peripheral equipment, nec; Engineering services; Process control instruments
HQ: Altra Industrial Motion Corp.
300 Granite St Ste 201
Braintree MA
781 917-0600

(P-2835)
PALO ALTO NETWORKS INC (PA)
3000 Tannery Way (95054-2832)
PHONE..................................408 753-4000
Nikesh Arora, *Ch Bd*
Mark D Mclaughlin, *V Ch Bd*
William Jenkins, *
Nir Zuk, *
Jean Compeau, *CAO*
EMP: 500 **EST:** 2005
SQ FT: 941,000
SALES (est): 6.89B
SALES (corp-wide): 6.89B **Publicly Held**
Web: www.paloaltonetworks.com
SIC: **3577** 7371 Computer peripheral equipment, nec; Computer software development and applications

(P-2836)
QUALITYLOGIC INC
2245 1st St Ste 103 (93065-0904)
PHONE..................................208 424-1905
Joe Walker, *Mgr*
EMP: 109
SALES (corp-wide): 10.89MM **Privately Held**
Web: www.qualitylogic.com

PRODUCTS & SERVICES SECTION

3599 - Industrial Machinery, Nec (P-2854)

SIC: 3577 8748 Computer peripheral equipment, nec; Testing services
PA: Qualitylogic, Inc.
9576 W Emerald St
Boise ID
208 424-1905

(P-2837)
SILICON GRAPHICS INTL CORP (HQ)
940 N Mccarthy Blvd (95035-5128)
PHONE..............................669 900-8000
Jorge L Titinger, CEO
Mack Asrat, *
Cassio Conceicao, *
Eng Lim Goh, *
Peter E Hilliard, CAO*
▲ EMP: 126 EST: 2002
SALES (est): 201.45MM
SALES (corp-wide): 28.5B Publicly Held
Web: www.hpe.com
SIC: 3577 7371 Computer peripheral equipment, nec; Computer software development and applications
PA: Hewlett Packard Enterprise Company
1701 E Mossy Oaks Rd
Spring TX
678 259-9860

(P-2838)
SYNAPTICS INCORPORATED (PA)
Also Called: SYNAPTICS
1109 Mckay Dr (95131-1706)
PHONE..............................408 904-1100
Michael Hurlston, Pr
Nelson C Chan, *
Dean Butler, Sr VP
Vikram Gupta, CPO
Saleel Awsare, Sr VP
EMP: 400 EST: 1986
SQ FT: 111,000
SALES (est): 1.36B
SALES (corp-wide): 1.36B Publicly Held
Web: www.synaptics.com
SIC: 3577 7372 Computer peripheral equipment, nec; Application computer software

(P-2839)
VIEWSONIC CORPORATION (PA)
Also Called: Viewsonic
10 Pointe Dr Ste 200 (92821-7620)
PHONE..............................909 444-8888
James Chu, Ch Bd
Jeff Volpe, *
Brian Igoe, *
Sung Yi, *
Bonny Cheng, *
◆ EMP: 140 EST: 1987
SQ FT: 298,050
SALES (est): 171.21MM
SALES (corp-wide): 171.21MM Privately Held
Web: www.viewsonic.com
SIC: 3577 3575 5045 Computer peripheral equipment, nec; Computer terminals, monitors and components; Computer peripheral equipment

(P-2840)
VOYETRA TURTLE BEACH INC (DH)
Also Called: Turtle Beach
11011 Via Frontera Ste 200 (92127-1752)
PHONE..............................914 345-2255
▲ EMP: 93 EST: 1986
SALES (est): 59.9MM Publicly Held

SIC: 3577 7371 Computer peripheral equipment, nec; Computer software development
HQ: Vtb Holdings, Inc.
100 Summit Lake Dr
Valhalla NY
914 345-2255

3578 Calculating And Accounting Equipment

(P-2841)
CLOVER NETWORK INC
415 N Mathilda Ave (94085-4222)
PHONE..............................650 210-7888
EMP: 65 EST: 2010
SQ FT: 8,200
SALES (est): 27.08MM
SALES (corp-wide): 17.74B Publicly Held
Web: www.clover.com
SIC: 3578 4813 Calculating and accounting equipment; Internet connectivity services
HQ: First Data Corporation
255 Fiserv Dr
Brookfield WI

3585 Refrigeration And Heating Equipment

(P-2842)
HUSSMANN CORPORATION
13770 Ramona Ave (91710-5423)
P.O. Box 5133 (91708-5133)
PHONE..............................909 590-4910
Mike Gleason, Genl Mgr
EMP: 350
Web: www.hussmann.com
SIC: 3585 7623 Refrigeration and heating equipment; Refrigeration service and repair
HQ: Hussmann Corporation
12999 St Charles Rock Rd
Bridgeton MO
314 291-2000

(P-2843)
MESTEK INC
Also Called: Anemostat Products
1220 E Watson Center Rd (90745-4206)
PHONE..............................310 835-7500
Chang Hung, Mgr
EMP: 200
SALES (corp-wide): 689.94MM Privately Held
Web: www.mestek.com
SIC: 3585 3549 3542 3354 Heating equipment, complete; Metalworking machinery, nec; Punching, shearing, and bending machines; Shapes, extruded aluminum, nec
PA: Mestek, Inc.
260 N Elm St
Westfield MA
470 898-4533

(P-2844)
R-COLD INC
1221 S G St (92570-2477)
PHONE..............................951 436-5476
Michael Mulcahy, Pr
Ernest Gaston, *
EMP: 65 EST: 1982
SQ FT: 28,000
SALES (est): 10.84MM Privately Held
Web: www.r-cold.com
SIC: 3585 1541 Refrigeration and heating equipment; Industrial buildings and warehouses

(P-2845)
THERMOCRAFT
2554 Commercial St (92113-1132)
PHONE..............................619 813-2985
Dean Rafiee, Pr
Dean Ideen Rafiee, *
EMP: 100 EST: 2016
SALES (est): 7.51MM Privately Held
SIC: 3585 5078 5031 Refrigeration and heating equipment; Commercial refrigeration equipment; Doors, garage

(P-2846)
VEGE-MIST INC
Also Called: Alco Designs
407 E Redondo Beach Blvd (90248-2312)
PHONE..............................310 353-2300
Samuel Cohen, CEO
▲ EMP: 61 EST: 1988
SQ FT: 8,000
SALES (est): 14.91MM Privately Held
Web: www.alcodesigns.com
SIC: 3585 2541 5074 2542 Humidifying equipment, except portable; Store and office display cases and fixtures; Water purification equipment; Partitions and fixtures, except wood

3589 Service Industry Machinery, Nec

(P-2847)
APPLIED MEMBRANES INC
Also Called: Wateranywhere
2450 Business Park Dr (92081-8847)
PHONE..............................760 727-3711
Gulshan Dhawan, CEO
◆ EMP: 178 EST: 1983
SQ FT: 55,000
SALES (est): 45.88MM Privately Held
Web: www.appliedmembranes.com
SIC: 3589 5074 Water purification equipment, household type; Water heaters and purification equipment

(P-2848)
J L WINGERT COMPANY
1298 N Blue Gum St (92806-2413)
P.O. Box 6207 (92846-6207)
PHONE..............................714 379-5519
Tommy Thomas, CEO
Reeve Thomas, *
EMP: 65 EST: 1965
SALES (est): 9.31MM Privately Held
Web: www.jlwingert.com
SIC: 3589 5084 Water treatment equipment, industrial; Industrial machinery and equipment

(P-2849)
SHEPARD BROS INC (PA)
503 S Cypress St (90631-6126)
PHONE..............................562 697-1366
Ronald Shepard, CEO
Duane Shepard, *
Jon Wynkoop, *
▲ EMP: 119 EST: 1976
SQ FT: 57,830
SALES (est): 30.98MM
SALES (corp-wide): 30.98MM Privately Held
Web: www.shepardbros.com
SIC: 3589 5169 Sewage and water treatment equipment; Chemicals and allied products, nec

3599 Industrial Machinery, Nec

(P-2850)
COLLEEN & HERB ENTERPRISES INC
Also Called: C & H Enterprises
46939 Bayside Pkwy (94538-6527)
PHONE..............................510 226-6083
Herbert Schmidt, CEO
Colleen Schmidt, *
Jake Schmidt, *
EMP: 115 EST: 1984
SQ FT: 50,000
SALES (est): 16.74MM Privately Held
Web: www.candhenterprises.com
SIC: 3599 7692 Machine shop, jobbing and repair; Welding repair

(P-2851)
DELAFIELD CORPORATION (PA)
Also Called: Delafield Fluid Technology
1520 Flower Ave (91010-2925)
PHONE..............................626 303-0740
Nik Ray, Pr
Jim Martin, *
Henry Custodia, *
◆ EMP: 120 EST: 1949
SQ FT: 90,000
SALES (est): 40.45MM
SALES (corp-wide): 40.45MM Privately Held
Web: www.dftcorp.com
SIC: 3599 5085 3498 3492 Hose, flexible metallic; Valves, pistons, and fittings; Tube fabricating (contract bending and shaping); Fluid power valves and hose fittings

(P-2852)
GEORGE FISCHER INC (HQ)
5462 Irwindale Ave Ste A (91706-2074)
PHONE..............................626 571-2770
Chris Blumer, CEO
Daniel Vaterlaus, VP
◆ EMP: 140 EST: 1954
SALES (est): 265.41MM Privately Held
Web: www.signet-gf.com
SIC: 3599 5074 3829 3559 Electrical discharge machining (EDM); Pipes and fittings, plastic; Testing equipment: abrasion, shearing strength, etc.; Foundry machinery and equipment
PA: Georg Fischer Ag
Amsler-Laffon-Strasse 9
Schaffhausen SH

(P-2853)
HAIG PRECISION MFG CORP
3616 Snell Ave (95136-1305)
PHONE..............................408 378-4920
Daniel S Sarkisian, CEO
Paul Sarkisian, *
▲ EMP: 60 EST: 1960
SQ FT: 26,000
SALES (est): 9.34MM Privately Held
Web: www.haigprecision.com
SIC: 3599 7692 Machine shop, jobbing and repair; Welding repair

(P-2854)
JL HALEY ENTERPRISES INC
3510 Luyung Dr (95742-6872)
PHONE..............................916 631-6375
James L Haley, CEO
◆ EMP: 140 EST: 1971
SQ FT: 67,000
SALES (est): 24.9MM
SALES (corp-wide): 138.57MM Privately Held

3599 - Industrial Machinery, Nec (P-2855)

Web: www.jlhaleyinc.com
SIC: **3599** 3312 7692 Machine shop, jobbing and repair; Blast furnaces and steel mills; Welding repair
PA: Vander-Bend Manufacturing, Inc.
2701 Orchard Pkwy
San Jose CA
408 245-5150

(P-2855)
PROCESS FAB INC
13153 Lakeland Rd (90670-4520)
P.O. Box 314 (90670)
PHONE..............................562 921-1979
EMP: 180
SIC: **3599** 8711 Machine shop, jobbing and repair; Industrial engineers

(P-2856)
VALLEY TOOL AND MACHINE CO INC
111 Explorer St (91768-3278)
PHONE..............................909 595-2205
Chuck Rogers, *CEO*
Jim Rogers, *
Nancy Larson, *
EMP: 68 EST: 1982
SQ FT: 34,000
SALES (est): 3.68MM **Privately Held**
Web: www.valleytool-inc.com
SIC: **3599** 7692 3544 Machine shop, jobbing and repair; Welding repair; Special dies, tools, jigs, and fixtures

(P-2857)
VANDER-BEND MANUFACTURING INC
Also Called: J.L. Haley
3510 Luyung Dr (95742-6872)
PHONE..............................916 631-6375
Steve Butts, *Brnch Mgr*
EMP: 140
SALES (corp-wide): 138.57MM **Privately Held**
Web: www.vander-bend.com
SIC: **3599** 3312 7692 Machine shop, jobbing and repair; Blast furnaces and steel mills; Welding repair
PA: Vander-Bend Manufacturing, Inc.
2701 Orchard Pkwy
San Jose CA
408 245-5150

(P-2858)
WELDMAC MANUFACTURING COMPANY
1451 N Johnson Ave (92020-1615)
PHONE..............................619 440-2300
Marshall J Rugg, *Pr*
Barbara Bloomfield, *
Robert L Rugg, *
EMP: 122 EST: 1968
SQ FT: 100,000
SALES (est): 29.66MM **Privately Held**
Web: www.weldmac.com
SIC: **3599** 3444 7692 Machine shop, jobbing and repair; Sheet metalwork; Brazing

3612 Transformers, Except Electric

(P-2859)
RING LLC (HQ)
12515 Cerise Ave (90250-4801)
PHONE..............................310 929-7085
Jamie Siminoff, *Managing Member*
▲ EMP: 300 EST: 2013
SQ FT: 40,000
SALES (est): 181.5MM **Publicly Held**
Web: www.ring.com
SIC: **3612** 5065 Doorbell transformers, electric; Security control equipment and systems
PA: Amazon.Com, Inc.
410 Terry Ave N
Seattle WA

3613 Switchgear And Switchboard Apparatus

(P-2860)
AEMI HOLDINGS LLC
6610 Cobra Way (92121-4107)
PHONE..............................858 481-0210
Daniel H Chang, *Pr*
Xiang Ming Li, *Sr VP*
Caili Chang, *
▲ EMP: 77 EST: 1986
SQ FT: 45,000
SALES (est): 18.98MM **Privately Held**
Web: www.aem-usa.com
SIC: **3613** 3677 7699 Fuses and fuse equipment; Inductors, electronic; Metal reshaping and replating services

(P-2861)
ROMAC SUPPLY CO INC
Also Called: Romac
17722 Neff Ranch Rd (92886-9013)
PHONE..............................323 721-5810
TOLL FREE: 800
David B Rosenfield, *Pr*
Lisa R Podolsky, *
Phillip Rosenfield, *
Edith Rosenfield, *
Victoria Rosenfield, *
EMP: 60 EST: 1955
SALES (est): 20.89MM **Privately Held**
Web: www.tauberaronsinc.com
SIC: **3613** 3621 3612 5063 Switchgear and switchgear accessories, nec; Motors and generators; Transformers, except electric; Motors, electric

(P-2862)
WEST COAST SWITCHGEAR (DH)
13837 Bettencourt St (90703-1009)
PHONE..............................562 802-3441
Alfred P Cisternelli, *CEO*
▲ EMP: 93 EST: 2003
SQ FT: 20,000
SALES (est): 17.56MM **Privately Held**
Web: www.westcoastswitchgear.com
SIC: **3613** 5063 Power circuit breakers; Switchgear
HQ: Resa Power, Llc
8723 Fallbrook Dr
Houston TX
832 900-8340

3621 Motors And Generators

(P-2863)
NANTENERGY LLC
2040 E Mariposa Ave (90245-5027)
PHONE..............................310 905-4866
EMP: 75 EST: 2019
SALES (est): 3.1MM **Privately Held**
SIC: **3621** 8731 Storage battery chargers, motor and engine generator type; Energy research

3625 Relays And Industrial Controls

(P-2864)
CRYDOM INC (DH)
2320 Paseo De Las Americas Ste 201 (92154-7273)
PHONE..............................619 210-1590
Bob Ciurczak, *Pr*
▲ EMP: 75 EST: 2005
SQ FT: 20,000
SALES (est): 112.36MM
SALES (corp-wide): 4.03B **Privately Held**
Web: www.sensata.com
SIC: **3625** 5065 3674 3643 Control equipment, electric; Electronic parts and equipment, nec; Semiconductors and related devices; Current-carrying wiring services
HQ: Sensata Technologies, Inc.
529 Pleasant St
Attleboro MA

(P-2865)
CURTISS-WRGHT CNTRLS ELCTRNIC (DH)
Also Called: Curtiss-Wrght Cntrls Elctrnic
28965 Avenue Penn (91355-4185)
PHONE..............................661 702-1494
Thomas P Quinly, *CEO*
David Dietz, *
EMP: 172 EST: 1985
SQ FT: 18,700
SALES (est): 53.65MM
SALES (corp-wide): 2.56B **Publicly Held**
Web: www.curtisswright.com
SIC: **3625** 8731 8711 3769 Relays and industrial controls; Commercial physical research; Consulting engineer; Space vehicle equipment, nec
HQ: Curtiss-Wright Controls, Inc.
201 Old Boiling Sprng Rd
Shelby NC
704 869-4600

(P-2866)
MICROSEMI FREQUENCY TIME CORP (DH)
3870 N 1st St (95134-1702)
PHONE..............................480 792-7200
Ganesh Moorthy, *Pr*
Steve Sanghi, *
J Eric Bjornholt, *
▲ EMP: 170 EST: 2001
SALES (est): 104.07MM
SALES (corp-wide): 8.44B **Publicly Held**
Web: www.microsemi.com
SIC: **3625** 7372 Timing devices, electronic; Business oriented computer software
HQ: Microsemi Corporation
11861 Western Ave
Garden Grove CA
949 380-6100

(P-2867)
MOOG INC
Also Called: Moog Jon Street Warehouse
1218 W Jon St (90502-1208)
PHONE..............................310 533-1178
Alberto Bilalon, *Mgr*
EMP: 500
SALES (corp-wide): 3.04B **Publicly Held**
Web: www.moog.com
SIC: **3625** 8711 3812 Relays and industrial controls; Aviation and/or aeronautical engineering; Aircraft/aerospace flight instruments and guidance systems
PA: Moog Inc.
400 Jamison Rd
Elma NY
716 652-2000

(P-2868)
S R C DEVICES INCCUSTOMER
6295 Ferris Sq Ste D (92121-3248)
PHONE..............................866 772-8668
Richard W Carlyle, *Pr*
Mark Mccabe, *Sr VP*
EMP: 303 EST: 2001
SQ FT: 2,000
SALES (est): 16.16MM **Privately Held**
SIC: **3625** 3643 5065 Switches, electronic applications; Current-carrying wiring services; Electronic parts and equipment, nec

3629 Electrical Industrial Apparatus

(P-2869)
COOPER BUSSMANN LLC
Also Called: Cooper Bussmann-Automotive
5735 W Las Positas Blvd Ste 100 (94588-4002)
PHONE..............................925 924-8500
Hundi Kamath, *Mgr*
EMP: 161
SIC: **3629** 5065 Capacitors and condensers; Capacitors, electronic
HQ: Cooper Bussmann, Llc
114 Old State Rd
Ellisville MO

3631 Household Cooking Equipment

(P-2870)
SUPERIOR EQUIPMENT SOLUTIONS
1085 Bixby Dr (91745-1704)
PHONE..............................323 722-7900
Jeffrey Bernstein, *CEO*
Stephan Bernstein, *
▲ EMP: 60 EST: 2001
SQ FT: 45,000
SALES (est): 750MM **Privately Held**
Web: www.alfrescogrills.com
SIC: **3631** 5046 Household cooking equipment; Restaurant equipment and supplies, nec

3645 Residential Lighting Fixtures

(P-2871)
B-K LIGHTING INC
40429 Brickyard Dr (93636-9515)
PHONE..............................559 438-5800
Douglas W Hagen, *Pr*
Nathan Sloan, *
▲ EMP: 90 EST: 1985
SQ FT: 70,000
SALES (est): 19.96MM **Privately Held**
Web: www.bklighting.com
SIC: **3645** 3646 5063 Residential lighting fixtures; Commercial lighting fixtures; Electrical apparatus and equipment

(P-2872)
FEIT ELECTRIC COMPANY INC (PA)
Also Called: Feit Electric
4901 Gregg Rd (90660-2108)
PHONE..............................562 463-2852
Aaron Feit, *CEO*

PRODUCTS & SERVICES SECTION
3661 - Telephone And Telegraph Apparatus (P-2889)

Alan Feit, *
Toby S Feit, *
John Mcmillin, *CFO*
◆ **EMP:** 182 **EST:** 1978
SQ FT: 300,000
SALES (est): 65.67MM
SALES (corp-wide): 65.67MM **Privately Held**
Web: www.feit.com
SIC: 3645 3641 5023 3646 Residential lighting fixtures; Electric light bulbs, complete; Homefurnishings; Commercial lighting fixtures

(P-2873)
WASHOE EQUIPMENT INC
Also Called: Sunoptics Prismatic Skylights
6201 27th St (95822-3712)
PHONE..................916 395-4700
TOLL FREE: 800
Jim Blomberg, *Pr*
Jerry Blomberg, *
Thomas Blomberg, *
Grant Grabble, *
▼ **EMP:** 1815 **EST:** 1978
SQ FT: 16,000
SALES (est): 8.55MM
SALES (corp-wide): 3.95B **Publicly Held**
Web: www.aessunoptics.com
SIC: 3645 3646 5031 Residential lighting fixtures; Commercial lighting fixtures; Skylights, all materials
PA: Acuity Brands, Inc.
1170 Peachtree St Ne # 23
Atlanta GA
404 853-1400

3646 Commercial Lighting Fixtures

(P-2874)
FOCUS INDUSTRIES INC
Also Called: Focus Landscape
25301 Commercentre Dr (92630-8808)
PHONE..................949 830-1350
Stan Shibata, *Pr*
June Shibata, *
▲ **EMP:** 100 **EST:** 1989
SQ FT: 40,000
SALES (est): 22.55MM **Privately Held**
Web: www.focusindustries.com
SIC: 3646 5063 Commercial lighting fixtures; Electrical apparatus and equipment

3648 Lighting Equipment, Nec

(P-2875)
CLEAR BLUE ENERGY CORP
Also Called: Cbec
17150 Via Del Campo Ste 203 (92127-2111)
P.O. Box 532086 (92153-2086)
PHONE..................858 451-1549
Paul Santina, *CEO*
Jim Kelly, *
EMP: 80 **EST:** 2009
SALES (est): 9.98MM **Privately Held**
Web: www.cbesco.com
SIC: 3648 1731 Lighting equipment, nec; Lighting contractor

(P-2876)
JIMWAY INC
Also Called: Altair Lighting
20101 S Santa Fe Ave (90221-5917)
PHONE..................310 886-3718
Hsing-min Keng, *CEO*
Irene Wang, *
▲ **EMP:** 100 **EST:** 1982
SQ FT: 200,000
SALES (est): 19.89MM **Privately Held**
Web: www.jimway.com
SIC: 3648 3221 5063 Lighting equipment, nec; Glass containers; Electrical apparatus and equipment

3651 Household Audio And Video Equipment

(P-2877)
ARLO TECHNOLOGIES INC (PA)
Also Called: ARLO
2200 Faraday Ave Ste 150 (92008-7224)
PHONE..................408 890-3900
Matthew Mcrae, *CEO*
Ralph E Faison, *Ch Bd*
Gordon Mattingly, *CFO*
Brian Busse, *Corporate Secretary*
EMP: 86 **EST:** 2014
SQ FT: 43,500
SALES (est): 490.41MM
SALES (corp-wide): 490.41MM **Publicly Held**
Web: www.arlo.com
SIC: 3651 7372 Household audio and video equipment; Application computer software

(P-2878)
DANA INNOVATIONS (PA)
Also Called: Sonance
991 Calle Amanecer (92673-6212)
PHONE..................949 492-7777
Ari Supran, *CEO*
Scott Struthers, *Pr*
Geoffrey L Spencer, *Sec*
Mike Simmons, *
◆ **EMP:** 156 **EST:** 1981
SQ FT: 42,320
SALES (est): 49.59MM
SALES (corp-wide): 49.59MM **Privately Held**
Web: www.sonance.com
SIC: 3651 5731 7629 Speaker systems; Radio, television, and electronic stores; Electrical repair shops

(P-2879)
DOLBY LABORATORIES INC (PA)
Also Called: Dolby
1275 Market St Fl 15 (94103-1426)
PHONE..................415 558-0200
Kevin Yeaman, *Pr*
Peter Gotcher, *
Andy Sherman, *Corporate Secretary*
Robert Park, *Sr VP*
Todd Pendleton, *CMO*
▲ **EMP:** 520 **EST:** 1965
SALES (est): 1.25B
SALES (corp-wide): 1.25B **Publicly Held**
Web: www.dolby.com
SIC: 3651 7819 6794 Audio electronic systems; Laboratory service, motion picture; Music licensing and royalties

(P-2880)
ISOLATION NETWORK INC (PA)
Also Called: Ingrooves
55 Francisco St Ste 350 (94133-2112)
PHONE..................818 212-2600
Robert D Roback, *CEO*
Adam Hiles, *
Clifton Wong, *
Vincent Freda, *
EMP: 79 **EST:** 2003
SQ FT: 5,000
SALES (est): 33.42MM
SALES (corp-wide): 33.42MM **Privately Held**
Web: www.ingrooves.com
SIC: 3651 7929 Music distribution apparatus ; Musical entertainers

(P-2881)
SONY ELECTRONICS INC (DH)
16535 Via Esprillo 1 (92127-1738)
PHONE..................858 942-2400
Shigeki Ishizuka, *Pr*
Phil Molyneux, *
Hideki Komiyama, *
Rintaro Miyoshi, *
William A Glaser, *
◆ **EMP:** 1000 **EST:** 1988
SALES (est): 1.41B **Privately Held**
Web: www.sony.com
SIC: 3651 5064 3695 3671 Household audio and video equipment; Electrical appliances, television and radio; Video recording tape, blank; Television tubes
HQ: Sony Corporation Of America
25 Madison Ave Fl 27
New York NY

(P-2882)
TOSHIBA AMER ELCTRNIC CMPNNTS (DH)
Also Called: Toshiba
5231 California Ave (92617-3235)
PHONE..................949 462-7700
Hideya Yamaguchi, *CEO*
Hitoshi Otsuka, *
Ichiro Hirata, *
Richard Tobias, *
Farhad Mafie, *
◆ **EMP:** 300 **EST:** 1998
SQ FT: 100,000
SALES (est): 412.02MM **Privately Held**
Web: www.toshiba.com
SIC: 3651 3631 3674 3679 Television receiving sets; Microwave ovens, including portable: household; Semiconductors and related devices; Electronic circuits
HQ: Toshiba America Inc
1251 Ave Of Amrcas Ste 41
New York NY
212 596-0600

(P-2883)
TOSHIBA AMERICA INC
5241 California Ave Ste 200 (92617-3052)
PHONE..................212 596-0600
EMP: 2058
Web: www.toshiba.com
SIC: 3651 3631 5075 3571 Television receiving sets; Microwave ovens, including portable: household; Compressors, air conditioning; Personal computers (microcomputers)
HQ: Toshiba America Inc
1251 Ave Of Amrcas Ste 41
New York NY
212 596-0600

3661 Telephone And Telegraph Apparatus

(P-2884)
ALTIGEN COMMUNICATIONS INC
670 N Mccarthy Blvd Ste 200 (95035-5119)
PHONE..................408 597-9000
Jeremiah J Fleming, *Pr*
Mike Plumer, *
Simon Chouldjian, *
Shirley Sun, *
Philip M Mcdermott, *CFO*
▲ **EMP:** 115 **EST:** 1994
SQ FT: 27,576
SALES (est): 16.94MM **Privately Held**
Web: www.altigen.com
SIC: 3661 1731 Telephone and telegraph apparatus; Communications specialization

(P-2885)
INFINERA CORPORATION (PA)
Also Called: Infinera
6373 San Ignacio Ave (95119-1200)
PHONE..................408 572-5200
David W Heard, *CEO*
George A Riedel, *
Nancy Erba, *CFO*
David L Teichmann, *CLO*
David F Welch, *CIO*
▼ **EMP:** 450 **EST:** 2000
SQ FT: 82,000
SALES (est): 1.57B
SALES (corp-wide): 1.57B **Publicly Held**
Web: www.infinera.com
SIC: 3661 7372 Fiber optics communications equipment; Prepackaged software

(P-2886)
INTERNTNAL CNNCTORS CABLE CORP
Also Called: I C C
2100 E Valencia Dr Ste D (92831-4811)
PHONE..................888 275-4422
Mike Lin, *Pr*
Mike Lin, *Pr*
Eugene Chyun Tsai, *Stockholder*
▲ **EMP:** 110 **EST:** 1984
SQ FT: 38,720
SALES (est): 9.41MM **Privately Held**
SIC: 3661 5065 Telephone and telegraph apparatus; Telephone and telegraphic equipment

(P-2887)
JETSTREAM COMMUNICATIONS INC
5400 Hellyer Ave (95138-1019)
PHONE..................408 361-7000
Sundi Sundaresh, *Pr*
David Frankel, *
John Niedermaier, *
Stephen Ashurkoff, *Worldwide Sales Vice President*
EMP: 100 **EST:** 1994
SALES (est): 10.49MM **Privately Held**
SIC: 3661 7371 Telephone and telegraph apparatus; Custom computer programming services

(P-2888)
NETGEAR INC (PA)
350 E Plumeria Dr (95134-1911)
PHONE..................408 907-8000
◆ **EMP:** 130 **EST:** 1996
SQ FT: 142,700
SALES (est): 932.47MM **Publicly Held**
Web: www.netgear.com
SIC: 3661 4813 Fiber optics communications equipment; Telephone communication, except radio

(P-2889)
OPTOPLEX CORPORATION
48500 Kato Rd (94538-7338)
PHONE..................510 490-9930
James C Sha, *Pr*
Dar-yuan Song, *Ex VP*
EMP: 300 **EST:** 2000
SQ FT: 16,000
SALES (est): 47.01MM **Privately Held**
Web: www.optoplex.com

3661 - Telephone And Telegraph Apparatus

SIC: **3661** 7361 3827 Fiber optics communications equipment; Employment agencies; Optical instruments and lenses

(P-2890)
VOX NETWORK SOLUTIONS INC
130 Produce Ave Ste C (94080-6523)
PHONE..................................650 989-1000
Scott Landis, *Pr*
Craig Schneider, *
Aaron Wilson, *
EMP: 150 **EST:** 2006
SALES (est): 78.14MM
SALES (corp-wide): 90.79MM **Privately Held**
Web: www.voxns.com
SIC: **3661** 8748 4813 Switching equipment, telephone; Telecommunications consultant; Internet host services
PA: Waterfield Technologies, Inc.
110 S Hartford Ave # 2502
Tulsa OK
918 858-6400

3663 Radio And T.v. Communications Equipment

(P-2891)
APPLE INC (PA)
Also Called: Apple
1 Apple Park Way (95014-0642)
PHONE..................................408 996-1010
Timothy D Cook, *CEO*
Arthur D Levinson, *Ch Bd*
Jeff Williams, *COO*
Lucca Maestri, *Sr VP*
Kate Adams, *Sr VP*
◆ **EMP:** 1310 **EST:** 1977
SALES (est): 383.29B
SALES (corp-wide): 383.29B **Publicly Held**
Web: www.apple.com
SIC: **3663** 3571 3575 3577 Mobile communication equipment; Personal computers (microcomputers); Computer terminals, monitors and components; Printers, computer

(P-2892)
ARUBA NETWORKS INC
390 W Caribbean Dr (94089-1010)
PHONE..................................408 227-4500
EMP: 622
SALES (corp-wide): 28.5B **Publicly Held**
Web: www.hpe.com
SIC: **3663** 3577 7371 Mobile communication equipment; Data conversion equipment, media-to-media: computer; Computer software development
HQ: Aruba Networks, Inc.
6280 America Center Dr
San Jose CA
408 941-4300

(P-2893)
LOCKHEED MARTIN CORPORATION
Also Called: Lockheed Martin
3130 Zanker Rd (95134-1965)
P.O. Box 3504 (94088-3504)
PHONE..................................408 473-3000
Magda Clyne, *Mgr*
EMP: 74
Web: www.lockheedmartin.com
SIC: **3663** 7373 8711 Satellites, communications; Computer integrated systems design; Engineering services
PA: Lockheed Martin Corporation
6801 Rockledge Dr
Bethesda MD

(P-2894)
MICRO-MODE PRODUCTS INC
1870 John Towers Ave (92020-1193)
PHONE..................................619 449-3844
Vincent De Marco, *Pr*
Michael Cuban, *
Ruby Marco, *
EMP: 170 **EST:** 1971
SALES (est): 49.31MM
SALES (corp-wide): 2.99B **Publicly Held**
Web: www.micromode.com
SIC: **3663** 3678 7389 Microwave communication equipment; Electronic connectors; Business Activities at Non-Commercial Site
PA: Itt Inc.
100 Washington Blvd Fl 6
Stamford CT
914 641-2000

(P-2895)
NAVCOM TECHNOLOGY INC (HQ)
20780 Madrona Ave (90503-3777)
PHONE..................................310 381-2000
Tony Thelen, *CEO*
Craig Fawcept, *
Michael Linzy, *
EMP: 100 **EST:** 1997
SQ FT: 55,000
SALES (est): 20.38MM
SALES (corp-wide): 52.58B **Publicly Held**
Web: www.navcomtech.com
SIC: **3663** 8748 Satellites, communications; Communications consulting
PA: Deere & Company
1 John Deere Pl
Moline IL
309 765-8000

(P-2896)
NOKIA INC
200 S Mathilda Ave (94086-6135)
P.O. Box 22720 (71903-2720)
PHONE..................................408 530-7600
▲ **EMP:** 2500
SIC: **3663** 5065 3661 3577 Cellular radio telephone; Mobile telephone equipment; Telephone and telegraph apparatus; Computer peripheral equipment, nec

(P-2897)
QUALCOMM INCORPORATED (PA)
Also Called: Qualcomm
5775 Morehouse Dr (92121-1714)
PHONE..................................858 587-1121
Cristiano R Amon, *Pr*
Mark D Mclaughlin, *Ch Bd*
Akash Palkhiwala, *CFO*
Heather Ace, *Chief Human Resources Officer*
Ann Cathcart Chaplin, *Corporate Secretary*
EMP: 1430 **EST:** 1985
SALES (est): 44.2B
SALES (corp-wide): 44.2B **Publicly Held**
Web: www.qualcomm.com
SIC: **3663** 3674 7372 6794 Mobile communication equipment; Semiconductors and related devices; Business oriented computer software; Patent buying, licensing, leasing

(P-2898)
RAYTHEON APPLIED SGNAL TECH IN
2000 E El Segundo Blvd (90245-4501)
PHONE..................................310 436-7000
John R Treichler, *CEO*
EMP: 71
SALES (corp-wide): 67.07B **Publicly Held**
Web: www.appsig.com
SIC: **3663** 8711 Radio and t.v. communications equipment; Engineering services
HQ: Raytheon Applied Signal Technology, Inc.
100 Headquarters Dr
San Jose CA
408 749-1888

(P-2899)
VIASAT INC (PA)
Also Called: Viasat
6155 El Camino Real (92009-1602)
PHONE..................................760 476-2200
Mark Dankberg, *Ch Bd*
K Guru Gowrappan, *Pr*
Kevin Harkenrider, *Ex VP*
Mark Miller, *Ex VP*
Shawn Duffy, *Sr VP*
▲ **EMP:** 711 **EST:** 1986
SALES (est): 2.56B
SALES (corp-wide): 2.56B **Publicly Held**
Web: www.viasat.com
SIC: **3663** 4899 Space satellite communications equipment; Data communication services

3669 Communications Equipment, Nec

(P-2900)
CARRIER FIRE SEC AMERICAS CORP
Also Called: Utc, Mas
2955 Red Hill Ave Ste 100 (92626-1207)
PHONE..................................949 737-7800
Shin Voeks, *Genl Mgr*
EMP: 113
SALES (corp-wide): 20.42B **Publicly Held**
Web: corporate.carrier.com
SIC: **3669** 5063 Burglar alarm apparatus, electric; Alarm systems, nec
HQ: Carrier Fire & Security Americas Corporation
13995 Pasteur Blvd
Palm Beach Gardens FL

(P-2901)
GENERAL MONITORS INC (DH)
16782 Von Karman Ave Ste 14 (92606-2417)
PHONE..................................949 581-4464
Nishan J Vartanian, *CEO*
Richard Lamishaw, *
◆ **EMP:** 110 **EST:** 1961
SALES (est): 49.75MM
SALES (corp-wide): 1.53B **Publicly Held**
Web: us.msasafety.com
SIC: **3669** 1799 3812 Fire detection systems, electric; Gas leakage detection; Infrared object detection equipment
HQ: Msa Safety Sales, Llc
1000 Cranberry Woods Dr
Cranberry Township PA
800 672-2222

(P-2902)
JOHNSON CNTRLS FIRE PRTCTION L
Also Called: Simplexgrinnell
3568 Ruffin Rd (92123-2597)
P.O. Box 23080 (92193-3080)
PHONE..................................858 633-9100
Bob Jamieson, *Brnch Mgr*
EMP: 150
SIC: **3669** 1731 1711 3873 Emergency alarms; Fire detection and burglar alarm systems specialization; Fire sprinkler system installation; Watches, clocks, watchcases, and parts
HQ: Johnson Controls Fire Protection Lp
6600 Congress Ave
Boca Raton FL
561 988-7200

(P-2903)
WALTON ELECTRIC CORPORATION
755 N Central Ave Ste A (91786-9475)
P.O. Box 1599 (91711-8599)
PHONE..................................909 981-5051
Tanyon D Dunkley, *CEO*
Don R Davis, *
Ron C Stickel, *
EMP: 150 **EST:** 1985
SQ FT: 10,150
SALES (est): 35.19MM **Privately Held**
Web: www.waltonelectriccorp.com
SIC: **3669** 1731 Fire alarm apparatus, electric; Electrical work

(P-2904)
ZETTLER COMPONENTS INC (PA)
75 Columbia (92868)
PHONE..................................949 831-5000
Kurt Rexius, *Genl Mgr*
▲ **EMP:** 250 **EST:** 1996
SQ FT: 27,000
SALES (est): 65.75MM **Privately Held**
Web: www.zettlercomponents.com
SIC: **3669** 5065 5087 Intercommunication systems, electric; Intercommunication equipment, electronic; Firefighting equipment

3672 Printed Circuit Boards

(P-2905)
ANC TECHNOLOGY INC
Also Called: Shanghai Anc Electronic Tech
10195 Stockton Rd (93021-9755)
PHONE..................................805 530-3958
▲ **EMP:** 100 **EST:** 1994
SQ FT: 60,000
SALES (est): 6.91MM **Privately Held**
Web: www.anctech.com
SIC: **3672** 5083 Printed circuit boards; Irrigation equipment

(P-2906)
ASTRONIC
2 Orion (92656-4200)
PHONE..................................949 454-1180
Sang H Choi, *CEO*
Ok Kay Choi, *Sec*
▲ **EMP:** 143 **EST:** 1976
SQ FT: 41,000
SALES (est): 22.41MM **Privately Held**
Web: www.astronic-ems.com
SIC: **3672** 1742 Printed circuit boards; Acoustical and insulation work

(P-2907)
HUGHES CIRCUITS INC (PA)
Also Called: Hci
546 S Pacific St (92078-4050)
PHONE..................................760 744-0300
Barbara Hughes, *CEO*
Jerry Hughes, *
Michelle Glatts, *
Joe Hughes, *
Steve Hughes, *

PRODUCTS & SERVICES SECTION
3674 - Semiconductors And Related Devices (P-2925)

EMP: 99 EST: 1999
SQ FT: 50,000
SALES (est): 36.08MM
SALES (corp-wide): 36.08MM Privately Held
Web: www.hughescircuits.com
SIC: 3672 3679 8711 3444 Printed circuit boards; Electronic circuits; Engineering services; Sheet metalwork

(P-2908)
MURRIETTA CIRCUITS
5000 E Landon Dr (92807-1978)
PHONE...................714 970-2430
Andrew Murrietta, CEO
Albert G Murrietta, *
Albert A Murrietta, *
Josh Murrietta, OK Vice President*
Helen Murrietta, *
EMP: 105 EST: 1992
SQ FT: 48,500
SALES (est): 22.67MM Privately Held
Web: www.murrietta.com
SIC: 3672 8711 Printed circuit boards; Engineering services

(P-2909)
ONCORE MANUFACTURING LLC
6600 Stevenson Blvd (94538-2471)
PHONE...................510 516-5488
James Liow, Brnch Mgr
EMP: 99
SALES (corp-wide): 1.43B Privately Held
Web: www.neotech.com
SIC: 3672 8711 Printed circuit boards; Electrical or electronic engineering
HQ: Oncore Manufacturing Llc
  9340 Owensmouth Ave
  Chatsworth CA

(P-2910)
SPECTRUM ASSEMBLY INC
Also Called: Spectrum Electronics
6300 Yarrow Dr Ste 100 (92011-1542)
PHONE...................760 930-4000
Ronald Topp, Pr
Ronald Tupp, *
Michael Baldwin, *
EMP: 147 EST: 1993
SQ FT: 20,000
SALES (est): 24.05MM Privately Held
Web: www.saicorp.com
SIC: 3672 3569 3315 3999 Printed circuit boards; Assembly machines, non-metalworking; Wire and fabricated wire products; Barber and beauty shop equipment

(P-2911)
XILINX INC (HQ)
Also Called: Xilinx
2100 Logic Dr (95124-4355)
PHONE...................408 559-7778
Lisa T Su, Pr
Devinder Kumar, Ex VP
Mark D Papermaster, Ex VP
Darren Grasby, CSO
Harry A Wolin, Corporate Secretary
EMP: 1069 EST: 1990
SQ FT: 588,000
SALES (est): 3.15B
SALES (corp-wide): 23.6B Publicly Held
Web: www.amd.com
SIC: 3672 3674 7372 Printed circuit boards; Microcircuits, integrated (semiconductor); Application computer software
PA: Advanced Micro Devices, Inc.
  2485 Augustine Dr
  Santa Clara CA
  408 749-4000

3674 Semiconductors And Related Devices

(P-2912)
ALTERA CORPORATION (HQ)
Also Called: Altera
101 Innovation Dr (95134-1941)
PHONE...................408 544-7000
John P Daane, Pr
Danny Biran, Senior Vice President Corporate Strategy*
William Y Hata, Senior Vice President Worldwide Operation*
Bradley Howe, Senior Vice President Research & Development*
Kevin H Lyman, Senior Vice President Human Resources*
▲ EMP: 253 EST: 1983
SQ FT: 505,000
SALES (est): 288.77MM
SALES (corp-wide): 63.05B Publicly Held
Web: www.intel.com
SIC: 3674 7371 Semiconductors and related devices; Computer software development and applications
PA: Intel Corporation
  2200 Mission College Blvd
  Santa Clara CA
  408 765-8080

(P-2913)
APTINA LLC
Also Called: Aptina Imaging
2660 Zanker Rd (95134-2100)
PHONE...................408 660-2699
Joseph Passarello, Managing Member
EMP: 650 EST: 2006
SALES (est): 55.76MM
SALES (corp-wide): 8.33B Publicly Held
Web: www.onsemi.com
SIC: 3674 7336 Semiconductors and related devices; Graphic arts and related design
PA: On Semiconductor Corporation
  5701 N Pima Rd
  Scottsdale AZ
  602 244-6600

(P-2914)
CHRONTEL INC (PA)
2210 Otoole Ave Ste 100 (95131-1300)
PHONE...................408 383-9328
Bruce Wooley, Ch Bd
David C Soo, Pr
James Lin, *
EMP: 70 EST: 1986
SQ FT: 40,000
SALES (est): 10.94MM Privately Held
Web: www.chrontel.com
SIC: 3674 8711 Integrated circuits, semiconductor networks, etc.; Engineering services

(P-2915)
CONEXANT HOLDINGS INC
4000 Macarthur Blvd (92660-2558)
PHONE...................415 983-2706
EMP: 600
SIC: 3674 5065 Semiconductors and related devices; Semiconductor devices

(P-2916)
DAYLIGHT SOLUTIONS INC (DH)
Also Called: Drs Daylight Solutions
16465 Via Esprillo Ste 100 (92127-1701)
PHONE...................858 432-7500
Timothy Day, CEO
Paul Larson, Pr
EMP: 167 EST: 2004
SALES (est): 40.72MM

SALES (corp-wide): 15.28B Publicly Held
Web: www.daylightsolutions.com
SIC: 3674 5084 3826 Molecular devices, solid state; Instruments and control equipment; Analytical instruments
HQ: Leonardo Drs, Inc.
  2345 Crystal Dr Ste 1000
  Arlington VA
  703 416-8000

(P-2917)
DRS NTWORK IMAGING SYSTEMS LLC
Also Called: Drs Network & Imaging Systems
10600 Valley View St (90630-4833)
PHONE...................714 220-3800
EMP: 100 EST: 2009
SALES (est): 23.98MM
SALES (corp-wide): 15.28B Publicly Held
Web: www.leonardodrs.com
SIC: 3674 8731 Infrared sensors, solid state; Commercial physical research
HQ: Leonardo Drs, Inc.
  2345 Crystal Dr Ste 1000
  Arlington VA
  703 416-8000

(P-2918)
DSP GROUP INC (HQ)
Also Called: Dsp Group
2055 Gateway Pl Ste 480 (95110-1019)
PHONE...................408 986-4300
Michael Hurlston, Pr
Dean Butler, *
Venkat Kodavati, *
Divyesh Shah, *
EMP: 67 EST: 1987
SQ FT: 1,723
SALES (est): 114.48MM
SALES (corp-wide): 1.36B Publicly Held
Web: www.dspg.com
SIC: 3674 7371 Integrated circuits, semiconductor networks, etc.; Computer software development
PA: Synaptics Incorporated
  1109 Mckay Dr
  San Jose CA
  408 904-1100

(P-2919)
ESPERANTO TECHNOLOGIES INC (PA)
800 W El Camino Real Ste 410 (94040)
PHONE...................650 319-7357
Art Swift, CEO
EMP: 91 EST: 2014
SALES (est): 9.98MM
SALES (corp-wide): 9.98MM Privately Held
Web: www.esperanto.ai
SIC: 3674 7371 Integrated circuits, semiconductor networks, etc.; Computer software development

(P-2920)
GREENLIANT SYSTEMS INC
3970 Freedom Cir Ste 100 (95054-1204)
PHONE...................408 217-7400
EMP: 105 EST: 2010
SALES (est): 14.45MM Privately Held
Web: www.greenliant.com
SIC: 3674 5065 Semiconductors and related devices; Electronic parts and equipment, nec

(P-2921)
HANERGY HOLDING (AMERICA) LLC (HQ)
1350 Bayshore Hwy Ste 825 (94010-1823)

PHONE...................650 288-3722
Yi Wu, CEO
EMP: 100 EST: 2010
SALES (est): 94.3MM Privately Held
SIC: 3674 6719 Solar cells; Investment holding companies, except banks
PA: Jinjiang Hydropower Group Co., Ltd.
  Room 105, No. 680, Tanghekou Street, Tanghekou Town, Huairou Dis
  Beijing BJ

(P-2922)
IC SENSORS INC
45738 Northport Loop W (94538-6476)
PHONE...................510 498-1570
Frank Guibone, Pr
Victor Chatigny, *
EMP: 86 EST: 1982
SQ FT: 34,000
SALES (est): 2.32MM Privately Held
SIC: 3674 8711 3625 Semiconductors and related devices; Engineering services; Switches, electronic applications
HQ: Measurement Specialties, Inc.
  1000 Lucas Way
  Hampton VA
  757 766-1500

(P-2923)
INTEL CORPORATION (PA)
Also Called: Intel
2200 Mission College Blvd (95054-1549)
P.O. Box 58119 (95052-8119)
PHONE...................408 765-8080
Patrick P Gelsinger, CEO
Frank Yeary, *
David A Zinsner, Ex VP
Christoph Schell, CMO
April Miller Boise, CLO
◆ EMP: 5900 EST: 1968
SALES (est): 63.05B
SALES (corp-wide): 63.05B Publicly Held
Web: www.intel.com
SIC: 3674 3577 7372 Microprocessors; Computer peripheral equipment, nec; Prepackaged software

(P-2924)
IXYS INTGRTED CRCITS DIV AV IN
145 Columbia (92656-1413)
PHONE...................949 831-4622
Nathan Zommer, Ch Bd
Uzi Sasson, *
EMP: 559 EST: 1983
SQ FT: 28,000
SALES (est): 11.82MM
SALES (corp-wide): 2.51B Publicly Held
SIC: 3674 7389 Microcircuits, integrated (semiconductor); Design services
HQ: Ixys, Llc
  1590 Buckeye Dr
  Milpitas CA
  408 457-9000

(P-2925)
KYOCERA INTERNATIONAL INC (HQ)
8611 Balboa Ave (92123-1501)
PHONE...................858 492-1456
Robert Whisler, Vice Chairman
Nick Huntalas, Pr
William Edwards, VP
George Woodworth, VP
Franklin Kim, Div VP
◆ EMP: 100 EST: 1969
SQ FT: 16,000
SALES (est): 113.45MM Privately Held
Web: global.kyocera.com

3674 - Semiconductors And Related Devices (P-2926)

SIC: 3674 5023 5731 Semiconductors and related devices; Kitchen tools and utensils, nec; Radio, television, and electronic stores
PA: Kyocera Corporation
6, Takedatobadonocho, Fushimi-Ku
Kyoto KYO

(P-2926)
MEGACHIPS LSI USA CORPORATION
910 E Hamilton Ave Ste 120 (95008-0612)
PHONE..............................408 570-0555
Ikuo Iwama, *CEO*
Akihide Maeda, *
EMP: 75 EST: 2018
SALES (est): 11.35MM **Privately Held**
Web: www.megachips.co.jp
SIC: 3674 5065 Semiconductors and related devices; Semiconductor devices
PA: Megachips Corporation
1-1-1, Miyahara, Yodogawa-Ku
Osaka OSK

(P-2927)
MIASOLE HI-TECH CORP (DH)
Also Called: Miasole
3211 Scott Blvd Ste 201 (95054-3010)
PHONE..............................408 919-5700
Jie Zhang, *CEO*
Lyndsey Zhang, *
Atiye Bayman, *
EMP: 250 EST: 2012
SALES (est): 69.78MM **Privately Held**
Web: www.miasole.com
SIC: 3674 5074 Solar cells; Heating equipment and panels, solar
HQ: Hanergy Holding (America) Llc
1350 Bayshore Hwy
Burlingame CA
650 288-3722

(P-2928)
MICROSEMI SOC CORP (DH)
3850 N 1st St (95134-1702)
PHONE..............................408 643-6000
James J Peterson, *CEO*
John W Hohener, *
Esmat Z Hamdy, *Senior Vice President Technology*
Fares N Mubarak, *Marketing*
David L Van De Hey, *
▲ EMP: 103 EST: 1985
SQ FT: 158,000
SALES (est): 147.55MM
SALES (corp-wide): 8.44B **Publicly Held**
Web: www.microsemi.com
SIC: 3674 7371 Microcircuits, integrated (semiconductor); Computer software development
HQ: Microsemi Corporation
11861 Western Ave
Garden Grove CA
949 380-6100

(P-2929)
PATRIOT MEMORY INC (PA)
Also Called: Patriot Memory
47027 Benicia St (94538-7331)
PHONE..............................510 979-1021
Paul Jones, *Managing Member*
Doug Diggs, *
▲ EMP: 125 EST: 1985
SALES (est): 23.09MM
SALES (corp-wide): 23.09MM **Privately Held**
Web: www.patriotmemory.com
SIC: 3674 5045 Semiconductors and related devices; Computers, nec

(P-2930)
PURE WAFER INC
Also Called: Wrs Materials
2240 Ringwood Ave (95131-1716)
PHONE..............................408 945-8112
Jerry Winters, *CEO*
EMP: 235
SALES (corp-wide): 50.03MM **Privately Held**
Web: www.purewafer.com
SIC: 3674 8742 Integrated circuits, semiconductor networks, etc.; Financial consultant
HQ: Pure Wafer, Inc.
2575 Melville Rd
Prescott AZ

(P-2931)
QUALCOMM ATHEROS INC (HQ)
1700 Technology Dr (95110-1383)
PHONE..............................408 773-5200
▲ EMP: 600 EST: 1998
SALES (est): 434.87MM
SALES (corp-wide): 44.2B **Publicly Held**
SIC: 3674 4899 Integrated circuits, semiconductor networks, etc.; Communication signal enhancement network services
PA: Qualcomm Incorporated
5775 Morehouse Dr
San Diego CA
858 587-1121

(P-2932)
QUALCOMM TECHNOLOGIES INC (HQ)
5775 Morehouse Dr (92121-1714)
P.O. Box 919042 (92191-9042)
PHONE..............................858 587-1121
Cristiano Amon, *CEO*
James Thompson, *
Kevin Frizzell, *
Jim Cathey, *CCO*
▲ EMP: 298 EST: 2011
SALES (est): 1.88B
SALES (corp-wide): 44.2B **Publicly Held**
Web: www.qualcomm.com
SIC: 3674 7372 Integrated circuits, semiconductor networks, etc.; Business oriented computer software; Patent buying, licensing, leasing
PA: Qualcomm Incorporated
5775 Morehouse Dr
San Diego CA
858 587-1121

(P-2933)
RAMBUS INC (PA)
Also Called: Rambus
4453 N 1st St Ste 100 (95134-1260)
PHONE..............................408 462-8000
Luc Seraphin, *Pr*
Charles Kissner, *Non-Executive Chairman of the Board*
Rahul Mathur, *VP Fin*
Sean Fan, *Sr VP*
John Shinn, *CCO*
◆ EMP: 274 EST: 1990
SALES (est): 454.79MM **Publicly Held**
Web: www.rambus.com
SIC: 3674 6794 Integrated circuits, semiconductor networks, etc.; Patent owners and lessors

(P-2934)
TESSERA TECHNOLOGIES INC (DH)
3025 Orchard Pkwy (95134-2017)
PHONE..............................408 321-6000
Tom Lacey, *CEO*

Jon E Kirchner, *Pr*
Robert Andersen, *CFO*
Kris M Graves, *Chief Human Resources Officer*
▲ EMP: 104 EST: 1990
SALES (est): 68.87MM
SALES (corp-wide): 438.93MM **Publicly Held**
Web: www.adeia.com
SIC: 3674 6794 Integrated circuits, semiconductor networks, etc.; Patent buying, licensing, leasing
HQ: Adeia Holdings Inc.
3025 Orchard Pkwy
San Jose CA
408 473-2500

(P-2935)
UMC GROUP (USA)
Also Called: Umc
488 De Guigne Dr (94085-3903)
PHONE..............................408 523-7800
Robert Tsao, *Ch*
Jason S Wang, *
Ing-dar Liu, *Vice Chairman*
Peter Chang, *
Fu Tai Liou, *
▲ EMP: 75 EST: 1997
SQ FT: 40,000
SALES (est): 24.87MM **Privately Held**
Web: www.umc.com
SIC: 3674 5065 Wafers (semiconductor devices); Electronic parts and equipment, nec
PA: United Microelectronics Corporation
3, Li-Shin 2nd Rd., Hsinchu Science Park,
Hsinchu City

(P-2936)
WAFER RECLAIM SERVICES LLC
Also Called: Wrs Materials
2240 Ringwood Ave (95131-1716)
PHONE..............................408 945-8112
▲ EMP: 182
Web: www.purewafer.com
SIC: 3674 8742 Integrated circuits, semiconductor networks, etc.; Financial consultant

3675 Electronic Capacitors

(P-2937)
JOHANSON TECHNOLOGY INC
4001 Calle Tecate (93012-5087)
PHONE..............................805 575-0124
Justin Greene, *Ex Dir*
John Petrinec, *
▲ EMP: 130 EST: 1991
SQ FT: 30,000
SALES (est): 23.75MM **Privately Held**
Web: www.johansontechnology.com
SIC: 3675 5065 3674 Electronic capacitors; Electronic parts and equipment, nec; Semiconductors and related devices
PA: Johanson Ventures, Inc.
4001 Calle Tecate
Camarillo CA

3678 Electronic Connectors

(P-2938)
JOSLYN SUNBANK COMPANY LLC
1740 Commerce Way (93446-3620)
PHONE..............................805 238-2840
Mark Thek, *Genl Mgr*
Mike Ritter, *Dir Opers*
Kirsten Park, *VP*

EMP: 500 EST: 1997
SQ FT: 80,000
SALES (est): 61.75MM **Privately Held**
Web: joslyn-sunbank-company-llc-in-paso-robles-ca.cityfos.com
SIC: 3678 3643 5065 Electronic connectors; Connectors and terminals for electrical devices; Connectors, electronic
HQ: Eaton Corporation
1000 Eaton Blvd
Cleveland OH
440 523-5000

3679 Electronic Components, Nec

(P-2939)
AVR GLOBAL TECHNOLOGIES INC (PA)
Also Called: Avr Global Tech
500 La Terraza Blvd Ste 150 (92025)
P.O. Box 3814 (92629-8814)
PHONE..............................949 391-1180
Andy Bowman, *CEO*
Andy Bowman, *Pr*
Val Pontes, *Treas*
EMP: 197 EST: 2016
SALES (est): 11.13MM
SALES (corp-wide): 11.13MM **Privately Held**
Web: www.avrglobaltech.com
SIC: 3679 3714 5065 5063 Harness assemblies, for electronic use: wire or cable; Automotive wiring harness sets; Electronic parts and equipment, nec; Wire and cable

(P-2940)
BI TECHNOLOGIES CORPORATION (HQ)
Also Called: TT Electronics
120 S State College Blvd Ste 175 (92821-5834)
PHONE..............................714 447-2300
▲ EMP: 260 EST: 1984
SALES (est): 110.16MM
SALES (corp-wide): 742.85MM **Privately Held**
Web: www.ttelectronics.com
SIC: 3679 5065 8711 Electronic circuits; Electronic parts and equipment, nec; Engineering services
PA: Tt Electronics Plc
4th Floor
Woking
193 282-5300

(P-2941)
COMPASS COMPONENTS INC (PA)
Also Called: Compass Manufacturing Service
48133 Warm Springs Blvd (94539-7498)
PHONE..............................510 656-4700
Jack Maxwell, *CEO*
Bob Duplantier, *
EMP: 110 EST: 1979
SQ FT: 36,000
SALES (est): 63.15MM
SALES (corp-wide): 63.15MM **Privately Held**
Web: www.compassmade.com
SIC: 3679 5065 Harness assemblies, for electronic use: wire or cable; Electronic parts

(P-2942)
GIGATERA COMMUNICATIONS
Also Called: KMW Communications
1818 E Orangethorpe Ave (92831-5324)

PRODUCTS & SERVICES SECTION

3699 - Electrical Equipment And Supplies, Nec (P-2960)

PHONE.....................714 515-1100
Duk Y Kim, *Ch Bd*
Duk Y Kim, *Pr*
Yeong Kim, *
Burton Calloway, *
▲ EMP: 65 EST: 1995
SQ FT: 4,500
SALES (est): 28.85MM **Privately Held**
Web: www.gteracom.com
SIC: 3679 5063 Electronic circuits; Electrical apparatus and equipment
PA: Kmw Inc.
    21 Dongtan-Daero 25-Gil
    Hwaseong

(P-2943)
JANCO CORPORATION
Also Called: Esterline Mason
13955 Balboa Blvd (91342-1084)
P.O. Box 3038 (91508-3038)
PHONE...........................818 361-3366
▼ EMP: 120 EST: 1947
SALES (est): 26.52MM
SALES (corp-wide): 6.58B **Publicly Held**
Web: www.transdigm.com
SIC: 3679 3825 3643 5088 Electronic switches; Shunts, electrical; Bus bars (electrical conductors); Aircraft and parts, nec
HQ: Esterline Technologies Corp
    1301 E 9th St Ste 3000
    Cleveland OH
    216 706-2960

(P-2944)
LUCIX CORPORATION (HQ)
Also Called: Lucix
800 Avenida Acaso Ste E (93012-8758)
PHONE...........................805 987-6645
Mark Shahriary, *Pr*
Cheryl Johnson, *
D Ick Fanucchi, *
▲ EMP: 83 EST: 1999
SQ FT: 48,000
SALES (est): 49.19MM **Publicly Held**
Web: www.lucix.com
SIC: 3679 8731 Microwave components; Commercial physical research
PA: Heico Corporation
    3000 Taft St
    Hollywood FL

(P-2945)
Q MICROWAVE INC
1591 Pioneer Way (92020-1637)
PHONE...........................619 258-7322
Eric Maat, *CEO*
Craig Higginson, *
Craig Shauan, *
EMP: 84 EST: 1998
SQ FT: 18,000
SALES (est): 14.9MM **Privately Held**
Web: www.qmicrowave.com
SIC: 3679 5065 Microwave components; Electronic parts and equipment, nec

(P-2946)
TELEDYNE TECHNOLOGIES INC
Also Called: Teledyne Controls
501 Continental Blvd (90245-5036)
P.O. Box 1026 (90245-1026)
PHONE...........................310 765-3600
Masood Hassan, *Brnch Mgr*
EMP: 300
SALES (corp-wide): 5.46B **Publicly Held**
Web: www.teledyne.com
SIC: 3679 8731 3812 3519 Electronic circuits ; Commercial physical research; Search and navigation equipment; Internal combustion engines, nec
PA: Teledyne Technologies Inc

1049 Camino Dos Rios
Thousand Oaks CA
805 373-4545

(P-2947)
WAVESTREAM CORPORATION (HQ)
545 W Terrace Dr (91773-2915)
PHONE...........................909 599-9080
Robert Huffman, *CEO*
Nimrod Itach, *
Lanis Bell, *
James Rosenberg, *
EMP: 103 EST: 2006
SQ FT: 33,000
SALES (est): 46.93MM **Privately Held**
Web: www.wavestream.com
SIC: 3679 8731 Microwave components; Commercial physical research
PA: Gilat Satellite Networks Ltd.
    21 Yegia Kapaim
    Petah Tikva

3691 Storage Batteries

(P-2948)
FLUX POWER HOLDINGS INC (PA)
2685 S Melrose Dr (92081-8783)
PHONE...........................877 505-3589
Ronald F Dutt, *Ch Bd*
Charles A Scheiwe, *CFO*
Jeffrey Mason, *VP Opers*
▲ EMP: 111 EST: 1998
SQ FT: 63,200
SALES (est): 66.34MM **Publicly Held**
Web: www.fluxpower.com
SIC: 3691 5063 Storage batteries; Storage batteries, industrial

(P-2949)
NATRON ENERGY INC
3542 Bassett St (95054-2704)
PHONE...........................408 498-5828
Colin Wessells, *CEO*
EMP: 60 EST: 2012
SQ FT: 2,500
SALES (est): 12.68MM **Privately Held**
Web: www.natron.energy
SIC: 3691 7389 Batteries, rechargeable; Business Activities at Non-Commercial Site

(P-2950)
TENERGY CORPORATION
Also Called: All-Battery.com
436 Kato Ter (94539-8332)
PHONE...........................510 687-0388
Xiangbing Li, *CEO*
Ling Ch Liang, *
▲ EMP: 90 EST: 2004
SALES (est): 11.93MM **Privately Held**
Web: www.tenergybattery.com
SIC: 3691 5063 Alkaline cell storage batteries; Batteries

3694 Engine Electrical Equipment

(P-2951)
MYOTEK INDUSTRIES INCORPORATED (DH)
1278 Glenneyre St Ste 431 (92651-3103)
PHONE...........................949 502-3776
▲ EMP: 90 EST: 1998
SQ FT: 1,800
SALES (est): 29.51MM
SALES (corp-wide): 180.46MM **Privately Held**

Web: www.fordledfog.com
SIC: 3694 5013 Automotive electrical equipment, nec; Automotive servicing equipment
HQ: Myotek Holdings, Inc.
    1176 Main St Ste B
    Irvine CA
    949 502-3776

3695 Magnetic And Optical Recording Media

(P-2952)
CD VIDEO MANUFACTURING INC
Also Called: C D Video
12650 Westminster Ave (92706-2139)
PHONE...........................714 265-0770
Minh T Nguyen, *Pr*
▲ EMP: 60 EST: 1995
SQ FT: 11,000
SALES (est): 13.55MM **Privately Held**
Web: www.cdvideomfg.com
SIC: 3695 3652 7819 Video recording tape, blank; Compact laser discs, prerecorded; Services allied to motion pictures

(P-2953)
TECHNICOLOR DISC SERVICES CORP (HQ)
3601 Calle Tecate Ste 120 (93012-5097)
PHONE...........................805 445-1122
▲ EMP: 200 EST: 1996
SALES (est): 49.93MM **Privately Held**
SIC: 3695 7361 Computer software tape and disks: blank, rigid, and floppy; Employment agencies
PA: Vantiva
    10 Boulevard De Grenelle
    Paris

(P-2954)
U-TECH MEDIA USA LLC
1105 Montague Expy (95035-6845)
PHONE...........................408 597-1600
▲ EMP: 220
SIC: 3695 7389 Computer software tape and disks: blank, rigid, and floppy; Packaging and labeling services

3699 Electrical Equipment And Supplies, Nec

(P-2955)
CONSTRUCTION INNOVATIONS LLC
Also Called: Ci
10630 Mather Blvd Ste 200 (95655-4125)
PHONE...........................855 725-9555
Larry A Devore, *Managing Member*
James B Littlejohn, *
EMP: 150 EST: 2012
SQ FT: 17,000
SALES (est): 51.92MM
SALES (corp-wide): 160MM **Privately Held**
Web: www.constructioninnovations.com
SIC: 3699 8711 Electrical equipment and supplies, nec; Consulting engineer
PA: Bdg Innovations, Llc
    6001 Outfall Cir
    Sacramento CA
    855 725-9555

(P-2956)
CUBIC DEFENSE APPLICATIONS INC
CMS Secure Comms
9233 Balboa Ave (92123-1513)
PHONE...........................858 505-2870
Jerry Madigan, *VP*
EMP: 200
SALES (corp-wide): 1.48B **Privately Held**
Web: www.cubic.com
SIC: 3699 7382 Security devices; Security systems services
HQ: Cubic Defense Applications, Inc.
    9233 Balboa Ave
    San Diego CA
    858 776-5664

(P-2957)
DOORKING INC (PA)
Also Called: Doorking
120 S Glasgow Ave (90301-1502)
PHONE...........................310 645-0023
Thomas Richmond, *Pr*
Pat Kochie, *
Susan Richmond, *
◆ EMP: 185 EST: 1948
SQ FT: 16,000
SALES (est): 98.13MM
SALES (corp-wide): 98.13MM **Privately Held**
Web: www.doorking.com
SIC: 3699 5065 3829 Security control equipment and systems; Security control equipment and systems; Measuring and controlling devices, nec

(P-2958)
GHANGOR CLOUD INC
2001 Gateway Pl Ste 710 (95110-1077)
PHONE...........................408 713-3303
Tarique Mustafa, *CEO*
Bhanu Panda, *
John Racioppi, *
EMP: 65 EST: 2014
SALES (est): 3.15MM **Privately Held**
Web: www.ghangorcloud.com
SIC: 3699 7371 Security devices; Software programming applications

(P-2959)
IWERKS ENTERTAINMENT INC
Also Called: Simex-Iwerks
25040 Avenue Tibbitts Ste F (91355-3946)
PHONE...........................661 678-1800
Gary Matus, *CEO*
Jeff Dahl, *
Mark Cornell, *
Donald Stults, *
EMP: 75 EST: 1986
SALES (est): 11.51MM
SALES (corp-wide): 17.76MM **Privately Held**
Web: www.simex-iwerks.com
SIC: 3699 7819 Electrical equipment and supplies, nec; Developing and printing of commercial motion picture film
PA: Simex Inc
    600-210 King St E
    Toronto ON
    416 597-1585

(P-2960)
MEGGITT SAFETY SYSTEMS INC (DH)
Also Called: Meggitt Ctrl Systms-Vntura Cnt
1785 Voyager Ave (93063-3363)
PHONE...........................805 584-4100
Dennis Hutton, *Pr*
Dolores Watai, *
▲ EMP: 210 EST: 1999

3699 - Electrical Equipment And Supplies, Nec (P-2961)

SQ FT: 180,000
SALES (est): 118.2MM
SALES (corp-wide): 19.07B Publicly Held
Web: www.meggitt.com
SIC: 3699 3724 3728 7389 Betatrons; Exhaust systems, aircraft; Aircraft parts and equipment, nec; Fire protection service other than forestry or public
HQ: Meggitt Limited
  Pilot Way
  Coventry W MIDLANDS
  247 708-7211

(P-2961)
ROMEO SYSTEMS INC
Also Called: Romeo Power Technology
5560 Katella Ave (90630-5001)
PHONE.........................323 675-2180
Michael Patterson, Ch
Lionel Selwood Junior, CEO
Lauren Webb, *
Criswell Choi, *
◆ EMP: 133 EST: 2014
SALES (est): 9.51MM
SALES (corp-wide): 50.83MM Publicly Held
SIC: 3699 8731 High-energy particle physics equipment; Energy research
HQ: Romeo Power, Inc.
  5560 Katella Ave
  Cypress CA
  833 467-2237

(P-2962)
SPECTRA-PHYSICS INC (DH)
Also Called: Laser Division
1565 Barber Ln (95035-7409)
P.O. Box 19607 (92623-9607)
PHONE.........................877 835-9620
Robert J Phillippy, CEO
▼ EMP: 90 EST: 1961
SQ FT: 129,500
SALES (est): 88.1MM
SALES (corp-wide): 3.55B Publicly Held
Web: www.esi.com
SIC: 3699 8731 Laser systems and equipment; Commercial physical research
HQ: Newport Corporation
  1791 Deere Ave
  Irvine CA
  949 863-3144

(P-2963)
SUSS MCRTEC PHTNIC SYSTEMS INC
2520 Palisades Dr (92882-0632)
PHONE.........................951 817-3700
Courtney T Sheets, CEO
Debora Blanchard, *
Debbie Brown, *
EMP: 90 EST: 1966
SALES (est): 18MM
SALES (corp-wide): 310.68MM Privately Held
Web: www.suss.com
SIC: 3699 7389 Electrical equipment and supplies, nec; Business services, nec
PA: SUss Microtec Se
  SchleiBheimer Str. 90
  Garching B. Munchen BY
  89320070

(P-2964)
UNDERSEA SYSTEMS INTL INC
Also Called: Ocean Technology Systems
3133 W Harvard St (92704-3912)
PHONE.........................714 754-7848
Michael R Pelissier, Pr
Jerry Peck, *
▲ EMP: 62 EST: 1987

SQ FT: 18,000
SALES (est): 12.95MM Privately Held
Web: www.oceantechnologysystems.com
SIC: 3699 8711 Underwater sound equipment; Acoustical engineering

(P-2965)
WESTGATE MFG INC
Also Called: Westgate Manufacturing
2462 E 28th St (90058-1402)
PHONE.........................323 826-9490
Isaac Hadjyan, CEO
Eryeh Hadjyan, *
Ebrahim Hadjyan, *
▲ EMP: 74 EST: 2008
SALES (est): 11.74MM Privately Held
Web: www.westgatemfg.com
SIC: 3699 5063 Electrical equipment and supplies, nec; Lighting fixtures

3711 Motor Vehicles And Car Bodies

(P-2966)
LUCID USA INC (HQ)
Also Called: Lucid Motors
7373 Gateway Blvd (94560-1149)
PHONE.........................510 648-3553
Peter Rawlinson, CEO
Derek Jenkins, *
Jonathan Butler, *
Sherry House, *
▲ EMP: 163 EST: 2007
SQ FT: 65,000
SALES (est): 527.5MM
SALES (corp-wide): 608.18MM Publicly Held
Web: www.lucidmotors.com
SIC: 3711 8711 Motor vehicles and car bodies; Engineering services
PA: Lucid Group, Inc.
  7373 Gateway Blvd
  Newark CA
  510 648-3553

(P-2967)
MILLENWORKS
1361 Valencia Ave (92780-6459)
PHONE.........................714 426-5500
▲ EMP: 75
SIC: 3711 5012 7549 8731 Military motor vehicle assembly; Commercial vehicles; Automotive customizing services, nonfactory basis; Electronic research

3713 Truck And Bus Bodies

(P-2968)
HARBOR TRUCK BODIES INC
Also Called: Harbor Truck Body
255 Voyager Ave (92821-6223)
PHONE.........................714 996-0411
Ken Lindt, Pr
EMP: 79 EST: 1973
SQ FT: 50,000
SALES (est): 22.13MM Privately Held
Web: www.harbortruckandvan.com
SIC: 3713 7532 Truck bodies (motor vehicles); Body shop, automotive

(P-2969)
VAHE ENTERPRISES INC
Also Called: Aa Leasing
750 E Slauson Ave (90011-5236)
PHONE.........................323 235-6657
Vahe Karapetian, CEO
▲ EMP: 90 EST: 1976

SQ FT: 60,000
SALES (est): 9.89MM Privately Held
Web: www.aacatertruck.com
SIC: 3713 7513 Truck bodies (motor vehicles); Truck leasing, without drivers

3714 Motor Vehicle Parts And Accessories

(P-2970)
ACHATES POWER INC
4060 Sorrento Valley Blvd Ste A (92121-1428)
PHONE.........................858 535-9920
David Crompton, Pr
David Johnson, CEO
John Koszewnik, Prin
Jerome Paye, Dir Opers
Carol Mottershead, Finance
EMP: 95 EST: 2003
SALES (est): 24.96MM Privately Held
Web: www.achatespower.com
SIC: 3714 8711 Motor vehicle engines and parts; Mechanical engineering

(P-2971)
AEVA TECHNOLOGIES INC (PA)
Also Called: AEVA
555 Ellis St (94043-2214)
PHONE.........................650 481-7070
Soroush Salehian Dardashti, CEO
Mina Rezk, Ch Bd
Saurabh Sinha, CFO
EMP: 222 EST: 2017
SALES (est): 4.19MM
SALES (corp-wide): 4.19MM Publicly Held
Web: www.aeva.com
SIC: 3714 7372 Motor vehicle parts and accessories; Prepackaged software

(P-2972)
C R LAURENCE CO INC (HQ)
Also Called: Crl
2503 E Vernon Ave (90058-1826)
PHONE.........................323 588-1281
Arty Feles, Pr
Barbara Haaksma, *
Shirin Khosravi, *
Jacque Maples, *
Steve Whitcomb, *
◆ EMP: 380 EST: 1963
SQ FT: 170,000
SALES (est): 483.56MM
SALES (corp-wide): 32.72B Privately Held
Web: www.crlaurence.com
SIC: 3714 5072 5039 Sun roofs, motor vehicle; Hand tools; Glass construction materials
PA: Crh Public Limited Company
  Stonemason S Way
  Rathfarnham
  14041000

(P-2973)
GIBSON PERFORMANCE CORPORATION
Also Called: Gibson Exhaust Systems
1270 Webb Cir (92879-5760)
PHONE.........................951 372-1220
Ronald Gibson, Pr
Julie Gibson, *
▲ EMP: 75 EST: 1990
SQ FT: 50,000
SALES (est): 9.72MM Privately Held
Web: www.gibsonperformance.com
SIC: 3714 5013 Exhaust systems and parts, motor vehicle; Motor vehicle supplies and new parts

(P-2974)
IMPCO TECHNOLOGIES INC (HQ)
Also Called: Impco
3030 S Susan St (92704-6435)
PHONE.........................714 656-1200
Massimo Fracchia, Genl Mgr
Peter Chase, *
◆ EMP: 160 EST: 1958
SQ FT: 108,000
SALES (est): 44.72MM
SALES (corp-wide): 305.7MM Privately Held
Web: www.impcotechnologies.com
SIC: 3714 3592 7363 Fuel systems and parts, motor vehicle; Carburetors; Engineering help service
PA: Westport Fuel Systems Inc
  1691 75th Ave
  Vancouver BC
  604 718-2000

(P-2975)
NORTHROP GRMMN SPCE & MSSN SYS
2501 Santa Fe Ave (90278-1117)
PHONE.........................310 812-4321
EMP: 334
SIC: 3714 7373 3663 3661 Motor vehicle parts and accessories; Computer integrated systems design; Radio and t.v. communications equipment; Telephone and telegraph apparatus
HQ: Northrop Grumman Space & Mission Systems Corp.
  6379 San Ignacio Ave
  San Jose CA
  703 280-2900

(P-2976)
PRIME WHEEL CORPORATION
23920 Vermont Ave (90710-1602)
PHONE.........................310 326-5080
Eddie Chen, Mgr
EMP: 453
SQ FT: 200,000
SALES (corp-wide): 315.67MM Privately Held
Web: www.primewheel.com
SIC: 3714 3471 5013 Motor vehicle wheels and parts; Plating and polishing; Automotive supplies and parts
PA: Prime Wheel Corporation
  17705 S Main St
  Gardena CA
  310 516-9126

(P-2977)
QF LIQUIDATION INC (PA)
Also Called: Quantum Technologies
25242 Arctic Ocean Dr (92630-8821)
PHONE.........................949 930-3400
W Brian Olson, Pr
Bradley J Timon, CFO
Kenneth R Lombardo, Corporate Secretary
Mark Arold, VP Opers
David M Mazaika, Development
◆ EMP: 155 EST: 2000
SQ FT: 156,000
SALES (est): 24.78MM Privately Held
Web: www.qtww.com
SIC: 3714 3764 8711 Motor vehicle parts and accessories; Space propulsion units and parts; Engineering services

PRODUCTS & SERVICES SECTION   3731 - Shipbuilding And Repairing (P-2994)

3715 Truck Trailers

(P-2978)
CIMC INTERMODAL EQUIPMENT LLC (HQ)
Also Called: Cimc Intermodal Equipment
10530 Sessler St (90280-7252)
PHONE.....................562 904-8600
▲ **EMP:** 70 **EST:** 2007
SALES (est): 43.48MM **Privately Held**
Web: www.ciemanufacturing.com
SIC: 3715 7539 Truck trailer chassis; Trailer repair
PA: China International Marine Containers (Group) Co., Ltd.
Floor 8, Zhongji Group Yanfa Center, No.2, Shekou Gangwan Avenue
Shenzhen GD

(P-2979)
COZAD TRAILER SALES LLC
4907 E Waterloo Rd (95215-2096)
PHONE.....................209 931-3000
Delores Pistacchio, *
Kara Kardashian, *
▲ **EMP:** 92 **EST:** 1953
SQ FT: 78,000
SALES (est): 17.32MM **Privately Held**
Web: www.cozadtrailers.com
SIC: 3715 7539 Trailer bodies; Trailer repair

(P-2980)
UTILITY TRAILER MFG CO
Tautliner Division
17295 Railroad St Ste A (91748-1043)
PHONE.....................909 594-6026
Linda Baker, Mgr
EMP: 141
SALES (corp-wide): 897.7MM **Privately Held**
Web: www.utilitytrailer.com
SIC: 3715 5199 Truck trailers; Tarpaulins
PA: Utility Trailer Manufacturing Company, Llc
17295 Railroad St Ste A
City Of Industry CA
626 965-1514

3721 Aircraft

(P-2981)
CHIPTON-ROSS INC
420 Culver Blvd (90293-7706)
PHONE.....................310 414-7800
Judith Hinkley, Pr
EMP: 100 **EST:** 1983
SQ FT: 6,000
SALES (est): 9.01MM **Privately Held**
Web: www.chiptonross.com
SIC: 3721 3731 8731 7363 Motorized aircraft; Military ships, building and repairing; Commercial physical research; Temporary help service

(P-2982)
NORTHROP GRUMMAN SYSTEMS CORP
Also Called: Aerospace Systems
1 Space Park Blvd (90278-1071)
PHONE.....................310 812-1089
EMP: 305
Web: www.northropgrumman.com
SIC: 3721 3761 3728 3812 Airplanes, fixed or rotary wing; Guided missiles, complete; Fuselage assembly, aircraft; Inertial guidance systems
HQ: Northrop Grumman Systems Corporation
2980 Fairview Park Dr
Falls Church VA
703 280-2900

(P-2983)
SCALED COMPOSITES LLC
1624 Flight Line (93501-1663)
PHONE.....................661 824-4541
Greg Morris, Pr
Mark Taylor, VP
Jennifer Santiago, Ex VP
Ben Diachun, VP
Jason Kelley, VP
EMP: 500 **EST:** 2000
SQ FT: 160,000
SALES (est): 98.52MM **Publicly Held**
Web: www.scaled.com
SIC: 3721 3999 8711 Aircraft; Models, except toy; Aviation and/or aeronautical engineering
HQ: Northrop Grumman Systems Corporation
2980 Fairview Park Dr
Falls Church VA
703 280-2900

(P-2984)
WORLDWIDE AEROS CORP
3971 Fredonia Dr (90068-1213)
PHONE.....................818 344-3999
Igor Pasternak, Pr
Carrie Cass, CFO
▲ **EMP:** 82 **EST:** 1987
SALES (est): 8.84MM **Privately Held**
SIC: 3721 8711 Airships; Aviation and/or aeronautical engineering

3724 Aircraft Engines And Engine Parts

(P-2985)
GKN AEROSPACE CHEM-TRONICS INC (DH)
Also Called: Chem-Tronics
1150 W Bradley Ave (92020-1504)
P.O. Box 1604 (92022-1604)
PHONE.....................619 258-5000
Marcus J Bryson, CEO
Michael A Beck, *
Les Emanuel, *
Stacey Clapp, *
▲ **EMP:** 648 **EST:** 1953
SQ FT: 400,000
SALES (est): 194.63MM
SALES (corp-wide): 9.07B **Privately Held**
Web: www.gknaerospace.com
SIC: 3724 7699 Aircraft engines and engine parts; Aircraft and heavy equipment repair services
HQ: Gkn Limited
2nd Floor, One Central Boulevard
Solihull W MIDLANDS
121 210-9800

3728 Aircraft Parts And Equipment, Nec

(P-2986)
ACE CLEARWATER ENTERPRISES INC (PA)
19815 Magellan Dr (90502-1107)
PHONE.....................310 323-2140
James D Dodson, Pr
Kellie Johnson, *
EMP: 100 **EST:** 1961
SALES (est): 46.01MM
SALES (corp-wide): 46.01MM **Privately Held**
Web: www.aceclearwater.com
SIC: 3728 3544 7692 3812 Aircraft parts and equipment, nec; Special dies, tools, jigs, and fixtures; Welding repair; Search and navigation equipment

(P-2987)
AIRBORNE TECHNOLOGIES INC
Also Called: Airborne Technologies
999 Avenida Acaso (93012-8700)
P.O. Box 2210 (93011-2210)
PHONE.....................805 389-3700
Greg Beason, CEO
Christopher Celtruda, *
Richard Drinkward, *
EMP: 232 **EST:** 1980
SQ FT: 40,000
SALES (est): 37.08MM
SALES (corp-wide): 89.76MM **Privately Held**
Web: www.goallclear.com
SIC: 3728 5088 7699 3812 Aircraft parts and equipment, nec; Aircraft equipment and supplies, nec; Aircraft and heavy equipment repair services; Search and navigation equipment
PA: Kellstrom Holding Corporation
100 N Pcf Cast Hwy Ste 19
El Segundo CA
561 222-7455

(P-2988)
AIRTECH INTERNATIONAL INC (PA)
Also Called: Airtech Advanced Mtls Group
5700 Skylab Rd (92647-2055)
PHONE.....................714 899-8100
Jeff Dahlgren, Pr
◆ **EMP:** 130 **EST:** 1973
SQ FT: 150,000
SALES (est): 95.6MM
SALES (corp-wide): 95.6MM **Privately Held**
Web: www.airtechintl.com
SIC: 3728 3081 5088 2673 Aircraft parts and equipment, nec; Unsupported plastics film and sheet; Aeronautical equipment and supplies; Bags: plastic, laminated, and coated

(P-2989)
AMRO FABRICATING CORPORATION (PA)
1430 Amro Way (91733-3046)
PHONE.....................626 579-2200
John Hammond, Pr
Michael Riley, *
EMP: 238 **EST:** 1977
SQ FT: 150,000
SALES (est): 45.24MM
SALES (corp-wide): 45.24MM **Privately Held**
Web: www.karman-sd.com
SIC: 3728 3769 3544 5088 Aircraft parts and equipment, nec; Space vehicle equipment, nec; Special dies, tools, jigs, and fixtures; Aircraft and space vehicle supplies and parts

(P-2990)
DUCOMMUN LABARGE TECH INC (HQ)
Also Called: American Electronics
23301 Wilmington Ave (90745-6209)
PHONE.....................310 513-7200
Stephen G Oswald, Pr
Christopher Wampler, VP
Jerry Redondo, VP
Michelle Stein, VP
Rajiv Tata, Sec

▲ **EMP:** 180 **EST:** 1958
SQ FT: 117,000
SALES (est): 74.16MM
SALES (corp-wide): 712.54MM **Publicly Held**
Web: www.ducommun.com
SIC: 3728 3769 5065 3812 Aircraft parts and equipment, nec; Space vehicle equipment, nec; Electronic parts and equipment, nec; Search and navigation equipment
PA: Ducommun Incorporated
200 Sandpointe Ave # 700
Santa Ana CA
657 335-3665

(P-2991)
IRISH INTERIORS INC (HQ)
Also Called: Lift By Encore
5511 Skylab Rd Ste 101 (92647-2071)
PHONE.....................949 559-0930
Thomas Mcfarland, Pr
Micheal Melancon, *
Karl Jonson, *
▲ **EMP:** 130 **EST:** 1972
SQ FT: 42,000
SALES (est): 81.25MM
SALES (corp-wide): 66.61B **Publicly Held**
Web: www.encoreaerospace.com
SIC: 3728 1799 Aircraft parts and equipment, nec; Renovation of aircraft interiors
PA: The Boeing Company
929 Long Bridge Dr
Arlington VA
703 414-6338

(P-2992)
PACIFIC CONTOURS CORPORATION
5340 E Hunter Ave (92807-2053)
PHONE.....................714 693-1260
Tom Rapacz, Pr
Tim Anderson, *
Jon Stannard, *
EMP: 60 **EST:** 1997
SQ FT: 36,000
SALES (est): 11.75MM **Privately Held**
Web: www.pacificcontours.com
SIC: 3728 5088 Aircraft assemblies, subassemblies, and parts, nec; Aircraft and parts, nec

(P-2993)
WOODWARD HRT INC
Also Called: Woodward Duarte
1700 Business Center Dr (91010-2859)
PHONE.....................626 359-9211
Don Grimes, Mgr
EMP: 250
SALES (corp-wide): 2.38B **Publicly Held**
SIC: 3728 5084 Aircraft parts and equipment, nec; Hydraulic systems equipment and supplies
HQ: Woodward Hrt, Inc.
25200 Rye Canyon Rd
Santa Clarita CA
661 294-6000

3731 Shipbuilding And Repairing

(P-2994)
LARSON AL BOAT SHOP
1046 S Seaside Ave (90731-7334)
PHONE.....................310 514-4100
Jack Wall, CEO
Gloria Wall, *
George Wall, *
▲ **EMP:** 70 **EST:** 1903

3751 - Motorcycles, Bicycles, And Parts (P-2995)

PRODUCTS & SERVICES SECTION

SQ FT: 65,000
SALES (est): 23.56MM **Privately Held**
Web: www.larsonboat.com
SIC: **3731** 4493 Military ships, building and repairing; Marinas

3751 Motorcycles, Bicycles, And Parts

(P-2995)
GLOBAL MOTORSPORT PARTS INC
15750 Vineyard Blvd Ste 100 (95037-7119)
PHONE..............................408 778-0500
Joseph F Keenan, *Ch Bd*
Seth Murdock, *CFO*
◆ EMP: 182 **EST**: 1998
SALES (est): 1.75MM **Privately Held**
Web: www.customchrome.com
SIC: **3751** 5013 Motorcycle accessories; Motorcycle parts
HQ: Dae-Il Usa, Inc.
    112 Robert Young Blvd
    Murray KY

(P-2996)
SPINERGY INC
1709 La Costa Meadows Dr (92078-5105)
PHONE..............................760 496-2121
Martin Connolly, *Pr*
▲ EMP: 80 **EST**: 1977
SQ FT: 63,000
SALES (est): 14.86MM **Privately Held**
Web: www.spinergy.com
SIC: **3751** 3949 7389 Bicycles and related parts; Exercise equipment; Design services

(P-2997)
V&H PERFORMANCE LLC
Also Called: Vance & Hines
13861 Rosecrans Ave (90670-5207)
PHONE..............................562 921-7461
Andrew Graves, *CEO*
Mike Kennedy, *
Terry Vance, *
Byron Hines, *Stockholder*
▼ EMP: 65 **EST**: 2010
SQ FT: 12,000
SALES (est): 31.63MM
SALES (corp-wide): 251.1MM **Privately Held**
Web: www.vanceandhines.com
SIC: **3751** 5013 Motorcycles, bicycles and parts; Motorcycle parts
PA: Motorsport Aftermarket Group, Inc.
    13861 Rosecrans Ave
    Santa Fe Springs CA
    917 838-4002

3761 Guided Missiles And Space Vehicles

(P-2998)
KRATOS DEF & SEC SOLUTIONS INC (PA)
Also Called: Kratos
10680 Treena St Ste 600 (92131-2440)
PHONE..............................858 812-7300
Eric Demarco, *Pr*
William Hoglund, *
Deanna Hom Lund, *
Marie Mendoza, *Sr VP*
Benjamin Goodwin, *Senior Vice President Corporate Development*
EMP: 166 **EST**: 1995
SALES (est): 898.3MM **Publicly Held**
Web: www.kratosdefense.com

SIC: **3761** 3663 7382 8711 Guided missiles and space vehicles; Microwave communication equipment; Security systems services; Engineering services

3799 Transportation Equipment, Nec

(P-2999)
DG PERFORMANCE SPC INC
4100 E La Palma Ave (92807-1818)
PHONE..............................714 961-8850
Mark W Dooley, *Pr*
William J Dooley, *
Joan K Dooley, *
EMP: 100 **EST**: 1972
SQ FT: 25,000
SALES (est): 8.68MM **Privately Held**
Web: www.dgperformance.com
SIC: **3799** 3751 5012 5961 Recreational vehicles; Motorcycles and related parts; Recreation vehicles, all-terrain; Fitness and sporting goods, mail order

3812 Search And Navigation Equipment

(P-3000)
AEROJET RCKETDYNE HOLDINGS INC (HQ)
222 N Pacific Coast Hwy Ste 500 (90245)
P.O. Box 537012 (95853-7012)
PHONE..............................310 252-8100
Ross Niebergall, *Pr*
Joseph Chontos, *VP*
EMP: 75 **EST**: 1915
SALES (est): 2.24B
SALES (corp-wide): 17.06B **Publicly Held**
Web: www.l3harris.com
SIC: **3812** 3764 3769 6552 Defense systems and equipment; Propulsion units for guided missiles and space vehicles; Space vehicle equipment, nec; Subdividers and developers, nec
PA: L3harris Technologies, Inc.
    1025 W Nasa Blvd
    Melbourne FL
    321 727-9100

(P-3001)
ASRC AEROSPACE CORP
Also Called: ASRC AEROSPACE CORP
Nasa Ames Research Center (94035)
PHONE..............................650 604-5946
Ted Price, *Mgr*
EMP: 348
SALES (corp-wide): 2.72B **Privately Held**
SIC: **3812** 7371 7373 5088 Search and navigation equipment; Custom computer programming services; Computer integrated systems design; Transportation equipment and supplies
HQ: Asrc Aerospace Corp.
    7000 Muirkirk Meadows Dr # 100
    Beltsville MD
    301 837-5500

(P-3002)
ATK SPACE SYSTEMS LLC
370 N Halstead St (91107-3122)
PHONE..............................626 351-0205
Joe Tellegrino, *Mgr*
EMP: 96
Web: www.northropgrumman.com
SIC: **3812** 3826 8711 Search and navigation equipment; Instruments measuring thermal properties; Engineering services
HQ: Atk Space Systems Llc

6033 Bandini Blvd
Commerce CA
323 722-0222

(P-3003)
CUBIC CORPORATION (HQ)
Also Called: Cubic
9233 Balboa Ave (92123-1513)
PHONE..............................858 277-6780
Stevan Slijepcevic, *Pr*
Anshooman Aga, *Ex VP*
Mark A Harrison, *CAO*
Grace G Lee, *Chief Human Resources Officer*
Hilary L Hageman, *Corporate Secretary*
EMP: 1243 **EST**: 1951
SQ FT: 265,000
SALES (est): 1.48B
SALES (corp-wide): 1.48B **Privately Held**
Web: www.cubic.com
SIC: **3812** 3699 7372 3724 Defense systems and equipment; Flight simulators (training aids), electronic; Application computer software; Aircraft engines and engine parts
PA: Atlas Cc Acquisition Corp.
    850 New Burton Rd Ste 201
    Dover DE
    858 277-6780

(P-3004)
EDO COMMUNICATIONS AND COUNTERMEASURES SYSTEMS INC
Also Called: Force Protection Systems
7821 Orion Ave (91406-2029)
PHONE..............................818 464-2475
EMP: 60
SIC: **3812** 3663 3612 7371 Search and navigation equipment; Radio and t.v. communications equipment; Signaling transformers, electric; Custom computer programming services

(P-3005)
MEGGITT (ORANGE COUNTY) INC
Also Called: Meggitt Aerospace
355 N Pastoria Ave (94085-4110)
PHONE..............................408 739-3533
Joseph Fragala, *Prin*
EMP: 68
SALES (corp-wide): 19.07B **Publicly Held**
Web: www.meggitt.com
SIC: **3812** 8731 3829 Search and navigation equipment; Commercial physical research; Measuring and controlling devices, nec
HQ: Meggitt (Orange County), Inc.
    4 Marconi
    Irvine CA

(P-3006)
NORTHROP GRUMMAN SYSTEMS CORP
Also Called: Northrop Grmman Def Mssion Sys
9326 Spectrum Center Blvd (92123-1443)
PHONE..............................410 765-5589
Steve Appel, *Brnch Mgr*
EMP: 1466
Web: www.northropgrumman.com
SIC: **3812** 7379 Search and navigation equipment; Computer related consulting services
HQ: Northrop Grumman Systems Corporation
    2980 Fairview Park Dr
    Falls Church VA
    703 280-2900

(P-3007)
NORTHROP GRUMMAN SYSTEMS CORP
15120 Innovation Dr (92128-3402)
PHONE..............................858 592-4518
Chris Willenborg, *Brnch Mgr*
EMP: 433
SQ FT: 211,000
Web: www.northropgrumman.com
SIC: **3812** 8711 7373 Search and navigation equipment; Engineering services; Computer integrated systems design
HQ: Northrop Grumman Systems Corporation
    2980 Fairview Park Dr
    Falls Church VA
    703 280-2900

(P-3008)
NORTHROP GRUMMAN SYSTEMS CORP
17066 Goldentop Rd (92127-2412)
PHONE..............................858 618-4349
Gerald Dufresne, *Mgr*
EMP: 223
Web: www.northropgrumman.com
SIC: **3812** 3761 7373 3721 Search and detection systems and instruments; Guided missiles, complete; Computer integrated systems design; Airplanes, fixed or rotary wing
HQ: Northrop Grumman Systems Corporation
    2980 Fairview Park Dr
    Falls Church VA
    703 280-2900

(P-3009)
RAYTHEON COMPANY
Also Called: Raytheon
1921 E Mariposa Ave (90245)
PHONE..............................310 647-1000
David Wajsgras, *Brnch Mgr*
EMP: 100
SALES (corp-wide): 67.07B **Publicly Held**
Web: www.rtx.com
SIC: **3812** 4899 Sonar systems and equipment; Satellite earth stations
HQ: Raytheon Company
    870 Winter St
    Waltham MA
    781 522-3000

(P-3010)
RAYTHEON COMPANY
Also Called: Raytheon
75 Coromar Dr (93117-3023)
PHONE..............................805 562-4611
EMP: 75
SALES (corp-wide): 67.07B **Publicly Held**
Web: www.rtx.com
SIC: **3812** 8731 3845 3825 Sonar systems and equipment; Commercial research laboratory; Electromedical equipment; Instruments to measure electricity
HQ: Raytheon Company
    870 Winter St
    Waltham MA
    781 522-3000

3821 Laboratory Apparatus And Furniture

(P-3011)
MINARIS MEDICAL AMERICA INC
630 Clyde Ct (94043-2239)
PHONE..............................800 233-6278

▲ = Import ▼ = Export
◆ = Import/Export

Takashi Miyamoto, *CEO*
Kazuyoshi Tsunoda, *
Keiichi Takeda, *
EMP: 190 **EST:** 1982
SQ FT: 31,000
SALES (est): 23.01MM **Privately Held**
Web: www.minarismedical.com
SIC: 3821 2835 8071 Laboratory measuring apparatus; In vitro diagnostics; Medical laboratories
HQ: Resonac Corporation
  1-9-1, Higashishimbashi
  Minato-Ku TKY

(P-3012)
TECAN SYSTEMS INC
Also Called: Tecan
  18635 Sutter Blvd (95037-2826)
PHONE..............................408 953-3100
David Martyr, *CEO*
Rudolf Eugster, *
Martin Brusdeilins, *
▲ **EMP:** 100 **EST:** 1972
SALES (est): 51.12MM **Privately Held**
Web: www.tecan.com
SIC: 3821 3829 3561 3494 Laboratory apparatus, except heating and measuring; Measuring and controlling devices, nec; Pumps and pumping equipment; Valves and pipe fittings, nec
HQ: Tecan U.S. Group, Inc.
  9401 Globe Center Dr # 140
  Morrisville NC
  919 361-5200

3822 Environmental Controls

(P-3013)
CHEVRON ENERGY SOLUTIONS LP
Also Called: Chevron Energy Solutions Co
  345 California St Fl 18 (94104-2650)
PHONE..............................415 894-4188
EMP: 300
SIC: 3822 6531 3823 3691 Energy cutoff controls, residential or commercial types; Buying agent, real estate; Process control instruments; Storage batteries

(P-3014)
NVENT THERMAL LLC (DH)
  899 Broadway St (94063-3104)
PHONE..............................650 474-7414
Brad Faulconer, *Pr*
◆ **EMP:** 300 **EST:** 2000
SQ FT: 65,000
SALES (est): 750MM **Privately Held**
Web: www.nvent.com
SIC: 3822 1711 Environmental controls; Heating and air conditioning contractors
HQ: Nvent Management Company
  1665 Utica Ave S Ste 700
  Saint Louis Park MN
  763 204-7700

(P-3015)
SIEMENS INDUSTRY INC
  7464 French Rd (95828-4600)
PHONE..............................916 681-3000
Oliver Hauck, *Brnch Mgr*
EMP: 200
SALES (corp-wide): 71.74B **Privately Held**
Web: new.siemens.com
SIC: 3822 5063 3669 1731 Air conditioning and refrigeration controls; Electric alarms and signaling equipment; Emergency alarms; Safety and security specialization
HQ: Siemens Industry, Inc.
  100 Technology Dr
  Alpharetta GA
  847 215-1000

3823 Process Control Instruments

(P-3016)
FUTEK ADVANCED SENSOR TECH INC
Also Called: Futek Advanced Sensor Tech
  10 Thomas (92618-2702)
PHONE..............................949 465-0900
Javad Mokhberi, *CEO*
Javad Mokhberi, *
▼ **EMP:** 140 **EST:** 1988
SQ FT: 23,000
SALES (est): 30MM **Privately Held**
Web: www.futek.com
SIC: 3823 8711 Process control instruments; Engineering services

(P-3017)
KEYSIGHT TECHNOLOGIES INC (PA)
  1400 Fountaingrove Pkwy (95403-1738)
  P.O. Box 4026 (95402-4026)
PHONE..............................800 829-4444
Satish C Dhanasekaran, *Pr*
Ronald S Nersesian, *.
Neil Dougherty, *Sr VP*
Ingrid Estrada, *PEOPLE*
Jeffrey Li, *Sr VP*
EMP: 960 **EST:** 1939
SALES (est): 5.42B
SALES (corp-wide): 5.42B **Publicly Held**
Web: www.keysight.com
SIC: 3823 3829 7629 Process control instruments; Measuring and controlling devices, nec; Electronic equipment repair

(P-3018)
MOORE INDUSTRIES-INTERNATIONAL INC (PA)
Also Called: Moore Industries
  16650 Schoenborn St (91343-6106)
PHONE..............................818 894-7111
▲ **EMP:** 200 **EST:** 1965
SALES (est): 39.36MM
SALES (corp-wide): 39.36MM **Privately Held**
Web: www.miinet.com
SIC: 3823 5084 Process control instruments; Industrial machinery and equipment

(P-3019)
ROHRBACK COSASCO SYSTEMS INC (DH)
  11841 Smith Ave (90670-3226)
PHONE..............................562 949-0123
Bryan Sanderlin, *CEO*
▼ **EMP:** 71 **EST:** 1977
SQ FT: 37,000
SALES (est): 17.49MM
SALES (corp-wide): 2.23B **Privately Held**
Web: www.cosasco.com
SIC: 3823 8742 Process control instruments; Industry specialist consultants
HQ: Halma Investment Holdings Limited
  Misbourne Court Rectory Way
  Amersham BUCKS

3824 Fluid Meters And Counting Devices

(P-3020)
BRITELAB INC
Also Called: Britex
  6341 San Ignacio Ave (95119-1202)
PHONE..............................650 961-0671
Robert De Neve, *CEO*
Paul Rogan, *
Saeed Seyed, *
Jae Jung, *CSO**
▲ **EMP:** 65 **EST:** 2007
SQ FT: 52,000
SALES (est): 14.42MM **Privately Held**
Web: www.britelab.com
SIC: 3824 8741 8742 Mechanical and electromechanical counters and devices; Management services; Management consulting services

(P-3021)
D & K ENGINEERING (PA)
Also Called: Decatur Electronics
  16990 Goldentop Rd (92127-2415)
PHONE..............................858 451-8999
Jeffrey Moss, *CEO*
Alex Kunczynski, *
Diane Law, *
Bill Suttner, *
Peter Ma, *VP*
▲ **EMP:** 105 **EST:** 2000
SQ FT: 60,000
SALES (est): 141.94MM **Privately Held**
Web: www.dkengineering.com
SIC: 3824 8711 Mechanical and electromechanical counters and devices; Acoustical engineering

(P-3022)
EXELIXIS INC
Division 1
  1851 Harbor Bay Pkwy (94502-3010)
PHONE..............................650 837-7000
Michael M Morrissey, *Pr*
EMP: 371
Web: www.exelixis.com
SIC: 3824 8731 Fluid meters and counting devices; Commercial physical research
PA: Exelixis, Inc.
  1851 Harbor Bay Pkwy
  Alameda CA

3825 Instruments To Measure Electricity

(P-3023)
ANRITSU US HOLDING INC (HQ)
Also Called: Anritsu Company
  490 Jarvis Dr (95037-2834)
PHONE..............................408 778-2000
Wade Hulon, *Pr*
▲ **EMP:** 500 **EST:** 1990
SQ FT: 244,000
SALES (est): 231.69MM **Privately Held**
SIC: 3825 3663 5065 Test equipment for electronic and electric measurement; Radio and t.v. communications equipment; Electronic parts and equipment, nec
PA: Anritsu Corporation
  5-1-1, Onna
  Atsugi KNG

(P-3024)
BAE SYSTEMS INFO ELCTRNIC SYST
Also Called: Bae Systems
  10920 Technology Pl (92127-1874)
PHONE..............................858 592-5000
Mark Gist, *Brnch Mgr*
EMP: 699
SALES (corp-wide): 25.59B **Privately Held**
Web: www.baesystems.com
SIC: 3825 7373 3812 Test equipment for electronic and electric measurement; Computer integrated systems design; Search and navigation equipment
HQ: Bae Systems Information And Electronic Systems Integration Inc.
  65 Spit Brook Rd
  Nashua NH
  603 885-4321

(P-3025)
BAE SYSTEMS NATIONAL SECURITY SOLUTIONS INC
  10920 Technology Pl (92127-1874)
  P.O. Box 509008 (92150-9008)
PHONE..............................858 592-5000
▲ **EMP:** 2200
SIC: 3825 7373 3812 Test equipment for electronic and electric measurement; Computer integrated systems design; Search and navigation equipment

(P-3026)
IXIA (HQ)
  26601 Agoura Rd (91302-1959)
PHONE..............................818 871-1800
Neil Dougherty, *Pr*
Jeffrey Li, *VP*
Jason Kary, *
Matthew S Alexander, *Corporate Secretary**
Stephen Williams, *
EMP: 275 **EST:** 1997
SQ FT: 116,000
SALES (est): 443.72MM
SALES (corp-wide): 5.42B **Publicly Held**
Web: www.keysight.com
SIC: 3825 7371 Network analyzers; Custom computer programming services
PA: Keysight Technologies, Inc.
  1400 Fountaingrove Pkwy
  Santa Rosa CA
  800 829-4444

(P-3027)
L3HARRIS INTERSTATE ELEC CORP
  3033 Science Park Rd (92121-1167)
PHONE..............................858 552-9500
Andrew Leuthe, *Prin*
EMP: 74
SALES (corp-wide): 17.06B **Publicly Held**
Web: www.l3harris.com
SIC: 3825 7379 5045 Test equipment for electronic and electric measurement; Computer related consulting services; Computer software
HQ: L3harris Interstate Electronics Corporation
  602 E Vermont Ave
  Anaheim CA
  714 758-0500

3826 Analytical Instruments

(P-3028)
AGILENT TECHNOLOGIES INC (PA)
Also Called: Agilent
  5301 Stevens Creek Blvd (95051-7201)
  P.O. Box 58059 (95052-8059)
PHONE..............................800 227-9770
Michael R Mcmullen, *Pr*
Koh Boon Hwee, *Non-Executive Chairman of the Board**
Padraig Mcdonnell, *CCO*
Robert W Mcmahon, *Sr VP*
Michael Tang, *Sr VP*
▲ **EMP:** 1657 **EST:** 1999
SALES (est): 6.85B
SALES (corp-wide): 6.85B **Publicly Held**
Web: www.agilent.com
SIC: 3826 7372 Analytical instruments; Prepackaged software

3826 - Analytical Instruments (P-3029)

(P-3029)
BRUKER CELLULAR ANALYSIS INC (HQ)
5858 Horton St Ste 320 (94608-2183)
PHONE................510 858-2855
Mark Munch, *Dir*
Gerald Herman, *Dir*
Brent Alldredge, *Dir*
EMP: 232 EST: 2011
SALES (est): 78.59MM
SALES (corp-wide): 2.53B **Publicly Held**
Web: www.berkeleylights.com
SIC: 3826 8733 Analytical instruments; Research institute
PA: Bruker Corporation
 40 Manning Rd
 Billerica MA
 978 663-3660

(P-3030)
HORIBA INSTRUMENTS INC (DH)
Also Called: Horiba Automotive Test Systems
9755 Research Dr (92618-4626)
PHONE................949 250-4811
Jai Hakhu, *Ch Bd*
▲ EMP: 195 EST: 1998
SQ FT: 80,000
SALES (est): 194.11MM **Privately Held**
Web: www.horiba.com
SIC: 3826 3829 3511 3825 Analytical instruments; Measuring and controlling devices, nec; Turbines and turbine generator sets; Instruments to measure electricity
HQ: Horiba Americas Holding Incorporated
 9755 Research Dr
 Irvine CA
 949 250-4811

(P-3031)
PASCO SCIENTIFIC (PA)
Also Called: Pasco Scientific
10101 Foothills Blvd (95747-7100)
PHONE................916 786-3800
◆ EMP: 155 EST: 1964
SALES (est): 27.33MM
SALES (corp-wide): 27.33MM **Privately Held**
Web: www.pasco.com
SIC: 3826 5049 3829 Analytical instruments; Scientific and engineering equipment and supplies; Measuring and controlling devices, nec

(P-3032)
QUEST DIAGNOSTICS NICHOLS INST (HQ)
Also Called: Quest Diagnostics
33608 Ortega Hwy (92675-2042)
PHONE................949 728-4000
Catherine T Doherty, *CEO*
Nicholas Conti, *
Timothy Sharpe, *
Dan Haemmerle, *
Mark Garawitz, *
EMP: 1000 EST: 1971
SQ FT: 240,000
SALES (est): 240.87MM
SALES (corp-wide): 9.88B **Publicly Held**
Web: www.questdiagnostics.com
SIC: 3826 8071 Analytical instruments; Testing laboratories
PA: Quest Diagnostics Incorporated
 500 Plaza Dr Ste G
 Secaucus NJ
 973 520-2700

(P-3033)
SEER INC (PA)
Also Called: Seer
3800 Bridge Pkwy Ste 102 (94065-1171)
PHONE................650 453-0000
Omid Farokhzad, *Ch Bd*
Omid Farokhzad, *Ch Bd*
David R Horn, *CFO*
Elona Kogan, *Corporate Secretary*
Scott D Thomas, *CCO*
EMP: 115 EST: 2017
SQ FT: 51,000
SALES (est): 15.49MM
SALES (corp-wide): 15.49MM **Publicly Held**
Web: www.seer.bio
SIC: 3826 8733 Analytical instruments; Medical research

(P-3034)
STANDARD BIOTOOLS INC (PA)
2 Tower Pl Ste 2000 (94080-1844)
PHONE................650 266-6000
Michael Egholm, *Pr*
Carlos V Paya, *
Hanjoon Alex Kim, *COO*
Bradley Kreger, *Senior Vice President Global Operations*
Nicholas Khadder, *Corporate Secretary*
EMP: 467 EST: 1999
SQ FT: 78,000
SALES (est): 97.95MM
SALES (corp-wide): 97.95MM **Publicly Held**
Web: www.standardbio.com
SIC: 3826 8731 Analytical instruments; Biotechnical research, commercial

3827 Optical Instruments And Lenses

(P-3035)
COHERENT AEROSPACE & DEF INC
14192 Chambers Rd (92780-6908)
PHONE................714 247-7100
Mark Maiberger, *Genl Mgr*
EMP: 60
SALES (corp-wide): 5.16B **Publicly Held**
Web: www.iiviad.com
SIC: 3827 7389 8748 Optical instruments and apparatus; Design services; Business consulting, nec
HQ: Coherent Aerospace & Defense, Inc.
 36570 Briggs Rd
 Murrieta CA
 951 926-2994

(P-3036)
GMTO CORPORATION
Also Called: Giant Mgllan Tlscope Orgnztion
300 N Lake Ave Fl 14 (91101-4164)
PHONE................626 204-0500
Robert Shelton, *Pr*
Alan Gordon, *
Amy Honbo, *
Doctor Robert N Shelton, *Pr*
Sara Lee Keller, *
▲ EMP: 70 EST: 2007
SALES (est): 8.77MM **Privately Held**
Web: www.giantmagellan.org
SIC: 3827 8733 Telescopes: elbow, panoramic, sighting, fire control, etc.; Noncommercial research organizations

(P-3037)
KLA CORPORATION (PA)
Also Called: KLA
1 Technology Dr (95035-7916)
PHONE................408 875-3000
Richard P Wallace, *Pr*
Bren D Higgins, *Ex VP*
Mary Beth Wilkinson, *CLO*
Brian Lorig, *Ex VP*
Virendra A Kirloskar, *CAO*
◆ EMP: 300 EST: 1975
SALES (est): 10.5B
SALES (corp-wide): 10.5B **Publicly Held**
Web: www.kla.com
SIC: 3827 3825 7699 7629 Optical instruments and lenses; Semiconductor test equipment; Optical instrument repair; Electronic equipment repair

(P-3038)
LIGHTWORKS OPTICS INC
14192 Chambers Rd (92780-6908)
PHONE................714 247-7100
EMP: 60
Web: www.iiviad.com
SIC: 3827 7389 8748 Optical instruments and apparatus; Design services; Business consulting, nec

3829 Measuring And Controlling Devices, Nec

(P-3039)
A D A C LABORATORIES (INC)
Also Called: Adac Medical Systems
3860 N 1st St (95134-1702)
PHONE................408 321-9100
▼ EMP: 732
SIC: 3829 3844 7373 3571 Medical diagnostic systems, nuclear; Radiographic X-ray apparatus and tubes; Turnkey vendors, computer systems; Computers, digital, analog or hybrid

(P-3040)
ALL WEATHER INC
Also Called: AWI
1065 National Dr Ste 1 (95834-1927)
PHONE................916 928-1000
Jason Hall, *Pr*
Bob Perrin, *
Adam Thomas, *
◆ EMP: 65 EST: 2000
SQ FT: 50,000
SALES (est): 20.17MM **Privately Held**
Web: www.allweatherinc.com
SIC: 3829 8999 3674 Weather tracking equipment; Weather related services; Radiation sensors

(P-3041)
APPLIED PHYSICS SYSTEMS INC (PA)
425 Clyde Ave (94043-2209)
PHONE................650 965-0500
William Goodman, *Pr*
Robert Goodman, *
Christine Goodman, *
EMP: 102 EST: 1978
SALES (est): 20.7MM
SALES (corp-wide): 20.7MM **Privately Held**
Web: www.appliedphysics.com
SIC: 3829 8711 Magnetometers; Consulting engineer

(P-3042)
APPLIED TECHNOLOGIES ASSOC INC (HQ)
Also Called: A T A
3025 Buena Vista Dr (93446-8555)
PHONE................805 239-9100
William B Wade, *Pr*
William B Wade, *Pr*
George Walker, *
▲ EMP: 127 EST: 1981
SALES (est): 32.25MM
SALES (corp-wide): 400.64MM **Privately Held**
Web: secure.scientificdrilling.com
SIC: 3829 1381 Surveying instruments and accessories; Drilling oil and gas wells
PA: Scientific Drilling International, Inc.
 16071 Grnspint Pk Dr Ste
 Houston TX
 281 443-3300

(P-3043)
OPTIVUS PROTON THERAPY INC
1475 Victoria Ct (92408-2831)
P.O. Box 608 (92354-0608)
PHONE................909 799-8300
Jon W Slater, *CEO*
Daryl L Anderson, *
EMP: 75 EST: 1992
SQ FT: 35,000
SALES (est): 15.85MM **Privately Held**
Web: www.optivus.com
SIC: 3829 7371 8742 3699 Nuclear radiation and testing apparatus; Custom computer programming services; Maintenance management consultant; Electrical equipment and supplies, nec

(P-3044)
TOPCON POSITIONING SYSTEMS INC (DH)
Also Called: Topcon
7400 National Dr (94550-7340)
PHONE................925 245-8300
Raymond O'connor, *Pr*
David Mudrick, *
M Yamazaki, *
James Orsino, *
◆ EMP: 122 EST: 1993
SQ FT: 80,000
SALES (est): 125.22MM **Privately Held**
Web: www.topconpositioning.com
SIC: 3829 3625 3823 3699 Surveying instruments and accessories; Relays and industrial controls; Process control instruments; Electrical equipment and supplies, nec
HQ: Topcon America Corporation
 111 Bauer Dr
 Oakland NJ
 201 599-5100

3841 Surgical And Medical Instruments

(P-3045)
ABBOTT LABORATORIES
Also Called: Abbott Vascular
3200 Lakeside Dr (95054-2807)
P.O. Box 58167 (95052-8167)
PHONE................408 845-3000
Jean Reyda, *Brnch Mgr*
EMP: 750
SALES (corp-wide): 43.65B **Publicly Held**
Web: www.abbott.com
SIC: 3841 8731 Surgical and medical instruments; Commercial physical research
PA: Abbott Laboratories
 100 Abbott Park Rd
 Abbott Park IL
 224 667-6100

PRODUCTS & SERVICES SECTION
3842 - Surgical Appliances And Supplies (P-3063)

(P-3046)
ACCRIVA DGNOSTICS HOLDINGS INC (DH)
Also Called: Itc Nexus Holding Company
6260 Sequence Dr (92121-4358)
PHONE.................................858 404-8203
Scott Cramer, *CEO*
Greg Tibbitts, *CFO*
Tom Whalen, *CSO*
EMP: 350 **EST:** 2010
SALES (est): 92.51MM **Privately Held**
Web: www.werfen.com
SIC: 3841 2835 6719 Diagnostic apparatus, medical; Blood derivative diagnostic agents; Investment holding companies, except banks
HQ: Instrumentation Laboratory Company
180 Hartwell Rd
Bedford MA

(P-3047)
ALCON VISION LLC
Also Called: Alcon Surgical
15800 Alton Pkwy (92618-3818)
P.O. Box 19587 (92623-9587)
PHONE.................................949 753-6488
Kenneth Lickel, *Mgr*
EMP: 600
SQ FT: 32,000
Web: www.alcon.com
SIC: 3841 3851 5049 Surgical and medical instruments; Ophthalmic goods; Optical goods
HQ: Alcon Vision, Llc
6201 South Fwy
Fort Worth TX
817 293-0450

(P-3048)
AMERICORE INC
Also Called: Americore
19705 August Ave (95324-9302)
P.O. Box 1353 (95324-1353)
PHONE.................................209 632-5679
Ryan Cunha, *Pr*
Ryan Marques Cunha, *
EMP: 60 **EST:** 2007
SALES (est): 5.92MM **Privately Held**
Web: www.americoremechanical.com
SIC: 3841 1796 3498 Diagnostic apparatus, medical; Millwright; Fabricated pipe and fittings

(P-3049)
BAXALTA US INC
1700 Rancho Conejo Blvd (91320-1424)
PHONE.................................805 498-8664
Paul Marshall, *Mgr*
EMP: 491
SIC: 3841 2835 2389 3842 Surgical and medical instruments; Blood derivative diagnostic agents; Hospital gowns; Surgical appliances and supplies
HQ: Baxalta Us Inc.
1200 Lakeside Dr
Bannockburn IL
224 948-2000

(P-3050)
CAREFUSION 207 INC
1100 Bird Center Dr (92262-8000)
PHONE.................................760 778-7200
Edward Borkowski, *CFO*
Carol Zilm, *INFUS & RESP**
Cathy Cooney, *
Neil Ryding, *GLOBAL MFG SUPPLY**
Joan Stafslien, *
▲ **EMP:** 327 **EST:** 2005
SALES (est): 55.32MM
SALES (corp-wide): 1.8B **Privately Held**
SIC: 3841 8741 Surgical and medical instruments; Nursing and personal care facility management
PA: Vyaire Holding Company
26125 N Riverwoods Blvd
Mettawa IL
872 757-0114

(P-3051)
EVOLVE MANUFACTURING TECH INC
47300 Bayside Pkwy (94538-6516)
PHONE.................................510 690-8959
Noreen King, *Pr*
Dave Devine, *
Douglas Fujii, *
Pete Pangelinan, *
James Han, *
▲ **EMP:** 65 **EST:** 1999
SQ FT: 45,000
SALES (est): 14.12MM **Privately Held**
Web: www.evolvemfg.com
SIC: 3841 3674 8731 Ultrasonic medical cleaning equipment; Semiconductors and related devices; Biotechnical research, commercial

(P-3052)
HEMODIALYSIS INC
Also Called: Hunnington Dialysis Center
806 S Fair Oaks Ave (91105-2601)
PHONE.................................626 792-0548
Susan Burkhart, *Mgr*
EMP: 75
SALES (corp-wide): 8.93MM **Privately Held**
Web: www.hemodialysis-inc.com
SIC: 3841 8011 Hemodialysis apparatus; Hematologist
PA: Hemodialysis, Inc.
710 W Wilson Ave
Glendale CA
818 500-8736

(P-3053)
INOGEN INC (PA)
301 Coromar Dr (93117-3286)
PHONE.................................805 562-0500
Nabil Shabshab, *Pr*
Elizabeth Mora, *
Alison Bauerlein, *Corporate Secretary*
George Parr, *CCO*
Jason M Somer, *Ex VP*
◆ **EMP:** 208 **EST:** 2001
SQ FT: 46,000
SALES (est): 377.24MM
SALES (corp-wide): 377.24MM **Publicly Held**
Web: www.inogen.com
SIC: 3841 3842 7352 Surgical and medical instruments; Surgical appliances and supplies; Medical equipment rental

(P-3054)
INTERFACE ASSOCIATES INC
Also Called: Interface Catheter Solutions
27721 La Paz Rd (92677-3948)
PHONE.................................949 448-7056
EMP: 175
Web: www.interfaceusa.com
SIC: 3841 5047 Surgical and medical instruments; Hospital equipment and furniture

(P-3055)
INVUITY INC
Also Called: Intelligent Photonics
444 De Haro St Ste 110 (94107-2350)
PHONE.................................415 665-2100
Kevin A Lobo, *Ch Bd*
James H Mackaness, *
▲ **EMP:** 172 **EST:** 2004
SQ FT: 38,135
SALES (est): 36.42MM
SALES (corp-wide): 18.45B **Publicly Held**
SIC: 3841 5047 Surgical instruments and apparatus; Surgical equipment and supplies
PA: Stryker Corporation
2825 Airview Blvd
Portage MI
269 385-2600

(P-3056)
KARL STORZ ENDSCPY-AMERICA INC (HQ)
2151 E Grand Ave (90245-5025)
PHONE.................................424 218-8100
Charles Wilhelm, *CEO*
Mark Green, *VP*
Sken Huang, *CFO*
Sonal Matai, *Mng Dir*
▲ **EMP:** 415 **EST:** 1971
SQ FT: 90,000
SALES (est): 280.88MM
SALES (corp-wide): 2.24B **Privately Held**
Web: www.karlstorz.com
SIC: 3841 5047 Surgical and medical instruments; Medical equipment and supplies
PA: Karl Storz Se & Co. Kg
Dr.-Karl-Storz-Str. 34
Tuttlingen BW
74617080

(P-3057)
MAHANA THERAPEUTICS INC (PA)
201 Mission St Ste 1200 (94105-1805)
PHONE.................................650 483-4720
Simon Levy, *CEO*
Myla Puyat, *
EMP: 76 **EST:** 2018
SALES (est): 13.29MM
SALES (corp-wide): 13.29MM **Privately Held**
Web: www.mahana.com
SIC: 3841 8082 7372 Surgical and medical instruments; Home health care services; Application computer software

(P-3058)
PRO-DEX INC (PA)
Also Called: Pro-Dex
2361 Mcgaw Ave (92614-5831)
PHONE.................................949 769-3200
Richard L Van Kirk, *Pr*
Nicholas J Swenson, *
Alisha K Charlton, *CFO*
EMP: 120 **EST:** 1978
SQ FT: 28,000
SALES (est): 46.09MM **Publicly Held**
Web: www.pro-dex.com
SIC: 3841 3843 7372 3594 Surgical and medical instruments; Dental equipment; Business oriented computer software; Motors, pneumatic

(P-3059)
RESMED INC (PA)
Also Called: Resmed
9001 Spectrum Center Blvd (92123-1438)
PHONE.................................858 836-5000
Michael Farrell, *CEO*
Peter C Farrell, *Non-Executive Chairman of the Board*
Rob Douglas, *Pr*
Brett Sandercock, *CFO*
David Pendarvis, *Global General Counsel*
EMP: 702 **EST:** 1989
SQ FT: 230,000
SALES (est): 4.22B **Publicly Held**
Web: www.resmed.com
SIC: 3841 7372 Diagnostic apparatus, medical; Application computer software

(P-3060)
THI INC
1525 E Edinger Ave (92705-4907)
PHONE.................................714 444-4643
Jim Willett, *CEO*
▲ **EMP:** 100 **EST:** 2000
SQ FT: 35,000
SALES (est): 21.72MM **Privately Held**
Web: www.tenacore.com
SIC: 3841 7699 Surgical instruments and apparatus; Surgical instrument repair

(P-3061)
VENUS CONCEPT INC
1800 Bering Dr (95112-4212)
PHONE.................................408 489-4925
Ryan Rhodes, *Pr*
EMP: 87
Web: www.venusconcept.com
SIC: 3841 5047 Surgical and medical instruments; Electro-medical equipment
HQ: Venus Concept Canada Corp
235 Yorkland Blvd Suite 900
Toronto ON
888 907-0115

3842 Surgical Appliances And Supplies

(P-3062)
ALPHATEC SPINE INC (HQ)
Also Called: Atec Spine
1950 Camino Vida Roble (92008-6505)
PHONE.................................760 431-9286
James M Corbett, *CEO*
Patrick Ryan, *
Thomas Mcleer, *Sr VP*
Ebun S Garner, *
Michael O'neill, *CFO*
▲ **EMP:** 250 **EST:** 1990
SALES (est): 93.43MM **Publicly Held**
Web: www.atecspine.com
SIC: 3842 8711 5047 Surgical appliances and supplies; Engineering services; Medical equipment and supplies
PA: Alphatec Holdings, Inc.
1950 Camino Vida Roble
Carlsbad CA

(P-3063)
BOSTON SCNTFIC NRMDLATION CORP (HQ)
25155 Rye Canyon Loop (91355-5004)
PHONE.................................661 949-4310
Michael F Mahoney, *CEO*
Kevin Ballinger, *
Wendy Carruthers, *
Supratim Bose, *
Jeffrey D Capello, *
▲ **EMP:** 450 **EST:** 1993
SQ FT: 26,000
SALES (est): 92.78MM
SALES (corp-wide): 12.68B **Publicly Held**
SIC: 3842 3841 5047 Hearing aids; Surgical and medical instruments; Medical and hospital equipment
PA: Boston Scientific Corporation
300 Boston Scientific Way
Marlborough MA
508 683-4000

3842 - Surgical Appliances And Supplies (P-3064)

(P-3064)
WEBER ORTHOPEDIC LP (PA)
Also Called: Hely & Weber Orthopedic
1185 E Main St (93060-2954)
P.O. Box 832 (93061-0832)
PHONE..................................800 221-5465
Jim Weber, *Pt*
Jim Weber, *Pr*
John P Hely, *
▲ **EMP:** 62 **EST:** 1982
SQ FT: 28,000
SALES (est): 9.25MM
SALES (corp-wide): 9.25MM Privately Held
Web: www.hely-weber.com
SIC: 3842 5047 Braces, orthopedic; Orthopedic equipment and supplies

(P-3065)
ZIMMER DENTAL INC
1900 Aston Ave (92008-7308)
PHONE..................................800 854-7019
EMP: 440 **EST:** 1981
SALES (est): 51.96MM
SALES (corp-wide): 6.94B Publicly Held
SIC: 3842 8021 3843 Implants, surgical; Offices and clinics of dentists; Dental equipment and supplies
HQ: Zimmer, Inc.
1800 W Center St
Warsaw IN
800 348-9500

3843 Dental Equipment And Supplies

(P-3066)
3M COMPANY
3M
2111 Mcgaw Ave (92614-0908)
PHONE..................................949 863-1360
David Goldinger, *Brnch Mgr*
EMP: 294
SQ FT: 77,656
SALES (corp-wide): 34.23B Publicly Held
Web: www.3m.com
SIC: 3843 5047 Dental equipment and supplies; Dental equipment and supplies
PA: 3m Company
3m Center
Saint Paul MN
651 733-1110

(P-3067)
BIEN AIR USA INC
Also Called: Bien Air
8861 Research Dr Ste 100 (92618-4255)
PHONE..................................949 477-6050
Arhur Mateen, *Pr*
Jean Claude Maeier, *
Arthur Mateen, *
EMP: 65 **EST:** 1959
SALES (est): 39.95MM Privately Held
Web: dental.bienair.com
SIC: 3843 7699 5047 Dental equipment; Dental instrument repair; Hospital equipment and furniture
HQ: Bien-Air Dental Sa
Langgasse 60
Biel-Bienne BE

(P-3068)
ORTHO ORGANIZERS INC
1822 Aston Ave (92008-7306)
PHONE..................................760 448-8600
David Parker, *Ch*
Russell J Bonafede, *
Robert Riley, *
Ted Dreifuss, *

Alison Weber, *
▲ **EMP:** 226 **EST:** 1975
SQ FT: 65,000
SALES (est): 33.76MM
SALES (corp-wide): 12.65B Publicly Held
Web: www.henryscheinortho.com
SIC: 3843 5047 Orthodontic appliances; Dental equipment and supplies
PA: Henry Schein, Inc.
135 Duryea Rd
Melville NY
631 843-5500

(P-3069)
SELANE PRODUCTS INC (PA)
Also Called: Sml Space Maintainers Labs
9129 Lurline Ave (91311-5922)
P.O. Box 2101 (91313-2101)
PHONE..................................818 998-7460
Rob Veis, *CEO*
▲ **EMP:** 60 **EST:** 1957
SQ FT: 12,000
SALES (est): 9.83MM
SALES (corp-wide): 9.83MM Privately Held
Web: www.smldent.com
SIC: 3843 8072 Orthodontic appliances; Dental laboratories

3844 X-ray Apparatus And Tubes

(P-3070)
CARL ZISS X-RAY MICROSCOPY INC
5300 Central Pkwy (94568-4999)
PHONE..................................925 701-3600
Bobby Blair, *CEO*
Peter Jackson, *
Timothy Hart, *
Jin Yoon, *
EMP: 66 **EST:** 2000
SALES (est): 23.26MM Privately Held
Web: www.team-dignitas.net
SIC: 3844 5047 X-ray apparatus and tubes; X-ray machines and tubes
HQ: Carl Zeiss Microscopy Gmbh
Carl-Zeiss-Promenade 10
Jena TH

3845 Electromedical Equipment

(P-3071)
AMPRONIX LLC
15 Whatney (92618-2808)
PHONE..................................949 273-8000
Burton Tripathi, *Managing Member*
◆ **EMP:** 62 **EST:** 1982
SQ FT: 58,000
SALES (est): 19.01MM Privately Held
Web: www.ampronix.com
SIC: 3845 5047 Electrotherapeutic apparatus; Diagnostic equipment, medical

(P-3072)
BIONESS INC
25103 Rye Canyon Loop (91355-5004)
PHONE..................................661 362-4850
Todd Cushman, *Pr*
Alfred E Mann, *Ch*
Jim Mchargue, *COO*
Dan Lutz, *Sr VP*
Perry Payne, *VP Opers*
▲ **EMP:** 190 **EST:** 2004
SQ FT: 29,000
SALES (est): 50.97MM
SALES (corp-wide): 512.12MM Publicly Held

Web: www.bionessrehab.com
SIC: 3845 5047 Transcutaneous electrical nerve stimulators (TENS); Medical and hospital equipment
PA: Bioventus Inc.
4721 Emperor Blvd Ste 100
Durham NC
919 474-6700

(P-3073)
CALA HEALTH INC
1800 Gateway Dr Ste 300 (94404-2467)
PHONE..................................415 890-3961
Renee Ryan, *CEO*
Kathryn Rosenbluth, *CSO**
EMP: 90 **EST:** 2013
SALES (est): 11.17MM Privately Held
Web: www.calahealth.com
SIC: 3845 7389 Transcutaneous electrical nerve stimulators (TENS); Business services, nec

(P-3074)
CAREFUSION CORPORATION (HQ)
Also Called: Bd Carefusion
3750 Torrey View Ct (92130-2622)
PHONE..................................858 617-2000
Thomas E Polen Junior, *Pr*
Christopher R Reidy, *
▲ **EMP:** 420 **EST:** 2009
SALES (est): 2.32B
SALES (corp-wide): 18.87B Publicly Held
Web: www.bd.com
SIC: 3845 8742 3841 Electromedical equipment; Hospital and health services consultant; Surgical instruments and apparatus
PA: Becton, Dickinson And Company
1 Becton Dr
Franklin Lakes NJ
201 847-6800

(P-3075)
EKO DEVICES INC
Also Called: Eko Devices
2100 Powell St Ste 300 (94608-1803)
PHONE..................................844 356-3384
Connor Landgraf, *CEO*
Adam Saltman, *Chief Medical Officer**
Tyler Crouch, *
EMP: 100 **EST:** 2013
SALES (est): 10.74MM Privately Held
Web: www.ekohealth.com
SIC: 3845 5047 3841 Electromedical equipment; Medical and hospital equipment; Diagnostic apparatus, medical

(P-3076)
HYPERBARIC TECHNOLOGIES INC
3224 Hoover Ave (91950-7224)
PHONE..................................619 336-2022
W T Gurnee, *Pr*
EMP: 80 **EST:** 1992
SQ FT: 15,000
SALES (est): 7.61MM Privately Held
SIC: 3845 3841 7352 3443 Electromedical equipment; Medical instruments and equipment, blood and bone work; Medical equipment rental; Fabricated plate work (boiler shop)

(P-3077)
SIEMENS MED SOLUTIONS USA INC
Also Called: Oncology Care Systems Group
4040 Nelson Ave (94520-1200)
PHONE..................................925 246-8200

Ajit Singh, *Pr*
EMP: 2460
SALES (corp-wide): 71.74B Privately Held
Web: new.siemens.com
SIC: 3845 3842 5047 Electromedical equipment; Surgical appliances and supplies; Hospital equipment and furniture
HQ: Siemens Medical Solutions Usa, Inc.
40 Liberty Blvd
Malvern PA
888 826-9702

(P-3078)
TOSHIBA AMERICA MRI INC
Also Called: Toshiba
280 Utah Ave Ste 200 (94080-6883)
PHONE..................................650 737-6686
▲ **EMP:** 190
SIC: 3845 8731 Magnetic resonance imaging device, nuclear; Commercial physical research

(P-3079)
VARIAN MEDICAL SYSTEMS INC (DH)
Also Called: Varian
3100 Hansen Way (94304-1030)
PHONE..................................650 493-4000
Christopher Toth, *CEO*
EMP: 1710 **EST:** 1948
SQ FT: 481,000
SALES (est): 3.42B
SALES (corp-wide): 71.74B Privately Held
Web: www.varian.com
SIC: 3845 7372 Electromedical equipment; Prepackaged software
HQ: Siemens Healthineers Ag
Siemensstr. 3
Forchheim BY
800 311-2244

3851 Ophthalmic Goods

(P-3080)
HOYA OPTICAL INC (PA)
1400 Carpenter Ln (95351-1102)
P.O. Box 580870 (95358-0016)
PHONE..................................209 579-7739
Fred Fink, *CEO*
EMP: 90 **EST:** 1954
SQ FT: 17,700
SALES (est): 4.55MM
SALES (corp-wide): 4.55MM Privately Held
Web: www.hoyavision.com
SIC: 3851 8011 5995 5048 Ophthalmic goods; Offices and clinics of medical doctors; Optical goods stores; Ophthalmic goods

(P-3081)
SPY INC (PA)
1896 Rutherford Rd (92008-7326)
PHONE..................................760 804-8420
Seth Hamot, *Interim Chief Executive Officer*
James Mcginty, *CFO*
Jim Sepanek, *Ex VP*
▲ **EMP:** 69 **EST:** 1994
SQ FT: 32,551
SALES (est): 13.91MM Privately Held
Web: www.spyoptic.com
SIC: 3851 5099 Glasses, sun or glare; Sunglasses

PRODUCTS & SERVICES SECTION

3861 Photographic Equipment And Supplies

(P-3082)
CAROLENSE ENTRMT GROUP LLC ✿
506 S Spring St (90013-3200)
PHONE.................................405 493-1120
Danesha Barber, *Managing Member*
EMP: 60 **EST:** 2022
SALES (est): 2.94MM **Privately Held**
SIC: 3861 7389 Film, sensitized motion picture, X-ray, still camera, etc.; Business Activities at Non-Commercial Site

(P-3083)
CHRISTIE DIGITAL SYSTEMS INC (HQ)
10550 Camden Dr (90630-4600)
PHONE.................................714 236-8610
Hideaki Onishi, *CEO*
Michael Phipps, *
EMP: 83 **EST:** 1999
SALES (est): 99.79MM **Privately Held**
Web: www.christiedigital.com
SIC: 3861 6719 Projectors, still or motion picture, silent or sound; Investment holding companies, except banks
PA: Ushio Inc.
 1-6-5, Marunouchi
 Chiyoda-Ku TKY

(P-3084)
GOPRO INC (PA)
Also Called: Gopro
3025 Clearview Way (94402-3709)
PHONE.................................650 332-7600
Nicholas Woodman, *Ch Bd*
Brian Mcgee, *Ex VP*
Eve Saltman, *CCO CLO*
Dean Jahnke, *Senior Vice President Global Sales*
Charles Lafrade, *CAO*
◆ **EMP:** 495 **EST:** 2004
SQ FT: 201,000
SALES (est): 1.09B
SALES (corp-wide): 1.09B **Publicly Held**
Web: www.gopro.com
SIC: 3861 7372 Cameras and related equipment; Prepackaged software

(P-3085)
MPO VIDEOTRONICS INC (PA)
5069 Maureen Ln (93021-7148)
PHONE.................................805 499-8513
Larry Kaiser, *Pr*
Julius Barron, *
Don Gaston, *
EMP: 75 **EST:** 1947
SALES (est): 9.6MM
SALES (corp-wide): 9.6MM **Privately Held**
Web: www.mpo-video.com
SIC: 3861 5065 7819 3823 Motion picture apparatus and equipment; Video equipment, electronic; Equipment rental, motion picture; Process control instruments

3911 Jewelry, Precious Metal

(P-3086)
AMINCO INTERNATIONAL USA INC
Also Called: California Premium Incentives
20571 Crescent Bay Dr (92630-8825)
PHONE.................................949 457-3261
Ann Wu, *Ex Dir*
William Wu, *
Ann Wu, *Treas*
▲ **EMP:** 62 **EST:** 1978
SQ FT: 35,000
SALES (est): 9.62MM **Privately Held**
Web: www.amincousa.com
SIC: 3911 5099 Jewelry, precious metal; Brass goods

3931 Musical Instruments

(P-3087)
RICO CORPORATION (HQ)
Also Called: Rico Products
8484 San Fernando Rd (91352-3227)
PHONE.................................818 394-2700
James D Addario, *CEO*
◆ **EMP:** 169 **EST:** 1928
SALES (est): 38.66MM
SALES (corp-wide): 169.13MM **Privately Held**
Web: www.daddario.com
SIC: 3931 5099 Reeds for musical instruments; Musical instruments
PA: D'addario & Company, Inc.
 595 Smith St
 Farmingdale NY
 631 439-3300

3942 Dolls And Stuffed Toys

(P-3088)
MOOSE TOYS LLC
Also Called: Moose
737 Campus Sq W (90245-2567)
PHONE.................................310 341-4642
Manny Stul, *Ch*
EMP: 95 **EST:** 2018
SALES (est): 24.17MM **Privately Held**
Web: www.moosetoys.com
SIC: 3942 3944 5092 7389 Dolls and stuffed toys; Electronic games and toys; Toys and hobby goods and supplies; Business Activities at Non-Commercial Site
HQ: Moose Toys Pty Ltd
 29 Grange Road
 Cheltenham VIC

(P-3089)
UPD INC
Also Called: United Pacific Designs
4507 S Maywood Ave (90058-2610)
PHONE.................................323 588-8711
Shahin Dardashty, *Pr*
Fred Dardashty, *
Ben Hooshim, *
◆ **EMP:** 60 **EST:** 1990
SQ FT: 140,000
SALES (est): 15.45MM **Privately Held**
Web: www.updinc.net
SIC: 3942 5112 3944 Dolls and stuffed toys; Pens and/or pencils; Puzzles

3944 Games, Toys, And Children's Vehicles

(P-3090)
HORIZON HOBBY LLC
4710 E Guasti Rd Ste A (91761-8121)
PHONE.................................909 390-9595
Yolanda Perry, *Brnch Mgr*
EMP: 67
SALES (corp-wide): 94.6MM **Privately Held**
Web: www.horizonhobby.com
SIC: 3944 5092 Automobile and truck models, toy and hobby; Hobby goods
PA: Horizon Hobby, Llc
 2904 Research Rd
 Champaign IL
 217 352-1913

3949 Sporting And Athletic Goods, Nec

(P-3091)
AMRON INTERNATIONAL INC (PA)
Also Called: Amron
1380 Aspen Way (92081-8349)
PHONE.................................760 208-6500
Debra L Ritchie, *CEO*
◆ **EMP:** 69 **EST:** 1979
SQ FT: 40,000
SALES (est): 10.62MM
SALES (corp-wide): 10.62MM **Privately Held**
Web: www.amronintl.com
SIC: 3949 5091 Skin diving equipment, scuba type; Diving equipment and supplies

(P-3092)
JOHNSON OUTDOORS INC
Scuba Pro
1166 Fesler St Ste A (92020-1813)
PHONE.................................619 402-1023
Joe Stella, *Brnch Mgr*
EMP: 114
SALES (corp-wide): 743.36MM **Publicly Held**
Web: www.johnsonoutdoors.com
SIC: 3949 5091 Skin diving equipment, scuba type; Diving equipment and supplies
PA: Johnson Outdoors Inc.
 555 Main St
 Racine WI
 262 631-6600

(P-3093)
ORCA ARMS LLC
Also Called: Orca Arms
9825 Carroll Centre Rd Ste 100 (92126)
PHONE.................................858 586-0503
Hamid R Ray Akhavan, *Managing Member*
Ardeshir Akhavan, *
▲ **EMP:** 68 **EST:** 2012
SQ FT: 5,500
SALES (est): 4.23MM **Privately Held**
Web: www.orcaarms.com
SIC: 3949 5099 Sporting and athletic goods, nec; Firearms and ammunition, except sporting

(P-3094)
ROSEN & ROSEN INDUSTRIES INC
Also Called: R & R Industries
204 Avenida Fabricante (92672-7538)
PHONE.................................949 361-9238
Richard Rosen, *Pr*
Daniel Rosen, *
▲ **EMP:** 80 **EST:** 1979
SQ FT: 22,500
SALES (est): 6.33MM **Privately Held**
Web: www.rrind.com
SIC: 3949 7389 Sporting and athletic goods, nec; Embroidery advertising

(P-3095)
STAR TRAC STRENGTH INC
Also Called: Star Trac Fitness
14410 Myford Rd (92606-1001)
Rural Route 300 (98662)
PHONE.................................714 669-1660
▲ **EMP:** 405
SIC: 3949 5091 Exercise equipment; Exercise equipment

(P-3096)
TOPGOLF CALLAWAY BRANDS CORP (PA)
2180 Rutherford Rd (92008-7328)
PHONE.................................760 931-1771
Oliver G Brewer Iii, *Pr*
John F Lundgren, *
Erik J Anderson, *
Rebecca Fine, *CPO*
Brian P Lynch, *CLO*
◆ **EMP:** 349 **EST:** 1982
SALES (est): 4B
SALES (corp-wide): 4B **Publicly Held**
Web: www.topgolfcallawaybrands.com
SIC: 3949 2329 2339 6794 Golf equipment; Men's and boys' sportswear and athletic clothing; Women's and misses' athletic clothing and sportswear; Patent buying, licensing, leasing

3955 Carbon Paper And Inked Ribbons

(P-3097)
ECMM SERVICES INC
1320 Valley Vista Dr # 204 (91765-3956)
PHONE.................................714 988-9388
Vincent Yang, *Pr*
Donald Sung, *
EMP: 250 **EST:** 2010
SALES (est): 23.4MM **Privately Held**
SIC: 3955 5045 Print cartridges for laser and other computer printers; Printers, computer
PA: Hon Hai Precision Industry Co., Ltd.
 No. 2, Ziyou St.
 New Taipei City TAP

(P-3098)
PLANET GREEN CARTRIDGES INC
Also Called: Planet Green
20724 Lassen St (91311-4507)
PHONE.................................818 725-2596
Sean Levi, *Pr*
Natalya Levi, *
◆ **EMP:** 84 **EST:** 2000
SQ FT: 29,699
SALES (est): 10.14MM **Privately Held**
Web: www.pginkjets.com
SIC: 3955 5093 Print cartridges for laser and other computer printers; Plastics scrap

3993 Signs And Advertising Specialties

(P-3099)
CALIFORNIA NEON PRODUCTS
Also Called: C N P Signs & Graphics
9944 Blossom Valley Rd (92021-2203)
PHONE.................................619 283-2191
Peter Mccarter, *CEO*
Robert Mccarter, *VP*
Richard Mccarter, *Sec*
EMP: 70 **EST:** 1939
SALES (est): 9.63MM **Privately Held**
Web: www.cnpsigns.com
SIC: 3993 1799 Electric signs; Sign installation and maintenance

(P-3100)
MARKETSHARE INC (PA)
2001 Tarob Ct (95035-6825)
PHONE.................................408 262-0677
Frederick Wilhelm, *CEO*
John Lovell, *
EMP: 65 **EST:** 1987
SQ FT: 16,000

3993 - Signs And Advertising Specialties (P-3101)

SALES (est): 11.84MM Privately Held
Web: www.marketshareonline.com
SIC: 3993 7312 Electric signs; Billboard advertising

(P-3101)
SIGNTECH ELECTRICAL ADVG INC
Also Called: Signtech
4444 Federal Blvd (92102-2505)
PHONE..................................619 527-6100
Harold E Schauer Junior, CEO
David E Schauer, *
Kimra Schauer, *
Art Navarro, *
Patty Soria, *
EMP: 120 EST: 1984
SQ FT: 25,000
SALES (est): 19.82MM Privately Held
Web: www.signtech.com
SIC: 3993 1799 Electric signs; Sign installation and maintenance

(P-3102)
SUPERIOR ELECTRICAL ADVG INC (PA)
1700 W Anaheim St (90813-1102)
PHONE..................................562 495-3808
Jim Sterk, CEO
Patti Skoglundadams, *
Doug Tokeshi, *
Stan Janocha, *
▲ EMP: 85 EST: 1962
SQ FT: 100,000
SALES (est): 15.72MM
SALES (corp-wide): 15.72MM Privately Held
Web: www.superiorsigns.com
SIC: 3993 7629 Electric signs; Electrical equipment repair services

(P-3103)
YOUNG ELECTRIC SIGN COMPANY
Also Called: Yesco
10235 Bellegrave Ave (91752-1919)
PHONE..................................909 923-7668
Duane Wardle, Brnch Mgr
EMP: 197
SQ FT: 8,500
SALES (corp-wide): 498.12MM Privately Held
Web: www.yesco.com
SIC: 3993 1799 Electric signs; Sign installation and maintenance
PA: Young Electric Sign Company Inc
2401 S Foothill Dr
Salt Lake City UT
801 464-4600

3996 Hard Surface Floor Coverings, Nec

(P-3104)
ALTRO USA INC
Also Called: Compass Flooring
12648 Clark St (90670-3950)
PHONE..................................562 944-8292
Al Boegh, Prin
EMP: 73
SALES (corp-wide): 194.81MM Privately Held
Web: www.altro.com
SIC: 3996 5023 Hard surface floor coverings, nec; Resilient floor coverings: tile or sheet
HQ: Altro Usa, Inc.
80 Industrial Way Ste 1
Wilmington MA
800 377-5597

3999 Manufacturing Industries, Nec

(P-3105)
BRITE INDUSTRIES INC
Also Called: Brite Labs
1746 13th St (94607-1510)
PHONE..................................510 250-9330
Brian Brown, CEO
EMP: 96 EST: 2017
SALES (est): 4.1MM Privately Held
SIC: 3999 5159

(P-3106)
DEVELOPLUS INC
1575 Magnolia Ave (92879-2073)
PHONE..................................951 738-8595
▲ EMP: 140 EST: 1990
SQ FT: 40,000
SALES (est): 32.67MM Privately Held
Web: www.developlus.com
SIC: 3999 5087 Hair and hair-based products ; Beauty parlor equipment and supplies

(P-3107)
HALONUS INC
6855 E Swarthmore Dr (92807-5118)
PHONE..................................714 345-0822
Steve Newhouse, CEO
EMP: 336 EST: 2018
SALES (est): 707.36K Privately Held
SIC: 3999 5099 5999 Fire extinguishers, portable; Fire extinguishers; Fire extinguishers
HQ: A-Gas Us Inc.
1100 Haskins Rd
Bowling Green OH
800 372-1301

(P-3108)
HOGAN MFG INC (PA)
1638 Main St (95320-1722)
P.O. Box 398 (95320-0398)
PHONE..................................209 838-7323
Mark Hogan, CEO
Joe Debiasio, *
Zach Hogan, *
Tyler Lucas, *
Bernice Hogan, *
▲ EMP: 150 EST: 1944
SQ FT: 43,000
SALES (est): 38.38MM
SALES (corp-wide): 38.38MM Privately Held
Web: www.hoganmfg.com
SIC: 3999 3441 3443 1791 Wheelchair lifts; Fabricated structural metal; Fabricated plate work (boiler shop); Structural steel erection

(P-3109)
LA SPAS INC
1325 N Blue Gum St (92806-1750)
PHONE..................................714 630-1150
▲ EMP: 130
Web: www.maaxspas.com
SIC: 3999 5091 Hot tubs; Fitness equipment and supplies

(P-3110)
MERCADO LATINO INC
Continental Candle Company
1420 W Walnut St (90220-5013)
PHONE..................................310 537-1062
EMP: 65
SALES (corp-wide): 87.08MM Privately Held
Web: www.continentalcandle.com
SIC: 3999 3641 7699 3645 Candles; Electric lamps; Restaurant equipment repair; Residential lighting fixtures
PA: Mercado Latino, Inc.
245 Baldwin Park Blvd
City Of Industry CA
626 333-6862

(P-3111)
PICNIC TIME INC
Also Called: Beach State
5131 Maureen Ln (93021-1783)
PHONE..................................805 529-7400
Gustavo Cosaro, CEO
◆ EMP: 77 EST: 1982
SQ FT: 20,000
SALES (est): 23.12MM Privately Held
Web: www.picnictime.com
SIC: 3999 5199 Handles, handbag and luggage; Bags, baskets, and cases

(P-3112)
SEGA HOLDINGS USA INC
9737 Lurline Ave (91311-4404)
PHONE..................................415 701-6000
◆ EMP: 1880
SIC: 3999 5045 Coin-operated amusement machines; Computers and accessories, personal and home entertainment

(P-3113)
TAG TOYS INC
1810 S Acacia Ave (90220-4927)
PHONE..................................310 639-4566
Lawrence Mestyanek, CEO
Judy Mestyanek, *
EMP: 65 EST: 1976
SQ FT: 60,000
SALES (est): 5.66MM Privately Held
Web: www.tagtoys.com
SIC: 3999 8351 3944 Education aids, devices and supplies; Child day care services; Games, toys, and children's vehicles

(P-3114)
ZOO MED LABORATORIES INC
3650 Sacramento Dr (93401-7113)
PHONE..................................805 542-9988
▲ EMP: 133 EST: 1977
SALES (est): 11.15MM Privately Held
Web: www.zoomed.com
SIC: 3999 5199 Pet supplies; Pets and pet supplies

4011 Railroads, Line-haul Operating

(P-3115)
CALIFRNIA HIGH SPEED RAIL AUTH
770 L St Ste 620 (95814-3313)
PHONE..................................916 324-1541
Dan Richard, Ch
EMP: 100 EST: 2010
SALES (est): 256.21K
SALES (corp-wide): 534.4MM Privately Held
Web: hsr.ca.gov
SIC: 4011 Railroads, line-haul operating
PA: State Of California
State Capital
Sacramento CA
916 445-2841

(P-3116)
LOS ANGELES JUNCTION RLWY CO
4433 Exchange Ave (90058-2622)
PHONE..................................323 277-2004
Chuck Potempa, CEO
Rob Rellyl, *
Rm Reilly, *
EMP: 103 EST: 1922
SALES (est): 5.84MM
SALES (corp-wide): 302.09B Publicly Held
SIC: 4011 Railroads, line-haul operating
HQ: Bnsf Railway Company
2650 Lou Menk Dr
Fort Worth TX
800 795-2673

(P-3117)
TRONA RAILWAY COMPANY
13068 Main St (93562-1911)
PHONE..................................760 372-2312
EMP: 590 EST: 1913
SQ FT: 30,000
SALES (est): 3.74MM Privately Held
SIC: 4011 Railroads, line-haul operating
HQ: Searles Valley Minerals Inc.
9401 Indian Creek Pkwy
Overland Park KS

(P-3118)
UNION PACIFIC RAILROAD COMPANY
Also Called: Union Pacific Lines
2401 E Sepulveda Blvd (90810-1945)
PHONE..................................562 490-7000
EMP: 300
SALES (corp-wide): 24.88B Publicly Held
Web: www.up.com
SIC: 4011 Railroads, line-haul operating
HQ: Union Pacific Railroad Company Inc
1400 Douglas St
Omaha NE
402 544-5000

4111 Local And Suburban Transit

(P-3119)
A-PARA TRANSIT CORP
Also Called: Yefllow Shttle Vtrans Sdan Svc
1400 Doolittle Dr (94577-2226)
PHONE..................................510 562-5500
Shiv D Kumar, Pr
EMP: 110 EST: 1992
SQ FT: 2,200
SALES (est): 24.64MM Privately Held
Web: www.aparatransit.com
SIC: 4111 Local and suburban transit

(P-3120)
ACCESS SERVICES
Also Called: ACCESS PARATRANSIT
3449 Santa Anita Ave (91731-2424)
P.O. Box 5728 (91734-1728)
PHONE..................................213 270-6000
Doran J Barnes, CEO
Shelly Verrinder, *
EMP: 80 EST: 1994
SALES (est): 176.28MM Privately Held
Web: www.accessla.org
SIC: 4111 Local and suburban transit

(P-3121)
AIRPORT CONNECTION INC
Also Called: Roadrunner Shuttle
95 Dawson Dr (93012-8001)
PHONE..................................805 389-8196
Sumaia Sandlin, CEO
Desmond P Sandlin, *
EMP: 180 EST: 1991
SQ FT: 3,500

PRODUCTS & SERVICES SECTION
4111 - Local And Suburban Transit (P-3143)

SALES (est): 18.98MM **Privately Held**
SIC: 4111 4119 Airport transportation; Limousine rental, with driver

(P-3122)
ALAMEDA-CONTRA COSTA TRNST DST (PA)
Also Called: AC Transit
1600 Franklin St (94612-2806)
P.O. Box 28507 (94604-8507)
PHONE..................510 891-4777
Michael Hursh, *Genl Mgr*
Kathleen Kelly, *Chief Brand Officer**
Nancy Skowbo, *General SERVICE Development**
Linda Nemeroff, *District Secretary**
Clarence Jhonson, *Media Affairs Manager**
▲ EMP: 250 EST: 1956
SQ FT: 100,000
SALES (est): 28.11MM
SALES (corp-wide): 28.11MM **Privately Held**
Web: www.actransit.org
SIC: 4111 Bus line operations

(P-3123)
BART
150 California St Ste 275 (94111-4538)
PHONE..................510 421-3768
EMP: 76 EST: 2018
SALES (est): 972.24K **Privately Held**
Web: www.bart.gov
SIC: 4111 Local and suburban transit

(P-3124)
BUTTE COUNTY ASSN GOVERNMENTS
326 Huss Dr Ste 150 (95928-8265)
PHONE..................530 809-4616
Jon Clark, *Ex Dir*
EMP: 65 EST: 2005
SQ FT: 42,100
SALES (est): 2.36MM **Privately Held**
Web: www.bcag.org
SIC: 4111 Local and suburban transit

(P-3125)
CALIFORNIA TRANSIT INC
1900 S Alameda St (90058-1014)
PHONE..................323 234-8750
Timmy Mardirossian, *Pr*
Eda Aghajanian, ***
Carol Story, ***
Sedik Mardirossian, ***
EMP: 76 EST: 2008
SALES (est): 4.81MM
SALES (corp-wide): 47.41MM **Privately Held**
SIC: 4111 Bus line operations
PA: San Gabriel Transit, Inc.
    3650 Rockwell Ave
    El Monte CA
    626 258-1310

(P-3126)
CITY OF FOLSOM
1300 Leidesdorff St (95630-2449)
PHONE..................916 355-8375
EMP: 112
SALES (corp-wide): 116.53MM **Privately Held**
Web: www.folsom.ca.us
SIC: 4111 Local and suburban transit
PA: City Of Folsom
    50 Natoma St
    Folsom CA
    916 355-7200

(P-3127)
CITY OF FRESNO
Fresno Area Express
2223 G St (93706-1631)
PHONE..................559 621-7433
Bruce Red, *Genl Mgr*
EMP: 460
SALES (corp-wide): 670.32MM **Privately Held**
Web: www.fresno.gov
SIC: 4111 Bus transportation
PA: City Of Fresno
    2600 Fresno St
    Fresno CA
    559 621-7001

(P-3128)
FIRST STUDENT INC
Also Called: Community Transit Services
4337 Rowland Ave (91731-1119)
PHONE..................626 448-9446
John Desmond, *Brnch Mgr*
EMP: 125
Web: www.firststudentinc.com
SIC: 4111 4119 Bus line operations; Local passenger transportation, nec
PA: First Student, Inc.
    600 Vine St Ste 1400
    Cincinnati OH

(P-3129)
FIRST TRANSIT INC
Also Called: First Group
1213 W Arbor Vitae St (90301-2903)
PHONE..................310 216-9584
EMP: 86
SALES (corp-wide): 4.23MM **Privately Held**
Web: www.transdevna.com
SIC: 4111 Local and suburban transit
HQ: First Transit, Inc.
    600 Vine St Ste 1400
    Cincinnati OH
    513 241-2200

(P-3130)
FIRST TRANSIT INC
9421 Feron Blvd Ste 101 (91730-4575)
PHONE..................909 948-3474
EMP: 72
SALES (corp-wide): 4.23MM **Privately Held**
Web: www.transdevna.com
SIC: 4111 Local and suburban transit
HQ: First Transit, Inc.
    600 Vine St Ste 1400
    Cincinnati OH
    513 241-2200

(P-3131)
FIRST TRANSIT INC
1717 E Via Burton (92806-1212)
PHONE..................714 644-9828
EMP: 72
SALES (corp-wide): 4.23MM **Privately Held**
Web: www.transdevna.com
SIC: 4111 Local and suburban transit
HQ: First Transit, Inc.
    600 Vine St Ste 1400
    Cincinnati OH
    513 241-2200

(P-3132)
FIRST TRANSIT INC
6671 Marine Way (92618-1724)
PHONE..................949 857-7211
EMP: 72
SALES (corp-wide): 4.23MM **Privately Held**
Web: www.transdevna.com
SIC: 4111 Local and suburban transit
HQ: First Transit, Inc.
    600 Vine St Ste 1400
    Cincinnati OH
    513 241-2200

(P-3133)
FIRST TRANSIT INC
Also Called: Laidlaw Transit Services
117 Fern St Ste 100 (95060-2155)
PHONE..................831 460-9911
Camilla Shaffer, *Mgr*
EMP: 115
SALES (corp-wide): 4.23MM **Privately Held**
Web: www.transdevna.com
SIC: 4111 Local and suburban transit
HQ: First Transit, Inc.
    600 Vine St Ste 1400
    Cincinnati OH
    513 241-2200

(P-3134)
FIRST TRANSIT INC
15730 S Figueroa St (90248-2429)
P.O. Box Figueroa (90248)
PHONE..................323 222-0010
John Britt, *Brnch Mgr*
EMP: 86
SALES (corp-wide): 4.23MM **Privately Held**
Web: www.transdevna.com
SIC: 4111 Local and suburban transit
HQ: First Transit, Inc.
    600 Vine St Ste 1400
    Cincinnati OH
    513 241-2200

(P-3135)
FIRST TRANSIT INC
4337 Rowland Ave (91731-1119)
PHONE..................626 307-7842
Kenneth Beard, *Mgr*
EMP: 72
SALES (corp-wide): 4.23MM **Privately Held**
Web: www.transdevna.com
SIC: 4111 Local and suburban transit
HQ: First Transit, Inc.
    600 Vine St Ste 1400
    Cincinnati OH
    513 241-2200

(P-3136)
FIRST TRANSIT INC
2047 Grogan Ave (95341-6440)
PHONE..................209 385-1226
Caryn Borba, *Brnch Mgr*
EMP: 86
SALES (corp-wide): 4.23MM **Privately Held**
Web: www.transdevna.com
SIC: 4111 Bus transportation
HQ: First Transit, Inc.
    600 Vine St Ste 1400
    Cincinnati OH
    513 241-2200

(P-3137)
FIRST TRANSIT INC
Also Called: Dispatch Office
407 High St (94601-3903)
PHONE..................510 437-8990
EMP: 129
SALES (corp-wide): 4.23MM **Privately Held**
Web: www.transdevna.com
SIC: 4111 Local and suburban transit
HQ: First Transit, Inc.
    600 Vine St Ste 1400
    Cincinnati OH
    513 241-2200

(P-3138)
FIRST TRANSIT INC
29 Prado Rd (93401-7314)
PHONE..................805 544-2730
Kim Blakeman, *Mgr*
EMP: 172
SALES (corp-wide): 4.23MM **Privately Held**
Web: www.transdevna.com
SIC: 4111 Bus transportation
HQ: First Transit, Inc.
    600 Vine St Ste 1400
    Cincinnati OH
    513 241-2200

(P-3139)
FORREST GROUP LLC (PA)
1422 N Curson Ave Apt 9 (90046-4037)
PHONE..................619 808-9798
Allen Forrest, *CEO*
EMP: 64 EST: 2016
SALES (est): 1.86MM
SALES (corp-wide): 1.86MM **Privately Held**
Web: www.tfgla.com
SIC: 4111 8742 7319 3532 Airport transportation; Food and beverage consultant; Display advertising service; Shuttle cars, underground

(P-3140)
GMJ AIR SHUTTLE LLC
5411 Luce Ave # 201 (95652-2447)
PHONE..................916 884-2001
Jerome Joondeph, *Managing Member*
EMP: 100 EST: 2012
SALES (est): 5.39MM **Privately Held**
Web: www.xojetaviation.com
SIC: 4111 Airport transportation

(P-3141)
GOLDEN EMPIRE TRANSIT DISTRICT (PA)
Also Called: Get-A-Lift Handicap Bus Trnsp
1830 Golden State Ave (93301-1012)
PHONE..................661 869-2438
Steven Woods, *CEO*
Karen King, ***
EMP: 232 EST: 1973
SALES (est): 49.74MM
SALES (corp-wide): 49.74MM **Privately Held**
Web: www.getbus.org
SIC: 4111 Bus line operations

(P-3142)
JEREMIAH PHILLIPS LLC
Also Called: Airline Coach Service
863 Malcolm Rd (94010-1406)
P.O. Box 4427 (94011-4427)
PHONE..................650 697-7733
Alex Morrison, *Managing Member*
Charles Morrison, ***
EMP: 99 EST: 2016
SQ FT: 10,000
SALES (est): 2.37MM **Privately Held**
SIC: 4111 Airport transportation

(P-3143)
KEOLIS TRANSIT AMERICA INC
14663 Keswick St (91405-1204)
PHONE..................818 616-5254
Steve Shaw, *Pr*
EMP: 175
SALES (corp-wide): 4.23MM **Privately Held**

4111 - Local And Suburban Transit (P-3144)

(P-3144)
KEOLIS TRANSIT AMERICA INC
Web: www.keolisna.com
SIC: 4111 Local and suburban transit
HQ: Keolis Transit America, Inc.
  53 State St Fl 11
  Boston MA

(P-3144)
KEOLIS TRANSIT AMERICA INC
660 W Avenue L (93534-7117)
PHONE..................661 341-3910
Steve Shaw, Pr
EMP: 90
SALES (corp-wide): 4.23MM Privately Held
Web: www.keolisna.com
SIC: 4111 Local and suburban transit
HQ: Keolis Transit America, Inc.
  53 State St Fl 11
  Boston MA

(P-3145)
KOTOBUKI-YA INC
Also Called: CPS
720 Woodside Way (94401-1610)
PHONE..................650 344-7955
Koichi Suyama, Pr
EMP: 70 EST: 1983
SALES (est): 2.45MM Privately Held
Web: www.kotobukiyausa.com
SIC: 4111 Airport transportation

(P-3146)
LONG BEACH PUBLIC TRNSP CO (PA)
Also Called: Long Beach Transit
1963 E Anaheim St (90813-3907)
PHONE..................562 599-8571
Kenneth A Mcdonald, CEO
Kenneth A Mcdonald, CEO
Laurence W Jackson, *
EMP: 570 EST: 1963
SQ FT: 10,000
SALES (est): 57.81MM
SALES (corp-wide): 57.81MM Privately Held
Web: www.ridelbt.com
SIC: 4111 Local and suburban transit

(P-3147)
LONG BEACH PUBLIC TRNSP CO
1300 Gardenia Ave (90804-3220)
PHONE..................562 591-2301
Laurence Jackson, Brnch Mgr
EMP: 80
SALES (corp-wide): 57.81MM Privately Held
Web: www.ridelbt.com
SIC: 4111 Bus line operations
PA: Long Beach Public Transportation Co Inc
  1963 E Anaheim St
  Long Beach CA
  562 599-8571

(P-3148)
LOS ANGLES CNTY MTRO TRNSP AUT
Also Called: Green Line Rail Eqp Maint
14724 Aviation Blvd (90260-1122)
PHONE..................310 643-3804
Ed Smith, Mgr
EMP: 354
SALES (corp-wide): 628.29MM Privately Held
Web: www.metro.net
SIC: 4111 Local and suburban transit
PA: Los Angeles County Metropolitan Transportation Authority
  1 Gateway Plz Fl 25
  Los Angeles CA
  323 466-3876

(P-3149)
LOS ANGLES CNTY MTRO TRNSP AUT (PA)
Also Called: Metro
1 Gateway Plz Fl 25 (90012-3745)
P.O. Box 512296 (90051-0296)
PHONE..................323 466-3876
Stephanie Wiggins, CEO
Rick Thorpe, CEO
Nalini Ahuja, Dir
Brian Boudreau, Ex Dir
Greg Kildare, Ex Dir
EMP: 900 EST: 1964
SALES (est): 628.29MM
SALES (corp-wide): 628.29MM Privately Held
Web: www.metro.net
SIC: 4111 Local and suburban transit

(P-3150)
LOS ANGLES CNTY MTRO TRNSP AUT
Also Called: Lacmta
470 Bauchet St (90012-2907)
PHONE..................213 922-5012
Jim Montoya, Brnch Mgr
EMP: 2132
SALES (corp-wide): 628.29MM Privately Held
Web: www.metro.net
SIC: 4111 Bus transportation
PA: Los Angeles County Metropolitan Transportation Authority
  1 Gateway Plz Fl 25
  Los Angeles CA
  323 466-3876

(P-3151)
LOS ANGLES CNTY MTRO TRNSP AUT
Also Called: Division 7
100 Sunset Ave (90291-2517)
PHONE..................310 392-8636
John Adams, Mgr
EMP: 533
SALES (corp-wide): 628.29MM Privately Held
Web: www.metro.net
SIC: 4111 Bus transportation
PA: Los Angeles County Metropolitan Transportation Authority
  1 Gateway Plz Fl 25
  Los Angeles CA
  323 466-3876

(P-3152)
LOS ANGLES CNTY MTRO TRNSP AUT
9201 Canoga Ave (91311-5839)
PHONE..................213 922-6308
Pat Orr, Mgr
EMP: 711
SALES (corp-wide): 628.29MM Privately Held
Web: www.metro.net
SIC: 4111 Bus line operations
PA: Los Angeles County Metropolitan Transportation Authority
  1 Gateway Plz Fl 25
  Los Angeles CA
  323 466-3876

(P-3153)
LOS ANGLES CNTY MTRO TRNSP AUT
900 Lyon St (90012-2913)
PHONE..................213 922-5887
John Drayton, Mgr
EMP: 533
SALES (corp-wide): 628.29MM Privately Held
Web: www.metro.net
SIC: 4111 Bus line operations
PA: Los Angeles County Metropolitan Transportation Authority
  1 Gateway Plz Fl 25
  Los Angeles CA
  323 466-3876

(P-3154)
LOS ANGLES CNTY MTRO TRNSP AUT
Also Called: Division 1
1130 E 6th St (90021-1108)
PHONE..................213 922-6301
Ron Reedy, Brnch Mgr
EMP: 355
SALES (corp-wide): 628.29MM Privately Held
Web: www.metro.net
SIC: 4111 Bus line operations
PA: Los Angeles County Metropolitan Transportation Authority
  1 Gateway Plz Fl 25
  Los Angeles CA
  323 466-3876

(P-3155)
LOS ANGLES CNTY MTRO TRNSP AUT
630 W Avenue 28 (90065-1502)
PHONE..................213 922-6203
Cheryl Brown, Mgr
EMP: 355
SALES (corp-wide): 628.29MM Privately Held
Web: www.metro.net
SIC: 4111 Bus line operations
PA: Los Angeles County Metropolitan Transportation Authority
  1 Gateway Plz Fl 25
  Los Angeles CA
  323 466-3876

(P-3156)
LOS ANGLES CNTY MTRO TRNSP AUT
1 Gateway Plaza Dr (90012-3745)
PHONE..................213 922-6202
Maria Japardi, Brnch Mgr
EMP: 533
SALES (corp-wide): 628.29MM Privately Held
Web: www.metro.net
SIC: 4111 Bus line operations
PA: Los Angeles County Metropolitan Transportation Authority
  1 Gateway Plz Fl 25
  Los Angeles CA
  323 466-3876

(P-3157)
LOS ANGLES CNTY MTRO TRNSP AUT
8800 Santa Monica Blvd (90069-4536)
PHONE..................213 922-6207
Grant Myers, Mgr
EMP: 711
SALES (corp-wide): 628.29MM Privately Held
Web: www.metro.net
SIC: 4111 Bus line operations
PA: Los Angeles County Metropolitan Transportation Authority
  1 Gateway Plz Fl 25
  Los Angeles CA
  323 466-3876

(P-3158)
LOS ANGLES CNTY MTRO TRNSP AUT
Also Called: Metro
11900 Branford St (91352-1003)
PHONE..................213 922-6215
Gary Stivack, Mgr
EMP: 888
SALES (corp-wide): 628.29MM Privately Held
Web: www.metro.net
SIC: 4111 Bus line operations
PA: Los Angeles County Metropolitan Transportation Authority
  1 Gateway Plz Fl 25
  Los Angeles CA
  323 466-3876

(P-3159)
LOS ANGLES CNTY MTRO TRNSP AUT
Also Called: Metro
720 E 15th St (90021-2122)
PHONE..................213 533-1506
Carla Aleman, Brnch Mgr
EMP: 533
SALES (corp-wide): 628.29MM Privately Held
Web: www.metro.net
SIC: 4111 Bus line operations
PA: Los Angeles County Metropolitan Transportation Authority
  1 Gateway Plz Fl 25
  Los Angeles CA
  323 466-3876

(P-3160)
LOS ANGLES CNTY MTRO TRNSP AUT
Also Called: Office of Inspector General
818 W 7th St Ste 500 (90017-3463)
PHONE..................213 244-6783
Arthur Sinai, Mgr
EMP: 533
SALES (corp-wide): 628.29MM Privately Held
Web: www.metro.net
SIC: 4111 Bus line operations
PA: Los Angeles County Metropolitan Transportation Authority
  1 Gateway Plz Fl 25
  Los Angeles CA
  323 466-3876

(P-3161)
LOS ANGLES CNTY MTRO TRNSP AUT
320 S Santa Fe Ave (90013-1812)
P.O. Box 194 (90078-0194)
PHONE..................213 626-4455
EMP: 711
SALES (corp-wide): 628.29MM Privately Held
Web: www.metro.net
SIC: 4111 Bus line operations
PA: Los Angeles County Metropolitan Transportation Authority
  1 Gateway Plz Fl 25
  Los Angeles CA
  323 466-3876

(P-3162)
METROPOLITAN TRNSP COMM (PA)
Also Called: M T C
375 Beale St Ste 800 (94105-2001)

PRODUCTS & SERVICES SECTION
4111 - Local And Suburban Transit (P-3185)

PHONE.................................415 778-6700
Steve Hieminger, *Ex Dir*
Jake Mackenzie, *
Therese Mcmillan, *POLICY*
Ann Flemer, *Department Executive Director**
Brian Mayhew, *
EMP: 103 **EST:** 1970
SQ FT: 21,000
SALES (est): 193.14MM
SALES (corp-wide): 193.14MM **Privately Held**
Web: mtc.ca.gov
SIC: 4111 Bus line operations

(P-3163)
MV TRANSPORTATION INC
13690 Vaughn St (91340-3017)
PHONE.................................323 666-0856
EMP: 239
SALES (corp-wide): 1.31B **Privately Held**
Web: www.mvtransit.com
SIC: 4111 Local and suburban transit
PA: Mv Transportation, Inc.
2711 N Haskell Ave # 150
Dallas TX
972 391-4600

(P-3164)
MV TRANSPORTATION INC
1944 Williams St (94577-2304)
PHONE.................................510 351-1603
Jay Jeter, *Brnch Mgr*
EMP: 171
SALES (corp-wide): 1.31B **Privately Held**
Web: www.mvtransit.com
SIC: 4111 Local and suburban transit
PA: Mv Transportation, Inc.
2711 N Haskell Ave # 150
Dallas TX
972 391-4600

(P-3165)
MV TRANSPORTATION INC
1242 Los Angeles St (91204-2404)
PHONE.................................818 409-3387
Jesse Saavedra, *Brnch Mgr*
EMP: 238
SALES (corp-wide): 1.31B **Privately Held**
Web: www.mvtransit.com
SIC: 4111 Local and suburban transit
PA: Mv Transportation, Inc.
2711 N Haskell Ave # 150
Dallas TX
972 391-4600

(P-3166)
MV TRANSPORTATION INC
1250 S Wilson Way Ste A1 (95205-7026)
PHONE.................................209 547-7879
Nick Harbut, *Brnch Mgr*
EMP: 238
SALES (corp-wide): 1.31B **Privately Held**
Web: www.mvtransit.com
SIC: 4111 Local and suburban transit
PA: Mv Transportation, Inc.
2711 N Haskell Ave # 150
Dallas TX
972 391-4600

(P-3167)
MV TRANSPORTATION INC
24 S Sacramento St (95240-2150)
PHONE.................................209 339-1972
Elizabeth Davidiaz, *Brnch Mgr*
EMP: 198
SALES (corp-wide): 1.31B **Privately Held**
Web: www.mvtransit.com
SIC: 4111 Local and suburban transit
PA: Mv Transportation, Inc.
2711 N Haskell Ave # 150
Dallas TX
972 391-4600

(P-3168)
MV TRANSPORTATION INC
Also Called: Mv Transit
34650 7th St (94587-3693)
PHONE.................................510 441-0698
David Brophy, *Brnch Mgr*
EMP: 238
SALES (corp-wide): 1.31B **Privately Held**
Web: www.mvtransit.com
SIC: 4111 Local and suburban transit
PA: Mv Transportation, Inc.
2711 N Haskell Ave # 150
Dallas TX
972 391-4600

(P-3169)
MV TRANSPORTATION INC
15677 Phoebe Ave (90638-5214)
PHONE.................................562 943-6776
EMP: 238
SALES (corp-wide): 1.31B **Privately Held**
Web: www.mvtransit.com
SIC: 4111 Local and suburban transit
PA: Mv Transportation, Inc.
2711 N Haskell Ave # 150
Dallas TX
972 391-4600

(P-3170)
MV TRANSPORTATION INC
501 Giuseppe Ct Ste F (95678-6310)
PHONE.................................916 788-3000
Elizabeth Thrasher, *Brnch Mgr*
EMP: 238
SALES (corp-wide): 1.31B **Privately Held**
Web: www.mvtransit.com
SIC: 4111 Local and suburban transit
PA: Mv Transportation, Inc.
2711 N Haskell Ave # 150
Dallas TX
972 391-4600

(P-3171)
MV TRANSPORTATION INC
265 S Rancho Rd (91361-5222)
PHONE.................................805 557-7372
Cheryl Seafert, *Brnch Mgr*
EMP: 198
SALES (corp-wide): 1.31B **Privately Held**
Web: www.mvtransit.com
SIC: 4111 Local and suburban transit
PA: Mv Transportation, Inc.
2711 N Haskell Ave # 150
Dallas TX
972 391-4600

(P-3172)
MV TRANSPORTATION INC
5420 W Jefferson Blvd (90016-3716)
PHONE.................................323 936-9783
EMP: 238
SALES (corp-wide): 1.31B **Privately Held**
Web: www.mvtransit.com
SIC: 4111 Local and suburban transit
PA: Mv Transportation, Inc.
2711 N Haskell Ave # 150
Dallas TX
972 391-4600

(P-3173)
MV TRANSPORTATION INC
Also Called: Mv Transportation
670 Lawrence Dr (91320-2205)
PHONE.................................805 375-5467
EMP: 198
SALES (corp-wide): 1.31B **Privately Held**
Web: www.mvtransit.com

(P-3174)
MV TRANSPORTATION INC
14011 S Central Ave (90059-3622)
PHONE.................................310 638-0556
EMP: 277
SALES (corp-wide): 1.31B **Privately Held**
Web: www.mvtransit.com
SIC: 4111 Local and suburban transit
PA: Mv Transportation, Inc.
2711 N Haskell Ave # 150
Dallas TX
972 391-4600

(P-3175)
MV TRANSPORTATION INC
303 Via Del Norte (92058-1231)
PHONE.................................760 400-0300
EMP: 238
SALES (corp-wide): 1.31B **Privately Held**
Web: www.mvtransit.com
SIC: 4111 Local and suburban transit
PA: Mv Transportation, Inc.
2711 N Haskell Ave # 150
Dallas TX
972 391-4600

(P-3176)
MV TRANSPORTATION INC
755 Norlak Ave (92025-2514)
PHONE.................................760 520-0118
EMP: 198
SALES (corp-wide): 1.31B **Privately Held**
Web: www.mvtransit.com
SIC: 4111 Local and suburban transit
PA: Mv Transportation, Inc.
2711 N Haskell Ave # 150
Dallas TX
972 391-4600

(P-3177)
MV TRANSPORTATION INC
16738 Stagg St (91406-1635)
PHONE.................................818 374-9145
Judy Smith, *Mgr*
EMP: 277
SALES (corp-wide): 1.31B **Privately Held**
Web: www.mvtransit.com
SIC: 4111 Local and suburban transit
PA: Mv Transportation, Inc.
2711 N Haskell Ave # 150
Dallas TX
972 391-4600

(P-3178)
MV TRANSPORTATION INC
3550 3rd St (94124-1404)
PHONE.................................415 206-7386
Tim Dumandan, *Mgr*
EMP: 277
SALES (corp-wide): 1.31B **Privately Held**
Web: www.mvtransit.com
SIC: 4111 Local and suburban transit
PA: Mv Transportation, Inc.
2711 N Haskell Ave # 150
Dallas TX
972 391-4600

(P-3179)
MV TRANSPORTATION INC
1612 State St (92311-4107)
PHONE.................................760 255-3330
Tom Conlon, *Mgr*
EMP: 238
SALES (corp-wide): 1.31B **Privately Held**

(P-3180)
MV TRANSPORTATION INC
7231 Rosecrans Ave (90723-2501)
PHONE.................................562 259-9911
EMP: 75
SALES (corp-wide): 1.31B **Privately Held**
Web: www.mvtransit.com
SIC: 4111 Local and suburban transit
PA: Mv Transportation, Inc.
2711 N Haskell Ave # 150
Dallas TX
972 391-4600

(P-3181)
MV TRANSPORTATION INC
10170 Croydon Way Ste A (95827-2104)
PHONE.................................916 854-2638
Roberta Collins, *Mgr*
EMP: 277
SALES (corp-wide): 1.31B **Privately Held**
Web: www.mvtransit.com
SIC: 4111 Local and suburban transit
PA: Mv Transportation, Inc.
2711 N Haskell Ave # 150
Dallas TX
972 391-4600

(P-3182)
MV TRANSPORTATION INC
3250 Dutton Ave (95407-7866)
PHONE.................................707 546-1999
EMP: 238
SALES (corp-wide): 1.31B **Privately Held**
Web: www.mvtransit.com
SIC: 4111 Local and suburban transit
PA: Mv Transportation, Inc.
2711 N Haskell Ave # 150
Dallas TX
972 391-4600

(P-3183)
NORTH COUNTY TRANSIT DISTRICT (PA)
Also Called: Nctd
810 Mission Ave (92054-2825)
PHONE.................................760 966-6500
Matt Tucker, *Ex Dir*
EMP: 60 **EST:** 1976
SQ FT: 7,000
SALES (est): 29.54MM
SALES (corp-wide): 29.54MM **Privately Held**
Web: www.gonctd.com
SIC: 4111 Bus transportation

(P-3184)
OMNITRANS (PA)
1700 W 5th St (92411-2499)
PHONE.................................909 379-7100
TOLL FREE: 800
EMP: 212 **EST:** 1976
SALES (est): 8.48MM
SALES (corp-wide): 8.48MM **Privately Held**
Web: www.omnitrans.org
SIC: 4111 Bus line operations

(P-3185)
OMNITRANS
4748 Arrow Hwy (91763-1208)
PHONE.................................909 379-7100
John Steffon, *Brnch Mgr*
EMP: 219

4111 - Local And Suburban Transit (P-3186)

SALES (corp-wide): 8.48MM Privately Held
Web: www.omnitrans.org
SIC: 4111 Bus line operations
PA: Omnitrans
1700 W 5th St
San Bernardino CA
909 379-7100

(P-3186)
ORANGE CNTY TRNSP AUTH SCHLRSH
11790 Cardinal Cir (92843-3839)
P.O. Box 14184 (92863-1584)
PHONE.................714 560-6282
Arthur Leahy, CEO
EMP: 83
SALES (corp-wide): 761.4MM Privately Held
Web: www.octa.net
SIC: 4111 Bus line operations
PA: Orange County Transportation Authority Scholarship Foundation, Inc.
550 S Main St
Orange CA
714 636-7433

(P-3187)
ORANGE CNTY TRNSP AUTH SCHLRSH (PA)
Also Called: Orange County Trnsp Auth
550 S Main St (92868-4506)
P.O. Box 14184 (92863-1584)
PHONE.................714 636-7433
Darrell Johnson, CEO
Don Hansen, *
John Dunning Junior, COO
Amy Wu, *
EMP: 350 EST: 1972
SQ FT: 77,000
SALES (est): 761.4MM
SALES (corp-wide): 761.4MM Privately Held
Web: www.octa.net
SIC: 4111 8711 Bus line operations; Construction and civil engineering

(P-3188)
ORANGE CNTY TRNSP AUTH SCHLRSH
Also Called: Octa
600 S Main St Ste 910 (92868-4689)
PHONE.................714 999-1726
EMP: 600
SALES (corp-wide): 761.4MM Privately Held
Web: www.octa.net
SIC: 4111 Bus line operations
PA: Orange County Transportation Authority Scholarship Foundation, Inc.
550 S Main St
Orange CA
714 636-7433

(P-3189)
PENINSULA CRRDOR JINT PWERS BD
Also Called: CALTRAIN
1250 San Carlos Ave (94070-2468)
P.O. Box 3006 (94070-1306)
PHONE.................650 508-6200
Michael J Scanlon, Ex Dir
Virginia Harrington, *
Chuck Harvey, *
Jose Cisneros, *
Malia Cohen, *
EMP: 105 EST: 1995
SALES (est): 37.69MM Privately Held
Web: www.caltrain.com

SIC: 4111 Local railway passenger operation

(P-3190)
PRIVATE SUITE LAX LLC
Also Called: PS
6871 W Imperial Hwy (90045-6311)
PHONE.................310 907-9950
Joshua Gausman, Managing Member
Amina Belouizdad, Managing Member*
Jordi Mena, *
EMP: 140 EST: 2017
SQ FT: 57,590
SALES (est): 22MM Privately Held
Web: www.reserveps.com
SIC: 4111 Airport transportation

(P-3191)
REDDING AERO ENTERPRISES INC
Also Called: Redding Jet Center
3775 Flight Ave Ste 100 (96002-9376)
PHONE.................530 224-2300
Jack Kilpatrick, *
Victor Clarke, *
Steve Hoppes, *
EMP: 60 EST: 1972
SQ FT: 31,000
SALES (est): 6.04MM Privately Held
Web: www.reddingjet.com
SIC: 4111 4581 Airport transportation services, regular route; Aircraft servicing and repairing

(P-3192)
RIVERSIDE TRANSIT AGENCY (PA)
Also Called: R T A
1825 3rd St (92507-3484)
P.O. Box 59968 (92517-1968)
PHONE.................951 565-5000
Larry Rubio, CEO
EMP: 350 EST: 1977
SQ FT: 10,400
SALES (est): 3.22MM
SALES (corp-wide): 3.22MM Privately Held
Web: www.riversidetransit.com
SIC: 4111 Bus transportation

(P-3193)
SACRAMENTO REGIONAL TRNST DIST (PA)
1400 29th St (95816-6406)
P.O. Box 2110 (95812-2110)
PHONE.................916 726-2877
Mike Wiley, Genl Mgr
▲ EMP: 700 EST: 1955
SQ FT: 10,000
SALES (est): 21MM
SALES (corp-wide): 21MM Privately Held
Web: www.sacrt.com
SIC: 4111 Bus line operations

(P-3194)
SAN BERNARDINO CNTY TRNSP AUTH
Also Called: SANBAG
1170 W 3rd St Fl 2 (92410-1724)
PHONE.................909 884-8276
Raymond Wolfe, Ex Dir
EMP: 125 EST: 1973
SALES (est): 672.67MM Privately Held
Web: www.gosbcta.com
SIC: 4111 Local and suburban transit

(P-3195)
SAN DIEGO METRO TRNST SYS
1255 Imperial Ave Ste 1000 (92101-7490)
PHONE.................619 231-1466

Sharon Cooney, CEO
Paul Jadlonski, *
Stan Abrams, *
EMP: 1600 EST: 1976
SQ FT: 40,000
SALES (est): 112.66MM Privately Held
Web: www.sandiego.com
SIC: 4111 Bus line operations

(P-3196)
SAN DIEGO TRANSIT CORPORATION (PA)
Also Called: San Diego Metro Trnst Sys
100 16th St (92101-7694)
PHONE.................619 238-0100
Langley Powell, Ex Dir
EMP: 650 EST: 1967
SQ FT: 20,000
SALES (est): 66.86MM
SALES (corp-wide): 66.86MM Privately Held
Web: www.sdmts.com
SIC: 4111 Commuter bus operation

(P-3197)
SAN DIEGO TROLLEY INC
Also Called: SAN DIEGO TROLLEY INC
1341 Commercial St (92113-1021)
PHONE.................619 595-4933
Bill Brown, Brnch Mgr
EMP: 483
SALES (corp-wide): 149MM Privately Held
Web: www.sdmts.com
SIC: 4111 Trolley operation
HQ: San Diego Trolley, Inc.
1255 Imperial Ave Ste 900
San Diego CA
619 595-4949

(P-3198)
SAN FRANCISCO BAY AREA RAPID
Also Called: Oakland Shops/Annex
601 E 8th St (94606-3606)
PHONE.................510 286-2893
Tom Delaney, Superintnt
EMP: 2000
SALES (corp-wide): 166.11MM Privately Held
Web: www.bart.gov
SIC: 4111 Local railway passenger operation
PA: San Francisco Bay Area Rapid Transit District
2150 Webster St
Oakland CA
510 464-6000

(P-3199)
SAN FRNCSCO BAY AREA RPID TRNS (PA)
Also Called: BART
2150 Webster St (94612-3012)
P.O. Box 12688 (94604-2688)
PHONE.................510 464-6000
Robert Powers, Genl Mgr
Scott Schroeder, *
Fola Dasilva, *
▲ EMP: 400 EST: 1957
SQ FT: 150,000
SALES (est): 166.11MM
SALES (corp-wide): 166.11MM Privately Held
Web: www.bart.gov
SIC: 4111 Local railway passenger operation

(P-3200)
SAN GABRIEL TRANSIT INC (PA)

Also Called: San Gabriel Valley Cab Co
3650 Rockwell Ave (91731-2322)
PHONE.................626 258-1310
Timmy Mardirossian, Pr
Sedik Mardirossian, *
Eda Aghajanian, *
EMP: 220 EST: 1953
SQ FT: 8,000
SALES (est): 47.41MM
SALES (corp-wide): 47.41MM Privately Held
Web: www.sgtransit.com
SIC: 4111 Local and suburban transit

(P-3201)
SAN JOAQUIN REGIONAL TRNST DST
Also Called: Sjrtd
421 E Weber Ave (95202-3024)
P.O. Box 201010 (95201-9010)
PHONE.................209 948-5566
Gloria G Salazar, CEO
Donna Kelsay, *
Gloria Salazar, *
Ciro Aguirre, *
EMP: 201 EST: 1964
SQ FT: 29,100
SALES (est): 48.32MM Privately Held
Web: www.sanjoaquinrtd.com
SIC: 4111 Bus line operations

(P-3202)
SAN LUIS OBSPO RGNAL TRNST AUT
Also Called: Slorta
253 Elks Ln (93401-5410)
PHONE.................805 781-4465
Omar Mcpherson, Prin
Geoff Straw, *
Tania Arnold, *
EMP: 90 EST: 1989
SALES (est): 8.91MM Privately Held
Web: www.slorta.org
SIC: 4111 Local and suburban transit

(P-3203)
SAN MATEO COUNTY TRANSIT DST (PA)
Also Called: SAMTRANS
1250 San Carlos Ave (94070-2420)
P.O. Box 3006 (94070-1306)
PHONE.................650 508-6200
Jim Hartnett, CEO
Virginia Harrington, *
R George Cameron, CAO*
C H Harvey, COO
Rita Haskin, CCO*
EMP: 250 EST: 1976
SQ FT: 20,000
SALES (est): 8.91MM
SALES (corp-wide): 8.91MM Privately Held
Web: www.smctd.com
SIC: 4111 Bus line operations

(P-3204)
SAN MATEO COUNTY TRANSIT DST
Also Called: Sam Trans
301 N Access Rd (94080-6901)
PHONE.................650 588-4860
John Gerbo, Brnch Mgr
EMP: 275
SQ FT: 2,000
SALES (corp-wide): 8.91MM Privately Held
Web: www.smctd.com
SIC: 4111 Bus line operations
PA: San Mateo County Transit District
1250 San Carlos Ave

PRODUCTS & SERVICES SECTION

4111 - Local And Suburban Transit (P-3224)

San Carlos CA
650 508-6200

(P-3205)
SANTA BARBARA METRO TRNST DST (PA)
Also Called: M T D
550 Olive St (93101-1610)
PHONE.................................805 963-3364
David Davis, *Ch*
John Britton, *
Chuck Mcquary, *Vice Chairman*
Bill Shelor, *
Roger Aceves, *
EMP: 85 **EST:** 1967
SQ FT: 8,500
SALES (est): 22.76MM
SALES (corp-wide): 22.76MM **Privately Held**
Web: www.sbmtd.gov
SIC: 4111 Bus line operations

(P-3206)
SANTA CLARA VALLEY TRNSP AUTH (PA)
Also Called: Santa Clara Vta
3331 N 1st St (95134-1906)
PHONE.................................408 321-2300
Carolyn Gonot, *CEO*
David Hill, *COO*
Greg Richardson, *CFO*
▲ **EMP:** 1053 **EST:** 1972
SQ FT: 217,000
SALES (est): 604.96MM
SALES (corp-wide): 604.96MM **Privately Held**
Web: www.vta.org
SIC: 4111 Local and suburban transit

(P-3207)
SANTA CLARA VALLEY TRNSP AUTH
Document Control-Central File
3331 N 1st St Bldg B (95134-1906)
PHONE.................................408 321-5559
Michael Burns, *Mgr*
EMP: 102
SALES (corp-wide): 604.96MM **Privately Held**
Web: www.vta.org
SIC: 4111 9621 Local and suburban transit; Regulation, administration of transportation, County government
PA: Santa Clara Valley Transportation Authority
3331 N 1st St
San Jose CA
408 321-2300

(P-3208)
SANTA CRUZ METRO TRNST DST
Also Called: Maintenance Dept
138 Golf Club Dr (95060-2121)
PHONE.................................831 429-5455
Tom Stickle, *Mgr*
EMP: 101
SALES (corp-wide): 8.25MM **Privately Held**
Web: www.scmtd.com
SIC: 4111 Local and suburban transit
PA: Santa Cruz Metropolitan Transit District
110 Vernon St
Santa Cruz CA
831 426-6143

(P-3209)
SANTA CRUZ METRO TRNST DST
Also Called: Fleet Maintenance Dept
110 Vernon St Ste B (95060-2130)
PHONE.................................831 469-1954
Tom Stickel, *Mgr*
EMP: 89
SALES (corp-wide): 8.25MM **Privately Held**
Web: www.scmtd.com
SIC: 4111 Local and suburban transit
PA: Santa Cruz Metropolitan Transit District
110 Vernon St
Santa Cruz CA
831 426-6143

(P-3210)
SANTA CRUZ METRO TRNST DST
135 Aviation Way Ste 2 (95076-2046)
PHONE.................................831 426-6080
EMP: 89
SALES (corp-wide): 8.25MM **Privately Held**
Web: www.scmtd.com
SIC: 4111 Local and suburban transit
PA: Santa Cruz Metropolitan Transit District
110 Vernon St
Santa Cruz CA
831 426-6143

(P-3211)
SFO AIRPORTER INC (PA)
Also Called: Compass Transportation Charter
1535 S 10th St (95112-2516)
PHONE.................................650 246-2734
Nicholas C Leonoudakis, *Ch Bd*
Jeffrey G Leonoudakis, *
Timothy K Leonoudakis, *
Stephan C Leonoudakis, *
▼ **EMP:** 100 **EST:** 1976
SALES (est): 19.23MM
SALES (corp-wide): 19.23MM **Privately Held**
Web: www.sfoairporter.com
SIC: 4111 4141 4131 Airport transportation; Local bus charter service; Intercity bus line

(P-3212)
SFO AIRPORTER INC
325 5th St (94107-1040)
PHONE.................................415 495-3909
Gordis Esposto, *Brnch Mgr*
EMP: 100
SALES (corp-wide): 19.23MM **Privately Held**
Web: www.sfoairporter.com
SIC: 4111 4141 4131 Airport transportation; Local bus charter service; Intercity bus line
PA: Sfo Airporter, Inc.
1535 S 10th St
San Jose CA
650 246-2734

(P-3213)
SHUTTLE SMART INC
6150 W 96th St (90045-5218)
PHONE.................................310 338-9466
Brian Clark, *Brnch Mgr*
EMP: 130
SALES (corp-wide): 1.8MM **Privately Held**
Web: www.shuttlesmart.net
SIC: 4111 Airport transportation
PA: Shuttle Smart, Inc.
25923 Washington Blvd Ne
Kingston WA
303 757-4870

(P-3214)
SMS TRANSPORTATION SVCS INC
865 S Figueroa St Ste 2750 (90017-2627)
PHONE.................................213 489-5367
John Harris, *CEO*
Delilah Lanoix, *
Danielle Wiltz, *
Jennifer Wiltz, *
EMP: 150 **EST:** 1994
SQ FT: 3,000
SALES (est): 14.74MM **Privately Held**
Web: www.smstransportation.net
SIC: 4111 Airport transportation

(P-3215)
SONOMA COUNTY AIRPORT EX INC
Also Called: Airport Express
5807 Old Redwood Hwy (95403-1167)
PHONE.................................707 837-8700
Howard Emigh, *Pr*
Tony Geraldi, *
EMP: 440 **EST:** 1981
SQ FT: 5,500
SALES (est): 6.55MM
SALES (corp-wide): 78.52MM **Privately Held**
Web: www.airportexpressinc.com
SIC: 4111 4141 Airport transportation services, regular route; Local bus charter service
PA: Groome Transportation, Incorporated
2201 W Broad St Ste 105
Richmond VA
804 222-7226

(P-3216)
SOUTHERN CAL RGIONAL RAIL AUTH
Also Called: Metrolink Doc
2704 N Garey Ave (91767-1810)
PHONE.................................213 808-7043
EMP: 143
Web: www.metrolinktrains.com
SIC: 4111 Commuter rail passenger operation
PA: Southern California Regional Rail Authority
900 Wilshire Blvd # 1500
Los Angeles CA

(P-3217)
SOUTHERN CAL RGIONAL RAIL AUTH (PA)
Also Called: Metrolink
900 Wilshire Blvd Ste 1500 (90017-3402)
P.O. Box 812060 (90081-0018)
PHONE.................................213 452-0200
Darren M Kettle, *CEO*
Stephanie Wiggins, *
Elissa Konove, *
Gary Lettengarver, *
Ronnie Campbell, *
EMP: 128 **EST:** 1991
SALES (est): 93.97MM **Privately Held**
Web: www.metrolinktrains.com
SIC: 4111 Commuter rail passenger operation

(P-3218)
SOUTHLAND TRANSIT INC (PA)
3650 Rockwell Ave (91731-2322)
PHONE.................................626 258-1310
Timmy Mardirossian, *CEO*
Dave Daley, *Pr*
EMP: 64 **EST:** 2001
SALES (est): 23.96MM
SALES (corp-wide): 23.96MM **Privately Held**
Web: www.southlandtransit.com
SIC: 4111 Local and suburban transit

(P-3219)
SUNLINE TRANSIT AGENCY (PA)
Also Called: STA
32505 Harry Oliver Trl (92276-3501)
PHONE.................................760 343-3456
Glenn Miller, *Ch*
Caroline Rude, *
Greg Pettis, *
EMP: 160 **EST:** 1977
SQ FT: 19,006
SALES (est): 48.63MM
SALES (corp-wide): 48.63MM **Privately Held**
Web: www.sunline.org
SIC: 4111 Local and suburban transit

(P-3220)
SUPERSHUTTLE INTERNATIONAL INC
323 S Canal St (94080-4605)
PHONE.................................650 246-2786
Eric Butler, *Prin*
EMP: 80
SALES (corp-wide): 4.23MM **Privately Held**
Web: www.supershuttle.com
SIC: 4111 Local and suburban transit
HQ: Supershuttle International, Inc.
14500 N Northsight Blvd # 329
Scottsdale AZ
800 258-3826

(P-3221)
SUPERSHUTTLE INTERNATIONAL INC
700 16th St (94158-2531)
PHONE.................................415 558-8500
Ruth T West, *Brnch Mgr*
EMP: 83
SALES (corp-wide): 4.23MM **Privately Held**
Web: www.supershuttle.com
SIC: 4111 Airport transportation services, regular route
HQ: Supershuttle International, Inc.
14500 N Northsight Blvd # 329
Scottsdale AZ
800 258-3826

(P-3222)
TRANSDEV SERVICES INC
326 Huss Dr (95928-8261)
PHONE.................................530 342-6851
EMP: 282
SALES (corp-wide): 4.23MM **Privately Held**
Web: www.transdevna.com
SIC: 4111 Local and suburban transit
HQ: Transdev Services, Inc.
720 E Bttrfeld Rd Ste 300
Lombard IL
630 571-7070

(P-3223)
TRANSITAMERICA SERVICES INC
93 Cahill St (95110-2501)
PHONE.................................408 961-4350
Robert J Smith, *CEO*
EMP: 77 **EST:** 2005
SALES (est): 25.43MM **Privately Held**
Web: www.herzog.com
SIC: 4111 Local and suburban transit

(P-3224)
VTA
787 Regent Park Dr (95123-1332)
PHONE.................................408 546-7777
Harvinder Saini, *Prin*

4111 - Local And Suburban Transit (P-3225)

EMP: 86 EST: 2010
SALES (est): 3.24MM **Privately Held**
Web: www.vta.org
SIC: **4111** Local and suburban transit

(P-3225)
WEST COUNTY TRNSP AGCY
367 W Robles Ave (95407-8126)
PHONE.................................707 206-9988
Chad Barksdale, *Ex Dir*
Michael Rea, *Prin*
EMP: 177 EST: 1998
SQ FT: 125,017
SALES (est): 18.1MM **Privately Held**
Web: www.schoolbusing.org
SIC: **4111** Local and suburban transit

4119 Local Passenger Transportation, Nec

(P-3226)
AIR METHODS
2885 U St (92408-0207)
PHONE.................................909 382-0045
EMP: 74 EST: 2019
SALES (est): 975.29K **Privately Held**
Web: www.airmethods.com
SIC: **4119** Ambulance service

(P-3227)
AMBULNZ HEALTH LLC
12531 Vanowen St (91605-5321)
PHONE.................................877 311-5555
EMP: 261
SALES (corp-wide): 18.79MM **Privately Held**
Web: www.ambulnz.com
SIC: **4119** Ambulance service
PA: Ambulnz Health, Llc
  3550 N Academy Blvd
  Colorado Springs CO
  877 311-5555

(P-3228)
AMERICAN MED RSPNSE AMBLNCE SV (DH)
Also Called: A M R
879 Marlborough Ave (92507-2133)
PHONE.................................303 495-1217
William A Sanger, *CEO*
Don Harvey, *Pr*
Randel Owen, *Ex VP*
EMP: 63 EST: 1993
SALES (est): 121.31MM **Privately Held**
SIC: **4119** Ambulance service
HQ: American Medical Response, Inc.
  6363 S Fiddlers Green Cir
  Greenwood Village CO

(P-3229)
AMERICAN MED RSPNSE INLAND EMP
4451 Caterpillar Rd Ste 1 (96003-1493)
PHONE.................................530 241-2686
John Lord, *Brnch Mgr*
EMP: 639
SIC: **4119** Ambulance service
HQ: American Medical Response Of Inland Empire
  879 Marlborough Ave
  Riverside CA

(P-3230)
AMERICAN MED RSPNSE INLAND EMP
116 Hubbard St (95060-2938)
PHONE.................................831 423-7030
David Zenker, *Brnch Mgr*
EMP: 639
SIC: **4119** Ambulance service
HQ: American Medical Response Of Inland Empire
  879 Marlborough Ave
  Riverside CA

(P-3231)
AMERICAN MED RSPNSE INLAND EMP (HQ)
879 Marlborough Ave (92507-2133)
PHONE.................................951 782-5200
Bill Fanger, *Pr*
EMP: 80 EST: 1962
SALES (est): 21.62MM **Privately Held**
SIC: **4119** Ambulance service
PA: Global Medical Response, Inc.
  6363 S Fiddlers Green Cir
  Greenwood Village CO

(P-3232)
AMERICAN MEDICAL RESPONSE INC
Also Called: American Medical Response
1111 Montalvo Way (92262-5440)
PHONE.................................760 883-5000
Wayne Dennis, *Prin*
EMP: 160
Web: www.amr.net
SIC: **4119** 8099 Ambulance service; Medical rescue squad
HQ: American Medical Response, Inc.
  6363 S Fiddlers Green Cir
  Greenwood Village CO

(P-3233)
AMERICAN MEDICAL RESPONSE INC
13992 Catalina St (94577-5506)
PHONE.................................415 794-9204
Thomas Wagner, *CEO*
EMP: 250 EST: 1992
SALES (est): 22.35MM **Publicly Held**
SIC: **4119** 7372 Ambulance service; Application computer software
HQ: Envision Healthcare Corporation
  1a Burton Hills Blvd
  Nashville TN
  615 665-1283

(P-3234)
AMERICAN PROF AMBULANCE CORP
16945 Sherman Way (91406-3614)
P.O. Box 7263 (91409-7263)
PHONE.................................818 996-2200
Lyubov Popok, *Pr*
EMP: 85 EST: 2002
SALES (est): 5.2MM **Privately Held**
Web: www.apa-ems.com
SIC: **4119** Ambulance service

(P-3235)
AMERICARE AMBULANCE
Also Called: AMERICARE AMBULANCE
10730 Thornmint Rd (92127-2700)
PHONE.................................760 739-9723
Mark Ewing, *Brnch Mgr*
EMP: 129
SALES (corp-wide): 912.35K **Privately Held**
SIC: **4119** Ambulance service
PA: Americare Ambulance Llc
  6524 Fremont Cir
  Huntington Beach CA
  310 835-9390

(P-3236)
AMERICARE MEDSERVICES INC
Also Called: Americare Ambulance Service
6524 Fremont Cir (92648-6637)
PHONE.................................310 632-1141
EMP: 70 EST: 1995
SQ FT: 10,000
SALES (est): 7.63MM **Privately Held**
Web: www.americare.org
SIC: **4119** Ambulance service

(P-3237)
ATLANTIC EXPRESS TRNSP
Also Called: Atlantic Express of California
2450 Long Beach Blvd (90806-3125)
PHONE.................................562 997-6868
Darinda Garnett, *Mgr*
EMP: 158
SALES (corp-wide): 301.19MM **Privately Held**
SIC: **4119** 8748 4151 Local passenger transportation, nec; Traffic consultant; School buses
HQ: Atlantic Express Transportation Corp
  7 North St
  Staten Island NY
  718 442-7000

(P-3238)
ATS MEDICAL SERVICES LLC
Also Called: Ats
720 Portal St (94931-3060)
P.O. Box 2549 (61132-2549)
PHONE.................................815 963-5001
Andrew T Schultz, *Pr*
Bradley Bull, *
EMP: 544 EST: 2005
SALES (est): 2.47MM
SALES (corp-wide): 249.05MM **Privately Held**
Web: www.atsambulance.com
SIC: **4119** Ambulance service
PA: Pt-1 Holdings, Llc
  720 Portal St
  Cotati CA
  707 665-4295

(P-3239)
BAUERS INTELLIGENT TRNSP INC (PA)
50 Pier (94158-2193)
PHONE.................................415 263-4020
Gary Bauer, *CEO*
Gary Schwartz, *
Dennis Jackson, *
EMP: 250 EST: 1989
SQ FT: 125,000
SALES (est): 55.35MM **Privately Held**
Web: www.bauersit.com
SIC: **4119** Limousine rental, with driver

(P-3240)
BAY MEDIC TRANSPORTATION INC
959 Detroit Ave (94518-2501)
PHONE.................................800 689-9511
Nesar Abdiani, *CEO*
Ali Abdani, *
EMP: 180 EST: 1995
SQ FT: 1,600
SALES (est): 9MM **Privately Held**
Web: www.baymedic.com
SIC: **4119** Ambulance service

(P-3241)
BLACK TIE TRANSPORTATION LLC
7080 Commerce Dr (94588-8021)
PHONE.................................925 847-0747
Bill Wheeler, *Managing Member*
Jennifer Wheeler, *
Debbie Moore, *
EMP: 130 EST: 1997
SQ FT: 18,000
SALES (est): 11.77MM **Privately Held**
Web: www.blacktietrans.com
SIC: **4119** 4724 Limousine rental, with driver; Travel agencies

(P-3242)
BLS LMSINE SVC LOS ANGELES INC
Also Called: B L S Limousine Service
2860 Fletcher Dr (90039-2452)
PHONE.................................323 644-7166
Jay D Okon, *Pr*
Phyllis Okon, *
EMP: 350 EST: 1988
SQ FT: 20,000
SALES (est): 8.7MM **Privately Held**
Web: www.blsco.com
SIC: **4119** Limousine rental, with driver

(P-3243)
CALIFORNIA MED RESPONSE INC
Also Called: Cal-Med Ambulance
1557 Santa Anita Ave (91733-3313)
PHONE.................................562 968-1818
Ronald A Marks, *Pr*
Ronald A Marks, *Pr*
Linda Marks, *
EMP: 80 EST: 2009
SALES (est): 7.05MM **Privately Held**
Web: www.calmedambulance.com
SIC: **4119** Ambulance service

(P-3244)
CALIFRNIA SHOCK TRUMA A RESCUE (PA)
Also Called: Calstar
4933 Bailey Loop (95652-2516)
PHONE.................................916 921-4000
Lynn Malmstrom, *Pr*
Sonja Vargas, *
EMP: 63 EST: 1983
SQ FT: 44,000
SALES (est): 35.94K
SALES (corp-wide): 35.94K **Privately Held**
Web: www.reachair.com
SIC: **4119** Ambulance service

(P-3245)
CALL-THE-CAR
3100 New York Dr Ste 100 (91107-1554)
P.O. Box 4114 (90640-9302)
PHONE.................................855 282-6968
Michelle Tyson, *CEO*
EMP: 89 EST: 2012
SALES (est): 9.5MM **Privately Held**
Web: www.callthecar.com
SIC: **4119** Local passenger transportation, nec

(P-3246)
CARE MEDICAL TRNSP INC
Also Called: Care Ambulance
9770 Candida St (92126-4536)
PHONE.................................858 653-4520
EMP: 190 EST: 1995
SQ FT: 14,000
SALES (est): 4.37MM **Privately Held**
SIC: **4119** Ambulance service

(P-3247)
CARRENTALSCOM INC
655 Montgomery St Ste 600 (94111-2627)
PHONE.................................866 468-9473

PRODUCTS & SERVICES SECTION

4119 - Local Passenger Transportation, Nec (P-3270)

EMP: 86
SALES (corp-wide): 11.67B **Publicly Held**
SIC: 4119 Automobile rental, with driver
HQ: Carrentals.Com, Inc.
  1111 Expedia Group Way W
  Seattle WA
  866 468-9473

(P-3248)
CAV INC
Also Called: Care A Van Transport
5931 Sea Lion Pl Ste 110 (92010-6622)
PHONE..................................760 729-5199
Richard Dripps, Pr
Robert Sneedon, *
Robert Newkirk, Operations*
Deana Mason, Marketing MNG*
EMP: 75 EST: 1993
SQ FT: 1,200
SALES (est): 5.14MM **Privately Held**
SIC: 4119 Ambulance service

(P-3249)
CLS TRNSPRTTION LOS ANGLES LLC (HQ)
Also Called: Empire Cls Wrldwide Chffred Sv
600 S Allied Way (90245-4727)
PHONE..................................310 414-8189
David Singler, Managing Member
William Minich, *
EMP: 150 EST: 1987
SALES (est): 22.82MM **Privately Held**
Web: www.empirecls.com
SIC: 4119 Limousine rental, with driver
PA: Gts Holdings, Inc.
  225 Meadowlands Pkwy
  Secaucus NJ

(P-3250)
CRUISE LLC (HQ)
1201 Bryant St (94103-4306)
PHONE..................................415 335-4097
Daniel Ammann, CEO
Gil West, *
EMP: 75 EST: 2016
SALES (est): 170.1MM **Publicly Held**
Web: www.getcruise.com
SIC: 4119 Automobile rental, with driver
PA: General Motors Company
  300 Renaissance Ctr L1
  Detroit MI

(P-3251)
DAV-EL RESERVATIONS SYSTEM INC
Also Called: Dav El Chuffeured Trnsp Networ
2025 Mckinnon Ave (94124-1608)
PHONE..................................415 206-7950
Irwin Rosnel, Mgr
EMP: 72
SALES (corp-wide): 6.77MM **Privately Held**
SIC: 4119 Limousine rental, with driver
PA: Dav-El Reservations System, Inc.
  200 2nd St
  Chelsea MA
  617 887-0900

(P-3252)
EAGLE AMBULANCE
3251 Franklin Canyon Rd (94572-2123)
PHONE..................................800 304-6985
Josh Burke, Pr
EMP: 99 EST: 2018
SALES (est): 600K **Privately Held**
Web: www.eagle-ambulance.com
SIC: 4119 Ambulance service

(P-3253)
EASTWESTPROTO INC
Also Called: Lifeline Ambulance
6605 E Washington Blvd (90040-1813)
PHONE..................................888 535-5728
Genady Gorin, CEO
Genia Gorin, *
EMP: 275 EST: 2002
SQ FT: 10,000
SALES (est): 28.48MM **Privately Held**
Web: www.lifeline-ems.com
SIC: 4119 Ambulance service

(P-3254)
EMERGENCY AMBULANCE SVC INC
3200 E Birch St Ste A (92821-6287)
PHONE..................................714 990-1331
Phillip E Davis, Pr
EMP: 80 EST: 1977
SALES (est): 15.3MM **Privately Held**
Web: www.emergencyambulance.com
SIC: 4119 Ambulance service

(P-3255)
ENLOE MEDICAL CENTER
Also Called: Tty-Deaf Hndcppd-Cmmnction Ctr
W 5th Av & Esplanade (95926)
PHONE..................................530 891-7347
Bob Quitu, Mgr
EMP: 82
SALES (corp-wide): 814.04MM **Privately Held**
Web: www.enloe.org
SIC: 4119 Ambulance service
PA: Enloe Medical Center
  1531 Esplanade
  Chico CA
  530 332-7300

(P-3256)
EXECUTIVE NETWORK ENTPS INC
1224 21st St Apt E (90404-1390)
PHONE..................................310 457-8822
Patricia Stephenson, Mgr
EMP: 520
SIC: 4119 Limousine rental, with driver
PA: Executive Network Enterprises, Inc.
  13440 Beach Ave
  Marina Del Rey CA

(P-3257)
EXECUTIVE NETWORK ENTPS INC (PA)
Also Called: Malibu Limousine Service
13440 Beach Ave (90292-5624)
PHONE..................................310 447-2759
Patricia Stephenson, Pr
Stori Stephenson, *
Trish Rudd, *
EMP: 80 EST: 2003
SQ FT: 5,000
SALES (est): 4.74MM **Privately Held**
SIC: 4119 Limousine rental, with driver

(P-3258)
FALCK MOBILE HEALTH CORP
212 S Atlantic Blvd Ste 102 (90022)
PHONE..................................323 720-1578
EMP: 444
SALES (corp-wide): 4.95B **Privately Held**
Web: www.falck.us
SIC: 4119 Ambulance service
HQ: Falck Mobile Health Corp.
  1517 W Braden Ct
  Orange CA
  714 288-3800

(P-3259)
FALCK MOBILE HEALTH CORP
8932 Katella Ave Ste 201 (92804-6299)
PHONE..................................714 828-7750
Dan Richardson, Prin
EMP: 444
SALES (corp-wide): 4.95B **Privately Held**
Web: www.falck.us
SIC: 4119 Ambulance service
HQ: Falck Mobile Health Corp.
  1517 W Braden Ct
  Orange CA
  714 288-3800

(P-3260)
FALCON CRTICAL CARE TRNSPT LLC
1600 S Main St Ste 215 (94596-5376)
PHONE..................................510 223-1171
Tyler Coats, CEO
EMP: 63 EST: 1998
SALES (est): 11.36MM **Privately Held**
Web: www.falconambulance.com
SIC: 4119 Ambulance service

(P-3261)
FILYN CORPORATION
Also Called: Lynch Ambulance Service
2950 E La Jolla St (92806-1307)
PHONE..................................714 632-0225
Walter John Lynch, CEO
Nancy Lynch, *
EMP: 200 EST: 1986
SALES (est): 19.48MM **Privately Held**
Web: www.lynchambulance.com
SIC: 4119 Ambulance service

(P-3262)
FIRST RESPONDER EMS INC
Also Called: Paradise Ambulance Service
333 Huss Dr Ste 100 (95928-8242)
PHONE..................................530 897-6345
Byron Parsons, Pr
EMP: 80 EST: 1988
SALES (est): 4.54MM **Privately Held**
Web: www.firstresponder.com
SIC: 4119 Ambulance service

(P-3263)
FIRSTMED AMBULANCE SVCS INC
8630 Tamarack Ave (91352-2504)
PHONE..................................818 982-8333
Kristina Bableyan, Pr
EMP: 62 EST: 2007
SALES (est): 7.83MM **Privately Held**
Web: www.firstmedambulance.com
SIC: 4119 Ambulance service

(P-3264)
FLIXBUS INC
12575 Beatrice St (90066-7001)
PHONE..................................925 577-4164
Pierre Gourdain, CEO
EMP: 104 EST: 2017
SALES (est): 6.73MM
SALES (corp-wide): 611.17MM **Privately Held**
Web: www.flixbus.com
SIC: 4119 Local rental transportation
HQ: Flix North America Inc.
  315 Continental Ave
  Dallas TX
  214 564-8215

(P-3265)
GARY CARDIFF ENTERPRISES INC
Also Called: Cardiff Transportation
75255 Sheryl Ave (92211-5129)
PHONE..................................760 568-1403
Gary Cardiff, CEO
Sharon Cardiff, *
EMP: 89 EST: 1990
SQ FT: 10,000
SALES (est): 8.46MM **Privately Held**
Web: www.cardifflimo.com
SIC: 4119 Limousine rental, with driver

(P-3266)
GLOBAL PARATRANSIT INC
400 W Compton Blvd (90248-1700)
PHONE..................................310 715-7550
Reza Nasrollahy, Pr
EMP: 300 EST: 2000
SQ FT: 17,000
SALES (est): 25.4MM **Privately Held**
Web: www.global-paratransit.com
SIC: 4119 Ambulance service

(P-3267)
HALL AMBULANCE SERVICE INC
2001 O St # O (93301-4724)
PHONE..................................661 322-8741
Harvy Hall, Pr
EMP: 73
SALES (corp-wide): 32.75MM **Privately Held**
Web: www.hallamb.com
SIC: 4119 Ambulance service
PA: Hall Ambulance Service, Inc.
  1001 21st St
  Bakersfield CA
  661 322-8741

(P-3268)
HALL AMBULANCE SERVICE INC (PA)
1001 21st St (93301-4708)
PHONE..................................661 322-8741
Harvey L Hall, Pr
Mary Kenny, *
EMP: 60 EST: 1971
SQ FT: 4,000
SALES (est): 32.75MM
SALES (corp-wide): 32.75MM **Privately Held**
Web: www.hallamb.com
SIC: 4119 4729 4789 Ambulance service; Transportation ticket offices; Cargo loading and unloading services

(P-3269)
KWPH ENTERPRISES
Also Called: American Ambulance
2911 E Tulare St (93721-1502)
PHONE..................................559 443-5900
Todd Valeri, Pr
Todd R Valeri, *
James Wampler, *
EMP: 700 EST: 1975
SQ FT: 22,000
SALES (est): 275MM **Privately Held**
Web: www.americanambulance.com
SIC: 4119 Ambulance service

(P-3270)
LANDJET (PA)
1090 Hall Ave (92509-1800)
PHONE..................................909 873-4636
Kevin Sacalas, CEO
EMP: 131 EST: 2018
SALES (est): 5.9MM
SALES (corp-wide): 5.9MM **Privately Held**
Web: www.landjet-inc.com
SIC: 4119 Local rental transportation

4119 - Local Passenger Transportation, Nec (P-3271)

(P-3271)
LEADER INDUSTRIES INC
Also Called: Leader Emergency Vehicles
10941 Weaver Ave (91733-2752)
PHONE.................................626 575-0880
Gary Hunter, *Prin*
EMP: 160 EST: 2001
SALES (est): 16.12MM **Privately Held**
Web: www.leaderambulance.com
SIC: **4119** 5046 3711 Ambulance service; Commercial equipment, nec; Motor vehicles and car bodies

(P-3272)
LIBERTY AMBULANCE LLC
9441 Washburn Rd (90242-2912)
PHONE.................................562 741-6230
EMP: 103 EST: 2008
SALES (est): 11.35MM **Privately Held**
Web: www.libertyambulance.com
SIC: **4119** Ambulance service

(P-3273)
LIFESTAR RESPONSE OF ALABAMA
Also Called: Care Ambulance
1517 W Braden Ct (92868-1125)
P.O. Box 241468 (36124-1468)
PHONE.................................800 449-4911
Charles Maymon, *CEO*
Michael Arguelles, *COO*
EMP: 72 EST: 2007
SALES (est): 9.79MM **Privately Held**
Web: www.care-ambulance.com
SIC: **4119** Ambulance service

(P-3274)
LYFT INC (PA)
Also Called: LYFT
185 Berry St Ste 400 (94107-1725)
PHONE.................................844 250-2773
David Risher, *CEO*
Logan Green, *
Prashant Aggarwal, *
John Zimmer, *
Lisa Blackwood-kapral, *CAO*
EMP: 490 EST: 2007
SQ FT: 309,000
SALES (est): 4.1B **Publicly Held**
Web: www.lyft.com
SIC: **4119** Local rental transportation

(P-3275)
MEDIC AMBULANCE SERVICE INC (PA)
506 Couch St (94590-2408)
P.O. Box 4467 (94590-0459)
PHONE.................................707 644-1761
Rodolfo Manfredi, *Pr*
Marissa Luchini, *
Helen Pierson, *
EMP: 130 EST: 1959
SQ FT: 7,000
SALES (est): 26.32MM
SALES (corp-wide): 26.32MM **Privately Held**
Web: www.medicambulance.net
SIC: **4119** Ambulance service

(P-3276)
MEDIC-1 AMBULANCE SERVICE INC
1305 W Arrow Hwy Ste 206 (91773-2338)
PHONE.................................909 592-8840
Gordon Shipp, *Pr*
Todd Duprey, *
Gary Sylvester, *
EMP: 92 EST: 2001
SALES (est): 4.53MM **Privately Held**
SIC: **4119** Ambulance service

(P-3277)
MEDIX AMBULANCE SERVICE INC (PA)
26021 Pala (92691-2705)
P.O. Box 1000 (92609-1000)
PHONE.................................949 470-8915
EMP: 157 EST: 1978
SALES (est): 9.17MM
SALES (corp-wide): 9.17MM **Privately Held**
SIC: **4119** Ambulance service

(P-3278)
MEDRESPONSE LLC
9961 Baldwin Pl (91731-2203)
PHONE.................................877 311-5555
Vince Pinsky, *Managing Member*
EMP: 75 EST: 2019
SALES (est): 1.23MM **Privately Held**
SIC: **4119** Local passenger transportation, nec

(P-3279)
MEDSTAR LLC
20 Business Park Way Ste 100 (95828-0965)
PHONE.................................916 669-0550
EMP: 65 EST: 1997
SALES (est): 2.98MM **Privately Held**
SIC: **4119** Ambulance service

(P-3280)
MEDTRANS INC
345 S Woods Ave (90022-1641)
PHONE.................................323 780-9500
Avetis Avetisyan, *CEO*
EMP: 75 EST: 2008
SALES (est): 2.21MM **Privately Held**
Web: www.medtrans.ai
SIC: **4119** Ambulance service

(P-3281)
MERCY MEDICAL TRNSP INC
27350 Valley Center Rd Ste A (92082-7220)
P.O. Box 530 (92082-0530)
PHONE.................................760 739-8026
Richard Roesch, *Pr*
EMP: 188 EST: 1993
SALES (est): 8.69MM **Privately Held**
Web: www.mercymedtrans.com
SIC: **4119** 8062 Ambulance service; General medical and surgical hospitals

(P-3282)
MISSION AMBULANCE INC
400 Ramona Ave (92879-1443)
P.O. Box 3111 (92878-3111)
PHONE.................................951 272-2300
Daniel Gold, *Pr*
EMP: 81 EST: 1999
SALES (est): 8.67MM **Privately Held**
Web: www.missionsafetyservices.com
SIC: **4119** Ambulance service

(P-3283)
MUSIC EXPRESS INC (PA)
2601 W Empire Ave (91504-3225)
PHONE.................................818 845-1502
EMP: 171 EST: 1973
SALES (est): 24.87MM
SALES (corp-wide): 24.87MM **Privately Held**
Web: www.musicexpress.com
SIC: **4119** Limousine rental, with driver

(P-3284)
NATIONAL EXPRESS LLC
880 Thornton Rd (95341-8003)
PHONE.................................209 201-9345
EMP: 776
Web: www.nellc.com
SIC: **4119** Vanpool operation
HQ: National Express Llc
  2601 Navistar Dr Bldg 4
  Lisle IL

(P-3285)
PARATRANSIT INCORPORATED (PA)
2501 Florin Rd (95822-4467)
P.O. Box 231100 (95823-0401)
PHONE.................................916 429-2009
Linda Jean Deavens, *CEO*
Steve Robinson-burmester, *CFO*
Ninh Dao-dickinson, *COO*
EMP: 208 EST: 1978
SQ FT: 250,000
SALES (est): 14.14MM
SALES (corp-wide): 14.14MM **Privately Held**
Web: www.paratransit.org
SIC: **4119** 7539 Ambulance service; Automotive repair shops, nec

(P-3286)
PREMIER MEDICAL TRANSPORT INC
Also Called: Premier Ambulance
260 N Palm St # 200 (92821-2870)
PHONE.................................805 340-5191
Adrian Dehghanmanesh, *CEO*
EMP: 117 EST: 2007
SALES (est): 12.93MM **Privately Held**
Web: www.premieramb.com
SIC: **4119** Ambulance service

(P-3287)
PRIORITY ONE MED TRNSPT INC (PA)
9327 Fairway View Pl Ste 300 (91730-0968)
PHONE.................................909 948-4400
Michael Parker, *Pr*
EMP: 70 EST: 1996
SQ FT: 7,000
SALES (est): 4.46MM
SALES (corp-wide): 4.46MM **Privately Held**
Web: www.priorityonemedical.com
SIC: **4119** Ambulance service

(P-3288)
PRN AMBULANCE LLC
8928 Sepulveda Blvd (91343-4306)
PHONE.................................818 810-3600
Mike Sechrist, *CEO*
Avo Avetisyan, *Pr*
Elena Whorton, *Pr*
Kevin Gorman, *CFO*
Michael Gorman, *COO*
EMP: 300 EST: 2001
SQ FT: 3,000
SALES (est): 58.95MM
SALES (corp-wide): 249.05MM **Privately Held**
Web: www.prnambulance.com
SIC: **4119** Ambulance service
PA: Pt-1 Holdings, Llc
  720 Portal St
  Cotati CA
  707 665-4295

(P-3289)
PROTRANSPORT-1 LLC (HQ)
Also Called: Protransport-1
720 Portal St (94931-3060)
PHONE.................................707 975-2386
Kelley Sechrist, *
Elena Whorton, *
Kurt Whorton, *
EMP: 170 EST: 2000
SQ FT: 2,600
SALES (est): 91.5MM
SALES (corp-wide): 249.05MM **Privately Held**
Web: www.protransport-1.com
SIC: **4119** Ambulance service
PA: Pt-1 Holdings, Llc
  720 Portal St
  Cotati CA
  707 665-4295

(P-3290)
PURE LUXURY LIMOUSINE SERVICE
Also Called: Pure Luxury Worldwide Trnsp
4246 Petaluma Blvd N (94952-1240)
P.O. Box 910 (94951-0910)
PHONE.................................800 626-5466
Gary L Buffo Junior, *CEO*
EMP: 111 EST: 1991
SQ FT: 35,000
SALES (est): 14.52MM **Privately Held**
Web: www.pureluxury.com
SIC: **4119** Limousine rental, with driver

(P-3291)
RM EXECUTIVE TRANSPORTATION
Also Called: Mosaic Global Transportation
525 Sunol St (95126-3752)
PHONE.................................650 260-1240
Maurice Brewster, *CEO*
Maurice Brewster, *Pr*
Rhonda Brewster, *
EMP: 139 EST: 2002
SALES (est): 14.77MM **Privately Held**
Web: www.mosaicglobaltransportation.com
SIC: **4119** Limousine rental, with driver

(P-3292)
ROYAL AMBULANCE INC
14472 Wicks Blvd (94577-6712)
PHONE.................................877 995-6161
Steve Grau, *CEO*
Steve Grau, *Pr*
Leon Botoshansky, *
EMP: 120 EST: 2005
SQ FT: 5,000
SALES (est): 10.86MM **Privately Held**
Web: www.royalambulance.com
SIC: **4119** Ambulance service

(P-3293)
RYANS EXPRESS TRNSP SVCS INC (PA)
Also Called: Ryan's Express
19500 Mariner Ave (90503-1644)
PHONE.................................310 219-2960
John Busskohl, *CEO*
Chris Sanchez, *
George Cohen, *
Alexander E Hansen, *
Daniel Azar, *
EMP: 80 EST: 1999
SQ FT: 20,000
SALES (est): 25.34MM
SALES (corp-wide): 25.34MM **Privately Held**
Web: www.ryanstransportation.com

SIC: 4119 Limousine rental, with driver

(P-3294)
SAN LUIS AMBULANCE SERVICE INC
3546 S Higuera St (93401-7304)
P.O. Box 954 (93406-0954)
PHONE.................................805 543-2626
Frank I Kelton, *Pr*
Betsy Kelton, *
EMP: 124 EST: 1967
SQ FT: 7,500
SALES (est): 9.65MM **Privately Held**
Web: www.sanlusambulance.info
SIC: 4119 Ambulance service

(P-3295)
SCHAEFER AMBULANCE SERVICE INC
Also Called: Gold Cross Ambulance
4627 Beverly Blvd (90004-3101)
P.O. Box 74609 (90004-0609)
PHONE.................................323 468-1642
TOLL FREE: 800
EMP: 463
Web: www.schaeferamb.com
SIC: 4119 Ambulance service

(P-3296)
SUNLINE TRANSIT AGENCY
790 Vine Ave (92236-1736)
PHONE.................................760 972-4059
EMP: 119
SALES (corp-wide): 48.63MM **Privately Held**
Web: www.sunline.org
SIC: 4119 Local passenger transportation, nec
PA: Sunline Transit Agency
    32505 Harry Oliver Trl
    Thousand Palms CA
    760 343-3456

(P-3297)
SUPERSHUTTLE INTERNATIONAL INC
160 S Linden Ave (94080-6419)
PHONE.................................650 246-2704
EMP: 77
SALES (corp-wide): 4.23MM **Privately Held**
Web: www.supershuttle.com
SIC: 4119 Limousine rental, with driver
HQ: Supershuttle International, Inc.
    14500 N Northsight Blvd # 329
    Scottsdale AZ
    800 258-3826

(P-3298)
TRANSDEV SERVICES INC
5640 Peck Rd (91006-5850)
PHONE.................................626 357-7912
EMP: 916
SALES (corp-wide): 4.23MM **Privately Held**
Web: www.transdevna.com
SIC: 4119 4121 Local passenger transportation, nec; Taxicabs
HQ: Transdev Services, Inc.
    720 E Bttrfeld Rd Ste 300
    Lombard IL
    630 571-7070

(P-3299)
TRANSDEV SERVICES INC
544 Vernon Way (92020-1935)
PHONE.................................619 401-3452
EMP: 176

Web: www.transdevna.com
SIC: 4119 Local passenger transportation, nec
HQ: Transdev Services, Inc.
    720 E Bttrfeld Rd Ste 300
    Lombard IL
    630 571-7070

(P-3300)
TRANSDEV SERVICES INC
2361 Airport Blvd (95110-1207)
PHONE.................................408 282-4706
EMP: 176
SALES (corp-wide): 4.23MM **Privately Held**
Web: www.transdevna.com
SIC: 4119 4121 Local passenger transportation, nec; Taxicabs
HQ: Transdev Services, Inc.
    720 E Bttrfeld Rd Ste 300
    Lombard IL
    630 571-7070

(P-3301)
TRIPLE R TRANSPORTATION INC
978 Rd 192 (93215)
P.O. Box 38 (93216-0038)
PHONE.................................661 725-6494
Joe Rodriguez, *Pr*
EMP: 80 EST: 2008
SALES (est): 3.89MM **Privately Held**
SIC: 4119 Local rental transportation

(P-3302)
UNIVERSAL LIMOUSINE & TRNSP CO
Also Called: Universal Charter Services
9944 Mills Station Rd Ste C (95827-2202)
PHONE.................................916 361-5466
EMP: 70 EST: 1994
SQ FT: 10,000
SALES (est): 3.8MM **Privately Held**
Web: www.universallimo.com
SIC: 4119 Limousine rental, with driver

(P-3303)
VIRGIN FISH INC (PA)
Also Called: Avalon Transportation Co
1000 Corporate Pointe Ste 150 (90230-7690)
PHONE.................................310 391-6161
Jeff Brush, *Prin*
Jeff Brush, *Pr*
David Dinwiddie, *
EMP: 150 EST: 1990
SQ FT: 3,000
SALES (est): 23.41MM **Privately Held**
Web: www.avalontrans.com
SIC: 4119 Limousine rental, with driver

(P-3304)
VOYAGE AUTO INC
333 Brannan St (94107-1810)
PHONE.................................917 588-1249
Oliver Cameron, *CEO*
EMP: 75 EST: 2017
SALES (est): 4.16MM **Publicly Held**
SIC: 4119 Local passenger transportation, nec
HQ: Cruise Llc
    1201 Bryant St
    San Francisco CA
    415 335-4097

(P-3305)
WESTMED AMBULANCE INC
Also Called: WESTMED AMBULANCE, INC
3872 Las Flores Canyon Rd (90265-5264)

PHONE.................................310 456-3830
EMP: 155
Web: www.westmedambulance.com
SIC: 4119 Ambulance service
PA: Westmed Ambulance, Inc.
    13933 Crenshaw Blvd
    Hawthorne CA

(P-3306)
WESTMED AMBULANCE INC
Also Called: WESTMED AMBULANCE, INC
2537 Old San Pasqual Rd (92027-4753)
PHONE.................................310 219-1779
Allen Cress, *Prin*
EMP: 155
Web: www.westmedambulance.com
SIC: 4119 Ambulance service
PA: Westmed Ambulance, Inc.
    13933 Crenshaw Blvd
    Hawthorne CA

4121 Taxicabs

(P-3307)
ADMINISTRATIVE SVCS COOP INC
1515 W 190th St Ste 200 (90248-4924)
PHONE.................................310 715-1968
Martiros Manukyan, *CEO*
Raymond Mcgreevy, *Pr*
EMP: 200 EST: 1992
SALES (est): 7.5MM **Privately Held**
SIC: 4121 Taxicabs

4131 Intercity And Rural Bus Transportation

(P-3308)
MONTEREY-SALINAS TRANSIT CORP
Also Called: MONTEREY-SALINAS TRANSIT CORPORATION
1375 Burton Ave (93901-4403)
PHONE.................................831 754-2804
Carl Sedoryk, *Brnch Mgr*
EMP: 140
SALES (corp-wide): 27.59MM **Privately Held**
Web: www.mst.org
SIC: 4131 Intercity and rural bus transportation
PA: Monterey-Salinas Transit District
    19 Upper Ragsdale Dr # 2
    Monterey CA
    888 678-2871

(P-3309)
SANTA BARBARA TRNSP CORP
Also Called: Student Transportation America
26501 Ruether Ave (91350-2600)
PHONE.................................661 259-7285
Richard Varner, *Dir*
EMP: 100
SALES (corp-wide): 2.01B **Privately Held**
SIC: 4131 4151 Intercity and rural bus transportation; School buses
HQ: Santa Barbara Transportation Corporation
    3349 Hwy 138 Ste C
    Wall Township NJ
    732 280-4200

(P-3310)
SANTA MONICA CITY OF
Santa Monica Big Blue Bus
1685 Main St (90401-3248)
PHONE.................................310 458-1975

Edward King, *Mgr*
EMP: 271
SALES (corp-wide): 502.49MM **Privately Held**
Web: www.santamonica.gov
SIC: 4131 Intercity and rural bus transportation
PA: City Of Santa Monica
    1685 Main St
    Santa Monica CA
    310 458-8411

4141 Local Bus Charter Service

(P-3311)
EMPIRE TRANSPORTATION INC
8800 Park St (90706-5529)
PHONE.................................562 529-2676
Miguel Oliver, *CEO*
Bertha Aguirre, *
Monica Escorza Oliver, *
EMP: 425 EST: 2005
SQ FT: 25,000
SALES (est): 35.8MM **Privately Held**
Web: www.emptransportation.com
SIC: 4141 7521 4111 Local bus charter service; Indoor parking services; Bus transportation

(P-3312)
MICHAELS TRNSP SVC INC
140 Yolano Dr (94589-2251)
PHONE.................................707 674-6013
Michael Brown, *Pr*
Paulette Brown, *
EMP: 95 EST: 1983
SQ FT: 26,000
SALES (est): 19.92MM **Privately Held**
Web: www.bustransportation.com
SIC: 4141 7363 8331 4111 Local bus charter service; Employee leasing service; Job training services; Bus transportation

(P-3313)
PEGASUS TRANSIT INC
210 Beedy St (93036-1006)
PHONE.................................805 988-1540
Maria Paseta, *Pr*
EMP: 60 EST: 2004
SALES (est): 9.07MM **Privately Held**
Web: www.pegasustransit.com
SIC: 4141 4522 8211 Local bus charter service; Nonscheduled charter services; Charter schools

(P-3314)
STORER TRANSPORTATION SERVICE (PA)
Also Called: Storer Travel Service
3519 Mcdonald Ave (95358-9771)
PHONE.................................209 521-8250
Donald Storer, *CEO*
Warren Storer, *
EMP: 275 EST: 1971
SQ FT: 6,000
SALES (est): 33.85MM
SALES (corp-wide): 33.85MM **Privately Held**
Web: www.storercoachways.com
SIC: 4141 4725 4724 4151 Local bus charter service; Tours, conducted; Travel agencies; School buses

4142 Bus Charter Service, Except Local

(P-3315)
AMADOR STAGE LINES INC
Also Called: Allen Transportation Co
1331 C St (95814-0913)
P.O. Box 15707 (95852-0707)
PHONE..................916 444-7880
W R Allen, *CEO*
Alex B Allen, *
William R Allen, *
R E Allen, *
EMP: 80 **EST:** 1947
SQ FT: 2,000
SALES (est): 11.63MM **Privately Held**
Web: www.amadorstagelines.com
SIC: 4142 Bus charter service, except local

(P-3316)
CERTIFIED TRNSP SVCS INC
Also Called: Certified Transportation
1038 N Custer St (92701-3915)
PHONE..................714 835-8676
David Gregory, *CEO*
EMP: 70 **EST:** 1990
SQ FT: 3,000
SALES (est): 10.07MM **Privately Held**
Web: www.ctsbus.com
SIC: 4142 Bus charter service, except local

(P-3317)
COACH USA INC
Also Called: Foothill Transit West Covina
5640 Peck Rd (91006-5850)
PHONE..................626 357-7912
Keith Whalen, *Brnch Mgr*
EMP: 100
Web: www.coachusa.com
SIC: 4142 Bus charter service, except local
HQ: Coach Usa, Inc.
160 S Route 17 N
Paramus NJ

(P-3318)
HOT DOGGER TOURS INC
Also Called: Gold Coast Tours
105 Gemini Ave (92821-3702)
PHONE..................714 988-4088
TOLL FREE: 800
John Hartley, *Pr*
Mark Wilkerson, *
EMP: 120 **EST:** 1976
SQ FT: 955
SALES (est): 14.23MM **Privately Held**
Web: www.goldcoasttours.com
SIC: 4142 4725 4141 Bus charter service, except local; Tours, conducted; Local bus charter service

(P-3319)
ORANGE BELT STAGES (PA)
Also Called: Orange Belt Adventures
2134 E Mineral King Ave (93292-6905)
P.O. Box 949 (93279-0949)
PHONE..................559 733-4408
Michael Haworth, *Pr*
Bruce Lynn, *
EMP: 65 **EST:** 1916
SQ FT: 10,000
SALES (est): 8.91MM
SALES (corp-wide): 8.91MM **Privately Held**
Web: www.orangebelt.com
SIC: 4142 4141 Bus charter service, except local; Local bus charter service

(P-3320)
ROYAL COACH TOURS (PA)
630 Stockton Ave (95126-2433)
PHONE..................408 279-4801
Sandra Allen, *CEO*
Daniel Smith, *
Joanne Smith Christian, *Stockholder*
EMP: 60 **EST:** 1960
SQ FT: 2,500
SALES (est): 23.48MM
SALES (corp-wide): 23.48MM **Privately Held**
Web: www.royal-coach.com
SIC: 4142 Bus charter service, except local

(P-3321)
SURERIDE CHARTER INC
Also Called: Sun Diego Charter
522 W 8th St (91950-1004)
PHONE..................619 336-9200
EMP: 120 **EST:** 1994
SQ FT: 60,000
SALES (est): 16.23MM **Privately Held**
Web: www.sundiegocharter.com
SIC: 4142 Bus charter service, except local

4151 School Buses

(P-3322)
ANTELOPE VLY SCHL TRNSP AGCY
670 W Avenue L8 (93534-7100)
PHONE..................661 952-3106
Morris Fuselier Iii, *CEO*
Gary Russell, *
Joanne Downen, *
EMP: 206 **EST:** 1980
SALES (est): 21.01MM **Privately Held**
Web: www.avsta.org
SIC: 4151 School buses

(P-3323)
CITY OF DOWNEY
7209 Rosecrans Ave (90723-2501)
PHONE..................562 529-5465
Judy Smith, *Brnch Mgr*
EMP: 63
SALES (corp-wide): 148.39MM **Privately Held**
Web: www.downeyca.org
SIC: 4151 School buses
PA: City Of Downey
11111 Brookshire Ave
Downey CA

(P-3324)
COUNTY OF LOS ANGELES
Also Called: Pupil Transportation
9402 Greenleaf Ave (90605-2700)
PHONE..................562 945-2581
Dan Ibarra, *Dir*
EMP: 224
SALES (corp-wide): 31.7B **Privately Held**
Web: www.lacounty.gov
SIC: 4151 9621 School buses; Regulation, administration of transportation
PA: County Of Los Angeles
500 W Temple St Ste 437
Los Angeles CA
213 974-1101

(P-3325)
DURHAM SCHOOL SERVICES L P
723 S Alameda St (90220-3809)
PHONE..................310 767-5820
Raphael Balonos, *Mgr*
EMP: 200
Web: www.durhamschoolservices.com
SIC: 4151 School buses
HQ: Durham School Services, L. P.
2601 Navistar Dr
Lisle IL
630 836-0292

(P-3326)
DURHAM SCHOOL SERVICES L P
8555 Flower Ave (90723-5602)
PHONE..................562 408-1206
Paul Wiggins, *Genl Mgr*
EMP: 114
Web: www.durhamschoolservices.com
SIC: 4151 School buses
HQ: Durham School Services, L. P.
2601 Navistar Dr
Lisle IL
630 836-0292

(P-3327)
DURHAM SCHOOL SERVICES L P
379 Earhart Way (94551-9509)
PHONE..................925 606-0871
Phillys Decia, *Mgr*
EMP: 114
Web: www.durhamschoolservices.com
SIC: 4151 School buses
HQ: Durham School Services, L. P.
2601 Navistar Dr
Lisle IL
630 836-0292

(P-3328)
DURHAM SCHOOL SERVICES L P
4029 Las Virgenes Rd (91302-3505)
PHONE..................818 880-4257
Nanette Nanzini, *Genl Mgr*
EMP: 200
Web: www.durhamschoolservices.com
SIC: 4151 School buses
HQ: Durham School Services, L. P.
2601 Navistar Dr
Lisle IL
630 836-0292

(P-3329)
DURHAM SCHOOL SERVICES L P
Also Called: Lidlaw Educational Services
12999 Victoria St (91739-9532)
PHONE..................909 899-1809
Laura Randals, *Mgr*
EMP: 114
Web: www.durhamschoolservices.com
SIC: 4151 School buses
HQ: Durham School Services, L. P.
2601 Navistar Dr
Lisle IL
630 836-0292

(P-3330)
DURHAM SCHOOL SERVICES L P
Also Called: Durham School Services
1506 White Oaks Rd (95008-6724)
PHONE..................833 698-7474
EMP: 171
Web: www.durhamschoolservices.com
SIC: 4151 School buses
HQ: Durham School Services, L. P.
2601 Navistar Dr
Lisle IL
630 836-0292

(P-3331)
DURHAM SCHOOL SERVICES L P
3151 W 5th St Ste A (93030-6415)
PHONE..................805 483-6076
Lee Philips, *Genl Mgr*
EMP: 171
Web: www.durhamschoolservices.com
SIC: 4151 School buses
HQ: Durham School Services, L. P.
2601 Navistar Dr
Lisle IL
630 836-0292

(P-3332)
DURHAM SCHOOL SERVICES L P
Also Called: Durham School Services
10701 E Bennett Rd (95945-9361)
P.O. Box 1393 (95945-1393)
PHONE..................530 273-7282
Paula Davidson, *Genl Mgr*
EMP: 171
Web: www.durhamschoolservices.com
SIC: 4151 4119 4111 School buses; Local passenger transportation, nec; Local and suburban transit
HQ: Durham School Services, L. P.
2601 Navistar Dr
Lisle IL
630 836-0292

(P-3333)
DURHAM SCHOOL SERVICES L P
2713 River Ave (91770-3303)
PHONE..................626 573-3769
David Gonzales, *Genl Mgr*
EMP: 1000
Web: www.durhamschoolservices.com
SIC: 4151 School buses
HQ: Durham School Services, L. P.
2601 Navistar Dr
Lisle IL
630 836-0292

(P-3334)
DURHAM SCHOOL SERVICES L P
2003 Laguna Canyon Rd (92651-1123)
PHONE..................949 376-0376
EMP: 114
Web: www.durhamschoolservices.com
SIC: 4151 School buses
HQ: Durham School Services, L. P.
2601 Navistar Dr
Lisle IL
630 836-0292

(P-3335)
ELK GROVE UNIFIED SCHOOL DST
Also Called: Transportation Department
8421 Gerber Rd (95828-3711)
PHONE..................916 686-7733
Jill Gayaldo, *Brnch Mgr*
EMP: 62
SALES (corp-wide): 741.91MM **Privately Held**
Web: www.egusd.net
SIC: 4151 School buses
PA: Grove Elk Unified School District
9510 Elk Grove Florin Rd
Elk Grove CA
916 686-5085

PRODUCTS & SERVICES SECTION

4173 - Bus Terminal And Service Facilities (P-3357)

(P-3336)
FIRST STUDENT INC
436 Parr Blvd (94801-1123)
PHONE..................................510 237-6677
Brian Rutford, Prin
EMP: 170
Web: www.firststudentinc.com
SIC: 4151 School buses
PA: First Student, Inc.
   600 Vine St Ste 1400
   Cincinnati OH

(P-3337)
FIRST STUDENT INC
59 Jordan St (94901-3918)
PHONE..................................415 455-9098
Cindy Srering, Brnch Mgr
EMP: 159
Web: www.firststudentinc.com
SIC: 4151 School buses
PA: First Student, Inc.
   600 Vine St Ste 1400
   Cincinnati OH

(P-3338)
FIRST STUDENT INC
Also Called: Laidlaw Educational Services
5006 E Calle San Raphael (92264-3452)
PHONE..................................760 320-4659
Mike Robertson, Mgr
EMP: 306
Web: www.firststudentinc.com
SIC: 4151 School buses
PA: First Student, Inc.
   600 Vine St Ste 1400
   Cincinnati OH

(P-3339)
FIRST STUDENT INC
2005 Navy Dr (95206-1142)
PHONE..................................209 466-7737
Drigden Summers, Mgr
EMP: 159
Web: www.firststudentinc.com
SIC: 4151 School buses
PA: First Student, Inc.
   600 Vine St Ste 1400
   Cincinnati OH

(P-3340)
FIRST STUDENT INC
2805 Se Ave (93725-1942)
PHONE..................................559 268-4077
EMP: 147
Web: www.firststudentinc.com
SIC: 4151 School buses
PA: First Student, Inc.
   600 Vine St Ste 1400
   Cincinnati OH

(P-3341)
FIRST STUDENT INC
2270 Jerrold Ave (94124-1012)
PHONE..................................415 647-9012
Bob Gonzales, Mgr
EMP: 193
Web: www.firststudentinc.com
SIC: 4151 School buses
PA: First Student, Inc.
   600 Vine St Ste 1400
   Cincinnati OH

(P-3342)
FIRST STUDENT INC
931 Remillard Ct (95122-2625)
PHONE..................................408 971-3466
Susan Moorehaed, Mgr
EMP: 147
Web: www.firststudentinc.com

SIC: 4151 School buses
PA: First Student, Inc.
   600 Vine St Ste 1400
   Cincinnati OH

(P-3343)
FIRST STUDENT INC
11233 San Fernando Rd (91340-3409)
PHONE..................................818 896-0333
Sue Wagnon, Brnch Mgr
EMP: 272
Web: www.firststudentinc.com
SIC: 4151 School buses
PA: First Student, Inc.
   600 Vine St Ste 1400
   Cincinnati OH

(P-3344)
FIRST STUDENT INC
Also Called: Cardinal Transportation
14800 S Avalon Blvd (90248-2012)
PHONE..................................310 769-2400
Ray Borales, Pr
Roy J Weber, *
▲ EMP: 5056 EST: 1987
SQ FT: 18,000
SALES (est): 10.01MM
SALES (corp-wide): 5.71B Privately Held
Web: www.firststudentinc.com
SIC: 4151 School buses
HQ: Firstgroup America, Inc.
   191 Rosa Parks St
   Cincinnati OH
   513 241-2200

(P-3345)
FRESNO CNTY SPRNTNDENT SCHOOLS
Also Called: Southwest Transportation Agcy
16644 S Elm Ave (93609-9757)
P.O. Box 785 (93656-0785)
PHONE..................................559 644-1000
Tony Mendes, Brnch Mgr
EMP: 198
SALES (corp-wide): 227.82MM Privately Held
Web: www.fcoe.org
SIC: 4151 School buses
PA: Fresno County Superintendent Of Schools
   1111 Van Ness Ave
   Fresno CA
   559 265-3000

(P-3346)
LONG BEACH UNIFIED SCHOOL DST
Also Called: Transportation Department
2700 Pine Ave (90806-2617)
PHONE..................................562 426-6176
Paul Bailey, Dir
EMP: 170
SALES (corp-wide): 788.46MM Privately Held
Web: www.lbschools.net
SIC: 4151 School buses
PA: Long Beach Unified School District
   1515 Hughes Way
   Long Beach CA
   562 997-8000

(P-3347)
MERCED TRANSPORTATION COMPANY
300 Grogan Ave (95341-6446)
PHONE..................................209 384-2575
TOLL FREE: 800
Curtis Riggs, Pr
Gaye Riggs, *

EMP: 67 EST: 1980
SQ FT: 8,000
SALES (est): 6.01MM Privately Held
SIC: 4151 School buses

(P-3348)
RIM OF WORLD UNIFIED SCHL DST
Also Called: Transportation
27614 Hwy 18 Across Building I (92352)
P.O. Box 430 (92352-0430)
PHONE..................................909 336-0330
Susie Hubbard, Dir
EMP: 75
SALES (corp-wide): 50.82MM Privately Held
Web: www.rimsd.k12.ca.us
SIC: 4151 School buses
PA: Rim Of The World Unified School District
   27315 N Bay Rd
   Blue Jay CA
   909 336-2031

(P-3349)
SANTA BARBARA TRNSP CORP
42138 7th St W (93534-7145)
PHONE..................................661 510-0566
EMP: 138
SALES (corp-wide): 2.01B Privately Held
SIC: 4151 School buses
HQ: Santa Barbara Transportation Corporation
   3349 Hwy 138 Ste C
   Wall Township NJ
   732 280-4200

(P-3350)
SANTA BARBARA TRNSP CORP
Also Called: Santa Barbara Transportation
1131 E Houston Ave (93292-3845)
PHONE..................................559 738-5780
Ray Delegard, VP
EMP: 103
SALES (corp-wide): 2.01B Privately Held
SIC: 4151 School buses
HQ: Santa Barbara Transportation Corporation
   3349 Hwy 138 Ste C
   Wall Township NJ
   732 280-4200

(P-3351)
SANTA BARBARA TRNSP CORP
Also Called: Student Transportation America
520 Gannon Pl (92025-2513)
PHONE..................................760 746-0850
EMP: 206
SALES (corp-wide): 2.01B Privately Held
SIC: 4151 School buses
HQ: Santa Barbara Transportation Corporation
   3349 Hwy 138 Ste C
   Wall Township NJ
   732 280-4200

(P-3352)
SANTA BARBARA TRNSP CORP
Also Called: Student Transportation America
6500 Hollister Ave Ste 100 (93117-3011)
PHONE..................................805 928-0402
EMP: 188
SALES (corp-wide): 2.01B Privately Held
SIC: 4151 4121 School buses; Taxicabs
HQ: Santa Barbara Transportation Corporation
   3349 Hwy 138 Ste C
   Wall Township NJ
   732 280-4200

(P-3353)
UNIVERSITY CALIFORNIA DAVIS
Also Called: Transportation Services
1 Shields Ave (95616-8500)
PHONE..................................530 752-8277
Cliff Contreras, Dir
EMP: 109
SALES (corp-wide): 534.4MM Privately Held
Web: www.ucdavis.edu
SIC: 4151 7521 School buses; Automobile parking
HQ: University Of California, Davis
   1 Shields Ave
   Davis CA

4173 Bus Terminal And Service Facilities

(P-3354)
ALAMEDA-CONTRA COSTA TRNST DST
A C Transit
10626 International Blvd (94603-3806)
PHONE..................................510 577-8816
Glen Andrade, Mgr
EMP: 980
SALES (corp-wide): 28.11MM Privately Held
Web: www.actransit.org
SIC: 4173 Maintenance facilities for motor vehicle passenger transport
PA: Alameda-Contra Costa Transit District
   1600 Franklin St
   Oakland CA
   510 891-4777

(P-3355)
DURHAM SCHOOL SERVICES L P
2818 W 5th St (92703-1824)
PHONE..................................714 542-8989
Debbie Williams, Mgr
EMP: 257
SQ FT: 4,843
Web: www.durhamschoolservices.com
SIC: 4173 4151 Maintenance facilities for motor vehicle passenger transport; School buses
HQ: Durham School Services, L. P.
   2601 Navistar Dr
   Lisle IL
   630 836-0292

(P-3356)
FIRST STUDENT INC
300 S Buena Vista Ave (92882-1937)
PHONE..................................951 736-3234
Jackie Mansperger, Mgr
EMP: 204
Web: www.firststudentinc.com
SIC: 4173 4151 Maintenance facilities, buses; School buses
PA: First Student, Inc.
   600 Vine St Ste 1400
   Cincinnati OH

(P-3357)
GREYHOUND LINES INC
1716 E 7th St (90021-1202)
PHONE..................................213 629-8400
Mark Jacobson, Prin
EMP: 96
SQ FT: 100,000
SALES (corp-wide): 611.17MM Privately Held
Web: www.greyhound.com

4173 - Bus Terminal And Service Facilities (P-3358)

SIC: 4173 Bus terminal operation
HQ: Greyhound Lines, Inc.
350 N Saint Paul St # 300
Dallas TX
214 849-8000

(P-3358)
SAN MATEO COUNTY TRANSIT DST
Also Called: Sam Trans
501 Pico Blvd (94070-2706)
PHONE..................650 508-6412
Ed Proctor, Mgr
EMP: 220
SALES (corp-wide): 8.91MM Privately Held
Web: www.smctd.com
SIC: 4173 4111 Maintenance facilities, buses ; Local and suburban transit
PA: San Mateo County Transit District
1250 San Carlos Ave
San Carlos CA
650 508-6200

4212 Local Trucking, Without Storage

(P-3359)
365 DELIVERY INC
440 E Huntington Dr Ste 300 (91006-3776)
PHONE..................818 815-5005
Bernardo Anders, Pr
Ariana Barrera, *
EMP: 100 EST: 2017
SALES (est): 2.45MM Privately Held
SIC: 4212 Delivery service, vehicular

(P-3360)
A & S METAL RECYCLING INC (PA)
2261 E 15th St (90021-2841)
PHONE..................213 623-9443
Alexander Scott, CEO
▼ EMP: 62 EST: 1984
SQ FT: 18,000
SALES (est): 14.16MM
SALES (corp-wide): 14.16MM Privately Held
Web: www.aandsmetal.com
SIC: 4212 5093 Hazardous waste transport; Scrap and waste materials

(P-3361)
A G HACIENDA INCORPORATED
32794 Sherwood Ave (93250-9626)
P.O. Box 367 (93250-0367)
PHONE..................661 792-2418
Xochilht Gonzalez, Pr
EMP: 400 EST: 1997
SALES (est): 9.77MM Privately Held
SIC: 4212 0761 4214 Local trucking, without storage; Farm labor contractors; Local trucking with storage

(P-3362)
A-1 DELIVERY CO
1777 S Vintage Ave (91761-3659)
P.O. Box 4210 (91761-8910)
PHONE..................909 444-1220
Joe Romine, Pr
Johnny Romine, *
William Turner, *
EMP: 75 EST: 1976
SQ FT: 10,000
SALES (est): 9.8MM Privately Held
Web: www.a1deliveryco.com
SIC: 4212 Delivery service, vehicular

(P-3363)
A-TEAM DELIVERS LLC
12127 Mall Blvd Ste A322 (92392-7665)
PHONE..................858 254-8401
Steve Ford, CEO
EMP: 80 EST: 2020
SALES (est): 2.55MM Privately Held
SIC: 4212 Delivery service, vehicular

(P-3364)
ACE RELOCATION SYSTEMS INC (PA)
Also Called: Ace Relocation Systems
5608 Eastgate Dr (92121-2816)
PHONE..................858 677-5500
Lawrence Lammers, CEO
Lawrence R Lammers, *
Daniel J Lammers, *
Laura Marion, *
Richard Clarke, *
▲ EMP: 69 EST: 1955
SQ FT: 48,000
SALES (est): 83.17MM
SALES (corp-wide): 83.17MM Privately Held
Web: www.acerelocation.com
SIC: 4212 Moving services

(P-3365)
ADVANCED CHEMICAL TRNSPT INC
600 Iowa St (92373-8047)
PHONE..................951 790-7989
EMP: 196
SALES (corp-wide): 95.12MM Privately Held
Web: www.actenviro.com
SIC: 4212 Hazardous waste transport
PA: Advanced Chemical Transport, Inc.
967 Mabury Rd
San Jose CA
408 548-5050

(P-3366)
AJR TRUCKING INC
435 E Weber Ave (90222-1424)
PHONE..................310 707-1120
Khachatur Khudikyan, CEO
Angel Reyes, *
Hakop Khudikyan, *
EMP: 84 EST: 1989
SQ FT: 12,000
SALES (est): 10.01MM Privately Held
Web: www.ajrtrucking.com
SIC: 4212 Mail carriers, contract

(P-3367)
ANCON MARINE LLC
Also Called: Ancon Services
2735 Rose Ave (90755-1927)
PHONE..................562 326-5900
EMP: 102
SALES (corp-wide): 113.73MM Privately Held
Web: www.anconservices.com
SIC: 4212 Local trucking, without storage
PA: Ancon Marine, Llc
10571 Los Alamitos Blvd
Los Alamitos CA
707 756-0286

(P-3368)
APEX BULK COMMODITIES INC (PA)
Also Called: Apex Bulk Commodities
12531 Violet Rd Ste A (92301-2731)
PHONE..................760 246-6077
EMP: 200 EST: 1967
SALES (est): 41.54MM
SALES (corp-wide): 41.54MM Privately Held
Web: www.apexbulk.com
SIC: 4212 4213 Liquid haulage, local; Trucking, except local

(P-3369)
ARAKELIAN ENTERPRISES INC
Also Called: Athens Services
11121 Pendleton St (91352-1513)
PHONE..................818 768-2644
Ron Arakelian Junior, CEO
EMP: 164
SALES (corp-wide): 199.65MM Privately Held
Web: www.athensservices.com
SIC: 4212 Garbage collection and transport, no disposal
PA: Arakelian Enterprises, Inc.
14048 Valley Blvd
City Of Industry CA
626 336-3636

(P-3370)
ASBURY ENVIRONMENTAL SERVICES (PA)
Also Called: World Oil Environmental Svcs
1300 S Santa Fe Ave (90221-4916)
PHONE..................310 886-3400
Steve Kerdoon, CEO
Bruce De Menno, *
Chris Mahoney, *
Anne Asbury, *
EMP: 75 EST: 1936
SQ FT: 22,000
SALES (est): 41.47MM
SALES (corp-wide): 41.47MM Privately Held
Web: www.asburyenv.com
SIC: 4212 Local trucking, without storage

(P-3371)
B & G DELIVERY SYSTEM INC
2549 Harris Ave (95838-3128)
P.O. Box 2486 (95677-8461)
PHONE..................916 921-4401
EMP: 125
Web: www.bgdelivery.com
SIC: 4212 4215 Delivery service, vehicular; Courier services, except by air

(P-3372)
BELSHIRE TRNSP SVCS INC
Also Called: Belshire
25971 Towne Centre Dr (92610-2462)
PHONE..................949 460-5200
Karen Cass, *
EMP: 125 EST: 2002
SALES (est): 9.48MM Privately Held
Web: www.belshire.com
SIC: 4212 Hazardous waste transport

(P-3373)
BFI WASTE SYSTEMS N AMER INC
Also Called: Site 915
1601 Dixon Landing Rd Bldg 1 (95035-8100)
PHONE..................408 432-1234
Desi Reno, Genl Mgr
EMP: 92
SALES (corp-wide): 13.51B Publicly Held
SIC: 4212 4959 4953 Garbage collection and transport, no disposal; Sanitary services, nec; Refuse systems
HQ: Bfi Waste Systems Of North America, Inc.
2394 E Camelback Rd
Phoenix AZ

(P-3374)
BURNS AND SONS TRUCKING INC
Also Called: Dependable Disposal and Recycl
9210 Olive Dr (91977-2305)
P.O. Box 1640 (91979-1640)
PHONE..................619 460-5394
TOLL FREE: 800
Eva N Burns, CEO
Jack Burns Senior, Pr
Tom Mcfarlane, Genl Mgr
Jim Burns, *
Jack Burns Junior, VP
EMP: 85 EST: 1977
SQ FT: 6,000
SALES (est): 15.08MM Privately Held
Web: www.burnsandsons.com
SIC: 4212 4214 Local trucking, without storage; Local trucking with storage

(P-3375)
C P S EXPRESS
4375 E Lowell St Ste G (91761-2227)
P.O. Box 248 (91752-0248)
PHONE..................951 685-1041
Kurt Allen, CEO
Timothy Pollock, *
Paul Anderson, *
EMP: 115 EST: 1980
SQ FT: 7,000
SALES (est): 23.73MM
SALES (corp-wide): 23.73MM Privately Held
Web: www.cpsexpress.com
SIC: 4212 4213 4214 Local trucking, without storage; Trucking, except local; Local trucking with storage
PA: Haddy, J G Sales Co, Inc
4375 E Lowell St Ste G
Ontario CA
951 685-4100

(P-3376)
C S TRANSPORT INC
Also Called: Southern California Carriers
425 E Heber Rd Ste 200 (92249-9660)
PHONE..................760 666-5661
Samuel Colin, Pr
EMP: 64 EST: 2006
SQ FT: 700
SALES (est): 2.44MM Privately Held
SIC: 4212 4731 Local trucking, without storage; Transportation agents and brokers

(P-3377)
CALIFORNIA TRANSPORT ENTERPRISES INC
2610 Wisconsin Ave (90280-5598)
P.O. Box 471 (90280-0471)
PHONE..................
EMP: 66 EST: 1978
SALES (est): 3.74MM Privately Held
Web: www.cteinc.net
SIC: 4212 Local trucking, without storage

(P-3378)
CARGO SOLUTION BROKERAGE INC
14587 Valley Blvd (92335-6248)
PHONE..................909 350-1644
Yudvinder S Kang, CEO
EMP: 200 EST: 2004
SALES (est): 4.61MM Privately Held
SIC: 4212 Local trucking, without storage

(P-3379)
CARTEL TRANSPORT LLC
154 Poppy Ave (95363-9717)
PHONE..................209 892-3880
Dominic Carlucci, Managing Member

EMP: 125
SALES (corp-wide): 4.77MM **Privately Held**
Web: www.carluccitransport.com
SIC: **4212** Local trucking, without storage
PA: Cartel Transport, Llc
    1487 13th St
    Firebaugh CA
    559 659-3981

(P-3380)
CATERED FIT CORP
13631 Saticoy St (91402-6301)
PHONE..................................855 400-2348
Adam Friden, *Genl Mgr*
EMP: 102
SALES (corp-wide): 6.72MM **Privately Held**
Web: www.cateredfit.com
SIC: **4212** 5812 Baggage transfer; Caterers
PA: Catered Fit Corp
    5150 N State Road 7
    Fort Lauderdale FL
    954 549-4693

(P-3381)
CENTRAL STATES LOGISTICS INC
Also Called: Diligent Delivery Systems
28338 Constellation Rd Ste 940 (91355-5012)
PHONE..................................661 295-7222
Larry Browne, *Brnch Mgr*
EMP: 181
SALES (corp-wide): 36.79MM **Privately Held**
Web: www.diligentusa.com
SIC: **4212** Delivery service, vehicular
PA: Central States Logistics, Inc.
    9200 Derrington Rd # 100
    Houston TX
    888 374-3354

(P-3382)
CENTRAL VALLEY CONCRETE INC (PA)
Also Called: Central Valley Trucking
3823 N State Highway 59 (95348-9370)
PHONE..................................209 723-8846
Scott Neal, *CEO*
EMP: 150 EST: 1975
SQ FT: 2,000
SALES (est): 34.42MM
SALES (corp-wide): 34.42MM **Privately Held**
Web: www.centralvalleyconcrete.com
SIC: **4212** 3273 Local trucking, without storage; Ready-mixed concrete

(P-3383)
CJ LOGISTICS AMERICA LLC
12350 Philadelphia Ave (91752-3228)
PHONE..................................909 605-7233
EMP: 190
Web: america.cjlogistics.com
SIC: **4212** 4213 4225 4731 Local trucking, without storage; Trucking, except local; General warehousing and storage; Freight consolidation
HQ: Cj Logistics America, Llc
    1750 S Wolf Rd
    Des Plaines IL

(P-3384)
CNET EXPRESS
15134 Indiana Ave Apt 38 (90723-3582)
PHONE..................................949 357-5475
Diana Diaz Vargas, *CEO*
Tamara Lupoe, *Prin*
Allen E Lupoe Junior, *Prin*

EMP: 102 EST: 2018
SALES (est): 3.08MM **Privately Held**
SIC: **4212** Delivery service, vehicular

(P-3385)
DAWSON DELIVERY LLC
27240 Turnberry Ln Ste 200 (91355-1045)
PHONE..................................505 385-1074
David Dawson, *Prin*
EMP: 60 EST: 2020
SALES (est): 2.7MM **Privately Held**
Web: www.dawsondeliveryca.com
SIC: **4212** Local trucking, without storage

(P-3386)
DELIVERY SOLUTIONS INC
Also Called: D S I
595 Tamarack Ave Ste D (92821-3206)
PHONE..................................800 335-6557
▲ EMP: 75
Web: www.deliverysolutions.com
SIC: **4212** Delivery service, vehicular

(P-3387)
DELUXE AUTO CARRIERS INC
Also Called: Excel Auto Transporting Towing
4788 Brookhollow Cir (92509-3072)
PHONE..................................909 746-0900
Jesus Holguin, *Pr*
Raul Silva, *
EMP: 60 EST: 2004
SALES (est): 15.94MM **Privately Held**
Web: www.deluxeac.com
SIC: **4212** Local trucking, without storage

(P-3388)
DLF LOGISTICS LLC
Also Called: Dlf Logistics
1019 S Rimpau Blvd (90019-1810)
P.O. Box 1929 (90801-1929)
PHONE..................................626 387-3797
Durran Felton, *Managing Member*
EMP: 81 EST: 2019
SALES (est): 2.51MM **Privately Held**
SIC: **4212** Local trucking, without storage

(P-3389)
FEATHER RIVER DISPOSAL INC
1166 Industrial Way (95971-9724)
PHONE..................................530 283-2065
Mike Clemetf, *Prin*
EMP: 266 EST: 1964
SALES (est): 1.77MM
SALES (corp-wide): 19.7B **Publicly Held**
SIC: **4212** Garbage collection and transport, no disposal
HQ: Waste Management Of Texas, Inc.
    1001 Fannin St Ste 4000
    Houston TX

(P-3390)
FOX TRANSPORTATION INC (PA)
8610 Helms Ave (91730-4520)
P.O. Box 3119 (91729-3119)
PHONE..................................909 291-4646
Michael K Fox, *CEO*
David Langrehr, *Sr VP*
David Burns, *VP*
Joey Ramirez, *Dir*
Mary Anne Fox, *Stockholder*
EMP: 73 EST: 2003
SALES (est): 10.43MM **Privately Held**
Web: www.foxtransportationinc.com
SIC: **4212** Local trucking, without storage

(P-3391)
FRANK GHIGLIONE INC (PA)
Also Called: Rodgers Trucking Co

1622 Moreland Dr (94501-3018)
PHONE..................................510 483-7000
Frank Ghiglione, *Pr*
Winifred Ghiglione, *
EMP: 80 EST: 1972
SALES: 8.6MM
SALES (corp-wide): 8.6MM **Privately Held**
Web: www.rodgerstrucking.com
SIC: **4212** Delivery service, vehicular

(P-3392)
FRANK GHIGLIONE INC
Also Called: Rogers Trucking
2972 Alvarado St Ste H (94577-5732)
PHONE..................................510 483-2063
Frank Ghiglione, *Mgr*
EMP: 80
SALES (corp-wide): 8.6MM **Privately Held**
Web: www.rodgerstrucking.com
SIC: **4212** 4214 Delivery service, vehicular; Local trucking with storage
PA: Frank Ghiglione, Inc.
    1622 Moreland Dr
    Alameda CA
    510 483-7000

(P-3393)
FRESGO LLC
Also Called: Kitchen United
219 S Fair Oaks Ave (91105-2005)
PHONE..................................626 389-3500
James Collins, *Managing Member*
EMP: 79 EST: 2019
SALES (est): 5.95MM **Privately Held**
SIC: **4212** Delivery service, vehicular

(P-3394)
GALE/TRIANGLE INC (PA)
Also Called: Triangle West
12816 Shoemaker Ave (90670-6346)
PHONE..................................562 741-1300
Michael Kaplan, *CEO*
Bob Kaplan, *Pr*
Craig Kaplan, *CEO*
▲ EMP: 94 EST: 1994
SQ FT: 40,000
SALES (est): 6.54MM **Privately Held**
SIC: **4212** 4214 Local trucking, without storage; Local trucking with storage

(P-3395)
GATEWAY LOGISTICS TECH LLC
11400 W Olympic Blvd (90064-1579)
PHONE..................................732 750-9000
Jim Deveau, *CEO*
EMP: 268 EST: 2020
SALES (est): 1.15MM
SALES (corp-wide): 58.62MM **Privately Held**
SIC: **4212** 4213 Local trucking, without storage; Trucking, except local
PA: Taylored Services Parent Co. Inc.
    1495 E Locust St
    Ontario CA
    909 510-4800

(P-3396)
GAZELLE TRANSPORTATION LLC
34915 Gazelle Ct (93308-9618)
PHONE..................................661 322-8868
EMP: 193 EST: 1992
SALES (est): 20.08MM **Privately Held**
Web: www.gazelletrans.com
SIC: **4212** Local trucking, without storage

(P-3397)
GENERAL LGSTICS SYSTEMS US INC

24305 Prielipp Rd (92595-7425)
PHONE..................................951 677-3972
EMP: 128
SALES (corp-wide): 14.47B **Privately Held**
Web: www.gls-us.com
SIC: **4212** Delivery service, vehicular
HQ: General Logistics Systems Us, Inc.
    4000 Executive Pkwy # 295
    San Ramon CA

(P-3398)
GENERAL LGSTICS SYSTEMS US INC
12300 Bell Ranch Dr (90670-3356)
PHONE..................................562 577-6037
EMP: 171
SALES (corp-wide): 14.47B **Privately Held**
Web: www.gls-us.com
SIC: **4212** Delivery service, vehicular
HQ: General Logistics Systems Us, Inc.
    4000 Executive Pkwy # 295
    San Ramon CA

(P-3399)
GILLIES TRUCKING INC
3931 Newton Rd (95205-2488)
P.O. Box 8303 (95208-0303)
PHONE..................................209 948-6268
Randy Gilles, *Pr*
Ken Gillies, *
James T Gillies, *
EMP: 76 EST: 1954
SQ FT: 5,000
SALES (est): 4.14MM **Privately Held**
Web: www.gilliestrucking.com
SIC: **4212** Local trucking, without storage

(P-3400)
GRIMMWAY ENTERPRISES INC
11646 Malaga Rd (93203-9641)
PHONE..................................307 302-0090
EMP: 87
SALES (corp-wide): 1.86B **Privately Held**
Web: www.grimmway.com
SIC: **4212** Farm to market haulage, local
PA: Grimmway Enterprises, Inc.
    14141 Di Giorgio Rd
    Arvin CA
    800 301-3101

(P-3401)
HANKS INC
Also Called: SUN EXPRESS
13866 Slover Ave (92337-7037)
PHONE..................................909 350-8365
Brenda Cash, *Admn*
Brian Bachar, *
Shirley Bachar, *
▲ EMP: 74 EST: 1961
SQ FT: 24,000
SALES (est): 13.44MM **Privately Held**
Web: www.shipsun.com
SIC: **4212** 4213 Local trucking, without storage; Trucking, except local

(P-3402)
HARTWICK & HAND INC (PA)
Also Called: H & H Truck Terminal
16953 N D St (92394-1417)
P.O. Box 1595 (92393-1595)
PHONE..................................760 245-1666
Stacy L Hand, *CEO*
Edward Perreria, *
EMP: 73 EST: 1961
SQ FT: 8,800
SALES (est): 4.44MM
SALES (corp-wide): 4.44MM **Privately Held**
SIC: **4212** Local trucking, without storage

4212 - Local Trucking, Without Storage (P-3403)

(P-3403)
HEAVY LOAD TRANSFER LLC
18735 S Ferris Pl (90220-6405)
PHONE....................310 816-0260
EMP: 75 EST: 2016
SALES (est): 3.74MM Privately Held
Web: www.ttsi.com
SIC: 4212 Local trucking, without storage

(P-3404)
HF COX INC
Also Called: Cox Petroleum Transport
8330 Atlantic Ave (90201-5808)
PHONE....................323 587-2359
Diane Judge, Brnch Mgr
EMP: 290
SALES (corp-wide): 683.25K Privately Held
Web: www.coxpetroleum.com
SIC: 4212 Petroleum haulage, local
PA: H.F. Cox, Inc.
  118 Cox Transport Way
  Bakersfield CA
  661 366-3236

(P-3405)
HIGH PERFORMANCE LOGISTICS LLC
7227 Central Ave (92504-1432)
PHONE....................702 300-4880
Michael Waters, Managing Member
EMP: 75 EST: 2018
SALES (est): 3.22MM Privately Held
SIC: 4212 Local trucking, without storage

(P-3406)
HUB GROUP TRUCKING INC
13867 Valley Blvd (92335-5230)
PHONE....................909 770-8950
Roy Sheredon, Brnch Mgr
EMP: 500
SALES (corp-wide): 5.34B Publicly Held
Web: www.hubgroup.com
SIC: 4212 Local trucking, without storage
HQ: Hub Group Trucking, Inc.
  2001 Hub Group Way
  Oak Brook IL
  630 271-3600

(P-3407)
J D L MOTOR EXPRESS
1250 Delevan Dr (92102-2437)
PHONE....................619 232-6136
John Lenore, Pr
Dorothy Lenore, Sec
Harold Gursky, VP
EMP: 72 EST: 1966
SALES (est): 633.63K
SALES (corp-wide): 45.4MM Privately Held
Web: www.johnlenore.com
SIC: 4212 4213 Local trucking, without storage; Automobiles, transport and delivery
PA: Lenore John & Co
  1250 Delevan Dr
  San Diego CA
  619 232-6136

(P-3408)
JOHN AGUILAR & COMPANY INC
Also Called: Vernon Transportation Company
1505 Navy Dr (95206-4104)
P.O. Box 31450 (95213-1450)
PHONE....................209 546-0171
Gregg Wilson, Pr
Dave Wilson, *
EMP: 85 EST: 1986
SQ FT: 5,600
SALES (est): 14.86MM Privately Held
Web: sugartrux.websitepro.hosting
SIC: 4212 Liquid haulage, local

(P-3409)
JS HOMEN TRUCKING INC
4224 Turlock Rd (95369-9729)
P.O. Box 382 (95369-0382)
PHONE....................209 723-9559
Joe Homen, Pr
Margaret Homen, *
EMP: 65 EST: 1989
SQ FT: 2,484
SALES (est): 2.18MM Privately Held
SIC: 4212 Local trucking, without storage

(P-3410)
KNIGHT TRANSPORTATION INC
4450 S Blackstone St (93274-7405)
PHONE....................559 685-9838
Mark Rogers, Prin
EMP: 65
SQ FT: 24,920
Web: www.knighttrans.com
SIC: 4212 4213 Local trucking, without storage; Trucking, except local
HQ: Knight Transportation, Inc.
  2002 W Wahalla Ln
  Phoenix AZ

(P-3411)
MAD DOG EXPRESS INC (PA)
299 Lawrence Ave (94080-6818)
P.O. Box 281585 (94128-1585)
PHONE....................650 588-1900
Steve Harth, Pr
John Coleman, *
EMP: 70 EST: 1989
SQ FT: 18,500
SALES (est): 3.88MM Privately Held
SIC: 4212 Local trucking, without storage

(P-3412)
MAMBA LOGISTICS INC
23749 Fitzgerald St (91304-5704)
PHONE....................661 234-8050
Danisha Danielle Wrighster, CEO
EMP: 65 EST: 2020
SALES (est): 1.89MM Privately Held
Web: www.mambalogistics.com
SIC: 4212 4215 Delivery service, vehicular; Package delivery, vehicular

(P-3413)
MISSION TRAIL WSTE SYSTEMS INC
Also Called: Recycle Waste
1060 Richard Ave (95050-2816)
PHONE....................408 727-5365
Louie Pellegrini, Pr
Robert Molinaro, *
William Dobert, *
Douglas Button, . *
EMP: 75 EST: 1960
SALES (est): 14.37MM Privately Held
Web: www.missiontrail.com
SIC: 4212 4953 Garbage collection and transport, no disposal; Recycling, waste materials

(P-3414)
MT DBLO RESOURCE RECOVERY LLC
4080 Mallard Dr (94520-1245)
PHONE....................925 682-9113
EMP: 300 EST: 2017
SALES (est): 8.2MM Privately Held
Web: www.mdrr.com
SIC: 4212 4953 Garbage collection and transport, no disposal; Liquid waste, collection and disposal

(P-3415)
NEAL TRUCKING INC
9749 Bellegrave Ave (92509-2642)
PHONE....................951 685-5048
Dianne Neal, CEO
Randy Neal, *
EMP: 65 EST: 1976
SQ FT: 1,500
SALES (est): 8.75MM Privately Held
Web: www.nealtrucking.com
SIC: 4212 Dump truck haulage

(P-3416)
NIPPON EX NEC LGSTICS AMER INC
Also Called: Nec Logistics America
18615 S Ferris Pl (90220-6452)
PHONE....................310 604-6100
Kazuhiko Takahashi, CEO
Hidehito Tachikawa, *
▲ EMP: 75 EST: 1990
SQ FT: 353,000
SALES (est): 24.43MM Privately Held
SIC: 4212 4213 4225 Local trucking, without storage; Trucking, except local; General warehousing and storage
HQ: Nec Corporation Of America
  3929 W John Carpenter Fwy
  Irving TX
  214 262-6000

(P-3417)
OCEAN BLUE ENVMTL SVCS INC (PA)
Also Called: Ocean Blue
925 W Esther St (90813-1423)
PHONE....................562 624-4120
Maria C Lee, CEO
Ron Dare, *
Moonho C Lee, *
EMP: 63 EST: 1994
SQ FT: 5,000
SALES (est): 8.7MM Privately Held
Web: www.ocean-blue.com
SIC: 4212 8734 Hazardous waste transport; Hazardous waste testing

(P-3418)
PG TRUCKING INC
7216 Cafe Rouge Dr (93312-5980)
P.O. Box 11330 (93389-1330)
PHONE....................661 301-4942
Paula Gonzales, Pr
EMP: 62 EST: 1989
SALES (est): 2.68MM Privately Held
SIC: 4212 Mail carriers, contract

(P-3419)
PSC INDUSTRIAL OUTSOURCING LP
Also Called: Hydrochempsc
62117 Railroad St (93450-8033)
P.O. Box 431 (93450-0431)
PHONE....................831 627-2595
EMP: 242
SALES (corp-wide): 5.17B Publicly Held
Web: www.hpc-industrial.com
SIC: 4212 Hazardous waste transport
HQ: Psc Industrial Outsourcing, Lp
  900 Georgia Ave
  Deer Park TX
  713 393-5600

(P-3420)
RDS LOGISTICS GROUP (PA)
8600 Banana Ave (92335-3033)
PHONE....................909 355-4100
Judi Girard, Ch Bd
Greg Stefflre, CEO
Sharon Brooks, Pr
EMP: 67 EST: 1981
SQ FT: 50,000
SALES (est): 21.96MM
SALES (corp-wide): 21.96MM Privately Held
Web: www.rdsrally.com
SIC: 4212 Moving services

(P-3421)
ROY MILLER FREIGHT LINES LLC (PA)
3165 E Coronado St (92806-1915)
P.O. Box 18419 (92817-8419)
PHONE....................714 632-5511
Danny Miller, Mng
Danny Miller, CEO
Wiley R Miller Junior, Managing Member
EMP: 100 EST: 1942
SALES (est): 19.14MM
SALES (corp-wide): 19.14MM Privately Held
Web: www.roymiller.com
SIC: 4212 Local trucking, without storage

(P-3422)
SAVAGE SERVICES CORPORATION
8636 Sorensen Ave (90670-2633)
PHONE....................562 400-2044
EMP: 78
SALES (corp-wide): 1.73B Privately Held
Web: www.savageco.com
SIC: 4212 Local trucking, without storage
HQ: Savage Services Corporation
  901 W Legacy Center Way
  Midvale UT

(P-3423)
SOUTH COAST TRNSP & DIST INC
Western Regional Delivery
1424 S Raymond Ave (92831-5235)
PHONE....................310 816-0280
Elias Youkhehpaz, Pr
EMP: 73
Web: www.wrds.com
SIC: 4212 Local trucking, without storage
PA: South Coast Transportation & Distribution, Inc.
  1424 S Raymond Ave
  Fullerton CA

(P-3424)
SOUTHERN COUNTIES TERMINALS
Also Called: Griley Air Freight
5341 W 104th St (90045-6009)
P.O. Box 92940 (90009-2940)
PHONE....................310 642-0462
EMP: 90 EST: 1973
SALES (est): 15.35MM Privately Held
Web: www.grileyair.com
SIC: 4212 Local trucking, without storage

(P-3425)
STANFORD TRANSPORTATION INC
10201 Alondra Dr (93311-4550)
PHONE....................661 302-3288
Gurjeet Singh, Pr
Navjot Singh, *

PRODUCTS & SERVICES SECTION

4213 - Trucking, Except Local (P-3447)

Charnhjit Badhesha, *
EMP: 60 EST: 2015
SALES (est): 7MM Privately Held
Web: transportation.stanford.edu
SIC: 4212 Local trucking, without storage

(P-3426)
TRAIL LINES INC
9415 Sorensen Ave (90670-2648)
P.O. Box 3567 (90670-1567)
PHONE...................562 758-6980
Ofer Shitrit, CEO
Reuven Spivak, *
EMP: 75 EST: 1994
SALES (est): 14.88MM Privately Held
Web: www.traillines.com
SIC: 4212 4789 Local trucking, without storage; Pipeline terminal facilities, independently operated

(P-3427)
TRANSPRTTION BRKG SPCLISTS INC
Also Called: Tbs
3151 Airway Ave Ste F208 (92626-4621)
PHONE...................714 754-4236
Ben Haeri, CEO
Steve Kennedy, *
Mike Owens, *
Lee Mayer, *
Fred Khac, *
EMP: 450 EST: 2016
SALES (est): 16.39MM Privately Held
SIC: 4212 Local trucking, without storage

(P-3428)
TT TRUCKING SERVICES LLC
Also Called: TT Trucking Services
12745 Jade Rd (92392-6256)
P.O. Box 6216 (92554-6216)
PHONE...................323 790-3408
Tiffany Taylor, Managing Member
Terry Taylor, Managing Member*
EMP: 76 EST: 2019
SALES (est): 2.08MM Privately Held
SIC: 4212 4215 Delivery service, vehicular; Courier services, except by air

(P-3429)
ULS EXPRESS INC
2850 E Del Amo Blvd (90221-6007)
P.O. Box 7547 (90807-0547)
PHONE...................310 631-0800
EMP: 157 EST: 1987
SQ FT: 220,000
SALES (est): 4.62MM Privately Held
Web: www.uwc-net.com
SIC: 4212 Local trucking, without storage
HQ: Universal Logistics System, Inc.
2850 Del Amo Blvd
Carson CA
310 631-0800

(P-3430)
UNIS TRANSPORTATION LLC
218 Machlin Ct Ste A (91789-3057)
PHONE...................626 271-9800
Jeff Wu, Brnch Mgr
EMP: 63
SALES (corp-wide): 14.02MM Privately Held
Web: www.unisco.com
SIC: 4212 Local trucking, without storage
PA: Unis Transportation, Llc
6800 Valley View St
Buena Park CA
626 271-9800

(P-3431)
UNITED PARCEL SERVICE INC
Also Called: UPS
1601 W Mckinley Ave (93728-1220)
PHONE...................559 442-2950
Michael Eskew, Brnch Mgr
EMP: 80
SALES (corp-wide): 100.34B Publicly Held
Web: www.ups.com
SIC: 4212 Delivery service, vehicular
HQ: United Parcel Service, Inc.
55 Glenlake Pkwy
Atlanta GA
404 828-6000

(P-3432)
UNITED PUMPING SERVICE INC
14000 Valley Blvd (91746-2801)
PHONE...................626 961-9326
Eduardo T Perry Senior, Pr
Daniel C Perry, *
Margaret Perry, *
Eduardo Perry Junior, Sec
EMP: 95 EST: 1970
SQ FT: 25,000
SALES (est): 21.71MM Privately Held
Web: www.unitedpumping.com
SIC: 4212 Hazardous waste transport

(P-3433)
VALLEY COURIERS INC
181 S Wineville Ave Ste O (91761-7888)
PHONE...................909 605-2999
Henry Kilantang, Mgr
EMP: 68
SALES (corp-wide): 4.1MM Privately Held
Web: www.valleycouriers.com
SIC: 4212 Delivery service, vehicular
PA: Valley Couriers, Inc.
23955 Park Granada
Calabasas CA

(P-3434)
WASTE MANAGEMENT RECYCLING
Also Called: Waste Management
9227 Tujunga Ave (91352-1542)
P.O. Box 7400 (91109-7400)
PHONE...................818 767-6180
EMP: 97 EST: 1955
SALES (est): 35.42MM
SALES (corp-wide): 19.7B Publicly Held
SIC: 4212 4953 Garbage collection and transport, no disposal; Sanitary landfill operation
PA: Waste Management, Inc.
800 Capitol St Ste 3000
Houston TX
713 512-6200

(P-3435)
WASTE MGT COLLECTN RECYCL INC
Also Called: Waste Management
2658 N Main St (94597-2729)
PHONE...................925 935-8900
Ronald J Proto, Mgr
EMP: 77
SALES (corp-wide): 19.7B Publicly Held
SIC: 4212 4953 Garbage collection and transport, no disposal; Refuse systems
HQ: Waste Management Collection And Recycling, Inc.
1001 Fannin St Ste 4000
Houston TX

(P-3436)
WATERS MOVING & STORAGE INC
37 Bridgehead Rd (94553-1300)
P.O. Box 1029 (94553-0102)
PHONE...................925 372-0914
TOLL FREE: 800
Ken Waters, CEO
Paulette Waters, *
EMP: 75 EST: 1975
SQ FT: 50,000
SALES (est): 8.02MM Privately Held
Web: www.watersmoving.com
SIC: 4212 Moving services

(P-3437)
WAVECO INC (PA)
Also Called: Valey Farm
8656 Sparling Ln (95620-9605)
P.O. Box 506 (95620-0506)
PHONE...................707 678-4404
EMP: 65 EST: 1965
SALES (est): 11.59MM
SALES (corp-wide): 11.59MM Privately Held
SIC: 4212 Farm to market haulage, local

(P-3438)
WESTERN MESSENGER SERVICE INC
Also Called: Western Attorney Services
75 Columbia Sq (94103-4099)
PHONE...................415 487-4229
Dennis Golladay, Pr
Dennis Golladay Prestreas, Prin
Raymond Crosetti, *
Patty Sokolecki, *
Joe Mcmanus, NV Operations President
EMP: 115 EST: 1979
SQ FT: 11,000
SALES (est): 8.88MM Privately Held
Web: www.westernmessenger.com
SIC: 4212 Delivery service, vehicular

(P-3439)
WETZEL & SONS MVG & STOR INC
Also Called: Wetzel Trucking
12400 Osborne St (91331-2002)
PHONE...................818 890-0992
Donald C Wetzel, Pr
Daniel S Wetzel, *
EMP: 70 EST: 1976
SQ FT: 146,000
SALES (est): 5.22MM Privately Held
Web: www.wetzelmovingandstorage.com
SIC: 4212 Moving services

(P-3440)
XPO CARTAGE INC
Also Called: Pacer
5800 Sheila St (90040-2322)
PHONE...................800 837-7584
EMP: 83
SIC: 4212 Local trucking, without storage

4213 Trucking, Except Local

(P-3441)
AMERICAN FREIGHTWAYS LP
10845 Rancho Bernardo Rd Ste 100 (92127-2113)
PHONE...................866 326-5902
Kirk Carmichael, Genl Pt
Mark Goodacre, Genl Pt
EMP: 62 EST: 2004
SQ FT: 10,000
SALES (est): 20.7MM Privately Held
Web: www.americanfreightways.net
SIC: 4213 Trucking, except local

(P-3442)
APPLE FREIGHT INC
223 W 5th St (95366-2771)
PHONE...................510 423-4000
Aman S Mangat, CEO
Aman Singh, *
EMP: 65 EST: 1981
SALES (est): 4.82MM Privately Held
Web: www.applefreightinc.com
SIC: 4213 4231 4789 Trucking, except local; Trucking terminal facilities; Cargo loading and unloading services

(P-3443)
ARDWIN INC
Also Called: Ardwin Freight
2940 N Hollywood Way (91505-1024)
P.O. Box 1609 (91507-1609)
PHONE...................818 767-7777
Edwin Sahakian, Pr
EMP: 130 EST: 1988
SQ FT: 10,000
SALES (est): 20.98MM Privately Held
Web: www.ardwin.com
SIC: 4213 Contract haulers

(P-3444)
ATECH WAREHOUSING & DIST INC (PA)
7 College Ave (95401-4702)
P.O. Box 6836 (95406-0836)
PHONE...................707 526-1910
Jesse E Amaral, Pr
Geri Amaral, *
EMP: 60 EST: 1993
SQ FT: 35,000
SALES (est): 8.52MM Privately Held
Web: www.atechlogistics.com
SIC: 4213 Less-than-truckload (LTL)

(P-3445)
AVERITT EXPRESS INC
3133 W 131st St (90250-5516)
PHONE...................310 970-9520
EMP: 64
Web: www.averitt.com
SIC: 4213 Trucking, except local
HQ: Averitt Express, Inc.
1415 Neal St
Cookeville TN
931 526-3306

(P-3446)
AVERY TRANSPORT INC
43120 Venture St (93535-4510)
PHONE...................661 948-3627
Jack Cole, Pr
Jeff Souleles, VP
EMP: 71 EST: 1967
SQ FT: 150,000
SALES (est): 2.45MM Publicly Held
Web: www.averytransport.com
SIC: 4213 Mobile homes transport
PA: Rev Group, Inc.
245 S Executive Dr # 100
Brookfield WI

(P-3447)
BERT E JESSUP TRANSPORTATION
Also Called: Jessup Transportation
641 Old Gilroy St (95020-6233)
PHONE...................408 848-3390
Leonard Milanowski, CEO
Robin Jessup, *
Len Milanowski, *

(PA)=Parent Co (HQ)=Headquarters
✪ = New Business established in last 2 years

4213 - Trucking, Except Local (P-3448)

EMP: 85 EST: 1967
SQ FT: 10,000
SALES (est): 4.81MM Privately Held
Web: www.jessup.net
SIC: 4213 Trucking, except local

(P-3448)
BEST OVERNITE EXPRESS INC (PA)
Also Called: Best Overnight Express
406 Live Oak Ave (91706-1314)
P.O. Box 90816 (91715-0816)
PHONE..................626 256-6340
William K Applebee, Pr
Mike White, *
Micah Applebee, *
EMP: 100 EST: 1988
SQ FT: 25,000
SALES (est): 32.1MM Privately Held
Web: www.bestovernite.com
SIC: 4213 Trucking, except local

(P-3449)
BULK TRANSPORTATION (PA)
415 S Lemon Ave (91789-2911)
P.O. Box 390 (91788-0390)
PHONE..................909 594-2855
Brett Richardson, Pr
George G Cross, *
Gary K Cross, *
Susan Duffield, *
▲ EMP: 60 EST: 1961
SQ FT: 3,500
SALES (est): 23.38MM
SALES (corp-wide): 23.38MM Privately Held
SIC: 4213 4789 Contract haulers; Cargo loading and unloading services

(P-3450)
BUTTON TRANSPORTATION INC
7000 Button Ln (95620-9116)
PHONE..................707 678-7434
Robert Button, Pr
Anthony Iten, *
EMP: 175 EST: 1975
SQ FT: 5,000
SALES (est): 39.98MM Privately Held
Web: www.buttontransportation.com
SIC: 4213 Contract haulers

(P-3451)
CALIFORNIA BULK INC
Also Called: Alegre Trucking
3939 Producers Dr (95206-4204)
PHONE..................209 983-1069
Robert Fowler, Mgr
EMP: 197
SIC: 4213 Trucking, except local
PA: California Bulk, Inc.
5100 W Highway 12
Lodi CA

(P-3452)
CARGO SOLUTION EXPRESS INC (PA)
14587 Valley Blvd # 89 (92335-6248)
PHONE..................909 350-1644
Balwinder Kaur Kang, Pr
EMP: 250 EST: 2002
SQ FT: 10,000
SALES (est): 99.15MM
SALES (corp-wide): 99.15MM Privately Held
Web: www.cargosolutionexpress.com
SIC: 4213 Trucking, except local

(P-3453)
CERTIFIED FRT LOGISTICS INC (PA)
1344 White Ct (93458-3732)
P.O. Box 5668 (93456-5668)
PHONE..................800 592-5906
James O Nelson, Pr
Edwin F Nelson Junior, VP
Jon Cramer, *
Scott Cramer, *
EMP: 120 EST: 1963
SQ FT: 40,000
SALES (est): 42.02MM
SALES (corp-wide): 42.02MM Privately Held
Web: www.certifiedfreightlogistics.com
SIC: 4213 Refrigerated products transport

(P-3454)
CJ LOGISTICS AMERICA LLC
1895 Marigold Ave (92374-5028)
PHONE..................909 363-4354
Greg Hart, Genl Pt
EMP: 95
Web: america.cjlogistics.com
SIC: 4213 4212 Trucking, except local; Local trucking, without storage
HQ: Cj Logistics America, Llc
1750 S Wolf Rd
Des Plaines IL

(P-3455)
COMPLETE LOGISTICS COMPANY
1207 Air Wing Rd (92154-7713)
PHONE..................619 661-9610
Roseles Ray, Mgr
EMP: 63
SALES (corp-wide): 45.07MM Privately Held
Web: www.logisticsinc.com
SIC: 4213 Trucking, except local
PA: The Complete Logistics Company
15895 Valley Blvd 200
Fontana CA
909 544-5040

(P-3456)
CONTRACT TRANSPORTATION SYS CO
Also Called: Certified Distribution Svcs
12500 Slauson Ave Ste B2 (90670-8618)
PHONE..................562 696-3262
Chuck Huff, Brnch Mgr
EMP: 64
SALES (corp-wide): 22.15B Publicly Held
SIC: 4213 Trucking, except local
HQ: Contract Transportation Systems Co.
101 W Prospect Ave
Cleveland OH
216 566-2000

(P-3457)
CONTRACTORS CARGO COMPANY (PA)
Also Called: Contractors Rigging & Erectors
7223 Alondra Blvd (90723-3901)
P.O. Box 5290 (90224-5290)
PHONE..................310 609-1957
Carla Ann Wheeler, CEO
Gerald D Wheeler, *
Kimberly Dorio, *
◆ EMP: 80 EST: 1959
SALES (est): 24.28MM
SALES (corp-wide): 24.28MM Privately Held
Web: www.contractorscargo.com

SIC: 4213 4731 1623 4741 Contract haulers; Freight transportation arrangement; Water, sewer, and utility lines; Rental of railroad cars

(P-3458)
COVENANT TRANSPORT INC
Also Called: Covenant Transport
1300 E Franklin Ave (91766-5416)
PHONE..................909 469-0130
Bill Furgess, Mgr
EMP: 660
Web: www.covenantlogistics.com
SIC: 4213 Contract haulers
HQ: Covenant Transport, Inc.
400 Birmingham Hwy
Chattanooga TN
423 821-1212

(P-3459)
CRST EXPEDITED INC
2577 W Yosemite Ave (95337-9641)
P.O. Box 1450 (95336-1148)
PHONE..................209 249-4403
Brad Manting, Mgr
EMP: 370
SALES (corp-wide): 980.15MM Privately Held
Web: www.crst.com
SIC: 4213 Trucking, except local
HQ: Crst Expedited, Inc.
201 1st St Se
Cedar Rapids IA
800 443-0940

(P-3460)
CRST EXPEDITED INC
1219 E Elm St (91761-4585)
PHONE..................909 563-5606
John Smith, Brnch Mgr
EMP: 500
SALES (corp-wide): 980.15MM Privately Held
Web: www.crst.com
SIC: 4213 4212 Trucking, except local; Local trucking, without storage
HQ: Crst Expedited, Inc.
201 1st St Se
Cedar Rapids IA
800 443-0940

(P-3461)
CRST EXPEDITED INC
Also Called: Gardner Logistics
9032 Merrill Ave (91708)
P.O. Box 747 (91708-0747)
PHONE..................909 563-5606
EMP: 189
SALES (corp-wide): 980.15MM Privately Held
Web: www.crst.com
SIC: 4213 Contract haulers
HQ: Crst Expedited, Inc.
201 1st St Se
Cedar Rapids IA
800 443-0940

(P-3462)
CUNHA DRAYING INC
1500 Madruga Rd (95330-9779)
PHONE..................209 858-1400
Paul Buttini, Pr
Peggy Deforest, *
EMP: 65 EST: 1977
SQ FT: 10,000
SALES (est): 8.48MM Privately Held
Web: www.cunhatruck.com
SIC: 4213 Contract haulers

(P-3463)
D C SHOWER DOORS INC
Also Called: Image Transfer
26121 Avenue Hall (91355-3490)
PHONE..................661 257-1177
Jason Shepard, Pr
EMP: 198 EST: 1996
SQ FT: 125,000
SALES (est): 1.04MM
SALES (corp-wide): 136.14MM Privately Held
Web: www.cwdoors.com
SIC: 4213 Trucking, except local
PA: Contractors Wardrobe, Inc.
26121 Avenue Hall
Valencia CA
661 257-1177

(P-3464)
DEPENDABLE COMPANIES
2555 E Olympic Blvd (90023-2605)
PHONE..................800 548-8608
Ron Massman, CEO
EMP: 116 EST: 2015
SALES (est): 9.9MM Privately Held
Web: www.godependable.com
SIC: 4213 Trucking, except local

(P-3465)
DEPENDABLE HIGHWAY EXPRESS INC (PA)
Also Called: Dependable Logistics Services
2555 E Olympic Blvd (90023-2605)
P.O. Box 58047 (90058-0047)
PHONE..................323 526-2200
Ronald Massman, Pr
Robert Massman, VP
Michael Dougan, CFO
◆ EMP: 300 EST: 1984
SQ FT: 1,680,000
SALES (est): 206.32MM
SALES (corp-wide): 206.32MM Privately Held
Web: www.godependable.com
SIC: 4213 4225 Contract haulers; General warehousing and storage

(P-3466)
DOUBLE EAGLE TRNSP CORP
12135 Scarbrough Ct (92344-9200)
PHONE..................760 956-3770
Gerald E Butcher, Pr
EMP: 140 EST: 1992
SQ FT: 10,125
SALES (est): 8.43MM Privately Held
SIC: 4213 4212 Contract haulers; Local trucking, without storage

(P-3467)
DOUDELL TRUCKING COMPANY (PA)
1505 N 4th St (95112-4607)
P.O. Box 5879 (95150-5879)
PHONE..................408 263-7300
Armand Kunde, Pr
EMP: 80 EST: 1944
SQ FT: 20,000
SALES (est): 5.85MM
SALES (corp-wide): 5.85MM Privately Held
SIC: 4213 4214 4212 Contract haulers; Local trucking with storage; Local trucking, without storage

(P-3468)
ED ROCHA LIVESTOCK TRNSP INC
Also Called: Rocha Transportation
2400 Nickerson Dr (95358-9409)

PRODUCTS & SERVICES SECTION

4213 - Trucking, Except Local (P-3490)

P.O. Box 40 (95307-0040)
PHONE.................................209 538-1302
Zachary Dirksen, *Pr*
Henry Dirksen, *
Corrie M Toste, *
Zachary Dirksen, *Treas*
EMP: 70 **EST:** 1963
SQ FT: 5,500
SALES (est): 12.48MM **Privately Held**
Web: www.rochatrans.com
SIC: 4213 Contract haulers

(P-3469)
ESPARZA ENTERPRISES INC
500 Workman St (93307-6871)
PHONE.................................661 631-0347
EMP: 792
SALES (corp-wide): 135MM **Privately Held**
Web: www.esparzainc.com
SIC: 4213 Trucking, except local
PA: Esparza Enterprises, Inc.
3851 Fruitvale Ave
Bakersfield CA
661 831-0002

(P-3470)
ESTES EXPRESS LINES
14727 Alondra Blvd (90638-5617)
PHONE.................................714 994-3770
Benjamin J Torman, *Brnch Mgr*
EMP: 152
SALES (corp-wide): 3.56B **Privately Held**
Web: www.estes-express.com
SIC: 4213 Contract haulers
PA: Estes Express Lines
3901 W Broad St
Richmond VA
804 353-1900

(P-3471)
ESTES EXPRESS LINES
120 Press Ln (91910-1012)
PHONE.................................619 425-4040
Craig Buker, *Brnch Mgr*
EMP: 89
SALES (corp-wide): 3.56B **Privately Held**
Web: www.estes-express.com
SIC: 4213 Contract haulers
PA: Estes Express Lines
3901 W Broad St
Richmond VA
804 353-1900

(P-3472)
ESTES EXPRESS LINES
1750 Adams Ave (94577-1002)
PHONE.................................510 635-0165
Bill Wardell, *Mgr*
EMP: 101
SALES (corp-wide): 3.56B **Privately Held**
Web: www.estes-express.com
SIC: 4213 Contract haulers
PA: Estes Express Lines
3901 W Broad St
Richmond VA
804 353-1900

(P-3473)
ESTES EXPRESS LINES
10736 Cherry Ave (92337-7196)
PHONE.................................909 427-9850
Mark Brown, *Mgr*
EMP: 114
SALES (corp-wide): 3.56B **Privately Held**
Web: www.estes-express.com
SIC: 4213 4212 Less-than-truckload (LTL);
Local trucking, without storage
PA: Estes Express Lines
3901 W Broad St

Richmond VA
804 353-1900

(P-3474)
ESTES EXPRESS LINES
Also Called: Estes
13327 Temple Ave (91746-1513)
PHONE.................................626 333-9090
Kieran O'carroll, *Mgr*
EMP: 89
SQ FT: 6,156
SALES (corp-wide): 3.56B **Privately Held**
Web: www.estes-express.com
SIC: 4213 4212 Less-than-truckload (LTL);
Local trucking, without storage
PA: Estes Express Lines
3901 W Broad St
Richmond VA
804 353-1900

(P-3475)
ESTES EXPRESS LINES
Also Called: Estes
4355 S Chestnut Ave (93725-9372)
PHONE.................................559 441-0915
Michael Haynes, *Mgr*
EMP: 89
SALES (corp-wide): 3.56B **Privately Held**
Web: www.estes-express.com
SIC: 4213 4212 Less-than-truckload (LTL);
Local trucking, without storage
PA: Estes Express Lines
3901 W Broad St
Richmond VA
804 353-1900

(P-3476)
FEDEX FREIGHT WEST INC
6411 Guadalupe Mines Rd (95120)
PHONE.................................775 356-7600
◆ **EMP:** 4500
SIC: 4213 4731 4212 Less-than-truckload
(LTL); Freight transportation arrangement;
Local trucking, without storage

(P-3477)
**FRANK C ALEGRE TRUCKING
INC (PA)**
5100 W Highway 12 (95242-9529)
P.O. Box 1508 (95241-1508)
PHONE.................................209 334-2112
Andress Alegre, *CEO*
Michelle Schultz, *
Robert Fowler, *
EMP: 185 **EST:** 1963
SQ FT: 34,200
SALES (est): 25.07MM
SALES (corp-wide): 25.07MM **Privately Held**
Web: www.alegretrucking.com
SIC: 4213 4212 Contract haulers; Dump
truck haulage

(P-3478)
FRIENDS GROUP EXPRESS INC
14520 Village Dr Apt 1013 (92337-0196)
P.O. Box 310488 (92331-0488)
PHONE.................................909 346-6814
Parmjit Singh Grewal, *Prin*
EMP: 78 **EST:** 2014
SQ FT: 700
SALES (est): 2.29MM **Privately Held**
SIC: 4213 4212 Trucking, except local; Local
trucking, without storage

(P-3479)
FTG CONSTRUCTION MTLS INC
5100 W Highway 12 (95242-9529)
P.O. Box 1508 (95241-1508)
PHONE.................................209 334-4038

Anthony J Alegre, *CEO*
Gary D Alegre, *Stockholder*
Frank C Alegre Junior, *Stockholder*
Michelle Shultz, *
EMP: 66 **EST:** 1973
SQ FT: 1,200
SALES (est): 2.72MM **Privately Held**
Web: www.ftgmaterials.com
SIC: 4213 Trucking, except local

(P-3480)
FUEL DELIVERY SERVICES INC
4895 S Airport Way (95206-3915)
P.O. Box 1369 (95201-1369)
PHONE.................................209 751-2185
Ronald M Vandepol, *CEO*
Tom V Depol, *Stockholder**
David Atwater, *Stockholder**
Mike Boswart, *Stockholder**
EMP: 94 **EST:** 1998
SQ FT: 2,000
SALES (est): 15.91MM **Privately Held**
Web: www.gofds.com
SIC: 4213 Liquid petroleum transport, non-
local

(P-3481)
GILLIG LLC
1100 Voyager St (94550-2551)
PHONE.................................510 264-5000
EMP: 255
SALES (corp-wide): 1.98B **Privately Held**
Web: www.gillig.com
SIC: 4213 Automobiles, transport and
delivery
HQ: Gillig Llc
451 Discovery Dr
Livermore CA
510 264-5000

(P-3482)
GILLSON TRUCKING INC
1801 E Dr Martin Luther King Jr Blvd
(95205-7013)
PHONE.................................925 400-9094
Harsimran Singh, *CEO*
Bikramjit Singh, *
Harsimran Singh, *Prin*
EMP: 250 **EST:** 2013
SALES (est): 24.56MM **Privately Held**
SIC: 4213 Trucking, except local

(P-3483)
GLS US FREIGHT INC (PA)
6750 Longe St Ste 100 (95206-4938)
P.O. Box 31357 (95213-1357)
PHONE.................................209 823-2168
Steven Bergan, *CEO*
Aaron Schulte, *
Mark Gunton, *
EMP: 100 **EST:** 1976
SALES (est): 89.98MM
SALES (corp-wide): 89.98MM **Privately Held**
Web: freight.gls-us.com
SIC: 4213 Contract haulers

(P-3484)
H & H TRANSPORTATION LLC
300 El Sobrante Rd (92879-5757)
P.O. Box 77697 (92877-0123)
PHONE.................................951 817-2300
EMP: 60 **EST:** 1998
SALES (est): 4.02MM **Privately Held**
SIC: 4213 4212 Trucking, except local; Local
trucking, without storage

(P-3485)
H RAUVEL INC
Also Called: Nova Transportation Services

501 W Walnut St (90220-5221)
PHONE.................................562 989-3333
Hector Velasco, *Mgr*
EMP: 180
SALES (corp-wide): 23.11MM **Privately Held**
Web: www.novafreight.net
SIC: 4213 Trucking, except local
PA: H. Rauvel, Inc.
1710 E Sepulveda Blvd
Carson CA
310 604-0060

(P-3486)
HAWK TRANSPORTATION INC
Also Called: Hawk
15238 Arrow Blvd (92335-3250)
PHONE.................................800 709-4295
Manprit K Sandhu, *CEO*
Jagtar Sandhu, *
Harry Bhangu, *
EMP: 60 **EST:** 2002
SQ FT: 1,300
SALES (est): 4.22MM **Privately Held**
SIC: 4213 Trucking, except local

(P-3487)
**HEARTLAND EXPRESS INC
IOWA**
Also Called: Heartland Express
10131 Redwood Ave (92335-6236)
PHONE.................................319 626-3600
Matthew Gonzalez, *Supervisor*
EMP: 549
SALES (corp-wide): 968MM **Publicly Held**
Web: www.heartlandexpress.com
SIC: 4213 Trucking, except local
HQ: Heartland Express, Inc. Of Iowa
901 Heartland Way
North Liberty IA
319 626-3600

(P-3488)
**HENDRICKSON TRUCK LINES
INC**
7080 Florin Perkins Rd (95828-2609)
P.O. Box 292219 (95829-2219)
PHONE.................................916 387-9614
William Hendrickson, *Ch*
Ward Hendrickson, *
Alban Lang, *
EMP: 148 **EST:** 2013
SALES (est): 9.1MM **Privately Held**
Web: www.htlines.com
SIC: 4213 Trucking, except local

(P-3489)
HENDRICKSON TRUCKING INC
7080 Florin Perkins Rd (95828-2609)
P.O. Box 292219 (95829-2219)
PHONE.................................916 387-9614
William Hendrickson, *CEO*
Ward Hendrickson, *
EMP: 280 **EST:** 1976
SQ FT: 5,480
SALES (est): 28.59MM **Privately Held**
Web: www.hendricksontrucking.com
SIC: 4213 Trucking, except local

(P-3490)
HF COX INC (PA)
Also Called: Cox Petroleum Transport
118 Cox Transportation Way (93307)
PHONE.................................661 366-3236
Dainiel L Mairs, *Pr*
Bruce Mckinnon, *VP*
Gwen Mairs, *
EMP: 60 **EST:** 1969
SQ FT: 5,000
SALES (est): 683.25K

4213 - Trucking, Except Local (P-3491)

SALES (corp-wide): 683.25K **Privately Held**
Web: www.coxpetroleum.com
SIC: **4213** 4212 Trucking, except local; Petroleum haulage, local

(P-3491)
HI PRO INC
4584 Adobe Rd (92277-1671)
P.O. Box 148 (92277-0148)
PHONE................................760 367-7734
Joshua Stoneback, *CEO*
EMP: 200 EST: 2012
SALES (est): 9.74MM **Privately Held**
Web: www.hiproinc.com
SIC: **4213** 7389 4212 Trucking, except local; Brokers, contract services; Delivery service, vehicular

(P-3492)
INDIAN RIVER TRANSPORT CO
8444 W Doe Ave (93291-9261)
PHONE................................209 664-0456
John J Harned Junior, *Brnch Mgr*
EMP: 153
SALES (corp-wide): 51.3MM **Privately Held**
Web: www.indianrivertransport.com
SIC: **4213** Contract haulers
PA: Indian River Transport Co.
    2580 Executive Rd
    Winter Haven FL
    863 324-2430

(P-3493)
INLAND STAR DIST CTRS INC (PA)
3146 S Chestnut Ave (93725-2606)
P.O. Box 2396 (93745-2396)
PHONE................................559 237-2052
Michael K Kelton, *CEO*
◆ EMP: 60 EST: 1985
SQ FT: 550,000
SALES (est): 48.2MM
SALES (corp-wide): 48.2MM **Privately Held**
Web: www.inlandstar.com
SIC: **4213** 4225 Trucking, except local; General warehousing

(P-3494)
J B HUNT TRANSPORT INC
2660 Loomis Rd (95205-8008)
PHONE................................209 235-1371
Shane O'connor, *Mgr*
EMP: 203
SALES (corp-wide): 14.81B **Publicly Held**
Web: www.jbhunt.com
SIC: **4213** Trucking, except local
HQ: J. B. Hunt Transport, Inc.
    615 Jb Hunt Corporate Dr
    Lowell AR
    479 820-0000

(P-3495)
J B HUNT TRANSPORT INC
3305 S Chestnut Ave (93725-2608)
PHONE................................385 226-4538
EMP: 135
SALES (corp-wide): 14.81B **Publicly Held**
Web: www.jbhunt.com
SIC: **4213** Trucking, except local
HQ: J. B. Hunt Transport, Inc.
    615 Jb Hunt Corporate Dr
    Lowell AR
    479 820-0000

(P-3496)
J B HUNT TRANSPORT INC
3170 Crow Canyon Pl Ste 180 (94583-1347)
PHONE................................866 759-1127
Arifa Tuzin, *Mgr*
EMP: 101
SALES (corp-wide): 14.81B **Publicly Held**
Web: www.jbhunt.com
SIC: **4213** Trucking, except local
HQ: J. B. Hunt Transport, Inc.
    615 Jb Hunt Corporate Dr
    Lowell AR
    479 820-0000

(P-3497)
JACK JONES TRUCKING INC
1090 E Belmont St (91761-4501)
PHONE................................909 456-2500
Valerie Liese, *Pr*
Erin Craig, *
Bob Liese, *
Kristy Richardson, *
Robert Liese, *
EMP: 100 EST: 1971
SQ FT: 3,000
SALES (est): 10.29MM **Privately Held**
Web: www.jjtinc.com
SIC: **4213** Trucking, except local

(P-3498)
KALWAY INC ✪
10156 Live Oak Ave (92335-6227)
PHONE................................800 303-0076
Sameer Pannu, *CEO*
EMP: 60 EST: 2022
SALES (est): 2.13MM
SALES (corp-wide): 66.11MM **Privately Held**
SIC: **4213** Trucking, except local
HQ: Kal Freight Inc
    600 109th St Ste B
    Arlington TX
    909 471-7026

(P-3499)
KINGS COUNTY TRUCK LINES (HQ)
754 S Blackstone St (93274-5757)
P.O. Box 1016 (93275-1016)
PHONE................................559 686-2857
Mark Tisdale, *VP*
Mark Tisdale, *General Vice President*
EMP: 162 EST: 1940
SQ FT: 45,000
SALES (est): 618.36K
SALES (corp-wide): 7.23MM **Privately Held**
SIC: **4213** Contract haulers
PA: Ruan Transportation Management Systems, Inc.
    666 Grand Ave Ste 3100
    Des Moines IA
    515 245-2500

(P-3500)
KLX LLC
1351 Charles Willard St (90746-4023)
P.O. Box 4438 (93278-4438)
PHONE................................559 684-1037
Ron Greenberg, *Pr*
Percy Greenberg, *
Jeff Peterson, *
EMP: 65 EST: 1983
SQ FT: 12,000
SALES (est): 5.1MM **Privately Held**
Web: www.klx-llc.com
SIC: **4213** Trucking, except local

(P-3501)
KS TRANS SERVICES CO
3190 S Elm Ave (93706-5619)
P.O. Box 12005 (93776-2005)
PHONE................................559 264-5650
Rajinder K Nijjar, *CEO*
Kevin Nijjar, *
EMP: 80 EST: 2010
SALES (est): 2.64MM **Privately Held**
SIC: **4213** Trucking, except local

(P-3502)
LANDFORCE CORPORATION
17201 N D St (92394-1401)
PHONE................................760 843-7839
Rajinder Bhangu, *CEO*
EMP: 120 EST: 2000
SALES (est): 8.63MM **Privately Held**
Web: www.landforcecorp.com
SIC: **4213** Trucking, except local

(P-3503)
LANDSTAR GLOBAL LOGISTICS INC
2313 E Philadelphia St Ste D (91761-8047)
PHONE................................909 266-0096
EMP: 62
Web: www.landstar.com
SIC: **4213** Trucking, except local
HQ: Landstar Global Logistics, Inc.
    13410 Sutton Park Dr S
    Jacksonville FL

(P-3504)
LAS VEGAS / LA EXPRESS INC (PA)
1000 S Cucamonga Ave (91761-3461)
PHONE................................909 972-3100
Ronald Cain Junior, *CEO*
Beverly A Adley, *
Michael P Adley, *
EMP: 170 EST: 1988
SQ FT: 163,000
SALES (est): 18.9MM **Privately Held**
Web: www.vegasexpress.com
SIC: **4213** Trucking, except local

(P-3505)
LEMORE TRANSPORTATION INC (PA)
Also Called: Royal Trucking
1420 Royal Industrial Way (94520-4914)
P.O. Box 6085 (94524-1085)
PHONE................................925 689-6444
Barbara Querio, *CEO*
Roy Querio, *
EMP: 73 EST: 1965
SQ FT: 6,000
SALES (est): 9.29MM
SALES (corp-wide): 9.29MM **Privately Held**
Web: www.royaltrucking.com
SIC: **4213** Contract haulers

(P-3506)
LIBERTY LINEHAUL WEST INC
1501 Chapin Rd (90640-6626)
PHONE................................323 728-8900
Greg Dubuque, *CEO*
EMP: 66 EST: 1997
SALES (est): 33.66MM
SALES (corp-wide): 27.34MM **Privately Held**
Web: www.libertylinehaul.com
SIC: **4213** Contract haulers
PA: Kriska Transportation Group Limited
    850 Sophia St
    Prescott ON
    613 925-5903

(P-3507)
LOAD DELIVERED LOGISTICS LLC
214 Main St (90291-2522)
PHONE................................310 822-0215
Michael Cherney, *Mgr*
EMP: 109
SALES (corp-wide): 1.18B **Privately Held**
SIC: **4213** Trucking, except local
HQ: Load Delivered Logistics Llc
    640 N Lasalle Ste 555
    Chicago IL
    877 930-5623

(P-3508)
LTL PROS INC
13610 S Archibald Ave (91761-7930)
PHONE................................909 350-1600
Manuel Vargas, *Pr*
EMP: 80 EST: 2017
SALES (est): 2.78MM **Privately Held**
Web: www.ltlpros.com
SIC: **4213** Trucking, except local

(P-3509)
MARK CLEMONS
Also Called: Mtc Transportation
4584 Adobe Rd (92277-1671)
P.O. Box 148 (92277-0148)
PHONE................................760 361-1531
Mark Clemons, *Owner*
Genevieve Clemons, *Mgr*
EMP: 200 EST: 1978
SALES (est): 7.35MM **Privately Held**
SIC: **4213** 4212 4513 4522 Heavy machinery transport; Local trucking, without storage; Air courier services; Air transportation, nonscheduled

(P-3510)
MASHBURN TRNSP SVCS INC
1423 Kern St (93268-4607)
P.O. Box 66 (93268-8066)
PHONE................................661 763-5724
Denise Mashburn, *Pr*
Michael Mashburn, *
EMP: 120 EST: 1987
SQ FT: 2,000
SALES (est): 16.63MM **Privately Held**
Web: www.mashburntransportation.com
SIC: **4213** 4212 Contract haulers; Local trucking, without storage

(P-3511)
MASUTA NATIONAL INC
65 Quinta Ct Ste C (95823-4344)
PHONE................................916 520-0904
Jasdeep Masuta, *CEO*
EMP: 200 EST: 2019
SALES (est): 4MM **Privately Held**
Web: www.masutanational.com
SIC: **4213** 7389 Trucking, except local; Business Activities at Non-Commercial Site

(P-3512)
MATHESON FAST FREIGHT INC
9785 Goethe Rd (95827-3559)
PHONE................................209 342-0184
Mark Matheson, *Brnch Mgr*
EMP: 265
SALES (corp-wide): 390.08MM **Privately Held**
Web: www.mathesoninc.com
SIC: **4213** Less-than-truckload (LTL)
HQ: Matheson Fast Freight, Inc.
    9780 Dino Dr
    Elk Grove CA
    916 686-4600

PRODUCTS & SERVICES SECTION

4213 - Trucking, Except Local (P-3534)

(P-3513)
MATHESON FAST FREIGHT INC (HQ)
9780 Dino Dr (95624-9477)
PHONE..................................916 686-4600
Robert B Matheson, *Ch Bd*
Mark B Matheson, *
Carole L Matheson, *
Donald G Brocca, *
Laurie Johnson, *
EMP: 70 **EST:** 1984
SQ FT: 7,200
SALES (est): 22.71MM
SALES (corp-wide): 390.08MM **Privately Held**
SIC: 4213 Less-than-truckload (LTL)
PA: Matheson Trucking, Inc.
9785 Goethe Rd
Sacramento CA
916 685-2330

(P-3514)
MCCOLLISTERS TRNSP GROUP INC
Also Called: United Van Lines
10672 Jasmine St (92337-8242)
PHONE..................................909 428-5700
Chris Ciofreddi, *Ofcr*
EMP: 72
SALES (corp-wide): 181.14MM **Privately Held**
Web: www.mccollisters.com
SIC: 4213 Trucking, except local
PA: Mccollister's Global Services, Inc.
8 Terri Ln
Burlington NJ
609 386-0600

(P-3515)
MEATHEAD MOVERS INC (PA)
3600 S Higuera St (93401-7306)
PHONE..................................805 544-6328
Evan Steed, *VP*
Aaron B Steed, *
EMP: 68 **EST:** 2001
SQ FT: 1,700
SALES (est): 20.08MM
SALES (corp-wide): 20.08MM **Privately Held**
Web: www.meatheadmovers.com
SIC: 4213 Household goods transport

(P-3516)
MICHAEL DUSI TRUCKING INC
4305 Second Wind Way (93446-6304)
P.O. Box 2339 (93447-2339)
PHONE..................................805 237-9499
EMP: 68
Web: www.michaeldusitrucking.com
SIC: 4213 Trucking, except local

(P-3517)
NATIONAL RETAIL TRNSP INC
400 Harley Knox Blvd (92571-7566)
PHONE..................................951 243-6110
EMP: 80
SALES (corp-wide): 496.65MM **Privately Held**
SIC: 4213 Trucking, except local
HQ: National Retail Transportation, Inc.
2820 16th St
North Bergen NJ
201 866-0462

(P-3518)
NATIONAL RETAIL TRNSP INC
355 W Carob St (90220-5212)
PHONE..................................310 605-3777
Manuel Villasenor, *Brnch Mgr*
EMP: 67
SALES (corp-wide): 496.65MM **Privately Held**
SIC: 4213 Trucking, except local
HQ: National Retail Transportation, Inc.
2820 16th St
North Bergen NJ
201 866-0462

(P-3519)
NEW LEGEND INC
Also Called: New Legend Logistics
1235 Oswald Rd (95991-9719)
PHONE..................................530 674-3100
Baveljit Singh Samara, *Brnch Mgr*
EMP: 500
Web: www.newlegendinc.com
SIC: 4213 4212 Trucking, except local; Local trucking, without storage
PA: New Legend, Inc.
811 S 59th Ave
Phoenix AZ

(P-3520)
NEW LEGEND INC
8613 Etiwanda Ave (91739-9611)
PHONE..................................855 210-2300
EMP: 229
Web: www.newlegendinc.com
SIC: 4213 4212 Trucking, except local; Local trucking, without storage
PA: New Legend, Inc.
811 S 59th Ave
Phoenix AZ

(P-3521)
NORTHERN RFRIGERATED TRNSP INC (PA)
2700 W Main St (95380-9537)
PHONE..................................209 664-3800
Richard Mello, *CEO*
John Doidge, *
Judi Mello, *
EMP: 120 **EST:** 1947
SQ FT: 25,000
SALES (est): 32.45MM
SALES (corp-wide): 32.45MM **Privately Held**
Web: www.northernrefrigerated.com
SIC: 4213 Refrigerated products transport

(P-3522)
NY TRANSPORT INC
10191 Redwood Ave (92335-6236)
P.O. Box 868 (92316-0868)
PHONE..................................909 355-9832
Nazario Yanez, *CEO*
Nazario Y Perez, *
EMP: 65 **EST:** 2005
SALES (est): 4.76MM **Privately Held**
SIC: 4213 Trucking, except local

(P-3523)
OZARK TRUCKING INC (PA)
4916 Dudley Blvd (95652-2521)
PHONE..................................916 561-5400
EMP: 150 **EST:** 1989
SALES (est): 20.34MM **Privately Held**
Web: www.ozarktruckinginc.com
SIC: 4213 4212 Trucking, except local; Local trucking, without storage

(P-3524)
PACIFIC DRAYAGE SERVICES LLC
Also Called: Pds
550 W Artesia Blvd (90220-5524)
PHONE..................................833 334-4622
Mark George, *Managing Member*
EMP: 210 **EST:** 2019
SALES (est): 13.69MM
SALES (corp-wide): 488.55MM **Privately Held**
Web: www.imcc.com
SIC: 4213 Trucking, except local
PA: Imc Companies - National Accounts, Llc
1305 Schilling Blvd W
Collierville TN
901 746-3700

(P-3525)
PAN PACIFIC PETROLEUM CO INC (PA)
9302 Garfield Ave (90280-3805)
P.O. Box 1966 (90280-1966)
PHONE..................................562 928-0100
Robert Roth, *CEO*
Dale Snyder, *
Steven Roth, *
EMP: 100 **EST:** 1962
SQ FT: 600
SALES (est): 7.33MM
SALES (corp-wide): 7.33MM **Privately Held**
SIC: 4213 5172 Liquid petroleum transport, non-local; Petroleum brokers

(P-3526)
PAN PACIFIC PETROLEUM CO INC
Also Called: Truck Terminal
1850 Coffee Rd (93308-5746)
PHONE..................................661 589-3200
Dave Palmer, *Mgr*
EMP: 20
SALES (corp-wide): 7.33MM **Privately Held**
SIC: 4213 Liquid petroleum transport, non-local
PA: Pan Pacific Petroleum Company, Inc.
9302 Garfield Ave
South Gate CA
562 928-0100

(P-3527)
POINTDIRECT TRANSPORT INC
19083 Mermack Ave (92532-2256)
PHONE..................................909 371-0837
Adolfo De La Herran, *Pr*
EMP: 100 **EST:** 2014
SALES (est): 2.46MM **Privately Held**
Web: www.point-direct.com
SIC: 4213 Trucking, except local

(P-3528)
POPPY STATE EXPRESS INC
2700 W Main St (95380-9537)
PHONE..................................209 664-3950
Richard D Mello, *Pr*
John Doidge, *
Daniel N Watson, *
Claudia Doidge, *
Judy Mello, *
EMP: 80 **EST:** 1980
SQ FT: 30,000
SALES (est): 7.47MM **Privately Held**
Web: www.northernrefrigerated.com
SIC: 4213 Refrigerated products transport

(P-3529)
PROGRESSIVE TRANSPORTATION INC
Also Called: PROGRESSIVE TRANSPORTATION, INC.
1210 E 223rd St Ste 328 (90745-4254)
PHONE..................................310 684-2100
Kevin Dukesherer, *Prin*
EMP: 72
Web: www.progressivetransportation.com
SIC: 4213 Contract haulers
HQ: Progressive Transportation, Llc
156535 E Wausau Ave
Wausau WI

(P-3530)
RCG LOGISTICS LLC
Also Called: Rcg Auto Logistics
9300 Tech Center Dr Ste 190 (95826-2575)
PHONE..................................916 999-1234
Vitaliy Kezmenko, *CEO*
Vitaliy Kuzmenko, *
Aleksandr Marinov, *
Donald Neverov, *
Melissa Burger, *Contrlr*
EMP: 95 **EST:** 2010
SALES (est): 15.32MM **Privately Held**
Web: www.rcgauto.com
SIC: 4213 4731 Automobiles, transport and delivery; Freight transportation arrangement

(P-3531)
REEVE TRUCKING COMPANY INC (PA)
Also Called: Reeve Trucking Company
5050 Carpenter Rd (95215-8105)
P.O. Box 5126 (95205-0126)
PHONE..................................209 948-4061
Lori J Reeve, *Pr*
Donald E Reeve, *VP*
Donald J Reeve Aka Spike, *VP*
▲ **EMP:** 70 **EST:** 1972
SQ FT: 100,000
SALES (est): 30.31MM
SALES (corp-wide): 30.31MM **Privately Held**
Web: www.reevetrucking.com
SIC: 4213 Contract haulers

(P-3532)
RELIANCE INTERMODAL INC
1919 Martin Luther King Ste A And B (95210)
P.O. Box 31238 (95213-1238)
PHONE..................................209 946-0200
Lakhbir S Deol, *CEO*
EMP: 65 **EST:** 2011
SALES (est): 2.18MM **Privately Held**
Web: www.relianceintermodal.com
SIC: 4213 Trucking, except local

(P-3533)
RENN TRANSPORTATION INC
8845 Forest St (95020-3651)
PHONE..................................408 842-3545
Brad E Renn, *Pr*
Robert Renn, *
Patricia Renn, *
EMP: 100 **EST:** 2005
SQ FT: 9,609
SALES (est): 11.48MM **Privately Held**
Web: www.renntransportation.com
SIC: 4213 Trucking, except local

(P-3534)
RPM TRANSPORTATION INC (DH)
11660 Arroyo Ave (92705-3057)
PHONE..................................714 388-3500
Shawn Duke, *Pr*
Andrew Lewes, *
▲ **EMP:** 110 **EST:** 1985
SQ FT: 175,000
SALES (est): 17.69MM
SALES (corp-wide): 1.16B **Privately Held**
Web: www.odysseylogistics.com

4213 - Trucking, Except Local (P-3535)

SIC: **4213** 4225 4214 Trailer or container on flat car (TOFC/COFC); General warehousing; Local trucking with storage
HQ: Rpm Consolidated Services, Inc.
1901 Raymer Ave
Fullerton CA
714 388-3500

(P-3535)
RUAN
830 W Glenwood Ave (95380-5751)
PHONE.....................209 634-4928
Bill Hagney, *Mgr*
EMP: 126
SALES (corp-wide): 4.9MM **Privately Held**
Web: www.ruan.com
SIC: **4213** Contract haulers
PA: Ruan
1354 S Blackstone St
Tulare CA
559 688-0591

(P-3536)
RUAN TRANSPORT CORPORATION
830 W Glenwood Ave (95380-5751)
PHONE.....................209 599-5000
Mike Elliott, *Brnch Mgr*
EMP: 62
SALES (corp-wide): 7.23MM **Privately Held**
Web: www.ruan.com
SIC: **4213** Contract haulers
HQ: Ruan Transport Corporation
666 Grand Ave Ste 3100
Des Moines IA
515 245-2500

(P-3537)
S & M MOVING SYSTEMS
Also Called: SM International
48551 Warm Springs Blvd (94539-7765)
PHONE.....................510 497-2300
Gerald P Stadler, *Prin*
John Stadler, *
▲ EMP: 60 EST: 1985
SQ FT: 38,000
SALES (est): 22.82MM
SALES (corp-wide): 48.8MM **Privately Held**
Web: www.smmoving.com
SIC: **4213** 4214 Trucking, except local; Local trucking with storage
PA: Torrance Van & Storage Company
12128 Burke St
Santa Fe Springs CA

(P-3538)
SAIA INC
Also Called: Saia S Reno Barbara K
1508 Wyant Way (95864-2642)
PHONE.....................916 483-8331
EMP: 122
SALES (corp-wide): 2.79B **Publicly Held**
Web: www.saia.com
SIC: **4213** Contract haulers
PA: Saia, Inc.
11465 Johns Creek Pkwy # 400
Johns Creek GA
770 232-5067

(P-3539)
SAIA MOTOR FREIGHT LINE LLC
14731 Santa Ana Ave (92337-7233)
PHONE.....................909 356-2808
Mike Ewing, *Mgr*
EMP: 64
SALES (corp-wide): 2.79B **Publicly Held**

SIC: **4213** 4212 Contract haulers; Local trucking, without storage
HQ: Saia Motor Freight Line, Llc
11465 Johns Creek Pkwy # 400
Duluth GA
770 232-5067

(P-3540)
SAIA MOTOR FREIGHT LINE LLC
9119 Elkmont Dr (95624-9706)
PHONE.....................916 690-8417
Joe Meyer, *Brnch Mgr*
EMP: 68
SALES (corp-wide): 2.79B **Publicly Held**
SIC: **4213** Contract haulers
HQ: Saia Motor Freight Line, Llc
11465 Johns Creek Pkwy # 400
Duluth GA
770 232-5067

(P-3541)
SAIA MOTOR FREIGHT LINE LLC
2550 E 28th St (90058-1430)
PHONE.....................323 277-2880
Gerard Francois, *Brnch Mgr*
EMP: 62
SALES (corp-wide): 2.79B **Publicly Held**
SIC: **4213** Contract haulers
HQ: Saia Motor Freight Line, Llc
11465 Johns Creek Pkwy # 400
Duluth GA
770 232-5067

(P-3542)
SCAN-VINO LLC (PA)
Also Called: Cherokee Freight Lines
5463 Cherokee Rd (95215-1128)
P.O. Box 5509 (95205-0509)
PHONE.....................209 931-3570
Leanne Scannavino, *Prin*
Jack Riella, *Prin*
EMP: 69 EST: 1965
SQ FT: 1,000
SALES (est): 27.6MM
SALES (corp-wide): 27.6MM **Privately Held**
Web: www.gocfl.com
SIC: **4213** Contract haulers

(P-3543)
SEA-LOGIX LLC
1425 Maritime St (94607-1022)
PHONE.....................510 271-1400
Mary Brown, *Area Superintendent*
EMP: 60
SALES (corp-wide): 494.24MM **Privately Held**
Web: www.sealogix.com
SIC: **4213** Trucking, except local
HQ: Sea-Logix, Llc.
4040 Civic Center Dr # 350
San Rafael CA
415 927-6400

(P-3544)
SIERRA AGRICULTURAL TRNSP INC
1316 W Center Ave (93291-5804)
P.O. Box 590 (93279-0590)
PHONE.....................559 738-5448
John M Rast, *Pr*
Cary Crum, *
John Rast, *
EMP: 69 EST: 2002
SQ FT: 1,600
SALES (est): 3.7MM **Privately Held**
Web: www.sierratrans.com

SIC: **4213** Contract haulers

(P-3545)
STANLEY G ALEXANDER INC (PA)
Also Called: Alexander's Moving & Storage
2942 Dow Ave (92780-7220)
PHONE.....................714 731-1658
EMP: 130 EST: 1953
SALES (est): 53.18MM
SALES (corp-wide): 53.18MM **Privately Held**
Web: www.alexanders.net
SIC: **4213** Trucking, except local

(P-3546)
STEVENS TRANSPORTATION INC
Also Called: Stevens Trucking
7100 E Brundage Ln (93307-3060)
PHONE.....................661 366-3286
EMP: 150 EST: 1984
SALES (est): 23.69MM **Privately Held**
Web: www.stibk.com
SIC: **4213** Refrigerated products transport

(P-3547)
SUNSET PACIFIC TRANSPORTATION INC (PA)
14522 Yorba Ave (91710-9208)
PHONE.....................909 464-1677
▲ EMP: 65 EST: 1980
SALES (est): 12.75MM
SALES (corp-wide): 12.75MM **Privately Held**
Web: www.sunsetpacific.com
SIC: **4213** 4214 Trucking, except local; Local trucking with storage

(P-3548)
SWIFT LEASING CO LLC
14392 Valley Blvd (92335-5240)
PHONE.....................909 347-0500
EMP: 288
Web: www.swifttrans.com
SIC: **4213** Contract haulers
HQ: Swift Leasing Co., Llc
2200 S 75th Ave
Phoenix AZ
602 269-9700

(P-3549)
T & T TRUCKING INC (PA)
11396 N Highway 99 (95240-6899)
PHONE.....................800 692-3457
Terry M Tarditi, *Pr*
John King, *
Mary Lou Tarditi, *
EMP: 107 EST: 1965
SQ FT: 25,000
SALES (est): 18.65MM
SALES (corp-wide): 18.65MM **Privately Held**
Web: www.tttrucking.com
SIC: **4213** Contract haulers

(P-3550)
TCI TRANSPORTATION SERVICES
14561 Merrill Ave Bldg B (92335-4219)
PHONE.....................909 355-8545
EMP: 194
SALES (corp-wide): 29.25MM **Privately Held**
Web: www.tcitransportation.com
SIC: **4213** Trucking, except local
PA: Tci Transportation Services
4950 Triggs St
Commerce CA
323 269-3033

(P-3551)
TIGER LINES LLC (HQ)
927 Black Diamond Way (95240-0738)
P.O. Box 1120 (95241-1120)
PHONE.....................209 334-4100
Dennis Altnow, *Managing Member*
Donald Altnow, *Managing Member**
EMP: 75 EST: 1935
SQ FT: 20,000
SALES (est): 26.87MM
SALES (corp-wide): 26.87MM **Privately Held**
Web: www.tigerlines.com
SIC: **4213** 4214 4212 Contract haulers; Local trucking with storage; Local trucking, without storage
PA: Lts Rentals, Llc
927 Black Diamond Way
Lodi CA
209 334-4100

(P-3552)
TIMMERMAN STARLITE TRCKG INC
3955 Starlite Dr (95307-9733)
P.O. Box 2710 (95307-7710)
PHONE.....................209 538-1706
Colby Bell, *CEO*
Agnes Timmerman, *
Geneveve Timmerman, *
EMP: 65 EST: 1976
SALES (est): 7.08MM **Privately Held**
Web: www.starlitetrucking.com
SIC: **4213** 4212 Trucking, except local; Farm to market haulage, local

(P-3553)
TMT INDUSTRIES INC
14774 Jurupa Ave (92337-7263)
P.O. Box 310123 (92331-0123)
PHONE.....................909 493-3441
Antonio Y Martinez, *CEO*
Tony Martinez Senior, *Pr*
Tony Martinez Junior, *VP*
Evelyn Martinez, *
EMP: 63 EST: 1966
SALES (est): 18.19MM **Privately Held**
SIC: **4213** 4212 Trucking, except local; Local trucking, without storage

(P-3554)
TQ LOGISTICS INC
700 Laurelwood Rd (95054-2422)
PHONE.....................408 565-0188
Andrew Reynolds, *Pr*
EMP: 72
SALES (corp-wide): 46.93MM **Privately Held**
Web: www.tqlogistics.com
SIC: **4213** Contract haulers
PA: Tq Logistics, Inc.
3698 Largent Way Nw # 104
Marietta GA
770 426-8050

(P-3555)
TRIPLE-E MACHINERY MOVING INC
3301 Gilman Rd (91732-3225)
PHONE.....................626 444-1137
Steve Englebrecht, *CEO*
Joe Englbrecht, *
EMP: 60 EST: 1974
SQ FT: 12,000
SALES (est): 8.7MM **Privately Held**
Web: www.tripleemachinery.com
SIC: **4213** Heavy machinery transport

PRODUCTS & SERVICES SECTION
4214 - Local Trucking With Storage (P-3577)

(P-3556)
TRIUS TRUCKING INC
4692 E Lincoln Ave (93625-9685)
P.O. Box 2700 (93745-2700)
PHONE..................................559 834-4000
Tehal Singh Thandi, *CEO*
EMP: 87 **EST:** 2002
SQ FT: 3,900
SALES (est): 13.48MM **Privately Held**
Web: www.triustrucking.com
SIC: 4213 Trucking, except local

(P-3557)
TRIWAYS INC
Also Called: Warehouse and Distribution
11201 Iberia St Ste B (91752-3280)
P.O. Box 9342 (91762-9342)
PHONE..................................951 361-4840
Juan M Jauregui, *Pr*
Bob Schwenig, *
Fredy R Jimenez, *
▲ **EMP:** 65 **EST:** 1978
SQ FT: 228,000
SALES (est): 11.23MM **Privately Held**
Web: www.triways.net
SIC: 4213 Trucking, except local

(P-3558)
U C L INCORPORATED (PA)
Also Called: United Cargo Logistics
620 S Hacienda Blvd (91745-1126)
PHONE..................................323 235-0099
Byung Y Chang, *CEO*
Chris Chang, *
Yong Ku, *
EMP: 100 **EST:** 1998
SQ FT: 16,000
SALES (est): 27.76MM
SALES (corp-wide): 27.76MM **Privately Held**
Web: www.uclinc.com
SIC: 4213 Trucking, except local

(P-3559)
U S XPRESS INC
363 Nina Lee Rd (92231-9527)
PHONE..................................760 768-6707
EMP: 302
Web: www.usxpress.com
SIC: 4213 Trucking, except local
HQ: U. S. Xpress, Inc.
    4080 Jenkins Rd
    Chattanooga TN
    866 266-7270

(P-3560)
VALLEY BULK INC
17649 Turner Rd (92394-8716)
P.O. Box 1100 (92393-1100)
PHONE..................................760 843-0574
Jeff W Golson, *Pr*
EMP: 85 **EST:** 1995
SALES (est): 7.83MM **Privately Held**
Web: www.valleybulkinc.com
SIC: 4213 Contract haulers

(P-3561)
VAN KING & STORAGE INC
Also Called: King Relocation Services
13535 Larwin Cir (90670-5032)
PHONE..................................562 921-0555
TOLL FREE: 800
Steve Komorous, *Pr*
Edwin Nabal, *
Keith Hindsley, *
EMP: 75 **EST:** 1955
SQ FT: 60,000
SALES (est): 23.33MM **Privately Held**
Web: www.kingvanstorage.com
SIC: 4213 4225 Trucking, except local; General warehousing and storage

(P-3562)
VENTURA TRANSFER COMPANY (PA)
2418 E 223rd St (90810-1697)
PHONE..................................310 549-1660
Randall J Clifford, *CEO*
Greg Clifford, *
Galen Clifford, *
Phyllis E Batchelor, *
Steven F Clifford, *
▲ **EMP:** 75 **EST:** 1927
SQ FT: 10,000
SALES (est): 20.11MM
SALES (corp-wide): 20.11MM **Privately Held**
Web: www.venturatransfercompany.com
SIC: 4213 4212 4214 Contract haulers; Local trucking, without storage; Local trucking with storage

(P-3563)
VITO TRUCKING LLC
2812 Nathan Ave (95354-4135)
PHONE..................................209 342-5104
Vito Ranuio, *Managing Member*
EMP: 60 **EST:** 2005
SALES (est): 2.29MM **Privately Held**
Web: www.vitotrucking.com
SIC: 4213 Trucking, except local

(P-3564)
WILLIAMS TANK LINES (PA)
1477 Tillie Lewis Dr (95206-1130)
PHONE..................................209 944-5613
Michael I Williams, *CEO*
Marlys A Williams, *
EMP: 90 **EST:** 1978
SQ FT: 15,000
SALES (est): 56.63MM
SALES (corp-wide): 56.63MM **Privately Held**
Web: www.williamstanklines.com
SIC: 4213 Liquid petroleum transport, non-local

(P-3565)
WILLIAMS TANK LINES
2148 Bricyn Ln (93308-6244)
PHONE..................................661 634-9755
Steve Bailey, *Brnch Mgr*
EMP: 67
SALES (corp-wide): 56.63MM **Privately Held**
Web: www.williamstanklines.com
SIC: 4213 Liquid petroleum transport, non-local
PA: Williams Tank Lines
    1477 Tillie Lewis Dr
    Stockton CA
    209 944-5613

(P-3566)
XPO LOGISTICS FREIGHT INC
4965 Convoy St (92111-1600)
PHONE..................................858 569-8921
Tim Tuerk, *Mgr*
EMP: 61
SQ FT: 20,344
SALES (corp-wide): 7.72B **Publicly Held**
Web: ext-web.ltl-xpo.com
SIC: 4213 Trucking, except local
HQ: Xpo Logistics Freight, Inc.
    2211 Old Earhart Rd # 100
    Ann Arbor MI
    800 755-2728

(P-3567)
XPO LOGISTICS FREIGHT INC
5475 S Airport Way (95206-3918)
PHONE..................................209 983-8285
Rudy Romo, *Mgr*
EMP: 100
SQ FT: 1,000
SALES (corp-wide): 7.72B **Publicly Held**
Web: ext-web.ltl-xpo.com
SIC: 4213 Contract haulers
HQ: Xpo Logistics Freight, Inc.
    2211 Old Earhart Rd # 100
    Ann Arbor MI
    800 755-2728

(P-3568)
XPO LOGISTICS FREIGHT INC
2171 Otoole Ave (95131-1314)
PHONE..................................408 435-3876
Jon Sullivan, *Brnch Mgr*
EMP: 87
SQ FT: 8,834
SALES (corp-wide): 7.72B **Publicly Held**
Web: ext-web.ltl-xpo.com
SIC: 4213 Contract haulers
HQ: Xpo Logistics Freight, Inc.
    2211 Old Earhart Rd # 100
    Ann Arbor MI
    800 755-2728

(P-3569)
XPO LOGISTICS FREIGHT INC
4195 E Central Ave (93725-9026)
PHONE..................................559 485-1164
Bud Whitney, *Prin*
EMP: 131
SQ FT: 39,620
SALES (corp-wide): 7.72B **Publicly Held**
Web: ext-web.ltl-xpo.com
SIC: 4213 Contract haulers
HQ: Xpo Logistics Freight, Inc.
    2211 Old Earhart Rd # 100
    Ann Arbor MI
    800 755-2728

(P-3570)
XPO LOGISTICS FREIGHT INC
2102 N Batavia St (92865-3104)
PHONE..................................714 282-7717
Tim Worner, *Mgr*
EMP: 87
SALES (corp-wide): 7.72B **Publicly Held**
Web: ext-web.ltl-xpo.com
SIC: 4213 Contract haulers
HQ: Xpo Logistics Freight, Inc.
    2211 Old Earhart Rd # 100
    Ann Arbor MI
    800 755-2728

(P-3571)
XPO LOGISTICS FREIGHT INC
3516 Kiessig Ave (95823-1036)
PHONE..................................916 399-8291
John Sullivan, *Brnch Mgr*
EMP: 100
SALES (corp-wide): 7.72B **Publicly Held**
Web: ext-web.ltl-xpo.com
SIC: 4213 Contract haulers
HQ: Xpo Logistics Freight, Inc.
    2211 Old Earhart Rd # 100
    Ann Arbor MI
    800 755-2728

(P-3572)
XPO LOGISTICS FREIGHT INC
20697 Prism Pl (92630-7803)
PHONE..................................949 581-9030
Joseph Tickford, *Brnch Mgr*
EMP: 61
SQ FT: 13,890
SALES (corp-wide): 7.72B **Publicly Held**
Web: ext-web.ltl-xpo.com
SIC: 4213 Contract haulers
HQ: Xpo Logistics Freight, Inc.
    2211 Old Earhart Rd # 100
    Ann Arbor MI
    800 755-2728

(P-3573)
XPO LOGISTICS FREIGHT INC
1955 E Washington Blvd (90021-3206)
PHONE..................................213 744-0664
Todd Liverman, *Brnch Mgr*
EMP: 157
SQ FT: 39,842
SALES (corp-wide): 7.72B **Publicly Held**
Web: ext-web.ltl-xpo.com
SIC: 4213 4212 4731 Contract haulers; Local trucking, without storage; Freight forwarding
HQ: Xpo Logistics Freight, Inc.
    2211 Old Earhart Rd # 100
    Ann Arbor MI
    800 755-2728

(P-3574)
XPO LOGISTICS FREIGHT INC
2200 Claremont Ct (94545-5002)
PHONE..................................510 785-6920
Terry Smith, *Mgr*
EMP: 100
SQ FT: 28,704
SALES (corp-wide): 7.72B **Publicly Held**
Web: ext-web.ltl-xpo.com
SIC: 4213 4212 4731 Contract haulers; Local trucking, without storage; Freight transportation arrangement
HQ: Xpo Logistics Freight, Inc.
    2211 Old Earhart Rd # 100
    Ann Arbor MI
    800 755-2728

(P-3575)
XPO LOGISTICS FREIGHT INC
13364 Marlay Ave (92337-6919)
PHONE..................................951 685-1244
EMP: 100
SALES (corp-wide): 7.72B **Publicly Held**
Web: ext-web.ltl-xpo.com
SIC: 4213 Contract haulers
HQ: Xpo Logistics Freight, Inc.
    2211 Old Earhart Rd # 100
    Ann Arbor MI
    800 755-2728

(P-3576)
XPO LOGISTICS FREIGHT INC
12903 Lakeland Rd (90670-4516)
PHONE..................................562 946-8331
EMP: 91
SALES (corp-wide): 7.72B **Publicly Held**
Web: ext-web.ltl-xpo.com
SIC: 4213 Contract haulers
HQ: Xpo Logistics Freight, Inc.
    2211 Old Earhart Rd # 100
    Ann Arbor MI
    800 755-2728

4214 Local Trucking With Storage

(P-3577)
17400 INC
17400 Chestnut St (91748-1013)
PHONE..................................626 913-1800
John W Miller, *CEO*
James R Miller, *
▲ **EMP:** 60 **EST:** 1933
SQ FT: 110,000

4214 - Local Trucking With Storage (P-3578)

SALES (est): 7.24MM **Privately Held**
Web: www.halbertbrothersinc.com
SIC: **4214** 1796 Local trucking with storage; Machine moving and rigging

(P-3578)
ALL CARTAGE TRANSPORTATION INC (PA)
Also Called: A C T
12621 Chadron Ave (90250-4809)
P.O. Box 90521 (90009-0521)
PHONE.................................310 970-0600
George Aiello, *Pr*
Jeff De Seire, *
EMP: 77 **EST:** 1979
SQ FT: 24,000
SALES (est): 14.98MM
SALES (corp-wide): 14.98MM **Privately Held**
Web: www.allcartage.com
SIC: **4214** 4449 Local trucking with storage; Transportation (freight) on bays and sounds of the ocean

(P-3579)
AMERICAN WEST WORLDWIDE EX INC (PA)
51 Zaca Ln Ste 120 (93401-7353)
PHONE.................................800 788-4534
Josh Brown, *CEO*
Cathie Brown, *
▲ **EMP:** 68 **EST:** 1986
SALES (est): 25.85MM **Privately Held**
Web: www.awest.com
SIC: **4214** 4213 4225 Local trucking with storage; Trucking, except local; General warehousing

(P-3580)
CITY MOVING INC (PA)
2507 Medford St (90033-1112)
PHONE.................................888 794-8808
Lior Oren, *CEO*
EMP: 150 **EST:** 2014
SALES (est): 9.88MM
SALES (corp-wide): 9.88MM **Privately Held**
Web: www.citymoving.com
SIC: **4214** Local trucking with storage

(P-3581)
COROVAN CORPORATION (PA)
12302 Kerran St (92064-6884)
PHONE.................................858 762-8100
Richard R Schmitz, *CEO*
Robert J Schmitz, *
Thomas A Schmitz, *
EMP: 175 **EST:** 1994
SQ FT: 80,000
SALES (est): 98.92MM **Privately Held**
Web: www.corovan.com
SIC: **4214** Local trucking with storage

(P-3582)
COROVAN MOVING & STORAGE CO (HQ)
12302 Kerran St (92064-6884)
PHONE.................................858 748-1100
Richard R Schmitz, *Pr*
Robert J Schmitz, *
Thomas A Schmitz, *
Jerry P Brothers, *
▲ **EMP:** 100 **EST:** 1948
SQ FT: 600,000
SALES (est): 65.6MM **Privately Held**
Web: www.corovan.com
SIC: **4214** 4213 Household goods moving and storage, local; Household goods transport

PA: Corovan Corporation
12302 Kerran St
Poway CA

(P-3583)
COVAN WORLD-WIDE MOVING INC
10015 Waples Ct Ste B (92121-2962)
PHONE.................................858 558-0439
Stewart Mcquinn, *Mgr*
EMP: 66
Web: www.covan.com
SIC: **4214** Household goods moving and storage, local
HQ: Covan World-Wide Moving, Incorporated
1 Eagle Ridge Dr
Midland City AL
334 983-6500

(P-3584)
CRUZ MODULAR INC (PA)
Also Called: Systechs
249 W Baywood Ave Ste B (92865-2604)
PHONE.................................714 283-2890
Linda Galleran, *CEO*
Vince Schlachter, *Pr*
Malcolm Craycroft, *VP*
EMP: 90 **EST:** 1991
SALES (est): 4.45MM **Privately Held**
Web: cruzmodulard.openfos.com
SIC: **4214** 7641 4226 1799 Furniture moving and storage, local; Reupholstery and furniture repair; Special warehousing and storage, nec; Office furniture installation

(P-3585)
DURKEE DRAYAGE COMPANY
Also Called: Go Durkee Logistics
539 Stone Rd (94510-1113)
PHONE.................................510 970-7550
Jeffrey J Fenton, *Pr*
Cathy Lashin, *
▲ **EMP:** 80 **EST:** 1933
SQ FT: 80,000
SALES (est): 9.04MM **Privately Held**
Web: www.durkeedrayage.com
SIC: **4214** Local trucking with storage

(P-3586)
FN LOGISTICS LLC
12588 Florence Ave (90670-3919)
PHONE.................................213 625-5900
Richard Saghian, *Pr*
EMP: 953
SIC: **4214** Local trucking with storage
HQ: Fn Logistics, Llc.
2801 E 46th St
Vernon CA
213 625-5900

(P-3587)
FOX TRANSPORTATION INC
18408 S Laurel Park Rd (90220-6015)
PHONE.................................310 971-0867
Luke Shire, *Mgr*
EMP: 227
Web: www.foxtransportationinc.com
SIC: **4214** 4225 Local trucking with storage; General warehousing and storage
PA: Fox Transportation, Inc.
8610 Helms Ave
Rancho Cucamonga CA

(P-3588)
GREAT AMRCN LOGISTICS DIST INC
13565 Larwin Cir (90670-5032)
PHONE.................................562 229-3601

TOLL FREE: 800
EMP: 85 **EST:** 1993
SQ FT: 120,000
SALES (est): 13.49MM **Privately Held**
Web: www.greatamerican-logistics.com
SIC: **4214** 4212 4213 6719 Household goods moving and storage, local; Moving services; Trucking, except local; Investment holding companies, except banks

(P-3589)
LEGACY TRANSPORTATION SVCS INC (PA)
Also Called: Legacy Global Logistics Svcs
935 Mclaughlin Ave (95122-2612)
PHONE.................................408 294-9800
John Migliozzi, *Pr*
Michael Quinn, *
Shelly J Mcallister, *VP*
Shelly Gipson, *
▲ **EMP:** 140 **EST:** 1991
SQ FT: 200,000
SALES (est): 57.76MM **Privately Held**
Web: www.legacytsi.com
SIC: **4214** 4213 Local trucking with storage; Trucking, except local

(P-3590)
MOVING SOLUTIONS INC
Also Called: North American Van Lines
7093 Central Ave (94560-4201)
PHONE.................................408 920-0110
Rick S Philpott, *CEO*
Janet Philpott, *
EMP: 150 **EST:** 1984
SQ FT: 200,000
SALES (est): 20.23MM **Privately Held**
Web: www.northamerican.com
SIC: **4214** 8742 7376 1799 Local trucking with storage; Construction project management consultant; Computer facilities management; Office furniture installation

(P-3591)
NOR-CAL MOVING SERVICES (PA)
Also Called: Allied Intl San Franisco
3129 Corporate Pl (94545-3915)
PHONE.................................510 371-4942
Peter Mazzetti Junior, *CEO*
Dennis D Goza, *
Dave Konecny, *
John Mizera, *
Louis Marchiorlatti, *
▲ **EMP:** 125 **EST:** 1982
SQ FT: 200,000
SALES (est): 24.39MM
SALES (corp-wide): 24.39MM **Privately Held**
Web: www.nor-calmoving.com
SIC: **4214** 4213 Household goods moving and storage, local; Household goods transport

(P-3592)
REDDING LUMBER TRANSPORT INC
Also Called: R L T
4301 Eastside Rd (96001-3801)
P.O. Box 492110 (96049-2110)
PHONE.................................530 241-8193
Albert Shufelberger, *Pr*
William Weber, *
EMP: 74 **EST:** 1972
SQ FT: 4,000
SALES (est): 10.27MM **Privately Held**
Web: www.rlttrucking.com
SIC: **4214** 4213 Local trucking with storage; Refrigerated products transport

(P-3593)
ROYAL EXPRESS INC (PA)
3545 E Date Ave (93725-1933)
PHONE.................................559 272-3500
Kirpal S Shiota, *CEO*
EMP: 111 **EST:** 1975
SQ FT: 435,600
SALES (est): 15.1MM
SALES (corp-wide): 15.1MM **Privately Held**
Web: www.smartwayexp.com
SIC: **4214** Local trucking with storage

(P-3594)
SAMUEL J PIAZZA & SON INC (PA)
Also Called: Piazza Trucking
9001 Rayo Ave (90280-3606)
PHONE.................................323 357-1999
Michael Piazza, *CEO*
Robert Piazza, *
William Piazza, *
EMP: 70 **EST:** 1970
SQ FT: 20,000
SALES (est): 18.83MM
SALES (corp-wide): 18.83MM **Privately Held**
Web: www.piazzatrucking.com
SIC: **4214** 4213 Local trucking with storage; Trucking, except local

(P-3595)
SCHICK MOVING & STORAGE CO (PA)
2721 Michelle Dr (92780-7018)
P.O. Box 3627 (92781-3627)
PHONE.................................714 731-5500
TOLL FREE: 800
Gordon C Schick, *Pr*
Arthur C Schick Junior, *VP*
Beverly C Schick, *
Gordon Schick, *
Lynne M Larson, *
EMP: 100 **EST:** 1956
SQ FT: 113,000
SALES (est): 6.9MM
SALES (corp-wide): 6.9MM **Privately Held**
Web: www.schickusa.com
SIC: **4214** Household goods moving and storage, local

(P-3596)
SPECIAL DISPATCH CAL INC (PA)
243 Newport Ave (90803-5920)
PHONE.................................714 521-8200
John Edward Dearing, *CEO*
Thomas Dearing, *
EMP: 60 **EST:** 1968
SALES (est): 22.13MM **Privately Held**
Web: www.specialdispatch.com
SIC: **4214** 4212 Local trucking with storage; Delivery service, vehicular

(P-3597)
SS SKIKOS INCORPORATED
1289 Sebastopol Rd (95407-6834)
PHONE.................................707 575-3000
EMP: 80 **EST:** 2002
SALES (est): 8.44MM **Privately Held**
Web: www.skikostrucking.com
SIC: **4214** Local trucking with storage

(P-3598)
THREE WAY INC
Also Called: 3-Way Air Charter
2940 Mead Ave (95051-0817)
P.O. Box 1806 (94538-0032)
PHONE.................................408 748-6902

PRODUCTS & SERVICES SECTION
4215 - Courier Services, Except By Air (P-3620)

▲ EMP: 250
SIC: 4214 4213 4731 Local trucking with storage; Trucking, except local; Freight transportation arrangement

(P-3599)
TRANSPORT EXPRESS INC
Also Called: Port Logistics Group
19801 S Santa Fe Ave (90221-5915)
PHONE..................................310 898-2000
Robert L Stull, *CEO*
Steven Senecal, *
William Meroth, *
Patricia Senecal, *
◆ EMP: 76 EST: 1977
SQ FT: 230,000
SALES (est): 4.71MM **Privately Held**
Web: www.transportexpress.com
SIC: 4214 4225 4731 Local trucking with storage; General warehousing; Brokers, shipping

(P-3600)
VALLEY RLCTION STOR NTHRN CAL
Also Called: Valley Northamerican
3230 Reed Ave (95605-1622)
PHONE..................................916 375-0001
Mark Palatier, *Brnch Mgr*
EMP: 74
SALES (corp-wide): 26.59MM **Privately Held**
Web: www.northamerican.com
SIC: 4214 Local trucking with storage
PA: Valley Relocation And Storage Of Northern California, Inc.
5000 Marsh Dr
Concord CA
925 230-2025

(P-3601)
VALLEY RLCTION STOR NTHRN CAL
Also Called: Valley Northamerican
835 Sinclair Frontage Rd (95035-0308)
PHONE..................................408 938-3672
Ralph Rojas, *Brnch Mgr*
EMP: 74
SALES (corp-wide): 26.59MM **Privately Held**
Web: www.northamerican.com
SIC: 4214 Local trucking with storage
PA: Valley Relocation And Storage Of Northern California, Inc.
5000 Marsh Dr
Concord CA
925 230-2025

(P-3602)
VAN TORRANCE & STORAGE COMPANY (PA)
Also Called: S & M Moving Systems
12128 Burke St (90670-2678)
TOLL FREE: 800
◆ EMP: 100 EST: 1918
SQ FT: 95,000
SALES (est): 48.8MM
SALES (corp-wide): 48.8MM **Privately Held**
Web: www.unitedvanlines.com
SIC: 4214 4213 Local trucking with storage; Trucking, except local

(P-3603)
VERNON CENTRAL WAREHOUSE INC
Also Called: Vernon Warehouse Co
2050 E 38th St (90058-1615)
P.O. Box 58426 (90058-0426)

PHONE..................................323 234-2200
Joseph E Tack, *CEO*
Robert L Shipp, *
Joe Tack, *
Jim Boltinghouse, *
Steve Shanklin, *
EMP: 125 EST: 1933
SQ FT: 100,000
SALES (est): 20.6MM **Privately Held**
Web: www.sweetenerproducts.com
SIC: 4214 5149 Local trucking with storage; Natural and organic foods

(P-3604)
W WHY W ENTERPRISES INC
Also Called: Atlas/Eastern Van Lines
2671 Pomona Blvd (91768-3221)
PHONE..................................626 969-4292
William Coffman, *Pr*
Yvonne Coffman, *
EMP: 60 EST: 1956
SALES (est): 2.35MM **Privately Held**
Web: www.easternvanlines.com
SIC: 4214 4213 Local trucking with storage; Household goods transport

---
4215 Courier Services, Except By Air

(P-3605)
ALL COUNTIES COURIER INC
1900 S State College Blvd Ste 450 (92806-6163)
PHONE..................................714 599-9300
Patricia Cochran, *Pr*
EMP: 200 EST: 1984
SALES (est): 20.26MM **Privately Held**
SIC: 4215 Package delivery, vehicular

(P-3606)
APOLLO COURIERS INC (PA)
1039 W Hillcrest Blvd (90301-2023)
PHONE..................................310 337-0377
Frank Ghamari, *Pr*
Fred Ghamarifard, *Pr*
Payman Khosravi, *CFO*
EMP: 69 EST: 1988
SQ FT: 2,200
SALES (est): 8.5MM **Privately Held**
Web: www.apollocouriers.com
SIC: 4215 Package delivery, vehicular

(P-3607)
BATTLE-TESTED STRATEGIES LLC
650 Commerce Ave Ste E (93551-3884)
PHONE..................................661 802-6509
Johnathon Ervin, *CEO*
EMP: 90 EST: 2018
SALES (est): 2.72MM **Privately Held**
SIC: 4215 7379 Package delivery, vehicular; Computer related services, nec

(P-3608)
DHB DELIVERY LLC
1134 N Chestnut Ln (91702-6867)
PHONE..................................626 588-7562
Daniel R Bourgault, *Managing Member*
EMP: 84 EST: 2019
SALES (est): 2.68MM **Privately Held**
SIC: 4215 Package delivery, vehicular

(P-3609)
DI OVERNITE LLC
Also Called: Deliver-It
1900 S State College Blvd Ste 450 (92806-6163)
PHONE..................................877 997-7447

EMP: 89 EST: 2013
SALES (est): 12.11MM **Privately Held**
Web: www.deliver-it.com
SIC: 4215 Package delivery, vehicular

(P-3610)
DIRECT PARCEL INC ✪
1768 Hardial Ct (95993-9436)
PHONE..................................303 381-4099
Sundip Sangha, *Pr*
EMP: 71 EST: 2023
SALES (est): 1.32MM **Privately Held**
SIC: 4215 7389 Courier services, except by air; Business Activities at Non-Commercial Site

(P-3611)
EXPRESS GROUP INCORPORATED (PA)
Also Called: Westwood Express Messenger Svc
10801 National Blvd Ste 104 (90064-4140)
PHONE..................................310 474-5999
David F Davoodian, *Pr*
Malek Neman, *
EMP: 74 EST: 1980
SQ FT: 4,000
SALES (est): 4.32MM
SALES (corp-wide): 4.32MM **Privately Held**
Web: www.deliverla.com
SIC: 4215 Courier services, except by air

(P-3612)
FUNNELCLOUDSALES
21758 Placeritos Blvd (91321-1830)
PHONE..................................661 284-6032
Timothy Kane, *Pr*
EMP: 90
SALES (est): 1.34MM **Privately Held**
SIC: 4215 7389 Package delivery, vehicular; Business Activities at Non-Commercial Site

(P-3613)
GENERAL LGSTICS SYSTEMS US INC
4601 Malat St (94601-4903)
PHONE..................................800 322-5555
Patrick Stoops, *Prin*
EMP: 171
SALES (corp-wide): 14.47B **Privately Held**
Web: www.gls-us.com
SIC: 4215 Package delivery, vehicular
HQ: General Logistics Systems Us, Inc.
4000 Executive Pkwy # 295
San Ramon CA

(P-3614)
GENERAL LGSTICS SYSTEMS US INC
827 N American St (93291-9337)
PHONE..................................559 651-1850
Dave Johnson, *Mgr*
EMP: 214
SALES (corp-wide): 14.47B **Privately Held**
Web: www.gls-us.com
SIC: 4215 4513 Package delivery, vehicular; Parcel delivery, private air
HQ: General Logistics Systems Us, Inc.
4000 Executive Pkwy # 295
San Ramon CA

(P-3615)
GENERAL LGSTICS SYSTEMS US INC
760 Cabin Dr (94941-3915)
PHONE..................................415 492-1112
Steve Koller, *Mgr*
EMP: 128

SALES (corp-wide): 14.47B **Privately Held**
Web: www.gls-us.com
SIC: 4215 4212 Package delivery, vehicular; Delivery service, vehicular
HQ: General Logistics Systems Us, Inc.
4000 Executive Pkwy # 295
San Ramon CA

(P-3616)
INTEGRATED PARCEL NETWORK
Also Called: Pacific Couriers
11135 Rush St Ste A (91733-3520)
PHONE..................................714 278-6100
Nadia Youssef, *CEO*
EMP: 275 EST: 1985
SALES (est): 4.49MM **Privately Held**
Web: www.iparcelnetwork.com
SIC: 4215 4214 7389 Package delivery, vehicular; Local trucking with storage; Courier or messenger service

(P-3617)
JET DELIVERY INC (PA)
2169 Wright Ave (91750-5835)
PHONE..................................800 716-7177
Michael Barbata, *Pr*
Jason Barbata, *CIO*
Mark Sur, *
EMP: 90 EST: 1950
SQ FT: 34,000
SALES (est): 24.73MM
SALES (corp-wide): 24.73MM **Privately Held**
Web: www.jetdelivery.com
SIC: 4215 4231 4212 4213 Package delivery, vehicular; Trucking terminal facilities; Local trucking, without storage; Trucking, except local

(P-3618)
KXP CARRIER SERVICES LLC
Also Called: Expak Logistics
11777 San Vicente Blvd (90049-5011)
PHONE..................................424 320-5300
Michael S Kraus, *CEO*
EMP: 140 EST: 2014
SQ FT: 1,500
SALES (est): 1.01MM
SALES (corp-wide): 24.03MM **Privately Held**
Web: www.expak.com
SIC: 4215 Parcel delivery, vehicular
PA: Kxp Advantage Services, Llc
11777 San Vicente Blvd # 747
Los Angeles CA
424 320-5300

(P-3619)
M & N CONSULTING INC
Also Called: A-LINE MESSENGER SERVICE
21358 Nordhoff St (91311-6921)
PHONE..................................818 349-9400
TOLL FREE: 800
Robin Anderson, *Pr*
EMP: 61 EST: 1990
SQ FT: 1,170
SALES (est): 3.64MM **Privately Held**
Web: www.alinems.com
SIC: 4215 Package delivery, vehicular

(P-3620)
MADDEN CORPORATION
Also Called: Pam's Delivery Svc & Nat Msgnr
2301 E Pacifica Pl (90220-6210)
PHONE..................................714 922-1670
Donald L Madden, *Pr*
EMP: 100 EST: 2003
SALES (est): 13.18MM **Privately Held**

4215 - Courier Services, Except By Air (P-3621)

SIC: **4215** Courier services, except by air

(P-3621)
MESSENGER EXPRESS (PA)
5435 Cahuenga Blvd Ste C (91601-2948)
PHONE..........................213 614-0475
Gilbert Kort, *Pr*
EMP: 143 EST: 1976
SALES (est): 4.48MM
SALES (corp-wide): 4.48MM Privately Held
Web: www.lightningmessengerexpress.com
SIC: **4215** 7389 4212 Package delivery, vehicular; Courier or messenger service; Delivery service, vehicular

(P-3622)
ON TRAC
1635 Main Ave Ste 3 (95838-2452)
PHONE..........................916 921-6016
Lloyd Layton, *Account Executive*
EMP: 73 EST: 2017
SALES (est): 918.62K Privately Held
SIC: **4215** Courier services, except by air

(P-3623)
ONTRAC LOGISTICS INC
1745 W Penhall Way (92801-6744)
PHONE..........................714 776-0363
EMP: 68
SALES (corp-wide): 735.78MM Privately Held
Web: www.ontrac.com
SIC: **4215** Courier services, except by air
HQ: Ontrac Logistics, Inc.
8401 Greensboro Dr Fl 7
Mc Lean VA

(P-3624)
ONTRAC LOGISTICS INC
Ontrac
11085 Olinda St (91352-3302)
PHONE..........................818 504-9043
EMP: 84
SALES (corp-wide): 735.78MM Privately Held
Web: www.ontrac.com
SIC: **4215** Courier services, except by air
HQ: Ontrac Logistics, Inc.
8401 Greensboro Dr Fl 7
Mc Lean VA

(P-3625)
ONTRAC LOGISTICS INC
Ontrac
9774 Calabash Ave (92335-5204)
PHONE..........................804 334-5000
EMP: 76
SALES (corp-wide): 735.78MM Privately Held
Web: www.ontrac.com
SIC: **4215** Package delivery, vehicular
HQ: Ontrac Logistics, Inc.
8401 Greensboro Dr Fl 7
Mc Lean VA

(P-3626)
PEACH INC
Also Called: Action Messenger Service
1311 N Highland Ave (90028-7608)
P.O. Box 69673 (90069-0673)
PHONE..........................323 654-2333
Arthur P Ruben, *Pr*
EMP: 125 EST: 1990
SQ FT: 3,500
SALES (est): 9.7MM Privately Held
Web: www.actionmessenger.com
SIC: **4215** 7389 Courier services, except by air; Courier or messenger service

(P-3627)
SABSAF LLC
Also Called: Sabsaf Logistics
17192 Murphy Ave Unit 18641 (92623-0519)
PHONE..........................951 266-6676
Saba Safiari, *Managing Member*
EMP: 75 EST: 2019
SALES (est): 5.72MM Privately Held
Web: www.sabsaf.com
SIC: **4215** Package delivery, vehicular

(P-3628)
SPEEDY EXPRESS LLC
4401 W Slauson Ave Ste A (90043-2267)
PHONE..........................818 300-7785
Kentrice Jones, *Prin*
EMP: 96 EST: 2020
SALES (est): 2.72MM Privately Held
SIC: **4215** Courier services, except by air

(P-3629)
SYNCTRUCK LLC
415 Darrell Rd (94010-6709)
PHONE..........................415 425-0447
Luis Toledo, *Prin*
EMP: 92
SALES (corp-wide): 9.87MM Privately Held
Web: www.synctruck.com
SIC: **4215** Package delivery, vehicular
PA: Synctruck Llc
510 Eccles Ave
South San Francisco CA
650 239-6231

(P-3630)
TOP PRIORITY COURIERS INC (PA)
1257 Columbia Ave Ste D1 (92507-2124)
P.O. Box 20376 (92516-0376)
PHONE..........................951 781-1000
Siroos Zakikhani, *Pr*
EMP: 60 EST: 1988
SQ FT: 6,000
SALES (est): 9.32MM Privately Held
Web: www.topprioritycouriers.com
SIC: **4215** Package delivery, vehicular

(P-3631)
UNITED PARCEL SERVICE INC
Also Called: UPS
716 Main St 1 (96093)
PHONE..........................530 623-3938
EMP: 158
SALES (corp-wide): 100.34B Publicly Held
Web: www.ups.com
SIC: **4215** Parcel delivery, vehicular
HQ: United Parcel Service, Inc.
55 Glenlake Pkwy
Atlanta GA
404 828-6000

(P-3632)
UNITED PARCEL SERVICE INC
Also Called: UPS
1601 Atlas Rd (94806-1101)
PHONE..........................510 262-2338
Jim Kelly, *Pr*
EMP: 320
SALES (corp-wide): 100.34B Publicly Held
Web: www.ups.com
SIC: **4215** 4513 Parcel delivery, vehicular; Air courier services
HQ: United Parcel Service, Inc.
55 Glenlake Pkwy
Atlanta GA
404 828-6000

(P-3633)
UNITED PARCEL SERVICE INC
Also Called: UPS
1380 Shore St (95691-3522)
PHONE..........................916 373-4076
Tom Karls, *Mgr*
EMP: 399
SALES (corp-wide): 100.34B Publicly Held
Web: www.ups.com
SIC: **4215** Parcel delivery, vehicular
HQ: United Parcel Service, Inc.
55 Glenlake Pkwy
Atlanta GA
404 828-6000

(P-3634)
UNITED PARCEL SERVICE INC
Also Called: UPS
22 Brookline (92656-1461)
PHONE..........................949 643-6634
EMP: 732
SALES (corp-wide): 100.34B Publicly Held
Web: www.ups.com
SIC: **4215** Parcel delivery, vehicular
HQ: United Parcel Service, Inc.
55 Glenlake Pkwy
Atlanta GA
404 828-6000

(P-3635)
UNITED PARCEL SERVICE INC
Also Called: UPS
17115 S Western Ave (90247-5299)
PHONE..........................310 217-2646
Randy Hulhellt, *Mgr*
EMP: 120
SALES (corp-wide): 100.34B Publicly Held
Web: www.ups.com
SIC: **4215** 4513 Parcel delivery, vehicular; Air courier services
HQ: United Parcel Service, Inc.
55 Glenlake Pkwy
Atlanta GA
404 828-6000

(P-3636)
UNITED PARCEL SERVICE INC
Also Called: UPS
3140 Jurupa St (91761)
PHONE..........................909 974-7212
Richard Ricardo, *Prin*
EMP: 892
SALES (corp-wide): 100.34B Publicly Held
Web: www.ups.com
SIC: **4215** Parcel delivery, vehicular
HQ: United Parcel Service, Inc.
55 Glenlake Pkwy
Atlanta GA
404 828-6000

(P-3637)
UNITED PARCEL SERVICE INC
Also Called: UPS
1999 S 7th St (95112-6009)
PHONE..........................408 291-2942
Frank Cademarti, *Mgr*
EMP: 67
SALES (corp-wide): 100.34B Publicly Held
Web: www.ups.com
SIC: **4215** Parcel delivery, vehicular
HQ: United Parcel Service, Inc.
55 Glenlake Pkwy
Atlanta GA
404 828-6000

(P-3638)
UNITED PARCEL SERVICE INC
UPS
2222 17th St (94103-5015)
PHONE..........................415 252-4564
Tom Dalto, *Mgr*
EMP: 1438
SALES (corp-wide): 100.34B Publicly Held
Web: www.ups.com
SIC: **4215** 4513 Parcel delivery, vehicular; Air courier services
HQ: United Parcel Service, Inc.
55 Glenlake Pkwy
Atlanta GA
404 828-6000

(P-3639)
UNITED PARCEL SERVICE INC
Also Called: UPS
16000 Arminta St (91406-1895)
PHONE..........................404 828-6000
EMP: 333
SALES (corp-wide): 100.34B Publicly Held
Web: www.ups.com
SIC: **4215** Parcel delivery, vehicular
HQ: United Parcel Service, Inc.
55 Glenlake Pkwy
Atlanta GA
404 828-6000

(P-3640)
UNITED PARCEL SERVICE INC
Also Called: UPS
7925 Ronson Rd (92111-1997)
PHONE..........................909 279-5111
EMP: 559
SALES (corp-wide): 100.34B Publicly Held
Web: www.ups.com
SIC: **4215** Parcel delivery, vehicular
HQ: United Parcel Service, Inc.
55 Glenlake Pkwy
Atlanta GA
404 828-6000

(P-3641)
UNITED PARCEL SERVICE INC
Also Called: UPS
8400 Pardee Dr (94621-1456)
PHONE..........................510 813-5662
EMP: 2690
SALES (corp-wide): 100.34B Publicly Held
Web: www.ups.com
SIC: **4215** Parcel delivery, vehicular
HQ: United Parcel Service, Inc.
55 Glenlake Pkwy
Atlanta GA
404 828-6000

(P-3642)
UNITED PARCEL SERVICE INC
Also Called: UPS
13233 Moore St (90703-2276)
PHONE..........................562 404-3236
Gary Mieredos, *Mgr*
EMP: 320
SALES (corp-wide): 100.34B Publicly Held
Web: www.ups.com
SIC: **4215** Parcel delivery, vehicular
HQ: United Parcel Service, Inc.
55 Glenlake Pkwy
Atlanta GA
404 828-6000

PRODUCTS & SERVICES SECTION
4222 - Refrigerated Warehousing And Storage (P-3662)

(P-3643)
UNITED PARCEL SERVICE INC
Also Called: UPS
1501 Rancho Conejo Blvd (91320-1410)
PHONE.................805 375-1832
Grant Nissan, *Brnch Mgr*
EMP: 67
SALES (corp-wide): 100.34B **Publicly Held**
Web: www.ups.com
SIC: 4215 Parcel delivery, vehicular
HQ: United Parcel Service, Inc.
    55 Glenlake Pkwy
    Atlanta GA
    404 828-6000

(P-3644)
UNITED PARCEL SERVICE INC
Also Called: UPS
2300 Boswell Ct (91914-3520)
PHONE.................619 482-8119
EMP: 107
SALES (corp-wide): 100.34B **Publicly Held**
Web: www.ups.com
SIC: 4215 Parcel delivery, vehicular
HQ: United Parcel Service, Inc.
    55 Glenlake Pkwy
    Atlanta GA
    404 828-6000

(P-3645)
UNITED PARCEL SERVICE INC
Also Called: UPS
1100 Baldwin Park Blvd (91706-5895)
PHONE.................626 814-6216
EMP: 466
SALES (corp-wide): 100.34B **Publicly Held**
Web: www.ups.com
SIC: 4215 4513 Parcel delivery, vehicular; Air courier services
HQ: United Parcel Service, Inc.
    55 Glenlake Pkwy
    Atlanta GA
    404 828-6000

(P-3646)
UNITY COURIER SERVICE INC (DH)
3231 Fletcher Dr (90065-2919)
P.O. Box 10909 (91510-0909)
PHONE.................323 255-9800
Ali Sharifi, *CEO*
Larry Lum, *
EMP: 200 EST: 1984
SQ FT: 11,000
SALES (est): 58.7MM
SALES (corp-wide): 2.89B **Privately Held**
SIC: 4215 Package delivery, vehicular
HQ: Tforce TI Holdings Usa, Inc.
    4701 E 32nd St
    Joplin MO
    877 396-2639

(P-3647)
UNITY COURIER SERVICE INC
1132 Beecher St (94577-1252)
PHONE.................510 568-8890
Michael Wynant, *Brnch Mgr*
EMP: 125
SALES (corp-wide): 2.89B **Privately Held**
SIC: 4215 Package delivery, vehicular
HQ: Unity Courier Service, Inc.
    3231 Fletcher Dr
    Los Angeles CA
    323 255-9800

(P-3648)
UPS EXPEDITED MAIL SVCS INC
Also Called: UPS
14390 Washington Ave (94578-3419)
PHONE.................510 297-4600
Mike Frete, *Genl Mgr*
EMP: 438
SALES (corp-wide): 100.34B **Publicly Held**
Web: www.ups.com
SIC: 4215 Parcel delivery, vehicular
HQ: Ups Expedited Mail Services, Inc.
    12380 Morris Rd
    Alpharetta GA
    404 828-6000

(P-3649)
UPS EXPEDITED MAIL SVCS INC
14500 Washington Ave (94578-3419)
PHONE.................510 297-5029
EMP: 438
SALES (corp-wide): 100.34B **Publicly Held**
Web: www.ups.com
SIC: 4215 Parcel delivery, vehicular
HQ: Ups Expedited Mail Services, Inc.
    12380 Morris Rd
    Alpharetta GA
    404 828-6000

4221 Farm Product Warehousing And Storage

(P-3650)
HONEYVILLE INC
11600 Dayton Dr (91730-5525)
PHONE.................909 980-9500
EMP: 85
SALES (corp-wide): 188.43MM **Privately Held**
Web: www.honeyville.com
SIC: 4221 5153 2045 2041 Grain elevator, storage only; Grains; Prepared flour mixes and doughs; Flour and other grain mill products
PA: Honeyville, Inc.
    1040 W 600 N
    Ogden UT
    435 494-4193

4222 Refrigerated Warehousing And Storage

(P-3651)
AMERICOLD LOGISTICS LLC
5401 Santa Ana St (91761-8626)
PHONE.................909 937-2200
Chris Mckeon, *Brnch Mgr*
EMP: 112
SALES (corp-wide): 2.91B **Publicly Held**
Web: www.americold.com
SIC: 4222 Warehousing, cold storage or refrigerated
HQ: Americold Logistics, Llc
    10 Glenlake Pkwy Ste 600
    Atlanta GA
    678 441-1400

(P-3652)
AMERICOLD LOGISTICS LLC
Also Called: Americold Realty
700 Malaga St (91761-8627)
P.O. Box 3967 (91761-0989)
PHONE.................909 390-4950
Jeff Canfield, *Mgr*
EMP: 91
SALES (corp-wide): 2.91B **Publicly Held**
Web: www.americold.com

SIC: 4222 Warehousing, cold storage or refrigerated
HQ: Americold Logistics, Llc
    10 Glenlake Pkwy Ste 600
    Atlanta GA
    678 441-1400

(P-3653)
CAL PACKING AND STORAGE LP
Also Called: Bravante Produce
1356 S Buttonwillow Ave (93654-9333)
PHONE.................559 638-2929
George Bravante, *Mng Pt*
EMP: 70 EST: 2005
SQ FT: 100,000
SALES (est): 12.71MM **Privately Held**
Web: www.bravanteproduce.com
SIC: 4222 7389 5148 Warehousing, cold storage or refrigerated; Packaging and labeling services; Fresh fruits and vegetables

(P-3654)
EXETER PACKERS INC
Also Called: Sun Pacific Cold Storage
33374 Lerdo Hwy (93308-9782)
PHONE.................661 399-0416
Richard Peters, *Mgr*
EMP: 118
SALES (corp-wide): 41.55MM **Privately Held**
Web: www.sunpacific.com
SIC: 4222 0172 Warehousing, cold storage or refrigerated; Grapes
PA: Exeter Packers, Inc.
    1250 E Myer Ave
    Exeter CA
    559 592-5168

(P-3655)
MIKE CAMPBELL & ASSOCIATES LTD
Also Called: Mike Campbell Assoc Logictics
10907 Downey Ave Ste 203 (90241-3737)
PHONE.................626 369-3981
Vickie J Campbell, *CEO*
James Heermans, *
Paul Trump, *
EMP: 1000 EST: 1983
SALES (est): 50.19MM **Privately Held**
SIC: 4222 4225 4214 4213 Storage, frozen or refrigerated goods; General warehousing and storage; Local trucking with storage; Trucking, except local

(P-3656)
POWERED BY FULFILLMENT INC
20880 Krameria Ave (92518-1512)
PHONE.................626 825-9841
Caleb Alexander Lee, *CEO*
EMP: 100 EST: 2020
SALES (est): 3.66MM **Privately Held**
SIC: 4222 Warehousing, cold storage or refrigerated

(P-3657)
PREFERRED FRZR SVCS - LBF LLC
4901 Bandini Blvd (90058-5400)
PHONE.................323 263-8811
Brian Beattie, *CEO*
▲ EMP: 100 EST: 2013
SALES (est): 2.57MM **Privately Held**
SIC: 4222 Warehousing, cold storage or refrigerated

(P-3658)
PREMIER COLD STORAGE & PKG LLC ✪
1071 E 233rd St (90745-6206)
PHONE.................949 444-8859
Steve Karo, *Pr*
EMP: 205 EST: 2022
SALES (est): 12.09MM **Privately Held**
SIC: 4222 3053 Warehousing, cold storage or refrigerated; Packing materials

(P-3659)
STANDARD-SOUTHERN CORPORATION
Also Called: Los Angeles Cold Storage Co
400 S Central Ave (90013-1712)
P.O. Box 54244 (90054-0244)
PHONE.................213 624-1831
Larry Rauch, *Mgr*
EMP: 80
SALES (corp-wide): 30.46MM **Privately Held**
Web: www.lacold.com
SIC: 4222 Warehousing, cold storage or refrigerated
PA: Standard-Southern Corporation
    4635 Suthwest Fwy Ste 910
    Houston TX
    713 627-1700

(P-3660)
STANDARD-SOUTHERN CORPORATION
Also Called: L.A. Cold Storage
440 S Central Ave (90013-1712)
PHONE.................213 624-1831
Larry Rauch, *Pr*
EMP: 181
SALES (corp-wide): 30.46MM **Privately Held**
Web: www.standardsouthern.com
SIC: 4222 Warehousing, cold storage or refrigerated
PA: Standard-Southern Corporation
    4635 Suthwest Fwy Ste 910
    Houston TX
    713 627-1700

(P-3661)
STANDARD-SOUTHERN CORPORATION
Also Called: Los Angeles Cold Storage
715 E 4th St (90013-1727)
PHONE.................213 624-1831
Thom Thomas, *Brnch Mgr*
EMP: 109
SALES (corp-wide): 30.46MM **Privately Held**
Web: www.standardsouthern.com
SIC: 4222 Warehousing, cold storage or refrigerated
PA: Standard-Southern Corporation
    4635 Suthwest Fwy Ste 910
    Houston TX
    713 627-1700

(P-3662)
UNIFIED GROCERS INC
U W G Northern California Div
1888 S East Ave (93721-3231)
P.O. Box 513396 (90051-1396)
PHONE.................559 268-8454
John Kelly, *Mgr*
EMP: 180
Web: www.unfi.com
SIC: 4222 4213 5149 Refrigerated warehousing and storage; Trucking, except local; Groceries and related products, nec
HQ: Unfi Grocers Distribution, Inc.

(PA)=Parent Co (HQ)=Headquarters
✪ = New Business established in last 2 years

4222 - Refrigerated Warehousing And Storage (P-3663)

2500 S Atlantic Blvd
Commerce CA
323 264-5200

(P-3663)
UNITED STATES COLD STORAGE INC
3500 W Canal Dr (95380)
P.O. Box 1863 (95381-1863)
PHONE..................................209 668-1636
EMP: 72
SALES (corp-wide): 17.24B Privately Held
Web: www.uscold.com
SIC: 4222 Warehousing, cold storage or refrigerated
HQ: United States Cold Storage, Inc.
2 Aquarium Dr Ste 400
Camden NJ
856 354-8181

(P-3664)
UNITED STATES COLD STORAGE INC
Also Called: United States Cold Storage Cal
6501 District Blvd (93313-2000)
P.O. Box 45001 (93384-5001)
PHONE..................................661 832-2653
Randall Dorrell, Mgr
EMP: 69
SALES (corp-wide): 17.24B Privately Held
Web: www.uscold.com
SIC: 4222 Warehousing, cold storage or refrigerated
HQ: United States Cold Storage, Inc.
2 Aquarium Dr Ste 400
Camden NJ
856 354-8181

(P-3665)
UNITED STATES COLD STORAGE INC
Also Called: U S Cold Storage
3936 Dudley Blvd (95652-2317)
PHONE..................................916 392-9160
Ed Ramos, Brnch Mgr
EMP: 65
SALES (corp-wide): 17.24B Privately Held
Web: www.uscold.com
SIC: 4222 Warehousing, cold storage or refrigerated
HQ: United States Cold Storage, Inc.
2 Aquarium Dr Ste 400
Camden NJ
856 354-8181

(P-3666)
UNITED STATES COLD STORAGE INC
1400 N Macarthur Dr Ste A (95376-2829)
PHONE..................................209 835-2653
Stan Moya, Brnch Mgr
EMP: 74
SALES (corp-wide): 17.24B Privately Held
Web: www.uscold.com
SIC: 4222 Warehousing, cold storage or refrigerated
HQ: United States Cold Storage, Inc.
2 Aquarium Dr Ste 400
Camden NJ
856 354-8181

(P-3667)
USKO EXPRESS INC
11290 Point East Dr Ste 200 (95742-6232)
PHONE..................................916 515-8065
Vladimir Skots, Pr
EMP: 80 EST: 2010
SALES (est): 22.35MM Privately Held
Web: www.uskoinc.com

SIC: 4222 4221 Refrigerated warehousing and storage; Farm product warehousing and storage

(P-3668)
WEBER DISTRIBUTION LLC (PA)
Also Called: Weber Logistics
13530 Rosecrans Ave (90670-5087)
PHONE..................................855 469-3237
Bob Lilja, CEO
Maggie Movius, CFO
EMP: 82 EST: 2004
SALES (est): 53.96MM Privately Held
Web: www.weberlogistics.com
SIC: 4222 4225 4213 4212 Refrigerated warehousing and storage; General warehousing and storage; Trucking, except local; Local trucking, without storage

---

4225 General Warehousing And Storage

(P-3669)
ACT FULFILLMENT INC (PA)
3155 Universe Dr (91752-3252)
PHONE..................................909 930-9083
Randolph Cox, CEO
Randolph Cox, Pr
Lydiann Cox, CFO
▲ EMP: 220 EST: 2004
SALES (est): 25.15MM Privately Held
Web: www.actfulfillment.com
SIC: 4225 General warehousing

(P-3670)
ADVANCED STRLZTION PDTS SVCS I
Also Called: Advanced Strlztion Pdts Lgstic
13135 Napa St (92335-2961)
PHONE..................................909 350-6987
EMP: 444
SALES (corp-wide): 5.83B Publicly Held
SIC: 4225 General warehousing and storage
HQ: Advanced Sterlization Products Services Inc.
33 Technology Dr
Irvine CA

(P-3671)
ADVANTAGE MEDIA SERVICES INC
Also Called: AMS Fulfillment
28220 Industry Dr (91355-4105)
PHONE..................................661 705-7588
John Bevacqua, VP
EMP: 210
SALES (corp-wide): 39.78MM Privately Held
Web: www.amsfulfillment.com
SIC: 4225 General warehousing
PA: Advantage Media Services, Inc.
29010 Commerce Center Dr
Valencia CA
661 775-0611

(P-3672)
ALBERTSONS LLC
Also Called: Albertson's Distribution Ctr
9300 Toledo Way (92618-1802)
PHONE..................................949 855-2465
Jim Rollins, Genl Mgr
EMP: 80
SALES (corp-wide): 77.65B Publicly Held
Web: www.albertsons.com
SIC: 4225 General warehousing and storage
HQ: Albertson's Llc
250 E Parkcenter Blvd
Boise ID
208 395-6200

(P-3673)
ALLEN DISTRIBUTION (PA)
4580 Logistics Dr (95215-8353)
PHONE..................................717 258-3040
Gary C Heishman, Pt
Ryan E Heishman, Genl Pt
EMP: 175 EST: 1988
SQ FT: 2,450,000
SALES (est): 121.89MM
SALES (corp-wide): 121.89MM Privately Held
Web: www.allendistribution.com
SIC: 4225 General warehousing

(P-3674)
AMAZONCOM INC
Also Called: Amazon.Com
1910 E Central Ave (92408-0123)
PHONE..................................626 260-6954
EMP: 89
Web: www.amazon.com
SIC: 4225 General warehousing and storage
PA: Amazon.Com, Inc.
410 Terry Ave N
Seattle WA

(P-3675)
APL LOGISTICS AMERICAS LTD
1550 N Chrisman Rd (95304-9396)
PHONE..................................209 836-0302
Riad Sweilem, Brnch Mgr
EMP: 90
Web: www.apllogistics.com
SIC: 4225 General warehousing and storage
HQ: Apl Logistics Americas, Ltd.
14350 N 87th St Ste 350
Scottsdale AZ
602 606-8861

(P-3676)
ASHLEY FURNITURE INDS LLC
Also Called: Ashley Furniture
2250 W Lugonia Ave (92374-5050)
PHONE..................................909 825-4900
EMP: 470
SALES (corp-wide): 4.17B Privately Held
Web: www.ashleyfurniture.com
SIC: 4225 5021 General warehousing; Furniture
PA: Ashley Furniture Industries, Llc
1 Ashley Way
Arcadia WI
608 323-3377

(P-3677)
BACO REALTY CORPORATION
6310 Stockton Blvd (95824-4003)
PHONE..................................916 974-9898
EMP: 84
SALES (corp-wide): 36.27MM Privately Held
Web: www.securitypublicstoragc.com
SIC: 4225 Warehousing, self storage
PA: Baco Realty Corporation
128 King St Ste 400
San Francisco CA
415 281-3700

(P-3678)
BACO REALTY CORPORATION
2071 Camino Ramon (94583-1378)
PHONE..................................925 275-0100
George Bamburg, Prin
EMP: 85
SQ FT: 48,000
SALES (corp-wide): 36.27MM Privately Held
Web: www.securitypublicstorage.com
SIC: 4225 Warehousing, self storage
PA: Baco Realty Corporation

128 King St Ste 400
San Francisco CA
415 281-3700

(P-3679)
C & B DELIVERY SERVICE
Also Called: Temco
1405 E Franklin Ave (91766-5453)
PHONE..................................909 623-4708
Virginia Templeton, Pr
EMP: 85 EST: 1967
SQ FT: 91,000
SALES (est): 2.33MM Privately Held
SIC: 4225 General warehousing

(P-3680)
C&S WHOLESALE GROCERS INC
Also Called: C&S WHOLESALE GROCERS, INC.
8301 Fruitridge Rd (95826-4806)
PHONE..................................916 383-5275
Ric Clark, Genl Mgr
EMP: 261
SALES (corp-wide): 15.34B Privately Held
Web: www.cswg.com
SIC: 4225 General warehousing
PA: C&S Wholesale Grocers, Llc
7 Corporate Dr
Keene NH
603 354-7000

(P-3681)
CARROLL SHELBY LICENSING INC
19021 S Figueroa St (90248-4510)
PHONE..................................310 914-1843
Tracey Smith, Pr
EMP: 78 EST: 2001
SQ FT: 69,247
SALES (est): 797.81K Privately Held
SIC: 4225 General warehousing
PA: Shelby Carroll International Inc
19021 S Figueroa St
Gardena CA

(P-3682)
CASAS INTERNATIONAL BRKG INC (PA)
Also Called: Casas
9355 Airway Rd Ste 4 (92154-7931)
PHONE..................................619 661-6162
Sylvia Casas, Pr
John Jolliffe, *
◆ EMP: 65 EST: 1984
SQ FT: 120,000
SALES (est): 21.99MM
SALES (corp-wide): 21.99MM Privately Held
Web: www.cphgroupusa.com
SIC: 4225 4731 General warehousing; Customhouse brokers

(P-3683)
CASESTACK LLC (HQ)
3000 Ocean Park Blvd Ste 1000 (90405-3070)
PHONE..................................310 473-8885
Daniel A Sanker, Pr
David Isaksen, *
Steve Sezna, *
Guillermo Pardon Cti, Prin
▲ EMP: 65 EST: 2007
SALES (est): 293.95MM
SALES (corp-wide): 5.34B Publicly Held
Web: www.hubgroup.com
SIC: 4225 4731 General warehousing and storage; Freight transportation arrangement
PA: Hub Group, Inc.

PRODUCTS & SERVICES SECTION **4225 - General Warehousing And Storage (P-3703)**

2001 Hub Group Way
Oak Brook IL
630 271-3600

(P-3684)
CHARLES MATOIAN ENTPS INC (PA)
Also Called: OK Produce
1888 Se Ave (93721-3231)
P.O. Box 12838 (93779-2838)
PHONE..................................559 445-8600
Matty Matoian, *Pr*
EMP: 197 EST: 1941
SQ FT: 70,000
SALES (est): 56.68MM
SALES (corp-wide): 56.68MM Privately Held
Web: www.okproduce.com
SIC: 4225 General warehousing

(P-3685)
CHINO-PACIFIC WAREHOUSE CORP (PA)
Also Called: Pcwc
3601 Jurupa St (91761-2905)
PHONE..................................909 545-8100
Jim Marcoly, *Pr*
David Boras, *
George Ramirez, *
David Strawn, *
Tony Gurrola, *
▲ EMP: 66 EST: 1987
SQ FT: 975,000
SALES (est): 24.86MM
SALES (corp-wide): 24.86MM Privately Held
Web: www.weberlogistics.com
SIC: 4225 General warehousing

(P-3686)
CJ LOGISTICS AMERICA LLC
1565 N Macarthur Dr (95376-2846)
PHONE..................................209 362-2232
Bob Justice, *Mgr*
EMP: 158
Web: america.cjlogistics.com
SIC: 4225 General warehousing and storage
HQ: Cj Logistics America, Llc
    1750 S Wolf Rd
    Des Plaines IL

(P-3687)
CJ LOGISTICS AMERICA LLC
3800 Fanucchi Way E. (93263)
PHONE..................................847-390-6800
Kevin Coleman, *CEO*
EMP: 63
Web: america.cjlogistics.com
SIC: 4225 General warehousing and storage
HQ: Cj Logistics America, Llc
    1750 S Wolf Rd
    Des Plaines IL

(P-3688)
COASTAL PACIFIC FD DISTRS INC
Also Called: Coastal Pacific Foods
1520 E Mission Blvd Ste B (91761-2124)
PHONE..................................909 947-2066
EMP: 83
SALES (corp-wide): 496.11MM Privately Held
Web: www.cpfd.com
SIC: 4225 General warehousing and storage
PA: Coastal Pacific Food Distributors, Inc.
    1015 Performance Dr
    Stockton CA
    909 947-2066

(P-3689)
COSTCO WHOLESALE CORPORATION
Also Called: Mira Loma Dry Depot
11600 Riverside Dr Ste A (91752-3700)
PHONE..................................951 361-3606
Rachell Aguire, *Brnch Mgr*
EMP: 613
SALES (corp-wide): 242.29B Publicly Held
Web: www.costco-locations.org
SIC: 4225 General warehousing and storage
PA: Costco Wholesale Corporation
    999 Lake Dr Ste 200
    Issaquah WA
    425 313-8100

(P-3690)
COUNTY OF LOS ANGELES
Also Called: Public Works, Dept of
1537 Alcazar St (90033-1001)
PHONE..................................626 458-1707
Shirely Gist, *Mgr*
EMP: 82
SALES (corp-wide): 31.7B Privately Held
Web: www.lacounty.gov
SIC: 4225 9511 General warehousing and storage; Air, water, and solid waste management
PA: County Of Los Angeles
    500 W Temple St Ste 437
    Los Angeles CA
    213 974-1101

(P-3691)
CUSTOM GOODS LLC
907 E 236th St (90745-6234)
PHONE..................................310 241-6700
EMP: 70
Web: www.custom-goods.com
SIC: 4225 General warehousing
PA: Custom Goods, Llc
    1035 E Watson Center Rd
    Carson CA

(P-3692)
CUSTOM GOODS LLC
809 E 236th St (90745-6232)
PHONE..................................310 241-6700
EMP: 70
Web: www.custom-goods.com
SIC: 4225 General warehousing
PA: Custom Goods, Llc
    1035 E Watson Center Rd
    Carson CA

(P-3693)
CV LOGISTICS INC
Also Called: Cvl
2741 Riverside Blvd (95818-2900)
P.O. Box 440 (96148-0440)
EMP: 70 EST: 1993
SALES (est): 6.43MM Privately Held
Web: www.cvlogistics.com
SIC: 4225 7389 4226 4214 General warehousing; Inventory stocking service; Special warehousing and storage, nec; Furniture moving and storage, local

(P-3694)
DALTON TRUCKING INC (PA)
13560 Whittram Ave (92335-2951)
P.O. Box 5025 (92334-5025)
PHONE..................................909 823-0663
Terry Klenske, *CEO*
Mathew Klenske, *
Eleanor Klenske, *
Roszetta Bautista, *
EMP: 159 EST: 1970
SQ FT: 11,000
SALES (est): 37.99MM
SALES (corp-wide): 37.99MM Privately Held
Web: www.daltontrucking.com
SIC: 4225 General warehousing and storage

(P-3695)
DART INTERNATIONAL A CORP (HQ)
Also Called: Dart Entities
1430 S Eastman Ave (90023-4006)
P.O. Box 23944 (90023-0944)
PHONE..................................323 264-8746
Terence Dedeaux, *CEO*
Paul Martin, *
William J Smollen, *
EMP: 110 EST: 1979
SQ FT: 50,000
SALES (est): 26.55MM
SALES (corp-wide): 114.71MM Privately Held
Web: www.dartentities.com
SIC: 4225 General warehousing
PA: Dart Transportation Service, A Corporation
    1430 S Eastman Ave Ste 1
    Commerce CA
    323 981-8205

(P-3696)
DART WAREHOUSE CORPORATION (HQ)
1430 S Eastman Ave (90023-4006)
PHONE..................................323 264-1011
Robert Anthony Santich, *CEO*
Raoul Dedeaux, *
Eileen Takahashi, *
Ashok Agarwal, *
Don Brown, *
▲ EMP: 255 EST: 1938
SALES (est): 57.34MM
SALES (corp-wide): 114.71MM Privately Held
Web: www.dartentities.com
SIC: 4225 General warehousing
PA: Dart Transportation Service, A Corporation
    1430 S Eastman Ave Ste 1
    Commerce CA
    323 981-8205

(P-3697)
DISTRIBUTION ALTERNATIVES INC
Also Called: Scholls
1990 S Cucamonga Ave (91761-5605)
PHONE..................................909 673-1000
Mark Chase, *Mgr*
EMP: 63
SALES (corp-wide): 95.6MM Privately Held
Web: www.daserv.com
SIC: 4225 7319 General warehousing; Distribution of advertising material or sample services
PA: Distribution Alternatives, Inc.
    6870 21st Ave
    Lino Lakes MN
    651 636-9167

(P-3698)
DISTRIBUTION ALTERNATIVES INC
10621 6th St (91730-5900)
PHONE..................................909 746-5600
EMP: 108
SALES (corp-wide): 95.6MM Privately Held
Web: www.daserv.com
SIC: 4225 General warehousing
PA: Distribution Alternatives, Inc.
    6870 21st Ave
    Lino Lakes MN
    651 636-9167

(P-3699)
DOT PRINTER INC
Also Called: DOT Printer Warehouse
9700 Toledo Way (92618-1810)
PHONE..................................714 335-7012
Jeff Shattuck, *Genl Mgr*
EMP: 60
SALES (corp-wide): 39.35MM Privately Held
Web: www.thedotcorp.com
SIC: 4225 General warehousing
PA: The Dot Printer Inc
    2424 Mcgaw Ave
    Irvine CA
    949 474-1100

(P-3700)
EMED TECHNOLOGIES CORPORATION
4814 Golden Foothill Pkwy (95762-9822)
PHONE..................................775 232-3287
EMP: 90
Web: www.emedtc.com
SIC: 4225 General warehousing and storage
PA: Emed Technologies Corporation
    1262 Hawks Flight Ct # 200
    El Dorado Hills CA

(P-3701)
F R T INTERNATIONAL INC
Also Called: Frontier Logistics Services
14439 S Avalon Blvd (90248-2005)
PHONE..................................310 329-5700
Daniel Park, *Brnch Mgr*
EMP: 74
SALES (corp-wide): 26.2MM Privately Held
Web: www.frontier-logistics.com
SIC: 4225 4731 4412 4214 General warehousing; Customhouse brokers; Deep sea foreign transportation of freight; Local trucking with storage
PA: F. R. T. International, Inc.
    1700 N Alameda St
    Compton CA
    310 604-8208

(P-3702)
F R T INTERNATIONAL INC (PA)
Also Called: Frontier Logistics Services
1700 N Alameda St (90222-4128)
PHONE..................................310 604-8208
Brian Chung, *CEO*
Joyce Chung, *
◆ EMP: 80 EST: 1983
SQ FT: 200,000
SALES (est): 26.2MM
SALES (corp-wide): 26.2MM Privately Held
SIC: 4225 4731 4412 4214 General warehousing; Customhouse brokers; Deep sea foreign transportation of freight; Local trucking with storage

(P-3703)
FASHION APPAREL SERVICE TRNSP
Also Called: Twe Logistics
6701 Koll Center Pkwy Ste 200 (94566-8061)
PHONE..................................866 835-1112
Chris Abraham, *Pr*
▲ EMP: 105 EST: 1990
SALES (est): 3.99MM Privately Held

4225 - General Warehousing And Storage (P-3704)

Web: www.twelogistics.com
SIC: 4225 Warehousing, self storage

(P-3704)
FASHION LOGISTICS INC
20550 Denker Ave (90501-1645)
PHONE..................424 201-4100
EMP: 130
SALES (corp-wide): 32.95MM Privately Held
Web: www.fashionlogistics.com
SIC: 4225 General warehousing
PA: Fashion Logistics, Inc.
621 Us Highway 46 W
Hasbrouck Heights NJ
201 596-0040

(P-3705)
FLOWSPACE INC
660 Baker St Ste B201 (92626-4409)
PHONE..................323 741-1325
Joseph Benjamin Eachus Junior, CEO
Jason Harbert, *
Anne Hallock, CRO*
EMP: 90 EST: 2016
SALES (est): 10.57MM Privately Held
Web: www.flow.space
SIC: 4225 General warehousing

(P-3706)
FOAMEX LP
Foamex
19201 S Reyes Ave (90221-5807)
PHONE..................323 774-5600
Dean Offerman, Brnch Mgr
EMP: 150
Web: www.fxi.com
SIC: 4225 General warehousing and storage
PA: Foamex L.P.
100 W Matsonford Rd # 5
Wayne PA

(P-3707)
FRESNO UNIFIED SCHOOL DISTRICT
Also Called: Fusd Central Warehouse
4498 N Brawley Ave (93722-3917)
PHONE..................559 457-3030
Isaac Rodriguez, Brnch Mgr
EMP: 113
SALES (corp-wide): 516.02MM Privately Held
Web: www.fresnounified.org
SIC: 4225 General warehousing and storage
PA: Fresno Unified School District
Educational Facilities Corporation
2309 Tulare St
Fresno CA
559 457-3000

(P-3708)
FTDI WEST INC
3375 Enterprise Dr (92316-3539)
PHONE..................909 473-1111
Alan Baum, Pr
Steve Rocha, *
EMP: 80 EST: 2008
SALES (est): 19.26MM Privately Held
Web: www.ftdiwest.com
SIC: 4225 Warehousing, self storage

(P-3709)
GENERAL ELECTRIC COMPANY
Also Called: GE
20005 Business Pkwy (91789-2944)
PHONE..................909 869-7404
Gary Anderson, Mgr
EMP: 95
SALES (corp-wide): 76.56B Publicly Held
Web: www.geappliances.com
SIC: 4225 4226 General warehousing; Special warehousing and storage, nec.
PA: General Electric Company
1 Financial Ctr Ste 3700
Boston MA
617 443-3000

(P-3710)
GENERATIONAL PROPERTIES INC
3141 E 44th St (90058-2405)
PHONE..................323 583-3163
Angelo V Antoci, Prin
Angelo V Antoci, Prin
Sam Perricone, *
EMP: 291 EST: 1950
SQ FT: 4,000
SALES (est): 22.29MM Privately Held
SIC: 4225 General warehousing and storage

(P-3711)
GXO LOGISTICS SUPPLY CHAIN INC
3520 S Cactus Ave (92316-3816)
PHONE..................336 309-6201
Christopher Cotto, Mgr
EMP: 1000
SALES (corp-wide): 8.99B Publicly Held
Web: www.gxo.com
SIC: 4225 General warehousing and storage
HQ: Gxo Logistics Supply Chain, Inc.
4035 Piedmont Pkwy
High Point NC
336 232-4100

(P-3712)
GXO LOGISTICS SUPPLY CHAIN INC
2163 S Riverside Ave (92324-3355)
PHONE..................951 512-1201
Miguel Moreno, Brnch Mgr
EMP: 100
SALES (corp-wide): 8.99B Publicly Held
Web: www.gxo.com
SIC: 4225 General warehousing
HQ: Gxo Logistics Supply Chain, Inc.
4035 Piedmont Pkwy
High Point NC
336 232-4100

(P-3713)
H RAUVEL INC (PA)
Also Called: Nova Container Freight Station
1710 E Sepulveda Blvd (90745-6142)
PHONE..................310 604-0060
Hector R Velasco, Pr
▼ EMP: 70 EST: 1978
SQ FT: 258,000
SALES (est): 23.11MM
SALES (corp-wide): 23.11MM Privately Held
Web: www.novafreight.net
SIC: 4225 4731 General warehousing; Agents, shipping

(P-3714)
HAULAWAY STORAGE CNTRS INC
11292 Western Ave (90680-2912)
P.O. Box 125 (90680-0125)
PHONE..................800 826-9040
Clifford Robert Ronnenberg, CEO
Daniel Letto, *
Joyce Amato, *
EMP: 436 EST: 2000
SALES (est): 18.56MM
SALES (corp-wide): 335.28MM Privately Held
Web: www.haulaway.com

SIC: 4225 4226 General warehousing; Special warehousing and storage, nec.
PA: Cr&R Incorporated
11292 Western Ave
Stanton CA
714 826-9049

(P-3715)
HOME DEPOT USA INC
Also Called: Home Depot, The
11650 Venture Dr (91752-3209)
PHONE..................951 361-1235
John Lawson, Brnch Mgr
EMP: 133
SALES (corp-wide): 157.4B Publicly Held
Web: www.homedepot.com
SIC: 4225 General warehousing and storage
HQ: Home Depot U.S.A., Inc.
2455 Paces Ferry Rd Se
Atlanta GA

(P-3716)
HOME DEPOT USA INC
Also Called: Home Depot, The
8535 Oakwood Pl Ste B (91730-4864)
PHONE..................909 483-8115
Rose Navares, Mgr
EMP: 104
SALES (corp-wide): 157.4B Publicly Held
Web: www.homedepot.com
SIC: 4225 General warehousing and storage
HQ: Home Depot U.S.A., Inc.
2455 Paces Ferry Rd Se
Atlanta GA

(P-3717)
HOME DEPOT USA INC
Also Called: Home Depot, The
13250 Gregg St Ste A2 (92064-7164)
PHONE..................858 859-4143
Greg Williams, Prin
EMP: 120
SALES (corp-wide): 157.4B Publicly Held
Web: www.homedepot.com
SIC: 4225 General warehousing and storage
HQ: Home Depot U.S.A., Inc.
2455 Paces Ferry Rd Se
Atlanta GA

(P-3718)
HOME DEPOT USA INC
Also Called: Home Depot, The
14659 Alondra Blvd Ste B (90638-5629)
PHONE..................714 522-8651
Maurice Martinez, Mgr
EMP: 91
SALES (corp-wide): 157.4B Publicly Held
Web: www.homedepot.com
SIC: 4225 General warehousing and storage
HQ: Home Depot U.S.A., Inc.
2455 Paces Ferry Rd Se
Atlanta GA

(P-3719)
HOME DEPOT USA INC
Also Called: Home Depot, The
1400 E Pescadero Ave (95304-8523)
PHONE..................209 855-7000
Gerry Balagtas, Brnch Mgr
EMP: 110
SALES (corp-wide): 157.4B Publicly Held
Web: www.homedepot.com
SIC: 4225 General warehousing and storage
HQ: Home Depot U.S.A., Inc.
2455 Paces Ferry Rd Se
Atlanta GA

(P-3720)
KAIR HARBOR EXPRESS LLC (PA)
1129 Canal Ave (90813-2623)
PHONE..................562 432-6800
Peter Wu, Managing Member
EMP: 80 EST: 2015
SQ FT: 50,000
SALES (est): 21.96MM
SALES (corp-wide): 21.96MM Privately Held
Web: www.kairharborexpress.com
SIC: 4225 4214 General warehousing and storage; Local trucking with storage

(P-3721)
KKW TRUCKING INC (PA)
3100 Pomona Blvd (91768-3230)
P.O. Box 2960 (91769-2960)
PHONE..................909 869-1200
Dennis W Firestone, CEO
Lynnette Brown, *
EMP: 550 EST: 1962
SQ FT: 150,000
SALES (est): 101.18MM
SALES (corp-wide): 101.18MM Privately Held
Web: www.kkwtrucks.com
SIC: 4225 4231 4226 4214 General warehousing and storage; Trucking terminal facilities; Special warehousing and storage, nec; Local trucking with storage

(P-3722)
KROGER CO
Also Called: Ralphs Logistics - Compton DC
2201 S Wilmington Ave (90220-5448)
PHONE..................859 630-6959
Lisa Allen, Brnch Mgr
EMP: 500
SALES (corp-wide): 148.26B Publicly Held
Web: www.thekrogerco.com
SIC: 4225 General warehousing and storage
PA: The Kroger Co
1014 Vine St Ste 1000
Cincinnati OH
513 762-4000

(P-3723)
LAMPS PLUS INC
Also Called: Warehouse
9425 California St (92374-5024)
PHONE..................909 801-5333
John Gelmini, Mgr
EMP: 64
SALES (corp-wide): 490.53MM Privately Held
Web: www.lampsplus.com
SIC: 4225 5063 5023 General warehousing and storage; Lighting fixtures; Lamps: floor, boudoir, desk
PA: Lamps Plus, Inc.
20250 Plummer St
Chatsworth CA
818 886-5267

(P-3724)
LAVA SCS LLC
218 Machlin Ct (91789-3048)
PHONE..................909 437-7881
Chris Deman, Brnch Mgr
EMP: 79
Web: www.lavascs.com
SIC: 4225 4731 General warehousing and storage; Truck transportation brokers
PA: Lava Scs, Llc
801 River Dr
North Sioux City SD

(P-3725)
LOCKHEED MARTIN CORPORATION
Also Called: Rotary and Miission Systems

PRODUCTS & SERVICES SECTION

4225 - General Warehousing And Storage (P-3747)

Bldg 821 South Loop (92310)
PHONE.............................760 386-2572
Kurt Pinkerton, *Mgr*
EMP: 142
Web: www.gyrocamsystems.com
SIC: 4225 General warehousing and storage
PA: Lockheed Martin Corporation
   6801 Rockledge Dr
   Bethesda MD

(P-3726)
LONGS DRUG STORES CAL LLC
Also Called: Longs Drug Store
2400 Keystone Pacific Pkwy (95363-8893)
PHONE.............................209 895-7839
Stephen Mccormick, *Mgr*
EMP: 18994
SALES (corp-wide): 322.47B **Publicly Held**
Web: www.cvs.com
SIC: 4225 General warehousing and storage
HQ: Longs Drug Stores California L.L.C.
   1 Cvs Dr
   Woonsocket RI

(P-3727)
LOWES HOME CENTERS LLC
Also Called: Lowe's
3984 Indian Ave (92571-3154)
PHONE.............................951 443-2500
Thomas Tucker, *Brnch Mgr*
EMP: 143
SALES (corp-wide): 97.06B **Publicly Held**
Web: www.lowes.com
SIC: 4225 General warehousing and storage
HQ: Lowe's Home Centers, Llc
   1000 Lowes Blvd
   Mooresville NC
   336 658-4000

(P-3728)
MAKESPACE LABS INC
3526 Hayden Ave (90232-2413)
PHONE.............................800 920-9440
Rahul Gandhi, *CEO*
Chang Paik, *
EMP: 200 EST: 2013
SALES (est): 8.62MM **Privately Held**
Web: www.clutter.com
SIC: 4225 General warehousing and storage

(P-3729)
MAXAR SPACE LLC
1140 Hamilton Ct (94025-1425)
PHONE.............................650 852-4000
Pat Downey, *Brnch Mgr*
EMP: 708
SALES (corp-wide): 1.6B **Privately Held**
Web: www.maxar.com
SIC: 4225 General warehousing
HQ: Maxar Space Llc
   3875 Fabian Way
   Palo Alto CA
   650 852-4000

(P-3730)
MCR PRINTING AND PACKG CORP
8830 Siempre Viva Rd (92154-6278)
PHONE.............................619 488-3012
EMP: 170
SALES (corp-wide): 10.12MM **Privately Held**
Web: www.mcrprintingandpackaging.com
SIC: 4225 General warehousing
PA: Mcr Printing And Packaging, Corp.
   113 W G St Pmb 438
   San Diego CA
   619 488-3169

(P-3731)
MIDAS EXPRESS LOS ANGELES INC
11854 Alameda St (90262-4019)
PHONE.............................310 609-0366
Jack Wu, *Pr*
Jacky Strong, *Stockholder**
▲ EMP: 200 EST: 1995
SQ FT: 90,000
SALES (est): 9.58MM **Privately Held**
Web: www.midasexpress.com
SIC: 4225 4731 4226 General warehousing and storage; Freight forwarding; Textile warehousing

(P-3732)
MOULTON LOGISTICS MANAGEMENT
7855 Hayvenhurst Ave (91406-1712)
P.O. Box 8191 (91409-8191)
PHONE.............................818 997-1800
◆ EMP: 175
Web: www.amwarelogistics.com
SIC: 4225 4822 General warehousing and storage; Electronic mail

(P-3733)
MSBLOUS LLC
11671 Dayton Dr (91730-5526)
PHONE.............................909 929-9689
Jiayi CU, *Mgr*
EMP: 84
SALES (corp-wide): 2.22MM **Privately Held**
SIC: 4225 General warehousing and storage
PA: Msblous Llc
   8 The Grn Ste 7360
   Dover DE
   909 908-1889

(P-3734)
NATIONAL DISTRIBUTION AGCY INC (HQ)
Also Called: Pacific Coast Warehouse Co
7025 Central Ave (94560-4201)
PHONE.............................510 487-6226
▲ EMP: 62 EST: 1982
SQ FT: 305,000
SALES (est): 5.13MM
SALES (corp-wide): 15.82MM **Privately Held**
SIC: 4225 General warehousing
PA: Public Investment Corporation
   4800 Ne Savannah Rd
   Jensen Beach FL
   310 451-5227

(P-3735)
NAUTILUS INTL HOLDG CORP
413 Luce Ave (95203)
PHONE.............................209 465-5713
EMP: 433
SALES (corp-wide): 64.26MM **Privately Held**
Web: www.nautilusintl.com
SIC: 4225 General warehousing and storage
PA: Nautilus International Holding Corporation
   3806 Worsham Ave
   Long Beach CA
   310 816-6500

(P-3736)
NAVY EXCHANGE SERVICE COMMAND
4250 Eucalyptus Ave (91710-9704)
PHONE.............................909 517-2640
Ron Patel, *Mgr*
EMP: 72

Web: www.mynavyexchange.com
SIC: 4225 9711 General warehousing and storage; Navy
HQ: Navy Exchange Service Command
   3280 Virginia Beach Blvd
   Virginia Beach VA
   757 463-6200

(P-3737)
NEOVIA LOGISTICS DIST LP
5750 E Francis St (91761-3607)
PHONE.............................909 657-4900
EMP: 96
SALES (corp-wide): 672.55MM **Privately Held**
Web: www.neovialogistics.com
SIC: 4225 General warehousing and storage
HQ: Neovia Logistics Distribution, Lp
   6363 N State Highway # 700
   Irving TX

(P-3738)
NORDSTROM INC
Also Called: Nordstrom
1600 S Milliken Ave (91761-2301)
PHONE.............................909 390-1040
Pat Smith, *Mgr*
EMP: 300
SALES (corp-wide): 15.53B **Publicly Held**
Web: www.nordstrom.com
SIC: 4225 4226 General warehousing and storage; Special warehousing and storage, nec
PA: Nordstrom, Inc.
   1617 6th Ave
   Seattle WA
   206 628-2111

(P-3739)
NORDSTROM INC
Also Called: Nordstrom
37599 Filbert St (94560-3537)
PHONE.............................510 794-5440
Dan Allen, *Mgr*
EMP: 150
SALES (corp-wide): 15.53B **Publicly Held**
Web: www.nordstrom.com
SIC: 4225 General warehousing and storage
PA: Nordstrom, Inc.
   1617 6th Ave
   Seattle WA
   206 628-2111

(P-3740)
NORTH BAY DISTRIBUTION INC (PA)
2050 Cessna Dr (95688-8712)
PHONE.............................707 452-9984
Lee Perry, *Pr*
EMP: 100 EST: 1997
SQ FT: 220,000
SALES (est): 51.42MM
SALES (corp-wide): 51.42MM **Privately Held**
Web: www.nbd3pl.com
SIC: 4225 General warehousing

(P-3741)
NUGGET MARKET INC
Also Called: Nugget Mkts Pharmacy
157 Main St (95695-2914)
PHONE.............................530 662-5479
Ray Munoz, *Mgr*
EMP: 135
SALES (corp-wide): 209.74MM **Privately Held**
Web: www.nuggetmarket.com
SIC: 4225 5411 5912 5461 General warehousing; Grocery stores; Drug stores and proprietary stores; Retail bakeries

PA: Nugget Market, Inc.
   311 Mace Blvd
   Davis CA
   530 399-3300

(P-3742)
OSRAM SYLVANIA INC
1651 S Archibald Ave (91761-7651)
PHONE.............................909 923-3003
Wayne Cansford, *Brnch Mgr*
EMP: 100
SALES (corp-wide): 5B **Privately Held**
Web: www.sylvania-automotive.com
SIC: 4225 Warehousing, self storage
HQ: Osram Sylvania Inc.
   200 Ballardvale St Bldg 2
   Wilmington MA
   978 570-3000

(P-3743)
PENNEY OPCO LLC
Also Called: JC Penney
5959 Palm Ave (92407-1844)
PHONE.............................972 431-2618
EMP: 66
SALES (corp-wide): 1.93B **Privately Held**
SIC: 4225 General warehousing and storage
HQ: Penney Opco Llc
   6501 Legacy Dr Ste B100
   Plano TX
   972 431-4746

(P-3744)
PRO-FORM MANUFACTURING LLC
521 Stone Rd (94510-1113)
PHONE.............................707 752-9010
Joseph Neal, *Genl Mgr*
EMP: 340
SALES (corp-wide): 358.89MM **Privately Held**
Web: www.inw-group.com
SIC: 4225 General warehousing and storage
HQ: Pro-Form Manufacturing, Llc
   5001 Industrial Way
   Benicia CA

(P-3745)
PRO-FORM MANUFACTURING LLC
4725 Industrial Way (94510-1041)
PHONE.............................707 752-9010
Joseph Neal, *Genl Mgr*
EMP: 340
SALES (corp-wide): 358.89MM **Privately Held**
Web: www.inw-group.com
SIC: 4225 General warehousing and storage
HQ: Pro-Form Manufacturing, Llc
   5001 Industrial Way
   Benicia CA

(P-3746)
QUICK BOX LLC
13838 S Figueroa St (90061-1026)
PHONE.............................310 436-6444
EMP: 108
SALES (corp-wide): 26.2MM **Privately Held**
Web: www.quickbox.com
SIC: 4225 General warehousing and storage
PA: Quick Box, Llc
   11551 E 45th Ave Unit C
   Denver CO
   303 757-6500

(P-3747)
QUILL LLC
Also Called: Quill Distribution Center

4225 - General Warehousing And Storage (P-3748)

1500 S Dupont Ave (91761-1406)
PHONE.................................909 390-0600
Rocky Velasquez, Mgr
EMP: 249
Web: www.quill.com
SIC: 4225 General warehousing and storage
HQ: Quill Llc
   300 Tri State Intl
   Lincolnshire IL
   800 982-3400

(P-3748)
RADIAL SOUTH LP
Also Called: Radial
2225 Alder Ave (92377-8513)
PHONE.................................610 491-7000
EMP: 418
SALES (corp-wide): 2.34B Privately Held
Web: www.radial.com
SIC: 4225 General warehousing
HQ: Radial South, L.P.
   935 1st Ave
   King Of Prussia PA
   610 491-7000

(P-3749)
ROADEX AMERICA INC
2132 E Dominguez St Ste B (90810-1006)
PHONE.................................310 878-9800
Nicholas Sim, Pr
Russle Loh, *
Johnny Kwan, *
▲ EMP: 100 EST: 2001
SALES (est): 24.54MM Privately Held
Web: www.roadexamerica.com
SIC: 4225 5113 4789 General warehousing and storage; Industrial and personal service paper; Cargo loading and unloading services

(P-3750)
RPM CONSOLIDATED SERVICES INC (HQ)
1901 Raymer Ave (92833-2512)
PHONE.................................714 388-3500
Shawn K Duke, CEO
Dan Laporte, *
▲ EMP: 100 EST: 2002
SQ FT: 15,000
SALES (est): 95.99MM
SALES (corp-wide): 1.16B Privately Held
Web: www.odysseylogistics.com
SIC: 4225 4214 General warehousing and storage; Local trucking with storage
PA: Odyssey Logistics & Technology Corporation
   100 Reserve Rd Ste Cc210
   Danbury CT
   203 448-3900

(P-3751)
SAN DIEGO GAS & ELECTRIC CO
Mirimar Storage
6875c Consolidated Way (92121-2602)
PHONE.................................858 547-2086
EMP: 101
SALES (corp-wide): 14.44B Publicly Held
Web: www.sdge.com
SIC: 4225 4932 4924 4911 General warehousing and storage; Gas and other services combined; Natural gas distribution; Electric services
HQ: San Diego Gas & Electric Company
   8330 Century Park Ct
   San Diego CA
   619 696-2000

(P-3752)
SCHNEIDER ELECTRIC USA INC
Also Called: Pelco By Schneider Electric
14725 Monte Vista Ave (91710-5732)
PHONE.................................909 438-2295
EMP: 100
SALES (corp-wide): 82.05K Privately Held
Web: www.se.com
SIC: 4225 General warehousing and storage
HQ: Schneider Electric Usa, Inc.
   1 Boston Pl Ste 2700
   Boston MA
   978 975-9600

(P-3753)
SMART & FINAL STORES LLC
5500 Sheila St (90040-1425)
PHONE.................................323 725-0791
Tom Bullici, Mgr
EMP: 205
SIC: 4225 General warehousing and storage
HQ: Smart & Final Stores Llc
   600 Citadel Dr
   Commerce CA

(P-3754)
SONOMA TILEMAKERS INC
7890 Bell Rd (95492-7413)
PHONE.................................707 837-8177
EMP: 73
SALES (corp-wide): 46.3MM Privately Held
Web: www.sonomatilemakers.com
SIC: 4225 General warehousing and storage
HQ: Sonoma Tilemakers, Inc.
   7750 Bell Rd
   Windsor CA

(P-3755)
SOVENA USA INC
705 E Whitmore Ave (95358-9317)
PHONE.................................209 210-0388
EMP: 144
Web: www.sovenagroup.com
SIC: 4225 Miniwarehouse, warehousing
HQ: Sovena Usa, Inc.
   1 Olive Grove St
   Rome NY

(P-3756)
SPROUTS FARMERS MARKET INC
280 De Berry St (92324-4404)
PHONE.................................888 577-7688
EMP: 190
SALES (corp-wide): 6.4B Publicly Held
Web: www.sprouts.com
SIC: 4225 5411 General warehousing and storage; Grocery stores
PA: Sprouts Farmers Market, Inc.
   5455 E High St Ste 111
   Phoenix AZ
   480 814-8016

(P-3757)
SST IV 8020 LAS VGAS BLVD S LL
Also Called: Smartstop Self Storage
10 Terrace Rd (92694-1182)
PHONE.................................949 429-6600
H Michael Schwartz, Managing Member
Paula Mathews, *
Wayne Johnson, *
Michael Terjung, *
EMP: 99 EST: 2018
SALES (est): 2.45MM Privately Held
Web: www.smartstopselfstorage.com
SIC: 4225 Warehousing, self storage

(P-3758)
STORAGEPRO INC
1205 Franklin St (94612-2610)
PHONE.................................510 900-5474
EMP: 69
Web: www.storagepro.com
SIC: 4225 Warehousing, self storage
PA: Storagepro, Inc
   1615 Bonanza St Ste 208
   Walnut Creek CA

(P-3759)
STORAGEPRO INC
601 N King Rd (95133-1707)
PHONE.................................408 560-0511
EMP: 69
Web: www.storagepro.com
SIC: 4225 Warehousing, self storage
PA: Storagepro, Inc
   1615 Bonanza St Ste 208
   Walnut Creek CA

(P-3760)
TAKANE USA INC
2055 S Haven Ave (91761-0736)
PHONE.................................909 923-5511
Masahiko Yamada, Manager
EMP: 129
Web: www.calicobrands.com
SIC: 4225 General warehousing and storage
HQ: Takane U.S.A., Inc.
   369 Van Ness Way Ste 715
   Torrance CA
   310 212-1411

(P-3761)
TANIMURA ANTLE FRESH FOODS INC
761 Commercial Ave (93030-7233)
PHONE.................................805 483-2358
Sergio Romero, Mgr
EMP: 125
SALES (corp-wide): 321.47MM Privately Held
Web: www.taproduce.com
SIC: 4225 Warehousing, self storage
PA: Tanimura & Antle Fresh Foods, Inc.
   1 Harris Rd
   Salinas CA
   831 455-2950

(P-3762)
TARGET CORPORATION
Also Called: T.com Ontario Fc T-9479
1505 S Haven Ave (91761-2928)
PHONE.................................909 937-5500
Jacqueline Yee, Brnch Mgr
EMP: 177
SALES (corp-wide): 50.09B Publicly Held
Web: www.target.com
SIC: 4225 General warehousing and storage
PA: Target Corporation
   1000 Nicollet Mall
   Minneapolis MN
   612 304-6073

(P-3763)
TARGET CORPORATION
Also Called: Target
14750 Miller Ave (92336-1685)
PHONE.................................909 355-6000
George Spreiser, Genl Mgr
EMP: 103
SALES (corp-wide): 50.09B Publicly Held
Web: www.target.com
SIC: 4225 General warehousing and storage
PA: Target Corporation
   1000 Nicollet Mall
   Minneapolis MN
   612 304-6073

(P-3764)
TARGET CORPORATION
Also Called: Target
2050 E Beamer St (95776-6213)
PHONE.................................530 666-3705
Dave Sartin, Mgr
EMP: 75
SALES (corp-wide): 50.09B Publicly Held
Web: www.target.com
SIC: 4225 General warehousing and storage
PA: Target Corporation
   1000 Nicollet Mall
   Minneapolis MN
   612 304-6073

(P-3765)
TAYLORED FMI LLC
1495 E Locust St (91761-4570)
PHONE.................................909 510-4800
Jim Deveau, CEO
EMP: 88 EST: 2020
SALES (est): 1.92MM
SALES (corp-wide): 58.62MM Privately Held
Web: www.tayloredservices.com
SIC: 4225 General warehousing
PA: Taylored Services Parent Co. Inc.
   1495 E Locust St
   Ontario CA
   909 510-4800

(P-3766)
TAYLORED SERVICES LLC (DH)
Also Called: Taylored Services
1495 E Locust St (91761-4570)
PHONE.................................909 510-4800
Jim Deveau, CEO
▲ EMP: 80 EST: 1992
SQ FT: 330,000
SALES (est): 102.44MM Privately Held
Web: www.tayloredservices.com
SIC: 4225 4731 General warehousing and storage; Agents, shipping
HQ: Taylored Services Holdings, Llc
   1495 E Locust St
   Ontario CA
   909 510-4800

(P-3767)
TAYLORED SERVICES HOLDINGS LLC (DH)
Also Called: Taylored Services
1495 E Locust St (91761-4570)
PHONE.................................909 510-4800
Mikhail Kholyavenko, CEO
EMP: 80 EST: 2008
SQ FT: 330,000
SALES (est): 112.03MM Privately Held
Web: www.tayloredservices.com
SIC: 4225 General warehousing and storage
HQ: Yusen Logistics (Americas) Inc.
   300 Lighting Way Ste 100
   Secaucus NJ
   201 553-3800

(P-3768)
TONYS EXPRESS INC (PA)
10613 Jasmine St (92337-8241)
PHONE.................................909 427-8700
John Ohle, CEO
▲ EMP: 127 EST: 1954
SQ FT: 180,000
SALES (est): 28.76MM
SALES (corp-wide): 28.76MM Privately Held
Web: www.tonysexpress.com
SIC: 4225 4214 4212 General warehousing and storage; Local trucking with storage; Local trucking, without storage

PRODUCTS & SERVICES SECTION
4226 - Special Warehousing And Storage, Nec (P-3789)

(P-3769)
TOTAL WAREHOUSE INC
2895 E Miraloma Ave (92806-1804)
PHONE...................................480 582-3954
Boyd Kiefus, CEO
Dawn Koopmann, *
EMP: 119 EST: 2017
SALES (est): 8.29MM Privately Held
Web: www.totalwarehouse.com
SIC: 4225 7699 3537 5046 Miniwarehouse, warehousing; Industrial equipment services ; Forklift trucks; Commercial equipment, nec

(P-3770)
TRI-MODAL DIST SVCS INC
22560 Lucerne St (90745-4303)
PHONE...................................310 522-1844
▲ EMP: 91
SALES (corp-wide): 29.27MM Privately Held
Web: www.abilitytrimodal.com
SIC: 4225 General warehousing and storage
PA: Tri-Modal Distribution Services, Inc.
2011 E Carson St
Carson CA
310 522-5506

(P-3771)
TROPICANA MANUFACTURING CO INC
Also Called: Dura Freight Lines
525 S Lemon Ave (91789-2912)
PHONE...................................909 444-1025
Clint Schaffer, Mgr
EMP: 74
SALES (corp-wide): 49.44MM Privately Held
SIC: 4225 General warehousing
PA: Patina Freight, Inc.
20405 Business Pkwy
Walnut CA

(P-3772)
TROPICANA MANUFACTURING CO INC
Also Called: St George Logistics
1650 S Central Ave (90220-5317)
PHONE...................................310 764-4395
EMP: 73
SALES (corp-wide): 49.44MM Privately Held
SIC: 4225 General warehousing
PA: Patina Freight, Inc.
20405 Business Pkwy
Walnut CA

(P-3773)
UNIFIED GROCERS INC
Also Called: U W G Southern California Div
457 E Martin Luther King Jr Blvd (90011-5650)
PHONE...................................323 232-6124
Maurice Ochua, Brnch Mgr
EMP: 74
Web: www.unfi.com
SIC: 4225 8742 2051 General warehousing and storage; Marketing consulting services; Bread, cake, and related products
HQ: Unfi Grocers Distribution, Inc.
2500 S Atlantic Blvd
Commerce CA
323 264-5200

(P-3774)
UNIS LLC
19914 S Via Baron (90220-6104)
PHONE...................................310 747-3388
Omar Garcia, Brnch Mgr
EMP: 90
SALES (corp-wide): 194.54MM Privately Held
Web: www.unisco.com
SIC: 4225 General warehousing and storage
PA: Unis, Llc
218 Machlin Ct Ste A
Walnut CA
909 839-2600

(P-3775)
UNITED NATURAL FOODS WEST INC (HQ)
Also Called: Unfi
1101 Sunset Blvd (95765-1304)
PHONE...................................916 625-4100
Kurt M Luttecke, CEO
Michael S Funk, *
Steven L Spinner, *
Eric A Dorne, *
Sean F Griffin, *
▲ EMP: 385 EST: 1976
SQ FT: 150,000
SALES (est): 207.89MM Publicly Held
Web: www.unfi.com
SIC: 4225 5141 General warehousing and storage; Groceries, general line
PA: United Natural Foods, Inc.
313 Iron Horse Way
Providence RI

(P-3776)
UNIVERSAL PACKG SYSTEMS INC
Also Called: Paklab
14570 Monte Vista Ave (91710-5743)
PHONE...................................909 517-2442
EMP: 125
SALES (corp-wide): 359.71MM Privately Held
SIC: 4225 General warehousing
PA: Universal Packaging Systems, Inc.
380 Townline Rd Ste 130
Hauppauge NY
631 543-2277

(P-3777)
UNIVERSITY CAL SAN FRANCISCO
Materiel Management
616 Forbes Blvd (94080-2009)
PHONE...................................510 987-0700
Diana Hopper, Prin
EMP: 83
SALES (corp-wide): 534.4MM Privately Held
Web: www.ucsf.edu
SIC: 4225 8221 9411 General warehousing and storage; University; Administration of educational programs
HQ: University Cal San Francisco
513 Parnassus Ave 115f
San Francisco CA

(P-3778)
WALMART INC
Also Called: Walmart
1001 Columbia Ave (92507-2135)
PHONE...................................951 320-5722
EMP: 107
SALES (corp-wide): 611.29B Publicly Held
Web: corporate.walmart.com
SIC: 4225 General warehousing and storage
PA: Walmart Inc.
702 Sw 8th St
Bentonville AR
479 640-8287

(P-3779)
WALMART INC
Also Called: Walmart
10815 State Highway 99w (96080-7747)
PHONE...................................530 529-0916
Darwyn Jones, Mgr
EMP: 621
SALES (corp-wide): 611.29B Publicly Held
Web: www.walmart.com
SIC: 4225 General warehousing and storage
PA: Walmart Inc.
702 Sw 8th St
Bentonville AR
479 640-8287

(P-3780)
WALMART INC
Also Called: Walmart
13231 11th Ave (93230-9591)
PHONE...................................559 583-6071
Michael Whitney, Mgr
EMP: 159
SALES (corp-wide): 611.29B Publicly Held
Web: corporate.walmart.com
SIC: 4225 General warehousing and storage
PA: Walmart Inc.
702 Sw 8th St
Bentonville AR
479 640-8287

(P-3781)
WAREHOUSE SPECIALISTS LLC
Also Called: Wsi
2743 Thompson Creek Rd (91767-1861)
PHONE...................................909 596-2566
Chris Thiel, Mgr
EMP: 63
SQ FT: 172,000
SALES (corp-wide): 236.89MM Privately Held
Web: www.wsinc.com
SIC: 4225 General warehousing
HQ: Warehouse Specialists, Llc
1160 N Mayflower Dr
Appleton WI
920 830-5000

(P-3782)
WESTERN WINE SERVICES INC (PA)
880 Hanna Dr (94503-9605)
PHONE...................................800 999-8463
Michael W Hodes, Pr
Bruce Cohen, *
Marc Cohen, *
Tad Franzman, *
▲ EMP: 99 EST: 1988
SALES (est): 28.22MM
SALES (corp-wide): 28.22MM Privately Held
Web: www.westerncarriers.com
SIC: 4225 General warehousing and storage

(P-3783)
WINCO FOODS LLC
4400 Crows Landing Rd (95358-9304)
P.O. Box 581770 (95358-0031)
PHONE...................................209 556-6040
Branden Frank, Brnch Mgr
EMP: 144
Web: www.wincofoods.com
SIC: 4225 1541 General warehousing; Industrial buildings and warehouses
HQ: Winco Foods, Llc
650 N Armstrong Pl
Boise ID
208 377-0110

(P-3784)
WORLD CLASS DISTRIBUTION INC
2121 Boeing Way (95206-4934)
PHONE...................................909 574-4140
Michael Campbell, Prin
EMP: 68
SALES (corp-wide): 355.83K Privately Held
SIC: 4225 General warehousing and storage
HQ: World Class Distribution Inc.
10288 Calabash Ave
Fontana CA

(P-3785)
WORLD CLASS DISTRIBUTION INC
800 S Shamrock Ave (91016-6346)
PHONE...................................909 574-4140
Charles Pilliter, Pr
EMP: 68
SALES (corp-wide): 355.83K Privately Held
SIC: 4225 General warehousing and storage
HQ: World Class Distribution Inc.
10288 Calabash Ave
Fontana CA

(P-3786)
WORLD CLASS DISTRIBUTION INC
343 S Lena Rd (92408-1601)
PHONE...................................909 574-4140
EMP: 68
SALES (corp-wide): 355.83K Privately Held
SIC: 4225 General warehousing and storage
HQ: World Class Distribution Inc.
10288 Calabash Ave
Fontana CA

(P-3787)
WTI DISTRIBUTION INC
5491 E Francis St (91761-3604)
PHONE...................................909 597-8410
Harpenau Officer Marcella, CEO
Marcella Harpenau, *
EMP: 60 EST: 2011
SALES (est): 2.19MM Privately Held
Web: www.wtidi.com
SIC: 4225 General warehousing

4226 Special Warehousing And Storage, Nec

(P-3788)
ACCESS INFO HOLDINGS LLC
12135 Davis St (92557-6369)
PHONE...................................909 459-1417
EMP: 724
SALES (corp-wide): 45.7MM Privately Held
Web: www.accesscorp.com
SIC: 4226 Document and office records storage
PA: Access Information Holdings, Llc
500 Unicorn Park Dr # 500
Woburn MA
925 583-0100

(P-3789)
CORODATA RECORDS MGT INC
12375 Kerran St (92064-6801)
PHONE...................................858 748-1100
EMP: 77 EST: 2011
SALES (est): 4.89MM
SALES (corp-wide): 50.44MM Privately Held

4226 - Special Warehousing And Storage, Nec (P-3790)

Web: www.corodata.com
SIC: 4226 Document and office records storage
PA: Corodata Corporation
12375 Kerran St
Poway CA
858 748-1100

(P-3790)
DSV SOLUTIONS LLC
Also Called: DSV
13032 Slover Ave Ste 200 (92337-6901)
PHONE..................................909 829-5804
EMP: 105
SALES (corp-wide): 32.91B Privately Held
Web: www.dsv.com
SIC: 4226 Textile warehousing
HQ: Dsv Solutions, Llc
200 Wood Ave S 300
Iselin NJ
732 850-8000

(P-3791)
EXPRESS IMAGING SERVICES INC
1805 W 208th St Ste 202 (90501-1808)
PHONE..................................888 846-8804
Paul Terry, Pr
Kenny Ly, *
Tan Ly, CIO*
Anni Ly, Leasing Manager*
EMP: 100 EST: 2004
SQ FT: 10,000
SALES (est): 8.71MM Privately Held
Web: www.eiscallcenter.com
SIC: 4226 Document and office records storage

(P-3792)
GRM INFORMATION MGT SVCS INC (PA)
Also Called: Guarantee Records Management
41099 Boyce Rd (94538-2434)
PHONE..................................201 798-7100
Avner Schneur, Pr
Yossi Harel, *
Chris Urinyi, *
EMP: 300 EST: 1988
SQ FT: 1,000,000
SALES (est): 49.66MM Privately Held
Web: www.grmdocumentmanagement.com
SIC: 4226 7389 Document and office records storage; Document storage service

(P-3793)
KINDER MRGAN TANK STOR TRMNALS
2000 E Sepulveda Blvd (90810-1937)
PHONE..................................713 369-9000
Richard D Kinder, Ch Bd
Jeff Armstrong, Pr
EMP: 68 EST: 1976
SALES (est): 4.06MM Publicly Held
Web: www.kindermorgan.com
SIC: 4226 Special warehousing and storage, nec
HQ: Kinder Morgan Liquids Terminals Llc
1001 La St Ste 1000
Houston TX
713 369-9000

(P-3794)
KW INTERNATIONAL INC
18724 S Broadwick St (90220-6426)
PHONE..................................213 703-6914
Allen Lee, Brnch Mgr
EMP: 62
Web: www.kwinternational.com

SIC: 4226 8744 4731 Special warehousing and storage, nec; Facilities support services; Freight forwarding
PA: Kw International, Inc.
18655 Bishop Ave
Carson CA

(P-3795)
PACIFIC CHEMICAL DIST CORP (HQ)
Also Called: Pacific Chemical
6250 Caballero Blvd (90620-1124)
PHONE..................................714 521-7161
James N Tausz, Pr
James Banister, *
Rhonda Tausz, *
◆ EMP: 100 EST: 1978
SQ FT: 144,000
SALES (est): 24.92MM
SALES (corp-wide): 552.56MM Privately Held
Web: www.pacchem.com
SIC: 4226 Special warehousing and storage, nec
PA: Quantix Scs, Llc
24 Waterway Ave Ste 450
The Woodlands TX
800 542-8058

(P-3796)
PRIDE INDUSTRIES (PA)
10030 Foothills Blvd (95747-7102)
P.O. Box 1200 (95677-7200)
PHONE..................................916 788-2100
TOLL FREE: 800
Jeffery Dern, Pr
Everett Crane, *
Tim Yamauchi, *
Peter Berghuis, *
Tina Oliveira, *
▲ EMP: 250 EST: 1966
SQ FT: 177,000
SALES (est): 278.16MM
SALES (corp-wide): 278.16MM Privately Held
Web: www.prideindustries.com
SIC: 4226 7349 3679 Special warehousing and storage, nec; Building maintenance services, nec; Electronic circuits

4412 Deep Sea Foreign Transportation Of Freight

(P-3797)
FOSS MARITIME CO INC
Pier D Berth 35 (90802)
PHONE..................................562 435-0171
Steve Scalzo, Pr
EMP: 93 EST: 1936
SQ FT: 50,000
SALES (est): 11.58MM
SALES (corp-wide): 2.33B Privately Held
Web: www.foss.com
SIC: 4412 Deep sea foreign transportation of freight
HQ: Foss Maritime Company, Llc.
450 Alaskan Way S Ste 706
Seattle WA
206 281-3800

(P-3798)
PATRIOT CONTRACT SERVICES LLC
Also Called: PCS
1320 Willow Pass Rd Ste 485 (94520-5285)
PHONE..................................925 296-2000
Judy Collins, Ex VP
Frank Angelacci, VP

EMP: 400 EST: 1997
SQ FT: 7,800
SALES (est): 27.99MM Privately Held
Web: www.patriotships.com
SIC: 4412 4424 4449 4481 Deep sea foreign transportation of freight; Deep sea domestic transportation of freight; Canal and intracoastal freight transportation; Deep sea passenger transportation, except ferry

4424 Deep Sea Domestic Transportation Of Freight

(P-3799)
PASHA HAWAII TRNSPT LINES LLC
1425 Maritime St (94607-1022)
PHONE..................................510 271-1400
Mary Brown, Off Mgr
EMP: 100
SALES (corp-wide): 16.63MM Privately Held
Web: www.pashagroup.com
SIC: 4424 4783 Deep sea domestic transportation of freight; Containerization of goods for shipping
PA: Pasha Hawaii Transport Lines Llc
4040 Civic Center Dr # 350
San Rafael CA
415 927-6400

(P-3800)
POLAR TANKERS INC
60 Berth (90731-7252)
PHONE..................................310 519-8260
Chris Adams, Brnch Mgr
EMP: 210
SALES (corp-wide): 82.16B Publicly Held
Web: www.polartankers.conocophillips.com
SIC: 4424 Deep sea domestic transportation of freight
HQ: Polar Tankers, Inc.
300 Oceangate
Long Beach CA
562 388-1400

(P-3801)
POLAR TANKERS INC (DH)
300 Oceangate (90802-6801)
PHONE..................................562 388-1400
John R Hennon, Pr
John L Sullivan, *
George Mcshea, VP Opers
▲ EMP: 75 EST: 1956
SALES (est): 46.71MM
SALES (corp-wide): 82.16B Publicly Held
Web: www.polartankers.conocophillips.com
SIC: 4424 4412 Deep sea domestic transportation of freight; Deep sea foreign transportation of freight
HQ: Conocophillips Company
925 N Eldridge Pkwy
Houston TX
281 293-1000

4449 Water Transportation Of Freight

(P-3802)
CHEEMA LOGISTICS
968 Sierra St Ste 130 (93631-1554)
PHONE..................................559 702-1444
Parminder Singh, Pr
EMP: 65 EST: 2014
SALES (est): 2.3MM Privately Held
SIC: 4449 Intracoastal (freight) transportation

(P-3803)
DEVINE & SON TRUCKING CO INC (PA)
Also Called: Devine Intermodal
3870 Channel Dr (95691-3466)
P.O. Box 980160 (95798-0160)
PHONE..................................559 486-7440
John Frederick Drewes, CEO
Richard Coyle, *
EMP: 200 EST: 1923
SQ FT: 6,000
SALES (est): 28.33MM
SALES (corp-wide): 28.33MM Privately Held
Web: www.devineintermodal.com
SIC: 4449 4213 Canal and intracoastal freight transportation; Trucking, except local

4481 Deep Sea Passenger Transportation, Except Ferry

(P-3804)
PRINCESS CRUISE LINES LTD (HQ)
Also Called: Princess Cruises
24305 Town Center Dr (91355-1329)
P.O. Box 959 (91380-9059)
PHONE..................................661 753-0000
Jan Swartz, CEO
John Padgett, *
Natalya Leahy, *
◆ EMP: 2000 EST: 1965
SALES (est): 1.52B
SALES (corp-wide): 3.94B Privately Held
Web: www.princess.com
SIC: 4481 4725 7011 Deep sea passenger transportation, except ferry; Tour operators; Hotels
PA: Carnival Plc
Carnival House
Southampton HANTS
238 065-6666

4489 Water Passenger Transportation

(P-3805)
BLUE AND GOLD FLEET
Also Called: Pier Restaurant
Pier 41 Marine Terminal (94133)
PHONE..................................415 705-8200
Ron Duckhorn, Pr
Patrick Murphy, *
Kent Mcgrath, VP
Molly South, *
Robert Moore, *
▲ EMP: 70 EST: 1979
SALES (est): 14MM
SALES (corp-wide): 40MM Privately Held
Web: www.blueandgoldfleet.com
SIC: 4489 4724 Excursion boat operators; Travel agencies
PA: Pier 39 Limited Partnership
Beach Embarcadero Level 3
San Francisco CA
415 705-5500

(P-3806)
CATALINA CHANNEL EXPRESS INC (HQ)
Also Called: Catalina Express Cruises
385 E Swinford St (90731-1002)
PHONE..................................310 519-7971
Greg Bombard, Pr
Douglas Bombard, *
EMP: 200 EST: 1981
SQ FT: 20,000

PRODUCTS & SERVICES SECTION
4493 - Marinas (P-3825)

SALES (est): 54.13MM
SALES (corp-wide): 54.13MM **Privately Held**
Web: www.catalinaexpress.com
SIC: **4489** Excursion boat operators
PA: Bombard Marine & Resort
   Management Services, Inc.
   95 Berth
   San Pedro CA
   310 519-7971

(P-3807)
COMMODORE DINING CRUISES INC
Also Called: COMMODORE DINING CRUISES INC
Mainers Sq (94501)
PHONE.................510 337-9000
Max Browatzki, *Brnch Mgr*
EMP: 95
SALES (corp-wide): 4.55MM **Privately Held**
Web: www.commodoreevents.com
SIC: **4489** Excursion boat operators
PA: Commodore Cruises & Events, Inc.
   2394 Mariner Square Dr A
   Alameda CA
   510 337-9000

(P-3808)
HORNBLOWER YACHTS LLC
Also Called: Hornblower Cruises & Events
2825 5th Ave (92103-6326)
PHONE.................619 686-8700
Jim Unger, *Brnch Mgr*
EMP: 95
SALES (corp-wide): 495.57MM **Privately Held**
Web: www.cityexperiences.com
SIC: **4489** 7299 4499 Excursion boat operators; Banquet hall facilities; Chartering of commercial boats
PA: Hornblower Yachts, Llc
   The Embarcadero Pier 3 St Pier
   San Francisco CA
   415 424-4309

(P-3809)
SO CAL SHIP SERVICES
Also Called: Ship Services
971 S Seaside Ave (90731-7331)
PHONE.................310 519-8411
Michael A Lanham, *Pr*
EMP: 85 EST: 1982
SQ FT: 10,000
SALES (est): 12.25MM **Privately Held**
SIC: **4489** Water taxis

4491 Marine Cargo Handling

(P-3810)
INTERNATIONAL TRNSP SVC LLC (PA)
1281 Pier G Way (90802-6353)
P.O. Box 22704 (90801-5704)
PHONE.................562 435-7781
Kim Holtermand, *CEO*
Sean Lindsay, *COO*
Louis Paul, *Bd of Dir*
Richard Nicholson, *Bd of Dir*
▲ EMP: 114 EST: 1971
SQ FT: 10,000
SALES (est): 26.45MM
SALES (corp-wide): 26.45MM **Privately Held**
Web: www.itslb.com
SIC: **4491** Marine loading and unloading services

(P-3811)
LBCT LLC
1171 Pier F Ave (90802-6252)
PHONE.................562 951-6000
Anthony Otto, *Mgr*
EMP: 90 EST: 1980
SALES (est): 4.83MM **Privately Held**
Web: www.lbct.com
SIC: **4491** Marine terminals

(P-3812)
MARINE TERMINALS CORPORATION
389 Terminal Way (90731-7430)
PHONE.................310 519-2300
◆ EMP: 300 EST: 1931
SALES (est): 48.68MM
SALES (corp-wide): 251B **Privately Held**
Web: www.portsamerica.com
SIC: **4491** Stevedoring
HQ: Mtc Holdings
   3 Embarcadero Ctr Ste 550
   San Francisco CA
   912 651-4000

(P-3813)
PORT DEPT CITY OF OAKLAND (PA)
Also Called: Port of Oakland
530 Water St 2nd Fl (94607-3746)
P.O. Box 2064 (94604-2064)
PHONE.................510 627-1100
Veteran Chris Lytle, *Ex Dir*
Alan Yee, *
Cestra Butner, *
Earl Hamlin, *
Michael Colbruno, *
EMP: 350 EST: 1927
SQ FT: 285,600
SALES (est): 196.21MM
SALES (corp-wide): 196.21MM **Privately Held**
Web: www.portofoakland.com
SIC: **4491** 4581 Marine cargo handling; Airport leasing, if operating airport

(P-3814)
PORT OF LONG BEACH
415 W Ocean Blvd (90802-4511)
P.O. Box 570 (90801-0570)
PHONE.................562 283-7000
Paula Grond, *Sec*
EMP: 467 EST: 2014
SALES (est): 31.27MM **Privately Held**
Web: www.polb.com
SIC: **4491** Docks, piers and terminals
PA: City Of Long Beach
   1800 E Wardlow Rd
   Long Beach CA
   562 570-6450

(P-3815)
PORT OF LOS ANGELES
425 S Palos Verdes St (90731-3309)
PHONE.................310 732-3508
Gene Seroka, *Ex Dir*
EMP: 266 EST: 2017
SALES (est): 627.84MM **Privately Held**
Web: www.portoflosangeles.org
SIC: **4491** Waterfront terminal operation

(P-3816)
SAN DIEGO UNIFIED PORT DST
1400 Tidelands Ave (91950-4224)
PHONE.................619 686-6200
EMP: 115
SALES (corp-wide): 167.04MM **Privately Held**
Web: www.portofsandiego.org

SIC: **4491** Marine cargo handling
PA: San Diego Unified Port District
   3165 Pacific Hwy
   San Diego CA
   619 686-6200

(P-3817)
SAN DIEGO UNIFIED PORT DST (PA)
Also Called: PORT OF SAN DIEGO
3165 Pacific Hwy (92101-1128)
P.O. Box 120488 (92112-0488)
PHONE.................619 686-6200
John Bolduc, *CEO*
Robert Deangelis, *
Karen Porteous, *
Randa Coniglio, *
Thomas Russell, *
EMP: 240 EST: 1962
SQ FT: 120,000
SALES (est): 167.04MM
SALES (corp-wide): 167.04MM **Privately Held**
Web: www.portofsandiego.org
SIC: **4491** Marine cargo handling

(P-3818)
STOCKTON PORT DISTRICT
Also Called: PORT OF STOCKTON
2201 W Washington St Ste 13 (95203-2991)
P.O. Box 2089 (95201-2089)
PHONE.................209 946-0246
Mark Tollini, *Department Director*
Steve Escobar Dip, *Dir*
EMP: 100 EST: 1933
SQ FT: 18,000
SALES (est): 67.18MM **Privately Held**
Web: www.portofstockton.com
SIC: **4491** 4225 Waterfront terminal operation ; Warehousing, self storage

(P-3819)
SUDERMAN CONTG STEVEDORES INC (PA)
Also Called: Metro Ports
3806 Worsham Ave (90808-1896)
PHONE.................409 762-8131
Robert Dickey, *Pr*
Robert Willett, *
Walter W Hansel, *
EMP: 100 EST: 1987
SQ FT: 4,500
SALES (est): 9.92MM **Privately Held**
Web: www.metroports.com
SIC: **4491** Stevedoring

(P-3820)
YUSEN TERMINALS LLC (DH)
Also Called: Yti
701 New Dock St (90731-7535)
PHONE.................310 548-8000
Patrick Burgoyne, *CEO*
Betsy Christie, *
▲ EMP: 63 EST: 1991
SALES (est): 24.99MM **Privately Held**
Web: www.yti.com
SIC: **4491** Marine terminals
HQ: Nyk Group Americas Inc.
   300 Lighting Way Ste 500
   Secaucus NJ

4492 Towing And Tugboat Service

(P-3821)
BRUSCO TUG & BARGE INC
170 E Port Hueneme Rd (93041-3213)

PHONE.................805 986-1600
David Brusco, *Brnch Mgr*
EMP: 125
SALES (corp-wide): 20.45MM **Privately Held**
Web: www.bruscotug.com
SIC: **4492** Tugboat service
PA: Brusco Tug & Barge, Inc.
   548 14th Ave
   Longview WA
   360 423-9856

(P-3822)
CROSS LINK INC
Also Called: Westar Marine Services
50 Pier Bldg C (94158-2193)
P.O. Box 78100 (94107-8100)
PHONE.................415 495-3191
Mary C Mcmillan, *CEO*
Wendy Heffron-morrow, *VP*
▲ EMP: 65 EST: 1975
SQ FT: 16,000
SALES (est): 9.59MM **Privately Held**
Web: www.westarmarineservices.com
SIC: **4492** Marine towing services

(P-3823)
PACIFIC MARITIME FREIGHT INC
Also Called: PACIFIC MARITIME FREIGHT, INC.
1512 Pier C St (90813-4043)
PHONE.................562 590-8188
EMP: 95
SALES (corp-wide): 41.59MM **Privately Held**
Web: www.pacificmaritimegroup.com
SIC: **4492** Tugboat service
PA: Pacific Maritime Group, Inc.
   1444 Cesar E Chavez Pkwy
   San Diego CA
   619 533-7932

4493 Marinas

(P-3824)
SHELTER POINTE LLC
Also Called: Shelter Pointe Hotel & Marina
1551 Shelter Island Dr (92106-3102)
PHONE.................619 221-8000
Jeff Foster, *Managing Member*
EMP: 221 EST: 1993
SALES (est): 10.8MM
SALES (corp-wide): 98.27MM **Privately Held**
Web: www.resortkonakai.com
SIC: **4493** 7011 7997 5812 Marinas; Resort hotel; Country club, membership; American restaurant
HQ: Pacifica Hotel Company
   39 Argonaut
   Aliso Viejo CA
   805 957-0095

(P-3825)
SHM MBYH LLC ✪
Also Called: Safe Hbr Marina Bay Yacht Hbr
1340 Marina Way S (94804-3747)
PHONE.................510 236-1013
EMP: 72 EST: 2022
SALES (est): 319.91K
SALES (corp-wide): 2.97B **Publicly Held**
SIC: **4493** Marinas
HQ: Safe Harbor Marinas, Llc
   14785 Preston Rd Ste 975
   Dallas TX
   972 488-1314

4499 Water Transportation Services, Nec

(P-3826)
HANJIN SHIPPING CO LTD
301 Hanjin Rd (90802)
PHONE.....................201 291-4600
Taisoo Suk, *Ex Dir*
◆ **EMP:** 691 **EST:** 1994
SALES (est): 31.81MM **Privately Held**
SIC: 4499 Steamship leasing

4512 Air Transportation, Scheduled

(P-3827)
AEROTRANSPORTE DE CARGE UNION
Also Called: Aerounion
5625 W Imperial Hwy (90045-6323)
PHONE.....................310 649-0069
Luis Ramo, *Pr*
Steven Connolly, *VP*
EMP: 400 **EST:** 2006
SALES (est): 9.64MM **Privately Held**
Web: pcola.gulf.net
SIC: 4512 Air cargo carrier, scheduled

(P-3828)
AIR NEW ZEALAND LIMITED
222 N Pacific Coast Hwy Ste 900 (90245-5629)
PHONE.....................310 648-7000
Roger Poulton, *VP*
EMP: 100
Web: www.airnewzealand.com
SIC: 4512 Air passenger carrier, scheduled
PA: Air New Zealand Limited
185 Fanshawe St
Auckland AUK

(P-3829)
AMERICAN AIRLINES INC
International Airport (94128)
P.O. Box 8277 (94128-2677)
PHONE.....................650 877-6000
Phillip Bock, *Mgr*
EMP: 98
SQ FT: 4,000
SALES (corp-wide): 48.97B **Publicly Held**
Web: www.aacargo.com
SIC: 4512 Air passenger carrier, scheduled
HQ: American Airlines, Inc.
1 Skyview Dr
Fort Worth TX
682 278-9000

(P-3830)
AMERICAN AIRLINES INC
400 World Way Ste F (90045-5863)
P.O. Box 92246 (90009-2246)
PHONE.....................310 646-4553
Sally Rabideau, *Owner*
EMP: 298
SALES (corp-wide): 48.97B **Publicly Held**
Web: www.aacreditunion.org
SIC: 4512 Air passenger carrier, scheduled
HQ: American Airlines, Inc.
1 Skyview Dr
Fort Worth TX
682 278-9000

(P-3831)
AMERIFLIGHT LLC
4700 W Empire Ave (91505-1098)
PHONE.....................818 847-0000
EMP: 130
SALES (corp-wide): 98.21MM **Privately Held**
Web: www.ameriflight.com
SIC: 4512 Air cargo carrier, scheduled
PA: Ameriflight, Llc
1515 W 20th St
Dfw Airport TX
800 800-4538

(P-3832)
CHINA AIRLINES LTD
5651 W 96th St (90045-5539)
PHONE.....................310 484-1818
EMP: 107
Web: www.china-airlines.com
SIC: 4512 Air passenger carrier, scheduled
HQ: China Airlines, Ltd.
11201 Aviation Blvd
Los Angeles CA

(P-3833)
CHINA AIRLINES LTD
Also Called: Baggage Service
380 World Way Ste S14 (90045-5890)
PHONE.....................310 646-4293
Tim Chan, *Mgr*
EMP: 107
Web: www.china-airlines.com
SIC: 4512 Air passenger carrier, scheduled
HQ: China Airlines, Ltd.
11201 Aviation Blvd
Los Angeles CA

(P-3834)
JETBLUE AIRWAYS INC
Also Called: Jet Blue
4100 E Donald Douglas Dr (90808-1754)
PHONE.....................562 394-4397
Alex Wilcox, *Dir*
EMP: 93 **EST:** 2004
SALES (est): 6.35MM
SALES (corp-wide): 9.16B **Publicly Held**
SIC: 4512 Air passenger carrier, scheduled
PA: Jetblue Airways Corporation
2701 Queens Plz N
Long Island City NY
718 286-7900

(P-3835)
KOREAN AIR LINES CO LTD
Also Called: Korean Air
380 World Way Ste S4 (90045-5847)
PHONE.....................310 646-4866
EMP: 175
Web: www.koreanair.com
SIC: 4512 Air passenger carrier, scheduled
PA: Korean Airlines Co., Ltd.
260 Haneul-Gil, Gangseo-Gu
Seoul

(P-3836)
KOREAN AIRLINES CO LTD
Also Called: Korean Arln Crgo Reservations
6101 W Imperial Hwy (90045-6305)
PHONE.....................310 410-2000
Jinkul Lee, *Pr*
EMP: 250
Web: www.koreanair.com
SIC: 4512 4513 Air passenger carrier, scheduled; Package delivery, private air
PA: Korean Airlines Co., Ltd.
260 Haneul-Gil, Gangseo-Gu
Seoul

(P-3837)
KOREAN AIRLINES CO LTD
Also Called: Korean Air
1813 Wilshire Blvd Ste 400 (90057-3600)
PHONE.....................213 484-1900
Kyung Kim, *Brnch Mgr*
EMP: 100
Web: www.koreanair.com
SIC: 4512 4729 Air passenger carrier, scheduled; Airline ticket offices
PA: Korean Airlines Co., Ltd.
260 Haneul-Gil, Gangseo-Gu
Seoul

(P-3838)
L A AIR INC
5933 W Century Blvd 500 (90045-5471)
PHONE.....................310 215-8245
Dennis W Altbrandt, *CEO*
Wayne Schoenfeld, *
Tim Clary, *MARKET PLANNING**
William J Wolf, *
EMP: 134 **EST:** 1980
SQ FT: 6,119
SALES (est): 4.08MM **Privately Held**
SIC: 4512 Air passenger carrier, scheduled

(P-3839)
NIPPON CARGO AIRLINES CO LTD
6501 W Imperial Hwy Hngr 8 (90045-6308)
PHONE.....................310 417-0801
EMP: 84
SIC: 4512 Air passenger carrier, scheduled
HQ: Nippon Cargo Airlines Co., Ltd.
663 N Access Rd
Chicago IL

(P-3840)
PIEDMONT AIRLINES INC
Also Called: American Airlines/Eagle
4100 E Donald Douglas Dr (90808-1754)
PHONE.....................562 421-1806
Sean Lucas, *Mgr*
EMP: 163
SALES (corp-wide): 48.97B **Publicly Held**
Web: www.piedmont-airlines.com
SIC: 4512 Air passenger carrier, scheduled
HQ: Piedmont Airlines, Inc.
5443 Airport Terminal Rd
Salisbury MD
410 572-5100

(P-3841)
PIEDMONT AIRLINES INC
Also Called: American Airlines/Eagle
5175 E Clinton Way (93727-2086)
PHONE.....................559 269-5694
Pete Ellgrande, *Mgr*
EMP: 118
SALES (corp-wide): 48.97B **Publicly Held**
Web: www.piedmont-airlines.com
SIC: 4512 Air passenger carrier, scheduled
HQ: Piedmont Airlines, Inc.
5443 Airport Terminal Rd
Salisbury MD
410 572-5100

(P-3842)
POLAR AIR CARGO LP
100 Oceangate Fl 15 (90802-4347)
PHONE.....................310 568-4551
FAX: 562 436-9333
EMP: 480
SALES (est): 13.37MM
SALES (corp-wide): 1.84B **Publicly Held**
SIC: 4512 Air cargo carrier, scheduled
PA: Atlas Air Worldwide Holdings, Inc.
2000 Westchester Ave
Purchase NY
914 701-8000

(P-3843)
SINGAPORE AIRLINES LIMITED
222 N Pacific Coast Hwy Ste 1600 (90245)
PHONE.....................310 647-1922
Tee Hooi Teoh, *Mgr*
EMP: 135
Web: www.singaporeair.com
SIC: 4512 Air passenger carrier, scheduled
PA: Singapore Airlines Limited
25 Airline Road
Singapore

(P-3844)
SKYWEST AIRLINES INC
Also Called: United Cargo
585 Mcdonnell Rd (94128-3162)
PHONE.....................650 827-7000
EMP: 286
SALES (corp-wide): 3B **Publicly Held**
Web: www.skywest.com
SIC: 4512 Air passenger carrier, scheduled
HQ: Skywest Airlines, Inc.
444 S River Rd
St George UT
435 634-3000

(P-3845)
SKYWEST AIRLINES INC
Also Called: Baggage & Air Freight Service
Fresno Air Terminal (93727)
PHONE.....................559 252-3400
Renae Kramer, *Brnch Mgr*
EMP: 232
SALES (corp-wide): 3B **Publicly Held**
Web: www.skywest.com
SIC: 4512 Air passenger carrier, scheduled
HQ: Skywest Airlines, Inc.
444 S River Rd
St George UT
435 634-3000

(P-3846)
SOUTHWEST AIRLINES CO
Also Called: Southwest Airlines
18601 Airport Way Ste 237 (92707-5257)
PHONE.....................949 252-5200
Larry Pits, *Mgr*
EMP: 80
SALES (corp-wide): 23.81B **Publicly Held**
Web: www.southwest.com
SIC: 4512 Air passenger carrier, scheduled
PA: Southwest Airlines Co.
2702 Love Field Dr
Dallas TX
214 792-4000

(P-3847)
UNITED AIRLINES INC
Also Called: Continental Airlines
7300 World Way W Rm 144 (90045-5829)
PHONE.....................310 258-3319
Ken Jaminson, *Mgr*
EMP: 89
SALES (corp-wide): 44.95B **Publicly Held**
SIC: 4512 Air passenger carrier, scheduled
HQ: United Airlines, Inc.
233 S Wacker Dr Ste 710
Chicago IL
872 825-4000

(P-3848)
UNITED COURIERS INC (DH)
Also Called: U C I Distribution Plus
3280 E Foothill Blvd (91107-3148)
PHONE.....................213 383-3611
Stephan Cretier, *CEO*
Richard R Irvin, *
Robert G Irvin, *
EMP: 200 **EST:** 1957
SQ FT: 25,000
SALES (est): 75.64MM
SALES (corp-wide): 175.11MM **Privately Held**

PRODUCTS & SERVICES SECTION
4522 - Air Transportation, Nonscheduled (P-3869)

SIC: **4512** 4215 4212 7381 Air cargo carrier, scheduled; Courier services, except by air; Local trucking, without storage; Armored car services
HQ: Ati Systems International, Inc.
2000 Nw Corp Blvd Ste 101
Boca Raton FL
561 939-7000

(P-3849)
UNITED PARCEL SERVICE INC
Also Called: UPS
1457 E Victoria Ave (92408-2923)
PHONE..................................800 742-5877
EMP: 120
SALES (corp-wide): 100.34B **Publicly Held**
Web: www.ups.com
SIC: **4512** Air cargo carrier, scheduled
HQ: United Parcel Service, Inc.
55 Glenlake Pkwy
Atlanta GA
404 828-6000

(P-3850)
UNITED PARCEL SERVICE INC
Also Called: UPS
26557 Danti Ct 1st Fl (94545-3917)
PHONE..................................510 264-8880
EMP: 107
SALES (corp-wide): 100.34B **Publicly Held**
Web: www.ups.com
SIC: **4512** Air cargo carrier, scheduled
HQ: United Parcel Service, Inc.
55 Glenlake Pkwy
Atlanta GA
404 828-6000

(P-3851)
UNITED PARCEL SERVICE INC
Also Called: UPS
3110 Jurupa St (91761-2902)
PHONE..................................909 605-7740
EMP: 120
SALES (corp-wide): 100.34B **Publicly Held**
Web: www.ups.com
SIC: **4512** Air cargo carrier, scheduled
HQ: United Parcel Service, Inc.
55 Glenlake Pkwy
Atlanta GA
404 828-6000

4513 Air Courier Services

(P-3852)
DHL EXPRESS (USA) INC
401 23rd St (94107-3102)
PHONE..................................415 826-7338
Jeffrey Funk, *Mgr*
EMP: 70
SALES (corp-wide): 98.08B **Privately Held**
SIC: **4513** Air courier services
HQ: Dhl Express (Usa), Inc.
16592 Collections Ctr Dr
Chicago IL
954 888-7000

(P-3853)
FEDERAL EXPRESS CORPORATION
Also Called: Fedex
8455 Pardee Dr (94621-1411)
PHONE..................................800 463-3339
EMP: 107
SALES (corp-wide): 90.16B **Publicly Held**
Web: www.fedex.com

SIC: **4513** 4215 Letter delivery, private air; Courier services, except by air
HQ: Federal Express Corporation
3610 Hacks Cross Rd
Memphis TN
901 369-3600

(P-3854)
FEDERAL EXPRESS CORPORATION
Also Called: Fedex
2500 Kimberly Ave (92831-5142)
PHONE..................................800 463-3339
EMP: 79
SALES (corp-wide): 90.16B **Publicly Held**
Web: www.fedex.com
SIC: **4513** Letter delivery, private air
HQ: Federal Express Corporation
3610 Hacks Cross Rd
Memphis TN
901 369-3600

(P-3855)
FEDERAL EXPRESS CORPORATION
Also Called: Fedex
3333 S Grand Ave (90007-4116)
PHONE..................................800 463-3339
EMP: 100
SALES (corp-wide): 90.16B **Publicly Held**
Web: www.fedex.com
SIC: **4513** Package delivery, private air
HQ: Federal Express Corporation
3610 Hacks Cross Rd
Memphis TN
901 369-3600

(P-3856)
LBC MUNDIAL CORPORATION (DH)
Also Called: LBC North America
3563 Investment Blvd Ste 3 (94545)
PHONE..................................650 873-0750
Miguel Angel Camahort, *Pr*
EMP: 60 **EST:** 1985
SQ FT: 25,000
SALES (est): 49.41MM **Privately Held**
Web: www.lbcexpress.com
SIC: **4513** 4215 6099 6221 Air courier services; Courier services, except by air; Foreign currency exchange; Commodity contracts brokers, dealers
HQ: Lbc Express Holdings, Inc.
Lbc Hangar, General Aviation Centre
Domestic Airport Road
Pasay City MAN

(P-3857)
MEJICO EXPRESS INC (PA)
Also Called: Grupoex
14849 Firestone Blvd Fl 1 (90638)
PHONE..................................714 690-8300
Jose Leon, *Pr*
EMP: 150 **EST:** 1988
SALES (est): 7.7MM **Privately Held**
SIC: **4513** Letter delivery, private air

(P-3858)
MENLO WORLDWIDE FORWARDING INC
Also Called: Menlo Worldwide Expedite
1 Lagoon Dr Ste 400 (94065-1564)
PHONE..................................650 596-9600
◆ **EMP:** 6500
SIC: **4513** 4215 4522 4731 Letter delivery, private air; Courier services, except by air; Flying charter service; Customhouse brokers

(P-3859)
UNITED PARCEL SERVICE INC
Also Called: UPS
3333 S Downey Rd (90058-4116)
PHONE..................................323 260-8957
Tony Peralta, *Mgr*
EMP: 226
SALES (corp-wide): 100.34B **Publicly Held**
Web: www.ups.com
SIC: **4513** 4215 Air courier services; Courier services, except by air
HQ: United Parcel Service, Inc.
55 Glenlake Pkwy
Atlanta GA
404 828-6000

(P-3860)
WEST AIR INC
5005 E Andersen Ave (93727-1502)
PHONE..................................559 454-7843
Tim Komberec, *CEO*
Thomas E Jordan, *
Robert Thompson, *
Lawrence W Olson, *
EMP: 70 **EST:** 1940
SQ FT: 10,000
SALES (est): 15.61MM **Privately Held**
Web: www.westair.net
SIC: **4513** Package delivery, private air
PA: Empire Holdings, Inc.
11559 N Atlas Rd
Hayden ID

(P-3861)
WING AVIATION LLC
1600 Amphitheatre Pkwy (94043-1351)
PHONE..................................650 224-1198
James Burgess, *CEO*
EMP: 120
SALES (est): 4.09MM **Privately Held**
SIC: **4513** Package delivery, private air

4522 Air Transportation, Nonscheduled

(P-3862)
ADVANCED AIR LLC
Also Called: Advanced Air
12101 Crenshaw Blvd Ste 100 (90250-3369)
PHONE..................................310 644-3344
Levi Stockton, *Pr*
EMP: 150 **EST:** 2005
SQ FT: 2,500
SALES (est): 24.34MM **Privately Held**
Web: www.advancedairlines.com
SIC: **4522** 4512 Air transportation, nonscheduled; Air transportation, scheduled

(P-3863)
AVJET CORPORATION (DH)
4301 W Empire Ave (91505-1109)
PHONE..................................818 841-6190
EMP: 80 **EST:** 1979
SALES (est): 15.66MM
SALES (corp-wide): 39.41B **Publicly Held**
Web: www.avjet.com
SIC: **4522** 5599 4581 Flying charter service; Aircraft, self-propelled; Aircraft cleaning and janitorial service
HQ: Jet Aviation Of America, Inc.
112 Chrles A Lndbrgh Dr T
Teterboro NJ
201 288-8400

(P-3864)
BOUTIQUE AIR INC (PA)
5 3rd St Ste 925 (94103-3220)
PHONE..................................415 449-0505
Shawn Simpson, *Pr*
Brian Murphy, *
EMP: 100 **EST:** 2007
SALES (est): 48.72MM **Privately Held**
Web: www.boutiqueair.com
SIC: **4522** 4512 Flying charter service; Air passenger carrier, scheduled

(P-3865)
J KENNETH FORESTER
7400 Flightline Dr (95403-9018)
PHONE..................................201 288-5040
Kenneth Forester, *Brnch Mgr*
EMP: 94
SALES (corp-wide): 3.33MM **Privately Held**
Web: www.meridian.aero
SIC: **4522** Flying charter service
PA: J Kenneth Forester Inc
485 Industrial Ave
Teterboro NJ
201 288-5040

(P-3866)
KAISERAIR INC (PA)
Also Called: Kaiserair
8735 Earhart Rd (94621-4547)
P.O. Box 2626 (94614-0626)
PHONE..................................510 569-9622
Ronald J Guerra, *Pr*
David A Mancebo, *VP*
Glenn Barrett, *VP*
Roby Guerra, *CFO*
David L Campbell, *Sec*
EMP: 148 **EST:** 1979
SQ FT: 970,000
SALES (est): 24.77MM
SALES (corp-wide): 24.77MM **Privately Held**
Web: www.kaiserair.com
SIC: **4522** Flying charter service

(P-3867)
PEGASUS ELITE AVIATION INC
7943 Woodley Ave (91406-1232)
PHONE..................................818 742-6666
EMP: 162 **EST:** 2007
SALES (est): 27.45MM
SALES (corp-wide): 27.45MM **Privately Held**
Web: www.pegjet.com
SIC: **4522** Flying charter service
PA: Prima Air Group Llc
800 E Colo Blvd Ste 888
Pasadena CA

(P-3868)
ROGERS HELICOPTERS INC
5508 E Aircorp Way (93727-1201)
PHONE..................................559 299-4903
Sandy Kilby, *Genl Mgr*
EMP: 88
SALES (corp-wide): 21.23MM **Privately Held**
Web: www.rogershelicopters.com
SIC: **4522** Flying charter service
PA: Rogers Helicopters, Inc.
5484 E Perimeter Rd
Fresno CA
559 299-4903

(P-3869)
SUN AIR JETS LLC
855 Aviation Dr Ste 200 (93010-8595)
PHONE..................................805 389-9301
Brian Counsil, *Pr*

4581 - Airports, Flying Fields, And Services (P-3870)

Steve Maloney, *
Rob Cox, OF Maintenance*
Ed Fares, *
EMP: 114 **EST:** 1999
SQ FT: 10,000
SALES (est): 20.39MM **Privately Held**
Web: www.sunairjets.com
SIC: 4522 4581 Flying charter service; Aircraft servicing and repairing

4581 Airports, Flying Fields, And Services

(P-3870)
ABM AVIATION INC
601 Gateway Blvd Ste 1145 (94080-7413)
PHONE.................................650 872-5400
Doug Kreuckamp, VP
EMP: 96
SALES (corp-wide): 7.81B **Publicly Held**
Web: www.abm.com
SIC: 4581 Airport
HQ: Abm Aviation, Inc.
 3399 Peachtree Rd Ne # 15
 Atlanta GA
 404 926-4200

(P-3871)
AEROGROUND INC (DH)
Also Called: Air Cargo Handling Service
270 Lawrence Ave (94080-6817)
PHONE.................................650 266-6965
Anthony Bonino, CEO
▲ **EMP:** 800 **EST:** 1989
SQ FT: 175,000
SALES (est): 131.03MM
SALES (corp-wide): 1.35B **Privately Held**
Web: mail.aeroground.com
SIC: 4581 4213 Air freight handling at airports; Trucking, except local
HQ: Menzies Aviation Limited
 Mw1 Building 557, Shoreham Road
 Hounslow MIDDX

(P-3872)
AIRPORT TERMINAL MGT INC
6851 W Imperial Hwy (90045-6311)
PHONE.................................310 988-1492
EMP: 321
SALES (corp-wide): 22.92MM **Privately Held**
Web: www.atmlax.com
SIC: 4581 Airport terminal services
PA: Airport Terminal Management, Inc.
 216 W Florence Ave
 Inglewood CA
 310 590-1650

(P-3873)
ALLIANCE GROUND INTL LLC
6181 W Imperial Hwy (90045-6305)
PHONE.................................310 646-2446
EMP: 1969
SALES (corp-wide): 478.27MM **Privately Held**
Web: www.allianceground.com
SIC: 4581 Airfreight loading and unloading services
HQ: Alliance Ground International, Llc
 9130 S Ddland Blvd Ste 18
 Miami FL
 305 740-3252

(P-3874)
ALLIANCE GROUND INTL LLC
648 West Field Rd (94128)
PHONE.................................650 821-0855
EMP: 422
SALES (corp-wide): 478.27MM **Privately Held**
Web: www.allianceground.com
SIC: 4581 Airfreight loading and unloading services
HQ: Alliance Ground International, Llc
 9130 S Ddland Blvd Ste 18
 Miami FL
 305 740-3252

(P-3875)
ATLANTIC AVIATION FBO INC
1250 Aviation Ave (95110-1119)
PHONE.................................408 297-7552
EMP: 124
SALES (corp-wide): 847MM **Privately Held**
Web: www.atlanticaviation.com
SIC: 4581 Aircraft maintenance and repair services
HQ: Atlantic Aviation Fbo Inc.
 5201 Tennyson Pkwy # 150
 Plano TX

(P-3876)
ATLANTIC AVIATION HOLDING CORP
2828 Donald Douglas Loop N Lbby (90405-2978)
PHONE.................................310 396-6770
Gregory Wain, Genl Mgr
EMP: 66
SALES (corp-wide): 847MM **Privately Held**
Web: www.atlanticaviation.com
SIC: 4581 Aircraft maintenance and repair services
HQ: Atlantic Aviation Holding Corporation
 6652 Pinecrest Dr Ste 300
 Plano TX
 972 905-2500

(P-3877)
AVIATION & DEFENSE INC
Also Called: ADI
255 S Leland Norton Way (92408-0103)
PHONE.................................909 382-3487
Daniel M Scanlon, CEO
Mike Scanlon, Pr
Dan Scanlon, VP
Kathy Meza, Contrlr
Jim Anderson, Sls Dir
EMP: 180 **EST:** 2011
SQ FT: 180,000
SALES (est): 24.47MM **Privately Held**
Web: www.adi.aero
SIC: 4581 Aircraft maintenance and repair services

(P-3878)
AVIATION CONSULTANTS INC
4900 Wing Way (93446-8522)
PHONE.................................805 596-0212
William Borgsmiller, Brnch Mgr
EMP: 76
SALES (corp-wide): 43.44MM **Privately Held**
Web: www.acijet.com
SIC: 4581 Airports, flying fields, and services
PA: Aviation Consultants, Inc.
 4751 Aviadores Way
 San Luis Obispo CA
 805 782-9722

(P-3879)
AVIATION CONSULTANTS INC
Also Called: Aci Jet
19301 Campus Dr (92707-5246)
PHONE.................................949 201-2550
William Borgsmiller, Brnch Mgr
EMP: 76
SALES (corp-wide): 43.44MM **Privately Held**
Web: www.acijet.com
SIC: 4581 Aircraft storage at airports
PA: Aviation Consultants, Inc.
 4751 Aviadores Way
 San Luis Obispo CA
 805 782-9722

(P-3880)
AVIATION MAINTENANCE GROUP INC
8352 Kimball Ave Hngr 3 (91708-9267)
PHONE.................................714 469-0515
Jeremy G Schuster, Pr
Doug Crowther, *
EMP: 85 **EST:** 1995
SALES (est): 4.85MM **Privately Held**
SIC: 4581 Aircraft maintenance and repair services

(P-3881)
CERTIFIED AVIATION SVCS LLC
612 West Field Rd (94128-3101)
PHONE.................................650 588-8665
EMP: 74
SIC: 4581 Aircraft maintenance and repair services
PA: Certified Aviation Services Llc
 1150 S Vineyard Ave
 Ontario CA

(P-3882)
CITY OF LONG BEACH
Also Called: Long Beach Airport
4100 E Donald Douglas Dr # 2 (90808-1798)
PHONE.................................562 570-2600
Chris Kunze, Mgr
EMP: 65
Web: www.longbeach.gov
SIC: 4581 9111 Airport; Mayors' office
PA: City Of Long Beach
 1800 E Wardlow Rd
 Long Beach CA
 562 570-6450

(P-3883)
CITY OF SAN JOSE
Also Called: Mineta San Jose Intl Arprt
1701 Airport Blvd Ste B1130 (95110)
PHONE.................................408 392-3600
William Sherry, Aviation Director
EMP: 69
SQ FT: 30,000
SALES (corp-wide): 2.14B **Privately Held**
Web: www.sanjoseca.gov
SIC: 4581 9199 Airport; General government administration, County government
PA: City Of San Jose
 200 E Santa Clara St 13th
 San Jose CA
 408 535-3500

(P-3884)
CITY OF SAN JOSE
Also Called: Airport
801 N 1st St (95110-1704)
PHONE.................................650 965-4156
Nina Grayson, Prin
EMP: 126 **EST:** 2009
SALES (est): 4.89MM
SALES (corp-wide): 2.14B **Privately Held**
Web: www.sanjoseca.gov
SIC: 4581 Airport
PA: City Of San Jose
 200 E Santa Clara St 13th
 San Jose CA
 408 535-3500

(P-3885)
CLAY LACY AVIATION INC (PA)
Also Called: C L A
7435 Valjean Ave (91406-2901)
PHONE.................................818 989-2900
TOLL FREE: 800
Brian Kirkdoffer, Pr
Hershel Clay Lacy, *
EMP: 317 **EST:** 1969
SQ FT: 18,000
SALES (est): 157.17MM
SALES (corp-wide): 157.17MM **Privately Held**
Web: www.claylacy.com
SIC: 4581 Airport terminal services

(P-3886)
COMAV LLC
Also Called: Comav Aviation
18260 Phantom W (92394-7971)
PHONE.................................760 523-5100
EMP: 103
SALES (corp-wide): 83.02MM **Privately Held**
Web: www.comav.com
SIC: 4581 Aircraft maintenance and repair services
PA: Comav, Llc
 18499 Phantom St Ste 17
 Victorville CA
 760 523-5100

(P-3887)
COMAV TECHNICAL SERVICES LLC
Also Called: S C A
18438 Readiness St (92394-7945)
PHONE.................................760 530-2400
Craig Garrick, CEO
Jon Day, *
▲ **EMP:** 223 **EST:** 1999
SQ FT: 47,625
SALES (est): 48.55MM
SALES (corp-wide): 83.02MM **Privately Held**
Web: www.comav.com
SIC: 4581 Aircraft maintenance and repair services
PA: Comav, Llc
 18499 Phantom St Ste 17
 Victorville CA
 760 523-5100

(P-3888)
COUNTY OF ORANGE
Also Called: John Wayne Airport
3160 Airway Ave (92626-4608)
PHONE.................................949 252-5006
Loan Leblow, Brnch Mgr
EMP: 135
SALES (corp-wide): 5.2B **Privately Held**
Web: www.ocgov.com
SIC: 4581 9621 Airport; Aircraft regulating agencies
PA: County Of Orange
 400 W Civic Center Dr G36
 Santa Ana CA
 714 834-6200

(P-3889)
COUNTY OF SACRAMENTO
Also Called: Airports Dept
6900 Airport Blvd (95837-1109)
PHONE.................................916 874-0912
Hardy Acree, Dir
EMP: 472
SALES (corp-wide): 3.56B **Privately Held**
Web: www.sacramento.aero
SIC: 4581 9621 Airport; Aircraft regulating agencies

PRODUCTS & SERVICES SECTION
4581 - Airports, Flying Fields, And Services (P-3911)

PA: County Of Sacramento
700 H St Ste 7650
Sacramento CA
916 874-8515

(P-3890)
DEPARTMENT OF ARPRTS OF THE CY
1 World Way (90045-5803)
PHONE.................................855 463-5252
EMP: 1507
SALES (est): 1.43MM
SALES (corp-wide): 1.38B **Privately Held**
Web: www.lawa.org
SIC: 4581 Airport
PA: Los Angeles World Airports
1 World Way
Los Angeles CA
855 463-5252

(P-3891)
DSD TRUCKING INC
2411 Santa Fe Ave (90278-1125)
PHONE.................................310 338-3395
Dan Cuevas, Pr
EMP: 100 EST: 1984
SQ FT: 300,000
SALES (est): 15.56MM **Privately Held**
Web: www.dsdcompanies.com
SIC: 4581 Air freight handling at airports

(P-3892)
F & E ARCFT MINT LOS ANGLES LL
531 Main St Ste 672 (90245-3006)
PHONE.................................310 338-0063
EMP: 350 EST: 1992
SALES (est): 17.58MM **Privately Held**
Web: www.feairmaintenance.com
SIC: 4581 7699 Aircraft servicing and repairing; Aircraft and heavy equipment repair services

(P-3893)
FLIGHTDOCS II LLC
6080 Center Dr Fl 6 (90045-9205)
PHONE.................................800 747-4560
EMP: 67
SALES (corp-wide): 22.39MM **Privately Held**
Web: www.veryon.com
SIC: 4581 Aircraft maintenance and repair services
HQ: Flightdocs Ii, Llc
382 Ne 191st St
Miami FL

(P-3894)
GAT - ARLN GROUND SUPPORT INC
2627 N Hollywood Way (91505-1062)
PHONE.................................818 847-9127
EMP: 221
Web: www.wearegat.net
SIC: 4581 Airports, flying fields, and services
PA: Gat - Airline Ground Support, Inc.
246 City Cir Ste 2000
Peachtree City GA

(P-3895)
GAT - ARLN GROUND SUPPORT INC
6701 Lindbergh Dr (95837-1138)
PHONE.................................916 923-2349
EMP: 276
Web: www.wearegat.net
SIC: 4581 Aircraft maintenance and repair services
PA: Gat - Airline Ground Support, Inc.

246 City Cir Ste 2000
Peachtree City GA

(P-3896)
KAISERAIR INC
Also Called: Santa Rosa Jet Center
2240 Airport Blvd (95403-1003)
PHONE.................................707 528-7400
Glenn Barrett, Mgr
EMP: 73
SALES (corp-wide): 24.77MM **Privately Held**
Web: www.kaiserair.com
SIC: 4581 Airport
PA: Kaiserair, Inc.
8735 Earhart Rd
Oakland CA
510 569-9622

(P-3897)
LOS ANGELES WORLD AIRPORTS (PA)
1 World Way (90045-5803)
P.O. Box 92216 (90009-2216)
PHONE.................................855 463-5252
Justin Erbacci, CEO
Michael Cummings, *
Robert L Gilbert, Chief Development Officer*
Arif Alikhan, *
EMP: 222 EST: 2010
SALES (est): 1.38B
SALES (corp-wide): 1.38B **Privately Held**
Web: www.lawa.org
SIC: 4581 Airport

(P-3898)
LOS ANGELES WORLD AIRPORTS
Also Called: Human Resources Services
7301 World Way W Fl 5 (90045-5828)
PHONE.................................424 646-5900
EMP: 452
SALES (corp-wide): 1.38B **Privately Held**
Web: www.lawa.org
SIC: 4581 Airport
PA: Los Angeles World Airports
1 World Way
Los Angeles CA
855 463-5252

(P-3899)
LOS ANGELES WORLD AIRPORTS
5312 W 99th Pl (90045-5722)
PHONE.................................424 646-9118
EMP: 226
SALES (corp-wide): 1.38B **Privately Held**
Web: www.lawa.org
SIC: 4581 Airport
PA: Los Angeles World Airports
1 World Way
Los Angeles CA
855 463-5252

(P-3900)
MENZIES AVIATION (TEXAS) INC
Also Called: Asig
1049 S Vineyard Ave (91761-8029)
P.O. Box 4178 (91761-1011)
PHONE.................................909 937-3998
Debbie Martin, Mgr
EMP: 74
SALES (corp-wide): 1.35B **Privately Held**
Web: www.menziesaviation.com
SIC: 4581 Airport
HQ: Menzies Aviation (Texas), Inc.
3500 William D Tate Ave # 200
Grapevine TX
469 281-8200

(P-3901)
NORMAN Y MNT-SAN JOSE INTL ARP
1701 Airport Blvd (95110-1202)
PHONE.................................408 392-3600
John Aitken, Dir
EMP: 250 EST: 2011
SALES (est): 177.74MM **Privately Held**
Web: www.flysanjose.com
SIC: 4581 Airport

(P-3902)
PACIFIC AVIATION CORPORATION
P.O. Box 250758 (94125-0758)
PHONE.................................650 821-1190
Addie E Castillo, Brnch Mgr
EMP: 524
Web: www.pacificaviation.com
SIC: 4581 Airport
PA: Pacific Aviation Corporation
201 Continental Blvd # 220
El Segundo CA

(P-3903)
PACIFIC AVIATION CORPORATION (PA)
201 Continental Blvd Ste 220 (90245-4500)
PHONE.................................310 646-4015
Evan Gobdel, CEO
Scott White, *
Robert Steinberger, *
EMP: 200 EST: 1995
SALES (est): 30.47MM **Privately Held**
Web: www.pacificaviation.com
SIC: 4581 Airport terminal services

(P-3904)
PHS / MWA
Also Called: Phs/Mwa Aviation Services
42374 Avenida Alvarado # A (92590)
PHONE.................................951 695-1008
Mary Bale, CEO
Bill Voetsch, *
EMP: 147 EST: 2003
SALES (est): 25.51MM **Publicly Held**
Web: www.wencor.com
SIC: 4581 3492 7629 Aircraft servicing and repairing; Control valves, aircraft: hydraulic and pneumatic; Electrical repair shops
HQ: Wencor Group, Llc
416 Dividend Dr
Peachtree City GA
678 490-0140

(P-3905)
PORT DEPT CITY OF OAKLAND
9532 Earhart Rd Ste 205 (94621-4551)
PHONE.................................510 563-3697
Mike Mantino, Mgr
EMP: 66
SALES (corp-wide): 196.21MM **Privately Held**
Web: www.portofoakland.com
SIC: 4581 Airport terminal services
PA: Port Department Of The City Of Oakland
530 Water St Fl 3
Oakland CA
510 627-1100

(P-3906)
PORT DEPT OF THE CY OAKLAND
Also Called: Metroplitan Oakland Intl Arprt
1 Airport Dr Ste 45 (94621-1476)
PHONE.................................510 563-3300
Bill Wade, Mgr
EMP: 66

SALES (corp-wide): 196.21MM **Privately Held**
Web: www.oaklandairport.com
SIC: 4581 Airport
PA: Port Department Of The City Of Oakland
530 Water St Fl 3
Oakland CA
510 627-1100

(P-3907)
PRIMEFLIGHT AVIATION SVCS INC
612 Mcdonald Rd Ste 100 (94128)
PHONE.................................650 877-1560
Robert Prescott, Mgr
EMP: 202
SALES (corp-wide): 240.13MM **Privately Held**
Web: www.primeflight.com
SIC: 4581 Airports, flying fields, and services
HQ: Primeflight Aviation Services, Inc.
7135 Charlotte Pike # 100
Nashville TN
615 312-7856

(P-3908)
ROTORCRAFT SUPPORT INC
67 D St (93015-1668)
PHONE.................................818 997-7667
Phillip G Difiore, Pr
Teri Neville, *
Jeffrey Teubner, *
▲ EMP: 63 EST: 1986
SQ FT: 10,000
SALES (est): 12.99MM **Privately Held**
Web: www.rotorcraftsupport.com
SIC: 4581 5088 5599 Aircraft maintenance and repair services; Helicopter parts; Aircraft instruments, equipment or parts

(P-3909)
SAN DEGO CNTY RGNAL ARPRT AUTH (PA)
Also Called: Sdcraa
3225 N Harbor Dr Fl 3 (92101-1045)
P.O. Box 82776 (92138-2776)
PHONE.................................619 400-2400
Thella F Bowens, CEO
EMP: 229 EST: 2003
SALES (est): 215.94MM
SALES (corp-wide): 215.94MM **Privately Held**
Web: www.san.org
SIC: 4581 Airport

(P-3910)
SAN DEGO CNTY RGNAL ARPRT AUTH
2320 Stillwater Rd (92101-1016)
PHONE.................................619 400-2404
EMP: 63
SALES (corp-wide): 215.94MM **Privately Held**
Web: www.san.org
SIC: 4581 Airport
PA: San Diego County Regional Airport Authority
3225 N Harbor Dr Fl 3
San Diego CA
619 400-2400

(P-3911)
SONOMA CNTY SCURITIZATION CORP
575 Administration Dr Rm 105a (95403-2823)
PHONE.................................707 565-2241
EMP: 76 EST: 2010

4581 - Airports, Flying Fields, And Services (P-3912)

SALES (est): 821.64K Privately Held
Web: sonomacounty.ca.gov
SIC: 4581 Airport

(P-3912)
SUNSET AVIATION LLC
7951 Earhart Rd (94621-4530)
PHONE.................................510 783-3584
EMP: 183
Web: www.solairus.aero
SIC: 4581 Airports, flying fields, and services
PA: Sunset Aviation Llc
201 1st St Ste 307
Petaluma CA

(P-3913)
SWISSPORT CARGO SERVICES LP
5757 W Century Blvd Ste 860 (90045-6401)
PHONE.................................703 742-4300
EMP: 66
SALES (corp-wide): 2.67MM Privately Held
Web: www.swissport.com
SIC: 4581 Air freight handling at airports
HQ: Swissport Cargo Services, L.P.
23723 Air Frt Ln Bldg 5
Dulles VA
703 742-4300

(P-3914)
SWISSPORT CARGO SERVICES LP
Also Called: Cargo Service Center
11001 Aviation Blvd (90045-6123)
PHONE.................................310 910-9541
Mark Wood, Genl Mgr
EMP: 154
SALES (corp-wide): 2.67MM Privately Held
Web: www.swissport.com
SIC: 4581 Airport terminal services
HQ: Swissport Cargo Services, L.P.
23723 Air Frt Ln Bldg 5
Dulles VA
703 742-4300

(P-3915)
SWISSPORT USA INC
Also Called: Employment Intake Training Ctr
7025 W Imperial Hwy (90045-6313)
PHONE.................................310 345-1986
Jerry Harris, Genl Mgr
EMP: 82
SALES (corp-wide): 2.67MM Privately Held
Web: www.swissport.com
SIC: 4581 Air freight handling at airports
HQ: Swissport Usa, Inc.
227 Fayetteville St # 900
Raleigh NC

(P-3916)
SWISSPORT USA INC
San Francisco Intl Airport (94128)
PHONE.................................650 821-6220
EMP: 62
SALES (corp-wide): 2.67MM Privately Held
Web: www.swissport.com
SIC: 4581 Airport terminal services
HQ: Swissport Usa, Inc.
227 Fayetteville St # 900
Raleigh NC

(P-3917)
SWISSPORT USA INC
11001 Aviation Blvd (90045-6123)
PHONE.................................310 910-9560
EMP: 67
SALES (corp-wide): 2.67MM Privately Held
Web: www.swissport.com
SIC: 4581 Airport terminal services
HQ: Swissport Usa, Inc.
227 Fayetteville St # 900
Raleigh NC

(P-3918)
TOTAL AIRPORT SERVICES LLC
3537 Branson Dr (94403-2901)
PHONE.................................650 358-0144
Ralph Eichenbaum, Brnch Mgr
EMP: 145
SALES (corp-wide): 155.31MM Privately Held
Web: www.totalairportservices.com
SIC: 4581 Aircraft maintenance and repair services
HQ: Total Airport Services, Llc
9130 S Dadeland Blvd # 1801
Miami FL
832 592-0048

(P-3919)
TRAVIS FLIGHT SERVICE INC
2112 Adams Ave (94577-1010)
P.O. Box Hh (94533-0657)
PHONE.................................707 437-4900
August John Loustau, Pr
Lillian Loustau, *
EMP: 60 **EST:** 1964
SQ FT: 5,000
SALES (est): 2.49MM Privately Held
SIC: 4581 Aircraft servicing and repairing

(P-3920)
TRUX TRANSPORT
237 Harbor Way (94080-6811)
P.O. Box 2505 (94083-2505)
PHONE.................................650 244-0200
Robert Simms, Pr
Edna Simms, *
▲ **EMP:** 100 **EST:** 1968
SQ FT: 50,000
SALES (est): 9.08MM Privately Held
Web: www.truxairlinecargo.com
SIC: 4581 Air freight handling at airports

(P-3921)
UNIVERSITY CALIFORNIA DAVIS
Also Called: Transportation Service Dept
1 Shields Ave (95616-8500)
PHONE.................................530 752-5435
EMP: 64
SALES (corp-wide): 534.4MM Privately Held
Web: www.ucdavis.edu
SIC: 4581 8221 9411 Airports, flying fields, and services; University; Administration of educational programs
HQ: University Of California, Davis
1 Shields Ave
Davis CA

(P-3922)
WORLD SVC WST/LA INFLGHT SVC L
Also Called: L.A. Inflight Service Company
1812 W 135th St (90249-2520)
PHONE.................................310 538-7000
Steven H Yoon, Managing Member
◆ **EMP:** 170 **EST:** 1988
SQ FT: 13,572
SALES (est): 2.08MM Privately Held
SIC: 4581 Aircraft cleaning and janitorial service

4613 Refined Petroleum Pipelines

(P-3923)
SFPP LP (DH)
1100 W Town And Country Rd Ste 600 (92868-4647)
PHONE.................................714 560-4400
Park Shaper, Genl Pt
Richard D Kinder, Genl Pt
EMP: 150 **EST:** 1998
SQ FT: 75,000
SALES (est): 319.91MM Publicly Held
Web: www.kindermorgan.com
SIC: 4613 Gasoline pipelines (common carriers)
HQ: Kinder Morgan Energy Partners, L.P.
1001 La St Ste 1000
Houston TX
713 369-9000

4724 Travel Agencies

(P-3924)
ALTOUR INTERNATIONAL INC (PA)
12100 W Olympic Blvd Ste 300 (90064-1051)
PHONE.................................310 571-6000
Alexander Chemla, Pr
David Sefton, *
EMP: 80 **EST:** 1995
SQ FT: 8,000
SALES (est): 25.7MM Privately Held
Web: www.altour.com
SIC: 4724 Travel agencies

(P-3925)
ALTOUR INTERNATIONAL INC
Also Called: Altour Travel Master
10635 Santa Monica Blvd Ste 200 (90025-8300)
PHONE.................................310 571-6000
EMP: 263
Web: www.altour.com
SIC: 4724 Travel agencies
PA: Altour International, Inc.
1270 Avenue Of The Flr 15
New York NY

(P-3926)
AMAWATERWAYS LLC (PA)
4500 Park Granada # 200 (91302-1677)
PHONE.................................800 626-0126
EMP: 245 **EST:** 2008
SALES (est): 86.22MM Privately Held
Web: www.amawaterways.com
SIC: 4724 Travel agencies

(P-3927)
AMERICAN TRAVEL SOLUTIONS LLC (PA)
Also Called: Amtrav
27509 Agoura Rd Ste 100 (91301-5150)
PHONE.................................818 359-6514
Jeff Klee, CEO
Craig Fichtelberg, COO
EMP: 65 **EST:** 1989
SALES (est): 9.75MM Privately Held
SIC: 4724 4729 Tourist agency arranging transport, lodging and car rental; Airline ticket offices

(P-3928)
AMERICANTOURS INTL LLC (HQ)
6053 W Century Blvd Ste 700 (90045-6430)
PHONE.................................310 641-9953
Michael Fitzpatrick, *
EMP: 105 **EST:** 2003
SQ FT: 20,000
SALES (est): 29.11MM
SALES (corp-wide): 29.11MM Privately Held
Web: www.americantours.com
SIC: 4724 4725 Travel agencies; Tour operators
PA: Americantours International Inc.
6053 W Century Blvd # 70
Los Angeles CA
310 641-9953

(P-3929)
BOOKING COM
5700 Wilshire Blvd Ste 285 (90036-3654)
PHONE.................................323 801-4200
Anthony Booking, Prin
EMP: 141 **EST:** 2013
SALES (est): 1.33MM Privately Held
Web: www.booking.com
SIC: 4724 Travel agencies

(P-3930)
FLIGHT CENTRE USA INC
888 W 6th St Ste 110 (90017-2728)
PHONE.................................310 458-3310
Robin Durham, Pr
EMP: 65
SIC: 4724 4729 Tourist agency arranging transport, lodging and car rental; Airline ticket offices
HQ: Flight Centre Usa, Inc.
1000 E Dominguez St # 200
Carson CA
213 346-0230

(P-3931)
HELLOWORLD TRAVEL SVCS USA INC
Also Called: Qantas Vctons Nwmans Vacations
6171 W Century Blvd Ste 160 (90045-5300)
PHONE.................................310 535-1005
Ross Webster, Pr
Gary Goeldner, *
EMP: 100 **EST:** 1985
SALES (est): 21.7MM Privately Held
Web: www.qantasvacations.com
SIC: 4724 Tourist agency arranging transport, lodging and car rental
PA: Helloworld Travel Limited
179 Normanby Rd
South Melbourne VIC

(P-3932)
HIPCAMP INC (PA)
965 Market St Ste 480 (94103-1701)
PHONE.................................242 377-8982
Alyssa Ravasio, CEO
EMP: 110 **EST:** 2013
SALES (est): 14.57MM
SALES (corp-wide): 14.57MM Privately Held
Web: www.hipcamp.com
SIC: 4724 Travel agencies

(P-3933)
HORNBLOWER GROUP INC (PA)
Pier 3 The Embarcadero (94111)
PHONE.................................415 635-2210
Terry Macrae, Ofcr
Kevin Rabbitt, CEO
Adam C Peakes, Ex VP
EMP: 494 **EST:** 2008
SALES (est): 63.63MM
SALES (corp-wide): 63.63MM Privately Held

PRODUCTS & SERVICES SECTION
4724 - Travel Agencies (P-3954)

Web: www.cityexperiences.com
SIC: 4724 Travel agencies

(P-3934)
HORNBLOWER YACHTS LLC (PA)
Also Called: California Hornblower
Pier 3 The Embarcadero (94111)
PHONE...............................415 424-4309
Terry Macrae, *Ch*
EMP: 250 EST: 1980
SALES (est): 495.57MM
SALES (corp-wide): 495.57MM **Privately Held**
Web: www.cityexperiences.com
SIC: 4724 Travel agencies

(P-3935)
HORNBLOWER YACHTS LLC
Also Called: Hornblower Cruisers and Events
2527 W Coast Hwy (92663-4709)
PHONE...............................949 650-2412
Kevin Lorton, *Brnch Mgr*
EMP: 552
SALES (corp-wide): 495.57MM **Privately Held**
Web: www.cityexperiences.com
SIC: 4724 Travel agencies
PA: Hornblower Yachts, Llc
   The Embarcadero Pier 3 St Pier
   San Francisco CA
   415 424-4309

(P-3936)
IDS INC
Also Called: IDS Technology
20300 Ventura Blvd Ste 200 (91364-2448)
PHONE...............................866 297-5757
Nathan Morad, *CEO*
Alberto Gamez, *CMO**
John Ledo, *
Gary Kurtz, *Legal Counsel**
EMP: 97 EST: 2009
SQ FT: 9,000
SALES (est): 4.25MM **Privately Held**
Web: www.idscontrols.com
SIC: 4724 7372 Travel agencies; Business oriented computer software

(P-3937)
JTB AMERICAS LTD (HQ)
3625 Del Amo Blvd Ste 260 (90503-1688)
PHONE...............................310 406-3121
Tsuneo Irita, *Pr*
Benny Harrell, *
EMP: 100 EST: 1963
SALES (est): 196.64MM **Privately Held**
Web: www.jtbamericas.com
SIC: 4724 Travel agencies
PA: Jtb Corp.
   2-3-11, Higashishinagawa
   Shinagawa-Ku TKY

(P-3938)
LBC HOLDINGS USA CORPORATION (PA)
362 E Grand Ave (94080-6210)
PHONE...............................650 873-0750
EMP: 164 EST: 1986
SQ FT: 25,000
SALES (est): 21.01MM **Privately Held**
SIC: 4724 4513 4412 Travel agencies; Air courier services; Deep sea foreign transportation of freight

(P-3939)
LBF TRAVEL INC
Also Called: Travelerhelpdesk.com
4545 Murphy Canyon Rd Ste 210 (92123-4318)
PHONE...............................858 429-7599
Michael H Thomas, *CEO*
Adrian Myram, *
EMP: 300 EST: 2010
SALES (est): 41.74MM **Privately Held**
Web: www.lbftravel.com
SIC: 4724 Tourist agency arranging transport, lodging and car rental

(P-3940)
MAGICAL CRUISE COMPANY LIMITED
500 S Buena Vista St (91521-0001)
PHONE...............................800 742-8939
EMP: 79
SALES (corp-wide): 261.49K **Privately Held**
Web: www.mmvbrandon.com
SIC: 4724 Tourist agency arranging transport, lodging and car rental
HQ: Magical Cruise Company, Limited
   3 Queen Caroline Street
   London

(P-3941)
NAVAN INC (PA)
3045 Park Blvd (94306-2231)
PHONE...............................888 505-8747
Ariel Cohen, *CEO*
Thomas Tuchscherer, *CFO*
EMP: 156 EST: 2015
SALES (est): 228.09MM
SALES (corp-wide): 228.09MM **Privately Held**
Web: www.navan.com
SIC: 4724 Travel agencies

(P-3942)
NIPPON TRAVEL AGENCY AMER INC
Also Called: Nta America
1411 W 190th St Ste 650 (90248-4369)
PHONE...............................310 768-1817
Tadashi Wakayama, *Pr*
EMP: 70 EST: 1999
SQ FT: 8,000
SALES (est): 10.78MM **Privately Held**
Web: www.ntaamerica.com
SIC: 4724 Tourist agency arranging transport, lodging and car rental
HQ: Nippon Travel Agency Co., Ltd.
   1-19-1, Nihombashi
   Chuo-Ku TKY

(P-3943)
NIPPON TRAVEL AGENCY PCF INC (DH)
Also Called: Nta Pacific
1411 W 190th St Ste 650 (90248-4369)
PHONE...............................310 768-0017
Tadashi Wakayama, *Pr*
Akio Tsuna, *
▲ EMP: 80 EST: 1973
SQ FT: 20,000
SALES (est): 48.73MM **Privately Held**
Web: www.ntaamerica.com
SIC: 4724 Tourist agency arranging transport, lodging and car rental
HQ: Nippon Travel Agency Co., Ltd.
   1-19-1, Nihombashi
   Chuo-Ku TKY

(P-3944)
ONELINK CORPORATION
1 Market Plz (94105-1101)
PHONE...............................415 293-8277
F W Guerin, *CEO*
EMP: 85 EST: 2002
SALES (est): 9.8MM **Privately Held**

SIC: 4724 Travel agencies

(P-3945)
OXY INC
Also Called: OXY-World Travel
10889 Wilshire Blvd (90024-4200)
PHONE...............................310 824-1315
Donald L Moore, *Pr*
EMP: 104 EST: 1974
SALES (est): 12.39MM
SALES (corp-wide): 37.09B **Publicly Held**
Web: www.oxy.com
SIC: 4724 Tourist agency arranging transport, lodging and car rental
PA: Occidental Petroleum Corporation
   5 Greenway Plz Ste 110
   Houston TX
   713 215-7000

(P-3946)
PINNACLE TRAVEL SERVICES LLC
390 N Pacific Coast Hwy (90245-4475)
PHONE...............................310 414-1787
Robert G Singh, *CEO*
EMP: 151 EST: 1999
SQ FT: 15,000
SALES (est): 23.23MM **Privately Held**
Web: www.ptsla.com
SIC: 4724 Tourist agency arranging transport, lodging and car rental

(P-3947)
PLEASANT HOLIDAYS LLC (HQ)
Also Called: Pleasant Hawaiian Holiday
2404 Townsgate Rd (91361-2505)
PHONE...............................818 991-3390
Jack E Richards, *CEO*
Duke Ah Moo, *
Bruce Rosenberg, *
EMP: 300 EST: 1998
SQ FT: 55,000
SALES (est): 154.34MM
SALES (corp-wide): 1.08B **Privately Held**
Web: beta.pleasantholidays.com
SIC: 4724 Tourist agency arranging transport, lodging and car rental
PA: Automobile Club Of Southern California
   2601 S Figueroa St
   Los Angeles CA
   213 741-3686

(P-3948)
PRINCESS CRUISE LINES LTD
Also Called: Princess Cruises
24833 Anza Dr (91355-1259)
P.O. Box 966 (91380-9066)
PHONE...............................661 753-2197
Princess Cruise, *Prin*
EMP: 1114
SALES (corp-wide): 3.94B **Privately Held**
Web: www.princess.com
SIC: 4724 Travel agencies
HQ: Princess Cruise Lines, Ltd.
   24305 Town Center Dr
   Santa Clarita CA
   661 753-0000

(P-3949)
PROTRAVEL INTERNATIONAL LLC
345 N Maple Dr (90210-3869)
PHONE...............................310 271-9566
Sara Sessa, *Brnch Mgr*
EMP: 100
SALES (corp-wide): 97.32MM **Privately Held**
Web: www.protravelinc.com
SIC: 4724 Travel agencies
PA: Protravel International Llc
   1633 Broadway Fl 35
   New York NY
   212 755-4550

(P-3950)
SEAT PLANNERS LLC
311 4th Ave Apt 509 (92101-6973)
PHONE...............................619 237-9434
Veronica Sosa, *Prin*
Antonio Sosa, *
EMP: 75 EST: 2019
SALES (est): 3.69MM **Privately Held**
Web: www.seatplanners.com
SIC: 4724 Travel agencies

(P-3951)
SKYLINK TRAVEL INC
18000 Studebaker Rd Ste 330 (90703-2674)
PHONE...............................212 380-2438
Moon K Lee, *Prin*
EMP: 103
SALES (corp-wide): 159.48MM **Publicly Held**
Web: www.skylinkus.com
SIC: 4724 Travel agencies
HQ: Skylink Travel Inc.
   15 W 36th St Fl 4
   New York NY
   212 380-2438

(P-3952)
SNAPCOMMERCE INC (PA)
Also Called: Snap Travel
18 Bartol St (94133-4501)
PHONE...............................917 704-4588
Hussein Fazal, *CEO*
Daniel Weisenfeld, *CFO*
Henry Shi, *COO*
EMP: 95 EST: 2016
SALES (est): 23.53MM
SALES (corp-wide): 23.53MM **Privately Held**
Web: www.snaptravel.com
SIC: 4724 Travel agencies

(P-3953)
TRANS-AMERICAN TRAVEL
Also Called: Trans AM Travel
4929 Wilshire Blvd Ste 310 (90010-3808)
PHONE...............................310 670-2111
EMP: 85
SALES (corp-wide): 159.48MM **Publicly Held**
Web: www.transamtravel.com
SIC: 4724 Tourist agency arranging transport, lodging and car rental
HQ: Trans Am Travel, Inc.
   4222 King St
   Alexandria VA
   703 880-4540

(P-3954)
TRAVEL STORE (PA)
Also Called: Travelstore
11601 Wilshire Blvd Ste 300 (90025-0509)
P.O. Box 6576 (90734-6576)
PHONE...............................310 575-5540
Wido Schaefer, *Pr*
Osvaldo Ramos, *
Dan Ilves, *
EMP: 70 EST: 1975
SQ FT: 7,000
SALES (est): 48.6MM
SALES (corp-wide): 48.6MM **Privately Held**
Web: www.travelstore.com
SIC: 4724 Tourist agency arranging transport, lodging and car rental

4724 - Travel Agencies (P-3955)

PRODUCTS & SERVICES SECTION

(P-3955)
TRAVEL WIZARD LLC
100 Smith Ranch Rd Ste 110 (94903-1900)
PHONE..................................415 446-5252
EMP: 67 **EST:** 1998
SALES (est): 16MM **Privately Held**
Web: www.travelwizard.com
SIC: 4724 Tourist agency arranging transport, lodging and car rental

(P-3956)
UBER
101 Jefferson Dr (94025-1114)
PHONE..................................866 440-6700
Brent Ritz, Ch Bd
EMP: 100 **EST:** 2004
SALES (est): 10.93MM **Privately Held**
Web: www.uberrealestate.com
SIC: 4724 7299 6531 Travel agencies; Information services, consumer; Real estate brokers and agents

4725 Tour Operators

(P-3957)
ACCENT HOSPITALITY GROUP LLC
Also Called: Nature Expeditions Africa
2830 I St Ste 104 (95816-4311)
PHONE..................................415 286-2867
EMP: 149 **EST:** 2016
SALES (est): 4.06MM **Privately Held**
SIC: 4725 Tour operators

(P-3958)
ALCATRAZ CRUISES LLC
Pier 33 Hornblower Alcatraz Landing (94111)
PHONE..................................415 981-7625
EMP: 66 **EST:** 2005
SALES (est): 21.43MM **Privately Held**
Web: www.cityexperiences.com
SIC: 4725 Tours, conducted

(P-3959)
ANTENNA AUDIO INC (PA)
Also Called: Antenna International
555 W 5th St Ste 3725 (90013-2670)
PHONE..................................203 523-0320
Janet Matricciani, CEO
Ira Morgenstern, *
▲ **EMP:** 796 **EST:** 1997
SALES (est): 20.98MM
SALES (corp-wide): 20.98MM **Privately Held**
Web: www.antenna-international.com
SIC: 4725 Tour operators

(P-3960)
BACKROADS (PA)
801 Cedar St (94710-1800)
PHONE..................................510 527-1555
Tom Hale, CEO
EMP: 100 **EST:** 1979
SQ FT: 10,000
SALES (est): 96.89MM
SALES (corp-wide): 96.89MM **Privately Held**
Web: www.backroads.com
SIC: 4725 4724 Sightseeing tour companies; Travel agencies

(P-3961)
BLUE BUS TOURS LLC
Also Called: Grayline of San Francisco
10 Industrial Way (94005-1002)
PHONE..................................415 353-5310
Xavier Valls Pinilla, CEO
EMP: 120 **EST:** 2011
SALES (est): 7.95MM **Privately Held**
Web: www.graylineofsanfrancisco.com
SIC: 4725 Tours, conducted

(P-3962)
CLASSIC VACATIONS LLC
Also Called: Classic Custom Vacations
5669 Snell Ave Ste 343 (95123-3328)
PHONE..................................408 287-4550
David Hu, Pr
EMP: 149 **EST:** 2005
SALES (est): 50.28MM **Privately Held**
Web: www.classicvacations.com
SIC: 4725 Arrangement of travel tour packages, wholesale
PA: Najafi Companies, Llc
    2525 E Camelback Rd Ste 8
    Phoenix AZ

(P-3963)
CONTIKI US HOLDINGS INC
Also Called: Contiki Holidays
5551 Katella Ave (90630-5002)
PHONE..................................714 935-0808
Christopher Mcconnell, Prin
Christopher Mcconnell, CFO
Richard Launder, *
EMP: 60 **EST:** 1981
SALES (est): 13.85MM **Privately Held**
Web: www.contiki.com
SIC: 4725 4724 Tours, conducted; Tourist agency arranging transport, lodging and car rental

(P-3964)
JOGURU INC
2600 El Camino Real Ste 416 (94306-1705)
PHONE..................................855 526-4332
Praveen Kumar, CEO
Saket Newaskar, *
EMP: 75 **EST:** 2014
SQ FT: 2,500
SALES (est): 4.83MM **Privately Held**
SIC: 4725 Arrangement of travel tour packages, wholesale

(P-3965)
PACIFIC COAST SIGHTSEEING TOUR
2001 S Manchester Ave (92802-3803)
PHONE..................................714 507-1157
Kristin Martinez, General Mng
Luis Silva, *
EMP: 230 **EST:** 2012
SALES (est): 23MM **Privately Held**
Web: www.anaheimoc.org
SIC: 4725 4173 Arrangement of travel tour packages, wholesale; Bus terminal operation
HQ: Coach Usa, Inc.
    160 S Route 17 N
    Paramus NJ

(P-3966)
PRINCESS CRUISE LINES LTD
24200 Magic Mountain Pkwy (91355-4886)
PHONE..................................661 753-0000
Barbara Potter, Brnch Mgr
EMP: 11523
SALES (corp-wide): 3.94B **Privately Held**
Web: www.princess.com
SIC: 4725 7011 4481 Tours, conducted; Hotels; Deep sea passenger transportation, except ferry
HQ: Princess Cruise Lines, Ltd.
    24305 Town Center Dr
    Santa Clarita CA
    661 753-0000

(P-3967)
SANTA BARBARA CITY OF
Also Called: Courthuse Tours-Docent Council
1100 Anacapa St Dept 3 (93101-6013)
PHONE..................................805 962-6464
Lori Bevon, Pr
EMP: 60
SALES (corp-wide): 233.22MM **Privately Held**
Web: www.santabarbaraca.gov
SIC: 4725 Tours, conducted
PA: City Of Santa Barbara
    735 Anacapa St
    Santa Barbara CA
    805 963-0611

(P-3968)
SANTA BARBARA ADVENTURE CO
Also Called: Santa Barbara Wine Cntry Tours
32 E Haley St (93101-2316)
P.O. Box 208 (93102-0208)
PHONE..................................805 884-9283
Michael T Cohen, CEO
EMP: 64 **EST:** 1998
SQ FT: 4,000
SALES (est): 6.86MM **Privately Held**
Web: www.sbadventureco.com
SIC: 4725 Tours, conducted

(P-3969)
SANTA CATALINA ISLAND COMPANY (PA)
Also Called: Scico
4 Park Plz Ste 420 (92614-5259)
P.O. Box 737 (90704-0737)
PHONE..................................310 510-2000
Randall Herrel Senior, CEO
Paxson H Offield, *
John T Dravinski, *
Ronald C Doutt, *
EMP: 114 **EST:** 1959
SALES (est): 78.14MM
SALES (corp-wide): 78.14MM **Privately Held**
Web: www.visitcatalinaisland.com
SIC: 4725 Sightseeing tour companies

(P-3970)
SCREAMLINE INVESTMENT CORP
Also Called: Tourcoach Transportation
2130 S Tubeway Ave (90040-1614)
PHONE..................................323 201-0114
Kamrouz Farhadi, CEO
Vahid Sapir, *
Farima Akopians, *
Shoeleh Sapir, *
▲ **EMP:** 120 **EST:** 1992
SQ FT: 8,000
SALES (est): 24.5MM **Privately Held**
Web: www.tourcoach.com
SIC: 4725 Sightseeing tour companies

(P-3971)
VIP TOURS OF CALIFORNIA INC
1419 E Maple Ave (90245-3302)
PHONE..................................310 216-7507
Marco Khorasani, Pr
Nicole J Khorasani, *
EMP: 70 **EST:** 2002
SALES (est): 9.87MM **Privately Held**
Web: www.viptoursofcalifornia.com
SIC: 4725 Tours, conducted

4729 Passenger Transportation Arrangement

(P-3972)
KOREAN AIRLINES CO LTD
Also Called: Korean Air
900 Wilshire Blvd Ste 1100 (90017-4701)
PHONE..................................213 484-5700
Kitaek Kang, Genl Mgr
EMP: 489
Web: www.koreanair.com
SIC: 4729 Airline ticket offices
PA: Korean Airlines Co., Ltd.
    260 Haneul-Gil, Gangseo-Gu
    Seoul

(P-3973)
MATRIX AVIATION SERVICES INC
6171 W Century Blvd Ste 100 (90045-5300)
PHONE..................................310 337-3037
Ramez Reno, CEO
Borseen Oushana, *
EMP: 175 **EST:** 2008
SQ FT: 3,000
SALES (est): 21.24MM **Privately Held**
Web: www.matrix-aviation.com
SIC: 4729 Airline ticket offices

4731 Freight Transportation Arrangement

(P-3974)
ABLE FREIGHT SERVICES LLC (PA)
5340 W 104th St (90045-6010)
PHONE..................................310 568-8883
◆ **EMP:** 90 **EST:** 1992
SALES (est): 30.82MM **Privately Held**
Web: www.ablefreight.com
SIC: 4731 Freight forwarding

(P-3975)
ADCOM EXPRESS INC
33830 Channel St (92592-5618)
PHONE..................................626 606-5160
EMP: 68
SALES (corp-wide): 1.09B **Publicly Held**
Web: www.adcomworldwide.com
SIC: 4731 Freight forwarding
HQ: Adcom Express, Inc.
    Triton Twers Two 700 S Ru
    Renton WA
    425 462-1094

(P-3976)
ADCOM EXPRESS INC
1404 E Walnut Ave # A (92831-4730)
PHONE..................................714 870-7447
EMP: 68
SALES (corp-wide): 1.09B **Publicly Held**
Web: www.adcomworldwide.com
SIC: 4731 Domestic freight forwarding
HQ: Adcom Express, Inc.
    Triton Twers Two 700 S Ru
    Renton WA
    425 462-1094

(P-3977)
ADVANTAGE LOGISTICS INC
Also Called: CTS Advantage Logistics
2071 Ringwood Ave Ste D (95131-1760)
P.O. Box 612438 (95161-2438)
PHONE..................................408 943-6300
▲ **EMP:** 185

PRODUCTS & SERVICES SECTION
4731 - Freight Transportation Arrangement (P-3998)

SIC: 4731 Freight transportation arrangement

(P-3978)
AGILITY HOLDINGS INC (DH)
Also Called: Agility Logistics
310 Commerce Ste 250 (92602-1399)
PHONE..................714 617-6300
◆ EMP: 80 EST: 1996
SALES (est): 1.01B
SALES (corp-wide): 32.91B Privately Held
SIC: 4731 4213 4214 Domestic freight forwarding; Household goods transport; Household goods moving and storage, local
HQ: Agility Logistics International B.V.
   Incheonweg 17
   Rozenburg Nh NH
   884360105

(P-3979)
AGILITY LOGISTICS CORP (DH)
Also Called: Global Integrated Logistics
310 Commerce Ste 250 (92602-1399)
PHONE..................714 617-6300
◆ EMP: 90 EST: 1973
SALES (est): 426.24MM
SALES (corp-wide): 32.91B Privately Held
Web: www.agility.com
SIC: 4731 7372 1381 Freight transportation arrangement; Prepackaged software; Drilling oil and gas wells
HQ: Agility Holdings, Inc.
   310 Commerce Ste 250
   Irvine CA

(P-3980)
AIR EXPRESS INTL USA INC
Also Called: Dhl Global Forwarding
19900 S Vermont Ave Ste A (90502-1147)
PHONE..................310 297-4401
Tim Robertson, Mgr
EMP: 85
SALES (corp-wide): 98.08B Privately Held
SIC: 4731 Freight forwarding
HQ: Air Express International Usa, Inc.
   1210 S Pine Island Rd
   Plantation FL
   786 264-3500

(P-3981)
AIR GROUP LEASING INC
1111 E Watson Center Rd Ste C (90745-4217)
PHONE..................310 684-4095
Victor Leigh, Pr
Thomas Bowling, *
▲ EMP: 1591 EST: 1992
SQ FT: 2,900
SALES (est): 5.93MM
SALES (corp-wide): 9.65B Publicly Held
SIC: 4731 4513 Freight forwarding; Package delivery, private air
PA: Alaska Air Group, Inc
   19300 International Blvd
   Seatac WA
   206 392-5040

(P-3982)
AIR-SEA FORWARDERS INC (PA)
9009 S La Cienega Blvd (90301-4459)
P.O. Box 90637 (90009-0637)
PHONE..................310 216-1616
Todd Hinkley, CEO
Paul Talley, *
Monica Villavicencio, *
Luisa Nakamura, *
◆ EMP: 60 EST: 1950
SQ FT: 42,000
SALES (est): 22.21MM
SALES (corp-wide): 22.21MM Privately Held

Web: www.airseainc.com
SIC: 4731 Foreign freight forwarding

(P-3983)
ALBA WHEELS UP INTL LLC
839 Mitten Rd (94066)
PHONE..................650 952-0815
Damien Stile, CEO
EMP: 68
SALES (corp-wide): 75.87MM Privately Held
Web: www.albawheelsup.com
SIC: 4731 8741 Customhouse brokers; Management services
HQ: Alba Wheels Up International, Llc
   1 E Lincoln Ave
   Valley Stream NY
   718 276-3000

(P-3984)
ALLEN LUND COMPANY LLC (HQ)
4529 Angeles Crest Hwy Ste 300 (91011-3247)
P.O. Box 1369 (91012-5369)
PHONE..................818 777-6142
David Lund, Mgr
Kathleen M Lund, *
Edward V Lund, *
Steve Doerfler, *
EMP: 70 EST: 1976
SQ FT: 16,000
SALES (est): 201.71MM Privately Held
Web: www.allenlund.com
SIC: 4731 Truck transportation brokers
PA: Allen Lund Corporation
   4529 Angeles Crest Hwy
   La Canada Flintridge CA

(P-3985)
APEX LOGISTICS INTL INC (PA)
Also Called: Apex USA
18554 S Susana Rd (90221-5620)
PHONE..................310 665-0288
Elsie Qian, CEO
Hui Qian, *
▲ EMP: 227 EST: 2003
SALES (est): 2.72B
SALES (corp-wide): 2.72B Privately Held
Web: www.apexglobe.com
SIC: 4731 Freight forwarding

(P-3986)
APM TERMINALS PACIFIC LLC
Also Called: Mearsk
2500 Navy Way Pier 400 (90731-7554)
PHONE..................310 221-4000
Milan D.o.s., Brnch Mgr
EMP: 401
SALES (corp-wide): 77.53B Privately Held
Web: www.apmterminals.com
SIC: 4731 Agents, shipping
HQ: Apm Terminals Pacific Llc
   9300 Arrowpoint Blvd
   Charlotte NC

(P-3987)
ATECH LOGISTICS INC
Also Called: Atech Logistics & Distribution
7 College Ave (95401-4702)
P.O. Box 6836 (95406-0836)
PHONE..................707 526-1910
Jesse E Amaral, Pr
Geri Amaral, *
EMP: 130 EST: 2002
SQ FT: 35,000
SALES (est): 31.83MM Privately Held
Web: www.atechlogistics.com
SIC: 4731 Freight forwarding

(P-3988)
BINEX LINE CORP (PA)
Also Called: BINEX
19515 S Vermont Ave (90502-1121)
PHONE..................310 416-8600
David Paek, Pr
Tim Park, *
Hyun K Cho, *
◆ EMP: 70 EST: 1995
SQ FT: 32,000
SALES (est): 271.3MM Privately Held
Web: www.binexline.com
SIC: 4731 Freight transportation arrangement

(P-3989)
BLACKROCK LOGISTICS INC (PA)
7031 Koll Center Pkwy Ste 250 (94566-3181)
PHONE..................925 523-3878
Larry T James, Pr
Mark J Polland, *
Jeff R Mitchell, *
Nora Schild, *
EMP: 63 EST: 2013
SALES (est): 44.52MM
SALES (corp-wide): 44.52MM Privately Held
Web: www.blackrock-logistics.net
SIC: 4731 Freight forwarding

(P-3990)
BLACKROCK LOGISTICS INC
Also Called: Blackrock Logistics
14601 Slover Ave (92337-7163)
PHONE..................909 259-5357
Larry T James, Pr
EMP: 114
SALES (corp-wide): 44.52MM Privately Held
Web: www.blackrock-logistics.net
SIC: 4731 Freight forwarding
PA: Blackrock Logistics Inc.
   7031 Koll Center Pkwy # 250
   Pleasanton CA
   925 523-3878

(P-3991)
CALIFORNIA NORTHERN RR CO
600 M St Ste 3 (95363-2100)
PHONE..................530 406-8981
Kurt Bedford, Brnch Mgr
EMP: 72
SALES (corp-wide): 2.17MM Privately Held
Web: www.woodlandchamber.org
SIC: 4731 Freight transportation arrangement
PA: California Northern Railroad Company
   1166 Oak Ave
   Woodland CA
   800 557-7387

(P-3992)
CAPABLE TRANSPORT INC
3528 Torrance Blvd Ste 220 (90503-4826)
PHONE..................310 697-0198
Steven Troyer, Pr
EMP: 70 EST: 2004
SALES (est): 4.7MM Privately Held
SIC: 4731 Truck transportation brokers

(P-3993)
CARGOMATIC INC (PA)
211 E Ocean Blvd Ste 350 (90802-4808)
PHONE..................866 513-2343
Richard Gerstein, CEO
Andrew Straub, *
Matt Hogan, *
Steve Jackson, CAO*
EMP: 129 EST: 2013

SALES (est): 95.65MM
SALES (corp-wide): 95.65MM Privately Held
Web: www.cargomatic.com
SIC: 4731 Transportation agents and brokers

(P-3994)
CARMICHAEL INTERNATIONAL SVC (DH)
Also Called: C I Container Line
1200 Corporate Center Dr Ste 200 (91754)
PHONE..................213 353-0800
John Salvo, Pr
Vince Salvo, *
Jim Ryan, *
◆ EMP: 100 EST: 1961
SQ FT: 19,000
SALES (est): 94.64MM Privately Held
Web: www.carmnet.com
SIC: 4731 Customhouse brokers
HQ: Kintetsu World Express, Inc.
   2-15-1, Konan
   Minato-Ku TKY

(P-3995)
CARROLL FULMER LOGISTICS CORP
13773 Algranti Ave (91342-2607)
PHONE..................626 435-9940
Josh Quijano, Brnch Mgr
EMP: 294
SALES (corp-wide): 182.11MM Privately Held
Web: www.cfulmer.com
SIC: 4731 Truck transportation brokers
HQ: Carroll Fulmer Logistics Corporation
   8340 American Way
   Groveland FL
   352 429-5000

(P-3996)
CEVA LOGISTICS LLC
19600 S Western Ave (90501-1117)
PHONE..................310 223-6500
Marvin O Schlanger, Mgr
EMP: 300
SALES (corp-wide): 31.16K Privately Held
Web: www.cevalogistics.com
SIC: 4731 Domestic freight forwarding
HQ: Ceva Logistics, Llc
   15350 Vickery Dr
   Houston TX
   281 618-3100

(P-3997)
CFR RINKENS LLC (PA)
Also Called: Cfr Rinknes
444 W Ocean Blvd Ste 1200 (90802-8128)
PHONE..................310 639-7725
Maximiliaan Hoes, Managing Member
Christoph Seitz, *
▼ EMP: 75 EST: 2012
SALES (est): 48MM
SALES (corp-wide): 48MM Privately Held
Web: www.cfrrinkens.com
SIC: 4731 Freight forwarding

(P-3998)
CJ LOGISTICS AMERICA LLC
5690 Industrial Pkwy (92407-1885)
PHONE..................540 377-2302
EMP: 190
Web: america.cjlogistics.com
SIC: 4731 Freight forwarding
HQ: Cj Logistics America, Llc
   1750 S Wolf Rd
   Des Plaines IL

4731 - Freight Transportation Arrangement (P-3999)

(P-3999)
CONNER LOGISTICS INC
Also Called: Conner Logistics
4069 W Shaw Ave Ste 103 (93722-6215)
PHONE..............................888 939-4637
Dave Conner, Pr
EMP: 90 EST: 2002
SALES (est): 11.64MM Privately Held
Web: www.connerlogistics.com
SIC: 4731 Freight forwarding

(P-4000)
COUNTY OF YOLO
Also Called: Yolo County Trnsp Dist
350 Industrial Way (95776-6011)
PHONE..............................530 661-0816
Terry Bassett, Dir
EMP: 169
SALES (corp-wide): 456.57MM Privately Held
Web: www.yolocounty.org
SIC: 4731 Transportation agents and brokers
PA: County Of Yolo
625 Court St Ste 102
Woodland CA
530 666-8190

(P-4001)
CROWLEY MARINE SERVICES INC
86 Berth 300 S Harbor Blvd (90731-3353)
PHONE..............................310 732-6500
Andrew Gauphier, Mgr
EMP: 431
Web: www.crowley.com
SIC: 4731 Freight transportation arrangement
HQ: Crowley Marine Services, Inc.
9487 Regency Square Blvd
Jacksonville FL

(P-4002)
DCW DCW INC
20500 Denker Ave (90501-1645)
PHONE..............................310 324-3147
Henry Mandil, CEO
EMP: 100 EST: 2020
SALES (est): 5.71MM Privately Held
SIC: 4731 4225 Freight transportation arrangement; General warehousing and storage

(P-4003)
DE WELL CONTAINER SHIPPING INC
Also Called: Logistics
5553 Bandini Blvd Unit A (90201-6421)
PHONE..............................310 735-8600
Yang Shi, CEO
▲ EMP: 90 EST: 2004
SALES (est): 27.42MM Privately Held
Web: www.de-well.com
SIC: 4731 Freight forwarding
PA: De Well Container Shipping Corp.
No.1568, Gangcheng Road, Pudong New District
Shanghai SH

(P-4004)
DEPENDABLE GLOBAL EXPRESS INC (PA)
Also Called: D G X
19201 S Susana Rd (90221-5710)
P.O. Box 513370 (90051-3370)
PHONE..............................310 537-2000
Ronald Massman, CEO
Bradley Dechter, *
Tim Rice, *
EMP: 144 EST: 2004
SALES (est): 24.8MM Privately Held
Web: www.dgxglobal.com
SIC: 4731 Freight forwarding

(P-4005)
DFDS INTERNATIONAL CORPORATION
Also Called: Dfds Transport US
898 Sepulveda Blvd, 6th Floor (90245-2705)
PHONE..............................310 414-1516
Tina Larsen, Genl Mgr
EMP: 80
SALES (corp-wide): 3.75B Privately Held
Web: www.dfdstransportusa.com
SIC: 4731 Foreign freight forwarding
HQ: Dfds International Corporation
100 Walnut Ave Ste 405
Clark NJ

(P-4006)
DHX-DEPENDABLE HAWAIIAN EX INC
3623 Munster St (94545-1646)
PHONE..............................510 686-2600
EMP: 89
SALES (corp-wide): 108.72MM Privately Held
Web: www.dhx.com
SIC: 4731 Freight forwarding
PA: Dhx-Dependable Hawaiian Express, Inc.
19201 S Susana Rd
Compton CA
310 537-2000

(P-4007)
DHX-DEPENDABLE HAWAIIAN EX INC (PA)
19201 S Susana Rd (90221-5710)
PHONE..............................310 537-2000
Ronald Massman, Ch
Annette Massman, *
Bradley Dechter, *
◆ EMP: 150 EST: 1980
SQ FT: 106,000
SALES (est): 108.72MM
SALES (corp-wide): 108.72MM Privately Held
Web: www.dhx.com
SIC: 4731 Foreign freight forwarding

(P-4008)
DIRECTED LLC
1 Viper Way Ste 1 (92081-7811)
PHONE..............................800 876-0800
Robert Struble, CEO
James Wiesen, *
Joseph Tristani, *
David Meisels, *
EMP: 164 EST: 2014
SQ FT: 83,057
SALES (est): 80MM Privately Held
Web: www.directed.com
SIC: 4731 Domestic freight forwarding

(P-4009)
DISPATCH TRUCKING LLC (PA)
14032 Santa Ana Ave (92337-7035)
PHONE..............................909 355-5531
Bruce L Degler, CEO
Jalayne Pugmire, *
EMP: 70 EST: 1991
SQ FT: 600
SALES (est): 11MM
SALES (corp-wide): 11MM Privately Held
SIC: 4731 Truck transportation brokers

(P-4010)
DSV SOLUTIONS LLC
Also Called: Corp., R.g Barry
13230 San Bernardino Ave (92335-5229)
PHONE..............................909 349-6100
EMP: 105
SALES (corp-wide): 32.91B Privately Held
Web: www.dsv.com
SIC: 4731 Freight forwarding
HQ: Dsv Solutions, Llc
200 Wood Ave S 300
Iselin NJ
732 850-8000

(P-4011)
DSV SOLUTIONS LLC
1670 Etiwanda Ave Ste A (91761-3641)
PHONE..............................909 390-4563
Bob Mccullough, Mgr
EMP: 105
SQ FT: 400,000
SALES (corp-wide): 32.91B Privately Held
Web: www.dsv.com
SIC: 4731 Freight forwarding
HQ: Dsv Solutions, Llc
200 Wood Ave S 300
Iselin NJ
732 850-8000

(P-4012)
DSV SOLUTIONS LLC
3454 E Miraloma Ave (92806-2101)
PHONE..............................714 630-0110
EMP: 90
SALES (corp-wide): 32.91B Privately Held
Web: www.dsv.com
SIC: 4731 Freight forwarding
HQ: Dsv Solutions, Llc
200 Wood Ave S 300
Iselin NJ
732 850-8000

(P-4013)
EMPIRE MED TRANSPORTATIONS LLC
Also Called: Unicare Medical Transportation
1433 W Linden St Ste M (92507-6816)
PHONE..............................877 473-6029
EMP: 83 EST: 2017
SALES (est): 800K Privately Held
SIC: 4731 Freight forwarding

(P-4014)
EXPEDITORS INTL OCEAN INC
5200 W Century Blvd Fl 6 (90045-5939)
PHONE..............................310 343-6200
EMP: 74
SALES (corp-wide): 16.52B Publicly Held
SIC: 4731 Freight forwarding
HQ: Expeditors International Ocean, Inc.
1015 3rd Ave Ste 1200
Seattle WA

(P-4015)
EXPEDITORS INTL WASH INC
19701 Hamilton Ave (90502-1352)
PHONE..............................310 343-6200
Eric Mooney, Brnch Mgr
EMP: 300
SALES (corp-wide): 16.52B Publicly Held
Web: www.expeditors.com
SIC: 4731 Freight forwarding
PA: Expeditors International Of Washington, Inc.
1015 3rd Ave
Seattle WA
206 674-3400

(P-4016)
EXPEDITORS INTL WASH INC
1470 Exposition Way Ste 110 (92154)
PHONE..............................619 710-1900
Trevor Moulton, Mgr
EMP: 60
SALES (corp-wide): 16.52B Publicly Held
Web: www.expeditors.com
SIC: 4731 Freight forwarding
PA: Expeditors International Of Washington, Inc.
1015 3rd Ave
Seattle WA
206 674-3400

(P-4017)
EXPEDITORS INTL WASH INC
12200 Wilkie Ave Ste 100 (90250-1838)
PHONE..............................323 781-1600
EMP: 66
SQ FT: 120,320
SALES (corp-wide): 16.52B Publicly Held
Web: www.expeditors.com
SIC: 4731 Freight forwarding
PA: Expeditors International Of Washington, Inc.
1015 3rd Ave
Seattle WA
206 674-3400

(P-4018)
EXPEDITORS INTL WASH INC
Also Called: Expeditors International
12200 Wilkie Ave # 100 (90250-1838)
PHONE..............................310 343-6200
EMP: 96
SALES (corp-wide): 16.52B Publicly Held
Web: www.expeditors.com
SIC: 4731 Foreign freight forwarding
PA: Expeditors International Of Washington, Inc.
1015 3rd Ave
Seattle WA
206 674-3400

(P-4019)
F R T INTERNATIONAL INC
Also Called: Frontier Logistics Services
2825 Jurupa St (91761-2903)
PHONE..............................909 390-4892
Steven Hall, Brnch Mgr
EMP: 74
SALES (corp-wide): 26.2MM Privately Held
SIC: 4731 Freight forwarding
PA: F. R. T. International, Inc.
1700 N Alameda St
Compton CA
310 604-8208

(P-4020)
FLOCK FREIGHT INC
Also Called: Auptix and Flock Freight
701 S Coast Highway 101 (92024-4441)
PHONE..............................855 744-7585
Oren Zaslansky, CEO
Pete Price, *
Luis Saenz, *
EMP: 120 EST: 2015
SALES (est): 58.1MM Privately Held
Web: www.flockfreight.com
SIC: 4731 Freight forwarding

(P-4021)
FNS INC (PA)
Also Called: FNS
1545 Francisco St (90501-1330)
PHONE..............................661 615-2300
Young Bin Kim, CEO
Dong Eon Kim, *

PRODUCTS & SERVICES SECTION
4731 - Freight Transportation Arrangement (P-4045)

◆ EMP: 100 EST: 1995
SQ FT: 100,000
SALES (est): 511.46MM **Privately Held**
Web: www.fnsusa.com
SIC: 4731 Freight forwarding

(P-4022)
FRITZ COMPANIES INC
Also Called: U P S
550-1 Eccles Ave (94101)
PHONE..............................650 635-2693
◆ EMP: 10000
SIC: 4731 Freight transportation arrangement

(P-4023)
GELS LOGISTICS INC (PA)
Also Called: 360zebra
437 Baldwin Park Blvd (91746-1408)
PHONE..............................626 340-6660
Xindi Hu, *CEO*
Ling Wang, *CFO*
EMP: 60 EST: 2013
SALES (est): 23.87MM
SALES (corp-wide): 23.87MM **Privately Held**
SIC: 4731 Transportation agents and brokers

(P-4024)
GLOBAL MAIL INC
921 W Artesia Blvd (90220-5105)
PHONE..............................310 735-0800
Eric Ricardo, *Brnch Mgr*
EMP: 214
SALES (corp-wide): 98.08B **Privately Held**
SIC: 4731 Freight transportation arrangement
HQ: Global Mail, Inc.
  2700 S Comm Pkwy Ste 300
  Weston FL
  800 805-9306

(P-4025)
GLOVIS AMERICA INC (HQ)
17305 Von Karman Ave Ste 200
(92614-6674)
PHONE..............................714 427-0944
Bong Jeong Ko, *CEO*
Scott Cornell, *
◆ EMP: 185 EST: 2002
SQ FT: 34,700
SALES (est): 856.58MM **Privately Held**
Web: www.glovisusa.com
SIC: 4731 Freight forwarding
PA: Hyundai Glovis Co.,Ltd
  83-21 Wangsimni-Ro, Seongdong-Gu
  Seoul

(P-4026)
GOLDEN HOUR DATA SYSTEMS INC
10052 Mesa Ridge Ct Ste 200
(92121-2971)
P.O. Box 19786 (92159-0786)
PHONE..............................858 768-2500
Kevin Hutton, *Pr*
Charles Haczewski, *
Peter Goutmann, *
Bill Dow, *
Eric Fleming, *CSO**
EMP: 120 EST: 1997
SQ FT: 14,000
SALES (est): 56.34MM **Privately Held**
Web: www.goldenhour.com
SIC: 4731 Transportation agents and brokers
HQ: Zoll Medical Corporation
  269 Mill Rd
  Chelmsford MA
  978 421-9655

(P-4027)
GRACE LOGISTICS INC
912 11th St Ste 201 (95354-2382)
PHONE..............................209 730-9800
Sam Dhillon, *CEO*
Daniel Evans, *Head OF Operations**
Nick Jordan, *VP*
EMP: 300 EST: 2021
SALES (est): 9.27MM **Privately Held**
SIC: 4731 Freight transportation arrangement

(P-4028)
GSC LOGISTICS INC
Also Called: Crowne Transportation
555 Maritime St (94607-1006)
PHONE..............................510 740-3151
Joel Lesser, *Brnch Mgr*
EMP: 73
SALES (corp-wide): 62MM **Privately Held**
Web: www.gsclogistics.com
SIC: 4731 Freight transportation arrangement
PA: Gsc Logistics, Inc.
  530 Water St Fl 5
  Oakland CA
  510 844-3700

(P-4029)
GXO LOGISTICS SUPPLY CHAIN INC
7140 Cajon Blvd. (92407-1898)
PHONE..............................909 838-5631
Luis Gonzales, *Mgr*
EMP: 100
SALES (corp-wide): 8.99B **Publicly Held**
Web: www.gxo.com
SIC: 4731 Freight forwarding
HQ: Gxo Logistics Supply Chain, Inc.
  4035 Piedmont Pkwy
  High Point NC
  336 232-4100

(P-4030)
GXO LOGISTICS SUPPLY CHAIN INC
2615 E 3rd St (92415-0001)
PHONE..............................909 253-5356
Sonja Lawson, *Mgr*
EMP: 70
SALES (corp-wide): 8.99B **Publicly Held**
Web: www.gxo.com
SIC: 4731 Freight forwarding
HQ: Gxo Logistics Supply Chain, Inc.
  4035 Piedmont Pkwy
  High Point NC
  336 232-4100

(P-4031)
HAM BROKERAGE
325 W Hospitality Ln Ste 102 (92408-3243)
PHONE..............................909 659-5392
Ruben Nunez, *CEO*
EMP: 75 EST: 2019
SALES (est): 4.47MM **Privately Held**
SIC: 4731 Freight transportation arrangement

(P-4032)
HANJIN TRANSPORTATION CO LTD
Also Called: Hanjin Global Logistics
15913 S Main St (90248-2550)
PHONE..............................310 522-5030
Bryce Dalziel, *Pr*
J B Park, *
EMP: 90 EST: 1996
SALES (est): 16.11MM **Privately Held**
Web: www.hanjinusa.com
SIC: 4731 Transportation agents and brokers

(P-4033)
HAPAG-LLOYD (AMERICA) LLC
555 E Ocean Blvd Ste 300 (90802-5052)
PHONE..............................562 435-0771
Oli Reichol, *Brnch Mgr*
EMP: 124
SQ FT: 5,000
SALES (corp-wide): 35.88B **Privately Held**
Web: www.hapag-lloyd.com
SIC: 4731 4412 4729 Agents, shipping;
  Deep sea foreign transportation of freight;
  Steamship ticket offices
HQ: Hapag-Lloyd (America) Llc
  3 Ravinia Dr Ste 1600
  Atlanta GA
  732 562-1800

(P-4034)
HITACHI TRANSPORT SYSTEM (AMERICA) LTD
21061 S Wstn Ave Ste 300 (90501)
P.O. Box 512046 (90051-0046)
PHONE..............................310 787-3420
▲ EMP: 283
SIC: 4731 Freight forwarding

(P-4035)
HOME EXPRESS DELIVERY SVC LLC
Also Called: Temco Logistics
25361 Commercentre Dr Ste 250 (92630)
PHONE..............................949 715-9844
EMP: 1000 EST: 2013
SALES (est): 35MM **Privately Held**
SIC: 4731 Freight transportation arrangement

(P-4036)
HUB GROUP LOS ANGELES LLC
Also Called: Hub City
1400 N Harbor Blvd # 300 (92835-4126)
P.O. Box 71357 (60694-1357)
PHONE..............................714 449-6300
▲ EMP: 85
SIC: 4731 Agents, shipping

(P-4037)
INLOG INC
6765 Westminster Blvd Ste 424
(92683-3769)
PHONE..............................949 212-3867
EMP: 85
SALES (corp-wide): 6.8MM **Privately Held**
SIC: 4731 Freight transportation arrangement
PA: Inlog, Inc.
  4760 Preston Rd
  Frisco TX
  949 212-5241

(P-4038)
INNOVEL SOLUTIONS INC
Also Called: Sears
521 Stone Rd (94510-1113)
PHONE..............................707 748-1940
Dixie Shaw, *Mgr*
EMP: 592
SALES (corp-wide): 4.18B **Privately Held**
Web: marketplace.sears.com
SIC: 4731 Agents, shipping
HQ: Innovel Solutions, Inc.
  3333 Beverly Rd
  Hoffman Estates IL
  847 286-2500

(P-4039)
INNOVEL SOLUTIONS INC
Also Called: Sears
960 Sherman St (92110-4013)
PHONE..............................619 497-1123
Steve Tiger, *Mgr*
EMP: 592
SALES (corp-wide): 4.18B **Privately Held**
Web: marketplace.sears.com
SIC: 4731 Agents, shipping
HQ: Innovel Solutions, Inc.
  3333 Beverly Rd
  Hoffman Estates IL
  847 286-2500

(P-4040)
INNOVEL SOLUTIONS INC
Also Called: Sears
5691 E Philadelphia St Ste 200
(91761-2805)
PHONE..............................909 605-1446
Derrick Daniel, *Mgr*
EMP: 592
SALES (corp-wide): 4.18B **Privately Held**
Web: marketplace.sears.com
SIC: 4731 Agents, shipping
HQ: Innovel Solutions, Inc.
  3333 Beverly Rd
  Hoffman Estates IL
  847 286-2500

(P-4041)
IRON MOUNTAIN INFO MGT LLC
441 N Oak St (90302-3314)
PHONE..............................818 848-9766
Jesse Ascencio, *Mgr*
EMP: 85
Web: www.bondednj.com
SIC: 4731 Freight forwarding
HQ: Iron Mountain Information
  Management, Llc
  3205 Burton Ave
  Burbank CA

(P-4042)
JAVELIN LOGISTICS COMPANY INC
7025 Central Ave (94560-4201)
PHONE..............................800 577-1060
Michael Bonino, *Pr*
Malcolm Winspear, *
Michael Sacrey, *
EMP: 225 EST: 2018
SALES (est): 20.76MM **Privately Held**
Web: www.javelinlogistics.com
SIC: 4731 Freight forwarding

(P-4043)
KLS AIR EXPRESS INC
Also Called: Freight Solution Providers
400 Capitol Mall Ste 2200 (95814-4421)
P.O. Box 4543 (95762-0020)
◆ EMP: 100
Web: www.klsairexpress.com
SIC: 4731 Freight forwarding

(P-4044)
KUEHNE + NAGEL INC
150 W Hill Pl (94005-1216)
PHONE..............................415 656-4100
Christian Herwig, *Brnch Mgr*
EMP: 121
Web: us.kuehne-nagel.com
SIC: 4731 Freight forwarding
HQ: Kuehne + Nagel Inc.
  10 Exchange Pl Fl 19-20
  Jersey City NJ
  201 413-5500

(P-4045)
KUEHNE + NAGEL INC
20000 S Western Ave (90501-1305)
PHONE..............................310 641-5500
Horst Gerjets, *Mgr*
EMP: 243
Web: home.kuehne-nagel.com

4731 - Freight Transportation Arrangement (P-4046)

SIC: 4731 Freight forwarding
HQ: Kuehne + Nagel Inc.
10 Exchange Pl Fl 19-20
Jersey City NJ
201 413-5500

(P-4046)
KW INTERNATIONAL INC
1457 Glenn Curtiss St (90746-4036)
PHONE..................310 354-6944
Dj Kim, *Brnch Mgr*
EMP: 77
Web: www.kwinternational.com
SIC: 4731 Freight forwarding
PA: Kw International, Inc.
18655 Bishop Ave
Carson CA

(P-4047)
KW INTERNATIONAL INC
18511 S Broadwick St (90220-6440)
PHONE..................310 747-1380
Dj Kim, *Mgr*
EMP: 70
Web: www.kwinternational.com
SIC: 4731 Freight forwarding
PA: Kw International, Inc.
18655 Bishop Ave
Carson CA

(P-4048)
L E COPPERSMITH INC (PA)
Also Called: Coppersmith Global Logistics
525 S Douglas St Ste 100 (90245-4810)
PHONE..................310 607-8000
Jeffrey Craig Coppersmith, *Pr*
Lew E Coppersmith Ii, *Sec*
Douglas S Walkley, *
Jim Rowley, *
◆ EMP: 80 EST: 1948
SQ FT: 40,000
SALES (est): 61.97MM
SALES (corp-wide): 61.97MM Privately Held
Web: www.coppersmith.com
SIC: 4731 4789 Customhouse brokers;
Cargo loading and unloading services

(P-4049)
LEE JENNINGS TARGET EX INC
Also Called: L J E Enterprises
815 Moffat Blvd (95336-5820)
PHONE..................209 823-0071
Lee Jennings Junior, *Mgr*
EMP: 66
SALES (corp-wide): 12.06MM Privately Held
Web: www.ljetarget.com
SIC: 4731 4213 Domestic freight forwarding;
Trucking, except local
PA: Lee Jennings Target Express, Inc.
1465 E Franklin Ave
Pomona CA
909 868-1040

(P-4050)
LOGISTEED AMERICA INC
Also Called: Logisteed Monterey Park
1000 Corporate Center Dr Ste 400 (91754)
PHONE..................323 263-8100
Tomoyuki Miyazaki, *Pr*
EMP: 100
Web: www.logisteed-america.com
SIC: 4731 Customhouse brokers
HQ: Logisteed America, Inc.
21061 S Wstrn Ave Ste 300
Torrance CA
310 787-3420

(P-4051)
LOMA LINDA UNIVERSITY MED CTR
Also Called: Warehouse and Receiving Center
1269 E San Bernardino Ave (92408-2943)
P.O. Box 2000 (92354-0200)
PHONE..................909 558-4000
Al Mendoza, *Dir*
EMP: 67
SALES (corp-wide): 388.6MM Privately Held
Web: www.lluh.org
SIC: 4731 Freight transportation arrangement
HQ: Loma Linda University Medical Center
11234 Anderson St
Loma Linda CA
909 558-4000

(P-4052)
LTL EX INC
11081 Cherry Ave (92337-7118)
PHONE..................951 255-1222
EMP: 60
SQ FT: 10,000
SALES (est): 11.43MM Privately Held
SIC: 4731 Freight transportation arrangement

(P-4053)
M-7 CONSOLIDATION INC
475 W Apra St (90220-5527)
PHONE..................310 898-3456
John J Brown, *Pr*
Harald Niehenke, *
John Brown, *
Kathleen Hogan, *
Harvey Turner, *
▼ EMP: 140 EST: 1994
SQ FT: 2,000
SALES (est): 24MM Privately Held
SIC: 4731 Foreign freight forwarding

(P-4054)
MAERSK WHSNG DIST SVCS USA LLC
1651 California St Ste A (92374-2904)
PHONE..................801 301-1732
EMP: 180
SALES (corp-wide): 77.53B Privately Held
Web: www.performanceteam.net
SIC: 4731 Freight forwarding
HQ: Maersk Warehousing & Distribution Services Usa Llc
2240 E Maple Ave
El Segundo CA
562 345-2200

(P-4055)
MAERSK WHSNG DIST SVCS USA LLC (HQ)
Also Called: Performance Team
2240 E Maple Ave (90245-6507)
PHONE..................562 345-2200
Cliff Katab, *
Michael B Kaplan, *
Tracy Kaplan, *
Linda Kaplan, *
◆ EMP: 200 EST: 1987
SALES (est): 507.16MM
SALES (corp-wide): 77.53B Privately Held
Web: www.performanceteam.net
SIC: 4731 4225 4213 Freight forwarding;
General warehousing and storage;
Trucking, except local
PA: A.P. Moller - Marsk A/S
Esplanaden 50
Kobenhavn K
33142990

(P-4056)
MAINFREIGHT INC (HQ)
1400 Glenn Curtiss St (90746-4030)
PHONE..................310 900-1974
John Hepworth, *Pr*
Ron Frady, *
◆ EMP: 90 EST: 1970
SQ FT: 100,000
SALES (est): 493.9MM Privately Held
Web: www.mainfreight.com
SIC: 4731 Domestic freight forwarding
PA: Mainfreight Limited
2 Railway Lane
Auckland AUK

(P-4057)
MAPCARGO GLOBAL LOGISTICS (PA)
2501 Santa Fe Ave (90278-1117)
PHONE..................310 297-8300
Marek Adam Panasewicz, *Pr*
◆ EMP: 74 EST: 1990
SQ FT: 20,000
SALES (est): 38.58MM Privately Held
Web: www.mapcargo.com
SIC: 4731 2448 Domestic freight forwarding;
Cargo containers, wood and wood with metal

(P-4058)
MARINE CORPS UNITED STATES
Traffic Management Office (92055)
P.O. Box 555004 (92055-5004)
PHONE..................760 725-3092
EMP: 72
Web: lejeune.marines.mil
SIC: 4731 9711 Transport clearinghouse;
Marine Corps
HQ: United States Marine Corps
Branch Hlth Clnic Bldg 5
Beaufort SC

(P-4059)
MIRAMAR TRANSPORTATION INC
Also Called: Pilot Freight Services
9340 Cabot Dr Ste I (92126-4397)
P.O. Box 502850 (92150-2850)
PHONE..................858 693-0071
Richard Evan Fore, *Pr*
Richard Evan Fore, *Pr*
Bob Mirinda, *
Carrie Jones, *
EMP: 100 EST: 1993
SALES (est): 22.16MM Privately Held
Web: www.miramartrans.com
SIC: 4731 Freight forwarding

(P-4060)
MODIVCARE SOLUTIONS LLC
7441 Lincoln Way # 225 (92841-1452)
PHONE..................714 503-6871
Kymblyn Brown, *Prin*
EMP: 123
SALES (corp-wide): 2.51B Publicly Held
Web: www.modivcare.com
SIC: 4731 Freight transportation arrangement
HQ: Modivcare Solutions, Llc
6900 E Layton Ave # 1200
Denver CO

(P-4061)
NATIONWIDE TRANS INC (PA)
11727 Eastend Ave (91710-1560)
P.O. Box 2558 (91708-2558)
PHONE..................909 355-3211
Kong Lee, *Pr*
Chris Bendigo, *

Max Paul, *
EMP: 100 EST: 2006
SALES (est): 9.47MM
SALES (corp-wide): 9.47MM Privately Held
SIC: 4731 Freight transportation arrangement

(P-4062)
NEX GROUP LLC
9018 Rancho Viejo Dr (93314-8547)
PHONE..................209 317-6677
Harpinder Sekhon, *Managing Member*
EMP: 70 EST: 2019
SALES (est): 4.92MM Privately Held
SIC: 4731 Freight forwarding

(P-4063)
NEXT TRUCKING INC
301 E Ocean Blvd Ste 1950 (90802-4878)
P.O. Box 7849 (90504-9249)
PHONE..................213 444-2250
Abhishek Kapur, *CEO*
EMP: 160 EST: 2016
SALES (est): 32.23MM Privately Held
Web: www.nexttrucking.com
SIC: 4731 4225 Freight forwarding; General warehousing and storage

(P-4064)
NFI INDUSTRIES
Also Called: Nfi
15750 Mountain Ave (91708-9120)
PHONE..................909 393-4471
▲ EMP: 85 EST: 2009
SALES (est): 11.92MM Privately Held
Web: www.nfiindustries.com
SIC: 4731 Freight transportation arrangement

(P-4065)
NIPPON EXPRESS
Also Called: Co Ltd, All Nippon Airways
21250 Hawthorne Blvd Fl 2 (90503-5513)
PHONE..................310 782-3000
EMP: 111 EST: 2011
SALES (est): 9MM Privately Held
Web: www.nipponexpress.com
SIC: 4731 Freight forwarding

(P-4066)
NIPPON EXPRESS USA INC
19500 S Vermont Ave (90502-1120)
PHONE..................310 527-4237
EMP: 70
Web: www.nipponexpress.com
SIC: 4731 Freight forwarding
HQ: Nippon Express U.S.A., Inc.
800 N Il Route 83
Wood Dale IL
708 304-9800

(P-4067)
NOATUM LOGISTICS USA LLC
1100 W Walnut St (90220-5114)
PHONE..................310 527-2104
▼ EMP: 242
Web: www.noatumlogistics.com
SIC: 4731 Freight forwarding
HQ: Noatum Logistics Usa, Llc
11501 Outlook St Ste 500
Overland Park KS

(P-4068)
NRI USA LLC (PA)
Also Called: Nri Distribution
13200 S Broadway (90061-1124)
PHONE..................323 345-6456
▲ EMP: 100 EST: 2011
SQ FT: 65,000
SALES (est): 60.01MM

▲ = Import ▼ = Export
◆ = Import/Export

PRODUCTS & SERVICES SECTION

4731 - Freight Transportation Arrangement (P-4091)

SALES (corp-wide): 60.01MM **Privately Held**
Web: www.nri3pl.com
SIC: **4731** Freight forwarding

(P-4069)
PACIFIC LOGISTICS CORP (PA)
Also Called: Paclo
7255 Rosemead Blvd (90660-4047)
PHONE......................562 478-4700
Douglas E Hockersmith, *Pr*
Timothy K Hewey, *
Diane J Hockersmith, *
▲ EMP: 208 EST: 1999
SQ FT: 206,000
SALES (est): 112.27MM
SALES (corp-wide): 112.27MM **Privately Held**
Web: www.pacific-logistics.com
SIC: **4731** Freight forwarding

(P-4070)
PACTRACK INC
11135 Rush St Ste A (91733-3520)
PHONE......................213 201-5856
Nabeil Hazu, *CEO*
Michael Vega, *
Nabeil Hazu, *VP*
EMP: 75 EST: 2014
SALES (est): 9.23MM **Privately Held**
Web: www.pactrack.com
SIC: **4731** 7389 Freight transportation arrangement; Courier or messenger service

(P-4071)
PANALPINA INC
19900 S Vermont Ave Ste A (90502-1147)
PHONE......................310 819-4060
Maurice Joseph, *Brnch Mgr*
EMP: 60
SALES (corp-wide): 32.91B **Privately Held**
Web: www.panalpina.com
SIC: **4731** Freight forwarding
HQ: Panalpina, Inc.
12430 Nw 25th St 100
Miami FL
305 894-1300

(P-4072)
PARAKEET LOGISTICS INC
1112 N Main St # 417 (95336-3208)
PHONE......................209 353-1818
Ajitpal Singh, *CEO*
EMP: 200 EST: 2017
SALES (est): 9.98MM **Privately Held**
Web: www.parakeetlogistics.com
SIC: **4731** Freight transportation arrangement

(P-4073)
PASHA GROUP (PA)
Also Called: Pasha Freight
4040 Civic Center Dr Ste 350 (94903-4187)
PHONE......................415 927-6400
George W Pasha Iv, *Pr*
George W Pasha Iii, *Ch Bd*
Amy Sherburne, *Sec*
Steve Hunter, *Treas*
James Britton, *CFO*
◆ EMP: 400 EST: 1973
SQ FT: 18,000
SALES (est): 494.24MM
SALES (corp-wide): 494.24MM **Privately Held**
Web: www.pashagroup.com
SIC: **4731** Freight forwarding

(P-4074)
PATRIOT BROKERAGE INC
7840 Foothill Blvd Ste H (91040-2907)
PHONE......................910 227-4142

Ross Tsarukyan, *Managing Member*
Liyan Tsarukyan, *
EMP: 84 EST: 2014
SQ FT: 13,000
SALES (est): 8.85MM **Privately Held**
SIC: **4731** Freight forwarding

(P-4075)
PEGASUS MARITIME INC
505 N Brand Blvd Ste 210 (91203-2877)
PHONE......................714 728-8565
Khurram Mahmood, *Pr*
Moazam Mahmood, *
Mookie Mahmood, *
Syed M Ali, *
EMP: 75 EST: 2000
SALES (est): 8.79MM **Privately Held**
Web: www.pegasusmaritime.com
SIC: **4731** Freight forwarding

(P-4076)
PORT LOGISTICS GROUP INC
19801 S Santa Fe Ave (90221-5915)
PHONE......................310 669-2551
Timothy Page, *Prin*
EMP: 344
Web: www.whiplash.com
SIC: **4731** Freight transportation arrangement
PA: Port Logistics Group, Inc.
288 S Mayo Ave
City Of Industry CA

(P-4077)
PREMIERE CUSTOMS BROKERS INC
5951 Skylab Rd (92647-2062)
PHONE......................310 410-6825
Richard K Lowery, *CEO*
EMP: 840 EST: 1994
SALES (est): 9.68MM
SALES (corp-wide): 1.44B **Publicly Held**
Web: www.premierechb.com
SIC: **4731** Customhouse brokers
HQ: Smart Modular Technologies Inc.
39870 Eureka Dr
Newark CA

(P-4078)
PRIME GLOBAL SOLUTIONS INC (PA)
Also Called: Pgs 360
15801 E Valley Blvd (91744-3929)
PHONE......................800 424-7746
Mike Katyal, *Pr*
Jorge Suria Dof, *Prin*
◆ EMP: 61 EST: 1989
SALES (est): 49.21MM **Privately Held**
Web: www.pgs360.com
SIC: **4731** 4225 Domestic freight forwarding; General warehousing and storage

(P-4079)
PRO LOADERS INC
14032 Santa Ana Ave (92337-7035)
PHONE......................909 355-5531
Bruce Degler, *Pr*
Kim Pugmire, *
Christopher Ebert, *
EMP: 200 EST: 1981
SQ FT: 600
SALES (est): 23.87MM **Privately Held**
SIC: **4731** 1629 7359 7519 Truck transportation brokers; Earthmoving contractor; Equipment rental and leasing, nec; Trailer rental

(P-4080)
PROFES NWFS INC
3559 Arden Rd (94545-3922)

PHONE......................510 780-0202
EMP: 68
SALES (corp-wide): 298.09K **Privately Held**
SIC: **4731** Domestic freight forwarding
PA: Profes Nwfs, Inc.
1071 Sneath Ln
San Bruno CA

(P-4081)
PROGISTICS DISTRIBUTION INC
480 Roland Way Ste 103 (94621-2013)
PHONE......................415 369-8845
Joel G Ritch, *CEO*
Julian Ludlow, *Pr*
James Liguori, *CFO*
EMP: 576 EST: 2012
SQ FT: 7,500
SALES (est): 91.13MM **Privately Held**
Web: www.progisticsdistribution.com
SIC: **4731** Freight transportation arrangement

(P-4082)
QUARTZ LOGISTICS INC
780 Nogales St Ste D (91748-1306)
PHONE......................626 606-2001
Tai Ruenn Wang, *CEO*
Sandy Chen, *
EMP: 60 EST: 2010
SQ FT: 12,000
SALES (est): 106.63MM **Privately Held**
Web: www.quartzlax.com
SIC: **4731** Freight forwarding

(P-4083)
QUIK PICK EXPRESS LLC
23610 Banning Blvd (90745-6220)
PHONE......................310 763-3000
Tom Boyle, *Managing Member*
EMP: 193
SALES (corp-wide): 40.63MM **Privately Held**
Web: www.quikpickexpress.com
SIC: **4731** Freight transportation arrangement
PA: Quik Pick Express Llc
1021 E 233rd St
Carson CA
310 763-3000

(P-4084)
R L JONES-SAN DIEGO INC (PA)
1778 Zinetta Rd Ste A (92231-9511)
P.O. Box 472 (92232-0472)
PHONE......................760 357-3177
Russell L Jones, *Pr*
Earl Roberts, *
EMP: 100 EST: 1952
SALES (est): 46.48MM
SALES (corp-wide): 46.48MM **Privately Held**
Web: www.rljones.com
SIC: **4731** 4225 Customhouse brokers; General warehousing and storage

(P-4085)
RK LOGISTICS GROUP INC
Also Called: THE RK LOGISTICS GROUP, INC
44951 Industrial Dr (94538-6486)
P.O. Box 610670 (95161-0670)
PHONE......................510 298-5128
EMP: 120
SALES (corp-wide): 27.24MM **Privately Held**
Web: www.rklogisticsgroup.com
SIC: **4731** Freight transportation arrangement
PA: The Rk Logistics Group Inc
41707 Christy St
Fremont CA
408 942-8107

(P-4086)
ROCK-IT CARGO USA LLC
5343 W Imperial Hwy Ste 900 (90045-6241)
PHONE......................310 410-0935
EMP: 193
Web: www.rockit.global
SIC: **4731** Freight forwarding
PA: Rock-It Cargo Usa Llc
201 Rock Lititz Blvd 2
Lititz PA

(P-4087)
RUN ROADLINES INC
1326 Como Dr (95337-8471)
P.O. Box 2006 (95336-1157)
PHONE......................209 681-3640
Manpreet Singh Randhawa, *Pr*
EMP: 60 EST: 2017
SALES (est): 5.24MM **Privately Held**
SIC: **4731** Freight forwarding

(P-4088)
RXO CSTOMS CLRNCE SLUTIONS LLC
400 Oyster Point Blvd Ste 307 (94080-1904)
PHONE......................650 589-8150
Elic Souzo, *Div Mgr*
EMP: 158
SALES (corp-wide): 82.96MM **Privately Held**
SIC: **4731** Freight forwarding
PA: Rxo Customs Clearance Solutions, Llc
1983 Marcus Ave Ste E100
New Hyde Park NY
614 923-1400

(P-4089)
RXO CSTOMS CLRNCE SLUTIONS LLC
2200 Claremont Ct 2nd Fl (94545-5002)
PHONE......................620 266-6315
EMP: 158
SALES (corp-wide): 82.96MM **Privately Held**
SIC: **4731** Freight forwarding
PA: Rxo Customs Clearance Solutions, Llc
1983 Marcus Ave Ste E100
New Hyde Park NY
614 923-1400

(P-4090)
RXO FREIGHT FORWARDING INC
32970 Alvarado Niles Rd (94587-8105)
PHONE......................630 795-1300
EMP: 2100
SALES (corp-wide): 4.8B **Publicly Held**
Web: www.xpo.com
SIC: **4731** Freight transportation arrangement
HQ: Rxo Freight Forwarding, Inc.
290 Gerzevske Ln
Carol Stream IL
630 795-1300

(P-4091)
SALSON LOGISTICS INC
1331 Torrance Blvd (90501-2351)
PHONE......................973 986-0200
Brian Howver, *Brnch Mgr*
EMP: 137
Web: www.salson.com
SIC: **4731** Freight forwarding
HQ: Salson Logistics, Inc.
888 Doremus Ave
Newark NJ
973 986-0200

4731 - Freight Transportation Arrangement (P-4092)

(P-4092)
SEAWORLD GLOBAL LOGISTICS
9350 Wilshire Blvd Ste 203 (90212-3214)
PHONE.................310 579-9164
Dhakshitha Gabriel, *Pr*
EMP: 385 EST: 2017
SALES (est): 20.62MM **Privately Held**
SIC: 4731 Foreign freight forwarding

(P-4093)
SELECT AIRCARGO SERVICES INC
12801 S Figueroa St (90061-1157)
PHONE.................310 851-8500
◆ EMP: 80
SIC: 4731 Foreign freight forwarding

(P-4094)
SHINE LOGISTICS LLC
Also Called: Freshdeals.co
9245 Laguna Springs Dr Ste 200 (95758-7987)
PHONE.................844 850-3391
Navjot Madahar, *Managing Member*
EMP: 120 EST: 2018
SALES (est): 32.65MM **Privately Held**
Web: www.shinelogisticsllc.com
SIC: 4731 Freight forwarding

(P-4095)
SILVER HAWK FREIGHT INC
Also Called: Titan Wolrdwide
16410 Bloomfield Ave (90703)
PHONE.................562 404-0226
Amar Durrani, *Pr*
EMP: 96 EST: 2011
SALES (est): 6.02MM **Privately Held**
Web: www.titan-worldwide.com
SIC: 4731 Freight forwarding

(P-4096)
SMD LOGISTICS INC
26710 Encinal Rd (93908-9763)
PHONE.................831 758-5300
Steve Scaroni, *Pr*
EMP: 131
SALES (corp-wide): 21.53MM **Privately Held**
Web: www.sfcos.com
SIC: 4731 Freight transportation arrangement
PA: Smd Logistics, Inc.
    101 E Main St
    Heber CA
    760 352-3194

(P-4097)
SOURCE LOGISTICS CENTER CORP
812 Union St (90640-6523)
PHONE.................323 887-3884
Marcelo Sada, *Pr*
Raul Villarrael, *VP*
Wendy Escobedo, *VP*
Fernando Ramirez, *Sec*
▲ EMP: 75 EST: 1999
SQ FT: 300,000
SALES (est): 7.84MM **Privately Held**
Web: www.sourcelogistics.com
SIC: 4731 Freight transportation arrangement

(P-4098)
SOURCEBLUE LLC
100 Bush St Ste 510 (94104-3908)
PHONE.................510 267-8100
EMP: 140
SIC: 4731 Freight forwarding
HQ: Sourceblue, Llc
    250 Pehle Ave
    Saddle Brook NJ
    201 722-3800

(P-4099)
STATES LOGISTICS SERVICES INC (PA)
5650 Dolly Ave (90621-1872)
PHONE.................714 521-6520
Daniel Monson, *CEO*
William Donovan, *
Kirk Hellofs, *
Jennifer Monson, *
▲ EMP: 140 EST: 1958
SQ FT: 900,000
SALES (est): 182.96MM **Privately Held**
Web: www.stateslogistics.com
SIC: 4731 Freight transportation arrangement

(P-4100)
STEVENS GLOBAL LOGISTICS INC (PA)
Also Called: Steven Global Freight Services
3700 Redondo Beach Ave (90278-1108)
P.O. Box 729 (90260-0729)
PHONE.................800 229-7284
Thomas J Petrizzio, *CEO*
Karl Chambers, *
Gary Hooper, *
◆ EMP: 95 EST: 1985
SQ FT: 48,000
SALES (est): 57.42MM
SALES (corp-wide): 57.42MM **Privately Held**
Web: www.stevensglobal.com
SIC: 4731 Freight forwarding

(P-4101)
STG LOGISTICS INC
5800 Sheila St (90040-2322)
PHONE.................323 869-6000
EMP: 65
SALES (corp-wide): 3.48B **Privately Held**
Web: www.stgusa.com
SIC: 4731 Freight transportation arrangement
HQ: Stg Logistics, Inc.
    6801 W Side Ave
    North Bergen NJ

(P-4102)
STRAIGHT FORWARDING INC
Also Called: Meow Logistics
20275 Business Pkwy (91789-2974)
PHONE.................909 594-3400
Yihsiang Wu, *CEO*
EMP: 100 EST: 2011
SALES (est): 78.88MM **Privately Held**
Web: www.sfi.com
SIC: 4731 Foreign freight forwarding

(P-4103)
SUPRA NATIONAL EXPRESS INC
1421 Charles Willard St (90746-4025)
PHONE.................310 549-7105
Daniel Linares, *CEO*
EMP: 125 EST: 2014
SALES (est): 25.32MM **Privately Held**
Web: www.snecorp.com
SIC: 4731 Truck transportation brokers

(P-4104)
SYNCREON AMERICA INC
Also Called: SYNCREON AMERICA INC.
14780 Bar Harbor Rd Ste B (92336-4254)
PHONE.................909 610-4511
EMP: 70
Web: www.syncreon.com
SIC: 4731 Freight transportation arrangement
HQ: Syncreon America Inc
    2851 High Meadow Cir # 25
    Auburn Hills MI
    248 377-4700

(P-4105)
TAYLORED SVCS PARENT CO INC (PA)
1495 E Locust St (91761-4570)
PHONE.................909 510-4800
Bill Butler, *CEO*
Michael Yusko, *
EMP: 80 EST: 2012
SQ FT: 330,000
SALES (est): 58.62MM
SALES (corp-wide): 58.62MM **Privately Held**
Web: www.tayloredservices.com
SIC: 4731 Agents, shipping

(P-4106)
THREE WAY LOGISTICS INC (PA)
Also Called: Three Way
42505 Christy St (94538-3993)
P.O. Box 1806 (94538-0032)
PHONE.................408 748-3929
Anthony J Bonino, *CEO*
Kevin Scherer, *
Stan Aikman, *
Michael Bonino, *
Philipp Scherer, *
▲ EMP: 60 EST: 2003
SQ FT: 135,000
SALES (est): 55.3MM
SALES (corp-wide): 55.3MM **Privately Held**
Web: www.threeway.com
SIC: 4731 Freight forwarding

(P-4107)
TOLL GLOBAL FWDG SCS USA INC
Also Called: TOLL GLOBAL FORWARDING SCS (USA) INC.
3355 Dulles Dr (91752-3244)
PHONE.................951 360-8310
Bryan Howber, *Sr VP*
EMP: 100
SIC: 4731 Freight forwarding
HQ: Toll Global Forwarding Scs (Usa) Inc.
    800 Federal Blvd Ste 2
    Carteret NJ
    732 750-9000

(P-4108)
TOLL GLOBAL FWDG SCS USA INC
Also Called: FMI International West 2
400 Westmont Dr 450 (90731)
PHONE.................732 750-9000
Gary Hecht, *Mgr*
EMP: 127
SIC: 4731 Freight forwarding
HQ: Toll Global Forwarding Scs (Usa) Inc.
    800 Federal Blvd Ste 2
    Carteret NJ
    732 750-9000

(P-4109)
TOTAL LOGISTICS ONLINE LLC
628 N Gilbert St (92833-2555)
PHONE.................714 526-3559
Ed Mock, *Brnch Mgr*
EMP: 78
SALES (corp-wide): 12.01B **Publicly Held**
Web: www.ryder.com
SIC: 4731 Freight transportation arrangement
HQ: Total Logistics Online L.L.C.
    4432 S Buttermilk Ct # 10
    Hudsonville MI

(P-4110)
TRANSIT AIR CARGO INC
2204 E 4th St (92705-3868)
P.O. Box 10053 (92711-0053)
PHONE.................714 571-0393
Gulnawaz Khodayar, *CEO*
Christy Colton, *
Michelle Nguyen, *
◆ EMP: 94 EST: 1989
SQ FT: 10,000
SALES (est): 24.63MM **Privately Held**
Web: www.transitair.com
SIC: 4731 Foreign freight forwarding

(P-4111)
TRI-TECH LOGISTICS LLC
1370 Brea Blvd Ste 200 (92835-4128)
PHONE.................855 373-7049
Gurdeep Singh Dhaliwal, *
Jeremy Engstrom, *
EMP: 210 EST: 2014
SALES (est): 23.13MM
SALES (corp-wide): 6.55MM **Privately Held**
Web: www.tritechlogistics.com
SIC: 4731 Freight forwarding
PA: Tri-Tech Logistics Ltd
    17660 65a Ave Unit 208
    Surrey BC
    604 415-9898

(P-4112)
TRICAP INTERNATIONAL LLC
19067 S Reyes Ave (90221-5813)
PHONE.................509 703-8780
Puneet Bawa Transpo, *Dir*
EMP: 78
SALES (corp-wide): 4.05MM **Privately Held**
Web: www.thetrianglegroup.com
SIC: 4731 Freight forwarding
PA: Tricap International, Llc
    9 Hackensack Ave Bldg 43
    Kearny NJ
    310 605-5089

(P-4113)
TRITON LOGISTICS CORPORATION
706 Steffy Rd (92065-3533)
PHONE.................619 822-8832
Jason Lawrence Foyer, *Prin*
EMP: 61
SALES (corp-wide): 9.84MM **Privately Held**
Web: www.tritonlogistics.us
SIC: 4731 Foreign freight forwarding
PA: Triton Logistics, Corporation
    6780 Miramar Rd Ste 200b
    San Diego CA
    619 822-8832

(P-4114)
UNIS LLC (PA)
Also Called: United Network Info Svcs
218 Machlin Ct Ste A (91789-3057)
PHONE.................909 839-2600
James Lin, *Pr*
Gracie Leung, *
EMP: 200 EST: 2012
SALES (est): 194.54MM
SALES (corp-wide): 194.54MM **Privately Held**
Web: www.unisco.com
SIC: 4731 Freight forwarding

(P-4115)
UPS WORLDWIDE LOGISTICS INC

PRODUCTS & SERVICES SECTION

4783 - Packing And Crating (P-4135)

Also Called: UPS
30336 Whipple Rd (94587-1525)
PHONE.................................510 476-4000
EMP: 100
SALES (corp-wide): 100.34B **Publicly Held**
Web: www.theupsstore.com
SIC: **4731** 4225 Freight forwarding; General warehousing and storage
HQ: Ups Worldwide Logistics Inc
  12380 Morris Rd
  Alpharetta GA

(P-4116)
US LINES LLC (DH)
Also Called: US Lines
3501 Jamboree Rd Ste 300 (92660-2936)
PHONE.................................714 751-3333
◆ EMP: 75 EST: 2004
SALES (est): 34.03MM
SALES (corp-wide): 31.16K **Privately Held**
SIC: **4731** Freight forwarding
HQ: Cma Cgm
  4 Boulevard J Saade
  Marseille
  488919000

(P-4117)
VANGUARD LGISTICS SVCS USA INC (HQ)
Also Called: Brennan International Trnspt
5000 Airport Plaza Dr Ste 200 (90815)
PHONE.................................310 847-3000
  Charles Brennan, *Ch*
  J Thurso Barendse, *VP*
  Therese Groff, *VP*
  Derek Moore, *TAX*
  Ank Deroos, *Dir*
◆ EMP: 100 EST: 1978
SALES (est): 227.78MM
SALES (corp-wide): 478.07MM **Privately Held**
Web: www.vanguardlogistics.com
SIC: **4731** Freight consolidation
PA: Naca Holdings, Inc.
  5000 Arprt Plz Dr Ste 200
  Long Beach CA
  310 847-3000

(P-4118)
VEG FRESH LOGISTICS LLC ✪
1400 W Rincon St (92878-9205)
PHONE.................................714 446-8800
EMP: 220 EST: 2022
SALES (est): 56.1MM **Privately Held**
Web: www.vegfresh.com
SIC: **4731** Transportation agents and brokers
PA: Veg-Fresh Farms, Llc
  1400 W Rincon St
  Corona CA

(P-4119)
WATCHPOINT LOGISTICS INC (PA)
700 Airport Blvd Ste 380 (94010-1931)
PHONE.................................800 486-8326
  Jay Bellin, *Pr*
  Julie Busch, *Dir*
  Michael Schweinberg, *Dir*
  Alec Binnie, *Dir*
◆ EMP: 110 EST: 1988
SQ FT: 35,000
SALES (est): 28.05MM
SALES (corp-wide): 28.05MM **Privately Held**
Web: www.watchpointlogistics.com
SIC: **4731** Freight forwarding

(P-4120)
XPO LOGISTICS SUPPLY CHAIN INC
5200b E Airport Dr (91761-8601)
PHONE.................................909 390-9799
FAX: 909 937-6089
EMP: 156
SALES (corp-wide): 14.62B **Publicly Held**
SIC: **4731** Freight transportation arrangement
HQ: Xpo Logistics Supply Chain, Inc.
  4035 Piedmont Pkwy
  High Point NC
  336 232-4100

(P-4121)
XPORT FORWARDING LLC
620 Newport Center Dr Ste 1100 (92660)
PHONE.................................949 354-0609
  Mario Bruendel, *Brnch Mgr*
EMP: 85
SALES (corp-wide): 3.37MM **Privately Held**
Web: www.xportforwarding.com
SIC: **4731** Freight forwarding
PA: Xport Forwarding, Llc
  2323 Main St
  Irvine CA
  949 668-1010

(P-4122)
YAMATO ENTERPRISES INC
Also Called: Julie's Hallmark
1773 Creek Dr (95125-1841)
PHONE.................................408 677-3554
  Victor Yamato, *Pr*
  Joanne Yamato, *
EMP: 80 EST: 1981
SALES (est): 4.22MM **Privately Held**
SIC: **4731** Foreign freight forwarding

(P-4123)
YUSEN LOGISTICS AMERICAS INC
2417 E Carson St Ste 100 (90810-1252)
PHONE.................................310 518-3008
  P Smith, *Brnch Mgr*
EMP: 200
SIC: **4731** Freight forwarding
HQ: Yusen Logistics (Americas) Inc.
  300 Lighting Way Ste 100
  Secaucus NJ
  201 553-3800

4783 Packing And Crating

(P-4124)
ADVANTAGE MEDIA SERVICES INC (PA)
Also Called: AMS Fulfillement
29010 Commerce Center Dr (91355-4188)
PHONE.................................661 775-0611
  Jay Catlin, *Pr*
  Ken Wiseman, *CEO*
  David Catlin, *Dir*
  Louise Aldrich, *Prin*
▲ EMP: 76 EST: 2002
SQ FT: 142,000
SALES (est): 39.78MM
SALES (corp-wide): 39.78MM **Privately Held**
Web: www.amsfulfillment.com
SIC: **4783** 4731 Packing goods for shipping; Agents, shipping

(P-4125)
ALOM TECHNOLOGIES CORPORATION (PA)
Also Called: Alom Technologies
48105 Warm Springs Blvd (94539-7498)
PHONE.................................510 360-3600
  Hannah Kain, *Pr*
  Jack Sexton, *
▲ EMP: 128 EST: 1997
SQ FT: 300,000
SALES (est): 94.95MM
SALES (corp-wide): 94.95MM **Privately Held**
Web: www.alom.com
SIC: **4783** 7389 7374 7331 Packing goods for shipping; Packaging and labeling services; Data processing and preparation; Direct mail advertising services

(P-4126)
CHANDLER PACKAGING A TRANSPAK COMPANY
Also Called: Fragile Handle With Care
7595 Raytheon Rd (92111-1506)
P.O. Box 421110 (92142-1110)
PHONE.................................858 292-5674
EMP: 64
Web: www.chanpack.com
SIC: **4783** 2449 3081 3086 Packing and crating; Wood containers, nec; Packing materials, plastics sheet; Packaging and shipping materials, foamed plastics

(P-4127)
DISNEYLAND RESORT
Also Called: Shipping Department
1020 W Ball Rd (92802-1804)
PHONE.................................714 781-7560
  Mark Steinmetz, *Brnch Mgr*
EMP: 742
SALES (corp-wide): 82.72B **Publicly Held**
Web: www.thewaltdisneycompany.com
SIC: **4783** Containerization of goods for shipping
HQ: Disneyland Resort
  1313 S Harbor Blvd
  Anaheim CA
  714 781-4000

(P-4128)
FRESHPOINT CENTRAL CAL INC
Also Called: Freshpoint Central California
5900 N Golden State Blvd (95382-9671)
PHONE.................................209 216-0200
  Jeffrey A Sacchini, *CEO*
  Brian M Sturgeon, *Pr*
EMP: 150 EST: 2000
SQ FT: 54,000
SALES (est): 21.16MM
SALES (corp-wide): 76.32MM **Publicly Held**
Web: www.freshpoint.com
SIC: **4783** Containerization of goods for shipping
HQ: Freshpoint, Inc.
  1390 Enclave Pkwy
  Houston TX

(P-4129)
INNOVATED PACKAGING CO INC
520 Marburg Way (95133-1619)
PHONE.................................510 745-8180
  Ben F Polando, *Pr*
  Adele Daszko, *
  Donna Fernandez, *
  Santina Polando, *
EMP: 75 EST: 1988
SALES (est): 20.21MM **Privately Held**
Web: www.innovpak.com
SIC: **4783** Packing and crating

(P-4130)
L&L FOODS HOLDINGS LLC
333 N Euclid Way (92801-6738)
PHONE.................................714 254-1430
EMP: 200
SIC: **4783** Packing goods for shipping

(P-4131)
MANN PACKING CO INC
Also Called: Mann Packing Pea Plant
1347 Harkins Rd (93901-4408)
PHONE.................................831 796-2670
EMP: 70
Web: www.veggiesmadeeasy.com
SIC: **4783** Packing and crating
HQ: Mann Packing Co., Inc.
  49 Katherine St
  Gonzales CA
  831 422-5341

(P-4132)
MEK ENTERPRISES INC
3517 Camino Del Rio S Ste 215 (92108)
PHONE.................................619 527-0957
  Marc Kranz, *CEO*
EMP: 100 EST: 2012
SALES (est): 10.44MM **Privately Held**
Web: www.4mek.com
SIC: **4783** 4214 Packing and crating; Furniture moving and storage, local

(P-4133)
MOONLIGHT PACKING CORPORATION
Also Called: Plant 04
17770 E Huntsman Ave (93654-9205)
PHONE.................................559 638-7799
EMP: 605
SIC: **4783** 5148 Packing and crating; Fruits, fresh
PA: Moonlight Packing Corporation
  17719 E Huntsman Ave
  Reedley CA

(P-4134)
PETCO ANIMAL SUPPLIES INC (DH)
Also Called: Petco
10850 Via Frontera (92127-1705)
PHONE.................................858 453-7845
  Ron Coughlin, *Ch*
  Brad Weston, *
  Charlie Piscitello, *
  Michael M Nuzzo, *
  Michael W Zuna, *Chief Marketing DIGITAL*
◆ EMP: 500 EST: 1965
SQ FT: 164,000
SALES (est): 2.15B
SALES (corp-wide): 298.02K **Privately Held**
Web: www.petco.com
SIC: **4783** 5999 5199 Crating goods for shipping; Pet supplies; Pet supplies
HQ: Petco Holdings, Inc. Llc
  10850 Via Frontera
  San Diego CA
  858 453-7845

(P-4135)
SUNTREAT PKG SHIPG A LTD PRTNR
Also Called: Suntreat
391 Oxford Ave (93247-2208)
P.O. Box 850 (93247-0850)
PHONE.................................559 562-4991
  Dennis A Griffith, *Mng Pt*
  Dwight J Griffith, *
EMP: 200 EST: 1958
SQ FT: 75,000
SALES (est): 21.24MM **Privately Held**
Web: www.suntreat.com

(PA)=Parent Co (HQ)=Headquarters
✪ = New Business established in last 2 years

4783 - Packing And Crating (P-4136)

SIC: **4783** 8742 Packing goods for shipping; Management consulting services

(P-4136)
UNIFIED AIRCRAFT SERVICES INC (PA)
1571 S Lilac Ave (92316-2141)
P.O. Box 401060 (89140-1060)
PHONE..................................909 877-0535
Ben C Warren, *Pr*
Benjamin T Warren, *
Venida L Warren, *
EMP: 65 EST: 1972
SQ FT: 14,500
SALES (est): 4.01MM
SALES (corp-wide): 4.01MM **Privately Held**
SIC: **4783** Packing goods for shipping

4785 Inspection And Fixed Facilities

(P-4137)
COFIROUTE USA LLC
Also Called: Cofiroute
100 Progress Ste 110 (92618-0353)
PHONE..................................949 754-0198
Gary Hausdorfer, *CEO*
Darla Casby, *
▲ EMP: 112 EST: 2002
SALES (est): 30.25MM
SALES (corp-wide): 16.98MM **Privately Held**
Web: www.cofirouteusa.com
SIC: **4785** Toll road operation
HQ: Vinci Concessions
    1973 Boulevard De La Defense
    Nanterre

(P-4138)
GOLDEN GATE BRDGE HWY TRNSP DS (PA)
Golden Gate Bridge Toll Plaza (94129)
PHONE..................................415 921-5858
James C Eddie, *Pr*
Kary H Witt, *
James Swindler, *
Dennis Mulligan, *
▲ EMP: 250 EST: 1928
SQ FT: 20,000
SALES (est): 145.69MM
SALES (corp-wide): 145.69MM **Privately Held**
Web: www.goldengate.org
SIC: **4785** 4131 4482 4111 Toll bridge operation; Interstate bus line; Ferries operating across rivers or within harbors; Bus transportation

(P-4139)
GOLDEN GATE BRDGE HWY TRNSP DS
Also Called: Golden Gate Ferry
101 E Sir Francis Drake Blvd (94939-1803)
PHONE..................................415 455-2000
David Clark, *Mgr*
EMP: 69
SALES (corp-wide): 145.69MM **Privately Held**
Web: www.goldengate.org
SIC: **4785** 4482 Toll bridge operation; Ferries operating across rivers or within harbors
PA: Golden Gate Bridge Highway & Transportation District
    Golden Gate Brdge Toll Pl
    San Francisco CA
    415 921-5858

(P-4140)
GOLDEN GATE BRIDGE HIGH
Also Called: Golden Gate Transit
1011 Andersen Dr (94901-5318)
PHONE..................................415 457-3110
Susan Chiaroni, *Mgr*
EMP: 535
SQ FT: 50,000
SALES (corp-wide): 145.69MM **Privately Held**
Web: www.goldengate.org
SIC: **4785** 4111 Toll bridge operation; Airport transportation services, regular route
PA: Golden Gate Bridge Highway & Transportation District
    Golden Gate Brdge Toll Pl
    San Francisco CA
    415 921-5858

4789 Transportation Services, Nec

(P-4141)
ACCORD LOGISTICS LLC ◆
3165 Indian Fig Dr (92115-8240)
PHONE..................................281 687-1181
Kubiat Akpan, *Managing Member*
EMP: 60 EST: 2022
SALES (est): 2.11MM **Privately Held**
SIC: **4789** 8742 Transportation services, nec ; Transportation consultant

(P-4142)
ADVANCED MULTIMODAL DIST INC
Also Called: Preferred Carrier California
14822 Central Ave (91710-9509)
PHONE..................................800 838-3058
Fredy Salvador Funes, *CEO*
EMP: 150 EST: 2017
SALES (est): 4.95MM **Privately Held**
SIC: **4789** 4731 Cargo loading and unloading services; Freight forwarding

(P-4143)
AMBIANCE TRANSPORTATION LLC
6901 San Fernando Rd (91201-1608)
PHONE..................................818 955-5757
EMP: 90 EST: 2018
SALES (est): 4.54MM **Privately Held**
SIC: **4789** Transportation services, nec

(P-4144)
AMERICAN TRANSPORTATION CO LLC
635 W Colorado St Ste 108a (91204)
PHONE..................................818 660-2343
Isaac Albekyan, *Prin*
EMP: 88 EST: 2012
SALES (est): 1.79MM **Privately Held**
SIC: **4789** Transportation services, nec

(P-4145)
CALIFRNIA DEPT INDUS RELATIONS
1515 Clay St Ste 1201 (94612-1474)
PHONE..................................510 286-7000
Robert Jones, *Dir*
EMP: 67
SALES (corp-wide): 534.4MM **Privately Held**
Web: dir.ca.gov
SIC: **4789** Pipeline terminal facilities, independently operated
HQ: California Department Of Industrial Relations

455 Golden Gate Ave Fl 10
San Francisco CA

(P-4146)
CAPSTONE LOGISTICS LLC
Also Called: Capstone Logistics
12661 Aldi Pl (92555-6703)
PHONE..................................770 414-1929
EMP: 149
SALES (corp-wide): 1.18B **Privately Held**
Web: www.capstonelogistics.com
SIC: **4789** Cargo loading and unloading services
PA: Capstone Logistics, Llc
    30 Technology Pkwy S # 2
    Peachtree Corners GA
    770 414-1929

(P-4147)
CAPSTONE LOGISTICS LLC
16888 Mckinley Ave (95330-9705)
PHONE..................................209 858-1401
EMP: 149
SALES (corp-wide): 1.18B **Privately Held**
Web: www.capstonelogistics.com
SIC: **4789** Cargo loading and unloading services
PA: Capstone Logistics, Llc
    30 Technology Pkwy S # 2
    Peachtree Corners GA
    770 414-1929

(P-4148)
CASA LOGISTICS LLC
1403 Jinette (92673-3473)
PHONE..................................949 636-3391
EMP: 60 EST: 2018
SALES (est): 2.94MM **Privately Held**
SIC: **4789** Transportation services, nec

(P-4149)
COMPREHENSIVE DIST SVCS INC
18726 S Western Ave Ste 300 (90248)
PHONE..................................310 523-1546
Sam Lee, *Pr*
EMP: 150 EST: 2010
SALES (est): 9.49MM **Privately Held**
SIC: **4789** Freight car loading and unloading

(P-4150)
DELIVERIMATES LLC
5311 Escover Ln (95118-3025)
PHONE..................................857 445-7736
EMP: 60 EST: 2020
SALES (est): 2.34MM **Privately Held**
Web: www.deliverimates.com
SIC: **4789** Transportation services, nec

(P-4151)
DRAKAINA LOGISTICS
958 Ryan Ave (93611-3423)
PHONE..................................559 765-1347
EMP: 70 EST: 2020
SALES (est): 2.23MM **Privately Held**
SIC: **4789** Transportation services, nec

(P-4152)
DREAMTEAM LOGISTICS LLC
8605 Santa Monica Blvd (90069-4109)
PHONE..................................818 300-7785
EMP: 75 EST: 2020
SALES (est): 1.8MM **Privately Held**
SIC: **4789** Transportation services, nec

(P-4153)
DTL TRANSPORT INC
4375 N Golden State Blvd (93722-3828)
PHONE..................................559 277-9075

Lakhvir Dosanjh, *CEO*
Lakhvir Singh, *
EMP: 99 EST: 2008
SQ FT: 1,700
SALES (est): 40.89MM **Privately Held**
Web: www.dtltrans.com
SIC: **4789** Cargo loading and unloading services

(P-4154)
DW MORGAN LLC
4185 Blackhawk Plaza Cir Ste 260 (94506-4906)
PHONE..................................925 460-2700
David W Morgan, *CEO*
EMP: 63 EST: 2013
SALES (est): 7.42MM **Privately Held**
Web: www.dwmorgan.com
SIC: **4789** 4731 4212 Cargo loading and unloading services; Domestic freight forwarding; Local trucking, without storage

(P-4155)
FLUOR FLTRON BLFOUR BTTY DRGDO
5901 W Century Blvd (90045-5411)
PHONE..................................949 420-5000
Kenneth Isett, *Prin*
Terry Gohde, *Prin*
EMP: 99 EST: 2018
SALES (est): 4.24MM **Privately Held**
Web: www.lalinxs.com
SIC: **4789** Transportation services, nec

(P-4156)
FULL SCALE LOGISTICS LLC
2722 Rocky Point Ct (91362-4943)
PHONE..................................805 279-6799
Kristen Infeld, *CEO*
EMP: 85 EST: 2020
SALES (est): 5.23MM **Privately Held**
SIC: **4789** Transportation services, nec

(P-4157)
GUNDERSON LLC
Also Called: Gunderson Modesto
884 Codoni Ave (95357-0500)
P.O. Box 959 (95319-0959)
PHONE..................................209 578-5154
Gordon Prich, *Mgr*
EMP: 112
SALES (corp-wide): 511.61MM **Privately Held**
SIC: **4789** Railroad car repair
HQ: Gunderson Llc
    4350 Nw Front Ave
    Portland OR
    503 972-5700

(P-4158)
GUNDERSON RAIL SERVICES LLC
Also Called: Greenbrier Rail Services
1475 Cooley Ct (92408-2830)
P.O. Box 1715 (92402-1715)
PHONE..................................909 478-0541
Kevin Johnson, *Contrlr*
EMP: 133
SQ FT: 64,248
SALES (corp-wide): 3.94B **Publicly Held**
Web: www.gbrx.com
SIC: **4789** Railroad car repair
HQ: Gunderson Rail Services Llc
    1 Centerpointe Dr Ste 200
    Lake Oswego OR
    503 684-7000

PRODUCTS & SERVICES SECTION

4812 - Radiotelephone Communication (P-4183)

(P-4159)
HYPERLOOP TECHNOLOGIES INC
Also Called: Hyperloop One
777 S Alameda St Ste 400 (90021-1657)
PHONE.................................213 800-3270
Sultan Ahmed Bin Sulayem, *Ch Bd*
Jay Walder, *
William Mulholland, *
Josh Giegel, *
Brent Callinicos, *
EMP: 197 EST: 2014
SALES (est): 99.68MM **Privately Held**
Web: www.hyperloop-one.com
SIC: **4789** Pipeline terminal facilities, independently operated

(P-4160)
JDM DELIVERIES INC
802 Cotter Ave (91010-1820)
PHONE.................................626 831-1876
EMP: 60 EST: 2019
SALES (est): 2.72MM **Privately Held**
SIC: **4789** Transportation services, nec

(P-4161)
JESSE ALEXANDER TRANSPORT
9338 Azurite Ave (92344-4611)
PHONE.................................760 669-0379
Jesus Gomez, *Managing Member*
EMP: 60 EST: 2014
SALES (est): 1.61MM **Privately Held**
SIC: **4789** Transportation services, nec

(P-4162)
JIT TRANSPORTATION INC
1075 Montague Express Way (95035-6826)
PHONE.................................408 232-4800
Gene Ashley, *Pr*
EMP: 350 EST: 2007
SALES (est): 25.05MM **Privately Held**
Web: www.jittransportation.com
SIC: **4789** Space flight operations, except government

(P-4163)
KAYDAN LOGISTICS LLC
45562 Ponderosa Ct (92592-2829)
PHONE.................................951 961-9000
Kirk Morrison, *CEO*
EMP: 91 EST: 2020
SALES (est): 4.99MM **Privately Held**
SIC: **4789** Transportation services, nec

(P-4164)
KHAIRA LOGISTICS INC
Also Called: Khaira Logistics
4451 Gateway Park Blvd (95834-2401)
PHONE.................................916 308-4740
Major Singh, *Pr*
EMP: 65 EST: 2016
SALES (est): 3.46MM **Privately Held**
SIC: **4789** Transportation services, nec

(P-4165)
LANDMARK DISTRIBUTION LLC
34 E Sola St (93101-2506)
PHONE.................................805 965-3058
EMP: 75
Web: www.landmarkglobal.com
SIC: **4789** 4731 Cargo loading and unloading services; Foreign freight forwarding

(P-4166)
LOCATION SERVICES LLC (PA)
Also Called: Pathfinder Services
2365 Iron Point Rd Ste 160 (95630-8713)
PHONE.................................800 588-0097
Lee Mccarty, *CEO*
Karen Gordon, *
EMP: 90 EST: 2014
SQ FT: 15,000
SALES (est): 23.93MM
SALES (corp-wide): 23.93MM **Privately Held**
Web: www.location-services.com
SIC: **4789** Car loading

(P-4167)
MERIDIAN RAIL ACQUISITION
Also Called: Greenbrier Rail
1475 Cooley Ct (92408-2830)
P.O. Box 1715 (92402-1715)
PHONE.................................909 478-0541
EMP: 203
SALES (corp-wide): 3.94B **Publicly Held**
Web: www.gbrx.com
SIC: **4789** Railroad car repair
HQ: Meridian Rail Acquisition Corp
   1 Centerpointe Dr Ste 400
   Lake Oswego OR
   503 684-7000

(P-4168)
MOTOGISTICS LOGISTICS INC
Also Called: Motogistics
1490 E Foothill Blvd Ste C (91786-4071)
PHONE.................................626 975-6470
Kelsey Hawkins, *Ex Dir*
EMP: 60 EST: 2021
SALES (est): 3.04MM **Privately Held**
SIC: **4789** Transportation services, nec

(P-4169)
NERYS LOGISTICS INC
9925 Airway Rd (92154-7932)
PHONE.................................619 616-2124
EMP: 124
SALES (corp-wide): 12.26MM **Privately Held**
SIC: **4789** Cargo loading and unloading services
PA: Nery's Logistics, Inc.
   774 Mays Blvd
   Incline Village NV
   775 338-7060

(P-4170)
PATRIOT LOGISTICS SERVICES LLC
1520 Independence Way (92084-3616)
PHONE.................................443 994-9660
Joshua Schraeder, *Prin*
Kenneth Dinsmore, *
EMP: 80 EST: 2020
SALES (est): 3.23MM **Privately Held**
SIC: **4789** Transportation services, nec

(P-4171)
POSTMATES INC (HQ)
950 23rd St (94107-3401)
PHONE.................................800 882-6106
Bastian Lehmann, *Ch*
Sean Plaice, *
Kristen Schaefer, *
Vivek Patel, *
EMP: 91 EST: 2011
SALES (est): 307.83MM
SALES (corp-wide): 31.88B **Publicly Held**
Web: www.postmates.com
SIC: **4789** Cargo loading and unloading services
PA: Uber Technologies, Inc.
   1515 3rd St
   San Francisco CA
   415 612-8582

(P-4172)
PRIME TRANSPORT INC
2404 S Grove Ave (91761-6224)
PHONE.................................909 972-1300
Angad Singh Pasricha, *Brnch Mgr*
EMP: 74
SALES (corp-wide): 831.18K **Privately Held**
Web: www.primetransport.com
SIC: **4789** Cargo loading and unloading services
PA: Prime Transport Inc.
   1252 Amaryllis Way
   Corona CA
   909 972-1300

(P-4173)
RIOLO TRANSPORTATION INC
2725 Jefferson St Ste 2d (92008-1705)
PHONE.................................760 729-4405
Gail Phipps, *Brnch Mgr*
EMP: 378
Web: www.riolo.com
SIC: **4789** Pipeline terminal facilities, independently operated
PA: Riolo Transportation, Inc.
   759 N Vulcan Ave
   Encinitas CA

(P-4174)
SECURE TRANSPORTATION CO INC
8304 Clairemont Mesa Blvd Ste 202 (92111-1315)
PHONE.................................858 790-3958
Shawana Walters, *Mgr*
EMP: 60
SALES (corp-wide): 29.79MM **Privately Held**
Web: www.securetransportation.com
SIC: **4789** Pipeline terminal facilities, independently operated
PA: Secure Transportation Company, Inc.
   12800 Center Court Dr S # 120
   Cerritos CA
   562 941-0107

(P-4175)
TAYLORED TRANSLOAD LLC
1495 E Locust St (91761-4570)
PHONE.................................909 510-4800
Jim Deveau, *Prin*
EMP: 79 EST: 2020
SALES (est): 939.28K
SALES (corp-wide): 58.62MM **Privately Held**
SIC: **4789** Cargo loading and unloading services
PA: Taylored Services Parent Co. Inc.
   1495 E Locust St
   Ontario CA
   909 510-4800

(P-4176)
TW SERVICES INC
1801 W Romneya Dr Ste 601 (92801-1828)
PHONE.................................714 441-2400
Charles An, *Pr*
Thomas Hwang, *
EMP: 300 EST: 2009
SALES (est): 28.82MM **Privately Held**
Web: www.twserviceinc.com
SIC: **4789** Freight car loading and unloading

(P-4177)
UPS FREIGHT
751 Nuttman St (95054-2623)
PHONE.................................408 727-0703
EMP: 187 EST: 2000
SALES (est): 1.01MM
SALES (corp-wide): 100.34B **Publicly Held**
SIC: **4789** Transportation services, nec
HQ: Ups Freight Services, Inc.
   1000 Semmes Ave
   Richmond VA
   804 231-8000

(P-4178)
WESTERN AG INCORPORATED
686 King Ave (95991-2808)
PHONE.................................530 713-7901
Mohammad Khan, *Pr*
EMP: 92 EST: 2015
SALES (est): 9.86MM **Privately Held**
Web: www.westernag.com
SIC: **4789** Pipeline terminal facilities, independently operated

(P-4179)
WHO DAT NATION TRNSP LLC
13186 Rincon Rd (92308-6214)
PHONE.................................760 403-7237
Ricky D Jones, *Managing Member*
EMP: 73 EST: 2017
SALES (est): 1.56MM **Privately Held**
SIC: **4789** Cargo loading and unloading services

4812 Radiotelephone Communication

(P-4180)
20/20 MOBILE CORP
3380 La Sierra Ave (92503-5271)
PHONE.................................909 587-2973
EMP: 83
SALES (corp-wide): 4.99MM **Privately Held**
SIC: **4812** Cellular telephone services
PA: 20/20 Mobile Corp
   10050 Magnolia Ave
   Riverside CA
   951 354-8100

(P-4181)
4G WIRELESS INC (PA)
Also Called: Verizon Wireless
775 Laguna Canyon Rd (92651-1838)
PHONE.................................949 748-6100
Mohammad Honarkar, *Pr*
EMP: 78 EST: 2005
SALES (est): 122.38MM **Privately Held**
Web: www.4g-ventures.com
SIC: **4812** Cellular telephone services

(P-4182)
AT&T CORP
330 R (94583)
PHONE.................................925 823-6949
EMP: 416
SALES (corp-wide): 120.74B **Publicly Held**
Web: www.att.com
SIC: **4812** Cellular telephone services
HQ: At&T Corp.
   1 At&T Way
   Bedminster NJ
   800 403-3302

(P-4183)
AT&T CORP
Rm 620 (92805)
PHONE.................................714 284-2878
EMP: 311
SALES (corp-wide): 120.74B **Publicly Held**
Web: www.att.com

4812 - Radiotelephone Communication (P-4184)

SIC: 4812 Cellular telephone services
HQ: At&T Corp.
1 At&T Way
Bedminster NJ
800 403-3302

(P-4184)
AT&T CORP
2260 E Imperial Hwy (90245-3501)
PHONE......................303 596-8431
Anne Chow, *CEO*
EMP: 94
SALES (corp-wide): 120.74B **Publicly Held**
Web: www.att.com
SIC: 4812 Cellular telephone services
HQ: At&T Corp.
28 Liberty St
New York NY

(P-4185)
BLACK DOT WIRELESS LLC
23456 Madero Ste 210 (92691-2783)
PHONE......................949 502-3800
Marc Anthony, *Managing Member*
Gary Arnett, *
EMP: 85 EST: 2004
SALES (est): 24.14MM **Privately Held**
Web: www.blackdotwireless.com
SIC: 4812 Cellular telephone services

(P-4186)
BLACKWATER CELLULAR CORP
Also Called: Cellular One
125 E Sir Francis Drake Blvd # 4 (94939-1860)
PHONE......................415 526-2200
Kevin Douglas, *Ch Bd*
Tim Mc Gaw, *
EMP: 150 EST: 1991
SALES (est): 7.65MM **Privately Held**
Web: www.cellularone.com
SIC: 4812 Cellular telephone services

(P-4187)
CELLCO PARTNERSHIP
Also Called: Verizon
2428 Las Positas Rd (94551-8838)
PHONE......................925 245-0494
Gary Larsen, *Mgr*
EMP: 71
SALES (corp-wide): 136.84B **Publicly Held**
Web: www.verizonwireless.com
SIC: 4812 Cellular telephone services
HQ: Cellco Partnership
1 Verizon Way
Basking Ridge NJ

(P-4188)
CELLCO PARTNERSHIP
Also Called: Verizon Wireless
682 Freeman Ln (95949-9616)
PHONE......................530 477-8042
EMP: 71
SALES (corp-wide): 136.84B **Publicly Held**
Web: www.verizonwireless.com
SIC: 4812 Cellular telephone services
HQ: Cellco Partnership
1 Verizon Way
Basking Ridge NJ

(P-4189)
CELLCO PARTNERSHIP
Also Called: Verizon Wireless
5815 Stockton Blvd Ste D (95824-3051)
PHONE......................916 838-9525
EMP: 71
SALES (corp-wide): 136.84B **Publicly Held**
Web: www.verizonwireless.com
SIC: 4812 Cellular telephone services
HQ: Cellco Partnership
1 Verizon Way
Basking Ridge NJ

(P-4190)
CELLCO PARTNERSHIP
Also Called: Verizon Wireless
691 S Main St Ste 80 (92868-5619)
PHONE......................714 564-0050
EMP: 71
SALES (corp-wide): 136.84B **Publicly Held**
Web: www.verizon.com
SIC: 4812 Cellular telephone services
HQ: Cellco Partnership
1 Verizon Way
Basking Ridge NJ

(P-4191)
CELLCO PARTNERSHIP
Also Called: Verizon Wireless
237 E Compton Blvd (90220-2412)
PHONE......................310 603-0101
EMP: 71
SALES (corp-wide): 136.84B **Publicly Held**
Web: www.verizonwireless.com
SIC: 4812 Cellular telephone services
HQ: Cellco Partnership
1 Verizon Way
Basking Ridge NJ

(P-4192)
CELLCO PARTNERSHIP
Also Called: Verizon Wireless
300 W Shaw Ave (93612-3680)
PHONE......................559 321-8116
EMP: 71
SALES (corp-wide): 136.84B **Publicly Held**
Web: www.verizonwireless.com
SIC: 4812 Cellular telephone services
HQ: Cellco Partnership
1 Verizon Way
Basking Ridge NJ

(P-4193)
CELLCO PARTNERSHIP
Also Called: Verizon
1440 41st Ave Ste B (95010-2940)
PHONE......................831 475-3100
Jeff Dehaven, *Mgr*
EMP: 71
SALES (corp-wide): 136.84B **Publicly Held**
Web: www.verizon.com
SIC: 4812 Cellular telephone services
HQ: Cellco Partnership
1 Verizon Way
Basking Ridge NJ

(P-4194)
CELLCO PARTNERSHIP
Also Called: Verizon
2500 E Imperial Hwy Ste 178 (92821-6122)
PHONE......................714 256-6015
Greg Schuler, *Mgr*
EMP: 71
SALES (corp-wide): 136.84B **Publicly Held**
Web: www.verizonwireless.com
SIC: 4812 Cellular telephone services
HQ: Cellco Partnership
1 Verizon Way
Basking Ridge NJ

(P-4195)
CELLCO PARTNERSHIP
Also Called: Verizon Wireless
258 N El Camino Real Ste A (92024)
PHONE......................760 642-0430
EMP: 71
SALES (corp-wide): 136.84B **Publicly Held**
Web: www.verizonwireless.com
SIC: 4812 Cellular telephone services
HQ: Cellco Partnership
1 Verizon Way
Basking Ridge NJ

(P-4196)
CELLCO PARTNERSHIP
Also Called: Verizon Wireless
26445 Bouquet Canyon Rd (91350-2396)
PHONE......................661 296-7585
Yesenia Alapisco, *Brnch Mgr*
EMP: 71
SALES (corp-wide): 136.84B **Publicly Held**
Web: www.verizonwireless.com
SIC: 4812 Cellular telephone services
HQ: Cellco Partnership
1 Verizon Way
Basking Ridge NJ

(P-4197)
CELLCO PARTNERSHIP
Also Called: Verizon Wireless
407 Kern St (93268-2812)
PHONE......................661 765-5397
EMP: 71
SALES (corp-wide): 136.84B **Publicly Held**
Web: www.verizonwireless.com
SIC: 4812 Cellular telephone services
HQ: Cellco Partnership
1 Verizon Way
Basking Ridge NJ

(P-4198)
CELLCO PARTNERSHIP
Also Called: Verizon Wireless
20 City Blvd W (92868-3100)
PHONE......................951 205-4170
Cvc Cellular, *Prin*
EMP: 71
SALES (corp-wide): 136.84B **Publicly Held**
Web: www.verizonwireless.com
SIC: 4812 Cellular telephone services
HQ: Cellco Partnership
1 Verizon Way
Basking Ridge NJ

(P-4199)
CELLCO PARTNERSHIP
Also Called: Verizon Wireless
2921 Los Feliz Blvd (90039-1539)
PHONE......................323 662-0009
Fernando Lara, *Prin*
EMP: 71
SALES (corp-wide): 136.84B **Publicly Held**
Web: www.wirelessplus.com
SIC: 4812 Cellular telephone services
HQ: Cellco Partnership
1 Verizon Way
Basking Ridge NJ

(P-4200)
CELLCO PARTNERSHIP
Also Called: Verizon Wireless
6965 Camino Arroyo Ste 60 (95020-7343)
PHONE......................408 846-5170
Ignacio Solorio, *Prin*
EMP: 71
SALES (corp-wide): 136.84B **Publicly Held**
Web: www.verizonwireless.com
SIC: 4812 Cellular telephone services
HQ: Cellco Partnership
1 Verizon Way
Basking Ridge NJ

(P-4201)
CELLCO PARTNERSHIP
Also Called: Verizon Wireless
71800 Highway 111 Ste A110 (92270-4492)
PHONE......................760 568-5542
Hicks Duana, *Prin*
EMP: 71
SALES (corp-wide): 136.84B **Publicly Held**
Web: www.verizonwireless.com
SIC: 4812 Cellular telephone services
HQ: Cellco Partnership
1 Verizon Way
Basking Ridge NJ

(P-4202)
CELLCO PARTNERSHIP
Also Called: Verizon Wireless
23718 El Toro Rd Ste A (92630-8908)
PHONE......................949 472-0700
Tracie Kemper, *Brnch Mgr*
EMP: 71
SALES (corp-wide): 136.84B **Publicly Held**
Web: www.verizon.com
SIC: 4812 Cellular telephone services
HQ: Cellco Partnership
1 Verizon Way
Basking Ridge NJ

(P-4203)
CELLCO PARTNERSHIP
Also Called: Verizon Wireless
2687 Park Ave (92782-2707)
PHONE......................714 258-8870
EMP: 71
SALES (corp-wide): 136.84B **Publicly Held**
Web: www.verizon.com
SIC: 4812 Cellular telephone services
HQ: Cellco Partnership
1 Verizon Way
Basking Ridge NJ

(P-4204)
CELLCO PARTNERSHIP
Also Called: Verizon Wireless
10952 Trinity Pkwy (95219-7297)
PHONE......................209 474-9071
EMP: 71
SALES (corp-wide): 136.84B **Publicly Held**
Web: www.verizonwireless.com
SIC: 4812 Cellular telephone services
HQ: Cellco Partnership
1 Verizon Way
Basking Ridge NJ

(P-4205)
CELLCO PARTNERSHIP
Also Called: Verizon Wireless
11902 Gem St (90650-2448)
PHONE......................562 244-8814
Jorge A Molina, *Prin*
EMP: 74
SALES (corp-wide): 136.84B **Publicly Held**
Web: www.verizonwireless.com
SIC: 4812 Cellular telephone services
HQ: Cellco Partnership
1 Verizon Way
Basking Ridge NJ

PRODUCTS & SERVICES SECTION
4812 - Radiotelephone Communication (P-4228)

(P-4206)
CELLCO PARTNERSHIP
Also Called: Verizon Wireless
12821 Main St (92345-9126)
PHONE..................760 662-5914
EMP: 71
SALES (corp-wide): 136.84B **Publicly Held**
Web: www.verizon.com
SIC: **4812** Cellular telephone services
HQ: Cellco Partnership
1 Verizon Way
Basking Ridge NJ

(P-4207)
CELLCO PARTNERSHIP
Also Called: Verizon Wireless
3825 Grand Ave (91710-5448)
PHONE..................909 591-9740
EMP: 71
SALES (corp-wide): 136.84B **Publicly Held**
Web: www.verizonwireless.com
SIC: **4812** Cellular telephone services
HQ: Cellco Partnership
1 Verizon Way
Basking Ridge NJ

(P-4208)
CLFRN/CLRD/FLRD/RGON I COMCAST
Also Called: Comcast
3011 Comcast Pl (94551-7594)
PHONE..................925 424-0273
EMP: 170 EST: 1996
SALES (est): 18.88MM
SALES (corp-wide): 121.43B **Publicly Held**
SIC: **4812** 4841 Radiotelephone communication; Cable television services
PA: Comcast Corporation
1 Comcast Ctr
Philadelphia PA
215 286-1700

(P-4209)
CONTRA COSTA COUNTY
30 Douglas Dr (94553-4068)
PHONE..................925 313-1323
EMP: 286 EST: 2016
SALES (est): 19.26MM **Privately Held**
Web: www.cchealth.org
SIC: **4812** Radiotelephone communication

(P-4210)
CREDO MOBILE INC
Also Called: Working Assets Long Distance
101 Market St Ste 700 (94105-1533)
P.O. Box 88878 (60188-0878)
PHONE..................415 369-2000
Michael Hall Kieschnick, *CEO*
Stephen Gunn, *
Douglas Moore, *
EMP: 100 EST: 1985
SQ FT: 21,000
SALES (est): 24.19MM **Privately Held**
Web: www.credomobile.com
SIC: **4812** Cellular telephone services

(P-4211)
CRICKET COMMUNICATIONS LLC (DH)
Also Called: Cricket Wireless
7337 Trade St (92121-2423)
EMP: 65 EST: 1999
SALES (est): 198.39MM
SALES (corp-wide): 120.74B **Publicly Held**
Web: www.cricketwireless.com
SIC: **4812** Cellular telephone services
HQ: Leap Wireless International, Inc.
7337 Trade St
San Diego CA
858 882-6000

(P-4212)
CUBIC SECURE COMMUNICATIONS I
9233 Balboa Ave (92123-1513)
PHONE..................858 505-2000
Steve Slijepcevic, *Managing Member*
EMP: 275
SALES (est): 10.8MM **Privately Held**
Web: www.cubic.com
SIC: **4812** Radiotelephone communication

(P-4213)
DIRECTV GROUP HOLDINGS LLC (HQ)
Also Called: Directv
2260 E Imperial Hwy (90245-3501)
PHONE..................310 964-5000
Michael White, *Pr*
Patrick Doyle, *Ex VP*
Larry Hunter, *Ex VP*
Joseph Bosch, *Chief Human Resources Officer*
Steven Adams, *CAO*
▲ EMP: 170 EST: 1977
SALES (est): 2.53B
SALES (corp-wide): 120.74B **Publicly Held**
SIC: **4812** Cellular telephone services
PA: At&T Inc.
208 S Akard St
Dallas TX
210 821-4105

(P-4214)
DISH WIRELESS LLC
Also Called: Boost Mobile
1190 N Chestnut Ave (93702-1709)
PHONE..................559 515-6866
EMP: 243
SIC: **4812** Cellular telephone services
HQ: Dish Wireless L.L.C.
9601 S Meridian Blvd
Englewood CO
303 723-1000

(P-4215)
EA MOBILE INC
5510 Lincoln Blvd (90094-2034)
PHONE..................310 754-7125
Mitch Lasky, *Ch Bd*
Michael Marchetti, *CFO*
Craig Gatarz, *COO*
Scott Lahman, *President Publishing*
Minard Hamilton, *Executive Distribution Vice President*
EMP: 96 EST: 2000
SQ FT: 23,000
SALES (est): 5.64MM
SALES (corp-wide): 7.43B **Publicly Held**
SIC: **4812** Cellular telephone services
PA: Electronic Arts Inc.
209 Redwood Shores Pkwy
Redwood City CA
650 628-1500

(P-4216)
ESCHAT ✪
3450 Broad St Ste 106 (93401-7214)
PHONE..................805 541-5044
EMP: 100 EST: 2023
SALES (est): 2.35MM **Privately Held**
SIC: **4812** Radiotelephone communication

(P-4217)
LETS TALKCOM INC
201 Mission St Ste 3000 (94105-1884)
PHONE..................415 357-7600
EMP: 100
Web: www.letstalk.com
SIC: **4812** 4813 Cellular telephone services; Telephone communication, except radio

(P-4218)
MBIT WIRELESS INC (PA)
4340 Von Karman Ave Ste 140 (92660-1201)
PHONE..................949 205-4559
Bhasker Patel, *Pr*
Mw Sohn, *
EMP: 131 EST: 2005
SALES (est): 9.98MM **Privately Held**
Web: www.mbitwireless.com
SIC: **4812** Cellular telephone services

(P-4219)
NEW CINGULAR WIRELESS SVCS INC
Also Called: AT&T
252 Broadway (92101-5004)
PHONE..................619 238-3638
Jason Cid, *Brnch Mgr*
EMP: 77
SALES (corp-wide): 120.74B **Publicly Held**
Web: www.att.com
SIC: **4812** 5999 Cellular telephone services; Mobile telephones and equipment
HQ: New Cingular Wireless Services, Inc.
7277 164th Ave Ne
Redmond WA
425 827-4500

(P-4220)
NEW CINGULAR WIRELESS SVCS INC
Also Called: AT&T
2166 Santa Rosa Ave (95407-7691)
PHONE..................707 535-0891
Jay Brooks, *Mgr*
EMP: 60
SALES (corp-wide): 120.74B **Publicly Held**
SIC: **4812** Cellular telephone services
HQ: New Cingular Wireless Services, Inc.
7277 164th Ave Ne
Redmond WA
425 827-4500

(P-4221)
NEXTEL COMMUNICATIONS INC
Also Called: Nextel
330 Commerce (92602-1398)
PHONE..................714 368-4509
Don Girkis, *VP*
EMP: 150
SALES (corp-wide): 79.57B **Publicly Held**
Web: www.sprint.com
SIC: **4812** Cellular telephone services
HQ: Nextel Communications, Inc.
12502 Sunrise Valley Dr
Reston VA
833 639-8353

(P-4222)
PACIFIC BELL TELEPHONE COMPANY
262 19th Ave (94403-1419)
PHONE..................650 572-6807
Carl Edwards, *Prin*
EMP: 4444
SALES (corp-wide): 120.74B **Publicly Held**

Web: www.att.com
SIC: **4812** Cellular telephone services
HQ: Pacific Bell Telephone Company
430 Bush St Fl 3
San Francisco CA
415 542-9000

(P-4223)
PACIFIC BELL TELEPHONE COMPANY
3847 Cardiff Ave (90232-2613)
PHONE..................310 515-2898
EMP: 4444
SALES (corp-wide): 120.74B **Publicly Held**
Web: www.att.com
SIC: **4812** Cellular telephone services
HQ: Pacific Bell Telephone Company
430 Bush St Fl 3
San Francisco CA
415 542-9000

(P-4224)
PACIFIC BELL TELEPHONE COMPANY
2040 Polk St 267 (94109-2520)
PHONE..................415 978-0881
EMP: 4444
SALES (corp-wide): 120.74B **Publicly Held**
Web: www.att.com
SIC: **4812** Cellular telephone services
HQ: Pacific Bell Telephone Company
430 Bush St Fl 3
San Francisco CA
415 542-9000

(P-4225)
RED POCKET INC
Also Called: Red Pocket Mobile
2060d E Avenida De Los Arboles Ste 288 (91362)
PHONE..................888 993-3888
Joshua Gordon, *Pr*
Steve Bowman, *
EMP: 75 EST: 2005
SALES (est): 14.09MM **Privately Held**
Web: www.redpocket.com
SIC: **4812** Cellular telephone services

(P-4226)
SLING MEDIA LLC
1051 E Hillsdale Blvd Ste 500 (94404-1640)
PHONE..................650 293-8000
Charles W Ergen, *CEO*
▲ EMP: 180 EST: 2004
SALES (est): 54.55MM **Publicly Held**
SIC: **4812** Radiotelephone communication
PA: Dish Network Corporation
9601 S Meridian Blvd
Englewood CO

(P-4227)
SPRINT COMMUNICATIONS CO LP
15582 Whittwood Ln (90603-2355)
PHONE..................562 943-8907
EMP: 149
SALES (corp-wide): 79.57B **Publicly Held**
SIC: **4812** Cellular telephone services
HQ: Sprint Communications Company L.P.
6391 Sprint Pkwy
Overland Park KS
800 829-0965

(P-4228)
SPRINT COMMUNICATIONS CO LP

4812 - Radiotelephone Communication (P-4229)

Also Called: Sprint
31754 Temecula Pkwy Ste A (92592-6805)
PHONE................................951 303-8501
EMP: 163
SALES (corp-wide): 79.57B Publicly Held
SIC: 4812 5065 4813 Cellular telephone services; Telephone and telegraphic equipment; Local and long distance telephone communications
HQ: Sprint Communications Company L.P.
    6391 Sprint Pkwy
    Overland Park KS
    800 829-0965

(P-4229)
SPRINT COMMUNICATIONS CO LP
5381 W Centinela Ave (90045-2003)
PHONE................................310 216-9093
EMP: 201
SALES (corp-wide): 79.57B Publicly Held
SIC: 4812 4813 Cellular telephone services; Local and long distance telephone communications
HQ: Sprint Communications Company L.P.
    6391 Sprint Pkwy
    Overland Park KS
    800 829-0965

(P-4230)
SPRINT COMMUNICATIONS CO LP
4225 Oceanside Blvd (92056-3472)
PHONE................................760 941-4535
EMP: 190
SALES (corp-wide): 79.57B Publicly Held
SIC: 4812 Cellular telephone services
HQ: Sprint Communications Company L.P.
    6391 Sprint Pkwy
    Overland Park KS
    800 829-0965

(P-4231)
SPRINT COMMUNICATIONS CO LP
23865 Clinton Keith Rd (92595-9829)
PHONE................................951 461-9786
EMP: 149
SALES (corp-wide): 79.57B Publicly Held
SIC: 4812 Cellular telephone services
HQ: Sprint Communications Company L.P.
    6391 Sprint Pkwy
    Overland Park KS
    800 829-0965

(P-4232)
SPRINT COMMUNICATIONS CO LP
3580 Grand Oaks (92881-4656)
PHONE................................951 340-1924
EMP: 161
SALES (corp-wide): 79.57B Publicly Held
SIC: 4812 4813 Cellular telephone services; Local and long distance telephone communications
HQ: Sprint Communications Company L.P.
    6391 Sprint Pkwy
    Overland Park KS
    800 829-0965

(P-4233)
SPRINT COMMUNICATIONS CO LP
44416 Valley Central Way (93536-6528)
PHONE................................661 951-8927
EMP: 190
SALES (corp-wide): 79.57B Publicly Held
SIC: 4812 Cellular telephone services
HQ: Sprint Communications Company L.P.
    6391 Sprint Pkwy
    Overland Park KS
    800 829-0965

(P-4234)
SPRINT COMMUNICATIONS CO LP
1270 W Redondo Beach Blvd (90247-3411)
PHONE................................310 515-0293
EMP: 149
SALES (corp-wide): 79.57B Publicly Held
SIC: 4812 Cellular telephone services
HQ: Sprint Communications Company L.P.
    6391 Sprint Pkwy
    Overland Park KS
    800 829-0965

(P-4235)
SPRINT CORPORATION
Also Called: Sprint
432 S Broadway (90013-1103)
PHONE................................213 613-4200
EMP: 110
SALES (corp-wide): 79.57B Publicly Held
Web: www.sprint.com
SIC: 4812 Cellular telephone services
HQ: Sprint Llc
    6200 Sprint Pkwy
    Overland Park KS
    855 848-3280

(P-4236)
SPRINT CORPORATION
Also Called: Sprint
4707 Firestone Blvd (90280-3403)
PHONE................................323 357-0797
EMP: 110
SALES (corp-wide): 79.57B Publicly Held
Web: www.sprint.com
SIC: 4812 Cellular telephone services
HQ: Sprint Llc
    6200 Sprint Pkwy
    Overland Park KS
    855 848-3280

(P-4237)
TKS WIRELESS INC
Also Called: Cricket Wireless
3320 Foothill Blvd (94601-3115)
P.O. Box 2225 (94587-7225)
PHONE................................510 227-6440
Sami D Aldajani, Pr
Khalid Aldajani, *
EMP: 200 EST: 2013
SALES (est): 10.11MM Privately Held
SIC: 4812 Cellular telephone services

(P-4238)
TRELLISWARE TECHNOLOGIES INC (HQ)
10641 Scripps Summit Ct Ste 100 (92131-3918)
PHONE................................858 753-1600
Metin Bayram, Pr
Steve Fisher, CFO
Paul Konopka, CCO
Anna Kochka, Pers/VP
Matt Fallows, Vice-President Global Business Development
EMP: 125 EST: 2000
SQ FT: 46,000
SALES (est): 44.36MM
SALES (corp-wide): 2.56B Publicly Held
Web: www.trellisware.com
SIC: 4812 4813 3663 Radiotelephone communication; Local and long distance telephone communications; Airborne radio communications equipment
PA: Viasat, Inc.
    6155 El Camino Real
    Carlsbad CA
    760 476-2200

(P-4239)
VERIZON BUS NETWRK SVCS LLC
Also Called: Verizon Business
11080 White Rock Rd Ste 100 (95670-6299)
PHONE................................916 779-5600
Bert C Roberts Junior, Brnch Mgr
EMP: 175
SALES (corp-wide): 136.84B Publicly Held
Web: www.verizonwireless.com
SIC: 4812 Cellular telephone services
HQ: Verizon Business Network Services Llc
    1 Verizon Way
    Basking Ridge NJ
    908 559-2000

(P-4240)
VERIZON BUS NETWRK SVCS LLC
Also Called: Verizon Business
1740 Creekside Oaks Dr Ste 200 (95833-3639)
PHONE................................916 569-5999
Suresh Madala, Prin
EMP: 175
SALES (corp-wide): 136.84B Publicly Held
Web: www.verizonwireless.com
SIC: 4812 Cellular telephone services
HQ: Verizon Business Network Services Llc
    1 Verizon Way
    Basking Ridge NJ
    908 559-2000

(P-4241)
VERIZON BUS NETWRK SVCS LLC
Also Called: Verizon Business
4340 Solar Way (94538-6335)
PHONE................................510 497-2500
Randy Cade, Mgr
EMP: 175
SALES (corp-wide): 136.84B Publicly Held
Web: www.verizonwireless.com
SIC: 4812 Cellular telephone services
HQ: Verizon Business Network Services Llc
    1 Verizon Way
    Basking Ridge NJ
    908 559-2000

(P-4242)
VERIZON COMMUNICATIONS INC
Also Called: Verizon
176 E Badillo St (91723-2113)
PHONE................................626 858-1739
Mark Clark, Dir
EMP: 60
SALES (corp-wide): 136.84B Publicly Held
Web: www.verizon.com
SIC: 4812 4813 Cellular telephone services; Telephone communication, except radio
PA: Verizon Communications Inc.
    1095 Ave Of The Americas
    New York NY
    212 395-1000

(P-4243)
VERIZON SERVICES CORP
Also Called: Verizon
2530 Wilshire Blvd Fl 1 (90403-4616)
PHONE................................310 315-1100
EMP: 332
SALES (corp-wide): 136.84B Publicly Held
Web: www.sitestar.net
SIC: 4812 Cellular telephone services
HQ: Verizon Services Corp.
    22001 Loudoun County Pkwy 125-100
    Ashburn VA
    703 729-5931

(P-4244)
VERIZON SOUTH INC
Also Called: Verizon
424 S Patterson Ave (93111-2404)
PHONE................................805 681-8527
Dennis Candini, Mgr
EMP: 207
SALES (corp-wide): 136.84B Publicly Held
SIC: 4812 Cellular telephone services
HQ: Verizon South Inc.
    600 Hidden Rdg
    Irving TX
    972 718-5600

(P-4245)
YOUR WIRELESS RETAILER INC
Also Called: Verizon Wireless
3540 Riverside Plaza Dr Ste 338 (92506-2707)
PHONE................................310 293-3706
Brooke Bennett, Pr
Herb Thompson, Mgr
Marcus Bradford, Pr
EMP: 65 EST: 2002
SQ FT: 1,800
SALES (est): 365.97K Privately Held
Web: www.wirelessplus.com
SIC: 4812 Cellular telephone services

4813 Telephone Communication, Except Radio

(P-4246)
11 MAIN INC
527 Flume St (95928-5608)
PHONE................................530 892-9191
Jeff Schlicht, CEO
Crystal Estes, *
Mike Effle, *
Ray Kaminski, *
Christina Liu, *
EMP: 105 EST: 2013
SALES (est): 15.21MM Privately Held
Web: www.11main.com
SIC: 4813 Online service providers
HQ: Alibaba.Com Us Llc
    525 Almanor Ave Ste 400
    Sunnyvale CA
    408 785-5580

(P-4247)
2WIRE INC (DH)
2450 Walsh Ave (95051-1303)
PHONE................................408 235-5500
Tim O'loughlin, CEO
Pasquale Romano, Pr
Tom Bohan, Sec
▲ EMP: 138 EST: 1998
SQ FT: 82,000
SALES (est): 67.73MM Publicly Held
Web: www.commscope.com
SIC: 4813 Internet connectivity services
HQ: Ruckus Wireless, Inc.
    350 W Java Dr
    Sunnyvale CA

PRODUCTS & SERVICES SECTION

4813 - Telephone Communication, Except Radio (P-4269)

(P-4248)
8X8 INC (PA)
Also Called: 8X8
675 Creekside Way (95008-0636)
PHONE.................................408 727-1885
Samuel Wilson, *CEO*
Jaswinder Pal Singh, *
Kevin Kraus, *CFO*
Hunter Middleton, *CPO*
Suzy Seandel, *CAO*
EMP: 1227 EST: 1987
SALES (est): 743.94MM
SALES (corp-wide): 743.94MM **Publicly Held**
Web: www.8x8.com
SIC: 4813 7372 Internet host services; Prepackaged software

(P-4249)
AB CELLULAR HOLDING LLC
Also Called: At & T Wireless Service
1452 Edinger Ave (92780-6246)
PHONE.................................562 468-6846
EMP: 2100
SIC: 4813 Local and long distance telephone communications

(P-4250)
ADCHEMY INC
1001 E Hillsdale Blvd Fl 7 (94404-1642)
PHONE.................................650 581-4600
EMP: 100
SIC: 4813 Online service providers

(P-4251)
ADICIO INC
5857 Owens Ave Ste 300 (92008-5507)
PHONE.................................760 602-9502
Richard Miller, *Pr*
Richette Lock, *
Mike Cavallo, *
EMP: 90 EST: 1997
SALES (est): 14.52MM **Privately Held**
Web: www.adicio.com
SIC: 4813 Internet host services

(P-4252)
AERIS COMMUNICATIONS INC (PA)
1731 Technology Dr Ste 800 (95110)
PHONE.................................408 557-1900
Marc Jones, *Ch*
Mark Cratsenburg Doctor, *VP Mktg*
John Molise, *
Syed Zaeem Hosain, *
Raj Kanaya, *
EMP: 249 EST: 2013
SQ FT: 30,000
SALES (est): 68.85MM **Privately Held**
Web: www.aeris.com
SIC: 4813 Local and long distance telephone communications

(P-4253)
ASIAINFO-LINKAGE INC
5201 Great America Pkwy Ste 4209 (95054-1122)
PHONE.................................408 970-9788
Steve Zhang, *
Steve Zhang, *CEO*
Ying Han, *
Lihua Yan, *
Yadong Jin, *
EMP: 1500 EST: 1994
SALES (est): 211.35MM **Privately Held**
Web: www.asiainfo-linkage.com
SIC: 4813 Internet connectivity services
HQ: Asiainfo Technologies (China), Inc.
Room 101, 1st Floor, Building 19, East District, No. 10, Northwe
Beijing BJ

(P-4254)
ASK MEDIA GROUP LLC
1955 Broadway Ste 350 (94612-2205)
PHONE.................................212 524-8716
Shane Mcgilloway, *CEO*
Nazly Hajjarian, *
EMP: 100 EST: 2017
SQ FT: 47,679
SALES (est): 7.92MM **Privately Held**
Web: www.askmediagroup.com
SIC: 4813 Web search portals

(P-4255)
BOLDYN NETWORKS US SERVICES LL
Also Called: Mobilitie Services, LLC
121 Innovation Dr Ste 200 (92617-3094)
PHONE.................................877 999-7070
Gary Jabara, *Ch*
Christos Karmis, *
Dissy Sarabosing, *
Dana Tardelli, *
EMP: 350 EST: 2015
SALES (est): 56.13MM
SALES (corp-wide): 72.96MM **Privately Held**
Web: www.boldyn.com
SIC: 4813 Local telephone communications
PA: Boardwalk Ig Management, Llc
1945 Placentia Ave Ste D
Costa Mesa CA

(P-4256)
BOLDYN NTWRKS US OPRATIONS LLC
121 Innovation Dr (92617-3091)
PHONE.................................949 515-1500
EMP: 145 EST: 2021
SALES (est): 7.87MM **Privately Held**
Web: www.boldyn.com
SIC: 4813 Online service providers

(P-4257)
BRAFTON INCORPORATED
220 Montgomery St Ste 917 (94104-3440)
PHONE.................................617 206-3040
EMP: 62
Web: www.brafton.com
SIC: 4813 Internet host services
PA: Brafton, Incorporated
2 Oliver St
Boston MA

(P-4258)
BROADVIEW NETWORKS INC
7731 Hayvenhurst Ave (91406-1735)
PHONE.................................818 939-0015
EMP: 86
SALES (corp-wide): 6.51B **Privately Held**
SIC: 4813 Local and long distance telephone communications
HQ: Broadview Networks, Inc.
4001 N Rodney Parham Rd
Little Rock AR

(P-4259)
CAL CONSOLDATED COMMUNICATIONS
Also Called: Consolidated Communications
211 Lincoln St (95678-2614)
P.O. Box 619969 (95661-0969)
PHONE.................................916 786-6141
Bob Udell, *CEO*
EMP: 477 EST: 1914
SQ FT: 21,500
SALES (est): 15.98MM
SALES (corp-wide): 1.19B **Publicly Held**
Web: www.consolidated.com
SIC: 4813 Local telephone communications
HQ: Surewest Communications
211 Lincoln St
Roseville CA
916 786-6141

(P-4260)
CALIFORNIA INTERNET LP (PA)
Also Called: Geolinks
251 Camarillo Ranch Rd (93012-5082)
PHONE.................................805 225-4638
Skyler Ditchfield, *Pt*
Ryan Adams, *
Phil Oseas, *
Ryan Hauf, *
EMP: 164 EST: 2011
SALES (est): 46.21MM
SALES (corp-wide): 46.21MM **Privately Held**
Web: www.geolinks.com
SIC: 4813 Internet connectivity services

(P-4261)
CALNET INC
4101 Wild Chaparral Dr (95682-8739)
P.O. Box 1041 (95682-1041)
PHONE.................................530 672-1078
John Lane, *CEO*
Ken Garnett, *
EMP: 78 EST: 1996
SALES (est): 46.98MM **Privately Held**
Web: www.cal.net
SIC: 4813 Internet connectivity services

(P-4262)
CASTLE ACCESS INC
Also Called: Kio Networks
9606 Aero Dr Ste 1900 (92123-1888)
PHONE.................................858 836-0200
EMP: 60
Web: www.castleaccess.com
SIC: 4813 Internet host services

(P-4263)
CBS MAXPREPS INC
Also Called: Maxpreps
4364 Town Center Blvd Ste 320 (95762-7127)
PHONE.................................530 676-6440
Andy Beal, *Pr*
EMP: 100 EST: 1993
SQ FT: 9,000
SALES (est): 1.91MM
SALES (corp-wide): 30.15B **Publicly Held**
Web: www.maxpreps.com
SIC: 4813 Web search portals
PA: Paramount Global
1515 Broadway
New York NY
212 258-6000

(P-4264)
CHANNEL INTELLIGENCE INC
1600 Amphitheatre Pkwy (94043-1351)
P.O. Box 534351 (30353-4351)
PHONE.................................321 939-5600
EMP: 150
Web: support.google.com
SIC: 4813 Internet host services

(P-4265)
CLEARCAPTIONS LLC
Also Called: Clearcaptions
3001 Lava Ridge Ct Ste 100 (95661-3094)
PHONE.................................866 868-8695
Robert Rae, *Pr*
Gordon L Ellis, *
Rita Beier Braman, *Tax Vice President*
Blaine Reeve, *
Corrine Perritano, *
EMP: 289 EST: 2014
SALES (est): 81.26MM
SALES (corp-wide): 99.68MM **Privately Held**
Web: www.clearcaptions.com
SIC: 4813 Internet connectivity services
PA: Purple Communications, Inc.
13620 Ranch Road 620 N C100
Austin TX
888 900-4780

(P-4266)
CONNEXITY INC (DH)
Also Called: Shopzilla.com
2120 Colorado Ave Ste 400 (90404-3504)
PHONE.................................310 571-1235
William Glass, *CEO*
Aaron Young, *CFO*
Blythe Holden, *Sr VP*
EMP: 203 EST: 2012
SALES (est): 94.72MM
SALES (corp-wide): 694.97MM **Privately Held**
Web: www.connexity.com
SIC: 4813 7383 7331 Online service providers; News syndicates; Direct mail advertising services
HQ: Symphony Technology Group, L.L.C.
428 University Ave
Palo Alto CA
650 935-9500

(P-4267)
DECENTRAL TV CORPORATION
Also Called: Kyte
442 Post St Fl 10 (94102-1524)
PHONE.................................415 480-6800
Daniel Graf, *CEO*
Anne Dorman, *CFO*
Gannon Hall, *COO*
Dan Fitzsimons, *CRO*
EMP: 66 EST: 2006
SQ FT: 2,000
SALES (est): 10.64MM
SALES (corp-wide): 22.71MM **Privately Held**
SIC: 4813 Internet host services
PA: Piksel, Inc.
2100 Powers Ferry Rd Se # 400
Atlanta GA
877 664-6137

(P-4268)
DIGITALMOJO INC
3111 Camino Del Rio N Ste 400 (92108-5724)
PHONE.................................800 413-5916
Martin Smith, *CEO*
Jerry Papazian, *
Martin Caverly, *
Michael Hart, *
Mary Khoury, *
EMP: 75 EST: 2005
SQ FT: 800
SALES (est): 9.49MM **Privately Held**
Web: www.digitalmojo.com
SIC: 4813 8742 Internet connectivity services; Marketing consulting services

(P-4269)
DIVERSFIED CMMNCTIONS SVCS INC
Also Called: D C S
1260 Pioneer St (92821-3725)
PHONE.................................714 888-2284
Steve Hurley, *CEO*
Steven Hurley, *
Bill Shields, *
▲ EMP: 63 EST: 1972

4813 - Telephone Communication, Except Radio (P-4270)

PRODUCTS & SERVICES SECTION

SQ FT: 19,000
SALES (est): 14.23MM **Privately Held**
Web: www.diversified.net
SIC: **4813** Telephone communications broker

(P-4270)
ENVIVIO INC
2795 Augustine Dr (95054-2957)
PHONE..................................650 243-2700
Julien Signes, *Pr*
Terry D Kramer, *
Erik E Miller, *CFO*
EMP: 163 EST: 2000
SALES (est): 46.12MM
SALES (corp-wide): 25.89B **Privately Held**
Web: www.mediakind.com
SIC: **4813** Telephone/video communications
HQ: Ericsson Inc.
    6300 Legacy Dr
    Plano TX
    972 583-0000

(P-4271)
ERICSSON INC
2755 Augustine Dr (95054-2919)
PHONE..................................408 750-5000
Kevin A Denuccio, *Mgr*
EMP: 1100
SALES (corp-wide): 25.89B **Privately Held**
Web: www.ericsson.com
SIC: **4813** Telephone communication, except radio
HQ: Ericsson Inc.
    6300 Legacy Dr
    Plano TX
    972 583-0000

(P-4272)
FILANITY CORPORATION
Also Called: Vietnumber
17011 Beach Blvd Ste 1440 (92647)
PHONE..................................714 475-3521
Frank Kim, *Pr*
Luan Kim, *Stockholder*
EMP: 60 EST: 2007
SQ FT: 2,800
SALES (est): 2.67MM **Privately Held**
SIC: **4813** Local and long distance telephone communications

(P-4273)
FORMAGRID INC (PA)
Also Called: Airtable
799 Market St Fl 8 (94103-2044)
PHONE..................................415 200-2040
Howard Liu, *CEO*
Andrew Ofstad, *
EMP: 495 EST: 2013
SQ FT: 10,000
SALES (est): 216MM
SALES (corp-wide): 216MM **Privately Held**
Web: www.airtable.com
SIC: **4813** 7371 7372 7373 Proprietary online service networks; Computer software development and applications; Utility computer software; Systems software development services

(P-4274)
FORTITUDE TECHNOLOGY INC
Also Called: Carinet
8929 Complex Dr Ste A (92123-1454)
PHONE..................................858 974-5080
Tim Caulfield, *CEO*
Joe Mcmillen, *Prin*
Michael C Robert, *
EMP: 85 EST: 1997
SQ FT: 40,000
SALES (est): 7.4MM **Privately Held**

SIC: **4813** Internet connectivity services

(P-4275)
FOX INTERACTIVE MEDIA INC
6100 Center Dr Ste 800 (90045-9201)
PHONE..................................310 969-7000
EMP: 128
SIC: **4813** Online service providers

(P-4276)
FREE CONFERENCING CORPORATION
Also Called: Freeconferencecall.com
4300 E Pacific Coast Hwy (90804-2114)
P.O. Box 41069 (90853-1069)
PHONE..................................562 437-1411
EMP: 116 EST: 2004
SQ FT: 10,000
SALES (est): 17.46MM **Privately Held**
Web: www.freeconferencecall.com
SIC: **4813** 7389 Voice telephone communications

(P-4277)
FRONTIER CALIFORNIA INC
Also Called: Verizon
510 Park Ave (91340-2527)
PHONE..................................818 365-0542
Gloria Caudill, *Brnch Mgr*
EMP: 373
SALES (corp-wide): 5.79B **Publicly Held**
SIC: **4813** Telephone communication, except radio
HQ: Frontier California Inc.
    401 Merritt 7
    Norwalk CT
    203 614-5600

(P-4278)
FRONTIER CALIFORNIA INC
Also Called: Verizon
295 Parkshore Dr (95630-4716)
PHONE..................................212 395-1000
Victor Andersen, *Brnch Mgr*
EMP: 373
SALES (corp-wide): 5.79B **Publicly Held**
SIC: **4813** Telephone communication, except radio
HQ: Frontier California Inc.
    401 Merritt 7
    Norwalk CT
    203 614-5600

(P-4279)
FRONTIER CALIFORNIA INC
Also Called: Verizon
1 Wellpoint Way (91362-3893)
PHONE..................................805 372-6000
Alex Stadler, *Prin*
EMP: 298
SALES (corp-wide): 5.79B **Publicly Held**
SIC: **4813** Telephone communication, except radio
HQ: Frontier California Inc.
    401 Merritt 7
    Norwalk CT
    203 614-5600

(P-4280)
FRONTIER CALIFORNIA INC
Also Called: Verizon
83793 Doctor Carreon Blvd (92201-7035)
PHONE..................................760 342-0500
EMP: 298
SALES (corp-wide): 5.79B **Publicly Held**
SIC: **4813** Local and long distance telephone communications
HQ: Frontier California Inc.
    401 Merritt 7
    Norwalk CT
    203 614-5600

(P-4281)
FRONTIER CALIFORNIA INC
Also Called: Verizon
7352 Slater Ave (92647-6227)
PHONE..................................714 375-6713
Patrick Dillon, *Mgr*
EMP: 335
SALES (corp-wide): 5.79B **Publicly Held**
SIC: **4813** 8721 5065 8711 Local and long distance telephone communications; Billing and bookkeeping service; Telephone and telegraphic equipment; Electrical or electronic engineering
HQ: Frontier California Inc.
    401 Merritt 7
    Norwalk CT
    203 614-5600

(P-4282)
FRONTIER CALIFORNIA INC
Also Called: Verizon
525 E Yosemite Ave (95336-5806)
P.O. Box 992 (95336-1139)
PHONE..................................209 239-4128
Luanne Weldon, *Brnch Mgr*
EMP: 298
SALES (corp-wide): 5.79B **Publicly Held**
SIC: **4813** 4812 Local telephone communications; Radiotelephone communication
HQ: Frontier California Inc.
    401 Merritt 7
    Norwalk CT
    203 614-5600

(P-4283)
FRONTIER CALIFORNIA INC
Also Called: Verizon
350 Lagoon St (93514-3406)
PHONE..................................760 872-0812
EMP: 298
SALES (corp-wide): 5.79B **Publicly Held**
SIC: **4813** Local telephone communications
HQ: Frontier California Inc.
    401 Merritt 7
    Norwalk CT
    203 614-5600

(P-4284)
FRONTIER CALIFORNIA INC
Also Called: Verizon
200 W Church St (93458-5005)
PHONE..................................805 925-0000
Carrie Ramsey, *Mgr*
EMP: 335
SALES (corp-wide): 5.79B **Publicly Held**
SIC: **4813** Long distance telephone communications
HQ: Frontier California Inc.
    401 Merritt 7
    Norwalk CT
    203 614-5600

(P-4285)
FUTUREWEI TECHNOLOGIES INC
2330 Central Expy (95050-2516)
PHONE..................................469 277-5700
EMP: 178
SALES (corp-wide): 31.02B **Privately Held**
Web: www.futurewei.com
SIC: **4813** Telephone communication, except radio
HQ: Futurewei Technologies, Inc.
    2220 Central Expy
    Santa Clara CA
    469 277-5700

(P-4286)
FUZE INC (PA)
675 Creekside Way (95008-0636)
PHONE..................................800 890-1553
Brian Day, *CEO*
Steven Kokinos, *
Aaron Evans, *
Thomas Lake, *
Brian Kardon, *
EMP: 173 EST: 2005
SALES (est): 97.37MM **Privately Held**
Web: de.fuze.com
SIC: **4813** Telephone cable service, land or submarine

(P-4287)
GAIA INTERACTIVE INC
Also Called: Gaia Online
5201 Great America Pkwy Ste 320 (95054-1140)
▲ EMP: 105 EST: 2003
SALES (est): 10.45MM **Privately Held**
Web: www.gaiainteractive.com
SIC: **4813** Internet host services

(P-4288)
GLOBAL DOMAINS INTL INC
Also Called: Worldsite.ws
701 Palomar Airport Rd (92011-1027)
PHONE..................................760 602-3000
Michael S Starr, *Pr*
Allen Ezier, *
EMP: 74 EST: 1999
SQ FT: 5,000
SALES (est): 3.1MM **Privately Held**
Web: www.website.ws
SIC: **4813** Internet connectivity services

(P-4289)
GOGRID LLC
Also Called: Coloserve
150 S 1st St Ste 101 (95113-2605)
PHONE..................................415 869-7444
John Keagy, *Managing Member*
David Hecht, *
Simon Tam, *
Brett Newsome, *
Jeff Samuels, *CMO*
EMP: 112 EST: 2001
SQ FT: 20,000
SALES (est): 16.43MM **Privately Held**
SIC: **4813** 7374 7375 7371 Internet connectivity services; Data processing and preparation; Data base information retrieval ; Computer software development and applications

(P-4290)
GOOGLE FIBER INC (DH)
1600 Amphitheatre Pkwy (94043-1351)
PHONE..................................650 253-0000
Dinni Jain, *CEO*
Milo Medin, *
Fleur Knowsley, *
Robert Andreatta, *
EMP: 74 EST: 2010
SALES (est): 184.18MM
SALES (corp-wide): 282.84B **Publicly Held**
Web: fiber.google.com
SIC: **4813** Internet host services
HQ: Google Llc
    1600 Amphitheatre Pkwy
    Mountain View CA
    650 253-0000

(P-4291)
GOOGLE INTERNATIONAL LLC (DH)
35018 Avenue D (92399-4407)

PRODUCTS & SERVICES SECTION
4813 - Telephone Communication, Except Radio (P-4312)

PHONE..................650 253-0000
Eric Schmidt, Ch Bd
Larry Page, *
David C Drummond, *
▼ EMP: 83 EST: 2014
SALES (est): 48.19MM
SALES (corp-wide): 282.84B Publicly Held
Web: www.google.com
SIC: 4813 7375 Internet connectivity services; Information retrieval services
HQ: Google Llc
1600 Amphitheatre Pkwy
Mountain View CA
650 253-0000

(P-4292)
GTT COMMUNICATIONS (MP) INC (DH)
Also Called: Megapath
6700 Koll Center Pkwy Ste 330 (94566-7022)
PHONE..................415 687-3870
Craig Young, Ch
Paul Milley, *
Steve Chisholm, *
Kurt Hoffman, *
David Williams, CRO*
EMP: 150 EST: 1997
SQ FT: 12,000
SALES (est): 87.46MM Privately Held
SIC: 4813 7375 Internet connectivity services; Information retrieval services
HQ: Gtt Americas, Llc
7900 Tysons One Pl Fl 14
Mc Lean VA
703 783-3124

(P-4293)
HIGHTAIL INC
1919 S Bascom Ave (95008-2220)
PHONE..................408 879-9118
EMP: 100
Web: www.hightail.com
SIC: 4813 Internet connectivity services

(P-4294)
HOTWIRE INC
Also Called: Hotwire.com
114 Sansome St Ste 400 (94104-3810)
PHONE..................415 343-8400
Dara Khosrowshahi, CEO
Clem Bason, *
Jen Roane, *
EMP: 175 EST: 1999
SALES (est): 2.31MM
SALES (corp-wide): 11.67B Publicly Held
Web: www.hotwire.com
SIC: 4813 Internet connectivity services
PA: Expedia Group, Inc.
1111 Expedia Group Way W
Seattle WA
206 481-7200

(P-4295)
HULU LLC
12312 W Olympic Blvd (90064)
PHONE..................888 631-4858
Mike Hopkins, CEO
EMP: 739
SALES (corp-wide): 82.72B Publicly Held
Web: www.hulu.com
SIC: 4813 4833 Internet host services; Television translator station
HQ: Hulu, Llc
2500 Broadway Ste 200
Santa Monica CA

(P-4296)
HULU LLC (HQ)
2500 Broadway Ste 200 (90404-3071)
PHONE..................310 571-4700
Randy Freer, CEO
Joe Earley, Pr
EMP: 250 EST: 2007
SALES (est): 1.88B
SALES (corp-wide): 82.72B Publicly Held
Web: www.hulu.com
SIC: 4813 4833 Internet host services; Television translator station
PA: The Walt Disney Company
500 S Buena Vista St
Burbank CA
818 560-1000

(P-4297)
INCOMNET COMMUNICATIONS CORP
2801 Main St (92614-5027)
PHONE..................949 251-8000
George P Blanco, Pr
John Hill, Ch Bd
Stephen A Garcia, CFO
Andrew Kalinowski, VP Mktg
EMP: 80 EST: 1983
SQ FT: 68,000
SALES (est): 7.73MM Privately Held
SIC: 4813 Long distance telephone communications

(P-4298)
INDIEGOGO INC
2261 Market St Ste 4731 (94114-1612)
PHONE..................866 641-4646
Andy Yang, CEO
EMP: 138 EST: 2007
SALES (est): 45.2MM Privately Held
Web: www.indie-gogo.com
SIC: 4813 7371 Internet host services; Computer code authors

(P-4299)
INFONET SERVICES CORPORATION (DH)
Also Called: BT Infonet
2160 E Grand Ave (90245-5024)
PHONE..................310 335-2600
David Andrew, CEO
Jose A Collazo, *
Paul Galleberg, *
Akbar H Firdosy, *
John C Hoffman, *
▲ EMP: 600 EST: 1988
SQ FT: 150,000
SALES (est): 202.89MM
SALES (corp-wide): 24.85B Privately Held
Web: www.infonet.com
SIC: 4813 7373 7375 Data telephone communications; Computer integrated systems design; Information retrieval services
HQ: British Telecommunications Public Limited Company
1 Braham Street
London
800 917-1017

(P-4300)
INGENIO INC
182 Howard St # 826 (94105-1611)
PHONE..................415 248-4000
Warren Heffelfinger, CEO
Mark Britto, *
EMP: 120 EST: 1999
SQ FT: 25,000
SALES (est): 26.12MM
SALES (corp-wide): 120.74B Publicly Held

SIC: 4813 Internet host services
PA: At&T Inc.
208 S Akard St
Dallas TX
210 821-4105

(P-4301)
JUSTANSWER LLC
38 Keyes Ave Ste 150 (94129-1709)
PHONE..................800 785-2305
Jeremy Liegl, CLO*
EMP: 247 EST: 2011
SALES (est): 10.56MM Privately Held
Web: www.pearl.com
SIC: 4813 Online service providers

(P-4302)
KIJIJI CLASSIFIEDS LLC
2125 Hamilton Ave (95125-5905)
PHONE..................669 213-9255
EMP: 66
SIC: 4813 Online service providers
HQ: Kijiji Classifieds, Llc
2065 Hamilton Ave
San Jose CA

(P-4303)
KIJIJI CLASSIFIEDS LLC
99 Fremont St (94105-2228)
PHONE..................408 376-4952
EMP: 66
SIC: 4813 Internet host services
HQ: Kijiji Classifieds, Llc
2065 Hamilton Ave
San Jose CA

(P-4304)
KIJIJI CLASSIFIEDS LLC (HQ)
2065 Hamilton Ave (95125-5904)
PHONE..................408 376-4952
EMP: 67 EST: 2008
SALES (est): 9.02MM Publicly Held
SIC: 4813 Internet host services
PA: Ebay Inc.
2025 Hamilton Ave
San Jose CA

(P-4305)
LAUNCH MEDIA INC (HQ)
Also Called: Tourdates.com
25 Taylor St (94102-3916)
PHONE..................310 593-6152
David Goldberg, Ch Bd
Robert Roback, Pr
Jeff Mickeal, CFO
EMP: 120 EST: 1994
SQ FT: 21,375
SALES (est): 24.5MM Privately Held
SIC: 4813 Internet host services
PA: Altaba Inc.
140 E 45th St Fl 15
New York NY

(P-4306)
LISTENCOM INC
2012 16th St (94103-4819)
PHONE..................415 934-2000
Rob Reid, CEO
Sean Ryan, *
EMP: 80 EST: 1998
SALES (est): 16.56MM
SALES (corp-wide): 58.18MM Privately Held
SIC: 4813 7375 Proprietary online service networks; Information retrieval services
HQ: Realnetworks Llc
1501 1st Ave S Ste 600
Seattle WA

(P-4307)
LMI NET
1700 Martin Luther King Jr Way (94709-2114)
PHONE..................510 843-6389
Douglas Hansen, Owner
Doug Hansen, Owner
EMP: 80 EST: 2001
SALES (est): 1.46MM Privately Held
Web: www.lmi.net
SIC: 4813 Internet connectivity services

(P-4308)
LOCAL LIGHTHOUSE CORP
1525 Mesa Verde Dr E Ste 225 (92626-5258)
PHONE..................888 370-8231
Eric Oakley, CEO
EMP: 61 EST: 2011
SALES (est): 867.23K Privately Held
Web: www.locallighthouse.com
SIC: 4813 8742 Internet host services; Marketing consulting services

(P-4309)
LUMEN TECH GVRNMENT SLTONS INC
2240 Douglas Blvd Ste 250 (95661-3874)
PHONE..................916 781-7772
Peter Kusendahl, Brnch Mgr
EMP: 5006
SALES (corp-wide): 17.48B Publicly Held
SIC: 4813 Local telephone communications
HQ: Lumen Technologies Government Solutions, Inc.
931 14th St Ste 1000b
Denver CO
303 992-1400

(P-4310)
MAILCENTRO INC
715 Sutter St Ste B (95630-2546)
PHONE..................916 985-4445
David Saykally, Pr
EMP: 120 EST: 2001
SALES (est): 534.22K Privately Held
SIC: 4813 Internet host services
PA: Computer Power Software Group Inc.
716 Figueroa St
Folsom CA

(P-4311)
MEDIA TEMPLE INC
12655 W Jefferson Blvd # 400 (90066-7008)
PHONE..................877 578-4000
Russell P Reeder, CEO
Marc Dumont, *
John Carey, *
Albert Lopez, *
Rod Stoddard, *
EMP: 203 EST: 1998
SALES (est): 48.87MM
SALES (corp-wide): 4.09B Publicly Held
Web: www.mediatemple.net
SIC: 4813 7371 Internet host services; Computer software development and applications
HQ: Godaddy.Com, Llc
2155 E Godaddy Way
Tempe AZ

(P-4312)
MEEBO INC
1600 Amphitheatre Pkwy (94043-1351)
P.O. Box 2050 (94042-2050)
PHONE..................650 253-0000
▲ EMP: 89
Web: www.meebo.com

4813 - Telephone Communication, Except Radio (P-4313)

SIC: 4813 Internet connectivity services

(P-4313)
MEGAPATH INC
6800 Koll Center Pkwy Ste 200
(94566-7053)
PHONE..................................877 611-6342
EMP: 1772 EST: 2000
SALES (est): 25.71MM **Privately Held**
SIC: 4813 Internet connectivity services

(P-4314)
MIS SCIENCES CORP
2550 N Hollywood Way Ste 404
(91505-1055)
PHONE..................................818 847-0213
EMP: 125 EST: 1996
SQ FT: 7,500
SALES (est): 9.67MM **Privately Held**
Web: www.mis-sciences.com
SIC: 4813 8748 7376 8742 Internet connectivity services; Systems engineering consultant, ex. computer or professional; Computer facilities management; Management information systems consultant

(P-4315)
MOBITV INC (PA)
345 California St Ste 2200 (94104-2670)
PHONE..................................510 981-1303
Charlie Nooney, *Ch Bd*
Paul Scanlan, *
David Brubeck, *
Ray Derenzo, *CMO*
Anders Norstrom, *
EMP: 99 EST: 2000
SALES (est): 43.97MM
SALES (corp-wide): 43.97MM **Privately Held**
Web: business.tivo.com
SIC: 4813 4899 Internet connectivity services.; Data communication services

(P-4316)
MP3COM INC
4790 Eastgate Mall (92121-2060)
PHONE..................................858 623-7000
Derrick Oien, *COO*
Michael Robertson, *Prin*
EMP: 81 EST: 1998
SQ FT: 61,000
SALES (est): 1.72MM
SALES (corp-wide): 30.15B **Publicly Held**
SIC: 4813 Internet host services
HQ: Cbs Interactive Inc.
680 Folsom St
San Francisco CA

(P-4317)
MPOWER HOLDING CORPORATION (HQ)
Also Called: Tpx Communications
515 S Flower St Fl 36 (90071-2201)
PHONE..................................866 699-8242
Richard A Jalkut, *CEO*
Richard A Jalkut, *Ch Bd*
Timothy J Medina, *
EMP: 89 EST: 1996
SALES (est): 502.8MM **Privately Held**
SIC: 4813 Internet connectivity services
PA: U.S. Telepacific Holdings Corp.
515 S Flower St Fl 47
Los Angeles CA

(P-4318)
MPULSE MOBILE INC (PA)
21255 Burbank Blvd (91367-6669)
PHONE..................................888 678-5735
Chris Nicholson, *CEO*
Ram Prayaga, *
Brian Chudleigh, *
Allison Gage, *ENGAGEMENT*
EMP: 78 EST: 2014
SALES (est): 36.67MM
SALES (corp-wide): 36.67MM **Privately Held**
Web: www.mpulsemobile.com
SIC: 4813 Data telephone communications

(P-4319)
NEW DREAM NETWORK LLC
Also Called: Dreamhost.com
707 Wilshire Blvd Ste 5050 (90017-3607)
PHONE..................................323 375-3842
EMP: 74
SALES (corp-wide): 7.07MM **Privately Held**
Web: www.dreamhost.com
SIC: 4813 Internet host services
PA: New Dream Network, Llc
417 Assod Rd Pmb 257 257 Pmb
Brea CA
626 644-9466

(P-4320)
NEXTPOINT INC (PA)
Also Called: Break Media
8750 Wilshire Blvd Ste 200 (90211-2700)
PHONE..................................310 360-5904
Keith Richman, *Pr*
Andrew Doyle, *
David Subar, *
EMP: 80 EST: 2005
SALES (est): 22.65MM **Privately Held**
Web: www.breakmedia.com
SIC: 4813 Internet connectivity services

(P-4321)
NEXXEN GROUP LLC (PA)
535 Mission St Fl 14 (94105-3253)
PHONE..................................425 279-1222
Amy Rosthstin, *Managing Member*
Yaniv Arvie, *
Sagi Niri, *
EMP: 179 EST: 2007
SALES (est): 41.19MM **Privately Held**
Web: www.rhythmone.com
SIC: 4813 2741 7319 Online service providers; Internet publishing and broadcasting; Display advertising service

(P-4322)
NUERA COMMUNICATIONS INC (DH)
9890 Towne Centre Dr Ste 150 (92121)
PHONE..................................858 625-2400
EMP: 75 EST: 1997
SQ FT: 48,709
SALES (est): 21.32MM **Privately Held**
Web: www.nuera.com
SIC: 4813 Telephone communication, except radio
HQ: Audiocodes, Inc.
80 Kingsbridge Rd
Piscataway NJ
732 469-0880

(P-4323)
O1 COMMUNICATIONS INC (PA)
Also Called: O1 Communications
4359 Town Center Blvd Ste 217
(95762-7113)
PHONE..................................888 444-1111
Bradley Jenkins, *CEO*
Max Seely, *Sr VP*
Jim Beausoleil, *CFO*
EMP: 77 EST: 1998
SQ FT: 20,000
SALES (est): 9.89MM
SALES (corp-wide): 9.89MM **Privately Held**
SIC: 4813 Data telephone communications

(P-4324)
PAC-WEST TELECOMM INC
4210 Coronado Ave (95204-2341)
PHONE..................................877 626-4325
EMP: 70
SIC: 4813 Local and long distance telephone communications

(P-4325)
PACIFIC BELL TELEPHONE COMPANY (HQ)
Also Called: Pacbell
430 Bush St Fl 3 (94108-3735)
PHONE..................................415 542-9000
TOLL FREE: 800
Kenneth P Mcneely, *CEO*
Ray Wilkins Junior, *Pr*
▲ EMP: 2000 EST: 1906
SQ FT: 500,000
SALES (est): 1B
SALES (corp-wide): 120.74B **Publicly Held**
Web: www.att.com
SIC: 4813 2741 4822 Local and long distance telephone communications; Directories, telephone: publishing only, not printed on site; Telegraph and other communications
PA: At&T Inc.
208 S Akard St
Dallas TX
210 821-4105

(P-4326)
PACNET SERVICES USA INC
435 Harriet St Fl 2 (94103-4914)
PHONE..................................415 287-2500
EMP: 203
SIC: 4813 Internet connectivity services
HQ: Pacnet Services Usa, Inc
40 Wall St Fl 44
New York NY

(P-4327)
PARETO NETWORKS INC
1183 Bordeaux Dr Ste 22 (94089-1201)
PHONE..................................877 727-8020
Daniel Ryan, *CEO*
EMP: 466 EST: 2008
SALES (est): 2.43MM **Publicly Held**
Web: www.extremenetworks.com
SIC: 4813 Proprietary online service networks
HQ: Aerohive Networks, Inc.
1011 Mccarthy Blvd
Milpitas CA

(P-4328)
PAYCHEX BENEFIT TECH INC
Also Called: Benetrac
2385 Northside Dr Ste 100 (92108-2716)
PHONE..................................800 322-7292
Martin Mucci, *CEO*
B Thomas Golisano, *
Jan Hawthorne, *
Susan Short, *
John B Gibson, *
EMP: 110 EST: 1986
SALES (est): 24.46MM
SALES (corp-wide): 5.01B **Publicly Held**
SIC: 4813 Online service providers
PA: Paychex, Inc.
911 Panorama Trl S
Rochester NY
585 385-6666

(P-4329)
PCS MOBILE SOLUTIONS LLC
3534 Tweedy Blvd (90280-6026)
PHONE..................................323 567-2490
EMP: 80
SALES (corp-wide): 48.68MM **Privately Held**
Web: www.pcsmobilesolutions.com
SIC: 4813 4812 Local and long distance telephone communications; Cellular telephone services
PA: Pcs Mobile Solutions, Llc
32000 Northwestern Hwy # 279
Farmington Hills MI
248 539-2221

(P-4330)
PHONECOM INC
14288 Danielson St (92064-8891)
PHONE..................................973 577-6380
EMP: 93 EST: 2013
SALES (est): 624.3K **Privately Held**
Web: www.phone.com
SIC: 4813 Internet connectivity services

(P-4331)
PUBLIC COMMUNICATIONS SVCS INC
11859 Wilshire Blvd Ste 600 (90025-6616)
P.O. Box 2868 (36652-2868)
PHONE..................................310 231-1000
Paul Jennings, *CEO*
Tommie Joe, *
Dennis Komai, *
EMP: 150 EST: 1987
SQ FT: 15,000
SALES (est): 16.92MM **Privately Held**
SIC: 4813 Local and long distance telephone communications

(P-4332)
QUALITY SPEAKS LLC (PA)
Also Called: Phonepower
9221 Corbin Ave Ste 260 (91324-1625)
PHONE..................................818 264-4400
Jim Murphy, *CEO*
Sam Ghahremanpour, *Pr*
Kevin Connor, *CFO*
EMP: 61 EST: 2010
SALES (est): 41.22MM
SALES (corp-wide): 41.22MM **Privately Held**
Web: www.phonepower.com
SIC: 4813 Local and long distance telephone communications

(P-4333)
QWEST CYBERSOLUTIONS LLC
Also Called: Qwest
3015 Winona Ave (91504-2541)
PHONE..................................818 729-2100
Gino Roa, *Dir*
EMP: 147
SALES (corp-wide): 17.48B **Publicly Held**
SIC: 4813 Telephone communication, except radio
HQ: Qwest Cyber.Solutions Llc
931 14th St
Denver CO
303 296-2787

(P-4334)
RACE TELECOMMUNICATIONS LLC (PA)
601 Gateway Blvd Ste 280 (94080-7074)
PHONE..................................650 246-8900
Raul Alcaraz, *CEO*
EMP: 60 EST: 2006
SALES (est): 10.89MM **Privately Held**

PRODUCTS & SERVICES SECTION

4813 - Telephone Communication, Except Radio (P-4354)

SIC: **4813** 7374 Internet connectivity services; Data processing and preparation

(P-4335)
RAKUTEN USA INC
800 Concar Dr Ste 175 (94402-7044)
PHONE..........................650 383-1328
Amit Patel, *CEO*
Hiroshi Mikitani, *Dir*
Ken Takayama, *Dir*
Reginald Rasch, *Sec*
Wai Yan Sun, *Treas*
EMP: **240** EST: 2006
SALES (est): **18.64MM Privately Held**
Web: global.rakuten.com
SIC: **4813** Internet connectivity services
PA: Rakuten Group, Inc.
    1-14-1, Tamagawa
    Setagaya-Ku TKY

(P-4336)
SCALEFAST INC (PA)
Also Called: Pepitastore
2100 E Grand Ave (90245-5024)
PHONE..........................310 595-4040
Nicolas Stehle, *CEO*
Yanick Turgeon, *
Olivier Schott, *
EMP: **103** EST: 2014
SALES (est): **41.9MM**
SALES (corp-wide): **41.9MM Privately Held**
Web: www.scalefast.com
SIC: **4813** Proprietary online service networks

(P-4337)
SENDMAIL INC
892 Ross Dr (94089-1443)
PHONE..........................510 594-5400
Gregory S Olson, *Prin*
Sandy Abbott, *
Gregory Shapiro, *
Stephanie Nevin, *
Sherry Walden, *
EMP: **110** EST: 2013
SQ FT: **30,000**
SALES (est): **47.46MM**
SALES (corp-wide): **1.05B Privately Held**
Web: www.proofpoint.com
SIC: **4813** 7371 7372 7373 Internet host services; Computer software development; Prepackaged software; Computer integrated systems design
HQ: Proofpoint, Inc.
    925 W Maude Ave
    Sunnyvale CA
    408 517-4710

(P-4338)
SIERRA TELEPHONE COMPANY INC
49150 Road 426 (93644-8702)
P.O. Box 219 (93644-0219)
PHONE..........................559 683-4611
Harry H Baker, *Pr*
John H Baker, *
Heidi D Baker, *
EMP: **190** EST: 1908
SALES (est): **46.75MM**
SALES (corp-wide): **97.86MM Privately Held**
Web: www.sierratel.com
SIC: **4813** Local telephone communications
PA: Sierra Tel Communications Group
    49150 Road 426
    Oakhurst CA
    559 683-4611

(P-4339)
SKYPE INC
One Microsoft Way, Redmond (94304)
PHONE..........................650 493-7900
Donald Albert, *Pr*
Laura Shesgreen, *
Shauna Kline, *
Tony Bates, *
▲ EMP: **70** EST: 2005
SQ FT: **90,698**
SALES (est): **10.64MM**
SALES (corp-wide): **211.91B Publicly Held**
Web: www.skype.com
SIC: **4813** Internet connectivity services
PA: Microsoft Corporation
    1 Microsoft Way
    Redmond WA
    425 882-8080

(P-4340)
SLASHSUPPORT INC
Also Called: SLASHSUPPORT, INC.
3175 Spring St (94063-3928)
PHONE..........................650 385-2000
Manish Tandon, *CEO*
EMP: **62**
Web: www.movate.com
SIC: **4813** Internet host services
HQ: Movate Inc.
    5600 Tennyson Pkwy # 255
    Plano TX
    408 985-4377

(P-4341)
SPOKEO INC
556 S Fair Oaks Ave Ste 1 (91105-2656)
PHONE..........................877 913-3088
EMP: **214**
Web: www.spokeo.com
SIC: **4813** Internet host services
PA: Spokeo, Inc.
    199 S Los Robles Ave # 711
    Pasadena CA

(P-4342)
SPRINT COMMUNICATIONS CO LP
Also Called: Sprint
12913 Harbor Blvd Ste Q4 (92840-5856)
PHONE..........................714 534-2107
EMP: **190**
SALES (corp-wide): **79.57B Publicly Held**
SIC: **4813** 4812 Local and long distance telephone communications; Cellular telephone services
HQ: Sprint Communications Company L.P.
    6391 Sprint Pkwy
    Overland Park KS
    800 829-0965

(P-4343)
SPRINT COMMUNICATIONS CO LP
1316 N Azusa Ave (91722-1259)
PHONE..........................626 339-0430
EMP: **149**
SALES (corp-wide): **79.57B Publicly Held**
SIC: **4813** 4812 Local and long distance telephone communications; Cellular telephone services
HQ: Sprint Communications Company L.P.
    6391 Sprint Pkwy
    Overland Park KS
    800 829-0965

(P-4344)
SPRINT COMMUNICATIONS CO LP
111 Universal Hollywood Dr (91608-1054)
PHONE..........................818 755-7100
Bill Henry, *Mgr*
EMP: **147**
SALES (corp-wide): **79.57B Publicly Held**
SIC: **4813** 4812 Long distance telephone communications; Radiotelephone communication
HQ: Sprint Communications Company L.P.
    6391 Sprint Pkwy
    Overland Park KS
    800 829-0965

(P-4345)
SPRINT COMMUNICATIONS CO LP
1505 E Enterprise Dr (92408-0159)
PHONE..........................909 382-6030
Bill Neece, *Mgr*
EMP: **149**
SALES (corp-wide): **79.57B Publicly Held**
SIC: **4813** 4812 Long distance telephone communications; Radiotelephone communication
HQ: Sprint Communications Company L.P.
    6391 Sprint Pkwy
    Overland Park KS
    800 829-0965

(P-4346)
SYDATA INC
6494 Weathers Pl Ste 100 (92121-2938)
PHONE..........................760 444-4368
Sindhura Thummalasetty, *CEO*
EMP: **125** EST: 2018
SALES (est): **9.03MM Privately Held**
Web: www.sydatainc.com
SIC: **4813** 7371 Internet connectivity services; Custom computer programming services

(P-4347)
SYNAPTICS INCORPORATED
3120 Scott Blvd (95054-3326)
PHONE..........................408 454-5100
EMP: **78**
SALES (corp-wide): **1.36B Publicly Held**
Web: www.synaptics.com
SIC: **4813** 4899 Data telephone communications; Data communication services
PA: Synaptics Incorporated
    1109 Mckay Dr
    San Jose CA
    408 904-1100

(P-4348)
TEKWORKS INC
12742 Knott St (92841-3904)
PHONE..........................877 835-9675
William E Bourgeois, *CEO*
EMP: **70**
SALES (corp-wide): **13.15MM Privately Held**
Web: www.paladintechnologies.com
SIC: **4813** 1731 Telephone communication, except radio; Communications specialization
PA: Paladin Technologies Inc
    1350-355 Burrard St
    Vancouver BC
    604 676-0136

(P-4349)
TELISIMO INTERNATIONAL CORP
2330 Shelter Island Dr Ste 210a (92106-3126)
PHONE..........................619 325-1593
Linda G Noda Hobbs, *Pr*
Mark D Wooster, *
▲ EMP: **400** EST: 1990
SQ FT: **15,000**
SALES (est): **25.71MM Privately Held**
Web: www.wirelessweb.com
SIC: **4813** Telephone communication, except radio

(P-4350)
TEMPO COMMUNICATIONS INC (PA)
1390 Aspen Way (92081-8349)
PHONE..........................800 642-2155
Jason Edward Butchko, *CEO*
John Parizek, *
David Collmann, *
EMP: **85** EST: 2019
SALES (est): **21.19MM**
SALES (corp-wide): **21.19MM Privately Held**
Web: www.tempocom.com
SIC: **4813** 3823 Telephone communication, except radio; Absorption analyzers: infrared, x-ray, etc.: industrial

(P-4351)
TOGETHER LABS INC
901 Marshall St # 200 (94063-2026)
P.O. Box 2772 (94064-2772)
PHONE..........................650 231-4688
Daren Tsui, *CEO*
Cary Rosenzweig, *
Kevin Henshaw, *
Lauren Bigelow, *CPO*
John Burris, *CDO*
EMP: **103** EST: 2005
SALES (est): **23.32MM Privately Held**
Web: secure.imvu.com
SIC: **4813** Internet connectivity services

(P-4352)
TRUCONNECT COMMUNICATIONS INC (PA)
Also Called: Telescape
1149 S Hill St Ste 400 (90015-2207)
PHONE..........................512 919-2641
Mathew Johnson, *CEO*
Robert A Yap, *
Nathan Johnson, *
EMP: **201** EST: 2001
SALES (est): **38.01MM**
SALES (corp-wide): **38.01MM Privately Held**
Web: www.truconnect.com
SIC: **4813** Internet host services

(P-4353)
USTREAM INC
410 Townsend St Fl 4 (94107-1581)
PHONE..........................415 489-9400
John Ham, *CEO*
Brad Hunstable, *
EMP: **65** EST: 2007
SALES (est): **10.37MM**
SALES (corp-wide): **60.53B Publicly Held**
Web: video.ibm.com
SIC: **4813** Internet host services
PA: International Business Machines Corporation
    1 New Orchard Rd Ste 1 # 1
    Armonk NY
    914 499-1900

(P-4354)
UVNV INC (HQ)
Also Called: Ultra Mobile
1550 Scenic Ave Ste 100 (92626-1420)
PHONE..........................888 777-0446
David Glickman, *CEO*
Tyler R Leshney, *
Dave Schofield, *

4813 - Telephone Communication, Except Radio (P-4355)

Chris Furlong, *
Rizwan Kassim, *
EMP: 73 **EST:** 2012
SQ FT: 8,600
SALES (est): 110.42MM
SALES (corp-wide): 79.57B **Publicly Held**
Web: www.ultramobile.com
SIC: 4813 Telephone communication, except radio
PA: T-Mobile Us, Inc.
   12920 Se 38th St
   Bellevue WA
   425 378-4000

(P-4355)
VERIZON BUS NETWRK SVCS LLC
Also Called: Verizon Business
2175 N California Blvd Ste 700 (94596-7344)
PHONE..................925 934-3030
Bill Berkowitz, *Brnch Mgr*
EMP: 175
SALES (corp-wide): 136.84B **Publicly Held**
Web: www.verizonwireless.com
SIC: 4813 4812 Long distance telephone communications; Radiotelephone communication
HQ: Verizon Business Network Services Llc
   1 Verizon Way
   Basking Ridge NJ
   908 559-2000

(P-4356)
VOLCANO COMMUNICATIONS COMPANY (PA)
Also Called: Volcano Telephone Company
20000 State Highway 88 (95665-9512)
P.O. Box 1070 (95665-1070)
PHONE..................209 296-7502
Sharon J Lundgren, *Pr*
John M Lundgren, *
Delia P Dede Harder, *
Elizabeth Lundgren, *
Angela Lundgren, *
EMP: 100 **EST:** 1903
SQ FT: 19,600
SALES (est): 29.21MM
SALES (corp-wide): 29.21MM **Privately Held**
Web: www.volcanocommunications.com
SIC: 4813 4841 Local telephone communications; Cable television services

(P-4357)
VTA TELEPHONE INFORMATION
3331 N 1st St (95134-1927)
PHONE..................408 321-7127
Ash Kalra, *Ch*
EMP: 358 **EST:** 2011
SALES (est): 10.4MM **Privately Held**
Web: www.vta.org
SIC: 4813 Local and long distance telephone communications

(P-4358)
WEBPASS INC
267 8th St (94103-3910)
PHONE..................415 233-4100
Dinni Jain, *CEO*
EMP: 75 **EST:** 2006
SQ FT: 8,000
SALES (est): 12.23MM
SALES (corp-wide): 282.84B **Publicly Held**
Web: www.gfiber.com
SIC: 4813 Internet connectivity services
HQ: Google Fiber Inc.
   1600 Amphitheatre Pkwy
   Mountain View CA
   650 253-0000

(P-4359)
XSOLLA (USA) INC (PA)
Also Called: Xsolla
15260 Ventura Blvd Ste 2230 (91403-5356)
PHONE..................818 435-6613
EMP: 540 **EST:** 2009
SQ FT: 30,000
SALES (est): 66.15MM **Privately Held**
Web: www.xsolla.com
SIC: 4813 Internet connectivity services

(P-4360)
YTEL INC
26632 Towne Centre Dr Ste 300 (92610)
PHONE..................800 382-4913
Nick Newsom, *CEO*
EMP: 100 **EST:** 2012
SALES (est): 11.42MM **Privately Held**
Web: www.ytel.com
SIC: 4813 Internet host services

(P-4361)
ZADAONET
685 Scofield Ave Apt 22 (94303-2350)
PHONE..................650 556-6377
Wenda Zhao, *Pr*
EMP: 60 **EST:** 2017
SALES (est): 983.84K **Privately Held**
SIC: 4813 Internet connectivity services

(P-4362)
ZENLAYER INC
21680 Gateway Center Dr Ste 350 (91765-2456)
P.O. Box 5709 (91765-7709)
PHONE..................909 718-3558
Joe Zhu, *CEO*
EMP: 408 **EST:** 2016
SALES (est): 48.05MM **Privately Held**
Web: www.zenlayer.com
SIC: 4813 Internet connectivity services

(P-4363)
ZYXEL COMMUNICATIONS INC
Also Called: Zyxel
1130 N Miller St (92806-2001)
PHONE..................714 632-0882
Howie Chu, *Pr*
◆ **EMP:** 80 **EST:** 1989
SQ FT: 32,000
SALES (est): 21.33MM **Privately Held**
Web: www.zyxel.com
SIC: 4813 Internet host services
HQ: Zyxel Communications Corporation
   No. 2, Gongye E. 9th Rd.,
   Baoshan Township HSI

4822 Telegraph And Other Communications

(P-4364)
DELUXE ENCORE INC
Also Called: A Deluxe Entrmt Svcs Group Co
2400 W Empire Ave Ste 400 (91504-3355)
PHONE..................323 466-7663
Warren Stein, *CEO*
EMP: 147 **EST:** 2013
SALES (est): 2.32MM **Privately Held**
SIC: 4822 Cable, telegram, and telex services

(P-4365)
INTRADO INTERACTIVE SVCS CORP
100 Enterprise Way Ste A300 (95066-3248)
PHONE..................888 527-5225
EMP: 89
SALES (corp-wide): 2.78B **Privately Held**
Web: www.intrado.com
SIC: 4822 Nonvocal message communications
HQ: Intrado Interactive Services Corporation
   11808 Miracle Hills Dr
   Omaha NE

(P-4366)
J2 CLOUD SERVICES LLC (HQ)
Also Called: Efax Corporate
700 S Flower St Fl 15 (90017-4101)
PHONE..................323 860-9200
EMP: 80 **EST:** 1995
SQ FT: 40,000
SALES (est): 668.5MM
SALES (corp-wide): 1.39B **Publicly Held**
Web: enterprise.efax.com
SIC: 4822 Telegraph and other communications
PA: Ziff Davis, Inc.
   114 5th Ave Fl 14
   New York NY
   212 503-3500

(P-4367)
RELIANCE COMMUNICATIONS LLC
Also Called: School Messenger
100 Enterprise Way Ste A3 (95066-3248)
PHONE..................408 827-4726
EMP: 89
Web: www.schoolmessenger.com
SIC: 4822 Nonvocal message communications

(P-4368)
WIN TELECOM GLOBAL CORPORATION
1735 Independence Blvd Apt #101 (93906-5351)
PHONE..................408 477-5672
Robert Marcus, *CEO*
EMP: 100 **EST:** 2009
SALES (est): 2.2MM **Privately Held**
Web: www.wintelecomglobal.com
SIC: 4822 Telegraph and other communications

4832 Radio Broadcasting Stations

(P-4369)
ABC CABLE NETWORKS GROUP (HQ)
Also Called: ABC
500 S Buena Vista St (91521-0007)
PHONE..................818 460-7477
Gary K Marsh, *CEO*
Anne M Sweeney, *
Patrick Lopker, *
▲ **EMP:** 200 **EST:** 1969
SALES (est): 506.25MM
SALES (corp-wide): 82.72B **Publicly Held**
Web: www.thewaltdisneycompany.com
SIC: 4832 4833 Radio broadcasting stations; Television broadcasting stations
PA: The Walt Disney Company
   500 S Buena Vista St
   Burbank CA
   818 560-1000

(P-4370)
ADELANTE MEDIA GROUP LLC
500 Media Pl (95815-3733)
PHONE..................801 908-8777
EMP: 60
Web: www.adelantemediagroup.com
SIC: 4832 Radio broadcasting stations

(P-4371)
AGM CALIFORNIA INC
1400 Easton Dr Ste 144 (93309-9404)
P.O. Box 2700 (93303-2700)
PHONE..................661 328-0118
Lawrence Rogers Brandon, *Pr*
EMP: 126 **EST:** 2010
SALES (est): 5.79MM **Privately Held**
Web: www.americangeneralmedia.com
SIC: 4832 Radio broadcasting stations

(P-4372)
AMAZING FACTS INTERNATIONAL
Also Called: AMAZING FACTS MINISTRIES
6615 Sierra College Blvd (95746-7366)
P.O. Box 1058 (95678-8058)
PHONE..................916 434-3880
Allen Hrenyk, *Prin*
Doug Batchelor, *
EMP: 85 **EST:** 2017
SALES (est): 34.24MM **Privately Held**
Web: www.amazingfacts.org
SIC: 4832 Radio broadcasting stations, except music format

(P-4373)
AUDACY INC
Also Called: Kseg-FM
3010 Lava Ridge Ct Ste 220 (95661-3075)
PHONE..................916 766-5000
John Geary, *Mgr*
EMP: 120
SALES (corp-wide): 1.25B **Publicly Held**
Web: www.audacy.com
SIC: 4832 7929 Radio broadcasting stations, music format; Entertainers and entertainment groups
PA: Audacy, Inc.
   2400 Market St Fl 4
   Philadelphia PA
   610 660-5610

(P-4374)
DASH RADIO INC
Also Called: Dash Radio
6230 Wilshire Blvd # 118 (90048-5126)
PHONE..................310 456-9993
Scott Keeney, *Pr*
Ron Goldie, *Sec*
EMP: 81 **EST:** 2014
SALES (est): 1.24MM **Privately Held**
Web: www.dashradio.com
SIC: 4832 Radio broadcasting stations

(P-4375)
DISNEY ENTERPRISES INC (DH)
Also Called: Disney
500 S Buena Vista St (91521-0001)
P.O. Box 3232 (92803-3232)
PHONE..................818 560-1000
Christine M Mccarthy, *Pr*
◆ **EMP:** 561 **EST:** 1986
SALES (est): 40.66B
SALES (corp-wide): 82.72B **Publicly Held**
Web: www.disney.com
SIC: 4832 6794 5331 7996 Radio broadcasting stations; Copyright buying and licensing; Variety stores; Theme park, amusement
HQ: Twdc Enterprises 18 Corp.
   500 S Buena Vista St
   Burbank CA

4832 - Radio Broadcasting Stations (P-4396)

(P-4376)
DISNEY STREAMING SERVICES LLC
500 S Buena Vista St (94105)
PHONE..................................818 560-1000
EMP: 120 EST: 2019
SALES (est): 27.11MM
SALES (corp-wide): 82.72B Publicly Held
Web: www.disneystreaming.com
SIC: 4832 5331 Radio broadcasting stations; Variety stores
HQ: Twdc Enterprises 18 Corp.
    500 S Buena Vista St
    Burbank CA

(P-4377)
EDUCATIONAL MEDIA FOUNDATION (PA)
Also Called: K-LOVE RADIO NETWORK
5700 West Oaks Blvd (95765-3719)
PHONE..................................916 251-1600
Todd Woods, CEO
Darrell Chambliss, *
Richard Jenkins, *
David Atkinson, *
Jon Taylor, *
EMP: 200 EST: 1981
SQ FT: 55,000
SALES (est): 238.35MM
SALES (corp-wide): 238.35MM Privately Held
Web: www.klove.com
SIC: 4832 Radio broadcasting stations

(P-4378)
EL DORADO BROADCASTERS LLC
11920 Hesperia Rd (92345-1851)
PHONE..................................760 241-1313
Tim Anderson, Prin
EMP: 92 EST: 2007
SALES (est): 4.28MM Privately Held
Web: www.edbroadcasters.com
SIC: 4832 Radio broadcasting stations, music format

(P-4379)
ENTERCOM MEDIA CORP
Also Called: CBS
900 E Washington St Ste 315 (92324-7111)
PHONE..................................909 825-9525
Kevin Murphy, Genl Mgr
EMP: 114
SALES (corp-wide): 1.25B Publicly Held
SIC: 4832 Radio broadcasting stations
HQ: Entercom Media Corp.
    345 Hudson St
    New York NY
    212 314-9200

(P-4380)
ENTERCOM MEDIA CORP
Also Called: CBS
1071 W Shaw Ave (93711-3702)
PHONE..................................559 490-0106
El Smith, Mgr
EMP: 65
SQ FT: 5,938
SALES (corp-wide): 1.25B Publicly Held
SIC: 4832 Radio broadcasting stations, music format
HQ: Entercom Media Corp.
    345 Hudson St
    New York NY
    212 314-9200

(P-4381)
ENTERCOM MEDIA CORP
Also Called: CBS
865 Battery St Fl 3 (94111-1503)
PHONE..................................415 765-4097
EMP: 140
SALES (corp-wide): 1.25B Publicly Held
SIC: 4832 Radio broadcasting stations, music format
HQ: Entercom Media Corp.
    345 Hudson St
    New York NY
    212 314-9200

(P-4382)
ENTERCOM MEDIA CORP
Also Called: CBS
5670 Wilshire Blvd Ste 200 (90036-5679)
PHONE..................................323 930-7317
Sials Marshall, Brnch Mgr
EMP: 130
SALES (corp-wide): 1.25B Publicly Held
Web: www.audacy.com
SIC: 4832 Radio broadcasting stations, music format
HQ: Entercom Media Corp.
    345 Hudson St
    New York NY
    212 314-9200

(P-4383)
ENTERCOM MEDIA CORP
Also Called: CBS
280 Commerce Cir (95815-4212)
PHONE..................................916 923-6800
EMP: 140
SALES (corp-wide): 1.25B Publicly Held
SIC: 4832 Radio broadcasting stations, music format
HQ: Entercom Media Corp.
    345 Hudson St
    New York NY
    212 314-9200

(P-4384)
FOOTHLL-DE ANZA CMNTY CLLEGE D
Also Called: Kfjc FM
12345 S El Monte Rd Ste 6202 (94022-4504)
PHONE..................................650 949-7260
Eric Johnson, Genl Mgr
EMP: 74
SALES (corp-wide): 115.04MM Privately Held
Web: www.fhda.edu
SIC: 4832 Radio broadcasting stations, music format
PA: Foothill-De Anza Community College District Financing Corporation
    12345 S El Monte Rd
    Los Altos Hills CA
    650 949-6100

(P-4385)
HENDRIE RADIO INC
2871 Instone Ct (91361-3712)
PHONE..................................818 259-8175
EMP: 61
SALES (corp-wide): 853.22K Privately Held
SIC: 4832 Radio broadcasting stations
PA: Hendrie Radio, Inc.
    1014 S Westlake Blvd
    Westlake Village CA

(P-4386)
IHEARTCOMMUNICATIONS INC
Also Called: Krzr 103 7 FM
83 E Shaw Ave Ste 150 (93710-7622)
PHONE..................................559 230-4300
Jeff Negrete, Brnch Mgr
EMP: 75
Web: www.iheartmedia.com
SIC: 4832 Radio broadcasting stations
HQ: Iheartcommunications, Inc.
    20880 Stone Oak Pkwy
    San Antonio TX
    210 822-2828

(P-4387)
K G O T V NEWS BUREAU
520 3rd St Ste 200 (94607-3505)
PHONE..................................510 451-4772
Ed Kosowski, Prin
EMP: 100 EST: 2002
SALES (est): 483.59K Privately Held
SIC: 4832 Radio broadcasting stations
HQ: San Francisco Radio Assets Llc
    750 Battery St Fl 2
    San Francisco CA

(P-4388)
K WAVE 1079
3000 W Macarthur Blvd Ste 500 (92704-6916)
PHONE..................................714 918-6207
Lance Emma, Genl Mgr
EMP: 69 EST: 1985
SALES (est): 473.95K
SALES (corp-wide): 31.18MM Privately Held
SIC: 4832 Radio broadcasting stations
PA: Calvary Chapel Of Costa Mesa
    3800 S Fairview St
    Santa Ana CA
    714 979-4422

(P-4389)
KIFM SMOOTH JAZZ 981 INC
1615 Murray Canyon Rd (92108-4314)
PHONE..................................619 297-3698
Mike Stafford, Pr
EMP: 110 EST: 1999
SQ FT: 12,000
SALES (est): 19.54MM
SALES (corp-wide): 1.25B Publicly Held
SIC: 4832 Radio broadcasting stations
HQ: Abe Entercom Holdings Llc
    401 E City Ave Ste 809
    Bala Cynwyd PA
    404 239-7211

(P-4390)
KRCA LICENSE LLC
1845 W Empire Ave (91504-9922)
PHONE..................................818 840-1400
EMP: 105 EST: 2001
SALES (est): 4.55MM
SALES (corp-wide): 283.69MM Privately Held
SIC: 4832 Radio broadcasting stations
HQ: Krca Television Llc
    1 Estrella Way
    Burbank CA

(P-4391)
KUIC INC
Also Called: Kuic-FM
555 Mason St Ste 245 (95688-4640)
PHONE..................................707 446-0200
James Levitt, Ch Bd
John F Levitt, *
EMP: 130 EST: 1969
SQ FT: 4,200
SALES (est): 502.72K
SALES (corp-wide): 7.06MM Privately Held
Web: www.kuic.com
SIC: 4832 2711 Radio broadcasting stations; Newspapers
PA: Coast Radio Company, Inc.
    555 Mason St Ste 245
    Vacaville CA
    707 446-0200

(P-4392)
LBI MEDIA HOLDINGS INC
3101 W 5th St (92703-1829)
PHONE..................................714 554-5000
Jesus Mar, Brnch Mgr
EMP: 334
SALES (corp-wide): 283.69MM Privately Held
SIC: 4832 Radio broadcasting stations
HQ: Lbi Media Holdings, Inc.
    1 Estrella Way
    Burbank CA

(P-4393)
LEARFIELD COMMUNICATIONS LLC
5291 California Ave Ste 100 (92617-3220)
PHONE..................................949 823-1729
EMP: 60
SALES (corp-wide): 461.62MM Privately Held
Web: www.learfield.com
SIC: 4832 Radio broadcasting stations
HQ: Learfield Communications, Llc
    2400 Dallas Pkwy Ste 510
    Plano TX
    336 464-0224

(P-4394)
LIBERMAN BROADCASTING INC (PA)
1845 W Empire Ave (91504-9922)
PHONE..................................818 729-5300
Lenard D Liberman, CEO
Jose Liberman, *
Frederic T Boyer, *
Eduardo Leon, *
Winter Horton, *
EMP: 83 EST: 2004
SALES (est): 283.69MM
SALES (corp-wide): 283.69MM Privately Held
Web: www.estrellamedia.com
SIC: 4832 Radio broadcasting stations

(P-4395)
LOCAL MEDIA SAN DIEGO LLC
Also Called: Magic 92.5
6160 Cornerstone Ct E Ste 150 (92121-3720)
PHONE..................................858 888-7000
Norman Mckee, CFO
EMP: 100 EST: 2009
SALES (est): 6.91MM Privately Held
Web: www.magic925.com
SIC: 4832 Radio broadcasting stations, music format

(P-4396)
LOTUS COMMUNICATIONS CORP (PA)
3301 Barham Blvd Ste 200 (90068-1403)
PHONE..................................323 512-2225
Howard Kalmenson, Pr
Jerry Roy, *
William H Shriftman, *
Jim Kalmenson, *
Jasmin Dorismond, *
EMP: 60 EST: 1959
SQ FT: 25,848
SALES (est): 89.02MM
SALES (corp-wide): 89.02MM Privately Held
Web: www.lotuscorp.com
SIC: 4832 Radio broadcasting stations

4832 - Radio Broadcasting Stations

(P-4397)
MULTICULTURAL RDO BRDCSTG INC
747 E Green St (91101-2145)
PHONE..................626 844-8882
EMP: 99
SALES (corp-wide): 49.85MM Privately Held
Web: www.mrbi.net
SIC: 4832 Radio broadcasting stations, music format
PA: Multicultural Radio Broadcasting, Inc.
  207 William St Fl 11 Flr 11
  New York NY
  212 966-1059

(P-4398)
NBCUNIVERSAL MEDIA LLC
Also Called: Universal Pictures Intl
100 Universal City Plz Bldg 2160 (91608)
PHONE..................818 777-1000
EMP: 534
SALES (corp-wide): 121.43B Publicly Held
Web: www.nbc.com
SIC: 4832 7812 Radio broadcasting stations; Motion picture production and distribution
HQ: Nbcuniversal Media, Llc
  30 Rockefeller Plz Fl 2
  New York NY

(P-4399)
PANDORA MEDIA LLC
3000 Ocean Park Blvd Ste 3050 (90405-3020)
PHONE..................424 653-6803
EMP: 237
SALES (corp-wide): 12.16B Publicly Held
Web: www.pandora.com
SIC: 4832 Radio broadcasting stations
HQ: Pandora Media, Llc
  2100 Franklin St Ste 700
  Oakland CA
  510 451-4100

(P-4400)
PANDORA MEDIA LLC (DH)
Also Called: Pandora
2100 Franklin St Ste 700 (94612-3145)
PHONE..................510 451-4100
Roger Lynch, Pr
Peter Ruzicka, Ch Bd
Naveen Chopra, CFO
David Gerbitz, COO
Kristen Robinson, Chief Human Resources Officer
EMP: 433 EST: 2000
SQ FT: 250,000
SALES (est): 894.01MM
SALES (corp-wide): 12.16B Publicly Held
Web: www.pandora.com
SIC: 4832 Radio broadcasting stations
HQ: Sirius Xm Radio Inc.
  1221 Ave Of The Amrcas 35
  New York NY

(P-4401)
RADIO DISNEY GROUP LLC
3800 W Alameda Ave Ste 1150 (91505-4331)
PHONE..................818 569-5000
EMP: 92 EST: 2003
SALES (est): 25.56MM
SALES (corp-wide): 82.72B Publicly Held
Web: radio.disney.com
SIC: 4832 Radio broadcasting stations
HQ: Abc Cable Networks Group
  500 S Buena Vista St
  Burbank CA
  818 460-7477

(P-4402)
SAN BRNRDINO CMNTY COLLEGE DST
Also Called: Kvcr, TV & FM
701 S Mount Vernon Ave (92410-2705)
PHONE..................909 384-4444
Larry Ciecalone, Pr
EMP: 136
SALES (corp-wide): 46.53MM Privately Held
Web: www.sbccd.edu
SIC: 4832 4833 Radio broadcasting stations; Television broadcasting stations
PA: San Bernardino Community College District
  550 E Hospitality Ln # 200
  San Bernardino CA
  909 382-4000

(P-4403)
SAN FRANCISCO RADIO ASSETS LLC (DH)
Also Called: Kgo 810am
750 Battery St Fl 2 (94111-1523)
PHONE..................415 216-1300
EMP: 150 EST: 1946
SQ FT: 51,000
SALES (est): 23.7MM Privately Held
SIC: 4832 Radio broadcasting stations
HQ: Cumulus Network Holdings Inc.
  3090 Nowitzki Way Ste 400
  Dallas TX

(P-4404)
SIRIUS XM RADIO INC
953 N Sycamore Ave (90038-2373)
PHONE..................323 802-1100
EMP: 127
SALES (corp-wide): 12.16B Publicly Held
Web: www.siriusxm.com
SIC: 4832 Radio broadcasting stations
HQ: Sirius Xm Radio Inc.
  1221 Ave Of The Amrcas 35
  New York NY

(P-4405)
SPANISH BRDCSTG SYS OF CAL
Also Called: Klax Radio Station
7007 Nw 77th Ave (90064)
PHONE..................310 203-0900
Raul Alarcon Senior, Ch Bd
Joseph Garcia, *
EMP: 70 EST: 1984
SALES (est): 9.18MM
SALES (corp-wide): 243.92MM Privately Held
Web: www.spanishbroadcasting.com
SIC: 4832 7313 Radio broadcasting stations; Radio advertising representative
HQ: Spanish Broadcasting System Of Greater Miami, Inc.
  7007 Nw 77th Ave
  Medley FL
  305 644-4800

(P-4406)
TRIAD BROADCASTING COMPANY (PA)
Also Called: Triad Broadcasting
2511 Garden Rd Ste A104 (93940-5376)
P.O. Box 7539 (93921-7539)
PHONE..................831 655-6350
David J Benjamin, Pr
Steve Feder, *
EMP: 140 EST: 1999
SALES (est): 22.33MM
SALES (corp-wide): 22.33MM Privately Held

SIC: 4832 Radio broadcasting stations

(P-4407)
TUNEIN INC
Also Called: Radio Time
475 Brannan St Ste 320 (94107-5420)
PHONE..................650 319-7100
EMP: 200 EST: 2010
SALES (est): 73.7MM Privately Held
Web: www.tunein.com
SIC: 4832 Radio broadcasting stations

(P-4408)
UNIVISION RADIO INC
600 W Broadway Ste 2150 (92101-3389)
PHONE..................619 744-4370
Peter Moore, Mgr
EMP: 60
SALES (corp-wide): 71.34K Privately Held
Web: www.univision.com
SIC: 4832 Radio broadcasting stations
HQ: Univision Radio, Inc.
  2323 Bryan St Ste 1900
  Dallas TX

4833 Television Broadcasting Stations

(P-4409)
ABC CABLE NETWORKS GROUP
Also Called: ABC
900 Front St (94111-1427)
PHONE..................415 954-7911
Lynn Dooley, Brnch Mgr
EMP: 200
SALES (corp-wide): 82.72B Publicly Held
SIC: 4833 Television broadcasting stations
HQ: Abc Cable Networks Group
  500 S Buena Vista St
  Burbank CA
  818 460-7477

(P-4410)
ABC SIGNATURE STUDIOS INC
500 S Buena Vista St (91521-0001)
PHONE..................818 560-1000
Linda A Bagley, CEO
EMP: 86 EST: 1989
SALES (est): 20.58MM
SALES (corp-wide): 82.72B Publicly Held
SIC: 4833 Television broadcasting stations
PA: The Walt Disney Company
  500 S Buena Vista St
  Burbank CA
  818 560-1000

(P-4411)
AMERICAN MULTIMEDIA TV USA
Also Called: Amtv USA
530 S Lake Ave Unit 368 (91101-3515)
PHONE..................626 466-1038
Jason Quin, Pr
EMP: 67 EST: 2004
SALES (est): 2.31MM Privately Held
Web: www.amtvusa.com
SIC: 4833 7372 Television broadcasting stations; Application computer software

(P-4412)
BAY CITY TELEVISION INC (PA)
8253 Ronson Rd (92111-2004)
P.O. Box 880083 (92168-0083)
PHONE..................858 279-6666
Jose Antonio Baston Patino, CEO
Robert Taylor, *
EMP: 100 EST: 1953
SQ FT: 12,000
SALES (est): 17.4MM
SALES (corp-wide): 17.4MM Privately Held
Web: www.sandiego6.com
SIC: 4833 7311 Television broadcasting stations; Advertising agencies

(P-4413)
BUZZTIME INC
2231 Rutherford Rd Ste 210 (92008-8811)
PHONE..................760 476-1976
Dario Santana, CEO
EMP: 130 EST: 2000
SALES (est): 634.23K Privately Held
Web: www.buzztime.com
SIC: 4833 Television broadcasting stations

(P-4414)
CALIFORNIA OREGON BROADCASTING (HQ)
Also Called: Kaef TV
755 Auditorium Dr (96001-0920)
PHONE..................530 243-7777
Sarah Smith, Genl Mgr
EMP: 60 EST: 1963
SQ FT: 14,000
SALES (est): 5.9MM
SALES (corp-wide): 17.33MM Privately Held
Web: www.krcrtv.com
SIC: 4833 Television broadcasting stations
PA: Appalachian Broadcasting Corp
  101 Lee St
  Bristol VA
  276 645-1555

(P-4415)
CATAMUNT BRDCSTG CHC-RDDING IN (PA)
Also Called: Khsl TV
3460 Silverbell Rd (95973-0388)
PHONE..................530 893-2424
Raymond Johns, Pr
EMP: 104 EST: 1950
SQ FT: 18,000
SALES (est): 11.45MM
SALES (corp-wide): 11.45MM Privately Held
Web: www.actionnewsnow.com
SIC: 4833 Television broadcasting stations

(P-4416)
CBS BROADCASTING INC
Also Called: CBS
855 Battery St (94111-1503)
PHONE..................415 765-0928
Bruno Cohen, Mgr
EMP: 97
SALES (corp-wide): 30.15B Publicly Held
Web: www.cbsnews.com
SIC: 4833 Television broadcasting stations
HQ: Cbs Broadcasting Inc.
  524 W 57th St
  New York NY
  212 975-4321

(P-4417)
CBS BROADCASTING INC
Also Called: CBS
4024 Radford Ave Bldg 4 (91604)
PHONE..................818 655-8500
Michael Klausman, Pr
EMP: 123
SALES (corp-wide): 30.15B Publicly Held
Web: www.cbs.com
SIC: 4833 Television broadcasting stations
HQ: Cbs Broadcasting Inc.
  524 W 57th St
  New York NY
  212 975-4321

PRODUCTS & SERVICES SECTION
4833 - Television Broadcasting Stations (P-4436)

(P-4418)
CBS FILMS INC
8560 W Sunset Blvd Fl 5 (90069-2342)
EMP: 71 **EST:** 2007
SALES (est): 11.03MM
SALES (corp-wide): 30.15B **Publicly Held**
Web: www.cbsfilms.com
SIC: 4833 Television broadcasting stations
PA: Paramount Global
   1515 Broadway
   New York NY
   212 258-6000

(P-4419)
CBS STUDIOS INC
Also Called: Csi Vegas
27420 Avenue Scott Ste A (91355-3450)
PHONE..........................661 964-6020
EMP: 469
SALES (corp-wide): 30.15B **Publicly Held**
Web: www.cbstelevisionstudios.com
SIC: 4833 Television broadcasting stations
HQ: Cbs Studios Inc.
   6100 Wilshire Blvd # 1000
   Los Angeles CA

(P-4420)
CHANNEL 40 INC
Also Called: Ktxl-Fox 40
4655 Fruitridge Rd (95820-5201)
PHONE..........................916 454-4422
Jerry Del Core, *General Vice President*
Jerry Del Core, *VP*
EMP: 105 **EST:** 1989
SQ FT: 25,000
SALES (est): 17.09MM
SALES (corp-wide): 5.21MM **Publicly Held**
Web: www.fox40.com
SIC: 4833 Television translator station
HQ: Tribune Media Company
   515 N State St Ste 2400
   Chicago IL
   312 222-3394

(P-4421)
CHRONICLE BROADCASTING CO
Also Called: Kron-TV
900 Front St (94111-1427)
PHONE..........................415 561-8000
Francis A Martin Iii, *Pr*
Ronald Ingram, *
Robert M Raymer, *
Glen Tom E Pickell, *Treas*
EMP: 400 **EST:** 1966
SQ FT: 90,000
SALES (est): 83.86MM
SALES (corp-wide): 4.29B **Privately Held**
Web: www.kron4.com
SIC: 4833 Television broadcasting stations
HQ: Hearst Communications, Inc.
   300 W 57th St
   New York NY
   212 649-2000

(P-4422)
CNN AMERICA INC
Also Called: Cnn
6430 W Sunset Blvd Ste 300 (90028-7901)
PHONE..........................323 993-5000
Suzanne Spurgeon, *Prin*
EMP: 182
SIC: 4833 Television broadcasting stations
HQ: Cnn America Inc
   190 Marietta St Nw 12s
   Atlanta GA

(P-4423)
COMCAST SPRTSNET BAY AREA HLDN
360 3rd St 2nd Fl (94107-2154)
PHONE..........................415 896-2557
Richard Cotton, *Managing Member*
EMP: 142 **EST:** 1989
SALES (est): 3.27MM
SALES (corp-wide): 121.43B **Publicly Held**
Web: www.nbcsports.com
SIC: 4833 Television broadcasting stations
HQ: Nbcuniversal Media, Llc
   30 Rockefeller Plz Fl 2
   New York NY

(P-4424)
CW NETWORK LLC (HQ)
Also Called: Cwtv
3300 W Olive Ave Fl 3 (91505-4640)
PHONE..........................818 977-2500
Dennis Miller, *Pr*
John Maatta, *
Mitchell Nedick, *
Tom Martin, *
Ashley Hovey, *Chief Digital Officer*
EMP: 210 **EST:** 2006
SALES (est): 112.21MM
SALES (corp-wide): 5.21MM **Publicly Held**
Web: www.cwtv.com
SIC: 4833 Television broadcasting stations
PA: Nexstar Media Group, Inc.
   545 E John Carpenter Fwy
   Irving TX
   972 373-8800

(P-4425)
DISNEY NETWORKS GROUP LLC
Also Called: Nat Geo TV
10201 W Pico Blvd Ste 100/3132 (90064-2606)
PHONE..........................310 369-5104
Brian Sullivan, *Pr*
EMP: 64
SALES (corp-wide): 82.72B **Publicly Held**
SIC: 4833 Television broadcasting stations
HQ: Disney Networks Group, Llc
   10201 W Pico Blvd Bldg 10
   Los Angeles CA
   310 369-1000

(P-4426)
DISNEY NETWORKS GROUP LLC (DH)
Also Called: Fox Network Center
10201 W Pico Blvd Bldg 101 (90064-2606)
P.O. Box 900 (90213-0900)
PHONE..........................310 369-1000
Brian Sullivan, *Pr*
EMP: 86 **EST:** 1996
SALES (est): 32.39MM
SALES (corp-wide): 82.72B **Publicly Held**
SIC: 4833 Television broadcasting stations
HQ: Fox Entertainment Group, Llc
   1211 Ave Of The Americas
   New York NY
   212 852-7000

(P-4427)
ENTRAVSION COMMUNICATIONS CORP
Also Called: K S S C - F M
5700 Wilshire Blvd Ste 250 (90036-3659)
PHONE..........................323 900-6100
Jeff Liberman, *Pr*
EMP: 100
Web: www.entravision.com

SIC: 4833 4832 Television broadcasting stations; Radio broadcasting stations
PA: Entravsion Communications Corporation
   2425 Olympic Blvd Ste 600
   Santa Monica CA

(P-4428)
ENTRAVSION COMMUNICATIONS CORP
Also Called: Kyue TV
72920 Parkview Dr (92260-9357)
P.O. Box 13750 (92255-3750)
PHONE..........................760 836-0466
Mario Carrera, *Dir*
Walter Ulloa, *
EMP: 68 **EST:** 1989
SQ FT: 3,000
SALES (est): 4.01MM **Publicly Held**
Web: www.entravision.com
SIC: 4833 Television broadcasting stations
PA: Entravsion Communications Corporation
   2425 Olympic Blvd Ste 600
   Santa Monica CA

(P-4429)
ENTRAVSION COMMUNICATIONS CORP (PA)
2425 Olympic Blvd Ste 6000w (90404-4030)
PHONE..........................310 447-3870
EMP: 114 **EST:** 1996
SQ FT: 16,000
SALES (est): 956.21MM **Publicly Held**
Web: www.entravision.com
SIC: 4833 4832 Television broadcasting stations; Radio broadcasting stations

(P-4430)
EW SCRIPPS COMPANY
Also Called: Kgtv
4600 Air Way (92102-2528)
PHONE..........................619 237-1010
Derek Dalton, *VP*
EMP: 187
SALES (corp-wide): 2.45B **Publicly Held**
Web: www.10news.com
SIC: 4833 Television broadcasting stations
PA: The E W Scripps Company
   312 Walnut St Ste 2800
   Cincinnati OH
   513 977-3000

(P-4431)
FOX INC (DH)
Also Called: Home Entertainment Div
10201 W Pico Blvd (90064-2606)
P.O. Box 900 (90213-0900)
PHONE..........................310 369-1000
K Rupert Murdoch, *Ch Bd*
Mike Dunn, *
Jay Itzkowitz, *
▲ **EMP:** 2000 **EST:** 1984
SQ FT: 25,000
SALES (est): 881.26MM
SALES (corp-wide): 82.72B **Publicly Held**
Web: www.fox.com
SIC: 4833 7812 Television broadcasting stations; Motion picture production and distribution
HQ: News America Incorporated
   1211 Ave Of The Americas
   New York NY
   212 852-7000

(P-4432)
FOX BROADCASTING COMPANY LLC (HQ)
10201 W Pico Blvd Bldg 1003220 (90064-2606)
P.O. Box 900 (90213-0900)
PHONE..........................310 369-1000
David F Devoe Junior, *CEO*
Nancy Utley, *
Sang Gong, *
Del Mayberry, *
Joe Earley, *
EMP: 200 **EST:** 1986
SQ FT: 41,000
SALES (est): 115.56MM
SALES (corp-wide): 14.91B **Publicly Held**
Web: www.fox.com
SIC: 4833 Television broadcasting stations
PA: Fox Corporation
   1211 Ave Of The Americas
   New York NY
   212 852-7000

(P-4433)
FOX SPORTS INC (DH)
Also Called: F O X
10201 W Pico Blvd (90064-2606)
PHONE..........................310 369-1000
Randy Freer, *CEO*
Eric Shanks, *
EMP: 131 **EST:** 1995
SALES (est): 192.62MM
SALES (corp-wide): 82.72B **Publicly Held**
Web: www.foxsports.com
SIC: 4833 Television broadcasting stations
HQ: Fox Entertainment Group, Llc
   1211 Ave Of The Americas
   New York NY
   212 852-7000

(P-4434)
FOX TELEVISION STATIONS INC (HQ)
Also Called: Fox Television Center
1999 S Bundy Dr (90025-5203)
PHONE..........................310 584-2000
Roger Ailes, *Ch Bd*
Murdock Lachlan, *
Bill Lamb, *
Amy Carney, *
Dick Slenker, *Operations*
▲ **EMP:** 300 **EST:** 1998
SALES (est): 871.03MM
SALES (corp-wide): 14.91B **Publicly Held**
Web: www.foxla.com
SIC: 4833 7313 Television broadcasting stations; Radio, television, publisher representatives
PA: Fox Corporation
   1211 Ave Of The Americas
   New York NY
   212 852-7000

(P-4435)
FOX US PRODUCTIONS 27 INC
1600 Rosecrans Ave Bldg 5a (90266-3708)
PHONE..........................310 727-2550
EMP: 128
SALES (est): 887.75K
SALES (corp-wide): 82.72B **Publicly Held**
SIC: 4833 Television broadcasting stations
HQ: Fox Entertainment Group, Llc
   1211 Ave Of The Americas
   New York NY
   212 852-7000

(P-4436)
GULF- CALIFORNIA BROADCAST CO
Also Called: Kesq TV
31276 Dunham Way (92276-3310)
PHONE..........................760 773-0342
John Kuenuke, *Pr*

4833 - Television Broadcasting Stations (P-4437)

PRODUCTS & SERVICES SECTION

EMP: 63 EST: 1984
SALES (est): 11.64MM
SALES (corp-wide): 181.04MM Privately Held
Web: www.kesq.com
SIC: 4833 7922 Television broadcasting stations; Theatrical producers and services
PA: News-Press & Gazette Company Inc
825 Edmond St
Saint Joseph MO
816 271-8500

(P-4437)
HALLMARK MEDIA US LLC (DH)
Also Called: Hallmark Channel
12700 Ventura Blvd Ste 100 (91604-2469)
PHONE.................................818 755-2400
EMP: 95 EST: 1995
SALES (est): 46.99MM
SALES (corp-wide): 2.72B Privately Held
Web: www.hallmark.com
SIC: 4833 Television broadcasting stations
HQ: Crown Media Holdings, Inc.
12700 Ventura Blvd # 100
Studio City CA
888 390-7474

(P-4438)
HEARST STATIONS INC
Also Called: Kcra
3 Television Cir (95814-0750)
PHONE.................................916 446-3333
E Proshinsky, Genl Mgr
EMP: 108
SALES (corp-wide): 4.29B Privately Held
Web: www.kcra.com
SIC: 4833 Television broadcasting stations
HQ: Hearst Stations Inc.
3 Television Cir
Sacramento CA
916 446-3333

(P-4439)
HEARST STATIONS INC
Also Called: K S B W- T V
238 John St (93901-3339)
P.O. Box 81651 (93912)
PHONE.................................831 758-8888
Joseph W Heston, Pr
EMP: 110
SQ FT: 31,681
SALES (corp-wide): 4.29B Privately Held
Web: www.ksbw.com
SIC: 4833 Television translator station
HQ: Hearst Stations Inc.
3 Television Cir
Sacramento CA
916 446-3333

(P-4440)
HERRING NETWORKS INC
Also Called: Awe
4757 Morena Blvd (92117-3462)
PHONE.................................858 270-6900
Charles P Herring, Pr
EMP: 130 EST: 2003
SALES (est): 13.6MM Privately Held
Web: www.awetv.com
SIC: 4833 Television broadcasting stations

(P-4441)
HUB TELEVISION NETWORKS LLC
2950 N Hollywood Way Ste 100 (91505)
PHONE.................................818 531-3600
EMP: 70
Web: www.hubworld.com
SIC: 4833 Television broadcasting stations

(P-4442)
INTERNATIONAL MEDIA GROUP INC
1990 S Bundy Dr Ste 850 (90025-5253)
PHONE.................................310 478-1818
Peter Mathes, Ch Bd
EMP: 60 EST: 1985
SQ FT: 17,000
SALES (est): 973.38K
SALES (corp-wide): 8.91MM Privately Held
SIC: 4833 Television broadcasting stations
PA: Asianmedia Group Llc
1990 S Bundy Dr Ste 850
Los Angeles CA
310 478-1818

(P-4443)
KFSN TELEVISION LLC
Also Called: ABC 30
1777 G St (93706-1688)
PHONE.................................559 442-1170
Dan Adams, Pr
EMP: 117 EST: 2005
SQ FT: 26,962
SALES (est): 14.07MM
SALES (corp-wide): 82.72B Publicly Held
Web: www.abc30.com
SIC: 4833 Television broadcasting stations
HQ: Disney Enterprises, Inc.
500 S Buena Vista St
Burbank CA
818 560-1000

(P-4444)
KING WORLD PRODUCTIONS INC
Also Called: King World
1575 N Gower St Ste 100 (90028-6488)
PHONE.................................310 264-3549
EMP: 161
SALES (corp-wide): 30.15B Publicly Held
SIC: 4833 Television broadcasting stations
HQ: King World Productions, Inc
51 W 52nd St Fl 24
New York NY
212 315-4000

(P-4445)
KMPH FOX 26
Also Called: Pappas Telecasting Company
5111 E Mckinley Ave (93727-2033)
PHONE.................................559 255-2600
Harry Pappas, Prin
EMP: 171 EST: 1971
SALES (est): 3.66MM
SALES (corp-wide): 3.93B Publicly Held
Web: www.kmph.com
SIC: 4833 Television broadcasting stations
PA: Sinclair Broadcast Group, Inc.
10706 Beaver Dam Rd
Hunt Valley MD
410 568-1500

(P-4446)
KQED INC (PA)
Also Called: KQED PUBLIC MEDIA
2601 Mariposa St (94110-1426)
P.O. Box 410865 (94141-0865)
PHONE.................................415 864-2000
John Boland, Pr
Donald W Derheim, *
William L Lowery, Legal Counsel*
Mitzie Kelley, *
EMP: 258 EST: 1952
SQ FT: 75,000
SALES (est): 109.65MM
SALES (corp-wide): 109.65MM Privately Held
Web: www.kqed.org

SIC: 4833 4832 Television broadcasting stations; Radio broadcasting stations

(P-4447)
KSBY COMMUNICATIONS LLC
1772 Calle Joaquin (93405-7210)
PHONE.................................805 541-6666
Kathleen Choal, Pr
EMP: 173 EST: 2005
SALES (est): 7.37MM
SALES (corp-wide): 2.45B Publicly Held
Web: www.ksby.com
SIC: 4833 Television broadcasting stations
PA: The E W Scripps Company
312 Walnut St Ste 2800
Cincinnati OH
513 977-3000

(P-4448)
KTSF CHANNEL 26
Also Called: Lincoln Broadcasting Company
100 Valley Dr (94005-1318)
PHONE.................................415 467-6397
Lincoln Howell, CEO
EMP: 71 EST: 1996
SALES (est): 4.8MM
SALES (corp-wide): 12.66MM Privately Held
Web: www.ktsf.com
SIC: 4833 Television broadcasting stations
PA: Lincoln Broadcasting Company, A California Limited Partnership
100 Valley Dr
Brisbane CA
415 508-1056

(P-4449)
KTVU PARTNERSHIP INC
Also Called: Ktvu Television Fox 2
2 Jack London Sq (94607-3727)
PHONE.................................510 834-1212
Murdock Lachlan, CEO
♦ EMP: 230 EST: 1963
SALES (est): 22.49MM
SALES (corp-wide): 14.91B Publicly Held
Web: wn.ktvu.com
SIC: 4833 Television broadcasting stations
HQ: Fox Television Stations, Inc.
1999 S Bundy Dr
Los Angeles CA
310 584-2000

(P-4450)
KVIE INC (PA)
Also Called: KVIE CHANNEL 6
2030 W El Camino Ave Ste 100 (95833)
P.O. Box 6 (95812-0006)
PHONE.................................916 929-5843
David Lowe, CEO
David Hosley, *
Julie Saqueton, *
Staci Orlando, *
EMP: 60 EST: 1955
SQ FT: 69,000
SALES (est): 16.54MM
SALES (corp-wide): 16.54MM Privately Held
Web: www.kvie.org
SIC: 4833 Television broadcasting stations

(P-4451)
KXTV INC
Also Called: K X T V Channel 10
400 Broadway (95818-2041)
PHONE.................................916 441-2345
Risa Omega, Pr
EMP: 160 EST: 1940
SQ FT: 29,000
SALES (est): 23.7MM
SALES (corp-wide): 3.28B Publicly Held

Web: www.abc10.com
SIC: 4833 Television broadcasting stations
PA: Tegna Inc.
8350 Broad St Ste 2000
Tysons VA
703 873-6600

(P-4452)
LIFETIME ENTRMT SVCS LLC
Also Called: Lifetime TV Network
2049 Century Park E Ste 840 (90067-3101)
PHONE.................................310 556-7500
Maryann Harris, Genl Mgr
EMP: 300
SALES (corp-wide): 82.72B Publicly Held
Web: www.mylifetime.com
SIC: 4833 5942 Television broadcasting stations; Book stores
HQ: Lifetime Entertainment Services, Llc
235 E 45th St
New York NY
212 424-7000

(P-4453)
MCKINNON PUBLISHING COMPANY
4575 Viewridge Ave (92123-1623)
PHONE.................................858 571-5151
Michael Mckinnon, Pr
EMP: 599 EST: 1993
SALES (est): 1.93MM Privately Held
Web: www.kusi.com
SIC: 4833 Television broadcasting stations
HQ: Mckinnon Broadcasting Company
4575 Viewridge Ave
San Diego CA
858 571-5151

(P-4454)
NBC SUBSIDIARY (KNBC-TV) LLC
Also Called: NBC
100 Universal City Plz Bldg 2120 (91608)
P.O. Box 66132 (90066-0132)
PHONE.................................818 684-5746
Todd Mokhtari, Pr
Jenik Badalian, *
EMP: 250 EST: 2009
SALES (est): 76.11MM
SALES (corp-wide): 121.43B Publicly Held
Web: www.nbcuniversal.com
SIC: 4833 Television broadcasting stations
PA: Comcast Corporation
1 Comcast Ctr
Philadelphia PA
215 286-1700

(P-4455)
NEWPORT TELEVISION LLC
Kget-TV
2120 L St (93301-2331)
PHONE.................................661 283-1700
Sandy Dipasquale, Pr
EMP: 671
SALES (corp-wide): 20.65MM Privately Held
Web: www.kget.com
SIC: 4833 Television translator station
PA: Newport Television Llc
460 Nichols Rd Ste 250
Kansas City MO
816 751-0200

(P-4456)
PAPPAS TELECASTING OF THE MIDLANDS LP
Also Called: Kptm-Tv Channel 42
500 S Chinowth St Ste C (93277-1653)

PRODUCTS & SERVICES SECTION
4841 - Cable And Other Pay Television Services (P-4476)

PHONE..............................559 733-7800
EMP: 253
SIC: 4833 Television broadcasting stations

(P-4457)
PARTICIPANT CHANNEL INC
331 Foothill Rd Fl 3 (90210-3609)
PHONE..............................310 550-7715
Evan Shapiro, Pr
Robert Murphy, *
Jeff Ivers, *
Gabriel Brakin, *
EMP: 63 EST: 2005
SALES (est): 9.1MM Privately Held
Web: www.participant.com
SIC: 4833 Television broadcasting stations

(P-4458)
PUBLIC MDIA GROUP SOUTHERN CAL (PA)
2900 W Alameda Ave Unit 600 (91505-4216)
PHONE..............................714 241-4100
Andrew Russell, Pr
Jamie Myers, *
Paul Nelson, *
Dawn Ariza, *
EMP: 100 EST: 1960
SQ FT: 50,000
SALES (est): 54.29MM
SALES (corp-wide): 54.29MM Privately Held
Web: www.kcet.org
SIC: 4833 Television broadcasting stations

(P-4459)
REVOLT MEDIA AND TV LLC
Also Called: Revolt
9200 W Sunset Blvd Fl 3 (90069-3502)
PHONE..............................323 645-3000
Detavio Samuels, CEO
Keith Clinkscales, *
EMP: 120 EST: 2010
SALES (est): 25.89MM Privately Held
Web: www.revolt.tv
SIC: 4833 Television broadcasting stations

(P-4460)
SACRAMENTO TELEVISION STNS INC (HQ)
Also Called: Kmax TV
2713 Kovr Dr (95605-1600)
PHONE..............................916 374-1452
Peter Dunn, CEO
EMP: 152 EST: 1954
SQ FT: 40,000
SALES (est): 34.07MM
SALES (corp-wide): 30.15B Publicly Held
Web: www.sacramentomediamarket.com
SIC: 4833 Television broadcasting stations
PA: Paramount Global
1515 Broadway
New York NY
212 258-6000

(P-4461)
SF BROADCASTING WISCONSIN INC
2425 Olympic Blvd (90404-4030)
PHONE..............................310 586-2410
EMP: 151 EST: 1994
SALES (est): 27.41MM
SALES (corp-wide): 3.19B Publicly Held
SIC: 4833 Television broadcasting stations
PA: Match Group, Inc.
8750 N Cntl Expy Ste 1400
Dallas TX
214 576-9352

(P-4462)
SMITH BROADCASTING GROUP INC
Also Called: Keyt Television
730 Miramonte Dr (93109-1417)
P.O. Box 729 (93102-0729)
PHONE..............................805 882-3933
Michael Granados, Genl Mgr
EMP: 332
SALES (corp-wide): 6.69MM Privately Held
Web: www.keyt.com
SIC: 4833 7313 Television broadcasting stations; Television and radio time sales
PA: Smith Broadcasting Group, Inc
2315 Red Rose Way
Santa Barbara CA
805 965-0400

(P-4463)
STATION VENTURE OPERATIONS LP
Also Called: NBC 7/Channel 39
9680 Granite Ridge Dr (92123-2673)
PHONE..............................619 231-3939
Dick Kelley, Genl Mgr
Jackie Bradford, Genl Mgr
▲ EMP: 76 EST: 1967
SQ FT: 23,000
SALES (est): 9.51MM
SALES (corp-wide): 121.43B Publicly Held
Web: www.nbcsandiego.com
SIC: 4833 Television broadcasting stations
HQ: Nbcuniversal, Llc
1221 Ave Of The Amrcas St
New York NY
212 664-4444

(P-4464)
TMZ PRODUCTIONS INC (HQ)
8033 W Sunset Blvd (90046-2401)
PHONE..............................818 972-8000
EMP: 65 EST: 2010
SALES (est): 25.83MM
SALES (corp-wide): 14.91B Publicly Held
Web: www.tmz.com
SIC: 4833 Television broadcasting stations
PA: Fox Corporation
1211 Ave Of The Americas
New York NY
212 852-7000

(P-4465)
TRINITY BRDCSTG NETWRK INC
Also Called: Trinity Christn Ctr Santa Ana
2442 Michelle Dr (92780-7015)
PHONE..............................714 665-3619
Paul F Crouch, Pr
EMP: 150 EST: 1987
SALES (est): 30.44MM
SALES (corp-wide): 120.98MM Privately Held
Web: www.tbn.org
SIC: 4833 Television broadcasting stations
PA: Trinity Christian Center Of Santa Ana, Inc.
13600 Heritage Pkwy # 200
Fort Worth TX
714 665-3619

(P-4466)
TWDC ENTERPRISES 18 CORP (HQ)
Also Called: Disney Financial Services
500 S Buena Vista St (91521-0001)
PHONE..............................818 560-1000
Robert Iger, CEO
Christine M Mccarthy, V

Alan N Braverman, *
Kevin A Mayer, CSO*
M Jayne Parker, Chief Human Resources Officer*
◆ EMP: 521 EST: 1925
SALES (est): 46.53B
SALES (corp-wide): 82.72B Publicly Held
Web: www.thewaltdisneycompany.com
SIC: 4833 4841 7011 7996 Television broadcasting stations; Cable television services; Resort hotel; Amusement parks
PA: The Walt Disney Company
500 S Buena Vista St
Burbank CA
818 560-1000

(P-4467)
TWENTETH CNTURY FOX INTL TV IN
10201 W Pico Blvd (90064-2606)
PHONE..............................310 369-1000
Peter Chernin, Ch Bd
EMP: 5980 EST: 1996
SALES (est): 20.44MM
SALES (corp-wide): 82.72B Publicly Held
SIC: 4833 Television broadcasting stations
HQ: Fox Entertainment Group, Llc
1211 Ave Of The Americas
New York NY
212 852-7000

(P-4468)
TWENTIETH TELEVISION INC
1999 S Bundy Dr (90025-5203)
PHONE..............................310 584-2000
EMP: 77
SALES (corp-wide): 82.72B Publicly Held
Web: www.mynetworktv.com
SIC: 4833 Television broadcasting stations
HQ: Twentieth Television, Inc.
10201 W Pico Blvd
Los Angeles CA

(P-4469)
VALLEYCREST PRODUCTIONS LTD
500 S Buena Vista St (91521-0001)
PHONE..............................818 560-5391
Joseph Santaniello, CEO
EMP: 100 EST: 1999
SALES (est): 47.48MM
SALES (corp-wide): 82.72B Publicly Held
SIC: 4833 Television broadcasting stations
HQ: Twdc Enterprises 18 Corp.
500 S Buena Vista St
Burbank CA

(P-4470)
WALT DISNEY COMPANY
7131 Tujunga Ave (91605-6217)
PHONE..............................818 560-4665
Robert A Iger, CEO
EMP: 70 EST: 2014
SALES (est): 533.92K Privately Held
Web: www.thewaltdisneycompany.com
SIC: 4833 Television broadcasting stations

(P-4471)
YOUNG BRDCSTG OF SAN FRANCISCO
Also Called: Kron-TV
900 Front St (94111-1427)
PHONE..............................415 441-4444
Deb Mcdermot, Pr
EMP: 69 EST: 2000
SALES (est): 4.29MM
SALES (corp-wide): 5.21MM Publicly Held
Web: www.kron4.com

SIC: 4833 Television broadcasting stations
HQ: Young Broadcasting, Llc
599 Lexington Ave
New York NY
517 372-8282

4841 Cable And Other Pay Television Services

(P-4472)
ABS-CBN INTERNATIONAL (DH)
432 N Canal St Ste 21 (94080-4666)
PHONE..............................800 527-2820
Eugenio Lopez Iii, CEO
▲ EMP: 140 EST: 1979
SALES (est): 605.15K Privately Held
SIC: 4841 7822 Cable and other pay television services; Television and video tape distribution
HQ: Abs-Cbn Interactive, Inc.
9th Floor Eugenio Lopez Jr., Communication Center
Quezon MAN

(P-4473)
BALLENA TECHNOLOGIES
1150 Ballena Blvd Ste 250 (94501-7313)
PHONE..............................510 521-0720
Richard Sherratt, CEO
EMP: 259 EST: 1999
SALES (est): 5.44MM
SALES (corp-wide): 121.43B Publicly Held
Web: www.seats3d.com
SIC: 4841 Subscription television services
HQ: Comcast Spectacor, Llc
3601 S Broad St Ste 2
Philadelphia PA
215 465-4500

(P-4474)
BDR INDUSTRIES INC (PA)
Also Called: R N D Enterprises
820 E Avenue L12 (93535-5403)
PHONE..............................661 940-8554
Scott Riddle, Pr
Edward Donovan, *
▲ EMP: 95 EST: 1984
SQ FT: 30,000
SALES (est): 24.38MM
SALES (corp-wide): 24.38MM Privately Held
Web: www.rndcable.com
SIC: 4841 Cable television services

(P-4475)
CALIFORNIA BROADCAST CTR LLC
3800 Via Oro Ave (90810-1866)
PHONE..............................310 233-2425
Bruce Churchill, CEO
EMP: 91 EST: 1955
SALES (est): 7.16MM
SALES (corp-wide): 120.74B Publicly Held
SIC: 4841 Cable and other pay television services
HQ: Directv Latin America, Llc
1 Rockefeller Plz
New York NY
212 205-0500

(P-4476)
CCO HOLDINGS LLC
1645 Countryside Dr (95380-9528)
PHONE..............................209 585-1001
EMP: 108
SALES (corp-wide): 54.02B Publicly Held

4841 - Cable And Other Pay Television Services (P-4477)

SIC: **4841** Cable television services
HQ: Cco Holdings, Llc
400 Atlantic St
Stamford CT
203 905-7801

(P-4477)
CCO HOLDINGS LLC
375 N Main St (93257-3739)
PHONE..................................559 560-5323
Dan Mcgough, *Mgr*
EMP: 179
SALES (corp-wide): 54.02B **Publicly Held**
SIC: **4841** Cable television services
HQ: Cco Holdings, Llc
400 Atlantic St
Stamford CT
203 905-7801

(P-4478)
CCO HOLDINGS LLC
3106 San Gabriel Blvd (91770-2579)
PHONE..................................626 500-1214
Steve Stannard, *Brnch Mgr*
EMP: 108
SALES (corp-wide): 54.02B **Publicly Held**
SIC: **4841** Cable television services
HQ: Cco Holdings, Llc
400 Atlantic St
Stamford CT
203 905-7801

(P-4479)
CCO HOLDINGS LLC
1636 Market St (96001-1021)
PHONE..................................530 646-4026
EMP: 108
SALES (corp-wide): 54.02B **Publicly Held**
SIC: **4841** Cable television services
HQ: Cco Holdings, Llc
400 Atlantic St
Stamford CT
203 905-7801

(P-4480)
CCO HOLDINGS LLC
23841 Malibu Rd (90265-4644)
PHONE..................................310 589-3008
EMP: 108
SALES (corp-wide): 54.02B **Publicly Held**
SIC: **4841** Cable television services
HQ: Cco Holdings, Llc
400 Atlantic St
Stamford CT
203 905-7801

(P-4481)
CCO HOLDINGS LLC
12319 Norwalk Blvd (90650-2039)
PHONE..................................562 239-2761
EMP: 108
SALES (corp-wide): 54.02B **Publicly Held**
SIC: **4841** Cable television services
HQ: Cco Holdings, Llc
400 Atlantic St
Stamford CT
203 905-7801

(P-4482)
CCO HOLDINGS LLC
825 W Henderson Ave (93257-1742)
PHONE..................................559 202-1001
EMP: 106
SALES (corp-wide): 54.02B **Publicly Held**
SIC: **4841** Cable television services
HQ: Cco Holdings, Llc
400 Atlantic St
Stamford CT
203 905-7801

(P-4483)
CCO HOLDINGS LLC
1151 N Azusa Ave (91702-2005)
PHONE..................................626 513-0204
EMP: 106
SALES (corp-wide): 54.02B **Publicly Held**
SIC: **4841** Cable television services
HQ: Cco Holdings, Llc
400 Atlantic St
Stamford CT
203 905-7801

(P-4484)
CCO HOLDINGS LLC
681 Leavesley Rd Ste 175 (95020-3657)
PHONE..................................408 413-0317
Krpinski Cindy, *Brnch Mgr*
EMP: 108
SALES (corp-wide): 54.02B **Publicly Held**
SIC: **4841** Cable television services
HQ: Cco Holdings, Llc
400 Atlantic St
Stamford CT
203 905-7801

(P-4485)
CCO HOLDINGS LLC
1128 W Branch St (93420-1906)
PHONE..................................805 904-1047
EMP: 108
SALES (corp-wide): 54.02B **Publicly Held**
SIC: **4841** Cable television services
HQ: Cco Holdings, Llc
400 Atlantic St
Stamford CT
203 905-7801

(P-4486)
CCO HOLDINGS LLC
1131 Creston Rd (93446-3031)
PHONE..................................805 400-1002
EMP: 108
SALES (corp-wide): 54.02B **Publicly Held**
SIC: **4841** Cable television services
HQ: Cco Holdings, Llc
400 Atlantic St
Stamford CT
203 905-7801

(P-4487)
CCO HOLDINGS LLC
21898 Us Highway 18 (92307-3916)
PHONE..................................760 810-4076
EMP: 108
SALES (corp-wide): 54.02B **Publicly Held**
SIC: **4841** Cable television services
HQ: Cco Holdings, Llc
400 Atlantic St
Stamford CT
203 905-7801

(P-4488)
CCO HOLDINGS LLC
5835 Eastside Rd (96001-4547)
PHONE..................................864 679-1745
EMP: 108
SALES (corp-wide): 54.02B **Publicly Held**
SIC: **4841** Cable television services
HQ: Cco Holdings, Llc
400 Atlantic St
Stamford CT
203 905-7801

(P-4489)
CCO HOLDINGS LLC
Also Called: Charter Communications
51 W Main St Ste F (93001-2566)
PHONE..................................805 232-5887
EMP: 108
SALES (corp-wide): 54.02B **Publicly Held**
SIC: **4841** Cable television services
HQ: Cco Holdings, Llc
400 Atlantic St
Stamford CT
203 905-7801

(P-4490)
CCO HOLDINGS LLC
Also Called: Charter Communications
2310 N Bellflower Blvd (90815-2019)
PHONE..................................562 228-1262
EMP: 107
SALES (corp-wide): 54.02B **Publicly Held**
SIC: **4841** Cable television services
HQ: Cco Holdings, Llc
400 Atlantic St
Stamford CT
203 905-7801

(P-4491)
CCO HOLDINGS LLC
2684 N Tustin St (92865-2438)
PHONE..................................714 509-5861
EMP: 108
SALES (corp-wide): 54.02B **Publicly Held**
SIC: **4841** 3663 3651 Cable television services; Radio and t.v. communications equipment; Household audio and video equipment
HQ: Cco Holdings, Llc
400 Atlantic St
Stamford CT
203 905-7801

(P-4492)
CCO HOLDINGS LLC
26827 Baseline St (92346-3059)
PHONE..................................909 742-8273
EMP: 108
SALES (corp-wide): 54.02B **Publicly Held**
SIC: **4841** 3663 3651 Cable television services; Radio and t.v. communications equipment; Household audio and video equipment
HQ: Cco Holdings, Llc
400 Atlantic St
Stamford CT
203 905-7801

(P-4493)
COMCAST CORPORATION
Also Called: Comcast
1205 S Dupont Ave (91761-1536)
PHONE..................................909 890-0886
Mike Shanter, *Brnch Mgr*
EMP: 100
SQ FT: 23,318
SALES (corp-wide): 121.43B **Publicly Held**
Web: corporate.comcast.com
SIC: **4841** Cable television services
PA: Comcast Corporation
1 Comcast Ctr
Philadelphia PA
215 286-1700

(P-4494)
COX COMMUNICATIONS CAL LLC
5159 Federal Blvd (92105-5428)
PHONE..................................619 262-1122
James Robbins, *CEO*
EMP: 380
SALES (corp-wide): 16.61B **Privately Held**
SIC: **4841** Cable television services
HQ: Cox Communications California, Llc
6205 Pachtree Dunwoody Rd
Atlanta GA
404 843-5000

(P-4495)
CROWN MEDIA HOLDINGS INC (HQ)
12700 Ventura Blvd Ste 200 (91604-2469)
PHONE..................................888 390-7474
William J Abbott, *Pr*
Andrew Rooke, *
Charles L Stanford, *
Laura Lee, *Executive Distribution Vice President*
Susanne Mcavoy, *VP Mktg*
EMP: 61 EST: 1999
SQ FT: 41,423
SALES (est): 107.5MM
SALES (corp-wide): 2.72B **Privately Held**
Web: www.hallmarkchannel.com
SIC: **4841** Cable television services
PA: Hallmark Cards, Incorporated
2501 Mcgee St
Kansas City MO
816 274-5111

(P-4496)
CYPRESS COMMUNICATIONS INC
1999 Harrison St Ste 101 (94612-3520)
PHONE..................................415 962-4500
EMP: 76
SIC: **4841** Cable and other pay television services
HQ: Cypress Communications, Inc.
75 Erieview Plz Fl 4
Cleveland OH

(P-4497)
DIRECTV
1655 W 110th Pl (90047-4826)
PHONE..................................323 810-2032
Geron Flynn, *Prin*
EMP: 99 EST: 2010
SALES (est): 762.77K **Privately Held**
Web: www.directv.com
SIC: **4841** Direct broadcast satellite services (DBS)

(P-4498)
DIRECTV INC
2260 E Imperial Hwy (90245-3501)
P.O. Box 105249 (30348-5249)
PHONE..................................888 388-4249
EMP: 476 EST: 2015
SALES (est): 45.31MM **Privately Held**
Web: www.directv.com
SIC: **4841** Cable and other pay television services

(P-4499)
DIRECTV ENTERPRISES LLC
2230 E Imperial Hwy (90245-3504)
P.O. Box 956 (90245-0956)
PHONE..................................310 535-5000
EMP: 16229 EST: 1995
SQ FT: 75,000
SALES (est): 13.6MM
SALES (corp-wide): 120.74B **Publicly Held**
SIC: **4841** Direct broadcast satellite services (DBS)
HQ: Directv Holdings Llc
2230 E Imperial Hwy
El Segundo CA
310 964-5000

(P-4500)
DIRECTV GROUP HOLDINGS LLC
140 Station Ave (93555-3838)
PHONE..................................760 375-8300
EMP: 139

PRODUCTS & SERVICES SECTION

4841 - Cable And Other Pay Television Services (P-4520)

SALES (corp-wide): 120.74B **Publicly Held**
SIC: **4841** Cable and other pay television services
HQ: Directv Group Holdings, Llc
2260 E Imperial Hwy
El Segundo CA

(P-4501)
DIRECTV GROUP HOLDINGS LLC
360 Cortez Cir (93012-8630)
PHONE..............................805 207-6675
EMP: 110
SALES (corp-wide): 120.74B **Publicly Held**
SIC: **4841** Cable television services
HQ: Directv Group Holdings, Llc
2260 E Imperial Hwy
El Segundo CA

(P-4502)
DIRECTV GROUP HOLDINGS LLC
715 E Avenue L8 Ste 101 (93535-5405)
PHONE..............................661 632-6562
EMP: 111
SALES (corp-wide): 120.74B **Publicly Held**
SIC: **4841** Direct broadcast satellite services (DBS)
HQ: Directv Group Holdings, Llc
2260 E Imperial Hwy
El Segundo CA

(P-4503)
DIRECTV GROUP INC (DH)
Also Called: Directv
2260 E Imperial Hwy (90245-3501)
PHONE..............................310 964-5000
Michael White, *CEO*
Patrick T Doyle, *
Romulo Pontual, *
John F Murphy, *CAO*
J William Little, *
▲ EMP: 128 EST: 1977
SALES (est): 1.87B
SALES (corp-wide): 120.74B **Publicly Held**
SIC: **4841** 6794 Direct broadcast satellite services (DBS); Franchises, selling or licensing
HQ: Directv Group Holdings, Llc
2260 E Imperial Hwy
El Segundo CA

(P-4504)
DIRECTV HOLDINGS LLC (DH)
2230 E Imperial Hwy (90245-3504)
PHONE..............................310 964-5000
Michael D White, *Pr*
Larry D Hunter, *Ex VP*
Patrick T Doyle, *Ex VP*
John F Murphy, *CAO*
◆ EMP: 71 EST: 2002
SALES (est): 1.29B
SALES (corp-wide): 120.74B **Publicly Held**
SIC: **4841** Direct broadcast satellite services (DBS)
HQ: The Directv Group Inc
2260 E Imperial Hwy
El Segundo CA
310 964-5000

(P-4505)
DIRECTV INTERNATIONAL INC (DH)
2230 E Imperial Hwy Fl 10 (90245-3504)
PHONE..............................310 964-6460
EMP: 150 EST: 1996
SALES (est): 494.29MM
SALES (corp-wide): 120.74B **Publicly Held**
SIC: **4841** Cable and other pay television services
HQ: The Directv Group Inc
2260 E Imperial Hwy
El Segundo CA
310 964-5000

(P-4506)
DIRECTV LATIN AMERICA LLC
2230 E Imperial Hwy (90245-3504)
PHONE..............................310 535-5000
Bruce Churchill, *CEO*
EMP: 73 EST: 1996
SALES (est): 1.24MM **Privately Held**
SIC: **4841** Cable television services

(P-4507)
E ENTERTAINMENT TELEVISION INC
Also Called: Style Network
5750 Wilshire Blvd # 500 (90036-3697)
PHONE..............................323 954-2400
EMP: 900
SIC: **4841** 4833 Cable television services; Television broadcasting stations

(P-4508)
FX NETWORKS LLC
10201 W Pico Blvd Bldg 103 (90064-2606)
P.O. Box 900 (90213-0900)
PHONE..............................310 369-1000
John Landgraf, *Managing Member*
Stephanie Gibbons, *
EMP: 150 EST: 1997
SALES (est): 53.25MM
SALES (corp-wide): 82.72B **Publicly Held**
Web: www.fxnetworks.com
SIC: **4841** Cable television services
HQ: Fox Entertainment Group, Llc
1211 Ave Of The Americas
New York NY
212 852-7000

(P-4509)
GAME SHOW NETWORK MUSIC LLC (DH)
Also Called: G S N
2150 Colorado Ave Ste 100 (90404-5514)
PHONE..............................310 255-6800
Mark Seldman, *Managing Member*
EMP: 244 EST: 1992
SALES (est): 89.95MM **Privately Held**
SIC: **4841** Cable television services
HQ: Sony Pictures Entertainment, Inc.
10202 Washington Blvd
Culver City CA
310 244-4000

(P-4510)
GLOBECAST AMERICA INCORPORATED
10525 Washington Blvd (90232-3311)
PHONE..............................310 845-3900
Lisa Coelho, *Brnch Mgr*
EMP: 205
SALES (corp-wide): 23.35B **Privately Held**
Web: www.globecast.com
SIC: **4841** Satellite master antenna systems services (SMATV)
HQ: Globecast America Incorporated
10525 Washington Blvd
Culver City CA
310 845-3900

(P-4511)
INTEL MEDIA INC
2200 Mission College Blvd M (95054-1537)
PHONE..............................408 765-0063
Erik Huggers, *Pr*
EMP: 350 EST: 1999
SALES (est): 116.54MM
SALES (corp-wide): 63.05B **Publicly Held**
Web: www.intel.com
SIC: **4841** Subscription television services
PA: Intel Corporation
2200 Mission College Blvd
Santa Clara CA
408 765-8080

(P-4512)
INTERNATIONAL FMLY ENTRMT INC (DH)
Also Called: Fox Family Channel
3800 W Alameda Ave (91505-4300)
PHONE..............................818 560-1000
Mel Woods, *Pr*
EMP: 144 EST: 1990
SALES (est): 102.39MM
SALES (corp-wide): 82.72B **Publicly Held**
SIC: **4841** 7812 7922 7999 Cable television services; Television film production; Theatrical producers; Recreation services
HQ: Abc Family Worldwide, Inc.
500 S Buena Vista St
Burbank CA
818 560-1000

(P-4513)
MLB ADVANCED MEDIA LP
Also Called: Visalia Rawhide
300 N Giddings St (93291-4745)
PHONE..............................559 625-0480
EMP: 536
SALES (corp-wide): 4.71MM **Privately Held**
Web: www.rawhidebaseball.com
SIC: **4841** 7313 7929 Subscription television services; Electronic media advertising representatives; Entertainment service
HQ: Mlb Advanced Media, L.P.
1271 Ave Of The Americas
New York NY
212 485-3444

(P-4514)
NDS AMERICAS INC (DH)
3500 Hyland Ave (92626-1459)
PHONE..............................714 434-2100
Abe Peled, *Pr*
Dov Rubin, *
Alex Gersh, *
EMP: 90 EST: 1992
SALES (est): 42.68MM
SALES (corp-wide): 57B **Publicly Held**
Web: www.synamedia.com
SIC: **4841** Cable television services
HQ: Nds Group Limited
9-11 New Square
Feltham MIDDX

(P-4515)
NETFLIX INC (PA)
Also Called: Netflix
121 Albright Way (95032-1801)
PHONE..............................408 540-3700
Ted Sarandos, *CCO**
Reed Hastings, *
Spencer Neumann, *CFO*
David Hyman, *CLO*
EMP: 166 EST: 1998
SALES (est): 31.62B **Publicly Held**
Web: www.netflix.com

SIC: **4841** 2741 Subscription television services; Internet publishing and broadcasting

(P-4516)
OC COMMUNICATIONS INC
2204 Kausen Dr Ste 100 (95758-7176)
PHONE..............................916 686-3700
EMP: 650
Web: www.occom.com
SIC: **4841** Cable and other pay television services

(P-4517)
OWN LLC
Also Called: Oprah Winfrey Network
4000 Warner Blvd (91522-0001)
PHONE..............................323 602-5500
Oprah Winfrey, *CRO*
Oprah Winfrey, *Chief Creative Officer*
Erik Logan, *
Sheri Salata, *
EMP: 140 EST: 2008
SALES (est): 97.31MM
SALES (corp-wide): 189.98MM **Privately Held**
Web: www.oprah.com
SIC: **4841** Cable television services
PA: Discovery Communications, Inc.
10100 Santa Monica Blvd
Los Angeles CA
310 975-5906

(P-4518)
PLAXO INC
Also Called: Comcast Slcon Vly Innvtion Ctr
1050 Enterprise Way # 200 (94089-1415)
PHONE..............................408 900-8701
Justin Miller, *Pr*
Preston Smalley, *
Jai Saxena, *
EMP: 80 EST: 2002
SALES (est): 24.36MM
SALES (corp-wide): 121.43B **Publicly Held**
SIC: **4841** Cable television services
PA: Comcast Corporation
1 Comcast Ctr
Philadelphia PA
215 286-1700

(P-4519)
ROKU INC (PA)
Also Called: ROKU
1155 Coleman Ave (95110-1104)
PHONE..............................408 556-9040
Anthony Wood, *Ch Bd*
Dan Jedda, *CFO*
Gil Fuchsberg, *Sr VP*
Stephen H Kay, *Sr VP*
▲ EMP: 250 EST: 2002
SALES (est): 3.13B **Publicly Held**
Web: www.roku.com
SIC: **4841** 7822 Cable and other pay television services; Motion picture and tape distribution

(P-4520)
SPECTRUM MGT HOLDG CO LLC
Also Called: Time Warner
3550 Wilshire Blvd (90010-2401)
PHONE..............................323 657-0899
EMP: 84
SALES (corp-wide): 54.02B **Publicly Held**
Web: www.spectrum.com
SIC: **4841** Cable television services
HQ: Spectrum Management Holding Company, Llc
400 Atlantic St

4841 - Cable And Other Pay Television Services (P-4521)

Stamford CT
203 905-7801

(P-4521)
SPECTRUM MGT HOLDG CO LLC
Time Warner
10450 Pacific Center Ct (92121-4338)
PHONE.................................858 695-3220
Jim Fellhauer, *Pr*
EMP: 78
SQ FT: 25,500
SALES (corp-wide): 54.02B **Publicly Held**
Web: www.spectrum.com
SIC: 4841 Cable television services
HQ: Spectrum Management Holding Company, Llc
400 Atlantic St
Stamford CT
203 905-7801

(P-4522)
SPECTRUM MGT HOLDG CO LLC
Also Called: Time Warner
5865 Friars Rd (92110-6009)
PHONE.................................619 684-6106
EMP: 86
SALES (corp-wide): 54.02B **Publicly Held**
Web: www.spectrum.com
SIC: 4841 Cable television services
HQ: Spectrum Management Holding Company, Llc
400 Atlantic St
Stamford CT
203 905-7801

(P-4523)
TIME WARNER CABLE ENTPS LLC
Also Called: Time Warner
3500 W Olive Ave Ste 1000 (91505-5515)
PHONE.................................818 972-0808
EMP: 64
SALES (corp-wide): 54.02B **Publicly Held**
SIC: 4841 Cable television services
HQ: Time Warner Cable Enterprises Llc
400 Atlantic St Ste 6
Stamford CT

(P-4524)
TIME WARNER CABLE ENTPS LLC
Also Called: Time Warner
4000 Warner Blvd (91526-0001)
PHONE.................................818 977-7840
Mark Pincus, *Brnch Mgr*
EMP: 79
SALES (corp-wide): 54.02B **Publicly Held**
Web: www.wbd.com
SIC: 4841 Cable television services
HQ: Time Warner Cable Enterprises Llc
400 Atlantic St Ste 6
Stamford CT

(P-4525)
TIME WARNER COMPANIES INC
Also Called: Time Warner
2939 Nebraska Ave (90404-4108)
PHONE.................................310 315-4437
Pauline Thomke, *Brnch Mgr*
EMP: 633
SIC: 4841 Cable television services
HQ: Time Warner Companies, Inc.
1 Time Warner Ctr
New York NY
212 484-8000

(P-4526)
VIDEO VICE DATA COMMUNICATIONS (PA)
Also Called: Vvd Communications
7391 Lincoln Way (92841-1428)
P.O. Box 91421 (90809-1421)
PHONE.................................714 897-6300
Bantofin Montoya, *Pr*
Annie Yonemura, *
EMP: 201 **EST:** 2002
SQ FT: 30,000
SALES (est): 36.81MM
SALES (corp-wide): 36.81MM **Privately Held**
Web: www.vvdservices.com
SIC: 4841 1731 Cable and other pay television services; Electrical work

(P-4527)
VUBIQUITY HOLDINGS INC (DH)
Also Called: Vubiquity
15301 Ventura Blvd Ste 3000 (91403-5837)
PHONE.................................818 526-5000
Darcy Antonellis, *CEO*
Doug Sylvester, *
William G Arendt, *
James P Riley, *
Stephen Holsten, *
EMP: 185 **EST:** 2006
SALES (est): 120.51MM
SALES (corp-wide): 4.58B **Privately Held**
Web: www.amdocs.com
SIC: 4841 Cable and other pay television services
HQ: Amdocs, Inc.
625 Mryvlle Cntre Dr Ste
Saint Louis MO
314 212-7000

4899 Communication Services, Nec

(P-4528)
ACTIVISION BLIZZARD MEDIA LLC
405 Howard St Ste 400 (94105-2672)
PHONE.................................206 890-4996
EMP: 78 **EST:** 2017
SALES (est): 499.95K **Privately Held**
Web: www.activisionblizzardmedia.com
SIC: 4899 Communication services, nec

(P-4529)
AXXCELERA BRDBAND WIRELESS INC
Also Called: Axxcelera
48389 Fremont Blvd (94538-6513)
PHONE.................................510 573-4708
EMP: 104
SALES (corp-wide): 84.02MM **Privately Held**
Web: www.axxcelera.com
SIC: 4899 Data communication services
HQ: Axxcelera Broadband Wireless, Inc.
82 Coromar Dr
Santa Barbara CA
805 968-9621

(P-4530)
CALIX INC (PA)
Also Called: Calix
2777 Orchard Pkwy (95134-2008)
PHONE.................................408 514-3000
Michael Weening, *Pr*
Carl Russo, *
Cory Sindelar, *CAO*
J Matthew Collins, *COMMERCIAL*
Shane Eleniak, *Chief Product Officer*
◆ **EMP:** 604 **EST:** 1999
SALES (est): 867.83MM
SALES (corp-wide): 867.83MM **Publicly Held**
Web: www.calix.com
SIC: 4899 7372 4813 Data communication services; Prepackaged software; Internet connectivity services

(P-4531)
CALLISTO MEDIA INC
918 Parker St (94710-2526)
PHONE.................................510 253-0500
Deepail Ajmani, *Prin*
EMP: 69 **EST:** 2012
SALES (est): 2.03MM **Privately Held**
Web: www.callistomedia.com
SIC: 4899 Communication services, nec

(P-4532)
CAMBIUM NETWORKS INC
2010 N 1st St (95131-2018)
PHONE.................................847 640-3809
EMP: 243
Web: www.cambiumnetworks.com
SIC: 4899 Data communication services
HQ: Cambium Networks, Inc.
3800 Golf Rd Ste 360
Rolling Meadows IL
888 863-5250

(P-4533)
CASELA TECHNOLOGIES USA
1525 Mccarthy Blvd Ste 1000 (95035-7451)
PHONE.................................650 892-8480
Tim Munks, *Ex Dir*
EMP: 85 **EST:** 2020
SALES (est): 2.57MM **Privately Held**
SIC: 4899 Communication services, nec

(P-4534)
COMMUNICATIONS SUPPLY CORP
6251 Knott Ave (90620-1010)
PHONE.................................714 670-7711
Michael Davis, *Genl Mgr*
EMP: 70
Web: www.wesco.com
SIC: 4899 1731 3577 3357 Data communication services; Communications specialization; Computer peripheral equipment, nec; Nonferrous wiredrawing and insulating
HQ: Communications Supply Corp
225 W Station Square Dr # 700
Pittsburgh PA
630 221-6400

(P-4535)
DISCOVERY COMMUNICATIONS INC (PA)
10100 Santa Monica Blvd Ste 1500 (90067-4002)
PHONE.................................310 975-5906
David Zazlov, *CEO*
EMP: 260 **EST:** 2014
SALES (est): 189.98MM
SALES (corp-wide): 189.98MM **Privately Held**
Web: www.discovery.com
SIC: 4899 Data communication services

(P-4536)
EXPERIOR LABORATORIES INC
1635 Ives Ave (93033-1890)
PHONE.................................805 483-3400
Lorenz Cartellieri, *CEO*
Lorenz Cartellieri, *Pr*
John Kim, *
EMP: 65 **EST:** 2003
SALES (est): 9.56MM **Privately Held**
Web: www.experiorlabs.com
SIC: 4899 8734 Communication signal enhancement network services; Testing laboratories

(P-4537)
HORIZON COMMUNICATION TECH INC
Also Called: Horizon Communication
13700 Alton Pkwy Ste 154-278 (92618-1628)
PHONE.................................714 982-3900
Nicolle Degraw, *CEO*
Micheal Degraw, *
Anthony Turrentine, *
Alex Hisa, *
EMP: 80 **EST:** 1998
SALES (est): 21.63MM **Privately Held**
SIC: 4899 Data communication services

(P-4538)
INTELPEER CLOUD CMMNCTIONS LLC (PA)
155 Bovet Rd Ste 405 (94402-3137)
PHONE.................................650 525-9200
Frank Fawzi, *Managing Member*
Phil Bronsdon, *Sr VP*
Haydar Haba, *VISIONARY*
Andre Simone, *CFO*
Matt Edic Cxo, *Prin*
EMP: 106 **EST:** 2002
SQ FT: 6,000
SALES (est): 47.79MM
SALES (corp-wide): 47.79MM **Privately Held**
Web: www.intelepeer.com
SIC: 4899 Data communication services

(P-4539)
INTELSAT US LLC
Also Called: Intell Set
1600 Forbes Way (90810-1830)
PHONE.................................310 525-5500
EMP: 105
SALES (corp-wide): 775.18MM **Privately Held**
Web: www.intelsat.com
SIC: 4899 Satellite earth stations
HQ: Intelsat Us Llc
7900 Tysons One Pl
Mc Lean VA

(P-4540)
ITRON NETWORKED SOLUTIONS INC (HQ)
230 W Tasman Dr (95134-1714)
PHONE.................................669 770-4000
Thomas L Deitrich, *Pr*
Catriona M Fallon, *Sr VP*
Robert Farrow, *
Shannon M Votava, *Sec*
▲ **EMP:** 400 **EST:** 2002
SQ FT: 191,800
SALES (est): 311.01MM
SALES (corp-wide): 1.8B **Publicly Held**
Web: www.itron.com
SIC: 4899 7372 Communication signal enhancement network services; Prepackaged software
PA: Itron, Inc.
2111 N Molter Rd
Liberty Lake WA
509 924-9900

(P-4541)
KRAMER MEDIA LLC
201 Mission St Fl 9 (94105-1886)

PRODUCTS & SERVICES SECTION

4911 - Electric Services (P-4564)

PHONE..............................415 439-4601
Andrew Kramer, Brnch Mgr
EMP: 62
SALES (corp-wide): 197.67K **Privately Held**
SIC: **4899** Data communication services
PA: Kramer Media, Llc
5000 Proctor Ave
Oakland CA
510 595-9252

(P-4542)
LEMONLIGHT
4063 Glencoe Ave # A (90292-5607)
PHONE..............................310 801-6487
EMP: 70 EST: 2015
SALES (est): 582.33K **Privately Held**
Web: www.lemonlight.com
SIC: **4899** Data communication services

(P-4543)
MAXAR SPACE LLC (HQ)
3875 Fabian Way (94303-4604)
PHONE..............................650 852-4000
John Celli, Pr
Bill Mccombe, Sr VP
David Bernstein, *
Richard Currier, *
Paul Estey, *
◆ EMP: 75 EST: 1892
SALES (est): 785.75MM
SALES (corp-wide): 1.6B **Privately Held**
Web: www.maxar.com
SIC: **4899** 3663 Satellite earth stations; Satellites, communications
PA: Maxar Technologies Inc.
1300 W 120th Ave
Westminster CO
303 684-7660

(P-4544)
MOBILEUM INC (PA)
20813 Stevens Creek Blvd Ste 200 (95014-2185)
PHONE..............................408 844-6600
Bobby Srinivasan, *
Andrew Warner, CFO
Avnish Chauhan, *
Bernardo Lucas, CMO*
Ron Haberman, CPO
EMP: 180 EST: 2000
SQ FT: 4,000
SALES (est): 192.66MM **Privately Held**
Web: www.mobileum.com
SIC: **4899** 7373 Data communication services; Computer systems analysis and design

(P-4545)
NEXUS IS INC
27202 Turnberry Ln Ste 100 (91355-1022)
PHONE..............................704 969-2200
EMP: 340
SIC: **4899** Data communication services

(P-4546)
PROSOFT TECHNOLOGY INC (HQ)
9201 Camino Media Ste 200 (93311-1362)
PHONE..............................661 716-5100
Thomas Crone, Pr
EMP: 101 EST: 1990
SALES (est): 51.24MM
SALES (corp-wide): 2.61B **Publicly Held**
Web: www.prosoft-technology.com
SIC: **4899** Data communication services
PA: Belden Inc.
1 N Brentwood Blvd Fl 15
Saint Louis MO
314 854-8000

(P-4547)
RELIGION OF SPORTS HQ
3310 Airport Ave (90405-6134)
PHONE..............................214 557-1766
Pietro Moro, COO
EMP: 60 EST: 2018
SALES (est): 636.99K **Privately Held**
Web: www.religionofsports.com
SIC: **4899** Communication services, nec

(P-4548)
SEFNCO COMMUNICATIONS INC
8615 Elder Creek Rd (95828-1800)
PHONE..............................925 271-2943
EMP: 60
SALES (corp-wide): 9.78B **Publicly Held**
Web: www.sefnco.com
SIC: **4899** Data communication services
HQ: Sefnco Communications, Inc.
777 Main St
Buckley WA
877 385-2903

(P-4549)
SHIFT NETWORK
101 San Antonio Rd (94952-9524)
PHONE..............................415 223-7560
EMP: 72 EST: 2011
SALES (est): 474.41K **Privately Held**
Web: www.theshiftnetwork.com
SIC: **4899** Communication services, nec

(P-4550)
SHONDALAND INC
2029 Century Park E Ste 1500 (90002-3076)
PHONE..............................323 468-8109
Shonda L Rhimes, CEO
EMP: 62 EST: 2010
SALES (est): 5.12MM **Privately Held**
Web: www.shondaland.com
SIC: **4899** Communication services, nec

(P-4551)
SIEGE MEDIA LLC
624 Broadway Ste 301 (92101-5421)
PHONE..............................858 751-4439
Ross Hudgens, Prin
EMP: 89 EST: 2016
SALES (est): 1.62MM **Privately Held**
Web: www.siegemedia.com
SIC: **4899** Communication services, nec

(P-4552)
SOCIALIVE
121 W Palm Ave Apt 3 (90245-2262)
PHONE..............................978 821-4637
Jonathan Macleod, Prin
EMP: 69 EST: 2017
SALES (est): 1.38MM **Privately Held**
Web: www.socialive.us
SIC: **4899** Communication services, nec

(P-4553)
SS8 NETWORKS INC (PA)
Also Called: S S 8
750 Tasman Dr (95035-7456)
PHONE..............................408 894-8400
Dennis Haar, CEO
Kam Wong, *
Cemal Dikmen, *
Keith Bhatia, *
EMP: 120 EST: 1999
SQ FT: 83,000
SALES (est): 43.6MM
SALES (corp-wide): 43.6MM **Privately Held**
Web: www.ss8.com

SIC: **4899** 7381 Communication signal enhancement network services; Detective services

(P-4554)
TELETRAC INC (PA)
Also Called: Fleet Mangement Solutions
310 Commerce Ste 100 (92602-1360)
PHONE..............................714 897-0877
Tj Chung, Pr
Tim Van Cleve, *
▲ EMP: 143 EST: 1995
SALES (est): 84.77MM
SALES (corp-wide): 84.77MM **Privately Held**
Web: www.teletracnavman.com
SIC: **4899** Data communication services

(P-4555)
THINKOM SOLUTIONS INC
4881 W 145th St (90250-6701)
PHONE..............................310 371-5486
Mark Silk, CEO
William W Milroy, *
Michael Burke, *
Stuart Coppedge, *
Matthew Turk, *
EMP: 116 EST: 2000
SQ FT: 74,000
SALES (est): 30.05MM **Privately Held**
Web: www.thinkom.com
SIC: **4899** Satellite earth stations

(P-4556)
TRANSON MEDIA LLC
548 Market St Ste 41895 (94104-5401)
PHONE..............................415 621-9830
Michael Transon, Pr
EMP: 70 EST: 2014
SALES (est): 5.27MM **Privately Held**
SIC: **4899** Communication services, nec

(P-4557)
TXTMEQUICKCOM
44 Montgomery St Fl 6 (94104-4602)
PHONE..............................703 596-8989
Ray Bolouri, CEO
Rey Bolouri, *
Herman Pippin, *
EMP: 186 EST: 2014
SQ FT: 3,400
SALES (est): 9.55MM **Privately Held**
SIC: **4899** Data communication services

(P-4558)
VERTICAL COMMUNICATION (HQ)
3979 Freedom Cir Ste 400 (95054-1257)
PHONE..............................408 969-9600
William Tauscher, CEO
▲ EMP: 65 EST: 1996
SALES (est): 18.42MM
SALES (corp-wide): 40MM **Privately Held**
Web: www.vertical.com
SIC: **4899** Data communication services
PA: Vertical Communications, Inc.
1000 Holcomb Woods Pkwy # 415
Roswell GA
877 837-8422

(P-4559)
WOVEXX HOLDINGS INC (DH)
Also Called: Redwood
10381 Jefferson Blvd (90232-3511)
PHONE..............................310 424-2080
EMP: 90 EST: 2010
SQ FT: 12,000
SALES (est): 46.91MM **Publicly Held**

SIC: **4899** 7929 Data communication services; Entertainment service
HQ: Warner Music Group Corp.
1633 Broadway
New York NY
212 275-2000

4911 Electric Services

(P-4560)
AES ALAMITOS LLC
Also Called: AES
690 N Studebaker Rd (90803-2221)
PHONE..............................562 493-7891
Weikko Wirta, Managing Member
EMP: 90 EST: 1997
SALES (est): 56.57MM
SALES (corp-wide): 12.62B **Publicly Held**
Web: www.aes.com
SIC: **4911** Generation, electric power
PA: The Aes Corporation
4300 Wilson Blvd Ste 1100
Arlington VA
703 522-1315

(P-4561)
ALAMEDA BUREAU ELEC IMPRV CORP (HQ)
Also Called: Alameda Municipal Power
2000 Grand St (94501-1228)
P.O. Box H (94501-0263)
PHONE..............................510 748-3902
Edwin Dankworth, CEO
Gregory Hamm, *
Margie Sherratt, *
Peter Holmes, *
Jane Chisaki, *
▲ EMP: 85 EST: 1882
SALES (est): 37.93MM **Privately Held**
Web: www.alamedamp.com
SIC: **4911** Distribution, electric power
PA: City Of Alameda
2263 Santa Clara Ave
Alameda CA
510 747-7400

(P-4562)
CALIFRNIA IND SYS OPRATOR CORP (PA)
Also Called: California ISO
250 Outcropping Way (95630-8773)
P.O. Box 639014 (95763-9014)
PHONE..............................916 351-4400
EMP: 450 EST: 1997
SQ FT: 79,000
SALES (est): 244.26MM **Privately Held**
Web: www.caiso.com
SIC: **4911** Distribution, electric power

(P-4563)
CHESTNUT RIDGE ENERGY COMPANY
18101 Von Karman Ave Ste 920 (92612-1012)
▲ EMP: 185 EST: 1998
SALES (est): 2.29MM
SALES (corp-wide): 408.14MM **Privately Held**
SIC: **4911** Generation, electric power
HQ: Edison Mission Holdings Co.
18101 Von Karman Ave # 1700
Irvine CA
949 752-5588

(P-4564)
CITY OF GLENDALE
Also Called: Power Plant
634 Bekins Way (91201-3013)
PHONE..............................818 548-3980

4911 - Electric Services (P-4565)

Larry Moorehouse, *Superintnt*
EMP: 75
SALES (corp-wide): 390.24MM **Privately Held**
Web: www.glendaleca.gov
SIC: 4911 Generation, electric power
PA: City Of Glendale
141 N Glendale Ave Fl 2
Glendale CA
818 548-2085

(P-4565)
CITY OF SANTA CLARA
Also Called: Silicon Valley Power
1500 Warburton Ave (95050-3796)
PHONE..............................408 615-2300
John Roukema, *Mgr*
EMP: 84
SALES (corp-wide): 321.79MM **Privately Held**
Web: www.santaclaraca.gov
SIC: 4911 Electric services
PA: City Of Santa Clara
1500 Warburton Ave
Santa Clara CA
408 615-2200

(P-4566)
CITY OF SANTA CLARA
Also Called: Electric Department
1705 Martin Ave (95050-2557)
PHONE..............................408 615-2046
EMP: 90
SQ FT: 15,000
SALES (corp-wide): 321.79MM **Privately Held**
Web: www.santaclaraca.gov
SIC: 4911 Electric power broker
PA: City Of Santa Clara
1500 Warburton Ave
Santa Clara CA
408 615-2200

(P-4567)
COSO OPERATING COMPANY LLC
2 Gill Station Coso Rd. (93542)
P.O. Box 1690 (93527-1690)
PHONE..............................760 764-1300
Jim Pagano, *CEO*
Joseph Greco, *
▲ **EMP:** 90 **EST:** 1999
SALES (est): 55.02MM **Privately Held**
Web: www.cosoenergy.com
SIC: 4911 Generation, electric power

(P-4568)
CYPRESS CREEK HOLDINGS LLC
3250 Ocean Park Blvd Ste 355 (90405-3208)
PHONE..............................310 581-6299
Ben Van De Bunt, *Ch*
Matthew Mcgovern, *CEO*
Michael Cohen, *
EMP: 100 **EST:** 2014
SALES (est): 13.64MM **Privately Held**
SIC: 4911

(P-4569)
CYPRESS CREEK RENEWABLES LLC
445 Bush St Fl 7 (94108-3728)
PHONE..............................415 306-5300
Matthew Mcgovern, *Brnch Mgr*
EMP: 60
SALES (corp-wide): 126.64MM **Publicly Held**
Web: www.ccrenew.com

SIC: 4911
HQ: Cypress Creek Renewables, Llc
3402 Pico Blvd
Santa Monica CA
310 581-6299

(P-4570)
DYNEGY MARKETING & TRADE LLC
Also Called: Dynegy
Hwy 1 & Dolan Rd (95039)
PHONE..............................831 633-6700
EMP: 75
SALES (corp-wide): 13.73B **Publicly Held**
Web: www.dynegy.com
SIC: 4911 4923 Generation, electric power; Gas transmission and distribution
HQ: Dynegy Marketing & Trade, Llc
6555 Sierra Dr
Irving TX
214 812-4600

(P-4571)
DYNEGY MOSS LANDING LLC
Also Called: Moss Landing Power Plant
7301 Highway 1 (95039-9716)
P.O. Box 690 (95039-0690)
PHONE..............................831 633-6618
Robert C Flexon, *CEO*
▲ **EMP:** 75 **EST:** 1997
SALES (est): 204.55MM
SALES (corp-wide): 13.73B **Publicly Held**
SIC: 4911 Electric services
PA: Vistra Corp.
6555 Sierra Dr
Irving TX
214 812-4600

(P-4572)
EDF RENEWABLES INC (PA)
15445 Innovation Dr (92128-3432)
P.O. Box 504080 (92150-4080)
PHONE..............................858 521-3300
Tristan Grimbert, *Pr*
Luis Silva, *CFO*
▲ **EMP:** 225 **EST:** 1987
SALES (est): 678.73MM **Privately Held**
Web: www.edf-re.com
SIC: 4911 Electric services

(P-4573)
EDISON CAPITAL
18101 Von Karman Ave Ste 1700 (92612-1012)
PHONE..............................909 594-3789
Thomas Mc Daniel, *Pr*
Larry Mount, *
Jim Phillipsen, *
Richard E Lucey, *
Phillip Dandridge, *
EMP: 103 **EST:** 1987
SQ FT: 12,000
SALES (est): 47.31MM
SALES (corp-wide): 17.22B **Publicly Held**
SIC: 4911 Electric services
HQ: Edison Mission Group Inc.
2244 Walnut Grove Ave
Rosemead CA
626 302-2222

(P-4574)
EDISON INTERNATIONAL (PA)
2244 Walnut Grove Ave (91770-3714)
P.O. Box 976 (91770-0976)
PHONE..............................626 302-2222
Pedro J Pizarro, *Pr*
William P Sullivan, *Non-Executive Chairman of the Board*
Maria Rigatti, *Ex VP*
Adam S Umanoff, *Ex VP*

Caroline Choi Senior, *Corporate Affairs Vice President*
EMP: 1092 **EST:** 1987
SALES (est): 17.22B
SALES (corp-wide): 17.22B **Publicly Held**
Web: www.edison.com
SIC: 4911 Electric services

(P-4575)
EDISON MISSION ENERGY (PA)
Also Called: Edison Mission
2244 Walnut Grove Ave (91770-3714)
PHONE..............................626 302-5778
Theodore F Craver Junior, *Dir*
Raymond W Vickers, *Dir*
John P Finneran Junior, *Dir*
Paul Jacob, *Dir*
W James Scilacci, *Dir*
▲ **EMP:** 143 **EST:** 2001
SQ FT: 71,000
SALES (est): 408.14MM
SALES (corp-wide): 408.14MM **Privately Held**
Web: www.edisonenergy.com
SIC: 4911 Electric services

(P-4576)
EDISON MSSION MIDWEST HOLDINGS
2244 Walnut Grove Ave (91770-3714)
PHONE..............................626 302-2222
Guy F Gorney, *Pr*
EMP: 1929 **EST:** 1999
SALES (est): 23.82MM
SALES (corp-wide): 17.22B **Publicly Held**
Web: www.edison.com
SIC: 4911 Electric services
HQ: Edison Mission Group Inc.
2244 Walnut Grove Ave
Rosemead CA
626 302-2222

(P-4577)
EDWARD W SCOTT ELECTRIC CO INC
1555 Burke Ave Ste L (94124-1442)
PHONE..............................415 206-7120
Eileen B Lynch, *Prin*
EMP: 107
SALES (corp-wide): 41.47MM **Privately Held**
Web: www.edwardwscottelectric.com
SIC: 4911 Electric services
PA: Edward W. Scott Electric Co., Inc.
500 W Ohio Ave
Richmond CA
415 206-7120

(P-4578)
ENPOWER MANAGEMENT CORP
2603 Camino Ramon Ste 263 (94583-9143)
PHONE..............................925 244-1100
Edward Tomeo, *Pr*
Alex Sugaoka, *
EMP: 79 **EST:** 1994
SALES (est): 886.87K
SALES (corp-wide): 35.23MM **Privately Held**
SIC: 4911 Generation, electric power
PA: Enpower Corp.
2603 Camino Ramon Ste 263
San Ramon CA
925 244-1100

(P-4579)
HANWHA Q CELLS USA CORP
300 Spectrum Center Dr Ste 1250 (92618-4925)
PHONE..............................949 748-5996

Jae Kyu Lee, *Pr*
EMP: 95 **EST:** 2000
SALES (est): 300MM **Privately Held**
Web: www.qcellsusa.com
SIC: 4911

(P-4580)
IMPERIAL IRRIGATION DISTRICT (PA)
Also Called: I I D
333 E Barioni Blvd (92251-1773)
P.O. Box 937 (92251-0937)
PHONE..............................800 303-7756
Stephen Benson, *Pr*
Anthony Sanchez, *
Stella Mendoza, *
Mike Abatti, *
Keven Kelly, *
▲ **EMP:** 700 **EST:** 1911
SQ FT: 10,000
SALES (est): 859.47MM
SALES (corp-wide): 859.47MM **Privately Held**
Web: www.iid.com
SIC: 4911 4971 4931 Hydro electric power generation; Water distribution or supply systems for irrigation; Electric and other services combined

(P-4581)
INSPIRE ENERGY HOLDINGS LLC
Also Called: Inspire Energy
3402 Pico Blvd Ste 300 (90405-2118)
PHONE..............................866 403-2620
Patrick Maloney, *CEO*
EMP: 138 **EST:** 2013
SALES (est): 55.21MM
SALES (corp-wide): 381.31B **Privately Held**
Web: www.inspirecleanenergy.com
SIC: 4911 Distribution, electric power
PA: Shell Plc
Shell Centre
London
800 731-8888

(P-4582)
JTI ELCTRCAL INSTRMNTATION LLC
3901 Fanucchi Way Unit 201 (93263-9589)
PHONE..............................661 393-5535
EMP: 65 **EST:** 2013
SALES (est): 5.81MM **Privately Held**
SIC: 4911 Electric services

(P-4583)
LEEMAH ELECTRONICS INC
Also Called: (415 Location)
1080 Samson St (94111-1308)
PHONE..............................415 394-1288
Jack Wang, *Mgr*
EMP: 105
SALES (corp-wide): 63.99MM **Privately Held**
Web: www.leemah.com
SIC: 4911 3672 3669 3571 Electric services; Printed circuit boards; Intercommunication systems, electric; Electronic computers
HQ: Leemah Electronics, Inc.
155 S Hill Dr
Brisbane CA

(P-4584)
LIBERTY UTLTIES CLPECO ELC LLC
Also Called: LIBERTY
701 National Ave (96148-9867)
PHONE..............................800 782-2506

PRODUCTS & SERVICES SECTION **4911 - Electric Services (P-4606)**

EMP: 60 EST: 2013
SQ FT: 10,000
SALES (est): 92.99MM **Privately Held**
SIC: **4911** Distribution, electric power

(P-4585)
MAAS ENERGY WORKS LLC
1730 South St (96001-1811)
PHONE.................................530 710-8545
Daryl Maas, *CEO*
EMP: 120 EST: 2010
SALES (est): 26.23MM **Privately Held**
Web: www.maasenergy.com
SIC: **4911** 3612 Electric services; Airport lighting transformers

(P-4586)
MARIN CLEAN ENERGY
Also Called: McE
1125 Tamalpais Ave (94901-3221)
PHONE.................................415 464-6028
Dawn Weisz, *CEO*
EMP: 75 EST: 2008
SQ FT: 10,000
SALES (est): 27.86MM **Privately Held**
Web: www.mcecleanenergy.org
SIC: **4911** Distribution, electric power

(P-4587)
MODESTO IRRIGATION DISTRICT
929 Woodland Ave (95351-1553)
P.O. Box 4060 (95352-4060)
PHONE.................................209 526-7373
Ellen Short, *Genl Mgr*
EMP: 88
SALES (corp-wide): 450.11MM **Privately Held**
Web: www.mid.org
SIC: **4911** 4971 Distribution, electric power; Irrigation systems
PA: Modesto Irrigation District (Inc)
    1231 11th St
    Modesto CA
    209 526-7337

(P-4588)
MODESTO IRRIGATION DISTRICT
Modesto Irrigation District
1231 11th St (95354-0701)
P.O. Box 4060 (95352-4060)
PHONE.................................209 526-7563
Don Durman, *Treas*
EMP: 88
SALES (corp-wide): 450.11MM **Privately Held**
Web: www.mid.org
SIC: **4911** 4941 Fossil fuel electric power generation; Water supply
PA: Modesto Irrigation District (Inc)
    1231 11th St
    Modesto CA
    209 526-7337

(P-4589)
MODESTO IRRIGATION DISTRICT (PA)
1231 11th St (95354-0701)
P.O. Box 4060 (95352-4060)
PHONE.................................209 526-7337
Allen Short, *Pr*
EMP: 175 EST: 1887
SQ FT: 90,000
SALES (est): 450.11MM
SALES (corp-wide): 450.11MM **Privately Held**
Web: www.mid.org

SIC: **4911** 4971 Fossil fuel electric power generation; Water distribution or supply systems for irrigation

(P-4590)
NATURAL GAS CORP CALIFORNIA
77 Beale St Fl 32 (94105-1814)
PHONE.................................415 973-7000
Jack F Jenkins-stark, *Prin*
EMP: 356 EST: 1937
SQ FT: 30,000
SALES (est): 9.52MM **Publicly Held**
SIC: **4911** Transmission, electric power
HQ: Pacific Gas And Electric Company
    300 Lakeside Dr Ste 210
    Oakland CA
    415 973-7000

(P-4591)
NORTHERN CALIFORNIA POWER AGCY (PA)
Also Called: Ncpa
651 Commerce Dr (95678-6411)
PHONE.................................916 781-3636
EMP: 65 EST: 1968
SQ FT: 17,400
SALES (est): 100.85MM
SALES (corp-wide): 100.85MM **Privately Held**
Web: www.ncpa.com
SIC: **4911** Transmission, electric power

(P-4592)
NRG CALIFORNIA SOUTH LP
Also Called: Etiwanda Power Plant
8996 Etiwanda Ave (91739-9662)
PHONE.................................909 899-7241
Lee Moore, *Brnch Mgr*
EMP: 220
SIC: **4911** Generation, electric power
HQ: Nrg California South Lp
    804 Carnegie Ctr
    Princeton NJ

(P-4593)
NRG CALIFORNIA SOUTH LP
Also Called: Coolwater Generating Station
37000 E Santa Fe St (92327)
PHONE.................................760 254-5241
Bob Ott, *Mgr*
EMP: 123
SIC: **4911** Generation, electric power
HQ: Nrg California South Lp
    804 Carnegie Ctr
    Princeton NJ

(P-4594)
NRG CALIFORNIA SOUTH LP
Also Called: Mandalay Generating Station
393 Harbor Blvd (93035-1108)
PHONE.................................805 984-5241
Thomas Di Ciolli, *Mgr*
EMP: 224
SIC: **4911** Fossil fuel electric power generation
HQ: Nrg California South Lp
    804 Carnegie Ctr
    Princeton NJ

(P-4595)
NRG EL SEGUNDO OPERATIONS INC
Also Called: El Segundo Energy Center
301 Vista Del Mar (90245-3650)
PHONE.................................310 615-6344
John Ragan, *Pr*
▲ EMP: 65 EST: 1998
SALES (est): 31.56MM **Publicly Held**

Web: www.elsegundo.org
SIC: **4911** Generation, electric power
PA: Nrg Energy, Inc.
    910 Louisiana St Ste B200
    Houston TX

(P-4596)
NRG SOLAR LLC
5790 Fleet St (92008-4703)
PHONE.................................760 710-2140
EMP: 129 EST: 2012
SALES (est): 13.44MM **Publicly Held**
SIC: **4911** Generation, electric power
HQ: Nrg Repowering Holdings Llc
    211 Carnegie Ctr
    Princeton NJ
    760 710-2140

(P-4597)
OHMCONNECT INC
Also Called: Ohmconnect
371 3rd St 2nd Fl (94607-4103)
PHONE.................................404 881-8659
Cisco Devries, *CEO*
Matthew Duesterberg, *CRO*
Curtis Tongue, *Corporate Secretary*
EMP: 85 EST: 2013
SALES (est): 33.53MM **Privately Held**
Web: www.ohmconnect.com
SIC: **4911** Electric services

(P-4598)
OUTSOURCE UTILITY CONTR CORP
8015 E Crystal Dr (92807-2523)
PHONE.................................714 238-9263
Heather Morgan, *Pr*
Joe Morgan, *
Josh Stewart, *
EMP: 200 EST: 2010
SALES (est): 47.03MM **Privately Held**
Web: www.outsourceucc.com
SIC: **4911** Distribution, electric power

(P-4599)
PACIFIC ENERGY FUELS COMPANY
Also Called: PG&e
77 Beale St Ste 100 (94105-1814)
PHONE.................................415 973-8200
Gordon Smith, *Pr*
EMP: 546 EST: 1988
SALES (est): 35.85MM **Publicly Held**
SIC: **4911** Transmission, electric power
HQ: Pacific Gas And Electric Company
    300 Lakeside Dr Ste 210
    Oakland CA
    415 973-7000

(P-4600)
PACIFIC GAS AND ELECTRIC CO
Also Called: PG&e
16001 Powerhouse Rd (95469-8771)
PHONE.................................707 743-1197
EMP: 63
SIC: **4911** Distribution, electric power
HQ: Pacific Gas And Electric Company
    300 Lakeside Dr Ste 210
    Oakland CA
    415 973-7000

(P-4601)
PACIFIC GAS AND ELECTRIC CO
Also Called: PG&e
5555 Florin Perkins Rd (95826-4815)
P.O. Box 997300 (95899-7300)
PHONE.................................916 275-2763
Maria Jordan, *Mgr*
EMP: 200

Web: www.pge.com
SIC: **4911** 4923 Distribution, electric power; Gas transmission and distribution
HQ: Pacific Gas And Electric Company
    300 Lakeside Dr Ste 210
    Oakland CA
    415 973-7000

(P-4602)
PACIFIC GAS AND ELECTRIC CO
Also Called: PG&e
2111 Hillcrest Ave (94509-2862)
PHONE.................................925 779-7745
Mike Diaz, *Mgr*
EMP: 254
Web: www.pge.com
SIC: **4911** 4922 4924 1311 Distribution, electric power; Pipelines, natural gas; Natural gas distribution; Crude petroleum production
HQ: Pacific Gas And Electric Company
    300 Lakeside Dr Ste 210
    Oakland CA
    415 973-7000

(P-4603)
PACIFIC GAS AND ELECTRIC CO (HQ)
Also Called: PG&E
300 Lakeside Dr (94612-3655)
P.O. Box 770000 (94177-0001)
PHONE.................................415 973-7000
Sumeet Singh, *Ex VP*
Cheryl F Campbell, *
Marlene M Santos, *CCO*
Jason M Glickman, *Ex VP*
Julius Cox, *Ex VP*
▲ EMP: 3000 EST: 1905
SALES (est): 21.68B **Publicly Held**
Web: www.pge.com
SIC: **4911** 4924 Generation, electric power; Natural gas distribution
PA: Pg&E Corporation
    300 Lakeside Dr Ste 210
    Oakland CA

(P-4604)
PACIFIC GAS AND ELECTRIC CO
Also Called: PG&e
6537 Foothill Blvd (94605-2016)
PHONE.................................510 437-2222
Audey Ford, *Mgr*
EMP: 165
Web: www.pge.com
SIC: **4911** 4924 Generation, electric power; Natural gas distribution
HQ: Pacific Gas And Electric Company
    300 Lakeside Dr Ste 210
    Oakland CA
    415 973-7000

(P-4605)
PACIFIC GAS AND ELECTRIC CO
Also Called: PG&e
650 O St (93721-2708)
PHONE.................................559 263-7361
C R Martin, *Brnch Mgr*
EMP: 838
Web: www.pge.com
SIC: **4911** 4922 Generation, electric power; Natural gas transmission
HQ: Pacific Gas And Electric Company
    300 Lakeside Dr Ste 210
    Oakland CA
    415 973-7000

(P-4606)
PACIFIC GAS AND ELECTRIC CO
Also Called: PG&e
3136 Boeing Way # 2447a (95206-4989)

4911 - Electric Services (P-4607)

PHONE..................209 942-1787
Robert Eggert, *Brnch Mgr*
EMP: 254
SQ FT: 138,000
Web: www.pge.com
SIC: 4911 4922 Generation, electric power; Natural gas transmission
HQ: Pacific Gas And Electric Company
300 Lakeside Dr Ste 210
Oakland CA
415 973-7000

(P-4607)
PACIFIC GAS AND ELECTRIC CO
Also Called: PG&e
2180 Harrison St (94110-1300)
PHONE..................415 695-3513
Dave Bradley, *Brnch Mgr*
EMP: 254
Web: www.pge.com
SIC: 4911 4922 4924 1311 Generation, electric power; Pipelines, natural gas; Natural gas distribution; Natural gas production
HQ: Pacific Gas And Electric Company
300 Lakeside Dr Ste 210
Oakland CA
415 973-7000

(P-4608)
PACIFIC GAS AND ELECTRIC CO
Also Called: PG&e
425 Beck Ave (94533-6808)
PHONE..................415 973-7000
Dana Mckiddin, *Prin*
EMP: 140
Web: www.pge.com
SIC: 4911 Transmission, electric power
HQ: Pacific Gas And Electric Company
300 Lakeside Dr Ste 210
Oakland CA
415 973-7000

(P-4609)
PACIFIC GAS AND ELECTRIC CO
Also Called: PG&e
885 Embarcadero Dr (95605-1503)
PHONE..................916 375-5005
Richard Yamacuchi, *Brnch Mgr*
EMP: 254
Web: www.pge.com
SIC: 4911 Transmission, electric power
HQ: Pacific Gas And Electric Company
300 Lakeside Dr Ste 210
Oakland CA
415 973-7000

(P-4610)
PACIFIC GAS AND ELECTRIC CO
Also Called: PG&e
P.O. Box 930 (95201-3093)
PHONE..................209 932-6550
EMP: 165
Web: www.pge.com
SIC: 4911 Transmission, electric power
HQ: Pacific Gas And Electric Company
300 Lakeside Dr Ste 210
Oakland CA
415 973-7000

(P-4611)
PACIFIC GAS AND ELECTRIC CO
Also Called: PG&e
8 E River Park Pl W (93720-1551)
PHONE..................209 726-7650
Sharla Jennings, *Treas*
EMP: 787
Web: www.pge.com
SIC: 4911 Transmission, electric power
HQ: Pacific Gas And Electric Company

300 Lakeside Dr Ste 210
Oakland CA
415 973-7000

(P-4612)
PACIFIC GAS AND ELECTRIC CO
Also Called: PG&e
350 Salem St (95928-5331)
P.O. Box 49 (95927-0049)
PHONE..................530 258-6215
Rodney J Strub, *Brnch Mgr*
EMP: 140
Web: www.pge.com
SIC: 4911 4932 Transmission, electric power; Gas and other services combined
HQ: Pacific Gas And Electric Company
300 Lakeside Dr Ste 210
Oakland CA
415 973-7000

(P-4613)
PACIFIC GAS AND ELECTRIC CO
Also Called: PG&e
2740 Gateway Oaks Dr (95833-3501)
PHONE..................916 923-7007
Russ Jackson, *Mgr*
EMP: 419
Web: www.pge.com
SIC: 4911 Transmission, electric power
HQ: Pacific Gas And Electric Company
300 Lakeside Dr Ste 210
Oakland CA
415 973-7000

(P-4614)
PACIFIC GAS AND ELECTRIC CO
PG&e
4525 Hollis St (94608-2911)
PHONE..................510 450-5744
G L Fairbanks, *Brnch Mgr*
EMP: 267
Web: jobs.pge.com
SIC: 4911 Transmission, electric power
HQ: Pacific Gas And Electric Company
300 Lakeside Dr Ste 210
Oakland CA
415 973-7000

(P-4615)
PACIFIC GAS AND ELECTRIC CO
PG&e
1970 Industrial Way (94002)
PHONE..................650 592-9411
Michele A Silva, *Brnch Mgr*
EMP: 89
Web: www.pge.com
SIC: 4911 4923 Transmission, electric power; Gas transmission and distribution
HQ: Pacific Gas And Electric Company
300 Lakeside Dr Ste 210
Oakland CA
415 973-7000

(P-4616)
PACIFIC GAS AND ELECTRIC CO
Also Called: PG&e
3965 Occidental Rd (95401-5898)
PHONE..................707 579-6337
Leo Conner, *Prin*
EMP: 76
Web: www.pge.com
SIC: 4911 Transmission, electric power
HQ: Pacific Gas And Electric Company
300 Lakeside Dr Ste 210
Oakland CA
415 973-7000

(P-4617)
PACIFIC GAS AND ELECTRIC CO
PG&e

3400 Crow Canyon Rd (94583-1308)
PHONE..................650 513-0700
Robert Kohne, *Brnch Mgr*
EMP: 200
SQ FT: 3,000
Web: www.pge.com
SIC: 4911 Transmission, electric power
HQ: Pacific Gas And Electric Company
300 Lakeside Dr Ste 210
Oakland CA
415 973-7000

(P-4618)
PACIFIC GAS AND ELECTRIC CO
Also Called: PG&e
777 Railroad Ave (94565-2651)
P.O. Box 590 (94565-0590)
PHONE..................925 757-2000
Barbara Corsi, *Brnch Mgr*
EMP: 63
Web: www.pge.com
SIC: 4911 Transmission, electric power
HQ: Pacific Gas And Electric Company
300 Lakeside Dr Ste 210
Oakland CA
415 973-7000

(P-4619)
PACIFIC GAS AND ELECTRIC CO
Also Called: PG&e
4340 Old Santa Fe Rd (93401-8160)
PHONE..................805 545-4562
Del Richie, *Mgr*
EMP: 178
Web: www.pge.com
SIC: 4911 Transmission, electric power
HQ: Pacific Gas And Electric Company
300 Lakeside Dr Ste 210
Oakland CA
415 973-7000

(P-4620)
PACIFIC GAS AND ELECTRIC CO
Also Called: PG&e
1220 Andersen Dr (94901-5332)
PHONE..................800 743-5000
Jeffrey Bleich, *Brnch Mgr*
EMP: 102
Web: www.pge.com
SIC: 4911 Transmission, electric power
HQ: Pacific Gas And Electric Company
300 Lakeside Dr Ste 210
Oakland CA
415 973-7000

(P-4621)
PACIFIC GAS AND ELECTRIC CO
Also Called: PG&e
3955 Arch Rd Ste 100 (95215-8328)
PHONE..................209 942-5142
Richard Kolodzie, *Prin*
EMP: 63
Web: www.pge.com
SIC: 4911 Transmission, electric power
HQ: Pacific Gas And Electric Company
300 Lakeside Dr Ste 210
Oakland CA
415 973-7000

(P-4622)
PACIFIC GAS AND ELECTRIC CO
Also Called: PG&e
210 Corona Rd (94954-1319)
PHONE..................707 765-5118
Tom Reimer, *Mgr*
EMP: 140
SQ FT: 168,577
Web: www.pge.com
SIC: 4911 Transmission, electric power
HQ: Pacific Gas And Electric Company

300 Lakeside Dr Ste 210
Oakland CA
415 973-7000

(P-4623)
PACIFIC GAS AND ELECTRIC CO
Also Called: PG&e
631 N Colusa St (95988-2209)
PHONE..................530 229-4164
Sam Burton, *Mgr*
EMP: 114
Web: www.pge.com
SIC: 4911 4922 Transmission, electric power; Natural gas transmission
HQ: Pacific Gas And Electric Company
300 Lakeside Dr Ste 210
Oakland CA
415 973-7000

(P-4624)
PACIFIC GAS AND ELECTRIC CO
PG&e
111 Stony Cir (95401-9599)
PHONE..................800 756-7243
Gary F Heitz, *Prin*
EMP: 381
SQ FT: 100,000
Web: www.pge.com
SIC: 4911 Transmission, electric power
HQ: Pacific Gas And Electric Company
300 Lakeside Dr Ste 210
Oakland CA
415 973-7000

(P-4625)
PACIFIC GAS AND ELECTRIC CO
Also Called: PG&e
4690 Evora Rd (94520-1004)
PHONE..................925 676-0948
John Glenn, *Brnch Mgr*
EMP: 178
Web: www.pge.com
SIC: 4911 Transmission, electric power
HQ: Pacific Gas And Electric Company
300 Lakeside Dr Ste 210
Oakland CA
415 973-7000

(P-4626)
PACIFIC GAS AND ELECTRIC CO
Also Called: PG&e
3050 Geneva Ave (94014-1640)
PHONE..................800 684-4648
EMP: 89
Web: www.pge.com
SIC: 4911 Transmission, electric power
HQ: Pacific Gas And Electric Company
300 Lakeside Dr Ste 210
Oakland CA
415 973-7000

(P-4627)
PACIFIC GAS AND ELECTRIC CO
Also Called: PG&e
390 E Alisal St (93901-4329)
PHONE..................800 684-4648
EMP: 63
Web: www.pge.com
SIC: 4911 Transmission, electric power
HQ: Pacific Gas And Electric Company
300 Lakeside Dr Ste 210
Oakland CA
415 973-7000

(P-4628)
PACIFIC GAS AND ELECTRIC CO
Also Called: PG&e
1850 Gateway Blvd Fl 7 (94520-3279)
PHONE..................925 818-7082
EMP: 63

PRODUCTS & SERVICES SECTION

4911 - Electric Services (P-4650)

Web: www.pge.com
SIC: 4911 Transmission, electric power
HQ: Pacific Gas And Electric Company
300 Lakeside Dr Ste 210
Oakland CA
415 973-7000

(P-4629)
PACIFIC GAS AND ELECTRIC CO
Also Called: PG&e
1745 2nd St (93662-3625)
P.O. Box 180 (93662-0180)
PHONE..................559 891-2143
Gary Truitt, Mgr
EMP: 63
Web: www.pge.com
SIC: 4911 Transmission, electric power
HQ: Pacific Gas And Electric Company
300 Lakeside Dr Ste 210
Oakland CA
415 973-7000

(P-4630)
PACIFIC GAS AND ELECTRIC CO
Also Called: PG&e
4636 Missouri Flat Rd (95667-6823)
PHONE..................530 621-7237
Gordon Smith, Brnch Mgr
EMP: 102
Web: www.pge.com
SIC: 4911 Transmission, electric power
HQ: Pacific Gas And Electric Company
300 Lakeside Dr Ste 210
Oakland CA
415 973-7000

(P-4631)
PACIFIC GAS AND ELECTRIC CO
Also Called: PG&e
1567 Huntoon St (95965-4921)
PHONE..................530 532-4093
Gene Murray, Brnch Mgr
EMP: 89
Web: www.pge.com
SIC: 4911 Transmission, electric power
HQ: Pacific Gas And Electric Company
300 Lakeside Dr Ste 210
Oakland CA
415 973-7000

(P-4632)
PACIFIC GAS AND ELECTRIC CO
Also Called: PG&e
9 Mi Nw Of Avila Bch (93424)
P.O. Box 56 (93424-0056)
PHONE..................805 506-5280
David Oatley, Brnch Mgr
EMP: 1400
Web: www.pge.com
SIC: 4911 Transmission, electric power
HQ: Pacific Gas And Electric Company
300 Lakeside Dr Ste 210
Oakland CA
415 973-7000

(P-4633)
PACIFIC GAS AND ELECTRIC CO
Also Called: PG&e
33995 Alta Bonny Nook Rd (95701)
P.O. Box 688 (95701-0688)
PHONE..................530 389-2202
Dave Barret, Frmn Supr
EMP: 76
Web: www.pge.com
SIC: 4911 Transmission, electric power
HQ: Pacific Gas And Electric Company
300 Lakeside Dr Ste 210
Oakland CA
415 973-7000

(P-4634)
PACIFIC GAS AND ELECTRIC CO
Also Called: PG&e
3600 Meadow View Dr (96002-9701)
PHONE..................530 365-7672
John Duncan, Mgr
EMP: 724
Web: www.pge.com
SIC: 4911 Transmission, electric power
HQ: Pacific Gas And Electric Company
300 Lakeside Dr Ste 210
Oakland CA
415 973-7000

(P-4635)
PACIFIC GAS AND ELECTRIC CO
Also Called: PG&e
31295 Manton Viola Rd (96059)
PHONE..................530 474-3333
Chip Stalica, Mgr
EMP: 63
Web: www.pge.com
SIC: 4911 Transmission, electric power
HQ: Pacific Gas And Electric Company
300 Lakeside Dr Ste 210
Oakland CA
415 973-7000

(P-4636)
PACIFIC GAS AND ELECTRIC CO
Also Called: PG&e
3395 Mcmaude Pl (95407-8120)
PHONE..................707 577-7283
Bob Murphy, Brnch Mgr
EMP: 63
Web: www.pge.com
SIC: 4911 Transmission, electric power
HQ: Pacific Gas And Electric Company
300 Lakeside Dr Ste 210
Oakland CA
415 973-7000

(P-4637)
PACIFIC GAS AND ELECTRIC CO
Also Called: PG&e
12840 Bill Clark Way (95602-9527)
PHONE..................530 889-3102
Steve Pennett, Mgr
EMP: 813
Web: www.pge.com
SIC: 4911 Transmission, electric power
HQ: Pacific Gas And Electric Company
300 Lakeside Dr Ste 210
Oakland CA
415 973-7000

(P-4638)
PACIFIC GAS AND ELECTRIC CO
Also Called: PG&e
202 Pearson Rd (95969-5046)
PHONE..................530 327-7633
Molly Williams, Brnch Mgr
EMP: 63
Web: www.pge.com
SIC: 4911 Transmission, electric power
HQ: Pacific Gas And Electric Company
300 Lakeside Dr Ste 210
Oakland CA
415 973-7000

(P-4639)
PACIFIC GAS AND ELECTRIC CO
Also Called: PG&e
4040 West Ln (95204-2436)
PHONE..................209 942-1523
Ken Wells, Mgr
EMP: 711
Web: www.pge.com
SIC: 4911 Transmission, electric power
HQ: Pacific Gas And Electric Company

300 Lakeside Dr Ste 210
Oakland CA
415 973-7000

(P-4640)
PACIFIC GAS AND ELECTRIC CO
Also Called: PG&e
2311 Garden Rd (93940-5325)
PHONE..................831 648-3231
Richard Brent, Brnch Mgr
EMP: 165
Web: www.pge.com
SIC: 4911 Transmission, electric power
HQ: Pacific Gas And Electric Company
300 Lakeside Dr Ste 210
Oakland CA
415 973-7000

(P-4641)
PACIFIC GAS AND ELECTRIC CO
Also Called: PG&e
42105 Boyce Rd (94538-3110)
PHONE..................510 770-2025
Gary Commick, Prin
EMP: 470
Web: www.pge.com
SIC: 4911 Transmission, electric power
HQ: Pacific Gas And Electric Company
300 Lakeside Dr Ste 210
Oakland CA
415 973-7000

(P-4642)
PACIFIC GAS AND ELECTRIC CO
Also Called: PG&e
1000 King Salmon Ave (95503-6859)
PHONE..................707 444-0700
Roy Willis, Mgr
EMP: 343
Web: www.pge.com
SIC: 4911 Transmission, electric power
HQ: Pacific Gas And Electric Company
300 Lakeside Dr Ste 210
Oakland CA
415 973-7000

(P-4643)
PACIFIC GAS AND ELECTRIC CO
Also Called: PG&e
33755 Old Mill Rd (93602-9655)
P.O. Box 425 (93602-0425)
PHONE..................559 855-6112
John Moore, Genl Mgr
EMP: 178
Web: www.pge.com
SIC: 4911 Transmission, electric power
HQ: Pacific Gas And Electric Company
300 Lakeside Dr Ste 210
Oakland CA
415 973-7000

(P-4644)
PACIFIC GAS AND ELECTRIC CO
Also Called: PG&e
1028 6th St (93635-4218)
PHONE..................209 826-5131
Stephen Rath, Brnch Mgr
EMP: 63
Web: www.pge.com
SIC: 4911 Transmission, electric power
HQ: Pacific Gas And Electric Company
300 Lakeside Dr Ste 210
Oakland CA
415 973-7000

(P-4645)
PACIFIC GAS AND ELECTRIC CO
Also Called: PG&e
35863 Fairview Rd (92347-9710)
PHONE..................760 253-2925

Dan Lytle, Mgr
EMP: 178
Web: www.pge.com
SIC: 4911 Transmission, electric power
HQ: Pacific Gas And Electric Company
300 Lakeside Dr Ste 210
Oakland CA
415 973-7000

(P-4646)
PACIFIC GAS AND ELECTRIC CO
Also Called: PG&e
1524 N Carpenter Rd (95351-1110)
PHONE..................209 576-6636
Sheila Radford, Brnch Mgr
EMP: 482
Web: www.pge.com
SIC: 4911 4923 4932 Transmission, electric power; Gas transmission and distribution; Gas and other services combined
HQ: Pacific Gas And Electric Company
300 Lakeside Dr Ste 210
Oakland CA
415 973-7000

(P-4647)
PACIFIC GAS AND ELECTRIC CO
Also Called: PG&e
811 W J St (95361-3669)
PHONE..................800 743-5000
Ross Leveretg, Mgr
EMP: 63
Web: www.pge.com
SIC: 4911 4923 4939 Transmission, electric power; Gas transmission and distribution; Combination utilities, nec
HQ: Pacific Gas And Electric Company
300 Lakeside Dr Ste 210
Oakland CA
415 973-7000

(P-4648)
PACIFIC GAS AND ELECTRIC CO
Also Called: PG&e
11239 Midway (95928-8219)
PHONE..................530 896-4318
Russ Bates, Brnch Mgr
EMP: 114
Web: www.pge.com
SIC: 4911 Transmission, electric power
HQ: Pacific Gas And Electric Company
300 Lakeside Dr Ste 210
Oakland CA
415 973-7000

(P-4649)
PACIFIC GAS AND ELECTRIC CO
Also Called: PG&e
2221 S Orange Ave (93725-1011)
PHONE..................559 263-7152
Robert Martin, Mgr
EMP: 495
Web: www.pge.com
SIC: 4911 Transmission, electric power
HQ: Pacific Gas And Electric Company
300 Lakeside Dr Ste 210
Oakland CA
415 973-7000

(P-4650)
PACIFIC GAS AND ELECTRIC CO
Also Called: PG&e
502 E Grant Line Rd (95376-2800)
P.O. Box 356 (95378-0356)
PHONE..................559 263-5438
Matt Storment, Brnch Mgr
EMP: 63
Web: www.pge.com
SIC: 4911 Transmission, electric power
HQ: Pacific Gas And Electric Company

4911 - Electric Services (P-4651)

300 Lakeside Dr Ste 210
Oakland CA
415 973-7000

(P-4651)
PACIFIC GAS AND ELECTRIC CO
Also Called: PG&e
5221 Quinn Rd (95688-9453)
PHONE.................707 452-1983
Del Harris, *Brnch Mgr*
EMP: 241
Web: www.pge.com
SIC: 4911 Transmission, electric power
HQ: Pacific Gas And Electric Company
300 Lakeside Dr Ste 210
Oakland CA
415 973-7000

(P-4652)
PACIFIC GAS AND ELECTRIC CO
Also Called: PG&e
800 Price Canyon Rd (93449-2722)
PHONE.................805 546-5267
Don Boatman, *Brnch Mgr*
EMP: 178
Web: www.pge.com
SIC: 4911 Transmission, electric power
HQ: Pacific Gas And Electric Company
300 Lakeside Dr Ste 210
Oakland CA
415 973-7000

(P-4653)
PACIFIC GAS AND ELECTRIC CO
Also Called: PG&e
3797 1st St (94551-4905)
PHONE.................925 373-2623
Kermit Pol, *Brnch Mgr*
EMP: 127
Web: www.pge.com
SIC: 4911 Transmission, electric power
HQ: Pacific Gas And Electric Company
300 Lakeside Dr Ste 210
Oakland CA
415 973-7000

(P-4654)
PACIFIC GAS AND ELECTRIC CO
Also Called: PG&e
316 L St (95616-4231)
PHONE.................530 757-5803
Gail Sanchez, *Mgr*
EMP: 673
Web: www.pge.com
SIC: 4911 Transmission, electric power
HQ: Pacific Gas And Electric Company
300 Lakeside Dr Ste 210
Oakland CA
415 973-7000

(P-4655)
PACIFIC GAS AND ELECTRIC CO
Also Called: PG&e
145453 National Trails Hway (92363)
P.O. Box 337 (92363-0267)
PHONE.................760 326-2615
Felix Vasquez, *Mgr*
EMP: 152
Web: www.pge.com
SIC: 4911 Transmission, electric power
HQ: Pacific Gas And Electric Company
300 Lakeside Dr Ste 210
Oakland CA
415 973-7000

(P-4656)
PACIFIC GAS AND ELECTRIC CO
Also Called: PG&e
66 Ranch Dr (95035-5103)
PHONE.................408 945-6215

Jeff Klotz, *Brnch Mgr*
EMP: 127
Web: www.pge.com
SIC: 4911 Transmission, electric power
HQ: Pacific Gas And Electric Company
300 Lakeside Dr Ste 210
Oakland CA
415 973-7000

(P-4657)
PACIFIC GAS AND ELECTRIC CO
Also Called: PG&e
28570 Tiger Creek Rd (95666-9646)
PHONE.................209 295-2651
EMP: 127
Web: www.pge.com
SIC: 4911 Transmission, electric power
HQ: Pacific Gas And Electric Company
300 Lakeside Dr Ste 210
Oakland CA
415 973-7000

(P-4658)
PACIFIC GAS AND ELECTRIC CO
Also Called: PG&e
4201 Arrow St (93308-4938)
PHONE.................661 398-5918
EMP: 178
Web: www.pge.com
SIC: 4911 Transmission, electric power
HQ: Pacific Gas And Electric Company
300 Lakeside Dr Ste 210
Oakland CA
415 973-7000

(P-4659)
PACIFIC GAS AND ELECTRIC CO
Also Called: PG&e
160 Cow Meadow Pl (93465)
PHONE.................805 434-4418
EMP: 89
Web: www.pge.com
SIC: 4911 Transmission, electric power
HQ: Pacific Gas And Electric Company
300 Lakeside Dr Ste 210
Oakland CA
415 973-7000

(P-4660)
PLACER COUNTY WATER AGENCY
Also Called: Power Systems Division
24625 Harrison St (95631-9328)
P.O. Box 667 (95631-0667)
PHONE.................530 367-6701
Stephen Jones, *Mgr*
EMP: 83
SALES (corp-wide): 103.28MM **Privately Held**
Web: www.pcwa.net
SIC: 4911 Electric services
PA: Placer County Water Agency
144 Ferguson Rd
Auburn CA
530 823-4850

(P-4661)
PLACER COUNTY WATER AGENCY (PA)
Also Called: Placer County Water Agency
144 Ferguson Rd (95603-3231)
P.O. Box 6570 (95604-6570)
PHONE.................530 823-4850
Andy Fecko, *Genl Mgr*
Ross Branch, *Public Affairs Manager*
EMP: 90 **EST:** 1957
SQ FT: 22,750
SALES (est): 103.28MM
SALES (corp-wide): 103.28MM **Privately Held**

Web: www.pcwa.net
SIC: 4911 4941 4971 Distribution, electric power; Water supply; Irrigation systems

(P-4662)
RRI ENERGY COOLWATER INC
37000 E Santa Fe St (92327)
PHONE.................760 254-5290
Mark Jacobs, *Pr*
EMP: 90 **EST:** 1997
SALES (est): 5.75MM **Publicly Held**
SIC: 4911 Generation, electric power
HQ: Reliant Energy Retail Holdings, Llc
1000 Main St
Houston TX
713 497-3000

(P-4663)
SACRAMENTO MUNICPL UTILITY DST (PA)
Also Called: S M U D
6201 S St (95817-1818)
P.O. Box 15830 (95852-0830)
PHONE.................916 452-3211
Arlen Orchard, *CEO*
Jim Tracy, *CFO*
▲ **EMP:** 710 **EST:** 1923
SQ FT: 118,000
SALES (est): 2.15B
SALES (corp-wide): 2.15B **Privately Held**
Web: www.smud.org
SIC: 4911 Distribution, electric power

(P-4664)
SACRAMENTO MUNICPL UTILITY DST
6201 S St (95817-1818)
PHONE.................916 452-3211
Carlos Diaz, *Brnch Mgr*
EMP: 205
SALES (corp-wide): 2.15B **Privately Held**
Web: www.smud.org
SIC: 4911 Generation, electric power
PA: Sacramento Municipal Utility District
6201 S St
Sacramento CA
916 452-3211

(P-4665)
SACRAMENTO MUNICPL UTILITY DST
Also Called: Smud Energy Services
6301 S St (95817-1816)
P.O. Box 15830 (95852-0830)
PHONE.................916 732-5155
Jan Schori, *Mgr*
EMP: 88
SALES (corp-wide): 2.15B **Privately Held**
Web: www.smud.org
SIC: 4911 Generation, electric power
PA: Sacramento Municipal Utility District
6201 S St
Sacramento CA
916 452-3211

(P-4666)
SACRAMENTO MUNICPL UTILITY DST
Also Called: Supply Change Services
6201 S St (95817-1818)
P.O. Box 15830 (95852-0830)
PHONE.................916 732-5616
Frankie Mcdermott, *Mgr*
EMP: 701
SALES (corp-wide): 2.15B **Privately Held**
Web: www.smud.org
SIC: 4911 Fossil fuel electric power generation
PA: Sacramento Municipal Utility District

6201 S St
Sacramento CA
916 452-3211

(P-4667)
SAN DIEGO GAS & ELECTRIC CO
Also Called: SDG&e
2300 Harveson Pl (92029-1965)
PHONE.................760 432-2508
Carl La Peter, *Prin*
EMP: 292
SALES (corp-wide): 14.44B **Publicly Held**
Web: www.sdge.com
SIC: 4911 Distribution, electric power
HQ: San Diego Gas & Electric Company
8330 Century Park Ct
San Diego CA
619 696-2000

(P-4668)
SAN DIEGO GAS & ELECTRIC CO
Also Called: SDG&e
5488 Overland Ave (92123-1205)
PHONE.................858 654-6377
E Dimuzio, *Brnch Mgr*
EMP: 323
SALES (corp-wide): 14.44B **Publicly Held**
Web: www.sdge.com
SIC: 4911 Distribution, electric power
HQ: San Diego Gas & Electric Company
8330 Century Park Ct
San Diego CA
619 696-2000

(P-4669)
SAN DIEGO GAS & ELECTRIC CO
Also Called: SDG&e
10975 Technology Pl (92127-1811)
PHONE.................858 613-3216
EMP: 111
SALES (corp-wide): 14.44B **Publicly Held**
Web: www.sdge.com
SIC: 4911 Distribution, electric power
HQ: San Diego Gas & Electric Company
8330 Century Park Ct
San Diego CA
619 696-2000

(P-4670)
SAN DIEGO GAS & ELECTRIC CO
Also Called: SDG&e
8306 Century Park Ct # Cp42c (92123-1530)
PHONE.................858 654-1289
Eric Llewellyn, *Brnch Mgr*
EMP: 81
SALES (corp-wide): 14.44B **Publicly Held**
Web: www.sdge.com
SIC: 4911 Distribution, electric power
HQ: San Diego Gas & Electric Company
8330 Century Park Ct
San Diego CA
619 696-2000

(P-4671)
SAN DIEGO GAS & ELECTRIC CO
Also Called: Eastern District Office
104 N Johnson Ave (92020-3181)
PHONE.................619 441-3834
Allan Marchart, *Mgr*
EMP: 267
SALES (corp-wide): 14.44B **Publicly Held**
Web: www.sdge.com

PRODUCTS & SERVICES SECTION

4911 - Electric Services (P-4691)

SIC: 4911 Distribution, electric power
HQ: San Diego Gas & Electric Company
8330 Century Park Ct
San Diego CA
619 696-2000

(P-4672)
SAN DIEGO GAS & ELECTRIC CO
Also Called: SDG&e
1801 S Atlantic Blvd (91754-5207)
PHONE..................................619 696-2000
J Walker Martin, *CEO*
EMP: 161
SALES (corp-wide): 14.44B Publicly Held
Web: www.sdge.com
SIC: 4911 Distribution, electric power
HQ: San Diego Gas & Electric Company
8330 Century Park Ct
San Diego CA
619 696-2000

(P-4673)
SAN DIEGO GAS & ELECTRIC CO
Project Construction Metro
701 33rd St (92102-3341)
PHONE..................................619 699-1018
Scott Furgerson, *Mgr*
EMP: 166
SALES (corp-wide): 14.44B Publicly Held
Web: www.sdge.com
SIC: 4911 Distribution, electric power
HQ: San Diego Gas & Electric Company
8330 Century Park Ct
San Diego CA
619 696-2000

(P-4674)
SAN DIEGO GAS & ELECTRIC CO
Also Called: SDG&ec
5488 Overland Ave (92123-1205)
P.O. Box 129007 (92112-9007)
PHONE..................................858 541-5920
Patrick Lee, *Mgr*
EMP: 126
SALES (corp-wide): 14.44B Publicly Held
Web: www.sdge.com
SIC: 4911 4924 Generation, electric power; Natural gas distribution
HQ: San Diego Gas & Electric Company
8330 Century Park Ct
San Diego CA
619 696-2000

(P-4675)
SEMPRA ENERGY
Also Called: Sempra Energy
9305 Lightwave Ave (92123-6463)
PHONE..................................619 696-2000
Sean Luko, *Bmch Mgr*
EMP: 1000
SALES (corp-wide): 14.44B Publicly Held
Web: www.sempra.com
SIC: 4911 4923 Distribution, electric power; Gas transmission and distribution
PA: Sempra
488 8th Ave
San Diego CA
619 696-2000

(P-4676)
SEMPRA ENERGY GLOBAL ENTPS
101 Ash St (92101-3017)
PHONE..................................619 696-2000
Mark Snell, *Pr*
Mark Fisher, *

Michael Allman, *
EMP: 1000 EST: 1997
SQ FT: 10,000
SALES (est): 480.01MM
SALES (corp-wide): 14.44B Publicly Held
Web: www.sempra.com
SIC: 4911 4924 Generation, electric power; Natural gas distribution
PA: Sempra
488 8th Ave
San Diego CA
619 696-2000

(P-4677)
SEMPRA ENERGY INTERNATIONAL
Also Called: Sempra Energy Utilities
101 Ash St (92101-3017)
PHONE..................................619 696-2000
Luis Eduardo Pawluszek, *CEO*
Donald E Felsinger, *
Mark A Snell, *
Javade Chaudhri, *
Randall L Clark, *
EMP: 1200 EST: 1998
SALES (est): 576.02MM
SALES (corp-wide): 14.44B Publicly Held
Web: www.sempra.com
SIC: 4911 Electric services
PA: Sempra
488 8th Ave
San Diego CA
619 696-2000

(P-4678)
SIEMENS ENERGY INC
3215 47th Ave (95824-2400)
PHONE..................................916 391-2993
Frank Miller, *Mgr*
EMP: 73
SALES (corp-wide): 28.9B Privately Held
Web: new.siemens.com
SIC: 4911 Generation, electric power
HQ: Siemens Energy, Inc.
4400 N Alafaya Trl
Orlando FL
407 736-2000

(P-4679)
SOLARRESERVE INC
520 Broadway Fl 6 (90401-2420)
PHONE..................................310 315-2200
Kevin B Smith, *CEO*
Stephen Mullennix, *
EMP: 99 EST: 2008
SQ FT: 20,000
SALES (est): 19.38MM Privately Held
SIC: 4911 Distribution, electric power

(P-4680)
SOLV ENERGY LLC (HQ)
16680 W Bernardo Dr (92127-1900)
PHONE..................................858 251-4888
George Hershman, *CEO*
Ben Catalano, *CFO*
EMP: 159 EST: 2015
SALES (est): 30.23MM Privately Held
Web: www.solvenergy.com
SIC: 4911
PA: American Securities Llc
590 Madison Ave Fl 38
New York NY

(P-4681)
SOUTHERN CALIFORNIA EDISON CO
Also Called: Northern Hydro
54205 Mt Poplar Ave (93605)
PHONE..................................559 893-3611
David Dormire, *Mgr*

EMP: 102
SALES (corp-wide): 17.22B Publicly Held
Web: www.sce.com
SIC: 4911 Electric services
HQ: Southern California Edison Company
2244 Walnut Grove Ave
Rosemead CA
626 302-1212

(P-4682)
SOUTHERN CALIFORNIA EDISON CO
Also Called: Monrovia Service Center
1440 S California Ave (91016-4211)
PHONE..................................626 303-8480
Robert Robinson, *Prin*
EMP: 190
SQ FT: 31,603
SALES (corp-wide): 17.22B Publicly Held
Web: www.sce.com
SIC: 4911 Electric services
HQ: Southern California Edison Company
2244 Walnut Grove Ave
Rosemead CA
626 302-1212

(P-4683)
SOUTHERN CALIFORNIA EDISON CO
3589 Foothill Dr (91361-2410)
PHONE..................................805 496-3406
EMP: 60
SALES (corp-wide): 17.22B Publicly Held
Web: www.sce.com
SIC: 4911 Electric services
HQ: Southern California Edison Company
2244 Walnut Grove Ave
Rosemead CA
626 302-1212

(P-4684)
SOUTHERN CALIFORNIA EDISON CO
2 Innovation Way Fl 1 (91768-2560)
PHONE..................................909 274-1925
EMP: 504
SALES (corp-wide): 17.22B Publicly Held
Web: www.sce.com
SIC: 4911 Electric services
HQ: Southern California Edison Company
2244 Walnut Grove Ave
Rosemead CA
626 302-1212

(P-4685)
SOUTHERN CALIFORNIA EDISON CO
Also Called: Thousand Oaks Service Center
3589 Foothill Dr (91361-2475)
PHONE..................................818 999-1880
Jerry Willaferd, *Bmch Mgr*
EMP: 87
SALES (corp-wide): 17.22B Publicly Held
Web: www.sce.com
SIC: 4911 8741 Electric services; Business management
HQ: Southern California Edison Company
2244 Walnut Grove Ave
Rosemead CA
626 302-1212

(P-4686)
SOUTHERN CALIFORNIA EDISON CO
Also Called: Irwindale 6000
6000 N Irwindale Ave Ste A (91702-3200)
PHONE..................................626 815-7296
Ray Maese, *Bmch Mgr*
EMP: 92

SALES (corp-wide): 17.22B Publicly Held
Web: www.sce.com
SIC: 4911 Electric services
HQ: Southern California Edison Company
2244 Walnut Grove Ave
Rosemead CA
626 302-1212

(P-4687)
SOUTHERN CALIFORNIA EDISON CO
265 Ne End Ave (91767-5803)
PHONE..................................909 469-0251
John Risen, *Bmch Mgr*
EMP: 609
SALES (corp-wide): 17.22B Publicly Held
Web: www.sce.com
SIC: 4911 Electric services
HQ: Southern California Edison Company
2244 Walnut Grove Ave
Rosemead CA
626 302-1212

(P-4688)
SOUTHERN CALIFORNIA EDISON CO
Also Called: Compton Service Center
1924 E Cashdan St (90220-6403)
PHONE..................................310 608-5029
Floyd Rich, *Bmch Mgr*
EMP: 269
SALES (corp-wide): 17.22B Publicly Held
Web: www.sce.com
SIC: 4911 Electric services
HQ: Southern California Edison Company
2244 Walnut Grove Ave
Rosemead CA
626 302-1212

(P-4689)
SOUTHERN CALIFORNIA EDISON CO
Also Called: N Trans/Sub Regional Office
28250 Gateway Village Dr (91355-1177)
PHONE..................................661 607-0207
EMP: 183
SALES (corp-wide): 17.22B Publicly Held
Web: www.sce.com
SIC: 4911 Electric services
HQ: Southern California Edison Company
2244 Walnut Grove Ave
Rosemead CA
626 302-1212

(P-4690)
SOUTHERN CALIFORNIA EDISON CO
Also Called: Southeastern Westminster
7300 Fenwick Ln (92683-5238)
PHONE..................................714 895-0420
Dee Pak Nanda, *VP*
EMP: 660
SALES (corp-wide): 17.22B Publicly Held
Web: www.sce.com
SIC: 4911 Electric services
HQ: Southern California Edison Company
2244 Walnut Grove Ave
Rosemead CA
626 302-1212

(P-4691)
SOUTHERN CALIFORNIA EDISON CO
Also Called: Saddleback Valley Service Ctr
14155 Bake Pkwy (92618-1818)
PHONE..................................949 587-5416
Robert Torres, *Mgr*
EMP: 133
SALES (corp-wide): 17.22B Publicly Held

4911 - Electric Services (P-4692)

PRODUCTS & SERVICES SECTION

Web: www.sce.com
SIC: 4911 Electric services
HQ: Southern California Edison Company
2244 Walnut Grove Ave
Rosemead CA
626 302-1212

(P-4692)
SOUTHERN CALIFORNIA EDISON CO
Also Called: Lightthipe Substation
6900 Orange Ave (90805-1599)
PHONE..................562 529-7301
Jim Hill, Mgr
EMP: 82
SQ FT: 38,928
SALES (corp-wide): 17.22B Publicly Held
Web: www.sce.com
SIC: 4911 Electric services
HQ: Southern California Edison Company
2244 Walnut Grove Ave
Rosemead CA
626 302-1212

(P-4693)
SOUTHERN CALIFORNIA EDISON CO
Also Called: Orange Coast Service Center
7333 Bolsa Ave (92683-5210)
PHONE..................714 895-0163
Jeff Lebow, Brnch Mgr
EMP: 101
SALES (corp-wide): 17.22B Publicly Held
Web: www.sce.com
SIC: 4911 Electric services
HQ: Southern California Edison Company
2244 Walnut Grove Ave
Rosemead CA
626 302-1212

(P-4694)
SOUTHERN CALIFORNIA EDISON CO
Also Called: Ridgecrest Service Center
510 S China Lake Blvd (93555-5006)
PHONE..................760 375-1821
Howell Applegrath, Mgr
EMP: 119
SALES (corp-wide): 17.22B Publicly Held
Web: www.sce.com
SIC: 4911 Electric services
HQ: Southern California Edison Company
2244 Walnut Grove Ave
Rosemead CA
626 302-1212

(P-4695)
SOUTHERN CALIFORNIA EDISON CO
13025 Los Angeles St (91706-2241)
PHONE..................626 814-4212
Ed Entillon, Brnch Mgr
EMP: 293
SQ FT: 21,000
SALES (corp-wide): 17.22B Publicly Held
Web: www.sce.com
SIC: 4911 Electric services
HQ: Southern California Edison Company
2244 Walnut Grove Ave
Rosemead CA
626 302-1212

(P-4696)
SOUTHERN CALIFORNIA EDISON CO
Also Called: Covina Service Center
800 W Cienega Ave (91773-2490)
PHONE..................909 592-3757
Gary Martinez, Brnch Mgr

EMP: 220
SALES (corp-wide): 17.22B Publicly Held
Web: www.sce.com
SIC: 4911 Electric services
HQ: Southern California Edison Company
2244 Walnut Grove Ave
Rosemead CA
626 302-1212

(P-4697)
SOUTHERN CALIFORNIA EDISON CO
Also Called: Whittier Service Center
9901 Geary Ave (90670-3251)
PHONE..................562 903-3191
Fred Swearingen, Prin
EMP: 298
SALES (corp-wide): 17.22B Publicly Held
Web: www.sce.com
SIC: 4911 Electric services
HQ: Southern California Edison Company
2244 Walnut Grove Ave
Rosemead CA
626 302-1212

(P-4698)
SOUTHERN CALIFORNIA EDISON CO
Also Called: Ctac Research 60901
6090 N Irwindale Ave (91702-3207)
PHONE..................626 812-7380
Diane Ronewko, Mgr
EMP: 243
SALES (corp-wide): 17.22B Publicly Held
Web: www.sce.com
SIC: 4911 Electric services
HQ: Southern California Edison Company
2244 Walnut Grove Ave
Rosemead CA
626 302-1212

(P-4699)
SOUTHERN CALIFORNIA EDISON CO
7400 Fenwick Ln (92683-5243)
PHONE..................714 895-0119
EMP: 60
SALES (corp-wide): 17.22B Publicly Held
Web: www.sce.com
SIC: 4911 Electric services
HQ: Southern California Edison Company
2244 Walnut Grove Ave
Rosemead CA
626 302-1212

(P-4700)
SOUTHERN CALIFORNIA EDISON CO
55481 Mt Poplar (93605)
P.O. Box 130 (93605-0130)
PHONE..................559 893-2037
Southern Edison, Brnch Mgr
EMP: 181
SALES (corp-wide): 17.22B Publicly Held
Web: www.sce.com
SIC: 4911 Distribution, electric power
HQ: Southern California Edison Company
2244 Walnut Grove Ave
Rosemead CA
626 302-1212

(P-4701)
SOUTHERN CALIFORNIA EDISON CO
Also Called: North Orange County Svc Ctr
1851 W Valencia Dr (92833-3215)
PHONE..................714 870-3225
David Kama, Dist Mgr
EMP: 412

SALES (corp-wide): 17.22B Publicly Held
Web: www.sce.com
SIC: 4911 Distribution, electric power
HQ: Southern California Edison Company
2244 Walnut Grove Ave
Rosemead CA
626 302-1212

(P-4702)
SOUTHERN CALIFORNIA EDISON CO
Also Called: Southern Cal Edson - Prvate Ch
2131 Walnut Grove Ave (91770-3769)
PHONE..................626 302-1212
Grant Thomas, Brnch Mgr
EMP: 306
SALES (corp-wide): 17.22B Publicly Held
Web: www.sce.com
SIC: 4911 Distribution, electric power
HQ: Southern California Edison Company
2244 Walnut Grove Ave
Rosemead CA
626 302-1212

(P-4703)
SOUTHERN CALIFORNIA EDISON CO (HQ)
Also Called: SCE
2244 Walnut Grove Ave (91770-3714)
P.O. Box 976 (91770-0976)
PHONE..................626 302-1212
Kevin M Payne, Pr
Steven D Powell, Ofcr
William M Petmecky Iii, Sr VP
Caroline Choi Senior, Corporate Affairs Vice President
Jacqueline Trapp, Senior Vice President Human Resources
▲ EMP: 1200 EST: 1909
SALES (est): 17.17B
SALES (corp-wide): 17.22B Publicly Held
Web: www.sce.com
SIC: 4911 Generation, electric power
PA: Edison International
2244 Walnut Grove Ave
Rosemead CA
626 302-2222

(P-4704)
SOUTHERN CALIFORNIA EDISON CO
4900 Rivergrade Rd Bldg 2b1 (91706-1401)
PHONE..................626 543-8081
Peter Quon, Brnch Mgr
EMP: 64
SALES (corp-wide): 17.22B Publicly Held
Web: www.sce.com
SIC: 4911 Generation, electric power
HQ: Southern California Edison Company
2244 Walnut Grove Ave
Rosemead CA
626 302-1212

(P-4705)
SOUTHERN CALIFORNIA EDISON CO
4000 Bishop Creek Rd (93514-7026)
PHONE..................760 873-0715
EMP: 183
SALES (corp-wide): 17.22B Publicly Held
Web: www.sce.com
SIC: 4911 Generation, electric power
HQ: Southern California Edison Company
2244 Walnut Grove Ave
Rosemead CA
626 302-1212

(P-4706)
SOUTHERN CALIFORNIA EDISON CO
Also Called: Valley Substation
26125 Menifee Rd (92585-9441)
PHONE..................800 336-2822
Henry Herrea, Brnch Mgr
EMP: 96
SALES (corp-wide): 17.22B Publicly Held
Web: www.sce.com
SIC: 4911 Generation, electric power
HQ: Southern California Edison Company
2244 Walnut Grove Ave
Rosemead CA
626 302-1212

(P-4707)
SOUTHERN CALIFORNIA EDISON CO
6042 N Irwindale Ave Ste A (91702-3250)
PHONE..................626 633-3070
Jami Mcdonald, Brnch Mgr
EMP: 60
SALES (corp-wide): 17.22B Publicly Held
Web: www.sce.com
SIC: 4911 Generation, electric power
HQ: Southern California Edison Company
2244 Walnut Grove Ave
Rosemead CA
626 302-1212

(P-4708)
SOUTHERN CALIFORNIA EDISON CO
Also Called: Western Division Regional Off
125 Elm Ave (90802-4918)
PHONE..................562 491-3803
Lorene Miller, Mgr
EMP: 247
SALES (corp-wide): 17.22B Publicly Held
Web: www.sce.com
SIC: 4911 Generation, electric power
HQ: Southern California Edison Company
2244 Walnut Grove Ave
Rosemead CA
626 302-1212

(P-4709)
SOUTHERN CALIFORNIA EDISON CO
Also Called: Villa Park Substation
1900 E Taft Ave (92865-4702)
PHONE..................714 283-8568
EMP: 69
SALES (corp-wide): 17.22B Publicly Held
Web: www.sce.com
SIC: 4911 Generation, electric power
HQ: Southern California Edison Company
2244 Walnut Grove Ave
Rosemead CA
626 302-1212

(P-4710)
SOUTHERN CALIFORNIA EDISON CO
Alhambra Combined Facility
501 S Marengo Ave (91803-1640)
P.O. Box 700 (91770-0700)
PHONE..................626 308-6193
EMP: 742
SALES (corp-wide): 17.22B Publicly Held
Web: www.sce.com
SIC: 4911 Generation, electric power
HQ: Southern California Edison Company
2244 Walnut Grove Ave
Rosemead CA
626 302-1212

▲ = Import ▼ = Export
◆ = Import/Export

PRODUCTS & SERVICES SECTION

4924 - Natural Gas Distribution (P-4731)

(P-4711)
SUNNOVA ENERGY CORPORATION
6531 Irvine Center Dr Ste 200 (92618-2146)
PHONE.................877 757-7697
EMP: 720
SALES (corp-wide): 176.35MM Privately Held
Web: www.sunnova.com
SIC: 4911
PA: Sunnova Energy Corporation
20 Greenway Plz Ste 540
Houston TX
281 985-9900

(P-4712)
TERABASE ENERGY INC
2222 Harold Way (94704-1425)
PHONE.................415 763-7181
Matthew Campbell, CEO
EMP: 80 EST: 2019
SQ FT: 1,500
SALES (est): 5.2MM Privately Held
Web: www.terabase.energy
SIC: 4911

(P-4713)
TRUCKEE DNNER PUB UTLITY DST F
Also Called: TRUCKEE DONNER PUD
11570 Donner Pass Rd (96161-4992)
PHONE.................530 587-3896
EMP: 68 EST: 1927
SQ FT: 48,000
SALES (est): 48.03MM Privately Held
Web: www.tdpud.org
SIC: 4911 4941 Distribution, electric power; Water supply

(P-4714)
TURLOCK IRRGTION DST EMPLYEES (PA)
333 E Canal Dr (95380-3946)
P.O. Box 949 (95381-0949)
PHONE.................209 883-8222
Joe Alamo, Pr
Jessie Kirschner, Finance*
EMP: 212 EST: 1887
SQ FT: 20,000
SALES (est): 342.97MM
SALES (corp-wide): 342.97MM Privately Held
Web: www.tid.org
SIC: 4911 Distribution, electric power

(P-4715)
TWIN OAKS POWER LP (HQ)
101 Ash St Hq10b (92101-3017)
PHONE.................619 696-2034
EMP: 100 EST: 2002
SALES (est): 72MM
SALES (corp-wide): 14.44B Publicly Held
SIC: 4911 4924 Generation, electric power; Natural gas distribution
PA: Sempra
488 8th Ave
San Diego CA
619 696-2000

(P-4716)
V3 ELECTRIC INC
4925 Robert J Mathews Pkwy Ste 100 (95762-5700)
PHONE.................916 597-2627
Joshua Collette, CEO
Alec Nethercott, *
Atul Raj, *
EMP: 184 EST: 2014
SQ FT: 15,000
SALES (est): 46.01MM Privately Held
Web: www.v3electric.com
SIC: 4911 1731
; Electric power systems contractors

(P-4717)
VEXILLUM INC
Also Called: EZ Electric
10636 Industrial Ave (95678-5902)
PHONE.................916 218-3815
Scott Zachman, Pr
EMP: 63
SALES (corp-wide): 24.78MM Privately Held
Web: www.ez-electric.com
SIC: 4911 Electric services
PA: Vexillum, Inc.
1250 Birchwood Dr
Sunnyvale CA
408 541-4245

(P-4718)
WATSON COGENERATION CO INC
22850 Wilmington Ave (90745-5021)
P.O. Box 6203 (90749-6203)
PHONE.................310 816-8100
Paul L Foster, Ofcr
EMP: 63 EST: 1986
SQ FT: 1,000
SALES (est): 45.47MM Publicly Held
SIC: 4911 Generation, electric power
HQ: Western Refining, Inc.
212 N Clark Dr
El Paso TX

(P-4719)
WEST COAST ELECTRIC & PWR INC
741 E Ball Rd Ste 206 (92805-5952)
PHONE.................562 447-3254
Sergio Zorio, CEO
EMP: 60 EST: 2017
SALES (est): 24.15MM Privately Held
Web: www.wcepinc.com
SIC: 4911 7389 8711 Electric services; Mapmaking or drafting, including aerial; Engineering services

4922 Natural Gas Transmission

(P-4720)
SAN DIEGO GAS & ELECTRIC CO
Also Called: South Bay Power Plant
990 Bay Blvd (91911-1651)
PHONE.................800 411-7343
Carl Creelman, Brnch Mgr
EMP: 71
SALES (corp-wide): 14.44B Publicly Held
Web: www.sdge.com
SIC: 4922 4911 Natural gas transmission; Generation, electric power
HQ: San Diego Gas & Electric Company
8330 Century Park Ct
San Diego CA
619 696-2000

(P-4721)
SOUTHERN CALIFORNIA GAS CO
9400 Oakdale Ave (91311-6511)
P.O. Box 513249 (90051-1249)
PHONE.................818 701-2592
EMP: 266
SALES (corp-wide): 14.44B Publicly Held

Web: www.socalgas.com
SIC: 4922 4923 Pipelines, natural gas; Gas transmission and distribution
HQ: Southern California Gas Company
555 W 5th St Ste 14h1
Los Angeles CA
213 244-1200

4924 Natural Gas Distribution

(P-4722)
CLEAN ENERGY
4675 Macarthur Ct Ste 800 (92660-1895)
PHONE.................949 437-1000
EMP: 832 EST: 1996
SALES (est): 811.08MM
SALES (corp-wide): 420.16MM Publicly Held
Web: www.cleanenergyfuels.com
SIC: 4924 Natural gas distribution
PA: Clean Energy Fuels Corp.
4675 Macarthur Ct Ste 800
Newport Beach CA
949 437-1000

(P-4723)
PACIFIC GAS AND ELECTRIC CO
Also Called: PG&e
24300 Clawiter Rd (94545-2218)
PHONE.................510 784-3253
Tom Webb, Brnch Mgr
EMP: 901
Web: www.pge.com
SIC: 4924 4911 Natural gas distribution; Distribution, electric power
HQ: Pacific Gas And Electric Company
300 Lakeside Dr Ste 210
Oakland CA
415 973-7000

(P-4724)
PACIFIC GAS AND ELECTRIC CO
Also Called: PG&e
460 Rio Lindo Ave (95926-1815)
PHONE.................530 894-4739
Todd Stewart, Mgr
EMP: 63
Web: www.pge.com
SIC: 4924 4911 4923 Natural gas distribution; Electric services; Gas transmission and distribution
HQ: Pacific Gas And Electric Company
300 Lakeside Dr Ste 210
Oakland CA
415 973-7000

(P-4725)
SAN DIEGO GAS & ELECTRIC CO
Also Called: SDG&e
14601 Virginia St (92555-8100)
PHONE.................951 243-2241
John Garcia, Mgr
EMP: 242
SALES (corp-wide): 14.44B Publicly Held
Web: www.sdge.com
SIC: 4924 Natural gas distribution
HQ: San Diego Gas & Electric Company
8330 Century Park Ct
San Diego CA
619 696-2000

(P-4726)
SOCALGAS
1981 W Lugonia Ave (92374-9720)
P.O. Box 513249 (90051-1249)
PHONE.................909 307-7022
EMP: 61 EST: 2018
SALES (est): 2.89MM Privately Held

Web: www.socalgas.com
SIC: 4924 Natural gas distribution

(P-4727)
SOUTHERN CALIFORNIA GAS CO (HQ)
555 W 5th St Ste 14h1 (90013-1010)
PHONE.................213 244-1200
Debra L Reed, Ch
Scott D Drury, CEO
Maryam Sabbaghian Brown, Pr
Steven D Davis, Ex VP
Joseph A Householder, Ex VP
EMP: 505 EST: 1910
SALES (est): 6.84B
SALES (corp-wide): 14.44B Publicly Held
Web: www.socalgas.com
SIC: 4924 4922 4932 Natural gas distribution; Natural gas transmission; Gas and other services combined
PA: Sempra
488 8th Ave
San Diego CA
619 696-2000

(P-4728)
SOUTHERN CALIFORNIA GAS CO
Also Called: Socalgas
12801 Tampa Ave (91326-1045)
PHONE.................818 363-8542
EMP: 342
SALES (corp-wide): 14.44B Publicly Held
Web: www.socalgas.com
SIC: 4924 Natural gas distribution
HQ: Southern California Gas Company
555 W 5th St Ste 14h1
Los Angeles CA
213 244-1200

(P-4729)
SOUTHERN CALIFORNIA GAS CO
1 Liberty (92656-3830)
PHONE.................714 634-7221
Bill Jameson, Brnch Mgr
EMP: 114
SALES (corp-wide): 14.44B Publicly Held
Web: www.socalgas.com
SIC: 4924 Natural gas distribution
HQ: Southern California Gas Company
555 W 5th St Ste 14h1
Los Angeles CA
213 244-1200

(P-4730)
SOUTHERN CALIFORNIA GAS CO
Also Called: Gas Company, The
9240 Firestone Blvd (90241-5388)
PHONE.................562 803-7500
EMP: 494
SALES (corp-wide): 14.44B Publicly Held
Web: www.socalgas.com
SIC: 4924 Natural gas distribution
HQ: Southern California Gas Company
555 W 5th St Ste 14h1
Los Angeles CA
213 244-1200

(P-4731)
SOUTHERN CALIFORNIA GAS CO
Also Called: Northern Reg. Sub Base
1510 N Chester Ave (93308-2559)
PHONE.................661 399-4431
James Pina, Mgr
EMP: 133

(PA)=Parent Co (HQ)=Headquarters
✪ = New Business established in last 2 years

4924 - Natural Gas Distribution (P-4732)

PRODUCTS & SERVICES SECTION

SALES (corp-wide): 14.44B **Publicly Held**
Web: www.socalgas.com
SIC: 4924 Natural gas distribution
HQ: Southern California Gas Company
　　555 W 5th St Ste 14h1
　　Los Angeles CA
　　213 244-1200

(P-4732)
SOUTHERN CALIFORNIA GAS CO
1801 S Atlantic Blvd (91754-5207)
PHONE..............................213 244-1200
W J Torres, *Brnch Mgr*
EMP: 684
SALES (corp-wide): 14.44B **Publicly Held**
Web: www.socalgas.com
SIC: 4924 Natural gas distribution
HQ: Southern California Gas Company
　　555 W 5th St Ste 14h1
　　Los Angeles CA
　　213 244-1200

(P-4733)
SOUTHERN CALIFORNIA GAS CO
Also Called: Southern Cal Nursing Academy
73700 Dinah Shore Dr Ste 106
(92211-0813)
PHONE..............................714 262-0091
Ryan Nuqui, *Brnch Mgr*
EMP: 76
SALES (corp-wide): 14.44B **Publicly Held**
Web: www.yourcprmd.com
SIC: 4924 Natural gas distribution
HQ: Southern California Gas Company
　　555 W 5th St Ste 14h1
　　Los Angeles CA
　　213 244-1200

(P-4734)
SOUTHERN CALIFORNIA GAS CO
Also Called: Regional Office
1981 W Lugonia Ave (92374-9720)
P.O. Box 513249 (90051-1249)
PHONE..............................909 335-7802
James Boland, *Mgr*
EMP: 342
SALES (corp-wide): 14.44B **Publicly Held**
Web: www.socalgas.com
SIC: 4924 Natural gas distribution
HQ: Southern California Gas Company
　　555 W 5th St Ste 14h1
　　Los Angeles CA
　　213 244-1200

(P-4735)
SOUTHERN CALIFORNIA GAS CO
Also Called: Industry Station
920 S Stimson Ave (91745-1640)
PHONE..............................213 244-1200
EMP: 114
SALES (corp-wide): 14.44B **Publicly Held**
Web: www.socalgas.com
SIC: 4924 Natural gas distribution
HQ: Southern California Gas Company
　　555 W 5th St Ste 14h1
　　Los Angeles CA
　　213 244-1200

(P-4736)
SOUTHERN CALIFORNIA GAS CO
25200 Trumble Rd (92585-9664)
PHONE..............................213 244-1200
EMP: 114
SALES (corp-wide): 14.44B **Publicly Held**

Web: www.socalgas.com
SIC: 4924 Natural gas distribution
HQ: Southern California Gas Company
　　555 W 5th St Ste 14h1
　　Los Angeles CA
　　213 244-1200

(P-4737)
SOUTHERN CALIFORNIA GAS CO
Also Called: La Jolla Station
3050 E La Jolla St (92806)
PHONE..............................213 244-1200
EMP: 114
SALES (corp-wide): 14.44B **Publicly Held**
Web: www.socalgas.com
SIC: 4924 4922 4932 Natural gas distribution
; Natural gas transmission; Gas and other services combined
HQ: Southern California Gas Company
　　555 W 5th St Ste 14h1
　　Los Angeles CA
　　213 244-1200

(P-4738)
SOUTHERN CALIFORNIA GAS CO
333 E Main St Ste J (91801-3914)
PHONE..............................323 881-3587
G H Chavez, *Brnch Mgr*
EMP: 114
SALES (corp-wide): 14.44B **Publicly Held**
Web: www.socalgas.com
SIC: 4924 Natural gas distribution
HQ: Southern California Gas Company
　　555 W 5th St Ste 14h1
　　Los Angeles CA
　　213 244-1200

(P-4739)
SOUTHERN CALIFORNIA GAS CO
6738 Bright Ave (90601-4306)
PHONE..............................562 803-3341
Richard Duran, *Brnch Mgr*
EMP: 95
SALES (corp-wide): 14.44B **Publicly Held**
Web: www.socalgas.com
SIC: 4924 Natural gas distribution
HQ: Southern California Gas Company
　　555 W 5th St Ste 14h1
　　Los Angeles CA
　　213 244-1200

(P-4740)
SOUTHERN CALIFORNIA GAS CO
8141 Gulana Ave (90293-7930)
PHONE..............................310 823-7945
James Wine, *Mgr*
EMP: 345
SALES (corp-wide): 14.44B **Publicly Held**
Web: www.socalgas.com
SIC: 4924 Natural gas distribution
HQ: Southern California Gas Company
　　555 W 5th St Ste 14h1
　　Los Angeles CA
　　213 244-1200

(P-4741)
SOUTHERN CALIFORNIA GAS CO
155 S G St (92410-3317)
PHONE..............................909 335-7941
Al Garcia, *Brnch Mgr*
EMP: 247
SALES (corp-wide): 14.44B **Publicly Held**
Web: www.socalgas.com

SIC: 4924 Natural gas distribution
HQ: Southern California Gas Company
　　555 W 5th St Ste 14h1
　　Los Angeles CA
　　213 244-1200

(P-4742)
SOUTHERN CALIFORNIA GAS CO
1600 Corporate Center Dr (91754-7607)
P.O. Box C (91756-0001)
PHONE..............................213 244-1200
Joe M Rivera, *Rgnl Mgr*
EMP: 223
SALES (corp-wide): 14.44B **Publicly Held**
Web: www.socalgas.com
SIC: 4924 Natural gas distribution
HQ: Southern California Gas Company
　　555 W 5th St Ste 14h1
　　Los Angeles CA
　　213 244-1200

(P-4743)
SOUTHERN CALIFORNIA GAS CO
1050 Overland Ct (91773-1704)
P.O. Box 513249 (90051-1249)
PHONE..............................909 305-8297
Janet Yee, *Mgr*
EMP: 266
SQ FT: 39,344
SALES (corp-wide): 14.44B **Publicly Held**
Web: www.socalgas.com
SIC: 4924 Natural gas distribution
HQ: Southern California Gas Company
　　555 W 5th St Ste 14h1
　　Los Angeles CA
　　213 244-1200

(P-4744)
SOUTHERN CALIFORNIA GAS CO
Also Called: Southern California Gas
3318 Shadylawn Dr (91010-1667)
PHONE..............................626 358-4700
Patrick Moore, *Prin*
EMP: 77
SALES (corp-wide): 14.44B **Publicly Held**
Web: www.socalgas.com
SIC: 4924 Natural gas distribution
HQ: Southern California Gas Company
　　555 W 5th St Ste 14h1
　　Los Angeles CA
　　213 244-1200

(P-4745)
SOUTHERN CALIFORNIA GAS CO
Also Called: Honor Rancho Station
23130 Valencia Blvd (91355-1716)
PHONE..............................800 427-2200
Dan Skope, *VP*
EMP: 133
SALES (corp-wide): 14.44B **Publicly Held**
Web: www.socalgas.com
SIC: 4924 Natural gas distribution
HQ: Southern California Gas Company
　　555 W 5th St Ste 14h1
　　Los Angeles CA
　　213 244-1200

(P-4746)
SOUTHERN CALIFORNIA GAS TOWER
555 W 5th St (90013-1010)
PHONE..............................213 244-1200
Ed Guiles, *Pr*
EMP: 1000 EST: 1987
SALES (est): 133.19MM

SALES (corp-wide): 14.44B **Publicly Held**
SIC: 4924 Natural gas distribution
HQ: Southern California Gas Company
　　555 W 5th St Ste 14h1
　　Los Angeles CA
　　213 244-1200

(P-4747)
STEELRVER INFRSTRCTURE FUND N (HQ)
Also Called: Steelrver Infrstrcture Prtners
1 Letterman Dr Bldg D (94129-1494)
PHONE..............................415 291-2200
Chris Kinney, *Pt*
Dennis Mahoney, *Head OF ORIGINATION*
John Anderson, *Head OF POWER Finance*
EMP: 200 EST: 2006
SALES (est): 143.26MM **Privately Held**
SIC: 4924 Natural gas distribution
PA: Steelriver Infrastructure Partners Lp
　　1 Harbor Dr Ste 101
　　Sausalito CA

4931 Electric And Other Services Combined

(P-4748)
CALPINE ENERGY SOLUTIONS LLC (DH)
401 W A St Ste 500 (92101-7991)
PHONE..............................877 273-6772
EMP: 104 EST: 2006
SALES (est): 403.3MM
SALES (corp-wide): 10.07B **Privately Held**
Web: www.calpinesolutions.com
SIC: 4931 4932 Electric and other services combined; Gas and other services combined
HQ: Calpine Corporation
　　717 Texas St Ste 1000
　　Houston TX
　　713 830-2000

(P-4749)
CITY OF BURBANK
Also Called: Burbank Water & Power
164 W Magnolia Blvd (91502-1772)
PHONE..............................818 238-3550
Ronald E Davis, *Brnch Mgr*
EMP: 315
SALES (corp-wide): 259.01MM **Privately Held**
Web: www.burbankwaterandpower.com
SIC: 4931 4941 4911 7389 Electric and other services combined; Water supply; Electric services; Interior design services
PA: City Of Burbank
　　275 E Olive Ave
　　Burbank CA
　　818 238-5800

(P-4750)
CITY OF CORONADO
Also Called: Public Services
101 B Ave (92118-1510)
PHONE..............................619 522-7380
Scott Huth, *Dir*
EMP: 115
SALES (corp-wide): 62.19MM **Privately Held**
Web: www.coronado.ca.us
SIC: 4931 9111 Electric and other services combined; Mayors' office
PA: City Of Coronado
　　1825 Strand Way
　　Coronado CA
　　619 522-7300

PRODUCTS & SERVICES SECTION

4941 - Water Supply (P-4767)

(P-4751)
SAN DIEGO GAS & ELECTRIC CO (DH)
Also Called: SDG&E
8330 Century Park Ct (92123-1530)
PHONE..................................619 696-2000
TOLL FREE: 800
Caroline A Winn, *CEO*
Jessie J Knight Junior, *Ch Bd*
Scott D Drury, *
Steven D Davis, *
J Chris Baker, *Chief Information Technology Officer*
◆ **EMP:** 252 **EST:** 1905
SALES (est): 5.84B
SALES (corp-wide): 14.44B **Publicly Held**
Web: www.sdge.com
SIC: 4931 4911 4924 Electric and other services combined; Generation, electric power; Natural gas distribution
HQ: Enova Corporation
 101 Ash St
 San Diego CA

(P-4752)
SAN DIEGO GAS & ELECTRIC CO
Also Called: Supplier Diversity
8315 Century Park Ct Ste Cp-21d (92123-1548)
PHONE..................................866 616-5565
EMP: 131
SALES (corp-wide): 14.44B **Publicly Held**
Web: www.sdge.com
SIC: 4931 4911 Electric and other services combined; Generation, electric power
HQ: San Diego Gas & Electric Company
 8330 Century Park Ct
 San Diego CA
 619 696-2000

(P-4753)
SAN DIEGO GAS & ELECTRIC CO
Also Called: Orange County Service Center
662 Camino De Los Mares (92673-2827)
PHONE..................................949 361-8090
James Valentine, *Brnch Mgr*
EMP: 144
SALES (corp-wide): 14.44B **Publicly Held**
Web: www.sdge.com
SIC: 4931 4911 Electric and other services combined; Electric services
HQ: San Diego Gas & Electric Company
 8330 Century Park Ct
 San Diego CA
 619 696-2000

(P-4754)
UNDERGROUND CNSTR CO INC
5145 Industrial Way (94510-1042)
PHONE..................................707 746-8800
Christopher Ronco, *Pr*
George R Bradshaw, *
Giff Ludwigsen, *
Loren Hudson, *
Jeff Tinsley, *
EMP: 250 **EST:** 1936
SQ FT: 32,946
SALES (est): 172.76MM
SALES (corp-wide): 17.07B **Publicly Held**
Web: www.undergroundconstruction.com
SIC: 4931 5172 4923 Electric and other services combined; Aircraft fueling services; Gas transmission and distribution
PA: Quanta Services, Inc.
 2727 North Loop W Ste 100
 Houston TX
 713 629-7600

4932 Gas And Other Services Combined

(P-4755)
CLEAN ENERGY FUELS CORP (PA)
4675 Macarthur Ct Ste 800 (92660-1895)
PHONE..................................949 437-1000
Stephen A Scully, *Ch Bd*
Andrew J Littlefair, *
Robert M Vreeland, *CFO*
Mitchell W Pratt, *Corporate Secretary*
Barclay F Corbus, *Senior Vice President Strategic Development*
▲ **EMP:** 77 **EST:** 2001
SQ FT: 48,000
SALES (est): 420.16MM
SALES (corp-wide): 420.16MM **Publicly Held**
Web: www.cleanenergyfuels.com
SIC: 4932 4924 4922 Gas and other services combined; Natural gas distribution; Natural gas transmission

(P-4756)
SEMPRA (PA)
488 8th Ave (92101-7123)
PHONE..................................619 696-2000
Jeffrey W Martin, *Ch Bd*
Karen L Sedgwick, *Chief Human Resources Officer*
Trevor I Mihalik, *Ex VP*
Kevin C Sagara, *Group President*
Peter R Wall, *CAO*
EMP: 1000 **EST:** 1998
SALES (est): 14.44B
SALES (corp-wide): 14.44B **Publicly Held**
Web: www.sempra.com
SIC: 4932 4911 5172 4922 Gas and other services combined; Electric services; Petroleum products, nec; Natural gas transmission

4939 Combination Utilities, Nec

(P-4757)
AGILE SOURCING PARTNERS INC
Also Called: Agile
2385 Railroad St (92878-5411)
PHONE..................................951 279-4154
Jeff Giffen, *CEO*
Maria Thompson, *
EMP: 225 **EST:** 2006
SQ FT: 2,300
SALES (est): 77.04MM **Privately Held**
Web: www.agilesourcingpartners.com
SIC: 4939 Combination utilities, nec

(P-4758)
IMPERIAL IRRIGATION DISTRICT
81600 58th Ave (92253-7663)
P.O. Box 1080 (92247-1080)
PHONE..................................760 398-5811
Charles Haskin, *Genl Mgr*
EMP: 120
SALES (corp-wide): 859.47MM **Privately Held**
Web: www.iid.com
SIC: 4939 4911 Combination utilities, nec; Electric services
PA: Imperial Irrigation District
 333 E Barioni Blvd
 Imperial CA
 800 303-7756

(P-4759)
LOS ANGELES DEPT WTR & PWR
Also Called: Scattergood Generation Plant
12700 Vista Del Mar (90293-8502)
PHONE..................................310 524-8500
Nazih Batarseh, *Brnch Mgr*
EMP: 1009
Web: www.ladwp.com
SIC: 4939 Combination utilities, nec
HQ: Los Angeles Department Of Water And Power
 111 N Hope St
 Los Angeles CA
 213 367-1320

(P-4760)
NOR-CAL CONTROLS ES INC
4790 Golden Foothill Pkwy Ste 110 (95762-9332)
PHONE..................................916 836-0800
Rob O Lopez, *CEO*
Nu Chareunrath, *
Lisa Bear, *Chief Human Resource Officer*
Carolyn Lopez, *
EMP: 92 **EST:** 2006
SALES (est): 31MM **Privately Held**
Web: www.norcalcontrols.net
SIC: 4939 7373 8711 Combination utilities, nec; Computer integrated systems design; Engineering services

(P-4761)
SAN DIEGO GAS & ELECTRIC CO
North Coast O & M Center
5016 Carlsbad Blvd (92008-4303)
PHONE..................................760 438-6200
Jim Boland, *Dir*
EMP: 197
SALES (corp-wide): 14.44B **Publicly Held**
Web: www.sdge.com
SIC: 4939 4924 4911 Combination utilities, nec; Natural gas distribution; Electric services
HQ: San Diego Gas & Electric Company
 8330 Century Park Ct
 San Diego CA
 619 696-2000

(P-4762)
SAN DIEGO GAS & ELECTRIC CO
Also Called: SDG&e
436 H St (91910-4308)
PHONE..................................858 654-1135
Charles Johnson, *Crdt Mgr*
EMP: 202
SALES (corp-wide): 14.44B **Publicly Held**
Web: www.sdge.com
SIC: 4939 Combination utilities, nec
HQ: San Diego Gas & Electric Company
 8330 Century Park Ct
 San Diego CA
 619 696-2000

4941 Water Supply

(P-4763)
ALAMEDA COUNTY WATER DISTRICT (PA)
Also Called: ACWD
43885 S Grimmer Blvd (94538-6348)
P.O. Box 5110 (94537-5110)
PHONE..................................510 668-4200
Walt Wadlow, *Genl Mgr*
Ed Stevenson, *
Martin L Koller Presidnet, *Prin*
James G Gunther, *
Judy C Huang, *
EMP: 182 **EST:** 1914
SQ FT: 60,000
SALES (est): 134.81MM
SALES (corp-wide): 134.81MM **Privately Held**
Web: www.acwd.org
SIC: 4941 Water supply

(P-4764)
AMERICAN STATES WATER COMPANY (PA)
Also Called: AWR
630 E Foothill Blvd (91773-1207)
PHONE..................................909 394-3600
Robert J Sprowls, *Pr*
Anne M Holloway, *
Eva G Tang, *Corporate Secretary*
EMP: 568 **EST:** 1929
SALES (est): 491.53MM
SALES (corp-wide): 491.53MM **Publicly Held**
Web: americanstateswatercompany.gcs-web.com
SIC: 4941 4911 Water supply; Electric services

(P-4765)
AZULWORKS INC
1400 Egbert Ave (94124-3222)
PHONE..................................415 558-1507
Sandra R Hernandez, *Pr*
Christopher Kahney, *
EMP: 103 **EST:** 2001
SALES (est): 24.94MM **Privately Held**
Web: www.azulworks.com
SIC: 4941 1623 1389 1622 Water supply; Water, sewer, and utility lines; Construction, repair, and dismantling services; Tunnel construction

(P-4766)
CALAVERAS COUNTY WATER DST
120 Toma Ct (95249-9335)
P.O. Box 608 (95249-0608)
PHONE..................................209 754-3543
Scott Ratterman, *Pr*
Jeff Davidson, *
EMP: 66 **EST:** 1946
SQ FT: 5,000
SALES (est): 12.65MM **Privately Held**
Web: www.ccwd.org
SIC: 4941 Water supply

(P-4767)
CALIFORNIA WATER SERVICE CO (HQ)
1720 N 1st St (95112-4508)
PHONE..................................408 367-8200
Martin A Kropelnicki, *CEO*
Michael P Ireland, *
Helen Del Grosso, *
Francis S Ferraro, *
Robert R Guzzetta, *
EMP: 160 **EST:** 1926
SQ FT: 43,000
SALES (est): 391.44MM
SALES (corp-wide): 846.43MM **Publicly Held**
Web: www.calwater.com
SIC: 4941 Water supply
PA: California Water Service Group
 1720 N 1st St
 San Jose CA
 408 367-8200

4941 - Water Supply (P-4768)

(P-4768)
CALIFORNIA WATER SERVICE GROUP (PA)
1720 N 1st St (95112-4598)
PHONE..............................408 367-8200
Martin A Kropelnicki, Pr
Peter C Nelson, Ch Bd
Thomas F Smegal Iii, VP
Michael B Luu, Chief Risk Officer
Lynne P Mcghee, VP
EMP: 74 **EST:** 1999
SALES (est): 846.43MM
SALES (corp-wide): 846.43MM **Publicly Held**
Web: www.calwatergroup.com
SIC: 4941 Water supply

(P-4769)
CALLEGUAS MNCPL WTR DST PUB FC
2100 E Olsen Rd (91360-6800)
PHONE..............................805 526-9323
Thomas Slosson, Pr
Andy Waters, Prin
Andres Santamaria, Prin
Steve Blois, Prin
Scott Quady, Prin
EMP: 62 **EST:** 1953
SQ FT: 8,000
SALES (est): 150.14MM **Privately Held**
Web: www.calleguas.com
SIC: 4941 Water supply

(P-4770)
CITY OF AZUSA
Also Called: Azusa Lights & Water Dept
729 N Azusa Ave (91702-2528)
PHONE..............................626 969-4408
Joseph Hsu, Mgr
EMP: 77
SQ FT: 2,515
SALES (corp-wide): 74.3MM **Privately Held**
Web: ci.azusa.ca.us
SIC: 4941 Water supply
PA: City Of Azusa
213 E Foothill Blvd
Azusa CA
626 812-5200

(P-4771)
CITY OF FAIRFIELD
Also Called: North Bay Regional Water
5110 Peabody Rd (94533-8908)
PHONE..............................707 428-7680
Ken Britz, Mgr
EMP: 136
SALES (corp-wide): 184.59MM **Privately Held**
Web: fairfield.ca.gov
SIC: 4941 Water supply
PA: City Of Fairfield
1000 Webster St
Fairfield CA
707 428-7569

(P-4772)
CITY OF FRESNO
Also Called: Water Division
1910 E University Ave (93703-2927)
PHONE..............................559 621-5300
Lon Martin, Mgr
EMP: 165
SALES (corp-wide): 670.32MM **Privately Held**
Web: www.fresno.gov
SIC: 4941 Water supply
PA: City Of Fresno
2600 Fresno St
Fresno CA
559 621-7001

(P-4773)
CITY OF GLENDALE
Also Called: Public Service Yard
800 Air Way (91201-3012)
PHONE..............................818 548-2011
Pat Reily, Mgr
EMP: 75
SALES (corp-wide): 390.24MM **Privately Held**
Web: www.glendaleca.gov
SIC: 4941 Water supply
PA: City Of Glendale
141 N Glendale Ave Fl 2
Glendale CA
818 548-2085

(P-4774)
CITY OF RIVERSIDE
Also Called: Public Utilities
3901 Orange St (92501-3610)
PHONE..............................951 826-5312
EMP: 65
SALES (corp-wide): 402.47MM **Privately Held**
Web: www.riversideca.gov
SIC: 4941 Water supply
PA: City Of Riverside
3900 Main St Fl 7
Riverside CA
951 826-5311

(P-4775)
CITY OF UKIAH
Also Called: Public Works Water Department
1320 Airport Rd (95482-6466)
PHONE..............................707 463-6233
George Borecky, Genl Mgr
EMP: 193
SALES (corp-wide): 33.78MM **Privately Held**
Web: www.cityofukiah.com
SIC: 4941 9111 Water supply; Mayors' office
PA: City Of Ukiah
300 Seminary Ave
Ukiah CA
707 463-6203

(P-4776)
COACHLLA VLY WTR DST PUB FCLTI (PA)
Also Called: Coachella Valley Water Dst
75515 Hovley Ln E (92211-5104)
P.O. Box 1058 (92236-1058)
PHONE..............................760 398-2651
TOLL FREE: 888
James M Barrett, Genl Mgr
Steve Robbins, Interim General Manager*
Amy Ammons, Finance*
Jim Barrett, *
Isabel Luna, *
▲ **EMP:** 225 **EST:** 1918
SALES (est): 185.22MM
SALES (corp-wide): 185.22MM **Privately Held**
Web: www.cvwd.org
SIC: 4941 4971 4952 7389 Water supply; Water distribution or supply systems for irrigation; Sewerage systems; Water softener service

(P-4777)
COACHLLA VLY WTR DST PUB FCLTI
75525 Hovley Ln E (92260)
PHONE..............................760 398-2651
Steve Robins, Brnch Mgr
EMP: 172
SALES (corp-wide): 185.22MM **Privately Held**
Web: www.cvwd.org

SIC: 4941 4952 4971 Water supply; Sewerage systems; Irrigation systems
PA: Coachella Valley Water District Public Facilities Corporation
75515 Hovley Ln E
Palm Desert CA
760 398-2651

(P-4778)
CONTRA COSTA WATER DISTRICT (PA)
Also Called: CCWD
1331 Concord Ave (94520-4907)
PHONE..............................925 688-8000
Lisa Borba, Pr
▲ **EMP:** 225 **EST:** 1936
SQ FT: 22,000
SALES (est): 114.25MM
SALES (corp-wide): 114.25MM **Privately Held**
Web: www.ccwater.com
SIC: 4941 Water supply

(P-4779)
COUNTY OF ALAMEDA
399 Elmhurst St (94544-1307)
PHONE..............................510 670-6466
EMP: 78
Web: www.acfloodcontrol.org
SIC: 4941 Water supply
PA: County Of Alameda
1221 Oak St Ste 555
Oakland CA
510 272-6691

(P-4780)
COUNTY OF LOS ANGELES
Also Called: Water & Power Department
6801 E 2nd St (90803-4324)
PHONE..............................213 367-3176
Victor Barra, Dir
EMP: 91
SALES (corp-wide): 31.7B **Privately Held**
Web: www.lacounty.gov
SIC: 4941 9511 9631 4939 Water supply; Air, water, and solid waste management; Regulation, administration of utilities; Combination utilities, nec
PA: County Of Los Angeles
500 W Temple St Ste 437
Los Angeles CA
213 974-1101

(P-4781)
COUNTY OF LOS ANGELES
Also Called: Department of Public Works
900 S Fremont Ave (91803-1331)
P.O. Box 1460 (91802-2460)
PHONE..............................626 458-4000
Gail Farber, Dir
EMP: 300
SALES (corp-wide): 31.7B **Privately Held**
Web: www.ladpw.org
SIC: 4941 9511 4971 Water supply; Air, water, and solid waste management; Irrigation systems
PA: County Of Los Angeles
500 W Temple St Ste 437
Los Angeles CA
213 974-1101

(P-4782)
COUNTY OF SOLANO
Also Called: Water Supply
810 Vaca Valley Pkwy Ste 203 (95688-8835)
PHONE..............................707 451-6090
David Okita, Mgr
EMP: 124
SALES (corp-wide): 856.43MM **Privately Held**

Web: www.solanocounty.com
SIC: 4941 8641 Water supply; Civic and social associations
PA: County Of Solano
675 Texas St Ste 2600
Fairfield CA
707 784-6706

(P-4783)
CUCAMONGA VALLEY WATER DST
10440 Ashford St (91730-3057)
P.O. Box 638 (91729-0638)
PHONE..............................909 987-2591
Martin Zvirbulis, CEO
Kathleen Tiegs, *
Oscar Gonzalez, *
EMP: 100 **EST:** 1955
SQ FT: 15,000
SALES (est): 105.19MM **Privately Held**
Web: www.cvwdwater.com
SIC: 4941 Water supply

(P-4784)
DESERT WATER AGENCY FING CORP
Also Called: DWA
1200 S Gene Autry Trl (92264-3533)
P.O. Box 1710 (92263-1710)
PHONE..............................760 323-4971
Patricia G Oyga, CEO
Craig Ewing Undtermined, Prin
EMP: 88 **EST:** 2007
SQ FT: 38,000
SALES (est): 41.87MM **Privately Held**
Web: www.dwa.org
SIC: 4941 Water supply

(P-4785)
DUBLIN SAN RAMON SERVICES DST (PA)
7051 Dublin Blvd (94568-3018)
PHONE..............................925 875-2276
Bert Michalczyk, CEO
Lori Rose, *
▲ **EMP:** 109 **EST:** 1953
SQ FT: 19,400
SALES (est): 75.75MM
SALES (corp-wide): 75.75MM **Privately Held**
Web: www.dsrsd.com
SIC: 4941 Water supply

(P-4786)
EAST BAY MNCPL UTLITY DST WSTW
Also Called: Ebmud
15083 Camanche Pkwy S (95252-8330)
PHONE..............................209 772-8204
Kent Lambert, Brnch Mgr
EMP: 187
SALES (corp-wide): 769.52MM **Privately Held**
Web: www.ebmud.com
SIC: 4941 Water supply
HQ: East Bay Municipal Utility District, Wastewater System
375 11th St
Oakland CA

(P-4787)
EAST BAY MNCPL UTLITY DST WTR (PA)
Also Called: Ebmud
375 11th St (94607-4246)
P.O. Box 24055 (94623-1055)
PHONE..............................866 403-2683
Alexander Coate, Genl Mgr
Rischa Cole, Corporate Secretary*

4941 - Water Supply (P-4806)

David Klein, *
Sophia Skoda, *
Craig Spencer, *
EMP: 629 **EST:** 1923
SQ FT: 264,427
SALES (est): 769.52MM
SALES (corp-wide): 769.52MM **Privately Held**
Web: www.ebmud.com
SIC: 4941 Water supply

(P-4788)
EAST VALLEY WATER DISTRICT
31111 Greenspot Rd (92346-4427)
P.O. Box 3427 (92413-3427)
PHONE..................909 889-9501
John Mura, *CEO*
Matt Levesque, *
Kip E Sturgeon, *
Donald D Goodin, *
Glenn R Lightfoot, *
EMP: 61 **EST:** 1954
SALES (est): 43.09MM **Privately Held**
Web: www.eastvalley.org
SIC: 4941 8734 Water supply; Water testing laboratory

(P-4789)
EASTERN MUNICIPAL WATER DST (PA)
2270 Trumble Rd (92572)
P.O. Box 8300 (92572-8300)
PHONE..................951 928-3777
Paul D Jones Ii, *CEO*
▲ **EMP:** 420 **EST:** 1950
SQ FT: 160,000
SALES (est): 298.85MM
SALES (corp-wide): 298.85MM **Privately Held**
Web: www.emwd.org
SIC: 4941 4952 Water supply; Sewerage systems

(P-4790)
EASTERN MUNICIPAL WATER DST
19750 Evans Rd (92571-7469)
PHONE..................951 657-7469
Paul D Jones Ii, *Brnch Mgr*
EMP: 200
SALES (corp-wide): 298.85MM **Privately Held**
Web: www.emwd.org
SIC: 4941 Water supply
PA: Eastern Municipal Water District
2270 Trumble Rd
Perris CA
951 928-3777

(P-4791)
EL DORADO IRRIGATION DISTRICT
2890 Mosquito Rd (95667-4700)
PHONE..................530 622-4513
George Osborne, *Pr*
Ane Deister, *
EMP: 300 **EST:** 1925
SQ FT: 27,000
SALES (est): 68.25MM **Privately Held**
Web: www.eid.org
SIC: 4941 4952 8741 4971 Water supply; Sewerage systems; Management services; Irrigation systems

(P-4792)
ELSINORE VLY MUNICPL WTR DST (PA)
31315 Chaney St (92530-2743)
P.O. Box 3000 (92531-3000)
PHONE..................951 674-3146
Andy Morris, *Pr*
Ronald Young, *General Vice President*
Phil Williams, *VP*
EMP: 65 **EST:** 1950
SQ FT: 4,000
SALES (est): 86.55MM
SALES (corp-wide): 86.55MM **Privately Held**
Web: www.evmwd.com
SIC: 4941 4971 4952 Water supply; Water distribution or supply systems for irrigation; Sewerage systems

(P-4793)
FALLBROOK PUBLIC UTILITY DST
990 E Mission Rd (92028-2232)
P.O. Box 2290 (92088-2290)
PHONE..................760 728-1125
Nick Hoskot, *Pr*
Mary Mcneil, *VP*
Ruth Resch, *
Marcie Eilers, *
EMP: 67 **EST:** 1922
SQ FT: 12,000
SALES (est): 32.51MM **Privately Held**
Web: www.fpud.com
SIC: 4941 Water supply

(P-4794)
GOLDEN STATE WATER COMPANY (HQ)
Also Called: AWR
630 E Foothill Blvd (91773-1207)
PHONE..................909 394-3600
Robert J Sprowls, *Pr*
Anne M Holloway, *
Eva G Tang, *Corporate Secretary*
Gladys M Farrow, *VP Fin*
EMP: 64 **EST:** 1929
SALES (est): 340.6MM
SALES (corp-wide): 491.53MM **Publicly Held**
Web: www.gswater.com
SIC: 4941 4911 Water supply; Distribution, electric power
PA: American States Water Company
630 E Foothill Blvd
San Dimas CA
909 394-3600

(P-4795)
INLAND EMPIRE UTLTIES AGCY A M (PA)
6075 Kimball Ave (91708-9174)
P.O. Box 9020 (91709-0902)
PHONE..................909 993-1600
Shivaji Deshmukh, *CEO*
Kati Parker, *
John Anderson, *
Michael Camacho, *
Wyatt Troxel, *
EMP: 92 **EST:** 1950
SQ FT: 60,000
SALES (est): 160.44MM
SALES (corp-wide): 160.44MM **Privately Held**
Web: www.ieua.org
SIC: 4941 Water supply

(P-4796)
IRVINE RANCH WATER DISTRICT (PA)
15600 Sand Canyon Ave (92618-3100)
P.O. Box 57000 (92619-7000)
PHONE..................949 453-5300
Paul Jones, *Genl Mgr*
Robert Jacobson, *
EMP: 110 **EST:** 1961
SQ FT: 52,000
SALES (est): 88.94MM
SALES (corp-wide): 88.94MM **Privately Held**
Web: www.irwd.com
SIC: 4941 4952 Water supply; Sewerage systems

(P-4797)
IRVINE RANCH WATER DISTRICT
3512 Michelson Dr (92612-1757)
P.O. Box 14128 (92623-4128)
PHONE..................949 453-5300
Carl Ballard, *Dir*
EMP: 205
SALES (corp-wide): 88.94MM **Privately Held**
Web: www.irwd.com
SIC: 4941 4952 Water supply; Sewerage systems
PA: Irvine Ranch Water District Inc
15600 Sand Canyon Ave
Irvine CA
949 453-5300

(P-4798)
JURUPA COMMUNITY SERVICES DST
11201 Harrel St (92509)
PHONE..................951 685-7073
EMP: 89
SALES (corp-wide): 13.88MM **Privately Held**
SIC: 4941 4952 Water supply; Sewerage systems
PA: Jurupa Community Services District
11201 Harrel St
Jurupa Valley CA
951 360-5770

(P-4799)
LAS VIRGENES MUNICIPAL WTR DST
4232 Las Virgenes Rd Lbby (91302-3594)
PHONE..................818 251-2100
Glen Peterson, *Pr*
Charles Caspary, *
Lee Renger, *
Jay Lewitt, *
Leonard E Polan, *
EMP: 125 **EST:** 1958
SQ FT: 10,000
SALES (est): 67.09MM **Privately Held**
Web: www.lvmwd.com
SIC: 4941 Water supply

(P-4800)
LIBERTY UTILITIES PK WTR CORP (DH)
9750 Washburn Rd (90241-5625)
PHONE..................562 923-0711
Greg Sorensen, *Pr*
Chris Alario, *
EMP: 68 **EST:** 1937
SQ FT: 15,000
SALES (est): 48.76MM
SALES (corp-wide): 2.77B **Privately Held**
Web: www.libertyutilities.com
SIC: 4941 Water supply
HQ: Liberty Utilities (Canada) Corp
2845 Bristol Cir
Oakville ON
905 465-4500

(P-4801)
LINDA YORBA WATER DISTRICT (PA)
1717 E Miraloma Ave (92870-6785)
P.O. Box 309 (92885-0309)
PHONE..................714 701-3000
Ken Vecchiarelli, *Genl Mgr*
Stephen Parker, *
▲ **EMP:** 60 **EST:** 1959
SQ FT: 7,900
SALES (est): 39.25MM
SALES (corp-wide): 39.25MM **Privately Held**
Web: www.ylwd.com
SIC: 4941 4952 Water supply; Sewerage systems

(P-4802)
LOS ANGELES DEPT WTR & PWR
300 Mandich St (93514-3449)
PHONE..................760 873-0299
EMP: 1009
Web: www.ladwp.com
SIC: 4941 Water supply
HQ: Los Angeles Department Of Water And Power
111 N Hope St
Los Angeles CA
213 367-1320

(P-4803)
LOS ANGELES DEPT WTR & PWR
4030 Crenshaw Blvd (90008-2533)
P.O. Box 51211 (90051-5511)
PHONE..................323 256-8079
EMP: 1682
Web: www.ladwp.com
SIC: 4941 4911 Water supply; Electric services
HQ: Los Angeles Department Of Water And Power
111 N Hope St
Los Angeles CA
213 367-1320

(P-4804)
LOS ANGELES DEPT WTR & PWR
11801 Sheldon St (91352-1508)
PHONE..................213 367-1342
Kirk Bergland, *Brnch Mgr*
EMP: 1009
Web: www.ladwp.com
SIC: 4941 Water supply
HQ: Los Angeles Department Of Water And Power
111 N Hope St
Los Angeles CA
213 367-1320

(P-4805)
LOS ANGELES DEPT WTR & PWR
1630 N Main St (90012-1936)
PHONE..................213 367-4211
Paul Abram, *Mgr*
▲ **EMP:** 841
Web: www.ladwp.com
SIC: 4941 4911 Water supply; Electric services
HQ: Los Angeles Department Of Water And Power
111 N Hope St
Los Angeles CA
213 367-1320

(P-4806)
LOS ANGELES DEPT WTR & PWR
Also Called: Ladwp
201 S Webster St (93526-1769)
PHONE..................760 878-2156

4941 - Water Supply (P-4807)

EMP: 1009
Web: www.ladwp.com
SIC: 4941 Water supply
HQ: Los Angeles Department Of Water And Power
111 N Hope St
Los Angeles CA
213 367-1320

(P-4807)
LOS ANGELES DEPT WTR & PWR (HQ)
Also Called: Ladwp
111 N Hope St (90012-2607)
P.O. Box 51111 (90051-5700)
PHONE..............................213 367-1320
Martin Adams, Genl Mgr
David H Wright, *
Joseph A Brajevich, *
▲ EMP: 897 EST: 1902
SALES (est): 1.06B Privately Held
Web: www.ladwp.com
SIC: 4941 4911 Water supply; Electric services
PA: City Of Los Angeles
200 N Spring St Ste 303
Los Angeles CA
213 978-0600

(P-4808)
LOS ANGELES DEPT WTR & PWR
1141 W 2nd St Bldg D (90012-2007)
PHONE..............................213 367-5706
Carol Tharp, Brnch Mgr
EMP: 1178
Web: www.ladwp.com
SIC: 4941 Water supply
HQ: Los Angeles Department Of Water And Power
111 N Hope St
Los Angeles CA
213 367-1320

(P-4809)
MESA CNSLD WTR DST IMPRV CORP (PA)
Also Called: MESA WATER DISTRICT
1965 Placentia Ave (92627-3420)
PHONE..............................949 631-1200
Lee Pearl, Dir
Coleen L Monteleone, *
James R Fisler, *
Shawn Dewane, *
EMP: 66 EST: 1960
SQ FT: 26,000
SALES (est): 41.07MM
SALES (corp-wide): 41.07MM Privately Held
Web: www.mesawater.org
SIC: 4941 Water supply

(P-4810)
METROPLTAN WTR DST OF STHERN C
Also Called: Robert B Diemer Trtmnt Plant
3972 Valley View Ave (92886-1828)
PHONE..............................714 577-5031
Trudi Loy, Mgr
EMP: 83
SALES (corp-wide): 597.83MM Privately Held
Web: www.mwdh2o.com
SIC: 4941 Water supply
PA: The Metropolitan Water District Of Southern California
700 N Alameda St
Los Angeles CA
213 217-6000

(P-4811)
METROPLTAN WTR DST OF STHERN C
Also Called: Metropolitan Water Lavern
700 Moreno Ave (91750-3303)
P.O. Box 54153 (90054-0153)
PHONE..............................909 593-7474
Wendell Williams, Brnch Mgr
EMP: 370
SALES (corp-wide): 597.83MM Privately Held
Web: www.mwdh2o.com
SIC: 4941 Water supply
PA: The Metropolitan Water District Of Southern California
700 N Alameda St
Los Angeles CA
213 217-6000

(P-4812)
MOULTON NGUEL WTR DST PUB FCLT
Also Called: MOULTON NIGUEL WATER DISTRICT
26161 Gordon Rd (92653-8224)
P.O. Box 30203 (92607-0203)
PHONE..............................949 831-2500
Richard Fiore, Pr
David Cain, *
John V Foley, *
EMP: 97 EST: 1960
SALES (est): 72.49MM Privately Held
Web: www.mnwd.com
SIC: 4941 4959 Water supply; Sanitary services, nec

(P-4813)
OLIVENHAIN MUNICIPAL WATER DST
1966 Olivenhain Rd (92024-5676)
PHONE..............................760 753-6466
Edmund Sprague, Pr
Robert F Topolavac, *
Kimberly A Thorner, *
George Briest, *
Rainy Selamat, *
EMP: 79 EST: 1959
SQ FT: 11,000
SALES (est): 64.53MM Privately Held
Web: www.olivenhain.com
SIC: 4941 4971 Water supply; Impounding reservoir, irrigation

(P-4814)
ORANGE COUNTY WATER DISTRICT (PA)
Also Called: OCWD
18700 Ward St (92708-6930)
P.O. Box 8300 (92728-8300)
PHONE..............................714 378-3200
EMP: 70 EST: 1933
SALES (est): 138.4MM
SALES (corp-wide): 138.4MM Privately Held
Web: www.ocwd.com
SIC: 4941 Water supply

(P-4815)
OTAY WATER DISTRICT
2554 Sweetwater Springs Blvd (91978-2004)
PHONE..............................619 670-2222
Gary Croucher, Pr
Jose Lopez, *
Mark Watton, *
German Alvarez, *
Manny Magana, *
EMP: 170 EST: 1956
SQ FT: 6,000
SALES (est): 108.75MM Privately Held
Web: www.otaywater.gov
SIC: 4941 1623 Water supply; Water, sewer, and utility lines

(P-4816)
PADRE DAM MUNICIPAL WATER DST (PA)
9300 Fanita Pkwy (92071-7906)
P.O. Box 719003 (92072-9003)
PHONE..............................619 258-4617
Allen Carlisle, CEO
Douglas S Wilson, *
William Pommering, *
August Caires, *
James Peasley, *
EMP: 63 EST: 1955
SQ FT: 10,000
SALES (est): 80.79MM
SALES (corp-wide): 80.79MM Privately Held
Web: www.padredam.org
SIC: 4941 4952 7033 Water supply; Sewerage systems; Campgrounds

(P-4817)
PADRE DAM MUNICIPAL WATER DST
9120 Carlton Oaks Dr (92071-2922)
P.O. Box 719003 (92072-9003)
PHONE..............................619 258-4662
Harold Bailey, Dir
EMP: 64
SALES (corp-wide): 80.79MM Privately Held
Web: www.padredam.org
SIC: 4941 4959 Water supply; Sanitary services, nec
PA: Padre Dam Municipal Water District
9300 Fanita Pkwy
Santee CA
619 258-4617

(P-4818)
PALMDALE WATER DISTRICT
2029 E Avenue Q (93550-4050)
PHONE..............................661 947-4111
Michael Williams, CFO
Dennis Hoffmeyer, *
EMP: 93 EST: 1991
SALES (est): 31.32MM Privately Held
Web: www.palmdalewater.org
SIC: 4941 Water supply

(P-4819)
PUBLIC AUTHORITY
401 Mile Of Cars Way Ste 200 (91950-6612)
PHONE..............................619 731-3705
Andrea Villa, Prin
EMP: 100 EST: 2016
SALES (est): 1.12MM Privately Held
Web: www.sdihsspa.com
SIC: 4941 Water supply

(P-4820)
RANCHO CALIFORNIA WATER DST (PA)
Also Called: RCWD
42135 Winchester Rd (92590-4800)
P.O. Box 9017 (92589-9017)
PHONE..............................951 296-6900
William E Plummer, Prin
Bennet Drake, Pr
Stephen J Corona, Pr
Ralph Daily, Pr
John E Hoagland, VP
EMP: 143 EST: 1965
SQ FT: 71,000
SALES (est): 72.48MM
SALES (corp-wide): 72.48MM Privately Held
Web: www.ranchowater.com
SIC: 4941 Water supply

(P-4821)
SACRAMNTO SUBN WTR DST FING CO
3701 Marconi Ave Ste 100 (95821-5303)
PHONE..............................916 972-7171
Daniel York, Genl Mgr
EMP: 60 EST: 1958
SQ FT: 13,500
SALES (est): 53.36MM Privately Held
Web: www.sswd.org
SIC: 4941 Water supply

(P-4822)
SAN DIEGO COUNTY WATER AUTH (PA)
4677 Overland Ave (92123-1233)
PHONE..............................858 522-6600
Maureen Stapleton, Genl Mgr
Dennis Cushman, *
Eric Sandler, *
Sandy Kerl, *
Mark Muir, *
▲ EMP: 96 EST: 1944
SQ FT: 26,000
SALES (est): 105.74MM
SALES (corp-wide): 105.74MM Privately Held
Web: www.sdcwa.org
SIC: 4941 Water supply

(P-4823)
SAN DIEGO COUNTY WATER AUTH
610 W 5th Ave (92025-4093)
PHONE..............................760 480-1991
Brendan Sheehan, Pr
EMP: 184
SALES (corp-wide): 105.74MM Privately Held
Web: www.sdcwa.org
SIC: 4941 Water supply
PA: San Diego County Water Authority
4677 Overland Ave
San Diego CA
858 522-6600

(P-4824)
SAN GABRIEL VALLEY WATER ASSN
725 N Azusa Ave (91702-2528)
PHONE..............................626 815-1305
EMP: 100 EST: 1955
SALES (est): 251.12K Privately Held
Web: www.sgvwa.org
SIC: 4941 Water supply

(P-4825)
SAN GABRIEL VALLEY WATER CO (PA)
Also Called: Fontana Water Company
11142 Garvey Ave (91733-2425)
P.O. Box 6010 (91734-2010)
PHONE..............................626 448-6183
R H Nicholson Junior, Ch Bd
Michael L Whitehead, Pr
David Batt, VP
Frank A Lo Guidice, VP Opers
T J Ryan, Sec
EMP: 125 EST: 1936
SQ FT: 30,000
SALES (est): 48.82MM
SALES (corp-wide): 48.82MM Privately Held

PRODUCTS & SERVICES SECTION

4941 - Water Supply (P-4844)

Web: www.sgvwater.com
SIC: 4941 Water supply

(P-4826)
SAN GABRIEL VALLEY WATER CO
8440 Nuevo Ave (92335-3824)
P.O. Box 987 (92334-0987)
PHONE..............................909 822-2201
Mike Mcgraw, *Mgr*
EMP: 116
SQ FT: 2,727
SALES (corp-wide): 48.82MM **Privately Held**
Web: www.sgvwater.com
SIC: 4941 Water supply
PA: San Gabriel Valley Water Co.
11142 Garvey Ave
El Monte CA
626 448-6183

(P-4827)
SAN JOSE WATER COMPANY (HQ)
Also Called: S J W
110 W Taylor St (95110-2131)
PHONE..............................408 288-5314
W Richard Roth, *CEO*
Charles Toeniskoetter, *
Geaorge Belhumeur, *
Richard Balocco, *
Scott Yoo, *
EMP: 140 EST: 1866
SQ FT: 5,000
SALES (est): 415.23MM
SALES (corp-wide): 620.7MM **Publicly Held**
Web: www.sjwater.com
SIC: 4941 Water supply
PA: Sjw Group
110 W Taylor St
San Jose CA
408 279-7800

(P-4828)
SAN JOSE WATER COMPANY
1221 S Bascom Ave (95128-3514)
PHONE..............................408 298-0364
Paul Schreiber, *Mgr*
EMP: 180
SALES (corp-wide): 620.7MM **Publicly Held**
Web: www.sjwater.com
SIC: 4941 Water supply
HQ: San Jose Water Company
110 W Taylor St
San Jose CA
408 288-5314

(P-4829)
SANTA CLARA VLY WTR DST PUB FC (PA)
Also Called: Santa Clara Valley Water Dst
5750 Almaden Expy (95118-3614)
P.O. Box 20670 (95160-0670)
PHONE..............................408 265-2600
Beau Goldie, *CEO*
Anita Ong, *
▲ EMP: 250 EST: 1951
SQ FT: 40,780
SALES (est): 190MM
SALES (corp-wide): 190MM **Privately Held**
Web: www.valleywater.org
SIC: 4941 Water supply

(P-4830)
SANTA CLARA VLY WTR DST PUB FC
Also Called: Penitencia Water Trtmnt Plant
3959 Whitman Way (95132-3168)
PHONE..............................408 630-2560
EMP: 150
SALES (corp-wide): 190MM **Privately Held**
Web: www.valleywater.org
SIC: 4941 Water supply
PA: Santa Clara Valley Water District Public Facilities Financing Corporation
5750 Almaden Expy
San Jose CA
408 265-2600

(P-4831)
SANTA CLARA VLY WTR DST PUB FC
400 More Ave (95032-1111)
PHONE..............................408 395-8121
Greg Gibson, *Brnch Mgr*
EMP: 150
SALES (corp-wide): 190MM **Privately Held**
Web: www.valleywater.org
SIC: 4941 Water supply
PA: Santa Clara Valley Water District Public Facilities Financing Corporation
5750 Almaden Expy
San Jose CA
408 265-2600

(P-4832)
SANTA CLARITA VALLEY WTR AGCY
Also Called: Santa Clarita Water Division
26521 Summit Cir (91350-3049)
PHONE..............................661 259-2737
Mauricio E Guardado Junior, *Prin*
EMP: 160
SALES (corp-wide): 87.54MM **Privately Held**
Web: www.yourscvwater.com
SIC: 4941 Water supply
PA: Santa Clarita Valley Water Agency
27234 Bouquet Canyon Rd
Santa Clarita CA
661 297-1600

(P-4833)
SANTA CLRITA VLY WTR AGCY FING
27234 Bouquet Canyon Rd (91350-2173)
PHONE..............................661 259-2737
Tom Campbell, *CEO*
Ronald J Kelly, *
April Jacobs, *
Dan Masnada, *
William Cooper, *
EMP: 120 EST: 1962
SQ FT: 1,000
SALES (est): 30.93MM **Privately Held**
Web: www.yourscvwater.com
SIC: 4941 Water supply

(P-4834)
SANTA MARGARITA WATER DISTRICT
26101 Antonio Pkwy (92688-5505)
P.O. Box 7005 (92690-7005)
PHONE..............................949 459-6400
Daniel Ferns, *Brnch Mgr*
EMP: 135
Web: www.smwd.com
SIC: 4941 Water supply
PA: Santa Margarita Water District
26111 Antonio Pkwy
Rcho Sta Marg CA
949 459-6400

(P-4835)
SJW GROUP (PA)
110 W Taylor St (95110-2131)
PHONE..............................408 279-7800
Eric W Thornburg, *Ch Bd*
James P Lynch, *CFO*
Suzy Papazian, *Corporate Secretary*
Wendy Avila-walker, *Contrlr*
Bruce A Hauk Ccdo, *CSO*
EMP: 362 EST: 1866
SALES (est): 620.7MM
SALES (corp-wide): 620.7MM **Publicly Held**
Web: www.sjwgroup.com
SIC: 4941 6531 Water supply; Real estate agent, commercial

(P-4836)
SONOMA COUNTY WATER AGENCY (PA)
404 Aviation Blvd (95403-9019)
PHONE..............................707 526-5370
Grant Davis, *Genl Mgr*
Spencer Bader, *Mgr*
James Jasperse, *Mgr*
Pamela Jeane, *Mgr*
Michael Thompson, *Mgr*
EMP: 200 EST: 1950
SQ FT: 57,000
SALES (est): 55.59MM
SALES (corp-wide): 55.59MM **Privately Held**
Web: www.sonomawater.org
SIC: 4941 Water supply

(P-4837)
SOUTH SAN JQUIN CNTY FIRE AUTH
Also Called: South County Fire
835 N Central Ave (95376-4105)
PHONE..............................209 831-6702
David Bramell, *Prin*
Jackie Heefner, *
Robert Rickman, *
EMP: 95 EST: 2018
SALES (est): 10.75MM **Privately Held**
Web: www.cityoftracy.org
SIC: 4941 Water supply

(P-4838)
SOUTH SAN JQUIN IRRIGATION DST
Also Called: Ssjid
11011 E Highway 120 (95336-9751)
P.O. Box 747 (95366-0747)
PHONE..............................209 249-4600
Betty Garcia, *Ex Sec*
Jeff Shields, *Prin*
Don Battles, *
EMP: 93 EST: 1909
SQ FT: 8,500
SALES (est): 31.23MM **Privately Held**
Web: www.ssjid.com
SIC: 4941 Water supply

(P-4839)
SWEETWTER AUTH EMPLYEES CMMTTE (PA)
505 Garrett Ave (91910-5505)
P.O. Box 2328 (91912-2328)
PHONE..............................619 420-1413
Mark Rogers, *Ex Dir*
James Smyth, *
Teresa Thomas, *
W D Pocklington, *
Margaret C Welsh, *
EMP: 112 EST: 2004
SALES (est): 55.39MM
SALES (corp-wide): 55.39MM **Privately Held**
Web: www.sweetwater.org
SIC: 4941 Water supply

(P-4840)
SWWC UTILITIES INC (DH)
1325 N Grand Ave Ste 100 (91724-4044)
EMP: 173 EST: 2007
SQ FT: 32,000
SALES (est): 94.48MM **Privately Held**
Web: www.swwc.com
SIC: 4941 4952 Water supply; Sewerage systems
HQ: Southwest Water Company
1325 N Grand Ave Ste 100
Covina CA
626 543-2500

(P-4841)
THE METROPOLITAN WATER DISTRICT OF SOUTHERN CALIFORNIA (PA)
Also Called: Mwd
700 N Alameda St (90012-2944)
P.O. Box 54153 (90054-0153)
PHONE..............................213 217-6000
EMP: 850 EST: 1928
SALES (est): 597.83MM
SALES (corp-wide): 597.83MM **Privately Held**
Web: www.mwdh2o.com
SIC: 4941 Water supply

(P-4842)
TUOLUMNE UTILITIES DISTRICT
Also Called: T U D
18885 Nugget Blvd (95370-9284)
PHONE..............................209 532-5536
Pet Kampa, *Genl Mgr*
EMP: 80 EST: 1947
SQ FT: 6,000
SALES (est): 22.46MM **Privately Held**
Web: www.tudwater.com
SIC: 4941 4952 Water supply; Sewerage systems

(P-4843)
VALLECITOS WATER DISTRICT FINANCING CORPORATION (HQ)
Also Called: Vallecitos Water District
201 Vallecitos De Oro (92069-1453)
PHONE..............................760 744-0460
EMP: 96 EST: 1955
SALES (est): 69.93MM **Privately Held**
Web: www.vwd.org
SIC: 4941 4952 Water supply; Sewerage systems
PA: Vallecitos Water District
201 Vallecitos De Oro
San Marcos CA

(P-4844)
VALLEY CTR MNCPL WTR DST FCLTI
29300 Valley Center Rd (92082-6207)
P.O. Box 67 (92082-0067)
PHONE..............................760 735-4500
Gary Broomell, *Pr*
Robert A Polito, *
Kathy Stetson, *
Bill Jeffrey, *
Robert Polito, *Prin*
EMP: 69 EST: 1954
SQ FT: 40,000
SALES (est): 23.88MM **Privately Held**
Web: www.vcmwd.org
SIC: 4941 Water supply

4952 Sewerage Systems

(P-4845)
ARIES INDUSTRIES INC
Also Called: Ccv Engineering & Mfg
5748 E Shields Ave Ste 101 (93727-7854)
PHONE...................................559 291-0383
Kevin Blackhurse, Mgr
EMP: 101
SALES (corp-wide): 27.91MM Privately Held
Web: www.ariesindustries.com
SIC: 4952 Sewerage systems
PA: Aries Industries, Inc.
550 Elizabeth St
Waukesha WI
800 234-7205

(P-4846)
CENTRAL CNTRA CSTA SANI DST EM
5019 Imhoff Pl (94553-4316)
PHONE...................................925 228-9500
Roger Bailey, CEO
Roger Bailey, Genl Mgr
EMP: 275 EST: 1946
SQ FT: 40,000
SALES (est): 89.24MM Privately Held
Web: www.centralsan.org
SIC: 4952 Sewerage systems

(P-4847)
CENTRAL CONTRA COSTA SANITARY DISTRICT FACILITIES FINANCING AUTHORITY
Also Called: C C C S D
5019 Imhoff Pl (94553-4316)
PHONE...................................925 228-9500
EMP: 250 EST: 1994
SALES (est): 85.68MM Privately Held
Web: www.centralsan.org
SIC: 4952 4959 Sewerage systems; Sanitary services, nec

(P-4848)
COUNTY OF LOS ANGELES
Also Called: Public Works, Dept of
45712 Division St (93535-1334)
PHONE...................................661 942-6042
John Feese, Superintnt
EMP: 63
SALES (corp-wide): 31.7B Privately Held
Web: www.lacounty.gov
SIC: 4952 9511 Sewerage systems; Air, water, and solid waste management
PA: County Of Los Angeles
500 W Temple St Ste 437
Los Angeles CA
213 974-1101

(P-4849)
FAIRFIELD-SUISUN SEWER DST
1010 Chadbourne Rd (94534-9700)
PHONE...................................707 429-8930
Richard F Luthy Junior, Genl Mgr
EMP: 65 EST: 1951
SQ FT: 15,000
SALES (est): 25.41MM Privately Held
Web: www.fssd.com
SIC: 4952 Sewerage systems

(P-4850)
SACRAMENTO REG CO SANIT DIST
Sacramento Regional Waste
8521 Laguna Station Rd (95758-9550)
PHONE...................................916 875-9000
Ruben Robles, Mgr
EMP: 500
SALES (corp-wide): 101.69MM Privately Held
Web: www.regionalsan.com
SIC: 4952 Sewerage systems
PA: Sacramento Regional County Sanitation District
10060 Goethe Rd
Sacramento CA
916 876-6000

(P-4851)
SILICON VALLEY CLEAN WATER
Also Called: Sbsa
1400 Radio Rd (94065-1220)
PHONE...................................650 591-7121
Ronald W Shepherd, Prin
Daniel T Child, Mgr
EMP: 79 EST: 1975
SQ FT: 180,000
SALES (est): 53.53MM Privately Held
Web: www.svcw.org
SIC: 4952 Sewerage systems

(P-4852)
SOUTH TAHOE PUBLIC UTILITY DST
1275 Meadow Crest Dr (96150-7401)
PHONE...................................530 544-6474
Richard Solbrig, Genl Mgr
Paul Sciuto, *
Paul Hughes, *
EMP: 113 EST: 1950
SALES (est): 26.21MM Privately Held
Web: www.stpud.us
SIC: 4952 4941 Sewerage systems; Water supply

(P-4853)
UNION SANITARY DISTRICT
Also Called: Usd
5072 Benson Rd (94587-2508)
PHONE...................................510 477-7500
Paul Eldredge, Prin
Paul Eldredge, Genl Mgr
Manny Fernandez, *
Anjali Lathi, *
Jennifer Toy, *
▲ EMP: 130 EST: 1918
SALES (est): 76.73MM Privately Held
Web: unionsanitary.ca.gov
SIC: 4952 Sewerage systems

(P-4854)
VALLEY CENTER MUNICPL WTR DST
29300 Valley Center Rd (92082-6207)
PHONE...................................760 735-4500
Gary Broomell, Pr
Jim Pugh, *
Wally Grabbe, *
Gary Arant, *
EMP: 64 EST: 1954
SQ FT: 5,000
SALES (est): 11.05MM Privately Held
Web: www.vcmwd.org
SIC: 4952 4941 Sewerage systems; Water supply

4953 Refuse Systems

(P-4855)
ALAMEDA COUNTY INDUSTRIES LLC
610 Aladdin Ave (94577-4302)
PHONE...................................510 357-7282
EMP: 70 EST: 1999
SQ FT: 5,400
SALES (est): 8.77MM Privately Held
Web: www.alamedacountyindustries.com
SIC: 4953 Recycling, waste materials

(P-4856)
ARACO ENTERPRISES LLC
Also Called: Athens Environmental Services
9189 De Garmo Ave (91352-2609)
PHONE...................................818 767-0675
Michael R Arakelian, *
EMP: 400 EST: 2017
SALES (est): 24.71MM Privately Held
SIC: 4953 Garbage: collecting, destroying, and processing

(P-4857)
ARAKELIAN ENTERPRISES INC
Also Called: Athens Services
15045 Salt Lake Ave (91746-3315)
PHONE...................................626 336-3636
Ron Arakelian Junior, Owner
EMP: 390
SALES (corp-wide): 199.65MM Privately Held
Web: www.athensservices.com
SIC: 4953 Rubbish collection and disposal
PA: Arakelian Enterprises, Inc.
14048 Valley Blvd
City Of Industry CA
626 336-3636

(P-4858)
ARAKELIAN ENTERPRISES INC
687 Iowa Ave (92507-1610)
PHONE...................................951 342-3300
Sal Orozco, Mgr
EMP: 118
SALES (corp-wide): 199.65MM Privately Held
Web: www.athensservices.com
SIC: 4953 Recycling, waste materials
PA: Arakelian Enterprises, Inc.
14048 Valley Blvd
City Of Industry CA
626 336-3636

(P-4859)
ARAKELIAN ENTERPRISES INC (PA)
Also Called: Athens Services
14048 Valley Blvd (91746-2801)
P.O. Box 60009 (91716-0009)
PHONE...................................626 336-3636
Ron Arakelian Junior, CEO
Michael Arakelian, *
Kevin Hanifin, *
Gary Clifford, *
Dennis Chiappetta, *
EMP: 311 EST: 1958
SQ FT: 10,000
SALES (est): 199.65MM
SALES (corp-wide): 199.65MM Privately Held
Web: www.athensservices.com
SIC: 4953 Recycling, waste materials

(P-4860)
ATHENS DISPOSAL COMPANY INC (PA)
14048 Valley Blvd (91746-2801)
P.O. Box 60009 (91716-0009)
PHONE...................................626 336-3636
Ron Arakelian Senior, Pr
Ron Arakelian Junior, VP
EMP: 350 EST: 1958
SALES (est): 78.22MM
SALES (corp-wide): 78.22MM Privately Held
SIC: 4953 Recycling, waste materials

(P-4861)
ATLAS DISPOSAL INDUSTRIES LLC
3035 Prospect Park Dr Ste 40 (95670-6070)
PHONE...................................916 455-2800
Dave Sikich, CEO
Dave Sikich, Managing Member
Dell Loy Hanson, Managing Member*
Nick Sikich, *
Robin Stuhr, *
EMP: 70 EST: 1998
SALES (est): 18.9MM Privately Held
Web: www.atlasdisposal.com
SIC: 4953 Garbage: collecting, destroying, and processing

(P-4862)
BAY AREA CONCRETE LLC
1580 Chabot Ct (94545-2423)
PHONE...................................510 294-0220
EMP: 100 EST: 2012
SALES (est): 8.23MM Privately Held
Web: www.bayareaconcreterecycling.com
SIC: 4953 1771 Recycling, waste materials; Concrete work

(P-4863)
BAY COUNTIES WASTE SVCS INC
Also Called: Specialty Solid Waste & Recycl
3355 Thomas Rd (95054-2060)
PHONE...................................408 565-9900
Robert J Molinaro, CEO
William Dobert, *
Jerry Nabhan, *
Douglas Button, *
▲ EMP: 80 EST: 1930
SQ FT: 2,000
SALES (est): 18.58MM Privately Held
Web: www.sswr.com
SIC: 4953 Recycling, waste materials

(P-4864)
BEST WAY DISPOSAL CO INC
Also Called: Advance Disposal Company
17105 Mesa St (92345-5155)
P.O. Box 400997 (92340-0997)
PHONE...................................760 244-9773
Robert Bath, Ch Bd
Sheila Bath, *
EMP: 103 EST: 1965
SALES (est): 12.66MM Privately Held
Web: www.advancedisposal.com
SIC: 4953 Garbage: collecting, destroying, and processing

(P-4865)
BFI WASTE SYSTEMS N AMER INC
Also Called: Site 916
42600 Boyce Rd (94538-3131)
P.O. Box 5013 (94537-5013)
PHONE...................................510 657-1350
Fred Penning, Mgr
EMP: 88
SALES (corp-wide): 13.51B Publicly Held
SIC: 4953 4212 Refuse collection and disposal services; Local trucking, without storage
HQ: Bfi Waste Systems Of North America, Inc.
2394 E Camelback Rd
Phoenix AZ

(P-4866)
BFI WASTE SYSTEMS N AMER INC

4953 - Refuse Systems (P-4885)

Also Called: Republic Services
271 Rianda St (93901-3725)
PHONE..............................831 775-3850
Doug Kenyon, *Mgr*
EMP: 68
SALES (corp-wide): 13.51B **Publicly Held**
SIC: **4953** Garbage: collecting, destroying, and processing
HQ: Bfi Waste Systems Of North America, Inc.
2394 E Camelback Rd
Phoenix AZ

(P-4867)
BFI WASTE SYSTEMS N AMER INC
Also Called: Site 906
9200 Glenoaks Blvd (91352-2613)
PHONE..............................323 321-1722
Doug Moore, *Mgr*
EMP: 64
SALES (corp-wide): 13.51B **Publicly Held**
SIC: **4953** Garbage: collecting, destroying, and processing
HQ: Bfi Waste Systems Of North America, Inc.
2394 E Camelback Rd
Phoenix AZ

(P-4868)
BROWNING-FERRIS INDS CAL INC
Also Called: Site 211
951 Waterbird Way (94553-1469)
PHONE..............................925 313-8901
Oscar Vase, *Mgr*
EMP: 84
SQ FT: 60,000
SALES (corp-wide): 13.51B **Publicly Held**
SIC: **4953** Refuse systems
HQ: Browning-Ferris Industries Of California, Inc.
9200 Glenoaks Blvd
Sun Valley CA
818 790-5410

(P-4869)
BROWNING-FERRIS INDS CAL INC
Also Called: Site L71
12310 San Mateo Rd (94019-7112)
PHONE..............................650 726-1819
Jim Gunderson, *Mgr*
EMP: 191
SALES (corp-wide): 13.51B **Publicly Held**
SIC: **4953** Sanitary landfill operation
HQ: Browning-Ferris Industries Of California, Inc.
9200 Glenoaks Blvd
Sun Valley CA
818 790-5410

(P-4870)
BURRTEC WASTE INDUSTRIES INC (HQ)
Also Called: Burrtec
9890 Cherry Ave (92335-5202)
PHONE..............................909 429-4200
Cole Burr, *Pr*
▲ EMP: 150 EST: 1978
SQ FT: 10,000
SALES (est): 307.49MM
SALES (corp-wide): 320.11MM **Privately Held**
Web: www.burrtec.com
SIC: **4953** 4212 Rubbish collection and disposal; Local trucking, without storage
PA: Burrtec Waste Group, Inc.
9890 Cherry Ave
Fontana CA
909 429-4200

(P-4871)
BURRTEC WASTE INDUSTRIES INC
Also Called: Jack's Disposal Inc
5455 Industrial Pkwy (92407-1803)
PHONE..............................909 889-1969
Cole Burr, *Pr*
James Avakian, *
Jack Avakian Junior, *Sec*
Joseph Avakian, *
EMP: 215 EST: 1951
SQ FT: 500
SALES (est): 3.38MM
SALES (corp-wide): 3.38MM **Privately Held**
Web: www.burrtec.com
SIC: **4953** Rubbish collection and disposal
PA: Burr Group, Inc.
9890 Cherry Ave
Fontana CA
909 429-4200

(P-4872)
CALIFORNIA MARINE CLEANING INC (PA)
2049 Main St (92113-2216)
P.O. Box 13653 (92170-3653)
PHONE..............................619 231-8788
Matthew R Carr, *Pr*
Hazel Carr, *
EMP: 110 EST: 1985
SQ FT: 10,000
SALES (est): 41.23MM
SALES (corp-wide): 41.23MM **Privately Held**
Web: www.marinecleaning.com
SIC: **4953** Hazardous waste collection and disposal

(P-4873)
CALIFORNIA WASTE SERVICES LLC
621 W 152nd St (90247-2732)
PHONE..............................310 538-5998
Eric Casper, *Pr*
EMP: 120 EST: 1999
SQ FT: 20,000
SALES (est): 24.33MM **Privately Held**
Web: www.californiawasteservices.com
SIC: **4953** Refuse collection and disposal services

(P-4874)
CALIFORNIA WASTE SOLUTIONS INC (PA)
1005 Timothy Dr (95133-1043)
PHONE..............................408 292-0830
David Duong, *CEO*
Victor Duong, *
Kristina Duong, *
Tina Aguilar Ctrl, *Prin*
Linda Duong, *
◆ EMP: 75 EST: 1992
SQ FT: 120,000
SALES (est): 34.93MM **Privately Held**
Web: www.calwaste.com
SIC: **4953** Recycling, waste materials

(P-4875)
CALMET INC (PA)
Also Called: Metropolitan Waste Disposal
7202 Petterson Ln (90723-2022)
PHONE..............................323 721-8120
Thomas K Blackman, *Pr*
William Kalpakoff, *VP*
Kris Kazarian, *Sec*
Gary Kazarian, *Treas*
EMP: 180 EST: 1953
SQ FT: 38,000
SALES (est): 14.63MM
SALES (corp-wide): 14.63MM **Privately Held**
Web: www.calmet.com
SIC: **4953** 4212 Rubbish collection and disposal; Local trucking, without storage

(P-4876)
CEDARWOOD-YOUNG COMPANY (PA)
Also Called: Allan Company
14620 Joanbridge St (91706-1750)
PHONE..............................626 962-4047
Jason Young, *Pr*
Stephen Young, *Ch*
Michael Ochniak, *CFO*
Richard Hubbard, *VP Opers*
Don Rogers, *VP Mktg*
◆ EMP: 175 EST: 1963
SQ FT: 4,350
SALES (est): 252.16MM
SALES (corp-wide): 252.16MM **Privately Held**
Web: www.allancompany.com
SIC: **4953** Recycling, waste materials

(P-4877)
CHEMICAL WASTE MANAGEMENT INC
Also Called: Waste Management
35251 Old Skyline Rd (93239-4534)
P.O. Box 471 (93239-0471)
PHONE..............................559 386-9711
Robert Henry, *Mgr*
EMP: 122
SQ FT: 5,000
SALES (corp-wide): 19.7B **Publicly Held**
SIC: **4953** Nonhazardous waste disposal sites
HQ: Chemical Waste Management, Inc.
1001 Fannin St Ste 4000
Houston TX
713 512-6200

(P-4878)
CITY OF SACRAMENTO
Also Called: Department of Public Works
2812 Meadowview Rd (95832-1441)
PHONE..............................916 808-4949
Terrance Davis, *Mgr*
EMP: 116
Web: www.cityofsacramento.gov
SIC: **4953** 4212 9511 Rubbish collection and disposal; Garbage collection and transport, no disposal; Air, water, and solid waste management, local government
PA: City Of Sacramento
915 I St Fl 5
Sacramento CA
916 808-5300

(P-4879)
CIVICORPS
6315 San Leandro St (94621-3727)
PHONE..............................510 992-7800
Bill Zenoni, *Brnch Mgr*
EMP: 144
Web: www.cvcorps.org
SIC: **4953** Recycling, waste materials
PA: Civicorps
101 Myrtle St
Oakland CA

(P-4880)
COUNTY OF YOLO
Also Called: County Landfill
44090 County Road 28h (95776-9101)
P.O. Box 292 (95776-0292)
PHONE..............................530 666-8729
Wendy Nelson, *Brnch Mgr*
EMP: 87
SALES (corp-wide): 456.57MM **Privately Held**
Web: www.yolocounty.org
SIC: **4953** 9511 Rubbish collection and disposal; Air, water, and solid waste management
PA: County Of Yolo
625 Court St Ste 102
Woodland CA
530 666-8190

(P-4881)
COVANTA LONG BCH RNWBLE ENRGY
118 Pier S Ave (90802-1039)
PHONE..............................562 436-0636
▲ EMP: 126 EST: 2013
SALES (est): 9.81MM
SALES (corp-wide): 1.91B **Privately Held**
SIC: **4953** Recycling, waste materials
HQ: Covanta Energy, Llc
445 South St
Morristown NJ
862 345-5000

(P-4882)
CR&R INCORPORATED
Also Called: Perris Disposal Company
1706 Goetz Rd (92570-6274)
P.O. Box 1208 (92572-1208)
PHONE..............................951 634-8079
TOLL FREE: 800
Ed Campos, *Brnch Mgr*
EMP: 73
SALES (corp-wide): 335.28MM **Privately Held**
Web: www.crrwasteservices.com
SIC: **4953** Recycling, waste materials
PA: Cr&R Incorporated
11292 Western Ave
Stanton CA
714 826-9049

(P-4883)
DOWNTOWN DIVERSION INC
Also Called: Waste Management
2424 E Olympic Blvd (90021-2902)
PHONE..............................213 612-5005
Luis Flores, *Brnch Mgr*
EMP: 60
SALES (corp-wide): 6.44MM **Privately Held**
SIC: **4953** Recycling, waste materials
PA: Downtown Diversion Inc.
9081 Tujunga Ave
Sun Valley CA
818 252-0019

(P-4884)
E J HARRISON & SONS INC
Also Called: Harrison, E J & Sons Recycling
1589 Lirio Ave (93004-3227)
PHONE..............................805 647-1414
TOLL FREE: 800
Ken Keys, *Genl Mgr*
EMP: 173
SALES (corp-wide): 24.61MM **Privately Held**
Web: www.ejharrison.com
SIC: **4953** 2611 Rubbish collection and disposal; Pulp mills
PA: E. J. Harrison & Sons, Inc.
5275 Colt St
Ventura CA
805 647-1414

(P-4885)
EARTH TECHNOLOGY CORP USA

4953 - Refuse Systems (P-4886)

300 S Grand Ave Ste 900 (90071-3135)
PHONE..................213 593-8000
Keenan Driscoll, *Pr*
EMP: 74 **EST:** 1987
SALES (est): 4.87MM
SALES (corp-wide): 13.15B **Publicly Held**
SIC: 4953 8748 8742 8711 Refuse systems; Environmental consultant; Management consulting services; Engineering services
PA: Aecom
13355 Noel Rd Ste 400
Dallas TX
972 788-1000

(P-4886)
EAST BAY MUNICIPL UTILTY DISTR
Also Called: Ebmud
2020 Wake Ave (94607-5100)
PHONE..................866 403-2683
Alexander Coate, *Genl Mgr*
EMP: 124
SALES (corp-wide): 769.52MM **Privately Held**
Web: www.ebmud.com
SIC: 4953 9511 Sewage treatment facility; Air, water, and solid waste management, local government
PA: East Bay Municipal Utility District, Water System
375 11th St
Oakland CA
866 403-2683

(P-4887)
ECOLOGY RECYCLING SERVICES LLC
785 E M St (92324-3911)
PHONE..................909 370-1318
EMP: 168
SALES (corp-wide): 12.79B **Publicly Held**
SIC: 4953 Recycling, waste materials
HQ: Ecology Recycling Services, Llc
16700 Valley View Ave # 340
La Mirada CA
562 921-9975

(P-4888)
ECS REFINING INC
2222 S Sinclair Ave (95215-7551)
PHONE..................209 774-5000
EMP: 250
SIC: 4953 Recycling, waste materials

(P-4889)
ECULLET INC
1 Vintage Ct (94062-2560)
PHONE..................650 493-7300
Craig J London, *CEO*
Farook Afsari, *
Mark D Muenchow, *
EMP: 100 **EST:** 1999
SALES (est): 11.18MM **Privately Held**
Web: www.ecullet.com
SIC: 4953 Recycling, waste materials

(P-4890)
EDCO DISPOSAL CORPORATION (PA)
Also Called: La Mesa Disposal
2755 California Ave (90755-3304)
PHONE..................619 287-7555
Steve South, *CEO*
Edward Burr, *
Sandra Burr, *
EMP: 250 **EST:** 1967
SQ FT: 8,000
SALES (est): 134.33MM
SALES (corp-wide): 134.33MM **Privately Held**
Web: www.edcodisposal.com
SIC: 4953 Rubbish collection and disposal

(P-4891)
ELECTRNIC RCYCLERS INTL - IND
Also Called: Electronic Recyclers
7815 N Palm Ave Ste 140 (93711-5531)
PHONE..................317 522-1414
John S Shegerian, *Pr*
Linda L Ramos, *
Tammy L Shegerian, *
▼ **EMP:** 99 **EST:** 2008
SALES (est): 19.28MM **Privately Held**
Web: www.eridirect.com
SIC: 4953 Recycling, waste materials
PA: Electronic Recyclers International Inc.
7815 N Palm Ave Ste 140
Fresno CA

(P-4892)
ELECTRONIC RECYCLERS INTL INC (PA)
Also Called: Eri
7815 N Palm Ave Ste 140 (93711-5531)
PHONE..................559 442-3960
John S Shegerian, *CEO*
Tammy Shegerian, *
▲ **EMP:** 157 **EST:** 2006
SQ FT: 75,000
SALES (est): 499.9MM **Privately Held**
Web: www.eridirect.com
SIC: 4953 Recycling, waste materials

(P-4893)
EVERGREEN ENVMTL SVCS INC
6880 Smith Ave (94560-4224)
PHONE..................510 795-4400
Gary Colbert, *Pr*
EMP: 179 **EST:** 1977
SQ FT: 10,000
SALES (est): 780.97K
SALES (corp-wide): 10.57MM **Privately Held**
SIC: 4953 Liquid waste, collection and disposal
PA: Evergreen Holdings Inc.
18952 Macarthur Blvd # 410
Irvine CA
949 757-7770

(P-4894)
FIBRES INTERNATIONAL INC
Also Called: Fibres Internation Recycling
88 Rowland Way Ste 300 (94945-5000)
PHONE..................425 455-9811
Tony Rounds, *Genl Mgr*
EMP: 75
SIC: 4953 4212 3341 3231 Refuse collection and disposal services; Local trucking, without storage; Secondary nonferrous metals; Products of purchased glass
PA: Fibres International, Inc.
88 Rowland Way Ste 300
Novato CA

(P-4895)
FLAT WHITE ECONOMY INV USA LLC
5151 California Ave Ste 100 (92626)
PHONE..................949 344-5013
EMP: 165 **EST:** 2016
SALES (est): 1MM **Privately Held**
SIC: 4953 Recycling, waste materials

(P-4896)
FORWARD INC
Also Called: Site 204
9999 S Austin Rd (95336-8924)
PHONE..................209 982-4298
Ruben Ramirez, *Mgr*
EMP: 110
SALES (corp-wide): 13.51B **Publicly Held**
Web: www.goforward.com
SIC: 4953 Sanitary landfill operation
HQ: Forward, Inc.
1145 W Charter Way
Stockton CA
209 466-4482

(P-4897)
GILTON SOLID WASTE MGT INC
755 S Yosemite Ave (95361-4039)
PHONE..................209 527-3781
Richard Gilton, *Pr*
Tedford Gilton, *
Karen Gilton Hardister, *
Donna Gilton Love, *
EMP: 136 **EST:** 1961
SQ FT: 3,000
SALES (est): 27.45MM **Privately Held**
Web: www.gilton.com
SIC: 4953 Recycling, waste materials

(P-4898)
HAZMAT TSDF INC (PA)
180 W Monte Ave (92376)
PHONE..................909 873-4141
Jon L Bennett Junior, *Pr*
Jim Arnold, *
Dianna Vepeda, *
Jim Goyich, *
▲ **EMP:** 63 **EST:** 1988
SQ FT: 33,000
SALES (est): 19.15MM
SALES (corp-wide): 19.15MM **Privately Held**
Web: www.usahazmat.com
SIC: 4953 Hazardous waste collection and disposal

(P-4899)
IMS ELECTRONICS RECYCLING INC
Also Called: I M S Electonics Recycling
12455 Kerran St Ste 300 (92064-8834)
PHONE..................858 679-1555
▼ **EMP:** 102
SIC: 4953 Recycling, waste materials

(P-4900)
IMS RECYCLING SERVICES INC (PA)
Also Called: IMS Recycling Services
2697 Main St (92113-3612)
P.O. Box 13666 (92170-3666)
PHONE..................619 231-2521
Robert M Davis, *CEO*
Ruth Davis, *
Theodora Davis Inman, *
Deborah Odle, *
▼ **EMP:** 70 **EST:** 1954
SQ FT: 25,000
SALES (est): 113.06MM
SALES (corp-wide): 113.06MM **Privately Held**
Web: www.cpmfg.com
SIC: 4953 Recycling, waste materials

(P-4901)
JOES SWEEPING INC
Also Called: Nationwide Environmental Svcs
11914 Front St (90650-2911)
PHONE..................562 929-4344
Never Samuelian, *Pr*
Joe Samuelian, *
Ani Samuelian, *
EMP: 65 **EST:** 1989
SQ FT: 10,500
SALES (est): 32.71MM **Privately Held**
Web: www.nes-sweeping.com
SIC: 4953 Street refuse systems

(P-4902)
KELLER CANYON LANDFILL COMPANY
Also Called: Site 212
901 Bailey Rd (94565-4309)
PHONE..................925 458-9800
Jeff D Andrews, *CEO*
Norm Christiansen, *
EMP: 237 **EST:** 1992
SQ FT: 50,000
SALES (est): 4.99MM
SALES (corp-wide): 13.51B **Publicly Held**
SIC: 4953 Sanitary landfill operation
HQ: Browning-Ferris Industries Of California, Inc.
9200 Glenoaks Blvd
Sun Valley CA
818 790-5410

(P-4903)
KOCHERGEN FARMS COMPOSTING
Also Called: KOCHERGEN FARMS COMPOSTING INC
2365 E North Ave (93725-2615)
P.O. Box 11006 (93771-1006)
PHONE..................559 266-2650
Mike Kochergen, *Pr*
EMP: 62
Web: www.greenvalleyrecycling.com
SIC: 4953 Recycling, waste materials
PA: Kochergen Farms Composting, Inc.
523 N Brawley Ave Ste B
Fresno CA

(P-4904)
LOONEY BINS INC (HQ)
12153 Montague St (91331-2210)
PHONE..................818 485-8200
Myan Spaccarelli, *Pr*
Phyllis Shukiar, *
Jerry Lucera, *
EMP: 70 **EST:** 1995
SQ FT: 1,000
SALES (est): 29.21MM
SALES (corp-wide): 19.7B **Publicly Held**
SIC: 4953 Garbage: collecting, destroying, and processing
PA: Waste Management, Inc.
800 Capitol St Ste 3000
Houston TX
713 512-6200

(P-4905)
MADERA DISPOSAL SYSTEMS INC (DH)
Also Called: M D S I
21739 Road 19 (93610-8218)
P.O. Box 12227 (93777-2227)
PHONE..................559 665-3099
TOLL FREE: 800
Ron Mittelstaedt, *Pr*
EMP: 85 **EST:** 1965
SQ FT: 1,200
SALES (est): 24.55MM
SALES (corp-wide): 7.21B **Privately Held**
SIC: 4953 4212 Street refuse systems; Local trucking, without storage
HQ: Waste Connections Us, Inc.
3 Waterway Square Pl # 110
The Woodlands TX

(P-4906)
MAIN STREET FIBERS INC
608 E Main St (91761-1711)

PRODUCTS & SERVICES SECTION
4953 - Refuse Systems (P-4927)

P.O. Box 51491 (91761-0091)
PHONE.................................909 986-6310
Gregory S Young, *CEO*
Wayne Young, *
Steve Young, *
EMP: 60 **EST:** 1984
SQ FT: 25,000
SALES (est): 15.56MM **Privately Held**
Web: www.mainstreetfibers.com
SIC: 4953 Recycling, waste materials

(P-4907)
MARBORG INDUSTRIES (PA)
728 E Yanonali St (93103-3233)
P.O. Box 4127 (93140-4127)
PHONE.................................805 963-1852
Mario Borgatello Junior, *Pr*
David Borgatello, *
EMP: 250 **EST:** 1974
SALES (est): 52.32MM
SALES (corp-wide): 52.32MM **Privately Held**
Web: www.marborg.com
SIC: 4953 7359 7699 4212 Rubbish collection and disposal; Portable toilet rental; Septic tank cleaning service; Local trucking, without storage

(P-4908)
MARBORG RECOVERY LP
14470 Calle Real (93117-9732)
PHONE.................................805 963-1852
Brian Borgatello, *Pt*
EMP: 250 **EST:** 2016
SALES (est): 51.57MM
SALES (corp-wide): 52.32MM **Privately Held**
Web: www.marborg.com
SIC: 4953 Recycling, waste materials
PA: Marborg Industries
    728 E Yanonali St
    Santa Barbara CA
    805 963-1852

(P-4909)
MARIN SANITARY SERVICE (PA)
Also Called: Marin Resource Recovery Center
1050 Andersen Dr (94901-5316)
P.O. Box 10067 (94912-0067)
PHONE.................................415 456-2601
Patricia Garbarino, *CEO*
EMP: 85 **EST:** 1948
SALES (est): 57.2MM
SALES (corp-wide): 57.2MM **Privately Held**
Web: www.marinsanitaryservice.com
SIC: 4953 5099 4212 Garbage: collecting, destroying, and processing; Wood chips; Local trucking, without storage

(P-4910)
MARIN SANITARY SERVICE
565 Jacoby St (94901-5305)
PHONE.................................415 485-5646
Ruben Valtierra, *Brnch Mgr*
EMP: 60
SALES (corp-wide): 57.2MM **Privately Held**
Web: www.marinsanitaryservice.com
SIC: 4953 Recycling, waste materials
PA: Marin Sanitary Service
    1050 Andersen Dr
    San Rafael CA
    415 456-2601

(P-4911)
MBA POLYMERS INC
500 W Ohio Ave (94804-2040)
PHONE.................................510 231-9031
▲ **EMP:** 90

Web: www.mbapolymers.com
SIC: 4953 Recycling, waste materials

(P-4912)
MONTEREY RGIONAL WASTE MGT DST
14201 Del Monte Blvd (93933)
P.O. Box 1670 (93933-1670)
PHONE.................................831 384-5313
William Merry, *Pr*
Charles Rees, *
Leo Laska, *
EMP: 120 **EST:** 1951
SQ FT: 5,500
SALES (est): 45.66MM **Privately Held**
Web: www.regenmonterey.org
SIC: 4953 4911 4931 Sanitary landfill operation; Generation, electric power; Electric and other services combined

(P-4913)
MP ENVIRONMENTAL SVCS INC (PA)
3400 Manor St (93308-1451)
P.O. Box 80358 (93380-0358)
PHONE.................................800 458-3036
Dawn Calderwood, *Pr*
▲ **EMP:** 117 **EST:** 1991
SQ FT: 8,000
SALES (est): 92.88MM **Privately Held**
Web: www.mpenviro.com
SIC: 4953 4213 8748 7699 Hazardous waste collection and disposal; Trucking, except local; Environmental consultant; Tank repair and cleaning services

(P-4914)
NORCAL WASTE SERVICES INC
3514 Emery St (90023-3908)
PHONE.................................626 357-8666
John Harabedian, *Genl Mgr*
EMP: 100 **EST:** 1982
SQ FT: 1,000
SALES (est): 6.11MM **Privately Held**
SIC: 4953 Rubbish collection and disposal

(P-4915)
NORTECH WASTE LLC
Also Called: Nortech
219 Reward St (95959-2913)
P.O. Box 1748 (95648-1445)
PHONE.................................916 645-5230
Paul Szura, *Managing Member*
Jerry Jackson, *Managing Member*
Arthur A Daniels, *
Donald M Moriel, *
Michael J Sangiacomo, *
EMP: 120 **EST:** 1992
SALES (est): 22.88MM **Privately Held**
Web: www.nortechwaste.com
SIC: 4953 3341 3312 3231 Sanitary landfill operation; Secondary nonferrous metals; Blast furnaces and steel mills; Products of purchased glass

(P-4916)
ORANGE COUNTY SANITATION (PA)
10844 Ellis Ave (92708-7018)
P.O. Box 8127 (92728-8127)
PHONE.................................714 962-2411
James Herberg, *Genl Mgr*
James Ruth, *
▲ **EMP:** 300 **EST:** 1954
SALES (est): 315.43MM
SALES (corp-wide): 315.43MM **Privately Held**
Web: www.ocsan.gov
SIC: 4953 Waste materials, disposal at sea

(P-4917)
PALM SPRINGS DISPOSAL SERVICES
4690 E Mesquite Ave (92264-3510)
P.O. Box 2711 (92263-2711)
PHONE.................................760 327-1351
Frederic Wade, *CEO*
James Cunningham, *
Ray Wade, *
Mike Jaycox, *
EMP: 82 **EST:** 1972
SQ FT: 2,000
SALES (est): 14.08MM **Privately Held**
Web: www.palmspringsdisposal.com
SIC: 4953 Recycling, waste materials

(P-4918)
PAVEMENT COATINGS CO
Also Called: Pavement Coatings Co
736 Mission Rock Rd (93060-9762)
PHONE.................................805 647-0693
EMP: 233
SALES (corp-wide): 53.85MM **Privately Held**
Web: www.pavementrecycling.com
SIC: 4953 Recycling, waste materials
PA: Pavement Coatings Co.
    10240 San Sevaine Way
    Jurupa Valley CA
    714 826-3011

(P-4919)
PENAS DISPOSAL INC
Also Called: Pena's Recycling Center
12094 Avenue 408 (93615-2055)
PHONE.................................559 528-3909
Gabriel Pena, *Pr*
Arthur Pena, *
Maria Pena, *
EMP: 91 **EST:** 1968
SQ FT: 1,000
SALES (est): 17.81MM **Privately Held**
Web: www.penasdisposal.com
SIC: 4953 Recycling, waste materials

(P-4920)
PJBS HOLDINGS INC (PA)
Also Called: Benz - One Complete Operation
1401 Goodrick Dr (93561-1532)
P.O. Box 1750 (93581-1750)
PHONE.................................661 822-5273
Paul Benz, *CEO*
Louis Visco, *
Joan Benz, *
EMP: 75 **EST:** 1975
SQ FT: 4,500
SALES (est): 23.34MM
SALES (corp-wide): 23.34MM **Privately Held**
Web: www.benz.blue
SIC: 4953 4212 Refuse collection and disposal services; Petroleum haulage, local

(P-4921)
POTENTIAL INDUSTRIES INC (PA)
720 East E St (90744-6014)
P.O. Box 293 (90748-0293)
PHONE.................................310 549-5901
Anthony J Fan, *Pr*
Phillip C Chen, *Vice Chairman*
Daniel J Domonoske, *
Henry J Chen, *
Jessie Chen, *
◆ **EMP:** 149 **EST:** 1975
SQ FT: 45,000
SALES (est): 42.15MM
SALES (corp-wide): 42.15MM **Privately Held**
Web: www.potentialindustries.com

SIC: 4953 5093 Recycling, waste materials; Scrap and waste materials

(P-4922)
R PLANET EARTH LLC
3200 Fruitland Ave (90058-3718)
PHONE.................................213 320-0601
EMP: 135 **EST:** 2013
SALES (est): 11.7MM **Privately Held**
Web: www.rplanetearth.com
SIC: 4953 2611 Recycling, waste materials; Pulp mills, mechanical and recycling processing

(P-4923)
RAINBOW DISPOSAL CO INC (HQ)
Also Called: Rainbow Refuse Recycling
17121 Nichols Ln (92647-5719)
P.O. Box 1026 (92647-1026)
PHONE.................................714 847-3581
Jerry Moffatt, *CEO*
Stan Tkaczyck, *
EMP: 115 **EST:** 1956
SQ FT: 6,000
SALES (est): 48.28MM
SALES (corp-wide): 13.51B **Publicly Held**
SIC: 4953 Garbage: collecting, destroying, and processing
PA: Republic Services, Inc.
    18500 N Allied Way # 100
    Phoenix AZ
    480 627-2700

(P-4924)
RECOLOGY INC (PA)
Also Called: Recology
50 California St Ste 2400 (94111-4796)
PHONE.................................415 875-1000
Sal Coniglio, *CEO*
Dennis Wu, *
Mark R Lomele, *
George P Mcgrath, *COO*
EMP: 60 **EST:** 1988
SQ FT: 25,000
SALES (est): 1.41B
SALES (corp-wide): 1.41B **Privately Held**
Web: www.recology.com
SIC: 4953 Garbage: collecting, destroying, and processing

(P-4925)
RECOLOGY INC
245 N 1st St (95620-3027)
PHONE.................................916 379-3300
EMP: 63
SALES (corp-wide): 1.41B **Privately Held**
Web: www.recology.com
SIC: 4953 Recycling, waste materials
PA: Recology Inc.
    50 California St Ste 2400
    San Francisco CA
    415 875-1000

(P-4926)
RECOLOGY LOS ANGELES
Also Called: Recology
9189 De Garmo Ave (91352-2609)
PHONE.................................818 767-0675
EMP: 400 **EST:** 2006
SALES (est): 22.28MM **Privately Held**
SIC: 4953 Garbage: collecting, destroying, and processing

(P-4927)
RECOLOGY SONOMA MARIN
3400 Standish Ave (95407-8112)
PHONE.................................707 586-8261
Fred Stemmler, *Genl Mgr*
EMP: 450 **EST:** 2017

4953 - Refuse Systems (P-4928)

SALES (est): 92.2MM
SALES (corp-wide): 1.41B Privately Held
Web: www.recology.com
SIC: 4953 Recycling, waste materials
PA: Recology Inc.
  50 California St Ste 2400
  San Francisco CA
  415 875-1000

(P-4928)
RECOLOGY SOUTH VALLEY (HQ)
1351 Pacheco Pass Hwy (95020-9579)
PHONE..............................408 842-3358
Robert Coyle, *Pr*
Mike Sanjiacomo, *
EMP: 65 **EST:** 1949
SQ FT: 6,000
SALES (est): 20.76MM
SALES (corp-wide): 1.41B Privately Held
Web: www.recology.com
SIC: 4953 Sanitary landfill operation
PA: Recology Inc.
  50 California St Ste 2400
  San Francisco CA
  415 875-1000

(P-4929)
RECOLOGY YUBA-SUTTER
300 4th St (95901-5908)
P.O. Box G (95901-0062)
PHONE..............................530 743-6933
Robert Coyle, *Ex VP*
EMP: 90 **EST:** 1974
SALES (est): 24.41MM
SALES (corp-wide): 1.41B Privately Held
Web: www.recology.com
SIC: 4953 4212 Garbage: collecting, destroying, and processing; Hazardous waste transport
PA: Recology Inc.
  50 California St Ste 2400
  San Francisco CA
  415 875-1000

(P-4930)
RECYCLER CORE COMPANY INC
Also Called: Northwest Recycler Core
2727 Kansas Ave (92507-2638)
PHONE..............................951 276-1687
Kenneth Meier, *Pr*
Gisela Meier, *
Ruth Harris, *
▲ **EMP:** 100 **EST:** 1984
SQ FT: 280,000
SALES (est): 16.01MM Privately Held
Web: www.rccauto.com
SIC: 4953 Recycling, waste materials

(P-4931)
RECYCLING INDUSTRIES INC
4741 Watt Ave (95660-5526)
PHONE..............................916 452-3961
Scott Kuhnen, *Pr*
David Kuhnen, *
EMP: 75 **EST:** 1981
SQ FT: 155,000
SALES (est): 8.74MM Privately Held
Web: www.recyclingindustries.com
SIC: 4953 Recycling, waste materials

(P-4932)
REDWOOD LANDFILL INC
8950 Redwood Hwy (94945-1435)
P.O. Box 793 (94948-0793)
PHONE..............................415 892-2851
Ramin Khany, *Mgr*
Jessica K Jones, *
Barry Skolnick, *

EMP: 105 **EST:** 1958
SALES (est): 38.34MM
SALES (corp-wide): 19.7B Publicly Held
Web: redwoodlandfill.wm.com
SIC: 4953 Sanitary landfill operation
PA: Waste Management, Inc.
  800 Capitol St Ste 3000
  Houston TX
  713 512-6200

(P-4933)
SA RECYCLING LLC (PA)
Also Called: SA Recycling
2411 N Glassell St (92865-2717)
PHONE..............................714 632-2000
George Adams, *CEO*
George Adams, *Managing Member*
Mark Sweetman, *
◆ **EMP:** 160 **EST:** 2007
SQ FT: 40,000
SALES (est): 742.73MM Privately Held
Web: www.sarecycling.com
SIC: 4953 Recycling, waste materials

(P-4934)
SANITEC INDUSTRIES INC
10700 Sherman Way (91505-1042)
PHONE..............................818 523-1942
James Harkess, *Pr*
▲ **EMP:** 75 **EST:** 2003
SQ FT: 200,000
SALES (est): 8.38MM Privately Held
Web: www.sanitecind.com
SIC: 4953 5047 Medical waste disposal; Medical and hospital equipment

(P-4935)
SANITTION DSTRCTS LOS ANGLES C
1955 Workman Mill Rd (90601-1415)
P.O. Box 4998 (90607-4998)
PHONE..............................562 908-4288
Steve Mcguin, *Mgr*
Grace Robinson Chan, *Genl Mgr*
EMP: 1698 **EST:** 2007
SALES (est): 467.68MM
SALES (corp-wide): 726.8MM Privately Held
Web: www.lacsd.org
SIC: 4953 Sanitary landfill operation
PA: Los Angeles County Sanitation Districts
  1955 Workman Mill Rd
  Whittier CA
  562 699-7411

(P-4936)
SILICON PROCESSING AND TRADING INC
Also Called: SRS
322 N Aviador St (93010-8302)
PHONE..............................805 388-8683
▲ **EMP:** 72
SIC: 4953 Recycling, waste materials

(P-4937)
SOLAG INCORPORATED
Also Called: Solag Disposal Co
31641 Ortega Hwy (92675)
PHONE..............................949 728-1206
Clifford Ronnenberg, *Ch Bd*
Patricia Leyes, *
EMP: 572 **EST:** 1958
SALES (est): 1.73MM
SALES (corp-wide): 335.28MM Privately Held
SIC: 4953 4212 Rubbish collection and disposal; Local trucking, without storage
PA: Cr&R Incorporated
  11292 Western Ave
  Stanton CA
  714 826-9049

(P-4938)
SOUTH SAN FRNCSCO SCVENGER INC
500 E Jamie Ct (94080-6222)
P.O. Box 348 (94083-0348)
PHONE..............................650 589-4020
Doug Button, *Pr*
Daniel Bertoldi Junior, *VP*
Michael Achiro, *
Ron Fornesi, *
Vince Fornesi, *
EMP: 71 **EST:** 1907
SQ FT: 10,000
SALES (est): 17.8MM Privately Held
Web: www.ssfscavenger.com
SIC: 4953 Garbage: collecting, destroying, and processing

(P-4939)
SOUTH TAHOE REFUSE CO
Also Called: Sierra Disposal Service
2140 Ruth Ave (96150-4330)
PHONE..............................530 541-5105
Jeffrey Tillman, *Pr*
John De Marchini, *
John Tillman, *
Gloria Lehman, *
EMP: 100 **EST:** 1962
SQ FT: 5,000
SALES (est): 17.22MM Privately Held
Web: www.southtahoerefuse.com
SIC: 4953 Garbage: collecting, destroying, and processing

(P-4940)
STAR SCRAP METAL COMPANY INC
1509 S Bluff Rd (90640-6601)
PHONE..............................562 921-5045
Rose Starow Stein, *Pr*
Allen Stein, *
▼ **EMP:** 70 **EST:** 1974
SQ FT: 600
SALES (est): 12.33MM Privately Held
Web: www.sarecycling.com
SIC: 4953 Recycling, waste materials

(P-4941)
STRATEGIC MATERIALS INC
Also Called: Strategic Materials
7000 Bandini Blvd (90040-3303)
PHONE..............................323 887-6831
EMP: 65
SALES (corp-wide): 2.19B Privately Held
Web: www.smi.com
SIC: 4953 Recycling, waste materials
HQ: Strategic Materials, Inc.
  17220 Katy Fwy Ste 150
  Houston TX

(P-4942)
SUNSET SCAVENGER COMPANY
Also Called: Recology Sunset Scavenger
250 Executive Park Blvd Ste 2100 (94134-3306)
PHONE..............................415 330-1300
Archie Humphrey, *COO*
Gary Kirk, *Admn*
EMP: 420 **EST:** 1920
SQ FT: 3,800
SALES (est): 51.87MM
SALES (corp-wide): 1.41B Privately Held
Web: www.recology.com
SIC: 4953 Recycling, waste materials
PA: Recology Inc.
  50 California St Ste 2400
  San Francisco CA
  415 875-1000

(P-4943)
TAHOE TRUCKEE DISPOSAL CO INC
Also Called: Eastern Rgnal Lndfll Mtl Rcve
900 Cabin Creek Rd (96161)
PHONE..............................530 583-7825
EMP: 63
SALES (corp-wide): 18.57MM Privately Held
Web: www.skydivetruckeetahoe.com
SIC: 4953 Garbage: collecting, destroying, and processing
PA: Tahoe Truckee Disposal Co., Inc.
  645 W Lake Blvd Ste 5
  Tahoe City CA
  530 583-7800

(P-4944)
TALCO PLASTICS INC (PA)
1000 W Rincon St (92878-9228)
PHONE..............................951 531-2000
John L Shedd Senior, *Ch*
John L Shedd Junior, *Pr*
Bob Shedd, *
Ron Petty, *
William O'grady, *VP*
EMP: 85 **EST:** 1972
SQ FT: 110,000
SALES (est): 22.23MM
SALES (corp-wide): 22.23MM Privately Held
Web: www.talcoplastics.com
SIC: 4953 2821 Recycling, waste materials; Plastics materials and resins

(P-4945)
TEMARRY RECYCLING INC
476 Tecate Rd (91980)
PHONE..............................619 270-9453
Matt Songer, *CEO*
Teresa Songer, *
EMP: 63 **EST:** 2004
SALES (est): 9.3MM Privately Held
Web: www.triumvirate.com
SIC: 4953 Recycling, waste materials

(P-4946)
TRACY DLTA SOLID WASTE MGT INC
Also Called: Delta Disposal Service Co
30703 S Macarthur Dr (95377-9170)
P.O. Box 274 (95378-0274)
PHONE..............................209 835-0601
Michael Repetto, *Pr*
Carl Repetto, *
Susan Hudson, *
EMP: 61 **EST:** 1951
SQ FT: 1,000
SALES (est): 12.04MM Privately Held
Web: www.tdswm.com
SIC: 4953 Garbage: collecting, destroying, and processing

(P-4947)
UNITED PACIFIC WASTE
4334 San Gabriel River Pkwy (90660-1837)
P.O. Box 2924 (92628-2924)
PHONE..............................562 699-7600
Michael Kandilian, *Pr*
Mike Kandilian, *
Shawna Kandilian, *
EMP: 70 **EST:** 2001
SQ FT: 3,500
SALES (est): 14.13MM Privately Held
Web: www.crrwasteservices.com
SIC: 4953 4213 Garbage: collecting, destroying, and processing; Contract haulers

▲ = Import ▼ = Export ◆ = Import/Export

4953 - Refuse Systems (P-4967)

(P-4948)
USA WASTE OF CALIFORNIA INC
Also Called: Los Angeles City Hauling
9081 Tujunga Ave (91352-1516)
P.O. Box 541 (90078-0541)
PHONE.................818 252-3112
Jim Fish, *CEO*
EMP: 100
SALES (corp-wide): 19.7B **Publicly Held**
SIC: 4953 Recycling, waste materials
HQ: Usa Waste Of California, Inc.
   11931 Foundation Pl # 200
   Gold River CA
   916 387-1400

(P-4949)
VALLEY GARBAGE RUBBISH CO INC
Also Called: Healtth Sanitation Services
1850 W Betteravia Rd (93455-1065)
PHONE.................805 614-1131
Keith Ramsey, *Prin*
EMP: 138 EST: 1957
SQ FT: 3,000
SALES (est): 50.39MM
SALES (corp-wide): 19.7B **Publicly Held**
Web: wmhss.wm.com
SIC: 4953 Garbage: collecting, destroying, and processing
PA: Waste Management, Inc.
   800 Capitol St Ste 3000
   Houston TX
   713 512-6200

(P-4950)
VARNER BROS INC
1808 Roberts Ln (93308-2228)
P.O. Box 80427 (93380-0427)
PHONE.................661 399-2944
Vernon Varner, *Sec*
Elvey L Varner, *
EMP: 124 EST: 1959
SQ FT: 12,000
SALES (est): 13.72MM **Privately Held**
SIC: 4953 Garbage: collecting, destroying, and processing

(P-4951)
WARE DISPOSAL INC
1451 Manhattan Ave (92831-5221)
PHONE.................714 834-0234
Judith Helaine Ware, *CEO*
Ben Ware, *
Jay Ware, *
EMP: 120 EST: 1970
SQ FT: 48,900
SALES (est): 30.3MM **Privately Held**
Web: www.waredisposal.com
SIC: 4953 Refuse collection and disposal services

(P-4952)
WASTE CONNECTIONS CAL INC (DH)
Also Called: Greenteam of San Jose
1333 Oakland Rd (95112-1364)
PHONE.................408 282-4400
Paul Nelson, *District Vice President*
Pual Nelson, *District Vice President**
Ron Mittelstaedt, *
EMP: 150 EST: 1976
SQ FT: 6,000
SALES (est): 38.65MM
SALES (corp-wide): 7.21B **Privately Held**
Web: www.greenteam.com
SIC: 4953 Garbage: collecting, destroying, and processing
HQ: Waste Connections Us, Inc.

3 Waterway Square Pl # 110
The Woodlands TX

(P-4953)
WASTE MANAGEMENT CAL INC (HQ)
Also Called: Waste Management
9081 Tujunga Ave (91352-1516)
PHONE.................877 836-6526
EMP: 230 EST: 1953
SQ FT: 35,000
SALES (est): 439.26MM
SALES (corp-wide): 19.7B **Publicly Held**
SIC: 4953 Garbage: collecting, destroying, and processing
PA: Waste Management, Inc.
   800 Capitol St Ste 3000
   Houston TX
   713 512-6200

(P-4954)
WASTE MANAGEMENT CAL INC
Also Called: Waste Management
2141 Oceanside Blvd (92054-4405)
PHONE.................760 439-2824
John Lusignan, *Mgr*
EMP: 126
SQ FT: 4,500
SALES (corp-wide): 19.7B **Publicly Held**
SIC: 4953 4212 Garbage: collecting, destroying, and processing; Local trucking, without storage
HQ: Waste Management Of California, Inc.
   9081 Tujunga Ave
   Sun Valley CA
   877 836-6526

(P-4955)
WASTE MANAGEMENT CAL INC
Also Called: Waste Management
10910 Dawson Canyon Rd (92883-5020)
PHONE.................951 277-1740
Damon De Frates, *Brnch Mgr*
EMP: 115
SALES (corp-wide): 19.7B **Publicly Held**
SIC: 4953 Garbage: collecting, destroying, and processing
HQ: Waste Management Of California, Inc.
   9081 Tujunga Ave
   Sun Valley CA
   877 836-6526

(P-4956)
WASTE MANAGEMENT CAL INC
Also Called: Waste Management
1200 W City Ranch Rd (93551-4456)
PHONE.................661 947-7197
Carl Mccarthy, *Mgr*
EMP: 126
SALES (corp-wide): 19.7B **Publicly Held**
SIC: 4953 Rubbish collection and disposal
HQ: Waste Management Of California, Inc.
   9081 Tujunga Ave
   Sun Valley CA
   877 836-6526

(P-4957)
WASTE MANAGEMENT CAL INC
Also Called: Waste Management
1001 W Bradley Ave (92020-1501)
PHONE.................619 596-5100
TOLL FREE: 800
Rex Buck, *Prin*
EMP: 160
SQ FT: 2,000
SALES (corp-wide): 19.7B **Publicly Held**
SIC: 4953 Recycling, waste materials
HQ: Waste Management Of California, Inc.
   9081 Tujunga Ave
   Sun Valley CA
   877 836-6526

(P-4958)
WASTE MANAGEMENT CAL INC
Also Called: Waste Management
2801 N Madera Rd (93065-6208)
PHONE.................805 522-7023
Scott Tignac, *Mgr*
EMP: 195
SALES (corp-wide): 19.7B **Publicly Held**
SIC: 4953 Recycling, waste materials
HQ: Waste Management Of California, Inc.
   9081 Tujunga Ave
   Sun Valley CA
   877 836-6526

(P-4959)
WASTE MANAGEMENT CAL INC
Waste Management
910 Coyote Creek Golf Dr (95037)
P.O. Box 1870 (95038-1870)
PHONE.................408 779-2206
Joe Morse, *Mgr*
EMP: 69
SALES (corp-wide): 19.7B **Publicly Held**
SIC: 4953 Recycling, waste materials
HQ: Waste Management Of California, Inc.
   9081 Tujunga Ave
   Sun Valley CA
   877 836-6526

(P-4960)
WASTE MGT ALAMEDA CNTY INC (HQ)
Also Called: Waste Management
172 98th Ave (94603-1004)
PHONE.................510 613-8710
Barry S Skolnick, *CEO*
James E Trevathan, *
James C Fish Junior, *Ex VP*
EMP: 550 EST: 1920
SALES (est): 310.37MM
SALES (corp-wide): 19.7B **Publicly Held**
SIC: 4953 Garbage: collecting, destroying, and processing
PA: Waste Management, Inc.
   800 Capitol St Ste 3000
   Houston TX
   713 512-6200

(P-4961)
WASTE MGT COLLECTN RECYCL INC
Also Called: Waste Management
219 Pudding Creek Rd (95437-8136)
PHONE.................707 964-9172
Robert Thornsberry, *Mgr*
EMP: 73
SALES (corp-wide): 19.7B **Publicly Held**
SIC: 4953 Garbage: collecting, destroying, and processing
HQ: Waste Management Collection And Recycling, Inc.
   1001 Fannin St Ste 4000
   Houston TX

(P-4962)
WASTE MGT COLLECTN RECYCL INC
Also Called: Waste Management
1324 Paddock Pl (95776-5919)
PHONE.................530 662-8748
John Duncan, *Mgr*
EMP: 152
SALES (corp-wide): 19.7B **Publicly Held**
SIC: 4953 Garbage: collecting, destroying, and processing
HQ: Waste Management Collection And Recycling, Inc.
   1001 Fannin St Ste 4000
   Houston TX

(P-4963)
WASTE MGT COLLECTN RECYCL INC
Also Called: Waste Management
1449 W Rosecrans Ave (90249-2639)
P.O. Box 1428 (90249-0428)
PHONE.................310 532-6511
Dave Hauser, *Prin*
EMP: 144
SALES (corp-wide): 19.7B **Publicly Held**
SIC: 4953 5064 Garbage: collecting, destroying, and processing; Garbage disposals
HQ: Waste Management Collection And Recycling, Inc.
   1001 Fannin St Ste 4000
   Houston TX

(P-4964)
WASTE MGT COLLECTN RECYCL INC
Also Called: Waste Management
1340 W Beach St (95076-5122)
P.O. Box 2347 (95077-2347)
PHONE.................831 768-9505
James Moresco, *Brnch Mgr*
EMP: 123
SALES (corp-wide): 19.7B **Publicly Held**
SIC: 4953 Garbage: collecting, destroying, and processing
HQ: Waste Management Collection And Recycling, Inc.
   1001 Fannin St Ste 4000
   Houston TX

(P-4965)
WASTE MGT COLLECTN RECYCL INC
Also Called: Waste Management
450 Orr Springs Rd (95482-3131)
PHONE.................707 462-0210
EMP: 72
SALES (corp-wide): 19.7B **Publicly Held**
SIC: 4953 Garbage: collecting, destroying, and processing
HQ: Waste Management Collection And Recycling, Inc.
   1001 Fannin St Ste 4000
   Houston TX

(P-4966)
WASTE MGT COLLECTN RECYCL INC
Also Called: Waste Management
13940 Live Oak Ave (91706-1321)
PHONE.................626 960-7551
Rick Decaiva, *Mgr*
EMP: 81
SALES (corp-wide): 19.7B **Publicly Held**
SIC: 4953 4212 Rubbish collection and disposal; Local trucking, without storage
HQ: Waste Management Collection And Recycling, Inc.
   1001 Fannin St Ste 4000
   Houston TX

(P-4967)
WASTE MGT COLLECTN RECYCL INC
Also Called: Waste Management
17700 Indian St (92551-9511)
PHONE.................951 242-0421
Scott Jenkins, *Mgr*
EMP: 117
SALES (corp-wide): 19.7B **Publicly Held**
SIC: 4953 Recycling, waste materials
HQ: Waste Management Collection And Recycling, Inc.
   1001 Fannin St Ste 4000

4953 - Refuse Systems (P-4968)

Houston TX

(P-4968)
WASTE MGT COLLECTN RECYCL INC
Also Called: Waste Management
16122 Construction Cir E (92606-4498)
PHONE..................................949 451-2600
EMP: 125
SALES (corp-wide): 19.7B Publicly Held
SIC: 4953 4212 Recycling, waste materials; Garbage collection and transport, no disposal
HQ: Waste Management Collection And Recycling, Inc.
1001 Fannin St Ste 4000
Houston TX

(P-4969)
WM HEALTHCARE SOLUTIONS INC
Also Called: Wmhs Bay Area
3670 Enterprise Ave (94545-3206)
PHONE..................................713 328-7350
EMP: 63
SALES (corp-wide): 19.7B Publicly Held
SIC: 4953 Refuse systems
HQ: Wm Healthcare Solutions, Inc.
800 Capitol St Ste 3000
Houston TX

(P-4970)
WM HEALTHCARE SOLUTIONS INC
Also Called: Wmhs Tri Cities
7010 Auto Mall Pkwy (94538-3117)
PHONE..................................713 328-7350
EMP: 63
SALES (corp-wide): 19.7B Publicly Held
SIC: 4953 Refuse systems
HQ: Wm Healthcare Solutions, Inc.
800 Capitol St Ste 3000
Houston TX

(P-4971)
WM HEALTHCARE SOLUTIONS INC
Also Called: Wmhs Sacramento
5337 Luce Ave (95652-2440)
PHONE..................................713 328-7350
EMP: 63
SALES (corp-wide): 19.7B Publicly Held
SIC: 4953 Recycling, waste materials
HQ: Wm Healthcare Solutions, Inc.
800 Capitol St Ste 3000
Houston TX

(P-4972)
YUCAIPA DISPOSAL INC
9890 Cherry Ave (92335-5202)
PHONE..................................909 429-4200
Cole Burr, Pr
David R Marriner, CFO
EMP: 98 EST: 1959
SQ FT: 1,500
SALES (est): 1.74MM
SALES (corp-wide): 320.11MM Privately Held
Web: www.burrtec.com
SIC: 4953 4212 Rubbish collection and disposal; Local trucking, without storage
PA: Burrtec Waste Group, Inc.
9890 Cherry Ave
Fontana CA
909 429-4200

(P-4973)
ZEREP MANAGEMENT CORPORATION (PA)
17445 Railroad St (91748-1026)
PHONE..................................626 855-5522
Manuel Perez, CEO
EMP: 245 EST: 1970
SQ FT: 4,000
SALES (est): 37.94MM
SALES (corp-wide): 37.94MM Privately Held
Web: www.valleyvistaservices.com
SIC: 4953 4212 Refuse collection and disposal services; Local trucking, without storage

4959 Sanitary Services, Nec

(P-4974)
AMPCO CONTRACTING INC
17991 Cowan (92614-6025)
PHONE..................................949 955-2255
Andrew Pennor, Ch
Tim Vitta, *
Reggie Kama, *
Joe Ha, *
EMP: 220 EST: 2004
SALES (est): 53.13MM Privately Held
Web: www.ampcocontracting.com
SIC: 4959 1795 1794 Environmental cleanup services; Wrecking and demolition work; Excavation and grading, building construction

(P-4975)
CLEANSTREET LLC
1918 W 169th St (90247-5254)
PHONE..................................800 225-7316
TOLL FREE: 800
Christopher Valerian, Pr
EMP: 194 EST: 1965
SALES (est): 25.56MM
SALES (corp-wide): 536.39MM Privately Held
Web: www.sweepingcorp.com
SIC: 4959 Sweeping service: road, airport, parking lot, etc.
HQ: Sca Of Ca, Llc
4141 Rockside Rd Ste 100
Seven Hills OH
216 777-2750

(P-4976)
COUNTY OF SANTA CLARA
101 Skyport Dr (95110-1302)
PHONE..................................408 573-2400
Michael Murdter, Dir
EMP: 444
SQ FT: 25,600
Web: home.sccgov.org
SIC: 4959 9621 Road, airport, and parking lot maintenance services; Regulation, administration of transportation
PA: County Of Santa Clara
70 W Hedding St
San Jose CA
408 299-5200

(P-4977)
COUNTY OF STANISLAUS
Also Called: East Side Msqito Abatement Dst
2000 Santa Fe Ave (95357-0650)
PHONE..................................209 522-4098
J Wakoli Wekesa, Brnch Mgr
EMP: 68
Web: www.eastsidemosquito.com
SIC: 4959 Mosquito eradication
PA: County Of Stanislaus
1010 10th St Ste 5100
Modesto CA
209 525-6398

(P-4978)
DELTA DIABLO SANITATION DISTRICT
2500 Pittsburg Antioch Hwy (94509-1373)
PHONE..................................925 756-1900
EMP: 80 EST: 1955
SALES (est): 20.09MM Privately Held
Web: www.deltadiablo.org
SIC: 4959 Sanitary services, nec

(P-4979)
ENGINRNG/RMDTION RSRCES GROUP (PA)
Also Called: Errg
4585 Pacheco Blvd Ste 200 (94553-2228)
PHONE..................................925 839-2200
Cynthia Liu, CEO
Cynthia A Liu, *
Todd Katz, *
EMP: 70 EST: 1997
SQ FT: 31,000
SALES (est): 58.92MM
SALES (corp-wide): 58.92MM Privately Held
Web: www.errg.com
SIC: 4959 8744 Environmental cleanup services; Environmental remediation

(P-4980)
JONSET LLC
Also Called: Sunset Property Services
16251 Construction Cir W (92606-4412)
PHONE..................................949 551-5151
John Howhannesian, Pr
EMP: 96 EST: 1968
SQ FT: 6,000
SALES (est): 9.64MM
SALES (corp-wide): 536.39MM Privately Held
SIC: 4959 7349 Sweeping service: road, airport, parking lot, etc.; Janitorial service, contract basis
HQ: Sca Of Ca, Llc
4141 Rockside Rd Ste 100
Seven Hills OH
216 777-2750

(P-4981)
LOS ANGLES CNTY SNTTION DSTRCT (PA)
Also Called: L.A.cO.
1955 Workman Mill Rd (90601-1415)
P.O. Box 4998 (90607-4998)
PHONE..................................562 699-7411
Stephen Maguin, Genl Mgr
EMP: 850 EST: 1924
SALES (est): 726.8MM
SALES (corp-wide): 726.8MM Privately Held
Web: www.lacsd.org
SIC: 4959 Sanitary services, nec

(P-4982)
NRC ENVIRONMENTAL SERVICES INC (DH)
1605 Ferry Pt (94501-5021)
PHONE..................................510 749-1390
Steven Candito, Pr
Sal Sacco, *
Neil Challis, *
Todd Roloff, *
Mike Reese, *
▲ EMP: 80 EST: 1988
SQ FT: 18,000
SALES (est): 108.75MM
SALES (corp-wide): 13.51B Publicly Held
Web: www.nrcc.com
SIC: 4959 Toxic or hazardous waste cleanup
HQ: National Response Corporation
3500 Sunrise Hwy Ste 200b
Great River NY

(P-4983)
SACRAMNTO RGNAL CNTY SNTTION D (PA)
Also Called: Srcsd
10060 Goethe Rd (95827-3553)
PHONE..................................916 876-6000
Prabhakar Somavarapu, Mng Dir
Phil Serna, *
EMP: 200 EST: 1973
SQ FT: 136,000
SALES (est): 101.69MM
SALES (corp-wide): 101.69MM Privately Held
Web: www.regionalsan.com
SIC: 4959 Sanitary services, nec

(P-4984)
SULLIVAN INTERNATIONAL GROUP INC
Also Called: Sullivan
2750 Womble Rd Ste 100 (92106-6111)
PHONE..................................619 260-1432
EMP: 132
SIC: 4959 Toxic or hazardous waste cleanup

4961 Steam And Air-conditioning Supply

(P-4985)
CGP HOLDINGS LLC
2 Gill Station Coastal Rd (93542)
PHONE..................................760 764-1300
Joe Greco, CEO
EMP: 82 EST: 2007
SALES (est): 7.52MM Privately Held
SIC: 4961 Steam supply systems, including geothermal

4971 Irrigation Systems

(P-4986)
CITY OF ANAHEIM
Anaheim City Utilities Div
201 S Anaheim Blvd (92805-3826)
P.O. Box 3069 (92803-3069)
PHONE..................................714 254-0125
Ed Aghjayan, Brnch Mgr
EMP: 100
Web: www.anaheim.net
SIC: 4971 9111 Water distribution or supply systems for irrigation; Mayors' office
PA: City Of Anaheim
200 S Anaheim Blvd
Anaheim CA
714 765-5162

(P-4987)
FRESNO IRRIGATION DISTRICT
2907 S Maple Ave (93725-2218)
PHONE..................................559 233-7161
Gary R Serrato, Genl Mgr
Deann Hailey, *
Laurence Kimura, *
EMP: 83 EST: 1920
SQ FT: 18,000
SALES (est): 24.07MM Privately Held
Web: www.fresnoirrigation.com
SIC: 4971 Water distribution or supply systems for irrigation

PRODUCTS & SERVICES SECTION
5012 - Automobiles And Other Motor Vehicles (P-5007)

(P-4988)
FRESNO VALVES & CASTINGS INC (PA)
7736 E Springfield Ave (93662-9408)
P.O. Box 40 (93662-0040)
PHONE.................559 834-2511
Jeffery Showalter, *CEO*
Jeffery Showalter, *Pr*
Kevin Follansbee, *
Joni Roam, *
◆ **EMP:** 165 **EST:** 1952
SALES (est): 90.4MM
SALES (corp-wide): 90.4MM **Privately Held**
Web: www.fresnovalves.com
SIC: 4971 3491 3498 3441 Water distribution or supply systems for irrigation; Industrial valves; Fabricated pipe and fittings; Fabricated structural metal

(P-4989)
HUNTER INDUSTRIES INCORPORATED (PA)
Also Called: Hunter
1940 Diamond St (92078-5190)
PHONE.................760 744-5240
Gregory R Hunter, *CEO*
Stephanie C Brownell, *
◆ **EMP:** 193 **EST:** 1993
SQ FT: 450,000
SALES (est): 538.15MM **Privately Held**
Web: www.hunterindustries.com
SIC: 4971 3089 Irrigation systems; Fittings for pipe, plastics

(P-4990)
MARIN MUNICIPAL WATER DISTRICT (PA)
220 Nellen Ave (94925-1169)
P.O. Box 994 (94976-0994)
PHONE.................415 945-1455
Krishna Kumar, *Pr*
EMP: 220 **EST:** 1912
SQ FT: 32,000
SALES (est): 103.43MM
SALES (corp-wide): 103.43MM **Privately Held**
Web: www.marinwater.org
SIC: 4971 4941 Irrigation systems; Water supply

(P-4991)
NEVADA IRRIGATION DISTRICT (PA)
Also Called: N I D
1036 W Main St (95945-5424)
PHONE.................530 273-6185
Remleh Scherzinger, *Genl Mgr*
Keane Sommers, *
John H Drew, *
Scott Miller, *
Marie Owens, *
▲ **EMP:** 160 **EST:** 1921
SQ FT: 11,050
SALES (est): 57.96MM
SALES (corp-wide): 57.96MM **Privately Held**
Web: www.nevadacemeterydistrict.com
SIC: 4971 4911 Water distribution or supply systems for irrigation; Generation, electric power

(P-4992)
OAK SPRINGS NURSERY INC
13761 Eldridge Ave (91342-1764)
P.O. Box 922906 (91392-2906)
PHONE.................818 367-5832
Manuel Cacho, *Pr*
EMP: 90 **EST:** 1993

SALES (est): 9.37MM **Privately Held**
SIC: 4971 0781 Irrigation systems; Landscape services

(P-4993)
PALO VERDE IRRIGATION DISTRICT
180 W 14th Ave (92225-2714)
PHONE.................760 922-3144
Ed Smith, *Genl Mgr*
Janice Love, *CLLTR**
EMP: 85 **EST:** 1923
SQ FT: 8,125
SALES (est): 14.02MM **Privately Held**
Web: www.pvid.org
SIC: 4971 Water distribution or supply systems for irrigation

(P-4994)
RAIN BIRD CORPORATION
2475 Paseo De Las Americas Ste A # 1318 (92154-7255)
PHONE.................619 661-4493
Catherine Wade, *Brnch Mgr*
EMP: 68
SALES (corp-wide): 433.78MM **Privately Held**
Web: www.rainbird.com
SIC: 4971 Irrigation systems
PA: Rain Bird Corporation
970 W Sierra Madre Ave
Azusa CA
626 812-3400

(P-4995)
SOLANO IRRIGATION DISTRICT
810 Vaca Valley Pkwy Ste 201 (95688-8834)
PHONE.................707 448-6847
Robert Hansen, *Pr*
Guido E Colla, *
EMP: 99 **EST:** 1948
SQ FT: 8,500
SALES (est): 20.3MM **Privately Held**
Web: www.sidwater.org
SIC: 4971 Irrigation systems

(P-4996)
UNITED IRRIGATION INC
44907 Golf Center Pkwy Ste 3 (92201-7303)
PHONE.................760 347-6161
Anthony Cunzio, *Pr*
Samantha Chisholm, *
EMP: 60 **EST:** 2002
SQ FT: 1,300
SALES (est): 6.21MM **Privately Held**
Web: www.unitedgli.com
SIC: 4971 Irrigation systems

(P-4997)
VISTA IRRIGATION DISTRICT
Also Called: Vid
1391 Engineer St (92081-8836)
PHONE.................760 597-3100
John Amodeo, *Genl Mgr*
Roy Coox, *
EMP: 99 **EST:** 1923
SQ FT: 2,500
SALES (est): 43.19MM **Privately Held**
Web: www.vidwater.org
SIC: 4971 Water distribution or supply systems for irrigation

5012 Automobiles And Other Motor Vehicles

(P-4998)
A-Z BUS SALES INC (PA)
Also Called: John Deere Authorized Dealer
1900 S Riverside Ave (92324-3344)
PHONE.................951 781-7188
Edwin John Landherr, *CEO*
James Reynolds, *
▼ **EMP:** 90 **EST:** 1984
SQ FT: 20,000
SALES (est): 49.64MM
SALES (corp-wide): 49.64MM **Privately Held**
Web: www.a-zbus.com
SIC: 5012 5082 Busses; Construction and mining machinery

(P-4999)
ABC BUS INC
1485 Dale Way (92626-3918)
PHONE.................714 444-5888
Dane Cornell, *CEO*
EMP: 112
SALES (corp-wide): 182.45MM **Privately Held**
SIC: 5012 4173 Busses; Bus terminal and service facilities
HQ: Abc Bus, Inc.
1506 30th St Nw
Faribault MN
507 334-1871

(P-5000)
ABC BUS INC
3508 Haven Ave (94063-4603)
PHONE.................650 368-3364
Mike Lawrence, *Mgr*
EMP: 63
SALES (corp-wide): 182.45MM **Privately Held**
SIC: 5012 4173 Busses; Bus terminal and service facilities
HQ: Abc Bus, Inc.
1506 30th St Nw
Faribault MN
507 334-1871

(P-5001)
ADESA CORPORATION LLC
Also Called: Adesa Auction
8649 Kiefer Blvd (95826-3907)
PHONE.................916 388-8899
Jim Sale, *Brnch Mgr*
EMP: 99
Web: www.adesa.com
SIC: 5012 Automobile auction
HQ: Adesa Corporation, Llc
11299 Illinois St
Carmel IN

(P-5002)
ADESA CORPORATION LLC
2175 Cactus Rd (92154-8002)
PHONE.................619 661-5565
EMP: 92
Web: www.adesa.com
SIC: 5012 5521 Automobile auction; Used car dealers
HQ: Adesa Corporation, Llc
11299 Illinois St
Carmel IN

(P-5003)
ALEXANDER DENNIS INCORPORATED
31566 Railroad Canyon Rd Ste 3 (92587-9446)

PHONE.................951 244-9429
Colin Robertson, *CEO*
Stephen Walsh, *
▲ **EMP:** 2000 **EST:** 2004
SALES (est): 56.4MM
SALES (corp-wide): 2.34B **Privately Held**
Web: www.alexander-dennis.com
SIC: 5012 Busses
HQ: Alexander Dennis Limited
9 Central Boulevard
Larbert

(P-5004)
AMERICAN HONDA MOTOR CO INC (HQ)
Also Called: American Honda
1919 Torrance Blvd (90501-2722)
P.O. Box 2200 (90509-2200)
PHONE.................310 783-2000
Noriya Kaihara, *CEO*
Lyle Shroyer, *VP*
Yuichi Shimizu, *Sec*
Mikio Himuro, *CFO*
◆ **EMP:** 2375 **EST:** 1959
SALES (est): 12.82B **Privately Held**
Web: www.honda.com
SIC: 5012 3732 Automobiles; Jet skis
PA: Honda Motor Co., Ltd.
2-1-1, Minamiaoyama
Minato-Ku TKY

(P-5005)
AQUIRECORPS NORWALK AUTO AUCTN
Also Called: Aquire
12405 Rosecrans Ave (90650-5056)
PHONE.................562 864-7464
Rj Romero, *Ch Bd*
Lou Rudich, *
Chuck Doskow, *
Steve Fleurant, *
EMP: 125 **EST:** 1979
SQ FT: 55,000
SALES (est): 34.08MM **Privately Held**
Web: www.norwalkautoauction.com
SIC: 5012 Automobile auction

(P-5006)
CALIFRNIA AUTO DALERS EXCH LLC
Also Called: Riverside Auto Auction
1320 N Tustin Ave (92807-1619)
PHONE.................714 996-2400
Tim Van Dam, *Genl Mgr*
EMP: 400 **EST:** 1985
SALES (est): 47.32MM
SALES (corp-wide): 16.61B **Privately Held**
SIC: 5012 Automobile auction
HQ: Manheim Investments, Inc.
6205 Pachtree Dunwoody Rd
Atlanta GA
866 626-4346

(P-5007)
E M THARP INC (PA)
Also Called: Golden Peterbilt
15243 Road 192 (93257-8967)
PHONE.................559 782-5800
Morris Tharp, *Pr*
Morris A Tharp, *
EMP: 86 **EST:** 1952
SALES (est): 50.24MM **Privately Held**
Web: www.emtharp.com
SIC: 5012 5013 5511 5531 Trucks, commercial; Truck parts and accessories; Trucks, tractors, and trailers: new and used; Truck equipment and parts

5012 - Automobiles And Other Motor Vehicles (P-5008)

(P-5008)
FRESNO AUTO DEALERS AUCTION
278 N Marks Ave (93706-1136)
PHONE.............................559 268-8051
Darryl Ceccolil, Pr
▼ EMP: 704 EST: 1975
SQ FT: 15,000
SALES (est): 8.53MM
SALES (corp-wide): 16.61B Privately Held
SIC: 5012 Automobile auction
HQ: Manheim Investments, Inc.
  6205 Pachtree Dunwoody Rd
  Atlanta GA
  866 626-4346

(P-5009)
FRESNO TRUCK CENTER
2727 E Central Ave (93725-2425)
P.O. Box 12346 (93777-2346)
PHONE.............................559 486-4310
Randy Moore, Mgr
EMP: 80
SQ FT: 40,000
SALES (corp-wide): 119.89MM Privately Held
Web: www.californiatruckcenters.com
SIC: 5012 5511 7538 5531 Truck tractors; Trucks, tractors, and trailers: new and used ; General truck repair; Truck equipment and parts
PA: Fresno Truck Center
  2727 E Central Ave
  Fresno CA
  559 486-4310

(P-5010)
FRESNO TRUCK CENTER
Also Called: Delta Truck Center
10182 S Harlan Rd (95231-9647)
P.O. Box 20 (95231-0020)
PHONE.............................209 983-2400
John Gannon, Mgr
EMP: 125
SALES (corp-wide): 119.89MM Privately Held
Web: www.californiatruckcenters.com
SIC: 5012 5013 7538 5531 Trucks, commercial; Automotive supplies and parts; General automotive repair shops; Truck equipment and parts
PA: Fresno Truck Center
  2727 E Central Ave
  Fresno CA
  559 486-4310

(P-5011)
HYUNDAI MOTOR AMERICA (HQ)
10550 Talbert Ave (92708-6032)
P.O. Box 20850 (92728-0850)
PHONE.............................714 965-3000
Randy Parker, CEO
Jerry Flannery, Legal
Brian Smith, COO
Youngil Ko, CFO
Angela Zepeda, CMO
◆ EMP: 454 EST: 1985
SQ FT: 469,000
SALES (est): 1.1B Privately Held
Web: www.hyundaiusa.com
SIC: 5012 5511 Automobiles and other motor vehicles; Automobiles, new and used
PA: Hyundai Motor Company
  12 Heolleung-Ro, Seocho-Gu
  Seoul

(P-5012)
INLAND KENWORTH INC (HQ)
9730 Cherry Ave (92335-5257)
PHONE.............................909 823-9955
TOLL FREE: 800
Leigh Parker, Ch
William Currie, *
Les Ziegler, *
Jim Beidrwieden, *
▼ EMP: 105 EST: 1934
SQ FT: 60,000
SALES (est): 104.26MM
SALES (corp-wide): 1.1MM Privately Held
Web: www.inland-group.com
SIC: 5012 7538 5013 7513 Trucks, commercial; Diesel engine repair: automotive; Truck parts and accessories; Truck rental and leasing, no drivers
PA: Inland Industries Ltd
  2482 Douglas Rd
  Burnaby BC
  604 291-6021

(P-5013)
INTERSTATE TRUCK CENTER LLC (PA)
Also Called: Valley Peterbilt
2110 S Sinclair Ave (95215-7556)
PHONE.............................209 944-5821
David T Morganson, Managing Member
Rick Coslett, *
EMP: 100 EST: 1974
SQ FT: 22,000
SALES (est): 47.34MM
SALES (corp-wide): 47.34MM Privately Held
Web: www.itctrucks.com
SIC: 5012 7513 Trucks, commercial; Truck rental, without drivers

(P-5014)
LOS ANGELES TRUCK CENTERS LLC
Also Called: Los Angeles Freightliner
13800 Valley Blvd (92335-5216)
PHONE.............................909 510-4000
Ricardo Flores, Mgr
EMP: 200
SALES (corp-wide): 233.56MM Privately Held
Web: www.velocitytruckcenters.com
SIC: 5012 5013 7538 5531 5511 Trucks, commercial; General automotive repair shops; Auto and home supply stores; New and used car dealers
PA: Los Angeles Truck Centers, Llc
  2429 Peck Rd
  Whittier CA
  562 447-1200

(P-5015)
MARATHON INDUSTRIES INC
Also Called: Marathon Truck Bodies
25597 Springbrook Ave (91350-2427)
P.O. Box 800279 (91380-0279)
PHONE.............................661 286-1520
Chad Hess, Pr
Roger K Hess, *
Tom Garcia, *
EMP: 145 EST: 1993
SQ FT: 75,000
SALES (est): 27.5MM Privately Held
Web: www.marathontruckbody.com
SIC: 5012 3713 Automobiles and other motor vehicles; Truck and bus bodies

(P-5016)
MIRAMAR FORD TRUCK SALES INC
Also Called: NationaLease
6066 Miramar Rd (92121-2591)
PHONE.............................619 272-5340
Michael Buscher, Pr
Richard Harrigan, *
Michael Maury, *
EMP: 74 EST: 1982
SQ FT: 22,000
SALES (est): 23.76MM
SALES (corp-wide): 233.56MM Privately Held
Web: www.velocitytrucktrailer.com
SIC: 5012 5013 7513 Trucks, commercial; Truck parts and accessories; Truck rental and leasing, no drivers
PA: Los Angeles Truck Centers, Llc
  2429 Peck Rd
  Whittier CA
  562 447-1200

(P-5017)
NISSAN NORTH AMERICA INC
Nissan Division
1683 Sunflower Ave (92626-1540)
P.O. Box 5555 (92628-5555)
PHONE.............................714 433-3700
FAX: 714 433-3746
EMP: 150
SALES (corp-wide): 103.12B Privately Held
SIC: 5012 Automotive brokers
HQ: Nissan North America Inc
  1 Nissan Way
  Franklin TN
  615 725-1000

(P-5018)
UTILITY TRLR SLS STHERN CAL LL (PA)
15567 Valley Blvd (92335-6351)
PHONE.............................877 275-4887
Craig M Bennett, *
Stephen F Bennet, *
Harold C Bennett, *
Jeffrey J Bennett, *
EMP: 100 EST: 2007
SALES (est): 20.94MM Privately Held
Web: www.utilitytrailersales.com
SIC: 5012 5013 5531 5561 Trailers for passenger vehicles; Automotive supplies and parts; Auto and truck equipment and parts; Travel trailers: automobile, new and used

(P-5019)
WIND RIVER ENTERPRISES INC
Also Called: North Bay Auto Auction
250 Dittmer Rd (94534-1621)
PHONE.............................707 864-1040
Don Morrow, Pr
Maureen Green, Sec
EMP: 95 EST: 1993
SQ FT: 20,000
SALES (est): 19.25MM Privately Held
Web: www.nbauto.com
SIC: 5012 Automobile auction

5013 Motor Vehicle Supplies And New Parts

(P-5020)
1-800 RADIATOR & A/C LLC (DH)
Also Called: 1-800-Radiator
4401 Park Rd (94510-1124)
PHONE.............................707 747-7400
Jonathan Fitzpatrick, CEO
Scott O'melia, Sec
◆ EMP: 100 EST: 1985
SALES (est): 79.86MM
SALES (corp-wide): 2.03B Publicly Held
Web: www.radiator.com
SIC: 5013 Radiators
HQ: Driven Brands, Inc.
  440 S Church St Ste 700
  Charlotte NC

(P-5021)
4 WHEEL PARTS WHOLESALERS LLC
400 W Artesia Blvd (90220-5501)
PHONE.............................310 900-7725
▼ EMP: 452 EST: 2010
SALES (est): 9.07MM Privately Held
Web: www.4wheelparts.com
SIC: 5013 Automotive supplies and parts

(P-5022)
APU INC (PA)
14939 Oxnard St (91411-2611)
PHONE.............................661 948-2880
John Christy Junior, Pr
EMP: 60 EST: 1978
SQ FT: 20,000
SALES (est): 8.23MM
SALES (corp-wide): 8.23MM Privately Held
SIC: 5013 5531 Automotive supplies and parts; Automotive parts

(P-5023)
APW KNOX-SEEMAN WAREHOUSE INC (HQ)
1073 E Artesia Blvd (90746-1601)
PHONE.............................310 604-4373
Tong Y Suhr, CEO
Susan Suhr, *
▲ EMP: 98 EST: 1972
SQ FT: 32,000
SALES (est): 47.91MM
SALES (corp-wide): 48.2MM Privately Held
Web: www.apwks.com
SIC: 5013 5531 Automotive supplies and parts; Automotive parts
PA: Auto Parts Warehouse, Inc.
  16941 Keegan Ave
  Carson CA
  800 913-6119

(P-5024)
ASIAN EUROPEAN PRODUCTS INC
Also Called: E P I
18071 Fitch Fl 250 (92614-6085)
P.O. Box 28989 (92799-8989)
PHONE.............................949 553-3900
▲ EMP: 150
SIC: 5013 Automotive supplies and parts

(P-5025)
AUTOMOTIVE AFTERMARKET INC
Also Called: Completes Plus
15912 Hawthorne Blvd (90260-2644)
PHONE.............................310 793-0046
Guy Cooper, Brnch Mgr
EMP: 72
SALES (corp-wide): 22.78MM Privately Held
Web: www.completesplus.com
SIC: 5013 Truck parts and accessories
PA: Automotive Aftermarket, Inc.
  10425 S La Cienega Blvd
  Los Angeles CA
  310 703-5700

(P-5026)
AUTOMOTIVE IMPORTING MANUFACTURING INC (PA)
Also Called: Aim Mail Centers
3920 Security Park Dr (95742-6915)
P.O. Box 100 (95741-0100)

PRODUCTS & SERVICES SECTION
5013 - Motor Vehicle Supplies And New Parts (P-5047)

PHONE..............................916 985-8505
▲ **EMP:** 300 **EST:** 1967
SALES (est): 21.24MM
SALES (corp-wide): 21.24MM **Privately Held**
Web: www.aimpartsonline.com
SIC: 5013 3714 Automotive supplies and parts; Motor vehicle parts and accessories

(P-5027)
AZIMC INVESTMENTS INC
Also Called: IMC
8901 Canoga Ave (91304-1512)
PHONE..............................818 678-1200
Kristen Wright, Sec
Thomas Kliman, *
William Giles, *
◆ **EMP:** 250 **EST:** 1962
SALES (est): 87.59MM
SALES (corp-wide): 495MM **Privately Held**
SIC: 5013 Automotive supplies and parts
HQ: Interamerican Motor, Llc
 8901 Canoga Ave
 Canoga Park CA
 800 874-8925

(P-5028)
BATTERY SYSTEMS INC
12322 Monarch St (92841-2909)
PHONE..............................714 667-9320
EMP: 109
SALES (corp-wide): 545.41MM **Privately Held**
Web: www.batterysystems.net
SIC: 5013 Motor vehicle supplies and new parts
PA: Battery Systems, Inc.
 8585 N Stemmons Fwy # 60
 Dallas TX
 310 667-9320

(P-5029)
BBK PERFORMANCE INC
Also Called: Gripp
27427 Bostik Ct (92590-3698)
PHONE..............................951 296-1771
Brian Murphy, Pr
Ken Murphy, *
EMP: 75 **EST:** 1988
SALES (est): 13.33MM **Privately Held**
Web: www.bbkperformance.com
SIC: 5013 5531 Automotive supplies and parts; Automotive parts

(P-5030)
BRAGG INVESTMENT COMPANY INC
Also Called: Coastline Equipment
1930 Lockwood St (93036-2679)
PHONE..............................805 485-2106
Buck Baird, Mgr
EMP: 97
SQ FT: 17,900
SALES (corp-wide): 489.53MM **Privately Held**
Web: www.braggcompanies.com
SIC: 5013 7629 7359 5082 Trailer parts and accessories; Business machine repair, electric; Lawn and garden equipment rental; Construction and mining machinery
PA: Bragg Investment Company, Inc.
 6251 N Paramount Blvd
 Long Beach CA
 562 984-2400

(P-5031)
CAL-STATE AUTO PARTS INC (PA)
Also Called: Auto Pride
1361 N Red Gum St (92806-1318)
PHONE..............................714 630-5950
Richard J Deblasi, CEO
Steven Brooker, *
John Mcmillin, CFO
▲ **EMP:** 105 **EST:** 1971
SQ FT: 76,000
SALES (est): 44.73MM
SALES (corp-wide): 44.73MM **Privately Held**
Web: www.calstateautoparts.com
SIC: 5013 Automotive supplies and parts

(P-5032)
CENKET INC
449 Littlefield Ave (94080-6106)
EMP: 100
SIC: 5013 Automotive supplies and parts

(P-5033)
CLUB ASSIST NORTH AMERICA INC (DH)
888 W 6th St Ste 300 (90017-2729)
PHONE..............................213 388-4333
Brett Davies, CEO
Scott Davies, *
Alex Leombruni, *
Candace Enman, *
Stuart Davies, *
▲ **EMP:** 64 **EST:** 2001
SALES (est): 81.62MM **Privately Held**
SIC: 5013 Automotive batteries
HQ: Club Assist Corporation Pty Ltd
 237-239 Frankston-Dandenong Rd
 Dandenong VIC

(P-5034)
CUSTOM CHROME MANUFACTURING
Also Called: Custom Chrome
15750 Vineyard Blvd Ste 100 (95037-7119)
PHONE..............................408 825-5000
Dan Cook, Prin
Dan Cook, CEO
Bill Prescott, *
◆ **EMP:** 289 **EST:** 1990
SALES (est): 28.15MM **Privately Held**
Web: www.customchrome.com
SIC: 5013 Motorcycle parts
HQ: Dae-Il Usa, Inc.
 112 Robert Young Blvd
 Murray KY

(P-5035)
DENSO PDTS & SVCS AMERICAS INC (DH)
Also Called: Dsca
3900 Via Oro Ave (90810-1868)
PHONE..............................310 834-6352
Yoshihiko Yamada, CEO
Hirokatsu Yamashita, Pr
Roy Nakaue, Ex VP
Peter Clotz, VP Sls
Eugene Stark, VP Prd
◆ **EMP:** 452 **EST:** 1971
SQ FT: 235,000
SALES (est): 221.87MM **Privately Held**
Web: www.densorobotics.com
SIC: 5013 7361 5075 3714 Automotive supplies and parts; Employment agencies; Warm air heating and air conditioning; Motor vehicle parts and accessories
HQ: Denso International America, Inc.
 24777 Denso Dr
 Southfield MI
 248 350-7500

(P-5036)
DNA SPECIALTY INC
200 W Artesia Blvd (90220-5500)
PHONE..............................310 767-4070
James Choi, Pr
▲ **EMP:** 90 **EST:** 1984
SQ FT: 80,000
SALES (est): 24.13MM **Privately Held**
Web: www.dnaspecialty.com
SIC: 5013 3714 Wheels, motor vehicle; Wheels, motor vehicle

(P-5037)
EMPI INC
301 E Orangethorpe Ave (92801-1032)
PHONE..............................714 446-9606
Peter Guile, CEO
Todd Tyler, CFO
EMP: 89 **EST:** 2018
SQ FT: 127,000
SALES (est): 28.78MM **Privately Held**
Web: www.empius.com
SIC: 5013 3713 Automotive supplies and parts; Specialty motor vehicle bodies

(P-5038)
FAST PRO INC
Also Called: Fast Undercar
2555 Lafayette St Ste 103 (95050-2644)
PHONE..............................408 566-0200
EMP: 60 **EST:** 1996
SQ FT: 13,000
SALES (est): 6.24MM **Privately Held**
Web: www.fastundercar.com
SIC: 5013 Automotive supplies

(P-5039)
FIND IT PARTS INC
Also Called: Finditparts
11858 La Grange Ave (90025-5230)
PHONE..............................888 312-8812
David Seewack, CEO
Scott Spiwak, *
Ron Hendrixson, CPO*
Mohammad Wardak, *
EMP: 75 **EST:** 2002
SALES (est): 15.05MM **Privately Held**
Web: www.finditparts.com
SIC: 5013 Automotive supplies and parts

(P-5040)
FORD MOTOR COMPANY
Ford
1269 Phoenix Dr (95336-6006)
P.O. Box 1666 (94802-0666)
PHONE..............................209 824-6600
William Stewart, Mgr
EMP: 104
SALES (corp-wide): 158.06B **Publicly Held**
Web: www.ford.com
SIC: 5013 5531 Automotive supplies and parts; Automotive parts
PA: Ford Motor Company
 1 American Rd
 Dearborn MI
 313 322-3000

(P-5041)
GILLIG LLC
25972 Eden Landing Rd (94545-3816)
PHONE..............................800 735-1500
EMP: 255
SALES (corp-wide): 1.98B **Privately Held**
Web: www.gillig.com
SIC: 5013 Automotive supplies and parts
HQ: Gillig Llc
 451 Discovery Dr
 Livermore CA
 510 264-5000

(P-5042)
HANSON DISTRIBUTING COMPANY (PA)
975 W 8th St (91702-2246)
PHONE..............................626 224-9800
Daniel Hanson, CEO
EMP: 115 **EST:** 1954
SQ FT: 160,000
SALES (est): 64.25MM
SALES (corp-wide): 64.25MM **Privately Held**
Web: www.hansondistributing.com
SIC: 5013 Automotive supplies and parts

(P-5043)
HANSON DISTRIBUTING COMPANY
7940 W Doe Ave (93291-9703)
PHONE..............................559 802-1198
EMP: 98
SALES (corp-wide): 64.25MM **Privately Held**
Web: www.hansondistributing.com
SIC: 5013 Automotive supplies and parts
PA: Hanson Distributing Company
 975 W 8th St
 Azusa CA
 626 224-9800

(P-5044)
HINO MOTORS MFG USA INC
4550 Wineville Ave (91752-3723)
PHONE..............................951 727-0286
Debra Martinas, Brnch Mgr
EMP: 98
Web: www.hmmusa.com
SIC: 5013 Truck parts and accessories
HQ: Hino Motors Manufacturing U.S.A., Inc.
 45501 W 12 Mile Rd
 Novi MI

(P-5045)
IAP WEST INC
Also Called: Durago
20036 S Via Baron (90220-6105)
PHONE..............................310 667-9720
Michel Berg, CEO
Louis Berg, Pr
Sharon Berg, Sec
John Kelley, CFO
◆ **EMP:** 71 **EST:** 1981
SQ FT: 80,000
SALES (est): 13.6MM **Privately Held**
Web: www.iapperformance.com
SIC: 5013 Automotive engines and engine parts

(P-5046)
JUST WHEELS & TIRES LLC
Also Called: T S W Alloy Wheels
3172 Nasa St (92821-6234)
◆ **EMP:** 67 **EST:** 2020
SALES (est): 60MM **Privately Held**
Web: www.tsw.com
SIC: 5013 Wheels, motor vehicle

(P-5047)
KEYSTONE AUTOMOTIVE WAREHOUSE
Also Called: KEYSTONE AUTOMOTIVE WAREHOUSE
15640 Cantu Galleano Ranch Rd (91752-1404)
PHONE..............................951 277-5237
Michael Decicco, Prin
EMP: 100
SALES (corp-wide): 12.79B **Publicly Held**
Web: www.keystoneautomotive.com
SIC: 5013 Radiators

(PA)=Parent Co (HQ)=Headquarters
○ = New Business established in last 2 years

5013 - Motor Vehicle Supplies And New Parts (P-5048)

HQ: Keystone Automotive Warehouse, Inc.
44 Tunkhannock Ave
Exeter PA
570 655-4514

(P-5048)
MERIDIAN RACK & PINION INC
Also Called: Meridian
9980 Huennekens St Ste 200 (92121-2968)
PHONE..................888 875-0026
Renee Thomas-jacobs, CEO
Dara Greaney, VP
Matt Glauber, Pr
Chris Struempler, CFO
▲ EMP: 130 EST: 1989
SALES (est): 24.98MM Privately Held
Web: www.buyautoparts.com
SIC: 5013 5961 Automotive supplies and parts; Mail order house, order taking office only

(P-5049)
METROPOLITAN AUTOMOTIVE WAREHOUSE
Also Called: Auto Value
535 Tennis Court Ln (92408-1615)
P.O. Box 1529 (92402-1529)
PHONE..................909 885-2886
▼ EMP: 700
SIC: 5013 Automotive supplies and parts

(P-5050)
MIKUNI AMERICAN CORPORATION (HQ)
Also Called: M A C
8910 Mikuni Ave (91324-3403)
PHONE..................310 676-0522
Jun Iida, CEO
Yutaka Fujita, *
Masashi Seike, *
▲ EMP: 64 EST: 1968
SQ FT: 50,000
SALES (est): 80.22MM Privately Held
Web: www.mikuni.com
SIC: 5013 5088 Automotive hardware; Aircraft engines and engine parts
PA: Mikuni Corporation
    6-13-11, Sotokanda
    Chiyoda-Ku TKY

(P-5051)
MOBIS PARTS AMERICA LLC (HQ)
Also Called: Mobis Ventures Sv
10550 Talbert Ave 4th Fl (92708-6031)
PHONE..................786 515-1101
Yun Dong Park, Managing Member
Tae Hwan Chung, *
Beomseo Koo, *
◆ EMP: 90 EST: 2003
SALES (est): 224.39MM Privately Held
Web: www.mobisusa.com
SIC: 5013 Automotive supplies and parts
PA: Hyundai Mobis Co., Ltd.
    203 Teheran-Ro, Gangnam-Gu
    Seoul

(P-5052)
NSV INTERNATIONAL CORP
1250 E 29th St (90755-1800)
P.O. Box 14660 (90853-4660)
PHONE..................562 438-3836
Victor Harris, CEO
Stephan Humphries, *
Isabel Palafox, *
EMP: 100 EST: 2011
SQ FT: 1,200
SALES (est): 4.98MM Privately Held
Web: www.nsvauto.com

SIC: 5013 Automotive supplies

(P-5053)
PARTS AUTHORITY LLC
Also Called: Fast Undercar
4277 Transport St (93003-5657)
PHONE..................805 676-3410
Randy Buller, Pr
EMP: 110
SALES (corp-wide): 495MM Privately Held
Web: www.fastundercar.com
SIC: 5013 Automotive supplies and parts
PA: Parts Authority, Llc
    3 Dakota Dr Ste 110
    New Hyde Park NY
    833 380-8511

(P-5054)
RALCO HOLDINGS INC (DH)
13861 Rosecrans Ave (90670-5207)
PHONE..................949 440-5500
Michael Moore, CEO
EMP: 159 EST: 2009
SALES (est): 305.57MM Privately Held
SIC: 5013 3751 Motorcycle parts; Motorcycle accessories
HQ: Velocity Pooling Vehicle, Llc
    651 Canyon Dr Ste 100
    Coppell TX

(P-5055)
RALLY HOLDINGS LLC
17771 Mitchell N (92614-6028)
PHONE..................817 919-6833
EMP: 1151 EST: 2006
SALES (est): 305.57MM Privately Held
SIC: 5013 3751 Motorcycle parts; Motorcycle accessories
HQ: Ralco Holdings, Inc.
    13861 Rosecrans Ave
    Santa Fe Springs CA
    949 440-5500

(P-5056)
REELS INC
Also Called: Mr Bug
301 E Orangethorpe Ave (92801-1032)
PHONE..................714 446-9606
▲ EMP: 80 EST: 1971
SALES (est): 10.48MM Privately Held
Web: www.empius.com
SIC: 5013 3714 Automotive supplies and parts; Motor vehicle parts and accessories

(P-5057)
RICHARD HUETTER INC
Also Called: Pacific Parts International
21050 Osborne St (91304-1744)
PHONE..................818 700-8001
Richard Huetter, CEO
Maria L Huetter, *
▲ EMP: 70 EST: 1982
SQ FT: 30,000
SALES (est): 9.37MM Privately Held
Web: www.pacificparts.net
SIC: 5013 Automotive supplies and parts

(P-5058)
SADDLEMEN CORPORATION
Also Called: Saddlemen
17801 S Susana Rd (90221-5411)
PHONE..................310 638-1222
David Echert, CEO
▲ EMP: 140 EST: 1987
SQ FT: 20,000
SALES (est): 12.75MM Privately Held
Web: www.saddlemen.com
SIC: 5013 3751 Motorcycle parts; Motorcycle accessories

(P-5059)
SCAT ENTERPRISES INC
1400 Kingsdale Ave (90278-3927)
PHONE..................310 370-5501
Philip T Lieb, Pr
Craig Schenasi, *
◆ EMP: 65 EST: 1960
SQ FT: 42,000
SALES (est): 24.68MM Privately Held
Web: www.scatenterprises.com
SIC: 5013 3714 Automotive supplies and parts; Motor vehicle parts and accessories

(P-5060)
SHRIN LLC
Also Called: Coverking
900 E Arlee Pl (92805-5645)
P.O. Box 9860 (92812-7860)
PHONE..................714 850-0303
Narendra Gupta, Managing Member
◆ EMP: 100 EST: 1988
SQ FT: 90,000
SALES (est): 24.35MM Privately Held
Web: www.coverking.com
SIC: 5013 3714 Automotive supplies and parts; Motor vehicle parts and accessories

(P-5061)
SILLA AUTOMOTIVE LLC
Also Called: Silla Cooling Systems
1217 W Artesia Blvd (90220-5305)
PHONE..................800 624-1499
▲ EMP: 200
SIC: 5013 Radiators

(P-5062)
SPECTRA PREMIUM (USA) CORP
2220 Almond Ave (92374-2073)
PHONE..................951 653-0640
Sergio Zapata, Brnch Mgr
EMP: 62
SALES (corp-wide): 49.81MM Privately Held
Web: www.spectrapremium.com
SIC: 5013 Automotive supplies and parts
PA: Spectra Premium (Usa) Corp.
    3052 N Distribution Way
    Greenfield IN
    317 891-1700

(P-5063)
SSF IMPORTED AUTO PARTS LLC (DH)
Also Called: S S F
437 Rozzi Pl (94080-1915)
PHONE..................800 203-9287
Thomas Beer, Managing Member
Dennis Kreuser, *
▲ EMP: 100 EST: 1976
SALES (est): 118.98MM
SALES (corp-wide): 1.73B Privately Held
Web: www.ssfautoparts.com
SIC: 5013 Automotive supplies and parts
HQ: Wm Se
    Pagenstecherstr. 121
    Osnabruck NI
    54199890

(P-5064)
TAP WORLDWIDE LLC (HQ)
Also Called: 4 Wheel Parts Performance Ctrs
400 W Artesia Blvd (90220-5501)
PHONE..................310 900-5500
◆ EMP: 134 EST: 2009
SALES (est): 487.43MM
SALES (corp-wide): 8.59B Publicly Held
Web: www.4wheelparts.com
SIC: 5013 Motor vehicle supplies and new parts
PA: Polaris Inc.

2100 Highway 55
Medina MN
763 542-0500

(P-5065)
UNITED PACIFIC INDUSTRIES INC
3788 E Conant St (90808-1783)
PHONE..................562 421-3888
Jack Lin, CEO
Major Lin, *
Cathy Lin, *
Wen Chung Lin, *
▲ EMP: 60 EST: 1984
SQ FT: 50,000
SALES (est): 24.2MM Privately Held
Web: www.upauto.com
SIC: 5013 5531 Automotive supplies and parts; Truck equipment and parts

(P-5066)
VGP HOLDINGS LLC
9520 John St (90670-2904)
PHONE..................562 906-6200
EMP: 288
SIC: 5013 Automotive engines and engine parts
HQ: Vgp Holdings Llc
    100 Valvoline Way Pmb 200
    Lexington KY
    859 357-7777

(P-5067)
WEBASTO CHARGING SYSTEMS INC (DH)
1333 S Mayflower Ave Ste 100 (91016-4066)
PHONE..................626 415-4000
John Thomas, CEO
Doug Mcelroy, CFO
EMP: 85 EST: 2018
SALES (est): 22.01MM
SALES (corp-wide): 4.2B Privately Held
SIC: 5013 Automobile service station equipment
HQ: Webasto Roof Systems Inc.
    2500 Executive Hills Dr
    Auburn Hills MI
    248 997-5100

(P-5068)
YOSHIMURA RES & DEV AMER INC
5420 Daniels St Ste A (91710-9012)
PHONE..................909 628-4722
Fujio Yoshimura, Pr
Suehiro Watanabe, *
Don Sakakura, *
▲ EMP: 100 EST: 1975
SQ FT: 12,000
SALES (est): 24.8MM Privately Held
Web: www.yoshimura-rd.com
SIC: 5013 Motorcycle parts

5014 Tires And Tubes

(P-5069)
FALKEN TIRE HOLDINGS INC
Also Called: Falken Tires
8656 Haven Ave (91730-9103)
PHONE..................800 723-2553
Richard Smallwood, Pr
▲ EMP: 80 EST: 2006
SALES (est): 22.76MM Privately Held
SIC: 5014 Automobile tires and tubes
PA: Sumitomo Rubber Industries, Ltd.
    3-6-9, Wakinohamacho, Chuo-Ku
    Kobe HYO

▲ = Import ▼ = Export
◆ = Import/Export

PRODUCTS & SERVICES SECTION

5021 - Furniture (P-5090)

(P-5070)
ITD ARIZONA INC
6737 E Washington Blvd (90040-1801)
PHONE..................323 722-8542
◆ EMP: 98
SIC: 5014 Tires and tubes

(P-5071)
LAKIN TIRE WEST INCORPORATED (PA)
Also Called: Lakin Tire of Calif
15305 Spring Ave (90670-5645)
PHONE..................562 802-2752
Robert Lakin, CEO
David Lakin, *
◆ EMP: 164 EST: 1973
SQ FT: 50,000
SALES (est): 52.31MM
SALES (corp-wide): 52.31MM Privately Held
Web: www.lakintire.com
SIC: 5014 5531 Tires, used; Auto and home supply stores

(P-5072)
PETES ROAD SERVICE INC
120 W Warner Ave (92707-3257)
PHONE..................714 545-5818
Dave Taylor, Mgr
EMP: 66
SALES (corp-wide): 35.91MM Privately Held
Web: www.petesrs.com
SIC: 5014 5531 Automobile tires and tubes; Auto and home supply stores
PA: Pete's Road Service, Inc.
  2230 E Orangethorpe Ave
  Fullerton CA
  714 446-1207

(P-5073)
SUMITOMO RUBBER NORTH AMER INC (HQ)
Also Called: Falken Tire
8656 Haven Ave (91730-9107)
PHONE..................909 466-1116
Richard Smallwood, CEO
Toby Beiner, *
◆ EMP: 120 EST: 1963
SQ FT: 190,000
SALES (est): 101.56MM Privately Held
Web: www.falkentire.com
SIC: 5014 Automobile tires and tubes
PA: Sumitomo Rubber Industries, Ltd.
  3-6-9, Wakinohamacho, Chuo-Ku
  Kobe HYO

(P-5074)
TIRECO INC (PA)
500 W 190th St Ste 600 (90248-4269)
PHONE..................310 767-7990
Justin R Liu, *
Mimi Liu, *
◆ EMP: 150 EST: 2000
SALES (est): 112.53MM
SALES (corp-wide): 112.53MM Privately Held
Web: www.tireco.com
SIC: 5014 5013 5051 Tires, used; Wheels, motor vehicle; Tubing, metal

(P-5075)
TOYO TIRE USA CORP (DH)
Also Called: Nitto Tyres
5665 Plaza Dr Ste 300 (90630-5066)
P.O. Box 6052 (90630-0052)
PHONE..................714 236-2080
◆ EMP: 71 EST: 1966
SALES (est): 121.38MM Privately Held
Web: www.toyotires.com
SIC: 5014 Truck tires and tubes
HQ: Toyo Tire Holdings Of Americas Inc.
  3565 Harbor Blvd
  Costa Mesa CA
  714 229-6100

(P-5076)
YOKOHAMA TIRE CORPORATION (DH)
Also Called: Yokohama Tire USA
1 Macarthur Pl Ste 800 (92707-5948)
P.O. Box 4550 (92834-4550)
PHONE..................714 870-3800
◆ EMP: 150 EST: 1969
SALES (est): 497.5MM Privately Held
Web: www.yokohamaotr.com
SIC: 5014 3011 Automobile tires and tubes; Automobile tires, pneumatic
HQ: Yokohama Corporation Of North America
  1 Macarthur Pl
  Santa Ana CA

5021 Furniture

(P-5077)
ABBYSON LIVING CORP
Also Called: Yellow Luxury
26500 Agoura Rd Ste 102 (91302-3571)
PHONE..................805 465-5500
Yavar Rafieha, Pr
EMP: 112 EST: 2008
SALES (est): 15.03MM Privately Held
Web: www.abbyson.com
SIC: 5021 Household furniture

(P-5078)
BENCHPRO INC
Also Called: Bench Depot
23949 Tecate Mission Rd (91980)
P.O. Box G (91980-0958)
PHONE..................619 478-9400
Jay David Lissner, Pr
▲ EMP: 188 EST: 2001
SQ FT: 155,000
SALES (est): 24.92MM Privately Held
Web: www.benchpro.com
SIC: 5021 Furniture

(P-5079)
BKM OFFICEWORKS LLC (PA)
Also Called: BKM Officeworks
4780 Eastgate Mall Ste 100 (92121)
PHONE..................858 569-4700
William Kuhnert, CEO
Jim Skidmore, *
EMP: 70 EST: 2003
SQ FT: 100,000
SALES (est): 68.51MM
SALES (corp-wide): 68.51MM Privately Held
Web: www.bkmofficeworks.com
SIC: 5021 Office furniture, nec

(P-5080)
BLUMENTHAL DISTRIBUTING INC (PA)
Also Called: Office Star Products
1901 S Archibald Ave (91761-8548)
P.O. Box 3520 (91761-0952)
PHONE..................909 930-2000
Richard Blumenthal, CEO
Richard Blumenthal, Pr
Rose Blumenthal, Stockholder*
Jennifer Blumenthal, *
◆ EMP: 150 EST: 1983
SQ FT: 200,000
SALES (est): 54.5MM
SALES (corp-wide): 54.5MM Privately Held
Web: www.officestar.net
SIC: 5021 2522 Office furniture, nec; Chairs, office: padded or plain: except wood

(P-5081)
CAMBIUM BUSINESS GROUP INC (PA)
Also Called: Fairmont Designs
6950 Noritsu Ave (90620-1311)
PHONE..................714 670-1171
George Tsai, Ch
Jason Liu, *
Kevin Fitzgerald, *
Mark Klingensmith, *
◆ EMP: 120 EST: 1984
SQ FT: 200,000
SALES (est): 39.46MM
SALES (corp-wide): 39.46MM Privately Held
Web: www.fairmontdesigns.com
SIC: 5021 2511 Household furniture; Wood household furniture

(P-5082)
CASABELLA HOLDINGS LLC
9409 Buffalo Ave (91730-6012)
PHONE..................845 348-0012
◆ EMP: 68 EST: 2006
SALES (est): 11.12MM Privately Held
Web: www.casabella.com
SIC: 5021 Household furniture

(P-5083)
CK IMPORTS INC
Also Called: Falkon Furniture
530 Alameda Del Prado Ste C10 (94949-9810)
PHONE..................915 225-5747
Jakob Mieritz, CEO
EMP: 100 EST: 2019
SALES (est): 8.71MM Privately Held
SIC: 5021 Furniture

(P-5084)
COMPLETE OFFICE CALIFORNIA INC
Also Called: Complete Office
12724 Moore St (90703-2121)
PHONE..................714 880-1222
Edward B Walter, CEO
Rick Israel, *
EMP: 62 EST: 1961
SQ FT: 28,000
SALES (est): 42.87MM
SALES (corp-wide): 8.49B Publicly Held
Web: www.officedepot.com
SIC: 5021 5112 Office furniture, nec; Office supplies, nec
HQ: Office Depot, Llc
  6600 N Military Trl
  Boca Raton FL
  561 438-4800

(P-5085)
CONTRACT INTERIORS SAN DIEGO
Also Called: Contract Interiors
4450 N Brawley Ave Ste 125 (93722-3952)
PHONE..................559 276-0561
Douglas Davidian, CEO
Douglas B Davidian, *
Robyn Davidian, *
EMP: 80 EST: 1985
SQ FT: 18,480
SALES (est): 12.97MM Privately Held
SIC: 5021 Office and public building furniture

(P-5086)
COPPEL CORPORATION
Also Called: Coppel
503 Scaroni Ave (92231-9791)
PHONE..................760 357-3707
David Coppel, CEO
Angel Olguin, *
Allan Lewis Ctrl, Prin
Joaquin Aguirre Ruiz, *
Rosana Armenta, *
▲ EMP: 75 EST: 1991
SQ FT: 70,000
SALES (est): 760.41MM Privately Held
SIC: 5021 5137 5136 Household furniture; Women's and children's clothing; Men's and boy's clothing
HQ: Coppel, S.A. De C.V.
  Republica Poniente No. 2855
  Culiacan SIN

(P-5087)
CUSTOM COMFORT MATTRESS CO INC (PA)
Also Called: Custom Comfort Mattress Co
581 N Batavia St (92868-1218)
P.O. Box 1769 (92856-0769)
PHONE..................714 693-6161
EMP: 72 EST: 1997
SALES (est): 9.09MM Privately Held
Web: www.customcomfortmattress.com
SIC: 5021 5712 Beds; Bedding and bedsprings

(P-5088)
EC GROUP INC (PA)
Also Called: Dennis & Leen
5960 Bowcroft St (90016-4302)
PHONE..................310 815-2700
Richard Hallberg, Pr
Daniel Cuevas, *
Barbara Wiseley, *
▲ EMP: 80 EST: 1985
SQ FT: 18,000
SALES (est): 23.58MM Privately Held
Web: www.dennisandleen.com
SIC: 5021 Furniture

(P-5089)
GOFORTH & MARTI (PA)
Also Called: G/M Business Interiors
110 W A St Ste 140 (92101-3702)
PHONE..................800 68? 6583
Stephen L Easley, Pr
Laurinda Easley, *
Stephen W Easley, CIO*
Josie Donley, *
▲ EMP: 90 EST: 1944
SQ FT: 38,000
SALES (est): 110MM
SALES (corp-wide): 110MM Privately Held
Web: www.gmbi.net
SIC: 5021 Office furniture, nec

(P-5090)
HOMELEGANCE INC (PA)
Also Called: A G A
48200 Fremont Blvd (94538-6509)
PHONE..................510 933-6888
Puhsien C Chao, CEO
Rosa Chao, *
Hutch Chao, *
◆ EMP: 67 EST: 1984
SQ FT: 800,000
SALES (est): 21MM
SALES (corp-wide): 21MM Privately Held
Web: www.homelegance.com
SIC: 5021 Household furniture

5021 - Furniture (P-5091)

(P-5091)
HWOOD GROUP
9229 W Sunset Blvd Ste 305 (90069-3402)
PHONE..................................310 859-1011
John Terzian, Prin
EMP: 95 EST: 2015
SALES (est): 10.08MM Privately Held
Web: www.hwoodgroup.com
SIC: 5021 Restaurant furniture, nec

(P-5092)
INTEX RECREATION CORP
4001 Via Oro Ave (90810-1400)
PHONE..................................310 549-5400
Tien P Zee, CEO
Jim Lai, *
Bill Smith, *
Bob Howe, *
◆ EMP: 100 EST: 1966
SQ FT: 330,000
SALES (est): 22.14MM Privately Held
Web: www.intexcorp.com
SIC: 5021 5092 5091 5162 Waterbeds; Toys, nec; Watersports equipment and supplies; Plastics materials and basic shapes
PA: Intex Corp.
4001 Via Oro Ave Ste 210
Long Beach CA

(P-5093)
JANUS ET CIE (PA)
12310 Greenstone Ave (90670-4737)
PHONE..................................310 601-2958
Janice K Feldman, CEO
Paul Warren, *
Greg Buscher, *
◆ EMP: 110 EST: 1977
SQ FT: 154,000
SALES (est): 53.47MM
SALES (corp-wide): 53.47MM Privately Held
Web: www.janusetcie.com
SIC: 5021 5712 Outdoor and lawn furniture, nec; Furniture stores

(P-5094)
LOGISTAR LLC
448 S Hill St Ste 1101 (90013-1138)
PHONE..................................323 274-9651
EMP: 60 EST: 2018
SALES (est): 12.99MM Privately Held
SIC: 5021 Furniture

(P-5095)
NEW TANGRAM LLC
Also Called: BKM Total Office of Texas
9200 Sorensen Ave (90670-2645)
PHONE..................................562 365-5000
Joseph P Lozowski, Brnch Mgr
EMP: 177
SALES (corp-wide): 185.06MM Privately Held
Web: www.tangraminteriors.com
SIC: 5021 Office furniture, nec
PA: New Tangram, Llc
9200 Sorensen Ave
Santa Fe Springs CA
562 365-5000

(P-5096)
OFFICE MASTER INC
Also Called: Om Smart Seating
1110 Mildred St (91761-3512)
PHONE..................................909 392-5678
◆ EMP: 60 EST: 1986
SALES (est): 17.98MM Privately Held
Web: www.omseating.com
SIC: 5021 2522 Office furniture, nec; Benches, office; except wood

(P-5097)
OMNIA ITALIAN DESIGN LLC
4900 Edison Ave (91710-5713)
PHONE..................................909 393-4400
Peter Zolferino, Managing Member
Luie Nastri, *
◆ EMP: 200 EST: 1989
SQ FT: 110,000
SALES (est): 37.72MM Privately Held
Web: www.omnialeather.com
SIC: 5021 Household furniture

(P-5098)
ONE WORKPLACE L FERRARI LLC (PA)
Also Called: One Workplace
2500 De La Cruz Blvd (95050-2617)
PHONE..................................669 800-2500
TOLL FREE: 888
▲ EMP: 150 EST: 1925
SALES (est): 329.18MM
SALES (corp-wide): 329.18MM Privately Held
Web: www.oneworkplace.com
SIC: 5021 8744 Office furniture, nec; Facilities support services

(P-5099)
PALECEK IMPORTS INC (PA)
Also Called: Palecek
601 Parr Blvd (94801-1316)
PHONE..................................510 236-7730
Allan Palecek, Pr
Andrew T Palecek, *
◆ EMP: 90 EST: 1972
SQ FT: 250,000
SALES (est): 36.96MM
SALES (corp-wide): 36.96MM Privately Held
Web: www.palecek.com
SIC: 5021 5023 Household furniture; Homefurnishings

(P-5100)
PARRON-HALL CORPORATION
Also Called: Parron Hall Office Interiors
9655 Granite Ridge Dr Ste 100 (92123)
PHONE..................................858 268-1212
James Herr, Pr
Brianna Scherer, *
EMP: 68 EST: 1947
SQ FT: 8,000
SALES (est): 43.18MM Privately Held
Web: www.parronhall.com
SIC: 5021 Office furniture, nec

(P-5101)
PORTFOLIO PRODUCTIONS INC
Also Called: Sitcom
850 42nd Ave (94601-4035)
PHONE..................................510 434-1600
◆ EMP: 60
SIC: 5021 Furniture

(P-5102)
POUNDEX ASSOCIATES CORPORATION
21490 Baker Pkwy (91789-5239)
PHONE..................................909 444-5878
Lionel Chen, Ch
◆ EMP: 100 EST: 1988
SQ FT: 55,000
SALES (est): 23.85MM Privately Held
Web: www.poundex.com
SIC: 5021 Household furniture

(P-5103)
PREMIERE RACK SOLUTIONS INC
4502 Brickell Privado St (91761-7827)
P.O. Box 2205 (94551-2205)
PHONE..................................909 605-6300
EMP: 76
SIC: 5021 Racks

(P-5104)
PRIVILEGE INTERNATIONAL INC
2323 Firestone Blvd (90280-2684)
PHONE..................................323 585-0777
Eddy Sarraf, CEO
Eddy Sarraf, Pr
Mark Darwish, *
Richard Darwish, *
◆ EMP: 75 EST: 1999
SQ FT: 350,000
SALES (est): 9.19MM Privately Held
Web: www.privilegeinc.com
SIC: 5021 Furniture

(P-5105)
SITONIT SEATING INC
6415 Katella Ave (90630-5245)
PHONE..................................714 995-4800
Paul Devries, CEO
◆ EMP: 88 EST: 2008
SALES (est): 11.93MM Privately Held
Web: www.sitonit.net
SIC: 5021 Office furniture, nec
PA: Exemplis Llc
6415 Katella Ave Ste 100
Cypress CA

(P-5106)
UNISOURCE SOLUTIONS INC (PA)
8350 Rex Rd (90660-3785)
PHONE..................................562 654-3500
James Kastner, CEO
Ken Kastner, Pr
Jim Kastner, Ch
Clem Nieto, CFO
▲ EMP: 105 EST: 1987
SQ FT: 186,000
SALES (est): 48.15MM
SALES (corp-wide): 48.15MM Privately Held
Web: www.unisourceit.com
SIC: 5021 Office furniture, nec

(P-5107)
VIRCO INC (HQ)
2027 Harpers Way (90501-1524)
PHONE..................................310 533-0474
Robert Virtue, CEO
Robert Dose, *
▼ EMP: 249 EST: 1998
SQ FT: 560,000
SALES (est): 48.89MM
SALES (corp-wide): 231.06MM Publicly Held
Web: www.virco.com
SIC: 5021 2599 Furniture; Factory furniture and fixtures
PA: Virco Mfg. Corporation
2027 Harpers Way
Torrance CA
310 533-0474

(P-5108)
WINNERS ONLY INC
1365 Park Center Dr (92081-8338)
PHONE..................................760 599-0300
Alex Shu, Ch
Sheue-wen Lee, CEO
Fred Dizon, *
◆ EMP: 200 EST: 1989
SALES (est): 26.11MM Privately Held
Web: www.winnersonly.com

SIC: 5021 Office furniture, nec

(P-5109)
ZOCALO
1551 Bancroft Ave 1508 (94124-3216)
PHONE..................................415 293-1600
Jeremy Sommer, Pr
Steve Fox, *
◆ EMP: 62 EST: 1995
SQ FT: 150,000
SALES (est): 8.95MM Privately Held
Web: www.zocalo.org
SIC: 5021 Furniture

5023 Homefurnishings

(P-5110)
B R FUNSTEN & CO
Also Called: BR Funsten
105 Industrial Park Dr (95337)
PHONE..................................209 825-5375
Rod Tilson, Brnch Mgr
EMP: 60
SALES (corp-wide): 384.11MM Privately Held
Web: www.brfunsten.com
SIC: 5023 5713 Resilient floor coverings: tile or sheet; Floor covering stores
PA: B. R. Funsten & Co.
2485 Courage Dr Ste 100
Fairfield CA
209 825-5375

(P-5111)
B T MANCINI CO INC
8571 23rd Ave (95826-4993)
P.O. Box 276128 (95827-6128)
PHONE..................................916 381-3660
Mike Quirk, Mgr
EMP: 118
SQ FT: 13,000
SALES (corp-wide): 51.63MM Privately Held
Web: www.btmancini.com
SIC: 5023 Floor coverings
PA: B. T. Mancini Co., Inc.
876 S Milpitas Blvd
Milpitas CA
408 942-7900

(P-5112)
BRADSHAW INTERNATIONAL INC (PA)
Also Called: Bradshaw Home
9409 Buffalo Ave (91730-6012)
PHONE..................................909 476-3884
James Hair, CEO
Steve Molineaux, *
Robert Michelson, *
Jeff Megorden, *
Gary Appel, *
◆ EMP: 280 EST: 2010
SQ FT: 313,048
SALES (est): 642.04MM
SALES (corp-wide): 642.04MM Privately Held
Web: www.bradshawhome.com
SIC: 5023 Kitchenware

(P-5113)
BUTLER-JOHNSON CORPORATION
2200 Zanker Rd Ste 130 (95131-1111)
P.O. Box 612110 (95161-2110)
PHONE..................................800 776-2167
▲ EMP: 160
Web: www.butler-johnson.com
SIC: 5023 5032 Floor coverings; Brick, stone, and related material

PRODUCTS & SERVICES SECTION

5023 - Homefurnishings (P-5135)

(P-5114)
CONTRACTORS FLRG SVC CAL INC
300 E Dyer Rd (92707-3740)
P.O. Box 15106 (92735-0106)
PHONE.....................714 556-6100
EMP: 110 **EST:** 1996
SQ FT: 10,000
SALES (est): 19.98MM **Privately Held**
Web: www.cfsofca.com
SIC: 5023 Floor coverings

(P-5115)
E & E CO LTD (PA)
Also Called: Jla Home
45875 Northport Loop E (94538-6414)
PHONE.....................510 490-9788
Edmund Jin, *CEO*
Jessica Jeng, *CFO*
Eva Lu, *Sec*
◆ **EMP:** 180 **EST:** 1994
SQ FT: 60,000
SALES (est): 249.48MM **Privately Held**
Web: www.ee1994.com
SIC: 5023 Sheets, textile

(P-5116)
ELIJAH TEXTILES INC
Also Called: Sharp Fabric
1251 E Olympic Blvd Ste 108 (90021-1859)
PHONE.....................310 666-3443
Kourosh Amirianfar, *Pr*
EMP: 82 **EST:** 2001
SQ FT: 100,000
SALES (est): 34MM **Privately Held**
SIC: 5023 5949 Sheets, textile; Fabric stores piece goods

(P-5117)
GA GERTMENIAN AND SONS LLC (PA)
300 W Avenue 33 (90031-3503)
PHONE.....................213 250-7777
▲ **EMP:** 149 **EST:** 1896
SALES (est): 24.13MM
SALES (corp-wide): 24.13MM **Privately Held**
Web: www.gertmenian.com
SIC: 5023 Rugs

(P-5118)
GALLEHER LLC (PA)
Also Called: Galleher
9303 Greenleaf Ave (90670-3029)
PHONE.....................562 944-8885
Ted Koziowski, *CEO*
Jeff Hamar, *Ofcr*
Todd Hamar, *Sr VP*
Rick Coates, *Sr VP*
Russell Rumley, *CFO*
▲ **EMP:** 110 **EST:** 1937
SQ FT: 100,000
SALES (est): 110.9MM
SALES (corp-wide): 110.9MM **Privately Held**
Web: www.galleher.com
SIC: 5023 Homefurnishings

(P-5119)
GALLEHER LLC
1741 Junction Ave (95112-1029)
PHONE.....................408 850-1990
EMP: 84
SALES (corp-wide): 110.9MM **Privately Held**
Web: www.galleher.com
SIC: 5023 Floor coverings
PA: Galleher Llc
9303 Greenleaf Ave
Santa Fe Springs CA
562 944-8885

(P-5120)
GIBSON OVERSEAS INC (PA)
Also Called: Gibson Homeware
2410 Yates Ave (90040-1918)
PHONE.....................323 832-8900
Sol Gabbay, *CEO*
Darioush Gabbay, *
Soloman Gabbay, *
◆ **EMP:** 325 **EST:** 1979
SQ FT: 850,000
SALES (est): 221.89MM
SALES (corp-wide): 221.89MM **Privately Held**
Web: www.gibsonusa.com
SIC: 5023 3269 2511 Glassware; Kitchen and table articles, coarse earthenware; Kitchen and dining room furniture

(P-5121)
LEDRA BRANDS INC
Also Called: Bruck Lighting Systems
88 Maxwell (92618-4641)
PHONE.....................714 259-9959
Alex Ladjevardi, *Pr*
Jade Turney, *
Farah Emami, *
David Derk, *
Jorg Westerheide, *
▲ **EMP:** 112 **EST:** 1993
SALES (est): 26.55MM **Privately Held**
Web: www.ledrabrands.com
SIC: 5023 Lamps: floor, boudoir, desk

(P-5122)
LION TRADING COMPANY LLC
835 Sinclair Frontage Rd (95035-6308)
PHONE.....................408 946-0888
EMP: 111
SALES (corp-wide): 670.09K **Privately Held**
SIC: 5023 Sheets, textile
PA: Lion Trading Company, Llc
1838 N Milpitas Blvd
Milpitas CA
408 946-0888

(P-5123)
MARIAK INDUSTRIES INC
Also Called: Mariak Window Fashion
879 W 190th St Ste 1050 (90248-4224)
PHONE.....................310 661-4400
Leo Elinson, *CEO*
▲ **EMP:** 269 **EST:** 1986
SALES (est): 55.55MM
SALES (corp-wide): 1.56B **Privately Held**
Web: www.mariak.com
SIC: 5023 2591 Vertical blinds; Blinds vertical
PA: Springs Window Fashions, Llc
7549 Graber Rd
Middleton WI
608 836-1011

(P-5124)
MIRAMA ENTERPRISES INC
Also Called: Aroma Housewares
6469 Flanders Dr (92121-4104)
PHONE.....................858 587-8866
Chung Yuan Chang, *Pr*
Peter Chang, *
Shiurun Chang, *
Wenbo Bozhuang, *Stockholder**
Tom Kao, *COO*
◆ **EMP:** 68 **EST:** 1996
SQ FT: 60,000
SALES (est): 13.58MM **Privately Held**
Web: www.aroma-housewares.com
SIC: 5023 Kitchenware

(P-5125)
MSRS INC
Also Called: Vm International
945 E Church St (92507-1103)
PHONE.....................310 952-9000
Moe Vazin, *CEO*
Roya Vazin, *CFO*
◆ **EMP:** 120 **EST:** 1996
SQ FT: 250,000
SALES (est): 33.12MM **Privately Held**
SIC: 5023 2821 Kitchenware; Plastics materials and resins

(P-5126)
NATIONAL FLOORING PRODUCTS INC
5003 Ontario Mills Pkwy (91764-5123)
PHONE.....................877 238-3225
Curtis Gordon, *CEO*
EMP: 61 **EST:** 2016
SALES (est): 10.02MM **Privately Held**
Web: www.my-nfp.com
SIC: 5023 Floor coverings

(P-5127)
NEXGRILL INDUSTRIES INC (PA)
Also Called: Nexgrill Industries
14050 Laurelwood Pl (91710-5454)
PHONE.....................909 598-8799
Sherman Lin, *CEO*
◆ **EMP:** 98 **EST:** 1993
SQ FT: 50,000
SALES (est): 27.26MM
SALES (corp-wide): 27.26MM **Privately Held**
Web: www.nexgrill.com
SIC: 5023 3631 Grills, barbecue; Barbecues, grills, and braziers (outdoor cooking)

(P-5128)
NORCAL POTTERY PRODUCTS INC
5700 E Airport Dr (91761-8620)
PHONE.....................909 390-3745
Carrie Roberts, *Mgr*
EMP: 135
SALES (corp-wide): 3.34B **Publicly Held**
SIC: 5023 Pottery
HQ: Norcal Pottery Products, Inc.
1000 Washington St
Foxboro MA
510 895-5966

(P-5129)
NORMAN INTERNATIONAL INC
Also Called: Norman Charter
28 Centerpointe Dr Ste 120 (90623-1028)
PHONE.....................562 946-0420
Ranjan Mada, *CEO*
◆ **EMP:** 70 **EST:** 2001
SALES (est): 46.46MM
SALES (corp-wide): 46.46MM **Privately Held**
Web: www.normanusa.com
SIC: 5023 Homefurnishings
PA: Norman International Dallas, Llc
28 Centerpointe Dr # 120
La Palma CA
562 946-0420

(P-5130)
OMEGA MOULDING WEST LLC
Also Called: Omega
5500 Lindbergh Ln (90201-6410)
PHONE.....................323 261-3510
Bernard Portnoy, *Managing Member*
◆ **EMP:** 130 **EST:** 1998
SQ FT: 130,000
SALES (est): 18.25MM **Privately Held**
Web: www.omegamoulding.com
SIC: 5023 Frames and framing, picture and mirror

(P-5131)
PEKING HANDICRAFT INC (PA)
Also Called: P H I
1388 San Mateo Ave (94080-6501)
PHONE.....................650 871-3788
Derrick Lo, *CEO*
Paul Lam, *
◆ **EMP:** 120 **EST:** 1977
SQ FT: 150,000
SALES (est): 43.17MM
SALES (corp-wide): 43.17MM **Privately Held**
Web: www.pkhc.com
SIC: 5023 Linens and towels

(P-5132)
R W SMITH & CO (HQ)
Also Called: Trimark R.W. Smith
10101 Old Grove Rd (92131-1650)
P.O. Box 26100 (92196-0160)
PHONE.....................858 530-1800
▲ **EMP:** 65 **EST:** 1935
SALES (est): 61.93MM **Privately Held**
Web: www.rwsmithco.com
SIC: 5023 Kitchenware
PA: Trimark Usa, Llc
9 Hampshire St
Mansfield MA

(P-5133)
REU DISTRIBUTION LLC
Also Called: Republic Floor
7227 Telegraph Rd (90640-6512)
PHONE.....................323 201-4200
Eliyahu Shuat, *
EMP: 700 **EST:** 2015
SALES (est): 175MM **Privately Held**
SIC: 5023 5211 2426 Wood flooring; Flooring, wood; Flooring, hardwood

(P-5134)
SOTO PROVISION INC
Also Called: Soto Food Service
488 Parriott Pl W (91745-1015)
PHONE.....................626 458-4600
John R Renna Senior, *Pr*
John R Renna Junior, *VP*
Russ Fischer, *CFO*
EMP: 70 **EST:** 1974
SQ FT: 35,000
SALES (est): 65.04MM **Privately Held**
Web: www.sotofoodservice.com
SIC: 5023 5046 Kitchen tools and utensils, nec; Commercial cooking and food service equipment

(P-5135)
TABLETOPS UNLIMITED INC (PA)
Also Called: Tabletops Unlimited
23000 Avalon Blvd (90745-5017)
PHONE.....................310 549-6000
Mohsen Asgari, *Dir*
Hamid Ebrahimi, *
Daryoush Molayem, *
Ali Alan Asgari, *
Masoud Tehrani, *
◆ **EMP:** 77 **EST:** 1983
SQ FT: 350,000
SALES (est): 50.24MM
SALES (corp-wide): 50.24MM **Privately Held**
Web: www.ttustore.com
SIC: 5023 Kitchenware

5023 - Homefurnishings (P-5136)

(P-5136)
TAE SOOK CHUNG
Also Called: Elim Bedding Town
21080 Golden Springs Dr (91789-3894)
PHONE.............................909 598-6255
Tae Sook Chung, Owner
EMP: 76 EST: 2002
SALES (est): 3.83MM Privately Held
SIC: 5023 Blankets

(P-5137)
TEST-RITE PRODUCTS CORP (DH)
1900 Burgundy Pl (91761-2308)
PHONE.............................909 605-9899
Kelly Ho, Pr
Jack Ho, *
◆ EMP: 80 EST: 1975
SQ FT: 400,000
SALES (est): 67.23MM Privately Held
SIC: 5023 Homefurnishings
HQ: Test-Rite International (U.S.) Co., Ltd.
1900 Burgundy Pl Ste X
Ontario CA

(P-5138)
TIFFANY DALE INC (PA)
14765 Firestone Blvd (90638-5918)
PHONE.............................714 739-2700
Ye H Chung, CEO
Connie Chung, *
▲ EMP: 83 EST: 1979
SALES (est): 12.37MM
SALES (corp-wide): 12.37MM Privately Held
Web: www.daletiffany.com
SIC: 5023 Lamps: floor, boudoir, desk

(P-5139)
TRANSPAC INC
1050 Aviator Dr (95688-8709)
PHONE.............................707 452-0600
◆ EMP: 90
Web: www.shoptii.com
SIC: 5023 Decorative home furnishings and supplies

(P-5140)
TRI-WEST LTD (PA)
12005 Pike St (90670-6100)
PHONE.............................562 692-9166
Allen Gage, Pr
Randy Sims, Pt
John Lubinxki, Pt
▲ EMP: 200 EST: 1976
SQ FT: 300,000
SALES (est): 98.7MM
SALES (corp-wide): 98.7MM Privately Held
Web: www.triwestltd.com
SIC: 5023 Floor coverings

(P-5141)
UMA ENTERPRISES INC (PA)
Also Called: Uma Home Decor
350 W Apra St (90220-5529)
PHONE.............................310 631-1166
Naval Bansal, CEO
Larry Woods, *
◆ EMP: 60 EST: 1986
SQ FT: 460,000
SALES (est): 64.2MM
SALES (corp-wide): 64.2MM Privately Held
Web: www.umainc.com
SIC: 5023 Decorative home furnishings and supplies

(P-5142)
VENUS GROUP INC (PA)
Also Called: Venus Textiles
25861 Wright St (92610-3504)
PHONE.............................949 609-1299
Kirit D Patel, CEO
Rajni D Patel, VP
◆ EMP: 78 EST: 1971
SALES (est): 35.59MM
SALES (corp-wide): 35.59MM Privately Held
Web: www.venusgroup.com
SIC: 5023 2392 5719 Towels; Towels, fabric and nonwoven: made from purchased materials; Towels

(P-5143)
W DIAMOND SUPPLY CO (DH)
Also Called: Diamond W Floorcovering
19321 E Walnut Dr N (91748-1436)
PHONE.............................909 859-8939
Louis J Bettitta, CEO
Mike Klingele, *
Daniel Erickson, *
Kandi Anderson, *
▲ EMP: 60 EST: 1948
SQ FT: 106,000
SALES (est): 25.65MM
SALES (corp-wide): 250.72K Privately Held
Web: www.diamondw.com
SIC: 5023 Floor coverings
HQ: Tarkett, Inc.
30000 Aurora Rd
Solon OH
800 899-8916

(P-5144)
ZWILLING JA HENCKELS LLC
Also Called: Z Willing J A Henckels
100 Citadel Dr Ste 575 (90040-1571)
PHONE.............................323 597-1421
EMP: 244
SALES (corp-wide): 4.51B Privately Held
Web: www.zwilling.com
SIC: 5023 Kitchenware
HQ: Zwilling J.A. Henckels, Llc
270 Marble Ave
Pleasantville NY
914 749-3400

5031 Lumber, Plywood, And Millwork

(P-5145)
ALL-COAST FOREST PRODUCTS INC (PA)
250 Asti Rd (95425)
P.O. Box 9 (95425-0009)
PHONE.............................707 894-4281
EMP: 80 EST: 1975
SALES (est): 25.91MM
SALES (corp-wide): 25.91MM Privately Held
Web: www.all-coast.com
SIC: 5031 2421 Lumber: rough, dressed, and finished; Resawing lumber into smaller dimensions

(P-5146)
ANFINSON LUMBER SALES INC (PA)
13041 Union Ave (92337-6952)
PHONE.............................951 681-4707
Richard Anfinson, Pr
Patricia J Anfinson, *
EMP: 60 EST: 1957
SQ FT: 48,000
SALES (est): 6.5MM
SALES (corp-wide): 6.5MM Privately Held
Web: www.anfinson.com
SIC: 5031 Lumber: rough, dressed, and finished

(P-5147)
ATRIUM DOOR & WIN CO ARIZ INC
5455 E La Palma Ave Ste A (92807-2006)
PHONE.............................714 693-0601
Gregory T Faherty, Pr
Jeff Hull, *
Randall S Fojtasek, *
EMP: 118 EST: 1960
SQ FT: 220,000
SALES (est): 8.74MM
SALES (corp-wide): 5.58B Privately Held
SIC: 5031 Windows
HQ: Atrium Windows And Doors, Inc.
9001 Ambassador Row
Dallas TX
214 583-1840

(P-5148)
AURA HARDWOOD LUMBER INC
620 Quinn Ave (95112-2604)
PHONE.............................800 411-2872
▲ EMP: 70
Web: www.aurahardwoods.com
SIC: 5031 5211 Lumber: rough, dressed, and finished; Lumber products

(P-5149)
BUILDERS FIRSTSOURCE INC
Also Called: Heritage One Door & Carpentry
4300 Jetway Ct (95660-5702)
PHONE.............................916 481-5030
John Dutter, Brnch Mgr
EMP: 350
SALES (corp-wide): 22.73B Publicly Held
Web: www.bldr.com
SIC: 5031 2431 Doors and windows; Windows and window parts and trim, wood
PA: Builders Firstsource, Inc.
6031 Connection Dr # 400
Irving TX
214 880-3500

(P-5150)
BUILDING MATERIAL DISTRS INC (PA)
Also Called: B M D
225 Elm Ave (95632-1558)
P.O. Box 606 (95632-0606)
PHONE.............................800 356-3001
TOLL FREE: 800
Mark Buri, CEO
Cynthia Thompson, *
◆ EMP: 170 EST: 1943
SQ FT: 100,000
SALES (est): 145.11MM
SALES (corp-wide): 145.11MM Privately Held
Web: www.bmdusa.com
SIC: 5031 Building materials, exterior

(P-5151)
CONTI MATERIALS SERVICE LLC
3932 Newton Rd (95205-2425)
P.O. Box 30248 (95213-0248)
PHONE.............................209 467-0626
EMP: 60 EST: 1986
SALES (est): 15.59MM Privately Held
Web: www.contimaterials.com
SIC: 5031 5211 4212 Building materials, exterior; Lumber and other building materials; Local trucking, without storage

(P-5152)
COUNTY BUILDING MATERIALS INC
Also Called: Ace Hardware
2927 S King Rd (95122-1597)
PHONE.............................408 274-4920
Jay Robert Williams Junior, CEO
Jay R William Senior, Pr
Harry Glaze, *
▲ EMP: 60 EST: 1974
SQ FT: 26,000
SALES (est): 11.41MM Privately Held
Web: www.paylesshardwareandrockery.com
SIC: 5031 5032 5261 5193 Building materials, exterior; Brick, stone, and related material; Nursery stock, seeds and bulbs; Nursery stock

(P-5153)
DISCOUNT BUILDERS SUPPLY
1695 Mission St (94103-2432)
PHONE.............................415 285-2800
Charles Goodman, Pr
▲ EMP: 69 EST: 1961
SQ FT: 40,000
SALES (est): 21.02MM Privately Held
Web: www.discountbuilderssupplysf.com
SIC: 5031 5211 Building materials, exterior; Lumber and other building materials

(P-5154)
EXPERT DRY WALL SYSTEMS INC
1141 Old Bayshore Hwy Ste 30ca (95112)
PHONE.............................408 271-5044
Laura Grabar, Prin
EMP: 70 EST: 2013
SALES (est): 5.04MM Privately Held
SIC: 5031 1742 Wallboard; Drywall

(P-5155)
EXPO INDUSTRIES INC
Also Called: Expo Builders Supply
7455 Carroll Rd (92121-2303)
P.O. Box 711 (92121)
PHONE.............................858 566-3110
EMP: 95
Web: www.expostucco.com
SIC: 5031 3299 Building materials, exterior; Stucco

(P-5156)
FLEETWOOD ALUMINUM PRODUCTS INC
Also Called: Fleetwood Windows and Doors
1 Fleetwood Way (92879-5101)
P.O. Box 1086 (92878-1086)
PHONE.............................800 736-7363
EMP: 250 EST: 1960
SALES (est): 40.89MM Privately Held
Web: www.fleetwoodusa.com
SIC: 5031 3442 Doors and windows; Metal doors, sash, and trim

(P-5157)
FOUNDATION BUILDING MTLS INC (HQ)
Also Called: Foundation Building Materials
2520 Redhill Ave (92705-5542)
PHONE.............................714 380-3127
Ruben Mendoza, Pr
John Gorey, *
Pete Welly, *
Onur Demirkaya, *
Richard J Tilley, *
EMP: 237 EST: 2016
SALES (est): 2.06B Privately Held

▲ = Import ▼ = Export
◆ = Import/Export

PRODUCTS & SERVICES SECTION

5031 - Lumber, Plywood, And Millwork (P-5176)

Web: www.fbmsales.com
SIC: **5031** 5033 5039 Building materials, interior; Roofing, siding, and insulation; Ceiling systems and products
PA: American Securities Llc
590 Madison Ave Fl 38
New York NY

(P-5158)
GOLDEN STATE LUMBER INC
38801 Cherry St (94560-4939)
PHONE..................................510 229-5500
Ed Minton, *Brnch Mgr*
EMP: 113
SALES (corp-wide): 493.04MM **Privately Held**
Web: www.goldenstatelumber.com
SIC: **5031** 5211 Lumber: rough, dressed, and finished; Lumber and other building materials
PA: Golden State Lumber, Inc.
855 Lakeville St Ste 200
Petaluma CA
707 206-4100

(P-5159)
GOLDEN STATE LUMBER INC
3033 S Airport Way (95206-3899)
P.O. Box 31810 (95213-1810)
PHONE..................................209 234-7700
Ralph Panttaja, *Brnch Mgr*
EMP: 83
SALES (corp-wide): 493.04MM **Privately Held**
Web: www.goldenstatelumber.com
SIC: **5031** 5211 Lumber: rough, dressed, and finished; Lumber and other building materials
PA: Golden State Lumber, Inc.
855 Lakeville St Ste 200
Petaluma CA
707 206-4100

(P-5160)
GROVE LUMBER & BLDG SUPS INC (PA)
27126 Watson Rd (92585-9792)
PHONE..................................909 947-0277
Raymond G Croll Junior, *CEO*
EMP: 190 EST: 1979
SQ FT: 3,000
SALES (est): 100.98MM
SALES (corp-wide): 100.98MM **Privately Held**
Web: www.grovelumber.com
SIC: **5031** 5211 Lumber: rough, dressed, and finished; Lumber products

(P-5161)
H - INVESTMENT COMPANY
Also Called: Golden State Flooring
6999 Southfront Rd (94551-8221)
P.O. Box HI (94596)
PHONE..................................925 245-4300
▲ EMP: 240
Web: www.higlum.com
SIC: **5031** Hardboard

(P-5162)
HARDWOODS SPECIALTY PDTS US LP
620 Quinn Ave (95112-2604)
PHONE..................................408 275-1990
Lance Blanco, *Mgr*
EMP: 70
SALES (corp-wide): 2.58B **Privately Held**
Web: www.hardwoods-inc.com
SIC: **5031** 5211 Lumber: rough, dressed, and finished; Lumber products
HQ: Hardwoods Specialty Products Us Lp

2700 Lind Ave Sw Ste 100
Renton WA
425 251-1213

(P-5163)
HARDY WINDOW COMPANY (PA)
1639 E Miraloma Ave (92870-6623)
PHONE..................................714 996-1807
Chance P Hardy, *Pr*
EMP: 141 EST: 1998
SQ FT: 14,000
SALES (est): 33.55MM
SALES (corp-wide): 33.55MM **Privately Held**
Web: www.orangecountywindowanddoor.com
SIC: **5031** Windows

(P-5164)
HEPPNER HARDWOODS INC
555 W Danlee St (91702-2342)
PHONE..................................626 969-7983
Lorraine Heppner, *Pr*
▲ EMP: 60 EST: 1972
SQ FT: 217,800
SALES (est): 10.39MM **Privately Held**
Web: www.heppnerhardwoods.com
SIC: **5031** Lumber: rough, dressed, and finished

(P-5165)
HERITAGE ONE DOOR CRPENTRY LLC
Also Called: Heritage One Door
4300 Jetway Ct (95660-5702)
P.O. Box 214609 (95821-0609)
PHONE..................................916 481-5030
Charles Gardemeyer, *Managing Member*
Geoff Hughes, *
John Dutter, *
John Ballou, *
Tyler Randolth, *Installation Manager*
EMP: 86 EST: 2011
SQ FT: 80,000
SALES (est): 9.61MM
SALES (corp-wide): 36.03MM **Privately Held**
SIC: **5031** 2431 Doors and windows; Windows and window parts and trim, wood
PA: Heritage Interests, Llc
4300 Jetway Ct
North Highlands CA
916 481-5030

(P-5166)
HERITAGE ONE WIN BLDG SLTONS L
Also Called: Heritage One
4300 Jetway Ct (95660-5702)
P.O. Box 214609 (95821-0609)
PHONE..................................916 481-5030
Charles Gardemeyer, *CEO*
Geoff Hughes, *
Stephen Beckham, *
John Ballou, *
Tyler Randolth, *Installation Manager*
EMP: 171 EST: 2012
SQ FT: 80,000
SALES (est): 24MM
SALES (corp-wide): 36.03MM **Privately Held**
Web: www.heritageonewindow.com
SIC: **5031** Doors and windows
PA: Heritage Interests, Llc
4300 Jetway Ct
North Highlands CA
916 481-5030

(P-5167)
HOSKIN & MUIR INC
Also Called: Hmi Cardinal
6611 Preston Ave Ste B (94551-5108)
PHONE..................................925 373-1135
EMP: 72
SALES (corp-wide): 48.83MM **Privately Held**
Web: www.hmiglass.com
SIC: **5031** Molding, all materials
PA: Hoskin & Muir, Inc.
4795 Shepherdsville Rd
Louisville KY
502 969-4059

(P-5168)
INTERNATIONAL WINDOW CORP
Also Called: Iwc
1320 Performance Dr (95206-4925)
PHONE..................................562 928-6411
Ridley Dix, *Prin*
EMP: 90 EST: 2012
SALES (est): 25.79MM **Privately Held**
Web: www.intlwindow.com
SIC: **5031** Windows
HQ: Universal Molding Extrusion Company, Inc.
9151 Imperial Hwy
Downey CA
562 401-1015

(P-5169)
JAMES HARDIE BUILDING PDTS INC
10901 Elm Ave (92337-7327)
PHONE..................................909 355-6500
Bob Mussleman, *Brnch Mgr*
EMP: 130
Web: www.jameshardie.com
SIC: **5031** 3272 Building materials, exterior; Areaways, basement window: concrete
HQ: James Hardie Building Products Inc.
231 S La Salle St # 2000
Chicago IL
312 291-5072

(P-5170)
JELD-WEN INC
Also Called: Jeld-Wen Windows
2760 Progress St Ste B (92081-8449)
PHONE..................................760 597-4201
Clint Honeycutt, *Genl Mgr*
EMP: 300
Web: www.jeld-wen.com
SIC: **5031** Doors and windows
HQ: Jeld-Wen, Inc.
2645 Silver Crescent Dr
Charlotte NC
800 535-3936

(P-5171)
JELD-WEN INC
Also Called: American Building Supply
120 S Cedar Ave (92376-9010)
PHONE..................................909 879-8700
Carlos Duran, *Brnch Mgr*
EMP: 104
Web: www.abs-abs.com
SIC: **5031** Doors, nec
HQ: Jeld-Wen, Inc.
2645 Silver Crescent Dr
Charlotte NC
800 535-3936

(P-5172)
MENDOCINO FOREST PDTS CO LLC
Also Called: Sawmill
850 Kunzler Ranch Rd (95482-7294)

P.O. Box 996 (95482-0996)
PHONE..................................707 468-1431
Dean Kerstetter, *Ex VP*
EMP: 200
SALES (corp-wide): 134.91MM **Privately Held**
Web: www.mfp.com
SIC: **5031** 2421 2499 Lumber: rough, dressed, and finished; Sawmills and planing mills, general; Fencing, docks, and other outdoor wood structural products
PA: Mendocino Forest Products Company Llc
3700 Old Redwood Hwy # 200
Santa Rosa CA
707 620-2961

(P-5173)
MILGARD MANUFACTURING LLC
Also Called: Milgard Windows
6050 88th St (95828-1119)
PHONE..................................916 387-0700
EMP: 83
SALES (corp-wide): 822.1MM **Privately Held**
Web: www.milgard.com
SIC: **5031** Windows
HQ: Milgard Manufacturing Llc
1010 54th Ave E
Tacoma WA
253 922-4343

(P-5174)
NICHOLS LUMBER & HARDWARE CO
Also Called: Ace Hardware
13470 Dalewood St (91706-5883)
PHONE..................................626 960-4802
Judith A Nichols, *Pr*
Charles Nichols, *
EMP: 75 EST: 1958
SALES (est): 24.91MM **Privately Held**
Web: www.nicholslumber.com
SIC: **5031** 5251 2421 Lumber: rough, dressed, and finished; Hardware stores; Sawmills and planing mills, general

(P-5175)
NOVO DISTRIBUTION LLC
31 Heron Ln (92507-1243)
PHONE..................................951 742-5273
Scott Price, *Brnch Mgr*
EMP: 79
SALES (corp-wide): 2.58B **Privately Held**
Web: www.empireco.com
SIC: **5031** Lumber, plywood, and millwork
HQ: Novo Distribution Llc
8181 Logistics Dr
Zeeland MI
616 772-7272

(P-5176)
NU FOREST PRODUCTS INC
280 Asti Rd (95425)
P.O. Box 189 (95425-0189)
PHONE..................................707 433-3313
Douglas Hart, *CEO*
▲ EMP: 73 EST: 1971
SALES (est): 22.39MM **Privately Held**
Web: www.iwpllc.com
SIC: **5031** Lumber: rough, dressed, and finished
PA: International Building Materials Llc
14421 Se 98th Ct
Clackamas OR

(PA)=Parent Co (HQ)=Headquarters
✪ = New Business established in last 2 years

2024 Directory of California WholeSalers and Service Companies

5031 - Lumber, Plywood, And Millwork (P-5177)

(P-5177)
OAKLAND PALLET COMPANY INC (PA)
2500 Grant Ave (94580-1810)
PHONE.....................510 278-1291
Jose G Padilla, *Pr*
Carlos Padilla, *
Javier Padilla, *
EMP: 130 **EST**: 1995
SALES (est): 45.19MM **Privately Held**
Web: www.oaklandpallet.com
SIC: 5031 7699 Pallets, wood; Pallet repair

(P-5178)
OREGON PCF BLDG PDTS CALIF INC
Also Called: Orepac Building Products
8185 Signal Ct Ste A (95824-2354)
PHONE.....................916 381-8051
John Dutter, *Mgr*
EMP: 94
SALES (corp-wide): 471.9MM **Privately Held**
Web: www.orepac.com
SIC: 5031 Building materials, exterior
HQ: Oregon Pacific Building Products (Calif.), Inc.
30170 Sw Ore Pac Ave
Wilsonville OR
503 685-5499

(P-5179)
OREGON PCF BLDG PDTS MAPLE INC
Also Called: Orepac Millwork Products
2401 E Philadelphia St (91761-7743)
PHONE.....................909 627-4043
Douglas Hart, *Pr*
▲ **EMP**: 125 **EST**: 1992
SALES (est): 23.89MM
SALES (corp-wide): 471.9MM **Privately Held**
Web: www.orepac.com
SIC: 5031 5032 Building materials, exterior; Brick, stone, and related material
PA: Orepac Holding Company
30170 Sw Ore Pac Ave
Wilsonville OR
503 685-5499

(P-5180)
PANORAMIC DOORS LLC
3265 Production Ave Ste A (92058-1361)
PHONE.....................760 722-1300
Raffy Timonian, *VP*
EMP: 103
SALES (corp-wide): 25.58MM **Privately Held**
Web: www.panoramicdoors.com
SIC: 5031 Windows
PA: Panoramic Doors Llc
15050 Frye Rd
Fort Worth TX
817 952-3500

(P-5181)
PJS LUMBER INC
Also Called: P J'S Construction Supplies
45055 Fremont Blvd (94538-6318)
PHONE.....................510 743-5300
Shane Mcmillan, *CEO*
Terry W Protto, *
Carlton J Mcmillan, *Pr*
Jeff Veilleux, *
EMP: 145 **EST**: 1984
SQ FT: 2,000
SALES (est): 26.79MM **Privately Held**
Web: www.pjsrebar.com
SIC: 5031 5051 Lumber: rough, dressed, and finished; Steel

(P-5182)
RELIABLE WHOLESALE LUMBER INC (PA)
7600 Redondo Cir (92648-1303)
P.O. Box 191 (92648-0191)
PHONE.....................714 848-8222
Jerome M Higman, *Pr*
Jerome M Higman, *Pr*
David Higman, *
Will Higman, *
Jerry Higman, *Prin*
EMP: 90 **EST**: 1970
SQ FT: 4,500
SALES (est): 101.05MM
SALES (corp-wide): 101.05MM **Privately Held**
Web: www.rwli.net
SIC: 5031 2421 Lumber: rough, dressed, and finished; Sawmills and planing mills, general

(P-5183)
ROSEBURG FOREST PRODUCTS CO
98 Mill St (96094-2251)
PHONE.....................530 938-2721
Tom Didgs, *Mgr*
EMP: 87
SQ FT: 180,000
SALES (corp-wide): 976.32MM **Privately Held**
Web: www.roseburg.com
SIC: 5031 Lumber: rough, dressed, and finished
HQ: Roseburg Forest Products Co
3660 Gateway St
Springfield OR
541 679-3311

(P-5184)
ROYAL PLYWOOD COMPANY LLC
6003 88th St Ste 100 (95828-1143)
P.O. Box 728 (90637-0728)
PHONE.....................916 426-3292
Gabriel N Marshi, *Managing Member*
EMP: 78
SALES (corp-wide): 62.2MM **Privately Held**
Web: www.royalplywood.com
SIC: 5031 Lumber: rough, dressed, and finished
PA: Royal Plywood Company, Llc
14171 Park Pl
Cerritos CA
562 404-2989

(P-5185)
ROYAL PLYWOOD COMPANY LLC (PA)
14171 Park Pl (90703-2463)
P.O. Box 728 (90637-0728)
PHONE.....................562 404-2989
Stephen Fuller, *
▲ **EMP**: 78 **EST**: 1999
SQ FT: 120,000
SALES (est): 62.2MM
SALES (corp-wide): 62.2MM **Privately Held**
Web: www.royalplywood.com
SIC: 5031 Lumber: rough, dressed, and finished

(P-5186)
SACRAMENTO A-1 DOOR
Also Called: A-1 Door & Building Solutions
4300 Jetway Ct (95660-5702)
P.O. Box 214446 (95821-0446)
PHONE.....................916 481-5030
▲ **EMP**: 109
Web: www.a-1doorco.com
SIC: 5031 Doors, nec

(P-5187)
SHAPP INTERNATIONAL TRDG INC
Also Called: Shapp Internatiooonal
6000 Reseda Blvd (91356-1571)
P.O. Box 893 (91365-0893)
PHONE.....................818 348-3000
Allan Shapiro, *Pr*
Louis Justin, *
EMP: 118 **EST**: 1991
SQ FT: 8,000
SALES (est): 10.27MM **Privately Held**
SIC: 5031 5064 5112 5021 Lumber, plywood, and millwork; Electrical appliances, major; Stationery and office supplies; Furniture

(P-5188)
SIERRA FOREST PRODUCTS
9000 Road 234 (93270-9560)
P.O. Box 10060 (93270-0060)
PHONE.....................559 535-4893
Dave Thomas, *CEO*
Seth Hokit, *
Greg Mitchell, *
EMP: 110 **EST**: 1964
SQ FT: 3,000
SALES (est): 23.66MM **Privately Held**
Web: www.ucfp.com
SIC: 5031 Lumber, plywood, and millwork

(P-5189)
STATES DRAWER BOX SPC LLC
1482 N Batavia St (92867-3505)
PHONE.....................714 744-4247
Cathy Blankenship, *Pr*
EMP: 60 **EST**: 1980
SALES (est): 14.74MM **Privately Held**
Web: www.dbsdrawers.com
SIC: 5031 Lumber: rough, dressed, and finished
PA: States Industries, Llc
29545 E Enid Rd
Eugene OR

(P-5190)
SUPER PALLET RECYCLING CORP (PA)
Also Called: Super Pallet Recycling Center
10401 Grant Line Rd (95624-9404)
P.O. Box 1832 (95759-1832)
PHONE.....................916 686-1700
Gyan Kalwani, *Pr*
EMP: 78 **EST**: 1994
SALES (est): 9.77MM **Privately Held**
SIC: 5031 Pallets, wood

(P-5191)
TRINITY RIVER LUMBER COMPANY (PA)
1375 Main St (96093)
P.O. Box 249 (96093-0249)
PHONE.....................530 623-5561
Frank A Schmidbauer, *CEO*
Dee Sanders, *
▲ **EMP**: 145 **EST**: 1983
SQ FT: 10,000
SALES (est): 24.47MM
SALES (corp-wide): 24.47MM **Privately Held**
Web: www.trinityriverlumbercompany.com
SIC: 5031 Lumber: rough, dressed, and finished

(P-5192)
USG INTERIORS LLC
Also Called: USG
2575 Loomis Rd (95205-8045)
PHONE.....................209 466-4636
Sandy Hirzel, *Mgr*
EMP: 314
SALES (corp-wide): 14.2B **Privately Held**
SIC: 5031 Building materials, exterior
HQ: Usg Interiors, Llc
125 S Franklin St
Chicago IL
800 874-4968

(P-5193)
WALNUT INVESTMENT CORP
Also Called: AMS
2940 E White Star Ave (92806-2627)
PHONE.....................714 238-9240
▲ **EMP**: 550
SIC: 5031 5039 5072 Building materials, exterior; Ceiling systems and products; Hardware

(P-5194)
WEYERHAEUSER COMPANY
11100 Hope St (90630-5236)
PHONE.....................714 523-3330
EMP: 77
SALES (corp-wide): 10.18B **Publicly Held**
Web: www.weyerhaeuser.com
SIC: 5031 Lumber: rough, dressed, and finished
PA: Weyerhaeuser Company
220 Occidental Ave S
Seattle WA
206 539-3000

5032 Brick, Stone, And Related Material

(P-5195)
ATLAS CONSTRUCTION SUPPLY INC (PA)
4640 Brinnell St (92111-2302)
PHONE.....................858 277-2100
Brian Quinn, *Pr*
James E Wright, *
Tom Vargas, *
▲ **EMP**: 75 **EST**: 1980
SQ FT: 30,000
SALES (est): 49.08MM
SALES (corp-wide): 49.08MM **Privately Held**
Web: www.atlasform.com
SIC: 5032 Concrete building products

(P-5196)
CARRARA MARBLE CO AMER INC (PA)
15939 Phoenix Dr (91745-1624)
PHONE.....................626 961-6010
William Cordova, *Pr*
James Hogan, *
▲ **EMP**: 70 **EST**: 1953
SQ FT: 30,000
SALES (est): 16.11MM
SALES (corp-wide): 16.11MM **Privately Held**
Web: www.carrara.com
SIC: 5032 1743 1741 Ceramic wall and floor tile, nec; Marble installation, interior; Masonry and other stonework

PRODUCTS & SERVICES SECTION

5033 - Roofing, Siding, And Insulation (P-5217)

(P-5197)
CEMEX CEMENT INC
1201 W Gladstone St (91702-5142)
P.O. Box 575 (91702-0575)
PHONE..............................626 969-1747
Steve Hayes, *Mgr*
EMP: 101
SIC: 5032 3273 3251 1411 Concrete mixtures; Ready-mixed concrete; Brick and structural clay tile; Dimension stone
HQ: Cemex Cement, Inc.
10100 Katy Fwy Ste 300
Houston TX
713 650-6200

(P-5198)
CEMEX CORP
22101 W Sunset Ave (93635-9683)
PHONE..............................800 992-3639
EMP: 204
SIC: 5032 3273 Cement; Ready-mixed concrete
HQ: Cemex Corp.
8888 E Raintree Dr # 250
Scottsdale AZ
602 416-2600

(P-5199)
CEMEX CORP
808 Gilman St (94710-1422)
PHONE..............................800 992-3639
EMP: 204
SIC: 5032 3273 Cement; Ready-mixed concrete
HQ: Cemex Corp.
8888 E Raintree Dr # 250
Scottsdale AZ
602 416-2600

(P-5200)
CLARK - PACIFIC CORPORATION (PA)
Also Called: Clark Pacific
710 Riverpoint Ct Ste 100 (95605-1690)
PHONE..............................916 371-0305
Robert Clark, *Pr*
Don Clark, *
▲ EMP: 300 EST: 1966
SALES (est): 243.72MM
SALES (corp-wide): 243.72MM **Privately Held**
Web: www.clarkpacific.com
SIC: 5032 3272 Brick, stone, and related material; Concrete products, precast, nec

(P-5201)
CONCRETE TIE INDUSTRIES INC (PA)
Also Called: Concrete Tie
130 E Oris St (90222-2714)
P.O. Box 5406 (90224-5406)
PHONE..............................310 628-2328
Paul J Schoendienst, *Pr*
Steve Sim, *
EMP: 70 EST: 1981
SQ FT: 280,000
SALES (est): 9.21MM
SALES (corp-wide): 9.21MM **Privately Held**
SIC: 5032 3452 Concrete and cinder building products; Bolts, nuts, rivets, and washers

(P-5202)
ELDORADO STONE LLC
24100 Orange Ave (92570-8791)
PHONE..............................951 601-3838
EMP: 657
Web: www.eldoradostone.com

SIC: 5032 Brick, stone, and related material
HQ: Eldorado Stone Llc
3817 Ocean Ranch Blvd # 114
Oceanside CA
800 925-1491

(P-5203)
EMSER INTERNATIONAL LLC (PA)
8431 Santa Monica Blvd (90069-4294)
PHONE..............................323 650-2000
Sam Ghodsian, *Managing Member*
Ehsan Ghodsian, *
▲ EMP: 70 EST: 1967
SQ FT: 50,000
SALES (est): 48.12MM
SALES (corp-wide): 48.12MM **Privately Held**
Web: www.emser.com
SIC: 5032 Ceramic wall and floor tile, nec

(P-5204)
EMSER TILE LLC (PA)
Also Called: Design Made Easy
8431 Santa Monica Blvd (90069-4209)
PHONE..............................323 650-2000
◆ EMP: 275 EST: 1968
SALES (est): 273.97MM
SALES (corp-wide): 273.97MM **Privately Held**
Web: www.emser.com
SIC: 5032 5211 Ceramic wall and floor tile, nec; Tile, ceramic

(P-5205)
GRANITE ROCK CO
303 Coral St (95060-2106)
PHONE..............................831 471-3440
Jim Holnquist, *Mgr*
EMP: 62
SALES (corp-wide): 521.49MM **Privately Held**
Web: www.graniterock.com
SIC: 5032 Brick, stone, and related material
PA: Granite Rock Co.
350 Technology Dr
Watsonville CA
831 768-2000

(P-5206)
GRANITE ROCK CO
540 W Beach St (95076-5125)
P.O. Box 50001 (95077-5001)
PHONE..............................831 724-3847
Mark Trainer, *Mgr*
EMP: 62
SALES (corp-wide): 521.49MM **Privately Held**
Web: www.graniterock.com
SIC: 5032 Brick, stone, and related material
PA: Granite Rock Co.
350 Technology Dr
Watsonville CA
831 768-2000

(P-5207)
M S INTERNATIONAL INC (PA)
Also Called: MSI Orange Showroom & Dist Ctr
2095 N Batavia St (92865-3101)
PHONE..............................714 685-7500
Manahar Shah, *CEO*
Rajesh Shah, *
Rutesh Shah, *
Chandrika Shah, *
◆ EMP: 266 EST: 1983
SQ FT: 500,000
SALES (est): 513.97MM
SALES (corp-wide): 513.97MM **Privately Held**

Web: www.msisurfaces.com
SIC: 5032 5023 Granite building stone; Floor coverings

(P-5208)
PACIFIC CLAY PRODUCTS INC
14741 Lake St (92530-1610)
PHONE..............................661 857-1401
Barry Coley, *Pr*
Kai Chin, *
Dale Kline, *
▲ EMP: 160 EST: 1930
SQ FT: 200,000
SALES (est): 48.16MM **Privately Held**
Web: www.pacificclay.com
SIC: 5032 3251 Tile and clay products; Paving brick, clay

(P-5209)
ROBERTSONS READY MIX LTD
16952 S D St (92395-3302)
PHONE..............................702 798-0568
EMP: 90
Web: www.rrmca.com
SIC: 5032 Gravel
HQ: Robertson's Ready Mix, Ltd., A California Limited Partnership
200 S Main St Ste 200 # 200
Corona CA
951 493-6500

(P-5210)
TRIANGLE ROCK PRODUCT INC
Also Called: Triangle Rock Products
22101 W Sunset Ave (93635-9683)
P.O. Box 1111 (93635-1111)
PHONE..............................209 826-5066
EMP: 258 EST: 1945
SALES (est): 13.04MM **Publicly Held**
SIC: 5032 3273 5211 Brick, stone, and related material; Ready-mixed concrete; Lumber and other building materials
HQ: Calmat Co.
500 N Brand Blvd Ste 500 # 500
Glendale CA
818 553-8821

(P-5211)
UGM CITATAH INC (PA)
Also Called: Ugmc
13220 Cambridge St (90670-4902)
PHONE..............................562 921-9549
Viken Dave Yaghjian, *Pr*
Bruce Feaster, *
Irmen Yaghjian, *
▲ EMP: 125 EST: 1987
SQ FT: 46,000
SALES (est): 19.08MM
SALES (corp-wide): 19.08MM **Privately Held**
Web: www.ugmcstone.com
SIC: 5032 1741 1743 Marble building stone; Stone masonry; Terrazzo, tile, marble and mosaic work

(P-5212)
VALORI SAND & GRAVEL COMPANY
Also Called: Thompson Building Materials
11027 Cherry Ave (92337-7118)
P.O. Box 950 (92334-0950)
PHONE..............................909 350-3000
Tom Rievley, *Brnch Mgr*
EMP: 250
SALES (corp-wide): 23.42MM **Privately Held**
Web: www.thompsonbldg.com
SIC: 5032 5211 Brick, stone, and related material; Cement
PA: Valori Sand & Gravel Company Inc

141 W Taft Ave
Orange CA
714 637-0104

(P-5213)
WALKER & ZANGER LLC (HQ)
Also Called: Walker & Zanger
16719 Schoenborn St (91343-6115)
PHONE..............................818 280-8300
Jonathan Zanger, *CEO*
Pat Petrocelli, *
◆ EMP: 60 EST: 1958
SQ FT: 30,000
SALES (est): 105.87MM
SALES (corp-wide): 127.59MM **Privately Held**
Web: shop.walkerzanger.com
SIC: 5032 Marble building stone
PA: Mosaic Companies, Llc
4341 W 108th St
Hialeah FL
305 372-9787

(P-5214)
WEST COAST SAND AND GRAVEL INC (PA)
Also Called: West Coast Materials
7282 Orangethorpe Ave (90621-3331)
P.O. Box 5067 (90622-5067)
PHONE..............................714 522-0282
TOLL FREE: 800
Daniel C Reyneveld, *CEO*
Marvin J Struiksma, *
John Struiksma, *
Robert Struiksma, *
Mike Struiksma, *Co-Secretary*
EMP: 71 EST: 1968
SQ FT: 4,200
SALES (est): 102.63MM
SALES (corp-wide): 102.63MM **Privately Held**
Web: www.wcsg.com
SIC: 5032 Sand, construction

(P-5215)
WESTERN PACIFIC DISTRG LLC
Also Called: Westpac Materials
341 W Meats Ave (92865-2623)
PHONE..............................714 974-6837
Mark Hamilton, *Managing Member*
EMP: 157 EST: 2001
SALES (est): 48.62MM **Privately Held**
Web: www.westpacmaterials.com
SIC: 5032 Drywall materials

(P-5216)
WESTLAKE ROYAL STONE LLC
3817 Ocean Ranch Blvd Ste 114 (92056-8607)
PHONE..............................770 645-4539
EMP: 1494
SIC: 5032 Building stone
HQ: Westlake Royal Stone Llc
2801 Post Oak Blvd # 600
Houston TX
770 645-4500

5033 Roofing, Siding, And Insulation

(P-5217)
ALL ROOFG MTLS LONG BCH INC
1435 Walter St (93003-5669)
PHONE..............................805 656-6319
Allen Hopper, *Mgr*
EMP: 69
SALES (corp-wide): 8.43B **Publicly Held**

(PA)=Parent Co (HQ)=Headquarters
✪ = New Business established in last 2 years

5033 - Roofing, Siding, And Insulation (P-5218)

Web: www.onlongbeach.com
SIC: 5033 Roofing, asphalt and sheet metal
HQ: A.L.L. Roofing Materials Of Long
    Beach, Inc.
    3645 Long Beach Blvd
    Long Beach CA
    562 595-7531

(P-5218)
ALL ROOFG MTLS LONG BCH INC
3100 Orange Ave (90755-5220)
PHONE..................................562 595-7377
TOLL FREE: 800
EMP: 69
SALES (corp-wide): 8.43B Publicly Held
Web: www.onlongbeach.com
SIC: 5033 Roofing, asphalt and sheet metal
HQ: A.L.L. Roofing Materials Of Long
    Beach, Inc.
    3645 Long Beach Blvd
    Long Beach CA
    562 595-7531

(P-5219)
BEACON PACIFIC INC
Also Called: Pacific Supply
675 N Batavia St (92868-1220)
PHONE..................................714 288-1974
EMP: 110
SIC: 5033 5211 Roofing, asphalt and sheet metal; Roofing material

(P-5220)
BURLINGAME INDUSTRIES INC
Also Called: Eagle Roofing Products
4555 Mckinley Ave (95206-4008)
PHONE..................................209 464-9001
EMP: 109
SALES (corp-wide): 120.4MM Privately Held
Web: www.eagleroofing.com
SIC: 5033 Roofing, siding, and insulation
PA: Burlingame Industries, Incorporated
    3546 N Riverside Ave
    Rialto CA
    909 355-7000

(P-5221)
GULFSIDE SUPPLY INC
Also Called: R & S Supply
5858 Westside Rd (96001-4448)
PHONE..................................530 241-1615
James S Resch, CEO
EMP: 181
SALES (corp-wide): 844.31MM Privately Held
Web: www.stuartscustomcycles.com
SIC: 5033 5211 Roofing and siding materials; Roofing material
PA: Gulfside Supply, Inc.
    2900 E 7th Ave Ste 100
    Tampa FL
    813 636-9808

(P-5222)
MAC ARTHUR CO
2855 Mandela Pkwy Ste D (94608-4051)
PHONE..................................510 251-2102
Joe Freitas, Brnch Mgr
EMP: 105
SALES (corp-wide): 672.99MM Privately Held
Web: www.macarthurco.com
SIC: 5033 5075 Insulation materials; Warm air heating and air conditioning
PA: Mac Arthur Co.
    2400 Wycliff St
    Saint Paul MN
    651 646-2773

(P-5223)
PACIFIC COAST SUPPLY LLC
Also Called: Pacific Supply
1155 N Emerald Ave (95351-1560)
P.O. Box 3717 (95352-3717)
PHONE..................................209 521-2466
Jason Rowe, Mgr
EMP: 63
SQ FT: 1,000
SALES (corp-wide): 1.19B Privately Held
Web: www.paccoast.com
SIC: 5033 5032 5211 Roofing and siding materials; Drywall materials; Roofing material
HQ: Pacific Coast Supply, Llc
    4290 Roseville Rd
    North Highlands CA
    916 971-2301

(P-5224)
REVCHEM COMPOSITES INC (PA)
Also Called: Revchem Plastics
2720 S Willow Ave # B (92316-3259)
P.O. Box 333 (92316-0333)
PHONE..................................909 877-8477
Douglas L Dennis, CEO
Gina L Dennis, *
◆ EMP: 66 EST: 1975
SALES (est): 31.41MM
SALES (corp-wide): 31.41MM Privately Held
Web: www.revchem.com
SIC: 5033 Fiberglass building materials

(P-5225)
STANDARD INDUSTRIES INC
Also Called: GAF Materials
6505 Zerker Rd (93263-9614)
PHONE..................................661 387-1110
Phil Halpin, Genl Mgr
EMP: 100
SALES (corp-wide): 6.27B Privately Held
Web: www.gaf.com
SIC: 5033 Roofing and siding materials
HQ: Standard Building Solutions Inc.
    1 Campus Dr
    Parsippany NJ

5039 Construction Materials, Nec

(P-5226)
BAKERSFIELD SHINGLES WHOLESALE INC
Also Called: Bsw Roofing Contractors
4 P St (93304-3192)
P.O. Box 70272 (93387-0272)
PHONE..................................661 327-3727
EMP: 85 EST: 1971
SALES (est): 11.25MM Privately Held
Web: www.bswroofing.com
SIC: 5039 1761 Eavestroughing, parts and supplies; Roofing contractor

(P-5227)
JENSEN ENTERPRISES INC
Also Called: Jensen Precast
5400 Raley Blvd (95838-1700)
PHONE..................................916 992-8301
TOLL FREE: 800
Mark Voiselle, Genl Mgr
EMP: 70
SALES (corp-wide): 237.25MM Privately Held
Web: www.jensenprecast.com
SIC: 5039 5211 Septic tanks; Masonry materials and supplies

PA: Jensen Enterprises, Inc.
    9895 Double R Blvd
    Reno NV
    775 352-2700

(P-5228)
LSF9 CYPRESS LP (PA)
2741 Walnut Ave Ste 200 (92780-7063)
PHONE..................................714 380-3127
Ruben Mendoza, Pr
EMP: 156 EST: 2015
SALES (est): 153.99MM
SALES (corp-wide): 153.99MM Privately Held
SIC: 5039 5031 5033 Ceiling systems and products; Wallboard; Insulation materials

(P-5229)
LSF9 CYPRESS PARENT 2 LLC
2741 Walnut Ave Ste 200 (92780-7063)
PHONE..................................714 380-3127
EMP: 3500 EST: 2016
SALES (est): 153.99MM
SALES (corp-wide): 153.99MM Privately Held
SIC: 5039 5031 5033 Ceiling systems and products; Wallboard; Insulation materials
PA: Lsf9 Cypress L.P.
    2741 Walnut Ave Ste 200
    Tustin CA
    714 380-3127

(P-5230)
MODERN ALLOYS INC
11172 Western Ave (90680-2911)
PHONE..................................714 893-0551
Ronald B Grey, Pr
Ronald B Grey, CEO
Scott Squires, *
EMP: 60 EST: 1960
SQ FT: 6,800
SALES (est): 12.41MM
SALES (corp-wide): 15.89MM Privately Held
SIC: 5039 Metal guardrails
PA: Mafab, Inc.
    1925 Century Park E # 650
    Los Angeles CA
    714 893-0551

(P-5231)
PERRYMAN MECHANICAL INC
514 Glide Ave (95691-2307)
P.O. Box 405 (95691-0405)
PHONE..................................916 371-8888
EMP: 70 EST: 1982
SALES (corp-wide): 12.72MM Privately Held
Web: www.pmi.ac
SIC: 5039 Metal buildings

(P-5232)
SECURITY CONTRACTOR SVCS INC (PA)
Also Called: S C S
5339 Jackson St (95660-5004)
PHONE..................................916 338-4200
Barry J Marrs, CEO
EMP: 60 EST: 1961
SQ FT: 50,000
SALES (est): 48.58MM
SALES (corp-wide): 48.58MM Privately Held
Web: www.scsfence.com
SIC: 5039 7359 3315 Wire fence, gates, and accessories; Equipment rental and leasing, nec; Steel wire and related products

(P-5233)
WHITE CAP SUPPLY GROUP INC
Also Called: White Cap 301
28255 Kelly Johnson Pkwy (91355-5080)
PHONE..................................661 294-7737
Julia Laguardia, Brnch Mgr
EMP: 3596
SALES (corp-wide): 7.35B Privately Held
SIC: 5039 5072 Air ducts, sheet metal; Hardware
HQ: White Cap Supply Group, Inc.
    6250 Brook Hllow Pkwy Ste
    Norcross GA

(P-5234)
WILLIAMS SCOTSMAN INC
Also Called: Williams Scotsman - Fresno
2829 S Chestnut Ave (93725-2224)
PHONE..................................559 441-8181
Rob Gebhard, Mgr
EMP: 143
SALES (corp-wide): 2.14B Publicly Held
Web: www.willscot.com
SIC: 5039 Mobile offices and commercial units
HQ: Williams Scotsman, Inc.
    4646 E Van Buren St # 40
    Phoenix AZ
    480 894-6311

5043 Photographic Equipment And Supplies

(P-5235)
CANON USA INC
15955 Alton Pkwy (92618-3731)
PHONE..................................949 753-4000
Glen Takahashi, Mgr
EMP: 350
Web: usa.canon.com
SIC: 5043 5044 5045 8741 Photographic cameras, projectors, equipment and supplies; Office equipment; Computers, nec; Management services
HQ: Canon U.S.A., Inc.
    1 Canon Park
    Melville NY
    516 328-5000

(P-5236)
CHRISTIE DGTAL SYSTEMS USA INC (HQ)
10550 Camden Dr (90630-4600)
PHONE..................................714 236-8610
Hideaki Onishi, Pr
Zoran Veselic, *
Jeff Stavro, *
◆ EMP: 68 EST: 1992
SQ FT: 85,000
SALES (est): 76.63MM Privately Held
Web: www.christiedigital.com
SIC: 5043 Projection apparatus, motion picture and slide
PA: Ushio Inc.
    1-6-5, Marunouchi
    Chiyoda-Ku TKY

(P-5237)
DAYMEN US INC
Also Called: Lowepro
1435 N Mcdowell Blvd Ste 200 (94954-6547)
PHONE..................................707 827-4053
▲ EMP: 65
Web: www.lowepro.com
SIC: 5043 Photographic equipment and supplies

PRODUCTS & SERVICES SECTION **5044 - Office Equipment (P-5259)**

(P-5238)
JK IMAGING LTD
17239 S Main St (90248-3129)
PHONE.....................310 755-6848
Joe Atick, *CEO*
Mike Feng, *
Shu-ping Wu, *CFO*
▲ **EMP:** 100 **EST:** 2012
SQ FT: 6,000
SALES (est): 10.46MM **Privately Held**
SIC: 5043 Cameras and photographic equipment

(P-5239)
NORITSU-AMERICA CORPORATION (HQ)
6900 Noritsu Ave (90620-1372)
P.O. Box 5039 (90622-5039)
PHONE.....................714 521-9040
Michiro Niikura, *CEO*
Kanichi Nishimoto, *
Akihiko Kuwabara, *
◆ **EMP:** 115 **EST:** 1978
SQ FT: 27,500
SALES (est): 69.13MM **Privately Held**
Web: www.noritsu.com
SIC: 5043 Photographic processing equipment
PA: Noritsu Koki Co., Ltd.
   1-10-10, Azabujuban
   Minato-Ku TKY

(P-5240)
PILGRIM OPERATIONS LLC
Also Called: Tailbroom Media Grop
12020 Chandler Blvd Ste 200 (91607)
PHONE.....................818 478-4500
Douglas Liechty, *Managing Member*
EMP: 400 **EST:** 2012
SALES (est): 22.06MM **Privately Held**
SIC: 5043 Motion picture studio and theater equipment

5044 Office Equipment

(P-5241)
ALLMODULAR SYSTEMS INC
21005 Cabot Blvd (94545-1109)
PHONE.....................510 887-9000
Donald Marquez, *Pr*
Vince Contreras, *
Juan P Valera, *
Abel Marquez, *
Rosa Pelayo, *
▲ **EMP:** 66 **EST:** 2008
SALES (est): 10.09MM **Privately Held**
Web: www.allmodularsystems.com
SIC: 5044 Office equipment

(P-5242)
ALLSTATE IMAGING INC (PA)
21621 Nordhoff St (91311-5828)
PHONE.....................818 678-4550
Alan Jurick, *Pr*
Richard Shapiro, *
Russel Leventhal, *
EMP: 80 **EST:** 1990
SALES (est): 14.98MM **Privately Held**
SIC: 5044 Office equipment

(P-5243)
CANON BUSINESS SOLUTIONS-WEST INC
110 W Walnut St (90248-3100)
P.O. Box 51075 (90074-1075)
PHONE.....................310 217-3000
EMP: 450

SIC: 5044 Office equipment

(P-5244)
CUSTOM BUSINESS SOLUTIONS INC (PA)
Also Called: Northstar
1 Studebaker (92618-2013)
PHONE.....................949 380-7674
▼ **EMP:** 68 **EST:** 1995
SALES (est): 27.78MM **Privately Held**
Web: www.cbsnorthstar.com
SIC: 5044 Cash registers

(P-5245)
DUPLO USA CORPORATION (PA)
Also Called: Duplo
3050 Daimler St (92705-5813)
PHONE.....................949 752-8222
Peter Tu, *Pr*
◆ **EMP:** 71 **EST:** 1979
SQ FT: 30,000
SALES (est): 19.95MM
SALES (corp-wide): 19.95MM **Privately Held**
Web: www.duplousa.com
SIC: 5044 Duplicating machines

(P-5246)
IMAGE IV SYSTEMS INC (PA)
512 S Varney St (91502-2196)
PHONE.....................818 841-0756
Terry Shayne, *CEO*
Ronald Warren, *
Sue Warren, *
Rickie Miyake Ctrl, *Prin*
EMP: 79 **EST:** 1984
SQ FT: 4,000
SALES (est): 18.19MM
SALES (corp-wide): 18.19MM **Privately Held**
Web: www.imageiv.com
SIC: 5044 Photocopy machines

(P-5247)
INTEGRUS LLC
Also Called: Advanced Office
14370 Myford Rd Ste 100 (92606-1015)
PHONE.....................949 538-9211
Mike Dixon, *CEO*
Richard Van Dyke, *Pr*
Tim Wickers, *VP*
EMP: 100 **EST:** 2011
SALES (est): 23.07MM **Privately Held**
SIC: 5044 Office equipment

(P-5248)
INTERNATIONAL BUS MCHS CORP
Also Called: IBM
425 Market St (94105-2532)
PHONE.....................415 545-4747
Wirt Cook, *CEO*
EMP: 208
SALES (corp-wide): 60.53B **Publicly Held**
Web: www.ibm.com
SIC: 5044 5045 3571 Office equipment; Computers, peripherals, and software; Electronic computers
PA: International Business Machines Corporation
   1 New Orchard Rd Ste 1 # 1
   Armonk NY
   914 499-1900

(P-5249)
KYOCERA DCMENT SOLUTIONS W LLC
14101 Alton Pkwy (92618-1815)
PHONE.....................800 996-9591

Norihiko Ina, *Managing Member*
Mike Graves, *
EMP: 150 **EST:** 2008
SALES (est): 24.47MM **Privately Held**
SIC: 5044 Office equipment
HQ: Kyocera Document Solutions America, Inc.
   225 Sand Rd
   Fairfield NJ
   973 808-8444

(P-5250)
MICROTEK LAB INC (HQ)
13337 South St (90703-7308)
PHONE.....................310 687-5823
Clark Hsu, *Pr*
Stewart Chow, *
▲ **EMP:** 110 **EST:** 1980
SQ FT: 126,000
SALES (est): 61.04MM **Privately Held**
Web: www.microtekusa.com
SIC: 5044 Copying equipment
PA: Microtek International Inc.
   No.6 Industry E. Road 3 Science-Based Industrial Park
   Hsinchu City

(P-5251)
MR COPY INC (DH)
Also Called: Mrc, Smart Tech Solutions
5657 Copley Dr (92111-7903)
PHONE.....................858 573-6300
EMP: 75 **EST:** 2009
SQ FT: 18,000
SALES (est): 84.96MM
SALES (corp-wide): 7.11B **Publicly Held**
Web: www.mrc360.com
SIC: 5044 Copying equipment
HQ: Xerox Business Solutions Inc
   8701 Florida Mining Blvd
   Tampa FL

(P-5252)
NATIONAL LINK INCORPORATED
2235 Auto Centre Dr (91740-6721)
PHONE.....................909 670-1900
Sam Kandah, *Pr*
Carol Kandah, *
Jim Scott, *
Mark Wasilow, *
EMP: 68 **EST:** 1992
SQ FT: 5,000
SALES (est): 16.33MM **Privately Held**
Web: www.nationallinkatm.com
SIC: 5044 7389 7359 Bank automatic teller machines; Credit card service; Electronic equipment rental, except computers

(P-5253)
NEW AGE ELECTRONICS INC
21950 Arnold Center Rd (90810-1646)
PHONE.....................310 549-0000
▲ **EMP:** 130
SIC: 5044 5045 Office equipment; Computers, peripherals, and software

(P-5254)
RICOH ELECTRONICS INC
1920 W Base Line Rd (92376-3016)
PHONE.....................714 566-2500
EMP: 94
Web: rei.ricoh.com
SIC: 5044 Photocopy machines
HQ: Ricoh Electronics, Inc.
   1125 Hurricane Shoals Rd
   Lawrenceville GA
   714 566-2500

(P-5255)
SAN DIEGO CASH REGISTER CO INC
Also Called: Sdcr
7940 Arjons Dr (92126-4340)
PHONE.....................858 790-7327
Matthew Richardson, *CEO*
EMP: 63 **EST:** 1967
SQ FT: 12,000
SALES (est): 19.65MM
SALES (corp-wide): 317.86MM **Publicly Held**
Web: www.i3pos.com
SIC: 5044 Office equipment
PA: I3 Verticals, Inc.
   40 Burton Hills Blvd # 415
   Nashville TN
   615 465-4487

(P-5256)
SOURCECORP BPS NTHRN CAL INC
900 Fortress St (95973-9514)
PHONE.....................530 893-7900
Steve Grieco, *CEO*
Katy Murray, *
Charles Gilbert, *
Russel Birk, *
EMP: 183 **EST:** 2013
SALES (est): 2.23MM
SALES (corp-wide): 1.08B **Publicly Held**
SIC: 5044 7389 Microfilm equipment; Microfilm recording and developing service
HQ: Sourcecorp Bps Inc.
   2701 E Grauwyler Rd
   Irving TX
   866 321-5854

(P-5257)
TOSHIBA AMER BUS SOLUTIONS INC (DH)
Also Called: Toshiba
25530 Commercentre Dr (92630-8855)
PHONE.....................949 462-6000
Scott Maccabe, *CEO*
Desmond Allen, *
Mark Mathews, *
Bill Lombard, *
Larry White, *
◆ **EMP:** 350 **EST:** 1999
SQ FT: 90,000
SALES (est): 1.38B **Privately Held**
Web: business.toshiba.com
SIC: 5044 Copying equipment
HQ: Toshiba Tec Corporation
   1-11-1, Osaki
   Shinagawa-Ku TKY

(P-5258)
UBEO WEST LLC (HQ)
3131 Esplanade (95973-0202)
PHONE.....................530 343-6065
TOLL FREE: 800
EMP: 105 **EST:** 1959
SALES (est): 109.63MM
SALES (corp-wide): 175.37MM **Privately Held**
Web: www.raymorgan.com
SIC: 5044 5999 Office equipment; Business machines and equipment
PA: Ubeo, Llc
   401 E Sonterra Blvd # 350
   San Antonio TX
   210 918-6000

(P-5259)
UNITED MERCHANT SVCS CAL INC
Also Called: Ums Banking

5044 - Office Equipment (P-5260)

750 Fairmont Ave Ste 201 (91203-1074)
PHONE..................................818 246-6767
Joyce Gaines, *Pr*
Lynda Neuman, *
Bruce Ferguson, *
EMP: 72 **EST:** 1987
SQ FT: 8,580
SALES (est): 17.29MM **Privately Held**
SIC: 5044 5065 7629 Office equipment; Electronic parts and equipment, nec; Electronic equipment repair

(P-5260)
UNITED RIBBON COMPANY INC
Also Called: United Imaging
21201 Oxnard St (91367-5015)
PHONE..................................818 716-1515
TOLL FREE: 800
Michael Cohen, *Pr*
Yigal Avrahamy, *
EMP: 85 **EST:** 1973
SQ FT: 22,000
SALES (est): 51.7MM **Privately Held**
Web: www.unitedimaging.com
SIC: 5044 5943 5021 7699 Office equipment; Office forms and supplies; Office and public building furniture; Office equipment and accessory customizing

(P-5261)
XEROX CORPORATION
Xerox
3333 Coyote Hill Rd (94304-1314)
PHONE..................................650 813-7138
David Smith, *VP*
EMP: 98
SALES (corp-wide): 7.11B **Publicly Held**
Web: www.xerox.com
SIC: 5044 Office equipment
HQ: Xerox Corporation
201 Merritt 7 Ste 20
Norwalk CT
203 849-5216

(P-5262)
XEROX EDUCATION SERVICES LLC (DH)
2277 E 220th St (90810-1639)
PHONE..................................310 830-9847
J Michael Peffer, *Managing Member*
Mike R Festa, *Managing Member**
EMP: 90 **EST:** 1970
SALES (est): 247.08MM
SALES (corp-wide): 3.86B **Publicly Held**
Web: www.afsa.com
SIC: 5044 Office equipment
HQ: Conduent Business Services, Llc
100 Campus Dr Ste 200
Florham Park NJ
973 261-7100

(P-5263)
YUBICO INC
5201 Great America Pkwy Ste 122 (95054-1125)
PHONE..................................408 774-4064
Stina Ehrensvard, *CEO*
Mattias Danielsson, *
EMP: 350 **EST:** 2007
SALES (est): 62.17MM **Privately Held**
Web: www.yubico.com
SIC: 5044 7379 Office equipment; Online services technology consultants

5045 Computers, Peripherals, And Software

(P-5264)
ABNORMAL SECURITY CORPORATION (PA)
185 Clara St Ste 100 (94107-4505)
PHONE..................................415 690-7347
Evan Reiser, *CEO*
Rami Habal, *CPO**
EMP: 473 **EST:** 2018
SALES (est): 52.06MM
SALES (corp-wide): 52.06MM **Privately Held**
Web: www.greylock.com
SIC: 5045 7382 7381 Computers, peripherals, and software; Security systems services; Guard services

(P-5265)
ADESSO INC
Also Called: ADS Techonlogy
20659 Valley Blvd (91789-2731)
PHONE..................................909 839-2929
Allen Ku, *Pr*
▲ **EMP:** 200 **EST:** 1994
SALES (est): 21.78MM **Privately Held**
Web: www.adesso.com
SIC: 5045 Computer peripheral equipment

(P-5266)
ADVANCED MICRO DEVICES INC (PA)
Also Called: AMD
2485 Augustine Dr (95054-3002)
PHONE..................................408 749-4000
Lisa T Su, *Ch Bd*
Jean Hu, *Ex VP*
Mark D Papermaster, *Ex VP*
Harry A Wolin, *Corporate Secretary*
Darla Smith, *Corporate Vice President*
EMP: 2923 **EST:** 1969
SALES (est): 23.6B
SALES (corp-wide): 23.6B **Publicly Held**
Web: www.amd.com
SIC: 5045 Computers, peripherals, and software

(P-5267)
ALLOY TECHNOLOGIES INC (PA)
548 Market St (94104-5401)
PHONE..................................415 990-5140
Joel Beal, *CEO*
EMP: 65 **EST:** 2015
SALES (est): 12.04MM
SALES (corp-wide): 12.04MM **Privately Held**
Web: www.alloy.ai
SIC: 5045 Computer software

(P-5268)
ALTAMETRICS HOSTING LLC
Also Called: Altametrics
3191 Red Hill Ave Ste 100 (92626-3451)
PHONE..................................800 676-1281
Mitesh Gala, *Pr*
Anand Gala, *
Ajay Shiv, *CIO**
EMP: 140 **EST:** 2001
SQ FT: 6,000
SALES (est): 34.92MM **Privately Held**
Web: www.altametrics.com
SIC: 5045 Computer software

(P-5269)
AMAX ENGINEERING CORPORATION (PA)
Also Called: Amax Computer
1565 Reliance Way (94539-6103)
PHONE..................................510 651-8886
Jerry Kc Shih, *CEO*
Jean Shih, *VP*
Chi-lei Ni, *VP*
▲ **EMP:** 150 **EST:** 1979
SQ FT: 110,000
SALES (est): 174.47MM
SALES (corp-wide): 174.47MM **Privately Held**
SIC: 5045 Computer peripheral equipment

(P-5270)
AMERICAN FUTURE TECH CORP
Also Called: Ibuypower
529 Baldwin Park Blvd (91746-1419)
PHONE..................................888 462-3899
Alex Hou, *CEO*
Darren Su, *
▲ **EMP:** 120 **EST:** 1997
SQ FT: 25,000
SALES (est): 133.76MM **Privately Held**
Web: www.ibuypower.com
SIC: 5045 Computer peripheral equipment

(P-5271)
AMERICAN PORTWELL TECH INC (PA)
Also Called: AP Tech
44200 Christy St (94538-3179)
PHONE..................................510 403-3399
Allen Lee, *CEO*
Joyce Wang, *
▲ **EMP:** 60 **EST:** 1999
SQ FT: 42,515
SALES (est): 36.47MM
SALES (corp-wide): 36.47MM **Privately Held**
Web: www.portwell.com
SIC: 5045 Computer peripheral equipment

(P-5272)
APP ORCHID INC
6111 Bollinger Canyon Rd Ste 570 (94583-5177)
PHONE..................................833 277-6724
Vaibhav Nadgauda, *CEO*
Catherine Cruzado, *
Shyam Chodapunedi, *CRO**
EMP: 185 **EST:** 2013
SALES (est): 13.88MM **Privately Held**
Web: www.apporchid.com
SIC: 5045 Computers, peripherals, and software

(P-5273)
ARBITECH LLC
Also Called: Tuksy
64 Fairbanks (92618-1602)
PHONE..................................949 376-6650
Jimmy Whalen, *Pr*
Doug Kari, *
David Walker, *
▲ **EMP:** 74 **EST:** 2000
SQ FT: 40,000
SALES (est): 119.81MM **Privately Held**
Web: www.arbitech.com
SIC: 5045 Computer peripheral equipment

(P-5274)
ARCHLYNK LLC (PA) ◆
550 S Winchester Blvd Ste 605 (95128-2545)
PHONE..................................408 214-3140
Sekhar Puli, *CEO*
Jiten Veghela, *VP*
EMP: 76 **EST:** 2022
SALES (est): 5.16MM
SALES (corp-wide): 5.16MM **Privately Held**
SIC: 5045 Computer software

(P-5275)
ASUS COMPUTER INTERNATIONAL
48720 Kato Rd (94538-7312)
PHONE..................................510 739-3777
▲ **EMP:** 130 **EST:** 1994
SQ FT: 13,000
SALES (est): 116MM **Privately Held**
Web: www.asus.com
SIC: 5045 3577 Computer peripheral equipment; Computer peripheral equipment, nec
PA: Asustek Computer Incorporation
No. 15, Li-Te Rd.
Taipei City TAP

(P-5276)
ATEN TECHNOLOGY INC
Also Called: Iogear
15365 Barranca Pkwy (92618-2216)
PHONE..................................949 453-8782
▲ **EMP:** 80 **EST:** 1996
SALES (est): 29.99MM **Privately Held**
Web: www.iogear.com
SIC: 5045 Computer peripheral equipment
PA: Aten International Co., Ltd.
3f, No. 125, Sec. 2, Datong Rd.
New Taipei City TAP

(P-5277)
ATTIVO NETWORKS INC
444 Castro St (94041-2008)
PHONE..................................510 623-1000
Tushar Kothari, *CEO*
Jilbert Washten, *
Ashok Shah, *
Tony Cole, *
EMP: 70 **EST:** 2011
SALES (est): 10.53MM
SALES (corp-wide): 422.18MM **Publicly Held**
Web: www.sentinelone.com
SIC: 5045 7371 7372 7373 Computers, peripherals, and software; Software programming applications; Prepackaged software; Systems software development services
PA: Sentinelone, Inc.
444 Castro St Ste 400
Mountain View CA
855 868-3733

(P-5278)
AXIOM MEMORY SOLUTIONS INC
16 Goodyear Ste 120 (92618-3743)
PHONE..................................949 581-1450
Keith Carpenter, *Pr*
EMP: 75 **EST:** 1995
SALES (est): 21.82MM **Privately Held**
Web: www.axiomupgrades.com
SIC: 5045 Computer peripheral equipment

(P-5279)
BAKER & TAYLOR HOLDINGS LLC
Also Called: Baker & Taylor Marketing Svc
10350 Barnes Canyon Rd (92121-2708)
PHONE..................................858 457-2500
EMP: 1436
SALES (corp-wide): 2.52B **Privately Held**

▲ = Import ▼ = Export
◆ = Import/Export

PRODUCTS & SERVICES SECTION

5045 - Computers, Peripherals, And Software (P-5300)

SIC: **5045** 5065 5192 7822 Computer software; Tapes, audio and video recording; Books; Television tape distribution
HQ: Baker & Taylor Holdings, Llc
2810 Coliseum Centre Dr # 300
Charlotte NC
704 998-3100

(P-5280)
BENQ AMERICA CORP (HQ)
Also Called: Benq
3200 Park Center Dr Ste 150 (92626-1982)
PHONE..................................714 559-4900
Lars Yoder, *Pr*
Ky Lee, *Ch*
Conway Lee, *Prin*
Ellin Lee, *
Peter Y F Huang, *Prin*
◆ **EMP:** 65 **EST:** 1997
SALES (est): 78.39MM **Privately Held**
Web: www.benq.com
SIC: **5045** Computer peripheral equipment
PA: Qisda Corporation
No. 157, 159, Shanying Rd.,
Taoyuan City TAY

(P-5281)
BIZCOM ELECTRONICS INC (HQ)
1361 El Camino Real (95050-4280)
PHONE..................................408 262-7877
Ray Chen, *CEO*
Duan Wang, *
▲ **EMP:** 140 **EST:** 1992
SALES (est): 42.7MM **Privately Held**
Web: www.bizcom-us.com
SIC: **5045** 7629 7378 Computers, nec; Telecommunication equipment repair (except telephones); Computer maintenance and repair
PA: Compal Electronics, Inc.
No. 581, 581-1, Ruiguang Rd.
Taipei City TAP

(P-5282)
BRAINSTORM CORPORATION
Also Called: Skytech Gaming
1620 Proforma Ave (91761-7605)
PHONE..................................888 370-8882
Kevin Hsu, *CEO*
◆ **EMP:** 200 **EST:** 2005
SALES (est): 79.31MM **Privately Held**
Web: www.brainstormco.com
SIC: **5045** 5065 Computer peripheral equipment; Electronic parts and equipment, nec
PA: Dfi Inc.
10f, No. 97, Xintai 5th Rd., Sec. 1
New Taipei City TAP

(P-5283)
BRAMASOL INC
5201 Great America Pkwy Ste 220 (95054-1121)
PHONE..................................408 831-0046
EMP: 80 **EST:** 1996
SALES (est): 20.06MM **Privately Held**
Web: www.bramasol.com
SIC: **5045** Computer software

(P-5284)
BROADWAY TYPEWRITER CO INC
Also Called: Arey Jones Eductl Solutions
1055 6th Ave Ste 101 (92101-5201)
PHONE..................................800 998-9199
Michael Scarpella, *Pr*
Peter Scarpella, *
David Scarpella, *
Margaret Scarpella, *
EMP: 80 **EST:** 1968
SQ FT: 40,000
SALES (est): 139.47MM **Privately Held**
Web: www.areyjones.com
SIC: **5045** 7378 Computers, peripherals, and software; Computer maintenance and repair

(P-5285)
BUSINESS OBJECTS INC
3410 Hillview Ave (94304-1395)
PHONE..................................650 849-4000
▲ **EMP:** 5208
Web: www.sapcrystalserver.com
SIC: **5045** Computer software

(P-5286)
COMMERCIAL INDUS DESIGN CO INC
Also Called: C I Design
20372 N Sea Cir (92630-8806)
PHONE..................................949 273-6199
Jeff Wu, *CEO*
Kae J Lee, *
▲ **EMP:** 60 **EST:** 1983
SALES (est): 9.85MM **Privately Held**
SIC: **5045** Computer peripheral equipment

(P-5287)
CONVRGD DATA TECH INC
999 Commercial St Ste 202 (94303-4909)
PHONE..................................650 461-4488
Akash Rajkumar Saraf, *CEO*
EMP: 110 **EST:** 2017
SALES (est): 8.22MM **Privately Held**
SIC: **5045** Computers, peripherals, and software

(P-5288)
CREATIVE LABS INC (DH)
1900 Mccarthy Blvd Ste 103 (95035-7413)
PHONE..................................408 428-6600
Keh Long Ng, *CEO*
Craig Mchugh, *Pr*
◆ **EMP:** 200 **EST:** 1988
SALES (est): 127.9MM **Privately Held**
Web: us.creative.com
SIC: **5045** 5734 3577 Computer peripheral equipment; Computer and software stores; Computer peripheral equipment, nec
HQ: Creative Holdings, Inc.
1900 Mccarthy Blvd # 103
Milpitas CA

(P-5289)
CURVATURE LLC (DH)
7418 Hollister Ave Ste 110 (93117-2675)
PHONE..................................800 230-6638
Christopher Adams, *Pr*
Betsy Dellinger, *
Andrew Gehrlein, *
◆ **EMP:** 300 **EST:** 2001
SALES (est): 251.01MM **Privately Held**
Web: www.curvature.com
SIC: **5045** 7379 Computer peripheral equipment; Computer related maintenance services
HQ: Nhr Newco Holdings Llc
6500 Hollister Ave # 210
Santa Barbara CA
805 964-9975

(P-5290)
CYARA SOLUTIONS CORP
Also Called: Cyara
805 Veterans Blvd Ste 105 (94063-1750)
PHONE..................................650 549-8522
EMP: 174 **EST:** 2010
SALES (est): 23.51MM **Privately Held**
Web: www.cyara.com
SIC: **5045** Computer software

(P-5291)
CYBERCSI INC
3511 Thomas Rd Ste 5 (95054-2039)
PHONE..................................408 727-2900
Dave Sanders, *CEO*
EMP: 95 **EST:** 1993
SQ FT: 11,000
SALES (est): 28.7MM **Privately Held**
Web: www.cybercsi.com
SIC: **5045** 7378 Computers, peripherals, and software; Computer maintenance and repair

(P-5292)
D-LINK SYSTEMS INCORPORATED
Also Called: D - Link
14420 Myford Rd Ste 100 (92606-1019)
PHONE..................................714 885-6000
William Brown, *Pr*
▲ **EMP:** 164 **EST:** 1986
SQ FT: 120,000
SALES (est): 52.65MM **Privately Held**
Web: us.dlink.com
SIC: **5045** 3577 Computers, nec; Computer peripheral equipment, nec
PA: D-Link Corporation
No. 289, Xinhu 3rd Rd.
Taipei City TAP

(P-5293)
DATA EXCHANGE CORPORATION (PA)
Also Called: D E X
3600 Via Pescador (93012-5035)
PHONE..................................805 388-1711
Sheldon Malchicoff, *CEO*
Alan Kheel, *
Burcak Sungur, *
▲ **EMP:** 300 **EST:** 1980
SQ FT: 100,000
SALES (est): 70.96MM
SALES (corp-wide): 70.96MM **Privately Held**
Web: www.dex.com
SIC: **5045** 7378 Computers, peripherals, and software; Computer and data processing equipment repair/maintenance

(P-5294)
DATALLEGRO INC
85 Enterprise Ste 200 (92656-2614)
PHONE..................................949 680-3000
Stuart Frost, *Ch Bd*
Mark Theissen, *
EMP: 100 **EST:** 2003
SQ FT: 16,000
SALES (est): 26.35MM
SALES (corp-wide): 211.91B **Publicly Held**
Web: www.datallegro.com
SIC: **5045** Computer software
PA: Microsoft Corporation
1 Microsoft Way
Redmond WA
425 882-8080

(P-5295)
DAZZ INC
2345 Yale St (94306-1448)
PHONE..................................800 956-8019
Natalie Kanfer, *Admn*
EMP: 69
SALES (est): 5.66MM **Privately Held**
SIC: **5045** Computer software

(P-5296)
DROBO INC
Also Called: Drobo
1289 Anvilwood Ave (94089-2204)
PHONE..................................408 454-4200
John Coughlan, *CFO*
Mihir H Shah, *CEO*
Tom Buiocchi, *Pr*
James Gardner, *VP Opers*
Mark Herbert, *VP Engg*
▲ **EMP:** 80 **EST:** 2005
SQ FT: 15,000
SALES (est): 19.31MM
SALES (corp-wide): 41.04MM **Privately Held**
Web: www.drobo.com
SIC: **5045** Computer software
PA: Storcentric, Inc.
1289 Anvilwood Ave
Sunnyvale CA

(P-5297)
ELITEGROUP COMPUTER SYSTEMS HO
Also Called: E C S-Elitegroup Cmpt Systems
6851 Mowry Ave (94560-4925)
PHONE..................................510 794-2952
Sam Tsai, *Pr*
Joseph Chang, *CFO*
Jon R Parsons, *Sec*
▲ **EMP:** 240 **EST:** 1999
SQ FT: 108,000
SALES (est): 53.66MM **Privately Held**
Web: www.ecs.com.tw
SIC: **5045** 3577 Computer peripheral equipment; Computer peripheral equipment, nec
PA: Hiyes International Co., Ltd.
7f., No.260, Dunhua N. Rd.,
Taipei City TAP

(P-5298)
ELO TOUCH SOLUTIONS INC (PA)
670 N Mccarthy Blvd Ste 100 (95035-5119)
PHONE..................................408 597-8000
Craig Witsoe, *CEO*
Roxi Wen, *
Kevin Cole, *
Bruno Thuillier, *
◆ **EMP:** 257 **EST:** 2012
SQ FT: 75,000
SALES (est): 150.4MM
SALES (corp-wide): 150.4MM **Privately Held**
Web: www.elotouch.com
SIC: **5045** Computers, peripherals, and software

(P-5299)
EN POINTE TECHNOLOGIES SLS LLC
200 N Pacific Coast Hwy Ste 1050 (90245-4340)
PHONE..................................310 337-6151
Frank Khulusi, *CEO*
Robert Miley, *
Brandon Laverne, *
EMP: 200 **EST:** 2015
SALES (est): 182.57MM **Publicly Held**
SIC: **5045** Computer peripheral equipment
HQ: Pcm, Inc.
200 N Pacific Coast Hwy # 1050
El Segundo CA
310 354-5600

(P-5300)
ENVIRONMENTAL SYSTEMS RESEARCH INSTITUTE INC (PA)

5045 - Computers, Peripherals, And Software (P-5301)

Also Called: Esri
380 New York St (92373-8118)
P.O. Box 7661 (92375-0661)
PHONE..................................909 793-2853
EMP: 1900 **EST:** 1973
SALES (est): 490.13MM
SALES (corp-wide): 490.13MM **Privately Held**
Web: www.esri.com
SIC: 5045 7371 Computer software; Computer software development and applications

(P-5301)
EON REALITY INC (PA)
18 Technology Dr Ste 110 (92618-2380)
PHONE..................................949 460-2000
Mats Johansson, *Pr*
EMP: 78 **EST:** 2002
SALES (est): 33.99MM
SALES (corp-wide): 33.99MM **Privately Held**
Web: www.eonreality.com
SIC: 5045 5734 Computer software; Computer software and accessories

(P-5302)
ESET LLC (HQ)
Also Called: Eset North America
610 W Ash St Ste 1700 (92101-3345)
PHONE..................................619 876-5400
Anton Zajac, *Pr*
Andrew Lee, *
Brett Stapleton, *
Brent Mccarty, *VP*
EMP: 123 **EST:** 1999
SQ FT: 57,000
SALES (est): 72.67MM **Privately Held**
PA: Eset, Spol. S R.O.
  Einsteinova 3541/24
  Bratislava-Petrzalka

(P-5303)
EVERTEK COMPUTER CORPORATION
Also Called: Evertek Computer Products
42301 Zevo Dr Ste A (92590-3731)
PHONE..................................951 252-8700
◆ **EMP:** 63 **EST:** 1990
SALES (est): 12.48MM **Privately Held**
Web: www.evertek.com
SIC: 5045 Computers and accessories, personal and home entertainment

(P-5304)
EWORKPLACE MANUFACTURING INC
Also Called: Batchmaster Software
9861 Irvine Center Dr (92618-4307)
PHONE..................................949 583-1646
Sahib Dudani, *Pr*
EMP: 200 **EST:** 1999
SQ FT: 5,000
SALES (est): 45.18MM **Privately Held**
Web: www.batchmaster.com
SIC: 5045 Computer software

(P-5305)
FINTECH OPEN SOURCE FOUNDATION
1117 California Ave (94304-1106)
PHONE..................................650 665-9773
Gabriele Columbro, *Ex Dir*
EMP: 268 **EST:** 2015
SALES (est): 1.55MM **Privately Held**
Web: www.finos.org
SIC: 5045 Computer software

(P-5306)
GAR ENTERPRISES (PA)
Also Called: Kgs Electronics
418 E Live Oak Ave (91006-5619)
PHONE..................................626 574-1175
Nathan Sugimoto, *CEO*
Pastor Kazuo G Sugimoto, *Prin*
EMP: 70 **EST:** 1960
SALES (est): 23.35MM
SALES (corp-wide): 23.35MM **Privately Held**
Web: www.kgselectronics.com
SIC: 5045 3728 Anti-static equipment and devices; Aircraft assemblies, subassemblies, and parts, nec

(P-5307)
GBT INC
Also Called: Gigabyte Technology
17358 Railroad St (91748-1023)
PHONE..................................626 854-9338
Eric C Lu, *Pr*
Eric C Lu, *Pr*
James Liao, *
▲ **EMP:** 130 **EST:** 1990
SQ FT: 35,000
SALES (est): 634.41MM **Privately Held**
SIC: 5045 Computers and accessories, personal and home entertainment
PA: Giga-Byte Technology Co., Ltd.
  No. 6, Baoqiang Rd.,
  New Taipei City TAP

(P-5308)
GENERAL MICRO SYSTEMS INC (PA)
Also Called: G M S
8358 Maple Pl (91730-3839)
P.O. Box 3689 (91729-3689)
PHONE..................................909 980-4863
Benjamin K Sharfi, *Pr*
EMP: 77 **EST:** 1979
SQ FT: 20,000
SALES (est): 54.91MM
SALES (corp-wide): 54.91MM **Privately Held**
Web: www.gms4sbc.com
SIC: 5045 Computers, peripherals, and software

(P-5309)
GENERAL PROCUREMENT INC (PA)
Also Called: Connect Computers
1964 W Corporate Way (92801-5373)
PHONE..................................949 679-7960
▲ **EMP:** 84 **EST:** 1991
SALES (est): 92.18MM **Privately Held**
Web: www.generalprocurement.com
SIC: 5045 5065 Computers, peripherals, and software; Electronic parts

(P-5310)
GENICA CORPORATION
43195 Business Park Dr (92590-3629)
PHONE..................................855 433-5747
▲ **EMP:** 334
Web: www.genica.com
SIC: 5045 5734 Computer peripheral equipment; Modems, monitors, terminals, and disk drives: computers

(P-5311)
GETAC INC
Also Called: Getac North America
15495 Sand Canyon Ave Ste 350 (92618-3152)
PHONE..................................949 681-2900
Ming-hang Hwang, *CEO*
Jim Rimay, *
▲ **EMP:** 90 **EST:** 1994
SQ FT: 12,000
SALES (est): 56.22MM **Privately Held**
Web: www.getac.com
SIC: 5045 Mainframe computers
PA: Getac Holdings Corporation
  Building A, 5f, No. 209. Sec. 1.
  Nangang Rd.
  Taipei City TAP

(P-5312)
HPM INCORPORATED
Also Called: Cancom USA
850 Auburn Ct (94538-7306)
PHONE..................................510 353-0770
Charles Miano, *CEO*
Shawn Scanlon, *
Alex Lindsay, *
◆ **EMP:** 67 **EST:** 1994
SQ FT: 11,000
SALES (est): 54.62MM
SALES (corp-wide): 1.34B **Privately Held**
Web: www.hpmnetworks.com
SIC: 5045 7378 Computer software; Computer peripheral equipment repair and maintenance
PA: Cancom Se
  Erika-Mann-Str. 69
  Munchen BY
  89540540

(P-5313)
I2C INC
100 Redwood Shores Pkwy (94065-1155)
PHONE..................................650 593-5400
Amir Wain, *CEO*
Khalid Hameed, *
Jon Round, *
Maryann Allison, *Industry Relations*
Steve Diamond, *Content Vice President*
EMP: 400 **EST:** 2000
SALES (est): 94.83MM **Privately Held**
Web: www.i2cinc.com
SIC: 5045 Computer software

(P-5314)
INGRAM MICRO INC (HQ)
Also Called: Im-Logstics An Ingram McRo Div
3351 Michelson Dr Ste 100 (92612-0697)
PHONE..................................714 566-1000
Paul Bay, *CEO*
Mike Zilis, *
Augusto Aragone, *
◆ **EMP:** 4000 **EST:** 1979
SALES (est): 32.76B **Privately Held**
Web: corp.ingrammicro.com
SIC: 5045 Computer software
PA: Platinum Equity, Llc
  360 N Crescent Dr Bldg S
  Beverly Hills CA

(P-5315)
INGRAM MICRO SERVICES LLC
3351 Michelson Dr Ste 100 (92612-0697)
PHONE..................................714 566-1000
EMP: 83 **EST:** 2014
SALES (est): 828.67K **Privately Held**
Web: www.ingrammicroservices.com
SIC: 5045 Computer software

(P-5316)
INSIDEVIEW TECHNOLOGIES INC
Also Called: Insideview Technologies
444 De Haro St Ste 210 (94107-2398)
PHONE..................................415 728-9309
Gabe Rogol, *CEO*
EMP: 150 **EST:** 2005
SALES (est): 47.11MM **Privately Held**
Web: www.demandbase.com
SIC: 5045 Computer software
PA: Demandbase, Inc.
  680 Folsom St Ste 400
  San Francisco CA

(P-5317)
IRON SYSTEMS INC (PA)
980 Mission Ct (94539-8202)
PHONE..................................408 943-8000
▲ **EMP:** 72 **EST:** 2002
SQ FT: 43,000
SALES (est): 47.35MM **Privately Held**
Web: www.ironsystems.com
SIC: 5045 Computers, peripherals, and software

(P-5318)
JANE TECHNOLOGIES INC
1347 Pacific Ave Ste 201 (95060-3940)
PHONE..................................617 285-2466
EMP: 93 **EST:** 2017
SALES (est): 10.36MM **Privately Held**
SIC: 5045 Computers, peripherals, and software

(P-5319)
JUNIPER SQUARE INC
555 Montgomery St Ste 1400 (94111-2589)
PHONE..................................415 841-2722
Alex Robinson, *CEO*
Stacy Bricker, *
EMP: 355 **EST:** 2014
SALES (est): 62.49MM **Privately Held**
Web: www.junipersquare.com
SIC: 5045 Computer software

(P-5320)
K-MICRO INC
Also Called: Corpinfo Services
1618 Stanford St (90404-5368)
PHONE..................................310 442-3200
Michael Sabourian, *Pr*
Ahmad Gramian, *
EMP: 96 **EST:** 1984
SQ FT: 25,000
SALES (est): 16.68MM **Privately Held**
Web: www.corpinfo.com
SIC: 5045 7378 7373 7371 Computers and accessories, personal and home entertainment; Computer maintenance and repair; Computer integrated systems design ; Custom computer programming services

(P-5321)
KAPOW TECHNOLOGIES INC
Also Called: Kapow Software
15211 Laguna Canyon Rd (92618-3146)
PHONE..................................800 805-0828
▲ **EMP:** 60
SIC: 5045 Computer software

(P-5322)
KINGSTON TECHNOLOGY COMPANY INC (PA)
17600 Newhope St (92708-4220)
PHONE..................................714 435-2600
◆ **EMP:** 780 **EST:** 1987
SALES (est): 418.24MM
SALES (corp-wide): 418.24MM **Privately Held**
Web: www.kingston.com
SIC: 5045 3674 Computer peripheral equipment; Random access memory (RAM)

(P-5323)
LEANDATA INC
2901 Patrick Henry Dr (95054-1831)
PHONE..................................669 600-5676

▲ = Import ▼ = Export
◆ = Import/Export

PRODUCTS & SERVICES SECTION
5045 - Computers, Peripherals, And Software (P-5344)

Taifu Liang, *CEO*
Hendrick Lee, *VP*
Karen Steele, *CMO*
Steve De Marco, *CRO*
EMP: 198 **EST:** 2012
SALES (est): 9.52MM **Privately Held**
Web: www.leandata.com
SIC: 5045 Computer software

(P-5324)
LEXAR MEDIA INC
47300 Bayside Pkwy (94538-6516)
PHONE.................510 413-1200
EMP: 160
SIC: 5045 Computers, peripherals, and software

(P-5325)
LITMUS AUTOMATION INC (PA)
2350 Mission College Blvd Ste 1020 (95054-1563)
PHONE.................765 418-7405
Vatsal Shah, *CEO*
Sacha Sawaya, *
John Younes, *
EMP: 73 **EST:** 2016
SQ FT: 3,500
SALES (est): 10.59MM
SALES (corp-wide): 10.59MM **Privately Held**
Web: www.litmus.io
SIC: 5045 7372 Computer software; Prepackaged software

(P-5326)
MA LABORATORIES INC (PA)
Also Called: MA Labs
2075 N Capitol Ave (95132-1009)
PHONE.................408 941-0808
◆ **EMP:** 350 **EST:** 1983
SALES (est): 226.21MM
SALES (corp-wide): 226.21MM **Privately Held**
Web: www.malabs.com
SIC: 5045 Computers, peripherals, and software

(P-5327)
MAGNELL ASSOCIATE INC (DH)
Also Called: A B S
17560 Rowland St (91748-1114)
PHONE.................800 685-3471
Robert Chang, *CEO*
◆ **EMP:** 130 **EST:** 1990
SALES (est): 472.79MM
SALES (corp-wide): 2.38B **Publicly Held**
Web: www.absgamingpc.com
SIC: 5045 Computers and accessories, personal and home entertainment
HQ: Newegg Inc.
17560 Rowland St
City Of Industry CA
626 271-9700

(P-5328)
MATTERPORT OPERATING LLC (HQ)
352 E Java Dr (94089-1328)
PHONE.................650 641-2241
EMP: 214 **EST:** 2011
SQ FT: 28,322
SALES (est): 61.28MM
SALES (corp-wide): 136.13MM **Publicly Held**
Web: www.matterport.com
SIC: 5045 Computer software
PA: Matterport, Inc.
352 E Java Dr
Sunnyvale CA
650 641-2241

(P-5329)
MEDIATEK USA INC
10188 Telesis Ct Ste 500 (92121-4761)
PHONE.................858 731-9200
EMP: 124
SIC: 5045 Computer software
HQ: Mediatek Usa Inc.
2840 Junction Ave
San Jose CA
408 526-1899

(P-5330)
MSI COMPUTER CORP (HQ)
901 Canada Ct (91748-1136)
PHONE.................626 913-0828
Andy Tung, *CEO*
Connie Chang, *
◆ **EMP:** 90 **EST:** 1998
SQ FT: 77,500
SALES (est): 51.95MM **Privately Held**
Web: www.msicomputer.com
SIC: 5045 Computer peripheral equipment
PA: Micro-Star International Co., Ltd.
No.69, Lide St.,
New Taipei City TAP

(P-5331)
MTC WORLDWIDE CORP
17837 Rowland St (91748-1122)
PHONE.................626 839-6800
Roy Han, *CEO*
▲ **EMP:** 79 **EST:** 1989
SQ FT: 42,500
SALES (est): 21.57MM
SALES (corp-wide): 39.29MM **Privately Held**
Web: www.mtcusa.com
SIC: 5045 3577 Computer peripheral equipment; Computer peripheral equipment, nec
PA: Mtc Direct, Inc.
17837 Rowland St
City Of Industry CA
626 839-6800

(P-5332)
PAYDARFAR INDUSTRIES INC
Also Called: Saratech
26054 Acero (92691-2768)
PHONE.................949 481-3267
Saeed Paydarfar Ph.d., *CEO*
EMP: 60 **EST:** 2002
SQ FT: 5,930
SALES (est): 21.9MM **Privately Held**
Web: www.saratech.com
SIC: 5045 8711 7372 7373 Computer software; Engineering services; Prepackaged software; Value-added resellers, computer systems

(P-5333)
PC SPECIALISTS INC (DH)
Also Called: Technology Integration Group
10620 Treena St Ste 300 (92131-1141)
PHONE.................858 566-1900
EMP: 117 **EST:** 1983
SALES (est): 517.23MM
SALES (corp-wide): 831.25MM **Privately Held**
Web: www.tig.com
SIC: 5045 3571 7371 Computers, peripherals, and software; Electronic computers; Custom computer programming services
HQ: Converge Technology Solutions Corp
85 Rue Victoria etage 2eme
Gatineau QC
416 360-3995

(P-5334)
PENGUIN COMPUTING INC (DH)
45800 Northport Loop W (94538-6413)
PHONE.................415 954-2800
Tom Coull, *Pr*
Lisa Cummins, *CFO*
▲ **EMP:** 85 **EST:** 1999
SQ FT: 86,000
SALES (est): 67.37MM
SALES (corp-wide): 1.44B **Publicly Held**
Web: www.penguinsolutions.com
SIC: 5045 7371 7379 Computer software; Custom computer programming services; Computer related maintenance services
HQ: Smart Modular Technologies (De), Inc.
45800 Northport Loop W
Fremont CA

(P-5335)
PRIVATE LABEL PC LLC
Also Called: Private Label
748 Epperson Dr (91748-1336)
PHONE.................626 965-8686
▲ **EMP:** 120 **EST:** 1987
SALES (est): 24.39MM **Privately Held**
Web: www.plpc.com
SIC: 5045 Computer peripheral equipment

(P-5336)
PROMISE TECHNOLOGY INC
39889 Eureka Dr (94560-4811)
PHONE.................408 645-3499
Tung-hsu Lin, *CEO*
James Lee, *Pr*
▲ **EMP:** 80 **EST:** 1988
SALES (est): 46.08MM **Privately Held**
Web: www.promise.com
SIC: 5045 7379 Computers, peripherals, and software; Data processing consultant
PA: Promise Technology Inc.
2f, No. 30, Gongye E. 9th Rd.,
Xinzhukexuegongyexueyuan District
Baoshan Township HSI

(P-5337)
QUANTA CLOUD TECH USA LLC
Also Called: Qct LLC
1010 Rincon Cir (95131-1325)
PHONE.................510 270-6111
Alan Lam, *Managing Member*
▲ **EMP:** 1000 **EST:** 2011
SALES (est): 86.61MM **Privately Held**
Web: www.qct.io
SIC: 5045 Computers, peripherals, and software
PA: Quanta Computer Inc.
No. 188, Wenhua 2nd Rd.
Taoyuan City TAY

(P-5338)
QVENTUS INC
2261 Market St Pmb 5023 (94114-1612)
PHONE.................585 690-9638
Mudit Garg, *CEO*
EMP: 130 **EST:** 2011
SALES (est): 16.31MM **Privately Held**
Web: www.qventus.com
SIC: 5045 Computer software

(P-5339)
RAPID ROBOTICS INC
100 Hooper St Ste 15 (94107-3918)
PHONE.................972 741-2627
Jordan Kretchmer, *CEO*
EMP: 79 **EST:** 2019
SALES (est): 8.65MM **Privately Held**
Web: www.rapidrobotics.com
SIC: 5045 Computer software

(P-5340)
RAVIG INC
Also Called: Salient Global Technologies
510 Garcia Ave Ste E (94565-7405)
PHONE.................925 526-1234
Ravikanth Ganapavarapu, *CEO*
EMP: 60 **EST:** 1999
SQ FT: 34,000
SALES (est): 24.3MM
SALES (corp-wide): 24.3MM **Privately Held**
SIC: 5045 7373 3571 Computers, peripherals, and software; Systems software development services; Electronic computers
PA: Salient Global Technologies
11252 Leo Ln
Dallas TX
925 526-1234

(P-5341)
REGAL TECHNOLOGY PARTNERS INC
2921 Daimler St (92705-5810)
PHONE.................714 835-1162
Allen Ronk, *Pr*
Paul Sorrentino, *
Jim Allen, *
◆ **EMP:** 65 **EST:** 1988
SQ FT: 26,000
SALES (est): 43.62MM **Privately Held**
Web: www.regaltechnology.com
SIC: 5045 7379 Computers, nec; Computer related consulting services

(P-5342)
RIPPEY CORPORATION
Also Called: ITW Rippey
5000 Hillsdale Cir (95762-5706)
PHONE.................916 939-4332
EMP: 70
Web: www.rippey.com
SIC: 5045 5065 3674 Computers, peripherals, and software; Electronic parts and equipment, nec; Semiconductor circuit networks

(P-5343)
RIVERBED TECHNOLOGY LLC (HQ)
680 Folsom St Ste 600 (94107-2155)
PHONE.................415 247-8800
Dave Donatelli, *CEO*
Dan Smoot, *
Subbu Iyer, *CMO**
Hansan Bae, *
John Tyler, *
▲ **EMP:** 70 **EST:** 2002
SQ FT: 167,000
SALES (est): 864.94MM
SALES (corp-wide): 912.58MM **Privately Held**
Web: www.riverbed.com
SIC: 5045 3577 Computer software; Computer peripheral equipment, nec
PA: Vector Capital Management, L.P.
1 Market St Ste 2300
San Francisco CA
415 293-5000

(P-5344)
SAMSUNG ELECTRONICS AMER INC
645 Clyde Ave (94043-2213)
PHONE.................646 651-2309
EMP: 121
Web: sra.samsung.com
SIC: 5045 Computers, peripherals, and software

5045 - Computers, Peripherals, And Software (P-5345)

HQ: Samsung Electronics America, Inc.
85 Challenger Rd
Ridgefield Park NJ
201 229-4000

(P-5345)
SAMSUNG RESEARCH AMERICA INC
18500 Von Karman Ave Ste 700 (92612-0504)
PHONE.................................949 468-1143
David Swanson, *Brnch Mgr*
EMP: 432
Web: sra.samsung.com
SIC: 5045 Computers, peripherals, and software
HQ: Samsung Research America, Inc.
665 Clyde Ave
Mountain View CA

(P-5346)
SAVVION INC
5104 Old Ironsides Dr Ste 205 (95054-1109)
PHONE.................................408 330-3400
EMP: 132 **EST:** 1994
SALES (est): 40.52MM
SALES (corp-wide): 602.01MM **Publicly Held**
Web: www.aurea.com
SIC: 5045 7371 8243 Computer software; Computer software development; Software training, computer
PA: Progress Software Corporation
15 Wayside Rd Ste 4
Burlington MA
781 280-4000

(P-5347)
SEGA OF AMERICA INC
350 Rhode Island St Ste 300 (94103-5188)
PHONE.................................415 701-6000
EMP: 165
Web: www.dreamcast.com
SIC: 5045 5092 Computers and accessories, personal and home entertainment; Video games

(P-5348)
SERVERS DIRECT LLC
20480 Business Pkwy (91789-2938)
PHONE.................................800 576-7931
Andy Juang, *CEO*
Howard Gilles, *
EMP: 108 **EST:** 2003
SALES (est): 2.39MM **Privately Held**
Web: www.serversdirect.com
SIC: 5045 Computers, peripherals, and software
PA: Equus Computer Systems, Inc.
201 General Mills Blvd
Minneapolis MN

(P-5349)
SK HYNIX AMERICA INC (HQ)
3101 N 1st St (95134-1934)
PHONE.................................408 232-8000
Kun Chul Suh, *CEO*
Jae H Park, *
▲ **EMP:** 80 **EST:** 1983
SQ FT: 190,000
SALES (est): 244.54MM **Privately Held**
Web: www.skhynix.com
SIC: 5045 5065 Computer peripheral equipment; Semiconductor devices
PA: Sk Hynix Inc.
2091 Gyeongchung-Daero, Bubal-Eup
Icheon

(P-5350)
SMC NETWORKS INC (HQ)
Also Called: Ignitenet
20 Mason (92618-2706)
PHONE.................................949 679-8029
Alex Kim, *CEO*
Frank Kuo, *
Inho Kim, *
Lane Ruoff, *
◆ **EMP:** 80 **EST:** 1971
SQ FT: 22,650
SALES (est): 23.84MM **Privately Held**
Web: www.smc.com
SIC: 5045 Computer peripheral equipment
PA: Accton Technology Corporation
1 Creation 3rd Rd., Hsinchu Science Park,
Hsinchu City

(P-5351)
SOLID STATE STOR TECH USA CORP
2610 Orchard Pkwy (95134-2020)
PHONE.................................510 687-1800
Ren-wu Michael Gong, *Pr*
Chin-sou Tsai Jean Hong, *CFO*
Yung-huei Clara Chen, *Dir*
▲ **EMP:** 100 **EST:** 2003
SALES (est): 16.55MM **Privately Held**
Web: www.ssstc.com
SIC: 5045 Computer peripheral equipment
HQ: Solid State Storage Technology Corporation
12f-14f, No. 392, Ruiguang Rd.
Taipei City TAP

(P-5352)
SOUTHLAND TECHNOLOGY INC
8053 Vickers St (92111-1917)
PHONE.................................858 694-0932
Grace Pedigo, *CEO*
Robert Pedigo, *
EMP: 65 **EST:** 2001
SQ FT: 16,000
SALES (est): 64.89MM **Privately Held**
Web: www.southlandtechnology.com
SIC: 5045 8748 7373 7379 Computer peripheral equipment; Systems engineering consultant, ex. computer or professional; Computer integrated systems design; Computer related maintenance services

(P-5353)
SPIN TECHNOLOGY INC
2100 Geng Rd (94303-3343)
PHONE.................................888 883-2993
Dumitru Dontov, *CEO*
EMP: 67 **EST:** 2013
SALES (est): 10.07MM **Privately Held**
Web: www.spin.ai
SIC: 5045 Computer software

(P-5354)
SPIRENT COMMUNICATIONS INC (HQ)
Also Called: Spirent Calabasas
27349 Agoura Rd (91301-2413)
PHONE.................................818 676-2300
Eric G Hutchinson, *CEO*
Bill Burns, *Pr*
▲ **EMP:** 350 **EST:** 1988
SALES (est): 598.51MM
SALES (corp-wide): 607.5MM **Privately Held**
Web: www.spirent.com
SIC: 5045 3663 3829 3825 Computers, peripherals, and software; Radio and t.v. communications equipment; Measuring and controlling devices, nec; Instruments to measure electricity
PA: Spirent Communications Plc
Origin One
Crawley W SUSSEX
129 376-7676

(P-5355)
SQUARE ENIX INC
999 N Pacific Coast Hwy Fl 3 (90245)
PHONE.................................310 846-0400
Mike Fischer, *Pr*
Clinton Foy, *COO*
Koichiro Hyashi, *Sec*
▲ **EMP:** 110 **EST:** 1998
SALES (est): 49.93MM **Privately Held**
Web: www.square-enix.com
SIC: 5045 7372 Computer software; Publisher's computer software
HQ: Square Enix Of America Holdings, Inc.
999 N Pacific Coast Hwy # 3
El Segundo CA

(P-5356)
SUNVALLEYTEK INTERNATIONAL INC
Also Called: Sunvalley
4260 N Harbor Blvd (92835-1017)
PHONE.................................888 456-8468
Caijin Sun, *CEO*
▲ **EMP:** 60 **EST:** 2007
SALES (est): 12.16MM **Privately Held**
Web: www.sunvalleytek.com
SIC: 5045 5961 Computer software; Computer equipment and electronics, mail order

(P-5357)
SUPER TALENT TECHNOLOGY CORP
2077 N Capitol Ave (95132-1009)
PHONE.................................408 957-8133
Abraham Ma, *Pr*
◆ **EMP:** 670 **EST:** 1991
SALES (est): 47.76MM **Privately Held**
Web: www.supertalent.com
SIC: 5045 Computer peripheral equipment

(P-5358)
SWITCHFLY LLC (PA)
500 3rd St Ste 215 (94107-1853)
PHONE.................................415 541-9100
Craig Brennan, *Managing Member*
Graham Blankenbaker, *
EMP: 100 **EST:** 2002
SALES (est): 24.07MM **Privately Held**
Web: www.switchfly.com
SIC: 5045 Computer software

(P-5359)
SYNERZIP LLC
5924 Roxie Ter (94555-3632)
PHONE.................................510 579-9673
Hemant Elhence, *Prin*
EMP: 63
Web: www.excellarate.com
SIC: 5045 Computer software
PA: Synerzip, Llc
940 W Valley Rd Ste 1500
Wayne PA

(P-5360)
SYSPRO IMPACT SOFTWARE INC
Also Called: Syspro
1775 Flight Way Ste 150 (92782-1844)
PHONE.................................714 437-1000
Brian Stein, *CEO*
Joey Benadretti, *
Kristin Valentyn, *CRO**
EMP: 200 **EST:** 1991

SALES (est): 47.65MM **Privately Held**
Web: us.syspro.com
SIC: 5045 7372 7371 Computer software; Prepackaged software; Custom computer programming services

(P-5361)
THUNDERHEAD ONE INC
6220 Stoneridge Mall Rd (94588-3260)
PHONE.................................877 838-8945
Glen Manchester, *CEO*
EMP: 71 **EST:** 2015
SALES (est): 8.5MM **Privately Held**
Web: www.medallia.com
SIC: 5045 Computer software

(P-5362)
TP-LINK USA CORPORATION
3760 Kilroy Airport Way Ste 600 (90806-2443)
PHONE.................................562 528-7700
Dana Knight, *Mktg Dir*
EMP: 86
Web: www.tp-link.com
SIC: 5045 Computer peripheral equipment
HQ: Tp-Link Usa Corporation
10 Mauchly
Irvine CA
626 333-0234

(P-5363)
TREND MICRO INCORPORATED
Also Called: Deep Security
3031 Tisch Way (95128-2584)
PHONE.................................408 257-1500
Dana L Testa, *Mgr*
EMP: 89
Web: www.trendmicro.com
SIC: 5045 7382 7372 Computer software; Security systems services; Prepackaged software
HQ: Trend Micro Incorporated
225 E John Carpenter Fwy # 1500
Irving TX

(P-5364)
TREND MICRO INCORPORATED
10101 N De Anza Blvd (95014-2264)
PHONE.................................408 257-1500
Anrew Lai, *Brnch Mgr*
EMP: 202
Web: www.trendmicro.com
SIC: 5045 7382 7372 Computer software; Security systems services; Prepackaged software
HQ: Trend Micro Incorporated
225 E John Carpenter Fwy # 1500
Irving TX

(P-5365)
TREY ARCH LLC
3420 Ocean Park Blvd Ste 2000 (90405-3304)
PHONE.................................310 581-4700
EMP: 392 **EST:** 1996
SALES (est): 29.26MM
SALES (corp-wide): 211.91B **Publicly Held**
SIC: 5045 5092 Computer software; Video games
HQ: Activision Blizzard, Inc.
2701 Olympic Blvd Bldg B
Santa Monica CA
310 255-2000

(P-5366)
TRIVAD INC
880 Mitten Rd Ste 107 (94010-1309)
PHONE.................................650 286-1086
Jenna Lim, *CEO*

PRODUCTS & SERVICES SECTION
5046 - Commercial Equipment, Nec (P-5388)

EMP: 230 **EST:** 2002
SALES (est): 87.91MM **Privately Held**
Web: www.trivad.com
SIC: 5045 7373 5734 3721 Computers, peripherals, and software; Computer integrated systems design; Computer and software stores; Airplanes, fixed or rotary wing

(P-5367)
TW SECURITY CORP (DH)
5 Park Plz Ste 400 (92614-8524)
PHONE.................................949 932-1000
John Vigouroux, *CEO*
Bruce Green, *
Rodney S Miller, *
William Kilmer, *CMO*
EMP: 120 **EST:** 2008
SQ FT: 28,000
SALES (est): 110.53MM **Privately Held**
SIC: 5045 Computer software
HQ: Trustwave Holdings, Inc.
70 W Madison St Ste 600
Chicago IL
312 750-0950

(P-5368)
VENTURE DESIGN SERVICES INC
6737 Mowry Ave (94560-4927)
PHONE.................................510 744-3770
Tomaka Washington, *Mgr*
EMP: 69
SALES (corp-wide): 10MM **Privately Held**
SIC: 5045 Printers, computer
PA: Venture Design Services Inc.
1051 S East St
Anaheim CA
714 765-3740

(P-5369)
VIRTIUM LLC
30052 Tomas (92688-2127)
PHONE.................................949 888-2444
Robert P Healy, *Managing Member*
Sean P Barrette, *
EMP: 100 **EST:** 2015
SALES (est): 23.85MM **Privately Held**
Web: www.virtium.com
SIC: 5045 Computers, peripherals, and software

(P-5370)
WHI SOLUTIONS INC
Also Called: D S T Macdonald
28470 Avenue Stanford Ste 200 (91355)
PHONE.................................661 257-2120
Bruce Adamson, *Brnch Mgr*
EMP: 140
Web: www.whisolutions.com
SIC: 5045 7371 Computers, nec; Computer software development
HQ: Whi Solutions, Inc.
2145 Hamilton Ave
San Jose CA
914 697-9301

(P-5371)
WRANGLER TOPCO LLC
555 California St Ste 2900 (94104-1503)
PHONE.................................415 439-1400
Andrey Filev, *CEO*
Ryan Atlas, *VP*
Patrick Severson, *VP*
EMP: 1225 **EST:** 2018
SALES (est): 276.07MM
SALES (corp-wide): 4.38B **Privately Held**
SIC: 5045 Computer peripheral equipment
HQ: Cloud Software Group Holdings, Inc.
851 W Cypress Creek Rd
Fort Lauderdale FL
954 267-3000

(P-5372)
WYSE TECHNOLOGY LLC (DH)
Also Called: Dell Wyse
5455 Great America Pkwy (95054-3645)
PHONE.................................800 438-9973
▲ **EMP:** 150 **EST:** 1981
SALES (est): 99.62MM **Publicly Held**
SIC: 5045 5734 Computers, peripherals, and software; Computer and software stores
HQ: Dell Inc.
1 Dell Way
Round Rock TX
800 289-3555

5046 Commercial Equipment, Nec

(P-5373)
AES HEAVY EQUIPMENT RENTAL INC
Also Called: AES Generator Depot
611 Gateway Blvd (94080-7017)
PHONE.................................817 615-1044
Mark Wright, *Prin*
V Thomas, *
Nancy Palmer, *
Gregory Hammond, *
William Franklyn, *
EMP: 67 **EST:** 2020
SALES (est): 3.21MM **Privately Held**
SIC: 5046 Commercial equipment, nec

(P-5374)
AES HEAVY EQUIPMENT RENTAL INC
Also Called: AES Generator Depot
1390 Market St (94102-5402)
PHONE.................................817 615-1044
Mark Wright, *Prin*
Brayln Becerra, *
Othello Martin, *
Jacqueline Carraway, *
EMP: 69 **EST:** 2020
SALES (est): 3.25MM **Privately Held**
SIC: 5046 Commercial equipment, nec

(P-5375)
BUYEFFICIENT LLC
903 Calle Amanecer Ste 200 (92673-6251)
PHONE.................................949 382-3129
Dennis Baker, *Pr*
EMP: 130 **EST:** 2000
SALES (est): 7.3MM **Publicly Held**
Web: www.avendra.com
SIC: 5046 Hotel equipment and supplies
HQ: Avendra, Llc
540 Gaither Rd Ste 200
Rockville MD
301 825-0500

(P-5376)
DEPENDBLE BREAK RM SLTIONS INC
1431 W 9th St Ste B (91786-5698)
PHONE.................................909 982-5933
Zachary Oliver, *Pr*
Mark Oliver, *
EMP: 80 **EST:** 1987
SALES (est): 10.79MM **Privately Held**
Web: www.dependablevend.com
SIC: 5046 7389 5963 5078 Vending machines, coin-operated; Coffee service; Bottled water delivery; Drinking water coolers, mechanical

(P-5377)
EAST BAY RESTAURANT SUPPLY INC (PA)
49 4th St (94607-4603)
PHONE.................................510 465-4300
TOLL FREE: 800
◆ **EMP:** 120 **EST:** 1934
SALES (est): 38.58MM
SALES (corp-wide): 38.58MM **Privately Held**
Web: www.eastbayrestaurantsupply.com
SIC: 5046 Restaurant equipment and supplies, nec

(P-5378)
HANNAM CHAIN USA INC (PA)
Also Called: Hannam Chain Super 1 Market
2740 W Olympic Blvd (90006-2633)
PHONE.................................213 382-2922
Kee W Ha, *CEO*
Kee W Ha, *CEO*
Jeong Wan Koo, *Pr*
▲ **EMP:** 105 **EST:** 1987
SQ FT: 22,000
SALES (est): 24.41MM
SALES (corp-wide): 24.41MM **Privately Held**
SIC: 5046 5411 Restaurant equipment and supplies, nec; Supermarkets, independent

(P-5379)
HEC ASSET MANAGEMENT INC
29341 Kimberlina Rd (93280-7617)
P.O. Box 1200 (93280-8100)
PHONE.................................661 587-2250
Keith B Gardiner, *CEO*
EMP: 100 **EST:** 2011
SALES (est): 13.66MM **Privately Held**
SIC: 5046 Commercial equipment, nec

(P-5380)
INTERSTATE ELECTRIC CO INC
Also Called: IEC
2240 Yates Ave (90040-1914)
PHONE.................................800 225-5432
Edward Urlik, *CEO*
▲ **EMP:** 85 **EST:** 1946
SQ FT: 72,000
SALES (est): 24.22MM **Privately Held**
Web: www.iecdelivers.com
SIC: 5046 Signs, electrical

(P-5381)
JETRO HOLDINGS LLC
7466 Carroll Rd Ste 100 (92121-2356)
PHONE.................................858 564-0466
Dan Camacho, *Brnch Mgr*
EMP: 275
Web: www.restaurantdepot.com
SIC: 5046 Restaurant equipment and supplies, nec
HQ: Jetro Holdings, Llc
1710 Whitestone Expy
Whitestone NY

(P-5382)
JETRO HOLDINGS LLC
1611 E Washington Blvd (90021-3133)
PHONE.................................213 516-0301
Javier Gomez, *Brnch Mgr*
EMP: 192
Web: www.restaurantdepot.com
SIC: 5046 Restaurant equipment and supplies, nec
HQ: Jetro Holdings, Llc
1710 Whitestone Expy
Whitestone NY

(P-5383)
JONES SIGNS CO INC
Also Called: Ultrasigns Electrical Advg
9025 Balboa Ave Ste 150 (92123-1522)
PHONE.................................858 569-1400
EMP: 120
Web: www.ultrasign.com
SIC: 5046 Signs, electrical

(P-5384)
JUSTMAN PACKAGING & DISPLAY (PA)
5819 Telegraph Rd (90040-1515)
PHONE.................................323 728-8888
Morley Justman, *Pr*
Russell Justman, *VP*
Barbara Cabaret, *CFO*
▲ **EMP:** 65 **EST:** 1989
SALES (est): 23.76MM
SALES (corp-wide): 23.76MM **Privately Held**
SIC: 5046 5113 2752 Display equipment, except refrigerated; Corrugated and solid fiber boxes; Commercial printing, lithographic

(P-5385)
KUBOTA INDUSTRIAL EQUIPMENT
3401 Del Amo Blvd (90503-1636)
PHONE.................................817 756-1171
EMP: 148 **EST:** 2017
SALES (est): 22.25MM **Privately Held**
Web: www.kubota.com
SIC: 5046 Commercial equipment, nec

(P-5386)
MYERS RESTAURANT SUPPLY LLC
Also Called: Myers Fdservice Eqp Sup Design
1599 Cleveland Ave (95401-4280)
PHONE.................................707 570-1200
Charlie Fusari, *CEO*
Rob Myers, *
EMP: 114 **EST:** 2011
SALES (est): 50.12MM
SALES (corp-wide): 707.36MM **Privately Held**
Web: www.myersrestaurantsupply.com
SIC: 5046 Restaurant equipment and supplies, nec
PA: Edward Don & Company, Llc
9801 Adam Don Pkwy
Woodridge IL
708 442-9400

(P-5387)
R W SMITH & CO
Also Called: Trimark R. W. Smith & Co.
10101 Old Grove Rd (92131-1650)
PHONE.................................858 530-1800
EMP: 74
Web: www.rwsmithco.com
SIC: 5046 Restaurant equipment and supplies, nec
HQ: R. W. Smith & Co.
10101 Old Grove Rd
San Diego CA
858 530-1800

(P-5388)
SHOPPER INC
2655 Park Center Dr Ste B (93065-6333)
PHONE.................................805 527-6700
Bill Bieda, *CEO*
Elliot Bieda, *
Eta Bieda, *
◆ **EMP:** 300 **EST:** 1992
SALES (est): 47.15MM **Privately Held**

5046 - Commercial Equipment, Nec (P-5389)

SIC: **5046** Store fixtures

(P-5389)
TOM DREHER SALES INC
Beach Cities Wholesalers
2021 W 17th St (90813-1011)
P.O. Box 41386 (90853-1386)
PHONE...................................562 355-4074
Tom Dreher, *Pr*
EMP: 77
SIC: **5046** 5145 Restaurant equipment and supplies, nec; Popcorn and supplies
PA: Tom Dreher Sales, Inc.
2021 W 17th St
Long Beach CA

(P-5390)
TRIMARK ERF INC (PA)
Also Called: Big Tray
1200 7th St (94107-2201)
PHONE...................................415 626-5611
▼ **EMP:** 100 **EST:** 1961
SALES (est): 21.7MM
SALES (corp-wide): 21.7MM **Privately Held**
Web: www.chefstoys.com
SIC: **5046** 8742 Restaurant equipment and supplies, nec; Incentive or award program consultant

(P-5391)
TRIMARK RAYGAL LLC
Also Called: Trimark Orange County
210 Commerce (92602-1318)
PHONE...................................949 474-1000
Michael Anthony Costanzo, *Pr*
Eric Smith, *
Dirk Hallett, *Corporate Secretary*
EMP: 220 **EST:** 1971
SQ FT: 62,850
SALES (est): 153MM **Privately Held**
Web: www.trimarkusa.com
SIC: **5046** Restaurant equipment and supplies, nec
PA: Trimark Usa, Llc
9 Hampshire St
Mansfield MA

(P-5392)
TRINITY EQUIPMENT INC
2650 S La Cadena Dr (92324-3708)
PHONE...................................951 790-1652
Eric Lewis, *CEO*
Robert Sandoval, *
EMP: 75 **EST:** 2016
SALES (est): 10.44MM **Privately Held**
Web: www.trinityequipmentinc.com
SIC: **5046** 7353 Commercial equipment, nec; Heavy construction equipment rental

(P-5393)
TRUST 1 SALES INC
Also Called: Sam Sung Fixtures
1737 S Vermont Ave (90006-4523)
PHONE...................................323 732-3300
Richard Kim, *CEO*
Young S Kim, *
▲ **EMP:** 100 **EST:** 1984
SQ FT: 12,000
SALES (est): 8.16MM **Privately Held**
Web: www.trust1sales.com
SIC: **5046** 7699 Restaurant equipment and supplies, nec; Restaurant equipment repair

5047 Medical And Hospital Equipment

(P-5394)
A PLUS INTERNATIONAL INC (PA)
5138 Eucalyptus Ave (91710-9254)
PHONE...................................909 591-5168
Wayne Lin, *Pr*
David Lee, *VP*
◆ **EMP:** 73 **EST:** 1988
SQ FT: 150,000
SALES (est): 22.69MM
SALES (corp-wide): 22.69MM **Privately Held**
Web: www.aplusgroup.net
SIC: **5047** 3842 Medical equipment and supplies; Surgical appliances and supplies

(P-5395)
AGILITI INC
960 Riverside Pkwy (95605-1515)
PHONE...................................952 465-9993
EMP: 112
SALES (corp-wide): 1.12B **Publicly Held**
Web: www.agilitihealth.com
SIC: **5047** Medical equipment and supplies
HQ: Agiliti, Inc.
11095 Viking Dr Ste 300
Eden Prairie MN
952 893-3200

(P-5396)
ALPHA INNOTECH CORP
3040 Oakmead Village Dr (95051-0808)
PHONE...................................408 510-5500
Jason Novi, *Brnch Mgr*
EMP: 137
SALES (corp-wide): 1.14B **Publicly Held**
SIC: **5047** 7372 Diagnostic equipment, medical; Prepackaged software
HQ: Alpha Innotech Corp.
81 Daggett Dr
San Jose CA

(P-5397)
AMERICAN MEDICAL TECH INC
17595 Cartwright Rd (92614-5847)
PHONE...................................949 553-0359
Jean Signore, *Pr*
Jerry Signore, *VP*
EMP: 100 **EST:** 1989
SALES (est): 25.06MM **Privately Held**
Web: www.amtwoundcare.com
SIC: **5047** Medical equipment and supplies

(P-5398)
AMERICAN TOOTH INDUSTRIES
1200 Stellar Dr (93033-2404)
PHONE...................................805 487-9868
Emilio Pozzi, *CEO*
Bruno Pozzi, *
Victoria Pozzi, *
Roberto Trada, *
Minda Darimbang, *
▲ **EMP:** 98 **EST:** 1985
SQ FT: 28,000
SALES (est): 20.55MM **Privately Held**
Web: www.americantooth.com
SIC: **5047** Dental equipment and supplies

(P-5399)
ARGONAUT MFG SVCS INC
2841 Loker Ave E (92010-6626)
PHONE...................................888 834-8892
Wayne Woodard, *CEO*
Patrick Yount, *
EMP: 75 **EST:** 2016
SQ FT: 31,000
SALES (est): 12.62MM **Privately Held**
Web: www.argonautms.com
SIC: **5047** Diagnostic equipment, medical

(P-5400)
ARJO INC
17502 Fabrica Way (90703-7014)
PHONE...................................714 412-1170
Harald Stock, *Brnch Mgr*
EMP: 284
SALES (corp-wide): 7.13B **Privately Held**
Web: www.arjo.com
SIC: **5047** Medical equipment and supplies
HQ: Arjo, Inc.
2349 W Lake St Ste 250
Addison IL
630 785-4490

(P-5401)
AVITA MEDICAL AMERICAS LLC
Also Called: Avita Medical
28159 Avenue Stanford Ste 220 (91355)
PHONE...................................661 367-9170
Michael Perry, *Managing Member*
▲ **EMP:** 114 **EST:** 2005
SQ FT: 23,000
SALES (est): 34.42MM **Privately Held**
Web: www.avitamedical.com
SIC: **5047** Medical and hospital equipment
HQ: Avita Medical Pty Limited
L 7 330 Collins St
Melbourne VIC

(P-5402)
BALT USA LLC
Also Called: Blockade Medical
29 Parker Ste 100 (92618-1667)
PHONE...................................949 788-1443
EMP: 90 **EST:** 2011
SQ FT: 47,000
SALES (est): 37.79MM
SALES (corp-wide): 198.3MM **Privately Held**
Web: www.baltgroup.com
SIC: **5047** 3841 Medical equipment and supplies; Surgical and medical instruments
HQ: Balt International
10 Rue De La Croix Vigneron
Montmorency
139894641

(P-5403)
BETTER NIGHT LLC
5471 Kearny Villa Rd Ste 200 (92123)
PHONE...................................619 299-6299
EMP: 90 **EST:** 2017
SALES (est): 8.67MM **Privately Held**
Web: www.betternightsolutions.com
SIC: **5047** Medical and hospital equipment

(P-5404)
BINDING SITE INC (HQ)
6730 Mesa Ridge Rd Ste B (92121-2951)
PHONE...................................858 453-9177
Doug Kurth, *Pr*
Doug Anderson, *
▲ **EMP:** 77 **EST:** 1987
SQ FT: 23,000
SALES (est): 24.07MM
SALES (corp-wide): 44.91B **Publicly Held**
Web: www.thermofisher.com
SIC: **5047** Diagnostic equipment, medical
PA: Thermo Fisher Scientific Inc.
168 3rd Ave
Waltham MA
781 622-1000

(P-5405)
BIOSITE INC
9975 Summers Ridge Rd (92121-2997)
PHONE...................................510 683-9063
Yonkin John, *Pr*
EMP: 106 **EST:** 2011
SALES (est): 6.05MM **Privately Held**
Web: www.biositesystems.com
SIC: **5047** Medical equipment and supplies

(P-5406)
BRADEN PRTNERS LP A CAL LTD PR (HQ)
Also Called: Pacific Pulmonary Services Co
1304 Southpoint Blvd Ste 130 (94954)
PHONE...................................415 893-1518
Jane Thomas, *CEO*
Tsutomu Igawa, *
▲ **EMP:** 65 **EST:** 1990
SALES (est): 194.07MM
SALES (corp-wide): 194.07MM **Privately Held**
SIC: **5047** Medical equipment and supplies
PA: Pps Hme Llc
320 Park Ave Fl 18
New York NY

(P-5407)
CAMERON HEALTH INC
905 Calle Amanecer # 300 (92673-6277)
PHONE...................................949 940-4000
EMP: 100
SIC: **5047** Medical equipment and supplies

(P-5408)
CANON MEDICAL SYSTEMS USA INC (DH)
Also Called: Video Sensing Division
2441 Michelle Dr (92780-7047)
P.O. Box 2068 (92781-2068)
PHONE...................................714 730-5000
Shuzo Yamamoto, *Pr*
Nader Rad, *VP*
Calum G Cunningham, *VP*
Scott Goodwin, *VP*
John Patterson, *CFO*
◆ **EMP:** 300 **EST:** 1989
SQ FT: 135,000
SALES (est): 496.54MM **Privately Held**
Web: us.medical.canon
SIC: **5047** X-ray machines and tubes
HQ: Canon Medical Systems Corporation
1385, Shimoishigami
Otawara TCG

(P-5409)
COLOR HEALTH INC
Also Called: Color Genomic Danny
831 Mitten Rd Ste 100 (94010-1303)
PHONE...................................650 651-7116
Othman Laraki, *Pr*
EMP: 513 **EST:** 2013
SQ FT: 2,000
SALES (est): 96.3MM **Privately Held**
Web: www.color.com
SIC: **5047** Medical and hospital equipment

(P-5410)
CONVAID PRODUCTS LLC
2830 California St (90503-3908)
P.O. Box 4209 (90274-9571)
PHONE...................................310 618-0111
Chris Braun, *CEO*
Mervyn M Watkins, *
◆ **EMP:** 89 **EST:** 1976
SALES (est): 30.7MM **Privately Held**
Web: www.etac.com
SIC: **5047** Medical equipment and supplies

PRODUCTS & SERVICES SECTION
5047 - Medical And Hospital Equipment (P-5433)

(P-5411)
DISCUS DENTAL LLC (PA)
12121 Bluff Creek Dr Ste 100 (90094-2994)
PHONE...................................310 845-8600
◆ EMP: 150 EST: 2007
SALES (est): 31.14MM Privately Held
Web: www.discusdental.com
SIC: 5047 Dental equipment and supplies

(P-5412)
ELECTROMED INC
4590 Ish Dr (93063-7678)
PHONE...................................805 523-7500
Terry Belford, *Brnch Mgr*
EMP: 86
SALES (corp-wide): 48.07MM Publicly Held
Web: www.smartvest.com
SIC: 5047 Medical equipment and supplies
PA: Electromed, Inc.
   500 6th Ave Nw
   New Prague MN
   952 758-9299

(P-5413)
ENDOSCOPIC TECHNOLOGIES INC
Also Called: Estech
2603 Camino Ramon Ste 100 (94583-9127)
PHONE...................................925 866-7111
EMP: 60
Web: www.estech.com
SIC: 5047 Medical equipment and supplies

(P-5414)
FISHER & PAYKEL HEALTHCARE INC
17400 Laguna Canyon Rd Ste 300 (92618-5425)
PHONE...................................949 453-4000
Justin Callahan, *Pr*
Tony Barclay, *
Bryan Goudzwaard, *
Paul Shearer, *
▲ EMP: 150 EST: 1995
SQ FT: 5,000
SALES (est): 90.27MM Privately Held
Web: www.fphcare.com
SIC: 5047 Medical equipment and supplies
HQ: Fisher & Paykel Healthcare
    Corporation Limited
    15 Maurice Paykel Pl
    Auckland AUK

(P-5415)
GENEO UNITED LLC ✪
2077 Gateway Pl Ste 300 (95110-1149)
PHONE...................................224 548-5854
EMP: 65 EST: 2022
SALES (est): 5.78MM Privately Held
SIC: 5047 Medical equipment and supplies

(P-5416)
GOLD STANDARD DIAGNOSTICS CORP
2795 2nd St Ste 300 (95618-6505)
PHONE...................................530 759-8000
John M Griffiths, *Pr*
James Thompson, *CFO*
▲ EMP: 75 EST: 2006
SQ FT: 2,750
SALES (est): 27.52MM
SALES (corp-wide): 220.81K Privately Held
Web: www.gsdx.us
SIC: 5047 Diagnostic equipment, medical
PA: Eurofins Scientific Se
    Val Fleuri 23
    Luxembourg
    2618531

(P-5417)
GOLDEN STATE MEDICAL SUP INC
5187 Camino Ruiz (93012-8601)
PHONE...................................805 477-9866
Benjamin Hall, *
Thomas S Weaver, *
Shiela Curran, *
Anita Wrublevski, *
Jim Mcmanimie, *Sr VP*
EMP: 150 EST: 1989
SQ FT: 95,500
SALES (est): 47.53MM
SALES (corp-wide): 47.53MM Privately Held
Web: www.gsms.us
SIC: 5047 Medical equipment and supplies
PA: Gsms, Inc.
    5187 Camino Ruiz
    Camarillo CA
    805 477-9866

(P-5418)
GORDIAN MEDICAL INC
Also Called: Restorixhealth
17595 Cartwright Rd (92614-5847)
PHONE...................................714 556-0200
EMP: 290 EST: 2007
SALES (est): 46.64MM Privately Held
Web: www.amtwoundcare.com
SIC: 5047 Medical equipment and supplies

(P-5419)
GRIFOLS USA LLC
13111 Temple Ave (91746-1500)
PHONE...................................626 435-2600
EMP: 511
Web: www.grifols.com
SIC: 5047 Diagnostic equipment, medical
HQ: Grifols Usa, Llc
    2410 Grifols Way
    Los Angeles CA
    323 225-2221

(P-5420)
H AND H DRUG STORES INC (PA)
Also Called: Western Drug
3604 San Fernando Rd (91204-2917)
PHONE...................................818 956-6691
Hagop Youredjian, *Ch Bd*
Haig Youredjian, *
Zarig Youredjian, *
EMP: 70 EST: 1977
SQ FT: 19,000
SALES (est): 61.72MM
SALES (corp-wide): 61.72MM Privately Held
Web: www.westerndrug.com
SIC: 5047 Medical equipment and supplies

(P-5421)
H AND H DRUG STORES INC
Also Called: Western Drug Medical Supply
4692 E Waterloo Rd (95215-2309)
PHONE...................................209 931-5200
Haig J Youredjian, *Prin*
EMP: 80
SALES (corp-wide): 61.72MM Privately Held
Web: www.westerndrug.com
SIC: 5047 Medical equipment and supplies
PA: H And H Drug Stores, Inc.
    3604 San Fernando Rd
    Glendale CA
    818 956-6691

(P-5422)
H AND H DRUG STORES INC
Also Called: Western Drug Medical Supply
114 E Airport Dr (92408-3473)
PHONE...................................909 890-9700
EMP: 80
SALES (corp-wide): 61.72MM Privately Held
Web: www.westerndrug.com
SIC: 5047 Medical equipment and supplies
PA: H And H Drug Stores, Inc.
    3604 San Fernando Rd
    Glendale CA
    818 956-6691

(P-5423)
HARDY DIAGNOSTICS INC (PA)
1430 W Mccoy Ln (93455-1005)
P.O. Box 645264 (45264-5264)
PHONE...................................805 346-2766
Jay R Hardy, *Pr*
Jeff Schroder, *
◆ EMP: 300 EST: 1980
SQ FT: 75,000
SALES (est): 95.87MM
SALES (corp-wide): 95.87MM Privately Held
Web: www.hardydiagnostics.com
SIC: 5047 2836 Medical equipment and supplies; Agar culture media

(P-5424)
HORIBAABX INC
Also Called: Horiba Medical
34 Bunsen (92618-4210)
PHONE...................................949 453-0500
▲ EMP: 108
Web: www.horiba.com
SIC: 5047 Medical and hospital equipment

(P-5425)
IHEALTH MANUFACTURING INC ✪
15715 Arrow Hwy (91706-2006)
PHONE...................................216 785-0107
EMP: 80 EST: 2022
SALES (est): 7.26MM Privately Held
Web: www.ihealthlabs.com
SIC: 5047 Medical and hospital equipment

(P-5426)
JB DENTAL SUPPLY CO INC (PA)
17000 Kingsview Ave (90746-1230)
PHONE...................................310 202-8855
TOLL FREE: 800
Joseph Berman, *Pr*
Manny Chada, *
EMP: 120 EST: 1973
SQ FT: 26,000
SALES (est): 22.86MM
SALES (corp-wide): 22.86MM Privately Held
SIC: 5047 Dental equipment and supplies

(P-5427)
KAISER FOUNDATION HOSPITALS
275 W Macarthur Blvd (94611-5641)
PHONE...................................510 752-6808
Anne Burnett, *Dir*
EMP: 88
SALES (corp-wide): 68.1B Privately Held
Web: www.kaisercenter.com
SIC: 5047 Medical equipment and supplies
HQ: Kaiser Foundation Hospitals Inc
    1 Kaiser Plz
    Oakland CA
    510 271-6611

(P-5428)
KLM LABORATORIES INC
Also Called: Klm Orthotic
28280 Alta Vista Ave (91355-0958)
PHONE...................................661 295-2600
Kirk Marshall, *Pr*
Scott Marshall, *
Kent Marshall, *
EMP: 100 EST: 1974
SQ FT: 35,000
SALES (est): 24.34MM Privately Held
Web: www.klmlabstore.com
SIC: 5047 3842 Medical laboratory equipment; Foot appliances, orthopedic

(P-5429)
LABCON NORTH AMERICA
3200 Lakeville Hwy (94954-5903)
PHONE...................................707 766-2163
EMP: 199
SALES (corp-wide): 221.17MM Privately Held
Web: www.labcon.com
SIC: 5047 Medical equipment and supplies
HQ: Labcon, North America
    3700 Lakeville Hwy # 200
    Petaluma CA
    707 766-2100

(P-5430)
LEVLAD LLC
9200 Mason Ave (91311-6005)
PHONE...................................818 882-2951
◆ EMP: 215 EST: 1973
SALES (est): 47.42MM Privately Held
Web: www.levlad.com
SIC: 5047 5122 Incontinent care products and supplies; Cosmetics
PA: Natural Products Group, Llc
    9400 Jeronimo Rd
    Irvine CA

(P-5431)
MCKESSON MDCL-SRGCAL TOP HLDNG
Also Called: Physician Sales & Service
1938 W Malvern Ave (92833-2105)
PHONE...................................800 300-4350
Mike Baker, *Brnch Mgr*
EMP: 313
SALES (corp-wide): 276.71B Publicly Held
Web: mms.mckesson.com
SIC: 5047 Medical equipment and supplies
HQ: Mckesson Medical-Surgical Top
    Holdings Inc.
    2054 Vista Pkwy Ste 400
    West Palm Beach FL
    904 332-3000

(P-5432)
MENTOR WORLDWIDE LLC
5425 Hollister Ave (93111-3341)
PHONE...................................805 681-6000
Diane Becker, *Mgr*
EMP: 500
SALES (corp-wide): 94.94B Publicly Held
Web: www.mentordirect.com
SIC: 5047 Medical and hospital equipment
HQ: Mentor Worldwide Llc
    31 Technology Dr Ste 200
    Irvine CA
    800 636-8678

(P-5433)
MY TRUE IMAGE MFG INC
Also Called: Design Veronique
999 Marina Way S (94804-3738)
PHONE...................................510 970-7990
Veronica C Smith, *Pr*

(PA)=Parent Co (HQ)=Headquarters
✪ = New Business established in last 2 years

5047 - Medical And Hospital Equipment (P-5434)

▲ EMP: 80 EST: 1987
SQ FT: 30,000
SALES (est): 8.89MM Privately Held
Web: www.designveronique.com
SIC: 5047 Medical equipment and supplies

(P-5434)
NANTBIOSCIENCE INC
9920 Jefferson Blvd (90232-3506)
PHONE.................310 883-1300
Patrick Soon-shiong, CEO
EMP: 89 EST: 2013
SALES (est): 4.73MM
SALES (corp-wide): 158.26K **Publicly Held**
SIC: 5047 8099 Medical laboratory equipment; Blood related health services
PA: Nantworks, Llc
  9920 Jefferson Blvd
  Culver City CA
  310 883-1300

(P-5435)
NIHON KOHDEN AMERICA LLC (HQ)
Also Called: Nihon Kohden America, Inc.
15353 Barranca Pkwy (92618-2216)
PHONE.................949 580-1555
Eiichi Tanaka, CEO
Shinya Hama, CCO*
Ken Kanzler, *
▲ EMP: 130 EST: 1979
SQ FT: 35,000
SALES (est): 166.95MM Privately Held
Web: us.nihonkohden.com
SIC: 5047 Electro-medical equipment
PA: Nihon Kohden Corporation
  1-31-4, Nishiochiai
  Shinjuku-Ku TKY

(P-5436)
OWENS & MINOR DISTRIBUTION INC
452 Sespe Ave (93015-2042)
PHONE.................805 524-0243
Michael Guelzow, Brnch Mgr
EMP: 619
Web: www.owens-minor.com
SIC: 5047 Medical equipment and supplies
HQ: Owens & Minor Distribution, Inc.
  9120 Lockwood Blvd
  Mechanicsville VA
  804 723-7000

(P-5437)
P M D HOLDING CORP
Also Called: Peerigon Medical Distribution
26672 Towne Centre Dr Ste 310 (92610-2818)
PHONE.................949 595-4777
Frank Schyving, Pr
Charles Kruger, *
Rick Hayes, *
Mike Shaunessy Technical Servi ces, Prin
EMP: 259 EST: 1996
SALES (est): 14.79MM Privately Held
SIC: 5047 Medical equipment and supplies

(P-5438)
PACIFIC MEDICAL GROUP INC
Also Called: Avante Health Solutions
212 Avenida Fabricante (92672-7538)
PHONE.................949 493-1030
Sterling Peloso, Pr
EMP: 100 EST: 2005
SALES (est): 24.49MM Privately Held
Web: www.pacificmedicalsupply.com
SIC: 5047 Medical equipment and supplies

(P-5439)
PARTER MEDICAL PRODUCTS INC
17015 Kingsview Ave (90746-1220)
PHONE.................310 327-4417
Hormonz Foroughi, Pr
Parviz Hassanzadeh, Stockholder*
▲ EMP: 160 EST: 1984
SQ FT: 40,000
SALES (est): 24.44MM Privately Held
Web: www.partermedical.com
SIC: 5047 Medical equipment and supplies

(P-5440)
PASSPORT TO LEARNING INC
Also Called: PASSPORT TO LEARNING INCORPORATED
41319 12th St W (93551-1414)
PHONE.................661 538-9200
Betty Walkes, Brnch Mgr
EMP: 65
SALES (corp-wide): 2.46MM Privately Held
Web: www.passport2learn.com
SIC: 5047 Technical aids for the handicapped
PA: Passport To Learning Incorporated
  1241 1/2 West Blvd
  Los Angeles CA
  323 549-9328

(P-5441)
PEARSON DENTAL SUPPLIES INC (PA)
Also Called: Pearson Surgical Supply Co
13161 Telfair Ave (91342-3574)
PHONE.................818 362-2600
Keyhan Kashfian, Pr
Parviz Kashfian, *
Nader Kashfian, *
▲ EMP: 105 EST: 1983
SQ FT: 88,000
SALES (est): 71.98MM
SALES (corp-wide): 71.98MM Privately Held
Web: www.pearsondental.com
SIC: 5047 Dental equipment and supplies

(P-5442)
PETER BRASSELER HOLDINGS LLC
Also Called: Comet Medical
4837 Mcgrath St Ste J (93003-8077)
PHONE.................805 650-5209
Orlando Deleon, Mgr
EMP: 73
SALES (corp-wide): 47.53MM Privately Held
Web: www.brasselerusa.com
SIC: 5047 3841 3843 Dental equipment and supplies; Surgical and medical instruments; Dental equipment
PA: Peter Brasseler Holdings, Llc
  1 Brasseler Blvd
  Savannah GA
  912 925-8525

(P-5443)
POM MEDICAL LLC
5456 Endeavour Ct (93021-1705)
PHONE.................805 306-2105
EMP: 99 EST: 2012
SALES (est): 5.21MM Privately Held
Web: www.proceduraloxygenmask.com
SIC: 5047 Oxygen therapy equipment

(P-5444)
PRI MEDICAL TECHNOLOGIES INC
Also Called: UHS Surgical Services
10939 Pendleton St (91352-1522)
PHONE.................818 394-2800
EMP: 78
Web: www.agilitihealth.com
SIC: 5047 7352 8741 Instruments, surgical and medical; Medical equipment rental; Administrative management

(P-5445)
QUAD-C JH HOLDINGS INC
1055 E Discovery Ln (92801-1147)
PHONE.................502 741-0421
EMP: 230
SALES (corp-wide): 101.03MM Privately Held
SIC: 5047 Medical and hospital equipment
PA: Quad-C Jh Holdings Inc.
  2430 Whthall Pk Dr Ste 10
  Charlotte NC
  800 826-0270

(P-5446)
QUAD-C JH HOLDINGS INC
4593 Ish Dr Ste 320 (93063-7696)
PHONE.................800 966-6662
EMP: 230
SALES (corp-wide): 101.03MM Privately Held
SIC: 5047 Medical equipment and supplies
PA: Quad-C Jh Holdings Inc.
  2430 Whthall Pk Dr Ste 10
  Charlotte NC
  800 826-0270

(P-5447)
RASHMAN CORPORATION
Also Called: Uniform Accessories
8600 Wilbur Ave (91324-4438)
PHONE.................818 993-3030
Richard Rashman, CEO
Roger Rashman, *
▲ EMP: 65 EST: 1969
SQ FT: 50,000
SALES (est): 21.31MM Privately Held
Web: www.mcflyofficial.com
SIC: 5047 Medical equipment and supplies

(P-5448)
SAKURA FINETEK USA INC (HQ)
1750 W 214th St (90501-2857)
PHONE.................310 972-7800
Takashi Tsuzuki, Ch Bd
Anthony C Marotti, *
Kam Patel, *
▲ EMP: 109 EST: 1986
SQ FT: 68,000
SALES (est): 98.64MM Privately Held
Web: www.sakuraus.com
SIC: 5047 Medical laboratory equipment
PA: Sakura Global Holding Co., Ltd.
  3-1-9, Nihombashihoncho
  Chuo-Ku TKY

(P-5449)
SHIELD-DENVER HEALTH CARE CTR (HQ)
Also Called: Shield Healthcare
27911 Franklin Pkwy (91355-4110)
PHONE.................661 294-4200
Jim Snell, Pr
Jeffery Thompson, *
Cheryl Hornberger, *
EMP: 200 EST: 1983
SQ FT: 95,000
SALES (est): 43.74MM Privately Held
SIC: 5047 Medical equipment and supplies
PA: Dharma Ventures Group, Inc
  24700 Ave Rockefeller
  Valencia CA

(P-5450)
SHIMADZU PRECISION INSTRS INC
Shimadzu Medical Systems
20101 S Vermont Ave (90502-1328)
PHONE.................310 217-8855
Akinori Yamaguchi, Pr
EMP: 80
Web: www.spi-inc.com
SIC: 5047 Medical equipment and supplies
HQ: Shimadzu Precision Instruments, Inc.
  3645 N Lakewood Blvd
  Long Beach CA
  562 420-6226

(P-5451)
SUNRISE RESPIRATORY CARE INC
1881 Langley Ave (92614-5623)
PHONE.................949 398-6555
Oscar Munoz, CEO
Oscar L Munoz, *
EMP: 110 EST: 2010
SALES (est): 17.26MM Privately Held
Web: www.sunriseresp.com
SIC: 5047 Medical equipment and supplies

(P-5452)
TEAM POST-OP INC
Also Called: Team Post-Op
17256 Red Hill Ave (92614-5628)
PHONE.................949 253-5500
Jeffrey Salamon, Pr
Lisa Salamon, *
EMP: 105 EST: 1988
SQ FT: 1,400
SALES (est): 14.01MM
SALES (corp-wide): 1.12B Privately Held
Web: www.orthokinetix.net
SIC: 5047 Orthopedic equipment and supplies
HQ: Hanger Prosthetics & Orthotics, Inc.
  10910 Domain Dr Ste 300
  Austin TX
  512 777-3800

(P-5453)
THE DOCTORS COMPANY
185 Greenwood Rd (94558-7540)
PHONE.................707 226-0289
EMP: 700
Web: www.thedoctors.com
SIC: 5047 Hospital equipment and supplies, nec

(P-5454)
THERAPAK LLC (DH)
651 Wharton Dr (91711-4819)
PHONE.................909 267-2000
Todd Gates, Pr
◆ EMP: 70 EST: 2000
SQ FT: 24,000
SALES (est): 94.38MM
SALES (corp-wide): 7.51B **Publicly Held**
Web: www.therapak.com
SIC: 5047 Medical equipment and supplies
HQ: Vwr Corporation
  100 W Matsonford Rd Ste 1
  Radnor PA
  610 386-1700

(P-5455)
TOSOH BIOSCIENCE INC
Also Called: Tosoh USA
6000 Shoreline Ct Ste 101 (94080-7606)
PHONE.................650 615-4970
Daisuke Omoto, CEO
Tasha Nguyen, *
Erika Dorman, *

PRODUCTS & SERVICES SECTION

5051 - Metals Service Centers And Offices (P-5475)

◆ EMP: 75 EST: 1989
SQ FT: 13,917
SALES (est): 14.12MM **Privately Held**
Web: diagnostics.us.tosohbioscience.com
SIC: **5047** Medical laboratory equipment
HQ: Tosoh America, Inc.
3600 Gantz Rd
Grove City OH

(P-5456)
TRACPATCH HEALTH INC
2020 L St Ste 220 (95811-4260)
PHONE..................................916 355-7123
Collen Gray, *Pr*
Paul Rugg, *
Carolyn Hayes, *
Steve Gage, *
Dan Richards, *
EMP: 82 EST: 1992
SQ FT: 25,000
SALES (est): 25.4MM **Privately Held**
Web: www.tracpatch.com
SIC: **5047** 3841 Medical equipment and supplies; Surgical and medical instruments

(P-5457)
TWIN MED INC
5900 Wilshire Blvd (90036-5013)
▲ EMP: 500
SIC: **5047** Medical equipment and supplies

(P-5458)
VETERINARY SERVICE INC
1607 N Plaza Dr (93291-8887)
PHONE..................................559 651-1633
Tom Babb, *Brnch Mgr*
EMP: 68
SALES (corp-wide): 180.15MM **Privately Held**
Web: www.vsi.cc
SIC: **5047** Veterinarians' equipment and supplies
PA: Veterinary Service, Inc.
4100 Bangs Ave
Modesto CA
209 545-5100

(P-5459)
VIDENT
Also Called: Vita North America
22705 Savi Ranch Pkwy (92887-4604)
PHONE..................................714 221-6700
Emanuel Rauter, *CEO*
James Mcguire, *Dir*
Janet Siwinski, *
▲ EMP: 70 EST: 1984
SQ FT: 43,000
SALES (est): 49.15MM
SALES (corp-wide): 355.83K **Privately Held**
Web: www.vitanorthamerica.com
SIC: **5047** Dental equipment and supplies
HQ: Vita - Zahnfabrik H. Rauter
Gesellschaft Mit Beschrankter Haftung & Co Kg
Spitalgasse 3
Bad Sackingen BW
77615620

(P-5460)
VIEWRAY TECHNOLOGIES INC
815 E Middlefield Rd (94043-4025)
PHONE..................................650 252-0920
EMP: 75
SALES (corp-wide): 102.21MM **Publicly Held**
Web: www.viewray.com
SIC: **5047** Medical and hospital equipment
HQ: Viewray Technologies, Inc.

2 Thermo Fisher Way
Oakwood Village OH
440 703-3210

(P-5461)
ZEST ANCHORS LLC
Also Called: Zest Dental Solutions
2230 Enterprise St (92029-2004)
PHONE..................................760 743-7744
EMP: 90
SALES (corp-wide): 14.24MM **Privately Held**
Web: www.zestdent.com
SIC: **5047** Dental equipment and supplies
PA: Zest Anchors, Llc
2875 Loker Ave E
Carlsbad CA
760 743-7744

5048 Ophthalmic Goods

(P-5462)
ABB/CON-CISE OPTICAL GROUP LLC
Also Called: ABB Optical Group
1750 N Loop Rd Ste 150 (94502-8013)
PHONE..................................510 483-9400
Angel Alvarez, *CEO*
EMP: 299
Web: www.abboptical.com
SIC: **5048** 5049 Ophthalmic goods; Optical goods
HQ: Abb/Con-Cise Optical Group Llc
12301 Nw 39th St
Coral Springs FL

5049 Professional Equipment, Nec

(P-5463)
ABB ENTERPRISE SOFTWARE INC
Also Called: ABB - Los Gatos Research
3055 Orchard Dr (95134-2005)
P.O. Box 80065 (27623-0065)
PHONE..................................408 770-8968
Doug Baer, *Genl Mgr*
EMP: 284
Web: new.abb.com
SIC: **5049** 3826 Analytical instruments; Analytical instruments
HQ: Abb Inc.
305 Gregson Dr
Cary NC

(P-5464)
ABC SCHOOL EQUIPMENT INC
Also Called: Platinum Visual Systems
1451 E 6th St (92879-1715)
PHONE..................................951 817-2200
Gary P Stell Junior, *CEO*
Thomas Mendez, *
EMP: 70 EST: 1964
SQ FT: 35,000
SALES (est): 20.5MM **Privately Held**
Web: www.abcse.com
SIC: **5049** 3861 2531 School supplies; Photographic equipment and supplies; Public building and related furniture

(P-5465)
CPI INTERNATIONAL
5580 Skylane Blvd (95403-1030)
PHONE..................................707 521-6327
Ryan Vice, *CEO*
Joseph Phillips, *
▲ EMP: 70 EST: 1996

SQ FT: 20,000
SALES (est): 18.78MM **Privately Held**
Web: www.cpiinternational.com
SIC: **5049** 3826 Analytical instruments; Analytical instruments

(P-5466)
INDIO PRODUCTS INC (PA)
Also Called: Seven Sisters of New Orleans
12910 Mulberry Dr Unit A (90602-3455)
PHONE..................................323 720-1188
▲ EMP: 130 EST: 2010
SALES (est): 25.3MM
SALES (corp-wide): 25.3MM **Privately Held**
Web: www.indioproducts.com
SIC: **5049** 3999 Religious supplies; Candles

(P-5467)
LEXICON MARKETING (USA) INC (PA)
Also Called: Lexicon Marketing
640 S San Vicente Blvd (90048-4654)
PHONE..................................323 782-8282
Valeria Rico, *Pr*
EMP: 81 EST: 1979
SALES (est): 62.07MM **Privately Held**
SIC: **5049** 5999 School supplies; Education aids, devices and supplies

(P-5468)
REM OPTICAL COMPANY INC
Also Called: REM Eye Wear
10941 La Tuna Canyon Rd (91352-2012)
PHONE..................................818 504-3950
Alessandro Baronti, *Pr*
Donna Gindy, *COO*
Donna Nakawaki, *CFO*
Claudio Ninotti, *VP*
◆ EMP: 149 EST: 1977
SQ FT: 42,000
SALES (est): 49.45MM
SALES (corp-wide): 525.12MM **Privately Held**
Web: www.derigo.us
SIC: **5049** Optical goods
HQ: De Rigo Vision Spa
Zona Industriale Villanova 12
Longarone BL

(P-5469)
SAPPHIRE CLEAN ROOMS LLC
2810 E Coronado St (92806-2503)
PHONE..................................714 316-5036
Hector Garibay, *Pr*
EMP: 136
SALES (corp-wide): 8.61MM **Privately Held**
SIC: **5049** Laboratory equipment, except medical or dental
PA: Sapphire Clean Rooms, Llc
505 Porter Way
Placentia CA
714 316-5036

(P-5470)
SOCIAL STUDIES SCHOOL SERVICE
Also Called: Writing Company
14401 S Main St (90248-1913)
P.O. Box 802 (90232-0802)
PHONE..................................310 839-2436
David Weiner, *CEO*
David M Weigner, *
Irwin Ledin, *
Sanford Weiner, *
Aarion Willis, *EDU*
▲ EMP: 65 EST: 1967
SALES (est): 20.54MM **Privately Held**
Web: www.socialstudies.com

SIC: **5049** School supplies

(P-5471)
TECAN SP INC
14180 Live Oak Ave (91706-1350)
P.O. Box 1608 (91706-7608)
PHONE..................................626 962-0010
▲ EMP: 84 EST: 1997
SALES (est): 46.32MM **Privately Held**
Web: www.tecan.com
SIC: **5049** Laboratory equipment, except medical or dental
PA: Tecan Group Ag
Seestrasse 103
MAnnedorf ZH

5051 Metals Service Centers And Offices

(P-5472)
ALPERT & ALPERT IRON & METAL INC (PA)
1815 S Soto St (90023-4210)
P.O. Box 23961 (90023-0961)
PHONE..................................323 265-4040
◆ EMP: 60 EST: 1930
SALES (est): 110.22MM
SALES (corp-wide): 110.22MM **Privately Held**
Web: www.alpertandalpert.com
SIC: **5051** Iron and steel (ferrous) products

(P-5473)
ALUMINUM PRECISION PDTS INC
1001 Mcwane Blvd (93033-9016)
PHONE..................................805 488-4401
Richard Hayes, *Brnch Mgr*
EMP: 125
SQ FT: 15,000
SALES (est): 80.17MM **Privately Held**
Web: www.aluminumprecision.com
SIC: **5051** Steel
PA: Aluminum Precision Products, Inc.
3333 W Warner Ave
Santa Ana CA
714 546-8125

(P-5474)
AOC TECHNOLOGIES INC
6900 Koll Center Pkwy Ste 401 (94566-3154)
PHONE..................................925 875-0808
Gordon Gu, *Pr*
◆ EMP: 315 EST: 1999
SALES (est): 48.29MM **Privately Held**
Web: www.aoctech.com
SIC: **5051** 3357 Metal wires, ties, cables, and screening; Fiber optic cable (insulated)

(P-5475)
ARCHITECTURAL GL & ALUM CO INC (PA)
Also Called: Architectural Glass & Aluminum
6400 Brisa St (94550-2516)
PHONE..................................925 583-2460
Joseph Brescia, *CEO*
John Buckley, *
William Coll Senior, *Sec*
William Coll Junior, *VP*
▲ EMP: 155 EST: 1970
SQ FT: 33,000
SALES (est): 73.5MM
SALES (corp-wide): 73.5MM **Privately Held**
Web: www.aga-ca.com

5051 - Metals Service Centers And Offices (P-5476)

SIC: 5051 1793 1791 3442 Aluminum bars, rods, ingots, sheets, pipes, plates, etc.; Glass and glazing work; Exterior wall system installation; Sash, door or window: metal

(P-5476)
ASC PROFILES LLC (DH)
Also Called: ASC Building Products
2110 Enterprise Blvd (95691-3428)
PHONE..........................916 376-2800
Sarah Deukmejian, CEO
Paul Warme, CFO
EMP: 85 EST: 1972
SQ FT: 87,120
SALES (est): 98.8MM Privately Held
Web: www.ascprofiles.com
SIC: 5051 Steel
HQ: Bluescope Steel North America Corporation
1540 Genessee St
Kansas City MO

(P-5477)
AURORA CASTING & ENGRG INC
1790 E Lemonwood Dr (93060-9510)
PHONE..........................805 933-2761
John Carlos Penrose, CEO
EMP: 65 EST: 1979
SQ FT: 25,000
SALES (est): 21.66MM Privately Held
Web: www.auroracasting.com
SIC: 5051 Steel

(P-5478)
B & B SURPLUS INC (PA)
Also Called: B & B Specialty Metals
7020 Rosedale Hwy (93308-5842)
PHONE..........................661 589-0381
Donice Boylan, Pr
Michael Georgino, *
Michelle Boylan-pisano, CFO
▲ EMP: 65 EST: 1963
SQ FT: 20,000
SALES (est): 67.44MM
SALES (corp-wide): 67.44MM Privately Held
Web: www.bbsurplus.com
SIC: 5051 Steel

(P-5479)
BLUE CHIP STAMPS INC
301 E Colorado Blvd Ste 300 (91101)
PHONE..........................626 585-6700
Robert H Bird, COO
Charles T Munger, CEO
Jeffrey L Jacobson, *
Kenneth E Wittmeyer, VP
EMP: 3074 EST: 1956
SQ FT: 123,732
SALES (est): 221.89MM
SALES (corp-wide): 302.09B Publicly Held
SIC: 5051 Steel
PA: Berkshire Hathaway Inc.
3555 Farnam St Ste 1440
Omaha NE
402 346-1400

(P-5480)
BPS SUPPLY GROUP (PA)
Also Called: Imperial Pipe & Supply
3301 Zachary Ave (93263-9424)
P.O. Box 639 (93302-0639)
PHONE..........................661 589-9141
Dwight Byrum, CEO
Dwight Byrumm, *
Dan Byrum, *
Kevin Hashim, *

Cary Evans, *
◆ EMP: 60 EST: 1968
SQ FT: 60,000
SALES (est): 115.34MM
SALES (corp-wide): 115.34MM Privately Held
Web: www.bpssg.com
SIC: 5051 5085 Pipe and tubing, steel; Valves and fittings

(P-5481)
CALIFORNIA STEEL AND TUBE
16049 Stephens St (91745-1717)
PHONE..........................626 968-5511
TOLL FREE: 800
Rick Hirsch, Pr
Ron Prichard, VP
EMP: 108 EST: 1952
SQ FT: 108,000
SALES (est): 27.37MM
SALES (corp-wide): 9.74B Privately Held
Web: www.californiasteelandtube.com
SIC: 5051 Steel
HQ: Kloeckner Metals Corporation
500 Colonial Center Pkwy # 500
Roswell GA

(P-5482)
CMC REBAR WEST
5160 Fulton Dr (94534-1639)
PHONE..........................707 759-1400
Howard Bennion, Brnch Mgr
EMP: 101
SIC: 5051 Steel
HQ: Cmc Rebar West
3880 Murphy Canyon Rd # 100
San Diego CA

(P-5483)
CMC REBAR WEST
5425 Industrial Pkwy (92407-1803)
PHONE..........................909 713-1130
Lee Albright, Mgr
EMP: 101
SIC: 5051 Steel
HQ: Cmc Rebar West
3880 Murphy Canyon Rd # 100
San Diego CA

(P-5484)
COAST ALUMINUM INC (PA)
Also Called: Coast Aluminum
10628 Fulton Wells Ave (90670-3740)
P.O. Box 2144 (90670-0440)
PHONE..........................562 946-6061
TOLL FREE: 800
Thomas C Clark, Pr
Bonnie Clark, Stockholder*
▲ EMP: 125 EST: 1982
SQ FT: 112,000
SALES (est): 482.99MM Privately Held
Web: www.coastaluminum.com
SIC: 5051 Miscellaneous nonferrous products

(P-5485)
COUNTY OF SOLANO
Also Called: Solano Cnty of Dept Rsrce MGT
3255 N Texas St (94533-9714)
PHONE..........................707 421-6055
Wayne Spencer, Mgr
EMP: 79
SALES (corp-wide): 856.43MM Privately Held
Web: www.solanocounty.com
SIC: 5051 9111 Steel; County supervisors' and executives' office
PA: County Of Solano
675 Texas St Ste 2600
Fairfield CA
707 784-6706

(P-5486)
CREST STEEL CORPORATION
Also Called: Crest Steel
6580 General Rd (92509-0103)
PHONE..........................951 727-2600
James Hoffman, CEO
Kris Farris, *
Dave Zertuche, *
Paul Worden, *
▲ EMP: 90 EST: 1964
SQ FT: 12,000
SALES (est): 60.93MM
SALES (corp-wide): 17.02B Publicly Held
Web: www.creststeel.com
SIC: 5051 Steel
PA: Reliance Steel & Aluminum Co.
16100 N 71st St Ste 400
Scottsdale AZ
480 564-5700

(P-5487)
DANIEL GERARD WORLDWIDE INC
Also Called: City Wire Cloth
13055 Jurupa Ave (92337-6982)
PHONE..........................951 361-1111
TOLL FREE: 800
Todd Snelbaker, Mgr
EMP: 71
SQ FT: 50,000
SALES (corp-wide): 52.43MM Privately Held
Web: www.gerarddaniel.com
SIC: 5051 3496 3356 3315 Wire, nec; Mesh, made from purchased wire; Nonferrous rolling and drawing, nec; Steel wire and related products
PA: Gerard Daniel Worldwide, Inc.
34 Barnhart Dr
Hanover PA
800 232-3332

(P-5488)
DOUGLAS STEEL SUPPLY INC (PA)
Also Called: DOUGLAS STEEL SUPPLY CO.
4804 Laurel Canyon Blvd (91607-3717)
PHONE..........................323 587-7676
Douglas Stein, CEO
Donal Hecht, *
EMP: 86 EST: 1972
SQ FT: 100,000
SALES (est): 88.5K
SALES (corp-wide): 88.5K Privately Held
SIC: 5051 Steel

(P-5489)
EARLE M JORGENSEN COMPANY (HQ)
Also Called: EMJ Corporate
10650 Alameda St (90262-1754)
PHONE..........................323 567-1122
◆ EMP: 120 EST: 2006
SALES (est): 544.68MM
SALES (corp-wide): 17.02B Publicly Held
Web: www.emjmetals.com
SIC: 5051 Metals service centers and offices
PA: Reliance Steel & Aluminum Co.
16100 N 71st St Ste 400
Scottsdale AZ
480 564-5700

(P-5490)
EARLE M JORGENSEN COMPANY
Also Called: EMJ Hayward
31100 Wiegman Rd (94544-7850)
PHONE..........................510 487-2700
Barbara Nemeth, Brnch Mgr

EMP: 139
SQ FT: 91,982
SALES (corp-wide): 17.02B Publicly Held
Web: www.emjmetals.com
SIC: 5051 Steel
HQ: Earle M. Jorgensen Company
10650 Alameda St
Lynwood CA
323 567-1122

(P-5491)
EARLE M JORGENSEN COMPANY
350 S Grand Ave Ste 5100 (90071-3421)
PHONE..........................323 567-1122
Janice Day, Mgr
EMP: 90
SALES (corp-wide): 17.02B Publicly Held
Web: www.emjmetals.com
SIC: 5051 Steel
HQ: Earle M. Jorgensen Company
10650 Alameda St
Lynwood CA
323 567-1122

(P-5492)
FRY STEEL COMPANY
13325 Molette St (90670-5568)
P.O. Box 4028 (90670-1028)
PHONE..........................562 802-2721
◆ EMP: 115 EST: 1945
SALES (est): 39.99MM
SALES (corp-wide): 17.02B Publicly Held
Web: www.frysteel.com
SIC: 5051 5099 Steel; Brass goods
PA: Reliance Steel & Aluminum Co.
16100 N 71st St Ste 400
Scottsdale AZ
480 564-5700

(P-5493)
GEORG FISCHER LLC (DH)
Also Called: Georg Fischer Piping
9271 Jeronimo Rd (92618-1906)
PHONE..........................714 731-8800
◆ EMP: 70 EST: 1967
SQ FT: 55,000
SALES (est): 59.96MM Privately Held
Web: www.gfps.com
SIC: 5051 5085 Pipe and tubing, steel; Valves and fittings
HQ: George Fischer, Inc.
5462 Irwindale Ave Ste A
Baldwin Park CA
626 571-2770

(P-5494)
GVS ITALY
8616 La Tijera Blvd (90045-3944)
PHONE..........................424 382-4343
Bruno Montesano, Mgr
EMP: 100 EST: 2016
SALES (est): 9.12MM Privately Held
SIC: 5051 Aluminum bars, rods, ingots, sheets, pipes, plates, etc.

(P-5495)
HANWA AMERICAN CORP
Also Called: Hanwa American Los Angeles BR
18100 Von Karman Ave Ste 320 (92612-0169)
PHONE..........................949 955-2780
Toru Nakatam, Brnch Mgr
EMP: 60
Web: www.hanwa-usa.com
SIC: 5051 Aluminum bars, rods, ingots, sheets, pipes, plates, etc.
HQ: Hanwa American Corp.
Parker Plz 400 Klby St Fl

PRODUCTS & SERVICES SECTION

5051 - Metals Service Centers And Offices (P-5516)

Fort Lee NJ
201 363-4500

(P-5496)
HARBOR PIPE AND STEEL INC
Also Called: James Metals
1495 Columbia Ave Bldg 10 (92507-2074)
PHONE..................951 369-3990
Joseph W Beattie, Pr
Martha Fournier, *
Teri Stevens, *
P Jay Peterson, *
Tom Liljegren, *
▲ EMP: 150 EST: 1962
SALES (est): 47.54MM Privately Held
Web: www.harborpipe.com
SIC: 5051 Steel

(P-5497)
HARTMAN INDUSTRIES
Also Called: Commercial Casting Co
20229 E Lorencita Dr (91724-3834)
PHONE..................909 428-0114
Brad J Hartman, CEO
Brett Hartman, *
Sean Hartman, *
▲ EMP: 60 EST: 1991
SALES (est): 16.79MM Privately Held
Web: www.sandcast-parts.com
SIC: 5051 Steel

(P-5498)
JAYEM ENTERPRISES INC
Also Called: Acme Metals
14930 S San Pedro St (90248-2036)
PHONE..................310 329-2263
Jack Goldberg, Ch
◆ EMP: 60 EST: 1988
SQ FT: 265,000
SALES (est): 22.08MM Privately Held
Web: www.acmemetalsonline.com
SIC: 5051 Steel

(P-5499)
JFE SHOJI AMERICA HOLDINGS INC (DH)
301 E Ocean Blvd Ste 1750 (90802-4827)
PHONE..................562 637-3500
Naosuke Oda, Pr
Hidehiko Ogawa, *
Toshihiro Kabasawa, *
◆ EMP: 85 EST: 1965
SQ FT: 7,500
SALES (est): 286.74MM Privately Held
Web: www.jfe-shoji-steel-america.com
SIC: 5051 Steel
HQ: Jfe Shoji Corporation
1-9-5, Otemachi
Chiyoda-Ku TKY

(P-5500)
JIMS SUPPLY CO INC (PA)
3500 Buck Owens Blvd (93308-4920)
P.O. Box 668 (93302-0668)
PHONE..................661 616-6977
TOLL FREE: 800
Clay Watson, CEO
Jennifer Drake, *
Jennice Boylan, *
Dan Drake, *
Bryan Boylan, *
▲ EMP: 82 EST: 1959
SQ FT: 25,300
SALES (est): 39.16MM
SALES (corp-wide): 39.16MM Privately Held
Web: www.jscagsupply.com
SIC: 5051 Steel

(P-5501)
KLOECKNER METALS CORPORATION
Also Called: Gary Steel Division
9804 Norwalk Blvd # A (90670-2901)
PHONE..................562 906-2020
John Ganem, CEO
EMP: 75
SALES (corp-wide): 9.74B Privately Held
Web: www.kloecknermetals.com
SIC: 5051 Steel
HQ: Kloeckner Metals Corporation
500 Colonial Center Pkwy # 500
Roswell GA

(P-5502)
NEXCOIL INCORPORATED
Also Called: Nexcoil San Diego Coil Center
8753 Kerns St (92154-6213)
PHONE..................619 671-9247
Kazushige Kato, Genl Mgr
EMP: 69
Web: www.sdvssc.com
SIC: 5051 Steel
PA: Nexcoil Incorporated
404 E 1st St 602
Long Beach CA

(P-5503)
NORMAN INDUSTRIAL MTLS INC (PA)
Also Called: Industrial Metal Supply Co
8300 San Fernando Rd (91352-3222)
PHONE..................818 729-3333
TOLL FREE: 800
Eric Steinhauer, CEO
David Pace, *
David Berkey, *
Dave Cohen, *
▲ EMP: 125 EST: 1945
SQ FT: 70,000
SALES (est): 150.06MM
SALES (corp-wide): 150.06MM Privately Held
Web: www.industrialmetalsupply.com
SIC: 5051 3441 3449 Metals service centers and offices; Fabricated structural metal; Miscellaneous metalwork

(P-5504)
NORMAN INDUSTRIAL MTLS INC
Also Called: Industrial Metal Supply Co
2481 Alton Pkwy (92606-5030)
PHONE..................949 250-3343
Jerry Entin, VP
EMP: 65
SQ FT: 40,000
SALES (corp-wide): 150.06MM Privately Held
Web: www.industrialmetalsupply.com
SIC: 5051 5099 3366 Steel; Brass goods; Bronze foundry, nec
PA: Norman Industrial Materials, Inc.
8300 San Fernando Rd
Sun Valley CA
818 729-3333

(P-5505)
PACIFIC REBAR INC
501 S Oaks Ave (91762-4020)
PHONE..................909 984-7199
Tim Herwehe, Pr
EMP: 60 EST: 1986
SQ FT: 3,000
SALES (est): 8.26MM Privately Held
Web: www.pacificrebarinc.com
SIC: 5051 Steel

(P-5506)
PACIFIC STEEL GROUP
2755 S Willow Ave (92316-3260)
PHONE..................858 449-7219
EMP: 411
SALES (corp-wide): 119.78MM Privately Held
Web: www.pacificsteelgroup.com
SIC: 5051 Iron and steel (ferrous) products
PA: Pacific Steel Group
4805 Murphy Canyon Rd
San Diego CA
858 251-1100

(P-5507)
PACIFIC STEEL GROUP
Bldg 411 Gilmore Ave (95203)
PHONE..................707 297-8922
EMP: 377
SALES (corp-wide): 119.78MM Privately Held
Web: www.pacificsteelgroup.com
SIC: 5051 Iron and steel (ferrous) products
PA: Pacific Steel Group
4805 Murphy Canyon Rd
San Diego CA
858 251-1100

(P-5508)
PDM STEEL SERVICE CENTERS INC (HQ)
Also Called: Specialty Steel Service
3535 E Myrtle St (95205-4721)
PHONE..................209 943-0555
Derick Halecky, Pr
William Nixon, *
Joseph Anderson, *
Randy H Kearns, *
Brad Blickle, *
▲ EMP: 100 EST: 1954
SALES (est): 214.55MM
SALES (corp-wide): 17.02B Publicly Held
Web: www.pdmsteel.com
SIC: 5051 Steel
PA: Reliance Steel & Aluminum Co.
16100 N 71st St Ste 400
Scottsdale AZ
480 564-5700

(P-5509)
PDM STEEL SERVICE CENTERS INC
9245 Laguna Springs Dr # 350 (95758-7987)
PHONE..................916 513-4548
Randy Kearns, Pr
EMP: 200
SALES (corp-wide): 17.02B Publicly Held
Web: www.pdmsteel.com
SIC: 5051 Steel
HQ: Pdm Steel Service Centers, Inc.
3535 E Myrtle St
Stockton CA
209 943-0555

(P-5510)
PJS REBAR INC
45055 Fremont Blvd (94538-6318)
PHONE..................510 490-0321
Stuart Lowe, CEO
EMP: 70 EST: 2015
SALES (est): 14MM Privately Held
Web: www.pjsrebar.com
SIC: 5051 Steel

(P-5511)
PROTERIAL AMERICA LTD
Also Called: PROTERIAL AMERICA, LTD
880 N Mccarthy Blvd Ste 200 (95035-5126)
PHONE..................408 467-8900
Rick Shigashara, Brnch Mgr
EMP: 139
Web: www.hitachimetals.com
SIC: 5051 Steel
HQ: Proterial America, Ltd.
2 Manhattanville Rd # 301
Purchase NY
914 694-9200

(P-5512)
PUSAN PIPE AMERICA INC
Also Called: Seah Steel America
2100 Main St Ste 100 (92614-6238)
PHONE..................949 655-8000
Byung Joon Lee, CEO
Jun Lee, *
▲ EMP: 357 EST: 1978
SALES (est): 34.64MM Privately Held
SIC: 5051 Steel

(P-5513)
RELIANCE STEEL & ALUMINUM CO
Reliance Metal Center
33201 Western Ave (94587-2208)
PHONE..................510 476-4400
Dave Buchanan, Mgr
EMP: 90
SQ FT: 137,757
SALES (corp-wide): 17.02B Publicly Held
Web: www.rsac.com
SIC: 5051 Steel
PA: Reliance Steel & Aluminum Co.
16100 N 71st St Ste 400
Scottsdale AZ
480 564-5700

(P-5514)
RELIANCE STEEL & ALUMINUM CO
Bralco Metals
15090 Northam St (90638-5757)
PHONE..................714 736-4800
TOLL FREE: 800
Michael Hubbart, Brnch Mgr
EMP: 118
SALES (corp-wide): 17.02B Publicly Held
Web: www.rsac.com
SIC: 5051 Steel
PA: Reliance Steel & Aluminum Co.
16100 N 71st St Ste 400
Scottsdale AZ
480 564-5700

(P-5515)
RELIANCE STEEL & ALUMINUM CO
Also Called: Reliance Steel Company
2537 E 27th St (90058-1284)
PHONE..................323 583-6111
John Becknell, Brnch Mgr
EMP: 200
SALES (corp-wide): 17.02B Publicly Held
Web: www.rsac.com
SIC: 5051 Steel
PA: Reliance Steel & Aluminum Co.
16100 N 71st St Ste 400
Scottsdale AZ
480 564-5700

(P-5516)
RELIANCE STEEL & ALUMINUM CO
Metal Center
12034 Greenstone Ave (90670-4727)
P.O. Box 2101 (90670-0013)
PHONE..................562 944-3322
Jay Rose, Brnch Mgr

5051 - Metals Service Centers And Offices (P-5517)

EMP: 80
SQ FT: 142,000
SALES (corp-wide): 17.02B **Publicly Held**
Web: www.rsac.com
SIC: **5051** Steel
PA: Reliance Steel & Aluminum Co.
16100 N 71st St Ste 400
Scottsdale AZ
480 564-5700

(P-5517)
ROSSIN STEEL INC
9102 Birch St (91977-4109)
PHONE..............................619 656-9200
Ted F Rossin, *CEO*
Jeffrey Clinkscleas, *
EMP: 110 EST: 2005
SALES (est): 30.59MM **Privately Held**
Web: www.rossinsteelinc.com
SIC: **5051** Steel

(P-5518)
SAC INTERNATIONAL STEEL INC (PA)
6130 Avalon Blvd (90003-1633)
PHONE..............................323 232-2467
◆ EMP: 74 EST: 1979
SALES (est): 22.44MM **Privately Held**
Web: www.sacsteel.com
SIC: **5051** Sheets, metal

(P-5519)
STAUB METALS LLC
7747 Rosecrans Ave (90723-2509)
P.O. Box 1425 (90723-1425)
PHONE..............................562 602-2200
EMP: 85 EST: 1980
SALES (est): 25.44MM **Privately Held**
Web: www.staubmetals.com
SIC: **5051** Steel

(P-5520)
STEEL UNLIMITED INC
Also Called: Sui Companies
3200 Myers St (92503-5530)
PHONE..............................909 873-1222
TOLL FREE: 800
Mike Frabotta, *Pr*
David Sunde, *
▲ EMP: 75 EST: 1996
SQ FT: 142,000
SALES (est): 36.32MM **Privately Held**
Web: www.steelunlimited.com
SIC: **5051** Steel

(P-5521)
TA CHEN INTERNATIONAL INC (HQ)
Also Called: Sunland Shutters
5855 Obispo Ave (90805-3715)
PHONE..............................562 808-8000
Johnny Hsieh, *CEO*
James Chang, *
John Hellighausen, *
Andrew Chang, *
◆ EMP: 172 EST: 1989
SQ FT: 200,000
SALES (est): 917.07MM **Privately Held**
Web: www.tachen.com
SIC: **5051** Steel
PA: Ta Chen Stainless Pipe Co., Ltd.
No. 125, Xintian 2nd St.
Tainan City

(P-5522)
TCI ALUMINUM/NORTH INC
2353 Davis Ave (94545-1111)
PHONE..............................510 786-3750
TOLL FREE: 800
Jeff Bordalampe, *Pr*
Jim Clifton, *
EMP: 60 EST: 1972
SQ FT: 60,000
SALES (est): 23.22MM **Privately Held**
Web: www.tcialuminum.com
SIC: **5051** Steel

(P-5523)
TELL STEEL INC
2345 W 17th St (90813-1017)
PHONE..............................562 435-4826
TOLL FREE: 800
Greg More, *Pr*
Pete V Trigt, *
▲ EMP: 60 EST: 1958
SQ FT: 100,000
SALES (est): 28.14MM
SALES (corp-wide): 31.47MM **Privately Held**
Web: www.tellsteel.com
SIC: **5051** Steel
PA: Tuffli Company Incorporated
2245 W 190th St
Torrance CA
310 326-4747

(P-5524)
THE E JORDAN BROOKES CO INC
Also Called: E Jordan Brookes Co.
10634 Shoemaker Ave (90670-4038)
P.O. Box 2220 (90670-0220)
PHONE..............................562 968-2100
◆ EMP: 69
Web: www.wieland-metalservices.com
SIC: **5051** Metals service centers and offices

(P-5525)
THYSSENKRUPP INDUS SVCS NA INC
Also Called: THYSSENKRUPP INDUSTRIAL SERVICES NA, INC.
201 Discovery Dr (94551-9532)
PHONE..............................209 395-9111
EMP: 235
SALES (corp-wide): 41.01B **Privately Held**
Web: www.thyssenkrupp-supply-chain.com
SIC: **5051** Steel
HQ: Thyssenkrupp Supply Chain Services Na, Inc.
22355 W 11 Mile Rd
Southfield MI
248 233-5600

(P-5526)
TMX AEROSPACE
12821 Carmenita Rd Unit F (90670-4805)
PHONE..............................562 215-4410
EMP: 120 EST: 2006
SALES (est): 14.04MM **Privately Held**
Web: www.thyssenkrupp-aerospace.com
SIC: **5051** Steel

(P-5527)
TOTTEN TUBES INC (PA)
500 W Danlee St (91702-2341)
PHONE..............................626 812-0220
Tracy N Totten, *CEO*
David Totten, *
Linda Furse, *
Jeffrey Totten, *
EMP: 60 EST: 1955
SQ FT: 73,000
SALES (est): 48.57MM
SALES (corp-wide): 48.57MM **Privately Held**
Web: www.tottentubes.com

SIC: **5051** 3498 Pipe and tubing, steel; Coils, pipe; fabricated from purchased pipe

(P-5528)
TRANSTAR METALS CORP
Also Called: Castle Metals Aerospace
14001 Orange Ave (90723-2017)
PHONE..............................562 630-1400
▲ EMP: 450
SIC: **5051** Aluminum bars, rods, ingots, sheets, pipes, plates, etc.

(P-5529)
VALLEY IRON INC (PA)
Also Called: Brislan
3114 S Cherry Ave (93706-5491)
P.O. Box 12024 (93776-2024)
PHONE..............................559 485-3900
▲ EMP: 80 EST: 1983
SALES (est): 98.25MM
SALES (corp-wide): 98.25MM **Privately Held**
Web: www.valleyiron.com
SIC: **5051** Metals service centers and offices

(P-5530)
VIKING INDUSTRIAL CORPORATION
Also Called: Viking Industrial
620 Clark Ave (94565-5000)
PHONE..............................925 427-2518
Spencer M Brog, *CEO*
David Berry, *Sr VP*
J M Martin, *Stockholder*
◆ EMP: 106 EST: 1986
SQ FT: 40,000
SALES (est): 15.23MM **Privately Held**
Web: www.vikingind.com
SIC: **5051** Steel

(P-5531)
WIELAND METAL SERVICES LLC
Also Called: Wieland Brookes
5100 S Archibald Ave (91762-7414)
PHONE..............................562 968-2100
EMP: 69
Web: www.wieland-metalservices.com
SIC: **5051** Metals service centers and offices
HQ: Wieland Metal Services, Llc
301 Metro Center Blvd # 204
Warwick RI
401 736-2600

5063 Electrical Apparatus And Equipment

(P-5532)
ABB INC
Also Called: ABB, INC.
6650 Goodyear Rd (94510-1250)
PHONE..............................808 497-7240
EMP: 70
Web: new.abb.com
SIC: **5063** Switchgear
HQ: Abb Inc.
305 Gregson Dr
Cary NC

(P-5533)
ADJ PRODUCTS LLC (PA)
6122 S Eastern Ave (90040-3402)
PHONE..............................323 582-2650
Toby Velasquez, *Managing Member*
EMP: 120 EST: 2012
SALES (est): 15.41MM
SALES (corp-wide): 15.41MM **Privately Held**

Web: www.adj.com
SIC: **5063** Lighting fixtures

(P-5534)
ALTERNTIVE PROTECTIVE SVCS INC
7301 Topanga Canyon Blvd Ste 350 (91303-3395)
PHONE..............................818 456-0989
John Chaverra, *CEO*
EMP: 65 EST: 2018
SALES (est): 3.64MM **Privately Held**
SIC: **5063** 7381 Electrical supplies, nec; Security guard service

(P-5535)
AMERICAN ELECTRIC SUPPLY INC (PA)
361 S Maple St (92878-4307)
P.O. Box 2710 (92878-2710)
PHONE..............................951 734-7910
Michael Pratt, *CEO*
Jerry Empson, *
Kevin Klinzing, *
▲ EMP: 68 EST: 1984
SQ FT: 13,086
SALES (est): 159.43MM
SALES (corp-wide): 159.43MM **Privately Held**
Web: www.amelect.com
SIC: **5063** Electrical supplies, nec

(P-5536)
AMERICAN WHOLESALE LTG INC
Also Called: Brilliant Lighting Products
1725 Rutan Dr (94551-7638)
PHONE..............................510 252-1088
Jeffrey David Jensen, *Pr*
Jeremy Adamson, *
Daisy Quesada, *
▲ EMP: 60 EST: 1985
SQ FT: 12,000
SALES (est): 26.1MM **Privately Held**
Web: www.awlighting.com
SIC: **5063** Lighting fixtures

(P-5537)
ANIXTER INC
Anixter
7140 Opportunity Rd (92111-2202)
PHONE..............................800 854-2088
Marshall Merrifield, *Brnch Mgr*
EMP: 76
Web: www.anixter.com
SIC: **5063** Electrical apparatus and equipment
HQ: Anixter Inc.
2301 Patriot Blvd
Glenview IL
800 323-8167

(P-5538)
APPLIMOTION INC
5915 Jetton Ln (95650-9594)
PHONE..............................916 652-3118
▲ EMP: 69
Web: www.celeramotion.com
SIC: **5063** 8711 3545 Motors, electric; Consulting engineer; Precision measuring tools

(P-5539)
ARCHIPELAGO LIGHTING INC
4615 State St (91763-6130)
PHONE..............................909 627-5333
Jia H Deng, *CEO*
Jian H Ma, *CFO*
EMP: 70 EST: 2005

PRODUCTS & SERVICES SECTION
5063 - Electrical Apparatus And Equipment (P-5561)

SQ FT: 40,000
SALES (est): 9.64MM **Privately Held**
Web: www.archipelagolighting.com
SIC: **5063** Lighting fixtures

(P-5540)
BARTCO LIGHTING INC
5761 Research Dr (92649-1616)
PHONE..............................714 230-3200
Robert Barton, *CEO*
Dana B Mcke, *Ex VP*
Brian Labbe, *
▲ EMP: 70 EST: 1998
SALES (est): 23.98MM **Privately Held**
Web: www.bartcolighting.com
SIC: **5063** 3648 Lighting fixtures, commercial and industrial; Airport lighting fixtures: runway approach, taxi, or ramp

(P-5541)
BATTERY SYSTEMS INC
16725 Roscoe Blvd (91343-6110)
PHONE..............................818 474-1500
EMP: 75
SALES (corp-wide): 545.41MM **Privately Held**
Web: www.batterysystems.net
SIC: **5063** Batteries
PA: Battery Systems, Inc.
8585 N Stemmons Fwy # 60
Dallas TX
310 667-9320

(P-5542)
BAY CITY EQUIPMENT INDS INC
Also Called: John Deere Authorized Dealer
13625 Danielson St (92064-6829)
PHONE..............................619 938-8200
Mark Loftin, *CEO*
Rodney Lee, *
Charles Loftin, *
EMP: 100 EST: 1932
SQ FT: 20,000
SALES (est): 56.26MM **Privately Held**
Web: www.bcew.com
SIC: **5063** 5082 Generators; Construction and mining machinery

(P-5543)
BEACON ELECTRIC SUPPLY
9630 Chesapeake Dr (92123-1307)
PHONE..............................858 279-9770
EMP: 74
SIC: **5063** Electrical construction materials

(P-5544)
CABLECONN INDUSTRIES INC
Also Called: Cableconn
7198 Convoy Ct (92111-1019)
PHONE..............................858 571-7111
Lisa Coffman, *Pr*
Roger Newman, *
Rod Coffman, *
EMP: 65 EST: 1991
SQ FT: 20,000
SALES (est): 22.72MM **Privately Held**
Web: www.cableconn.com
SIC: **5063** 3678 3643 Building wire and cable ; Electronic connectors; Current-carrying wiring services

(P-5545)
CENTRAL WHOLESALE ELECTRICAL DISTRIBUTORS INC
6611 Preston Ave Ste E (94551-5108)
P.O. Box 5040 (94566-0901)
PHONE..............................925 245-9310
EMP: 90

SIC: **5063** Electrical supplies, nec

(P-5546)
CHESTER C LEHMANN CO INC (PA)
Also Called: Electrical Distributors Co
1135 Auzerais Ave (95126-3402)
P.O. Box 26830 (95159-6830)
PHONE..............................408 293-5818
Chester C Lehmann Iii, *CEO*
Scott Lehmann, *
▼ EMP: 65 EST: 1948
SQ FT: 80,000
SALES (est): 181.09MM
SALES (corp-wide): 181.09MM **Privately Held**
SIC: **5063** Electrical supplies, nec

(P-5547)
CITY ELECTRIC SUPPLY
360 Tesconi Cir (95401-4677)
PHONE..............................707 523-4600
Steve Acuri, *Mgr*
EMP: 151 EST: 2009
SALES (est): 10.01MM **Privately Held**
Web: ces-santarosa.portalced.com
SIC: **5063** 3699 3634 Electrical supplies, nec ; Electrical equipment and supplies, nec; Electric housewares and fans

(P-5548)
COMMERCIAL LIGHTING INDS INC
Also Called: Cli
81161 Indio Blvd (92201-1931)
PHONE..............................800 755-0155
Frank Halcovich, *CEO*
▼ EMP: 74 EST: 1991
SQ FT: 81,000
SALES (est): 30.92MM **Privately Held**
Web: www.commercial-lighting.net
SIC: **5063** Light bulbs and related supplies

(P-5549)
CORDELIA LIGHTING INC
20101 S Santa Fe Ave (90221-5917)
PHONE..............................310 886-3490
James Keng, *Pr*
Li-wei Wang, *VP*
▲ EMP: 106 EST: 1985
SQ FT: 200,000
SALES (est): 23.82MM **Privately Held**
Web: www.cordelia.com
SIC: **5063** Lighting fixtures

(P-5550)
COUNTY WHL ELC CO LOS ANGELES
Also Called: C E D
560 N Main St (92868-1102)
PHONE..............................714 633-3801
Joe Mihelich, *Prin*
EMP: 76 EST: 1986
SALES (est): 22.56MM
SALES (corp-wide): 1.5B **Privately Held**
Web: www.countywholesale.com
SIC: **5063** Electrical supplies, nec
PA: Consolidated Electrical Distributors, Inc.
1920 Westridge Dr
Irving TX
972 582-5300

(P-5551)
CUSTOM POWER LLC
10910 Talbert Ave (92708-6038)
PHONE..............................714 962-7600
▲ EMP: 70 EST: 1965
SALES (est): 24.69MM

SALES (corp-wide): 152.02MM **Privately Held**
Web: www.custompower.com
SIC: **5063** Batteries, dry cell
PA: Solid State Plc
Hedera Road Ravensbank Business Park
Redditch WORCS
152 783-0800

(P-5552)
DAHL-BECK ELECTRIC CO
2775 Goodrick Ave (94801-1109)
PHONE..............................510 237-2325
Roger Beck, *CEO*
William R Beck, *Pr*
Gerald Vaio, *VP*
James Ross, *Sec*
▲ EMP: 65 EST: 1932
SQ FT: 75,000
SALES (est): 21.87MM **Privately Held**
Web: www.dahlbeckelectric.com
SIC: **5063** 1731 Electrical supplies, nec; General electrical contractor

(P-5553)
DAVIS WHOLESALE ELECTRIC INC
11581 Vanowen St (91605-6225)
PHONE..............................818 392-2400
EMP: 60
SIC: **5063** Electrical supplies, nec

(P-5554)
EATON AEROSPACE LLC
Eaton Aerospace
4690 Colorado Blvd (90039-1106)
PHONE..............................818 409-0200
Stephanie Stewart, *Brnch Mgr*
EMP: 256
SQ FT: 41,117
SIC: **5063** 3492 Electrical apparatus and equipment; Fluid power valves and hose fittings
HQ: Eaton Aerospace Llc
1000 Eaton Blvd
Cleveland OH
216 523-5000

(P-5555)
ECOSENSE LIGHTING INC (PA)
837 N Spring St Ste 103 (90012-2323)
PHONE..............................855 632-6736
Mark Reynoso, *CEO*
George Mueller, *
Neil Gamble, *
Steven Gelsomini, *
Robert T Mcculley, *VP*
▲ EMP: 95 EST: 2008
SALES (est): 45.79MM
SALES (corp-wide): 45.79MM **Privately Held**
Web: www.ecosenselighting.com
SIC: **5063** Lighting fixtures

(P-5556)
ELECTRIC MOTOR SHOP
Also Called: Electric Motor & Supply Co.
250 Broadway St (93721-3103)
P.O. Box 446 (93709-0446)
PHONE..............................559 233-1153
Dicks Caglia, *Pr*
EMP: 148
SQ FT: 1,296
SALES (corp-wide): 62.51MM **Privately Held**
Web: www.electricmotorshop.com
SIC: **5063** Electrical supplies, nec
PA: Electric Motor Shop
253 Fulton St

Fresno CA
559 233-1153

(P-5557)
FACILITY SOLUTIONS GROUP INC
801 Richfield Rd (92870-6731)
PHONE..............................714 993-3966
Jeff Johnson, *Dist Mgr*
EMP: 64
SALES (corp-wide): 787.76MM **Privately Held**
Web: www.fsg.com
SIC: **5063** 1731 Lighting fixtures, commercial and industrial; Electrical work
PA: Facility Solutions Group, Inc.
4401 West Gate Blvd # 310
Austin TX
512 440-7985

(P-5558)
GRANITE ELECTRICAL SUPPLY INC
Also Called: Ges
1701 National Dr Ste 200 (95834-2951)
P.O. Box 348450 (95159)
PHONE..............................916 648-3900
EMP: 75
SIC: **5063** Electrical supplies, nec

(P-5559)
GRAYBAR ELECTRIC COMPANY INC
Also Called: Graybar
1370 Valley Vista Dr Ste 100 (91765-3921)
PHONE..............................909 451-4300
Bruce Spencer, *Brnch Mgr*
EMP: 153
SALES (corp-wide): 8.77B **Privately Held**
Web: www.graybar.com
SIC: **5063** 5065 Electrical supplies, nec; Telephone equipment
PA: Graybar Electric Company, Inc.
34 N Meramec Ave
Saint Louis MO
314 573-9200

(P-5560)
GRAYBAR ELECTRIC COMPANY INC
1211 Fee Dr (95815-3979)
PHONE..............................916 561-1900
Greg Langehaug, *Brnch Mgr*
EMP: 62
SALES (corp-wide): 8.77B **Privately Held**
Web: www.graybar.com
SIC: **5063** Electrical supplies, nec
PA: Graybar Electric Company, Inc.
34 N Meramec Ave
Saint Louis MO
314 573-9200

(P-5561)
GRAYBAR ELECTRIC COMPANY INC
8606 Miralani Dr (92126-4353)
PHONE..............................858 578-8606
Chris Ruperto, *Mgr*
EMP: 89
SQ FT: 42,973
SALES (corp-wide): 8.77B **Privately Held**
Web: www.graybar.com
SIC: **5063** Electrical supplies, nec
PA: Graybar Electric Company, Inc.
34 N Meramec Ave
Saint Louis MO
314 573-9200

5063 - Electrical Apparatus And Equipment (P-5562)

(P-5562)
GRAYBAR ELECTRIC COMPANY INC
3089 Whipple Rd (94587-1236)
PHONE..............................925 557-3000
Eric Ortega, Brnch Mgr
EMP: 62
SQ FT: 117,648
SALES (corp-wide): 8.77B Privately Held
Web: www.graybar.com
SIC: 5063 5065 Electrical supplies, nec; Telephone equipment
PA: Graybar Electric Company, Inc.
   34 N Meramec Ave
   Saint Louis MO
   314 573-9200

(P-5563)
GREATLINK INTERNATIONAL INC
44168 S Grimmer Blvd (94538-6310)
PHONE..............................510 657-1667
Anjee Huang, CEO
▲ EMP: 659 EST: 1997
SQ FT: 10,000
SALES (est): 64MM Privately Held
Web: www.greatlinkus.com
SIC: 5063 Cable conduit
PA: Greatlink Electronics Taiwan Ltd.
   5f, 7, Ln. 45, Baoxing Rd.,
   New Taipei City TAP

(P-5564)
HERNING ENTERPRISES INC
Also Called: Herning Underground Supply
23144 Clawiter Rd (94545-1320)
PHONE..............................510 782-5330
Michael D Herning, Pr
EMP: 128 EST: 1987
SQ FT: 12,000
SALES (est): 13.06MM Privately Held
SIC: 5063 Electrical apparatus and equipment

(P-5565)
HOCHIKI AMERICA CORPORATION (HQ)
Also Called: Hochiki
7051 Village Dr Ste 100 (90621-2262)
P.O. Box 514689 (90051-4689)
PHONE..............................714 522-2246
Hisham Harake, CEO
Hiroshi Kamei, *
Sunichi Shoji V Pes, Prin
Michel Nader, *
◆ EMP: 95 EST: 1972
SQ FT: 30,000
SALES (est): 48.18MM Privately Held
Web: www.hochikiamerica.com
SIC: 5063 3669 Fire alarm systems; Fire detection systems, electric
PA: Hochiki Corporation
   2-10-43, Kamiosaki
   Shinagawa-Ku TKY

(P-5566)
INDEPENDENT ELECTRIC SUP INC
4351 Northgate Blvd (95834-1104)
PHONE..............................916 924-4848
Don Bispo, Mgr
EMP: 62
SALES (corp-wide): 12.53MM Privately Held
SIC: 5063 Electrical supplies, nec
HQ: Independent Electric Supply Inc.
   2001 Marina Blvd
   San Leandro CA
   510 877-9850

(P-5567)
INDEPENDENT ELECTRIC SUP INC
Also Called: I E S
1565 Venture Ln (95380-5761)
PHONE..............................209 667-2659
TOLL FREE: 800
Dave Crew, Mgr
EMP: 63
SQ FT: 5,000
SALES (corp-wide): 12.53MM Privately Held
SIC: 5063 Electrical supplies, nec
HQ: Independent Electric Supply Inc.
   2001 Marina Blvd
   San Leandro CA
   510 877-9850

(P-5568)
INDEPENDENT ELECTRIC SUP INC
Also Called: Independent
1575 Burke Ave (94124-1428)
PHONE..............................415 734-4700
Marc Reisfelt, Mgr
EMP: 62
SALES (corp-wide): 12.53MM Privately Held
SIC: 5063 Electrical supplies, nec
HQ: Independent Electric Supply Inc.
   2001 Marina Blvd
   San Leandro CA
   510 877-9850

(P-5569)
JELIGHT COMPANY INC (PA)
2 Mason (92618-2513)
PHONE..............................949 380-8774
Marinko Jelic, Pr
Renata Jelic, *
▲ EMP: 62 EST: 1978
SQ FT: 27,000
SALES (est): 23.91MM
SALES (corp-wide): 23.91MM Privately Held
Web: www.jelight.com
SIC: 5063 Lighting fixtures

(P-5570)
JME INC (PA)
Also Called: T M B
527 Park Ave (91340-2557)
PHONE..............................201 896-8600
Colin R Waters, CEO
Thomas M Bissett, *
◆ EMP: 80 EST: 1982
SQ FT: 34,000
SALES (est): 38.15MM
SALES (corp-wide): 38.15MM Privately Held
Web: www.tmb.com
SIC: 5063 Lighting fittings and accessories

(P-5571)
KOBERT & COMPANY INC
Also Called: L.H. Dottie Co
6131 Garfield Ave (90040-3610)
PHONE..............................323 725-1000
▲ EMP: 90 EST: 1965
SALES (est): 29.43MM Privately Held
Web: www.lhdottie.com
SIC: 5063 5074 Electrical supplies, nec; Plumbing fittings and supplies

(P-5572)
KOFFLER ELEC MECH APPRTUS REPR
Also Called: Koffler Electrical Mechanical
527 Whitney St (94577-1113)
PHONE..............................510 567-0630
Lari Koffler, Pr
Wayne Berner, *
Charles H Koffler, *
Michael Bucedi, *
Kerry Koffler, *
▲ EMP: 80 EST: 1994
SQ FT: 77,548
SALES (est): 27.03MM Privately Held
Web: www.koffler.com
SIC: 5063 7694 Motors, electric; Electric motor repair

(P-5573)
LGE ELECTRICAL SALES INC
755 E Evelyn Ave (94086-6527)
P.O. Box 1263 (94070-1263)
PHONE..............................408 992-4145
Ray Landgraf, Mgr
EMP: 110
SALES (corp-wide): 12.53MM Privately Held
Web: www.lgesales.com
SIC: 5063 Electrical supplies, nec
HQ: Lge Electrical Sales, Inc.
   650 University Ave # 218
   Sacramento CA
   916 563-2737

(P-5574)
LIGHTING TECHNOLOGIES INTL LLC
13700 Live Oak Ave (91706-1319)
PHONE..............................626 480-0755
▲ EMP: 190 EST: 2016
SALES (est): 24.12MM Privately Held
Web: www.ltilighting.com
SIC: 5063 3648 Lighting fixtures; Lighting equipment, nec

(P-5575)
LOS ANGELES LTG MFG CO INC
Also Called: L A Lighting
10141 Olney St (91731-2311)
PHONE..............................626 454-8300
William D Shapiro, Pr
Mieko Shapiro, VP
◆ EMP: 70 EST: 1988
SQ FT: 50,000
SALES (est): 22.27MM Privately Held
Web: www.lalighting.com
SIC: 5063 3646 Lighting fixtures; Ceiling systems, luminous

(P-5576)
MAGNETIKA INC (PA)
2041 W 139th St (90249-2409)
PHONE..............................310 527-8100
Francis Ishida, Pr
Basil P Caloyeras, *
EMP: 80 EST: 1960
SQ FT: 40,000
SALES (est): 31.93MM
SALES (corp-wide): 31.93MM Privately Held
Web: www.magnetika.com
SIC: 5063 3612 Transformers, electric; Ballasts for lighting fixtures

(P-5577)
MAIN ELECTRIC SUPPLY CO LLC (PA)
Also Called: Main Electric Supply Company
3600 W Segerstrom Ave (92704-6408)
P.O. Box 25750 (92799-5750)
PHONE..............................949 833-3052
Karen Morris, CFO
▲ EMP: 69 EST: 1946
SQ FT: 35,000
SALES (est): 464.19MM
SALES (corp-wide): 464.19MM Privately Held
Web: www.mainelectricsupply.com
SIC: 5063 Electrical supplies, nec

(P-5578)
MAXIM LIGHTING INTL INC (PA)
Also Called: Maxim Lighting
253 Vineland Ave (91746-2319)
PHONE..............................626 956-4200
Jacob Sperling, CEO
Zvi Sperling, *
Michael S Andrews, *
▲ EMP: 200 EST: 1999
SQ FT: 26,000
SALES (est): 56.17MM
SALES (corp-wide): 56.17MM Privately Held
Web: www.maximlighting.com
SIC: 5063 Lighting fixtures

(P-5579)
MINKA LIGHTING LLC (PA)
Also Called: Minka Group
1151 Bradford Cir (92882-7166)
PHONE..............................951 735-9220
William S Brundage, Managing Member
Ian T Graham, *
Marian Tang, *
Kurt Schulzman, *
◆ EMP: 70 EST: 1982
SQ FT: 350,000
SALES (est): 89.88MM
SALES (corp-wide): 89.88MM Privately Held
Web: www.minkagroup.net
SIC: 5063 Lighting fixtures

(P-5580)
MOTIVE ENERGY INC (PA)
17260 Newhope St (92708-4210)
PHONE..............................714 888-2525
Robert J Istwan, Pr
▼ EMP: 80 EST: 1979
SQ FT: 35,000
SALES (est): 43.24MM
SALES (corp-wide): 43.24MM Privately Held
Web: www.motiveenergy.com
SIC: 5063 Storage batteries, industrial

(P-5581)
MPOWER ELECTRONICS INC
2910 Scott Blvd (95054-3312)
PHONE..............................408 320-1266
Hong Tao Sun, Pr
Peter Hsi, *
Weimin Cai, *
◆ EMP: 60 EST: 2018
SALES (est): 2.7MM Privately Held
Web: www.mpowerinc.com
SIC: 5063 3829 3624 Fire alarm systems; Gas detectors; Carbon and graphite products

(P-5582)
MULTIQUIP INC (DH)
Also Called: Mq Power
6141 Katella Ave Ste 200 (90630-5202)
PHONE..............................310 537-3700
Robert J Graydon, CEO
James Henehan, *
◆ EMP: 300 EST: 1973
SALES (est): 214.36MM Privately Held
Web: www.multiquip.com
SIC: 5063 5082 3645 Generators; General construction machinery and equipment; Garden, patio, walkway and yard lighting fixtures; electric
HQ: Itochu International Inc.

▲ = Import ▼ = Export
◆ = Import/Export

PRODUCTS & SERVICES SECTION
5064 - Electrical Appliances, Television And Radio (P-5602)

1251 Ave Of The Amrcas Fl
New York NY
212 818-8000

(P-5583)
NELSON & ASSOCIATES INC
12816 Leffingwell Ave (90670-6343)
PHONE..................................562 921-4423
Brian Haupt, *Pr*
Todd James Nelson, *
Kurt Nelson, *
Brian Haupt, *Ex VP*
▲ **EMP:** 65 **EST:** 1977
SQ FT: 120,000
SALES (est): 44.45MM **Privately Held**
Web: www.nelsonreps.com
SIC: 5063 Electrical supplies, nec

(P-5584)
NORA LIGHTING INC
6505 Gayhart St (90040-2507)
PHONE..................................323 767-2600
Fred Farzan, *CEO*
Jill Farzan, *
Neda Farzan, *
◆ **EMP:** 150 **EST:** 1989
SQ FT: 150,000
SALES (est): 90MM **Privately Held**
Web: www.noralighting.com
SIC: 5063 3648 5719 Lighting fixtures; Lighting fixtures, except electric: residential; Lighting fixtures

(P-5585)
ORBIT INDUSTRIES INC
7533 Garfield Ave (90201-4817)
PHONE..................................213 745-8884
Saeed Nikayin, *CEO*
John Alexandrovic, *
▲ **EMP:** 98 **EST:** 1965
SALES (est): 35.87MM **Privately Held**
Web: www.orbitelectric.com
SIC: 5063 Electrical apparatus and equipment
HQ: Element Materials Technology Group Limited
Davidson Building, 5 Southampton Street
London
800 470-3598

(P-5586)
ORIENTAL MOTOR USA CORPORATION (DH)
570 Alaska Ave Ste A (90503-3915)
PHONE..................................310 715-3300
Ryan Kanemura, *Pr*
Jake Kitayama, *
Pete Derose, *
Greg Johnston, *
◆ **EMP:** 60 **EST:** 1978
SQ FT: 31,600
SALES (est): 26.25MM **Privately Held**
Web: www.orientalmotor.com
SIC: 5063 Motors, electric
HQ: Oriental Motor Co., Ltd.
4-8-1, Higashiueno
Taito-Ku TKY

(P-5587)
PRECISION FLUORESCENT WEST INC (DH)
Also Called: Precision Energy Efficient Ltg
23281 La Palma Ave (92887-4768)
PHONE..................................352 692-5900
Raymond Pustinger, *Pr*
Dan Rodriguez, *
▲ **EMP:** 67 **EST:** 1995
SQ FT: 31,000
SALES (est): 47.09MM

SALES (corp-wide): 1.6B **Privately Held**
SIC: 5063 Electrical supplies, nec
HQ: Hli Solutions, Inc.
701 Millennium Blvd
Greenville SC

(P-5588)
REGENCY ENTERPRISES INC (PA)
Also Called: Regency Supply
9261 Jordan Ave (91311-5739)
PHONE..................................818 901-0255
Ron Regenstreif, *CEO*
Scott Anderson, *
Isaac Regenstreif, *
Judah Regenstreif, *
Mike Goldstone, *
◆ **EMP:** 272 **EST:** 1981
SALES (est): 104.14MM
SALES (corp-wide): 104.14MM **Privately Held**
Web: www.regencysupply.com
SIC: 5063 Light bulbs and related supplies

(P-5589)
SELECTA PRODUCTS INC (PA)
Also Called: Selecta Switch
1200 E Tehachapi Blvd (93561-8129)
P.O. Box 888 (93581-0888)
PHONE..................................661 823-7050
John Kenyon, *Pr*
Charles Kenyon, *
James Kenyon, *
Charlotte Tathwell, *
Dorothy Kenyon, *
▼ **EMP:** 60 **EST:** 1978
SQ FT: 20,000
SALES (est): 33.08MM
SALES (corp-wide): 33.08MM **Privately Held**
Web: www.selectainc.com
SIC: 5063 5065 Electrical supplies, nec; Electronic parts

(P-5590)
SGGH LLC
15301 Ventura Blvd Ste 400 (91403-6629)
PHONE..................................805 435-1255
EMP: 838 **EST:** 2014
SALES (est): 1.04MM
SALES (corp-wide): 133.24MM **Publicly Held**
SIC: 5063 6162 Circuit breakers; Mortgage bankers and loan correspondents
PA: Elah Holdings, Inc.
8214 Westchester Dr # 950
Dallas TX
805 435-1255

(P-5591)
SIEMENS INDUSTRY INC
6141 Katella Ave (90630-5202)
PHONE..................................714 761-2200
Eric Ackerman, *Genl Mgr*
EMP: 80
SALES (corp-wide): 71.74B **Privately Held**
Web: new.siemens.com
SIC: 5063 Electrical apparatus and equipment
HQ: Siemens Industry, Inc.
100 Technology Dr
Alpharetta GA
847 215-1000

(P-5592)
SITEONE LANDSCAPE SUPPLY LLC (DH)
10291 Ophir Rd (95658-9504)
PHONE..................................770 255-2100
Doug Black, *CEO*

Jeff Lanahan, *Sr VP*
Michael Harring, *Sec*
James Davlin, *Treas*
▲ **EMP:** 100 **EST:** 2001
SQ FT: 20,000
SALES (est): 1.08B
SALES (corp-wide): 4.01B **Publicly Held**
Web: www.lesco.com
SIC: 5063 5193 5083 Light bulbs and related supplies; Nursery stock; Irrigation equipment
HQ: Siteone Landscape Supply Holding, Llc
300 Colonial Center Pkwy # 6
Roswell GA
770 255-2100

(P-5593)
SOLARWORLD AMERICAS LLC
4650 Adohr Ln (93012-8508)
PHONE..................................503 844-3400
◆ **EMP:** 75
SIC: 5063 Electrical apparatus and equipment

(P-5594)
STEVEN ENGINEERING INC (HQ)
Also Called: Steven Engineering
230 Ryan Way (94080-6308)
PHONE..................................650 588-9200
Bryan J Wolfgram, *CEO*
Paul E Burk Iii, *Pr*
◆ **EMP:** 93 **EST:** 1975
SQ FT: 66,000
SALES (est): 72.47MM
SALES (corp-wide): 8.77B **Privately Held**
Web: www.stevenengineering.com
SIC: 5063 Electrical apparatus and equipment
PA: Graybar Electric Company, Inc.
34 N Meramec Ave
Saint Louis MO
314 573-9200

(P-5595)
SUMITOMO ELC INTRCNNECT PDTS I
915 Armorlite Dr (92069-1440)
PHONE..................................760 761-0600
Nobuyoshi Fujinama, *Pr*
▲ **EMP:** 60 **EST:** 1985
SQ FT: 55,000
SALES (est): 37.19MM **Privately Held**
Web: www.seipusa.com
SIC: 5063 Electrical supplies, nec
HQ: Sumitomo Electric Fine Polymer, Inc.
1-950, Asashironishi, Kumatoricho
Sennan-Gun OSK

(P-5596)
USHIO AMERICA INC (HQ)
5440 Cerritos Ave (90630-4567)
PHONE..................................714 236-8600
William Mackenzie, *CEO*
Shinji Kameda, *CFO*
Ako Shimada, *Sec*
Yuichi Asaka, *Prin*
◆ **EMP:** 90 **EST:** 1967
SQ FT: 70,000
SALES (est): 57.83MM **Privately Held**
Web: www.ushio.com
SIC: 5063 Lighting fixtures, commercial and industrial
PA: Ushio Inc.
1-6-5, Marunouchi
Chiyoda-Ku TKY

(P-5597)
WINDY CY WIRE CBLE TECH PDTS L
8024 Central Ave (94560-3450)

PHONE..................................510 284-3956
EMP: 217
SALES (corp-wide): 1.19B **Privately Held**
Web: www.smartwire.com
SIC: 5063 Wire and cable
HQ: Windy City Wire Cable And Technology Products, Llc
386 Internationale Dr H
Bolingbrook IL

(P-5598)
ZSPACE INC
55 Nicholson Ln Ste 2 (95134-1366)
PHONE..................................408 498-4050
Paul Kellenberger, *CEO*
Joseph Powers, *
EMP: 69 **EST:** 2006
SALES (est): 19.89MM **Privately Held**
Web: www.zspace.com
SIC: 5063 Transformers, electric

5064 Electrical Appliances, Television And Radio

(P-5599)
ATLAS SALES AND RENTALS INC
47233 Fremont Blvd (94538-6502)
P.O. Box 15100 (94539-2200)
PHONE..................................510 713-3313
EMP: 60
SIC: 5064 Air conditioning appliances

(P-5600)
AUTOMATIC LEASING INC (PA)
Also Called: Alco Service
445 S Figueroa St (90071-1602)
PHONE..................................213 746-4117
Peter Pierre Iii, *Pr*
Peter Pierre Senior, *VP*
EMP: 67 **EST:** 1959
SQ FT: 13,000
SALES (est): 22.17MM
SALES (corp-wide): 22.17MM **Privately Held**
Web: www.alcoservices.com
SIC: 5064 7359 Electrical appliances, major; Appliance rental

(P-5601)
DRAGON TRADE INTL CORP
614 5th Ave Ste D (92101-6964)
PHONE..................................619 816-6062
Jorge Petit, *CEO*
Carlos Hermida, *
Manuel Hermida Rodriguez, *
EMP: 200 **EST:** 2014
SALES (est): 40MM **Privately Held**
SIC: 5064 Electrical appliances, major

(P-5602)
E & S INTERNATIONAL ENTPS INC (PA)
Also Called: Import Direct
7801 Hayvenhurst Ave (91406-1712)
PHONE..................................818 887-0700
Philip Asherian, *CEO*
Farshad Asherian, *Pr*
Mike Rad, *COO*
Mark Barron, *CFO*
◆ **EMP:** 136 **EST:** 1983
SQ FT: 60,000
SALES (est): 71.5MM
SALES (corp-wide): 71.5MM **Privately Held**
Web: www.esintl.com
SIC: 5064 Electrical appliances, television and radio

5064 - Electrical Appliances, Television And Radio (P-5603)

(P-5603)
EPSILON ELECTRONICS INC (PA)
Also Called: Power Acoustik Electronics
1550 S Maple Ave (90640-6508)
PHONE..................323 722-3333
Jack Rochel, Pr
Mossa Rochel, *
◆ EMP: 77 EST: 1983
SQ FT: 69,000
SALES (est): 21.65MM
SALES (corp-wide): 21.65MM Privately Held
Web: www.epsilonelectronicsinc.com
SIC: 5064 Electrical entertainment equipment

(P-5604)
ETEKCITY CORPORATION
Also Called: Etekcity
1202 N Miller St Unit A (92806-1956)
PHONE..................855 686-3835
Grace Yang, CEO
Phillip Chen, *
Sean Yang, CIO*
EMP: 125 EST: 2011
SALES (est): 41.51MM Privately Held
Web: www.vesync.com
SIC: 5064 Electrical appliances, television and radio

(P-5605)
FUJITSU TEN CORP OF AMERICA
19600 S Vermont Ave (90502-1122)
PHONE..................310 327-2151
Masanori Yamamoto, Pr
EMP: 64
Web: www.denso-ten.com
SIC: 5064 7539 Radios, motor vehicle; Automotive repair shops, nec
HQ: Denso Ten Limited.
    1-2-28, Goshodoori, Hyogo-Ku
    Kobe HYO

(P-5606)
HARMAN-KARDON INCORPORATED
Also Called: Harman-Kardon
8500 Balboa Blvd (91329-0003)
P.O. Box 2200 (91328-2200)
PHONE..................818 841-4600
Tom Mcloughlin, Pr
Chet Simon, VP Fin
▲ EMP: 275 EST: 1949
SALES (est): 62.81MM Privately Held
Web: www.harman.com
SIC: 5064 3651 High fidelity equipment; Household audio and video equipment
HQ: Harman International Industries Incorporated
    400 Atlantic St Ste 15
    Stamford CT
    203 328-3500

(P-5607)
HOMELAND HOUSEWARES LLC
Also Called: Magic Bullet
10900 Wilshire Blvd Ste 900 (90024-6500)
PHONE..................310 996-7200
Rich Krause, CEO
▲ EMP: 80 EST: 2003
SALES (est): 14.8MM
SALES (corp-wide): 65.12MM Privately Held
Web: homeland-housewares.pissedconsumer.com
SIC: 5064 5963 Electrical appliances, major; Appliance sales, house-to-house
HQ: Capital Brands, Llc
    11601 Wilshire Blvd # 360
    Los Angeles CA

(P-5608)
MEMOREX PRODUCTS INC
17777 Center Court Dr N Ste 800 (90703-9320)
PHONE..................562 653-2800
Michael Golacinski, Pr
Allan Yap, *
Mae Higa, *
Kevin Mcdonnell, Sr VP
▲ EMP: 159 EST: 1993
SQ FT: 212,000
SALES (est): 7.95MM Publicly Held
SIC: 5064 5065 5045 3652 Electrical entertainment equipment; Radio and television equipment and parts; Computer peripheral equipment; Prerecorded records and tapes
PA: Glassbridge Enterprises, Inc.
    18 E 50th St Ste 700
    New York NY

(P-5609)
PAULS TV LLC
Also Called: Warehouse
900 Glenneyre St (92651-2707)
PHONE..................949 596-8800
EMP: 60
Web: www.paulstvcompany.com
SIC: 5064 Television sets

(P-5610)
PHILIPS NORTH AMERICA LLC
Also Called: Innercool Therapies
3721 Valley Centre Dr (92130-3329)
PHONE..................858 677-6390
EMP: 90
SALES (corp-wide): 133.64MM Privately Held
Web: usa.philips.com
SIC: 5064 Television sets
HQ: Philips North America Llc
    222 Jacobs St Fl 3
    Cambridge MA
    617 245-5900

(P-5611)
PURCELL-MURRAY COMPANY INC (PA)
235 Kansas St Fl 1 (94103-5170)
PHONE..................415 468-6620
Matthew David Murray, CEO
Timothy J Murray, *
Laurence D Purcell, *
Kevin William Murray, *
▲ EMP: 67 EST: 1981
SALES (est): 47.64MM
SALES (corp-wide): 47.64MM Privately Held
Web: www.purcellmurray.com
SIC: 5064 5074 Electrical appliances, major; Plumbing fittings and supplies

(P-5612)
R & B WHOLESALE DISTRS INC (PA)
2350 S Milliken Ave (91761-2332)
PHONE..................909 230-5400
Robert O Burggraf, Pr
Masako Burggraf, *
Shamsul Hyder, *
◆ EMP: 75 EST: 1968
SQ FT: 72,000
SALES (est): 97.96MM
SALES (corp-wide): 97.96MM Privately Held
Web: www.rbdist.com
SIC: 5064 Electrical appliances, major

(P-5613)
SAMSUNG ELECTRONICS AMER INC
5601 E Slauson Ave Ste 200 (90040-2953)
PHONE..................323 374-6300
EMP: 162
Web: www.samsung.com
SIC: 5064 Electrical appliances, television and radio
HQ: Samsung Electronics America, Inc.
    85 Challenger Rd
    Ridgefield Park NJ
    201 229-4000

(P-5614)
SIERRA SELECT DISTRIBUTORS INC
Also Called: Sierra Select
4320 Roseville Rd (95660-5711)
PHONE..................916 483-9295
Patrick Russell Tatro, CEO
John Tatro, *
Michael W Tatro, *
▲ EMP: 65 EST: 1982
SQ FT: 54,000
SALES (est): 39.05MM Privately Held
Web: www.sierraselect.com
SIC: 5064 Radios, nec

(P-5615)
TTE TECHNOLOGY INC
Also Called: Tcl Electronics
189 Technology Dr (92618-2402)
PHONE..................877 300-8837
Mark Zhang, Pr
Nicole Feng, Dir Fin
▲ EMP: 150 EST: 2004
SQ FT: 50,000
SALES (est): 169.46MM
SALES (corp-wide): 4.15MM Privately Held
Web: www.tcl.com
SIC: 5064 Television sets
HQ: Tcl Electronics Holdings Limited
    C/O Maples Corporate Services Limited
    George Town GR CAYMAN

(P-5616)
TV GUIDE ENTRMT GROUP LLC
2700 Colorado Ave Ste 200 (90404-5502)
PHONE..................310 360-1441
EMP: 80 EST: 1998
SALES (est): 78.41MM
SALES (corp-wide): 30.15B Publicly Held
SIC: 5064 Electrical entertainment equipment
HQ: Cbs Interactive Inc.
    680 Folsom St
    San Francisco CA

5065 Electronic Parts And Equipment, Nec

(P-5617)
ABX ENGINEERING INC
875 Stanton Rd (94010-1403)
PHONE..................650 552-2300
Paul Leininger Ii, CEO
EMP: 100 EST: 1980
SQ FT: 16,000
SALES (est): 37.49MM Privately Held
Web: www.abxengineering.com
SIC: 5065 7373 3672 Electronic parts; Turnkey vendors, computer systems; Printed circuit boards

(P-5618)
ACE WIRELESS & TRADING INC
3031 Orange Ave Ste B (92707-4246)
PHONE..................949 748-5700
◆ EMP: 375
SIC: 5065 Electronic parts

(P-5619)
ADVANCED MNLYTHIC CERAMICS INC
Also Called: AMC
15191 Bledsoe St (91342-2710)
PHONE..................818 364-9800
N Eric Johanson, Ch Bd
Phu Luu, Pr
Steve Makl, Prin
▲ EMP: 62 EST: 1994
SQ FT: 35,000
SALES (est): 18.26MM Privately Held
SIC: 5065 Electronic parts and equipment, nec
HQ: Johanson Dielectrics, Inc.
    4001 Calle Tecate
    Camarillo CA
    805 575-0124

(P-5620)
ADVANCED MP TECHNOLOGY LLC (DH)
27271 Las Ramblas Ste 300 (92691-8042)
PHONE..................800 492-3113
Homayoun Shorooghi, Pr
◆ EMP: 126 EST: 1994
SALES (est): 48.39MM
SALES (corp-wide): 410.29MM Privately Held
Web: www.a2globalelectronics.com
SIC: 5065 Electronic parts
HQ: America Ii Electronics, Llc
    2500 118th Ave N
    Saint Petersburg FL
    727 573-0900

(P-5621)
ADVANTEST AMERICA CORPORATION (HOLDING CO)
3061 Zanker Rd (95134-2127)
PHONE..................408 456-3600
EMP: 320 EST: 1997
SALES (est): 37.72MM Privately Held
Web: www.advantest.com
SIC: 5065 8731 7373 Semiconductor devices; Computer (hardware) development; Systems software development services
PA: Advantest Corporation
    1-6-2, Marunouchi
    Chiyoda-Ku TKY

(P-5622)
ADVANTEST AMERICA INC
3201 Scott Blvd (95054-3008)
PHONE..................408 988-7700
EMP: 270
SIC: 5065 3825 Semiconductor devices; Instruments to measure electricity

(P-5623)
AIR ELECTRO INC (PA)
9452 De Soto Ave (91311-4910)
P.O. Box 2231 (91313-2231)
PHONE..................818 407-5400
EMP: 85 EST: 1951
SALES (est): 26.76MM
SALES (corp-wide): 26.76MM Privately Held
Web: www.airelectro.com
SIC: 5065 3674 Electronic parts; Computer logic modules

PRODUCTS & SERVICES SECTION
5065 - Electronic Parts And Equipment, Nec (P-5645)

(P-5624)
ALIPHCOM
Also Called: Aliph
99 Rhode Island St Fl 3 (94103-5232)
PHONE..............................415 230-7600
▲ EMP: 300
Web: www.jawbone.com
SIC: **5065** 5999 Sound equipment, electronic
; Electronic parts and equipment

(P-5625)
AP GLOBAL INC
Also Called: Accessory Power
2326 Townsgate Rd (91361-2501)
PHONE..............................818 707-3167
Robert Breines, *Pr*
Gail Breines, *
EMP: 60 **EST:** 2013
SALES (est): 9.84MM **Privately Held**
Web: www.accessorypower.com
SIC: **5065** Electronic parts and equipment, nec

(P-5626)
AVAGO TECHNOLOGIES US INC (HQ)
Also Called: Avago Technologies
1320 Ridder Park Dr (95131-2313)
P.O. Box 3643 (95055-3643)
PHONE..............................800 433-8778
Hock Tan, *Pr*
Dick Chang, *
Douglas Bettinger, *
Jeff Henderson, *
Tze Siong Chong, *
▲ **EMP:** 400 **EST:** 2005
SALES (est): 1.88MM
SALES (corp-wide): 33.2B **Publicly Held**
SIC: **5065** 3674 Semiconductor devices; Semiconductor diodes and rectifiers
PA: Broadcom Inc.
1320 Ridder Park Dr
San Jose CA
408 433-8000

(P-5627)
BATTERY SYSTEMS INC
26151 Jefferson Ave Ste A (92562-9560)
PHONE..............................951 894-2960
Mikel Sides, *Brnch Mgr*
EMP: 81
SALES (corp-wide): 545.41MM **Privately Held**
Web: www.batterysystems.net
SIC: **5065** Electronic parts and equipment, nec
PA: Battery Systems, Inc.
8585 N Stemmons Fwy # 60
Dallas TX
310 667-9320

(P-5628)
BEAR COMMUNICATIONS INC
Also Called: Bearcom Wireless Worldwide
8290 Vickers St Ste D (92111-2116)
PHONE..............................619 263-2159
Rick Andrews, *Brnch Mgr*
EMP: 85
SALES (corp-wide): 809.13MM **Privately Held**
Web: www.bearcom.com
SIC: **5065** Communication equipment
HQ: Bear Communications, Inc.
4009 Dist Dr Ste 200
Garland TX

(P-5629)
BEAR COMMUNICATIONS INC
Also Called: Bearcom Wireless Worldwide
8584 Venice Blvd (90034-2549)
PHONE..............................310 854-2327
TOLL FREE: 800
Stan Cameron, *Brnch Mgr*
EMP: 85
SALES (corp-wide): 809.13MM **Privately Held**
Web: www.bearcom.com
SIC: **5065** Communication equipment
HQ: Bear Communications, Inc.
4009 Dist Dr Ste 200
Garland TX

(P-5630)
BEAR COMMUNICATIONS INC
Also Called: Bearcom Wireless Worldwide
150 N Hill Dr Ste 19 (94005-1018)
PHONE..............................415 656-2327
EMP: 85
SALES (corp-wide): 809.13MM **Privately Held**
Web: www.bearcom.com
SIC: **5065** 5999 Communication equipment; Telephone and communication equipment
HQ: Bear Communications, Inc.
4009 Dist Dr Ste 200
Garland TX

(P-5631)
BISCO INC
5065 E Hunter Ave (92807-6001)
P.O. Box 3005 (90408-3005)
PHONE..............................714 693-2901
Michael Levinrad, *Pr*
EMP: 146 **EST:** 2010
SALES (est): 13.53MM **Privately Held**
Web: www.biscoind.com
SIC: **5065** Electronic parts

(P-5632)
BISCO INDUSTRIES INC (HQ)
Also Called: Fastcor
5065 E Hunter Ave (92807-6001)
PHONE..............................800 323-1232
▲ **EMP:** 85 **EST:** 1973
SALES (est): 160.95MM
SALES (corp-wide): 292.56MM **Publicly Held**
Web: www.biscoind.com
SIC: **5065** Electronic parts
PA: Eaco Corporation
5065 E Hunter Ave
Anaheim CA
714 876-2490

(P-5633)
BITCENTRAL INC
Also Called: Bitcentral
4340 Von Karman Ave # 410 (92660-2085)
PHONE..............................949 253-9000
EMP: 85
SIC: **5065** Communication equipment

(P-5634)
BRAEMAC (CA) LLC
43134 Osgood Rd (94539-5608)
PHONE..............................510 687-1000
Ben Kingsley, *Managing Member*
Raymond Ford, *
◆ **EMP:** 80 **EST:** 1997
SQ FT: 16,000
SALES (est): 24.28MM **Privately Held**
Web: www.braemacca.com
SIC: **5065** Semiconductor devices

(P-5635)
BRIX GROUP INC (PA)
Also Called: Pana-Pacific
838 N Laverne Ave (93727-6868)
PHONE..............................559 457-4700
Harrison Brix, *CEO*
John Trenberth, *
Kristina Reed, *
John Tingleff, *
Harrison Brix, *Sec*
▲ **EMP:** 80 **EST:** 1973
SQ FT: 35,000
SALES (est): 113.03MM
SALES (corp-wide): 113.03MM **Privately Held**
Web: www.thebrixgroup.com
SIC: **5065** 5013 Mobile telephone equipment
; Motor vehicle supplies and new parts

(P-5636)
BROWNSTONE COMPANIES INC
Also Called: Brownstone Security
2629 Manhattan Beach Blvd # 100 (90278-1604)
PHONE..............................310 297-3600
EMP: 700
SIC: **5065** Security control equipment and systems

(P-5637)
BUYERS CONSULTATION SVC INC (PA)
Also Called: B C S
8735 Remmet Ave (91304-1519)
P.O. Box 8427 (91372-8427)
PHONE..............................818 341-4820
Jo Manhan, *Pr*
▲ **EMP:** 75 **EST:** 1988
SQ FT: 40,000
SALES (est): 47.65MM **Privately Held**
Web: www.scrapdr.com
SIC: **5065** 7389 5093 4953 Electronic parts and equipment, nec; Auctioneers, fee basis ; Metal scrap and waste materials; Recycling, waste materials

(P-5638)
CAL SOUTHERN SOUND IMAGE INC (PA)
Also Called: Sound Image
2425 Auto Park Way (92029-1222)
PHONE..............................760 737-3900
David R Shadoan, *CEO*
Ralph Wagner, *
EMP: 65 **EST:** 1984
SQ FT: 28,000
SALES (est): 49.52MM
SALES (corp-wide): 49.52MM **Privately Held**
Web: www.sound-image.com
SIC: **5065** 3651 5064 Sound equipment, electronic; Speaker systems; Electrical appliances, television and radio

(P-5639)
CALIFORNIA EASTERN LABS INC (PA)
5201 Great America Pkwy Ste 320 (95054-1122)
PHONE..............................408 919-2500
Paul Minton, *CEO*
Jerry A Arden, *
Paul A S Minton, *
Kevin Beber, *
Mark A Sargent, *
▲ **EMP:** 80 **EST:** 1959
SQ FT: 42,000
SALES (est): 37.14MM
SALES (corp-wide): 37.14MM **Privately Held**
Web: www.cel.com
SIC: **5065** Semiconductor devices

(P-5640)
CBOL CORPORATION
19850 Plummer St (91311-5652)
PHONE..............................818 704-8200
Howard Nam, *COO*
Kenneth Cheung, *
Lynn Turk, *
Spencer H Kim, *
◆ **EMP:** 131 **EST:** 1987
SQ FT: 69,820
SALES (est): 99.45MM **Privately Held**
Web: www.cbol.com
SIC: **5065** 5072 5013 5088 Electronic parts and equipment, nec; Hardware; Motor vehicle supplies and new parts; Transportation equipment and supplies

(P-5641)
CICOIL LLC
24960 Avenue Tibbitts (91355-3426)
PHONE..............................661 295-1295
Jeffrey T Crane, *CEO*
John Palahnuk, *
Patrick H Albert, *
EMP: 120 **EST:** 1956
SQ FT: 16,000
SALES (est): 31.3MM **Privately Held**
Web: www.cicoil.com
SIC: **5065** Electronic parts and equipment, nec

(P-5642)
CNET TECHNOLOGY CORPORATION
26291 Production Ave Ste 205 (94545)
PHONE..............................408 392-9966
Simon J Chang, *Pr*
▲ **EMP:** 250 **EST:** 1987
SQ FT: 50,000
SALES (est): 45.87MM **Privately Held**
Web: www.cnetusa.com
SIC: **5065** 3661 3577 Communication equipment; Telephone and telegraph apparatus; Computer peripheral equipment, nec
PA: Kmc (Kuei Meng) International Inc.
8f-5, No. 425, Jhonghua Rd.
Tainan City

(P-5643)
CP DOCUMENT TECHNOLOGIES LLC (PA)
Also Called: Copypage
800 W 6th St Ste 1400 (90017-2718)
PHONE..............................213 617-4040
EMP: 70 **EST:** 1992
SQ FT: 8,350
SALES (est): 23.32MM **Privately Held**
SIC: **5065** 7334 7374 Electronic parts; Photocopying and duplicating services; Optical scanning data service

(P-5644)
CYAN INC
1383 N Mcdowell Blvd # 300 (94954-1190)
PHONE..............................707 735-2300
EMP: 200
SIC: **5065** Mobile telephone equipment

(P-5645)
DECISION SCIENCES INTL CORP
Also Called: Decision Sciences
12345 First American Way Ste 100 (92064-6828)
PHONE..............................858 571-1900
Dwight Johnson, *Pr*
Mike Goll, *
▼ **EMP:** 60 **EST:** 2009
SALES (est): 23.27MM **Privately Held**

5065 - Electronic Parts And Equipment, Nec (P-5646)

Web: www.decisionsciences.com
SIC: 5065 Radar detectors

(P-5646)
DELTA AMERICA LTD (HQ)
Also Called: Delta Products
46101 Fremont Blvd (94538-6468)
PHONE.................................510 668-5100
Ming H Huang, Pr
Yao Chou, Sec
◆ EMP: 130 EST: 1988
SALES (est): 465.66MM Privately Held
Web: www.deltabreez.com
SIC: 5065 3679 8731 Electronic parts and equipment, nec; Switches, stepping; Electronic research
PA: Delta Electronics, Inc.
186, Ruey Kuang Rd.
Taipei City TAP

(P-5647)
EFORCITY CORPORATION
Also Called: Ascend Distribution
18525 Railroad St (91748-1316)
PHONE.................................626 442-3168
◆ EMP: 60
Web: www.juvoplus.com
SIC: 5065 Telephone equipment

(P-5648)
EQUITY INTERNATIONAL INC
Also Called: B & W
5541 Fermi Ct (92008-7348)
PHONE.................................978 664-2712
Joseph Atkins, Pr
Stephen Curran, *
Cindy Hughes, *
EMP: 574 EST: 1993
SALES (est): 107.37MM Privately Held
Web: www.bowerswilkins.com
SIC: 5065 Radio and television equipment and parts
HQ: B & W Group Ltd
Dale Road
Worthing W SUSSEX
190 322-1500

(P-5649)
EXAR INTERNATIONAL INC
48760 Kato Rd (94538-7312)
PHONE.................................949 753-8108
Ronald W Guire, CFO
Thomas R Melendrez, *
Ronald W Guire, VP
Donald Ciffone, *
Barbara Hoff, *
EMP: 118 EST: 1984
SALES (est): 4.64MM
SALES (corp-wide): 1.12B Publicly Held
SIC: 5065 Semiconductor devices
HQ: Exar Corporation
1060 Rincon Cir
San Jose CA
669 265-6100

(P-5650)
EXPONENTIAL TECH GROUP INC
Also Called: Rfmw
188 Martinvale Ln (95119-1356)
PHONE.................................408 414-1450
Joel Levine, Brnch Mgr
EMP: 80
SALES (corp-wide): 302.09B Publicly Held
Web: www.rfmw.com
SIC: 5065 Electronic parts
HQ: Exponential Technology Group, Inc.
2441 Northeast Pkwy
Fort Worth TX
817 804-3870

(P-5651)
FOREIGN TRADE CORPORATION
Also Called: Technocel
685 Cochran St Ste 200 (93065-1921)
PHONE.................................805 823-8400
▲ EMP: 115
SIC: 5065 Mobile telephone equipment

(P-5652)
FORTRON/SOURCE CORPORATION
4231 Business Center Dr Ste 7 (94538)
PHONE.................................510 440-0188
EMP: 89
SALES (corp-wide): 4.87MM Privately Held
SIC: 5065 Electronic parts
PA: Fortron/Source Corporation
23181 Antonio Pkwy
Rcho Sta Marg CA
949 766-9240

(P-5653)
GLOBALFOUNDRIES AMERICAS INC
Also Called: Globalfoundries
2600 Great America Way (95054-1169)
PHONE.................................408 462-3900
EMP: 132
SIC: 5065 Semiconductor devices

(P-5654)
HARMAN INTERNATIONAL INDS INC
Also Called: Los Angeles Sales Office
8500 Balboa Blvd (91329-0003)
PHONE.................................818 893-8411
Jan Quaglia, Brnch Mgr
EMP: 2591
Web: www.harman.com
SIC: 5065 Radio parts and accessories, nec
HQ: Harman International Industries Incorporated
400 Atlantic St Ste 15
Stamford CT
203 328-3500

(P-5655)
HEC INC
Also Called: Total Garments
30961 Agoura Rd Ste 311 (91361-5607)
PHONE.................................818 879-7414
Shaukat H Zaidi, CEO
Shamim Zaidi, VP
EMP: 338 EST: 1996
SQ FT: 4,500
SALES (est): 21.84MM Privately Held
Web: www.hoorayusa.com
SIC: 5065 Electronic parts

(P-5656)
HIGH TECH PET PRODUCTS
2111 Portola Rd # A (93003-7723)
PHONE.................................805 644-1797
Nicholas Donge, Pr
▲ EMP: 60 EST: 1980
SALES (est): 5.07MM Privately Held
Web: www.hitecpet.com
SIC: 5065 2399 Electronic parts and equipment, nec; Pet collars, leashes, etc.: non-leather

(P-5657)
HIRSCH ELECTRONICS LLC
1900 Carnegie Ave Ste B (92705-5557)
PHONE.................................949 250-8888
John Picc, Managing Member
John Piccininni, Managing Member*
Stephen D Healy, Managing Member*
EMP: 85 EST: 1981
SQ FT: 34,600
SALES (est): 17.44MM Publicly Held
Web: www.identiv.com
SIC: 5065 Security control equipment and systems
PA: Identiv, Inc.
2201 Walnut Ave Ste 100
Fremont CA

(P-5658)
HITACHI HIGH-TECH AMERICA INC
5960 Inglewood Dr Ste 200 (94588-8611)
PHONE.................................925 218-2800
Bob Gordon, Mgr
EMP: 70
Web: www.hitachi-hightech.com
SIC: 5065 Electronic parts
HQ: Hitachi High-Tech America, Inc.
10 N Martingale Rd # 500
Schaumburg IL
847 273-4141

(P-5659)
HM ELECTRONICS INC (PA)
Also Called: H M E
2848 Whiptail Loop (92010-6708)
PHONE.................................858 535-6000
Harrison Y Miyahira, Ch Bd
Charles Miyahira, CEO
◆ EMP: 315 EST: 1971
SQ FT: 73,000
SALES (est): 452.77MM
SALES (corp-wide): 452.77MM Privately Held
Web: www.hme.com
SIC: 5065 Electronic parts and equipment, nec

(P-5660)
HYPERCEL CORPORATION
Also Called: Naztech
28385 Constellation Rd (91355-5048)
PHONE.................................661 310-1000
David Nazar, Pr
▲ EMP: 60 EST: 1995
SQ FT: 16,800
SALES (est): 21.81MM Privately Held
Web: www.hypercel.com
SIC: 5065 5999 Mobile telephone equipment ; Mobile telephones and equipment

(P-5661)
I C CLASS COMPONENTS CORP (PA)
Also Called: Classic Components
23605 Telo Ave (90505-4028)
PHONE.................................310 539-5500
Jeffrey Klein, Pr
Kris Klein, Ex VP
Daniel Lee, VP
Mike Thomas, VP
▲ EMP: 100 EST: 1985
SQ FT: 53,000
SALES (est): 95.8MM
SALES (corp-wide): 95.8MM Privately Held
Web: www.class-ic.com
SIC: 5065 Electronic parts

(P-5662)
IDEC CORPORATION (HQ)
1175 Elko Dr (94089-2209)
PHONE.................................408 747-0550
Toshiyuki Funaki, CEO
Mikio Funaki, *
Donald L Scrivner, *
▲ EMP: 89 EST: 1975
SQ FT: 84,000
SALES (est): 48.53MM Privately Held
Web: us.idec.com
SIC: 5065 Electronic parts
PA: Idec Corporation
2-6-64, Nishimiyahara, Yodogawa-Ku
Osaka OSK

(P-5663)
INSULECTRO (PA)
20362 Windrow Dr (92630-8140)
PHONE.................................949 587-3200
Patrick Redfern, CEO
Sean M Redfern, *
Brad Biddle, *
Kenneth Parent, *
Kevin M Miller, *
▲ EMP: 70 EST: 1991
SQ FT: 40,000
SALES (est): 115.66MM
SALES (corp-wide): 115.66MM Privately Held
Web: www.insulectro.com
SIC: 5065 Electronic parts

(P-5664)
INTELLIPOWER INC
Also Called: Ametek Intellipower
1746 N Saint Thomas Cir (92865-4247)
PHONE.................................714 921-1580
G W Bill Shipman, CEO
Dan Rieth, *
Oscar Tang, *
Dan Johnson, *
EMP: 100 EST: 1988
SQ FT: 22,000
SALES (est): 44.08MM
SALES (corp-wide): 6.15B Publicly Held
Web: www.intellipower.com
SIC: 5065 Electronic parts and equipment, nec
PA: Ametek, Inc.
1100 Cassatt Rd
Berwyn PA
610 647-2121

(P-5665)
JEB HOLDINGS CORP (PA)
54125 Maranatha Dr (92549-0075)
P.O. Box 67 (92549-0067)
PHONE.................................951 659-2183
Gordon Brown Senior, CEO
EMP: 75 EST: 1957
SQ FT: 80,000
SALES (est): 23.43MM
SALES (corp-wide): 23.43MM Privately Held
Web: www.southbaycable.com
SIC: 5065 Electronic parts

(P-5666)
JIT CORPORATION
Also Called: J I T Supply
2790 Valley View Ave (92860-2349)
PHONE.................................805 238-5000
Brent Smith, Pr
Sharon Smith, *
EMP: 60 EST: 1986
SQ FT: 30,000
SALES (est): 11.01MM Privately Held
SIC: 5065 Electronic parts

(P-5667)
JVCKENWOOD USA CORPORATION (HQ)
4001 Worsham Ave (90808-1976)
P.O. Box 22745 (90801-5745)
PHONE.................................310 639-9000
Kuhiro Aigami, Pr
Joseph Glassett, *

PRODUCTS & SERVICES SECTION
5065 - Electronic Parts And Equipment, Nec (P-5687)

Kazuhiro Aigami, *Pr*
Mark Jasin, *
Craig Geiger, *
▲ **EMP:** 160 **EST:** 1961
SQ FT: 238,000
SALES (est): 80.58MM **Privately Held**
Web: us.jvckenwood.com
SIC: 5065 Electronic parts and equipment, nec
PA: Jvckenwood Corporation
    3-12, Moriyacho, Kanagawa-Ku
    Yokohama KNG

(P-5668)
L3HARRIS INTERSTATE ELEC CORP
707 E Vermont Ave A (92805-5612)
PHONE..........................714 758-0500
EMP: 149
SALES (corp-wide): 17.06B **Publicly Held**
Web: www.l3harris.com
SIC: 5065 Electronic parts
HQ: L3harris Interstate Electronics Corporation
    602 E Vermont Ave
    Anaheim CA
    714 758-0500

(P-5669)
LEMO USA INC
635 Park Ct (94928-7940)
P.O. Box 2408 (94927-2408)
PHONE..........................707 206-3700
Dinshaw Pohwala, *CEO*
EMP: 100 **EST:** 1972
SQ FT: 55,000
SALES (est): 47.13MM **Privately Held**
Web: www.lemo.com
SIC: 5065 3678 Connectors, electronic; Electronic connectors
HQ: Interlemo U.S.A. Inc.
    635 Park Ct
    Rohnert Park CA

(P-5670)
LG DISPLAY AMERICA INC (HQ)
2540 N 1st St Ste 400 (95131-1016)
PHONE..........................408 350-0190
Chris Min, *Pr*
Davis Lee, *
James Jeong, *
Cheol D Ong Jeong, *
Sang Deog Yeo, *
▲ **EMP:** 70 **EST:** 1999
SQ FT: 1,000
SALES (est): 42.63MM **Privately Held**
Web: www.lgphilips-lcd.com
SIC: 5065 Modems, computer
PA: Lg Display Co., Ltd.
    128 Yeoui-Daero, Yeongdeungpo-Gu
    Seoul

(P-5671)
LINKSYS LLC
120 Theory (92617-3210)
PHONE..........................408 526-4000
EMP: 156
Web: www.linksys.com
SIC: 5065 Electronic parts and equipment, nec
HQ: Linksys Llc
    121 Theory Ste 150
    Irvine CA
    310 751-5100

(P-5672)
LINKSYS LLC
121 Theory Ste 150 (92617-3204)
PHONE..........................310 751-5100
EMP: 194

Web: www.linksys.com
SIC: 5065 Electronic parts and equipment, nec
HQ: Linksys Llc
    121 Theory Ste 150
    Irvine CA
    310 751-5100

(P-5673)
LINKSYS USA INC
121 Theory (92617-3209)
PHONE..........................949 270-8500
Harry Dewhirst, *CEO*
EMP: 100 **EST:** 2018
SALES (est): 27.07MM
SALES (corp-wide): 4.42B **Publicly Held**
Web: www.linksys.com
SIC: 5065 3577 Communication equipment; Data conversion equipment, media-to-media: computer
PA: Fortinet, Inc.
    899 Kifer Rd
    Sunnyvale CA
    408 235-7700

(P-5674)
MAURY MICROWAVE INC (PA)
2900 Inland Empire Blvd (91764-4804)
PHONE..........................909 987-4715
Michael Howo, *CEO*
▲ **EMP:** 200 **EST:** 1957
SQ FT: 6,000
SALES (est): 61.84MM
SALES (corp-wide): 61.84MM **Privately Held**
Web: www.maurymw.com
SIC: 5065 Electronic parts and equipment, nec

(P-5675)
METRIC EQUIPMENT SALES INC
Also Called: Microlease
25841 Industrial Blvd Ste 200 (94545-2991)
PHONE..........................510 264-0887
TOLL FREE: 800
Nigel Brown, *CEO*
Mike Clark, *
David Sherve, *
Gordon Curwen, *
Nathan Hurst, *
EMP: 70 **EST:** 1992
SQ FT: 25,000
SALES (est): 25.68MM
SALES (corp-wide): 254.4MM **Privately Held**
SIC: 5065 5084 7359 3825 Electronic parts; Measuring and testing equipment, electrical ; Electronic equipment rental, except computers; Instruments to measure electricity
HQ: Microlease Inc.
    6060 Sepulveda Blvd
    Van Nuys CA
    866 520-0200

(P-5676)
MITSUBISHI ELECTRIC US INC (DH)
Also Called: Meus
5900 Katella Ave Ste A (90630-5019)
P.O. Box 6007 (90630-0007)
PHONE..........................714 220-2500
Mike Corbo, *Pr*
Masahiro Oya, *
Mike Corbo, *Pr*
Jared Baker, *
Perry Pappous, *
◆ **EMP:** 200 **EST:** 2000
SQ FT: 10,400
SALES (est): 931.5MM **Privately Held**

Web: us.mitsubishielectric.com
SIC: 5065 3534 1796 3669 Electronic parts; Escalators, passenger and freight; Elevator installation and conversion; Visual communication systems
HQ: Mitsubishi Electric Us Holdings, Inc.
    5900 Katella Ave Ste A
    Cypress CA
    714 220-2500

(P-5677)
MOBILE LINE COMMUNICATIONS CORPORATION
1402 Morgan Cir (92780-6423)
▲ **EMP:** 75
SIC: 5065 Telephone equipment

(P-5678)
MOTOROLA MOBILITY LLC
Also Called: Motorola
6450 Sequence Dr (92121-4376)
PHONE..........................858 455-1500
Rick Neal, *Brnch Mgr*
EMP: 73
SQ FT: 30,000
Web: www.motorola.com
SIC: 5065 3663 Communication equipment; Radio and t.v. communications equipment
HQ: Motorola Mobility Llc
    222 Mdse Mart Plz # 1800
    Chicago IL

(P-5679)
NALLATECH INC
Also Called: Nallatech
741 Flynn Rd (93012-8056)
PHONE..........................805 383-8997
Colin Rutherford, *Ch*
William P Miller, *
Allan Cantle, *
Ed Hennessy, *
EMP: 64 **EST:** 2008
SALES (est): 30.05MM
SALES (corp-wide): 36.93B **Privately Held**
Web: www.bittware.com
SIC: 5065 Electronic parts and equipment, nec
HQ: Interconnect Systems International, Llc
    741 Flynn Rd
    Camarillo CA
    805 482-2870

(P-5680)
NEST LABS INC
3400 Hillview Ave (94304-1346)
PHONE..........................855 469-6378
◆ **EMP:** 70 **EST:** 2010
SALES (est): 19.85MM
SALES (corp-wide): 282.84B **Publicly Held**
SIC: 5065 5999 Electronic parts and equipment, nec; Electronic parts and equipment
HQ: Google Llc
    1600 Amphitheatre Pkwy
    Mountain View CA
    650 253-0000

(P-5681)
NILES AUDIO CORPORATION
1690 Corporate Cir (94954-6912)
P.O. Box 9003 (94954)
PHONE..........................760 710-0992
▲ **EMP:** 75
Web: www.nilesaudio.com
SIC: 5065 5064 Video equipment, electronic; High fidelity equipment

(P-5682)
NISCAYAH INC
Hamilton Pacific
751 N Todd Ave (91702-2244)
PHONE..........................626 683-8167
Diane Frank, *Brnch Mgr*
EMP: 95
SALES (corp-wide): 16.95B **Publicly Held**
SIC: 5065 Security control equipment and systems
HQ: Niscayah, Inc.
    2400 Commerce Ave Ste 500
    Duluth GA
    678 474-1720

(P-5683)
NITTO DENKO AMERICA INC
48500 Fremont Blvd (94538-6579)
PHONE..........................510 445-5400
◆ **EMP:** 60
SIC: 5065 5162 Electronic parts; Plastics products, nec

(P-5684)
NOVACAP LLC
25111 Anza Dr (91355-3416)
PHONE..........................661 295-5920
Mark Skoog, *CEO*
Shelley Mears, *
▲ **EMP:** 280 **EST:** 1980
SQ FT: 38,000
SALES (est): 55.8MM
SALES (corp-wide): 764.7MM **Publicly Held**
Web: www.novacap.ca
SIC: 5065 Electronic parts and equipment, nec
PA: Knowles Corporation
    1151 Maplewood Dr
    Itasca IL
    630 250-5100

(P-5685)
NUVOTON TECHNOLOGY CORP AMER
2727 N 1st St (95134-2029)
PHONE..........................408 544-1718
Arthur Yu-cheng Chiao, *Ch*
Robert Hsu, *
Bor-yuan Hwang, *VP*
Stephen Rei-min Huang, *VP*
Hsi-jung Tsai, *VP*
EMP: 60 **EST:** 2008
SALES (est): 21.92MM **Privately Held**
Web: www.nuvoton.com
SIC: 5065 Semiconductor devices
HQ: Nuvoton Technology Corporation
    No. 4, Yanxin 3rd Rd.,
    Hsinchu City

(P-5686)
OMNITRON SYSTEMS TECH INC
38 Tesla (92618-4603)
PHONE..........................949 250-6510
Arie Goldberg, *CEO*
Heidi Cairns, *VP*
EMP: 75 **EST:** 1985
SQ FT: 15,000
SALES (est): 22.66MM **Privately Held**
Web: www.omnitron-systems.com
SIC: 5065 Electronic parts and equipment, nec

(P-5687)
PARADE TECHNOLOGIES INC
2720 Orchard Pkwy (95134-2012)
PHONE..........................408 329-5540
Ji Zhao, *CEO*
EMP: 80 **EST:** 2005
SQ FT: 5,500

5065 - Electronic Parts And Equipment, Nec (P-5688)

SALES (est): 19.22MM Privately Held
Web: www.paradetech.com
SIC: 5065 Semiconductor devices
PA: Parade Technologies, Ltd
C/O: Maples Corporate Services Limited
George Town GR CAYMAN

(P-5688)
PERFORMANCE DESIGNED PDTS LLC (PA)
9179 Aero Dr (92123-2411)
PHONE..................................800 331-3844
Brad Wildes, CEO
Navin Kumar, CMO*
Ryan O'desky, CFO
Dave Mason, *
Tom Roberts, *
◆ EMP: 64 EST: 1990
SQ FT: 18,000
SALES (est): 54.41MM Privately Held
Web: www.pdp.com
SIC: 5065 Video equipment, electronic

(P-5689)
PRESIDIO COMPONENTS INC
7169 Construction Ct (92121-2615)
PHONE..................................858 578-9390
Violet Devoe, Pr
Daniel Devoe, *
Alan Devoe, *
Lambert Devoe, *
▲ EMP: 120 EST: 1980
SQ FT: 35,000
SALES (est): 55.32MM Privately Held
Web: www.presidiocomponents.com
SIC: 5065 Electronic parts and equipment, nec

(P-5690)
Q TECH CORPORATION
6161 Chip Ave (90630-5213)
PHONE..................................310 836-7900
Sally Phillips, Pr
Richard Taylor, *
EMP: 200 EST: 1972
SALES (est): 42.77MM Privately Held
Web: www.q-tech.com
SIC: 5065 Electronic parts and equipment, nec

(P-5691)
QUINSTAR TECHNOLOGY INC
24085 Garnier St (90505-5319)
PHONE..................................310 320-1111
Leo Fong, Pr
John Kuno, *
▲ EMP: 72 EST: 1993
SALES (est): 37.82MM Privately Held
Web: www.quinstar.com
SIC: 5065 3671 Electronic parts and equipment, nec; Cathode ray tubes, including rebuilt

(P-5692)
R&M USA INC (DH)
Also Called: Realm
840 Yosemite Way (95035-6360)
PHONE..................................408 945-6626
Paulo Campos, CEO
Christopher Stratas, *
Kimberly Horowitz, *
Patrick Steiner, *
Michel Riva, *
▲ EMP: 99 EST: 1999
SQ FT: 34,865
SALES (est): 43.51MM Privately Held
Web: www.rdm.com
SIC: 5065 Communication equipment
HQ: Reichle & De-Massari Ag
Binzstrasse 32
Wetzikon ZH

(P-5693)
RANTEC POWER SYSTEMS INC (HQ)
1173 Los Olivos Ave (93402-3230)
PHONE..................................805 596-6000
Michael C Bickel, Pr
Michael C Bickel, Pr
Frank Janku, *
EMP: 97 EST: 1963
SQ FT: 40,000
SALES (est): 49.58MM
SALES (corp-wide): 56.3MM Privately Held
Web: www.rantec.com
SIC: 5065 Electronic parts and equipment, nec
PA: Rps Holdings, Inc.
1173 Los Olivos Ave
Los Osos CA
805 596-6000

(P-5694)
RAYTHEON CMMAND CTRL SLTONS LL (DH)
1801 Hughes Dr (92833-2200)
P.O. Box 34055 (92834-9455)
PHONE..................................714 446-3118
Alex Cresswell, *
Don Johnson, *
▲ EMP: 700 EST: 2001
SALES (est): 312.6K
SALES (corp-wide): 67.07B Publicly Held
SIC: 5065 Security control equipment and systems
HQ: Raytheon Company
870 Winter St
Waltham MA
781 522-3000

(P-5695)
RENESAS ELECTRONICS AMERICA INC
2801 Scott Blvd (95050-2549)
P.O. Box 58062 (95052-8062)
PHONE..................................408 588-6000
▲ EMP: 1169
SIC: 5065 8731 5731 5045 Semiconductor devices; Electronic research; Radio, television, and electronic stores; Computers, peripherals, and software

(P-5696)
RFMW LTD
Also Called: Rfmw
188 Martinvale Ln (95119-1356)
PHONE..................................408 414-1450
EMP: 80
SIC: 5065 Electronic parts

(P-5697)
SAMSUNG ELECTRONICS AMER INC
Also Called: Samsung Electronics
665 Clyde Ave (94043-2235)
PHONE..................................650 210-1000
Evan Maxei, Dir
EMP: 1000
SQ FT: 395
Web: www.samsung.com
SIC: 5065 Electronic parts and equipment, nec
HQ: Samsung Electronics America, Inc.
85 Challenger Rd
Ridgefield Park NJ
201 229-4000

(P-5698)
SAMSUNG SEMICONDUCTOR INC (DH)
Also Called: Samsung
3655 N 1st St (95134-1707)
PHONE..................................408 544-4000
Young Chang Bae, Pr
Tom Quinn, *
Damian Huh, *
Angela Cheong, *
◆ EMP: 216 EST: 1979
SQ FT: 206,816
SALES (est): 715.31MM Privately Held
Web: semiconductor.samsung.com
SIC: 5065 5045 Semiconductor devices; Computers, peripherals, and software
HQ: Samsung Electronics America, Inc.
85 Challenger Rd
Ridgefield Park NJ
201 229-4000

(P-5699)
SL POWER ELECTRONICS CORP (HQ)
27001 Agoura Rd Ste 325 (91301-5339)
PHONE..................................800 235-5929
Karim Alhusseini, Pr
◆ EMP: 65 EST: 1978
SALES (est): 162.87MM
SALES (corp-wide): 1.85B Publicly Held
Web: www.slpower.com
SIC: 5065 Electronic parts and equipment, nec
PA: Advanced Energy Industries, Inc.
1595 Wynkoop St Ste 800
Denver CO
970 407-6626

(P-5700)
SOL REPUBLIC INC
1000 Van Ness Ave (94109-6971)
PHONE..................................877 400-0310
EMP: 100
SIC: 5065 5731 Electronic parts and equipment, nec; Consumer electronic equipment, nec

(P-5701)
STEREN ELECTRONICS INTL LLC (PA)
Also Called: Steren Electronic Solutions
8445 Camino Santa Fe (92121-2650)
PHONE..................................800 266-3333
David Shteremberg, *
Vick Soffer, *
Jose Zyman, *
◆ EMP: 100 EST: 1956
SALES (est): 35.8MM
SALES (corp-wide): 35.8MM Privately Held
Web: www.sterenusa.com
SIC: 5065 Connectors, electronic

(P-5702)
SUMITOMO ELC DVC INNVTONS USA
2355 Zanker Rd (95131-1109)
PHONE..................................408 232-9500
Mike Nishiguchi, CEO
Eddie Tsumura, *
John Wyatt, *
▲ EMP: 80 EST: 2000
SQ FT: 52,600
SALES (est): 26.14MM Privately Held
Web: www.sei-device.com
SIC: 5065 Electronic parts
PA: Sumitomo Electric Industries, Ltd.
4-5-33, Kitahama, Chuo-Ku
Osaka OSK

(P-5703)
SUPERIOR COMMUNICATIONS INC (PA)
Also Called: Puregear
5027 Irwindale Ave Ste 900 (91706-2187)
PHONE..................................877 522-4727
Solomon Chen, *
Jeffrey Banks, CEO
Robert Chen, *
Keith Kam, *
Jennifer Ju, Legal Counsel*
▲ EMP: 248 EST: 1991
SQ FT: 11,000
SALES (est): 93.98MM Privately Held
Web: www.superiorcommunications.com
SIC: 5065 Communication equipment

(P-5704)
SWANN COMMUNICATIONS USA INC
Also Called: Swann
12636 Clark St (90670-3950)
PHONE..................................562 777-2551
Michael Lucas, CEO
Kimberly Banducci, *
▲ EMP: 70 EST: 2000
SQ FT: 45,000
SALES (est): 26.32MM Privately Held
Web: us.swann.com
SIC: 5065 Video equipment, electronic

(P-5705)
TABULA INC
1100 La Avenida St (94043-1452)
PHONE..................................408 986-9140
Dennis Segers, CEO
Steven Teig, *
EMP: 100 EST: 2003
SALES (est): 22.13MM Privately Held
Web: www.tabula.com
SIC: 5065 Semiconductor devices

(P-5706)
TALLEY INC (PA)
Also Called: Talley & Associates
12976 Sandoval St (90670-4061)
P.O. Box 3123 (90670-0123)
PHONE..................................562 906-8000
John R Talley, CEO
Mark D Talley, *
Elizabeth J Talley, *
Jeffrey R Talley, *
Richard M Talley, *
◆ EMP: 110 EST: 1968
SQ FT: 80,000
SALES (est): 100.18MM
SALES (corp-wide): 100.18MM Privately Held
Web: www.talleycom.com
SIC: 5065 Communication equipment

(P-5707)
TAOGLAS
2106 Orange Ave (92029-4301)
PHONE..................................760 855-4580
Dermot Oshea, Prin
EMP: 61 EST: 2010
SALES (est): 572.63K Privately Held
Web: www.taoglas.com
SIC: 5065 Electronic parts and equipment, nec

(P-5708)
TDK-LAMBDA AMERICAS INC
401 Mile Of Cars Way Ste 325 (91950-6610)
PHONE..................................619 575-4400
Pascal Shauson, CEO
EMP: 200

PRODUCTS & SERVICES SECTION
5072 - Hardware (P-5728)

Web: us.tdk-lambda.com
SIC: 5065 Electronic parts and equipment, nec
HQ: Tdk-Lambda Americas Inc.
405 Essex Rd
Tinton Falls NJ
732 795-4100

(P-5709)
TECH SYSTEMS INC
7372 Walnut Ave Ste J (90620-1718)
PHONE.................................714 523-5404
Raymond Downs, *Mgr*
EMP: 210
SALES (corp-wide): 88.57MM Privately Held
Web: www.techsystemsinc.com
SIC: 5065 Closed circuit TV
PA: Tech Systems, Inc.
4942 Summer Oak Dr
Buford GA
770 495-8700

(P-5710)
TECOM INDUSTRIES INCORPORATED
375 Conejo Ridge Ave (91361-4928)
PHONE.................................805 267-0100
◆ EMP: 160
Web: www.smithsinterconnect.com
SIC: 5065 Electronic parts

(P-5711)
TELIT WIRELESS SOLUTIONS INC
7700 Irvine Center Dr (92618-2923)
PHONE.................................949 461-7150
EMP: 131
Web: www.telit.com
SIC: 5065 Electronic parts
PA: Telit Wireless Solutions, Inc.
5425 Page Rd Ste 120
Durham NC

(P-5712)
TILE INC (HQ)
1900 S Norfolk St Ste 310 (94403-1150)
PHONE.................................650 274-0676
Charles Prober, *CEO*
Robert O'hare, *CFO*
Kristen Daru, *Sec*
▲ EMP: 196 EST: 2012
SQ FT: 4,000
SALES (est): 64.93MM
SALES (corp-wide): 228.31MM Privately Held
Web: www.thetileapp.com
SIC: 5065 Security control equipment and systems
PA: Life360, Inc.
1900 S Norfolk St Ste 310
San Mateo CA

(P-5713)
TPS AVIATION INC (PA)
1515 Crocker Ave (94544-7038)
PHONE.................................510 475-1010
George Sozaburo Kujiraoka, *CEO*
◆ EMP: 100 EST: 1963
SQ FT: 58,700
SALES (est): 48.89MM
SALES (corp-wide): 48.89MM Privately Held
Web: www.tpsaviation.com
SIC: 5065 3728 3429 5088 Electronic parts; Aircraft parts and equipment, nec; Hardware, nec; Aircraft and parts

(P-5714)
WENZLAU ENGINEERING INC
2950 E Harcourt St (90221-5502)
PHONE.................................310 604-3400
William D Wenzlau Junior, *CEO*
◆ EMP: 64 EST: 1956
SQ FT: 40,000
SALES (est): 28.04MM Privately Held
Web: www.wenzlau.com
SIC: 5065 8711 5511 Electronic parts; Consulting engineer; Trucks, tractors, and trailers: new and used

(P-5715)
WEXLER CORPORATION
Also Called: Wexler Video
1111 S Victory Blvd (91502-2550)
PHONE.................................818 846-9381
EMP: 1645 EST: 1980
SALES (est): 45.67MM Privately Held
Web: www.reesewexler.com
SIC: 5065 7359 Video equipment, electronic; Equipment rental and leasing, nec
HQ: H.I.G. Capital, Inc.
1450 Brickell Ave Fl 31
Miami FL
305 379-2322

(P-5716)
WINBOND ELECTRONICS CORP AMER
2727 N 1st St (95134-2029)
PHONE.................................408 943-6666
Yuan Mou Shu, *Prin*
▲ EMP: 60 EST: 1990
SQ FT: 50,000
SALES (est): 24.23MM Privately Held
SIC: 5065 8731 3674 Electronic parts; Commercial physical research; Semiconductors and related devices
PA: Winbond Electronics Corporation
8, Keya 1st Rd.,
Taichung City

(P-5717)
XCERRA CORPORATION
Also Called: Western Region
880 N Mccarthy Blvd Ste 100 (95035-5126)
PHONE.................................408 635-4300
Ken Daub, *Brnch Mgr*
EMP: 200
SALES (corp-wide): 812.77MM Publicly Held
Web: www.cohu.com
SIC: 5065 Semiconductor devices
HQ: Xcerra Corporation
825 University Ave
Norwood MA
781 461-1000

(P-5718)
XP POWER LLC (DH)
990 Benecia Ave (94085-2804)
PHONE.................................408 732-7777
Gavin Griggs, *CEO*
▲ EMP: 60 EST: 1991
SQ FT: 58,000
SALES (est): 332.25MM Privately Held
Web: www.xppower.com
SIC: 5065 Electronic parts and equipment, nec
HQ: Forx Inc
990 Benecia Ave
Sunnyvale CA
408 732-7777

(P-5719)
YUNEEC USA INC
Also Called: Yuneec USA
9227 Haven Ave Ste 210 (91730-5473)
P.O. Box 970 (94566-0970)
PHONE.................................855 284-8888
Mike Kahn, *CEO*
Larry Liu, *
Ryan Borders, *
▲ EMP: 70 EST: 2013
SALES (est): 54MM Privately Held
Web: www.yuneec.online
SIC: 5065 7629 Video equipment, electronic; Electrical equipment repair services
HQ: Yuneec International Co., Limited
Rm D 10/F Billion Ctr Twr A
Kowloon Bay KLN

5072 Hardware

(P-5720)
AMERICAN KAL ENTERPRISES INC (PA)
Also Called: Pro America Premium Tools
4265 Puente Ave (91706-3420)
PHONE.................................626 338-7308
John Toshima, *Pr*
Mila Bierotte, *
▲ EMP: 90 EST: 1966
SQ FT: 32,000
SALES (est): 23.68MM
SALES (corp-wide): 23.68MM Privately Held
SIC: 5072 3546 3463 3462 Hand tools; Power-driven handtools; Nonferrous forgings; Iron and steel forgings

(P-5721)
ASSA ABLOY RSDENTIAL GROUP INC (HQ)
Also Called: Emtek Products
12801 Schabarum Ave (91706-6808)
PHONE.................................626 961-0413
Lucas Boselli, *CEO*
Thomas Millar, *
◆ EMP: 200 EST: 1979
SALES (est): 157.72MM
SALES (corp-wide): 4.72B Publicly Held
Web: www.emtek.com
SIC: 5072 Hardware
PA: Fortune Brands Innovations, Inc.
520 Lake Cook Rd
Deerfield IL
847 484-4400

(P-5722)
ASSA ABLOY RSDENTIAL GROUP INC
600 Baldwin Park Blvd (91746)
PHONE.................................626 369-4718
Birk Sorennsen, *Mgr*
EMP: 597
SALES (corp-wide): 4.72B Publicly Held
Web: www.emtek.com
SIC: 5072 Hardware
HQ: Assa Abloy Residential Group, Inc.
12801 Schabarum Ave
Irwindale CA
626 961-0413

(P-5723)
B & B SPECIALTIES INC
G S Aerospace Division
4321 E La Palma Ave (92807-1887)
PHONE.................................714 985-3075
Tom Rutan, *Mgr*
EMP: 100
SALES (corp-wide): 22.69MM Privately Held
SIC: 5072 3429 Miscellaneous fasteners; Hardware, nec
PA: B & B Specialties, Inc.
4321 E La Palma Ave
Anaheim CA
714 985-3000

(P-5724)
CAMSTAR INTERNATIONAL INC
939 W 9th St (91786-4543)
PHONE.................................909 931-2540
Bingqing Li, *Pr*
▲ EMP: 75 EST: 2007
SQ FT: 1,500
SALES (est): 10.93MM Privately Held
Web: www.camstarusa.com
SIC: 5072 Security devices, locks
PA: Yuxin Technology Company
Dayao Village
Weifang SD

(P-5725)
CHARLES MCMURRAY CO (PA)
2520 N Argyle Ave (93727-1302)
P.O. Box 569 (93709-0569)
PHONE.................................559 292-5751
Charles Mcmurray, *CEO*
Louis Mc Murray, *Pr*
▲ EMP: 62 EST: 1946
SQ FT: 58,000
SALES (est): 38.36MM
SALES (corp-wide): 38.36MM Privately Held
Web: www.charlesmcmurray.com
SIC: 5072 Builders' hardware, nec

(P-5726)
CLARENDON SPECIALTY FAS INC
2180 Temple Ave (90804-1020)
PHONE.................................714 842-2603
Arnaud Zemmour, *Admn*
Michael Lang, *
Jeff Heywood, *
▲ EMP: 90 EST: 1985
SQ FT: 4,000
SALES (est): 23.06MM Privately Held
Web: www.clarendonsf.com
SIC: 5072 3444 Miscellaneous fasteners; Sheet metalwork

(P-5727)
CORONA CLIPPER INC
Also Called: Corona Tools
22440 Temescal Canyon Rd Ste 102 (92883-4200)
PHONE.................................951 737-6515
Stephen J Erickson, *CEO*
Al Schulten, *
John Reisveck, *
◆ EMP: 86 EST: 1927
SQ FT: 85,000
SALES (est): 45.24MM
SALES (corp-wide): 26.64MM Privately Held
Web: www.coronatoolsusa.com
SIC: 5072 3524 Hand tools; Lawn and garden equipment
PA: Natt Tools Group Inc
460 Sherman Ave N
Hamilton ON
905 549-7433

(P-5728)
HAMPTON PRODUCTS INTL CORP (PA)
50 Icon (92610-3000)
PHONE.................................949 472-4256
Gregory J Gluchowski, *Junior President*
Gregory J Gluchowski Junior, *Pr*
▲ EMP: 100 EST: 1973
SQ FT: 160,000
SALES (est): 87.89MM
SALES (corp-wide): 87.89MM Privately Held

5072 - Hardware (P-5729)

Web: www.hamptonproducts.com
SIC: 5072 Hardware

(P-5729)
HD SUPPLY DISTRIBUTION SERVICES LLC
Also Called: Crown Bolt
26940 Aliso Viejo Pkwy (92656-2622)
PHONE..................................949 643-4700
◆ EMP: 1078
Web: www.hdsupplyhardwaresolutions.com
SIC: 5072 Screws

(P-5730)
JACKSONS HARDWARE INC
Also Called: Marin Industrial Distributors
435 Du Bois St. At Andersen Dr (94901-3910)
P.O. Box 10247 (94912-0247)
PHONE..................................415 870-4083
Matthew R Olson, Pr
Anna Buss, *
EMP: 61 EST: 1964
SQ FT: 50,000
SALES (est): 16.05MM Privately Held
Web: www.jacksonshardware.com
SIC: 5072 5251 Hardware; Hardware stores

(P-5731)
MAKITA USA INC (HQ)
Also Called: Makita
14930 Northam St (90638-5753)
PHONE..................................714 522-8088
Sean Okada, Pr
Yuhei Iwanaga, CFO
◆ EMP: 250 EST: 1970
SQ FT: 130,000
SALES (est): 468.51MM Privately Held
Web: www.makitatools.com
SIC: 5072 Power handtools
PA: Makita Corporation
   3-11-8, Sumiyoshicho
   Anjo AIC

(P-5732)
PORTEOUS ENTERPRISES INC (DH)
1040 E Watson Center Rd (90745-4202)
PHONE..................................310 549-9180
◆ EMP: 175 EST: 1969
SALES (est): 32.24MM Privately Held
SIC: 5072 Nuts (hardware)
HQ: Brighton-Best International, Inc.
   5855 Obispo Ave
   Long Beach CA
   562 808-8000

(P-5733)
ROK INC
Also Called: Rok Hardware & Cabinets
10 Lakeview (92604-3681)
PHONE..................................714 322-8563
EMP: 65
SALES (corp-wide): 2.63MM Privately Held
SIC: 5072 Hardware
PA: Rok Inc.
   1351 N Kraemer Blvd
   Anaheim CA
   800 763-8390

(P-5734)
SEVILLE CLASSICS INC (PA)
19401 Harborgate Way (90501-1322)
PHONE..................................310 533-3800
Jackson Yang, CEO
Julie Yang, *
◆ EMP: 157 EST: 1979
SQ FT: 10,000

SALES (est): 35.66MM
SALES (corp-wide): 35.66MM Privately Held
Web: www.sevilleclassics.com
SIC: 5072 5199 Hardware; General merchandise, non-durable

(P-5735)
SUNKIST ENTERPRISES
1308 Rollins Rd (94010-2410)
PHONE..................................650 347-3900
EMP: 75 EST: 1983
SQ FT: 6,000
SALES (est): 4.87MM Privately Held
Web: www.se.supply
SIC: 5072 5031 Hardware; Lumber, plywood, and millwork

(P-5736)
TIME MOTION TOOLS INC
12778 Brookprinter Pl (92064-6810)
PHONE..................................858 679-0303
EMP: 60
SIC: 5072 Hardware

(P-5737)
TOMARCO CONTRACTOR SPC INC (PA)
Also Called: Tomarco Fastening Systems
14848 Northam St (90638-5747)
PHONE..................................714 523-1771
William Thompson, CEO
Keith Watkins, *
▲ EMP: 60 EST: 1977
SQ FT: 33,000
SALES (est): 45.83MM
SALES (corp-wide): 45.83MM Privately Held
Web: www.tomarco.com
SIC: 5072 Hand tools

(P-5738)
WILDENRADT-MCMURRAY INC
Also Called: Macmurray Pacific
568 7th St (94103-4710)
PHONE..................................510 835-5500
Eric Wildenradt, VP
Theodore Wildenradt, *
Vernelle Wildenradt, *
▲ EMP: 70 EST: 1951
SQ FT: 25,000
SALES (est): 15.01MM Privately Held
Web: www.macpac1.com
SIC: 5072 Builders' hardware, nec

(P-5739)
WORLDWIDE INTGRTED RSURCES INC
7171 Telegraph Rd (90640-6511)
PHONE..................................323 838-8938
Fred Morad, Pr
Sina Salamat, *
Susan Morad, *
◆ EMP: 60 EST: 1991
SQ FT: 20,000
SALES (est): 13.51MM Privately Held
Web: www.papercraftsarts.com
SIC: 5072 5087 Hardware; Janitors' supplies

(P-5740)
WURTH LOUIS AND COMPANY (DH)
895 Columbia St (92821-2917)
P.O. Box 2253 (92822-2253)
PHONE..................................714 529-1771
Vito Mancini, Pr
Tom Mauss, *
Ed Mcgraw, VP
▲ EMP: 90 EST: 1975

SQ FT: 116,000
SALES (est): 84.42MM
SALES (corp-wide): 20.7B Privately Held
Web: www.wurthlac.com
SIC: 5072 5198 Furniture hardware, nec; Stain
HQ: Wurth Group Of North America Inc.
   93 Grant St
   Ramsey NJ

5074 Plumbing And Hydronic Heating Supplies

(P-5741)
BRITA PRODUCTS COMPANY
Also Called: Brita
1221 Broadway Ste 290 (94612-1838)
P.O. Box 24305 (94623-1305)
PHONE..................................510 271-7000
Greg Frank, Pr
EMP: 85 EST: 1988
SALES (est): 46.93MM
SALES (corp-wide): 7.39B Publicly Held
SIC: 5074 Water purification equipment
PA: The Clorox Company
   1221 Broadway Ste 1300
   Oakland CA
   510 271-7000

(P-5742)
BUILDCOM INC
Also Called: Faucetdirect.com
402 Otterson Dr Ste 100 (95928-8206)
PHONE..................................800 375-3403
Christian B Friedland, Pr
Lindsay Fee, *
Brandon Proctor, *
Nick Strachan, *
Danielle Porto Mohn, CMO*
▼ EMP: 380 EST: 2000
SQ FT: 22,100
SALES (est): 221.89MM
SALES (corp-wide): 2.67MM Privately Held
Web: www.handlesets.com
SIC: 5074 5999 Plumbing fittings and supplies; Plumbing and heating supplies
HQ: Ferguson Enterprises, Llc
   751 Lakefront Cmns
   Newport News VA
   757 969-4011

(P-5743)
BURKE ENGINEERING CO
9700 Factorial Way (91733-1725)
P.O. Box 928 (92075-0928)
PHONE..................................626 579-6763
EMP: 100
Web: www.burkehvacr.com
SIC: 5074 5084 5075 Heating equipment (hydronic); Controlling instruments and accessories; Warm air heating and air conditioning

(P-5744)
CAL-STEAM SUPPLY
1595 Crocker Ave (94544-7038)
P.O. Box 1004c (15650-4004)
PHONE..................................510 512-7700
EMP: 88
SIC: 5074 Plumbing fittings and supplies

(P-5745)
DI-SEP SYSTEMS INTL INC (HQ)
15519 Blackburn Ave (90650-6846)
PHONE..................................562 407-3432
James Ellis, Pr
Bob Robury, CEO
EMP: 72 EST: 1979

SQ FT: 1,300
SALES (est): 943.17K
SALES (corp-wide): 78.2MM Privately Held
SIC: 5074 Water purification equipment
PA: Smith & Loveless, Inc.
   14040 Santa Fe Trail Dr
   Shawnee Mission KS
   913 888-5201

(P-5746)
ELMCO SALES INC (PA)
15070 Proctor Ave (91746-3305)
P.O. Box 3787 (91744-0787)
PHONE..................................626 855-4831
Donald E Morris, Ch Bd
Kristin E Kahle, *
EMP: 90 EST: 1944
SQ FT: 49,650
SALES (est): 23.24MM
SALES (corp-wide): 23.24MM Privately Held
Web: www.elmcoaz.com
SIC: 5074 Plumbing fittings and supplies

(P-5747)
EPS CORPORATE HOLDINGS INC
1235 S Lewis St (92805-6429)
PHONE..................................714 635-3131
Greg Boiko, Mgr
EMP: 60
SIC: 5074 1711 Plumbing fittings and supplies; Plumbing contractors
HQ: Eps Corporate Holdings, Inc.
   3100 Dnald Dglas Loop Hng
   Santa Monica CA

(P-5748)
FERGUSON FIRE FABRICATION INC (DH)
Also Called: Pacific Fire Safety
2750 S Towne Ave (91766-6205)
PHONE..................................909 517-3085
Leo J Klien, Pr
Leo J Klien, *
Dave Keltner, *
▲ EMP: 100 EST: 1987
SQ FT: 120,000
SALES (est): 232.98MM
SALES (corp-wide): 2.67MM Privately Held
Web: www.ferguson.com
SIC: 5074 5099 Plumbing fittings and supplies; Safety equipment and supplies
HQ: Ferguson Enterprises, Llc
   751 Lakefront Cmns
   Newport News VA
   757 969-4011

(P-5749)
FERGUSON FIRE FABRICATION INC
235 N Joy St (92879-1323)
PHONE..................................951 272-8803
EMP: 60
SALES (corp-wide): 2.67MM Privately Held
Web: www.ferguson.com
SIC: 5074 Plumbing fittings and supplies
HQ: Ferguson Fire & Fabrication, Inc.
   2750 S Towne Ave
   Pomona CA
   909 517-3085

(P-5750)
GLOBAL PLUMBING & FIRE SUPPLY
723 Sonora Ave (91201-2431)

PRODUCTS & SERVICES SECTION
5075 - Warm Air Heating And Air Conditioning (P-5771)

PHONE..........................818 550-8444
Armond Sarkissian, *CEO*
EMP: 112 **EST:** 2016
SALES (est): 9.5MM **Privately Held**
Web: www.firesprinklerstore.com
SIC: 5074 Plumbing fittings and supplies

(P-5751)
GREAT WESTERN SALES INC
Also Called: Mega Western Sales
8737 Dice Rd (90670-2513)
P.O. Box 3427 (90703-3427)
PHONE..........................310 323-7900
▲ **EMP:** 76 **EST:** 1971
SALES (est): 22.24MM **Privately Held**
Web: www.megawestern.com
SIC: 5074 Plumbing fittings and supplies

(P-5752)
H20 INNOVATION USA HOLDING INC
1048 La Mirada Ct (92081-7874)
PHONE..........................760 639-4400
Coley Ali, *Brnch Mgr*
EMP: 86
SALES (corp-wide): 119.63MM **Privately Held**
SIC: 5074 7389 Water softeners; Water softener service
HQ: H20 Innovation Usa Holding, Inc.
8900 109th Ave N Ste 1000
Champlin MN
763 566-8961

(P-5753)
HARRINGTON INDUSTRIAL PLAS LLC (PA)
14480 Yorba Ave (91710-5766)
P.O. Box 5128 (91708-5128)
PHONE..........................909 597-8641
Eben Lenderking, *CEO*
Dave Abercrombie, *Pr*
Mike Tourtelot, *CFO*
▼ **EMP:** 85 **EST:** 1959
SQ FT: 50,000
SALES (est): 600.66MM
SALES (corp-wide): 600.66MM **Privately Held**
Web: www.hipco.com
SIC: 5074 Pipes and fittings, plastic

(P-5754)
LARSEN SUPPLY CO (PA)
Also Called: Lasco
12055 Slauson Ave (90670-2601)
PHONE..........................562 698-0731
John Palumbo, *CEO*
Rella Bodinus, *
Ruth Larsen, *Stockholder*
◆ **EMP:** 100 **EST:** 1930
SQ FT: 60,000
SALES (est): 22.97MM
SALES (corp-wide): 22.97MM **Privately Held**
Web: www.lasco.net
SIC: 5074 5075 Plumbing fittings and supplies; Warm air heating and air conditioning

(P-5755)
MITTAL RAM
100 E Hillcrest Blvd (90301-2415)
PHONE..........................310 769-6669
Ram Mittal, *Owner*
Lillian Mittal, *Prin*
EMP: 95 **EST:** 1989
SALES (est): 5.43MM **Privately Held**
SIC: 5074 Heating equipment and panels, solar

(P-5756)
MMA RENEWABLE VENTURES LLC
44 Montgomery St Ste 2200 (94104-4709)
PHONE..........................415 229-8817
EMP: 100 **EST:** 2005
SALES (est): 2.1B
SALES (corp-wide): 42.01MM **Privately Held**
SIC: 5074 Heating equipment and panels, solar
HQ: Fp Acquisition Company 3.5 Llc
745 5th Ave Fl 25
New York NY
855 650-6932

(P-5757)
NANOSOLAR INC
2434 Rock St Apt 14 (94043-2671)
▲ **EMP:** 254
Web: www.nanosolar.com
SIC: 5074 3674 Plumbing and hydronic heating supplies; Solar cells

(P-5758)
PACE SUPPLY CORP (PA)
Also Called: Premier Pump and Supply
6000 State Farm Dr Ste 200 (94928-2133)
P.O. Box 6407 (94927-6407)
PHONE..........................707 755-2499
Keith Hubbard, *Pr*
Ted M Green, *
Albert Bacci, *
▲ **EMP:** 80 **EST:** 1994
SQ FT: 10,000
SALES (est): 161.12MM **Privately Held**
Web: www.pacesupply.com
SIC: 5074 Plumbing fittings and supplies

(P-5759)
RYAN HERCO PRODUCTS CORP (DH)
Also Called: Ryan Herco Flow Solutions
3010 N San Fernando Blvd (91504-2524)
PHONE..........................818 841-1141
Randy Beckwith, *CEO*
◆ **EMP:** 60 **EST:** 1948
SQ FT: 48,000
SALES (est): 148.9MM
SALES (corp-wide): 664.84MM **Privately Held**
Web: www.rhfs.com
SIC: 5074 5162 Pipes and fittings, plastic; Plastics materials and basic shapes
HQ: Sunsource Holdings, Inc.
2301 W Windsor Ct
Addison IL

(P-5760)
SOLARNET LLC
Also Called: DC Power Systems
1500 Valley House Dr Ste 210 (94928-4937)
PHONE..........................707 992-3100
◆ **EMP:** 108
Web: www.soligent.net
SIC: 5074 Heating equipment and panels, solar

(P-5761)
SOLIGENT LEASING LLC
1500 Valley House Dr (94928-4937)
PHONE..........................707 992-3100
Tosh Fujioka, *CEO*
EMP: 171 **EST:** 2013
SALES (est): 3.35MM
SALES (corp-wide): 25.09MM **Privately Held**
Web: www.soligent.net

SIC: 5074 Heating equipment and panels, solar
PA: Soligent Holdings Inc.
1500 Valley House Dr
Rohnert Park CA
707 992-3100

(P-5762)
SONATA SOLAR LLC
1500 Valley House Dr # 210 (94928-4937)
PHONE..........................707 992-3100
EMP: 170
SIC: 5074 Heating equipment and panels, solar

(P-5763)
WATERSTONE FAUCETS LLC
Also Called: Waterstone Faucets
41180 Raintree Ct (92562-7020)
P.O. Box 1240 (92593-1240)
PHONE..........................951 304-0520
Christopher G Kuran, *Managing Member*
Steve Kliewer, *
Bob Santella, *
▲ **EMP:** 131 **EST:** 1999
SQ FT: 42,000
SALES (est): 23.78MM **Privately Held**
Web: www.waterstoneco.com
SIC: 5074 3432 Plumbing fittings and supplies; Faucets and spigots, metal and plastic

(P-5764)
WESTERN NEVADA SUPPLY CO
10990 Industrial Way Ste A (96161-0257)
PHONE..........................530 582-5009
Theodore Reviglio, *Brnch Mgr*
EMP: 70
SALES (corp-wide): 267.59MM **Privately Held**
Web: www.goblueteam.com
SIC: 5074 Plumbing fittings and supplies
PA: Western Nevada Supply Co.
950 S Rock Blvd
Sparks NV
775 359-5800

5075 Warm Air Heating And Air Conditioning

(P-5765)
AC PRO INC (PA)
Also Called: MSI Hvac
11700 Industry Ave (92337-6934)
PHONE..........................951 360-7849
Dion Quinn, *CEO*
EMP: 250 **EST:** 1986
SQ FT: 80,000
SALES (est): 107.01MM
SALES (corp-wide): 107.01MM **Privately Held**
Web: www.acpro.com
SIC: 5075 3444 Air conditioning and ventilation equipment and supplies; Sheet metalwork

(P-5766)
AIR TREATMENT CORPORATION (PA)
Also Called: Air Treatment
640 N Puente St (92821-2830)
PHONE..........................909 869-7975
Mark Hartman, *Ch Bd*
Craig Domagala, *
Deborah Hudson, *
Jay Olson, *
▲ **EMP:** 65 **EST:** 1990
SQ FT: 45,000
SALES (est): 124.76MM **Privately Held**

Web: www.airtreatment.com
SIC: 5075 Electrical heating equipment

(P-5767)
EDWARD B WARD & COMPANY INC
Valair Division
2345 Los Angeles St (93721-3115)
PHONE..........................559 487-1860
Paul Caputi, *Mgr*
EMP: 85
SALES (corp-wide): 20.42B **Publicly Held**
SIC: 5075 Air conditioning equipment, except room units, nec
HQ: Edward B. Ward & Company, Inc.
99 S Hill Dr Ste B
Brisbane CA
415 330-6600

(P-5768)
FLORENCE FILTER CORPORATION
530 W Manville St (90220-5510)
PHONE..........................310 637-1137
Adrian M Anhood, *CEO*
Floriana A Anhood, *
Erika A Anhood, *
▲ **EMP:** 60 **EST:** 1971
SQ FT: 55,000
SALES (est): 10.68MM **Privately Held**
Web: www.florencefilter.com
SIC: 5075 3564 5211 Air filters; Filters, air: furnaces, air conditioning equipment, etc.; Lumber and other building materials

(P-5769)
HEAT TRANSFER PDTS GROUP LLC
Also Called: Htpghnl
1933 S Vineyard Ave (91761-7747)
PHONE..........................909 786-3669
EMP: 145
Web: www.htpg.com
SIC: 5075 Warm air heating and air conditioning
HQ: Heat Transfer Products Group, Llc
3885 Crestwood Pkwy Nw # 50
Duluth GA

(P-5770)
NORMAN S WRGHT MECH EQP CRPRTN (PA)
99 S Hill Dr Ste A (94005-1282)
PHONE..........................415 467-7600
Richard F Leao, *Pr*
Robert L Beyer, *Ex VP*
Salvatore M Giglio, *Ex VP*
EMP: 80 **EST:** 1906
SQ FT: 50,000
SALES (est): 127.87MM
SALES (corp-wide): 127.87MM **Privately Held**
Web: www.normanwright.com
SIC: 5075 1711 Warm air heating equipment and supplies; Heating and air conditioning contractors

(P-5771)
SIERRA PCF HM & COMFORT INC
Also Called: Sierra Pacific Htg & Air-Solar
2550 Mercantile Dr Ste D (95742-8202)
PHONE..........................916 638-0543
Jason Hanson, *Pr*
Mike Loer, *
EMP: 75 **EST:** 1984
SALES (est): 30.28MM **Privately Held**
Web: www.sierrapacifichome.com

5075 - Warm Air Heating And Air Conditioning

SIC: **5075** 5074 Warm air heating and air conditioning; Heating equipment and panels, solar

(P-5772)
SLAKEY BROTHERS INC (PA)
2215 Kausen Dr Ste 1 (95758-7172)
P.O. Box 15647 (95852-0647)
PHONE..................916 478-2000
◆ EMP: 95 EST: 1939
SALES (est): 262.21MM
SALES (corp-wide): 262.21MM **Privately Held**
Web: www.slakey.com
SIC: **5075** 5074 5078 Warm air heating equipment and supplies; Plumbing fittings and supplies; Refrigeration equipment and supplies

(P-5773)
SPECIALTY A/C PRODUCTS INC (PA)
Also Called: Trane
310 Soquel Way (94085-4101)
PHONE..................408 481-3611
EMP: 70 EST: 1986
SALES (est): 21.78MM
SALES (corp-wide): 21.78MM **Privately Held**
Web: www.hvac-marketing.com
SIC: **5075** Electrical heating equipment

(P-5774)
TRANE US INC
Also Called: Trane
4145 Delmar Ave Ste 2 (95677-4041)
PHONE..................916 577-1100
Tyler Clemmer, *Mgr*
EMP: 67
Web: www.trane.com
SIC: **5075** Air conditioning and ventilation equipment and supplies
HQ: Trane U.S. Inc.
    800 Beaty St Ste E
    Davidson NC
    704 655-4000

(P-5775)
US AIRCONDITIONING DISTRIBUTORS INC (PA)
Also Called: U.S. Airconditioning Distrs
16900 Chestnut St (91748-1012)
P.O. Box 1111 (91749-1111)
PHONE..................626 854-4500
◆ EMP: 150 EST: 1964
SALES (est): 87.8MM **Privately Held**
Web: www.us-ac.com
SIC: **5075** 1711 Air conditioning equipment, except room units, nec; Plumbing, heating, air-conditioning

5078 Refrigeration Equipment And Supplies

(P-5776)
BEVERAGES & MORE INC
6820 Katella Ave (90630-5108)
PHONE..................714 891-1242
Jeff Ruffelo, *Brnch Mgr*
EMP: 113
SALES (corp-wide): 1.61B **Privately Held**
Web: www.bevmo.com
SIC: **5078** Refrigerated beverage dispensers
HQ: Beverages & More, Inc.
    1401 Willow Pass Rd # 90
    Concord CA

(P-5777)
CUSTOM COOLER INC (HQ)
420 E Arrow Hwy (91773-3340)
PHONE..................909 592-1111
Sangyup Steve Lee, *Pr*
Ray Tolcher, *VP*
▲ EMP: 78 EST: 2006
SALES (est): 23.03MM
SALES (corp-wide): 276.77MM **Privately Held**
Web: www.customcooler.com
SIC: **5078** Refrigeration equipment and supplies
PA: Kps Global Llc
    4201 N Beach St
    Fort Worth TX
    817 281-5121

(P-5778)
HILL PHOENIX INC
Walk-Ins Western Operations
14680 Monte Vista Ave (91710-5744)
PHONE..................909 592-8830
Sangyup Steve Lee, *Mgr*
EMP: 83
SALES (corp-wide): 8.51B **Publicly Held**
Web: www.hillphoenix.com
SIC: **5078** Refrigeration equipment and supplies
HQ: Hill Phoenix, Inc.
    2016 Gees Mill Rd Ne
    Conyers GA

(P-5779)
KONOIKE-E STREET INC
901 E E St (90744-6144)
PHONE..................310 233-7300
Richard Burke, *CEO*
Wayne Lamb, *Pr*
▲ EMP: 63 EST: 2011
SALES (est): 8.62MM **Privately Held**
Web: www.kpaccoldstorage.com
SIC: **5078** Cold storage machinery
HQ: Konoike-Pacific (California), Inc.
    1420 Coil Ave
    Wilmington CA

(P-5780)
OMNITEAM INC
4380 Ayers Ave (90058-4306)
PHONE..................562 923-9660
Kans Haasis Junior, *CEO*
Robert Davis, *
Don Hyatt Senior, *VP*
EMP: 125 EST: 1999
SALES (est): 24.11MM **Privately Held**
Web: www.omniteaminc.com
SIC: **5078** Commercial refrigeration equipment

(P-5781)
REFRIGERATION SUPPLIES DISTRIBUTOR (PA)
Also Called: R S D
26021 Atlantic Ocean Dr (92630-8831)
PHONE..................949 380-7878
▲ EMP: 70 EST: 1907
SALES (est): 193.04MM
SALES (corp-wide): 193.04MM **Privately Held**
Web: www.rsd.net
SIC: **5078** 5075 Refrigeration equipment and supplies; Air conditioning and ventilation equipment and supplies

5082 Construction And Mining Machinery

(P-5782)
ASOMEO ENVMTL RSTRTION INDUST
2151 River Plaza Dr Ste 105 (95833-3881)
PHONE..................530 434-6869
Akan Ismaili, *Pr*
EMP: 90 EST: 2018
SALES (est): 9.32MM **Privately Held**
Web: www.aeri-ca.com
SIC: **5082** 5083 Logging and forestry machinery and equipment; Landscaping equipment

(P-5783)
BOUTON CONSTRUCTION INC
420 E Mcglincy Ln (95008-4905)
PHONE..................408 375-0829
Chad Bouton, *CEO*
EMP: 89 EST: 2010
SALES (est): 9.6MM **Privately Held**
SIC: **5082** 1799 1741 1611 Road construction equipment; Waterproofing; Retaining wall construction; Surfacing and paving

(P-5784)
CAMERON WEST COAST INC
Also Called: Cameron Surface Systems
4315 Yeager Way (93313-2018)
▲ EMP: 90 EST: 1992
SQ FT: 48,000
SALES (est): 22.56MM **Publicly Held**
SIC: **5082** 1389 7353 Oil field equipment; Oil field services, nec; Oil field equipment, rental or leasing
HQ: Cameron International Corporation
    1333 West Loop S Ste 1700
    Houston TX

(P-5785)
CASE POWER AND EQUIPMENT
Also Called: Case Dealer Holding Company
1751 Bell Ave (95838-2862)
PHONE..................916 649-0096
EMP: 199
SIC: **5082** 7353 General construction machinery and equipment; Heavy construction equipment rental

(P-5786)
DENARDI MACHINERY INC
Also Called: D3 Equipment
1475 Pioneer Way (92020-1627)
PHONE..................619 749-0039
EMP: 102
SIC: **5082** 7699 General construction machinery and equipment; Construction equipment repair

(P-5787)
EVERPAC
1499 Palmyrita Ave (92507-1600)
PHONE..................951 774-3274
William R Johnson Junior, *Pr*
EMP: 71 EST: 2002
SALES (est): 2.18MM
SALES (corp-wide): 49.45MM **Privately Held**
Web: www.quinncompany.com
SIC: **5082** General construction machinery and equipment
PA: Johnson Machinery Co.
    800 E La Cadena Dr
    Riverside CA
    951 686-4560

(P-5788)
GAMA CONTRACTING SERVICES INC
1835 Floradale Ave (91733-3605)
PHONE..................626 442-7200
Jose Sergio Duenas, *Pr*
EMP: 140 EST: 2008
SALES (est): 19.35MM **Privately Held**
Web: www.gamacsi.com
SIC: **5082** 1795 8744 General construction machinery and equipment; Wrecking and demolition work; Environmental remediation

(P-5789)
GOODFELLOW CORPORATION
590 Crane St (92530-2737)
PHONE..................909 874-2700
Lynn Goodfellow, *Brnch Mgr*
EMP: 69
SALES (corp-wide): 54.2MM **Privately Held**
Web: www.goodfellowcorp.com
SIC: **5082** General construction machinery and equipment
PA: Goodfellow Corporation
    12451 Us 95
    Boulder City NV
    702 293-7504

(P-5790)
GOTTSTEIN CORPORATION
3500 Chester Ave (93301-1630)
PHONE..................661 322-8934
Scott Gottstein, *Brnch Mgr*
EMP: 210
SALES (corp-wide): 57MM **Privately Held**
Web: www.gottsteincorporation.com
SIC: **5082** General construction machinery and equipment
PA: Gottstein Corporation
    39 Elm Rd
    Hazle Township PA
    570 454-7162

(P-5791)
HOLT OF CALIFORNIA (HQ)
Also Called: Holt CA
7310 Pacific Ave (95668-9708)
PHONE..................916 991-8200
TOLL FREE: 800
Victor Wykoff Junior, *Ch Bd*
Gordon Beatie Co, *V Ch Bd*
Kenneth Monroe, *
Ronald Monroe, *
Daniel Johns, *
◆ EMP: 155 EST: 1998
SQ FT: 160,000
SALES (est): 292.81MM
SALES (corp-wide): 292.81MM **Privately Held**
Web: www.holtca.com
SIC: **5082** 5084 5083 7359 General construction machinery and equipment; Materials handling machinery; Agricultural machinery, nec; Equipment rental and leasing, nec
PA: Hoc Holdings, Inc.
    7310 Pacific Ave
    Pleasant Grove CA
    916 921-8950

(P-5792)
HOLT OF CALIFORNIA
Also Called: Caterpillar Authorized Dealer
3850 Channel Dr (95691-3466)
PHONE..................916 373-4100
TOLL FREE: 888
Carry Roulet, *Mgr*
EMP: 150
SALES (corp-wide): 292.81MM **Privately Held**

PRODUCTS & SERVICES SECTION
5083 - Farm And Garden Machinery (P-5811)

Web: www.holtca.com
SIC: **5082** 5083 5084 General construction machinery and equipment; Agricultural machinery and equipment; Materials handling machinery
HQ: Holt Of California
7310 Pacific Ave
Pleasant Grove CA
916 991-8200

(P-5793)
HOLT OF CALIFORNIA
Also Called: Caterpillar Authorized Dealer
1521 W Charter Way (95206-1112)
PHONE...............................209 466-6000
Kenman Row, *Mgr*
EMP: 106
SALES (corp-wide): 292.81MM **Privately Held**
Web: www.holtca.com
SIC: **5082** 5083 5084 General construction machinery and equipment; Agricultural machinery and equipment; Industrial machinery and equipment
HQ: Holt Of California
7310 Pacific Ave
Pleasant Grove CA
916 991-8200

(P-5794)
JOHNSON MACHINERY CO (PA)
Also Called: Caterpillar Authorized Dealer
800 E La Cadena Dr (92507-8715)
P.O. Box 351 (92502-0351)
PHONE...............................951 686-4560
William Johnson Junior, *Pr*
Kevin Kelly, *
Matt Merickel, *
◆ EMP: 175 EST: 1940
SQ FT: 70,000
SALES (est): 49.45MM
SALES (corp-wide): 49.45MM **Privately Held**
Web: www.johnson-machinery.com
SIC: **5082** General construction machinery and equipment

(P-5795)
NAUMANN/HOBBS MTL HDLG CORP II
Also Called: Hawthorne Lift Systems
86998 Avenue 52 (92236-2710)
PHONE...............................866 266-2244
EMP: 105
SALES (corp-wide): 90MM **Privately Held**
SIC: **5082** 5084 General construction machinery and equipment; Industrial machinery and equipment
PA: Naumann/Hobbs Material Handling Corporation Ii, Inc.
4336 S 43rd Pl
Phoenix AZ
602 437-1331

(P-5796)
PETERSON HOLDING COMPANY (PA)
Also Called: Peterson Cat
955 Marina Blvd (94577-3440)
PHONE...............................510 357-6200
Duane S Doyle, *CEO*
EMP: 70 EST: 1977
SALES (est): 543.5MM **Privately Held**
Web: www.petersonholding.com
SIC: **5082** 7699 General construction machinery and equipment; Agricultural equipment repair services

(P-5797)
PETERSON MACHINERY CO
Also Called: Peterson Cat
5100 Caterpillar Rd (96003-1411)
PHONE...............................530 243-5410
EMP: 585
Web: www.petersoncat.com
SIC: **5082** Construction and mining machinery
HQ: Peterson Machinery Co.
955 Marina Blvd
San Leandro CA

(P-5798)
QUINN COMPANY
Also Called: Caterpillar Authorized Dealer
510 Pickerell Ave (93212)
P.O. Box 578 (93212-0578)
PHONE...............................559 992-2193
Greg Thomas, *Mgr*
EMP: 68
SQ FT: 10,000
SALES (corp-wide): 472.61MM **Privately Held**
Web: www.quinncompany.com
SIC: **5082** 5083 5084 7353 General construction machinery and equipment; Farm and garden machinery; Industrial machinery and equipment; Heavy construction equipment rental
HQ: Quinn Company
10006 Rose Hills Rd
City Of Industry CA
562 463-4000

(P-5799)
QUINN COMPANY
1300 Abbott St (93901-4507)
PHONE...............................831 758-8461
Jesse Sandoval, *Brnch Mgr*
EMP: 62
SALES (corp-wide): 472.61MM **Privately Held**
Web: www.quinncompany.com
SIC: **5082** General construction machinery and equipment
HQ: Quinn Company
10006 Rose Hills Rd
City Of Industry CA
562 463-4000

(P-5800)
QUINN COMPANY
Also Called: Caterpillar Authorized Dealer
2200 Pegasus Dr (93308-6801)
PHONE...............................661 393-5800
Steve Eucce, *Brnch Mgr*
EMP: 93
SALES (corp-wide): 472.61MM **Privately Held**
Web: www.quinncompany.com
SIC: **5082** 5083 5084 7353 General construction machinery and equipment; Farm and garden machinery; Industrial machinery and equipment; Heavy construction equipment rental
HQ: Quinn Company
10006 Rose Hills Rd
City Of Industry CA
562 463-4000

(P-5801)
QUINN COMPANY
Also Called: Caterpillar Authorized Dealer
801 Del Norte Blvd (93030-8966)
PHONE...............................805 485-2171
Jay Ervine, *Brnch Mgr*
EMP: 74
SALES (corp-wide): 472.61MM **Privately Held**
Web: www.quinncompany.com
SIC: **5082** 5083 5084 7353 General construction machinery and equipment; Farm and garden machinery; Industrial machinery and equipment; Heavy construction equipment rental
HQ: Quinn Company
10006 Rose Hills Rd
City Of Industry CA
562 463-4000

(P-5802)
QUINN COMPANY
Also Called: Caterpillar Authorized Dealer
1655 Carlotti Dr (93454-1503)
PHONE...............................805 925-8611
Dan Hunt, *Mgr*
EMP: 68
SALES (corp-wide): 472.61MM **Privately Held**
Web: www.quinncompany.com
SIC: **5082** 5083 5084 7353 General construction machinery and equipment; Farm and garden machinery; Industrial machinery and equipment; Heavy construction equipment rental
HQ: Quinn Company
10006 Rose Hills Rd
City Of Industry CA
562 463-4000

(P-5803)
QUINN SHEPHERD MACHINERY
Also Called: Caterpillar Authorized Dealer
10006 Rose Hills Rd (90601-1702)
P.O. Box 226789 (90022-6789)
PHONE...............................562 463-6000
Blake Quinn, *Pr*
▲ EMP: 287 EST: 1924
SQ FT: 163,000
SALES (est): 97.6MM
SALES (corp-wide): 472.61MM **Privately Held**
Web: www.quinncompany.com
SIC: **5082** 5084 General construction machinery and equipment; Industrial machinery and equipment
PA: Quinn Group, Inc.
10006 Rose Hills Rd
City Of Industry CA
562 463-4000

(P-5804)
SOUND-CRETE CONTRACTORS INC
530 Opper St Ste A (92029-1034)
PHONE...............................760 291-1240
Louis Fisher, *Pr*
Terry Russo, *
Jim Dorsey, *
EMP: 65 EST: 2005
SALES (est): 7.46MM **Privately Held**
Web: www.soundcrete.us
SIC: **5082** General construction machinery and equipment

5083 Farm And Garden Machinery

(P-5805)
ALSCO - GEYER IRRIGATION INC
700 5th St (95912-9550)
P.O. Box 111 (95912-0111)
PHONE...............................530 476-2253
Charles Geyer, *Pr*
Marjoria Martinez, *
Andy Geyer, *Prin*
EMP: 90 EST: 1996
SQ FT: 3,000
SALES (est): 22.84MM **Privately Held**
Web: www.alscogeyerirrigation.com
SIC: **5083** Irrigation equipment

(P-5806)
B J T C INC
Also Called: Agricultural Supply
1435 Simpson Way (92029-1312)
P.O. Box 1383 (92227-1383)
PHONE...............................760 737-2442
EMP: 60
SIC: **5083** Farm and garden machinery

(P-5807)
CASCADE TURF LLC
Also Called: Aa Equipment
4811 Brooks St (91763-4733)
PHONE...............................909 626-8586
EMP: 79
SIC: **5083** Agricultural machinery and equipment

(P-5808)
EURODRIP USA INC
7545 Carroll Rd (92121-2401)
PHONE...............................559 674-2670
◆ EMP: 80 EST: 1996
SALES (est): 32.77MM **Privately Held**
Web: www.eurodripusa.com
SIC: **5083** 3084 Irrigation equipment; Plastics pipe
HQ: Rivulis S.A.
Athinon - Lamias National Rd (55th Km), P.O. Box 34
Oinofyta

(P-5809)
GREEN ACRES NURSERY & SUP LLC (PA)
604 Sutter St Ste 350 (95630-2698)
PHONE...............................916 673-9720
▲ EMP: 90 EST: 2002
SALES (est): 26.66MM
SALES (corp-wide): 26.66MM **Privately Held**
Web: www.idiggreenacres.com
SIC: **5083** 5261 Irrigation equipment; Nursery stock, seeds and bulbs

(P-5810)
I BRANDS LLC
2617 N Sepulveda Blvd (90266-2737)
PHONE...............................424 336-5216
EMP: 140 EST: 2010
SALES (est): 8.7MM **Privately Held**
Web: www.tomaro.com
SIC: **5083** Agricultural machinery and equipment

(P-5811)
NETAFIM IRRIGATION INC (HQ)
Also Called: Netafim USA
5470 E Home Ave (93727-2107)
PHONE...............................559 453-6800
Igal Aisenberg, *Pr*
Lauri Hanover, *
Michael Dowgert, *
◆ EMP: 260 EST: 1965
SQ FT: 100,000
SALES (est): 98.04MM **Privately Held**
Web: www.netafimusa.com
SIC: **5083** 3523 Irrigation equipment; Irrigation equipment, self-propelled
PA: Netafim Ltd
10 Hashalom Rd.
Tel Aviv-Jaffa

5083 - Farm And Garden Machinery (P-5812)

(P-5812)
SPEARS MANUFACTURING CO (PA)
15853 Olden St (91342-1249)
P.O. Box 9203 (91392-9203)
PHONE.................................818 364-1611
Robert Wayne Spears, *CEO*
Wayne Spears, *
Michael Valasquez, *General Vice President*
Ken Ruggles, *
◆ **EMP:** 134 **EST:** 1970
SQ FT: 119,088
SALES (est): 1.37B
SALES (corp-wide): 1.37B **Privately Held**
Web: www.spearsmanufacturing.com
SIC: 5083 3494 Irrigation equipment; Valves and pipe fittings, nec

(P-5813)
TDR DEVELOPMENT INC
Also Called: T D R
1819 S Walnut Rd (95380-9219)
P.O. Box 1530 (95381-1530)
PHONE.................................209 667-6455
Mathew Anthony Bruno, *CEO*
Tony Bruno, *
EMP: 100 **EST:** 1972
SQ FT: 10,000
SALES (est): 25.73MM **Privately Held**
Web: www.tdr-inc.com
SIC: 5083 7699 1542 Dairy machinery and equipment; Industrial equipment services; Nonresidential construction, nec

(P-5814)
UNITED GREEN MARK INC
Also Called: Sprinkler Irrgtion Specialists
1145 N 13th St (95112-2903)
PHONE.................................408 295-3376
Dave Usher, *Mgr*
EMP: 77
SALES (corp-wide): 4.01B **Publicly Held**
SIC: 5083 Lawn and garden machinery and equipment
HQ: United Green Mark Inc
    650 Stephenson Hwy
    Troy MI
    248 588-2100

(P-5815)
VALLEY TRUCK AND TRACTOR INC
Also Called: John Deere Authorized Dealer
Hwy 113 (95676)
P.O. Box 256 (95676-0256)
PHONE.................................530 738-4421
Mike Cardoza, *Mgr*
EMP: 66
SALES (corp-wide): 90MM **Privately Held**
Web: agriculture.papemachinery.com
SIC: 5083 5261 Agricultural machinery and equipment; Lawnmowers and tractors
PA: Valley Truck And Tractor Inc.
    1003 Stabler Ln
    Yuba City CA
    530 673-4615

(P-5816)
VUCOVICH INC (PA)
Also Called: John Deere Authorized Dealer
4288 S Bagley Ave (93725-9014)
P.O. Box 2513 (93745-2513)
PHONE.................................559 486-8020
Marsha Vucovich, *Pr*
EMP: 60 **EST:** 1961
SQ FT: 42,800
SALES (est): 23.43MM
SALES (corp-wide): 23.43MM **Privately Held**
Web: www.fresnoequipment.com

SIC: 5083 Farm equipment parts and supplies

5084 Industrial Machinery And Equipment

(P-5817)
AIRGAS USA LLC
3737 Worsham Ave (90808-1774)
P.O. Box 7423 (91109-7423)
PHONE.................................562 497-1991
Douglas L Jones, *Reg Pr*
EMP: 1726
SALES (corp-wide): 109.44MM **Privately Held**
Web: www.airgas.com
SIC: 5084 Welding machinery and equipment
HQ: Airgas Usa, Llc
    259 N Radnor Chester Rd
    Radnor PA
    216 642-6600

(P-5818)
AMADA AMERICA INC (HQ)
7025 Firestone Blvd (90621-1869)
PHONE.................................714 739-2111
TOLL FREE: 800
Mike Guarin, *CEO*
Koa Nakata, *CFO*
▲ **EMP:** 75 **EST:** 1971
SQ FT: 103,000
SALES (est): 185.26MM **Privately Held**
Web: www.amada.com
SIC: 5084 6159 Metalworking machinery; Machinery and equipment finance leasing
PA: Amada Co., Ltd.
    200, Ishida
    Isehara KNG

(P-5819)
ANRITSU AMERICAS SALES COMPANY
490 Jarvis Dr (95037-2834)
PHONE.................................408 778-2000
Hirokazu Hamada, *CEO*
EMP: 540 **EST:** 2018
SQ FT: 250,000
SALES (est): 66.14MM **Privately Held**
Web: www.anritsu.com
SIC: 5084 Measuring and testing equipment, electrical
HQ: Anritsu U.S. Holding, Inc.
    490 Jarvis Dr
    Morgan Hill CA
    408 778-2000

(P-5820)
BEJAC CORPORATION (PA)
569 S Van Buren St (92870-6613)
PHONE.................................714 528-6224
Ron Barlet, *Pr*
Peggy Barlet, *
Kim Smith-grime, *CFO*
▼ **EMP:** 66 **EST:** 1953
SQ FT: 2,000
SALES (est): 49.58MM
SALES (corp-wide): 49.58MM **Privately Held**
Web: www.bejac.com
SIC: 5084 7353 Industrial machinery and equipment; Heavy construction equipment rental

(P-5821)
BIG JOE CALIFORNIA NORTH INC (PA)
Also Called: Big Joe Handling Systems
25932 Eden Landing Rd (94545-3816)
PHONE.................................510 785-6900
Boyd J Kiefus, *CEO*
Rod D Kiefus, *
EMP: 110 **EST:** 2003
SQ FT: 52,000
SALES (est): 43.23MM
SALES (corp-wide): 43.23MM **Privately Held**
Web: www.bigjoelift.com
SIC: 5084 5999 7359 8331 Lift trucks and parts; Business machines and equipment; Equipment rental and leasing, nec; Job training services

(P-5822)
BLUE WHITE ROBOTICS US INC (PA)
Also Called: Bluewhite
3731 W Ashcroft Ave (93722-4257)
PHONE.................................559 731-2239
EMP: 193 **EST:** 2020
SALES (est): 17.72MM
SALES (corp-wide): 17.72MM **Privately Held**
Web: www.bluewhiterobotics.com
SIC: 5084 Industrial machinery and equipment

(P-5823)
BUCKEYE FIRE EQUIPMENT COMPANY
2416 Teagarden St (94577-4336)
PHONE.................................510 483-1815
Mark Libardos, *Prin*
EMP: 291
SALES (corp-wide): 113.98MM **Privately Held**
Web: www.buckeyef.com
SIC: 5084 Industrial machinery and equipment
PA: Buckeye Fire Equipment Company
    110 Kings Rd
    Kings Mountain NC
    704 739-7415

(P-5824)
CAPITOL BARRICADE INC (PA)
6001 Elvas Ave (95819-4357)
PHONE.................................916 451-5176
Joseph Reihl, *Pr*
Suzanne Reihl, *
Todd Woolford, *
◆ **EMP:** 60 **EST:** 1966
SQ FT: 3,200
SALES (est): 73.71K
SALES (corp-wide): 73.71K **Privately Held**
Web: www.capitolbarricade.com
SIC: 5084 7359 Safety equipment; Equipment rental and leasing, nec

(P-5825)
CDS MOVING EQUIPMENT INC (PA)
Also Called: Cds Packing Solutions
375 W Manville St (90220-5617)
PHONE.................................310 631-1100
TOLL FREE: 800
Allen J Sidor, *Pr*
▲ **EMP:** 80 **EST:** 1981
SQ FT: 100,000
SALES (est): 57.92MM
SALES (corp-wide): 57.92MM **Privately Held**
Web: www.cds-usa.com
SIC: 5084 Materials handling machinery

(P-5826)
CLARKLIFT-WEST INC
Also Called: Team Power Forklift
4750 Illinois Ave (95628-6313)
PHONE.................................916 381-5674
▲ **EMP:** 121
SIC: 5084 7699 7359 Lift trucks and parts; Industrial truck repair; Industrial truck rental

(P-5827)
CROMER INC
Also Called: Cromer Material Handling
4701 Oakport St (94601-4906)
PHONE.................................510 534-6566
Matthew A Adams, *Pr*
EMP: 339 **EST:** 2021
SALES (est): 14.65MM
SALES (corp-wide): 192.89MM **Privately Held**
Web: www.cromer.com
SIC: 5084 Materials handling machinery
PA: Gnco, Inc.
    1395 Valley Belt Rd
    Brooklyn Heights OH
    216 706-2349

(P-5828)
CUMMINS WEST INC
Also Called: Cummins
14775 Wicks Blvd (94577-6717)
P.O. Box 3005 (47202-3005)
PHONE.................................510 351-6101
TOLL FREE: 800
▲ **EMP:** 325
Web: www.cumminswestinc.com
SIC: 5084 7629 5063 3519 Engines and parts, diesel; Electrical repair shops; Electrical apparatus and equipment; Internal combustion engines, nec

(P-5829)
DSI PROCESS SYSTEMS LLC
Also Called: Statco
7595 Reynolds Cir (92647-6787)
PHONE.................................314 382-1525
EMP: 136 **EST:** 2010
SALES (est): 19.92MM **Privately Held**
Web: www.statco-dsi.com
SIC: 5084 Industrial machinery and equipment

(P-5830)
DYNAPOWER COMPANY LLC
2913 Whipple Rd (94587-1207)
PHONE.................................802 860-7200
EMP: 101
SALES (corp-wide): 4.03B **Privately Held**
Web: www.dynapower.com
SIC: 5084 Conveyor systems
HQ: Dynapower Company Llc
    85 Meadowland Dr
    South Burlington VT
    802 860-7200

(P-5831)
ELEVATOR EQUIPMENT CORPORATION (PA)
Also Called: Eeco
4035 Goodwin Ave (90039-1109)
P.O. Box 39714 (90039-0714)
PHONE.................................323 245-0147
Abe Salehpour, *CEO*
Abdul Mozayeni, *
◆ **EMP:** 75 **EST:** 1944
SQ FT: 20,000
SALES (est): 25.64MM
SALES (corp-wide): 25.64MM **Privately Held**
Web: www.elevatorequipment.com
SIC: 5084 Elevators

5084 - Industrial Machinery And Equipment (P-5851)

(P-5832)
ELLISON TECHNOLOGIES INC
9912 Pioneer Blvd (90670-3250)
PHONE..................................562 949-8311
EMP: 67
Web: www.ellisontechnologies.com
SIC: 5084 Machine tools and accessories
HQ: Ellison Technologies, Inc.
   9828 Arlee Ave
   Santa Fe Springs CA
   562 949-8311

(P-5833)
EQUIPMENT DEPOT INC
Also Called: Southern California Mtl Hdlg
12393 Slauson Ave (90606-2824)
PHONE..................................562 949-1000
David Turner, Pr
EMP: 150
Web: www.eqdepot.com
SIC: 5084 Conveyor systems
HQ: Equipment Depot, Inc.
   16330 Air Center Blvd
   Houston TX
   713 365-2530

(P-5834)
FARM PUMP & IRRIGATION CO INC (PA)
Also Called: F P I
535 N Shafter Ave (93263-1900)
P.O. Box 1477 (93263-1477)
PHONE..................................661 589-6901
John Gargan, CEO
Kathy Gargan, *
EMP: 60 EST: 1983
SQ FT: 4,000
SALES (est): 23.51MM
SALES (corp-wide): 23.51MM Privately Held
Web: www.fpi-co.com
SIC: 5084 5083 Pumps and pumping equipment, nec; Irrigation equipment

(P-5835)
FUELING AND SERVICE TECH INC
Also Called: Fastech
7050 Village Dr Ste D (90621-2263)
PHONE..................................714 523-0194
M Dan Mcgill, CEO
EMP: 75 EST: 1994
SQ FT: 15,000
SALES (est): 36.83MM Privately Held
Web: www.fastechus.com
SIC: 5084 Petroleum industry machinery

(P-5836)
GENMARK AUTOMATION (DH)
46723 Lakeview Blvd (94538-6528)
PHONE..................................510 897-3400
Yuji Shioga, CEO
▼ EMP: 98 EST: 1985
SQ FT: 86,000
SALES (est): 43.43MM Privately Held
Web: www.genmarkautomation.com
SIC: 5084 3674 Industrial machinery and equipment; Wafers (semiconductor devices)
HQ: Nidec Instruments Corporation
   5329, Shimosuwamachi
   Suwa-Gun NAG

(P-5837)
GOLDEN EAGLE DISTRIBUTING CORP
1251 Tinker Rd (95765-1311)
P.O. Box 1560 (95677-7560)
PHONE..................................916 645-6600
Gary Bussell, CEO
Steven L Clark, *
◆ EMP: 100 EST: 1946
SQ FT: 90,000
SALES (est): 42.07MM Privately Held
Web: www.goldeneagledist.com
SIC: 5084 Chainsaws
HQ: Echo, Incorporated
   400 Oakwood Rd
   Lake Zurich IL
   847 540-8400

(P-5838)
GRAY LIFT INC
Also Called: Warehouse Sys
4646 E Jensen Ave (93725-1699)
P.O. Box 2808 (93745-2808)
PHONE..................................559 268-6621
EMP: 86
Web: www.graylift.com
SIC: 5084 7699 7359 Industrial machinery and equipment; Industrial equipment services; Equipment rental and leasing, nec

(P-5839)
HITACHI AMERICA LTD (HQ)
Also Called: Hitachi
2535 Augustine Dr (95054-3003)
PHONE..................................914 332-5800
◆ EMP: 125 EST: 1959
SALES (est): 1.58B Privately Held
Web: www.hitachi.us
SIC: 5084 5065 3577 5063 Industrial machinery and equipment; Electronic parts and equipment, nec; Computer peripheral equipment, nec; Generators
PA: Hitachi, Ltd.
   1-6-6, Marunouchi
   Chiyoda-Ku TKY

(P-5840)
INDUSTRIAL PARTS DEPOT LLC (HQ)
Also Called: Ipd
1550 Charles Willard St (90746-4039)
PHONE..................................310 530-1900
Michael Badar, Pr
Russell Kneipp, Managing Member*
◆ EMP: 70 EST: 1955
SALES (est): 26.55MM
SALES (corp-wide): 77.26MM Privately Held
Web: www.ipdparts.com
SIC: 5084 3519 Engines and parts, diesel; Parts and accessories, internal combustion engines
PA: Storm Industries, Inc.
   23223 Normandie Ave
   Torrance CA
   310 534-5232

(P-5841)
INOXPA USA INC
6145 State Farm Dr (94928-2147)
PHONE..................................707 585-3900
Candi Granes Campasol, Pr
▲ EMP: 300 EST: 2004
SALES (est): 24.65MM Privately Held
Web: www.inoxpausa.com
SIC: 5084 Pumps and pumping equipment, nec
HQ: Inoxpa Sau
   Calle Dels Telers 60
   Banyoles GI

(P-5842)
JOHN TILLMAN COMPANY (DH)
1300 W Artesia Blvd (90220-5307)
PHONE..................................310 764-0110
Phillip Mcgreevy, Pr
▲ EMP: 100 EST: 1928
SQ FT: 25,000
SALES (est): 37.94MM
SALES (corp-wide): 14.5B Privately Held
Web: www.jtillman.com
SIC: 5084 3842 3548 Safety equipment; Personal safety equipment; Welding apparatus
HQ: Bunzl Distribution Inc.
   1 Cityplace Dr Ste 200
   Saint Louis MO

(P-5843)
LAKOS CORPORATION (HQ)
Also Called: Lakos
1365 N Clovis Ave (93727-2282)
P.O. Box 398936 (94139-8936)
PHONE..................................559 255-1601
Scott Marion, CEO
Eric Arneson, *
Brian Ketcham, *
Kathy Colby, *
◆ EMP: 90 EST: 1972
SQ FT: 100,000
SALES (est): 27.79MM
SALES (corp-wide): 27.79MM Privately Held
Web: www.lakos.com
SIC: 5084 3491 Industrial machinery and equipment; Pressure valves and regulators, industrial
PA: Lakos Acquisition Holdco, Llc
   1365 N Clovis Ave
   Fresno CA
   559 255-1601

(P-5844)
MATERIAL HANDLING SUPPLY INC (HQ)
12900 Firestone Blvd (90670-5405)
PHONE..................................562 921-7715
TOLL FREE: 800
Alexander Stephen Lynn, CEO
Donn C Lynn Junior, Ch Bd
John Hanson, *
EMP: 80 EST: 1962
SQ FT: 85,000
SALES (est): 19.08MM
SALES (corp-wide): 19.08MM Privately Held
Web: www.mhs-ca.com
SIC: 5084 7629 5046 Food industry machinery; Electrical repair shops; Commercial equipment, nec
PA: Envicor
   12900 Firestone Blvd
   Santa Fe Springs CA
   562 921-7715

(P-5845)
MAXON LIFT CORP (PA)
11921 Slauson Ave (90670-2221)
PHONE..................................562 464-0099
Casey Lugash, Pr
Brenda Leung, VP Fin
▲ EMP: 110 EST: 1957
SQ FT: 30,000
SALES (est): 66.93MM Privately Held
Web: www.maxonlift.com
SIC: 5084 3537 3534 Lift trucks and parts; Industrial trucks and tractors; Elevators and moving stairways

(P-5846)
MCGRATH RENTCORP (PA)
Also Called: Mobile Mdlar MGT Corp Prnce Gr
5700 Las Positas Rd (94551-7806)
PHONE..................................925 606-9200
Joseph F Hanna, Pr
Ronald H Zech, Non-Executive Chairman of the Board*
Keith E Pratt, Ex VP
David M Whitney, CAO
Kay Dashner, Pers/VP
EMP: 128 EST: 1979
SQ FT: 26,000
SALES (est): 733.82MM
SALES (corp-wide): 733.82MM Publicly Held
Web: www.mgrc.com
SIC: 5084 7359 Measuring and testing equipment, electrical; Electronic equipment rental, except computers

(P-5847)
NAN FANG DIST GROUP INC
Also Called: Nan Fang
2100 Williams St (94577-3225)
PHONE..................................510 297-5382
Ze Pan, CEO
Zhen Patrick Poon, VP
▲ EMP: 100 EST: 1994
SALES (est): 12.73MM Privately Held
SIC: 5084 Engines and parts, diesel

(P-5848)
NIKON PRECISION INC (DH)
1399 Shoreway Rd (94002-4107)
PHONE..................................650 508-4674
Yoshiyuki Takabatake, CEO
▲ EMP: 250 EST: 1982
SQ FT: 30,000
SALES (est): 161.21MM Privately Held
Web: www.nikonprecision.com
SIC: 5084 5065 Industrial machinery and equipment; Electronic parts and equipment, nec
HQ: Nikon Americas Inc.
   1300 Walt Whitman Rd Fl 2
   Melville NY

(P-5849)
OL OLD COMPANY
Also Called: Accuret Equipment
404 E Commercial St (91767-5508)
PHONE..................................800 492-6864
Scott Tredinnick, Pr
▲ EMP: 60 EST: 1980
SQ FT: 2,300
SALES (est): 22.44MM Privately Held
Web: www.reladyne.com
SIC: 5084 5172 Materials handling machinery; Lubricating oils and greases
HQ: Reladyne Llc
   8280 Montgomery Rd # 101
   Cincinnati OH
   513 489-6000

(P-5850)
OLIVER HEALTHCARE PACKAGING CO
Also Called: Clean Cut Technologies
1145 N Ocean Cir (92806-1939)
PHONE..................................714 864-3500
Mike Benevento, Pr
EMP: 100
SALES (corp-wide): 2.13B Privately Held
Web: www.oliverhcp.com
SIC: 5084 5199 3053 Processing and packaging equipment; Packaging materials; Packing materials
HQ: Oliver Healthcare Packaging Company
   445 6th St Nw
   Grand Rapids MI
   616 456-7711

(P-5851)
ONEIL DATA SYSTEMS LLC
12655 Beatrice St (90066-7300)
PHONE..................................310 448-6400
▲ EMP: 150

5084 - Industrial Machinery And Equipment (P-5852)

PRODUCTS & SERVICES SECTION

SIC: 5084 Fans, industrial

(P-5852)
OTIS ELEVATOR COMPANY
470 Lakeside Dr Ste D (94085-4720)
PHONE.....................408 727-1231
Ed Persiclo, *Mgr*
EMP: 103
SQ FT: 2,500
SALES (corp-wide): 13.69B **Publicly Held**
Web: www.otis.com
SIC: 5084 7699 3534 1796 Elevators; Elevators: inspection, service, and repair; Elevators and moving stairways; Installing building equipment
HQ: Otis Elevator Company
1 Carrier Pl
Farmington CT
860 674-3000

(P-5853)
OTIS ELEVATOR COMPANY
512 Paula Ave Ste A (91201-2363)
PHONE.....................818 241-2828
Sam Goe, *Brnch Mgr*
EMP: 250
SQ FT: 15,000
SALES (corp-wide): 13.69B **Publicly Held**
Web: www.otis.com
SIC: 5084 7699 Elevators; Elevators: inspection, service, and repair
HQ: Otis Elevator Company
1 Carrier Pl
Farmington CT
860 674-3000

(P-5854)
OTIS ELEVATOR COMPANY
Also Called: United Technologies
711 E Ball Rd Ste 200 (92805-5960)
PHONE.....................714 758-9593
Bob Mcleese, *Brnch Mgr*
EMP: 101
SALES (corp-wide): 13.69B **Publicly Held**
Web: www.otis.com
SIC: 5084 1796 Elevators; Elevator installation and conversion
HQ: Otis Elevator Company
1 Carrier Pl
Farmington CT
860 674-3000

(P-5855)
OTIS ELEVATOR COMPANY
444 Spear St Ste 100 (94105-1642)
PHONE.....................415 546-0880
Rob Neill, *Brnch Mgr*
EMP: 104
SALES (corp-wide): 13.69B **Publicly Held**
Web: www.otis.com
SIC: 5084 1796 Elevators; Elevator installation and conversion
HQ: Otis Elevator Company
1 Carrier Pl
Farmington CT
860 674-3000

(P-5856)
PAPE MATERIAL HANDLING INC
2615 Pellissier Pl (90601-1508)
PHONE.....................562 463-8000
Jordan Pape, *Brnch Mgr*
EMP: 200
Web: www.papemh.com
SIC: 5084 7699 7359 Lift trucks and parts; Industrial machinery and equipment repair; Industrial truck rental
HQ: Pape' Material Handling, Inc.
355 Goodpasture Island Rd
Eugene OR

(P-5857)
PAPE MATERIAL HANDLING INC
47132 Kato Rd (94538-7333)
PHONE.....................510 659-4100
Ken Mader, *Brnch Mgr*
EMP: 80
SQ FT: 37,536
Web: www.papemh.com
SIC: 5084 8743 7359 5082 Materials handling machinery; Sales promotion; Stores and yards equipment rental; Contractor's materials
HQ: Pape' Material Handling, Inc.
355 Goodpasture Island Rd
Eugene OR

(P-5858)
PARKER-HANNIFIN CORPORATION
Customer Support Military Div
14300 Alton Pkwy (92618-1898)
PHONE.....................949 465-4519
Edwin Feick, *Brnch Mgr*
EMP: 119
SALES (corp-wide): 19.07B **Publicly Held**
Web: www.parker.com
SIC: 5084 Hydraulic systems equipment and supplies
PA: Parker-Hannifin Corporation
6035 Parkland Blvd
Cleveland OH
216 896-3000

(P-5859)
POWELL WORKS INC
Also Called: Powell Works
17807 Maclaren St Ste B (91744-5700)
PHONE.....................909 861-6699
Jerry Wang, *Pr*
▲ **EMP:** 256 **EST:** 2015
SQ FT: 2,500
SALES (est): 18.54MM **Privately Held**
SIC: 5084 Compressors, except air conditioning

(P-5860)
POWER GENERATION ENTPS INC
26764 Oak Ave (91351-2409)
PHONE.....................818 484-8550
Vartan Seropian, *CEO*
EMP: 110 **EST:** 2014
SALES (est): 9.39MM **Privately Held**
Web: www.powergenenterprises.com
SIC: 5084 Industrial machinery and equipment

(P-5861)
PRO SAFETY INC
20503 Belshaw Ave (90746-3505)
PHONE.....................562 364-7450
Catherina Zember, *Pr*
EMP: 148 **EST:** 2015
SQ FT: 88,000
SALES (est): 22.88MM **Privately Held**
Web: www.airprotarservices.com
SIC: 5084 8331 Industrial machinery and equipment; Job training and related services

(P-5862)
R F MACDONALD CO (PA)
25920 Eden Landing Rd (94545-3816)
PHONE.....................510 784-0110
James T Macdonald, *
Chris Sentner, *
Robert Sygiel, *
Patricia Fuetsch, *
EMP: 76 **EST:** 1956
SQ FT: 25,000
SALES (est): 97.16MM
SALES (corp-wide): 97.16MM **Privately Held**
Web: www.rfmacdonald.com
SIC: 5084 7699 5074 Pumps and pumping equipment, nec; Industrial machinery and equipment repair; Boilers, power (industrial)

(P-5863)
RAYMOND HANDLING SOLUTIONS INC (DH)
9939 Norwalk Blvd (90670-3321)
P.O. Box 3683 (90670-1683)
PHONE.....................562 944-8067
James Wilcox, *CEO*
EMP: 188 **EST:** 2002
SQ FT: 5,000
SALES (est): 118.87MM **Privately Held**
Web: www.raymondwest.com
SIC: 5084 7699 7359 Materials handling machinery; Industrial machinery and equipment repair; Industrial truck rental
HQ: The Raymond Corporation
22 S Canal St
Greene NY
607 656-2311

(P-5864)
REBAS INC
Also Called: Toyota Material Hdlg Solutions
12907 Imperial Hwy (90670-4715)
PHONE.....................562 941-4155
Shankar Basu, *Ch Bd*
Simon Walker, *
▲ **EMP:** 104 **EST:** 1990
SQ FT: 103,000
SALES (est): 37.91MM **Privately Held**
Web: www.toyotamhs.com
SIC: 5084 Materials handling machinery

(P-5865)
RELIABLE ROBOTICS CORPORATION
950 N Rengstorff Ave Ste E (94043-1746)
PHONE.....................650 336-0608
Kevin Sagis, *Sr VP*
EMP: 97 **EST:** 2017
SALES (est): 10.37MM **Privately Held**
Web: www.reliable.co
SIC: 5084 Robots, industrial

(P-5866)
REPLANET LLC
800 N Haven Ave Ste 120 (91764-4951)
P.O. Box 2893 (95344-0893)
PHONE.....................951 520-1700
EMP: 600
Web: www.replanet.com
SIC: 5084 4953 Recycling machinery and equipment; Refuse systems

(P-5867)
RJMS CORPORATION
Also Called: Toyota Material Hdlg Nthrn CA
773 Vertin Ave (93901-4581)
PHONE.....................831 757-1091
Edward Jacobs, *Mgr*
EMP: 110
SQ FT: 1,500
SALES (corp-wide): 115.11MM **Privately Held**
Web: www.tmhnc.com
SIC: 5084 Materials handling machinery
PA: Rjms Corporation
6999 Southfront Rd
Livermore CA
510 675-0500

(P-5868)
RL SURGENER INC
Also Called: Rls Industries
4201 Armour Ave (93308-4551)
P.O. Box 5096 (93388-5096)
PHONE.....................661 322-0153
EMP: 65
Web: www.rlsind.com
SIC: 5084 7699 Pumps and pumping equipment, nec; Mechanical instrument repair

(P-5869)
SOUTHERN CALIFORNIA MATERIAL HANDLING INC
Also Called: Scmh
12393 Slauson Ave (90606-2824)
P.O. Box 80770 (91118-8770)
PHONE.....................562 949-1006
▲ **EMP:** 150
SIC: 5084 Conveyor systems

(P-5870)
STAINLESS STL FABRICATORS INC
Also Called: Cook King
15120 Desman Rd (90638-5737)
PHONE.....................714 739-9904
Craig Miller, *Pr*
Dave Hart, *
Glenna Miller, *
Jennifer Arcos, *Prin*
EMP: 60 **EST:** 1985
SQ FT: 11,204
SALES (est): 23.48MM **Privately Held**
Web: www.ssfab.net
SIC: 5084 3444 Industrial machinery and equipment; Restaurant sheet metalwork

(P-5871)
SWARCO MCCAIN INC (DH)
2365 Oak Ridge Way (92081-8348)
PHONE.....................760 727-8100
Jo Ann Mills, *CEO*
▲ **EMP:** 250 **EST:** 1987
SQ FT: 6,700
SALES (est): 157.67MM
SALES (corp-wide): 2.67MM **Privately Held**
Web: www.mccain-inc.com
SIC: 5084 3444 3669 Industrial machinery and equipment; Sheet metalwork; Traffic signals, electric
HQ: Swarco Ag
Blattenwaldweg 8
Wattens
522458770

(P-5872)
TESTEQUITY INC
Also Called: Testequity
6100 Condor Dr (93021-2608)
PHONE.....................805 498-9933
EMP: 85
SIC: 5084 Measuring and testing equipment, electrical

(P-5873)
TK ELEVATOR CORPORATION
14400 Catalina St (94577-5516)
PHONE.....................510 476-1900
Ed Persico, *Mgr*
EMP: 224
SALES (corp-wide): 2.67MM **Privately Held**
Web: www.tkelevator.com
SIC: 5084 1796 3534 Elevators; Elevator installation and conversion; Elevators and moving stairways

PRODUCTS & SERVICES SECTION

5085 - Industrial Supplies (P-5894)

HQ: Tk Elevator Corporation
   788 Cir 75 Pkwy Se # 500
   Atlanta GA
   678 319-3240

(P-5874)
TK ELEVATOR CORPORATION
1965 Gillespie Way Ste 101 (92020-0505)
PHONE.................................619 596-7220
Jeff Hansen, *Mgr*
EMP: 105
SALES (corp-wide): 2.67MM **Privately Held**
Web: www.tkelevator.com
SIC: 5084 Elevators
HQ: Tk Elevator Corporation
   788 Cir 75 Pkwy Se # 500
   Atlanta GA
   678 319-3240

(P-5875)
TRI TOOL INC (HQ)
3041 Sunrise Blvd (95742-6502)
PHONE.................................916 288-6100
Christopher M Belle, *CEO*
George J Wernette Iii, *Pr*
Jerri Wernette, *
Chris Soriano, *
▲ **EMP:** 101 **EST:** 1972
SQ FT: 125,000
SALES (est): 74.9MM
SALES (corp-wide): 74.9MM **Privately Held**
Web: www.tritool.com
SIC: 5084 3548 3541 Industrial machinery and equipment; Welding apparatus; Pipe cutting and threading machines
PA: The Wernette Family Limited Partnership Of 1995
   3041 Sunrise Blvd
   Rancho Cordova CA
   916 288-6100

(P-5876)
UNITED MATERIAL HANDLING INC
4160 Temescal Canyon Rd (92883-4615)
PHONE.................................951 657-4900
Ryan Bartlett, *Pr*
Brook Bartlett, *
▲ **EMP:** 61 **EST:** 2011
SALES (est): 23.95MM **Privately Held**
Web: www.unitedmh.com
SIC: 5084 Materials handling machinery

(P-5877)
UNIVERSAL ROBOTS USA INC
101 Pacifica Ste 350 (92618-3330)
PHONE.................................949 230-3642
EMP: 61
SALES (corp-wide): 3.04MM **Privately Held**
Web: www.universal-robots.com
SIC: 5084 Industrial machinery and equipment
PA: Universal Robots Usa Inc
   27175 Haggerty Rd
   Novi MI
   844 462-6268

(P-5878)
VALIN CORPORATION (PA)
Also Called: Valin
5225 Hellyer Ave Ste 250 (95138-1023)
PHONE.................................408 730-9850
Joseph C Nettemeyer, *Pr*
David Hefler, *
John Pregenzer, *
◆ **EMP:** 96 **EST:** 1974
SALES (est): 132.13MM
SALES (corp-wide): 132.13MM **Privately Held**
Web: www.valin.com
SIC: 5084 Materials handling machinery

(P-5879)
VALLEY POWER SYSTEMS INC (PA)
Also Called: John Deere Authorized Dealer
425 S Hacienda Blvd (91745-1123)
PHONE.................................626 333-1243
TOLL FREE: 800
Hampton Clark Lee, *Ch Bd*
Michael Barnett, *Pr*
Robert K Humphryes, *CFO*
Richard Kickliter, *VP*
Bruce Noble, *Marketing*
◆ **EMP:** 100 **EST:** 1949
SQ FT: 49,000
SALES (est): 178.72MM
SALES (corp-wide): 178.72MM **Privately Held**
Web: www.valleypowersystems.com
SIC: 5084 Engines and parts, diesel

(P-5880)
VALLEY POWER SYSTEMS INC
Also Called: Valley Detriot Diesel
4000 Rosedale Hwy (93308-6131)
PHONE.................................661 325-9001
Ken Relyea, *Brnch Mgr*
EMP: 92
SALES (corp-wide): 178.72MM **Privately Held**
Web: www.valleypowersystems.com
SIC: 5084 Engines and parts, diesel
PA: Valley Power Systems, Inc.
   425 S Hacienda Blvd
   City Of Industry CA
   626 333-1243

(P-5881)
VANTAGE ELEVATION LLC
Also Called: Vantage Elevation- Sacramento
6201 Warehouse Way (95826-4909)
PHONE.................................916 426-2347
EMP: 73
SALES (corp-wide): 13.78MM **Privately Held**
Web: www.vantageelevation.com
SIC: 5084 Elevators
PA: Vantage Elevation Llc
   50 E 153rd St
   Bronx NY
   347 226-4558

(P-5882)
WASSCO
Also Called: Wassco Sales
12778 Brookprinter Pl (92064-6810)
P.O. Box 856 (60076-0856)
PHONE.................................858 679-0444
EMP: 106
SIC: 5084 Machine tools and metalworking machinery

(P-5883)
WESTAIR GASES & EQUIPMENT INC
Also Called: Westair Gases & Equipment
3901 Buck Owens Blvd (93308-4927)
PHONE.................................661 387-6800
Steve Castiglione, *Mgr*
EMP: 160
SALES (corp-wide): 100.78MM **Privately Held**
Web: www.westairgases.com
SIC: 5084 Welding machinery and equipment
PA: Westair Gases & Equipment, Inc.
   2505 Congress St
   San Diego CA
   866 937-8247

(P-5884)
WESTERN REFINING INC
2619 S East Ave (93706-5409)
PHONE.................................602 286-1400
EMP: 79
Web: www.wnr.com
SIC: 5084 Metalworking machinery
HQ: Western Refining, Inc.
   212 N Clark Dr
   El Paso TX

(P-5885)
WESTERN REFINING INC
1201 Baker St (92626-3916)
PHONE.................................714 708-2200
EMP: 63
Web: www.wnr.com
SIC: 5084 2911 Metalworking machinery; Petroleum refining
HQ: Western Refining, Inc.
   212 N Clark Dr
   El Paso TX

(P-5886)
WIGGINS LIFT CO INC
2571 Cortez St (93036-1642)
P.O. Box 5187 (93031-5187)
PHONE.................................805 485-7821
Hattie Wiggins, *Ch Bd*
Michael M Wiggins, *
Paul Hurbace, *
Jack Mc Dowell, *General Vice President*
Michelle Mc Dowell, *
◆ **EMP:** 70 **EST:** 1951
SQ FT: 55,000
SALES (est): 20MM **Privately Held**
Web: www.wigginslift.com
SIC: 5084 Materials handling machinery

(P-5887)
YALE/CHASE EQUIPMENT AND SERVICES INC
2615 Pellissier Pl (90601-1508)
P.O. Box 1231 (91749-1231)
PHONE.................................562 463-8000
TOLL FREE: 800
◆ **EMP:** 200
Web: www.papemh.com
SIC: 5084 7699 7359 Lift trucks and parts; Industrial machinery and equipment repair; Industrial truck rental

---

5085 Industrial Supplies

(P-5888)
ALLIED HIGH TECH PRODUCTS INC
16207 Carmenita Rd (90703-2212)
P.O. Box 4608 (90224-4608)
PHONE.................................310 635-2466
Clayton A Smith, *Pr*
Shirley A Smith, *
▲ **EMP:** 70 **EST:** 1983
SQ FT: 34,000
SALES (est): 43.01MM **Privately Held**
Web: www.alliedhightech.com
SIC: 5085 Abrasives

(P-5889)
AMERICAN INDUSTRIAL SOURCE INC
15759 Strathern St Ste 1 (91406-1345)
P.O. Box 8011 (91409-8011)
PHONE.................................800 661-0622
Boris Kofsman, *Pr*
EMP: 90 **EST:** 2005
SALES (est): 8MM **Privately Held**
Web: www.americanindustrialsource.com
SIC: 5085 Industrial supplies

(P-5890)
ARCONIX/USA INC
Also Called: Arconix USA
880 Avenida Acaso Ste 100 (93012-8721)
PHONE.................................805 388-2525
Allen Kay, *Pr*
Mark G Harris, *
John R Danzi, *
Cameron Hill, *
EMP: 106 **EST:** 1948
SALES (est): 2.34MM **Privately Held**
SIC: 5085 Fasteners, industrial: nuts, bolts, screws, etc.
HQ: Penn Engineering & Manufacturing Corp.
   5190 Old Easton Rd
   Danboro PA
   800 237-4736

(P-5891)
BAY STANDARD INC
24485 Marsh Creek Rd (94513-4319)
P.O. Box 801 (94513-0801)
PHONE.................................925 634-1181
Gary W Landgraf, *Pr*
Karen Landgraf, *
Tom Landgraf, *
▲ **EMP:** 100 **EST:** 1966
SALES (est): 15.21MM **Privately Held**
Web: www.baystandard.com
SIC: 5085 3965 Fasteners and fastening equipment; Fasteners

(P-5892)
BDI INC
9917 Gidley St Unit A (91731-1136)
PHONE.................................626 442-8948
EMP: 103
SALES (corp-wide): 1.51B **Privately Held**
Web: www.bdiexpress.com
SIC: 5085 Hydraulic and pneumatic pistons and valves
HQ: Bdi, Inc.
   8000 Hub Pkwy
   Cleveland OH
   216 642-9100

(P-5893)
BEACON ROOFING SUPPLY INC
8501 Telfair Ave (91352-3928)
PHONE.................................818 768-4661
EMP: 60
SALES (corp-wide): 8.43B **Publicly Held**
Web: www.becn.com
SIC: 5085 5169 Industrial supplies; Sealants
PA: Beacon Roofing Supply, Inc.
   505 Huntmar Park Dr # 300
   Herndon VA
   571 323-3939

(P-5894)
CENTRAL PURCHASING LLC (HQ)
Also Called: Harbor Freight Tools
26677 Agoura Rd (91302-1959)
P.O. Box 6010 (93011-6010)
PHONE.................................800 444-3353
Allan Smidt, *
◆ **EMP:** 500 **EST:** 1968
SQ FT: 277,000
SALES (est): 1.85B
SALES (corp-wide): 1.99B **Privately Held**
Web: go.harborfreight.com

5085 - Industrial Supplies (P-5895)

SIC: **5085** 5961 5251 Tools, nec; Tools and hardware, mail order; Tools
PA: Harbor Freight Tools Usa, Inc.
   26677 Agoura Rd
   Calabasas CA
   818 836-5001

(P-5895)
CLOVER ENVMTL SOLUTIONS LLC
Also Called: Color Laser R&D
9414 Eton Ave (91311-5862)
PHONE..............................815 431-8100
EMP: 677
SALES (corp-wide): 173.68MM **Privately Held**
Web: www.cloverimaging.com
SIC: **5085** Ink, printer's
PA: Clover Environmental Solutions Llc
   4200 Columbus St
   Ottawa IL
   866 734-6548

(P-5896)
COLUMBIA SPECIALTY COMPANY INC
Also Called: Plumbing World
5875 Obispo Ave (90805-3715)
PHONE..............................562 634-6425
▲ EMP: 78
Web: www.tristarind.com
SIC: **5085** Valves and fittings

(P-5897)
CURIOSITY INK MEDIA LLC
478 Ellis St (91105-1617)
PHONE..............................561 287-5776
EMP: 127 EST: 2017
SALES (est): 157.49K
SALES (corp-wide): 5.43MM **Publicly Held**
SIC: **5085** Ink, printer's
PA: Grom Social Enterprises, Inc.
   2060 Nw Boca Raton Blvd
   Boca Raton FL
   561 287-5776

(P-5898)
D & D SAW WORKS INC
Also Called: D & D Tool & Supply
1445 Engineer St Ste 110 (92081-8846)
EMP: 126
SIC: **5085** Industrial supplies

(P-5899)
DELTA RUBBER CO INC
2648 Teepee Dr (95205-2419)
PHONE..............................209 948-0511
▲ EMP: 80
SIC: **5085** 3535 3052 Rubber goods, mechanical; Conveyors and conveying equipment; Rubber and plastics hose and beltings

(P-5900)
ENCORE GLASS INC
2925 Cordelia Rd (94534-4224)
PHONE..............................707 745-4444
▲ EMP: 62 EST: 1975
SALES (est): 26.98MM **Privately Held**
Web: www.encoreglass.com
SIC: **5085** Glass bottles

(P-5901)
ERIKS NORTH AMERICA INC
Also Called: Valley Rubber & Gasket
10182 Croydon Way (95827-2102)
PHONE..............................916 366-9340
Les A Shively, CEO
EMP: 98
SALES (corp-wide): 484.16MM **Privately Held**
Web: www.eriksna.com
SIC: **5085** 3053 3052 Hose, belting, and packing; Gaskets; packing and sealing devices; Rubber and plastics hose and beltings
PA: Eriks North America, Inc.
   650 Washington Rd Ste 500
   Pittsburgh PA
   412 787-2400

(P-5902)
FASTENER TECHNOLOGY CORP
7415 Fulton Ave (91605-4116)
PHONE..............................818 764-6467
Dennis Suedkamp, CEO
Thomas Boat, *
EMP: 125 EST: 1979
SQ FT: 24,000
SALES (est): 23.09MM
SALES (corp-wide): 128.24MM **Privately Held**
Web: www.ftc-usa.com
SIC: **5085** 3812 5251 Fasteners, industrial: nuts, bolts, screws, etc.; Aircraft/aerospace flight instruments and guidance systems; Tools
HQ: Avantus Aerospace, Inc.
   29101 The Old Rd
   Valencia CA
   661 295-8620

(P-5903)
GENERAL TOOL INC
Also Called: Gt Diamond
2025 Alton Pkwy (92606-4904)
PHONE..............................949 261-2322
Jae Woo Kim, CEO
▲ EMP: 90 EST: 1984
SQ FT: 40,000
SALES (est): 24.47MM **Privately Held**
Web: www.gtdiamond.com
SIC: **5085** Diamonds, industrial: natural, crude

(P-5904)
HOWMET GLOBL FSTNING SYSTEMS I (HQ)
Also Called: Howmet Fastening Systems
3990a Heritage Oak Ct (93063-6711)
PHONE..............................805 426-2270
Vagner Finelli, Pr
▲ EMP: 120 EST: 1977
SQ FT: 37,000
SALES (est): 1.11B
SALES (corp-wide): 5.66B **Publicly Held**
SIC: **5085** 5072 5065 Fasteners and fastening equipment; Hardware; Electronic parts and equipment, nec
PA: Howmet Aerospace Inc.
   201 Isabella St Ste 200
   Pittsburgh PA
   412 553-1950

(P-5905)
HOWMET GLOBL FSTNING SYSTEMS I
Also Called: Fullerton Operations Plant 1
800 S State College Blvd (92831-5334)
PHONE..............................714 871-1550
Craig Brown, Mgr
EMP: 71
SQ FT: 153,604
SALES (corp-wide): 5.66B **Publicly Held**
Web: www.howmet.com
SIC: **5085** Fasteners and fastening equipment
HQ: Howmet Global Fastening Systems Inc.
   3990a Heritage Oak Ct
   Simi Valley CA
   805 426-2270

(P-5906)
HOWMET GLOBL FSTNING SYSTEMS I
3000 Lomita Blvd (90505-5103)
PHONE..............................310 784-0700
Kenneth Paine, Mgr
EMP: 60
SALES (corp-wide): 5.66B **Publicly Held**
Web: www.howmet.com
SIC: **5085** Fasteners, industrial: nuts, bolts, screws, etc.
HQ: Howmet Global Fastening Systems Inc.
   3990a Heritage Oak Ct
   Simi Valley CA
   805 426-2270

(P-5907)
LONESTAR SIERRA LLC
1820 W Orangewood Ave (92868-2043)
PHONE..............................866 575-5680
EMP: 225 EST: 2016
SALES (est): 19.81MM **Privately Held**
Web: www.lonestarsierra.com
SIC: **5085** Refractory material

(P-5908)
LORD & SONS INC
10504 Pioneer Blvd (90670-3704)
PHONE..............................562 529-2500
Lawrence James, Mgr
EMP: 97
SALES (corp-wide): 355.83K **Privately Held**
Web: www.lordandsons.com
SIC: **5085** Fasteners, industrial: nuts, bolts, screws, etc.
HQ: Lord & Sons, Inc.
   430 E Trimble Rd
   San Jose CA
   408 293-4841

(P-5909)
LOWRYS INC
8501 Telfair Ave (91352-3928)
PHONE..............................818 768-4661
EMP: 60
SIC: **5085** 5169 Industrial supplies; Sealants

(P-5910)
MASTER FASTENERS INTERNATIONAL LLC
Also Called: Fastener Source
724 W Cowles St (90813-1419)
P.O. Box 606 (95632-0606)
PHONE..............................562 279-0150
▲ EMP: 68
SIC: **5085** Fasteners and fastening equipment

(P-5911)
MCMASTER-CARR SUPPLY COMPANY
9630 Norwalk Blvd (90670-2932)
P.O. Box 54960 (90054-0960)
PHONE..............................562 692-5911
EMP: 491
SALES (corp-wide): 621.02MM **Privately Held**
Web: www.mcmaster.com
SIC: **5085** Industrial supplies
PA: Mcmaster-Carr Supply Company
   600 N County Line Rd
   Elmhurst IL
   630 834-9600

(P-5912)
MIDLAND INDUSTRIES
659 E Ball Rd (92805-5910)
PHONE..............................800 821-5725
Vince Hodes, Owner
EMP: 100 EST: 2020
SALES (est): 5.12MM **Privately Held**
SIC: **5085** Valves, pistons, and fittings

(P-5913)
MILLENNIA STAINLESS INC
10016 Romandel Ave (90670-3424)
PHONE..............................562 946-3545
Ching-po Li, CEO
▲ EMP: 75 EST: 1996
SQ FT: 10,500
SALES (est): 23.75MM **Privately Held**
Web: www.millenniastainless.com
SIC: **5085** 5065 5051 Industrial supplies; Coils, electronic; Steel
PA: Chain Chon Industrial Co., Ltd.
   No.178, Ta Guan Rd.,
   Taoyuan City TAY

(P-5914)
MILLS IRON WORKS
14834 S Maple Ave (90248-1936)
PHONE..............................323 321-6520
Jeffrey Griffith, CEO
Kenneth E Berger, *
EMP: 75 EST: 1905
SQ FT: 48,000
SALES (est): 19.56MM **Privately Held**
Web: www.millsiron.com
SIC: **5085** Valves and fittings

(P-5915)
NELSON STUD WELDING INC
Also Called: Automatic Screw Mch Pdts Co
630 E Lambert Rd (92821-4119)
P.O. Box 1608 (35602-1608)
PHONE..............................256 353-1931
Mike Selby, Genl Mgr
EMP: 113
SALES (corp-wide): 16.95B **Publicly Held**
Web: www.stanleyengineeredfastening.com
SIC: **5085** Fasteners, industrial: nuts, bolts, screws, etc.
HQ: Nelson Stud Welding, Inc.
   7900 W Ridge Rd
   Elyria OH
   440 329-0400

(P-5916)
NSK PRECISION AMERICA INC
Also Called: NSK Prcsion Amer Snta Fe Sprng
13921 Bettencourt St (90703-1011)
PHONE..............................562 968-1000
EMP: 84
SIC: **5085** Bearings
HQ: Nsk Precision America, Inc.
   3450 Bearing Dr
   Franklin IN
   317 738-5000

(P-5917)
PACIFIC ECHO INC
23540 Telo Ave (90505-4098)
PHONE..............................310 539-1822
Yasuo Ogami, CEO
▲ EMP: 90 EST: 1967
SQ FT: 110,000
SALES (est): 40.15MM **Privately Held**
Web: www.pacificecho.com
SIC: **5085** Hose, belting, and packing
HQ: Kakuichi Co., Ltd.
   1415, Midoricho, Tsuruga
   Nagano NAG

PRODUCTS & SERVICES SECTION
5087 - Service Establishment Equipment (P-5939)

(P-5918)
PENTACON INC
21123 Nordhoff St (91311-5816)
PHONE..................818 727-8000
EMP: 300
SIC: 5085 5063 Fasteners and fastening equipment; Electrical fittings and construction materials

(P-5919)
POMWONDERFUL LLC
5286 S Del Rey Ave (93616-9700)
P.O. Box 509 (93616-0509)
PHONE..................559 888-8500
Chris Bennett, *Brnch Mgr*
EMP: 79
SALES (corp-wide): 2.04B **Privately Held**
Web: www.pomwonderful.com
SIC: 5085 5148 Bottler supplies; Fruits, fresh
HQ: Pomwonderful Llc
  11444 W Olympic Blvd
  Los Angeles CA
  310 966-5800

(P-5920)
PRECISION FLUID CONTROLS INC
1751 Aviation Blvd Ste 200 (95648)
PHONE..................916 626-3029
Peggy Stevens, *Pr*
EMP: 70 **EST:** 2004
SALES (est): 16.89MM **Privately Held**
Web: www.precisionfluidcontrols.com
SIC: 5085 3728 Valves and fittings; Accumulators, aircraft propeller

(P-5921)
RBC TRANSPORT DYNAMICS CORP
3131 W Segerstrom Ave (92704-5811)
PHONE..................203 267-7001
Michael Harnett, *Pr*
▲ **EMP:** 185 **EST:** 1992
SQ FT: 75,000
SALES (est): 51.24MM
SALES (corp-wide): 1.47B **Publicly Held**
Web: www.rbcbearings.com
SIC: 5085 3728 Bearings; Aircraft assemblies, subassemblies, and parts, nec
HQ: Roller Bearing Company Of America, Inc.
  102 Willenbrock Rd
  Oxford CT
  203 267-7001

(P-5922)
ROPE PARTNER INC
125 Mcpherson St Ste B (95060-5883)
PHONE..................831 460-9448
Eric Stanfield, *Pr*
Chris Bley, *
EMP: 65 **EST:** 2001
SQ FT: 1,900
SALES (est): 9.64MM **Privately Held**
Web: www.ropepartner.com
SIC: 5085 Rope, cord, and thread

(P-5923)
RUTLAND TOOL & SUPPLY CO (HQ)
Also Called: MSC Metalworking
2225 Workman Mill Rd (90601-1437)
PHONE..................562 566-5000
TOLL FREE: 800
Thomas J Neri, *CEO*
Andrew Verey, *
◆ **EMP:** 140 **EST:** 2005
SALES (est): 56.07MM **Publicly Held**
SIC: 5085 5251 Industrial supplies; Tools
PA: Msc Industrial Direct Co., Inc.
  515 Broadhollow Rd # 1000
  Melville NY

(P-5924)
S & S TOOL & SUPPLY INC (HQ)
Also Called: S & S Supplies and Solutions
2700 Maxwell Way (94534-9708)
P.O. Box 1111 (94553-0111)
PHONE..................800 430-8665
Tracy Tomkovicz, *CEO*
Tanya Powell, *
▲ **EMP:** 100 **EST:** 1983
SQ FT: 90,000
SALES (est): 153.23MM
SALES (corp-wide): 950.58MM **Privately Held**
Web: igate2.suppliesandsolutions.com
SIC: 5085 7699 5072 7359 Industrial tools; Industrial equipment services; Hand tools; Equipment rental and leasing, nec
PA: Total Safety U.S., Inc.
  4210 Malone Dr
  Pasadena TX
  713 353-7100

(P-5925)
SO CAL SANDBAGS INC
12620 Bosley Ln (92883-6358)
PHONE..................951 277-3404
Peter Rasinski, *Pr*
EMP: 100 **EST:** 1986
SALES (est): 29.1MM **Privately Held**
Web: www.socalsandbags.com
SIC: 5085 5999 Industrial supplies; Safety supplies and equipment

(P-5926)
SOLAR LINK INTERNATIONAL INC
4652 E Brickell St Ste A (91761-1593)
P.O. Box 56 (91773-0056)
PHONE..................909 605-7789
Chien Hui Liu Eeo, *Prin*
Johnny Tsai, *
▲ **EMP:** 218 **EST:** 1998
SALES (est): 22.43MM **Privately Held**
Web: www.solar-link.com
SIC: 5085 Industrial supplies

(P-5927)
SOUTHERN CALIFORNIA VALVE INC
Also Called: Scv
13903 Maryton Ave (90670-4924)
PHONE..................562 404-2246
◆ **EMP:** 70 **EST:** 1972
SALES (est): 15.91MM **Privately Held**
SIC: 5085 Valves and fittings

(P-5928)
SPS TECHNOLOGIES LLC
Shur-Lok Company
2541 White Rd (92614-6235)
PHONE..................949 474-6000
Damian Moreau, *Mgr*
EMP: 422
SALES (corp-wide): 302.09B **Publicly Held**
Web: www.shur-lok.com
SIC: 5085 Fasteners, industrial: nuts, bolts, screws, etc.
HQ: Sps Technologies, Llc
  301 Highland Ave
  Jenkintown PA
  215 572-3000

(P-5929)
SPS TECHNOLOGIES LLC
Also Called: Pb Fasteners
1700 W 132nd St (90249-2008)
PHONE..................310 323-6222
EMP: 260
SALES (corp-wide): 302.09B **Publicly Held**
Web: www.pccfasteners.com
SIC: 5085 Fasteners, industrial: nuts, bolts, screws, etc.
HQ: Sps Technologies, Llc
  301 Highland Ave
  Jenkintown PA
  215 572-3000

(P-5930)
TEN DAYS MANUFACTURING
Also Called: Daily Manufacturing
1615 Yeager Ave (91750-5854)
PHONE..................888 222-1575
Mohammed Shabeer Humkar, *CEO*
EMP: 103 **EST:** 2020
SALES (est): 9.83MM **Privately Held**
SIC: 5085 Plastic bottles

(P-5931)
TITAN NEWMAN INC
Also Called: Newman Flange & Fitting Co
1649 L St (95360-1048)
P.O. Box 905 (95360-0905)
PHONE..................209 862-2977
Samuel Liebelt, *Pr*
Helmut Liebelt, *
Penny Mello, *BOARD**
◆ **EMP:** 70 **EST:** 1974
SQ FT: 1,800
SALES (est): 17.79MM **Privately Held**
Web: www.newmanflange.com
SIC: 5085 Valves and fittings

(P-5932)
TRISTAR INDUSTRIAL LLC
Also Called: Columbia Spclty A Trstar Indus
5875 Obispo Ave (90805-3715)
PHONE..................562 634-6425
Michael Taylor, *Brnch Mgr*
EMP: 78
Web: www.tristarind.com
SIC: 5085 Valves and fittings
PA: Tristar Industrial, Llc
  1645 W Buckeye Rd
  Phoenix AZ

(P-5933)
TSC AUTO ID TECHNOLOGY AMERICA (HQ)
3040 Saturn St Ste 200 (92821-6231)
PHONE..................909 468-0100
Hank Wang, *Pr*
▲ **EMP:** 120 **EST:** 2008
SALES (est): 21.93MM **Privately Held**
SIC: 5085 Ink, printer's
PA: Tsc Auto Id Technology Co.,Ltd.
  9f, No. 95, Minquan Rd.
  New Taipei City TAP

(P-5934)
VALLEY RUBBER & GASKET COMPANY INC
Also Called: Lewisgoetz
10182 Croydon Way (95827-2102)
PHONE..................916 369-8885
▲ **EMP:** 98
SIC: 5085 3053 3052 Hose, belting, and packing; Gaskets; packing and sealing devices; Rubber and plastics hose and beltings

5087 Service Establishment Equipment

(P-5935)
AMERICAN SANITARY SUPPLY INC
3800 E Miraloma Ave (92806-2108)
P.O. Box 6436 (92816-0436)
PHONE..................714 632-3010
Luis Salazar, *CEO*
Silvia Salazar, *
▲ **EMP:** 75 **EST:** 1983
SQ FT: 20,000
SALES (est): 21.77MM **Privately Held**
Web: www.amersan.com
SIC: 5087 Janitors' supplies

(P-5936)
CHIRO INC (PA)
Also Called: Mr Clean Maintenance Systems
2260 S Vista Ave (92316-2908)
P.O. Box 31 (92324-0031)
PHONE..................909 879-1160
Arthur Rose, *Pr*
Timothy Russell, *
EMP: 130 **EST:** 1980
SQ FT: 10,000
SALES (est): 47.97MM
SALES (corp-wide): 47.97MM **Privately Held**
Web: www.mrcleansystems.com
SIC: 5087 7349 5169 Cleaning and maintenance equipment and supplies; Cleaning service, industrial or commercial; Chemicals and allied products, nec

(P-5937)
CSE HOLDINGS INC
650 Brennan St (95131-1204)
P.O. Box 105843 (30348-5843)
PHONE..................408 436-1907
TOLL FREE: 800
▲ **EMP:** 250
SIC: 5087 5084 7699 5113 Janitors' supplies; Cleaning equipment, high pressure, sand or steam; Industrial machinery and equipment repair; Industrial and personal service paper

(P-5938)
ETTORE PRODUCTS CO
Also Called: Ettore
2100 N Loop Rd (94502-8010)
P.O. Box 2164 (94621-0064)
PHONE..................510 748-4130
Michael A Smahlik, *CEO*
Diane Smahlik, *
▲ **EMP:** 65 **EST:** 1958
SQ FT: 30,000
SALES (est): 23.93MM **Privately Held**
Web: www.ettore.com
SIC: 5087 Janitors' supplies

(P-5939)
GLAMOUR INDUSTRIES CO
100 Wilshire Blvd Ste 700 (90401-3602)
PHONE..................213 687-8600
EMP: 100
SALES (corp-wide): 110.3MM **Privately Held**
Web: www.aiibeauty.com
SIC: 5087 Beauty parlor equipment and supplies
PA: Glamour Industries, Co.
  2220 Gaspar Ave
  Commerce CA
  323 728-2999

5087 - Service Establishment Equipment (P-5940)

(P-5940)
HAAKER EQUIPMENT COMPANY (PA)
Also Called: Total Clean
2070 N White Ave (91750-5679)
PHONE..............................909 598-2706
Robin Haaker, Pr
▼ EMP: 60 EST: 1972
SQ FT: 50,000
SALES (est): 28.38MM
SALES (corp-wide): 28.38MM **Privately Held**
Web: www.haaker.com
SIC: **5087** 5999 Cleaning and maintenance equipment and supplies; Cleaning equipment and supplies

(P-5941)
HD SUPPLY FACILITIES MAINT LTD
21651 Baker Pkwy (91789-5235)
PHONE..............................909 594-3843
Mary Sullivan, Brnch Mgr
EMP: 62
SALES (corp-wide): 157.4B **Publicly Held**
Web: www.hdsupplysolutions.com
SIC: **5087** Cleaning and maintenance equipment and supplies
HQ: Hd Supply Facilities Maintenance, Ltd.
3400 Cumberland Blvd Se
Atlanta GA
770 852-9000

(P-5942)
HD SUPPLY FACILITIES MAINT LTD
2754 W Winton Ave (94545-1120)
PHONE..............................510 783-4019
EMP: 72
SALES (corp-wide): 157.4B **Publicly Held**
Web: www.hdsupplysolutions.com
SIC: **5087** Cleaning and maintenance equipment and supplies
HQ: Hd Supply Facilities Maintenance, Ltd.
3400 Cumberland Blvd Se
Atlanta GA
770 852-9000

(P-5943)
HYDRO TEK SYSTEMS INC
Also Called: Hydro Tek
2353 Almond Ave (92374-2035)
PHONE..............................909 799-9222
TOLL FREE: 800
John S Koen, Pr
Andrea S Koen, *
◆ EMP: 63 EST: 1985
SQ FT: 45,000
SALES (est): 19.71MM
SALES (corp-wide): 1.11B **Privately Held**
Web: www.hydrotek.us
SIC: **5087** 3589 5084 Service establishment equipment; Commercial cleaning equipment; Industrial machinery and equipment
HQ: Nilfisk A/S
Marmorvej 8
Kobenhavn O
43238100

(P-5944)
LN CURTIS AND SONS (PA)
Also Called: Curtis
185 Lennon Ln # 110 (94598-2422)
P.O. Box 60000 (94160-0001)
PHONE..............................510 839-5111
Paul F Curtis Cffo, Prin
Paul F Curtis, CFO
Tim Henderson, *
John Viboch, *
Roger Curtis, *
▲ EMP: 65 EST: 1929
SQ FT: 25,000
SALES (est): 138.14MM
SALES (corp-wide): 138.14MM **Privately Held**
Web: www.lncurtis.com
SIC: **5087** 5099 Firefighting equipment; Safety equipment and supplies

(P-5945)
MAINTEX INC
13575 Gregg St (92064-7136)
PHONE..............................858 513-8286
Rich Russel, Mgr
EMP: 61
SQ FT: 21,729
SALES (corp-wide): 35.04MM **Privately Held**
Web: www.maintex.com
SIC: **5087** Janitors' supplies
PA: Maintex, Inc.
13300 Nelson Ave
City Of Industry CA
800 446-1888

(P-5946)
MALYS OF CALIFORNIA INC
28145 Harrison Pkwy (91355-4165)
PHONE..............................661 295-8317
EMP: 500
SIC: **5087** Barber shop equipment and supplies

(P-5947)
NIKKEN GLOBAL INC (HQ)
18301 Von Karman Ave Ste 120 (92612-1009)
PHONE..............................949 789-2000
Tom Toshizo Watanabe, Ch Bd
Kendall Cho, *
▲ EMP: 155 EST: 1996
SALES (est): 92.01MM **Privately Held**
SIC: **5087** 5023 5013 5122 Stress reducing equipment, electric; Bedspreads; Seat covers; Vitamins and minerals
PA: Nikken International, Inc.
18301 Von Karman Ave
Irvine CA

(P-5948)
SPILO WORLDWIDE INC
Also Called: Spilo Worldwide
100 Wilshire Blvd Ste 700 (90401-3602)
PHONE..............................213 687-8600
Marc Spilo, CEO
◆ EMP: 100 EST: 1977
SALES (est): 9.65MM
SALES (corp-wide): 1.56B **Publicly Held**
SIC: **5087** Beauty parlor equipment and supplies
PA: Enovis Corporation
2711 Centerville Rd # 400
Wilmington DE
301 252-9160

(P-5949)
SWEIS INC (PA)
20000 Mariner Ave (90503-7140)
PHONE..............................310 375-0558
EMP: 70 EST: 2000
SALES (est): 23.12MM **Privately Held**
Web: www.sweisinc.com
SIC: **5087** 2844 Beauty parlor equipment and supplies; Hair preparations, including shampoos

(P-5950)
UNITED FABRICARE SUPPLY INC (PA)
1237 W Walnut St (90220-5009)
P.O. Box 1796 (90001-0796)
PHONE..............................310 537-2096
Steve S Hong, CEO
W David Weimer, *
Hae S Hong, *
Mike Fahar, *
Kirby Schnebly, *
▲ EMP: 75 EST: 1946
SQ FT: 50,000
SALES (est): 33.62MM
SALES (corp-wide): 33.62MM **Privately Held**
Web: www.unitedfabricaresupply.com
SIC: **5087** Laundry equipment and supplies

(P-5951)
WAXIES ENTERPRISES LLC
Also Called: Waxie
905 Wineville Ave (91764-8508)
P.O. Box 5926 (92412)
PHONE..............................909 942-3100
Jeff Roberts, Brnch Mgr
EMP: 60
Web: info.waxie.com
SIC: **5087** Janitors' supplies
HQ: Waxie's Enterprises, Llc
9353 Waxie Way
San Diego CA
800 995-4466

(P-5952)
WAXIES ENTERPRISES LLC (DH)
Also Called: Waxie Sanitary Supply
9353 Waxie Way (92123-1350)
P.O. Box 60227 (90060-0227)
PHONE..............................800 995-4466
TOLL FREE: 800
EMP: 140 EST: 1945
SALES (est): 250.63MM **Privately Held**
Web: info.waxie.com
SIC: **5087** Janitors' supplies
HQ: Envoy Solutions, Llc
2101 Claire Ct
Glenview IL
847 832-4000

(P-5953)
WEST COAST BEAUTY SUPPLY CO
5001 Industrial Way (94510-1017)
PHONE..............................707 748-4800
TOLL FREE: 800
▲ EMP: 1000
SIC: **5087** 3069 Beauty parlor equipment and supplies; Capes, vulcanized rubber or rubberized fabric

5088 Transportation Equipment And Supplies

(P-5954)
AIREY ENTERPRISES LLC
Also Called: A Transportation
5530 Corbin Ave Ste 325 (91356-6037)
P.O. Box 17328 (91416-7328)
PHONE..............................818 530-3362
EMP: 160 EST: 2015
SALES (est): 10.01MM **Privately Held**
SIC: **5088** Transportation equipment and supplies

(P-5955)
APICAL INDUSTRIES INC
Also Called: Dart Aerospace
3030 Enterprise Ct Ste A (92081-8358)
PHONE..............................760 724-5300
Alain Madore, CEO
EMP: 100 EST: 1995
SQ FT: 30,000
SALES (est): 35.53MM
SALES (corp-wide): 6.58B **Publicly Held**
Web: www.apicalindustries.com
SIC: **5088** 3728 Helicopter parts; Aircraft landing assemblies and brakes
HQ: Dart Aerospace Company
9900 Boul Cavendish Suite 310
Saint-Laurent QC
514 907-5959

(P-5956)
COM DEV USA LLC
2333 Utah Ave (90245-4818)
PHONE..............................424 456-8000
EMP: 100
Web: www.comdev-usa.com
SIC: **5088** 3679 Aircraft equipment and supplies, nec; Microwave components

(P-5957)
FALCON AEROSPACE HOLDINGS LLC
Also Called: Wesco Aircraft
27727 Avenue Scott (91355-1219)
PHONE..............................661 775-7200
Randy J Snyder, Ch Bd
Gregory A Hann, *
Tommy Lee, *
EMP: 1250 EST: 2006
SALES (est): 221.89MM **Privately Held**
Web: www.incora.com
SIC: **5088** Aircraft and parts, nec

(P-5958)
INTEGRATED PROCUREMENT TECH (PA)
Also Called: Ipt
7230 Hollister Ave (93117-2807)
PHONE..............................805 682-0842
◆ EMP: 85 EST: 1996
SQ FT: 26,000
SALES (est): 82.14MM **Privately Held**
Web: www.iptsb.com
SIC: **5088** 5065 Aircraft and parts, nec; Communication equipment

(P-5959)
JCM ENGINEERING CORP
2690 E Cedar St (91761-8533)
PHONE..............................909 923-3730
Robert Schenkkan, Pr
Myrna Lamar, *
Ken Safford, *
EMP: 85 EST: 1979
SQ FT: 140,000
SALES (est): 23.33MM **Privately Held**
Web: www.jcmcorp.com
SIC: **5088** Aeronautical equipment and supplies

(P-5960)
KETTENBURG MARINE CORPORATION
2810 Carleton St (92106-2792)
P.O. Box 6448 (92166-0448)
PHONE..............................619 224-8211
Tom Fetter, Pr
Jane T Fetter, *
▼ EMP: 140 EST: 1919
SQ FT: 30,000
SALES (est): 12.93MM **Privately Held**
SIC: **5088** 7699 Marine supplies; Boat repair

(P-5961)
LJ WALCH CO INC
6600 Preston Ave (94551-5132)
P.O. Box 2798 (94551-2798)
PHONE..............................925 449-9252

PRODUCTS & SERVICES SECTION

5091 - Sporting And Recreation Goods (P-5981)

Ron Luty, CEO
Tony Ippolito, *
Tom Walch, *
Mark Nelson, *
Bill Luty, Supply Vice President*
▲ EMP: 60 EST: 1953
SQ FT: 38,500
SALES (est): 24.97MM Privately Held
Web: www.ljwalch.com
SIC: 5088 7629 Aircraft and parts, nec; Aircraft electrical equipment repair

(P-5962)
LOGISTICAL SUPPORT LLC
20409 Prairie St (91311-6029)
PHONE..................818 341-3344
Joseph Lucan, *
Jerry Hill, *
EMP: 120 EST: 1997
SQ FT: 14,600
SALES (est): 22.07MM
SALES (corp-wide): 35.16MM Privately Held
Web: www.rtcaerospace.com
SIC: 5088 Aircraft and parts, nec
PA: Rtc Aerospace Llc
 7215 45th Street Ct E
 Fife WA
 918 407-0291

(P-5963)
ONTIC ENGINEERING AND MFG INC (PA)
20400 Plummer St (91311-5372)
P.O. Box 2424 (91313-2424)
PHONE..................818 678-6555
Gareth Hall, CEO
Greth Hall, CEO
Peg Billson, Pr
EMP: 95 EST: 1986
SQ FT: 54,000
SALES (est): 450.6MM
SALES (corp-wide): 450.6MM Privately Held
Web: www.ontic.com
SIC: 5088 3728 3812 3563 Aircraft equipment and supplies, nec; Aircraft parts and equipment, nec; Search and navigation equipment; Air and gas compressors

(P-5964)
PACIFIC AEROSPACE RESOURCES & TECHNOLOGIES LLC
18284 Readiness St (92394-7947)
▲ EMP: 62
Web: www.pacificaerospacegroup.com
SIC: 5088 Aircraft equipment and supplies, nec

(P-5965)
PROPONENT INC (PA)
Also Called: Proponent
3120 Enterprise St (92821-6236)
PHONE..................714 223-5400
Andrew Todhunter, Pr
Steven Frields, *
Corey Yarnell, *
▲ EMP: 175 EST: 1972
SALES (est): 127.06MM
SALES (corp-wide): 127.06MM Privately Held
Web: www.proponent.com
SIC: 5088 3728 Aircraft and parts, nec; Aircraft parts and equipment, nec

(P-5966)
RAYTHEON LGSTICS SPPORT TRNING
2000 E El Segundo Blvd (90245-4501)
PHONE..................310 647-9438
EMP: 337
SALES (corp-wide): 67.07B Publicly Held
SIC: 5088 Aeronautical equipment and supplies
HQ: Raytheon Logistics Support & Training Company
 180 Hartwell Rd
 Bedford MA
 310 647-9438

(P-5967)
REGENT AEROSPACE CORPORATION (PA)
Also Called: Regent
28110 Harrison Pkwy (91355-4109)
PHONE..................661 257-3000
Reza Soltanianzadeh, CEO
Reza Soltanian, *
Tim Garvin, *
▲ EMP: 200 EST: 1993
SQ FT: 90,000
SALES (est): 100.28MM Privately Held
Web: www.regentaerospace.com
SIC: 5088 3728 Aircraft and parts, nec; Aircraft parts and equipment, nec

(P-5968)
SHIMADZU PRECISION INSTRS INC (DH)
Also Called: Shimadzu Medical Systems USA
3645 N Lakewood Blvd (90808-1797)
PHONE..................562 420-6226
Takashi Ishii, CEO
Tina Kang, CFO
Tsuyosh Hirai, Sec
▲ EMP: 70 EST: 1979
SQ FT: 60,000
SALES (est): 98.03MM Privately Held
Web: www.spi-inc.com
SIC: 5088 5047 5084 Aircraft equipment and supplies, nec; Medical equipment and supplies; Industrial machinery and equipment
HQ: Shimadzu America, Inc.
 7102 Riverwood Dr
 Columbia MD

(P-5969)
SVENDSENS BOAT WORKS INC
Also Called: Svendsen Marine Distributing
2900 Main St Ste 1900 (94501-7265)
PHONE..................510 522-2886
▲ EMP: 70 EST: 1963
SALES (est): 23.46MM
SALES (corp-wide): 23.46MM Privately Held
Web: www.svendsens.com
SIC: 5088 5551 3732 Marine supplies; Marine supplies, nec; Sailboats, building and repairing
PA: Bay Maritime Corp
 2900 Main St Ste 2100
 Alameda CA
 510 337-9122

(P-5970)
UNITED STATES MARINE CORPS
Also Called: Marine Aviation Logistics
Marine Corps Air Stn Bldg 23122 (Camp Pendleton) (92049)
PHONE..................760 725-3564
EMP: 100
Web: www.marines.mil
SIC: 5088 9711 Marine supplies; Marine Corps
HQ: United States Marine Corps
 Branch Hlth Clnic Bldg 5
 Beaufort SC

(P-5971)
WESCO AIRCRAFT HARDWARE CORP
27727 Avenue Scott (91355-3909)
PHONE..................661 775-7200
Steve Halford, Brnch Mgr
EMP: 400
SALES (corp-wide): 1.7B Privately Held
Web: www.incora.com
SIC: 5088 Aircraft and parts, nec
HQ: Wesco Aircraft Hardware Corp.
 2601 Meacham Blvd Ste 400
 Fort Worth TX
 817 284-4449

5091 Sporting And Recreation Goods

(P-5972)
AFTCO MFG CO INC
Also Called: Bluewater Wear
2400 S Garnsey St (92707-3335)
PHONE..................949 660-8757
William D Shedd, CEO
Casey Shedd, *
Cody Shedd, *
◆ EMP: 75 EST: 1957
SQ FT: 24,000
SALES (est): 26.72MM Privately Held
Web: www.aftco.com
SIC: 5091 Fishing tackle

(P-5973)
BIKES ONLINE INC
2711 Loker Ave W (92010-6601)
PHONE..................650 272-3378
Andre Batista, Dir Opers
EMP: 95 EST: 2019
SALES (est): 9.96MM Privately Held
Web: www.bikesonline.com
SIC: 5091 Bicycles

(P-5974)
CHEM QUIP INC
Also Called: White House Sales
2551 Land Ave (95815-2363)
PHONE..................800 821-1678
Don Aston, CEO
Greg Durkee, *
Steve Hubbard, *
Brain Long, *
EMP: 62 EST: 1961
SQ FT: 20,000
SALES (est): 11.52MM Privately Held
Web: www.poolcorp.com
SIC: 5091 5169 Swimming pools, equipment and supplies; Chlorine

(P-5975)
CREATIVE RECRTL SYSTEMS INC
2377 Gold Meadow Way Ste 100 (95670-4405)
PHONE..................916 638-5375
Paul Stanfel, CEO
EMP: 67 EST: 1972
SALES (est): 8.83MM Privately Held
Web: www.creativesystems.com
SIC: 5091 Sporting and recreation goods

(P-5976)
DAIWA CORPORATION
Also Called: Daiwa Golf Company Division
20155 Ellipse (92610-3002)
P.O. Box 6600 (90630-0066)
PHONE..................562 375-6800
Carey Graves, Pr
Tomoaki Komatsu, *
Tad Suzuki, *
Cynthia Young, *
William Steiner, *
◆ EMP: 65 EST: 1966
SALES (est): 26.61MM Privately Held
Web: www.daiwa.us
SIC: 5091 Fishing tackle
PA: Globeride, Inc.
 3-14-16, Maesawa
 Higashi Kurume TKY

(P-5977)
EASTON DIAMOND SPORTS LLC
3500 Willow Ln (91361-4921)
PHONE..................800 632-7866
Ed Kinnaly, CEO
EMP: 100 EST: 2017
SALES (est): 20.36MM Privately Held
Web: easton.rawlings.com
SIC: 5091 Sporting and recreation goods

(P-5978)
INTER VALLEY POOL SUPPLY INC
Also Called: Intervalley Pools
1415 E 3rd St (91766-2241)
PHONE..................626 969-5657
John A Fry, Pr
EMP: 60 EST: 1985
SQ FT: 23,000
SALES (est): 10.76MM
SALES (corp-wide): 149.04MM Privately Held
SIC: 5091 5963 Swimming pools, equipment and supplies; Bottled water delivery
PA: Hasa, Inc.
 23119 Drayton St
 Saugus CA
 661 259-5848

(P-5979)
INTEX PROPERTIES S BAY CORP (PA)
4001 Via Oro Ave Ste 210 (90810-1400)
PHONE..................310 549-5400
Tien P Zee, Pr
◆ EMP: 108 EST: 1970
SQ FT: 80,000
SALES (est): 91.03MM
SALES (corp-wide): 91.03MM Privately Held
Web: www.intexcorp.com
SIC: 5091 5092 5021 3081 Watersports equipment and supplies; Toys, nec; Waterbeds; Vinyl film and sheet

(P-5980)
SHIMANO NORTH AMER HOLDG INC (HQ)
Also Called: Shimano North America Bicycle
1 Holland (92618-2506)
PHONE..................949 951-5003
Hiroshi Matsui, CEO
Jim Lafrance, *
Gerriet O'neill, Contrlr
▲ EMP: 150 EST: 1986
SQ FT: 122,000
SALES (est): 91.38MM Privately Held
SIC: 5091 Bicycle parts and accessories
PA: Shimano Inc.
 77, 3cho, Oimatsucho, Sakai-K
 Sakai OSK

(P-5981)
SPECIALIZED BICYCLE COMPONENTS HOLDING COMPANY INC (PA)
15130 Concord Cir (95037-5428)
PHONE..................408 779-6229

(PA)=Parent Co (HQ)=Headquarters
◆ = New Business established in last 2 years

5091 - Sporting And Recreation Goods (P-5982)

◆ EMP: 300 EST: 1974
SALES (est): 524.96MM
SALES (corp-wide): 524.96MM Privately Held
Web: www.specialized.com
SIC: 5091 Bicycle equipment and supplies

(P-5982)
TITAN MFG & DISTRG INC
480 E North Ave Ste 101 (93706-5466)
PHONE..................................559 475-0882
EMP: 65
SALES (corp-wide): 32.52MM Privately Held
Web: www.titangreatoutdoors.com
SIC: 5091 5961 Fitness equipment and supplies; Electronic shopping
PA: Titan Manufacturing And Distributing, Inc.
3839 Frest Hl Irene Rd St
Memphis TN
901 850-1500

(P-5983)
TROY LEE DESIGNS LLC (DH)
155 E Rincon St (92879-1328)
PHONE..................................951 371-5219
Jason William Steris, *CEO*
▲ EMP: 79 EST: 1981
SQ FT: 6,000
SALES (est): 42.06MM
SALES (corp-wide): 857.59K Privately Held
Web: www.troyleedesigns.com
SIC: 5091 7336 Sporting and recreation goods; Graphic arts and related design
HQ: 2 Ride Holding
Zac De La Valentine
*Marseille

5092 Toys And Hobby Goods And Supplies

(P-5984)
2K GAMES INC
10 Hamilton Landing (94949-8207)
EMP: 172 EST: 2004
SALES (est): 19.7MM Publicly Held
Web: www.2k.com
SIC: 5092 Video games
PA: Take-Two Interactive Software, Inc.
110 W 44th St
New York NY

(P-5985)
AURORA WORLD INC
Also Called: Aurora
8820 Mercury Ln (90660-6706)
PHONE..................................562 205-1222
TOLL FREE: 800
Heui-yul Noh, *CEO*
Kee Sun Hong, *
◆ EMP: 110 EST: 1991
SQ FT: 100,000
SALES (est): 49.38MM Privately Held
Web: www.auroragift.com
SIC: 5092 Toys, nec
PA: Aurora World Corporation
624 Teheran-Ro, Gangnam-Gu
Seoul

(P-5986)
BANDAI NAMCO ENTRMT AMER INC
Also Called: Ndga
23 Odyssey (92618-3144)
PHONE..................................408 235-2000
Naoki Katashima, *CEO*
Masaaki Tsuji, *
Graeme Bayless, *
Shuji Nakata, *
Hide Irie, *
▲ EMP: 200 EST: 1990
SQ FT: 51,118
SALES (est): 96.33MM Privately Held
Web: www.bandainamcoent.com
SIC: 5092 Video games
HQ: Bandai Namco Holdings Usa Inc.
2120 Park Pl Ste 120
El Segundo CA

(P-5987)
CAPCOM ENTERTAINMENT INC
Also Called: Capcom U.S.a
185 Berry St (94107-5705)
PHONE..................................650 350-6500
Kazuhiro Abe, *CEO*
Hiroshi Tobisawa, *
Mark Beaumont, *NORTH AMERICA EUROPE*
▲ EMP: 80 EST: 1995
SALES (est): 50.34MM Privately Held
Web: www.capcom.com
SIC: 5092 Video games
HQ: Capcom U.S.A. Inc
185 Berry St Ste 1200
San Francisco CA
650 350-6500

(P-5988)
CAPCOM U S A INC (HQ)
185 Berry St Ste 1200 (94107-1794)
PHONE..................................650 350-6500
Koko Ishikawa, *Pr*
Rob Dyer, *
▲ EMP: 180 EST: 1985
SALES (est): 94.19MM Privately Held
Web: news.capcomusa.com
SIC: 5092 7993 7372 Video games; Arcades; Prepackaged software
PA: Capcom Co., Ltd.
3-1-3, Uchihiranomachi, Chuo-Ku
Osaka OSK

(P-5989)
DELTA CREATIVE INC
2690 Pellissier Pl (90601-1507)
PHONE..................................800 423-4135
William B George, *Pr*
Alexander Ritchie, *
Martina Mueller, *
▲ EMP: 105 EST: 1974
SQ FT: 112,000
SALES (est): 29.21MM Privately Held
Web: www.plaidonline.com
SIC: 5092 5198 Arts and crafts equipment and supplies; Paints
HQ: Dk Household Brands Holding Ag
Muhlebachstrasse 20
ZUrich ZH

(P-5990)
FAO ROC HOLDINGS LLC
Also Called: Fao Schwarz
7755 Irvine Center Dr Ste 100 (92618-2903)
PHONE..................................949 900-6501
David Conn, *CEO*
David Niggli, *CMO*
Robert Tuscano, *VP Opers*
EMP: 170 EST: 2017
SALES (est): 14.62MM Privately Held
SIC: 5092 7371 Toys and hobby goods and supplies; Computer software development and applications

(P-5991)
ME & MY BIG IDEAS LLC
Also Called: Happy Planner, The
6261 Katella Ave (90630-5249)
PHONE..................................240 348-5240
Tom Shaw, *CEO*
Stephanie Rahmatulla, *
▲ EMP: 101 EST: 1998
SALES (est): 26.31MM Privately Held
Web: www.thehappyplanner.com
SIC: 5092 Arts and crafts equipment and supplies

(P-5992)
MERCHSOURCE LLC (DH)
Also Called: Threesixty Group
7755 Irvine Center Dr (92618-2903)
PHONE..................................800 374-2744
Johann Clapp, *Managing Member*
Mike Roberts, *
◆ EMP: 115 EST: 2011
SALES (est): 97.9MM
SALES (corp-wide): 1.44MM Privately Held
Web: www.merchsource.com
SIC: 5092 Toys and hobby goods and supplies
HQ: Threesixty Group Limited
28/F Harbourside Hq
Kowloon Bay KLN

(P-5993)
MGA ENTERTAINMENT INC
9220 Winnetka Ave (91311-8172)
PHONE..................................800 222-4685
Isaac Larian, *CEO*
Steve Schultz, *
Elizabeth Risha, *
◆ EMP: 2100 EST: 1980
SALES (est): 310.11MM Privately Held
SIC: 5092 Toys, nec

(P-5994)
PAISLEY CRAFTS LLC
Also Called: Ilovetocreate
5673 E Shields Ave (93727-7819)
PHONE..................................559 291-4444
Larry Hermansen, *Pr*
EMP: 130 EST: 2021
SALES (est): 31.91MM
SALES (corp-wide): 445.67MM Privately Held
SIC: 5092 Arts and crafts equipment and supplies
HQ: Plaid Enterprises, Inc.
3225 Westech Dr
Norcross GA

(P-5995)
RN CHIDAKASHI TECHNOLOGIES INC
Also Called: Miko
6200 Stoneridge Mall Rd Ste 300 (94588)
PHONE..................................415 687-6145
Sneh Vaswani, *CEO*
Rakesh Kakaya, *CSO*
EMP: 150 EST: 2019
SALES (est): 66.63MM Privately Held
Web: www.miko.ai
SIC: 5092 Toys and games
PA: Rn Chidakashi Technologies Private Limited
Flat No 4, Stambhtirth Building,
Mumbai MH

(P-5996)
SEGA OF AMERICA INC
250 E Olive Ave Ste 200 (91502-1211)
PHONE..................................747 477-3708
EMP: 270
Web: www.sega.com
SIC: 5092 Video games
HQ: Sega Of America, Inc.

140 Progress Ste 100
Irvine CA
949 788-0455

(P-5997)
SMC PRODUCTS INC
Also Called: Hpi Racing
22651 Lambert St Ste 105 (92630-1611)
PHONE..................................949 753-1099
▲ EMP: 68
SIC: 5092 3944 Toys and hobby goods and supplies; Electronic toys

(P-5998)
SONY INTERACTIVE ENTERTAINMENT AMERICA LLC
Also Called: Sony Computer Entrmt Amer
2207 Bridgepointe Pkwy (94404-5060)
P.O. Box 5888 (94402-5888)
PHONE..................................650 655-8000
▲ EMP: 1500
Web: www.playstation.com
SIC: 5092 Video games

(P-5999)
SUPER7 RETAIL INC
Also Called: Super7
777 Florida St Ste 202 (94110-2025)
PHONE..................................415 374-7190
Brian Flynn, *Pr*
EMP: 78 EST: 2018
SALES (est): 7.78MM Privately Held
Web: www.super7.com
SIC: 5092 Toys and hobby goods and supplies

(P-6000)
ULTRA PRO INTERNATIONAL LLC
Also Called: Jolly Roger Games
6049 E Slauson Ave (90040-3007)
PHONE..................................323 890-2100
Marc Lieberman, *
Herman Lee, *
▲ EMP: 122 EST: 2011
SALES (est): 53.46MM Privately Held
Web: www.ultrapro.com
SIC: 5092 3944 Toys and hobby goods and supplies; Games, toys, and children's vehicles

(P-6001)
VICTORY INTL GROUP LLC
Also Called: M Z J
14748 Pipeline Ave Ste B (91709-6024)
PHONE..................................949 407-5888
Dawson Fan, *Pr*
▲ EMP: 230 EST: 2001
SQ FT: 4,960
SALES (est): 896MM Privately Held
Web: www.victoryintlgroup.com
SIC: 5092 3843 2389 3842 Toys and hobby goods and supplies; Dental equipment and supplies; Hospital gowns; Respiratory protection equipment, personal

5093 Scrap And Waste Materials

(P-6002)
AADLEN BROS AUTO WRECKING INC (PA)
11590 Tuxford St (91352-3186)
PHONE..................................323 875-1400
Sam Adlen, *Pr*
Samuel Lewinstein, *
EMP: 79 EST: 1951
SALES (est): 4.05MM

PRODUCTS & SERVICES SECTION

5094 - Jewelry And Precious Stones (P-6023)

SALES (corp-wide): 4.05MM **Privately Held**
Web: www.aadlenbros.com
SIC: **5093** Metal scrap and waste materials

(P-6003)
ADAMS INTERNATIONAL MTLS CORP
3200 E Frontera St (92806-2822)
P.O. Box 6258 (92816-0258)
PHONE..................714 630-8901
George Adams Senior, *Ch Bd*
EMP: 60 **EST:** 1987
SALES (est): 3.62MM **Privately Held**
SIC: **5093** Ferrous metal scrap and waste

(P-6004)
ALCO IRON & METAL CO (PA)
2140 Davis St (94577-2202)
PHONE..................510 562-1107
Kem Kantor, *Pr*
Kevin Kantor, *
Keith Kantor, *
Tony Nam, *
◆ **EMP:** 100 **EST:** 1955
SQ FT: 35,000
SALES (est): 59.47MM
SALES (corp-wide): 59.47MM **Privately Held**
Web: www.alcometals.com
SIC: **5093** 5051 Metal scrap and waste materials; Steel

(P-6005)
CASS INC (PA)
2730 Peralta St (94607-1707)
P.O. Box 24222 (94623-1222)
PHONE..................510 893-6476
Edward B Kangeter Iv, *CEO*
Chal Sulprizio, *
◆ **EMP:** 60 **EST:** 1973
SQ FT: 20,000
SALES (est): 48.26MM
SALES (corp-wide): 48.26MM **Privately Held**
Web: www.customalloy.com
SIC: **5093** Nonferrous metals scrap

(P-6006)
CITY FIBERS INC (PA)
2500 E 24th St (90058-1206)
P.O. Box 58646 (90058-0646)
PHONE..................323 583-1013
David T Jones, *Pr*
Kipp Jones, *
EMP: 60 **EST:** 1984
SQ FT: 55,000
SALES (est): 10.51MM
SALES (corp-wide): 10.51MM **Privately Held**
Web: www.cityfibers.com
SIC: **5093** 4953 Waste paper; Recycling, waste materials

(P-6007)
FIRMA PLASTIC CO INC
9309 Rayo Ave (90280-3612)
PHONE..................323 567-7767
David A Carpenter, *VP*
EMP: 240 **EST:** 1990
SALES (est): 1.48MM **Privately Held**
SIC: **5093** Metal scrap and waste materials
HQ: Metal Management, Inc.
2425 S Wood St
Chicago IL
773 890-4210

(P-6008)
GLOBAL PLASTICS INC
145 Malbert St (92570-8624)
PHONE..................951 657-5466
Nadim Salim Bahou, *Pr*
Patti Gilmour, *
▲ **EMP:** 120 **EST:** 1996
SQ FT: 55,000
SALES (est): 24.21MM **Privately Held**
Web: www.globalpetinc.com
SIC: **5093** 4953 3053 Plastics scrap; Recycling, waste materials; Packing materials

(P-6009)
GREENPATH RECOVERY WEST INC
Also Called: Greenpath Recovery Recycl Svcs
330 W Citrus St Ste 250 (92324-1422)
PHONE..................909 954-0686
Joe Castro, *Pr*
EMP: 60 **EST:** 2012
SQ FT: 90,000
SALES (est): 8.01MM **Privately Held**
Web: www.greenpathrecovery.com
SIC: **5093** 3089 2821 Scrap and waste materials; Plastics processing; Plastics materials and resins

(P-6010)
JUNK KING FRNCHISE SYSTEMS LLC
1616 Gilbreth Rd (94010-1405)
PHONE..................888 888-5865
EMP: 127 **EST:** 2019
SALES (est): 22.52MM **Privately Held**
SIC: **5093** Junk and scrap

(P-6011)
KINSBURSKY BROS SUPPLY INC (PA)
Also Called: Kinsbursky Brothers
125 E Commercial St Ste A (92801-1214)
PHONE..................714 738-8516
Steven Kinsbursky, *Pr*
Scott Kinsbursky, *
Aaron Zisman, *
Todd Coy, *
▲ **EMP:** 65 **EST:** 1958
SQ FT: 35,000
SALES (est): 25.07MM
SALES (corp-wide): 25.07MM **Privately Held**
Web: www.kbirecycling.com
SIC: **5093** Metal scrap and waste materials

(P-6012)
PAVEMENT RECYCLING SYSTEMS INC (PA)
Also Called: Prsi
10240 San Sevaine Way (91752-1100)
PHONE..................951 682-1091
Richard W Gove, *Pr*
Stephen Concannon, *
Nathan Beyler, *Prin*
▲ **EMP:** 125 **EST:** 1989
SQ FT: 40,000
SALES (est): 72.5MM **Privately Held**
Web: www.pavementrecycling.com
SIC: **5093** 1611 Scrap and waste materials; Surfacing and paving

(P-6013)
PICK PULL AUTO DISMANTLING INC
7600 Stockton Blvd (95823-3917)
PHONE..................916 689-1446
Tom Klauer, *Brnch Mgr*
EMP: 63
SALES (corp-wide): 2.88B **Publicly Held**
SIC: **5093** 5015 Automotive wrecking for scrap; Automotive parts and supplies, used
HQ: Pick And Pull Auto Dismantling, Inc.
10850 Gold Center Dr # 325
Rancho Cordova CA
916 689-2000

(P-6014)
SCHNITZER FRESNO INC
2727 S Chestnut Ave (93725-2114)
P.O. Box 12085 (93776-2085)
PHONE..................559 233-3211
Leonard Schnitzer, *CEO*
Barry Rosen, *
Gary Schnitzer, *
Gilbert Schnitzer, *
EMP: 77 **EST:** 1917
SQ FT: 2,400
SALES (est): 4.41MM
SALES (corp-wide): 2.88B **Publicly Held**
SIC: **5093** Junk and scrap
PA: Schnitzer Steel Industries, Inc.
299 Sw Clay St Ste 400
Portland OR
503 224-9900

(P-6015)
SELF SERVE AUTO DISMANTLERS (PA)
Also Called: Adams Steel
3200 E Frontera St (92806-2822)
P.O. Box 6258 (92816-0258)
PHONE..................714 630-8901
George Adams Junior, *Pr*
Mike Adams, *
Terry Adams, *
Wendy Adams, *
◆ **EMP:** 120 **EST:** 1987
SQ FT: 41,000
SALES (est): 21.73MM **Privately Held**
SIC: **5093** Ferrous metal scrap and waste

(P-6016)
SIERRA INTERNATIONAL MCHY LLC
1620 E Brundage Ln Frnt (93307-2756)
P.O. Box 1340 (93302-1340)
PHONE..................661 327-7073
Phillip Sacco, *Managing Member*
Ben Sacco, *
John Sacco, *
◆ **EMP:** 65 **EST:** 1946
SQ FT: 15,000
SALES (est): 45.99MM **Privately Held**
Web: www.sierraintl.com
SIC: **5093** 5084 Nonferrous metals scrap; Industrial machinery and equipment

(P-6017)
SIMS GROUP USA CORPORATION (DH)
Also Called: Simsmetal America
600 S 4th St (94804-3504)
PHONE..................510 412-5300
Alistair Field, *CEO*
Bob Kelman, *
Myles Partridge, *
Jimmie Buckland, *
John Crabb, *
◆ **EMP:** 100 **EST:** 1987
SQ FT: 4,000
SALES (est): 142.18MM **Privately Held**
Web: www.simsmm.com
SIC: **5093** 4953 Ferrous metal scrap and waste; Recycling, waste materials
HQ: Sims Group Usa Holdings Corp
200 W Madison St Ste 3950
Chicago IL
212 604-0710

5094 Jewelry And Precious Stones

(P-6018)
A-MARK PRECIOUS METALS INC (PA)
Also Called: A-Mark
2121 Rosecrans Ave Ste 6300 (90245-7528)
PHONE..................310 587-1477
Gregory N Roberts, *CEO*
Jeffrey D Benjamin, *Ch Bd*
Thor G Gjerdrum, *Pr*
Brian Aquilino, *COO*
Kathleen Simpson Taylor, *Ex VP*
▲ **EMP:** 92 **EST:** 1965
SQ FT: 9,000
SALES (est): 9.29B
SALES (corp-wide): 9.29B **Publicly Held**
Web: www.amark.com
SIC: **5094** Jewelry

(P-6019)
BLISS WORLD LLC
39 Pier (94133-1006)
PHONE..................415 217-7047
Ori Kedem, *Brnch Mgr*
EMP: 70
Web: www.blissworld.com
SIC: **5094** Jewelry
HQ: Bliss World Llc
42 W 39th St Fl 9
New York NY
212 931-6383

(P-6020)
C&C JEWELRY MFG INC
323 W 8th St Fl 4 (90014-3109)
PHONE..................213 623-6800
Mikhail Chekhman, *Pr*
Robert Connolly, *
Dmitriy Moskalenko Ctrl, *Prin*
▲ **EMP:** 75 **EST:** 2001
SQ FT: 3,000
SALES (est): 28.36MM **Privately Held**
SIC: **5094** 3915 Jewelry; Jewel preparing: instruments, tools, watches, and jewelry

(P-6021)
CITIZEN WATCH COMPANY OF AMERICA INC (HQ)
Also Called: Citizen Watch America
1000 W 190th St (90502-1040)
PHONE..................800 321-1023
▲ **EMP:** 150 **EST:** 1975
SALES (est): 97.29MM **Privately Held**
SIC: **5094** Watches and parts
PA: Citizen Watch Co., Ltd.
6-1-12, Tanashicho
Nishitokyo TKY

(P-6022)
GOLDCO DIRECT LLC
Also Called: Goldco
24025 Park Sorrento Ste 210 (91302-4025)
PHONE..................818 343-0186
EMP: 80 **EST:** 2006
SALES (est): 40MM **Privately Held**
Web: www.goldco.com
SIC: **5094** Precious metals

(P-6023)
MEL BERNIE AND COMPANY INC (PA)
Also Called: 1928 Jewelry Company

3000 W Empire Ave (91504-3109)
PHONE..................................818 841-1928
Melvyn Bernie, CEO
▲ EMP: 250 EST: 1968
SQ FT: 65,000
SALES (est): 46.13MM
SALES (corp-wide): 46.13MM Privately Held
Web: www.1928.com
SIC: 5094 Jewelry

(P-6024)
NER PRECIOUS METALS INC
640 St Hill St Ste 450 (90014)
PHONE..................................310 367-3179
Pedram Shamekh, CEO
▲ EMP: 60 EST: 2017
SQ FT: 900
SALES (est): 4.82MM Privately Held
SIC: 5094 5131 5085 Precious metals; Piece goods and other fabrics; Industrial supplies

(P-6025)
NIXON INC (PA)
Also Called: Nixon Watches
2810 Whiptail Loop Ste 1 (92010-6754)
Rural Route 2810 Whiptail (92010)
PHONE..................................888 455-9200
Andrew Laats, *
▲ EMP: 120 EST: 1997
SALES (est): 49.35MM
SALES (corp-wide): 49.35MM Privately Held
Web: www.nixon.com
SIC: 5094 5611 5136 Watches and parts; Clothing accessories: men's and boys'; Leather and sheep lined clothing, men's and boys'

(P-6026)
SIMON GOLUB & SONS INC (DH)
Also Called: Lorenzo USA
514 Via De La Valle Ste 210 (92075)
▲ EMP: 90 EST: 1923
SQ FT: 40,000
SALES (est): 37.92MM Privately Held
Web: www.portlandjewelrysupplies.com
SIC: 5094 3911 Jewelry; Jewelry, precious metal
HQ: Astral Holdings Inc
    5506 6th Ave S
    Seattle WA

(P-6027)
SWEDA COMPANY LLC
Also Called: Sweda
17411 E Valley Blvd (91744-5159)
PHONE..................................626 357-9999
Brandon Mackay, CEO
Seidler Sweda, *
Paul Beck, *
Scott Pearson, *
Kellie Claudio, *
◆ EMP: 273 EST: 1976
SQ FT: 350,000
SALES (est): 56.55MM Privately Held
SIC: 5094 5044 Watches and parts; Calculators, electronic

(P-6028)
TOUCAN INC (PA)
Also Called: Tomas Jewelry
824 L St Ste 6 (95521-5766)
P.O. Box 4899 (95518-4899)
PHONE..................................707 822-6662
Thomas S Perrett, Pr
▲ EMP: 80 EST: 1980
SQ FT: 25,000
SALES (est): 18.5MM
SALES (corp-wide): 18.5MM Privately Held
Web: www.toucan-inc.com
SIC: 5094 Jewelry

5099 Durable Goods, Nec

(P-6029)
BOSSA NOVA ROBOTICS INC (HQ)
610 22nd St Ste 250 (94107-3119)
P.O. Box 590979 (94159-0979)
PHONE..................................415 234-5136
Bruce Mcwilliams, CEO
▼ EMP: 70 EST: 2011
SQ FT: 5,000
SALES (est): 48.67MM Privately Held
Web: www.bossanova.com
SIC: 5099 Robots, service or novelty
PA: Bossa Nova Robotics Holding Corp.
    610 22nd St Ste 250
    San Francisco CA

(P-6030)
BOSSA NOVA ROBOTICS INC
709 N Shoreline Blvd (94043-3208)
P.O. Box 590979 (94159-0979)
PHONE..................................415 234-5136
EMP: 101
Web: www.bossanova.com
SIC: 5099 Robots, service or novelty
HQ: Bossa Nova Robotics, Inc.
    610 22nd St Ste 250
    San Francisco CA
    415 234-5136

(P-6031)
BURGETT INCORPORATED (PA)
Also Called: Piano Disc
4111a N Freeway Blvd (95834-1209)
PHONE..................................916 567-9999
Gary Burgett, CEO
Kirk Burgett, *
▲ EMP: 62 EST: 1977
SQ FT: 48,000
SALES (est): 17.8MM
SALES (corp-wide): 17.8MM Privately Held
Web: www.pianodiscremote.com
SIC: 5099 3429 3931 3651 Pianos; Piano hardware; Musical instruments; Household audio and video equipment

(P-6032)
C D LISTENING BAR INC
Also Called: Super D Phantom Distribution
17822 Gillette Ave Ste A (92614-0527)
PHONE..................................949 225-1170
EMP: 730
Web: www.criticschoiceonline.com
SIC: 5099 Compact discs

(P-6033)
CAPTAIN KIRK SERVICES INC
Also Called: Airfield Supply Co
1190 Coleman Ave (95110-1190)
PHONE..................................408 320-0230
Marc Matulich, Prin
EMP: 100 EST: 2017
SALES (est): 9.61MM Privately Held
Web: www.airfieldsupplyco.com
SIC: 5099 Durable goods, nec

(P-6034)
CELLMARK INC (DH)
Also Called: United International
88 Rowland Way Ste 300 (94945-5049)
PHONE..................................415 927-1700
Christer A Simren, CEO
◆ EMP: 65 EST: 1984
SQ FT: 13,000
SALES (est): 530.26MM Privately Held
Web: www.cellmark.com
SIC: 5099 5093 5111 Pulpwood; Waste paper; Fine paper
HQ: Cellmark Ab
    Lilla Bommen 3c
    GOteborg
    31100300

(P-6035)
CELLMARK PULP & PAPER INC
22 Pelican Way (94901-5545)
PHONE..................................415 927-1700
◆ EMP: 70
SIC: 5099 5111 Pulpwood; Fine paper

(P-6036)
CENTERLINE WOOD PRODUCTS
15447 Anacapa Rd Ste 102 (92392-2481)
PHONE..................................760 246-4530
Michael Rodriguez, Pr
EMP: 99 EST: 2017
SALES (est): 5.8MM Privately Held
Web: www.cwp.cab
SIC: 5099 Wood and wood by-products

(P-6037)
CORE & MAIN INC
939 Broadway St (94063-3106)
PHONE..................................650 366-3833
EMP: 124
SALES (corp-wide): 6.65B Publicly Held
Web: www.coreandmain.com
SIC: 5099 Safety equipment and supplies
PA: Core & Main, Inc.
    1830 Craig Park Ct
    Saint Louis MO
    314 432-4700

(P-6038)
CORE & MAIN INC
1425 E Beamer St (95776-6014)
PHONE..................................530 662-7700
EMP: 340
SALES (corp-wide): 6.65B Publicly Held
Web: www.coreandmain.com
SIC: 5099 Safety equipment and supplies
PA: Core & Main, Inc.
    1830 Craig Park Ct
    Saint Louis MO
    314 432-4700

(P-6039)
D J AMERICAN SUPPLY INC
Also Called: American Dj Group of Companies
6122 S Eastern Ave (90040-3402)
PHONE..................................323 582-2650
Charles Davies, Pr
Alfred Gonzales, Pr
Toby Velazquez, Pr
◆ EMP: 126 EST: 1985
SQ FT: 100,000
SALES (est): 24.32MM Privately Held
Web: www.americandjsupply.com
SIC: 5099 5719 5999 Firearms and ammunition, except sporting; Lighting fixtures; Theatrical equipment and supplies

(P-6040)
FAM PPE LLC
5553-B Bandini Blvd B (90201)
PHONE..................................323 888-7755
Frank M Zarabi, Managing Member
EMP: 223 EST: 2020
SALES (est): 327.37K Privately Held
SIC: 5099 Safety equipment and supplies
PA: Fam, Llc
    5553 B Bandini Blvd
    Bell CA

(P-6041)
FOX LUGGAGE INC
221 N Orange Ave (91744-3433)
PHONE..................................323 588-1688
Wayne Wang, CEO
Sherrishan H Lee, *
▲ EMP: 65 EST: 1999
SALES (est): 6.43MM Privately Held
Web: www.foxluggage.com
SIC: 5099 Luggage

(P-6042)
FT 2 INC
1211 N Miller St (92806-1933)
PHONE..................................714 765-5555
◆ EMP: 170
SIC: 5099 2393 3161 Carrying cases; Textile bags; Luggage

(P-6043)
GENIUS PRODUCTS INC
3301 Exposition Blvd Ste 100 (90404)
PHONE..................................310 453-1222
Trevor Drinkwater, Pr
Stephen K Bannon, *
Edward J Byrnes, *
▲ EMP: 222 EST: 2005
SQ FT: 40,520
SALES (est): 25.76MM Privately Held
Web: www.geniusproducts.com
SIC: 5099 3652 7819 Video and audio equipment; Prerecorded records and tapes; Video tape or disk reproduction

(P-6044)
GOLDEN STATE MEDICAL SUPPLY
5247 Camino Ruiz (93012-8602)
PHONE..................................805 477-8966
Benjamin Hall, CEO
Thomas Weaver, CFO
EMP: 99 EST: 2017
SALES (est): 2.42MM Privately Held
Web: www.gsms.us
SIC: 5099 Durable goods, nec

(P-6045)
GUTHY-RENKER LLC
Also Called: Guthy-Renker Direct
3340 Ocean Park Blvd Fl 2 (90405-3204)
PHONE..................................310 581-6250
EMP: 80
Web: www.guthy-renker.com
SIC: 5099 7812 5999 Tapes and cassettes, prerecorded; Commercials, television: tape or film; Cosmetics
PA: Guthy-Renker Llc
    100 N Pcf Cast Hwy Ste 16
    El Segundo CA

(P-6046)
MONSTER INC (PA)
Also Called: Monster Products
601 Gateway Blvd Ste 900 (94080-7070)
P.O. Box 435 (94005-0435)
PHONE..................................415 840-2000
Noel Lee, Pr
Irene Baron, *
◆ EMP: 330 EST: 1978
SQ FT: 50,000
SALES (est): 150.7MM
SALES (corp-wide): 150.7MM Privately Held
Web: www.monsterstore.com
SIC: 5099 4841 3679 Video and audio equipment; Cable and other pay television services; Headphones, radio

PRODUCTS & SERVICES SECTION
5112 - Stationery And Office Supplies (P-6065)

(P-6047)
OLIVET INTERNATIONAL INC (PA)
11015 Hopkins St (91752-3248)
PHONE..................951 681-8888
Sean Lin, *Managing Member*
Lydia Hsu, *
David Yu, *
Pei Te Lin, *
▼ **EMP:** 89 **EST:** 1984
SQ FT: 456,000
SALES (est): 172.9MM
SALES (corp-wide): 172.9MM **Privately Held**
Web: www.olivetintl.com
SIC: 5099 3161 Luggage; Luggage

(P-6048)
PLATINUM DISC LLC
Also Called: Echo Bridge Home Entertainment
10203 Santa Monica Blvd Fl 5 (90067-6416)
PHONE..................608 784-6620
Nate Hart, *Pr*
Nathan Hart, *
▼ **EMP:** 91 **EST:** 1995
SALES (est): 24.03MM
SALES (corp-wide): 24.03MM **Privately Held**
SIC: 5099 Compact discs
PA: Echo Bridge Entertainment, Llc
75 2nd Ave Ste 500
Needham MA
781 444-6767

(P-6049)
RGGD INC (PA)
Also Called: Crystal Art Gallery
4950 S Santa Fe Ave (90058-2106)
PHONE..................323 581-6617
Randy Greenberg, *CEO*
Douglas Song, *
◆ **EMP:** 79 **EST:** 1994
SQ FT: 120,000
SALES (est): 26.79MM
SALES (corp-wide): 26.79MM **Privately Held**
Web: www.crystalartgallery.com
SIC: 5099 3441 Wood and wood by-products; Fabricated structural metal

(P-6050)
ROLAND CORPORATION US (HQ)
5100 S Eastern Ave (90040-2938)
P.O. Box 910921 (90091-0921)
PHONE..................323 890-3700
Christopher Bristol, *CEO*
Dennis M Houlihan, *
Mark S Malbon, *
Charles L Wright, *
Junpei Yamato, *
◆ **EMP:** 165 **EST:** 1953
SQ FT: 50,000
SALES (est): 70.96MM **Privately Held**
Web: www.roland.com
SIC: 5099 5045 3931 Musical instruments; Computer peripheral equipment; Organs, all types: pipe, reed, hand, electronic, etc.
PA: Roland Corporation
2036-1, Hosoechonakagawa, Kita-Ku
Hamamatsu SZO

(P-6051)
ROSEN ELECTRONICS LLC
Also Called: Rosen Electronics
2500 E Francis St (91761-7730)
PHONE..................951 898-9808
W Thomas Clements, *Pr*
▲ **EMP:** 75 **EST:** 2003

SALES (est): 21.56MM
SALES (corp-wide): 75.4MM **Privately Held**
SIC: 5099 3679 Video and audio equipment; Liquid crystal displays (LCD)
PA: Aamp Of Florida, Inc.
15500 Lightwave Dr # 202
Clearwater FL
727 572-9255

(P-6052)
SOUVENIR COFFEE CORPORATION
3084 Claremont Ave (94705-2630)
PHONE..................510 450-0505
EMP: 85
SALES (corp-wide): 6.52MM **Privately Held**
Web: www.souvenir-coffee.com
SIC: 5099 Souvenirs
PA: Souvenir Coffee Corporation
2849 Garber St
Berkeley CA
510 919-2777

(P-6053)
SUN COAST MERCHANDISE CORP
6405 Randolph St (90040-3511)
PHONE..................323 720-9700
Kumar C Bhavnani, *Pr*
Dilip Bhavnani, *
Vidya Bhavnani, *
◆ **EMP:** 250 **EST:** 1943
SQ FT: 120,000
SALES (est): 24.59MM **Privately Held**
Web: www.sunscopeusa.com
SIC: 5099 Brass goods

(P-6054)
SUNSCAPE EYEWEAR INC
17526 Von Karman Ave Ste A (92614-4258)
PHONE..................949 553-0590
Ali Adam Rizza, *Pr*
Adam Rizza, *CFO*
Wally Rizza, *VP*
▲ **EMP:** 78 **EST:** 1999
SQ FT: 10,500
SALES (est): 6.13MM **Privately Held**
Web: www.isunscape.com
SIC: 5099 Sunglasses

(P-6055)
SUPPLYWORKS
650 Brennan St (95131-1204)
PHONE..................408 954-1234
EMP: 61 **EST:** 2015
SALES (est): 2.43MM **Privately Held**
Web: www.supplyworks.com
SIC: 5099 Durable goods, nec

(P-6056)
TAYLOR-LISTUG INC (PA)
Also Called: Taylor Guitars
1980 Gillespie Way (92020-1096)
PHONE..................619 258-1207
Kurt Listug, *CEO*
Robert Taylor, *
▲ **EMP:** 245 **EST:** 1968
SQ FT: 86,000
SALES (est): 180.56MM
SALES (corp-wide): 180.56MM **Privately Held**
Web: www.taylorguitars.com
SIC: 5099 5736 3931 Musical instruments; Musical instrument stores; Guitars and parts, electric and nonelectric

(P-6057)
UNITED STATES LUGGAGE CO LLC
13300 Carmenita Rd (90670-4815)
PHONE..................562 293-4400
Anthony Fortunato, *Mgr*
EMP: 71
SALES (corp-wide): 34.62MM **Privately Held**
Web: www.usluggage.com
SIC: 5099 Luggage
PA: United States Luggage Company, Llc
400 Wireless Blvd
Hauppauge NY
631 434-7070

(P-6058)
YAMAHA CORPORATION OF AMERICA (HQ)
Also Called: Yamaha Music Corporation U S A
6600 Orangethorpe Ave (90620-1396)
PHONE..................714 522-9011
Hitoshi Fukutome, *CEO*
Terry Lewis, *
Brian Jemelian, *
◆ **EMP:** 300 **EST:** 1958
SALES (est): 427.4MM **Privately Held**
Web: usa.yamaha.com
SIC: 5099 5065 5091 3931 Musical instruments; Sound equipment, electronic; Sporting and recreation goods; Musical instruments
PA: Yamaha Corporation
10-1, Nakazawacho, Naka-Ku
Hamamatsu SZO

5111 Printing And Writing Paper

(P-6059)
CLEANSMART SOLUTIONS INC (DH)
47422 Kato Rd (94538-7319)
PHONE..................510 413-4700
▲ **EMP:** 85 **EST:** 1956
SALES (est): 49MM
SALES (corp-wide): 1.33B **Privately Held**
SIC: 5111 5113 5087 Printing paper; Industrial and personal service paper; Janitors' supplies
HQ: Kelly Spicers Inc.
12310 Slauson Ave
Santa Fe Springs CA

(P-6060)
KELLY SPICERS INC (HQ)
Also Called: Kelly Spicers Packaging North
12310 Slauson Ave (90670-2629)
PHONE..................562 698-1199
Janice Gottesman, *Pr*
Rick Anderson, *
▲ **EMP:** 180 **EST:** 1965
SQ FT: 365,000
SALES (est): 606.41MM
SALES (corp-wide): 1.33B **Privately Held**
Web: www.kellyspicers.com
SIC: 5111 5199 5087 Fine paper; Packaging materials; Janitors' supplies
PA: Central National Gottesman Inc.
3 Manhattanville Rd # 301
Purchase NY
914 696-9000

5112 Stationery And Office Supplies

(P-6061)
5 DAY BUSINESS FORMS MFG INC
2921 E La Cresta Ave (92806-1873)
PHONE..................714 632-8674
Lesley Messick, *Brnch Mgr*
EMP: 62
SALES (corp-wide): 22.66MM **Privately Held**
Web: www.5daybf.com
SIC: 5112 Business forms
PA: 5 Day Business Forms Mfg., Inc.
2910 E La Cresta Ave
Anaheim CA
213 623-3577

(P-6062)
BANGKIT (USA) INC
Also Called: Bazic Product
10511 Valley Blvd (91731-2403)
PHONE..................626 672-0888
Handy Hioe, *CEO*
Anita Handojo, *
◆ **EMP:** 76 **EST:** 1998
SQ FT: 195,000
SALES (est): 39.09MM **Privately Held**
Web: www.bazicproducts.com
SIC: 5112 Office supplies, nec

(P-6063)
BLUE SKY THE CLOR IMGNTION LLC
Also Called: Day Designer
410 Exchange Ste 250 (92602-1392)
PHONE..................714 389-7700
James E Freeman Iii, *CEO*
Warren Vidovich, *Managing Member*
Jeannie M Alich, *
Dennis Marquardt, *
▲ **EMP:** 85 **EST:** 2002
SALES (est): 42.98MM **Privately Held**
Web: www.bluesky.com
SIC: 5112 5943 Stationery and office supplies; Stationery stores

(P-6064)
CENVEO WORLDWIDE LIMITED
705 Baldwin Park Blvd (91746-1504)
PHONE..................626 369-4921
Timothy Hollywood, *Brnch Mgr*
EMP: 456
SALES (corp-wide): 1.04B **Privately Held**
Web: www.cenveo.com
SIC: 5112 Stationery and office supplies
HQ: Cenveo Worldwide Limited
200 First Stamford Pl
Stamford CT
203 595-3000

(P-6065)
ESSENDANT CO
Also Called: United Stationers
918 S Stimson Ave (91745-1640)
PHONE..................626 961-0011
Terry Deines, *Mgr*
EMP: 130
Web: www.essendant.com
SIC: 5112 5044 5021 5943 Office supplies, nec; Office equipment; Furniture; Office forms and supplies
HQ: Essendant Co.
1 Parkway North Blvd # 100
Deerfield IL
847 627-7000

5112 - Stationery And Office Supplies

(P-6066)
IMAGE SOURCE INC (PA)
Also Called: Bluebird Office Supplies
2110 Pontius Ave (90025-5726)
P.O. Box 642380 (90064-8094)
PHONE..............................310 477-0700
Faramarz Sadeghi, CEO
Ramin Sadeghi, Treas
▲ EMP: 181 EST: 1982
SQ FT: 5,000
SALES (est): 19.23MM
SALES (corp-wide): 19.23MM Privately Held
Web: imagesourceusa.visualedgeit.com
SIC: 5112 5943 Office supplies, nec; Office forms and supplies

(P-6067)
MINTED LLC (PA)
747 Front St Fl 2 (94111-1917)
PHONE..............................415 399-1100
Mariam Naficy, CEO
Melissa Kim, Dir
Vlad Kuznetsov, VP
Namrata Patel, VP
Brady Wood, VP
▲ EMP: 180 EST: 2007
SALES (est): 453.09MM
SALES (corp-wide): 453.09MM Privately Held
Web: www.minted.com
SIC: 5112 Social stationery and greeting cards

(P-6068)
OFFICEMAX NORTH AMERICA INC
Also Called: OfficeMax
1800 Oakdale Rd Ste B (95355-2988)
PHONE..............................209 551-9700
Lee Blankenship, Brnch Mgr
EMP: 117
SALES (corp-wide): 8.49B Publicly Held
SIC: 5112 5943 Stationery and office supplies; Office forms and supplies
HQ: Officemax North America, Inc.
    263 Shuman Blvd Ste 145
    Naperville IL
    630 717-0791

(P-6069)
PENTEL OF AMERICA LTD (HQ)
2715 Columbia St (90503-3861)
PHONE..............................310 320-3831
Chotaro Koumi, Pr
Norikazu Hasegama, *
Nobuo Aihara, CMO*
Toshiro Hemmi, *
◆ EMP: 132 EST: 1966
SQ FT: 46,000
SALES (est): 97.63MM Privately Held
Web: www.pentel.com
SIC: 5112 3951 5199 3952 Pens and/or pencils; Pens and mechanical pencils; Artists' materials; Artists' materials, except pencils and leads
PA: Pentel Co., Ltd.
    7-2, Nihombashikoamicho
    Chuo-Ku TKY

(P-6070)
PUNCH STUDIO LLC (PA)
6025 W Slauson Ave (90230-6507)
P.O. Box 3663 (90231-3663)
PHONE..............................310 390-9900
Todd Brian Kirshner, CEO
Nathalie Carrer, *
◆ EMP: 230 EST: 2001
SQ FT: 106,000
SALES (est): 57.91MM Privately Held

Web: www.punchstudio.com
SIC: 5112 Greeting cards

(P-6071)
VIKING OFFICE PRODUCTS INC (DH)
3366 E Willow St (90755-2311)
PHONE..............................562 490-1000
M Bruce Nelson, Pr
Mark R Brown, Vice-President Information Systems*
Ronald W Weissman, Senior Vice President Logistics*
▲ EMP: 292 EST: 1960
SQ FT: 187,000
SALES (est): 349.49MM
SALES (corp-wide): 8.49B Publicly Held
Web: www.officedepot.com
SIC: 5112 5021 5045 5087 Office supplies, nec; Office furniture, nec; Computers, peripherals, and software; Janitors' supplies
HQ: Office Depot, Llc
    6600 N Military Trl
    Boca Raton FL
    561 438-4800

(P-6072)
XSE GROUP INC
92 Argonaut Ste 235 (92656-4112)
PHONE..............................888 272-8340
EMP: 199
SALES (corp-wide): 96.92MM Privately Held
Web: www.xsegroup.com
SIC: 5112 Office supplies, nec
PA: Xse Group, Inc.
    35 Phil Mack Dr
    Middletown CT
    888 272-8340

5113 Industrial And Personal Service Paper

(P-6073)
ANDWIN CORPORATION (PA)
Also Called: Andwin Scientific
167 W Cochran St (93065-6217)
P.O. Box 689 (91365-0689)
PHONE..............................818 999-2828
Natalie Sarraf, CEO
Jesse Palaganas, *
▲ EMP: 62 EST: 1950
SALES (est): 59.75MM
SALES (corp-wide): 59.75MM Privately Held
Web: www.andwinclinical.com
SIC: 5113 5199 5087 5047 Shipping supplies ; Art goods and supplies; Janitors' supplies; Hospital equipment and furniture

(P-6074)
BUNZL DISTRIBUTION CAL LLC (DH)
Also Called: Bunzl
3310 E Miraloma Ave (92806-1911)
PHONE..............................714 688-1900
Derek R Goodin, *
Scot Gregory, *
◆ EMP: 98 EST: 1989
SQ FT: 150,000
SALES (est): 87.38MM
SALES (corp-wide): 14.5B Privately Held
Web: www.bunzldistribution.com
SIC: 5113 Paper, wrapping or coarse, and products
HQ: Bunzl Distribution Usa, Llc
    1 Cityplace Dr Ste 200
    Saint Louis MO

(P-6075)
CALIFORNIA BOX II
8949 Toronto Ave (91730-5412)
PHONE..............................909 944-9202
John Widera, CEO
Mackey Davis, *
EMP: 80 EST: 1990
SQ FT: 100,000
SALES (est): 10.58MM
SALES (corp-wide): 33.56MM Privately Held
Web: www.calbox.com
SIC: 5113 2653 Corrugated and solid fiber boxes; Boxes, corrugated: made from purchased materials
PA: California Box Company
    13901 Carmenita Rd
    Santa Fe Springs CA
    562 921-1223

(P-6076)
CALIFORNIA SUPPLY INC
491 E Compton Blvd (90248-2078)
P.O. Box 3906 (90247-7598)
PHONE..............................310 532-2500
Mark Weinstein, CEO
Michael Rosson, *
◆ EMP: 69 EST: 1975
SQ FT: 75,000
SALES (est): 36.39MM Privately Held
Web: www.calsupply.com
SIC: 5113 5087 Industrial and personal service paper; Janitors' supplies

(P-6077)
FRICK PAPER COMPANY LLC
Also Called: Paper Mart Indus & Ret Packg
2164 N Batavia St (92865-3104)
PHONE..............................714 787-4900
Tom Frick, Managing Member
John Frick, *
◆ EMP: 106 EST: 1921
SQ FT: 210,000
SALES (est): 83.52MM Privately Held
Web: www.papermart.com
SIC: 5113 Paper, wrapping or coarse, and products

(P-6078)
GEORGIA-PACIFIC LLC
Also Called: Georgia-Pacific
9206 Santa Fe Springs Rd (90670-2618)
PHONE..............................562 861-6226
EMP: 275
SALES (corp-wide): 36.93B Privately Held
Web: www.gp.com
SIC: 5113 2653 Corrugated and solid fiber boxes; Boxes, corrugated: made from purchased materials
HQ: Georgia-Pacific Llc
    133 Peachtree St Nw
    Atlanta GA
    404 652-4000

(P-6079)
IMPERIAL BAG & PAPER CO LLC
Also Called: Paper Company, The
2825 Warner Ave (92606-4443)
PHONE..............................800 834-6248
Julie Scheibe, VP Opers
EMP: 98
SALES (corp-wide): 1.6B Privately Held
Web: www.imperialdade.com
SIC: 5113 5199 Containers, paper and disposable plastic; Packaging materials
PA: Imperial Bag & Paper Co. Llc
    255 Route 1 And 9
    Jersey City NJ
    201 437-7440

(P-6080)
NEWAY PACKAGING CORP (PA)
1973 E Via Arado (90220-6102)
PHONE..............................602 454-9000
Russell E Freebury, Pr
Sarah D Giles-bell, VP
Carole Freebury, *
◆ EMP: 60 EST: 1977
SQ FT: 36,000
SALES (est): 49.92MM
SALES (corp-wide): 49.92MM Privately Held
Web: www.newaypkgshop.com
SIC: 5113 5084 Shipping supplies; Packaging machinery and equipment

(P-6081)
OAK PAPER PRODUCTS CO INC (PA)
Also Called: Acorn Paper Products Co.
3686 E Olympic Blvd (90023-3146)
P.O. Box 23965 (90023-0965)
PHONE..............................323 268-0507
TOLL FREE: 800
David Weissberg, CEO
Max Weissberg, *
▲ EMP: 174 EST: 1959
SQ FT: 250,000
SALES (est): 91.84MM
SALES (corp-wide): 91.84MM Privately Held
Web: www.acorn-paper.com
SIC: 5113 5199 5087 2653 Shipping supplies ; Packaging materials; Janitors' supplies; Corrugated and solid fiber boxes

(P-6082)
OAKLAND PAPER & SUPPLY INCORPORATED (PA)
Also Called: Oakland Packaging and Supply
3200 Regatta Blvd Ste F (94804-4592)
PHONE..............................510 307-4242
▲ EMP: 105 EST: 1930
SALES (est): 48.02MM
SALES (corp-wide): 48.02MM Privately Held
Web: www.oakpackaging.com
SIC: 5113 5087 Boxes and containers; Moving equipment and supplies

(P-6083)
OASIS BRANDS INC
100 S Anaheim Blvd Ste 280 (92805-3848)
PHONE..............................540 658-2830
▲ EMP: 75 EST: 2009
SALES (est): 6.84MM Privately Held
SIC: 5113 Napkins, paper

(P-6084)
ORORA PACKAGING SOLUTIONS (HQ)
Also Called: Orora North America
6600 Valley View St (90620-1145)
PHONE..............................714 562-6000
Bernardino Salvatore, Pr
Bernardino Salvatorre, *
David Conley, *
Lara Coons, *
◆ EMP: 100 EST: 1951
SQ FT: 300,000
SALES (est): 1.88B Privately Held
Web: www.ororapackagingsolutions.com
SIC: 5113 2653 Paper, wrapping or coarse, and products; Boxes, corrugated: made from purchased materials
PA: Orora Limited
    109 Burwood Rd
    Hawthorn VIC

▲ = Import ▼ = Export
◆ = Import/Export

PRODUCTS & SERVICES SECTION
5122 - Drugs, Proprietaries, And Sundries (P-6103)

(P-6085)
ORORA PACKAGING SOLUTIONS
Also Called: Landsberg Los Angeles Div 1001
1640 S Greenwood Ave (90640-6538)
P.O. Box 800 (90640-0800)
PHONE..................................323 832-2000
Jed Wockenfuss, *Mgr*
EMP: 168
Web: www.ororapackagingsolutions.com
SIC: 5113 2653 Paper, wrapping or coarse, and products; Boxes, corrugated: made from purchased materials
HQ: Orora Packaging Solutions
6600 Valley View St
Buena Park CA
714 562-6000

(P-6086)
ORORA PACKAGING SOLUTIONS
Landsberg Sacramento Div 1020
1221 Tara Ct (95765-1200)
PHONE..................................916 645-8100
Dan Davis, *Brnch Mgr*
EMP: 78
Web: www.ororapackagingsolutions.com
SIC: 5113 2653 Paper, wrapping or coarse, and products; Boxes, corrugated: made from purchased materials
HQ: Orora Packaging Solutions
6600 Valley View St
Buena Park CA
714 562-6000

(P-6087)
ORORA PACKAGING SOLUTIONS
Also Called: Corru Kraft Buena Pk Div 5058
6200 Caballero Blvd (90620-1124)
PHONE..................................714 562-6002
Jim Wilczek, *Brnch Mgr*
EMP: 149
Web: www.ororapackagingsolutions.com
SIC: 5113 2653 Paper, wrapping or coarse, and products; Boxes, corrugated: made from purchased materials
HQ: Orora Packaging Solutions
6600 Valley View St
Buena Park CA
714 562-6000

(P-6088)
P & R PAPER SUPPLY CO INC (HQ)
1898 E Colton Ave (92374-9798)
P.O. Box 590 (92373-0201)
PHONE..................................909 389-1807
Robert Tillis, *CEO*
Joe Maiberger, *
Luke Maiberger, *
Chris Dirx, *
Paul Cervino, *
▼ **EMP:** 90 **EST:** 1965
SQ FT: 75,000
SALES (est): 81.69MM
SALES (corp-wide): 1.6B Privately Held
Web: www.prpaper.com
SIC: 5113 5169 5149 5072 Paper, wrapping or coarse, and products; Chemicals and allied products, nec; Groceries and related products, nec; Hardware
PA: Imperial Bag & Paper Co. Llc
255 Route 1 And 9
Jersey City NJ
201 437-1400

(P-6089)
PACKAGING INNOVATORS LLC
6850 Brisa St (94550-2521)
P.O. Box 1110 (94551-1110)
PHONE..................................925 371-2000
TOLL FREE: 800
William E Mazzocco, *Pr*
Beverly J Flynt, *
▲ **EMP:** 90 **EST:** 1975
SALES (est): 48.11MM
SALES (corp-wide): 317.12MM Privately Held
Web: www.goldenwestpackaging.com
SIC: 5113 2653 3993 Shipping supplies; Corrugated and solid fiber boxes; Signs and advertising specialties
PA: Golden West Packaging Group Llc
15400 Don Julian Rd
City Of Industry CA
888 501-5893

(P-6090)
PERRIN BERNARD SUPOWITZ LLC (HQ)
Also Called: Fergadis Enterprises
5496 Lindbergh Ln (90201-6409)
PHONE..................................323 981-2800
Ken Sweder, *Ch*
Ron Margolis, *CFO*
EMP: 132 **EST:** 1926
SQ FT: 175,000
SALES (est): 276.73MM
SALES (corp-wide): 1.01B Privately Held
Web: www.individualfoodservice.com
SIC: 5113 Industrial and personal service paper
PA: Kelso & Company, L.P.
299 Park Ave Fl 30
New York NY
212 350-7700

(P-6091)
UNISOURCE PACKAGING INC
4225 Hacienda Dr Ste A (94588-2720)
P.O. Box 8803 (94588)
PHONE..................................925 227-6000
Allan Dragone, *CEO*
▲ **EMP:** 112 **EST:** 1993
SALES (est): 42.44MM
SALES (corp-wide): 7.15B Privately Held
SIC: 5113 Shipping supplies
HQ: Veritiv Operating Company
1000 Abernathy Rd Bldg 4
Atlanta GA
770 391-8200

(P-6092)
USED CARDBOARD BOXES INC
4032 Wilshire Blvd Ste 402 (90010-3413)
PHONE..................................323 724-2500
Marty Metro, *CEO*
▲ **EMP:** 125 **EST:** 2006
SALES (est): 58.85MM Privately Held
Web: www.usedcardboardboxes.com
SIC: 5113 Corrugated and solid fiber boxes

(P-6093)
VERITIV OPERATING COMPANY
Also Called: International Paper
7337 Las Positas Rd (94551-5110)
PHONE..................................925 245-6060
EMP: 151
SALES (corp-wide): 7.15B Privately Held
Web: www.veritivcorp.com
SIC: 5113 Industrial and personal service paper
HQ: Veritiv Operating Company
1000 Abernathy Rd Bldg 4
Atlanta GA
770 391-8200

5122 Drugs, Proprietaries, And Sundries

(P-6094)
AMERISOURCEBERGEN DRUG CORP
Also Called: ABC Valencia
1851 California Ave (92881-6477)
PHONE..................................951 371-2000
Ron Green, *Mgr*
EMP: 150
SALES (corp-wide): 238.59B Publicly Held
Web: www.amerisourcebergendrug.com
SIC: 5122 4225 Pharmaceuticals; General warehousing and storage
HQ: Amerisourcebergen Drug Corporation
1 W 1st Ave
Conshohocken PA
610 727-7000

(P-6095)
AMERISOURCEBERGEN DRUG CORP
Also Called: ABC Sacramento Striker
1325 W Striker Ave (95834-1164)
PHONE..................................916 830-4500
Bruce Bennett, *Brnch Mgr*
EMP: 102
SALES (corp-wide): 238.59B Publicly Held
Web: www.amerisourcebergendrug.com
SIC: 5122 Pharmaceuticals
HQ: Amerisourcebergen Drug Corporation
1 W 1st Ave
Conshohocken PA
610 727-7000

(P-6096)
BAXTER HEALTHCARE CORPORATION
1 Baxter Way Ste 100 (91362-3813)
PHONE..................................805 372-3000
John Bacich, *Pr*
EMP: 130
SALES (corp-wide): 15.11B Publicly Held
Web: www.baxter.com
SIC: 5122 2834 2836 5047 Drugs, proprietaries, and sundries; Solutions, pharmaceutical; Biological products, except diagnostic; Medical equipment and supplies
HQ: Baxter Healthcare Corporation
1 Baxter Pkwy
Deerfield IL
224 948-2000

(P-6097)
BEAUTY 21 COSMETICS INC
Also Called: L A Girl
2021 S Archibald Ave (91761-8535)
PHONE..................................909 945-2220
Lan Jack Yu, *CEO*
Chafe Yu Trinh, *
Mahon So Yu, *
◆ **EMP:** 175 **EST:** 1985
SQ FT: 250,000
SALES (est): 45.25MM Privately Held
Web: www.lagirlusa.com
SIC: 5122 2844 Cosmetics; Perfumes, cosmetics and other toilet preparations

(P-6098)
BENEFIT COSMETICS LLC (DH)
225 Bush St Fl 20 (94104-4279)
PHONE..................................415 781-8153
Christie Fleischer, *CEO*
Antonio Belloni, *Managing Member*
Anish Melwani, *Managing Member*
▲ **EMP:** 100 **EST:** 1976
SQ FT: 800
SALES (est): 193.06MM
SALES (corp-wide): 503.87MM Privately Held
Web: www.benefitcosmetics.com
SIC: 5122 5999 Cosmetics; Cosmetics
HQ: Lvmh Moet Hennessy Louis Vuitton Inc.
19 E 57th St
New York NY
212 931-2700

(P-6099)
CARDINAL HEALTH INC
3238 Dwight Rd (95758-6439)
PHONE..................................916 372-9880
Trey Almonza, *Mgr*
EMP: 75
SALES (corp-wide): 205.01B Publicly Held
Web: www.cardinalhealth.com
SIC: 5122 Pharmaceuticals
PA: Cardinal Health, Inc.
7000 Cardinal Pl
Dublin OH
614 757-5000

(P-6100)
CARDINAL HEALTH INC
Also Called: Whitmire Distribution
27680 Avenue Mentry (91355-1452)
PHONE..................................661 295-6100
EMP: 64
SALES (corp-wide): 205.01B Publicly Held
Web: www.cardinalhealth.com
SIC: 5122 Pharmaceuticals
PA: Cardinal Health, Inc.
7000 Cardinal Pl
Dublin OH
614 757-5000

(P-6101)
CENCORA INC
1368 Metropolitan Dr (92868)
P.O. Box 247 (08086-0247)
PHONE..................................610 727-7000
Daniel Ramirez, *Mgr*
EMP: 249
SALES (corp-wide): 238.59B Publicly Held
Web: www.amerisourcebergen.com
SIC: 5122 Pharmaceuticals
PA: Cencora, Inc.
1 W 1st Ave
Conshohocken PA
610 727-7000

(P-6102)
COLORESCIENCE INC
2141 Palomar Airport Rd Ste 200 (92011-1423)
PHONE..................................866 426-5673
Mary Fisher, *CEO*
Josie Juncal, *CCO*
Ted Ebel, *Chief Business Officer*
Steve P Loomis, *
▲ **EMP:** 111 **EST:** 2000
SQ FT: 15,000
SALES (est): 31.05MM Privately Held
Web: www.colorescience.com
SIC: 5122 2844 Cosmetics; Cosmetic preparations

(P-6103)
CONQUISTADOR INTERNATIONAL LLC
Also Called: Posh'n Bae
21200 Oxnard St Ste 492 (91365-7301)
PHONE..................................424 249-9304

5122 - Drugs, Proprietaries, And Sundries (P-6104)

Andrew Andrew, *Managing Member*
EMP: 100 **EST:** 2018
SALES (est): 10.19MM **Privately Held**
SIC: 5122 Cosmetics

(P-6104)
DAKO NORTH AMERICA INC
6392 Via Real (93013-2921)
P.O. Box 58059 (93013)
PHONE...........................805 566-6655
◆ **EMP:** 325
SIC: 5122 3841 Biologicals and allied products; Diagnostic apparatus, medical

(P-6105)
DISTRIBUTION ALTERNATIVES INC
1979 Renaissance Pkwy (92376-2403)
PHONE...........................909 770-8900
EMP: 90
SALES (corp-wide): 95.6MM **Privately Held**
Web: www.daserv.com
SIC: 5122 Cosmetics
PA: Distribution Alternatives, Inc.
  6870 21st Ave
  Lino Lakes MN
  651 636-9167

(P-6106)
E MANAGEMENT SERVICES LLC
20010 Ventura Blvd (91364-2632)
PHONE...........................818 835-9525
Kevin Krivitsky, *Prin*
Kevin Krivitsky, *Prin*
EMP: 75 **EST:** 2019
SALES (est): 5.9MM **Privately Held**
SIC: 5122 Drugs, proprietaries, and sundries

(P-6107)
FAIRN & SWANSON INC
Also Called: Baja Duty Free
400 Lancaster St (94601-2827)
PHONE...........................510 533-8260
◆ **EMP:** 200
Web: www.fairn.com
SIC: 5122 5182 Cosmetics; Liquor

(P-6108)
FFF ENTERPRISES INC (PA)
44000 Winchester Rd (92590-2578)
PHONE...........................951 296-2500
Patrick M Schmidt, *CEO*
Wayne Talleur, *CFO*
Chris Ground, *COO*
Jonathan Hahn, *CIO*
Michael J Alkire, *Bd of Dir*
EMP: 300 **EST:** 1988
SQ FT: 162,000
SALES (est): 539.81MM
SALES (corp-wide): 539.81MM **Privately Held**
Web: www.fffenterprises.com
SIC: 5122 Pharmaceuticals

(P-6109)
GLAMOUR INDUSTRIES CO (PA)
Also Called: American International Inds
2220 Gaspar Ave (90040-1516)
PHONE...........................323 728-2999
Zvi Ryzman, *Pr*
Theresa Cooper, *Ex VP*
Charlie Loveless, *VP*
Betty Ryzman, *Sec*
EMP: 400 **EST:** 1971
SQ FT: 224,000
SALES: 110.3MM
SALES (corp-wide): 110.3MM **Privately Held**
Web: www.aiibeauty.com

SIC: 5122 2844 Cosmetics; Cosmetic preparations

(P-6110)
GOLDEN N-LIFE DIAMITE INTL INC (PA)
4555 Great America Pkwy Ste 220 (95054-1243)
PHONE...........................510 651-0405
Roget Uys, *CEO*
Daniel L Lewis, *
Robert Galano, *
▲ **EMP:** 80 **EST:** 1958
SQ FT: 66,000
SALES (est): 44.19MM
SALES (corp-wide): 44.19MM **Privately Held**
SIC: 5122 Cosmetics

(P-6111)
H D SMITH LLC
1370 E Victoria St (90746-7501)
P.O. Box 6231 (90749-6231)
PHONE...........................310 641-1885
Bob Schwartz, *Mgr*
EMP: 100
SALES (corp-wide): 238.59B **Publicly Held**
SIC: 5122 5047 Pharmaceuticals; Medical and hospital equipment
HQ: H. D. Smith, Llc
  1 W 1st Ave Ste 100
  Conshohocken PA
  866 232-1222

(P-6112)
HATCHBEAUTY PRODUCTS LLC (PA)
Also Called: Hatchbeauty
355 S Grand Ave (90071-3152)
P.O. Box 641415 (90064-6415)
PHONE...........................310 396-7070
Tracy Holland, *Managing Member*
Benjamin Bennett, *
◆ **EMP:** 83 **EST:** 2009
SALES (est): 38.75MM
SALES (corp-wide): 38.75MM **Privately Held**
Web: www.hatchcltv.com
SIC: 5122 Cosmetics, perfumes, and hair products

(P-6113)
INTEGRATED HEALTH CONCEPTS INC
Also Called: Conversio Health
720 Aerovista Pl Ste D (93401-8726)
PHONE...........................866 239-3784
Taylor Cline, *CEO*
Debra Henderson, *
EMP: 64 **EST:** 2001
SQ FT: 25,000
SALES (est): 12.94MM **Privately Held**
Web: www.conversiohealth.com
SIC: 5122 Pharmaceuticals

(P-6114)
IRISYS INC
6828 Nancy Ridge Dr Ste 100 (92121)
PHONE...........................858 623-1520
EMP: 86 **EST:** 2001
SQ FT: 10,000
SALES (est): 20.33MM **Privately Held**
Web: www.societalcdmo.com
SIC: 5122 8748 Pharmaceuticals; Business consulting, nec

(P-6115)
JAPONESQUE LLC
Also Called: Japonesque
12647 Alcosta Blvd Ste 375 (94583-4774)
PHONE...........................925 866-6670
Simon Worraker, *CEO*
▲ **EMP:** 80 **EST:** 2002
SALES (est): 31.41MM **Privately Held**
Web: www.japonesque.com
SIC: 5122 2844 Cosmetics; Cosmetic preparations

(P-6116)
JARROW FORMULAS INC (PA)
15233 Ventura Blvd Fl 900 (91403-2250)
PHONE...........................310 204-6936
Ojesh Bhalla, *CEO*
Jarrow L Rogovin, *
Michael Jacobs, *
Peilin Guo, *
Clayton Dubose, *
◆ **EMP:** 80 **EST:** 1977
SQ FT: 37,000
SALES (est): 52.95MM
SALES (corp-wide): 52.95MM **Privately Held**
Web: www.jarrow.com
SIC: 5122 Vitamins and minerals

(P-6117)
JESSICA COSMETICS INTL INC
Also Called: Jessica's Cosmetics
13209 Saticoy St (91605-3405)
PHONE...........................818 759-1050
Jessica Vartoughian, *Pr*
▲ **EMP:** 60 **EST:** 1968
SALES (est): 11.75MM **Privately Held**
Web: www.jessicacosmetics.com
SIC: 5122 7231 Cosmetics; Beauty shops

(P-6118)
JORDANA COSMETICS LLC
Also Called: Jordana Cosmetics
2035 E 49th St (90058-2801)
P.O. Box 8382 (90008-0382)
PHONE...........................310 730-4400
Laurie Minc, *Pr*
Ralph Bijou, *Prin*
◆ **EMP:** 65 **EST:** 1986
SQ FT: 30,000
SALES (est): 22.24MM **Privately Held**
Web: www.jordanacosmetics.com
SIC: 5122 5961 Cosmetics; Catalog and mail-order houses

(P-6119)
KOI CBD LLC
Also Called: Wholesale
14631 Best Ave (90650-5258)
PHONE...........................562 650-4673
Malinda Ridenour, *Managing Member*
EMP: 65 **EST:** 2016
SALES (est): 5.57MM **Privately Held**
Web: www.koicbd.com
SIC: 5122 Vitamins and minerals

(P-6120)
KUSH SUPPLY CO LLC
7375 Chapman Ave (92841-2104)
PHONE...........................714 243-4023
EMP: 97
SALES (corp-wide): 10.04MM **Privately Held**
Web: www.kushco.com
SIC: 5122 Pharmaceuticals
PA: Kush Supply Co. Llc
  6261 Katella Ave Ste 250
  Cypress CA
  714 243-4098

(P-6121)
LIFETECH RESOURCES LLC
Also Called: International Research Labs
700 Science Dr (93021-2012)
PHONE...........................805 944-1199
Richard Carieri, *Ch Bd*
Susan Mccarthy, *Pr*
Anna Carieri, *
▲ **EMP:** 85 **EST:** 1990
SQ FT: 152,000
SALES (est): 46MM **Privately Held**
Web: www.lifetechresources.com
SIC: 5122 5149 Cosmetics; Health foods

(P-6122)
LINA GALE (USA) INC (PA)
Also Called: Markwins Beauty Brands
22067 Ferrero (91789-5214)
PHONE...........................909 595-8898
John Chen, *CEO*
Lina Chen, *
▲ **EMP:** 60 **EST:** 1991
SALES (est): 23.19MM
SALES (corp-wide): 23.19MM **Privately Held**
Web: www.markwinsbeauty.com
SIC: 5122 Cosmetics

(P-6123)
MARKWINS BEAUTY BRANDS INC (PA)
22067 Ferrero (91789-5214)
PHONE...........................909 595-8898
Lina Chen, *CEO*
John Chen, *
◆ **EMP:** 150 **EST:** 1984
SQ FT: 320,000
SALES (est): 270.93MM
SALES (corp-wide): 270.93MM **Privately Held**
Web: www.markwinsbeauty.com
SIC: 5122 Cosmetics

(P-6124)
MARKWINS BEAUTY PRODUCTS INC
Also Called: Wet N Wild Los Angeles
22067 Ferrero (91789-5214)
PHONE...........................909 595-8898
Eric Chen, *Pr*
James Koeppl, *
Shawn Haynes, *
Michael Shaw, *
◆ **EMP:** 66 **EST:** 2003
SQ FT: 200,000
SALES (est): 42.23MM
SALES (corp-wide): 270.93MM **Privately Held**
Web: www.wetnwildbeauty.com
SIC: 5122 Cosmetics
PA: Markwins Beauty Brands, Inc.
  22067 Ferrero
  City Of Industry CA
  909 595-8898

(P-6125)
MCKESSON CORPORATION
3000 Colby St (94705-2083)
PHONE...........................510 666-0854
Micah Wakamatsu, *Brnch Mgr*
EMP: 66
SALES (corp-wide): 276.71B **Publicly Held**
Web: www.mckesson.com
SIC: 5122 Pharmaceuticals
PA: Mckesson Corporation
  6555 State Highway 161
  Irving TX
  972 446-4800

PRODUCTS & SERVICES SECTION
5122 - Drugs, Proprietaries, And Sundries (P-6146)

(P-6126)
MCKESSON CORPORATION
Also Called: McKesson Drug Company
9501 Norwalk Blvd (90670-2929)
P.O. Box 2116 (90670-0116)
PHONE..................................562 463-2100
Todd Kleinow, *Mgr*
EMP: 108
SALES (corp-wide): 276.71B **Publicly Held**
Web: www.mckesson.com
SIC: 5122 Pharmaceuticals
PA: Mckesson Corporation
6555 State Highway 161
Irving TX
972 446-4800

(P-6127)
MCKESSON CORPORATION
Also Called: Drohan Trade Center
11000 Trade Center Dr (95670-6153)
PHONE..................................916 636-8700
Donna Draher, *Brnch Mgr*
EMP: 73
SQ FT: 3,000
SALES (corp-wide): 276.71B **Publicly Held**
Web: www.mckesson.com
SIC: 5122 Pharmaceuticals
PA: Mckesson Corporation
6555 State Highway 161
Irving TX
972 446-4800

(P-6128)
MCKESSON MDCL-SRGCAL MDMART IN
Also Called: McKesson
2800 E Philadelphia St (91761-8523)
PHONE..................................800 755-2090
Tom Cummings, *Brnch Mgr*
EMP: 62
SALES (corp-wide): 276.71B **Publicly Held**
SIC: 5122 Pharmaceuticals
HQ: Mckesson Medical-Surgical Medimart Inc.
8121 10th Ave N
Minneapolis MN
763 595-6000

(P-6129)
MCKESSON PROPERTY COMPANY INC
Also Called: McKesson
1 Post St (94104-5284)
PHONE..................................415 983-8300
Frank Robinson, *Pr*
EMP: 245 **EST:** 1979
SQ FT: 300,000
SALES (est): 69.15MM
SALES (corp-wide): 276.71B **Publicly Held**
SIC: 5122 Pharmaceuticals
PA: Mckesson Corporation
6555 State Highway 161
Irving TX
972 446-4800

(P-6130)
MEDICAL RESEARCH INSTITUTE
Also Called: M R I
21411 Prairie St (91311-5829)
PHONE..................................818 739-6000
Chirag Patel, *CEO*
Patrick S Mccullough, *Pr*
Jenia G Khudagulyan, *
Alfred Baumeler, *CMO* *
Kevin J Dwyer, *
EMP: 242 **EST:** 1997
SALES (est): 8.27MM **Privately Held**
SIC: 5122 Vitamins and minerals
HQ: Natrol Llc
21411 Prairie St
Chatsworth CA
818 739-6000

(P-6131)
METAGENICS LLC (PA)
25 Enterprise Ste 200 (92656-2713)
PHONE..................................949 366-0818
Pat Smallcombe, *Pr*
Jean M Bellin, *
Dave Tuit, *
John Troup, *CSO**
Sara Gottfried, *CMO**
◆ **EMP:** 150 **EST:** 1983
SQ FT: 88,000
SALES (est): 188.55MM
SALES (corp-wide): 188.55MM **Privately Held**
Web: www.metagenics.com
SIC: 5122 Vitamins and minerals

(P-6132)
MURAD LLC
1340 Storm Pkwy (90501-5041)
PHONE..................................310 726-3300
EMP: 115
SALES (est): 62.39B **Privately Held**
Web: www.murad.com
SIC: 5122 Cosmetics
HQ: Murad, Llc
2121 Park Pl Fl 1
El Segundo CA

(P-6133)
N QIAGEN AMERCN HOLDINGS INC (HQ)
27220 Turnberry Ln Ste 200 (91355-1005)
PHONE..................................800 426-8157
Peer Schatz, *Pr*
EMP: 250 **EST:** 2000
SALES (est): 476.32MM **Privately Held**
SIC: 5122 Biologicals and allied products
PA: Qiagen N.V.
Hulsterweg 82
Venlo LI

(P-6134)
NATURES PRODUCTS INC (DH)
1221 Broadway (94612-1837)
PHONE..................................954 233-3300
Jose Minski, *Pr*
Meyer Minski, *VP*
Ruben Minski, *VP*
◆ **EMP:** 156 **EST:** 1986
SALES (est): 97.34MM
SALES (corp-wide): 7.39B **Publicly Held**
SIC: 5122 5499 Vitamins and minerals; Health and dietetic food stores
HQ: Nutranext, Llc
1301 Sawgrs Corp Pkwy
Sunrise FL

(P-6135)
NATUREWARE INC
6590 Darin Way (90630-5121)
PHONE..................................714 251-4510
Eun Ah Shin, *CEO*
Han C Shin, *
EMP: 96 **EST:** 2006
SALES (est): 22.65MM **Privately Held**
SIC: 5122 Vitamins and minerals

(P-6136)
NEW MILANI GROUP LLC
Also Called: Milani Cosmetics
10000 Washington Blvd Ste 210 (90232-2782)
P.O. Box 58585 (90058-0585)
PHONE..................................323 582-9404
Mary Van Praag, *CEO*
Lindsay Shumlas, *CFO*
Evelyn Wang, *CMO*
▲ **EMP:** 93 **EST:** 2001
SQ FT: 11,893
SALES (est): 32.98MM **Privately Held**
Web: www.milanicosmetics.com
SIC: 5122 Cosmetics

(P-6137)
PAUL MITCHELL JOHN SYSTEMS (PA)
Also Called: Paul Mitchell
20705 Centre Pointe Pkwy (91350-2967)
P.O. Box 10597 (90213-3597)
PHONE..................................800 793-8790
John Paul Dejoria, *Ch Bd*
Michaeline Dejoria, *CEO*
◆ **EMP:** 80 **EST:** 1980
SQ FT: 90,000
SALES (est): 100.53MM
SALES (corp-wide): 100.53MM **Privately Held**
Web: www.paulmitchell.com
SIC: 5122 5999 Hair preparations; Hair care products

(P-6138)
PIXI INC
Also Called: Pixi Beauty
10351 Santa Monica Blvd Ste 410 (90025-6908)
PHONE..................................310 670-7767
Felix Strand, *Pr*
Anthony Oppe, *
Petra Strand Oppe, *
Sjon Dowell, *
EMP: 64 **EST:** 2007
SQ FT: 8,400
SALES (est): 22.99MM **Privately Held**
SIC: 5122 Cosmetics

(P-6139)
PPHM INC
Also Called: Avid Biosciences
14282 Franklin Ave (92780-7009)
PHONE..................................714 508-6100
Nicholas Green, *CEO*
Daniel Hart, *CFO*
Jeffrey Masten, *VP*
EMP: 100 **EST:** 2002
SALES (est): 40.96MM
SALES (corp-wide): 149.27MM **Publicly Held**
SIC: 5122 Pharmaceuticals
PA: Avid Biosciences, Inc.
14191 Myford Rd
Tustin CA
714 508-6100

(P-6140)
PRIMAL ELEMENTS INC
Also Called: Primal Elements
18062 Redondo Cir (92648-1326)
PHONE..................................714 899-0757
▲ **EMP:** 99 **EST:** 1993
SQ FT: 56,500
SALES (est): 25.37MM **Privately Held**
Web: www.primalelements.com
SIC: 5122 2841 Cosmetics; Detergents, synthetic organic or inorganic alkaline

(P-6141)
QYK BRANDS LLC
12821 Western Ave (92841-4027)
PHONE..................................949 312-7119
EMP: 189 **EST:** 2017
SALES (est): 20.76MM **Privately Held**
Web: www.qyk.us
SIC: 5122 2842 3842 2023 Pharmaceuticals; Disinfectants, household or industrial plant; Respiratory protection equipment, personal; Dietary supplements, dairy and non-dairy based

(P-6142)
RUGBY LABORATORIES INC (DH)
311 Bonnie Cir (92878-5182)
PHONE..................................951 270-1400
David C Hsia Ph.d., *Pr*
Michael E Boser, *
Chato Abad, *
Frederick Wilkinson, *
Michel J Feldman, *
EMP: 90 **EST:** 1961
SALES (est): 92.61MM
SALES (corp-wide): 205.01B **Publicly Held**
SIC: 5122 2834 Pharmaceuticals; Pharmaceutical preparations
HQ: The Harvard Drug Group L L C
341 Mason Rd
La Vergne TN
800 616-2471

(P-6143)
SCIENCE OF SKINCARE LLC
Also Called: Innovative Skin Care
3333 N San Fernando Blvd (91504-2531)
PHONE..................................818 254-7961
C Bryan Johns, *Managing Member*
Alec Call, *
◆ **EMP:** 84 **EST:** 2003
SQ FT: 36,000
SALES (est): 26.51MM **Privately Held**
Web: www.isclinical.com
SIC: 5122 Cosmetics

(P-6144)
SCILEX INC (HQ)
960 San Antonio Rd (94303-4922)
PHONE..................................650 516-4310
Jaisim Shah, *CEO*
EMP: 65 **EST:** 2019
SALES (est): 38.03MM
SALES (corp-wide): 62.84MM **Publicly Held**
Web: www.scilexholding.com
SIC: 5122 Pharmaceuticals
PA: Sorrento Therapeutics, Inc.
4955 Directors Pl Ste 100
San Diego CA
858 203-4100

(P-6145)
SGII INC (PA)
Also Called: Senegence International
19651 Alter (92610-2507)
PHONE..................................949 521-6161
Joni Rogers Kante, *CEO*
Philippe Guerreau, *
Ben Kante, *
▲ **EMP:** 244 **EST:** 1997
SQ FT: 49,415
SALES (est): 89.75MM
SALES (corp-wide): 89.75MM **Privately Held**
Web: web.senegence.com
SIC: 5122 Cosmetics

(P-6146)
SV LABS CORPORATION (PA)
Also Called: Sinclair & Valentine
480 Airport Blvd (95076-2002)
PHONE..................................831 722-9526
Graham Orriss, *CEO*
Jeffrey K Slaboden, *

5122 - Drugs, Proprietaries, And Sundries (P-6147)

▲ EMP: 75 EST: 1979
SQ FT: 55,000
SALES (est): 97.52MM
SALES (corp-wide): 97.52MM Privately Held
Web: www.svnaturally.com
SIC: 5122 2844 Cosmetics; Perfumes, cosmetics and other toilet preparations

(P-6147)
UNITE EUROTHERAPY INC
2870 Whiptail Loop Ste 100 (92010-6709)
PHONE.................................760 585-1800
Andrew Dale, Pr
Andrew Dale, CEO
Jerry Trombetta, *
▲ EMP: 80 EST: 2002
SALES (est): 23MM Privately Held
Web: www.unitehair.com
SIC: 5122 Hair preparations

(P-6148)
URBAN DECAY COSMETICS LLC
Also Called: Urban Decay
833 W 16th St (92663-2801)
PHONE.................................949 631-4504
▲ EMP: 370 EST: 2000
SALES (est): 5.57MM
SALES (corp-wide): 5.95B Privately Held
SIC: 5122 Cosmetics
PA: L'oreal
    Mugler Beaute
    Paris
    140206000

(P-6149)
VALLEY OF SUN COSMETICS LLC
Also Called: Valley of The Sun Labs
535 Patrice Pl (90248-4232)
PHONE.................................310 327-9062
Ajmal Shehzad, *
◆ EMP: 156 EST: 1994
SQ FT: 10,000
SALES (est): 22.79MM Privately Held
Web: www.hollywoodstyleusa.com
SIC: 5122 Cosmetics

(P-6150)
VALLEY WHOLESALE DRUG CO LLC
Also Called: Valley Wholesale Drug
1401 W Fremont St (95203-2627)
P.O. Box 247 (08086-0247)
PHONE.................................209 466-0131
Henry Dale Smith, CEO
Dan Matteoli, *
Angelo Grande, *
EMP: 75 EST: 1948
SQ FT: 10,000
SALES (est): 25.42MM
SALES (corp-wide): 238.59B Publicly Held
Web: www.smartsourcerx.com
SIC: 5122 Pharmaceuticals
HQ: H. D. Smith, Llc
    1 W 1st Ave Ste 100
    Conshohocken PA
    866 232-1222

(P-6151)
VIVA LIFE SCIENCE INC
350 Paularino Ave (92626-4616)
PHONE.................................949 645-6100
David Fan, Pr
EMP: 220 EST: 1987
SQ FT: 60,000
SALES (est): 2.43MM
SALES (corp-wide): 22.12MM Privately Held

Web: www.vivalife.com
SIC: 5122 2833 Vitamins and minerals; Medicinals and botanicals
PA: Westar Nutrition Corp.
    350 Paularino Ave
    Costa Mesa CA
    949 645-6100

(P-6152)
WELLA OPERATIONS US LLC
4500 Park Granada Ste 100 (91302-1665)
PHONE.................................818 999-5112
Sennen Pamich, Sr VP
EMP: 500 EST: 2020
SALES (est): 106.83MM
SALES (corp-wide): 261.21MM Privately Held
SIC: 5122 Cosmetics, perfumes, and hair products
PA: Wella Germany Gmbh
    Berliner Allee 65-65a
    Darmstadt HE
    61513022301

5131 Piece Goods And Notions

(P-6153)
CHARMING TRIM & PACKAGING
5889 Rickenbacker Rd (90040-3027)
PHONE.................................415 302-7021
Richard Ringeisen, Pr
Barry Chan, *
EMP: 1000 EST: 2011
SALES (est): 40.49MM Privately Held
Web: www.charmingtrim.com
SIC: 5131 3111 Trimmings, apparel; Garment leather

(P-6154)
DESIGN COLLECTION INC
2209 S Santa Fe Ave (90058-1109)
PHONE.................................323 277-9200
Simon Barlava, CEO
Morris Barlava, *
Sohail Hussain, *
◆ EMP: 60 EST: 1987
SQ FT: 67,000
SALES (est): 18.53MM Privately Held
Web: www.designcollection.com
SIC: 5131 5023 Trimmings, apparel; Sheets, textile

(P-6155)
J ROBERT SCOTT INC (PA)
722 N La Cienega Blvd (90069-5086)
▲ EMP: 120 EST: 1972
SALES (est): 24.19MM
SALES (corp-wide): 24.19MM Privately Held
Web: www.jrobertscott.com
SIC: 5131 2512 2511 Textiles, woven, nec; Upholstered household furniture; Wood household furniture

(P-6156)
L & R DISTRIBUTORS INC
9292 9th St (91730-4407)
PHONE.................................909 980-3807
EMP: 272
SALES (corp-wide): 465.97MM Privately Held
Web: www.lrdist.com
SIC: 5131 Notions, nec
PA: L. & R. Distributors, Inc.
    88 35th St Ste 4
    Brooklyn NY
    718 272-2100

(P-6157)
M M FAB INC
Also Called: South Seas Imports
2300 E Gladwick St (90220-6208)
PHONE.................................310 763-3800
Richard Friedman, Prin
▲ EMP: 85 EST: 1988
SQ FT: 110,000
SALES (est): 14.94MM Privately Held
Web: www.southseasimports.com
SIC: 5131 Textiles, woven, nec

(P-6158)
MORGAN FABRICS CORPORATION (PA)
Also Called: Morgan Fabrics
4265 Exchange Ave (90058-2604)
P.O. Box 58523 (90058-0523)
PHONE.................................323 583-9981
Arnold Gittelson, Ch
Michael Gittelson, Pr
Robert Gittelson, VP
Ken Yang, CFO
◆ EMP: 60 EST: 1956
SQ FT: 50,000
SALES (est): 23.53MM
SALES (corp-wide): 23.53MM Privately Held
Web: www.morgan-fabrics.com
SIC: 5131 2759 Textiles, woven, nec; Commercial printing, nec

(P-6159)
PHOENIX TEXTILE INC (PA)
Also Called: Level 99
14600 S Broadway (90248-1812)
PHONE.................................310 715-7090
Dominic Poon, Pr
Joseph Tse, Treas
◆ EMP: 87 EST: 1984
SQ FT: 39,000
SALES (est): 23.57MM
SALES (corp-wide): 23.57MM Privately Held
Web: www.phoenixla.com
SIC: 5131 7389 Textiles, woven, nec; Sewing contractor

(P-6160)
PINDLER & PINDLER INC (PA)
Also Called: Pindler
11910 Poindexter Ave (93021-1748)
P.O. Box 8007 (93020-8007)
PHONE.................................805 531-9090
Curt R Pindler, Pr
S L Crawford Junior, Ex VP
Barbara Bick, *
▲ EMP: 95 EST: 1939
SQ FT: 75,000
SALES (est): 46.18MM
SALES (corp-wide): 46.18MM Privately Held
Web: www.pindler.com
SIC: 5131 Drapery material, woven

(P-6161)
RADIX TEXTILE INC
Also Called: Radix
600 E Washington Blvd Ste C2 (90015-3739)
PHONE.................................323 234-1667
Arad Shemirani, CEO
▲ EMP: 99 EST: 2007
SALES (est): 9.27MM Privately Held
SIC: 5131 2211 Piece goods and other fabrics; Broadwoven fabric mills, cotton

(P-6162)
SPECIALTY TEXTILE SERVICES LLC
1333 30th St Ste A (92154-3484)
PHONE.................................619 476-8750
Mark Wilstine, Mgr
EMP: 155
Web: www.specialtytextileservices.com
SIC: 5131 Textiles, woven, nec
PA: Specialty Textile Services Llc
    737 W Buchanan St
    Phoenix AZ

(P-6163)
STEVEN LABEL CORPORATION (PA)
11926 Burke St (90670-2546)
P.O. Box 3688 (90670-1688)
PHONE.................................562 698-9971
EMP: 119 EST: 1954
SALES (est): 23.33MM
SALES (corp-wide): 23.33MM Privately Held
Web: www.stevenlabel.com
SIC: 5131 3643 Labels; Electric switches

(P-6164)
UNICOLORS INC
3251 E 26th St (90058-8007)
PHONE.................................323 307-9878
Nader Pazirandeh, CEO
David Shu, *
▲ EMP: 60 EST: 1995
SQ FT: 35,000
SALES (est): 9.28MM Privately Held
Web: www.unicolors.net
SIC: 5131 Piece goods and other fabrics

(P-6165)
ZABIN INDUSTRIES INC (PA)
3957 S Hill St Ste A (90037-1343)
P.O. Box 15218 (90015-0218)
PHONE.................................213 749-1215
Alan Faiola, Pr
Virginia Acosta, *
▲ EMP: 70 EST: 1940
SQ FT: 43,000
SALES (est): 8.93MM
SALES (corp-wide): 8.93MM Privately Held
Web: www.zabin.com
SIC: 5131 Zippers

5136 Men's And Boy's Clothing

(P-6166)
BLACK BOX INC
371 2nd St Ste 1 (92024-3524)
PHONE.................................760 804-3300
▲ EMP: 100
SIC: 5136 5137 Men's and boy's clothing; Women's and children's clothing

(P-6167)
BOARDRIDERS WHOLESALE LLC (DH)
Also Called: Quiksilver
5600 Argosy Ave Ste 100 (92649-1063)
PHONE.................................714 889-2200
Arne Arens, CEO
◆ EMP: 73 EST: 1969
SALES (est): 100.9MM Privately Held
Web: www.quiksilver.com
SIC: 5136 5091 Men's and boy's clothing; Surfing equipment and supplies
HQ: Boardriders, Inc.
    5600 Argosy Ave Ste 100

PRODUCTS & SERVICES SECTION

5136 - Men's And Boy's Clothing (P-6189)

Huntington Beach CA
714 889-5404

(P-6168)
BRIXTON LLC
3821 Ocean Ranch Blvd (92056-2601)
PHONE..................866 264-4245
Raphael Peck, *Managing Member*
Jason Young, *
David Stoddard, *
▲ **EMP:** 79 **EST:** 2004
SQ FT: 10,000
SALES (est): 46.78MM
SALES (corp-wide): 677.57MM **Privately Held**
Web: www.brixton.com
SIC: 5136 5611 5137 5621 Work clothing, men's and boys'; Clothing accessories: men's and boys'; Fur clothing, women's and children's; Women's specialty clothing stores
PA: Altamont Capital Partners Llc
400 Hamilton Ave Ste 230
Palo Alto CA
650 264-7750

(P-6169)
CALIFORNIA SHIRT PRINTER INC
12221 Monarch St (92841-2906)
P.O. Box 801 (92038-0801)
PHONE..................714 898-9946
Suresh Khemlani, *Pr*
Sylvia Johnson, *
▲ **EMP:** 60 **EST:** 1980
SQ FT: 47,000
SALES (est): 9.8MM **Privately Held**
Web: www.calshirtprinter.com
SIC: 5136 7336 Shirts, men's and boys'; Silk screen design

(P-6170)
CHEF WORKS INC (PA)
12325 Kerran St # A (92064-6801)
PHONE..................858 643-5600
Neil R Gross, *CEO*
Joshua C Gross, *Pr*
David Roth, *COO*
David Forster, *CFO*
▲ **EMP:** 137 **EST:** 1994
SQ FT: 50,000
SALES (est): 116.22MM **Privately Held**
Web: www.chefworks.com
SIC: 5136 5137 Uniforms, men's and boys'; Uniforms, women's and children's

(P-6171)
COLOSSEUM ATHLETICS CORP
Also Called: Colosseum Athletics
2400 S Wilmington Ave (90220-5403)
PHONE..................310 667-8341
Stuart Whang, *CEO*
◆ **EMP:** 85 **EST:** 1992
SQ FT: 64,227
SALES (est): 36.14MM **Privately Held**
Web: www.colosseumusa.com
SIC: 5136 5137 Sportswear, men's and boys'; Sportswear, women's and children's

(P-6172)
DORFMAN MILANO COMPANY (HQ)
Also Called: Dorfman Pacific
2615 Boeing Way (95206-3984)
P.O. Box 213005 (95213-9005)
PHONE..................209 982-1400
Michael Binnie, *Pr*
Richard L Highsmith, *
◆ **EMP:** 140 **EST:** 1921
SQ FT: 275,000
SALES (est): 90.9MM **Privately Held**
Web: www.dorfmanmilano.com
SIC: 5136 5137 Caps, men's and boys'; Caps and gowns
PA: Young An Hat Co., Ltd.
215 Ojeong-Ro
Bucheon

(P-6173)
FASHION WORLD INCORPORATED
Also Called: Bijan
420 N Rodeo Dr (90210-4502)
PHONE..................310 273-6544
Manigeh Messa, *Mgr*
EMP: 128
SALES (corp-wide): 4.71MM **Privately Held**
SIC: 5136 Men's and boy's clothing
PA: Fashion World, Incorporated
421 N Rodeo Dr Ph
Beverly Hills CA
310 273-6544

(P-6174)
FORIA INTERNATIONAL INC
18689 Arenth Ave (91748-1302)
PHONE..................626 912-8836
◆ **EMP:** 111
Web: www.foria.com
SIC: 5136 Men's and boy's clothing

(P-6175)
GONZALES PARK LLC
Also Called: Fifth Sun
495 Ryan Ave (95973-8846)
PHONE..................530 343-8725
Daniel Gonzales, *Managing Member*
▲ **EMP:** 192 **EST:** 1995
SQ FT: 26,000
SALES (est): 98.1MM
SALES (corp-wide): 638.25MM **Privately Held**
Web: www.5sun.com
SIC: 5136 2326 5699 Shirts, men's and boys'; Men's and boy's work clothing; T-shirts, custom printed
HQ: Mad Engine Global, Llc
6740 Cobra Way Ste 100
San Diego CA
858 558-5270

(P-6176)
HELMET HOUSE LLC (PA)
Also Called: Tour Master
26855 Malibu Hills Rd (91301-5100)
PHONE..................800 421-7247
Robert M Miller, *CEO*
Philip Bellomy, *
Randy Hutchings, *
◆ **EMP:** 84 **EST:** 1969
SQ FT: 80,000
SALES (est): 40.34MM
SALES (corp-wide): 40.34MM **Privately Held**
Web: www.helmethouse.com
SIC: 5136 3949 3751 Men's and boy's clothing; Helmets, athletic; Motorcycle accessories

(P-6177)
HYBRID PROMOTIONS LLC (PA)
Also Called: Hybrid Promotions
10700 Valley View St (90630-4835)
PHONE..................714 952-3866
William Scott Hutchison, *CEO*
Faith Garcia-ross, *COO*
Ed Massura Csco, *Prin*
◆ **EMP:** 136 **EST:** 1999
SALES (est): 252.15MM
SALES (corp-wide): 252.15MM **Privately Held**
Web: www.hybridapparel.com
SIC: 5136 5137 5611 Sportswear, men's and boys'; Women's and children's clothing; Men's and boys' clothing stores

(P-6178)
KILAM INC
Also Called: Kilam
47685 Lakeview Blvd (94538-6544)
PHONE..................510 943-4040
Sunil Kilam, *Pr*
▼ **EMP:** 160 **EST:** 2006
SALES (est): 20.9MM **Privately Held**
Web: www.eastessence.com
SIC: 5136 5137 3842 5047 Apparel belts, men's and boys'; Apparel belts, women's and children's; Gloves, safety; Medical equipment and supplies

(P-6179)
LLC NOBLE RIDER (PA)
Also Called: Noble Outfitters
4300 Spyres Way (95356-9259)
PHONE..................209 566-7800
Dan J Costa, *Managing Member*
▲ **EMP:** 99 **EST:** 2012
SALES (est): 10.19MM
SALES (corp-wide): 10.19MM **Privately Held**
Web: www.nobleoutfitters.com
SIC: 5136 5137 7389 Sportswear, men's and boys'; Sportswear, women's and children's; Apparel designers, commercial

(P-6180)
M & S TRADING INC
Also Called: 7 Diamonds Clothing
15778 Gateway Cir (92780-6469)
PHONE..................714 241-7190
Sami Khalil, *CEO*
▲ **EMP:** 71 **EST:** 1991
SQ FT: 36,000
SALES (est): 7.37MM **Privately Held**
SIC: 5136 5137 Sportswear, men's and boys'; Women's and children's clothing

(P-6181)
MOTENG INC
Also Called: Rax Alar Products
12220 Parkway Centre Dr (92064-6867)
PHONE..................858 715-2500
▲ **EMP:** 70
SIC: 5136 5137 5072 5139 Men's and boy's clothing; Women's and children's clothing; Hardware; Footwear

(P-6182)
MOUNTAIN GEAR CORPORATION
Also Called: Tri-Mountain
4889 4th St (91706-2194)
PHONE..................626 851-2488
Daniel Tsai, *CEO*
Rosie Tsai, *
▲ **EMP:** 125 **EST:** 1994
SQ FT: 300,000
SALES (est): 21.76MM **Privately Held**
Web: www.trimountain.com
SIC: 5136 Sportswear, men's and boys'

(P-6183)
PRANA LIVING LLC (HQ)
Also Called: Prana
3209 Lionshead Ave (92010-4710)
PHONE..................866 915-6457
Monica Mirro, *Pr*
▲ **EMP:** 89 **EST:** 1992
SALES (est): 27.64MM
SALES (corp-wide): 3.46B **Publicly Held**
Web: www.prana.com
SIC: 5136 5137 Men's and boy's clothing; Women's and children's clothing
PA: Columbia Sportswear Company
14375 Nw Science Park Dr
Portland OR
503 985-4000

(P-6184)
QUAKE CITY CASUALS INC
Also Called: Quake City Caps
1800 S Flower St (90015-3424)
PHONE..................213 746-0540
John Glucksman, *CEO*
▲ **EMP:** 125 **EST:** 1977
SQ FT: 11,500
SALES (est): 20.32MM **Privately Held**
Web: www.capstoneheadwear.com
SIC: 5136 Men's and boy's clothing

(P-6185)
RICK SOLOMON ENTERPRISES INC (PA)
Also Called: Axis
8460 Higuera St (90232-2520)
P.O. Box 266 (90078-0266)
PHONE..................310 280-3700
Richard Solomon, *Pr*
Barbara Baskin, *
◆ **EMP:** 64 **EST:** 1983
SQ FT: 14,058
SALES (est): 9.99MM
SALES (corp-wide): 9.99MM **Privately Held**
Web: www.resmechanical.com
SIC: 5136 Sportswear, men's and boys'

(P-6186)
ROOCHI TRADERS INCORPORATED
Also Called: Cotton Heritage
6393 E Washington Blvd (90040-1817)
PHONE..................323 722-5592
▲ **EMP:** 75 **EST:** 1982
SALES (est): 33.92MM **Privately Held**
SIC: 5136 Sportswear, men's and boys'

(P-6187)
STR WORLDWIDE INC
Also Called: Silver Star Distribution
17462 Von Karman Ave (92614-6206)
PHONE..................949 276-5990
Luke Burrett, *Pr*
▲ **EMP:** 5035 **EST:** 1991
SQ FT: 2,000
SALES (est): 5.43MM **Privately Held**
SIC: 5136 Sportswear, men's and boys'
PA: Authentic Brands Group Llc
1411 Broadway Fl 4
New York NY

(P-6188)
STUSSY INC
Also Called: Stussy
17426 Daimler St (92614-5514)
PHONE..................949 474-9255
Frank Sinatra, *CEO*
▲ **EMP:** 90 **EST:** 1985
SQ FT: 30,000
SALES (est): 60.88MM **Privately Held**
Web: www.stussy.com
SIC: 5136 Men's and boy's clothing

(P-6189)
TOPWIN CORPORATION (PA)
Also Called: People's Place
1808 Abalone Ave (90501-3703)
PHONE..................310 325-2255

5136 - Men's And Boy's Clothing (P-6190)

Tomokazu Yoshimura, *CEO*
◆ **EMP:** 60 **EST:** 1984
SQ FT: 22,000
SALES (est): 22.33MM
SALES (corp-wide): 22.33MM **Privately Held**
Web: www.topwin.com
SIC: 5136 5137 5611 5621 Men's and boy's clothing; Women's and children's clothing; Men's and boys' clothing stores; Women's clothing stores

(P-6190)
TRLGGC SERVICES LLC
1888 Rosecrans Ave (90266-3712)
PHONE..............................323 266-3072
EMP: 256 **EST:** 2015
SALES (est): 958.45K
SALES (corp-wide): 350MM **Privately Held**
SIC: 5136 5137 Work clothing, men's and boys'; Women's and children's dresses, suits, skirts, and blouses
HQ: True Religion Sales, Llc
500 W 190th St Ste 300
Gardena CA

(P-6191)
TWIN HILL ACQUISITION CO INC
Also Called: Men's Wearhouse
6100 Stevenson Blvd (94538-2490)
PHONE..............................281 776-7000
Stuart Graham, *CEO*
EMP: 84 **EST:** 2001
SALES (est): 44.03MM
SALES (corp-wide): 2.52B **Privately Held**
Web: www.tailoredbrands.com
SIC: 5136 Sportswear, men's and boys'
HQ: The Men's Wearhouse Llc
6380 Rogerdale Rd
Houston TX
281 776-7000

(P-6192)
UNI HOSIERY CO INC (PA)
1911 E Olympic Blvd (90021-2421)
PHONE..............................213 228-0100
Harry Hayog Chung, *CEO*
◆ **EMP:** 120 **EST:** 1988
SQ FT: 500,000
SALES (est): 24.55MM
SALES (corp-wide): 24.55MM **Privately Held**
Web: www.unihosiery.com
SIC: 5136 5137 Hosiery, men's and boys'; Hosiery: women's, children's, and infants'

(P-6193)
VANTAGE CUSTOM CLASSICS INC
Also Called: Vantage Apparel
3321 S Susan St (92704-6858)
PHONE..............................714 755-1133
Patty Venny, *Mgr*
EMP: 117
SALES (corp-wide): 45.64MM **Privately Held**
Web: www.vantageapparel.com
SIC: 5136 2397 2395 Sportswear, men's and boys'; Schiffli machine embroideries; Pleating and stitching
PA: Vantage Custom Classics, Inc.
100 Vantage Dr
Avenel NJ
732 340-3000

5137 Women's And Children's Clothing

(P-6194)
ALSTYLE AP & ACTIVEWEAR MGT CO (HQ)
1501 E Cerritos Ave (92805-6400)
PHONE..............................714 765-0400
Rauf Gajiani, *CEO*
Amin Amdani, *
◆ **EMP:** 1800 **EST:** 2001
SQ FT: 715,000
SALES (est): 447.65MM
SALES (corp-wide): 3.24B **Privately Held**
SIC: 5137 Women's and children's clothing
PA: Les Vetements De Sport Gildan Inc
600 Boul De Maisonneuve O 33eme Etage
Montreal QC
514 735-2023

(P-6195)
BP CLOTHING LLC
Also Called: Baby Phat
3424 Garfield Ave (90040-3104)
▲ **EMP:** 150
SIC: 5137 Women's and children's clothing

(P-6196)
CALIFORNIA RAIN COMPANY INC
Also Called: California Rain
1213 E 14th St (90021-2215)
PHONE..............................213 623-6061
Jack Jhy C Jang, *Pr*
◆ **EMP:** 90 **EST:** 1986
SQ FT: 8,600
SALES (est): 15.82MM **Privately Held**
Web: www.californiarainla.com
SIC: 5137 5136 5699 Sportswear, women's and children's; Sportswear, men's and boys'; Customized clothing and apparel

(P-6197)
DELTA GALIL USA INC
Also Called: Loomworks Apparel
16912 Von Karman Ave (92606-4972)
PHONE..............................949 296-0380
EMP: 244
Web: www.deltagalil.com
SIC: 5137 Women's and children's lingerie and undergarments
HQ: Delta Galil Usa Inc.
1 Harmon Plz Fl 5
Secaucus NJ
201 902-0055

(P-6198)
EDGEMINE INC
Also Called: Mine
1801 E 50th St (90058-1940)
PHONE..............................323 267-8222
Kevin Chang Kang, *CEO*
Kristen Han, *Pr*
Sarah King, *VP*
Daniel Kang, *CFO*
▲ **EMP:** 130 **EST:** 1994
SQ FT: 200,000
SALES (est): 95MM **Privately Held**
Web: www.edgemine.com
SIC: 5137 5621 5961 Women's and children's clothing; Women's specialty clothing stores; Electronic shopping

(P-6199)
FOX HEAD INC (HQ)
Also Called: Fox Racing
16752 Armstrong Ave (92606-4912)
PHONE..............................949 757-9500
Jeff Mcguane, *CEO*
Tanya Fischesser, *
◆ **EMP:** 492 **EST:** 1974
SALES (est): 211.34MM
SALES (corp-wide): 3.08B **Publicly Held**
Web: www.foxracing.com
SIC: 5137 5699 5136 5961 Sportswear, women's and children's; Sports apparel; Sportswear, men's and boys'; Mail order house, nec
PA: Vista Outdoor Inc.
1 Vista Way
Anoka MN
763 433-1000

(P-6200)
INTERFOCUS INC (PA)
Also Called: Patpat
440 N Wolfe Rd E089 (94085-3869)
PHONE..............................844 972-8728
Can Wang, *CEO*
Can Gao, *CFO*
EMP: 79 **EST:** 2014
SALES (est): 15.71MM
SALES (corp-wide): 15.71MM **Privately Held**
Web: us.patpat.com
SIC: 5137 5961 Women's and children's clothing; Catalog and mail-order houses

(P-6201)
JOHNNY WAS LLC
395 Santa Monica Blvd # 124 (90401-2205)
PHONE..............................310 656-0600
Eli Levite, *Brnch Mgr*
EMP: 98
SALES (corp-wide): 1.41B **Publicly Held**
Web: www.johnnywas.com
SIC: 5137 2339 Women's and children's clothing; Women's and misses' accessories
HQ: Johnny Was, Llc
2423 E 23rd St
Los Angeles CA
323 582-1005

(P-6202)
KAREN KANE INC (PA)
2275 E 37th St (90058-1427)
PHONE..............................323 588-0000
Michael Kane, *CEO*
Lonnie Kane, *CFO*
Karen Kane, *Sec*
Cecelia Jenkins, *Treas*
▲ **EMP:** 130 **EST:** 1979
SQ FT: 96,000
SALES (est): 92.98MM
SALES (corp-wide): 92.98MM **Privately Held**
Web: www.karenkane.com
SIC: 5137 Women's and children's clothing

(P-6203)
KASH APPAREL LLC
Also Called: Socialite Clothing
1437 E 20th St (90011-1301)
PHONE..............................213 747-8885
Stephanie Kleinjan, *Managing Member*
Adir Haroni, *
▲ **EMP:** 62 **EST:** 2011
SQ FT: 10,000
SALES (est): 15.68MM **Privately Held**
Web: www.shopsocialite.com
SIC: 5137 Women's and children's accessories

(P-6204)
LDLA CLOTHING LLC
Also Called: Living Doll
13071 Temple Ave (91746-1418)
PHONE..............................323 312-2805
EMP: 60 **EST:** 2009
SALES (est): 7.5MM **Privately Held**
SIC: 5137 Women's and children's clothing

(P-6205)
LYMI INC (PA)
Also Called: Reformation, The
2744 E 11th St (90023-3404)
PHONE..............................855 756-0560
Hali Borenstein, *CEO*
Jennifer Maclellan, *
Yael Alfalo, *
▲ **EMP:** 100 **EST:** 2013
SQ FT: 120,000
SALES (est): 272.4MM
SALES (corp-wide): 272.4MM **Privately Held**
Web: www.thereformation.com
SIC: 5137 Women's and children's clothing

(P-6206)
MAD ENGINE GLOBAL LLC
6740 Cobra Way Ste 100 (92121-4102)
PHONE..............................858 558-5270
EMP: 306 **EST:** 2020
SALES (est): 33.73MM **Privately Held**
SIC: 5137 Women's and children's clothing

(P-6207)
MATESTA CORPORATION
5620 Knott Ave (90621-1808)
P.O. Box 5395 (90622-5395)
PHONE..............................949 874-6052
Salim Saeed, *CEO*
Robert Abraham, *CFO*
▲ **EMP:** 106 **EST:** 2017
SALES (est): 62MM **Privately Held**
Web: www.matesta.com
SIC: 5137 5136 Women's and children's clothing; Men's and boy's clothing

(P-6208)
MIAS FASHION MFG CO INC
Also Called: California Basic
12623 Cisneros Ln (90670-3373)
PHONE..............................562 906-1060
Peter D Anh, *Pr*
Brian Song, *
◆ **EMP:** 252 **EST:** 1999
SALES (est): 83MM **Privately Held**
Web: www.miasfashion.com
SIC: 5137 Women's and children's clothing

(P-6209)
MISOPE U S A INC
Also Called: I Joah
1100 S San Pedro St Ste A7 (90015-2343)
PHONE..............................213 746-0888
Peter Song, *Pr*
▲ **EMP:** 60 **EST:** 1997
SALES (est): 6.35MM **Privately Held**
SIC: 5137 Women's and children's clothing

(P-6210)
NEWPORT APPAREL CORPORATION (PA)
Also Called: I N G
1215 W Walnut St (90220-5009)
PHONE..............................310 605-1900
James Kim, *Pr*
Kimberly Kim, *
▲ **EMP:** 62 **EST:** 1988
SQ FT: 38,500
SALES (est): 21.36MM
SALES (corp-wide): 21.36MM **Privately Held**
Web: www.newportapparel.com

PRODUCTS & SERVICES SECTION

5139 - Footwear (P-6232)

SIC: 5137 Sportswear, women's and children's

(P-6211)
NHN GLOBAL INC (HQ)
Also Called: Fashiongo.com
2250 Maple Ave (90011-1190)
PHONE.................................424 672-1177
Daniel Lee, *CEO*
EMP: 109 EST: 2005
SALES (est): 50.67MM **Privately Held**
Web: www.nhnglobal.com
SIC: 5137 7389 Women's and children's clothing
PA: Nhn Corporation
   16 Daewangpangyo-Ro 645beon-Gil,
   Bundang-Gu
   Seongnam

(P-6212)
NYDJ APPAREL LLC
Also Called: Not Your Daughters Jeans
5401 S Soto St (90058-3618)
PHONE.................................323 581-9040
Lisa Collier, *Pr*
Steve Brink, *
▲ EMP: 200 EST: 2003
SQ FT: 6,000
SALES (est): 44.59MM **Privately Held**
Web: www.nydj.com
SIC: 5137 Women's and children's clothing

(P-6213)
O & K INC (PA)
Also Called: One Clothing
2121 E 37th St (90058-1416)
PHONE.................................323 846-5700
Chang Ho Ok, *CEO*
Seongeun Kim, *
Chang Ho, *
▲ EMP: 134 EST: 1989
SQ FT: 55,000
SALES (est): 23.69MM **Privately Held**
Web: www.oneclothing.com
SIC: 5137 Women's and children's clothing

(P-6214)
PARADISE LINGERIE INC
Also Called: Honeydew Intimates
20830 Dearborn St (91311-5915)
PHONE.................................818 717-9717
Motty Zafrani, *CFO*
▲ EMP: 61 EST: 1985
SQ FT: 13,000
SALES (est): 9.6MM **Privately Held**
Web: www.honeydewintimates.com
SIC: 5137 5136 Lingerie; Underwear, men's and boys'

(P-6215)
PARAGON TEXTILES INC
Also Called: Samiyatex
13003 S Figueroa St (90061-1136)
PHONE.................................310 323-7500
Murtaza Haji, *CEO*
Murtaza Haji, *Pr*
Farhana Haji, *
▼ EMP: 65 EST: 1992
SQ FT: 42,500
SALES (est): 23.41MM **Privately Held**
Web: www.samiyatex.com
SIC: 5137 Women's and children's clothing

(P-6216)
PIEGE CO (PA)
Also Called: Buffalo
20120 Plummer St (91311-5448)
PHONE.................................818 727-9100
Kambiz Zarabi, *CEO*
Morad Zarabi, *
Michael Zarabi, *
Nara Estpanian, *
▲ EMP: 95 EST: 1981
SQ FT: 48,000
SALES (est): 41.83MM
SALES (corp-wide): 41.83MM **Privately Held**
Web: www.felina.com
SIC: 5137 5136 5632 Lingerie; Men's and boys' suits and trousers; Lingerie and corsets (underwear)

(P-6217)
PRINCESS CRUISE LINES LTD
1242 E 25th St (90011-1708)
PHONE.................................213 745-0314
Delcino Fernandez, *Brnch Mgr*
EMP: 186
SALES (corp-wide): 3.94B **Privately Held**
Web: www.princess.com
SIC: 5137 Infants' wear
HQ: Princess Cruise Lines, Ltd.
   24305 Town Center Dr
   Santa Clarita CA
   661 753-0000

(P-6218)
SAK BRAND GROUP
400 Alabama St (94110-1315)
PHONE.................................415 486-1200
EMP: 65
Web: www.thesak.com
SIC: 5137 5632 3171 Women's and children's clothing; Women's accessory and specialty stores; Women's handbags and purses
PA: The Sak Brand Group
   339 5th Ave Fl 2
   New York NY

(P-6219)
SAME SWIM LLC
2333 E 49th St (90058-2820)
PHONE.................................323 582-2588
EMP: 90 EST: 2015
SALES (est): 4.07MM **Privately Held**
SIC: 5137 Women's and children's sportswear and swimsuits

(P-6220)
SEVEN LICENSING COMPANY LLC
Also Called: Seven7 Brands
801 S Figueroa St Ste 2500 (90017-5504)
PHONE.................................323 780-8250
▲ EMP: 102 EST: 2002
SALES (est): 38.76MM **Privately Held**
Web: www.sunrisebrands.com
SIC: 5137 Women's and children's accessories
PA: Sunrise Brands, Llc
   5401 S Soto St
   Vernon CA

(P-6221)
SIGNAL PRODUCTS INC (PA)
Also Called: Signal Products/Guess Handbags
5600 W Adams Blvd Ste 200 (90016-2563)
PHONE.................................213 748-0990
▲ EMP: 90 EST: 1992
SALES (est): 21.8MM **Privately Held**
Web: www.signalbrands.com
SIC: 5137 Handbags

(P-6222)
STANCE INC (PA)
Also Called: Stance
197 Avenida La Pata (92673-6307)
PHONE.................................949 391-9030
John Wilson, *CEO*
Brian Shea, *
▲ EMP: 215 EST: 2009
SALES (est): 84.98MM
SALES (corp-wide): 84.98MM **Privately Held**
Web: www.stance.com
SIC: 5137 Women's and children's clothing

(P-6223)
SWATFAME INC (PA)
Also Called: Kut From The Kloth
16425 Gale Ave (91745-1722)
PHONE.................................626 961-7928
Mitchell Quaranta, *CEO*
Jonathan Greenberg, *
Brian Min, *
▲ EMP: 290 EST: 1978
SQ FT: 233,000
SALES (est): 88.04MM
SALES (corp-wide): 88.04MM **Privately Held**
Web: www.swatfame.com
SIC: 5137 2211 2339 Dresses; Denims; Women's and misses' outerwear, nec

(P-6224)
TARRANT APPAREL GROUP
Also Called: Fashion Resources
5401 S Soto St (90058-3618)
PHONE.................................323 780-8250
Gerard Guez, *Ch Bd*
Todd Kay, *
Peter Akaradian, *
▲ EMP: 94 EST: 1988
SALES (est): 14.26MM **Privately Held**
Web: www.sunrisebrands.com
SIC: 5137 Women's and children's clothing
PA: Sunrise Brands, Llc
   5401 S Soto St
   Vernon CA

(P-6225)
THIRDLOVE INC
Also Called: Thirdlove
555 Market St Fl 13 (94105-2806)
PHONE.................................415 692-0089
Heidi Zak, *CEO*
Jenny Oh, *CFO*
Phillip Spector, *
EMP: 230 EST: 2012
SALES (est): 99.36MM **Privately Held**
Web: www.thirdlove.com
SIC: 5137 2342 Underwear: women's, children's, and infants'; Brassieres

5139 Footwear

(P-6226)
ACI INTERNATIONAL (PA)
844 Moraga Dr (90049-1632)
PHONE.................................310 889-3400
Steven Jackson, *CEO*
David Mankowitz, *
Anna Liau, *
▲ EMP: 80 EST: 1952
SQ FT: 40,000
SALES (est): 62.71MM
SALES (corp-wide): 62.71MM **Privately Held**
Web: www.acifootwear.com
SIC: 5139 3021 Shoes; Rubber and plastics footwear

(P-6227)
ASICS AMERICA CORPORATION (HQ)
Also Called: Asics Tiger
7755 Irvine Center Dr Ste 400 (92618-2904)
PHONE.................................949 453-8888
Gene Mccarthy, *Pr*
Seiho Gohashi, *
Kenji Sakai, *
◆ EMP: 109 EST: 1973
SALES (est): 882.54MM **Privately Held**
Web: www.asics.com
SIC: 5139 5136 5137 2369 Footwear, athletic; Sportswear, men's and boys'; Sportswear, women's and children's; Girl's and children's outerwear, nec
PA: Asics Corporation
   7-1-1, Minatojimanakamachi, Chuo-Ku
   Kobe HYO

(P-6228)
AYLESVA INC
14537 Garfield Ave (90723-3425)
PHONE.................................562 688-0592
Jose Luis Solorcano, *Pr*
EMP: 120 EST: 2013
SALES (est): 4.55MM **Privately Held**
Web: aylesva-com-inc.hub.biz
SIC: 5139 5661 5651 5137 Shoes; Shoe stores; Family clothing stores; Coordinate sets: women's, children's, and infants'

(P-6229)
BIRKENSTOCK USA LP
100 Wood Hollow Dr Ste 100 (94945)
PHONE.................................415 884-3200
Stephan Birkenstock, *Pt*
Bernd Hillen, *Pt*
▲ EMP: 250 EST: 1971
SQ FT: 15,000
SALES (est): 76.33MM
SALES (corp-wide): 861.84MM **Privately Held**
Web: www.birkenstock.com
SIC: 5139 Footwear
HQ: Ockenfels Services Gmbh
   Burg Ockenfels
   Linz RP
   26459420

(P-6230)
BLOWFISH LLC
Also Called: Blowfish Footwear
6065 Bristol Pkwy # 100 (90230-6601)
PHONE.................................310 566-5700
Don Weiss, *Pr*
Stephen Hoyt, *
Greg Kearns, *
▲ EMP: 77 EST: 2006
SALES (est): 20.82MM
SALES (corp-wide): 2.97B **Publicly Held**
Web: www.blowfishshoes.com
SIC: 5139 Shoes
PA: Caleres, Inc.
   8300 Maryland Ave
   Saint Louis MO
   314 854-4000

(P-6231)
CONVERSE INC
1437 3rd Street Promenade 39 (90401)
PHONE.................................310 451-0314
EMP: 89
SALES (corp-wide): 51.22B **Publicly Held**
Web: www.converse.com
SIC: 5139 5661 Footwear, athletic; Footwear, athletic
HQ: Converse Inc.
   1 Lovejoy Wharf
   Boston MA
   617 248-9530

(P-6232)
FORTUNE DYNAMIC INC
21923 Ferrero (91789-5210)

5139 - Footwear (P-6233)

PHONE..................909 979-8318
Carol Lee, Pr
James Lee, *
◆ EMP: 90 EST: 1986
SQ FT: 150,000
SALES (est): 19.78MM **Privately Held**
Web: www.fortunedynamic.com
SIC: 5139 Shoes

(P-6233)
OSATA ENTERPRISES INC
Also Called: Globe Shoes
18105 Bishop Ave (90746-4020)
PHONE.....................888 445-6237
Matthew Hill, Pr
Gary Valentine, *
▲ EMP: 100 EST: 1997
SQ FT: 30,000
SALES (est): 32.67MM **Privately Held**
SIC: 5139 Shoes
PA: Globe International Limited
1 Fennell St
Port Melbourne VIC

(P-6234)
SOUTH CONE INC
Also Called: Reef
5935 Darwin Ct (92008-7302)
PHONE.....................760 431-2300
Mike Jensen, CEO
◆ EMP: 120 EST: 1984
SQ FT: 37,583
SALES (est): 26.68MM
SALES (corp-wide): 11.61B **Publicly Held**
Web: www.reef.com
SIC: 5139 3144 3143 Shoes; Women's footwear, except athletic; Men's footwear, except athletic
PA: V.F. Corporation
1551 Wewatta St
Denver CO
720 778-4000

5141 Groceries, General Line

(P-6235)
ACOSTA INC
Also Called: Acosta Sales & Marketing
480 Apollo St Ste C (92821-3121)
PHONE.....................714 988-1500
Rick Nist, Brnch Mgr
EMP: 150
SALES (corp-wide): 1.88B **Privately Held**
Web: www.acosta.com
SIC: 5141 Food brokers
HQ: Acosta Inc.
6600 Corporate Ctr Pkwy
Jacksonville FL
904 281-9800

(P-6236)
ACOSTA INC
Acosta Sales & Marketing
5735 W Las Positas Blvd Ste 300 (94588-4002)
PHONE.....................925 600-3500
Tony Mello, Dir
EMP: 96
SALES (corp-wide): 1.88B **Privately Held**
Web: www.acosta.com
SIC: 5141 Food brokers
HQ: Acosta Inc.
6600 Corporate Ctr Pkwy
Jacksonville FL
904 281-9800

(P-6237)
ADVANTAGE-CROWN SLS & MKTG LLC (DH)
1400 S Douglass Rd Ste 200 (92806-6904)
P.O. Box 66010 (92816-6010)
PHONE.....................714 780-3000
Bob Vesley, CFO
▲ EMP: 1100 EST: 1995
SALES (est): 340.5MM
SALES (corp-wide): 4.71B **Publicly Held**
SIC: 5141 Food brokers
HQ: Advantage Sales & Marketing Llc
15310 Barranca Pkwy # 100
Irvine CA
949 797-2900

(P-6238)
AFC DISTRIBUTION CORP
19205 S Laurel Park Rd (90220-6032)
PHONE.....................310 604-3630
Sadamu Taniguch, CEO
EMP: 250 EST: 2016
SALES (est): 89.31MM **Privately Held**
Web: www.afcsushi.com
SIC: 5141 Groceries, general line
PA: Zensho Holdings Co., Ltd.
2-18-1, Konan
Minato-Ku TKY

(P-6239)
AMK FOODSERVICES INC
Also Called: Kaney Foods
830 Capitolio Way (93401-7122)
P.O. Box 1188 (93406-1188)
PHONE.....................805 544-7600
John P Kaney, CEO
EMP: 130 EST: 1988
SQ FT: 35,000
SALES (est): 25.36MM **Privately Held**
SIC: 5141 Food brokers

(P-6240)
ANSAR GALLERY INC
2505 El Camino Rd (92782)
PHONE.....................949 220-0000
Ali Akbar Feroozesh, Prin
Hussein Saadat, *
▲ EMP: 200 EST: 2013
SQ FT: 120,000
SALES (est): 36.44MM **Privately Held**
Web: www.ansargallery.us
SIC: 5141 Food brokers
PA: Ansar Gallery Llc Branch
Office No M, Al-Ittihad Street-Ansar Mall, Al-Nahda
Sharjah

(P-6241)
BI-RITE RESTAURANT SUP CO INC
Also Called: Bi-Rite Foodservice Distrs
123 S Hill Dr (94005-1203)
PHONE.....................415 656-0187
William Barulich, CEO
Steve Barulich, Pr
Nathan Barulich, VP
Zachary Barulich, CFO
Zack Barulich, CFO
◆ EMP: 300 EST: 1941
SQ FT: 220,000
SALES (est): 173.96MM **Privately Held**
Web: www.birite.com
SIC: 5141 5147 5148 5023 Groceries, general line; Meats and meat products; Fresh fruits and vegetables; Kitchenware

(P-6242)
BUFFALO MARKET INC
Also Called: Buffalo Market
1439 N Highland Ave (90028-7622)
PHONE.....................650 337-0078
Adam Olejniczak, CEO
Charmaine Button, *
Sean Howell, *
EMP: 140 EST: 2019
SALES (est): 22MM **Privately Held**
Web: www.buffalomarket.com
SIC: 5141 Groceries, general line

(P-6243)
C&S WHOLESALE GROCERS INC
Also Called: C&S WHOLESALE GROCERS, INC.
2797 S Orange Ave (93725-1919)
P.O. Box 11097 (93771-1097)
PHONE.....................559 442-4700
Randy Wood, Brnch Mgr
EMP: 138
SALES (corp-wide): 15.34B **Privately Held**
Web: www.cswg.com
SIC: 5141 Food brokers
PA: C&S Wholesale Grocers, Llc
7 Corporate Dr
Keene NH
603 354-7000

(P-6244)
CANTON FOOD CO INC
750 S Alameda St (90021-1624)
PHONE.....................213 688-7707
Shiu Lit Kwan, CEO
Shui Lit Kwan, *
Cho W Kwan, *
Wai Kam Kwan, *
▲ EMP: 106 EST: 1979
SQ FT: 96,000
SALES (est): 29.65MM **Privately Held**
Web: www.cantonfoodco.com
SIC: 5141 5146 5411 5421 Food brokers; Seafoods; Grocery stores; Seafood markets

(P-6245)
CERENZIA FOODS INC
8585 White Oak Ave (91730-5146)
P.O. Box 3719 (91729-3719)
PHONE.....................909 989-4000
Joseph F Annunziato, CEO
Tony Tony Annunziato, Prin
▲ EMP: 60 EST: 1984
SQ FT: 75,000
SALES (est): 47.36MM **Privately Held**
Web: www.cerenziafoods.com
SIC: 5141 Food brokers

(P-6246)
COASTAL PACIFIC FD DISTRS INC (PA)
1015 Performance Dr (95206-4925)
P.O. Box 30910 (95213-0910)
PHONE.....................909 947-2066
Terrence Wood, CEO
David Jared, Vice Chairman
Wayne Duncan, Sec
John Payne, Treas
Edmond Jared, VP
◆ EMP: 220 EST: 1986
SQ FT: 500,000
SALES (est): 496.11MM
SALES (corp-wide): 496.11MM **Privately Held**
Web: www.cpfd.com
SIC: 5141 5149 Groceries, general line; Bakery products

(P-6247)
CONCORD FOODS INC (HQ)
4601 E Guasti Rd (91761-8105)
PHONE.....................909 975-2000
Nick J Sciortino Junior, Pr
John Sciortino, *
Roy Sciortino, *
EMP: 89 EST: 1985
SQ FT: 67,000
SALES (est): 51.77MM
SALES (corp-wide): 76.32MM **Publicly Held**
Web: www.concordfoodsinc.com
SIC: 5141 Food brokers
PA: Sysco Corporation
1390 Enclave Pkwy
Houston TX
281 584-1390

(P-6248)
DEL MONACO FOODS LLC
Also Called: Del Monaco Foods, Inc.
18675 Madrone Pkwy Ste 150 (95037-2868)
PHONE.....................408 500-4100
Ernestine Del Monaco, Ch Bd
Vic Del Monaco, *
Tony Del Monaco, *
EMP: 88 EST: 1998
SQ FT: 18,000
SALES (est): 15.1MM
SALES (corp-wide): 105MM **Privately Held**
SIC: 5141 Food brokers
PA: Kettle Cuisine, Llc
330 Lynnway
Lynn MA
617 409-1100

(P-6249)
DELIVERR INC
307 S Wilson Ave Apt 6 (91106-3238)
PHONE.....................213 534-8686
EMP: 415
SALES (corp-wide): 504.44MM **Privately Held**
Web: www.deliveer.com
SIC: 5141 Groceries, general line
HQ: Deliverr, Inc.
110 Sutter St Fl 9
San Francisco CA
415 475-9175

(P-6250)
DOT FOODS INC
2200 Nickerson Dr (95358-9489)
PHONE.....................209 581-9090
EMP: 145
SALES (corp-wide): 1.09B **Privately Held**
Web: www.dotfoods.com
SIC: 5141 Food brokers
PA: Dot Foods, Inc.
1 Dot Way
Mount Sterling IL
217 773-4411

(P-6251)
DPI SPECIALTY FOODS WEST INC (DH)
Also Called: Dpi Specialty Foods
601 S Rockefeller Ave (91761-7871)
PHONE.....................909 975-1019
John Jordan, CEO
Donna Robbins, *
James De Keyser, *
Larry Noble, *
Conor Crowley, *
◆ EMP: 102 EST: 1951
SQ FT: 250,000
SALES (est): 477.21MM
SALES (corp-wide): 2.4B **Privately Held**
Web: www.dpispecialtyfoods.com
SIC: 5141 Food brokers
HQ: Dpi Specialty Foods, Inc.
601 S Rockefeller Ave
Ontario CA

▲ = Import ▼ = Export
◆ = Import/Export

PRODUCTS & SERVICES SECTION
5141 - Groceries, General Line (P-6272)

(P-6252)
DPI SPECIALTY FOODS WEST INC
Also Called: Dpi West
930 S Rockefeller Ave (91761-8149)
PHONE...................909 975-1019
EMP: 233
SALES (corp-wide): 2.4B **Privately Held**
Web: www.dpispecialtyfoods.com
SIC: 5141 Food brokers
HQ: Dpi Specialty Foods West, Inc.
601 S Rockefeller Ave
Ontario CA
909 975-1019

(P-6253)
FOOD SALES WEST INC
235 Baker St (92626-4504)
P.O. Box 19738 (92623-9738)
PHONE...................714 966-2900
David Lyons, *CEO*
Carl Scharffenberger, *
Mary Ellen Scharffenberger, *
Robert Watkins, *
Michael Berkson, *
EMP: 85 **EST:** 1973
SQ FT: 12,000
SALES (est): 18.88MM **Privately Held**
SIC: 5141 Food brokers

(P-6254)
FOOTHILL PACKING INC
2255 S Broadway (93454-7871)
PHONE...................805 925-7900
Jorge Rivera, *Pr*
EMP: 489
SALES (corp-wide): 46.83MM **Privately Held**
Web: www.foothillpacking.com
SIC: 5141 Food brokers
PA: Foothill Packing, Inc.
1582 Moffett St
Salinas CA
831 784-1453

(P-6255)
GOURMET FOODS INC (PA)
2910 E Harcourt St (90221-5502)
PHONE...................310 632-3300
Marcel Lagnaz, *Managing Member*
Mitch Rosen, *Managing Member*
◆ **EMP:** 81 **EST:** 1986
SQ FT: 35,000
SALES (est): 51.21MM
SALES (corp-wide): 51.21MM **Privately Held**
Web: www.gourmetfoodsinc.com
SIC: 5141 5812 2099 Food brokers; Eating places; Food preparations, nec

(P-6256)
GRAND SUPERCENTER INC
8550 Chetle Ave Ste B (90606-2662)
PHONE...................562 318-3451
Ilyeon Kwon, *CEO*
EMP: 90
SALES (corp-wide): 485.87MM **Privately Held**
SIC: 5141 5499 Groceries, general line; Juices, fruit or vegetable
HQ: Grand Supercenter Inc.
300 Chubb Ave
Lyndhurst NJ
201 507-9900

(P-6257)
HIGHLAND WHOLESALE FOODS INC
Also Called: Highland Wholesale Foods
1604 Tillie Lewis Dr (95206-1170)
PHONE...................209 933-0580
T Gregory Stagnitto, *Pr*
Tommy Sodaro, *
Cliff Coler, *
▼ **EMP:** 80 **EST:** 1999
SQ FT: 240,000
SALES (est): 28.29MM **Privately Held**
Web: www.highlandwholesalefoods.com
SIC: 5141 Food brokers

(P-6258)
ICPK CORPORATION
Also Called: Hpp Food Services
1130 W C St (90744-5102)
PHONE...................310 830-8020
EMP: 70
SALES (corp-wide): 17.78MM **Privately Held**
Web: www.hppfs.com
SIC: 5141 2035 Groceries, general line; Dressings, salad: raw and cooked (except dry mixes)
PA: Icpk Corporation
16700 Valley View Ave # 170
La Mirada CA
714 321-7025

(P-6259)
ITALFOODS INC
205 Shaw Rd (94080-6605)
P.O. Box 2563 (94083-2563)
PHONE...................650 877-0724
Georgette Guerra, *CEO*
▲ **EMP:** 80 **EST:** 1978
SQ FT: 114,000
SALES (est): 31.28MM **Privately Held**
Web: www.italfoodsinc.com
SIC: 5141 Food brokers

(P-6260)
LASSEN CANYON NURSERY INC (PA)
1300 Salmon Creek Rd (96003-8267)
P.O. Box 992400 (96099-2400)
PHONE...................530 223-1075
Elizabeth Elwood Ponce, *CEO*
Kenneth Elwood Junior, *Pr*
▼ **EMP:** 125 **EST:** 1964
SQ FT: 3,000
SALES (est): 46.53MM
SALES (corp-wide): 46.53MM **Privately Held**
Web: www.lassencanyonnursery.com
SIC: 5141 5191 0171 Groceries, general line; Hay; Raspberry farm

(P-6261)
LEE BROS FOODSERVICES INC (PA)
Also Called: Lee Industrial Catering
660 E Gish Rd (95112-2707)
PHONE...................408 275-0700
Chieu Van Le, *CEO*
Huong Le, *
Jimmy Lee, *
▲ **EMP:** 100 **EST:** 1985
SQ FT: 15,000
SALES (est): 49.32MM
SALES (corp-wide): 49.32MM **Privately Held**
SIC: 5141 5142 Food brokers; Packaged frozen goods

(P-6262)
LUKES LOCAL INC
960 Cole St (94117-4316)
PHONE...................415 742-4207
Luke Oppenheim, *CEO*
Luke Chappell, *
Toms Gutierrez, *
EMP: 90 **EST:** 2009
SALES (est): 15.5MM **Privately Held**
Web: www.lukeslocal.com
SIC: 5141 5411 Groceries, general line; Grocery stores

(P-6263)
MARQUEZ BROTHERS ENTPS INC
15480 Valley Blvd (91746-3325)
PHONE...................626 330-3310
Gustavo Marquez, *Pr*
Juan Marquez, *
Jaime Marquez, *
◆ **EMP:** 200 **EST:** 1993
SQ FT: 200,000
SALES (est): 22.87MM **Privately Held**
SIC: 5141 Food brokers

(P-6264)
MARQUEZ BROTHERS INTL INC (PA)
Also Called: M B
5801 Rue Ferrari (95138-1857)
PHONE...................408 960-2700
Marquez Gustavo Junior, *CEO*
Gustavo Marquez, *
Lara Franciso, *VP*
Jaime Marquez, *
Jerry Santamaria, *
◆ **EMP:** 150 **EST:** 1981
SQ FT: 160,000
SALES (est): 104.16MM
SALES (corp-wide): 104.16MM **Privately Held**
Web: www.marquezbrothers.com
SIC: 5141 Food brokers

(P-6265)
MARTIN-BROWER COMPANY LLC
4704 Fite Ct (95215-8308)
P.O. Box 547 (97378-0547)
PHONE...................209 466-2980
EMP: 260
Web: www.martinbrower.com
SIC: 5141 Food brokers
HQ: The Martin-Brower Company, L.L.C.
6250 N River Rd Ste 9000
Rosemont IL
847 227-6500

(P-6266)
MCLANE FOODSERVICE INC
14813 Meridian Pkwy (92518-3004)
PHONE...................951 867-3555
Richard Arzinger, *Genl Mgr*
EMP: 234
SALES (corp-wide): 302.09B **Publicly Held**
Web: www.mclaneco.com
SIC: 5141 Groceries, general line
HQ: Mclane Foodservice, Inc.
2085 Midway Rd
Carrollton TX
972 364-2054

(P-6267)
MCLANE/PACIFIC INC
Also Called: McLane
3876 E Childs Ave (95341-9520)
P.O. Box 2107 (95344-0107)
PHONE...................209 725-2500
William G Rosier, *CEO*
Mike Youngblood, *Pr*
Jim Kent, *Ex VP*
Kevin Koch, *Treas*
▲ **EMP:** 498 **EST:** 1983
SQ FT: 220,000
SALES (est): 92.57MM
SALES (corp-wide): 302.09B **Publicly Held**
SIC: 5141 Food brokers
HQ: Mclane Company, Inc.
4747 Mclane Pkwy
Temple TX
254 771-7500

(P-6268)
MERCADO LATINO INC (PA)
245 Baldwin Park Blvd (91746-1404)
P.O. Box 6168 (91734-6168)
PHONE...................626 333-6862
Roberto Rodriguez, *CEO*
Richard Rodriguez, *
Jorge Rodriguez, *
Angelita Rodriguez, *
◆ **EMP:** 100 **EST:** 1963
SQ FT: 105,000
SALES (est): 87.08MM
SALES (corp-wide): 87.08MM **Privately Held**
Web: www.mercadolatinoinc.com
SIC: 5141 5148 Food brokers; Fresh fruits and vegetables

(P-6269)
MERCADO LATINO INC
33430 Western Ave (94587-3202)
PHONE...................510 475-5500
Robert Rodriguez, *Prin*
EMP: 65
SALES (corp-wide): 87.08MM **Privately Held**
Web: www.mercadolatinoinc.com
SIC: 5141 Food brokers
PA: Mercado Latino, Inc.
245 Baldwin Park Blvd
City Of Industry CA
626 333-6862

(P-6270)
NAFTA DISTRIBUTORS
5120 Santa Ana St (91761-8632)
PHONE...................800 956-2382
Samuel Madikians, *CEO*
▲ **EMP:** 75 **EST:** 1994
SQ FT: 12,000
SALES (est): 28.28MM **Privately Held**
Web: www.naftadistributors.com
SIC: 5141 Food brokers

(P-6271)
NASSER COMPANY INC (PA)
Also Called: Nasser Company of Arizona
22720 Savi Ranch Pkwy (92887-4614)
PHONE...................714 279-2100
Burhan Nasser, *Pr*
Mary Beth Nasser, *
Becky Salazar, *
EMP: 60 **EST:** 1984
SQ FT: 17,445
SALES (est): 52.23MM
SALES (corp-wide): 52.23MM **Privately Held**
Web: www.nasserco.com
SIC: 5141 Food brokers

(P-6272)
NONGSHIM AMERICA INC (HQ)
Also Called: Nongshim
12155 6th St (91730-6115)
PHONE...................909 481-3698
Dong Y Shin, *CEO*
Joon Park, *
Jongmin Chung, *
Chris Gepford, *
◆ **EMP:** 250 **EST:** 1994

5141 - Groceries, General Line (P-6273)

SALES (est): 83.03MM **Privately Held**
Web: www.nongshimusa.com
SIC: **5141** 2098 Food brokers; Noodles (e.g. egg, plain, and water), dry
PA: Nongshim Co., Ltd.
   112 Yeouidaebang-Ro, Dongjak-Gu
   Seoul

(P-6273)
OAKHURST INDUSTRIES INC
Also Called: Freund Baking Co
3265 Investment Blvd (94545-3806)
PHONE...............................510 265-2400
EMP: 130
SQ FT: 67,896
Web: www.oakhurstmetals.com
SIC: **5141** 2051 Groceries, general line; Bread, cake, and related products
PA: Oakhurst Industries, Inc.
   2050 S Tubeway Ave
   Commerce CA

(P-6274)
OTASTY FOODS INC
160 S Hacienda Blvd (91745-1101)
PHONE...............................626 330-1229
Ming Chao Huang, *Pr*
Ken Chen, *
◆ EMP: 91 EST: 1994
SQ FT: 58,000
SALES (est): 27.82MM **Privately Held**
Web: www.otastyfoods.com
SIC: **5141** Food brokers

(P-6275)
PALISADES RANCH INC
Also Called: Goldberg and Solovy Foods Inc
5925 Alcoa Ave (90058-3920)
PHONE...............................323 581-6161
Paul Paget, *CEO*
Earl Goldberg, *Pr*
EMP: 285 EST: 1974
SQ FT: 70,000
SALES (est): 93.67MM
SALES (corp-wide): 76.32MM **Publicly Held**
Web: www.gsfoods.com
SIC: **5141** 5149 5046 5169 Food brokers; Groceries and related products, nec; Restaurant equipment and supplies, nec; Chemicals and allied products, nec
PA: Sysco Corporation
   1390 Enclave Pkwy
   Houston TX
   281 584-1390

(P-6276)
PERFORMANCE FOOD GROUP INC
Also Called: Vistar Northern California
7587 Las Positas Rd (94551-8202)
PHONE...............................804 287-8097
EMP: 500
SALES (corp-wide): 57.25B **Publicly Held**
Web: www.pfgc.com
SIC: **5141** Food brokers
HQ: Performance Food Group, Inc.
   12500 West Creek Pkwy
   Richmond VA
   804 484-7700

(P-6277)
PERFORMANCE FOOD GROUP INC
Also Called: Performnce Foodservice-Ledyard
1047 17th Ave (95062-3033)
PHONE...............................831 462-4400
EMP: 101
SALES (corp-wide): 57.25B **Publicly Held**
Web: www.performancefoodservice.com
SIC: **5141** 5046 5087 Food brokers; Restaurant equipment and supplies, nec; Janitors' supplies
HQ: Performance Food Group, Inc.
   12500 West Creek Pkwy
   Richmond VA
   804 484-7700

(P-6278)
PIVEG INC
3525 Del Mar Heights Rd Ste 1069 (92130-2199)
PHONE...............................858 436-3070
Roberto L Espinoza, *CEO*
▲ EMP: 220 EST: 2004
SALES (est): 57.3MM **Privately Held**
Web: www.piveg.com
SIC: **5141** Food brokers

(P-6279)
PREMIER FOOD SERVICES INC
14359 Amargosa Rd Ste F (92392-2334)
PHONE...............................760 843-8000
David Lopez, *Brnch Mgr*
EMP: 450
SALES (corp-wide): 422MM **Privately Held**
Web: www.premierfoodservices.com
SIC: **5141** Groceries, general line
HQ: Premier Food Services, Inc.
   9500 Gilman Dr
   La Jolla CA

(P-6280)
RDM EXPRESS INC
2000 Mckinnon Ave (94124-1621)
PHONE...............................415 642-4916
Michael Hin, *Prin*
EMP: 81
SALES (corp-wide): 956.97K **Privately Held**
Web: www.rdmexpress.com
SIC: **5141** Food brokers
PA: Rdm Express Inc.
   750 La Playa St
   San Francisco CA
   415 642-4916

(P-6281)
REAL MEX FOODS INC
Also Called: El Torito Franchising Company
5660 Katella Ave Ste 200 (90630-5059)
PHONE...............................714 523-0031
EMP: 100
SIC: **5141** 5182 5087 2099 Food brokers; Wine and distilled beverages; Restaurant supplies; Food preparations, nec

(P-6282)
RETAIL REALM DISTRIBUTION INC (PA)
454 W Napa St # B (95476-6519)
PHONE...............................707 996-5400
Afshin Amir Alikhani, *Pr*
EMP: 80 EST: 2009
SALES (est): 8.38MM
SALES (corp-wide): 8.38MM **Privately Held**
Web: www.retailrealm.com
SIC: **5141** Food brokers

(P-6283)
ROBERT KINSELLA INC
15375 Barranca Pkwy Ste G107 (92618-2217)
PHONE...............................949 453-9533
Robert Kinsella, *Owner*
EMP: 77
SALES (corp-wide): 4.41MM **Privately Held**
SIC: **5141** Food brokers
PA: Robert Kinsella, Inc.
   535 S Nolen Dr Ste 100
   Southlake TX
   214 260-8670

(P-6284)
SALADINOS INC (PA)
Also Called: Saladino's Foodservice
3325 W Figarden Dr (93711-3909)
P.O. Box 12266 (93777-2266)
PHONE...............................559 271-3700
Craig A Saladino, *CEO*
Don Saladino, *
Tim Christoni, *
Mark Schuh, *CFO*
Patrick Peters, *
EMP: 113 EST: 1944
SQ FT: 40,000
SALES (est): 288.61MM
SALES (corp-wide): 288.61MM **Privately Held**
Web: www.saladinos.com
SIC: **5141** 2099 Food brokers; Food preparations, nec

(P-6285)
SHOEI FOODS (USA) INC
1900 Feather River Blvd (95961-9709)
PHONE...............................530 742-7866
Don Soetaert, *CEO*
Sumio Kawanabe, *
Tall Matsushima, *
◆ EMP: 100 EST: 1985
SQ FT: 68,000
SALES (est): 83.22MM **Privately Held**
Web: www.shoeifoodsusa.com
SIC: **5141** Food brokers
PA: Shoei Foods Corporation
   5-7, Akihabara
   Taito-Ku TKY

(P-6286)
SIMCO FOODS INC
Also Called: Wipeout Bar & Grill
39 Pier Ste A202 (94133-1067)
PHONE...............................415 982-5872
Sandra Fletcher, *VP*
Caroline Simmons, *
Nancy Simmons, *
Warren Simmons, *
EMP: 60 EST: 1986
SALES (est): 4.65MM **Privately Held**
Web: www.wipeoutbarandgrill.com
SIC: **5141** Groceries, general line

(P-6287)
SMART & FINAL STORES INC
Also Called: SMART & FINAL STORES, INC.
9870 N Magnolia Ave (92071-1901)
PHONE...............................619 449-2396
EMP: 331
SALES (corp-wide): 4.74B **Privately Held**
SIC: **5141** Groceries, general line
HQ: Smart Stores Operations Llc
   600 Citadel Dr
   Commerce CA
   323 869-7500

(P-6288)
SMART & FINAL STORES INC
Also Called: SMART & FINAL STORES, INC.
4550 W Pico Blvd (90019-4257)
PHONE...............................323 549-9586
EMP: 221
SALES (corp-wide): 4.74B **Privately Held**
SIC: **5141** Groceries, general line
HQ: Smart Stores Operations Llc
   600 Citadel Dr
   Commerce CA
   323 869-7500

(P-6289)
SMART & FINAL STORES INC
Also Called: SMART & FINAL STORES, INC.
1005 W Arrow Hwy (91773-2422)
PHONE...............................909 592-2190
EMP: 331
SALES (corp-wide): 4.74B **Privately Held**
SIC: **5141** Groceries, general line
HQ: Smart Stores Operations Llc
   600 Citadel Dr
   Commerce CA
   323 869-7500

(P-6290)
SMART & FINAL STORES INC
Also Called: SMART & FINAL STORES, INC.
13346 Limonite Ave (92880-3360)
PHONE...............................909 773-1813
EMP: 221
SALES (corp-wide): 4.74B **Privately Held**
SIC: **5141** Groceries, general line
HQ: Smart Stores Operations Llc
   600 Citadel Dr
   Commerce CA
   323 869-7500

(P-6291)
SMART & FINAL STORES INC
Also Called: SMART & FINAL STORES, INC.
150 B Ave (92118-1511)
PHONE...............................619 522-2014
EMP: 221
SALES (corp-wide): 4.74B **Privately Held**
SIC: **5141** Groceries, general line
HQ: Smart Stores Operations Llc
   600 Citadel Dr
   Commerce CA
   323 869-7500

(P-6292)
SMART & FINAL STORES INC
Also Called: SMART & FINAL STORES, INC.
7223 Fair Oaks Blvd (95608-6410)
PHONE...............................916 486-6315
EMP: 331
SALES (corp-wide): 4.74B **Privately Held**
SIC: **5141** Groceries, general line
HQ: Smart Stores Operations Llc
   600 Citadel Dr
   Commerce CA
   323 869-7500

(P-6293)
SMART & FINAL STORES INC
Also Called: SMART & FINAL STORES, INC.
850 Linden Ave (93013-2043)
PHONE...............................805 566-2174
EMP: 331
SALES (corp-wide): 4.74B **Privately Held**
SIC: **5141** Groceries, general line
HQ: Smart Stores Operations Llc
   600 Citadel Dr
   Commerce CA
   323 869-7500

(P-6294)
SMART & FINAL STORES INC
Also Called: SMART & FINAL STORES, INC.
1308 W Edinger Ave (92704-4306)
PHONE...............................714 549-2362
EMP: 331
SALES (corp-wide): 4.74B **Privately Held**
SIC: **5141** Groceries, general line
HQ: Smart Stores Operations Llc
   600 Citadel Dr
   Commerce CA
   323 869-7500

PRODUCTS & SERVICES SECTION

5141 - Groceries, General Line (P-6318)

(P-6295)
SMART & FINAL STORES INC
Also Called: SMART & FINAL STORES, INC.
13439 Camino Canada (92021-8811)
PHONE.................................619 390-1738
EMP: 331
SALES (corp-wide): 4.74B **Privately Held**
SIC: **5141** Groceries, general line
HQ: Smart Stores Operations Llc
    600 Citadel Dr
    Commerce CA
    323 869-7500

(P-6296)
SMART & FINAL STORES INC
Also Called: SMART & FINAL STORES, INC.
15427 Amar Rd (91744-2803)
PHONE.................................626 330-2495
Robert Terry, *Brnch Mgr*
EMP: 331
SALES (corp-wide): 4.74B **Privately Held**
SIC: **5141** Groceries, general line
HQ: Smart Stores Operations Llc
    600 Citadel Dr
    Commerce CA
    323 869-7500

(P-6297)
SMART & FINAL STORES INC
Also Called: SMART & FINAL STORES, INC.
18555 Devonshire St (91324-1308)
PHONE.................................818 368-6409
Marie Teolis, *Brnch Mgr*
EMP: 331
SALES (corp-wide): 4.74B **Privately Held**
SIC: **5141** Groceries, general line
HQ: Smart Stores Operations Llc
    600 Citadel Dr
    Commerce CA
    323 869-7500

(P-6298)
SMART & FINAL STORES INC
Also Called: SMART & FINAL STORES, INC.
1180 S King Rd (95122-2143)
PHONE.................................408 251-0109
EMP: 221
SALES (corp-wide): 4.74B **Privately Held**
SIC: **5141** Groceries, general line
HQ: Smart Stores Operations Llc
    600 Citadel Dr
    Commerce CA
    323 869-7500

(P-6299)
SMART & FINAL STORES INC
Also Called: SMART & FINAL STORES, INC.
644 Redondo Ave (90814-1453)
PHONE.................................562 438-0450
EMP: 221
SALES (corp-wide): 4.74B **Privately Held**
SIC: **5141** Groceries, general line
HQ: Smart Stores Operations Llc
    600 Citadel Dr
    Commerce CA
    323 869-7500

(P-6300)
SMART & FINAL STORES INC
Also Called: SMART & FINAL STORES, INC.
1845 W Vista Way (92083-6119)
PHONE.................................760 732-1480
EMP: 331
SALES (corp-wide): 4.74B **Privately Held**
SIC: **5141** Groceries, general line
HQ: Smart Stores Operations Llc
    600 Citadel Dr
    Commerce CA
    323 869-7500

(P-6301)
SMART & FINAL STORES INC
Also Called: SMART & FINAL STORES, INC.
2121 Spring St (93446-1455)
PHONE.................................805 237-0323
EMP: 331
SALES (corp-wide): 4.74B **Privately Held**
SIC: **5141** Groceries, general line
HQ: Smart Stores Operations Llc
    600 Citadel Dr
    Commerce CA
    323 869-7500

(P-6302)
SMART & FINAL STORES INC
Also Called: SMART & FINAL STORES, INC.
955 Carlsbad Village Dr (92008-1802)
PHONE.................................760 434-2449
EMP: 221
SALES (corp-wide): 4.74B **Privately Held**
SIC: **5141** Groceries, general line
HQ: Smart Stores Operations Llc
    600 Citadel Dr
    Commerce CA
    323 869-7500

(P-6303)
SMART & FINAL STORES INC
Also Called: SMART & FINAL STORES, INC.
933 Sweetwater Rd (91977-4837)
PHONE.................................619 668-9039
EMP: 331
SALES (corp-wide): 4.74B **Privately Held**
SIC: **5141** Groceries, general line
HQ: Smart Stores Operations Llc
    600 Citadel Dr
    Commerce CA
    323 869-7500

(P-6304)
SMART & FINAL STORES INC
Also Called: SMART & FINAL STORES, INC.
26911 Trabuco Rd (92691-3506)
PHONE.................................949 581-1212
EMP: 331
SALES (corp-wide): 4.74B **Privately Held**
SIC: **5141** Groceries, general line
HQ: Smart Stores Operations Llc
    600 Citadel Dr
    Commerce CA
    323 869-7500

(P-6305)
SMART & FINAL STORES INC
Also Called: SMART & FINAL STORES, INC.
2825 Grass Valley Hwy (95603-2542)
PHONE.................................530 823-1205
EMP: 331
SALES (corp-wide): 4.74B **Privately Held**
SIC: **5141** Groceries, general line
HQ: Smart Stores Operations Llc
    600 Citadel Dr
    Commerce CA
    323 869-7500

(P-6306)
SMART & FINAL STORES INC
Also Called: SMART & FINAL STORES, INC.
2235 University Ave (92104-2717)
PHONE.................................619 291-1842
EMP: 331
SALES (corp-wide): 4.74B **Privately Held**
SIC: **5141** Groceries, general line
HQ: Smart Stores Operations Llc
    600 Citadel Dr
    Commerce CA
    323 869-7500

(P-6307)
SMART & FINAL STORES INC
Also Called: SMART & FINAL STORES, INC.
615 N Pacific Coast Hwy (90277-2107)
PHONE.................................323 497-8528
EMP: 221
SALES (corp-wide): 4.74B **Privately Held**
SIC: **5141** Groceries, general line
HQ: Smart Stores Operations Llc
    600 Citadel Dr
    Commerce CA
    323 869-7500

(P-6308)
SMART & FINAL STORES INC
Also Called: SMART & FINAL STORES, INC.
240 S Diamond Bar Blvd (91765-1605)
PHONE.................................323 855-8434
EMP: 221
SALES (corp-wide): 4.74B **Privately Held**
SIC: **5141** Groceries, general line
HQ: Smart Stores Operations Llc
    600 Citadel Dr
    Commerce CA
    323 869-7500

(P-6309)
SMART & FINAL STORES INC
Also Called: SMART & FINAL STORES, INC.
3830 W Verdugo Ave (91505-3441)
PHONE.................................818 954-8631
EMP: 221
SALES (corp-wide): 4.74B **Privately Held**
SIC: **5141** Groceries, general line
HQ: Smart Stores Operations Llc
    600 Citadel Dr
    Commerce CA
    323 869-7500

(P-6310)
SMART & FINAL STORES INC
Also Called: SMART & FINAL STORES, INC.
5038 W Avenue N (93551-5729)
PHONE.................................661 722-6210
Danny Omada, *Brnch Mgr*
EMP: 331
SALES (corp-wide): 4.74B **Privately Held**
SIC: **5141** Groceries, general line
HQ: Smart Stores Operations Llc
    600 Citadel Dr
    Commerce CA
    323 869-7500

(P-6311)
SMART & FINAL STORES INC
Also Called: SMART & FINAL STORES, INC.
5770 Lindero Canyon Rd (91362-4088)
PHONE.................................818 889-8253
EMP: 221
SALES (corp-wide): 4.74B **Privately Held**
SIC: **5141** Groceries, general line
HQ: Smart Stores Operations Llc
    600 Citadel Dr
    Commerce CA
    323 869-7500

(P-6312)
SMART & FINAL STORES INC
Also Called: SMART & FINAL STORES, INC.
7800 Telegraph Rd (93004-1503)
PHONE.................................805 647-4276
Brian Gillman, *Brnch Mgr*
EMP: 331
SALES (corp-wide): 4.74B **Privately Held**
SIC: **5141** Groceries, general line
HQ: Smart Stores Operations Llc
    600 Citadel Dr
    Commerce CA
    323 869-7500

(P-6313)
SMART & FINAL STORES INC
Also Called: SMART & FINAL STORES, INC.
2800 Fletcher Pkwy (92020-2111)
PHONE.................................619 589-7000
EMP: 331
SALES (corp-wide): 4.74B **Privately Held**
SIC: **5141** Groceries, general line
HQ: Smart Stores Operations Llc
    600 Citadel Dr
    Commerce CA
    323 869-7500

(P-6314)
SMART & FINAL STORES INC
Also Called: SMART & FINAL STORES, INC.
10740 Westview Pkwy (92126-2962)
PHONE.................................858 578-7343
EMP: 331
SALES (corp-wide): 4.74B **Privately Held**
SIC: **5141** Groceries, general line
HQ: Smart Stores Operations Llc
    600 Citadel Dr
    Commerce CA
    323 869-7500

(P-6315)
SMART & FINAL STORES INC
Also Called: SMART & FINAL STORES, INC.
13003 Whittier Blvd (90602-3046)
PHONE.................................562 907-7037
David Hirs, *Brnch Mgr*
EMP: 331
SALES (corp-wide): 4.74B **Privately Held**
SIC: **5141** Groceries, general line
HQ: Smart Stores Operations Llc
    600 Citadel Dr
    Commerce CA
    323 869-7500

(P-6316)
SMART & FINAL STORES INC
Also Called: SMART & FINAL STORES, INC.
303 E Foothill Blvd (91702-2516)
PHONE.................................626 334-5189
EMP: 221
SALES (corp-wide): 4.74B **Privately Held**
SIC: **5141** Groceries, general line
HQ: Smart Stores Operations Llc
    600 Citadel Dr
    Commerce CA
    323 869-7500

(P-6317)
SMART & FINAL STORES INC
Also Called: SMART & FINAL STORES, INC.
2425 N Blackstone Avenue (93703-1748)
PHONE.................................559 229-2944
EMP: 331
SALES (corp-wide): 4.74B **Privately Held**
SIC: **5141** Groceries, general line
HQ: Smart Stores Operations Llc
    600 Citadel Dr
    Commerce CA
    323 869-7500

(P-6318)
SMART & FINAL STORES INC
Also Called: SMART & FINAL STORES, INC.
401 Jacklin Rd (95035-3226)
PHONE.................................408 941-9642
EMP: 331
SALES (corp-wide): 4.74B **Privately Held**
SIC: **5141** Groceries, general line
HQ: Smart Stores Operations Llc
    600 Citadel Dr
    Commerce CA
    323 869-7500

(PA)=Parent Co (HQ)=Headquarters
✧ = New Business established in last 2 years

5141 - Groceries, General Line (P-6319)

(P-6319)
SMART & FINAL STORES INC
Also Called: SMART & FINAL STORES, INC.
5135 E Los Angeles Ave (93063-3431)
PHONE................................805 520-6035
EMP: 221
SALES (corp-wide): 4.74B Privately Held
SIC: 5141 Groceries, general line
HQ: Smart Stores Operations Llc
 600 Citadel Dr
 Commerce CA
 323 869-7500

(P-6320)
SMART & FINAL STORES INC
Also Called: SMART & FINAL STORES, INC.
790 W Shaw Ave (93612-3216)
PHONE................................559 297-9376
EMP: 331
SALES (corp-wide): 4.74B Privately Held
SIC: 5141 Groceries, general line
HQ: Smart Stores Operations Llc
 600 Citadel Dr
 Commerce CA
 323 869-7500

(P-6321)
SMART & FINAL STORES LLC
Also Called: Smart & Final
5555 Wilshire Blvd (90036-3808)
PHONE................................323 939-0946
Erik Hofmeister, Mgr
EMP: 72
SIC: 5141 Groceries, general line
HQ: Smart & Final Stores Llc
 600 Citadel Dr
 Commerce CA

(P-6322)
SMART & FINAL STORES LLC
350 7th Ave (94118-2322)
PHONE................................415 751-9951
Michael Gin, Mgr
EMP: 60
SIC: 5141 Groceries, general line
HQ: Smart & Final Stores Llc
 600 Citadel Dr
 Commerce CA

(P-6323)
SMART & FINAL STORES LLC
744 W Hammer Ln (95210-3748)
PHONE................................209 952-1030
Eric Pool, Brnch Mgr
EMP: 60
SIC: 5141 Groceries, general line
HQ: Smart & Final Stores Llc
 600 Citadel Dr
 Commerce CA

(P-6324)
SMART & FINAL STORES LLC
2511 Daly St (90031-2222)
PHONE................................323 539-2400
EMP: 60
SIC: 5141 Groceries, general line
HQ: Smart & Final Stores Llc
 600 Citadel Dr
 Commerce CA

(P-6325)
SMART & FINAL STORES LLC
Also Called: Smart & Final 508
2749 Calloway Dr Ste 500 (93312-2639)
PHONE................................661 589-2579
EMP: 60
SIC: 5141 Groceries, general line
HQ: Smart & Final Stores Llc
 600 Citadel Dr
 Commerce CA

(P-6326)
SMART & FINAL STORES LLC
1737 Oceanside Blvd (92054-3453)
PHONE................................760 439-3489
Roy Degroot, Brnch Mgr
EMP: 60
SIC: 5141 Groceries, general line
HQ: Smart & Final Stores Llc
 600 Citadel Dr
 Commerce CA

(P-6327)
SMART & FINAL STORES LLC
15930 Bellflower Blvd (90706-4602)
PHONE................................562 920-6268
EMP: 60
SIC: 5141 Groceries, general line
HQ: Smart & Final Stores Llc
 600 Citadel Dr
 Commerce CA

(P-6328)
SMART & FINAL STORES LLC
Also Called: Smart & Final
10893 San Fernando Rd (91331-2629)
PHONE................................818 896-6212
Mario Sanchez, Mgr
EMP: 72
SIC: 5141 Groceries, general line
HQ: Smart & Final Stores Llc
 600 Citadel Dr
 Commerce CA

(P-6329)
SMART & FINAL STORES LLC
5001 E Ramon Rd Bldg 4 (92264-1554)
PHONE................................760 322-8639
Angel Robles, Brnch Mgr
EMP: 60
SIC: 5141 Groceries, general line
HQ: Smart & Final Stores Llc
 600 Citadel Dr
 Commerce CA

(P-6330)
SMART & FINAL STORES LLC
Also Called: Smart & Final
3708 W Burbank Blvd (91505-2239)
PHONE................................818 562-3234
Sue Laymond, Brnch Mgr
EMP: 60
SQ FT: 15,367
SIC: 5141 Groceries, general line
HQ: Smart & Final Stores Llc
 600 Citadel Dr
 Commerce CA

(P-6331)
SMART & FINAL STORES LLC
Also Called: Smart & Final
1180 N Main St Ste 101c (93514-2472)
PHONE................................760 873-7181
William Goodman, Mgr
EMP: 60
SIC: 5141 Groceries, general line
HQ: Smart & Final Stores Llc
 600 Citadel Dr
 Commerce CA

(P-6332)
SMART & FINAL STORES LLC
Also Called: Smart & Final
3901 Sonoma Blvd (94589-2204)
PHONE................................707 644-4281
John Wamble, Mgr
EMP: 60

(P-6333)
SMART & FINAL STORES LLC
2475 E Chapman Ave (92831-3603)
PHONE................................714 441-1069
Derin Collet, Mgr
EMP: 60
SIC: 5141 Groceries, general line
HQ: Smart & Final Stores Llc
 600 Citadel Dr
 Commerce CA

(P-6334)
SMART & FINAL STORES LLC
Also Called: Smart & Final
23631a El Toro Rd (92630-4780)
PHONE................................949 770-8281
Mike Mckanin, Mgr
EMP: 60
SIC: 5141 Groceries, general line
HQ: Smart & Final Stores Llc
 600 Citadel Dr
 Commerce CA

(P-6335)
SMART & FINAL STORES LLC
Also Called: Smart & Final
1804 Girard St (93215-1082)
PHONE................................661 721-2163
Patrick Lim, Mgr
EMP: 60
SIC: 5141 Groceries, general line
HQ: Smart & Final Stores Llc
 600 Citadel Dr
 Commerce CA

(P-6336)
SMART & FINAL STORES LLC
Also Called: Smart & Final
6601 Laurel Canyon Blvd (91606-1522)
PHONE................................818 982-6202
Laurie Lombardo, Mgr
EMP: 60
SQ FT: 34,014
SIC: 5141 Groceries, general line
HQ: Smart & Final Stores Llc
 600 Citadel Dr
 Commerce CA

(P-6337)
SMART & FINAL STORES LLC
Also Called: Smart & Final
6882 Edinger Ave (92647-3402)
PHONE................................714 842-4637
Tony Quintanar, Mgr
EMP: 60
SIC: 5141 Groceries, general line
HQ: Smart & Final Stores Llc
 600 Citadel Dr
 Commerce CA

(P-6338)
SMART & FINAL STORES LLC
Also Called: Smart & Final
210 N Verdugo Rd (91206-3938)
PHONE................................818 243-4239
Art Marroquin, Mgr
EMP: 60
SQ FT: 31,125
SIC: 5141 Groceries, general line
HQ: Smart & Final Stores Llc
 600 Citadel Dr
 Commerce CA

(P-6339)
SMART & FINAL STORES LLC
Also Called: Smart & Final
11110 Ramona Blvd (91731-3139)
PHONE................................626 443-1381
Victor Vios, Mgr
EMP: 60
SIC: 5141 Groceries, general line
HQ: Smart & Final Stores Llc
 600 Citadel Dr
 Commerce CA

(P-6340)
SMART & FINAL STORES LLC
Also Called: Smart & Final
79770 Highway 111 (92253-4538)
PHONE................................760 342-1646
Mario Saldivar, Mgr
EMP: 72
SIC: 5141 Groceries, general line
HQ: Smart & Final Stores Llc
 600 Citadel Dr
 Commerce CA

(P-6341)
SMART & FINAL STORES LLC
Also Called: Smart & Final
720 15th St (92101-7320)
PHONE................................619 239-3377
Robert Brennon, Mgr
EMP: 72
SQ FT: 12,000
SIC: 5141 Groceries, general line
HQ: Smart & Final Stores Llc
 600 Citadel Dr
 Commerce CA

(P-6342)
SMART & FINAL STORES LLC
2065 El Camino Real (95050-4054)
PHONE................................408 296-3293
Haley Bonduant, Mgr
EMP: 72
SIC: 5141 Groceries, general line
HQ: Smart & Final Stores Llc
 600 Citadel Dr
 Commerce CA

(P-6343)
SMART & FINAL STORES LLC
1840 S Norfolk St (94403-1102)
PHONE................................650 345-1335
Jason Nickles, Mgr
EMP: 60
SIC: 5141 Groceries, general line
HQ: Smart & Final Stores Llc
 600 Citadel Dr
 Commerce CA

(P-6344)
SMART & FINAL STORES LLC
5281 Prospect Rd (95129-5026)
PHONE................................408 517-8803
Brett D'anicl, Mgr
EMP: 72
SIC: 5141 Groceries, general line
HQ: Smart & Final Stores Llc
 600 Citadel Dr
 Commerce CA

(P-6345)
SMART & FINAL STORES LLC
Also Called: Smart and Final Stores
480 Diablo Rd (94526-3503)
PHONE................................925 552-8153
EMP: 60
SIC: 5141 Groceries, general line
HQ: Smart & Final Stores Llc
 600 Citadel Dr

PRODUCTS & SERVICES SECTION
5141 - Groceries, General Line (P-6372)

(P-6346)
SMART & FINAL STORES LLC
Also Called: Smart & Final
2750 E Main St (93003-2875)
PHONE.................................805 643-5556
Marian Bosse, *Mgr*
EMP: 60
SIC: **5141** Groceries, general line
HQ: Smart & Final Stores Llc
600 Citadel Dr
Commerce CA

(P-6347)
SMART & FINAL STORES LLC
3310 Vine St (92507-4149)
PHONE.................................951 341-8230
Michael Camero, *Mgr*
EMP: 60
SIC: **5141** Groceries, general line
HQ: Smart & Final Stores Llc
600 Citadel Dr
Commerce CA

(P-6348)
SMART & FINAL STORES LLC
1516 S Pacific Coast Hwy (90277-5201)
PHONE.................................310 540-6157
EMP: 60
SIC: **5141** Groceries, general line
HQ: Smart & Final Stores Llc
600 Citadel Dr
Commerce CA

(P-6349)
SMART & FINAL STORES LLC
2021 N Oxnard Blvd (93036-2963)
PHONE.................................805 485-2051
EMP: 60
SIC: **5141** Groceries, general line
HQ: Smart & Final Stores Llc
600 Citadel Dr
Commerce CA

(P-6350)
SMART & FINAL STORES LLC
Also Called: Smart & Final
1401 E Katella Ave (92867-5023)
PHONE.................................714 771-1470
Rich Bretton, *Prin*
EMP: 72
SIC: **5141** Groceries, general line
HQ: Smart & Final Stores Llc
600 Citadel Dr
Commerce CA

(P-6351)
SMART & FINAL STORES LLC
2795 S Paradise Ave Ste 170 (95304-8529)
PHONE.................................323 219-6352
Neil Cueva, *Mgr*
EMP: 60
SIC: **5141** Groceries, general line
HQ: Smart & Final Stores Llc
600 Citadel Dr
Commerce CA

(P-6352)
SMART & FINAL STORES LLC
Also Called: Smart & Final
600 W Center St (93291-6018)
PHONE.................................559 625-9044
Joe Souza, *Brnch Mgr*
EMP: 60
SIC: **5141** Groceries, general line
HQ: Smart & Final Stores Llc
600 Citadel Dr
Commerce CA

(P-6353)
SMART & FINAL STORES LLC
Also Called: Smart & Final
10833 Long Beach Blvd (90262-1912)
PHONE.................................310 631-8639
Phillip White, *Mgr*
EMP: 60
SIC: **5141** Groceries, general line
HQ: Smart & Final Stores Llc
600 Citadel Dr
Commerce CA

(P-6354)
SMART & FINAL STORES LLC
160 W Willow St (91768-1828)
PHONE.................................909 622-3321
Fernando Villaltandel, *Mgr*
EMP: 60
SIC: **5141** 5411 Groceries, general line;
Grocery stores, independent
HQ: Smart & Final Stores Llc
600 Citadel Dr
Commerce CA

(P-6355)
SMART & FINAL STORES LLC
Also Called: Smart & Final
760 N Main St (92878-5839)
PHONE.................................951 737-4151
John Baubispa, *Mgr*
EMP: 72
SIC: **5141** 5411 Groceries, general line;
Grocery stores
HQ: Smart & Final Stores Llc
600 Citadel Dr
Commerce CA

(P-6356)
SMART & FINAL STORES LLC
Also Called: Smart & Final
10113 Venice Blvd (90034-5809)
PHONE.................................310 559-1722
Eddie Preciado, *Mgr*
EMP: 131
SQ FT: 19,886
SIC: **5141** Groceries, general line
HQ: Smart & Final Stores Llc
600 Citadel Dr
Commerce CA

(P-6357)
SMART & FINAL STORES LLC
Also Called: Smart & Final
2949 W Pico Blvd (90006-3879)
PHONE.................................323 732-9101
Cuate De Rosa, *Mgr*
EMP: 60
SQ FT: 11,457
SIC: **5141** Groceries, general line
HQ: Smart & Final Stores Llc
600 Citadel Dr
Commerce CA

(P-6358)
SMART & FINAL STORES LLC
Also Called: Smart & Final
939 N Western Ave (90029-3246)
PHONE.................................323 466-9289
Joe Simmons, *Mgr*
EMP: 96
SQ FT: 30,381
SIC: **5141** Groceries, general line
HQ: Smart & Final Stores Llc
600 Citadel Dr
Commerce CA

(P-6359)
SMART & FINAL STORES LLC
Also Called: Smart & Final
319 E Market St (93901-3706)
PHONE.................................831 754-1068
Jose Gonzales, *Mgr*
EMP: 96
SIC: **5141** Groceries, general line
HQ: Smart & Final Stores Llc
600 Citadel Dr
Commerce CA

(P-6360)
SMART & FINAL STORES LLC
Also Called: Smart & Final
8137 S Vermont Ave (90044-3535)
PHONE.................................323 758-5734
Tony Saldana, *Mgr*
EMP: 72
SQ FT: 12,000
SIC: **5141** Groceries, general line
HQ: Smart & Final Stores Llc
600 Citadel Dr
Commerce CA

(P-6361)
SMART & FINAL STORES LLC
Also Called: Smart & Final 341
1125 E El Segundo Blvd (90059-3101)
PHONE.................................323 569-7148
Rodney Peete, *Mgr*
EMP: 96
SIC: **5141** Groceries, general line
HQ: Smart & Final Stores Llc
600 Citadel Dr
Commerce CA

(P-6362)
SMART & FINAL STORES LLC
Also Called: Smart & Final
12210 Santa Monica Blvd (90025-2518)
PHONE.................................310 207-8688
Jerry Miyamoto, *Mgr*
EMP: 217
SQ FT: 18,263
SIC: **5141** Groceries, general line
HQ: Smart & Final Stores Llc
600 Citadel Dr
Commerce CA

(P-6363)
SMART & FINAL STORES LLC
Also Called: Smart & Final
5700 N Blackstone Ave (93710-5006)
PHONE.................................559 439-5954
Brent Reed, *Mgr*
EMP: 108
SIC: **5141** Groceries, general line
HQ: Smart & Final Stores Llc
600 Citadel Dr
Commerce CA

(P-6364)
SMART & FINAL STORES LLC
Also Called: Smart & Final
395 N Escondido Blvd (92025-2624)
PHONE.................................760 746-5490
Ron Graves, *Prin*
EMP: 60
SIC: **5141** Groceries, general line
HQ: Smart & Final Stores Llc
600 Citadel Dr
Commerce CA

(P-6365)
SMART & FINAL STORES LLC
Also Called: Smart & Final
7930 Valley View St (90620-2354)
PHONE.................................714 521-3680
Art Valencia, *Mgr*
EMP: 60
SQ FT: 25,604

(P-6366)
SMART & FINAL STORES LLC
1725 Golden State Ave (93301-1009)
PHONE.................................661 326-7945
Louis Mandisaball, *Mgr*
EMP: 72
SIC: **5141** Groceries, general line
HQ: Smart & Final Stores Llc
600 Citadel Dr
Commerce CA

(P-6367)
SMART & FINAL STORES LLC
2971 W Ramsey St (92220-3721)
PHONE.................................951 849-5658
Louise Gomez, *Mgr*
EMP: 60
SIC: **5141** Groceries, general line
HQ: Smart & Final Stores Llc
600 Citadel Dr
Commerce CA

(P-6368)
SMART & FINAL STORES LLC
21600 S Vermont Ave (90502-1940)
PHONE.................................310 328-3023
Kevin Witt, *Mgr*
EMP: 60
SIC: **5141** Groceries, general line
HQ: Smart & Final Stores Llc
600 Citadel Dr
Commerce CA

(P-6369)
SMART & FINAL STORES LLC
Also Called: Smart & Final 355
6235 El Cajon Blvd (92115-3917)
PHONE.................................619 286-0688
Jeff Ewing, *Mgr*
EMP: 60
SIC: **5141** Groceries, general line
HQ: Smart & Final Stores Llc
600 Citadel Dr
Commerce CA

(P-6370)
SMART & FINAL STORES LLC
Also Called: Smart & Final
5195 Clairemont Mesa Blvd (92117-1446)
PHONE.................................858 541-2090
Brett Hollywood, *Mgr*
EMP: 72
SIC: **5141** Groceries, general line
HQ: Smart & Final Stores Llc
600 Citadel Dr
Commerce CA

(P-6371)
SMART & FINAL STORES LLC
Also Called: Smart & Final
5029 Florence Ave (90201-3802)
PHONE.................................323 562-3421
Yolanda Van Gelder, *Mgr*
EMP: 60
SIC: **5141** Groceries, general line
HQ: Smart & Final Stores Llc
600 Citadel Dr
Commerce CA

(P-6372)
SMART & FINAL STORES LLC
(DH)
Also Called: Smart & Final
600 Citadel Dr (90040-1562)

5141 - Groceries, General Line (P-6373)

PHONE..................323 869-7500
David G Hirz, *Pr*
EMP: 97 **EST:** 1991
SALES (est): 1.53B **Privately Held**
SIC: 5141 Groceries, general line
HQ: Chedraui Usa, Inc.
  600 Citadel Dr
  Commerce CA
  323 869-7500

(P-6373)
SMART & FINAL STORES LLC
Also Called: Smart & Final
2308 E 4th St (90033-4306)
PHONE..................323 268-9179
Juan Garcia, *Mgr*
EMP: 143
SQ FT: 11,648
SIC: 5141 Groceries, general line
HQ: Smart & Final Stores Llc
  600 Citadel Dr
  Commerce CA

(P-6374)
SMART & FINAL STORES LLC
Also Called: Smart & Final
725 E Main St (91801-4053)
PHONE..................626 281-2049
Ben Skiezel, *Mgr*
EMP: 60
SIC: 5141 Groceries, general line
HQ: Smart & Final Stores Llc
  600 Citadel Dr
  Commerce CA

(P-6375)
SMART & FINAL STORES LLC
1216 Compton Ave (90021-2331)
PHONE..................213 747-6697
Lisa Mesias, *Mgr*
EMP: 96
SQ FT: 14,160
SIC: 5141 Groceries, general line
HQ: Smart & Final Stores Llc
  600 Citadel Dr
  Commerce CA

(P-6376)
SMART & FINAL STORES LLC
Also Called: Smart & Final
1090 Fletcher Pkwy (92020-1822)
PHONE..................619 562-4151
Pat Wiggins, *Mgr*
EMP: 72
SIC: 5141 Groceries, general line
HQ: Smart & Final Stores Llc
  600 Citadel Dr
  Commerce CA

(P-6377)
SMART & FINAL STORES LLC
4039 Tyler St (92503-3401)
PHONE..................951 352-5715
Teri Henricks, *Mgr*
EMP: 60
SIC: 5141 Groceries, general line
HQ: Smart & Final Stores Llc
  600 Citadel Dr
  Commerce CA

(P-6378)
SMART & FINAL STORES LLC
Also Called: Smart & Final 463
3141 Main St (91911-5705)
PHONE..................619 427-0202
Robert Agnew, *Mgr*
EMP: 60
SQ FT: 13,392
SIC: 5141 Groceries, general line
HQ: Smart & Final Stores Llc
  600 Citadel Dr
  Commerce CA

(P-6379)
SMART & FINAL STORES LLC
Also Called: Smart & Final
1290 N Imperial Ave (92243-1300)
PHONE..................760 352-0811
Jerry Marlborough, *Mgr*
EMP: 60
SIC: 5141 Groceries, general line
HQ: Smart & Final Stores Llc
  600 Citadel Dr
  Commerce CA

(P-6380)
SMART & FINAL STORES LLC
Also Called: Smart & Final
1856 Erringer Rd (93065-3523)
PHONE..................805 582-9231
Scott Davis, *Mgr*
EMP: 60
SIC: 5141 Groceries, general line
HQ: Smart & Final Stores Llc
  600 Citadel Dr
  Commerce CA

(P-6381)
SMART & FINAL STORES LLC
28207 Newhall Ranch Rd (91355-0986)
PHONE..................661 775-1416
Brian Ginsburg, *Brnch Mgr*
EMP: 60
SIC: 5141 Groceries, general line
HQ: Smart & Final Stores Llc
  600 Citadel Dr
  Commerce CA

(P-6382)
SMART & FINAL STORES LLC
250 E 10th St # 589 (95020-6579)
PHONE..................408 846-7020
EMP: 60
SIC: 5141 Groceries, general line
HQ: Smart & Final Stores Llc
  600 Citadel Dr
  Commerce CA

(P-6383)
SMART & FINAL STORES LLC
Also Called: Smart & Final
16847 Ventura Blvd (91436-1703)
PHONE..................818 789-0242
Diana Briggs, *Mgr*
EMP: 60
SIC: 5141 Groceries, general line
HQ: Smart & Final Stores Llc
  600 Citadel Dr
  Commerce CA

(P-6384)
SMART & FINAL STORES LLC
1243 42nd Ave (94601-4007)
PHONE..................510 536-7494
Michael Laplaca, *Mgr*
EMP: 72
SIC: 5141 5411 Groceries, general line; Grocery stores
HQ: Smart & Final Stores Llc
  600 Citadel Dr
  Commerce CA

(P-6385)
SMART & FINAL STORES LLC
Also Called: Smart & Final
23640 Lyons Ave (91321-2513)
PHONE..................661 255-9822
Tony Interante, *Brnch Mgr*
EMP: 60

600 Citadel Dr
Commerce CA

SIC: 5141 Groceries, general line
HQ: Smart & Final Stores Llc
  600 Citadel Dr
  Commerce CA

(P-6386)
SMART & FINAL STORES LLC
Also Called: Smart & Final
6555 Foothill Blvd (91042-2728)
PHONE..................818 352-9399
EMP: 60
SIC: 5141 Groceries, general line
HQ: Smart & Final Stores Llc
  600 Citadel Dr
  Commerce CA

(P-6387)
SMART & FINAL STORES LLC
Also Called: Smart & Final 389
707 W 19th St (92627-3516)
PHONE..................949 548-8473
Don Sickel, *Mgr*
EMP: 60
SIC: 5141 Food brokers
HQ: Smart & Final Stores Llc
  600 Citadel Dr
  Commerce CA

(P-6388)
SMART & FINAL STORES LLC
Also Called: Smart & Final 306
28500 S Western Ave (90275-1436)
PHONE..................310 832-4179
Orlando Novoa, *Mgr*
EMP: 60
SIC: 5141 Food brokers
HQ: Smart & Final Stores Llc
  600 Citadel Dr
  Commerce CA

(P-6389)
SMART & FINAL STORES LLC
Also Called: Smart & Final
114 N Azusa Ave (91722-3604)
PHONE..................626 915-6619
Danny Henricks, *Mgr*
EMP: 60
SIC: 5141 Food brokers
HQ: Smart & Final Stores Llc
  600 Citadel Dr
  Commerce CA

(P-6390)
SMART STORES OPERATIONS LLC
12339 Poway Rd (92064-4218)
PHONE..................858 748-0101
EMP: 221
SALES (corp-wide): 4.74B **Privately Held**
SIC: 5141 Groceries, general line
HQ: Smart Stores Operations Llc
  600 Citadel Dr
  Commerce CA
  323 869-7500

(P-6391)
SMART STORES OPERATIONS LLC (DH)
Also Called: Smart & Final
600 Citadel Dr (90040-1562)
PHONE..................323 869-7500
David B Kaplan, *Ch Bd*
David G Hirz, *
Richard N Phegley, *
Leland P Smith, *
Edward Wong, *Senior Vice President Supply Chain*
EMP: 447 **EST:** 1900
SQ FT: 81,000

SALES (est): 4.74B
SALES (corp-wide): 4.74B **Privately Held**
SIC: 5141 Groceries, general line
HQ: Smart & Final Holdings, Inc.
  600 Citadel Dr
  Commerce CA
  800 894-0511

(P-6392)
SOUTHWEST TRADERS INCORPORATED
4747 Frontier Way (95215-9671)
PHONE..................209 462-1607
Jerry Alestra, *Brnch Mgr*
EMP: 97
SALES (corp-wide): 398.79MM **Privately Held**
Web: www.southwesttraders.com
SIC: 5141 Food brokers
PA: Southwest Traders Incorporated
  27565 Diaz Rd
  Temecula CA
  951 699-7800

(P-6393)
SOUTHWEST TRADERS INCORPORATED (PA)
Also Called: Swt Stockton
27565 Diaz Rd (92590-3411)
PHONE..................951 699-7800
Ken Smith, *CEO*
Lynne Bredemeier, *
▲ **EMP:** 180 **EST:** 1977
SQ FT: 130,000
SALES (est): 398.79MM
SALES (corp-wide): 398.79MM **Privately Held**
Web: www.southwesttraders.com
SIC: 5141 Food brokers

(P-6394)
SPROUTS FARMERS MARKET INC
1700 Mchenry Ave (95350-4373)
PHONE..................209 527-7575
Andrew Jhawar, *Brnch Mgr*
EMP: 234
SALES (corp-wide): 6.4B **Publicly Held**
Web: www.sprouts.com
SIC: 5141 Groceries, general line
PA: Sprouts Farmers Market, Inc.
  5455 E High St Ste 111
  Phoenix AZ
  480 814-8016

(P-6395)
SUNFOODS LLC (HQ)
Also Called: Hinode
1620 E Kentucky Ave (95776-6110)
P.O. Box 8729 (95776-8729)
PHONE..................530 661-1923
Matt Alonso, *CEO*
John Koury, *
Clyde Uchida, *
Jacqueline Hartshorn, *
◆ **EMP:** 70 **EST:** 2008
SQ FT: 1,600
SALES (est): 30.79MM **Privately Held**
Web: www.hinoderice.com
SIC: 5141 Food brokers
PA: Ricegrowers Limited
  57 Yanco Ave
  Leeton NSW

(P-6396)
SUPERIOR FOODS INC
Also Called: Superior Foods Companies, The
275 Westgate Dr (95076-2470)
PHONE..................831 728-3691

David E Moore, *Ch Bd*
R Neil Happee, *
Mateo Lettunich, *
H Monroe Howser Iii, *CFO*
◆ **EMP:** 100 **EST:** 1980
SQ FT: 10,782
SALES (est): 47.09MM **Privately Held**
Web: www.superiorfoods.com
SIC: 5141 Food brokers

(P-6397)
SYGMA NETWORK INC
Also Called: Sygma
46905 47th St W (93536-8527)
PHONE.................................661 723-0405
Mike Wren, *Brnch Mgr*
EMP: 162
SALES (corp-wide): 76.32MM **Publicly Held**
Web: www.sygmanetwork.com
SIC: 5141 Food brokers
HQ: The Sygma Network Inc
5550 Blazer Pkwy Ste 300
Dublin OH

(P-6398)
SYGMA NETWORK INC
Also Called: Sygma
3741 Gold River Ln (95215-9669)
PHONE.................................209 932-5300
John Rivers, *Mgr*
EMP: 237
SALES (corp-wide): 76.32MM **Publicly Held**
Web: www.sygmanetwork.com
SIC: 5141 Food brokers
HQ: The Sygma Network Inc
5550 Blazer Pkwy Ste 300
Dublin OH

(P-6399)
SYSCO CENTRAL CALIFORNIA INC
Also Called: Sysco
136 Mariposa Rd (95354-4122)
P.O. Box 729 (95353-0729)
PHONE.................................209 527-7700
Elizabeth Aspray, *Pr*
Robin Kawashima, *
▲ **EMP:** 312 **EST:** 1938
SQ FT: 177,000
SALES (est): 130.45MM
SALES (corp-wide): 76.32MM **Publicly Held**
SIC: 5141 5142 5046 5148 Food brokers; Meat, frozen: packaged; Restaurant equipment and supplies, nec; Fruits, fresh
PA: Sysco Corporation
1390 Enclave Pkwy
Houston TX
281 584-1390

(P-6400)
SYSCO LOS ANGELES INC
Also Called: Sysco
20701 Currier Rd (91789-2904)
PHONE.................................909 595-9595
TOLL FREE: 800
Daniel S Haag, *CEO*
John Kao, *Sr VP*
Sal Adelberg, *
◆ **EMP:** 1000 **EST:** 1988
SALES (est): 305.77MM
SALES (corp-wide): 76.32MM **Publicly Held**
Web: www.sysco.com
SIC: 5141 5084 Groceries, general line; Food industry machinery
PA: Sysco Corporation
1390 Enclave Pkwy
Houston TX
281 584-1390

(P-6401)
SYSCO RIVERSIDE INC
15750 Meridian Pkwy (92518-3001)
PHONE.................................951 601-5300
Saul Adelsberg, *CEO*
EMP: 375 **EST:** 2009
SALES (est): 198.23MM
SALES (corp-wide): 76.32MM **Publicly Held**
Web: www.sysco-riverside.com
SIC: 5141 5142 5143 5144 Food brokers; Packaged frozen goods; Dairy products, except dried or canned; Poultry and poultry products
PA: Sysco Corporation
1390 Enclave Pkwy
Houston TX
281 584-1390

(P-6402)
SYSCO SACRAMENTO INC
Also Called: Sysco
7062 Pacific Ave (95668-9731)
P.O. Box 138007 (95813-8007)
PHONE.................................916 275-2714
Jackie L Ward, *Ch Bd*
Bill Delaney, *
Brian Beach, *
Greg Bertrand, *
Tom Bene, *
▼ **EMP:** 393 **EST:** 2000
SQ FT: 350,000
SALES (est): 221.89MM
SALES (corp-wide): 76.32MM **Publicly Held**
Web: www.sysco.com
SIC: 5141 5142 Food brokers; Packaged frozen goods
PA: Sysco Corporation
1390 Enclave Pkwy
Houston TX
281 584-1390

(P-6403)
SYSCO SAN DIEGO INC
Also Called: Sysco
12180 Kirkham Rd (92064-6879)
PHONE.................................858 513-7300
Kevin Mangan, *CEO*
Debra Morey, *
◆ **EMP:** 370 **EST:** 1996
SQ FT: 250,000
SALES (est): 204.66MM
SALES (corp-wide): 76.32MM **Publicly Held**
Web: www.sysco.com
SIC: 5141 5142 5147 5148 Food brokers; Packaged frozen goods; Meats and meat products; Fresh fruits and vegetables
PA: Sysco Corporation
1390 Enclave Pkwy
Houston TX
281 584-1390

(P-6404)
SYSCO SAN FRANCISCO INC
Also Called: Sysco
5900 Stewart Ave (94538-3134)
P.O. Box 5019 (94537-5019)
PHONE.................................510 226-3000
TOLL FREE: 800
James Ehlers, *Pr*
Bruce Luong, *
Jane Brett, *
Patrick Bily, *
Frank Tognotti, *
▼ **EMP:** 650 **EST:** 1939
SQ FT: 470,000
SALES (est): 221.89MM
SALES (corp-wide): 76.32MM **Publicly Held**
Web: www.syscosf.com
SIC: 5141 5147 5142 Food brokers; Meats, fresh; Packaged frozen goods
PA: Sysco Corporation
1390 Enclave Pkwy
Houston TX
281 584-1390

(P-6405)
SYSCO VENTURA INC
Also Called: Sysco
3100 Sturgis Rd (93030-7276)
PHONE.................................805 205-7000
Jerry L Barash, *Pr*
Manny Fernandez, *
Bill Delaney, *
Brian Beach, *
Twila Day, *
EMP: 300 **EST:** 2003
SQ FT: 370,000
SALES (est): 91.71MM
SALES (corp-wide): 76.32MM **Publicly Held**
Web: www.sysco.com
SIC: 5141 Food brokers
PA: Sysco Corporation
1390 Enclave Pkwy
Houston TX
281 584-1390

(P-6406)
TAPIA ENTERPRISES INC (PA)
Also Called: Tapia Brothers Co
6067 District Blvd (90270-3560)
PHONE.................................323 560-7415
Raul Tapia, *CEO*
Francisco Tapia, *Treas*
Ramon Tapia, *Sec*
▲ **EMP:** 95 **EST:** 1985
SQ FT: 40,000
SALES (est): 86.67MM
SALES (corp-wide): 86.67MM **Privately Held**
Web: www.tapiabrothers.com
SIC: 5141 Groceries, general line

(P-6407)
UNIFIED GROCERS INC
Also Called: Unified Grocers, Inc.
800 E Pescadero Ave (95304-9799)
P.O. Box 60753 (95376)
PHONE.................................209 832-6200
Ralph Mitles, *Brnch Mgr*
EMP: 150
Web: www.unfi.com
SIC: 5141 Groceries, general line
HQ: Unfi Grocers Distribution, Inc.
2500 S Atlantic Blvd
Commerce CA
323 264-5200

(P-6408)
UNION SUP COMSY SOLUTIONS INC
2301 E Pacifica Pl (90220-6210)
PHONE.................................785 357-5005
Guy Steele, *CFO*
Kyle Deere, *
EMP: 298 **EST:** 2012
SALES (est): 45.73MM **Publicly Held**
Web: www.unionsupply.com
SIC: 5141 5661 2252 Food brokers; Footwear, athletic; Men's, boys', and girls' hosiery
HQ: Union Supply Group, Inc.
2500 Regent Blvd Ste 100
Dallas TX

(P-6409)
US FOODS INC
300 Lawrence Dr Frnt (94551-5139)
PHONE.................................925 606-3525
Phil Collins, *Brnch Mgr*
EMP: 500
Web: www.usfoods.com
SIC: 5141 Food brokers
HQ: Us Foods, Inc.
9399 W Higgins Rd # 100
Rosemont IL

(P-6410)
US FOODS INC
15155 Northam St (90638-5754)
P.O. Box 29283 (85038-9283)
PHONE.................................714 670-3500
David Patterson, *Brnch Mgr*
EMP: 172
Web: www.usfoods.com
SIC: 5141 5046 3556 2099 Food brokers; Commercial equipment, nec; Food products machinery; Food preparations, nec
HQ: Us Foods, Inc.
9399 W Higgins Rd # 100
Rosemont IL

(P-6411)
USFI INC
Also Called: Social Talkie
108 W Walnut St Ste 221 (90248-3102)
PHONE.................................424 260-9210
Gary Place, *Pr*
Byung Hak Erick Yoo, *
Steven Choi, *
William Baek, *
▲ **EMP:** 75 **EST:** 1998
SQ FT: 4,000
SALES (est): 23.69MM **Privately Held**
Web: www.usfifoods.com
SIC: 5141 5149 Food brokers; Groceries and related products, nec

(P-6412)
VIELE & SONS INC (PA)
Also Called: Viele & Sons Instnl Groc
1820 E Valencia Dr (92831-4847)
PHONE.................................714 447-3663
TOLL FREE: 800
Anthony J Viele, *Pr*
Anthony Viele Junior, *VP*
Mike Viele, *VP*
Joseph Viele, *Treas*
Frances Viele, *Sec*
EMP: 90 **EST:** 1958
SQ FT: 95,000
SALES (est): 48.93MM
SALES (corp-wide): 48.93MM **Privately Held**
Web: www.vieleandsons.com
SIC: 5141 Food brokers

(P-6413)
VITCO DISTRIBUTORS INC
Also Called: Vitco Food Service
715 E California St (91761-1814)
PHONE.................................909 355-1300
Kostas Vitakis, *Pr*
Emmanuel Vitakis, *
EMP: 199 **EST:** 2001
SQ FT: 20,000
SALES (est): 98.58MM **Privately Held**
Web: www.vitcofoods.com
SIC: 5141 Food brokers

(P-6414)
WISMETTAC ASIAN FOODS INC (HQ)
Also Called: Wismettac Fresh Fish
13409 Orden Dr (90670-6336)

5141 - Groceries, General Line (P-6415)

PHONE...................562 802-1900
Yoshiro Susaki, *Ch*
Yuji Sasa, *
Hiroyuki Shinkai, *
Toshiyuki Nishikawa, *
◆ **EMP:** 200 **EST:** 1960
SQ FT: 225,000
SALES (est): 496.09MM **Privately Held**
Web: www.wismettacusa.com
SIC: 5141 Groceries, general line
PA: Nishimoto Co., Ltd.
3-2-1, Nihombashimuromachi
Chuo-Ku TKY

(P-6415)
WORLD-WIDE FOODS
Also Called: Divine Specialties
501 Library St (91340-2523)
PHONE...................818 887-1338
Scott Michael Roysner, *CEO*
Blossom Roysner, *Pr*
Scott Roysner, *VP*
Steven Roysner, *CFO*
EMP: 68 **EST:** 1983
SQ FT: 10,000
SALES (est): 13.92MM **Privately Held**
Web: www.divinespecialties.com
SIC: 5141 Groceries, general line

5142 Packaged Frozen Goods

(P-6416)
ARTISAN BISTRO FOODS INC
Also Called: Food Collective
1882 Mcgaw Ave Ste A (92614-5741)
PHONE...................949 797-0014
▲ **EMP:** 60
Web: www.act1diabetes.org
SIC: 5142 Packaged frozen goods

(P-6417)
CONTESSA LIQUIDATING CO INC
222 W 6th St Fl 8 (90731-3345)
P.O. Box 1950 (90733-1950)
◆ **EMP:** 113
SIC: 5142 5146 Packaged frozen goods; Seafoods

(P-6418)
CONTESSA PREMIUM FOODS INC
5980 Alcoa Ave (90058-3925)
PHONE...................310 832-8000
EMP: 250
SIC: 5142 5146 Packaged frozen goods; Fish and seafoods

(P-6419)
DISCOVERY FOODS INC
2395 American Ave (94545-1807)
◆ **EMP:** 80
SIC: 5142 Packaged frozen goods

(P-6420)
EL PRIMO FOODS INC
608 Monterey Pass Rd (91754-2419)
PHONE...................626 289-5054
EMP: 225
SIC: 5142 Packaged frozen goods

(P-6421)
GOLDEN WEST TRADING INC
Also Called: Royal Poultry
4401 S Downey Rd (90058-2518)
P.O. Box 58161 (90058-0161)
PHONE...................323 581-3663
Erik Litmanovich, *CEO*
Tony Cimolino, *
Levi Litmanovich, *
Josh Solovy, *
Zack Levenson, *
▲ **EMP:** 180 **EST:** 1992
SQ FT: 40,000
SALES (est): 205.16MM
SALES (corp-wide): 452.76MM **Privately Held**
Web: www.gwfg.com
SIC: 5142 Meat, frozen: packaged
PA: Golden West Food Group, Inc.
4401 S Downey Rd
Vernon CA
888 807-3663

(P-6422)
MARIE CLLENDER WHOLESALERS INC
170 E Rincon St (92879-1327)
PHONE...................951 737-6760
Phillip Ratner, *Pr*
Gerald Tanaka, *
Kurt Schweickhart, *
EMP: 4152 **EST:** 1968
SQ FT: 28,000
SALES (est): 22.84MM
SALES (corp-wide): 421.81MM **Privately Held**
SIC: 5142 Bakery products, frozen
HQ: Castle Harlan Partners Iii Lp
150 E 58th St Fl 38
New York NY
212 644-8600

(P-6423)
MCLANE FOODSERVICE DIST INC
Also Called: M B M
5675 Sunol Blvd (94566-7765)
PHONE...................252 985-7200
Al Monceaux, *Mgr*
EMP: 81
SALES (corp-wide): 302.09B **Publicly Held**
Web: www.mbmcareers.com
SIC: 5142 Packaged frozen goods
HQ: Mclane Foodservice Distribution, Inc.
4747 Mclane Pkwy
Temple TX
252 985-7200

(P-6424)
MOONLIGHT PACKING CORPORATION
1300 I St (93654-3318)
PHONE...................559 638-7799
Kary Martinez, *Brnch Mgr*
EMP: 605
SIC: 5142 Frozen vegetables and fruit products
PA: Moonlight Packing Corporation
17719 E Huntsman Ave
Reedley CA

(P-6425)
PACIFIC SFOOD - SACRAMENTO LLC
Also Called: Pacific Fresh Seafood
1420 National Dr (95834-1967)
PHONE...................916 419-5500
Frank Dominic Dulcich, *Pr*
Tim Horgan, *COO*
◆ **EMP:** 180 **EST:** 1989
SQ FT: 50,000
SALES (est): 45.57MM
SALES (corp-wide): 647.74MM **Privately Held**
Web: www.pacificseafood.com
SIC: 5142 5146 Fish, frozen: packaged; Fish, fresh
HQ: Pacific Seafood Distribution, Llc
16797 Se 130th Ave
Clackamas OR
503 905-4500

(P-6426)
PRODUCERS DAIRY FOODS INC (PA)
250 E Belmont Ave (93701-1405)
PHONE...................559 264-6583
Lawrence A Shehadey, *Ch Bd*
Richard Shehadey, *
▲ **EMP:** 200 **EST:** 1932
SALES (est): 199.85MM
SALES (corp-wide): 199.85MM **Privately Held**
Web: www.producersdairy.com
SIC: 5142 5143 Fruit juices, frozen; Dairy products, except dried or canned

(P-6427)
WEI-CHUAN USA INC (PA)
13031 Temple Ave (91746-1418)
PHONE...................626 225-7168
Steve Lin, *Pr*
William Huang, *Treas*
Benny Chang, *Sec*
◆ **EMP:** 120 **EST:** 1972
SQ FT: 38,000
SALES (est): 92.64MM
SALES (corp-wide): 92.64MM **Privately Held**
Web: www.weichuanusa.com
SIC: 5142 2038 Packaged frozen goods; Dinners, frozen and packaged

(P-6428)
WEST PICO FOODS INC
5201 S Downey Rd (90058-3703)
P.O. Box 58107 (90058-0107)
PHONE...................323 586-9050
Elias Naghi, *Pr*
Don Lubitz, *
▲ **EMP:** 125 **EST:** 1969
SQ FT: 42,000
SALES (est): 34.78MM **Privately Held**
Web: www.westpicofoods.com
SIC: 5142 5144 Packaged frozen goods; Poultry: live, dressed or frozen (unpackaged)

5143 Dairy Products, Except Dried Or Canned

(P-6429)
ARYA ICE CREAM DISTRG CO INC
914 E 31st St (90011-2502)
P.O. Box 456 (90710-0456)
PHONE...................323 234-2994
Ali Pakravan, *CEO*
Hossein Sahabi, *
Mansour Azizian, *Stockholder**
Mansour Sahabi, *Stockholder**
Farhad Karamati, *Stockholder**
▲ **EMP:** 60 **EST:** 1990
SQ FT: 46,000
SALES (est): 24.84MM **Privately Held**
Web: www.aryaicecream.com
SIC: 5143 Ice cream and ices

(P-6430)
CACIQUE DISTRIBUTORS US
Also Called: Cacique
14923 Proctor Ave (91746-3206)
P.O. Box 1047 (91017-1047)
PHONE...................626 961-3399
EMP: 240
SIC: 5143 Cheese

(P-6431)
CACIQUE FOODS LLC
Also Called: Cacique
14923 Proctor Ave (91746-3206)
P.O. Box 1047 (91017-1047)
PHONE...................626 961-3399
EMP: 240
SALES (corp-wide): 129.03MM **Privately Held**
Web: www.caciquefoods.com
SIC: 5143 Cheese
PA: Cacique Foods Llc
1410 Westridge Cir N
Irving TX
626 961-3399

(P-6432)
CALIFORNIA DAIRIES INC
11894 Avenue 120 (93256-9748)
P.O. Box 837 (93272-0837)
PHONE...................559 752-5200
Steve Cooper, *Brnch Mgr*
EMP: 176
SALES (corp-wide): 33.2B **Privately Held**
Web: www.californiadairies.com
SIC: 5143 Dairy products, except dried or canned
PA: California Dairies, Inc.
2000 N Plaza Dr
Visalia CA
559 625-2200

(P-6433)
CENTRAL VALLEY CHEESE INC
115 S Kilroy Rd (95380-9531)
PHONE...................209 664-1080
Antranik Baghdassarian, *CEO*
EMP: 70 **EST:** 1999
SALES (est): 53.58MM **Privately Held**
Web: www.centralvalleycheese.com
SIC: 5143 Cheese
PA: Karoun Dairies, Inc.
13023 Arroyo St
San Fernando CA

(P-6434)
DFA DAIRY BRANDS FLUID LLC
17851 Railroad St (91748-1118)
PHONE...................800 395-7004
EMP: 326
SALES (corp-wide): 24.52B **Privately Held**
SIC: 5143 Dairy products, except dried or canned
HQ: Dfa Dairy Brands Fluid, Llc
1405 N 98th St
Kansas City KS
816 801-6455

(P-6435)
DREYERS GRAND ICE CREAM INC
Also Called: Nestle Dsd - Manteca DC
1351 Dupont Ct (95336-6004)
PHONE...................209 823-4343
Maria Lundblad, *Brnch Mgr*
EMP: 256
SALES (corp-wide): 2.67MM **Privately Held**
Web: www.dreyersgrandicecream.com
SIC: 5143 Ice cream and ices
HQ: Dreyer's Grand Ice Cream, Inc.
5929 College Ave
Oakland CA
510 594-9466

PRODUCTS & SERVICES SECTION   **5145 - Confectionery (P-6455)**

(P-6436)
DREYERS GRND ICE CREAM HLDNGS (DH)
5929 College Ave (94618-1325)
PHONE..............................510 652-8187
Michael T Mitchell, *CEO*
Steve Barbour, *
◆ **EMP:** 230 **EST:** 2002
SQ FT: 64,000
SALES (est): 1.1B
SALES (corp-wide): 2.67MM **Privately Held**
Web: www.dreyersinc.com
SIC: 5143 5451 2024 Frozen dairy desserts; Ice cream (packaged); Ice cream and frozen deserts
HQ: Froneri International Limited
   Richmond House
   Northallerton
   167 742-3397

(P-6437)
FOSTER DAIRY FARMS (PA)
Also Called: Crystal Creamery
529 Kansas Ave (95351-1515)
PHONE..............................209 576-3400
Dennis Roberts, *Pr*
Mark Shaw, *
▼ **EMP:** 800 **EST:** 1958
SALES (est): 459.3MM
SALES (corp-wide): 459.3MM **Privately Held**
Web: www.crystalcreamery.com
SIC: 5143 2026 Dairy products, except dried or canned; Fluid milk

(P-6438)
INDEPENDENT DAR PRODUCERS INC
21522 Geer Ave (95324-9721)
P.O. Box 279 (95324-0279)
PHONE..............................209 667-6076
EMP: 298 **EST:** 2011
SALES (est): 373.63K
SALES (corp-wide): 264.32MM **Privately Held**
SIC: 5143 Dairy products, except dried or canned
PA: Hilmar Cheese Company, Inc.
   8901 Lander Ave
   Hilmar CA
   209 667-6076

(P-6439)
KLM MANAGEMENT COMPANY
Also Called: Amcom Food Service
14120 Valley Blvd (91746-2802)
PHONE..............................626 330-3479
Ted Degroot, *Pr*
Curtis Degroot, *
▼ **EMP:** 79 **EST:** 1993
SQ FT: 91,000
SALES (est): 20.68MM **Privately Held**
Web: www.am-com.net
SIC: 5143 Dairy products, except dried or canned

(P-6440)
LOS ALTOS FOOD PRODUCTS LLC
Also Called: Los Altos
450 Baldwin Park Blvd (91746-1407)
PHONE..............................626 330-6555
Raul Andrade, *Pr*
Raul Andrade, *Pr*
Gloria Andrade, *
EMP: 105 **EST:** 1988
SQ FT: 38,000
SALES (est): 91.8MM **Privately Held**
Web: www.losaltosfoods.com
SIC: 5143 Cheese

(P-6441)
NESTLE ICE CREAM COMPANY
7301 District Blvd (93313-2042)
PHONE..............................661 398-3500
James L Dintaman, *CEO*
▲ **EMP:** 1920 **EST:** 1993
SALES (est): 396.25K **Privately Held**
SIC: 5143 5451 Ice cream and ices; Ice cream (packaged)
HQ: Nestle Usa, Inc.
   1812 N Moore St
   Arlington VA
   703 682-4600

(P-6442)
PACIFIC CHEESE CO INC (PA)
21090 Cabot Blvd (94545-1110)
P.O. Box 56598 (94545-6598)
PHONE..............................510 784-8800
Stephen B Gaddis, *Pr*
June M Gaddis, *
◆ **EMP:** 230 **EST:** 1966
SQ FT: 107,000
SALES (est): 1B
SALES (corp-wide): 1B **Privately Held**
Web: www.pacificcheese.com
SIC: 5143 Cheese

(P-6443)
TONYS FINE FOODS (HQ)
3575 Reed Ave (95605-1628)
P.O. Box 1501 (95605-0698)
PHONE..............................916 374-4000
TOLL FREE: 800
Karl Berger, *Pr*
▲ **EMP:** 390 **EST:** 1934
SQ FT: 143,000
SALES (est): 443.29MM **Publicly Held**
Web: www.unifresh.com
SIC: 5143 5149 Cheese; Groceries and related products, nec
PA: United Natural Foods, Inc.
   313 Iron Horse Way
   Providence RI

5144 Poultry And Poultry Products

(P-6444)
HIDDEN VILLA RANCH PRODUCE INC (HQ)
Also Called: Hidden Villa Ranch
310 N Harbor Blvd Ste 205 (92832-1954)
P.O. Box 34001 (92834-9411)
PHONE..............................714 680-3447
Tim E Luberski, *Pr*
Don Lawson, *
Greg Schneider, *
Michael Sencer, *
Robert J Kelly Bob, *Ex VP*
◆ **EMP:** 270 **EST:** 1995
SQ FT: 21,619
SALES (est): 410MM
SALES (corp-wide): 410MM **Privately Held**
Web: www.hiddenvilla.com
SIC: 5144 Eggs
PA: Luberski, Inc.
   310 N Harbor Blvd Ste 205
   Fullerton CA
   714 680-3447

(P-6445)
INTERSTATE FOODS INC
310 S Long Beach Blvd (90221-3400)
PHONE..............................310 635-2442
Carlos Velasco, *CEO*
EMP: 145 **EST:** 1999
SQ FT: 13,000
SALES (est): 42.59MM **Privately Held**
SIC: 5144 Poultry products, nec

(P-6446)
LEHAR SALES CO
477 Forbes Blvd (94080-2017)
PHONE..............................510 465-3255
Harold J De Luca, *CEO*
Rick Charles, *
Tarry Winfrey, *
Claire Venturini, *
Hariette Young, *
EMP: 70 **EST:** 1949
SALES (est): 1.14MM
SALES (corp-wide): 40.81MM **Privately Held**
Web: www.pacagri.com
SIC: 5144 Poultry: live, dressed or frozen (unpackaged)
PA: Pacific Agri-Products, Inc.
   477 Forbes Blvd
   South San Francisco CA
   650 873-0440

(P-6447)
NULAID FOODS INC (PA)
200 W 5th St (95366-2793)
PHONE..............................209 599-2121
David K Crockett, *Pr*
Scott Hennecke, *
EMP: 79 **EST:** 1963
SQ FT: 5,000
SALES (est): 47.01MM
SALES (corp-wide): 47.01MM **Privately Held**
Web: www.nulaid.com
SIC: 5144 2047 2015 2023 Eggs; Dog food; Egg processing; Cream substitutes

(P-6448)
RACE STREET PARTNERS INC (PA)
967 W Hedding St (95126-1257)
PHONE..............................408 294-6161
TOLL FREE: 800
Gino Barsanti, *Ch*
Dan Barsanti, *VP*
Michael Barsanti, *Sec*
James Riparbelli, *VP*
David Riparbelli, *VP*
EMP: 80 **EST:** 1946
SQ FT: 63,000
SALES (est): 9.58MM
SALES (corp-wide): 9.58MM **Privately Held**
Web: www.racestreetpartners.com
SIC: 5144 5146 5147 5142 Poultry and poultry products; Fish and seafoods; Meats and meat products; Packaged frozen goods

(P-6449)
ROGERS POULTRY CO (PA)
5050 S Santa Fe Ave (90058-2124)
PHONE..............................323 585-0802
TOLL FREE: 800
George V Saffarrans, *CEO*
John C Butler, *
EMP: 100 **EST:** 1979
SQ FT: 15,000
SALES (est): 40.15MM
SALES (corp-wide): 40.15MM **Privately Held**
Web: www.rogerspoultry.com
SIC: 5144 Poultry products, nec

(P-6450)
ROGERS POULTRY CO
2020 E 67th St (90001-2169)
PHONE..............................800 585-0802
John C Butler, *COO*
EMP: 80
SALES (corp-wide): 40.15MM **Privately Held**
Web: www.rogerspoultry.com
SIC: 5144 Poultry products, nec
PA: Roger's Poultry Co.
   5050 S Santa Fe Ave
   Vernon CA
   323 585-0802

(P-6451)
SUNRISE FARMS LLC
395 Liberty Rd (94952-2811)
PHONE..............................707 778-6450
James Carlson, *Mgr*
Al Nissen, *
Richard Weber, *
Arnold Riebli, *
▲ **EMP:** 65 **EST:** 1966
SQ FT: 10,000
SALES (est): 8.29MM **Privately Held**
SIC: 5144 2015 Eggs: cleaning, oil treating, packing, and grading; Poultry slaughtering and processing

5145 Confectionery

(P-6452)
A & R WHOLESALE DISTRS INC
1765 W Penhall Way (92801-6728)
PHONE..............................714 777-7742
Martin R Alsobrooks, *CEO*
Ron Paz, *
Jeff Kuriel, *
EMP: 60 **EST:** 1986
SALES (est): 20.14MM
SALES (corp-wide): 519.54MM **Privately Held**
Web: www.anrwholesale.com
SIC: 5145 Snack foods
HQ: Gold Star Foods, Inc.
   3781 E Airport Dr
   Ontario CA
   909 843-9600

(P-6453)
AMERICAN NUTS LLC
12950 San Fernando Rd (91342-3601)
PHONE..............................818 364-8855
Duncan Lavery, *CEO*
Nate Willits, *CFO*
EMP: 138 **EST:** 2018
SALES (est): 64.78MM **Privately Held**
Web: www.americannuts.com
SIC: 5145 2034 Nuts, salted or roasted; Dried and dehydrated fruits

(P-6454)
AMERICAN TRADING INTL INC
Also Called: ATI
10780 Santa Monica Blvd Ste 370 (90025-4720)
PHONE..............................310 445-2000
Seth Merrick Wilen, *CEO*
Seth Merrick Wilen, *Pr*
◆ **EMP:** 60 **EST:** 1995
SALES (est): 52.49MM **Privately Held**
Web: www.american-trading.com
SIC: 5145 5141 Confectionery; Food brokers

(P-6455)
AWESOME OFFICE INC
Also Called: Snacknation
3415 S Sepulveda Blvd Ste 1100
(90034-6009)

5145 - Confectionery (P-6456)

PRODUCTS & SERVICES SECTION

PHONE.................310 845-7750
Sean Kelly, CEO
EMP: 73 EST: 2015
SALES (est): 24.11MM Privately Held
Web: www.snacknation.com
SIC: 5145 Snack foods

(P-6456)
CALBEE AMERICA INCORPORATED
3625 Del Amo Blvd Ste 235 (90503-1696)
PHONE.................310 370-2500
EMP: 60
Web: www.calbeeamerica.com
SIC: 5145 Confectionery
HQ: Calbee America Incorporated
2600 Maxwell Way
Fairfield CA
707 427-2500

(P-6457)
CANTEEN VENDING - SAN DIEGO
Also Called: Rainbow Vending & Distributing
5515 Market St (92114-2218)
PHONE.................619 527-1900
Greg Karron, Pr
Greg Carron, *
Don Martin, *
EMP: 1627 EST: 1968
SQ FT: 10,300
SALES (est): 9.28MM
SALES (corp-wide): 29.97B Privately Held
Web: www.canteensd.com
SIC: 5145 5149 5962 Snack foods; Soft drinks; Candy and snack food vending machines
HQ: Compass Group Usa, Inc.
2400 Yorkmont Rd
Charlotte NC

(P-6458)
CENTURY SNACKS LLC
5560 E Slauson Ave (90040-2921)
PHONE.................323 278-9578
Valerie Oswalt, CEO
David Lowe, Ch
Tiffany Obenchain, VP
Mel Deane, Vice Chairman
Stephen Famolaro, CFO
EMP: 330 EST: 1999
SQ FT: 280,000
SALES (est): 99.97MM
SALES (corp-wide): 177.61MM Privately Held
Web: www.centurysnacks.com
SIC: 5145 2064 Nuts, salted or roasted; Nuts, candy covered
HQ: Scncs, Llc
5560 E Slauson Ave
Commerce CA
323 278-9578

(P-6459)
CONSOLIDATED SVC DISTRS INC
Also Called: Jacks Candy
777 S Central Ave (90021-1507)
PHONE.................908 687-5800
Steven Simon, Pr
Herbert Lefkowitz, *
Mark Leskowitz, *
Bill German, *
▲ EMP: 85 EST: 1937
SALES (est): 23.93MM Privately Held
Web: www.jackscandy.com
SIC: 5145 5194 Candy; Tobacco and tobacco products

(P-6460)
ENERGY CLUB INC
Also Called: Energy Club
12950 Pierce St (91331-2526)
▲ EMP: 80 EST: 1984
SALES (est): 25.51MM
SALES (corp-wide): 25.51MM Privately Held
SIC: 5145 2099 Confectionery; Food preparations, nec
PA: Shackleton Equity Partners Llc
4119 Guardian St
Simi Valley CA
310 733-5658

(P-6461)
FRITO-LAY NORTH AMERICA INC
Also Called: Frito-Lay
9535 Archibald Ave (91730-5737)
PHONE.................909 941-6214
Brian Birrell, Mgr
EMP: 500
SALES (corp-wide): 86.39B Publicly Held
Web: www.fritolay.com
SIC: 5145 Snack foods
HQ: Frito-Lay North America, Inc.
7701 Legacy Dr
Plano TX

(P-6462)
FRITO-LAY NORTH AMERICA INC
Also Called: Frito-Lay
28801 Highway 58 (93314-9584)
PHONE.................661 328-6034
Jason Audler, Mgr
EMP: 245
SALES (corp-wide): 86.39B Publicly Held
Web: www.fritolay.com
SIC: 5145 Snack foods
HQ: Frito-Lay North America, Inc.
7701 Legacy Dr
Plano TX

(P-6463)
POINDEXTER NUT COMPANY INC
5414 E Floral Ave (93662-9621)
PHONE.................559 834-1555
▼ EMP: 325 EST: 2013
SALES (est): 59.85MM Privately Held
Web: www.poindexternut.com
SIC: 5145 Nuts, salted or roasted

(P-6464)
S&E GOURMET CUTS INC
Also Called: Country Archer Jerky
1055 E Cooley Ave (92408-2819)
PHONE.................909 370-0155
Eugene Kang, CEO
Susan Kang, *
EMP: 150 EST: 2011
SALES (est): 45.02MM Privately Held
Web: www.countryarcher.com
SIC: 5145 2013 Snack foods; Cured meats, from purchased meat

5146 Fish And Seafoods

(P-6465)
ANTONELLI & SONS FISH & POULTRY
119 S Linden Ave (94080-6410)
PHONE.................650 952-7413
EMP: 65
SIC: 5146 5148 5421 5431 Fish and seafoods; Fresh fruits and vegetables; Fish and seafood markets; Fruit and vegetable markets

(P-6466)
CALIFORNIA SHELLFISH CO INC
Point St George Fisheries
1280 Columbus Ave #300r (94133-1302)
P.O. Box 1386 (95402-1386)
PHONE.................707 542-9490
Tony Delima, Brnch Mgr
EMP: 233
SALES (corp-wide): 89.26MM Privately Held
SIC: 5146 Fish, fresh
PA: California Shellfish Company, Inc.
818 E Broadway C
San Gabriel CA
415 923-7400

(P-6467)
CATALINA OFFSHORE PRODUCTS INC
5202 Lovelock St (92110-4011)
PHONE.................619 297-9797
EMP: 90 EST: 1975
SALES (est): 14.1MM Privately Held
Web: www.catalinaop.com
SIC: 5146 Seafoods

(P-6468)
CENTRAL COAST SEAFOODS
5495 Traffic Way (93422-4246)
PHONE.................805 462-3474
Giovanni Comin, Pr
Molly Comin, *
EMP: 156 EST: 1973
SQ FT: 10,000
SALES (est): 2.5MM
SALES (corp-wide): 91.81MM Privately Held
Web: www.ccseafood.com
SIC: 5146 Seafoods
PA: Santa Monica Seafood Company
18531 S Broadwick St
Rancho Dominguez CA
310 886-7900

(P-6469)
DEL MAR SEAFOODS INC
1449 Spinnaker Dr (93001-4355)
PHONE.................805 850-0421
EMP: 185
Web: www.delmarseafoods.com
SIC: 5146 Seafoods
PA: Del Mar Seafoods, Inc.
331 Ford St
Watsonville CA

(P-6470)
H & N FOODS INTERNATIONAL INC (HQ)
Also Called: H & N Fish Co.
5580 S Alameda St (90058-3426)
PHONE.................323 586-9300
Hua Thanh Ngo, Pr
Christine Ngo, *
Bobby Ngo, *
Dat Trieu, *
◆ EMP: 125 EST: 1981
SQ FT: 45,000
SALES (est): 48.37MM
SALES (corp-wide): 57.39MM Privately Held
Web: www.hngroup.com
SIC: 5146 Seafoods
PA: H & N Group, Inc.
5580 S Alameda St
Vernon CA
323 586-9388

(P-6471)
IMP FOODS INC
1650 Delta Ct (94544-7043)
PHONE.................510 429-4600
▲ EMP: 60
Web: www.impfoods.com
SIC: 5146 Fish, frozen, unpackaged

(P-6472)
KINGS SEAFOOD COMPANY LLC
7691 Edinger Ave (92647-3604)
PHONE.................714 793-1177
Malia Cappuccio, Brnch Mgr
EMP: 612
Web: www.kingsseafood.com
SIC: 5146 Seafoods
PA: King's Seafood Company, Llc
3185 Airway Ave Ste J
Costa Mesa CA

(P-6473)
LUSAMERICA FOODS INC (PA)
16480 Railroad Ave (95037-5210)
PHONE.................408 778-7200
Fernando Luis Frederico, CEO
Anna Frederico, *
▲ EMP: 84 EST: 1976
SQ FT: 40,000
SALES (est): 50.82MM
SALES (corp-wide): 50.82MM Privately Held
Web: www.lusamerica.com
SIC: 5146 5142 Fish, fresh; Packaged frozen goods

(P-6474)
MARUHIDE MARINE PRODUCTS INC
Also Called: M M P
2145 W 17th St (90813-1013)
PHONE.................562 435-6509
Hideo Kawamura, Pr
EMP: 60 EST: 1975
SQ FT: 14,352
SALES (est): 7.97MM Privately Held
Web: www.maruhideusa.com
SIC: 5146 Seafoods

(P-6475)
OCEAN GROUP INC (PA)
Also Called: Ocean Fresh Fish Seafood Mktg
1100 S Santa Fe Ave (90021-1743)
PHONE.................213 622-3677
Young Won Kim, Pr
Katie Chung Yeh, *
◆ EMP: 60 EST: 1983
SQ FT: 20,000
SALES (est): 40MM Privately Held
Web: www.oceanfreshinc.com
SIC: 5146 Seafoods

(P-6476)
PLD ENTERPRISES INC
Also Called: Superior Seafood Co
440 Stanford Ave (90013-2121)
PHONE.................213 626-4444
Chip Mezin, Genl Mgr
EMP: 70
SIC: 5146 Fish and seafoods
PA: P.L.D. Enterprises, Inc.
1621 W 25th St Ste 228
San Pedro CA

(P-6477)
PROSPECT ENTERPRISES INC (PA)
Also Called: American Fish and Seafood

PRODUCTS & SERVICES SECTION

5147 - Meats And Meat Products (P-6497)

625 Kohler St (90021-1023)
PHONE.....................213 599-5700
Ernest Y Doizaki, *Ch Bd*
Jack King, *
Paula Eberhardt, *
◆ **EMP:** 160 **EST:** 1947
SQ FT: 20,000
SALES (est): 99.24MM
SALES (corp-wide): 99.24MM **Privately Held**
Web: www.kansasmarine.com
SIC: 5146 2092 Fish, fresh; Fresh or frozen packaged fish

(P-6478)
QUALY PAK SPECIALTY FOODS INC
2208 Signal Pl (90731-7227)
PHONE.....................310 541-3023
◆ **EMP:** 85
Web: www.qualypak.com
SIC: 5146 5142 Fish, fresh; Fish, frozen: packaged

(P-6479)
RED CHAMBER CO (PA)
1912 E Vernon Ave (90058-1611)
PHONE.....................323 234-9000
Shan Chun Kou, *Ch Bd*
Shu Chin Kou, *Ch Bd*
Ming Bin Kou, *CEO*
◆ **EMP:** 341 **EST:** 1974
SQ FT: 15,000
SALES (est): 94.16MM
SALES (corp-wide): 94.16MM **Privately Held**
Web: www.redchamber.com
SIC: 5146 4222 Seafoods; Warehousing, cold storage or refrigerated

(P-6480)
SEAFOOD FAMILY PARTNERS LP
1123 Cory Ave (90069-1701)
PHONE.....................310 761-1500
Anthony J Cigliano, *Prin*
EMP: 165 **EST:** 2008
SALES (est): 10.35MM **Privately Held**
SIC: 5146 Seafoods

(P-6481)
SHINING OCEAN INC
10888 7th St (91730-5421)
PHONE.....................253 826-3700
Daryl Gormley, *CEO*
Michael Beauregard, *
Matthew Lacki, *
◆ **EMP:** 140 **EST:** 1985
SALES (est): 22.52MM
SALES (corp-wide): 22.52MM **Privately Held**
Web: www.kanimi.com
SIC: 5146 Seafoods
PA: Aquamar Holdings, Inc.
10888 7th St
Rancho Cucamonga CA
909 481-4700

(P-6482)
SJ DISTRIBUTORS LLC (PA)
625 Vista Way (95035-5433)
PHONE.....................888 988-2328
Scott Chun Ho Suen, *CEO*
Jerry Yeung, *
Jenny Lin, *
EMP: 71 **EST:** 2005
SQ FT: 60,000
SALES (est): 610.06MM **Privately Held**
Web: www.sjfood.com

SIC: 5146 5149 5148 5142 Seafoods; Canned goods: fruit, vegetables, seafood, meats, etc.; Fresh fruits and vegetables; Meat, frozen: packaged

(P-6483)
SLADE GORTON & CO INC
1 Centerpointe Dr Ste 311 (90623-2512)
PHONE.....................714 676-4200
Holly Hunt, *Mgr*
EMP: 66
Web: www.sladegorton.com
SIC: 5146 Fish, fresh
HQ: Slade Gorton & Co Inc
255 Bear Hill Rd Ste 401
Waltham MA
800 225-1573

(P-6484)
SSC INC (HQ)
Also Called: Sunnyvale Seafood
2910 Faber St (94587-1214)
PHONE.....................510 477-0008
Gary Mason, *CEO*
▲ **EMP:** 85 **EST:** 1983
SQ FT: 74,000
SALES (est): 49.6MM **Privately Held**
Web: www.sunnyvaleseafood.com
SIC: 5146 5147 Seafoods; Meats, fresh
PA: Zhanjiang Guolian Aquatic Products Co.,Ltd.
No.6 , Industrial Avenue, Huayu Industry Zhuanyi Industrial Park
Zhanjiang GD

(P-6485)
STAGNARO BROS SEAFOOD INC
320 Washington St (95060-4929)
PHONE.....................831 423-1188
Giovanni Stagnaro, *Ch Bd*
Ernest M Stagnaro, *
Robert Tara, *
Robert Mc Pherson, *
Virginia Stagnaro, *
EMP: 73 **EST:** 1937
SQ FT: 12,000
SALES (est): 19.61MM **Privately Held**
Web: www.stagnarobrothers.com
SIC: 5146 5812 5421 Seafoods; Seafood restaurants; Seafood markets

(P-6486)
TRI-MARINE FISH COMPANY LLC
220 Cannery St (90731-7308)
PHONE.....................310 547-1144
Vince Torre, *Managing Member*
◆ **EMP:** 75 **EST:** 2001
SQ FT: 30,000
SALES (est): 21.26MM **Privately Held**
SIC: 5146 Seafoods

(P-6487)
TRI-UNION SEAFOODS LLC (DH)
Also Called: Chicken of Sea International
2150 E Grand Ave (90245-5024)
P.O. Box 85568 (92186-5568)
PHONE.....................424 397-8556
Valentin Ramirez, *CEO*
Christie Fleming, *
Jim Cox, *
Ignatius Dharma, *
David E Roszmann, *
◆ **EMP:** 69 **EST:** 1996
SQ FT: 24,000
SALES (est): 75.25MM **Privately Held**
SIC: 5146 2091 Seafoods; Tuna fish: packaged in cans, jars, etc.
HQ: Thai Union North America, Inc.

2150 E Grand Ave
El Segundo CA
424 397-8556

(P-6488)
TRUE WRLD FODS SAN FRNCSCO LLC
1815 Williams St (94577-2301)
PHONE.....................510 352-8140
Shinryo Shimada, *Managing Member*
David Miller, *
Makoto Kikuchi, *
◆ **EMP:** 62 **EST:** 1978
SQ FT: 27,000
SALES (est): 33.8MM
SALES (corp-wide): 1.21B **Privately Held**
Web: www.trueworldfoods.com
SIC: 5146 Seafoods
HQ: True World Holdings Llc
24 Link Dr Unit D
Rockleigh NJ
201 750-0024

5147 Meats And Meat Products

(P-6489)
BICARA LTD
318 Avenue I Ste 65 (90277-5601)
PHONE.....................310 316-6222
William Jeffrey Hughes, *CEO*
William D Hughes, *
Raymond Rosenthal, *
◆ **EMP:** 300 **EST:** 1948
SQ FT: 105,000
SALES (est): 24.62MM **Privately Held**
SIC: 5147 5146 5141 Meats and meat products; Seafoods; Groceries, general line

(P-6490)
BRIDGFORD MARKETING COMPANY (DH)
1308 N Patt St (92801-2551)
P.O. Box 3773 (92803-3773)
PHONE.....................714 526-5533
Allan L Bridgford, *Ch*
Allan L Bridgford Senior, *Ch*
William L Bridgford, *
John Simmons, *
Ray Lancey, *
EMP: 89 **EST:** 1957
SQ FT: 100,000
SALES (est): 84.74MM
SALES (corp-wide): 265.9MM **Publicly Held**
Web: www.bridgford.com
SIC: 5147 5149 Meats and meat products; Bakery products
HQ: Bridgford Foods Corporation
1707 S Good Latimer Expy
Dallas TX
714 526-5533

(P-6491)
DEL MAR HOLDING LLC
1022 Bay Marina Dr 10 (91950-6398)
PHONE.....................313 659-7300
Leon Bergmann, *CEO*
Joel Jorgensen, *
EMP: 1600 **EST:** 2016
SALES (est): 86.51MM **Privately Held**
SIC: 5147 Meats and meat products

(P-6492)
HARVEST MEAT COMPANY INC
Also Called: HARVEST MEAT COMPANY, INC.
1022 Bay Marina Dr Ste 106 (91950-6327)

PHONE.....................619 477-0185
Jonathan Leavy, *Brnch Mgr*
EMP: 100
SALES (corp-wide): 535.73MM **Privately Held**
Web: www.harvestfooddistributors.com
SIC: 5147 Meats, fresh
HQ: Harvest Meat Company Inc
1000 Bay Marina Dr
National City CA

(P-6493)
HARVEST MEAT COMPANY INC (HQ)
Also Called: Harvest Food Distributors
1000 Bay Marina Dr (91950-6302)
PHONE.....................619 477-0185
Leon Bergmann, *CEO*
◆ **EMP:** 80 **EST:** 1994
SQ FT: 60,000
SALES (est): 226.66MM
SALES (corp-wide): 535.73MM **Privately Held**
Web: www.harvestfooddistributors.com
SIC: 5147 Meats, fresh
PA: Del Mar Holdings, L.L.C.
12499 Evergreen Ave
Detroit MI
313 659-7300

(P-6494)
HEARTLAND MEAT COMPANY INC
Also Called: H M C
3461 Main St (91911-5828)
PHONE.....................619 407-3668
TOLL FREE: 800
Joseph E Stidman, *CEO*
James Methey, *
Stephanie Stidman, *
EMP: 70 **EST:** 1971
SQ FT: 49,000
SALES (est): 23.4MM **Privately Held**
Web: www.heartlandmeat.com
SIC: 5147 2013 Meats, fresh; Sausages and other prepared meats

(P-6495)
HV RANDALL FOODS LLC
2900 Ayers Ave (90058-4304)
P.O. Box 2669 (90255-8069)
PHONE.....................323 261-6565
M Scott Dineen, *CEO*
Alan Cutler, *
EMP: 140 **EST:** 2020
SALES (est): 27.17MM **Privately Held**
Web: www.randallfoods.com
SIC: 5147 Meats and meat products

(P-6496)
JENSEN MEAT COMPANY INC
2550 Britannia Blvd Ste 101 (92154-7404)
PHONE.....................619 754-6400
Abel Olivera, *CEO*
Sam Acuna, *
Jeff Hamann, *
EMP: 95 **EST:** 1958
SQ FT: 25,000
SALES (est): 95.16MM **Privately Held**
Web: www.jensenmeat.com
SIC: 5147 Meats, fresh

(P-6497)
JETRO CASH AND CARRY ENTPS LLC
Also Called: Restaurant Depot
1709 Main St (92113-1025)
PHONE.....................619 233-0200
Frank Shapiro, *Brnch Mgr*

5147 - Meats And Meat Products (P-6498)

EMP: 100
Web: www.restaurantdepot.com
SIC: 5147 5141 5142 5181 Meats, fresh; Groceries, general line; Packaged frozen goods; Beer and other fermented malt liquors
HQ: Jetro Cash And Carry Enterprises, Llc
1710 Whitestone Expy
Whitestone NY
718 762-8700

(P-6498)
L & T MEAT CO
3050 E 11th St (90023-3606)
PHONE......................323 262-2815
EMP: 80 **EST:** 1995
SQ FT: 20,000
SALES (est): 23.02MM **Privately Held**
Web: www.ltmeat.com
SIC: 5147 Meats, fresh

(P-6499)
MPCI HOLDINGS INC
Also Called: Monterrey The Natural Choice
7850 Waterville Rd (92154-8219)
P.O. Box 81046 (92138-1046)
PHONE......................619 294-2222
TOLL FREE: 800
▲ **EMP:** 130
SIC: 5147 5143 5148 5113 Meats, fresh; Cheese; Fresh fruits and vegetables; Disposable plates, cups, napkins, and eating utensils

(P-6500)
NEWPORT MEAT SOUTHERN CAL INC
Also Called: Newport Meat Company
16691 Hale Ave (92606-5025)
PHONE......................949 399-4200
Timothy K Hussman, *CEO*
Denise Van Voorhis, *
EMP: 227 **EST:** 1976
SQ FT: 92,000
SALES (est): 94.5MM
SALES (corp-wide): 76.32MM **Publicly Held**
Web: www.newportmeat.com
SIC: 5147 5142 Meats, fresh; Packaged frozen goods
PA: Sysco Corporation
1390 Enclave Pkwy
Houston TX
281 584-1390

(P-6501)
RANCHO FOODS INC
2528 E 37th St (90058-1725)
P.O. Box 58504 (90058-0504)
PHONE......................323 585-0503
Annette Mac Donald, *Pr*
John Mac Donald, *VP*
EMP: 100 **EST:** 1972
SQ FT: 26,000
SALES (est): 29.1MM **Privately Held**
Web: www.ranchofoods.com
SIC: 5147 2013 Meats, fresh; Sausages and other prepared meats

(P-6502)
RITE-WAY MEAT PACKERS INC
5151 Alcoa Ave (90058-3715)
PHONE......................323 826-2144
Irwin Miller, *Pr*
Carol Miller, *
▲ **EMP:** 69 **EST:** 1961
SQ FT: 64,000
SALES (est): 29.76MM **Privately Held**
Web: www.roseandshore.com
SIC: 5147 Meats, fresh

(P-6503)
RW ZANT LLC (DH)
1470 E 4th St (90033-4236)
PHONE......................323 980-5457
Robert W Zant, *Pr*
William Zant, *
▲ **EMP:** 90 **EST:** 1950
SQ FT: 42,000
SALES (est): 47.3MM
SALES (corp-wide): 1.24B **Privately Held**
Web: www.rwzant.com
SIC: 5147 5146 5144 4222 Meats, fresh; Fish and seafoods; Poultry and poultry products; Cheese warehouse
HQ: Honor Holdings Inc.
5505 Tacony St
Philadelphia PA
215 236-1700

(P-6504)
STROUK GROUP LLC
Also Called: Monsieur Marcel
6333 W 3rd St Ste 150 (90036-3154)
PHONE......................323 939-7792
Stephane Strouk, *Pr*
Katrin Strouk, *
EMP: 105 **EST:** 1998
SALES (est): 13.9MM **Privately Held**
Web: www.mrmarcel.com
SIC: 5147 5143 5812 Meats and meat products; Cheese; French restaurant

(P-6505)
SYDNEY & ANNE BLOOM FARMS INC
Also Called: Randall Farms
2900 Ayers Ave (90058-4304)
P.O. Box 2669 (90255-8069)
PHONE......................323 261-6565
EMP: 545 **EST:** 1952
SALES (est): 98.62MM **Privately Held**
Web: www.randallfoods.com
SIC: 5147 7299 Meats and meat products; Butcher service, processing only - does not sell meat

(P-6506)
THREE SONS INC
Also Called: Merit Day Food Service
5201 Industry Ave (90660-2505)
P.O. Box 6 (90660-0006)
PHONE......................562 801-4100
Michael Shannon Day, *CEO*
John Brenan, *
David Day, *Stockholder*
Mariellen Day, *Stockholder*
Michael Day, *Stockholder*
▲ **EMP:** 87 **EST:** 1975
SQ FT: 40,000
SALES (est): 21.29MM **Privately Held**
Web: www.americanmeatcompanies.com
SIC: 5147 2013 2011 Meats, cured or smoked; Sausages and other prepared meats; Meat packing plants

(P-6507)
WAYNE PROVISION CO INC (PA)
Also Called: Premier Meat Company
5030 Gifford Ave (90058-2726)
P.O. Box 58183 (90058-0183)
PHONE......................323 277-5888
Naftali Greenberg, *CEO*
Eldad Hadar, *
Terry Hanks, *
▼ **EMP:** 92 **EST:** 1975
SQ FT: 7,822
SALES (est): 49.99MM
SALES (corp-wide): 49.99MM **Privately Held**
Web: www.premiermeatcompany.com

SIC: 5147 5144 Meats, fresh; Poultry and poultry products

(P-6508)
WEBERS QUALITY MEATS INC
Also Called: Butcher's Brand
990 Carden St (94577-1164)
PHONE......................510 635-9892
Stefan Weber, *Pr*
Linda Weber, *
EMP: 60 **EST:** 1979
SQ FT: 10,000
SALES (est): 24.87MM **Privately Held**
SIC: 5147 5142 Meats, fresh; Meat, frozen: packaged

(P-6509)
YOSEMITE FOODS INC
4221 E Mariposa Rd (95215-8158)
P.O. Box 31480 (95213-1480)
PHONE......................209 990-5400
Michael Lau, *Ex Dir*
EMP: 120 **EST:** 2016
SALES (est): 20.87MM **Privately Held**
Web: www.yosemitefoods.com
SIC: 5147 Meats and meat products

(P-6510)
YOSEMITE MEAT COMPANY INC
601 Zeff Rd (95351-3942)
P.O. Box 31480 (95213-1480)
PHONE......................209 524-5117
Johnnie F Lau, *Pr*
Gay Lau, *
▲ **EMP:** 100 **EST:** 1974
SQ FT: 3,600
SALES (est): 24.05MM **Privately Held**
Web: www.yosemitemeat.com
SIC: 5147 2013 Meats, fresh; Bacon, side and sliced: from purchased meat

5148 Fresh Fruits And Vegetables

(P-6511)
4 EARTH FARMS LLC (PA)
Also Called: McL Fresh
5555 E Olympic Blvd (90022-5129)
PHONE......................323 201-5800
David Lake, *CEO*
Robert Lake, *
◆ **EMP:** 329 **EST:** 1993
SQ FT: 165,000
SALES (est): 69.45MM **Privately Held**
Web: www.4earthfarms.com
SIC: 5148 4783 Fresh fruits and vegetables; Containerization of goods for shipping

(P-6512)
AGRI-EMPIRE
630 W 7th St (92583-4015)
P.O. Box 490 (92581-0490)
PHONE......................951 654-7311
Larry J Minor, *Pr*
EMP: 120 **EST:** 1943
SQ FT: 5,000
SALES (est): 23.48MM **Privately Held**
Web: www.agri-empire.com
SIC: 5148 Potatoes, fresh

(P-6513)
ALL ABOUT PRODUCE COMPANY
712 Fiero Ln Ste 30 (93401-8705)
PHONE......................805 543-9000
EMP: 63 **EST:** 1993
SALES (est): 7.87MM **Privately Held**
SIC: 5148 Fruits, fresh

PA: The Berry Man Inc
205 W Montecito St
Santa Barbara CA

(P-6514)
BAY CITIES PRODUCE INC
2109 Williams St (94577-3224)
PHONE......................510 346-4943
EMP: 160 **EST:** 1947
SALES (est): 37.4MM **Privately Held**
Web: www.baycitiesproduce.com
SIC: 5148 5142 Fruits, fresh; Fruits, frozen

(P-6515)
BERRY MAN INC
Also Called: THE BERRY MAN, INC
712 Fiero Ln (93401-8938)
PHONE......................805 543-9000
Mark Shackelford, *Prin*
EMP: 69
Web: www.theberryman.com
SIC: 5148 Fruits
PA: The Berry Man Inc
205 W Montecito St
Santa Barbara CA

(P-6516)
BLAZERWILKINSONGEE LLC
19040 Portola Dr (93908-1213)
P.O. Box 7428 (93962-7428)
PHONE......................831 455-3700
EMP: 300 **EST:** 1996
SQ FT: 25,000
SALES (est): 49.37MM **Privately Held**
Web: www.bwgberries.com
SIC: 5148 Fresh fruits and vegetables

(P-6517)
BORG PRODUCE SALES LLC
1601 E Olympic Blvd Ste 100 (90021-1940)
P.O. Box 21008 (90021-0008)
PHONE......................213 624-2674
▲ **EMP:** 170
SIC: 5148 Fresh fruits and vegetables

(P-6518)
BOSKOVICH FRESH CUT LLC
711 Diaz Ave (93030-7247)
P.O. Box 1272 (93032-1272)
PHONE......................805 487-2299
George Boskovich, *CEO*
George Boskovich, *Managing Member*
Lina Perez, *
EMP: 250 **EST:** 2018
SALES (est): 24.49MM **Privately Held**
SIC: 5148 Vegetables, fresh

(P-6519)
BRAGA FRESH FAMILY FARMS INC
Also Called: Braga Fresh Gonzales 2
500 S Alta St (93926)
PHONE......................831 675-2361
EMP: 217
SALES (corp-wide): 150MM **Privately Held**
Web: www.bragafresh.com
SIC: 5148 Fresh fruits and vegetables
PA: Braga Fresh Family Farms, Inc.
33750 Moranda Rd
Soledad CA
831 675-2154

(P-6520)
BUY FRESH PRODUCE INC
6636 E 26th St (90040-3216)
PHONE......................323 796-0127
Ted Kasnetsis, *Pr*
Traci Kasnetsis, *

PRODUCTS & SERVICES SECTION

5148 - Fresh Fruits And Vegetables (P-6541)

EMP: 80 EST: 2005
SQ FT: 23,500
SALES (est): 22.65MM **Privately Held**
Web: www.buyfreshproduceinc.com
SIC: 5148 Fruits, fresh

(P-6521)
CALIFORNIA VEGETABLE SPC INC
Also Called: California Endive Farm
15 Poppy House Rd (94571-1201)
P.O. Box 638 (94571-0638)
PHONE.....................707 374-2111
Alexandre Pierron-darbonne, *CEO*
Luc Darbonne, *CEO*
Richard Collins, *Pr*
Jose Arias, *VP*
▲ EMP: 70 EST: 1987
SQ FT: 11,000
SALES (est): 25.35MM **Privately Held**
Web: www.endive.com
SIC: 5148 Fresh fruits and vegetables

(P-6522)
CAPAY INCORPORATED (PA)
Also Called: Capay Fruits and Vegetables
23804 State Highway 16 (95607-9739)
PHONE.....................530 796-0730
Thaddeus Barsotti, *CEO*
Noah Barnes, *
Moyra Barsotti, *
EMP: 98 EST: 1979
SALES (est): 41.89MM
SALES (corp-wide): 41.89MM **Privately Held**
Web: www.capayorganic.com
SIC: 5148 Fresh fruits and vegetables

(P-6523)
CATANIA WORLDWIDE
Also Called: Stellar Distributing, Inc.
21801 Ave Ste 16 (93637)
PHONE.....................559 664-8400
Paul Catania Junior, *Pr*
Robert Farnam, *
◆ EMP: 350 EST: 1988
SQ FT: 30,000
SALES (est): 48.26MM **Privately Held**
Web: www.cataniaworldwide.com
SIC: 5148 Vegetables, fresh

(P-6524)
CECELIA PACKING CORPORATION
24780 E South Ave (93646-9426)
PHONE.....................559 626-5000
James J Cotter, *CEO*
David G Roth, *
Randy Jacobson, *
◆ EMP: 130 EST: 1937
SQ FT: 55,000
SALES (est): 29.51MM **Privately Held**
Web: www.ceceliapack.com
SIC: 5148 Fresh fruits and vegetables

(P-6525)
CHICO PRODUCE INC (PA)
Also Called: Pro Pacific Fresh
70 Pepsi Way (95938-9798)
P.O. Box 1069 (95938-1069)
PHONE.....................530 893-0596
Terry Richardson, *CEO*
Bruce Parks, *
▼ EMP: 141 EST: 1983
SQ FT: 70,000
SALES (est): 72.6MM
SALES (corp-wide): 72.6MM **Privately Held**
Web: www.ppf-foods.com

SIC: 5148 5149 4783 Fruits, fresh; Dried or canned foods; Containerization of goods for shipping

(P-6526)
CHURCH BROTHERS LLC (PA)
19065 Portola Dr Ste C (93908-1250)
P.O. Box 509 (93902-0509)
PHONE.....................831 796-1000
Steve Church, *
Jay Brown, *
EMP: 95 EST: 1999
SQ FT: 1,000
SALES (est): 505MM
SALES (corp-wide): 505MM **Privately Held**
Web: www.churchbrothers.com
SIC: 5148 Fresh fruits and vegetables

(P-6527)
COAST CITRUS DISTRIBUTORS (PA)
Also Called: Coast Tropical
7597 Bristow Ct (92154-7419)
P.O. Box 530369 (92153-0369)
PHONE.....................619 661-7950
James M Alvarez, *Ch Bd*
Margarita Alvarez, *
◆ EMP: 100 EST: 1950
SQ FT: 80,000
SALES (est): 122.73MM
SALES (corp-wide): 122.73MM **Privately Held**
Web: www.coasttropical.com
SIC: 5148 Fruits, fresh

(P-6528)
COAST PRODUCE COMPANY (PA)
1791 Bay St (90021-1655)
P.O. Box 86468 (90086-0468)
PHONE.....................213 955-4900
Mike Ito, *CEO*
John K Dunn, *
Rick Uyeno, *
▲ EMP: 165 EST: 1955
SQ FT: 80,000
SALES (est): 47.07MM
SALES (corp-wide): 47.07MM **Privately Held**
Web: www.coastproduce.com
SIC: 5148 Fruits, fresh

(P-6529)
CUSTOM PRODUCE SALES (HQ)
13475 E Progress Dr (93648-9674)
P.O. Box 977 (93631-0977)
PHONE.....................559 254-5800
Minyi Xu, *CEO*
▲ EMP: 180 EST: 1995
SALES (est): 50.23MM
SALES (corp-wide): 297.68MM **Privately Held**
Web: www.customproducesales.com
SIC: 5148 Fruits, fresh
PA: Grubmarket, Inc.
  395 Oyster Point Blvd # 515
  South San Francisco CA
  415 986-0523

(P-6530)
D&D WHOLESALE DISTRIBUTORS LLC
777 Baldwin Park Blvd (91746-1504)
PHONE.....................626 333-2111
Joe Dupree, *Pr*
Pamela Dupree, *
EMP: 90 EST: 1979
SQ FT: 20,000

SALES (est): 31.09MM **Privately Held**
Web: www.ddwholesale.com
SIC: 5148 5143 Fruits, fresh; Dairy products, except dried or canned

(P-6531)
DAIRYLAND PRODUCE LLC
Also Called: Green Leaf Produce
453 Valley Dr (94005-1209)
PHONE.....................415 647-2991
Frank Ballentine, *Brnch Mgr*
EMP: 146
SIC: 5148 5451 Fruits, fresh; Dairy products stores
HQ: Dairyland Produce, Llc
  1005 N Cockrell Hill Rd
  Dallas TX
  214 426-5666

(P-6532)
DAVALAN SALES INC
Also Called: Davalan Fresh
1601 E Olympic Blvd Ste 325 (90021-1957)
PHONE.....................213 623-2500
Alan Frick, *Pr*
Dave Bouton, *
▲ EMP: 200 EST: 1983
SQ FT: 15,000
SALES (est): 23.92MM **Privately Held**
Web: www.davalanfresh.com
SIC: 5148 Fruits, fresh

(P-6533)
DAYLIGHT FOODS INC
30200 Whipple Rd (94587-1524)
PHONE.....................510 931-4207
Chris Vlahopouliotis, *Pr*
Paul Jennings, *
▲ EMP: 120 EST: 2003
SALES (est): 36.53MM
SALES (corp-wide): 297.68MM **Privately Held**
Web: www.daylightfoods.com
SIC: 5148 Fruits, fresh
PA: Grubmarket, Inc.
  395 Oyster Point Blvd # 515
  South San Francisco CA
  415 986-0523

(P-6534)
DRISCOLLS INC (PA)
345 Westridge Dr (95076-4169)
P.O. Box 50045 (95077-5045)
PHONE.....................831 424-0506
Miles Reiter, *CEO*
Joseph Miles Reiter, *
John Siletto, *
Jerry D'amore, *VP*
Dorn Wenninger, *
◆ EMP: 60 EST: 1953
SQ FT: 19,932
SALES (est): 647.53MM
SALES (corp-wide): 647.53MM **Privately Held**
Web: www.driscolls.com
SIC: 5148 5431 Fruits, fresh; Fruit and vegetable markets

(P-6535)
DRISCOLLS INC
150 Westridge Dr (95076-6709)
PHONE.....................800 871-3333
EMP: 75
SALES (corp-wide): 647.53MM **Privately Held**
Web: www.driscolls.com
SIC: 5148 Fruits, fresh
PA: Driscoll's, Inc.
  345 Westridge Dr
  Watsonville CA
  831 424-0506

(P-6536)
EARLS ORGANIC PRODUCE
Also Called: Earl's Organic Produce
2101 Jerrold Ave Ste 100 (94124-1009)
PHONE.....................415 824-7419
Earl Herrick, *CEO*
▲ EMP: 78 EST: 1989
SALES (est): 25.3MM **Privately Held**
Web: www.earlsorganic.com
SIC: 5148 Fresh fruits and vegetables

(P-6537)
EVOLUTION FRESH INC
Also Called: Evolution Juice
11655 Jersey Blvd Ste A (91730-4903)
PHONE.....................800 794-9986
Chris Bruzzo, *CEO*
Ricki Reves, *
▲ EMP: 180 EST: 2010
SQ FT: 70,000
SALES (est): 72.22MM
SALES (corp-wide): 1.33B **Privately Held**
Web: www.evolutionfresh.com
SIC: 5148 2037 Fruits, fresh; Frozen fruits and vegetables
HQ: Wm. Bolthouse Farms, Inc.
  7200 E Brundage Ln
  Bakersfield CA
  661 366-7209

(P-6538)
FAMILY TREE PRODUCE INC
5510 E La Palma Ave (92807-2108)
PHONE.....................714 693-5688
Fidel Guzman, *Pr*
Christy Guzman, *
EMP: 115 EST: 1975
SQ FT: 33,000
SALES (est): 37.41MM **Privately Held**
Web: www.familytreeproduce.com
SIC: 5148 Fruits, fresh

(P-6539)
FAMOUS VINEYARDS LLC
20715 Ave 8 (93261)
PHONE.....................661 392-5000
Joe Butkiewicz, *Managing Member*
EMP: 100 EST: 2019
SALES (est): 9.36MM **Privately Held**
SIC: 5148 Fruits, fresh

(P-6540)
FARMERS LINK INC
2858 E 26th St (90058-8005)
P.O. Box 86086 (90086-0223)
PHONE.....................213 623-5242
Saul G Pinon, *Pr*
EMP: 82
SALES (corp-wide): 4.67MM **Privately Held**
SIC: 5148 Vegetables
PA: Farmers Link, Inc
  1601 E Olympic Blvd
  Los Angeles CA
  213 623-5242

(P-6541)
FIELD FRESH FARMS LLC
320 Industrial Rd (95076-5116)
P.O. Box 2731 (95077-2731)
PHONE.....................831 722-1422
Steven Dobler, *
Craig Dobler, *
EMP: 80 EST: 2005
SQ FT: 66,000
SALES (est): 49MM **Privately Held**
Web: www.fieldfreshproduce.com
SIC: 5148 Fruits, fresh

5148 - Fresh Fruits And Vegetables (P-6542)

(P-6542)
FIELD FRESH FOODS INCORPORATED
14805 S San Pedro St (90248-2030)
P.O. Box 3877 (90247-7577)
PHONE.............................310 719-8422
EMP: 600 EST: 1994
SALES (est): 70.34MM **Privately Held**
Web: www.fieldfresh.com
SIC: **5148** Vegetables, fresh

(P-6543)
FRESH INNOVATIONS CAL LLC
7735 S Highway 99 (95215-9623)
PHONE.............................209 983-9700
Timothy Stejskal, *CEO*
Richard Turner, *CFO*
EMP: 135 EST: 2006
SALES (est): 25.08MM
SALES (corp-wide): 112.56MM **Privately Held**
Web: www.fresh-innovations.com
SIC: **5148** Fruits
PA: Peterson Farms, Inc.
   3104 W Baseline Rd
   Shelby MI
   231 861-6333

(P-6544)
FRESHKO PRODUCE SERVICES INC
2155 E Muscat Ave (93725-2326)
P.O. Box 11097 (93771-1097)
PHONE.............................559 497-7000
Manny Robles, *Prin*
Randall Shepherd, *
EMP: 142 EST: 2002
SQ FT: 47,000
SALES (est): 43.99MM
SALES (corp-wide): 15.34B **Privately Held**
Web: www.freshkoproduce.com
SIC: **5148** 5499 Fruits, fresh; Juices, fruit or vegetable
PA: C&S Wholesale Grocers, Llc
   7 Corporate Dr
   Keene NH
   603 354-7000

(P-6545)
FRESHPOINT INC
Also Called: Freshpoint Las Vegas
155 N Orange Ave (91744-3432)
PHONE.............................626 855-1400
Terry Owen, *Pr*
EMP: 191
SALES (corp-wide): 76.32MM **Publicly Held**
Web: www.freshpoint.com
SIC: **5148** Fresh fruits and vegetables
HQ: Freshpoint, Inc.
   1390 Enclave Pkwy
   Houston TX

(P-6546)
FRESHPOINT SOUTHERN CAL INC
Also Called: Freshpoint Southern California
155 N Orange Ave (91744-3432)
PHONE.............................626 855-1400
Verne L Lusby Junior, *CEO*
Robert Gordon, *
Jim Procuniar, *
Rich Dachman, *
Jeff Ronk, *
EMP: 208 EST: 1921
SQ FT: 97,000
SALES (est): 67.52MM
SALES (corp-wide): 76.32MM **Publicly Held**
Web: www.freshpoint.com
SIC: **5148** 5142 Fruits, fresh; Packaged frozen goods
PA: Sysco Corporation
   1390 Enclave Pkwy
   Houston TX
   281 584-1390

(P-6547)
FRIEDAS INC
Also Called: Friedas Specialty Produce
4465 Corporate Center Dr (90720-2540)
PHONE.............................714 826-6100
Karen Caplan, *Pr*
Jackie Caplan-wiggins, *VP*
▲ EMP: 75 EST: 1962
SQ FT: 81,306
SALES (est): 34.67MM **Privately Held**
Web: www.friedas.com
SIC: **5148** 5499 7389 Vegetables, fresh; Dried fruit; Labeling bottles, cans, cartons, etc.

(P-6548)
FRUIT FILLINGS LLC
2531 E Edgar Ave (93706-5410)
PHONE.............................559 237-4715
Stephen Norcross, *Pr*
Keith Siemens, *
◆ EMP: 109 EST: 1983
SQ FT: 3,600
SALES (est): 47.74MM
SALES (corp-wide): 578.75MM **Privately Held**
Web: www.fruitfillings.com
SIC: **5148** Fruits, fresh
PA: Bakemark Usa Llc
   7351 Crider Ave
   Pico Rivera CA
   562 949-1054

(P-6549)
FRUIT GROWERS SUPPLY COMPANY
225 S Wineville Ave (91761-7891)
PHONE.............................909 390-0190
Steve Moore, *Mgr*
EMP: 60
SALES (corp-wide): 222.6MM **Privately Held**
Web: www.fruitgrowers.com
SIC: **5148** Fruits, fresh
PA: Fruit Growers Supply Company Inc
   27770 N Entrmt Dr Fl 3 Flr 3
   Valencia CA
   888 997-4855

(P-6550)
GALLI PRODUCE COMPANY
1650 Old Bayshore Hwy (95112-4304)
P.O. Box 612620 (95161-2620)
PHONE.............................408 436-6100
Gerald Pieracci, *Pr*
Joseph Vanni, *
Kristin Killin, *
Dennis Tinucci, *
Jeff Pieracci, *
EMP: 60 EST: 1950
SQ FT: 10,000
SALES (est): 19.7MM **Privately Held**
Web: www.galliproduce.com
SIC: **5148** 5142 Fruits, fresh; Fruits, frozen

(P-6551)
GENERAL PROD A CAL LTD PARTNR (PA)
7625 Lone Tree Rd (95837-9331)
P.O. Box 308 (95812-0308)
PHONE.............................916 441-6431
Jeff Sacchini, *CEO*
Dan Chan, *
Don Weersing, *
Sheryl Weichert, *
◆ EMP: 200 EST: 1933
SALES (est): 80.12MM
SALES (corp-wide): 80.12MM **Privately Held**
Web: www.generalproduce.com
SIC: **5148** Fruits, fresh

(P-6552)
GIFTING COMPANY LLC (PA)
Also Called: Manhattan Fruitier
6011 E Pine St (95240-0815)
P.O. Box 1264 (95241-1264)
PHONE.............................209 365-2300
▲ EMP: 150 EST: 2008
SQ FT: 47,200
SALES (est): 63.78MM
SALES (corp-wide): 63.78MM **Privately Held**
Web: www.californiafruitexchange.com
SIC: **5148** 5499 Fruits; Food gift baskets

(P-6553)
GIUMARRA AGRICOM INTL LLC
15651 Old Milky Way (92027-7104)
PHONE.............................760 480-8502
Don Corsaro, *Brnch Mgr*
EMP: 1990
SALES (corp-wide): 134.67MM **Privately Held**
Web: www.giumarra.com
SIC: **5148** Fruits
HQ: Giumarra Agricom International Llc
   1601 E Olympic Blvd
   Los Angeles CA

(P-6554)
GIUMARRA BROS FRUIT CO INC (PA)
Also Called: Giumarra International Berry
1601 E Olympic Blvd Ste 400 (90021-1921)
P.O. Box 861449 (90086-1449)
PHONE.............................213 627-2900
Donald Corsaro, *Ch*
John Giumarra Junior, *Treas*
John Corsaro, *
◆ EMP: 74 EST: 1950
SQ FT: 8,000
SALES (est): 59.39MM
SALES (corp-wide): 59.39MM **Privately Held**
Web: www.giumarra.com
SIC: **5148** Fresh fruits and vegetables

(P-6555)
GOURMET SPECIALTIES INC
2120 E 25th St (90058-1126)
PHONE.............................323 587-1734
EMP: 75 EST: 2010
SALES (est): 12.34MM **Privately Held**
SIC: **5148** Fresh fruits and vegetables

(P-6556)
GREEN FARMS INC
Also Called: Worldwide Produce
2652 Long Beach Ave (90058-1323)
PHONE.............................858 831-7701
Abbas Ghulam, *Brnch Mgr*
EMP: 89
SALES (corp-wide): 114.14MM **Privately Held**
Web: www.wwproduce.com
SIC: **5148** Fresh fruits and vegetables
HQ: Green Farms California, Llc
   2652 Long Beach Ave Ste 2
   Los Angeles CA

(P-6557)
GREEN THUMB PRODUCE INC
2648 W Ramsey St (92220-3716)
P.O. Box 1357 (92220-0010)
PHONE.............................951 849-4711
EMP: 250 EST: 1996
SALES (est): 45.31MM **Privately Held**
Web: www.greenthumbproduce.com
SIC: **5148** Fresh fruits and vegetables

(P-6558)
GRIMMWAY ENTERPRISES INC
Also Called: Cal-Organic Farms
12000 Main St (93241-2836)
P.O. Box 81498 (93380-1498)
PHONE.............................661 845-3758
EMP: 266
SALES (corp-wide): 1.86B **Privately Held**
Web: www.calorganicfarms.com
SIC: **5148** Vegetables, fresh
PA: Grimmway Enterprises, Inc.
   14141 Di Giorgio Rd
   Arvin CA
   800 301-3101

(P-6559)
INGARDIA BROS PRODUCE INC
700 S Hathaway St (92705-4126)
PHONE.............................949 645-1365
EMP: 190 EST: 1973
SALES (est): 36.47MM **Privately Held**
Web: www.ingardiabros.com
SIC: **5148** 5146 Fresh fruits and vegetables; Seafoods

(P-6560)
LA SPECIALTY PRODUCE CO (PA)
Also Called: Vesta Foodservice
13527 Orden Dr (90670-6338)
P.O. Box 2293 (90670-0293)
PHONE.............................562 741-2200
Michael Glick, *CEO*
Scott Parra-matthews, *CFO*
EMP: 375 EST: 1985
SQ FT: 188,000
SALES (est): 210.39MM
SALES (corp-wide): 210.39MM **Privately Held**
Web: www.vestafoodservice.com
SIC: **5148** Fruits, fresh

(P-6561)
LEGACY FARMS LLC
1765 W Penhall Way (92801-6728)
PHONE.............................714 736-1800
Nick Cancellieri, *Managing Member*
Ron Shimizu, *Managing Member*
Michael Sanders, *Managing Member*
▲ EMP: 100 EST: 1991
SQ FT: 95,000
SALES (est): 50.51MM **Privately Held**
Web: www.legacyproduce.com
SIC: **5148** Fruits, fresh

(P-6562)
LIBERTY PACKING COMPANY LLC (PA)
Also Called: Morning Star Company The
724 Main St (95695-3491)
PHONE.............................209 826-7100
▲ EMP: 80 EST: 2001
SALES (est): 215.3MM
SALES (corp-wide): 215.3MM **Privately Held**
SIC: **5148** 2033 Vegetables; Tomato products, packaged in cans, jars, etc.

PRODUCTS & SERVICES SECTION **5148 - Fresh Fruits And Vegetables (P-6582)**

(P-6563)
MOONLIGHT PACKING CORPORATION (PA)
Also Called: Moonlight Companies
17719 E Huntsman Ave (93654-9205)
P.O. Box 846 (93654-0846)
PHONE..................................559 638-7799
Russell Tavlan, *Pr*
Ty Tavlan, *
▲ **EMP:** 185 **EST:** 1992
SQ FT: 80,000
SALES (est): 443.18MM **Privately Held**
SIC: 5148 4783 Fruits, fresh; Packing and crating

(P-6564)
MORADA PRODUCE COMPANY LP
500 N Jack Tone Rd (95215-9214)
P.O. Box 659 (95236-0659)
PHONE..................................209 546-0426
Henry Foppiano, *Pt*
◆ **EMP:** 1500 **EST:** 2003
SQ FT: 98,000
SALES (est): 221.89MM **Privately Held**
Web: www.moradaproduce.com
SIC: 5148 Fresh fruits and vegetables

(P-6565)
NATURES PRODUCE
3305 Bandini Blvd (90058-4130)
P.O. Box 58366 (90058-0366)
PHONE..................................323 235-4343
Rick Polisky, *CEO*
▲ **EMP:** 110 **EST:** 2000
SALES (est): 48.11MM **Privately Held**
Web: www.naturesproduce.com
SIC: 5148 Fruits, fresh

(P-6566)
NEWSTAR FRESH FOODS LLC (PA)
850 Work St Ste 101 (93901-4378)
P.O. Box 2627 (93902-2627)
PHONE..................................888 782-7220
Anthony Vasquez, *CEO*
Mitch Secondo, *
Carl Wiseman, *
▼ **EMP:** 200 **EST:** 1996
SQ FT: 1,300,000
SALES (est): 83.31MM **Privately Held**
Web: www.newstarfresh.com
SIC: 5148 Fresh fruits and vegetables

(P-6567)
NOR-CAL PRODUCE INC
2995 Oates St (95691-5902)
P.O. Box 980188 (95798-0188)
PHONE..................................916 373-0830
Todd Achondo, *CEO*
▼ **EMP:** 130 **EST:** 1972
SQ FT: 85,000
SALES (est): 45.32MM **Publicly Held**
Web: www.unifresh.com
SIC: 5148 Fruits, fresh
PA: United Natural Foods, Inc.
   313 Iron Horse Way
   Providence RI

(P-6568)
PACIFIC TRELLIS FRUIT LLC (PA)
Also Called: Borg Produce Sales
2301 E 7th St Ste C200 (90023-1041)
PHONE..................................323 859-9600
Josh Leichter, *CEO*
David Sullivan, *
▲ **EMP:** 130 **EST:** 1999
SQ FT: 10,000
SALES (est): 90.36MM
SALES (corp-wide): 90.36MM **Privately Held**
Web: www.dulcinea.com
SIC: 5148 Fruits, fresh

(P-6569)
PREMIER MUSHROOMS LP (PA)
2880 Niagara Ave (95932)
PHONE..................................530 458-2700
John Ashbaugh, *Pt*
Rex Pugh, *
▲ **EMP:** 68 **EST:** 2006
SQ FT: 10,000
SALES (est): 33.37MM **Privately Held**
Web: www.premiermushrooms.com
SIC: 5148 Fresh fruits and vegetables

(P-6570)
PRIMETIME INTERNATIONAL INC
47110 Washington St Ste 103 (92253-2186)
PHONE..................................760 399-4166
Mark Nickerson, *Managing Member**
Mike Way, *Managing Member**
Jeff Taylor, *Managing Member**
▲ **EMP:** 95 **EST:** 1994
SALES (est): 19.81MM **Privately Held**
Web: www.primetimeproduce.com
SIC: 5148 4783 Vegetables, fresh; Packing goods for shipping
PA: Sun And Sands Enterprises, Llc
   47110 Washington St # 103
   La Quinta CA

(P-6571)
PRO ACT LLC
40 Ragsdale Dr Ste 200 (93940-5774)
PHONE..................................831 655-4250
Harold Walker Iii, *CEO*
Loffredo Produce, *Managing Member**
Pacific Coast Fruit, *Managing Member**
Capitol City Produce, *Managing Member**
Produce One, *Managing Member**
▲ **EMP:** 75 **EST:** 1990
SALES (est): 27.03MM **Privately Held**
Web: www.proactusa.com
SIC: 5148 5431 Fruits, fresh; Fruit and vegetable markets

(P-6572)
PRODUCE EXCHANGE INCORPORATED (DH)
7407 Southfront Rd (94551-8224)
PHONE..................................925 454-8700
Marty Mazzanti, *Prin*
Samuel E Jones Junior, *Pr*
Don Held, *Prin*
▲ **EMP:** 65 **EST:** 1980
SQ FT: 10,000
SALES (est): 47.41MM
SALES (corp-wide): 346.39MM **Privately Held**
Web: www.lipmanfamilyfarms.com
SIC: 5148 Fruits, fresh
HQ: Lipman-Texas, Llc
   11990 Shiloh Rd
   Dallas TX
   214 367-6500

(P-6573)
PROFESSIONAL PRODUCE
2570 E 25th St (90058-1211)
P.O. Box 58308 (90058-0308)
PHONE..................................323 277-1550
Ted Kaplan, *CEO*
Maribel Reyes, *
◆ **EMP:** 99 **EST:** 1994
SQ FT: 5,000
SALES (est): 40.35MM **Privately Held**
Web: www.profproduce.com
SIC: 5148 Fruits, fresh

(P-6574)
READY PAC FOODS INC
125 Railroad Ave Ste 203 (94526-3835)
PHONE..................................925 552-0400
EMP: 99
SALES (corp-wide): 2.67MM **Privately Held**
Web: www.readypac.com
SIC: 5148 Fresh fruits and vegetables
HQ: Ready Pac Foods, Inc.
   4401 Foxdale St
   Irwindale CA
   626 856-8686

(P-6575)
READY PAC PRODUCE INC (DH)
Also Called: Ready Pac Foods
4401 Foxdale St (91706-2161)
PHONE..................................800 800-4088
Tony Sarsam, *CEO*
Jay Ellis, *
Bob Estes, *CIO**
Dan Redfern, *
Tristan Simpson, *CMO**
▲ **EMP:** 239 **EST:** 1969
SQ FT: 480,000
SALES (est): 256.43MM
SALES (corp-wide): 2.67MM **Privately Held**
Web: www.readypac.com
SIC: 5148 2099 Fresh fruits and vegetables; Salads, fresh or refrigerated
HQ: Ready Pac Foods, Inc.
   4401 Foxdale St
   Irwindale CA
   626 856-8686

(P-6576)
RIVER RANCH FRESH FOODS LLC (PA)
911 Blanco Cir Ste B (93901-4449)
PHONE..................................831 758-1390
John Bowman, *
Brian Thure, *
Ped Mills, *
Tom Welch, *
▲ **EMP:** 450 **EST:** 1993
SALES (est): 103.9MM **Privately Held**
Web: www.riverranchfreshfoods.com
SIC: 5148 Vegetables, fresh

(P-6577)
SAMBAZON INC (PA)
Also Called: Sambazon
209 Avenida Fabricante Ste 200 (92672)
PHONE..................................877 726-2296
Ryan Black, *CEO*
Ed Nichols, *
Jeremy Black, *
Travis Baumgardner, *
Bruce Peasland, *
◆ **EMP:** 60 **EST:** 2000
SQ FT: 10,000
SALES (est): 51.69MM
SALES (corp-wide): 51.69MM **Privately Held**
Web: www.sambazon.com
SIC: 5148 5499 Fruits; Juices, fruit or vegetable

(P-6578)
SEASON PRODUCE CO INC
1601 E Olympic Blvd Ste 315 (90021-1942)
PHONE..................................213 689-0008
Patrick R Horwath, *Pr*
Daniel Horwath, *
Timothy R Horwath, *
EMP: 353 **EST:** 1958
SQ FT: 20,000
SALES (est): 23.87MM
SALES (corp-wide): 23.87MM **Privately Held**
SIC: 5148 Fresh fruits and vegetables
PA: S & H Packing & Sales Co., Inc.
   2590 Harriet St
   Los Angeles CA
   323 581-7172

(P-6579)
SFFI COMPANY INC (PA)
Also Called: Simply Fresh Fruit
11020 White Rock Rd Ste 100 (95670-6402)
PHONE..................................323 586-0000
William T Sander, *Pr*
Jaxon Potter, *VP*
Bruce Spiro, *VP*
▲ **EMP:** 76 **EST:** 1999
SALES (est): 23.68MM
SALES (corp-wide): 23.68MM **Privately Held**
SIC: 5148 Fresh fruits and vegetables

(P-6580)
SHAPIRO-GILMAN-SHANDLER CO
Also Called: S G S Produce
739 Decatur St (90021-1649)
PHONE..................................213 593-1200
Minyi Xu, *CEO*
Carol C Shandler, *
Morris Shander, *
Muriel Shandler, *
▲ **EMP:** 101 **EST:** 1907
SQ FT: 50,000
SALES (est): 44.42MM
SALES (corp-wide): 297.68MM **Privately Held**
Web: www.sgsproduce.com
SIC: 5148 Fruits, fresh
PA: Grubmarket, Inc.
   395 Oyster Point Blvd # 515
   South San Francisco CA
   415 986-0523

(P-6581)
SIMPLY FRESH FRUIT INC
11020 White Rock Rd # 100 (95670-6402)
PHONE..................................323 586-0000
Gustavo Fernandez, *CEO*
William Sander, *
Jaxon Potter, *
Bruce Spiro, *
◆ **EMP:** 99 **EST:** 1983
SALES (est): 18.37MM
SALES (corp-wide): 23.68MM **Privately Held**
SIC: 5148 Fresh fruits and vegetables
PA: Sffi Company, Inc.
   11020 White Rock Rd Ste 1
   Rancho Cordova CA
   323 586-0000

(P-6582)
SUN AND SANDS ENTERPRISES LLC (PA)
Also Called: Prime Time International
47110 Washington St Ste 103 (92253-2186)
PHONE..................................760 399-4166
Chares Hodges, *Managing Member**
Sandra Gayle Hodges, *
Mark Nickerson, *
Chuck Hodges, *
▲ **EMP:** 64 **EST:** 1986
SALES (est): 72.57MM **Privately Held**

5148 - Fresh Fruits And Vegetables (P-6583)

Web: www.primetimeproduce.com
SIC: 5148 Fresh fruits and vegetables

(P-6583)
SUN PACIFIC MARKETING COOP INC
20715 Ave 8 (93261)
PHONE.................................559 784-6845
EMP: 395
SALES (corp-wide): 92.65MM Privately Held
Web: www.sunpacific.com
SIC: 5148 Fresh fruits and vegetables
PA: Sun Pacific Marketing Cooperative, Inc.
1095 E Green St
Pasadena CA
213 612-9957

(P-6584)
SUN PACIFIC MARKETING COOP INC
Also Called: Sun Pacific Farming
31452 Old River Rd (93311-9621)
PHONE.................................661 847-1015
Bob Dipiazza, Brnch Mgr
EMP: 395
SALES (corp-wide): 92.65MM Privately Held
Web: www.sunpacific.com
SIC: 5148 Fresh fruits and vegetables
PA: Sun Pacific Marketing Cooperative, Inc.
1095 E Green St
Pasadena CA
213 612-9957

(P-6585)
SUNBERRY GROWERS LLC
Also Called: Sunberry Growers
710 La Guardia St Ste A (93905-3347)
PHONE.................................805 922-9888
Carlos Ramirez, Managing Member
EMP: 2602 EST: 2014
SALES (est): 970.95K
SALES (corp-wide): 125.53MM Privately Held
SIC: 5148 Fresh fruits and vegetables
PA: Ramco Enterprises, L.P.
710 La Guardia St
Salinas CA
831 758-5272

(P-6586)
SUNKIST GROWERS INC (PA)
27770 Entertainment Dr (91355-1091)
PHONE.................................661 290-8900
Russell Hanlin Ii, Pr
Richard G French, VP
Michael Woottton, Sr VP
John Mc Guigan, VP
Russell L Hanlin Ii, VP
◆ EMP: 223 EST: 1893
SQ FT: 50,000
SALES (est): 1.15B
SALES (corp-wide): 1.15B Privately Held
Web: www.sunkist.com
SIC: 5148 2033 2037 2899 Fruits, fresh; Fruit juices: packaged in cans, jars, etc.; Fruit juice concentrates, frozen; Lemon oil (edible)

(P-6587)
SUNRISE GROWERS INC
701 W Kimberly Ave # 210 (92870-6330)
PHONE.................................714 706-6090
EMP: 140
SIC: 5148 Fruits

(P-6588)
V & L PRODUCE INC
Also Called: General Produce
2550 E 25th St (90058-1211)
PHONE.................................323 589-3125
Victor Mendoza, Pr
▲ EMP: 140 EST: 1984
SQ FT: 12,000
SALES (est): 29.6MM Privately Held
Web: www.vlproduce.com
SIC: 5148 Fresh fruits and vegetables

(P-6589)
VAL-PRO INC
Also Called: Continental Sales Co.
1661 Mcgarry St (90021-3116)
PHONE.................................213 689-0844
Joe Vidal, Brnch Mgr
EMP: 60
SALES (corp-wide): 35.49MM Privately Held
Web: www.valleyproduce.com
SIC: 5148 Fruits, fresh
PA: Val-Pro, Inc.
1601 E Olympic Blvd # 300
Los Angeles CA
213 627-8736

(P-6590)
VAL-PRO INC (PA)
Also Called: Valley Fruit & Produce Co
1601 E Olympic Blvd Ste 300 (90021-1942)
PHONE.................................213 627-8736
◆ EMP: 170 EST: 1920
SALES (est): 35.49MM
SALES (corp-wide): 35.49MM Privately Held
Web: www.valleyproduce.com
SIC: 5148 Fruits, fresh

(P-6591)
VEG-FRESH FARMS LLC (PA)
Also Called: Veg Fresh
1400 W Rincon St (92878-9205)
PHONE.................................800 422-5535
EMP: 134 EST: 1989
SQ FT: 94,000
SALES (est): 56.1MM Privately Held
Web: www.vegfresh.com
SIC: 5148 Vegetables, fresh

(P-6592)
VEGIWORKS INC
6 Viewmont Ter (94080-1570)
PHONE.................................415 643-8686
Shing Ho, CFO
Calvin Leong, *
Phillip Woo, *
EMP: 65 EST: 1992
SALES (est): 8.44MM Privately Held
Web: www.vegiworks.com
SIC: 5148 Fresh fruits and vegetables

(P-6593)
VENTURA COUNTY LEMON COOP
Also Called: Ventura Pacific Co
2620 Sakioka Dr (93030-5647)
P.O. Box 6986 (93031-6986)
PHONE.................................805 385-3345
Donald Dames, Pr
Milton Daily, Ch Bd
James H Gill, Sec
Jim Waters, Treas
EMP: 80 EST: 1943
SALES (est): 19.98MM Privately Held
Web: www.venturapacific.com

SIC: 5148 4783 3999 Fruits, fresh; Containerization of goods for shipping; Fruits, artificial and preserved

(P-6594)
WATSONVILLE COAST PRODUCE INC
275 Kearney Ext Frnt (95076-4223)
P.O. Box 490 (95077-0490)
PHONE.................................831 722-3851
Gary L Manfre, CEO
John Burkett, *
Frank L Capurro, *
Douglas Peterson, *
EMP: 75 EST: 1952
SQ FT: 40,000
SALES (est): 25.56MM Privately Held
Web: www.coastpro.com
SIC: 5148 Fruits, fresh

(P-6595)
WAWONA PACKING CO LLC
Also Called: Gerawan Farming Partners
7700 N Palm Ave Ste 206 (93711-5894)
▼ EMP: 1400 EST: 1999
SQ FT: 16,000
SALES (est): 455.35MM
SALES (corp-wide): 498.13MM Privately Held
Web: www.prima.com
SIC: 5148 Fresh fruits and vegetables
HQ: Mvk Intermediate Holdings Llc
7700 N Palm Ave Ste 206
Fresno CA

(P-6596)
WEST CENTRAL PRODUCE INC
Also Called: West Central Food Service
12840 Leyva St (90650-6852)
P.O. Box 4664 (90607-4664)
PHONE.................................213 629-3600
Michael Dodo, CEO
Jamie Purcell, *
Lance Shiring, *
▲ EMP: 400 EST: 1970
SQ FT: 34,000
SALES (est): 92.57MM Privately Held
Web: www.westcentralfoodservice.com
SIC: 5148 5147 5149 5146 Fruits, fresh; Meats and meat products; Dairy products, dried or canned; Seafoods

(P-6597)
WIEMAR DISTRIBUTORS INC
Also Called: M & M Distributors
1953 S Alameda St (90058-1013)
PHONE.................................213 747-7036
Marco Moreno, Pr
Rosa Moreno, *
▲ EMP: 65 EST: 1992
SQ FT: 31,000
SALES (est): 23.9MM Privately Held
Web: www.mm-farms.com
SIC: 5148 Fruits, fresh

(P-6598)
WORLD VARIETY PRODUCE INC
Also Called: Melissas World Variety Produce
5325 S Soto St (90058-3624)
P.O. Box 514599 (90051-2599)
PHONE.................................800 588-0151
Joe V Hernandez, Prin
Joe V Hernandez, Pr
Sharon Hernandez, *
David Shafer, *
◆ EMP: 325 EST: 1983
SQ FT: 244,000
SALES (est): 80.3MM Privately Held
Web: www.melissas.com
SIC: 5148 Fruits, fresh

5149 Groceries And Related Products, Nec

(P-6599)
AMERICAN BOTTLING COMPANY
2009 Farallon Dr (94577-6601)
PHONE.................................510 346-3777
Ken Dippy, Mgr
EMP: 87
Web: www.keurigdrpepper.com
SIC: 5149 Beverages, except coffee and tea
HQ: The American Bottling Company
6425 Hall Of Fame Ln
Frisco TX

(P-6600)
ANNIES HOMEGROWN INC
1610 5th St (94710-1715)
PHONE.................................510 558-7500
John Foraker, CEO
Stephen Palmer, *
Sandy Cortez, *
▼ EMP: 75 EST: 1997
SQ FT: 10,000
SALES (est): 31.39MM
SALES (corp-wide): 20.09B Publicly Held
Web: www.annies.com
SIC: 5149 Natural and organic foods
HQ: Annie's, Inc.
1610 5th St
Berkeley CA

(P-6601)
APP WHOLESALE LLC
3686 E Olympic Blvd (90023-3146)
PHONE.................................323 980-8315
EMP: 500 EST: 2013
SQ FT: 220,000
SALES (est): 84.69MM Privately Held
Web: www.app-wholesale.com
SIC: 5149 2741 Specialty food items; Business service newsletters: publishing and printing

(P-6602)
ARTISAN BAKERS
940 Riverside Pkwy Ste 50 (95605-1513)
PHONE.................................707 939-1765
Bill Dozier, CEO
Craig Ponsford, *
Sharon Ponsford, *
Elizabeth Ponsford, *
Chris Jones, *
EMP: 60 EST: 1992
SALES (est): 23.86MM Privately Held
Web: www.artisanbakers.com
SIC: 5149 5461 Bakery products; Retail bakeries

(P-6603)
ASHBURY MARKET INC
179 Starlite St (94080-6313)
PHONE.................................650 952-8889
Arnold E Wong, Pr
Richard Wong, *
EMP: 80 EST: 1993
SQ FT: 10,000
SALES (est): 24.62MM Privately Held
Web: www.raisondetrebakery.com
SIC: 5149 Bakery products

(P-6604)
ASPIRE BAKERIES LLC
6501 District Blvd (93313-2000)
PHONE.................................661 832-0409
EMP: 392
SALES (corp-wide): 1.77B Privately Held

PRODUCTS & SERVICES SECTION
5149 - Groceries And Related Products, Nec (P-6624)

Web: www.aspirebakeries.com
SIC: 5149 Bakery products
HQ: Aspire Bakeries Llc
6701 Center Dr W Ste 850
Los Angeles CA
844 992-7747

(P-6605)
ASPIRE BAKERIES LLC
Also Called: Fresh Start Bakeries
1220 S Baker Ave (91761-7739)
P.O. Box 1283 (91802-1283)
PHONE..................................909 472-3500
Rob Crawford, Genl Mgr
EMP: 197
SALES (corp-wide): 1.77B **Privately Held**
Web: www.aspirebakeries.com
SIC: 5149 Bakery products
HQ: Aspire Bakeries Llc
6701 Center Dr W Ste 850
Los Angeles CA
844 992-7747

(P-6606)
ASPIRE BAKERIES LLC
6500 Overlake Pl (94560-1083)
PHONE..................................510 494-1700
EMP: 321
SALES (corp-wide): 1.77B **Privately Held**
Web: www.aspirebakeries.com
SIC: 5149 Bakery products
HQ: Aspire Bakeries Llc
6701 Center Dr W Ste 850
Los Angeles CA
844 992-7747

(P-6607)
BAKEMARK USA LLC (PA)
Also Called: Bakemark
7351 Crider Ave (90660-3705)
PHONE..................................562 949-1054
Jim Parker, Managing Member
◆ EMP: 102 EST: 1928
SQ FT: 275,000
SALES (est): 578.75MM
SALES (corp-wide): 578.75MM **Privately Held**
Web: www.bakemark.com
SIC: 5149 2045 3556 2099 Bakery products; Flours and flour mixes, from purchased flour ; Food products machinery; Food preparations, nec

(P-6608)
BAKERY EX SOUTHERN CAL LLC
1910 W Malvern Ave (92833-2105)
PHONE..................................714 446-9470
EMP: 100 EST: 2001
SQ FT: 28,000
SALES (est): 23.54MM **Privately Held**
SIC: 5149 Bakery products

(P-6609)
BAY BREAD LLC
Also Called: La Boulange
2325 Pine St (94115-2714)
PHONE..................................415 440-0356
Pascal Rigo, Managing Member
Fred Estrada, *
Lori Goodman, *
EMP: 70 EST: 2003
SALES (est): 27.69MM
SALES (corp-wide): 32.25B **Publicly Held**
Web: www.laboulangeriesf.com
SIC: 5149 Breading mixes
PA: Starbucks Corporation
2401 Utah Ave S
Seattle WA
206 447-1575

(P-6610)
BLUETRITON BRANDS INC
Also Called: Arrowhead Water
619 N Main St (92868-1103)
PHONE..................................714 532-6220
Dan Miller, Mgr
EMP: 106
SQ FT: 16,312
SALES (corp-wide): 1.3B **Privately Held**
Web: local.readyrefresh.com
SIC: 5149 5499 5963 5078 Water, distilled; Water: distilled mineral or spring; Bottled water delivery; Refrigeration equipment and supplies
HQ: Bluetriton Brands, Inc.
900 Long Ridge Rd Bldg 2
Stamford CT

(P-6611)
BOBOLI INTERNATIONAL LLC
Also Called: Boboli International
5530 El Greco Dr (95212-9228)
PHONE..................................209 473-3507
▲ EMP: 85
Web: www.boboli-intl.com
SIC: 5149 Sauces

(P-6612)
BUENA VISTA FOOD PRODUCTS INC (DH)
823 W 8th St (91702-2247)
PHONE..................................626 815-8859
Laura Trujillo, Pr
Michelle Reitzin-bass, Prin
Peter Woods, Prin
Mike Likovich, Prin
EMP: 115 EST: 1991
SALES (est): 50.51MM **Privately Held**
Web: www.bvfoods.com
SIC: 5149 Bakery products
HQ: Sterling Foods, Llc
1075 Arion Pkwy
San Antonio TX
210 490-1669

(P-6613)
CALIFORNIA BAKING COMPANY
Also Called: California Bread Co.
681 Anita St (91911-4663)
PHONE..................................619 591-8289
Abraham Levy, Pr
EMP: 300 EST: 2002
SALES (est): 24.87MM **Privately Held**
Web: www.californiabaking.com
SIC: 5149 2051 Bakery products; Sponge goods, bakery: except frozen

(P-6614)
CLOVER-STORNETTA FARMS LLC (PA)
Also Called: Clover Sonoma
1800 S Mcdowell Boulevard Ext Ste 100 (94954-6962)
P.O. Box 750369 (94975-0369)
PHONE..................................707 769-3282
TOLL FREE: 800
Marcus Benedetti, Pr
Dan Benedetti, *
Mike Keifer, *
Mkulima Britt, *
Gene Benedetti, *
EMP: 180 EST: 1977
SQ FT: 80,000
SALES (est): 96.07MM
SALES (corp-wide): 96.07MM **Privately Held**
Web: www.cloversonoma.com

SIC: 5149 5143 2026 Juices; Dairy products, except dried or canned; Milk and cream, except fermented, cultured, and flavored

(P-6615)
COASTAL COCKTAILS INC (PA)
Also Called: Modern Gourmet Foods
1920 E Deere Ave Ste 100 (92705-5717)
PHONE..................................949 250-8951
Boaz Shonfeld, CEO
▲ EMP: 60 EST: 2009
SALES (est): 39MM **Privately Held**
Web: www.coastalcocktails.com
SIC: 5149 2086 Food gift baskets; Bottled and canned soft drinks

(P-6616)
COLUSA PRODUCE CORPORATION
1954 Progress Rd (95957-9643)
PHONE..................................530 696-0121
Jim Wallace, Pr
◆ EMP: 78 EST: 1990
SQ FT: 5,000
SALES (est): 23.54MM **Privately Held**
SIC: 5149 5159 5148 Spices and seasonings ; Broomcorn; Fresh fruits and vegetables

(P-6617)
COMPLETELY FRESH FOODS INC
4401 S Downey Rd (90058-2518)
P.O. Box 58667 (90058-0667)
PHONE..................................323 722-9136
Josh Solovy, Pr
Levi Litmanovich, *
Eric Litmanovich, *
EMP: 200 EST: 2006
SQ FT: 15,000
SALES (est): 46.35MM
SALES (corp-wide): 452.76MM **Privately Held**
Web: www.gwfg.com
SIC: 5149 5046 Specialty food items; Commercial equipment, nec
PA: Golden West Food Group, Inc.
4401 S Downey Rd
Vernon CA
888 807-3663

(P-6618)
CORE-MARK INTERNATIONAL INC
200 Coremark Ct (93307-8402)
P.O. Box 70458 (93387-0458)
PHONE..................................661 366-2673
Caral Parker, Pr
EMP: 211
SALES (corp-wide): 57.25B **Publicly Held**
Web: www.core-mark.com
SIC: 5149 Groceries and related products, nec
HQ: Core-Mark International, Inc.
1500 Solana Blvd Ste 3400
Westlake TX
650 589-9445

(P-6619)
CORE-MARK INTERNATIONAL INC
2311 E 48th St (90058-2007)
PHONE..................................323 583-6531
Julian Puentes, Brnch Mgr
EMP: 174
SALES (corp-wide): 57.25B **Publicly Held**
Web: www.core-mark.com
SIC: 5149 5194 5145 Groceries and related products, nec; Tobacco and tobacco products; Confectionery

HQ: Core-Mark International, Inc.
1500 Solana Blvd Ste 3400
Westlake TX
650 589-9445

(P-6620)
CORE-MARK INTERNATIONAL INC
3970 Pell Cir (95838-2511)
PHONE..................................509 535-9768
Christopher Ladesich, Prin
EMP: 79
SQ FT: 25,000
SALES (corp-wide): 57.25B **Publicly Held**
Web: www.core-mark.com
SIC: 5149 5194 5141 Groceries and related products, nec; Tobacco and tobacco products; Groceries, general line
HQ: Core-Mark International, Inc.
1500 Solana Blvd Ste 3400
Westlake TX
650 589-9445

(P-6621)
CORE-MARK INTERNATIONAL INC
31300 Medallion Dr (94544-7902)
PHONE..................................510 487-3000
Bob Norton, Mgr
EMP: 102
SALES (corp-wide): 57.25B **Publicly Held**
Web: www.core-mark.com
SIC: 5149 5194 5145 5141 Groceries and related products, nec; Tobacco and tobacco products; Confectionery; Groceries, general line
HQ: Core-Mark International, Inc.
1500 Solana Blvd Ste 3400
Westlake TX
650 589-9445

(P-6622)
CREATIVE ENERGY FOODS INC
9957 Medford Ave Ste 4 (94603-2309)
PHONE..................................510 638-8668
Richard C Dwinell, CEO
Wesley Felton, *
George Jewell, *
Jacker Wong, *
◆ EMP: 95 EST: 1998
SQ FT: 105,000
SALES (est): 42.22MM **Privately Held**
Web: www.creativeenergyfoods.com
SIC: 5149 2026 Health foods; Dips, sour cream based

(P-6623)
CULINARY HISPANIC FOODS INC
Also Called: Productos Chata
805 Bow St (91914)
PHONE..................................619 955-6101
Jorge Aguilar, CEO
Carlos Machado, *
▲ EMP: 1458 EST: 2011
SQ FT: 4,000
SALES (est): 70.89MM **Privately Held**
SIC: 5149 Canned goods: fruit, vegetables, seafood, meats, etc.

(P-6624)
DEL MONTE FOODS INC (HQ)
Also Called: Del Monte Foods
205 N Wiget Ln (94598-2458)
PHONE..................................925 949-2772
Greg Longstreet, Pr
Bibie Wu, CMO
Parag Schadeva, COO
William Sawyers, CCO

5149 - Groceries And Related Products, Nec (P-6625)

◆ EMP: 125 EST: 2013
SALES (est): 784.65MM Privately Held
Web: www.delmontefoods.com
SIC: 5149 2033 Groceries and related products, nec; Canned fruits and specialties
PA: Del Monte Pacific Limited
17 Bukit Pasoh Road
Singapore

(P-6625)
DESERT VALLEY DATE LLC
86740 Industrial Way (92236-2718)
PHONE.................................760 398-0999
Greg Willsey, *Managing Member*
EMP: 85 EST: 2020
SALES (est): 10.1MM Privately Held
Web: www.desertvalleydate.com
SIC: 5149 5148 Organic and diet food; Fruits

(P-6626)
DOMINO FOODS INC
830 Loring Ave (94525-1104)
PHONE.................................510 787-2121
David Koncelik, *CEO*
EMP: 115
SALES (corp-wide): 2.16B Privately Held
SIC: 5149 Groceries and related products, nec
HQ: Domino Foods Inc.
99 Wood Ave S Ste 901
Iselin NJ
732 590-1173

(P-6627)
EL GUAPO SPICES INC (PA)
Also Called: El Guapo Spices and Herbs Pkg
6200 E Slauson Ave (90040-3012)
PHONE.................................213 312-1300
Dan Terrazas, *Pr*
EMP: 100 EST: 1982
SALES (est): 9.18MM
SALES (corp-wide): 9.18MM Privately Held
SIC: 5149 Spices and seasonings

(P-6628)
GALASSOS BAKERY (PA)
Also Called: Galasso's Bakery
10820 San Sevaine Way (91752-1116)
PHONE.................................951 360-1211
Jeannette Galasso, *Pr*
Mark Bailey, *
Pearl Denault, *
Rick Vargas, *Operations*
EMP: 180 EST: 1923
SQ FT: 110,000
SALES (est): 95.32MM
SALES (corp-wide): 95.32MM Privately Held
Web: www.galassos.com
SIC: 5149 Bakery products

(P-6629)
GANO EXCEL (USA) INC
8652 Kimball Ave (91708-9612)
P.O. Box 9275 (91226-0275)
PHONE.................................626 338-8081
Matthew Nguyen, *Pr*
Soon Seng Leow, *
Ruben Cardenas, *
Chang Ching Lew, *
Chin Iakooi, *
▲ EMP: 67 EST: 2002
SALES (est): 23.26MM Privately Held
Web: www.ganoexcel.us
SIC: 5149 Coffee, green or roasted

(P-6630)
GLOBAL BAKERIES INC
13336 Paxton St (91331-2339)
PHONE.................................818 896-0525
▲ EMP: 60
SIC: 5149 Bakery products

(P-6631)
GOGLANIAN BAKERIES INC (HQ)
Also Called: Goglanian
3401 W Segerstrom Ave (92704-6404)
PHONE.................................714 338-1145
◆ EMP: 300 EST: 1978
SQ FT: 71,500
SALES (est): 55.7MM
SALES (corp-wide): 4.81B Privately Held
Web: www.richsusa.com
SIC: 5149 Bakery products
PA: Rich Products Corporation
1 Robert Rich Way
Buffalo NY
716 878-8000

(P-6632)
GOURMET INDIA FOOD COMPANY LLC
12220 Rivera Rd Ste A (90606-6206)
PHONE.................................562 698-9763
▲ EMP: 75 EST: 2000
SALES (est): 9.47MM Privately Held
Web: www.aqualitytemp.com
SIC: 5149 Bakery products

(P-6633)
HARRIS FREEMAN & CO INC (PA)
Also Called: Harris Tea Company
3110 E Miraloma Ave (92806-1906)
PHONE.................................714 765-7525
Anil J Shah, *CEO*
Kevin Shah, *
Meena Shah, *
◆ EMP: 500 EST: 1981
SQ FT: 58,000
SALES (est): 150K
SALES (corp-wide): 150K Privately Held
Web: www.harrisfreeman.com
SIC: 5149 2099 Tea; Spices, including grinding

(P-6634)
IRIS USA INC
3021 Boeing Way (95206-4920)
PHONE.................................209 982-9100
Kenji Megero, *Mgr*
▲ EMP: 109
Web: www.irisusainc.com
SIC: 5149 5099 5191 Dog food; Luggage; Soil, potting and planting
HQ: Iris Usa, Inc.
13423 W Cactus Rd
Surprise AZ

(P-6635)
J & D MEAT COMPANY
Also Called: JD Food
4671 E Edgar Ave (93725-1676)
P.O. Box 12051 (93776-2051)
PHONE.................................559 445-1123
Mark K Ford, *Pr*
Robert Maxey, *
Steven Maxey, *
EMP: 115 EST: 1974
SQ FT: 51,000
SALES (est): 59.2MM Privately Held
Web: www.jdfood.com
SIC: 5149 5147 5148 5143 Groceries and related products, nec; Meats and meat products; Fresh fruits and vegetables; Dairy products, except dried or canned

(P-6636)
JAGPREET ENTERPRISES LLC
Also Called: Quick-N-Ezee Indian Foods
3374 Enterprise Ave (94545-3228)
PHONE.................................510 336-8376
Sukhjeet K Singh, *CEO*
Dalbir Singh, *
Cecilia Huffstutler, *
▲ EMP: 150 EST: 1992
SQ FT: 30,000
SALES (est): 30.24MM Privately Held
Web: www.sukhis.com
SIC: 5149 Groceries and related products, nec

(P-6637)
JAVA CITY (HQ)
1300 Del Paso Rd (95834-1168)
PHONE.................................916 565-5500
Brendan Mcdonnell, *CEO*
Jeff Hill, *
Paul Bork, *
Cheryl Dominguez, *
Kim Peterson, *
▲ EMP: 80 EST: 1984
SQ FT: 11,200
SALES (est): 85.61MM Privately Held
Web: www.javacity.com
SIC: 5149 Coffee, green or roasted
PA: Bewley's Limited
Northern Cross
Dublin

(P-6638)
JFC INTERNATIONAL INC (HQ)
7101 E Slauson Ave (90040-3622)
P.O. Box 875349 (90087-0449)
PHONE.................................323 721-6100
Yoshiyuki Ishigaki, *CEO*
Hiroyuki Enomoto, *
◆ EMP: 203 EST: 1948
SALES (est): 604.95MM Privately Held
Web: www.jfc.com
SIC: 5149 7389 Specialty food items; Labeling bottles, cans, cartons, etc.
PA: Kikkoman Corporation
2-1-1, Nishishimbashi
Minato-Ku TKY

(P-6639)
JFC INTERNATIONAL INC
Also Called: Los Angeles Branch
7140 Bandini Blvd (90040-3325)
PHONE.................................323 721-6900
Tamaki Saijo, *Brnch Mgr*
EMP: 165
Web: www.jfc.com
SIC: 5149 Specialty food items
HQ: Jfc International Inc.
7101 E Slauson Ave
Commerce CA
323 721-6100

(P-6640)
K T LUCKY CO INC
10925 Schmidt Rd (91733-2707)
PHONE.................................626 579-7272
Hang Huynh, *Pr*
▲ EMP: 70 EST: 1986
SQ FT: 12,000
SALES (est): 10MM Privately Held
SIC: 5149 Macaroni

(P-6641)
KALIOCOMMERCE INC
19330 Stevens Creek Blvd (95014-2551)
PHONE.................................408 550-8040
Larry Kavanagh, *Brnch Mgr*
EMP: 75
SALES (corp-wide): 5.5MM Privately Held
Web: www.kaliocommerce.com
SIC: 5149 Tea
PA: Kaliocommerce, Inc.
4340 Stevens Creek Blvd # 250
San Jose CA
408 550-8040

(P-6642)
LA PROVENCE INC
Also Called: La Provence Bakery
1370 W San Marcos Blvd Ste 130 (92078-1601)
PHONE.................................760 736-3299
Philip Dardaine, *CEO*
Thierry Bouchereau, *
Karen Dardaine, *
EMP: 95 EST: 1990
SQ FT: 6,000
SALES (est): 26.31MM Privately Held
Web: www.laprovenceinc.com
SIC: 5149 Bakery products

(P-6643)
LA TORTILLA FACTORY INC (PA)
3300 Westwind Blvd (95403-8273)
PHONE.................................707 586-4000
Samuel Carlos Tamayo, *CEO*
Carlos Tamayo, *
Sam Tamayo, *
Carlos G Tamayo, *
Jonna Greene, *
EMP: 280 EST: 1977
SALES (est): 97.79MM
SALES (corp-wide): 97.79MM Privately Held
Web: www.latortillafactory.com
SIC: 5149 2051 Specialty food items; Bread, cake, and related products

(P-6644)
LENORE JOHN & CO (PA)
1250 Delevan Dr (92102-2437)
PHONE.................................619 232-6136
John G Lenore, *CEO*
Jamie Lenore, *
Karl Hurlbert, *
◆ EMP: 120 EST: 1966
SQ FT: 50,000
SALES (est): 45.4MM
SALES (corp-wide): 45.4MM Privately Held
Web: www.johnlenore.com
SIC: 5149 5182 5181 Soft drinks; Wine; Beer and other fermented malt liquors

(P-6645)
MHH HOLDINGS INC
5653 Alton Pkwy (92618-4058)
PHONE.................................949 651-9903
Cynthia Espere, *Brnch Mgr*
EMP: 216
SALES (corp-wide): 23.68MM Privately Held
SIC: 5149 Tea
PA: Mhh Holdings, Inc.
4580 Calle Alto
Camarillo CA
805 484-7924

(P-6646)
MHH HOLDINGS INC
415 S Lake Ave Ste 108 (91101-5047)
PHONE.................................626 744-9370
Xiomara Bellido, *Prin*
EMP: 217
SALES (corp-wide): 23.68MM Privately Held
SIC: 5149 Tea
PA: Mhh Holdings, Inc.
4580 Calle Alto

PRODUCTS & SERVICES SECTION

5149 - Groceries And Related Products, Nec (P-6667)

Camarillo CA
805 484-7924

(P-6647)
MIGHTY LEAF TEA
100 Smith Ranch Rd Ste 120 (94903-1900)
PHONE..................................415 491-2650
▲ **EMP:** 65 **EST:** 1998
SQ FT: 5,000
SALES (est): 48.95MM **Privately Held**
Web: www.peets.com
SIC: 5149 5499 Tea; Tea
HQ: Peet's Coffee & Tea, Llc
  1400 Park Ave
  Emeryville CA
  510 594-2100

(P-6648)
MONDELEZ GLOBAL LLC
Also Called: Nabisco
5815 Clark St (91761-3676)
PHONE..................................909 605-0140
Botie Magee, *Brnch Mgr*
EMP: 61
Web: www.mondelezinternational.com
SIC: 5149 2099 2052 Crackers, cookies, and bakery products; Food preparations, nec; Cookies and crackers
HQ: Mondelez Global Llc
  905 W Fulton Market # 200
  Chicago IL
  847 943-4000

(P-6649)
MONSTER ENERGY COMPANY (HQ)
Also Called: Monster Energy
1 Monster Way (92879-7101)
PHONE..................................866 322-4466
Rodney C Sacks, *CEO*
Hilton H Scholsberg, *V Ch Bd*
Thomas J Kelly, *CFO*
◆ **EMP:** 258 **EST:** 1992
SQ FT: 300,000
SALES (est): 577.37K
SALES (corp-wide): 6.31B **Publicly Held**
Web: www.monsterbevcorp.com
SIC: 5149 Juices
PA: Monster Beverage Corporation
  1 Monster Way
  Corona CA
  951 739-6200

(P-6650)
MUTUAL TRADING CO INC (DH)
4200 Shirley Ave (91731-1130)
PHONE..................................213 626-9458
Masatoshi Ohata, *Dir*
Atsuko Kanai, *
Yoshihiro Sakata, *
Ami Nakanishi, *Dir*
Minori Mori, *
◆ **EMP:** 105 **EST:** 1926
SALES (est): 191.56MM **Privately Held**
Web: www.lamtc.com
SIC: 5149 5141 5023 Groceries and related products, nec; Groceries, general line; Homefurnishings
HQ: Takara Shuzo International Co., Ltd.
  20, Naginatabokocho, Higashiiru, Karasuma, Shijodoori, Shimogyo-Kyoto KYO

(P-6651)
NATIONAL BEVERAGE CORP
Also Called: Shasta Beverages
26901 Industrial Blvd (94545-3346)
PHONE..................................510 783-3200
EMP: 65
SALES (corp-wide): 1.17B **Publicly Held**

Web: www.nationalbeverage.com
SIC: 5149 Soft drinks
PA: National Beverage Corp.
  8100 Sw 10th St Ste 4000
  Plantation FL
  954 581-0922

(P-6652)
NATURAL BALANCE PET FOODS INC
Also Called: Natural Balance Pet Foods, Inc.
50 Elsie St (94110-5107)
P.O. Box 193575 (94119-3575)
PHONE..................................415 247-3020
EMP: 68
SIC: 5149 Pet foods
PA: Natural Balance Pet Foods, Llc
  2358 University Ave # 2280
  San Diego CA

(P-6653)
NATURES BEST
6 Pointe Dr Ste 300 (92821-6323)
P.O. Box 2248 (92822-2248)
PHONE..................................714 255-4600
▲ **EMP:** 360
SIC: 5149 Health foods

(P-6654)
NEUROBRANDS LLC
Also Called: Neuro Drinks
15303 Ventura Blvd Ste 675 (91403-6608)
P.O. Box 55245 (91413-0245)
PHONE..................................310 393-6444
Diana Jenkins, *CEO*
Scott Laporta, *
Greg Buscher, *
▲ **EMP:** 125 **EST:** 2009
SALES (est): 42.36MM **Privately Held**
Web: www.drinkneuro.com
SIC: 5149 Soft drinks

(P-6655)
NEW DESSERTS INC
Also Called: Just Desserts
5000 Fulton Dr (94534-1677)
PHONE..................................415 780-6860
Michael Mendes, *CEO*
John Wohlgemuth, *
Leighton Mue, *
EMP: 71 **EST:** 1974
SQ FT: 73,500
SALES (est): 30.44MM
SALES (corp-wide): 121.93MM **Privately Held**
Web: www.justdesserts.com
SIC: 5149 2024 Bakery products; Ice cream and frozen deserts
HQ: Rubicon Bakers Llc
  154 S 23rd St
  Richmond CA
  510 779-3010

(P-6656)
PASTA SHOP (PA)
Also Called: Market Hall Foods
5655 College Ave Ste 201 (94618-1583)
PHONE..................................510 250-6005
Sara Wilson, *Mng Pt*
Anthony Wilson, *Pt*
Peter Wilson, *Pt*
▲ **EMP:** 80 **EST:** 1981
SQ FT: 4,500
SALES (est): 46.26MM
SALES (corp-wide): 46.26MM **Privately Held**
Web: www.rockridgemarkethall.com
SIC: 5149 5411 5812 5431 Pasta and rice; Delicatessen stores; Caterers; Fruit and vegetable markets

(P-6657)
PERFECT BAR LLC
Also Called: Perfect Snacks
3931 Sorrento Valley Blvd Ste 100 (92121-1402)
PHONE..................................866 628-8548
Bill Keith, *CEO*
EMP: 200 **EST:** 2005
SQ FT: 16,000
SALES (est): 96.39MM **Publicly Held**
Web: www.perfectsnacks.com
SIC: 5149 Health foods
PA: Mondelez International, Inc.
  905 W Fulton Market # 200
  Chicago IL

(P-6658)
POMWONDERFUL LLC
23154 Lerdo Hwy (93206-9503)
PHONE..................................559 258-4834
Ashish Pandit, *Dir*
EMP: 60
SALES (corp-wide): 2.04B **Privately Held**
Web: www.pomwonderful.com
SIC: 5149 Groceries and related products, nec
HQ: Pomwonderful Llc
  11444 W Olympic Blvd
  Los Angeles CA
  310 966-5800

(P-6659)
POMWONDERFUL LLC
900 Airport Blvd (93640-2441)
PHONE..................................310 966-5800
Larry Isonio, *Brnch Mgr*
EMP: 100
SALES (corp-wide): 2.04B **Privately Held**
Web: www.pomwonderful.com
SIC: 5149 5148 5085 Beverage concentrates; Fruits, fresh; Plastic bottles
HQ: Pomwonderful Llc
  11444 W Olympic Blvd
  Los Angeles CA
  310 966-5800

(P-6660)
PREMIER NUTRITION COMPANY LLC (HQ)
Also Called: Joint Juice
1222 67th St Ste 210 (94608-1121)
PHONE..................................415 814-9410
Darcy Davenport, *CEO*
David Ritterbush, *
Marty Lambrechts, *
Mark Levine, *
David Cooper, *
◆ **EMP:** 159 **EST:** 1999
SQ FT: 45,000
SALES (est): 116.8MM **Publicly Held**
Web: www.premiernutrition.com
SIC: 5149 Specialty food items
PA: Post Holdings, Inc.
  2503 S Hanley Rd
  Saint Louis MO

(P-6661)
PULMUONE USA INC
5755 Rossi Ln (95020-7063)
PHONE..................................714 361-0806
▲ **EMP:** 290
Web: www.pulmuonefoodsusa.com
SIC: 5149 Natural and organic foods
HQ: Pulmuone U.S.A., Inc.
  2315 Moore Ave
  Fullerton CA

(P-6662)
ROCKVIEW DAIRIES INC (PA)
Also Called: Motive Nation
7011 Stewart And Gray Rd (90241-4347)
P.O. Box 668 (90241-0668)
PHONE..................................562 927-5511
Egbert Jim Degroot, *CEO*
Ted De Groot, *
Joe Valadez, *
◆ **EMP:** 188 **EST:** 1966
SALES (est): 87.42MM
SALES (corp-wide): 87.42MM **Privately Held**
Web: www.rockviewfarms.com
SIC: 5149 5143 2026 Dried or canned foods; Milk; Fluid milk

(P-6663)
ROYAL CROWN ENTERPRISES INC
780 Epperson Dr (91748-1336)
PHONE..................................626 854-8080
◆ **EMP:** 150
SIC: 5149 5141 Canned goods: fruit, vegetables, seafood, meats, etc.; Groceries, general line

(P-6664)
SAN FRANCISCO HERB & NATURAL FOOD CO INC
Also Called: San Francisco Herb Tea & Spice
47444 Kato Rd (94538-7319)
PHONE..................................510 770-1215
◆ **EMP:** 85
Web: www.herbspicetea.com
SIC: 5149 2833 2099 Tea; Medicinals and botanicals; Food preparations, nec

(P-6665)
SEMIFREDDIS INC (PA)
Also Called: Semifreddi's Bakery
1980 N Loop Rd (94502-3540)
PHONE..................................510 596-9930
Thomas Frainier, *Pr*
Michael Rose, *
Bill F, *
EMP: 110 **EST:** 1984
SQ FT: 36,000
SALES (est): 23.81MM
SALES (corp-wide): 23.81MM **Privately Held**
Web: www.semifreddis.com
SIC: 5149 5461 Bakery products; Retail bakeries

(P-6666)
SHAMROCK FOODS COMPANY
856 National Dr (95834-1173)
PHONE..................................602 819-1654
EMP: 257
SALES (corp-wide): 5.7B **Privately Held**
Web: www.shamrockfoods.com
SIC: 5149 Groceries and related products, nec
PA: Shamrock Foods Company
  3900 E Camelback Rd # 300
  Phoenix AZ
  602 233-6400

(P-6667)
SHAMROCK FOODS COMPANY
12400 Riverside Dr (91752-1004)
PHONE..................................951 685-6314
EMP: 703
SALES (corp-wide): 5.7B **Privately Held**
Web: www.shamrockfoods.com
SIC: 5149 Groceries and related products, nec
PA: Shamrock Foods Company

5149 - Groceries And Related Products, Nec (P-6668)

3900 E Camelback Rd # 300
Phoenix AZ
602 233-6400

(P-6668)
SHAW BAKERS LLC
14490 Catalina St (94577-5516)
PHONE..................650 273-1440
EMP: 133
SALES (corp-wide): 22.72MM Privately Held
SIC: 5149 5142 2053 Bakery products; Bakery products, frozen; Frozen bakery products, except bread
PA: Shaw Bakers Llc
320b Shaw Rd
South San Francisco CA
650 273-1440

(P-6669)
SOOFER CO INC
Also Called: Sadaf Foods
2828 S Alameda St (90058-1347)
PHONE..................323 234-6666
Dariush Soofer, CEO
Jamshid Soofer, *
Dariush Soofer, VP
Behrooz David Soofer, *
Ramon Sentimental, *
◆ **EMP:** 75 **EST:** 1981
SQ FT: 70,000
SALES (est): 38.84MM Privately Held
Web: www.sadaffoods.com
SIC: 5149 Spices and seasonings

(P-6670)
SPECIALTY BAKING INC
Also Called: Specialty Baking Co.
3134 Capelaw Ct (95135-1101)
PHONE..................408 298-6950
Robert Murillo, CEO
Manual Escobar, *
Mark Murillo, *
Robert Murillo Junior, Sec
EMP: 70 **EST:** 1978
SQ FT: 10,000
SALES (est): 9.08MM Privately Held
Web: www.perfectdomain.com
SIC: 5149 2051 Bakery products; Bread, cake, and related products

(P-6671)
STARWEST BOTANICALS LLC (PA)
161 Main Ave (95838-2080)
PHONE..................916 638-8100
Van Joerger, Pr
▼ **EMP:** 92 **EST:** 1975
SQ FT: 68,400
SALES (est): 37.34MM
SALES (corp-wide): 37.34MM Privately Held
Web: www.starwest-botanicals.com
SIC: 5149 Tea

(P-6672)
SUGAR FOODS CORPORATION
33378 Transit Ave (94587-2014)
PHONE..................510 441-0311
EMP: 74
SALES (corp-wide): 286.33MM Privately Held
Web: www.sugarfoods.com
SIC: 5149 Bakery products
PA: Sugar Foods Corporation
950 3rd Ave Fl 21
New York NY
212 753-6900

(P-6673)
SUN-MAID GROWERS CALIFORNIA (PA)
6795 N Palm Ave Ste 200 (93704-1082)
PHONE..................559 896-8000
Harry J Overly, CEO
Steve Loftus, CDO
Braden Bender, VP
Kayhan Hazrati, VP
Rick Stark, Sec
◆ **EMP:** 750 **EST:** 1912
SALES (est): 394.98MM
SALES (corp-wide): 394.98MM Privately Held
Web: www.sunmaid.com
SIC: 5149 Groceries and related products, nec

(P-6674)
SUNFOOD CORPORATION
Also Called: Sunfood Superfoods
1830 Gillespie Way Ste 101 (92020-0922)
PHONE..................619 596-7979
Robert Deupree, CEO
▲ **EMP:** 95 **EST:** 2009
SALES (est): 48.45MM Privately Held
Web: www.sunfood.com
SIC: 5149 Natural and organic foods

(P-6675)
SUPER STORE INDUSTRIES
Also Called: Ssi
2800 W March Ln Ste 210 (95219-8200)
P.O. Box 549 (95330-0549)
PHONE..................209 858-3365
Tom Hughes, Brnch Mgr
EMP: 400
Web: www.ssica.com
SIC: 5149 5141 4225 Groceries and related products, nec; Groceries, general line; General warehousing and storage
PA: Super Store Industries
16888 Mckinley Ave
Lathrop CA

(P-6676)
SURGE GLOBL BKRIES HLDINGS LLC (PA)
Also Called: Global Bakeries
13336 Paxton St (91331-2339)
PHONE..................818 896-0525
Chris Botticella, CEO
Ash Aghasi, COO
EMP: 98 **EST:** 2018
SQ FT: 44,000
SALES (est): 22.62MM
SALES (corp-wide): 22.62MM Privately Held
Web: www.globalbakeriesllc.com
SIC: 5149 Bakery products

(P-6677)
TADIN INC
Also Called: Tadin Herb & Tea Co.
3345 E Slauson Ave (90058-3914)
PHONE..................213 406-8880
▲ **EMP:** 95
Web: www.tadin.com
SIC: 5149 Tea

(P-6678)
TAMA TRADING COMPANY
1920 E 20th St (90058-1076)
PHONE..................213 748-8262
William A Sauro, CEO
Sandra Sauro, *
◆ **EMP:** 61 **EST:** 1926
SQ FT: 60,000
SALES (est): 25.2MM Privately Held

Web: www.tamatrading.com
SIC: 5149 5143 5147 5145 Specialty food items; Cheese; Meats and meat products; Candy

(P-6679)
TANAKA FARMS
5380 University Dr (92612-2944)
PHONE..................949 653-2100
Glenn Tannaka, Owner
EMP: 60 **EST:** 1975
SALES (est): 9.77MM Privately Held
Web: www.tanakafarms.com
SIC: 5149 Groceries and related products, nec

(P-6680)
TL MONTGOMERY & ASSOCIATES INC
2833 Leonis Blvd Ste 205 (90058-2909)
PHONE..................323 583-1645
▼ **EMP:** 110
SIC: 5149 Pet foods

(P-6681)
TLD ACQUISITION CO LLC
Also Called: Tld Distribution Co
505 S 7th Ave (91746-3121)
▲ **EMP:** 150
SIC: 5149 5023 5145 5046 Beverages, except coffee and tea; Glassware; Snack foods; Restaurant equipment and supplies, nec

(P-6682)
TRAINA DRIED FRUIT INC
Also Called: Traina Foods
280 S 1st St (95363-2822)
PHONE..................209 892-5472
EMP: 160
Web: www.trainafoods.com
SIC: 5149 Fruits, dried
PA: Traina Dried Fruit, Inc.
337 Lemon Ave
Patterson CA

(P-6683)
TRAINA DRIED FRUIT INC (PA)
Also Called: Traina Foods
337 Lemon Ave (95363-9634)
P.O. Box 157 (95363-0157)
PHONE..................209 892-5472
William Traina, CEO
Justin A Traina, *
Joseph Traina, *
Josephine Traina, *
◆ **EMP:** 80 **EST:** 1926
SQ FT: 5,000
SALES (est): 61.59MM Privately Held
Web: www.trainafoods.com
SIC: 5149 Fruits, dried

(P-6684)
TRINIDAD/BENHAM CORP
12400 Wilshire Blvd Ste 1180 (90025-1019)
PHONE..................626 723-2300
EMP: 72
SALES (corp-wide): 468.79MM Privately Held
Web: www.trinidadbenham.com
SIC: 5149 Pasta and rice
HQ: Trinidad/Benham Corp.
3650 S Yosemite St # 300
Denver CO
303 220-1400

(P-6685)
TRINITY FRESH DISTRIBUTION LLC

8200 Berry Ave Ste 140 (95828-1612)
P.O. Box 619 (95683-0619)
PHONE..................916 714-7368
EMP: 70
SIC: 5149 Dairy products, dried or canned

(P-6686)
US FOODS INC
Also Called: General Cold Stg 4145
8457 Eastern Ave (90201-7137)
PHONE..................562 806-2445
EMP: 159
Web: www.usfoods.com
SIC: 5149 Dried or canned foods
HQ: Us Foods, Inc.
9399 W Higgins Rd # 100
Rosemont IL

(P-6687)
US FOODS INC
Also Called: Central Prcss 4140
636 Stanford Ave (90021-1006)
PHONE..................213 623-4150
EMP: 159
Web: www.usfoods.com
SIC: 5149 Dried or canned foods
HQ: Us Foods, Inc.
9399 W Higgins Rd # 100
Rosemont IL

(P-6688)
US FOODS INC
Also Called: SF Outsd Stg 4117
4671 Las Positas Rd Ste B (94551-9631)
PHONE..................925 606-1919
EMP: 159
Web: www.usfoods.com
SIC: 5149 Dried or canned foods
HQ: Us Foods, Inc.
9399 W Higgins Rd # 100
Rosemont IL

(P-6689)
US FOODS INC
Also Called: P&O Stg-Carson 4150
1610 E Sepulveda Blvd (90745-6120)
PHONE..................310 632-6265
EMP: 159
Web: www.usfoods.com
SIC: 5149 Dried or canned foods
HQ: Us Foods, Inc.
9399 W Higgins Rd # 100
Rosemont IL

(P-6690)
US FOODS INC
Also Called: U.S. Foodservice 4114
1320 W Weber Ave (95203-3132)
PHONE..................209 948-0793
EMP: 159
Web: www.usfoods.com
SIC: 5149 Dried or canned foods
HQ: Us Foods, Inc.
9399 W Higgins Rd # 100
Rosemont IL

(P-6691)
VINH - SANH TRADING CORP
13500 Nelson Ave (91746-2334)
PHONE..................626 968-6888
Timothy Chen, CEO
Kan Wang Chen, *
Stacy Tran, *
▲ **EMP:** 77 **EST:** 1998
SQ FT: 178,000
SALES (est): 23.71MM Privately Held
Web: www.vinhsanh.com
SIC: 5149 Groceries and related products, nec

5169 - Chemicals And Allied Products, Nec (P-6711)

5153 Grain And Field Beans

(P-6692)
GRAIN TO GREEN INC
301 N El Camino Real (92672-4716)
P.O. Box 1697 (92018-1697)
PHONE..................................760 845-6107
Gina Marsaglia, *Prin*
EMP: 111
SALES (corp-wide): 6.27MM **Privately Held**
SIC: 5153 Grains
PA: Grain To Green Inc
2730 Gateway Rd Ste 100
Carlsbad CA
760 707-1655

(P-6693)
PACIFIC GRAIN & FOODS LLC (PA)
Also Called: Pacific Grain and Foods
4067 W Shaw Ave Ste 116 (93722-6214)
P.O. Box 3928 (93650-3928)
PHONE..................................559 276-2580
Lee Perkins, *Pr*
Karen Perkins, *
◆ **EMP:** 87 **EST:** 1982
SQ FT: 172,000
SALES (est): 29.04MM **Privately Held**
Web: www.pacificgrainandfoods.com
SIC: 5153 7389 5149 Grains; Packaging and labeling services; Spices and seasonings

(P-6694)
RIVIANA FOODS INC
Also Called: Inharvest
2870 Niagara Rd (95932)
P.O. Box 910 (95932-0910)
PHONE..................................530 458-8512
Cruz Gonzalez, *Brnch Mgr*
EMP: 80
Web: www.riviana.com
SIC: 5153 5149 2099 2098 Grain and field beans; Rice, polished; Food preparations, nec; Macaroni and spaghetti
HQ: Riviana Foods Inc.
2777 Allen Pkwy Fl 15
Houston TX
713 529-3251

5159 Farm-product Raw Materials, Nec

(P-6695)
FLUIDS MANUFACTURING INC
11941 Vose St (91605-5750)
P.O. Box 16297 (91615-6297)
PHONE..................................818 264-4657
Stephan Sutton, *CEO*
EMP: 150 **EST:** 2015
SALES (est): 12.29MM **Privately Held**
SIC: 5159

(P-6696)
MINTURN HULLER COOPERATIVE INC
9080 S Minturn Rd (93610-9317)
P.O. Box 760 (93610-0760)
PHONE..................................559 665-1185
Mark Wolfshorndl, *Pr*
Sterling Alexander, *
Kitt Kahl, *
Jeff Hamilton, *
Daniel Clendenin, *
EMP: 76 **EST:** 1966
SQ FT: 25,000
SALES (est): 24MM **Privately Held**
Web: www.minturnhuller.com
SIC: 5159 0723 Nuts and nut by-products; Almond hulling and shelling services

(P-6697)
SOUTH VALLEY ALMOND CO LLC
Also Called: South Valley Farms
15443 Beech Ave (93280-7604)
PHONE..................................661 391-9000
Paul C Genho, *Managing Member*
Merrill Dibble, *Managing Member*
◆ **EMP:** 200 **EST:** 2007
SQ FT: 4,000
SALES (est): 24.86MM **Privately Held**
Web: www.southvalleyfarms.com
SIC: 5159 Nuts and nut by-products

5162 Plastics Materials And Basic Shapes

(P-6698)
EDGEBANDING SERVICES INC (PA)
Also Called: E S I
828 W Cienega Ave (91773-2459)
PHONE..................................909 599-2336
◆ **EMP:** 75 **EST:** 1988
SALES (est): 45.93MM **Privately Held**
Web: www.edgebanding-services.com
SIC: 5162 5031 Plastics products, nec; Structural assemblies, prefabricated: wood

(P-6699)
ELKAY PLASTICS CO INC (PA)
6000 Sheila St (90040-2405)
PHONE..................................323 722-7073
Louis Chertkow, *Pr*
Geoffrey Pankau, *
▲ **EMP:** 100 **EST:** 1966
SQ FT: 175,000
SALES (est): 101.9MM
SALES (corp-wide): 101.9MM **Privately Held**
Web: www.lkpkg.com
SIC: 5162 Plastics products, nec

5169 Chemicals And Allied Products, Nec

(P-6700)
ACCESS BUSINESS GROUP LLC
Also Called: Access Logistics
12825 Leffingwell Ave (90670-6339)
PHONE..................................808 422-9482
Hee Douglas, *Brnch Mgr*
EMP: 281
SIC: 5169 Chemicals and allied products, nec
HQ: Access Business Group Llc
7575 Fulton St E
Ada MI

(P-6701)
ACCESS BUSINESS GROUP LLC
5600 Beach Blvd (90621-2007)
P.O. Box 5940 (90622-5940)
PHONE..................................714 562-6200
Steve Vanandel, *BD*
EMP: 475
SIC: 5169 Chemicals and allied products, nec
HQ: Access Business Group Llc
7575 Fulton St E
Ada MI

(P-6702)
ACCESS BUSINESS GROUP LLC
Also Called: Nutrilite
5609 River Way (90621-1709)
PHONE..................................714 562-7914
EMP: 292
SIC: 5169 Chemicals and allied products, nec
HQ: Access Business Group Llc
7575 Fulton St E
Ada MI

(P-6703)
AIR PRODUCTS AND CHEMICALS INC
Also Called: Air Products
1515 Norman Ave Frnt (95054-2029)
PHONE..................................408 988-6263
John Mclaine, *CEO*
EMP: 96
SALES (corp-wide): 12.7B **Publicly Held**
Web: www.airproducts.com
SIC: 5169 Chemicals and allied products, nec
PA: Air Products And Chemicals, Inc.
1940 Air Products Blvd
Allentown PA
610 481-4911

(P-6704)
AIRGAS SPECIALTY PRODUCTS INC
Also Called: Airgas
6270 Wilderness Ave (92504-1055)
PHONE..................................951 353-2390
Joe Ennes, *Brnch Mgr*
EMP: 68
SALES (corp-wide): 109.44MM **Privately Held**
Web: www.airgasspecialtyproducts.com
SIC: 5169 Ammonia
HQ: Airgas Specialty Products, Inc.
2530 Sever Rd Ste 300
Lawrenceville GA

(P-6705)
APPLIED SILICONE COMPANY LLC
Also Called: Applied Silicone
1050 Cindy Ln (93013-2906)
PHONE..................................805 525-5657
Ralph Alastair Winn, *Pr*
Phil Galarnau, *
▲ **EMP:** 81 **EST:** 1987
SQ FT: 20,000
SALES (est): 42.8MM
SALES (corp-wide): 7.51B **Publicly Held**
SIC: 5169 Chemicals and allied products, nec
HQ: Nusil Technology Llc
1050 Cindy Ln
Carpinteria CA
805 684-8780

(P-6706)
BRENNTAG PACIFIC INC (DH)
10747 Patterson Pl (90670-4043)
PHONE..................................562 903-9626
David Eckelbarger, *CEO*
Steven Pozzi, *Pr*
H Edward Boyadjian, *Ex VP*
Julia Tu, *Contrlr*
Leslie Lenhardt, *Sec*
▲ **EMP:** 93 **EST:** 2003
SALES (est): 388.96MM **Privately Held**
SIC: 5169 Chemicals, industrial and heavy
HQ: Brenntag North America, Inc.
5083 Pottsville Pike
Reading PA
610 926-6100

(P-6707)
CHEMBRIDGE CORPORATION (PA)
11199 Sorrento Valley Rd Ste 206 (92121-1334)
PHONE..................................858 451-7400
Eugene Vaisberg, *CEO*
Sergey Altshteyn, *Pr*
EMP: 260 **EST:** 1993
SQ FT: 26,000
SALES (est): 29.83MM **Privately Held**
Web: www.chembridge.com
SIC: 5169 Chemicals and allied products, nec

(P-6708)
ENVIRO TECH CHEMICAL SVCS INC (DH)
500 Winmoore Way (95358-5750)
PHONE..................................209 581-9576
Michael S Harvey, *Pr*
Michael B Archibald, *
◆ **EMP:** 102 **EST:** 1991
SQ FT: 136,551
SALES (est): 64.49MM **Privately Held**
Web: www.envirotech.com
SIC: 5169 2842 Industrial chemicals; Specialty cleaning
HQ: Arxada Ag
Lonzastrasse 2
Visp VS

(P-6709)
GROVE COLLABORATIVE INC ✪
1301 Sansome St (94111-1231)
PHONE..................................800 231-8527
EMP: 130 **EST:** 2022
SALES (est): 27.53MM
SALES (corp-wide): 321.53MM **Publicly Held**
SIC: 5169 Specialty cleaning and sanitation preparations
PA: Grove Collaborative Holdings, Inc.
1301 Sansome St
San Francisco CA
800 231-8527

(P-6710)
HENKEL US OPERATIONS CORP
5800 Bristol Pkwy (90230-6696)
PHONE..................................424 308-0505
Thomas Keller, *Brnch Mgr*
EMP: 72
SALES (corp-wide): 23.26B **Privately Held**
Web: www.henkel.com
SIC: 5169 5099 Adhesives and sealants; Firearms and ammunition, except sporting
HQ: Henkel Us Operations Corporation
1 Henkel Way
Rocky Hill CT
860 571-5100

(P-6711)
HILL BROTHERS CHEMICAL COMPANY (PA)
Also Called: Hill Brothers Chemical
3000 E Birch St Ste 108 (92821-6261)
PHONE..................................714 998-8800
Adam Hill, *Pr*
Matthew Thorne, *
Thomas F James, *
Kathryn J Waters, *
▲ **EMP:** 150 **EST:** 1935
SALES (est): 125.44MM
SALES (corp-wide): 125.44MM **Privately Held**
Web: www.hillbrothers.com

5169 - Chemicals And Allied Products, Nec (P-6712)

SIC: 5169 2819 Acids; Calcium chloride and hypochlorite

(P-6712)
HYDRITE CHEMICAL CO
1603 Clancy Ct (93291-9253)
PHONE.................................559 651-3450
Steve Reid, Opers
EMP: 97
SALES (corp-wide): 424.27MM Privately Held
Web: www.hydrite.com
SIC: 5169 Industrial chemicals
PA: Hydrite Chemical Co.
   17385 Golf Pkwy
   Brookfield WI
   262 792-1450

(P-6713)
R D ABBOTT CO INC
11958 Monarch St (92841-2112)
PHONE.................................562 944-5354
Keith Arthur Thomas, CEO
▲ EMP: 91 EST: 1949
SALES (est): 57.75MM Privately Held
Web: www.rdabbott.com
SIC: 5169 Chemicals and allied products, nec

(P-6714)
UNIVAR SOLUTIONS USA INC
2600 Garfield Ave (90040-2608)
P.O. Box 512062 (90040)
PHONE.................................323 727-7005
Gary Cramer, Brnch Mgr
EMP: 175
SALES (corp-wide): 11.48B Privately Held
Web: www.univarsolutions.com
SIC: 5169 Industrial chemicals
HQ: Univar Solutions Usa Inc.
   3075 Highland Pkwy # 200
   Downers Grove IL
   331 777-6000

(P-6715)
VALEANT BIOMEDICALS INC (DH)
1 Enterprise (92656-2606)
PHONE.................................949 461-6000
Tim Tyson, Pr
EMP: 100 EST: 1983
SQ FT: 55,000
SALES (est): 93.84MM
SALES (corp-wide): 8.12B Privately Held
SIC: 5169 2835 8731 3826 Chemicals and allied products, nec; Diagnostic substances; Biotechnical research, commercial; Analytical instruments
HQ: Bausch Health Americas, Inc.
   400 Somerset Corp Blvd
   Bridgewater NJ
   908 927-1400

(P-6716)
ZEP INC
Selig Chemical Industries
1000 Railroad St (92882-1947)
PHONE.................................877 428-9937
Mike Saults, Mgr
EMP: 158
SALES (corp-wide): 978.45MM Privately Held
Web: www.zep.com
SIC: 5169 Industrial chemicals
HQ: Zep Inc.
   600 Galleria Pkwy Se # 1500
   Atlanta GA
   877 428-9937

5171 Petroleum Bulk Stations And Terminals

(P-6717)
R E GOODSPEED AND SONS DISTRIBUTING INC
Also Called: Goodspeed Distributing
11211 G Ave (92345-5134)
P.O. Box 401924 (92340-1924)
PHONE.................................760 949-3356
EMP: 65
SIC: 5171 Petroleum bulk stations

(P-6718)
SHASTA-SISKIYOU TRANSPORT
Also Called: Sst Oil
2370 Wyndham Ln (96001-3815)
P.O. Box 990327 (96099-0327)
PHONE.................................530 241-1167
EMP: 60 EST: 1928
SALES (est): 21.82MM Privately Held
Web: www.sstoil.com
SIC: 5171 Petroleum bulk stations

(P-6719)
SOUTHERN COUNTIES OIL CO (DH)
Also Called: SC Fuels
1800 W Katella Ave Ste 210 (92867-3417)
P.O. Box 4159 (92863-4159)
PHONE.................................714 744-7140
TOLL FREE: 800
Shameek Konar, CEO
Mimi Taylor, *
David Larimer, *
EMP: 95 EST: 1969
SALES (est): 960.53MM
SALES (corp-wide): 3.84B Privately Held
Web: www.scfuels.com
SIC: 5171 5541 5172 Petroleum bulk stations; Gasoline service stations; Petroleum products, nec
HQ: Pilot Travel Centers Llc
   5508 Lonas Dr
   Knoxville TN
   877 866-7378

(P-6720)
ZECO SYSTEMS INC
Also Called: Greenlots
767 S Alameda St Ste 200 (90021-1660)
PHONE.................................888 751-8560
Andreas Lips, CEO
Brett Hauser, *
Lin-dhuang Khoo, Sr VP
Harmeet Singh, *
Ron Mahabir, *
EMP: 95 EST: 2012
SQ FT: 10,000
SALES (est): 53.36MM
SALES (corp-wide): 381.31B Privately Held
Web: www.shellrecharge.com
SIC: 5171 Petroleum bulk stations and terminals
HQ: Zeco Holdings, Inc.
   925 N La Brea Ave
   West Hollywood CA
   888 751-8560

5172 Petroleum Products, Nec

(P-6721)
ADVANCED LUBRICATION SPC INC
Also Called: Advanced Lubrication Spc
810 Wright Ave (94804-3640)
PHONE.................................215 244-2114
EMP: 92
SALES (corp-wide): 100.64MM Privately Held
Web: www.advancedlubes.com
SIC: 5172 Lubricating oils and greases
PA: Advanced Lubrication Specialties, Inc.
   420 Imperial Ct
   Bensalem PA
   215 244-2114

(P-6722)
ALL-POINTS PETROLEUM LLC
640 Noyes Ct (94510-1229)
P.O. Box 2658 (97528-0240)
PHONE.................................707 745-1116
EMP: 61 EST: 1993
SQ FT: 4,000
SALES (est): 25.7MM Privately Held
Web: www.allpointspetroleum.com
SIC: 5172 Gasoline

(P-6723)
ASTRA OIL COMPANY INC
301 Main St Ste 201 (92648-5171)
PHONE.................................714 969-6569
◆ EMP: 160
Web: www.astraoil.com
SIC: 5172 Petroleum products, nec

(P-6724)
CASEY COMPANY (PA)
180 E Ocean Blvd Ste 1010 (90802-4711)
PHONE.................................562 436-9685
Larry Delpit Senior, Ch
Betty Jane Blanchette, *
Barbara Odom, *
EMP: 129 EST: 1982
SQ FT: 4,000
SALES (est): 101.77MM
SALES (corp-wide): 101.77MM Privately Held
SIC: 5172 Petroleum products, nec

(P-6725)
COAST OIL COMPANY LLC
4250 Williams Rd (95129-3344)
PHONE.................................408 252-7720
EMP: 70
Web: www.coastoil.com
SIC: 5172 Gasoline

(P-6726)
COMMERCIAL FUELING NETWORK
1510 Fashion Island Blvd Ste 130 (94404-5055)
PHONE.................................800 899-2236
EMP: 81
SALES (corp-wide): 958.61K Privately Held
Web: www.cfnfleetwide.com
SIC: 5172 Petroleum products, nec
PA: Commercial Fueling Network
   2003 Western Ave Ste 203
   Seattle WA
   206 441-7877

(P-6727)
EASY FUEL INC
1346 E Taylor St (95133-1040)
PHONE.................................408 280-5235
EMP: 80
SIC: 5172 Diesel fuel

(P-6728)
EFUEL LLC
Also Called: Easy Fuel
65 Enterprise 3rd Fl (92656-2601)
PHONE.................................949 330-7145
Donald Harper, CEO
EMP: 90 EST: 2016
SALES (est): 43.99MM
SALES (corp-wide): 175.7B Publicly Held
Web: www.efuelco.com
SIC: 5172 Petroleum products, nec
PA: Phillips 66
   2331 Citywest Blvd
   Houston TX
   832 765-3010

(P-6729)
EMPIRE OIL CO
2756 S Riverside Ave (92316-3500)
PHONE.................................909 877-0226
Richard Alden Senior, CEO
Richard Scott Alden Junior, Pr
Donald Welker, *
EMP: 146 EST: 1961
SQ FT: 2,300
SALES (est): 2.42MM Publicly Held
SIC: 5172 Diesel fuel
HQ: Northern Tier Energy Lp
   1250 W Washington St # 300
   Tempe AZ
   602 302-5450

(P-6730)
GENERAL PETROLEUM LLC (HQ)
Also Called: G P Resources
19501 S Santa Fe Ave (90221-5913)
P.O. Box 2136 (76099-2136)
PHONE.................................562 983-7300
James A Halsam Iii, CEO
Michael Ruehring, *
Sean Kha, *
▲ EMP: 150 EST: 1946
SQ FT: 5,000
SALES (est): 46.98MM
SALES (corp-wide): 66.45MM Privately Held
SIC: 5172 Crude oil
PA: Pecos, Inc.
   19501 S Santa Fe Ave
   Compton CA
   310 356-2300

(P-6731)
JANKOVICH COMPANY LLC
961 E Harbor Dr (92101-7808)
PHONE.................................619 232-4939
Harvey Valier, Brnch Mgr
EMP: 76
SALES (corp-wide): 2.33B Privately Held
Web: www.thejankovichcompany.com
SIC: 5172 Petroleum products, nec
HQ: The Jankovich Company Llc
   307 W 22nd St
   San Pedro CA
   310 547-3305

(P-6732)
KAG WEST LLC
Also Called: Kag West
4076 Seaport Blvd (95691-3417)
P.O. Box 1496 (95691-1496)
PHONE.................................916 371-4581
EMP: 89 EST: 2003
SALES (est): 10.41MM Privately Held
SIC: 5172 Petroleum products, nec

(P-6733)
M O DION & SONS INC (DH)
Also Called: F & L Racing Fuel
1543 W 16th St (90813-1210)
PHONE.................................562 432-3946
TOLL FREE: 888

PRODUCTS & SERVICES SECTION
5181 - Beer And Ale (P-6753)

Pat Cullen, *CEO*
Patrick B Cullen, *
Matt Cullen, *
Bill Frank, *
EMP: 60 **EST:** 1930
SQ FT: 85,000
SALES (est): 201.96MM
SALES (corp-wide): 246.25B **Publicly Held**
Web: www.amberresources.com
SIC: 5172 Gasoline
HQ: Renewable Energy Group, Inc.
    416 S Bell Ave
    Ames IA
    515 239-8000

(P-6734)
POMA HOLDING COMPANY INC
571 W Slover Ave (92316-2454)
PHONE....................909 877-2441
EMP: 118
Web: www.pomacos.com
SIC: 5172 Petroleum products, nec

(P-6735)
PREMIER FUEL DISTRIBUTORS INC
Also Called: Premier Fuel Delivery Service
156 E La Cadena Dr (92507-8699)
PHONE....................760 423-3610
Hugo Rodriguez, *CEO*
EMP: 150 **EST:** 2013
SALES (est): 19.06MM **Privately Held**
SIC: 5172 2869 Petroleum products, nec; Fuels

(P-6736)
REDWOOD COAST PETROLEUM INC
444 Yolanda Ave Ste A (95404-8090)
P.O. Box 428 (95402-0428)
PHONE....................707 546-0766
EMP: 70
Web: www.flyersenergy.com
SIC: 5172 3569 Petroleum products, nec; Lubrication equipment, industrial

(P-6737)
SACRAMENTO INTL JET CTR INC
6133 Freeport Blvd (95822-3534)
PHONE....................916 428-8292
Scott Powell, *CEO*
Scott Powell, *Pr*
Becky Watts, *
EMP: 75 **EST:** 2006
SALES (est): 14.18MM **Privately Held**
Web: www.sacjet.com
SIC: 5172 4581 Aircraft fueling services; Airport hangar rental

(P-6738)
SASOL WAX NORTH AMERICA CORPORATION
Also Called: Sasol Wax
3563 Inv Blvd Ste 2 (94545)
PHONE....................510 783-9295
◆ **EMP:** 100
SIC: 5172 5169 Lubricating oils and greases; Waxes, except petroleum

(P-6739)
SOCO GROUP INC
Also Called: Soco Petroleum
350 E Main St (92243-2618)
P.O. Box 1905 (92244-1905)
PHONE....................760 352-4683
Mark Schultz, *Brnch Mgr*
EMP: 67

SALES (corp-wide): 72.12MM **Privately Held**
Web: www.scfuels.com
SIC: 5172 Petroleum products, nec
PA: The Soco Group Inc
    5962 Priestly Dr
    Carlsbad CA
    760 804-8460

(P-6740)
SOCO GROUP INC
Also Called: Soco Petroleum Group
240 E 1st St (92570-2215)
PHONE....................951 657-2350
Ron Lamb, *Mgr*
EMP: 67
SALES (corp-wide): 72.12MM **Privately Held**
Web: www.scfuels.com
SIC: 5172 Gasoline
PA: The Soco Group Inc
    5962 Priestly Dr
    Carlsbad CA
    760 804-8460

(P-6741)
STURDY OIL COMPANY
721 Vertin Ave (93901-4526)
PHONE....................831 970-9897
EMP: 72
SALES (corp-wide): 67.91MM **Privately Held**
Web: www.sturdyoil.com
SIC: 5172 Gasoline
PA: Sturdy Oil Company
    1511 Abbott St
    Salinas CA
    831 422-8801

(P-6742)
TESORO REFINING & MKTG CO LLC
2101 E Pacific Coast Hwy (90744-2914)
PHONE....................877 837-6762
James Nichols, *Brnch Mgr*
EMP: 244
SIC: 5172 Service station supplies, petroleum
HQ: Tesoro Refining & Marketing Company Llc
    19100 Ridgewood Pkwy
    San Antonio TX
    210 626-6000

(P-6743)
VALLEY PACIFIC PETRO SVCS INC
1083 Madison Ln (93907-1815)
PHONE....................209 461-3635
EMP: 69
SALES (corp-wide): 105.95MM **Privately Held**
Web: www.valleypacific.com
SIC: 5172 Petroleum products, nec
PA: Valley Pacific Petroleum Services, Inc.
    152 Frank West Cir # 100
    Stockton CA
    209 948-9412

(P-6744)
VALLEY PACIFIC PETRO SVCS INC (PA)
Also Called: Valley Pacific
152 Frank West Cir Ste 100 (95206-4003)
PHONE....................209 948-9412
TOLL FREE: 800
Nathan Crum, *Pr*
Diane E Crum, *
Dan Elmer, *COMMERCIAL* *

Dale Heinze, *Retail Vice President* *
Christy Appleton, *
EMP: 60 **EST:** 1954
SQ FT: 10,000
SALES (est): 105.95MM
SALES (corp-wide): 105.95MM **Privately Held**
Web: www.valleypacific.com
SIC: 5172 Gasoline

(P-6745)
VALLEY PACIFIC PETRO SVCS INC
9521 Enos Ln (93314-8007)
PHONE....................661 746-7737
Kat Bowen, *Brnch Mgr*
EMP: 68
SALES (corp-wide): 105.95MM **Privately Held**
Web: www.valleypacific.com
SIC: 5172 Gasoline
PA: Valley Pacific Petroleum Services, Inc.
    152 Frank West Cir # 100
    Stockton CA
    209 948-9412

(P-6746)
VAN DE POL ENTERPRISES INC (PA)
Also Called: Shell
4895 S Airport Way (95206-3915)
P.O. Box 1107 (95201-1107)
PHONE....................209 465-3421
TOLL FREE: 800
Lee Atwater, *Ch Bd*
Ronald M Vandepol, *
Jon Rosman, *
Curtis Thornhill, *
Scott Macewan, *
EMP: 75 **EST:** 1959
SQ FT: 10,000
SALES (est): 131.81MM
SALES (corp-wide): 131.81MM **Privately Held**
Web: www.vandepol.us
SIC: 5172 Gasoline

(P-6747)
WFI EQUIPMENT INC
2200 E Brundage Ln (93307-2806)
P.O. Box 82277 (93380-2277)
PHONE....................661 327-4900
Charles Mccan, *Pr*
Tom Jamieson, *
Brian Bucassa, *
EMP: 63 **EST:** 1982
SQ FT: 5,000
SALES (est): 118.83MM **Privately Held**
Web: www.wholesalefuels.com
SIC: 5172 Gasoline

5181 Beer And Ale

(P-6748)
ADVANCE BEVERAGE CO INC
5200 District Blvd (93313-2330)
P.O. Box 9517 (93389-9517)
PHONE....................661 833-3783
William K Lazzerini Senior, *Ch Bd*
William K Lazzerini Junior, *Pr*
Anthony Lazzerini, *
◆ **EMP:** 90 **EST:** 1952
SQ FT: 93,000
SALES (est): 41.54MM **Privately Held**
Web: www.advancebeverage.com
SIC: 5181 5182 Beer and other fermented malt liquors; Wine

(P-6749)
ALLIED COMPANY HOLDINGS INC (PA)
Also Called: Best-Way Distributing Co
13235 Golden State Rd (91342-1129)
PHONE....................818 493-6400
Kevin Williams, *CEO*
William L Larson, *
Erin S Gabler, *
Earl J Whitehead, *
◆ **EMP:** 98 **EST:** 1953
SQ FT: 240,000
SALES (est): 47.07MM
SALES (corp-wide): 47.07MM **Privately Held**
Web: www.alliedbeverages.com
SIC: 5181 Beer and other fermented malt liquors

(P-6750)
ALLIED COMPANY HOLDINGS INC
28311 Constellation Rd (91355-5048)
P.O. Box 129 (92398-0129)
PHONE....................661 510-6533
Kevin R Williams, *Brnch Mgr*
EMP: 186
SALES (corp-wide): 47.07MM **Privately Held**
SIC: 5181 Beer and other fermented malt liquors
PA: Allied Company Holdings, Inc.
    13235 Golden State Rd
    Sylmar CA
    818 493-6400

(P-6751)
BASSO DISTRIBUTING CO INC
2505 Pleasant Valley Rd (93012-8505)
P.O. Box 1019 (93011-1019)
PHONE....................805 656-1946
James L Basso, *Pr*
Steve Basso, *
▲ **EMP:** 65 **EST:** 1940
SQ FT: 68,000
SALES (est): 9MM **Privately Held**
SIC: 5181 5812 5182 Beer and other fermented malt liquors; Soda fountain; Wine

(P-6752)
BEAUCHAMP DISTRIBUTING COMPANY
1911 S Santa Fe Ave (90221-5306)
PHONE....................310 639-5320
Patrick L Beauchamp, *Pr*
Mary S Beauchamp, *
Stacee L Beauchamp, *
Peter J Gumpert, *
▲ **EMP:** 100 **EST:** 1971
SQ FT: 100,000
SALES (est): 47.24MM **Privately Held**
Web: www.beauchampdist.com
SIC: 5181 5149 Beer and other fermented malt liquors; Groceries and related products, nec

(P-6753)
BOTTOMLEY DISTRIBUTING CO INC
755 Yosemite Dr (95035-5436)
PHONE....................408 945-0660
Donald A Bottomley, *Pr*
◆ **EMP:** 90 **EST:** 1965
SQ FT: 96,000
SALES (est): 24.73MM **Privately Held**
Web: www.bottomleydistributing.com
SIC: 5181 Beer and other fermented malt liquors

5181 - Beer And Ale (P-6754)

(P-6754)
CAPITAL BEVERAGE COMPANY (PA)
2500 Del Monte St (95691-3835)
P.O. Box 914 (95691-0914)
PHONE..........................916 371-8164
Kenneth M Adamson, *Pr*
Joyce Adamson, *
◆ **EMP:** 110 **EST:** 1960
SQ FT: 130,000
SALES (est): 10.61MM
SALES (corp-wide): 10.61MM **Privately Held**
SIC: 5181 5182 5149 Beer and other fermented malt liquors; Wine coolers, alcoholic; Juices

(P-6755)
CENTRAL COAST DISTRIBUTING LLC
815 S Blosser Rd (93458-4915)
PHONE..........................805 922-2108
▲ **EMP:** 90 **EST:** 2001
SQ FT: 51,651
SALES (est): 19.29MM **Privately Held**
Web: www.greatbeer.us
SIC: 5181 Beer and other fermented malt liquors

(P-6756)
CLASSIC BEV SOUTHERN CAL LLC
120 Puente Ave (91746-2301)
PHONE..........................626 934-3700
Carlos Joseph Sanchez, *CEO*
John Thomas, *
▲ **EMP:** 261 **EST:** 1978
SQ FT: 102,000
SALES (est): 49.29MM **Privately Held**
Web: www.classicdist.com
SIC: 5181 Beer and other fermented malt liquors

(P-6757)
CREST BEVERAGE LLC
1348 47th St (92102-2510)
PHONE..........................858 452-2300
Steven S Sourapas, *Managing Member*
▲ **EMP:** 400 **EST:** 2009
SALES (est): 49.99MM **Privately Held**
Web: www.crestbeverage.com
SIC: 5181 Beer and other fermented malt liquors

(P-6758)
CREST BEVERAGE COMPANY INC
3840 Via De La Valle Ste 300 (92014-4268)
P.O. Box 9160 (92067-4160)
PHONE..........................858 452-2300
Steven S Sourapas Senior, *Pr*
▲ **EMP:** 170 **EST:** 1956
SQ FT: 160,000
SALES (est): 19.82MM **Privately Held**
Web: www.crestbeverage.com
SIC: 5181 5182 5149 Beer and other fermented malt liquors; Wine; Groceries and related products, nec

(P-6759)
DBI BEVERAGE SAN FRANCISCO
245 S Spruce Ave Ste 100 (94080-4520)
PHONE..........................415 643-9900
David Ingram, *Ch Bd*
Bob Stahl, *
Rick Guida, *
▲ **EMP:** 250 **EST:** 1934

SALES (est): 55.56MM
SALES (corp-wide): 88MM **Privately Held**
SIC: 5181 5149 Beer and other fermented malt liquors; Soft drinks
PA: Dbi Beverage Inc.
2 Ingram Blvd
La Vergne TN
615 793-2337

(P-6760)
DELTA SIERRA BEVERAGE LLC
3700 Finch Rd (95357-4140)
PHONE..........................209 522-9011
EMP: 275 **EST:** 1919
SALES (est): 17.2MM **Privately Held**
Web: www.dsbeverage.com
SIC: 5181 Beer and other fermented malt liquors

(P-6761)
DONAGHY SALES INC (PA)
2363 S Cedar Ave (93725-1078)
PHONE..........................559 486-0901
Edward Donaghy, *CEO*
Janis Donaghy, *Sec*
▲ **EMP:** 223 **EST:** 1968
SQ FT: 75,000
SALES (est): 84.99MM
SALES (corp-wide): 84.99MM **Privately Held**
Web: www.donaghysales.com
SIC: 5181 Beer and other fermented malt liquors

(P-6762)
FRESNO BEVERAGE COMPANY INC
Also Called: Valley Wide Beverage Company
3525 S East Ave (93725-9000)
PHONE..........................559 650-1500
Louis J Amendola, *CEO*
◆ **EMP:** 180 **EST:** 1985
SQ FT: 140,000
SALES (est): 55.42MM **Privately Held**
Web: www.valleywidebeverage.com
SIC: 5181 Beer and other fermented malt liquors

(P-6763)
GATE CITY BEVERAGE DISTRS (PA)
2505 Steele Rd (92408-3913)
PHONE..........................909 799-0281
Leona Aronoff, *Pr*
Barry Aronoff, *
▲ **EMP:** 294 **EST:** 1940
SQ FT: 280,000
SALES (est): 47.89MM
SALES (corp-wide): 47.89MM **Privately Held**
Web: www.gatecitybeverage.com
SIC: 5181 5149 5145 Beer and other fermented malt liquors; Soft drinks; Confectionery

(P-6764)
HARALAMBOS BEVERAGE CO
26717 Palmetto Ave (92374-1513)
PHONE..........................562 347-4300
H T Haralambos, *CEO*
Anthony Haralambos, *
Thomas Haralambos, *
Sally Haralambos, *
▲ **EMP:** 300 **EST:** 1933
SALES (est): 56.73MM **Privately Held**
SIC: 5181 5149 Beer and other fermented malt liquors; Beverages, except coffee and tea

(P-6765)
HARBOR DISTRIBUTING LLC (HQ)
Also Called: Golden Brands
5901 Bolsa Ave (92647-2053)
PHONE..........................714 933-2400
Jude Reyes, *
Chris Reyes, *
▲ **EMP:** 200 **EST:** 1989
SQ FT: 150,000
SALES (est): 893.68MM **Privately Held**
Web: www.harbordistributingllc.com
SIC: 5181 Beer and other fermented malt liquors
PA: Reyes Holdings, L.L.C.
6250 N River Rd Ste 9000
Rosemont IL

(P-6766)
HARBOR DISTRIBUTING LLC
Also Called: Golden Brands
3500 Carlin Dr (95691-5872)
PHONE..........................916 373-5700
Kimberly Clift, *Brnch Mgr*
EMP: 300
Web: www.harbordistributingllc.com
SIC: 5181 Beer and other fermented malt liquors
HQ: Harbor Distributing, L.L.C
5901 Bolsa Ave
Huntington Beach CA
714 933-2400

(P-6767)
HARBOR DISTRIBUTING LLC
6450 Lockheed Dr (96002-9000)
PHONE..........................530 691-5811
Duke Reyes, *Mgr*
EMP: 73 **EST:** 2021
SALES (est): 4.61MM **Privately Held**
Web: www.harbordistributingllc.com
SIC: 5181 Beer and other fermented malt liquors

(P-6768)
HARBOR DISTRIBUTING LLC
Also Called: Harbor Distributing Co
16407 S Main St (90248-2823)
PHONE..........................310 538-5483
David Reyes, *Brnch Mgr*
EMP: 81
Web: www.harbordistributingllc.com
SIC: 5181 Beer and other fermented malt liquors
HQ: Harbor Distributing, L.L.C
5901 Bolsa Ave
Huntington Beach CA
714 933-2400

(P-6769)
JORDANOS INC (PA)
Also Called: Jordano's Food Service
550 S Patterson Ave (93111-2498)
P.O. Box 6803 (93160-6803)
PHONE..........................805 964-0611
Peter Jordano, *CEO*
Michael F Sieckowski, *VP*
Jeffrey S Jordano, *Ex VP*
▲ **EMP:** 250 **EST:** 1915
SQ FT: 80,000
SALES (est): 315.61MM
SALES (corp-wide): 315.61MM **Privately Held**
Web: www.jordanos.com
SIC: 5181 5182 5149 5141 Beer and other fermented malt liquors; Wine; Soft drinks; Groceries, general line

(P-6770)
LE VECKE CORPORATION (PA)
Also Called: Le Vecke Group
10810 Inland Ave (91752-3235)
PHONE..........................951 681-8600
Neil Levecke, *Pr*
◆ **EMP:** 62 **EST:** 1949
SALES (est): 87.9MM
SALES (corp-wide): 87.9MM **Privately Held**
Web: www.levecke.com
SIC: 5181 Beer and other fermented malt liquors

(P-6771)
LIQUID INVESTMENTS INC (PA)
3840 Via De La Valle Ste 300 (92014-4268)
PHONE..........................858 509-8510
Ron L Fowler, *CEO*
Terry L Harris, *
Mark Herculson, *
▲ **EMP:** 170 **EST:** 1981
SQ FT: 190,000
SALES (est): 55.15MM
SALES (corp-wide): 55.15MM **Privately Held**
Web: www.nextsolutions.us
SIC: 5181 5145 5182 Beer and other fermented malt liquors; Fountain supplies; Wine

(P-6772)
MARKSTEIN BEV CO SACRAMENTO
Also Called: Markstein Beverage Company
60 Main Ave (95838-2034)
P.O. Box 15379 (95851-0379)
PHONE..........................916 920-3911
Hayden Markstein, *VP*
Steve Markstein, *
Richard Markstein, *
▲ **EMP:** 150 **EST:** 1974
SALES (est): 49.35MM **Privately Held**
Web: www.marksteinbev.com
SIC: 5181 5149 Beer and other fermented malt liquors; Soft drinks

(P-6773)
MARKSTEIN BEVERAGE CO
845 Rio Claro Ct (92057-6323)
PHONE..........................760 744-9100
▲ **EMP:** 120 **EST:** 1919
SALES (est): 18.8MM **Privately Held**
SIC: 5181 Beer and other fermented malt liquors

(P-6774)
MARKSTEIN SALES COMPANY
Also Called: Markstein Beverage Co
1645 Drive In Way (94509-8507)
PHONE..........................925 755-1919
Laura Lee Markstein, *Pr*
Robert C Markstein, *
▲ **EMP:** 130 **EST:** 1955
SQ FT: 5,000
SALES (est): 56.91MM **Privately Held**
Web: www.marksteinsalescompany.com
SIC: 5181 Beer and other fermented malt liquors

(P-6775)
MATAGRANO INC
25858 Clawiter Rd (94545-3213)
P.O. Box 2588 (94083-2588)
PHONE..........................650 829-4829
Louis Matagrano, *Pr*
Frank Matagrano Junior, *VP*
Tom Haas, *
William Hill, *
Trevor Bartlett, *

PRODUCTS & SERVICES SECTION

5182 - Wine And Distilled Beverages (P-6794)

▲ **EMP:** 175 **EST:** 1972
SALES (est): 43.22MM **Privately Held**
Web: www.matagrano.com
SIC: **5181** 5149 Beer and other fermented malt liquors; Mineral or spring water bottling

(P-6776)
ME FOX & COMPANY INC
128 Component Dr (95131-1180)
P.O. Box 2336 (95070-0336)
PHONE.................................408 435-8510
▲ **EMP:** 111
Web: www.mefox.com
SIC: **5181** 5149 Beer and other fermented malt liquors; Soft drinks

(P-6777)
MESA DISTRIBUTING CO INC (HQ)
3840 Via De La Valle Ste 300 (92014)
PHONE.................................858 452-2300
Ronald Fowler, *Ch Bd*
Ron L Fowler, *Ch Bd*
Jack F Studebaker, *Sec*
▲ **EMP:** 225 **EST:** 1978
SQ FT: 190,000
SALES (est): 22.53MM
SALES (corp-wide): 55.15MM **Privately Held**
SIC: **5181** 0182 5182 Beer and other fermented malt liquors; Vegetable crops, grown under cover; Wine and distilled beverages
PA: Liquid Investments, Inc.
  3840 Via De La Valle # 300
  Del Mar CA
  858 509-8510

(P-6778)
MORRIS DISTRIBUTING
3800a Lakeville Hwy (94954-5673)
P.O. Box 5699 (94955-5699)
PHONE.................................707 769-7294
Ronald L Morris, *CEO*
Joe Netter, *
▲ **EMP:** 80 **EST:** 1933
SQ FT: 13,500
SALES (est): 24.43MM **Privately Held**
Web: www.morrisdistributing.com
SIC: **5181** 5149 Beer and other fermented malt liquors; Mineral or spring water bottling

(P-6779)
NOR-CAL BEVERAGE CO INC (PA)
2150 Stone Blvd (95691-4049)
PHONE.................................916 372-0600
Shannon Deary-bell, *Pr*
Donald Deary, *
Grant Deary, *
Tim Deary, *
Mike Montroni, *
◆ **EMP:** 280 **EST:** 1937
SQ FT: 152,000
SALES (est): 231.77MM
SALES (corp-wide): 231.77MM **Privately Held**
Web: www.ncbev.com
SIC: **5181** 2086 Beer and other fermented malt liquors; Soft drinks: packaged in cans, bottles, etc.

(P-6780)
REYES HOLDINGS LLC
Also Called: Golden Brands
1729 Seabright Ave Ste A (95062-2120)
PHONE.................................831 761-6400
David Reyes, *Brnch Mgr*
EMP: 103
Web: www.reyesholdings.com

SIC: **5181** 5149 Beer and other fermented malt liquors; Beverages, except coffee and tea
PA: Reyes Holdings, L.L.C.
  6250 N River Rd Ste 9000
  Rosemont IL

(P-6781)
SACCANI DISTRIBUTING COMPANY
2600 5th St (95818-2848)
P.O. Box 1764 (95812-1764)
PHONE.................................916 441-0213
Gary Saccani, *Pr*
Roland Saccani, *
Steven Fishman, *
▲ **EMP:** 90 **EST:** 1933
SQ FT: 40,000
SALES (est): 25.35MM **Privately Held**
Web: www.saccanidist.com
SIC: **5181** 5149 Beer and other fermented malt liquors; Soft drinks

(P-6782)
SEQUOIA BEVERAGE COMPANY LP
Also Called: Bueno Beverage Company
2122 N Plaza Dr (93291-9358)
P.O. Box 5025 (93278-5025)
PHONE.................................559 651-2444
Dan Bueno, *Pt*
Joan Carpenter, *Pt*
Rose Bueno, *Pt*
EMP: 101 **EST:** 1939
SQ FT: 100,000
SALES (est): 22.03MM **Privately Held**
Web: www.buenobev.com
SIC: **5181** Beer and other fermented malt liquors

(P-6783)
STRAUB DISTRIBUTING CO LTD (PA)
4633 E La Palma Ave (92807-1909)
PHONE.................................714 779-4000
Michael L Cooper, *Genl Pt*
Don Beightol, *Pt*
Robert K Adams, *Pt*
▲ **EMP:** 150 **EST:** 1948
SQ FT: 32,000
SALES (est): 55.82MM
SALES (corp-wide): 55.82MM **Privately Held**
Web: www.straubdistributing.com
SIC: **5181** Beer and other fermented malt liquors

(P-6784)
T F LOUDERBACK INC
Also Called: Bay Area Beverage Company
700 National Ct (94804-2008)
PHONE.................................510 965-6120
Thomas J Louderback, *Pr*
Ron Bishop, *
Todd Rovelstad, *
Michael J Marver Ctrl, *Prin*
◆ **EMP:** 102 **EST:** 1969
SQ FT: 65,000
SALES (est): 23.92MM **Privately Held**
Web: www.bayareabev.com
SIC: **5181** 5149 2037 2033 Beer and other fermented malt liquors; Beverages, except coffee and tea; Frozen fruits and vegetables; Canned fruits and specialties

(P-6785)
TRIANGLE DISTRIBUTING CO
Also Called: Heimark Distributing
12065 Pike St (90670-2964)

PHONE.................................562 699-3424
▲ **EMP:** 270
SIC: **5181** Beer and other fermented malt liquors

(P-6786)
VARNI BROTHERS CORPORATION (PA)
Also Called: Stanislaus Distributing Co
400 Hosmer Ave (95351-3920)
PHONE.................................209 521-1777
Michael Attilio Varni, *Pr*
Fred Varni, *
◆ **EMP:** 80 **EST:** 1960
SQ FT: 80,000
SALES (est): 80.15MM
SALES (corp-wide): 80.15MM **Privately Held**
Web: www.vbcbottling.com
SIC: **5181** 2086 5182 Beer and other fermented malt liquors; Bottled and canned soft drinks; Wine

5182 Wine And Distilled Beverages

(P-6787)
BREAKTHRU BEVERAGE CAL LLC (HQ)
6550 E Washington Blvd (90040-1822)
P.O. Box 910900 (90091-0900)
PHONE.................................800 331-2829
James P Myerson, *Pr*
◆ **EMP:** 350 **EST:** 1966
SQ FT: 135,000
SALES (est): 363.76MM
SALES (corp-wide): 2.8B **Privately Held**
Web: www.breakthrubevca.com
SIC: **5182** Wine
PA: Breakthru Beverage Group, Llc
  60 E 42nd St Ste 1915
  New York NY
  212 699-7000

(P-6788)
BREAKTHRU BEVERAGE CAL LLC
Also Called: Wine Warehouse
912 Harbour Way S (94804-3615)
P.O. Box 45616 (94145-0616)
PHONE.................................510 236-2233
Michael Cimino, *Mgr*
EMP: 67
SALES (corp-wide): 2.8B **Privately Held**
Web: www.breakthrubevca.com
SIC: **5182** 5181 Liquor; Beer and ale
HQ: Breakthru Beverage California, Llc
  6550 E Washington Blvd
  Commerce CA
  800 331-2829

(P-6789)
BRONCO WINE COMPANY (PA)
Also Called: Classic Wines of California
6342 Bystrum Rd (95307-6652)
P.O. Box 789 (95307-0789)
PHONE.................................209 538-3131
◆ **EMP:** 200 **EST:** 1973
SALES (est): 69.71MM
SALES (corp-wide): 69.71MM **Privately Held**
Web: www.broncowine.com
SIC: **5182** 2084 Wine; Wines

(P-6790)
CANANDAIGUA WINE COMPANY INC
12667 Road 24 (93637-9020)

PHONE.................................559 673-7071
Marvin Sands, *Ch Bd*
Richard Sands, *
Robert Sands, *
Bertram E Silk, *
Lynn K Fetterman, *
◆ **EMP:** 84 **EST:** 1937
SALES (est): 28.66MM
SALES (corp-wide): 9.45B **Publicly Held**
Web: www.cbrands.com
SIC: **5182** Wine
PA: Constellation Brands, Inc.
  207 High Point Dr # 100
  Victor NY
  585 678-7100

(P-6791)
CENTRAL COAST WINE COMPANY
Also Called: Winebow
4301 Industrial Way (94510-1227)
PHONE.................................707 745-8500
Eugenia Keegan, *Brnch Mgr*
EMP: 110
SALES (corp-wide): 515.73MM **Privately Held**
Web: www.winebow.com
SIC: **5182** Wine
HQ: Central Coast Wine Company
  4301 Industrial Way
  Benicia CA
  707 745-8500

(P-6792)
CONSTLLTION BRNDS US OPRTONS I
Also Called: Beatbox Beverages
5950 E Woodbridge Rd (95220-9429)
PHONE.................................209 294-4110
Cathy Olson, *Brnch Mgr*
EMP: 80
SALES (corp-wide): 9.45B **Publicly Held**
Web: www.cbrands.com
SIC: **5182** Wine
HQ: Constellation Brands U.S. Operations, Inc.
  235 N Bloomfield Rd
  Canandaigua NY
  585 396-7600

(P-6793)
CONSTLLTION BRNDS US OPRTONS I
Also Called: Mission Bell Winery
12667 Road 24 (93637-9020)
PHONE.................................559 485-0141
Michael Othites, *Brnch Mgr*
EMP: 773
SALES (corp-wide): 9.45B **Publicly Held**
Web: www.cbrands.com
SIC: **5182** Wine
HQ: Constellation Brands U.S. Operations, Inc.
  235 N Bloomfield Rd
  Canandaigua NY
  585 396-7600

(P-6794)
DIAGEO NORTH AMERICA INC
Also Called: Diageno Chateau & Estate Wines
555 Gateway Dr (94558-6291)
PHONE.................................707 299-2600
Ray Chadwick, *Genl Mgr*
EMP: 74
SALES (corp-wide): 21.15B **Privately Held**
SIC: **5182** Wine
HQ: Diageo North America Inc.
  3 World Trade Ctr
  New York NY
  212 202-1800

(PA)=Parent Co (HQ)=Headquarters
✿ = New Business established in last 2 years

5182 - Wine And Distilled Beverages (P-6795)

(P-6795)
DIAGEO NORTH AMERICA INC
21468 8th St E (95476-9767)
PHONE..........................707 939-6200
Claudia Schubert, *Brnch Mgr*
EMP: 119
SALES (corp-wide): 21.15B **Privately Held**
SIC: 5182 Wine
HQ: Diageo North America Inc.
3 World Trade Ctr
New York NY
212 202-1800

(P-6796)
FRANK-LIN DISTILLERS PDTS LTD (PA)
2455 Huntington Dr (94533-9734)
PHONE..........................408 259-8900
Frank J Maestri, *Pr*
Michael Maestri, *
Vincent Maestri, *
Lindley Maestri, *
Michael Wasteney, *
◆ EMP: 110 EST: 1966
SQ FT: 54,216
SALES (est): 42.56MM
SALES (corp-wide): 42.56MM **Privately Held**
Web: www.frank-lin.com
SIC: 5182 2085 Wine; Distilled and blended liquors

(P-6797)
GUARACHI WINE PARTNERS INC
Also Called: Parker Station
27001 Agoura Rd Ste 285 (91301-5141)
PHONE..........................818 225-5100
Alejandro Guarachi, *CEO*
▲ EMP: 80 EST: 1988
SQ FT: 5,000
SALES (est): 23.23MM **Privately Held**
Web: www.guarachiwinepartners.com
SIC: 5182 Wine

(P-6798)
HENRY WINE GROUP LLC (HQ)
Also Called: Henry Wine Group of C.A., The
4301 Industrial Way (94510-1227)
PHONE..........................707 745-8500
Ed Hogan, *Pr*
Kent Fitzgerald, *
Stephanie O'brien, *CFO*
▲ EMP: 297 EST: 2003
SALES (est): 42.98MM
SALES (corp-wide): 515.73MM **Privately Held**
SIC: 5182 Wine
PA: The Winebow Group Llc
4800 Cox Rd Ste 300
Glen Allen VA
804 752-3670

(P-6799)
HOPE FAMILY WINES
4280 Second Wind Way (93446-6309)
PHONE..........................805 238-6979
EMP: 60
SALES (corp-wide): 10.16MM **Privately Held**
Web: www.hopefamilywines.com
SIC: 5182 Wine
PA: Hope Family Wines
1585 Live Oak Rd
Paso Robles CA
805 238-4112

(P-6800)
HORIZON BEVERAGE COMPANY
8380 Pardee Dr (94621-1481)
P.O. Box 2163 (94621-0063)
PHONE..........................800 332-8358
Ces Butner, *Pt*
Denny Suzuki, *Pt*
EMP: 76 EST: 1987
SQ FT: 20,000
SALES (est): 6.48MM **Privately Held**
Web: www.horizonbeverage.com
SIC: 5182 Wine

(P-6801)
LLC WILSON DANIELS
1300 Main St Ste 300 (94559-1946)
P.O. Box 441 (94574-0441)
PHONE..........................707 963-9661
Benjy Kirschner, *Sr VP*
Kevin Murphy, *Sr VP*
EMP: 93 EST: 2016
SALES (est): 21.4MM
SALES (corp-wide): 439.37MM **Privately Held**
Web: www.wilsondaniels.com
SIC: 5182 Wine
HQ: Infinium Spirits Inc.
510 Market St
San Diego CA
949 425-8627

(P-6802)
MONTESQUIEU CORP
Also Called: Montesquieu Vins & Domaines
888 W E St (92101-5915)
PHONE..........................877 705-5669
Fonda Hopkins, *Pr*
Frank Kryger, *
▲ EMP: 100 EST: 1991
SALES (est): 18.49MM **Privately Held**
Web: www.montesquieu.com
SIC: 5182 8743 Wine; Promotion service

(P-6803)
NEW PARROTT & CO
Also Called: Parrott & Co
5565 Tesla Rd (94550-9149)
PHONE..........................925 456-2286
Tyson Overton, *CEO*
Eric Wente, *Dir*
Peter Chouinard, *CFO*
Rich Archer, *Contrlr*
◆ EMP: 136 EST: 1977
SALES (est): 1.2MM
SALES (corp-wide): 88.64MM **Privately Held**
SIC: 5182 Wine
PA: Wente Bros.
5565 Tesla Rd
Livermore CA
925 456-2300

(P-6804)
REGAL III LLC
Also Called: Regal Wine Co
421 Aviation Blvd (95403-1069)
PHONE..........................707 836-2100
Donald M Hartford Junior, *Managing Member*
◆ EMP: 141 EST: 2010
SQ FT: 8,000
SALES (est): 11.28MM **Privately Held**
Web: www.regalwineco.com
SIC: 5182 Wine

(P-6805)
REPUBLIC NAT DISTRG CO LLC (PA)
Also Called: Rndc
14402 Franklin Ave (92780-7013)
P.O. Box 37100 (40233-7100)
PHONE..........................714 368-4615
Jay Johnson, *Managing Member*
Nicholas Mehall, *
Robert Hendrickson, *
Robert Cornella, *
Sean Halligan, *Co-Executive Vice President*
▲ EMP: 144 EST: 1998
SALES (est): 1.4B
SALES (corp-wide): 1.4B **Privately Held**
Web: www.rndc-usa.com
SIC: 5182 Wine

(P-6806)
SOUTH BAY WINE GROUP LLC
Also Called: Castle Rock Winery
389 4th St E (95476-5717)
PHONE..........................310 465-0551
Gregory Popovich, *Brnch Mgr*
EMP: 66
SALES (corp-wide): 2.59MM **Privately Held**
Web: www.thefamilycoppola.com
SIC: 5182 Wine
PA: South Bay Wine Group, Llc
300 Via Archimedes
Geyserville CA
310 465-0551

(P-6807)
SOUTHERN GLZERS WINE SPRITS LL
Also Called: Sgws of CA
33321 Dowe Ave (94587-2033)
P.O. Box 5001 (94587-8501)
PHONE..........................510 477-5500
EMP: 350
SALES (corp-wide): 7.22B **Privately Held**
Web: www.southernglazers.com
SIC: 5182 Wine
PA: Southern Glazer's Wine And Spirits, Llc
1600 Nw 163rd St
Miami FL
866 375-9555

(P-6808)
SOUTHERN GLZERS WINE SPRITS LL
Also Called: Southern Glzers Wine Sprits Ca
17101 Valley View Ave (90703-2413)
PHONE..........................562 926-2000
EMP: 500
SALES (corp-wide): 7.22B **Privately Held**
Web: www.southernglazers.com
SIC: 5182 5181 Wine; Beer and ale
PA: Southern Glazer's Wine And Spirits, Llc
1600 Nw 163rd St
Miami FL
866 375-9555

(P-6809)
VARNI BROTHERS CORPORATION
Also Called: Stanislaus Distributing
416 Hosmer Ave (95351-3920)
PHONE..........................209 526-5513
Dianne Varni, *Mgr*
EMP: 85
SQ FT: 2,000
SALES (corp-wide): 80.15MM **Privately Held**
Web: www.vbcbottling.com
SIC: 5182 5181 Wine; Beer and other fermented malt liquors
PA: Varni Brothers Corporation
400 Hosmer Ave
Modesto CA
209 521-1777

(P-6810)
VINO FARMS LLC
1377 E Lodi Ave (95240-0840)
PHONE..........................209 334-6975
John Ledbetter, *
EMP: 450 EST: 2008
SQ FT: 5,000
SALES (est): 82.01MM **Privately Held**
Web: www.vinofarms.net
SIC: 5182 Wine

(P-6811)
WINE INDUSTRY NETWORK LLC
155 Foss Creek Cir (95448-4288)
PHONE..........................707 953-9672
EMP: 60 EST: 2019
SALES (est): 1.07MM **Privately Held**
Web: www.wineindustrynetwork.com
SIC: 5182 Wine

(P-6812)
WORLD WINE ESTATES
1250 Cuttings Wharf Rd (94559-9738)
PHONE..........................707 257-5300
Douglas Roberts, *Brnch Mgr*
EMP: 133
Web: www.tweglobal.com
SIC: 5182 Wine
PA: Treasury Wine Estates Limited
L 8 161 Collins St
Melbourne VIC

(P-6813)
YOUNGS HOLDINGS INC (PA)
15 Enterprise Ste 100 (92656-2654)
PHONE..........................714 368-4615
Chris Underwood, *CEO*
Vernon Underwood Junior, *Ch Bd*
EMP: 100 EST: 1973
SALES (est): 439.37MM
SALES (corp-wide): 439.37MM **Privately Held**
Web: www.youngsholdings.com
SIC: 5182 Wine

(P-6814)
YOUNGS MARKET COMPANY LLC (HQ)
14402 Franklin Ave (92780-7013)
PHONE..........................800 317-6150
Chris Underwood, *CEO*
Dennis Hamann, *
◆ EMP: 350 EST: 1888
SQ FT: 250,000
SALES (est): 1.06B
SALES (corp-wide): 1.4B **Privately Held**
Web: www.rndc-usa.com
SIC: 5182 Wine
PA: Republic National Distributing Company, Llc
14402 Franklin Ave
Tustin CA
714 368-4615

(P-6815)
YOUNGS MARKET COMPANY LLC
850 Jarvis Dr (95037-2846)
PHONE..........................408 782-3121
Ken Feroli, *Mgr*
EMP: 216
SALES (corp-wide): 1.4B **Privately Held**
Web: www.rndc-usa.com
SIC: 5182 Wine
HQ: Young's Market Company, Llc
14402 Franklin Ave
Tustin CA
800 317-6150

(P-6816)
YOUNGS MARKET COMPANY LLC

PRODUCTS & SERVICES SECTION

5191 - Farm Supplies (P-6836)

Also Called: Wine Dept
500 S Central Ave (90013-1715)
PHONE..................213 629-3929
Mark Sneed, *Brnch Mgr*
EMP: 495
SALES (corp-wide): 1.4B **Privately Held**
Web: www.rndc-usa.com
SIC: 5182 Wine
HQ: Young's Market Company, Llc
 14402 Franklin Ave
 Tustin CA
 800 317-6150

5191 Farm Supplies

(P-6817)
A L GILBERT COMPANY (PA)
Also Called: Berry Seed & Feed
304 N Yosemite Ave (95361-3140)
P.O. Box 38 (95361-0038)
PHONE..................209 847-1721
◆ EMP: 75 EST: 1892
SALES (est): 345.84MM
SALES (corp-wide): 345.84MM **Privately Held**
Web: www.farmerswarehouse.com
SIC: 5191 Animal feeds

(P-6818)
ACX INTERMODAL INC
920 E Pacific Coast Hwy (90744-2725)
PHONE..................310 241-6229
John Gombos, *Pr*
▼ EMP: 111 EST: 1983
SALES (est): 4.11MM **Privately Held**
Web: www.acxintermodal.com
SIC: 5191 Animal feeds
HQ: Al Dahra Acx, Inc.
 920 E Pacific Coast Hwy
 Wilmington CA

(P-6819)
AFC-BPI INC
729 Green Valley Rd (95076-1226)
PHONE..................541 441-2847
EMP: 325
SALES (corp-wide): 1.15B **Privately Held**
SIC: 5191 Farm supplies
HQ: Afc-Bpi, Inc.
 1727 Highway 223
 Union Springs AL

(P-6820)
AG RX (PA)
Also Called: Mountain View Transportation
751 S Rose Ave (93030-5146)
P.O. Box 2008 (93034-2008)
PHONE..................805 487-0696
Ken Burdullis, *Pr*
EMP: 92 EST: 1993
SQ FT: 45,000
SALES (est): 54.03MM **Privately Held**
Web: www.agrx.com
SIC: 5191 Fertilizer and fertilizer materials

(P-6821)
AHERN AGRIBUSINESS INC
Also Called: Ahern International
9465 Customhouse Plz Ste G (92154-7631)
PHONE..................619 661-9450
Roee Tamari, *Ch Bd*
Kevin Ahern, *
Brianna Ahern, *
Martin Pulido, *
◆ EMP: 63 EST: 1981
SQ FT: 7,000
SALES (est): 46.17MM **Privately Held**
Web: www.ahernseeds.com

SIC: 5191 Seeds: field, garden, and flower
HQ: Ahern Internacional De Mexico, S.A. De C.V.
 Francisco Eusebio Kino No. 17523
 Tijuana BCN

(P-6822)
BORDER VALLEY TRADING LTD
Also Called: Border Valley Trading
604 Mead Rd (92227-9748)
P.O. Box 62 (92227-0062)
PHONE..................760 344-6700
Greg Braun, *Pr*
Robert Presley, *
Paul Cameron, *
◆ EMP: 68 EST: 1990
SQ FT: 1,200
SALES (est): 23.13MM **Privately Held**
Web: www.bordervalley.com
SIC: 5191 Hay

(P-6823)
E B STONE & SON INC
Also Called: Greenall
6111 Lambie Rd (94585-9789)
P.O. Box 550 (94585-0550)
PHONE..................707 426-2500
Bradford G Crandall, *CEO*
Bradford G Crandall Junior, *Pr*
Lynne Crandall, *
EMP: 65 EST: 1918
SQ FT: 79,000
SALES (est): 24.85MM **Privately Held**
Web: www.ebstone.org
SIC: 5191 2873 2875 3423 Fertilizer and fertilizer materials; Nitrogenous fertilizers; Fertilizers, mixing only; Hand and edge tools, nec

(P-6824)
EXCEL GARDEN PRODUCTS
1340 Treat Blvd Ste 600 (94597-7578)
PHONE..................925 948-4000
Charlie Nausch, *Prin*
EMP: 207
SALES (corp-wide): 3.34B **Publicly Held**
Web: www.centralgarden.com
SIC: 5191 Garden supplies
HQ: Excel Garden Products
 10708 Norwalk Blvd
 Santa Fe Springs CA

(P-6825)
FOSTER POULTRY FARMS
Also Called: FOSTER POULTRY FARMS
4107 Ave 360 (93673)
PHONE..................559 457-6509
Larry Ficken, *Manager*
EMP: 68
SALES (corp-wide): 1.25B **Privately Held**
Web: www.fosterfarms.com
SIC: 5191 Farm supplies
PA: Foster Poultry Farms, Llc
 1000 Davis St
 Livingston CA
 209 394-7901

(P-6826)
HART CHEMICALS INC
Also Called: Pacific Coast Chemicals Co.
2424 4th St (94710-2404)
PHONE..................510 549-3535
◆ EMP: 75
SIC: 5191 5169 Farm supplies; Chemicals and allied products, nec

(P-6827)
L & L NURSERY SUPPLY INC (HQ)
Also Called: Unigro

2552 Shenandoah Way (92407-1845)
PHONE..................909 591-0461
Lloyd Swindell, *Ch Bd*
Tom Medhurst, *
▲ EMP: 150 EST: 1953
SQ FT: 107,000
SALES (est): 98.18MM
SALES (corp-wide): 183.31MM **Privately Held**
Web: www.bfgsupply.com
SIC: 5191 2875 2449 5193 Insecticides; Potting soil, mixed; Wood containers, nec; Flowers and florists supplies
PA: Bfg Supply Co., Llc
 14500 Kinsman Rd
 Burton OH
 800 883-0234

(P-6828)
L A HEARNE COMPANY (PA)
512 Metz Rd (93930-2503)
PHONE..................831 385-5441
Francis Giudici, *Pr*
Dennis Hearne, *
Francis Giudici, *Pr*
Larry Hearne, *
Tim Hearne, *
◆ EMP: 70 EST: 1938
SQ FT: 220,000
SALES (est): 47.22MM
SALES (corp-wide): 47.22MM **Privately Held**
Web: www.hearneco.com
SIC: 5191 0723 5699 4214 Fertilizers and agricultural chemicals; Bean cleaning services; Western apparel; Local trucking with storage

(P-6829)
NEWCO DISTRIBUTORS INC
9060 Rochester Ave (91730-5522)
P.O. Box 1449 (91729-1449)
PHONE..................909 291-2240
Randall Barb, *CEO*
EMP: 60 EST: 1959
SQ FT: 60,000
SALES (est): 43.19MM **Privately Held**
Web: www.newcopet.com
SIC: 5191 5149 Animal feeds; Pet foods

(P-6830)
PIONEER HI-BRED INTL INC
Also Called: Pioneer
18285 County Road 96 (95695-9340)
PHONE..................530 666-1084
Glen Cole, *Brnch Mgr*
EMP: 69
SALES (corp-wide): 17.45B **Publicly Held**
Web: www.pioneer.com
SIC: 5191 Seeds: field, garden, and flower
HQ: Pioneer Hi-Bred International, Inc.
 7100 Nw 62nd Ave
 Johnston IA
 515 535-3200

(P-6831)
SAKATA SEED AMERICA INC (HQ)
18095 Serene Dr (95037-2833)
P.O. Box 880 (95038-0880)
PHONE..................408 778-7758
David Armstrong, *CEO*
Koichi Matsunaga, *
Eduardo Flores, *
▲ EMP: 90 EST: 1977
SQ FT: 48,000
SALES (est): 108.4MM **Privately Held**
Web: www.sakata.com

SIC: 5191 0182 Seeds: field, garden, and flower; Vegetable crops, grown under cover
PA: Sakata Seed Corporation
 2-7-1, Nakamachidai, Tsuzuki-Ku
 Yokohama KNG

(P-6832)
SEEDS OF CHANGE INC
Also Called: Sustainable Agriculture
31 Mountain Laurel (92679-4216)
P.O. Box 4908 (90224-4908)
PHONE..................310 764-7700
Will Righeimer, *CEO*
◆ EMP: 120 EST: 1997
SALES (est): 21.91MM
SALES (corp-wide): 42.84B **Privately Held**
Web: www.seedsofchange.com
SIC: 5191 0723 Seeds: field, garden, and flower; Crop preparation services for market
HQ: Mars Food Us, Llc
 2001 E Cashdan St Ste 201
 Rancho Dominguez CA
 310 933-0670

(P-6833)
SEMINIS VEGETABLE SEEDS INC (DH)
Also Called: Seminis
2700 Camino Del Sol (93030-7967)
PHONE..................855 733-3834
Michael J Frank, *CEO*
Kerry Preete, *
◆ EMP: 600 EST: 1962
SQ FT: 370,000
SALES (est): 463.76MM
SALES (corp-wide): 52.7B **Privately Held**
Web: www.seminis-us.com
SIC: 5191 0723 Seeds: field, garden, and flower; Crop preparation services for market
HQ: Bayer Northern Production Co., Llc
 800 N Lindbergh Blvd
 Saint Louis MO
 314 694-1000

(P-6834)
STANISLAUS FARM SUPPLY COMPANY (PA)
Also Called: Stan Farm
624 E Service Rd (95358-9451)
PHONE..................209 538-7070
Nickolas J Biscay, *CEO*
Espiridion Ixta, *
EMP: 61 EST: 1949
SQ FT: 4,000
SALES (est): 55.56MM
SALES (corp-wide): 55.56MM **Privately Held**
Web: www.farmsupply.com
SIC: 5191 Fertilizer and fertilizer materials

(P-6835)
TARGET SPECIALTY PRODUCTS INC
15415 Marquardt Ave (90670-5711)
P.O. Box 3408 (90670-1408)
PHONE..................562 865-9541
EMP: 100
Web: www.target-specialty.com
SIC: 5191 Chemicals, agricultural

(P-6836)
TENCATE ADVANCED COMPOSITE
Also Called: TenCate Advanced Composites USA, Inc.
2450 Cordelia Rd (94534-1651)
PHONE..................707 359-3400
EMP: 129
Web: www.toraytac.com

5191 - Farm Supplies (P-6837)

SIC: 5191 Garden supplies
HQ: Toray Advanced Composites Usa Inc.
    18255 Sutter Blvd
    Morgan Hill CA

(P-6837)
VOLOAGRI INC
41970 E Main St (95776-9508)
PHONE..................805 547-9391
Alois Van Vliet, *CEO*
EMP: 150 EST: 2012
SALES (est): 9.81MM **Privately Held**
Web: www.voloagri.com
SIC: 5191 Seeds: field, garden, and flower

(P-6838)
WILBUR-ELLIS COMPANY LLC (DH)
Also Called: Red Zone Technologies
345 California St Fl 27 (94104-2644)
PHONE..................415 772-4000
John Buckley, *Pr*
Daniel Pres-agribusiness R Vra denburg, *Prin*
Steven J Dietze, *
David P Granoff, *
Michael J Hunter, *
EMP: 300 EST: 2016
SALES (est): 2.11B
SALES (corp-wide): 3.22B **Privately Held**
Web: www.wilburellis.com
SIC: 5191 0711 Fertilizer and fertilizer materials; Fertilizer application services
HQ: Wilbur-Ellis Holdings Ii, Inc.
    345 California St Fl 27
    San Francisco CA
    415 772-4000

(P-6839)
ZOOLOGICAL SOCIETY SAN DIEGO
123 Camino De La Reina Ste 100s (92108)
PHONE..................619 718-3000
Tina Pinard, *Mgr*
EMP: 61
SALES (corp-wide): 422.09MM **Privately Held**
Web: www.sandiegozoowildlifealliance.org
SIC: 5191 Farm supplies
PA: Zoological Society Of San Diego
    2920 Zoo Dr
    San Diego CA
    619 231-1515

5192 Books, Periodicals, And Newspapers

(P-6840)
BAKER & TAYLOR LLC
10350 Barnes Canyon Rd Ste 100 (92121-2708)
PHONE..................858 457-2500
James Leidich, *Dir*
EMP: 178
Web: www.baker-taylor.com
SIC: 5192 5099 5199 5045 Books; Tapes and cassettes, prerecorded; Calendars; Computer software
PA: Baker & Taylor, Llc
    2810 Clseum Cntre Dr Ste
    Charlotte NC

(P-6841)
EL AVISO MAGAZINE
4850 Gage Ave (90201-1409)
P.O. Box 3360 (90202-3360)
PHONE..................323 586-9199
Jose Zepeda, *CEO*
EMP: 83 EST: 1988
SALES (est): 2.47MM **Privately Held**
Web: www.elaviso.com
SIC: 5192 2721 Magazines; Magazines: publishing and printing

(P-6842)
GREAT ATLANTIC NEWS LLC
Also Called: News Group, The
1575 N Main St (92867-3439)
PHONE..................770 863-9000
EMP: 109
SALES (corp-wide): 10.3B **Privately Held**
SIC: 5192 5994 Periodicals; Magazine stand
HQ: Great Atlantic News L.L.C.
    1962 Highway 160 W # 102
    Fort Mill SC

(P-6843)
HAY HOUSE INC (PA)
2591 Pioneer Ave Ste A (92081-8415)
P.O. Box 5100 (92018-5100)
PHONE..................760 431-7695
Louise L Hay, *Ch Bd*
Reid Tracy, *
◆ EMP: 62 EST: 1987
SALES (est): 33.77MM
SALES (corp-wide): 33.77MM **Privately Held**
Web: www.hayhouse.com
SIC: 5192 5099 5942 5735 Books; Tapes and cassettes, prerecorded; Book stores; Audio tapes, prerecorded

(P-6844)
MADER NEWS INC
508 S Varney St (91502-2126)
PHONE..................818 551-5000
Avan Mader, *Pr*
EMP: 100 EST: 1972
SALES (est): 12.28MM **Privately Held**
Web: www.madernews.com
SIC: 5192 Newspapers

(P-6845)
WHITE DIGITAL MEDIA INC
Also Called: Wdm Group
3394 Carmel Mountain Rd Ste 250 (92121-1065)
PHONE..................760 827-7800
Brian Smith, *CEO*
Glen White, *
Matthew P Melucci, *Chief Content Officer* *
EMP: 150 EST: 2007
SALES (est): 19.03MM **Privately Held**
SIC: 5192 Magazines

(P-6846)
ZYANTE INC
Also Called: Zybooks
41 E Main St (95030-6907)
PHONE..................510 541-4434
Smita Bakshi, *CEO*
EMP: 91 EST: 2012
SALES (est): 23.46MM
SALES (corp-wide): 2.02B **Publicly Held**
Web: www.zybooks.com
SIC: 5192 Newspapers
PA: John Wiley & Sons, Inc.
    111 River St Ste 2000
    Hoboken NJ
    201 748-6000

5193 Flowers And Florists Supplies

(P-6847)
ALTMAN SPECIALTY PLANTS LLC
20460 Spence Rd (93908-9723)
PHONE..................831 758-4850
Matt Altman, *Prin*
EMP: 650
SALES (corp-wide): 865.96MM **Privately Held**
Web: www.altmanplants.com
SIC: 5193 Nursery stock
PA: Altman Specialty Plants, Llc
    3742 Blue Bird Canyon Rd
    Vista CA
    800 348-4881

(P-6848)
ALTMAN SPECIALTY PLANTS LLC (PA)
Also Called: Altman Plants
3742 Blue Bird Canyon Rd (92084-7432)
PHONE..................800 348-4881
Ken Altman, *CEO*
Deena Altman, *
▲ EMP: 800 EST: 1973
SQ FT: 4,000
SALES (est): 865.96MM
SALES (corp-wide): 865.96MM **Privately Held**
Web: www.altmanplants.com
SIC: 5193 3999 Nursery stock; Atomizers, toiletry

(P-6849)
ALTMAN SPECIALTY PLANTS LLC
Also Called: Altman Flowers
2575 Olive Hill Rd (92028-9557)
PHONE..................800 348-4881
EMP: 433
SALES (corp-wide): 865.96MM **Privately Held**
Web: www.altmanplants.com
SIC: 5193 Nursery stock
PA: Altman Specialty Plants, Llc
    3742 Blue Bird Canyon Rd
    Vista CA
    800 348-4881

(P-6850)
B & B NURSERIES INC
Also Called: Landscape Center
9505 Cleveland Ave (92503-6241)
P.O. Box 7399 (92513-7399)
PHONE..................951 352-8383
Mark Barrett, *CEO*
EMP: 109 EST: 1985
SALES (est): 13.18MM **Privately Held**
Web: www.tlcnurseries.com
SIC: 5193 0781 Flowers and nursery stock; Landscape counseling services

(P-6851)
BANDY RANCH FLORAL CORP
2755 Dos Aarons Way Ste B (92081-8359)
PHONE..................805 757-9905
Steve Dodge, *CEO*
EMP: 115 EST: 2015
SALES (est): 32.25MM **Privately Held**
Web: www.bandyranchfloral.com
SIC: 5193 Flowers, fresh

(P-6852)
BELLA TERRA NURSERY INC
Also Called: Terra Bella Nursery
302 Hollister St (92154-4700)
P.O. Box 551 (91912-0551)
PHONE..................619 585-1118
Jose L Ramos, *Pr*
EMP: 100 EST: 2007
SALES (est): 9.7MM **Privately Held**
Web: www.terrabellanursery.com
SIC: 5193 Flowers and florists supplies

(P-6853)
BOUQS COMPANY
Also Called: Thebouqs.com
4094 Glencoe Ave (90292-5608)
PHONE..................888 320-2687
Kimberly Tobman, *CEO*
John Tabis, *Ch Bd*
Jp Montfar, *COO*
EMP: 87 EST: 2012
SALES (est): 14.66MM **Privately Held**
Web: www.bouqs.com
SIC: 5193 Flowers, fresh

(P-6854)
BUSHNELL GARDENS
Also Called: Bushnell's Landscape Creations
5255 Douglas Blvd (95746-6204)
PHONE..................916 791-4199
David Bushnell, *Owner*
EMP: 80 EST: 1979
SQ FT: 1,040
SALES (est): 14.95MM **Privately Held**
Web: www.bushnellgardens.com
SIC: 5193 0781 0782 5261 Nursery stock; Landscape architects; Lawn and garden services; Retail nurseries

(P-6855)
CAMFLOR INC
2364 Riverside Rd (95076-9430)
PHONE..................831 726-1330
Daniel Campos, *Pr*
Zandra Campos, *
▲ EMP: 110 EST: 1986
SALES (est): 24.73MM **Privately Held**
Web: www.camflor.com
SIC: 5193 Flowers, fresh

(P-6856)
COUNTRY FLORAL SUPPLY INC (PA)
Also Called: Country Furnishings
3802 Weatherly Cir (91361-3821)
PHONE..................805 520-8026
Mark Reese, *Pr*
Debbie Reese, *
▲ EMP: 80 EST: 1982
SQ FT: 60,000
SALES (est): 8.94MM
SALES (corp-wide): 8.94MM **Privately Held**
SIC: 5193 5999 Artificial flowers; Artificial flowers

(P-6857)
DELTA FLORAL DISTRIBUTORS INC
6810 West Blvd (90043-4668)
PHONE..................323 751-8116
Foti Defterios, *Pr*
▲ EMP: 200 EST: 1984
SQ FT: 30,000
SALES (est): 23.13MM **Privately Held**
SIC: 5193 Flowers, fresh

▲ = Import ▼ = Export
◆ = Import/Export

5193 - Flowers And Florists Supplies (P-6878)

(P-6858)
FISHERS NURSERY
24081 S Austin Rd (95366-9646)
P.O. Box 657 (95366-0657)
PHONE..................................209 599-3412
Jerry Fisher, *Pr*
Mary Fisher, *
▲ **EMP:** 75 **EST:** 1968
SQ FT: 450,000
SALES (est): 8.22MM **Privately Held**
SIC: 5193 Nursery stock

(P-6859)
GREEN THUMB INTERNATIONAL INC
21812 Sherman Way (91303-1940)
PHONE..................................818 340-6400
Del Berquist, *Prin*
EMP: 87
SALES (corp-wide): 24.03MM **Privately Held**
Web: www.greenthumb.com
SIC: 5193 5261 0782 0181 Nursery stock; Retail nurseries and garden stores; Lawn and garden services; Ornamental nursery products
PA: Green Thumb International Inc
7105 Jordan Ave
Canoga Park CA
818 340-6400

(P-6860)
GRINGO VENTURES LLC
Also Called: Dos Gringos
3260 Corporate Vw (92081-8528)
PHONE..................................760 477-7999
EMP: 354 **EST:** 1995
SALES (est): 47.6MM **Privately Held**
Web: www.dosgringos.com
SIC: 5193 0181 Flowers and florists supplies; Ornamental nursery products

(P-6861)
GROLINK PLANT COMPANY INC (PA)
Also Called: Grolink
4107 W Gonzales Rd (93036-7783)
P.O. Box 5506 (93031-5506)
PHONE..................................805 984-7958
Anthony Vollering, *CEO*
Art Gordijin, *
Jerry Van Wingerden, *
Harry Van Wingerden, *Stockholder*
Ton Vallering, *
▲ **EMP:** 149 **EST:** 1985
SQ FT: 400,000
SALES (est): 17.87MM
SALES (corp-wide): 17.87MM **Privately Held**
Web: www.grolink.com
SIC: 5193 0181 Nursery stock; Ornamental nursery products

(P-6862)
HEADSTART NURSERY INC (PA)
4860 Monterey Rd (95020-9511)
PHONE..................................408 842-3030
Steven H Costa, *Pr*
Randy Costa, *
Don Christopher, *
William A Christopher, *
▲ **EMP:** 85 **EST:** 1977
SQ FT: 3,000
SALES (est): 50.98MM
SALES (corp-wide): 50.98MM **Privately Held**
Web: www.headstartnursery.com
SIC: 5193 5261 Plants, potted; Retail nurseries and garden stores

(P-6863)
KENDAL FLORAL SUPPLY LLC (PA)
Also Called: Kendal North Bouquet Co
1960 Kellogg Ave (92008-6581)
PHONE..................................888 828-9875
Kenneth X Baca, *Pr*
▲ **EMP:** 80 **EST:** 1973
SALES (est): 51.67MM
SALES (corp-wide): 51.67MM **Privately Held**
Web: www.sheilafrankllc.com
SIC: 5193 Flowers, fresh

(P-6864)
MELLANO & CO
Also Called: Melano Enterprises
734 Wilshire Rd (92057-2111)
P.O. Box 100 (92068-0100)
PHONE..................................760 433-9550
Harry M Mellano, *Owner*
EMP: 108
SALES (corp-wide): 49.4MM **Privately Held**
Web: www.mellano.com
SIC: 5193 Flowers, fresh
PA: Mellano & Company
766 Wall St
Los Angeles CA
213 622-0796

(P-6865)
MELLANO & COMPANY (PA)
Also Called: Mellano Enterprises
766 Wall St (90014-2316)
P.O. Box 100 (92068-0100)
PHONE..................................213 622-0796
Michael Anthony Mellano, *CEO*
H Mike Mellano Senior, *VP*
Michelle Castellano, *
Bob Mellano, *
EMP: 75 **EST:** 1975
SALES (est): 49.4MM
SALES (corp-wide): 49.4MM **Privately Held**
Web: www.mellano.com
SIC: 5193 Flowers, fresh

(P-6866)
NAKASE BROTHERS WHL NURS LP (PA)
9441 Krepp Dr (92646-2799)
PHONE..................................949 855-4388
Shigeo Gary Nakase, *Managing Member*
▲ **EMP:** 100 **EST:** 1965
SALES (est): 22.88MM
SALES (corp-wide): 22.88MM **Privately Held**
Web: www.nakasebros.com
SIC: 5193 Nursery stock

(P-6867)
NAKASE BROTHERS WHOLESALE NURS
Also Called: NAKASE BROTHERS WHOLESALE NURSERY
20621 Lake Forest Dr (92630-7743)
PHONE..................................949 855-4388
Joann Shurlock, *Mgr*
EMP: 180
SALES (corp-wide): 22.88MM **Privately Held**
Web: www.nakasebros.com
SIC: 5193 Nursery stock
PA: Nakase Brothers Wholesale Nursery Lp
9441 Krepp Dr
Huntington Beach CA
949 855-4388

(P-6868)
NORMANS NURSERY INC
5800 Via Real (93013-2610)
PHONE..................................805 684-5442
EMP: 142
SALES (corp-wide): 95.85MM **Privately Held**
Web: www.nngrower.com
SIC: 5193 Nursery stock
PA: Norman's Nursery, Inc.
8665 Duarte Rd
San Gabriel CA
626 285-9795

(P-6869)
NORMANS NURSERY INC
Also Called: Norman's Nursery
20500 Ramona Blvd (91706)
PHONE..................................626 285-9795
Ricardo Goodman, *Mgr*
EMP: 143
SALES (corp-wide): 95.85MM **Privately Held**
Web: www.nngrower.com
SIC: 5193 Nursery stock
PA: Norman's Nursery, Inc.
8665 Duarte Rd
San Gabriel CA
626 285-9795

(P-6870)
NORMANS NURSERY INC
Also Called: Norman's
6250 N Escalon Bellota Rd (95236-9428)
P.O. Box 959 (95236-0959)
PHONE..................................209 887-2033
Barbara Hayes, *Mgr*
EMP: 143
SALES (corp-wide): 95.85MM **Privately Held**
Web: www.normansnursery.com
SIC: 5193 0181 Nursery stock; Nursery stock, growing of
PA: Norman's Nursery, Inc.
8665 Duarte Rd
San Gabriel CA
626 285-9795

(P-6871)
PARDEE TREE NURSERY
30970 Via Puerta Del Sol (92057)
P.O. Box 240 (92003-0240)
PHONE..................................760 630-5400
Lauren Davis, *Pr*
EMP: 75 **EST:** 1999
SALES (est): 12.49MM **Privately Held**
Web: www.pardeetree.com
SIC: 5193 Nursery stock

(P-6872)
PONTO NURSERY
2545 Ramona Dr (92084-1632)
P.O. Box 536 (92085-0536)
PHONE..................................760 724-6003
William Ponto, *Pr*
Judy Ponto, *
EMP: 70 **EST:** 1956
SQ FT: 2,000
SALES (est): 7.7MM **Privately Held**
Web: www.pontonursery.com
SIC: 5193 Nursery stock

(P-6873)
SPECTRUM EQUIPMENT LLC
Also Called: Spectrum Floral Service
2505 Commerce Way (92081-8420)
PHONE..................................760 599-8849
Gene Aschbrenner, *Managing Member*
Sarah Aschbrenner, *
William Simon, *
EMP: 80 **EST:** 2017
SQ FT: 16,000
SALES (est): 10.24MM **Privately Held**
SIC: 5193 Flowers, fresh

(P-6874)
SUNSHINE FLORAL INC
4595 Foothill Rd (93013-3096)
PHONE..................................805 684-1177
Henry Vanwingerden, *Pr*
Anthony Vollering, *
▲ **EMP:** 70 **EST:** 1972
SALES (est): 10.56MM **Privately Held**
Web: www.sunshinefloral.com
SIC: 5193 Flowers, fresh

(P-6875)
SUNSHINE FLORAL LLC
1070 S Rice Ave Ste 1 (93033-2110)
P.O. Box 728 (93014-0728)
PHONE..................................805 982-8822
Anthony Vollering, *Managing Member*
Ton Vollering, *Managing Member*
Henry Van Wingerden, *Managing Member*
▲ **EMP:** 60 **EST:** 1985
SQ FT: 10,000
SALES (est): 9.61MM **Privately Held**
Web: www.sunshinefloral.com
SIC: 5193 Flowers, fresh

(P-6876)
T - Y NURSERY INC
15335 Highway 76 (92061-9583)
P.O. Box 424 (92061-0424)
PHONE..................................760 742-2151
Alfonso Ramos, *Mgr*
EMP: 200
SALES (corp-wide): 23.67MM **Privately Held**
Web: www.tynursery.com
SIC: 5193 5261 Plants, potted; Retail nurseries
PA: T - Y Nursery, Inc.
5221 Arvada St
Torrance CA
310 370-2561

(P-6877)
VILLAGE NURSERIES WHL LLC
6901 Bradshaw Rd (95829-9303)
PHONE..................................916 993-2292
Steve Sawyer, *Brnch Mgr*
EMP: 271
SALES (corp-wide): 47.24MM **Privately Held**
Web: www.everde.com
SIC: 5193 Nursery stock
PA: Village Nurseries Wholesale, Llc
1589 N Main St
Orange CA
714 279-3100

(P-6878)
VILLAGE NURSERIES WHL LLC
20099 Santa Rosa Mine Rd (92570-7774)
PHONE..................................951 657-3940
Joseph Jensen, *Brnch Mgr*
EMP: 272
SALES (corp-wide): 47.24MM **Privately Held**
Web: www.everde.com
SIC: 5193 Nursery stock
PA: Village Nurseries Wholesale, Llc
1589 N Main St
Orange CA
714 279-3100

5194 Tobacco And Tobacco Products

(P-6879)
FLAWLESS VAPE WHL & DIST INC
1021 E Orangethorpe Ave (92801-1135)
PHONE..................714 406-2933
Jason Grace, *Pr*
EMP: 60 **EST:** 2015
SALES (est): 30MM Privately Held
Web: www.flawlessvapedistro.com
SIC: 5194 Cigarettes

(P-6880)
KRETEK INTERNATIONAL INC (DH)
5449 Endeavour Ct (93021-1712)
PHONE..................805 531-8888
Hugh R Cassar, *CEO*
Lynn K Cassar, *
Sean Cassar, *
Donald Gormley, *
Eliot Suied, *
◆ **EMP:** 90 **EST:** 1983
SQ FT: 80,000
SALES (est): 76.31MM Privately Held
Web: www.kretek.com
SIC: 5194 Cigarettes
HQ: Pt. Djarum
   Jl. Ahmad Yani No. 28
   Kabupaten Kudus JT

(P-6881)
PACIFIC GROSERVICE INC
Also Called: Pitco Foods
567 Cinnabar St (95110-2306)
PHONE..................408 727-4826
Pericles Navab, *Ch Bd*
David Luttway, *Pr*
Azadeh Hariri, *Stockholder*
Parviz Maboudi, *Stockholder*
Esmael Maboudi, *Stockholder*
▲ **EMP:** 360 **EST:** 1982
SQ FT: 85,000
SALES (est): 84.67MM Privately Held
Web: www.pitcofoods.com
SIC: 5194 5145 5141 5113 Tobacco and tobacco products; Candy; Groceries, general line; Industrial and personal service paper

5198 Paints, Varnishes, And Supplies

(P-6882)
ADAS INVESTMENT HOLDINGS INC
1114 Industrial Ave (93030-7408)
PHONE..................805 483-2341
EMP: 69
SIC: 5198 5231 Paints; Paint and painting supplies

(P-6883)
BERG LACQUER CO (PA)
Also Called: Pacific Coast Lacquer
3150 E Pico Blvd (90023-3632)
PHONE..................323 261-8114
Sandra Berg, *Pr*
Robert O Berg, *
Donna Berg, *
▲ **EMP:** 65 **EST:** 1934
SQ FT: 85,000
SALES (est): 23.85MM
SALES (corp-wide): 23.85MM Privately Held
SIC: 5198 2851 Paints; Paints and paint additives

(P-6884)
TCP GLOBAL CORPORATION
Also Called: Autobody Depot
6695 Rasha St (92121-2240)
PHONE..................858 909-2110
Dean A Faucett, *Pr*
Dean Faucett, *
Todd Faucett, *
Rick Faucett, *
◆ **EMP:** 67 **EST:** 1979
SQ FT: 38,000
SALES (est): 27.12MM Privately Held
Web: www.tcpglobal.com
SIC: 5198 5231 Paints; Paint

5199 Nondurable Goods, Nec

(P-6885)
99 CENTS ONLY STORES LLC (HQ)
Also Called: 99 Cents Only Stores
4000 Union Pacific Ave (90023-3202)
PHONE..................323 980-8145
Barry J Feld, *CEO*
Felicia Thornton, *V Ch Bd*
Michael Kvitko, *CMO*
Ashok Walia, *CFO*
◆ **EMP:** 500 **EST:** 1965
SALES (est): 730.02MM
SALES (corp-wide): 730.02MM Privately Held
Web: www.99only.com
SIC: 5199 5331 4224 General merchandise, non-durable; Variety stores; General warehousing and storage
PA: Number Holdings, Inc.
   4000 Union Pacific Ave
   Commerce CA
   323 980-8145

(P-6886)
AJM PACKAGING CORPORATION
1160 Vernon Way (92020-1837)
PHONE..................619 448-4007
Joe Marcelynas, *Prin*
EMP: 63
SALES (corp-wide): 495.55MM Privately Held
Web: www.ajmpack.com
SIC: 5199 Packaging materials
PA: A.J.M. Packaging Corporation
   4111 Andover Rd Ste 100e
   Bloomfield Township MI
   248 901-0040

(P-6887)
ALLAQUARIA LLC
Also Called: Quality Marine
5420 W 104th St (90045-6012)
P.O. Box 2439 (90051-0439)
PHONE..................310 645-1107
G Christopher Bverner, *Managing Member*
Mary L Buerner, *
▲ **EMP:** 60 **EST:** 2003
SQ FT: 45,000
SALES (est): 20.11MM Privately Held
Web: www.qualitymarine.com
SIC: 5199 Tropical fish

(P-6888)
AMERICAN PAPER & PLASTICS LLC
Also Called: American Paper & Provisions
550 S 7th Ave (91746-3120)
PHONE..................626 444-0000
Daniel Emrani, *CEO*
EMP: 119 **EST:** 1982
SQ FT: 300,000
SALES (est): 48.7MM
SALES (corp-wide): 1.6B Privately Held
Web: www.appinc.com
SIC: 5199 Packaging materials
PA: Imperial Bag & Paper Co. Llc
   255 Route 1 And 9
   Jersey City NJ
   201 437-7440

(P-6889)
ATA RETAIL SERVICES LLC
7133 Koll Center Pkwy Ste 100 (94566-3203)
PHONE..................925 621-4700
▲ **EMP:** 1000
SIC: 5199 General merchandise, non-durable

(P-6890)
B2B INDUSTRIAL PRODUCTS LLC
23271 Eichler St (94545-5302)
PHONE..................510 887-4586
Michael Theriault, *Brnch Mgr*
EMP: 82
SALES (corp-wide): 130.44MM Privately Held
Web: www.b2bind.com
SIC: 5199 Packaging materials
PA: B2b Industrial Products Llc
   313 S Rohlwing Rd
   Addison IL
   630 396-6200

(P-6891)
B2B INDUSTRIAL PRODUCTS LLC
340 El Camino Real S Ste 35b (93901)
PHONE..................630 396-6300
EMP: 102
SALES (corp-wide): 130.44MM Privately Held
Web: www.b2bind.com
SIC: 5199 Packaging materials
PA: B2b Industrial Products Llc
   313 S Rohlwing Rd
   Addison IL
   630 396-6200

(P-6892)
BAGGU CORPORATION
2415 3rd St Ste 239 (94107-3177)
PHONE..................800 605-0759
Emily Hall Sugihara, *CEO*
EMP: 65 **EST:** 2007
SALES (est): 7.41MM Privately Held
Web: www.baggu.com
SIC: 5199 5137 General merchandise, non-durable; Handbags

(P-6893)
BLUEMARK INC
27909 Hancock Pkwy (91355-4116)
PHONE..................323 230-0770
Joseph Shusterman, *CEO*
Yosef Shusterman, *
EMP: 112 **EST:** 2009
SALES (est): 24.7MM Privately Held
Web: www.bluemark.com
SIC: 5199 Advertising specialties

(P-6894)
BTG S CORP (PA)
Also Called: Four Seasons General Mdse
2801 E Vernon Ave (90058-1803)
PHONE..................323 582-4444
◆ **EMP:** 85 **EST:** 1985
SALES (est): 37.58MM
SALES (corp-wide): 37.58MM Privately Held
Web: www.4sgm.com
SIC: 5199 General merchandise, non-durable

(P-6895)
CALVEY INCORPORATED
Also Called: Ernest Packaging Solutions
8670 Fruitridge Rd Ste 300 (95826-9735)
PHONE..................916 681-4800
A Charles Wilson, *Ch*
Tim Wilson, *
▲ **EMP:** 60 **EST:** 1946
SQ FT: 155,000
SALES (est): 21.4MM
SALES (corp-wide): 189.32MM Privately Held
SIC: 5199 Packaging materials
PA: Ernest Packaging
   5777 Smithway St
   Commerce CA
   800 233-7788

(P-6896)
CELMOL INC
Also Called: Mark Roberts
1611 E Saint Andrew Pl (92705-4932)
PHONE..................714 259-1000
Mark Rees, *Pr*
▲ **EMP:** 60 **EST:** 1983
SQ FT: 36,000
SALES (est): 9.87MM Privately Held
Web: www.markrobertswholesale.com
SIC: 5199 5193 Christmas novelties; Flowers, fresh

(P-6897)
CLOUDRADIANT CORP (PA)
Also Called: Enbiz International
12 Fuchsia (92630-1431)
PHONE..................408 256-1527
Anil Rao, *Pr*
◆ **EMP:** 128 **EST:** 2010
SALES (est): 23.69MM
SALES (corp-wide): 23.69MM Privately Held
SIC: 5199 8748 7371 8711 General merchandise, non-durable; Business consulting, nec; Computer software systems analysis and design, custom; Consulting engineer

(P-6898)
CLOUDRADIANT CORP
Also Called: Enbiz International
1111 Di Napoli Dr (95129-4014)
PHONE..................408 256-1527
Anil Rao, *Pr*
EMP: 726
SALES (corp-wide): 23.69MM Privately Held
SIC: 5199 8748 General merchandise, non-durable; Business consulting, nec
PA: Cloudradiant Corp.
   12 Fuchsia
   Lake Forest CA
   408 256-1527

(P-6899)
CROSSROAD SERVICES INC
2360 Alvarado St (94577-4314)
PHONE..................714 728-3915
Adam Parrish, *CEO*
Steven Scheiner, *
Feroun Khan, *
EMP: 419 **EST:** 1984
SQ FT: 5,000
SALES (est): 16.28MM Privately Held
Web: www.mycsm.com

PRODUCTS & SERVICES SECTION

5199 - Nondurable Goods, Nec (P-6923)

SIC: 5199 Variety store merchandise

(P-6900)
DOLPHIN HKG LTD (PA)
Also Called: Dolphin International
1125 W Hillcrest Blvd (90301-2021)
P.O. Box 91081 (90009-1081)
PHONE..............................310 215-3356
Steven Lundblad, *Pr*
Helen Lundblad, *
◆ EMP: 70 EST: 1970
SQ FT: 12,000
SALES (est): 9.56MM
SALES (corp-wide): 9.56MM Privately Held
Web: www.dolphin-int.com
SIC: 5199 Tropical fish

(P-6901)
DYNAMIC TRADES INC
4617 Weed Patch Ct (95635-9507)
PHONE..............................530 701-8138
EMP: 65
SALES (corp-wide): 9.73MM Privately Held
Web: www.dynamictrades.com
SIC: 5199 General merchandise, non-durable
PA: Dynamic Trades, Inc.
   470 Nevada St Ste 110
   Auburn CA
   530 333-0695

(P-6902)
EMERALD PACKAGING INC
Also Called: E P
33050 Western Ave (94587-2157)
PHONE..............................510 429-5700
Kevin Kelly, *CEO*
James P Kelly Senior, *Ch Bd*
James M Kelly Junior, *Ex VP*
Maura Kelly Koberlein, *VP*
Mary Anne Lothrot, *Ex Sec*
▲ EMP: 250 EST: 1963
SQ FT: 80,000
SALES (est): 94.73MM Privately Held
Web: www.empack.com
SIC: 5199 2673 Packaging materials; Food storage and frozen food bags, plastic

(P-6903)
EMPIRE WEST SOLUTIONS LLC
340 El Camino Real S # 35b (93901-4553)
PHONE..............................831 783-1649
Bill Drake, *Pr*
EMP: 102 EST: 2016
SALES (est): 547.45K
SALES (corp-wide): 130.44MM Privately Held
SIC: 5199 Packaging materials
PA: B2b Industrial Products Llc
   313 S Rohlwing Rd
   Addison IL
   630 396-6200

(P-6904)
EPSILON PLASTICS INC
3100 E Harcourt St (90221-5506)
PHONE..............................310 609-1320
Jim Gifford, *Mgr*
EMP: 75
SQ FT: 39,863
Web: www.sigmaplasticsgroup.com
SIC: 5199 Packaging materials
HQ: Epsilon Plastics Inc.
   Page & Schuyler Ave 8
   Lyndhurst NJ
   201 933-6000

(P-6905)
ERNEST PACKAGING (PA)
Also Called: Ernest Paper
5777 Smithway St (90040-1507)
PHONE..............................800 233-7788
Charles Wilson, *Ch Bd*
Timothy Wilson, *
▲ EMP: 130 EST: 1947
SQ FT: 300,000
SALES (est): 189.32MM
SALES (corp-wide): 189.32MM Privately Held
Web: www.ernestpackaging.com
SIC: 5199 7389 5113 Packaging materials; Cosmetic kits, assembling and packaging; Shipping supplies

(P-6906)
EVERGREEN PACKAGING LLC
Also Called: Turlock Plant
1500 W Main St (95380-3704)
PHONE..............................209 664-3426
Ed Sanfrancisco, *Contrlr*
EMP: 233
Web: www.pactiveevergreen.com
SIC: 5199 Packaging materials
HQ: Evergreen Packaging Llc
   5350 Poplar Ave Ste 400
   Memphis TN

(P-6907)
FLEXPORT INC
1420 N Mckinley Ave (90059-3534)
PHONE..............................323 524-7132
EMP: 72 EST: 2018
SALES (est): 920.04K Privately Held
Web: www.flexport.com
SIC: 5199 Nondurable goods, nec

(P-6908)
FOAM DISTRIBUTORS INCORPORATED
Also Called: Foam Fabrication For Packaging
31009 San Antonio St (94544-7903)
PHONE..............................510 441-8377
Stephanie Wright, *Ch*
Stephanie Wright, *Ch*
Steve M Doyle, *
EMP: 75 EST: 1977
SQ FT: 72,000
SALES (est): 24.88MM Privately Held
Web: www.foamdist.com
SIC: 5199 Packaging materials

(P-6909)
G3 ENTERPRISES INC (PA)
502 E Whitmore Ave (95358-9411)
PHONE..............................209 341-7515
Tom Cook, *Pr*
Craig Hardy, *
▲ EMP: 610 EST: 1961
SQ FT: 10,000
SALES (est): 116.51MM
SALES (corp-wide): 116.51MM Privately Held
Web: www.g3enterprises.com
SIC: 5199 4225 4731 6512 General merchandise, non-durable; General warehousing and storage; Freight forwarding; Nonresidential building operators

(P-6910)
GAJU MARKET CORPORATION
450 S Western Ave (90020-4120)
PHONE..............................213 382-9444
David Rhee, *CEO*
EMP: 135 EST: 2015
SQ FT: 2,000
SALES (est): 25MM Privately Held
Web: www.gajumarketplace.com
SIC: 5199 General merchandise, non-durable

(P-6911)
GIFTING GROUP LLC
42210 Zevo Dr (92590-3732)
PHONE..............................951 296-0310
▲ EMP: 75 EST: 2011
SQ FT: 24,575
SALES (est): 4.27MM Privately Held
Web: www.aldercreekgiftbaskets.com
SIC: 5199 5149 5145 5947 Gifts and novelties; Food gift baskets; Candy; Gift baskets

(P-6912)
GRAPHIC PACKAGING INTL LLC
1600 Barranca Pkwy (92606-4823)
PHONE..............................949 250-0900
Wendy Shute, *Brnch Mgr*
EMP: 100
Web: www.graphicpkg.com
SIC: 5199 Packaging materials
HQ: Graphic Packaging International, Llc
   1500 Riveredge Pkwy # 100
   Atlanta GA

(P-6913)
GRAPHIC PACKAGING INTL LLC
Also Called: International Paper
1600 Kelsey Rd (93291)
P.O. Box 4349 (93278-4349)
PHONE..............................559 651-3535
Robert E Eades, *Mgr*
EMP: 150
Web: www.graphicpkg.com
SIC: 5199 Packaging materials
HQ: Graphic Packaging International, Llc
   1500 Riveredge Pkwy # 100
   Atlanta GA

(P-6914)
GRHT INC
Also Called: Foam Co, The
14818 Raymer St (91405-1219)
PHONE..............................323 873-6393
Gil Rosky, *Pr*
Hossein Tehrani, *
EMP: 60 EST: 1978
SQ FT: 11,000
SALES (est): 9.74MM Privately Held
SIC: 5199 Foam rubber

(P-6915)
HOOD PACKAGING CORPORATION
Also Called: Coveris
10801 Iona Ave (93230-9415)
PHONE..............................559 585-2040
Walter Gerst, *Brnch Mgr*
EMP: 140
Web: www.hoodpkg.com
SIC: 5199 Packaging materials
HQ: Hood Packaging Corporation
   25 Woodgreen Pl
   Madison MS
   601 853-7260

(P-6916)
HUHTAMAKI INC
8450 Gerber Rd (95828-3712)
PHONE..............................916 688-4938
EMP: 87
SALES (corp-wide): 4.65B Privately Held
Web: www.huhtamaki.com
SIC: 5199 Packaging materials
HQ: Huhtamaki, Inc.
   9201 Packaging Dr
   De Soto KS
   913 583-3025

(P-6917)
IMPORT COLLECTION (PA)
Also Called: Tic
7885 Nelson Rd (91402-6829)
PHONE..............................818 782-3060
David Mehdyzadeh, *CEO*
Sammy Mehdizadeh, *
Sina Mehdyzadeh, *
◆ EMP: 65 EST: 1971
SQ FT: 160,000
SALES (est): 17.91MM
SALES (corp-wide): 17.91MM Privately Held
Web: www.kavanadecor.com
SIC: 5199 5023 Gifts and novelties; Decorative home furnishings and supplies

(P-6918)
JEWELSCENT INC
955 W Imperial Hwy Ste 120 (92821-3812)
P.O. Box 8965 (92822-5965)
PHONE..............................800 550-1762
Nga Nguyen, *CEO*
EMP: 86 EST: 2013
SALES (est): 2.49MM Privately Held
Web: www.jewelscent.com
SIC: 5199 Candles

(P-6919)
JON RENAU COLLECTION INC
Also Called: Easihair
2640 Business Park Dr (92081-7842)
PHONE..............................760 598-0067
John Reynolds, *Pr*
Stella Reynolds, *
▲ EMP: 68 EST: 1984
SALES (est): 9.49MM Privately Held
Web: www.jonrenau.com
SIC: 5199 Wigs

(P-6920)
KATZKIN LEATHER INC (PA)
6868 W Acco St (90640-5441)
PHONE..............................323 725-1243
Brook Mayberry, *Pr*
Scott Briskie, *
▲ EMP: 200 EST: 1998
SQ FT: 50,000
SALES (est): 48.6MM
SALES (corp-wide): 48.6MM Privately Held
Web: www.katzkin.com
SIC: 5199 2531 Leather and cut stock; Seats, automobile

(P-6921)
KHW ENTERPRISES INC
8550 Chetle Ave Ste A (90606-2697)
PHONE..............................562 236-8440
◆ EMP: 75
SIC: 5199 Pets and pet supplies

(P-6922)
KOLE IMPORTS
Also Called: Basket Basics
24600 Main St (90745-6332)
PHONE..............................310 834-0004
Robert Kole, *CEO*
Dan Kole, *
◆ EMP: 78 EST: 1985
SQ FT: 150,000
SALES (est): 30.82MM Privately Held
Web: www.koleimports.com
SIC: 5199 General merchandise, non-durable

(P-6923)
LANE WINPAK INC (HQ)
Also Called: Winpak
1365 N Ayala Dr (92376-3101)

5199 - Nondurable Goods, Nec (P-6924)

PHONE...............................909 386-1762
Bruce J Berry, CEO
Ted Torrens, *
M G Johnston, *
▲ EMP: 69 EST: 1996
SALES (est): 53.4MM
SALES (corp-wide): 1.18B Privately Held
Web: www.winpak.com
SIC: 5199 Packaging materials
PA: Winpak Ltd
100 Saulteaux Cres
Winnipeg MB
204 889-1015

(P-6924)
LEE-MAR AQUARIUM & PET SUPS
Also Called: Lee Mar Aquarium & Pet Sups
2459 Dogwood Way (92081-8421)
PHONE...............................760 727-1300
Terran R Boyd, Pr
▲ EMP: 100 EST: 1971
SQ FT: 67,000
SALES (est): 8.82MM Privately Held
Web: www.leemarpet.com
SIC: 5199 3999 Pet supplies; Pet supplies

(P-6925)
LIFESTREET CORPORATION
Also Called: Lifestreet Media
98 Battery St, St 504 (94070)
PHONE...............................650 508-2220
Mitchell Wiesman, CEO
EMP: 75 EST: 2008
SALES (est): 9.53MM Privately Held
Web: www.lifestreet.com
SIC: 5199 Advertising specialties

(P-6926)
LOGOMARK INC
Also Called: Valumark
1201 Bell Ave (92780-6420)
PHONE...............................714 675-6100
Trevor Gnesin, Pr
▲ EMP: 250 EST: 1992
SQ FT: 200,000
SALES (est): 92.77MM Privately Held
Web: www.logomark.com
SIC: 5199 Advertising specialties

(P-6927)
MANUFACTURED PACKAGING PDTS
33463 Western Ave (94587-3201)
PHONE...............................510 487-1211
EMP: 70 EST: 2011
SALES (est): 6.33MM Privately Held
Web: www.mppmfg.com
SIC: 5199 Packaging materials

(P-6928)
MIDWAY INTERNATIONAL INC
Also Called: Bobbi Boss
13131 166th St (90703-2202)
PHONE...............................800 826-2383
Ha Chung, CEO
◆ EMP: 97 EST: 1985
SQ FT: 32,700
SALES (est): 31.59MM Privately Held
Web: www.bobbiboss.com
SIC: 5199 5047 Wigs; Medical equipment and supplies

(P-6929)
MISA IMPORTS INC
2343 Saybrook Ave (90040-1721)
PHONE...............................562 281-6773
EMP: 100
SALES (corp-wide): 345.56MM Privately Held
Web: www.misaimports.com
SIC: 5199 Art goods and supplies
PA: Misa Imports Inc.
1502 Viceroy Dr
Dallas TX
972 235-3834

(P-6930)
MISSION PETS LLC
Also Called: Mission Pets, Inc.
986 Mission St Fl 5 (94103-2970)
PHONE...............................415 904-9914
Adam Kellogg, CEO
Domenic Grisanzio, *
▲ EMP: 66 EST: 1999
SQ FT: 10,000
SALES (est): 23.73MM
SALES (corp-wide): 23.73MM Privately Held
Web: www.mission-pets.com
SIC: 5199 Pet supplies
PA: Harren Equity Partners, Llc
200 Garrett St Ste F
Charlottesville VA
434 245-5800

(P-6931)
MUTUAL TRADING CO INC
843 E 4th St (90013-1801)
PHONE...............................213 229-9393
EMP: 72
Web: www.lamtc.com
SIC: 5199 Advertising specialties
HQ: Mutual Trading Co., Inc.
4200 Shirley Ave
El Monte CA
213 626-9458

(P-6932)
NW PACKAGING LLC (PA)
Also Called: NW Packaging
1201 E Lexington Ave (91766-5520)
P.O. Box 357 (92871-0357)
PHONE...............................909 706-3627
Robert E Sliter, Admn
EMP: 100 EST: 2012
SALES (est): 19.33MM
SALES (corp-wide): 19.33MM Privately Held
Web: www.nwpackagingonline.com
SIC: 5199 Packaging materials

(P-6933)
P2F HOLDINGS
Also Called: Mulen
1760 Apollo Ct (90740-5617)
PHONE...............................562 296-1055
▲ EMP: 75
SIC: 5199 General merchandise, non-durable

(P-6934)
PACTIV LLC
12500 Slauson Ave Ste H1 (90670-8639)
PHONE...............................562 693-1451
Craig Snedden, Mgr
EMP: 61
Web: www.pactiv.com
SIC: 5199 Packaging materials
HQ: Pactiv Llc
1900 W Field Ct
Lake Forest IL
847 482-2000

(P-6935)
PHD MARKETING INC
1373 Ridgeway St (91768-2701)
PHONE...............................909 620-1000
Thaer Ahmad, Pr
John Kamar, *
▲ EMP: 60 EST: 2010
SQ FT: 20,000
SALES (est): 7.76MM Privately Held
SIC: 5199 5399 General merchandise, non-durable; Army-Navy goods stores

(P-6936)
POLYVORE INC
701 First Ave (94089-1019)
PHONE...............................650 968-1195
Jessica Lee, CEO
EMP: 60 EST: 2007
SALES (est): 28.38MM
SALES (corp-wide): 600K Privately Held
Web: www.ssense.com
SIC: 5199 Advertising specialties
HQ: Groupe Atallah Inc
333 Rue Chabanel O Bureau 900
Montreal QC
514 384-1906

(P-6937)
PREMIERE PACKAGING INDS INC
Also Called: P P I
12202 Slauson Ave (90670-2628)
PHONE...............................562 799-9200
John Luyben, CEO
Christi Luyben, *
▲ EMP: 77 EST: 1999
SALES (est): 24.87MM
SALES (corp-wide): 1.33B Privately Held
SIC: 5199 Packaging materials
HQ: Kelly Spicers Inc.
12310 Slauson Ave
Santa Fe Springs CA

(P-6938)
PRO SPECIALTIES GROUP INC
8221 Arjons Dr Ste F (92126-4305)
PHONE...............................858 541-1100
Cheng Shun Li, Pr
I Chin Li, Sec
▲ EMP: 70 EST: 1997
SQ FT: 23,000
SALES (est): 24.75MM Privately Held
Web: www.psginc.com
SIC: 5199 Advertising specialties

(P-6939)
PROACTIVE PACKG & DISPLAY LLC
602 S Rockefeller Ave Ste A (91761-8190)
PHONE...............................909 390-5624
Richard Hartman, CEO
▲ EMP: 72 EST: 1994
SQ FT: 164,000
SALES (est): 42MM
SALES (corp-wide): 679.24MM Privately Held
Web: www.proactivepkg.com
SIC: 5199 Packaging materials
HQ: New-Indy Containerboard Llc
3500 Porsche Way Ste 150
Ontario CA
909 296-3400

(P-6940)
PROJECT FUSION LLC
495 Ryan Ave (95973-8846)
PHONE...............................530 343-8725
EMP: 233 EST: 2021
SALES (est): 21.82MM Privately Held
SIC: 5199 General merchandise, non-durable

(P-6941)
QUAKER PET GROUP INC
160 Mitchell Blvd (94903-2044)
PHONE...............................415 721-7400
▲ EMP: 100 EST: 2010
SQ FT: 11,000
SALES (est): 34.3MM
SALES (corp-wide): 1.22B Privately Held
SIC: 5199 Pet supplies
HQ: Worldwise, Inc.
6 Hamilton Landing # 150
Novato CA

(P-6942)
REDBARN PET PRODUCTS INC (PA)
Also Called: Redbarn Premium Pet Products
3229 E Spring St Ste 310 (90806-2478)
PHONE...............................562 495-7315
◆ EMP: 236 EST: 1994
SQ FT: 50,000
SALES (est): 57.4MM Privately Held
Web: www.redbarn.com
SIC: 5199 2047 Pet supplies; Dog and cat food

(P-6943)
REVOLTION CNSMR SLTIONS CA LLC (DH)
Also Called: Command Packaging
3840 E 26th St (90058-4107)
PHONE...............................323 980-0918
◆ EMP: 112 EST: 1989
SQ FT: 170,000
SALES (est): 84.55MM
SALES (corp-wide): 803.37MM Privately Held
Web: www.commandpackaging.com
SIC: 5199 Packaging materials
HQ: Delta Plastics Of The South, Llc
8801 Frazier Pike
Little Rock AR

(P-6944)
ROYAL IMEX INC
12605 Clark St (90670-3951)
PHONE...............................562 777-9787
Jin Chul Jhung, CEO
◆ EMP: 60 EST: 1980
SQ FT: 55,000
SALES (est): 10.65MM Privately Held
Web: www.royalimex.com
SIC: 5199 Wigs

(P-6945)
ROYAL PAPER BOX CO CALIFORNIA (PA)
1105 S Maple Ave (90640-6007)
P.O. Box 458 (90640-0458)
PHONE...............................323 728-7041
Jim Hodges, CEO
Darryl Carlson, VP
Scott Larson, VP
Andy Polanco, VP
Steve Perez, VP
▲ EMP: 197 EST: 1940
SQ FT: 172,500
SALES (est): 900.5K
SALES (corp-wide): 900.5K Privately Held
Web: www.royalpaperbox.com
SIC: 5199 Packaging materials

(P-6946)
SAXCO-DEMPTOS INC
Also Called: Demptos Glass
1855 Gateway Blvd Ste 400 (94520-3289)
PHONE...............................707 422-9999
◆ EMP: 150
SIC: 5199 Packaging materials

(P-6947)
SCHROFF INC
7328 Trade St (92121-3435)
PHONE...............................858 740-2400

PRODUCTS & SERVICES SECTION

5211 - Lumber And Other Building Materials (P-6968)

Robert Bradley, *Brnch Mgr*
EMP: 1281
Web: schroff.nvent.com
SIC: 5199 Packaging materials
HQ: Schroff, Inc.
170 Commerce Dr
Warwick RI
763 204-7700

(P-6948)
SHIMS BARGAIN INC (PA)
Also Called: J C Sales
2600 S Soto St (90058-8015)
PHONE.............................323 881-0099
Sesilia Song, *CEO*
Kenneth Suh, *
James Shim, *
Bj Chang, *CFO*
◆ **EMP:** 100 **EST:** 1993
SQ FT: 420,000
SALES (est): 90.41MM **Privately Held**
Web: www.jcsalesweb.com
SIC: 5199 General merchandise, non-durable

(P-6949)
SMITH PACKING INC
680 S Simas Rd (93455-9700)
P.O. Box 1338 (93456-1338)
PHONE.............................805 348-1817
Alvaro Quesada, *Prin*
EMP: 118
SALES (corp-wide): 9.23MM **Privately Held**
Web: www.smithpackinginc.com
SIC: 5199 Packaging materials
PA: Smith Packing, Inc.
111 W Chapel St
Santa Maria CA
805 348-1818

(P-6950)
SP IMAGES INC
6049 E Slauson Ave (90040-3007)
P.O. Box 30340 (79120-0340)
PHONE.............................508 530-3225
Joel Weinshanker, *Pr*
John Capuano, *
Michael Sosidka, *
EMP: 65 **EST:** 2014
SALES (est): 3.66MM **Privately Held**
Web: www.spimages.com
SIC: 5199 Gifts and novelties

(P-6951)
SPORTS IMAGES INC
Also Called: Sports Images
6049 E Slauson Ave (90040-3007)
PHONE.............................508 530-3225
Joel Weinshanker, *Pr*
John Capuano, *
Michael Sosidka, *
▲ **EMP:** 65 **EST:** 1989
SALES (est): 5.95MM **Privately Held**
Web: www.spimages.com
SIC: 5199 Gifts and novelties

(P-6952)
TARGUS INTERNATIONAL LLC (PA)
Also Called: Targus
1211 N Miller St (92806-1933)
PHONE.............................714 765-5555
Mikel H Williams, *CEO*
Bill Oppenlander, *
Victor C Streufert, *
◆ **EMP:** 175 **EST:** 1995
SQ FT: 200,656
SALES (est): 97.3MM
SALES (corp-wide): 97.3MM **Privately Held**

Web: us.targus.com
SIC: 5199 5065 Bags, baskets, and cases; Electronic parts and equipment, nec

(P-6953)
THORO--PACKAGING (DH)
1467 Davril Cir (92878-4357)
PHONE.............................951 278-2100
Janet Dabek Steiner, *Pr*
EMP: 125 **EST:** 1967
SQ FT: 56,000
SALES (est): 48.87MM **Privately Held**
Web: www.autajon.com
SIC: 5199 Packaging materials
HQ: Autajon Cs
Chemin De Fontjarus Pt Pelican
Montelimar
475002000

(P-6954)
UNIX PACKAGING LLC
5361 Alexander St (90040-3062)
PHONE.............................213 627-5050
EMP: 278
SALES (corp-wide): 93.6MM **Privately Held**
Web: www.unixpackaging.com
SIC: 5199 Packaging materials
PA: Unix Packaging, Llc
9 Minson Way
Montebello CA
213 627-5050

(P-6955)
VENIDA PACKING COMPANY
19823 Avenue 300 (93221-9771)
P.O. Box 212 (93221-0212)
PHONE.............................559 592-2816
Verne Crookshanks, *CEO*
Michael Murray, *
George Tantua, *
EMP: 125 **EST:** 1977
SQ FT: 50,000
SALES (est): 18.83MM **Privately Held**
Web: www.venidapacking.com
SIC: 5199 Packaging materials

(P-6956)
VICTORY FOAM INC (PA)
3 Holland (92618-2506)
PHONE.............................949 474-0690
Frank M Comerford, *CEO*
Myles Comerford, *
Helen Comerford, *
▲ **EMP:** 94 **EST:** 1982
SQ FT: 53,000
SALES (est): 37.51MM
SALES (corp-wide): 37.51MM **Privately Held**
Web: www.victoryfoam.com
SIC: 5199 3086 Packaging materials; Cups and plates, foamed plastics

(P-6957)
WORLDWISE INC (DH)
6 Hamilton Landing Ste 150 (94949-8268)
P.O. Box 3360 (94912-3360)
PHONE.............................415 721-7400
▲ **EMP:** 99 **EST:** 1991
SALES (est): 150MM
SALES (corp-wide): 1.22B **Privately Held**
Web: www.petwisebrands.com
SIC: 5199 3999 Pet supplies; Pet supplies
HQ: Alvarez & Marsal Capital, Llc
289 Greenwich Ave Ste 2
Greenwich CT
203 742-5880

5211 Lumber And Other Building Materials

(P-6958)
BOISE CASCADE COMPANY
Also Called: Boise Cascade
7145 Arlington Ave (92503-1508)
PHONE.............................951 343-3000
Mike Bland, *Mgr*
EMP: 94
SALES (corp-wide): 8.39B **Publicly Held**
Web: www.bc.com
SIC: 5211 5031 Lumber products; Lumber: rough, dressed, and finished
PA: Boise Cascade Company
1111 W Jefferson St # 100
Boise ID
208 384-6161

(P-6959)
DIXIELINE LUMBER COMPANY LLC
2625 Durahart St (92507-2654)
PHONE.............................951 224-8491
EMP: 628
SALES (corp-wide): 22.73B **Publicly Held**
Web: www.dixieline.com
SIC: 5211 5251 2439 5072 Lumber and other building materials; Builders' hardware ; Trusses, wooden roof; Hardware
HQ: Dixieline Lumber Company Llc
3250 Sports Arena Blvd
San Diego CA
619 224-4120

(P-6960)
FAMILY TIES HOME CARE LLC
1350 Lafitte Dr (91377-4718)
PHONE.............................818 565-9147
EMP: 75 **EST:** 2020
SALES (est): 4.06MM **Privately Held**
Web: www.familytieshomecare.com
SIC: 5211 8059 Home centers; Personal care home, with health care

(P-6961)
GANAHL LUMBER COMPANY
Also Called: Benjamin Moore Authorized Ret
150 W Blaine St (92878-4047)
P.O. Box 1326 (92878-1326)
PHONE.............................951 278-4000
Mark Ganahl, *Prin*
EMP: 67
SALES (corp-wide): 781.96MM **Privately Held**
Web: www.ganahllumber.com
SIC: 5211 2431 5031 1751 Millwork and lumber; Millwork; Lumber: rough, dressed, and finished; Window and door (prefabricated) installation
PA: Ganahl Lumber Company
1220 E Ball Rd
Anaheim CA
714 772-5444

(P-6962)
HOME DEPOT USA INC
Also Called: Home Depot, The
5859 Antelope Rd (95842-3902)
PHONE.............................916 726-0620
Chris Ludwig, *Mgr*
EMP: 108
SALES (corp-wide): 157.4B **Publicly Held**
Web: www.homedepot.com
SIC: 5211 7359 Home centers; Tool rental
HQ: Home Depot U.S.A., Inc.
2455 Paces Ferry Rd Se
Atlanta GA

(P-6963)
HOME DEPOT USA INC
Also Called: Home Depot, The
7121 Firestone Blvd (90241-4104)
PHONE.............................562 776-2200
Max Hernandez, *Mgr*
EMP: 344
SALES (corp-wide): 157.4B **Publicly Held**
Web: www.homedepot.com
SIC: 5211 7359 Home centers; Tool rental
HQ: Home Depot U.S.A., Inc.
2455 Paces Ferry Rd Se
Atlanta GA

(P-6964)
HOME DEPOT USA INC
Also Called: Home Depot, The
16800 Roscoe Blvd (91406-1105)
PHONE.............................818 780-5448
John Cruz, *Mgr*
EMP: 120
SALES (corp-wide): 157.4B **Publicly Held**
Web: www.homedepot.com
SIC: 5211 7359 Home centers; Tool rental
HQ: Home Depot U.S.A., Inc.
2455 Paces Ferry Rd Se
Atlanta GA

(P-6965)
HOME DEPOT USA INC
Also Called: Home Depot, The
10801 Garden Grove Blvd (92843-1201)
PHONE.............................714 539-0319
Chris Murray, *Mgr*
EMP: 134
SALES (corp-wide): 157.4B **Publicly Held**
Web: www.homedepot.com
SIC: 5211 7359 Home centers; Tool rental
HQ: Home Depot U.S.A., Inc.
2455 Paces Ferry Rd Se
Atlanta GA

(P-6966)
HOME DEPOT USA INC
Also Called: Home Depot, The
3323 Madison St (92504-4132)
PHONE.............................951 358-1370
Brian Lay, *Mgr*
EMP: 127
SALES (corp-wide): 157.4B **Publicly Held**
Web: www.homedepot.com
SIC: 5211 7359 Home centers; Tool rental
HQ: Home Depot U.S.A., Inc.
2455 Paces Ferry Rd Se
Atlanta GA

(P-6967)
HOME DEPOT USA INC
Also Called: Home Depot, The
2001 Chess Dr (94404-1567)
PHONE.............................650 525-9343
Cliff Calderan, *Mgr*
EMP: 133
SALES (corp-wide): 157.4B **Publicly Held**
Web: www.homedepot.com
SIC: 5211 7359 Home centers; Tool rental
HQ: Home Depot U.S.A., Inc.
2455 Paces Ferry Rd Se
Atlanta GA

(P-6968)
HOME DEPOT USA INC
Also Called: Home Depot, The
10001 Fairway Dr (95678-1955)
PHONE.............................916 787-0201
Lucretia M Heath, *Mgr*
EMP: 107
SALES (corp-wide): 157.4B **Publicly Held**
Web: www.homedepot.com

5211 - Lumber And Other Building Materials (P-6969)

(P-6969)
HOME DEPOT USA INC
Also Called: Home Depot, The
1750 E Edinger Ave (92705-5031)
PHONE..................................714 259-1030
Rudy Teralta, *Mgr*
EMP: 128
SALES (corp-wide): 157.4B **Publicly Held**
Web: www.homedepot.com
SIC: **5211** 7359 Home centers; Tool rental
HQ: Home Depot U.S.A., Inc.
2455 Paces Ferry Rd Se
Atlanta GA

(P-6970)
HOME DEPOT USA INC
Also Called: Home Depot, The
3040 E Slauson Ave (90255-3138)
PHONE..................................323 587-5520
Ross Manzo, *Mgr*
EMP: 101
SALES (corp-wide): 157.4B **Publicly Held**
Web: www.homedepot.com
SIC: **5211** 7359 Home centers; Tool rental
HQ: Home Depot U.S.A., Inc.
2455 Paces Ferry Rd Se
Atlanta GA

(P-6971)
HOME DEPOT USA INC
Also Called: Home Depot, The
3363 W Century Blvd (90303-1366)
PHONE..................................310 677-1944
Kim Dixon, *Mgr*
EMP: 111
SQ FT: 107,421
SALES (corp-wide): 157.4B **Publicly Held**
Web: www.homedepot.com
SIC: **5211** 7359 Home centers; Tool rental
HQ: Home Depot U.S.A., Inc.
2455 Paces Ferry Rd Se
Atlanta GA

(P-6972)
HOME DEPOT USA INC
Also Called: Home Depot, The
5010 Feather River Dr (95219-8001)
PHONE..................................209 474-8285
Debhra Dates, *Brnch Mgr*
EMP: 127
SALES (corp-wide): 157.4B **Publicly Held**
Web: www.homedepot.com
SIC: **5211** 7359 Home centers; Tool rental
HQ: Home Depot U.S.A., Inc.
2455 Paces Ferry Rd Se
Atlanta GA

(P-6973)
HOME DEPOT USA INC
Also Called: Home Depot, The
8000 Folsom Blvd (95826-2613)
PHONE..................................916 381-3181
Kip Armstrong, *Mgr*
EMP: 87
SALES (corp-wide): 157.4B **Publicly Held**
Web: www.homedepot.com
SIC: **5211** 7359 Home centers; Tool rental
HQ: Home Depot U.S.A., Inc.
2455 Paces Ferry Rd Se
Atlanta GA

(P-6974)
HOME DEPOT USA INC
Also Called: Home Depot, The
1625 S Mountain Ave (91016-4205)
PHONE..................................626 256-0580
Mako Kapaska, *Mgr*
EMP: 151
SALES (corp-wide): 157.4B **Publicly Held**
Web: www.homedepot.com
SIC: **5211** 7359 Home centers; Tool rental
HQ: Home Depot U.S.A., Inc.
2455 Paces Ferry Rd Se
Atlanta GA

(P-6975)
HOME DEPOT USA INC
Also Called: Home Depot, The
635 W Capitol Expy (95136-4070)
PHONE..................................408 978-1099
Art Miner, *Mgr*
EMP: 123
SALES (corp-wide): 157.4B **Publicly Held**
Web: www.homedepot.com
SIC: **5211** 7359 Home centers; Tool rental
HQ: Home Depot U.S.A., Inc.
2455 Paces Ferry Rd Se
Atlanta GA

(P-6976)
HOME DEPOT USA INC
Also Called: Home Depot, The
43900 Ice House Ter (94538-6046)
PHONE..................................510 490-0191
Jasmine Gonzalez, *Mgr*
EMP: 81
SALES (corp-wide): 157.4B **Publicly Held**
Web: www.homedepot.com
SIC: **5211** 7359 Home centers; Tool rental
HQ: Home Depot U.S.A., Inc.
2455 Paces Ferry Rd Se
Atlanta GA

(P-6977)
HOME DEPOT USA INC
Also Called: Home Depot, The
6280 Hembree Ln (95492-6839)
PHONE..................................707 836-0377
Mark E Dennis, *Mgr*
EMP: 89
SALES (corp-wide): 157.4B **Publicly Held**
Web: www.homedepot.com
SIC: **5211** 7359 Home centers; Tool rental
HQ: Home Depot U.S.A., Inc.
2455 Paces Ferry Rd Se
Atlanta GA

(P-6978)
HOME DEPOT USA INC
Also Called: Home Depot, The
1151 W Lugonia Ave (92374-2000)
PHONE..................................909 748-0505
Kade Kasner, *Brnch Mgr*
EMP: 141
SALES (corp-wide): 157.4B **Publicly Held**
Web: www.homedepot.com
SIC: **5211** 7359 Home centers; Tool rental
HQ: Home Depot U.S.A., Inc.
2455 Paces Ferry Rd Se
Atlanta GA

(P-6979)
HOME DEPOT USA INC
Also Called: Home Depot, The
1177 Great Mall Dr (95035-8005)
PHONE..................................408 942-7301
Chris Rumnell, *Mgr*
EMP: 120
SQ FT: 131,994
SALES (corp-wide): 157.4B **Publicly Held**
Web: www.homedepot.com
SIC: **5211** 7359 Home centers; Tool rental
HQ: Home Depot U.S.A., Inc.
2455 Paces Ferry Rd Se
Atlanta GA

(P-6980)
HOME DEPOT USA INC
Also Called: Home Depot, The
225 Soscol Ave (94559-4007)
PHONE..................................707 251-0162
Ernie Linsay, *Mgr*
EMP: 74
SALES (corp-wide): 157.4B **Publicly Held**
Web: www.homedepot.com
SIC: **5211** 7359 Home centers; Tool rental
HQ: Home Depot U.S.A., Inc.
2455 Paces Ferry Rd Se
Atlanta GA

(P-6981)
HOME DEPOT USA INC
Also Called: Home Depot, The
1830 W Slauson Ave (90047-1126)
PHONE..................................323 292-1397
John Cruz, *Mgr*
EMP: 219
SQ FT: 110,000
SALES (corp-wide): 157.4B **Publicly Held**
Web: www.homedepot.com
SIC: **5211** 7359 Home centers; Tool rental
HQ: Home Depot U.S.A., Inc.
2455 Paces Ferry Rd Se
Atlanta GA

(P-6982)
HOME DEPOT USA INC
Also Called: Home Depot, The
21787 Hesperian Blvd (94541-7027)
PHONE..................................510 887-8544
Andrew Tucker, *Brnch Mgr*
EMP: 104
SALES (corp-wide): 157.4B **Publicly Held**
Web: www.homedepot.com
SIC: **5211** 7359 Home centers; Tool rental
HQ: Home Depot U.S.A., Inc.
2455 Paces Ferry Rd Se
Atlanta GA

(P-6983)
HOME DEPOT USA INC
Also Called: Home Depot, The
401 W Ventura Blvd (93010-9122)
PHONE..................................805 389-9918
Michael Curbelo, *Mgr*
EMP: 149
SALES (corp-wide): 157.4B **Publicly Held**
Web: www.homedepot.com
SIC: **5211** 7359 Home centers; Tool rental
HQ: Home Depot U.S.A., Inc.
2455 Paces Ferry Rd Se
Atlanta GA

(P-6984)
HOME DEPOT USA INC
Also Called: Home Depot, The
27401 La Paz Rd (92677-3739)
PHONE..................................949 831-3698
Dan Schneid, *Brnch Mgr*
EMP: 97
SALES (corp-wide): 157.4B **Publicly Held**
Web: www.homedepot.com
SIC: **5211** 7359 Home centers; Tool rental
HQ: Home Depot U.S.A., Inc.
2455 Paces Ferry Rd Se
Atlanta GA

(P-6985)
HOME DEPOT USA INC
Also Called: Home Depot, The
2500 Las Positas Rd (94551-8810)
PHONE..................................925 243-1212
Peter Mullins, *Mgr*
EMP: 136
SALES (corp-wide): 157.4B **Publicly Held**
Web: www.homedepot.com
SIC: **5211** 7359 Home centers; Tool rental
HQ: Home Depot U.S.A., Inc.
2455 Paces Ferry Rd Se
Atlanta GA

(P-6986)
HOME DEPOT USA INC
Also Called: Home Depot, The
2055 N Figueroa St (90065-1021)
PHONE..................................323 342-9495
Laud Ashbar, *Mgr*
EMP: 273
SQ FT: 107,880
SALES (corp-wide): 157.4B **Publicly Held**
Web: www.homedepot.com
SIC: **5211** 7359 Home centers; Tool rental
HQ: Home Depot U.S.A., Inc.
2455 Paces Ferry Rd Se
Atlanta GA

(P-6987)
HOME DEPOT USA INC
Also Called: Home Depot, The
625 S Placentia Ave (92831-5199)
PHONE..................................714 459-4909
Pete Canscale, *Mgr*
EMP: 119
SALES (corp-wide): 157.4B **Publicly Held**
Web: www.homedepot.com
SIC: **5211** 7359 Home centers; Tool rental
HQ: Home Depot U.S.A., Inc.
2455 Paces Ferry Rd Se
Atlanta GA

(P-6988)
HOME DEPOT USA INC
Also Called: Home Depot, The
7150 N Abby St (93720-2920)
PHONE..................................559 431-9860
Randy Martin, *Brnch Mgr*
EMP: 113
SALES (corp-wide): 157.4B **Publicly Held**
Web: www.homedepot.com
SIC: **5211** 7359 Home centers; Tool rental
HQ: Home Depot U.S.A., Inc.
2455 Paces Ferry Rd Se
Atlanta GA

(P-6989)
HOME DEPOT USA INC
Also Called: Home Depot, The
6400 Alondra Blvd (90723-3726)
PHONE..................................562 272-8055
Raul M Rodriguez, *Brnch Mgr*
EMP: 123
SALES (corp-wide): 157.4B **Publicly Held**
Web: www.homedepot.com
SIC: **5211** 7359 Home centers; Tool rental
HQ: Home Depot U.S.A., Inc.
2455 Paces Ferry Rd Se
Atlanta GA

(P-6990)
HOME DEPOT USA INC
Also Called: Home Depot, The
750 S Jaye St (93257-5310)
PHONE..................................559 782-4611
Scott Sherwood, *Mgr*
EMP: 133
SALES (corp-wide): 157.4B **Publicly Held**
Web: www.homedepot.com
SIC: **5211** 7359 Home centers; Tool rental
HQ: Home Depot U.S.A., Inc.
2455 Paces Ferry Rd Se
Atlanta GA

(P-6991)
HOME DEPOT USA INC
Also Called: Home Depot, The
355 Marketplace Ave (92113-1960)

PRODUCTS & SERVICES SECTION

5211 - Lumber And Other Building Materials (P-7013)

PHONE..............................619 263-1533
Brian Farwell, *Mgr*
EMP: 94
SALES (corp-wide): 157.4B **Publicly Held**
Web: www.homedepot.com
SIC: 5211 7359 Home centers; Tool rental
HQ: Home Depot U.S.A., Inc.
    2455 Paces Ferry Rd Se
    Atlanta GA

(P-6992)
HOME DEPOT USA INC
Also Called: Home Depot, The
1475 E Valley Pkwy (92027-2313)
PHONE..............................760 233-1285
Marco Bernardino, *Mgr*
EMP: 101
SALES (corp-wide): 157.4B **Publicly Held**
Web: www.homedepot.com
SIC: 5211 7359 Home centers; Tool rental
HQ: Home Depot U.S.A., Inc.
    2455 Paces Ferry Rd Se
    Atlanta GA

(P-6993)
HOME DEPOT USA INC
Also Called: Home Depot, The
401 W Esplanade Dr (93036-1298)
PHONE..............................805 983-0653
Chris Barajas, *Mgr*
EMP: 121
SALES (corp-wide): 157.4B **Publicly Held**
Web: www.homedepot.com
SIC: 5211 7359 Home centers; Tool rental
HQ: Home Depot U.S.A., Inc.
    2455 Paces Ferry Rd Se
    Atlanta GA

(P-6994)
HOME DEPOT USA INC
Also Called: Home Depot, The
4864 E Kings Canyon Rd (93727-3809)
PHONE..............................559 455-9124
Tim Archangeles, *Mgr*
EMP: 118
SALES (corp-wide): 157.4B **Publicly Held**
Web: www.homedepot.com
SIC: 5211 7359 Home centers; Tool rental
HQ: Home Depot U.S.A., Inc.
    2455 Paces Ferry Rd Se
    Atlanta GA

(P-6995)
HOME DEPOT USA INC
Also Called: Home Depot, The
6140 Hamner Ave (91752-3121)
PHONE..............................951 727-0324
Otto Torres, *Mgr*
EMP: 94
SALES (corp-wide): 157.4B **Publicly Held**
Web: www.homedepot.com
SIC: 5211 7359 Home centers; Tool rental
HQ: Home Depot U.S.A., Inc.
    2455 Paces Ferry Rd Se
    Atlanta GA

(P-6996)
HOME DEPOT USA INC
Also Called: Home Depot, The
575 N China Lake Blvd (93555-3581)
PHONE..............................760 375-4614
Garbriel Garcia, *Mgr*
EMP: 116
SALES (corp-wide): 157.4B **Publicly Held**
Web: www.homedepot.com
SIC: 5211 7359 Home centers; Tool rental
HQ: Home Depot U.S.A., Inc.
    2455 Paces Ferry Rd Se
    Atlanta GA

(P-6997)
HOME DEPOT USA INC
Also Called: Home Depot, The
1625 Sycamore Ave (94547-1707)
PHONE..............................510 245-9572
Christian Hexsinger, *Mgr*
EMP: 80
SALES (corp-wide): 157.4B **Publicly Held**
Web: www.homedepot.com
SIC: 5211 7359 Home centers; Tool rental
HQ: Home Depot U.S.A., Inc.
    2455 Paces Ferry Rd Se
    Atlanta GA

(P-6998)
HOME DEPOT USA INC
Also Called: Home Depot, The
5631 Lone Tree Way (94513-5307)
PHONE..............................925 513-6060
Kerry Snyder, *Mgr*
EMP: 110
SALES (corp-wide): 157.4B **Publicly Held**
Web: www.homedepot.com
SIC: 5211 7359 Home centers; Tool rental
HQ: Home Depot U.S.A., Inc.
    2455 Paces Ferry Rd Se
    Atlanta GA

(P-6999)
HOME DEPOT USA INC
Also Called: Home Depot, The
15975 Perris Blvd (92551-4692)
PHONE..............................951 485-5400
Maribel Reyes, *Mgr*
EMP: 98
SALES (corp-wide): 157.4B **Publicly Held**
Web: www.homedepot.com
SIC: 5211 7359 Home centers; Tool rental
HQ: Home Depot U.S.A., Inc.
    2455 Paces Ferry Rd Se
    Atlanta GA

(P-7000)
HOME DEPOT USA INC
Also Called: Home Depot, The
2155 N Schnoor Ave (93637-5014)
PHONE..............................559 675-0127
Darien Steele, *Mgr*
EMP: 121
SALES (corp-wide): 157.4B **Publicly Held**
Web: www.homedepot.com
SIC: 5211 7359 Home centers; Tool rental
HQ: Home Depot U.S.A., Inc.
    2455 Paces Ferry Rd Se
    Atlanta GA

(P-7001)
HOME DEPOT USA INC
Also Called: Home Depot, The
1095 N Pullman St (92807-2516)
PHONE..............................714 921-1215
Rob Sholte, *Mgr*
EMP: 99
SALES (corp-wide): 157.4B **Publicly Held**
Web: www.homedepot.com
SIC: 5211 7359 Home centers; Tool rental
HQ: Home Depot U.S.A., Inc.
    2455 Paces Ferry Rd Se
    Atlanta GA

(P-7002)
HOME DEPOT USA INC
Also Called: Home Depot, The
860 E Dunne Ave (95037-4609)
PHONE..............................408 779-9755
Holly Martindale, *Mgr*
EMP: 114
SALES (corp-wide): 157.4B **Publicly Held**
Web: www.homedepot.com

SIC: 5211 7359 Home centers; Tool rental
HQ: Home Depot U.S.A., Inc.
    2455 Paces Ferry Rd Se
    Atlanta GA

(P-7003)
HOME DEPOT USA INC
Also Called: Home Depot, The
350 N Orchard Ave (95482-4536)
PHONE..............................707 462-3009
Chris Keggereis, *Brnch Mgr*
EMP: 84
SALES (corp-wide): 157.4B **Publicly Held**
Web: www.homedepot.com
SIC: 5211 7359 Home centers; Tool rental
HQ: Home Depot U.S.A., Inc.
    2455 Paces Ferry Rd Se
    Atlanta GA

(P-7004)
HOME DEPOT USA INC
Also Called: Home Depot, The
1320 Eastlake Pkwy (91915-4116)
PHONE..............................619 421-0639
Emil Isvanca, *Mgr*
EMP: 109
SALES (corp-wide): 157.4B **Publicly Held**
Web: www.homedepot.com
SIC: 5211 7359 Home centers; Tool rental
HQ: Home Depot U.S.A., Inc.
    2455 Paces Ferry Rd Se
    Atlanta GA

(P-7005)
HOME DEPOT USA INC
Also Called: Home Depot, The
3200 Puente Ave (91706-5526)
PHONE..............................626 813-7131
Chip Dazies, *Mgr*
EMP: 107
SQ FT: 105,920
SALES (corp-wide): 157.4B **Publicly Held**
Web: www.homedepot.com
SIC: 5211 7359 Home centers; Tool rental
HQ: Home Depot U.S.A., Inc.
    2455 Paces Ferry Rd Se
    Atlanta GA

(P-7006)
HOME DEPOT USA INC
Also Called: Home Depot, The
298 Fletcher Pkwy (92020-2506)
PHONE..............................619 401-6610
Bill Walker, *Brnch Mgr*
EMP: 100
SALES (corp-wide): 157.4B **Publicly Held**
Web: www.homedepot.com
SIC: 5211 7359 Home centers; Tool rental
HQ: Home Depot U.S.A., Inc.
    2455 Paces Ferry Rd Se
    Atlanta GA

(P-7007)
HOME DEPOT USA INC
Also Called: Home Depot, The
600 S Harbor Blvd (90631-6166)
PHONE..............................562 690-6006
Merna Rosas, *Mgr*
EMP: 99
SALES (corp-wide): 157.4B **Publicly Held**
Web: www.homedepot.com
SIC: 5211 7359 Home centers; Tool rental
HQ: Home Depot U.S.A., Inc.
    2455 Paces Ferry Rd Se
    Atlanta GA

(P-7008)
HOME DEPOT USA INC
Also Called: Home Depot, The
110 E Sepulveda Blvd (90745-6301)

PHONE..............................310 835-7547
Emily R Simpson, *Mgr*
EMP: 139
SALES (corp-wide): 157.4B **Publicly Held**
Web: www.homedepot.com
SIC: 5211 7359 Home centers; Tool rental
HQ: Home Depot U.S.A., Inc.
    2455 Paces Ferry Rd Se
    Atlanta GA

(P-7009)
HOME DEPOT USA INC
Also Called: Home Depot, The
12322 Washington Blvd (90606-2503)
PHONE..............................562 789-4121
Ben Deardudin, *Mgr*
EMP: 122
SALES (corp-wide): 157.4B **Publicly Held**
Web: www.homedepot.com
SIC: 5211 7359 Home centers; Tool rental
HQ: Home Depot U.S.A., Inc.
    2455 Paces Ferry Rd Se
    Atlanta GA

(P-7010)
HOME DEPOT USA INC
Also Called: Home Depot, The
3500 W Macarthur Blvd (92704-6808)
PHONE..............................714 966-8551
Beatrice Celazeo, *Genl Mgr*
EMP: 110
SALES (corp-wide): 157.4B **Publicly Held**
Web: www.homedepot.com
SIC: 5211 7359 Home centers; Tool rental
HQ: Home Depot U.S.A., Inc.
    2455 Paces Ferry Rd Se
    Atlanta GA

(P-7011)
HOME DEPOT USA INC
Also Called: Home Depot, The
14603 Ocean Gate Ave (90250-6744)
PHONE..............................310 644-9600
Jason Oaks, *Mgr*
EMP: 116
SALES (corp-wide): 157.4B **Publicly Held**
Web: www.homedepot.com
SIC: 5211 7359 Home centers; Tool rental
HQ: Home Depot U.S.A., Inc.
    2455 Paces Ferry Rd Se
    Atlanta GA

(P-7012)
HOME DEPOT USA INC
Also Called: Home Depot, The
435 W Katella Ave (92867-4603)
PHONE..............................714 538-9600
Michelle Fromholz, *Mgr*
EMP: 120
SALES (corp-wide): 157.4B **Publicly Held**
Web: www.homedepot.com
SIC: 5211 1752 1751 Home centers; Carpet laying; Window and door installation and erection
HQ: Home Depot U.S.A., Inc.
    2455 Paces Ferry Rd Se
    Atlanta GA

(P-7013)
HOME DEPOT USA INC
Also Called: Home Depot, The
25100 Madison Ave (92562-8907)
PHONE..............................951 698-1555
Maria Tub, *Mgr*
EMP: 130
SALES (corp-wide): 157.4B **Publicly Held**
Web: www.homedepot.com
SIC: 5211 7359 Home centers; Tool rental
HQ: Home Depot U.S.A., Inc.
    2455 Paces Ferry Rd Se

5211 - Lumber And Other Building Materials (P-7014)

Atlanta GA

(P-7014)
HOME DEPOT USA INC
Also Called: Home Depot, The
1617 N Carpenter Rd (95351-1146)
PHONE.................................209 491-0200
Cary Teruya, *Mgr*
EMP: 117
SALES (corp-wide): 157.4B **Publicly Held**
Web: www.homedepot.com
SIC: **5211** 7359 Home centers; Tool rental
HQ: Home Depot U.S.A., Inc.
2455 Paces Ferry Rd Se
Atlanta GA

(P-7015)
HOME DEPOT USA INC
Also Called: Home Depot, The
1355 E Ontario Ave (92881-6604)
PHONE.................................951 808-0327
Vanessa Muenoz, *Brnch Mgr*
EMP: 126
SALES (corp-wide): 157.4B **Publicly Held**
Web: www.homedepot.com
SIC: **5211** 7359 Home centers; Tool rental
HQ: Home Depot U.S.A., Inc.
2455 Paces Ferry Rd Se
Atlanta GA

(P-7016)
HOME DEPOT USA INC
Also Called: Home Depot, The
2300 Harbor Blvd Ste F (92626-6200)
PHONE.................................949 646-4220
Marcella Kinsey, *Mgr*
EMP: 120
SALES (corp-wide): 157.4B **Publicly Held**
Web: www.homedepot.com
SIC: **5211** 7359 Home centers; Tool rental
HQ: Home Depot U.S.A., Inc.
2455 Paces Ferry Rd Se
Atlanta GA

(P-7017)
HOME DEPOT USA INC
Also Called: Home Depot, The
20021 Lake Forest Dr (92630-8703)
PHONE.................................949 609-0221
Elizabeth Capippi, *Mgr*
EMP: 103
SALES (corp-wide): 157.4B **Publicly Held**
Web: www.homedepot.com
SIC: **5211** 7359 Home centers; Tool rental
HQ: Home Depot U.S.A., Inc.
2455 Paces Ferry Rd Se
Atlanta GA

(P-7018)
HOME DEPOT USA INC
Also Called: Home Depot, The
15150 Bear Valley Rd (92395-8709)
PHONE.................................760 955-2999
Jyll Cowdell, *Mgr*
EMP: 131
SALES (corp-wide): 157.4B **Publicly Held**
Web: www.homedepot.com
SIC: **5211** 7359 Home centers; Tool rental
HQ: Home Depot U.S.A., Inc.
2455 Paces Ferry Rd Se
Atlanta GA

(P-7019)
HOME DEPOT USA INC
Also Called: Home Depot, The
7015 Telegraph Rd (90040-3225)
PHONE.................................323 727-9600
Sal Prieto, *Mgr*
EMP: 321
SALES (corp-wide): 157.4B **Publicly Held**

Web: www.homedepot.com
SIC: **5211** 7359 Home centers; Tool rental
HQ: Home Depot U.S.A., Inc.
2455 Paces Ferry Rd Se
Atlanta GA

(P-7020)
HOME DEPOT USA INC
Also Called: Home Depot, The
12975 W Jefferson Blvd (90066-7023)
PHONE.................................310 822-3330
Bj Powers, *Mgr*
EMP: 211
SALES (corp-wide): 157.4B **Publicly Held**
Web: www.homedepot.com
SIC: **5211** 7359 Home centers; Tool rental
HQ: Home Depot U.S.A., Inc.
2455 Paces Ferry Rd Se
Atlanta GA

(P-7021)
HOME DEPOT USA INC
Also Called: Home Depot, The
27952 Hillcrest (92692-3637)
PHONE.................................949 364-1900
Dionne Kiloh, *Mgr*
EMP: 94
SALES (corp-wide): 157.4B **Publicly Held**
Web: www.homedepot.com
SIC: **5211** 7359 Home centers; Tool rental
HQ: Home Depot U.S.A., Inc.
2455 Paces Ferry Rd Se
Atlanta GA

(P-7022)
HOME DEPOT USA INC
Also Called: Home Depot, The
12960 Foothill Blvd (91342-4928)
PHONE.................................818 365-7662
Gil Camarena, *Mgr*
EMP: 130
SALES (corp-wide): 157.4B **Publicly Held**
Web: www.homedepot.com
SIC: **5211** 7359 Home centers; Tool rental
HQ: Home Depot U.S.A., Inc.
2455 Paces Ferry Rd Se
Atlanta GA

(P-7023)
HOME DEPOT USA INC
Also Called: Home Depot, The
20642 Golden Triangle Rd (91351-2419)
PHONE.................................661 252-7800
Jeff Rogers, *Mgr*
EMP: 204
SALES (corp-wide): 157.4B **Publicly Held**
Web: www.homedepot.com
SIC: **5211** 7359 Home centers; Tool rental
HQ: Home Depot U.S.A., Inc.
2455 Paces Ferry Rd Se
Atlanta GA

(P-7024)
HOME DEPOT USA INC
Also Called: Home Depot, The
7530 Broadway (91945-1604)
PHONE.................................619 589-2999
Terry Ouellette, *Mgr*
EMP: 137
SALES (corp-wide): 157.4B **Publicly Held**
Web: www.homedepot.com
SIC: **5211** 7359 Home centers; Tool rental
HQ: Home Depot U.S.A., Inc.
2455 Paces Ferry Rd Se
Atlanta GA

(P-7025)
HOME DEPOT USA INC
Also Called: Home Depot, The
2450 Cherry Ave (90755-3706)

PHONE.................................562 595-9200
Nick Crooks, *Mgr*
EMP: 87
SALES (corp-wide): 157.4B **Publicly Held**
Web: www.homedepot.com
SIC: **5211** 7359 Home centers; Tool rental
HQ: Home Depot U.S.A., Inc.
2455 Paces Ferry Rd Se
Atlanta GA

(P-7026)
HOME DEPOT USA INC
Also Called: Home Depot, The
14549 Ramona Ave (91710-5647)
PHONE.................................909 393-5205
EMP: 138
SALES (corp-wide): 157.4B **Publicly Held**
Web: www.homedepot.com
SIC: **5211** 7359 Home centers; Tool rental
HQ: Home Depot U.S.A., Inc.
2455 Paces Ferry Rd Se
Atlanta GA

(P-7027)
HOME DEPOT USA INC
Also Called: Home Depot, The
111 Shoreline Pkwy (94901-5521)
PHONE.................................415 458-8675
EMP: 83
SALES (corp-wide): 157.4B **Publicly Held**
Web: www.homedepot.com
SIC: **5211** 7359 Home centers; Tool rental
HQ: Home Depot U.S.A., Inc.
2455 Paces Ferry Rd Se
Atlanta GA

(P-7028)
HOME DEPOT USA INC
Also Called: Home Depot, The
11884 Foothill Blvd (91730-3900)
PHONE.................................909 948-9200
EMP: 126
SALES (corp-wide): 157.4B **Publicly Held**
Web: www.homedepot.com
SIC: **5211** 7359 Home centers; Tool rental
HQ: Home Depot U.S.A., Inc.
2455 Paces Ferry Rd Se
Atlanta GA

(P-7029)
J B WHL ROOFG BLDG SUPS INC (DH)
Also Called: J B
21524 Nordhoff St (91311-5822)
P.O. Box 5289 (91313-5289)
PHONE.................................818 998-0440
W Keith Jones, *Pr*
Brian Jones, *Sec*
EMP: 70 EST: 1981
SQ FT: 2,000
SALES (est): 48.89MM **Privately Held**
Web: www.jbwholesale.com
SIC: **5211** 5033 Roofing material; Shingles, except wood
HQ: Srs Distribution Inc.
7440 S Hwy 121
Mckinney TX

(P-7030)
LOWES HOME CENTERS LLC
Also Called: Lowe's
7651 N Blackstone Ave (93720-4306)
PHONE.................................559 436-6266
Dale Delmanowski, *Mgr*
EMP: 168
SQ FT: 136,597
SALES (corp-wide): 97.06B **Publicly Held**
Web: www.lowes.com

SIC: **5211** 5031 5722 5064 Home centers; Building materials, exterior; Household appliance stores; Electrical appliances, television and radio
HQ: Lowe's Home Centers, Llc
1000 Lowes Blvd
Mooresville NC
336 658-4000

(P-7031)
LOWES HOME CENTERS LLC
Also Called: Lowe's
3801 Pelandale Ave Side Frnt (95356)
PHONE.................................209 545-7676
Rick Christman, *Brnch Mgr*
EMP: 175
SALES (corp-wide): 97.06B **Publicly Held**
Web: www.lowes.com
SIC: **5211** 5031 5722 5064 Home centers; Building materials, exterior; Household appliance stores; Electrical appliances, television and radio
HQ: Lowe's Home Centers, Llc
1000 Lowes Blvd
Mooresville NC
336 658-4000

(P-7032)
LOWES HOME CENTERS LLC
Also Called: Lowe's
11399 Foothill Blvd (91730-7626)
PHONE.................................909 476-9697
Jeniffer Lang, *Mgr*
EMP: 123
SALES (corp-wide): 97.06B **Publicly Held**
Web: www.lowes.com
SIC: **5211** 5031 5722 5064 Home centers; Building materials, exterior; Household appliance stores; Electrical appliances, television and radio
HQ: Lowe's Home Centers, Llc
1000 Lowes Blvd
Mooresville NC
336 658-4000

(P-7033)
LOWES HOME CENTERS LLC
Also Called: Lowe's
30481 Avenida De Las Flores (92688)
PHONE.................................949 589-5005
Pete Bradley, *Brnch Mgr*
EMP: 66
SALES (corp-wide): 97.06B **Publicly Held**
Web: www.lowes.com
SIC: **5211** 5031 5722 5064 Home centers; Building materials, exterior; Household appliance stores; Electrical appliances, television and radio
HQ: Lowe's Home Centers, Llc
1000 Lowes Blvd
Mooresville NC
336 658-4000

(P-7034)
LOWES HOME CENTERS LLC
Also Called: Lowe's
2318 Northside Dr (92108-2704)
PHONE.................................619 584-5500
Rebecca Young, *Mgr*
EMP: 115
SALES (corp-wide): 97.06B **Publicly Held**
Web: www.lowes.com
SIC: **5211** 5031 5722 5064 Home centers; Building materials, exterior; Household appliance stores; Electrical appliances, television and radio
HQ: Lowe's Home Centers, Llc
1000 Lowes Blvd
Mooresville NC
336 658-4000

PRODUCTS & SERVICES SECTION
5211 - Lumber And Other Building Materials (P-7052)

(P-7035)
LOWES HOME CENTERS LLC
Also Called: Lowe's
14333 Bear Valley Rd (92392-5403)
PHONE.................................760 949-9565
Shawn Pierson, *Mgr*
EMP: 89
SALES (corp-wide): 97.06B **Publicly Held**
Web: www.lowes.com
SIC: **5211** 5031 5722 5064 Home centers; Building materials, exterior; Household appliance stores; Electrical appliances, television and radio
HQ: Lowe's Home Centers, Llc
    1000 Lowes Blvd
    Mooresville NC
    336 658-4000

(P-7036)
LOWES HOME CENTERS LLC
Also Called: Lowe's
13500 Paxton St (91331-2352)
PHONE.................................818 686-4300
Mario Garza, *Brnch Mgr*
EMP: 98
SALES (corp-wide): 97.06B **Publicly Held**
Web: www.lowes.com
SIC: **5211** 5031 5722 5064 Home centers; Building materials, exterior; Household appliance stores; Electrical appliances, television and radio
HQ: Lowe's Home Centers, Llc
    1000 Lowes Blvd
    Mooresville NC
    336 658-4000

(P-7037)
LOWES HOME CENTERS LLC
Also Called: Lowe's
491 Bay Shore Blvd (94124-1508)
PHONE.................................415 486-8611
EMP: 125
SALES (corp-wide): 97.06B **Publicly Held**
Web: www.lowes.com
SIC: **5211** 5031 5722 5064 Home centers; Building materials, exterior; Household appliance stores; Electrical appliances, television and radio
HQ: Lowe's Home Centers, Llc
    1000 Lowes Blvd
    Mooresville NC
    336 658-4000

(P-7038)
LOWES HOME CENTERS LLC
Also Called: Lowe's
30472 Haun Rd (92584-6810)
PHONE.................................951 723-1930
Dave Jenkins, *Brnch Mgr*
EMP: 112
SALES (corp-wide): 97.06B **Publicly Held**
Web: www.lowes.com
SIC: **5211** 5031 5722 5064 Home centers; Building materials, exterior; Household appliance stores; Electrical appliances, television and radio
HQ: Lowe's Home Centers, Llc
    1000 Lowes Blvd
    Mooresville NC
    336 658-4000

(P-7039)
LOWES HOME CENTERS LLC
Also Called: Lowe's
2445 Golden Hill Rd (93446-6285)
PHONE.................................805 602-9051
EMP: 182
SALES (corp-wide): 97.06B **Publicly Held**
Web: www.lowes
SIC: **5211** 5031 5722 5064 Home centers; Building materials, exterior; Household appliance stores; Electrical appliances, television and radio
HQ: Lowe's Home Centers, Llc
    1000 Lowes Blvd
    Mooresville NC
    336 658-4000

(P-7040)
LOWES HOME CENTERS LLC
Also Called: Lowe's
800 E Bidwell St (95630-3350)
PHONE.................................916 984-7979
Dave Ward, *Ofcr*
EMP: 115
SALES (corp-wide): 97.06B **Publicly Held**
Web: www.lowes.com
SIC: **5211** 5031 5722 5064 Home centers; Building materials, exterior; Household appliance stores; Electrical appliances, television and radio
HQ: Lowe's Home Centers, Llc
    1000 Lowes Blvd
    Mooresville NC
    336 658-4000

(P-7041)
LOWES HOME CENTERS LLC
Also Called: Lowe's
907 Avenida Pico (92673-3908)
PHONE.................................949 369-4644
Sonya Olmedo, *Mgr*
EMP: 179
SALES (corp-wide): 97.06B **Publicly Held**
Web: www.lowes.com
SIC: **5211** 5031 5722 5064 Home centers; Building materials, exterior; Household appliance stores; Electrical appliances, television and radio
HQ: Lowe's Home Centers, Llc
    1000 Lowes Blvd
    Mooresville NC
    336 658-4000

(P-7042)
LOWES HOME CENTERS LLC
Also Called: Lowe's
775 Ridder Park Dr (95131-2489)
PHONE.................................408 518-4165
EMP: 81
SALES (corp-wide): 97.06B **Publicly Held**
Web: www.lowes.com
SIC: **5211** 5031 5722 5064 Home centers; Building materials, exterior; Household appliance stores; Electrical appliances, television and radio
HQ: Lowe's Home Centers, Llc
    1000 Lowes Blvd
    Mooresville NC
    336 658-4000

(P-7043)
LOWES HOME CENTERS LLC
Also Called: Lowe's
9851 Magnolia Ave (92503-3528)
PHONE.................................951 509-5500
Daniel Mergio, *Brnch Mgr*
EMP: 142
SALES (corp-wide): 97.06B **Publicly Held**
Web: www.lowes.com
SIC: **5211** 5031 5722 5064 Home centers; Building materials, exterior; Household appliance stores; Electrical appliances, television and radio
HQ: Lowe's Home Centers, Llc
    1000 Lowes Blvd
    Mooresville NC
    336 658-4000

(P-7044)
LOWES HOME CENTERS LLC
Also Called: Lowe's
78865 Highway 111 (92253-2003)
PHONE.................................760 771-5566
Ron Stewart, *Mgr*
EMP: 112
SALES (corp-wide): 97.06B **Publicly Held**
Web: www.lowes.com
SIC: **5211** 5031 5722 5064 Home centers; Building materials, exterior; Household appliance stores; Electrical appliances, television and radio
HQ: Lowe's Home Centers, Llc
    1000 Lowes Blvd
    Mooresville NC
    336 658-4000

(P-7045)
LOWES HOME CENTERS LLC
Also Called: Lowe's
14873 Carmenita Rd (90650-5232)
PHONE.................................562 926-0826
Patrick Cosley, *Mgr*
EMP: 79
SALES (corp-wide): 97.06B **Publicly Held**
Web: www.lowes.com
SIC: **5211** 5031 5722 5064 Home centers; Building materials, exterior; Household appliance stores; Electrical appliances, television and radio
HQ: Lowe's Home Centers, Llc
    1000 Lowes Blvd
    Mooresville NC
    336 658-4000

(P-7046)
LOWES HOME CENTERS LLC
Also Called: Lowe's
3400 N Texas St (94533-7242)
PHONE.................................707 207-2070
Susan Moores, *Brnch Mgr*
EMP: 139
SALES (corp-wide): 97.06B **Publicly Held**
Web: www.lowes.com
SIC: **5211** 5064 5722 Home centers; Electrical appliances, television and radio; Household appliance stores
HQ: Lowe's Home Centers, Llc
    1000 Lowes Blvd
    Mooresville NC
    336 658-4000

(P-7047)
LOWES HOME CENTERS LLC
Also Called: Lowe's
1751 E Monte Vista Ave (95688-3103)
PHONE.................................707 455-4400
EMP: 62
SALES (corp-wide): 97.06B **Publicly Held**
Web: www.lowes.com
SIC: **5211** 5031 5722 5064 Home centers; Building materials, exterior; Household appliance stores; Electrical appliances, television and radio
HQ: Lowe's Home Centers, Llc
    1000 Lowes Blvd
    Mooresville NC
    336 658-4000

(P-7048)
LOWES HOME CENTERS LLC
Also Called: Lowe's
1951 Auto Center Dr (94509-3100)
PHONE.................................925 756-0370
Chris Cool, *Mgr*
EMP: 97
SALES (corp-wide): 97.06B **Publicly Held**
Web: www.lowes.com

(P-7049)
LOWES HOME CENTERS LLC
Also Called: Lowe's
8383 Topanga Canyon Blvd (91304-2343)
PHONE.................................818 610-1960
Pete Reed, *Brnch Mgr*
EMP: 143
SALES (corp-wide): 97.06B **Publicly Held**
Web: www.lowes.com
SIC: **5211** 5031 5722 5064 Home centers; Building materials, exterior; Household appliance stores; Electrical appliances, television and radio
HQ: Lowe's Home Centers, Llc
    1000 Lowes Blvd
    Mooresville NC
    336 658-4000

(P-7050)
LOWES HOME CENTERS LLC
Also Called: Lowe's
1659 W Foothill Blvd (91786-3533)
PHONE.................................909 982-4795
Dan Caganap, *Mgr*
EMP: 75
SALES (corp-wide): 97.06B **Publicly Held**
Web: www.lowes.com
SIC: **5211** 5031 5722 5064 Home centers; Building materials, exterior; Household appliance stores; Electrical appliances, television and radio
HQ: Lowe's Home Centers, Llc
    1000 Lowes Blvd
    Mooresville NC
    336 658-4000

(P-7051)
LOWES HOME CENTERS LLC
Also Called: Lowe's
32040 Union Lndg (94587-1769)
PHONE.................................510 476-0600
Nick Perry, *Mgr*
EMP: 97
SALES (corp-wide): 97.06B **Publicly Held**
Web: www.lowes.com
SIC: **5211** 5031 7389 Home centers; Building materials, exterior; Interior designer
HQ: Lowe's Home Centers, Llc
    1000 Lowes Blvd
    Mooresville NC
    336 658-4000

(P-7052)
LOWES HOME CENTERS LLC
Also Called: Lowe's
1340 El Camino Real (94066-1304)
PHONE.................................650 616-7800
Chris Marino, *Mgr*
EMP: 105
SALES (corp-wide): 97.06B **Publicly Held**
Web: www.lowes.com
SIC: **5211** 5031 5722 5064 Home centers; Building materials, exterior; Household appliance stores; Electrical appliances, television and radio
HQ: Lowe's Home Centers, Llc
    1000 Lowes Blvd
    Mooresville NC
    336 658-4000

5211 - Lumber And Other Building Materials (P-7053)

(P-7053)
LOWES HOME CENTERS LLC
Also Called: Lowe's
5201 E Ramon Rd (92264-3600)
PHONE..................760 866-1901
Robert Richmond, Brnch Mgr
EMP: 143
SALES (corp-wide): 97.06B **Publicly Held**
Web: www.lowes.com
SIC: **5211** 5031 5722 5064 Home centers; Building materials, exterior; Household appliance stores; Electrical appliances, television and radio
HQ: Lowe's Home Centers, Llc
1000 Lowes Blvd
Mooresville NC
336 658-4000

(P-7054)
LOWES HOME CENTERS LLC
Also Called: Lowe's
10201 Fairway Dr (95678-1969)
PHONE..................916 771-7111
Chris Ralls, Brnch Mgr
EMP: 66
SALES (corp-wide): 97.06B **Publicly Held**
Web: www.lowes.com
SIC: **5211** 5031 5722 5064 Home centers; Building materials, exterior; Household appliance stores; Electrical appliances, television and radio
HQ: Lowe's Home Centers, Llc
1000 Lowes Blvd
Mooresville NC
336 658-4000

(P-7055)
LOWES HOME CENTERS LLC
Also Called: Lowe's
4255 1st St (94551-4967)
PHONE..................925 245-2440
Steve Harada, Mgr
EMP: 98
SALES (corp-wide): 97.06B **Publicly Held**
Web: www.lowes.com
SIC: **5211** 5031 5722 5064 Home centers; Building materials, exterior; Household appliance stores; Electrical appliances, television and radio
HQ: Lowe's Home Centers, Llc
1000 Lowes Blvd
Mooresville NC
336 658-4000

(P-7056)
LOWES HOME CENTERS LLC
Also Called: Lowe's
8369 Power Inn Rd (95624-3464)
PHONE..................916 688-1922
Barry Wood, Brnch Mgr
EMP: 108
SALES (corp-wide): 97.06B **Publicly Held**
Web: www.lowes.com
SIC: **5211** 5031 5722 5064 Home centers; Building materials, exterior; Household appliance stores; Electrical appliances, television and radio
HQ: Lowe's Home Centers, Llc
1000 Lowes Blvd
Mooresville NC
336 658-4000

(P-7057)
LOWES HOME CENTERS LLC
Also Called: Lowe's
2350 Forest Ave (95928-7600)
PHONE..................530 895-5130
Mike Marrs, Brnch Mgr
EMP: 75
SALES (corp-wide): 97.06B **Publicly Held**
Web: www.lowes.com
SIC: **5211** 5031 5722 5064 Home centers; Building materials, exterior; Household appliance stores; Electrical appliances, television and radio
HQ: Lowe's Home Centers, Llc
1000 Lowes Blvd
Mooresville NC
336 658-4000

(P-7058)
LOWES HOME CENTERS LLC
Also Called: Lowe's
2000 W Empire Ave (91504-3434)
PHONE..................818 557-2300
Chris Mcgilroy, Mgr
EMP: 129
SALES (corp-wide): 97.06B **Publicly Held**
Web: www.lowes.com
SIC: **5211** 5031 5722 5064 Home centers; Building materials, exterior; Household appliance stores; Electrical appliances, television and radio
HQ: Lowe's Home Centers, Llc
1000 Lowes Blvd
Mooresville NC
336 658-4000

(P-7059)
LOWES HOME CENTERS LLC
Also Called: Lowe's
1500 N Lemon St (92801-1204)
PHONE..................714 447-6140
Brian Hefel, Brnch Mgr
EMP: 92
SALES (corp-wide): 97.06B **Publicly Held**
Web: www.lowes.com
SIC: **5211** 5031 5722 5064 Home centers; Building materials, exterior; Household appliance stores; Electrical appliances, television and radio
HQ: Lowe's Home Centers, Llc
1000 Lowes Blvd
Mooresville NC
336 658-4000

(P-7060)
LOWES HOME CENTERS LLC
Also Called: Lowe's
155 Old Grove Rd (92057-1216)
PHONE..................760 966-7140
Mike Shratz, Mgr
EMP: 102
SALES (corp-wide): 97.06B **Publicly Held**
Web: www.lowes.com
SIC: **5211** 5031 5722 5064 Home centers; Building materials, exterior; Household appliance stores; Electrical appliances, television and radio
HQ: Lowe's Home Centers, Llc
1000 Lowes Blvd
Mooresville NC
336 658-4000

(P-7061)
LOWES HOME CENTERS LLC
Also Called: Lowe's
3645 E Hammer Ln (95212-2823)
PHONE..................209 956-7200
Rose Rozich, Brnch Mgr
EMP: 74
SALES (corp-wide): 97.06B **Publicly Held**
Web: www.lowes.com
SIC: **5211** 5031 5722 5064 Home centers; Building materials, exterior; Household appliance stores; Electrical appliances, television and radio
HQ: Lowe's Home Centers, Llc
1000 Lowes Blvd
Mooresville NC
336 658-4000

(P-7062)
LOWES HOME CENTERS LLC
Also Called: Lowe's
24701 Madison Ave (92562-9763)
PHONE..................951 461-8916
Scott Holland, Mgr
EMP: 109
SALES (corp-wide): 97.06B **Publicly Held**
Web: www.lowes.com
SIC: **5211** 5031 5722 5064 Home centers; Building materials, exterior; Household appliance stores; Electrical appliances, television and radio
HQ: Lowe's Home Centers, Llc
1000 Lowes Blvd
Mooresville NC
336 658-4000

(P-7063)
LOWES HOME CENTERS LLC
Also Called: Lowe's
151 Vista Village Dr (92083-4974)
PHONE..................760 631-6255
Bill Mobley, Brnch Mgr
EMP: 98
SALES (corp-wide): 97.06B **Publicly Held**
Web: www.lowes.com
SIC: **5211** 5031 5722 5064 Home centers; Building materials, exterior; Household appliance stores; Electrical appliances, television and radio
HQ: Lowe's Home Centers, Llc
1000 Lowes Blvd
Mooresville NC
336 658-4000

(P-7064)
LOWES HOME CENTERS LLC
Also Called: Hawthorne Lowe's
2800 W 120th St (90250-3338)
PHONE..................323 327-4000
Mike Bryant, Mgr
EMP: 135
SALES (corp-wide): 97.06B **Publicly Held**
Web: www.lowes.com
SIC: **5211** 5031 5722 5064 Home centers; Building materials, exterior; Household appliance stores; Electrical appliances, television and radio
HQ: Lowe's Home Centers, Llc
1000 Lowes Blvd
Mooresville NC
336 658-4000

(P-7065)
LOWES HOME CENTERS LLC
Also Called: Lowe's
8600 Washington Blvd (90660-3790)
PHONE..................562 942-9909
Jose Rodriquez, Brnch Mgr
EMP: 110
SALES (corp-wide): 97.06B **Publicly Held**
Web: www.lowes.com
SIC: **5211** 5031 5722 5064 Home centers; Building materials, exterior; Household appliance stores; Electrical appliances, television and radio
HQ: Lowe's Home Centers, Llc
1000 Lowes Blvd
Mooresville NC
336 658-4000

(P-7066)
LOWES HOME CENTERS LLC
Also Called: Lowe's
12400 Day St (92553-7501)
PHONE..................951 656-1859
David Jenkins, Mgr
EMP: 67
SALES (corp-wide): 97.06B **Publicly Held**
Web: www.lowes.com
SIC: **5211** 5031 5722 5064 Home centers; Building materials, exterior; Household appliance stores; Electrical appliances, television and radio
HQ: Lowe's Home Centers, Llc
1000 Lowes Blvd
Mooresville NC
336 658-4000

(P-7067)
LOWES HOME CENTERS LLC
Also Called: Lowe's
7151 Camino Arroyo (95020-7308)
PHONE..................408 413-6000
Joe Solis, Mgr
EMP: 72
SQ FT: 146,682
SALES (corp-wide): 97.06B **Publicly Held**
Web: www.lowes.com
SIC: **5211** 5031 5722 5064 Home centers; Building materials, exterior; Household appliance stores; Electrical appliances, television and radio
HQ: Lowe's Home Centers, Llc
1000 Lowes Blvd
Mooresville NC
336 658-4000

(P-7068)
LOWES HOME CENTERS LLC
Also Called: Lowe's
7840 Greenback Ln (95610-5910)
PHONE..................916 728-7800
Ron Latta, Mgr
EMP: 89
SALES (corp-wide): 97.06B **Publicly Held**
Web: www.lowes.com
SIC: **5211** 5031 5722 5064 Home centers; Building materials, exterior; Household appliance stores; Electrical appliances, television and radio
HQ: Lowe's Home Centers, Llc
1000 Lowes Blvd
Mooresville NC
336 658-4000

(P-7069)
LOWES HOME CENTERS LLC
Also Called: Lowe's
1380 S Beach Blvd (90631-6374)
PHONE..................562 690-5122
Ken Konkel, Mgr
EMP: 109
SALES (corp-wide): 97.06B **Publicly Held**
Web: www.lowes.com
SIC: **5211** 5031 5722 5064 Home centers; Building materials, exterior; Household appliance stores; Electrical appliances, television and radio
HQ: Lowe's Home Centers, Llc
1000 Lowes Blvd
Mooresville NC
336 658-4000

(P-7070)
LOWES HOME CENTERS LLC
Also Called: Lowe's
39500 Lowes Dr (93551-3754)
PHONE..................661 267-9888
Veronica Pinkui, Mgr
EMP: 74
SQ FT: 133,410
SALES (corp-wide): 97.06B **Publicly Held**
Web: www.lowes.com
SIC: **5211** 5031 5722 5064 Home centers; Building materials, exterior; Household appliance stores; Electrical appliances, television and radio
HQ: Lowe's Home Centers, Llc
1000 Lowes Blvd

PRODUCTS & SERVICES SECTION
5211 - Lumber And Other Building Materials (P-7088)

Mooresville NC
336 658-4000

(P-7071)
LOWES HOME CENTERS LLC
Also Called: Lowe's
40390 Winchester Rd (92591-5519)
PHONE..................951 296-1618
Rose Burns, *Mgr*
EMP: 141
SALES (corp-wide): 97.06B **Publicly Held**
Web: www.lowes.com
SIC: **5211** 5031 5722 5064 Home centers; Building materials, exterior; Household appliance stores; Electrical appliances, television and radio
HQ: Lowe's Home Centers, Llc
1000 Lowes Blvd
Mooresville NC
336 658-4000

(P-7072)
LOWES HOME CENTERS LLC
Also Called: Lowe's
22255 S Western Ave (90501-4106)
PHONE..................310 787-1469
Ricky Garcia, *Mgr*
EMP: 118
SALES (corp-wide): 97.06B **Publicly Held**
Web: www.lowes.com
SIC: **5211** 5031 5722 5064 Home centers; Building materials, exterior; Household appliance stores; Electrical appliances, television and radio
HQ: Lowe's Home Centers, Llc
1000 Lowes Blvd
Mooresville NC
336 658-4000

(P-7073)
LOWES HOME CENTERS LLC
Also Called: Lowe's
4144 S Mooney Blvd (93277-9144)
PHONE..................559 624-4300
Scott Roy, *Mgr*
EMP: 107
SQ FT: 134,561
SALES (corp-wide): 97.06B **Publicly Held**
Web: www.lowes.com
SIC: **5211** 5031 5722 5064 Home centers; Building materials, exterior; Household appliance stores; Electrical appliances, television and radio
HQ: Lowe's Home Centers, Llc
1000 Lowes Blvd
Mooresville NC
336 658-4000

(P-7074)
LOWES HOME CENTERS LLC
Also Called: Lowe's
2225 Otay Lakes Rd (91915-1001)
PHONE..................619 739-9060
EMP: 131
SALES (corp-wide): 97.06B **Publicly Held**
Web: www.lowes.com
SIC: **5211** 5031 5722 5064 Home centers; Building materials, exterior; Household appliance stores; Electrical appliances, television and radio
HQ: Lowe's Home Centers, Llc
1000 Lowes Blvd
Mooresville NC
336 658-4000

(P-7075)
LOWES HOME CENTERS LLC
Also Called: Lowe's
500 S Mills Rd (93003-3459)
PHONE..................805 675-8800
Glen Sueishi, *Mgr*
EMP: 97
SALES (corp-wide): 97.06B **Publicly Held**
Web: www.lowes.com
SIC: **5211** 5031 5722 5064 Home centers; Building materials, exterior; Household appliance stores; Electrical appliances, television and radio
HQ: Lowe's Home Centers, Llc
1000 Lowes Blvd
Mooresville NC
336 658-4000

(P-7076)
LOWES HOME CENTERS LLC
Also Called: Lowe's
1750 W Olive Ave (95348-1201)
PHONE..................209 385-5000
Terry Stewart, *Mgr*
EMP: 110
SALES (corp-wide): 97.06B **Publicly Held**
Web: www.lowes.com
SIC: **5211** 5031 5722 5064 Home centers; Building materials, exterior; Household appliance stores; Electrical appliances, television and radio
HQ: Lowe's Home Centers, Llc
1000 Lowes Blvd
Mooresville NC
336 658-4000

(P-7077)
LOWES HOME CENTERS LLC
Also Called: Lowe's
16851 Sierra Lakes Pkwy (92336-1226)
PHONE..................909 350-7900
Jan Hardy, *Mgr*
EMP: 162
SALES (corp-wide): 97.06B **Publicly Held**
Web: www.lowes.com
SIC: **5211** 5031 5722 5064 Home centers; Building materials, exterior; Household appliance stores; Electrical appliances, television and radio
HQ: Lowe's Home Centers, Llc
1000 Lowes Blvd
Mooresville NC
336 658-4000

(P-7078)
LOWES HOME CENTERS LLC
Also Called: Lowe's
875 Shaw Ave (93612-3911)
PHONE..................559 322-3000
John Metcalf, *Brnch Mgr*
EMP: 162
SALES (corp-wide): 97.06B **Publicly Held**
Web: www.lowes.com
SIC: **5211** 5031 5722 5064 Home centers; Building materials, exterior; Household appliance stores; Electrical appliances, television and radio
HQ: Lowe's Home Centers, Llc
1000 Lowes Blvd
Mooresville NC
336 658-4000

(P-7079)
LOWES HOME CENTERS LLC
Also Called: Lowe's
1285 Magnolia Ave (92879-2092)
PHONE..................951 256-9004
Jeff Fowler, *Brnch Mgr*
EMP: 80
SALES (corp-wide): 97.06B **Publicly Held**
Web: www.lowes.com
SIC: **5211** 5031 5722 5064 Home centers; Building materials, exterior; Household appliance stores; Electrical appliances, television and radio
HQ: Lowe's Home Centers, Llc
1000 Lowes Blvd
Mooresville NC
336 658-4000

(P-7080)
LOWES HOME CENTERS LLC
Also Called: Lowe's
1389 S Lower Sacramento Rd (95242)
PHONE..................209 339-2600
Erik Hajek, *Mgr*
EMP: 142
SALES (corp-wide): 97.06B **Publicly Held**
Web: www.lowes.com
SIC: **5211** 5031 5722 5064 Home centers; Building materials, exterior; Household appliance stores; Electrical appliances, television and radio
HQ: Lowe's Home Centers, Llc
1000 Lowes Blvd
Mooresville NC
336 658-4000

(P-7081)
LOWES HOME CENTERS LLC
Also Called: Lowe's
350 S Sanderson Ave (92545-9014)
PHONE..................951 492-7000
Randy Scott, *Mgr*
EMP: 79
SALES (corp-wide): 97.06B **Publicly Held**
Web: www.lowes.com
SIC: **5211** 5031 5722 5064 Home centers; Building materials, exterior; Household appliance stores; Electrical appliances, television and radio
HQ: Lowe's Home Centers, Llc
1000 Lowes Blvd
Mooresville NC
336 658-4000

(P-7082)
LOWES HOME CENTERS LLC
Also Called: Lowe's
9416 Mission Gorge Rd (92071-3847)
P.O. Box 710909 (92072-0909)
PHONE..................619 212-4100
Jim Andrews, *Mgr*
EMP: 110
SALES (corp-wide): 97.06B **Publicly Held**
Web: www.lowes.com
SIC: **5211** 5031 5722 5064 Home centers; Building materials, exterior; Household appliance stores; Electrical appliances, television and radio
HQ: Lowe's Home Centers, Llc
1000 Lowes Blvd
Mooresville NC
336 658-4000

(P-7083)
LOWES HOME CENTERS LLC
Also Called: Lowe's
1725 W Redlands Blvd (92373-8012)
PHONE..................909 307-8883
Jim Riley, *Mgr*
EMP: 92
SALES (corp-wide): 97.06B **Publicly Held**
Web: www.lowes.com
SIC: **5211** 5031 5722 5064 Home centers; Building materials, exterior; Household appliance stores; Electrical appliances, television and radio
HQ: Lowe's Home Centers, Llc
1000 Lowes Blvd
Mooresville NC
336 658-4000

(P-7084)
LOWES HOME CENTERS LLC
Also Called: Lowe's
730 W Avenue K (93534-6001)
PHONE..................661 341-9000
Pete Reed, *Genl Mgr*
EMP: 75
SALES (corp-wide): 97.06B **Publicly Held**
Web: www.lowes.com
SIC: **5211** 5031 5722 5064 Home centers; Building materials, exterior; Household appliance stores; Electrical appliances, television and radio
HQ: Lowe's Home Centers, Llc
1000 Lowes Blvd
Mooresville NC
336 658-4000

(P-7085)
LOWES HOME CENTERS LLC
Also Called: Lowe's
43612 Pacific Commons Blvd (94538-3808)
PHONE..................510 344-4920
Jason Mcnutt, *Mgr*
EMP: 87
SALES (corp-wide): 97.06B **Publicly Held**
Web: www.lowes.com
SIC: **5211** 5031 5722 5064 Home centers; Building materials, exterior; Household appliance stores; Electrical appliances, television and radio
HQ: Lowe's Home Centers, Llc
1000 Lowes Blvd
Mooresville NC
336 658-4000

(P-7086)
LOWES HOME CENTERS LLC
Also Called: Lowe's
2053 N Imperial Ave (92243-1324)
PHONE..................760 337-6700
Chad Manley, *Mgr*
EMP: 100
SALES (corp-wide): 97.06B **Publicly Held**
Web: www.lowes.com
SIC: **5211** 5031 5722 5064 Home centers; Building materials, exterior; Household appliance stores; Electrical appliances, television and radio
HQ: Lowe's Home Centers, Llc
1000 Lowes Blvd
Mooresville NC
336 658-4000

(P-7087)
LOWES HOME CENTERS LLC
Also Called: Lowe's
12189 Apple Valley Rd (92308-6702)
PHONE..................760 961-3000
Chris Horan, *Mgr*
EMP: 100
SALES (corp-wide): 97.06B **Publicly Held**
Web: www.lowes.com
SIC: **5211** 5031 5722 5064 Home centers; Building materials, exterior; Household appliance stores; Electrical appliances, television and radio
HQ: Lowe's Home Centers, Llc
1000 Lowes Blvd
Mooresville NC
336 658-4000

(P-7088)
LOWES HOME CENTERS LLC
Also Called: Lowe's
29335 Central Ave (92532-2212)
PHONE..................951 253-6000
A Nuseibtel, *Prin*
EMP: 120
SALES (corp-wide): 97.06B **Publicly Held**
Web: www.lowes.com

5211 - Lumber And Other Building Materials (P-7089)

SIC: **5211** 5031 5722 5064 Home centers; Building materials, exterior; Household appliance stores; Electrical appliances, television and radio
HQ: Lowe's Home Centers, Llc
    1000 Lowes Blvd
    Mooresville NC
    336 658-4000

(P-7089)
LOWES HOME CENTERS LLC
Also Called: Lowe's
1275 Simi Town Center Way (93065-0513)
PHONE.................................805 426-2780
Bob Derr, *Mgr*
EMP: 98
SALES (corp-wide): 97.06B **Publicly Held**
Web: www.lowes.com
SIC: **5211** 5031 5722 5064 Home centers; Building materials, exterior; Household appliance stores; Electrical appliances, television and radio
HQ: Lowe's Home Centers, Llc
    1000 Lowes Blvd
    Mooresville NC
    336 658-4000

(P-7090)
LOWES HOME CENTERS LLC
Also Called: Lowe's
19601 Nordhoff St (91324-2422)
PHONE.................................818 477-9022
Mark Harrison, *Store Mgr*
EMP: 75
SALES (corp-wide): 97.06B **Publicly Held**
Web: www.lowes.com
SIC: **5211** 5031 5722 5064 Home centers; Building materials, exterior; Household appliance stores; Electrical appliances, television and radio
HQ: Lowe's Home Centers, Llc
    1000 Lowes Blvd
    Mooresville NC
    336 658-4000

(P-7091)
LOWES HOME CENTERS LLC
Also Called: Lowe's
7921 Redwood Dr (94931-3032)
PHONE.................................707 242-5000
Dave Berlin, *Mgr*
EMP: 74
SALES (corp-wide): 97.06B **Publicly Held**
Web: www.lowes.com
SIC: **5211** 5031 5722 5064 Home centers; Building materials, exterior; Household appliance stores; Electrical appliances, television and radio
HQ: Lowe's Home Centers, Llc
    1000 Lowes Blvd
    Mooresville NC
    336 658-4000

(P-7092)
LOWES HOME CENTERS LLC
Also Called: Lowe's
12071 Industry Blvd (95642-9310)
PHONE.................................209 223-6140
EMP: 89
SALES (corp-wide): 97.06B **Publicly Held**
Web: www.lowes.com
SIC: **5211** 5031 5722 5064 Home centers; Building materials, exterior; Household appliance stores; Electrical appliances, television and radio
HQ: Lowe's Home Centers, Llc
    1000 Lowes Blvd
    Mooresville NC
    336 658-4000

(P-7093)
LOWES HOME CENTERS LLC
Also Called: Lowe's
811 E Arques Ave (94085-4523)
PHONE.................................408 470-1680
EMP: 131
SALES (corp-wide): 97.06B **Publicly Held**
Web: www.lowes.com
SIC: **5211** 5031 5722 5064 Home centers; Building materials, exterior; Household appliance stores; Electrical appliances, television and radio
HQ: Lowe's Home Centers, Llc
    1000 Lowes Blvd
    Mooresville NC
    336 658-4000

(P-7094)
LOWES HOME CENTERS LLC
Also Called: Lowe's
1200 E Cypress Ave (96002-1162)
PHONE.................................530 351-0181
Kevin Lowe, *Ofcr*
EMP: 62
SALES (corp-wide): 97.06B **Publicly Held**
Web: www.lowes.com
SIC: **5211** 5031 5722 5064 Home centers; Building materials, exterior; Household appliance stores; Electrical appliances, television and radio
HQ: Lowe's Home Centers, Llc
    1000 Lowes Blvd
    Mooresville NC
    336 658-4000

(P-7095)
LOWES HOME CENTERS LLC
Also Called: Lowe's
2390 S Grove Ave (91761-4808)
PHONE.................................909 969-9053
Myarna Zega, *Mgr*
EMP: 120
SALES (corp-wide): 97.06B **Publicly Held**
Web: www.lowes.com
SIC: **5211** 5031 5722 5064 Home centers; Building materials, exterior; Household appliance stores; Electrical appliances, television and radio
HQ: Lowe's Home Centers, Llc
    1000 Lowes Blvd
    Mooresville NC
    336 658-4000

(P-7096)
LOWES HOME CENTERS LLC
Also Called: Lowe's
1145 E Prosperity Ave (93274-8030)
PHONE.................................559 366-5000
Eric Locke, *Mgr*
EMP: 64
SALES (corp-wide): 97.06B **Publicly Held**
Web: www.lowes.com
SIC: **5211** 5031 5722 5064 Home centers; Building materials, exterior; Household appliance stores; Electrical appliances, television and radio
HQ: Lowe's Home Centers, Llc
    1000 Lowes Blvd
    Mooresville NC
    336 658-4000

(P-7097)
LOWES HOME CENTERS LLC
Also Called: Lowe's
620 W Mission Ave (92025-1611)
PHONE.................................760 484-5113
Bill Mobley, *Mgr*
EMP: 146
SALES (corp-wide): 97.06B **Publicly Held**
Web: www.lowes.com

(P-7098)
LOWES HOME CENTERS LLC
Also Called: Lowe's
935 Tharp Rd (95993-8998)
PHONE.................................530 844-5000
Matt Heichlinger, *Mgr*
EMP: 61
SALES (corp-wide): 97.06B **Publicly Held**
Web: www.lowes.com
SIC: **5211** 5031 5722 5064 Home centers; Building materials, exterior; Household appliance stores; Electrical appliances, television and radio
HQ: Lowe's Home Centers, Llc
    1000 Lowes Blvd
    Mooresville NC
    336 658-4000

(P-7099)
LOWES HOME CENTERS LLC
Also Called: Lowe's
3303 Entertainment Way (95380-8437)
PHONE.................................209 656-3020
Rick Christman, *Mgr*
EMP: 97
SALES (corp-wide): 97.06B **Publicly Held**
Web: www.lowes.com
SIC: **5211** 5031 5722 5064 Home centers; Building materials, exterior; Household appliance stores; Electrical appliances, television and radio
HQ: Lowe's Home Centers, Llc
    1000 Lowes Blvd
    Mooresville NC
    336 658-4000

(P-7100)
LOWES HOME CENTERS LLC
Also Called: Lowe's
1601 Columbus St (93305-2133)
PHONE.................................661 889-9000
Francisco Dubon, *Brnch Mgr*
EMP: 146
SALES (corp-wide): 97.06B **Publicly Held**
Web: www.lowes.com
SIC: **5211** 5031 5722 5064 Home centers; Building materials, exterior; Household appliance stores; Electrical appliances, television and radio
HQ: Lowe's Home Centers, Llc
    1000 Lowes Blvd
    Mooresville NC
    336 658-4000

(P-7101)
LOWES HOME CENTERS LLC
Also Called: Lowe's
17789 Castleton St (91748-1706)
PHONE.................................626 217-1133
Robert Dominguez, *Brnch Mgr*
EMP: 66
SALES (corp-wide): 97.06B **Publicly Held**
Web: www.lowes.com
SIC: **5211** 5031 5722 5064 Home centers; Building materials, exterior; Household appliance stores; Electrical appliances, television and radio
HQ: Lowe's Home Centers, Llc
    1000 Lowes Blvd
    Mooresville NC
    336 658-4000

(P-7102)
LOWES HOME CENTERS LLC
Also Called: Lowe's
3251 Zinfandel Dr (95670-6378)
PHONE.................................916 267-2850
Randy Sergeant, *Brnch Mgr*
EMP: 139
SALES (corp-wide): 97.06B **Publicly Held**
Web: www.lowes.com
SIC: **5211** 5031 5722 5064 Home centers; Building materials, exterior; Household appliance stores; Electrical appliances, television and radio
HQ: Lowe's Home Centers, Llc
    1000 Lowes Blvd
    Mooresville NC
    336 658-4000

(P-7103)
LOWES HOME CENTERS LLC
Also Called: Lowe's
2500 Park Ave (92782-2712)
PHONE.................................714 913-2663
Nico Zavala, *Mgr*
EMP: 107
SALES (corp-wide): 97.06B **Publicly Held**
Web: www.lowes.com
SIC: **5211** 5031 5722 5064 Home centers; Building materials, exterior; Household appliance stores; Electrical appliances, television and radio
HQ: Lowe's Home Centers, Llc
    1000 Lowes Blvd
    Mooresville NC
    336 658-4000

(P-7104)
LOWES HOME CENTERS LLC
Also Called: Lowe's
3750 Dublin Blvd (94568-7352)
PHONE.................................925 241-3082
Sly Renard, *Genl Mgr*
EMP: 79
SALES (corp-wide): 97.06B **Publicly Held**
Web: www.lowes.com
SIC: **5211** 5031 5722 5064 Home centers; Building materials, exterior; Household appliance stores; Electrical appliances, television and radio
HQ: Lowe's Home Centers, Llc
    1000 Lowes Blvd
    Mooresville NC
    336 658-4000

(P-7105)
LOWES HOME CENTERS LLC
Also Called: Lowe's
500 W Vandalia Ave (93257-5912)
PHONE.................................559 306-5000
Bryan Bernard, *Mgr*
EMP: 120
SALES (corp-wide): 97.06B **Publicly Held**
Web: www.lowes.com
SIC: **5211** 5031 5722 5064 Home centers; Building materials, exterior; Household appliance stores; Electrical appliances, television and radio
HQ: Lowe's Home Centers, Llc
    1000 Lowes Blvd
    Mooresville NC
    336 658-4000

(P-7106)
LOWES HOME CENTERS LLC
Also Called: Lowe's
2100 W Cleveland Ave (93637-8756)
PHONE.................................559 416-4000
Jay Mahabir, *Brnch Mgr*
EMP: 80
SALES (corp-wide): 97.06B **Publicly Held**

PRODUCTS & SERVICES SECTION — 5251 - Hardware Stores (P-7124)

Web: www.lowes.com
SIC: **5211** 5031 5722 5064 Home centers; Building materials, exterior; Household appliance stores; Electrical appliances, television and radio
HQ: Lowe's Home Centers, Llc
1000 Lowes Blvd
Mooresville NC
336 658-4000

(P-7107)
LOWES HOME CENTERS LLC
Also Called: Lowe's
4777 Chino Hills Pkwy (91709-5849)
PHONE..................................909 438-9000
EMP: 123
SALES (corp-wide): 97.06B **Publicly Held**
Web: www.lowes.com
SIC: **5211** 5031 5722 5064 Home centers; Building materials, exterior; Household appliance stores; Electrical appliances, television and radio
HQ: Lowe's Home Centers, Llc
1000 Lowes Blvd
Mooresville NC
336 658-4000

(P-7108)
LOWES HOME CENTERS LLC
Also Called: Lowe's
19001 Golden Valley Rd (91387-1471)
PHONE..................................661 678-4430
Veronica January, *Brnch Mgr*
EMP: 109
SALES (corp-wide): 97.06B **Publicly Held**
Web: www.lowes.com
SIC: **5211** 5031 5722 5064 Home centers; Building materials, exterior; Household appliance stores; Electrical appliances, television and radio
HQ: Lowe's Home Centers, Llc
1000 Lowes Blvd
Mooresville NC
336 658-4000

(P-7109)
LOWES HOME CENTERS LLC
Also Called: Lowe's
1955 W Lacey Blvd (93230-7439)
PHONE..................................559 410-9000
Garrett Barth, *Brnch Mgr*
EMP: 162
SALES (corp-wide): 97.06B **Publicly Held**
Web: www.lowes.com
SIC: **5211** 5031 5722 5064 Home centers; Building materials, exterior; Household appliance stores; Electrical appliances, television and radio
HQ: Lowe's Home Centers, Llc
1000 Lowes Blvd
Mooresville NC
336 658-4000

(P-7110)
LOWES HOME CENTERS LLC
Also Called: Lowe's
27847 Greenspot Rd (92346-4381)
PHONE..................................909 557-9010
EMP: 74
SALES (corp-wide): 97.06B **Publicly Held**
Web: www.lowes.com
SIC: **5211** 5031 5722 5064 Home centers; Building materials, exterior; Household appliance stores; Electrical appliances, television and radio
HQ: Lowe's Home Centers, Llc
1000 Lowes Blvd
Mooresville NC
336 658-4000

(P-7111)
LOWES HOME CENTERS LLC
Also Called: Lowe's
1935 Arnold Industrial Way (94520-5312)
PHONE..................................925 566-9000
EMP: 87
SALES (corp-wide): 97.06B **Publicly Held**
Web: www.lowes.com
SIC: **5211** 5031 5722 5064 Home centers; Building materials, exterior; Household appliance stores; Electrical appliances, television and radio
HQ: Lowe's Home Centers, Llc
1000 Lowes Blvd
Mooresville NC
336 658-4000

(P-7112)
PARAGON INDUSTRIES INC
Also Called: Bedrosian's Tiles & Stone
1515 E Winston Rd (92805-6445)
PHONE..................................714 778-1800
Diana Kelly, *Pr*
EMP: 100
SALES (corp-wide): 251.57MM **Privately Held**
Web: www.bedrosians.com
SIC: **5211** 5032 Tile, ceramic; Brick, stone, and related material
PA: Paragon Industries, Inc.
4285 N Golden State Blvd
Fresno CA
559 275-5000

(P-7113)
WESTERN BUILDING MATERIALS CO (PA)
4620 E Olive Ave (93702-1660)
PHONE..................................559 454-8500
Peter Hastrup, *Pr*
EMP: 60 EST: 1967
SQ FT: 32,000
SALES (est): 12.85MM
SALES (corp-wide): 12.85MM **Privately Held**
Web: western-building-materials-co-in-fresno-ca.cityfos.com
SIC: **5211** 1742 Millwork and lumber; Acoustical and ceiling work

---

5231 Paint, Glass, And Wallpaper Stores

(P-7114)
DONS MOBILE GLASS INC (PA)
Also Called: Wardrobe and Bath Specialties
3800 Finch Rd (95357-4100)
PHONE..................................209 548-7000
TOLL FREE: 800
Stephen W Mort, *Pr*
Bill Manuel, *
Robert Serpa, *
Clinton Mort, *
▲ EMP: 60 EST: 1960
SQ FT: 60,000
SALES (est): 47.56MM
SALES (corp-wide): 47.56MM **Privately Held**
Web: www.donsmobileglass.com
SIC: **5231** 5039 Glass; Glass construction materials

5251 Hardware Stores

(P-7115)
C B TOOL & SUPPLY INC
Also Called: Peninsula Power Tool
1045 Memorex Dr (95050-2809)
PHONE..................................916 568-7514
TOLL FREE: 800
▲ EMP: 70
SIC: **5251** 5084 Tools, hand; Industrial machinery and equipment

(P-7116)
CHA-DOR REALTY LLC
Also Called: Meek's
2763 Lake Tahoe Blvd (96150-7724)
P.O. Box 7647 (96158-0647)
PHONE..................................530 544-2237
Mike Willford, *Brnch Mgr*
EMP: 101
SQ FT: 28,515
SALES (corp-wide): 23.63MM **Privately Held**
Web: www.doitbest.com
SIC: **5251** 5031 Hardware stores; Lumber: rough, dressed, and finished
PA: Cha-Dor Realty Llc
1651 Response Rd Ste 200
Sacramento CA
916 565-1586

(P-7117)
D & J LUMBER CO INC (PA)
Also Called: Ace Hardware
600 Tennant Ave (95037-5519)
P.O. Box 7 (95038-0007)
PHONE..................................408 778-1550
Michael Johnson, *Pr*
Michael Seda, *
EMP: 70 EST: 1980
SQ FT: 20,000
SALES (est): 24.37MM
SALES (corp-wide): 24.37MM **Privately Held**
Web: www.johnson-lumber.com
SIC: **5251** 5031 5231 Hardware stores; Lumber: rough, dressed, and finished; Paint, glass, and wallpaper stores

(P-7118)
FOOTHILL HOME IMPROVEMENT CENTER INC
Also Called: Ace Hardware
15825 Foothill Blvd (92335-8046)
PHONE..................................909 355-3655
EMP: 60
SIC: **5251** 5072 5211 5031 Builders' hardware; Builders' hardware, nec; Lumber and other building materials; Lumber, plywood, and millwork

(P-7119)
GANAHL LUMBER COMPANY
Also Called: Benjamin Moore Authorized Ret
6586 Beach Blvd (90621-2903)
PHONE..................................714 522-2864
Chad Kidder, *Mgr*
EMP: 68
SALES (corp-wide): 781.96MM **Privately Held**
Web: www.ganahllumber.com
SIC: **5251** 5031 5231 Hardware stores; Lumber: rough, dressed, and finished; Paint, glass, and wallpaper stores
PA: Ganahl Lumber Company
1220 E Ball Rd
Anaheim CA
714 772-5444

(P-7120)
GANAHL LUMBER COMPANY
Also Called: Benjamin Moore Authorized Ret
10742 Los Alamitos Blvd (90720-2331)
PHONE..................................562 346-2100
Tom Barkley, *Brnch Mgr*
EMP: 68
SALES (corp-wide): 781.96MM **Privately Held**
Web: www.ganahllumber.com
SIC: **5251** 5231 5031 1751 Hardware stores; Paint; Lumber: rough, dressed, and finished ; Window and door (prefabricated) installation
PA: Ganahl Lumber Company
1220 E Ball Rd
Anaheim CA
714 772-5444

(P-7121)
GANAHL LUMBER COMPANY
Also Called: Benjamin Moore Authorized Ret
23132 Orange Ave (92630-4881)
PHONE..................................949 830-3600
EMP: 68
SALES (corp-wide): 781.96MM **Privately Held**
Web: www.ganahllumber.com
SIC: **5251** 5231 5211 5031 Hardware stores; Paint; Lumber products; Lumber: rough, dressed, and finished
PA: Ganahl Lumber Company
1220 E Ball Rd
Anaheim CA
714 772-5444

(P-7122)
HILLS FLAT LUMBER CO (PA)
380 Railroad Ave (95945-5909)
P.O. Box 1630 (95713-1630)
PHONE..................................530 273-6171
Edward J Pardini Junior, *CEO*
Jason Pardini, *
Kennan Pardini, *
Sandra Pardini, *
Edward J Pardini Junior, *Prin*
EMP: 80 EST: 1921
SQ FT: 12,000
SALES (est): 47.57MM
SALES (corp-wide): 47.57MM **Privately Held**
Web: www.hillsflatlumber.com
SIC: **5251** 5031 5193 5999 Hardware stores; Doors and windows; Nursery stock; Plumbing and heating supplies

(P-7123)
LUMBER CITY CORP
Also Called: Do It Center
2695 Cochran St (93065-2664)
PHONE..................................805 522-0533
Mike Mckenzie, *Mgr*
EMP: 69
SALES (corp-wide): 51.36MM **Privately Held**
Web: www.doitbest.com
SIC: **5251** 5211 0181 Hardware stores; Lumber and other building materials; Ornamental nursery products
PA: Lumber City Corp.
20525 Nordhoff St Ste 210
Chatsworth CA
818 407-3888

(P-7124)
MORRIS LEVIN AND SON
Also Called: Morris Levin Rentl & Parts Ctr
1816 S K St (93274-6842)
PHONE..................................559 686-8665
Paul Atlas, *Pr*

5261 - Retail Nurseries And Garden Stores (P-7125)

Marilyn Atlas, *
David Atlas, *
EMP: 125 **EST:** 1934
SQ FT: 40,000
SALES (est): 22.95MM **Privately Held**
Web: www.morrislevin.com
SIC: 5251 1711 7359 Hardware stores; Plumbing, heating, air-conditioning; Rental store, general

5261 Retail Nurseries And Garden Stores

(P-7125)
DESCANSO GARDENS GUILD INC
1418 Descanso Dr (91011-3102)
PHONE..............................818 952-4408
David Brown, *CEO*
EMP: 65 **EST:** 1960
SQ FT: 1,000
SALES (est): 16.7MM **Privately Held**
Web: www.descansogardens.org
SIC: 5261 8399 Retail nurseries and garden stores; Fund raising organization, non-fee basis

(P-7126)
GREEN THUMB INTERNATIONAL INC
Also Called: Green Thumb Nurseries
23734 Newhall Ave (91321-3125)
PHONE..............................661 259-1071
Bryan Payne, *Mgr*
EMP: 86
SALES (corp-wide): 24.03MM **Privately Held**
Web: www.greenthumb.com
SIC: 5261 5712 5193 0782 Nursery stock, seeds and bulbs; Outdoor and garden furniture; Nursery stock; Sodding contractor
PA: Green Thumb International Inc
   7105 Jordan Ave
   Canoga Park CA
   818 340-6400

5271 Mobile Home Dealers

(P-7127)
PACIFIC HOUSING GROUP LLC
1356 S Buttonwillow Ave (93654-9333)
PHONE..............................559 651-1133
George Bravante Junior, *Pt*
EMP: 70 **EST:** 1997
SALES (est): 2.37MM **Privately Held**
SIC: 5271 1799 Mobile home dealers; Mobile home site set up and tie down

5311 Department Stores

(P-7128)
PENNEY OPCO LLC
Also Called: JCP
2115 S Mooney Blvd (93277-6242)
PHONE..............................559 732-4171
Tommy Ramirez, *Genl Mgr*
EMP: 77
SALES (corp-wide): 1.93B **Privately Held**
SIC: 5311 7231 7221 Department stores, non-discount; Beauty shops; Photographic studios, portrait
HQ: Penney Opco Llc
   6501 Legacy Dr Ste B100
   Plano TX
   972 431-4746

(P-7129)
PENNEY OPCO LLC
Also Called: JC Penney
1695 Arden Way (95815-4004)
PHONE..............................916 564-0315
Wayne Schlaefli, *Mgr*
EMP: 205
SQ FT: 200,000
SALES (corp-wide): 1.93B **Privately Held**
SIC: 5311 7231 Department stores, non-discount; Beauty shops
HQ: Penney Opco Llc
   6501 Legacy Dr Ste B100
   Plano TX
   972 431-4746

(P-7130)
PENNEY OPCO LLC
Also Called: JC Penney
400 S Baldwin Ave Lowr (91007-1909)
PHONE..............................626 445-6454
Jeff Paige, *Mgr*
EMP: 104
SALES (corp-wide): 1.93B **Privately Held**
SIC: 5311 7231 Department stores, non-discount; Beauty shops
HQ: Penney Opco Llc
   6501 Legacy Dr Ste B100
   Plano TX
   972 431-4746

(P-7131)
PENNEY OPCO LLC
Also Called: JC Penney
280 W Hillcrest Dr (91360-4210)
PHONE..............................805 497-6811
M Kline, *Brnch Mgr*
EMP: 131
SALES (corp-wide): 1.93B **Privately Held**
SIC: 5311 7231 5995 Department stores, non-discount; Beauty shops; Optical goods stores
HQ: Penney Opco Llc
   6501 Legacy Dr Ste B100
   Plano TX
   972 431-4746

(P-7132)
PENNEY OPCO LLC
Also Called: JC Penney
4915 Claremont Ave (95207-5707)
PHONE..............................209 951-1110
Ralph Carino, *Mgr*
EMP: 170
SALES (corp-wide): 1.93B **Privately Held**
SIC: 5311 7231 7221 5995 Department stores, non-discount; Beauty shops; Photographic studios, portrait; Optical goods stores
HQ: Penney Opco Llc
   6501 Legacy Dr Ste B100
   Plano TX
   972 431-4746

(P-7133)
PENNEY OPCO LLC
Also Called: JC Penney 1505
1203 Plaza Dr (91790-2885)
PHONE..............................626 960-3711
Bob Watanabe, *Brnch Mgr*
EMP: 170
SALES (corp-wide): 1.93B **Privately Held**
SIC: 5311 7231 5995 Department stores, non-discount; Beauty shops; Optical goods stores
HQ: Penney Opco Llc
   6501 Legacy Dr Ste B100
   Plano TX
   972 431-4746

(P-7134)
PENNEY OPCO LLC
Also Called: JC Penney
1932 E 20th St (95928-6342)
PHONE..............................530 899-8160
Dave Oliver, *Mgr*
EMP: 166
SALES (corp-wide): 1.93B **Privately Held**
SIC: 5311 7231 5961 Department stores, non-discount; Beauty shops; Catalog and mail-order houses
HQ: Penney Opco Llc
   6501 Legacy Dr Ste B100
   Plano TX
   972 431-4746

(P-7135)
WALMART INC
Also Called: Walmart
1366 S Riverside Ave (92376-7608)
PHONE..............................909 820-9912
James Wright, *Mgr*
EMP: 243
SQ FT: 180,839
SALES (corp-wide): 611.29B **Publicly Held**
Web: corporate.walmart.com
SIC: 5311 7384 Department stores, discount; Film developing services
PA: Walmart Inc.
   702 Sw 8th St
   Bentonville AR
   479 640-8287

5331 Variety Stores

(P-7136)
CPL HOLDINGS LLC
12181 Bluff Creek Dr Ste 250 (90094-2992)
PHONE..............................310 348-6800
Patrick Gregory, *CFO*
Stephen Krenzer, *
EMP: 200 **EST:** 2012
SQ FT: 40,000
SALES (est): 22.35MM **Privately Held**
Web: www.coredigitalmedia.com
SIC: 5331 6719 5961 Variety stores; Investment holding companies, except banks; Electronic shopping

(P-7137)
GOODWILL INDS SOUTHERN CAL (PA)
342 N San Fernando Rd (90031-1730)
PHONE..............................323 223-1211
Patrick Mcclenahan, *Pr*
Michelle Tan, *
▲ **EMP:** 880 **EST:** 1919
SQ FT: 200,000
SALES (est): 279.59MM
SALES (corp-wide): 279.59MM **Privately Held**
Web: www.goodwillsocal.org
SIC: 5331 8331 Variety stores; Vocational rehabilitation agency

(P-7138)
NUMBER HOLDINGS INC (PA)
4000 Union Pacific Ave (90023-3202)
PHONE..............................323 980-8145
Frank J Schools, *
▲ **EMP:** 175 **EST:** 2011
SALES (est): 730.02MM
SALES (corp-wide): 730.02MM **Privately Held**
Web: www.99only.com
SIC: 5331 5199 Variety stores; General merchandise, non-durable

(P-7139)
PG USA LLC
Also Called: Pricegrabber.com
5150 W Goldleaf Cir (90056-1662)
PHONE..............................310 954-1040
◆ **EMP:** 85 **EST:** 1999
SALES (est): 11.82MM
SALES (corp-wide): 694.97MM **Privately Held**
SIC: 5331 4813 Variety stores; Online service providers
HQ: Connexity, Inc.
   2120 Colorado Ave Ste 400
   Santa Monica CA

5399 Miscellaneous General Merchandise

(P-7140)
COSTCO WHOLESALE CORPORATION
Also Called: Costco
1345 N Montebello Blvd (90640-2585)
PHONE..............................323 890-1904
EMP: 205
SIC: 5399 5014 Warehouse club stores; Automobile tires and tubes

(P-7141)
SMART & FINAL STORES LLC
Also Called: Smart & Final
10935 Firestone Blvd (90650-2242)
PHONE..............................562 868-0794
Jackie Turcios, *Mgr*
EMP: 84
SIC: 5399 4225 Warehouse club stores; General warehousing
HQ: Smart & Final Stores Llc
   600 Citadel Dr
   Commerce CA

5411 Grocery Stores

(P-7142)
BEL AIR MART
Also Called: Bel Air Market 525
9435 Elk Grove Blvd (95624-5013)
PHONE..............................916 714-6996
Gary Larrabee, *Mgr*
EMP: 97
SALES (corp-wide): 2.33B **Privately Held**
Web: www.raleys.com
SIC: 5411 4311 6099 Supermarkets, chain; U.S. postal service; Money order issuance
HQ: Bel Air Mart
   500 W Capitol Ave
   West Sacramento CA

(P-7143)
GROCERY OUTLET HOLDING CORP (PA)
5650 Hollis St (94608-2597)
PHONE..............................510 845-1999
Robert J Sheedy Junior, *Pr*
Eric J Lindberg Junior, *Ch Bd*
Charles C Bracher, *Ex VP*
Andrea R Bortner, *Chief Human Resources Officer*
Luke D Thompson, *Sr VP*
EMP: 470 **EST:** 1946
SALES (est): 3.58B
SALES (corp-wide): 3.58B **Publicly Held**
Web: www.groceryoutlet.com
SIC: 5411 5141 Grocery stores, independent; Groceries, general line

▲ = Import ▼ = Export
◆ = Import/Export

PRODUCTS & SERVICES SECTION

5499 - Miscellaneous Food Stores (P-7163)

(P-7144)
HOLZHEUS EL RANCHO MARKET INC
2886 Mission Dr (93463-9408)
PHONE.....................805 688-4300
EMP: 100 EST: 1966
SALES (est): 9.8MM Privately Held
Web: www.californiafreshmarket.com
SIC: 5411 5147 Grocery stores, independent ; Meats, fresh

(P-7145)
LUCKY STORES II LLC
Also Called: Save Mart
875 S Tracy Blvd (95376-4744)
PHONE.....................209 830-1977
EMP: 80 EST: 2011
SALES (est): 4.91MM Privately Held
SIC: 5411 5122 Grocery stores, chain; Pharmaceuticals

(P-7146)
MAJOR MARKET INC
Also Called: Major Market-Ftd Florist
845 S Main Ave (92028-3347)
PHONE.....................760 723-0857
John Elkon, Mgr
EMP: 122
SALES (corp-wide): 24.34MM Privately Held
Web: www.majormarketgrocery.com
SIC: 5411 7336 Supermarkets, chain; Commercial art and graphic design
PA: Major Market, Inc.
     845 S Main Ave
     Fallbrook CA
     760 723-0857

(P-7147)
PRESTIGE STATIONS INC (DH)
Also Called: Am/PM Mini Market
4 Centerpointe Dr (90623-1015)
PHONE.....................714 670-5145
John Lannan, VP
EMP: 200 EST: 1974
SQ FT: 7,000
SALES (est): 270.65MM
SALES (corp-wide): 241.39B Privately Held
Web: www.ampm.com
SIC: 5411 7549 5541 Convenience stores, chain; Automotive maintenance services; Filling stations, gasoline
HQ: Atlantic Richfield Company Inc
     4 Centerpointe Dr Ste 200
     La Palma CA
     800 333-3991

(P-7148)
ROF FERRARI LENDING 1 LLC
Also Called: A.G. Ferrari Foods
14234 Catalina St (94577-5512)
PHONE.....................510 351-5520
▲ EMP: 190
SIC: 5411 5149 2032 Grocery stores; Natural and organic foods; Italian foods, nec: packaged in cans, jars, etc.

(P-7149)
SAVE MART SUPERMARKETS DISC
Also Called: Save Mart
6797 N Milburn Ave (93722-2132)
PHONE.....................559 261-4123
Rick Hancock, Mgr
EMP: 89
SALES (corp-wide): 4.1B Privately Held
Web: www.savemart.com

SIC: 5411 7319 Supermarkets, chain; Shopping news, advertising and distributing service
PA: Save Mart Supermarkets Llc
     1800 Standiford Ave
     Modesto CA
     209 577-1600

(P-7150)
SAVE MART SUPERMARKETS DISC
Also Called: Save Mart
2237 Claribel Rd (95367-9473)
PHONE.....................209 863-1480
Tony Angoletta, Mgr
EMP: 99
SALES (corp-wide): 4.1B Privately Held
Web: www.savemart.com
SIC: 5411 5141 Supermarkets, chain; Groceries, general line
PA: Save Mart Supermarkets Llc
     1800 Standiford Ave
     Modesto CA
     209 577-1600

(P-7151)
SAVE MART SUPERMARKETS LLC (PA)
Also Called: S-Mart
1800 Standiford Ave (95350-0180)
P.O. Box 4278 (95352-4278)
PHONE.....................209 577-1600
Chris Mcgarry, CEO
Shane Sampson, *
Ali Sadiq, *
Hal Levitt Senior, Retail Operations Vice President
EMP: 250 EST: 1953
SQ FT: 34,000
SALES (est): 4.1B
SALES (corp-wide): 4.1B Privately Held
Web: www.thesavemartcompanies.com
SIC: 5411 5141 4213 4212 Supermarkets, chain; Groceries, general line; Refrigerated products transport; Local trucking, without storage

(P-7152)
SMART & FINAL STORES LLC
Also Called: Smart & Final
3400 White Ln (93309-6821)
PHONE.....................661 832-4540
Luis Mendizabel, Mgr
EMP: 60
SIC: 5411 5141 Supermarkets; Groceries, general line
HQ: Smart & Final Stores Llc
     600 Citadel Dr
     Commerce CA

(P-7153)
SUPER CENTER CONCEPTS INC
Also Called: Superior Super Warehouse
7300 Atlantic Ave (90201-4305)
PHONE.....................323 562-8980
Peter Buyn, Brnch Mgr
EMP: 122
Web: www.superiorgrocers.com
SIC: 5411 5421 2052 2051 Grocery stores, independent; Meat and fish markets; Cookies and crackers; Bread, cake, and related products
PA: Super Center Concepts, Inc.
     15510 Carmenita Rd
     Santa Fe Springs CA

(P-7154)
VONS COMPANIES INC
Also Called: Vons 2407
475 W Main St (92227-2244)

PHONE.....................760 351-3002
Frank Huerta, Mgr
EMP: 132
SALES (corp-wide): 77.65B Publicly Held
SIC: 5411 5912 2051 7384 Supermarkets, chain; Drug stores; Bread, cake, and related products; Photofinish laboratories
HQ: The Vons Companies Inc
     5918 Stoneridge Mall Rd
     Pleasanton CA
     925 467-3000

(P-7155)
WOOLTARI USA INC
17022 Montanero Ave Ste 2 (90746-1340)
PHONE.....................310 933-8648
Minhyuk Kim, CEO
EMP: 69
SALES (corp-wide): 6.53MM Privately Held
SIC: 5411 4225 Grocery stores; Miniwarehouse, warehousing
PA: Wooltari Usa, Inc.
     860 E 238th St
     Carson CA
     636 497-0550

5431 Fruit And Vegetable Markets

(P-7156)
CDF PARKWAY LLC (PA)
Also Called: Zanger Vineyards
10021 Pacheco Pass Hwy (95023-9541)
PHONE.....................408 842-7282
▲ EMP: 142 EST: 1908
SALES (est): 23.29MM
SALES (corp-wide): 23.29MM Privately Held
Web: www.casadefruta.com
SIC: 5431 0175 5812 5541 Fruit stands or markets; Deciduous tree fruits; Eating places; Gasoline service stations

(P-7157)
HERMAN PRODUCE SALES LLC
2370 W Cleveland Ave # 108 (93637-8742)
PHONE.....................559 661-8253
EMP: 98
SALES (corp-wide): 4.87MM Privately Held
SIC: 5431 5148 Fruit and vegetable markets; Fresh fruits and vegetables
PA: Herman Produce Sales Llc
     2985 Airport Dr
     Madera CA
     559 871-3161

5441 Candy, Nut, And Confectionery Stores

(P-7158)
GHIRARDELLI CHOCOLATE COMPANY (DH)
Also Called: Ghirardelli
1111 139th Ave (94578-2616)
PHONE.....................510 483-6970
Martin Thompson, CEO
◆ EMP: 375 EST: 1852
SQ FT: 210,000
SALES (est): 137.91MM Privately Held
Web: www.ghirardelli.com
SIC: 5441 2066 5812 5149 Candy; Chocolate ; Soda fountain; Chocolate
HQ: Lindt & Sprungli (Usa) Inc.
     1 Fine Chocolate Pl
     Stratham NH
     603 778-8100

5461 Retail Bakeries

(P-7159)
MADONNA INN INC
100 Madonna Rd (93405-5408)
PHONE.....................805 543-3000
Phyllis Madonna, CEO
EMP: 200 EST: 1951
SQ FT: 9,200
SALES (est): 24.31MM Privately Held
Web: www.madonnainn.com
SIC: 5461 5812 5813 7991 Retail bakeries; Cafe; Bar (drinking places); Spas

(P-7160)
MAMOLOS CNTNTL BAILEY BAKERIES
Also Called: Viktor Benes Bakeries
2734 Townsgate Rd (91361-2906)
PHONE.....................805 496-0045
Manigeh Tabataba, Mgr
EMP: 141
SALES (corp-wide): 9.89MM Privately Held
Web: www.viktorbenesbakery.com
SIC: 5461 5149 Cakes; Bakery products
PA: Mamolo's Continental & Bailey Bakeries Inc
     703 S Main St
     Burbank CA
     818 841-9347

5499 Miscellaneous Food Stores

(P-7161)
IHERB LLC (PA)
Also Called: Iherb House Brands
22780 Harley Knox Blvd Unit 101 (92570)
PHONE.....................951 616-3600
Emun Zabihi, *
◆ EMP: 1501 EST: 2001
SQ FT: 336,000
SALES (est): 1.64B
SALES (corp-wide): 1.64B Privately Held
Web: www.iherb.com
SIC: 5499 5122 Vitamin food stores; Drugs, proprietaries, and sundries

(P-7162)
PEETS COFFEE INC (DH)
Also Called: Peet's Coffee
1400 Park Ave (94608-3520)
P.O. Box 12509 (94712-3509)
PHONE.....................510 594-2100
David Burwick, Pr
Gerald Baldwin, Ch Bd
Patrick Odea, Pr
Shawn Conway, VP
Tom Cawley, VP
EMP: 75 EST: 1966
SQ FT: 60,000
SALES (est): 113.15MM Privately Held
Web: www.peets.com
SIC: 5499 2095 5149 Coffee; Roasted coffee ; Cat food
HQ: Peet's Coffee & Tea, Llc
     1400 Park Ave
     Emeryville CA
     510 594-2100

(P-7163)
TRIFECTA NUTRITION INC
428 J St Ste 800 (95814-2329)
PHONE.....................530 564-8388
Gregory Connolly, CEO
EMP: 85 EST: 2019
SALES (est): 14.38MM Privately Held

5511 - New And Used Car Dealers (P-7164)

Web: www.trifectanutrition.com
SIC: 5499 8099 Health foods; Nutrition services

5511 New And Used Car Dealers

(P-7164)
ADVANTAGE FORD LINCOLN MERCURY
Also Called: Advantage Ford
1031 Central Ave (91010-2424)
PHONE..................626 305-9188
Gary W Hoecker, *Pr*
EMP: 97 EST: 1997
SQ FT: 20,280
SALES (est): 21.57MM **Privately Held**
Web: www.advantageford.com
SIC: 5511 7532 Automobiles, new and used; Top and body repair and paint shops

(P-7165)
ALBANY FORD INC (PA)
Also Called: Albany Subaru
718 San Pablo Ave (94706-1131)
PHONE..................510 528-1244
John Nakamura, *Pr*
Donald Val Strough, *
Laurie Bush, *
EMP: 60 EST: 1990
SQ FT: 20,000
SALES (est): 27.89MM **Privately Held**
Web: www.albanyford.com
SIC: 5511 7538 Automobiles, new and used; General automotive repair shops

(P-7166)
ALHAMBRA MOTORS INC
Also Called: Goudy Honda
1400 W Main St (91801-1952)
PHONE..................626 576-1114
TOLL FREE: 800
EMP: 156 EST: 1958
SALES (est): 45.89MM **Privately Held**
Web: www.goudyhonda.com
SIC: 5511 7521 Automobiles, new and used; Automobile parking

(P-7167)
ALLEN GWYNN CHEVROLET INC
Also Called: Allen Gwynn Chevrolet
1400 S Brand Blvd (91204-2895)
PHONE..................818 240-0000
Gwynn G Bacon, *Pr*
James Bacon, *Prin*
Virginia Bacon, *Prin*
EMP: 76 EST: 1930
SALES (est): 31.69MM **Privately Held**
Web: www.lovemychevy.com
SIC: 5511 7515 Automobiles, new and used; Passenger car leasing

(P-7168)
ALLEN/CLARK CADILLAC
Also Called: Crestview Cadillac
2700 E Garvey Ave S (91791-2114)
PHONE..................626 966-7441
TOLL FREE: 800
Scott Allen, *Pr*
▲ EMP: 68 EST: 1957
SQ FT: 10,000
SALES (est): 17.97MM **Privately Held**
Web: www.crestview-cadillac.com
SIC: 5511 5531 7549 Automobiles, new and used; Automotive parts; Do-it-yourself garages

(P-7169)
AMERICAN SUZUKI MOTOR CORPORATION
3251 E Imperial Hwy (92821-6722)
P.O. Box 1100 (92822-1100)
PHONE..................714 996-7040
◆ EMP: 382
SIC: 5511 5571 5091 5013 Automobiles, new and used; Motorcycle dealers; Outboard motors; Motor vehicle supplies and new parts

(P-7170)
BARGAIN RENT-A-CAR
Also Called: Lexus of Cerritos
18800 Studebaker Rd (90703-5339)
PHONE..................562 865-7447
Afshin Kahensohayegh, *Mgr*
Lewis M Webb, *
Jerry Heuer, *Acting Secretary*
EMP: 130 EST: 1960
SALES (est): 50.96MM
SALES (corp-wide): 26.98B **Publicly Held**
Web: www.cerritoslexus.com
SIC: 5511 5521 5012 Automobiles, new and used; Used car dealers; Automobiles and other motor vehicles
HQ: Webb Automotive Group, Inc.
200 Sw 1st Ave
Fort Lauderdale FL
954 769-7000

(P-7171)
BERBERIAN BROS INC
Also Called: Volvo
3755 Nw Ln (95204-2431)
P.O. Box 8790 (95208-0790)
PHONE..................209 944-5514
Brian Marricci, *Mgr*
EMP: 62
SALES (corp-wide): 24.4MM **Privately Held**
Web: www.mbusa.com
SIC: 5511 7538 Automobiles, new and used; Engine repair
PA: Berberian Bros., Inc.
5200 N Palm Ave Ste 203
Fresno CA
559 230-0134

(P-7172)
BIG VALLEY FORD INC
Also Called: Quick Lane
3282 Auto Center Cir (95212-2836)
P.O. Box 690398 (95269-0398)
PHONE..................209 870-4400
Paul Joseph Umdenstock, *Pr*
Darlene Gibbons, *
EMP: 150 EST: 1982
SQ FT: 10,000
SALES (est): 51.17MM **Privately Held**
Web: www.bigvalleyford.biz
SIC: 5511 7538 Automobiles, new and used; General automotive repair shops

(P-7173)
BOB BAKER VOLKSWAGEN
Also Called: Bob Baker Chrysler-Plymouth
5500 Paseo Del Norte (92008-4428)
P.O. Box 2129 (92067-2129)
PHONE..................760 438-2200
Michael Baker, *Pr*
Micheal Baker, *
Tom Solomon, *
William Kornik, *General Vice President*
Michelle Wagstaff, *
EMP: 90 EST: 1975
SALES (est): 22.65MM
SALES (corp-wide): 111.45MM **Privately Held**
Web: www.autonationvolkswagencarlsbad.com
SIC: 5511 7538 5531 Automobiles, new and used; General automotive repair shops; Automotive parts
PA: Bob Baker Enterprises, Inc.
591 Camino De La Reina
San Diego CA
619 683-5591

(P-7174)
BOB STALL CHEVROLET
7601 Alvarado Rd (91942-8211)
P.O. Box 339 (91944-0339)
PHONE..................619 460-1311
John Stall, *CEO*
Thomas Stall, *
EMP: 110 EST: 1958
SALES (est): 25.02MM **Privately Held**
Web: www.bobstall.com
SIC: 5511 7538 Automobiles, new and used; General automotive repair shops

(P-7175)
BONANDER AUTO TRUCK & TRLR INC (PA)
Also Called: Bonander Pontiac-Buick-Gmc
231 S Center St (95380-4918)
PHONE..................209 632-8871
Donald E Bonander, *Pr*
Eileen Weston, *
EMP: 60 EST: 1937
SQ FT: 15,000
SALES (est): 49.85MM
SALES (corp-wide): 49.85MM **Privately Held**
Web: www.bonanderbuickgmc.com
SIC: 5511 7539 5012 Automobiles, new and used; Automotive repair shops, nec; Trailers for trucks, new and used

(P-7176)
BOULEVARD AUTOMOTIVE GROUP (PA)
Also Called: Boulevard Collision Center
2850 Cherry Ave (90755-1909)
PHONE..................562 492-1000
EMP: 83 EST: 1961
SALES (est): 16.05MM
SALES (corp-wide): 16.05MM **Privately Held**
Web: www.boulevard4u.com
SIC: 5511 7538 Automobiles, new and used; General automotive repair shops

(P-7177)
BRECHT ENTERPRISES INC
Also Called: Brecht BMW
1555 Auto Park Way (92029-2003)
P.O. Box 461089 (92046-1089)
PHONE..................760 745-3000
TOLL FREE: 888
EMP: 100 EST: 1985
SQ FT: 56,000
SALES (est): 33.49MM **Privately Held**
Web: www.bmwofescondido.com
SIC: 5511 5571 6159 5013 Automobiles, new and used; Motorcycle dealers; Equipment and vehicle finance leasing companies; Automotive supplies and parts

(P-7178)
CABE BROTHERS
Also Called: Cabe Toyota
2895 Long Beach Blvd (90806-1533)
PHONE..................562 595-7411
John Cabe, *Pr*
Marilyn Gidden, *
Glenda Favilla, *
Myra Cabe, *
EMP: 81 EST: 1956
SQ FT: 11,080
SALES (est): 40.6MM **Privately Held**
Web: www.cabetoyota.com
SIC: 5511 7538 Automobiles, new and used; General automotive repair shops

(P-7179)
CAPITOLA IMPORTS INC
Also Called: Toyota of Santa Cruz
4200 Auto Plaza Dr (95010-2073)
PHONE..................831 462-4200
Charles L Canfield, *Pr*
EMP: 140 EST: 1985
SALES (est): 23.35MM **Privately Held**
Web: www.toyota.com
SIC: 5511 7549 Automobiles, new and used; Automotive maintenance services

(P-7180)
CENTER AUTOMOTIVE INC
Also Called: Center B M W
5201 Van Nuys Blvd (91401-5618)
P.O. Box 3870 (91031-6870)
PHONE..................818 907-9995
EMP: 85 EST: 1968
SQ FT: 50,000
SALES (est): 27.92MM **Privately Held**
Web: www.bmwshermanoaks.com
SIC: 5511 5012 Automobiles, new and used; Automobiles and other motor vehicles

(P-7181)
CENTRAL VALLEY TRLR REPR INC
Also Called: Cvtr
2974 S East Ave (93725-1911)
P.O. Box 12427 (93777-2427)
PHONE..................559 233-8444
TOLL FREE: 800
Michael L Shuemake, *Pr*
Lou Shuemake, *
EMP: 80 EST: 1984
SQ FT: 24,000
SALES (est): 40.97MM **Privately Held**
Web: www.cvtr.com
SIC: 5511 7538 7539 5531 Trucks, tractors, and trailers: new and used; General truck repair; Trailer repair; Truck equipment and parts

(P-7182)
CENTURY WEST LLC
4245 Lankershim Blvd (91602-2802)
PHONE..................818 432-5800
Dennis Lin, *Pr*
EMP: 92 EST: 1995
SALES (est): 30.88MM **Privately Held**
Web: www.centurywestbmw.com
SIC: 5511 7538 Automobiles, new and used; General automotive repair shops

(P-7183)
CHASE CHEVROLET CO INC
Also Called: Chase Chvrlet Chevy Trck World
6441 Holman Rd (95212-2703)
P.O. Box 8349 (95208-0349)
PHONE..................209 475-6600
John W Chase, *Pr*
Ron Bearian, *
EMP: 100 EST: 1944
SALES (est): 49.65MM **Privately Held**
Web: www.chasechevrolet.com
SIC: 5511 5531 7538 5521 Automobiles, new and used; Automotive parts; General automotive repair shops; Used car dealers

5511 - New And Used Car Dealers (P-7203)

(P-7184)
CITRUS MOTORS ONTARIO INC (PA)
Also Called: Citrus Ford
1375 S Woodruff Way (91761-2233)
P.O. Box 4270 (91761-8970)
PHONE..................................909 390-0930
Dennis Shannon, Pr
Alice Van Dentoorn, *
EMP: 211 EST: 1950
SALES (est): 49.18MM
SALES (corp-wide): 49.18MM **Privately Held**
Web: www.citrusmotors.com
SIC: 5511 7538 Automobiles, new and used; General automotive repair shops

(P-7185)
CJM AUTOMOTIVE GROUP INC
Also Called: Bakersfield Mazda
3101 Cattle Dr (93313-2651)
P.O. Box 41117 (93384-1117)
PHONE..................................661 832-3000
Masoud Bashirtash, Pr
James Haddad, *
Farhad Bashirtash, *
Ali Reza Bashirtash, *
EMP: 70 EST: 1960
SALES (est): 24.22MM **Privately Held**
Web: www.drivecj.com
SIC: 5511 7538 Automobiles, new and used; General automotive repair shops

(P-7186)
COUNTY FORD NORTH INC (PA)
Also Called: North County GMC
450 W Vista Way (92083-5829)
PHONE..................................760 945-9900
James E Crowley, Pr
Sean Crowley, *
Jeffrey Friestedt, *
Joseph Weir, *
Scott Crowley, *
▼ EMP: 213 EST: 1992
SALES (est): 62.08MM **Privately Held**
Web: www.northcountyford.net
SIC: 5511 5521 7538 7515 Automobiles, new and used; Used car dealers; General automotive repair shops; Passenger car leasing

(P-7187)
COURTESY CHEVROLET CENTER
Also Called: Geo Sales-Courtesy Chevrolet
750 Camino Del Rio N (92108-3207)
PHONE..................................619 297-4321
TOLL FREE: 877
William R Gruwell, Pr
EMP: 86 EST: 1961
SQ FT: 60,000
SALES (est): 18.97MM **Privately Held**
Web: www.courtesysandiego.com
SIC: 5511 7538 5531 7515 Automobiles, new and used; General automotive repair shops; Auto and home supply stores; Passenger car leasing

(P-7188)
COURTESY MOTORS AUTO CTR INC
Also Called: Volvo
2520 Cohasset Rd (95973-1307)
PHONE..................................530 345-9444
Ron Faria, Pr
Stephen W Wade, *
EMP: 100 EST: 1975
SQ FT: 30,000
SALES (est): 33.34MM **Privately Held**
Web: www.chicocourtesy.com
SIC: 5511 7538 7532 Automobiles, new and used; General automotive repair shops; Top and body repair and paint shops

(P-7189)
CREVIER CLASSICS LLC
1500 Auto Mall Dr (92705-4743)
PHONE..................................714 835-3171
EMP: 320 EST: 1971
SALES (est): 32.76MM **Privately Held**
Web: www.crevierbmw.com
SIC: 5511 5521 5531 7538 Automobiles, new and used; Automobiles, used cars only ; Auto and home supply stores; General automotive repair shops

(P-7190)
D LONGO INC
Also Called: Longo Scion
3534 Peck Rd (91731-3526)
PHONE..................................626 580-6000
Greg Penske, Pr
EMP: 380 EST: 1967
SALES (est): 168.53MM
SALES (corp-wide): 5.16B **Privately Held**
Web: www.longotoyota.com
SIC: 5511 7538 Automobiles, new and used; General automotive repair shops
PA: Penske Corporation
2555 S Telegraph Rd
Bloomfield Hills MI
248 648-2000

(P-7191)
DAVID A CAMPBELL CORPORATION
Also Called: B M W of Riverside
3060 Adams St (92504-4014)
P.O. Box 4007 (92514-4007)
PHONE..................................951 785-4444
Allen David Franklin, CEO
Steven Campbell, *
Patrick Campbell, *
EMP: 150 EST: 1975
SQ FT: 45,000
SALES (est): 28.19MM **Privately Held**
Web: www.bmwofriverside.com
SIC: 5511 7538 Automobiles, new and used; General automotive repair shops

(P-7192)
DCH ACURA OF TEMECULA
Also Called: Lithia
26705 Ynez Rd (92591-4693)
P.O. Box 9043 (92589-9043)
PHONE..................................877 847-9532
Kenneth Colson, VP
EMP: 100 EST: 2014
SALES (est): 10.98MM **Privately Held**
Web: www.ohacura.com
SIC: 5511 7539 5531 Automobiles, new and used; Automotive repair shops, nec; Automotive parts

(P-7193)
DCH CALIFORNIA MOTORS INC
Also Called: Toyota of Oxnard
1631 Auto Center Dr (93036-8972)
PHONE..................................805 988-7900
Shau-wai Lam, Pr
Scott Borg, *
EMP: 95 EST: 1991
SALES (est): 23.52MM
SALES (corp-wide): 28.19B **Publicly Held**
Web: www.toyotaofoxnard.com
SIC: 5511 7538 7532 Automobiles, new and used; General automotive repair shops; Top and body repair and paint shops
HQ: Dch North America Inc.
955 Rte 9 N
South Amboy NJ
732 727-9168

(P-7194)
DCH GARDENA HONDA
Also Called: Gardena Honda
15541 S Western Ave (90249-4320)
P.O. Box 3220 (90247-1420)
PHONE..................................310 515-5700
TOLL FREE: 800
Shauwai Lam, Prin
EMP: 140 EST: 1979
SQ FT: 290,000
SALES (est): 45.27MM
SALES (corp-wide): 28.19B **Publicly Held**
Web: www.gardenahonda.com
SIC: 5511 7538 Automobiles, new and used; General automotive repair shops
HQ: Dch North America Inc.
955 Rte 9 N
South Amboy NJ
732 727-9168

(P-7195)
DICK DEWESE CHEVROLET INC
Also Called: Tom Bell Chevrolet
800 Alabama St (92374-2806)
PHONE..................................909 793-2681
Tom O Bell, Pr
Derek Hanson, *
Lynn Drysdale, *
EMP: 102 EST: 1951
SQ FT: 10,000
SALES (est): 32.85MM **Privately Held**
Web: www.tombellchevrolet.com
SIC: 5511 7538 5531 5521 Automobiles, new and used; General automotive repair shops; Auto and home supply stores; Used car dealers

(P-7196)
DREW FORD
Also Called: Drew Hyundai
8970 La Mesa Blvd (91942-0849)
P.O. Box 188 (91944-0188)
PHONE..................................619 464-7777
William J Drew, Pr
EMP: 250 EST: 1927
SQ FT: 90,000
SALES (est): 51.99MM **Privately Held**
Web: www.drewauto.com
SIC: 5511 7538 Automobiles, new and used; General automotive repair shops

(P-7197)
DUBLIN VOLKSWAGEN
Also Called: Dublin Dodge
6085 Scarlett Ct (94568-3102)
P.O. Box 9099 (95157-0099)
PHONE..................................925 829-0800
Craig Perry, Genl Mgr
EMP: 75 EST: 1997
SQ FT: 22,161
SALES (est): 20.13MM
SALES (corp-wide): 14B **Publicly Held**
Web: www.dublinvolkswagen.com
SIC: 5511 7538 Automobiles, new and used; General automotive repair shops
PA: Sonic Automotive, Inc.
4401 Colwick Rd
Charlotte NC
704 566-2400

(P-7198)
EL CENTRO MOTORS
Also Called: Ford Lincoln Mercury
1520 Ford Dr (92243-1603)
P.O. Box 3250 (92244-3250)
PHONE..................................760 336-2100
EMP: 95 EST: 1901
SALES (est): 39.31MM **Privately Held**
Web: www.elcentromotors.net
SIC: 5511 7538 5531 Automobiles, new and used; General automotive repair shops; Automotive parts

(P-7199)
EL MONTE AUTOMOTIVE GROUP INC
Also Called: Longo Lexus
3530 Peck Rd (91731-3526)
PHONE..................................626 580-6200
Greg Penske, Pr
EMP: 104 EST: 1989
SALES (est): 33.75MM **Privately Held**
Web: www.longolexus.com
SIC: 5511 7532 7515 5521 Automobiles, new and used; Top and body repair and paint shops; Passenger car leasing; Used car dealers

(P-7200)
EL MONTE AUTOMOTIVE GROUP LLC
Also Called: Nelson Honda
3464 Peck Rd (91731-3253)
PHONE..................................626 444-0321
TOLL FREE: 800
EMP: 80 EST: 1960
SALES (est): 19.43MM **Privately Held**
SIC: 5511 7538 7515 5531 Automobiles, new and used; General automotive repair shops; Passenger car leasing; Auto and home supply stores

(P-7201)
ENVIRNMENTAL TRNSP SPECIALISTS
Also Called: University Honda
4343 Chiles Rd (95618-4342)
PHONE..................................916 442-4971
Douglas Malinoff, Pr
EMP: 63 EST: 1978
SQ FT: 21,000
SALES (est): 12.42MM **Privately Held**
Web: www.honda.com
SIC: 5511 7538 5531 Automobiles, new and used; General automotive repair shops; Automotive parts

(P-7202)
ESCONDIDO MOTORS LLC
Also Called: Mercedes Benz of Escondido
1101 W 9th Ave (92025-3843)
PHONE..................................760 745-5000
Simon Sarriedine, CEO
Jack Manukyan, *
EMP: 80 EST: 1988
SALES (est): 25.03MM **Privately Held**
Web: www.mbescondido.com
SIC: 5511 5521 7515 5531 Automobiles, new and used; Automobiles, used cars only ; Passenger car leasing; Auto and home supply stores

(P-7203)
EUROPA AUTO IMPORTS INC
Also Called: Mercedes Benz of San Diego
4750 Kearny Mesa Rd (92111-2405)
PHONE..................................858 569-6900
Ora Smith, Pr
Judy Antrim, *
Duayne Hancock, *
▼ EMP: 116 EST: 1957
SQ FT: 10,000
SALES (est): 30.76MM **Privately Held**
Web: www.mbsd.com

5511 - New And Used Car Dealers (P-7204)

SIC: 5511 5521 7538 Automobiles, new and used; Used car dealers; General automotive repair shops

(P-7204)
FAA BEVERLY HILLS INC
Also Called: Beverly Hills BMW
5070 Wilshire Blvd (90036-4381)
PHONE.................................323 801-1430
Step Jones, Genl Mgr
EMP: 85 EST: 1991
SQ FT: 4,000
SALES (est): 33.27MM
SALES (corp-wide): 14B Publicly Held
Web: www.bmwofbeverlyhills.com
SIC: 5511 7538 Automobiles, new and used; General automotive repair shops
PA: Sonic Automotive, Inc.
4401 Colwick Rd
Charlotte NC
704 566-2400

(P-7205)
FAA CONCORD T INC
Also Called: Concord Toyota
1090 Concord Ave (94520-5601)
PHONE.................................925 682-7131
Thomas A Price, Pr
W Bruce Bercovich, *
EMP: 85 EST: 1970
SQ FT: 25,000
SALES (est): 26.73MM
SALES (corp-wide): 14B Publicly Held
Web: www.concordtoyota.com
SIC: 5511 7538 5531 5521 Automobiles, new and used; General automotive repair shops; Auto and home supply stores; Used car dealers
PA: Sonic Automotive, Inc.
4401 Colwick Rd
Charlotte NC
704 566-2400

(P-7206)
FELIX CHEVROLET LP (PA)
Also Called: Felix Chevrolet
714 W Olympic Blvd Ste 1124 (90015-1425)
PHONE.................................213 748-6141
Nicholas N Shammas, Pt
George Damaa, Pt
EMP: 113 EST: 1921
SALES (est): 52.74MM
SALES (corp-wide): 52.74MM Privately Held
Web: www.felixchevrolet.com
SIC: 5511 7538 7532 5531 Automobiles, new and used; General automotive repair shops; Top and body repair and paint shops ; Auto and home supply stores

(P-7207)
FIESTA FORD INC
Also Called: Fiesta Ford Lincoln-Mercury
79015 Avenue 40 (92203-9499)
PHONE.................................760 775-7777
Paul J Thiel, CEO
EMP: 126 EST: 1966
SQ FT: 304,920
SALES (est): 49.21MM Privately Held
Web: www.quicklane.com
SIC: 5511 7538 Automobiles, new and used; General automotive repair shops

(P-7208)
FORD FUTURE INC
Also Called: Future Ford Lincon
650 Automall Dr (95661-3022)
PHONE.................................916 786-3673
EMP: 176 EST: 1981

SALES (est): 23.59MM Privately Held
Web: www.futureford.com
SIC: 5511 7538 Automobiles, new and used; General automotive repair shops

(P-7209)
FORD OF SANTA MONICA INC
Also Called: Ford
1402 Santa Monica Blvd (90404-1710)
PHONE.................................310 451-1588
Ron Davis, CEO
EMP: 92 EST: 1948
SALES (est): 36.46MM Privately Held
Web: www.smford.com
SIC: 5511 5012 Automobiles, new and used; Ambulances

(P-7210)
FORD OF SIMI VALLEY INC
Also Called: Ford
2440 1st St (93065-0916)
PHONE.................................805 583-0333
Larry Hibbler, Pr
Kathleen Lindsey, *
EMP: 70 EST: 2001
SQ FT: 28,000
SALES (est): 30.39MM Privately Held
Web: www.quicklane.com
SIC: 5511 7538 Automobiles, new and used; General automotive repair shops

(P-7211)
FORD STORE MORGAN HILL INC
17045 Condit Rd (95037-3301)
PHONE.................................408 782-8201
Timothy Paulus, Pr
EMP: 70 EST: 2004
SALES (est): 28.22MM Privately Held
Web: www.fordstoremorganhill.com
SIC: 5511 5521 7515 Automobiles, new and used; Used car dealers; Passenger car leasing

(P-7212)
FOX HILLS AUTO INC (PA)
Also Called: Airport Marina Ford
5880 W Centinela Ave (90045-1504)
PHONE.................................310 649-3673
Norris J Bishton Junior, CEO
▲ EMP: 140 EST: 1989
SQ FT: 35,000
SALES (est): 70.01MM Privately Held
Web: www.ford.com
SIC: 5511 7538 5531 5521 Automobiles, new and used; General automotive repair shops; Auto and home supply stores; Used car dealers

(P-7213)
FREEMAN MOTORS INC
Also Called: Freeman Toyota Rent-A-Car
2875 Corby Ave (95407-7878)
P.O. Box 1704 (95402-1704)
PHONE.................................707 542-1791
Stephen C Freeman, CEO
Donald E Woodruff, *
Betty E Freeman, *
EMP: 185 EST: 1961
SQ FT: 65,000
SALES (est): 17.62MM Privately Held
Web: www.freemanmotors.com
SIC: 5511 7538 Automobiles, new and used; General automotive repair shops

(P-7214)
FRESNO CHRYSLER JEEP INC
Also Called: Fresno Chrysler Ddge Jeep Ram
6162 N Blackstone Ave (93710-5010)
PHONE.................................559 431-4000

Timothy Allen Finegan, Pr
Tim Finegan Senior, Pr
Tim Finegan Junior, VP
Annette Diggs, *
EMP: 85 EST: 1976
SQ FT: 5,000
SALES (est): 24.14MM Privately Held
Web: www.fresnochryslerjeep.com
SIC: 5511 5531 7538 Automobiles, new and used; Automotive parts; General automotive repair shops

(P-7215)
FRESNO TRUCK CENTER (PA)
Also Called: Lee Financial Services
2727 E Central Ave (93725-2425)
P.O. Box 12346 (93777-2346)
PHONE.................................559 486-4310
EMP: 112 EST: 1959
SALES (est): 119.89MM
SALES (corp-wide): 119.89MM Privately Held
Web: www.californiatruckcenters.com
SIC: 5511 5521 5531 5012 Trucks, tractors, and trailers: new and used; Trucks, tractors, and trailers: used; Truck equipment and parts; Trailers for trucks, new and used

(P-7216)
FRONTIER FORD (PA)
Also Called: Frontier Rent-A-Car
3701 Stevens Creek Blvd (95051-7335)
PHONE.................................408 241-1800
James F Landes, CEO
E Robert Breech Junior, VP
Harold D Arnon, *
Andrew L Breech, *
▲ EMP: 140 EST: 1960
SQ FT: 10,000
SALES (est): 55.76MM
SALES (corp-wide): 55.76MM Privately Held
Web: www.frontierford.com
SIC: 5511 5521 5012 Automobiles, new and used; Used car dealers; Automobiles and other motor vehicles

(P-7217)
FUTURE FORD OF CONCORD LLC
Also Called: Future Ford Lncoln Mrcury Cnco
2285 Diamond Blvd (94520-5705)
PHONE.................................925 686-5000
Gary Steven Pleau, Managing Member
Henry C Hansel, *
EMP: 80 EST: 2004
SALES (est): 32.37MM Privately Held
Web: www.futurefordofconcord.com
SIC: 5511 7539 Automobiles, new and used; Automotive repair shops, nec

(P-7218)
GALPIN MOTORS INC (PA)
Also Called: Galpin Ford
15505 Roscoe Blvd (91343-6503)
PHONE.................................818 787-3800
Herbert F Boeckman li, Pr
Karl L Boeckmann, *
Bradley M Boeckmann, *
Alan J Skobin, *
Jane Boeckmann, *
▼ EMP: 500 EST: 1946
SQ FT: 175,000
SALES (est): 372.23MM
SALES (corp-wide): 372.23MM Privately Held
Web: www.galpin.com

SIC: 5511 5521 7538 7515 Automobiles, new and used; Used car dealers; General automotive repair shops; Passenger car leasing

(P-7219)
GEORGE CHEVROLET
Also Called: George Chevrolet
17000 Lakewood Blvd (90706-5523)
PHONE.................................562 925-2500
Jeffery Estabrooks, Pr
Patricia Estabrooks, *
EMP: 100 EST: 1961
SQ FT: 56,000
SALES (est): 41.44MM Privately Held
Web: www.chevrolet.com
SIC: 5511 7515 7538 Automobiles, new and used; Passenger car leasing; General automotive repair shops

(P-7220)
GERMAN MOTORS CORPORATION
Also Called: BMW of San Francisco
1675 Howard St (94103-2526)
PHONE.................................415 590-3773
Henry Schmitt, CEO
Henry Schmitt, Pr
Michele Schmitt, *
Michael Greening, *
▲ EMP: 240 EST: 1964
SQ FT: 112,000
SALES (est): 91.45MM Privately Held
Web: www.sfgermanmotors.com
SIC: 5511 7532 Automobiles, new and used; Top and body repair and paint shops

(P-7221)
GOLDEN GATE FREIGHTLINER INC (HQ)
Also Called: Golden Gate Truck Center
8200 Baldwin St (94621-1910)
P.O. Box 6038 (94603-0038)
PHONE.................................559 486-4310
TOLL FREE: 800
Gary L Howard, Pr
Doug Howard, *
Brian Nicholson, *
EMP: 122 EST: 1977
SQ FT: 50,000
SALES (est): 106.02MM
SALES (corp-wide): 119.89MM Privately Held
Web: www.goldengatetruck.com
SIC: 5511 5531 7538 Trucks, tractors, and trailers: new and used; Truck equipment and parts; General truck repair
PA: Fresno Truck Center
2727 E Central Ave
Fresno CA
559 486-4310

(P-7222)
GORDON TURNER MOTORS
Also Called: Turner Volvo
2535 Arden Way (95825-2413)
P.O. Box 254490 (95865-4490)
PHONE.................................916 488-2400
EMP: 166
SIC: 5511 5531 7538 Automobiles, new and used; Automotive parts; General automotive repair shops

(P-7223)
GPI CA-NIII INC
Also Called: Performance Nissan
1434 Buena Vista St (91010-2402)
PHONE.................................626 305-3000
John C Rickel, CEO
Frank Grese Junior, Prin

PRODUCTS & SERVICES SECTION
5511 - New And Used Car Dealers (P-7241)

EMP: 85 EST: 1991
SALES (est): 6.71MM Publicly Held
Web: www.perfnissan.com
SIC: 5511 7538 7515 5531 Automobiles, new and used; General automotive repair shops; Passenger car leasing; Auto and home supply stores
PA: Group 1 Automotive, Inc.
800 Gessner Rd Ste 500
Houston TX

(P-7224)
GREGORY CONSULTING INC (PA)
6350 Leland St (93003-8585)
PHONE..................805 642-0111
TOLL FREE: 888
Robert Gregory, Pr
Nancy Gregory, *
EMP: 135 EST: 1986
SQ FT: 54,000
SALES (est): 42.99MM
SALES (corp-wide): 42.99MM Privately Held
Web: www.paradisechevrolet.com
SIC: 5511 7538 5521 Automobiles, new and used; General automotive repair shops; Used car dealers

(P-7225)
H W HUNTER INC (PA)
Also Called: Hunter Dodge Chrysler Jeep Ram
1130 Auto Mall Dr (93534-6302)
P.O. Box 4324 (93539-4324)
PHONE..................661 948-8411
Timothy H Fuller, CEO
EMP: 80 EST: 1956
SQ FT: 5,000
SALES (est): 23.73MM
SALES (corp-wide): 23.73MM Privately Held
Web: www.hunterdodgechryslerjeep.net
SIC: 5511 7538 Automobiles, new and used; General automotive repair shops

(P-7226)
HABERFELDE FORD (PA)
Also Called: Jim Burke Ford
2001 Oak St (93301-3010)
P.O. Box 2088 (93303-2088)
PHONE..................661 328-3600
Daniel George Hay, Pr
Michelle Hay, *
Beverly Burke, *
Joe Hay, *
EMP: 236 EST: 1913
SQ FT: 102,000
SALES (est): 49.31MM
SALES (corp-wide): 49.31MM Privately Held
Web: www.jimburkeford.com
SIC: 5511 7538 Automobiles, new and used; General automotive repair shops

(P-7227)
HABERFELDE FORD
Also Called: Jim Burke Ford
5300 Gasoline Alley Dr (93313-3213)
PHONE..................661 837-6400
Joe Hay, Brnch Mgr
EMP: 64
SALES (corp-wide): 49.31MM Privately Held
Web: www.jimburkelincoln.com
SIC: 5511 7538 Automobiles, new and used; General automotive repair shops
PA: Ford Haberfelde
2001 Oak St
Bakersfield CA
661 328-3600

(P-7228)
HALREC INC
Also Called: Stevens Creek Toyota
4202 Stevens Creek Blvd (95129-1336)
P.O. Box 9099 (95157-0099)
PHONE..................408 984-1234
Harold Cornelius, Ch Bd
Stephen C Cornelius, *
Mark Feldman, *
EMP: 250 EST: 1966
SQ FT: 11,500
SALES (est): 71.84MM Privately Held
Web: www.stevenscreektoyota.com
SIC: 5511 7539 7538 7532 Automobiles, new and used; Automotive repair shops, nec; General automotive repair shops; Top and body repair and paint shops

(P-7229)
HANSEL - PRESTIGE INC
Also Called: Hansel BMW of Santa Rosa
2925 Corby Ave (95407-7846)
PHONE..................707 578-4717
EMP: 154
Web: www.bmwgroup.com
SIC: 5511 5013 7539 Automobiles, new and used; Motor vehicle supplies and new parts ; Automotive repair shops, nec
HQ: Hansel - Prestige, Inc.
3075 Corby Ave
Santa Rosa CA
707 545-6602

(P-7230)
HARBILL INC
Also Called: Crest Chevrolet
909 W 21st St (92405-3201)
P.O. Box 501 (92402-0501)
PHONE..................909 883-8833
D William Bader, CEO
Robert Bader, *
Douglas Bader, *
Patty Bader, *
EMP: 93 EST: 1958
SQ FT: 20,000
SALES (est): 26.56MM Privately Held
Web: www.daliaauto.com
SIC: 5511 5012 5531 5521 Automobiles, new and used; Automobiles and other motor vehicles; Auto and home supply stores; Used car dealers

(P-7231)
HARVEY & MADDING INC
Also Called: Dublin Honda
6300 Dublin Blvd (94568-7657)
PHONE..................925 828-8030
Kenneth C Harvey, CEO
Brenda S Harvey, *
EMP: 100 EST: 1977
SQ FT: 332,576
SALES (est): 85.46MM Privately Held
Web: www.dublinhonda.com
SIC: 5511 7538 5015 5013 Automobiles, new and used; General automotive repair shops; Motor vehicle parts, used; Motor vehicle supplies and new parts

(P-7232)
HENDRICK AUTOMOTIVE GROUP
Also Called: Acura Pleasanton
4355 Rosewood Dr (94588-3003)
P.O. Box 9050 (94566-9050)
PHONE..................925 463-4700
Bob Slapp, Genl Mgr
EMP: 100
SQ FT: 16,967
SALES (corp-wide): 78.7MM Privately Held
Web: www.hendrickcars.com
SIC: 5511 5012 Automobiles, new and used; Automobiles and other motor vehicles
PA: Hendrick Automotive Group
6000 Monroe Rd Ste 100
Charlotte NC
704 568-5550

(P-7233)
HOEHN COMPANY INC
Also Called: Hoehn Honda
5454 Paseo Del Norte (92008-4426)
P.O. Box 789 (92018-0789)
PHONE..................760 438-1818
TOLL FREE: 888
Robert A Hoehn, Pr
T William Hoehn Iii, VP
Gloria Rediker, *
EMP: 80 EST: 1993
SQ FT: 3,000
SALES (est): 22.4MM Privately Held
Web: www.hoehnhonda.com
SIC: 5511 7538 Automobiles, new and used; General automotive repair shops

(P-7234)
HONDA WORLD WESTMINSTER
13600 Beach Blvd (92683-3202)
PHONE..................714 890-8900
Jim Kitzmiller, Pr
Tom Chadwell, *
EMP: 175 EST: 1989
SQ FT: 6,000
SALES (est): 62.1MM
SALES (corp-wide): 102.66MM Privately Held
Web: www.honda.com
SIC: 5511 7539 5015 5012 Automobiles, new and used; Automotive repair shops, nec; Motor vehicle parts, used; Automobiles and other motor vehicles
PA: Piercey Management Services, Inc.
16901 Millikan Ave
Irvine CA
949 379-3701

(P-7235)
IDEALAB (HQ)
130 W Union St (91103-3628)
PHONE..................626 356-3654
▲ EMP: 82 EST: 1996
SQ FT: 30,000
SALES (est): 138.99MM
SALES (corp-wide): 146.11MM Privately Held
Web: www.idealab.com
SIC: 5511 6726 New and used car dealers; Investment offices, nec
PA: Idealab Holdings, L.L.C.
130 W Union St
Pasadena CA
626 585-6900

(P-7236)
ISUZU NORTH AMERICA CORP (HQ)
1400 S Douglass Rd Ste 100 (92806-6901)
PHONE..................714 935-9300
Masanori Katayama, Pr
Shinichi Takahashi, *
Masatoshi Ito, *
◆ EMP: 150 EST: 1975
SQ FT: 64,000
SALES (est): 535.14MM Privately Held
Web: www.isuzu.com
SIC: 5511 5084 5013 5015 Automobiles, new and used; Engines and parts, diesel; Automotive supplies and parts; Motor vehicle parts, used
PA: Isuzu Motors Limited
1-2-5, Takashima, Nishi-Ku
Yokohama KNG

(P-7237)
J M FREMONT MOTORS LLC
43191 Boscell Rd (94538-5129)
PHONE..................510 403-3700
Fletcher Jones Junior, CEO
Keith May, Pr
Fletcher Jones Iii, COO
EMP: 65 EST: 2017
SALES (est): 9.26MM Privately Held
Web: www.audifremont.com
SIC: 5511 7538 5531 Automobiles, new and used; General automotive repair shops; Automotive parts

(P-7238)
JACK GOSCH FORD INC
Also Called: Gosch Ford Lincoln Mercury
150 Carriage Cir (92545-9610)
PHONE..................951 658-3181
TOLL FREE: 800
Jack E Gosch, Pr
Mark E Gosch, *
Eric Gosch, *
Marc Gosch, *
Richard Rodgers, *
EMP: 100 EST: 1964
SQ FT: 35,000
SALES (est): 41.25MM Privately Held
Web: www.goschauto.com
SIC: 5511 7538 Automobiles, new and used; General automotive repair shops

(P-7239)
JACK PWELL CHRYSLER - DDGE INC
Also Called: Jack Pwell Chrysler Ddge Jeep
1625 Auto Park Way (92029-2008)
PHONE..................760 745-2880
Jack Powell Junior, Pr
Jack Powell Junior, Pr
Judith Powell, *
EMP: 85 EST: 1958
SQ FT: 28,000
SALES (est): 31.67MM Privately Held
Web: www.jeep.com
SIC: 5511 7538 5531 Automobiles, new and used; General automotive repair shops; Auto and home supply stores

(P-7240)
JEEP CHRYSLER OF ONTARIO
Also Called: Jeep Chrysler Ddge Ram Ontario
1202 Auto Center Dr (91761-2208)
PHONE..................909 390-9898
Richard D Romero, Ch Bd
R J Romero, *
Kathy Brown, *
Valerie Romero, *
J B Butterwick, *
EMP: 95 EST: 1993
SQ FT: 30,000
SALES (est): 18.52MM Privately Held
Web: www.jcofontario.com
SIC: 5511 7538 5531 Automobiles, new and used; General automotive repair shops; Auto and home supply stores

(P-7241)
JOHN L SLLIVAN INVESTMENTS INC (PA)
Also Called: Roseville Toyota
6200 Northfront Rd (94551-9507)
PHONE..................916 969-5911
John L Sullivan, Pr
David Rodgers, *
Steve Ruckels, *
EMP: 220 EST: 1980

5511 - New And Used Car Dealers (P-7242)

SQ FT: 15,000
SALES (est): 64.06MM
SALES (corp-wide): 64.06MM Privately Held
Web: www.toyota.com
SIC: 5511 7538 Automobiles, new and used; General automotive repair shops

(P-7242)
JOHN L SULLIVAN CHEVROLET INC
350 Automall Dr (95661-3019)
P.O. Box 1028 (95678-8028)
PHONE..................................916 742-7663
John L Sullivan, Pr
David Rogers, *
Steve A Ruckels, *
EMP: 150 EST: 1950
SQ FT: 70,000
SALES (est): 29.69MM Privately Held
Web: www.myrosevillechevrolet.com
SIC: 5511 7539 5531 5521 Automobiles, new and used; Automotive repair shops, nec; Auto and home supply stores; Used car dealers

(P-7243)
JOHNSON FORD (PA)
Also Called: Antelope Valley Lincoln
1155 Auto Mall Dr (93534-5867)
PHONE..................................888 483-0454
Michael H Johnson, Pr
Doug Killebrew, *
Brooke Powell, *
Bob Heninger, *
EMP: 120 EST: 1957
SQ FT: 70,000
SALES (est): 43.31MM
SALES (corp-wide): 43.31MM Privately Held
Web: www.diamondfordav.com
SIC: 5511 7538 5561 Automobiles, new and used; General automotive repair shops; Camper and travel trailer dealers

(P-7244)
JVAC INC
Also Called: Keller Lincoln Ford
1073 Cadillac Ln (93230-4966)
PHONE..................................559 584-5531
Jon Keller, Pr
Valerie Keller, *
EMP: 70 EST: 2008
SALES (est): 14.36MM Privately Held
Web: www.quicklane.com
SIC: 5511 7538 Automobiles, new and used; General automotive repair shops

(P-7245)
KEN GRODY REDLANDS LLC
Also Called: Ken Grody Ford - Redlands
1121 W Colton Ave (92374-2935)
PHONE..................................909 793-3211
William Raymond, *
Brandi Desherlia, *
EMP: 85 EST: 2019
SALES (est): 16.84MM Privately Held
Web: www.kengrodyfordredlands.com
SIC: 5511 7538 New and used car dealers; General automotive repair shops

(P-7246)
KEYES MOTORS INC (PA)
Also Called: Keyes Toyota
5855 Van Nuys Blvd (91401-4219)
PHONE..................................818 782-0172
Howard Keyes, Pr
Lawrence Abramson, *
EMP: 80 EST: 1968
SQ FT: 20,000

SALES (est): 97.87MM
SALES (corp-wide): 97.87MM Privately Held
Web: www.keyestoyota.com
SIC: 5511 7538 7515 5012 Automobiles, new and used; General automotive repair shops; Passenger car leasing; Automobiles and other motor vehicles

(P-7247)
KEYLEX INC (PA)
Also Called: Keyes Lexus
5905 Van Nuys Blvd (91401-3624)
PHONE..................................818 379-4000
Howard Keyes, Pr
EMP: 87 EST: 1989
SQ FT: 32,376
SALES (est): 39.62MM Privately Held
Web: www.keyeslexus.com
SIC: 5511 7538 7515 5531 Automobiles, new and used; General automotive repair shops; Passenger car leasing; Auto and home supply stores

(P-7248)
KEYSTONE FORD INC (PA)
12000 Firestone Blvd (90650-2907)
PHONE..................................562 868-0825
TOLL FREE: 800
Norman P Stutzke, Pr
Lamberto Colon, *
Paul Stutzke, *
EMP: 130 EST: 1968
SQ FT: 14,000
SALES (est): 8.56MM
SALES (corp-wide): 8.56MM Privately Held
Web: www.ford.com
SIC: 5511 5531 7514 Automobiles, new and used; Automotive parts; Rent-a-car service

(P-7249)
LAKE CHEVROLET
31201 Auto Center Dr (92530-4424)
P.O. Box 4000 (92531-4000)
PHONE..................................951 674-3116
EMP: 133
Web: www.andersonchevroletca.com
SIC: 5511 7515 5521 Automobiles, new and used; Passenger car leasing; Used car dealers

(P-7250)
LARRY HOPKINS INC
Also Called: Larry Hopkins Honda
1048 W El Camino Real (94087-1024)
PHONE..................................408 720-1888
Steven E Hopkins, Pr
Terry Hopkins, Stockholder*
EMP: 100 EST: 1947
SQ FT: 13,000
SALES (est): 25.93MM Privately Held
Web: www.honda.com
SIC: 5511 7538 5531 5521 Automobiles, new and used; General automotive repair shops; Auto and home supply stores; Used car dealers

(P-7251)
LEO HOFFMAN CHEVROLET INC (PA)
Also Called: Puente Hills Chevrolet
17300 E Gale Ave (91748-1512)
P.O. Box 90428 (91715-0428)
PHONE..................................626 968-8411
Thomas L Hoffman, Pr
Gary A Campbell, *
Kurt Hoffman, *
EMP: 71 EST: 1944
SQ FT: 75,000

SALES (est): 38.5MM
SALES (corp-wide): 38.5MM Privately Held
Web: www.chevroletofpuentehills.com
SIC: 5511 7515 Automobiles, new and used; Passenger car leasing

(P-7252)
LITHIA MOTORS INC
Also Called: Lithia Ford Mzda Suzuki Fresno
195 E Auto Center Dr (93710-5100)
PHONE..................................559 435-8400
Ron Kirby, Mgr
EMP: 150
SALES (corp-wide): 28.19B Publicly Held
Web: www.quicklane.com
SIC: 5511 7515 5521 7538 Automobiles, new and used; Passenger car leasing; Used car dealers; General automotive repair shops
PA: Lithia Motors, Inc.
150 N Bartlett St Ste 148
Medford OR
541 776-6401

(P-7253)
LOS FELIZ FORD INC (PA)
Also Called: Star Ford Lincoln Mercury
1101 S Brand Blvd (91204-2313)
PHONE..................................818 502-1901
Steve Bussjaeger, Pr
Tad Okumoto, *
Agnes Gurida, *
EMP: 80 EST: 1970
SQ FT: 75,000
SALES (est): 31.57MM
SALES (corp-wide): 31.57MM Privately Held
Web: www.starford.com
SIC: 5511 7515 Automobiles, new and used; Passenger car leasing

(P-7254)
M K SMITH CHEVROLET
12845 Central Ave (91710-4120)
P.O. Box 455 (91708-0455)
PHONE..................................909 628-8961
Marc Smith, CEO
Carolyn Coble, *
Cheryl Smith, *
Marc Smith, Ex VP
EMP: 120 EST: 1941
SALES (est): 42.49MM Privately Held
Web: www.mksmithchevrolet.com
SIC: 5511 7549 5531 Automobiles, new and used; Automotive maintenance services; Automotive parts

(P-7255)
MAGIC ACQUISITION CORP
Also Called: Autonation Ford Valencia
23920 Creekside Rd (91355-1701)
PHONE..................................661 382-4700
EMP: 350 EST: 1996
SALES (est): 44.93MM
SALES (corp-wide): 26.98B Publicly Held
Web: www.autonationfordvalencia.com
SIC: 5511 7538 5531 New and used car dealers; General automotive repair shops; Auto and home supply stores
HQ: Magic Acquisition Holding, Llc
200 Sw 1st Ave
Fort Lauderdale FL
954 769-7000

(P-7256)
MARTIN CHEVROLET
23505 Hawthorne Blvd (90505-4739)
P.O. Box 2895 (90509-2895)
PHONE..................................323 772-6494

TOLL FREE: 888
Joe Giacomin, Pr
Fran Williams, *
EMP: 100 EST: 1947
SQ FT: 10,000
SALES (est): 28.99MM Privately Held
Web: www.martinchevrolet.com
SIC: 5511 7538 Automobiles, new and used; General automotive repair shops

(P-7257)
MEL RAPTON INC
Also Called: Mel Rapton Honda
2329 Fulton Ave (95825-0374)
PHONE..................................916 514-4050
EMP: 132
SALES (corp-wide): 48.35MM Privately Held
Web: www.honda.com
SIC: 5511 7699 Automobiles, new and used; Battery service and repair
PA: Mel Rapton, Inc.
3630 Fulton Ave
Sacramento CA
916 436-8364

(P-7258)
MILLER AUTOMOTIVE GROUP INC (HQ)
Also Called: Miller Nissan
5425 Van Nuys Blvd (91401-5628)
PHONE..................................818 787-8400
Fred Miller, Ch Bd
Michael Miller, *
Mark Miller, *
Doug Stewart, *
▲ EMP: 350 EST: 1989
SQ FT: 40,000
SALES (est): 138.97MM Publicly Held
Web: www.nissanofvannuys.com
SIC: 5511 7538 5521 Automobiles, new and used; General automotive repair shops; Automobiles, used cars only
PA: Group 1 Automotive, Inc.
800 Gessner Rd Ste 500
Houston TX

(P-7259)
MISSION VLY FORD TRCK SLS INC
Also Called: Mission Vly Ford String Trcks
780 E Brokaw Rd (95112-1007)
P.O. Box 611150 (95161-1150)
PHONE..................................408 933-2300
Ernest A Speno, Pr
Jeffrey A Speno, *
Jeff Speno, *
EMP: 80 EST: 1986
SQ FT: 90,000
SALES (est): 25.69MM Privately Held
Web: www.missionvalleyford.com
SIC: 5511 5531 7513 7538 Automobiles, new and used; Truck equipment and parts; Truck leasing, without drivers; General truck repair

(P-7260)
MISSION VOLKSWAGEN INC
Also Called: Capistrano Volkswagen
32922 Valle Rd (92675-4802)
PHONE..................................949 493-4511
Miles Braden, Pr
Miles Brandon, *
EMP: 80 EST: 1993
SQ FT: 3,997
SALES (est): 26.6MM Privately Held
Web: www.capovw.com
SIC: 5511 7538 Automobiles, new and used; General automotive repair shops

PRODUCTS & SERVICES SECTION
5511 - New And Used Car Dealers (P-7281)

(P-7261)
MOSSY AUTOMOTIVE GROUP INC (PA)
Also Called: Mossy Toyota
4555 Mission Bay Dr (92109-4920)
PHONE..............................858 581-4000
Philip Mossy, Pr
Peter Mossy, *
EMP: 100 EST: 2002
SALES (est): 68.2MM **Privately Held**
Web: www.mossytoyota.com
SIC: **5511** 7538 Automobiles, new and used; General automotive repair shops

(P-7262)
MOSSY FORD INC
Also Called: Quick Lane
4570 Mission Bay Dr (92109-4985)
PHONE..............................858 273-7500
Phillip Mossy, Pr
John Epps, *
▼ EMP: 200 EST: 1988
SQ FT: 10,000
SALES (est): 42.99MM **Privately Held**
Web: www.mossyford.com
SIC: **5511** 7538 7532 7515 Automobiles, new and used; General automotive repair shops; Top and body repair and paint shops; Passenger car leasing

(P-7263)
MOSSY NISSAN INC
Also Called: Mossy Nissan Kearlly Mesa
8118 Clairemont Mesa Blvd (92111-1998)
PHONE..............................858 565-6608
Mike Obeso, Mgr
EMP: 100
Web: www.mossynissan.com
SIC: **5511** 5521 7515 Automobiles, new and used; Used car dealers; Passenger car leasing
HQ: Nissan Mossy Inc
    2700 National City Blvd
    National City CA
    619 474-1011

(P-7264)
NGP MOTORS INC
Also Called: Sunrise Ford
5500 Lankershim Blvd (91601-2724)
P.O. Box 908 (92334-0908)
PHONE..............................818 980-9800
Robert Burncati, Pr
Maureen Burncati, *
EMP: 131 EST: 1979
SQ FT: 75,000
SALES (est): 42.33MM **Privately Held**
Web: www.quicklane.com
SIC: **5511** 7539 7538 Automobiles, new and used; Automotive repair shops, nec; General automotive repair shops

(P-7265)
NICHOLAS K CORPORATION
Also Called: Ford Store San Leandro
1111 Marina Blvd (94577-3364)
PHONE..............................510 352-2000
Robert Knezevich, CEO
EMP: 109 EST: 1954
SQ FT: 60,000
SALES (est): 20.15MM **Privately Held**
Web: www.fordsanleandro.com
SIC: **5511** 7515 Automobiles, new and used; Passenger car leasing

(P-7266)
NICK ALEXANDER IMPORTS
6333 S Alameda St (90001-1812)
PHONE..............................800 800-6425
TOLL FREE: 800
Elizabeth Alexander, CEO
Mary Alexander, *
EMP: 110 EST: 1978
SQ FT: 32,500
SALES (est): 57.56MM **Privately Held**
Web: www.alexanderbmw.com
SIC: **5511** 7549 Automobiles, new and used; Automotive maintenance services

(P-7267)
NIELLO IMPORTS II INC
Also Called: Neillo Audi
2350 Auburn Blvd (95821-1756)
PHONE..............................916 480-2800
Richard L Neillo Junior, Pr
EMP: 150 EST: 2005
SALES (est): 49.6MM **Privately Held**
Web: audi.niello.com
SIC: **5511** 7538 Automobiles, new and used; General automotive repair shops

(P-7268)
NISSAN OF TUSTIN
Also Called: Tustin Saab
30 Auto Center Dr (92782-8401)
PHONE..............................714 669-8282
James H Parkinson, Pr
Mark Parkinson, *
EMP: 149 EST: 1972
SQ FT: 30,000
SALES (est): 45.07MM **Privately Held**
Web: www.nissanoftustin.com
SIC: **5511** 6159 Automobiles, new and used; Automobile finance leasing

(P-7269)
NOARUS INVESTMENTS INC
Also Called: Airport Honda
5850 W Centinela Ave (90045-1504)
PHONE..............................310 649-2440
Norris J Bishton, Pr
EMP: 100 EST: 1998
SALES (est): 27.63MM **Privately Held**
Web: www.honda.com
SIC: **5511** 5521 5531 7538 Automobiles, new and used; Automobiles, used cars only; Automotive parts; General automotive repair shops

(P-7270)
NOARUS TGG
Also Called: Toyota Scion Place
9444 Trask Ave (92844-2824)
PHONE..............................714 895-5595
Norris J Bishton, Pr
Gary Alwood, *
William Hurst, General Vice President*
EMP: 97 EST: 1979
SQ FT: 30,000
SALES (est): 37.16MM **Privately Held**
Web: www.toyota.com
SIC: **5511** 5531 7538 Automobiles, new and used; Automotive parts; General automotive repair shops

(P-7271)
OCEANSIDE AUTO COUNTRY INC (PA)
Also Called: Toyota Carlsbad
6030 Avenida Encinas Ste 200 (92011-1001)
PHONE..............................760 438-2000
Judith Jones-cone, CEO
Olen Woods, *
Michael W Wear, *
EMP: 116 EST: 1972
SQ FT: 3,500
SALES (est): 62.34MM
SALES (corp-wide): 62.34MM **Privately Held**
Web: www.toyota.com
SIC: **5511** 7538 7532 Automobiles, new and used; General automotive repair shops; Top and body repair and paint shops

(P-7272)
ONTARIO AUTOMOTIVE LLC
Also Called: Penske Honda Ontario
1401 Auto Center Dr (91761-2221)
PHONE..............................909 974-3800
Roger Penske, Ch Bd
Greg Penske, *
Brian Kobus, *
EMP: 125 EST: 1990
SALES (est): 23.81MM
SALES (corp-wide): 5.16B **Privately Held**
Web: www.penskehondaontario.com
SIC: **5511** 5521 5012 Automobiles, new and used; Used car dealers; Automobiles and other motor vehicles
PA: Penske Corporation
    2555 S Telegraph Rd
    Bloomfield Hills MI
    248 648-2000

(P-7273)
P A MOTORCARS LLC
Also Called: Penske Motorcars
2016 E Garvey Ave S (91791-1911)
PHONE..............................877 433-3517
Greg Penske, Pr
Dave Summers, *
EMP: 1429 EST: 1995
SQ FT: 23,909
SALES (est): 4.22MM
SALES (corp-wide): 5.16B **Privately Held**
SIC: **5511** 5521 7539 7538 Automobiles, new and used; Used car dealers; Automotive repair shops, nec; General automotive repair shops
PA: Penske Corporation
    2555 S Telegraph Rd
    Bloomfield Hills MI
    248 648-2000

(P-7274)
PALM SPRINGS MOTORS INC
Also Called: Palm Sprng Ford Lncoln Mercury
69-200a Highway 111 (92234)
PHONE..............................760 699-6695
Paul J Thiel, CEO
William S Torrance, *
Joseph A Gibbs, *
EMP: 200 EST: 1950
SALES (est): 47.99MM **Privately Held**
Web: www.quicklane.com
SIC: **5511** 7538 Automobiles, new and used; General automotive repair shops

(P-7275)
PARK PLACE FORD LLC
Also Called: Ford
555 W Foothill Blvd (91786-3853)
PHONE..............................909 946-5555
EMP: 83 EST: 2012
SQ FT: 15,000
SALES (est): 21.46MM **Privately Held**
Web: www.ford.com
SIC: **5511** 7532 7549 5561 Automobiles, new and used; Collision shops, automotive; Emissions testing without repairs, automotive; Travel trailers: automobile, new and used

(P-7276)
PEARSON FORD CO (PA)
5900 Sycamore Canyon Blvd (92507-0719)
PHONE..............................877 743-0421
John Mccallan, Pr
EMP: 180 EST: 1940
SQ FT: 275,000
SALES (est): 38.09MM
SALES (corp-wide): 38.09MM **Privately Held**
Web: www.ford.com
SIC: **5511** 7539 7538 5521 Automobiles, new and used; Automotive repair shops, nec; General automotive repair shops; Used car dealers

(P-7277)
PERFORMANCE CHEVROLET INC
8757 Auburn Folsom Rd (95746-0350)
P.O. Box 41469 (95841-0469)
PHONE..............................916 338-7300
John A Mcmichael, CEO
Valerie Mcmichael, VP
EMP: 109 EST: 1965
SALES (est): 21.58MM **Privately Held**
Web: www.futurechevyofsac.com
SIC: **5511** 7538 7532 5531 Automobiles, new and used; General automotive repair shops; Body shop, automotive; Automotive parts

(P-7278)
PERRY FORD OF POWAY LLC
Also Called: Perry Ford
12740 Poway Rd (92064-4404)
PHONE..............................858 748-1400
Perry Falk, Managing Member
EMP: 100 EST: 1995
SQ FT: 50,000
SALES (est): 26.44MM **Privately Held**
Web: www.aaronfordofpoway.com
SIC: **5511** 7538 5531 5521 Automobiles, new and used; General automotive repair shops; Auto and home supply stores; Used car dealers

(P-7279)
PIERCEY NORTH INC
Also Called: Piercey Toyota
525 E Bayshore Rd (94063-2717)
PHONE..............................408 240-1400
William R Piercey, CEO
Artus V Whicker, *
Tom A Chadwell, *
EMP: 110 EST: 1969
SALES (est): 29.06MM
SALES (corp-wide): 102.66MM **Privately Held**
Web: www.toyotamilpitas.com
SIC: **5511** 5531 5521 5013 Automobiles, new and used; Auto and home supply stores; Used car dealers; Motor vehicle supplies and new parts
PA: Piercey Management Services, Inc.
    16901 Millikan Ave
    Irvine CA
    949 379-3701

(P-7280)
PMB MOTORCARS LLC
1829 E Garvey Ave N (91791-1403)
PHONE..............................626 384-3600
EMP: 2304
SALES (corp-wide): 5.16B **Privately Held**
Web: www.mbusa.com
SIC: **5511** 7538 Automobiles, new and used; General automotive repair shops
HQ: Pmb Motorcars, Llc
    2010 E Garvey Ave S
    West Covina CA
    626 859-1200

(P-7281)
POWAY TOYOTA SCION INC
Also Called: Poway Toyota

5511 - New And Used Car Dealers (P-7282)

13631 Poway Rd (92064-4703)
PHONE..................................858 486-2900
TOLL FREE: 800
Tim Moran, Genl Mgr
EMP: 129 EST: 1996
SQ FT: 10,000
SALES (est): 18.79MM **Privately Held**
Web: www.toyotaofpoway.com
SIC: 5511 7538 7515 Automobiles, new and used; General automotive repair shops; Passenger car leasing

(P-7282)
PRICE-SIMMS FORD LLC
Also Called: Ford Lincoln Fairfield
3050 Auto Mall Ct (94534-4184)
PHONE..................................707 421-3300
EMP: 70 EST: 2010
SALES (est): 38.52MM **Privately Held**
Web: www.fordfairfield.com
SIC: 5511 7538 Automobiles, new and used; General automotive repair shops

(P-7283)
PUTNAM MOTORS INC
Also Called: Putnam Lexus
390 Convention Way (94063-1405)
P.O. Box 2219 (94064-2219)
PHONE..................................650 381-3152
Marty Putnam, Pr
Ellen Beller, *
▼ EMP: 75 EST: 1989
SALES (est): 39.29MM **Privately Held**
Web: www.putnamlexus.com
SIC: 5511 7539 Automobiles, new and used; Automotive repair shops, nec

(P-7284)
R E BARBER-FORD
Also Called: Barber Volkeswagen
3440 E Main St (93003-5012)
P.O. Box 1628 (93002-1628)
PHONE..................................805 656-4259
EMP: 135
SIC: 5511 7538 7532 5521 New and used car dealers; General automotive repair shops; Top and body repair and paint shops ; Used car dealers

(P-7285)
RACEWAY FORD INC
Also Called: Quick Lane
5900 Sycamore Canyon Blvd (92507-0719)
PHONE..................................951 571-9300
John Barry Mccallan Junior, Pr
EMP: 145 EST: 1956
SALES (est): 52.88MM **Privately Held**
Web: www.racewayford.com
SIC: 5511 7538 Automobiles, new and used; General automotive repair shops

(P-7286)
RANCHO FORD INC
Also Called: Rancho
26895 Ynez Rd (92591-4695)
PHONE..................................951 699-1302
Eric Gosch, Pr
Marc L Gosch, *
Issac Lizarrago, *
EMP: 124 EST: 1984
SQ FT: 40,000
SALES (est): 48.47MM **Privately Held**
Web: www.goschfordtemecula.com
SIC: 5511 7532 7515 5521 Automobiles, new and used; Top and body repair and paint shops; Passenger car leasing; Used car dealers

(P-7287)
RESEDA DODGE SALES INC
Also Called: Simi Valley Chrysler
4470 Winnetka Ave (91364-4608)
PHONE..................................805 581-9090
Salem Aranout, Mgr
EMP: 69
SALES (corp-wide): 9.36MM **Privately Held**
Web: www.chrysler.com
SIC: 5511 7538 5531 Automobiles, new and used; General automotive repair shops; Automotive parts
PA: Reseda Dodge Sales, Inc.
4470 Winnetka Ave
Woodland Hills CA
818 345-4001

(P-7288)
RHI INC (PA)
Also Called: Robertson Honda
5841 Lankershim Blvd (91601-1035)
PHONE..................................818 508-3800
TOLL FREE: 800
Robert Robertson, Pr
▼ EMP: 97 EST: 1970
SQ FT: 130,000
SALES (est): 46.72MM
SALES (corp-wide): 46.72MM **Privately Held**
Web: www.victoryautomotivegroup.com
SIC: 5511 7538 7532 5531 Automobiles, new and used; General automotive repair shops; Body shop, automotive; Automotive parts

(P-7289)
RIVERVIEW INTL TRCKS LLC (PA)
2445 Evergreen Ave (95691-3011)
P.O. Box 716 (95691-0716)
PHONE..................................916 372-8541
Lyle Bassett, Mng Pt
Eric Bassett, *
EMP: 76 EST: 1945
SQ FT: 25,000
SALES (est): 51.61MM
SALES (corp-wide): 51.61MM **Privately Held**
Web: www.riverviewinternational.com
SIC: 5511 5531 7538 7532 Trucks, tractors, and trailers: new and used; Truck equipment and parts; General truck repair; Body shop, trucks

(P-7290)
RJMS CORPORATION (PA)
Also Called: Toyota Material Hdlg Nthrn Cal
6999 Southfront Rd (94551-8221)
PHONE..................................510 675-0500
TOLL FREE: 800
Richard Andres, CEO
Mark Andres, *
Stephen Andres, *
▲ EMP: 100 EST: 1921
SQ FT: 45,000
SALES (est): 115.11MM
SALES (corp-wide): 115.11MM **Privately Held**
Web: www.tmhnc.com
SIC: 5511 5085 7699 Automobiles, new and used; Industrial supplies; Industrial machinery and equipment repair

(P-7291)
ROTOLO CHEVROLET INC
16666 S Highland Ave (92336-1213)
P.O. Box 457 (92334-0457)
PHONE..................................866 756-9776
Marie Waddingham, Pr
Nina Rotolo, *
Darinda Madeiros, *
EMP: 137 EST: 1971
SQ FT: 51,000
SALES (est): 197.8MM **Privately Held**
Web: www.rotolochevy.com
SIC: 5511 5521 7538 Automobiles, new and used; Used car dealers; General automotive repair shops

(P-7292)
RPM LUXURY AUTO SALES INC
Also Called: Lexus of Roseville
300 Automall Dr (95661-3019)
P.O. Box 41529 (95841-0529)
PHONE..................................916 783-9111
Roger Karker, Brnch Mgr
EMP: 106
SALES (corp-wide): 83.37MM **Privately Held**
Web: www.lexus.com
SIC: 5511 7539 7538 Automobiles, new and used; Automotive repair shops, nec; General automotive repair shops
PA: Rpm Luxury Auto Sales, Inc.
2600 Fulton Ave
Sacramento CA
916 485-3987

(P-7293)
SAN DIEGO V INC (PA)
Also Called: San Diego Volvo
5350 Kearny Mesa Rd (92111-1802)
PHONE..................................888 308-2260
TOLL FREE: 800
Stephen Hinkle, CEO
Wesley G Hinkle, *
Robin Seal, *
EMP: 85 EST: 1956
SQ FT: 9,200
SALES (est): 34.3MM
SALES (corp-wide): 34.3MM **Privately Held**
Web: www.volvocarssandiego.com
SIC: 5511 7532 Automobiles, new and used; Top and body repair and paint shops

(P-7294)
SAN FERNANDO VALLEY AUTO LLC
Also Called: Rydell Chevrolet-Northridge
18600 Devonshire St (91324-1309)
PHONE..................................818 832-1600
Kelly Cashman, Dir
EMP: 189
SALES (corp-wide): 98.64MM **Privately Held**
Web: www.rydells.com
SIC: 5511 7538 7532 Automobiles, new and used; General automotive repair shops; Body shop, automotive
PA: San Fernando Valley Automotive, Llc
6001 Van Nuys Blvd
Van Nuys CA
818 817-4600

(P-7295)
SANBORN CHEVROLET INC
Also Called: Sanborn Collision Center
1210 S Cherokee Ln (95240-5994)
P.O. Box 1057 (95241-1057)
PHONE..................................209 334-5000
Kini Sanborn, Pr
EMP: 88 EST: 1971
SQ FT: 31,500
SALES (est): 38.15MM **Privately Held**
Web: www.sanbornchevrolet.com

SIC: 5511 7538 7532 5521 Automobiles, new and used; General automotive repair shops; Body shop, automotive; Automobiles, used cars only

(P-7296)
SEIDNER-MILLER INC
Also Called: Toyota of Glendora
1949 Auto Centre Dr (91740-6714)
PHONE..................................909 305-2000
Murrey Seidner, Pr
Peter Miller, *
EMP: 180 EST: 1993
SQ FT: 65,000
SALES (est): 44.48MM **Privately Held**
Web: www.toyotaofglendora.com
SIC: 5511 7532 7515 5521 Automobiles, new and used; Top and body repair and paint shops; Passenger car leasing; Used car dealers

(P-7297)
SELMAN CHEVROLET COMPANY
1800 E Chapman Ave (92867-7704)
P.O. Box 31 (92856-9031)
PHONE..................................714 633-3521
TOLL FREE: 800
William H Selman Junior, CEO
William H Selman Iii, VP
Daisy Kan, *
EMP: 107 EST: 1951
SQ FT: 4,000
SALES (est): 46.67MM **Privately Held**
Web: www.selmanchevy.com
SIC: 5511 7515 Automobiles, new and used; Passenger car leasing

(P-7298)
SIMPSON AUTOMOTIVE INC
Also Called: Simpson Buick Pontiac GMC
6600 Auto Center Dr (90621-2927)
PHONE..................................714 690-6200
David A Simpson, Pr
Dianna Ramsey, *
EMP: 91 EST: 1951
SQ FT: 46,000
SALES (est): 50.48MM **Privately Held**
Web: www.simpsonbuickgmcbuenapark.com
SIC: 5511 5531 7539 Automobiles, new and used; Auto and truck equipment and parts; Automotive repair shops, nec

(P-7299)
SOUTH BAY FORD INC (PA)
Also Called: Quick Lane
5100 W Rosecrans Ave (90250-6620)
P.O. Box 1550 (90251-1550)
PHONE..................................310 644-0211
TOLL FREE: 800
Gary Premeaux, CEO
Steve Wood, *
▼ EMP: 150 EST: 1993
SALES (est): 77.08MM
SALES (corp-wide): 77.08MM **Privately Held**
Web: www.southbayford.com
SIC: 5511 5531 7538 5521 Automobiles, new and used; Automotive parts; General automotive repair shops; Used car dealers

(P-7300)
SOUTH BAY TOYOTA
18416 S Western Ave (90248-3823)
PHONE..................................310 323-7800
David Wilson, Pr
David Ortiz, General Vice President*
EMP: 141 EST: 1989
SQ FT: 33,000
SALES (est): 48.98MM **Privately Held**

PRODUCTS & SERVICES SECTION
5511 - New And Used Car Dealers (P-7320)

Web: www.southbaytoyota.com
SIC: **5511** 7538 7515 Automobiles, new and used; General automotive repair shops; Passenger car leasing

(P-7301)
SOUTH CNTY LXUS AT MSSION VEJO
28242 Marguerite Pkwy (92692-3704)
PHONE..........................949 347-3400
Patrick Lustin, *Genl Mgr*
EMP: 200 **EST**: 2013
SALES (est): 37.3MM **Privately Held**
Web: www.southcountylexus.com
SIC: **5511** 7549 Automobiles, new and used; Automotive maintenance services

(P-7302)
SOUTHBAY EUROPEAN INC
Also Called: Southbay BMW
18800 Hawthorne Blvd (90504-5507)
PHONE..........................310 939-7300
Fritz Hitchcock, *Pr*
Peter Boesen, *
EMP: 100 **EST**: 1968
SQ FT: 150,000
SALES (est): 36.36MM **Privately Held**
Web: www.southbaybmw.com
SIC: **5511** 5531 7539 Automobiles, new and used; Automotive parts; Automotive repair shops, nec

(P-7303)
SOUTHWEST MATERIAL HDLG INC (PA)
Also Called: Southwest Toyota Lift
3725 Nobel Ct (91752-3267)
P.O. Box 1070 (91752-8070)
PHONE..........................951 727-0477
Kirt Little, *CEO*
Joseph G Little, *
▲ **EMP**: 115 **EST**: 1962
SQ FT: 10,000
SALES (est): 91.04MM
SALES (corp-wide): 91.04MM **Privately Held**
Web: www.swwarehousesolutions.com
SIC: **5511** 7389 7699 7359 Automobiles, new and used; Design, commercial and industrial; Industrial machinery and equipment rental and leasing, nec

(P-7304)
STERLING MOTORS LTD
Also Called: Sterling BMW
3000 W Coast Hwy (92663-4004)
PHONE..........................949 645-5900
Wayne Minor, *CEO*
John Belanger, *
Steve Army, *
Jim Hutton, *
Doug Janco, *
EMP: 80 **EST**: 1955
SQ FT: 27,000
SALES (est): 32.25MM **Privately Held**
Web: www.sterlingbmw.com
SIC: **5511** 7515 Automobiles, new and used; Passenger car leasing

(P-7305)
STINSON ENTERPRISES INC
Also Called: Modesto Scion World
4513 Mchenry Ave (95356-9546)
P.O. Box 576921 (95357-6725)
PHONE..........................209 529-2933
TOLL FREE: 800
Lynn H Stinson, *Pr*
Kevin H Stinson, *
EMP: 125 **EST**: 1969

SQ FT: 45,000
SALES (est): 24.08MM **Privately Held**
Web: www.modestotoyota.com
SIC: **5511** 7539 Automobiles, new and used; Automotive repair shops, nec

(P-7306)
SUNLAND FORD INC
Also Called: Sunland Ford-Lincoln-Mercury
15330 Palmdale Rd (92392-2498)
PHONE..........................760 241-7751
Ken Chambers, *Pr*
EMP: 90 **EST**: 1969
SQ FT: 10,000
SALES (est): 22.82MM **Privately Held**
Web: www.sunlandfordinc.com
SIC: **5511** 7538 5531 5521 Automobiles, new and used; General automotive repair shops; Auto and home supply stores; Used car dealers

(P-7307)
SUNRISE FORD
Also Called: Quick Lane
16005 Valley Blvd (92335-6419)
P.O. Box 2469 (92334-2469)
PHONE..........................909 822-4401
Robert Bruncati, *CEO*
Maureen Bruncati, *
EMP: 200 **EST**: 1944
SQ FT: 100,000
SALES (est): 59.69MM **Privately Held**
Web: www.quicklane.com
SIC: **5511** 5012 7538 Automobiles, new and used; Automobiles and other motor vehicles ; General automotive repair shops

(P-7308)
SYMES CADILLAC INC
Also Called: Symes Cadillac of Pasadena
3475 E Colorado Blvd (91107-3879)
PHONE..........................626 689-4386
John C Symes Ii, *CEO*
Bill Symes, *
Peter C Symes, *
EMP: 64 **EST**: 1948
SQ FT: 40,000
SALES (est): 29.48MM **Privately Held**
Web: www.cadillacpasadena.com
SIC: **5511** 7538 5521 Automobiles, new and used; General automotive repair shops; Automobiles, used cars only

(P-7309)
TED FORD JONES INC
Also Called: Ken Grody Ford
5555 Paseo Del Norte (92008-4429)
P.O. Box 1576 (92018-1576)
PHONE..........................760 438-9171
Kurt Maletych, *Brnch Mgr*
EMP: 150
SALES (corp-wide): 45.03MM **Privately Held**
Web: www.ford.com
SIC: **5511** 7538 5521 5012 Automobiles, new and used; General automotive repair shops; Used car dealers; Automobiles and other motor vehicles
PA: Ted Jones Ford, Inc.
  6211 Beach Blvd
  Buena Park CA
  714 521-3110

(P-7310)
TED STEVENS INC
Also Called: Marin Acura
5860 Paradise Dr (94925-1203)
P.O. Box 218 (94976-0218)
PHONE..........................415 927-5664
Theodore Stevens, *Pr*

EMP: 67 **EST**: 1985
SALES (est): 19.53MM **Privately Held**
Web: www.acura.com
SIC: **5511** 7515 Automobiles, new and used; Passenger car leasing

(P-7311)
THEODORE ROBINS INC
Also Called: Theodore Robins Ford
2060 Harbor Blvd (92627-2673)
P.O. Box 5055 (92628-5055)
PHONE..........................949 642-0010
James M Robins, *Pr*
David Robins, *
Dave Robins Used, *Vice Manager*
EMP: 78 **EST**: 1921
SQ FT: 65,000
SALES (est): 25.29MM **Privately Held**
Web: www.robinsford.com
SIC: **5511** 5012 Automobiles, new and used; Automobiles and other motor vehicles

(P-7312)
THOMAS BAVARIAN MTR WORKS INC
Also Called: Steve Thomas BMW
411 E Daily Dr (93010-5818)
PHONE..........................805 482-8878
TOLL FREE: 800
Steve Thomas, *Pr*
Mary Schroeder, *
Christine Thomas, *
Steve Thomas Junior, *VP*
Robert Schroeder, *
EMP: 69 **EST**: 1983
SQ FT: 21,000
SALES (est): 27.03MM **Privately Held**
Web: www.stevethomasbmw.com
SIC: **5511** 7538 Automobiles, new and used; General automotive repair shops

(P-7313)
THREE-WAY CHEVROLET CO (PA)
4501 Wible Rd (93313-2639)
P.O. Box 9609 (93389-9609)
PHONE..........................661 847-6400
EMP: 180 **EST**: 1947
SALES (est): 157.35MM
SALES (corp-wide): 157.35MM **Privately Held**
Web: www.3waychevrolet.com
SIC: **5511** 5531 7538 7515 Automobiles, new and used; Automotive parts; General automotive repair shops; Passenger car leasing

(P-7314)
TOMS TRUCK CENTER INC
Also Called: Isuzu Truck Services
1008 E 4th St (92701-4779)
P.O. Box 88 (92702-0088)
PHONE..........................714 835-1978
TOLL FREE: 800
K C Heidler, *Brnch Mgr*
EMP: 177
SALES (corp-wide): 76.55MM **Privately Held**
Web: www.ttruck.com
SIC: **5511** 5012 Automobiles, new and used; Automobiles and other motor vehicles
PA: Tom's Truck Center, Inc.
  909 N Grand Ave
  Santa Ana CA
  800 238-9308

(P-7315)
TOWNE MOTOR COMPANY
Also Called: Towne Ford Sales
1 Bair Island Rd (94063-2764)

P.O. Box 670 (94064-0670)
PHONE..........................650 366-5744
Benjamin Kopf Junior, *Pr*
Marian Kopf, *
Robert Kopf, *
▼ **EMP**: 102 **EST**: 1926
SALES (est): 32.94MM **Privately Held**
Web: www.towneford.com
SIC: **5511** 7539 7549 Automobiles, new and used; Automotive repair shops, nec; Automotive customizing services, nonfactory basis

(P-7316)
TOYOTA OF ORANGE INC
1400 N Tustin St (92867-3995)
PHONE..........................714 639-6750
David Wilson, *Pr*
EMP: 135 **EST**: 1972
SQ FT: 38,000
SALES (est): 60.86MM
SALES (corp-wide): 60.86MM **Privately Held**
Web: www.toyotaoforange.com
SIC: **5511** 5521 5012 Automobiles, new and used; Used car dealers; Automobiles and other motor vehicles
PA: D W W Co., Inc.
  1400 N Tustin St
  Orange CA
  714 516-3111

(P-7317)
TOYOTA OF RIVERSIDE INC
7870 Indiana Ave (92504-4109)
PHONE..........................951 687-1622
David Wilson, *Pr*
EMP: 109 **EST**: 1969
SQ FT: 100,000
SALES (est): 52.1MM **Privately Held**
Web: www.toyotaofriverside.com
SIC: **5511** 5531 7538 5521 Automobiles, new and used; Automotive parts; General automotive repair shops; Used car dealers

(P-7318)
TRACY AUTO LP
Also Called: Tracy Toyota
2895 Naglee Rd (95304-7307)
PHONE..........................209 834-1111
Keena Turner, *Pt*
Ronnie Lott, *Pt*
EMP: 68 **EST**: 1999
SALES (est): 27.64MM **Privately Held**
Web: www.tracytoyota.com
SIC: **5511** 7514 Automobiles, new and used; Rent-a-car service

(P-7319)
TRANSWEST TRUCK CENTER LLC
10150 Cherry Ave (92335-5222)
PHONE..........................909 770-5170
EMP: 75 **EST**: 1975
SQ FT: 4,000
SALES (est): 21.98MM
SALES (corp-wide): 233.56MM **Privately Held**
Web: www.trans-west.com
SIC: **5511** 5531 5013 Automobiles, new and used; Automotive parts; Motor vehicle supplies and new parts
PA: Los Angeles Truck Centers, Llc
  2429 Peck Rd
  Whittier CA
  562 447-1200

(P-7320)
TUTTLE-CLICK FORD INC
Also Called: Tuttle Click Ford

(PA)=Parent Co (HQ)=Headquarters
✿ = New Business established in last 2 years

5511 - New And Used Car Dealers (P-7321)

43 Auto Center Dr (92618-2898)
PHONE..............................949 855-1704
Bob Tuttle, Pr
James H Click, *
Chris Cotter, *
Elvia Morales, *
EMP: 225 EST: 1980
SQ FT: 50,000
SALES (est): 49.04MM Privately Held
Web: www.quicklane.com
SIC: 5511 5521 7538 Automobiles, new and used; Used car dealers; General automotive repair shops

(P-7321)
VAHI TOYOTA INC (PA)
Also Called: Valley-HI Toyota Honda
14612 Valley Center Dr (92395-4205)
P.O. Box 1508 (92393-1508)
PHONE..............................760 241-6484
Kent Browning, Pr
EMP: 120 EST: 1971
SQ FT: 17,000
SALES (est): 26.35MM
SALES (corp-wide): 26.35MM Privately Held
Web: www.valleyhitoyota.com
SIC: 5511 7538 5561 5531 Automobiles, new and used; General automotive repair shops; Recreational vehicle dealers; Auto and home supply stores

(P-7322)
VALLEY AUTO SALES & LSG LLC
Also Called: Madera Chevy, Olds, Toyota
1300 Country Club Dr (93638-1573)
PHONE..............................559 674-9000
Henry M Mayfohrt Junior, Managing Member
EMP: 60 EST: 2000
SALES (est): 3MM Privately Held
Web: www.maderatoyota.com
SIC: 5511 7538 Automobiles, new and used; General automotive repair shops

(P-7323)
VILLA FORD INC
Also Called: David Wilson's Villa Ford
2550 N Tustin St (92865-3099)
PHONE..............................714 637-8222
TOLL FREE: 888
Peggy Baldwin-butler, Pr
Brian Butler, *
Peggy Butler, *
Karen Baldwin, *
EMP: 132 EST: 1970
SQ FT: 38,745
SALES (est): 47.31MM Privately Held
Web: www.villaford.com
SIC: 5511 7532 7549 Automobiles, new and used; Body shop, automotive; Automotive maintenance services

(P-7324)
VISTA FORD INC
Also Called: Vista Ford of Oxnard
1501 Auto Center Dr (93036-7916)
PHONE..............................805 983-5611
Randy Haddock, Mgr
EMP: 77
SALES (corp-wide): 99.66MM Privately Held
Web: www.envisionfordoxnard.com
SIC: 5511 5521 7538 Automobiles, new and used; Used car dealers; General automotive repair shops
PA: Vista Ford Inc.
21501 Ventura Blvd
Woodland Hills CA
818 884-7600

(P-7325)
VOLKSWAGEN OF VAN NUYS INC
300 Hitchcock Way (93105-4002)
PHONE..............................323 873-3311
Ludwig Pflock, Pr
EMP: 100 EST: 1991
SALES (est): 25.38MM Privately Held
Web: www.vw.com
SIC: 5511 7538 Automobiles, new and used; General automotive repair shops

(P-7326)
VOLKSWAGEN SANTA MONICA INC (PA)
Also Called: Lexus Santa Monica
2440 Santa Monica Blvd (90404-2039)
PHONE..............................310 829-1888
TOLL FREE: 888
Michael Sullivan, *
Kerry Sullivan, *
Hazel R Sullivan, *
EMP: 170 EST: 1964
SQ FT: 10,000
SALES (est): 110.91MM
SALES (corp-wide): 110.91MM Privately Held
Web: www.volkswagensantamonica.com
SIC: 5511 7532 7538 Automobiles, new and used; Body shop, automotive; General automotive repair shops

(P-7327)
WALNUT CREEK ASSOCIATES 2 INC
Also Called: Walnut Creek Honda
1707 N Main St (94596-4104)
P.O. Box 5500 (94596-1500)
PHONE..............................925 934-0530
David Robb, Pr
Ralph Robb, *
Nancy Robb, *
Terri Stuart, *
EMP: 86 EST: 1964
SALES (est): 25.78MM Privately Held
Web: www.walnutcreekhonda.com
SIC: 5511 7538 Automobiles, new and used; General automotive repair shops

(P-7328)
WALTER TIMMONS ENTERPRISES INC
Also Called: Timmons Volkswagen
3940 Cherry Ave (90807-3727)
PHONE..............................562 595-4601
Erika Timmons, Pr
Greg Timmons, *
EMP: 60 EST: 1971
SQ FT: 32,000
SALES (est): 31.43MM Privately Held
Web: www.timmonslongbeach.com
SIC: 5511 7538 5531 Automobiles, new and used; General automotive repair shops; Auto and truck equipment and parts

(P-7329)
WALTERS AUTO SALES AND SVC INC
Also Called: Mercedes Benz of Riverside
3213 Adams St (92504-4002)
PHONE..............................888 316-4097
Steve Kienle, Genl Mgr
Helga Kienle, *
Lothar Wacker, *
EMP: 248 EST: 1964
SQ FT: 14,000
SALES (est): 53.09MM Privately Held
Web: walters.mercedesdealer.com

SIC: 5511 5012 Automobiles, new and used; Automobiles and other motor vehicles

(P-7330)
WAYNE GOSSETT FORD INC
Also Called: Encinitas Ford
1424 Encinitas Blvd (92024-2930)
P.O. Box 230945 (92023-0945)
PHONE..............................760 753-6286
TOLL FREE: 800
Mark S Wheeler, Pr
EMP: 95 EST: 1960
SALES (est): 36.68MM Privately Held
Web: www.encinitasford.com
SIC: 5511 7549 Automobiles, new and used; Do-it-yourself garages

(P-7331)
WEATHERFORD MOTORS INC
Also Called: Weatherford BMW
1967 Market St (94520-2626)
PHONE..............................510 654-8280
Luis Garcia, CEO
Mitsunori Umebayashi, *
Kathleen Ingrim, *
Jenn Bishop, *
Rich Deeds, *
EMP: 112 EST: 1971
SQ FT: 23,000
SALES (est): 45.06MM Privately Held
Web: www.weatherfordbmw.com
SIC: 5511 7538 Automobiles, new and used; General automotive repair shops
HQ: Sojitz Corporation of America
1120 Avenue Of The Americ
New York NY
212 704-6500

(P-7332)
WEBER MOTORS FRESNO INC
Also Called: BMW Fresno
7171 N Palm Ave (93650-1082)
PHONE..............................559 447-6700
Yrma Rico, Pr
Shahram Mihantajouh, *
Al Monjazeb, *
EMP: 65 EST: 1970
SQ FT: 17,000
SALES (est): 25.19MM Privately Held
Web: www.bmwgroup.com
SIC: 5511 7549 7538 Automobiles, new and used; Automotive maintenance services; General automotive repair shops

(P-7333)
WESLEY B LASHER INV CORP (PA)
Also Called: Lasher Wes ADI/ Ddg/ Volkswagen
5800 Florin Rd (95823-2301)
PHONE..............................916 290-8500
Mark Lasher, Pr
Scott Lasher, *
EMP: 100 EST: 1955
SQ FT: 10,000
SALES (est): 52.21MM
SALES (corp-wide): 52.21MM Privately Held
Web: www.dodge.com
SIC: 5511 7538 5521 Automobiles, new and used; General automotive repair shops; Used car dealers

(P-7334)
WESTRUP-SADLER INC
Also Called: Reliable Pntiac Cdllac Bick GM
400 Automall Dr (95661-3020)
PHONE..............................916 783-2077
Bruce W Westrup, Pr
Joy H Westrup, *

EMP: 89 EST: 1969
SQ FT: 41,000
SALES (est): 9.29MM Privately Held
Web: www.reliabledealer.com
SIC: 5511 7515 Automobiles, new and used; Passenger car leasing

(P-7335)
WESTRUX INTERNATIONAL INC (PA)
15555 Valley View Ave (90670-5718)
PHONE..............................562 404-1020
David M Kenney, Pr
John M Reynolds, *
▲ EMP: 70 EST: 1982
SALES (est): 97.23MM
SALES (corp-wide): 97.23MM Privately Held
Web: www.westrux.com
SIC: 5511 5531 7513 7538 Trucks, tractors, and trailers: new and used; Truck equipment and parts; Truck rental, without drivers; Truck engine repair, except industrial

(P-7336)
YORK ENTERPRISES SOUTH INC
Also Called: Huntington Beach Ford
18255 Beach Blvd (92648-1351)
PHONE..............................714 842-6611
Oscar Bakhtiari, CEO
Donna Graham, *
EMP: 100 EST: 1989
SALES (est): 24.02MM Privately Held
Web: www.huntingtonbeachford.com
SIC: 5511 7538 Automobiles, new and used; General automotive repair shops

5521 Used Car Dealers

(P-7337)
CARMAX INC
25560 Madison Ave (92562-9095)
PHONE..............................951 387-3887
EMP: 115
SALES (corp-wide): 29.68B Publicly Held
Web: www.carmax.com
SIC: 5521 7539 Automobiles, used cars only; Automotive repair shops, nec
PA: Carmax, Inc.
12800 Tuckahoe Creek Pkwy
Richmond VA
804 747-0422

(P-7338)
K MOTORS INC
Also Called: Toyota of El Cajon
965 Arnele Ave (92020-3001)
PHONE..............................619 270-3000
Robert Kaminsky, Pr
Gary Kaminsky, *
Greg Kaminsky, *
Kim Kaminsky, *
Gregory Kaminsky, *
EMP: 186 EST: 1956
SQ FT: 29,497
SALES (est): 53.04MM Privately Held
Web: www.toyota.com
SIC: 5521 5013 5511 Automobiles, used cars only; Automotive supplies and parts; Automobiles, new and used

5531 - Auto And Home Supply Stores (P-7358)

5531 Auto And Home Supply Stores

(P-7339)
AKH COMPANY INC
Also Called: Discount Tire Center 038
1647 W Redlands Blvd Ste C (92373)
PHONE.............................909 748-5016
Marc Fortin, *Mgr*
EMP: 88
SALES (corp-wide): 31.08MM **Privately Held**
Web: www.discounttires.com
SIC: **5531** 7539 5014 Automotive tires; Wheel alignment, automotive; Automobile tires and tubes
PA: Akh Company, Inc.
 1160 N Anaheim Blvd
 Anaheim CA
 800 999-2878

(P-7340)
AKH COMPANY INC
Also Called: Discount Tire Center 077
23316 Sunnymead Blvd (92553-5227)
PHONE.............................951 924-5356
Juan Valdes, *Mgr*
EMP: 110
SALES (corp-wide): 31.08MM **Privately Held**
Web: www.discounttires.com
SIC: **5531** 5014 7539 Automotive tires; Automobile tires and tubes; Wheel alignment, automotive
PA: Akh Company, Inc.
 1160 N Anaheim Blvd
 Anaheim CA
 800 999-2878

(P-7341)
AM-PAC TIRE DIST INC (DH)
Also Called: Tire Pros
51 Moreland Rd (93065-1662)
P.O. Box 1949 (28070-1949)
▲ EMP: 75 EST: 1999
SALES (est): 110.83MM
SALES (corp-wide): 1.82B **Privately Held**
Web: www.amr1.com
SIC: **5531** 5014 Automotive tires; Tires and tubes
HQ: American Tire Distributors, Inc.
 12200 Herbert Wayne Ct # 150
 Huntersville NC
 704 992-2000

(P-7342)
ATV CANTER LLC (PA)
Also Called: American Tire Depot
4490 Ayers Ave (90058-4317)
PHONE.............................562 977-8565
Ara Tchaghlassian, *Pr*
Craig Anderson, *
◆ EMP: 70 EST: 1994
SQ FT: 15,000
SALES (est): 265.96MM **Privately Held**
Web: www.americantiredepot.com
SIC: **5531** 7538 Automotive tires; General automotive repair shops

(P-7343)
AUTOZONE INC
Also Called: Autozone
1361 W 190th St (90248-4306)
PHONE.............................310 525-2333
Raul Luna, *Brnch Mgr*
EMP: 60
SALES (corp-wide): 17.46B **Publicly Held**
Web: www.autozonepro.com
SIC: **5531** 5013 Automotive parts; Automotive supplies and parts
PA: Autozone, Inc.
 123 S Front St
 Memphis TN
 901 495-6500

(P-7344)
BI WAREHOUSING INC (PA)
Also Called: Anheuser-Busch
5404 Pacific St (95677-2714)
PHONE.............................916 624-0654
Bart W Riebes, *CEO*
Mel Todd, *
EMP: 83 EST: 1992
SQ FT: 30,000
SALES (est): 63.82MM
SALES (corp-wide): 63.82MM **Privately Held**
Web: www.napaonline.com
SIC: **5531** 5013 7539 Automotive parts; Automotive supplies and parts; Machine shop, automotive

(P-7345)
BI WAREHOUSING INC
Also Called: Riebe's Auto Parts
5404 Pacific St Ste B (95677-2714)
PHONE.............................916 624-0654
Mel Todd, *Genl Mgr*
EMP: 141
SALES (corp-wide): 63.82MM **Privately Held**
Web: www.napaonline.com
SIC: **5531** 5013 Automotive parts; Automotive supplies and parts
PA: Bi Warehousing, Inc.
 5404 Pacific St
 Rocklin CA
 916 624-0654

(P-7346)
CLASSIC CAMARO INC
Also Called: Classic Firebird
18460 Gothard St (92648-1229)
PHONE.............................714 847-6887
Jeffrey M Leonard, *CEO*
▲ EMP: 115 EST: 1977
SQ FT: 30,000
SALES (est): 24.18MM **Privately Held**
Web: www.classicindustries.com
SIC: **5531** 5013 Automotive accessories; Automotive supplies and parts

(P-7347)
FORNACA INC (PA)
Also Called: Frank Toyota & Scion
2400 National City Blvd (91950-6628)
P.O. Box 540 (91951-0540)
PHONE.............................866 308-9461
James Fornaca, *CEO*
Gary Fenelli, *
Ronald Fornaca, *
EMP: 140 EST: 1978
SQ FT: 150,000
SALES (est): 44.01MM **Privately Held**
Web: www.frankmotors.com
SIC: **5531** 5511 7532 Auto and home supply stores; Automobiles, new and used; Top and body repair and paint shops

(P-7348)
FRED M BOERNER MOTOR CO (PA)
Also Called: Boerner Truck Center
3620 E Florence Ave (90255-5905)
PHONE.............................323 560-3882
▼ EMP: 86 EST: 1926
SALES (est): 20.52MM
SALES (corp-wide): 20.52MM **Privately Held**
SIC: **5531** 7538 5012 Truck equipment and parts; General truck repair; Truck bodies

(P-7349)
GLOBAL TRADE ALLIANCE INC
Also Called: Action Crash Parts
13642 Orden Dr (90670-6353)
PHONE.............................562 944-6422
Todd Hanson, *Mgr*
EMP: 114
SALES (corp-wide): 12.79B **Publicly Held**
SIC: **5531** 5013 Automotive parts; Automotive supplies and parts
HQ: Global Trade Alliance, Inc.
 2040 S Hamilton Rd
 Columbus OH
 614 751-3100

(P-7350)
GOODYEAR COML TIRE & SVC CTRS
Also Called: Goodyear Coml Tire & Svc Ctrs
3085 W Capitol Ave (95691-2912)
PHONE.............................479 788-6400
Nicholas Stone, *Mgr*
EMP: 264
SALES (corp-wide): 20.8B **Publicly Held**
Web: www.goodyear.com
SIC: **5531** 7538 Automotive tires; General automotive repair shops
HQ: Goodyear Commercial Tire And Service Centers
 1000 S 21st St
 Fort Smith AR
 479 788-6400

(P-7351)
HANSON DISTRIBUTING COMPANY
19154 San Jose Ave (91748-1415)
PHONE.............................626 839-4026
EMP: 65
SALES (corp-wide): 64.25MM **Privately Held**
Web: www.hansondistributing.com
SIC: **5531** 5099 Auto and home supply stores ; Brass goods
PA: Hanson Distributing Company
 975 W 8th St
 Azusa CA
 626 224-9800

(P-7352)
KRACO ENTERPRISES LLC
505 E Euclid Ave (90222-2890)
PHONE.............................310 639-0666
◆ EMP: 164
Web: www.kraco.com
SIC: **5531** 3069 5013 Automotive accessories; Hard rubber and molded rubber products; Motor vehicle supplies and new parts

(P-7353)
MOSS MOTORS LTD (PA)
400 Rutherford St (93117-3702)
PHONE.............................805 967-4546
◆ EMP: 130 EST: 1948
SALES (est): 24.14MM
SALES (corp-wide): 24.14MM **Privately Held**
Web: www.mossmotors.com
SIC: **5531** 5013 Automotive parts; Automotive supplies and parts

(P-7354)
PARKHOUSE TIRE SERVICE INC (PA)
Also Called: Parkhouse Tire
6006 Shull St (90201-6237)
P.O. Box 2430 (90202-2430)
PHONE.............................562 928-0421
◆ EMP: 75 EST: 1971
SALES (est): 140.36MM
SALES (corp-wide): 140.36MM **Privately Held**
Web: www.parkhousetire.com
SIC: **5531** 5014 7534 Automotive tires; Automobile tires and tubes; Rebuilding and retreading tires

(P-7355)
RAMONA AUTO SERVICES INC
Also Called: Firestone
2451 S Euclid Ave (91762-6617)
P.O. Box 960 (92546-0960)
PHONE.............................909 986-1785
Chris Wyborny, *Brnch Mgr*
EMP: 74
Web: www.ramonatire.com
SIC: **5531** 7538 Automotive tires; General automotive repair shops
PA: Ramona Auto Services, Inc.
 2350 W Menlo Ave
 Hemet CA

(P-7356)
SANTA MARIA TIRE INC (PA)
Also Called: SM Tire
2170 Hutton Rd Bldg A (93444-9717)
P.O. Box 6007 (93456-6007)
PHONE.............................805 347-4793
Craig Stephens, *Pr*
Brenee Stephens, *
C Kent Stephens, *
Cameron Stephens, *
Conrad Stephens Attorney, *Prin*
EMP: 75 EST: 1946
SALES (est): 20.64MM
SALES (corp-wide): 20.64MM **Privately Held**
Web: www.smtire.com
SIC: **5531** 7534 Automotive tires; Rebuilding and retreading tires

(P-7357)
SOUTHERN CAL DISC TIRE CO INC
Also Called: Discount Tire
34734 Alvarado Niles Rd (94587-4502)
PHONE.............................510 429-1977
Mike Balestreri, *Brnch Mgr*
EMP: 122
SALES (corp-wide): 3.69B **Privately Held**
Web: www.discounttire.com
SIC: **5531** 5014 5013 Automotive tires; Automobile tires and tubes; Wheels, motor vehicle
HQ: Southern California Discount Tire Co., Inc.
 16100 N Grnway Hyden Loop
 Scottsdale AZ
 602 996-0201

(P-7358)
SOUTHERN CAL DISC TIRE CO INC
Also Called: Discount Tire
11127 Folsom Blvd (95670-6132)
PHONE.............................916 638-2388
Dave Tagliaferi, *Mgr*
EMP: 81
SALES (corp-wide): 3.69B **Privately Held**
Web: www.discounttire.com
SIC: **5531** 5013 Automotive tires; Wheels, motor vehicle
HQ: Southern California Discount Tire Co., Inc.
 16100 N Grnway Hyden Loop

5531 - Auto And Home Supply Stores (P-7359)
PRODUCTS & SERVICES SECTION

Scottsdale AZ
602 996-0201

(P-7359)
SOUTHERN CAL DISC TIRE CO INC
Also Called: Discount Tire
600 W Florida Ave (92543-4009)
PHONE..........................951 929-2130
Josh Mccartner, *Mgr*
EMP: 122
SALES (corp-wide): 3.69B **Privately Held**
Web: www.discounttire.com
SIC: **5531** 5013 Automotive tires; Wheels, motor vehicle
HQ: Southern California Discount Tire Co., Inc.
16100 N Grnway Hyden Loop
Scottsdale AZ
602 996-0201

(P-7360)
SOUTHERN CAL DISC TIRE CO INC
Also Called: Discount Tire
550 N Broadway (92025-2720)
PHONE..........................760 741-9805
David Benibedez, *Mgr*
EMP: 122
SALES (corp-wide): 3.69B **Privately Held**
Web: www.discounttire.com
SIC: **5531** 5014 5013 Automotive tires; Automobile tires and tubes; Wheels, motor vehicle
HQ: Southern California Discount Tire Co., Inc.
16100 N Grnway Hyden Loop
Scottsdale AZ
602 996-0201

(P-7361)
SOUTHERN CAL DISC TIRE CO INC
Also Called: Discount Tire
15672 Springdale St (92649-1315)
PHONE..........................714 901-8226
Joe Ortiz, *Mgr*
EMP: 108
SALES (corp-wide): 3.69B **Privately Held**
Web: www.discounttire.com
SIC: **5531** 5013 Automotive tires; Wheels, motor vehicle
HQ: Southern California Discount Tire Co., Inc.
16100 N Grnway Hyden Loop
Scottsdale AZ
602 996-0201

(P-7362)
SOUTHERN CAL DISC TIRE CO INC
Also Called: Discount Tire
705 S Grand Ave (91740-4141)
PHONE..........................626 335-2883
Abel Ariola, *Mgr*
EMP: 95
SALES (corp-wide): 3.69B **Privately Held**
Web: www.discounttire.com
SIC: **5531** 5013 Automotive tires; Wheels, motor vehicle
HQ: Southern California Discount Tire Co., Inc.
16100 N Grnway Hyden Loop
Scottsdale AZ
602 996-0201

(P-7363)
SOUTHERN CAL DISC TIRE CO INC
Also Called: Discount Tire
780 Grand Ave (92078-1249)
PHONE..........................760 744-3526
Brett Harris, *Mgr*
EMP: 95
SALES (corp-wide): 3.69B **Privately Held**
Web: www.discounttire.com
SIC: **5531** 5014 Automotive tires; Automobile tires and tubes
HQ: Southern California Discount Tire Co., Inc.
16100 N Grnway Hyden Loop
Scottsdale AZ
602 996-0201

(P-7364)
SOUTHERN CAL DISC TIRE CO INC
Also Called: Discount Tire
4640 Telephone Rd (93003-5630)
PHONE..........................805 639-0166
Thomas Gensen, *Mgr*
EMP: 95
SQ FT: 4,500
SALES (corp-wide): 3.69B **Privately Held**
Web: www.discounttire.com
SIC: **5531** 7538 Automotive tires; General automotive repair shops
HQ: Southern California Discount Tire Co., Inc.
16100 N Grnway Hyden Loop
Scottsdale AZ
602 996-0201

(P-7365)
SOUTHERN CAL DISC TIRE CO INC
Also Called: Discount Tire
209 S Escondido Blvd (92025-4116)
PHONE..........................760 741-3801
Pat Fuller, *Mgr*
EMP: 122
SALES (corp-wide): 3.69B **Privately Held**
Web: www.discounttire.com
SIC: **5531** 5014 5013 Automotive tires; Automobile tires and tubes; Wheels, motor vehicle
HQ: Southern California Discount Tire Co., Inc.
16100 N Grnway Hyden Loop
Scottsdale AZ
602 996-0201

(P-7366)
SOUTHERN CAL DISC TIRE CO INC
Also Called: Discount Tire
685 San Rodolfo Dr (92075-2001)
PHONE..........................858 481-6387
Bruce Hopple, *Brnch Mgr*
EMP: 122
SALES (corp-wide): 3.69B **Privately Held**
Web: www.discounttire.com
SIC: **5531** 5014 Automotive tires; Automobile tires and tubes
HQ: Southern California Discount Tire Co., Inc.
16100 N Grnway Hyden Loop
Scottsdale AZ
602 996-0201

(P-7367)
SOUTHERN CAL DISC TIRE CO INC
Also Called: Discount Tire
12651 Poway Rd (92064-4415)
PHONE..........................858 486-3600
Alan Birse, *Brnch Mgr*
EMP: 122
SALES (corp-wide): 3.69B **Privately Held**
Web: www.discounttire.com
SIC: **5531** 5014 5013 Automotive tires; Automobile tires and tubes; Wheels, motor vehicle
HQ: Southern California Discount Tire Co., Inc.
16100 N Grnway Hyden Loop
Scottsdale AZ
602 996-0201

(P-7368)
SOUTHERN CAL DISC TIRE CO INC
Also Called: Discount Tire
1037 S Coast Hwy (92054-5004)
PHONE..........................760 439-8539
John Toonds, *Mgr*
EMP: 122
SALES (corp-wide): 3.69B **Privately Held**
Web: www.discounttire.com
SIC: **5531** 5014 Automotive tires; Automobile tires and tubes
HQ: Southern California Discount Tire Co., Inc.
16100 N Grnway Hyden Loop
Scottsdale AZ
602 996-0201

(P-7369)
SOUTHERN CAL DISC TIRE CO INC
Also Called: Discount Tire
6434 Florin Rd (95823-2327)
PHONE..........................916 427-1961
Amos Bennett, *Mgr*
EMP: 122
SALES (corp-wide): 3.69B **Privately Held**
Web: www.discounttire.com
SIC: **5531** 5013 Automotive tires; Wheels, motor vehicle
HQ: Southern California Discount Tire Co., Inc.
16100 N Grnway Hyden Loop
Scottsdale AZ
602 996-0201

(P-7370)
SOUTHERN CAL DISC TIRE CO INC
Also Called: Discount Tire
1610 Broadway St (94063-2402)
PHONE..........................650 366-4003
Dan Richards, *Brnch Mgr*
EMP: 108
SALES (corp-wide): 3.69B **Privately Held**
Web: www.discounttire.com
SIC: **5531** 5014 5013 Automotive tires; Automobile tires and tubes; Wheels, motor vehicle
HQ: Southern California Discount Tire Co., Inc.
16100 N Grnway Hyden Loop
Scottsdale AZ
602 996-0201

(P-7371)
SOUTHERN CAL DISC TIRE CO INC
Also Called: Discount Tire
32 W El Camino Real (94040-2602)
PHONE..........................650 988-9611
Dan Appleman, *Brnch Mgr*
EMP: 122
SALES (corp-wide): 3.69B **Privately Held**
Web: www.discounttire.com
SIC: **5531** 5014 5013 Automotive tires; Automobile tires and tubes; Wheels, motor vehicle
HQ: Southern California Discount Tire Co., Inc.
16100 N Grnway Hyden Loop
Scottsdale AZ
602 996-0201

(P-7372)
SOUTHERN CAL DISC TIRE CO INC
Also Called: Discount Tire
107 N El Camino Real (92024-2802)
PHONE..........................760 634-2202
Alan Brise, *Brnch Mgr*
EMP: 122
SALES (corp-wide): 3.69B **Privately Held**
Web: www.discounttire.com
SIC: **5531** 7534 Automotive tires; Tire repair shop
HQ: Southern California Discount Tire Co., Inc.
16100 N Grnway Hyden Loop
Scottsdale AZ
602 996-0201

(P-7373)
SOUTHERN CAL DISC TIRE CO INC
Also Called: Discount Tire
980 E Hamilton Ave (95008-0615)
PHONE..........................408 377-5010
Marlon Arevall, *Mgr*
EMP: 108
SALES (corp-wide): 3.69B **Privately Held**
Web: www.discounttire.com
SIC: **5531** 5014 Automotive tires; Automobile tires and tubes
HQ: Southern California Discount Tire Co., Inc.
16100 N Grnway Hyden Loop
Scottsdale AZ
602 996-0201

(P-7374)
SOUTHERN CAL DISC TIRE CO INC
Also Called: Discount Tire
536 E Brokaw Rd (95112-1003)
PHONE..........................408 436-8274
Tracy Stevens, *Prin*
EMP: 122
SALES (corp-wide): 3.69B **Privately Held**
Web: www.discounttire.com
SIC: **5531** 5014 5013 Automotive tires; Automobile tires and tubes; Wheels, motor vehicle
HQ: Southern California Discount Tire Co., Inc.
16100 N Grnway Hyden Loop
Scottsdale AZ
602 996-0201

(P-7375)
SOUTHERN CAL DISC TIRE CO INC
Also Called: Discount Tire
3935 Convoy St (92111-3723)
PHONE..........................858 278-0661
Mark Leisenring, *Off Mgr*
EMP: 122
SALES (corp-wide): 3.69B **Privately Held**
Web: www.discounttire.com
SIC: **5531** 5014 Automotive tires; Automobile tires and tubes
HQ: Southern California Discount Tire Co., Inc.
16100 N Grnway Hyden Loop
Scottsdale AZ
602 996-0201

PRODUCTS & SERVICES SECTION

5551 - Boat Dealers (P-7393)

(P-7376)
SOUTHERN CAL DISC TIRE CO INC
Also Called: Discount Tire
20741 Avalon Blvd (90746-3313)
PHONE..................310 324-2569
Arnel Ramos, Mgr
EMP: 122
SALES (corp-wide): 3.69B Privately Held
Web: www.discounttire.com
SIC: 5531 5014 5013 Automotive tires; Automobile tires and tubes; Wheels, motor vehicle
HQ: Southern California Discount Tire Co., Inc.
16100 N Grnway Hyden Loop
Scottsdale AZ
602 996-0201

(P-7377)
SOUTHERN TIRE MART LLC
GCR Tires & Service 859
1401 Richards Blvd (95811-0423)
PHONE..................916 447-4220
Christopher Chadwick, Mgr
EMP: 71
SALES (corp-wide): 607.12MM Privately Held
Web: www.stmtires.com
SIC: 5531 5014 Automotive tires; Truck tires and tubes
PA: Southern Tire Mart, Llc
800 Highway 98 Byp
Columbia MS
601 424-3200

(P-7378)
TBC SHARED SERVICES LLC
742 S Main St (95472-4275)
PHONE..................707 829-9864
EMP: 2170
SIC: 5531 7534 Automotive tires; Tire retreading and repair shops

(P-7379)
TIRES WAREHOUSE LLC
18203 Mount Baldy Cir (92708-6117)
PHONE..................714 432-8851
Terry Ahlstrom, Brnch Mgr
EMP: 261
SALES (corp-wide): 1.56B Privately Held
Web: www.usautoforce.com
SIC: 5531 5014 Automotive tires; Tires and tubes
HQ: Tire's Warehouse, Llc
1820 Fullerton Ave # 300
Corona CA
951 808-0111

(P-7380)
TOYOTA DOWNTOWN LA
Also Called: Toyota of Downtown L.A.
714 W Olympic Blvd Ste 1131 (90015-1425)
PHONE..................213 342-3646
EMP: 154 EST: 1970
SALES (est): 19.82MM Privately Held
SIC: 5531 7538 5511 5521 Batteries, automotive and truck; General automotive repair shops; Automobiles, new and used; Used car dealers

(P-7381)
TRANSAMERICAN DISSOLUTION LLC (HQ)
Also Called: Four Wheel Parts Wholesalers
400 W Artesia Blvd (90220-5501)
PHONE..................310 900-5500
Greg Adler, Managing Member
◆ EMP: 200 EST: 1959
SQ FT: 120,000
SALES (est): 479.89MM
SALES (corp-wide): 8.59B Publicly Held
Web: www.4wheelparts.com
SIC: 5531 5013 Automotive parts; Automotive supplies and parts
PA: Polaris Inc.
2100 Highway 55
Medina MN
763 542-0500

(P-7382)
WHEELER AUTO GROUP INC
Also Called: Wheeler Chevrolet
350 Colusa Ave (95991-4201)
P.O. Box 1150 (95992-1150)
PHONE..................530 673-3765
Michael Wheeler, Pr
David W Wheeler, *
Ellen J Wheeler, *
EMP: 65 EST: 1960
SQ FT: 6,250
SALES (est): 9.08MM Privately Held
Web: www.yubacityquicklube.com
SIC: 5531 7538 5511 5012 Automotive parts; General automotive repair shops; Automobiles, new and used; Automobiles and other motor vehicles

5541 Gasoline Service Stations

(P-7383)
ATLANTIC RICHFIELD COMPANY (DH)
Also Called: A R C O
4 Centerpointe Dr (90623-1074)
PHONE..................800 333-3991
Robert A Malone, Pr
Ian Springett, *
▲ EMP: 2200 EST: 1870
SALES (est): 559.71MM
SALES (corp-wide): 241.39B Privately Held
Web: www.arco.com
SIC: 5541 1321 2911 Filling stations, gasoline; Natural gas liquids; Petroleum refining
HQ: Bp America Inc
4101 Winfield Rd Ste 200
Warrenville IL
214 210-4835

(P-7384)
C W BROWER INC (PA)
Also Called: Stop 'n' Save Liquors
413 S Riverside Dr Ste A (95354-4079)
PHONE..................209 523-1828
Libby Pomeroy, Pr
EMP: 65 EST: 1962
SQ FT: 100,000
SALES (est): 75.1MM
SALES (corp-wide): 75.1MM Privately Held
SIC: 5541 5921 5141 5411 Filling stations, gasoline; Hard liquor; Groceries, general line; Convenience stores, independent

(P-7385)
CHEVRON CORPORATION
Also Called: Chevron
324 W El Segundo Blvd (90245-3635)
PHONE..................310 615-5000
William Simok, Ex Dir
EMP: 812
SALES (corp-wide): 246.25B Publicly Held
Web: www.chevron.com
SIC: 5541 1311 1382 1321 Filling stations, gasoline; Crude petroleum production; Oil and gas exploration services; Natural gas liquids
PA: Chevron Corporation
6001 Bollinger Canyon Rd
San Ramon CA
925 326-2189

(P-7386)
CHEVRON SHIPPING COMPANY LLC
Also Called: Chevron
6001 Bollinger Canyon Rd (94583-5737)
PHONE..................925 842-1000
John S Watson, CEO
George L Kirkland, Ex VP
▲ EMP: 96 EST: 1997
SALES (est): 101.02MM
SALES (corp-wide): 246.25B Publicly Held
Web: www.chevron.com
SIC: 5541 4731 Filling stations, gasoline; Brokers, shipping
PA: Chevron Corporation
6001 Bollinger Canyon Rd
San Ramon CA
925 326-2189

(P-7387)
CHEVRON STATIONS INC
Also Called: Chevron
755 S Tracy Blvd (95376-4753)
PHONE..................209 830-0370
Kathy Carter, Mgr
EMP: 139
SALES (corp-wide): 246.25B Publicly Held
Web: www.chevron.com
SIC: 5541 5144 Filling stations, gasoline; Poultry and poultry products
HQ: Chevron Stations, Inc.
6001 Bollinger Canyon Rd
San Ramon CA
925 842-1000

(P-7388)
CHEVRON STATIONS INC
Also Called: Chevron
18060 San Ramon Valley Blvd (94583-4405)
PHONE..................925 328-0292
Mark Howard, Mgr
EMP: 139
SQ FT: 4,250
SALES (corp-wide): 246.25B Publicly Held
Web: www.chevron.com
SIC: 5541 5144 Filling stations, gasoline; Poultry and poultry products
HQ: Chevron Stations, Inc.
6001 Bollinger Canyon Rd
San Ramon CA
925 842-1000

(P-7389)
PAQ INC
Also Called: Food 4 Less
1465 Creston Rd (93446-3218)
PHONE..................805 227-1660
EMP: 85
SALES (corp-wide): 148.26B Publicly Held
Web: www.myfood4less.com
SIC: 5541 5411 5141 Gasoline service stations; Grocery stores, chain; Groceries, general line
HQ: Paq, Inc
3021 Reynolds Ranch Pkwy # 230
Lodi CA

(P-7390)
RAMOS OIL CO INC (PA)
1515 S River Rd (95691-2882)
P.O. Box 401 (95691-0401)
PHONE..................916 371-2570
Kent Ramos, Pr
William Ramos, *
Kyle Ramos, *
John Bailey, *
Janet Bard, *
EMP: 100 EST: 1951
SQ FT: 3,200
SALES (est): 182.8MM
SALES (corp-wide): 182.8MM Privately Held
Web: www.ramosoil.com
SIC: 5541 5172 Filling stations, gasoline; Lubricating oils and greases

(P-7391)
TEXACO INC (HQ)
Also Called: Texaco
6001 Bollinger Canyon Rd (94583-2324)
PHONE..................925 842-1000
David O'reilly, Ch Bd
Kari H Endries, *
◆ EMP: 800 EST: 1902
SQ FT: 110,000
SALES (est): 572.4MM
SALES (corp-wide): 246.25B Publicly Held
Web: www.texaco.com
SIC: 5541 5511 1321 4612 Filling stations, gasoline; Automobiles, new and used; Natural gas liquids production; Crude petroleum pipelines
PA: Chevron Corporation
6001 Bollinger Canyon Rd
San Ramon CA
925 326-2189

(P-7392)
UNITED EL SEGUNDO INC (PA)
Also Called: United Oil
4130 Cover St (90808-1885)
PHONE..................310 323-3992
Ronald Appel, Pr
Jeff Appel, *
EMP: 60 EST: 1954
SQ FT: 3,500
SALES (est): 102.04MM
SALES (corp-wide): 102.04MM Privately Held
Web: www.rocketstores.com
SIC: 5541 6531 Filling stations, gasoline; Real estate leasing and rentals

5551 Boat Dealers

(P-7393)
E & B MARINE INC (HQ)
Also Called: E & B Marine
500 Westridge Dr (95076-6710)
PHONE..................831 728-2700
Randolph K Repass, Ch Bd
Peter Harris, Pr
▲ EMP: 100 EST: 1956
SQ FT: 200,000
SALES (est): 97.18MM
SALES (corp-wide): 1.03B Privately Held
SIC: 5551 5961 5088 Marine supplies, nec; Mail order house, nec; Marine supplies
PA: West Marine, Inc.
1 E Broward Blvd Ste 200
Fort Lauderdale FL
831 728-2700

(PA)=Parent Co (HQ)=Headquarters
✪ = New Business established in last 2 years

5561 - Recreational Vehicle Dealers (P-7394)

PRODUCTS & SERVICES SECTION

5561 Recreational Vehicle Dealers

(P-7394)
GIANT INLAND EMPIRE RV CTR INC (PA)
Also Called: Giant Rv
9150 Benson Ave (91763-1688)
PHONE..................909 981-0444
TOLL FREE: 800
Behzad Barouti, *CEO*
Nasser Etebar, *
EMP: 125 EST: 1986
SQ FT: 50,000
SALES (est): 64.05MM
SALES (corp-wide): 64.05MM **Privately Held**
Web: www.giantrv.com
SIC: 5561 7538 Recreational vehicle parts and accessories; Recreational vehicle repairs

(P-7395)
LA MESA R V CENTER INC (PA)
Also Called: Rec Van
7430 Copley Park Pl (92111-1122)
PHONE..................858 874-8000
James R Kimbrell, *CEO*
James Walters, *
EMP: 130 EST: 1972
SALES (est): 209.29MM
SALES (corp-wide): 209.29MM **Privately Held**
Web: www.lamesarv.com
SIC: 5561 7538 Motor homes; Recreational vehicle repairs

5571 Motorcycle Dealers

(P-7396)
BESTOP BAJA LLC
Also Called: Baja Designs
2950 Norman Strasse Rd (92069-5946)
PHONE..................760 560-2252
John Larson, *Managing Member*
▲ EMP: 115 EST: 1992
SQ FT: 14,000
SALES (est): 24.57MM
SALES (corp-wide): 95.76MM **Privately Held**
Web: www.bajadesigns.com
SIC: 5571 3714 5013 Motorcycle parts and accessories; Motor vehicle electrical equipment; Motorcycle parts
PA: Bestop, Inc.
   333 Centennial Pkwy Ste B
   Louisville CO
   303 464-2548

(P-7397)
KAWASAKI MOTORS CORP USA (HQ)
26972 Burbank (92610-2506)
P.O. Box 25252 (92799-5252)
PHONE..................949 837-4683
Eigo Konya, *Pr*
Terunori Kitajima, *
Richard N Beattie, *Chief Marketing*
◆ EMP: 400 EST: 1967
SQ FT: 40,000
SALES (est): 267.77MM **Privately Held**
Web: www.kawasaki.com
SIC: 5571 5013 5084 5091 Motorcycle dealers; Motorcycle parts; Engines, gasoline; Boats, canoes, watercrafts, and equipment
PA: Kawasaki Heavy Industries, Ltd.
   1-1-1, Higashikawasakicho, Chuo-Ku
   Kobe HYO

(P-7398)
OCELOT ENGINEERING INC
Also Called: Chaparral Motorsports
555 S H St (92410-3415)
PHONE..................800 841-2960
David S Damron, *Pr*
James E Damron, *
Linda J Damron, *
◆ EMP: 160 EST: 1973
SALES (est): 44.2MM **Privately Held**
Web: www.chapmoto.com
SIC: 5571 5551 5013 3751 Motorcycles; Jet skis; Motorcycle parts; Motorcycle accessories

(P-7399)
YAMAHA MOTOR CORPORATION USA (HQ)
6555 Katella Ave (90630-5101)
PHONE..................714 761-7300
Mike Chrzanowski, *Pr*
Takuwy Watanabe, *
Jeff Young, *
◆ EMP: 400 EST: 1955
SQ FT: 200,000
SALES (est): 1.47B **Privately Held**
Web: www.yamaha-motor.com
SIC: 5571 5013 5091 5012 Motorcycle dealers; Motor vehicle supplies and new parts; Boats, canoes, watercrafts, and equipment; Motorcycles
PA: Yamaha Motor Co., Ltd.
   2500, Shingai
   Iwata SZO

5599 Automotive Dealers, Nec

(P-7400)
IRWIN INTERNATIONAL INC (PA)
Also Called: Aircraft Spruce Speciality Co
225 Airport Cir (92878-5027)
P.O. Box 4000 (92878-4000)
PHONE..................951 372-9555
James J Irwin, *Pr*
Elizabeth Irwin, *
▼ EMP: 95 EST: 1965
SQ FT: 5,000
SALES (est): 146.72MM
SALES (corp-wide): 146.72MM **Privately Held**
Web: www.aircraftspruce.com
SIC: 5599 5088 Aircraft instruments, equipment or parts; Aircraft and parts, nec

5611 Men's And Boys' Clothing Stores

(P-7401)
GURU DENIM LLC (DH)
Also Called: True Religion Apparel
500 W 190th St Ste 300 (90248-4269)
PHONE..................323 266-3072
Michael Buckley, *Managing Member*
▲ EMP: 150 EST: 2002
SALES (est): 84.38MM
SALES (corp-wide): 350MM **Privately Held**
Web: www.truereligion.com
SIC: 5611 5137 Clothing accessories: men's and boys'; Women's and children's clothing
HQ: True Religion Apparel, Inc.
   500 W 190th St Ste 300
   Gardena CA
   323 266-3072

(P-7402)
HUB DISTRIBUTING INC (HQ)
Also Called: Anchor Blue
1260 Corona Pointe Ct (92879-5013)
PHONE..................951 340-3149
Thomas Sands, *CEO*
Elaine Gregg, *
Thomas Shaw, *
▲ EMP: 300 EST: 1947
SQ FT: 500,000
SALES (est): 37.53MM
SALES (corp-wide): 3.46B **Privately Held**
SIC: 5611 5621 5632 5137 Men's and boys' clothing stores; Women's clothing stores; Apparel accessories; Women's and children's clothing
PA: Sun Capital Partners, Inc.
   5200 Town Center Cir # 450
   Boca Raton FL
   561 394-0550

5621 Women's Clothing Stores

(P-7403)
AMERICAN RAG COMPAGNIE
150 S La Brea Ave (90036-2910)
PHONE..................323 935-3154
Mark Werts Senior, *CEO*
Mark Werts Junior, *CFO*
▲ EMP: 100 EST: 1984
SQ FT: 15,000
SALES (est): 4.67MM **Privately Held**
Web: www.americanrag.com
SIC: 5621 5932 5137 5611 Ready-to-wear apparel, women's; Clothing, secondhand; Women's and children's clothing; Clothing, male: everyday, except suits and sportswear

(P-7404)
TOPSON DOWNS CALIFORNIA INC (PA)
Also Called: Topson Downs
3840 Watseka Ave (90232-2633)
PHONE..................310 558-0300
John Poyer, *Pr*
Joe Wirht, *
Daniel Abramovitch, *
▲ EMP: 250 EST: 1971
SQ FT: 42,000
SALES (est): 62.4MM
SALES (corp-wide): 62.4MM **Privately Held**
Web: www.topsondowns.com
SIC: 5621 5136 2211 2221 Women's clothing stores; Shirts, men's and boys'; Apparel and outerwear fabrics, cotton; Apparel and outerwear fabric, manmade fiber or silk

5632 Women's Accessory And Specialty Stores

(P-7405)
SOUTH SUN PRODUCTS INC
8601 Aero Dr (92123)
PHONE..................858 694-0910
▲ EMP: 65
Web: www.southsunproducts.com
SIC: 5632 5094 Costume jewelry; Beads

5651 Family Clothing Stores

(P-7406)
BURLINGTON COAT FCTRY WHSE OF
Also Called: Burlington Coat Factory
1201 S Baldwin Ave (91007-7582)
PHONE..................626 447-8784
Kathy Stewart, *Mgr*
EMP: 194 EST: 1996
SALES (est): 1.86MM
SALES (corp-wide): 8.7B **Publicly Held**
Web: www.burlington.com
SIC: 5651 5632 5661 5719 Family clothing stores; Women's accessory and specialty stores; Shoe stores; Miscellaneous homefurnishings
HQ: Burlington Coat Factory Warehouse Corporation
   1830 N Route 130
   Burlington NJ
   609 387-7800

(P-7407)
J & M SALES INC
Also Called: Fallas Discount Stores
15001 S Figueroa St (90248-1721)
PHONE..................310 324-9962
▲ EMP: 2500
SIC: 5651 6531 Unisex clothing stores; Real estate listing services

(P-7408)
NORDSTROM INC
Also Called: Nordstrom
1200 Broadway Plz (94596-5115)
PHONE..................925 930-7959
Brian Lee, *Brnch Mgr*
EMP: 163
SALES (corp-wide): 15.53B **Publicly Held**
Web: www.nordstrom.com
SIC: 5651 8741 Family clothing stores; Restaurant management
PA: Nordstrom, Inc.
   1617 6th Ave
   Seattle WA
   206 628-2111

(P-7409)
WALKING COMPANY HOLDINGS INC (PA)
Also Called: Big Dog Sportswear
1800 Avenue Of The Stars Ste 300 (90067-4204)
PHONE..................805 963-8727
Andrew D Feshbach, *CEO*
Fred Kayne, *
Roberta J Morris, *
Anthony J Wall, *Executive Business Affairs Vice President*
Lee M Cox Senior, *Retail Operations Vice President*
▲ EMP: 160 EST: 1993
SQ FT: 24,000
SALES (est): 307.79MM **Privately Held**
Web: www.thewalkingcompany.com
SIC: 5651 5961 5136 5137 Family clothing stores; Clothing, mail order (except women's); Sportswear, men's and boys'; Sportswear, women's and children's

5661 Shoe Stores

(P-7410)
CHARLES DAVID OF CALIFORNIA (PA)
Also Called: CD
5731 Buckingham Pkwy (90230-6985)
PHONE..................310 348-5050
Charles Malka, *Pr*
David Lann, *
▲ EMP: 62 EST: 1987
SQ FT: 33,000
SALES (est): 24.92MM

▲ = Import ▼ = Export
◆ = Import/Export

PRODUCTS & SERVICES SECTION

5713 - Floor Covering Stores (P-7431)

SALES (corp-wide): 24.92MM **Privately Held**
Web: www.charlesdavid.com
SIC: **5661** 5139 Women's shoes; Shoes

(P-7411)
T AND B BOOTS INC
Also Called: Takken's Comfort Shoes
72 S Main St B (93465-9787)
PHONE.............................805 434-9904
EMP: 80
SIC: **5661** 7251 Men's boots; Shoe repair shop

5699 Miscellaneous Apparel And Accessories

(P-7412)
AURELIO FELIX BARRETO III
Also Called: C-28
169 Radio Rd (92879-1724)
PHONE.............................951 354-9528
▲ EMP: 125
Web: www.c28.com
SIC: **5699** 5136 5137 Customized clothing and apparel; Men's and boy's clothing; Women's and children's clothing

(P-7413)
CINTAS CORPORATION
Also Called: Cintas Fire
4320 E Miraloma Ave (92807-1886)
P.O. Box 636525 (45263-6525)
PHONE.............................714 646-2550
Winter Barry, *Genl Mgr*
EMP: 80
SALES (corp-wide): 8.82B **Publicly Held**
Web: www.cintas.com
SIC: **5699** 7389 8711 Uniforms; Fire protection service other than forestry or public; Fire protection engineering
PA: Cintas Corporation
6800 Cintas Blvd
Cincinnati OH
513 459-1200

(P-7414)
CINTAS CORPORATION NO 3
Also Called: Cintas
675 32nd St (92102-3301)
PHONE.............................619 239-1001
Kevin Nolan, *Brnch Mgr*
EMP: 198
SQ FT: 7,000
SALES (corp-wide): 8.82B **Publicly Held**
Web: www.cintas.com
SIC: **5699** 7213 Uniforms; Uniform supply
HQ: Cintas Corporation No. 3
6800 Cintas Blvd
Mason OH

(P-7415)
CINTAS CORPORATION NO 3
Also Called: Cintas
2829 Workman Mill Rd (90601-1549)
PHONE.............................562 692-8741
Bryce Littlejohn, *Genl Mgr*
EMP: 91
SALES (corp-wide): 8.82B **Publicly Held**
Web: www.cintas.com
SIC: **5699** 7218 Uniforms; Industrial launderers
HQ: Cintas Corporation No. 3
6800 Cintas Blvd
Mason OH

(P-7416)
CINTAS CORPORATION NO 3
Also Called: Cintas
1877 Industrial Dr (95206-4975)
PHONE.............................209 922-0500
Randy Galvin, *Brnch Mgr*
EMP: 130
SALES (corp-wide): 8.82B **Publicly Held**
Web: www.cintas.com
SIC: **5699** 5713 7213 7359 Uniforms; Floor covering stores; Uniform supply; Equipment rental and leasing, nec
HQ: Cintas Corporation No. 3
6800 Cintas Blvd
Mason OH

(P-7417)
CREATEME TECHNOLOGIES LLC
Also Called: Createme
6701 Mowry Ave (94560-4927)
PHONE.............................646 880-8625
Thomas Myers, *CEO*
Jim Dadosky, *
EMP: 170 EST: 2019
SALES (est): 18.77MM **Privately Held**
Web: www.createme.com
SIC: **5699** 7371 7389 Customized clothing and apparel; Computer software development; Personal service agents, brokers, and bureaus

5712 Furniture Stores

(P-7418)
ABC HOME FURNISHINGS INC (PA)
Also Called: A.B.C. Carpet & Home
11111 Santa Monica Blvd (90025-0437)
PHONE.............................212 473-3000
Aaron Rose, *CEO*
Paulette Cole, *
▲ EMP: 525 EST: 1985
SALES (est): 55.6MM
SALES (corp-wide): 55.6MM **Privately Held**
Web: www.abchome.com
SIC: **5712** 5719 5023 Furniture stores; Beddings and linens; Homefurnishings

(P-7419)
AMES CONSTRUCTION INC
391 N Main St Ste 302 (92878-4006)
PHONE.............................951 356-1275
EMP: 286
SALES (corp-wide): 1.31B **Privately Held**
Web: www.amesconstruction.com
SIC: **5712** 1751 1522 1521 Customized furniture and cabinets; Cabinet building and installation; Residential construction, nec; Single-family housing construction
PA: Ames Construction, Inc.
2500 County Road 42 W
Burnsville MN
952 435-7106

(P-7420)
CONCRETEWORKS STUDIO INC
1998 Republic Ave (94577-4224)
PHONE.............................510 534-7141
Mark Rogero, *CEO*
EMP: 84 EST: 2015
SALES (est): 10.12MM **Privately Held**
Web: www.concreteworks.com
SIC: **5712** 5051 Custom made furniture, except cabinets; Forms, concrete construction (steel)

(P-7421)
LIVING SPACES FURNITURE LLC
Also Called: Living Spaces Furniture
250 Floresta Blvd (94578-4164)
PHONE.............................510 351-6783
Grover Geiselman, *Brnch Mgr*
EMP: 77
SALES (corp-wide): 774.22MM **Privately Held**
Web: www.livingspaces.com
SIC: **5712** 5021 Mattresses; Furniture
PA: Living Spaces Furniture, Llc
14501 Artesia Blvd
La Mirada CA
714 523-2000

(P-7422)
LIVING SPACES FURNITURE LLC
1900 University Dr (92083-7773)
PHONE.............................760 945-6805
EMP: 154
SALES (corp-wide): 774.22MM **Privately Held**
Web: www.livingspaces.com
SIC: **5712** 5021 Mattresses; Furniture
PA: Living Spaces Furniture, Llc
14501 Artesia Blvd
La Mirada CA
714 523-2000

(P-7423)
LIVING SPACES FURNITURE LLC (PA)
14501 Artesia Blvd (90638-5805)
P.O. Box 2309 (90621-0809)
PHONE.............................714 523-2000
Grover Geiselman, *CEO*
▲ EMP: 234 EST: 2003
SQ FT: 136,000
SALES (est): 774.22MM
SALES (corp-wide): 774.22MM **Privately Held**
Web: www.livingspaces.com
SIC: **5712** 5021 Mattresses; Furniture

(P-7424)
MILES TREASTER & ASSOCIATES
Also Called: M T A
1810 13th St (95811-7149)
PHONE.............................916 373-1800
Joseanna Tse, *CEO*
Therese Kingsbury, *
Joseanna Tse, *VP*
Ken Dinsmore, *
EMP: 75 EST: 1958
SQ FT: 16,500
SALES (est): 24.01MM **Privately Held**
Web: www.mtaoffice.com
SIC: **5712** 1799 Office furniture; Office furniture installation

(P-7425)
PIVOT INTERIORS INC (PA)
3355 Scott Blvd Ste 110 (95054-3103)
PHONE.............................408 432-5600
TOLL FREE: 888
Kenneth Baugh, *Pr*
▲ EMP: 191 EST: 1973
SQ FT: 24,000
SALES (est): 91.38MM
SALES (corp-wide): 91.38MM **Privately Held**
Web: www.pivotinteriors.com
SIC: **5712** 7389 7299 Office furniture; Interior design services; Home improvement and renovation contractor agency

(P-7426)
THE SONORA J S WEST & CO INC
Also Called: J S West Prokrane Gas
501 9th St (95354-3420)
PHONE.............................209 577-3221
EMP: 300
SIC: **5712** 5984 5171 Furniture stores; Propane gas, bottled; Petroleum bulk stations

5713 Floor Covering Stores

(P-7427)
ABC CARPET CO INC (PA)
Also Called: A B C Design Rugs
11111 Santa Monica Blvd (90025-0437)
PHONE.............................212 473-3000
Aaron Rose, *CEO*
Paul Chapman, *
◆ EMP: 75 EST: 1897
SALES (est): 49.23MM
SALES (corp-wide): 49.23MM **Privately Held**
Web: www.abchome.com
SIC: **5713** 5023 Floor covering stores; Floor coverings

(P-7428)
CARPET USA LTD (PA)
9310 S La Cienega Blvd (90301-4410)
PHONE.............................310 390-8570
Giora Agam, *CEO*
Jerry Agam, *
EMP: 65 EST: 1974
SQ FT: 25,000
SALES (est): 18.99MM
SALES (corp-wide): 18.99MM **Privately Held**
Web: www.carpetusafloors.com
SIC: **5713** 5023 Carpets; Carpets

(P-7429)
CHRISTIAN BROS FLRG INTRORS IN
Also Called: Christian Bros Flrg Interiors
12086 Woodside Ave (92040-2916)
PHONE.............................619 443-9500
Yvonne Castelli, *CEO*
Michael Castelli, *
Mike Sally, *
EMP: 80 EST: 1987
SQ FT: 2,800
SALES (est): 22.52MM **Privately Held**
Web: www.cbfloorsinc.com
SIC: **5713** 1752 Carpets; Carpet laying

(P-7430)
FAIRPRICE ENTERPRISES INC
Also Called: Fair Price Carpets
1070 Center St (92507-1016)
PHONE.............................951 684-8578
Kurt Ritz, *CEO*
Donovan Ritz, *
Marlene Ritz, *
EMP: 60 EST: 1957
SQ FT: 28,000
SALES (est): 4.68MM **Privately Held**
Web: www.fairpricecarpets.com
SIC: **5713** 3281 2426 5032 Carpets; Granite, cut and shaped; Flooring, hardwood; Ceramic wall and floor tile, nec

(P-7431)
FLOOR & DECOR OUTLETS AMER INC
1700 Fairway Dr (94577-5628)
PHONE.............................510 394-9976

(PA)=Parent Co (HQ)=Headquarters
✿ = New Business established in last 2 years

5713 - Floor Covering Stores (P-7432)

EMP: 89
SALES (corp-wide): 4.26B **Publicly Held**
Web: www.flooranddecor.com
SIC: 5713 1771 Floor covering stores; Concrete work
HQ: Floor And Decor Outlets Of America, Inc.
2500 Windy Ridge Pkwy Se
Atlanta GA
404 471-1634

(P-7432)
HOMESITE SVCS INC A CAL CORP (PA)
6611 Preston Ave Ste E (94551-5108)
PHONE.....................925 237-3050
Tina Tomei, *CEO*
Darryl Phelps, *
▲ **EMP:** 61 **EST:** 2004
SALES (est): 50.44MM **Privately Held**
Web: www.homesiteservices.net
SIC: 5713 5211 5023 Floor covering stores; Counter tops; Window covering parts and accessories

(P-7433)
PROVENZA FLOORS INC (PA)
15541 Mosher Ave (92780-6424)
PHONE.....................949 788-0900
Mohammadreza Jozi, *CEO*
▲ **EMP:** 70 **EST:** 2006
SALES (est): 23.69MM **Privately Held**
Web: www.provenzafloors.com
SIC: 5713 1771 Floor covering stores; Flooring contractor

5719 Miscellaneous Homefurnishings

(P-7434)
ANNAS LINENS INC
Also Called: Annas Linens
3550 Hyland Ave (92626-1438)
PHONE.....................714 850-0504
◆ **EMP:** 2500
Web: www.annaslinens.com
SIC: 5719 5714 5023 Linens; Drapery and upholstery stores; Window covering parts and accessories

(P-7435)
ARCHITECTURAL WINDOW SHADES
9900 Gidley St (91731-1112)
PHONE.....................626 578-1936
Tom Robertson, *Genl Mgr*
EMP: 60 **EST:** 2016
SALES (est): 12.78MM **Privately Held**
Web: www.awshades.com
SIC: 5719 5023 Window shades, nec; Window covering parts and accessories
HQ: Hunter Douglas N.V.
Dokweg 19
Willemstad

(P-7436)
BUDGET BLINDS LLC (DH)
19000 Macarthur Blvd Ste 100 (92612-1438)
PHONE.....................949 404-1100
Shirin Behzadi, *Managing Member*
EMP: 65 **EST:** 1992
SALES (est): 19.87MM
SALES (corp-wide): 1.49B **Privately Held**
Web: www.budgetblinds.com
SIC: 5719 7389 Window furnishings; Business services, nec
HQ: Home Franchise Concepts, Llc
777 International Pkwy
Flower Mound TX
949 404-1100

(P-7437)
COOKINGCOM INC
1960 E Grand Ave Ste 60 (90245-5099)
PHONE.....................310 664-1283
Tracy Randall, *Pr*
Bryan Handlen, *
Larry Sales, *
Laura Shaff, *
Sarah Cohen, *Content Vice President*
EMP: 150 **EST:** 1998
SQ FT: 8,000
SALES (est): 22.26MM **Privately Held**
Web: www.cooking.com
SIC: 5719 5046 Cookware, except aluminum ; Commercial cooking and food service equipment

(P-7438)
GOOD FELLAS INDUSTRIES INC
Also Called: G F I
4400 Bandini Blvd (90058-4310)
P.O. Box 861657 (90086-1657)
PHONE.....................323 924-9495
Judd A Shipper, *CEO*
◆ **EMP:** 85 **EST:** 1997
SQ FT: 40,000
SALES (est): 15.25MM **Privately Held**
Web: www.gfi-inc.net
SIC: 5719 1799 2591 Bedding (sheets, blankets, spreads, and pillows); Drapery track installation; Shade, curtain, and drapery hardware

(P-7439)
NORTH RANCH MANAGEMENT CORP
9754 Deering Ave (91311-4301)
PHONE.....................800 410-2153
Richard Goldman, *CEO*
▲ **EMP:** 70 **EST:** 2000
SALES (est): 9.88MM **Privately Held**
Web: www.dreamproducts.com
SIC: 5719 3171 3172 4813 Housewares, nec : Women's handbags and purses; Wallets; Online service providers

5722 Household Appliance Stores

(P-7440)
JOHNSTONE SUPPLY INC
Also Called: Johnson Contrls Authorized Dlr
8040 Slauson Ave (90640-6620)
PHONE.....................323 722-2859
William J Salpaka, *Pr*
EMP: 94
SALES (corp-wide): 1.18B **Privately Held**
Web: www.johnsoncontrols.com
SIC: 5722 3585 5075 Gas household appliances; Parts for heating, cooling, and refrigerating equipment; Warm air heating and air conditioning
HQ: Johnstone Supply, Llc
11632 Ne Ainsworth Cir
Portland OR
503 256-3663

5734 Computer And Software Stores

(P-7441)
COAST TO COAST CMPT PDTS INC
4277 Valley Fair St (93063-2940)
PHONE.....................805 244-9500
Rick Roussin, *Pr*
Wendy Roussin, *
Stacy Schulman, *
▼ **EMP:** 110 **EST:** 1985
SQ FT: 8,800
SALES (est): 49.36MM **Privately Held**
Web: www.coastcoast.com
SIC: 5734 7373 7371 5112 Magnetic disks; Computer systems analysis and design; Computer software systems analysis and design, custom; Stationery and office supplies

(P-7442)
E LA CARTE INC
Also Called: Sales Mkt Mfg Smart Dining Sys
985 Industrial Rd Ste 205 (94070-4157)
PHONE.....................650 468-0680
Rajat Suri, *Pr*
Mark Belinsky, *
EMP: 60 **EST:** 2008
SALES (est): 20.77MM **Privately Held**
Web: www.presto.com
SIC: 5734 7371 Computer software and accessories; Computer software development

(P-7443)
EKC ENTERPRISES INC
Also Called: Act Computer Services
4658 E Weathermaker Ave (93703-4430)
P.O. Box 6487 (93703-6487)
PHONE.....................559 438-0330
EMP: 94 **EST:** 2003
SALES (est): 10.95MM **Privately Held**
Web: www.ekccorp.com
SIC: 5734 1799 5999 Computer and software stores; Athletic and recreation facilities construction; Audio-visual equipment and supplies

(P-7444)
GOLDEN STAR TECHNOLOGY INC (PA)
Also Called: G S T
12881 166th St (90703-2103)
PHONE.....................562 345-8700
Jia Peir Wang, *CEO*
Alice Wang, *
Dennise Wang, *
▲ **EMP:** 70 **EST:** 1985
SQ FT: 55,000
SALES (est): 197.26MM
SALES (corp-wide): 197.26MM **Privately Held**
Web: www.gstinc.com
SIC: 5734 7378 5045 Computer peripheral equipment; Computer maintenance and repair; Computers, peripherals, and software

(P-7445)
GOSECURE INC (PA)
13220 Evening Creek Dr S Ste 107 (92128-4103)
PHONE.....................301 442-3432
Neal Creighton, *CEO*
Neal Creighton, *Pr*
Robert J Mccullen, *Ofcr*
Richard Miller, *COO*
Thalia Gietzen, *CFO*
EMP: 178 **EST:** 2004
SALES (est): 22.51MM **Privately Held**
Web: www.gosecure.net
SIC: 5734 7382 7372 7373 Computer software and accessories; Protective devices, security; Publisher's computer software; Computer systems analysis and design

(P-7446)
MESSAGESOLUTION INC
6690 Amador Plaza Rd Ste 255 (94568-2938)
PHONE.....................925 833-8000
Shuzhen Zhang, *VP*
EMP: 95 **EST:** 2004
SALES (est): 4.7MM **Privately Held**
Web: www.messagesolution.com
SIC: 5734 7379 7371 Computer and software stores; Computer related maintenance services; Custom computer programming services

(P-7447)
NOMIS SOLUTIONS INC (PA)
611 Gateway Blvd Ste 120 (94080-7015)
PHONE.....................650 588-9800
Greg Demas, *Pr*
George Neal, *CPO*
Nick Pessimisis, *
▼ **EMP:** 90 **EST:** 2002
SALES (est): 23.65MM
SALES (corp-wide): 23.65MM **Privately Held**
Web: www.nomissolutions.com
SIC: 5734 7371 Software, business and non-game; Computer software development and applications

(P-7448)
PC CLUB INC (HQ)
Also Called: Enpower Innovation
18537 Gale Ave (91748-1338)
PHONE.....................626 839-8080
Jackson Lan, *Pr*
Rudy Velasquez, *
▲ **EMP:** 60 **EST:** 1991
SQ FT: 30,000
SALES (est): 9.03MM **Privately Held**
Web: www.pcclub.com
SIC: 5734 5045 Computer and software stores; Computers, peripherals, and software
PA: National Appliance Of China Group Holdings
5900 Wilshire Blvd # 900
Los Angeles CA

(P-7449)
TD SYNNEX CORPORATION (PA)
Also Called: Td Synnex
44201 Nobel Dr (94538-3178)
PHONE.....................510 656-3333
Richard T Hume, *Pr*
Dennis Polk, *
Robert Kalsow-ramos, *V Ch Bd*
Marshall Witt, *CFO*
David Vetter, *CLO*
◆ **EMP:** 150 **EST:** 1980
SALES (est): 62.34B
SALES (corp-wide): 62.34B **Publicly Held**
Web: www.tdsynnex.com
SIC: 5734 7373 Computer and software stores; Computer integrated systems design

(P-7450)
TINYCO INC
225 Bush St Ste 1900 (94104-4292)
PHONE.....................415 644-8101
Saleman Ali, *CEO*
EMP: 125 **EST:** 2011
SALES (est): 27.81MM
SALES (corp-wide): 59.07MM **Privately Held**
SIC: 5734 7372 7371 Software, computer games; Application computer software; Software programming applications
PA: Jam City, Inc.
3562 Eastham Dr

PRODUCTS & SERVICES SECTION
5812 - Eating Places (P-7472)

Culver City CA
310 205-4800

(P-7451)
VELARO INCORPORATED
1234 N La Brea Ave (90038-1179)
PHONE..............................800 983-5276
Alex Bloom, *CEO*
Jasen Fici, *
Alex Bloom, *VP*
EMP: 95 **EST:** 2000
SALES (est): 4.42MM **Privately Held**
Web: www.velaro.com
SIC: 5734 7371 Software, business and non-game; Computer software development and applications

5812 Eating Places

(P-7452)
ACAPULCO RESTAURANTS INC
Also Called: Acapulco Mxican Rest Y Cantina
12625 Frederick St Ste T (92553-5236)
PHONE..............................951 653-8809
Fernando Correa, *Mgr*
EMP: 72
SALES (corp-wide): 493.81MM **Privately Held**
SIC: 5812 7299 Mexican restaurant; Banquet hall facilities
HQ: Acapulco Restaurants, Inc.
4001 Via Oro Ave Ste 200
Long Beach CA
310 513-7538

(P-7453)
ACAPULCO RESTAURANTS INC
Also Called: Acapulco Mxican Rest Escondido
1541 E Valley Pkwy (92027-2315)
PHONE..............................562 346-1200
Mark Shultden, *Genl Mgr*
EMP: 72
SALES (corp-wide): 493.81MM **Privately Held**
SIC: 5812 7299 Mexican restaurant; Banquet hall facilities
HQ: Acapulco Restaurants, Inc.
4001 Via Oro Ave Ste 200
Long Beach CA
310 513-7538

(P-7454)
ACCOR CORP
Also Called: Sofitel Los Angeles
8555 Beverly Blvd (90048-3303)
PHONE..............................310 278-5444
Gunter Zweimuller, *Pr*
EMP: 200 **EST:** 1986
SQ FT: 380,000
SALES (est): 24.41MM
SALES (corp-wide): 713.02MM **Privately Held**
Web: www.sofitel-los-angeles.com
SIC: 5812 7011 Eating places; Hotels
PA: Accor
82 Rue Henry Farman
Issy Les Moulineaux
146429193

(P-7455)
ALTA MIRA RECOVERY CTRS LLC
Also Called: Alta Mira Hotel & Restaurant
125 Bulkley Ave (94965-2231)
PHONE..............................415 332-1350
Tom Adams, *Mgr*
Phyllis Green, *
EMP: 84 **EST:** 1948
SQ FT: 5,000
SALES (est): 5.14MM **Privately Held**
Web: www.altamirarecovery.com
SIC: 5812 5813 7011 Eating places; Bar (drinking places); Hotels

(P-7456)
APPLE FARM COLLECTIONS-SLO INC (PA)
2015 Monterey St (93401-2617)
PHONE..............................805 544-2040
John E King, *Pr*
Carole D King, *
▼ **EMP:** 290 **EST:** 1977
SQ FT: 51,000
SALES (est): 11.74MM
SALES (corp-wide): 11.74MM **Privately Held**
Web: www.applefarm.com
SIC: 5812 7011 5947 Restaurant, family: independent; Motor inn; Gift shop

(P-7457)
ARDEN HILLS COUNTRY CLUB INC
Also Called: Arden Hills
1220 Arden Hills Ln (95864-5378)
PHONE..............................916 482-6111
Jeralyn Favero, *Pr*
Brett Favero, *
EMP: 60 **EST:** 1985
SALES (est): 8.78MM **Privately Held**
Web: www.ardenhills.club
SIC: 5812 5813 7991 Eating places; Drinking places; Physical fitness facilities

(P-7458)
BELLEVUE CLUB
525 Bellevue Ave (94610-5096)
PHONE..............................510 451-1000
Barbara Maroney, *Mgr*
Henry Johns, *
EMP: 126 **EST:** 1926
SQ FT: 1,080,000
SALES (est): 5.6MM **Privately Held**
Web: www.manufactureny.org
SIC: 5812 8641 American restaurant; Social club, membership

(P-7459)
BENIHANA INC
Also Called: Benihana 24
16226 Ventura Blvd (91436-2271)
PHONE..............................818 788-7121
Shugo Kanai, *Genl Mgr*
EMP: 95
SALES (corp-wide): 2.14B **Privately Held**
Web: www.benihana.com
SIC: 5812 7299 5813 Japanese restaurant; Banquet hall facilities; Cocktail lounge
HQ: Benihana Inc.
21500 Biscayne Blvd # 100
Miami FL
305 593-0770

(P-7460)
BEYOND FRANCHISE GROUP INC
Also Called: Pokeworks
220 Technology Dr Ste 120 (92618-2456)
PHONE..............................949 398-7338
EMP: 190 **EST:** 2017
SALES (est): 1.77MM **Privately Held**
Web: www.pokeworks.com
SIC: 5812 6794 Ethnic food restaurants; Franchises, selling or licensing

(P-7461)
BOILING CRAB OPERATIONS LLC
Also Called: Boiling Crab, The
5811 Mcfadden Ave (92649-1323)
PHONE..............................714 636-4885
Dada Ngo, *Managing Member*
Sinh Nguyen, *
Angela Nguyen, *
Hai Nguyen, *
EMP: 270 **EST:** 2013
SALES (est): 12.39MM **Privately Held**
Web: www.theboilingcrab.com
SIC: 5812 6794 Cajun restaurant; Franchises, selling or licensing

(P-7462)
BW HOTEL LLC
Also Called: Buffalo Wild Wings
9500 Wilshire Blvd (90212-2405)
PHONE..............................310 275-5200
Kathleen Taylor, *CEO*
▲ **EMP:** 820 **EST:** 1928
SALES (est): 53.98MM **Privately Held**
Web: www.buffalowildwings.com
SIC: 5812 7011 Grills (eating places); Hotels and motels

(P-7463)
CARLS JR RESTAURANTS LLC
Also Called: Carl's Jr.
6307 Carpinteria Ave Ste A (93013-2908)
PHONE..............................805 684-6388
EMP: 61 **EST:** 2013
SALES (est): 5.29MM
SALES (corp-wide): 8.04B **Privately Held**
Web: www.carlsjr.com
SIC: 5812 6794 Fast-food restaurant, chain; Franchises, selling or licensing
HQ: Cke Restaurants Holdings, Inc.
6700 Tower Cir Ste 1000
Franklin TN

(P-7464)
CARPENTERS SOUTHWEST ADM CORP
Also Called: Pea Soup Andersen's Restaurant
376 Avenue Of The Flags (93427-9704)
P.O. Box 195 (93427-0195)
PHONE..............................805 688-5581
Ed Sarbinie, *Mgr*
EMP: 239
SALES (corp-wide): 45.94MM **Privately Held**
Web: www.peasoupandersens.net
SIC: 5812 7299 Eating places; Banquet hall facilities
PA: Carpenters Southwest Administrative Corporation
533 S Fremont Ave
Los Angeles CA
213 386-8590

(P-7465)
CHICK-FIL-A INC
Also Called: Chick-Fil-A
5080 Redwood Dr (94928-7905)
PHONE..............................707 585-7462
James Bains, *Brnch Mgr*
EMP: 73
SALES (corp-wide): 1.21B **Privately Held**
Web: www.chick-fil-a.com
SIC: 5812 8741 Fast-food restaurant, chain; Restaurant management
PA: Chick-Fil-A, Inc.
5200 Buffington Rd
Atlanta GA
404 765-8038

(P-7466)
CHOP STOP INC
601 N Glendale Ave (91206-2408)
PHONE..............................818 369-7350
Mark Kulkis, *CEO*
EMP: 97 **EST:** 2010
SALES (est): 5.36MM **Privately Held**
Web: www.chopstop.com
SIC: 5812 6794 Fast food restaurants and stands; Franchises, selling or licensing

(P-7467)
CITADEL PANDA EXPRESS INC
Also Called: Panda Express
899 El Centro St Ste 201 (91030-3101)
PHONE..............................626 799-9898
EMP: 88 **EST:** 1990
SQ FT: 10,000
SALES (est): 2.06MM
SALES (corp-wide): 1.64B **Privately Held**
Web: www.pandaexpress.com
SIC: 5812 6794 Chinese restaurant; Franchises, selling or licensing
HQ: Panda Express, Inc.
1683 Walnut Grove Ave
Rosemead CA

(P-7468)
CITRUS RESTAURANT LLC
8110 Aero Dr (92123-1715)
PHONE..............................858 277-8888
Kate Mendez, *Genl Mgr*
EMP: 145 **EST:** 2010
SALES (est): 4.38MM **Privately Held**
SIC: 5812 7011 American restaurant; Hotels

(P-7469)
COUNTER HOSPITALITY GROUP LLC
Also Called: Heirloom
8398 N Fresno St Ste 101 (93720-1599)
PHONE..............................559 228-9735
EMP: 85 **EST:** 2019
SALES (est): 6.5MM **Privately Held**
Web: www.heirloom-eats.com
SIC: 5812 7372 American restaurant; Application computer software

(P-7470)
COX & YOUNG VENTURES LLC
Also Called: Classic Catering
447 Figueroa St (93940-3008)
PHONE..............................831 647-0114
Cheryl Cox, *Prin*
Dean Young, *
EMP: 80 **EST:** 2007
SALES (est): 4.44MM **Privately Held**
Web: www.eventsbyclassic.com
SIC: 5812 7299 Contract food services; Facility rental and party planning services

(P-7471)
CUCINA HOLDINGS INC (DH)
Also Called: Java City
1300 Del Paso Rd (95834-1168)
PHONE..............................916 565-5500
▲ **EMP:** 350 **EST:** 1969
SALES (est): 20.99MM **Privately Held**
Web: www.javacity.com
SIC: 5812 5149 Cafe; Coffee and tea
HQ: Bewley's CafE Grafton Street Limited
78/79 Grafton Street
Dublin
18160600

(P-7472)
DEL TACO RESTAURANTS INC (PA)
Also Called: Del Taco
25521 Commercentre Dr Ste 200 (92630-8872)
PHONE..............................949 462-9300
Lawrence F Levy, *Ch Bd*

5812 - Eating Places (P-7473)

PRODUCTS & SERVICES SECTION

Chad Gretzema, *Pr*
Steven L Brake, *Ex VP*
David A Pear, *VP Opers*
M Barry Westrum, *CMO*
EMP: 169 **EST:** 1964
SQ FT: 37,500
SALES (est): 527.36MM
SALES (corp-wide): 527.36MM **Privately Held**
Web: www.deltaco.com
SIC: 5812 6794 Fast-food restaurant, chain; Franchises, selling or licensing

(P-7473)
DINAHS GARDEN HOTEL INC
Also Called: Dinah's Garden Hotel
4261 El Camino Real (94306-4405)
PHONE.................................650 493-2844
TOLL FREE: 800
Julie Handley, *Pr*
Michael Simon, *
EMP: 99 **EST:** 1956
SQ FT: 51,370
SALES (est): 12.99MM **Privately Held**
Web: www.dinahshotel.com
SIC: 5812 7011 Eating places; Hotels

(P-7474)
DINE BRANDS GLOBAL INC (PA)
Also Called: Dine Brands Global
10 W Walnut St Fl 5 (91103-3633)
PHONE.................................818 240-6055
Stephen P Joyce, *CEO*
Richard J Dahl, *
Thomas H Song, *CFO*
Bryan R Adel, *Senior Vice President Legal*
Justin Skelton, *CIO*
EMP: 500 **EST:** 1958
SALES (est): 909.4MM
SALES (corp-wide): 909.4MM **Publicly Held**
Web: www.dinebrands.com
SIC: 5812 6794 Restaurant, family: chain; Franchises, selling or licensing

(P-7475)
EATALY INC
10250 Santa Monica Blvd (90067-6404)
PHONE.................................213 310-8000
Majid Mogharehabed, *CEO*
EMP: 60 **EST:** 2016
SALES (est): 1.35MM **Privately Held**
Web: www.eataly.com
SIC: 5812 5141 Italian restaurant; Groceries, general line

(P-7476)
EL POLLO LOCO HOLDINGS INC (PA)
3535 Harbor Blvd Ste 100 (92626-1494)
PHONE.................................714 599-5000
Laurance Roberts, *Pr*
Laurance Roberts, *Pr*
Michael G Maselli, *
Ira Fils, *Ex VP*
Maria Hollandsworth, *COO*
EMP: 156 **EST:** 1980
SQ FT: 29,880
SALES (est): 469.96MM **Publicly Held**
Web: www.elpolloloco.com
SIC: 5812 6794 Eating places; Franchises, selling or licensing

(P-7477)
EPICUREAN GROUP
111 Main St Ste 3 (94022-2914)
PHONE.................................650 947-6800
Mary Clark Bartlett, *CEO*
Reynaldo Hernandez, *
Marvin Rodriguez, *

EMP: 500 **EST:** 2003
SALES (est): 39.56MM **Privately Held**
Web: www.epicurean-group.com
SIC: 5812 8741 Contract food services; Business management

(P-7478)
EVENTS MANAGEMENT INC
Also Called: McCalls Catering
1798 Bryant St (94110-1406)
PHONE.................................415 487-9114
Stephen Denison, *Pr*
Dan Mccall, *CEO*
EMP: 300 **EST:** 1984
SALES (est): 25.69MM **Privately Held**
Web: www.mccallssf.com
SIC: 5812 5813 7299 Caterers; Bar (drinking places); Party planning service

(P-7479)
FAHETAS LLC
Also Called: Green Tomato Grill
1419 N Tustin St Ste A (92867-3922)
PHONE.................................949 280-1983
Kyle Markt, *Managing Member*
Chris Stern, *
Michael Moore, *
Bruce Whistnant, *
Nicole Piscetelli, *
EMP: 100 **EST:** 2012
SALES (est): 4MM **Privately Held**
Web: www.greentomatogrill.com
SIC: 5812 7371 Fast-food restaurant, chain; Computer software development and applications

(P-7480)
FAT BRANDS INC (PA)
9720 Wilshire Blvd Ste 500 (90212-2021)
PHONE.................................310 319-1850
Andrew A Wiederhorn, *Ch Bd*
James C Neuhauser, *Ex Ch Bd*
Edward H Rensi, *V Ch Bd*
EMP: 332 **EST:** 2017
SQ FT: 9,052
SALES (est): 407.22MM
SALES (corp-wide): 407.22MM **Publicly Held**
Web: www.fatbrands.com
SIC: 5812 6794 Restaurant, family: chain; Franchises, selling or licensing

(P-7481)
FISH HOUSE PARTNERS ONE LLC
Also Called: Restaurants Bars & Food Svcs
5955 Melrose Ave (90038-3623)
PHONE.................................323 460-4170
Michael Cimarusti, *Managing Member*
Cristina Echiverri, *
EMP: 96 **EST:** 2015
SALES (est): 1.53MM **Privately Held**
SIC: 5812 6799 Seafood restaurants; Investors, nec

(P-7482)
FOOD SPECIALISTS INC
Also Called: Scott's Seafood Grill & Bar
2 Broadway (94607-3748)
PHONE.................................510 444-3456
Raymond Gallagher, *Pr*
EMP: 340 **EST:** 1972
SALES (est): 16.54MM **Privately Held**
Web: www.scottsjls.com
SIC: 5812 6519 Restaurant, family: independent; Real property lessors, nec

(P-7483)
GAIGAEW INC
1002 George St (93401-4112)
PHONE.................................805 545-5996
G Sirisophonwatthanaku, *Brnch Mgr*
EMP: 62
SALES (corp-wide): 245.89K **Privately Held**
SIC: 5812 7389 Chinese restaurant; Business services, nec
PA: Gaigaew Inc.
1815 Osos St
San Luis Obispo CA
310 227-6500

(P-7484)
GAMEWORKS ENTERTAINMENT LLC (PA)
9737 Lurline Ave (91311-4404)
PHONE.................................206 521-0952
EMP: 620
SALES (est): 16.39MM
SALES (corp-wide): 16.39MM **Privately Held**
SIC: 5812 7993 Eating places; Video game arcade

(P-7485)
HARMAN MANAGEMENT CORPORATION (PA)
Also Called: A&W Restaurant
595 Millich Dr Ste 106 (95008-0550)
PHONE.................................650 941-5681
James Jackson, *Pr*
Vern Wardle, *
EMP: 211 **EST:** 1966
SQ FT: 10,000
SALES (est): 333.73MM
SALES (corp-wide): 333.73MM **Privately Held**
Web: www.harmans.biz
SIC: 5812 5046 8741 Fast-food restaurant, chain; Restaurant equipment and supplies, nec; Management services

(P-7486)
HIDEAWAY
80440 Hideaway Club Ct (92253-7867)
PHONE.................................760 777-7400
Shawn Ygnatowiz, *Genl Mgr*
Mike Finnell, *Prin*
EMP: 150 **EST:** 2006
SALES (est): 2.37MM **Privately Held**
Web: www.hideawaygolfclub.com
SIC: 5812 7041 Grills (eating places); Residence club, organization

(P-7487)
IL FORNAIO (AMERICA) LLC
16932 Valley View Ave Ste A (90638-5826)
PHONE.................................714 752-7052
Luis Espinoza, *Brnch Mgr*
EMP: 146
SALES (corp-wide): 8.04B **Privately Held**
Web: www.ilfornaio.com
SIC: 5812 5813 5149 2051 Italian restaurant; Drinking places; Bakery products; Bread, cake, and related products
HQ: Il Fornaio (America) Llc
770 Tamalpais Dr Ste 208
Corte Madera CA
415 945-0500

(P-7488)
INTERNATIONAL COFFEE & TEA LLC (HQ)
Also Called: Coffee Bean & Tea Leaf, The
5700 Wilshire Blvd Ste 120 (90036-3644)
PHONE.................................310 237-2326

John Fuller, *Pr*
Jeff Harris, *
Sunny Sassoon, *
Jacques Wizman, *
Mel Elias, *
▲ **EMP:** 75 **EST:** 1963
SQ FT: 20,000
SALES (est): 150.82MM **Privately Held**
Web: www.coffeebean.com
SIC: 5812 5499 6794 Coffee shop; Coffee; Franchises, selling or licensing
PA: Jollibee Foods Corporation
5th-10th Floor Jollibee Plaza Building
Pasig MAN

(P-7489)
JACK IN BOX INC (PA)
Also Called: Jack In The Box
9357 Spectrum Center Blvd (92123-1524)
P.O. Box 23447 (92193-3447)
PHONE.................................858 571-2121
Darin S Harris, *CEO*
David L Goebel, *Non-Executive Chairman of the Board*
Dawn E Hooper, *Interim Chief Financial Officer*
Ryan Ostrom, *CMO*
Tony Darden, *Sr VP*
▲ **EMP:** 546 **EST:** 1951
SQ FT: 70,000
SALES (est): 1.47B
SALES (corp-wide): 1.47B **Publicly Held**
Web: www.jackinthebox.com
SIC: 5812 6794 Fast-food restaurant, chain; Franchises, selling or licensing

(P-7490)
JMJ ENTERPRISES INC
Also Called: Someone's In The Kitchen
5973 Reseda Blvd (91356-1505)
PHONE.................................818 343-5151
Joann Roth Oseary, *Pr*
Jason Perel, *
EMP: 120 **EST:** 1981
SQ FT: 6,000
SALES (est): 5.36MM **Privately Held**
Web: www.sitk.com
SIC: 5812 7299 7359 Caterers; Party planning service; Sound and lighting equipment rental

(P-7491)
LAWRYS RESTAURANTS II INC
Also Called: Tam O'Shanter Inn
2980 Los Feliz Blvd (90039-1524)
PHONE.................................323 664-0228
Bryan Lytle, *Mgr*
EMP: 177
SALES (corp-wide): 25.93MM **Privately Held**
Web: www.lawrysonline.com
SIC: 5812 7299 Steak restaurant; Banquet hall facilities
PA: Lawry's Restaurants Ii, Inc.
100 N La Cienega Blvd
Beverly Hills CA
626 440-5234

(P-7492)
LOS ALAMITOS RACE COURSE
Also Called: Vessels Club Restaurant
4961 Katella Ave (90720-2721)
PHONE.................................714 820-2800
Edward Allred, *Pt*
EMP: 200 **EST:** 1943
SQ FT: 2,000
SALES (est): 9.23MM **Privately Held**
Web: www.losalamitos.com
SIC: 5812 7948 5813 5963 Eating places; Horses, racing; Bar (drinking places); Direct selling establishments

5812 - Eating Places (P-7511)

(P-7493)
LOVE AT FIRST BITE CATERING
Also Called: Premere Event Services
18281 Gothard St Ste 108 (92648-1205)
PHONE...............................714 369-0561
John Labrake, *Pr*
EMP: 70 **EST:** 1982
SQ FT: 2,600
SALES (est): 2.2MM **Privately Held**
Web: www.lafbcatering.com
SIC: 5812 7299 Caterers; Party planning service

(P-7494)
MAGIC CASTLES INC
7001 Franklin Ave (90028-8600)
PHONE...............................323 851-3313
Milton P Larsen, *CEO*
Ron Wilson, *
Bruce Cervon, *
EMP: 100 **EST:** 1962
SQ FT: 20,000
SALES (est): 7.93MM **Privately Held**
Web: www.magiccastle.com
SIC: 5812 7997 7991 Eating places; Membership sports and recreation clubs; Physical fitness facilities

(P-7495)
MEADOWOOD ASSOC A LTD PARTNR (PA)
Also Called: Meadowood Resort and Cntry CLB
900 Meadowood Ln (94574-9620)
PHONE...............................707 963-3646
Bob Ringstab, *Pt*
H William Harland, *Pt*
EMP: 160 **EST:** 1957
SALES (est): 38.12MM
SALES (corp-wide): 38.12MM **Privately Held**
Web: www.meadowood.com
SIC: 5812 7011 7997 Eating places; Resort hotel; Country club, membership

(P-7496)
MEXICALI INC
Also Called: Mexicali Restaurant
631 18th St (93301-4934)
PHONE...............................661 327-3861
Sunny Crews, *Mgr*
EMP: 115
SALES (corp-wide): 4.39MM **Privately Held**
Web: www.mexicalirestaurants.com
SIC: 5812 5813 7299 Mexican restaurant; Bar (drinking places); Banquet hall facilities
PA: Mexicali, Inc.
419 Baker St
Bakersfield CA
661 327-4218

(P-7497)
MOSSER VCTRIAN HT ARTS MUS INC
Also Called: Annabelles Bar & Bistro
68 4th St (94103-3102)
PHONE...............................415 777-1200
Greg Quinn, *Mgr*
EMP: 120
SALES (corp-wide): 17.33MM **Privately Held**
Web: www.themosser.com
SIC: 5812 7011 American restaurant; Hotels and motels
HQ: Mosser Victorian Hotel Of Arts And Music, Inc.
308 Jessie St
San Francisco CA
415 986-4400

(P-7498)
MSR DESERT RESORT LP
Also Called: Hotel Associates Palm Springs
49499 Eisenhower Dr (92253-2722)
P.O. Box 659 (92247-0659)
PHONE...............................760 564-5730
Michael Shannon, *Pt*
John Saer, *VP*
Nola Dyal, *VP*
Stephen Elliott, *VP*
Larry Scheerer, *VP*
▲ **EMP:** 1500 **EST:** 1926
SALES (est): 48.84MM **Privately Held**
Web: www.laquintavilla.com
SIC: 5812 7011 7997 5813 Eating places; Motel, franchised; Tennis club, membership; Drinking places

(P-7499)
ORIGINAL MELS INC (PA)
Also Called: Original Mels Diner
3941 Park Dr Ste 20-369 (95762-4549)
PHONE...............................916 458-6014
▲ **EMP:** 70 **EST:** 1994
SALES (est): 24.63MM **Privately Held**
Web: www.originalmels.com
SIC: 5812 6794 Caterers; Franchises, selling or licensing

(P-7500)
OSF INTERNATIONAL INC
Also Called: Old Spagetti Factory
111 N Twin Oaks Valley Rd (92069-2950)
PHONE...............................760 471-0155
EMP: 60
SALES (corp-wide): 145.43MM **Privately Held**
Web: www.osf.com
SIC: 5812 7299 Italian restaurant; Banquet hall facilities
PA: Osf International, Inc.
715 S Bancroft St
Portland OR
503 222-5375

(P-7501)
PANDA SYSTEMS INC
Also Called: Panda Express
1683 Walnut Grove Ave (91770-3711)
P.O. Box 1159 (91770-1011)
PHONE...............................626 799-9898
Andrew J Cherng, *Ch Bd*
Peggy T Cherng, *
EMP: 130 **EST:** 1988
SQ FT: 10,000
SALES (est): 9.44MM
SALES (corp-wide): 1.64B **Privately Held**
Web: www.pandaexpress.com
SIC: 5812 6794 Chinese restaurant; Franchises, selling or licensing
PA: Panda Restaurant Group, Inc.
1683 Walnut Grove Ave
Rosemead CA
626 799-9898

(P-7502)
PHOENIX CLB GRMAN ASSN IN ORNG
Also Called: German Association Orange Cnty
1340 S Sanderson Ave (92806-5629)
PHONE...............................714 224-0194
Hans Fiebelkorn, *Pr*
Walter Bretthauer, *
EMP: 60 **EST:** 1961
SALES (est): 2.24MM **Privately Held**
Web: www.thephoenixclub.com
SIC: 5812 8641 American restaurant; Fraternal associations

(P-7503)
PINES RESORTS OF CALIFORNIA (PA)
Also Called: Ducey's On The Lake
54449 Road 432 (93604-9762)
P.O. Box 109 (93604-0109)
PHONE...............................559 642-3121
Stephen R Welch, *Ex VP*
Stephen R Welch, *VP*
Rudolph Schulte, *
James H Franzen, *
EMP: 120 **EST:** 1974
SQ FT: 20,000
SALES (est): 13.16MM
SALES (corp-wide): 13.16MM **Privately Held**
Web: www.basslake.com
SIC: 5812 7011 5411 5813 Restaurant, family: independent; Tourist camps, cabins, cottages, and courts; Grocery stores, independent; Cocktail lounge

(P-7504)
PORTCO INC
Also Called: Bay Company, The
496 Jefferson St (94109-1315)
PHONE...............................415 771-5200
Arthur N Hoppe, *Pr*
David Berbey, *
Rhoda Berbey, *
EMP: 60 **EST:** 2003
SQ FT: 6,000
SALES (est): 4.34MM **Privately Held**
SIC: 5812 5651 5091 Eating places; Unisex clothing stores; Boat accessories and parts

(P-7505)
QDOBA RESTAURANT CORPORATION (HQ)
Also Called: Qdoba Mexican Grill
350 Camino De La Reina Fl 4 (92108)
PHONE...............................858 766-4900
Susan Daggett, *CFO*
EMP: 125 **EST:** 1995
SALES (est): 128.18MM
SALES (corp-wide): 407.13MM **Privately Held**
Web: www.qdoba.com
SIC: 5812 6794 Mexican restaurant; Franchises, selling or licensing
PA: Modern Restaurant Concepts Holdings, Llc
3001 Brighton Blvd
Denver CO
917 667-7972

(P-7506)
RED ROBIN INTERNATIONAL INC
Also Called: Red Robin
4545 La Jolla Village Dr (92122-1241)
PHONE...............................858 202-1651
Bill Clark, *Mgr*
EMP: 63
SALES (corp-wide): 1.27B **Publicly Held**
Web: www.redrobin.com
SIC: 5812 6794 Restaurant, family: chain; Patent owners and lessors
HQ: Red Robin International, Inc.
6312 S Fiddlers Green Cir 200n
Greenwood Village CO
303 846-6000

(P-7507)
ROUND TABLE PIZZA INC (DH)
Also Called: Round Table Pizza
1390 Willow Pass Rd Ste 300 (94520-5200)
PHONE...............................800 866-5866
Robert Mccourt, *Pr*
Nick Fletcher, *
Thomas Guilford, *
Matthew Dowling, *
EMP: 65 **EST:** 1972
SQ FT: 18,000
SALES (est): 99.51MM
SALES (corp-wide): 407.22MM **Publicly Held**
Web: www.roundtablepizza.com
SIC: 5812 6794 Pizzeria, chain; Franchises, selling or licensing
HQ: Global Franchise Group, Llc
9720 Wilshire Blvd Fl 5
Beverly Hills CA

(P-7508)
SEVERSON GROUP LLC
Also Called: Severson Group, The
950 Boardwalk Ste 202 (92078-2600)
PHONE...............................760 550-9976
Robert Severson, *Managing Member*
EMP: 200 **EST:** 2006
SQ FT: 10,000
SALES (est): 9.41MM **Privately Held**
Web: www.theseversongroup.com
SIC: 5812 8741 8742 8748 Contract food services; Management services; Management consulting services; Systems engineering consultant, ex. computer or professional

(P-7509)
SPECIALTY RESTAURANTS CORP
Also Called: Castaway Restaurant, The
1250 E Harvard Rd (91501-1002)
PHONE...............................818 843-5013
Saeed Fazeli, *Genl Mgr*
EMP: 235
SALES (corp-wide): 201.1MM **Privately Held**
Web: www.castawayburbank.com
SIC: 5812 7299 American restaurant; Banquet hall facilities
PA: Specialty Restaurants Corporation
150 Paularino Ave Bldg C
Costa Mesa CA
714 279-6100

(P-7510)
SUDWERK PRIVATBRAUEREI HUBSCH
Also Called: Sudwerk
2001 2nd St (95618-5474)
PHONE...............................530 756-2739
Ron Broward, *Pr*
EMP: 65 **EST:** 1989
SQ FT: 27,000
SALES (est): 2.28MM **Privately Held**
Web: www.sudwerkbrew.com
SIC: 5812 5813 2082 5181 American restaurant; Beer garden (drinking places); Malt beverages; Beer and ale

(P-7511)
SUTTERS PLACE INC (PA)
Also Called: Bay 101
1801 Bering Dr (95112-4207)
PHONE...............................408 451-8888
Timothy Bumb, *CEO*
George Bumb Junior, *Sec*
EMP: 84 **EST:** 1911
SQ FT: 80,000
SALES (est): 24.93MM
SALES (corp-wide): 24.93MM **Privately Held**
Web: www.bay101.com
SIC: 5812 5813 7999 Eating places; Bar (drinking places); Card rooms

5812 - Eating Places (P-7512)

(P-7512)
SYCUAN TRIBAL DEVELOPMENT
Also Called: Sycuan Resort
1530 Hilton Head Rd Ste 210 (92019-4655)
PHONE..................619 442-3425
Daniel Tucker, *Ch Bd*
Glen Quiroga, *
Codey Martinez, *
EMP: 250 **EST:** 2001
SALES (est): 8.77MM **Privately Held**
SIC: 5812 7992 7011 Eating places; Public golf courses; Hotels and motels
PA: Sycuan Band Of Kumeyaay Nation
3007 Dehesa Rd
El Cajon CA
619 445-6002

(P-7513)
TACO BELL CORP (HQ)
Also Called: Taco Bell
1 Glen Bell Way (92618-3344)
PHONE..................949 863-4500
Mark King, *CEO*
Nikki Lawson Global, *Chief Brand Officer*
▲ **EMP:** 1025 **EST:** 1962
SQ FT: 278,000
SALES (est): 508.54MM
SALES (corp-wide): 6.84B **Publicly Held**
Web: www.tacobell.com
SIC: 5812 6794 Fast-food restaurant, chain; Franchises, selling or licensing
PA: Yum Brands, Inc.
1441 Gardiner Ln
Louisville KY
502 874-8300

(P-7514)
TRE VENEZIE INC
Also Called: Ca'del Sole
4100 Cahuenga Blvd (91602-2831)
PHONE..................818 985-4669
Rodolfo Costela, *Pr*
Jean Louis De Mori, *
Rodolfo Costello, *General Vice President**
EMP: 73 **EST:** 1994
SQ FT: 7,000
SALES (est): 2.41MM **Privately Held**
Web: www.cadelsole.com
SIC: 5812 7299 Italian restaurant; Wedding consultant

(P-7515)
VALLEY MANAGEMENT ASSOCIATES (PA)
Also Called: McDonald's
18747 Sherman Way Frnt (91335-4055)
PHONE..................818 881-6801
Kenneth Lopaty, *Pr*
Fred Tillman, *VP*
Ronald Lopaty, *
Leroy Ratliff, *VP*
EMP: 60 **EST:** 1968
SQ FT: 10,000
SALES (est): 8.88MM
SALES (corp-wide): 8.88MM **Privately Held**
Web: www.mcdonalds.com
SIC: 5812 6371 Fast-food restaurant, chain; Union welfare, benefit, and health funds

(P-7516)
WARNER FOOD MANAGEMENT CO INC
4917 Genesta Ave (91316-3438)
PHONE..................818 285-2160
Sudesh Sood, *Pr*
Terry O'herrick, *Sec*
EMP: 125 **EST:** 1989
SQ FT: 2,000
SALES (est): 4.33MM **Privately Held**
SIC: 5812 8742 Fast-food restaurant, chain; Restaurant and food services consultants

(P-7517)
WINE & ROSES LLC
Also Called: Wine & Roses Hotel and Rest
2505 W Turner Rd (95242-4643)
PHONE..................209 334-6988
Kathy Munson, *
EMP: 190 **EST:** 1999
SQ FT: 22,000
SALES (est): 10.68MM **Privately Held**
Web: www.winerose.com
SIC: 5812 7011 7299 5813 American restaurant; Hotels and motels; Banquet hall facilities; Bars and lounges

(P-7518)
WKS RESTAURANT CORPORATION (PA)
Also Called: El Pollo Loco
5856 Corporate Ave Ste 200 (90630)
P.O. Box 39 (90714-0039)
PHONE..................562 425-1402
Roland Spongberg, *Pr*
Paul Tanner, *CFO*
EMP: 243 **EST:** 1987
SQ FT: 1,200
SALES (est): 200.55MM
SALES (corp-wide): 200.55MM **Privately Held**
Web: www.wksusa.com
SIC: 5812 6794 Mexican restaurant; Franchises, selling or licensing

(P-7519)
YADAV ENTERPRISES INC
Also Called: Jack In The Box
3550 Mowry Ave Ste 301 (94538-1461)
PHONE..................510 792-3393
EMP: 61 **EST:** 2008
SALES (est): 5.71MM **Privately Held**
Web: www.jackinthebox.com
SIC: 5812 6794 Restaurant, family: chain; Franchises, selling or licensing

5813 Drinking Places

(P-7520)
LEVITY OF BREA LLC
180 S Brea Blvd (92821-4989)
PHONE..................714 482-0700
Alireza Ghaemian, *Prin*
EMP: 92 **EST:** 2015
SALES (est): 2.23MM **Privately Held**
Web: www.improv.com
SIC: 5813 7997 5812 Bars and lounges; Membership sports and recreation clubs; Buffet (eating places)

(P-7521)
PALOS VERDES GOLF CLUB
Also Called: Palos Verdes Golf & Cntry CLB
3301 Via Campesina (90274-1468)
PHONE..................310 375-2759
Gerald Kouzmanoff, *CEO*
EMP: 100 **EST:** 1967
SQ FT: 55,000
SALES (est): 9.96MM **Privately Held**
Web: www.pvgc.com
SIC: 5813 5941 7997 5812 Bar (drinking places); Golf goods and equipment; Golf club, membership; Eating places

(P-7522)
SBE ENTERTAINMENT GROUP LLC (HQ)
2535 Las Vegas Blvd S (90036)
PHONE..................323 655-8000
Sam Nazarian, *Managing Member*
Nikki Mark, *
Sam Bakhshandehpour, *
EMP: 75 **EST:** 2002
SQ FT: 11,000
SALES (est): 213.5MM
SALES (corp-wide): 713.02MM **Privately Held**
Web: www.sbe.com
SIC: 5813 7011 5812 Night clubs; Hotels; American restaurant
PA: Accor
82 Rue Henry Farman
Issy Les Moulineaux
146429193

(P-7523)
TEN 15 INC
1015 Folsom St (94103-4016)
PHONE..................415 431-1200
Ira J Sandler, *Pr*
EMP: 80 **EST:** 1990
SQ FT: 15,000
SALES (est): 4.48MM **Privately Held**
Web: www.1015.com
SIC: 5813 6512 Night clubs; Auditorium and hall operation

(P-7524)
TWIN PINE CASINO & HOTEL
22223 Rancheria Rd Hwy 29 (95461)
P.O. Box 789 (95461-0789)
PHONE..................707 987-0197
Moke Simon, *Ch*
EMP: 100 **EST:** 2006
SALES (est): 8.98MM **Privately Held**
Web: www.twinpine.com
SIC: 5813 7011 Drinking places; Casino hotel

5912 Drug Stores And Proprietary Stores

(P-7525)
KERN VALLEY HOSP FOUNDATION (PA)
Also Called: KERN VALLEY HOSPITAL
6412 Laurel Ave (93240-9529)
P.O. Box 1628 (93240-1628)
PHONE..................760 379-2681
Clarence Semonious, *Pr*
Anne Litz, *
Sally Partin, *
Kay Knight, *
Mary Completo, *
EMP: 300 **EST:** 1964
SQ FT: 65,000
SALES (est): 49.64K
SALES (corp-wide): 49.64K **Privately Held**
Web: www.kvhd.org
SIC: 5912 8051 Drug stores; Extended care facility

(P-7526)
SANSUM CLINIC
Also Called: Santa Brbara Med Fndtion Clnic
215 Pesetas Ln (93110-1416)
P.O. Box 1200 (93102-1200)
PHONE..................805 681-7500
Kut Ransolhoff, *CEO*
EMP: 90
SALES (corp-wide): 365.94MM **Privately Held**
Web: www.sansumclinic.org
SIC: 5912 8011 Drug stores and proprietary stores; Offices and clinics of medical doctors
PA: Sansum Clinic
470 S Patterson Ave
Santa Barbara CA
805 681-7700

(P-7527)
SHARP HEALTHCARE (PA)
8695 Spectrum Center Blvd (92123-1489)
PHONE..................858 499-4000
Christopher Howard, *Managing Member*
Michael Murphy, *Managing Member**
Ann Pumpian, *Managing Member**
Daniel L Gross, *Managing Member**
Alison J Fleury, *Managing Member**
EMP: 760 **EST:** 1946
SQ FT: 15,700
SALES (est): 2.37B
SALES (corp-wide): 2.37B **Privately Held**
Web: www.sharp.com
SIC: 5912 8741 6324 8011 Drug stores; Hospital management; Hospital and medical service plans; Offices and clinics of medical doctors

(P-7528)
SHARP HEALTHCARE ACO LLC
Also Called: Sharp Rees-Stealy Pharmacy
2929 Health Center Dr (92123-2762)
PHONE..................619 688-3543
Christopher Howard, *Brnch Mgr*
EMP: 64
SQ FT: 27,810
SALES (corp-wide): 2.37B **Privately Held**
Web: www.sharp.com
SIC: 5912 8011 Drug stores; Orthopedic physician
PA: Sharp Healthcare
8695 Spectrum Center Blvd
San Diego CA
858 499-4000

(P-7529)
TOMMIES MEDICAL CTR PHRM INC
Also Called: Tommie's Home Health Care
410 Cloverleaf Dr (91706-6511)
PHONE..................714 961-7930
Thomasine R Kalman, *Pr*
Gerry Carnevali, *
EMP: 60 **EST:** 1979
SQ FT: 2,300
SALES (est): 3.77MM **Privately Held**
SIC: 5912 8082 Drug stores; Home health care services

5921 Liquor Stores

(P-7530)
BEVERAGES & MORE INC
875 E Birch St Ste A (92821-5769)
PHONE..................714 990-2060
Kerry Christopher, *Mgr*
EMP: 113
SALES (corp-wide): 1.61B **Privately Held**
Web: www.bevmo.com
SIC: 5921 5149 Wine; Soft drinks
HQ: Beverages & More, Inc.
1401 Willow Pass Rd # 90
Concord CA

(P-7531)
BEVERAGES & MORE INC
2000 N Tustin St (92865-3902)
PHONE..................714 279-8131
Lisa Young, *Mgr*
EMP: 113

PRODUCTS & SERVICES SECTION

5944 - Jewelry Stores (P-7550)

SALES (corp-wide): 1.61B **Privately Held**
Web: www.bevmo.com
SIC: **5921** 5149 Hard liquor; Soft drinks
HQ: Beverages & More, Inc.
  1401 Willow Pass Rd # 90
  Concord CA

5932 Used Merchandise Stores

(P-7532)
DESERT AREA RESOURCES TRAINING (PA)
Also Called: DART
  201 E Ridgecrest Blvd (93555-3919)
  PHONE.........................760 375-9787
Jinny Deangelis, *CEO*
Robert Beecroft, *
Jeannie Luke, *
Chris Bridges Cof Clieants, *Prin*
EMP: 100 **EST:** 1961
SQ FT: 10,800
SALES (est): 3.07MM
SALES (corp-wide): 3.07MM **Privately Held**
Web: www.dartontarget.org
SIC: **5932** 7349 8322 Clothing and shoes, secondhand; Janitorial service, contract basis; Association for the handicapped

(P-7533)
FRIANT & ASSOCIATES LLC (PA)
  1980 W Avenue 140th (94577-5608)
  P.O. Box 2399 (94614-0399)
  PHONE.........................510 535-5113
◆ **EMP:** 93 **EST:** 1990
SQ FT: 150,000
SALES (est): 21.96MM **Privately Held**
Web: www.friant.com
SIC: **5932** 1799 7641 Office furniture, secondhand; Office furniture installation; Office furniture repair and maintenance

(P-7534)
GOODWILL CENTRAL COAST (PA)
  1566 Moffett St (93905-3342)
  PHONE.........................831 423-8611
EMP: 135 **EST:** 1952
SALES (est): 43.26MM
SALES (corp-wide): 43.26MM **Privately Held**
Web: www.ccgoodwill.org
SIC: **5932** 8322 Used merchandise stores; Rehabilitation services

(P-7535)
GOODWILL CENTRAL COAST
Also Called: Goodwill Industries 15
  1045 N Main St (93906-3808)
  PHONE.........................831 755-8668
Jules Koester, *Brnch Mgr*
EMP: 92
SALES (corp-wide): 43.26MM **Privately Held**
Web: www.ccgoodwill.org
SIC: **5932** 8322 Used merchandise stores; Rehabilitation services
PA: Goodwill Central Coast
  1566 Moffett St
  Salinas CA
  831 423-8611

(P-7536)
GOODWILL CENTRAL COAST
Also Called: Goodwill Inds San Luis Obispo
  880 Industrial Way (93401-7666)
  PHONE.........................805 544-0542

James Burke, *Brnch Mgr*
EMP: 244
SALES (corp-wide): 43.26MM **Privately Held**
Web: www.ccgoodwill.org
SIC: **5932** 8322 Used merchandise stores; Rehabilitation services
PA: Goodwill Central Coast
  1566 Moffett St
  Salinas CA
  831 423-8611

(P-7537)
GOODWILL INDS OF GRTER E BAY I (PA)
  1301 30th Ave (94601-2208)
  PHONE.........................510 698-7200
John Latchford, *Pr*
John B Latchford, *
Michael Conlon, *
Patricia Salmon, *
John Schorman, *
EMP: 100 **EST:** 1919
SQ FT: 47,000
SALES (est): 43.78MM
SALES (corp-wide): 43.78MM **Privately Held**
Web: www.sfgoodwill.org
SIC: **5932** 8331 Clothing, secondhand; Job training and related services

(P-7538)
GOODWILL INDS OF RDWOOD EMPIRE (PA)
  651 Yolanda Ave (95404-6324)
  PHONE.........................707 523-0550
Mark Ihde, *Pr*
▲ **EMP:** 100 **EST:** 1974
SQ FT: 14,000
SALES (est): 19.4MM
SALES (corp-wide): 19.4MM **Privately Held**
Web: www.gire.org
SIC: **5932** 8331 Clothing, secondhand; Vocational rehabilitation agency

(P-7539)
GOODWILL INDS SAN JQUIN VLY FN (PA)
  4533 Alitalia Way (95206-3996)
  PHONE.........................209 466-2311
David L Miller, *Pr*
Linda Huntley, *
EMP: 100 **EST:** 1902
SALES (est): 19.74MM
SALES (corp-wide): 19.74MM **Privately Held**
Web: www.goodwill-sjv.org
SIC: **5932** 8322 Clothing, secondhand; Helping hand service (Big Brother, etc.)

(P-7540)
GOODWILL OF THE SAN FRANCISCO (PA)
  750 Post St (94109-6106)
  PHONE.........................415 575-2101
Maureen Sedonaen, *Pr*
Terry Fitzpatrick, *
▲ **EMP:** 350 **EST:** 1916
SALES (est): 66.47MM
SALES (corp-wide): 66.47MM **Privately Held**
Web: www.sfgoodwill.org
SIC: **5932** 8331 8641 Clothing, secondhand; Skill training center; Civic and social associations

5941 Sporting Goods And Bicycle Shops

(P-7541)
FELT RACING LLC
  30452 Esperanza (92688-2144)
  PHONE.........................949 452-9050
▲ **EMP:** 65
Web: www.feltracing.com
SIC: **5941** 8711 Bicycle and bicycle parts; Engineering services

(P-7542)
GROUP ROSSIGNOL USA INC
Also Called: Felt Bicycles
  30161 Avenida De Las Bandera Ste A (92688)
  PHONE.........................949 452-9050
EMP: 65
SALES (corp-wide): 1.78MM **Privately Held**
Web: www.feltbicycles.com
SIC: **5941** 8711 Bicycle and bicycle parts; Engineering services
HQ: Group Rossignol Usa, Inc.
  1413 Center Dr
  Park City UT
  435 252-3300

(P-7543)
ONTRAC LOGISTICS INC
  3830 Cypress Dr (94954-5613)
  PHONE.........................707 773-1564
EMP: 67
SALES (corp-wide): 735.78MM **Privately Held**
Web: www.ontrac.com
SIC: **5941** 4215 Sporting goods and bicycle shops; Courier services, except by air
HQ: Ontrac Logistics, Inc.
  8401 Greensboro Dr Fl 7
  Mc Lean VA

(P-7544)
SEQUOYAH COUNTRY CLUB
Also Called: SEQUOYAH GOLF SHOP
  4550 Heafey Rd (94605-4627)
  PHONE.........................510 632-2900
John Farquhar, *Pr*
EMP: 125 **EST:** 1913
SQ FT: 20,000
SALES (est): 8.56MM **Privately Held**
Web: www.sequoyahcc.com
SIC: **5941** 7997 5812 5813 Golf goods and equipment; Golf club, membership; American restaurant; Bar (drinking places)

5942 Book Stores

(P-7545)
ASSOCTED STDNTS CAL STATE UNIV (PA)
  101 Hazel St Rm 218 (95928)
  PHONE.........................530 898-6815
Susan Jennings, *Ex Dir*
EMP: 600 **EST:** 1942
SQ FT: 55,000
SALES (est): 14.18MM
SALES (corp-wide): 14.18MM **Privately Held**
Web: as.csuchico.edu
SIC: **5942** 5812 7999 7991 College book stores; Contract food services; Recreation center; Physical fitness facilities

(P-7546)
FAMILY CHRISTIAN STORES LLC (PA)
Also Called: Family Christian Stores
  3945 Freedom Cir Ste 560 (95054-1269)
  PHONE.........................616 554-8700
Charles Bengochea, *CEO*
Chuck Bengochea, *
▲ **EMP:** 100 **EST:** 1994
SQ FT: 61,212
SALES (est): 133.77MM **Privately Held**
SIC: **5942** 5735 5947 5699 Books, religious; Compact discs; Greeting cards; Customized clothing and apparel

(P-7547)
FORTY-NINER SHOPS INC
Also Called: UNIVERSITY BOOKSTORE
  6049 E 7th St (90840-0007)
  PHONE.........................562 985-5093
Don Penrod, *CEO*
Doctor Mary Ann Takemoto, *Ch*
Ms. Mary Stephens, *Treas*
EMP: 550 **EST:** 1949
SQ FT: 36,000
SALES (est): 18.72MM **Privately Held**
Web: www.fortyninershops.net
SIC: **5942** 5943 5812 7021 College book stores; School supplies; Cafeteria; Dormitory, commercially operated

(P-7548)
NORTH ORNGE CNTY CMNTY CLLEGE
Also Called: Fullerton College Bookstore
  330 E Chapman Ave (92832-2087)
  PHONE.........................714 992-7008
Nick Karvia, *Brnch Mgr*
EMP: 363
SALES (corp-wide): 103.05MM **Privately Held**
Web: www.nocccd.edu
SIC: **5942** 5045 College book stores; Computers, peripherals, and software
PA: North Orange County Community College District
  1830 W Romneya Dr
  Anaheim CA
  714 808-4500

(P-7549)
PSYCHIC EYE BOOK SHOPS INC (PA)
  13435 Ventura Blvd (91423-3812)
  PHONE.........................818 906-8263
Robert Leysen, *CEO*
Mary Karahalios, *
EMP: 80 **EST:** 1984
SQ FT: 5,000
SALES (est): 9.92MM
SALES (corp-wide): 9.92MM **Privately Held**
Web: www.pebooksandgifts.com
SIC: **5942** 5947 7999 Book stores; Gift shop; Fortune tellers

5944 Jewelry Stores

(P-7550)
DIAMOND GOLDENWEST CORPORATION (PA)
Also Called: Jewelry Exchange, The
  15732 Tustin Village Way (92780-4924)
  PHONE.........................714 542-9000
William S Doddridge, *Pr*
Sylvia Trujillo, *
EMP: 150 **EST:** 1977
SQ FT: 25,000

5944 - Jewelry Stores (P-7551)

SALES (est): 32.72MM
SALES (corp-wide): 32.72MM **Privately Held**
Web: www.jewelryexchange.com
SIC: **5944** 5094 Jewelry, precious stones and precious metals; Jewelry

(P-7551)
M & G JEWELERS INC
10823 Edison Ct (91730-3868)
PHONE....................909 989-2929
Juan Guevara, *Pr*
Michael Insalago, *
EMP: 68 **EST:** 1991
SQ FT: 8,432
SALES (est): 11.28MM **Privately Held**
Web: www.mandgjewelers.com
SIC: **5944** 3911 7631 Jewelry, precious stones and precious metals; Jewelry, precious metal; Watch repair

(P-7552)
MONEX DEPOSIT A CAL LTD PARTNR
Also Called: Monex
4910 Birch St (92660-8100)
PHONE....................949 752-1400
Mike Carabini, *Mng Pt*
Louis E Carabini, *Pt*
EMP: 100 **EST:** 1987
SALES (est): 8.32MM **Privately Held**
SIC: **5944** 6722 3324 Jewelry, precious stones and precious metals; Management investment, open-end; Steel investment foundries

5946 Camera And Photographic Supply Stores

(P-7553)
FREESTYLE SALES CO LTD PARTNR
Also Called: Freestyle
12231 Florence Ave (90670-3805)
P.O. Box 27924 (90027-0924)
PHONE....................323 660-3460
Ronald M Resch, *Pt*
Leonore King, *Pt*
▲ **EMP:** 90 **EST:** 1946
SALES (est): 9.55MM **Privately Held**
Web: www.freestylephoto.com
SIC: **5946** 5043 Photographic supplies; Photographic equipment and supplies

(P-7554)
SAMYS CAMERA INC (PA)
Also Called: Samy's Digital Imaging
12636 Beatrice St (90066-7312)
P.O. Box 48126 (90048-0126)
PHONE....................310 591-2100
▲ **EMP:** 104 **EST:** 1976
SALES (est): 58.23MM
SALES (corp-wide): 58.23MM **Privately Held**
Web: www.samys.com
SIC: **5946** 5731 7699 Cameras; Video recorders, players, disc players, and accessories; Camera repair shop

5947 Gift, Novelty, And Souvenir Shop

(P-7555)
ARENA STUART RENTALS INC
454 S Abbott Ave (95035-5258)
PHONE....................408 856-3232
Michael Berman, *Pr*
EMP: 150 **EST:** 2018
SALES (est): 5.22MM **Privately Held**
Web: www.stuartrental.com
SIC: **5947** 7359 Party favors; Party supplies rental services

(P-7556)
HALLMARK LABS LLC
3130 Wilshire Blvd Ste 400 (90403-2300)
PHONE....................424 210-3600
Steven Hawn, *Pr*
Jeff Mcmillen, *VP*
Dwight C Arn, *
Jill Marchant, *
Albert P Mauro Junior, *VP*
EMP: 117 **EST:** 2017
SQ FT: 22,831
SALES (est): 13.32MM
SALES (corp-wide): 2.72B **Privately Held**
Web: www.hallmarklabs.com
SIC: **5947** 2741 8999 Greeting cards; Internet publishing and broadcasting; Personal services
PA: Hallmark Cards, Incorporated
2501 Mcgee St
Kansas City MO
816 274-5111

(P-7557)
HOUDINI INC (PA)
Also Called: Wine Country Gift Baskets
4225 N Palm St (92835-1045)
PHONE....................714 525-0325
Timothy J Dean, *CEO*
John Obrien, *
Michelle Xavier Dean, *
Dan Maguire, *
◆ **EMP:** 60 **EST:** 1984
SQ FT: 300,000
SALES (est): 60.51MM
SALES (corp-wide): 60.51MM **Privately Held**
Web: www.winecountrygiftbaskets.com
SIC: **5947** 5199 Gift baskets; Gift baskets

(P-7558)
SSD MANAGEMENT LLC
Also Called: Sheraton
1380 Harbor Island Dr (92101-1007)
PHONE....................619 291-2900
Joe Tursey, *Prin*
EMP: 67 **EST:** 2006
SQ FT: 75,000
SALES (est): 25.87MM
SALES (corp-wide): 4.91B **Publicly Held**
Web: www.sheratonsandiegohotel.com
SIC: **5947** 7011 5812 5813 Gift, novelty, and souvenir shop; Hotels; Eating places; Drinking places
PA: Host Hotels & Resorts, Inc.
4747 Bethesda Ave # 1300
Bethesda MD
240 744-1000

5949 Sewing, Needlework, And Piece Goods

(P-7559)
MICHAEL LEVINE INC (PA)
920 Maple Ave (90015-1812)
PHONE....................213 622-6259
Laurence A Freidin, *Prin*
Laurence A Freidin, *Prin*
Laurence Freidin, *
▲ **EMP:** 60 **EST:** 2011
SQ FT: 60,000
SALES (est): 4.71MM
SALES (corp-wide): 4.71MM **Privately Held**
Web: www.lowpricefabric.com
SIC: **5949** 5131 Fabric, remnants; Upholstery fabrics, woven

5961 Catalog And Mail-order Houses

(P-7560)
E-FILLIATE INC
Also Called: West Coast Office & Dist Ctr
11321 White Rock Rd (95742-6505)
PHONE....................916 858-1000
Wesley Sumida, *CEO*
◆ **EMP:** 69 **EST:** 1987
SQ FT: 62,000
SALES (est): 23.73MM **Privately Held**
Web: www.efilliate.com
SIC: **5961** 5045 Computers and peripheral equipment, mail order; Computer peripheral equipment

(P-7561)
JAMES ELECTRONICS LIMITED
Also Called: Jameco Electronics
1355 Shoreway Rd (94002-4105)
PHONE....................650 592-6718
TOLL FREE: 800
Dennis D Farrey, *CEO*
Dennis D Farrey, *Ch Bd*
James Farrey, *CEO*
▲ **EMP:** 70 **EST:** 1973
SQ FT: 50,000
SALES (est): 22.26MM **Privately Held**
Web: www.jameco.com
SIC: **5961** 5065 5063 Electronic kits and parts, mail order; Electronic parts and equipment, nec; Electrical apparatus and equipment

(P-7562)
PCM INC (HQ)
200 N Pacific Coast Hwy Ste 1050 (90245-5605)
PHONE....................310 354-5600
Glynis A Bryan, *CFO*
EMP: 812 **EST:** 1987
SALES (est): 2.16B **Publicly Held**
Web: www.insight.com
SIC: **5961** 5731 5045 5734 Computer equipment and electronics, mail order; Radio, television, and electronic stores; Computers, peripherals, and software; Personal computers
PA: Insight Enterprises, Inc.
2701 E Insight Way Ste 1
Chandler AZ

(P-7563)
PERFORMANCE AUTOMOTIVE WHL INC (PA)
Also Called: Paw
20235 Nordhoff St (91311-6213)
P.O. Box 829 (91319-0829)
PHONE....................805 499-8973
Keith E Harvie, *CEO*
Brian Mcelroy, *Pr*
EMP: 100 **EST:** 1978
SALES (est): 5.15MM
SALES (corp-wide): 5.15MM **Privately Held**
Web: www.pawinc.com
SIC: **5961** 5013 Automotive supplies and equipment, mail order; Automotive supplies and parts

5963 Direct Selling Establishments

(P-7564)
AVERY GROUP INC
8941 Dalton Ave (90047-3631)
PHONE....................310 217-1070
Leatora Jefferson, *Pr*
EMP: 300 **EST:** 2006
SALES (est): 10.66MM **Privately Held**
Web: www.averygroup-inc.com
SIC: **5963** 7349 Food services, direct sales; Janitorial service, contract basis

(P-7565)
MCLANE FOODSERVICE DIST INC
Also Called: Mbm
1051 Wineville Ave Ste 100 (91764-5388)
PHONE....................252 955-9547
Fred Lowrey, *Brnch Mgr*
EMP: 102
SALES (corp-wide): 302.09B **Publicly Held**
Web: www.mbmcareers.com
SIC: **5963** 4226 Direct selling establishments; Special warehousing and storage, nec
HQ: Mclane Foodservice Distribution, Inc.
4747 Mclane Pkwy
Temple TX
252 985-7200

5992 Florists

(P-7566)
FOREST LAWN MEMORIAL-PARK ASSN (PA)
Also Called: Forest Lawn Mem Parks Mortuary
1712 S Glendale Ave (91205-3320)
PHONE....................323 254-3131
TOLL FREE: 800
Darin B Drabing, *CEO*
Darin B Drabing, *Pr*
Thomas Mckernan, *Ch Bd*
John Llewellyn, *
R Scott Jenkins, *
▲ **EMP:** 300 **EST:** 1906
SQ FT: 450,000
SALES (est): 214.25MM
SALES (corp-wide): 214.25MM **Privately Held**
Web: www.forestlawn.com
SIC: **5992** 6553 7261 Flowers, fresh; Cemetery association; Funeral service and crematories

5994 News Dealers And Newsstands

(P-7567)
DELAVE INC (PA)
Also Called: Delave Periodicals
311 E Reed St Apt 13 (95112-3886)
PHONE....................408 293-7200
Frank De La Cruz, *Pr*
Javier Vega, *
EMP: 65 **EST:** 1983
SQ FT: 40,000
SALES (est): 3.54MM
SALES (corp-wide): 3.54MM **Privately Held**
Web: www.delave.net
SIC: **5994** 5199 5611 Magazine stand; Advertising specialties; Clothing, sportswear, men's and boys'

PRODUCTS & SERVICES SECTION
5999 - Miscellaneous Retail Stores, Nec (P-7588)

5995 Optical Goods Stores

(P-7568)
CONNECTICUT CTR PLASTIC SURG
73260 El Paseo Ste 2b (92260-4270)
PHONE..................................760 779-9595
Gary Price Md, *Brnch Mgr*
EMP: 76
SIC: 5995 8011 8042 Optical goods stores; Physicians' office, including specialists; Specialized optometrists
PA: Connecticut Center For Plastic Surgery
330 Orchard St Ste 211
New Haven CT

5999 Miscellaneous Retail Stores, Nec

(P-7569)
ADVANCED GASES AND EQP INC
4639 Missouri Flat Rd (95667-6816)
PHONE..................................530 344-0771
Clif Brewer, *Brnch Mgr*
EMP: 62
SALES (corp-wide): 11.08MM **Privately Held**
Web: www.advancedgases.com
SIC: 5999 5084 Welding supplies; Industrial machinery and equipment
PA: Advanced Gases And Equipment Inc.
520 Houston St
West Sacramento CA
916 374-0771

(P-7570)
ADVANTEL INCORPORATED
Also Called: Advantel Networks
48377 Fremont Blvd # 117 (94538-6565)
PHONE..................................800 377-4911
TOLL FREE: 800
EMP: 130
SIC: 5999 7629 7371 Communication equipment; Telecommunication equipment repair (except telephones); Computer software development and applications

(P-7571)
AMERICAN CONSERVATORY THEATER (PA)
Also Called: A C T
30 Grant Ave Fl 7 (94108-5880)
PHONE..................................415 749-2228
Heather Kitchen, *Ex Dir*
Carey Perloff, *Dir*
EMP: 91 **EST:** 1966
SALES (est): 17.43MM **Privately Held**
Web: www.act-sf.org
SIC: 5999 8299 7299 6512 Theater programs ; Dramatic school; Costume rental; Theater building, ownership and operation

(P-7572)
BABYCENTER LLC (DH)
163 Freelon St (94107-1624)
PHONE..................................415 537-0900
EMP: 69 **EST:** 2001
SALES (est): 32.76MM
SALES (corp-wide): 94.94B **Publicly Held**
Web: www.babycenter.com
SIC: 5999 7299 Infant furnishings and equipment; Information services, consumer
HQ: Johnson & Johnson Consumer Inc.
199 Grandview Rd
Skillman NJ
908 874-1000

(P-7573)
BAYBERRY INC
Also Called: BAYBERRY INC
15120 Lakeshore Dr # C (95422-8392)
PHONE..................................707 995-1643
Lora Heise, *Brnch Mgr*
EMP: 71
SALES (corp-wide): 6.89MM **Privately Held**
Web: www.bayberryinc.org
SIC: 5999 8051 Medical apparatus and supplies; Mental retardation hospital
PA: Bayberry, Inc.
1700 2nd St Ste 350
Napa CA
707 252-5587

(P-7574)
CINEMA SECRETS INC
6639 Odessa Ave (91406-5746)
PHONE..................................818 846-0579
Barbara Stein, *Pr*
Maurice Stein, *
Michael Stein, *
Daniel Stein, *
▲ **EMP:** 60 **EST:** 1985
SALES (est): 11.08MM **Privately Held**
Web: www.cinemasecrets.com
SIC: 5999 5699 2389 5122 Cosmetics; Costumes, masquerade or theatrical; Costumes; Cosmetics

(P-7575)
CMC RESCUE INC
Also Called: CMC
6740 Cortona Dr (93117-5574)
PHONE..................................805 562-9120
James A Frank, *Ch*
Richard M Phillips, *
Elizabeth Henry, *
▲ **EMP:** 65 **EST:** 1978
SQ FT: 23,000
SALES (est): 16.6MM **Privately Held**
Web: www.cmcpro.com
SIC: 5999 5099 3842 8299 Safety supplies and equipment; Safety equipment and supplies; Personal safety equipment; Educational services

(P-7576)
COSMETIC LABORATORIES OF AMERICA LLC
Also Called: Cosmetic Laboratories America
20245 Sunburst St (91311-6219)
PHONE..................................818 717-6140
▲ **EMP:** 400
SIC: 5999 5122 2844 2833 Cosmetics; Cosmetics; Perfumes, cosmetics and other toilet preparations; Medicinals and botanicals

(P-7577)
DHARMA VENTURES GROUP INC (PA)
24700 Avenue Rockefeller (91355-3465)
PHONE..................................661 294-4200
Jim Snell, *Pr*
Cheryl Horn Berger, *
EMP: 280 **EST:** 2006
SQ FT: 75,000
SALES (est): 43.74MM **Privately Held**
SIC: 5999 6719 Medical apparatus and supplies; Personal holding companies, except banks

(P-7578)
DOCUSOURCE INC
Also Called: Equipment Brokers Unlimited
13100 Alondra Blvd Ste 108 (90703-2278)
PHONE..................................562 447-2600
▼ **EMP:** 80
SIC: 5999 7699 5943 Photocopy machines; Photocopy machine repair; Office forms and supplies

(P-7579)
FARM WATER TECHNOLOGICAL SERVICES INC
Also Called: Water Tech
1620 Jones St (92227-1774)
P.O. Box 1383 (92227-1383)
PHONE..................................760 344-8000
▲ **EMP:** 60
Web: www.rdoequipment.com
SIC: 5999 7359 1711 Farm machinery, nec; Lawn and garden equipment rental; Irrigation sprinkler system installation

(P-7580)
GARTON TRACTOR INC (PA)
Also Called: Kubota Authorized Dealer
2400 N Golden State Blvd (95382-9408)
P.O. Box 1849 (95381-1849)
PHONE..................................209 632-3931
William L Garton, *Pr*
Thomas Garton, *
Craig Hanshew, *
▲ **EMP:** 63 **EST:** 1953
SQ FT: 20,000
SALES (est): 57.25MM
SALES (corp-wide): 57.25MM **Privately Held**
Web: www.gartontractor.com
SIC: 5999 5083 Farm machinery, nec; Farm and garden machinery

(P-7581)
GREATCALL INC
Also Called: Jitterbug
10945 Vista Sorrento Pkwy Ste 120 (92130-8649)
P.O. Box 4428 (92018-4428)
PHONE..................................800 733-6632
David Inns, *CEO*
Bill Yates, *CMO*
Lynn Herrick, *CLO*
Bryan Adams, *CCO*
Anne Murphy, *CIO*
EMP: 501 **EST:** 2005
SQ FT: 29,000
SALES (est): 98.39MM
SALES (corp-wide): 46.3B **Publicly Held**
Web: www.lively.com
SIC: 5999 4812 Mobile telephones and equipment; Cellular telephone services
PA: Best Buy Co., Inc.
7601 Penn Ave S
Richfield MN
612 291-1000

(P-7582)
GUARDIAN SAFETY AND SUPPLY LLC
Also Called: Enviro Safety Products
8248 W Doe Ave (93291-9263)
PHONE..................................559 651-0919
John Maly, *Managing Member*
Matt Ridenour, *
Jennifer Barbee, *General Vice President*
◆ **EMP:** 65 **EST:** 1996
SQ FT: 20,000
SALES (est): 13.5MM
SALES (corp-wide): 13.5MM **Privately Held**
Web: www.guardiansafety.com
SIC: 5999 5199 Safety supplies and equipment; First aid supplies
PA: Gmp Holdings, Llc
25763 Calle Ct
Valencia CA
559 651-0919

(P-7583)
GUTHY-RENKER LLC (PA)
Also Called: Proactiv
100 N Pacific Coast Hwy Ste 1600 (90245)
P.O. Box 13670 (92255-3670)
PHONE..................................760 773-9022
Greg Renker, *Ch*
Bill Guthy, *
◆ **EMP:** 60 **EST:** 1988
SQ FT: 15,000
SALES (est): 79.45MM **Privately Held**
Web: www.guthy-renker.com
SIC: 5999 8742 Cosmetics; Marketing consulting services

(P-7584)
INNOVATIVE DIALYSIS PARTNERS INC
1 World Trade Ctr (90831-0002)
PHONE..................................562 495-8075
EMP: 350
SIC: 5999 8092 Medical apparatus and supplies; Kidney dialysis centers

(P-7585)
INTELL DETECTION SYSTEMS INC
Also Called: Intell Security Systems
3092 Sly Park Rd (95726-9504)
PHONE..................................530 644-1904
FAX: 916 962-7392
EMP: 60
SQ FT: 2,000
SALES (est): 3.67MM **Privately Held**
SIC: 5999 1731 Alarm and safety equipment stores; Safety and security specialization

(P-7586)
JAM FIRE PROTECTION INC
8254 Ronson Rd (92111-2015)
PHONE..................................858 495-2335
EMP: 64
Web: www.jamcorporation.com
SIC: 5999 1711 Alarm and safety equipment stores; Fire sprinkler system installation
PA: Jam Fire Protection, Inc.
1930 S Myrtle Ave
Monrovia CA

(P-7587)
NAPOLEON PERDIS COSMETICS INC
16825 Saticoy St (91406-2728)
PHONE..................................323 817-3611
Napoleon Perdis, *Pr*
Soula-marie Perdis, *Sec*
◆ **EMP:** 93 **EST:** 2005
SALES (est): 13.7MM **Privately Held**
Web: www.napoleonperdis.com
SIC: 5999 5122 Cosmetics; Cosmetics

(P-7588)
PETCO HEALTH & WELLNESS CO INC
10850 Via Frontera (92127-1705)
PHONE..................................858 453-7845
Ronald Coughlin Junior, *Ch Bd*
Brian Larose, *CFO*
Ilene Eskenazi, *CLO Chief Human Resources Officer*
John Zavada, *Chief*
EMP: 29000 **EST:** 2015
SQ FT: 257,000
SALES (est): 6.04B **Privately Held**
Web: corporate.petco.com

5999 - Miscellaneous Retail Stores, Nec (P-7589)

(P-7589)
PLAYBOY ENTERPRISES INC (HQ)
Also Called: Playboy
10960 Wilshire Blvd Fl 22 (90024-3808)
PHONE..............................310 424-1800
Ben Kohn, *Pr*
Suhail Rizvi, *
David Israel, *CFO*
▲ EMP: 77 EST: 1953
SQ FT: 45,000
SALES (est): 147MM
SALES (corp-wide): 266.93MM **Publicly Held**
Web: www.plbygroup.com
SIC: **5999** 5169 Toiletries, cosmetics, and perfumes; Silicon lubricants
PA: Plby Group, Inc.
 10960 Wilshire Blvd Fl 22
 Los Angeles CA
 310 424-1800

(P-7590)
POTTERY WORLD INC
Also Called: Jim Rodda Pottery World Owner
4419 Granite Dr (95677-2131)
PHONE..............................916 624-8080
James W Rodda, *CEO*
Bill Rodda, *
Sharon L Rodda, *
▲ EMP: 65 EST: 1974
SQ FT: 40,000
SALES (est): 9.05MM **Privately Held**
Web: www.potteryworld.com
SIC: **5999** 5719 5023 5193 Artificial flowers; Pottery; Pottery; Artificial flowers

(P-7591)
PRESENTATION PRODUCTS INC (PA)
Also Called: Spinitar
16751 Knott Ave (90638-6013)
PHONE..............................714 367-2900
Joseph J Rogina Junior, *CEO*
James Jeffrey Irvin, *Pr*
David Taccone, *VP Fin*
Scott Kroeze, *OF ENTERPRISE*
Dan Tompkins, *VP Sls*
▲ EMP: 80 EST: 1986
SQ FT: 18,000
SALES (est): 36.25MM
SALES (corp-wide): 36.25MM **Privately Held**
Web: www.spinitar.com
SIC: **5999** 7373 7622 Audio-visual equipment and supplies; Computer systems analysis and design; Tape recorder repair

(P-7592)
SAFETY NETWORK INC (PA)
1345 N Rabe Ave (93727-2249)
PHONE..............................559 291-8000
Russ Johnson, *Pr*
EMP: 100 EST: 1988
SALES (est): 21.32MM **Privately Held**
Web: www.safetynetworkinc.com
SIC: **5999** 5084 Safety supplies and equipment; Safety equipment

(P-7593)
SAN JOSE BLUPRT SVC & SUP CO
821 Martin Ave (95050-2903)
PHONE..............................408 295-5770
David Dignam, *Pr*

Miles Cowherd, *
Bernice E Cowherd, *
EMP: 150 EST: 1931
SQ FT: 10,000
SALES (est): 11.9MM **Privately Held**
SIC: **5999** 7334 Drafting equipment and supplies; Blueprinting service

(P-7594)
SEA DWELLING CREATURES INC
5515 W 104th St (90045-6013)
PHONE..............................310 676-9697
Bradford Remmer, *Pr*
Eric Cohen, *
Scott Cohen, *
◆ EMP: 70 EST: 1993
SQ FT: 24,000
SALES (est): 11.9MM **Privately Held**
Web: www.seadwelling.com
SIC: **5999** 5199 Tropical fish; Pets and pet supplies

(P-7595)
TIMBERLAKE CORPORATION
Also Called: Timberlake Medical Gas Supply
8322 Ferguson Ave (95828-0902)
PHONE..............................916 423-2198
Steve Vinci, *Genl Mgr*
EMP: 73 EST: 1982
SALES (est): 9.98MM
SALES (corp-wide): 14.77B **Privately Held**
Web: www.sutterhealth.org
SIC: **5999** 7352 Medical apparatus and supplies; Medical equipment rental
HQ: Sutter Ambulatory Care Corp
 1 Capitol Mall Ste 390
 Sacramento CA
 916 733-8800

(P-7596)
UNITED ACCESS LLC
4797 Ruffner St (92111-1519)
PHONE..............................623 879-0800
Richard May, *Pr*
EMP: 70
SALES (corp-wide): 9.84MM **Privately Held**
SIC: **5999** 5521 7538 Medical apparatus and supplies; Used car dealers; General automotive repair shops
HQ: United Access, L.L.C.
 9389 Natural Bridge Rd
 Saint Louis MO
 877 501-8267

(P-7597)
USA SELLER CO LLC
2840 Countryside Dr (95380-8405)
PHONE..............................209 656-7085
Diane Kline, *Brnch Mgr*
EMP: 653
Web: www.petsuppliesplus.com
SIC: **5999** 0752 Pets and pet supplies; Dog pounds
HQ: Usa Seller Co., Llc
 17197 N Laurel Park Dr
 Livonia MI
 734 793-6600

(P-7598)
USOC MEDICAL LLC
Also Called: Usoc Bio-Medical Services
20 Morgan (92618-2022)
PHONE..............................949 243-7109
Ali Nazem Youssef, *CEO*
Safwan Youssef, *COO*
EMP: 60 EST: 2010
SALES (est): 11.86MM
SALES (corp-wide): 11.86MM **Privately Held**

Web: www.usocmedical.com
SIC: **5999** 7699 Medical apparatus and supplies; Medical equipment repair, non-electric
PA: Csat Solutions Holdings Llc
 4949 Windfern Rd
 Houston TX
 713 934-5200

(P-7599)
VCA INC (DH)
Also Called: VCA
12401 W Olympic Blvd (90064-1022)
PHONE..............................310 571-6500
Doug Drew, *CEO*
Arthur J Antin, *
EMP: 102 EST: 1987
SQ FT: 81,000
SALES (est): 2.21B
SALES (corp-wide): 42.84B **Privately Held**
Web: www.vcahospitals.com
SIC: **5999** 5047 0742 Pets and pet supplies; Veterinarians' equipment and supplies; Animal hospital services, pets and other animal specialties
HQ: Mmi Holdings, Inc.
 18101 Se 6th Way
 Vancouver WA
 360 784-5422

(P-7600)
WAXIES ENTERPRISES LLC
Also Called: Waxie Sanitary Supply
3220 S Fairview St (92704-6509)
PHONE..............................714 545-8441
TOLL FREE: 800
Laura Maloney, *Brnch Mgr*
EMP: 88
SQ FT: 78,582
Web: info.waxie.com
SIC: **5999** 5191 5169 5087 Cleaning equipment and supplies; Farm supplies; Chemicals and allied products, nec; Service establishment equipment
HQ: Waxie's Enterprises, Llc
 9353 Waxie Way
 San Diego CA
 800 995-4466

(P-7601)
WILBUR-ELLIS HOLDINGS II INC (HQ)
345 California St Fl 27 (94104-2644)
PHONE..............................415 772-4000
John L Buckley, *Pr*
John P Thacher, *Ofcr*
Anne E Cleary, *VP*
David P Granoff, *VP*
Troy M Hackett, *VP*
◆ EMP: 70 EST: 2015
SQ FT: 27,000
SALES (est): 3.11B
SALES (corp-wide): 3.22B **Privately Held**
Web: www.wilburellis.com
SIC: **5999** 5191 5169 Feed and farm supply; Chemicals, agricultural; Industrial chemicals
PA: Wilbur-Ellis Holdings, Inc.
 345 California St Fl 27
 San Francisco CA
 415 772-4000

6011 Federal Reserve Banks

(P-7602)
FEDERAL RSRVE BNK SAN FRNCISCO
Also Called: Los Angeles Branch
950 S Grand Ave Fl 1 (90015-4202)
P.O. Box 512077 (90051-0077)

PHONE..............................213 683-2300
Mark Mullinix, *Mgr*
EMP: 640
Web: www.frbsf.org
SIC: **6011** Federal Reserve branches
HQ: Federal Reserve Bank Of San Francisco
 101 Market St
 San Francisco CA
 415 974-2000

6021 National Commercial Banks

(P-7603)
BANA HOME LOAN SERVICING
31303 Agoura Rd (91361-4635)
PHONE..............................213 345-7975
Rachel Fiorillo, *Sr VP*
EMP: 900 EST: 2016
SALES (est): 44.33MM **Privately Held**
SIC: **6021** National commercial banks

(P-7604)
BANC AMERICA LSG & CAPITL LLC (DH)
Also Called: Tai Capital Company
555 California St Fl 4 (94104-1506)
PHONE..............................415 765-7349
Daniel Monberg, *
EMP: 150 EST: 1975
SALES (est): 404.7MM
SALES (corp-wide): 94.95B **Publicly Held**
SIC: **6021** National commercial banks
HQ: Bank Of America, National Association
 100 N Tryon St
 Charlotte NC
 704 386-5681

(P-7605)
BANC CALIFORNIA NATIONAL ASSN (HQ)
3 Macarthur Pl Ste 100 (92707-6067)
PHONE..............................877 770-2262
Robert Franko, *Pr*
Sean Casey, *
Lynn Sullivan, *CRCRO**
Joseph Kauder, *
Debora Vrana, *Chief Communication Officer**
EMP: 89 EST: 1941
SALES (est): 309.46MM
SALES (corp-wide): 390.12MM **Publicly Held**
Web: www.bancofcal.com
SIC: **6021** National commercial banks
PA: Banc Of California, Inc.
 3 Macarthur Pl Ste 100
 Santa Ana CA
 855 361-2262

(P-7606)
BANC OF CALIFORNIA INC (PA)
3 Macarthur Pl Ste 100 (92707-6068)
P.O. Box 61452 (92602-6048)
PHONE..............................855 361-2262
Jared M Wolff, *Pr*
Robert D Sznewajs, *
Ido Dotan, *Corporate Secretary*
Robert G Dyck, *CCO*
Diana Hanson, *CAO*
EMP: 120 EST: 2002
SALES (est): 390.12MM
SALES (corp-wide): 390.12MM **Publicly Held**
Web: www.bancofcal.com
SIC: **6021** National commercial banks

PRODUCTS & SERVICES SECTION
6021 - National Commercial Banks (P-7628)

(P-7607)
BANK OF HOPE (HQ)
3200 Wilshire Blvd Ste 1400 (90010-1325)
PHONE.................213 639-1700
Kevin S Kim, *CEO*
Min J Kim, *Pr*
Scott Yoon-suk Whang, *Ch Bd*
Julianna Balicka, *Ex VP*
▲ EMP: 108 EST: 1985
SALES (est): 769.88MM
SALES (corp-wide): 767.51MM **Publicly Held**
Web: www.bankofhope.com
SIC: 6021 National commercial banks
PA: Hope Bancorp, Inc.
    3200 Wilshire Blvd # 1400
    Los Angeles CA
    213 639-1700

(P-7608)
BBCN BANK
Also Called: California Center Bank
3731 Wilshire Blvd (90010-2828)
PHONE.................213 251-2222
▲ EMP: 704
SIC: 6021 National commercial banks

(P-7609)
BNY MELLON NATIONAL ASSN
Also Called: Mellon
10250 Constellation Blvd Ste 2100 (90067-6200)
PHONE.................310 551-7600
Tiffany L Barbara, *Dir*
EMP: 618
SALES (corp-wide): 19.99B **Publicly Held**
Web: www.bnymellon.com
SIC: 6021 National commercial banks
HQ: Bny Mellon, National Association
    500 Grant St
    Pittsburgh PA
    412 234-5000

(P-7610)
CHASE INC
Also Called: Chase
3754 W Holland Ave (93722-7836)
PHONE.................559 275-7331
EMP: 100 EST: 1993
SALES (est): 22.46MM **Privately Held**
Web: www.chase.com
SIC: 6021 National commercial banks

(P-7611)
CIT BANK NA
2827 Main St (90405-4009)
PHONE.................310 399-9262
EMP: 63
SALES (corp-wide): 3.09B **Publicly Held**
SIC: 6021 National commercial banks
HQ: Cit Bank, N.A.
    75 N Fair Oaks Ave
    Pasadena CA

(P-7612)
CIT BANK NA (HQ)
75 N Fair Oaks Ave Ste C (91103-3647)
P.O. Box 7056 (91109-7056)
PHONE.................626 859-5400
Ellen R Alemany, *Ch Bd*
Joseph Otting, *
Kenneth A Brause, *
Stacey Goodman, *
Carol Hayles, *
EMP: 75 EST: 2009
SALES (est): 621.29MM
SALES (corp-wide): 5.55B **Publicly Held**
Web: www.firstcitizens.com
SIC: 6021 National commercial banks
PA: First Citizens Bancshares Inc
    4300 Six Forks Rd
    Raleigh NC
    919 716-7000

(P-7613)
CITIBANK FSB (HQ)
Also Called: Citibank
1 Sansome St (94104-4448)
PHONE.................415 627-6000
David A Brooks, *Ch Bd*
Edgar Ancona, *Treas*
EMP: 300 EST: 1921
SQ FT: 20,000
SALES (est): 165.07MM
SALES (corp-wide): 101.08B **Publicly Held**
Web: www.citigroup.com
SIC: 6021 National commercial banks
PA: Citigroup Inc.
    388 Greenwich St Fl 38
    New York NY
    212 559-1000

(P-7614)
CITIBANK FSB
Also Called: Citibank
1 World Trade Ctr Ste 100 (90831-0100)
PHONE.................562 999-3453
Jim Drake, *Brnch Mgr*
EMP: 134
SALES (corp-wide): 101.08B **Publicly Held**
Web: www.citigroup.com
SIC: 6021 National commercial banks
HQ: Citibank, F.S.B.
    1 Sansome St
    San Francisco CA
    415 627-6000

(P-7615)
CITIBANK FSB
Also Called: Citibank
2000 Irving St (94122-1716)
PHONE.................415 649-6971
EMP: 134
SALES (corp-wide): 101.08B **Publicly Held**
Web: www.citigroup.com
SIC: 6021 National commercial banks
HQ: Citibank, F.S.B.
    1 Sansome St
    San Francisco CA
    415 627-6000

(P-7616)
CITY NATIONAL BANK (DH)
555 S Flower St Ste 2500 (90071-2326)
PHONE.................310 888-6000
Kelly Coffey, *CEO*
Christopher J Warmuth, *
Christopher J Carey, *
Cary Walker, *Corporate Manager*
Richard Shier, *
▲ EMP: 300 EST: 1968
SQ FT: 80,000
SALES (est): 3.3B
SALES (corp-wide): 35.59B **Privately Held**
Web: www.cnb.com
SIC: 6021 6022 National commercial banks;
    State commercial banks
HQ: Rbc Usa Holdco Corporation
    3 World Financial Ctr
    New York NY
    212 858-7200

(P-7617)
CITY NATIONAL BANK
18111 Von Karman Ave Ste 100 (92612-7117)
PHONE.................949 223-4000
James Mccloskey, *Prin*
EMP: 72
SALES (corp-wide): 35.59B **Privately Held**
Web: locations.cnb.com
SIC: 6021 National commercial banks
HQ: City National Bank
    555 S Flower St Ste 2500
    Los Angeles CA
    310 888-6000

(P-7618)
CITY NATIONAL BANK
Also Called: C N B Commercial Banking Ctr
3484 Central Ave (92506-2156)
PHONE.................951 276-8800
Bruce Wachtel, *Mgr*
EMP: 66
SALES (corp-wide): 35.59B **Privately Held**
Web: locations.cnb.com
SIC: 6021 National commercial banks
HQ: City National Bank
    555 S Flower St Ste 2500
    Los Angeles CA
    310 888-6000

(P-7619)
CITY NATIONAL BANK
Also Called: C N B Commercial Banking Ctr
1450 Chapin Ave Fl 100 (94010-4044)
PHONE.................650 696-6404
Veronica Morsello, *Prin*
EMP: 66
SALES (corp-wide): 35.59B **Privately Held**
Web: locations.cnb.com
SIC: 6021 National commercial banks
HQ: City National Bank
    555 S Flower St Ste 2500
    Los Angeles CA
    310 888-6000

(P-7620)
CITY NATIONAL BANK
Also Called: Head Office Banking 1
400 N Roxbury Dr (90210-5000)
PHONE.................310 888-6150
Thomas Caballerd, *Brnch Mgr*
EMP: 65
SALES (corp-wide): 35.59B **Privately Held**
Web: www.cnb.com
SIC: 6021 National commercial banks
HQ: City National Bank
    555 S Flower St Ste 2500
    Los Angeles CA
    310 888-6000

(P-7621)
CITY NATIONAL BANK
Also Called: C N B Real Estate Group
555 S Flower St Ste 2500 (90071-2326)
P.O. Box 5581 (90209-5581)
PHONE.................310 888-6500
EMP: 140
SALES (corp-wide): 35.59B **Privately Held**
Web: www.cnb.com
SIC: 6021 National commercial banks
HQ: City National Bank
    555 S Flower St Ste 2500
    Los Angeles CA
    310 888-6000

(P-7622)
CITY NATIONAL CORPORATION
555 S Flower St (90071-2326)
▲ EMP: 3566
SIC: 6021 National commercial banks

(P-7623)
CITY NATIONAL SECURITIES INC
400 N Roxbury Dr Ste 400 (90210-5021)
PHONE.................310 888-6393
Michael Nunnelee, *Pr*
EMP: 103 EST: 2005
SALES (est): 9.51MM
SALES (corp-wide): 35.59B **Privately Held**
Web: www.cnb.com
SIC: 6021 National commercial banks
HQ: City National Bank
    555 S Flower St Ste 2500
    Los Angeles CA
    310 888-6000

(P-7624)
FIRST BANK AND TRUST
4040 Atlantic Ave (90807-2908)
PHONE.................562 595-8775
Kennith P Maness, *Ch Bd*
David Goren, *
Ronald F Clark, *
Clement W Morin, *
EMP: 76 EST: 1982
SQ FT: 2,880
SALES (est): 4.55MM **Privately Held**
SIC: 6021 National trust companies with deposits, commercial

(P-7625)
FIRST COMMUNITY BANCORP
5900 La Place Ct Ste 200 (92008-8832)
PHONE.................858 756-3023
Andrew Colker, *Prin*
EMP: 99 EST: 2018
SALES (est): 13.68MM
SALES (corp-wide): 1.63B **Privately Held**
SIC: 6021 National commercial banks
PA: Pacwest Bancorp
    9701 Wilshire Blvd # 700
    Beverly Hills CA
    310 887-8500

(P-7626)
FIRST NATIONAL BANK
Also Called: First National Bank
6110 El Tordo (92067)
P.O. Box 2388 (92067-2388)
PHONE.................858 756-3023
Matthew P Wagner, *CEO*
Robert Borgman, *
Lynn M Hopkins, *
Sali Tice, *
EMP: 262 EST: 1982
SQ FT: 7,000
SALES (est): 37.07MM
SALES (corp-wide): 1.63B **Privately Held**
Web: www.pacwest.com
SIC: 6021 6153 National commercial banks;
    Purchasers of accounts receivable and commercial paper
PA: Pacwest Bancorp
    9701 Wilshire Blvd # 700
    Beverly Hills CA
    310 887-8500

(P-7627)
FIRST NATIONAL BANK OF NORTHERN CALIFORNIA
Also Called: First National Bank
975 El Camino Real (94080-3203)
PHONE.................650 583-8450
TOLL FREE: 800
EMP: 184
Web: www.tcbk.com
SIC: 6021 National commercial banks

(P-7628)
HOPE BANCORP INC (PA)
3200 Wilshire Blvd Ste 1400 (90010-1333)
PHONE.................213 639-1700
Kevin S Kim, *Ch Bd*
Julianna Balicka, *Ex VP*

6021 - National Commercial Banks (P-7629)

EMP: 83 EST: 2000
SALES (est): 767.51MM
SALES (corp-wide): 767.51MM Publicly Held
Web: www.ir-hopebancorp.com
SIC: 6021 National commercial banks

(P-7629)
MANHATTAN BANCORP
2141 Rosecrans Ave # 1100 (90245-4747)
PHONE.................................310 606-8000
EMP: 187
SIC: 6021 National commercial banks

(P-7630)
MERRILL LYNCH PRCE FNNER SMITH
Also Called: Merrill Lynch
101 California St Fl 21 (94111-5891)
PHONE.................................415 676-2500
EMP: 80
SALES (corp-wide): 94.95B Publicly Held
Web: www.ml.com
SIC: 6021 National commercial banks
HQ: Merrill Lynch, Pierce, Fenner & Smith Incorporated
111 8th Ave
New York NY
800 637-7455

(P-7631)
MERRILL LYNCH PRCE FNNER SMITH
Also Called: Merrill Lynch
9595 Wilshire Blvd (90212-2512)
PHONE.................................310 858-1500
EMP: 80
SALES (corp-wide): 94.95B Publicly Held
Web: www.ml.com
SIC: 6021 National commercial banks
HQ: Merrill Lynch, Pierce, Fenner & Smith Incorporated
111 8th Ave
New York NY
800 637-7455

(P-7632)
MISSION COMMUNITY BANCORP
3380 S Higuera St (93401-6926)
PHONE.................................805 782-5000
EMP: 111
SIC: 6021 National commercial banks

(P-7633)
MUFG AMERICAS HOLDINGS CORP
1221 Broadway Fl 8 (94612-1837)
PHONE.................................212 782-5911
EMP: 450
SIC: 6021 National commercial banks
HQ: Mufg Americas Holdings Corporation
1251 Ave Of The Americas
New York NY
212 782-6800

(P-7634)
MUFG UNION BANK FOUNDATION
445 S Figueroa St (90071-1630)
PHONE.................................213 236-5000
Masashi Oka, Pr
John F Harrigan, *
W H Wofford, *
David Anderson, *
Charles D Kenny, *
EMP: 4200 EST: 1967
SALES (est): 8.3MM Privately Held
SIC: 6021 National commercial banks

(P-7635)
NORTHERN TRUST OF CALIFORNIA (INC)
Also Called: Northern Trust
201 S Lake Ave Ste 600 (91101-3016)
EMP: 285
SIC: 6021 National commercial banks

(P-7636)
PACIFIC WESTERN BANK
Also Called: Rancho Santa Fe
6110 El Tordo (92067)
PHONE.................................858 756-3023
EMP: 262
SALES (corp-wide): 1.63B Privately Held
Web: www.pacwest.com
SIC: 6021 6153 National commercial banks; Purchasers of accounts receivable and commercial paper
HQ: Pacific Western Bank
9701 Wilshire Blvd # 700
Beverly Hills CA
310 887-8500

(P-7637)
PACWEST BANCORP (PA)
9701 Wilshire Blvd Ste 700 (90212-2007)
PHONE.................................310 887-8500
Matthew P Wagner, Pr
John M Eggemeyer Iii, Ch Bd
James J Pieczynski, V Ch Bd
Bart R Olson, Ex VP
Mark T Yung, Ex VP
EMP: 133 EST: 1999
SALES (est): 1.63B
SALES (corp-wide): 1.63B Privately Held
Web: www.pacwestbancorp.com
SIC: 6021 National commercial banks

(P-7638)
UNIONBANCAL MORTGAGE CORP
400 California St (94104-1302)
PHONE.................................415 705-7350
William Baner, Pr
EMP: 90 EST: 1993
SALES (est): 934.86K
SALES (corp-wide): 27.4B Publicly Held
SIC: 6021 National commercial banks
PA: U.S. Bancorp
800 Nicollet Mall # 1500
Minneapolis MN
651 466-3000

(P-7639)
WELLS FARGO & COMPANY (PA)
Also Called: Wells Fargo
420 Montgomery St (94104-1207)
P.O. Box 63750 (94163-0001)
PHONE.................................866 249-3302
Charles W Scharf, Pr
Steven D Black, *
Derek A Flowers, CRO
EMP: 1268 EST: 1929
SQ FT: 400,000
SALES (est): 82.86B
SALES (corp-wide): 82.86B Publicly Held
Web: www.wellsfargo.com
SIC: 6021 National commercial banks

(P-7640)
WELLS FARGO BANK LTD
333 S Grand Ave Ste 500 (90071-1569)
PHONE.................................213 253-6227
EMP: 74 EST: 2013
SALES (est): 444.76MM
SALES (corp-wide): 82.86B Publicly Held
Web: www.wellsfargo.com

SIC: 6021 National commercial banks
HQ: Wfc Holdings, Llc
420 Montgomery St
San Francisco CA
415 396-7392

(P-7641)
WELLS FARGO BANK NATIONAL ASSN
5798 Stone Ridge Mall (94588-2862)
PHONE.................................925 463-1983
Richard Thornton, Brnch Mgr
EMP: 84
SALES (corp-wide): 82.86B Publicly Held
Web: www.wellsfargo.com
SIC: 6021 National commercial banks
HQ: Wells Fargo Bank, National Association
420 Montgomery St San
San Francisco CA
605 575-6900

(P-7642)
WELLS FARGO BANK NATIONAL ASSN
2220 Mountain Blvd Ste 160 (94611-2950)
P.O. Box 1559 (94604-1559)
PHONE.................................510 530-3095
Ellen Thomas, Mgr
EMP: 65
SALES (corp-wide): 82.86B Publicly Held
Web: www.wellsfargo.com
SIC: 6021 National commercial banks
HQ: Wells Fargo Bank, National Association
420 Montgomery St San
San Francisco CA
605 575-6900

(P-7643)
WELLS FARGO BANK NATIONAL ASSN (HQ)
Also Called: Wells Fargo
420 Montgomery St Frnt San (94104-1298)
PHONE.................................605 575-6900
Charles W Scharf, Pr
Howard Atkins, *
Patricia R Callahan, *
John A Berg Exec V, President North Central
David J Munio, *
▲ EMP: 223 EST: 1870
SALES (est): 63.15B
SALES (corp-wide): 82.86B Publicly Held
Web: www.wellsfargo.com
SIC: 6021 6159 National trust companies with deposits, commercial; General and industrial loan institutions
PA: Wells Fargo & Company
420 Montgomery St
San Francisco CA
866 249-3302

(P-7644)
WELLS FARGO CENTER FOR ARTS
50 Mark West Springs Rd Ofc (95403-1476)
PHONE.................................707 527-7006
Richard Nowlin, Ex Dir
EMP: 72 EST: 2015
SALES (est): 1.82MM Privately Held
Web: www.wellsfargocenterarts.org
SIC: 6021 National commercial banks

(P-7645)
WELLS FARGO INVESTMENTS LLC
603 14th St (90266-4838)
PHONE.................................310 546-4235
John H Busby, Prin

EMP: 88
SALES (corp-wide): 82.86B Publicly Held
SIC: 6021 National commercial banks
HQ: Wells Fargo Investments, Llc
420 Montgomery St Frnt
San Francisco CA

(P-7646)
WELLS FARGO INVESTMENTS LLC
401 B St Ste 101 (92101-4270)
PHONE.................................619 702-6949
EMP: 88
SALES (corp-wide): 82.86B Publicly Held
SIC: 6021 National commercial banks
HQ: Wells Fargo Investments, Llc
420 Montgomery St Frnt
San Francisco CA

(P-7647)
WELLS FARGO SECURITIES LLC
Also Called: Barrington Associates
1800 Century Park E Ste 1100 (90067-1501)
PHONE.................................310 479-3500
Jim Freedman, Brnch Mgr
EMP: 1076
SALES (corp-wide): 82.86B Publicly Held
Web: www.wellsfargoadvisors.com
SIC: 6021 National commercial banks
HQ: Wells Fargo Securities, Llc
550 S Tryon St
Charlotte NC

(P-7648)
WELLS FRGO BNK NA AS TRSTEE FO
1330 N Broadway Ste C (94596-4646)
PHONE.................................925 765-6316
Andrew Camera, Prin
EMP: 99 EST: 2019
SALES (est): 4.02MM Privately Held
SIC: 6021 National commercial banks

(P-7649)
WFC HOLDINGS LLC (HQ)
420 Montgomery St (94104-1207)
PHONE.................................415 396-7392
Richard M Kovacevich, Ch Bd
EMP: 200 EST: 1998
SQ FT: 750,000
SALES (est): 516.62MM
SALES (corp-wide): 82.86B Publicly Held
SIC: 6021 National commercial banks
PA: Wells Fargo & Company
420 Montgomery St
San Francisco CA
866 249-3302

6022 State Commercial Banks

(P-7650)
1ST CENTURY BANCSHARES INC
1875 Century Park E Ste 1400 (90067-2572)
PHONE.................................310 270-9500
EMP: 71
Web: www.1stcenturybank.com
SIC: 6022 State commercial banks

(P-7651)
AMERICAN BUSINESS BANK
3633 Inland Empire Blvd Ste 720 (91764-4922)
PHONE.................................909 919-2040
Elaine Lopez, Brnch Mgr

6022 - State Commercial Banks (P-7673)

EMP: 88
SALES (corp-wide): 134.55MM **Publicly Held**
Web: www.americanbb.bank
SIC: 6022 State commercial banks
PA: American Business Bank
    400 S Hope St Ste 300
    Los Angeles CA
    213 430-4000

(P-7652)
AMERICAN BUSINESS BANK
970 W 190th St Ste 850 (90502-1059)
PHONE..................310 808-1200
Debbie Dm, *Mgr*
EMP: 89
SALES (corp-wide): 134.55MM **Publicly Held**
Web: www.cbbank.com
SIC: 6022 State trust companies accepting deposits, commercial
PA: American Business Bank
    400 S Hope St Ste 300
    Los Angeles CA
    213 430-4000

(P-7653)
AMERICAN SECURITY BANK
1401 Dove St Ste 100 (92660-2425)
PHONE..................949 440-5200
EMP: 90
SIC: 6022 State commercial banks

(P-7654)
AVIDBANK HOLDINGS INC
1732 N 1st St Fl 6 (95112-4544)
PHONE..................408 200-7390
Mark Mordell, *CEO*
Robert Holden, *Pr*
William Phillips, *Ex VP*
Geoff Butner, *CCO*
Porter Mckay, *Sr VP*
EMP: 107 EST: 2003
SALES (est): 17.92MM **Privately Held**
Web: www.avidbank.com
SIC: 6022 State commercial banks

(P-7655)
BANK OF MARIN BANCORP (PA)
504 Redwood Blvd Ste 100 (94947-6923)
P.O. Box 2039 (94948-2039)
PHONE..................415 763-4520
Russell A Colombo, *CEO*
Brian M Sobel, *
William H Mcdevitt Junior, *V Ch Bd*
Timothy D Myers, *Pr*
Tani Girton, *Ex VP*
EMP: 132 EST: 2007
SALES (est): 140.95MM **Publicly Held**
Web: www.bankofmarin.com
SIC: 6022 State trust companies accepting deposits, commercial

(P-7656)
BANK OF ORIENT FOUNDATION (HQ)
100 Pine St Ste 600 (94111-5108)
P.O. Box 2489 (94126-2489)
PHONE..................415 338-0668
Ernest L Go, *Ch Bd*
Basil Yeung, *Sr VP*
Brock Williamson, *Sr VP*
John Ng, *Ex VP*
Yvonne Go, *Sr VP*
▲ EMP: 65 EST: 1970
SQ FT: 20,000
SALES (est): 45.93MM
SALES (corp-wide): 40.53MM **Privately Held**
Web: www.bankorient.com

SIC: 6022 State trust companies accepting deposits, commercial
PA: Orient Bancorporation
    100 Pine St Ste 600
    San Francisco CA
    415 567-1554

(P-7657)
BANK OF SIERRA (HQ)
90 N Main St (93257-3712)
P.O. Box 1930 (93258-1930)
PHONE..................559 782-4300
Kevin Mcphaill, *Pr*
Morris Tharp, *
Kenneth E Goodwin, *
Matthew Macia, *Chief Risk Officer*
EMP: 105 EST: 1977
SQ FT: 37,000
SALES (est): 151.01MM
SALES (corp-wide): 152.59MM **Publicly Held**
Web: www.bankofthesierra.com
SIC: 6022 State commercial banks
PA: Sierra Bancorp
    86 N Main St
    Porterville CA
    559 782-4900

(P-7658)
BANK OF STOCKTON (HQ)
Also Called: BANK OF STOCKTON
301 E Miner Ave (95202-2501)
P.O. Box 1110 (95201-3003)
PHONE..................209 929-1600
Robert M Eberhardt, *Pr*
Douglass M Eberhardt, *
John Dentoni, *
EMP: 180 EST: 1867
SQ FT: 15,000
SALES (est): 151.5MM **Privately Held**
Web: www.bankofstockton.com
SIC: 6022 State trust companies accepting deposits, commercial
PA: 1867 Western Financial Corp
    301 E Miner Ave
    Stockton CA

(P-7659)
BIG POPPY HOLDINGS INC
6580 Oakmont Dr Ste A (95409-5917)
PHONE..................707 636-9020
EMP: 136
Web: www.poppy.bank
SIC: 6022 State commercial banks
PA: Big Poppy Holdings, Inc.
    438 1st St Ste 100
    Santa Rosa CA

(P-7660)
BIG POPPY HOLDINGS INC
9230 Old Redwood Hwy (95492-9282)
PHONE..................707 836-1588
EMP: 136
Web: www.poppy.bank
SIC: 6022 State commercial banks
PA: Big Poppy Holdings, Inc.
    438 1st St Ste 100
    Santa Rosa CA

(P-7661)
BMO BANK NA
180 Montgomery St (94104-4205)
PHONE..................415 765-4886
Auguchian Dekerverheau, *Ex VP*
EMP: 200
SALES (corp-wide): 24.49B **Privately Held**
SIC: 6022 State commercial banks
HQ: Bmo Bank N.A.
    320 S Canal St
    Chicago IL
    312 461-2323

(P-7662)
BNY MELLON NATIONAL ASSN
Also Called: Mellon
1600 Newport Center Dr Ste 200 (92660)
PHONE..................877 420-6377
Carrie Gibson, *Prin*
EMP: 562
SALES (corp-wide): 19.99B **Publicly Held**
Web: www.bnymellon.com
SIC: 6022 State commercial banks
HQ: Bny Mellon, National Association
    500 Grant St
    Pittsburgh PA
    412 234-5000

(P-7663)
BRIDGE BANK NATIONAL ASSOCIATION
55 Almaden Blvd Ste 200 (95113-1619)
PHONE..................408 423-8500
▲ EMP: 70
SIC: 6022 8742 State commercial banks; Management consulting services

(P-7664)
BUSA SERVICING INC (PA)
787 W 5th St (90071-2003)
PHONE..................310 203-3400
Manuel Sanchez Lugo, *Ch Bd*
Rebecca Macieira-kaufmann, *CEO*
Thomas Levine, *Senior Vice President Legal*
Roger Johnston, *
Francisco Moreno, *
▲ EMP: 200 EST: 1963
SALES (est): 46.34MM
SALES (corp-wide): 46.34MM **Privately Held**
Web: www.citigroup.com
SIC: 6022 State commercial banks

(P-7665)
CALIFORNIA BANCORP (PA)
1300 Clay St Ste 500 (94612-1427)
PHONE..................510 457-3737
Steven E Shelton, *CEO*
Thomas A Sa, *Pr*
Stephen A Cortese, *Ch Bd*
EMP: 125 EST: 2017
SALES (est): 89.65MM
SALES (corp-wide): 89.65MM **Publicly Held**
Web: www.bankcbc.com
SIC: 6022 State commercial banks

(P-7666)
CALIFORNIA BANK & TRUST
11622 El Camino Real (92130-2051)
PHONE..................801 844-7637
David Blackford, *CEO*
Gene Louie, *
Steven Borg, *
Frank Lee, *
◆ EMP: 1910 EST: 1952
SALES (est): 157.72MM
SALES (corp-wide): 3.34B **Publicly Held**
SIC: 6022 State trust companies accepting deposits, commercial
HQ: Zions Bancorporation
    1 S Main St Fl 15
    Salt Lake City UT
    801 844-7637

(P-7667)
CALIFORNIA REPUBLIC BANK
18400 Von Karman Ave # 630 (92612-0544)
P.O. Box 25085 (92799-5085)
PHONE..................949 270-9700
EMP: 270

SIC: 6022 State commercial banks

(P-7668)
CAPITALSOURCE BANK
130 S State College Blvd (92821-5807)
P.O. Box 2485 (92822-2485)
PHONE..................714 989-4600
EMP: 250
SIC: 6022 State commercial banks

(P-7669)
CATHAY BANK (HQ)
777 N Broadway (90012-2819)
PHONE..................626 279-3698
Dunson K Cheng, *Ch Bd*
Perry P Oei, *
James R Brewer, *
Heng W Chen, *
Irwin Wong, *
▲ EMP: 125 EST: 1962
SALES (est): 908.87MM **Publicly Held**
Web: www.cathaybank.com
SIC: 6022 State trust companies accepting deposits, commercial
PA: Cathay General Bancorp
    777 N Broadway
    Los Angeles CA

(P-7670)
CATHAY CAPITAL TRUST II
9650 Flair Dr (91731-3005)
PHONE..................213 625-4700
EMP: 79 EST: 2013
SALES (est): 1.59MM **Publicly Held**
Web: www.cathaybank.com
SIC: 6022 State commercial banks
PA: Cathay General Bancorp
    777 N Broadway
    Los Angeles CA

(P-7671)
CATHAY GENERAL BANCORP (PA)
777 N Broadway (90012-2819)
PHONE..................213 625-4700
Chang M Liu, *Pr*
Dunson K Cheng, *Ex Ch Bd*
Peter Wu, *V Ch Bd*
Anthony M Tang, *V Ch Bd*
Heng W Chen, *Ex VP*
EMP: 142 EST: 1990
SALES (est): 908.1MM **Publicly Held**
Web: www.cathaybank.com
SIC: 6022 State commercial banks

(P-7672)
CENTRAL VALLEY CMNTY BANCORP (PA)
7100 N Financial Dr Ste 101 (93720)
PHONE..................559 298-1775
James M Ford, *Pr*
Daniel J Doyle, *
Shannon R Avrett, *CFO*
Patrick J Carman, *CCO*
Steven D Mcdonald, *Sec*
EMP: 231 EST: 2000
SALES (est): 88.04MM
SALES (corp-wide): 88.04MM **Publicly Held**
Web: ir.cvcb.com
SIC: 6022 State commercial banks

(P-7673)
CENTRAL VALLEY COMMUNITY BANK (HQ)
7100 N Financial Dr Ste 101 (93720)
PHONE..................800 298-1775
Daniel J Doyle, *CEO*
James M Ford, *

6022 - State Commercial Banks (P-7674)

David A Kinross, *
Thomas L Sommer, *
Gary Litzsinger, *
EMP: 117 **EST:** 1979
SQ FT: 11,400
SALES (est): 90.63MM
SALES (corp-wide): 88.04MM **Publicly Held**
Web: www.cvcb.com
SIC: 6022 State trust companies accepting deposits, commercial
PA: Central Valley Community Bancorp
7100 N Fincl Dr Ste 101
Fresno CA
559 298-1775

(P-7674)
CITIZENS BUSINESS BANK (HQ)
701 N Haven Ave Ste 280 (91764-4920)
P.O. Box 51000 (91761-1087)
PHONE................................909 980-4030
TOLL FREE: 877
Christopher D Myers, Pr
Hal W Oswalt, *
E Allen Nicholson, *
David C Harvey, *
David F Farnsworth, CCO*
▲ **EMP:** 150 **EST:** 1973
SQ FT: 23,000
SALES (est): 566.96MM **Publicly Held**
Web: www.cbbank.com
SIC: 6022 State trust companies accepting deposits, commercial
PA: Cvb Financial Corp.
701 N Haven Ave Ste 350
Ontario CA

(P-7675)
COMMUNITY BANK
460 Sierra Madre Villa Ave (91107-2967)
PHONE................................626 577-1700
▲ **EMP:** 300
SIC: 6022 6029 State trust companies accepting deposits, commercial; Commercial banks, nec

(P-7676)
CONTINENTAL PACIFIC BANK
555 Mason St Ste 280 (95688-4611)
P.O. Box 297 (95696-0297)
PHONE................................707 448-1200
Walter O Sunderman, Pr
Walter O Sunderman, Pr
Andrew S Popovich, CAO
Ronald A Alfstad, Ex VP
Larry Fletcher, Sr VP
EMP: 98 **EST:** 1983
SQ FT: 4,500
SALES (est): 5.39MM **Privately Held**
SIC: 6022 State commercial banks

(P-7677)
CVB FINANCIAL CORP (PA)
701 N Haven Ave Ste 350 (91764-4920)
PHONE................................909 980-4030
David A Brager, CEO
Hal W Oswalt, Ch Bd
George A Borba Junior, V Ch Bd
E Allen Nicholson, CFO
Richard H Wohl, Ex VP
EMP: 104 **EST:** 1981
SALES (est): 564.66MM **Publicly Held**
Web: www.cbbank.com
SIC: 6022 State commercial banks

(P-7678)
EAST WEST BANCORP INC (PA)
Also Called: EAST WEST
135 N Los Robles Ave Fl 7 (91101-4525)
PHONE................................626 768-6000
Dominic Ng, Ch Bd
Douglas P Krause, Vice Chairman
Irene H Oh, CRO
Parker Shi, Ex VP
Lisa L Kim, Corporate Secretary
◆ **EMP:** 270 **EST:** 1998
SALES (est): 2.62B
SALES (corp-wide): 2.62B **Publicly Held**
Web: www.eastwestbank.com
SIC: 6022 State commercial banks

(P-7679)
EAST WEST BANK (HQ)
Also Called: EAST WEST
135 N Los Robles Ave Ste 100 (91101-4526)
PHONE................................626 768-6000
Dominic Ng, CEO
Donald S Chow, Ex VP
Douglas P Krause, Ex VP
Thomas J Tolda, CFO
Irene Oh, Sr VP
◆ **EMP:** 300 **EST:** 1973
SQ FT: 18,000
SALES (est): 2.62B
SALES (corp-wide): 2.62B **Publicly Held**
Web: www.eastwestbank.com
SIC: 6022 State commercial banks
PA: East West Bancorp, Inc.
135 N Los Robles Ave Fl 7
Pasadena CA
626 768-6000

(P-7680)
ENTERPRISE BANK & TRUST
11939 Rancho Bernardo Rd Ste 200 (92128)
PHONE................................858 432-7000
Stephen Marsh, Brnch Mgr
EMP: 118
Web: www.enterprisebank.com
SIC: 6022 State trust companies accepting deposits, commercial
HQ: Enterprise Bank & Trust
150 N Meramec Ave Ste 300
Saint Louis MO
314 725-5500

(P-7681)
ENTERPRISE BANK & TRUST
17785 Center Court Dr N # 750 (90703-9310)
PHONE................................562 345-9092
EMP: 184
SIC: 6022 State trust companies accepting deposits, commercial
HQ: Enterprise Bank & Trust
150 N Meramec Ave Ste 300
Saint Louis MO
314 725-5500

(P-7682)
FARMERS & MERCHANTS BANCORP (PA)
111 W Pine St (95240-2110)
PHONE................................209 367-2300
Kent A Steinwert, Ch Bd
Bart R Olson, Ex VP
Kenneth W Smith, Senior Credit Officer
Barbara Britenriker, CFO
Katrina Degroff, CAO
EMP: 330 **EST:** 1999
SALES (est): 204.59MM
SALES (corp-wide): 204.59MM **Publicly Held**
Web: www.fmbonline.com
SIC: 6022 State commercial banks

(P-7683)
FARMERS MERCHANTS BNK LONG BCH (HQ)
Also Called: F&M Bank
302 Pine Ave (90802-2326)
P.O. Box 1370 (90801-1370)
PHONE................................562 437-0011
W Henry Walker, CEO
Kenneth G Walker, *
John Hinrichs, *
Danile K Walker, *
Michael Hess, *
▲ **EMP:** 130 **EST:** 1907
SQ FT: 150,000
SALES (est): 325.95MM **Privately Held**
Web: www.fmb.com
SIC: 6022 6029 State trust companies accepting deposits, commercial; Commercial banks, nec
PA: Palomar Enterprises, Llc
302 Pine Ave
Long Beach CA

(P-7684)
FB CORPORATION
1211 E Valley Blvd (91801-5235)
PHONE................................626 300-0880
Tim Wang, Mgr
EMP: 377
SALES (corp-wide): 551.63MM **Privately Held**
Web: www.first.bank
SIC: 6022 State commercial banks
PA: Fb Corporation
135 N Meramec Ave
Saint Louis MO
314 854-4600

(P-7685)
FIRST FOUNDATION INC (PA)
Also Called: FFI
18101 Von Karman Ave Ste 700 (92612-1012)
PHONE................................949 202-4160
Scott F Kavanaugh, V Ch Bd
Ulrich E Keller Junior, Ex Ch Bd
Amy Djou, Interim Chief Financial Officer
Kelly Rentzel, Ex VP
EMP: 160 **EST:** 2006
SALES (est): 452.11MM **Publicly Held**
Web: www.firstfoundationinc.com
SIC: 6022 State commercial banks

(P-7686)
FIRST REPUB SECURITIES CO LLC
111 Pine St Fl 2 (94111-5606)
PHONE................................877 348-5576
James Herbert Ii, Ch
EMP: 67 **EST:** 2007
SALES (est): 2.44MM **Privately Held**
Web: www.firstrepublic.com
SIC: 6022 State commercial banks

(P-7687)
FIRST REPUBLIC TRUST COMPANY
111 Pine St (94111-5699)
PHONE................................415 392-1400
EMP: 230
SALES (est): 25.73MM **Privately Held**
Web: www.firstrepublic.com
SIC: 6022 State commercial banks

(P-7688)
FNB BANCORP
975 El Camino Real (94080-3203)
PHONE................................650 588-6800
EMP: 167
Web: www.tcbk.com
SIC: 6022 State trust companies accepting deposits, commercial

(P-7689)
FREMONT BANK (HQ)
39150 Fremont Blvd (94538-1316)
P.O. Box 5101 (94537-5101)
PHONE................................510 505-5226
Morris Hyman, Ch Bd
Andy Mastorakis, Pr
Alan L Hyman, V Ch Bd
Michael J Wallace, Ch
Gloria Villasana Fuerniss, Asst VP
EMP: 250 **EST:** 1964
SQ FT: 20,000
SALES (est): 274.12MM
SALES (corp-wide): 276.87MM **Privately Held**
Web: www.fremontbank.com
SIC: 6022 State commercial banks
PA: Fremont Bancorporation
39150 Fremont Blvd
Fremont CA
510 792-2300

(P-7690)
FREMONT BANK
1679 Industrial Pkwy W (94544-7046)
PHONE................................510 512-1900
Carrie Alejandre, Mgr
EMP: 80
SALES (corp-wide): 276.87MM **Privately Held**
Web: www.fremontbank.com
SIC: 6022 State commercial banks
HQ: Fremont Bank
39150 Fremont Blvd
Fremont CA
510 505-5226

(P-7691)
FREMONT BANK
210 Railroad Ave (94526-3818)
PHONE................................925 314-1420
Guy Greco, Mgr
EMP: 80
SALES (corp-wide): 276.87MM **Privately Held**
Web: www.fremontbank.com
SIC: 6022 State commercial banks
HQ: Fremont Bank
39150 Fremont Blvd
Fremont CA
510 505-5226

(P-7692)
HERITAGE BANK OF COMMERCE (HQ)
224 Airport Pkwy Ste 100 (95110-2020)
PHONE................................408 947-6900
Walter Kaczmarek, CEO
Robertson Jones, *
William Del Biaggio Junior, Ex VP
Lawrence D Mcgovern, Ex VP
Michael Benito, *
EMP: 120 **EST:** 1993
SQ FT: 36,000
SALES (est): 198.93MM
SALES (corp-wide): 198.94MM **Publicly Held**
Web: www.heritagebankofcommerce.bank
SIC: 6022 State trust companies accepting deposits, commercial
PA: Heritage Commerce Corp
224 Airport Pkwy Ste 100
San Jose CA
408 947-6900

▲ = Import ▼ = Export
◆ = Import/Export

PRODUCTS & SERVICES SECTION
6022 - State Commercial Banks (P-7715)

(P-7693)
HERITAGE OAKS BANCORP
1222 Vine St (93446-2332)
PHONE..................805 369-5200
EMP: 283
SIC: 6022 State commercial banks

(P-7694)
HERITAGE OAKS BANK
1222 Vine St (93446-2268)
PHONE..................805 239-5200
EMP: 220
SIC: 6022 State commercial banks

(P-7695)
MANUFACTURERS BANK (DH)
Also Called: Smbc Manubank
515 S Figueroa St 4th Fl (90071-3313)
PHONE..................213 489-6200
Mitsugu Serizawa, *CEO*
Naresh Sheth, *
Adrian Danescu, *
Ted Mergenthaler, *
Leslie A Lyons, *
▲ EMP: 164 EST: 1962
SQ FT: 69,206
SALES (est): 83.86MM **Privately Held**
Web: www.manufacturersbank.com
SIC: 6022 State commercial banks
HQ: Sumitomo Mitsui Banking Corporation
    1-1-2, Marunouchi
    Chiyoda-Ku TKY

(P-7696)
MECHANICS BANK (DH)
1111 Civic Dr Ste 290 (94596-8203)
PHONE..................800 797-6324
Mark Borrecco, *
Rauly Butler, *
Larry Fountain, *
Scott Givans, *
EMP: 110 EST: 1905
SQ FT: 77,000
SALES (est): 703.23MM
SALES (corp-wide): 1.2MM **Privately Held**
Web: www.mechanicsbank.com
SIC: 6022 State commercial banks
HQ: Eb Acquisition Company Llc
    6565 Hillcrest Ave
    Dallas TX
    214 871-5151

(P-7697)
MERCHANTS BANK CALIFORNIA N A
1 Civic Plaza Dr Ste 200 (90745-7958)
P.O. Box 6008 (90806-0008)
PHONE..................310 549-4350
Joyce Yamasaki, *CEO*
Daniel K Roberts, *
EMP: 75 EST: 1989
SQ FT: 5,551
SALES (est): 9.36MM **Privately Held**
Web: www.merchantsbankca.com
SIC: 6022 State commercial banks

(P-7698)
MORGAN STNLEY SMITH BARNEY LLC
74199 El Paseo Ste 201 (92260-4151)
PHONE..................760 568-3500
Anthony Maddlina, *Mgr*
EMP: 124
SALES (corp-wide): 53.67B **Publicly Held**
Web: www.morganstanley.com
SIC: 6022 State commercial banks
HQ: Morgan Stanley Smith Barney, Llc
    1585 Broadway
    New York NY

(P-7699)
MORGAN STNLEY SMITH BARNEY LLC
Also Called: Morgan Stanley Smith Barney
28202 Cabot Rd Ste 150 (92677-1250)
PHONE..................800 490-5412
EMP: 67
SALES (corp-wide): 53.67B **Publicly Held**
Web: us.etrade.com
SIC: 6022 State commercial banks
HQ: Morgan Stanley Smith Barney, Llc
    1585 Broadway
    New York NY

(P-7700)
NORTH VALLEY BANCORP
300 Park Marina Cir (96001-0964)
PHONE..................530 226-2900
EMP: 319
SIC: 6022 State commercial banks

(P-7701)
NORTH VALLEY BANK
Also Called: N V B
1327 South St (96001-1911)
P.O. Box 994630 (96099-4630)
PHONE..................530 226-2920
EMP: 177
SIC: 6022 State commercial banks

(P-7702)
OP BANCORP (PA)
1000 Wilshire Blvd Ste 500 (90017-2462)
PHONE..................213 892-9999
Min J Kim, *Pr*
Brian Choi, *Ch Bd*
Christine Y Oh, *Ex VP*
EMP: 105 EST: 2016
SQ FT: 15,239
SALES (est): 105.83MM
SALES (corp-wide): 105.83MM **Publicly Held**
SIC: 6022 State commercial banks

(P-7703)
PACIFIC COAST BANKERS BANK
1676 N California Blvd Ste 300 (94596-4185)
PHONE..................415 399-1900
Steve Brown, *Pr*
Nino Petroni, *
Eric Davis, *CIO**
EMP: 60 EST: 1997
SALES (est): 57.22MM
SALES (corp-wide): 49.94MM **Privately Held**
Web: www.pcbb.com
SIC: 6022 State commercial banks
PA: Pacific Coast Bankers' Bancshares
    1676 N Calif Blvd Ste 300
    Walnut Creek CA
    415 399-1900

(P-7704)
PACIFIC COMMERCE BANK
420 E 3rd St Ste 100 (90013-1645)
PHONE..................213 617-0082
EMP: 65
Web: www.enterprisebank.com
SIC: 6022 State commercial banks

(P-7705)
PACIFIC PREMIER BANCORP INC
3403 10th St Ste 100 (92501-3635)
PHONE..................951 274-2400
Joe Servi, *Brnch Mgr*

EMP: 99
Web: www.ppbi.com
SIC: 6022 State commercial banks
PA: Pacific Premier Bancorp, Inc.
    17901 Von Karman Ave # 1
    Irvine CA

(P-7706)
PACIFIC PREMIER BANCORP INC (PA)
17901 Von Karman Ave Ste 1200 (92614-6297)
PHONE..................949 864-8000
EMP: 123 EST: 1996
SALES (est): 857.33MM **Publicly Held**
Web: www.ppbi.com
SIC: 6022 State commercial banks

(P-7707)
PACIFIC PREMIER BANK
333 S Grand Ave Ste 3580 (90071-3477)
PHONE..................213 626-0085
EMP: 78
Web: www.ppbi.com
SIC: 6022 State trust companies accepting deposits, commercial
HQ: Pacific Premier Bank
    17901 Von Karman Ave # 1
    Irvine CA
    714 431-4000

(P-7708)
PCB BANCORP (PA)
3701 Wilshire Blvd Ste 100 (90010-2804)
PHONE..................213 210-2000
Henry Kim, *Pr*
Sang Young Lee, *Ch Bd*
Timothy Chang, *Corporate Secretary*
EMP: 245 EST: 2007
SALES (est): 116.25MM
SALES (corp-wide): 116.25MM **Publicly Held**
Web: www.mypcbbank.com
SIC: 6022 State commercial banks

(P-7709)
PCB BANK (HQ)
3701 Wilshire Blvd Ste 900 (90010-2871)
PHONE..................213 210-2000
Hae Young Cho, *CEO*
Henry Kim, *
Heo Young Cho, *
Andrew Chung, *
Mike Kim, *Chief Lending Officer**
▲ EMP: 152 EST: 2003
SALES (est): 116.25MM
SALES (corp-wide): 116.25MM **Publicly Held**
Web: www.mypcbbank.com
SIC: 6022 State commercial banks
PA: Pcb Bancorp
    3701 Wilshire Blvd # 100
    Los Angeles CA
    213 210-2000

(P-7710)
PORREY PINES BANK INC
Also Called: Western Alliance Bank
1951 Webster St (94612-2909)
PHONE..................510 899-7500
Larry Fountain, *Mgr*
Dianne Williams, *Mgr*
EMP: 227 EST: 2006
SALES (est): 7.02MM
SALES (corp-wide): 3.02B **Publicly Held**
Web: www.westernalliancebancorporation.com
SIC: 6022 State commercial banks
PA: Western Alliance Bancorporation
    1 E Wshington St Ste 1400
    Phoenix AZ
    602 389-3500

(P-7711)
PREMIER COMMERCIAL BANCORP
2400 E Katella Ave Ste 125 (92806-5920)
PHONE..................714 978-2400
Kenneth J Cosgrove, *Ch Bd*
Ashokkumar Patel, *
Stephen W Pihl, *
Viktor R Uehlinger, *
EMP: 64 EST: 2004
SALES (est): 22.38MM **Privately Held**
SIC: 6022 State commercial banks

(P-7712)
RABOBANK NATIONAL ASSOCIATION
Also Called: Rabobank North America
915 Highland Pointe Dr (95678-5419)
P.O. Box 1845 (92244-1845)
EMP: 1700
SIC: 6022 State commercial banks

(P-7713)
RCB CORPORATION (PA)
Also Called: RIVER CITY BANK
2480 Natomas Park Dr (95833-2979)
P.O. Box 15247 (95851-0247)
PHONE..................916 567-2600
Stephen Fleming, *Pr*
Anker Christensen, *
Shawn Devlin, *
Jon Kelly, *
EMP: 80 EST: 1981
SALES (est): 2MM
SALES (corp-wide): 2MM **Privately Held**
Web: www.rivercitybank.com
SIC: 6022 State commercial banks

(P-7714)
RIVER CITY BANK (HQ)
Also Called: RIVER CITY BANK
2480 Natomas Park Dr Ste 100 (95833-2979)
P.O. Box 15247 (95851-0247)
PHONE..................916 567-2600
Stephen A Fleming, *Pr*
Amii Barnard-bahn, *Sr VP*
Jim Kimball, *
Rebecca Fabisch Miller, *
Brian Killeen, *
▲ EMP: 80 EST: 1973
SALES (est): 140.25MM
SALES (corp-wide): 2MM **Privately Held**
Web: www.rivercitybank.com
SIC: 6022 State commercial banks
PA: Rcb Corporation
    2480 Natomas Park Dr
    Sacramento CA
    916 567-2600

(P-7715)
SAVINGS BANK MENDOCINO COUNTY (PA)
Also Called: Sbmc
200 N School St (95482-4811)
P.O. Box 3600 (95482-3600)
PHONE..................707 462-6613
Stacy Starkey, *Pr*
Charles B Mannon, *Chief Executive Officer Tech**
Bruce Little, *
Nancy Burris, *TO BRD**
Noreen Evans, *
▲ EMP: 130 EST: 1903
SALES (est): 49.03MM
SALES (corp-wide): 49.03MM **Privately Held**

6022 - State Commercial Banks (P-7716)

Web: www.savingsbank.com
SIC: **6022** State trust companies accepting deposits, commercial

(P-7716)
SEACOAST CMMERCE BANC HOLDINGS
11939 Rancho Bernardo Rd (92128-2072)
PHONE.................................858 432-7000
Richard Sanborn, *CEO*
Scott R Andrews, *CAO*
S Alan Rosen, *Admn*
EMP: 200 EST: 2014
SALES (est): 49MM **Publicly Held**
Web: www.scbholdings.com
SIC: **6022** State commercial banks
PA: Enterprise Financial Services Corp
    150 N Meramec Ave Ste 350
    Saint Louis MO

(P-7717)
STANDARD CHARTERED BANK
601 S Figueroa St Ste 2775 (90017-5877)
PHONE.................................626 639-8000
Jim Mc Cabe, *CEO*
EMP: 84
SALES (corp-wide): 24.84B **Privately Held**
Web: www.sc.com
SIC: **6022** 6282 6029 State trust companies accepting deposits, commercial; Investment advisory service; Commercial banks, nec
HQ: Standard Chartered Bank
    1 Basinghall Avenue
    London
    207 885-8888

(P-7718)
SVB FINANCIAL GROUP (PA)
3003 Tasman Dr (95054-1191)
PHONE.................................408 654-7400
Greg W Becker, *Pr*
Daniel J Beck, *CFO*
Philip Cox, *COO*
Michelle Draper, *Chief Marketing*
Christopher Edmonds-waters, *Chief Human Resources Officer*
EMP: 609 EST: 1999
SQ FT: 157,177
SALES (est): 7.4B
SALES (corp-wide): 7.4B **Publicly Held**
Web: www.svb.com
SIC: **6022** State commercial banks

(P-7719)
TRICO BANCSHARES (PA)
63 Constitution Dr (95973-4937)
PHONE.................................530 898-0300
Richard P Smith, *Ch Bd*
Michael W Koehnen, *V Ch Bd*
Peter G Wiese, *Ex VP*
John S Fleshood, *Ex VP*
Daniel K Bailey, *Chief Business Officer*
EMP: 150 EST: 1981
SALES (est): 418.55MM
SALES (corp-wide): 418.55MM **Publicly Held**
Web: www.tcbk.com
SIC: **6022** State commercial banks

(P-7720)
US BANK EQUIPMENT FINANCE
Also Called: US Bank
801 Larkspur Landing Cir (94939-1706)
PHONE.................................415 461-4600
EMP: 85
SIC: **6022** 6021 State commercial banks; National commercial banks

(P-7721)
VALLEY BUSINESS BANK
701 W Main St (93291-6145)
PHONE.................................559 622-9000
▲ EMP: 70
Web: www.cbbank.com
SIC: **6022** State commercial banks

(P-7722)
VALLEY COMMERCE BANCORP
701 W Main St (93291-6145)
PHONE.................................559 622-9000
EMP: 83
Web: www.cbbank.com
SIC: **6022** State commercial banks

(P-7723)
WELLS FARGO FINANCING CORPORATION
Also Called: Wells Fargo
420 Montgomery St Frnt (94104-1205)
PHONE.................................415 222-4292
EMP: 158880
SIC: **6022** 6021 State commercial banks; National commercial banks

(P-7724)
WESTAMERICA BANCORPORATION (PA)
1108 5th Ave (94901-2916)
P.O. Box 1200 (94585-1200)
PHONE.................................707 863-6000
David L Payne, *Ch Bd*
Robert Thorson, *CFO*
EMP: 72 EST: 1972
SALES (est): 266.88MM
SALES (corp-wide): 266.88MM **Publicly Held**
Web: www.westamerica.com
SIC: **6022** State commercial banks

(P-7725)
WESTERN ALLIANCE BANK
Also Called: Bridge Bank
55 Almaden Blvd Ste 200 (95113-1619)
PHONE.................................408 423-8500
Lee Shodiss, *VP*
EMP: 70
SALES (corp-wide): 3.02B **Publicly Held**
Web: www.westernalliancebancorporation.com
SIC: **6022** 8742 State commercial banks; Management consulting services
HQ: Western Alliance Bank
    1 E Wshington St Ste 1400
    Phoenix AZ

(P-7726)
WILSHIRE BANCORP INC
3200 Wilshire Blvd (90010-1333)
PHONE.................................213 387-3200
EMP: 547
SIC: **6022** State commercial banks

(P-7727)
WILSHIRE BANK
Also Called: Wilshire State Bank
3200 Wilshire Blvd Fl 10 (90010-1311)
PHONE.................................213 427-1000
▲ EMP: 349
SIC: **6022** State commercial banks

6029 Commercial Banks, Nec

(P-7728)
BANK OF MANHATTAN
2141 Rosecrans Ave Ste 1100 (90245-4747)
PHONE.................................310 606-8000
EMP: 187
SIC: **6029** Commercial banks, nec

(P-7729)
CHASES LLC
2079 Bonita Ave (91750-4442)
PHONE.................................909 596-6810
EMP: 60 EST: 2011
SALES (est): 6.62MM **Privately Held**
Web: www.chaseslaverne.com
SIC: **6029** Commercial banks, nec

(P-7730)
COMMERCIAL FIN LSG BNK CRDIFF
Also Called: Bank of Cardiff
12626 High Bluff Dr Ste 370 (92130-2070)
P.O. Box 2562 (92014-1862)
PHONE.................................888 234-0166
Vadim Garry Lyulkin, *Pr*
William S Stern, *
Dean G Lyulkin, *
EMP: 65 EST: 2003
SALES (est): 20.7MM **Privately Held**
Web: www.cardiff.co
SIC: **6029** Commercial banks, nec

(P-7731)
FEDERAL LAND BNK ASSN NTHRN CA
3435 Silverbell Rd (95973-0386)
P.O. Box 929 (95927-0929)
PHONE.................................530 895-8698
Bruce Strickler, *Pr*
Daniel Stevenson, *CCO**
Robert O'sullivan, *CCO*
EMP: 81 EST: 1990
SQ FT: 4,000
SALES (est): 415.23K **Privately Held**
SIC: **6029** Commercial banks, nec

(P-7732)
FIRST FOUNDATION INC
301 N Lake Ave Ste 100 (91101-4108)
PHONE.................................626 993-1300
Carol Golbranson, *Brnch Mgr*
EMP: 231
Web: www.firstfoundationinc.com
SIC: **6029** Commercial banks, nec
PA: First Foundation Inc.
    18101 Von Karman Ave # 7
    Irvine CA

(P-7733)
OPUS BANK
19900 Macarthur Blvd Ste 1200 (92612-8427)
PHONE.................................949 250-9800
TOLL FREE: 800
▲ EMP: 607
Web: www.ppbi.com
SIC: **6029** Commercial banks, nec

(P-7734)
PATENT AND TRADEMARK OFFICE US
26 S 4th St (95112-3526)
PHONE.................................831 332-7127
EMP: 280
Web: www.uspto.gov
SIC: **6029** Commercial banks, nec
HQ: United States Patent And Trademark Office
    600 Dulany St Ste 1
    Alexandria VA
    571 272-4100

(P-7735)
PLAZA BANK
18200 Von Kaman Ave Ste 5 (92612)
PHONE.................................949 502-4300
EMP: 78
Web: www.ppbi.com
SIC: **6029** Commercial banks, nec

(P-7736)
PREMIER VALLEY BANK
255 E River Park Cir Ste 180 (93720)
PHONE.................................559 438-2002
EMP: 102
SIC: **6029** Commercial banks, nec

(P-7737)
STANDARD CHARTERED BANK
9 Great Oaks Blvd (95119-1242)
PHONE.................................408 629-3219
EMP: 159
SALES (corp-wide): 24.84B **Privately Held**
Web: www.sc.com
SIC: **6029** 6021 Commercial banks, nec; National commercial banks
HQ: Standard Chartered Bank
    1 Basinghall Avenue
    London
    207 885-8888

(P-7738)
STANDARD CHARTERED BANK
50 Fremont St Ste 2210 (94105-6631)
PHONE.................................877 308-2182
EMP: 93
SALES (corp-wide): 24.84B **Privately Held**
Web: www.sc.com
SIC: **6029** Commercial banks, nec
HQ: Standard Chartered Bank
    1 Basinghall Avenue
    London
    207 885-8888

(P-7739)
SUMITOMO MITSUI BANKING CORP
601 S Figueroa St Ste 1800 (90017-5723)
PHONE.................................213 452-7800
EMP: 115
Web: www.smbc.co.jp
SIC: **6029** Commercial banks, nec
HQ: Sumitomo Mitsui Banking Corporation
    1-1-2, Marunouchi
    Chiyoda-Ku TKY

(P-7740)
TRI COUNTIES BANK (HQ)
63 Constitution Dr (95973-4937)
PHONE.................................530 898-0300
William J Casey, *Ch Bd*
Richard P Smith, *
Richard O'sullivan, *US Sales Vice President*
Craig Carney, *Senior Credit Officer**
Robert Steveson, *
EMP: 75 EST: 1974
SALES (est): 420.17MM
SALES (corp-wide): 418.55MM **Publicly Held**
Web: www.tcbk.com
SIC: **6029** 6163 Commercial banks, nec; Loan brokers
PA: Trico Bancshares
    63 Constitution Dr
    Chico CA
    530 898-0300

(P-7741)
TRI COUNTIES BANK
975 El Camino Real (94080-3203)
PHONE.................................650 583-8450

PRODUCTS & SERVICES SECTION
6061 - Federal Credit Unions (P-7760)

EMP: 184
SALES (corp-wide): 418.55MM **Publicly Held**
Web: www.tcbk.com
SIC: 6029 Commercial banks, nec
HQ: Tri Counties Bank
63 Constitution Dr
Chico CA
530 898-0300

6035 Federal Savings Institutions

(P-7742)
BANK OF SACRAMENTO
1750 Howe Ave Ste 100 (95825-3356)
PHONE.................................916 648-2100
EMP: 70
SIC: 6035 Federal savings banks

(P-7743)
GREENBOX LOANS INC
Also Called: Greenbox
3250 Wilshire Blvd Ste 1900 (90010-1605)
PHONE.................................800 919-1086
Raymond Eshaghian, CEO
EMP: 81 **EST:** 2000
SALES (est): 48.78MM **Privately Held**
Web: www.greenboxloans.com
SIC: 6035 6162 Federal savings and loan associations; Loan correspondents

(P-7744)
ONEWEST BANK GROUP LLC
888 E Walnut St (91101-1895)
P.O. Box 7056 (91109-7056)
PHONE.................................626 535-4870
EMP: 850
SIC: 6035 Federal savings banks

(P-7745)
PACIFIC TRUST BANK
18500 Von Karman Ave Ste 1100 (92612-0504)
P.O. Box 61452 (92602-6048)
PHONE.................................949 236-5211
Robert M Franko, CEO
Al Majors, *
Hans Ganz, *
James P Sheehy, *
Marangal Domingo, *
EMP: 107 **EST:** 1941
SALES (est): 83.94MM
SALES (corp-wide): 390.12MM **Publicly Held**
SIC: 6035 Federal savings banks
PA: Banc Of California, Inc.
3 Macarthur Pl Ste 100
Santa Ana CA
855 361-2262

(P-7746)
PAN AMERICAN BANK FSB
18191 Von Karman Ave Ste 300 (92612-7106)
PHONE.................................949 224-1917
Jim Vagim, Pr
EMP: 350 **EST:** 1994
SQ FT: 20,000
SALES (est): 96.49MM
SALES (corp-wide): 1.95B **Publicly Held**
SIC: 6035 Federal savings and loan associations
HQ: Vroom Automotive Finance Corporation
1071 Camelback St Ste 100
Newport Beach CA
949 224-1226

(P-7747)
PFF BANCORP INC (PA)
2058 N Mills Ave Ste 139 (91711-2812)
PHONE.................................213 683-6393
EMP: 852 **EST:** 1995
SALES (est): 46.19MM **Privately Held**
SIC: 6035 Federal savings and loan associations

6036 Savings Institutions, Except Federal

(P-7748)
EXCHANGE BANK (PA)
Also Called: Eb
545 4th St (95401-6323)
P.O. Box 403 (95402-0403)
PHONE.................................707 524-3000
Gary T Hartwick, CEO
William R Schrader, Pr
Bruce Decrona, Sr VP
Greg Jahn, Sr VP
Gary Searby, CIO
EMP: 135 **EST:** 1890
SQ FT: 50,000
SALES (est): 118.95MM
SALES (corp-wide): 118.95MM **Privately Held**
Web: www.exchangebank.com
SIC: 6036 8741 6022 State savings banks, not federally chartered; Management services; State commercial banks

(P-7749)
MIZUHO BANK LTD
Also Called: MIZUHO BANK LTD
350 S Grand Ave Ste 1500 (90071-3471)
PHONE.................................213 243-4500
Geoffrey Matsunaga, Admn
EMP: 124
Web: www.mizuhogroup.com
SIC: 6036 Savings institutions, except federal
HQ: Mizuho Bank, Ltd.
1271 Ave Of The Americas
New York NY
212 282-3000

6061 Federal Credit Unions

(P-7750)
1ST UNITED CREDIT UNION (PA)
5901 Gibraltar Dr (94588-2718)
P.O. Box 11746 (94588-1746)
PHONE.................................800 649-0193
Victor Quint, Pr
Victoria Pipkin, *
Shirley Sifuentes, *
Greg Pulliam, CAO*
Ed Renteria, CIO*
▲ **EMP:** 60 **EST:** 1932
SQ FT: 20,000
SALES (est): 44.84MM
SALES (corp-wide): 44.84MM **Privately Held**
Web: www.1stunitedcu.com
SIC: 6061 Federal credit unions

(P-7751)
ALLIED HALTHCARE FEDERAL CR UN
Also Called: AHFCU
2801 Atlantic Ave (90806-1701)
P.O. Box 93124 (90809-3124)
PHONE.................................562 933-0370
Charles Baldwin, Pr
Dennis Hayes, VP
EMP: 73 **EST:** 1956
SQ FT: 3,600
SALES (est): 2.45MM **Privately Held**
Web: www.ahfcu.org
SIC: 6061 Federal credit unions

(P-7752)
ALTAONE FEDERAL CREDIT UNION (PA)
Also Called: Alta One Fcu
701 S China Lake Blvd (93555-5027)
P.O. Box 1209 (93556-1209)
PHONE.................................760 371-7000
Stephanie Sievers, Pr
Denise Mattice, *
EMP: 114 **EST:** 1947
SQ FT: 33,000
SALES (est): 19.98MM
SALES (corp-wide): 19.98MM **Privately Held**
Web: www.altaone.org
SIC: 6061 Federal credit unions

(P-7753)
AMERICAN FIRST CREDIT UNION (PA)
6 Pointe Dr Ste 400 (92821-6322)
PHONE.................................562 691-1112
TOLL FREE: 800
Jon Shigematsu, Prin
Jon Shigematsu, CEO
Julie Glance, *
Brian Thompson, CAO*
EMP: 96 **EST:** 1956
SALES (est): 25.2MM
SALES (corp-wide): 25.2MM **Privately Held**
Web: www.amerfirst.org
SIC: 6061 Federal credit unions

(P-7754)
AMERICAS CHRISTIAN CREDIT UN (PA)
Also Called: Accu
2100 E Route 66 Ste 100 (91740-4623)
PHONE.................................626 208-5400
Mendell Thompson, Pr
Terri Snyder, *
Nicolette Harms, *
Richard H Mathews, Chief Human Resources Officer*
EMP: 61 **EST:** 1958
SQ FT: 22,000
SALES (est): 17.27MM
SALES (corp-wide): 17.27MM **Privately Held**
Web: www.americaschristiancu.com
SIC: 6061 Federal credit unions

(P-7755)
ARROWHEAD CENTRAL CREDIT UNION (PA)
8686 Haven Ave (91730-9107)
P.O. Box 4100 (91729-4100)
PHONE.................................866 212-4333
Darin Woinarowicz, CEO
Marie A Alonzo, Ch
Susan Conjurski, Ex VP
Doug Hallen, Treas
Raymond Mesler, CFO
EMP: 301 **EST:** 1949
SQ FT: 40,000
SALES (est): 41.12MM
SALES (corp-wide): 41.12MM **Privately Held**
Web: www.arrowheadcu.org
SIC: 6061 Federal credit unions

(P-7756)
BAY FEDERAL CREDIT UNION (PA)
3333 Clares St (95010-2564)
PHONE.................................831 479-6000
Dennis Osmer, Ch
H Duane Smith, *
Michael Leung, *
Ivonne J Guzman, *
EMP: 70 **EST:** 1957
SALES (est): 34.92MM
SALES (corp-wide): 34.92MM **Privately Held**
Web: www.bayfed.com
SIC: 6061 Federal credit unions

(P-7757)
CAL TECH EMPLYEES FDERAL CR UN (PA)
Also Called: CALTECH EFCU
528 Foothill Blvd (91011-3506)
P.O. Box 11001 (91012-6001)
PHONE.................................818 952-4444
Richard Harris, Prin
Stephen L Proia, *
Willis Chapman, *
Richard L Harris, *
Dlorah Gonzales, *
EMP: 64 **EST:** 1955
SALES (est): 36.45MM
SALES (corp-wide): 36.45MM **Privately Held**
Web: www.caltechefcu.org
SIC: 6061 Federal credit unions

(P-7758)
CALIFORNIA CREDIT UNION
503 Telegraph Canyon Rd (91910-6436)
P.O. Box 85833 (92186-5833)
PHONE.................................858 769-7369
Lisa Barker, Prin
EMP: 69
SALES (corp-wide): 152.71MM **Privately Held**
Web: www.ccu.com
SIC: 6061 Federal credit unions
PA: The California Credit Union
701 N Brand Blvd Fl 7
Glendale CA
818 291-6700

(P-7759)
COAST CENTRAL CREDIT UNION (PA)
2650 Harrison Ave (95501-3223)
PHONE.................................707 445-8801
Dean Christensen, Pr
Ches Meierding, *
Tom Noonan, *
EMP: 65 **EST:** 1932
SQ FT: 17,000
SALES (est): 40.52MM
SALES (corp-wide): 40.52MM **Privately Held**
Web: www.coastccu.org
SIC: 6061 Federal credit unions

(P-7760)
COMMONWEALTH CENTRAL CREDIT UN (PA)
5890 Silver Creek Valley Rd (95138-1027)
P.O. Box 641690 (95164-1690)
PHONE.................................408 531-3100
Craig Weber, CEO
EMP: 69 **EST:** 1959
SQ FT: 36,432
SALES (est): 17.43MM
SALES (corp-wide): 17.43MM **Privately Held**
Web: www.wealthcu.org
SIC: 6061 Federal credit unions

6061 - Federal Credit Unions (P-7761)

(P-7761)
CREDIT UNION SOUTHERN CAL (PA)
8101 E Kaiser Blvd Ste 300 (92808-2243)
P.O. Box 200 (90608-0200)
PHONE..............................562 698-8326
Dave Gunderson, *Pr*
Peter Putnam, *CFO*
Ed Fost, *COO*
Debbie Childs, *Ex VP*
▲ **EMP:** 77 **EST:** 1954
SQ FT: 12,000
SALES (est): 62.11MM
SALES (corp-wide): 62.11MM **Privately Held**
Web: www.cusocal.org
SIC: 6061 Federal credit unions

(P-7762)
EDUCATIONAL EMPLOYEES CR UN (PA)
2222 W Shaw Ave Ste 100 (93711-3419)
PHONE..............................559 437-7700
Barbara Thomas, *Ch*
Elizabeth Dooley, *
Rick Browning, *
EMP: 110 **EST:** 1934
SQ FT: 44,000
SALES (est): 140.03MM
SALES (corp-wide): 140.03MM **Privately Held**
Web: www.myeecu.org
SIC: 6061 Federal credit unions

(P-7763)
EDUCATIONAL EMPLOYEES CR UN
3488 W Shaw Ave (93711-3216)
P.O. Box 5242 (93755-5242)
PHONE..............................559 896-0222
TOLL FREE: 800
Bruce L Barnett, *Pr*
EMP: 67
SQ FT: 17,939
SALES (corp-wide): 140.03MM **Privately Held**
Web: www.myeecu.org
SIC: 6061 Federal credit unions
PA: Educational Employees Credit Union
2222 W Shaw Ave
Fresno CA
559 437-7700

(P-7764)
EXCITE CREDIT UNION (PA)
265 Curtner Ave (95125-1404)
P.O. Box 18460 (95158-8460)
PHONE..............................800 232-8669
Brian Dorcy, *CEO*
Brian Dorcy, *Pr*
Deborah Sunderman, *
EMP: 73 **EST:** 1952
SQ FT: 40,000
SALES (est): 18.68MM
SALES (corp-wide): 18.68MM **Privately Held**
Web: www.excitecu.org
SIC: 6061 Federal credit unions

(P-7765)
F & A FEDERAL CREDIT UNION
2625 Corporate Pl (91754-7645)
P.O. Box 30831 (90030-0831)
PHONE..............................213 268-1226
Richard Andrews, *Pr*
EMP: 70 **EST:** 1936
SQ FT: 43,000
SALES (est): 32.84MM **Privately Held**
Web: www.fafcu.org
SIC: 6061 Federal credit unions

(P-7766)
FARMERS INSUR GROUP FDRAL CR U (PA)
Also Called: FARMERS INSURANCE
2255 N Ontario St Ste 320 (91504-3191)
P.O. Box 2723 (90509-2723)
PHONE..............................323 209-6000
Mark Herter, *CEO*
Laszlo Haredy, *
Jan Larson, *
Laura Campbell, *
EMP: 70 **EST:** 1936
SQ FT: 12,000
SALES (est): 57.98MM
SALES (corp-wide): 57.98MM **Privately Held**
Web: www.figfcu.org
SIC: 6061 Federal credit unions

(P-7767)
FINANCIAL PARTNERS CREDIT UN (PA)
Also Called: Financial Partners Credit Un
7800 Imperial Hwy (90242-3457)
P.O. Box 7005 (90241-7005)
PHONE..............................562 904-3000
John Crites, *Ch Bd*
Nader Moghaddam, *
Michael Patterson, *
Mary Torsney, *
Wanda Williams, *
EMP: 73 **EST:** 1937
SQ FT: 32,000
SALES (est): 50.06MM
SALES (corp-wide): 50.06MM **Privately Held**
Web: www.fpcu.org
SIC: 6061 Federal credit unions

(P-7768)
FIREFIGHTERS FIRST CREDIT UN (PA)
1520 W Colorado Blvd (91105-1413)
PHONE..............................323 254-1700
Dixie Abramian, *CEO*
EMP: 138 **EST:** 1935
SALES (est): 45.52MM
SALES (corp-wide): 45.52MM **Privately Held**
Web: www.firefightersfirstcu.org
SIC: 6061 Federal credit unions

(P-7769)
FIRST ENTERTAINMENT CREDIT UN (PA)
6735 Forest Lawn Dr Ste 100 (90068-1001)
P.O. Box 100 (90078-0100)
PHONE..............................323 851-3673
Charles A Bruen, *Pr*
Lucy Wander-perna, *Ch*
Dennis Tange, *
Michael Edwards, *Vice Chairman**
Irwin Jacobson, *
EMP: 80 **EST:** 1998
SQ FT: 57,000
SALES (est): 54.43MM
SALES (corp-wide): 54.43MM **Privately Held**
Web: www.firstent.org
SIC: 6061 Federal credit unions

(P-7770)
FIRST FINANCIAL FEDERAL CR UN
650 Sierra Madre Villa Ave Ste 300 (91107-2013)
PHONE..............................800 537-8491
SIC: 6061 Federal credit unions

Dietmar Huesch, *CFO*
EMP: 140 **EST:** 1974
SALES (est): 10.94MM **Privately Held**
SIC: 6061 Federal credit unions

(P-7771)
FIRST TECHNOLOGY FEDERAL CR UN
19960 Stevens Creek Blvd (95014-2306)
PHONE..............................408 863-6240
Dennis Nakpil, *Mgr*
EMP: 69
SALES (corp-wide): 605.64MM **Privately Held**
Web: www.firsttechfed.com
SIC: 6061 Federal credit unions
PA: First Technology Federal Credit Union
2702 Orchard Pkwy
San Jose CA
855 855-8805

(P-7772)
FIRST TECHNOLOGY FEDERAL CR UN (PA)
Also Called: First Tech Federal Credit Un
2702 Orchard Pkwy (95134-2012)
PHONE..............................855 855-8805
Gregory A Mitchell, *CEO*
Scott Jenner, *
Marangal Marito Domingo, *CFO*
Phil Campbell, *
Monique Little, *CPO**
EMP: 100 **EST:** 1952
SALES (est): 605.64MM
SALES (corp-wide): 605.64MM **Privately Held**
Web: www.firsttechfed.com
SIC: 6061 Federal credit unions

(P-7773)
FIRST TECHNOLOGY FEDERAL CR UN
1011 Sunset Blvd Ste 210 (95765-3782)
PHONE..............................855 855-8805
EMP: 86
SALES (corp-wide): 605.64MM **Privately Held**
Web: www.firsttechfed.com
SIC: 6061 Federal credit unions
PA: First Technology Federal Credit Union
2702 Orchard Pkwy
San Jose CA
855 855-8805

(P-7774)
FRONTWAVE CREDIT UNION (PA)
1278 Rocky Point Dr (92056-5867)
PHONE..............................760 430-7511
Bill Birnie, *Pr*
Shilpa Edlabadkar, *
Paul Leonhardt, *CLO**
Jennifer Williams, *
EMP: 107 **EST:** 1953
SQ FT: 22,000
SALES (est): 31.72MM
SALES (corp-wide): 31.72MM **Privately Held**
Web: www.frontwavecu.com
SIC: 6061 Federal credit unions

(P-7775)
ILWU FEDERAL CREDIT UNION
3447 Atlantic Ave (90807-4513)
P.O. Box 7629 (90807-0629)
PHONE..............................310 834-6411
Ralph Ruiz, *Pr*
Devric Thomas, *
Kimberly Mathis, *

Robert York, *
EMP: 61 **EST:** 1954
SQ FT: 10,000
SALES (est): 12.19MM **Privately Held**
Web: www.ilwucu.org
SIC: 6061 Federal credit unions

(P-7776)
KERN FEDERAL CREDIT UNION
1717 Truxtun Ave (93301-5102)
PHONE..............................661 327-9461
Brandon Ivie, *CEO*
EMP: 87 **EST:** 1949
SQ FT: 17,000
SALES (est): 10.46MM **Privately Held**
Web: www.stratacu.org
SIC: 6061 6163 Federal credit unions; Loan brokers

(P-7777)
KEYPOINT CREDIT UNION (PA)
2150 Trade Zone Blvd Ste 200 (95131-1730)
PHONE..............................408 731-4100
T Bradford Canfield, *CEO*
Timothy M Kramer, *
John Herrick, *
EMP: 123 **EST:** 1979
SALES (est): 41.34MM
SALES (corp-wide): 41.34MM **Privately Held**
Web: www.kpcu.com
SIC: 6061 Federal credit unions

(P-7778)
KINECTA FEDERAL CREDIT UNION (PA)
Also Called: Kinecta
1440 Rosecrans Ave (90266-3702)
P.O. Box 10003 (90267-7503)
PHONE..............................310 643-5400
Keith Sultemeier, *CEO*
Teresa Freeborn, *
Joseph E Whitaker, *
Steven J Glouberman, *
Sharon Moseley, *
EMP: 250 **EST:** 1940
SQ FT: 80,000
SALES (est): 161.89MM
SALES (corp-wide): 161.89MM **Privately Held**
Web: www.kinecta.org
SIC: 6061 Federal credit unions

(P-7779)
LOGIX FEDERAL CREDIT UNION (PA)
2340 N Hollywood Way (91505-1124)
P.O. Box 4130 (91310-4130)
PHONE..............................888 718-5328
Ana Fonseca, *CEO*
Jan Franklin, *
Tim Boland, *
Dave Styler, *
Ana Fonseca, *CFO*
EMP: 210 **EST:** 1937
SQ FT: 75,000
SALES (est): 230.72MM
SALES (corp-wide): 230.72MM **Privately Held**
Web: www.logixbanking.com
SIC: 6061 Federal credit unions

(P-7780)
LOS ANGELES FEDERAL CREDIT UN (PA)
Also Called: Los Angeles Federal Credit Un
300 S Glendale Ave Ste 100 (91205-1752)
PHONE..............................818 242-8640

PRODUCTS & SERVICES SECTION
6061 - Federal Credit Unions (P-7799)

John T Dea, *CEO*
Richard Lie, *
Leta Cook, *
Anthony Cuevas, *
EMP: 100 **EST:** 1936
SQ FT: 40,000
SALES (est): 35.44MM
SALES (corp-wide): 35.44MM **Privately Held**
Web: www.lafcu.org
SIC: 6061 Federal credit unions

(P-7781)
MERIWEST CREDIT UNION (PA)
5615 Chesbro Ave Ste 100 (95123-3047)
P.O. Box 530953 (95153-5353)
PHONE.................................408 363-3200
TOLL FREE: 877
Julie A Kirsch, *Prin*
Christopher Owen, *
Hudson Lee, *
Steven G Johnson, *
Mark Antonioli, *
EMP: 130 **EST:** 1961
SQ FT: 61,000
SALES (est): 53.81MM
SALES (corp-wide): 53.81MM **Privately Held**
Web: www.meriwest.com
SIC: 6061 Federal credit unions

(P-7782)
MISSION FEDERAL CREDIT UNION
4250 Clairemont Mesa Blvd Ste B (92117-2747)
P.O. Box 910557 (92191-0557)
PHONE.................................858 531-5106
EMP: 218
SALES (corp-wide): 119.62MM **Privately Held**
Web: www.missionfed.com
SIC: 6061 Federal credit unions
PA: Mission Federal Credit Union
5785 Oberlin Dr Ste 312
San Diego CA
858 546-2184

(P-7783)
MISSION FEDERAL CREDIT UNION (PA)
5785 Oberlin Dr Ste 312 (92121-1724)
PHONE.................................858 546-2184
Debra Schwartz, *CEO*
Ron Araujo, *CFO*
Sheila Carpizo, *Acctg Mgr*
EMP: 75 **EST:** 2015
SQ FT: 59,956
SALES (est): 119.62MM
SALES (corp-wide): 119.62MM **Privately Held**
Web: www.missionfed.com
SIC: 6061 Federal credit unions

(P-7784)
MISSION FEDERAL SERVICES LLC (PA)
10325 Meanley Dr (92131-3011)
P.O. Box 919023 (92191-9023)
PHONE.................................858 524-2850
Debra Schwartz, *CEO*
Rose Hartley, *
Richard Hartley, *
Gary M Devan Senior, *Vice-President Information Systems*
Elaine Ziegler, *Senior Vice President Human Resources*
EMP: 150 **EST:** 1961
SQ FT: 55,000
SALES (est): 109.72MM
SALES (corp-wide): 109.72MM **Privately Held**
Web: www.missionfed.com
SIC: 6061 Federal credit unions

(P-7785)
NOBLE CREDIT UNION
2580 W Shaw Ln Frnt (93711-2776)
P.O. Box 8027 (93747-8027)
PHONE.................................559 252-5000
Susan Ryan, *Mgr*
EMP: 69
SALES (corp-wide): 30.87MM **Privately Held**
Web: www.noblecu.com
SIC: 6061 Federal credit unions
PA: Noble Credit Union
2550 W Shaw Ave
Fresno CA
559 252-5000

(P-7786)
NORTHROP GRUMMAN FEDERAL CR UN (PA)
879 W 190th St Ste 800 (90248-4205)
PHONE.................................310 808-4000
Stanley R Swenson Junior, *Pr*
Georgetta A Wolff, *
Kathi Harper, *
Stephen Considine, *Vice Chairman*
EMP: 60 **EST:** 1946
SALES (est): 44.3MM
SALES (corp-wide): 44.3MM **Privately Held**
Web: www.ngfcu.us
SIC: 6061 Federal credit unions

(P-7787)
NUVISION FINCL FEDERAL CR UN (PA)
7812 Edinger Ave Ste 100 (92647-3727)
P.O. Box 1220 (92647-1220)
PHONE.................................714 375-8000
Roger Ballard, *CEO*
John Afdem, *CFO*
Robert Geraci, *Treas*
EMP: 137 **EST:** 1935
SALES (est): 98.79MM
SALES (corp-wide): 98.79MM **Privately Held**
Web: www.nuvisionfederal.com
SIC: 6061 Federal credit unions

(P-7788)
ORANGE COUNTYS CREDIT UNION (PA)
1721 E Saint Andrew Pl (92705-4934)
P.O. Box 11777 (92711-1777)
PHONE.................................714 755-5900
Lucy Ito, *Interim Chief Executive Officer*
Dan Dillon, *
EMP: 157 **EST:** 1938
SALES (est): 53.13MM
SALES (corp-wide): 53.13MM **Privately Held**
Web: www.orangecountyscu.org
SIC: 6061 Federal credit unions

(P-7789)
PACIFIC SERVICE CREDIT UNION (PA)
1355 Willow Way Ste 200 (94520-5721)
P.O. Box 8191 (94596-8191)
PHONE.................................888 858-6878
Jenna Lampson, *Pr*
Lawrence Labonte, *
Vicki Turano, *
David Sena, *
EMP: 76 **EST:** 1936
SALES (est): 35.89MM
SALES (corp-wide): 35.89MM **Privately Held**
Web: www.pacificservice.org
SIC: 6061 Federal credit unions

(P-7790)
PARTNERS FEDERAL CREDIT UNION (PA)
100 N First St Ste 400 (91502-1818)
PHONE.................................800 948-6677
Ricky Otey, *Pr*
Rick Wise, *
EMP: 73 **EST:** 1968
SQ FT: 26,000
SALES (est): 65.93MM
SALES (corp-wide): 65.93MM **Privately Held**
Web: www.partnersfcu.org
SIC: 6061 6163 Federal credit unions; Loan brokers

(P-7791)
PATELCO CREDIT UNION (PA)
3 Park Pl (94568-7983)
P.O. Box 8020 (94588-8601)
PHONE.................................800 358-8228
Erin Mendez, *CEO*
Alison Jones, *
Sue Gruber, *
Kevin Landel, *CIO*
Richard Wada, *CLO*
EMP: 250 **EST:** 1936
SALES (est): 208.87MM
SALES (corp-wide): 208.87MM **Privately Held**
Web: www.patelco.org
SIC: 6061 Federal credit unions

(P-7792)
POLICE CREDIT UNION OF CAL (PA)
1250 Grundy Ln (94066-3032)
P.O. Box 1087 (94066-7087)
PHONE.................................415 242-2142
Eddie C Young, *CEO*
Michael Sordelli, *
Rosalyn Reilly, *
EMP: 70 **EST:** 1958
SQ FT: 18,561
SALES (est): 24.84MM
SALES (corp-wide): 24.84MM **Privately Held**
Web: www.thepolicecu.org
SIC: 6061 Federal credit unions

(P-7793)
REDWOOD CREDIT UNION (PA)
3033 Cleveland Ave Ste 100 (95403-2126)
P.O. Box 6104 (95406-0104)
PHONE.................................707 545-4000
Brett Martinez, *Pr*
Michelle Anderson, *CLO*
EMP: 190 **EST:** 1950
SQ FT: 20,000
SALES (est): 179.9MM
SALES (corp-wide): 179.9MM **Privately Held**
Web: www.redwoodcu.org
SIC: 6061 Federal credit unions

(P-7794)
REDWOOD CREDIT UNION
100 Van Ness Ave 10th Fl (94102-5209)
PHONE.................................415 861-7928
Jacob Roberts, *Mgr*
EMP: 81
SALES (corp-wide): 179.9MM **Privately Held**
Web: www.redwoodcu.org
SIC: 6061 Federal credit unions
PA: Redwood Credit Union
3033 Cleveland Ave # 100
Santa Rosa CA
707 545-4000

(P-7795)
SAFE CREDIT UNION (PA)
2295 Iron Point Rd Ste 100 (95630-8767)
PHONE.................................916 979-7233
Dave Roughton, *CEO*
EMP: 160 **EST:** 1940
SQ FT: 57,000
SALES (est): 98MM
SALES (corp-wide): 98MM **Privately Held**
Web: www.safecu.org
SIC: 6061 Federal credit unions

(P-7796)
SAN DIEGO COUNTY CREDIT UNION (PA)
Also Called: Sdccu
6545 Sequence Dr (92121-4363)
PHONE.................................877 732-2848
Irene Oberbauer, *Pr*
Robert Marchand, *
Heather Moshier, *
Theresa Halleck, *
Tracey Curran, *
▲ **EMP:** 239 **EST:** 1938
SQ FT: 50,000
SALES (est): 210.99MM
SALES (corp-wide): 210.99MM **Privately Held**
Web: www.sdccu.com
SIC: 6061 Federal credit unions

(P-7797)
SAN FRANCISCO FEDERAL CR UN (PA)
770 Golden Gate Ave (94102-3194)
PHONE.................................415 775-5377
William Wolverton, *CEO*
Steve Ho, *
Heidi Goldstein, *CAO*
Melissa Palwick, *EXPERIENCE*
▲ **EMP:** 70 **EST:** 1953
SQ FT: 35,500
SALES (est): 24.15MM
SALES (corp-wide): 24.15MM **Privately Held**
Web: www.sanfranciscofcu.com
SIC: 6061 Federal credit unions

(P-7798)
SAN MATEO CREDIT UNION
525 Middlefield Rd (94063-1853)
P.O. Box 910 (94064-0910)
PHONE.................................650 363-1725
Barry Jolette, *CEO*
EMP: 100
SALES (corp-wide): 59.34MM **Privately Held**
Web: www.smcu.org
SIC: 6061 Federal credit unions
PA: San Mateo Credit Union
350 Convention Way # 300
Redwood City CA
650 363-1725

(P-7799)
SAN MATEO CREDIT UNION
1515 S El Camino Real Ste 100 (94402)
P.O. Box 910 (94064-0910)
PHONE.................................650 363-1725
Preston Monroe, *Prin*
EMP: 184 **EST:** 2008
SALES (est): 1.47MM
SALES (corp-wide): 59.34MM **Privately Held**

6061 - Federal Credit Unions (P-7800)

Web: www.smcu.org
SIC: 6061 Federal credit unions
PA: San Mateo Credit Union
350 Convention Way # 300
Redwood City CA
650 363-1725

(P-7800)
SCE FEDERAL CREDIT UNION (PA)
Also Called: SCE FCU
12701 Schabarum Ave (91706-6807)
P.O. Box 8017 (91734-2317)
PHONE..................................626 960-6888
Dennis Huber, CEO
George Poitou, *
Daniel Rader, *
EMP: 90 EST: 1952
SQ FT: 30,000
SALES (est): 28.29MM
SALES (corp-wide): 28.29MM Privately Held
Web: www.scefcu.org
SIC: 6061 Federal credit unions

(P-7801)
SCHOOLS FINANCIAL CREDIT UNION (PA)
1485 Response Rd Ste 126 (95815-4803)
P.O. Box 11547 (92711-1547)
PHONE..................................916 569-5400
James P Jordan Iii, Pr
James P Jordan Iii, Pr
Tim Marriott, *
EMP: 150 EST: 1933
SQ FT: 56,000
SALES (est): 71.36MM
SALES (corp-wide): 71.36MM Privately Held
Web: www.schoolsfirstfcu.org
SIC: 6061 Federal credit unions

(P-7802)
SCHOOLSFIRST FEDERAL CREDIT UN (PA)
2115 N Broadway (92706-2613)
P.O. Box 11547 (92711-1547)
PHONE..................................714 258-4000
Bill Cheney, CEO
Jose Lara, *
Jim Phillips, *
Jill Meznarich, Chief Auditor*
EMP: 270 EST: 1934
SALES (est): 335.16MM
SALES (corp-wide): 335.16MM Privately Held
Web: www.schoolsfirstfcu.org
SIC: 6061 Federal credit unions

(P-7803)
SCHOOLSFIRST FEDERAL CREDIT UN
Also Called: Consumer Loan Dept
15442 Del Amo Ave (92780-6445)
P.O. Box 11547 (92711-1547)
PHONE..................................480 777-5995
Rudy Tafoya, Dir
EMP: 66
SQ FT: 61,058
SALES (corp-wide): 335.16MM Privately Held
Web: www.schoolsfirstfcu.org
SIC: 6061 Federal credit unions
PA: Schoolsfirst Federal Credit Union
2115 N Broadway
Santa Ana CA
714 258-4000

(P-7804)
SESLOC FEDERAL CREDIT UNION (PA)
3855 Broad St (93401-7109)
P.O. Box 5360 (93403-5360)
PHONE..................................805 543-1816
Bertha Foxford, Pr
Andy Bechinsky, *
Micki Myall, *
EMP: 77 EST: 1942
SQ FT: 19,700
SALES (est): 29.15MM
SALES (corp-wide): 29.15MM Privately Held
Web: www.sesloc.org
SIC: 6061 Federal credit unions

(P-7805)
SIERRA CENTRAL CREDIT UNION (PA)
1351 Harter Pkwy (95993-2604)
PHONE..................................530 671-3009
John Cassidy, CEO
Ron Sweeney, *
EMP: 90 EST: 1955
SQ FT: 8,000
SALES (est): 39.62MM
SALES (corp-wide): 39.62MM Privately Held
Web: www.sierracentral.com
SIC: 6061 Federal credit unions

(P-7806)
SOUTHLAND CREDIT UNION (PA)
10701 Los Alamitos Blvd (90720-2353)
P.O. Box 3003 (90720-1303)
PHONE..................................562 862-6831
Ferris R Foster, CEO
Tom Lent, *
EMP: 60 EST: 1999
SALES (est): 33.87MM
SALES (corp-wide): 33.87MM Privately Held
Web: www.southlandcu.org
SIC: 6061 Federal credit unions

(P-7807)
STANFORD FEDERAL CREDIT UNION (PA)
Also Called: SFCU
1860 Embarcadero Rd (94303-3308)
P.O. Box 10690 (94303-0843)
PHONE..................................650 725-1000
Jane S Duperrault, Ch Bd
Michael A Hindery, *
Timothy R Warner, *
Tana Hutchison, *
Jerry L Jobe, *
EMP: 61 EST: 1959
SALES (est): 88.52MM
SALES (corp-wide): 88.52MM Privately Held
Web: www.sfcu.org
SIC: 6061 Federal credit unions

(P-7808)
STAR ONE CREDIT UNION (PA)
1306 Bordeaux Dr (94089-1005)
P.O. Box 3643 (94088-3643)
PHONE..................................408 543-5202
TOLL FREE: 800
Rick Heldebrant, Pr
EMP: 107 EST: 1956
SQ FT: 25,000
SALES (est): 183.03MM
SALES (corp-wide): 183.03MM Privately Held
Web: www.starone.org

SIC: 6061 Federal credit unions

(P-7809)
SUN COMMUNITY FEDERAL CR UN
1001 E Us Highway 98 (92231-9759)
PHONE..................................760 337-4200
Lolie Escalante, Brnch Mgr
EMP: 67
SALES (corp-wide): 18.62MM Privately Held
Web: www.suncommunity.com
SIC: 6061 Federal credit unions
PA: Sun Community Federal Credit Union
1068 Broadway Ave
El Centro CA
760 336-8622

(P-7810)
TECHNOLOGY CREDIT UNION (PA)
2010 N 1st St Ste 200 (95131-2001)
P.O. Box 1409 (95109-1409)
PHONE..................................408 451-9111
Todd Harris, CEO
Harold Roundtree, Member Services Vice President*
Steve Fisher, *
Suzan Windnagler, *
Ted Thames, *
EMP: 133 EST: 1960
SQ FT: 23,000
SALES (est): 173.21MM
SALES (corp-wide): 173.21MM Privately Held
Web: www.techcu.com
SIC: 6061 Federal credit unions

(P-7811)
TELESIS COMMUNITY CREDIT UNION (PA)
9301 Winnetka Ave (91311-6069)
PHONE..................................818 885-1226
Grace Mayo, Pr
Jean Faenza, *
EMP: 90 EST: 1993
SQ FT: 17,000
SALES (est): 8.96MM Privately Held
Web: www.telesiscu.com
SIC: 6061 6163 Federal credit unions; Loan brokers

(P-7812)
TRAVIS CREDIT UNION (PA)
1 Travis Way (95687-3276)
P.O. Box 2069 (95696-2069)
PHONE..................................707 449-4000
Patsy Vanouwerkerk, CEO
Catherine Johnson, *
EMP: 300 EST: 1951
SQ FT: 12,000
SALES (est): 140.99MM
SALES (corp-wide): 140.99MM Privately Held
Web: www.traviscu.org
SIC: 6061 Federal credit unions

(P-7813)
UNIFY FINCL CR UN PROF CORP (PA)
2305b W 190th St (90504-6003)
P.O. Box 10018 (90267-7518)
PHONE..................................877 254-9328
Gordon M Howe, CEO
EMP: 80 EST: 1958
SALES (est): 118.97MM
SALES (corp-wide): 118.97MM Privately Held
Web: www.unifyfcu.com

SIC: 6061 Federal credit unions

(P-7814)
UNITED SVCS AMER FEDERAL CR UN (PA)
Also Called: USA Federal Credit Union
9999 Willow Creek Rd (92131-1117)
PHONE..................................858 831-8100
TOLL FREE: 800
Martin Cassell, Pr
Ron Davis, *
Jim Bedinger, *
EMP: 90 EST: 1953
SQ FT: 42,000
SALES (est): 19.03MM
SALES (corp-wide): 19.03MM Privately Held
Web: www.navyfederal.org
SIC: 6061 Federal credit unions

(P-7815)
UNIVERSITY CREDIT UNION
1500 S Sepulveda Blvd (90025-3312)
PHONE..................................310 477-6628
Charles Bumbarger, Pr
Tristan Dion Chen, CMO*
EMP: 104 EST: 1945
SALES (est): 25.46MM Privately Held
Web: www.ucu.org
SIC: 6061 Federal credit unions

(P-7816)
V A DESERT PCF FEDERAL CR UN
5901 E 7th St (90822-5201)
PHONE..................................562 498-1250
Cindy Glessner, CEO
Charles Feistman, Ch Bd
Christine Wood, COO
Craig Kasper, Sec
Marion G Smith, Sec
EMP: 81 EST: 1947
SQ FT: 2,500
SALES (est): 3.57MM Privately Held
Web: www.vadpfcu.org
SIC: 6061 Federal credit unions

(P-7817)
VALLEY STRONG CREDIT UNION (PA)
Also Called: Ksfcu
11500 Bolthouse Dr (93311-8822)
P.O. Box 9506 (93389-9506)
PHONE..................................661 833-7900
TOLL FREE: 800
Stephen P Renock Iv, CEO
Stephen P Renock Iv, Pr
Shari Butler, *
Neil Marshall, *
Shelli Anglim, *
EMP: 60 EST: 1940
SQ FT: 18,000
SALES (est): 79.85MM
SALES (corp-wide): 79.85MM Privately Held
Web: www.valleystrong.com
SIC: 6061 Federal credit unions

(P-7818)
VENTURA COUNTY CREDIT UNION (PA)
2575 Vista Del Mar Dr Ste 100 (93001-3900)
PHONE..................................805 477-4000
Joseph Schroeder, Pr
Linda Rossi, *
Gavin Bradley, *
Linda Sim, *
EMP: 84 EST: 1950

SQ FT: 22,500
SALES (est): 30.73MM
SALES (corp-wide): 30.73MM **Privately Held**
Web: www.vccuonline.net
SIC: **6061** Federal credit unions

6062 State Credit Unions

(P-7819)
ADELFI CREDIT UNION
Also Called: Eccu
955 W Imperial Hwy Ste 100 (92821-3812)
P.O. Box 2400 (92822-2400)
PHONE..................714 671-5700
Abel Pomar, *CEO*
Gregory Talbott, *
Susan Rushing, *
Patty Staples, *
Tom Honan, *
EMP: 147 EST: 1964
SQ FT: 125,000
SALES (est): 17.48MM **Privately Held**
Web: www.adelfibanking.com
SIC: **6062** State credit unions, not federally chartered

(P-7820)
CALIFORNIA COAST CREDIT UNION (PA)
9201 Spectrum Center Blvd Ste 300 (92123-1442)
P.O. Box 502080 (92150-2080)
PHONE..................858 495-1600
Marla Shepard, *CEO*
Ruth Peshkoff, *
Carol Walker, *
Charles Wallace, *
Frederick Schwartz, *
EMP: 74 EST: 1929
SALES (est): 81.41MM
SALES (corp-wide): 81.41MM **Privately Held**
Web: www.calcoastcu.org
SIC: **6062** 6163 State credit unions, not federally chartered; Loan brokers

(P-7821)
CALIFORNIA CREDIT UNION (PA)
701 N Brand Blvd Fl 7 (91203-1218)
P.O. Box 29100 (91209-9100)
PHONE..................818 291-6700
Steve O'Connell, *CEO*
Rebecca Collier, *
Hudson Lee, *
EMP: 120 EST: 1933
SALES (est): 152.71MM
SALES (corp-wide): 152.71MM **Privately Held**
Web: www.ccu.com
SIC: **6062** 6061 State credit unions, not federally chartered; Federal credit unions

(P-7822)
CHRISTIAN COMMUNITY CREDIT UN (PA)
255 N Lone Hill Ave (91773-2308)
P.O. Box 3012 (91722-9012)
PHONE..................626 915-7551
Marji Hughes, *Interim Chief Executive Officer*
John T Walling, *
David Estridge, *
Linda Tashiro, *
Marji Hughes, *Ex VP*
EMP: 70 EST: 1957
SQ FT: 24,000
SALES (est): 28.67MM
SALES (corp-wide): 28.67MM **Privately Held**

Web: www.mycccu.com
SIC: **6062** State credit unions, not federally chartered

(P-7823)
COASTHILLS CREDIT UNION (PA)
Also Called: Cscu
1075 E Betteravia Rd (93454-7023)
P.O. Box 8000 (93456-8000)
PHONE..................805 733-7600
Jeff York, *Pr*
Dave Upham, *
Scott Coe, *
Marty Chatham, *
Dal Widick, *
EMP: 80 EST: 1958
SQ FT: 30,000
SALES (est): 52.93MM
SALES (corp-wide): 52.93MM **Privately Held**
Web: www.coasthills.coop
SIC: **6062** State credit unions, not federally chartered

(P-7824)
CU COOPERATIVE SYSTEMS INC (PA)
Also Called: Co-Op Solutions
9692 Haven Ave (91730-0101)
PHONE..................909 948-2500
Dean Michaels, *Pr*
Grace Mayo, *Vice Chairman*
Tom Sargent, *Ch Bd*
John Bommarito, *Treas*
James Hanisch, *Ex VP*
▲ EMP: 285 EST: 1981
SALES (est): 185.31MM
SALES (corp-wide): 185.31MM **Privately Held**
Web: www.co-opfs.org
SIC: **6062** State credit unions, not federally chartered

(P-7825)
GOLDEN 1 CREDIT UNION
7770 College Town Dr (95826-2343)
PHONE..................916 732-2900
Wayne Moore, *Brnch Mgr*
EMP: 63
SALES (corp-wide): 403.88MM **Privately Held**
Web: www.golden1.com
SIC: **6062** State credit unions, not federally chartered
PA: Golden 1 Credit Union
    8945 Cal Center Dr
    Sacramento CA
    916 732-2900

(P-7826)
GOLDEN 1 CREDIT UNION (PA)
8945 Cal Center Dr (95826-3239)
P.O. Box 15966 (95852-0966)
PHONE..................916 732-2900
Teresa Halleck, *Pr*
EMP: 400 EST: 1933
SQ FT: 100,000
SALES (est): 403.88MM
SALES (corp-wide): 403.88MM **Privately Held**
Web: www.golden1.com
SIC: **6062** State credit unions, not federally chartered

(P-7827)
LBS FINANCIAL CREDIT UNION (PA)
5505 Garden Grove Blvd Ste 500 (92683-1894)

PHONE..................562 598-9007
Sean Hardeman, *CEO*
Sean M Hardeman, *
Gene Allen, *
Dug Woog, *
EMP: 120 EST: 1935
SQ FT: 63,000
SALES (est): 64.22MM
SALES (corp-wide): 64.22MM **Privately Held**
Web: www.lbsfcu.org
SIC: **6062** State credit unions, not federally chartered

(P-7828)
LOS ANGELES POLICE CREDIT UN (PA)
Also Called: L A P F C U
16150 Sherman Way (91406-3907)
P.O. Box 10188 (91410-0188)
PHONE..................818 787-6520
Tyler E Izen, *Ch Bd*
G Michael Padgett, *
Warren D Spayth, *
Angelino Cayanan, *
EMP: 100 EST: 1936
SQ FT: 30,000
SALES (est): 39.68MM
SALES (corp-wide): 39.68MM **Privately Held**
Web: www.lapfcu.org
SIC: **6062** 6061 State credit unions, not federally chartered; Federal credit unions

(P-7829)
NORTH ISLAND FINANCIAL CREDIT UNION
Also Called: North Island Credit Union
5898 Copley Dr Ste 100 (92111-7917)
P.O. Box 85833 (92186-5833)
PHONE..................619 656-6525
EMP: 353
SIC: **6062** State credit unions

(P-7830)
PREMIER AMERICA CREDIT UNION (PA)
Also Called: Premier Amer Wealth MGT Group
19867 Prairie St Lbby (91311-6532)
P.O. Box 2178 (91313-2178)
PHONE..................818 772-4000
John M Merlo, *Pr*
James Anderson, *
Nancy Wheeler-chandler, *Vice Chairman*
Liz Condercuri, *
Marge Mcnaught, *Sr VP*
EMP: 135 EST: 1957
SQ FT: 80,000
SALES (est): 107.51MM
SALES (corp-wide): 107.51MM **Privately Held**
Web: www.premieramerica.com
SIC: **6062** 6163 State credit unions, not federally chartered; Loan brokers

(P-7831)
PROVIDENT CREDIT UNION (PA)
303 Twin Dolphin Dr (94065-1409)
P.O. Box 8007 (94063-0907)
PHONE..................650 508-0300
Maurice Schmid, *Ch*
Ludelle Morrow, *
Connie Finch, *
Fred Gomes, *
Heidi Parks, *
EMP: 130 EST: 1951
SQ FT: 150,000
SALES (est): 114.63MM
SALES (corp-wide): 114.63MM **Privately Held**

Web: www.providentcu.org
SIC: **6062** State credit unions, not federally chartered

(P-7832)
SACRAMENTO CREDIT UNION (PA)
800 H St (95814-2603)
P.O. Box 2351 (95812-2351)
PHONE..................916 444-6070
TOLL FREE: 888
Bhavnesh Makin, *CEO*
James Batson, *
Blake Cairney, *
EMP: 64 EST: 1935
SQ FT: 39,138
SALES (est): 13.96MM
SALES (corp-wide): 13.96MM **Privately Held**
Web: www.sactocu.org
SIC: **6062** 6163 State credit unions, not federally chartered; Loan brokers

(P-7833)
VISTERRA CREDIT UNION
23520 Cactus Ave (92553-8906)
P.O. Box 9500 (92552-9500)
PHONE..................951 656-4411
EMP: 107
Web: www.visterracu.org
SIC: **6062** State credit unions

(P-7834)
WESCOM CENTRAL CREDIT UNION (PA)
123 S Marengo Ave (91101-2428)
P.O. Box 7058 (91109-7058)
PHONE..................888 493-7266
TOLL FREE: 888
Darren Williams, *Prin*
Jane P Wood, *Prin*
Keith Pipes, *Prin*
Jonathon Bauman, *Prin*
Jeanne Brown, *Prin*
EMP: 425 EST: 1934
SQ FT: 90,000
SALES (est): 112.52MM
SALES (corp-wide): 112.52MM **Privately Held**
Web: www.wescom.org
SIC: **6062** State credit unions, not federally chartered

6081 Foreign Bank And Branches And Agencies

(P-7835)
FUJI BANK LTD
601 California St Ste 400 (94108-2809)
PHONE..................415 362-4740
Kenji Matsuo, *Brnch Mgr*
EMP: 88
Web: www.mizuhobank.co.jp
SIC: **6081** Agencies of foreign banks
HQ: Mizuho Bank, Ltd.
    1-5-5, Otemachi
    Chiyoda-Ku TKY

6082 Foreign Trade And International Banks

(P-7836)
PARIBAS ASSET MANAGEMENT INC
1 Front St 23rd Fl (94111-5331)
PHONE..................415 772-1300
Francois Denis, *Prin*

6091 Nondeposit Trust Facilities

(P-7837)
DEUTSCHE BANK NATIONAL TR CO
1761 E Saint Andrew Pl (92705-4934)
PHONE..................................714 247-6054
F Jim Della Sala, *Prin*
David West, *
EMP: 75 **EST:** 2007
SALES (est): 25.92MM
SALES (corp-wide): 2.3B **Privately Held**
SIC: 6091 6021 Nondeposit trust facilities; National commercial banks
HQ: Deutsche Bank Trust Company Americas
60 Wall St
New York NY
212 250-2500

(P-7838)
SUNAMERICA INC (HQ)
Also Called: SunAmerica
1 Sun America Ctr Fl 38 (90067-6121)
PHONE..................................310 772-6000
Eli Broad, *Ch*
Jay S Wintrob, *CEO*
James R Belardi, *Ex VP*
Michael J Akers, *Sr VP*
Mary L Cavanaugh, *Sr VP*
▲ **EMP:** 1000 **EST:** 1957
SQ FT: 95,845
SALES (est): 459.86MM
SALES (corp-wide): 56.44B **Publicly Held**
Web: www.liveatwestfield.com
SIC: 6091 6311 6211 6282 Nondeposit trust facilities; Life insurance carriers; Mutual funds, selling by independent salesperson; Manager of mutual funds, contract or fee basis
PA: American International Group, Inc.
1271 Ave Of The Americas
New York NY
212 770-7000

6099 Functions Related To Depository Banking

(P-7839)
AIRBNB PAYMENTS INC
888 Brannan St (94103-4928)
PHONE..................................415 861-2325
Sam Shrauger, *CEO*
David Bernstein, *CFO*
EMP: 66 **EST:** 2013
SALES (est): 7.12MM **Privately Held**
Web: www.airbnb.com
SIC: 6099 Electronic funds transfer network, including switching

(P-7840)
ASSOCTED FGN EXCH HOLDINGS INC (HQ)
21045 Califa St (91367-5104)
PHONE..................................818 386-2702
Irving Barr, *Ch*
Jan Vliestra, *

Fred Kunik, *
EMP: 89 **EST:** 2006
SALES (est): 112.61MM **Publicly Held**
SIC: 6099 Foreign currency exchange
PA: Fleetcor Technologies, Inc.
3280 Peachtree Rd Ne # 2400
Atlanta GA

(P-7841)
BLACKHAWK NETWORK INC (DH)
6220 Stoneridge Mall Rd (94588-3260)
PHONE..................................925 226-9990
Talbott Roche, *Pr*
EMP: 625 **EST:** 2003
SALES (est): 650.1MM
SALES (corp-wide): 2.23B **Privately Held**
Web: www.blackhawknetwork.com
SIC: 6099 Electronic funds transfer network, including switching
HQ: Blackhawk Network Holdings, Inc.
6220 Stoneridge Mall Rd
Pleasanton CA

(P-7842)
BLACKHAWK NETWORK HOLDINGS INC (HQ)
Also Called: Blackhawk
6220 Stoneridge Mall Rd (94588-3260)
PHONE..................................925 226-9990
Talbott Roche, *Pr*
Chuck Garner, *
Sachin Dhawan, *
Charles O Garner, *
Joan Lockie, *Chief Accounting Officer*
EMP: 500 **EST:** 2001
SQ FT: 149,000
SALES (est): 1.84B
SALES (corp-wide): 2.23B **Privately Held**
Web: www.blackhawknetwork.com
SIC: 6099 Electronic funds transfer network, including switching
PA: Bhn Holdings, Inc.
6220 Stoneridge Mall Rd
Pleasanton CA
925 226-9990

(P-7843)
CONTINENTAL CURRENCY SVCS INC (PA)
Also Called: Cash It Here
1108 E 17th St (92701-2600)
P.O. Box 10970 (92711-0970)
PHONE..................................714 667-6699
Fred Kunik, *Pr*
Irving Barr, *
David Wilder, *
EMP: 80 **EST:** 1977
SQ FT: 12,500
SALES (est): 244.72MM
SALES (corp-wide): 244.72MM **Privately Held**
Web: www.continentalcurrencyservices.com
SIC: 6099 Check cashing agencies

(P-7844)
CONTINENTAL EXCH SOLUTIONS INC
14601 Lakewood Blvd (90723-3602)
PHONE..................................562 790-8532
EMP: 61
Web: us.riafinancial.com
SIC: 6099 Check cashing agencies
HQ: Continental Exchange Solutions Inc.
6565 Knott Ave
Buena Park CA

(P-7845)
CONTINENTAL EXCH SOLUTIONS INC
12891 Harbor Blvd (92840-5808)
PHONE..................................714 530-3582
Victoria Rodriguez, *Genl Mgr*
EMP: 61
Web: us.riafinancial.com
SIC: 6099 Electronic funds transfer network, including switching
HQ: Continental Exchange Solutions Inc.
6565 Knott Ave
Buena Park CA

(P-7846)
CONTINENTAL EXCH SOLUTIONS INC (HQ)
Also Called: Ria Financial Service
6565 Knott Ave (90620-1139)
PHONE..................................714 522-7044
Juan C Bianchi, *CEO*
Timothy A Fanning, *
Shawn D Fielder, *
EMP: 94 **EST:** 1987
SALES (est): 377.87MM **Publicly Held**
Web: us.riafinancial.com
SIC: 6099 Electronic funds transfer network, including switching
PA: Euronet Worldwide, Inc.
11400 Tomahawk Crk Pkwy # 300
Leawood KS

(P-7847)
CONTINENTAL EXCH SOLUTIONS INC
2796 Mission St (94110-3104)
PHONE..................................415 824-4280
EMP: 61
Web: us.riafinancial.com
SIC: 6099 Foreign currency exchange
HQ: Continental Exchange Solutions Inc.
6565 Knott Ave
Buena Park CA

(P-7848)
CONTINENTAL EXCH SOLUTIONS INC
662 Oller St (93640-2317)
PHONE..................................559 655-7583
EMP: 61
Web: us.riafinancial.com
SIC: 6099 Foreign currency exchange
HQ: Continental Exchange Solutions Inc.
6565 Knott Ave
Buena Park CA

(P-7849)
CONTINENTAL EXCH SOLUTIONS INC
1575 E Holt Ave (91767-5823)
PHONE..................................909 622-0500
EMP: 61
Web: us.riafinancial.com
SIC: 6099 Foreign currency exchange
HQ: Continental Exchange Solutions Inc.
6565 Knott Ave
Buena Park CA

(P-7850)
CONTINENTAL EXCH SOLUTIONS INC
860 E Alisal St Ste D (93905-2606)
PHONE..................................562 345-2156
EMP: 61
Web: us.riafinancial.com
SIC: 6099 Foreign currency exchange
HQ: Continental Exchange Solutions Inc.
6565 Knott Ave

Buena Park CA

(P-7851)
CONTINENTAL EXCH SOLUTIONS INC
960 W Arrow Hwy (91722-1252)
PHONE..................................626 969-4130
EMP: 61
Web: us.riafinancial.com
SIC: 6099 Money order issuance
HQ: Continental Exchange Solutions Inc.
6565 Knott Ave
Buena Park CA

(P-7852)
DEBISYS INC (PA)
Also Called: Emida Technologies
27442 Portola Pkwy Ste 150 (92610-2823)
PHONE..................................949 699-1401
Dennis Andrews, *CEO*
Jim Wodach, *
EMP: 80 **EST:** 1977
SQ FT: 10,000
SALES (est): 53.23MM
SALES (corp-wide): 53.23MM **Privately Held**
Web: www.emida.com
SIC: 6099 Automated teller machine (ATM) network

(P-7853)
E Z SERVICES
Also Called: Super Services
1101 W Lincoln Ave Ste 145 (92805-3590)
PHONE..................................714 635-7599
Rosalva Sepulveda, *Brnch Mgr*
EMP: 95
SIC: 6099 Check cashing agencies
PA: E Z Services
1221 E 17th St
Santa Ana CA

(P-7854)
FCTI INC (PA)
11766 Wilshire Blvd Ste 300 (90025-6538)
PHONE..................................310 405-0022
EMP: 86 **EST:** 1993
SALES (est): 36.76MM **Privately Held**
Web: www.fcti.com
SIC: 6099 Automated teller machine (ATM) network

(P-7855)
FINASTRA MERCHANT SERVICES INC (PA)
333 Bush St Fl 26 (94104-2806)
PHONE..................................415 277-9900
Reuven Ben Menachem, *CEO*
Edward Ho, *
Mierzwa Dennis, *
Santo Manna, *
Bryan Schreiber, *
EMP: 60 **EST:** 1999
SQ FT: 14,000
SALES (est): 19.76MM
SALES (corp-wide): 19.76MM **Privately Held**
SIC: 6099 Electronic funds transfer network, including switching

(P-7856)
HAPPY MONEY INC
Also Called: Payoff
21515 Hawthorne Blvd Ste 200 (90503-6512)
PHONE..................................949 430-0630
EMP: 351 **EST:** 2009
SALES (est): 11.97MM **Privately Held**
Web: www.happymoney.com

PRODUCTS & SERVICES SECTION
6141 - Personal Credit Institutions (P-7876)

SIC: 6099 Functions related to deposit banking

(P-7857)
LENLYN LTD WHICH WILL DO BUS I (HQ)
Also Called: Ice Currency Services USA
6151 W Century Blvd Ste 1108 (90045-5310)
P.O. Box 92192 (90009-2192)
PHONE.................310 417-3432
Bharat Shah, CEO
EMP: 75 EST: 1984
SQ FT: 1,000
SALES (est): 25.28MM Privately Held
SIC: 6099 Foreign currency exchange
PA: Lenlyn Holdings Limited
1st Floor
London

(P-7858)
OKCOIN USA INC
Also Called: Okx
115 Sansome St (94104-3626)
PHONE.................415 991-2033
Tim Byun, CEO
EMP: 219 EST: 2017
SALES (est): 28.22MM Privately Held
Web: www.okcoin.com
SIC: 6099 Automated clearinghouses

(P-7859)
POPULUS FINANCIAL GROUP INC
Also Called: Ace Cash Express
6302 Van Buren Blvd (92503-2051)
PHONE.................951 509-3506
Michael Mc Knight, Brnch Mgr
EMP: 105
Web: www.acecashexpress.com
SIC: 6099 Check cashing agencies
HQ: Populus Financial Group, Inc.
300 E John Carpenter Fwy # 900
Irving TX
972 550-5000

(P-7860)
SAN MNUEL BAND MISSION INDIANS
101 Pure Water Ln (92346-6711)
PHONE.................909 425-4682
EMP: 118
Web: www.sanmanuel-nsn.gov
SIC: 6099 Check clearing services
PA: San Manuel Band Of Mission Indians
26569 Community Center Dr
Highland CA
909 864-8933

(P-7861)
SERFIN FUNDS TRANSFER (PA)
1000 S Fremont Ave Bldg A-O (91803-8800)
PHONE.................626 457-3070
EMP: 100 EST: 1994
SALES (est): 9.74MM Privately Held
SIC: 6099 Electronic funds transfer network, including switching

(P-7862)
XOOM CORPORATION
425 Market St Ste 1200 (94105-5404)
PHONE.................415 777-4800
John Kunze, Pr
Ryno Blignaut, Interim Chief Financial Officer*
Julian King, *
Christopher G Ferro, CCO*
EMP: 190 EST: 2001
SQ FT: 35,552
SALES (est): 78.83MM
SALES (corp-wide): 27.52B Publicly Held
Web: www.xoom.com
SIC: 6099 Electronic funds transfer network, including switching
HQ: Paypal, Inc.
2211 N 1st St
San Jose CA
877 981-2163

6111 Federal And Federally Sponsored Credit

(P-7863)
DEUTSCHE BANK NATIONAL TR CO
1999 Avenue Of The Stars Ste 3750 (90067-6022)
PHONE.................310 788-6200
EMP: 100 EST: 1983
SALES (est): 161.96MM
SALES (corp-wide): 23B Privately Held
SIC: 6111 National Consumer Cooperative Bank
HQ: Deutsche Bank Trust Company Americas
60 Wall St
New York NY
212 250-2500

(P-7864)
EDUCATIONAL CREDIT MGT CORP
Also Called: Ecmc-CA
P.O. Box 64909 (55164-0909)
PHONE.................800 367-1590
EMP: 293
SALES (corp-wide): 164.74MM Privately Held
Web: www.ecmcfoundation.org
SIC: 6111 Federal and federally sponsored credit agencies
PA: Educational Credit Management Corporation
111 Washington Ave S # 1400
Minneapolis MN
651 221-0566

(P-7865)
FEDERAL HM LN BNK SAN FRNCISCO (PA)
333 Bush St Fl 27 (94104-2806)
PHONE.................415 616-1000
John F Luikart, Ch Bd
Brian M Riley, V Ch Bd
Greg Seibly, Pr
Kenneth C Miller, Sr VP
David H Martens, CRO
▲ EMP: 227 EST: 1932
SQ FT: 108,147
SALES (est): 2.09B
SALES (corp-wide): 2.09B Privately Held
Web: www.fhlbsf.com
SIC: 6111 Federal and federally sponsored credit agencies

(P-7866)
LAW SCHOOL FINANCIAL INC
Also Called: Law School Loans
175 S Lake Ave Unit 200 (91101-2629)
PHONE.................626 243-1800
EMP: 190
SQ FT: 25,000
SALES (est): 15.5MM Privately Held
Web: www.lawschoolloans.com
SIC: 6111 Student Loan Marketing Association

(P-7867)
TUITIONIO INC
10960 Wilshire Blvd Ste 1420 (90024-3702)
P.O. Box 810 (94401-0810)
PHONE.................855 353-9395
Scott Thompson, CEO
EMP: 65 EST: 2012
SALES (est): 5.1MM Privately Held
Web: www.tuition.io
SIC: 6111 Student Loan Marketing Association

(P-7868)
YOSEMITE FARM CREDIT ACA (PA)
806 W Monte Vista Ave (95382-7242)
P.O. Box 3278 (95381-3278)
PHONE.................209 667-2366
Leonard Van Eldern, Pr
Tracy Sparks, *
EMP: 60 EST: 1917
SQ FT: 9,000
SALES (est): 24.36MM
SALES (corp-wide): 24.36MM Privately Held
Web: www.yosemitefarmcredit.com
SIC: 6111 Federal Land Banks

6141 Personal Credit Institutions

(P-7869)
AMERICAN HONDA FINANCE CORP (DH)
Also Called: AMERICAN HONDA
1919 Torrance Blvd (90501-2722)
P.O. Box 2200 (90509-2200)
PHONE.................310 972-2239
Hideo Tamaka, CEO
John Weisickle, *
Stephan Smith, *
EMP: 200 EST: 1980
SALES (est): 2.5B Privately Held
Web: www.honda.com
SIC: 6141 Financing: automobiles, furniture, etc., not a deposit bank
HQ: American Honda Motor Co., Inc.
1919 Torrance Blvd
Torrance CA
310 783-2000

(P-7870)
ASSOCIATES FIRST CAPITAL CORP
Also Called: Avco Financial
3634 5th Ave (91214-2444)
PHONE.................818 248-7055
EMP: 76
SALES (corp-wide): 101.08B Publicly Held
SIC: 6141 Consumer finance companies
HQ: Associates First Capital Corporation
4000 Regent Blvd
Irving TX
800 922-6235

(P-7871)
CASHCALL INC
Also Called: Chapter Seven Lending
1 City Blvd W Ste 102 (92868-3621)
P.O. Box 66007 (92816-6007)
PHONE.................949 752-4600
John Paul Reddam, CEO
Ethan Taub, CMO*
EMP: 1400 EST: 2000
SALES (est): 323.43MM Privately Held
Web: www.cashcall.com

SIC: 6141 Personal finance licensed loan companies, small

(P-7872)
CIG FINANCIAL LLC
Also Called: Autonation Finance
6 Executive Cir Ste 100 (92614-6732)
P.O. Box 19795 (92623-9795)
PHONE.................877 244-4442
Greg Skjonsby, Pr
EMP: 102 EST: 2011
SALES (est): 60.2MM
SALES (corp-wide): 26.98B Publicly Held
Web: www.cigfinancial.com
SIC: 6141 7389 Consumer finance companies; Financial services
PA: Autonation, Inc.
200 Sw 1st Ave Ste 1700
Fort Lauderdale FL
954 769-6000

(P-7873)
CITIFINANCIAL CREDIT COMPANY
Also Called: Citifinancial
1054 Harter Pkwy Ste 4 (95993-2653)
PHONE.................530 671-7970
EMP: 96
SALES (corp-wide): 101.08B Publicly Held
SIC: 6141 Consumer finance companies
HQ: Citifinancial Credit Company
300 Saint Paul Pl Fl 3
Baltimore MD
410 332-3000

(P-7874)
CITIFINANCIAL CREDIT COMPANY
Also Called: Citifinancial
2655 Del Vista Dr (91745-5244)
PHONE.................626 712-8780
EMP: 95
SALES (corp-wide): 101.08B Publicly Held
SIC: 6141 Consumer finance companies
HQ: Citifinancial Credit Company
300 Saint Paul Pl Fl 3
Baltimore MD
410 332-3000

(P-7875)
HYUNDAI PROTECTION PLAN INC
3161 Michelson Dr Ste 1900 (92612-4400)
PHONE.................949 468-4000
Jwa Jin Cho, Prin
EMP: 297 EST: 2015
SALES (est): 4.51MM Privately Held
SIC: 6141 Automobile loans, including insurance
HQ: Hyundai Capital America
3161 Michelson Dr # 1900
Irvine CA

(P-7876)
LENDINGCLUB CORPORATION (PA)
Also Called: Lendingclub
595 Market St Fl 4 (94105-2802)
PHONE.................415 632-5600
Scott Sanborn, CEO
John C Morris, Non-Executive Chairman of the Board
Thomas Casey, CFO
Annie Armstrong, CRO
Brandon Pace, Corporate Secretary
EMP: 411 EST: 2006
SALES (est): 1.27B Publicly Held

6141 - Personal Credit Institutions (P-7877)

Web: www.lendingclub.com
SIC: **6141** 7389 6153 Personal credit institutions; Financial services; Working capital financing

(P-7877)
LOAN FACTORY INC
Also Called: Loan Factory
2195 Tully Rd (95122-1346)
PHONE.................................408 646-6662
Thuan Nguyen, *Admn*
EMP: 61 **EST:** 2017
SALES (est): 4.96MM **Privately Held**
Web: www.loanfactory.com
SIC: **6141** Personal credit institutions

(P-7878)
MITSUBISHI MOTORS CR AMER INC (DH)
Also Called: Mmca
6400 Katella Ave (90630-5208)
P.O. Box 689040 (37068-9040)
PHONE.................................714 799-4730
Dan Booth, *Pr*
Charles Tredway, *
Ellen Gleberman, *
Hideyuki Kitamura, *
EMP: 394 **EST:** 1990
SQ FT: 32,256
SALES (est): 151.85MM **Privately Held**
Web: www.mitsubishicars.com
SIC: **6141** 6159 Automobile loans, including insurance; Truck finance leasing
HQ: Mitsubishi Motors North America, Inc.
4031 Aspen Grove Dr
Franklin TN
714 799-4730

(P-7879)
MONTEREY FINANCIAL SVCS INC (PA)
Also Called: Monterey Collection Services
4095 Avenida De La Plata (92056-5802)
P.O. Box 5199 (92052-5199)
PHONE.................................760 639-3500
Robert Steinke, *Pr*
Mike Gray, *
Kathi Steinke, *
EMP: 110 **EST:** 1989
SQ FT: 27,000
SALES (est): 21.84MM **Privately Held**
Web: www.montereyfinancial.com
SIC: **6141** 8721 7322 8742 Consumer finance companies; Billing and bookkeeping service; Collection agency, except real estate; Financial consultant

(P-7880)
NATIONAL PLANNING CORPORATION
100 N Pacific Coast Hwy Ste 1800 (90245-5612)
PHONE.................................800 881-7174
John C Johnson, *Pr*
Sarah Corce, *
Jim Dafalco, *
Patricia Mccallop, *CCO*
EMP: 150 **EST:** 1998
SALES (est): 21.42MM **Privately Held**
Web: www.nationalplanningholdings.com
SIC: **6141** Automobile and consumer finance companies

(P-7881)
NEW AMERICAN FUNDING LLC (PA)
Also Called: Naf
14511 Myford Rd Ste 100 (92780-7057)
PHONE.................................949 430-7029
Rick Arvielo, *CEO*
Patricia Arvielo, *
Christy Bunce, *
Scott Frommert, *
EMP: 650 **EST:** 2002
SALES (est): 408.95MM **Privately Held**
Web: www.newamericanfunding.com
SIC: **6141** 7371 Licensed loan companies, small; Computer software development and applications

(P-7882)
NORTH AMERICAN ACCEPTANCE CORP
Also Called: An Open Check
3191 Red Hill Ave Ste 100 (92626-3451)
PHONE.................................714 868-3195
Marco J Rasic, *CEO*
Mary Clancey Rasic, *
EMP: 123 **EST:** 2002
SQ FT: 24,000
SALES (est): 11.18MM **Privately Held**
SIC: **6141** 6719 Automobile and consumer finance companies; Personal holding companies, except banks

(P-7883)
OPORTUN FINANCIAL CORPORATION (PA)
Also Called: Oportun
2 Circle Star Way (94070-6200)
PHONE.................................650 810-8823
Raul Vazquez, *CEO*
Jonathan Coblentz, *CAO*
Matthew Jenkins, *General LOANS & AUTO LOANS*
David Needham, *CPO*
Patrick Kirscht, *CCO*
EMP: 577 **EST:** 2005
SALES (est): 640.66MM **Publicly Held**
SIC: **6141** Personal credit institutions

(P-7884)
PAYOFF INC
Also Called: Happy Money
3200 Park Center Dr Ste 800 (92626-7163)
PHONE.................................949 430-0630
Scott Saunders, *CEO*
Christopher Hilliard, *CCO**
Adam Zarlengo, *CPO**
EMP: 89 **EST:** 2012
SQ FT: 19,500
SALES (est): 24.89MM **Privately Held**
Web: www.happymoney.com
SIC: **6141** Personal credit institutions

(P-7885)
PROFESSIONAL CR REPORTING INC
3560 Hyland Ave (92626-1438)
PHONE.................................714 556-1570
Tim Nguyen, *Admn*
EMP: 253 **EST:** 2016
SALES (est): 1.88MM
SALES (corp-wide): 288.05MM **Publicly Held**
Web: www.profcredit.com
SIC: **6141** Personal credit institutions
PA: Meridianlink, Inc.
3560 Hyland Ave Ste 200
Costa Mesa CA
714 708-6950

(P-7886)
SAVVYMONEY INC
4160 Dublin Blvd Ste 250 (94568-7751)
PHONE.................................415 684-7261
Todd Marksberry, *Prin*
Taras Shram, *Dir*
EMP: 70 **EST:** 2008
SALES (est): 10.06MM **Privately Held**
Web: www.savvymoney.com
SIC: **6141** Personal credit institutions

(P-7887)
UPSTART NETWORK INC
Also Called: Upstart
2950 S Delaware St Ste 300 (94403)
P.O. Box 1503 (94070-7503)
PHONE.................................650 204-1000
Dave Girouard, *CEO*
Paul Gu, *
Anna Mongayt, *
EMP: 135 **EST:** 2012
SALES (est): 24.88MM **Privately Held**
Web: www.upstart.com
SIC: **6141** Personal finance licensed loan companies, small

6153 Short-term Business Credit

(P-7888)
AFFIRM INC (HQ)
Also Called: Affirm Identity
650 California St Fl 12 (94108-2716)
PHONE.................................415 984-0490
Max Levchin, *CEO*
Huey Lin, *
Rob Pfeifer, *
Carl Gish, *CMO**
EMP: 193 **EST:** 2003
SALES (est): 110.24MM
SALES (corp-wide): 1.59B **Publicly Held**
Web: www.affirm.com
SIC: **6153** Working capital financing
PA: Affirm Holdings, Inc.
650 California St Fl 12
San Francisco CA
415 984-0490

(P-7889)
AFFIRM HOLDINGS INC (PA)
Also Called: Affirm
650 California St Fl 12 (94108-2716)
PHONE.................................415 984-0490
Max Levchin, *Ch Bd*
Libor Michalek, *Pr*
Michael Linford, *CFO*
Katherine Adkins, *CLO*
Silvija Martincevic, *CCO*
EMP: 2319 **EST:** 2012
SALES (est): 1.59B
SALES (corp-wide): 1.59B **Publicly Held**
SIC: **6153** Working capital financing

(P-7890)
AMWEST FUNDING CORP
6 Pointe Dr Ste 300 (92821-6323)
PHONE.................................714 831-3333
Ryan Kim, *Pr*
EMP: 112 **EST:** 2017
SALES (est): 17.23MM **Privately Held**
Web: www.amwestfunding.com
SIC: **6153** Working capital financing

(P-7891)
BALBOA CAPITAL CORPORATION (DH)
575 Anton Blvd Ste 1200 (92626-7685)
PHONE.................................949 756-0800
H Palmer Proctor Junior, *CEO*
EMP: 200 **EST:** 1988
SQ FT: 24,000
SALES (est): 144.3MM
SALES (corp-wide): 1.18B **Publicly Held**
Web: www.balboacapital.com
SIC: **6153** Working capital financing
HQ: Ameris Bank
305 S Main St
Moultrie GA
800 845-5219

(P-7892)
BANKAMERICA FINANCIAL INC
Also Called: Bank of America
315 Montgomery St (94104-1856)
PHONE.................................415 622-3521
James A Dern, *Pr*
John Carson, *Sr VP*
Dana Flynn, *VP*
Paul Ogorzelec, *Sr VP*
Claudia Chan-schaffer, *VP*
EMP: 91 **EST:** 1990
SALES (est): 9.31MM
SALES (corp-wide): 94.95B **Publicly Held**
SIC: **6153** 6141 6282 Factors of commercial paper; Consumer finance companies; Investment advisory service
PA: Bank Of America Corporation
100 N Tryon St Ste 2650
Charlotte NC
704 386-5681

(P-7893)
ENCORE CAPITAL GROUP INC (PA)
Also Called: Encore
350 Camino De La Reina Ste 100 (92108)
PHONE.................................877 445-4581
Ashish Masih, *Pr*
Michael P Monaco, *Non-Executive Chairman of the Board*
Jonathan C Clark, *Ex VP*
Gregory L Call, *Corporate Secretary*
Monique Dumais, *CIO*
EMP: 528 **EST:** 1990
SQ FT: 118,000
SALES (est): 1.4B
SALES (corp-wide): 1.4B **Publicly Held**
Web: www.encorecapital.com
SIC: **6153** Purchasers of accounts receivable and commercial paper

(P-7894)
HANA COMMERCIAL FINANCE LLC
1000 Wilshire Blvd Ste 570 (90017-2462)
PHONE.................................213 240-1234
Sunnie Kim, *Managing Member*
EMP: 85 **EST:** 2016
SALES (est): 6.9MM **Privately Held**
Web: www.hanafinancial.com
SIC: **6153** Factoring services

(P-7895)
INPUT 1 LLC
6200 Canoga Ave Ste 400 (91367-2459)
PHONE.................................818 340-0030
Todd Greenbaum, *Managing Member*
Jeffrey S Greenbaum, *
EMP: 110 **EST:** 1984
SQ FT: 24,000
SALES (est): 18.93MM **Privately Held**
Web: www.input1.com
SIC: **6153** 7371 Short-term business credit institutions, except agricultural; Computer software development and applications

(P-7896)
MIDLAND CREDIT MANAGEMENT INC
Also Called: Midland Credit Management
350 Camino De La Reina Ste 100 (92108)
P.O. Box 939069 (92193-9069)
PHONE.................................877 240-2377

PRODUCTS & SERVICES SECTION
6159 - Miscellaneous Business Credit (P-7918)

Kenneth A Vecchione, *CEO*
Carl Gregory, *
Robin Pruitt, *
Monique Dumais, *CIO**
EMP: 1800 **EST:** 1953
SALES (est): 454.67MM
SALES (corp-wide): 1.4B **Publicly Held**
Web: www.midlandcredit.com
SIC: 6153 Short-term business credit institutions, except agricultural
PA: Encore Capital Group, Inc.
350 Cmino De La Rina Ste Reina
San Diego CA
877 445-4581

(P-7897)
MORGAN STNLEY SMITH BARNEY LLC
9665 Wilshire Blvd Ste 600 (90212-2340)
PHONE 310 285-4800
Joel Davidman, *Prin*
EMP: 73
SALES (corp-wide): 53.67B **Publicly Held**
Web: www.morganstanley.com
SIC: 6153 Working capital financing
HQ: Morgan Stanley Smith Barney, Llc
1585 Broadway
New York NY

(P-7898)
NATIONAL FUNDING INC (PA)
Also Called: Moneyjet
9530 Towne Centre Dr Ste 120 (92121-1972)
PHONE 888 733-2383
EMP: 120 **EST:** 1999
SALES (est): 14.65MM
SALES (corp-wide): 14.65MM **Privately Held**
Web: www.nationalfunding.com
SIC: 6153 6159 7389 Working capital financing; Machinery and equipment finance leasing; Financial services

(P-7899)
NEW AMERICA FUNDING LLC
Also Called: New American Funding
19300 Rinaldi St Ste M (91326-3785)
PHONE 818 235-0640
Harry Zakarian, *Brnch Mgr*
EMP: 70
Web: www.newamericanfunding.com
SIC: 6153 Working capital financing
PA: New American Funding, Llc
14511 Myford Rd Ste 100
Tustin CA

(P-7900)
NEW AMERICA FUNDING LLC
Also Called: New American Funding
55 S Market St Ste 1600 (95113-2327)
PHONE 408 429-2085
Chris Macnaughton, *Mgr*
EMP: 71
Web: www.newamericanfunding.com
SIC: 6153 Working capital financing
PA: New American Funding, Llc
14511 Myford Rd Ste 100
Tustin CA

(P-7901)
PACIFIC LIFE GLOBAL FUNDING
700 Newport Center Dr (92660-6307)
PHONE 949 219-3011
William Gross, *Prin*
EMP: 72 **EST:** 2007
SALES (est): 1.53MM
SALES (corp-wide): 12.84B **Privately Held**
SIC: 6153 Short-term business credit institutions, except agricultural
HQ: Pacific Life Insurance Company
700 Newport Center Dr
Newport Beach CA
949 219-3011

(P-7902)
PAR CONSULTING LLC
Also Called: US Business Funding
4500 Campus Dr Ste 380 (92660-1815)
PHONE 949 461-1140
EMP: 70 **EST:** 2008
SQ FT: 100
SALES (est): 1.06MM **Privately Held**
SIC: 6153 Working capital financing

(P-7903)
PURPOSE FUNDING INC
27651 La Paz Rd # 200 (92677-3917)
PHONE 949 456-7899
Walter A Styck, *CEO*
EMP: 65 **EST:** 2005
SALES (est): 9.41MM **Privately Held**
Web: www.purposefunding.com
SIC: 6153 Working capital financing

(P-7904)
RELIANT SERVICES GROUP LLC
Also Called: Reliant Funding Group
9540 Towne Centre Dr Ste 100 (92121)
PHONE 877 850-0998
Steve Kietz, *CEO*
Adam Stettner, *
Paul Norman, *
EMP: 180 **EST:** 2000
SALES (est): 46.65MM **Privately Held**
Web: www.reliantfunding.com
SIC: 6153 Working capital financing

(P-7905)
RETIREMENT FNDING SOLUTIONS INC
3131 Camino Del Rio N Ste 190 (92108)
PHONE 802 238-4216
EMP: 62 **EST:** 2017
SALES (est): 1.33MM **Privately Held**
Web: www.rfslends.com
SIC: 6153 Working capital financing

(P-7906)
RIVIERA FINANCE OF TEXAS INC
10430 Pioneer Blvd Ste 1 (90670-8245)
PHONE 562 777-1300
Sandy Newman, *Brnch Mgr*
EMP: 88
Web: www.rivierafinance.com
SIC: 6153 Factors of commercial paper
PA: Riviera Finance Of Texas, Inc
220 Avenue I
Redondo Beach CA

(P-7907)
SEQUOIA RESIDENTIAL FUNDING
1 Belvedere Pl Ste 330 (94941-2493)
PHONE 415 389-7373
George Bull, *CEO*
EMP: 90 **EST:** 2004
SALES (est): 45.55MM **Publicly Held**
SIC: 6153 7389 Working capital financing; Financial services
PA: Redwood Trust, Inc.
1 Belvedere Pl Ste 300
Mill Valley CA

(P-7908)
SKYVIEW CAPITAL LLC
2000 Avenue Of The Stars Ste 810 (90067-4702)
PHONE 310 273-6000
Alex Soltani, *CEO*
EMP: 99 **EST:** 2002
SALES (est): 16.32MM **Privately Held**
Web: www.skyviewcapital.com
SIC: 6153 Direct working capital financing

(P-7909)
STANISLAUS CNTY TOBACCO FUNDNG
1010 10th St Ste 6400 (95354-0882)
PHONE 209 525-6376
Gordon B Ford, *Prin*
EMP: 213 **EST:** 2007
SALES (est): 2.42MM **Privately Held**
SIC: 6153 Working capital financing
PA: County Of Stanislaus
1010 10th St Ste 5100
Modesto CA
209 525-6398

(P-7910)
STARTENGINE CROWDFUNDING INC
750 N San Vicente Blvd Ste 800w (90069-5788)
PHONE 800 317-2200
Howard Marks, *CEO*
Ron Miller, *Ofcr*
Josh Amster, *VP*
EMP: 78 **EST:** 2014
SALES (est): 24.36MM **Privately Held**
Web: www.startengine.com
SIC: 6153 Working capital financing

(P-7911)
TOPMARK FUNDING LLC
516 Gibson Dr Ste 160 (95678-5792)
PHONE 866 627-6644
James Daniel Summers, *Managing Member*
Evan Lang, *Managing Member*
EMP: 79 **EST:** 2015
SALES (est): 19.17MM **Privately Held**
Web: www.topmarkfunding.com
SIC: 6153 6159 Working capital financing; Truck finance leasing

(P-7912)
WELLS FARGO COML DIST FIN LLC
3100 Zinfandel Dr Ste 255 (95670-6391)
PHONE 916 636-2020
EMP: 114
SALES (corp-wide): 82.86B **Publicly Held**
SIC: 6153 Mercantile financing
HQ: Wells Fargo Commercial Distribution Finance, Llc
10 S Wacker Dr
Chicago IL
847 747-6800

6159 Miscellaneous Business Credit

(P-7913)
AMERICAN AGCREDIT FLCA (PA)
400 Aviation Blvd Ste 100 (95403-1181)
P.O. Box 1120 (95402-1120)
PHONE 707 545-1200
Ron Carli, *CEO*
Byron Enix, *
Floyd Ridenhour, *
Christopher Call, *
EMP: 91 **EST:** 1925
SQ FT: 26,000
SALES (est): 157.85MM
SALES (corp-wide): 157.85MM **Privately Held**
Web: www.agloan.com
SIC: 6159 Agricultural credit institutions

(P-7914)
AMERICAN CAPITAL GROUP INC
Also Called: A C G
23382 Mill Creek Dr # 115 (92653-1682)
PHONE 949 271-5800
Carl Heaton, *Pr*
Carl J Heaton, *
EMP: 64 **EST:** 1995
SALES (est): 20.9MM
SALES (corp-wide): 20.9MM **Privately Held**
Web: www.acgcapital.com
SIC: 6159 Equipment and vehicle finance leasing companies
PA: Nationwide Capital Holdings, Inc.
31726 Rncho Viejo Ste 111
San Juan Capistrano CA
949 271-5816

(P-7915)
ATEL 14 LLC
600 California St Fl 6 (94108-2733)
PHONE 415 989-8800
EMP: 63 **EST:** 2009
SALES (est): 2.54MM **Privately Held**
Web: www.atel.com
SIC: 6159 Machinery and equipment finance leasing
PA: Atel Associates 14, Llc
600 California St Fl 9
San Francisco CA

(P-7916)
ATEL CAPITAL GROUP (PA)
Also Called: Leasing Equipment
505 Montgomery St Fl 11 (94111-2585)
PHONE 800 543-2835
Dean L Cash, *Ch*
Paritosh K Choksi, *
Vasco H Morais, *Secretary General**
Russell H Wilder, *
Russ Wilder, *CCO**
EMP: 80 **EST:** 1977
SALES (est): 77.28MM **Privately Held**
Web: www.atel.com
SIC: 6159 Machinery and equipment finance leasing

(P-7917)
CAPITALSOURCE INC
633 W 5th St 33rd Fl (90071-2005)
PHONE 213 443-7700
EMP: 515
SIC: 6159 General and industrial loan institutions

(P-7918)
CAPNET FINANCIAL SERVICES INC (PA)
Also Called: Capital Network Funding Svcs
11901 Santa Monica Blvd (90025-2767)
PHONE 877 980-0558
John Armstrnog, *CEO*
Blake Johnson, *
Michael Kromnick, *
Armita Dalal, *Head**
EMP: 90 **EST:** 2001
SQ FT: 23,000
SALES (est): 12.09MM
SALES (corp-wide): 12.09MM **Privately Held**

6159 - Miscellaneous Business Credit (P-7919)

(P-7919)
ELECTRONIC COMMERCE LLC
Also Called: Electronic Commerce
4100 Newport Place Dr Ste 500 (92660)
PHONE..............................800 770-5520
Darnell Ponder, *Mng Pt*
Khaazra Maaranu, *
EMP: 85 **EST:** 2013
SALES (est): 8.6MM **Privately Held**
SIC: 6159 Intermediate investment banks

(P-7920)
INVESTBANK CORP
4231 Balboa Ave # 1077 (92117-5504)
PHONE..............................858 225-7825
EMP: 64
SALES (corp-wide): 3.83MM **Privately Held**
Web: www.investbankcorp.com
SIC: 6159 Intermediate investment banks
PA: Investbank Corp.
  848 N Rainbow Blvd 1584
  Las Vegas NV
  800 445-1550

(P-7921)
MOTOLEASE FUNDING LLC
10866 Wilshire Blvd (90024-4350)
PHONE..............................310 601-4779
Maurice M Salter, *Ch Bd*
Emre Ucer, *
EMP: 70 **EST:** 2018
SALES (est): 4.35MM **Privately Held**
Web: motolease-llc.business.site
SIC: 6159 Automobile finance leasing

(P-7922)
NATIONS FIRST CAPITAL LLC
Also Called: Go Capital
516 Gibson Dr Ste 160 (95678-5792)
PHONE..............................855 396-3600
Evan Lang, *Managing Member*
Evan Lang, *Managing Member*
Dan Summers, *
EMP: 70 **EST:** 2013
SALES (est): 8.43MM **Privately Held**
Web: www.gocapitalusa.com
SIC: 6159 Equipment and vehicle finance leasing companies

(P-7923)
SECURE CHOICE LENDING
1650 Spruce St Ste 100 (92507-7403)
PHONE..............................951 733-8925
Mark Hossler, *Pr*
EMP: 75 **EST:** 2017
SALES (est): 3.9MM **Privately Held**
Web: www.securechoicelending.com
SIC: 6159 General and industrial loan institutions

(P-7924)
TRINITY CAPITAL CORPORATION
475 Sansome St Fl 19 (94111-3112)
PHONE..............................415 956-5174
EMP: 85
SIC: 6159 8741 Machinery and equipment finance leasing; Management services

(P-7925)
WELLS FARGO CAPITAL FIN LLC (DH)
2450 Colorado Ave Ste 3000w (90404)
PHONE..............................310 453-7300
Sean Spring, *

EMP: 99 **EST:** 2002
SALES (est): 129.33MM
SALES (corp-wide): 82.86B **Publicly Held**
Web: www.wellsfargocapitalfinance.com
SIC: 6159 General and industrial loan institutions
HQ: Wells Fargo Bank, National Association
  420 Montgomery St San
  San Francisco CA
  605 575-6900

(P-7926)
WESTLAKE SERVICES LLC (HQ)
Also Called: Westlake Financial Services
4751 Wilshire Blvd Ste 100 (90010-3847)
P.O. Box 76809 (90076-0809)
PHONE..............................323 692-8800
Don Hankey, *Ch Bd*
James Vagim, *Pr*
Kent Hagan, *VP*
Ian Anderson, *Pr*
Paul Kerwin, *CFO*
EMP: 123 **EST:** 1988
SQ FT: 22,000
SALES (est): 286.86MM
SALES (corp-wide): 352.68MM **Privately Held**
Web: www.westlakefinancial.com
SIC: 6159 6141 Automobile finance leasing; Personal credit institutions
PA: Hankey Investment Company, Lp
  4751 Wilshire Blvd # 110
  Los Angeles CA
  323 692-4008

6162 Mortgage Bankers And Correspondents

(P-7927)
AMERICAN FINANCIAL NETWORK INC (PA)
Also Called: Gateway Home Realty
10 Pointe Dr Ste 330 (92821-7620)
PHONE..............................714 831-4000
John B Sherman, *Pr*
John R Sherman, *
▲ **EMP:** 200 **EST:** 2001
SQ FT: 8,000
SALES (est): 201.91MM
SALES (corp-wide): 201.91MM **Privately Held**
Web: www.afncorp.com
SIC: 6162 Mortgage bankers

(P-7928)
AMERICAN INTERNET MORTGAGE INC
Also Called: Aimloan.com, A Direct Lender
4121 Camino Del Rio S Ste 200 (92108-4103)
PHONE..............................888 411-4246
Vincent J Kasperick, *Pr*
EMP: 106 **EST:** 1998
SQ FT: 4,500
SALES (est): 22.56MM **Privately Held**
Web: www.aimloan.com
SIC: 6162 Mortgage bankers

(P-7929)
AMERICAN PACIFIC MORTGAGE CORP (PA)
Also Called: Big Valley Mortgage
3000 Lava Ridge Ct Ste 200 (95661-2800)
PHONE..............................916 960-1325
EMP: 120 **EST:** 1996
SQ FT: 35,000
SALES (est): 335.1K **Privately Held**
Web: www.apmortgage.com

SIC: 6162 Mortgage bankers

(P-7930)
AMERIHOME INC
1 Baxter Way Ste 300 (91362-3888)
PHONE..............................888 469-0810
James S Furash, *Ch*
John Hedlund, *
Garrett Galati, *
Josh Adler, *
Mark Miller, *CRO*
EMP: 738 **EST:** 2020
SALES (est): 215.13MM
SALES (corp-wide): 215.13MM **Privately Held**
Web: www.amerihome.com
SIC: 6162 Mortgage bankers and loan correspondents
PA: A-A Mortgage Opportunities, L.P.
  1 Baxter Way
  Thousand Oaks CA
  888 469-0810

(P-7931)
AMNET ESOP CORPORATION
Also Called: American Mortgage Network
347 Third Ave Fl 2 (91910-3929)
PHONE..............................877 354-1110
Joseph Sal Restivo, *CEO*
Shawn Stougard, *
EMP: 144 **EST:** 2019
SALES (est): 12MM **Privately Held**
Web: www.amnetmtg.com
SIC: 6162 Mortgage bankers

(P-7932)
AMNET MORTGAGE LLC
10421 Wateridge Cir Ste 250 (92121)
PHONE..............................858 909-1200
John M Robbins, *CEO*
Jay M Fuller, *Parts Vice President*
Lisa Falk, *
EMP: 759 **EST:** 1997
SQ FT: 40,400
SALES (est): 187.13MM
SALES (corp-wide): 82.86B **Publicly Held**
SIC: 6162 Mortgage bankers and loan correspondents
HQ: Wells Fargo Bank, National Association
  420 Montgomery St San
  San Francisco CA
  605 575-6900

(P-7933)
ANCHOR LOANS LP
Also Called: Anchor Nationwide Loans
1 Baxter Way # 220 (91362-3817)
PHONE..............................310 395-0010
Stephen Pollack, *CEO*
Bryan Thompson, *CFO*
EMP: 200 **EST:** 2015
SALES (est): 41.48MM **Privately Held**
Web: www.anchorloans.com
SIC: 6162 Mortgage bankers and loan correspondents

(P-7934)
ARCS COMMERCIAL MORTGAGE CO LP (DH)
Also Called: Arcs Commercial Mortgage
26901 Agoura Rd Ste 200 (91301-5109)
PHONE..............................818 676-3274
Timothy White, *CEO*
▲ **EMP:** 110 **EST:** 1995
SQ FT: 15,000
SALES (est): 21.62MM
SALES (corp-wide): 23.54B **Publicly Held**
SIC: 6162 Mortgage bankers
HQ: Pnc Bank, National Association
  300 5th Ave
  Pittsburgh PA
  877 762-2000

(P-7935)
ATHAS CAPITAL GROUP INC
27001 Agoura Rd Ste 200 (91301-5357)
PHONE..............................877 877-1477
Brian O'shaughnessy, *CEO*
EMP: 126 **EST:** 2007
SALES (est): 15.35MM **Privately Held**
Web: www.athascapital.com
SIC: 6162 Mortgage bankers and loan correspondents

(P-7936)
BERKSHIRE HTHWAY HM SVCS CAL P
2365 Northside Dr Ste 200 (92108-2720)
PHONE..............................619 302-8082
EMP: 110
SALES (corp-wide): 302.09B **Publicly Held**
Web: www.bhhscalifornia.com
SIC: 6162 Mortgage bankers and loan correspondents
HQ: Berkshire Hathaway Home Services California Properties
  12770 El Cmino Real Ste 1
  San Diego CA
  858 792-6085

(P-7937)
BLEND INSURANCE AGENCY INC
Also Called: Blend
415 Kearny St (94108-2803)
PHONE..............................650 550-4810
Crystal Sumner, *Pr*
EMP: 189 **EST:** 2018
SALES (est): 14.13MM **Privately Held**
Web: insurance.blend.com
SIC: 6162 Loan correspondents

(P-7938)
BLUFI LENDING CORPORATION
9909 Mira Mesa Blvd # 160 (92131-3002)
EMP: 120
SIC: 6162 Loan correspondents

(P-7939)
CAKE MORTGAGE CORP
Also Called: Millennial Home Lending
9200 Oakdale Ave Ste 501 (91311-6562)
PHONE..............................818 812-5150
David Arshak Abelyan, *CEO*
EMP: 70 **EST:** 2018
SALES (est): 11.24MM **Privately Held**
Web: www.cakehome.com
SIC: 6162 Mortgage bankers and loan correspondents

(P-7940)
CAL COAST FINANCIAL INC
39355 California St Ste 101 (94538-1447)
PHONE..............................510 683-9850
Roger Bakshi, *CEO*
EMP: 70 **EST:** 1990
SALES (est): 5MM **Privately Held**
Web: www.calcoastmtg.com
SIC: 6162 Mortgage bankers and loan correspondents

(P-7941)
CAL MUTUAL INC
34077 Temecula Creek Rd (92592-5646)
PHONE..............................888 700-4650
Dennis Shane Dailey, *Pr*
EMP: 87 **EST:** 2013
SALES (est): 5.54MM **Privately Held**

PRODUCTS & SERVICES SECTION

6162 - Mortgage Bankers And Correspondents (P-7964)

Web: www.calmutualmortgage.com
SIC: **6162** 6531 Mortgage bankers and loan correspondents; Real estate agent, residential

(P-7942)
CALIBER HOME LOANS INC
3700 Hilborn Rd Ste 700 (94534-7997)
PHONE...................707 432-1000
Sanjiv Das, *Prin*
EMP: 84
SALES (corp-wide): 4.73B **Publicly Held**
Web: www.caliberhomeloans.com
SIC: **6162** Mortgage bankers and loan correspondents
HQ: Caliber Home Loans, Inc.
    1525 S Belt Line Rd
    Coppell TX

(P-7943)
CARRINGTON MRTG HOLDINGS LLC
1600 S Douglass Rd Ste 110 (92806-5948)
PHONE...................888 267-0584
EMP: 123 EST: 2001
SQ FT: 192,000
SALES (est): 59.5MM
SALES (corp-wide): 107.6MM **Privately Held**
SIC: **6162** Mortgage bankers and loan correspondents
PA: Carrington Capital Management Llc
    1700 E Putnam Ave Ste 501
    Old Greenwich CT
    203 661-6186

(P-7944)
CHANGE LENDING LLC
523 Capitola Ave (95010-2824)
PHONE...................831 460-0202
Peter Gaeckle, *Brnch Mgr*
EMP: 92
Web: www.changemtg.com
SIC: **6162** Mortgage bankers and loan correspondents
PA: Change Lending, Llc
    175 N Riverview Dr
    Anaheim CA

(P-7945)
CHANGE LENDING LLC
32 Discovery Ste 160 (92618-3156)
PHONE...................949 769-3526
EMP: 92
Web: www.changemtg.com
SIC: **6162** Mortgage bankers and loan correspondents
PA: Change Lending, Llc
    175 N Riverview Dr
    Anaheim CA

(P-7946)
CHANGE LENDING LLC
970 Executive Way (96002-0630)
PHONE...................530 282-1166
Gretchen Wilson, *Brnch Mgr*
EMP: 91
Web: www.changemtg.com
SIC: **6162** Mortgage bankers and loan correspondents
PA: Change Lending, Llc
    175 N Riverview Dr
    Anaheim CA

(P-7947)
CHANGE LENDING LLC (PA)
Also Called: Change Home Loans
175 N Riverview Dr (92808-1225)
PHONE...................949 423-6814
Mario De Tomasi, *CEO*

Scott Simonich, *
Theodore Ray, *
Kari Hallowell, *
Alan Lindeke, *
EMP: 60 EST: 1994
SALES (est): 101.38MM **Privately Held**
Web: www.changemtg.com
SIC: **6162** Mortgage bankers and loan correspondents

(P-7948)
CHASE MANHATTAN MORTGAGE CORP
Also Called: Chase Manhattan
2245 Mendocino Ave Ste 202 (95403-3112)
PHONE...................707 525-5060
Randy Blankenbaker, *Mgr*
EMP: 120
SALES (corp-wide): 154.79B **Publicly Held**
SIC: **6162** Mortgage bankers and loan correspondents
HQ: Chase Manhattan Mortgage Corp
    343 Thornall St Ste 7
    Edison NJ
    732 205-0600

(P-7949)
CHASE MANHATTAN MORTGAGE CORP
Also Called: Chase Manhattan
560 Mission St Fl 2 (94105-2915)
PHONE...................858 605-3300
Cindy Dunks, *Mgr*
EMP: 120
SALES (corp-wide): 154.79B **Publicly Held**
SIC: **6162** Mortgage bankers
HQ: Chase Manhattan Mortgage Corp
    343 Thornall St Ste 7
    Edison NJ
    732 205-0600

(P-7950)
CLEAREDGE LENDING
65 Enterprise (92656-2705)
PHONE...................562 708-7706
EMP: 94 EST: 2019
SALES (est): 7.16MM **Privately Held**
Web: www.clearedgelending.com
SIC: **6162** Mortgage bankers and loan correspondents

(P-7951)
CMG FINANCIAL SERVICES
3160 Crow Canyon Rd Ste 400 (94583-1368)
PHONE...................925 983-3073
Christopher M George, *CEO*
EMP: 1841 EST: 2003
SALES (est): 454.67MM **Privately Held**
Web: www.cmgfi.com
SIC: **6162** Mortgage bankers and loan correspondents

(P-7952)
COUNTRY CLUB MORTGAGE INC
Also Called: Premier Home Loan Group
525 N Hall St # B (93291-4639)
PHONE...................559 636-3333
William C Rose, *Pr*
Gary Smee, *VP*
EMP: 70 EST: 2001
SALES (est): 5.21MM **Privately Held**
Web: www.countryclubmortgage.com
SIC: **6162** Mortgage bankers and loan correspondents

(P-7953)
COUNTRYWIDE HOME LOANS INC (HQ)
Also Called: Countrywide
225 W Hillcrest Dr (91360-7883)
EMP: 700 EST: 1969
SQ FT: 220,000
SALES (est): 513.39MM
SALES (corp-wide): 94.95B **Publicly Held**
Web: www.bankofamerica.com
SIC: **6162** Mortgage bankers
PA: Bank Of America Corporation
    100 N Tryon St Ste 2650
    Charlotte NC
    704 386-5681

(P-7954)
COUNTRYWIDE HOME LOANS INC
Also Called: Countrywide
801 N Brand Blvd Ste 750 (91203-3218)
PHONE...................818 550-8700
Lynda Martinlawley, *Mgr*
EMP: 1567
SALES (corp-wide): 94.95B **Publicly Held**
Web: www.bankofamerica.com
SIC: **6162** Mortgage bankers
HQ: Countrywide Home Loans, Inc.
    225 W Hillcrest Dr
    Thousand Oaks CA

(P-7955)
DIGNIFIED HOME LOANS LLC
1 Baxter Way Ste 120 (91362-3809)
PHONE...................818 421-7753
Preston James, *Prin*
EMP: 85 EST: 2013
SALES (est): 4.89MM **Privately Held**
Web: www.dignifiedhomeloans.com
SIC: **6162** Mortgage bankers and loan correspondents

(P-7956)
E&S FINANCIAL GROUP INC
Also Called: Capital Mortgage Services
700 E Main St (93001-2906)
PHONE...................805 644-1621
Jordan Eller, *Pr*
EMP: 70 EST: 2008
SALES (est): 10.29MM **Privately Held**
SIC: **6162** Mortgage bankers and loan correspondents

(P-7957)
EC CLOSING CORP
Also Called: Cal Western Foreclosure Svcs
525 E Main St (92020-4007)
P.O. Box 22004 (92022-9004)
PHONE...................800 546-1531
EMP: 80
Web: www.rickpatterson.com
SIC: **6162** Loan correspondents

(P-7958)
ECC CAPITAL CORPORATION (PA)
2600 E Coast Hwy Ste 250 (92625-2144)
PHONE...................949 954-7060
Steven G Holder, *Ch Bd*
Roque A Santi, *Pr*
Larry Moretti, *Ex VP*
EMP: 68 EST: 2004
SALES (est): 51.84MM
SALES (corp-wide): 51.84MM **Privately Held**
Web: www.ecccapital.com
SIC: **6162** Mortgage bankers and loan correspondents

(P-7959)
EMET LENDING GROUP INC
Also Called: Dream Mortgage Group
2601 Saturn St Ste 200 (92821-6702)
PHONE...................714 933-9800
Julie Ahn, *CEO*
EMP: 80 EST: 2015
SALES (est): 6.39MM **Privately Held**
Web: www.emetlending.com
SIC: **6162** Mortgage bankers

(P-7960)
EMPIRE HOME LOANS INC
4401 Hazel Ave Ste 135 (95628-6695)
PHONE...................916 715-1974
Anthony Lombardo, *Pr*
Leo Whitton, *
Julie Yarbrough, *
EMP: 130 EST: 2019
SALES (est): 10MM **Privately Held**
Web: www.empirehomeloans.com
SIC: **6162** Mortgage brokers, using own money

(P-7961)
EQUITY SMART HOME LOANS INC
1499 Huntington Dr Ste 500 (91030-5473)
PHONE...................626 864-8774
Pablo Martinez, *CEO*
EMP: 87 EST: 2016
SALES (est): 13.16MM **Privately Held**
Web: www.equitysmartloans.com
SIC: **6162** Mortgage bankers

(P-7962)
FEDERAL HOME LOAN MRTG CORP
Also Called: Freddie Mac
444 S Flower St Fl 44 (90071-2944)
PHONE...................213 337-4200
Steve Griffin, *Mgr*
EMP: 727
SALES (corp-wide): 86.72B **Publicly Held**
Web: www.freddiemac.com
SIC: **6162** Mortgage bankers and loan correspondents
PA: Federal Home Loan Mortgage Corporation
    8200 Jones Branch Dr
    Mc Lean VA
    703 903-2000

(P-7963)
FIN-WEST GROUP
5740 Ralston St Ste 130 (93003-6038)
PHONE...................805 658-7435
Bob Davis, *Brnch Mgr*
EMP: 305
SALES (corp-wide): 11.57MM **Privately Held**
SIC: **6162** Mortgage bankers and loan correspondents
PA: Fin-West Group
    1131 W 6th St Ste 250
    Ontario CA
    909 595-1996

(P-7964)
FIRST MORTGAGE CORPORATION
1131 W 6th St Ste 300 (91762-1118)
PHONE...................909 595-1996
EMP: 430
SIC: **6162** Mortgage bankers

6162 - Mortgage Bankers And Correspondents (P-7965)

(P-7965)
FIRST PRIORITY FINANCIAL INC
3700 Hilborn Rd Ste 700 (94534-7997)
PHONE.............................707 432-1000
Timothy Kearns, Pr
David Soldati, *
Michael Soldati, *
EMP: 300 EST: 1977
SQ FT: 4,500
SALES (est): 52.41MM Privately Held
Web: www.firstpriorityfinancial.com
SIC: 6162 Mortgage bankers and loan correspondents

(P-7966)
GENHOME MORTGAGE CORPORATION
Also Called: Generation Home Mortgage
16815 Von Karman Ave Ste 200 (92606-2403)
P.O. Box 17059 (92623-7059)
PHONE.............................949 561-0412
EMP: 62 EST: 2019
SALES (est): 10.14MM Privately Held
Web: www.genhomemortgage.com
SIC: 6162 Mortgage bankers and loan correspondents

(P-7967)
GFS CAPITAL HOLDINGS
6499 Havenwood Cir Ste 720 (92648-6621)
PHONE.............................714 720-3918
EMP: 280
SIC: 6162 Mortgage brokers, using own money

(P-7968)
GOAL FINANCIAL LLC
401 W A St Ste 1300 (92101-7906)
PHONE.............................619 684-7600
EMP: 250 EST: 2004
SALES (est): 36.02MM Privately Held
Web: www.goalfinancial.net
SIC: 6162 Loan correspondents

(P-7969)
GOLDEN EMPIRE MORTGAGE INC (PA)
Also Called: Gem Mortgage
1200 Discovery Dr Ste 300 (93309-7036)
PHONE.............................661 328-1600
John Copeland, Prin
EMP: 80 EST: 2006
SALES (est): 91.08MM Privately Held
Web: www.gemcorp.com
SIC: 6162 7371 Mortgage bankers; Computer software development

(P-7970)
GOLDEN EMPIRE MORTGAGE INC (PA)
2130 Chester Ave (93301-4471)
PHONE.............................661 328-1600
Howard Kootstra, CEO
EMP: 100 EST: 1987
SQ FT: 25,000
SALES (est): 56.06MM Privately Held
Web: www.gemcorp.com
SIC: 6162 Mortgage bankers

(P-7971)
GOLDEN EMPIRE MORTGAGE INC
Also Called: Gem
41331 12th St W Ste 102 (93551-1423)
PHONE.............................661 949-3388
Jane Lawrence, Brnch Mgr
EMP: 254

Web: bcontreras.gemcorp.com
SIC: 6162 Mortgage bankers
PA: Golden Empire Mortgage, Inc.
2130 Chester Ave
Bakersfield CA

(P-7972)
GOODLEAP LLC
4200 Douglas Blvd (95746-5902)
PHONE.............................916 290-9999
Hayes Barnard, Pr
EMP: 100
SALES (corp-wide): 150.56MM Privately Held
Web: www.goodleap.com
SIC: 6162 Mortgage bankers
PA: Goodleap, Llc
8781 Sierra College Blvd
Roseville CA
916 290-9999

(P-7973)
GOODLEAP LLC
Also Called: Goodleap
22 Executive Park Ste 100 (92614-2700)
PHONE.............................916 290-9999
Hayes Barnard, Pr
EMP: 100
SALES (corp-wide): 150.56MM Privately Held
Web: www.goodleap.com
SIC: 6162 Mortgage bankers
PA: Goodleap, Llc
8781 Sierra College Blvd
Roseville CA
916 290-9999

(P-7974)
GOODLEAP LLC (PA)
Also Called: Paramount Equity
8781 Sierra College Blvd (95661-5920)
PHONE.............................916 290-9999
Hayes Barnard, Pr
EMP: 196 EST: 2003
SALES (est): 150.56MM
SALES (corp-wide): 150.56MM Privately Held
Web: www.goodleap.com
SIC: 6162 Mortgage bankers

(P-7975)
GUARANTEED RATE INC
230 Commerce (92602-1337)
PHONE.............................424 354-5344
EMP: 149
Web: www.rate.com
SIC: 6162 Mortgage bankers and loan correspondents
PA: Guaranteed Rate, Inc.
3940 N Ravenswood Ave
Chicago IL

(P-7976)
GUARANTEED RATE INC
1065 Higuera St Ste 100 (93401-3786)
PHONE.............................805 550-6933
EMP: 149
Web: www.rate.com
SIC: 6162 Mortgage bankers and loan correspondents
PA: Guaranteed Rate, Inc.
3940 N Ravenswood Ave
Chicago IL

(P-7977)
GUARANTEED RATE INC
915 Highland Pointe Dr (95678-5419)
PHONE.............................916 501-3919
EMP: 149
Web: www.rate.com

SIC: 6162 Mortgage bankers and loan correspondents
PA: Guaranteed Rate, Inc.
3940 N Ravenswood Ave
Chicago IL

(P-7978)
GUARANTEED RATE INC
1455 Frazee Rd Ste 500 (92108-4350)
PHONE.............................760 310-6008
Trent Annicharico, Brnch Mgr
EMP: 149
Web: www.rate.com
SIC: 6162 Mortgage bankers
PA: Guaranteed Rate, Inc.
3940 N Ravenswood Ave
Chicago IL

(P-7979)
GUILD HOLDINGS COMPANY (PA)
Also Called: Guild Mortgage
5887 Copley Dr (92111-7906)
PHONE.............................858 560-6330
Mary Ann Mcgarry, CEO
Patrick J Duffy, Ch Bd
Terry L Schmidt, Pr
David M Neylan, Ex VP
Barry H Horn, Ex VP
EMP: 267 EST: 2020
SALES (est): 1.16B
SALES (corp-wide): 1.16B Publicly Held
Web: ir.guildmortgage.com
SIC: 6162 Mortgage bankers and loan correspondents

(P-7980)
HOME MRTG ALIANCE CORP HMAC (PA)
Also Called: Scion Lending
4 Hutton Centre Dr Ste 500 (92707-8710)
PHONE.............................800 900-7040
Hanan Hanna, CEO
EMP: 408 EST: 2013
SALES (est): 48.27MM
SALES (corp-wide): 48.27MM Privately Held
Web: www.homemac.com
SIC: 6162 Mortgage bankers and loan correspondents

(P-7981)
HOMEQ SERVICING CORPORATION (DH)
4837 Watt Ave (95660-5108)
PHONE.............................916 339-6192
Arthur Lyon, Pr
Keith G Becher, *
Mark K Metz, *
EMP: 1000 EST: 1967
SALES (est): 361.82MM
SALES (corp-wide): 953.9MM Publicly Held
Web: www.homeq.com
SIC: 6162 6163 6111 6159 Mortgage bankers ; Agents, farm or business loan; Student Loan Marketing Association; Automobile finance leasing
HQ: Ocwen Loan Servicing, Llc
1661 Worthington Rd # 100
West Palm Beach FL
561 682-8000

(P-7982)
HOMEXPRESS MORTGAGE CORP
1936 E Deere Ave Ste 200 (92705-5733)
PHONE.............................714 944-3022
EMP: 192 EST: 2018

SALES (est): 13.22MM Privately Held
Web: www.homexmortgage.com
SIC: 6162 Mortgage bankers and loan correspondents

(P-7983)
IMPAC MORTGAGE CORP
Also Called: Impac Mortgage
19500 Jamboree Rd Ste 100 (92612-2426)
PHONE.............................949 475-3600
EMP: 298 EST: 2008
SALES (est): 7.86MM Privately Held
Web: www.cashcallmortgage.com
SIC: 6162 Mortgage bankers
PA: Impac Mortgage Holdings, Inc.
19500 Jamboree Rd Ste 100
Irvine CA

(P-7984)
INTEGRITY MORTGAGE GROUP
Also Called: Champion Mortgage
9747 Businesspark Ave (92131-1653)
PHONE.............................858 225-5000
Alexander Vari, Pr
EMP: 100 EST: 2001
SALES (est): 2.96MM Privately Held
Web: www.integrity-loans.com
SIC: 6162 Mortgage bankers and loan correspondents

(P-7985)
ISERVE RESIDENTIAL LENDING LLC
Also Called: Idirect Home Loans
10920 Via Frontera Ste 520 (92127-1733)
PHONE.............................858 486-4169
EMP: 100 EST: 2011
SALES (est): 30.86MM Privately Held
Web: www.iservelending.com
SIC: 6162 Bond and mortgage companies

(P-7986)
JMAC LENDING INC
Also Called: Jmac Home Loans
2510 Redhill Ave (92705-5542)
PHONE.............................949 345-1508
Mai Christina Pham, Pr
EMP: 60 EST: 2007
SALES (est): 20.47MM Privately Held
Web: www.jmaclending.com
SIC: 6162 Mortgage bankers and loan correspondents

(P-7987)
LENDERS INVESTMENT CORP
18101 Von Karman Ave Ste 400 (92612-1012)
PHONE.............................714 540-4747
Kerry M Smith, Pr
Bill Ammerman, *
EMP: 86 EST: 2003
SQ FT: 14,000
SALES (est): 5.33MM Privately Held
SIC: 6162 Mortgage bankers

(P-7988)
LENDSURE MORTGAGE CORP
Also Called: Talis Lending
15253 Avenue Of Science (92128-3437)
PHONE.............................888 707-7811
Joseph John Lydon, Prin
EMP: 224 EST: 2016
SALES (est): 3.1MM Privately Held
Web: www.lendsure.com
SIC: 6162 Mortgage bankers and loan correspondents

PRODUCTS & SERVICES SECTION
6162 - Mortgage Bankers And Correspondents (P-8010)

(P-7989)
LENDUS LLC
Also Called: Venice Team, The
3240 Stone Valley Rd W (94507-1555)
PHONE..........................925 295-9300
EMP: 720 EST: 2017
SALES (est): 79.48MM Privately Held
Web: www.crosscountrymortgage.com
SIC: 6162 Mortgage bankers and loan correspondents

(P-7990)
LENOX FINANCIAL MORTGAGE CORP
Also Called: Weslend Financial
200 Sandpointe Ave Ste 800 (92707-5751)
PHONE..........................949 428-5100
Wesley C Hoaglund, CEO
EMP: 251 EST: 1999
SALES (est): 77.01MM Privately Held
Web: www.lenoxhomeloans.com
SIC: 6162 Mortgage bankers

(P-7991)
LOANDEPOT INC
3555 Deer Park Dr (95219-2377)
PHONE..........................209 323-7900
EMP: 471
SALES (corp-wide): 1.26B Publicly Held
Web: www.loandepot.com
SIC: 6162 Mortgage bankers and loan correspondents
PA: Loandepot, Inc.
   6561 Irvine Center Dr
   Irvine CA
   888 337-6888

(P-7992)
LOANDEPOT INC (PA)
Also Called: Loandepot
6561 Irvine Center Dr (92618-2118)
PHONE..........................888 337-6888
Frank Martell, Pr
Anthony Hsieh, Ofcr
David Hayes, CFO
Joseph Grassi, CRO
Jeff Dergurahian, Executive Capital Markets Vice President
EMP: 492 EST: 2010
SQ FT: 144,398
SALES (est): 1.26B
SALES (corp-wide): 1.26B Publicly Held
Web: www.loandepot.com
SIC: 6162 Mortgage bankers and loan correspondents

(P-7993)
LOANDEPOT INC
2080 Otay Lakes Rd # 101 (91913-1362)
PHONE..........................619 245-0115
EMP: 314
SALES (corp-wide): 1.26B Publicly Held
Web: www.loandepot.com
SIC: 6162 Mortgage bankers and loan correspondents
PA: Loandepot, Inc.
   6561 Irvine Center Dr
   Irvine CA
   888 337-6888

(P-7994)
LOANDEPOT INC
25500 Commercentre Dr (92630-8855)
PHONE..........................949 470-6263
EMP: 471
SALES (corp-wide): 1.26B Publicly Held
Web: www.loandepot.com
SIC: 6162 Mortgage bankers and loan correspondents
PA: Loandepot, Inc.
   6561 Irvine Center Dr
   Irvine CA
   888 337-6888

(P-7995)
LOANDEPOT INC
3555 Deer Park Dr Ste 100 (95219-2379)
PHONE..........................209 229-4120
EMP: 314
SALES (corp-wide): 1.26B Publicly Held
Web: www.loandepot.com
SIC: 6162 Mortgage bankers
PA: Loandepot, Inc.
   6561 Irvine Center Dr
   Irvine CA
   888 337-6888

(P-7996)
LOANDEPOTCOM LLC
1020 15th St Ste 20 (95354-1132)
PHONE..........................209 846-6400
Shareen Carnes, Brnch Mgr
EMP: 511
SALES (corp-wide): 1.26B Publicly Held
Web: www.franklinloancenter.com
SIC: 6162 Mortgage bankers and loan correspondents
HQ: Loandepot.Com, Llc
   26642 Towne Centre Dr
   Foothill Ranch CA

(P-7997)
LOANDEPOTCOM LLC
42455 10th St W Ste 109 (93534-7060)
PHONE..........................661 202-1700
EMP: 851
SALES (corp-wide): 1.26B Publicly Held
Web: www.franklinloancenter.com
SIC: 6162 Loan correspondents
HQ: Loandepot.Com, Llc
   26642 Towne Centre Dr
   Foothill Ranch CA

(P-7998)
LOANDEPOTCOM LLC
901 N Palm Canyon Dr Ste 107 (92262-4449)
PHONE..........................760 797-6000
EMP: 681
SALES (corp-wide): 1.26B Publicly Held
Web: www.franklinloancenter.com
SIC: 6162 Mortgage bankers
HQ: Loandepot.Com, Llc
   26642 Towne Centre Dr
   Foothill Ranch CA

(P-7999)
LOANDEPOTCOM LLC (DH)
Also Called: Customer Loan Depot
26642 Towne Centre Dr (92610-2808)
PHONE..........................888 337-6888
Andrew Dodson, Pr
David Norris, *
Bryan Sullivan, Ex VP
Peter Macdonald, Ex VP
Harold Gonzalez, Sr VP
EMP: 963 EST: 2009
SALES (est): 986.92MM
SALES (corp-wide): 1.26B Publicly Held
Web: www.movement.com
SIC: 6162 Mortgage bankers
HQ: Ld Holdings Group Llc
   26642 Towne Centre Dr
   Foothill Ranch CA
   888 337-6888

(P-8000)
MASON MCDUFFIE MORTGAGE CORP (PA)
Also Called: Unifirst Mortgage Lending
12647 Alcosta Blvd Ste 300 (94583-5102)
PHONE..........................925 242-4400
Chuck Iverson, Pr
Herb Tasker, *
Jack Radin, *
Bill Godfrey, *
Kevin Conlon, SED Vice President*
EMP: 83 EST: 1887
SALES (est): 54.36MM Privately Held
Web: www.masonmac.com
SIC: 6162 Mortgage bankers

(P-8001)
METROPOLITAN HOME MORTGAGE INC
Also Called: Intelliloan
3090 Bristol St Ste 600 (92626-7318)
PHONE..........................949 428-0161
Daryl Preedge, Pr
EMP: 100 EST: 1993
SQ FT: 5,000
SALES (est): 20.7MM Privately Held
Web: www.metrohmc.com
SIC: 6162 Mortgage bankers and loan correspondents

(P-8002)
MISSION HILLS MORTGAGE CORP (HQ)
Also Called: Mission Hills Mortgage Bankers
18500 Von Karman Ave Ste 1100 (92612-0546)
PHONE..........................714 972-3832
Jay Ledbetter, Pr
EMP: 140 EST: 1969
SQ FT: 27,000
SALES (est): 86.13MM
SALES (corp-wide): 145.44MM Privately Held
Web: www.mhmb.com
SIC: 6162 Mortgage bankers and loan correspondents
PA: Tarbell Financial Corporation
   1403 N Tustin Ave Ste 380
   Santa Ana CA
   714 972-0988

(P-8003)
MORTGAGE SOLUTIONS FCS INC
Also Called: Client Direct Mortgage
2700 Ygnacio Valley Rd Ste 255 (94598-3455)
PHONE..........................925 954-8364
Ramon Von Walker, CEO
EMP: 60 EST: 2012
SALES (est): 5.62MM Privately Held
SIC: 6162 Mortgage bankers and loan correspondents

(P-8004)
MOUNTAIN WEST FINANCIAL INC (PA)
Also Called: Mortgage Works Financial
31 W Stuart Ave (92374-3244)
PHONE..........................909 793-1500
Gary H Martell Junior, Pr
Michael W Douglas, *
EMP: 391 EST: 1990
SALES (est): 102.05MM Privately Held
Web: www.mwfinc.com
SIC: 6162 Mortgage bankers

(P-8005)
NETWORK CAPITAL FUNDING CORP (PA)
Also Called: Network Capital
7700 Irvine Center Dr Fl 3 (92618-2923)
PHONE..........................949 442-0060
Tri Nguyen, Pr
▲ EMP: 345 EST: 2002
SALES (est): 52.59MM
SALES (corp-wide): 52.59MM Privately Held
Web: www.networkcapital.com
SIC: 6162 Mortgage bankers

(P-8006)
NEW CENTURY MORTGAGE CORP
Also Called: New Century Mortgage
18400 Von Karman Ave Ste 1000 (92612-1514)
PHONE..........................949 440-7030
Brad A Morrice, Pr
Brad A Morrice, CEO
Patrick Flanagan, *
Patti M Dodge, *
Daniel P Sussman, *
EMP: 3261 EST: 1995
SALES (est): 109.24MM Privately Held
SIC: 6162 Mortgage bankers and loan correspondents

(P-8007)
OCMBC INC
Also Called: Ocmban
19000 Macarthur Blvd Ste 200 (92612-1420)
PHONE..........................949 679-7400
Rabi H Aziz, CEO
Madelina L Colon, *
EMP: 301 EST: 2001
SQ FT: 12,500
SALES (est): 61.94MM Privately Held
Web: www.lsmortgage.com
SIC: 6162 Mortgage bankers

(P-8008)
PARKSIDE LENDING LLC
180 Redwood St Ste 250 (94102-3283)
PHONE..........................415 771-3700
Matthew Ostander, *
EMP: 60 EST: 2004
SQ FT: 5,097
SALES (est): 26.46MM Privately Held
Web: www.parksidelending.com
SIC: 6162 Mortgage bankers and loan correspondents

(P-8009)
PENNYMAC BROKER DIRECT
112 S Lakeview Canyon Rd Ste 130 (91362)
PHONE..........................614 288-5126
EMP: 60 EST: 2017
SALES (est): 787.96K Privately Held
Web: tpo.pennymac.com
SIC: 6162 Mortgage bankers and loan correspondents

(P-8010)
PENNYMAC FINANCIAL SVCS INC (PA)
Also Called: Pennymac
3043 Townsgate Rd (91361-3027)
PHONE..........................818 224-7442
David A Spector, Ch Bd
Andrew S Chang, Sr Mng Dir
Daniel S Perotti, Sr Mng Dir
Vandad Fartaj, CIO
EMP: 60 EST: 2008
SQ FT: 66,000
SALES (est): 1.99B
SALES (corp-wide): 1.99B Publicly Held
Web: www.gopennymac.com
SIC: 6162 6282 Mortgage bankers and loan correspondents; Investment advice

---

(PA)=Parent Co (HQ)=Headquarters
✪ = New Business established in last 2 years

6162 - Mortgage Bankers And Correspondents (P-8011)

(P-8011)
PNMAC HOLDINGS INC (HQ)
3043 Townsgate Rd (91361-3027)
PHONE..................818 224-7442
David A Spector, *Pr*
Stanford L Kurland, *Ch Bd*
Andrew S Chang, *Sr Mng Dir*
EMP: 65 EST: 2008
SQ FT: 60,000
SALES (est): 1.1B
SALES (corp-wide): 1.99B **Publicly Held**
Web: pfsi.pennymac.com
SIC: 6162 6282 Mortgage bankers and loan correspondents; Investment advice
PA: Pennymac Financial Services, Inc.
3043 Townsgate Rd
Westlake Village CA
818 224-7442

(P-8012)
PRIVATE NAT MRTG ACCPTANCE LLC (DH)
Also Called: Pennymac
6101 Condor Dr (91301)
PHONE..................818 224-7401
Jeff Grogin, *CLO*
Steve Bailey, *CSO*
Doug Jones Cclo, *Prin*
EMP: 800 EST: 2008
SALES (est): 575.74MM
SALES (corp-wide): 1.99B **Publicly Held**
Web: www.pennymac.com
SIC: 6162 Mortgage bankers
HQ: Pnmac Holdings, Inc.
3043 Townsgate Rd
Westlake Village CA
818 224-7442

(P-8013)
PROVIDENT FUNDING ASSOC LP
1235 N Dutton Ave Ste A (95401-4666)
PHONE..................707 568-2420
Mark Mast, *Mgr*
EMP: 80
Web: www.provident.com
SIC: 6162 Mortgage bankers
PA: Provident Funding Associates, L.P.
851 Traeger Ave Ste 100
San Bruno CA

(P-8014)
REAL ESTATE EQUITY EXCHANGE
Also Called: Unison
650 California St Fl 1800 (94108-2722)
PHONE..................415 992-4200
Thomas Stonholtz, *Ch*
EMP: 75 EST: 2013
SALES (est): 9.67MM **Privately Held**
SIC: 6162 Mortgage bankers and loan correspondents

(P-8015)
RENEW FINANCIAL CORP II
Also Called: Afc First Consumer Discount Co
555 12th St Ste 1650 (94607-3623)
PHONE..................610 433-7486
Peter J Krajsa, *CEO*
John M Hayes, *
Laura Nelson, *
EMP: 232 EST: 1947
SALES (est): 10.58MM **Privately Held**
Web: www.renewfinancial.com
SIC: 6162 6036 Bond and mortgage companies; Savings institutions, except federal
PA: Renew Financial Holdings Inc.
555 12th St Ste 1650
Oakland CA

(P-8016)
RPM MORTGAGE INC
3240 Stone Valley Rd W (94507-1555)
PHONE..................925 295-9300
EMP: 238
SIC: 6162 Mortgage bankers and loan correspondents

(P-8017)
RUSHMORE LOAN MGT SVCS LLC (PA)
Also Called: Rushmore Crrspndent Lnding Svc
15480 Laguna Canyon Rd Ste 100 (92618-2132)
P.O. Box 514707 (90051-4707)
PHONE..................949 727-4798
Terry Smith, *Managing Member*
EMP: 839 EST: 2008
SQ FT: 3,000
SALES (est): 165.78MM **Privately Held**
Web: www.rushmorelm.com
SIC: 6162 Mortgage bankers and loan correspondents

(P-8018)
SCENIC OAKS FUNDING INC
1156 Scenic Dr (95350-6161)
PHONE..................209 572-2301
Tony T Avilla, *Pr*
Michael Zagaris, *
Paula Leffler, *
Jon Zagaris, *Stockholder*
EMP: 71 EST: 2009
SALES (est): 9.82MM **Privately Held**
Web: www.scenicoaks.com
SIC: 6162 Mortgage bankers and loan correspondents

(P-8019)
SEA BREEZE FINANCIAL SVCS INC
Also Called: Sea Breeze Mortgage Services
18191 Von Karman Ave Ste 150 (92612-7102)
P.O. Box 19079 (92817-9079)
PHONE..................949 223-9700
Leonard Hamilton, *Pr*
Curtis Green, *
EMP: 150 EST: 1985
SQ FT: 50,000
SALES (est): 17.62MM **Privately Held**
SIC: 6162 Mortgage bankers

(P-8020)
SECURITY NAT MSTR HOLDG CO LLC (PA)
323 5th St (95501-0305)
P.O. Box 1028 (95502-1028)
PHONE..................707 442-2818
Robin P Arkley Ii, *CEO*
EMP: 140 EST: 2002
SQ FT: 15,000
SALES (est): 114.43MM
SALES (corp-wide): 114.43MM **Privately Held**
Web: www.snsc.com
SIC: 6162 Mortgage bankers and loan correspondents

(P-8021)
SIERRA PACIFIC MORTGAGE CO INC (PA)
Also Called: Gen Lending
950 Glenn Dr (95630-3190)
PHONE..................916 932-1700
James Coffrini, *Pr*
Chuck Iverson, *
Janet Lewis, *
Curtis Dair, *
Joseph Moran, *Chief Compliance Officer*
EMP: 580 EST: 1986
SALES (est): 217.88MM
SALES (corp-wide): 217.88MM **Privately Held**
Web: loans.sierrapacificmortgage.com
SIC: 6162 Mortgage bankers

(P-8022)
SN SERVICING CORPORATION
323 5th St (95501-0305)
P.O. Box 35 (95502-0035)
PHONE..................707 445-9883
Robin P Arkley, *Prin*
EMP: 63
SALES (corp-wide): 114.43MM **Privately Held**
Web: www.snsc.com
SIC: 6162 6211 Mortgage bankers and loan correspondents; Security brokers and dealers
HQ: Sn Servicing Corporation
3050 Westfork Dr
Baton Rouge LA

(P-8023)
STEARNS HOLDINGS LLC
2600 E Bidwell St Ste 160 (95630-6449)
PHONE..................916 358-9170
EMP: 136
SIC: 6162 6141 Mortgage bankers and loan correspondents; Personal credit institutions
HQ: Stearns Holdings, Llc
401 E Corp Dr Ste 150
Lewisville TX
714 513-7273

(P-8024)
THRIVE MORTGAGE LLC
Also Called: Georgetown Mortgage
9587 Foothill Blvd (91730-3506)
PHONE..................909 527-3736
EMP: 80
Web: www.thrivemortgage.com
SIC: 6162 Mortgage bankers and loan correspondents
PA: Thrive Mortgage, Llc
4819 Williams Dr
Georgetown TX

(P-8025)
TURNKEY FOUNDATION INC
Also Called: Nationwide
1805 E Garry Ave Ste 130 (92705-5851)
PHONE..................949 557-6203
Ryan O'kane, *Pr*
David Arvidson, *CEO*
EMP: 84 EST: 2004
SALES (est): 11.87MM **Privately Held**
Web: www.arborfinancialgroup.net
SIC: 6162 6531 6411 Mortgage bankers and loan correspondents; Real estate agents and managers; Insurance agents, brokers, and service

(P-8026)
UNIVERSAL AMERICAN MRTG CO CAL
1420 Rocky Ridge Dr Ste 320 (95661-2830)
PHONE..................916 773-2722
Kathleen Connelly, *Mgr*
EMP: 653
SALES (corp-wide): 33.67B **Publicly Held**
SIC: 6162 Mortgage bankers
HQ: Universal American Mortgage Company Of California
700 Nw 107th Ave Fl 3
Miami FL
305 551-7001

(P-8027)
WALKER & DUNLOP INC
12100 Wilshire Blvd Ste 300 (90025-7120)
PHONE..................301 215-5500
Willy Walker, *Mgr*
EMP: 63
Web: www.walkerdunlop.com
SIC: 6162 6411 6531 Mortgage bankers; Insurance agents, brokers, and service; Real estate agents and managers
PA: Walker & Dunlop, Inc.
7272 Wscnsin Ave Ste 1300
Bethesda MD

(P-8028)
XANDER MORTGAGE & REAL ESTATE
Also Called: Real Estate & Mortgage Broker
2520 W Shaw Ln Ste 106 (93711-2768)
PHONE..................855 905-2575
Mohan Cheema, *Pr*
EMP: 71 EST: 2019
SALES (est): 5.7MM **Privately Held**
Web: www.goxander.com
SIC: 6162 Mortgage bankers and loan correspondents

6163 Loan Brokers

(P-8029)
5 ARCHES LLC
19800 Macarthur Blvd (92612-2421)
PHONE..................949 387-8092
Shawn Miller, *CEO*
Gene Clark, *
Steven Davis, *
EMP: 95 EST: 2012
SALES (est): 24.66MM **Publicly Held**
SIC: 6163 Mortgage brokers arranging for loans, using money of others
PA: Redwood Trust, Inc.
1 Belvedere Pl Ste 300
Mill Valley CA

(P-8030)
BLUEVINE CAPITAL INC
Also Called: Bluevine
401 Warren St Ste 300 (94063-1536)
PHONE..................888 216-9619
Eyal Lifshitz, *CEO*
Pimentel Ben, *Head OF CONTENT*
Brad Brodigan, *CCO*
Patrick Adams, *
Steve Allocca, *
EMP: 300 EST: 2013
SALES (est): 72.82MM **Privately Held**
Web: www.bluevine.com
SIC: 6163 Agents, farm or business loan

(P-8031)
CARNEGIE MORTGAGE LLC
Also Called: Ovation Home Loans
15480 Laguna Canyon Rd Ste 100 (92618-2132)
PHONE..................949 379-7000
EMP: 300
Web: www.carnegiemtg.com
SIC: 6163 Mortgage brokers arranging for loans, using money of others
PA: Carnegie Mortgage Llc
2297 Highway 33
Trenton NJ

PRODUCTS & SERVICES SECTION
6163 - Loan Brokers (P-8054)

(P-8032)
CHANGE LENDING LLC
6265 Greenwich Dr Ste 215 (92122-5917)
PHONE..................858 500-3060
EMP: 91
Web: www.changemtg.com
SIC: 6163 Mortgage brokers arranging for loans, using money of others
PA: Change Lending, Llc
     175 N Riverview Dr
     Anaheim CA

(P-8033)
CHANGE LENDING LLC
100 Stony Point Rd Ste 290 (95401-4117)
PHONE..................707 596-5111
Scott Simonich, Brnch Mgr
EMP: 91
Web: www.changemtg.com
SIC: 6163 Mortgage brokers arranging for loans, using money of others
PA: Change Lending, Llc
     175 N Riverview Dr
     Anaheim CA

(P-8034)
CLEAR MORTGAGE CAPITAL INC
Also Called: Blackink.
19800 Macarthur Blvd (92612-2484)
PHONE..................866 239-8068
Nathan Kowarsky, CEO
EMP: 64 EST: 2020
SALES (est): 4.18MM Privately Held
Web: www.clearmortgagecapital.com
SIC: 6163 7371 Loan brokers; Computer software development and applications

(P-8035)
CLEARPATH LENDING
Also Called: Clearpath Lending
15635 Alton Pkwy Ste 300 (92618-7332)
PHONE..................949 502-3577
Amir Ali Omid, CEO
EMP: 130 EST: 2012
SALES (est): 24.26MM Privately Held
Web: www.clearpathlending.com
SIC: 6163 Mortgage brokers arranging for loans, using money of others

(P-8036)
CMG MORTGAGE INC (PA)
Also Called: Cmg
3160 Crow Canyon Rd Ste 400 (94583-1368)
PHONE..................619 554-1327
Christopher M George, CEO
EMP: 349 EST: 1993
SQ FT: 5,500
SALES (est): 132.27MM Privately Held
Web: www.cmgfi.com
SIC: 6163 Mortgage brokers arranging for loans, using money of others

(P-8037)
CONVENTUS LENDING LLC
111 Potrero Ave (94103-4812)
PHONE..................415 923-8069
Keith Tomao, Prin
EMP: 66 EST: 2016
SALES (est): 10.78MM Privately Held
Web: www.cvlending.com
SIC: 6163 Mortgage brokers arranging for loans, using money of others

(P-8038)
DANA CAPITAL GROUP INC (PA)
300 Spectrum Center Dr Ste 1200 (92618-2938)
PHONE..................949 789-0200
EMP: 65 EST: 1995
SQ FT: 12,259
SALES (est): 24.8MM Privately Held
SIC: 6163 Mortgage brokers arranging for loans, using money of others

(P-8039)
E-LOAN INC (DH)
6230 Stoneridge Mall Rd (94588-3260)
PHONE..................925 847-6200
Mark E Lefanowicz, Pr
EMP: 850 EST: 1992
SQ FT: 118,000
SALES (est): 191.95MM
SALES (corp-wide): 3.36B Publicly Held
Web: www.eloan.com
SIC: 6163 6162 Mortgage brokers arranging for loans, using money of others; Mortgage bankers and loan correspondents
HQ: Popular Finance Inc
     326 Slud St El Snrial Con El Senorial Cond
     Ponce PR
     787 844-2760

(P-8040)
EARNEST OPERATIONS LLC
Also Called: Earnest
535 Mission St Ste 1663 (94105-2997)
PHONE..................888 601-2801
Louis Beryl, CEO
Benjamin Hutchinson, *
EMP: 73 EST: 2013
SQ FT: 2,500
SALES (est): 28.51MM
SALES (corp-wide): 3.84B Publicly Held
Web: www.earnest.com
SIC: 6163 Mortgage brokers arranging for loans, using money of others
HQ: Earnest Llc
     10 W Broadway Ste 800
     Salt Lake City UT
     888 601-2801

(P-8041)
EMERY FINANCIAL INC (PA)
Also Called: Wjbradley Mortgage Capital
625 Kings Rd (92663-5711)
PHONE..................949 219-0640
Bradford Sarvak, Pr
EMP: 60 EST: 1993
SALES (est): 10.26MM Privately Held
Web: www.emeryfinancial.com
SIC: 6163 Mortgage brokers arranging for loans, using money of others

(P-8042)
FIGURE LENDING LLC
Also Called: Figure
650 California St Fl 2700 (94108-2608)
PHONE..................888 819-6388
EMP: 333 EST: 2018
SALES (est): 11.61MM Privately Held
Web: www.figure.works
SIC: 6163 Loan brokers

(P-8043)
GUARANTEE MORTGAGE CORPORATION
Also Called: Security First Loan
505 Montgomery St Ste 1275 (94111-6549)
PHONE..................415 441-5050
EMP: 225
Web: www.guaranteemortgage.com
SIC: 6163 Mortgage brokers arranging for loans, using money of others

(P-8044)
HOMEBRIDGE FINANCIAL SVCS INC
15301 Ventura Blvd Ste D300 (91403-6665)
PHONE..................818 981-0606
Douglas Rotella, Pr
EMP: 1700
Web: www.homebridge.com
SIC: 6163 Mortgage brokers arranging for loans, using money of others
PA: Homebridge Financial Services, Inc.
     194 Wood Ave S Fl 9
     Iselin NJ

(P-8045)
LENDINGCLUB ASSET MGT LLC
71 Stevenson St Ste 300 (94105-2985)
PHONE..................415 632-5600
Russ Elmer, Prin
EMP: 71 EST: 2010
SALES (est): 4.08MM Publicly Held
Web: www.lendingclub.com
SIC: 6163 Loan brokers
PA: Lendingclub Corporation
     595 Market St Ste 200
     San Francisco CA

(P-8046)
LIBERTY AMERICAN MORTGAGE CORP (PA)
193 Blue Ravine Rd # 240 (95630-4756)
PHONE..................916 780-3000
Frank A Sousa, Pr
Patrick White, *
Brian Messier, *
Jayne Metz, *
John Cunningham, *
EMP: 92 EST: 1985
SQ FT: 18,000
SALES (est): 9.79MM
SALES (corp-wide): 9.79MM Privately Held
SIC: 6163 6162 Mortgage brokers arranging for loans, using money of others; Mortgage bankers

(P-8047)
LMB OPCO LLC
Also Called: Lowermybills.com
12181 Bluff Creek Dr Ste 250 (90094-2992)
PHONE..................310 348-6800
Jeff Hughes, CEO
EMP: 320 EST: 2016
SALES (est): 65.16MM Privately Held
Web: www.quickencompare.com
SIC: 6163 7389 Mortgage brokers arranging for loans, using money of others; Financial services

(P-8048)
ML MORTGAGE CORP
Also Called: ML Mortgage
8270 Aspen St (91730-3271)
PHONE..................909 652-0780
Kamran Akbar, Pr
Jamal Akber, *
EMP: 75 EST: 2007
SQ FT: 1,200
SALES (est): 11.12MM Privately Held
Web: www.mlmortgage.net
SIC: 6163 Mortgage brokers arranging for loans, using money of others

(P-8049)
PACIFIC BAY LENDING GROUP
Also Called: Bay Valley Mortgage
15020 La Mirada Blvd (90638-4743)
PHONE..................714 367-5125
John Nelson, CEO
Christine Kim, *
EMP: 100 EST: 2011
SALES (est): 13.83MM Privately Held
Web: www.valleyviewhomeloans.com
SIC: 6163 Mortgage brokers arranging for loans, using money of others

(P-8050)
PENNYMAC CORP
27001 Agoura Rd (91301-5339)
PHONE..................818 878-8416
EMP: 355 EST: 2010
SALES (est): 4.45MM Publicly Held
Web: www.pennymac.com
SIC: 6163 Loan brokers
PA: Pennymac Mortgage Investment Trust
     6101 Condor Dr
     Moorpark CA

(P-8051)
PLATINUM CAPITAL GROUP (PA)
3500 N Sepulveda Blvd Ste E (90266-3639)
PHONE..................310 406-3505
Mark Moses, CEO
Brett Dillenberg, *
Jack Daly E, Development
John Bastis, *
EMP: 78 EST: 1993
SQ FT: 24,000
SALES (est): 53.87MM Privately Held
Web: investnow.proiwebsites.com
SIC: 6163 Mortgage brokers arranging for loans, using money of others

(P-8052)
POPE MORTGAGE & ASSOCIATES INC
2980 Inland Empire Blvd Unit 100 (91764-6531)
PHONE..................909 466-5380
Paul Pope, Pr
EMP: 72 EST: 2003
SQ FT: 14,000
SALES (est): 9.72MM Privately Held
SIC: 6163 Mortgage brokers arranging for loans, using money of others

(P-8053)
PROSPER MARKETPLACE INC (PA)
221 Main St Fl 3 (94105-1906)
PHONE..................415 593-5400
David Kimball, Ch Bd
Usama Ashraf, Pr
Melinda Marchesi, CMO
EMP: 116 EST: 2005
SQ FT: 50,000
SALES (est): 199.88MM Privately Held
Web: www.prosper.com
SIC: 6163 Loan brokers

(P-8054)
RMR FINANCIAL LLC (DH)
Also Called: Online Capital
610 Newport Center Dr (92660-6419)
PHONE..................408 355-2000
EMP: 84 EST: 2000
SQ FT: 11,300
SALES (est): 28.4MM
SALES (corp-wide): 953.9MM Publicly Held
SIC: 6163 6162 Mortgage brokers arranging for loans, using money of others; Mortgage bankers
HQ: Phh Corporation
     3000 Leadenhall Rd
     Mount Laurel NJ
     856 917-1744

6163 - Loan Brokers (P-8055)

(P-8055)
SAND CANYON CORPORATION (HQ)
7595 Irvine Center Dr Ste 120 (92618-2957)
P.O. Box 57080 (92619-7080)
PHONE..........................949 727-9425
Robert Dubrish, *Pr*
William O'neill, *CFO*
Steve Nadon, *
Dale M Sugimoto, *
EMP: 100 **EST:** 1992
SALES (est): 116.72MM
SALES (corp-wide): 3.47B **Publicly Held**
Web: www.sandcanyondentistry.com
SIC: 6163 6162 Loan brokers; Mortgage bankers and loan correspondents
PA: H & R Block, Inc.
1 H And R Block Way
Kansas City MO
816 854-3000

(P-8056)
SECURED FUNDING CORPORATION
2955 Red Hill Ave (92626-5907)
PHONE..........................714 689-6749
Lorne Lahodny, *Pr*
John R Lynch Junior, *VP*
Phil Dandrige, *
Joe Lindsay, *CIO*
EMP: 800 **EST:** 1993
SQ FT: 60,000
SALES (est): 46.83MM **Privately Held**
SIC: 6163 Mortgage brokers arranging for loans, using money of others

(P-8057)
SOCIAL FINANCE INC
Also Called: SOCIAL FINANCE, INC
375 Healdsburg Ave # 280 (95448-4150)
PHONE..........................707 473-9889
EMP: 453
SALES (corp-wide): 1.09B **Publicly Held**
SIC: 6163 Loan brokers
HQ: Social Finance, Inc.
234 1st St
San Francisco CA
415 930-4467

(P-8058)
STRATUS REAL ESTATE INC
Also Called: Stratus Realestate
435 Garfield Ave (91030-2249)
PHONE..........................626 441-5549
Steve Heighmler, *Pr*
EMP: 99
SALES (corp-wide): 678.49MM **Privately Held**
Web: www.stratusrealestate.com
SIC: 6163 Loan brokers
HQ: Stratus Real Estate, Inc.
5311 Topanga Canyon Blvd # 3
Woodland Hills CA

(P-8059)
STRATUS REAL ESTATE INC
Banning Villa Apartments
1100 N Banning Blvd Apt 111 (90744-3530)
PHONE..........................310 549-7028
Bernadette Saunder, *Mgr*
EMP: 99
SALES (corp-wide): 678.49MM **Privately Held**
Web: www.stratusrealestate.com
SIC: 6163 6513 Loan brokers; Apartment building operators
HQ: Stratus Real Estate, Inc.
5311 Topanga Canyon Blvd # 3
Woodland Hills CA

(P-8060)
TARBELL FINANCIAL CORPORATION (PA)
1403 N Tustin Ave Ste 380 (92705-8691)
PHONE..........................714 972-0988
Donald Tarbell, *CEO*
Tina Jimov, *
Elizabeth Tarbell, *
Ronald Tarbell, *
Jin Lee, *
EMP: 100 **EST:** 1982
SQ FT: 60,000
SALES (est): 145.44MM
SALES (corp-wide): 145.44MM **Privately Held**
Web: www.tarbellcareers.com
SIC: 6163 6531 6099 Mortgage brokers arranging for loans, using money of others; Real estate brokers and agents; Escrow institutions other than real estate

(P-8061)
TRANSGLOBAL HOLDING COMPANY
1045 W Huntington Dr Ste 200 (91007-8840)
PHONE..........................626 447-7888
Philip C K Hu, *Admn*
EMP: 98 **EST:** 2016
SALES (est): 1.38MM **Privately Held**
Web: www.transglobalus.com
SIC: 6163 Loan brokers

(P-8062)
UNITED VISION FINANCIAL INC
16027 Ventura Blvd # 200 (91436-2728)
PHONE..........................818 285-0211
Dan Michaels, *Pr*
EMP: 180 **EST:** 2003
SQ FT: 3,000
SALES (est): 13.08MM **Privately Held**
SIC: 6163 Mortgage brokers arranging for loans, using money of others

(P-8063)
VILLA VENETIA
2775 Mesa Verde Dr E (92626-4957)
PHONE..........................714 540-1800
United Dominion, *Pr*
EMP: 278 **EST:** 2001
SALES (est): 3.06MM
SALES (corp-wide): 678.49MM **Privately Held**
SIC: 6163 Loan brokers
HQ: Stratus Real Estate, Inc.
5311 Topanga Canyon Blvd # 3
Woodland Hills CA

6211 Security Brokers And Dealers

(P-8064)
AH CAPITAL MANAGEMENT LLC
Also Called: Andreessen Horowitz
2865 Sand Hill Rd Ste 101 (94025-7022)
PHONE..........................650 798-5800
EMP: 532 **EST:** 2009
SALES (est): 58.06MM **Privately Held**
Web: www.a16z.com
SIC: 6211 Security brokers and dealers

(P-8065)
AMERIHOME MORTGAGE COMPANY LLC
Also Called: Amerihome Mortgage
1 Baxter Way Ste 300 (91362-3811)
PHONE..........................888 469-0810
James Furash, *CEO*
Thomas Smith, *
Todd Taylor, *
EMP: 704 **EST:** 2014
SALES (est): 168.88MM
SALES (corp-wide): 3.02B **Publicly Held**
Web: www.amerihome.com
SIC: 6211 Mortgages, buying and selling
PA: Western Alliance Bancorporation
1 E Wshington St Ste 1400
Phoenix AZ
602 389-3500

(P-8066)
BBAM US LP
Also Called: Bbam Arcft Holdings 139 Labuan
50 California St Fl 14 (94111-4683)
PHONE..........................415 267-1600
Steve Vissis, *CEO*
EMP: 320 **EST:** 1993
SALES (est): 19.57MM
SALES (corp-wide): 219.01MM **Privately Held**
Web: www.bbam.com
SIC: 6211 Investment bankers
PA: Bbam Llc
50 California St Fl 14
San Francisco CA
415 267-1600

(P-8067)
BLACKSTONE TECHNOLOGY GROUP (PA)
1141 Capuchino Ave (94010-3509)
PHONE..........................415 837-1400
David Mysona, *CEO*
Casey Courneen, *
Rakesh Agrawal, *
Ken Hans, *
Patrick James, *
EMP: 100 **EST:** 2000
SALES (est): 79.95MM
SALES (corp-wide): 79.95MM **Privately Held**
Web: www.bstonetech.com
SIC: 6211 Security brokers and dealers

(P-8068)
BTIG LLC (PA)
Also Called: Baypoint Trading
600 Montgomery St Fl 6 (94111-2708)
PHONE..........................415 248-2200
Kevin Chessen, *
Brian Endres, *
Pawan Misra, *
EMP: 77 **EST:** 2003
SALES (est): 139.2MM
SALES (corp-wide): 139.2MM **Privately Held**
Web: www.btig.com
SIC: 6211 Investment firm, general brokerage

(P-8069)
CANACCORD GENUITY LLC
44 Montgomery St Ste 1600 (94104-4703)
PHONE..........................415 229-7171
EMP: 191
SALES (corp-wide): 1.11B **Privately Held**
Web: www.canaccordgenuity.com
SIC: 6211 Investment bankers
HQ: Canaccord Genuity Llc
99 High St Ste 1200
Boston MA
617 371-3900

(P-8070)
CANYON PARTNERS INCORPORATED (HQ)
Also Called: Canyon
2000 Ave Of The Strs 11 Fl (90067)
PHONE..........................310 272-1000
Joshua S Friedman, *CEO*
John Simpson, *
Mitchell R Julis, *
John Plaga, *
Todd Lemkin, *
EMP: 60 **EST:** 1990
SQ FT: 5,500
SALES (est): 97.12MM
SALES (corp-wide): 97.12MM **Privately Held**
Web: www.canyonpartners.com
SIC: 6211 Investment firm, general brokerage
PA: Canyon Partners, Llc
2000 Avenue Of The Stars # 11
Los Angeles CA
310 272-1000

(P-8071)
CARRINGTON MORTGAGE SVCS LLC
7600 N Ingram Ave Ste 205 (93711-5824)
PHONE..........................559 261-1724
Lenard Lujan, *Brnch Mgr*
EMP: 152
Web: www.carringtonwholesale.com
SIC: 6211 6162 6141 Mortgages, buying and selling; Loan correspondents; Personal credit institutions
PA: Carrington Mortgage Services, Llc
1600 S Douglass Rd 200a
Anaheim CA

(P-8072)
CARRINGTON MORTGAGE SVCS LLC
10370 Commerce Center Dr Ste 140 (91730-5806)
PHONE..........................909 226-7963
Jaleh Jenkins, *Brnch Mgr*
EMP: 152
Web: www.carringtonwholesale.com
SIC: 6211 6163 Mortgages, buying and selling; Loan brokers
PA: Carrington Mortgage Services, Llc
1600 S Douglass Rd 200a
Anaheim CA

(P-8073)
CASEY SECURITIES INC (PA)
301 Pine St (94104-3301)
PHONE..........................415 544-5030
Richard Casey C H B C E O, *Prin*
Richard Casey, *Ch Bd*
George Gasparini, *
Kathleen Gallagher, *
Scott Nelson, *
EMP: 67 **EST:** 1976
SQ FT: 800
SALES (est): 7.51MM
SALES (corp-wide): 7.51MM **Privately Held**
Web: www.caseysec.com
SIC: 6211 Brokers, security

(P-8074)
CENTURION GROUP INC (PA)
Also Called: Coast Group Financial
365 S Rancho Santa Fe Rd (92078-2338)
PHONE..........................760 471-8536
Jack Heilbron, *Pr*
Mary Lamoges, *
EMP: 125 **EST:** 1982
SQ FT: 9,000
SALES (est): 13.27MM
SALES (corp-wide): 13.27MM **Privately Held**
SIC: 6211 8111 Brokers, security; Legal services

PRODUCTS & SERVICES SECTION
6211 - Security Brokers And Dealers (P-8096)

(P-8075)
CHARGER INVESTMENT PARTNERS LP
880 Apollo St Ste 347 (90245-4752)
PHONE.................310 372-5525
Aaron Perlmutter, Pt
Chris Boyle, Pt
Kimberly Pollack, Pt
EMP: 93 EST: 2019
SALES (est): 7.91MM Privately Held
Web: www.chargerinv.com
SIC: 6211 Investment bankers

(P-8076)
CHARLES SCHWAB CORPORATION
Also Called: Charles Schwab
27580 Ynez Rd Ste A (92591-4667)
PHONE.................800 435-4000
Mark Morgan, Mgr
EMP: 154
SALES (corp-wide): 20.76B Publicly Held
Web: www.schwab.com
SIC: 6211 6282 Brokers, security; Investment advice
PA: The Charles Schwab Corporation
3000 Schwab Way
Westlake TX
817 859-5000

(P-8077)
CHARLES SCHWAB CORPORATION
Also Called: Charles Schwab
1900 Avenue Of The Stars Ste 101 (90067-4302)
PHONE.................800 435-4000
Jane E Fry, Brnch Mgr
EMP: 62
SALES (corp-wide): 20.76B Publicly Held
Web: www.schwab.com
SIC: 6211 Brokers, security
PA: The Charles Schwab Corporation
3000 Schwab Way
Westlake TX
817 859-5000

(P-8078)
CHARLES SCHWAB CORPORATION
Also Called: Charles Schwab
3741 Douglas Blvd Ste 190 (95661-4357)
PHONE.................916 789-2120
Kevin Rose, Prin
EMP: 62
SALES (corp-wide): 20.76B Publicly Held
Web: www.schwab.com
SIC: 6211 Brokers, security
PA: The Charles Schwab Corporation
3000 Schwab Way
Westlake TX
817 859-5000

(P-8079)
CHARLES SCHWAB CORPORATION
Also Called: Charles Schwab
7510 Hazard Center Dr Ste 407 (92108-4525)
PHONE.................800 435-4000
Jim Croutch, Prin
EMP: 86
SALES (corp-wide): 20.76B Publicly Held
Web: www.schwab.com
SIC: 6211 Brokers, security
PA: The Charles Schwab Corporation
3000 Schwab Way
Westlake TX
817 859-5000

(P-8080)
CITIGROUP GLOBAL MARKETS INC
Also Called: Smith Barney
225 W Santa Clara St Ste 900 (95113-1723)
PHONE.................408 947-2200
David Perez, Mgr
EMP: 75
SALES (corp-wide): 101.08B Publicly Held
Web: www.citigroup.com
SIC: 6211 Security brokers and dealers
HQ: Citigroup Global Markets Inc.
388 Greenwich St Fl 18
New York NY
212 816-6000

(P-8081)
CONIFER SECURITIES LLC
1 Ferry Building Ste 255 (94111-4243)
PHONE.................415 677-1500
EMP: 75
SIC: 6211 Security brokers and dealers

(P-8082)
EMMETT A LARKIN COMPANY INC (PA)
22 Battery St Ste 806 (94111-5522)
PHONE.................415 986-2332
EMP: 85 EST: 1959
SQ FT: 10,000
SALES (est): 8.35MM
SALES (corp-wide): 8.35MM Privately Held
Web: www.internettrading.com
SIC: 6211 8742 6282 Stock brokers and dealers; Management consulting services; Investment advice

(P-8083)
FIRST ALLIED SECURITIES INC (HQ)
Also Called: First Allied
655 W Broadway Fl 11 (92101-8561)
P.O. Box 85549 (92186-5549)
PHONE.................619 702-9600
Adam Antoniades, CEO
Frank Campanale, Vice Chairman*
Joel Marks, *
Kevin Keefe, *
Gregg S Glaser, *
EMP: 75 EST: 1994
SALES (est): 1.26MM Privately Held
Web: www.cetera.com
SIC: 6211 Brokers, security
PA: Cetera Financial Group, Inc.
655 W Broadway Ste 1680
San Diego CA

(P-8084)
FOREX CAPITAL MARKETS LLC
201 Mission St Ste 290 (94105-1859)
PHONE.................415 343-4874
Chris Pelton, Brnch Mgr
EMP: 153
SALES (corp-wide): 101.07MM Privately Held
Web: www.fxcm.com
SIC: 6211 Brokers, security
PA: Forex Capital Markets L.L.C.
55 Water St Fl 50
New York NY
212 897-7660

(P-8085)
FRANKLIN TMPLETON INV SVCS LLC (DH)
Also Called: Franklin Templeton Investment
3344 Quality Dr (95670-7361)
P.O. Box 2258 (95741-2258)
PHONE.................916 463-1500
Charles B Johnson, Ch Bd
Basil Fox, *
Robert Smith, *
EMP: 1200 EST: 1981
SQ FT: 40,000
SALES (est): 585.42MM
SALES (corp-wide): 7.85B Publicly Held
SIC: 6211 6282 Traders, security; Investment advisory service
HQ: Templeton Worldwide, Inc.
500 E Broward Blvd # 900
Fort Lauderdale FL

(P-8086)
FREMONT GROUP MANAGEMENT LLC
405 Howard St (94105-2261)
PHONE.................415 284-8500
David Covin, Pr
Alam M Dachs, *
David R Covin, *
Tanya Cota, *
EMP: 160 EST: 1999
SALES (est): 14.54MM Privately Held
SIC: 6211 Investment firm, general brokerage

(P-8087)
GLOBAL INVSTMENTS ARICOR GROUP
667 Clay St (94111-2501)
PHONE.................415 735-9191
Fabricio Fabiani Gonzales, CEO
EMP: 500 EST: 1994
SALES (est): 35.3MM Privately Held
Web: www.globalygroupusa.com
SIC: 6211 Investment firm, general brokerage

(P-8088)
GOLD PARENT LP
11111 Santa Monica Blvd (90025-3333)
PHONE.................310 954-0444
Jonathan D Sokoloff, Prin
EMP: 3400 EST: 2016
SALES (est): 68.41MM Privately Held
SIC: 6211 Investment bankers

(P-8089)
GOLDMAN SACHS & CO LLC
Also Called: Goldman Sachs
555 California St Ste 4500 (94104-1675)
PHONE.................415 393-7500
TOLL FREE: 800
Eff Martin, Genl Mgr
EMP: 146
SALES (corp-wide): 68.71B Publicly Held
Web: www.goldmansachs.com
SIC: 6211 6282 Investment bankers; Investment advice
HQ: Goldman Sachs & Co. Llc
200 West St
New York NY
212 902-1000

(P-8090)
GOLDMAN SACHS & CO LLC
Also Called: Goldman Sachs
2121 Avenue Of The Stars Ste 2600 (90067-5050)
PHONE.................310 407-5700
John Mallory, Brnch Mgr
EMP: 120
SALES (corp-wide): 68.71B Publicly Held
Web: www.goldmansachs.com
SIC: 6211 Investment bankers
HQ: Goldman Sachs & Co. Llc
200 West St
New York NY
212 902-1000

(P-8091)
GORES GROUP LLC (PA)
9800 Wilshire Blvd (90212-1804)
PHONE.................310 209-3010
Alec Gores, CEO
Vance Diggens, *
Frank Stefanik, *
Catherine Scanlon, *
Joseph Page, *
EMP: 60 EST: 2003
SALES (est): 1.81B
SALES (corp-wide): 1.81B Privately Held
Web: www.gores.com
SIC: 6211 7372 5734 Investment firm, general brokerage; Prepackaged software; Computer software and accessories

(P-8092)
GRIGSBY LABEL LLC
4995 Hillsdale Cir (95762-5707)
PHONE.................916 933-4991
EMP: 123 EST: 2010
SALES (est): 10.4MM
SALES (corp-wide): 116.51MM Privately Held
Web: www.g3enterprises.com
SIC: 6211 Investment firm, general brokerage
PA: G3 Enterprises, Inc.
502 E Whitmore Ave
Modesto CA
209 341-7515

(P-8093)
HYUNDAI ABS FUNDING LLC
3161 Michelson Dr (92612-4400)
PHONE.................949 732-2697
EMP: 157 EST: 2016
SALES (est): 8.55MM Privately Held
SIC: 6211 Security brokers and dealers
HQ: Hyundai Capital America
3161 Michelson Dr # 1900
Irvine CA

(P-8094)
IMPERIAL CAPITAL LLC (PA)
10100 Santa Monica Blvd Ste 2400 (90067-4136)
PHONE.................310 246-3700
Randall Wooster, CEO
Jason W Reese, Ch
Randall E Wooster, CEO
Timothy Sullivan, Pr
Mark Martis, COO
EMP: 85 EST: 1997
SALES (est): 49.63MM
SALES (corp-wide): 49.63MM Privately Held
Web: www.imperialcapital.com
SIC: 6211 Investment bankers

(P-8095)
INTERLINK SECURITIES CORP
20750 Ventura Blvd Ste 300 (91364-2338)
P.O. Box 4323 (91365-4323)
PHONE.................818 992-6700
Barry Wolfe, Pr
EMP: 100 EST: 1992
SALES (est): 8.98MM Privately Held
SIC: 6211 6722 Security brokers and dealers; Management investment, open-end

(P-8096)
JMP GROUP LLC (HQ)
600 Montgomery St Ste 1100 (94111-2701)
PHONE.................415 835-8900
Joseph A Jolson, Ch Bd
Raymond S Jackson, CFO
Craig R Johnson, V Ch Bd
EMP: 65 EST: 2000
SQ FT: 51,730

6211 - Security Brokers And Dealers (P-8097)

SALES (est): 121.89MM
SALES (corp-wide): 9.07B **Publicly Held**
Web: www.jmpg.com
SIC: 6211 Investment bankers
PA: Citizens Financial Group, Inc.
1 Citizens Plz Ste 1 # 1
Providence RI
203 900-6715

(P-8097)
LEAR CAPITAL INC
1990 S Bundy Dr Ste 600 (90025-5256)
PHONE.............................310 571-0190
John Ohanesian, *Pr*
Kevin Demeritt, *
EMP: 72 EST: 1997
SQ FT: 4,500
SALES (est): 26.31MM **Privately Held**
Web: www.learcapital.com
SIC: 6211 Mineral, oil, and gas leasing and royalty dealers

(P-8098)
LEONARD GREEN & PARTNERS LP (PA)
11111 Santa Monica Blvd Ste 2000 (90025-3353)
PHONE.............................310 954-0444
Jonathan Sokoloff, *Pt*
John Danhakl, *
Peter Nolan, *
Jonathan Seiffer, *
John Baumer, *
▲ EMP: 93 EST: 1989
SQ FT: 15,000
SALES (est): 3.41B **Privately Held**
Web: www.leonardgreen.com
SIC: 6211 Investment firm, general brokerage

(P-8099)
LERETA LLC (PA)
901 Corporate Center Dr (91768-2642)
PHONE.............................626 543-1765
John Walsh, *CEO*
Tyler Page, *
James V Micali, *
Cody Tillack, *
Chris Masten, *
EMP: 350 EST: 2009
SALES (est): 272.05MM **Privately Held**
Web: www.lereta.com
SIC: 6211 6541 6361 Tax certificate dealers; Title search companies; Real estate title insurance

(P-8100)
LPL FINANCIAL HOLDINGS INC (PA)
Also Called: Lplfh
4707 Executive Dr (92121-3091)
PHONE.............................800 877-7210
Dan H Arnold, *Pr*
James S Putnam, *Non-Executive Chairman of the Board*
Matthew J Audette, *CFO*
Greg Gates, *Technology*
Michelle Oroschakoff, *CLO*
EMP: 476 EST: 1989
SQ FT: 420,000
SALES (est): 8.6B **Publicly Held**
Web: www.lpl.com
SIC: 6211 6282 6091 Brokers, security; Investment advisory service; Nondeposit trust facilities

(P-8101)
M L STERN & CO LLC (DH)
8350 Wilshire Blvd Ste 300 (90211-2327)
PHONE.............................323 658-4400
Stephen F Kempa, *

EMP: 117 EST: 1980
SQ FT: 8,100
SALES (est): 40.29MM
SALES (corp-wide): 1.42B **Publicly Held**
Web: www.mlstern.com
SIC: 6211 Brokers, security
HQ: Hilltop Securities Holdings Llc
200 Crescent Ct Ste 1330
Dallas TX
214 855-2177

(P-8102)
MAP ENERGY LLC
988 Howard Ave (94010-8019)
PHONE.............................650 324-9095
EMP: 85 EST: 2018
SALES (est): 9.63MM **Privately Held**
Web: www.map-energy.com
SIC: 6211 Security brokers and dealers

(P-8103)
MERRILL LYNCH PIERCE FENNER
Also Called: Merrill Lynch Wealth MGT
560 S Winchester Blvd (95128-2560)
PHONE.............................408 260-6001
Bill Yates, *Prin*
EMP: 100
SALES (corp-wide): 94.95B **Publicly Held**
Web: www.ml.com
SIC: 6211 6411 Security brokers and dealers; Insurance agents and brokers
HQ: Merrill Lynch, Pierce, Fenner & Smith Incorporated
111 8th Ave
New York NY
800 637-7455

(P-8104)
MERRILL LYNCH PRCE FNNER SMITH
Also Called: Merrill Lynch
21215 Burbank Blvd Ste 600 (91367-7090)
PHONE.............................818 340-9500
EMP: 60
SALES (corp-wide): 94.95B **Publicly Held**
Web: www.ml.com
SIC: 6211 Security brokers and dealers
HQ: Merrill Lynch, Pierce, Fenner & Smith Incorporated
111 8th Ave
New York NY
800 637-7455

(P-8105)
MERRILL LYNCH PRCE FNNER SMITH
Also Called: Merrill Lynch
650 Town Center Dr # 500 (92626-1989)
PHONE.............................714 429-2800
EMP: 88
SALES (corp-wide): 93.85B **Publicly Held**
Web: www.ml.com
SIC: 6211 8742 Security brokers and dealers; Financial consultant
HQ: Merrill Lynch, Pierce, Fenner & Smith Incorporated
111 8th Ave
New York NY
800 637-7455

(P-8106)
MERRILL LYNCH PRCE FNNER SMITH
Also Called: Merrill Lynch
292 Hemsted Dr Ste 100 (96002-0946)
PHONE.............................530 223-3005
Gregory Debord, *Mgr*
EMP: 60

SALES (corp-wide): 94.95B **Publicly Held**
Web: www.ml.com
SIC: 6211 Security brokers and dealers
HQ: Merrill Lynch, Pierce, Fenner & Smith Incorporated
111 8th Ave
New York NY
800 637-7455

(P-8107)
MERRILL LYNCH PRCE FNNER SMITH
Also Called: Merrill Lynch
24200 Magic Mountain Pkwy Ste 115 (91355-4886)
PHONE.............................661 802-0764
Ann Johnson, *Brnch Mgr*
EMP: 60
SALES (corp-wide): 94.95B **Publicly Held**
Web: www.ml.com
SIC: 6211 Security brokers and dealers
HQ: Merrill Lynch, Pierce, Fenner & Smith Incorporated
111 8th Ave
New York NY
800 637-7455

(P-8108)
MERRILL LYNCH PRCE FNNER SMITH
Also Called: Merrill Lynch
74800 Us Highway 111 (92210-7116)
PHONE.............................760 862-1400
Robert O Braun, *Brnch Mgr*
EMP: 120
SALES (corp-wide): 94.95B **Publicly Held**
Web: www.ml.com
SIC: 6211 Security brokers and dealers
HQ: Merrill Lynch, Pierce, Fenner & Smith Incorporated
111 8th Ave
New York NY
800 637-7455

(P-8109)
MERRILL LYNCH PRCE FNNER SMITH
Also Called: Merrill Lynch
3075a Hansen Way (94304-1000)
PHONE.............................650 842-2440
Huert Chang, *Brnch Mgr*
EMP: 120
SALES (corp-wide): 94.95B **Publicly Held**
Web: www.ml.com
SIC: 6211 Security brokers and dealers
HQ: Merrill Lynch, Pierce, Fenner & Smith Incorporated
111 8th Ave
New York NY
800 637-7455

(P-8110)
MERRILL LYNCH PRCE FNNER SMITH
Also Called: Merrill Lynch
520 Newport Center Dr Ste 1900 (92660)
PHONE.............................949 467-3760
David Gunta, *Brnch Mgr*
EMP: 120
SALES (corp-wide): 94.95B **Publicly Held**
Web: www.ml.com
SIC: 6211 Security brokers and dealers
HQ: Merrill Lynch, Pierce, Fenner & Smith Incorporated
111 8th Ave
New York NY
800 637-7455

(P-8111)
MERRILL LYNCH PRCE FNNER SMITH
Also Called: Merrill Lynch
28202 Cabot Rd (92677-1222)
PHONE.............................949 456-8082
EMP: 60
SALES (corp-wide): 94.95B **Publicly Held**
Web: www.ml.com
SIC: 6211 Security brokers and dealers
HQ: Merrill Lynch, Pierce, Fenner & Smith Incorporated
111 8th Ave
New York NY
800 637-7455

(P-8112)
MERRILL LYNCH PRCE FNNER SMITH
Also Called: Merrill Lynch
100 Wilshire Blvd Ste 300 (90401-1110)
PHONE.............................310 477-3400
Baldwin Chin, *Mgr*
EMP: 60
SALES (corp-wide): 94.95B **Publicly Held**
Web: www.ml.com
SIC: 6211 Security brokers and dealers
HQ: Merrill Lynch, Pierce, Fenner & Smith Incorporated
111 8th Ave
New York NY
800 637-7455

(P-8113)
MERRILL LYNCH PRCE FNNER SMITH
Also Called: Merrill Lynch
555 California St Fl 9 (94104-1512)
PHONE.............................415 955-3700
Jim Dullanty, *Brnch Mgr*
EMP: 150
SALES (corp-wide): 94.95B **Publicly Held**
Web: www.ml.com
SIC: 6211 6282 Security brokers and dealers; Investment advice
HQ: Merrill Lynch, Pierce, Fenner & Smith Incorporated
111 8th Ave
New York NY
800 637-7455

(P-8114)
MERRILL LYNCH PRCE FNNER SMITH
Also Called: Merrill Lynch
701 B St Ste 2350 (92101-8101)
PHONE.............................619 699-3700
Quinton Ellis, *Brnch Mgr*
EMP: 221
SALES (corp-wide): 94.95B **Publicly Held**
Web: www.ml.com
SIC: 6211 8742 Security brokers and dealers; Financial consultant
HQ: Merrill Lynch, Pierce, Fenner & Smith Incorporated
111 8th Ave
New York NY
800 637-7455

(P-8115)
MERRILL LYNCH PRCE FNNER SMITH
Also Called: Merrill Lynch
901 Via Piemonte Ste 503 (91764-8507)
PHONE.............................909 476-5100
TOLL FREE: 800
Chris Barney, *Mgr*
EMP: 60
SALES (corp-wide): 94.95B **Publicly Held**

PRODUCTS & SERVICES SECTION
6211 - Security Brokers And Dealers (P-8133)

Web: www.ml.com
SIC: **6211** Security brokers and dealers
HQ: Merrill Lynch, Pierce, Fenner & Smith Incorporated
111 8th Ave
New York NY
800 637-7455

(P-8116)
MERRILL LYNCH PRCE FNNER SMITH
Also Called: Merrill Lynch
1096 Coast Village Rd (93108-0723)
PHONE.................................805 695-7028
EMP: 80
SALES (corp-wide): 94.95B **Publicly Held**
Web: www.ml.com
SIC: **6211** 6021 Security brokers and dealers; National commercial banks
HQ: Merrill Lynch, Pierce, Fenner & Smith Incorporated
111 8th Ave
New York NY
800 637-7455

(P-8117)
MERRILL LYNCH PRCE FNNER SMITH
Also Called: Merrill Lynch
801 10th St Fl 7-1 (95354-2311)
PHONE.................................209 578-2600
Stanly Oneil, Owner
EMP: 80
SALES (corp-wide): 94.95B **Publicly Held**
Web: fa.ml.com
SIC: **6211** Security brokers and dealers
HQ: Merrill Lynch, Pierce, Fenner & Smith Incorporated
111 8th Ave
New York NY
800 637-7455

(P-8118)
MERRILL LYNCH PRCE FNNER SMITH
Also Called: Merrill Lynch
2998 Douglas Blvd Ste 290 (95661-4229)
PHONE.................................916 984-3200
EMP: 70
SALES (corp-wide): 93.85B **Publicly Held**
Web: www.ml.com
SIC: **6211** Security brokers and dealers
HQ: Merrill Lynch, Pierce, Fenner & Smith Incorporated
111 8th Ave
New York NY
800 637-7455

(P-8119)
MERRILL LYNCH PRCE FNNER SMITH
Also Called: Merrill Lynch
50 W San Fernando St Ste 1600 (95113-2420)
PHONE.................................408 283-3000
Patricia Williams, Mgr
EMP: 141
SALES (corp-wide): 94.95B **Publicly Held**
Web: www.ml.com
SIC: **6211** 6282 Security brokers and dealers; Investment advice
HQ: Merrill Lynch, Pierce, Fenner & Smith Incorporated
111 8th Ave
New York NY
800 637-7455

(P-8120)
MERRILL LYNCH PRCE FNNER SMITH
Also Called: Merrill Lynch
5951 La Sendita A (92067)
P.O. Box 7297 (92067-7297)
PHONE.................................800 403-8796
EMP: 60
SALES (corp-wide): 94.95B **Publicly Held**
Web: www.ml.com
SIC: **6211** Security brokers and dealers
HQ: Merrill Lynch, Pierce, Fenner & Smith Incorporated
111 8th Ave
New York NY
800 637-7455

(P-8121)
MERRILL LYNCH PRCE FNNER SMITH
Also Called: Merrill Lynch Prce Fnner Smith
555 Capitol Mall Ste 1400 (95814-4504)
PHONE.................................916 648-6200
EMP: 60
SALES (corp-wide): 94.95B **Publicly Held**
Web: www.ml.com
SIC: **6211** Security brokers and dealers
HQ: Merrill Lynch, Pierce, Fenner & Smith Incorporated
111 8th Ave
New York NY
800 637-7455

(P-8122)
MERRILL LYNCH PRCE FNNER SMITH
Also Called: Merrill Lynch
212 E Main St Ste 101 (93291-6356)
PHONE.................................559 741-9033
EMP: 60
SALES (corp-wide): 94.95B **Publicly Held**
Web: www.ml.com
SIC: **6211** Security brokers and dealers
HQ: Merrill Lynch, Pierce, Fenner & Smith Incorporated
111 8th Ave
New York NY
800 637-7455

(P-8123)
MERRILL LYNCH PRCE FNNER SMITH
Also Called: Merrill Lynch
4900 Hopyard Rd Ste 140 (94588-3345)
PHONE.................................925 227-6600
Uwe Ruttke, Mgr
EMP: 100
SALES (corp-wide): 94.95B **Publicly Held**
Web: www.ml.com
SIC: **6211** Security brokers and dealers
HQ: Merrill Lynch, Pierce, Fenner & Smith Incorporated
111 8th Ave
New York NY
800 637-7455

(P-8124)
MERRILL LYNCH PRCE FNNER SMITH
Also Called: Merrill Lynch
1424 State St (93101-2512)
PHONE.................................805 963-0333
Frederick Burrows, Brnch Mgr
EMP: 120
SALES (corp-wide): 94.95B **Publicly Held**
Web: www.ml.com
SIC: **6211** Security brokers and dealers
HQ: Merrill Lynch, Pierce, Fenner & Smith Incorporated
111 8th Ave
New York NY
800 637-7455

(P-8125)
MERRILL LYNCH PRCE FNNER SMITH
Also Called: Merrill Lynch
5080 California Ave Ste 102 (93309-1698)
P.O. Box 9788 (93389-9788)
PHONE.................................661 326-7700
Gary Sampson, Mgr
EMP: 141
SALES (corp-wide): 94.95B **Publicly Held**
Web: www.ml.com
SIC: **6211** Security brokers and dealers
HQ: Merrill Lynch, Pierce, Fenner & Smith Incorporated
111 8th Ave
New York NY
800 637-7455

(P-8126)
MERRILL LYNCH PRCE FNNER SMITH
Also Called: Merrill Lynch
145 S State College Blvd Ste 300 (92821-5818)
PHONE.................................714 257-4400
TOLL FREE: 800
Robert Max, Mgr
EMP: 141
SALES (corp-wide): 94.95B **Publicly Held**
Web: www.ml.com
SIC: **6211** Security brokers and dealers
HQ: Merrill Lynch, Pierce, Fenner & Smith Incorporated
111 8th Ave
New York NY
800 637-7455

(P-8127)
MERRILL LYNCH PRCE FNNER SMITH
Also Called: Merrill Lynch
3255 W March Ln Ste 110 (95219-2353)
PHONE.................................209 472-3500
Philip B Benson, Mgr
EMP: 100
SALES (corp-wide): 94.95B **Publicly Held**
Web: www.ml.com
SIC: **6211** 8742 Security brokers and dealers; Financial consultant
HQ: Merrill Lynch, Pierce, Fenner & Smith Incorporated
111 8th Ave
New York NY
800 637-7455

(P-8128)
MERRILL LYNCH PRCE FNNER SMITH
Also Called: Merrill Lynch
90 S E St Frnt (95404-6511)
PHONE.................................707 575-6374
Matthew Davis, Mgr
EMP: 100
SALES (corp-wide): 94.95B **Publicly Held**
Web: www.ml.com
SIC: **6211** Security brokers and dealers
HQ: Merrill Lynch, Pierce, Fenner & Smith Incorporated
111 8th Ave
New York NY
800 637-7455

(P-8129)
MERRILL LYNCH PRCE FNNER SMITH
Also Called: Merrill Lynch
2301 Rosecrans Ave Ste 3150 (90245-4967)
PHONE.................................310 536-1600
Shawn Soroush, Mgr
EMP: 60
SALES (corp-wide): 94.95B **Publicly Held**
Web: www.ml.com
SIC: **6211** Security brokers and dealers
HQ: Merrill Lynch, Pierce, Fenner & Smith Incorporated
111 8th Ave
New York NY
800 637-7455

(P-8130)
MERRILL LYNCH PRCE FNNER SMITH
Also Called: Merrill Lynch
1331 N California Blvd Ste 400 (94596-4561)
PHONE.................................925 945-4800
Michael Dunn, Brnch Mgr
EMP: 85
SALES (corp-wide): 94.95B **Publicly Held**
Web: www.ml.com
SIC: **6211** 8742 Security brokers and dealers; Financial consultant
HQ: Merrill Lynch, Pierce, Fenner & Smith Incorporated
111 8th Ave
New York NY
800 637-7455

(P-8131)
MERRILL LYNCH PRCE FNNER SMITH
Also Called: Merrill Lynch Carlsbad Office
1000 Aviara Dr Ste 200 (92011-4218)
PHONE.................................760 930-3100
Nick Givogri, Mgr
EMP: 80
SALES (corp-wide): 94.95B **Publicly Held**
Web: www.ml.com
SIC: **6211** Security brokers and dealers
HQ: Merrill Lynch, Pierce, Fenner & Smith Incorporated
111 8th Ave
New York NY
800 637-7455

(P-8132)
MERRILL LYNCH PRCE FNNER SMITH
Also Called: Merrill Lynch
800 E Colorado Blvd Ste 400 (91101)
PHONE.................................800 637-7455
Mark Mixon, Mgr
EMP: 201
SALES (corp-wide): 94.95B **Publicly Held**
Web: www.ml.com
SIC: **6211** Security brokers and dealers
HQ: Merrill Lynch, Pierce, Fenner & Smith Incorporated
111 8th Ave
New York NY
800 637-7455

(P-8133)
MERRILL LYNCH PRCE FNNER SMITH
Also Called: Merrill Lynch
5260 N Palm Ave Ste 100 (93704-2220)
P.O. Box 11217 (93772-1217)
PHONE.................................559 436-0919
Leonard Kirgorian, Dir
EMP: 100
SALES (corp-wide): 94.95B **Publicly Held**
Web: www.ml.com

6211 - Security Brokers And Dealers (P-8134)

SIC: **6211** Security brokers and dealers
HQ: Merrill Lynch, Pierce, Fenner & Smith
Incorporated
111 8th Ave
New York NY
800 637-7455

(P-8134)
MERRILL LYNCH PRCE FNNER SMITH
Also Called: Merrill Lynch
200 E Franklin St (93940-3057)
PHONE.................................831 625-2700
Michael Vollstebt, *Mgr*
EMP: 141
SALES (corp-wide): 94.95B **Publicly Held**
Web: www.ml.com
SIC: **6211** Security brokers and dealers
HQ: Merrill Lynch, Pierce, Fenner & Smith
Incorporated
111 8th Ave
New York NY
800 637-7455

(P-8135)
MERRILL LYNCH PRCE FNNER SMITH
Also Called: Merrill Lynch
3010 Old Ranch Pkwy Ste 150
(90740-2764)
PHONE.................................562 493-1300
Julie Danaho, *Mgr*
EMP: 80
SALES (corp-wide): 94.95B **Publicly Held**
Web: www.ml.com
SIC: **6211** Security brokers and dealers
HQ: Merrill Lynch, Pierce, Fenner & Smith
Incorporated
111 8th Ave
New York NY
800 637-7455

(P-8136)
MERRILL LYNCH PRCE FNNER SMITH
Also Called: Merrill Lynch
11811 Bernardo Plaza Ct (92128-2401)
PHONE.................................858 673-6700
John Lohrenc, *Mgr*
EMP: 100
SALES (corp-wide): 94.95B **Publicly Held**
Web: www.ml.com
SIC: **6211** Security brokers and dealers
HQ: Merrill Lynch, Pierce, Fenner & Smith
Incorporated
111 8th Ave
New York NY
800 637-7455

(P-8137)
MERRILL LYNCH PRCE FNNER SMITH
Also Called: Merrill Lynch
101 S Ellsworth Ave Fl 4 (94401-3956)
PHONE.................................650 579-3050
Peter Soltesz, *Mgr*
EMP: 141
SALES (corp-wide): 94.95B **Publicly Held**
Web: www.ml.com
SIC: **6211** Security brokers and dealers
HQ: Merrill Lynch, Pierce, Fenner & Smith
Incorporated
111 8th Ave
New York NY
800 637-7455

(P-8138)
MERRILL LYNCH PRCE FNNER SMITH
Also Called: Merrill Lynch
2815 Townsgate Rd Ste 300 (91361-3094)
PHONE.................................805 381-2600
TOLL FREE: 800
Brian Riley, *Mgr*
EMP: 100
SALES (corp-wide): 94.95B **Publicly Held**
Web: www.ml.com
SIC: **6211** Security brokers and dealers
HQ: Merrill Lynch, Pierce, Fenner & Smith
Incorporated
111 8th Ave
New York NY
800 637-7455

(P-8139)
MERRILL LYNCH PRCE FNNER SMITH
Also Called: Merrill Lynch
2 Belvedere Pl Ste 100 (94941-2486)
PHONE.................................415 289-8800
EMP: 100
SALES (corp-wide): 94.95B **Publicly Held**
Web: www.ml.com
SIC: **6211** Security brokers and dealers
HQ: Merrill Lynch, Pierce, Fenner & Smith
Incorporated
111 8th Ave
New York NY
800 637-7455

(P-8140)
MERRILL LYNCH PRCE FNNER SMITH
Also Called: Merrill Lynch
7825 Fay Ave Ste 300 (92037-4255)
PHONE.................................858 456-3600
EMP: 100
SALES (corp-wide): 94.95B **Publicly Held**
Web: www.ml.com
SIC: **6211** Security brokers and dealers
HQ: Merrill Lynch, Pierce, Fenner & Smith
Incorporated
111 8th Ave
New York NY
800 637-7455

(P-8141)
MERRILL LYNCH PRCE FNNER SMITH
Also Called: Merrill Lynch
12830 El Camino Real Ste 300 (92130)
PHONE.................................858 677-1300
EMP: 80
SALES (corp-wide): 94.95B **Publicly Held**
Web: www.ml.com
SIC: **6211** Security brokers and dealers
HQ: Merrill Lynch, Pierce, Fenner & Smith
Incorporated
111 8th Ave
New York NY
800 637-7455

(P-8142)
MERRILL LYNCH PRCE FNNER SMITH
Also Called: Merrill Lynch
1020 Marsh St (93401-3630)
PHONE.................................805 596-2222
EMP: 60
SALES (corp-wide): 94.95B **Publicly Held**
Web: www.ml.com
SIC: **6211** Security brokers and dealers
HQ: Merrill Lynch, Pierce, Fenner & Smith
Incorporated
111 8th Ave
New York NY
800 637-7455

(P-8143)
MERRILL LYNCH PRCE FNNER SMITH
Also Called: Merrill Lynch
100 Spectrum Center Dr (92618-4940)
PHONE.................................949 235-5050
C De Lorm, *Brnch Mgr*
EMP: 60
SALES (corp-wide): 94.95B **Publicly Held**
Web: www.ml.com
SIC: **6211** Stock brokers and dealers
HQ: Merrill Lynch, Pierce, Fenner & Smith
Incorporated
111 8th Ave
New York NY
800 637-7455

(P-8144)
MORGAN STNLEY SMITH BARNEY LLC
650 Castro St (94041-2055)
PHONE.................................650 316-6788
Mitchell Baker, *Pr*
EMP: 130
SALES (corp-wide): 53.67B **Publicly Held**
Web: www.morganstanley.com
SIC: **6211** 6282 Security brokers and dealers
; Investment advice
HQ: Morgan Stanley Smith Barney, Llc
1585 Broadway
New York NY

(P-8145)
MORGAN STNLEY SMITH BARNEY LLC
1225 Prospect St Ste 202 (92037-3687)
PHONE.................................212 761-4000
Emily Temporal, *Brnch Mgr*
EMP: 103
SALES (corp-wide): 53.67B **Publicly Held**
Web: www.morganstanley.com
SIC: **6211** Security brokers and dealers
HQ: Morgan Stanley Smith Barney, Llc
1585 Broadway
New York NY

(P-8146)
MORGAN STNLEY SMITH BARNEY LLC
3750 University Ave Ste 600 (92501-3323)
PHONE.................................951 682-1181
James Gibson, *Mgr*
EMP: 109
SALES (corp-wide): 53.67B **Publicly Held**
Web: www.morganstanley.com
SIC: **6211** Security brokers and dealers
HQ: Morgan Stanley Smith Barney, Llc
1585 Broadway
New York NY

(P-8147)
MORGAN STNLEY SMITH BARNEY LLC
6004 La Madrona Dr (95060-1040)
PHONE.................................831 440-5200
Stephanie Tucker, *Brnch Mgr*
EMP: 62
SALES (corp-wide): 53.67B **Publicly Held**
Web: www.morganstanley.com
SIC: **6211** Security brokers and dealers
HQ: Morgan Stanley Smith Barney, Llc
1585 Broadway
New York NY

(P-8148)
MORGAN STNLEY SMITH BARNEY LLC
555 California St Fl 35 (94104-1615)
PHONE.................................415 984-6500
Greg M Desmond, *Brnch Mgr*
EMP: 181
SALES (corp-wide): 53.67B **Publicly Held**
Web: www.morganstanley.com
SIC: **6211** Security brokers and dealers
HQ: Morgan Stanley Smith Barney, Llc
1585 Broadway
New York NY

(P-8149)
MORGAN STNLEY SMITH BARNEY LLC
444 S Flower St Ste 2700 (90071-2971)
PHONE.................................213 891-3200
Bruce Brereton, *Brnch Mgr*
EMP: 119
SALES (corp-wide): 53.67B **Publicly Held**
Web: www.morganstanley.com
SIC: **6211** Security brokers and dealers
HQ: Morgan Stanley Smith Barney, Llc
1585 Broadway
New York NY

(P-8150)
MORGAN STNLEY SMITH BARNEY LLC
21650 Oxnard St Ste 1800 (91367-4944)
PHONE.................................818 715-1800
Fred Rucker Esq, *Brnch Mgr*
EMP: 103
SALES (corp-wide): 53.67B **Publicly Held**
Web: www.morganstanley.com
SIC: **6211** Stock brokers and dealers
HQ: Morgan Stanley Smith Barney, Llc
1585 Broadway
New York NY

(P-8151)
MORGAN STNLEY SMITH BARNEY LLC
5796 Armada Dr Ste 200 (92008-4694)
PHONE.................................760 438-5100
John Condos, *Prin*
EMP: 130
SALES (corp-wide): 53.67B **Publicly Held**
Web: www.morganstanley.com
SIC: **6211** Stock brokers and dealers
HQ: Morgan Stanley Smith Barney, Llc
1585 Broadway
New York NY

(P-8152)
MORGAN STNLEY SMITH BARNEY LLC
10 Pointe Dr Ste 400 (92821-7620)
PHONE.................................714 674-4100
Vincent Daigneault, *Prin*
EMP: 103
SALES (corp-wide): 53.67B **Publicly Held**
Web: www.morganstanley.com
SIC: **6211** Stock brokers and dealers
HQ: Morgan Stanley Smith Barney, Llc
1585 Broadway
New York NY

(P-8153)
MORGAN STNLEY SMITH BARNEY LLC
225 W Santa Clara St Ste 900
(95113-1723)
PHONE.................................408 346-0105
David Perez, *Brnch Mgr*
EMP: 103
SALES (corp-wide): 53.67B **Publicly Held**
Web: www.morganstanley.com
SIC: **6211** Stock brokers and dealers
HQ: Morgan Stanley Smith Barney, Llc
1585 Broadway

PRODUCTS & SERVICES SECTION

6211 - Security Brokers And Dealers (P-8175)

(P-8154)
MORGAN STNLEY SMITH BARNEY LLC
1014 Santa Barbara St (93101-2126)
PHONE......................805 963-3381
Walter Harris, *Pr*
EMP: 103
SALES (corp-wide): 53.67B **Publicly Held**
Web: www.morganstanley.com
SIC: 6211 Stock brokers and dealers
HQ: Morgan Stanley Smith Barney, Llc
1585 Broadway
New York NY

(P-8155)
MORGAN STNLEY SMITH BARNEY LLC
Also Called: Morgan Stanley Smith Barney
101 W Broadway Ste 1800 (92101-8298)
PHONE......................619 238-1226
Nozomi Ward, *Sr VP*
EMP: 119
SALES (corp-wide): 53.67B **Publicly Held**
Web: www.morganstanley.com
SIC: 6211 Stock brokers and dealers
HQ: Morgan Stanley Smith Barney, Llc
1585 Broadway
New York NY

(P-8156)
MURIEL SIEBERT & CO INC
9378 Wilshire Blvd Ste 300 (90212-3168)
PHONE......................800 993-2015
Joseph M Ramos, *Ex VP*
EMP: 100
SALES (corp-wide): 67.51MM **Publicly Held**
Web: www.siebert.com
SIC: 6211 Brokers, security
HQ: Muriel Siebert & Co., Inc.
15 Exchange Pl Ste 615
Jersey City NJ
212 644-2400

(P-8157)
NATIONAL FINANCIAL SVCS LLC
19200 Von Karman Ave Ste 400
(92612-8553)
PHONE......................949 476-0157
Lawrence Goodkind, *Brnch Mgr*
EMP: 861
SALES (corp-wide): 4.35B **Privately Held**
Web: www.mybrokerageinfo.com
SIC: 6211 Investment firm, general brokerage
HQ: National Financial Services Llc
200 Seaport Blvd Ste 630
Boston MA
800 471-0382

(P-8158)
NORTH PT MRGERS ACQSITIONS INC
580 California St Ste 2000 (94104-1004)
PHONE......................415 358-3500
David Jacquin, *CEO*
EMP: 66 **EST:** 2003
SALES (est): 8.67MM **Privately Held**
Web: www.nptma.com
SIC: 6211 Security brokers and dealers

(P-8159)
PACIFIC SELECT DISTRS INC
700 Newport Center Dr Fl 4 (92660-6307)
PHONE......................949 219-3011
Gerald W Robinson, *Pr*
Audrey L Milfs, *
Edward R Byrd, *
Kathy R Gough, *Assistant Vice President Compliance**
Thomas C Sutton, *
EMP: 96 **EST:** 1969
SQ FT: 300,000
SALES (est): 10.67MM
SALES (corp-wide): 12.84B **Privately Held**
Web: www.pacificlife.com
SIC: 6211 Brokers, security
HQ: Pacific Life Insurance Company
700 Newport Center Dr
Newport Beach CA
949 219-3011

(P-8160)
PALISADES GROUP LLC
11755 Wilshire Blvd Ste 1700 (90025-1500)
PHONE......................424 280-7560
Stephen Kirch, *CEO*
Jack Macdowell Junior, *CIO*
Justin Bodiya, *COO*
Sally Kawana, *CFO*
EMP: 143 **EST:** 2012
SALES (est): 4.87MM
SALES (corp-wide): 4.87MM **Privately Held**
Web: palisades.us.com
SIC: 6211 Investment firm, general brokerage
PA: The Palisades Holdings I Llc
11755 Wilshire Blvd # 17
Los Angeles CA
424 280-7560

(P-8161)
PLAZA HOME MORTGAGE INC
9808 Scranton Rd (92121-3704)
PHONE......................858 346-1208
Kevin Parra, *Pr*
EMP: 108
SALES (corp-wide): 117.8MM **Privately Held**
Web: www.plazahomemortgage.com
SIC: 6211 6162 Mortgages, buying and selling; Loan correspondents
PA: Plaza Home Mortgage, Inc.
4820 Eastgate Mall # 100
San Diego CA
858 346-1200

(P-8162)
POINT DIGITAL FINANCE INC
Also Called: Point
444 High St Fl 4 (94301-1670)
P.O. Box 192 (94302-0192)
PHONE......................888 764-6823
Edward Lim, *CEO*
EMP: 183 **EST:** 2014
SALES (est): 10.04MM **Privately Held**
Web: www.point.com
SIC: 6211 Investment firm, general brokerage

(P-8163)
ROBINHOOD MARKETS INC (PA)
Also Called: Robinhood
85 Willow Rd (94025-3656)
PHONE......................844 428-5411
Vladimir Tenev, *Ch Bd*
Gretchen Howard, *COO*
Jason Warnick, *CFO*
Baiju Bhatt, *CCO**
Daniel Gallagher, *CLO*
EMP: 1976 **EST:** 2013
SALES (est): 958MM
SALES (corp-wide): 958MM **Publicly Held**
Web: www.robinhood.com
SIC: 6211 Stock brokers and dealers

(P-8164)
ROTH CAPITAL PARTNERS LLC (PA)
Also Called: Roth Mkm
888 San Clemente Dr (92660-6369)
PHONE......................800 678-9147
Byron Roth, *Ch*
Byron Roth, *CEO*
Gordon Roth, *COO*
Warren Dunnavant Ii, *VP*
EMP: 100 **EST:** 1984
SQ FT: 52,000
SALES (est): 52.8MM
SALES (corp-wide): 52.8MM **Privately Held**
Web: www.roth.com
SIC: 6211 Investment bankers

(P-8165)
SCHWAB PRVATE CLENT INV ADVSOR
211 Main St (94105-1905)
PHONE......................415 667-0820
Terri R Kallsen, *Pr*
EMP: 1171 **EST:** 2014
SALES (est): 4.36MM
SALES (corp-wide): 20.76B **Publicly Held**
Web: www.schwab.com
SIC: 6211 Brokers, security
PA: The Charles Schwab Corporation
3000 Schwab Way
Westlake TX
817 859-5000

(P-8166)
SUTTER SECURITIES INC
6 Venture Ste 395 (92618-7315)
PHONE......................415 352-6300
Robert Muh, *CEO*
Frank Soriano, *Pr*
Joseph M Ducote, *Dir*
Ashford D Wood, *Dir*
Frederick Selinger, *Dir*
EMP: 111 **EST:** 1992
SALES (est): 6.06MM
SALES (corp-wide): 6.06MM **Privately Held**
Web: www.suttersecurities.com
SIC: 6211 Investment bankers
PA: Sutter Securities Group, Inc.
6 Venture Ste 395
Irvine CA
310 504-3706

(P-8167)
SVB SECURITIES LLC
255 California St Fl 12 (94111-4923)
PHONE......................800 778-1164
Jeffrey Leerink, *CEO*
EMP: 87
SALES (corp-wide): 7.4B **Publicly Held**
Web: www.svbsecurities.com
SIC: 6211 Brokers, security
HQ: Svb Securities Llc
53 State St Ste 40
Boston MA

(P-8168)
THOMAS WEISEL PARTNERS LLC (DH)
1 Montgomery St Ste 3700 (94104-5537)
PHONE......................415 364-2500
Bob West, *
Blake Jorgensen, *
EMP: 300 **EST:** 1998
SALES (est): 98.09MM
SALES (corp-wide): 4.59B **Publicly Held**
Web: www.twp-stifel.com
SIC: 6211 Investment bankers
HQ: Thomas Weisel Partners Group Inc.
1 Montgomery St Fl 36
San Francisco CA

(P-8169)
TRUST COMPANY OF WEST
865 S Figueroa St Ste 1800 (90017-2543)
PHONE......................213 244-0000
EMP: 515
SIC: 6211 Bond dealers and brokers

(P-8170)
UBS AMERICAS INC
600 W Broadway Ste 2800 (92101-0906)
PHONE......................619 557-2400
EMP: 155
Web: www.ubs.com
SIC: 6211 Security brokers and dealers
HQ: Ubs Americas Inc.
600 Washington Blvd
Stamford CT
203 719-3000

(P-8171)
US VENTURE PARTNERS
1460 El Camino Real Ste 100
(94025-4123)
PHONE......................650 854-9080
Arati Prabhakar, *Pt*
EMP: 64 **EST:** 2013
SALES (est): 1.22MM **Privately Held**
Web: www.usvp.com
SIC: 6211 Investment bankers

(P-8172)
VECTOR CAPITAL MANAGEMENT LP (PA)
1 Market St Ste 2300 (94105-1414)
PHONE......................415 293-5000
Alex Slusky, *CIO*
David Baylor, *COO*
James Murray, *CFO*
EMP: 84 **EST:** 1998
SQ FT: 8,000
SALES (est): 912.58MM
SALES (corp-wide): 912.58MM **Privately Held**
Web: www.vectorcapital.com
SIC: 6211 6799 Security brokers and dealers ; Venture capital companies

(P-8173)
VEEV GROUP INC
Also Called: Dragonfly Investments Group
2701 W Winton Ave (94545-1125)
PHONE......................650 292-0752
Amit Haller, *CEO*
Gordon Heneweer, *
Sean Freeberg, *
EMP: 210 **EST:** 2018
SALES (est): 49.74MM **Privately Held**
Web: www.veev.com
SIC: 6211 Investment firm, general brokerage

(P-8174)
W R HAMBRECHT CO INC (PA)
Pier 1, Bay 3 (94111)
PHONE......................415 551-8600
William R Hambrecht, *Ch Bd*
Clay Corbus, *
Jonathan Fayman, *
Gordon Palumbo, *VP*
EMP: 60 **EST:** 1998
SQ FT: 25,000
SALES (est): 22.45MM
SALES (corp-wide): 22.45MM **Privately Held**
Web: www.hambrechtcapital.com
SIC: 6211 Investment bankers

(P-8175)
WEDBUSH SECURITIES INC (HQ)
1000 Wilshire Blvd Ste 900 (90017-1774)

6211 - Security Brokers And Dealers (P-8176)

P.O. Box 30014 (90030-0014)
PHONE.....................213 688-8000
Edward W Wedbush, Pr
Thomas Ringer, *
Peter Allman-ward, CFO
Earl I Feldhorn, *
V Thomas Hale, *
EMP: 300 EST: 1955
SQ FT: 100,000
SALES (est): 224.6MM
SALES (corp-wide): 254.49MM Privately Held
Web: www.wedbush.com
SIC: 6211 Brokers, security
PA: Wedbush Capital
1000 Wilshire Blvd
Los Angeles CA
213 688-8080

(P-8176)
WELLS FARGO INVESTMENTS LLC
3550 Round Barn Blvd Ste 307 (95403-0922)
PHONE.....................707 521-1232
Lisa Franchetti, Brnch Mgr
EMP: 88
SALES (corp-wide): 82.86B Publicly Held
SIC: 6211 6799 Security brokers and dealers; Investors, nec
HQ: Wells Fargo Investments, Llc
420 Montgomery St Frnt
San Francisco CA

(P-8177)
WELLS FARGO PRIME SERVICES LLC
45 Fremont St Ste 3000 (94105-2256)
PHONE.....................415 848-0269
Robert Garrett, *
EMP: 65 EST: 2004
SALES (est): 24.53MM
SALES (corp-wide): 82.86B Publicly Held
Web: www.mfpcapital.com
SIC: 6211 Security brokers and dealers
HQ: Everen Capital Corporation
301 S College St
Charlotte NC

(P-8178)
WILLIAM ONEIL & CO INC (PA)
12655 Beatrice St (90066-7302)
PHONE.....................310 448-6800
Willaim J Oneil, CEO
Don Drake, CFO
Randy Watts, CIS
EMP: 243 EST: 2010
SQ FT: 5,000
SALES (est): 84.74MM
SALES (corp-wide): 84.74MM Privately Held
Web: www.williamoneil.com
SIC: 6211 6282 Brokers, security; Investment advisory service

6221 Commodity Contracts Brokers, Dealers

(P-8179)
ARTISAN PARTNERS LTD PARTNR
100 Pine St Ste 2950 (94111-5200)
PHONE.....................415 283-2444
Vickey Harris, Mgr
EMP: 313
Web: www.artisanpartners.com
SIC: 6221 Commodity dealers, contracts
PA: Artisan Partners Limited Partnership
875 E Wscnsin Ave Ste 800
Milwaukee WI

(P-8180)
CT COMMODITIES INC
217 W Terra Bella Ave (93256-9631)
P.O. Box 44 (93256-0044)
PHONE.....................559 757-3996
Randal Lee Terrel, Pr
EMP: 61 EST: 2012
SALES (est): 7.87MM Privately Held
SIC: 6221 Commodity contracts brokers, dealers

6231 Security And Commodity Exchanges

(P-8181)
NYSE ARCA INC
115 Sansome St (94104-3601)
PHONE.....................415 393-4000
Philip D Defeo, Ch
Peter Armstrong, *
Paul N Koutoulas, *
James Yee, CIO*
Thomas Connaghan, Senior Executive Vice-President Operations*
▲ EMP: 113 EST: 1882
SALES (est): 42.07MM
SALES (corp-wide): 7.29B Publicly Held
Web: www.nyse.com
SIC: 6231 Stock exchanges
HQ: Nyse Group, Inc.
11 Wall St
New York NY

6282 Investment Advice

(P-8182)
ADVICEPERIOD
2121 Avenue Of The Stars Ste 2400 (90067-5010)
PHONE.....................424 281-3600
Allison Schaengold, Prin
EMP: 83 EST: 2014
SALES (est): 4.84MM Privately Held
Web: www.adviceperiod.com
SIC: 6282 Investment advisory service

(P-8183)
AL HEWITT INC
4009 Mission Oaks Blvd (93012-5156)
PHONE.....................661 945-7050
Alan Hewitt, CEO
EMP: 161 EST: 2005
SALES (est): 2.36MM
SALES (corp-wide): 164.45MM Privately Held
Web: www.merceradvisors.com
SIC: 6282 Investment advisory service
PA: Mercer Global Advisors, Inc.
1200 17th St Ste 500
Denver CO
888 885-8101

(P-8184)
ALLIANZ GLOBAL INVESTORS OF AMERICA LP
680 Nwport Ctr Dr Ste 250 (92660)
PHONE.....................949 219-2200
EMP: 1800
SIC: 6282 Investment advisory service

(P-8185)
ALLSPRING FUNDS DISTR LLC
525 Market St Fl 10 (94105-2718)
PHONE.....................415 396-8000
EMP: 77
SALES (est): 1.03MM
SALES (corp-wide): 109.16MM Privately Held
SIC: 6282 Investment advisory service
PA: Allspring Global Investments, Llc
1415 Vantage Park Dr Fl 3
Charlotte NC
415 396-8000

(P-8186)
ANDERSON KAYNE CAPITAL
1800 Avenue Of The Stars Ste 200 # 3rd (90067)
PHONE.....................800 231-7414
Richard Kayne, Ch
Robert Sinnott, CEO
Edward Cerny, Mng Pt
EMP: 300 EST: 1994
SALES (est): 24.32MM Privately Held
Web: www.kaynecapitalfoundation.org
SIC: 6282 Investment advisory service

(P-8187)
ATLAS CAPITAL GROUP LLC
1318 E 7th St Ste 200 (90021-1123)
PHONE.....................213 988-8890
EMP: 80
Web: www.atlas-cap.com
SIC: 6282 Investment advisory service
PA: Atlas Capital Group, Llc
450 Park Ave Fl 4
New York NY

(P-8188)
BAM ADVISOR SERVICES LLC
Also Called: Loring Ward
10 Almaden Blvd Fl 15 (95113-2226)
PHONE.....................800 366-7266
EMP: 60
Web: www.buckinghamstrategicpartners.com
SIC: 6282 Investment advisory service
PA: Bam Advisor Services, Llc
8182 Maryland Ave Ste 500
Saint Louis MO

(P-8189)
BEATING WALL STREET INC (PA)
20121 Ventura Blvd Ste 305 (91364-2559)
PHONE.....................818 332-9696
Hamed Khorsand, Pr
EMP: 230 EST: 2000
SALES (est): 24.71MM
SALES (corp-wide): 24.71MM Privately Held
Web: www.bwsfinancial.com
SIC: 6282 Investment advisory service

(P-8190)
BEL AIR INV ADVISORS LLC
1999 Avenue Of The Stars Ste 2800 (90067-6041)
PHONE.....................310 229-1500
David Sadkin, Pr
Reed Halladay, *
EMP: 67 EST: 1997
SALES (est): 23.14MM
SALES (corp-wide): 58.22MM Privately Held
Web: www.belair-llc.com
SIC: 6282 Investment advisory service
HQ: Hightower Advisors, Llc
200 W Madison St Ste 2500
Chicago IL

(P-8191)
BRANDES INV PARTNERS INC (PA)
11988 El Camino Real Ste 300 (92131-6123)
P.O. Box 919048 (92191-9048)
PHONE.....................858 755-0239
Charles H Brandes, Ch Bd
Brent V Woods, *
Glenn R Carlson, *
Jeffrey A Busby, *
Gary Iwamura, *
EMP: 250 EST: 1974
SQ FT: 27,000
SALES (est): 96.26MM
SALES (corp-wide): 96.26MM Privately Held
Web: www.brandes.com
SIC: 6282 Investment advisory service

(P-8192)
C2 FINANCIAL CORPORATION
3000 Citrus Cir Ste 118 (94598-2694)
PHONE.....................925 938-1300
Star Darden, Brnch Mgr
EMP: 163
SALES (corp-wide): 94.73MM Privately Held
Web: www.c2financial.com
SIC: 6282 Investment advice
PA: C2 Financial Corporation
10509 Vista Sorrento Pkwy # 400
San Diego CA
858 312-4900

(P-8193)
C2 FINANCIAL CORPORATION
Also Called: C2 Financial
978 Burlingame Ave (93612-0464)
PHONE.....................559 824-2300
EMP: 162
SALES (corp-wide): 94.73MM Privately Held
Web: www.c2financial.com
SIC: 6282 Investment advice
PA: C2 Financial Corporation
10509 Vista Sorrento Pkwy # 400
San Diego CA
858 312-4900

(P-8194)
C2 FINANCIAL CORPORATION
703 Sunset Ct (92109-7024)
PHONE.....................858 220-2112
EMP: 162
SALES (corp-wide): 94.73MM Privately Held
Web: www.c2financial.com
SIC: 6282 Investment advice
PA: C2 Financial Corporation
10509 Vista Sorrento Pkwy # 400
San Diego CA
858 312-4900

(P-8195)
CALLAN LLC (PA)
1 Bush St (94104-4491)
PHONE.....................415 974-5060
Ronald D Peyton, CEO
Ronald Peyton, CEO
Gregory C Allen, Pr
James Callahan, Ex VP
Janet Becker-wold, Sr VP
EMP: 120 EST: 1973
SALES (est): 60.08MM
SALES (corp-wide): 60.08MM Privately Held
Web: www.callan.com
SIC: 6282 8742 Investment advisory service; Banking and finance consultant

▲ = Import ▼ = Export
◆ = Import/Export

PRODUCTS & SERVICES SECTION

6282 - Investment Advice (P-8215)

(P-8196)
CAPITAL GROUP COMPANIES INC (PA)
Also Called: Capital Group, The
333 S Hope St Fl 55 (90071-3061)
PHONE.................................213 486-9200
Tim Armour, *Ch*
Jody Jonsson, *Vice Chairman*
Rob Klausner, *
Matt O'connor, *Distributor*
EMP: 800 EST: 1931
SQ FT: 106,000
SALES (est): 5.43B
SALES (corp-wide): 5.43B Privately Held
Web: www.capitalgroup.com
SIC: 6282 6091 6722 8741 Investment advice; Nondeposit trust facilities; Mutual fund sales, on own account; Management services

(P-8197)
CAPITAL RESEARCH AND MGT CO (HQ)
333 S Hope St Fl 55 (90071-3061)
PHONE.................................213 486-9200
R Michael Shanahan, *Ch Bd*
James F Rothenberg, *Ch Bd*
Timothy Armour, *CEO*
Gordon Crawford, *Sr VP*
Gina Despres, *Sr VP*
EMP: 500 EST: 1944
SALES (est): 600.28MM
SALES (corp-wide): 5.43B Privately Held
SIC: 6282 Investment research
PA: The Capital Group Companies Inc
    333 S Hope St Fl 55
    Los Angeles CA
    213 486-9200

(P-8198)
FISHER INVESTMENTS INC
13100 Skyline Blvd (94062-4542)
PHONE.................................888 823-9566
EMP: 107
SALES (corp-wide): 974.75MM Privately Held
Web: www.fisherinvestments.com
SIC: 6282 Investment advisory service
PA: Fisher Investments, Inc.
    5525 Nw Fisher Creek Dr
    Camas WA
    888 823-9566

(P-8199)
FORWARD MANAGEMENT LLC
Also Called: Webster Investment Management
244 California St Ste 200 (94111-4308)
P.O. Box 1345 (80201-1345)
PHONE.................................415 869-6300
John Blaisdell, *CEO*
Jeffrey P Cusack, *
Darrell Davis, *
David Chow, *
James Halligan, *
EMP: 100 EST: 1998
SQ FT: 22,000
SALES (est): 24.77MM
SALES (corp-wide): 51.88MM Privately Held
SIC: 6282 Investment advisory service
PA: Salient Partners, L.P.
    4265 San Felipe St Fl 8
    Houston TX
    713 993-4675

(P-8200)
FRANKLIN RESOURCES INC (PA)
Also Called: FRANKLIN
1 Franklin Pkwy (94403-1906)
PHONE.................................650 312-2000
Jennifer M Johnson, *Pr*
Gregory E Johnson, *Ofcr*
Rupert H Johnson Junior, *V Ch Bd*
Matthew Nicholls, *Ex VP*
Thomas C Merchant, *Corporate Secretary*
EMP: 268 EST: 1947
SQ FT: 743,793
SALES (est): 7.85B
SALES (corp-wide): 7.85B Publicly Held
Web: www.franklinresources.com
SIC: 6282 6722 6726 Investment advice; Management investment, open-end; Management investment funds, closed-end

(P-8201)
FRANKLIN TMPLETON INV SVCS LLC
5130 Hacienda Dr Fl 4 (94568-7598)
PHONE.................................925 875-2619
Priscilla Voyer, *Mgr*
EMP: 162
SALES (corp-wide): 7.85B Publicly Held
SIC: 6282 Investment advisory service
HQ: Franklin Templeton Investor Services, Llc
    3344 Quality Dr
    Rancho Cordova CA
    916 463-1500

(P-8202)
HIGHMARK CAPITAL MGT INC
350 California St 12th Fl (94104-1402)
PHONE.................................800 582-4734
Earle Malm, *Pr*
EMP: 93 EST: 1998
SALES (est): 966.02K
SALES (corp-wide): 27.4B Publicly Held
SIC: 6282 Investment advisory service
PA: U.S. Bancorp
    800 Nicollet Mall # 1500
    Minneapolis MN
    651 466-3000

(P-8203)
HOULIHAN LOKEY INC (PA)
10250 Constellation Blvd Fl 5 (90067-6260)
PHONE.................................310 788-5200
Scott L Beiser, *CEO*
Irwin N Gold, *
Scott J Adelson, *
David A Preiser, *
J Lindsey Alley, *CFO*
EMP: 300 EST: 1972
SALES (est): 1.81B
SALES (corp-wide): 1.81B Publicly Held
Web: www.hl.com
SIC: 6282 6211 Investment advice; Security brokers and dealers

(P-8204)
INDEPENDENT FINCL GROUP INC
12636 High Bluff Dr Ste 100 (92130-2022)
PHONE.................................858 436-3180
Scott Heising, *CEO*
EMP: 88 EST: 2003
SALES (est): 8.45MM Privately Held
Web: www.ifgsd.com
SIC: 6282 Investment advice

(P-8205)
JORDAN PARK GROUP LLC
100 Pine St Ste 2600 (94111-5212)
PHONE.................................415 417-3000
Frank Ghali, *Mgr*
EMP: 149 EST: 2017
SALES (est): 5.82MM Privately Held
Web: www.jordanpark.com
SIC: 6282 Investment advisory service

(P-8206)
MARLIN EQUITY PARTNERS LLC (PA)
1301 Manhattan Ave (90254-3654)
PHONE.................................310 364-0100
David Mcgovern, *Managing Member*
Nick Kaiser, *
Peter Spasov, *
George Kase, *
Steve Johnson, *
EMP: 80 EST: 2005
SALES (est): 2.15B Privately Held
Web: www.marlinequity.com
SIC: 6282 3661 Investment advisory service; Telephones and telephone apparatus

(P-8207)
MCMORGAN & COMPANY LLC (HQ)
1 Front St Ste 500 (94111-5327)
PHONE.................................415 788-9300
EMP: 90 EST: 1966
SALES (est): 24.88MM
SALES (corp-wide): 32.05B Privately Held
Web: www.mcmorgan.com
SIC: 6282 Investment advisory service
PA: New York Life Insurance Company
    51 Madison Ave Bsmt 1b
    New York NY
    212 576-7000

(P-8208)
MERCER GLOBAL SECURITIES LLC
Also Called: Mercer Global Securities
1801 E Cabrillo Blvd Ste A (93108-2897)
PHONE.................................805 565-1681
Gene Dongieux, *Mgr*
EMP: 77 EST: 1995
SALES (est): 4.47MM Privately Held
Web: www.merceradvisors.com
SIC: 6282 Investment advisory service

(P-8209)
MORGAN STNLEY SMITH BARNEY LLC
2421 Buhne St (95501-3206)
PHONE.................................707 443-3071
Edward Vaccaro, *Brnch Mgr*
EMP: 62
SALES (corp-wide): 53.67B Publicly Held
Web: www.morganstanley.com
SIC: 6282 Investment advisory service
HQ: Morgan Stanley Smith Barney, Llc
    1585 Broadway
    New York NY

(P-8210)
NATIONAL FINANCIAL SVCS LLC
44 Montgomery St Ste 1900 (94104-4706)
PHONE.................................415 912-2805
Jay Penn, *Prin*
EMP: 861
SALES (corp-wide): 4.35B Privately Held
Web: www.mybrokerageinfo.com
SIC: 6282 Investment advisory service
HQ: National Financial Services Llc
    200 Seaport Blvd Ste 630
    Boston MA
    800 471-0382

(P-8211)
OAKTREE CAPITAL MANAGEMENT LP (DH)
333 S Grand Ave Fl 28 (90071-1530)
PHONE.................................213 830-6300
Jay Wintrob, *CEO*
Todd Molz, *COO*
EMP: 120 EST: 2007
SALES (est): 4.86B
SALES (corp-wide): 69.06B Privately Held
Web: www.oaktreecapital.com
SIC: 6282 6722 6211 Investment advisory service; Management investment, open-end; Security brokers and dealers
HQ: Brookfield Asset Management Llc
    250 Vesey St Fl 15
    New York NY

(P-8212)
PACIFIC ALTRNTIVE ASSET MGT LL (HQ)
Also Called: Paamco
660 Newport Center Dr Ste 930 (92660)
PHONE.................................949 261-4900
Jane Buchan, *CEO*
EMP: 94 EST: 2000
SALES (est): 31.66MM
SALES (corp-wide): 59.99MM Privately Held
Web: www.paamcoprisma.com
SIC: 6282 Investment advisory service
PA: Paamco Prisma Holdings, Llc
    660 Nwport Ctr Dr Ste 930
    Newport Beach CA
    949 261-4900

(P-8213)
PANTHEON VENTURES (US) LP
555 California St Ste 3450 (94104-1503)
PHONE.................................415 249-6200
EMP: 133
SALES (corp-wide): 14.15MM Privately Held
Web: www.pantheon.com
SIC: 6282 Investment advisory service
HQ: Pantheon Ventures (Us) Lp
    11 Times Sq Fl 35
    New York NY

(P-8214)
PAYDEN & RYGEL (PA)
333 S Grand Ave Ste 4000 (90071-1507)
PHONE.................................213 625-1900
Joan Payden, *CEO*
Scott J Weiner, *Managing Principal GLOBAL*
Brian Matthews, *Managing Principal GLOBAL*
Brad Hersh, *
EMP: 140 EST: 1983
SALES (est): 60.97MM
SALES (corp-wide): 60.97MM Privately Held
Web: www.payden.com
SIC: 6282 6211 Investment counselors; Security brokers and dealers

(P-8215)
PERMIRA ADVISERS LLC
3000 Sand Hill Rd Ste 1-170 (94025-7162)
PHONE.................................650 681-4701
Richard Sanders, *Brnch Mgr*
EMP: 662
SALES (corp-wide): 220.02MM Privately Held
Web: www.permira.com
SIC: 6282 Investment advisory service
HQ: Permira Advisers Llc
    320 Park Ave Fl 28
    New York NY
    212 386-7480

6282 - Investment Advice (P-8216)

(P-8216)
PLAN MEMBER FINANCIAL CORP
Also Called: Planmember Services
6187 Carpinteria Ave (93013-2805)
PHONE...............................800 874-6910
Jon Ziehl, *CEO*
Terry Janeway, *
Bill Kemble, *
Trish Stone-damon, *Sec*
EMP: 100 **EST:** 1990
SQ FT: 6,000
SALES (est): 34.06MM **Privately Held**
Web: www.planmember.com
SIC: 6282 Investment counselors

(P-8217)
PROSPECT FINANCIAL GROUP INC
Also Called: Homefinance.com
7825 Fay Ave Ste 160 (92037-4241)
PHONE...............................858 605-0952
Jason Vondrak, *CEO*
EMP: 71 **EST:** 2011
SALES (est): 7.98MM **Privately Held**
Web: www.prospecthomefinance.com
SIC: 6282 Investment advice

(P-8218)
RESEARCH AFFILIATES CAPITAL LP
Also Called: Research Affiliates
620 Newport Center Dr Ste 900 (92660)
PHONE...............................949 325-8700
EMP: 82 **EST:** 2002
SALES (est): 21.79MM **Privately Held**
Web: www.researchaffiliates.com
SIC: 6282 Investment advisory service

(P-8219)
RESEARCH AFFILIATES MGT LLC
Also Called: Research Affiliates
620 Newport Center Dr Ste 900 (92660)
PHONE...............................949 325-8700
Rob Arnott, *CEO*
Jason Hsu, *CIO*
Katrina Sherrerd, *COO*
EMP: 80 **EST:** 2002
SALES (est): 8.23MM **Privately Held**
Web: www.researchaffiliates.com
SIC: 6282 Investment counselors

(P-8220)
RNC CAPITAL MANAGEMENT LLC
Also Called: Rnc Genter Capital Management
11601 Wilshire Blvd (90025)
PHONE...............................310 477-6543
Manny Gutierrez, *
EMP: 65 **EST:** 1968
SQ FT: 20,000
SALES (est): 17.05MM **Privately Held**
Web: www.gentercapitalmanagement.com
SIC: 6282 Investment counselors

(P-8221)
SHAMROCK HOLDINGS INC (PA)
Also Called: Shamrock Holdings California
4444 W Lakeside Dr Ste 150 (91505)
P.O. Box 7774 (91510-7774)
PHONE...............................818 845-4444
Stanley P Gold, *Pr*
Roy E Disney, *
Robert Moskowitz, *
George Buchler, *
▲ **EMP:** 60 **EST:** 1966
SQ FT: 12,000
SALES (est): 14.75MM
SALES (corp-wide): 14.75MM **Privately Held**
Web: www.shamrock.com
SIC: 6282 Manager of mutual funds, contract or fee basis

(P-8222)
TARRANT CAPITAL IP LLC (PA)
Also Called: Tpg Growth
345 California St Ste 3300 (94104-2606)
PHONE...............................415 743-1500
EMP: 5040 **EST:** 2007
SALES (est): 1.38B **Privately Held**
Web: www.tpg.com
SIC: 6282 7372 Manager of mutual funds, contract or fee basis; Prepackaged software

(P-8223)
TCW GROUP INC (PA)
865 S Figueroa St Ste 1800 (90017-2543)
PHONE...............................213 244-0000
David Lippman, *Pr*
Richard M Villa, *
Meredith S Jackson, *
David S Devito, *
Jeffrey Engelsman Global, *Chief Compliance Officer*
EMP: 450 **EST:** 1971
SALES (est): 232.19MM **Privately Held**
SIC: 6282 6211 Investment advisory service; Security brokers and dealers

(P-8224)
THE RROMEO CORPORATION
Also Called: Rreef
101 California St Fl 24 (94111-5898)
PHONE...............................415 781-3300
EMP: 131
SIC: 6282 Investment advisory service

(P-8225)
THOMAS JAMES CAPITAL INC
26940 Aliso Viejo Pkwy Ste 100 (92656-2650)
PHONE...............................949 481-7026
Thomas L Beadel, *Pr*
James Quandt, *
EMP: 150 **EST:** 2006
SQ FT: 1,400
SALES (est): 27.67MM **Privately Held**
Web: www.tjh.com
SIC: 6282 6798 Investment advisory service; Real estate investment trusts

(P-8226)
U S TRUST COMPANY NA
Also Called: US Trust
515 S Flower St Ste 2700 (90071-2216)
PHONE...............................213 861-5000
Tim Leach, *CEO*
EMP: 350 **EST:** 1982
SQ FT: 65,000
SALES (est): 49.71MM
SALES (corp-wide): 94.95B **Publicly Held**
SIC: 6282 6022 Investment advice; State commercial banks
HQ: Bank Of America Pvt Wealth Management
114 W 47th St Ste C-1
New York NY
800 878-7878

(P-8227)
USCF ADVISERS LLC
1999 Harrison St Ste 1530 (94612-4730)
PHONE...............................510 522-9600
Stuart Crumbaugh, *Prin*
EMP: 328 **EST:** 2013
SALES (est): 881.19K **Publicly Held**
Web: www.uscfinvestments.com
SIC: 6282 Investment advisory service
HQ: Wainwright Holdings, Inc.
103 Foulk Rd Ste 202
Wilmington DE
302 656-1950

(P-8228)
WETHERBY ASSET MANAGEMENT LLC
580 California St Fl 8 (94104-1029)
PHONE...............................415 399-9159
Debra L Wetherby, *Pr*
Allan Jacobi, *
Chris Hauswirth, *
EMP: 76 **EST:** 1990
SALES (est): 19.15MM **Privately Held**
Web: www.wetherby.com
SIC: 6282 Investment advisory service

6289 Security And Commodity Service

(P-8229)
AMERICAN FUNDS SERVICE COMPANY (DH)
Also Called: Capital Group
6455 Irvine Center Dr (92618-4518)
PHONE...............................949 975-5000
EMP: 300 **EST:** 1968
SALES (est): 318.47MM
SALES (corp-wide): 5.43B **Privately Held**
Web: www.capitalgroup.com
SIC: 6289 6211 Security transfer agents; Security brokers and dealers
HQ: Capital Research And Management Company
333 S Hope St Fl 55
Los Angeles CA
213 486-9200

(P-8230)
COMPUTERSHARE INC
2335 Alaska Ave (90245-4808)
PHONE...............................800 522-6645
EMP: 240
Web: www.computershare.com
SIC: 6289 Stock transfer agents
HQ: Computershare Inc.
150 Royall St Ste 205
Canton MA

6311 Life Insurance

(P-8231)
ALTERRA SPCALTY INSUR SVCS LTD
201 California St (94111-5002)
PHONE...............................415 490-4615
EMP: 148
SALES (corp-wide): 11.68B **Publicly Held**
SIC: 6311 Life insurance
HQ: Alterra Specialty Insurance Services Limited
9020 Stony Point Pkwy # 32
Richmond VA

(P-8232)
BEST LIFE AND HEALTH INSUR CO
2435 E Coast Hwy Ste 4 (92625-2004)
P.O. Box 19721 (92623-9721)
PHONE...............................949 253-4080
Donald R Lawrenz, *Ch Bd*
Alfred Stoefell, *Stockholder*
EMP: 60 **EST:** 1972
SALES (est): 22.58MM
SALES (corp-wide): 22.58MM **Privately Held**
Web: www.bestlife.com
SIC: 6311 6324 Life insurance carriers; Hospital and medical service plans
PA: Pension Administrators Inc
17701 Mitchell N
Irvine CA
949 253-4080

(P-8233)
GOLDEN STATE MUTL LF INSUR CO (PA)
1999 W Adams Blvd (90018-3514)
P.O. Box 26894 (94126-6894)
PHONE...............................713 526-4361
Larkin Teasley, *Pr*
EMP: 100 **EST:** 1925
SQ FT: 57,000
SALES (est): 48.33MM
SALES (corp-wide): 48.33MM **Privately Held**
SIC: 6311 Mutual association life insurance

(P-8234)
GUARDIAN LIFE INSUR CO AMER
975 San Pasqual St (91106-3368)
PHONE...............................626 792-1935
Bob Daignault, *Brnch Mgr*
EMP: 70
SALES (corp-wide): 3.42B **Privately Held**
Web: www.guardianlife.com
SIC: 6311 Life insurance
PA: Guardian Life Insurance Company Of America
10 Hudson Yards Fl 22
New York NY
212 598-8000

(P-8235)
GUARDIAN LIFE INSUR CO AMER
510 W 6th St Ste 815 (90014-1309)
PHONE...............................213 624-2002
Charles Bogue, *Brnch Mgr*
EMP: 71
SALES (corp-wide): 3.42B **Privately Held**
Web: www.guardianlife.com
SIC: 6311 Life insurance
PA: Guardian Life Insurance Company Of America
10 Hudson Yards Fl 22
New York NY
212 598-8000

(P-8236)
JOHN ALDEN LIFE INSURANCE CO
20950 Warner Center Ln Ste A (91367-6560)
PHONE...............................818 595-7600
Thomas Christenson, *Brnch Mgr*
EMP: 104
SALES (corp-wide): 10.19B **Publicly Held**
SIC: 6311 Life insurance
HQ: Alden John Life Insurance Company
501 W Michigan St
Milwaukee WI
414 271-3011

(P-8237)
JOHN HANCOCK LIFE INSUR CO USA
5000 Birch St Ste 120 (92660-8117)
PHONE...............................949 254-1440
EMP: 94
SALES (corp-wide): 32.83B **Privately Held**
Web: www.johnhancock.com

▲ = Import ▼ = Export
◆ = Import/Export

PRODUCTS & SERVICES SECTION
6321 - Accident And Health Insurance (P-8257)

SIC: 6311 Life insurance
HQ: John Hancock Life Insurance
    Company (U.S.A.)
    865 S Figueroa St # 3320
    Los Angeles CA
    213 689-0813

(P-8238)
KAPOR CENTER FOR SOCIAL IMPACT
2148 Broadway (94612-2310)
PHONE.................510 488-6600
Mitch Kapor, *CEO*
Freada Kapor Klein, *Pt*
Benjamin Todd Jealous, *Pt*
EMP: 70 EST: 2012
SALES (est): 25.99MM **Privately Held**
Web: www.kaporcenter.org
SIC: 6311 Benevolent insurance associations

(P-8239)
MASSACHUSETTS MUTL LF INSUR CO
Also Called: Massmutual
8383 Wilshire Blvd Ste 600 (90211-2425)
PHONE.................323 965-6339
Grant D Fraser, *Brnch Mgr*
EMP: 60
SALES (corp-wide): 10.36B **Privately Held**
Web: www.fraserfinancialgroup.com
SIC: 6311 Life insurance
PA: Massachusetts Mutual Life Insurance
    Company
    1295 State St
    Springfield MA
    413 744-8411

(P-8240)
MASSMUTUAL PACIFIC
Also Called: MASSMUTUAL PACIFIC
1435 River Park Dr Ste 410 (95815-4509)
PHONE.................916 437-1713
EMP: 127
SALES (corp-wide): 8.28MM **Privately Held**
Web: northerncalifornia.massmutual.com
SIC: 6311 Life insurance carriers
PA: Massmutual Pacific, Inc.
    3003 Oak Rd Ste 250
    Walnut Creek CA
    925 949-7400

(P-8241)
NEW FIRST FINCL RESOURCES LLC
100 Spectrum Center Dr Ste 400
(92618-4962)
PHONE.................949 223-2160
EMP: 212 EST: 1987
SALES (est): 23.6MM **Privately Held**
Web: www.ffrmembers.com
SIC: 6311 Life insurance

(P-8242)
NORTHWESTERN MUTL FINCL NETWRK (PA)
4225 Executive Sq Ste 1250 (92037-9122)
PHONE.................619 234-3111
Garrett J Bleakley, *Owner*
EMP: 100 EST: 1952
SALES (est): 43.25MM **Privately Held**
Web: www.northwesternmutual.com
SIC: 6311 Life insurance

(P-8243)
PACIFIC ASSET HOLDING LLC
700 Newport Center Dr (92660-6307)
PHONE.................949 219-3011
EMP: 237 EST: 1997
SALES (est): 8.48MM
SALES (corp-wide): 12.84B **Privately Held**
SIC: 6311 6371 6321 Life insurance carriers;
    Pension funds; Accident insurance carriers
HQ: Pacific Life Insurance Company
    700 Newport Center Dr
    Newport Beach CA
    949 219-3011

(P-8244)
PACIFIC LIFE & ANNUITY COMPANY
700 Newport Center Dr (92660-6307)
P.O. Box 9000 (92658-9030)
PHONE.................949 219-3011
James Morris, *Pr*
Khanh T Tran, *
Audrey L Milfs, *
Brian Klemens, *
EMP: 650 EST: 1982
SQ FT: 125,000
SALES (est): 203.9MM
SALES (corp-wide): 12.84B **Privately Held**
Web: www.pacificlife.com
SIC: 6311 6411 Life insurance carriers;
    Insurance agents, brokers, and service
HQ: Pacific Life Insurance Company
    700 Newport Center Dr
    Newport Beach CA
    949 219-3011

(P-8245)
PATRA CORPORATION (PA)
1107 Investment Blvd Ste 100 (95762)
PHONE.................415 595-9987
Dan Easterlin, *Pr*
Bob Murphy, *
EMP: 90 EST: 2007
SALES (est): 887.89MM
SALES (corp-wide): 887.89MM **Privately Held**
Web: www.patracorp.com
SIC: 6311 Life insurance

(P-8246)
PROVIDENT LF ACCIDENT INSUR CO
Also Called: Provident
1277 Treat Blvd Ste 300 (94597-7952)
PHONE.................925 944-4700
Peggy Hill, *Mgr*
EMP: 69
SQ FT: 1,200
Web: www.unum.com
SIC: 6311 Life insurance
HQ: Provident Life & Accident Insurance
    Company
    1 Fountain Sq Ste 1 # 1
    Chattanooga TN
    423 755-1011

(P-8247)
SUNAMERICA LIFE INSURANCE COMPANY
Also Called: SunAmerica
1 Sun America Ctr Fl 36 (90067-6100)
PHONE.................310 772-6000
EMP: 225
SIC: 6311 Life insurance

(P-8248)
TRANSAMERICA CORPORATION
600 Montgomery St Fl 16 (94111-2704)
PHONE.................415 392-9742
Frank Herringer, *Prin*
EMP: 64
Web: www.transamerica.com
SIC: 6311 Life insurance

HQ: Transamerica Corporation
    4333 Edgewood Rd
    Cedar Rapids IA
    319 398-8511

(P-8249)
TRANSAMERICA FINANCE CORP (DH)
600 Montgomery St Fl 16 (94111-2718)
PHONE.................415 983-4000
Robert A Watson, *Ch Bd*
Robert R Mcduff, *Sr VP*
Phillip Rice, *
Thomas G Bastian, *
Stephen H Foltz, *
EMP: 112 EST: 1931
SALES (est): 60.52MM **Privately Held**
SIC: 6311 Life insurance
HQ: Transamerica Corporation
    4333 Edgewood Rd
    Cedar Rapids IA
    319 398-8511

(P-8250)
TRANSAMERICA OCCIDENTAL LIFE INSURANCE COMPANY
1150 S Olive St Fl 23 (90015-2477)
P.O. Box 2101 (90078-2101)
PHONE.................213 742-2111
EMP: 3700
SIC: 6311 6371 6321 6324 Life insurance
    carriers; Pension funds; Health insurance
    carriers; Group hospitalization plans

(P-8251)
TRUCK UNDERWRITERS ASSOCIATION
Farmers Insurance
6303 Owensmouth Ave Fl 1 (91367-2200)
PHONE.................323 932-3200
Jane Franklin, *VP*
EMP: 1078
SQ FT: 275,000
Web: www.farmers.com
SIC: 6311 6331 6321 Life insurance; Fire,
    marine, and casualty insurance; Accident
    and health insurance
HQ: Truck Underwriters Association
    4680 Wilshire Blvd
    Los Angeles CA
    323 932-3200

(P-8252)
WCF SELECT INSURANCE COMPANY
1465 N Mcdowell Blvd Ste 100
(94954-6569)
P.O. Box 970 (63366-0970)
PHONE.................415 899-2000
D Andrew Torrance, *Ch*
Jill E Paterson, *Ex VP*
Cynthia L Pevehouse, *Sr VP*
Linda E Wright, *Sr VP*
EMP: 131 EST: 1922
SQ FT: 240,000
SALES (est): 3.51MM
SALES (corp-wide): 27.99B **Privately Held**
SIC: 6311 6321 6331 6351 Life insurance
    carriers; Accident insurance carriers; Fire,
    marine and casualty insurance and carriers;
    Surety insurance
HQ: Fireman's Fund Insurance Company
    1 Progress Point Pkwy # 200
    O Fallon MO
    415 899-2000

(P-8253)
WESTERN NATIONAL LIFE INSUR CO
Also Called: AIG
1395 Creekside Dr (94596-7412)
PHONE.................925 946-5100
Elaine Woolery, *Mgr*
EMP: 247
SALES (corp-wide): 56.44B **Publicly Held**
Web: www.aig.com
SIC: 6311 Life insurance
HQ: Western National Life Insurance
    Company
    2929 Allen Pkwy Ste 3800
    Houston TX
    713 522-1111

6321 Accident And Health Insurance

(P-8254)
21ST CENTURY LF & HLTH CO INC (PA)
Also Called: Lifecare Assurance Company
21600 Oxnard St Ste 1500 (91367-4972)
P.O. Box 4243 (91365-4243)
PHONE.................818 887-4436
James M Glickman, *Pr*
Alan S Hughes, *
Daniel J Di Sipio, *
Jay R Peters Fsa, *Ex VP*
Pete Diffley, *
▲ EMP: 241 EST: 1980
SQ FT: 50,000
SALES (est): 326.99MM **Privately Held**
Web: www.lifecareassurance.com
SIC: 6321 Health insurance carriers

(P-8255)
ADVISE HEALTH HOLDINGS LLC
476 Jackson St Fl 2 (94111-1623)
PHONE.................415 723-1723
EMP: 84
SALES (corp-wide): 81.91K **Privately Held**
SIC: 6321 Health insurance carriers
PA: Advise Health Holdings, Llc
    2200 Atlantic St Ste 300
    Stamford CT
    203 717-1350

(P-8256)
AGENT FRANCHISE LLC
9518 9th St Ste C2 (91730-4546)
PHONE.................949 930-5025
EMP: 101 EST: 2014
SQ FT: 14,980
SALES (est): 22.4MM **Privately Held**
Web: www.agentfranchise.com
SIC: 6321 Accident and health insurance

(P-8257)
ALLIANZ REINSURANCE AMER INC
1465 N Mcdowell Blvd (94954-6570)
P.O. Box 750039 (94975-0039)
PHONE.................415 899-2000
Joe Beneducci, *Pr*
EMP: 287 EST: 1956
SQ FT: 240,000
SALES (est): 61.4MM
SALES (corp-wide): 27.99B **Privately Held**
SIC: 6321 Reinsurance carriers, accident
    and health
HQ: Fireman's Fund Insurance Company
    1 Progress Point Pkwy # 200
    O Fallon MO
    415 899-2000

6321 - Accident And Health Insurance (P-8258)

(P-8258)
AUTO CLUB ENTERPRISES (PA)
3333 Fairview Rd Ms A451 (92626-1610)
P.O. Box 25001 (92799-5001)
PHONE.................................714 850-5111
Robert T Bouttier, *CEO*
Thomas Mc Kernon, *
Henry Reza Toofanian, *
John F Boyle, *
Avery Brown, *
EMP: 1200 **EST:** 1912
SQ FT: 700,000
SALES (est): 1.37B
SALES (corp-wide): 1.37B **Privately Held**
SIC: 6321 Accident and health insurance

(P-8259)
AUTO CLUB ENTERPRISES
8761 Santa Monica Blvd (90069-4538)
PHONE.................................310 914-8500
Bob Szhwab, *Mgr*
EMP: 500
SALES (corp-wide): 1.37B **Privately Held**
SIC: 6321 Accident and health insurance
PA: Auto Club Enterprises
    3333 Fairview Rd Msa451
    Costa Mesa CA
    714 850-5111

(P-8260)
CARE 1ST HEALTH PLAN (PA)
601 Potrero Grande Dr Fl 2 (91755-7430)
PHONE.................................323 889-6638
Maureen Tyson, *Pr*
Anna Tran, *
Janet Jan, *
Michael Rowan, *
Jamie Ueoka, *
EMP: 165 **EST:** 1994
SALES (est): 169.66MM **Privately Held**
Web: www.blueshieldca.com
SIC: 6321 Health insurance carriers

(P-8261)
CARELON MED BENEFITS MGT INC
505 N Brand Blvd (91203-1906)
PHONE.................................847 310-0366
EMP: 586
SALES (corp-wide): 156.59B **Publicly Held**
Web: www.careloninsights.com
SIC: 6321 Health insurance carriers
HQ: Carelon Medical Benefits
    Management, Inc.
    8600 W Bryn Mawr Ave Tw
    Chicago IL

(P-8262)
CAREMORE HEALTH PLAN (HQ)
Also Called: Caremore Insurance Services
12900 Park Plaza Dr Ste 150 (90703-9329)
PHONE.................................562 622-2950
TOLL FREE: 888
Leeba R Lessin, *Sup Chief Executive Officer*
Allan Hoops, *CEO*
Sergio Zaldivar, *Senior Vice President Corporate Development*
John Kao, *OF MANAGEMENT SERVICES ORGANIZATION*
Doctor Ken Kin Md, *Chief Medical Officer*
EMP: 148 **EST:** 1996
SALES (est): 111.92MM
SALES (corp-wide): 156.59B **Publicly Held**
Web: www.caremore.com
SIC: 6321 Health insurance carriers
PA: Elevance Health, Inc.
    220 Virginia Ave
    Indianapolis IN
    800 331-1476

(P-8263)
DOCTORS COMPANY FOUNDATION
185 Greenwood Rd (94558-6270)
PHONE.................................800 421-2368
Richard E Anderson, *CEO*
EMP: 755 **EST:** 2014
SALES (est): 580K **Privately Held**
Web: www.thedoctors.com
SIC: 6321 Health insurance carriers

(P-8264)
EMPOWER ANNUITY INSUR CO AMER
Also Called: Great-West Healthcare
500 N Central Ave Ste 220 (91203-1928)
PHONE.................................818 409-0880
Steven Ferri, *Brnch Mgr*
EMP: 79
SALES (corp-wide): 48.16B **Privately Held**
Web: www.empower.com
SIC: 6321 Accident and health insurance
HQ: Empower Annuity Insurance Company Of America
    8515 E Orchard Rd
    Greenwood Village CO
    866 317-6586

(P-8265)
HI-Q INC
Also Called: Health Iq
2513 Charleston Rd (94043-1634)
PHONE.................................800 549-1664
Min Kyu Lee, *CEO*
Debbie Hee Lee, *Sec*
EMP: 288 **EST:** 1987
SALES (est): 63.45MM **Privately Held**
Web: www.healthequitylabs.com
SIC: 6321 Accident and health insurance

(P-8266)
INLAND EMPIRE HEALTH PLAN (PA)
Also Called: Iehp
10801 6th St Ste 120 (91730-5987)
P.O. Box 1400 (91729-1400)
PHONE.................................909 890-2000
Jarrod Mcnaughton, *CEO*
Bob Buster, *
Chet Uma, *
Supriya Sood, *
Randee Roberts, *
EMP: 850 **EST:** 1994
SQ FT: 72,000
SALES (est): 715.81MM **Privately Held**
Web: www.iehp.org
SIC: 6321 6324 Health insurance carriers; Health Maintenance Organization (HMO), insurance only

(P-8267)
LIFECARE ASSURANCE COMPANY
21600 Oxnard St Fl 16 (91367-4976)
PHONE.................................818 887-4436
James Glickman, *Pr*
Alan S Hughes, *
Daniel J Disipio, *
Peter Diffley, *
Dick Sato, *
EMP: 246 **EST:** 1988
SQ FT: 35,000
SALES (est): 326.99MM **Privately Held**
Web: www.lifecareassurance.com
SIC: 6321 6411 6311 Accident and health insurance; Insurance agents, brokers, and service; Life insurance
PA: 21st Century Life And Health Company, Inc.
    21600 Oxnard St Ste 1500
    Woodland Hills CA

(P-8268)
MD CARE INC
Also Called: MD Care Healthplan
1640 E Hill St (90755-3612)
P.O. Box 14165 (40512-4165)
PHONE.................................562 344-3400
EMP: 75 **EST:** 2004
SALES (est): 18.29MM
SALES (corp-wide): 54.38B **Publicly Held**
SIC: 6321 Health insurance carriers
PA: Humana Inc.
    500 W Main St Ste 300
    Louisville KY
    502 580-1000

(P-8269)
MOLINA HLTHCARE CAL PRTNER PLA
200 Oceangate Ste 100 (90802-4317)
PHONE.................................562 435-3666
Richard Chambers, *CEO*
J Mario Molina, *
John Kotal, *
Doctor James Howatt, *Chief Medical Officer*
Terry Bayer, *
EMP: 314 **EST:** 1980
SALES (est): 4.31M
SALES (corp-wide): 31.97B **Publicly Held**
Web: www.molinahealthcare.com
SIC: 6321 8011 Health insurance carriers; Clinic, operated by physicians
PA: Molina Healthcare, Inc.
    200 Oceangate Ste 100
    Long Beach CA
    562 435-3666

(P-8270)
SANTA BRBARA SAN LUIS OBSPO RG
Also Called: Cencal Health
4050 Calle Real (93110-3413)
PHONE.................................800 421-2560
Robert Freeman, *CEO*
Kashina Bishop, *
EMP: 140 **EST:** 2009
SALES (est): 66.19MM **Privately Held**
Web: www.cencalhealth.org
SIC: 6321 Accident and health insurance

(P-8271)
SANTE HEALTH SYSTEM INC (PA)
Also Called: Sante Community Physicians
7370 N Palm Ave Ste 101 (93711-5782)
P.O. Box 1507 (93716-1507)
PHONE.................................559 228-5400
Mateo F Desoto, *CEO*
Scott Wells, *
Debbie Keena, *
Chris Cheney, *
EMP: 85 **EST:** 1994
SQ FT: 20,000
SALES (est): 171.94MM **Privately Held**
Web: www.santehealth.net
SIC: 6321 7371 Accident and health insurance; Computer software development and applications

(P-8272)
STATE COMPENSATION INSUR FUND
2901 N Ventura Rd Ste 100 (93036-1126)
PHONE.................................888 782-8338
Martin Goldman, *Mgr*
EMP: 90
SALES (corp-wide): 2.76B **Privately Held**
Web: www.statefundca.com
SIC: 6321 9651 Disability health insurance; Insurance commission, government
PA: State Compensation Insurance Fund
    333 Bush St Ste 800
    San Francisco CA
    888 782-8338

(P-8273)
WESTERN HEALTH ADVANTAGE
2349 Gateway Oaks Dr Ste 100 (95833-4244)
PHONE.................................916 567-1950
Garry Maisel, *Pr*
Rita Ruecker, *
EMP: 100 **EST:** 1995
SQ FT: 25,000
SALES (est): 674.43MM **Privately Held**
Web: www.westernhealth.com
SIC: 6321 Health insurance carriers

6324 Hospital And Medical Service Plans

(P-8274)
ADMAR CORPORATION
1551 N Tustin Ave Ste 300 (92705-8638)
P.O. Box 1049 (92702-1049)
PHONE.................................714 953-9600
Kraig Boysen, *Pr*
Virginia Pascual, *
Ed Evans, *
EMP: 160 **EST:** 1973
SQ FT: 37,000
SALES (est): 62.76MM
SALES (corp-wide): 1.08B **Publicly Held**
SIC: 6324 Hospital and medical service plans
PA: Multiplan Corporation
    640 5th Ave Fl 12
    New York NY
    212 380-7500

(P-8275)
AETNA HEALTH CALIFORNIA INC (DH)
Also Called: Aetna
1401 Willow Pass Rd Ste 600 (94520-7927)
P.O. Box 818024 (44181-8024)
PHONE.................................925 543-9223
Kristen Ann Miranda, *CEO*
Edward Chung-i Lee, *Sec*
Tracy Louis Smith, *
EMP: 198 **EST:** 1979
SALES (est): 383.17MM
SALES (corp-wide): 322.47B **Publicly Held**
Web: www.aetna.com
SIC: 6324 Health Maintenance Organization (HMO), insurance only
HQ: Aetna Inc.
    151 Farmington Ave
    Hartford CT

(P-8276)
ALAMEDA ALLIANCE FOR HEALTH
1240 S Loop Rd (94502-7084)
PHONE.................................510 747-4555
EMP: 135 **EST:** 1993
SQ FT: 50,000
SALES (est): 86.85MM **Privately Held**
Web: www.alamedaalliance.org

6324 - Hospital And Medical Service Plans (P-8295)

SIC: 6324 Health Maintenance Organization (HMO), insurance only

(P-8277)
ALIGNMENT HEALTH PLAN
Also Called: Citizens Choice Health Plan
1100 W Town And Country Rd Ste 1600 (92868-4600)
PHONE.................................323 728-7232
Chuck Weber, *Pr*
Elizabeth Tejada, *
Charlotte Leblanc, *CAO**
EMP: 90 EST: 2003
SALES (est): 23.16MM
SALES (corp-wide): 1.43B **Publicly Held**
Web: www.alignmenthealthplan.com
SIC: 6324 Health Maintenance Organization (HMO), insurance only
PA: Alignment Healthcare, Inc.
   1100 W Twn Cntry Rd # 1600
   Orange CA
   844 310-2247

(P-8278)
ALIGNMENT HEALTHCARE INC (PA)
Also Called: Alignment Health
1100 W Town And Country Rd Ste 1600 (92868-4698)
PHONE.................................844 310-2247
John Kao, *CEO*
Joseph Konowiecki, *Ch Bd*
Thomas Freeman, *CFO*
Dinesh Kumar, *CMO*
Richard Cross, *Sr VP*
EMP: 64 EST: 2013
SQ FT: 89,000
SALES (est): 1.43B
SALES (corp-wide): 1.43B **Publicly Held**
Web: www.alignmenthealth.com
SIC: 6324 7372 Hospital and medical service plans; Prepackaged software

(P-8279)
AMERICAN SPCLTY HLTH GROUP INC
10221 Wateridge Cir Ste 201 (92121-2702)
PHONE.................................858 754-2000
George T Devries, *CEO*
Robert White, *COO*
Kevin E Kujawa, *CIO*
Marcel Danko, *CFO*
▲ EMP: 500 EST: 1987
SQ FT: 148,000
SALES (est): 105.93MM **Privately Held**
Web: www.ashcompanies.com
SIC: 6324 Hospital and medical service plans
PA: American Specialty Health Incorporated
   12800 N Meridian St # 190
   Carmel IN

(P-8280)
ANTHEM INSURANCE COMPANIES INC
Also Called: Anthem
5260 N Palm Ave Ste 215 (93704-2209)
PHONE.................................559 230-6200
EMP: 94
SALES (corp-wide): 156.59B **Publicly Held**
Web: www.anthem.com
SIC: 6324 Hospital and medical service plans
HQ: Anthem Insurance Companies, Inc.
   220 Virginia Ave
   Indianapolis IN
   317 488-6000

(P-8281)
ANTHEM INSURANCE COMPANIES INC
Also Called: Anthem
2 Embarcadero Ctr Ste 1310 (94111-3823)
PHONE.................................415 617-1700
EMP: 94
SALES (corp-wide): 156.59B **Publicly Held**
Web: www.anthem.com
SIC: 6324 Hospital and medical service plans
HQ: Anthem Insurance Companies, Inc.
   220 Virginia Ave
   Indianapolis IN
   317 488-6000

(P-8282)
BLUE CROSS OF CALIFORNIA (HQ)
Also Called: Blue Cross
21215 Burbank Blvd Ste 630 (91367-7091)
PHONE.................................805 557-6050
Mark Morgan, *Pr*
Thomas C Geiser, *
Kenneth C Zurek, *
EMP: 118 EST: 1992
SQ FT: 427,104
SALES (est): 84.43MM
SALES (corp-wide): 156.59B **Publicly Held**
SIC: 6324 6411 Health Maintenance Organization (HMO), insurance only; Insurance agents, brokers, and service
PA: Elevance Health, Inc.
   220 Virginia Ave
   Indianapolis IN
   800 331-1476

(P-8283)
BLUE SHIELD CAL LF HLTH INSUR
4005 Manzanita Ave Ste 6 (95608-1779)
P.O. Box 629015 (95762-9015)
PHONE.................................800 660-3007
EMP: 1324
SALES (corp-wide): 8.08B **Privately Held**
Web: www.blueshieldca.com
SIC: 6324 Hospital and medical service plans
HQ: Blue Shield Of California Life & Health Insurance Co
   50 Beale St Ste 2000
   San Francisco CA
   415 229-5000

(P-8284)
BLUE SHIELD CAL LF HLTH INSUR
2275 Rio Bonito Way Ste 250 (92108-1685)
PHONE.................................619 686-4200
Matthew Leming, *Prin*
EMP: 1324
SALES (corp-wide): 8.08B **Privately Held**
Web: www.blueshieldca.com
SIC: 6324 Hospital and medical service plans
HQ: Blue Shield Of California Life & Health Insurance Co
   50 Beale St Ste 2000
   San Francisco CA
   415 229-5000

(P-8285)
BLUE SHIELD OF CA
3300 Zinfandel Dr (95670-6043)
PHONE.................................916 841-0584
Rhonda Meredith, *Prin*
EMP: 72 EST: 2016
SALES (est): 1.52MM **Privately Held**
Web: www.blueshieldca.com

SIC: 6324 Hospital and medical service plans

(P-8286)
CALIFORNIA PHYSICIANS SERVICE (PA)
Also Called: Blue Shield of California
601 12th St (94607-3885)
P.O. Box 272540 (95927-2540)
PHONE.................................510 607-2000
Paul Markovich, *Pr*
Paul Markovich, *Pr*
Sandra Clarke, *
Jeffrey Robertson, *CMO**
Lisa Davis, *CIO**
EMP: 900 EST: 1939
SQ FT: 120,000
SALES (est): 8.08B
SALES (corp-wide): 8.08B **Privately Held**
Web: www.blueshieldca.com
SIC: 6324 Hospital and medical service plans

(P-8287)
CALIFORNIA PHYSICIANS SERVICE
4700 Bechelli Ln (96002-3506)
PHONE.................................530 351-6115
EMP: 70
SALES (corp-wide): 8.08B **Privately Held**
Web: www.blueshieldca.com
SIC: 6324 Hospital and medical service plans
PA: California Physicians' Service
   601 12th St
   Oakland CA
   510 607-2000

(P-8288)
CALIFORNIA PHYSICIANS SERVICE
Also Called: Blue Shield of California
3840 Kilroy Airport Way (90806-2452)
PHONE.................................310 744-2668
Aubrey Chernick, *Brnch Mgr*
EMP: 88
SALES (corp-wide): 8.08B **Privately Held**
Web: www.blueshieldca.com
SIC: 6324 Hospital and medical service plans
PA: California Physicians' Service
   601 12th St
   Oakland CA
   510 607-2000

(P-8289)
CALIFORNIA PHYSICIANS SERVICE
Also Called: Blue Shield of California
6300 Canoga Ave Ste A (91367-8000)
PHONE.................................818 598-8000
John Headberg, *Brnch Mgr*
EMP: 210
SALES (corp-wide): 8.08B **Privately Held**
Web: www.blueshieldca.com
SIC: 6324 Hospital and medical service plans
PA: California Physicians' Service
   601 12th St
   Oakland CA
   510 607-2000

(P-8290)
CALIFORNIA PHYSICIANS SERVICE
Also Called: Blue Shield of California
5250 N Palm Ave Ste 120 (93704-2200)
PHONE.................................559 440-4000
Mark Turley, *Dir*
EMP: 88
SALES (corp-wide): 8.08B **Privately Held**
Web: www.blueshieldca.com
SIC: 6324 Hospital and medical service plans
PA: California Physicians' Service
   601 12th St
   Oakland CA
   510 607-2000

(P-8291)
CENTER FOR ELDERS INDEPENDENCE
Also Called: C E I
510 17th St Ste 400 (94612-1504)
PHONE.................................510 433-1150
Peter Szutu, *Pr*
EMP: 225 EST: 1981
SALES (est): 110.88MM **Privately Held**
Web: cei.elders.org
SIC: 6324 Hospital and medical service plans

(P-8292)
CIGNA BEHAVIORAL HEALTH OF CAL
Also Called: Cigna
450 N Brand Blvd Ste 500 (91203-4414)
PHONE.................................800 753-0540
EMP: 401 EST: 2014
SALES (est): 3.97MM
SALES (corp-wide): 180.52B **Publicly Held**
SIC: 6324 Health Maintenance Organization (HMO), insurance only
HQ: Evernorth Behavioral Health, Inc
   11095 Viking Dr Ste 350
   Eden Prairie MN

(P-8293)
CIGNA HEALTHCARE CAL INC (DH)
Also Called: Cigna
400 N Brand Blvd Ste 400 (91203-2306)
P.O. Box 188045 (37422-8045)
PHONE.................................818 500-6262
TOLL FREE: 800
Leroy Volberding, *Pr*
David Yeager, *Contrlr*
EMP: 400 EST: 1968
SQ FT: 110,000
SALES (est): 259.02MM
SALES (corp-wide): 180.52B **Publicly Held**
Web: www.cigna.com
SIC: 6324 Health Maintenance Organization (HMO), insurance only
HQ: Healthsource, Inc.
   1750 Elm St Ste 800
   Manchester NH
   603 268-7000

(P-8294)
COUNTY OF LOS ANGELES
Also Called: Community Hlth Plan Off MGT Ca
1000 S Fremont Ave Unit 4 (91803-8859)
PHONE.................................626 299-5300
Dave Beck, *Dir*
EMP: 91
SALES (corp-wide): 31.7B **Privately Held**
Web: www.lacounty.gov
SIC: 6324 9431 Hospital and medical service plans; Mental health agency administration, government
PA: County Of Los Angeles
   500 W Temple St Ste 437
   Los Angeles CA
   213 974-1101

(P-8295)
DELTA DENTAL OF CALIFORNIA (PA)
560 Mission St Ste 1300 (94105-0938)
PHONE.................................415 972-8300
Mike Castro, *CEO*

6324 - Hospital And Medical Service Plans (P-8296)

Sarah Chavarria, *Pr*
Nilesh Patel, *Ex VP*
Charles Lamont, *Ex VP*
EMP: 487 **EST:** 1955
SQ FT: 241,000
SALES (est): 5.41B
SALES (corp-wide): 5.41B **Privately Held**
Web: www.deltadentalins.com
SIC: 6324 Dental insurance

(P-8296)
DELTA DENTAL OF CALIFORNIA
Also Called: Delta Dental Plan
11155 International Dr (95826)
PHONE.................................916 853-7373
EMP: 94
SALES (corp-wide): 5.41B **Privately Held**
Web: www.deltadental.com
SIC: 6324 Dental insurance
PA: Delta Dental Of California
560 Mission St Ste 1300
San Francisco CA
415 972-8300

(P-8297)
DENTISTS INSURANCE COMPANY (HQ)
Also Called: Tdic
1201 K St Ste 1600 (95814-3906)
P.O. Box 1582 (95812-1582)
PHONE.................................916 443-4567
Mark Soeth, *Pr*
EMP: 118 **EST:** 1979
SQ FT: 12,000
SALES (est): 15.76MM
SALES (corp-wide): 15.89MM **Privately Held**
Web: www.tdicinsurance.com
SIC: 6324 Dental insurance
PA: California Dental Association Inc
1201 K St Fl 14
Sacramento CA
916 443-0505

(P-8298)
HEALTH NET LLC (HQ)
21650 Oxnard St (91367-7829)
PHONE.................................818 676-6000
Jay M Gellert, *Pr*
James E Woys, *Interim Treasurer**
Juanell Hefner, ***
Angelee F Bouchard, ***
Rich Hall, *ACTURIAL**
EMP: 250 **EST:** 2015
SQ FT: 115,488
SALES (est): 1.52B **Publicly Held**
Web: www.healthnet.com
SIC: 6324 6311 Hospital and medical service plans; Life insurance carriers
PA: Centene Corporation
7700 Forsyth Blvd Ste 800
Saint Louis MO

(P-8299)
HEALTH NET LLC
6013 Niles St (93306-4696)
PHONE.................................661 321-3904
EMP: 168
Web: www.healthnet.com
SIC: 6324 Hospital and medical service plans
HQ: Health Net, Llc
21650 Oxnard St Fl 25
Woodland Hills CA
818 676-6000

(P-8300)
HEALTH NET FEDERAL SVCS LLC (DH)
Also Called: Health Net
10730 International Dr (95670-7359)
P.O. Box 989734 (95798-9734)
PHONE.................................916 935-5000
Thomas F Carrato, *Pr*
EMP: 700 **EST:** 1989
SQ FT: 100,000
SALES (est): 472.86MM **Publicly Held**
Web: www.healthnetfederalservices.com
SIC: 6324 Hospital and medical service plans
HQ: Health Net Of California, Inc.
7700 Forsyth Blvd
Saint Louis MO
818 676-6775

(P-8301)
HEALTH NET INC
21650 Oxnard St Fl 25 (91367-7829)
PHONE.................................818 676-6000
EMP: 8014
SIC: 6324 6311 Hospital and medical service plans; Life insurance carriers

(P-8302)
HEALTH NET PHARMACEUTICAL SVCS
Also Called: Health Net
2868 Prospect Park Dr (95670-6020)
PHONE.................................800 977-7532
EMP: 126 **EST:** 2019
SALES (est): 18.23MM **Publicly Held**
Web: www.healthnet.com
SIC: 6324 Hospital and medical service plans
PA: Centene Corporation
7700 Forsyth Blvd Ste 800
Saint Louis MO

(P-8303)
HEALTH PLAN OF SAN JOAQUIN
7751 S Manthey Rd (95231-9802)
PHONE.................................209 942-6300
Michael Schrader, *CEO*
EMP: 120 **EST:** 1994
SALES (est): 67.05MM **Privately Held**
Web: www.hpsj.com
SIC: 6324 Health Maintenance Organization (HMO), insurance only

(P-8304)
INLAND EMPIRE HEALTH PLAN
805 W 2nd St Ste C (92410-3255)
P.O. Box 1800 (91729-1800)
PHONE.................................866 228-4347
EMP: 1945
Web: www.iehp.org
SIC: 6324 8742 Health Maintenance Organization (HMO), insurance only; Hospital and health services consultant
PA: Inland Empire Health Plan
10801 6th St Ste 120
Rancho Cucamonga CA

(P-8305)
KAISER FNDTION HLTH PLAN GA IN
1850 California Ave (92881-3378)
PHONE.................................951 270-1200
Anita Ward, *Mgr*
EMP: 379
SALES (corp-wide): 68.1B **Privately Held**
Web: www.kaiserpermanente.org
SIC: 6324 Hospital and medical service plans
HQ: Kaiser Foundation Health Plan Of Georgia, Inc.
3495 Piedmont Rd Ne # 9
Atlanta GA
404 364-7000

(P-8306)
KAISER FNDTION HOSP GIFT SHPPE
Also Called: Dept of Cardiologist
6041 Cadillac Ave (90034-1702)
PHONE.................................323 857-3290
Ron Golden, *Mgr*
EMP: 171
SALES (corp-wide): 2.75MM **Privately Held**
Web: www.kaiserpermanentelocations.net
SIC: 6324 Hospital and medical service plans
PA: Kaiser Foundation Hospital Gift Shoppe
200 Muir Rd
Martinez CA
925 372-1000

(P-8307)
KAISER FOUNDATION HOSPITALS
Also Called: Kaiser Permanente
3750 Grand Ave (91710-5478)
PHONE.................................888 750-0036
Jonathan Rothchild, *Mgr*
EMP: 114
SALES (corp-wide): 68.1B **Privately Held**
Web: www.kaisercenter.com
SIC: 6324 Hospital and medical service plans
HQ: Kaiser Foundation Hospitals Inc
1 Kaiser Plz
Oakland CA
510 271-6611

(P-8308)
KAISER FOUNDATION HOSPITALS
4785 N 1st St Fl 2 (93726-0513)
PHONE.................................559 448-4620
EMP: 61
SALES (corp-wide): 68.1B **Privately Held**
Web: www.kaisercenter.com
SIC: 6324 Hospital and medical service plans
HQ: Kaiser Foundation Hospitals Inc
1 Kaiser Plz
Oakland CA
510 271-6611

(P-8309)
KAISER FOUNDATION HOSPITALS
270 International Cir (95119-1130)
PHONE.................................408 972-6560
EMP: 64
SALES (corp-wide): 68.1B **Privately Held**
Web: www.kaisercenter.com
SIC: 6324 Hospital and medical service plans
HQ: Kaiser Foundation Hospitals Inc
1 Kaiser Plz
Oakland CA
510 271-6611

(P-8310)
KAISER FOUNDATION HOSPITALS
Also Called: Kaiser Foundation Health Plan
9201 Big Horn Blvd (95758-1240)
PHONE.................................916 478-5000
Calvin Tong-fong, *Mgr*
EMP: 196
SALES (corp-wide): 68.1B **Privately Held**
Web: www.kaiserpermanente.org
SIC: 6324 Hospital and medical service plans
HQ: Kaiser Foundation Hospitals Inc
1 Kaiser Plz
Oakland CA
510 271-6611

(P-8311)
KAISER FOUNDATION HOSPITALS
Also Called: Kaiser Permanente
1011 Baldwin Park Blvd (91706-5806)
PHONE.................................626 851-1011
Linda Margarita Gutierrez, *Prin*
EMP: 793
SALES (corp-wide): 68.1B **Privately Held**
Web: www.starbucks.com
SIC: 6324 Hospital and medical service plans
HQ: Kaiser Foundation Hospitals Inc
1 Kaiser Plz
Oakland CA
510 271-6611

(P-8312)
KAISER FOUNDATION HOSPITALS
Also Called: Kaiser Prmnente Downey Med Ctr
9333 Imperial Hwy (90242-2812)
PHONE.................................562 657-9000
Gemma Abad, *Brnch Mgr*
EMP: 410
SALES (corp-wide): 68.1B **Privately Held**
Web: www.kaisercenter.com
SIC: 6324 Hospital and medical service plans
HQ: Kaiser Foundation Hospitals Inc
1 Kaiser Plz
Oakland CA
510 271-6611

(P-8313)
KAISER FOUNDATION HOSPITALS
Also Called: Kaiser Foundation Health Plan
1761 Broadway St Ste 210 (94589-2227)
PHONE.................................707 645-2720
Cynthia Chandler, *Dir*
EMP: 306
SALES (corp-wide): 68.1B **Privately Held**
Web: www.kaiserpermanente.org
SIC: 6324 Hospital and medical service plans
HQ: Kaiser Foundation Hospitals Inc
1 Kaiser Plz
Oakland CA
510 271-6611

(P-8314)
KAISER FOUNDATION HOSPITALS
Also Called: Kaiser Foundation Health Plan
10305 Promenade Pkwy (95757-9400)
PHONE.................................916 544-6000
EMP: 85
SALES (corp-wide): 68.1B **Privately Held**
Web: www.kaiserpermanente.org
SIC: 6324 Hospital and medical service plans
HQ: Kaiser Foundation Hospitals Inc
1 Kaiser Plz
Oakland CA
510 271-6611

(P-8315)
KAISER FOUNDATION HOSPITALS
Also Called: Kaiser Fndtion Rhblitation Ctr
975 Sereno Dr (94589-2441)
PHONE.................................707 651-1000
Steve Allen, *Dir*
EMP: 146
SALES (corp-wide): 68.1B **Privately Held**
Web: www.kaiserpermanente.org
SIC: 6324 Hospital and medical service plans
HQ: Kaiser Foundation Hospitals Inc
1 Kaiser Plz
Oakland CA
510 271-6611

(P-8316)
KAISER FOUNDATION HOSPITALS

6324 - Hospital And Medical Service Plans (P-8335)

Also Called: La Mesa Medical Offices
8080 Parkway Dr (91942-2104)
PHONE..................619 528-5000
Caroline Wu, *Prin*
EMP: 111
SALES (corp-wide): 68.1B **Privately Held**
Web: www.kaisercenter.com
SIC: 6324 Hospital and medical service plans
HQ: Kaiser Foundation Hospitals Inc
1 Kaiser Plz
Oakland CA
510 271-6611

(P-8317)
KAISER FOUNDATION HOSPITALS
Also Called: Kaiser Permanente
1249 S Sunset Ave (91790-3960)
PHONE..................866 319-4269
Jane Lau, *Mgr*
EMP: 76
SALES (corp-wide): 68.1B **Privately Held**
Web: www.kaisercenter.com
SIC: 6324 Hospital and medical service plans
HQ: Kaiser Foundation Hospitals Inc
1 Kaiser Plz
Oakland CA
510 271-6611

(P-8318)
KAISER FOUNDATION HOSPITALS
Also Called: Novato Medical Offices
97 San Marin Dr (94945-1100)
PHONE..................415 899-7400
Margaret R Hill, *Prin*
EMP: 120
SALES (corp-wide): 68.1B **Privately Held**
Web: www.kaisercenter.com
SIC: 6324 Hospital and medical service plans
HQ: Kaiser Foundation Hospitals Inc
1 Kaiser Plz
Oakland CA
510 271-6611

(P-8319)
KAISER FOUNDATION HOSPITALS
Also Called: Kaiser Permanente Division RES
2000 Brdwy (94612)
PHONE..................510 891-3400
Joe Shelby Md, *Dir*
EMP: 292
SQ FT: 86,875
SALES (corp-wide): 68.1B **Privately Held**
Web: www.kaisercenter.com
SIC: 6324 Hospital and medical service plans
HQ: Kaiser Foundation Hospitals Inc
1 Kaiser Plz
Oakland CA
510 271-6611

(P-8320)
KAISER FOUNDATION HOSPITALS
Also Called: Kaiser Foundation Health Plan
25 N Via Monte (94598-2510)
PHONE..................925 926-3000
Phil Newbold, *Prin*
EMP: 70
SQ FT: 79,360
SALES (corp-wide): 68.1B **Privately Held**
Web: www.kaiserpermanente.org
SIC: 6324 Hospital and medical service plans
HQ: Kaiser Foundation Hospitals Inc
1 Kaiser Plz
Oakland CA
510 271-6611

(P-8321)
KAISER FOUNDATION HOSPITALS
Also Called: Kaiser Prmnnte S Scrmnto Med C
6600 Bruceville Rd (95823-4671)
PHONE..................916 688-2000
Sarah Krevans, *Brnch Mgr*
EMP: 3600
SALES (corp-wide): 68.1B **Privately Held**
Web: www.kpcosmeticservices.com
SIC: 6324 Hospital and medical service plans
HQ: Kaiser Foundation Hospitals Inc
1 Kaiser Plz
Oakland CA
510 271-6611

(P-8322)
KAISER FOUNDATION HOSPITALS
Also Called: Kaiser Permanente
12470 Whittier Blvd (90602-1017)
PHONE..................866 340-5974
Beth Lopez, *Prin*
EMP: 143
SALES (corp-wide): 68.1B **Privately Held**
Web: www.kaisercenter.com
SIC: 6324 Hospital and medical service plans
HQ: Kaiser Foundation Hospitals Inc
1 Kaiser Plz
Oakland CA
510 271-6611

(P-8323)
KAISER FOUNDATION HOSPITALS
Also Called: Kaiser Foundation Health Plan
2071 Herndon Ave (93611-6101)
PHONE..................559 324-5100
Angela H Kuo Md, *Brnch Mgr*
EMP: 123
SQ FT: 67,465
SALES (corp-wide): 68.1B **Privately Held**
Web: www.kaiserpermanente.org
SIC: 6324 Hospital and medical service plans
HQ: Kaiser Foundation Hospitals Inc
1 Kaiser Plz
Oakland CA
510 271-6611

(P-8324)
KAISER FOUNDATION HOSPITALS
Also Called: Kaiser Foundation Health Plan
395 Hickey Blvd (94015-2770)
PHONE..................650 301-5860
Arthur Chin, *Prin*
EMP: 67
SALES (corp-wide): 68.1B **Privately Held**
Web: www.kaiserpermanente.org
SIC: 6324 Hospital and medical service plans
HQ: Kaiser Foundation Hospitals Inc
1 Kaiser Plz
Oakland CA
510 271-6611

(P-8325)
KAISER FOUNDATION HOSPITALS
Also Called: Kaiser Foundation Health Plan
5900 State Farm Dr Ste 100 (94928-2149)
PHONE..................707 206-3000
Noel Smith, *Brnch Mgr*
EMP: 87
SALES (corp-wide): 68.1B **Privately Held**
Web: www.kaiserpermanente.org
SIC: 6324 Hospital and medical service plans
HQ: Kaiser Foundation Hospitals Inc
1 Kaiser Plz
Oakland CA
510 271-6611

(P-8326)
KAISER FOUNDATION HOSPITALS
Also Called: Kaiser Foundation Health Plan
1539 W Garvey Ave N (91790-2139)
PHONE..................626 856-3045
Kwame Okoreeh, *Mgr*
EMP: 82
SQ FT: 10,403
SALES (corp-wide): 68.1B **Privately Held**
Web: www.kaiserpermanente.org
SIC: 6324 Hospital and medical service plans
HQ: Kaiser Foundation Hospitals Inc
1 Kaiser Plz
Oakland CA
510 271-6611

(P-8327)
KAISER FOUNDATION HOSPITALS
Also Called: Kaiser Foundation Health Plan
9961 Sierra Ave (92335-6720)
P.O. Box None (92335)
PHONE..................909 427-3910
Gerald Mc Call, *Brnch Mgr*
EMP: 347
SALES (corp-wide): 68.1B **Privately Held**
Web: www.kaiserpermanente.org
SIC: 6324 Hospital and medical service plans
HQ: Kaiser Foundation Hospitals Inc
1 Kaiser Plz
Oakland CA
510 271-6611

(P-8328)
KAISER FOUNDATION HOSPITALS
Also Called: Kaiser Foundation Health Plan
12200 Bellflower Blvd (90242-2804)
PHONE..................562 622-4190
Jim Harrington, *Brnch Mgr*
EMP: 143
SALES (corp-wide): 68.1B **Privately Held**
Web: www.kaiserpermanente.org
SIC: 6324 Hospital and medical service plans
HQ: Kaiser Foundation Hospitals Inc
1 Kaiser Plz
Oakland CA
510 271-6611

(P-8329)
KAISER FOUNDATION HOSPITALS
Also Called: Kaiser Foundation Health Plan
2345 Fair Oaks Blvd (95825-4708)
PHONE..................916 973-5000
Jerry Newman, *Mgr*
EMP: 129
SALES (corp-wide): 68.1B **Privately Held**
Web: www.kaiserpermanente.org
SIC: 6324 Hospital and medical service plans
HQ: Kaiser Foundation Hospitals Inc
1 Kaiser Plz
Oakland CA
510 271-6611

(P-8330)
KAISER FOUNDATION HOSPITALS
Also Called: Kaiser Foundation Health Plan
5755 Cottle Rd (95123-3640)
PHONE..................408 972-3376
Donald D Mordecai, *Brnch Mgr*
EMP: 102
SALES (corp-wide): 68.1B **Privately Held**
Web: www.kp2020.org
SIC: 6324 8011 6321 Hospital and medical service plans; Offices and clinics of medical doctors; Accident and health insurance
HQ: Kaiser Foundation Hospitals Inc
1 Kaiser Plz
Oakland CA
510 271-6611

(P-8331)
KAISER FOUNDATION HOSPITALS
Also Called: Kaiser Foundation Health Plan
11666 Sherman Way (91605-5831)
PHONE..................818 503-7082
Charles Ford, *Mgr*
EMP: 163
SALES (corp-wide): 68.1B **Privately Held**
Web: www.kaiserpermanente.org
SIC: 6324 Hospital and medical service plans
HQ: Kaiser Foundation Hospitals Inc
1 Kaiser Plz
Oakland CA
510 271-6611

(P-8332)
KAISER FOUNDATION HOSPITALS
Also Called: Kaiser Foundation Health Plan
7520 Arroyo Cir (95020-7303)
PHONE..................408 848-4600
Gary Zuselt, *Brnch Mgr*
EMP: 347
SQ FT: 62,360
SALES (corp-wide): 68.1B **Privately Held**
Web: www.kaiserpermanente.org
SIC: 6324 Hospital and medical service plans
HQ: Kaiser Foundation Hospitals Inc
1 Kaiser Plz
Oakland CA
510 271-6611

(P-8333)
KAISER FOUNDATION HOSPITALS
Also Called: Kaiser Foundation Health Plan
7300 N Fresno St (93720-2941)
PHONE..................559 44. 4500
Jeffrey Collins, *Mgr*
EMP: 2356
SALES (corp-wide): 68.1B **Privately Held**
Web: www.kaisercenter.com
SIC: 6324 Hospital and medical service plans
HQ: Kaiser Foundation Hospitals Inc
1 Kaiser Plz
Oakland CA
510 271-6611

(P-8334)
KAISER FOUNDATION HOSPITALS
Also Called: Kaiser Permanente
1795 2nd St (94710-1704)
PHONE..................510 559-5362
David Newkom, *Dir*
EMP: 726
SALES (corp-wide): 68.1B **Privately Held**
Web: www.kaisercenter.com
SIC: 6324 Health Maintenance Organization (HMO), insurance only
HQ: Kaiser Foundation Hospitals Inc
1 Kaiser Plz
Oakland CA
510 271-6611

(P-8335)
KAISER FOUNDATION HOSPITALS
Also Called: Kaiser Foundation Health Plan
1625 I St (95354-1121)

6324 - Hospital And Medical Service Plans (P-8336)

P.O. Box 577680 (95357-7680)
PHONE..................................209 557-1000
EMP: 269
SALES (corp-wide): 68.1B **Privately Held**
Web: www.kaiserpermanente.org
SIC: 6324 Health Maintenance Organization (HMO), insurance only
HQ: Kaiser Foundation Hospitals Inc
1 Kaiser Plz
Oakland CA
510 271-6611

(P-8336)
KAISER FUNDATION HLTH PLAN INC
Also Called: Kaiser Foundation Health Plan
4460 Hacienda Dr (94588-2761)
PHONE..................................510 271-5800
Linsey Dicks, *Mgr*
EMP: 100
SALES (corp-wide): 68.1B **Privately Held**
Web: www.kaiserpermanente.org
SIC: 6324 Health Maintenance Organization (HMO), insurance only
PA: Kaiser Foundation Health Plan, Inc.
1 Kaiser Plz
Oakland CA
510 271-5800

(P-8337)
KAISER PERMANENTE
5105 W Goldleaf Cir (90056-1269)
PHONE..................................323 298-3100
EMP: 63 EST: 2017
SALES (est): 4.74MM **Privately Held**
Web: thrive.kaiserpermanente.org
SIC: 6324 Hospital and medical service plans

(P-8338)
KAISER PERMANENTE
9985 Sierra Ave (92335-6720)
PHONE..................................909 427-3910
Terry Bellmonte, *Prin*
EMP: 164 EST: 2002
SALES (est): 18.36MM **Privately Held**
SIC: 6324 Hospital and medical service plans

(P-8339)
LIBERTY DENTAL PLAN CAL INC
340 Commerce Ste 100 (92602-1358)
PHONE..................................949 223-0007
Amir Hossein Neshat, *Prin*
Maja Kapic, *
EMP: 300 EST: 2001
SALES (est): 64.64MM **Privately Held**
Web: www.libertydentalplan.com
SIC: 6324 Dental insurance

(P-8340)
LIBERTY DENTAL PLAN CORP (PA)
340 Commerce Ste 100 (92602-1358)
PHONE..................................888 703-6999
Marti Lolli, *Pr*
Rohan C Reid, *
Amir Neshat, *
Rosa Roldan, *Chief Dental Officer**
EMP: 99 EST: 2007
SALES (est): 98.23MM
SALES (corp-wide): 98.23MM **Privately Held**
Web: www.libertydentalplan.com
SIC: 6324 Dental insurance

(P-8341)
LOCAL INTTIVE HLTH AUTH FOR LO (PA)
Also Called: L.A. Care Health Plan
1055 W 7th St Fl 10 (90017-2750)
PHONE..................................213 694-1250
John Baackes, *CEO*
Richard Seidman, *CMO**
Dino Kasdagly, *
Marie Montgomery, *
EMP: 894 EST: 1995
SALES (est): 701.73MM **Privately Held**
Web: www.lacare.org
SIC: 6324 Health Maintenance Organization (HMO), insurance only

(P-8342)
MANAGED DENTAL CARE
Also Called: Managed Dental Care California
6200 Canoga Ave Ste 100 (91367-2426)
PHONE..................................818 598-6599
Michael Gould, *Pr*
EMP: 184 EST: 1990
SALES (est): 1.71MM
SALES (corp-wide): 3.42B **Privately Held**
Web: www.manageddentalcare.net
SIC: 6324 Dental insurance
PA: Guardian Life Insurance Company Of America
10 Hudson Yards Fl 22
New York NY
212 598-8000

(P-8343)
MANAGED HEALTH NETWORK
Also Called: Managed Health
7755 Center Ave Ste 700 (92647-9126)
PHONE..................................714 934-5519
Carol Mclean, *Brnch Mgr*
EMP: 257
Web: www.mhn.com
SIC: 6324 Hospital and medical service plans
HQ: Managed Health Network
2370 Kerner Blvd
San Rafael CA

(P-8344)
MANAGED HEALTH NETWORK
Also Called: Managed Health
625 Ellis St Ste 100 (94043-2225)
PHONE..................................650 988-4842
David Mccourt, *Brnch Mgr*
EMP: 240
Web: www.mhn.com
SIC: 6324 Hospital and medical service plans
HQ: Managed Health Network
2370 Kerner Blvd
San Rafael CA

(P-8345)
MANAGED HEALTH NETWORK (DH)
Also Called: Managed Health
2370 Kerner Blvd (94901-5613)
P.O. Box 10207 (94912-0207)
PHONE..................................415 460-8168
Jeffrey Bairstow, *CEO*
Steven Sell, *Pr*
Nancy Diamond, *Sec*
John Volkober, *Treas*
Jonathan Wormhoudt, *COO*
EMP: 500 EST: 1982
SQ FT: 97,314
SALES (est): 335.72MM **Publicly Held**
Web: www.mhn.com
SIC: 6324 8099 8093 8011 Hospital and medical service plans; Medical services organization; Specialty outpatient clinics, nec; Offices and clinics of medical doctors
HQ: Health Net, Llc
21650 Oxnard St Fl 25
Woodland Hills CA
818 676-6000

(P-8346)
MOLINA HEALTHCARE INC
1500 Hughes Way (90810-1870)
PHONE..................................310 221-3031
EMP: 63
SALES (corp-wide): 31.97B **Publicly Held**
Web: www.molinahealthcare.com
SIC: 6324 6321 Hospital and medical service plans; Accident and health insurance
PA: Molina Healthcare, Inc.
200 Oceangate Ste 100
Long Beach CA
562 435-3666

(P-8347)
ON LOK SENIOR HEALTH SERVICES (PA)
Also Called: On Lok Lifeways
1333 Bush St (94109-5691)
PHONE..................................415 292-8888
Robert Edmondson, *CEO*
Sue Wong, *
Eileen Kunz, *
Grace Li, *COO*
Valorie Villela, *
EMP: 570 EST: 1971
SQ FT: 40,000
SALES (est): 210.34MM
SALES (corp-wide): 210.34MM **Privately Held**
Web: www.onlok.org
SIC: 6324 8082 Health Maintenance Organization (HMO), insurance only; Home health care services

(P-8348)
OPTUMRX INC
Also Called: Prescription Solutions
2858 Loker Ave E Ste 100 (92010-6673)
P.O. Box 2975 (66201-1375)
PHONE..................................760 804-2399
Sean O'rourke, *Mgr*
EMP: 400
SALES (corp-wide): 324.16B **Publicly Held**
Web: www.optumrx.com
SIC: 6324 Hospital and medical service plans
HQ: Optumrx, Inc.
2300 Main St
Irvine CA

(P-8349)
OPTUMRX INC (DH)
Also Called: Optumrx PBM Administrator Cal
2300 Main St (92614-6223)
P.O. Box 509075 (92150-9075)
PHONE..................................714 825-3600
John Michael Prince, *CEO*
Timothy Wicks, *Pr*
Jeff Park, *COO*
Jeffrey Grosklags, *CFO*
EMP: 300 EST: 1990
SALES (est): 23.01B
SALES (corp-wide): 324.16B **Publicly Held**
Web: www.optumrx.com
SIC: 6324 6321 Hospital and medical service plans; Accident and health insurance
HQ: Optum, Inc.
11000 Optum Cir
Eden Prairie MN
952 936-1300

(P-8350)
PACIFCARE HLTH PLAN ADMNSTRTOR (DH)
Also Called: Pacificare
3120 W Lake Center Dr (92704-6917)
P.O. Box 25186 (92799-5186)
PHONE..................................714 825-5200
David Reed, *Ch Bd*
Coy F Baugh, *Treas*
EMP: 400 EST: 1975
SQ FT: 220,000
SALES (est): 1.02B
SALES (corp-wide): 324.16B **Publicly Held**
SIC: 6324 Group hospitalization plans
HQ: Pacificare Health Systems, Llc
5995 Plaza Dr
Cypress CA

(P-8351)
PARTNERSHIP HEALTH PLAN CAL
4665 Business Center Dr (94534-1675)
PHONE..................................707 863-4100
Jack Horn, *CEO*
Gary Erickson, *
Liz Gibboney, *
EMP: 290 EST: 1994
SQ FT: 75,000
SALES (est): 188.2MM **Privately Held**
Web: www.partnershiphp.org
SIC: 6324 Health Maintenance Organization (HMO), insurance only

(P-8352)
PERMANENTE KAISER INTL (HQ)
Also Called: Kp International
1 Kaiser Plz (94612-3610)
PHONE..................................510 271-5910
Raymond J Baxter, *CEO*
Kathy Lancaster, *
Bechara Choucair, *CCHO**
Nari Gopala, *Chief Digital Officer**
Greg Holmes, *Chief Human Resources Officer**
EMP: 352 EST: 2009
SALES (est): 526.66MM
SALES (corp-wide): 68.1B **Privately Held**
SIC: 6324 Hospital and medical service plans
PA: Kaiser Foundation Health Plan, Inc.
1 Kaiser Plz
Oakland CA
510 271-5800

(P-8353)
PERMANENTE MEDICAL GROUP INC
220 Oyster Point Blvd (94080-1911)
PHONE..................................650 827-6500
Milan Patel, *Brnch Mgr*
EMP: 418
SALES (corp-wide): 68.1B **Privately Held**
Web: www.permanente.org
SIC: 6324 Hospital and medical service plans
HQ: The Permanente Medical Group Inc
1950 Franklin St Fl 7th
Oakland CA
866 858-2226

(P-8354)
PERMANENTE MEDICAL GROUP INC
900 Veterans Blvd Ste 400 (94063-1742)
PHONE..................................650 598-2852
Diana Patino, *Brnch Mgr*
EMP: 522
SALES (corp-wide): 68.1B **Privately Held**
Web: www.permanente.org
SIC: 6324 Hospital and medical service plans
HQ: The Permanente Medical Group Inc
1950 Franklin St Fl 7th
Oakland CA
866 858-2226

PRODUCTS & SERVICES SECTION
6324 - Hospital And Medical Service Plans (P-8373)

(P-8355)
PERMANENTE MEDICAL GROUP INC
1725 Eastshore Hwy (94710-1703)
PHONE.................510 559-5119
Susan Yee, Admn
EMP: 522
SALES (corp-wide): 68.1B Privately Held
Web: www.permanente.org
SIC: 6324 Hospital and medical service plans
HQ: The Permanente Medical Group Inc
1950 Franklin St Fl 7th
Oakland CA
866 858-2226

(P-8356)
PERMANENTE MEDICAL GROUP INC
3555 Whipple Rd (94587-1507)
PHONE.................510 675-4010
Deana Medinas, Dir
EMP: 731
SALES (corp-wide): 68.1B Privately Held
Web: www.permanente.org
SIC: 6324 Hospital and medical service plans
HQ: The Permanente Medical Group Inc
1950 Franklin St Fl 7th
Oakland CA
866 858-2226

(P-8357)
PRIVATE MEDICAL-CARE INC
12898 Towne Center Dr (90703-8546)
PHONE.................562 924-8311
Robert Elliott, Pr
EMP: 1689 EST: 1970
SALES (est): 4.62MM
SALES (corp-wide): 5.41MM Privately Held
SIC: 6324 Dental insurance
PA: Delta Dental Of California
560 Mission St Ste 1300
San Francisco CA
415 972-8300

(P-8358)
SAFEGUARD HEALTH ENTPS INC (HQ)
95 Enterprise Ste 100 (92656-2605)
PHONE.................800 880-1800
Steven J Baileys D.d.s., Ch Bd
James E Buncher, Pr
Stephen J Baker, Ex VP
Ronald I Brendzel, Sr VP
Dennis L Gates, Sr VP
EMP: 355 EST: 1974
SQ FT: 68,000
SALES (est): 92.41MM
SALES (corp-wide): 69.9B Publicly Held
Web: www.metlife.com
SIC: 6324 Dental insurance
PA: Metlife, Inc.
200 Park Ave Fl 1200
New York NY
212 578-9500

(P-8359)
SCAN GROUP (PA)
3800 Kilroy Airport Way Ste 100 (90806-2494)
PHONE.................562 308-2733
Sachin H Jain, Pr
Linda Rosenstock, *
Janet Kornblatt, *
Michael Plumb, *
Deepa Sheth, Chief Corporate Development Officer*
EMP: 306 EST: 1983
SALES (est): 6.11MM
SALES (corp-wide): 6.11MM Privately Held

Web: www.scanhealthplan.com
SIC: 6324 Health Maintenance Organization (HMO), insurance only

(P-8360)
SENIOR CARE (PA)
Also Called: Scan Health Plan
3800 Kilroy Airport Way (90806-2494)
P.O. Box 22616 (90801-5616)
PHONE.................562 989-5100
David Schmidt, CEO
Dennis Eder, *
EMP: 650 EST: 1978
SQ FT: 119,219
SALES (est): 113.83MM
SALES (corp-wide): 113.83MM Privately Held
Web: www.scanhealthplan.com
SIC: 6324 Health Maintenance Organization (HMO), insurance only

(P-8361)
SHARP HEALTH PLAN
8520 Tech Way Ste 200 (92123-1450)
PHONE.................858 499-8300
Melissa Hayden-cook, Pr
Rita Datko, *
Leslie Pels-beck, VP
Michael Byrd, Chief Business Development Officer*
Doctor Cary Shames, Chief Medical Officer
EMP: 98 EST: 1992
SALES (est): 918.72MM
SALES (corp-wide): 2.37B Privately Held
Web: www.sharphealthplan.com
SIC: 6324 Health Maintenance Organization (HMO), insurance only
PA: Sharp Healthcare
8695 Spectrum Center Blvd
San Diego CA
858 499-4000

(P-8362)
SOUTHERN CAL PRMNNTE MED GROUP
13652 Cantara St (91402-5423)
PHONE.................800 272-3500
Arthur Phelps, Brnch Mgr
EMP: 468
SALES (corp-wide): 68.1B Privately Held
Web: www.permanente.org
SIC: 6324 Hospital and medical service plans
HQ: Southern California Permanente Medical Group
393 Walnut Dr
Pasadena CA
626 405-5704

(P-8363)
SOUTHERN CAL PRMNNTE MED GROUP
Also Called: Southern California Permanente Medical Group
10800 Magnolia Ave (92505-3043)
PHONE.................866 984-7483
Jeffrey A Weisz, Prin
EMP: 158
SALES (corp-wide): 68.1B Privately Held
Web: www.permanente.org
SIC: 6324 Hospital and medical service plans
HQ: Southern California Permanente Medical Group
393 Walnut Dr
Pasadena CA
626 405-5704

(P-8364)
SOUTHERN CAL PRMNNTE MED GROUP

1511 W Garvey Ave N (91790-2138)
PHONE.................626 960-4844
EMP: 283
SALES (corp-wide): 68.1B Privately Held
Web: www.permanente.org
SIC: 6324 Hospital and medical service plans
HQ: Southern California Permanente Medical Group
393 Walnut Dr
Pasadena CA
626 405-5704

(P-8365)
SOUTHERN CAL PRMNNTE MED GROUP
Also Called: Tustin Executive Center
17542 17th St Ste 300 (92780-1960)
PHONE.................714 734-4500
Adamma Agufoh, Dir
EMP: 223
SALES (corp-wide): 68.1B Privately Held
Web: www.permanente.org
SIC: 6324 Hospital and medical service plans
HQ: Southern California Permanente Medical Group
393 Walnut Dr
Pasadena CA
626 405-5704

(P-8366)
SOUTHERN CAL PRMNNTE MED GROUP
Also Called: S C P M G
1255 W Arrow Hwy (91773-2340)
PHONE.................909 394-2505
EMP: 182
SALES (corp-wide): 68.1B Privately Held
Web: www.permanente.org
SIC: 6324 Hospital and medical service plans
HQ: Southern California Permanente Medical Group
393 Walnut Dr
Pasadena CA
626 405-5704

(P-8367)
SOUTHERN CAL PRMNNTE MED GROUP
Also Called: SOUTHERN CALIFORNIA PERMANENTE MEDICAL GROUP
6860 Avenida Encinas (92011-3201)
PHONE.................619 528-5000
Walter Borschel, Admn
EMP: 182
SALES (corp-wide): 68.1B Privately Held
Web: www.permanente.org
SIC: 6324 Hospital and medical service plans
HQ: Southern California Permanente Medical Group
393 Walnut Dr
Pasadena CA
626 405-5704

(P-8368)
SOUTHERN CAL PRMNNTE MED GROUP
Also Called: Kaiser Foundation Health Plan
5855 Copley Dr Ste 250 (92111-7908)
PHONE.................858 974-1000
Tom Cooper, Mgr
EMP: 367
SQ FT: 89,984
SALES (corp-wide): 68.1B Privately Held
Web: www.kaiserpermanente.org
SIC: 6324 Health Maintenance Organization (HMO), insurance only
HQ: Southern California Permanente Medical Group
393 Walnut Dr
Pasadena CA
626 405-5704

(P-8369)
SOUTHERN CAL PRMNNTE MED GROUP (HQ)
Also Called: Kaiser Permanente
393 Walnut St (91107-4922)
PHONE.................626 405-5704
Gregory Adams, Ch
Anthony A Barrueta, Prin
Vanessa M Benavides, Prin
Chuck Columbus, Prin
Ramin Davidoff, Ch Bd
EMP: 60 EST: 1981
SQ FT: 600,000
SALES (est): 1.78B
SALES (corp-wide): 68.1B Privately Held
Web: www.permanente.org
SIC: 6324 8741 Health Maintenance Organization (HMO), insurance only; Management services
PA: Kaiser Foundation Health Plan, Inc.
1 Kaiser Plz
Oakland CA
510 271-5800

(P-8370)
UHC OF CALIFORNIA (DH)
Also Called: Pacificare Health Systems
5995 Plaza Dr (90630-5028)
PHONE.................952 936-6615
Brad A Bowlus, Principal Health Plan
Joseph S Konowiecki, *
Michael Montevideo, *
EMP: 800 EST: 1975
SALES (est): 478.68MM
SALES (corp-wide): 324.16B Publicly Held
SIC: 6324 8732 Health Maintenance Organization (HMO), insurance only; Commercial nonphysical research
HQ: Pacificare Health Systems, Llc
5995 Plaza Dr
Cypress CA

(P-8371)
VALLEY HEALTH PLAN
2480 N 1st St Ste 160 (95131-1014)
P.O. Box 26160 (95159-6160)
PHONE.................408 885-4760
Greg Price, CEO
EMP: 561 EST: 1986
SALES (est): 10.05MM Privately Held
Web: www.valleyhealthplan.org
SIC: 6324 Hospital and medical service plans
PA: County Of Santa Clara
70 W Hedding St
San Jose CA
408 299-5200

(P-8372)
VISION SERVICE PLAN (PA)
Also Called: C V S Optical Lab Div
3333 Quality Dr (95670-7985)
PHONE.................916 851-5000
Michael J Guyette, Pr
Chris Warren, CLO*
Kate Renwick-espinosa, CIO
Alec Mahmood, *
▲ EMP: 1600 EST: 1955
SQ FT: 300,000
SALES (est): 1.89B
SALES (corp-wide): 1.89B Privately Held
Web: www.vsp.com
SIC: 6324 5048 Hospital and medical service plans; Ophthalmic goods

(P-8373)
VIVIO HEALTH INC
1933 Davis St Ste 274 (94577-1263)
PHONE.................925 365-6600
Pramod John, CEO

6331 Fire, Marine, And Casualty Insurance

EMP: 60 EST: 2016
SALES (est): 11.12MM **Privately Held**
Web: www.viviohealth.com
SIC: 6324 Hospital and medical service plans

(P-8374)
ALLIANZ GLOBL RISKS US INSUR
Also Called: Allianz Insurance Company
1465 N Mcdowell Blvd (94954-6569)
PHONE................................415 899-3758
Lori Oaks, Mgr
EMP: 400
SALES (corp-wide): 27.99B **Privately Held**
Web: commercial.allianz.com
SIC: 6331 Fire, marine, and casualty insurance
HQ: Allianz Global Risks Us Insurance Company
 2350 W Empire Ave
 Burbank CA

(P-8375)
ALLIANZ GLOBL RISKS US INSUR (DH)
Also Called: Allianz Insurance Company
2350 W Empire Ave Ste 200 (91504-3350)
P.O. Box 970 (63366-0970)
EMP: 175 EST: 1938
SQ FT: 20,000
SALES (est): 243.05MM
SALES (corp-wide): 27.99B **Privately Held**
Web: commercial.allianz.com
SIC: 6331 Property damage insurance
HQ: Fireman's Fund Insurance Company
 1 Progress Point Pkwy # 200
 O Fallon MO
 415 899-2000

(P-8376)
ALLIED INSURANCE
1601 Exposition Blvd (95815-5103)
P.O. Box 182171 (43218-2171)
PHONE................................916 924-4000
EMP: 500
Web: www.nationwide.com
SIC: 6331 Fire, marine, and casualty insurance

(P-8377)
ARROWHEAD GEN INSUR AGCY INC (HQ)
701 B St Ste 2100 (92101-8197)
PHONE................................619 881-8600
Chris L Walker, CEO
Steve Boydm, Prin
Steve Boyd, *
Scott Marshall, *
Stephen M Lesieur, *
EMP: 240 EST: 1983
SQ FT: 74,000
SALES (est): 145.88MM
SALES (corp-wide): 3.05B **Publicly Held**
Web: www.arrowheadgrp.com
SIC: 6331 6411 Automobile insurance; Insurance agents, brokers, and service
PA: Brown & Brown, Inc.
 300 N Beach St
 Daytona Beach FL
 386 252-9601

(P-8378)
BERKSHIRE HATHAWAY HOME SERVIC
11409 Carson St (90715-2512)
PHONE................................562 809-1331
EMP: 82
SALES (corp-wide): 2.56MM **Privately Held**
Web: www.brucemulhearn.com
SIC: 6331 Property damage insurance
PA: Berkshire Hathaway Home Services Ca Roperties
 18000 Studebaker Rd # 600
 Cerritos CA
 562 860-2625

(P-8379)
CALIFORNIA CAPITAL INSUR CO (HQ)
Also Called: Capital Insurance Group
2300 Garden Rd (93940-5326)
P.O. Box 3110 (93942-3110)
PHONE................................831 233-5500
Lindsay Chatterton, Pr
Thomas Scherff, Claims Vice President*
Walter Benett, Underwriting Vice President*
Radhakrishna Mydam, CIO*
Davis Tyndall, *
EMP: 142 EST: 1898
SQ FT: 50,000
SALES (est): 252.59MM
SALES (corp-wide): 2.41B **Privately Held**
SIC: 6331 Fire, marine and casualty insurance and carriers
PA: Auto-Owners Insurance Company
 6101 Anacapri Blvd
 Lansing MI
 517 323-1200

(P-8380)
CALIFORNIA CASUALTY MGT CO (HQ)
Also Called: California Casualty
1875 S Grant St Ste 800 (94402-2647)
PHONE................................650 574-4000
Carl B Brown, Ch Bd
Joseph L Volponi, Pr
Michael Ray, Ex VP
James R Englese, Sr VP
▲ EMP: 135 EST: 1917
SALES (est): 126.89MM
SALES (corp-wide): 239.88MM **Privately Held**
Web: www.calcas.com
SIC: 6331 8741 Reciprocal interinsurance exchanges: fire, marine, casualty; Management services
PA: California Casualty Indemnity Exchange
 1900 Almeda De Las Pulgas
 San Mateo CA
 650 574-4000

(P-8381)
CALIFRNIA CSLTY INDEMNITY EXCH (PA)
1900 Alameda De Las Pulgas (94403-1222)
PHONE................................650 574-4000
Thomas R Brown, Ch
Mike Ray, *
EMP: 130 EST: 1914
SQ FT: 90,000
SALES (est): 239.88MM
SALES (corp-wide): 239.88MM **Privately Held**
SIC: 6331 Workers' compensation insurance

(P-8382)
COMPWEST INSURANCE COMPANY
100 Pringle Ave Ste 515 (94596-3558)
PHONE................................415 593-5100
William J Mudge, Pr
Patrick Persse, *
EMP: 140 EST: 2004
SALES (est): 33.93MM **Privately Held**
Web: www.compwestinsurance.com
SIC: 6331 Reciprocal interinsurance exchanges: fire, marine, casualty

(P-8383)
GEOVERA SPECIALTY INSURANCE CO
1455 Oliver Rd (94534-3472)
PHONE................................707 863-3700
EMP: 60 EST: 1996
SALES (est): 23.44MM **Privately Held**
Web: www.geovera.com
SIC: 6331 Property damage insurance
PA: Geovera Holdings, Inc.
 4820 Bsneca Ctr Dr Ste 20
 Fairfield CA

(P-8384)
GOLDEN EAGLE INSURANCE CORP (DH)
Also Called: Golden Eagle
525 B St Ste 1300 (92101-4421)
P.O. Box 85826 (92186-5826)
PHONE................................619 744-6000
J Paul Condrin Iii, CEO
Frank J Kotarba, *
EMP: 250 EST: 1997
SALES (est): 206.53MM
SALES (corp-wide): 20.63B **Privately Held**
SIC: 6331 Property damage insurance
HQ: Liberty Mutual Insurance Company
 175 Berkeley St
 Boston MA
 617 357-9500

(P-8385)
HARTFORD CASUALTY INSURANCE CO
Also Called: Hartford
101 Montgomery St Ste 2700 (94104-4179)
PHONE................................415 836-4800
William Reynolds, Mgr
EMP: 115
SIC: 6331 Fire, marine, and casualty insurance: mutual
HQ: Hartford Casualty Insurance Company
 1 Hartford Plz
 Hartford CT
 860 547-5000

(P-8386)
HMC ASSETS LLC
2015 Manhattan Beach Blvd Ste 200 (90278-1226)
PHONE................................310 535-9293
EMP: 114 EST: 2010
SALES (est): 9.84MM
SALES (corp-wide): 147.22MM **Privately Held**
Web: www.wedgewoodloanassets.com
SIC: 6331 Property damage insurance
PA: Wedgewood Inc.
 2015 Manhattan Beach Blvd # 102
 Redondo Beach CA
 310 640-3070

(P-8387)
ICW GROUP HOLDINGS INC (PA)
15025 Innovation Dr (92128-3456)
P.O. Box 509039 (92150-9039)
PHONE................................858 350-2400
Kevin M Prior, CEO
Ernest Rady, *
Sariborz Rostamian, *
EMP: 234 EST: 1974
SQ FT: 160,000
SALES (est): 610.35MM
SALES (corp-wide): 610.35MM **Privately Held**
Web: www.icwgroup.com
SIC: 6331 6411 Fire, marine and casualty insurance and carriers; Insurance brokers, nec

(P-8388)
INSURANCE COMPANY OF WEST
11455 El Camino Real Ste 200 (92130)
PHONE................................858 350-2400
Greg Hermie, Brnch Mgr
EMP: 63
SALES (corp-wide): 610.35MM **Privately Held**
Web: www.icwgroup.com
SIC: 6331 6411 Fire, marine and casualty insurance; Insurance agents, nec
HQ: Insurance Company Of West
 15025 Innovation Dr
 San Diego CA
 858 350-2400

(P-8389)
KRAMER-WILSON COMPANY INC (PA)
Also Called: Century National
340 N Westlake Blvd Ste 210 (91362-7034)
P.O. Box 3999 (91609-0599)
PHONE................................818 760-0880
Weldon Wilson, CEO
Kevin Wilson, *
Daniel Sherrin, *
Mary Ann Wagner, *
◆ EMP: 240 EST: 1969
SALES (est): 79.91MM
SALES (corp-wide): 79.91MM **Privately Held**
SIC: 6331 Fire, marine insurance and carriers

(P-8390)
MERCURY CASUALTY COMPANY (HQ)
Also Called: M C C
555 W Imperial Hwy (92821-4802)
P.O. Box 54600 (90054-0600)
PHONE................................323 937-1060
Gabriel Tirador, CEO
George Joseph, *
EMP: 600 EST: 1962
SALES (est): 765.86MM
SALES (corp-wide): 3.64B **Publicly Held**
Web: www.mercuryinsurance.com
SIC: 6331 6351 Automobile insurance; Warranty insurance, home
PA: Mercury General Corporation
 4484 Wilshire Blvd
 Los Angeles CA
 323 937-1060

(P-8391)
MERCURY GENERAL CORPORATION (PA)
Also Called: Mercury General
4484 Wilshire Blvd (90010-3710)
P.O. Box 36662 (90036-0662)
PHONE................................323 937-1060
Gabriel Tirador, Pr
George Joseph, *
Theodore R Stalick, Sr VP
Christopher Graves, VP
Abby Hosseini, VP
EMP: 634 EST: 1961
SQ FT: 41,000
SALES (est): 3.64B
SALES (corp-wide): 3.64B **Publicly Held**
Web: www.mercuryinsurance.com

PRODUCTS & SERVICES SECTION

6331 - Fire, Marine, And Casualty Insurance (P-8409)

SIC: **6331** 6411 Automobile insurance; Insurance agents, brokers, and service

(P-8392)
MERCURY INSURANCE COMPANY
Also Called: Mercury Insurance Group
555 W Imperial Hwy (92821-4839)
P.O. Box 1150 (92822-1150)
PHONE..................714 671-6700
Gave Tirador, *Pr*
EMP: 89
SALES (corp-wide): 3.64B **Publicly Held**
Web: www.mercuryinsurance.com
SIC: **6331** 6411 Fire, marine, and casualty insurance; Insurance agents, brokers, and service
HQ: Mercury Insurance Company
4484 Wilshire Blvd
Los Angeles CA
323 937-1060

(P-8393)
MERCURY INSURANCE COMPANY
Also Called: Mercury Insurance Group
104 Woodmere Rd (95630-4705)
PHONE..................916 353-4859
Beverly Ramm, *VP*
EMP: 549
SALES (corp-wide): 3.64B **Publicly Held**
Web: www.mercuryinsurance.com
SIC: **6331** 6411 Fire, marine, and casualty insurance; Insurance claim processing, except medical
HQ: Mercury Insurance Company
4484 Wilshire Blvd
Los Angeles CA
323 937-1060

(P-8394)
MERCURY INSURANCE COMPANY
Also Called: Mercury Insurance Broker
1433 Santa Monica Blvd (90404-1709)
PHONE..................310 451-4943
Ken Donaldson, *Owner*
EMP: 308
SALES (corp-wide): 3.64B **Publicly Held**
Web: www.mercuryinsurance.com
SIC: **6331** 6411 Fire, marine, and casualty insurance; Insurance agents, brokers, and service
HQ: Mercury Insurance Company
4484 Wilshire Blvd
Los Angeles CA
323 937-1060

(P-8395)
MERCURY INSURANCE COMPANY
1700 Greenbriar Ln (92821-5971)
PHONE..................714 255-5000
Ken Kitzmiller, *Brnch Mgr*
EMP: 1000
SALES (corp-wide): 3.64B **Publicly Held**
Web: www.mercuryinsurance.com
SIC: **6331** Fire, marine, and casualty insurance
HQ: Mercury Insurance Company
4484 Wilshire Blvd
Los Angeles CA
323 937-1060

(P-8396)
MERCURY INSURANCE COMPANY (HQ)
4484 Wilshire Blvd (90010-3710)
P.O. Box 54600 (90054-0600)
PHONE..................323 937-1060
Gabe Tirador, *CEO*
George Joseph, *
Ted Stalick, *
Judith Walters, *
EMP: 160 EST: 1972
SQ FT: 40,809
SALES (est): 1.21B
SALES (corp-wide): 3.64B **Publicly Held**
Web: www.mercuryinsurance.com
SIC: **6331** Fire, marine, and casualty insurance
PA: Mercury General Corporation
4484 Wilshire Blvd
Los Angeles CA
323 937-1060

(P-8397)
MERCURY INSURANCE COMPANY
9635 Granite Ridge Dr Ste 200 (92123)
P.O. Box 10730 (92711-0730)
PHONE..................858 694-4100
Randy Petro, *Mgr*
EMP: 564
SALES (corp-wide): 3.64B **Publicly Held**
Web: www.mercuryinsurance.com
SIC: **6331** 6399 Fire, marine, and casualty insurance; Warranty insurance, automobile
HQ: Mercury Insurance Company
4484 Wilshire Blvd
Los Angeles CA
323 937-1060

(P-8398)
MERCURY INSURANCE COMPANY
27200 Tourney Rd Ste 400 (91355-4997)
P.O. Box 10730 (92711-0730)
PHONE..................661 291-6470
David Levy, *Mgr*
EMP: 586
SALES (corp-wide): 3.64B **Publicly Held**
Web: www.mercuryinsurance.com
SIC: **6331** Fire, marine, and casualty insurance
HQ: Mercury Insurance Company
4484 Wilshire Blvd
Los Angeles CA
323 937-1060

(P-8399)
MERCURY INSURANCE SERVICES LLC
4484 Wilshire Blvd (90010-3710)
PHONE..................323 937-1060
Gabriel Tirador, *CEO*
EMP: 2977 EST: 2000
SALES (est): 31.86MM
SALES (corp-wide): 3.64B **Publicly Held**
Web: www.mercuryinsurance.com
SIC: **6331** Property damage insurance
HQ: Mercury Casualty Company
555 W Imperial Hwy
Brea CA
323 937-1060

(P-8400)
METROMILE OPERATING COMPANY (DH)
Also Called: Metromile
425 Market St Ste 700 (94105-5418)
PHONE..................888 244-1702
Dan Preston, *CEO*
Carrie Dolan, *CFO*
EMP: 80 EST: 2013
SALES (est): 83.04MM
SALES (corp-wide): 256.7MM **Publicly Held**
Web: www.metromile.com
SIC: **6331** Automobile insurance
HQ: Metromile, Llc
425 Market St Ste 700
San Francisco CA
888 242-5204

(P-8401)
MID-CENTURY INSURANCE COMPANY
6303 Owensmouth Ave Fl 1 (91367-2200)
PHONE..................323 932-7116
Ron Coble, *Sr VP*
Bob Woudstra, *
EMP: 250 EST: 1953
SALES (est): 95.59MM
SALES (corp-wide): 71.15B **Privately Held**
Web: www.farmers.com
SIC: **6331** 6351 Automobile insurance; Fidelity insurance
HQ: Farmers Insurance Exchange
6301 Owensmouth Ave # 750
Woodland Hills CA
888 327-6335

(P-8402)
ORION INDEMNITY COMPANY
714 W Olympic Blvd Ste 800 (90015-1425)
PHONE..................213 742-8700
Jeanette Shammas, *Ch Bd*
Nicholas J Lannotti, *
Denise M Tyson, *
EMP: 100 EST: 1949
SALES (est): 53.17MM
SALES (corp-wide): 3.64B **Publicly Held**
Web: www.orionindemnity.com
SIC: **6331** Fire, marine, and casualty insurance
PA: Mercury General Corporation
4484 Wilshire Blvd
Los Angeles CA
323 937-1060

(P-8403)
REPUBLIC INDEMNITY CO AMER
100 Pine St Fl 14 (94111-5116)
P.O. Box 7878 (94120-7878)
PHONE..................415 981-3200
Darryl Yim, *VP*
EMP: 100
Web: www.republicindemnity.com
SIC: **6331** Workers' compensation insurance
HQ: Republic Indemnity Company Of America
4500 Park Granada Ste 300
Calabasas CA
818 990-9860

(P-8404)
REPUBLIC INDEMNITY CO AMER (DH)
Also Called: Rica
4500 Park Granada Ste 300 (91302-1667)
P.O. Box 20036 (91416-0036)
PHONE..................818 990-9860
Dwayne Marioni, *CEO*
Marion Chappel, *
EMP: 129 EST: 1973
SQ FT: 70,000
SALES (est): 703.47MM **Publicly Held**
Web: www.republicindemnity.com
SIC: **6331** Workers' compensation insurance
HQ: Pennsylvania Company Inc
1 E 4th St
Cincinnati OH
513 579-2121

(P-8405)
REPUBLIC INDEMNITY COMPANY CAL
15821 Ventura Blvd Ste 370 (91436-2909)
P.O. Box 4275 (91365-4275)
PHONE..................818 990-9860
Dwayne T Marioni, *Pr*
Shila Euper, *
EMP: 127 EST: 1982
SALES (est): 22.4MM **Publicly Held**
Web: www.republicindemnity.com
SIC: **6331** Fire, marine, and casualty insurance
HQ: Republic Indemnity Company Of America
4500 Park Granada Ste 300
Calabasas CA
818 990-9860

(P-8406)
ROYAL SPECIALTY UNDWRT INC
Also Called: Rsui Group
15303 Ventura Blvd Ste 500 (91403-6619)
PHONE..................818 922-6700
Christine Chinen, *Admn*
EMP: 103
SALES (corp-wide): 302.09B **Publicly Held**
SIC: **6331** 6411 Fire, marine, and casualty insurance; Insurance agents, brokers, and service
HQ: Royal Specialty Underwriting, Inc.
945 E Paces Ferry Rd Ne
Atlanta GA

(P-8407)
STATE COMPENSATION INSUR FUND (PA)
Also Called: State Fund
333 Bush St Ste 800 (94104-2845)
P.O. Box 8192 (94588-8792)
PHONE..................888 782-8338
Vern Steiner, *CEO*
Brian Watson, *
Andreas Acker, *
Beatriz Sanchez, *
Shaun Coyne, *CIO**
EMP: 75 EST: 1914
SALES (est): 2.76B
SALES (corp-wide): 2.76B **Privately Held**
Web: www.statefundca.com
SIC: **6331** Workers' compensation insurance

(P-8408)
STATE COMPENSATION INSUR FUND
1030 Vaquero Cir (95688-8804)
PHONE..................415 565-1222
Maria C Castanares, *Prin*
EMP: 234
SALES (corp-wide): 2.76B **Privately Held**
Web: www.statefundca.com
SIC: **6331** Workers' compensation insurance
PA: State Compensation Insurance Fund
333 Bush St Ste 800
San Francisco CA
888 782-8338

(P-8409)
STATE COMPENSATION INSUR FUND
Also Called: Santa Ana District Office
1750 E 4th St Fl 3 (92705-3929)
PHONE..................714 565-5000
Liz Glidden, *Mgr*
EMP: 241
SALES (corp-wide): 2.76B **Privately Held**
Web: www.statefundca.com
SIC: **6331** 9651 Workers' compensation insurance; Insurance commission, government
PA: State Compensation Insurance Fund
333 Bush St Ste 800

6331 - Fire, Marine, And Casualty Insurance (P-8410)

San Francisco CA
888 782-8338

(P-8410)
STATE COMPENSATION INSUR FUND
Also Called: Bakersfield District Office
9801 Camino Media Ste 101 (93311-1312)
P.O. Box 21810 (93390-1810)
PHONE..................661 664-4000
Robert Kean, *Mgr*
EMP: 91
SALES (corp-wide): 2.76B **Privately Held**
Web: www.statefundca.com
SIC: 6331 9651 Workers' compensation insurance; Insurance commission, government
PA: State Compensation Insurance Fund
333 Bush St Ste 800
San Francisco CA
888 782-8338

(P-8411)
STATE COMPENSATION INSUR FUND
Also Called: San Jose District Office
2275 Gateway Oaks Dr (95833-3224)
PHONE..................888 782-8338
Jerry Madden, *Mgr*
EMP: 210
SALES (corp-wide): 2.76B **Privately Held**
Web: www.statefundca.com
SIC: 6331 9651 Workers' compensation insurance; Insurance commission, government
PA: State Compensation Insurance Fund
333 Bush St Ste 800
San Francisco CA
888 782-8338

(P-8412)
STATE COMPENSATION INSUR FUND
Also Called: San Diego District Office
10105 Pacific Heights Blvd Ste 120 (92121)
PHONE..................888 782-8338
Lisa Middleton, *Mgr*
EMP: 235
SALES (corp-wide): 2.76B **Privately Held**
Web: www.statefundca.com
SIC: 6331 9651 Workers' compensation insurance; Insurance commission, government
PA: State Compensation Insurance Fund
333 Bush St Ste 800
San Francisco CA
888 782-8338

(P-8413)
STATE COMPENSATION INSUR FUND
Also Called: Fresno District Office
10 E River Park Pl E Ste 110 (93720)
PHONE..................559 433-2700
John Putnam, *Dist Mgr*
EMP: 231
SALES (corp-wide): 2.76B **Privately Held**
Web: www.statefundca.com
SIC: 6331 9651 Workers' compensation insurance; Insurance commission, government
PA: State Compensation Insurance Fund
333 Bush St Ste 800
San Francisco CA
888 782-8338

(P-8414)
STATE COMPENSATION INSUR FUND
Also Called: Santa Rosa District Office
1450 Neotomas Ave (95405-7537)
PHONE..................888 782-8338
Richard Schultz, *Mgr*
EMP: 330
SQ FT: 51,000
SALES (corp-wide): 2.76B **Privately Held**
Web: www.statefundca.com
SIC: 6331 9651 Workers' compensation insurance; Insurance commission, government
PA: State Compensation Insurance Fund
333 Bush St Ste 800
San Francisco CA
888 782-8338

(P-8415)
STATE COMPENSATION INSUR FUND
Also Called: Sacramento District Office
2275 Gateway Oaks Dr (95833-3224)
PHONE..................916 924-5100
Gary Dunlap, *Mgr*
EMP: 235
SALES (corp-wide): 2.76B **Privately Held**
Web: www.statefundca.com
SIC: 6331 9651 Workers' compensation insurance; Insurance commission, government
PA: State Compensation Insurance Fund
333 Bush St Ste 800
San Francisco CA
888 782-8338

(P-8416)
STATE COMPENSATION INSUR FUND
Also Called: Eureka District Office
800 W Harris St Ste 37 (95503-3929)
PHONE..................707 443-9721
Steve Mackey, *Brnch Mgr*
EMP: 208
SALES (corp-wide): 2.76B **Privately Held**
Web: www.statefundca.com
SIC: 6331 9651 Workers' compensation insurance; Insurance commission, government
PA: State Compensation Insurance Fund
333 Bush St Ste 800
San Francisco CA
888 782-8338

(P-8417)
STATE COMPENSATION INSUR FUND
21300 Victory Blvd Ste 600 (91367-2525)
P.O. Box 1950 (91365)
PHONE..................818 888-4750
Mary Powers, *Brnch Mgr*
EMP: 510
SALES (corp-wide): 2.76B **Privately Held**
Web: www.statefundca.com
SIC: 6331 9651 Workers' compensation insurance; Insurance commission, government
PA: State Compensation Insurance Fund
333 Bush St Ste 800
San Francisco CA
888 782-8338

(P-8418)
STATE COMPENSATION INSUR FUND
Also Called: Riverside District Office
6301 Day St (92507-0902)
PHONE..................888 782-8338
Barbara Katzka, *Mgr*
EMP: 208
SALES (corp-wide): 2.76B **Privately Held**
Web: www.statefundca.com

SIC: 6331 9651 Workers' compensation insurance; Insurance commission, government
PA: State Compensation Insurance Fund
333 Bush St Ste 800
San Francisco CA
888 782-8338

(P-8419)
STATE COMPENSATION INSUR FUND
5890 Owens Dr (94588-3900)
PHONE..................888 782-8338
Alicia Reyes, *Prin*
EMP: 102
SALES (corp-wide): 2.76B **Privately Held**
Web: www.statefundca.com
SIC: 6331 9651 Workers' compensation insurance
PA: State Compensation Insurance Fund
333 Bush St Ste 800
San Francisco CA
888 782-8338

(P-8420)
STATE COMPENSATION INSUR FUND
Also Called: Los Angles Dst Off Policy Svcs
900 Corporate Center Dr (91754-7620)
P.O. Box 65005 (93650-5005)
PHONE..................323 266-5000
Joe Codron, *Brnch Mgr*
EMP: 224
SALES (corp-wide): 2.76B **Privately Held**
Web: www.statefundca.com
SIC: 6331 9651 Workers' compensation insurance; Insurance commission, government
PA: State Compensation Insurance Fund
333 Bush St Ste 800
San Francisco CA
888 782-8338

(P-8421)
STATE COMPENSATION INSUR FUND
Also Called: State Contract Office
5900 State Farm Dr (94928-2149)
P.O. Box 3171 (94585-6171)
PHONE..................888 782-8338
EMP: 120
SALES (corp-wide): 2.76B **Privately Held**
Web: www.statefundca.com
SIC: 6331 9651 Workers' compensation insurance; Insurance commission, government
PA: State Compensation Insurance Fund
333 Bush St Ste 800
San Francisco CA
888 782-8338

(P-8422)
SWISS RE SOLUTIONS HOLDG CORP
111 Sutter St Ste 400 (94105-1206)
PHONE..................415 834-2200
Ken Brandt, *Mgr*
EMP: 86
SIC: 6331 Property damage insurance
HQ: Swiss Re Solutions Holding Corporation
5200 Metcalf Ave
Overland Park KS
913 676-5200

(P-8423)
TRISTAR INSURANCE GROUP INC (PA)
Also Called: Tristar Risk Management
100 Oceangate Ste 700 (90802-4368)
PHONE..................562 495-6600
Thomas J Veale, *Pr*
Russ O'donnell, *Sec*
Joseph Mclaughlin, *Sr VP*
Denise J Cotter, *CFO*
EMP: 700 **EST:** 1982
SQ FT: 9,000
SALES (est): 515.57MM
SALES (corp-wide): 515.57MM **Privately Held**
Web: www.tristargroup.net
SIC: 6331 8741 Workers' compensation insurance; Management services

(P-8424)
WESTERN GENERAL INSURANCE CO
5230 Las Virgenes Rd Ste 100 (91302-3447)
P.O. Box 26894 (94126-6894)
PHONE..................818 880-9070
Robert M Ehrlich, *Pr*
Daniel Mallut, *
John Albanese, *
Denise M Tyson, *
Marleen Kushner, *
EMP: 165 **EST:** 1971
SQ FT: 51,000
SALES (est): 38.35MM **Privately Held**
Web: www.westerngeneral.com
SIC: 6331 Automobile insurance

(P-8425)
WESTERN MUTUAL INSURANCE CO
27489 Agoura Rd (91301-2419)
PHONE..................818 879-2142
Joe Crail, *Pr*
EMP: 70 **EST:** 1942
SALES (est): 7.18MM **Privately Held**
SIC: 6331 Fire, marine, and casualty insurance: mutual

(P-8426)
ZENITH INSURANCE COMPANY (DH)
Also Called: Zenith A Fairfax Company, The
21255 Califa St (91367-5021)
P.O. Box 9055 (91409-9055)
PHONE..................818 713-1000
Stanley R Zax, *Ch Bd*
Jack D Miller, *Pr*
Paul Ramont, *Chief Underwriting Officer*
EMP: 400 **EST:** 1950
SQ FT: 120,000
SALES (est): 1.01B
SALES (corp-wide): 19.79B **Privately Held**
Web: www.thezenith.com
SIC: 6331 Workers' compensation insurance
HQ: Zenith National Insurance Corp.
21255 Califa St
Woodland Hills CA
818 713-1000

6351 Surety Insurance

(P-8427)
AMERICAN CONTRS INDEMNITY CO (DH)
Also Called: HCC Surety Group
801 S Figueroa St Ste 700 (90017-2523)
PHONE..................213 330-1309
Adam S Pessin, *Pr*
Michael Budnitsky, *
EMP: 150 **EST:** 1990
SALES (est): 104.02MM **Privately Held**
Web: www.tmhcc.com
SIC: 6351 Surety insurance bonding
HQ: Hcc Insurance Holdings, Inc.

PRODUCTS & SERVICES SECTION

6361 - Title Insurance (P-8447)

13403 Northwest Fwy
Houston TX

(P-8428)
CAMICO MUTUAL INSURANCE CO (PA)
1800 Gateway Dr Ste 200 (94404-4072)
PHONE..................................800 652-1772
Ricardo R Rosario, *Pr*
Andrew M Eassa, *
Jay H Stewart, *
Suzanne M Holl, *LOSS PREVENTION SERVICES*
Stephen W Dixon, *ADMINISTRATIVE SERVICES*
EMP: 79 EST: 1986
SALES (est): 57.25MM
SALES (corp-wide): 57.25MM **Privately Held**
Web: www.camico.com
SIC: **6351** Liability insurance

(P-8429)
CAP-MPT (PA)
333 S Hope St Fl 8 (90071-3001)
PHONE..................................213 473-8600
Jim Weidner, *CEO*
Michael Wormley Md, *Ch Bd*
Thomas Andre, *
Cindy Belcher, *
Nancy Brusegaard Johnson, *
EMP: 140 EST: 1977
SALES (est): 23.03MM
SALES (corp-wide): 23.03MM **Privately Held**
Web: www.capphysicians.com
SIC: **6351** Liability insurance

(P-8430)
DEVELOPERS SURETY INDEMNITY CO (DH)
Also Called: Insco Dico Group , The
17771 Cowan Ste 100 (92614-6044)
P.O. Box 19725 (92623-9725)
PHONE..................................949 263-3300
Walter Crowell, *Pr*
Harry C Crowell, *
David Rhodes, *
EMP: 70 EST: 1936
SQ FT: 25,000
SALES (est): 56.56MM
SALES (corp-wide): 5.96B **Privately Held**
Web: www.amtrustfinancial.com
SIC: **6351** Fidelity or surety bonding
HQ: Insco Insurance Services, Inc.
  17771 Cowan Ste 100
  Irvine CA
  949 263-3415

(P-8431)
DOCTORS COMPANY INSURANCE SVCS
Also Called: Doctors Insurance Agcy of Cal
185 Greenwood Rd (94558-7540)
P.O. Box 2900 (94558-0900)
PHONE..................................707 226-0100
Manuel F Puebla, *Ch Bd*
Jack Meyer, *
EMP: 300 EST: 1994
SALES (est): 91.16MM
SALES (corp-wide): 663.78MM **Privately Held**
Web: www.thedoctors.com
SIC: **6351** 6331 Liability insurance; Fire, marine, and casualty insurance
PA: The Doctors' Company An Interinsurance Exchange
  185 Greenwood Rd
  Napa CA
  707 226-0100

(P-8432)
FAR WEST BOND SERVICES CAL INC (PA)
5230 Las Virgenes Rd (91302-3448)
P.O. Box 4500 (91365-4500)
PHONE..................................818 704-1111
John Savage, *Pr*
Neal Pomp, *
Steve Kay, *
▼ EMP: 300 EST: 1974
SALES (est): 86.45MM
SALES (corp-wide): 86.45MM **Privately Held**
SIC: **6351** 6331 Surety insurance; Fire, marine, and casualty insurance

(P-8433)
NMI HOLDINGS INC (PA)
2100 Powell St 12th Fl (94608-1894)
PHONE..................................855 530-6642
Adam Pollitzer, *Pr*
Bradley M Shuster, *Ch Bd*
Ravi Mallela, *Ex VP*
Robert Smith, *CRO*
Patrick Mathis, *Information Technology*
EMP: 97 EST: 2011
SQ FT: 47,000
SALES (est): 523.35MM
SALES (corp-wide): 523.35MM **Publicly Held**
Web: www.nationalmi.com
SIC: **6351** Mortgage guarantee insurance

(P-8434)
SELECT HOME WARRANTY CA INC
222 W 6th St Ste 400 (90731-3345)
PHONE..................................732 835-0110
Joseph Shrem, *CEO*
EMP: 325 EST: 2019
SALES (est): 25MM **Privately Held**
SIC: **6351** Warranty insurance, home

(P-8435)
XL SPECIALTY INSURANCE COMPANY
1340 Treat Blvd (94597-2101)
P.O. Box 8098 (94596-8098)
PHONE..................................925 942-6142
Jim Bily, *Asst VP*
EMP: 281
SALES (corp-wide): 4.5MM **Privately Held**
Web: www.allunderoneroofkc.com
SIC: **6351** Surety insurance
HQ: Xl Specialty Insurance Company
  190 S La Salle St # 3900
  Chicago IL
  847 517-2990

6361 Title Insurance

(P-8436)
CHICAGO TITLE COMPANY
Also Called: Chicago Title
675 N 1st St Ste 400 (95112-5111)
PHONE..................................408 292-4212
Randy Couurk, *Owner*
Madeline G M Lovejoy, *
EMP: 114 EST: 2010
SALES (est): 12.9MM **Privately Held**
Web: santaclara.ctic.com
SIC: **6361** Real estate title insurance

(P-8437)
CHICAGO TITLE INSURANCE CO
Also Called: Chicago Title
1500 E Hamilton Ave Ste 104 (95008-0834)
PHONE..................................408 371-4100
Mary Dm, *Brnch Mgr*
EMP: 1007
Web: www.ctic.com
SIC: **6361** Real estate title insurance
HQ: Chicago Title Insurance Company
  10 S Lasalle St Ste 2850
  Chicago IL
  312 223-2402

(P-8438)
CHICAGO TITLE INSURANCE CO (HQ)
Also Called: Chicago Title
4050 Calle Real (93110-3413)
PHONE..................................805 565-6900
William Halvorsen Junior, *Pr*
A Larry Sisk, *
Peter G Leemputte, *
EMP: 150 EST: 1984
SQ FT: 44,637
SALES (est): 1.02B **Publicly Held**
SIC: **6361** Real estate title insurance
PA: Fidelity National Financial, Inc.
  601 Riverside Ave Fl 4
  Jacksonville FL

(P-8439)
FIDELITY NATIONAL TITLE CO
Also Called: Fidelity National
42544 10th St W Ste C (93534-7079)
PHONE..................................818 881-7800
Cynthia L Fried, *Brnch Mgr*
EMP: 65
SALES (corp-wide): 3.01MM **Privately Held**
Web: www.fntic.com
SIC: **6361** Real estate title insurance
PA: Fidelity National Title Company
  8525 Madison Ave Ste 110
  Fair Oaks CA
  916 646-6057

(P-8440)
FIRST AMERICAN FINANCIAL CORP (PA)
1 First American Way (92707-5913)
PHONE..................................714 250-3000
EMP: 656 EST: 1889
SQ FT: 490,000
SALES (est): 7.61B **Publicly Held**
Web: www.firstam.com
SIC: **6361** 6351 Title insurance; Surety insurance

(P-8441)
FIRST AMERICAN MORTGAGE SVCS
3 First American Way (92707-5913)
PHONE..................................714 250-4210
EMP: 350 EST: 2009
SALES (est): 28.1MM **Privately Held**
Web: www.firstam.com
SIC: **6361** Title insurance

(P-8442)
FIRST AMERICAN TITLE INSUR CO
330 Soquel Ave (95062-2300)
PHONE..................................831 426-6500
James Boxdell, *Brnch Mgr*
EMP: 85
Web: www.firstam.com
SIC: **6361** Title insurance
HQ: First American Title Insurance Company
  1 First American Way
  Santa Ana CA
  800 854-3643

(P-8443)
FIRST AMERICAN TITLE INSUR CO (HQ)
Also Called: First American Mortgage Svcs
1 First American Way (92707-5913)
P.O. Box 267 (92702-0267)
PHONE..................................800 854-3643
Curt G Johnson, *V Ch Bd*
Curt Caspersen, *
Mark R Amesen, *
Max Weldex, *
Kurt Pfotenhauer, *Vice Chairman*
EMP: 485 EST: 1889
SALES (est): 3.64B **Publicly Held**
Web: www.firstam.com
SIC: **6361** 7371 Real estate title insurance; Computer software development
PA: First American Financial Corporation
  1 First American Way
  Santa Ana CA

(P-8444)
LAWYERS TITLE INSURANCE CORP
2751 Park View Ct (93036-5452)
PHONE..................................805 484-2701
John Arnold, *Mgr*
EMP: 325
Web: www.ltic.com
SIC: **6361** Guarantee of titles
HQ: Lawyers Title Insurance Corporation
  601 Riverside Ave
  Jacksonville FL
  888 866-3684

(P-8445)
LAWYERS TITLE INSURANCE CORP
530 El Camino Real Ste A (94070-2454)
PHONE..................................650 445-6300
EMP: 117
Web: www.ltic.com
SIC: **6361** Real estate title insurance
HQ: Lawyers Title Insurance Corporation
  601 Riverside Ave
  Jacksonville FL
  888 866-3684

(P-8446)
LAWYERS TITLE INSURANCE CORP
Also Called: Lawyers Title Escrow
5000 Birch St (92660-2138)
PHONE..................................949 223-5575
Dan Williams, *Owner*
EMP: 117
Web: www.ltic.com
SIC: **6361** Real estate title insurance
HQ: Lawyers Title Insurance Corporation
  601 Riverside Ave
  Jacksonville FL
  888 866-3684

(P-8447)
LAWYERS TITLE INSURANCE CORP
20630 Patio Dr (94546-5606)
PHONE..................................510 733-2250
EMP: 89
Web: www.ltic.com
SIC: **6361** Real estate title insurance
HQ: Lawyers Title Insurance Corporation
  601 Riverside Ave
  Jacksonville FL
  888 866-3684

6361 - Title Insurance (P-8448)

(P-8448)
LAWYERS TITLE INSURANCE CORP
18551 Von Karman Ave Ste 100 (92612-1552)
PHONE.................................949 223-5575
EMP: 89
Web: www.ltic.com
SIC: 6361 6541 Real estate title insurance; Title and trust companies
HQ: Lawyers Title Insurance Corporation
   601 Riverside Ave
   Jacksonville FL
   888 866-3684

(P-8449)
MOTHER LODE HOLDING CO
9085 Foothills Blvd (95747-7130)
PHONE.................................916 624-8141
Marsha A Emmett, Brnch Mgr
EMP: 99
Web: www.placertitle.com
SIC: 6361 Real estate title insurance
HQ: Mother Lode Holding Co.
   189 Fulweiler Ave
   Auburn CA

(P-8450)
MOTHER LODE HOLDING CO (HQ)
189 Fulweiler Ave (95603-4507)
PHONE.................................530 887-2410
Jerry Adams, CEO
Marsha Emmett, Pr
Andy French, Sec
David Philipp, CFO
EMP: 106 EST: 1987
SQ FT: 10,000
SALES (est): 344.41MM Publicly Held
Web: www.mlhc.org
SIC: 6361 6531 7389 Real estate title insurance; Escrow agent, real estate; Courier or messenger service
PA: First American Financial Corporation
   1 First American Way
   Santa Ana CA

(P-8451)
OLD REPUBLIC TITLE COMPANY
Also Called: Old Republic
3425 Brookside Rd Ste C (95219-2366)
PHONE.................................209 951-9460
Brenda Dontath, Brnch Mgr
EMP: 65
SALES (corp-wide): 8.08B Publicly Held
Web: www.ortconline.com
SIC: 6361 6541 Real estate title insurance; Title abstract offices
HQ: Old Republic Title Company
   275 Battery St Ste 1500
   San Francisco CA
   415 421-3500

(P-8452)
OLD REPUBLIC TITLE HOLDG INC
Also Called: Old Republic
3558 Deer Park Dr (95219-2350)
PHONE.................................209 956-7663
Gang Huang, Brnch Mgr
EMP: 80
SALES (corp-wide): 8.08B Publicly Held
Web: www.orcig.com
SIC: 6361 Real estate title insurance
HQ: Old Republic Title Holding Company, Inc.
   275 Battery St Ste 1500
   San Francisco CA
   415 421-3500

(P-8453)
OLD REPUBLIC TITLE HOLDG INC
Also Called: Old Republic
7451 N Remington Ave Ste 102 (93711-5870)
PHONE.................................559 440-9249
EMP: 109
SALES (corp-wide): 8.08B Publicly Held
Web: www.ortconline.com
SIC: 6361 Real estate title insurance
HQ: Old Republic Title Holding Company, Inc.
   275 Battery St Ste 1500
   San Francisco CA
   415 421-3500

(P-8454)
OLD RPBLIC TITLE INFO CONCEPTS
524 Gibson Dr (95678-5799)
PHONE.................................916 781-4100
Robert Matanane, Sr VP
EMP: 273 EST: 1973
SQ FT: 15,000
SALES (est): 23.34MM
SALES (corp-wide): 8.08B Publicly Held
SIC: 6361 6531 Real estate title insurance; Escrow agent, real estate
HQ: Old Republic Title Holding Company, Inc.
   275 Battery St Ste 1500
   San Francisco CA
   415 421-3500

(P-8455)
STEWART TITLE CALIFORNIA INC (DH)
7676 Hazard Center Dr Ste 1400 (92108-4501)
PHONE.................................619 692-1600
Shari Schneider, Pr
Brian Glaze, VP
Gregg Unrath, VP
Linda Mundy, Sec
EMP: 140 EST: 1996
SQ FT: 44,000
SALES (est): 127.18MM
SALES (corp-wide): 3.07B Publicly Held
Web: www.stewart.com
SIC: 6361 Guarantee of titles
HQ: Stewart Title Company
   1360 Post Oak Blvd Ste 10
   Houston TX
   713 625-8100

6371 Pension, Health, And Welfare Funds

(P-8456)
ASSOCIATED THIRD PARTY ADMINISTRATORS INC
Also Called: Atpa
222 N Pacific Coast Hwy # 2000 (90245-5648)
EMP: 390
SIC: 6371 6411 Union welfare, benefit, and health funds; Insurance agents, brokers, and service

(P-8457)
CAL SOUTHERN UNITED FOOD
Also Called: U F C Pension Trust Fund
6425 Katella Ave Ste 100 (90630-5246)
P.O. Box 6010 (90630-0010)
PHONE.................................714 220-2297
P Thompson, Admn
EMP: 240 EST: 1957

SQ FT: 36,000
SALES (est): 42.82MM Privately Held
Web: www.scufcwfunds.com
SIC: 6371 Pension funds

(P-8458)
CALIFRNIA PUB EMPLYEES RTRMENT (DH)
Also Called: Califrnia Gvrnment Oprtons Agc
400 Q St (95811-6201)
P.O. Box 942706 (94229-2706)
PHONE.................................916 795-3000
EMP: 1600 EST: 1932
SALES (est): 1.15B
SALES (corp-wide): 534.4MM Privately Held
Web: calpers.ca.gov
SIC: 6371 9441 Pension funds; Admnistration of social and manpower programs
HQ: California Government Operations Agency
   915 Capitol Mall Ste 200
   Sacramento CA

(P-8459)
CALIFRNIA STATE TCHERS RTRMENT (DH)
Also Called: Cal Strs
100 Waterfront Pl (95605-2807)
P.O. Box 15275 (95851-0275)
PHONE.................................858 258-5077
James D Mosman, CEO
Dana Dillon, *
Sharon Hendricks, *
EMP: 322 EST: 1913
SQ FT: 100,000
SALES (est): 7.74B
SALES (corp-wide): 534.4MM Privately Held
Web: www.calstrs.com
SIC: 6371 9441 Pension, health, and welfare funds; Administration of social and manpower programs
HQ: California Government Operations Agency
   915 Capitol Mall Ste 200
   Sacramento CA

(P-8460)
CHELBAY SCHULER & CHELBAY (PA)
Also Called: United Administrative Services
6800 Santa Teresa Blvd Ste 100 (95119-1238)
P.O. Box 5057 (95150-5057)
PHONE.................................408 288-4400
Robert J Bradley, Pr
David Andresen, *
Sharon Crist, *
EMP: 100 EST: 1951
SQ FT: 35,000
SALES (est): 24.63MM
SALES (corp-wide): 24.63MM Privately Held
Web: www.uastpa.com
SIC: 6371 Pension funds

(P-8461)
HEALTH SVCS BNEFT ADMNSTRTORS (PA)
Also Called: Hsba
4160 Dublin Blvd Ste 400 (94568-7735)
PHONE.................................925 833-7300
Stanley R Fisher, Pr
David Haumesser, *
Michael Taime, *
Angela Rampone, *
Mary Callahan, *
EMP: 67 EST: 1989

SQ FT: 12,500
SALES (est): 28.44MM Privately Held
Web: www.hsba.com
SIC: 6371 Union welfare, benefit, and health funds

(P-8462)
LIPMAN INSUR ADMNSTRATORS INC
39420 Liberty St Ste 260 (94538-2297)
P.O. Box 5820 (94537-5820)
PHONE.................................510 796-4676
Frederic J Lipman, Pr
Margaret Epstein, *
Janet Sylvester C F O, Prin
EMP: 100 EST: 1987
SQ FT: 14,000
SALES (est): 23.98MM Privately Held
Web: www.lipmantpa.com
SIC: 6371 Union welfare, benefit, and health funds

(P-8463)
LOS ANGLES CNTY EMPLYEES RTRME (PA)
Also Called: Lacera
300 N Lake Ave Ste 720 (91101-5674)
P.O. Box 7060 (91109-7060)
PHONE.................................626 564-6000
Gregg Rademather, CEO
EMP: 200 EST: 1938
SQ FT: 85,000
SALES (est): 2.06B
SALES (corp-wide): 2.06B Privately Held
Web: www.lacera.com
SIC: 6371 Pension funds

(P-8464)
MOTION PCTURE INDUST PNSION HL
11365 Ventura Blvd Ste 300 (91604-3148)
PHONE.................................818 769-0007
David Wescoe, CEO
Chuck Killian, *
EMP: 150 EST: 1954
SQ FT: 12,500
SALES (est): 48.89MM Privately Held
SIC: 6371 Pension, health, and welfare funds

(P-8465)
PRODUCR-WRTERS GILD AMER PNSIO
2900 W Alameda Ave Unit 1100 (91505-4220)
PHONE.................................818 846-1015
Jim Hedges, Admn
Wendy Pagnone, Admn
EMP: 70 EST: 1960
SQ FT: 30,000
SALES (est): 18.46MM Privately Held
Web: www.wgaplans.org
SIC: 6371 Pension funds

(P-8466)
PUBLIC EMPLOYEES RETIREMENT
Also Called: Calpers
400 Q St (95811-6201)
PHONE.................................916 795-3400
Russell Fong, Brnch Mgr
EMP: 331
SALES (corp-wide): 534.4MM Privately Held
Web: calpers.ca.gov
SIC: 6371 9441 Pension funds; Administration of social and manpower programs
HQ: California Public Employees' Retirement System

PRODUCTS & SERVICES SECTION
6411 - Insurance Agents, Brokers, And Service (P-8486)

400 Q St
Sacramento CA

(P-8467)
RREEF MANAGEMENT COMPANY
101 California St # 2400 (94111-5802)
PHONE.................415 781-3300
EMP: 179
SIC: 6371 Pension funds

(P-8468)
SCREEN ACTORS GUILD - AMERICAN
Also Called: Screen Actors Guild-Producers
3601 W Olive Ave Fl 2 (91505-4662)
P.O. Box 7830 (91510-7830)
PHONE.................818 954-9400
EMP: 100
SALES (corp-wide): 79.3MM **Privately Held**
Web: www.sagaftraplans.org
SIC: 6371 6411 Pensions; Pension and retirement plan consultants
PA: Screen Actors Guild - American Federation Of Television And Radio Artists
5757 Wilshire Blvd Fl 7
Los Angeles CA
415 391-7510

(P-8469)
SOUTHWEST ADMINISTRATORS INC
466 Foothill Blvd (91011-3503)
EMP: 300
SIC: 6371 Pension funds

(P-8470)
WOODMONT REALTY ADVISORS INC
1050 Ralston Ave (94002-2240)
PHONE.................650 592-3960
Ronald V Granville, CEO
Ronald V Granville, Ch Bd
Howard Friedman, *
Caryn Kali, *
EMP: 294 EST: 1987
SQ FT: 10,000
SALES (est): 2.18MM **Privately Held**
Web: www.woodmontrealtyadvisors.com
SIC: 6371 Pension funds
PA: Woodmont Real Estate Services, L.P.
1050 Ralston Ave
Belmont CA

6399 Insurance Carriers, Nec

(P-8471)
AMWINS CONNECT INSUR SVCS LLC
2677 N Main St Ste 800 (92705-6687)
PHONE.................714 460-5153
Philip Lebherz, Brnch Mgr
EMP: 73
SALES (corp-wide): 54.79MM **Privately Held**
Web: www.amwinsconnect.com
SIC: 6399 Deposit insurance
PA: Amwins Connect Insurance Services, Llc
1600 W Hillsdale Blvd
San Mateo CA
650 348-4131

(P-8472)
FEDERAL DEPOSIT INSURANCE CORP
Also Called: FDIC-San Frncisco Regional Off
25 Jessie St At Ecker Sq Ste 2300 (94105-2780)
PHONE.................415 546-0160
Stan Ivie, Brnch Mgr
EMP: 122
SQ FT: 127,215
SALES (corp-wide): 7.21B **Privately Held**
Web: www.fdic.gov
SIC: 6399 9311 Federal Deposit Insurance Corporation (FDIC); Finance, taxation, and monetary policy
PA: Federal Deposit Insurance Corporation
550 17th St Nw
Washington DC
877 275-3342

(P-8473)
SQUARETRADE INC (DH)
2000 Sierra Point Pkwy Ste 300 (94005-1857)
PHONE.................415 541-1000
EMP: 117 EST: 1999
SALES (est): 403.26MM **Publicly Held**
Web: www.squaretrade.com
SIC: 6399 Warranty insurance, product; except automobile
HQ: Allstate Non-Insurance Holdings, Inc.
2775 Sanders Rd Ste D
Northbrook IL
847 402-5000

(P-8474)
UNITRIN DIRECT INSURANCE CO (HQ)
80 Blue Ravine Rd Ste 200 (95630-4715)
PHONE.................760 603-3276
Scott Carter, Pr
EMP: 62 EST: 2000
SALES (est): 20.24MM **Publicly Held**
SIC: 6399 Warranty insurance, automobile
PA: Kemper Corporation
200 E Randolph St # 3300
Chicago IL

6411 Insurance Agents, Brokers, And Service

(P-8475)
21ST CENTURY LIFE INSURANCE CO (DH)
Also Called: 21st Century Insurance
6301 Owensmouth Ave Ste 700 (91367-2208)
PHONE.................877 310-5687
Glenn A Pfeil, CEO
Michael J Cassanego, *
Dean E Stark, *
Richard R Andre, *
Kathy Doyle, *
EMP: 1800 EST: 1955
SQ FT: 412,000
SALES (est): 415.03MM **Privately Held**
Web: www.21st.com
SIC: 6411 Insurance agents, brokers, and service
HQ: 21st Century North America Insurance Company
3 Beaver Valley Rd
Wilmington DE
877 310-5687

(P-8476)
ABD INSURANCE & FINCL SVCS INC (PA)
Also Called: Nationwide
777 Mariners Island Blvd Ste 250 (94404-1562)
PHONE.................650 488-8565
Brian M Hetherington, Ch
Kurt De Grosz, *
Michael F Mccloskey, CFO
Edward I Cha, *
Andrea M Trudeau, *
EMP: 70 EST: 2009
SQ FT: 14,000
SALES (corp-wide): 93.55MM **Privately Held**
Web: www.newfront.com
SIC: 6411 Insurance brokers, nec

(P-8477)
ACCLAMATION INSURANCE MGT SVCS
4450 N Brawley Ave (93722-3952)
P.O. Box 26597 (93729-6597)
PHONE.................559 227-9891
Kenneth Wilkerson, Mgr
EMP: 78
Web: www.aims4claims.com
SIC: 6411 Insurance agents, nec
PA: Acclamation Insurance Management Services
10445 Old Placerville Rd
Sacramento CA

(P-8478)
ADMINSURE INC
3380 Shelby St (91764-5567)
PHONE.................909 718-1200
Alithia Vargas-flores, Pr
EMP: 130 EST: 1982
SQ FT: 30,000
SALES (est): 19.66MM **Privately Held**
Web: www.adminsure.com
SIC: 6411 Insurance agents, nec

(P-8479)
AFLAC
4325 Main St (95451-8952)
PHONE.................800 992-3522
EMP: 108 EST: 2015
SALES (est): 700.32K **Privately Held**
Web: www.aflac.com
SIC: 6411 Insurance agents, brokers, and service

(P-8480)
AGIA INC (PA)
Also Called: Agia Affinity
1155 Eugenia Pl (93013-2062)
PHONE.................805 566-9191
J Christopher Burke, Pr
Julie L Capritto, Sr VP
Andrew Dowen, Sr VP
Susan Roe, VP Mktg
Carl A Adamek, Senior Vice President Accounting
EMP: 231 EST: 1965
SQ FT: 18,000
SALES (est): 97.42MM **Privately Held**
Web: www.agia.com
SIC: 6411 Medical insurance claim processing, contract or fee basis

(P-8481)
AIG DIRECT INSURANCE SVCS INC
Also Called: Matrix Direct Insurance Svcs
9640 Granite Ridge Dr Ste 200 (92123)
PHONE.................858 309-3000
Ron Harris, CEO
Laura Huffman, *
Kevin Wilshusen, *
Patty Karstein, *
EMP: 275 EST: 1995
SQ FT: 24,000
SALES (est): 105.94MM
SALES (corp-wide): 56.44B **Publicly Held**
Web: www.aigdirect.com
SIC: 6411 Insurance agents, nec
HQ: American General Life Insurance Company
2727 Allen Pkwy Ste A
Houston TX
713 522-1111

(P-8482)
ALAMEDA CNTY EMPLYEES RTRMENT
Also Called: Acera
475 14th St Ste 1000 (94612-1916)
PHONE.................510 628-3000
Charles Conrad, Genl Mgr
Catherine Walker, *
EMP: 70 EST: 1948
SALES (est): 15.68MM **Privately Held**
Web: www.acera.org
SIC: 6411 Pension and retirement plan consultants

(P-8483)
ALLSTATE FINANCIAL SVCS LLC
Also Called: Allstate
5161 Pomona Blvd Ste 212 (90022-1749)
PHONE.................323 981-8520
Carlos Godinez, Prin
EMP: 96
Web: www.allstate.com
SIC: 6411 Insurance agents, brokers, and service
HQ: Allstate Financial Services, Llc
2920 S 84th St
Lincoln NE
402 328-6700

(P-8484)
ALLSTATE FLORAL INC
15928 Commerce Way (90703-2319)
PHONE.................562 926-2989
EMP: 223
SALES (corp-wide): 53.44MM **Privately Held**
Web: www.allstatefloral.com
SIC: 6411 Insurance agents and brokers
PA: Allstate Floral, Inc.
14101 Park Pl
Cerritos CA
562 926-2302

(P-8485)
AMERICAN CMMRCAL CLIMS ADMNSTR
1200 Fulsome St (94104)
PHONE.................415 782-3933
Louis Rovens, CEO
Bryon Kerns, Stockholder*
Raul Panello, Stockholder*
EMP: 125 EST: 1997
SQ FT: 2,400
SALES (est): 43.73MM
SALES (corp-wide): 302.09B **Publicly Held**
SIC: 6411 Insurance claim adjusters, not employed by insurance company
HQ: Columbia Insurance Company
1314 Douglas St Ste 1400
Omaha NE
402 536-3000

(P-8486)
AMERICAN HERITAGE LF INSUR CO

6411 - Insurance Agents, Brokers, And Service (P-8487)

Also Called: American Heritage
400 Exchange Ste 210 (92602-1340)
PHONE..................................800 753-9227
EMP: 67
Web: www.allstate.com
SIC: 6411 Insurance agents, brokers, and service
HQ: American Heritage Life Insurance Co Inc
1776 Amercn Heritg Lf Dr
Jacksonville FL
904 992-1776

(P-8487)
AMERICAN SPCLTY HLTH PLANS CAL
10221 Wateridge Cir (92121-2702)
PHONE..................................619 297-8100
George Devries, Pr
Robert White, *
Marcel Danko, CFO
EMP: 500 EST: 1999
SALES (est): 50.46MM Privately Held
Web: www.ashcompanies.com
SIC: 6411 Insurance information and consulting services
PA: American Specialty Health Incorporated
12800 N Meridian St # 190
Carmel IN

(P-8488)
AMWINS CONNECT INSUR SVCS LLC (PA)
1600 W Hillsdale Blvd Ste 201 (94402-3768)
PHONE..................................650 348-4131
Philip Lebherz, Ch Bd
Becky Patel, *
Tamara Henderson, *
Peter Diaz, *
Ken Doyle, *
EMP: 60 EST: 1976
SQ FT: 18,000
SALES (est): 54.79MM
SALES (corp-wide): 54.79MM Privately Held
Web: www.amwinsconnect.com
SIC: 6411 Insurance agents, nec

(P-8489)
AMWINS INSURANCE BRKG CAL LLC (HQ)
Also Called: Amwins Brkg Wash Henrico Co
21550 Oxnard St Ste 1100 (91367-7106)
PHONE..................................818 772-1774
Scott M Purviance, *
George Maggay, *
Ron Benigno, *
EMP: 60 EST: 1981
SQ FT: 16,000
SALES (est): 21.72MM
SALES (corp-wide): 726.22MM Privately Held
Web: www.amwins.com
SIC: 6411 Insurance brokers, nec
PA: Amwins Group, Inc.
4725 Piedmont Row Dr # 600
Charlotte NC
704 749-2700

(P-8490)
ANCHOR GENERAL INSUR AGCY INC
10256 Meanley Dr (92131-3009)
P.O. Box 509020 (92150-9020)
PHONE..................................858 527-3600
Abdulla Badani, Pr
EMP: 203 EST: 1995
SALES (est): 44.65MM Privately Held

Web: www.anchorgeneral.com
SIC: 6411 Insurance agents, nec

(P-8491)
AON CONSULTING & INSUR SVCS
Also Called: AON
199 Fremont St Fl 14 (94105-2253)
PHONE..................................415 486-7500
Judy Vukovich, Sr VP
EMP: 111 EST: 1988
SALES (est): 7.67MM Privately Held
Web: www.aon.com
SIC: 6411 8742 Insurance brokers, nec; Management consulting services
HQ: Aon Consulting, Inc.
200 E Randolph St Ll3
Chicago IL
312 381-1000

(P-8492)
AON/ALBERT G RUBEN INSUR SVCS (DH)
Also Called: AON
10880 Wilshire Blvd Ste 700 (90024-4101)
PHONE..................................310 234-6800
Paul Jones, Dir
EMP: 62 EST: 1960
SALES (est): 49.73MM
SALES (corp-wide): 1.98B Privately Held
Web: www.aon.com
SIC: 6411 Insurance brokers, nec
HQ: Aon Group, Inc.
200 E Randolph St Fl 5
Chicago IL

(P-8493)
ARTHUR J GALLAGHER & CO
Also Called: Nationwide
500 N Brand Blvd Ste 100 (91203-3931)
PHONE..................................818 539-2300
Scott Firestone, Brnch Mgr
EMP: 60
SALES (corp-wide): 8.55B Publicly Held
Web: www.ajg.com
SIC: 6411 Insurance brokers, nec
PA: Arthur J. Gallagher & Co.
2850 Golf Rd Ste 600
Rolling Meadows IL
630 773-3800

(P-8494)
ARTHUR J GALLAGHER & CO
Also Called: Nationwide
501 W Main St (93291-6149)
PHONE..................................559 733-1181
EMP: 90
SALES (corp-wide): 8.55B Publicly Held
Web: www.ajg.com
SIC: 6411 Insurance brokers, nec
PA: Arthur J. Gallagher & Co.
2850 Golf Rd Ste 600
Rolling Meadows IL
630 773-3800

(P-8495)
ARTHUR J GALLAGHER RISK MGMT
Also Called: Nationwide
500 N Brand Blvd Ste 100 (91203-3931)
PHONE..................................818 539-2300
Gregory S Chapman, Pr
Gerald S Chapman, *
Paulette Chapman, *
EMP: 80 EST: 1973
SALES (est): 9.47MM
SALES (corp-wide): 8.55B Publicly Held
Web: www.ajg.com

SIC: 6411 Insurance brokers, nec
PA: Arthur J. Gallagher & Co.
2850 Golf Rd Ste 600
Rolling Meadows IL
630 773-3800

(P-8496)
ASPIRE GENERAL INSURANCE CO
2721 Citrus Rd Ste B (95742-6313)
P.O. Box 870 (91729-0870)
PHONE..................................877 789-4742
Byron Storms, Pr
Brad Hinkle, Chief Claims Officer
EMP: 60 EST: 1980
SALES (est): 9.67MM Privately Held
Web: www.aspiregeneral.com
SIC: 6411 Insurance agents, nec

(P-8497)
ASSURED INSURANCE TECH INC
650 Page Mill Rd (94304-1001)
PHONE..................................650 753-1070
Justin Lewis-weber, CEO
EMP: 63 EST: 2019
SALES (est): 4.99MM Privately Held
Web: www.assured.claims
SIC: 6411 Insurance brokers, and service

(P-8498)
AT-BAY SPECIALTY INSURANCE CO
1 Post St Fl 14 (94104-5218)
PHONE..................................888 338-9522
Gregg Davis, Dir
Rob Glanville, Dir
EMP: 174 EST: 2008
SALES (est): 308.9K
SALES (corp-wide): 5.72MM Privately Held
SIC: 6411 Loss prevention services, insurance
PA: At-Bay, Inc.
1 Post St Fl 14
San Francisco CA
888 338-9522

(P-8499)
ATHENS INSURANCE SERVICE INC
Also Called: Athens Administrators
2552 Stanwell Dr Ste 100 (94520-4851)
P.O. Box 4029 (94524-4029)
PHONE..................................925 826-1000
James C Jenkins, Ch Bd
James R Jenkins, *
Jodi Ellington, *
Jane Catelani, *
EMP: 250 EST: 1976
SALES (est): 25.26MM Privately Held
Web: www.athensadmin.com
SIC: 6411 Insurance claim adjusters, not employed by insurance company

(P-8500)
ATLAS GENERAL INSUR SVCS LLC
Also Called: Nationwide
6165 Greenwich Dr Ste 200 (92122-5911)
PHONE..................................858 529-6700
EMP: 153 EST: 2008
SALES (est): 32.88MM
SALES (corp-wide): 8.55B Publicly Held
Web: atlas.us.com
SIC: 6411 Insurance agents, nec
PA: Arthur J. Gallagher & Co.
2850 Golf Rd Ste 600

SIC: 6411 Insurance brokers, nec
PA: Arthur J. Gallagher & Co.
2850 Golf Rd Ste 600
Rolling Meadows IL
630 773-3800

(P-8501)
AUTO INSURANCE SPECIALISTS LLC (DH)
Also Called: Nationwide
17785 Center Court Dr N Ste 110 (90703-8573)
PHONE..................................562 345-6247
EMP: 210 EST: 1968
SQ FT: 45,000
SALES (est): 59.77MM
SALES (corp-wide): 3.64B Publicly Held
Web: www.aisinsurance.com
SIC: 6411 Insurance brokers, nec
HQ: Ais Management, Llc
17785 Center Court Dr N # 250
Cerritos CA

(P-8502)
AUTOMOBILE CLUB SOUTHERN CAL
Also Called: A A A Automobile Club So Cal
13331 Jamboree Rd (92602)
P.O. Box 11763 (92711-1763)
PHONE..................................714 973-1211
Sid Munger, Mgr
EMP: 175
SALES (corp-wide): 1.08B Privately Held
Web: ace.aaa.com
SIC: 6411 Insurance agents, brokers, and service
PA: Automobile Club Of Southern California
2601 S Figueroa St
Los Angeles CA
213 741-3686

(P-8503)
AUTOMOBILE CLUB SOUTHERN CAL
Also Called: AAA
2033b S Broadway (93454-7809)
P.O. Box 1308 (93456-1308)
PHONE..................................805 922-5731
Keith Pierce, Mgr
EMP: 78
SALES (corp-wide): 1.08B Privately Held
Web: ace.aaa.com
SIC: 6411 Insurance agents, brokers, and service
PA: Automobile Club Of Southern California
2601 S Figueroa St
Los Angeles CA
213 741-3686

(P-8504)
AUTOMOBILE CLUB SOUTHERN CAL
Also Called: AAA Auto Club
3333 Fairview Rd (92626-1698)
PHONE..................................714 885-1343
Becky Martinez, Brnch Mgr
EMP: 200
SALES (corp-wide): 1.08B Privately Held
Web: ace.aaa.com
SIC: 6411 Insurance agents, brokers, and service
PA: Automobile Club Of Southern California
2601 S Figueroa St
Los Angeles CA
213 741-3686

(P-8505)
AUTOMOBILE CLUB SOUTHERN CAL (PA)
Also Called: A A A Automobile Club So Cal
2601 S Figueroa St (90007-3254)
P.O. Box 25001 (92799-5001)

PRODUCTS & SERVICES SECTION
6411 - Insurance Agents, Brokers, And Service (P-8524)

PHONE..................................213 741-3686
John F Boyle, *CEO*
Zoo Babies, *
Peter R Mcdonald, *Sr VP*
Robert T Bouttier, *
EMP: 150 **EST:** 1900
SQ FT: 425,000
SALES (est): 1.08B
SALES (corp-wide): 1.08B **Privately Held**
Web: ace.aaa.com
SIC: 6411 8699 Insurance agents, nec; Automobile owners' association

(P-8506)
B&C LIQUIDATING CORP (HQ)
Also Called: Nationwide
3475 E Foothill Blvd Ste 100 (91107)
P.O. Box 6030 (91102-6030)
PHONE..................................626 799-7000
EMP: 123 **EST:** 1931
SALES (est): 23.58MM
SALES (corp-wide): 474.73MM **Privately Held**
Web: www.boltonco.com
SIC: 6411 Insurance agents, nec
PA: The Ima Financial Group Inc
430 E Douglas Ave Ste 400
Wichita KS
316 267-9221

(P-8507)
BARNEY & BARNEY INC
Also Called: Loss and Risk Advisors
9171 Twne Cntre Dr 500 (92122)
P.O. Box 85638 (92186-5638)
PHONE..................................800 321-4696
EMP: 200
SIC: 6411 Property and casualty insurance agent

(P-8508)
BENEFIT & RISK MANAGEMENT SVCS
80 Iron Point Cir Ste 200 (95630-8593)
P.O. Box 2140 (95763-2140)
PHONE..................................888 326-2555
Matthew Allen Schafer, *CEO*
Paul Schafer, *
Luke Schafer, *
EMP: 130 **EST:** 1993
SQ FT: 15,000
SALES (est): 25.85MM **Privately Held**
Web: www.brmsonline.com
SIC: 6411 Insurance brokers, nec

(P-8509)
BENEFITSTREET INC
12677 Alcosta Blvd (94583-4423)
PHONE..................................925 831-0800
EMP: 96 **EST:** 1993
SALES (est): 6.77MM **Privately Held**
Web: www.benefitstreet.com
SIC: 6411 Pension and retirement plan consultants

(P-8510)
BENETECH INC (PA)
3841 N Freeway Blvd Ste 185 (95834-1949)
P.O. Box 348570 (95834-8570)
PHONE..................................916 484-6811
Robert L Brandon, *Pr*
James Casalegno, *Sr VP*
Wes Jones, *VP*
Charles Walker, *VP*
Paula Emison, *VP*
EMP: 60 **EST:** 1974
SQ FT: 20,000
SALES (est): 21.01MM
SALES (corp-wide): 21.01MM **Privately Held**
Web: www.benetechinc.com
SIC: 6411 Pension and retirement plan consultants

(P-8511)
BERKSHIRE HATHAWAY HOMESTATES (HQ)
1 California St Ste 600 (94111-5403)
P.O. Box 881716 (94188-1716)
PHONE..................................415 433-1650
Louis B Rovens, *Pr*
EMP: 180 **EST:** 1998
SQ FT: 51,000
SALES (est): 95.33MM
SALES (corp-wide): 302.09B **Publicly Held**
Web: www.bhhc.com
SIC: 6411 Insurance claim processing, except medical
PA: Berkshire Hathaway Inc.
3555 Farnam St Ste 1440
Omaha NE
402 346-1400

(P-8512)
BICKMORE AND ASSOCIATES INC (DH)
Also Called: Bickmore Risk Svcs Consulting
1750 Creekside Oaks Dr Ste 200 (95833-3628)
PHONE..................................916 244-1100
Greg L Trout, *CEO*
John Alltop, *ACTURIAL & CONSULTING SOLUTIONS**
L Robert Kramer, *Program Administrator**
Jeffrey C Grubbs, *
EMP: 70 **EST:** 1984
SQ FT: 25,500
SALES (est): 12.48MM
SALES (corp-wide): 2.39B **Privately Held**
Web: www.bickmoreactuarial.net
SIC: 6411 Insurance information and consulting services
HQ: York Risk Services Group, Inc.
1 Upper Pond Rd Bldg F
Parsippany NJ
973 404-1200

(P-8513)
BITCO CNSTR INSUR AGCY INC
Also Called: Old Republic
225 S Lake Ave Ste 1050 (91101-4820)
PHONE..................................626 683-5200
Joan Miles, *CEO*
EMP: 90 **EST:** 2006
SALES (est): 18.06MM
SALES (corp-wide): 8.08B **Publicly Held**
Web: www.orcig.com
SIC: 6411 Insurance agents, brokers, and service
HQ: Old Republic General Insurance Group, Inc.
307 N Michigan Ave # 1418
Chicago IL

(P-8514)
BUILDERS TRDSMENS INSUR SVCS I
Also Called: Unitas Insurance Services
6610 Sierra College Blvd (95677-4306)
PHONE..................................916 772-9200
Norbert Hohlbein, *Pr*
Paul Hohlbein, *
Jeff Hohlbein, *
Lisa Erickson, *
Jeff Erickson, *
EMP: 75 **EST:** 1998
SQ FT: 15,000
SALES (est): 24.48MM
SALES (corp-wide): 5.96B **Privately Held**
Web: my.btisinc.com
SIC: 6411 Insurance brokers, nec
HQ: Amtrust Financial Services, Inc.
59 Maiden Ln Fl 43
New York NY

(P-8515)
BURNHAM BENEFITS INSUR SVCS
Also Called: Burnham Risk Insurance
15901 Hawthorne Blvd Ste 200 (90260-2655)
PHONE..................................310 370-5000
Kristen Allison, *Brnch Mgr*
EMP: 74
SALES (corp-wide): 99.6MM **Privately Held**
Web: www.burnhambenefits.com
SIC: 6411 Insurance agents, nec
PA: Burnham Benefits Insurance Services, Llc
2211 Michelson Dr # 1200
Irvine CA
805 772-7965

(P-8516)
BURNHAM BNEFITS INSUR SVCS LLC (PA)
Also Called: Life Plans
2211 Michelson Dr Ste 1200 (92612-0304)
PHONE..................................805 772-7965
Kristen Mauger Allison, *Pr*
Scott Aston, *
Janet Vreeland, *
Nooshin George, *
Chris Krusiewicz, *
EMP: 72 **EST:** 1995
SALES (est): 99.6MM
SALES (corp-wide): 99.6MM **Privately Held**
Web: www.burnhambenefits.com
SIC: 6411 Insurance agents, nec

(P-8517)
CAL INSURANCE AND ASSOC INC
Also Called: Nationwide
2311 Taraval St (94116-2253)
PHONE..................................415 661-6500
Scott Hauge, *Pr*
Joe Be Lotchi, *
Richard Miller, *
EMP: 76 **EST:** 1961
SQ FT: 8,000
SALES (est): 9.73MM **Privately Held**
Web: www.mycalteam.com
SIC: 6411 Insurance agents, nec

(P-8518)
CALIFORNIA FAIR PLAN ASSN
725 S Figueroa St Ste 3900 (90017-5439)
PHONE..................................213 487-0111
Stuart M Wilkinson, *Pr*
EMP: 80 **EST:** 1968
SALES (est): 16.69MM **Privately Held**
Web: www.cfpnet.com
SIC: 6411 Insurance agents, nec

(P-8519)
CALIFRNIA INSUR GUARANTEE ASSN
Also Called: C I G A
330 N Brand Blvd Ste 500 (91203-2304)
P.O. Box 29066 (91209-9066)
PHONE..................................818 844-4300
Lawrence E Mulryan, *Dir*
Wayne Wilson, *
EMP: 110 **EST:** 1969
SALES (est): 25.42MM **Privately Held**
Web: www.ciga.org
SIC: 6411 Insurance agents, brokers, and service

(P-8520)
CARELON BHAVIORAL HLTH CAL INC
Also Called: Valueoptions of California Inc
12898 Towne Center Dr (90703-8546)
PHONE..................................800 228-1286
Juan Molina, *VP Opers*
Jolene Myrter, *
Steve Rockowitz, *
EMP: 637 **EST:** 1989
SALES (est): 2.18MM
SALES (corp-wide): 156.59B **Publicly Held**
Web: www.carelonbehavioralhealthca.com
SIC: 6411 6321 Insurance agents, nec; Accident and health insurance
HQ: Fhc Health Systems, Inc
240 Corporate Blvd # 212
Norfolk VA
757 459-5100

(P-8521)
CARNEGIE AGENCY INC
Also Called: Carnegie General Insur Agcy
2535 W Hillcrest Dr (91320-2457)
P.O. Box 2595 (91319-2595)
PHONE..................................805 445-1470
John Smith, *Pr*
Chuck Smith, *
EMP: 75 **EST:** 1988
SALES (est): 7.85MM **Privately Held**
SIC: 6411 Insurance agents, brokers, and service

(P-8522)
CARTEL MARKETING INC
Also Called: Insure Express Insurance Svc
5230 Las Virgenes Rd Ste 250 (91302-3448)
PHONE..................................818 483-1130
Robert M Humphreys, *Ch Bd*
Jack Edelstein, *
William Russell, *
EMP: 101 **EST:** 1984
SQ FT: 14,000
SALES (est): 9.02MM
SALES (corp-wide): 54.49MM **Privately Held**
Web: www.cartel.net
SIC: 6411 Insurance agents, nec
HQ: Expresslink, Inc.
16501 Ventura Blvd # 300
Encino CA
818 788-5555

(P-8523)
CBIZ LIFE INSUR SOLUTIONS INC
13500 Evening Creek Dr N Ste 450 (92128-8111)
PHONE..................................858 444-3100
Timothy Moynihan, *Pr*
EMP: 121 **EST:** 1974
SALES (est): 26.17MM **Publicly Held**
Web: lifeinsurance.cbiz.com
SIC: 6411 Insurance brokers, nec
PA: Cbiz, Inc.
6050 Oak Tree Blvd # 500
Cleveland OH

(P-8524)
CENTURY-NATIONAL INSURANCE CO (DH)
16650 Sherman Way Ste 200 (91406-3782)
PHONE..................................818 760-0880

6411 - Insurance Agents, Brokers, And Service (P-8525)

Weldon Wilson, *CEO*
Marie Balicki, *
Judy Osborn, *
EMP: 260 **EST:** 1955
SQ FT: 41,000
SALES (est): 91.53MM **Publicly Held**
Web: www.cnico.com
SIC: 6411 Insurance agents, nec
HQ: National General Holdings Corp.
  59 Maiden Ln Fl 38
  New York NY

(P-8525)
CHIVAROLI & ASSOC INC
200 N Westlake Blvd Ste 101 (91362-3784)
PHONE.....................208 338-6640
Roger Jones, *Brnch Mgr*
EMP: 97
SALES (corp-wide): 1.31MM **Privately Held**
Web: www.chivaroli.com
SIC: 6411 Insurance agents, nec
PA: Chivaroli & Assoc Inc
  4500 Kruse Way Ste 100
  Lake Oswego OR
  503 675-0255

(P-8526)
CHOIC ADMINI INSUR SERVI
Also Called: California Choice
721 S Parker St Ste 200 (92868-4772)
PHONE.....................714 542-4200
Michael Close, *Pr*
John M Word, *
Raymond D Godeke, *
Brenda Scott, *
EMP: 500 **EST:** 1984
SALES (est): 50.26MM **Privately Held**
Web: www.choicebuilder.com
SIC: 6411 Insurance agents, nec

(P-8527)
CLAIMS MANAGEMENT INC
1101 Creekside Ridge Dr Ste 100 (95678-3567)
P.O. Box 619079 (95661-9079)
PHONE.....................916 631-1250
Kathy Peterson, *Pr*
EMP: 117 **EST:** 1981
SQ FT: 23,000
SALES (est): 2.87MM **Privately Held**
Web: www.cmi-mba.com
SIC: 6411 Insurance claim adjusters, not employed by insurance company

(P-8528)
COACTION SPCLTY INSUR GROUP IN
Also Called: Coaction
101 N Brand Blvd Ste 1900 (91203-2634)
PHONE.....................818 230-8200
EMP: 61
SALES (corp-wide): 816.11MM **Privately Held**
Web: www.coactionspecialty.com
SIC: 6411 Insurance brokers, nec
HQ: Coaction Specialty Insurance Group, Inc.
  412 Mount Kemble Ave 300c
  Morristown NJ

(P-8529)
COLLECTIVEHEALTH INC (PA)
Also Called: Collective Health
45 Fremont St Ste 1200 (94105-2204)
PHONE.....................844 265-3288
Ali Diab, *CEO*
EMP: 172 **EST:** 2013
SALES (est): 129.35MM
SALES (corp-wide): 129.35MM **Privately Held**
Web: www.collectivehealth.com
SIC: 6411 7379 7372 Medical insurance claim processing, contract or fee basis; Online services technology consultants; Business oriented computer software

(P-8530)
COMMERCIAL CRRERS INSUR AGCY I
4 Centerpointe Dr Ste 300 (90623-1074)
PHONE.....................562 404-4900
Charles J Escalante, *Pr*
Henry H Escalante, *
Shannon S Walker, *
Helen M Escalante, *
EMP: 89 **EST:** 1979
SQ FT: 16,000
SALES (est): 2.16MM
SALES (corp-wide): 8.55B **Publicly Held**
Web: www.cciainsurance.com
SIC: 6411 Insurance agents, nec
HQ: Meadowbrook,
  26255 American Dr
  Southfield MI
  248 358-1100

(P-8531)
CONEXIS BNFITS ADMNSTRATORS LP (HQ)
721 S Parker St Ste 300 (92868-4732)
PHONE.....................714 835-5006
EMP: 120 **EST:** 1988
SQ FT: 57,000
SALES (est): 53.17MM
SALES (corp-wide): 105.94MM **Privately Held**
Web: www.cleanandpure.net
SIC: 6411 Insurance information and consulting services
PA: Word & Brown, Insurance Administrators, Inc.
  721 S Parker St Ste 300
  Orange CA
  714 835-5006

(P-8532)
CONFIE HOLDING II CO (PA)
Also Called: Confie
7711 Center Ave Ste 200 (92647-9124)
PHONE.....................714 252-2500
Cesar Soriano, *CEO*
Michael Kaplan, *
Darrin Silveria, *CSO*
Tim Clark, *Chief Human Resource Officer*
Joshua Marder, *CMO*
EMP: 160 **EST:** 2007
SALES (est): 109.15MM
SALES (corp-wide): 109.15MM **Privately Held**
Web: www.nationwide.com
SIC: 6411 Insurance agents, nec

(P-8533)
COVERANCE INSUR SOLUTIONS INC
1343 6th St (90266-6041)
PHONE.....................310 856-9925
EMP: 190
SALES (corp-wide): 15.49MM **Privately Held**
Web: www.coveranceis.com
SIC: 6411 Insurance agents, brokers, and service
PA: Coverance Insurance Solutions, Inc.
  100 W Broadway Ste 3000
  Long Beach CA
  231 218-6100

(P-8534)
CRC INSURANCE SERVICES INC
Also Called: Crump Insurance
50 California St Ste 2000 (94111-4703)
PHONE.....................415 986-5050
Garrett Koehn, *Genl Mgr*
EMP: 78
SALES (corp-wide): 25.36B **Publicly Held**
Web: www.crcgroup.com
SIC: 6411 Insurance brokers, nec
HQ: Crc Insurance Services, Llc
  1 Metroplex Dr Ste 400
  Birmingham AL
  205 870-7790

(P-8535)
CREST FINANCIAL CORPORATION (DH)
12641 166th St (90703-2101)
P.O. Box 3190 (90703-3190)
PHONE.....................562 733-6500
Susan Scurti, *Pr*
Shannon S Walker, *
Michael Costello, *
Walter E Erker, *
EMP: 62 **EST:** 1983
SQ FT: 15,000
SALES (est): 9.23MM
SALES (corp-wide): 439.84K **Privately Held**
SIC: 6411 7311 Insurance agents, nec; Advertising agencies
HQ: Ameritrust Group, Inc.
  26255 American Dr
  Southfield MI

(P-8536)
CSAA INSURANCE EXCHANGE (PA)
3055 Oak Rd (94597-2098)
P.O. Box 23392 (94623-0392)
PHONE.....................925 279-2300
Thomas Troy, *Pr*
Stephen O'connor, *Mgr*
Michael Zukerman, *
EMP: 97 **EST:** 1914
SALES (est): 2.04B
SALES (corp-wide): 2.04B **Privately Held**
Web: csaa-insurance.aaa.com
SIC: 6411 Insurance agents, nec

(P-8537)
CSAA INSURANCE SERVICES INC (HQ)
Also Called: Csaa Insurance Group
3055 Oak Rd (94597-2098)
P.O. Box 23392 (94623-0392)
PHONE.....................925 279-3153
Thomas M Troy, *CEO*
Michael Day, *CFO*
Greg Meyer, *COO*
Paul Acevedo, *CIO*
Marlys Rodgers Ciso, *Prin*
EMP: 62 **EST:** 2015
SALES (est): 115.84MM
SALES (corp-wide): 2.04B **Privately Held**
Web: csaa-insurance.aaa.com
SIC: 6411 Insurance agents, brokers, and service
PA: Csaa Insurance Exchange
  3055 Oak Rd
  Walnut Creek CA
  925 279-2300

(P-8538)
CSAC EXCESS INSURANCE AUTH
75 Iron Point Cir Ste 200 (95630-8813)
PHONE.....................916 850-7300
Michael Fleming, *CEO*
EMP: 60 **EST:** 1979
SQ FT: 13,613
SALES (est): 9.25MM **Privately Held**
Web: www.prismrisk.gov
SIC: 6411 Insurance agents, nec

(P-8539)
CUSTOMZED SVCS ADMNSTRTORS INC
Also Called: Global Care Travel
9797 Aero Dr Ste 300 (92123-1891)
P.O. Box 939057 (92193-9057)
PHONE.....................858 810-2004
Christopher Carnicelli, *CEO*
John Martini, *
EMP: 140 **EST:** 1991
SALES (est): 50.22MM
SALES (corp-wide): 4.18B **Privately Held**
Web: www.generalitravelinsurance.com
SIC: 6411 4724 Insurance agents, nec; Travel agencies
HQ: Generali Global Assistance, Inc.
  4330 East West Hwy # 1000
  Bethesda MD
  240 330-1000

(P-8540)
CYBERPOLICY INC
19584 Pine Valley Ave (91326-1408)
PHONE.....................877 626-9991
Keith Moore, *CEO*
EMP: 103 **EST:** 2016
SALES (est): 4.49MM **Privately Held**
Web: www.cyberpolicy.com
SIC: 6411 Insurance agents, brokers, and service

(P-8541)
CYPRESS PNT-RROWHEAD GEN INSUR
2365 Northside Dr Ste 450 (92108-2719)
PHONE.....................619 681-0560
Bill Trzos, *Pr*
EMP: 75 **EST:** 2001
SQ FT: 6,000
SALES (est): 3.38MM **Privately Held**
SIC: 6411 Insurance agents, brokers, and service

(P-8542)
DEALEY RENTON AND ASSOCIATES
530 Water St 7th Fl (94607-3547)
P.O. Box 12675 (94604-2675)
PHONE.....................510 465-3090
Morgan West, *Prin*
EMP: 63 **EST:** 2014
SALES (est): 8.58MM **Privately Held**
Web: www.assuredpartners.com
SIC: 6411 Insurance brokers, nec

(P-8543)
DEDICTED DFNED BENEFT SVCS LLC
550 N Brand Blvd Ste 1610 (91203-1964)
P.O. Box 219800 (64121-9800)
PHONE.....................415 931-1990
Karen Shapiro, *CEO*
EMP: 119 **EST:** 2006
SALES (est): 2.04MM
SALES (corp-wide): 947.08MM **Privately Held**
Web: www.dedicated-db.com
SIC: 6411 Pension and retirement plan consultants
PA: Ascensus, Llc
  200 Dryden Rd E Ste 1000
  Dresher PA
  215 648-8000

PRODUCTS & SERVICES SECTION
6411 - Insurance Agents, Brokers, And Service (P-8564)

(P-8544)
DEWITT STERN GROUP INC
5990 Sepulvda Blvd # 550 (91411-2536)
PHONE..................................818 933-2700
Jolyon F Stern, *Brnch Mgr*
EMP: 137
SALES (corp-wide): 1.04B Privately Held
Web: www.dewittstern.com
SIC: 6411 Insurance brokers, nec
HQ: Dewitt Stern Group, Inc.
 420 Lexington Ave Rm 2700
 New York NY
 212 867-3550

(P-8545)
DIBUDUO DFENDIS INSUR BRKS LLC (PA)
Also Called: Nationwide
6873 Nw Ave St 101 (93711-4308)
P.O. Box 5479 (93755-5479)
PHONE..................................559 432-0222
Matt Defendis, *Pt*
Mike De Fendis, *
EMP: 93 EST: 1960
SQ FT: 22,000
SALES (est): 40.89MM
SALES (corp-wide): 40.89MM Privately Held
Web: www.dibu.com
SIC: 6411 Insurance agents, nec

(P-8546)
DMA CLAIMS MANAGEMENT INC
Also Called: David Morse & Assoc.
330 N Brand Blvd Ste 230 (91203-2380)
P.O. Box 26004 (91222-6004)
PHONE..................................323 342-6800
Dan Mara, *Brnch Mgr*
EMP: 77
SALES (corp-wide): 51.21MM Privately Held
Web: www.dmaclaims.com
SIC: 6411 Insurance claim adjusters, not employed by insurance company
PA: Dma Claims Management, Inc.
 330 N Brand Blvd Ste 230
 Glendale CA
 323 342-6800

(P-8547)
DOCTORS MANAGEMENT COMPANY (HQ)
185 Greenwood Rd (94558-6270)
P.O. Box 2900 (94558-0900)
PHONE..................................707 226-0100
Richard E Anderson, *CEO*
Michael Yacob, *
Eugene M Bullis, *
Kenneth R Chrisman, *
William J Gallagher, *
EMP: 200 EST: 1976
SQ FT: 72,000
SALES (est): 232.28MM
SALES (corp-wide): 663.78MM Privately Held
Web: www.thedoctors.com
SIC: 6411 Insurance information and consulting services
PA: The Doctors' Company An Interinsurance Exchange
 185 Greenwood Rd
 Napa CA
 707 226-0100

(P-8548)
EDGEWOOD PARTNERS INSUR CTR
Also Called: Nationwide
3000 Executive Pkwy Ste 325 (94583-4335)
PHONE..................................925 244-7700
EMP: 96
Web: www.nationwide.com
SIC: 6411 Insurance agents, nec
PA: Edgewood Partners Insurance Center
 1 California St Ste 400
 San Francisco CA

(P-8549)
EDGEWOOD PARTNERS INSUR CTR
Also Called: Nationwide
4675 Macarthur Ct (92660-1875)
PHONE..................................949 263-0606
Dan Ryan, *Brnch Mgr*
EMP: 206
Web: www.epicbrokers.com
SIC: 6411 Insurance brokers, nec
PA: Edgewood Partners Insurance Center
 1 California St Ste 400
 San Francisco CA

(P-8550)
EDGEWOOD PARTNERS INSUR CTR
Also Called: Edgewood Partners Insur Ctr
3001 Executive Pkwy Ste 325 (94583)
PHONE..................................925 244-7700
Brian Quinn, *Mgr*
EMP: 137
Web: www.epicbrokers.com
SIC: 6411 Insurance brokers, nec
PA: Edgewood Partners Insurance Center
 1 California St Ste 400
 San Francisco CA

(P-8551)
EDGEWOOD PARTNERS INSUR CTR (PA)
Also Called: Nationwide
1 California St Ste 400 (94111-5402)
P.O. Box 5900 (94402-5900)
PHONE..................................415 365-8000
EMP: 65 EST: 1994
SALES (est): 832.27MM Privately Held
Web: www.epicbrokers.com
SIC: 6411 Insurance brokers, nec

(P-8552)
EHEALTH INC (PA)
Also Called: EHEALTH
2625 Augustine Dr Fl 2 (95054-2956)
PHONE..................................650 584-2700
Scott N Flanders, *CEO*
David K Francis, *COO*
Timothy C Hannan, *CMO*
Derek N Yung, *Sr VP*
EMP: 150 EST: 1997
SQ FT: 32,492
SALES (est): 405.36MM Publicly Held
Web: www.ehealthinsurance.com
SIC: 6411 Insurance agents, nec

(P-8553)
EHEALTHINSURANCE SERVICES INC (HQ)
Also Called: Ehealth
2625 Augustine Dr Ste 201 (95054-2956)
PHONE..................................650 584-2700
Ellen O Tausche, *Prin*
Scott N Flanders, *Prin*
Bill Shaughnessy, *
Dave Francis, *Prin*
Samuel C Gibbs Iii, *Sr VP*
EMP: 100 EST: 1997
SALES (est): 88.29MM Publicly Held
SIC: 6411 Insurance agents, nec
PA: Ehealth, Inc.
 2625 Augustine Dr Fl 2
 Santa Clara CA

(P-8554)
EPISOURCE LLC
500 W 190th St Ste 400 (90248-4290)
PHONE..................................714 452-1961
Sishir Reddy, *Prin*
Erik Simonsen, *
EMP: 6600 EST: 2006
SALES (est): 612.89MM Privately Held
Web: www.episource.com
SIC: 6411 Medical insurance claim processing, contract or fee basis

(P-8555)
EPSTEIN WHITE RTRMENT INCOME S
9740 Appaloosa Rd Ste 150 (92131-1600)
PHONE..................................858 564-8036
EMP: 81 EST: 2013
SALES (est): 2.07MM
SALES (corp-wide): 164.45MM Privately Held
Web: www.epsteinandwhite.com
SIC: 6411 Pension and retirement plan consultants
PA: Mercer Global Advisors, Inc.
 1200 17th St Ste 500
 Denver CO
 888 885-8101

(P-8556)
ESURANCE INSURANCE SVCS INC (HQ)
Also Called: PNC
650 Davis St (94111-1904)
PHONE..................................415 875-4500
Gary C Tolman, *CEO*
Jean Bernard Duler, *
Jonathan Adkisson, *
Elinor Mackinnon, *CIO*
Alan Gellman, *CMO*
EMP: 92 EST: 1999
SQ FT: 10,000
SALES (est): 148.92MM Publicly Held
Web: www.esurance.com
SIC: 6411 Insurance agents, nec
PA: The Allstate Corporation
 3100 Sanders Rd
 Northbrook IL

(P-8557)
FARMERS GROUP INC (HQ)
Also Called: Farmers Insurance
6301 Owensmouth Ave (91367-2268)
P.O. Box 2450 (49501-2450)
PHONE..................................323 932-3200
Raul Vargas, *Pr*
Giles Harrison, *
Melissa Joye, *CMO*
▲ EMP: 2100 EST: 1927
SALES (est): 4.96B Privately Held
Web: www.farmers.com
SIC: 6411 Insurance agents, brokers, and service
PA: Zurich Insurance Group Ag
 C/O Zurich Versicherungs-Gesellschaft Ag
 ZUrich ZH

(P-8558)
FARMERS INSURANCE
Also Called: Farmers Insurance
6303 Owensmouth Ave Fl 1 (91367-2200)
PHONE..................................818 876-3400
Steve Wampler, *Mgr*
EMP: 316 EST: 2011
SALES (est): 3.14MM Privately Held
Web: www.farmers.com
SIC: 6411 Insurance agents, brokers, and service

(P-8559)
FARMERS INSURANCE
27433 Tourney Rd Ste 170 (91355-5399)
PHONE..................................661 257-0844
Corrine Mirone, *Prin*
EMP: 179
Web: www.farmers.com
SIC: 6411 Insurance agents, brokers, and service
HQ: Farmers Insurance
 6600 Sw Hampton St
 Portland OR
 503 372-2000

(P-8560)
FARMERS INSURANCE
3600 Lime St Ste 122 (92501-0911)
PHONE..................................951 681-1068
Lucinda Metcalfe, *Brnch Mgr*
EMP: 179
Web: www.statefarm.com
SIC: 6411 Insurance agents, brokers, and service
HQ: Farmers Insurance
 6600 Sw Hampton St
 Portland OR
 503 372-2000

(P-8561)
FARMERS INSURANCE
113 Avondale Ave (91754-1797)
PHONE..................................626 288-0870
Yvone Ti, *Brnch Mgr*
EMP: 179
Web: www.farmers.com
SIC: 6411 Insurance agents and brokers
HQ: Farmers Insurance
 6600 Sw Hampton St
 Portland OR
 503 372-2000

(P-8562)
FARMERS INSURANCE BEELINE
Also Called: Farmers Insurance
4601 Wilshire Blvd (90010-3894)
PHONE..................................909 997-4734
EMP: 74 EST: 2018
SALES (est): 419.01K Privately Held
Web: www.farmers.com
SIC: 6411 Insurance agents, brokers, and service

(P-8563)
FARMERS INSURANCE EXCHANGE
2344 Merced St (94577-4209)
PHONE..................................510 895-6000
EMP: 232
Web: www.farmers.com
SIC: 6411 Insurance agents, brokers, and service
HQ: Farmers Insurance Exchange
 6301 Owensmouth Ave # 750
 Woodland Hills CA
 888 327-6335

(P-8564)
FARMERS INSURANCE EXCHANGE
Also Called: Farmers Insurance
411 E Pine St Ste A (93221-1800)
PHONE..................................559 594-4149
Sammy Harrell, *Brnch Mgr*
EMP: 232

6411 - Insurance Agents, Brokers, And Service (P-8565)

Web: www.farmers.com
SIC: 6411 Insurance agents, brokers, and service
HQ: Farmers Insurance Exchange
6301 Owensmouth Ave # 750
Woodland Hills CA
888 327-6335

(P-8565)
FARMERS INSURANCE EXCHANGE (DH)
Also Called: Farmers Insurance
6301 Owensmouth Ave (91367-2212)
PHONE.....................888 327-6335
Jeff Pailey, CEO
Thomas Noh, *
Eric Kappler, CPO*
EMP: 3000 EST: 1928
SQ FT: 210,000
SALES (est): 1.71B Privately Held
Web: www.farmers.com
SIC: 6411 Insurance agents and brokers
HQ: Farmers Group, Inc.
6301 Owensmouth Ave # 300
Woodland Hills CA
323 932-3200

(P-8566)
FINANCIAL GROUP INC
Also Called: Finan Group
12432 Oxnard St (91606-4510)
PHONE.....................818 308-8527
Andres Saavedra, Prin
EMP: 130
SALES (corp-wide): 1.47B Publicly Held
SIC: 6411 Insurance agents, brokers, and service
HQ: The Financial Group Inc
2555 Severn Ave Ste 100
Metairie LA
504 456-0101

(P-8567)
FINANCIAL PACIFIC INSURANCE CO
3850 Atherton Rd (95765-3700)
PHONE.....................916 630-5000
EMP: 161 EST: 2011
SALES (est): 616.5K Publicly Held
SIC: 6411 Insurance agents, brokers, and service
HQ: Financial Pacific Insurance Group, Inc
3880 Atherton Rd
Rocklin CA

(P-8568)
FIRE INSURANCE EXCHANGE (PA)
6301 Owensmouth Ave (91367-2216)
PHONE.....................323 932-3200
Martin Feinstein, Pr
John Harrington, *
Doren Hohl, *
Ron Myhan, *
EMP: 2300 EST: 1942
SALES (est): 941.33MM
SALES (corp-wide): 941.33MM Privately Held
Web: www.farmers.com
SIC: 6411 Insurance agents, brokers, and service

(P-8569)
FIRST AMRCN PRPRTY INSUR CSLTY
114 E 5th St (92701-4642)
PHONE.....................949 474-7500
Dirk Mcnamee, Pr
EMP: 138 EST: 1930

SALES (est): 1.74MM Publicly Held
SIC: 6411 Insurance agents, nec
HQ: First American Specialty Insurance Company
4 First American Way
Santa Ana CA
949 474-7500

(P-8570)
FLEXPORT INC (PA)
760 Market St Fl 8 (94102-2300)
PHONE.....................415 231-5252
Ryan Petersen, CEO
Christopher Ferro, *
Sandy Manders, *
Paige Delacey, CPO*
Mehmet Goker, Chief Data Officer*
EMP: 245 EST: 2013
SALES (est): 504.44MM
SALES (corp-wide): 504.44MM Privately Held
Web: www.flexport.com
SIC: 6411 Insurance agents and brokers

(P-8571)
FMC FINANCIAL GROUP (PA)
4675 Macarthur Ct Ste 1250 (92660-1875)
PHONE.....................949 225-9369
James Chapel, Owner
▲ EMP: 75 EST: 1981
SALES (est): 8.95MM Privately Held
Web: www.fmcfg.com
SIC: 6411 Insurance agents and brokers

(P-8572)
FREEWAY INSURANCE (PA)
Also Called: South Coast Auto Insurance
7711 Center Ave Ste 200 (92647-9124)
P.O. Box 669 (90630-0669)
PHONE.....................714 252-2500
Elias Assaf, Pr
John Klaeb, *
Norm Hudson, *
EMP: 120 EST: 1988
SQ FT: 20,000
SALES (est): 51.45MM
SALES (corp-wide): 51.45MM Privately Held
Web: www.freeway.com
SIC: 6411 Insurance agents, nec

(P-8573)
GEICO GENERAL INSURANCE CO
Also Called: Geico
5211 Madison Ave (95841-3053)
PHONE.....................916 923-5050
EMP: 281
SALES (corp-wide): 302.09B Publicly Held
Web: www.geico.com
SIC: 6411 Insurance agents, nec
HQ: Geico General Insurance Company
1 Geico Plz
Washington DC

(P-8574)
GEICO GENERAL INSURANCE CO
Also Called: Geico
14111 Danielson St (92064-6886)
PHONE.....................858 848-8200
Elizabeth Shew, Prin
EMP: 2370
SALES (corp-wide): 302.09B Publicly Held
Web: www.geico.com
SIC: 6411 Insurance agents, nec
HQ: Geico General Insurance Company
1 Geico Plz

Washington DC

(P-8575)
GNET AGENCY
5455 Wilshire Blvd Ste 2200 (90036-4272)
PHONE.....................323 951-9399
Johnathan Rosenberg, Pr
EMP: 86 EST: 2017
SALES (est): 2.61MM Privately Held
Web: www.gnet.agency
SIC: 6411 Insurance agents, brokers, and service

(P-8576)
GROSSLIGHT INSURANCE INC
Also Called: Nationwide
21300 Victory Blvd Ste 700 (91367-7726)
PHONE.....................310 473-9611
Joan Schiewe, CEO
Steven Schiewe, *
EMP: 60 EST: 1950
SALES (est): 21.12MM
SALES (corp-wide): 135.13MM Privately Held
Web: www.grosslight.com
SIC: 6411 Insurance agents, nec
PA: Pcf Insurance Services Of The West, Llc
2500 W Executive Pkwy # 200
Lehi UT
818 703-8057

(P-8577)
GROSVENOR INV MGT US INC
155 Montgomery St Ste 611 (94104-4111)
PHONE.....................415 773-0275
John Ford, Prin
EMP: 80
SALES (corp-wide): 7.85B Publicly Held
SIC: 6411 Pension and retirement plan consultants
HQ: Grosvenor Investment Management Us Inc.
10 New King St Ste 214
White Plains NY
914 683-3710

(P-8578)
GROSVENOR INV MGT US INC
2308 Chelsea Rd (90274-2606)
PHONE.....................310 265-0297
Stephen Waddell, Brnch Mgr
EMP: 80
SALES (corp-wide): 7.85B Publicly Held
SIC: 6411 Pension and retirement plan consultants
HQ: Grosvenor Investment Management Us Inc.
10 New King St Ste 214
White Plains NY
914 683-3710

(P-8579)
GS LEVINE INSURANCE SVCS INC
10505 Sorrento Valley Rd Ste 200 (92121-1618)
PHONE.....................858 481-8692
Gary S Levine, CEO
Ross Afsahi, *
Dick Avakian, *
EMP: 62 EST: 1985
SQ FT: 17,000
SALES (est): 26.79MM
SALES (corp-wide): 8.55B Publicly Held
SIC: 6411 Insurance brokers, nec
PA: Arthur J. Gallagher & Co.
2850 Golf Rd Ste 600
Rolling Meadows IL
630 773-3800

(P-8580)
H & H AGENCY INC (PA)
1403 N Tustin Ave Ste 280 (92705-8691)
PHONE.....................949 260-8840
Michael Weinstein, CEO
EMP: 88 EST: 1969
SQ FT: 25,000
SALES (est): 9.48MM
SALES (corp-wide): 9.48MM Privately Held
Web: www.hhagency.com
SIC: 6411 Insurance agents, nec

(P-8581)
HAMILTON BRWART INSUR AGCY LLC
1282 W Arrow Hwy (91786-5040)
P.O. Box 1949 (91785-1949)
PHONE.....................909 920-3250
EMP: 67 EST: 1976
SQ FT: 12,000
SALES (est): 7.71MM Privately Held
Web: www.dailybulletin.com
SIC: 6411 Insurance agents, nec

(P-8582)
HAZELRIGG CLAIMS MGT SVCS INC (HQ)
15345 Fairfield Ranch Rd Ste 250 (91710)
P.O. Box 669 (91708-0669)
PHONE.....................909 606-6373
Arlene Hazelrigg, Pr
EMP: 60 EST: 1991
SQ FT: 5,000
SALES (est): 25.25MM
SALES (corp-wide): 515.57MM Privately Held
Web: www.hazelriggclaims.com
SIC: 6411 Insurance claim adjusters, not employed by insurance company
PA: Tristar Insurance Group, Inc.
100 Oceangate Ste 700
Long Beach CA
562 495-6600

(P-8583)
HEALTHCOMP LLC (PA)
Also Called: Healthcomp Administrators
621 Santa Fe Ave (93721-2724)
P.O. Box 45018 (93718-5018)
PHONE.....................559 499-2450
EMP: 258 EST: 1994
SQ FT: 50,000
SALES (est): 116.63MM Privately Held
Web: www.healthcomp.com
SIC: 6411 Medical insurance claim processing, contract or fee basis

(P-8584)
HEALTHSMART MANAGEMENT SERVICE
10855 Business Center Dr Ste C (90630)
P.O. Box 6300 (90630-0063)
PHONE.....................714 947-8600
Carol Houchins, Pr
EMP: 90 EST: 1996
SALES (est): 9.51MM Privately Held
Web: www.healthsmartmso.com
SIC: 6411 8741 8721 Medical insurance claim processing, contract or fee basis; Hospital management; Billing and bookkeeping service

(P-8585)
HEFFERNAN INSURANCE BROKERS (PA)
Also Called: Nationwide
1350 Carlback Ave (94596-7231)
P.O. Box 5608 (94596-1608)

PRODUCTS & SERVICES SECTION
6411 - Insurance Agents, Brokers, And Service (P-8603)

PHONE.................................925 934-8500
TOLL FREE: 800
EMP: 500 EST: 1978
SALES (est): 65.76MM
SALES (corp-wide): 65.76MM Privately Held
Web: www.heffernanfoundation.org
SIC: 6411 Insurance brokers, nec

(P-8586)
HOWARDS MBS INC
23909 Sylvan St (91367-1246)
PHONE.................................202 570-4074
Ketsha Thompson, CEO
EMP: 75 EST: 2006
SALES (est): 2.67MM Privately Held
SIC: 6411 7929 Education services, insurance; Entertainers and entertainment groups

(P-8587)
HUB INTRNTIONAL INSUR SVCS INC
Also Called: Der Manouel Insurance Group
548 W Cromwell Ave Ste 101 (93711-5714)
PHONE.................................559 447-4600
EMP: 71
Web: www.dmig.com
SIC: 6411 Insurance agents, nec
HQ: Hub International Insurance Services Inc.
3390 University Ave # 300
Riverside CA

(P-8588)
INDEMNITY COMPANY CALIFORNIA (DH)
17771 Cowan Ste 100 (92614-6044)
P.O. Box 19725 (92623-9725)
PHONE.................................949 263-3300
Harry C Crowell, Ch
Walter A Crowell, Sec
Sam Zaza, Treas
Fern Haberman, CFO
EMP: 71 EST: 1967
SQ FT: 50,000
SALES (est): 24.11MM
SALES (corp-wide): 5.96B Privately Held
SIC: 6411 Insurance agents, nec
HQ: Insco Insurance Services, Inc.
17771 Cowan Ste 100
Irvine CA
949 263-3415

(P-8589)
INSCO INSURANCE SERVICES INC (DH)
Also Called: Developers Surety Indemnity Co
17771 Cowan Ste 100 (92614-6044)
P.O. Box 19725 (92623-9725)
PHONE.................................949 263-3415
Harry Crowell, Ch Bd
EMP: 70 EST: 1970
SQ FT: 50,000
SALES (est): 80.67MM
SALES (corp-wide): 5.96B Privately Held
Web: comingsoon.markmonitor.com
SIC: 6411 6351 Property and casualty insurance agent; Surety insurance bonding
HQ: Amtrust Financial Services, Inc.
59 Maiden Ln Fl 43
New York NY

(P-8590)
INSURANCE COMPANY OF WEST (HQ)
Also Called: I C W
15025 Innovation Dr (92128-3409)
P.O. Box 509039 (92150-9039)
PHONE.................................858 350-2400
Kevin Prior, Pr
Ernest Rady, *
H Michael Freet, *
EMP: 92 EST: 1972
SQ FT: 150,000
SALES (est): 216.83MM
SALES (corp-wide): 610.35MM Privately Held
Web: www.icwgroup.com
SIC: 6411 Insurance agents, nec
PA: Icw Group Holdings, Inc.
15025 Innovation Dr # 200
San Diego CA
858 350-2400

(P-8591)
INSURANCE COMPANY OF WEST
6140 Stoneridge Mall Rd Ste 390 (94588)
P.O. Box 509039 (92150-9039)
PHONE.................................925 474-2800
Dan Diaz, Brnch Mgr
EMP: 63
SALES (corp-wide): 610.35MM Privately Held
Web: www.icwgroup.com
SIC: 6411 Insurance agents, nec
HQ: Insurance Company Of West
15025 Innovation Dr
San Diego CA
858 350-2400

(P-8592)
INSURANCE INC SOUTHERN CAL
Also Called: Nationwide
3400 Central Ave Ste 220 (92506-2180)
PHONE.................................951 300-9333
Timothy Dean, Pr
Nowel Milik, VP
◆ EMP: 92 EST: 1958
SALES (est): 4.88MM Privately Held
Web: www.insuranceinc.com
SIC: 6411 Insurance agents, nec

(P-8593)
INTERWEST INSURANCE SVCS LLC
Also Called: Nationwide
5 Sierra Gate Plz 2nd Fl (95678-6637)
PHONE.................................916 784-1008
EMP: 60
SALES (corp-wide): 150.2MM Privately Held
Web: www.nationwide.com
SIC: 6411 Insurance agents, nec
PA: Interwest Insurance Services, Llc
8950 Cal Center Dr # 200
Sacramento CA
916 488-3100

(P-8594)
INTERWEST INSURANCE SVCS LLC (PA)
Also Called: Kemper Insurance
8950 Cal Center Dr Bldg 3 # 200 (95826-3262)
PHONE.................................916 488-3100
Tom Williams, Ch
Keith Schuler, CEO
Thomas Williams, Pr
William O'keefe, Ex VP
Richard Pratt, Sec
EMP: 173 EST: 2014
SQ FT: 20,000
SALES (est): 150.2MM
SALES (corp-wide): 150.2MM Privately Held
Web: www.iwins.com
SIC: 6411 Insurance brokers, nec

(P-8595)
JAMES C JENKINS INSUR SVC INC
Also Called: Athens Insurance
1390 Willow Pass Rd Ste 800 (94520-5200)
PHONE.................................925 798-3334
John Hahn, CEO
Peter Garvey, *
Karman Chan, *
Michael Gonthier, CAO*
EMP: 125 EST: 1977
SQ FT: 30,000
SALES (est): 41.08MM Privately Held
SIC: 6411 Insurance brokers, nec
PA: Edgewood Partners Insurance Center
1 California St Ste 400
San Francisco CA

(P-8596)
JAMES G PARKER INSURANCE ASSOC (PA)
Also Called: Nationwide
1753 E Fir Ave (93720-3840)
P.O. Box 3947 (93650-3947)
PHONE.................................559 222-7722
James G Parker, Pr
Jon Parker, *
Gerald Thompson, *
Leroy Berrett, *
Paul Thompson, *
EMP: 70 EST: 1978
SQ FT: 13,000
SALES (est): 41.84MM
SALES (corp-wide): 41.84MM Privately Held
Web: www.jgparker.com
SIC: 6411 Insurance agents, nec

(P-8597)
JOHN HANCOCK LIFE INSUR CO USA (DH)
Also Called: John Hancock
865 S Figueroa St Ste 3320 (90017-2507)
PHONE.................................213 689-0813
Emeritus D'alessandro, CEO
David F D'alessandro, Pr
Robert R Reitano, *
Gregory P Winn, *
▲ EMP: 2000 EST: 1862
SQ FT: 3,600,000
SALES (est): 653.33MM
SALES (corp-wide): 32.83B Privately Held
Web: www.manulife.com
SIC: 6411 6351 6371 6321 Insurance agents and brokers; Mortgage guarantee insurance; Pensions; Accident insurance carriers
HQ: John Hancock Financial Services, Inc.
200 Clarendon St
Boston MA
617 572-6000

(P-8598)
JOHN HANCOCK LIFE INSUR CO USA
Also Called: John Hancock
10180 Telesis Ct (92121-2705)
PHONE.................................858 292-1667
EMP: 125
SALES (corp-wide): 32.83B Privately Held
Web: www.johnhancock.com
SIC: 6411 Insurance agents and brokers
HQ: John Hancock Life Insurance Company (U.S.A.)
865 S Figueroa St # 3320
Los Angeles CA
213 689-0813

(P-8599)
KASPICK & CO LLC (DH)
203 Redwood Shores Pkwy Ste 300 (94065-1198)
PHONE.................................650 585-4100
Lindy Sherwood, Managing Member
EMP: 60 EST: 1989
SALES (est): 23.61MM
SALES (corp-wide): 32.66B Privately Held
Web: www.kaspick.com
SIC: 6411 Insurance agents, brokers, and service
HQ: Teachers Insurance And Annuity Association-College Retirement Equities Fund
730 3rd Ave Ste 2a
New York NY
212 490-9000

(P-8600)
KEENAN & ASSOCIATES
1111 Broadway Ste 2000 (94607-4021)
PHONE.................................510 986-6750
John Scatterday, Mgr
EMP: 66
Web: www.keenan.com
SIC: 6411 Insurance brokers, nec
HQ: Keenan & Associates
2355 Crenshaw Blvd # 200
Torrance CA
310 212-3344

(P-8601)
KEENAN & ASSOCIATES (HQ)
2355 Crenshaw Blvd Ste 200 (90501-3325)
P.O. Box 4328 (90510-4328)
PHONE.................................310 212-3344
John Keenan, Ch Bd
Sean Smith, *
Henry Loubet, Senior Vice President Strategic Planning*
Keith Pippard, *
Davis Seres, *
EMP: 339 EST: 1972
SQ FT: 80,000
SALES (est): 389.29MM Privately Held
Web: www.keenan.com
SIC: 6411 Insurance brokers, nec
PA: Assuredpartners, Inc.
450 S Orange Ave Fl 4
Orlando FL

(P-8602)
LEAVITT UNITED INSUR SVCS INC
301 S Shepherd St (95370-5037)
PHONE.................................209 532-6951
Brandy Busch, Operations
EMP: 67
SALES (corp-wide): 306.15MM Privately Held
Web: www.leavitt.com
SIC: 6411 Insurance agents, nec
HQ: Leavitt United Insurance Services, Inc.
2358 Maritime Dr Ste 100
Elk Grove CA
916 691-5555

(P-8603)
LEXISNEXIS RISK ASSETS INC
Also Called: Choicepoint
2112 Business Center Dr Ste 150 (92614)
PHONE.................................949 222-0028
Tim Coon, Owner
EMP: 112
SALES (corp-wide): 10.3B Privately Held
Web: risk.lexisnexis.com
SIC: 6411 Information bureaus, insurance
HQ: Lexisnexis Risk Assets Inc.
1105 N Market St Ste 501

(PA)=Parent Co (HQ)=Headquarters
✿ = New Business established in last 2 years

6411 - Insurance Agents, Brokers, And Service (P-8604)

Wilmington DE
800 458-9410

(P-8604)
LOCKTON CMPNIES LLC - PCF SRIE (HQ)
Also Called: Lockton Insurance Brokers
777 S Figueroa St Ste 5200 (90017-5800)
PHONE.............................213 689-0500
Timothy J Noonan, *Pr*
Nate Mundy, *
Leonard G Fodemski, *
EMP: 294 **EST:** 2016
SQ FT: 72,300
SALES (est): 213.82MM
SALES (corp-wide): 1.61B **Privately Held**
Web: global.lockton.com
SIC: 6411 Insurance brokers, nec
PA: Lockton, Inc.
  444 W 47th St Ste 900
  Kansas City MO
  816 960-9000

(P-8605)
MARKEL CORP
Also Called: Associated Intl Insur Co
21600 Oxnard St Ste 900 (91367-7834)
PHONE.............................818 595-0600
Anthony Markel, *Pr*
Alan Kirshner, *
Steven Markel, *
EMP: 278 **EST:** 1972
SQ FT: 32,000
SALES (est): 4.73MM
SALES (corp-wide): 11.68B **Publicly Held**
Web: www.markel.com
SIC: 6411 Insurance agents, brokers, and service
HQ: Markel North America, Inc.
  4521 Highwoods Pkwy
  Glen Allen VA
  804 747-0136

(P-8606)
MARSH & MCLENNAN AGENCY LLC
Also Called: Marsh
9171 Towne Centre Dr Ste 500
(92122-1234)
PHONE.............................858 457-3414
Paul Hering, *Brnch Mgr*
EMP: 200
SALES (corp-wide): 20.72B **Publicly Held**
Web: www.marshmma.com
SIC: 6411 Insurance brokers, nec
HQ: Marsh & Mclennan Agency Llc
  9850 Nw 41st St Ste 100
  Doral FL

(P-8607)
MARSH RISK & INSURANCE SVCS
Also Called: MMC
633 W 5th St Ste 1200 (90071-2095)
PHONE.............................213 624-5555
Melody Schwartz, *Sr VP*
EMP: 687 **EST:** 1883
SALES (est): 93.35MM
SALES (corp-wide): 20.72B **Publicly Held**
SIC: 6411 Insurance brokers, nec
PA: Marsh & Mclennan Companies, Inc.
  1166 Ave Of The Americas
  New York NY
  212 345-5000

(P-8608)
MC GRAW COMMERCIAL INSUR SVC (PA)
3601 Haven Ave (94025-1064)
PHONE.............................650 780-4800
Michael J Mc Graw, *Pr*
John M Mc Graw, *
Joan D Mc Graw, *
EMP: 90 **EST:** 1984
SQ FT: 20,000
SALES (est): 8.73MM
SALES (corp-wide): 8.73MM **Privately Held**
SIC: 6411 Insurance agents, nec

(P-8609)
MEDICAL EYE SERVICES INC
Also Called: Mesvision
345 Baker St (92626-4518)
P.O. Box 25209 (92799-5209)
PHONE.............................714 619-4660
Aspasia Shappet, *Pr*
EMP: 91 **EST:** 1976
SQ FT: 12,000
SALES (est): 23.26MM
SALES (corp-wide): 23.26MM **Privately Held**
Web: www.mesvision.com
SIC: 6411 Insurance claim processing, except medical
PA: The Eye Care Network Of California Inc
  345 Baker St
  Costa Mesa CA
  714 619-4660

(P-8610)
MEDICAL UNDERWRITERS CAL INC (PA)
Also Called: Medical Insurance Exchange
6250 Claremont Ave (94618-1324)
PHONE.............................510 428-9411
William K Scheuber, *Pr*
Ron Neupauer, *
Stephen Stimel, *
L Richard Mello Cfosec, *Treas*
EMP: 79 **EST:** 1975
SQ FT: 13,000
SALES (est): 24.82MM
SALES (corp-wide): 24.82MM **Privately Held**
Web: www.miec.com
SIC: 6411 Insurance agents, nec

(P-8611)
MELITA-MCDONALD INSUR SVCS INC
Also Called: Melita Group, The
75 E Santa Clara St Ste 1200 (95113-1834)
P.O. Box 610520 (95161-0520)
PHONE.............................408 882-0800
Paul Mifsud, *Pr*
Lisa Mccormack, *Ex VP*
Greg St Geme, *VP*
EMP: 71 **EST:** 1993
SQ FT: 11,500
SALES (est): 5.16MM **Privately Held**
Web: www.melitagroup.com
SIC: 6411 Insurance brokers, nec

(P-8612)
MESA INSURANCE SOLUTIONS INC
50 Castilian Dr (93117-3080)
PHONE.............................805 308-6308
EMP: 203 **EST:** 2017
SALES (est): 456.47K
SALES (corp-wide): 471.88MM **Publicly Held**
SIC: 6411 Insurance agents, brokers, and service
PA: Appfolio, Inc.
  70 Castilian Dr
  Santa Barbara CA
  805 364-6093

(P-8613)
MOMENTOUS INSURANCE BRKG INC
5990 Sepulveda Blvd Ste 550 (91411-2536)
PHONE.............................818 933-2700
Diane Brinson Schiele, *Pr*
Michelle Boyer, *Prin*
Carla Cave, *Prin*
Erin Gaston, *Sr VP*
David Oliver, *Sr VP*
EMP: 75 **EST:** 2008
SALES (est): 18.71MM
SALES (corp-wide): 20.72B **Publicly Held**
Web: www.momentousins.com
SIC: 6411 Insurance agents, nec
PA: Marsh & Mclennan Companies, Inc.
  1166 Ave Of The Americas
  New York NY
  212 345-5000

(P-8614)
MONARCH E & S INSURANCE SVCS
2540 Foothill Blvd # 101 (91214-4573)
PHONE.............................559 226-0200
EMP: 70
SALES (est): 12.77MM **Privately Held**
SIC: 6411 Insurance information and consulting services

(P-8615)
MONY LIFE INSURANCE COMPANY
Also Called: Mony Life
333 S Anita Dr Ste 750 (92868-3322)
PHONE.............................714 939-6669
Joseph Moore, *Mgr*
EMP: 72
Web: www.equitable.com
SIC: 6411 Insurance agents, brokers, and service
HQ: Mony Life Insurance Company
  1740 Broadway
  New York NY
  800 487-6669

(P-8616)
MORRIS GRRITANO INSUR AGCY INC
Also Called: Nationwide
1122 Laurel Ln (93401-5895)
P.O. Box 1189 (93406-1189)
PHONE.............................805 543-6887
Brendan Morris, *CEO*
Gene Garritano, *
Gabe Garcia, *
David Morgan, *Stockholder*
Kelly Morgan, *Stockholder*
EMP: 85 **EST:** 1916
SQ FT: 14,000
SALES (est): 22.71MM **Privately Held**
Web: www.morrisgarritano.com
SIC: 6411 Insurance agents, nec

(P-8617)
MULLIN TBG INSUR AGCY SVCS LLC (DH)
Also Called: Mullintbg
3333 Michelson Dr Ste 820 (92612-0655)
EMP: 185 **EST:** 1987
SALES (est): 96.87MM
SALES (corp-wide): 60.05B **Publicly Held**
SIC: 6411 Insurance information and consulting services
HQ: The Prudential Insurance Company Of America
  751 Broad St Fl 21
  Newark NJ
  973 802-6000

(P-8618)
NATIONAL INSURANCE CRIME BUR
15545 Devonshire St Ste 309 (91345-2655)
PHONE.............................818 895-2867
Bob Jones, *Dir*
EMP: 82
SALES (corp-wide): 59.53MM **Privately Held**
Web: www.nicb.org
SIC: 6411 Insurance agents, brokers, and service
PA: National Insurance Crime Bureau, Inc
  1111 E Touhy Ave Ste 400
  Des Plaines IL
  847 544-7000

(P-8619)
NAU COUNTRY INSURANCE COMPANY
120 Main St (95695-3100)
PHONE.............................530 662-7466
Greg Deal, *Pr*
EMP: 194
Web: sorry.naucountry.com
SIC: 6411 6399 Insurance agents, nec; Health insurance for pets
HQ: Nau Country Insurance Company
  7333 Sunwood Dr Nw
  Ramsey MN

(P-8620)
NAU COUNTRY INSURANCE COMPANY
7485 N Palm Ave Ste 105 (93711-5764)
PHONE.............................559 252-7400
Rick Guestin, *Owner*
EMP: 227
Web: sorry.naucountry.com
SIC: 6411 Insurance agents, nec
HQ: Nau Country Insurance Company
  7333 Sunwood Dr Nw
  Ramsey MN

(P-8621)
NETWORKED INSURANCE AGENTS LLC
Also Called: Nationwide
1410 Rocky Ridge Dr (95661-2811)
PHONE.............................800 682-8476
George Biancardi, *Pr*
Kelly Mcrae, *CFO*
Larry Oslie, *Ex VP*
EMP: 110 **EST:** 2013
SALES (est): 22.87MM
SALES (corp-wide): 726.22MM **Privately Held**
Web: www.amwins.com
SIC: 6411 Insurance agents, nec
PA: Amwins Group, Inc.
  4725 Piedmont Row Dr # 600
  Charlotte NC
  704 749-2700

(P-8622)
NEW YORK LIFE RE INVESTORS
Also Called: New York Life
50 California St (94111-4621)
PHONE.............................415 402-4117
EMP: 97 **EST:** 2017
SALES (est): 908.81K **Privately Held**
Web: www.newyorklife.com
SIC: 6411 Insurance agents and brokers

(P-8623)
NEWPORT GROUP INC
35 Iron Point Cir Ste 300 (95630-8589)
PHONE.............................925 328-4540
Gregory W Tschider, *Brnch Mgr*

PRODUCTS & SERVICES SECTION

6411 - Insurance Agents, Brokers, And Service (P-8642)

EMP: 285
SALES (corp-wide): 947.08MM Privately Held
Web: www.newportgroup.com
SIC: 6411 Pension and retirement plan consultants
HQ: Newport Group, Inc.
35 Iron Point Cir Ste 300
Folsom CA

(P-8624)
NEWPORT GROUP INC (HQ)
Also Called: Newport Retirement Services
35 Iron Point Cir Ste 300 (95630-8589)
PHONE.................................925 328-4540
EMP: 106 EST: 1985
SALES (est): 574.28MM
SALES (corp-wide): 947.08MM Privately Held
Web: www.newportgroup.com
SIC: 6411 Pension and retirement plan consultants
PA: Ascensus, Llc
200 Dryden Rd E Ste 1000
Dresher PA
215 648-8000

(P-8625)
NEXT INSURANCE INC
490 California Ave Ste 300 (94306-1900)
PHONE.................................855 222-5919
EMP: 193
SALES (corp-wide): 62.92MM Privately Held
Web: www.nextinsurance.com
SIC: 6411 Insurance agents, nec
PA: Next Insurance, Inc.
975 California Ave
Palo Alto CA
855 222-5919

(P-8626)
NNA INSURANCE SERVICES LLC
9350 De Soto Ave (91311-4926)
P.O. Box 2402 (91313-2402)
PHONE.................................818 739-4071
Milton G Valera, Ch Bd
Deborah M Thaw, *
Thomas A Heymann, *
Robert A Clarke, *
▲ EMP: 204 EST: 1957
SQ FT: 55,000
SALES (est): 24.4MM Privately Held
Web: www.nationalnotary.org
SIC: 6411 Insurance agents, brokers, and service

(P-8627)
NORCAL INSURANCE COMPANY (HQ)
Also Called: Norcal
575 Market St Fl 10 (94105-2844)
PHONE.................................415 735-2000
Ned Rand, Pr
EMP: 285 EST: 1975
SALES (est): 106.56MM
SALES (corp-wide): 1.11B Publicly Held
Web: www.norcal-group.com
SIC: 6411 6331 Insurance agents, nec; Fire, marine, and casualty insurance
PA: Proassurance Corporation
100 Brookwood Pl
Birmingham AL
205 877-4400

(P-8628)
NORTHWEST ADMINISTRATORS INC
1000 Marina Blvd Ste 400 (94005-1841)
PHONE.................................650 570-7300
William Riker, Prin
EMP: 65
SALES (corp-wide): 89.51MM Privately Held
Web: www.nwadmin.com
SIC: 6411 Pension and retirement plan consultants
PA: Northwest Administrators, Inc.
2323 Eastlake Ave E
Seattle WA
206 329-4900

(P-8629)
NORTHWESTERN MUTL INV MGT LLC
Also Called: Northwestern Mutual Investment
610 Newport Center Dr Ste 850 (92660)
PHONE.................................949 759-5555
Gary Farmer, Ex Dir
EMP: 435
SALES (corp-wide): 16.13B Privately Held
Web: www.northwesternmutual.com
SIC: 6411 6282 Insurance agents, brokers, and service; Investment advice
HQ: Northwestern Mutual Investment Management Company, Llc
720 E Wisconsin Ave
Milwaukee WI
414 271-1444

(P-8630)
OAK RIVER INSURANCE COMPANY
1 California St Ste 600 (94111-5403)
P.O. Box 881236 (94188-1236)
PHONE.................................800 661-6029
EMP: 180
SALES (corp-wide): 302.09B Publicly Held
Web: www.bhhc.com
SIC: 6411 Insurance agents, brokers, and service
HQ: Oak River Insurance Company
1314 Douglas St
Omaha NE

(P-8631)
OLD REPUBLIC HM PROTECTION INC
Also Called: Old Republic
2 Annabel Ln Ste 112 (94583-1377)
P.O. Box 5017 (94583-0917)
PHONE.................................925 866-1500
Frank Caballero, Pr
Frank Caballero, Sr VP
Lorna Mello, VP
EMP: 305 EST: 1974
SQ FT: 39,500
SALES (est): 243.98MM
SALES (corp-wide): 8.08B Publicly Held
Web: www.orhp.com
SIC: 6411 Insurance agents, brokers, and service
PA: Old Republic International Corporation
307 N Michigan Ave
Chicago IL
312 346-8100

(P-8632)
ORBA INSURANCE SERVICES INC
Also Called: Orba Financial & Inter SEC
2339 Gold Meadow Way Ste 200 (95670)
PHONE.................................916 858-1222
Gary Curry, Pr
Susan Curry, *
EMP: 91 EST: 1979
SQ FT: 2,600
SALES (est): 6.72MM Privately Held
SIC: 6411 Insurance agents and brokers

(P-8633)
PACIFIC COMPENSATION INSUR CO
3011 Townsgate Rd Ste 120 (91361-5876)
P.O. Box 5034 (91359-5034)
PHONE.................................818 575-8500
Marc E Schmittlein, Pr
EMP: 150 EST: 2002
SALES (est): 58.09MM
SALES (corp-wide): 808.75MM Privately Held
Web: www.copperpoint.com
SIC: 6411 Insurance agents, nec
HQ: Pacific Compensation Corporation
3011 Townsgate Rd Ste 120
Westlake Village CA

(P-8634)
PACIFIC INDEMNITY COMPANY
Also Called: Chubb
555 S Flower St Ste 300 (90071-2427)
PHONE.................................213 622-2334
John Fennigan, Pr
EMP: 300 EST: 1926
SALES (est): 92.59MM Privately Held
Web: www.chubb.com
SIC: 6411 6331 6351 Property and casualty insurance agent; Fire, marine, and casualty insurance; mutual; Surety insurance
HQ: Ina Chubb Holdings Inc
436 Walnut St
Philadelphia PA
215 640-1000

(P-8635)
PACIFIC PIONEER INSUR GROUP (PA)
Also Called: Nationwide
6363 Katella Ave (90630-5205)
PHONE.................................714 228-7888
EMP: 80 EST: 1989
SQ FT: 32,000
SALES (est): 13.74MM Privately Held
Web: www.ucageneral.com
SIC: 6411 Insurance agents, nec

(P-8636)
PATHPOINT INC
Also Called: Pathpoint Insurance Services
548 Market St (94104-5401)
PHONE.................................914 500-7154
Ralph Blust, CRO
EMP: 66 EST: 2016
SALES (est): 2.78MM Privately Held
Web: www.pathpoint.com
SIC: 6411 Insurance agents, brokers, and service

(P-8637)
PEGASUS RISK MANAGEMENT INC (PA)
Also Called: Status Medical Management
642 Galaxy Way (95356-9606)
P.O. Box 5038 (95352-5038)
PHONE.................................209 574-2800
Ray Simon, Pr
Brian Bergstrom, *
EMP: 70 EST: 1995
SQ FT: 10,000
SALES (est): 8.93MM Privately Held
Web: www.simon-companies.com
SIC: 6411 Insurance claim processing, except medical

(P-8638)
PENNBROOK INSURANCE SERVICE
Also Called: Nationwide
300 Montgomery Ste 450 (94104-1906)
P.O. Box 26849 (94126-0849)
PHONE.................................415 820-2200
Clayton Wiens, Pr
EMP: 99 EST: 1982
SQ FT: 5,200
SALES (est): 6.71MM Privately Held
Web: www.kemper.com
SIC: 6411 Insurance agents, nec

(P-8639)
PETRA RISK SOLUTIONS
5927 Priestly Dr Ste 102 (92008-8800)
PHONE.................................800 466-8951
EMP: 67
SALES (corp-wide): 24.66MM Privately Held
Web: www.petrarisksolutions.com
SIC: 6411 Insurance brokers, nec
PA: Petra Risk Solutions
770 The City Dr S # 1500
Orange CA
800 466-8951

(P-8640)
PLANPRESCRIBER INC
440 E Middlefield Rd (94043-4006)
PHONE.................................650 584-2700
Bruce A Telkamp, CEO
EMP: 239 EST: 2012
SALES (est): 921.88K Publicly Held
SIC: 6411 Insurance agents, brokers, and service
PA: Ehealth, Inc.
2625 Augustine Dr Fl 2
Santa Clara CA

(P-8641)
POLISEEK AIS INSUR SLTIONS INC
Also Called: Nationwide
17785 Center Court Dr N Ste 250 (90703-8573)
PHONE.................................866 480-7335
Mark Ribisi, Pr
Chris Bremer, CAO*
Romayne Levee, *
Lani Elkin, *
Mark Casas, *
EMP: 85 EST: 2008
SALES (est): 2MM
SALES (corp-wide): 3.64B Publicly Held
Web: www.nationwide.com
SIC: 6411 Insurance agents, nec
HQ: Ais Management, Llc
17785 Center Court Dr N # 250
Cerritos CA

(P-8642)
PRECEPT ADVISORY GROUP LLC (DH)
Also Called: Precept Group The
130 Theory Ste 200 (92617-3065)
PHONE.................................949 955-1430
Wade R Olson, Pr
Alex Wasilewski, Ex VP
Steve Zarate, COO
Christopher H Coulter, CMO
Mercedes Meseck, VP
EMP: 90 EST: 1987
SQ FT: 32,000
SALES (est): 28.16MM
SALES (corp-wide): 25.36B Publicly Held
Web: www.bbt.com

6411 - Insurance Agents, Brokers, And Service (P-8643)

SIC: 6411 Insurance brokers, nec
HQ: Mcgriff Insurance Services, Inc.
3201 Beechleaf Ct Ste 200
Raleigh NC
919 716-9907

(P-8643)
PREFERRED EMPLOYERS INSUR CO
9797 Aero Dr Ste 200 (92123-1829)
P.O. Box 85478 (92186-5478)
PHONE..................................619 688-3900
Linda R Smith, CEO
Steven A Gallacher, *
Dennis J Levesque, Pr
EMP: 86 EST: 1997
SALES (est): 24.62MM
SALES (corp-wide): 11.17B Publicly Held
Web: www.peiwc.com
SIC: 6411 Insurance information and consulting services
PA: W. R. Berkley Corporation
475 Steamboat Rd Fl 1
Greenwich CT
203 629-3000

(P-8644)
PREMIER DEALER SERVICES INC
9449 Balboa Ave Ste 300 (92123-4395)
PHONE..................................858 810-1700
John R Topits, Pr
Kurt Wolery, *
A Kurt Wolery, *
EMP: 100 EST: 1998
SALES (est): 9.31MM Privately Held
Web: www.pdsadm.com
SIC: 6411 Insurance agents, brokers, and service

(P-8645)
QUALITAS INSURANCE COMPANY
Also Called: Qualitas Premier Insur Svcs
4545 Murphy Canyon Rd Fl 3 (92123-4363)
PHONE..................................619 876-4355
Eduardo Pedrero, CEO
Robert Blanchard, *
EMP: 70 EST: 2014
SALES (est): 10.78MM Privately Held
Web: www.qualitasinsurance.com
SIC: 6411 Insurance agents, brokers, and service

(P-8646)
QUALITY CLAIMS MANAGEMENT CORP
2763 Camino Del Rio S (92108-3708)
PHONE..................................619 450-8600
Ronald Reitz, Pr
Thomas Holthus, *
Kevin Mccarthy, CFO
EMP: 60 EST: 2007
SQ FT: 8,000
SALES (est): 8.56MM Privately Held
Web: www.qualityclaims.com
SIC: 6411 Insurance claim adjusters, not employed by insurance company

(P-8647)
R MC CLOSKEY INSURANCE AGENCY
Also Called: Tax and Financial Group
4001 Macarthur Blvd Ste 300 (92660-2505)
PHONE..................................949 223-8100
Richard Mc Closkey, Pr
EMP: 120 EST: 1969
SQ FT: 15,000
SALES (est): 20.39MM Privately Held

Web: www.tfgroup.com
SIC: 6411 Insurance agents, nec

(P-8648)
RELATION INSURANCE INC (PA)
Also Called: Relation Insurance Services
1277 Treat Blvd Ste 400 (94597-7962)
PHONE..................................925 937-5858
Tim Hall, CEO
Edward Nathan Page, *
Timothy J Hall, *
Russell Brown, *
EMP: 86 EST: 2007
SQ FT: 1,695
SALES (est): 260.93MM
SALES (corp-wide): 260.93MM Privately Held
Web: www.relationinsurance.com
SIC: 6411 Insurance brokers, nec

(P-8649)
ROBERT MORENO INSURANCE SVCS
3110 E Guasti Rd Ste 500 (91761-1228)
PHONE..................................714 578-3318
Robert B Moreno, Owner
EMP: 140 EST: 1978
SALES (est): 20.49MM Privately Held
Web: rmis.informins.com
SIC: 6411 Insurance agents, nec

(P-8650)
SACRAMNTO HSING RDVLPMENT AGCY
630 I St Fl 3 (95814-2404)
PHONE..................................916 440-1376
La Shelle Dozier, Brnch Mgr
EMP: 270
SALES (corp-wide): 48.94MM Privately Held
Web: www.shra.org
SIC: 6411 Insurance agents, brokers, and service
PA: Sacramento Housing And Redevelopment Agency
801 12th St
Sacramento CA
916 440-1390

(P-8651)
SAFECO INSURANCE COMPANY AMER
Safeco
330 N Brand Blvd Ste 680 (91203-2385)
PHONE..................................818 956-4250
Don Chambers, Mgr
EMP: 145
SALES (corp-wide): 20.63B Privately Held
Web: www.safeco.com
SIC: 6411 Insurance agents, nec
HQ: Safeco Insurance Company Of America
1001 4th Ave Ste 800
Seattle WA
206 545-5000

(P-8652)
SANTOS LEGACY BUILDERS LLC
2829 Watt Ave # 101 (95821-6200)
PHONE..................................916 439-2777
Ernesto Santos, Managing Member
Ernesto David Santos, Managing Member*
EMP: 99 EST: 2014
SALES (est): 1.93MM Privately Held
SIC: 6411 Insurance agents, brokers, and service

(P-8653)
SEDGWICK CLAIMS MGT SVCS INC
Also Called: Sedgwick
2101 Webster St (94612-3011)
PHONE..................................510 302-3000
Athanasios Soha, Brnch Mgr
EMP: 79
SALES (corp-wide): 2.39B Privately Held
Web: www.sedgwick.com
SIC: 6411 Insurance claim adjusters, not employed by insurance company
PA: Sedgwick Claims Management Services, Inc.
1100 Ridgeway Loop Rd # 2
Memphis TN
248 649-2100

(P-8654)
SEDGWICK CLAIMS MGT SVCS INC
Also Called: Sedgwick
1851 Heritage Ln (95815-4926)
PHONE..................................916 568-7394
EMP: 70
SALES (corp-wide): 14.95B Publicly Held
SIC: 6411 Insurance claim adjusters, not employed by insurance company
HQ: Sedgwick Claims Management Services, Inc.
8125 Sedgwick Way
Memphis TN
901 415-7400

(P-8655)
SEDGWICK CMS HOLDINGS INC
Also Called: Sedgwick
3633 Inland Empire Blvd (91764-4922)
PHONE..................................909 477-5500
Kim Pech, Brnch Mgr
EMP: 254
Web: www.sedgwick.com
SIC: 6411 Insurance claim adjusters, not employed by insurance company
PA: Sedgwick Cms Holdings, Inc.
1100 Ridgeway Loop Rd # 2
Memphis TN

(P-8656)
SELECTQOTE AUTO HM INSUR SVCS
595 Market St Fl 10 (94105-2809)
PHONE..................................415 977-1300
Timothy Danker, Prin
EMP: 1679
SALES (corp-wide): 1B Publicly Held
Web: homeandauto.selectquote.com
SIC: 6411 Insurance agents, nec
HQ: Selectquote Auto & Home Insurance Services, Llc
6800 W 115th St Ste 2511
Overland Park KS
888 220-5450

(P-8657)
SENECA FAMILY OF AGENCIES
Also Called: Cys Knship Sneca Tstin Wrprund
1801 Park Court Pl Bldg H (92701-5028)
PHONE..................................714 881-8600
EMP: 108
SALES (corp-wide): 150.1MM Privately Held
Web: www.senecafoa.org
SIC: 6411 Insurance agents, brokers, and service
PA: Seneca Family Of Agencies
8945 Golf Links Rd
Oakland CA
510 317-1444

(P-8658)
SENTRY LIFE INSURANCE COMPANY
535 Main St Fl 2 (94553-1102)
PHONE..................................925 370-7339
EMP: 239
SALES (corp-wide): 3.62B Privately Held
Web: www.sentry.com
SIC: 6411 Insurance agents, brokers, and service
HQ: Sentry Life Insurance Company
1800 N Point Dr
Stevens Point WI
715 346-6000

(P-8659)
SENTRY LIFE INSURANCE COMPANY
4720 Aliso Way (92057-6821)
PHONE..................................661 274-4018
Jay Ottersen, Mgr
EMP: 191
SALES (corp-wide): 3.62B Privately Held
Web: www.sentry.com
SIC: 6411 Insurance agents, brokers, and service
HQ: Sentry Life Insurance Company
1800 N Point Dr
Stevens Point WI
715 346-6000

(P-8660)
SEQUOIA BNEFITS INSUR SVCS LLC (PA)
Also Called: Sequoia Benefits
1850 Gateway Dr Ste 600 (94404-4064)
PHONE..................................650 369-0200
EMP: 68 EST: 2001
SQ FT: 2,000
SALES (est): 26.87MM
SALES (corp-wide): 26.87MM Privately Held
Web: www.sequoia.com
SIC: 6411 Insurance agents, brokers, and service

(P-8661)
SOUTHERN CALIFORNIA PERMANENTE
393 E Walnut St (91188-0001)
PHONE..................................626 405-5722
EMP: 76 EST: 2014
SALES (est): 1.1MM Privately Held
Web: www.scpmgphysiciancareers.com
SIC: 6411 Pension and retirement plan consultants

(P-8662)
STANDARD INSURANCE COMPANY
1600 Riviera Ave Ste 150 (94596-7117)
PHONE..................................925 947-3950
Vicky Toroian, Mgr
EMP: 71
Web: www.standard.com
SIC: 6411 Insurance agents, nec
HQ: Standard Insurance Company
900 Sw 5th Ave Ste 400
Portland OR
971 321-7000

(P-8663)
STATE FARM GENERAL INSUR CO
Also Called: State Farm Insurance
945 Otay Lakes Rd Ste K (91913-3055)
PHONE..................................619 227-5777
Mark Witcher, Owner

PRODUCTS & SERVICES SECTION
6411 - Insurance Agents, Brokers, And Service (P-8684)

EMP: 99
SALES (corp-wide): 27.88B **Privately Held**
Web: www.statefarm.com
SIC: 6411 Insurance agents and brokers
HQ: State Farm General Insurance Co Inc
 1 State Farm Plz
 Bloomington IL
 309 766-2311

(P-8664)
STATE FARM MUTL AUTO INSUR CO
Also Called: State Farm Insurance
900 Old River Rd 400 (93311-9501)
PHONE...........................309 766-2311
EMP: 72
SALES (corp-wide): 39.59B **Privately Held**
SIC: 6411 Insurance agents and brokers
PA: State Farm Mutual Automobile
 Insurance Company
 1 State Farm Plz
 Bloomington IL
 309 766-2311

(P-8665)
SUNLAND INSURANCE AGENCY
Also Called: Sunland
4961 E Kings Canyon Rd (93727-3812)
P.O. Box 779 (93613-0779)
PHONE...........................559 251-7861
Michael Denman, Owner
EMP: 105 **EST:** 1974
SALES (est): 575.29K
SALES (corp-wide): 3.64B **Publicly Held**
SIC: 6411 Insurance agents, nec
HQ: Mercury Insurance Company
 4484 Wilshire Blvd
 Los Angeles CA
 323 937-1060

(P-8666)
SURECO HLTH LF INSUR AGCY INC
201 Sandpointe Ave Ste 600 (92707-5778)
PHONE...........................949 333-0263
Marc Steven Bablot, CEO
EMP: 75 **EST:** 2016
SALES (est): 10.31MM **Privately Held**
Web: www.sureco.com
SIC: 6411 7379 7311 Insurance agents, brokers, and service; Online services technology consultants; Advertising agencies

(P-8667)
SYMPHONY RISK SLTONS INSUR SVC
Also Called: Nationwide
44 Montgomery St Ste 1700 (94104-4704)
PHONE...........................415 957-0600
Van Maroevich, CEO
Theresa M Maroevich, *
Laura Cornaggia, *
Jerry Clifford, *
Gerald Clifford, *
EMP: 60 **EST:** 1969
SQ FT: 10,000
SALES (est): 11.73MM **Privately Held**
Web: www.nationwide.com
SIC: 6411 Insurance agents, nec

(P-8668)
TBG INSURANCE SERVICES CORP
100 N Pacific Coast Hwy Ste 500 (90245-5658)
PHONE...........................310 203-8770
Michael R Shute, CEO
Michael Glickman, *
EMP: 72 **EST:** 1983
SALES (est): 11.48MM
SALES (corp-wide): 60.05B **Publicly Held**
SIC: 6411 8111 Insurance agents, brokers, and service; Legal services
PA: Prudential Financial, Inc.
 751 Broad St
 Newark NJ
 973 802-6000

(P-8669)
TEACHERS PENSION & INSUR SVCS
213 S Sierra Ave (95361-4013)
PHONE...........................800 474-1440
Erik James Neville, Pr
Jodi Michelle Neville, Sec
EMP: 85 **EST:** 2008
SALES (est): 5.95MM **Privately Held**
Web: www.tpensions.com
SIC: 6411 Insurance agents, brokers, and service

(P-8670)
TEAGUE INSURANCE AGENCY INC
Also Called: Nationwide
4700 Spring St Ste 400 (91942-0275)
PHONE...........................619 464-6851
Walter Johnston, Pr
Elizabeth Bonilla, *
EMP: 61 **EST:** 1968
SQ FT: 4,500
SALES (est): 9.72MM **Privately Held**
Web: www.teagueins.com
SIC: 6411 Insurance agents, nec

(P-8671)
THI HOLDINGS (DELAWARE) INC
2140 E Palmdale Blvd Ste O (93550-1202)
PHONE...........................661 266-7423
Lewis Pelser, Mgr
EMP: 401
SALES (corp-wide): 18.35B **Privately Held**
SIC: 6411 Insurance agents, nec
HQ: Thi Holdings (Delaware), Inc.
 5915 Landerbrook Dr
 Cleveland OH

(P-8672)
TM CLAIMS SERVICE INC
Also Called: Tokio Marine Michido
800 E Colorado Blvd (91101-2103)
P.O. Box 7216 (91109-7316)
PHONE...........................626 568-7800
Tommy Hasegawa, Mgr
EMP: 96
Web: www.tmamerica.com
SIC: 6411 Insurance brokers, nec
HQ: Tm Claims Service, Inc.
 499 Wshngton Blvd Ste 150
 Jersey City NJ

(P-8673)
TOKIO MARINE HIGHLAND INSURANCE SERVICES INC (DH)
Also Called: Tm Highland Insurance Services
899 El Centro St (91030-3101)
PHONE...........................626 463-6486
EMP: 100 **EST:** 1962
SALES (est): 84.01MM **Privately Held**
Web: www.tokiomarinehighland.com
SIC: 6411 Insurance agents, nec
HQ: Tokio Marine Kiln Insurance Limited
 20 Fenchurch Street
 London
 207 886-9000

(P-8674)
TOPA INSURANCE COMPANY (HQ)
1800 Avenue Of The Stars Ste 1200 (90067-4200)
PHONE...........................310 201-0451
John E Anderson, Ch Bd
Harry W Degner, *
Noshirwan Marfatia, *
William S Anderson, *
Dan Sherrin, *
EMP: 79 **EST:** 1979
SALES (est): 24.39MM
SALES (corp-wide): 251.02MM **Privately Held**
Web: www.topains.com
SIC: 6411 Insurance agents, nec
PA: Topa Equities, Ltd.
 1900 Avenue Of The Stars # 1050
 Los Angeles CA
 310 203-9199

(P-8675)
TRAVELERS PROPERTY CSLTY CORP
Also Called: Travelers Insurance
401 Lennon Ln (94598-2508)
P.O. Box 13089 (95813-3089)
PHONE...........................925 945-4000
Julie Weisert, Brnch Mgr
EMP: 187
SALES (corp-wide): 36.88B **Publicly Held**
Web: www.travelers.com
SIC: 6411 Insurance agents, nec
HQ: Travelers Property Casualty Insurance Company
 1 Tower Sq
 Hartford CT

(P-8676)
TRG INSURANCE SERVICES
Also Called: The Rule Group
4675 Macarthur Ct (92660-8891)
PHONE...........................949 474-1550
EMP: 221 **EST:** 1983
SALES (est): 1.76MM **Privately Held**
SIC: 6411 Insurance brokers, nec
HQ: Integro Usa Inc.
 1 State St Fl 9
 New York NY
 212 295-8000

(P-8677)
TRI-AD
221 W Crest St Ste 300 (92025-1737)
PHONE...........................760 743-7555
EMP: 104 **EST:** 2019
SALES (est): 6.42MM **Privately Held**
Web: www.tri-ad.com
SIC: 6411 Pension and retirement plan consultants

(P-8678)
UNITED AGENCIES INC (PA)
Also Called: Nationwide
301 E Colorado Blvd Ste 200 (91101)
P.O. Box 7139 (91109-7139)
PHONE...........................818 952-8818
TOLL FREE: 800
Thomas Hays, Ch Bd
Gary Conkey, Pr
J O Youngfleish Iii, VP
Robert W Bader, VP
EMP: 66 **EST:** 1962
SQ FT: 5,900
SALES (est): 26.41MM
SALES (corp-wide): 26.41MM **Privately Held**
Web: www.unitedagencies.com

SIC: 6411 Insurance agents, nec

(P-8679)
VALLEY INSURANCE SERVICE INC
Also Called: Brower Hale
23181 Verdugo Dr Ste 100b (92653-1313)
PHONE...........................949 707-4080
Debbie Hale, Mgr
EMP: 554
SALES (corp-wide): 306.15MM **Privately Held**
SIC: 6411 Insurance agents, brokers, and service
HQ: Valley Insurance Service, Inc.
 4695 Macarthur Ct Ste 600
 Newport Beach CA
 626 966-3664

(P-8680)
VAN BEURDEN INSURANCE SVCS INC (PA)
Also Called: Kemper Insurance
1600 Draper St (93631-1911)
P.O. Box 67 (93631-0067)
PHONE...........................559 634-7125
William J Van Beurden, Pr
Chris Van Beurden, *
EMP: 67 **EST:** 1934
SQ FT: 20,000
SALES (est): 19.19MM
SALES (corp-wide): 19.19MM **Privately Held**
Web: www.vanbeurden.com
SIC: 6411 Insurance agents, nec

(P-8681)
VETERINARY PET INSURANCE SERVICES INC
Also Called: Dvm Insurance Agency
1800 E Imperial Hwy Ste 145 (92821)
P.O. Box 2344 (92822-2344)
PHONE...........................714 989-0555
EMP: 420
Web: www.petinsurance.com
SIC: 6411 Insurance agents, brokers, and service

(P-8682)
VETERINARY PET SERVICES INC
3060 Saturn St (92821-1732)
PHONE...........................714 989-0555
EMP: 106 **EST:** 2014
SALES (est): 2.66MM **Privately Held**
SIC: 6411 Insurance agents, brokers, and service

(P-8683)
WATERIDGE INSURANCE SVCS INC
Also Called: Nationwide
9655 Granite Ridge Dr (92123-2669)
PHONE...........................858 452-2200
Jeff Byroads, Mng Pt
John Clanton, *
EMP: 61 **EST:** 1984
SALES (est): 24.81MM **Privately Held**
Web: www.assuredpartners.com
SIC: 6411 Insurance agents, nec
PA: Assuredpartners, Inc.
 450 S Orange Ave Fl 4
 Orlando FL

(P-8684)
WELLS FRGO INSUR SVCS MINN INC
4141 Inland Empire Blvd (91764-5004)

6411 - Insurance Agents, Brokers, And Service (P-8685)

PHONE....................909 481-3802
EMP: 103
SALES (corp-wide): 94.18B Publicly Held
SIC: 6411 Insurance agents, brokers, and service
HQ: Wells Fargo Insurance Services Of Minnesota, Inc.
400 Highway 169 S Ste 800
Minneapolis MN
952 563-0600

(P-8685)
WEST COVINA FOSTER FAMILY AGCY
Also Called: A SUNRISE HORIZON
527 E Rowland St Ste 100 (91723-3230)
PHONE....................626 814-9085
Sukhwinder Singh, Ex Dir
Emmanuel Azariah, *
EMP: 70 EST: 1994
SALES (est): 5.23MM Privately Held
Web: www.westcovina.org
SIC: 6411 Insurance agents, brokers, and service

(P-8686)
WESTERN PENN AAA INSUR AGCY
3712 State St (93105-3104)
PHONE....................805 682-5811
EMP: 370
SALES (corp-wide): 1.08B Privately Held
SIC: 6411 Insurance agents, nec
HQ: Western Penn Aaa Insurance Agency Inc
5900 Baum Blvd Ste 2
Pittsburgh PA
412 362-3300

(P-8687)
WESTWOOD INSURANCE AGENCY LLC (HQ)
6320 Canoga Ave (91367-7799)
PHONE....................818 990-9715
John Flynn, Pr
Mark Nettleton, *
EMP: 89 EST: 1952
SALES (est): 17.7MM
SALES (corp-wide): 980.72MM Publicly Held
Web: www.westwoodinsurance.com
SIC: 6411 Insurance agents, nec
PA: Brp Group, Inc.
4211 W Boy Scout Blvd
Tampa FL
866 279-0698

(P-8688)
WINTON-IRELAND INSUR AGCY INC (PA)
Also Called: Nationwide
627 E Canal Dr (95380-4022)
P.O. Box 3277 (95381-3277)
PHONE....................209 667-0995
Michael Ireland, Pr
Jeff Quinn, *
Ted Green, *
EMP: 80 EST: 1913
SQ FT: 10,000
SALES (est): 21.16MM
SALES (corp-wide): 21.16MM Privately Held
Web: www.wisg.com
SIC: 6411 Insurance brokers, nec

(P-8689)
WM MICHAEL STEMLER INC (PA)
Also Called: Delta Health Systems
3244 Brookside Rd Ste 200 (95219-2384)
P.O. Box 1227 (95201-1227)
PHONE....................209 948-8483
William M Stemler, CEO
Richard Roge, *
Patti Silva, *
EMP: 110 EST: 1968
SQ FT: 30,100
SALES (est): 21.23MM
SALES (corp-wide): 21.23MM Privately Held
Web: www.deltahealthsystems.com
SIC: 6411 Medical insurance claim processing, contract or fee basis

(P-8690)
WM MICHAEL STEMLER INC
7110 N Fresno St Ste 350 (93720-2933)
PHONE....................559 228-4144
Robert Maes, Brnch Mgr
EMP: 80
SALES (corp-wide): 21.23MM Privately Held
Web: www.deltahealthsystems.com
SIC: 6411 Medical insurance claim processing, contract or fee basis
PA: Wm. Michael Stemler, Incorporated
3244 Brookside Rd Ste 200
Stockton CA
209 948-8483

(P-8691)
WOOD GUTMANN BOGART INSUR BRKG
Also Called: Nationwide
15901 Red Hill Ave Ste 100 (92780-7317)
PHONE....................714 505-7000
Kevin S Bogart, CEO
EMP: 93 EST: 1984
SALES (est): 23.83MM Privately Held
Web: www.burnhamwgb.com
SIC: 6411 Insurance agents, nec

(P-8692)
WOOD GUTMANN BOGART INSUR BRKS
Also Called: Burnham Wgb Insur Solutions
15901 Red Hill Ave Ste 100 (92780-7318)
PHONE....................714 505-7000
EMP: 130 EST: 1985
SQ FT: 5,500
SALES (est): 10.46MM
SALES (corp-wide): 99.6MM Privately Held
Web: www.burnhamwgb.com
SIC: 6411 Insurance brokers, nec
PA: Burnham Benefits Insurance Services, Llc
2211 Michelson Dr # 1200
Irvine CA
805 772-7965

(P-8693)
WOODRUFF-SAWYER & CO (PA)
Also Called: Nationwide
50 California St Fl 12 (94111-4646)
PHONE....................415 391-2141
Andy Barrengos, CEO
Melody Silberstein, Sr VP
Charles Shoemaker, Sr VP
Stephen Gaitley, Sr VP
Kristine Furrer, Sr VP
EMP: 240 EST: 1966
SQ FT: 54,000
SALES (est): 163.33MM
SALES (corp-wide): 163.33MM Privately Held
Web: www.woodruffsawyer.com
SIC: 6411 Insurance brokers, nec

(P-8694)
WORD & BROWN INSURANCE ADMINISTRATORS INC (PA)
Also Called: Cobrapro
721 S Parker St Ste 300 (92868-4732)
PHONE....................714 835-5006
EMP: 430 EST: 1977
SALES (est): 105.94MM
SALES (corp-wide): 105.94MM Privately Held
Web: www.wordandbrown.com
SIC: 6411 Insurance brokers, nec

(P-8695)
WORKERS CMPNSTION INSUR RTING (PA)
Also Called: Wcirb
1901 Harrison St 17th Fl (94612-3508)
PHONE....................888 229-2472
William Mudge, Pr
David Bellusci, *
Timothy Benjamin, *
Brenda Keys, *
Sean Cooper, *
EMP: 160 EST: 1915
SALES (est): 38.29MM
SALES (corp-wide): 38.29MM Privately Held
Web: www.wcirb.com
SIC: 6411 Insurance agents, brokers, and service

(P-8696)
WORLDWIDE HOLDINGS INC (PA)
725 S Figueroa St Ste 1900 (90017-5496)
PHONE....................213 236-4500
Donald R Davis, Ch
Davis D Moore, *
Daniel Colacurcio, *
EMP: 85 EST: 1970
SQ FT: 23,000
SALES (est): 45.29MM
SALES (corp-wide): 45.29MM Privately Held
SIC: 6411 Insurance brokers, nec

6512 Nonresidential Building Operators

(P-8697)
6500 HLLISTER AVE PARTNERS LLC
6500 Hollister Ave (93117-3011)
PHONE....................805 722-1362
EMP: 100 EST: 2014
SALES (est): 4MM Privately Held
SIC: 6512 Commercial and industrial building operation

(P-8698)
ABBEY-PROPERTIES LLC (PA)
12447 Lewis St Ste 203 (92840-6601)
PHONE....................562 435-2100
▲ EMP: 75 EST: 1989
SQ FT: 276,000
SALES (est): 14.52MM Privately Held
SIC: 6512 Commercial and industrial building operation

(P-8699)
ALLIANCE RESIDENTIAL LLC
Also Called: Royal Equestrian Apartments
1200 W Riverside Dr Ofc (91506-3113)
PHONE....................818 841-2441
David Page, Brnch Mgr
EMP: 65
SALES (corp-wide): 192.76MM Privately Held
Web: www.allresco.com
SIC: 6512 Commercial and industrial building operation
PA: Alliance Residential, Llc
2525 E Camelback Rd # 500
Phoenix AZ
602 778-2800

(P-8700)
ALPINE VILLAGE
Also Called: Alpine Inn Restaurant
23670 Hawthorne Blvd (90505-5904)
PHONE....................310 327-4384
Ursula Wilson, CEO
EMP: 250 EST: 1968
SALES (est): 9.92MM Privately Held
SIC: 6512 Commercial and industrial building operation

(P-8701)
AMERICARE HLTH RETIREMENT INC
Also Called: Silvergate San Marcos
1550 Security Pl Ofc (92078-4063)
PHONE....................760 744-4484
Melba Dunn, Admn
EMP: 150
SQ FT: 51,071
SALES (corp-wide): 8.84MM Privately Held
Web: www.silvergaterr.com
SIC: 6512 8051 Nonresidential building operators; Skilled nursing care facilities
PA: Americare Health & Retirement, Inc.
140 Lomas Santa Fe Dr # 1
Solana Beach CA
858 792-0696

(P-8702)
ARDEN REALTY INC
11601 Wilshire Blvd Fl 5 (90025-0509)
PHONE....................310 966-2600
EMP: 300
Web: www.ardenrealty.com
SIC: 6512 Commercial and industrial building operation

(P-8703)
BPR PROPERTIES BERKELEY LLC
Also Called: Hotel Shattuck Plaza
953 Industrial Ave Ste 100 (94303-4923)
PHONE....................650 424-1400
EMP: 67 EST: 2006
SALES (est): 8.84MM Privately Held
Web: www.bprhotels.com
SIC: 6512 Nonresidential building operators

(P-8704)
BROADWAY SACRAMENTO
1419 H St (95814-1901)
PHONE....................916 446-5880
Laura Mattice, Brnch Mgr
EMP: 165
Web: www.broadwaysacramento.com
SIC: 6512 Theater building, ownership and operation
PA: Broadway Sacramento
1510 J St Ste 200
Sacramento CA

(P-8705)
C & D WAX INC
9353 Waxie Way (92123-1036)
P.O. Box 23506 (92193-3506)
PHONE....................858 292-5954
David Wax, Ex VP

PRODUCTS & SERVICES SECTION
6512 - Nonresidential Building Operators (P-8726)

Charles Wax, *
EMP: 160 **EST:** 1987
SALES (est): 4.76MM **Privately Held**
SIC: 6512 Nonresidential building operators

(P-8706)
CALIFORNIA KIT CAB DOOR CORP
105 Cochrane Cir (95037-2832)
PHONE.................408 776-1105
EMP: 87
SALES (corp-wide): 51.21MM **Privately Held**
SIC: 6512 Commercial and industrial building operation
PA: California Kitchen Cabinet Door Corporation
610 Jarvis Dr Ste 200
Morgan Hill CA
408 782-5700

(P-8707)
CB RICHARD ELLIS STRGC PRTNERS
515 S Flower St Ste 3100 (90071-2201)
PHONE.................213 683-4200
EMP: 100 **EST:** 2000
SALES (est): 7.4MM **Publicly Held**
SIC: 6512 Nonresidential building operators
PA: Cbre Group, Inc.
2100 Mckinney Ave # 1250
Dallas TX

(P-8708)
CDCF III PCF LNDMARK SCRMNTO L
Also Called: Colony Dstrssed Cr Spcial Stto
515 S Flower St 44th Fl (90071-2201)
PHONE.................310 552-7211
EMP: 95 **EST:** 2016
SALES (est): 4.52MM **Privately Held**
SIC: 6512 Commercial and industrial building operation

(P-8709)
CITY OF ANAHEIM
Also Called: Anaheim Arena
2695 E Katella Ave (92806-5904)
PHONE.................714 704-2400
Tim Ryan, *Mgr*
EMP: 80
Web: www.anaheimteamstore.com
SIC: 6512 7941 Nonresidential building operators; Sports field or stadium operator, promoting sports events
PA: City Of Anaheim
200 S Anaheim Blvd
Anaheim CA
714 765-5162

(P-8710)
COINLIST
900 Kearny St Ste 500 (94133-5100)
P.O. Box 7775 (94120-7775)
PHONE.................408 230-4375
EMP: 65 **EST:** 2019
SALES (est): 3.05MM **Privately Held**
Web: queue.coinlist.co
SIC: 6512 Commercial and industrial building operation

(P-8711)
COLLINS & COLLINS
Also Called: Leal, Jennifer A
790 E Colorado Blvd Ste 600 (91101)
PHONE.................626 243-1100
John J Collins, *Pt*
Sameul Muir, *Pt*
Robert Traver, *Pt*
EMP: 69 **EST:** 1980
SALES (est): 6.78MM **Privately Held**
Web: www.ccllp.law
SIC: 6512 Commercial and industrial building operation

(P-8712)
COLONY MB PARTNERS LP
1999 Avenue Of The Stars Ste 1200 (90067-6022)
PHONE.................310 282-8820
EMP: 60 **EST:** 1993
SALES (est): 2.53MM **Privately Held**
SIC: 6512 Commercial and industrial building operation

(P-8713)
CRMLS LLC
15325 Fairfield Ranch Rd Ste 200 (91709)
PHONE.................909 859-2040
Art Carter, *CEO*
Edward Zorn, *VP*
Adrese Roundree, *COO*
Ray Ewing, *Chief*
EMP: 106 **EST:** 2019
SALES (est): 4.73MM **Privately Held**
Web: go.crmls.org
SIC: 6512 Nonresidential building operators

(P-8714)
DAVID D BOHANNON ORGANIZATION (PA)
Also Called: San Lorenzo Village Shopg Ctr
60 31st Ave (94403-3404)
PHONE.................650 345-8222
David D Bohannon Ii, *Pr*
Frances E Nelson, *
Scott Bohannon, *
Ernest Lotti Junior, *VP*
EMP: 60 **EST:** 1946
SQ FT: 5,000
SALES (est): 9.92MM
SALES (corp-wide): 9.92MM **Privately Held**
Web: www.ddbo.com
SIC: 6512 6552 Commercial and industrial building operation; Subdividers and developers, nec

(P-8715)
DESERT HOT SPRNG REAL PRPTS IN
Also Called: Desert Hot Springs Spa Hotel
10805 Palm Dr (92240-2511)
PHONE.................760 329-6000
Lynn Byrnes, *CEO*
EMP: 85 **EST:** 1988
SQ FT: 44,070
SALES (est): 2.44MM **Privately Held**
Web: www.dhsspa.com
SIC: 6512 Nonresidential building operators

(P-8716)
DONAHUE SCHRIBER RLTY GROUP LP (PA)
Also Called: Ds Lakeshore
200 Baker St Ste 100 (92626-4551)
PHONE.................714 545-1400
Patrick S Donahue, *CEO*
Lisa L Hirose, *Ex VP*
Lawrence P Casey, *Pr*
Mark L Whitfield, *Ex VP*
EMP: 100 **EST:** 1969
SQ FT: 44,805
SALES (est): 22.01MM
SALES (corp-wide): 22.01MM **Privately Held**
SIC: 6512 Shopping center, property operation only

(P-8717)
ENTREPRENEURIAL CAPITAL CORP
4100 Newport Place Dr Ste 400 (92660)
PHONE.................949 809-3900
John K Abel, *Prin*
EMP: 240
SALES (corp-wide): 33.22MM **Privately Held**
SIC: 6512 Commercial and industrial building operation
PA: Entrepreneurial Capital Corporation
4100 Newport Place Dr # 400
Newport Beach CA
949 809-3900

(P-8718)
ESKATON (PA)
5105 Manzanita Ave Ste D (95608-0523)
PHONE.................916 334-0296
Todd Murch, *CEO*
Sheri Peifer, *
Trevor Hammond, *
Constance Batterson, *
William Pace, *
EMP: 100 **EST:** 1968
SQ FT: 27,000
SALES (est): 156.38MM
SALES (corp-wide): 156.38MM **Privately Held**
Web: www.eskaton.org
SIC: 6512 8051 Commercial and industrial building operation; Convalescent home with continuous nursing care

(P-8719)
ESKATON
Also Called: Falconer House
5701 Falconer Way (95824-1517)
PHONE.................916 395-1722
Leslie Eck, *Brnch Mgr*
EMP: 216
SALES (corp-wide): 156.38MM **Privately Held**
Web: www.eskaton.org
SIC: 6512 8051 Commercial and industrial building operation; Convalescent home with continuous nursing care
PA: Eskaton
5105 Manzanita Ave Ste D
Carmichael CA
916 334-0296

(P-8720)
FORD MOTOR LAND DEV CORP
Also Called: Ford
3 Glen Bell Way Ste 100 (92618-3390)
PHONE.................949 242-6606
Dan Werbin, *Ex Dir*
EMP: 213
SALES (corp-wide): 158.06B **Publicly Held**
Web: www.fordland.com
SIC: 6512 Commercial and industrial building operation
HQ: Ford Motor Land Development Corporation
17000 Rotunda Dr Fl 1
Dearborn MI
248 200-8804

(P-8721)
FREEDOM PROPERTIES-HEMET LLC
Also Called: Village The
27122b Paseo Espada Ste 1024 (92675-5706)
PHONE.................949 489-0430
Cheryl L Roskamp, *Managing Member*
Ms. Cheryl L Roskamp, *Managing Member*
EMP: 250 **EST:** 1999
SALES (est): 6.95MM **Privately Held**
SIC: 6512 Nonresidential building operators

(P-8722)
GLENDALE ASSOCIATES LTD
Also Called: Apple Store Glendale Galleria
100 W Broadway Ste 100 (91210-1230)
PHONE.................818 246-6737
EMP: 100 **EST:** 1976
SALES (est): 5.33MM **Privately Held**
Web: www.glendalegalleria.com
SIC: 6512 Shopping center, property operation only

(P-8723)
GUMBINER SAVETT INC
Also Called: Gumbiner Svett Fnkel Fnglson R
1723 Cloverfield Blvd (90404-4017)
PHONE.................310 828-9798
Louis Savett, *Ch Bd*
Charles Gumbiner, *
Gary Finkel, *
David Rose, *
Rodney Fingleson, *
EMP: 90 **EST:** 1950
SQ FT: 25,000
SALES (est): 10.49MM **Privately Held**
Web: www.gscpa.com
SIC: 6512 Nonresidential building operators

(P-8724)
HEALTH CARE WORKERS UNION (PA)
Also Called: Local 250 Health Care Wkrs Un
560 Thomas L Berkley Way (94612-1602)
PHONE.................510 251-1250
Sal Rosselli, *Pr*
EMP: 70 **EST:** 1991
SQ FT: 25,777
SALES (est): 9.66MM **Privately Held**
Web: www.seiu-uhw.org
SIC: 6512 8631 Commercial and industrial building operation; Labor organizations

(P-8725)
ICW VALENCIA LLC
11455 El Camino Real Ste 200 (92130)
PHONE.................858 350-2600
John Chamberlain, *Prin*
EMP: 224 **EST:** 2013
SALES (est): 727.07K
SALES (corp-wide): 88.5MM **Privately Held**
SIC: 6512 Nonresidential building operators
PA: American Assets, Inc.
11455 El Cmno Rl Ste 140
San Diego CA
858 350-2600

(P-8726)
INSIGNIA/ESG HT PARTNERS INC (DH)
11150 Santa Monica Blvd Ste 220 (90025-3380)
PHONE.................310 765-2600
Mary Ann Tighe, *CEO*
John Powers, *Pr*
EMP: 325 **EST:** 1993
SALES (est): 211.51MM **Publicly Held**
SIC: 6512 Property operation, retail establishment
HQ: Cb Richard Ellis Real Estate Services, Llc
200 Park Ave Fl 19
New York NY
212 984-8000

6512 - Nonresidential Building Operators (P-8727)

(P-8727)
INSTRUMENTAL GLOBAL HQ
777 California Ave Ste 150 (94304-1179)
PHONE..................................650 681-9361
EMP: 74 EST: 2019
SALES (est): 1.31MM Privately Held
Web: www.instrumental.com
SIC: 6512 Commercial and industrial building operation

(P-8728)
INTEX RECREATION CORP
Also Called: INTEX RECREATION CORP
1665 Hughes Way (90810-1835)
PHONE..................................310 549-5400
EMP: 152
SALES (corp-wide): 91.03MM Privately Held
Web: www.intexcorp.com
SIC: 6512 Nonresidential building operators
PA: Intex Properties South Bay Corp.
    4001 Via Oro Ave Ste 210
    Long Beach CA
    310 549-5400

(P-8729)
JOHNSON SERVICE GROUP INC
950 S Bascom Ave (95128-3539)
PHONE..................................408 728-9510
EMP: 1388
SALES (corp-wide): 62.45MM Privately Held
Web: www.jsginc.com
SIC: 6512 Commercial and industrial building operation
PA: Johnson Service Group, Inc.
    1 E Oakhill Dr Ste 200
    Westmont IL
    630 590-6511

(P-8730)
KATELLA PROPERTIES
10140 Grayling Ave (90603-2607)
PHONE..................................562 704-8695
Paige Harrison, Brnch Mgr
EMP: 85
SALES (corp-wide): 8.82MM Privately Held
Web: www.katellaseniorliving.com
SIC: 6512 Nonresidential building operators
PA: Katella Properties
    3952 Katella Ave
    Los Alamitos CA
    562 596-2773

(P-8731)
LA COUNTY
5530 W 83rd St (90045-3309)
PHONE..................................310 417-5184
EMP: 84 EST: 2017
SALES (est): 1.13MM Privately Held
Web: www.musiccenter.org
SIC: 6512 Commercial and industrial building operation

(P-8732)
LERETA LLC
10760 4th St (91730-0975)
PHONE..................................626 332-1942
EMP: 186
Web: www.lereta.com
SIC: 6512 Commercial and industrial building operation
PA: Lereta, Llc
    901 Corporate Center Dr
    Pomona CA

(P-8733)
LOS ANGELES CONVEN AND EXH
Also Called: Los Angeles Dept Convetion Tou
1201 S Figueroa St (90015-1308)
PHONE..................................213 741-1151
Brad Gessner, Genl Mgr
EMP: 288 EST: 1968
SQ FT: 867,000
SALES (est): 23.19MM Privately Held
Web: www.lacclink.com
SIC: 6512 Commercial and industrial building operation

(P-8734)
MALIBU CONFERENCE CENTER INC
327 Latigo Canyon Rd (90265-2708)
PHONE..................................818 889-6440
Glen Gerson, Pr
EMP: 500 EST: 1985
SALES (est): 22.71MM Privately Held
Web: www.calamigos.com
SIC: 6512 Commercial and industrial building operation

(P-8735)
MILLS CORPORATION
Also Called: Ontario Mills Shopping Center
1 Mills Cir Ste 1 (91764-5215)
PHONE..................................909 484-8300
Laurence Siegel, Brnch Mgr
EMP: 91
Web: www.thefixsolutions.com
SIC: 6512 Shopping center, property operation only
HQ: The Mills Corporation
    5425 Wisconsin Ave # 300
    Chevy Chase MD
    301 968-6000

(P-8736)
MILWOOD HEALTHCARE INC
Also Called: MAYWOOD ACRES HEALTHCARE
2641 S C St (93033-4502)
PHONE..................................626 274-4345
Alger Brion, CEO
EMP: 97 EST: 2007
SQ FT: 10,000
SALES (est): 2.46MM Privately Held
Web: www.maywoodacres.com
SIC: 6512 Nonresidential building operators

(P-8737)
MMI REALTY SERVICES INC
260 California St 4th Fl (94111-4396)
PHONE..................................415 288-6888
John Mendelsohn, Brnch Mgr
EMP: 98
SALES (corp-wide): 5.22MM Privately Held
Web: www.mmirealty.com
SIC: 6512 Shopping center, property operation only
PA: Mmi Realty Services, Inc.
    99 S Lake Ave Ste 209
    Pasadena CA
    626 577-8660

(P-8738)
NEVINS/ADAMS PROPERTIES INC (PA)
Also Called: Nevins Adams Properties
920 Garden St Ste A (93101-7465)
PHONE..................................805 963-2884
Henry Nevins, Pr
David Adams, *
EMP: 250 EST: 1992
SALES (est): 9.2MM
SALES (corp-wide): 9.2MM Privately Held
SIC: 6512 Commercial and industrial building operation

(P-8739)
OLEN COMMERCIAL REALTY CORP
Also Called: Olen Residential Realty
7 Corporate Plaza Dr (92660-7904)
PHONE..................................949 644-6536
Igor M Olenicoff, Pr
Andrei Olenicoff, *
EMP: 400 EST: 1974
SQ FT: 44,000
SALES (est): 23.36MM Privately Held
SIC: 6512 Commercial and industrial building operation

(P-8740)
ORANGE BAKERY INC
75 Parker (92618-1605)
PHONE..................................949 454-1247
EMP: 139
Web: www.orangebakery.com
SIC: 6512 Commercial and industrial building operation
HQ: Orange Bakery, Inc.
    17751 Cowan
    Irvine CA
    949 863-1377

(P-8741)
ORMOND BEACH LP
1259 E Thousand Oaks Blvd (91362-2818)
PHONE..................................805 496-4948
Derrick Wada, Pt
Rick Schroeder, Pt
EMP: 80 EST: 2016
SALES (est): 4.15MM Privately Held
SIC: 6512 Nonresidential building operators

(P-8742)
PACIFIC STHWEST CNFRNCE OF EVA
Also Called: Mission Springs Conf Cntr
1050 Lockhart Gulch Rd (95066-2934)
PHONE..................................831 335-9133
Bryan Hayes, Dir
EMP: 139
SQ FT: 15,000
SALES (corp-wide): 4.75MM Privately Held
Web: www.pswc.org
SIC: 6512 Auditorium and hall operation
PA: Pacific Southwest Conference Of The Evangelical Covenant Church
    1333 Willow Pass Rd # 212
    Concord CA
    925 677-2140

(P-8743)
PARTHENON-EY
555 California St Ste 4375 (94104-1503)
PHONE..................................617 478-2550
EMP: 83 EST: 2019
SALES (est): 492.73K Privately Held
Web: parthenon.ey.com
SIC: 6512 Commercial and industrial building operation

(P-8744)
PIER 39 LIMITED PARTNERSHIP (PA)
Beach & Embarcadero Level 3 (94133)
PHONE..................................415 705-5500
Robert A Moor, Genl Pt
Molly M South, *
EMP: 60 EST: 1968
SQ FT: 200,000
SALES (est): 40MM
SALES (corp-wide): 40MM Privately Held
Web: www.pier39.com
SIC: 6512 Commercial and industrial building operation

(P-8745)
PM REALTY GROUP LP
3 Park Plz Ste 450 (92614-2572)
PHONE..................................949 390-5500
Jim Proehl, VP
EMP: 85
Web: www.madisonmarquette.com
SIC: 6512 7349 Nonresidential building operators; Building maintenance services, nec
HQ: Pm Realty Group, L.P.
    1000 Main St Ste 2400
    Houston TX
    713 209-5800

(P-8746)
POWERSCHOOL
150 Parkshore Dr (95630-4710)
PHONE..................................877 873-1550
EMP: 454 EST: 2018
SALES (est): 2.99MM Privately Held
Web: www.powerschool.com
SIC: 6512 Commercial and industrial building operation

(P-8747)
PREMIUM OUTLET PARTNERS LP
Camarillo Premium Outlets
740 Ventura Blvd (93010-5842)
PHONE..................................805 445-8520
Brian Hassett, Genl Mgr
EMP: 95
Web: www.simon.com
SIC: 6512 Shopping center, property operation only
HQ: Premium Outlet Partners, L.P.
    225 W Washington St
    Indianapolis IN

(P-8748)
PREMIUM OUTLET PARTNERS LP
Folsom Premium Outlets
13000 Folsom Blvd Ste 309 (95630-8002)
PHONE..................................916 985-0312
Brenda Sprouse, Brnch Mgr
EMP: 95
Web: www.simon.com
SIC: 6512 Shopping center, property operation only
HQ: Premium Outlet Partners, L.P.
    225 W Washington St
    Indianapolis IN

(P-8749)
PREMIUM OUTLET PARTNERS LP
Factory Stres/ Vcvlle Prmium O
321 Nut Tree Rd Ste 2 (95687-3242)
PHONE..................................707 448-3661
Larry Wallin, Mgr
EMP: 95
Web: www.simon.com
SIC: 6512 Shopping center, property operation only
HQ: Premium Outlet Partners, L.P.
    225 W Washington St
    Indianapolis IN

PRODUCTS & SERVICES SECTION
6512 - Nonresidential Building Operators (P-8771)

(P-8750)
PREMIUM OUTLET PARTNERS LP
Also Called: Carlsbad Premium Outlets
5620 Paseo Del Norte Ste 100 (92008)
PHONE...................760 804-9045
Caren Buksbaum, *Mgr*
EMP: 95
Web: www.simon.com
SIC: 6512 Shopping center, property operation only
HQ: Premium Outlet Partners, L.P.
225 W Washington St
Indianapolis IN

(P-8751)
PREMIUM OUTLET PARTNERS LP
Gilroy Premium Outlets
681 Leavesley Rd (95020-3647)
PHONE...................408 842-3729
Jennifer Bradley, *Brnch Mgr*
EMP: 95
Web: www.simon.com
SIC: 6512 Shopping center, property operation only
HQ: Premium Outlet Partners, L.P.
225 W Washington St
Indianapolis IN

(P-8752)
PREMIUM OUTLET PARTNERS LP
Desert Hills Premium Outlets
48400 Seminole Dr (92230-2125)
PHONE...................951 849-6641
EMP: 95
SQ FT: 430,000
Web: www.simon.com
SIC: 6512 Shopping center, property operation only
HQ: Premium Outlet Partners, L.P.
225 W Washington St
Indianapolis IN

(P-8753)
PROPERTY SHOP LA AT BERKSHIRE
1714 Hillhurst Ave (90027-4419)
PHONE...................310 497-3654
EMP: 65 EST: 2016
SALES (est): 1.23MM Privately Held
SIC: 6512 Nonresidential building operators

(P-8754)
REALTY INCOME CORPORATION (PA)
Also Called: Realty Income
11995 El Camino Real (92130-2539)
PHONE...................858 284-5000
Sumit Roy, *Pr*
Michael D Mckee, *Non-Executive Chairman of the Board*
Christie B Kelly, *Ex VP*
Michelle Bushore, *CLO*
Michael R Pfeiffer, *Ex VP*
EMP: 74 EST: 1969
SALES (est): 1.49B Publicly Held
Web: www.realtyincome.com
SIC: 6512 6798 Nonresidential building operators; Real estate investment trusts

(P-8755)
SAN DIEGO THEATRES INC
Also Called: CIVIC THEATRE
233 A St Ste 900 (92101-4003)
P.O. Box 124920 (92112-4920)
PHONE...................619 615-4007
Carol Wallace, *CEO*
Donald M Telford, *
EMP: 200 EST: 2003
SALES (est): 3.53MM Privately Held
Web: www.sandiegotheatres.org
SIC: 6512 Theater building, ownership and operation

(P-8756)
SCP HORTON OWNER 1 LLC
10850 Wilshire Blvd Ste 1050 (90024-4305)
PHONE...................310 693-4400
Jennifer Gattey, *Prin*
Steven Yari, *
EMP: 70 EST: 2018
SALES (est): 3.75MM Privately Held
SIC: 6512 Nonresidential building operators

(P-8757)
SDMV HOTEL PARTNERS LP
520 Newport Center Dr # 2 (92660-7020)
PHONE...................949 516-0088
Marshall Young, *Pt*
Li Hui Lo, *Pt*
Peiing Lee, *Pt*
EMP: 71 EST: 2019
SALES (est): 2.47MM Privately Held
SIC: 6512 Nonresidential building operators

(P-8758)
SHEA LA QUINTA LLC
Also Called: Shea Homes
655 Brea Canyon Rd (91789-3078)
PHONE...................909 594-9500
John F Shea, *CEO*
EMP: 71 EST: 2013
SALES (est): 959.79K
SALES (corp-wide): 2.1B Privately Held
Web: www.jfshea.com
SIC: 6512 Nonresidential building operators
HQ: Shea Homes Limited Partnership, A California Limited Partnership
655 Brea Canyon Rd
Walnut CA

(P-8759)
SHEA PROPERTIES MGT CO INC
Also Called: Shea Properties
130 Vantis Dr Ste 200 (92656-2691)
P.O. Box 62814 (92602-6093)
PHONE...................949 389-7000
Colm Macken, *CEO*
EMP: 347 EST: 2003
SQ FT: 48,000
SALES (est): 24.36MM
SALES (corp-wide): 2.1B Privately Held
Web: www.sheaproperties.com
SIC: 6512 Nonresidential building operators
PA: J. F. Shea Co., Inc.
655 Brea Canyon Rd
Walnut CA
909 594-9500

(P-8760)
SHORENSTEIN PROPERTIES LLC (PA)
235 Montgomery St Fl 16 (94104-3104)
PHONE...................415 772-7000
Glenn A Shannon, *
Richard A Chicotel, *
Robert S Underhill, *Co-Vice President*
Katie Mcgettigan, *Sr VP*
EMP: 125 EST: 1924
SQ FT: 20,000
SALES (est): 294.8MM
SALES (corp-wide): 294.8MM Privately Held
Web: www.shorenstein.com
SIC: 6512 Commercial and industrial building operation

(P-8761)
SKYWALKER PROPERTIES LTD LLC
1110 Gorgas Ave (94129-1406)
PHONE...................415 746-5296
George Lucas, *Brnch Mgr*
EMP: 63
SALES (corp-wide): 4.45MM Privately Held
SIC: 6512 Nonresidential building operators
PA: Skywalker Properties Ltd. Llc
1 Letterman Dr Bldg B
San Francisco CA
415 746-5059

(P-8762)
SMG HOLDINGS LLC
Also Called: Long Beach Convention Center
300 E Ocean Blvd (90802-4825)
PHONE...................562 499-7611
Charles Beirne, *Genl Mgr*
EMP: 69
SALES (corp-wide): 422MM Privately Held
Web: www.asmglobal.com
SIC: 6512 Nonresidential building operators
HQ: Smg Holdings, Llc
300 Cnshohckn State Rd # 450
Conshohocken PA

(P-8763)
SOLARI ENTERPRISES INC
1507 W Yale Ave (92867-3447)
PHONE...................714 282-2520
Johrita Solari, *Pr*
Bruce Solari, *
EMP: 140 EST: 1986
SQ FT: 8,400
SALES (est): 23.89MM Privately Held
Web: www.solari-ent.com
SIC: 6512 Property operation, retail establishment

(P-8764)
SOUTH COAST PLAZA LLC
Also Called: South Coast Plaza Mall
3333 Bristol St Ofc (92626-1811)
PHONE...................714 435-2000
David Grant, *Mgr*
EMP: 112
SALES (corp-wide): 44.46MM Privately Held
Web: www.southcoastplaza.com
SIC: 6512 Shopping center, property operation only
PA: South Coast Plaza, Llc
3333 Bristol St Ofc
Costa Mesa CA
714 546-0110

(P-8765)
STRAND HILL PROPERTIES
1131 Morningside Dr (90266-5319)
PHONE...................310 545-0707
EMP: 60 EST: 2019
SALES (est): 1.01MM Privately Held
Web: www.strandhill.com
SIC: 6512 Nonresidential building operators

(P-8766)
STRATEGIC ASSET SERVICES LLC
27422 Portola Pkwy Ste 150 (92610-2831)
PHONE...................949 713-0053
Young Hong, *Prin*
EMP: 92 EST: 2012
SALES (est): 2.51MM Privately Held
Web: www.strategicproperty.com

SIC: 6512 Nonresidential building operators

(P-8767)
SUNSET DEVELOPMENT COMPANY (PA)
Also Called: Bishop Ranch
2600 Camino Ramon Ste 201 (94583-5000)
P.O. Box 640 (94583-0640)
PHONE...................925 277-1700
Alexander R Mehran, *Pr*
Alex Mehran Senior, *Ch*
James Clancy, *Ex VP*
Edward Hagopian, *Ex VP*
David Claveau, *Sr VP*
EMP: 146 EST: 1954
SQ FT: 15,000
SALES (est): 41.46MM
SALES (corp-wide): 41.46MM Privately Held
Web: www.bishopranch.com
SIC: 6512 6552 6799 6519 Commercial and industrial building operation; Land subdividers and developers, commercial; Real estate investors, except property operators; Real property lessors, nec

(P-8768)
TEGTMEIER ASSOCIATES INC
14 Mansion Ct (94025-6657)
P.O. Box 776 (94026-0776)
PHONE...................650 847-1639
John Tegtmeier, *Pr*
EMP: 60 EST: 1959
SALES (est): 2.28MM Privately Held
SIC: 6512 7841 5049 Theater building, ownership and operation; Video disk/tape rental to the general public; Theatrical equipment and supplies

(P-8769)
TITAN LED
11959 Discovery Ct (93021-7120)
PHONE...................805 523-7500
Patrick Neff, *Pr*
EMP: 86 EST: 2017
SALES (est): 1.01MM Privately Held
Web: www.titanledus.com
SIC: 6512 Commercial and industrial building operation

(P-8770)
TOPA PROPERTY GROUP INC (HQ)
1800 Avenue Of The Stars Ste 1400 (90067-4200)
PHONE...................310 203-9199
James Brooks, *CEO*
Jim Brooks, *
Paul Gienger, *
Carol Shane, *
Darren Bell, *
EMP: 158 EST: 1981
SALES (est): 47.17MM
SALES (corp-wide): 251.02MM Privately Held
Web: www.andersonholdings.com
SIC: 6512 Commercial and industrial building operation
PA: Topa Equities, Ltd.
1900 Avenue Of The Stars # 1050
Los Angeles CA
310 203-9199

(P-8771)
TRIAD PROPERTIES
995 Riverside St (93001-1636)
PHONE...................805 648-5008
Denise Wise, *Prin*
Edward L Moses, *Prin*

6512 - Nonresidential Building Operators (P-8772)

Jim White, Ch
John Polanskey, Vice Chairman
Oscar Hernandez, Dir
EMP: 60 **EST:** 2004
SALES (est): 430.46K **Privately Held**
SIC: 6512 Nonresidential building operators

(P-8772)
UNIBAL-RODAMCO-WESTFIELD GROUP
2049 Century Park E 41st Fl (90067-3101)
PHONE...................................310 478-4456
EMP: 210 **EST:** 2019
SALES (est): 10.67MM **Privately Held**
Web: www.urw.com
SIC: 6512 Shopping center, property operation only

(P-8773)
UNIVERSAL SHOPPING PLAZA A CA
6281 Regio Ave (90620-1023)
PHONE...................................714 521-8899
Ho Yuan Chen, Genl Pt
EMP: 200 **EST:** 1987
SALES (est): 9.62MM **Privately Held**
SIC: 6512 Shopping center, property operation only

(P-8774)
UNIVERSITY BUSINESS CTR ASSOC
5383 Hollister Ave Ste 120 (93111-2304)
PHONE...................................601 354-3555
David H Hoster Ii, CEO
EMP: 80 **EST:** 1996
SALES (est): 4.37MM
SALES (corp-wide): 487.02MM **Publicly Held**
SIC: 6512 Commercial and industrial building operation
PA: Eastgroup Properties, Inc.
400 W Parkway Pl Ste 100
Ridgeland MS
601 354-3555

(P-8775)
VIRGA INVESTMENT PROPERTY
430 S George Wash Blvd (95993-9154)
PHONE...................................530 755-4409
Larry S Virga, Owner
EMP: 143 **EST:** 2010
SALES (est): 300K **Privately Held**
SIC: 6512 Nonresidential building operators

(P-8776)
WATT PROPERTIES INC (PA)
Also Called: Watt Commercial Properties
2716 Ocean Park Blvd Ste 2025 (90405-5207)
PHONE...................................310 314-2430
Janet Watt Van Huisen, Ch Bd
James Maginn, *
Susan Rorison, *
J Scott Watt, *
EMP: 78 **EST:** 1973
SQ FT: 8,700
SALES (est): 23.58MM
SALES (corp-wide): 23.58MM **Privately Held**
SIC: 6512 6531 6552 Shopping center, property operation only; Real estate managers; Land subdividers and developers, commercial

(P-8777)
WELLNEST
3787 S Vermont Ave (90007-4203)
PHONE...................................323 766-2345
EMP: 98 **EST:** 2020
SALES (est): 1.98MM **Privately Held**
Web: www.wellnestla.org
SIC: 6512 Commercial and industrial building operation

(P-8778)
WELLTOWER OM GROUP LLC
301 W Huntington Dr Ste 5 (91007-3462)
PHONE...................................626 254-0552
Heidy Giron, Brnch Mgr
EMP: 138
SALES (corp-wide): 5.86B **Publicly Held**
SIC: 6512 Commercial and industrial building operation
HQ: Welltower Om Group Llc
4500 Dorr St
Toledo OH
419 247-2800

(P-8779)
WEST SIDE REHAB CORPORATION
1755 E Martin Luther King Jr Blvd (90069-1512)
PHONE...................................323 231-4174
Dean Foley, Pr
EMP: 200 **EST:** 1973
SQ FT: 1,500
SALES (est): 5.83MM **Privately Held**
SIC: 6512 Commercial and industrial building operation

(P-8780)
WESTFIELD LLC (DH)
2049 Century Park E 41st Fl (90067-3101)
PHONE...................................310 478-4456
Peter Lowy, CEO
Gregory Miles, *
Mark Stefanel, *
Rory A Packer, *
EMP: 400 **EST:** 1978
SQ FT: 120,000
SALES (est): 535.37MM
SALES (corp-wide): 206.9MM **Privately Held**
Web: www.westfield.com
SIC: 6512 Shopping center, property operation only
HQ: Westfield America, Inc.
2049 Century Park E Fl 41
Los Angeles CA
310 478-4456

(P-8781)
WESTFIELD AMERICA INC (HQ)
2049 Century Park E 41st Fl (90067-3101)
PHONE...................................310 478-4456
Peter S Lowy, CEO
Jean Marie Tritant, *
Peter R Schwartz, *
Elizabeth Westman, *
Mark A Stefanek, *
EMP: 200 **EST:** 1924
SALES (est): 634.76MM
SALES (corp-wide): 206.9MM **Privately Held**
Web: www.urw.com
SIC: 6512 Shopping center, property operation only
PA: Unibail-Rodamco-Westfield Se
Unibail Rodamco
Paris
145051082

(P-8782)
WESTFIELD AMERICA LTD PARTNR
2049 Century Park E Ste 4100 (90067-3101)
PHONE...................................310 277-3898
EMP: 500 **EST:** 1998
SALES (est): 97.48MM
SALES (corp-wide): 206.9MM **Privately Held**
Web: www.westfield.com
SIC: 6512 Shopping center, property operation only
HQ: Westfield, Llc
2049 Century Park E Fl 41
Los Angeles CA

(P-8783)
WESTLAKE DEVELOPMENT GROUP LLC (PA)
520 S El Camino Real Ste 900 (94402-1726)
PHONE...................................650 579-1010
T M Chang, Managing Member
William H C Chang, *
EMP: 75 **EST:** 1972
SQ FT: 80,000
SALES (est): 17.8MM
SALES (corp-wide): 17.8MM **Privately Held**
Web: www.westlake-realty.com
SIC: 6512 6513 6531 Shopping center, property operation only; Apartment building operators; Real estate agents and managers

(P-8784)
WILSHIRE KINGSLEY INC
Also Called: Bcd Tofu House
3575 Wilshire Blvd (90010-2303)
PHONE...................................213 382-6677
Edward S Lee, Pr
Hee Sook Lee, *
EMP: 100 **EST:** 2001
SALES (est): 4.42MM **Privately Held**
Web: www.bcdtofuhouse.com
SIC: 6512 Commercial and industrial building operation

(P-8785)
YAMAMOTO OF ORIENT INC (HQ)
Also Called: Yamamotoyama of America
122 Voyager St (91768-3252)
PHONE...................................909 594-7356
Nami Yamamoto, CEO
Kahei Yamamoto, Ch Bd
Hisayuki Nakagawa, Pr
Kaichiro Yamamoto, Sec
Kazuya Aburano, Sec
◆ **EMP:** 130 **EST:** 1975
SQ FT: 60,000
SALES (est): 62.64MM **Privately Held**
Web: www.yamamotoyama.com
SIC: 6512 5812 5149 Shopping center, property operation only; Eating places; Tea
PA: Yamamotoyama Co., Ltd.
2-5-1, Nihombashi
Chuo-Ku TKY

6513 Apartment Building Operators

(P-8786)
10632 BOLSA AVENUE LP
Also Called: SYCAMORE COURT APT
500 Nwport Ctr Dr Ste 200 (92660)
P.O. Box 13326 (92658-5093)
PHONE...................................949 673-1221
Shawn Boyd, Prin
EMP: 62 **EST:** 2017
SALES (est): 1.66MM **Privately Held**
SIC: 6513 Apartment building operators

(P-8787)
4TH & FOLSOM ASSOCIATES LP
201 Eddy St (94102-2715)
PHONE...................................415 417-3086
Donald S Falk, Pt
Hermandeep Kaur, Pt
EMP: 431 **EST:** 2019
SALES (est): 8.16MM **Privately Held**
SIC: 6513 Apartment building operators

(P-8788)
A COMMUNITY OF FRIENDS
3701 Wilshire Blvd Ste 700 (90010-2813)
PHONE...................................213 480-0809
Dora Leong Gallo, CEO
EMP: 60 **EST:** 1988
SQ FT: 5,800
SALES (est): 16.48MM **Privately Held**
Web: www.acof.org
SIC: 6513 Apartment building operators

(P-8789)
ADVENTIST HEALTH SYSTEM/ WEST
Also Called: ADVENTIST HEALTH SYSTEM/ WEST
2700 E 4th St (91950-3006)
PHONE...................................619 475-5040
EMP: 82
SALES (corp-wide): 789.42MM **Privately Held**
Web: www.generationsllc.com
SIC: 6513 Retirement hotel operation
PA: Adventist Health System/West, Corporation
1 Adventist Health Way
Roseville CA
844 574-5686

(P-8790)
APERTO PROPERTY MANAGEMENT INC
17351 Main St (91744-5155)
PHONE...................................626 965-1961
EMP: 353
SALES (corp-wide): 15.89MM **Privately Held**
Web: www.apertoliving.com
SIC: 6513 Apartment building operators
PA: Aperto Property Management, Inc.
2 Venture Ste 525
Irvine CA
949 873-4200

(P-8791)
BARKER MANAGEMENT INCORPORATED
Also Called: Senior Garden APT
438 3rd Ave Apt 312 (92101-6876)
PHONE...................................619 236-8130
Peter Barker, Pr
EMP: 75
SALES (corp-wide): 24.16MM **Privately Held**
Web: www.barkermgt.com
SIC: 6513 Retirement hotel operation
PA: Barker Management, Incorporated
1101 E Orangewood Ave # 200
Anaheim CA
714 533-3450

(P-8792)
BAY VISTA SENIOR HOUSING
Also Called: HUMANGOOD
1900 Huntington Dr (91010-2694)
PHONE...................................925 924-7100
Grace Chrisostomo, Governor
Linda Coleman, *
Andrew Mcdonald, Governor

PRODUCTS & SERVICES SECTION
6513 - Apartment Building Operators (P-8814)

Susan Tolentino, *
EMP: 342 EST: 2012
SALES (est): 492.48K
SALES (corp-wide): 27.02MM Privately Held
SIC: 6513 Retirement hotel operation
HQ: Humangood Affordable Housing
1900 Huntington Dr
Duarte CA
925 924-7163

(P-8793)
BV GENERAL INC
Also Called: Leisure Vale Retirement Hotel
413 E Cypress St (91205-3334)
PHONE.................................818 244-2323
Polita Barnes, Dir
EMP: 75
SQ FT: 10,000
Web: www.leisurevale.com
SIC: 6513 Retirement hotel operation
PA: B.V. General, Inc.
1332 S Glendale Ave
Glendale CA

(P-8794)
CALIFRNIA ODD FLLOWS HSING NAP (PA)
Also Called: MEADOWS OF NAPA VALLEY
1800 Atrium Pkwy (94559-4837)
PHONE.................................707 257-7885
Wayne Panchesson, Ex Dir
EMP: 100 EST: 1992
SQ FT: 219,000
SALES (est): 22.17MM
SALES (corp-wide): 22.17MM Privately Held
SIC: 6513 8051 8322 Retirement hotel operation; Convalescent home with continuous nursing care; Old age assistance

(P-8795)
CALIFRNIA ODD FLLOWS HSING NAP
Also Called: Meadows Nappa Valley Care Ctr
1800 Atrium Pkwy (94559-4837)
PHONE.................................707 257-7885
EMP: 68
SQ FT: 30,000
SALES (corp-wide): 22.17MM Privately Held
SIC: 6513 8051 Retirement hotel operation; Skilled nursing care facilities
PA: California Odd Fellows Housing Of Napa, Incorporated
1800 Atrium Pkwy
Napa CA
707 257-7885

(P-8796)
CALIFRNIA-NEVADA METHDST HOMES
Also Called: Forest Hill Manor
551 Gibson Ave (93950-4330)
PHONE.................................831 657-5200
Beverly Power, Brnch Mgr
EMP: 105
SALES (corp-wide): 22.94MM Privately Held
Web: www.cnmh.org
SIC: 6513 Retirement hotel operation
PA: California-Nevada Methodist Homes
201 19th St Ste 100
Oakland CA
510 893-8989

(P-8797)
CASA SANDOVAL LLC
Also Called: Casa Sandoval

1200 Russell Way (94541-7708)
PHONE.................................510 727-1700
EMP: 90 EST: 1995
SQ FT: 215,000
SALES (est): 4.96MM Privately Held
Web: www.morningstarseniorliving.com
SIC: 6513 Retirement hotel operation

(P-8798)
CHARLES & CYNTHIA EBERLY INC
Also Called: The Eberly Company
8383 Wilshire Blvd Ste 906 (90211-2425)
PHONE.................................323 937-6468
Charles Eberly, Pr
Cynthia Eberly, *
EMP: 90 EST: 1986
SALES (est): 8.16MM Privately Held
Web: www.eberlyco.com
SIC: 6513 Apartment building operators

(P-8799)
CHATEAU LK SAN MRCOS HMWNERS A
1502 Circa Del Lago (92078-7201)
PHONE.................................760 471-0083
Chris Arvanitis, Pr
EMP: 75 EST: 1985
SQ FT: 240,000
SALES (est): 4.33MM Privately Held
Web: www.chateaulakesanmarcos.com
SIC: 6513 Retirement hotel operation

(P-8800)
CHRISTIAN CHURCH HOMES
Also Called: Sr. Thea Bowman Manor
6400 San Pablo Ave (94608-1274)
PHONE.................................510 420-8802
Sharon Jacob, Mgr
EMP: 73
SALES (corp-wide): 25.11MM Privately Held
Web: www.cchnc.org
SIC: 6513 Retirement hotel operation
PA: Christian Church Homes
1855 Olympic Blvd Ste 300
Walnut Creek CA
510 632-6712

(P-8801)
DOMINICAN OAKS CORPORATION
3400 Paul Sweet Rd Ofc (95065-1559)
PHONE.................................831 462-6257
Patience Beck, Mgr
Sister Julie Hyer, *
EMP: 80 EST: 1986
SALES (est): 12.67MM Privately Held
Web: www.dominicanoaks.com
SIC: 6513 Retirement hotel operation

(P-8802)
DOMINO REALTY MANAGEMENT CO
Also Called: Versailles On The Lake
3700 S Plaza Dr Ofc (92704-7465)
PHONE.................................714 556-0466
Phil Noden, Prin
EMP: 68
SALES (corp-wide): 9.84MM Privately Held
Web: www.dominorealty.com
SIC: 6513 Apartment building operators
PA: Domino Realty Management Company
9990 Santa Monica Blvd
Beverly Hills CA
310 712-1700

(P-8803)
EAH ELENA GARDENS LP
Also Called: Elena Gardens Apartments
2169 Francisco Blvd E Ste B (94901-5509)
PHONE.................................415 295-8840
EMP: 101
SALES (est): 3.4MM
SALES (corp-wide): 53.75MM Privately Held
Web: www.eahhousing.org
SIC: 6513 Apartment building operators
PA: Eah Inc.
22 Pelican Way
San Rafael CA
415 258-1800

(P-8804)
EAST BAY ASIAN LOCAL DEV CORP
1825 San Pablo Ave Ste 200 (94612-1517)
PHONE.................................510 267-1917
Lina Sheth, Interim Chief Executive Officer
Jeremy Liu, *
EMP: 109 EST: 1975
SQ FT: 78,000
SALES (est): 23.96MM Privately Held
Web: www.ebaldc.org
SIC: 6513 Apartment building operators

(P-8805)
EDEN HOUSING RESIDENT SVCS INC
22645 Grand St (94541-5031)
PHONE.................................510 582-1460
Yolanda York, Ex Dir
EMP: 99 EST: 2008
SALES (est): 4.76MM Privately Held
Web: www.edenhousing.org
SIC: 6513 Apartment building operators

(P-8806)
EMERITUS CORPORATION
Also Called: Creston Village
1919 Creston Rd Ofc (93446-4475)
PHONE.................................805 239-1313
Tonya Hogue, Dir
EMP: 208
SALES (corp-wide): 2.83B Publicly Held
Web: www.brookdaleliving.com
SIC: 6513 Retirement hotel operation
HQ: Emeritus Corporation
6737 W Wa St Ste 2300
Milwaukee WI

(P-8807)
ENCORE SENIOR LIVING III LLC
Also Called: Valley Crest Residential
18524 Corwin Rd (92307-2302)
PHONE.................................760 242-3188
Janna Herrera, Mgr
EMP: 63
SIC: 6513 Retirement hotel operation
PA: Encore Senior Living Iii, Llc
400 Locust St Ste 820
Des Moines IA

(P-8808)
ENCORE SENIOR LIVING III LLC
Also Called: Encore Senior Vlg At Riverside
6280 Clay St (92509-6005)
PHONE.................................951 360-1616
EMP: 79
SIC: 6513 Retirement hotel operation
PA: Encore Senior Living Iii, Llc
400 Locust St Ste 820
Des Moines IA

(P-8809)
ESSEX PORTFOLIO LP (HQ)
Also Called: EPLP
1100 Park Pl Ste 200 (94403-7107)
PHONE.................................650 655-7800
EMP: 316 EST: 1994
SALES (est): 1.61B
SALES (corp-wide): 1.61B Publicly Held
Web: www.essexapartmenthomes.com
SIC: 6513 Apartment building operators
PA: Essex Property Trust, Inc.
1100 Park Pl Ste 200
San Mateo CA
650 655-7800

(P-8810)
ESSEX PROPERTY TRUST INC (PA)
1100 Park Pl Ste 200 (94403-7107)
PHONE.................................650 655-7800
Michael J Schall, Pr
George M Marcus, *
Keith R Guericke, *
Barb Pak, Ex VP
EMP: 316 EST: 1994
SQ FT: 39,600
SALES (est): 1.61B
SALES (corp-wide): 1.61B Publicly Held
Web: www.essexapartmenthomes.com
SIC: 6513 6798 Apartment hotel operation; Real estate investment trusts

(P-8811)
FAIRWOOD ASSOCIATES APTS
Also Called: Fairwood Apartments
8893 Fair Oaks Blvd Ofc (95608-2672)
PHONE.................................916 944-0152
Leeann Morein, Prin
Arthur F Evans, Pt
Joanette Stiron, Mgr
EMP: 99 EST: 1980
SALES (est): 500K Publicly Held
SIC: 6513 Apartment building operators
PA: Apartment Investment & Management Company
4582 S Ulster St Ste 1450
Denver CO

(P-8812)
FFRT RESIDENTIAL LLC
Also Called: Fairfield Properties
5510 Morehouse Dr Ste 200 (92121-3722)
PHONE.................................858 457-2123
EMP: 135
SIC: 6513 6552 6531 1522 Apartment building operators; Subdividers and developers, nec; Real estate agents and managers; Residential construction, nec

(P-8813)
FRONT PORCH COMMUNITIES & SVCS
Also Called: Casa De Manana
849 Coast Blvd (92037-4223)
PHONE.................................858 454-2151
Justin Weber, Brnch Mgr
EMP: 146
Web: www.casademanana.org
SIC: 6513 8052 8361 Retirement hotel operation; Intermediate care facilities; Residential care
PA: Front Porch Communities And Services
800 N Brand Blvd Fl 19
Glendale CA

(P-8814)
FRONT PORCH COMMUNITIES & SVCS
Also Called: Carlsbad By The Sea

6513 - Apartment Building Operators (P-8815)

PRODUCTS & SERVICES SECTION

2855 Carlsbad Blvd (92008-2902)
PHONE.................760 729-4983
Tim Wetzel, Brnch Mgr
EMP: 186
Web: www.frontporch.net
SIC: 6513 Retirement hotel operation
PA: Front Porch Communities And Services
800 N Brand Blvd Fl 19
Glendale CA

(P-8815)
GREYSTAR LP
2580 California St (94040-2725)
PHONE.................650 386-6438
EMP: 5843
SALES (corp-wide): 117.7K Privately Held
Web: www.greystar.com
SIC: 6513 Apartment building operators
PA: Greystar, Lp
465 Meeting St Ste 500
Charleston SC
843 579-9400

(P-8816)
HARVEST MANAGEMENT SUB LLC
Also Called: Las Brisas
1299 Briarwood Dr (93401-5965)
PHONE.................805 543-0187
EMP: 3223
SALES (corp-wide): 389.7MM Privately Held
Web: www.holidayseniorliving.com
SIC: 6513 Retirement hotel operation
PA: Harvest Management Sub Llc
300 E Market St Ste 100
Louisville KY
503 370-7070

(P-8817)
HG FENTON COMPANY
7577 Mission Valley Rd Ste 200 (92108-4432)
PHONE.................619 400-0120
Mike Neal, *
Robert Gottlieb, *
Henry Hunte, *
EMP: 232 EST: 2008
SALES (est): 25.52MM Privately Held
Web: www.hgfenton.com
SIC: 6513 6519 Apartment building operators ; Real property lessors, nec

(P-8818)
HIGNELL INCORPORATED
Also Called: Sierra Manor Apts
1836 Laburnum Ave (95926-2375)
PHONE.................530 345-1965
Becky Nelson, Brnch Mgr
EMP: 60
SALES (corp-wide): 19.23MM Privately Held
Web: www.hignell.com
SIC: 6513 Apartment building operators
PA: Hignell, Incorporated
1750 Humboldt Rd
Chico CA
530 894-0404

(P-8819)
HILLCREST SENIOR HOUSING CORP
35 Hillcrest Dr (94014-1098)
PHONE.................650 757-1737
Susan Ruan, Prin
David A Grant, *
EMP: 293 EST: 2005
SALES (est): 389.75K
SALES (corp-wide): 27.02MM Privately Held

SIC: 6513 Retirement hotel operation
HQ: Humangood Affordable Housing
1900 Huntington Dr
Duarte CA
925 924-7163

(P-8820)
HUMANGOOD NORCAL
Also Called: Piedmont Gardens
110 41st St Ofc (94611-5219)
PHONE.................510 654-7172
Reginald Nyles, Brnch Mgr
EMP: 126
SALES (corp-wide): 27.02MM Privately Held
Web: www.humangood.org
SIC: 6513 Retirement hotel operation
HQ: Humangood Norcal
1900 Huntington Dr
Duarte CA
925 924-7100

(P-8821)
HUMANGOOD NORCAL (HQ)
Also Called: Rosewood Mmory Care Asssted Lv
1900 Huntington Dr (91010-2694)
PHONE.................925 924-7100
David B Ferguson, CEO
Christopher A Vito, *
Randy Stamper, *
Sloan Bentley, *
Jeff Glaze, *
EMP: 60 EST: 1955
SALES (est): 194.54MM
SALES (corp-wide): 27.02MM Privately Held
Web: www.humangood.org
SIC: 6513 Retirement hotel operation
PA: Humangood
1900 Huntington Dr
Duarte CA
602 906-4024

(P-8822)
HUMANGOOD SOCAL
Also Called: Regents Point
19191 Harvard Ave Ofc (92612-8624)
PHONE.................949 854-9500
Melinda Forney, Mgr
EMP: 107
SALES (corp-wide): 27.02MM Privately Held
Web: www.humangood.org
SIC: 6513 8052 8051 Retirement hotel operation; Intermediate care facilities; Skilled nursing care facilities
HQ: Humangood Socal
1900 Huntington Dr
Duarte CA
925 924-7138

(P-8823)
HUMANGOOD SOCAL
Also Called: Windsor Manor
1230 E Windsor Rd Ofc (91205-2674)
PHONE.................818 244-7219
Marc Herrera, Brnch Mgr
EMP: 107
SQ FT: 139,840
SALES (corp-wide): 27.02MM Privately Held
Web: www.humangood.org
SIC: 6513 Retirement hotel operation
HQ: Humangood Socal
1900 Huntington Dr
Duarte CA
925 924-7138

(P-8824)
HUMANGOOD SOCAL
Also Called: Royal Oaks
1763 Royal Oaks Dr Ofc (91010-1989)
PHONE.................626 357-1632
Tina Heaney, Mgr
EMP: 90
SALES (corp-wide): 27.02MM Privately Held
Web: www.humangood.org
SIC: 6513 Retirement hotel operation
HQ: Humangood Socal
1900 Huntington Dr
Duarte CA
925 924-7138

(P-8825)
HUNT ENTERPRISES INC
Also Called: Summer Glen Apartments
23200 Western Ave Ofc (90710-1000)
PHONE.................310 530-3733
Lauren Johnson, Genl Mgr
EMP: 66
SALES (corp-wide): 13.19MM Privately Held
Web: www.huntenterprises.net
SIC: 6513 Apartment building operators
PA: Hunt Enterprises, Inc.
4416 W 154th St
Lawndale CA
310 675-3555

(P-8826)
HUNTINGTON BCH SENIOR HSING LP
Also Called: Huntington Gardens
18765 Florida St (92648-1999)
PHONE.................714 842-4006
Don Jones, Pt
EMP: 165 EST: 2008
SALES (est): 235.43K
SALES (corp-wide): 8.57MM Privately Held
SIC: 6513 Apartment building operators
PA: Living Opportunities Management Company, Llc
3787 Worsham Ave
Long Beach CA
562 595-7567

(P-8827)
INTEGRAL SENIOR LIVING LLC (PA)
2333 State St Ste 300 (92008-1621)
PHONE.................760 547-2863
Tracee Degrande, *
Collette Valentine, *
Suzanne Foley, *
Vince Limburg, *
EMP: 148 EST: 2000
SALES (est): 115.87MM
SALES (corp-wide): 115.87MM Privately Held
Web: www.islllc.com
SIC: 6513 Retirement hotel operation

(P-8828)
INTERVEST PROPERTY MGT INC
Also Called: Southwood Garden Apartments
5601 N Paramount Blvd (90805-5124)
PHONE.................562 634-5672
Debbie Ward, Brnch Mgr
EMP: 60
SALES (corp-wide): 282.75K Privately Held
SIC: 6513 Apartment building operators
PA: Intervest Property Management, Inc.
2201 Dupont Dr Ste 300
Irvine CA
949 833-1554

(P-8829)
IRVINE APT COMMUNITIES LP
299 N State College Blvd (92868-1703)
PHONE.................714 937-8900
EMP: 201
SALES (corp-wide): 579.21MM Privately Held
Web: www.irvinecompanyapartments.com
SIC: 6513 Apartment building operators
HQ: Irvine Apartment Communities, Lp
110 Innovation Dr
Irvine CA

(P-8830)
IRVINE APT COMMUNITIES LP
Also Called: 1221 Ocean Ave Apartments
1221 Ocean Ave (90401-1034)
PHONE.................310 255-1221
Stephanie Van Dermotter, Mgr
EMP: 200
SALES (corp-wide): 579.21MM Privately Held
Web: www.1221oceanavenue.com
SIC: 6513 6531 Apartment building operators ; Rental agent, real estate
HQ: Irvine Apartment Communities, Lp
110 Innovation Dr
Irvine CA

(P-8831)
IRVINE APT COMMUNITIES LP
146 Berkeley (92612-4618)
PHONE.................949 854-4942
Kevin Baldridge, Brnch Mgr
EMP: 200
SALES (corp-wide): 579.21MM Privately Held
Web: www.irvinecompany.com
SIC: 6513 Apartment building operators
HQ: Irvine Apartment Communities, Lp
110 Innovation Dr
Irvine CA

(P-8832)
IRVINE APT COMMUNITIES LP
39 Rio Robles E (95134-1629)
PHONE.................408 943-1595
Donald Bren, Brnch Mgr
EMP: 200
SALES (corp-wide): 579.21MM Privately Held
SIC: 6513 Apartment building operators
HQ: Irvine Apartment Communities, Lp
110 Innovation Dr
Irvine CA

(P-8833)
IRVINE APT COMMUNITIES LP
13212 Magnolia St Ofc (92844-1368)
PHONE.................714 537-8500
Mike Conway, Brnch Mgr
EMP: 200
SALES (corp-wide): 579.21MM Privately Held
SIC: 6513 Apartment building operators
HQ: Irvine Apartment Communities, Lp
110 Innovation Dr
Irvine CA

(P-8834)
IRVINE APT COMMUNITIES LP (HQ)
Also Called: I A C
110 Innovation Dr (92617-3040)
PHONE.................949 720-5600
Raymond Watson, Vice Chairman
Mike Ellis, Ex VP
EMP: 200 EST: 1993
SQ FT: 8,316

PRODUCTS & SERVICES SECTION
6513 - Apartment Building Operators (P-8855)

SALES (est): 103.05MM
SALES (corp-wide): 579.21MM **Privately Held**
Web: www.irvinecompanyapartments.com
SIC: **6513** 6552 6798 Apartment building operators; Subdividers and developers, nec ; Real estate investment trusts
PA: The Irvine Company Llc
550 Newport Center Dr
Newport Beach CA
949 720-2000

(P-8835)
IRVINE APT COMMUNITIES LP
Also Called: Rancho Monterey Apartments
100 Robinson Dr (92782-1095)
PHONE..............................714 505-7181
EMP: 267
SALES (corp-wide): 579.21MM **Privately Held**
Web: www.irvinecompanyapartments.com
SIC: **6513** Apartment building operators
HQ: Irvine Apartment Communities, Lp
110 Innovation Dr
Irvine CA

(P-8836)
JOHN COLLINS CO INC
5155 Cedarwood Rd (91902-1942)
PHONE..............................818 227-2190
EMP: 97
SALES (corp-wide): 2.18MM **Privately Held**
Web: www.palmtowers.com
SIC: **6513** Apartment building operators
PA: The John Collins Co Inc
5135 N Harbor Dr
San Diego CA

(P-8837)
JOHN STEWART COMPANY
Also Called: Meadow Glen Apartments
2451 Meadowview Rd (95832-1467)
PHONE..............................415 345-4400
David Lawler, *Mgr*
EMP: 96
SALES (corp-wide): 100.41MM **Privately Held**
Web: www.jsco.net
SIC: **6513** Apartment building operators
PA: John Stewart Company
1388 Sutter St Ste 1100
San Francisco CA
415 345-4400

(P-8838)
KISCO SENIOR LIVING LLC
Also Called: KRC Santa Margarita
21952 Buena Suerte (92688-3903)
PHONE..............................949 888-2250
Rick Lansford, *Brnch Mgr*
EMP: 67
SALES (corp-wide): 138.27MM **Privately Held**
Web: www.kiscoseniorliving.com
SIC: **6513** Retirement hotel operation
PA: Senior Kisco Living Llc
5790 Fleet St Ste 300
Carlsbad CA
760 804-5900

(P-8839)
KISCO SENIOR LIVING LLC
Also Called: KRC Orange
620 S Glassell St (92866-3000)
PHONE..............................714 997-5355
Bruce Hoggan, *Ex Dir*
EMP: 125
SALES (corp-wide): 138.27MM **Privately Held**

Web: www.kiscoseniorliving.com
SIC: **6513** Retirement hotel operation
PA: Senior Kisco Living Llc
5790 Fleet St Ste 300
Carlsbad CA
760 804-5900

(P-8840)
KISCO SENIOR LIVING LLC
Also Called: Oak View Snoma Hlls Apartments
1350 Oak View Cir (94928-6411)
PHONE..............................707 585-1800
Kim Healis, *Brnch Mgr*
EMP: 74
SALES (corp-wide): 138.27MM **Privately Held**
Web: www.oakviewapts.com
SIC: **6513** Retirement hotel operation
PA: Senior Kisco Living Llc
5790 Fleet St Ste 300
Carlsbad CA
760 804-5900

(P-8841)
KISCO SENIOR LIVING LLC
Also Called: KRC Los Altos
1174 Los Altos Ave Ofc (94022-1059)
PHONE..............................650 948-7337
Felora Lotfi, *Brnch Mgr*
EMP: 67
SALES (corp-wide): 138.27MM **Privately Held**
Web: www.kiscoseniorliving.com
SIC: **6513** Retirement hotel operation
PA: Senior Kisco Living Llc
5790 Fleet St Ste 300
Carlsbad CA
760 804-5900

(P-8842)
MARINA CITY CLUB LP A CALI
4333 Admiralty Way (90292-5469)
PHONE..............................310 822-0611
J H Snyder, *Pt*
Lewis Geyser, *Pt*
Milton Swimmer, *Pt*
Lon Snyder, *Pt*
EMP: 125 EST: 1969
SQ FT: 10,000
SALES (est): 4.6MM **Privately Held**
Web: www.marinacityclub.net
SIC: **6513** 7997 4493 Apartment building operators; Membership sports and recreation clubs; Marinas

(P-8843)
MICHAELS MNGMNT-AFFORDABLE LLC
Also Called: Park Kngsburg Snior Apartments
333 Kern St Apt 101 (93631-9235)
PHONE..............................559 897-5885
Rita Rodriguez, *Mgr*
EMP: 136
SALES (corp-wide): 1.03MM **Privately Held**
Web: www.tmo.com
SIC: **6513** Retirement hotel operation
PA: Michaels Management-Affordable, Llc
2 Cooper St
Camden NJ
856 596-0500

(P-8844)
MONARK LP
2804 W El Segundo Blvd (90249-1551)
PHONE..............................310 769-6669
EMP: 99
SALES (est): 1.91MM **Privately Held**

SIC: **6513** Apartment building operators

(P-8845)
MONTEREY PINE APARTMENTS
680 S 37th St (94804-4207)
PHONE..............................510 215-1926
Brian Arnold, *Mgr*
EMP: 132 EST: 2002
SALES (est): 550.77K
SALES (corp-wide): 41.99MM **Privately Held**
Web: www.themontereypines.com
SIC: **6513** Apartment hotel operation
PA: A. F. Evans Company, Inc.
2033 N Main St Ste 340
Walnut Creek CA
510 891-9400

(P-8846)
NATIONAL COMMUNITY RENAISSANCE
Also Called: Heritage Pointe
8590 Malven Ave (91730-4669)
PHONE..............................909 948-7579
EMP: 108
SALES (corp-wide): 330 **Privately Held**
Web: www.nationalcore.org
SIC: **6513** Apartment building operators
PA: National Community Renaissance
9692 Haven Ave Ste 100
Rancho Cucamonga CA
909 483-2444

(P-8847)
NOMAD TEMPORARY HOUSING INC (PA)
Also Called: Lodging
16835 W Bernardo Dr Ste 100 (92127-1603)
PHONE..............................619 313-4300
Gavan James, *CEO*
Gavan James, *Pr*
Heather James, *
EMP: 75 EST: 2010
SQ FT: 3,400
SALES (est): 5.52MM
SALES (corp-wide): 5.52MM **Privately Held**
Web: www.nomadtemphousing.com
SIC: **6513** Apartment building operators

(P-8848)
OAK CREEK APARTMENTS
Also Called: Gerson Bakar & Associates
1600 Sand Hill Rd (94304-2047)
PHONE..............................650 327-1600
Gerson Bakar, *Pt*
A S Wilsey, *Genl Pt*
EMP: 237 EST: 1968
SQ FT: 300,000
SALES (est): 2.26MM
SALES (corp-wide): 22.33MM **Privately Held**
Web: www.oakcreekapts.com
SIC: **6513** Apartment hotel operation
PA: Jalson Co., Inc.
201 Filbert St Ste 700
San Francisco CA
415 391-1313

(P-8849)
OCONNER WOODS A CALIFORNIA
3400 Wagner Heights Rd Ofc (95209-4843)
PHONE..............................209 956-3400
Scot Sinclair, *CEO*
EMP: 106 EST: 1990
SQ FT: 3,000
SALES (est): 1.26MM **Privately Held**

Web: www.eskaton.org
SIC: **6513** Retirement hotel operation
PA: St. Joseph's Regional Housing Corporation
3400 Wagner Heights Rd
Stockton CA

(P-8850)
OCONNOR WOODS HOUSING CORP
Also Called: O'Connor Woods
3400 Wagner Heights Rd (95209-4843)
PHONE..............................209 956-3400
Edward G Schoeder, *Pr*
Scot Sinclair, *
EMP: 100 EST: 1991
SALES (est): 33.05MM **Privately Held**
Web: www.eskaton.org
SIC: **6513** Retirement hotel operation
PA: St. Joseph's Regional Housing Corporation
3400 Wagner Heights Rd
Stockton CA

(P-8851)
P MONTEREY LP
Also Called: Park Lane, The
47 Via Cimarron (93940-4332)
PHONE..............................831 250-6159
EMP: 70 EST: 2007
SALES (est): 4.73MM **Privately Held**
SIC: **6513** Retirement hotel operation

(P-8852)
PACIFICA SENIOR LIVING MGT LLC
1775 Hancock St Ste 200 (92110-2036)
PHONE..............................619 296-9000
Deepak Israni, *Managing Member*
EMP: 98 EST: 2011
SALES (est): 7.97MM **Privately Held**
Web: www.pacificaseniorliving.com
SIC: **6513** Retirement hotel operation

(P-8853)
PARK NEWPORT LTD (PA)
Also Called: Park Newport Apartments
1 Park Newport (92660-5004)
PHONE..............................949 644-1900
Gerson Bakar, *Owner*
EMP: 75 EST: 1970
SQ FT: 10,000
SALES (est): 2.38MM
SALES (corp-wide): 2.38MM **Privately Held**
Web: www.parknewportapts.com
SIC: **6513** Apartment hotel operation

(P-8854)
PRC MULTI-FAMILY LLC
Also Called: Park Regency Club Apts
10000 Imperial Hwy (90242-3243)
PHONE..............................562 803-5000
David Lifschitz, *CEO*
Alfred Somekh, *
EMP: 68 EST: 1984
SALES (est): 1.36MM
SALES (corp-wide): 123.67MM **Privately Held**
SIC: **6513** Apartment building operators
HQ: Gehr Development Corporation
7400 E Slauson Ave
Commerce CA

(P-8855)
PRESIDIO GATE APARTMENTS
2770 Lombard St (94123-2446)
PHONE..............................415 567-1050
EMP: 166

6513 - Apartment Building Operators (P-8856)

SALES (corp-wide): 1.37MM **Privately Held**
Web: www.covia.org
SIC: 6513 7389 Retirement hotel operation; Business Activities at Non-Commercial Site
PA: Presidio Gate Apartments
2185 N Calif Blvd Ste 215
Walnut Creek CA
925 956-7400

(P-8856)
PROPEL INC
Also Called: Re/Max
14824 Wicks Blvd (94577-6606)
PHONE.................510 733-1700
Steve Kirsch, *CEO*
Tim C Fiebig, *
Francine Fiebig, *
Steve Manser, *
Adriaan Theron, *Worldwide Sales Vice President*
EMP: 67 **EST:** 1990
SQ FT: 12,000
SALES (est): 3.21MM **Privately Held**
Web: www.remax.com
SIC: 6513 Apartment building operators

(P-8857)
RANCE KING PROPERTIES INC (PA)
Also Called: R K Properties
3737 E Broadway (90803-6104)
PHONE.................562 240-1000
William Rance King Junior, *Pr*
Steven King, *
EMP: 104 **EST:** 1978
SQ FT: 5,000
SALES (est): 17.97MM
SALES (corp-wide): 17.97MM **Privately Held**
Web: www.rkprop.com
SIC: 6513 Apartment building operators

(P-8858)
SAGE APARTMENT COMMUNITIES INC
18006 Sky Park Cir (92614-6406)
PHONE.................949 440-2300
Brian L Fitterer, *CEO*
EMP: 77 **EST:** 2013
SALES (est): 2.25MM **Privately Held**
Web: www.ipgliving.com
SIC: 6513 Apartment building operators

(P-8859)
SAN DIMAS RETIREMENT CENTER (PA)
Also Called: Longwood Management
834 W Arrow Hwy (91772-2418)
PHONE.................909 599-8441
Frankie Ramirez, *Admn*
Frankie Ramirez, *Admn*
EMP: 70 **EST:** 1965
SALES (est): 7.77MM
SALES (corp-wide): 7.77MM **Privately Held**
SIC: 6513 8059 Retirement hotel operation; Personal care home, with health care

(P-8860)
SELTZER - DOREN MGT CO INC
Also Called: Seltzer-Doren Company
20201 Sherman Way Ste 209 (91306-3269)
PHONE.................818 709-5210
Sheldon Seltzer, *Sec*
Gerald Doren, *
EMP: 65 **EST:** 1970
SQ FT: 3,275
SALES (est): 2.02MM **Privately Held**

SIC: 6513 6552 Apartment building operators; Subdividers and developers, nec

(P-8861)
SILVERADO ORCHARDS LLC (PA)
Also Called: Management Associates
601 Pope St Ofc (94574-1275)
P.O. Box 102 (94574-0102)
PHONE.................707 963-1461
Alan Baldwin, *Genl Pt*
L Meade Baldwin, *Genl Pt*
EMP: 75 **EST:** 1975
SQ FT: 80,000
SALES (est): 2.46MM
SALES (corp-wide): 2.46MM **Privately Held**
Web: www.silveradoorchards.com
SIC: 6513 Retirement hotel operation

(P-8862)
SMITH RNCH HMES HMEOWNERS ASSN
Also Called: Smith Ranch Homes
500 Deer Valley Rd (94903-5504)
PHONE.................415 492-4900
John Patrick Maura, *CEO*
EMP: 85 **EST:** 1989
SALES (est): 3.2MM **Privately Held**
Web: www.smithranchhomes.org
SIC: 6513 Retirement hotel operation

(P-8863)
STONESFAIR FINANCIAL CORP
577 Airport Blvd Ste 700 (94010-2024)
PHONE.................650 347-0442
EMP: 60 **EST:** 1993
SALES (est): 2.45MM **Privately Held**
Web: www.stonesfair.com
SIC: 6513 6514 Apartment building operators; Residential building, four or fewer units: operation

(P-8864)
THE PINES LTD
1423 E Washington Ave (92019-2559)
PHONE.................619 447-1880
EMP: 111
SALES (est): 4.1MM **Privately Held**
SIC: 6513 Apartment building operators

(P-8865)
TRAMMELL CROW RESIDENTIAL CO
Also Called: Tcr SC Construc 1 Ltd Ptr
949 S Coast Dr Ste 400 (92626-7836)
PHONE.................714 966-9355
Tina Meyer, *Mgr*
EMP: 68
Web: www.crowholdings.com
SIC: 6513 Apartment building operators
PA: Trammell Crow Residential Company
3819 Maple Ave
Dallas TX

(P-8866)
TRULIA INC
116 New Montgomery St (94105-3607)
PHONE.................415 648-4358
Oleg Salnik, *Brnch Mgr*
EMP: 666
SALES (corp-wide): 1.96B **Publicly Held**
Web: www.trulia.com
SIC: 6513 Apartment building operators
HQ: Trulia, Inc.
535 Mission St Fl 7
San Francisco CA

(P-8867)
VASONA MANAGEMENT INC
Also Called: Marina Breeze
13949 Doolittle Dr (94577-5548)
PHONE.................510 352-8728
Willie Johnson, *Prin*
EMP: 174
SALES (corp-wide): 22.22MM **Privately Held**
Web: www.vasonamanagement.com
SIC: 6513 Apartment building operators
PA: Vasona Management, Inc.
1500 E Hamilton Ave # 210
Campbell CA
408 354-4200

(P-8868)
VINTAGE SENIOR MANAGEMENT INC
Also Called: Vintage
91 Napa Rd (95476-7691)
PHONE.................707 595-0009
EMP: 832
SIC: 6513 Retirement hotel operation
PA: Senior Vintage Management Inc
23 Corporate Plaza Dr # 190
Newport Beach CA

(P-8869)
WAMC COMPANY INC
Also Called: Cal West Enterprises
7420 Clairemont Mesa Blvd (92111-1546)
PHONE.................858 454-2753
EMP: 94 **EST:** 1995
SALES (est): 2.33MM **Privately Held**
SIC: 6513 Apartment building operators

(P-8870)
WATERMARK RTRMENT CMMNTIES INC
Also Called: Rosewood Gardens
35 Fenton St (94550-4185)
PHONE.................925 344-5661
EMP: 100
Web: www.watermarkcommunities.com
SIC: 6513 Retirement hotel operation
HQ: Watermark Retirement Communities, Inc.
2020 W Rudasill Rd
Tucson AZ

(P-8871)
WATERMARK RTRMENT CMMNTIES INC
Also Called: Fountains At The Sea Bluffs
25411 Sea Bluffs Dr (92629-2190)
PHONE.................949 443-9543
EMP: 65
Web: www.watermarkcommunities.com
SIC: 6513 Retirement hotel operation
HQ: Watermark Retirement Communities, Inc.
2020 W Rudasill Rd
Tucson AZ

(P-8872)
WESTLAKE DEVELOPMENT GROUP LLC
Valley Palms Apartments
2155 Lanai Ave Apt 60 (95122-2409)
PHONE.................408 251-2746
Fong Nguyen, *Mgr*
EMP: 89
SALES (corp-wide): 17.8MM **Privately Held**
Web: www.westlake-realty.com
SIC: 6513 Apartment building operators
PA: Westlake Development Group, Llc
520 S El Camino Real # 900
San Mateo CA
650 579-1010

(P-8873)
WILLIAM WARREN PROPERTIES INC
Also Called: Access Self Storage SE
201 Wilshire Blvd Ste 102 (90401-1201)
PHONE.................310 454-1500
William Hobin, *Pr*
EMP: 100 **EST:** 2000
SALES (est): 9.56MM
SALES (corp-wide): 84.59MM **Privately Held**
Web: www.williamwarren.com
SIC: 6513 Apartment building operators
PA: The William Warren Group Inc
100 Wilshire Blvd Ste 400
Santa Monica CA
310 451-2130

(P-8874)
WILLMARK CMMNTIES UNIV VLG INC (PA)
9948 Hibert St Ste 210 (92131-1034)
PHONE.................858 271-0582
Mark Schmidt, *Pr*
EMP: 78 **EST:** 1984
SQ FT: 2,000
SALES (est): 14.38MM
SALES (corp-wide): 14.38MM **Privately Held**
SIC: 6513 1522 Apartment building operators; Multi-family dwellings, new construction

6514 Dwelling Operators, Except Apartments

(P-8875)
ACTION PROPERTY MANAGEMENT INC (PA)
Also Called: Action Property Management
2603 Main St Ste 500 (92614-4261)
PHONE.................949 450-0202
Matthew Holbrook, *CEO*
Marianne Simek, *
EMP: 90 **EST:** 1980
SQ FT: 18,000
SALES (est): 90.39MM
SALES (corp-wide): 90.39MM **Privately Held**
Web: www.actionlife.com
SIC: 6514 8641 Residential building, four or fewer units: operation; Homeowners' association

(P-8876)
DAYTON DMH INC
121 Spinnaker Ct (92014-3218)
PHONE.................858 350-4400
Donald Ambrose, *Pr*
EMP: 172 **EST:** 1995
SALES (est): 3.11MM **Privately Held**
SIC: 6514 Dwelling operators, except apartments

(P-8877)
EAH INC (PA)
Also Called: Eah Housing
22 Pelican Way (94901-5545)
PHONE.................415 258-1800
Laura Hall, *Pr*
Alvin Bonnett, *
Karen Belanger, *
EMP: 70 **EST:** 1968
SQ FT: 30,000
SALES (est): 53.75MM
SALES (corp-wide): 53.75MM **Privately Held**

PRODUCTS & SERVICES SECTION

6531 - Real Estate Agents And Managers (P-8896)

Web: www.eahhousing.org
SIC: 6514 Residential building, four or fewer units: operation

(P-8878)
MENLO GATEWAY INC
Also Called: Midpen Housing
303 Vintage Park Dr Ste 250 (94404-1166)
PHONE..............................650 356-2900
Mark Battey, Ch
Peter Villareal, *
Luina Palchak, *
EMP: 99 EST: 1986
SALES (est): 50.94MM **Privately Held**
Web: www.midpen-housing.org
SIC: 6514 6513 Residential building, four or fewer units: operation; Apartment building operators
PA: Stanford Mid-Peninsula Urban Coalition
303 Vintage Park Dr # 250
Foster City CA

6515 Mobile Home Site Operators

(P-8879)
CAREFREE COMMUNITIES INC
Also Called: Carefree Communities
1251 Old Conejo Rd (91320-1031)
PHONE..............................805 498-2612
EMP: 125
SALES (corp-wide): 2.97B **Publicly Held**
Web: www.carefreervresorts.com
SIC: 6515 Mobile home site operators
HQ: Carefree Communities Inc.
6991 E Camelback Rd B310
Scottsdale AZ
480 423-5700

(P-8880)
MOBILEHOME COMMUNITIES AMERICA
Also Called: Chateau La Salle
2681 Monterey Hwy (95111-3097)
PHONE..............................408 298-3230
Jodi Damon Cookson, Mgr
EMP: 116
SALES (corp-wide): 8.01MM **Privately Held**
SIC: 6515 Mobile home site operators
PA: Mobilehome Communities Of America
1122 Willow St Ste 200
San Jose CA
408 279-5200

(P-8881)
R C ROBERTS & CO (PA)
Also Called: Sands Rv Resort
801 A St (94901-3010)
PHONE..............................415 456-8600
EMP: 216 EST: 1977
SQ FT: 3,000
SALES (est): 11.06MM
SALES (corp-wide): 11.06MM **Privately Held**
Web: www.rroberts.co.uk
SIC: 6515 7011 6531 Mobile home site operators; Resort hotel; Real estate agents and managers

(P-8882)
WATERHOUSE MANAGEMENT CORP
500 Giuseppe Ct Ste 2 (95678-6305)
PHONE..............................916 772-4918
Kenneth Watershouse, Pr
EMP: 150 EST: 1997
SQ FT: 10,000
SALES (est): 4.17MM **Privately Held**
Web: www.waterhousemgmt.com
SIC: 6515 Mobile home site operators

6519 Real Property Lessors, Nec

(P-8883)
DREISBACH ENTERPRISES INC
2530 E 11th St (94601-1425)
PHONE..............................510 533-6600
Ray Guy, Brnch Mgr
EMP: 84
SALES (corp-wide): 41.55MM **Privately Held**
Web: www.dreisbach.com
SIC: 6519 1541 4222 4225 Real property lessors, nec; Industrial buildings and warehouses; Warehousing, cold storage or refrigerated; General warehousing and storage
PA: Dreisbach Enterprises, Inc.
575 Maritime St
Oakland CA
510 533-6600

(P-8884)
FREMONT REALTY CAPITAL LP
Also Called: Fremont
199 Fremont St Fl 19 (94105-2255)
PHONE..............................415 284-8665
Claude J Zinngrabe Junior, Mng Pt
Victor Kwok, *
Stuart I Blackie, *
Ashminder Singh, *
Tran Tran, *
EMP: 91 EST: 1997
SQ FT: 100,000
SALES (est): 9.46MM
SALES (corp-wide): 50.09MM **Privately Held**
Web: www.fremontrealtycapital.com
SIC: 6519 8742 Real property lessors, nec; Real estate consultant
PA: Fremont Group, L.L.C.
405 Howard St Fl 2
San Francisco CA
415 284-8500

(P-8885)
HG FENTON PROPERTY COMPANY (PA)
Also Called: Silverton Business Center
7577 Mission Valley Rd Ste 200 (92108)
PHONE..............................619 400-0120
Mike Neal, Pr
Jennifer Tokatyan, *
Geoffrey Swortwood, *
Allen Jones, *
Kevin Hill, *
EMP: 200 EST: 1920
SALES (est): 28.99MM
SALES (corp-wide): 28.99MM **Privately Held**
Web: www.hgfenton.com
SIC: 6519 Real property lessors, nec

(P-8886)
LAACO LTD (HQ)
Also Called: Storage West
4469 Admiralty Way (90292-5415)
PHONE..............................213 622-1254
Karen L Hathaway, Pr
John K Hathaway, *
Steven K Hathaway, *
Bryan J Cusworth, *
EMP: 125 EST: 1986
SALES (est): 6.3MM **Publicly Held**
Web: www.laac.com

SIC: 6519 7997 7011 5812 Real property lessors, nec; Yacht club, membership; Hotels; Eating places
PA: Cubesmart
5 Old Lancaster Rd
Malvern PA

(P-8887)
LYON REALTY
4340 Golden Center Dr Ste A (95667-6254)
PHONE..............................530 295-4444
EMP: 140
Web: www.golyon.com
SIC: 6519 6531 Real property lessors, nec; Real estate brokers and agents
PA: Lyon Realty
2280 Del Paso Rd Ste 100
Sacramento CA

(P-8888)
MAXIMUS REAL ESTATE PARTNERS
1 Maritime Plz Ste 1900 (94111-3509)
PHONE..............................415 584-4832
Robert Rosania, CEO
Seth Mallen, *
EMP: 100 EST: 2013
SALES (est): 11.84MM **Privately Held**
Web: www.maximusrepartners.com
SIC: 6519 Sub-lessors of real estate

(P-8889)
OLYMPUS PROPERTY
3411 State Rd (93308-4537)
PHONE..............................661 393-1700
Chandler Wonderly, Owner
EMP: 266
SALES (corp-wide): 36.79MM **Privately Held**
Web: www.olympusproperty.com
SIC: 6519 1741 Real property lessors, nec; Foundation building
PA: Olympus Property
500 Throckmorton St # 300
Fort Worth TX
817 795-4900

(P-8890)
PACIFIC YGNACIO CORPORATION
201 California St Ste 500 (94111-5028)
PHONE..............................925 939-3275
Robin Andrews, Mgr
EMP: 165 EST: 1998
SQ FT: 105,495
SALES (est): 1.96MM **Privately Held**
SIC: 6519 Real property lessors, nec
PA: Pacific Eagle Holdings Corporation
58 Tehama St
San Francisco CA

(P-8891)
UNIVERSITY CAL SAN FRANCISCO
Also Called: Umspe
2120 N Winery Ave Ste 102 (93703-4809)
PHONE..............................559 251-3033
EMP: 62
SALES (corp-wide): 534.4MM **Privately Held**
Web: www.ucsf.edu
SIC: 6519 Real property lessors, nec
HQ: University Cal San Francisco
513 Parnassus Ave 115f
San Francisco CA

6531 Real Estate Agents And Managers

(P-8892)
ABBOTT MANCO INC
100 Clock Tower Pl Ste 210 (93923-8774)
PHONE..............................831 250-7397
EMP: 91
SALES (corp-wide): 24.28MM **Privately Held**
Web: www.mancoabbott.com
SIC: 6531 Real estate managers
PA: Abbott Manco Inc
6051 N Fresno St Ste 110
Fresno CA
559 435-1756

(P-8893)
ABODE COMMUNITIES LLC
1149 S Hill St Fl 7 (90015-2207)
PHONE..............................213 629-2702
Robin Hughes, Pr
Rick Saperstein, *
Kenneth Krug, *
Sandra Kulli, Vice Chairman*
Holly Benson, *
▲ EMP: 150 EST: 1968
SQ FT: 10,094
SALES (est): 18.1MM **Privately Held**
Web: www.abodecommunities.org
SIC: 6531 8712 8711 Housing authority operator; Architectural services; Engineering services

(P-8894)
ABSOLUTELY ZERO CORPORATION
1 City Blvd W Ste 1000 (92868-3611)
PHONE..............................949 269-3300
Ronald Radziminsky, Pr
EMP: 275 EST: 2018
SALES (est): 24.92MM **Privately Held**
Web: www.owning.com
SIC: 6531 Real estate brokers and agents
PA: Guaranteed Rate, Inc.
3940 N Ravenswood Ave
Chicago IL

(P-8895)
ACCO MANAGEMENT COMPANY
Also Called: Spring Creek Apartments
100 Buckingham Dr Ofc (95051-7151)
PHONE..............................408 241-3000
Margie Misner, Mgr
EMP: 102
SALES (corp-wide): 8.65MM **Privately Held**
Web: www.springcreek-apartments.com
SIC: 6531 6513 Real estate managers; Apartment building operators
PA: Acco Management Company
130 E Dana St
Mountain View CA
650 961-8330

(P-8896)
ALL CALIFORNIA TITLE ESCROW CO
1001 Wilshire Blvd (90017-2415)
PHONE..............................800 626-0106
Radmila Vasile, Prin *
EMP: 71 EST: 2016
SALES (est): 587.39K **Privately Held**
Web: www.allcaltitle.com
SIC: 6531 Real estate managers

6531 - Real Estate Agents And Managers (P-8897)

(P-8897)
ALLIANT ASSET MGT CO LLC (HQ)
26050 Mureau Rd (91302-3174)
PHONE.................................818 668-2805
Shawn Horwitz, *Managing Member*
Scott Koticks, *
Brian Goldberg, *Managing Member*
EMP: 81 EST: 1997
SALES (est): 27.96MM **Publicly Held**
SIC: 6531 Real estate managers
PA: Walker & Dunlop, Inc.
7272 Wscnsin Ave Ste 1300
Bethesda MD

(P-8898)
ALLMARK INC (PA)
10070 Arrow Rte (91730-4194)
PHONE.................................909 989-7556
Wayne Slavitt, *CEO*
Pat Price, *
Michael Krcelic, *
Matt Duffy, *
Michael Payne, *
EMP: 65 EST: 1971
SQ FT: 3,167
SALES (est): 11.31MM
SALES (corp-wide): 11.31MM **Privately Held**
Web: www.allmarkproperties.com
SIC: 6531 Real estate managers

(P-8899)
AMERICAN DEVELOPMENT CORP (PA)
3605 Long Beach Blvd Ste 410 (90807-4013)
PHONE.................................562 989-3730
Marco Gomez, *Pr*
EMP: 87 EST: 1994
SQ FT: 8,000
SALES (est): 3.27MM **Privately Held**
SIC: 6531 Real estate agents and managers

(P-8900)
AMERICAN MARKETING SYSTEMS INC
Also Called: Amsi Real Estate Services
2800 Van Ness Ave (94109-1426)
PHONE.................................800 747-7784
Zoya Lee Smithton, *Dir*
Robb Fleischer, *
EMP: 75 EST: 1970
SQ FT: 8,000
SALES (est): 8.67MM **Privately Held**
Web: www.amsires.com
SIC: 6531 Real estate brokers and agents

(P-8901)
ARDENBROOK INC
Also Called: Ardenwood Rental Condominiums
5016 Paseo Padre Pkwy (94555-3416)
PHONE.................................510 794-1020
Ben Cisneros, *Mgr*
EMP: 62
Web: www.ardenwoodforest.com
SIC: 6531 6513 Real estate agents and managers; Apartment building operators
PA: Ardenbrook, Inc.
4725 Thornton Ave
Fremont CA

(P-8902)
ARGENT MANAGEMENT LLC (PA)
Also Called: Suncal
4131 S Main St (92707-5758)
PHONE.................................949 777-4000
Steve Elieff, *Managing Member*
Bruce Elieff, *Prin*
EMP: 68 EST: 2003
SALES (est): 28.49MM **Privately Held**
Web: www.argentdevco.com
SIC: 6531 Real estate agents and managers

(P-8903)
ARGENT MANAGEMENT LLC
4131 S Main St (92707-5758)
PHONE.................................949 777-4070
EMP: 72 EST: 2000
SALES (est): 2.52MM **Privately Held**
SIC: 6531 Rental agent, real estate

(P-8904)
ATLAS HOSPITALITY GROUP
1901 Main St Ste 175 (92614-0517)
PHONE.................................949 622-3400
Alan Reay, *Pr*
S Shah, *VP*
EMP: 90 EST: 1991
SALES (est): 5.53MM **Privately Held**
Web: www.atlashospitality.com
SIC: 6531 Real estate agent, commercial

(P-8905)
AUCTIONCOM INC
Also Called: Auction.com
1 Mauchly Ste 27 (92618-2305)
PHONE.................................800 499-6199
Jeffrey Frieden, *CEO*
James Corum, *
Virginia Pierce, *
Annamarie Giagunto, *
Joseph Joffrion, *
EMP: 200 EST: 1990
SQ FT: 18,000
SALES (est): 4.87MM **Privately Held**
SIC: 6531 Auction, real estate

(P-8906)
AUCTIONCOM LLC (PA)
Also Called: Auction.com
1 Mauchly (92618-2305)
PHONE.................................949 859-2777
Jeffrey Frieden, *
Keith Mclane, *Pr*
Eva Tapia, *
Eric Andrew, *
EMP: 142 EST: 2008
SALES (est): 162.88MM **Privately Held**
Web: www.auction.com
SIC: 6531 Real estate agents and managers

(P-8907)
AUCTIONCOM LLC
Also Called: Ten-X
2121 S El Camino Real Ste 900 (94403)
PHONE.................................949 609-5376
EMP: 125
Web: www.auction.com
SIC: 6531 Real estate brokers and agents
PA: Auction.Com, Llc
1 Mauchly
Irvine CA

(P-8908)
BAKERSFIELD WESTWIND CORP
Also Called: Coldwell Banker
1810 Westwind Dr (93301-3027)
PHONE.................................661 327-2121
John Garone, *Pr*
EMP: 145 EST: 1972
SALES (est): 9.46MM **Privately Held**
Web: www.coldwellbanker.com
SIC: 6531 Real estate agent, residential

(P-8909)
BARCELON ASSOCIATES MGT CORP
590 Lennon Ln Ste 110 (94598-5923)
PHONE.................................925 627-7000
Mark Barcelon, *CEO*
Sandy Barcelon, *
EMP: 250 EST: 1979
SQ FT: 3,000
SALES (est): 10.46MM **Privately Held**
Web: www.barcelon.com
SIC: 6531 Real estate managers

(P-8910)
BENNION DEVILLE FINE HOMES INC
Also Called: Windermere RE Coachella Vly
74850 Us Highway 111 (92210-7116)
PHONE.................................760 674-3452
Rick Fisk, *Brnch Mgr*
EMP: 378
SALES (corp-wide): 24.87MM **Privately Held**
Web: www.bdhomes.com
SIC: 6531 Real estate brokers and agents
PA: Bennion & Deville Fine Homes, Inc.
71691 Highway 111
Rancho Mirage CA
760 770-6801

(P-8911)
BERKSHIRE HTHWAY HM SVCS CA RP
9836 Atlantic Ave (90280-5219)
PHONE.................................562 307-5636
EMP: 82
SALES (corp-wide): 2.56MM **Privately Held**
Web: www.brucemulhearn.com
SIC: 6531 Real estate agent, residential
PA: Berkshire Hathaway Home Services Ca Roperties
18000 Studebaker Rd # 600
Cerritos CA
562 860-2625

(P-8912)
BEST SAC HOMES GRP AT BIG BLCK
550 Howe Ave Ste 150 (95825-5414)
PHONE.................................916 891-2641
EMP: 93 EST: 2019
SALES (est): 271.01K **Privately Held**
Web: www.seesacramentohomesnow.com
SIC: 6531 Real estate brokers and agents

(P-8913)
BEVERLY AND COMPANY INC
15301 Ventura Blvd B305 (91403-3102)
PHONE.................................323 422-3253
Max Edward Mcdermott, *CEO*
EMP: 93 EST: 2018
SALES (est): 515.15K **Privately Held**
Web: www.beverlycompany.com
SIC: 6531 Real estate brokers and agents

(P-8914)
BGK EQUITIES INC (HQ)
2000 Avenue Of The Stars (90067-4700)
PHONE.................................505 982-2184
Michael Mahony, *COO*
Ian Brownlow, *
EMP: 70 EST: 1995
SALES (est): 9.79MM **Privately Held**
Web: www.geminirosemont.com
SIC: 6531 Real estate agent, commercial
PA: Rosemont Realty, Llc
2000 Avenue Of The Stars # 550
Los Angeles CA

(P-8915)
BKM DIABLO 227 LLC
1701 Quail St Ste 100 (92660-2796)
PHONE.................................602 688-6409
Brian K Malliet, *Prin*
Rene Velasquez, *
EMP: 85 EST: 2018
SALES (est): 3.49MM **Privately Held**
Web: www.bkmmanagementco.com
SIC: 6531 Real estate managers

(P-8916)
BRIDGE HOUSING CORPORATION (PA)
600 California St Fl 900 (94108-9800)
PHONE.................................415 989-1111
Cynthia Parker, *Pr*
Lydia Tan, *Ex VP*
Susan Johnson, *Ex VP*
▲ EMP: 90 EST: 1982
SQ FT: 12,000
SALES (est): 54.14MM
SALES (corp-wide): 54.14MM **Privately Held**
Web: www.bridgehousing.com
SIC: 6531 Real estate agents and managers

(P-8917)
BUCHANAN STREET PARTNERS LP
3501 Jamboree Rd Ste 4200 (92660-2958)
PHONE.................................949 721-1414
Robert Brunswick, *CEO*
Timothy Ballard, *
James Gill, *
EMP: 85 EST: 2000
SALES (est): 10.16MM **Privately Held**
Web: www.buchananstreet.com
SIC: 6531 Real estate agents and managers

(P-8918)
BURLEIGH POINT LLC
Also Called: Burleigh Point, Ltd.
5600 Argosy Ave Ste 100 (92649-1063)
PHONE.................................949 428-3200
◆ EMP: 200
SIC: 6531 6513 Real estate agent, residential; Residential hotel operation

(P-8919)
C B COAST NEWPORT PROPERTIES
Also Called: Coldwell Bnkr Rsdntial Rfrral
840 Newport Center Dr Ste 100 (92660)
PHONE.................................949 644-1600
Daniel F Bibb, *Pr*
Tom Queen, *
Gary Legrand, *
EMP: 3448 EST: 1990
SQ FT: 7,300
SALES (est): 4.77MM **Publicly Held**
Web: www.coldwellbanker.com
SIC: 6531 Real estate agent, residential
HQ: Coldwell Banker Residential Referral Network
27271 Las Ramblas
Mission Viejo CA
949 367-1800

(P-8920)
CALIENTE CREEK PRTNERS A CAL L (PA)
8445 W Elowin Ct (93291-9262)
P.O. Box 6520 (93290-6520)
PHONE.................................559 651-1000
Thomas Collishaw, *CEO*
EMP: 88 EST: 1998

PRODUCTS & SERVICES SECTION
6531 - Real Estate Agents And Managers (P-8942)

SALES (est): 41.61MM
SALES (corp-wide): 41.61MM Privately Held
Web: www.selfhelpenterprises.org
SIC: 6531 6411 Real estate agent, residential; Insurance agents, brokers, and service

(P-8921)
CAMDEN DEVELOPMENT INC
27261 Las Ramblas (92691-6441)
PHONE..................................949 427-4674
EMP: 142
Web: www.camdenliving.com
SIC: 6531 Real estate agent, commercial
HQ: Camden Development, Inc.
 11 Greenway Plz Ste 2400
 Houston TX

(P-8922)
CARLYLE GROUP INC (PA)
9073 Nemo St Ste 100 (90069-5511)
PHONE..................................310 550-8656
Ronald Singer, CEO
Karen Burcombe-vogogel, VP
Charles Moore, Prin
David Lam, VP
▲ EMP: 86 EST: 1975
SQ FT: 3,000
SALES (est): 42.14MM
SALES (corp-wide): 42.14MM Privately Held
Web: www.carlyle.com
SIC: 6531 6799 Buying agent, real estate; Investors, nec

(P-8923)
CARMEL RLTY CARMEL VLY SLS OFF
4 E Carmel Valley Rd (93924-9753)
PHONE..................................831 622-1000
EMP: 92 EST: 2014
SALES (est): 2.78MM Privately Held
Web: www.carmelrealtycompany.com
SIC: 6531 Real estate agent, residential

(P-8924)
CARUSO MGT LTD A CAL LTD PRTNR (PA)
Also Called: Commons At Calabasas, The
101 The Grove Dr (90036-6221)
PHONE..................................323 900-8100
Rick Caruso, CEO
EMP: 99 EST: 1991
SALES (est): 24.62MM
SALES (corp-wide): 24.62MM Privately Held
Web: www.caruso.com
SIC: 6531 Rental agent, real estate

(P-8925)
CBABR INC (PA)
Also Called: Coldwell Banker
31620 Railroad Canyon Rd Ste A (92587-9476)
PHONE..................................951 640-7056
Budge Huskey, CEO
Dennis M Mccoy, Pr
Margaret Mccoy, Sec
Jody Regus, *
EMP: 73 EST: 1983
SQ FT: 4,000
SALES (est): 8.26MM Privately Held
Web: www.coldwellbanker.com
SIC: 6531 Real estate agent, residential

(P-8926)
CBRE INC
500 Capitol Mall Ste 2400 (95814-4752)
PHONE..................................916 446-6800
David Brennan, Mgr
EMP: 100
Web: www.cbre.com
SIC: 6531 Real estate agent, commercial
HQ: Cbre, Inc.
 2100 Mckinney Ave # 1250
 Dallas TX
 866 225-3099

(P-8927)
CBRE INC
4301 La Jolla Village Dr # 3000 (92122-1484)
PHONE..................................858 546-4600
EMP: 160
Web: www.cbre.us
SIC: 6531 Real estate agent, commercial
HQ: Cbre, Inc.
 400 S Hope St Ste 25
 Los Angeles CA
 213 613-3333

(P-8928)
CBRE GLOBL VALUE INVESTORS LLC (DH)
Also Called: Global Innovation Partner
601 S Figueroa St Ste 49 (90017-5253)
PHONE..................................213 683-4200
Ritson Ferguson, CEO
Gil Borok, *
Maurice Voskuilen, *
EMP: 150 EST: 1972
SALES (est): 95.44MM Publicly Held
Web: www.cbreim.com
SIC: 6531 Real estate agent, commercial
HQ: Cbre, Inc.
 2100 Mckinney Ave # 1250
 Dallas TX
 866 225-3099

(P-8929)
CBRE GLOBL VALUE INVESTORS LLC
Also Called: Cbre
3501 Jamboree Rd Ste 100 (92660-2940)
PHONE..................................949 725-8500
Steven Swerdlow, Prin
EMP: 151
Web: www.cbreim.com
SIC: 6531 Real estate agent, commercial
HQ: Cbre Global Value Investors, Llc
 601 S Figueroa St Ste 49
 Los Angeles CA
 213 683-4200

(P-8930)
CENTURY 21 A BETTER SVC RLTY
Also Called: Century 21
5831 Firestone Blvd Ste J (90280-3718)
PHONE..................................562 806-1000
EMP: 97
SQ FT: 4,000
SALES (est): 3.76MM Privately Held
Web: www.c21abetterservice.com
SIC: 6531 Real estate agents and managers

(P-8931)
CHARLES DUNN RE SVCS INC (PA)
800 W 6th St Ste 600 (90017-2702)
PHONE..................................213 270-6200
Walter Conn, CEO
Patrick Conn, *
EMP: 86 EST: 1995
SQ FT: 30,000
SALES (est): 10.55MM
SALES (corp-wide): 10.55MM Privately Held
Web: www.charlesdunn.com
SIC: 6531 Real estate brokers and agents

(P-8932)
CHILD DEVELOPMENT INCORPORATED
17341 Jacquelyn Ln (92647-5713)
PHONE..................................714 842-4064
EMP: 362
SALES (corp-wide): 49.76MM Privately Held
Web: www.catalystkids.org
SIC: 6531 Real estate agents and managers
PA: Child Development Incorporated
 350 Woodview Ave
 Morgan Hill CA
 408 556-7300

(P-8933)
CIRRUS ASSET MANAGEMENT INC (PA)
20720 Ventura Blvd Ste 300 (91364-6266)
PHONE..................................818 222-4840
Steve Heimler, CEO
Carrie E Roth, CFO
EMP: 77 EST: 2007
SALES (est): 23.31MM
SALES (corp-wide): 23.31MM Privately Held
SIC: 6531 Real estate managers

(P-8934)
CITISCAPE PRPRTY MGT GROUP LLC
Also Called: Citiscape
3450 3rd St Ste 1a (94124-1444)
PHONE..................................415 401-2000
Edward Dale, *
Robert Simms, *
EMP: 96 EST: 1999
SQ FT: 11,000
SALES (est): 17.21MM Privately Held
Web: www.citiscapesf.com
SIC: 6531 Real estate managers

(P-8935)
CITIVEST INC
Also Called: Hydrotech Construction Group
4350 Von Karman Ave Ste 200 (92660-2041)
PHONE..................................949 705-0420
Dana Haynes, Pr
EMP: 90 EST: 1987
SALES (est): 9.57MM Privately Held
Web: www.citivestinc.com
SIC: 6531 Real estate managers

(P-8936)
COASTAL ALLIANCE HOLDINGS INC
Also Called: Coldwell Banker Coastl Aliance
1650 Ximeno Ave Ste 120 (90804-2179)
PHONE..................................562 370-1000
Jack Irvin, Pr
EMP: 140 EST: 2003
SALES (est): 6.58MM Privately Held
Web: www.cbcoastalalliance.com
SIC: 6531 Real estate agent, residential

(P-8937)
COLDWELL BANKER HOME SOURCE
Also Called: Coldwell Banker
15500 W Sand St Ste 2 (92392-2931)
PHONE..................................760 684-8100
EMP: 60 EST: 2012
SALES (est): 4.67MM Privately Held
Web: www.cbcinland.com
SIC: 6531 Real estate agent, residential

(P-8938)
COLDWELL BANKER PREMIER PRPTS
Also Called: Coldwell Banker
1498 E Valley Rd (93108-1241)
PHONE..................................805 565-2200
Chuck Farish, Pr
EMP: 68 EST: 1998
SALES (est): 994.88K Privately Held
Web: www.coldwellbanker.com
SIC: 6531 Real estate agent, residential

(P-8939)
COLDWELL BANKER RE LLC
Also Called: Coldwell Banker
1712 Meridian Ave Ste C (95125-5587)
PHONE..................................408 723-3300
James Nichols, Managing Member
Joe Brown, Mgr
EMP: 60 EST: 2003
SALES (est): 11.23MM Publicly Held
Web: www.coldwellbanker.com
SIC: 6531 Real estate agent, residential
PA: Anywhere Real Estate Inc.
 175 Park Ave
 Madison NJ

(P-8940)
COLDWELL BANKER RESIDENTIAL (DH)
Also Called: Coldwell Banker
27742 Vista Del Lago Ste J1 (92692-1119)
PHONE..................................949 837-5700
Robert M Becker, Pr
Gregory S Campbell, *
Robert J Arrigoni, *
Bruce Zipf, *
Gregory Blackburn, *
EMP: 75 EST: 1987
SALES (est): 95.46MM Publicly Held
Web: www.coldwellbanker.com
SIC: 6531 Real estate agent, residential
HQ: Nrt Commercial Utah Llc
 175 Park Ave
 Madison NJ

(P-8941)
COLDWELL BANKER RESIDENTIAL RE
Also Called: Coldwell Banker
15 E Foothill Blvd (91006-2399)
PHONE..................................626 445-5500
Jack Cooley, Prin
EMP: 149 EST: 2003
SALES (est): 2.3MM Privately Held
Web: www.coldwellbanker.com
SIC: 6531 Real estate agent, residential

(P-8942)
COLDWELL BNKR RESIDENTIAL BRKG (DH)
Also Called: Coldwell Banker
1855 Gateway Blvd Ste 750 (94520-3290)
PHONE..................................925 275-3000
Bruce G Zipf, CEO
Avram Goldman, *
EMP: 100 EST: 1965
SALES (est): 105.85K Publicly Held
Web: www.coldwellbanker.com
SIC: 6531 Real estate agent, residential
HQ: Nrt Commercial Utah Llc
 175 Park Ave
 Madison NJ

6531 - Real Estate Agents And Managers (P-8943)

(P-8943)
COLDWELL BNKR RSDNTIAL RE SVCS
Also Called: Coldwell Banker
500 Sir Francis Drake Blvd (94904-2347)
PHONE..............................415 461-2020
Kate Hamilton, Mgr
EMP: 379
Web: www.coldwellbanker.com
SIC: 6531 Real estate agent, residential
HQ: Coldwell Banker Residential Real Estate Services, Inc.
27742 Vista Del Lago # 1
Mission Viejo CA

(P-8944)
COLDWELL BNKR RSDNTIAL RFRRAL (DH)
Also Called: Coldwell Banker
27271 Las Ramblas (92691-8041)
PHONE..............................949 367-1800
Robert Becker, Pr
Dan Happer, CFO
EMP: 410 EST: 1984
SQ FT: 6,000
SALES (est): 75.05MM **Publicly Held**
Web: www.coldwellbanker.com
SIC: 6531 Real estate agent, residential
HQ: Nrt Commercial Utah Llc
175 Park Ave
Madison NJ

(P-8945)
COLDWELL BNKR RSDNTIAL RFRRAL
Also Called: Coldwell Banker
201 Marine Ave (92662-1203)
P.O. Box 68 (92662-0068)
PHONE..............................949 673-8700
Steve Sutherland, Mgr
EMP: 805
Web: www.coldwellbanker.com
SIC: 6531 Real estate agent, residential
HQ: Coldwell Banker Residential Referral Network
27271 Las Ramblas
Mission Viejo CA
949 367-1800

(P-8946)
COLLEGE PARK REALTY INC (PA)
Also Called: Re/Max
10791 Los Alamitos Blvd (90720-2309)
PHONE..............................562 594-6753
Barry Binder, Pr
Carol Treadway, *
Betty Binder, *
EMP: 80 EST: 1974
SQ FT: 5,000
SALES (est): 11.93MM
SALES (corp-wide): 11.93MM **Privately Held**
Web: www.remaxcollegepark.com
SIC: 6531 Real estate agent, residential

(P-8947)
COLLIERS INTERNATIONAL
101 2nd St Ste 1100 (94105-3652)
PHONE..............................415 788-3100
Herbert Damner Junior, Pt
Scott Harper, Dir
EMP: 65 EST: 1979
SALES (est): 19.5MM
SALES (corp-wide): 4.46B **Privately Held**
SIC: 6531 Real estate agent, commercial
HQ: Colliers International New England, Llc
100 Federal St
Boston MA
617 330-8000

(P-8948)
COMMERCIAL PROPERTY MGT INC (PA)
3251 W 6th St Ste 109 (90020-5018)
PHONE..............................213 739-2000
David Soufer, Pr
EMP: 64 EST: 1990
SQ FT: 4,500
SALES (est): 4.55MM **Privately Held**
Web: www.cpmusa.com
SIC: 6531 Real estate managers

(P-8949)
COMMON GROUNDS HOLDINGS LLC
6790 Embarcadero Ln Ste 100 (92011-3277)
PHONE..............................760 206-7861
Jacob Bates, Prin
EMP: 90 EST: 2017
SALES (est): 2.21MM **Privately Held**
Web: www.cgworkplace.com
SIC: 6531 8742 Real estate leasing and rentals; Real estate consultant

(P-8950)
COMPASS
9454 Wilshire Blvd (90212-2907)
PHONE..............................818 629-9776
EMP: 83 EST: 2018
SALES (est): 1.57MM **Privately Held**
Web: www.compass.com
SIC: 6531 Real estate brokers and agents

(P-8951)
CONAM MANAGEMENT CORPORATION (PA)
3990 Ruffin Rd Ste 100 (92123-4805)
PHONE..............................858 614-7200
J Bradley Forrester, CEO
Daniel Epstein, *
Frazier Crawford, *
Rob Singh, *
E Scott Dupree, *
EMP: 142 EST: 1975
SQ FT: 45,634
SALES (est): 96.15MM **Privately Held**
Web: www.conam.com
SIC: 6531 Real estate managers

(P-8952)
CORE REALTY HOLDINGS MGT INC
Also Called: Crh Management
1600 Dove St Ste 450 (92660-2447)
PHONE..............................949 863-1031
EMP: 99 EST: 2010
SALES (est): 7.22MM **Privately Held**
Web: www.crhmi.com
SIC: 6531 Real estate agent, commercial

(P-8953)
CORTLANDT LIQUIDATING LLC
Also Called: Century 21 Showcase
13117 Highway 9 (95006-9120)
PHONE..............................831 338-4500
John Carver, Brnch Mgr
EMP: 211
SALES (corp-wide): 478.13MM **Privately Held**
Web: www.c21showcase.com
SIC: 6531 Real estate agent, residential
HQ: Cortlandt Liquidating Llc
22 Cortland St
New York NY

(P-8954)
CSL BERKSHIRE OPERATING CO LLC
Also Called: Clearwater Living
5000 Birch St Ste 400 (92660-8125)
PHONE..............................949 333-8580
Anthony Ferrero, Pr
EMP: 64 EST: 2017
SALES (est): 584.22K **Privately Held**
SIC: 6531 Real estate agents and managers

(P-8955)
CUBEWORKCOM INC
Also Called: Cubework
900 Turnbull Canyon Rd (91745-1404)
PHONE..............................909 991-6669
James Chang, CEO
Christine Wei, CCO
EMP: 200 EST: 2018
SALES (est): 9.65MM **Privately Held**
Web: www.cubework.com
SIC: 6531 Real estate leasing and rentals

(P-8956)
CUSHMAN & WAKEFIELD INC
Also Called: Nai BT Commercial
425 Market St Ste 2300 (94105-5410)
PHONE..............................415 781-8100
Eve Rouxton, Prin
EMP: 70
SALES (corp-wide): 10.11B **Privately Held**
Web: www.cushmanwakefield.com
SIC: 6531 Real estate agent, commercial
HQ: Cushman & Wakefield, Inc.
225 W Wacker Dr Ste 3000
Chicago IL
312 470-1800

(P-8957)
CUSHMAN & WAKEFIELD CAL INC (DH)
Also Called: Cushman & Wakefield
1 Maritime Plz Ste 900 (94111-3412)
PHONE..............................408 275-6730
John Forrester, CEO
EMP: 110 EST: 1887
SQ FT: 26,500
SALES (est): 75.44K
SALES (corp-wide): 10.11B **Privately Held**
Web: www.cushmanwakefield.com
SIC: 6531 Real estate brokers and agents
HQ: Cushman & Wakefield, Inc.
225 W Wacker Dr Ste 3000
Chicago IL
312 470-1800

(P-8958)
CUSHMAN & WAKEFIELD CAL INC
Also Called: Corporate Real Estate Advisors
12830 El Camino Real Ste 100 (92130)
PHONE..............................858 452-6500
Steve Rosetta, Mgr
EMP: 676
SALES (corp-wide): 10.11B **Privately Held**
Web: www.cushmanwakefield.com
SIC: 6531 8742 8732 Real estate agent, commercial; Real estate consultant; Market analysis, business, and economic research
HQ: Cushman & Wakefield Of California, Inc.
1 Maritime Plz Ste 900
San Francisco CA
408 275-6730

(P-8959)
CUSHMAN & WAKEFIELD CAL INC
3011 Townsgate Rd (91361-5820)
PHONE..............................805 418-5811
EMP: 360
SALES (corp-wide): 10.11B **Privately Held**
Web: www.cushmanwakefield.com
SIC: 6531 Real estate agent, commercial
HQ: Cushman & Wakefield Of California, Inc.
1 Maritime Plz Ste 900
San Francisco CA
408 275-6730

(P-8960)
CUSHMAN & WAKEFIELD CAL INC
Also Called: Cushman & Wakefield California
7281 Garden Grove Blvd Ste G (92841-4212)
PHONE..............................714 591-0451
EMP: 315
SALES (corp-wide): 10.11B **Privately Held**
Web: www.cushmanwakefield.com
SIC: 6531 Real estate agent, commercial
HQ: Cushman & Wakefield Of California, Inc.
1 Maritime Plz Ste 900
San Francisco CA
408 275-6730

(P-8961)
CUSHMAN & WAKEFIELD CAL INC
1357 Hillcrest Dr (95120-5618)
PHONE..............................408 572-4134
Robby Perrino, Prin
EMP: 405
SALES (corp-wide): 10.11B **Privately Held**
Web: www.cushmanwakefield.com
SIC: 6531 Real estate agent, commercial
HQ: Cushman & Wakefield Of California, Inc.
1 Maritime Plz Ste 900
San Francisco CA
408 275-6730

(P-8962)
CUSHMAN & WAKEFIELD CAL INC
555 12th St Ste 1400 (94607-4061)
PHONE..............................510 763-4900
Samuel C Swan, Dir
EMP: 721
SALES (corp-wide): 10.11B **Privately Held**
Web: www.cushmanwakefield.com
SIC: 6531 Real estate agent, commercial
HQ: Cushman & Wakefield Of California, Inc.
1 Maritime Plz Ste 900
San Francisco CA
408 275-6730

(P-8963)
CUSHMAN & WAKEFIELD CAL INC
770 Paseo Camarillo 315 (93010-6064)
PHONE..............................805 322-7244
EMP: 360
SALES (corp-wide): 10.11B **Privately Held**
Web: www.cushmanwakefield.com
SIC: 6531 Real estate agent, commercial
HQ: Cushman & Wakefield Of California, Inc.
1 Maritime Plz Ste 900
San Francisco CA
408 275-6730

(P-8964)
CUSHMAN & WAKEFIELD CAL INC
Also Called: Cushman & Wakefield

PRODUCTS & SERVICES SECTION
6531 - Real Estate Agents And Managers (P-8987)

560 S Winchester Blvd Ste 200
(95128-2500)
PHONE..............................408 436-5500
Joseph Cook Ii, *Prin*
EMP: 450
SALES (corp-wide): 10.11B **Privately Held**
Web: www.cushmanwakefield.com
SIC: 6531 Real estate agent, commercial
HQ: Cushman & Wakefield Of California, Inc.
    1 Maritime Plz Ste 900
    San Francisco CA
    408 275-6730

(P-8965)
CUSHMAN & WAKEFIELD CAL INC
Also Called: Cushman & Wakefield
3800 Concours Ste 300 (91764-5907)
PHONE..............................909 483-0077
EMP: 360
SALES (corp-wide): 10.11B **Privately Held**
Web: www.cushmanwakefield.com
SIC: 6531 Real estate agent, commercial
HQ: Cushman & Wakefield Of California, Inc.
    1 Maritime Plz Ste 900
    San Francisco CA
    408 275-6730

(P-8966)
CUSHMAN & WAKEFIELD CAL INC
901 Via Piemonte Ste 200 (91764-6597)
PHONE..............................909 980-3781
Luanne Alleman, *Mgr*
EMP: 450
SALES (corp-wide): 10.11B **Privately Held**
Web: www.cushmanwakefield.com
SIC: 6531 Real estate agent, commercial
HQ: Cushman & Wakefield Of California, Inc.
    1 Maritime Plz Ste 900
    San Francisco CA
    408 275-6730

(P-8967)
CUSHMAN & WAKEFIELD CAL INC
1333 N California Blvd Ste 550
(94596-4557)
PHONE..............................925 935-0770
Jill Campbell, *Mgr*
EMP: 315
SALES (corp-wide): 10.11B **Privately Held**
Web: www.cushmanwakefield.com
SIC: 6531 Real estate agent, commercial
HQ: Cushman & Wakefield Of California, Inc.
    1 Maritime Plz Ste 900
    San Francisco CA
    408 275-6730

(P-8968)
CUSHMAN & WAKEFIELD CAL INC
10250 Constellation Blvd Ste 2200
(90067-6255)
PHONE..............................310 556-1805
Eric Olosson, *Mgr*
EMP: 405
SALES (corp-wide): 10.11B **Privately Held**
Web: www.cushmanwakefield.com
SIC: 6531 Real estate agent, commercial
HQ: Cushman & Wakefield Of California, Inc.
    1 Maritime Plz Ste 900
    San Francisco CA
    408 275-6730

(P-8969)
CUSHMAN & WAKEFIELD CAL INC
3760 Kilroy Airport Way (90806-2443)
PHONE..............................562 276-1400
Joe Vargus, *Mgr*
EMP: 495
SALES (corp-wide): 10.11B **Privately Held**
Web: www.cushmanwakefield.com
SIC: 6531 Real estate agent, commercial
HQ: Cushman & Wakefield Of California, Inc.
    1 Maritime Plz Ste 900
    San Francisco CA
    408 275-6730

(P-8970)
CUSHMAN & WAKEFIELD CAL INC
18111 Von Karman Ave Ste 1000
(92612-7101)
PHONE..............................949 474-4004
Dee Shipley, *Mgr*
EMP: 811
SALES (corp-wide): 10.11B **Privately Held**
Web: www.cushmanwakefield.com
SIC: 6531 Real estate agent, commercial
HQ: Cushman & Wakefield Of California, Inc.
    1 Maritime Plz Ste 900
    San Francisco CA
    408 275-6730

(P-8971)
CUSHMAN & WAKEFIELD CAL INC
2125 Hamilton Ave (95125-5905)
PHONE..............................415 397-1700
EMP: 405
SALES (corp-wide): 10.11B **Privately Held**
Web: www.cushmanwakefield.com
SIC: 6531 Real estate agent, commercial
HQ: Cushman & Wakefield Of California, Inc.
    1 Maritime Plz Ste 900
    San Francisco CA
    408 275-6730

(P-8972)
CUSHMAN & WAKEFIELD CAL INC
455 Market St Ste 530 (94105-2455)
PHONE..............................415 828-1923
Mary Husnagel, *Brnch Mgr*
EMP: 540
SALES (corp-wide): 10.11B **Privately Held**
Web: www.cushmanwakefield.com
SIC: 6531 Real estate agent, commercial
HQ: Cushman & Wakefield Of California, Inc.
    1 Maritime Plz Ste 900
    San Francisco CA
    408 275-6730

(P-8973)
CUSHMAN REALTY CORPORATION
601 S Figueroa St Ste 4700 (90017-5752)
PHONE..............................213 627-4700
EMP: 200
SIC: 6531 Real estate brokers and agents

(P-8974)
DAISO CALIFORNIA LLC
7000 El Cerrito Plz (94530-4020)
PHONE..............................510 679-5121
EMP: 83
Web: www.daisorecall.com
SIC: 6531 Real estate agents and managers
PA: Daiso California Llc
    16400 Trojan Way
    La Mirada CA

(P-8975)
DAYMARK REALTY ADVISORS INC
Also Called: Daymark Properties Realty
750 B St Ste 2620 (92101-8172)
PHONE..............................714 975-2999
Todd A Mikles, *CEO*
EMP: 400 EST: 2010
SALES (est): 25.06MM **Privately Held**
SIC: 6531 Real estate brokers and agents

(P-8976)
DEASY PENNER PODLEY
Also Called: Dpp Real Estate
30 N Baldwin Ave (91024-1956)
PHONE..............................626 408-1280
Mike Deasy, *Ch Bd*
George Penner, *
EMP: 223 EST: 2019
SALES (est): 4.91MM **Privately Held**
Web: www.margaretgaremore.com
SIC: 6531 Real estate brokers and agents

(P-8977)
DELEON REALTY INC
1717 Embarcadero Rd Ste 5000
(94303-3357)
PHONE..............................650 543-8500
Michael Repka, *CEO*
EMP: 75 EST: 2011
SALES (est): 10.56MM **Privately Held**
Web: www.deleonrealty.com
SIC: 6531 Real estate agent, residential

(P-8978)
DENOVA HOME SALES INC
Also Called: Denova Homes
1500 Willow Pass Ct (94520-1009)
PHONE..............................925 852-0545
David Sanson, *Pr*
Lori Sanson, *
EMP: 84 EST: 1991
SQ FT: 1,850
SALES (est): 16.87MM **Privately Held**
Web: www.denovahomes.com
SIC: 6531 Real estate brokers and agents

(P-8979)
DG REAL ESTATE INC
4766 Park Granada Ste 214 (91302-3334)
PHONE..............................818 591-8800
EMP: 86
SIC: 6531 Real estate agent, commercial
PA: Dg Real Estate Inc.
    1030 Foothill Blvd Fl 1
    La Canada CA

(P-8980)
DIABLO REALTY
Also Called: Pacific Mortgage Resources
1301 Ygnacio Valley Rd Ste 100
(94598-2851)
PHONE..............................925 933-9300
Linda Jean Anderson, *Pr*
Moses Guillory, *
EMP: 114 EST: 1977
SALES (est): 10.7MM **Privately Held**
Web: windermerediablo.withwre.com
SIC: 6531 6163 Real estate agent, residential ; Mortgage brokers arranging for loans, using money of others

(P-8981)
DIAMOND RIDGE CORPORATION
Also Called: Re/Max
121 S Mountain Ave (91786-6257)
PHONE..............................909 949-0605
Jennifer Lynn Puglisi, *CEO*
EMP: 165 EST: 2001
SALES (est): 9.53MM **Privately Held**
Web: www.remax.com
SIC: 6531 Real estate agent, residential

(P-8982)
DICK JAMES & ASSOCIATES INC
Also Called: James Nevada Properties
2990 Lava Ridge Ct Ste 240 (95661-3076)
PHONE..............................916 332-7430
Michelle Amaral, *CFO*
EMP: 246 EST: 1998
SALES (est): 4.95MM **Privately Held**
SIC: 6531 Real estate managers

(P-8983)
DIEZ & LEIS RE GROUP INC
Also Called: Prudential Norcal Realty
5120 Manzanita Ave Ste 120 (95608-0558)
PHONE..............................916 487-4287
EMP: 605 EST: 1993
SQ FT: 10,000
SALES (est): 2.83MM
SALES (corp-wide): 60.05B **Publicly Held**
SIC: 6531 Real estate agent, residential
HQ: Brer Affiliates Llc
    18500 Von Karman Ave # 4
    Irvine CA
    949 794-7900

(P-8984)
DIGITAL REALTY
365 Main St (94105-2009)
PHONE..............................415 738-6500
EMP: 162 EST: 2016
SALES (est): 7.04MM **Privately Held**
Web: www.digitalrealty.com
SIC: 6531 Real estate agents and managers

(P-8985)
DILBECK INC (PA)
Also Called: Dilbeck Realtors
1030 Foothill Blvd (91011-3285)
PHONE..............................818 790-6774
Mark Dilbeck, *Ch Bd*
Mark Dilbeck, *Ch Bd*
Bruce Dilbeck, *
EMP: 70 EST: 1963
SQ FT: 9,000
SALES (est): 25.37MM
SALES (corp-wide): 25.37MM **Privately Held**
Web: www.dilbeck.com
SIC: 6531 Real estate agent, commercial

(P-8986)
DONAHUE SCHRBER RLTY GROUP INC (PA)
200 Baker St Ste 100 (92626-4551)
PHONE..............................714 545-1400
Thomas Schriber, *Ch Bd*
Patrick S Donahue, *
Larry Casey, *
EMP: 80 EST: 1954
SQ FT: 20,000
SALES (est): 27.92MM
SALES (corp-wide): 27.92MM **Privately Held**
SIC: 6531 Real estate agent, commercial

(P-8987)
DOROTHY SARKOZY
Also Called: Coldwell Banker Residential BR

6531 - Real Estate Agents And Managers (P-8988)

3810 Valley Centre Dr Ste 906
(92130-3308)
PHONE...................858 259-0555
Dorothy Sarkozy, Prin
EMP: 105 EST: 2003
SALES (est): 1.1MM Privately Held
Web: www.coldwellbanker.com
SIC: 6531 Real estate agent, residential

(P-8988)
E & S RING MANAGEMENT CORP
Also Called: Mariner's Village
4600 Via Marina Apt 209 (90292-7231)
PHONE...................310 821-4916
Christine Valentino, Mgr
EMP: 76
SALES (corp-wide): 43.5MM Privately Held
Web: www.esring.com
SIC: 6531 6513 Real estate managers; Apartment building operators
PA: E & S Ring Management Corp.
6601 Center Dr W Ste 600
Culver City CA
310 337-5400

(P-8989)
EAM ENTERPRISES INC
Also Called: Century 21 Crest
8307 Foothill Blvd (91040-2809)
PHONE...................818 951-6464
Razmik Mira, Owner
EMP: 71
Web: www.century21.com
SIC: 6531 Real estate agent, residential
PA: E.A.M. Enterprises Inc.
4005 Foothill Blvd
La Crescenta CA

(P-8990)
EAM ENTERPRISES INC (PA)
Also Called: Crest R E O & Relocation
4005 Foothill Blvd (91214-1623)
PHONE...................818 248-9100
Razmik Mirzakhanian, CEO
EMP: 100 EST: 1991
SQ FT: 5,000
SALES (est): 10.89MM Privately Held
Web: www.century21.com
SIC: 6531 Real estate agent, residential

(P-8991)
EAPPRAISEIT LLC (PA)
12395 First American Way (92064-6897)
PHONE...................800 281-6200
Devid Feildman, Prin
EMP: 65 EST: 2002
SALES (est): 4.96MM
SALES (corp-wide): 4.96MM Privately Held
Web: www.eappraiseit.com
SIC: 6531 Appraiser, real estate

(P-8992)
EC2002 INC
Also Called: Empire Realty Associates, Inc.
380 Diablo Rd (94526-3461)
PHONE...................925 217-5000
Judi Keenholtz, CEO
EMP: 1124 EST: 2002
SALES (est): 4MM Privately Held
Web: www.empirerealty.com
SIC: 6531 Real estate agent, residential
PA: Pacific Union International, Inc.
1 Letterman Dr Bldg C
San Francisco CA

(P-8993)
ENGEL & VOELKERS NEWPORT BEACH
3636 E Coast Hwy Ste B (92625-2554)
PHONE...................949 207-3101
EMP: 60 EST: 2015
SALES (est): 790.47K Privately Held
Web: newportbeach.evrealestate.com
SIC: 6531 Real estate brokers and agents

(P-8994)
ESSEX PROPERTIES LLC
18012 Sky Park Cir Ste 100 (92614-6671)
PHONE...................949 798-8100
Jim Niger, Pr
Burrel D Magnusson, *
Linda Webber, *
EMP: 75 EST: 1987
SALES (est): 2.26MM Privately Held
SIC: 6531 Real estate agent, commercial

(P-8995)
ETHAN CONRAD PROPERTIES INC (PA)
1300 National Dr Ste 100 (95834-1981)
PHONE...................916 779-1000
Ethan Conrad, Pr
Kenneth Miller, *
EMP: 89 EST: 2000
SQ FT: 45,063
SALES (est): 23.53MM
SALES (corp-wide): 23.53MM Privately Held
Web: www.ethanconradprop.com
SIC: 6531 Real estate agent, commercial

(P-8996)
EVOQ PROPERTIES INC
1318 E 7th St Ste 200 (90021-1128)
PHONE...................213 988-8890
Martin Caveroy, CEO
John Charles Maddux, *
Lynn Beckemeyer, Executive Development Vice President*
Todd Nielsen, Corporate Secretary*
Andrew Murray, *
EMP: 82 EST: 2006
SALES (est): 5.89MM Privately Held
Web: www.evoqproperties.com
SIC: 6531 Real estate agent, commercial

(P-8997)
EVR LENDING INC
Also Called: EVR LENDING INC
1397 Calle Avanzado (92673-6351)
PHONE...................949 492-4868
EMP: 77
Web: www.homesmart.com
SIC: 6531 Real estate agent, residential
PA: Evr Lending, Inc.
9901 Irvine Center Dr
Irvine CA

(P-8998)
EXCLUSIVE LIFESTYLES INC (PA)
Also Called: Corcoran Global Living
27762 Antonio Pkwy (92694-1140)
PHONE...................702 996-3030
Michael Mahon, CEO
Matthew Borland, COO
EMP: 68 EST: 2019
SALES (est): 2.02MM
SALES (corp-wide): 2.02MM Privately Held
SIC: 6531 6799 Real estate brokers and agents; Real estate investors, except property operators

(P-8999)
EXP REALTY
7100 Hillside Ave Apt 601 (90046-2316)
PHONE...................213 308-2927
Doris Fannin, Prin
EMP: 61 EST: 2018
SALES (est): 532K Privately Held
Web: www.mtolympus-lahomes.com
SIC: 6531 Real estate brokers and agents

(P-9000)
F M TARBELL CO
Also Called: Tarbel Realtors
39028 Winchester Rd Ste 101 (92563-3505)
PHONE...................951 677-3565
Joe Mcallen, Genl Mgr
EMP: 61
SALES (corp-wide): 145.44MM Privately Held
Web: www.jen4homes.com
SIC: 6531 Real estate agent, commercial
HQ: F. M. Tarbell Co.
1403 N Tustin Ave Ste 380
Santa Ana CA
714 972-0988

(P-9001)
F M TARBELL CO (HQ)
Also Called: Tarbell Realtors
1403 N Tustin Ave Ste 380 (92705-8691)
PHONE...................714 972-0988
TOLL FREE: 800
Tina Jimov, Pr
Donald M Tarbell, *
EMP: 110 EST: 1956
SQ FT: 60,000
SALES (est): 53.8MM
SALES (corp-wide): 145.44MM Privately Held
Web: www.jen4homes.com
SIC: 6531 Real estate agent, residential
PA: Tarbell Financial Corporation
1403 N Tustin Ave Ste 380
Santa Ana CA
714 972-0988

(P-9002)
FELSON COMPANIES INC
1290 B St Ste 210 (94541-2996)
PHONE...................510 538-1150
Joseph Felson, Pr
Joseph Lee Felson, *
Victor Richard Felson, *
Elliot Felson, *
EMP: 90 EST: 1955
SQ FT: 4,000
SALES (est): 8.78MM Privately Held
Web: www.felson.com
SIC: 6531 Real estate managers

(P-9003)
FIRST & LA REALTY CORP (PA)
Also Called: Century 21 Hill Top Realtors
1301 E Los Angeles Ave (93065-2882)
PHONE...................805 581-0021
Robert Connlee, Pr
Susan Hill, *
Pat Connlee, *
EMP: 67 EST: 1983
SQ FT: 2,600
SALES (est): 3.98MM
SALES (corp-wide): 3.98MM Privately Held
Web: www.century21.com
SIC: 6531 Real estate agent, residential

(P-9004)
FIRST AMERCN PROF RE SVCS INC (HQ)
200 Commerce (92602-5000)
PHONE...................714 250-1400
Larry Davidson, Pr
EMP: 240 EST: 1997
SQ FT: 28,000
SALES (est): 24.2MM Publicly Held
Web: www.smscorp.com
SIC: 6531 Real estate agents and managers
PA: First American Financial Corporation
1 First American Way
Santa Ana CA

(P-9005)
FIRST AMERICAN DATA CO LLC
Also Called: First American Data Tree
4 First American Way (92707-5913)
PHONE...................714 250-6594
Robert Karraa, COO
EMP: 63 EST: 1998
SALES (est): 8.84MM Publicly Held
Web: dna.firstam.com
SIC: 6531 Real estate listing services
PA: First American Financial Corporation
1 First American Way
Santa Ana CA

(P-9006)
FIRST AMERICAN TEAM REALTY INC (PA)
Also Called: Best Financial, The
2501 Cherry Ave Ste 100 (90755-2039)
PHONE...................562 427-7765
Steve S Vong, Pr
EMP: 150 EST: 1995
SQ FT: 3,300
SALES (est): 9.59MM Privately Held
Web: www.firstamericanteam.com
SIC: 6531 Real estate agent, residential

(P-9007)
FIRST TEAM RE - ORANGE CNTY
4 Corporate Plaza Dr Ste 100 (92660-7906)
PHONE...................949 759-5747
Jennifer Berman, Off Mgr
EMP: 68
SALES (corp-wide): 486 Privately Held
Web: www.firstteam.com
SIC: 6531 Real estate brokers and agents
PA: First Team Real Estate - Orange County
108 Pacifica Ste 300
Irvine CA
949 988-3000

(P-9008)
FIRST TEAM RE - ORANGE CNTY
200 S Main St Ste 100 (92882-2213)
PHONE...................951 270-2800
Linda Rocha, Prin
EMP: 68
SALES (corp-wide): 486 Privately Held
Web: www.firstteam.com
SIC: 6531 Real estate brokers and agents
PA: First Team Real Estate - Orange County
108 Pacifica Ste 300
Irvine CA
949 988-3000

(P-9009)
FIRST TEAM RE - ORANGE CNTY
Also Called: First Team Real Estate
8028 E Santa Ana Canyon Rd (92808-1108)
PHONE...................714 974-9191
EMP: 102
SALES (corp-wide): 486 Privately Held
Web: www.firstteam.com
SIC: 6531 Real estate brokers and agents
PA: First Team Real Estate - Orange County

PRODUCTS & SERVICES SECTION   **6531 - Real Estate Agents And Managers (P-9030)**

108 Pacifica Ste 300
Irvine CA
949 988-3000

(P-9010)
FIRST TEAM RE - ORANGE CNTY
Also Called: First Team Real Estate
26711 Aliso Creek Rd Ste 200a
(92656-4820)
PHONE..................................949 389-0004
EMP: 150
SALES (corp-wide): 486 **Privately Held**
Web: www.firstteam.com
SIC: **6531** Real estate brokers and agents
PA: First Team Real Estate - Orange
County
108 Pacifica Ste 300
Irvine CA
949 988-3000

(P-9011)
FIRST TEAM RE - ORANGE CNTY
12501 Seal Beach Blvd Ste 100
(90740-2763)
PHONE..................................562 596-9911
Judy Sharp, Mgr
EMP: 272
SALES (corp-wide): 486 **Privately Held**
Web: www.firstteam.com
SIC: **6531** Real estate agent, residential
PA: First Team Real Estate - Orange
County
108 Pacifica Ste 300
Irvine CA
949 988-3000

(P-9012)
FIRST TEAM RE - ORANGE CNTY (PA)
Also Called: First Team Walk-In Realty
108 Pacifica Ste 300 (92618-7435)
PHONE..................................949 988-3000
Cameron Merage, CEO
Michele Harrington, *
EMP: 160 **EST**: 1976
SQ FT: 8,000
SALES (est): 486
SALES (corp-wide): 486 **Privately Held**
Web: www.firstteam.com
SIC: **6531** Real estate agent, residential

(P-9013)
FIRST TEAM RE - ORANGE CNTY
42 64th Pl (90803-5676)
PHONE..................................562 346-5088
EMP: 68
SALES (corp-wide): 486 **Privately Held**
Web: www.firstteam.com
SIC: **6531** Real estate agent, residential
PA: First Team Real Estate - Orange
County
108 Pacifica Ste 300
Irvine CA
949 988-3000

(P-9014)
FIRST TEAM RE - ORANGE CNTY
32451 Golden Lantern Ste 210
(92677-5344)
PHONE..................................949 240-7979
Mark Kojac, Genl Mgr
EMP: 272
SALES (corp-wide): 486 **Privately Held**
Web: www.firstteam.com
SIC: **6531** Real estate agent, residential
PA: First Team Real Estate - Orange
County
108 Pacifica Ste 300
Irvine CA
949 988-3000

(P-9015)
FIRST TEAM RE - ORANGE CNTY
Also Called: 1st Team Real Estate
17240 17th St (92780-1945)
PHONE..................................714 544-5456
Michael Hampton, Mgr
EMP: 238
SALES (corp-wide): 486 **Privately Held**
Web: www.firstteam.com
SIC: **6531** Real estate agent, residential
PA: First Team Real Estate - Orange
County
108 Pacifica Ste 300
Irvine CA
949 988-3000

(P-9016)
FIRSTSRVICE RSIDENTIAL CAL INC (DH)
9130 Anaheim Pl Ste 110 (91730-8540)
P.O. Box 1510 (91785-1510)
PHONE..................................909 981-4131
Glennon Gray, Pr
James Gray, *
EMP: 69 **EST**: 1986
SALES (est): 20.46MM
SALES (corp-wide): 3.75B **Privately Held**
Web: www.fsresidential.com
SIC: **6531** Real estate managers
HQ: Firstservice Residential, Inc.
1855 Griffin Rd Ste A330
Dania Beach FL

(P-9017)
FIRSTSRVICE RSIDENTIAL CAL LLC (HQ)
Also Called: Merit Companies The
15241 Laguna Canyon Rd (92618-3146)
PHONE..................................949 448-6000
Bob Cardoza, Pr
Katie Ward, Prin
EMP: 200 **EST**: 1980
SQ FT: 21,000
SALES (est): 2.89MM
SALES (corp-wide): 3.75B **Privately Held**
Web: www.fsresidential.com
SIC: **6531** Real estate managers
PA: Firstservice Corporation
1255 Bay St Suite 600
Toronto ON
416 960-9566

(P-9018)
FPI MANAGEMENT INC
1124 F St (95616-2045)
PHONE..................................530 756-5332
EMP: 128
SALES (corp-wide): 249.98MM **Privately Held**
Web: www.fpimgt.com
SIC: **6531** Real estate managers
PA: Fpi Management, Inc.
800 Iron Point Rd
Folsom CA
916 357-5300

(P-9019)
FPI MANAGEMENT INC
Also Called: Hilltop Estates
131 Eureka St Ofc (95945-6361)
PHONE..................................530 272-5274
Guy Strange Administor, Brnch Mgr
EMP: 128
SALES (corp-wide): 249.98MM **Privately Held**
Web: www.fpimgt.com
SIC: **6531** 6513 Real estate managers;
Apartment building operators
PA: Fpi Management, Inc.
800 Iron Point Rd
Folsom CA
916 357-5300

(P-9020)
FUSION GROWTH PARTNERS INC
Also Called: Fusion Real Estate Network
1300 National Dr Ste 170 (95834-1991)
PHONE..................................916 448-3174
EMP: 90 **EST**: 2001
SQ FT: 4,400
SALES (est): 6.41MM **Privately Held**
Web: www.fusionrealestatenetwork.com
SIC: **6531** Real estate agent, residential

(P-9021)
GEMMM CORPORATION (PA)
Also Called: Prudential
2860 E Thousand Oaks Blvd (91362-3201)
PHONE..................................805 496-0555
TOLL FREE: 800
Robert L Majorino, Pr
Robert Hamilton, *
Anthony Principe, *
Lynn Gilbert, *
EMP: 100 **EST**: 1990
SQ FT: 12,500
SALES (est): 20.67MM
SALES (corp-wide): 20.67MM **Privately Held**
Web: www.bhhscalhomes.com
SIC: **6531** Real estate agent, residential

(P-9022)
GIC REAL ESTATE INC (DH)
1 Bush St Ste 1100 (94104-4417)
PHONE..................................415 229-1800
Adam Gallistel, CEO
EMP: 60 **EST**: 1985
SQ FT: 10,000
SALES (est): 52.71MM **Privately Held**
Web: www.gic.com.sg
SIC: **6531** 6799 Real estate managers; Real
estate investors, except property operators
HQ: Gic Private Limited
168 Robinson Road
Singapore

(P-9023)
GK MANAGEMENT CO INC (PA)
5150 Overland Ave (90230-4914)
PHONE..................................310 204-2050
Carole Glodney, CEO
Jona Goldrich, *
EMP: 150 **EST**: 1972
SALES (est): 64.47MM
SALES (corp-wide): 64.47MM **Privately Held**
Web: www.goldrichkest.com
SIC: **6531** Real estate managers

(P-9024)
GLENBOROUGH LLC (PA)
400 S El Camino Real Ste 1100
(94402-1706)
PHONE..................................650 343-9300
Terri Garnick, *
EMP: 60 **EST**: 1995
SALES (est): 7.48MM **Privately Held**
SIC: **6531** Real estate managers

(P-9025)
GOLDEN RAIN FOUNDATION (PA)
Also Called: Rossmoor
1001 Golden Rain Rd (94595-2412)
P.O. Box 2070 (94595-0070)
PHONE..................................925 988-7700
Stephen Adams, CEO

EMP: 75 **EST**: 1963
SQ FT: 5,000
SALES (est): 24.44MM
SALES (corp-wide): 24.44MM **Privately Held**
Web: www.rossmoor.com
SIC: **6531** 8011 2711 7997 Real estate
managers; Offices and clinics of medical
doctors; Newspapers; Golf club,
membership

(P-9026)
GRAND PACIFIC RESORTS INC (PA)
5900 Pasteur Ct Ste 200 (92008-7336)
P.O. Box 4068 (92018-4068)
PHONE..................................760 431-8500
Timothy J Stripe, CEO
David Brown, *
EMP: 250 **EST**: 1993
SQ FT: 22,000
SALES (est): 101.28MM **Privately Held**
Web: www.grandpacificresorts.com
SIC: **6531** 7011 Time-sharing real estate
sales, leasing and rentals; Hotels and
motels

(P-9027)
GREENBRIAR MANAGEMENT COMPANY
Also Called: Greenbriar Homes Community
26969 Beaver Ln (94022-1901)
PHONE..................................510 497-8200
Gilbert M Meyer, CEO
Carol Meyer, *
EMP: 100 **EST**: 1984
SALES (est): 5.71MM **Privately Held**
SIC: **6531** Cooperative apartment manager

(P-9028)
GREYSTAR MANAGEMENT SVCS LP
6320 Canoga Ave Ste 1512 (91367-2526)
PHONE..................................818 596-2180
Grace White, Owner
EMP: 138
Web: www.greystar.com
SIC: **6531** Real estate brokers and agents
PA: Greystar Management Services, L.P.
750 Bering Dr Ste 300
Houston TX

(P-9029)
GREYSTAR MANAGEMENT SVCS LP
Also Called: Greystar
620 Newport Center Dr 15th Fl (92660)
PHONE..................................949 705-0010
Kevin Kaverna, Dir
EMP: 809
Web: www.greystar.com
SIC: **6531** Real estate managers
PA: Greystar Management Services, L.P.
750 Bering Dr Ste 300
Houston TX

(P-9030)
GROSVENOR PROPERTIES LTD
Also Called: Grosvenor House
899 Pine St Apt 103 (94108-3027)
PHONE..................................415 421-1899
Paul Herbert, Mgr
EMP: 404
SALES (corp-wide): 29.62MM **Privately Held**
Web: www.grosvenorproperties.com
SIC: **6531** 6513 7389 7011 Real estate
managers; Apartment hotel operation;
Relocation service; Hotels

6531 - Real Estate Agents And Managers (P-9031)

PA: Grosvenor Properties Ltd.
222 Front St Fl 7
San Francisco CA
415 421-5940

(P-9031)
GRUBB & ELLIS COMPANY
1551 N Tustin Ave Ste 300 (92705-8621)
PHONE...................714 667-8252
◆ EMP: 4500
SIC: 6531 8742 6162 Real estate agent, commercial; Real estate consultant; Mortgage brokers, using own money

(P-9032)
GRUBB & ELLIS MANAGEMENT SERVICES INC
1551 N Tustin Ave Ste 300 (92705-8638)
PHONE...................412 201-8200
EMP: 1800
SIC: 6531 Real estate agents and managers

(P-9033)
GRUPE COMPANY (PA)
Also Called: Village West Interiors
3255 W March Ln Ste 400 (95219-2352)
P.O. Box 7576 (95267-0576)
PHONE...................209 473-6000
Frank A Passadore, Pr
Greenlaw Grupe Junior, Ch Bd
EMP: 60 EST: 1960
SQ FT: 7,000
SALES (est): 42.59MM
SALES (corp-wide): 42.59MM Privately Held
Web: www.grupe.com
SIC: 6531 1542 Real estate agent, residential ; Commercial and office building, new construction

(P-9034)
GUARANTEE REAL ESTATE
756 W Shaw Ave (93704-2223)
PHONE...................559 650-6030
Sandy Darling, VP
J Scott Leonard, *
EMP: 68 EST: 2000
SALES (est): 1.04MM Privately Held
Web: www.guarantee.com
SIC: 6531 Real estate brokers and agents

(P-9035)
HALL AND CHAMBERS INC
1625 W Glenoaks Blvd (91201-1826)
PHONE...................818 476-3000
Rick Bonyadi, Pr
EMP: 74 EST: 2015
SALES (est): 1.43MM Privately Held
Web: www.cbhallmark.com
SIC: 6531 Real estate agent, commercial

(P-9036)
HANKEN CONO ASSAD & CO INC
Also Called: Wintergreen Apts
1504 Oro Vista Rd Apt 145 (92154-4069)
PHONE...................619 575-3100
Martha Alonso, Mgr
EMP: 113
SALES (corp-wide): 16.83MM Privately Held
Web: www.sdrenting.com
SIC: 6531 6513 Condominium manager; Apartment building operators
PA: Hanken Cono Assad & Co., Inc.
5550 Baltimore Dr Ste 200
La Mesa CA
619 698-4770

(P-9037)
HANU REDDY REALTY
16251 Laguna Canyon Rd Ste 100 (92618-3624)
PHONE...................949 450-8800
Hanu Reddy, CEO
Ranjit Narasimhan, *
EMP: 70 EST: 1984
SALES (est): 2.41MM Privately Held
Web: www.hanureddy.com
SIC: 6531 Real estate agent, residential

(P-9038)
HELM MANAGEMENT CO (PA)
Also Called: Helm, The
4668 Nebo Dr Ste A (91941-5200)
PHONE...................619 589-6222
Tom Hensley, Pr
EMP: 70 EST: 1979
SQ FT: 1,176
SALES (est): 8.79MM
SALES (corp-wide): 8.79MM Privately Held
Web: www.helmmanagement.com
SIC: 6531 Real estate managers

(P-9039)
HINES INTERESTS LTD PARTNR
1 Hacker Way Bldg 10 (94025-1550)
PHONE...................650 518-6139
EMP: 170
SALES (corp-wide): 1.38B Privately Held
Web: www.hines.com
SIC: 6531 Real estate agent, commercial
PA: Hines Interests Limited Partnership
845 Texas Ave Houston
Houston TX
713 621-8000

(P-9040)
HOMEGAINCOM INC
12667 Alcosta Blvd Ste 200 (94583-5272)
PHONE...................925 983-2852
Tim Fagan, CEO
Mandy Grace, *
EMP: 65 EST: 1999
SQ FT: 13,000
SALES (est): 192.4K
SALES (corp-wide): 899.82K Privately Held
SIC: 6531 Real estate agent, residential
PA: One Planet Ops Inc.
1820 Bonanza St
Walnut Creek CA
925 983-2800

(P-9041)
HOUSE SEVEN GABLES RE INC
Also Called: Cole, Norman Anne
5753 E Santa Ana Canyon Rd Ste P (92807-3230)
PHONE...................714 282-0306
EMP: 95
SALES (corp-wide): 22.27MM Privately Held
Web: www.sevengables.com
SIC: 6531 Real estate brokers and agents
PA: House Of Seven Gables Real Estate, Inc.
12651 Newport Ave
Tustin CA
714 731-3777

(P-9042)
HOUSE SEVEN GABLES RE INC
19440 Goldenwest St (92648-2116)
PHONE...................714 500-3300
Terry Reay, Mgr
EMP: 60
SALES (corp-wide): 22.27MM Privately Held
Web: www.sevengables.com
SIC: 6531 Real estate agent, residential
PA: House Of Seven Gables Real Estate, Inc.
12651 Newport Ave
Tustin CA
714 731-3777

(P-9043)
HSF AFFILIATES LLC (PA)
Also Called: Prudential
18500 Von Karman Ave Ste 400 (92612-1511)
PHONE...................949 794-7900
Chris Stuart, CEO
Allan Dalton, CFO
Gino Blefari, Ch
EMP: 93 EST: 2012
SALES (est): 36.37MM
SALES (corp-wide): 36.37MM Privately Held
Web: www.hsfaffiliates.com
SIC: 6531 Real estate agent, residential

(P-9044)
HUNT ENTERPRISES INC
Also Called: Shibui Apartments
2270 Sepulveda Blvd Apt 50 (90501-5304)
PHONE...................310 325-1496
EMP: 67
SQ FT: 53,813
SALES (corp-wide): 13.19MM Privately Held
Web: www.huntenterprises.net
SIC: 6531 Real estate leasing and rentals
PA: Hunt Enterprises, Inc.
4416 W 154th St
Lawndale CA
310 675-3555

(P-9045)
HYDE & COMPANY INC
3330 W Mineral King Ave Ste F (93291-5763)
PHONE...................559 741-3636
Brian Hyde, Pr
EMP: 99 EST: 2015
SALES (est): 1.61MM Privately Held
SIC: 6531 Real estate agents and managers

(P-9046)
I D PROPERTY CORPORATION
Also Called: Property I D
1001 Wilshire Blvd Ste 100 (90017-2415)
PHONE...................213 625-0100
Carlos Siderman, Pr
▲ EMP: 120 EST: 1983
SALES (est): 9.85MM Privately Held
Web: www.propertyid.com
SIC: 6531 8742 Real estate listing services; Real estate consultant

(P-9047)
IDS REAL ESTATE GROUP (PA)
Also Called: I S D
515 S Figueroa St Ste 1600 (90071-3301)
PHONE...................213 627-9937
Murad M Siam, CEO
David G Mgrubllan, *
Mickey Siam, *
Jeff Newman, *
Lauren Cain, *
EMP: 60 EST: 1986
SQ FT: 20,000
SALES (est): 17.54MM
SALES (corp-wide): 17.54MM Privately Held
Web: www.idsrealestate.com
SIC: 6531 Real estate agent, commercial

(P-9048)
INCEPTION HOMES INC
1850 Hacienda Dr Ste 15 (92081-4545)
PHONE...................760 726-4302
Cindy Su, Brnch Mgr
EMP: 62
SALES (corp-wide): 9.76MM Privately Held
Web: www.advantagehomes.com
SIC: 6531 Real estate agents and managers
PA: Inception Homes, Inc.
2890 Monterey Hwy
San Jose CA
408 239-4859

(P-9049)
INSIDE REAL ESTATE
580 4th St (94107-1620)
PHONE...................415 525-4913
EMP: 65 EST: 2019
SALES (est): 3.62MM Privately Held
Web: www.legacysfhomes.com
SIC: 6531 Real estate brokers and agents

(P-9050)
INSIGNIA/ESG HT PARTNERS INC
225 W Santa Clara St Ste 250 (95113-1723)
PHONE...................408 288-2900
Pamela Cotta, Mgr
EMP: 440
SIC: 6531 Real estate agent, commercial
HQ: Insignia/Esg Hotel Partners, Inc.
11150 Santa Monica Blvd # 220
Los Angeles CA

(P-9051)
INSIGNIA/ESG HT PARTNERS INC
101 California St (94111-5802)
PHONE...................415 772-0123
EMP: 293
SIC: 6531 Real estate agent, commercial
HQ: Insignia/Esg Hotel Partners, Inc.
11150 Santa Monica Blvd # 220
Los Angeles CA

(P-9052)
INTERNET ESCROW SERVICES INC
Also Called: Escrow.com
180 Montgomery St Ste 650 (94104-4208)
PHONE...................888 511-8600
Robert Barrie, CEO
Neil Katz, *
EMP: 69 EST: 1999
SALES (est): 4.93MM Privately Held
Web: www.escrow.com
SIC: 6531 Escrow agent, real estate
PA: Freelancer Limited
'grosvenor Place' Level 37 225 George Street
Sydney NSW

(P-9053)
INVESERVE CORPORATION
812 W Las Tunas Dr (91776-1021)
PHONE...................626 458-3435
Norman Chang, Pr
Amy Chang, *
Michael Fang, *
EMP: 80 EST: 1987
SALES (est): 2.77MM Privately Held
Web: www.inveserve.com
SIC: 6531 Real estate agent, commercial

PRODUCTS & SERVICES SECTION
6531 - Real Estate Agents And Managers (P-9076)

(P-9054)
INVITATION HOMES INC
680 E Colorado Blvd (91101-6143)
PHONE..................805 372-2900
Luke Kochniuk, *Brnch Mgr*
EMP: 80
SALES (corp-wide): 2.24B **Publicly Held**
Web: www.invitationhomes.com
SIC: 6531 Real estate agents and managers
PA: Invitation Homes Inc.
  1717 Main St Ste 2000
  Dallas TX
  972 421-3600

(P-9055)
J BARON INC
Also Called: Re/Max
5299 Alton Pkwy (92604-8604)
PHONE..................949 451-1200
Tom Baron, *Pr*
EMP: 77 **EST:** 1988
SALES (est): 4.67MM **Privately Held**
Web: www.remax.com
SIC: 6531 Real estate agent, residential

(P-9056)
J H SNYDER COMPANY LLC
5757 Wilshire Blvd Ph 30 (90036-3690)
PHONE..................323 857-5546
EMP: 60 **EST:** 1997
SALES (est): 8.69MM **Privately Held**
Web: www.jhsnyder.net
SIC: 6531 Buying agent, real estate

(P-9057)
JAMBOREE REALTY CORP (PA)
Also Called: Jamboree Management
22982 Mill Creek Dr (92653-1214)
PHONE..................949 380-0300
Fred G Sparks, *Pr*
Richard M Tucker, *
Kathleen Tucker, *
EMP: 120 **EST:** 1982
SALES (est): 8.3MM
SALES (corp-wide): 8.3MM **Privately Held**
Web: www.jamboreemanagement.com
SIC: 6531 Real estate managers

(P-9058)
JMS REALTORS LTD (PA)
Also Called: Realty Concepts
575 E Alluvial Ave Ste 101 (93720-2800)
PHONE..................559 490-1500
John M Shamshoian, *CEO*
EMP: 172 **EST:** 1991
SALES (est): 14.87MM
SALES (corp-wide): 14.87MM **Privately Held**
Web: www.realtyconcepts.com
SIC: 6531 7389 Selling agent, real estate; Brokers, contract services

(P-9059)
JOHN STEWART COMPANY
1796 Tribute Rd Ste 100 (95815-4319)
PHONE..................916 561-0323
Steve Mcelroy, *Dir*
EMP: 153
SALES (corp-wide): 100.41MM **Privately Held**
Web: www.jsco.net
SIC: 6531 6552 6726 Real estate managers; Subdividers and developers, nec; Investors syndicates
PA: John Stewart Company
  1388 Sutter St Ste 1100
  San Francisco CA
  415 345-4400

(P-9060)
JOHN STEWART COMPANY
104 Whispering Pines Dr Ste 200 (95066-4799)
PHONE..................831 438-5725
Mari Tustin, *VP*
EMP: 120
SALES (corp-wide): 100.41MM **Privately Held**
Web: www.jsco.net
SIC: 6531 6552 6726 Real estate managers; Subdividers and developers, nec; Investors syndicates
PA: John Stewart Company
  1388 Sutter St Ste 1100
  San Francisco CA
  415 345-4400

(P-9061)
JOHN STEWART COMPANY (PA)
1388 Sutter St Ste 1100 (94109-5454)
PHONE..................415 345-4400
John K Stewart, *Ch*
Jack D Gardner, *
Mari Tustin, *
Dan Levine, *
Michael Smith-heimer, *CFO*
EMP: 80 **EST:** 1978
SQ FT: 15,000
SALES (est): 100.41MM
SALES (corp-wide): 100.41MM **Privately Held**
Web: www.jsco.net
SIC: 6531 6552 6726 Real estate managers; Subdividers and developers, nec; Investors syndicates

(P-9062)
JONES LANG LA SALLE
515 S Flower St Fl 13 (90071-2201)
PHONE..................213 239-6000
EMP: 67
SALES (est): 1.8MM **Privately Held**
Web: us.jll.com
SIC: 6531 Real estate agent, commercial

(P-9063)
JORDAN - LINK & COMPANY (PA)
Also Called: Century 21
2300 W Whitendale Ave (93277-6131)
PHONE..................559 733-9696
Bill Jordan, *Pr*
Steve Mcfadden, *VP*
Curt Link, *Sec*
EMP: 92 **EST:** 1976
SALES (est): 10.52MM
SALES (corp-wide): 10.52MM **Privately Held**
Web: www.jordanlink.com
SIC: 6531 Real estate agent, residential

(P-9064)
KELLER WLLAMS RLTY BVRLY HILLS
Also Called: Keller Williams Realtors
439 N Canon Dr Ste 300 (90210-3909)
PHONE..................310 432-6400
Paul Morris, *Prin*
EMP: 90 **EST:** 2005
SALES (est): 8.1MM **Privately Held**
Web: www.kwbeverlyhills.com
SIC: 6531 Real estate agent, residential

(P-9065)
KENNEDY-WILSON INC (PA)
151 El Camino Dr (90212-2704)
PHONE..................310 887-6400
William Mcmorrow, *Ch Bd*
Justin Enbody, *CFO*
Matt Windisch, *Pr*
John Pradhu, *VP*
EMP: 103 **EST:** 1977
SALES (est): 109.72MM **Privately Held**
Web: www.kennedywilson.com
SIC: 6531 6799 Auction, real estate; Real estate investors, except property operators

(P-9066)
KLAIR REAL ESTATE INC
Also Called: Exit Realty Consultants
3018 E Service Rd Ste 104& (95307)
PHONE..................209 484-8075
EMP: 120
Web: www.exithome.com
SIC: 6531 Real estate agent, residential
PA: Klair Real Estate, Inc.
  600 E Main St Ste 300
  Turlock CA

(P-9067)
LA CIENEGA ASSOCIATES
Also Called: Beverly Center
8500 Beverly Blvd Ste 501 (90048-6277)
PHONE..................310 854-0071
Laurel Crary-globus, *Genl Mgr*
A Alfred Taubman, *Pt*
Sheldon Gordon, *Pt*
EMP: 75 **EST:** 1982
SQ FT: 2,500
SALES (est): 6.49MM **Privately Held**
Web: www.beverlycenter.com
SIC: 6531 6512 Real estate brokers and agents; Auditorium and hall operation

(P-9068)
LAGUNA WOODS VILLAGE
24351 El Toro Rd (92637-4901)
P.O. Box 2220 (92654-2220)
PHONE..................949 597-4267
Milton John, *Dir*
Russ Disbro, *Dir*
EMP: 1000 **EST:** 1964
SALES (est): 18.77K **Privately Held**
Web: www.lagunawoodsvillage.com
SIC: 6531 Real estate agents and managers

(P-9069)
LANDMARK DIVIDEND LLC (PA)
Also Called: Landmark Dividend
400 Continental Blvd Ste 500 (90245-5076)
PHONE..................323 306-2683
Karen Delarosa, *Mgr*
Jeff Knyal, *CEO*
Oliver Piclo, *VP*
Brazy Pjr Arthur, *Managing Member*
George Doyle, *CFO*
EMP: 77 **EST:** 2010
SQ FT: 7,500
SALES (est): 76.63MM
SALES (corp-wide): 76.63MM **Privately Held**
Web: www.landmarkdividend.com
SIC: 6531 Real estate agent, commercial

(P-9070)
LAPHAM COMPANY INC
Also Called: Lapham Company Management
4844 Telegraph Ave (94609-2010)
PHONE..................510 531-6000
Jon Shahoian, *Pr*
Jon M Shahoian, *
EMP: 85 **EST:** 1947
SQ FT: 10,500
SALES (est): 9.38MM **Privately Held**
Web: www.laphamcompany.com
SIC: 6531 Real estate agent, residential

(P-9071)
LARAMAR GROUP LLC
Also Called: Fillmore Center, The
1475 Fillmore St (94115-4114)
PHONE..................415 292-1800
Steve Boyack, *Brnch Mgr*
EMP: 68
Web: www.thefillmorecenter.com
SIC: 6531 Cooperative apartment manager
PA: The Laramar Group L L C
  222 S Riverside Plz
  Chicago IL

(P-9072)
LASALLE JONES LANG
655 Redwood Hwy Frontage Rd Ste 177 (94941-3009)
PHONE..................415 388-4460
EMP: 91
SALES (corp-wide): 5.84MM **Privately Held**
Web: us.jll.com
SIC: 6531 Real estate agent, commercial
PA: Jones Lang Lasalle
  1 Front St Ste 1100
  San Francisco CA
  415 395-4900

(P-9073)
LEE & ASSOCIATES CENTRAL VLY
Also Called: Lee & Associates
241 Frank West Cir Ste 300 (95206-4226)
PHONE..................209 983-1111
Ernest J Pearson, *Ch*
Thomas D Davis, *Pr*
Tim Martin, *Sr VP*
Mark Reckers, *VP*
EMP: 93 **EST:** 1993
SALES (est): 6.63MM **Privately Held**
Web: www.lee-associates.com
SIC: 6531 Real estate agent, commercial

(P-9074)
LION CREEK SENIOR HOUSING PART
Also Called: Lion Creek Crossing V
6710 Lion Way (94621-3370)
PHONE..................510 878-9120
Jim Brooks, *Contrlr*
EMP: 99 **EST:** 2014
SALES (est): 2.01MM **Privately Held**
SIC: 6531 Real estate agents and managers

(P-9075)
LOAN SIGNING SYSTEM LLC
5694 Mission Center Rd (92108-4355)
PHONE..................619 878-3431
EMP: 76 **EST:** 2017
SALES (est): 679.17K **Privately Held**
Web: www.loansigningsystem.com
SIC: 6531 Real estate agents and managers

(P-9076)
LOIS LAUER REALTY (PA)
Also Called: Century 21
1998 Orange Tree Ln (92374-2841)
P.O. Box 524 (92373-0161)
PHONE..................909 748-7000
TOLL FREE: 800
David Coy, *Pr*
Shirley Harrington, *VP*
Ann Bryan, *Sec*
James H Lauer, *Dir*
EMP: 220 **EST:** 1976
SQ FT: 17,000
SALES (est): 20.49MM
SALES (corp-wide): 20.49MM **Privately Held**

6531 - Real Estate Agents And Managers (P-9077)

Web: www.loislauer.com
SIC: 6531 Real estate agent, residential

(P-9077)
LOWE ENTERPRISES RLTY SVCS INC
Also Called: Encino Financial Center
16133 Ventura Blvd Ste 535 (91436-2403)
PHONE..................818 990-9555
Karla Akins, *Brnch Mgr*
EMP: 2184
SALES (corp-wide): 367.25MM **Privately Held**
SIC: 6531 Real estate managers
HQ: Lowe Enterprises Realty Services, Inc.
11777 San Vicente Blvd
Los Angeles CA
310 820-6661

(P-9078)
LOYDA YU REAL ESTATE INC
860 Kuhn Dr Ste 200 (91914-4517)
PHONE..................619 475-7777
Loyda Calvano, *Pr*
EMP: 60 EST: 2014
SALES (est): 2.47MM **Privately Held**
Web: www.loydayu.com
SIC: 6531 Real estate agent, residential

(P-9079)
LRES CORPORATION (PA)
Also Called: Guardian Solutions
765 The City Dr S (92868-4942)
PHONE..................714 520-5737
Roger Beane, *Pr*
Don Mask, *CAO*
Alice Sorenson, *Ex VP*
Paul Abbamonto, *COO*
Richard Cimino, *Sr VP*
EMP: 91 EST: 2001
SALES (est): 19.15MM
SALES (corp-wide): 19.15MM **Privately Held**
Web: www.lres.com
SIC: 6531 Real estate managers

(P-9080)
LUXRE REALTY INC
222 Avenida Del Mar (92672-4005)
PHONE..................949 498-3702
Deborah Gietter, *CEO*
EMP: 71 EST: 2011
SALES (est): 4.89MM **Privately Held**
Web: www.luxrerealty.com
SIC: 6531 Real estate agent, residential

(P-9081)
LYON REALTY
2220 Douglas Blvd Ste 100 (95661-3822)
PHONE..................916 784-1500
Chris Sheffer, *Prin*
EMP: 140
Web: www.golyon.com
SIC: 6531 Real estate agent, residential
PA: Lyon Realty
2280 Del Paso Rd Ste 100
Sacramento CA

(P-9082)
LYON REALTY
2580 Fair Oaks Blvd Ste 20 (95825-7631)
PHONE..................916 481-3840
Jim Waters, *Off Mgr*
EMP: 140
Web: www.golyon.com
SIC: 6531 Real estate agent, residential
PA: Lyon Realty
2280 Del Paso Rd Ste 100
Sacramento CA

(P-9083)
LYON REALTY
851 Pleasant Grove Blvd Ste 150 (95678-6177)
PHONE..................916 787-7700
EMP: 140
Web: www.golyon.com
SIC: 6531 Real estate agent, residential
PA: Lyon Realty
2280 Del Paso Rd Ste 100
Sacramento CA

(P-9084)
LYON REALTY
8814 Madison Ave (95628-3908)
PHONE..................916 962-0111
EMP: 140
Web: www.golyon.com
SIC: 6531 Real estate agent, residential
PA: Lyon Realty
2280 Del Paso Rd Ste 100
Sacramento CA

(P-9085)
LYON REALTY
3900 Park Dr (95762-4553)
PHONE..................916 939-5300
EMP: 140
Web: www.golyon.com
SIC: 6531 Real estate agent, residential
PA: Lyon Realty
2280 Del Paso Rd Ste 100
Sacramento CA

(P-9086)
LYON REALTY (PA)
2280 Del Paso Rd Ste 100 (95834-9701)
PHONE..................916 574-8800
Patrick Shey, *Pr*
EMP: 60 EST: 2007
SALES (est): 36.82MM **Privately Held**
Web: www.golyon.com
SIC: 6531 6519 Real estate agent, residential; Real property lessors, nec

(P-9087)
LYON STAHL INVESTMENT RE INC
239 Oregon St (90245-4215)
PHONE..................310 425-9838
EMP: 88 EST: 2017
SALES (est): 2.2MM **Privately Held**
Web: www.lyonstahl.com
SIC: 6531 Real estate agent, commercial

(P-9088)
M & S ACQUISITION CORPORATION (PA)
707 Wilshire Blvd Ste 5200 (90017-3501)
PHONE..................213 385-1515
Mark Santarsiero, *CFO*
Mark Santarsiero, *CEO*
Robert Kerslake, *
Merle Atkins, *
Fred Thomas, *
EMP: 115 EST: 1993
SALES (est): 12.92MM
SALES (corp-wide): 12.92MM **Privately Held**
SIC: 6531 8742 Appraiser, real estate; Management consulting services

(P-9089)
MAIN STREET MANAGEMENT LLC (PA)
2015 Manhattan Beach Blvd Ste 100 (90278-1226)
PHONE..................310 640-3100
EMP: 78 EST: 1998
SQ FT: 3,550
SALES (est): 5.22MM
SALES (corp-wide): 5.22MM **Privately Held**
SIC: 6531 Rental agent, real estate

(P-9090)
MAINSTREET REALTORS
8577 Haven Ave Ste 101 (91730-4850)
PHONE..................909 373-3821
EMP: 79 EST: 2009
SALES (est): 2.6MM **Privately Held**
Web: www.mainstreetgroup.com
SIC: 6531 6519 Real estate brokers and agents; Real property lessors, nec

(P-9091)
MAJESTIC REALTY CO (PA)
Also Called: Majestic Management Co.
13191 Crossroads Pkwy N Ste 600 (91746)
PHONE..................562 692-9581
EMP: 150 EST: 1948
SALES (est): 640.33K
SALES (corp-wide): 640.33K **Privately Held**
Web: www.majesticrealty.com
SIC: 6531 6552 Real estate agent, commercial; Subdividers and developers, nec

(P-9092)
MANGOLD PROPERTY MGT INC
575 Calle Principal (93940-2811)
PHONE..................831 372-1338
Thomas Mangold, *Owner*
EMP: 65 EST: 1983
SQ FT: 13,000
SALES (est): 7.31MM **Privately Held**
Web: www.mangoldproperties.com
SIC: 6531 Real estate managers

(P-9093)
MARCUS & MILLICHAP INC (PA)
Also Called: Marcus & Millichap
23975 Park Sorrento Ste 400 (91302-4014)
PHONE..................818 212-2250
Hessam Nadji, *Pr*
Mitchell R Labar, *
Steve Degennaro, *
Christopher J Zorbas, *
Andrew Strockis, *CMO*
EMP: 106 EST: 1971
SQ FT: 24,028
SALES (est): 1.3B
SALES (corp-wide): 1.3B **Publicly Held**
Web: www.marcusmillichap.com
SIC: 6531 Real estate agent, commercial

(P-9094)
MARCUS MILLICHAP CORP RE SVCS (HQ)
2626 Hanover St (94304-1132)
PHONE..................650 391-1700
William Millichap, *Ch Bd*
EMP: 60 EST: 1982
SQ FT: 12,509
SALES (est): 4.48MM
SALES (corp-wide): 150.35K **Privately Held**
SIC: 6531 Real estate agent, commercial
PA: The Marcus & Millichap Company
777 California Ave
Palo Alto CA
650 494-1400

(P-9095)
MARSHALL REDDICK REALTY INC
Also Called: Marshall Reddick RE Netwrk
4299 Macarthur Blvd Ste 102 (92660-2019)
P.O. Box 10311 (92711-0311)
PHONE..................949 885-8180
Marshall Reddick, *CEO*
EMP: 142 EST: 2005
SQ FT: 3,800
SALES (est): 2.7MM **Privately Held**
Web: www.marshallreddick.com
SIC: 6531 Real estate brokers and agents

(P-9096)
MEMCO HOLDINGS INC
10390 Santa Monica Blvd # 210 (90025-5058)
PHONE..................310 277-0057
Mitchell Stein, *Pr*
EMP: 130 EST: 1987
SALES (est): 5.04MM **Privately Held**
SIC: 6531 Real estate managers

(P-9097)
MERIDIAN MANAGEMENT GROUP
1145 Bush St (94109-5919)
PHONE..................415 434-9700
Randall Chapman, *Pr*
Gil Dowd, *
Russell Flynn, *
James R Wilson, *
EMP: 160 EST: 1984
SQ FT: 6,200
SALES (est): 16.88MM **Privately Held**
Web: www.mmgprop.com
SIC: 6531 Real estate managers

(P-9098)
MESA MANAGEMENT INC
1451 Quail St Ste 201 (92660-2725)
P.O. Box 2990 (92658-9018)
PHONE..................949 851-0995
Steve Mensinger, *Pr*
Robert Lucas, *
EMP: 70 EST: 1977
SQ FT: 5,000
SALES (est): 9.5MM **Privately Held**
Web: www.mesamanagement.net
SIC: 6531 Real estate managers

(P-9099)
METROPOLITAN REALTY MGT INC
11254 Atlantic Ave Ste 4 (90262-3062)
PHONE..................310 537-5441
EMP: 70
SALES (corp-wide): 69.9B **Publicly Held**
SIC: 6531 Real estate brokers and agents
HQ: Metropolitan Realty Management, Inc.
1 Madison Ave Lbby
New York NY
212 578-2211

(P-9100)
MISSION-BISHOP REAL ESTATE INC
Also Called: Century 21
39180 Liberty St Ste 205 (94538-2586)
PHONE..................510 796-2100
EMP: 67 EST: 1988
SQ FT: 18,000
SALES (est): 1.65MM **Privately Held**
Web: www.century21.com
SIC: 6531 6163 Real estate agent, residential; Mortgage brokers arranging for loans, using money of others

(P-9101)
MOONSTONE MANAGEMENT CORP (PA)

PRODUCTS & SERVICES SECTION

6531 - Real Estate Agents And Managers (P-9123)

Also Called: Moonstone Hotel Properties
2905 Burton Dr (93428-4001)
PHONE.................805 927-4200
EMP: 175 EST: 1995
SQ FT: 5,000
SALES (est): 12.72MM Privately Held
Web: www.moonstonehotels.com
SIC: 6531 Real estate managers

(P-9102)
MOSS & COMPANY INC (PA)
15300 Ventura Blvd Ste 405 (91403-3140)
PHONE.................310 453-0911
Cindy Gray, Pr
Ronald Tamkin, Executive Partner*
Chris Gray, *
EMP: 70 EST: 1957
SQ FT: 10,000
SALES (est): 13.28MM
SALES (corp-wide): 13.28MM Privately Held
SIC: 6531 Real estate managers

(P-9103)
MOSS MANAGEMENT SERVICES INC
15300 Ventura Blvd # 405 (91403-3103)
PHONE.................818 990-5999
Cindy Gray, Pr
Chris Gray, Ex VP
Henriette Saffron, CFO
EMP: 124 EST: 2006
SALES (est): 5.48MM Privately Held
SIC: 6531 Real estate managers

(P-9104)
MOVE INC (HQ)
Also Called: Realsuite SM
3315 Scott Blvd (95054-3139)
PHONE.................408 558-7100
Damian Eales, CEO
Bryan Charap, *
Michael Lam, *
James Caulfield, *
EMP: 500 EST: 1993
SQ FT: 32,405
SALES (est): 142.41MM
SALES (corp-wide): 9.88B Publicly Held
Web: www.move.com
SIC: 6531 Real estate listing services
PA: News Corporation
    1211 Ave Of The Americas
    New York NY
    212 416-3400

(P-9105)
MOVE SALES INC (DH)
Also Called: Homestore Apartments & Rentals
3315 Scott Blvd (95054-3139)
PHONE.................805 557-2300
Steve Berkowitz, CEO
Maria Pietrosorte, Pr
Kristin Pudwill, VP
EMP: 75 EST: 1996
SALES (est): 36.32MM
SALES (corp-wide): 9.88B Publicly Held
Web: www.realtor.com
SIC: 6531 Real estate brokers and agents
HQ: Move, Inc.
    3315 Scott Blvd
    Santa Clara CA
    408 558-7100

(P-9106)
MSE ENTERPRISES INC (PA)
Also Called: Marshall S Ezralow & Assoc
23622 Calabasas Rd Ste 200 (91302-1549)
PHONE.................818 223-3500
Marshall S Ezralow, Pr
EMP: 90 EST: 1974

SALES (est): 4.85MM
SALES (corp-wide): 4.85MM Privately Held
SIC: 6531 Real estate managers

(P-9107)
MURCOR INC
Also Called: Pcv Murcor Real Estate Svcs
740 Corporate Center Dr Ste 100 (91768)
PHONE.................909 623-4001
Keith D Murray, Pr
Jon D Van Deuren, *
Richard J Barkley, *
Tim Scherf, *
Cindy Nasser, *
EMP: 225 EST: 1981
SALES (est): 26.2MM Privately Held
Web: www.pcvmurcor.com
SIC: 6531 Appraiser, real estate

(P-9108)
NEW HOME PROFESSIONALS
Also Called: Estate Investment Group
6500 Dublin Blvd Ste 201 (94568-3152)
P.O. Box 2398 (94568-0239)
PHONE.................925 556-1555
Jay Lange, Pr
EMP: 86 EST: 1984
SALES (est): 4.38MM Privately Held
Web: www.newhomeprofessionals.com
SIC: 6531 Real estate brokers and agents

(P-9109)
NICK SADEK SOTHEBYS INTL RLTY
9217 Sierra College Blvd (95661-5919)
PHONE.................916 257-3229
EMP: 97 EST: 2018
SALES (est): 1.01MM Privately Held
Web: www.nicksadeksir.com
SIC: 6531 Real estate brokers and agents

(P-9110)
NIJJAR REALTY INC (PA)
4900 Santa Anita Ave Ste 2c (91731-1498)
P.O. Box 6085 (91734-2085)
PHONE.................626 575-0062
Daljit Kler, Prin
Mike Nijjar, *
Peter Nijjar, *
Swaranjit S Nijjar, *
EMP: 70 EST: 1949
SQ FT: 2,000
SALES (est): 2.35MM
SALES (corp-wide): 2.35MM Privately Held
SIC: 6531 Real estate brokers and agents

(P-9111)
NMS PROPERTIES INC
10960 Wilshire Blvd (90024-3711)
PHONE.................310 656-2700
Naum Shekhter, CEO
Margot Shekhter, *
Kurt Lietz, *
Scott Walter, *
Dino Ciarmoli, *
EMP: 95 EST: 1997
SALES (est): 11.27MM Privately Held
Web: www.nmsproperties.com
SIC: 6531 Real estate managers

(P-9112)
ON CENTRAL REALTY INC
1648 Colorado Blvd (90041-1403)
PHONE.................323 543-8500
Vazrik Bonyadi, Brnch Mgr
EMP: 314
Web: www.coldwellbanker.com

SIC: 6531 6519 Real estate brokers and agents; Real property lessors, nec
PA: On Central Realty, Inc.
    1625 W Glenoaks Blvd
    Glendale CA

(P-9113)
ONERENT INC
Also Called: Poplar Homes
3031 Tisch Way Ste 110pw (95128-2561)
PHONE.................408 675-5490
Gregory Michael Toschi, CEO
EMP: 68 EST: 2018
SALES (est): 6.34MM Privately Held
Web: www.poplarhomes.com
SIC: 6531 Real estate brokers and agents

(P-9114)
OPENDOOR LABS INC
Also Called: Opendoor Property
8880 Cal Center Dr Ste 400 (95826-3222)
PHONE.................888 352-7075
EMP: 102
SALES (corp-wide): 192.59MM Privately Held
Web: www.opendoor.com
SIC: 6531 Buying agent, real estate
PA: Opendoor Labs Inc.
    410 N Scottsdale Rd # 1600
    Tempe AZ
    415 510-7213

(P-9115)
OPPENHEIM GROUP INC
Also Called: Oppenheim Group Real Estate
8606 W Sunset Blvd (90069-2302)
PHONE.................310 927-7048
EMP: 72 EST: 2017
SALES (est): 3.82MM Privately Held
Web: www.ogroup.com
SIC: 6531 Real estate agent, commercial

(P-9116)
ORCHARD HOLDINGS GROUP INC
1 Venture Ste 300 (92618-7416)
PHONE.................949 502-8300
James Saccacio, Pr
Bud Reynolds, *
Larry Spencer, *
EMP: 60 EST: 2001
SQ FT: 1,300
SALES (est): 5.33MM Privately Held
SIC: 6531 Real estate brokers and agents

(P-9117)
PACIFIC HOUSING MANAGEMENT (PA)
945 Katella St (92651-3705)
PHONE.................714 508-1777
Richard Hall, Pr
EMP: 60 EST: 1985
SALES (est): 1.61MM Privately Held
SIC: 6531 Real estate managers

(P-9118)
PACIFIC MONARCH RESORTS INC (PA)
Also Called: Vacation Interval Realty
4000 Macarthur Blvd Ste 600 (92660-2558)
PHONE.................949 609-2400
Mark D Post, CEO
Carlton Post, *
Nick Baldwin, *
EMP: 100 EST: 1987
SQ FT: 20,000
SALES (est): 79.14MM
SALES (corp-wide): 79.14MM Privately Held

Web: www.pacificmonarchresorts.com
SIC: 6531 7011 Time-sharing real estate sales, leasing and rentals; Vacation lodges

(P-9119)
PACIFIC UNION CO
1550 Tiburon Blvd Ste U (94920-2516)
PHONE.................415 789-8686
EMP: 67
SALES (corp-wide): 49.06MM Privately Held
Web: www.pacificunion.com
SIC: 6531 Real estate brokers and agents
PA: Pacific Union Co.
    1699 Van Ness Ave 2
    San Francisco CA
    415 929-7100

(P-9120)
PACIFIC UNION CO
1699 Van Ness Ave (94109-3608)
PHONE.................415 474-6600
EMP: 66
SALES (corp-wide): 49.06MM Privately Held
Web: www.pacificunion.com
SIC: 6531 6552 Real estate brokers and agents; Subdividers and developers, nec
PA: Pacific Union Co.
    1699 Van Ness Ave 2
    San Francisco CA
    415 929-7100

(P-9121)
PACIFIC UNION CO
Also Called: Pacific Union Residential Brkg
51 Moraga Way Ste 1 (94563-3022)
PHONE.................925 258-0090
Linda Kaneko, VP
EMP: 66
SALES (corp-wide): 49.06MM Privately Held
Web: www.pacificunion.com
SIC: 6531 Real estate agent, residential
PA: Pacific Union Co.
    1699 Van Ness Ave 2
    San Francisco CA
    415 929-7100

(P-9122)
PACIFIC UNION RE GROUP (DH)
1699 Van Ness Ave # 2 (94109-3608)
PHONE.................415 929-7100
Sandy Shaffer, Pr
EMP: 80 EST: 1987
SQ FT: 700
SALES (est): 23.29MM
SALES (corp-wide): 314.05MM Privately Held
Web: www.pacunion.com
SIC: 6531 6163 8741 Real estate agent, commercial; Mortgage brokers arranging for loans, using money of others; Financial management for business
HQ: Gmac Home Services, Inc.
    4 Walnut Grove Dr
    Horsham PA
    215 682-4600

(P-9123)
PALANGING INTERNATIONAL INC
Also Called: Coldwell Banker Royal Realty
861 Anchorage Pl (91914-4535)
PHONE.................619 948-2459
EMP: 127 EST: 1986
SQ FT: 2,568
SALES (est): 8.59MM Privately Held
Web: www.coldwellbanker.com

6531 - Real Estate Agents And Managers (P-9124)

SIC: 6531 Real estate agent, residential

(P-9124)
PALM REALTY BOUTIQUE INC
401 Manhattan Beach Blvd Ste B (90266-5342)
PHONE...................310 545-2490
Cary Brett Zebrowski, *Prin*
EMP: 89 EST: 2007
SALES (est): 3.08MM Privately Held
Web: www.prbhomes.com
SIC: 6531 Real estate brokers and agents

(P-9125)
PANGO GROUP INC
6100 San Fernando Rd (91201-2240)
PHONE...................818 502-0400
Scott Akerley, *CEO*
Brett Yates, *CFO*
EMP: 71 EST: 2009
SQ FT: 6,500
SALES (est): 4.98MM Privately Held
Web: www.pangogroup.com
SIC: 6531 Real estate brokers and agents

(P-9126)
PAPOLA ENTERPRISES INC
Also Called: Network Real Estate
167 S Auburn St (95945-6516)
PHONE...................530 272-8885
William Papola Junior, *Pr*
EMP: 68 EST: 1981
SALES (est): 13.19MM Privately Held
Web: www.papola.com
SIC: 6531 Real estate agent, residential

(P-9127)
PARK REGENCY INC
10146 Balboa Blvd (91344-7408)
PHONE...................818 363-6116
Joseph Alexander, *Pr*
Ken Engeron, *
Patrick Pace, *
EMP: 70 EST: 1980
SQ FT: 4,500
SALES (est): 9.27MM Privately Held
Web: www.parkregency.com
SIC: 6531 Real estate agent, residential

(P-9128)
PARKMERCED MANAGEMENT CORP
Also Called: Parkmerced Apartment Community
3711 19th Ave (94132-2641)
PHONE...................415 405-4600
Paulita Borroughs, *Genl Mgr*
EMP: 61 EST: 1940
SQ FT: 950,000
SALES (est): 2.51MM Privately Held
Web: www.parkmerced.com
SIC: 6531 Real estate managers

(P-9129)
PATHSTONE FAMILY OFFICE LLC
Also Called: Pathstone Federal Street
1900 Avenue Of The Stars Ste 970 (90067-4661)
PHONE...................888 750-7284
Steve Braverman, *Prin*
EMP: 84
SALES (corp-wide): 4.91MM Privately Held
Web: www.pathstone.com
SIC: 6531 Appraiser, real estate
PA: Pathstone Family Office, Llc
50 Park Row W Ste 113
Providence RI
888 750-7284

(P-9130)
PCS PROPERTY MANAGMENT LLC
11859 Wilshire Blvd Ste 600 (90025-6616)
PHONE...................310 231-1000
Michael Ross, *Brnch Mgr*
EMP: 141
Web: www.pcsnorthvalley.com
SIC: 6531 Real estate managers
PA: Pcs Property Managment Llc
4500 Woodman Ave Ofc
Sherman Oaks CA

(P-9131)
PERSONAL
914 Sanchez St (94114-3323)
PHONE...................321 219-9161
Len Rand, *Sls Dir*
EMP: 69 EST: 2018
SALES (est): 884.25K Privately Held
Web: www.persona-sf.com
SIC: 6531 Real estate agents and managers

(P-9132)
PHASE TEN STRATEGIC CORP
Also Called: Marketing Design Group
2445 5th Ave Ste 450 (92101-1670)
PHONE...................619 298-1445
Kimberly Hardcastle, *Prin*
EMP: 83 EST: 2014
SALES (est): 5.02MM Privately Held
Web: www.mdg.agency
SIC: 6531 7311 Real estate agents and managers; Advertising agencies

(P-9133)
PINNACLE ESTATE PROPERTIES (PA)
Also Called: Pinnacle Escrow Company
9137 Reseda Blvd (91324-3039)
PHONE...................818 993-4707
Dana Potter, *Pr*
Jeff Black, *
EMP: 120 EST: 1985
SQ FT: 13,000
SALES (est): 33.08MM
SALES (corp-wide): 33.08MM Privately Held
Web: www.pinnacleestate.com
SIC: 6531 Real estate agent, residential

(P-9134)
PITTS & BACHMANN REALTORS INC
1482 E Valley Rd Ste 44 (93108-1200)
P.O. Box 50816 (93150-0816)
PHONE...................805 969-5005
Dennis Walsh, *Owner*
EMP: 77
SALES (corp-wide): 4.25MM Privately Held
SIC: 6531 Real estate brokers and agents
PA: Pitts & Bachmann Realtors Inc
1165 Coast Village Rd K
Santa Barbara CA
805 682-6415

(P-9135)
PITTS & BACHMANN REALTORS INC
1436 State St (93101-2512)
PHONE...................805 963-1391
Patty Tunnicliffe, *Mgr*
EMP: 78
SALES (corp-wide): 4.25MM Privately Held
SIC: 6531 Real estate agent, residential
PA: Pitts & Bachmann Realtors Inc
1165 Coast Village Rd K
Santa Barbara CA
805 682-6415

(P-9136)
PLG ESTATES
9877 Santa Monica Blvd (90212-1604)
PHONE...................310 788-0700
Andrew Dinsky, *Prin*
EMP: 61 EST: 2014
SALES (est): 875.37K Privately Held
Web: www.plgestatesinc.com
SIC: 6531 Real estate brokers and agents

(P-9137)
PM REALTY GROUP LP
4680 Macarthur Ct (92660-1870)
PHONE...................949 553-8246
EMP: 61
Web: www.madisonmarquette.com
SIC: 6531 Real estate agent, commercial
HQ: Pm Realty Group, L.P.
1000 Main St Ste 2400
Houston TX
713 209-5800

(P-9138)
PREFERRED BROKERS INC (PA)
Also Called: Coldwell Banker
9100 Ming Ave Ste 100 (93311-1329)
PHONE...................661 836-2345
John Mackessey, *Pr*
Gary Belter, *
EMP: 70 EST: 1990
SQ FT: 8,000
SALES (est): 9.72MM Privately Held
Web: www.coldwellbanker.com
SIC: 6531 Real estate agent, residential

(P-9139)
PRO GROUP INC
Also Called: Keller Williams Realtors
4160 Temescal Canyon Rd Ste 500 (92883-4625)
PHONE...................951 271-3000
James Brown, *Pr*
Jim Brown, *
David Clark, *
Joseph Regan, *
EMP: 195 EST: 2003
SQ FT: 18,000
SALES (est): 9.71MM Privately Held
Web: www.pgescrow.com
SIC: 6531 Real estate agent, residential

(P-9140)
PROFESSIONAL CMNTY MGT CAL INC
11860 Pierce St Ste 100 (92505-5178)
PHONE...................951 359-2840
EMP: 97
SALES (corp-wide): 49.19MM Privately Held
Web: www.associaonline.com
SIC: 6531 6514 Real estate managers; Dwelling operators, except apartments
PA: Professional Community Management Of California, Inc.
27051 Twne Cntre Dr Ste 2
Foothill Ranch CA
800 369-7260

(P-9141)
PROFESSIONAL CMNTY MGT CAL INC
Also Called: P C M
850 Country Club Dr (92220-5306)
PHONE...................951 845-2191
Mike Bennett, *Mgr*
EMP: 317
SALES (corp-wide): 49.19MM Privately Held
Web: www.pcminternet.com
SIC: 6531 Real estate managers
PA: Professional Community Management Of California, Inc.
27051 Twne Cntre Dr Ste 2
Foothill Ranch CA
800 369-7260

(P-9142)
PROFESSIONAL CMNTY MGT CAL INC
Also Called: Pcm
24351 El Toro Rd (92637-4901)
PHONE...................949 206-0580
Milt Johns, *Mgr*
EMP: 183
SALES (corp-wide): 49.19MM Privately Held
Web: www.lagunawoodsvillage.com
SIC: 6531 Real estate managers
PA: Professional Community Management Of California, Inc.
27051 Twne Cntre Dr Ste 2
Foothill Ranch CA
800 369-7260

(P-9143)
PROFESSIONAL CMNTY MGT CAL INC
Also Called: Professional Community MGT
906 Sycamore Ave Ste 210 (92081-7851)
P.O. Box 201 (92085-0201)
PHONE...................760 918-8040
Jim Fraker, *VP*
EMP: 98
SALES (corp-wide): 49.19MM Privately Held
Web: www.pcminternet.com
SIC: 6531 Real estate managers
PA: Professional Community Management Of California, Inc.
27051 Twne Cntre Dr Ste 2
Foothill Ranch CA
800 369-7260

(P-9144)
PROFESSIONAL CMNTY MGT CAL INC
Also Called: Leisure World Resales
23522 Paseo De Valencia (92653)
P.O. Box 2220 (92654-2220)
PHONE...................949 597-4200
EMP: 146
SALES (corp-wide): 49.19MM Privately Held
Web: www.pcminternet.com
SIC: 6531 Real estate managers
PA: Professional Community Management Of California, Inc.
27051 Twne Cntre Dr Ste 2
Foothill Ranch CA
800 369-7260

(P-9145)
PROLAND PROPERTY MANAGMENT LLC (PA)
Also Called: Hollingshead Management
2510 W 7th St 2nd Fl (90057-3802)
PHONE...................213 738-8175
EMP: 80 EST: 1998
SQ FT: 5,000
SALES (est): 2.41MM
SALES (corp-wide): 2.41MM Privately Held
SIC: 6531 Real estate managers

PRODUCTS & SERVICES SECTION

6531 - Real Estate Agents And Managers (P-9169)

(P-9146)
PROMETHEUS RE GROUP INC (PA)
1900 S Norfolk St Ste 150 (94403-1150)
PHONE.................................650 931-3400
Sanford N Diller, CEO
Jackie Safier, *
John Ghio, *
Bill Levia, *
EMP: 140 EST: 1965
SALES (est): 232.19MM
SALES (corp-wide): 232.19MM Privately Held
Web: www.prometheusapartments.com
SIC: 6531 6552 Real estate managers; Land subdividers and developers, commercial

(P-9147)
PROPERTY MANAGEMENT ASSOC INC (PA)
Also Called: Capital Commercial Property
6011 Bristol Pkwy (90230-6601)
PHONE.................................323 295-2000
Thomas Spear, Pr
Joshua Fein, *
Patrick Lacey, *
EMP: 130 EST: 1991
SQ FT: 6,500
SALES (est): 12.12MM Privately Held
Web: www.wemanageproperties.com
SIC: 6531 Real estate managers

(P-9148)
RA SNYDER PROPERTIES INC (PA)
2399 Camino Del Rio S Ste 200 (92108)
PHONE.................................619 297-0274
Richard Snyder, Pr
Marietta Robinson, *
EMP: 210 EST: 1987
SQ FT: 2,400
SALES (est): 16.76MM
SALES (corp-wide): 16.76MM Privately Held
Web: www.rasnyder.com
SIC: 6531 Real estate managers

(P-9149)
RAD DIVERSIFIED REIT INC
3110 E Guasti Rd Ste 300 (91761-1262)
PHONE.................................813 723-7348
Dutch Mendenhall, CEO
Taylor Green, Prin
EMP: 80 EST: 2017
SALES (est): 1.3MM Privately Held
SIC: 6531 Real estate agents and managers

(P-9150)
RANCHO MISSION VIEJO LLC
28811 Ortega Hwy (92675-2023)
PHONE.................................949 240-3363
EMP: 60 EST: 1996
SALES (est): 1.72MM Privately Held
Web: www.ranchomissionviejo.com
SIC: 6531 Real estate agents and managers

(P-9151)
RE/MAX
Also Called: Re/Max
9454 Wilshire Blvd Ste 150 (90212-2931)
PHONE.................................310 205-0050
Victoria Berenbau, Prin
EMP: 119 EST: 2010
SALES (est): 5.19MM Privately Held
Web: www.remax.com
SIC: 6531 Real estate agent, residential

(P-9152)
RE/MAX EXECUTIVE
Also Called: Re/Max
220 Standiford Ave Ste A (95350-1159)
PHONE.................................209 499-7772
Matthew Enriquez, Prin
EMP: 65 EST: 2017
SALES (est): 1.6MM Privately Held
Web: www.remax.com
SIC: 6531 Real estate agent, residential

(P-9153)
RE/MAX OF VALENCIA INC (PA)
Also Called: Re/Max
25101 The Old Rd (91381-2206)
PHONE.................................661 255-2650
John O'hare, Pr
John Ohare, Pr
Alice O'hare, VP
EMP: 123 EST: 1985
SQ FT: 10,000
SALES (est): 17.22MM
SALES (corp-wide): 17.22MM Privately Held
Web: www.remax-valencia-ca.com
SIC: 6531 8742 Real estate agent, residential; Real estate consultant

(P-9154)
REALMANAGE LLC
1701 Novato Blvd Ste 209 (94947-3030)
PHONE.................................415 444-1600
Cris Oneill, Brnch Mgr
EMP: 73
SALES (corp-wide): 124.58K Privately Held
Web: www.realmanage.com
SIC: 6531 Real estate managers
PA: Realmanage, Llc
    6400 Intl Pkwy Ste 1000
    Plano TX
    866 473-2573

(P-9155)
REALSELECT INC
3063 W Chapman Ave Apt 6207 (92868-1738)
PHONE.................................661 803-5188
Ashley Ivey, Brnch Mgr
EMP: 151
SALES (corp-wide): 9.88B Publicly Held
Web: www.realtor.com
SIC: 6531 Real estate brokers and agents
HQ: Realselect, Inc.
    30700 Russell Ranch Rd
    Westlake Village CA

(P-9156)
REALTY ONE GROUP INC
19322 Jesse Ln (92508-5072)
PHONE.................................951 565-8105
EMP: 60
SALES (corp-wide): 88.41K Privately Held
Web: www.realtyonegroup.com
SIC: 6531 Real estate agent, residential
PA: Realty One Group, Inc.
    23811 Aliso Creek Rd
    Laguna Niguel CA
    949 596-4300

(P-9157)
REALTY ONE GROUP BMC ASSOC
2355 San Ramon Valley Blvd (94583-1523)
PHONE.................................925 230-0700
Alicia Muniz, Prin
EMP: 63 EST: 2014
SALES (est): 855.2K Privately Held
Web: www.rogfuture.com
SIC: 6531 Real estate agent, residential

(P-9158)
RED TAIL RESIDENTIAL LLC (PA) ✪
2082 Michelson Dr Fl 4 (92612-1212)
PHONE.................................949 399-2510
EMP: 70 EST: 2022
SALES (est): 16.2MM
SALES (corp-wide): 16.2MM Privately Held
Web: www.rtacq.com
SIC: 6531 Real estate agents and managers

(P-9159)
REGENCY REAL ESTATE BRKS INC
Also Called: Regency Real Estate Brokers
25950 Acero Ste 100 (92691-2781)
PHONE.................................949 707-4400
Julie Zetland, Pr
EMP: 128 EST: 1994
SALES (est): 4.79MM Privately Held
Web: www.regencyrealestate.com
SIC: 6531 Real estate brokers and agents

(P-9160)
REMAX 100
Also Called: Re/Max
4311 Wilshire Blvd Ste 110 (90010-3708)
PHONE.................................323 933-4567
Sue Choi, Pr
EMP: 62 EST: 1995
SALES (est): 465.94K Privately Held
Web: www.remax.com
SIC: 6531 8742 Real estate agent, residential; Real estate consultant

(P-9161)
REMAX EXEC KING HARBOR
Also Called: Re/Max
23740 Hawthorne Blvd (90505-8206)
PHONE.................................310 378-9889
Sandra Sanders, Owner
EMP: 95 EST: 2001
SALES (est): 2.45MM Privately Held
Web: www.cmiyukihomes.com
SIC: 6531 Real estate agent, residential

(P-9162)
REMAX OLSON & ASSOCIATES INC
Also Called: Re/Max
11141 Tampa Ave (91326-2254)
PHONE.................................818 366-3300
Todd C Olson, CEO
Keith Myers, Ex VP
EMP: 193 EST: 1987
SQ FT: 30,000
SALES (est): 5.55MM Privately Held
Web: www.olsonmax.com
SIC: 6531 Real estate agent, residential

(P-9163)
REMN INC
3400 Central Ave Ste 330 (92506-2164)
PHONE.................................951 697-8135
EMP: 94
Web: www.homebridge.com
SIC: 6531 6211 Real estate agents and managers; Mortgages, buying and selling
PA: Remn , Inc
    194 Wood Ave S Fl 9
    Iselin NJ

(P-9164)
RETIREMENT HOUSING FOUNDATION (PA)
Also Called: Retirement Housing
911 N Studebaker Rd Ste 100 (90815-4980)
PHONE.................................562 257-5100
Laverne R Joseph, CEO
Deborah J Stouff, *
Frank G Jahrling, *
Raymond East, *
Christina E Potter, Vice Chairman*
EMP: 65 EST: 1961
SALES (est): 49.8MM
SALES (corp-wide): 49.8MM Privately Held
Web: www.rhf.org
SIC: 6531 Real estate agents and managers

(P-9165)
REXFORD INDUSTRIAL LLC
9340 Cabot Dr (92126-4397)
PHONE.................................858 536-8914
EMP: 60
SALES (corp-wide): 42.11MM Privately Held
Web: www.rexfordindustrial.com
SIC: 6531 Real estate agents and managers
PA: Rexford Industrial, Llc
    11620 Wilshire Blvd Fl 10
    Los Angeles CA
    310 966-1680

(P-9166)
REXFORD INDUSTRIAL LLC
Also Called: Rexford Industries
10860 6th St (91730-5902)
PHONE.................................909 987-2174
EMP: 60
SALES (corp-wide): 42.11MM Privately Held
Web: www.rexfordindustrial.com
SIC: 6531 Real estate brokers and agents
PA: Rexford Industrial, Llc
    11620 Wilshire Blvd Fl 10
    Los Angeles CA
    310 966-1680

(P-9167)
RGC SERVICES INC (PA)
Also Called: Re/Max
5720 Ralston St Ste 100 (93003-7845)
PHONE.................................805 644-1242
Glenn Sipes, Pr
Michael Sipes, *
Jerry Beebe, *
EMP: 110 EST: 1994
SQ FT: 35,000
SALES (est): 24.56MM Privately Held
Web: www.remax.com
SIC: 6531 Real estate agent, residential

(P-9168)
RGC SERVICES INC
Also Called: Re/Max
601 E Daily Dr Ste 102 (93010-5838)
PHONE.................................805 484-1600
EMP: 89
Web: www.remax.com
SIC: 6531 Real estate agent, residential
PA: Rgc Services, Inc.
    5720 Ralston St Ste 100
    Ventura CA

(P-9169)
RICHARD REALTY GROUP INC
Also Called: Realty Group San Diego
5946 Priestly Dr (92008-8848)
PHONE.................................760 603-8377
Bill Richard, CEO
Jan Richard, *
Janis Richard, *
EMP: 60 EST: 2009

(PA)=Parent Co (HQ)=Headquarters
✪ = New Business established in last 2 years

2024 Directory of California WholeSalers and Service Companies

6531 - Real Estate Agents And Managers (P-9170)

SALES (est): 2.25MM **Privately Held**
Web: www.billrichardhomes.com
SIC: 6531 Real estate agent, residential

(P-9170)
RODEO REALTY INC (PA)
Also Called: Paramount Properties
9171 Wilshire Blvd Ste 321 (90210-5562)
PHONE.....................818 349-9997
Sydney Leibovitch, *CEO*
Linda Leibovitch, *
EMP: 76 EST: 1986
SQ FT: 5,000
SALES (est): 58.91MM **Privately Held**
Web: www.rodeore.com
SIC: 6531 Real estate agent, residential

(P-9171)
ROMAN CTHLIC BSHP OF SAN DIEGO
Also Called: Holy Cross Cemetary
4470 Hilltop Dr (92102-3651)
PHONE.....................619 264-3127
Mario Deblasio, *Brnch Mgr*
EMP: 91
SALES (corp-wide): 48.57MM **Privately Held**
Web: www.holycrosssd.com
SIC: 6531 Cemetery management service
PA: The Roman Catholic Bishop Of San Diego
3888 Paducah Dr
San Diego CA
858 490-8200

(P-9172)
ROW MANAGEMENT LTD INC
499 N Canon Dr (90210-4887)
PHONE.....................310 887-3671
Kevin Shahin, *Brnch Mgr*
EMP: 305
SALES (corp-wide): 38.02MM **Privately Held**
Web: www.aboardtheworld.com
SIC: 6531 Real estate agents and managers
PA: Row Management Ltd. Inc.
1551 Sawgrs Corp Pkwy
Sunrise FL
954 538-8400

(P-9173)
S&J STADTLER INC
Also Called: Remax Accord
5980 Stoneridge Dr Ste 122 (94588-4518)
PHONE.....................925 847-8900
Jerry Stadtler, *Owner*
EMP: 330
SALES (corp-wide): 22MM **Privately Held**
Web: www.remaxaccord.com
SIC: 6531 Real estate agent, residential
PA: S&J Stadtler, Inc.
313 Sycamore Valley Rd W
Danville CA
925 838-4100

(P-9174)
SACRAMNTO HSING RDVLPMENT AGCY
Also Called: Housing Auth of The Cy Scrmnto
801 12th St (95814-2947)
P.O. Box 1834 (95812-1834)
PHONE.....................916 440-1399
Lashelle Dozier, *Ex Dir*
EMP: 157
SALES (corp-wide): 48.94MM **Privately Held**
Web: www.shra.org
SIC: 6531 Real estate agents and managers
PA: Sacramento Housing And Redevelopment Agency
801 12th St
Sacramento CA
916 440-1390

(P-9175)
SATELLITE MANAGEMENT CO (PA)
Also Called: Ccts
1010 E Chestnut Ave (92701-6497)
PHONE.....................714 558-2411
Ronald Jensen, *CEO*
Mary E Conzelman, *
Helen M Jensen, *
EMP: 121 EST: 1963
SQ FT: 800
SALES (est): 21.42MM
SALES (corp-wide): 21.42MM **Privately Held**
Web: www.satellitemanagement.com
SIC: 6531 Real estate managers

(P-9176)
SFII FOS HLDNGS 1333 BRDWAY LL
260 California St # 1100 (94111-4396)
PHONE.....................925 771-8198
Meredith Murphy, *
EMP: 100 EST: 2019
SALES (est): 4.55MM **Privately Held**
SIC: 6531 Real estate brokers and agents

(P-9177)
SFT REALTY GALWAY DOWNS LLC
Also Called: Kentina
38801 Los Corralitos Rd (92592)
P.O. Box 4404 Jeremie Dr (92592)
PHONE.....................951 232-1880
Kenneth C Smith, *Managing Member*
EMP: 70 EST: 2013
SQ FT: 2,000
SALES (est): 2.2MM **Privately Held**
Web: www.galwaydowns.com
SIC: 6531 Real estate agents and managers

(P-9178)
SHE MANAGES PROPERTIES INC (PA)
9340 Hazard Way Ste B2 (92123-1228)
PHONE.....................619 291-6300
Karen Martinez, *Pr*
Jorge Martinez, *
EMP: 65 EST: 1988
SQ FT: 1,700
SALES (est): 13.14MM **Privately Held**
SIC: 6531 Real estate managers

(P-9179)
SIDE INC
Also Called: Luminary Group The
580 4th St (94107-1620)
PHONE.....................415 525-4913
Guy Gal, *CEO*
Edward Wu, *Pr*
Armin Shahabi, *Prin*
EMP: 228 EST: 2014
SALES (est): 10.83MM **Privately Held**
Web: www.side.com
SIC: 6531 Real estate brokers and agents

(P-9180)
SKYHILL FINANCIAL INC
5762 Bolsa Ave Ste 110 (92649-1172)
PHONE.....................714 657-3938
Rosanne Covy, *Pr*
Angela Hess, *
EMP: 60 EST: 2008
SALES (est): 5.39MM **Privately Held**
Web: www.skyhillfinancial.com
SIC: 6531 8741 Real estate managers; Administrative management

(P-9181)
SOLANO PACIFIC CORPORATION
Also Called: Coldwell Banker Solano Pacific
900 1st St (94510-3218)
PHONE.....................707 745-6000
Richard A Bortolazzo, *CEO*
Joseph Banuat, *Pr*
EMP: 97 EST: 1981
SQ FT: 5,000
SALES (est): 4.97MM **Privately Held**
Web: solanopacific.sites.cbmoxi.com
SIC: 6531 Real estate agent, residential

(P-9182)
SOUTHERN CAL PIPE TRADES ADM
Also Called: Marina Village
1936 Quivira Way Bldg G (92109-8315)
PHONE.....................619 224-3125
Gerald Pharest, *Genl Mgr*
EMP: 92
SALES (corp-wide): 24.6MM **Privately Held**
Web: www.scptac.org
SIC: 6531 Real estate agents and managers
PA: Southern California Pipe Trades Administrative Corp
501 Shatto Pl Ste 500
Los Angeles CA
213 385-6161

(P-9183)
SPUS7 125 CAMBRIDGEPARK LP
515 S Flower St Ste 3100 (90071-2233)
PHONE.....................213 683-4200
EMP: 121 EST: 2014
SALES (est): 1.88MM **Publicly Held**
SIC: 6531 Real estate agent, commercial
HQ: Cbre Global Value Investors, Llc
601 S Figueroa St Ste 49
Los Angeles CA
213 683-4200

(P-9184)
SPUS7 150 CAMBRIDGEPARK LP
515 S Flower St Ste 3100 (90071-2233)
PHONE.....................213 683-4200
EMP: 137 EST: 2014
SALES (est): 4.27MM **Publicly Held**
SIC: 6531 Real estate agent, commercial
HQ: Cbre Global Value Investors, Llc
601 S Figueroa St Ste 49
Los Angeles CA
213 683-4200

(P-9185)
SRHT PROPERTY HOLDING LLC
Also Called: Skid Row Housing Trust
1317 E 7th St (90021-1101)
PHONE.....................213 683-0522
Jerrick Holloway, *Pr*
EMP: 150 EST: 2005
SALES (est): 3.91MM **Privately Held**
Web: tpv.72e.myftpupload.com
SIC: 6531 Real estate managers

(P-9186)
STARPINT 1031 PROPERTY MGT LLC
Also Called: Vision Realty Managements
450 N Roxbury Dr Ste 1050 (90210-4235)
PHONE.....................310 247-0550
EMP: 110 EST: 1997
SALES (est): 12.1MM **Privately Held**
Web: www.starpointproperties.com
SIC: 6531 Real estate agent, commercial

(P-9187)
STEADFAST MANAGEMENT CO INC (PA)
Also Called: Steadfast Companies
18100 Von Karman Ave Ste 500 (92612-0162)
PHONE.....................949 748-3000
Rodney F Emery, *CEO*
Dinesh K Davar, *
Michael Brown, *
EMP: 82 EST: 2000
SALES (est): 67.86MM
SALES (corp-wide): 67.86MM **Privately Held**
Web: www.irtliving.com
SIC: 6531 Real estate managers

(P-9188)
STRATEGIC PROPERTY MANAGEMENT
2055 3rd Ave Ste 200 (92101-2058)
PHONE.....................619 295-2211
Don Clausson, *Prin*
EMP: 75 EST: 2000
SALES (est): 2.43MM **Privately Held**
Web: www.stratprop.com
SIC: 6531 Real estate managers

(P-9189)
TAHOE SSONS RSORT TIME INTRVAL
Also Called: Tahoe Seasons Resort
3901 Saddle Rd (96150-8707)
P.O. Box 16300 (96151-6300)
PHONE.....................530 541-6700
Michael Presley, *Genl Mgr*
EMP: 123 EST: 1983
SALES (est): 4.88MM **Privately Held**
Web: www.tahoeseasons.com
SIC: 6531 7011 5813 5812 Time-sharing real estate sales, leasing and rentals; Hotels and motels; Drinking places; Eating places

(P-9190)
TEN-X LLC
Also Called: TEN-X, LLC
1301 Shoreway Rd Ste 425 (94002-4154)
PHONE.....................800 793-6107
Monte J M Koch, *Brnch Mgr*
EMP: 153
Web: www.auction.com
SIC: 6531 Real estate brokers and agents
PA: Auction.Com, Llc
1 Mauchly
Irvine CA

(P-9191)
TEN-X FINANCE INC
Also Called: Ten-X
15295 Alton Pkwy (92618-2315)
PHONE.....................949 465-8523
Steve Jacobs, *CEO*
EMP: 111 EST: 2013
SALES (est): 529.03K
SALES (corp-wide): 2.18B **Publicly Held**
SIC: 6531 Real estate agents and managers
HQ: Ten-X, Inc.
15295 Alton Pkwy
Irvine CA
949 465-8523

PRODUCTS & SERVICES SECTION
6531 - Real Estate Agents And Managers (P-9215)

(P-9192)
TENDERLOIN HOUSING CLINIC INC (PA)
126 Hyde St (94102-3606)
PHONE.....................415 771-9850
Randall Shaw, *Pr*
EMP: 75 EST: 1980
SALES (est): 59.76MM Privately Held
Web: www.thclinic.org
SIC: 6531 8111 Real estate agents and managers; Legal services

(P-9193)
TERRA VISTA MANAGEMENT INC
Also Called: Terra Vista Management
2211 Pacific Beach Dr (92109-5626)
PHONE.....................858 581-4200
Micheal Gelfand, *Brnch Mgr*
EMP: 459
SALES (corp-wide): 20.52MM Privately Held
Web: www.campland.com
SIC: 6531 7033 4225 4226 Real estate managers; Trailer parks and campsites; General warehousing and storage; Special warehousing and storage, nec
PA: Vista Terra Management Inc
445 Marine View Ave # 110
Del Mar CA
323 954-5900

(P-9194)
THOMAS JAMES HOMES INC
26880 Aliso Viejo Pkwy Ste 100 (92656-2619)
PHONE.....................949 424-2356
EMP: 135 EST: 2019
SALES (est): 9.66MM Privately Held
Web: www.tjh.com
SIC: 6531 Real estate brokers and agents

(P-9195)
THOMAS PROPERTIES GROUP INC
515 S Flower St Fl 6 (90071-2241)
PHONE.....................213 613-1900
▲ EMP: 141
SIC: 6531 Real estate agent, commercial

(P-9196)
TRAMMELL CROW CENTL TEXAS LTD
2221 Rosecrans Ave (90245-4931)
PHONE.....................310 765-2600
Robert Ruth, *Prin*
EMP: 64
Web: www.trammellcrow.com
SIC: 6531 Real estate agent, commercial
HQ: Trammell Crow Central Texas, Ltd.
2001 Ross Ave Ste 325
Dallas TX

(P-9197)
TRG INC
Also Called: Rosenthal Group, The
1350 Abbot Kinney Blvd # 101 (90291-3893)
P.O. Box 837 (90294-0837)
PHONE.....................310 396-6750
EMP: 100
SALES (est): 3.32MM Privately Held
Web: www.trgnational.com
SIC: 6531 Real estate agents and managers

(P-9198)
TRIMONT LAND COMPANY (DH)
Also Called: Northstar-At-Tahoe
5001 Northstar Dr (96161-4236)
P.O. Box 129 (96160-0129)
PHONE.....................530 562-1010
Robert A Katz, *CEO*
Michael Barkin, *
▲ EMP: 300 EST: 1966
SALES (est): 35.12MM Publicly Held
Web: www.northstarcalifornia.com
SIC: 6531 7011 Real estate managers; Ski lodge
HQ: The Vail Corporation
390 Interlocken Cres # 10
Broomfield CO

(P-9199)
TRIYAR SV LLC (PA)
10850 Wilshire Blvd Ste 1050 (90024-4305)
PHONE.....................310 234-2888
EMP: 370 EST: 2012
SALES (est): 23.77MM Privately Held
Web: www.triyar.com
SIC: 6531 Buying agent, real estate

(P-9200)
TROOP REAL ESTATE INC
4165 E Thousand Oaks Blvd Ste 100 (91362)
PHONE.....................805 402-3028
Jeff Rosenblum, *Brnch Mgr*
EMP: 122
SALES (corp-wide): 23.18MM Privately Held
Web: www.suzankozman.com
SIC: 6531 Real estate agent, residential
PA: Troop Real Estate, Inc.
1308 Madera Rd Ste 8
Simi Valley CA
805 581-3200

(P-9201)
TROOP REAL ESTATE INC (PA)
1308 Madera Rd Ste 8 (93065-4044)
PHONE.....................805 581-3200
Brian C Troop, *CEO*
Laura Lee Anthony, *
Deborah Mccarthy, *COO*
EMP: 95 EST: 1987
SALES (est): 23.18MM
SALES (corp-wide): 23.18MM Privately Held
Web: www.joebarkey.net
SIC: 6531 Real estate agent, residential

(P-9202)
TROOP REAL ESTATE INC
586 W Main St (93060-3209)
PHONE.....................805 921-0030
Brian Troop, *Owner*
EMP: 101
SALES (corp-wide): 23.18MM Privately Held
Web: www.karentroop.com
SIC: 6531 Real estate agent, residential
PA: Troop Real Estate, Inc.
1308 Madera Rd Ste 8
Simi Valley CA
805 581-3200

(P-9203)
TROOP REAL ESTATE INC
236 W Ojai Ave Ste 100 (93023-3274)
PHONE.....................805 640-1440
Barry Snyder, *Brnch Mgr*
EMP: 121
SALES (corp-wide): 23.18MM Privately Held
Web: www.karentroop.com
SIC: 6531 Real estate agent, residential
PA: Troop Real Estate, Inc.
1308 Madera Rd Ste 8
Simi Valley CA
805 581-3200

(P-9204)
TRULINE REALTY
714 W Olympic Blvd Ste 622 (90015-1438)
PHONE.....................323 389-5432
EMP: 65 EST: 2017
SALES (est): 758.38K Privately Held
Web: www.trulinerealty.com
SIC: 6531 Real estate brokers and agents

(P-9205)
US REAL ESTATE SERVICES INC
Also Called: Res.net
27442 Portola Pkwy Ste 300 (92610-2823)
PHONE.....................949 598-9920
EMP: 90 EST: 1994
SQ FT: 37,000
SALES (est): 22.15MM Privately Held
Web: www.usres.com
SIC: 6531 Real estate brokers and agents

(P-9206)
USA MULTIFAMILY MANAGEMENT INC
3200 Douglas Blvd Ste 200 (95661-4238)
PHONE.....................916 773-6060
Karen Mccurdy, *Pr*
EMP: 130 EST: 1984
SQ FT: 5,020
SALES (est): 8.57MM
SALES (corp-wide): 49.85MM Privately Held
Web: www.usapropfund.com
SIC: 6531 Real estate managers
PA: Usa Properties Fund, Inc.
3200 Douglas Blvd Ste 200
Roseville CA
916 773-6060

(P-9207)
V TROTH INC
Also Called: Berkshire Hthway Hmsrvces Trot
1801 W Avenue K Ste 101 (93534-5999)
P.O. Box 2024 (93539-2024)
PHONE.....................661 948-4646
Debra K Anderson, *Pr*
Donald L Anderson, *
Mark A Troth, *
EMP: 75 EST: 1965
SALES (est): 9.64MM Privately Held
Web: www.bhhstroth.com
SIC: 6531 8742 Real estate agent, residential; Real estate consultant

(P-9208)
WALSH VINEYARDS MANAGEMENT INC
1125 Golden Gate Dr (94558-6188)
PHONE.....................707 258-1500
Tim Rodgers, *Pr*
Brian Shepard, *
Vicki Thorpe, *
EMP: 250 EST: 1980
SQ FT: 6,000
SALES (est): 23.15MM Privately Held
Web: www.wvmgmt.com
SIC: 6531 Real estate managers

(P-9209)
WAYPOINT REAL ESTATE GROUP LLC
1999 Harrison St Fl 24 (94612-3520)
PHONE.....................510 250-2200
EMP: 82 EST: 2011
SALES (est): 9.01MM Privately Held
SIC: 6531 Real estate brokers and agents

(P-9210)
WELLS & BENNETT INC (PA)
1451 Leimert Blvd (94602-1896)
PHONE.....................510 531-7000
Barton W Bennett, *Owner*
Jeannine Nelson, *
EMP: 65 EST: 1924
SQ FT: 5,000
SALES (est): 8.87MM
SALES (corp-wide): 8.87MM Privately Held
Web: www.wellsandbennett.com
SIC: 6531 6512 Real estate agent, commercial; Nonresidential building operators

(P-9211)
WEST EDGE INC
Also Called: West Edge
1061 Tierra Del Rey (91910-7821)
PHONE.....................619 475-4095
EMP: 88
Web: www.coldwellbankerwesthomes.com
SIC: 6531 Real estate agent, residential
PA: West Edge, Inc.
4538 Bonita Rd
Bonita CA

(P-9212)
WEST SHORES REALTY INC
449 Silver Spur Rd (90274-3574)
PHONE.....................310 541-8000
Amir Amir Al-khayat, *CEO*
EMP: 205 EST: 2015
SALES (est): 6.42MM Privately Held
Web: www.westshoresrealty.com
SIC: 6531 Real estate agent, residential

(P-9213)
WESTCO EQUITIES INC (PA)
Also Called: RPM Services
1625 E Shaw Ave Ste 116 (93710-8100)
PHONE.....................559 228-6788
Lee Brand, *Pr*
Ken Warkentin, *
Dwayne Welch, *
EMP: 88 EST: 1979
SALES (est): 9.39MM
SALES (corp-wide): 9.39MM Privately Held
Web: www.west-co.com
SIC: 6531 1522 Real estate managers; Remodeling, multi-family dwellings

(P-9214)
WESTCOE REALTORS INC
Also Called: Westcoe Escrow Division
7191 Magnolia Ave (92504-3805)
PHONE.....................951 784-2500
Rich Simonin, *Mgr*
Susan Simonin, *
Richard Simonin, *
EMP: 65 EST: 1985
SQ FT: 11,200
SALES (est): 7.37MM Privately Held
Web: www.westcoerealtors.com
SIC: 6531 Real estate agent, residential

(P-9215)
WESTERN NATIONAL GROUP LP
Also Called: Wng
8 Executive Cir (92614-6746)
PHONE.....................949 862-6200
EMP: 71 EST: 1994
SALES (est): 12.53MM Privately Held
Web: www.wng.com
SIC: 6531 Real estate managers

6531 - Real Estate Agents And Managers (P-9216)

(P-9216)
WESTERN NATIONAL SECURITIES (PA)
Also Called: Ramada By Wyndham
8 Executive Cir (92614-6746)
P.O. Box 19528 (92623-9528)
PHONE.....................949 862-6200
Michael K Hayde, *CEO*
David Stone, *Ch*
Jeff Scott, *CFO*
James Gilly, *
Jerry Lapointe, *
EMP: 120 **EST:** 1981
SQ FT: 35,000
SALES (est): 223.07MM
SALES (corp-wide): 223.07MM Privately Held
Web: www.wyndhamhotels.com
SIC: 6531 7011 Real estate managers; Hotels and motels

(P-9217)
WESTLAKE REALTY GROUP INC (PA)
Also Called: Westlake Realty
520 S El Camino Real Ste 900 (94402)
PHONE.....................650 579-1010
EMP: 98 **EST:** 2002
SALES (est): 8.02MM Privately Held
Web: www.westlake-realty.com
SIC: 6531 Real estate agent, commercial

(P-9218)
WHV RESORT GROUP INC (HQ)
Also Called: Welk Resort Center
300 Rancheros Dr Ste 310 (92069-2969)
PHONE.....................760 652-4913
Larry Welk, *CEO*
EMP: 242 **EST:** 1999
SALES (est): 158.46MM Publicly Held
Web: www.welkresorts.com
SIC: 6531 6552 7992 7011 Time-sharing real estate sales, leasing and rentals; Subdividers and developers, nec; Public golf courses; Hotels and motels
PA: Marriott Vacations Worldwide Corporation
9002 San Marco Ct
Orlando FL

(P-9219)
WILLIAM L LYON & ASSOC INC
Also Called: Lyon & Associates Realtors
2801 J St (95816-4315)
PHONE.....................916 447-7878
Laure Woodgundlach, *Mgr*
EMP: 345
SALES (corp-wide): 164.49MM Privately Held
Web: www.golyon.com
SIC: 6531 Real estate agent, residential
HQ: L Lyon William & Associates Inc
3640 Amrcn Rver Dr Ste 10
Sacramento CA
916 978-4200

(P-9220)
WILLIAM L LYON & ASSOC INC
Also Called: Lyon Realtors
8814 Madison Ave (95628-3908)
PHONE.....................916 535-0356
EMP: 331
SALES (corp-wide): 164.49MM Privately Held
Web: www.golyon.com
SIC: 6531 Real estate agent, residential
HQ: L Lyon William & Associates Inc
3640 Amrcn Rver Dr Ste 10
Sacramento CA
916 978-4200

(P-9221)
WILMARK MANAGEMENT SVCS INC (PA)
Also Called: Wilmark Development
9948 Hibert St Ste 210 (92131-1034)
PHONE.....................858 271-0583
Mark S Schmidt, *Pr*
EMP: 65 **EST:** 1978
SALES (est): 2.46MM Privately Held
SIC: 6531 Real estate managers

(P-9222)
WOODMAN REALTY INC
Also Called: Sierra Springs Apartments
26030 Base Line St Apt 97 (92410-7066)
PHONE.....................909 425-5324
Kelly Fox, *Mgr*
EMP: 243
SIC: 6531 Real estate agent, commercial
HQ: Woodman Realty Inc.
2016 Riverside Dr
Los Angeles CA

(P-9223)
WORLDWIDE INC
9601 Wilshire Blvd (90210-5213)
PHONE.....................310 276-7171
Steve Lewis, *Pr*
EMP: 60 **EST:** 2006
SQ FT: 9,800
SALES (est): 4.51MM Privately Held
Web: www.mlslimo.com
SIC: 6531 Real estate brokers and agents

(P-9224)
YLOPO LLC
4712 Admiralty Way 548 (90292-6905)
PHONE.....................818 915-9150
Howard Tager, *CEO*
EMP: 147 **EST:** 2014
SALES (est): 14.31MM Privately Held
Web: www.ylopo.com
SIC: 6531 Real estate agents and managers

(P-9225)
ZAPLABS LLC (DH)
2000 Powell St Ste 700 (94608-1805)
▲ **EMP:** 62 **EST:** 2004
SQ FT: 23,803
SALES (est): 30.27MM Publicly Held
Web: www.anywhere.re
SIC: 6531 7375 Real estate brokers and agents; Information retrieval services
HQ: Anywhere Real Estate Group Llc
175 Park Ave
Madison NJ

(P-9226)
ZEPHYR REALESTATE
4040 24th St (94114-3716)
PHONE.....................415 552-9500
Deborah Udin, *Prin*
EMP: 73 **EST:** 2010
SALES (est): 839.16K Privately Held
SIC: 6531 Real estate agent, residential

6541 Title Abstract Offices

(P-9227)
CORINTHIAN TITLE COMPANY INC
5030 Camino De La Siesta Ste 100 (92108)
PHONE.....................619 299-4800
Robert Romano, *
Larry Vinti, *
Michael Godwin, *
EMP: 70 **EST:** 2006
SQ FT: 6,000
SALES (est): 10.52MM Privately Held
Web: www.corinthiantitle.com
SIC: 6541 Title and trust companies

(P-9228)
EQUITY TITLE COMPANY (DH)
801 N Brand Blvd Ste 400 (91203-3261)
PHONE.....................818 291-4400
TOLL FREE: 800
Jim Cossell, *Pr*
EMP: 80 **EST:** 1979
SALES (est): 9.99MM Publicly Held
Web: www.equitytitle.com
SIC: 6541 Title and trust companies
HQ: Anywhere Integrated Services Llc
1000 Bishops Gate Blvd # 100
Mount Laurel NJ

(P-9229)
FIDELITY NAT HM WARRANTY CO
1850 Gateway Blvd Ste 400 (94520-8446)
PHONE.....................925 356-0194
Bill Jensen, *Mgr*
EMP: 150
Web: www.homewarranty.com
SIC: 6541 Title and trust companies
HQ: Fidelity National Home Warranty Company
2950 Buskirk Ave Ste 201
Walnut Creek CA

(P-9230)
FIDELITY NAT TITLE INSUR CO NY
Also Called: Fidelity National
950 Hampshire Rd (91361-2805)
PHONE.....................805 370-1400
EMP: 1437
Web: newyork.fntic.com
SIC: 6541 Title and trust companies
HQ: Fidelity National Title Insurance Co Of New York
1 Pak Ave Ste 1402
New York NY
904 854-8100

(P-9231)
FIRST AMERCN HM WARRANTY CORP
8521 Fallbrook Ave Ste 340 (91304)
P.O. Box 8030 (91309-8030)
PHONE.....................818 781-5050
Jeff Powell, *COO*
EMP: 490 **EST:** 2009
SALES (est): 389.22MM Publicly Held
Web: www.firstam.com
SIC: 6541 Title and trust companies
HQ: First American Home Buyers Protection Corporation
8521 Fallbrook Ave
West Hills CA
818 781-5050

(P-9232)
FIRST AMERICAN HOME WARRANTY
1244 Apollo Way (95407-6777)
PHONE.....................707 596-5151
Tracy Berger, *Prin*
EMP: 83 **EST:** 2019
SALES (est): 6.01MM Privately Held
Web: www.firstam.com
SIC: 6541 Title and trust companies

(P-9233)
FIRST AMERICAN TITLE COMPANY
1 First American Way (92707-5913)
PHONE.....................714 250-3109
EMP: 6000 **EST:** 1964
SALES (est): 167.12MM Privately Held
Web: www.firstam.com
SIC: 6541 Title and trust companies

(P-9234)
FIRST AMRCN APPRAISAL SVCS INC (DH)
12395 First American Way (92064-6897)
PHONE.....................619 938-7078
Anand Nallathambi, *Pr*
Joe Cuffaro Junior, *Ex VP*
EMP: 66 **EST:** 1977
SQ FT: 7,000
SALES (est): 23.01MM
SALES (corp-wide): 1.64B Privately Held
SIC: 6541 Title and trust companies
HQ: Corelogic, Inc.
40 Pacifica Ste 900
Irvine CA
866 873-3651

(P-9235)
GREENHEDGE ESCROW
2015 Manhattan Beach Blvd (90278-1226)
PHONE.....................310 640-3040
David Wehrly, *Prin*
EMP: 222 **EST:** 2016
SALES (est): 2.38MM
SALES (corp-wide): 147.22MM Privately Held
Web: www.greenhedgeescrow.com
SIC: 6541 Title and trust companies
PA: Wedgewood Inc.
2015 Manhattan Beach Blvd # 102
Redondo Beach CA
310 640-3070

(P-9236)
GUARDIAN TITLE COMPANY
300 Commerce (92602-1308)
PHONE.....................949 495-9306
E Neil Gulley, *CEO*
James Kozel, *
Gregory Blackburn, *
EMP: 100 **EST:** 1975
SALES (est): 21.17K Publicly Held
SIC: 6541 Title and trust companies
HQ: Nrt Commercial Utah Llc
175 Park Ave
Madison NJ

(P-9237)
MID VALLEY TITLE AND ESCROW CO
2295 Feather River Blvd Ste A (95965)
PHONE.....................530 533-6680
Angie Mastelotto, *Brnch Mgr*
EMP: 81
SQ FT: 6,000
Web: www.firstam.com
SIC: 6541 6531 Title search companies; Escrow agent, real estate
HQ: Mid Valley Title And Escrow Company
601 Main St
Chico CA
530 893-5644

(P-9238)
PROPERTY INSIGHT LLC
2510 Redhill Ave (92705-5542)
PHONE.....................877 747-2537
John Walsh, *Managing Member*
Ron Sree, *
EMP: 4197 **EST:** 2004
SALES (est): 1.14MM
SALES (corp-wide): 7.29B Publicly Held
Web: www.propertyinsight.biz

PRODUCTS & SERVICES SECTION
6552 - Subdividers And Developers, Nec (P-9259)

SIC: 6541 Title search companies
HQ: Black Knight Real Estate Data Solutions, Llc
 121 Theory Ste 100
 Irvine CA
 626 808-9000

(P-9239)
STEWART TITLE CALIFORNIA INC
525 N Brand Blvd Ste 200 (91203-3993)
PHONE..................818 502-2700
Steve Lessack, *Group President*
EMP: 125
SALES (corp-wide): 3.07B **Publicly Held**
Web: www.stewart.com
SIC: 6541 Title and trust companies
HQ: Stewart Title Of California, Inc.
 7676 Hazard Center Dr # 1400
 San Diego CA
 619 692-1600

(P-9240)
TITLE RESOURCE GROUP LLC
Also Called: TITLE RESOURCE GROUP LLC
801 N Brand Blvd (91203-1237)
PHONE..................818 291-4400
EMP: 75
Web: www.anywhereis.re
SIC: 6541 Title and trust companies
HQ: Anywhere Integrated Services Llc
 1000 Bishops Gate Blvd # 100
 Mount Laurel NJ

(P-9241)
WFG NATIONAL TITLE INSUR CO (PA)
Also Called: Alliance Title
700 N Brand Blvd Ste 1100 (91203-1208)
PHONE..................818 476-4000
Jeffrey Fox, *CEO*
Roberto Olivera, *
Art Cheyne, *
Rhio H Weir, *
James Lokay, *
EMP: 75 EST: 1980
SQ FT: 15,000
SALES (est): 26MM
SALES (corp-wide): 26MM **Privately Held**
Web: www.wfgtitle.com
SIC: 6541 Title and trust companies

6552 Subdividers And Developers, Nec

(P-9242)
A F EVANS DEVELOPMENT INC
2033 N Main St Ste 340 (94596-3727)
PHONE..................510 267-4612
Arthur F Evans, *Pr*
EMP: 264 EST: 1999
SQ FT: 2,500
SALES (est): 2.18MM
SALES (corp-wide): 41.99MM **Privately Held**
SIC: 6552 Land subdividers and developers, residential
PA: A. F. Evans Company, Inc.
 2033 N Main St Ste 340
 Walnut Creek CA
 510 891-9400

(P-9243)
A M S PARTNERSHIP (PA)
Also Called: La Mancha Development
1517 S Sepulveda Blvd (90025-3311)
PHONE..................310 312-6698
Marvin B Levine, *Pt*

Samuel Bachner, *Pt*
EMP: 60 EST: 1981
SQ FT: 2,500
SALES (est): 3.23MM
SALES (corp-wide): 3.23MM **Privately Held**
SIC: 6552 6512 Subdividers and developers, nec; Commercial and industrial building operation

(P-9244)
ALLEN DEVELOPMENT PARTNERS LLC (PA)
125 Sbridge 100 (93291)
PHONE..................559 732-5425
EMP: 60 EST: 1993
SALES (est): 3.55MM
SALES (corp-wide): 3.55MM **Privately Held**
SIC: 6552 Subdividers and developers, nec

(P-9245)
ARCHIPELAGO DEVELOPMENT INC
P.O. Box 7050 (92067-7050)
PHONE..................858 699-6272
Mark Edward Benjamin, *CEO*
EMP: 100 EST: 2008
SALES (est): 4.94MM **Privately Held**
SIC: 6552 Subdividers and developers, nec

(P-9246)
BOSTON PROPERTIES LTD PARTNR
4 Embarcadero Ctr Lbby Level (94111-4106)
PHONE..................415 772-0700
Robert Pester, *Mgr*
EMP: 61
SALES (corp-wide): 3.11B **Publicly Held**
Web: www.bxp.com
SIC: 6552 6531 Land subdividers and developers, commercial; Real estate agents and managers
HQ: Boston Properties Limited Partnership
 800 Boylston St Ste 1900
 Boston MA
 617 236-3300

(P-9247)
BROOKFELD BAY AREA HLDINGS LLC
Also Called: Brookfield Homes
12657 Alcosta Blvd (94583-4438)
PHONE..................925 743-8000
John J Ryan, *Managing Member*
EMP: 60 EST: 2000
SALES (est): 8.95MM **Privately Held**
SIC: 6552 Land subdividers and developers, residential

(P-9248)
CENTURY PACIFIC REALTY CORP
9401 Wilshire Blvd Ste 1250 (90212-2926)
PHONE..................310 729-9922
Irwin J Deutch, *Pr*
Charles L Schwennessen, *
Eric Maman, *
EMP: 250 EST: 1987
SQ FT: 3,500
SALES (est): 5.28MM **Privately Held**
SIC: 6552 Subdividers and developers, nec

(P-9249)
COLRICH COMMUNITIES INC
444 W Beech St Ste 300 (92101-2942)
PHONE..................858 350-7672

Richard Gabriel, *Ch Bd*
Colin Seid, *
Maggie Lucas, *
EMP: 60 EST: 1992
SALES (est): 11.68MM **Privately Held**
Web: www.colrich.com
SIC: 6552 Subdividers and developers, nec

(P-9250)
DEL WEBB CORPORATION
Summerset Orchards
772 Centennial Pl (94513-6965)
PHONE..................925 513-2640
Judy Gerry, *Mgr*
EMP: 101
SALES (corp-wide): 16.23B **Publicly Held**
Web: www.delwebb.com
SIC: 6552 1521 Land subdividers and developers, residential; New construction, single-family houses
HQ: Del Webb Corporation
 16767 N Perimeter Dr # 100
 Scottsdale AZ
 480 391-6000

(P-9251)
EDAW INC (HQ)
300 California St Fl 5 (94104-1411)
PHONE..................415 955-2800
Joseph E Brown, *CEO*
Jason Prior, *Pr*
Dana Waymire, *Sr VP*
Jason Bowen, *Contrlr*
▲ EMP: 120 EST: 1939
SQ FT: 18,072
SALES (est): 41.71MM
SALES (corp-wide): 13.15B **Publicly Held**
SIC: 6552 0781 Subdividers and developers, nec; Landscape architects
PA: Aecom
 13355 Noel Rd Ste 400
 Dallas TX
 972 788-1000

(P-9252)
GOLDRICH & KEST INDUSTRIES LLC (PA)
5150 Overland Ave (90230-4914)
P.O. Box 3623 (90231-3623)
PHONE..................310 204-2050
EMP: 750 EST: 1957
SQ FT: 5,000
SALES (est): 46.55MM
SALES (corp-wide): 46.55MM **Privately Held**
Web: www.goldrichkest.com
SIC: 6552 Subdividers and developers, nec

(P-9253)
GOLDRICH KEST HIRSCH STERN LLC (PA)
5150 Overland Ave (90230-4914)
P.O. Box 3623 (90231-3623)
PHONE..................310 204-2050
Jona Goldrich, *Pr*
Sol Kest, *
EMP: 250 EST: 1963
SQ FT: 5,000
SALES (est): 34.88MM
SALES (corp-wide): 34.88MM **Privately Held**
Web: www.goldrichkest.com
SIC: 6552 Land subdividers and developers, commercial

(P-9254)
GRUPE COMMERCIAL COMPANY
Also Called: Grupe Huber Company

1203 N Grant St (95202-1895)
P.O. Box 7576 (95267-0576)
PHONE..................209 473-6000
Kevin Huber, *Pr*
EMP: 119 EST: 1989
SALES (est): 11.67MM
SALES (corp-wide): 42.59MM **Privately Held**
Web: www.grupehuber.com
SIC: 6552 Land subdividers and developers, commercial
PA: The Grupe Company
 3255 W March Ln Ste 400
 Stockton CA
 209 473-6000

(P-9255)
HIGNELL INCORPORATED
Also Called: Courtyard Little Chico Creek
1770 Humboldt Rd (95928-8104)
PHONE..................530 342-0707
Vicky Reed, *Admn*
EMP: 60
SQ FT: 22,799
SALES (corp-wide): 19.23MM **Privately Held**
Web: www.hignell.com
SIC: 6552 6531 Land subdividers and developers, commercial; Real estate agents and managers
PA: Hignell, Incorporated
 1750 Humboldt Rd
 Chico CA
 530 894-0404

(P-9256)
KING VENTURES
285 Bridge St (93401-5510)
PHONE..................805 544-4444
John E King, *Owner*
EMP: 126 EST: 1977
SQ FT: 10,000
SALES (est): 7.22MM **Privately Held**
Web: www.kingventures.net
SIC: 6552 6512 Land subdividers and developers, commercial; Commercial and industrial building operation

(P-9257)
LAHONTAN LLC
Also Called: Lahontan Golf Club
11253 Brockway Rd Ste 201 (96161-3360)
PHONE..................530 550-2990
EMP: 75 EST: 1996
SQ FT: 1,500
SALES (est): 6.11MM **Privately Held**
Web: www.lahontangolf.com
SIC: 6552 6531 Land subdividers and developers, residential; Real estate agents and managers

(P-9258)
LAND SERVICES LDSCP CONTRS INC
901 Brown Rd (94539-7089)
PHONE..................510 656-8101
John Ahner, *Pr*
EMP: 80 EST: 1980
SQ FT: 11,000
SALES (est): 4.8MM **Privately Held**
Web: www.landservices.net
SIC: 6552 Subdividers and developers, nec

(P-9259)
LINCOLN PRPRTY NO 2087 LTD PRT
7777 Center Ave Ste 150 (92647-3096)
PHONE..................214 740-3300
Mack Pogue, *Ch Bd*
EMP: 131 EST: 2003

6552 - Subdividers And Developers, Nec (P-9260)

SALES (est): 691.51K
SALES (corp-wide): 1.32B **Privately Held**
SIC: **6552** 6531 Land subdividers and developers, commercial; Real estate managers
PA: Lincoln Property Company
2000 Mckinney Ave # 1000
Dallas TX
214 740-3300

(P-9260)
LOWE ENTERPRISES RE GROUP
Also Called: Lowe Enterprises
11777 San Vicente Blvd Ste 900 (90049-5084)
PHONE.............................310 820-6661
Bob Lowe, *Pr*
EMP: 199 EST: 1994
SQ FT: 10,000
SALES (est): 4.51MM
SALES (corp-wide): 367.25MM **Privately Held**
Web: www.lowe-re.com
SIC: **6552** 6531 Land subdividers and developers, commercial; Real estate managers
PA: Lowe Enterprises, Inc.
11777 San Vicente Blvd # 900
Los Angeles CA
310 820-6661

(P-9261)
LPC COMMERCIAL SERVICES INC
Also Called: LPC COMMERCIAL SERVICES, INC.
915 Wilshire Blvd Ste 250 (90017-3409)
PHONE.............................213 362-9080
David Binswangar, *Brnch Mgr*
EMP: 191
SALES (corp-wide): 1.32B **Privately Held**
Web: www.lpc.com
SIC: **6552** 6531 Land subdividers and developers, commercial; Real estate brokers and agents
HQ: Lpc Commercial Services Llc
2000 Mckinney Ave # 1000
Dallas TX

(P-9262)
MAKAR PROPERTIES LLC (PA)
Also Called: Makallon La Jolla Properties
4100 Macarthur Blvd Ste 150 (92660-2001)
P.O. Box 7080 (92658-7080)
PHONE.............................949 255-1100
Paul P Makarechian, *CEO*
Peter Ciaccia, *Pr*
EMP: 75 EST: 2001
SALES (est): 44.92MM
SALES (corp-wide): 44.92MM **Privately Held**
Web: www.makarproperties.com
SIC: **6552** 1542 Land subdividers and developers, commercial; Commercial and office building, new construction

(P-9263)
MEDA CYPRESS RIDGE LP
2235 Meda Ave (95404-5646)
PHONE.............................707 526-9782
Charles Cornell, *Pt*
EMP: 101 EST: 2004
SALES (est): 325.39K
SALES (corp-wide): 16.26MM **Privately Held**
SIC: **6552** Subdividers and developers, nec
PA: Burbank Housing Development Corporation
1425 Corporate Cntr Pkwy
Santa Rosa CA
707 526-9782

(P-9264)
MIDPEN HOUSING CORPORATION
303 Vintage Park Dr Ste 250 (94404-1166)
PHONE.............................650 356-2900
EMP: 300 EST: 1971
SQ FT: 20,000
SALES (est): 22.35MM **Privately Held**
Web: www.midpen-housing.org
SIC: **6552** Land subdividers and developers, residential

(P-9265)
NATIONAL CMNTY RENAISSANCE CAL
8265 Aspen St Ste 100 (91730-3291)
PHONE.............................619 223-9222
Rebecca Clark, *Mgr*
EMP: 231
Web: www.nationalcore.org
SIC: **6552** Subdividers and developers, nec
PA: National Community Renaissance Of California
9692 Haven Ave Ste 100
Rancho Cucamonga CA

(P-9266)
NATIONAL CMNTY RENAISSANCE CAL (PA)
9692 Haven Ave Ste 100 (91730-0101)
PHONE.............................909 483-2444
Steven J Pontell, *CEO*
Sebastiano Sterpa, *
Orlando Cabrera, *
Tracy Thomas, *
Doretta Bryan, *
EMP: 100 EST: 1992
SALES (est): 47.76MM **Privately Held**
Web: www.nationalcore.org
SIC: **6552** Subdividers and developers, nec

(P-9267)
OCEAN COLONY PARTNERS LLC
Also Called: Half Moon Bay Golf Links
2450 Cabrillo Hwy S Ste 200 (94019-2266)
PHONE.............................650 726-5764
William E Barrett, *Pt*
EMP: 175 EST: 1988
SQ FT: 6,000
SALES (est): 18.38MM **Privately Held**
Web: www.halfmoonbaygolf.com
SIC: **6552** 7992 7389 Subdividers and developers, nec; Public golf courses; Telephone services

(P-9268)
OLSON COMPANY LLC (PA)
Also Called: Olson Homes
3010 Old Ranch Pkwy Ste 100 (90740-2750)
PHONE.............................562 596-4770
EMP: 99 EST: 2014
SALES (est): 24.12MM
SALES (corp-wide): 24.12MM **Privately Held**
Web: www.olsonhomes.com
SIC: **6552** Subdividers and developers, nec

(P-9269)
OLSON URBAN HOUSING LLC
Also Called: Olson Company, The
3010 Old Ranch Pkwy Ste 100 (90740-2750)
PHONE.............................562 596-4770
Stephen E Olson, *
Mario A Urzua, *
Scott Laurie, *
Todd J Olson, *
EMP: 60 EST: 1988
SALES (est): 7.57MM **Privately Held**
Web: www.olsonhomes.com
SIC: **6552** Subdividers and developers, nec

(P-9270)
PACIFIC UNION HOMES INC (PA)
675 Hartz Ave Ste 300 (94526-3859)
PHONE.............................925 314-3800
Jeffrey W Abramson, *Pr*
Matt Tunney, *
Todd Deutscher, *
Tammy Reyes, *
EMP: 75 EST: 1996
SALES (est): 4.21MM
SALES (corp-wide): 4.21MM **Privately Held**
SIC: **6552** Subdividers and developers, nec

(P-9271)
PANATTONI DEVELOPMENT CO INC (PA)
2442 Dupont Dr (92612-1523)
PHONE.............................916 381-1561
Carl Panattoni, *Ch*
Dudley Mitchell, *
Jacklyn Shelby, *
Greg Thurman, *
Adon Panattoni, *
EMP: 90 EST: 1986
SALES (est): 36.08MM
SALES (corp-wide): 36.08MM **Privately Held**
Web: www.panattoni.com
SIC: **6552** Subdividers and developers, nec

(P-9272)
RANCHO SAN CARLOS PARTNERSHIP LP
Also Called: Santa Lucia Preserve
1 Rancho San Carlos Rd (93923-7999)
PHONE.............................831 626-8200
EMP: 150
SIC: **6552** Land subdividers and developers, residential

(P-9273)
SHAPELL INDUSTRIES LLC (HQ)
Also Called: S & S Construction Co
8383 Wilshire Blvd Ste 700 (90211-2425)
PHONE.............................323 655-7330
EMP: 100 EST: 1955
SQ FT: 25,000
SALES (est): 43.64MM
SALES (corp-wide): 10.28B **Publicly Held**
SIC: **6552** 6514 1522 Land subdividers and developers, residential; Residential building, four or fewer units: operation; Residential construction, nec
PA: Toll Brothers, Inc.
1140 Virginia Dr
Fort Washington PA
215 938-8000

(P-9274)
SILVER SADDLE RANCH & CLUB INC
Also Called: McQ
7635 N San Fernando Rd (91505-1073)
PHONE.............................818 768-8808
Thomas Maney, *Pr*
Justin Child, *
Terry Hansen, *Stockholder*
EMP: 100 EST: 1986
SQ FT: 5,500
SALES (est): 4.74MM **Privately Held**
SIC: **6552** 7041 Land subdividers and developers, residential; Residence club, organization

(P-9275)
STEELWAVE INC (PA)
999 Baker Way Ste 200 (94404-1568)
PHONE.............................650 571-2200
Barry S Diraimondo, *CEO*
C Preston Butcher, *
Rick Wada, *
EMP: 175 EST: 2004
SALES (est): 98.14MM
SALES (corp-wide): 98.14MM **Privately Held**
Web: www.steelwavellc.com
SIC: **6552** 8741 6531 6512 Land subdividers and developers, commercial; Financial management for business; Real estate agents and managers; Nonresidential building operators

(P-9276)
STEELWAVE LLC
4553 Glencoe Ave Ste 300 (90292-7914)
PHONE.............................310 821-1111
EMP: 578
SALES (corp-wide): 43.06MM **Privately Held**
Web: www.steelwavellc.com
SIC: **6552** Land subdividers and developers, commercial
PA: Steelwave, Llc
999 Baker Way Ste 200
San Mateo CA
650 571-2200

(P-9277)
STEELWAVE LLC
333 W San Carlos St Ste 200 (95110-2730)
PHONE.............................408 564-7678
EMP: 578
SALES (corp-wide): 43.06MM **Privately Held**
Web: www.steelwavellc.com
SIC: **6552** Land subdividers and developers, commercial
PA: Steelwave, Llc
999 Baker Way Ste 200
San Mateo CA
650 571-2200

(P-9278)
UNIWELL CORPORATION
2233 Ventura St (93721-2915)
PHONE.............................559 268-1000
Steve Klein, *Mgr*
EMP: 150
SALES (corp-wide): 17.64MM **Privately Held**
Web: www.uniwell.com
SIC: **6552** Subdividers and developers, nec
PA: Uniwell Corporation
21172 Figueroa St
Carson CA
310 782-8888

(P-9279)
VOIT REAL ESTATE SERVICES LLC
2020 Main St (92614-8200)
PHONE.............................949 851-5100
Robert D Voit, *Managing Member*
Robert Voit, *Pt*
EMP: 223 EST: 2007
SALES (est): 13.07MM **Privately Held**
Web: www.voitco.com
SIC: **6552** 6519 6531 Subdividers and developers, nec; Real property lessors, nec; Real estate agents and managers

PRODUCTS & SERVICES SECTION **6719 - Holding Companies, Nec (P-9298)**

(P-9280)
WEBB DEL CALIFORNIA CORP (DH)
39755 Berkey Dr (92211-1106)
PHONE..................760 772-5300
Nancy E Abbott, *Prin*
EMP: 300 EST: 1965
SQ FT: 14,000
SALES (est): 46.74MM
SALES (corp-wide): 16.23B **Publicly Held**
SIC: 6552 Subdividers and developers, nec
HQ: Pulte Home Company, Llc
    3350 Peachtree Rd Ne # 15
    Atlanta GA
    248 647-2750

6553 Cemetery Subdividers And Developers

(P-9281)
BETTER PLACE FORESTS
3727 Buchanan St Fl 4 (94123-1779)
PHONE..................888 958-7674
John Collins, *CEO*
EMP: 62 EST: 2019
SALES (est): 9.67MM **Privately Held**
Web: www.betterplaceforests.com
SIC: 6553 Cemeteries, real estate operation

(P-9282)
CHAPEL OF CHIMES (DH)
Also Called: Alameda Chapel of The Chimes
32992 Mission Blvd (94544-8277)
PHONE..................510 471-3363
Andy Bryant, *Pr*
Gordon Swallow, *
EMP: 71 EST: 1965
SQ FT: 10,000
SALES (est): 167.88K
SALES (corp-wide): 119.3M **Publicly Held**
Web: hayward.chapelofthechimes.com
SIC: 6553 7261 Cemeteries, real estate operation; Funeral home
HQ: Skylawn
    32992 Mission Blvd
    Hayward CA
    510 471-3363

(P-9283)
CHAPEL OF CHIMES
Also Called: Skylawn Memorial Park
10600 Skyline Blvd (94062-4592)
P.O. Box 5070 (94402-0070)
PHONE..................650 349-4411
Rich Mcgown, *Genl Mgr*
EMP: 80
SALES (corp-wide): 119.3M **Publicly Held**
Web: hayward.chapelofthechimes.com
SIC: 6553 7261 Cemeteries, real estate operation; Crematory
HQ: Chapel Of The Chimes
    32992 Mission Blvd
    Hayward CA
    510 471-3363

(P-9284)
CONGREGATION EMANU-EL
Also Called: Home of Peace Cemetery
1299 El Camino Real (94014-3238)
PHONE..................650 755-4700
James Carlson, *Genl Mgr*
EMP: 122
SALES (est): 11.16MM **Privately Held**
Web: www.jcemsf.org
SIC: 6553 Cemeteries, real estate operation
PA: The Congregation Emanu-El

2 Lake St
San Francisco CA
415 751-2535

(P-9285)
CYPRESS LAWN CEMETERY ASSN
Also Called: CYPRESS LAWN MEMORIAL PARK
1370 El Camino Real (94014-3239)
P.O. Box 397 (94014-0397)
PHONE..................650 755-0580
Kenneth E Varner, *CEO*
Barbara Dryg, *
EMP: 95 EST: 1892
SALES (est): 5.36MM **Privately Held**
Web: www.cypresslawn.com
SIC: 6553 Cemeteries, real estate operation

(P-9286)
FOREST LAWN CO
1712 S Glendale Ave (91205-3320)
PHONE..................818 241-4151
John Llewellyn, *Pr*
EMP: 150 EST: 1906
SQ FT: 50,000
SALES (est): 17.35MM **Privately Held**
Web: www.forestlawn.com
SIC: 6553 Real property subdividers and developers, cemetery lots only

(P-9287)
INGLEWOOD PARK CEMETERY (PA)
720 E Florence Ave (90301-1482)
P.O. Box 6042 (90312-6042)
PHONE..................310 412-6500
Daniel Villa, *Pr*
Cheryl Lewis, *
David Wharmby, *
Kevin Brown, *
Chris Winners, *
EMP: 152 EST: 1905
SQ FT: 14,000
SALES (est): 19.11MM
SALES (corp-wide): 19.11MM **Privately Held**
Web: www.inglewoodparkcemetery.com
SIC: 6553 Cemeteries, real estate operation

(P-9288)
OAKDALE MEMORIAL PARK (PA)
1401 S Grand Ave (91740-5406)
PHONE..................626 335-0281
Genny Delgado, *Mgr*
Genny Delgado, *Genl Mgr*
EMP: 75 EST: 1890
SQ FT: 10,000
SALES (est): 2.23MM
SALES (corp-wide): 2.23MM **Privately Held**
Web: www.oakdalemortuaryglendora.com
SIC: 6553 Cemeteries, real estate operation

(P-9289)
ROMAN CTHLIC BISHP OF SAN JOSE
Also Called: Gate of Heaven Cemetery
22555 Cristo Rey Dr (94024-7424)
PHONE..................833 304-0763
April Ouellette, *Prin*
EMP: 64
SALES (corp-wide): 51.08MM **Privately Held**
Web: www.cfcssanjose.org
SIC: 6553 Cemeteries, real estate operation
PA: The Roman Catholic Bishop Of San Jose
    1150 N 1st St Ste 100

San Jose CA
408 983-0100

(P-9290)
ROMAN CTHLIC DIOCESE OF ORANGE
Also Called: Good Shepherd Cemetery
8301 Talbert Ave (92646-1546)
PHONE..................714 847-8546
Lupe Ramirez, *Mgr*
EMP: 62
SALES (corp-wide): 92.62MM **Privately Held**
Web: www.occem.org
SIC: 6553 Cemeteries, real estate operation
PA: The Roman Catholic Diocese Of Orange
    13280 Chapman Ave
    Garden Grove CA
    714 282-3000

(P-9291)
ROMAN CTHLIC DIOCESE OF ORANGE
Also Called: Holy Sepulcher Cemetery
7845 E Santiago Canyon Rd (92869-1830)
PHONE..................714 532-6551
Mike Wessner, *Dir*
EMP: 132
SALES (corp-wide): 92.62MM **Privately Held**
Web: www.occem.org
SIC: 6553 Cemeteries, real estate operation
PA: The Roman Catholic Diocese Of Orange
    13280 Chapman Ave
    Garden Grove CA
    714 282-3000

(P-9292)
ROSE HILLS COMPANY (DH)
Also Called: Rose Hills Mem Pk & Mortuary
3888 Workman Mill Rd (90601-1626)
PHONE..................562 699-0921
TOLL FREE: 800
Dennis Poulsen, *Ch Bd*
Kenton Woods, *
Mary Guzman, *
EMP: 595 EST: 1996
SQ FT: 143,950
SALES (est): 77.92MM
SALES (corp-wide): 4.11B **Publicly Held**
Web: www.rosehills.com
SIC: 6553 Real property subdividers and developers, cemetery lots only
HQ: Rose Hills Holdings Corp.
    3888 Workman Mill Rd
    Whittier CA
    562 699-0921

(P-9293)
ROSE HILLS HOLDINGS CORP (HQ)
Also Called: Rose Hills Mem Pk & Mortuary
3888 Workman Mill Rd (90601-1626)
PHONE..................562 699-0921
Pat Monroe, *CEO*
EMP: 500 EST: 1996
SQ FT: 143,950
SALES (est): 87.18MM
SALES (corp-wide): 4.11B **Publicly Held**
Web: www.rosehills.com
SIC: 6553 Cemeteries, real estate operation
PA: Service Corporation International
    1929 Allen Pkwy
    Houston TX
    713 522-5141

6712 Bank Holding Companies

(P-9294)
BANAMEX USA BANCORP (DH)
787 W 5th St (90071-2003)
PHONE..................310 203-3440
Salvador Villar Junior, *Pr*
Francisco Moreno Senior, *VP*
▲ EMP: 210 EST: 1977
SALES (est): 96.96MM
SALES (corp-wide): 101.08B **Publicly Held**
Web: www.citigroup.com
SIC: 6712 6029 6022 Bank holding companies; Commercial banks, nec; State commercial banks
HQ: Banco Nacional De Mexico, S.A., Integrante Del Grupo Financiero Banamex
    Isabel La Catolica No. 44
    Ciudad De Mexico CMX

(P-9295)
SOCIAL FINANCE INC (HQ)
Also Called: Sofi
234 1st St (94105-2624)
PHONE..................415 930-4467
Anthony Noto, *CEO*
Chris Lapointe, *
EMP: 160 EST: 2011
SQ FT: 20,000
SALES (est): 259.13MM
SALES (corp-wide): 1.76B **Publicly Held**
Web: www.sofi.com
SIC: 6712 6022 6163 Bank holding companies; State commercial banks; Loan brokers
PA: Sofi Technologies, Inc.
    234 1st St
    San Francisco CA
    855 456-7634

6719 Holding Companies, Nec

(P-9296)
ALDON INC
1333 E 223rd St (90745-4314)
▲ EMP: 75 EST: 1974
SQ FT: 10,000
Web: www.toyota.com
SIC: 6719 Investment holding companies, except banks

(P-9297)
ALTERGY SYSTEMS
140 Blue Ravine Rd (95630-4703)
PHONE..................916 458-8590
Eric S Mettler, *Pr*
Nate Cammack, *
Richard J Burant, *
▲ EMP: 62 EST: 2001
SQ FT: 37,000
Web: www.altergy.com
SIC: 6719 Investment holding companies, except banks

(P-9298)
AME-GYU CO LTD
20000 Mariner Ave Ste 500 (90503-1670)
PHONE..................310 214-9572
Ryo Tozu, *CEO*
Hidekazu Seo, *
Hiratsugu Aiba, *
EMP: 1100 EST: 2016
SIC: 6719 5812 Investment holding companies, except banks; Japanese restaurant

6719 - Holding Companies, Nec (P-9299)

(P-9299)
AMERICAN ACADEMIC HLTH SYS LLC
222 N Pacific Coast Hwy Ste 900 (90245-5648)
PHONE..................310 414-7200
EMP: 2850 EST: 2017
SALES (est): 60.53MM Privately Held
Web: www.americanacademic.com
SIC: 6719 8062 Investment holding companies, except banks; General medical and surgical hospitals

(P-9300)
ASP HENRY HOLDINGS INC
999 N Pacific Coast Hwy Ste 800 (90245)
PHONE..................310 955-9200
Frank Ready, CEO
EMP: 600 EST: 2016
SALES (corp-wide): 6.59B Publicly Held
SIC: 6719 2952 Investment holding companies, except banks; Roof cement: asphalt, fibrous, or plastic
PA: Carlisle Companies Incorporated
16430 N Scottsdale Rd
Scottsdale AZ
480 781-5000

(P-9301)
BARRACUDA HOLDINGS LLC
3175 Winchester Blvd (95008-6557)
PHONE..................408 342-5400
Seth Boro, Pr
EMP: 1490 EST: 2017
SIC: 6719 Investment holding companies, except banks
PA: Thoma Bravo, L.P.
150 N Riverside Plz # 2800
Chicago IL

(P-9302)
BETHAR CORPORATION
17625 Railroad St (91748-1110)
P.O. Box 8445 (91748-0445)
▲ EMP: 180 EST: 1945
SQ FT: 80,000
SIC: 6719 Investment holding companies, except banks

(P-9303)
BPAZ HOLDINGS 18 LLC
1 Sansome St Fl 15 (94104-4448)
P.O. Box 2689 (94126-2689)
PHONE..................972 354-6250
Rob Saidi, Managing Member
EMP: 60 EST: 2018
SIC: 6719 Holding companies, nec

(P-9304)
BPAZ HOLDINGS 6 LLC
1 Sansome St Ste 1500 (94104-4449)
PHONE..................415 295-8080
Rob Saidi, VP
EMP: 80 EST: 2018
SIC: 6719 Holding companies, nec

(P-9305)
BRIDGE GROUP HH INC
3636 Nobel Dr Ste 450 (92122-1062)
PHONE..................858 455-5000
Jason Murray, CEO
EMP: 126 EST: 2016
SIC: 6719 Investment holding companies, except banks

(P-9306)
CCC PROPERTY HOLDINGS LLC
Also Called: Contractors Cargo Company
7223 Alondra Blvd (90723-3901)
P.O. Box 5290 (90224-5290)
PHONE..................310 609-1957
Gerald Wheeler, Ch Bd
Kim Dorio, *
Carla Ann Wheeler, *
Jerry Wheeler, *
EMP: 121 EST: 2009
SIC: 6719 Investment holding companies, except banks

(P-9307)
COADNA HOLDINGS INC
1020 Stewart Dr (94085-3914)
PHONE..................408 736-1100
Jim Yuan, Pr
Irene Yum, *
Oliver Lu, Chief Commercial Officer*
EMP: 80 EST: 2000
SALES (corp-wide): 5.16B Publicly Held
Web: www.coadna.com
SIC: 6719 3661 Investment holding companies, except banks; Fiber optics communications equipment
PA: Coherent Corp.
375 Saxonburg Blvd
Saxonburg PA
724 352-4455

(P-9308)
CONDOR TRADING LP
600 Montgomery St Fl 6 (94111-2708)
PHONE..................415 248-2200
Scott Kovalik, CEO
Brian Endres, *
Yojna Verma, *
EMP: 560 EST: 2002
SIC: 6719 Investment holding companies, except banks

(P-9309)
CRONOS USA CLIENT SERVICES LLC
322 Culver Blvd (90293-7704)
PHONE..................323 843-2741
EMP: 69 EST: 2019
SIC: 6719 Investment holding companies, except banks

(P-9310)
DMS UE ACQISITION HOLDINGS INC
225 Broadway Ste 2200 (92101-5011)
PHONE..................800 466-4178
Joe Marinucci, CEO
EMP: 100 EST: 2019
SIC: 6719 7311 7371 Investment holding companies, except banks; Advertising consultant; Computer software development

(P-9311)
ETS-ESC HOLDINGS LLC
2001 Crow Canyon Rd Ste 110 (94583-5368)
PHONE..................925 314-7100
Gary M Cappa, Pr
James Backman, COO
Charles Brice, CFO
EMP: 470 EST: 2017
SQ FT: 10,000
SALES (corp-wide): 1.47B Privately Held
SIC: 6719 Investment holding companies, except banks
HQ: Atlas Technical Consultants Llc
13215 Bee Cave Pkwy B230
Austin TX
866 858-4499

(P-9312)
FORTRESS HOLDING GROUP LLC
5500 E Santa Ana Canyon Rd Ste 220 (92807-3154)
PHONE..................714 202-8710
Luis Perez, Ch
Adam Forbs, Pr
EMP: 90 EST: 2009
SIC: 6719 Investment holding companies, except banks

(P-9313)
GATEWAY FRESH LLC
Also Called: Baja Fresh
3660 Grand Ave Ste A (91709-1477)
P.O. Box 1456 (91709-0049)
PHONE..................951 378-5439
FAX: 909 548-6602
EMP: 190
SQ FT: 5,000
SIC: 6719 Investment holding companies, except banks

(P-9314)
GCM HOLDING CORPORATION
1350 Atlantic St (94587-2004)
PHONE..................510 475-0404
Seamus Meagher, Pr
EMP: 300 EST: 2014
SIC: 6719 8711 3444 3541 Investment holding companies, except banks; Machine tool design; Sheet metalwork; Machine tools, metal cutting type
PA: Avista Capital Holdings, L.P.
65 E 55th St Fl 18
New York NY

(P-9315)
GGC ADMINISTRATION LLC
Also Called: Golden Gate Capital
1 Embarcadero Ctr Fl 39 (94111-3714)
PHONE..................415 983-2700
EMP: 8590 EST: 2000
SIC: 6719 Personal holding companies, except banks

(P-9316)
GH GROUP INC
Also Called: Glass House Group
3645 Long Beach Blvd (90807-4018)
PHONE..................562 264-5078
Kyle Kazan, CEO
Graham Farrar, *
Daryl Kato, *
Derrek Higgins, *
EMP: 250 EST: 2006
Web: www.gh-group.com
SIC: 6719 Investment holding companies, except banks

(P-9317)
HCO HOLDING I CORPORATION (HQ)
999 N Pacific Coast Hwy Ste 800 (90245-2715)
PHONE..................323 583-5000
Mike Kenny, *
Brian C Strauss, Parent Chief Executive Officer*
Dori M Reap, *
James F Barry, *
Robert D Armstrong, Senior Vice President Human Resources*
◆ EMP: 100 EST: 2005
SALES (est): 249.72MM
SALES (corp-wide): 254.17MM Privately Held

SIC: 6719 Investment holding companies, except banks
PA: Hnc Parent, Inc.
999 N Pacific Coast Hwy # 80
El Segundo CA
310 955-9200

(P-9318)
HIRSCH3667 CORP
5700 Hannum Ave Ste 250 (90230-6548)
PHONE..................310 641-6690
EMP: 140
SIC: 6719 Investment holding companies, except banks

(P-9319)
KELLY TOYS HOLDINGS LLC
Also Called: Kelly Toys
4811 S Alameda St (90058-2805)
PHONE..................323 923-1300
Jonathan Kelly, Pr
Matthew Siesel, *
David Neustein, *
EMP: 100 EST: 2020
SQ FT: 150,000
SALES (corp-wide): 302.09B Publicly Held
Web: www.squishmallows.com
SIC: 6719 5092 Investment holding companies, except banks; Toys and hobby goods and supplies
HQ: Jazwares, Llc
1067 Shotgun Rd
Sunrise FL

(P-9320)
MAFAB INC (PA)
1925 Century Park E Ste 650 (90067-2752)
PHONE..................714 893-0551
Ronald B Grey, Pr
Ronald Grey, *
EMP: 60 EST: 1972
SQ FT: 3,600
SALES (est): 15.89MM
SALES (corp-wide): 15.89MM Privately Held
SIC: 6719 Personal holding companies, except banks

(P-9321)
MILESTONE HOLDCO INC
901 Mariners Island Blvd (94404-1592)
PHONE..................650 376-2300
Steve Lucas, CEO
EMP: 949 EST: 2016
SALES (corp-wide): 17.61B Publicly Held
SIC: 6719 7371 7372 Investment holding companies, except banks; Custom computer programming services; Prepackaged software
HQ: Milestone Topco, Inc.
901 Mariners Island Blvd
San Mateo CA
650 376-2300

(P-9322)
MLIM HOLDINGS LLC
350 Camino De La Reina (92108-3003)
PHONE..................619 299-3131
Douglas Manchester, Ch
John Lynch, Vice Chairman*
EMP: 768 EST: 2011
SIC: 6719 Investment holding companies, except banks

(P-9323)
N2 ACQUISITION COMPANY INC
Also Called: N2 Imaging Systems
14440 Myford Rd (92606-1001)
PHONE..................714 942-3563

6719 - Holding Companies, Nec (P-9348)

Tony Bacarella, *CEO*
Timothy Boyle, *CFO*
EMP: 92 **EST:** 2019
SIC: 6719 Investment holding companies, except banks

(P-9324)
NRP HOLDING CO INC (PA)
1 Mauchly (92618-2305)
PHONE.................949 583-1000
Jeffrey P Frieden, *Pr*
Robert Friedman, *
EMP: 200 **EST:** 2003
SQ FT: 40,000
SALES (est): 44.87MM **Privately Held**
Web: www.auction.com
SIC: 6719 Investment holding companies, except banks

(P-9325)
NXS HOLDING CORP
2025 Gateway Pl Ste 160 (95110-1059)
PHONE.................408 791-3300
EMP: 230
SIC: 6719 Investment holding companies, except banks

(P-9326)
ON-TECH ENTERPRISES
EMP: 135 **EST:** 1994
SIC: 6719 Personal holding companies, except banks

(P-9327)
PLATINUM GROUP COMPANIES INC (PA)
Also Called: Top Finance Company
22560 La Quilla Dr (91311-1221)
P.O. Box 280518 (91328-0518)
PHONE.................818 721-3800
David Mandel, *CEO*
Sandy To, *
EMP: 125 **EST:** 2005
SQ FT: 20,000
SALES (est): 39.69MM **Privately Held**
SIC: 6719 Personal holding companies, except banks

(P-9328)
PROJECT FORTRESS PARENT LLC ✪
201 Mission St Ste 2900 (94105-1858)
PHONE.................415 599-1100
Seth Boro, *Managing Member*
EMP: 950 **EST:** 2022
SIC: 6719 7371 Investment holding companies, except banks; Computer software systems analysis and design, custom

(P-9329)
PROJECT SKYLINE INTERMEDIATE H
360 N Crescent Dr Bldg S (90210-2529)
PHONE.................310 712-1850
Tom Gores, *Pr*
EMP: 2020 **EST:** 2009
SIC: 6719 Investment holding companies, except banks

(P-9330)
PROSPECT MORTGAGE LLC
EMP: 1700 **EST:** 1999
SIC: 6719 Investment holding companies, except banks

(P-9331)
RODOLO INC
212 Industrial Dr (95206-3905)
EMP: 75 **EST:** 1985
SQ FT: 3,900
Web: www.hheng.com
SIC: 6719 Investment holding companies, except banks

(P-9332)
RON RICK HOLDINGS MONTANA LLC
80795 Vista Bonita Trl (92253-7525)
PHONE.................406 493-5606
Rick Kerscher, *Pr*
Rick Kerscherm, *Pr*
EMP: 100 **EST:** 2007
SQ FT: 7,000
SIC: 6719 Personal holding companies, except banks

(P-9333)
RSG GROUP USA INC
Also Called: Gold's Gym
7007 Romaine St Ste 101 (90038-2439)
PHONE.................214 574-4653
Sebastian Schoepe, *CEO*
EMP: 2000 **EST:** 2020
SALES (corp-wide): 242.12K **Privately Held**
Web: www.goldsgym.com
SIC: 6719 7991 Investment holding companies, except banks; Physical fitness facilities
HQ: Rsg Group Gmbh
    Tannenberg 4
    Schlusselfeld BY
    308 379-5500

(P-9334)
SABAN CAPITAL GROUP LLC
11301 W Olympic Blvd Ste 121601 (90064-1653)
PHONE.................310 557-5100
Adam Chesnoss, *COO*
Adam Chesnonss, *COO*
Haim Saban, *Ch*
EMP: 70 **EST:** 2003
SIC: 6719 Holding companies, nec

(P-9335)
SHRYNE GROUP INC
728 E Commercial St (90012-3412)
PHONE.................323 614-4558
Jon Avidor, *CEO*
Tak Sato, *
Elisabeth Baron, *CMO*
John Malone, *
Cary Berger, *CLO*
EMP: 2500 **EST:** 2019
Web: www.shrynegroup.com
SIC: 6719 Holding companies, nec

(P-9336)
SKEFFINGTON ENTERPRISES INC
2200 S Yale St (92704-4427)
PHONE.................714 540-1700
William J Skeffington, *Pr*
John Skeffington, *
EMP: 100 **EST:** 1951
SQ FT: 180,000
Web: www.bensasphalt.com
SIC: 6719 Personal holding companies, except banks

(P-9337)
SOLARIANT CAPITAL LLC
301 N Lake Ave Ste 950 (91101-5105)
PHONE.................626 544-0279
Daniel Kim, *Managing Member*
EMP: 180 **EST:** 2012
Web: www.solariantcapital.com
SIC: 6719 1629 6722 Investment holding companies, except banks; Power plant construction; Management investment, open-end

(P-9338)
SPR OP CO INC
70 W Ohio Ave Ste H (94804-2033)
PHONE.................510 232-5030
Matt Guelfi, *Pr*
Matthew Guelfi, *
Michael Guelfi, *
EMP: 150 **EST:** 1975
SQ FT: 105,000
Web: www.hartmannstudios.com
SIC: 6719 Investment holding companies, except banks

(P-9339)
STANTEC HOLDINGS DEL III INC
Also Called: Stantec Oil and Gas
5500 Ming Ave Ste 300 (93309-4683)
PHONE.................661 396-3770
Robert Gomes, *Pr*
EMP: 460 **EST:** 2005
SALES (corp-wide): 4.23B **Privately Held**
SIC: 6719 Investment holding companies, except banks
PA: Stantec Inc
    10220 103 Ave Nw Ste 300
    Edmonton AB
    866 782-6832

(P-9340)
STEELRVER INFRSTRCTURE PRTNERS (PA)
1 Harbor Dr Ste 101 (94965-1433)
P.O. Box 751074 (94975-1074)
PHONE.................415 512-1515
Christopher P Kinney, *Pt*
Dennis Mahoney, *Head OF ORIGINATION*
John Anderson, *Head OF POWER Finance*
EMP: 200 **EST:** 2009
SALES (est): 143.76MM **Privately Held**
SIC: 6719 Investment holding companies, except banks

(P-9341)
SWDS HOLDINGS INC
Also Called: Swds
8659 Research Dr (92618-4204)
PHONE.................800 395-5277
Vernon Leake, *CEO*
Michael Okada, *
Aaron Lodge, *
Jill Zack, *
EMP: 317 **EST:** 1987
Web: www.acrisurepg.com
SIC: 6719 Holding companies, nec

(P-9342)
THYME HOLDINGS LLC
Also Called: Westgate Gardens Care Center
4525 W Tulare Ave (93277-1560)
PHONE.................559 733-0901
Mark Hancock, *
EMP: 99 **EST:** 2011
SALES (corp-wide): 1.53B **Privately Held**
Web: www.westgategardenscarecenter.com
SIC: 6719 Holding companies, nec
HQ: California Opco, Llc
    100 E San Marcos Blvd
    San Marcos CA

(P-9343)
TRADESHIFT HOLDINGS INC (PA)
221 Main St Ste 250 (94105-1907)
PHONE.................800 381-3585
Christian Lanng, *CEO*
Jeppe Rindom, *
Peter Van Pruissen, *
Jigish Avalani, *
Mikkel Hippe Brun, *Prin*
EMP: 80 **EST:** 2011
SALES (est): 102MM
SALES (corp-wide): 102MM **Privately Held**
Web: www.tradeshift.com
SIC: 6719 Investment holding companies, except banks

(P-9344)
TRANSOM POST MIDCO LLC ✪
100 N Pacific Coast Hwy # 17 (90245-4359)
PHONE.................312 254-3300
Russell Roenick, *Managing Member*
EMP: 200 **EST:** 2022
SIC: 6719 Personal holding companies, except banks

(P-9345)
TYDG ENTERPRISES INC
10232 Palm Dr (90670-3368)
PHONE.................562 903-9030
Michael Rashtchi, *CEO*
George Abi-aad, *Pr*
Marianne Abi-aad, *Ex VP*
Johnathan Soon, *VP Opers*
▲ **EMP:** 95 **EST:** 1985
SQ FT: 65,000
Web: www.royalcorporation.com
SIC: 6719 Investment holding companies, except banks

(P-9346)
USB SLRCITY MSTR TNANT 2009 LL
393 Vintage Park Dr Ste 140 (94404-1140)
PHONE.................650 963-5693
EMP: 99 **EST:** 2010
SALES (corp-wide): 81.46B **Publicly Held**
SIC: 6719 Holding companies, nec
PA: Tesla, Inc.
    1 Tesla Rd
    Austin TX
    512 516-8177

(P-9347)
VISIONARY INTGRTION PRFSSNALS (PA)
Also Called: VIP
80 Iron Point Cir Ste 100 (95630-8592)
PHONE.................916 985-9625
Jonna Ward, *Pr*
Jennifer Salazar, *Dir*
EMP: 154 **EST:** 1996
SQ FT: 9,000
SALES (est): 89.18MM **Privately Held**
Web: www.trustvip.com
SIC: 6719 Personal holding companies, except banks

(P-9348)
WILBUR CURTIS CO INC
6913 W Acco St (90640-5403)
PHONE.................800 421-6150
Ray Peden, *CEO*
Michael A Curtis, *Ex VP*
Norman Fujitaki, *CFO*
Joe Laws, *COO*
Shubham Kumar, *Finance*

6719 - Holding Companies, Nec (P-9349)

◆ EMP: 280 EST: 1941
SQ FT: 175,000
SALES (corp-wide): 2.67MM **Privately Held**
Web: www.wilburcurtis.com
SIC: 6719 3589 Investment holding companies, except banks; Coffee brewing equipment
HQ: Groupe Seb Retailing
112 Chemin Du Moulin Carron
Ecully

(P-9349)
YF ART HOLDINGS GP LLC
9130 W Sunset Blvd (90069-3110)
PHONE.................................678 441-1400
Fred Boehler, Pr
EMP: 10600 EST: 2014
SIC: 6719 Investment holding companies, except banks

6722 Management Investment, Open-ended

(P-9350)
ABSOLUTE RETURN PORTFOLIO
700 Newport Center Dr (92660-6307)
P.O. Box 9000 (92658-9030)
PHONE.................................800 800-7646
EMP: 1437 EST: 2015
SALES (est): 2.41MM
SALES (corp-wide): 12.84B **Privately Held**
SIC: 6722 Money market mutual funds
HQ: Pacific Life Fund Advisors Llc
700 Newport Center Dr
Newport Beach CA

(P-9351)
ALLIANCEBERNSTEIN LP
Also Called: Bernstein
1999 Avenue Of The Stars Ste 2150 (90067-6022)
PHONE.................................310 286-6000
Alan D Croll, Brnch Mgr
EMP: 123
SALES (corp-wide): 14.02B **Publicly Held**
Web: www.alliancebernstein.com
SIC: 6722 Money market mutual funds
HQ: Alliancebernstein L.P.
501 Commerce St
Nashville TN
212 969-1000

(P-9352)
AMERICAN FUNDS DISTRS INC (DH)
333 S Hope St Ste Levb (90071-3003)
PHONE.................................213 486-9200
Michael Johnston, Ch Bd
Larry Clemmensen, *
J Kelly Webb, *
Dorine Darnell, *
EMP: 116 EST: 1972
SQ FT: 6,000
SALES (est): 111.21MM
SALES (corp-wide): 5.43B **Privately Held**
Web: www.capitalgroup.com
SIC: 6722 Mutual fund sales, on own account
HQ: Capital Research And Management Company
333 S Hope St Fl 55
Los Angeles CA
213 486-9200

(P-9353)
AMERICAN MUTUAL FUND
333 S Hope St Fl 51 (90071-1420)
PHONE.................................213 486-9200
Jonathan B Lovelace Junior, Ch Bd
James K Dunton, *
James W Ratzlaff, *
Robert G O'donnell, Pr
Joyce Gordon, *
EMP: 200 EST: 1949
SQ FT: 5,000
SALES (est): 2.09B **Privately Held**
SIC: 6722 Money market mutual funds

(P-9354)
ARES MANAGEMENT CORPORATION (PA)
Also Called: Ares
2000 Avenue Of The Stars Fl 12 (90067-4733)
PHONE.................................310 201-4100
Michael J Arougheti, Pr
Antony P Ressler, Ex Ch Bd
Jarrod Phillips, CFO
Ryan Berry, Chief Marketing
Naseem Sagati Aghili, Corporate Secretary
EMP: 102 EST: 1997
SALES (est): 3.06B
SALES (corp-wide): 3.06B **Publicly Held**
Web: www.aresmgmt.com
SIC: 6722 6282 Management investment, open-end; Investment advice

(P-9355)
ARES MANAGEMENT LLC (HQ)
2000 Avenue Of The Stars Fl 12 (90067-4733)
PHONE.................................310 201-4100
Antony Ressler, Managing Member
John Kissick, *
Matt Cwiertnia, *
David Kaplan, *
Bennett Rosenthal, *
EMP: 60 EST: 2001
SALES (est): 878.95MM
SALES (corp-wide): 3.06B **Publicly Held**
Web: www.aresmgmt.com
SIC: 6722 Management investment, open-end
PA: Ares Management Corporation
2000 Avenue Of The Stars # 12
Los Angeles CA
310 201-4100

(P-9356)
ARISTOTLE CREDIT PARTNERS LLC
11100 Santa Monica Blvd Ste 1700 (90025-3384)
PHONE.................................310 478-4005
Howard Gleicher, Prin
EMP: 68 EST: 2014
SALES (est): 4.77MM **Privately Held**
Web: www.aristotlecap.com
SIC: 6722 Money market mutual funds

(P-9357)
AXA ROSENBERG INV MGT LLC
4 Orinda Way Bldg E (94563-2523)
PHONE.................................925 253-3300
Jeremy Baskin, Managing Member
EMP: 131 EST: 1998
SALES (est): 41.51MM
SALES (corp-wide): 4.5MM **Privately Held**
Web: www.axa-im.com
SIC: 6722 Money market mutual funds
PA: Axa
Direction Juridique Centrale
Paris

(P-9358)
BELLOTA US CORP
22440 Temescal Canyon Rd (92883-4200)
PHONE.................................951 737-6515
▲ EMP: 150
SIC: 6722 Money market mutual funds

(P-9359)
BLACKROCK FUNDS III
400 Howard St (94105-9876)
PHONE.................................415 597-2000
Mike Sobel, Prin
EMP: 113 EST: 2006
SALES (est): 8.12MM **Privately Held**
Web: www.blackrock.com
SIC: 6722 Money market mutual funds

(P-9360)
BLACKROCK GLOBAL INVESTORS
400 Howard St (94105-2618)
PHONE.................................415 670-2000
Patricia Dunn, CEO
Blake Grossman, *
Carter Lyons, *
EMP: 1100 EST: 1995
SQ FT: 65,000
SALES (est): 98.91MM **Publicly Held**
SIC: 6722 Money market mutual funds
PA: Blackrock, Inc.
50 Hudson Yards
New York NY

(P-9361)
BLACKROCK INSTNL TR NAT ASSN (HQ)
Also Called: Ishares
400 Howard St (94105-9876)
PHONE.................................415 597-2000
Laurence D Fink, CEO
James Parsons, *
Robert S Kapito, *
EMP: 600 EST: 1973
SQ FT: 65,000
SALES (est): 1.4B **Publicly Held**
Web: www.blackrock.com
SIC: 6722 Money market mutual funds
PA: Blackrock, Inc.
50 Hudson Yards
New York NY

(P-9362)
BROADRACH CPITL PRTNERS FUND I
248 Homer Ave (94301-2722)
PHONE.................................650 331-2500
EMP: 2369 EST: 2014
SALES (est): 602.63K
SALES (corp-wide): 51.42MM **Privately Held**
SIC: 6722 Money market mutual funds
PA: Broadreach Capital Partners Llc
885 Oak Grove Ave Ste 206
Menlo Park CA
650 331-2500

(P-9363)
CARMEL PARTNERS LLC
530 Wilshire Blvd Ste 203 (90401-1427)
PHONE.................................916 479-5286
EMP: 108
SALES (corp-wide): 71.55MM **Privately Held**
Web: www.carmelpartners.com
SIC: 6722 Management investment, open-end
HQ: Carmel Partners, Llc
1000 Sansome St Fl 1
San Francisco CA
415 273-2900

(P-9364)
CAUSEWAY CAPITAL MGT LLC
11111 Santa Monica Blvd Fl 15 (90025-3349)
PHONE.................................310 231-6100
Gracie Fermelia, Managing Member
Sarah Ketterer, *
Harry Hartford, *
EMP: 109 EST: 2001
SALES (est): 34.35MM **Privately Held**
Web: www.causewaycap.com
SIC: 6722 Money market mutual funds

(P-9365)
CHARLES SCHWAB FAMILY OF FUNDS
211 Main St (94105-1901)
PHONE.................................415 627-7000
EMP: 462 EST: 2021
SALES (est): 6.8MM
SALES (corp-wide): 20.76B **Publicly Held**
Web: www.schwab.com
SIC: 6722 Management investment, open-end
PA: The Charles Schwab Corporation
3000 Schwab Way
Westlake TX
817 859-5000

(P-9366)
CLEARLAKE CAPITAL GROUP LP (PA)
233 Wilshire Blvd Ste 800 (90401-1207)
PHONE.................................310 400-8800
EMP: 258 EST: 2006
SALES (est): 3.89B **Privately Held**
Web: www.clearlake.com
SIC: 6722 Management investment, open-end

(P-9367)
DODGE & COX
555 California St 40th Fl (94104-1503)
PHONE.................................415 981-1710
Dana M Emery, CEO
John A Gunn, *
Dana Amery, *
Charles Poll, *
John Loll, *
EMP: 195 EST: 1930
SQ FT: 45,000
SALES (est): 110.5MM **Privately Held**
Web: www.dodgeandcox.com
SIC: 6722 Money market mutual funds

(P-9368)
FARALLON CAPITAL PARTNERS LP (PA)
1 Maritime Plz Ste 2100 (94111-3528)
PHONE.................................415 421-2132
Chun R Ding, Managing Member
EMP: 80 EST: 2003
SQ FT: 8,000
SALES (est): 33.88MM
SALES (corp-wide): 33.88MM **Privately Held**
Web: www.farralloncapital.com
SIC: 6722 Money market mutual funds

(P-9369)
FRANKLIN ADVISERS INC
1 Franklin Pkwy (94403-1906)
PHONE.................................650 312-2000
Charles B Johnson, Ch Bd
EMP: 1700 EST: 1985
SQ FT: 120,000
SALES (est): 53.39MM
SALES (corp-wide): 7.85B **Publicly Held**

PRODUCTS & SERVICES SECTION

6722 - Management Investment, Open-ended (P-9391)

SIC: 6722 Money market mutual funds
PA: Franklin Resources, Inc.
1 Franklin Pkwy
San Mateo CA
650 312-2000

(P-9370)
FRANKLIN TEMPLETON SVCS LLC
1 Franklin Pkwy Bldg 970 (94403-1906)
PHONE..................................650 312-3000
Martin L Flanagan, *Pr*
Charles B Johnson, *
EMP: 2500 EST: 1996
SALES (est): 460.54MM
SALES (corp-wide): 7.85B **Publicly Held**
SIC: 6722 Money market mutual funds
PA: Franklin Resources, Inc.
1 Franklin Pkwy
San Mateo CA
650 312-2000

(P-9371)
FRANKLIN TMPLETON INV SVCS LLC
3366 Quality Dr Fl 1 (95670-7363)
PHONE..................................650 312-4053
Bavel Fox, *Brnch Mgr*
EMP: 289
SALES (corp-wide): 7.85B **Publicly Held**
SIC: 6722 Money market mutual funds
HQ: Franklin Templeton Investor Services, Llc
3344 Quality Dr
Rancho Cordova CA
916 463-1500

(P-9372)
FRANKLIN TMPLETON INV SVCS LLC
1 Franklin Pkwy (94403-1906)
PHONE..................................650 312-2100
EMP: 144
SALES (corp-wide): 7.85B **Publicly Held**
SIC: 6722 Money market mutual funds
HQ: Franklin Templeton Investor Services, Llc
3344 Quality Dr
Rancho Cordova CA
916 463-1500

(P-9373)
GUGGENHEIM PRTNERS INV MGT LLC
100 Wilshire Blvd 5th Fl (90401-1110)
PHONE..................................310 576-1270
Robert Daviduk, *Dir*
EMP: 112
SALES (est): 27.56MM
SALES (corp-wide): 1.8B **Privately Held**
Web: www.guggenheimpartners.com
SIC: 6722 Money market mutual funds
PA: Guggenheim Partners, Llc
330 Madison Ave Rm 201
New York NY
212 739-0700

(P-9374)
HALL CAPITAL PARTNERS LLC (PA)
1 Maritime Plz Fl 5 (94111-3408)
PHONE..................................415 288-0544
Kathryn A Hall, *CEO*
Morris Offit, *
William Powers, *
John W Buoymaster, *
EMP: 78 EST: 1995
SQ FT: 6,000
SALES (est): 31.12MM **Privately Held**
Web: www.hallcapital.com
SIC: 6722 Management investment, open-end

(P-9375)
HUNT CAPITAL PARTNERS TAX CRDT
15910 Ventura Blvd Ste 1100 (91436-2802)
PHONE..................................818 380-6100
EMP: 67
SALES (est): 3.37MM **Privately Held**
Web: www.huntcapitalpartners.com
SIC: 6722 Money market mutual funds

(P-9376)
KAYNE ANDRSON RDNICK INV MGT L
2000 Avenue Of The Stars Fl 11 (90067-4700)
PHONE..................................310 229-9260
Jeannine Vanian, *
Robert Schwarzkopf, *
Sheryl Sadis, *
EMP: 60 EST: 1995
SQ FT: 20,000
SALES (est): 48.18MM **Publicly Held**
Web: www.kayne.com
SIC: 6722 Management investment, open-end
HQ: Virtus Partners, Inc.
755 Main St
Hartford CT

(P-9377)
LOS ANGELES CAPITAL MGT LLC (PA)
Also Called: La Capital
11150 Santa Monica Blvd Ste 200 (90025-0418)
PHONE..................................310 479-9998
Thomas Stevens, *Ch Bd*
Thomas D Stevens, *
Hal Reynolds, *
David Borger, *
Stuart Matsuda, *
EMP: 80 EST: 2002
SQ FT: 10,192
SALES (est): 105.64K
SALES (corp-wide): 105.64K **Privately Held**
Web: www.lacapm.com
SIC: 6722 8741 8211 6282 Management investment, open-end; Management services; Elementary and secondary schools; Investment advice

(P-9378)
MALK PARTNERS
7911 Herschel Ave Ste 400 (92037-4412)
PHONE..................................858 914-1125
Max Hong, *CEO*
EMP: 95 EST: 2017
SALES (est): 2.31MM **Privately Held**
Web: www.malk.com
SIC: 6722 Management investment, open-end

(P-9379)
MCMILLIN MANAGEMENT SVCS LP (HQ)
Also Called: McMillin Homes
2750 Womble Rd Ste 102 (92106-6114)
P.O. Box 21010 (92021-0980)
PHONE..................................619 477-4117
Scott Mcmillin, *Genl Pt*
Mark Mcmillin, *Pt*
EMP: 62 EST: 1998
SALES (est): 6.21MM
SALES (corp-wide): 33.68MM **Privately Held**
Web: www.mcmillin.com
SIC: 6722 8611 Management investment, open-end; Business associations
PA: Mcmillin Companies, Llc
2750 Womble Rd Ste 102
San Diego CA
619 477-4117

(P-9380)
MELLON GLOBAL OPRTNTY FUND LLC
Also Called: Mellon Capital Management
50 Fremont St Ste 3900 (94105-2240)
PHONE..................................415 546-6056
EMP: 83 EST: 2014
SALES (est): 2.62MM **Privately Held**
Web: www.mellon.com
SIC: 6722 Money market mutual funds

(P-9381)
METWEST TOTAL RETURN BOND FUND
865 S Figueroa St (90017-2543)
PHONE..................................800 241-4671
EMP: 74 EST: 2016
SALES (est): 974.46K **Privately Held**
SIC: 6722 Money market mutual funds
HQ: Metropolitan West Asset Management, Llc
865 S Figueroa St
Los Angeles CA
213 244-0000

(P-9382)
OAKTREE HOLDINGS INC
333 S Grand Ave Fl 28 (90071)
PHONE..................................213 830-6300
EMP: 944 EST: 2014
SALES (est): 2.14MM **Privately Held**
SIC: 6722 Management investment, open-end
PA: Oaktree Capital Group Holdings, L.P.
333 S Grand Ave Fl 28
Los Angeles CA

(P-9383)
OAKTREE REAL ESTATE OPPRTNTIES
333 S Grand Ave Fl 28 (90071-1530)
PHONE..................................213 830-6300
EMP: 708 EST: 2014
SALES (est): 9.2MM **Privately Held**
Web: www.oaktreecapital.com
SIC: 6722 Money market mutual funds
PA: Oaktree Capital Group Holdings, L.P.
333 S Grand Ave Fl 28
Los Angeles CA

(P-9384)
OAKTREE STRATEGIC INCOME LLC
333 S Grand Ave Fl 28 (90071-1530)
PHONE..................................213 830-6300
EMP: 1023 EST: 2015
SALES (est): 9.37MM **Privately Held**
Web: www.oaktreespecialtylending.com
SIC: 6722 Money market mutual funds
PA: Oaktree Capital Group Holdings, L.P.
333 S Grand Ave Fl 28
Los Angeles CA

(P-9385)
OCM REAL ESTATE OPPRTNTIES FUN
333 S Grand Ave Fl 28 (90071-1504)
PHONE..................................213 830-6300
EMP: 551 EST: 2014
SALES (est): 919.41K **Privately Held**
SIC: 6722 Money market mutual funds
PA: Oaktree Capital Group Holdings, L.P.
333 S Grand Ave Fl 28
Los Angeles CA

(P-9386)
PACIFIC INVESTMENT MGT CO LLC (DH)
Also Called: Pimco
650 Newport Center Dr (92660-6392)
P.O. Box 6430 (92658-6430)
PHONE..................................949 720-6000
Emmanuel Roman, *CEO*
Jeremie Banet, *
Sai S Devabhaktuni, *Head OF CORP DISTRESSED PORTFOLIO MGMNT*
Mohamed A El-erian, *Managing Member*
Jay Jacobs, *
EMP: 240 EST: 1969
SQ FT: 25,000
SALES (est): 503.48MM
SALES (corp-wide): 27.99B **Privately Held**
Web: www.pimco.com
SIC: 6722 Money market mutual funds
HQ: Allianz Asset Management Of America Llc
650 Newport Center Dr
Newport Beach CA
949 219-2200

(P-9387)
PIMCO CYMAN TRST PMCO CYMAN GL
650 Newport Center Dr (92660-6424)
PHONE..................................949 720-6000
EMP: 191 EST: 2005
SALES (est): 1.82MM **Privately Held**
Web: www.pimco.com
SIC: 6722 Money market mutual funds

(P-9388)
PW FUND B LP
555 Capitol Mall (95814-4504)
PHONE..................................916 379-3852
Brian Marty, *Mgr*
EMP: 80 EST: 2017
SALES (est): 19.07MM **Privately Held**
SIC: 6722 Money market mutual funds

(P-9389)
RS INVESTMENT MANAGEMENT LP
1 Bush St Ste 900 (94104-4425)
PHONE..................................415 591-2700
EMP: 163
SIC: 6722 Mutual fund sales, on own account

(P-9390)
SHAMROCK CAPITAL ADVISORS LLC
1100 Glendon Ave Ste 1600 (90024-3567)
PHONE..................................310 974-6600
EMP: 400 EST: 2010
SALES (est): 67.9MM **Privately Held**
Web: www.shamrockcap.com
SIC: 6722 Management investment, open-end

(P-9391)
TCW ABSOLUTE RETURN CREDIT LLC
865 S Figueroa St Ste 2100 (90017-2543)
PHONE..................................213 244-0000
Richard Clotfelter, *CEO*
EMP: 74 EST: 2007
SALES (est): 2.2MM **Privately Held**
SIC: 6722 Money market mutual funds
HQ: Tcw Asset Management Company

6722 - Management Investment, Open-ended (P-9392)

865 S Figueroa St # 1800
Los Angeles CA
213 244-0000

(P-9392)
TCW FUNDS MANAGEMENT INC
865 S Figueroa St Ste 2100 (90017-2588)
PHONE..............................213 244-0000
Thomas Larkin, *Ch*
Thomas Larkin, *Ch Bd*
Marc I Stern, *INTNL**
Michael Cahill, *Secretary General**
Ron Robinson, ***
EMP: 64 **EST:** 1987
SALES (est): 4.06MM **Privately Held**
SIC: 6722 Money market mutual funds
PA: The Tcw Group Inc
865 S Figueroa St # 1800
Los Angeles CA

(P-9393)
WESTERN ASSET CORE PLUS BOND P
385 E Colorado Blvd (91101-1923)
PHONE..............................626 844-9400
Larry Clark, *Prin*
EMP: 147 **EST:** 2012
SALES (est): 35.47K
SALES (corp-wide): 7.85B **Publicly Held**
Web: www.westernasset.com
SIC: 6722 Money market mutual funds
HQ: Western Asset Management Company
385 E Colorado Blvd # 100
Pasadena CA
626 844-9265

(P-9394)
WILSHIRE 2015 FUND
1299 Ocean Ave Ste 700 (90401-1061)
PHONE..............................310 451-3051
EMP: 66
SALES (est): 1.15MM **Privately Held**
Web: www.wilshire.com
SIC: 6722 Money market mutual funds

(P-9395)
WILSHIRE INCOME OPPORTUNITIES
1299 Ocean Ave Ste 700 (90401-1061)
PHONE..............................310 451-3051
EMP: 62 **EST:** 2017
SALES (est): 983.02K
SALES (corp-wide): 51.6MM **Privately Held**
Web: www.wilshire.com
SIC: 6722 Money market mutual funds
PA: Wilshire Advisors Llc
1299 Ocean Ave Ste 700
Santa Monica CA
310 451-3051

6726 Investment Offices, Nec

(P-9396)
ACORNS GROW INCORPORATED (PA)
Also Called: Acorns
5300 California Ave (92617-3038)
PHONE..............................949 251-0095
Noah Kerner, *CEO*
David Hijirida, *Pr*
Seth Wunder, *CIO*
Kennedy Reynolds, *EDUCATION CONTENT*
EMP: 384 **EST:** 2012
SQ FT: 2,500
SALES (est): 100.74MM
SALES (corp-wide): 100.74MM **Privately Held**
Web: www.acorns.com
SIC: 6726 Investment offices, nec

(P-9397)
AIG CAPITAL SERVICES INC
21650 Oxnard St Ste 750 (91367-4997)
PHONE..............................800 445-7862
EMP: 60
SALES (est): 1.75MM
SALES (corp-wide): 56.44B **Publicly Held**
SIC: 6726 Management investment funds, closed-end
HQ: Sunamerica Asset Management, Llc
185 Hudson St Ste 3300
Jersey City NJ
800 858-8850

(P-9398)
BRIDGEWEST VENTURES LLC (PA)
Also Called: Bridgewest Group, The
7310 Miramar Rd Ste 500 (92126-4222)
P.O. Box 928769 (92192-8769)
PHONE..............................858 529-6600
Masood Tayebi, *CEO*
Massih Tayebi, *Ch*
Kevin M Russell, *Chief Legal Counsel*
Saum Vahdat, *CFO*
EMP: 624 **EST:** 2014
SALES (est): 23.17MM
SALES (corp-wide): 23.17MM **Privately Held**
Web: www.bridgewestgroup.com
SIC: 6726 Management investment funds, closed-end

(P-9399)
CENTURY PK CAPITL PARTNERS LLC (PA)
2101 Rosecrans Ave Ste 4275 (90245-4749)
PHONE..............................310 867-2210
Paul J Wolf, ***
Charles W Roellig, ***
Guy Zaczepinski, ***
Gina Yang, ***
EMP: 160 **EST:** 2005
SALES (est): 98.49MM **Privately Held**
Web: www.centuryparkcapital.com
SIC: 6726 3569 3086 3448 Management investment funds, closed-end; Firefighting and related equipment; Carpet and rug cushions, foamed plastics; Ramps, prefabricated metal

(P-9400)
CHARLES SCHWAB CORPORATION
Also Called: Charles Schwab
10920 Via Frontera Ste 100 (92127-1730)
PHONE..............................800 435-4000
EMP: 92
SALES (corp-wide): 20.76B **Publicly Held**
Web: www.schwab.com
SIC: 6726 6211 Investment offices, nec; Brokers, security
PA: The Charles Schwab Corporation
3000 Schwab Way
Westlake TX
817 859-5000

(P-9401)
JASPER RIDGE PARTNERS
2885 Sand Hill Rd Ste 100 (94025-7022)
PHONE..............................650 494-4800
Maura Bowman, *Off Mgr*
EMP: 72 **EST:** 2012
SALES (est): 16.2MM **Privately Held**
Web: www.jasperridge.com
SIC: 6726 Management investment funds, closed-end

(P-9402)
KINGSWOOD CAPITAL MGT LP
11111 Santa Monica Blvd Ste 1700 (90025-3333)
PHONE..............................424 744-8238
Alexander Wolf, *Pt*
EMP: 200 **EST:** 2019
SALES (est): 18.7MM **Privately Held**
Web: www.kingswood-capital.com
SIC: 6726 Investment offices, nec

(P-9403)
MILLENNIUM MANAGEMENT LLC
2 Embarcadero Ctr # 1640 (94111-3823)
PHONE..............................415 844-4048
EMP: 2274
SALES (corp-wide): 508.01MM **Privately Held**
Web: www.mlp.com
SIC: 6726 Management investment funds, closed-end
PA: Millennium Management, Llc
399 Park Ave
New York NY
212 841-4100

(P-9404)
NETAPP CAPITAL SOLUTIONS INC
3060 Olsen Dr (95128-2155)
PHONE..............................408 822-6000
Matthew Fawcett, *CEO*
EMP: 99 **EST:** 2005
SALES (est): 26.69MM **Publicly Held**
Web: www.netapp.com
SIC: 6726 Investment offices, nec
PA: Netapp, Inc.
3060 Olsen Dr
San Jose CA

(P-9405)
NOOSPHERE VENTURE PARTNERS LP (PA)
800 W El Camino Real Ste 180 (94040)
PHONE..............................650 605-5684
Zoya Grishashvili, *Pt*
EMP: 117 **EST:** 2014
SALES (est): 19.61MM
SALES (corp-wide): 19.61MM **Privately Held**
Web: www.noosphereventures.com
SIC: 6726 Investment offices, nec

(P-9406)
OASIS WEST REALTY LLC
1800 Century Park E Ste 500 (90067-1508)
PHONE..............................310 274-8066
Samuel Surloff, ***
EMP: 502 **EST:** 2003
SALES (est): 50.15MM **Privately Held**
Web: www.alagemcapital.com
SIC: 6726 5947 5813 5812 Investment offices, nec; Gift shop; Drinking places; Eating places

(P-9407)
OPENGATE CAPITAL GROUP LLC
10250 Constellation Blvd Fl 17 (90067-6272)
PHONE..............................310 432-7000
EMP: 68 **EST:** 2008
SALES (est): 10.22MM **Privately Held**
Web: www.opengatecapital.com

(P-9408)
PACIFIC AVE CPITL PARTNERS LLC (PA)
2447 Pacific Coast Hwy Ste 101 (90254)
PHONE..............................424 254-9774
Christopher R Sznewajs, *Managing Member*
Joseph Villanueva, *CFO*
EMP: 418 **EST:** 2018
SALES (est): 97.68MM
SALES (corp-wide): 97.68MM **Privately Held**
Web: www.pacificavenuecapital.com
SIC: 6726 Investment offices, nec

(P-9409)
SILVER LAKE PARTNERS VII LP
2775 Sand Hill Rd Ste 100 (94025-7085)
PHONE..............................650 233-8120
Egon Durban, *Mng Pt*
Greg Mondre, *Mng Pt*
EMP: 180 **EST:** 2021
SALES (est): 10.39MM **Privately Held**
SIC: 6726 Investment offices, nec

(P-9410)
WESTERN ASSETS MANAGEMENT CO
Also Called: Pacific American Income Shares
385 E Colorado Blvd (91101-1931)
P.O. Box 983 (91102-0983)
PHONE..............................626 844-9400
James W Hirschmann, *Prin*
Kent Engel, *VP*
Ilene S Harker, *Sec*
James W Hirschmann, *Pr*
Steven Walsh, *VP*
EMP: 77 **EST:** 1971
SALES (est): 9.9MM **Privately Held**
SIC: 6726 Management investment funds, closed-end

6732 Trusts: Educational, Religious, Etc.

(P-9411)
CALIFRNIA MRTIME ACDEMY FNDTIO
200 Maritime Academy Dr (94590-8181)
PHONE..............................707 654-1000
Tom Cropper, *CEO*
Beverly Byl, ***
EMP: 200 **EST:** 1972
SALES (est): 17.46MM **Privately Held**
Web: www.csum.edu
SIC: 6732 Educational trust management

(P-9412)
COMMUNITY PARTNERS INTL
580 California St Fl 16 (94104-1068)
PHONE..............................510 225-9676
EMP: 117 **EST:** 2011
SALES (est): 10.47MM **Privately Held**
Web: www.cpintl.org
SIC: 6732 Trusts: educational, religious, etc.

(P-9413)
COUNTY OF LOS ANGELES
Also Called: Extension Services
6300 E State University Dr Ste 104 (90815-4666)
PHONE..............................562 985-4687
Marilyn Crego, *Dean*
EMP: 82
SALES (corp-wide): 31.7B **Privately Held**
Web: www.lacounty.gov

PRODUCTS & SERVICES SECTION
6733 - Trusts, Nec (P-9435)

SIC: **6732** 9111 Educational trust management; Executive offices
PA: County Of Los Angeles
500 W Temple St Ste 437
Los Angeles CA
213 974-1101

(P-9414)
EMPOWER OUR YOUTH
Also Called: Eoy
6767 W Sunset Blvd 8-188 (90028-7317)
PHONE.................................323 203-5436
Ihkisha Levell, *Prin*
EMP: 99 EST: 2008
SALES (est): 1.27MM **Privately Held**
SIC: **6732** Trusts: educational, religious, etc.

(P-9415)
GREATER LOS ANGLES VTRANS RES
11301 Wilshire Blvd Bldg 114 (90073-1003)
PHONE.................................310 312-1554
Jane Cheung, *Ex Dir*
Thoyd Ellis, *
Bonita Krall, *CPO**
Ron Waldorf, *
Leila Ghayouri, *
EMP: 90 EST: 2018
SALES (est): 7.08MM **Privately Held**
SIC: **6732** Trusts: educational, religious, etc.

(P-9416)
OAKLAND PROMISE
484 9th St (94607-4048)
PHONE.................................510 836-8900
Andrew Fremder, *Prin*
EMP: 70 EST: 2010
SALES (est): 5.12MM **Privately Held**
Web: www.eastbaycollegefund.org
SIC: **6732** Educational trust management

(P-9417)
OAKLAND PUBLIC EDUCATION FUND
520 3rd St Ste 109 (94607-3503)
P.O. Box 71005 (94612-7105)
PHONE.................................510 221-6968
Brian Stanley, *
Robert Spencer, *
EMP: 95 EST: 2003
SALES (est): 29.14MM **Privately Held**
Web: www.oaklandedfund.org
SIC: **6732** Trusts: educational, religious, etc.

(P-9418)
UCLA FOUNDATION
10889 Wilshire Blvd Ste 1100 (90024-4200)
PHONE.................................310 794-3193
Craig Ehrlich, *Ch*
Peter Hayashida, *
Neal Axelrod, *
Jocelyn Smith, *
EMP: 317 EST: 1945
SALES (est): 636.37MM **Privately Held**
Web: www.uclafoundation.org
SIC: **6732** Educational trust management

6733 Trusts, Nec

(P-9419)
2100 TRUST LLC (PA)
625 N Grand Ave (92701-4347)
PHONE.................................877 469-7344
Erek J Delorenzi, *Prin*
EMP: 200 EST: 2010
SALES (est): 1.04B
SALES (corp-wide): 1.04B **Privately Held**
Web: www.socalnewsgroup.com

SIC: **6733** Trusts, nec

(P-9420)
ADVENTIST HEALTH DELANO
Also Called: Wasco Medical Plaza
2300 7th St (93280-1585)
PHONE.................................661 758-4184
Bahram Ghaffari, *Brnch Mgr*
EMP: 98
SALES (corp-wide): 789.42MM **Privately Held**
Web: www.adventisthealth.org
SIC: **6733** 8011 Trusts, nec; Clinic, operated by physicians
HQ: Adventist Health Delano
1401 Garces Hwy Bldg A
Delano CA
661 725-4800

(P-9421)
BENEFITS PRGRAM ADMINSITRATION
Also Called: Gciu Employer Retirement Fund
13191 Concords Pkwy N Ste 205 (91746)
PHONE.................................562 463-5000
Mathew Wenner, *Admn*
EMP: 95 EST: 1955
SALES (est): 469.56K
SALES (corp-wide): 9.95MM **Privately Held**
SIC: **6733** Trusts, except educational, religious, charity: management
PA: Management Applied Programming, Inc.
13191 Crssroads Pkwy N Ste
City Of Industry CA
562 463-5000

(P-9422)
CAPITAL GUARDIAN TRUST COMPANY (HQ)
333 S Hope St Fl 52 (90071-3061)
PHONE.................................213 486-9200
Richard C Barker, *Ch Bd*
Robert Ronus, *
EMP: 100 EST: 1968
SQ FT: 6,000
SALES (est): 51.89MM
SALES (corp-wide): 5.43B **Privately Held**
SIC: **6733** Trusts, except educational, religious, charity: management
PA: The Capital Group Companies Inc
333 S Hope St Fl 55
Los Angeles CA
213 486-9200

(P-9423)
CARPENTER FNDS ADMNSTRTIVE OFF
265 Hegenberger Rd Ste 100 (94621-1443)
PHONE.................................510 633-0333
David Lee, *CEO*
EMP: 79 EST: 1953
SQ FT: 60,956
SALES (est): 13.11MM **Privately Held**
Web: www.carpenterfunds.com
SIC: **6733** Trusts, except educational, religious, charity: management

(P-9424)
COHESITY INC
1880 Fallen Leaf Ln (94024-6218)
PHONE.................................650 968-4470
EMP: 246
SALES (corp-wide): 221.15MM **Privately Held**
Web: www.cohesity.com
SIC: **6733** Trusts, nec
PA: Cohesity, Inc.

300 Park Ave Ste 1700
San Jose CA
855 926-4374

(P-9425)
EPIDAURUS
Also Called: Amity Foundation
3745 S Grand Ave (90007-4332)
PHONE.................................213 743-9075
Mark Schettenger, *Pr*
EMP: 272
SIC: **6733** Trusts, nec
PA: Epidaurus
721 N 4th Ave
Tucson AZ

(P-9426)
FORGE TRUST CO
3050 S Delaware St Ste 202 (94403-2394)
P.O. Box 7080 (94070-7080)
PHONE.................................650 591-3335
EMP: 60 EST: 2013
SALES (est): 11.42MM **Privately Held**
Web: www.forgetrust.com
SIC: **6733** Trusts, nec

(P-9427)
GUILD MORTGAGE COMPANY LLC (HQ)
Also Called: Guild Mortgage
5887 Copley Dr (92111-7906)
P.O. Box 85304 (92186-5304)
PHONE.................................800 365-4441
EMP: 200 EST: 1960
SALES (est): 901.22MM
SALES (corp-wide): 1.16B **Publicly Held**
Web: www.guildmortgage.com
SIC: **6733** 6162 Trusts, except educational, religious, charity: management; Mortgage bankers
PA: Guild Holdings Company
5887 Copley Dr
San Diego CA
858 560-6330

(P-9428)
IMPAC SECURED ASSETS CORP
19500 Jamboree Rd (92612-2411)
PHONE.................................949 475-3600
Ronald Martin Morrison, *Admn*
EMP: 99 EST: 2008
SALES (est): 2.39MM **Privately Held**
SIC: **6733** Trusts, nec
HQ: Impac Funding Corporation
19500 Jamboree Rd
Irvine CA

(P-9429)
IRONWRKER EMPLYEES BENEFT CORP
Also Called: IRONWORKERS UNION
131 N El Molino Ave Ste 330 (91101-1873)
PHONE.................................626 792-7337
Dick Zampa, *Pr*
EMP: 65 EST: 1977
SQ FT: 19,000
SALES (est): 2.06MM **Privately Held**
Web: www.ironworkerbenny.com
SIC: **6733** Trusts, except educational, religious, charity: management

(P-9430)
KAISER FOUNDATION HOSPITALS
Also Called: Kaiser Permanente
4647 Zion Ave (92120-2507)
PHONE.................................619 528-5888
Kathy Roper, *Mgr*
EMP: 1242

SALES (corp-wide): 68.1B **Privately Held**
Web: www.kaisercenter.com
SIC: **6733** 8062 Trusts, nec; General medical and surgical hospitals
HQ: Kaiser Foundation Hospitals Inc
1 Kaiser Plz
Oakland CA
510 271-6611

(P-9431)
KAISER FOUNDATION HOSPITALS
Also Called: Martinez Medical Offices
200 Muir Rd (94553-4672)
PHONE.................................925 372-1000
Bryan Fong, *Prin*
EMP: 2910
SALES (corp-wide): 68.1B **Privately Held**
Web: www.kaisercenter.com
SIC: **6733** 8011 Trusts, nec; General and family practice, physician/surgeon
HQ: Kaiser Foundation Hospitals Inc
1 Kaiser Plz
Oakland CA
510 271-6611

(P-9432)
KAISER FOUNDATION HOSPITALS
Also Called: Kaiser Permanente
5119 Pomona Blvd (90022-1711)
PHONE.................................323 881-5516
Judy Nantes, *Mgr*
EMP: 96
SALES (corp-wide): 68.1B **Privately Held**
Web: www.kaisercenter.com
SIC: **6733** Trusts, nec
HQ: Kaiser Foundation Hospitals Inc
1 Kaiser Plz
Oakland CA
510 271-6611

(P-9433)
KAISER FOUNDATION HOSPITALS
Also Called: Moreno Valley Heacock Med Offs
12815 Heacock St (92553-2836)
PHONE.................................951 601-6174
Mark Ituah, *Prin*
EMP: 85
SALES (corp-wide): 68.1B **Privately Held**
Web: www.kaisercenter.com
SIC: **6733** Trusts, nec
HQ: Kaiser Foundation Hospitals Inc
1 Kaiser Plz
Oakland CA
510 271-6611

(P-9434)
KAISER FOUNDATION HOSPITALS
Also Called: Kaiser Permanente
789 E Cooley Dr (92324-4007)
PHONE.................................909 427-5521
Barry A Wolfman, *Prin*
EMP: 64
SQ FT: 23,088
SALES (corp-wide): 68.1B **Privately Held**
Web: www.kaisercenter.com
SIC: **6733** Trusts, nec
HQ: Kaiser Foundation Hospitals Inc
1 Kaiser Plz
Oakland CA
510 271-6611

(P-9435)
KAISER FOUNDATION HOSPITALS
Also Called: Orange County-Irvine Med Ctr

6733 - Trusts, Nec (P-9436)

6640 Alton Pkwy (92618-3734)
PHONE..................................949 932-5000
EMP: 336
SALES (corp-wide): 68.1B Privately Held
Web: www.kaisercenter.com
SIC: 6733 Trusts, nec
HQ: Kaiser Foundation Hospitals Inc
    1 Kaiser Plz
    Oakland CA
    510 271-6611

(P-9436)
KAISER FOUNDATION HOSPITALS
Also Called: Kaiser Permanente
3285 Claremont Way (94558-3313)
PHONE..................................707 258-2500
Debby Bacon, Brnch Mgr
EMP: 132
SALES (corp-wide): 68.1B Privately Held
Web: www.kaisercenter.com
SIC: 6733 8093 8062 Trusts, except educational, religious, charity: management; Specialty outpatient clinics, nec; General medical and surgical hospitals
HQ: Kaiser Foundation Hospitals Inc
    1 Kaiser Plz
    Oakland CA
    510 271-6611

(P-9437)
LOMA LINDA UNIV CHLD HOSP
Also Called: LLUCH
11234 Anderson St (92354-2804)
P.O. Box 2000 (92354-0200)
PHONE..................................909 558-8000
EMP: 219 EST: 2011
SALES (est): 584.94MM Privately Held
Web: www.lluch.org
SIC: 6733 Trusts, nec

(P-9438)
MINISTRY SERVICES OF THE DAUGH
Also Called: Daughters Charity Health Sys
26000 Altamont Rd (94022-4317)
PHONE..................................650 917-4500
Ernie Wallerstein, CEO
James F Dover, Pr
Carol Furgurson, Admn
EMP: 180 EST: 2014
SALES (est): 10.03MM Privately Held
Web: www.daughtersofcharity.com
SIC: 6733 6732 Trusts, nec; Religious trust management

(P-9439)
MOELIS & COMPANY LLC
1999 Avenue Of The Stars Ste 1900 (90067-6022)
PHONE..................................310 443-2300
Stella Hoe, Brnch Mgr
EMP: 114
SALES (corp-wide): 985.3MM Publicly Held
Web: www.moelis.com
SIC: 6733 6282 Private estate, personal investment and vacation fund trusts; Investment advisory service
HQ: Moelis & Company Llc
    399 Park Ave Fl 5
    New York NY

(P-9440)
OPERATING ENGINEERS FUNDS INC (PA)
100 Corson St (91103-3892)
P.O. Box 7063 (91109-7063)
PHONE..................................866 400-5200

Mike Roddy, CEO
Matt Erieg, *
Chuck Killian, *
EMP: 135 EST: 1971
SQ FT: 84,600
SALES (est): 314.23K
SALES (corp-wide): 314.23K Privately Held
Web: www.oefi.org
SIC: 6733 Trusts, except educational, religious, charity: management

(P-9441)
PMT CRDIT RISK TRNSF TR 2015-1
3043 Townsgate Rd (91361-3027)
PHONE..................................818 224-7028
EMP: 96 EST: 2017
SALES (est): 456.76K Publicly Held
SIC: 6733 Trusts, nec
PA: Pennymac Mortgage Investment Trust
    6101 Condor Dr
    Moorpark CA

(P-9442)
PMT CRDIT RISK TRNSF TR 2015-2
3043 Townsgate Rd (91361-3027)
PHONE..................................818 224-7442
EMP: 202 EST: 2017
SALES (est): 968.86K Publicly Held
Web: www.pennymac.com
SIC: 6733 Trusts, nec
PA: Pennymac Mortgage Investment Trust
    6101 Condor Dr
    Moorpark CA

(P-9443)
PMT CRDIT RISK TRNSF TR 2019-2
3043 Townsgate Rd (91361-3027)
PHONE..................................818 224-7028
EMP: 86 EST: 2019
SALES (est): 416.95K Publicly Held
Web: pmt.pennymac.com
SIC: 6733 Trusts, nec
PA: Pennymac Mortgage Investment Trust
    6101 Condor Dr
    Moorpark CA

(P-9444)
PMT CRDIT RISK TRNSF TR 2020-1
3043 Townsgate Rd (91361-3027)
PHONE..................................818 224-7028
EMP: 115 EST: 2020
SALES (est): 987.58K Publicly Held
SIC: 6733 Trusts, nec
PA: Pennymac Mortgage Investment Trust
    6101 Condor Dr
    Moorpark CA

(P-9445)
PNMAC GMSR ISSUER TRUST
3043 Townsgate Rd (91361-3027)
PHONE..................................818 746-2271
EMP: 2339 EST: 2017
SALES (est): 7.1MM
SALES (corp-wide): 1.99B Publicly Held
SIC: 6733 Trusts, nec
HQ: Pnmac Holdings, Inc.
    3043 Townsgate Rd
    Westlake Village CA
    818 224-7442

(P-9446)
QUALITY LOAN SERVICE CORP
2763 Camino Del Rio S (92108-3708)
PHONE..................................619 645-7711

Kevin R Mccarthy, CEO
Thomas J Holthus, *
John R Valkus, *
Dave Owen, *
Victoria Logan, *
EMP: 384 EST: 1988
SALES (est): 83.78MM Privately Held
Web: www.qualityloan.com
SIC: 6733 Trusts, except educational, religious, charity: management

(P-9447)
SOUTHERN CAL PIPE TRADES ADM (PA)
Also Called: Southern Cal Pipe Trades ADM
501 Shatto Pl Ste 500 (90020-1730)
PHONE..................................213 385-6161
Milton D Johnson, Pr
EMP: 70 EST: 1956
SQ FT: 70,000
SALES (est): 24.6MM
SALES (corp-wide): 24.6MM Privately Held
Web: www.scptac.org
SIC: 6733 6513 Trusts, except educational, religious, charity: management; Retirement hotel operation

(P-9448)
TRUST WILL
961 W Laurel St (92101-1224)
PHONE..................................415 246-4503
EMP: 68 EST: 2019
SALES (est): 3.4MM Privately Held
Web: www.trustandwill.com
SIC: 6733 Trusts, nec

(P-9449)
UFCW & EMPLOYERS TRUST LLC (PA)
1000 Burnett Ave Ste 110 (94520-5713)
PHONE..................................800 552-2400
Jody Osterweil, Admn
EMP: 110 EST: 1957
SQ FT: 57,600
SALES (est): 559.66MM
SALES (corp-wide): 559.66MM Privately Held
Web: www.ufcwtrust.com
SIC: 6733 Trusts, nec

(P-9450)
VARNER FAMILY LTD PARTNERSHIP (PA)
5900 E Lerdo Hwy (93263-4023)
PHONE..................................661 399-1163
James Varner, Genl Pt
EMP: 80 EST: 2000
SALES (est): 55.84MM
SALES (corp-wide): 55.84MM Privately Held
SIC: 6733 Private estate, personal investment and vacation fund trusts

(P-9451)
WATTS HEALTH FOUNDATION INC
Also Called: Watts Health Center
10300 Compton Ave (90002-3628)
PHONE..................................323 357-6688
Clyde W Oden, Mgr
EMP: 63
SALES (corp-wide): 70.19MM Privately Held
Web: www.wattshealth.org
SIC: 6733 8322 8011 Trusts, nec; Individual and family services; Offices and clinics of medical doctors
HQ: Watts Health Foundation, Inc.

3405 W Imperial Hwy # 304
Inglewood CA
310 424-2220

6794 Patent Owners And Lessors

(P-9452)
BRER AFFILIATES LLC (DH)
Also Called: Prudential
18500 Von Karman Ave Ste 400 (92612-0504)
PHONE..................................949 794-7900
John Vanderwall, Pr
Patti Ray, *
EMP: 208 EST: 2004
SQ FT: 55,500
SALES (est): 116.65MM
SALES (corp-wide): 60.05B Publicly Held
SIC: 6794 6531 Franchises, selling or licensing; Real estate agents and managers
HQ: The Prudential Insurance Company Of America
    751 Broad St Fl 21
    Newark NJ
    973 802-6000

(P-9453)
LEVINE LCHTMAN CPITL PRTNERS S
Also Called: Levine Lchtman Capitl Partners
345 N Maple Dr Ste 300 (90210-5183)
PHONE..................................310 275-5335
EMP: 60 EST: 2010
SALES (est): 8.74MM
SALES (corp-wide): 148.42MM Privately Held
Web: www.llcp.com
SIC: 6794 Franchises, selling or licensing
PA: Levine Leichtman Capital Partners, Llc
    345 N Maple Dr Ste 300
    Beverly Hills CA
    310 275-5335

(P-9454)
QUALCOMM INTERNATIONAL INC (HQ)
Also Called: Qualcomm
5775 Morehouse Dr (92121-1714)
PHONE..................................858 587-1121
Steve Altman, Pr
Derek Aberle, *
EMP: 4000 EST: 1993
SALES (est): 253.04MM
SALES (corp-wide): 44.2B Publicly Held
SIC: 6794 Patent buying, licensing, leasing
PA: Qualcomm Incorporated
    5775 Morehouse Dr
    San Diego CA
    858 587-1121

(P-9455)
RISK MANAGEMENT SOLUTIONS INC (HQ)
Also Called: RMS
7575 Gateway Blvd Ste 300 (94560-1196)
PHONE..................................510 505-2500
Karen White, CEO
Stephen Robertson, CFO
Paul Dali, Ch Bd
EMP: 140 EST: 1988
SALES (est): 153.72MM
SALES (corp-wide): 5.47B Publicly Held
Web: www.rms.com
SIC: 6794 6411 Patent owners and lessors; Insurance information and consulting services
PA: Moody's Corporation
    250 Greenwich St

PRODUCTS & SERVICES SECTION

6798 - Real Estate Investment Trusts (P-9476)

New York NY
212 553-0300

(P-9456)
RPX CORPORATION (HQ)
Also Called: Rpx
4 Embarcadero Ctr Ste 4000 (94111-4100)
PHONE..................866 779-7641
Dan Mccurdy, CEO
Mallun Yen, *
Robert H Heath, VP Fin
Martin E Roberts, Sr VP
EMP: 95 EST: 2008
SQ FT: 67,000
SALES (est): 67.09MM
SALES (corp-wide): 67.09MM Privately Held
Web: www.rpxcorp.com
SIC: 6794 8741 Patent owners and lessors; Business management
PA: Riptide Parent, Llc
1950 University Ave # 350
East Palo Alto CA

(P-9457)
TENSILICA INC (HQ)
3393 Octavius Dr (95054-3004)
P.O. Box 202769 (75320-2769)
PHONE..................408 986-8000
Jack Guedj, Pr
Chris Rowen, *
Keith Van Sickle, *
Beatrice Fu, *
Dan Weed, *
◆ EMP: 80 EST: 1998
SQ FT: 20,000
SALES (est): 27.17MM
SALES (corp-wide): 3.56B Publicly Held
Web: www.cadence.com
SIC: 6794 9621 Patent owners and lessors; Licensing agencies
PA: Cadence Design Systems, Inc.
2655 Seely Ave Bldg 5
San Jose CA
408 943-1234

(P-9458)
TIVO CORPORATION (HQ)
Also Called: Tivo
2160 Gold St (95002-3700)
PHONE..................408 519-9100
David Shull, Pr
James E Meyer, *
Raghavendra Rau, *
Peter Halt, CFO
Pamela Sergeeff, CCO
EMP: 95 EST: 1997
SQ FT: 127,000
SALES (est): 668.13MM
SALES (corp-wide): 438.93MM Publicly Held
Web: www.tivo.com
SIC: 6794 7374 Patent owners and lessors; Computer graphics service
PA: Adeia Inc.
3025 Orchard Pkwy
San Jose CA
408 473-2500

(P-9459)
UNIVERSAL STDIOS LICENSING LLC
100 Universal City Plz (91608-1002)
PHONE..................818 695-1273
Sheetal Madadi, Mgr
Gabriela Kornzweig, Sec
EMP: 150 EST: 2010
SALES (est): 60.27MM
SALES (corp-wide): 121.43B Publicly Held

SIC: 6794 Copyright buying and licensing
HQ: Nbcuniversal Media, Llc
30 Rockefeller Plz Fl 2
New York NY

(P-9460)
WSM INVESTMENTS LLC
Also Called: Topco Sales
3990b Heritage Oak Ct (93063-6716)
PHONE..................818 332-4600
Scott Tucker, CEO
Martin Tucker, *
Michael Siegel, *
▲ EMP: 145 EST: 2009
SQ FT: 150,000
SALES (est): 39.75MM Privately Held
SIC: 6794 5122 5099 4731 Performance rights, publishing and licensing; Cosmetics; Novelties, durable; Freight forwarding
PA: Lover Health Science And Technology Incorporated Co., Ltd
No.1208, Taihu Ave., Changxing Economic Development Zone, Changx Huzhou ZJ

6798 Real Estate Investment Trusts

(P-9461)
5525 E PACIFIC COAST HWY INC
2016 Riverside Dr (90039-3707)
PHONE..................323 669-9090
Anil Mehta, Pr
EMP: 60 EST: 2004
SALES (est): 3.4MM Privately Held
SIC: 6798 Real estate investment trusts

(P-9462)
BIOMED REALTY TRUST INC (PA)
Also Called: Biomed Realty
4570 Executive Dr Ste 400 (92121-3074)
PHONE..................858 207-2513
Alan D Gold, Ch Bd
R Kent Griffin Junior, Pr
Greg N Lubushkin, CFO
Gary A Kreitzer, Ex VP
Charlie Piscitello, CPO
EMP: 375 EST: 2004
SQ FT: 61,286
SALES (est): 264.45MM
SALES (corp-wide): 264.45MM Privately Held
Web: www.biomedrealty.com
SIC: 6798 Real estate investment trusts

(P-9463)
BRE PROPERTIES INC
525 Market St Fl 4 (94105-2712)
PHONE..................415 445-6530
EMP: 617
Web: www.essexapartmenthomes.com
SIC: 6798 Real estate investment trusts

(P-9464)
CANYON VIEW CAPITAL INC
Also Called: Canyon View Capital
331 Soquel Ave Ste 100 (95062-2330)
PHONE..................831 480-6335
Robert J Davidson, CEO
Alison Ruday, *
Gary Rauscher, *
EMP: 80 EST: 2005
SALES (est): 9.91MM Privately Held
Web: www.canyonviewcapital.com
SIC: 6798 Real estate investment trusts

(P-9465)
CORESITE LLC
624 S Grand Ave Ste 1800 (90023-1629)
PHONE..................213 327-1231
Thomas Ray, Brnch Mgr
EMP: 323
Web: www.coresite.com
SIC: 6798 Real estate investment trusts
HQ: Coresite, L.L.C.
1001 17th St Ste 500
Denver CO
866 777-2673

(P-9466)
EQUINIX INC (PA)
Also Called: Equinix
1 Lagoon Dr Ste 400 (94065-1564)
PHONE..................650 598-6000
Charles Meyers, Pr
Peter F Van Camp, *
Keith D Taylor, CFO
Mike Campbell, CSO
Brandi Galvin Morandi, Legal
EMP: 220 EST: 1998
SALES (est): 7.26B
SALES (corp-wide): 7.26B Publicly Held
Web: www.equinix.com
SIC: 6798 7374 Real estate investment trusts; Computer processing services

(P-9467)
EXCEL TRUST INC
17140 Bernardo Center Dr (92128-2093)
PHONE..................858 613-1800
EMP: 67
SIC: 6798 Real estate investment trusts

(P-9468)
GATEWAY PORTFOLIO HOLDINGS LLC
601 Gateway Blvd Ste 930 (94080-7013)
PHONE..................626 578-0777
Joel Marcus, Managing Member
EMP: 99 EST: 2020
SALES (est): 4.94MM
SALES (corp-wide): 3.11B Publicly Held
SIC: 6798 Real estate investment trusts
HQ: Boston Properties Limited Partnership
800 Boylston St Ste 1900
Boston MA
617 236-3300

(P-9469)
HUDSON PACIFIC PROPERTIES INC (PA)
11601 Wilshire Blvd Ste 1600 (90025-0509)
PHONE..................310 445-5700
EMP: 71 EST: 2009
SALES (est): 1.03B Publicly Held
Web: www.hudsonpacificproperties.com
SIC: 6798 Real estate investment trusts

(P-9470)
IRVINE EASTGATE OFFICE II LLC
Also Called: Irvine Company Office Property
550 Newport Center Dr (92660-7010)
P.O. Box 2460 (92658-8960)
PHONE..................949 720-2000
Pam Van Nort, VP
EMP: 3000 EST: 2013
SQ FT: 3,000
SALES (est): 302.84MM Privately Held
Web: www.irvinecompany.com
SIC: 6798 Real estate investment trusts

(P-9471)
KIAVI INC (PA)
2 Allegheny Ctr Ste 200 (94105-5860)
PHONE..................844 415-4663

Michael Bourque, CEO
Matthew Humphrey, *
Bruce Schuman, *
Cherie Yu, CMO*
Carrie Weber, CRO*
EMP: 320 EST: 2013
SALES (est): 86.59MM
SALES (corp-wide): 86.59MM Privately Held
Web: www.kiavi.com
SIC: 6798 Real estate investment trusts

(P-9472)
KILROY REALTY CORPORATION (PA)
12200 W Olympic Blvd Ste 200 (90064-1044)
PHONE..................310 481-8400
John Kilroy, Ch Bd
Tyler Rose, Pr
Heidi Roth, Ex VP
Eliott Trencher, CIO
EMP: 68 EST: 1996
SQ FT: 150,832
SALES (est): 1.1B
SALES (corp-wide): 1.1B Publicly Held
Web: www.kilroyrealty.com
SIC: 6798 Real estate investment trusts

(P-9473)
MACERICH COMPANY (PA)
Also Called: MACERICH
401 Wilshire Blvd Ste 700 (90401-1452)
PHONE..................310 394-6000
Thomas E O'hern, CEO
Edward C Coppola, *
Scott W Kingsmore, Ex VP
Ann C Menard, CLO
Douglas J Healey, Head OF Leasing
EMP: 80 EST: 1965
SALES (est): 859.16MM
SALES (corp-wide): 859.16MM Publicly Held
Web: www.macerich.com
SIC: 6798 Real estate investment trusts

(P-9474)
MPG OFFICE TRUST INC
355 S Grand Ave Ste 3300 (90071-1592)
PHONE..................213 626-3300
EMP: 70
SIC: 6798 Real estate investment trusts

(P-9475)
PACIFICA COMPANIES LLC (PA)
Also Called: Pacifica Companies
1775 Hancock St Ste 200 (92110-2036)
PHONE..................619 296-9000
Deepak Israni, Pr
Ashok Israni, *
EMP: 78 EST: 2004
SALES (est): 442.68MM Privately Held
Web: www.pacificacompanies.com
SIC: 6798 6512 Real estate investment trusts; Nonresidential building operators

(P-9476)
PRIME ADMINISTRATION LLC
Also Called: Prime Group
357 S Curson Ave (90036-5201)
P.O. Box 360859 (90036-1359)
PHONE..................323 549-7155
Daniel H James, Ch
John C Atwater, CEO
EMP: 522 EST: 2004
SALES (est): 96.75MM Privately Held
Web: www.primegrp.com
SIC: 6798 Real estate investment trusts

6798 - Real Estate Investment Trusts (P-9477)

PRODUCTS & SERVICES SECTION

(P-9477)
PROLOGIS INC (PA)
Also Called: PROLOGIS
Pier 1 Bay 1 (94111)
PHONE..........................415 394-9000
Hamid R Moghadam, *Ch Bd*
Eugene F Reilly, *Vice Chairman*
Daniel S Letter, *Pr*
Timothy D Arndt, *CFO*
Gary E Anderson, *COO*
EMP: 460 **EST:** 1997
SALES (est): 5.97B
SALES (corp-wide): 5.97B **Publicly Held**
Web: www.prologis.com
SIC: 6798 Real estate investment trusts

(P-9478)
PROLOGIS LP (HQ)
Also Called: PROLOGIS
Pier 1 Bay 1 (94111)
PHONE..........................415 394-9000
Hamid R Moghadam, *Ch Bd*
Thomas S Olinger, *CFO*
Lori A Palazzolo, *CAO*
EMP: 452 **EST:** 1997
SALES (est): 5.97B
SALES (corp-wide): 5.97B **Publicly Held**
Web: www.prologis.com
SIC: 6798 Real estate investment trusts
PA: Prologis, Inc.
Bay 1 Pier 1
San Francisco CA
415 394-9000

(P-9479)
PUBLIC STORAGE (PA)
701 Western Ave (91201-2349)
PHONE..........................818 244-8080
Joseph D Russell Junior, *Pr*
Ronald L Havner Junior, *Ch Bd*
H Thomas Boyle, *CIO*
Natalia N Johnson, *Chief*
Nathaniel A Vitan, *CLO*
EMP: 430 **EST:** 1980
SALES (est): 4.18B
SALES (corp-wide): 4.18B **Publicly Held**
Web: www.publicstorage.com
SIC: 6798 Real estate investment trusts

(P-9480)
WESTERN ASSET MRTG CAPITL CORP
385 E Colorado Blvd (91101-1923)
PHONE..........................626 844-9400
EMP: 804 **EST:** 2012
SALES (est): 74.25MM **Privately Held**
Web: www.westernassetmcc.com
SIC: 6798 Real estate investment trusts

6799 Investors, Nec

(P-9481)
500 STARTUPS MANAGEMENT CO LLC
Also Called: Spacer.com
3478 Buskirk Ave Ste 1000 (94523-4378)
PHONE..........................650 743-4738
EMP: 120 **EST:** 2010
SALES (est): 75.65MM **Privately Held**
Web: www.500.co
SIC: 6799 Venture capital companies
HQ: Spacer.Com.Au Pty Ltd
Level 3 55 Pyrmont Bridge Road
Pyrmont NSW

(P-9482)
7TH & C INVESTMENTS LLC
404 14th St (92101-7508)
PHONE..........................619 233-7327
James W Brennan, *Prin*
EMP: 140 **EST:** 2010
SALES (est): 4.64MM
SALES (corp-wide): 573.83MM **Publicly Held**
Web: www.taogroup.com
SIC: 6799 Investors, nec
PA: Sphere Entertainment Co.
2 Penn Plz
New York NY
725 258-0001

(P-9483)
ABS CAPITAL PARTNERS III LP
101 California St Fl 24 (94111-5898)
PHONE..........................415 617-2800
John Mallon, *Brnch Mgr*
EMP: 431
Web: www.abscapital.com
SIC: 6799 Venture capital companies
PA: Abs Capital Partners Iii, L.P.
201 Intrntl Cir Ste 150
Cockeysville MD

(P-9484)
ACCEL-KKR COMPANY LLC (PA)
Also Called: Accel-KKR
2180 Sand Hill Rd Ste 300 (94025-6947)
PHONE..........................650 289-2460
Thomas Barnds, *Managing Member*
Park Durrett, *
Maurice Hernandez, *
EMP: 114 **EST:** 2000
SQ FT: 7,000
SALES (est): 83.97MM
SALES (corp-wide): 83.97MM **Privately Held**
Web: www.accel-kkr.com
SIC: 6799 Venture capital companies

(P-9485)
AH PARALLEL FUND V LP
2865 Sand Hill Rd Ste 101 (94025-7022)
PHONE..........................650 798-3900
Balaji Srinivasan, *Prin*
EMP: 338 **EST:** 2015
SALES (est): 15.69MM **Privately Held**
SIC: 6799 Investors, nec

(P-9486)
ALPINE INVSTORS CNFRNCE CALL H
Also Called: Telshare
3 Embarcadero Ctr Ste 2330 (94111-4003)
PHONE..........................415 392-9100
EMP: 86 **EST:** 2002
SALES (est): 1.02MM **Privately Held**
Web: www.alpineinvestors.com
SIC: 6799 Investors, nec

(P-9487)
ARABELLA PHILANTHROPIC
Also Called: ARABELLA PHILANTHROPIC INVESTMENT ADVISORS, LLC
340 Pine St Ste 401 (94104-3238)
PHONE..........................415 677-9700
Eric Kessler, *Brnch Mgr*
EMP: 109
Web: www.arabellaadvisors.com
SIC: 6799 Investors, nec
PA: Arabella Advisors, Llc
1828 L St Nw Ste 300
Washington DC

(P-9488)
ARE/CAL-SD REGION NO 62 LLC
26 N Euclid Ave (91101-1961)
PHONE..........................626 578-0777
Mark Butcher, *
EMP: 99 **EST:** 2019
SALES (est): 5.13MM **Privately Held**
SIC: 6799 Investors, nec

(P-9489)
B CAPITAL GROUP US LLC
1240 Rosecrans Ave Ste 120 (90266-2558)
PHONE..........................310 698-1270
Virginia Schmitt, *CFO*
EMP: 79 **EST:** 2016
SALES (est): 10.89MM **Privately Held**
Web: www.bcapgroup.com
SIC: 6799 Venture capital companies

(P-9490)
BACKBONE CAPITAL ADVISORS LLC
4084 Camellia Ave (91604-3006)
PHONE..........................818 769-8016
Britt Terrell, *Prin*
EMP: 127 **EST:** 2011
SALES (est): 412.15K
SALES (corp-wide): 9.21MM **Privately Held**
Web: www.backbonecap.com
SIC: 6799 Investors, nec
PA: Palm Tree Llc
11755 Wilshire Blvd
Los Angeles CA
424 220-6800

(P-9491)
BAIN CAPITL VENTR PARTNERS LLC
590 Howard St (94105-3002)
PHONE..........................415 213-2400
EMP: 231
Web: www.baincapitalventures.com
SIC: 6799 Venture capital companies
PA: Bain Capital Venture Partners, Llc
200 Clarendon St
Boston MA

(P-9492)
BROADREACH CAPITL PARTNERS LLC
6430 W Sunset Blvd Ste 504 (90028-7901)
PHONE..........................310 691-5760
Andre Ramillon, *Brnch Mgr*
EMP: 789
SALES (corp-wide): 51.42MM **Privately Held**
Web: www.broadreachcp.com
SIC: 6799 Investors, nec
PA: Broadreach Capital Partners Llc
885 Oak Grove Ave Ste 206
Menlo Park CA
650 331-2500

(P-9493)
BROADREACH CAPITL PARTNERS LLC (PA)
885 Oak Grove Ave Ste 206 (94025-4441)
PHONE..........................650 331-2500
John A Foster, *Dir*
Craig G Vought, *
Philip Flip F Maritz, *
Eli Khari, *
EMP: 60 **EST:** 2002
SALES (est): 51.42MM
SALES (corp-wide): 51.42MM **Privately Held**
Web: www.broadreachcp.com
SIC: 6799 Investors, nec

(P-9494)
BROADREACH CAPITL PARTNERS LLC
235 Montgomery St Ste 1018 (94104-2902)
PHONE..........................415 354-4640
John A Foster, *Brnch Mgr*
EMP: 790
SALES (corp-wide): 51.42MM **Privately Held**
Web: www.broadreachcp.com
SIC: 6799 Investors, nec
PA: Broadreach Capital Partners Llc
885 Oak Grove Ave Ste 206
Menlo Park CA
650 331-2500

(P-9495)
CALL TO ACTION PARTNERS LLC (PA)
11601 Wilshire Blvd Fl 23 (90025-0509)
PHONE..........................310 996-7200
Colin Sapire, *Managing Member*
Lenny Sands, *
Richard Kam, *
▲ **EMP:** 100 **EST:** 2009
SQ FT: 9,500
SALES (est): 33MM
SALES (corp-wide): 33MM **Privately Held**
SIC: 6799 Investors, nec

(P-9496)
CAPITAL INTL INVESTORS
333 S Hope St Ste 2500 (90071-1406)
PHONE..........................213 486-9200
Tim Armour, *Ch*
Phil De Toledo, *Pr*
Rob Lovelace, *Vice Chairman*
Rob Klausner, *COO*
Matt Chmn Ceo Distriibution O' connor, *Prin*
EMP: 69 **EST:** 2012
SALES (est): 484.12K **Privately Held**
SIC: 6799 Investors, nec

(P-9497)
CCCC GROWTH FUND LLC
899 El Centro St (91030-3101)
PHONE..........................626 441-8770
Carl L Herrmann Junior, *Managing Member*
EMP: 61 **EST:** 2001
SQ FT: 10,000
SALES (est): 4.77MM **Privately Held**
Web: www.ccccgrowthfund.com
SIC: 6799 6411 Investors, nec; Insurance agents, brokers, and service

(P-9498)
CENTERLINE MORTGAGE CAPITL INC
18300 Von Karman Ave Ste 600 (92612-1057)
PHONE..........................949 221-6685
Andy Mackay, *Brnch Mgr*
EMP: 366
SALES (corp-wide): 661.26MM **Privately Held**
Web: www.lument.com
SIC: 6799 Investors, nec
HQ: Centerline Mortgage Capital, Inc.
100 Church St Fl 15
New York NY
212 317-5700

(P-9499)
CENTURY PK CAPITL PARTNERS LLC
1010 El Camino Real Ste 300 (94025-2339)
PHONE..........................650 324-1956
Charles Roellig, *Mgr*

▲ = Import ▼ = Export
◆ = Import/Export

PRODUCTS & SERVICES SECTION

6799 - Investors, Nec (P-9523)

EMP: 90
Web: www.centuryparkcapital.com
SIC: 6799 Investors, nec
PA: Century Park Capital Partners, Llc
2101 Rosecrans Ave # 4275
El Segundo CA

(P-9500)
CITADEL ENTP AMERICAS LLC
1 Market Spear Fl 38 (94105)
PHONE..................................415 354-7200
Mitchell Cone, Brnch Mgr
EMP: 253
Web: www.citadel.com
SIC: 6799 Investors, nec
PA: Citadel Enterprise Americas Llc
131 S Dearborn St Ste 200
Chicago IL

(P-9501)
CLEARVIEW CAPITAL LLC
12100 Wilshire Blvd Ste 800 (90025-7140)
PHONE..................................310 806-9555
Larry Simon, Brnch Mgr
EMP: 916
SALES (corp-wide): 244.66MM Privately Held
Web: www.clearviewcap.com
SIC: 6799 Venture capital companies
PA: Clearview Capital, Llc
1010 Washington Blvd 2-9
Stamford CT
203 698-2777

(P-9502)
CORRIDOR CAPITAL LLC (PA)
12400 Wilshire Blvd Ste 645 (90025-1260)
PHONE..................................310 442-7000
Craig L Enenstein, CEO
Edward A Monnier, *
Cameron Reilly, *
Jessamyn Davis, *
EMP: 126 EST: 2005
SALES (est): 97.56MM Privately Held
Web: www.corridor-capital.com
SIC: 6799 Venture capital companies

(P-9503)
CPPIB AMERICA INC (DH)
Also Called: Canada Pension Plan Inv Bd
100 1st St Ste 2600 (94105-3081)
PHONE..................................646 564-4900
Mark Machin, Pr
John Graham, CEO
EMP: 100 EST: 2013
SALES (est): 22.88MM
SALES (corp-wide): 251B Privately Held
Web: www.cppinvestments.com
SIC: 6799 Investors, nec
HQ: Canada Pension Plan Investment
Board Financial Products Inc
One Queen St E Suite 2500
Toronto ON
416 868-4075

(P-9504)
CRESTMONT CAPITAL LLC
1422 Edinger Ave Ste 210 (92780-6298)
PHONE..................................949 537-3882
EMP: 250 EST: 2015
SALES (est): 22.59MM Privately Held
Web: www.crestmontcapital.com
SIC: 6799 Investors, nec

(P-9505)
CVF CAPITAL PARTNERS INC
Also Called: Central Valley Fund, The
1590 Drew Ave Ste 110 (95618-7849)
PHONE..................................530 757-7004
Jose C Blanco, CEO

Edward Mcnulty, Pr
Chris Carleson, *
EMP: 150 EST: 2012
SALES (est): 8.48MM Privately Held
Web: www.cvfcapitalpartners.com
SIC: 6799 Investors, nec

(P-9506)
DCM VENTURES LLC
2420 Sand Hill Rd (94025-6943)
PHONE..................................650 233-1400
EMP: 93 EST: 2016
SALES (est): 1.27MM Privately Held
Web: www.dcm.com
SIC: 6799 Venture capital companies

(P-9507)
EMP III INC
Also Called: Duarte Manor
1755 Mrtn Lthr Kng Jr Blv (90058-1522)
PHONE..................................323 231-4174
EMP: 80 EST: 2010
SALES (est): 2.47MM Privately Held
SIC: 6799 Real estate investors, except property operators

(P-9508)
FIRST ROUND CAPITAL LLC
595 Pacific Ave Fl 4 (94133-4685)
PHONE..................................415 646-0072
Josh Kopelman, Brnch Mgr
EMP: 176
Web: www.firstround.com
SIC: 6799 Venture capital companies
PA: First Round Capital, Llc
4040 Locust St
Philadelphia PA

(P-9509)
FRANCISCO PARTNERS MGT LP (PA)
Also Called: Francisco Partners
1 Letterman Dr Ste 410 (94129-1495)
PHONE..................................415 418-2900
Dipanjan Deb, CEO
David Golob, CIO
Tom Ludwig, COO
EMP: 177 EST: 1999
SQ FT: 15,000
SALES (est): 2.68B
SALES (corp-wide): 2.68B Privately Held
Web: www.franciscopartners.com
SIC: 6799 7372 Venture capital companies; Application computer software

(P-9510)
FULL STACK FINANCE
2701 Ocean Park Blvd Ste 210 (90405-5241)
PHONE..................................800 941-0356
EMP: 78 EST: 2018
SALES (est): 2.32MM Privately Held
Web: www.fullstackfinance.com
SIC: 6799 Investors, nec

(P-9511)
GITSIT SOLUTIONS LLC (PA)
333 S Anita Dr Ste 400 (92868-3314)
PHONE..................................714 352-2038
John Kontouis, Pr
Michael Corasaniti, CEO
EMP: 63 EST: 2007
SALES (est): 48.57MM Privately Held
Web: www.gitsitusa.com
SIC: 6799 Investors, nec

(P-9512)
GOLDEN GATE PRIVATE EQUITY INC (PA)

Also Called: Golden Gate Capital
1 Embarcadero Ctr Fl 39 (94111-3714)
PHONE..................................415 983-2706
David Dominik, Dir
Jesse Rogers, Dir
Prescott Ashe, Dir
Ken Diekroeger, Dir
Stefan Kaluzny, Dir
EMP: 66 EST: 2000
SQ FT: 7,800
SALES (est): 1.71B
SALES (corp-wide): 1.71B Privately Held
Web: www.goldengatecap.com
SIC: 6799 3534 Investors, nec; Elevators and moving stairways

(P-9513)
GOLDEN INTERNATIONAL
424 S Los Angeles St Ste 2 (90013-1470)
PHONE..................................213 628-1388
Gi Hanbae, Brnch Mgr
EMP: 2968
SALES (corp-wide): 20.03MM Privately Held
SIC: 6799 Investors, nec
PA: Golden International
36720 Palmdale Rd
Rancho Mirage CA
760 568-1912

(P-9514)
GRANITE RICK CO
5225 Hellyer Ave Ste 220 (95138-1021)
PHONE..................................831 768-2000
EMP: 152 EST: 2017
SALES (est): 1.12MM
SALES (corp-wide): 521.49MM Privately Held
SIC: 6799 Investors, nec
PA: Granite Rock Co.
350 Technology Dr
Watsonville CA
831 768-2000

(P-9515)
GROVES CAPITAL INC
4025 Stonebridge Ln (92091-4602)
PHONE..................................619 519-4453
EMP: 202 EST: 2019
SALES (est): 5.73MM Privately Held
Web: www.grovescapital.com
SIC: 6799 Investors, nec

(P-9516)
GRYPHON INVESTORS INC (PA)
1 Maritime Plz Ste 2300 (94111-3513)
PHONE..................................415 217-7400
▲ EMP: 130 EST: 1995
SALES (est): 1.32B Privately Held
Web: www.gryphon-inv.com
SIC: 6799 Venture capital companies

(P-9517)
GSA DES PLAINES LLC
10100 Santa Monica Blvd Ste 2600 (90067-4003)
PHONE..................................310 557-5100
Daniel Goldstone, Managing Member
EMP: 70 EST: 2012
SQ FT: 100
SALES (est): 1.59MM Privately Held
SIC: 6799 Real estate investors, except property operators

(P-9518)
HGGC LLC (PA)
1950 University Ave Ste 350 (94303-2250)
PHONE..................................650 321-4910
Rich Lawson, Managing Member
Tanner Ainge, *

Shamus Ankrom, *
Jared Archibald, *
Harv N Barenz, *
EMP: 253 EST: 2011
SALES (est): 609.02MM
SALES (corp-wide): 609.02MM Privately Held
Web: www.hggc.com
SIC: 6799 Commodity investors

(P-9519)
HIGHLAND CAPITAL PARTNERS LLC
537 Hamilton Ave (94301-2012)
PHONE..................................650 687-3800
Peter Bell, Genl Pt
EMP: 152
Web: www.hcp.com
SIC: 6799 Venture capital companies
PA: Highland Capital Partners Llc
1 Broadway Ste 16
Cambridge MA

(P-9520)
IDEALAB HOLDINGS LLC (PA)
130 W Union St (91103-3628)
PHONE..................................626 585-6900
Brent Novak, *
Marcia Goodstein, *
Craig Chrisney, *
Kristen Ding, *
EMP: 626 EST: 1996
SALES (est): 146.11MM
SALES (corp-wide): 146.11MM Privately Held
Web: www.idealab.com
SIC: 6799 5045 5734 Venture capital companies; Computer software; Computer software and accessories

(P-9521)
IMPERIAL CAPITAL GROUP LLC (PA)
2000 Avenue Of The Stars Ste 900s (90067-4700)
PHONE..................................310 246-3700
Lenny Bianco, Sr VP
EMP: 70 EST: 1989
SQ FT: 14,909
SALES (est): 12.84MM Privately Held
Web: www.imperialcapital.com
SIC: 6799 Investors, nec

(P-9522)
INTREPID INV BANKERS LLC
11755 Wilshire Blvd Ste 2200 (90025-1567)
PHONE..................................310 478-9000
Ed Bagdasarian, CEO
EMP: 5079 EST: 2010
SALES (est): 10.45MM Privately Held
Web: www.intrepidib.com
SIC: 6799 Investors, nec
HQ: Mufg Americas Holdings Corporation
1251 Ave Of The Americas
New York NY
212 782-6800

(P-9523)
INVENTURE CAPITAL CORPORATION (PA)
Also Called: Tala
429 Santa Monica Blvd Ste 450 (90401-3455)
PHONE..................................213 262-6903
Shivani B Siroya, CEO
EMP: 542 EST: 2014
SALES (est): 70.33MM
SALES (corp-wide): 70.33MM Privately Held

6799 - Investors, Nec (P-9524)

Web: www.tala.co
SIC: 6799 Venture capital companies

(P-9524)
JMG INVESTMENTS INC
23041 Hatteras St (91367-4236)
PHONE..................................818 519-0670
EMP: 60 EST: 2017
SALES (est): 4.51MM Privately Held
Web: www.harmonyplace.com
SIC: 6799 Investors, nec

(P-9525)
KINGFISH GROUP INC
601 California St Ste 1250 (94108-2817)
PHONE..................................650 980-0200
Christian Dubiel, Pr
EMP: 61 EST: 2008
SALES (est): 1.48MM Privately Held
Web: www.kingfishgroup.com
SIC: 6799 Venture capital companies

(P-9526)
LD ACQUISITION COMPANY 16 LLC
400 Continental Blvd Ste 500 (90245-5076)
PHONE..................................310 294-8160
Tim Brazy, CEO
George Doyle, *
Dan Parsons, *
Josef Bobek, *
EMP: 99 EST: 2017
SALES (est): 3.79MM Privately Held
SIC: 6799 Investors, nec

(P-9527)
LIFE SCIENCE ANGELS INC
1230 Bordeaux Dr (94089-1202)
PHONE..................................408 541-1152
Dorcy Kaplan, CEO
EMP: 68 EST: 2012
SALES (est): 1.24MM Privately Held
Web: www.lifescienceangels.com
SIC: 6799 Investors, nec

(P-9528)
M & H REALTY PARTNERS LP
353 Sacramento St Fl 21 (94111-3620)
PHONE..................................415 693-9000
EMP: 70
SALES (est): 4.2MM Privately Held
SIC: 6799 Real estate investors, except property operators

(P-9529)
MAKENA CAPITAL MANAGEMENT LLC
2755 Sand Hill Rd Ste 200 (94025-7086)
PHONE..................................650 926-0510
William Miller, Prin
EMP: 97 EST: 2005
SALES (est): 10.11MM Privately Held
Web: www.makenacap.com
SIC: 6799 Investors, nec

(P-9530)
MARLIN EQUITY PARTNERS III LP (PA)
1301 Manhattan Ave (90254-3654)
PHONE..................................310 364-0100
David Mcgovern, Pt
Nick Kaiser, Managing Member
EMP: 181 EST: 2009
SALES (est): 41.94MM Privately Held
Web: www.marlinequity.com
SIC: 6799 Venture capital companies

(P-9531)
MATSUSHITA INTERNATIONAL CORP (PA)
1141 Via Callejon (92673-6230)
PHONE..................................949 498-1000
Hiroyuki Matsushita, Pr
EMP: 80 EST: 1990
SALES (est): 21.11MM Privately Held
SIC: 6799 3711 3714 Real estate investors, except property operators; Automobile assembly, including specialty automobiles; Motor vehicle parts and accessories

(P-9532)
MCMILLIN COMPANIES LLC (PA)
Also Called: McMillin Homes
2750 Womble Rd Ste 102 (92106-6114)
P.O. Box 21010 (92021-0980)
PHONE..................................619 477-4117
EMP: 80 EST: 1998
SALES (est): 33.68MM
SALES (corp-wide): 33.68MM Privately Held
Web: www.mcmillin.com
SIC: 6799 Real estate investors, except property operators

(P-9533)
MEDIMPACT HOLDINGS INC (PA)
10181 Scripps Gateway Ct (92131-5152)
PHONE..................................858 566-2727
EMP: 817 EST: 2010
SALES (est): 473.33MM Privately Held
Web: www.medimpact.com
SIC: 6799 Investors, nec

(P-9534)
MIRAMAR ACQUISITION CO LLC
Also Called: Rosewood Miramar Bch Montecito
1759 S Jameson Ln (93108-2925)
PHONE..................................805 900-8338
Rick J Caruso, Prin
EMP: 157 EST: 2015
SALES (est): 25.91MM Privately Held
Web: www.rosewoodhotels.com
SIC: 6799 Investors, nec

(P-9535)
MORGENTHLER MGT PRTNERS VI LLC
Also Called: Morgenthaler Ventures
2710 Sand Hill Rd Ste 100 (94025-7140)
PHONE..................................650 388-7600
Gary Morgenthaler, Brnch Mgr
EMP: 2023
SALES (corp-wide): 166.44MM Privately Held
Web: www.mpepartners.com
SIC: 6799 Venture capital companies
PA: Morgenthaler Management Partners Vi, Llc
600 Superior Ave E # 2500
Cleveland OH
216 416-7500

(P-9536)
MSR HOTELS & RESORTS INC
Also Called: Sheraton Inn Bakersfield
5101 California Ave Ste 204 (93309-1623)
PHONE..................................661 325-9700
Kole Siefken, Mgr
EMP: 125
SALES (corp-wide): 53.67B Publicly Held
Web: www.cnl.com
SIC: 6799 Investors, nec
HQ: Msr Hotels & Resorts, Inc.
450 S Orange Ave
Orlando FL
407 650-1000

(P-9537)
MSR HOTELS & RESORTS INC
Also Called: Embassy Suites- Santa Clara
2885 Lakeside Dr (95054-2805)
PHONE..................................408 496-6400
Teri Owens, Brnch Mgr
EMP: 125
SALES (corp-wide): 53.67B Publicly Held
Web: www.cnl.com
SIC: 6799 Investors, nec
HQ: Msr Hotels & Resorts, Inc.
450 S Orange Ave
Orlando FL
407 650-1000

(P-9538)
NATIONAL FINANCIAL SVCS LLC
1411 Chapin Ave (94010-4002)
PHONE..................................650 343-6775
James Stevenson, Prin
EMP: 957
SALES (corp-wide): 4.35B Privately Held
Web: www.mybrokerageinfo.com
SIC: 6799 Investors, nec
HQ: National Financial Services Llc
200 Seaport Blvd Ste 630
Boston MA
800 471-0382

(P-9539)
NAVITAS SEMICONDUCTOR CORP (PA)
3520 Challenger St (90503-1640)
PHONE..................................901 685-2865
Gene Sheridan, Ch Bd
Ron Shelton, Sr VP
Ranbir Singh, Ex VP
EMP: 165 EST: 2020
SALES (est): 37.94MM
SALES (corp-wide): 37.94MM Privately Held
Web: www.navitassemi.com
SIC: 6799 Investors, nec

(P-9540)
NEXUS CAPITAL MANAGEMENT LP
11100 Santa Monica Blvd (90025-3384)
PHONE..................................424 330-8820
EMP: 925 EST: 2016
SALES (est): 71MM Privately Held
Web: www.nexuslp.com
SIC: 6799 Investors, nec

(P-9541)
NIGHTDRAGON ACQUISITION CORP (PA)
101 2nd St Ste 1275 (94105-3628)
PHONE..................................510 306-7780
Morgan Kyauk, Corporate Secretary
David G Dewalt, Ch Bd
Mark Garrett, V Ch Bd
Steve Simonian, CFO
EMP: 79 EST: 2020
Web: www.ndac.com
SIC: 6799 Investors, nec

(P-9542)
NNN REALTY INVESTORS LLC
19700 Fairchild Ste 300 (92612-2515)
PHONE..................................714 667-8252
Jeffrey T Hanson, CIO
Todd A Mikles, *
EMP: 458 EST: 1998
SQ FT: 18,800
SALES (est): 13.35MM Privately Held

SIC: 6799 6531 Investors, nec; Real estate managers

(P-9543)
NOGALES INVESTORS LLC
9229 W Sunset Blvd Ste 900 (90069-3410)
PHONE..................................310 276-7439
Luis Nogales, Managing Member
EMP: 275 EST: 2001
SQ FT: 2,500
SALES (est): 368.87K Privately Held
SIC: 6799 Investors, nec
PA: Nogales Investors Management, Llc
9229 W Sunset Blvd # 900
Los Angeles CA

(P-9544)
NORWEST VENTURE PARTNERS VI LP
525 University Ave Ste 800 (94301-1922)
PHONE..................................650 289-2243
EMP: 60 EST: 2009
SALES (est): 9.7MM
SALES (corp-wide): 82.86B Publicly Held
Web: www.nvp.com
SIC: 6799 Venture capital companies
PA: Wells Fargo & Company
420 Montgomery St
San Francisco CA
866 249-3302

(P-9545)
NRLL LLC
Also Called: Land Disposition Company
1 Mauchly (92618-2305)
P.O. Box 15534 (92623-5534)
PHONE..................................949 768-7777
EMP: 360 EST: 1995
SQ FT: 18,000
SALES (est): 978.11K Privately Held
Web: www.landauction.com
SIC: 6799 Real estate investors, except property operators
PA: Nrp Holding Co., Inc.
1 Mauchly
Irvine CA

(P-9546)
OAK HILL CAPITAL MGT LLC
Also Called: Oak Hill Capital Partners
3000 Sand Hill Rd Bldg 2 (94025-7113)
PHONE..................................650 234-0500
EMP: 5020 EST: 2004
SALES (est): 8.43MM
SALES (corp-wide): 1.14B Privately Held
Web: www.oakhill.com
SIC: 6799 Venture capital companies
PA: Oak Hill Capital Partners, L.P.
65 E 55th St Fl 32
New York NY
212 527-8400

(P-9547)
OAKTREE CAPITAL MANAGEMENT LP
Also Called: Gfi Energy Group
11611 San Vicente Blvd Ste 710 (90049-5106)
PHONE..................................310 442-0542
EMP: 60
SALES (corp-wide): 69.06B Privately Held
Web: www.oaktreecapital.com
SIC: 6799 4911 Investors, nec; Electric power broker
HQ: Oaktree Capital Management, L.P.
333 S Grand Ave Fl 28
Los Angeles CA

PRODUCTS & SERVICES SECTION
6799 - Investors, Nec (P-9572)

(P-9548)
OTTS ASIA MOORER DEVON
Also Called: Newshire Investment
10015 Baring Cross St (90044-4511)
PHONE.................323 603-6959
Asia Otts, *Owner*
Devon Moorer, *Owner*
EMP: 105 EST: 2016
SALES (est): 2.11MM **Privately Held**
SIC: 6799 Investors, nec

(P-9549)
PARTHENON CAPITAL LLC
4 Embarcadero Ctr Ste 2500 (94111-4106)
PHONE.................415 913-3900
Robert Hood, *Prin*
EMP: 1041
SALES (corp-wide): 214.12MM **Privately Held**
Web: www.parthenoncapital.com
SIC: 6799 Venture capital companies
PA: Parthenon Capital, Llc
399 Boylston St Ste 28
Boston MA
617 960-4000

(P-9550)
PMC CAPITAL PARTNERS LLC
12243 Branford St (91352-1010)
PHONE.................818 896-1101
Michel Tamer, *Mng Pt*
EMP: 1000 EST: 2019
SALES (est): 34.54MM **Privately Held**
Web: www.pmcsg.com
SIC: 6799 Venture capital companies

(P-9551)
PROVIDENCE REST PARTNERS LLC
Also Called: Restaurant Investment
5955 Melrose Ave (90038-3623)
PHONE.................323 460-4170
EMP: 88 EST: 2004
SALES (est): 3.45MM **Privately Held**
Web: www.providencela.com
SIC: 6799 5963 Investors, nec; Food services, direct sales

(P-9552)
PYRAMID PEAK CORPORATION
1401 Avocado Ave Ste 709 (92660-8714)
PHONE.................949 769-8600
Cindy Ragsdale, *Pr*
EMP: 70 EST: 2002
SALES (est): 5.93MM **Privately Held**
SIC: 6799 Investors, nec

(P-9553)
QATALYST PARTNERS LP
1 Maritime Plz Ste 2400 (94111-3542)
PHONE.................415 844-7700
EMP: 74 EST: 2008
SALES (est): 4.95MM **Privately Held**
Web: www.qatalyst.com
SIC: 6799 Investors, nec

(P-9554)
REGENT LP (PA)
9720 Wilshire Blvd Fl 6 (90212-2025)
PHONE.................310 299-4100
Michael A Reinstein, *CEO*
Roxanna Sassanian, *CFO*
EMP: 85 EST: 2017
SALES (est): 2.19B
SALES (corp-wide): 2.19B **Privately Held**
Web: www.regentlp.com
SIC: 6799 Investors, nec

(P-9555)
RENEWCARE OF SCOTTSDALE INC
27101 Puerta Real Ste 450 (92691-8566)
PHONE.................949 487-9500
Puerta Albrechtson, *Prin*
EMP: 60 EST: 2014
SALES (est): 2.75MM
SALES (corp-wide): 3.03B **Publicly Held**
SIC: 6799 Investors, nec
PA: The Ensign Group Inc
29222 Rncho Vejo Rd Ste 1
San Juan Capistrano CA
949 487-9500

(P-9556)
ROLL PROPERTIES INTL INC
Also Called: Paramout Farms
13646 Highway 33 (93249-9719)
PHONE.................661 797-6500
Bill Bowers, *Mgr*
EMP: 121
SALES (corp-wide): 27.25MM **Privately Held**
SIC: 6799 Real estate investors, except property operators
PA: Roll Properties International, Inc.
11444 W Olympic Blvd # 10
Los Angeles CA
310 966-5700

(P-9557)
RUSTIC CANYON GROUP LLC
Also Called: Rustic Canyon Partners
1025 Westwood Blvd (90024-2902)
PHONE.................310 998-8000
Nate Redmond, *Managing Member*
David Travers, *
Renee Labran, *
John Staenberg, *
Michael Kim, *
EMP: 75 EST: 2000
SALES (est): 9.31MM **Privately Held**
Web: www.rusticcanyonrestaurant.com
SIC: 6799 Venture capital companies

(P-9558)
SABAL CAPITAL PARTNERS LLC
680 E Colorado Blvd Ste 350 (91101)
PHONE.................949 255-1007
Pat Jackson, *CEO*
EMP: 130 EST: 2015
SALES (est): 130.47K
SALES (corp-wide): 7.53B **Publicly Held**
Web: www.regions.com
SIC: 6799 Investors, nec
HQ: Regions Bank
1900 5th Ave N Ste 2264
Birmingham AL
205 264-5523

(P-9559)
SAINTS MANAGEMENT LLC (PA)
475 Sansome St Ste 1850 (94111-3131)
PHONE.................415 773-2080
David Quinlivian, *Managing Member*
Lilian Shackelford Murray, *Managing Member*
EMP: 695 EST: 2004
SALES (est): 67.45MM
SALES (corp-wide): 67.45MM **Privately Held**
SIC: 6799 Venture capital companies

(P-9560)
SEQUOIA CAPITAL OPERATIONS LLC (PA)
Also Called: Sequoia Capital
2800 Sand Hill Rd Ste 101 (94025-7079)
PHONE.................650 854-3927
Donald Valentine, *Managing Member*
Gordon W Russell, *
Pierre Lamond, *
Mark Stevens, *
EMP: 75 EST: 1963
SQ FT: 6,000
SALES (est): 57.85MM
SALES (corp-wide): 57.85MM **Privately Held**
Web: www.sequoiacap.com
SIC: 6799 Venture capital companies

(P-9561)
SERENT CAPITAL LLC
44 Montgomery St Ste 3450 (94104-4819)
PHONE.................415 343-1050
Mark Shang, *CFO*
EMP: 69 EST: 2016
SALES (est): 4.58MM **Privately Held**
Web: www.serentcapital.com
SIC: 6799 Investors, nec

(P-9562)
SFIII LAKE LLC
260 California St # 1100 (94111-4396)
PHONE.................415 395-9701
Christopher Peatross, *Prin*
Olga Ornelas, *
EMP: 75 EST: 2019
SALES (est): 3.46MM **Privately Held**
SIC: 6799 Investors, nec

(P-9563)
SOLIS CAPITAL PARTNERS LLC
3371 Calle Tres Vistas Ste 100 (92024-6679)
PHONE.................760 309-9436
Daniel J Lubeck, *Brnch Mgr*
EMP: 86
SALES (corp-wide): 9.68MM **Privately Held**
Web: www.soliscapital.com
SIC: 6799 Venture capital companies
PA: Solis Capital Partners, Llc
23 Corporate Plaza Dr # 215
Newport Beach CA
949 296-2440

(P-9564)
SPECTRA SERVICES ACQUISITION L
1646 N California Blvd Ste 342 (94596-4124)
PHONE.................510 734-8394
EMP: 406 EST: 2019
SALES (est): 13.33MM **Privately Held**
SIC: 6799 Investors, nec

(P-9565)
STARWOOD CAPITAL GROUP LLC
100 Pine St Ste 3000 (94111-5216)
PHONE.................415 247-1220
Mark Davison, *Mgr*
EMP: 66
Web: www.starwoodcapital.com
SIC: 6799 Investors, nec
PA: Starwood Capital Group, L.L.C.
2340 Collins Ave
Miami Beach FL

(P-9566)
STONECALIBRE LLC (PA)
2049 Century Park E Ste 2550 (90067-3110)
PHONE.................310 774-0014
Brian Wall, *Pr*
EMP: 100 EST: 2012
SALES (est): 61.82MM **Privately Held**
Web: www.stonecalibre.com
SIC: 6799 Investors, nec

(P-9567)
SUNSTONE PARTNERS LLC
Also Called: Sunstone Partners
400 S El Camino Real Ste 300 (94402)
PHONE.................650 289-4400
Scott Hammack, *Operating Partner*
Jeff Rich, *Operating Partner*
Jennifer Gunn, *
EMP: 83 EST: 2004
SALES (est): 8.98MM **Privately Held**
Web: www.sunstonepartners.com
SIC: 6799 Venture capital companies

(P-9568)
SUNSTONE PARTNERS MGT LLC
Also Called: Sunstone Partners
400 S El Camino Real Ste 300 (94402)
PHONE.................650 289-4400
Gus Alberelli, *
John Moragne, *
EMP: 65 EST: 2015
SALES (est): 4.29MM **Privately Held**
Web: www.sunstonepartners.com
SIC: 6799 Venture capital companies

(P-9569)
SWANDER PACE CAPITAL LLC (PA)
101 Mission St Ste 1900 (94105-1726)
PHONE.................415 477-8500
Andrew Richards, *CEO*
Heather Fraser, *
Virginia Calvo, *CCO*
Tyler Matlock, *
Alex Litt, *
EMP: 567 EST: 1996
SQ FT: 5,000
SALES (est): 50.18MM
SALES (corp-wide): 50.18MM **Privately Held**
Web: www.spcap.com
SIC: 6799 Venture capital companies

(P-9570)
SWIFT REAL ESTATE PARTNERS LLC
260 California St Ste 1100 (94111-4322)
PHONE.................415 395-9701
Douglas D Abbey, *Ch*
EMP: 77 EST: 2015
SALES (est): 11.67MM **Privately Held**
Web: www.swiftrp.com
SIC: 6799 Real estate investors, except property operators

(P-9571)
TAPETECH TOOL COMPANY
Also Called: Tapetech Tool Company
7360 Convoy Ct (92111-1110)
PHONE.................858 268-0656
EMP: 633
SALES (corp-wide): 5.33B **Publicly Held**
Web: www.amestools.com
SIC: 6799 Investors, nec
HQ: Ames Tools Corporation
1327 Northbrook Pkwy # 400
Suwanee GA

(P-9572)
TCG CAPITAL MANAGEMENT LP
12180 Millennium Ste 500 (90094-2948)
PHONE.................310 633-2900
Peter Chernin, *CEO*
EMP: 135 EST: 2018

6799 - Investors, Nec (P-9573)

SALES (est): 9.86MM **Privately Held**
SIC: **6799** Investors, nec

(P-9573)
TENNENBAUM CAPITL PARTNERS LLC (HQ)
Also Called: T C P
2951 28th St Ste 1000 (90405-2993)
PHONE.................310 566-1000
Lee Landrum, *Mng Pt*
Michael Leitner, *
Rajneesh Vig, *
Howard Levkowitz, *
Philip Tseng, *
EMP: 70 EST: 1999
SQ FT: 15,850
SALES (est): 63.56MM **Publicly Held**
SIC: **6799** Venture capital companies
PA: Blackrock, Inc.
50 Hudson Yards
New York NY

(P-9574)
TRANSOM CAPITAL GROUP LLC (PA)
10990 Wilshire Blvd Ste 440 (90024-3927)
PHONE.................424 293-2818
Ken Firtel, *Managing Member*
Justin Gilson, *VP*
Nathan Dastic, *CFO*
EMP: 64 EST: 2007
SALES (est): 1.32B
SALES (corp-wide): 1.32B **Privately Held**
Web: www.transomcap.com
SIC: **6799** 5112 5943 3951 Investors, nec; Pens and/or pencils; Writing supplies; Fountain pens and fountain pen desk sets

(P-9575)
TRUAMERICA MULTIFAMILY LLC
Also Called: Solis FL Owner
10100 Santa Monica Blvd Ste 400 (90067-4002)
PHONE.................424 325-2750
EMP: 73 EST: 2013
SALES (est): 11.23MM **Privately Held**
Web: www.truamerica.com
SIC: **6799** Investors, nec

(P-9576)
USA ENTERPRISE INC
9777 Wilshire Blvd Ste 400 (90212-1910)
PHONE.................310 750-4246
Ahmed Sharif, *CEO*
EMP: 350 EST: 1999
SALES (est): 24.01MM **Privately Held**
Web: www.usaenterpriseinc.com
SIC: **6799** Real estate investors, except property operators

(P-9577)
VANTAGEPOINT MANAGEMENT INC (PA)
Also Called: Vantagepoint Capital Partners
1505 E Valley Rd Ste E (93108-2155)
PHONE.................650 866-3100
EMP: 65 EST: 1996
SALES (est): 7.27MM **Privately Held**
Web: www.vpcp.com
SIC: **6799** Venture capital companies

(P-9578)
WEDGEWOOD INC (PA)
2015 Manhattan Beach Blvd Ste 100 (90278-1230)
PHONE.................310 640-3070
Gregory L Geiser, *CEO*
David Wehrly, *
Michele Tasker, *

EMP: 81 EST: 1985
SQ FT: 3,200
SALES (est): 147.22MM
SALES (corp-wide): 147.22MM **Privately Held**
Web: www.wedgewood-inc.com
SIC: **6799** Real estate investors, except property operators

(P-9579)
WESTCORE DELTA VENTURE LLC
Also Called: Westcore Croydon
4350 La Jolla Village Dr Ste 900 (92122-1243)
P.O. Box 844405 (90084-4405)
PHONE.................858 625-4100
Don Ankeny, *CEO*
Marc Brutten, *Ch Bd*
EMP: 60 EST: 2013
SQ FT: 14,000
SALES (est): 2.44MM **Privately Held**
SIC: **6799** Real estate investors, except property operators

(P-9580)
WESTERN MILLING LLC (HQ)
Also Called: O.H. Kruse Grain and Milling
31120 West St (93227)
P.O. Box 1029 (93227-1029)
PHONE.................559 302-1000
Kevin Kruse, *CEO*
Kevin Kruse, *Managing Member*
Phil Shanon, *
Bob Berczynski, *
Ejnar Knudsen, *
▼ EMP: 243 EST: 2000
SALES (est): 587.31MM
SALES (corp-wide): 587.31MM **Privately Held**
Web: www.westernmilling.com
SIC: **6799** 5191 6221 Real estate investors, except property operators; Animal feeds; Commodity dealers, contracts
PA: Kruse Investment Company, Inc.
31120 W St
Goshen CA
559 302-1000

(P-9581)
WESTPORT CAPITAL PARTNERS LLC
2121 Rosecrans Ave Ste 4325 (90245-4744)
PHONE.................310 294-1234
Russel S Bernard, *Brnch Mgr*
EMP: 66
Web: www.westportcp.com
SIC: **6799** Investors, nec
PA: Westport Capital Partners Llc
300 Atlantic St Ste 110
Stamford CT

(P-9582)
WINDJMMER CPITL INVSTORS III L
Also Called: Westwind Equity Investors
610 Newport Center Dr Ste 1100 (92660)
PHONE.................949 706-9989
J Derek Watson, *
Mike Wattles, *
Jeff Miehe, *
Matt Anderson, *
EMP: 724 EST: 1990
SALES (est): 25.65MM **Privately Held**
Web: www.windjammercapital.com
SIC: **6799** Investors, nec

(P-9583)
WINDJMMER CPITL INVSTORS IV LP
610 Newport Center Dr Ste 1100 (92660)
PHONE.................919 706-9989
Bill Herkamp, *Pt*
EMP: 450 EST: 2011
SALES (est): 16.68MM **Privately Held**
Web: www.windjammercapital.com
SIC: **6799** Investors, nec

(P-9584)
XOJET SALES LLC
2000 Sierra Point Pkwy Ste 200 (94005-1846)
PHONE.................877 599-6538
EMP: 126 EST: 2018
SALES (est): 2.15MM **Privately Held**
Web: www.flyxo.com
SIC: **6799** Investors, nec

7011 Hotels And Motels

(P-9585)
1260 BB PROPERTY LLC
Also Called: Four Ssons Rsort Santa Barbara
1260 Channel Dr (93108-2805)
PHONE.................805 969-2261
H Ty Warner, *CEO*
▲ EMP: 500 EST: 1986
SALES (est): 58.51MM
SALES (corp-wide): 140.91MM **Privately Held**
SIC: **7011** Resort hotel
HQ: Fsb Cal Corp.
280 Chestnut Ave
Westmont IL
630 920-1515

(P-9586)
1651 TIBURON HOTEL LLC
Also Called: Lodge At Tiburon
1651 Tiburon Blvd (94920-2511)
PHONE.................401 946-4600
EMP: 80 EST: 2019
SALES (est): 3.57MM **Privately Held**
Web: www.lodgeattiburon.com
SIC: **7011** Hotels

(P-9587)
1835 COLUMBIA STREET LP
Also Called: Porto Vista Hotel
1835 Columbia St (92101-2505)
PHONE.................619 564-3993
Moe Siry, *Pt*
EMP: 80 EST: 1992
SALES (est): 5MM **Privately Held**
Web: www.portovistasd.com
SIC: **7011** Hotels

(P-9588)
1855 S HBR BLVD DRV HLDNGS LLC
Also Called: Sheraton Pk Ht At Anaheim Rsort
1855 S Harbor Blvd (92802-3509)
PHONE.................714 750-1811
Kunthea Hang, *Prin*
Tony Bruno, *
Ian Gee, *
EMP: 250 EST: 2012
SALES (est): 4.68MM **Privately Held**
Web: four-points.marriott.com
SIC: **7011** Hotels

(P-9589)
23627 CALABASAS ROAD LLC
Also Called: Anza A Calabasas Hotel, The
23627 Calabasas Rd (91302-1502)

PHONE.................818 222-5300
Mona Rigdon, *Prin*
James Mccrimmon, *Prin*
EMP: 65 EST: 2016
SALES (est): 2.19MM **Privately Held**
SIC: **7011** Hotels

(P-9590)
417 STOCKTON ST LLC
1180 S Beverly Dr Ste 508 (90035-1157)
PHONE.................323 327-9656
Jim Ciki, *Dir Fin*
EMP: 60 EST: 2018
SALES (est): 816.36K **Privately Held**
SIC: **7011** Hotels and motels

(P-9591)
4290 EL CAMINO PROPERTIES LP
Also Called: Cabana Hotel
4290 El Camino Real (94306-4404)
PHONE.................650 857-0787
Bhupendra B Patel, *Pt*
EMP: 146 EST: 1996
SALES (est): 5.4MM **Privately Held**
Web: www.cabanapaloalto.com
SIC: **7011** Hotels

(P-9592)
48123 CA INVESTORS LLC
Also Called: Ventana Inn & Spa
48123 Highway 1 (93920-9538)
PHONE.................831 667-2331
Kent L Colwell, *Managing Member*
John D Benzie, *
EMP: 152 EST: 1975
SALES (est): 11.16MM **Privately Held**
Web: www.ventanabigsur.com
SIC: **7011** 5812 Bed and breakfast inn; Eating places

(P-9593)
51ST ST & 8TH AVE CORP
Also Called: Loews Coronado Bay Resort
4000 Coronado Bay Rd (92118-3290)
PHONE.................619 424-4000
Johnathan M Tish, *CEO*
▲ EMP: 206 EST: 1994
SALES (est): 25.08MM **Privately Held**
Web: www.loewshotels.com
SIC: **7011** Hotels

(P-9594)
550 FLOWER ST OPERATIONS LLC
Also Called: Delphi Downtown La, The
550 S Flower St (90071-2501)
PHONE.................213 892-8080
EMP: 200 EST: 2002
SQ FT: 172,197
SALES (est): 10.59MM **Privately Held**
SIC: **7011** 5812 5813 Hotels; Eating places; Drinking places

(P-9595)
6417 SELMA HOTEL LLC
Also Called: Dream Hollywood
6417 Selma Ave (90028-7310)
PHONE.................323 844-6417
Richard Heyman, *Managing Member*
EMP: 250 EST: 2017
SALES (est): 15.12MM **Privately Held**
Web: www.dreamhotels.com
SIC: **7011** Hotels

(P-9596)
8110 AERO HOLDING LLC
Also Called: Sheraton
8110 Aero Dr (92123-1715)

PRODUCTS & SERVICES SECTION

7011 - Hotels And Motels (P-9618)

PHONE..................................858 277-8888
Lucy Burni, *Managing Member*
Nabih Geha, *
EMP: 210 EST: 2019
SALES (est): 7.99MM **Privately Held**
Web: www.fourpointssandiegohotel.com
SIC: 7011 5813 5812 Hotels and motels;
  Drinking places; Eating places

(P-9597)
901 WEST OLYMPIC BLVD LTD PRTN
Also Called: Residence Inn By Marriott
901 W Olympic Blvd (90015-1327)
PHONE..................................347 992-5707
Greg Steinhauer, *Pt*
Homer Williams, *Pt*
EMP: 110 EST: 2011
SQ FT: 286,000
SALES (est): 4.87MM **Privately Held**
Web: residence-inn.marriott.com
SIC: 7011 Hotels and motels

(P-9598)
ACCOR SERVICES US LLC (HQ)
Also Called: Fairmont Hotel
950 Mason St (94108-6000)
PHONE..................................415 772-5000
◆ EMP: 1000 EST: 2007
SQ FT: 2,100
SALES (est): 770.31MM
SALES (corp-wide): 713.02MM **Privately Held**
Web: www.fairmont.com
SIC: 7011 Hotels
PA: Accor
  82 Rue Henry Farman
  Issy Les Moulineaux
  146429193

(P-9599)
AGUA CLNTE BAND CHILLA INDIANS
Also Called: Agua Caliente Casino & Resort
32250 Bob Hope Dr (92270-2704)
PHONE..................................760 321-2000
Ken Kettler, *Brnch Mgr*
EMP: 1000
SALES (corp-wide): 83.82MM **Privately Held**
Web: www.aguacalientecasinos.com
SIC: 7011 Casino hotel
PA: Agua Caliente Band Of Cahuilla
  Indians
  5401 Dinah Shore Dr
  Palm Springs CA
  760 699-6800

(P-9600)
AGUA CLNTE BAND CHILLA INDIANS
Also Called: Spa Resort Casino
401 E Amado Rd (92262-6403)
PHONE..................................800 854-1279
EMP: 462
SALES (corp-wide): 83.82MM **Privately Held**
Web: www.aguacalientecasinos.com
SIC: 7011 7991 Casino hotel; Spas
PA: Agua Caliente Band Of Cahuilla
  Indians
  5401 Dinah Shore Dr
  Palm Springs CA
  760 699-6800

(P-9601)
AIRPORT BLVD HOTELS LLC
Also Called: Crowne Plaza San Francisco Int
1177 Airport Blvd (94010-1909)
PHONE..................................650 342-9200
EMP: 140
SIC: 7011 Hotels and motels

(P-9602)
ALOFT HT SAN FRANCISCO ARPRT
Also Called: Aloft
401 E Millbrae Ave (94030-3111)
PHONE..................................650 443-5500
Jason Kwan, *Prin*
EMP: 60 EST: 2018
SALES (est): 1.84MM **Privately Held**
Web: www.aloftsanfranciscoairport.com
SIC: 7011 Hotels

(P-9603)
AMENITIES DEVELOPMENT CO
Also Called: Ramada Inn
1089 Santa Anita Ave (91733-3864)
PHONE..................................626 350-9588
Judy Shieh, *Prin*
EMP: 112
SALES (corp-wide): 946.93K **Privately Held**
Web: www.wyndhamhotels.com
SIC: 7011 Hotels and motels
PA: Amenities Development Co.
  401 E Valley Blvd Ste 200
  San Gabriel CA
  626 571-6843

(P-9604)
AMERICAN KOYU CORPORATION
1733 S Anaheim Blvd (92805-6518)
P.O. Box 1145 (92878-1145)
PHONE..................................626 793-0669
Yoichi Erikawa, *Pr*
EMP: 150 EST: 2002
SALES (est): 19.24MM **Privately Held**
Web: koyucorp.jimdofree.com
SIC: 7011 Hotels

(P-9605)
AMERICAN PROPERTY MANAGEMENT
Also Called: Pleasanton Hilton Hotel
7050 Johnson Dr (94588-3328)
PHONE..................................925 463-8000
Han-ching Lin, *Pr*
Hui-ying Chou, *VP*
EMP: 143 EST: 1985
SQ FT: 191,112
SALES (est): 3.01MM **Privately Held**
SIC: 7011 5813 5812 Resort hotel; Drinking
  places; Eating places

(P-9606)
AMERICAN PRPRTY-MNAGEMENT CORP
Also Called: U. S. Grant Hotel
326 Broadway (92101-4812)
PHONE..................................619 232-3121
John Gallegon, *Mgr*
EMP: 1548
SALES (corp-wide): 74.7MM **Privately Held**
Web: www.wyndhamhotels.com
SIC: 7011 Hotels
PA: American Property-Management
  Corporation
  8910 University Center Ln # 100
  San Diego CA
  858 964-5500

(P-9607)
ANABELLE HOTEL INC
2011 W Olive Ave (91506-2641)
PHONE..................................818 845-7800
Tony Garibian, *Owner*
EMP: 78 EST: 2000
SALES (est): 323.99K **Privately Held**
Web: www.coasthotels.com
SIC: 7011 Hotels

(P-9608)
ANAHEIM - 1855 S HBR BLVD OWNE
Also Called: Sheraton
1855 S Harbor Blvd (92802-3509)
PHONE..................................714 750-1811
Ian Gee, *Prin*
EMP: 99 EST: 2019
SALES (est): 2.57MM **Privately Held**
Web: four-points.marriott.com
SIC: 7011 Hotels

(P-9609)
ANAHEIM CA LLC
Also Called: Doubltree Ht Anhim-Orange Cnty
100 The City Dr S (92868-3204)
PHONE..................................714 634-4500
Denise Pflum, *Mgr*
EMP: 65 EST: 2011
SALES (est): 6.33MM **Privately Held**
Web: www.hilton.com
SIC: 7011 Hotels and motels

(P-9610)
ANAHEIM PARK HOTEL
Also Called: Wyndham Hotels & Resorts
222 W Houston Ave (92832-3453)
PHONE..................................714 992-1700
Fred Menoufi, *Pt*
EMP: 197 EST: 1989
SQ FT: 174,123
SALES (est): 1.53MM **Privately Held**
Web: www.wyndhamhotels.com
SIC: 7011 YWCA/YWHA hotel

(P-9611)
ANAHEIM PLAZA HOTEL INC
Also Called: Anaheim Hotel, The
1700 S Harbor Blvd (92802-2316)
PHONE..................................714 772-5900
Saroj Patel, *CEO*
Saroj Patel, *Pr*
Rajni Patel, *VP*
EMP: 96 EST: 1961
SQ FT: 5,600
SALES (est): 8.99MM **Privately Held**
Web: www.theanaheimhotel.com
SIC: 7011 5812 5813 Motels; Eating places;
  Drinking places

(P-9612)
ANDAZ WEST HOLLYWOOD
8401 W Sunset Blvd (90069-1909)
PHONE..................................323 656-1234
Sulynn Jew, *Prin*
EMP: 87 EST: 2010
SALES (est): 19.21MM **Publicly Held**
Web: westhollywood.andaz.hyatt.com
SIC: 7011 Resort hotel
HQ: Hyatt Corporation
  250 Vesey St Fl 15
  New York NY
  312 750-1234

(P-9613)
ART PICCADILLY SHAW LLC
Also Called: Piccadilly Inn Airport
5115 E Mckinley Ave (93727-2033)
PHONE..................................559 375-7760
Kathy Bell, *Brnch Mgr*
EMP: 142
SALES (corp-wide): 8.84MM **Privately Held**
SIC: 7011 5813 5812 Hotels; Drinking places
  ; Eating places
PA: Art Piccadilly Shaw Llc
  2305 W Shaw Ave
  Fresno CA
  559 348-5520

(P-9614)
ART PICCADILLY SHAW LLC
Piccadilly Inn-University
4961 N Cedar Ave (93726-1062)
PHONE..................................559 224-4200
Theresa Cross, *Brnch Mgr*
EMP: 130
SALES (corp-wide): 8.84MM **Privately Held**
Web: www.hotel-piccadilly.com
SIC: 7011 Hotels
PA: Art Piccadilly Shaw Llc
  2305 W Shaw Ave
  Fresno CA
  559 348-5520

(P-9615)
ARVEE BROS INC
Also Called: Millwood Inn
1375 El Camino Real (94030-1410)
P.O. Box 970 (94030-0970)
PHONE..................................650 583-3935
Vijay R Patel, *Pr*
Reeta Patel, *VP*
EMP: 74 EST: 1953
SQ FT: 20,000
SALES (est): 1.62MM **Privately Held**
Web: www.millbrae.com
SIC: 7011 7389 Motels; Office facilities and
  secretarial service rental

(P-9616)
ASCOT HOTEL LP
Also Called: Hotel Angeleno
170 N Church Ln (90049-2044)
PHONE..................................310 476-6411
Mark Beccaria, *Pt*
EMP: 125 EST: 2008
SALES (est): 16.58MM **Privately Held**
Web: www.hotelangeleno.com
SIC: 7011 Hotels

(P-9617)
ASHFORD TRS FREMONT LLC
Also Called: Fremont Marriott Silicon Vly
46100 Landing Pkwy (94538-6437)
PHONE..................................510 413-3700
Deric Eubanks, *Pr*
EMP: 130 EST: 2019
SALES (est): 5.04MM **Privately Held**
Web: www.marriott.com
SIC: 7011 Hotels

(P-9618)
ASHFORD TRS SEVEN LLC
Also Called: Residence Inn Palm Desert
38305 Cook St (92211-1794)
PHONE..................................760 776-0050
EMP: 91
SQ FT: 80,290
SALES (corp-wide): 445.85K **Privately Held**
Web: courtyard.marriott.com
SIC: 7011 Hotels and motels
PA: Ashford Trs Seven Llc
  74895 Frank Sinatra Dr
  Palm Desert CA
  760 776-4150

7011 - Hotels And Motels (P-9619)

(P-9619)
ATLAS HOTELS INC
Also Called: Town and Country
500 Hotel Cir N (92108-3005)
PHONE..................619 291-2232
EMP: 1023
SIC: **7011** 5812 5813 Hotels; Eating places; Cocktail lounge

(P-9620)
ATRIUM FINANCE I LP
Also Called: Holiday Inn
300 J St (95814-2210)
PHONE..................916 446-0100
Liz Tavernese, *Genl Pt*
EMP: 4653 EST: 2005
SALES (est): 3.52MM **Privately Held**
Web: www.holidayinn.com
SIC: **7011** Hotels and motels
HQ: Atrium Hospitality Lp
    12735 Morris Road Ext # 400
    Alpharetta GA
    678 762-0005

(P-9621)
ATRIUM PLAZA LLC
Also Called: San Mateo Marriott
1770 S Amphlett Blvd (94402-2708)
PHONE..................650 653-6000
Neil Korsgaard, *Mgr*
EMP: 79 EST: 2000
SALES (est): 11.77MM **Privately Held**
SIC: **7011** Hotels

(P-9622)
AVIARA FSRC ASSOCIATES LIMITED
7100 Aviara Resort Dr (92011-4908)
PHONE..................760 603-6800
Robert Cima, *Genl Mgr*
Aviara Resort Club, *
EMP: 1200 EST: 1995
SALES (est): 21.49MM **Publicly Held**
SIC: **7011** Resort hotel
HQ: Aviara Resort Associates Limited Partnership, A California Limited Partnership
    7100 Aviara Resort Dr
    Carlsbad CA

(P-9623)
AVR SAN JOSE DOWNTOWN HT LLC
Also Called: AC Hotel San Jose Downtown
350 W Santa Clara St (95113-1501)
PHONE..................408 924-0900
Mona Rigdon, *Prin*
Allan Rose, *
EMP: 60 EST: 2019
SALES (est): 2.29MM **Privately Held**
Web: www.marriott.com
SIC: **7011** Hotels

(P-9624)
AYRES - PASO ROBLES LP
Also Called: Allegretto Vineyard Resort
2700 Buena Vista Dr (93446-9530)
PHONE..................714 850-0409
EMP: 120 EST: 2015
SALES (est): 6.88MM **Privately Held**
Web: www.allegrettovineyardresort.com
SIC: **7011** Hotels

(P-9625)
AYRES GROUP
Also Called: Ayres Suites Mission Viejo
28941 Los Alisos Blvd (92692-5934)
PHONE..................949 455-2545
Jeannie Flippin, *Dir*
EMP: 60
Web: www.ayreshotels.com
SIC: **7011** Hotels
PA: Ayres Group
    355 Bristol St
    Costa Mesa CA

(P-9626)
AYRES GROUP
Also Called: Ayres Hotel Manhattan Beach
14400 Hindry Ave (90250-6740)
PHONE..................310 220-6447
Ann Williams, *Mgr*
EMP: 93
SQ FT: 85,082
Web: www.ayreshotels.com
SIC: **7011** Hotels
PA: Ayres Group
    355 Bristol St
    Costa Mesa CA

(P-9627)
B H R OPERATIONS LLC
Also Called: Crown Plaza
777 Bellew Dr (95035-7900)
PHONE..................408 321-9500
Roy Escobar, *Managing Member*
Winnie Kwok, *
EMP: 4163 EST: 1987
SQ FT: 250,000
SALES (est): 2.3MM **Privately Held**
Web: www.crowneplaza.com
SIC: **7011** Hotels
HQ: Bristol Hotel & Resorts Inc.
    3 Ravinia Dr Ste 100
    Atlanta GA

(P-9628)
BAKERSFIELD HOSPITALITY LLC
6141 Knudsen Dr (93308-2904)
PHONE..................661 393-1277
Mahendra Patel, *Brnch Mgr*
EMP: 80
SALES (corp-wide): 234.48K **Privately Held**
SIC: **7011** Hotels and motels
PA: Bakersfield Hospitality Llc
    16609 Honeybee Dr
    Tustin CA

(P-9629)
BAKERSFIELD INN INC
Also Called: Marriott
801 Truxtun Ave (93301-4726)
PHONE..................661 323-1900
Bernard E Cooke, *Pr*
Vanessa Emo, *Dir*
EMP: 79 EST: 1979
SALES (est): 9.19MM **Privately Held**
Web: www.marriott.com
SIC: **7011** Hotels and motels

(P-9630)
BALDWIN HOSPITALITY LLC
Also Called: Courtyard By Marriott
14635 Baldwin Park Towne Ctr (91706-5548)
PHONE..................626 446-2988
Lina Mita, *Managing Member*
EMP: 80 EST: 1997
SALES (est): 2.53MM **Privately Held**
Web: courtyard.marriott.com
SIC: **7011** Hotels and motels

(P-9631)
BARONA RESORT & CASINO
1932 Wildcat Canyon Rd (92040-1553)
PHONE..................619 443-2300
Dean Allen, *Sr VP*
Linda Jordan, *Sr VP*
Nick Dillon, *Ex VP*
Troy Simpson, *Ex VP*
Rick Salinas, *Genl Mgr*
EMP: 3500 EST: 2005
SALES (est): 171.97MM **Privately Held**
Web: www.barona.com
SIC: **7011** Resort hotel

(P-9632)
BARTELL HOTELS
Also Called: Hilton San Diego Airport/Hrbr
1960 Harbor Island Dr (92101-1013)
PHONE..................619 291-6700
Luis Barrios, *Genl Mgr*
EMP: 100
SALES (corp-wide): 41.61MM **Privately Held**
Web: www.bartellhotels.com
SIC: **7011** Hotels
PA: Bartell Hotels, A California Limited Partnership
    4875 N Harbor Dr
    San Diego CA
    619 224-1556

(P-9633)
BAVARIAN LION COMPANY CAL (PA)
Also Called: Flamingo Resort Hotel
2777 4th St (95405-4795)
PHONE..................707 545-8530
Pierre Ehret, *Pr*
EMP: 200 EST: 1976
SQ FT: 32,000
SALES (est): 15.28MM
SALES (corp-wide): 15.28MM **Privately Held**
Web: www.montecitoheights.com
SIC: **7011** 7991 Resort hotel; Health club

(P-9634)
BAYVIEW PROPERTIES INC (PA)
Also Called: Best Western, The Beach Resort
2600 Sand Dunes Dr (93940-3838)
PHONE..................831 394-3321
Theodore Richter, *Pr*
EMP: 99 EST: 1986
SALES (est): 5.04MM
SALES (corp-wide): 5.04MM **Privately Held**
Web: www.bestwestern.com
SIC: **7011** Motels

(P-9635)
BCRA RESORT SERVICES INC
Also Called: Bacara Resorts and Spa
8301 Hollister Ave (93117-2474)
PHONE..................805 571-3176
EMP: 150
SIC: **7011** Hotels

(P-9636)
BEAR RIVER CASINO
Also Called: Bear River Casino Hotel
11 Bear Paws Way (95551-9684)
PHONE..................707 733-9644
John Mcginnis, *Asstg*
EMP: 238
Web: www.bearrivercasino.com
SIC: **7011** Casino hotel
PA: Bear River Casino
    27 Bear River Dr
    Loleta CA

(P-9637)
BEHRINGER HARVARD WILSHIRE BLV
Also Called: Hotel Palomar
10740 Wilshire Blvd (90024-4493)
PHONE..................310 475-8711
Ravi Sikand, *Pt*
EMP: 99 EST: 2006
SALES (est): 4.68MM **Privately Held**
Web: www.hotelpalomar-beverlyhills.com
SIC: **7011** 6531 Hotels; Real estate agents and managers

(P-9638)
BELVEDERE HOTEL PARTNERSHIP
Also Called: Peninsula Beverly Hill's
9882 Santa Monica Blvd (90212-1605)
PHONE..................310 551-2888
Ali Kasikci, *Mgr*
EMP: 442
SIC: **7011** 6512 5813 5812 Hotels; Nonresidential building operators; Drinking places; Eating places
PA: The Belvedere Hotel Partnership
    421 N Beverly Dr Ste 350
    Beverly Hills CA

(P-9639)
BELVEDERE PARTNERSHIP
Also Called: Peninsula Beverly Hills, The
9882 Santa Monica Blvd (90212-1605)
PHONE..................310 551-2888
Robert Zarnegan, *Pr*
▲ EMP: 400 EST: 2005
SALES (est): 25.24MM **Privately Held**
SIC: **7011** Bed and breakfast inn

(P-9640)
BENBOW VALLEY INVESTMENTS LLC
Also Called: Benbow Gifts
445 Lake Benbow Dr (95542-3616)
PHONE..................707 923-2124
John Porter, *Pt*
Jack Mac Donald, *Pt*
EMP: 61 EST: 1926
SALES (est): 8.53MM **Privately Held**
Web: www.benbowinn.com
SIC: **7011** 5812 5813 5947 Resort hotel; Eating places; Cocktail lounge; Gift shop

(P-9641)
BERKELEY
2086 Allston Way (94704-1430)
PHONE..................510 845-7300
Greg Maultin, *Genl Mgr*
EMP: 271 EST: 1998
SALES (est): 1.15MM **Privately Held**
Web: www.berkeley.edu
SIC: **7011** Hotels and motels

(P-9642)
BERKELEY DOWNTOWN HT OWNER LLC
Also Called: Residnce Inn By Mrriot Brkeley
2121 Center St (94704-1394)
PHONE..................510 982-2100
Bruce Carlton, *Managing Member*
EMP: 75 EST: 2021
SALES (est): 2.46MM **Privately Held**
Web: www.marriott.com
SIC: **7011** Hotel, franchised

(P-9643)
BEST REST MANAGEMENT INC
Also Called: Comfort Inn
1955 San Diego Ave (92110-2105)
PHONE..................619 543-1130
Victor Salem, *Pr*
EMP: 63 EST: 1989
SQ FT: 53,357

PRODUCTS & SERVICES SECTION

7011 - Hotels And Motels (P-9665)

SALES (est): 519.98K **Privately Held**
Web: www.choicehotels.com
SIC: **7011** Hotels and motels

(P-9644)
BEST WESTERN HOTEL TOMO
Also Called: Best Western
1800 Sutter St (94115-3220)
PHONE.................................415 921-4000
Sean Salera, *CFO*
EMP: 157 EST: 2007
SALES (est): 516.73K
SALES (corp-wide): 1.23MM **Privately Held**
Web: www.bestwestern.com
SIC: **7011** Hotels and motels
PA: Khp Iii Sf Sutter Llc
   1800 Sutter St
   San Francisco CA
   415 921-4000

(P-9645)
BEST WESTERN STOVALLS INN (PA)
Also Called: Anaheim Inn
1110 W Katella Ave (92802-2805)
PHONE.................................714 956-4430
James Stovall, *Pt*
Robert Stovall, *Pt*
Minta Pettis-stovall, *Pt*
Bill O'connell, *Pt*
EMP: 90 EST: 1966
SQ FT: 4,800
SALES (est): 22.46MM
SALES (corp-wide): 22.46MM **Privately Held**
Web: www.bestwestern.com
SIC: **7011** Hotels and motels

(P-9646)
BEVERLY HILLS COLLECTION
604 N Arden Dr (90210-3510)
PHONE.................................310 276-1022
EMP: 73 EST: 2018
SALES (est): 102.55K **Privately Held**
Web: www.thebeverlyhillscollection.com
SIC: **7011** Hotels

(P-9647)
BEVERLY HILLS LUXURY HOTEL LLC
1801 Century Park E Ste 1200 (90067-2301)
PHONE.................................310 274-9999
Kenneth Bordewick, *Managing Member*
EMP: 450 EST: 2002
SALES (est): 33.02MM **Privately Held**
SIC: **7011** Resort hotel

(P-9648)
BH PARTNERSHIP LP (PA)
Also Called: Bahia Resort Hotels
998 W Mission Bay Dr (92109-7803)
PHONE.................................858 539-7635
Anne L Evans, *Genl Pt*
William L Evans, *Pt*
Anthony Belefm, *Chief Human Resources Officer*
EMP: 300 EST: 1945
SALES (est): 58.24MM
SALES (corp-wide): 58.24MM **Privately Held**
Web: www.bahiahotel.com
SIC: **7011** 6531 5812 Resort hotel; Real estate managers; Eating places

(P-9649)
BHR OPERATIONS LLC
Also Called: Holiday Inn
495 Bay St (94133-1860)
PHONE.................................415 771-9000
Sheila Martin, *Genl Mgr*
EMP: 139
SALES (corp-wide): 1.19B **Privately Held**
Web: www.holidayinn.com
SIC: **7011** Hotels and motels
HQ: Bhr Operations, L.L.C.
   125 E John Carpenter Fwy
   Irving TX
   972 444-4900

(P-9650)
BHR OPERATIONS LLC
Also Called: Wyndham San Diego Bayside
1355 N Harbor Dr (92101-3321)
PHONE.................................619 232-3861
Joe Eustice, *Genl Mgr*
EMP: 139
SALES (corp-wide): 1.19B **Privately Held**
Web: www.wyndhamhotels.com
SIC: **7011** Hotels
HQ: Bhr Operations, L.L.C.
   125 E John Carpenter Fwy
   Irving TX
   972 444-4900

(P-9651)
BHR TRS TAHOE LLC
Also Called: Ritz-Carlton Lake Tahoe, The
13031 Ritz Carlton Highlands Ct (96161-4306)
PHONE.................................530 562-3045
Chris Stevens, *Asst Mgr*
EMP: 248 EST: 2018
SALES (est): 20.57MM
SALES (corp-wide): 669.59MM **Privately Held**
Web: www.ritzcarlton.com
SIC: **7011** Hotels
PA: Braemar Hotels & Resorts Inc.
   14185 Dallas Pkwy # 1100
   Dallas TX
   972 490-9600

(P-9652)
BISHOP PAIUTE GAMING CORP
Also Called: Paiute Palace Casino
2742 N Sierra Hwy (93514-2218)
P.O. Box 1325 (93515-1325)
PHONE.................................760 872-6005
Gloriana Bailey, *Pr*
EMP: 98 EST: 1995
SALES (est): 9.84MM **Privately Held**
Web: www.paiutegaming.com
SIC: **7011** Casino hotel

(P-9653)
BLUE LAKE CASINO
777 Casino Way Blue Lake (95525)
P.O. Box 1128 (95525-1128)
PHONE.................................707 668-5101
Eric Ramos, *Pr*
EMP: 81 EST: 2012
SALES (est): 6.03MM **Privately Held**
Web: www.bluelakecasino.com
SIC: **7011** Casino hotel

(P-9654)
BOREAL RIDGE CORPORATION
Also Called: Boreal Ski Area
19749 Boreal Ridge Rd (95728)
P.O. Box 39 (96160-0039)
PHONE.................................530 426-1012
John Cumming, *Pr*
Jodi Church,
EMP: 110 EST: 1964
SQ FT: 10,000
SALES (est): 11.55MM
SALES (corp-wide): 325.03MM **Privately Held**
Web: www.rideboreal.com
SIC: **7011** 7999 Ski lodge; Ski rental concession
PA: Powdr Corp.
   1794 Olympic Pkwy Ste 210
   Park City UT
   435 658-5500

(P-9655)
BOYKIN MGT CO LTD LBLTY CO
Also Called: Hampton Inn
3888 Greenwood St (92110-4412)
PHONE.................................619 299-6633
Tom Whelan, *Prin*
EMP: 69
SALES (corp-wide): 22.87MM **Privately Held**
Web: www.hilton.com
SIC: **7011** Hotels and motels
PA: Boykin Management Company Limited Liability Company
   8015 W Kenton Cir Ste 220
   Huntersville NC
   704 896-2880

(P-9656)
BOYKIN MGT CO LTD LBLTY CO
Also Called: Radisson Inn
200 Marina Blvd (94710-1608)
PHONE.................................510 548-7920
Neil Pasan, *Mgr*
EMP: 75
SALES (corp-wide): 22.87MM **Privately Held**
Web: www.boykin.com
SIC: **7011** 5812 5813 Hotels and motels; Eating places; Drinking places
PA: Boykin Management Company Limited Liability Company
   8015 W Kenton Cir Ste 220
   Huntersville NC
   704 896-2880

(P-9657)
BRAEMAR PARTNERSHIP
Also Called: Catamaran Resort Hotel
3999 Mission Blvd (92109-6959)
PHONE.................................858 488-1081
Robert Gleason, *CFO*
Anne L Evans, *Mgr*
EMP: 350 EST: 1959
SALES (est): 17.99MM **Privately Held**
Web: www.catamaranresort.com
SIC: **7011** 5812 5813 Resort hotel; American restaurant; Cocktail lounge

(P-9658)
BRE/JAPANTOWN OWNER LLC
Also Called: Hotel Kabuki
1625 Post St (94115-3603)
PHONE.................................415 922-3200
Craig Walterman, *Genl Mgr*
EMP: 100 EST: 2014
SALES (est): 9.81MM **Privately Held**
Web: www.sfmusictech.com
SIC: **7011** Hotels

(P-9659)
BRIDGE BAY RESORT & MARINA
Also Called: Bridge Bay Resort
10300 Bridge Bay Rd (96003-9419)
PHONE.................................530 275-3021
EMP: 75 EST: 2013
SALES (est): 11.87MM
SALES (corp-wide): 12.49MM **Privately Held**
Web: www.bridgebayhouseboats.com
SIC: **7011** Resort hotel
PA: Peloria Marinas Investors Llc
   2550 Via Tejon Ste 2b
   Palos Verdes Estates CA
   310 363-7775

(P-9660)
BRISAM LAX (DE) LLC
Also Called: Holiday Inn
9901 S La Cienega Blvd (90045-5915)
PHONE.................................310 649-5151
Steve Hostetter, *Genl Mgr*
EMP: 95 EST: 2007
SALES (est): 5.17MM **Privately Held**
Web: www.holidayinn.com
SIC: **7011** Hotels and motels

(P-9661)
BRISAN LLC
Also Called: Holiday Inn Fresno Downtown
1055 Van Ness Ave (93721-2006)
PHONE.................................559 233-6650
EMP: 89
Web: www.holidayinnfresno.com
SIC: **7011** Hotels and motels

(P-9662)
BROADMOOR HOTEL (PA)
Also Called: The Broadmoore
1499 Sutter St (94109-5417)
PHONE.................................415 776-7034
Irene Lieberman, *Pr*
◆ EMP: 75 EST: 1969
SALES (est): 4.75MM
SALES (corp-wide): 4.75MM **Privately Held**
Web: www.broadmoorsf.com
SIC: **7011** Resort hotel

(P-9663)
BROADMOOR HOTEL
Gaylord Suites
1465 65th St Apt 274 (94608-1168)
PHONE.................................415 673-8445
Tony Daviduskis, *Brnch Mgr*
EMP: 71
SQ FT: 85,619
SALES (corp-wide): 4.75MM **Privately Held**
Web: www.broadmoorsf.com
SIC: **7011** 6513 Resort hotel; Apartment hotel operation
PA: Broadmoor Hotel
   1499 Sutter St
   San Francisco CA
   415 776-7034

(P-9664)
BROADMOOR HOTEL
Also Called: Granada Hotel
1000 Sutter St (94109-5818)
PHONE.................................415 673-2511
EMP: 72
SALES (corp-wide): 4.75MM **Privately Held**
Web: www.broadmoorsf.com
SIC: **7011** Resort hotel
PA: Broadmoor Hotel
   1499 Sutter St
   San Francisco CA
   415 776-7034

(P-9665)
BUENA VISTA GAMING AUTHORITY
Also Called: Harrah's Northern California
4640 Coal Mine Rd (95640-9626)
PHONE.................................866 915-0777
Jc Rieger, *Genl Mgr*
EMP: 420 EST: 2019
SALES (est): 19.79MM **Privately Held**
SIC: **7011** Casino hotel

7011 - Hotels And Motels (P-9666)

(P-9666)
BURBANK PARTNERS LLC
Also Called: Courtyard By Marriott
15433 Ventura Blvd (91403-3003)
PHONE.....................................818 263-8704
EMP: 107 EST: 1968
SALES (est): 5.94MM **Privately Held**
Web: www.marriott.com
SIC: **7011** 5813 5812 7299 Hotels and motels; Cocktail lounge; Eating places; Banquet hall facilities

(P-9667)
BURTON WAY HOTELS LLC
Also Called: Four Seasons Hotels Limited
300 S Doheny Dr (90048-3704)
PHONE.....................................310 273-2222
Isadore Sharp, Ch
EMP: 92 EST: 2015
SALES (est): 16.56MM **Privately Held**
SIC: **7011** Hotels

(P-9668)
BURTON WAY HTELS LTD A CAL LTD
Also Called: Four Seasons Ht Westlake Vlg
2 Dole Dr (91362-7300)
PHONE.....................................818 575-3000
Robert Cima, Brnch Mgr
EMP: 215
SALES (corp-wide): 24.05MM **Privately Held**
SIC: **7011** Hotels
PA: Burton Way Hotels, Ltd., A California Limited Partnership
2029 Century Park E # 2200
Los Angeles CA
310 552-6623

(P-9669)
BURTON-WAY HOUSE LTD A CA
Also Called: Four Seasons Hotel
300 S Doheny Dr (90048-3704)
PHONE.....................................310 273-2222
Mehdi Efpekari, Genl Mgr
EMP: 215
SALES (corp-wide): 24.05MM **Privately Held**
SIC: **7011** 5812 Hotels; Eating places
PA: Burton Way Hotels, Ltd., A California Limited Partnership
2029 Century Park E # 2200
Los Angeles CA
310 552-6623

(P-9670)
BY THE BLUE SEA LLC
Also Called: Shutters On The Beach
1 Pico Blvd (90405-1063)
PHONE.....................................310 458-0030
Tim Dubois, Pr
Klaus Mennekes, *
EMP: 350 EST: 2001
SALES (est): 25.47MM **Privately Held**
Web: www.shuttersonthebeach.com
SIC: **7011** Hotels

(P-9671)
C N L HOTEL DEL PARTNERS LP
1500 Orange Ave (92118-2918)
PHONE.....................................619 522-8299
Todd Shallan, Pt
EMP: 81 EST: 2004
SALES (est): 912.91K **Privately Held**
Web: www.hoteldel.com
SIC: **7011** Resort hotel

(P-9672)
C W HOTELS LTD
Also Called: JW Marriott Le Merigot
1740 Ocean Ave (90401-3214)
PHONE.....................................310 395-9700
Damien Hirsch, Genl Mgr
EMP: 150
SALES (corp-wide): 23.2MM **Privately Held**
Web: jw-marriott.marriott.com
SIC: **7011** Hotels
PA: C W Hotels Ltd
740 Centre View Blvd
Crestview Hills KY
859 578-1100

(P-9673)
CABAZON BAND MISSION INDIANS
Fantasy Spring Resort Casino
84245 Indio Springs Dr (92203-3405)
PHONE.....................................760 342-5000
Jim Mccannon, Mgr
EMP: 520
Web: www.fantasyspringsresort.com
SIC: **7011** Casino hotel
PA: Cabazon Band Of Cahuilla Indians
84245 Indio Springs Dr
Indio CA

(P-9674)
CACHE CREEK CASINO RESORT
14455 State Highway 16 (95606-9707)
P.O. Box 65 (95606-0065)
PHONE.....................................530 796-3118
Leland Kinter, Prin
Mark Pirruccello, *
EMP: 2000 EST: 2007
SALES (est): 105.78MM **Privately Held**
Web: www.cachecreek.com
SIC: **7011** Casino hotel
PA: Yocha Dehe Wintun Nation, California
18960 County Rd 75 A
Brooks CA
530 796-3400

(P-9675)
CALHOT ILLINIOS LLC
Also Called: Ramada Inn
5250 W El Segundo Blvd (90250-4142)
PHONE.....................................310 536-9800
Fred Groth, Genl Mgr
Kairey Choi, Asst Mgr
EMP: 92 EST: 1990
SALES (est): 319.99K **Privately Held**
Web: www.wyndhamhotels.com
SIC: **7011** 5812 Hotels and motels; Eating places

(P-9676)
CALIFORNIA COMMERCE CLUB INC
Also Called: Commerce Casino
6131 Telegraph Rd (90040-2501)
PHONE.....................................323 721-2100
Haig Papaian, CEO
Ralph Wong, CAO*
Dante Oliveto, *
Harvey Ross, *
Deborah Payne, *
▲ EMP: 2600 EST: 1982
SQ FT: 350,000
SALES (est): 126.32MM **Privately Held**
Web: www.commercecasino.com
SIC: **7011** 5812 Casino hotel; Eating places

(P-9677)
CANTERBURY HOTEL CORP
Also Called: Wyndham Cntrbury At San Frncsc
750 Sutter St (94109-6417)
PHONE.....................................415 345-3200
Dean Lehr, Pr
Jon Lehr, *
Jacqueline W Lehr, *
Frederick T Smith, *
EMP: 91 EST: 1932
SQ FT: 98,410
SALES (est): 2.47MM **Privately Held**
Web: wyndham-canterbury-at-san-francisco-hotel.at-hotels.com
SIC: **7011** 5812 6531 Resort hotel; Eating places; Time-sharing real estate sales, leasing and rentals

(P-9678)
CAPITOL REGENCY LLC
Also Called: Hyatt Regency Sacramento
1209 L St (95814-3936)
PHONE.....................................916 443-1234
EMP: 360 EST: 1996
SALES (est): 24.84MM **Privately Held**
Web: www.hyatt.com
SIC: **7011** Hotels and motels

(P-9679)
CARLSBAD PROPERTIES INC
Also Called: Holiday Inn
850 Palomar Airport Rd (92011-4443)
PHONE.....................................760 438-7880
Andrew Warren, Pr
EMP: 67 EST: 1988
SALES (est): 10.09MM **Privately Held**
Web: www.carlsbadbytheseahotel.com
SIC: **7011** 5812 5813 7299 Resort hotel; Family restaurants; Bar (drinking places); Banquet hall facilities

(P-9680)
CARNEROS INN LLC
Also Called: Poumtjack Hotels
4048 Sonoma Hwy (94559-9745)
PHONE.....................................707 299-4880
EMP: 350 EST: 1998
SQ FT: 50,000
SALES (est): 40.18MM **Privately Held**
Web: www.carnerosresort.com
SIC: **7011** Resort hotel

(P-9681)
CARPENTERS SOUTHWEST ADM CORP (PA)
533 S Fremont Ave (90071-1706)
P.O. Box 17969 (90017-0969)
PHONE.....................................213 386-8590
Douglas Mccarron, CEO
EMP: 70 EST: 1982
SQ FT: 25,000
SALES (est): 45.94MM
SALES (corp-wide): 45.94MM **Privately Held**
Web: www.carpenterssw.org
SIC: **7011** Hotels and motels

(P-9682)
CARSON OPERATING COMPANY LLC
Also Called: Doubletree By Hilton Carson
2 Civic Plaza Dr (90745-2231)
PHONE.....................................310 830-9200
Greg Guthrie, Genl Mgr
Leroy Russell, *
EMP: 90 EST: 2015
SALES (est): 2.79MM **Privately Held**
Web: www.hilton.com
SIC: **7011** Hotels

(P-9683)
CASA MADRONA HOTEL AND SPA LLC
Also Called: Casa Madrona Hotel and Spa
801 Bridgeway (94965-2186)
PHONE.....................................415 332-0502
Brian Kelley, *
EMP: 1915 EST: 1951
SQ FT: 18,000
SALES (est): 9.29MM **Privately Held**
Web: www.casamadrona.com
SIC: **7011** 5812 Hotels; Eating places
PA: Olympus Real Estate Corp
5080 Spectrum Dr
Addison TX

(P-9684)
CASTLEHILL PROPERTIES INC
Also Called: Courtyard By Marriott Stockton
3252 W March Ln (95219-2341)
PHONE.....................................209 472-9700
Shawn Williams, Mgr
EMP: 84
SALES (corp-wide): 2.32MM **Privately Held**
Web: courtyard.marriott.com
SIC: **7011** Hotels and motels
PA: Castlehill Properties, Inc.
3240 W March Ln
Stockton CA
209 472-9800

(P-9685)
CAVALIER INN INC
Also Called: Cavalier Oceanfront Resort
9415 Hearst Dr (93452-9724)
PHONE.....................................805 927-4688
Mona Rigdon, Prin
Michael Hanchett, *
EMP: 80 EST: 2016
SALES (est): 2.09MM **Privately Held**
Web: www.cavalierresort.com
SIC: **7011** Motels

(P-9686)
CB-1 HOTEL
Also Called: Four Seasons Hotel
757 Market St (94103-2001)
PHONE.....................................415 633-3838
Douglas Housley, Genl Mgr
EMP: 99 EST: 2005
SQ FT: 59,300
SALES (est): 9.61MM **Privately Held**
SIC: **7011** Hotels

(P-9687)
CCHH BURLINGAME LLC
Also Called: Hyatt Rgncy San Frncisco Arprt
1333 Bayshore Hwy (94010-1804)
PHONE.....................................650 696-2607
EMP: 70 EST: 1998
SALES (est): 1.28MM
SALES (corp-wide): 4.91B **Publicly Held**
Web: www.hyatt.com
SIC: **7011** Hotels and motels
PA: Host Hotels & Resorts, Inc.
4747 Bethesda Ave # 1300
Bethesda MD
240 744-1000

(P-9688)
CDC SAN FRANCISCO LLC
Also Called: Intercontinental San Francisco
888 Howard St (94103-3011)
PHONE.....................................415 616-6512
EMP: 99 EST: 2007
SALES (est): 9.28MM **Privately Held**
Web: www.icsanfrancisco.com
SIC: **7011** Hotels

PRODUCTS & SERVICES SECTION

7011 - Hotels And Motels (P-9712)

(P-9689)
CELEBRITY CASINOS INC
Also Called: Crystal Casino & Hotel
123 E Artesia Blvd (90220-4921)
PHONE..................310 631-3838
Mark A Kelegian, Pr
Haig Kelegian Junior, CFO
Haig Kelegian Senior, CEO
EMP: 400 **EST:** 2005
SQ FT: 190,000
SALES (est): 23.37MM **Privately Held**
Web: www.thecrystalcasino.com
SIC: 7011 Casino hotel

(P-9690)
CENTURY GAMING MANAGEMENT INC
Also Called: Hollywood Park Casino
3883 W Century Blvd (90303-1003)
PHONE..................310 330-2800
▲ **EMP:** 710
SIC: 7011 5813 5812 Casino hotel; Drinking places; Eating places

(P-9691)
CENTURY NATIONAL PROPERTIES (PA)
Also Called: Daytona Surfsie
12200 Sylvan St Ste 250 (91606-3229)
PHONE..................818 760-0880
Weldon Wilson, Pr
Marie Balicki, *
Judith Osborne, *
EMP: 61 **EST:** 1983
SQ FT: 92,000
SALES (est): 4.42MM
SALES (corp-wide): 4.42MM **Privately Held**
Web: www.ihg.com
SIC: 7011 Hotels

(P-9692)
CHA LA MIRADA LLC
Also Called: Holiday Inn La Mirada
14299 Firestone Blvd (90638-5523)
PHONE..................714 739-8500
Regina Stryker, Prin
Jay Macaluso, Prin
EMP: 120 **EST:** 1984
SALES (est): 9.24MM **Privately Held**
Web: www.holidayinn.com
SIC: 7011 Hotels and motels

(P-9693)
CHAMINADE LTD
Also Called: Chaminade At Santa Cruz
1 Chaminade Ln (95065-1524)
PHONE..................831 475-5600
Tom O'shea, Genl Mgr
James Birpo, Genl Pt
James Greggs, Genl Pt
Don Murchanson, Genl Pt
EMP: 200 **EST:** 1979
SQ FT: 12,000
SALES (est): 23.6MM **Privately Held**
Web: www.chaminade.com
SIC: 7011 Resort hotel

(P-9694)
CHAMPION INVESTMENT CORP
12809 Oakfield Way (92064-1520)
PHONE..................917 712-7807
Chia-sheng Hou, Pr
Pi-lien Hou, VP
EMP: 100 **EST:** 1993
SALES (est): 2.06MM **Privately Held**
Web: www.hilton.com
SIC: 7011 Resort hotel

(P-9695)
CHASE SUITE HOTEL
12555 High Bluff Dr Ste 330 (92130-2040)
PHONE..................858 314-7910
Karen Gagnon, Owner
EMP: 63 **EST:** 1999
SALES (est): 821.49K **Privately Held**
Web: www.chasesuitehotels.com
SIC: 7011 Hotels

(P-9696)
CHEN & HUANG PARTNERS LP
Also Called: Travelodge
1400 S Bristol St (92704-3426)
PHONE..................714 557-8700
James Chen, Pt
Yi-ho Huang, Pt
EMP: 81 **EST:** 1978
SQ FT: 50,000
SALES (est): 927.41K **Privately Held**
Web: www.wyndhamhotels.com
SIC: 7011 Hotels and motels

(P-9697)
CHESAPEAKE LODGING TRUST
Also Called: Le Meridien Hotel
333 Battery St Lbby (94111-3234)
PHONE..................415 296-2900
Joel Myers, Dir
EMP: 127 **EST:** 2007
SALES (est): 25.31MM **Privately Held**
Web: le-meridien.marriott.com
SIC: 7011 7021 Hotels; Lodging house, except organization

(P-9698)
CHSP TRS FISHERMAN WHARF LLC
Also Called: Hyatt Fshrmans Wharf San Frncs
555 N Point St (94133-1311)
PHONE..................415 563-1234
Michael Kapoulis, *
Matheaw Dicello, *
EMP: 500 **EST:** 2013
SALES (est): 21.44MM
SALES (corp-wide): 2.5B **Publicly Held**
SIC: 7011 5813 5812 Hotels and motels; Bars and lounges; Eating places
HQ: Pk Domestic Sub Llc
4300 Wilson Blvd Ste 625
Arlington VA

(P-9699)
CHUKCHANSI GOLD RESORT CASINO
711 Lucky Ln (93614-8206)
PHONE..................866 794-6946
Richard Williams, CFO
EMP: 1400 **EST:** 2010
SQ FT: 489,000
SALES (est): 88.49MM **Privately Held**
Web: www.chukchansigold.com
SIC: 7011 Casino hotel

(P-9700)
CIM GROUP LP (PA)
Also Called: Commercial Inv MGT Group
4700 Wilshire Blvd Ste 1 (90010-3831)
PHONE..................323 860-4900
Avraham Shemesch, Pt
Eric P Rubenfeld, Pt
EMP: 223 **EST:** 2000
SALES (est): 217.89MM
SALES (corp-wide): 217.89MM **Privately Held**
Web: www.cimgroup.com
SIC: 7011 6798 6552 Hotels and motels; Real estate investment trusts; Land subdividers and developers, commercial

(P-9701)
CIM/H & H HOTEL LP
Also Called: Renaissance Hollywood Ht & Spa
1755 N Highland Ave (90028-4403)
PHONE..................323 856-1200
EMP: 350
Web: www.renaissancehollywood.com
SIC: 7011 Hotels

(P-9702)
CIM/OAKLAND CITY CENTER LLC
Also Called: City Center Grill
1001 Broadway (94607-4019)
PHONE..................510 451-4000
John Mazzoni, Genl Mgr
Avraham Shemesh, *
EMP: 99 **EST:** 2006
SALES (est): 3.22MM **Privately Held**
SIC: 7011 Hotels and motels

(P-9703)
CINDERELLA MOTEL
Also Called: Candy Cane Inn
1747 S Harbor Blvd (92802-2315)
PHONE..................559 432-0118
Ralph Kazarian, Pr
EMP: 81
SQ FT: 65,542
SALES (corp-wide): 6.06MM **Privately Held**
Web: www.candycaneinn.net
SIC: 7011 Motels
PA: Cinderella Motel
2416 W Shaw Ave Ste 109
Fresno CA
559 432-0118

(P-9704)
CITRUS NORTH VENTURE LLC
6591 Collins Dr Ste E11 (93021-1493)
PHONE..................256 428-2000
Marc Pierguidi, Sec
EMP: 99 **EST:** 2017
SALES (est): 1.52MM **Privately Held**
SIC: 7011 Hotel, franchised

(P-9705)
CLAREMONT HOTEL PROPERTIES LLC
Also Called: Claremont Hotel Club & Spa
41 Tunnel Rd (94705-2429)
PHONE..................510 843-3000
EMP: 550 **EST:** 2008
SALES (est): 48.46MM
SALES (corp-wide): 713.02MM **Privately Held**
Web: www.claremontresort.com
SIC: 7011 Resort hotel
HQ: Accor Services Us Llc
950 Mason St
San Francisco CA
415 772-5000

(P-9706)
CLASSIC RSDENCE MGT LTD PARTNR
Also Called: Hyatt Hotel
200 Glenwood Cir Ofc (93940-6773)
PHONE..................831 373-0101
Deann Daniel, Ex Dir
EMP: 64 **EST:** 1990
SQ FT: 196,000
SALES (est): 5.44MM **Privately Held**
Web: www.hyatt.com
SIC: 7011 8322 Hotels and motels; Senior citizens' center or association

(P-9707)
CLEAR GROUP INC
Also Called: The Clear Group Inc
408 N Avalon Blvd (90074-0001)
PHONE..................603 325-5600
Chris Barone, Brnch Mgr
EMP: 121
SALES (corp-wide): 249.45K **Privately Held**
SIC: 7011 Resort hotel
PA: The Clear Group Inc
1069 E Wardlow Rd
Long Beach CA

(P-9708)
CLUB ONE CASINO INC
Also Called: Club One Casino
3950 N Cedar Ave Ste 101 (93726-5273)
PHONE..................559 497-3000
Kyle R Kirkland, Pr
George Sarantos, *
EMP: 325 **EST:** 1995
SALES (est): 11.36MM **Privately Held**
Web: www.clubonecasino.com
SIC: 7011 Casino hotel

(P-9709)
CNCML A CALIFORNIA LTD PARTNR
Also Called: Plumpjack The
1920 Squaw Valley Rd (96146-1030)
P.O. Box 2407 (96146-2407)
PHONE..................530 583-1578
Hilary Newsom, Pr
Jeremy Scherer, Ex VP
Milham D Wakin, VP
EMP: 100 **EST:** 1975
SQ FT: 20,000
SALES (est): 4.93MM **Privately Held**
Web: www.plumpjackinn.com
SIC: 7011 5812 Resort hotel; Eating places

(P-9710)
CNI THL PROPCO FE LLC
Also Called: Four Points Bakersfield
5101 California Ave (93309-1623)
PHONE..................661 325-9700
EMP: 80 **EST:** 2017
SALES (est): 2.92MM **Privately Held**
Web: www.fourpointsbakersfield.com
SIC: 7011 Hotels and motels

(P-9711)
COLONY PALMS HOTEL LLC
572 N Indian Canyon Dr (92262-6030)
PHONE..................760 969-1800
Al Wertheimer, Prin
EMP: 70 **EST:** 2011
SALES (est): 5.11MM **Privately Held**
Web: www.colonypalmshotel.com
SIC: 7011 Resort hotel

(P-9712)
COLUMBIA HOSPITALITY INC
665 Bush St (94108-3510)
PHONE..................415 362-8878
S C Huang, Brnch Mgr
EMP: 265
SALES (corp-wide): 107.44MM **Privately Held**
Web: www.columbiahospitality.com
SIC: 7011 Hotels
PA: Columbia Hospitality Inc
2200 Alaskan Way Ste 200
Seattle WA
206 441-6666

(PA)=Parent Co (HQ)=Headquarters
✪ = New Business established in last 2 years

7011 - Hotels And Motels (P-9713)

(P-9713)
COLUMBIA HOSPITALITY INC
Also Called: Inns of Monterey
652 Cannery Row (93940-1021)
PHONE.....................831 646-8900
Randy Bernard, *Mgr*
EMP: 606
SALES (corp-wide): 107.44MM **Privately Held**
Web: www.spindriftinn.com
SIC: 7011 5813 5812 Hotels; Drinking places; Eating places
PA: Columbia Hospitality Inc
2200 Alaskan Way Ste 200
Seattle WA
206 441-6666

(P-9714)
COLUMBIA HOSPITALITY INC
Also Called: Hotel Pacific
300 Pacific St (93940-2418)
PHONE.....................831 373-5700
Randy Venard, *Mgr*
EMP: 531
SALES (corp-wide): 107.44MM **Privately Held**
Web: www.hotelpacific.com
SIC: 7011 Hotels
PA: Columbia Hospitality Inc
2200 Alaskan Way Ste 200
Seattle WA
206 441-6666

(P-9715)
COLUMBIA HOSPITALITY INC
242 Cannery Row (93940-1437)
PHONE.....................630 366-2309
EMP: 265
SALES (corp-wide): 107.44MM **Privately Held**
Web: www.montereybayinn.com
SIC: 7011 Inns
PA: Columbia Hospitality Inc
2200 Alaskan Way Ste 200
Seattle WA
206 441-6666

(P-9716)
COMFORT CALIFORNIA INC
Also Called: Comfort Inn
2775 Van Ness Ave (94109-1423)
PHONE.....................415 928-5000
Todd Symynuk, *Brnch Mgr*
EMP: 149
SALES (corp-wide): 96.75MM **Privately Held**
Web: www.choicehotels.com
SIC: 7011 Hotels and motels
HQ: Comfort California, Inc.
8171 Maple Lawn Blvd # 380
Fulton MD

(P-9717)
COMFORT CALIFORNIA INC
Also Called: Clarion Hotel
616 W Convention Way (92802-3401)
PHONE.....................714 750-3131
Mike Thomas, *Brnch Mgr*
EMP: 149
SALES (corp-wide): 96.75MM **Privately Held**
Web: www.choicehotels.com
SIC: 7011 Hotels and motels
HQ: Comfort California, Inc.
8171 Maple Lawn Blvd # 380
Fulton MD

(P-9718)
COMFORT INN PALO ALTO
Also Called: Comfort Inn
3945 El Camino Real (94306-3319)
PHONE.....................650 493-3142
EMP: 67 **EST:** 2004
SALES (est): 1.48MM **Privately Held**
Web: www.choicehotels.com
SIC: 7011 Hotels and motels

(P-9719)
CONCORD HOTEL LLC
Also Called: Crowne Plaza Concord
45 John Glenn Dr (94520-5604)
PHONE.....................925 521-3751
EMP: 95 **EST:** 2006
SALES (est): 5.57MM **Privately Held**
Web: www.concordplazahotel.com
SIC: 7011 Hotels

(P-9720)
CORE/RELATED GALA RETAIL LLC
Also Called: Conrad Los Angeles
100 S Grand Ave (90012-4794)
PHONE.....................213 349-8585
EMP: 61 **EST:** 2018
SQ FT: 1,800
SALES (est): 1.38MM **Privately Held**
SIC: 7011 Hotels and motels

(P-9721)
COUNTRYSIDE INN-CORONA LP
Also Called: Ayres Hotel Laguna Woods
24341 El Toro Rd (92637-4901)
PHONE.....................949 588-0131
Vince Neale, *Mgr*
EMP: 61
SALES (corp-wide): 24.29MM **Privately Held**
Web: www.ayreshotels.com
SIC: 7011 Resort hotel
PA: Countryside Inn-Corona, L.P.
1900 Frontage Rd
Corona CA
714 540-6060

(P-9722)
COURTYARD BY MARRIOTT
18090 San Ramon Valley Blvd (94583-4405)
PHONE.....................925 866-2900
Lisa Definney, *Genl Mgr*
Linda Robles, *Prin*
Erica Chasco, *Sls Mgr*
EMP: 79 **EST:** 2007
SALES (est): 2.24MM
SALES (corp-wide): 20.77B **Publicly Held**
Web: courtyard.marriott.com
SIC: 7011 Hotels and motels
HQ: Courtyard Management Llc
7750 Wisconsin Ave
Bethesda MD

(P-9723)
COURTYARD BY MARRIOTT/LAX
Also Called: Courtyard By Marriott
6161 W Century Blvd (90045-5310)
PHONE.....................310 981-2350
Patricia Marks, *Dir Fin*
EMP: 63 **EST:** 2010
SALES (est): 2.35MM **Privately Held**
Web: www.marriott.com
SIC: 7011 Hotels and motels

(P-9724)
COURTYARD LA LLC
3302 Griffith Park Blvd (90027-2211)
PHONE.....................917 913-8333
EMP: 70
SALES (corp-wide): 32.59K **Privately Held**
SIC: 7011 Hotels and motels
PA: Courtyard La Llc
824 S Los Angeles St # 5
Los Angeles CA

(P-9725)
COURTYARD MANAGEMENT CORP
Also Called: Courtyard By Marriott Irvine
7955 Irvine Center Dr (92618-3207)
PHONE.....................949 453-1033
Audun Poulsen, *Genl Mgr*
EMP: 70
SALES (corp-wide): 20.77B **Publicly Held**
Web: www.marriott.com
SIC: 7011 Hotels and motels
HQ: Courtyard Management Llc
7750 Wisconsin Ave
Bethesda MD

(P-9726)
COURTYARD OXNARD
600 E Esplanade Dr (93036-2480)
PHONE.....................805 988-3600
Patricia Tewes, *Genl Mgr*
EMP: 80 **EST:** 2009
SALES (est): 2.36MM **Privately Held**
SIC: 7011 Hotels and motels

(P-9727)
CPH MONARCH HOTEL LLC
Also Called: Waldorf Astoria Mnrc Bch Rsort
1 Monarch Beach Resort (92629-4085)
PHONE.....................949 234-3200
Paul Makarechian, *Pr*
▲ **EMP:** 1100 **EST:** 2001
SQ FT: 300,000
SALES (est): 48.14MM
SALES (corp-wide): 97.93MM **Privately Held**
Web: www.waldorfastoriamonarchbeach.com
SIC: 7011 Resort hotel
PA: Waldorf Astoria Management Llc
7930 Jones Branch Dr # 1100
Mc Lean VA
703 883-1000

(P-9728)
CRESTLINE HOTELS & RESORTS INC (HQ)
Also Called: Kyoto Grand Hotel and Gardens
120 S Los Angeles St 11 (90012-3724)
PHONE.....................213 629-1200
Richard Gaines, *Genl Mgr*
EMP: 130 **EST:** 1974
SALES (est): 4.22MM
SALES (corp-wide): 370.56MM **Privately Held**
Web: www.kyotograndhotel.com
SIC: 7011 5812 5813 Hotels; Restaurant, family: independent; Drinking places
PA: Crestline Hotels & Resorts, Llc
3950 University Dr # 301
Fairfax VA
571 529-6100

(P-9729)
CROWN MANAGEMENT SERVICES INC
Also Called: Green Shutter Plaza
22660 Main St (94541-5112)
PHONE.....................510 537-8470
Sanjay Bakshi, *CEO*
EMP: 74 **EST:** 1981
SALES (est): 486.49K **Privately Held**
SIC: 7011 Hotels and motels

(P-9730)
CRP CENTINELA LP
Also Called: Doubltree Los Angeles Westside
6161 W Centinela Ave (90230-6306)
PHONE.....................901 821-4117
Larry M Mills, *Pt*
EMP: 70 **EST:** 2008
SALES (est): 174.56MM
SALES (corp-wide): 4.44B **Publicly Held**
SIC: 7011 Hotels and motels
PA: The Carlyle Group Inc
1001 Pennsylvania Ave Nw 220s
Washington DC
202 729-5626

(P-9731)
CTC GROUP INC (DH)
Also Called: Doubletree Hotel
21333 Hawthorne Blvd (90503-5602)
PHONE.....................310 540-0500
John Huang, *CEO*
EMP: 145 **EST:** 1989
SALES (est): 33.28MM
SALES (corp-wide): 2.5B **Publicly Held**
Web: www.hilton.com
SIC: 7011 Hotels and motels
HQ: Gringteam Inc
21725 Gateway Center Dr
Diamond Bar CA

(P-9732)
CUPERTINO HSPITALITY ASSOC LLC
Also Called: Hilton Garden Inn Cupertino
10741 N Wolfe Rd (95014-0613)
PHONE.....................408 777-8787
Melanie Strother, *Brnch Mgr*
EMP: 168
SALES (corp-wide): 2.42MM **Privately Held**
Web: www.hilton.com
SIC: 7011 Resort hotel
PA: Cupertino Hospitality Associates, Llc
489 S El Camino Real
San Mateo CA

(P-9733)
CUPERTINO LESSEE LLC
Also Called: Juniper Hotel
10050 S De Anza Blvd (95014-2128)
PHONE.....................908 253-8900
Peggy Chen, *Genl Mgr*
EMP: 120 **EST:** 2017
SALES (est): 8.55MM
SALES (corp-wide): 2.5B **Publicly Held**
SIC: 7011 5812 Hotels; American restaurant
PA: Park Hotels & Resorts Inc.
1775 Tysons Blvd Fl 7
Tysons VA
571 302-5757

(P-9734)
CUSTOM HOTEL LLC
Also Called: Hotel June, The
8639 Lincoln Blvd (90045-3503)
PHONE.....................310 645-0400
Alisa Matthews, *
EMP: 461 **EST:** 2005
SALES (est): 13.14MM
SALES (corp-wide): 83.61MM **Privately Held**
Web: www.thehoteljune.com
SIC: 7011 Hotels
PA: Joie De Vivre Hospitality, Llc
1750 Geary Blvd
San Francisco CA
415 922-6000

7011 - Hotels And Motels (P-9756)

(P-9735)
CUSTOM HOUSE HOTEL LP
Also Called: Portola Hotel & Spa
2 Portola Plz (93940-2419)
PHONE..................831 649-4511
EMP: 208 EST: 1985
SALES (est): 31.14MM Privately Held
Web: www.portolahotel.com
SIC: 7011 Bed and breakfast inn

(P-9736)
CVR HSGE LLC
Also Called: Carmel Valley Ranch
1 Old Ranch Rd (93923-8551)
PHONE..................831 625-9500
Thomas Becker, Genl Mgr
Ulrich Samietz, *
EMP: 250 EST: 1993
SALES (est): 24.61MM Privately Held
Web: www.carmelvalleyranch.com
SIC: 7011 7997 6552 Resort hotel; Tennis club, membership; Subdividers and developers, nec

(P-9737)
CY GASLAMP LLC
Also Called: Courtyard San Dego Gslmp/Cnvnt
453 6th Ave (92101-7007)
PHONE..................619 544-1004
Tim Billing, Genl Mgr
EMP: 65 EST: 2015
SALES (est): 2.29MM Privately Held
SIC: 7011 Hotels

(P-9738)
CY SAC OPERATOR LLC
Also Called: Courtyard Sacramento-Midtown
4422 Y St (95817-2220)
PHONE..................916 455-6800
EMP: 67 EST: 2013
SALES (est): 2.31MM Privately Held
SIC: 7011 Hotels and motels

(P-9739)
DAVIDSON HOTEL PARTNERS LP
Also Called: Agoura Hills Renaissance Hotel
30100 Agoura Rd (91301-2004)
PHONE..................818 707-1220
Larry Mills, Pt
EMP: 1477
Web: www.davidsonhospitality.com
SIC: 7011 Hotels and motels
PA: Davidson Hotel Partners, L.P
1 Ravinia Dr Ste 1600
Atlanta GA

(P-9740)
DESTINATION RESIDENCES LLC
Also Called: Shadow Mtn Rsort Rcquet CLB Tn
45750 San Luis Rey Ave (92260-4728)
PHONE..................760 346-4647
Sindy Calhoun, Mgr
EMP: 342
SALES (corp-wide): 367.25MM Privately Held
Web: www.destinationhotels.com
SIC: 7011 5699 6531 Resort hotel; Sports apparel; Condominium manager
HQ: Destination Residences Llc
10333 E Dry Creek Rd
Englewood CO
303 799-3180

(P-9741)
DIAMOND MOUNTAIN CASINO
900 Skyline Dr (96130-6071)
P.O. Box 1327 (96130-1327)
PHONE..................530 252-1100
Campbell Jamieson, Mgr
Campbell Jamieson, CEO
Jill Ault, *
EMP: 135 EST: 1996
SQ FT: 24,000
SALES (est): 9.36MM Privately Held
Web: www.dmcah.com
SIC: 7011 Resort hotel

(P-9742)
DIAMOND RESORTS LLC
Also Called: Palm Canyon Resort & Spa
2800 S Palm Canyon Dr (92264-9337)
PHONE..................760 866-1800
Allison Wickerham, Managing Member
Carl Ellis, *
EMP: 100 EST: 2004
SALES (est): 300K Privately Held
Web: www.tophotelreservations.com
SIC: 7011 5812 7991 Resort hotel; American restaurant; Spas

(P-9743)
DIAMONDROCK SAN DEGO TNANT LLC
Also Called: Westin San Diego
400 W Broadway (92101-3504)
PHONE..................619 239-4500
EMP: 300 EST: 2012
SQ FT: 337,717
SALES (est): 25.58MM
SALES (corp-wide): 1B Publicly Held
Web: www.westinsandiego.com
SIC: 7011 Hotels
HQ: Diamondrock Hospitality Limited Partnership
3 Bethesda Metro Ctr
Bethesda MD

(P-9744)
DISNEY ENTERPRISES INC
Also Called: Disney
1150 W Magic Way (92802-2247)
PHONE..................714 778-6600
Michael D Eisner, Pr
EMP: 3500
SALES (corp-wide): 82.72B Publicly Held
Web: www.disney.com
SIC: 7011 Resort hotel
HQ: Disney Enterprises, Inc.
500 S Buena Vista St
Burbank CA
818 560-1000

(P-9745)
DISNEYLAND INTERNATIONAL
Also Called: Disneyland
1580 S Disneyland Dr (92802-2294)
PHONE..................714 956-6746
EMP: 5000
SALES (corp-wide): 82.72B Publicly Held
Web: disneyland.disney.go.com
SIC: 7011 Resort hotel
HQ: Disneyland International
1313 S Harbor Blvd
Anaheim CA
714 781-4565

(P-9746)
DISNEYLAND RESORT (DH)
1313 S Harbor Blvd (92802-2309)
P.O. Box 4708 (92803-4708)
PHONE..................714 781-4000
Micheal Colglazier, Pr
Ken Potrock, Pr
▲ EMP: 148 EST: 2011
SALES (est): 51.4MM
SALES (corp-wide): 82.72B Publicly Held

(P-9747)
DJONT OPERATIONS LLC
Also Called: Embassy Suites
150 Anza Blvd (94010-1924)
PHONE..................650 342-4600
Ernie Catanzaro, Genl Mgr
EMP: 120
SALES (corp-wide): 1.19B Privately Held
Web: www.hilton.com
SIC: 7011 Hotels and motels
HQ: Djont Operations, L.L.C.
125 E Houston St
San Antonio TX

(P-9748)
DJONT OPERATIONS LLC
Also Called: Embassy Stes - Mlpts/Slcon Vly
901 E Calaveras Blvd (95035-5419)
PHONE..................408 942-0400
Teri Owens, Genl Mgr
EMP: 120
SALES (corp-wide): 1.19B Privately Held
Web: www.hilton.com
SIC: 7011 Hotels and motels
HQ: Djont Operations, L.L.C.
125 E Houston St
San Antonio TX

(P-9749)
DJONT OPERATIONS LLC
Also Called: Embassy Suites - Lax Airport S
1440 E Imperial Ave (90245-2623)
PHONE..................310 640-3600
Shar Franklin, Genl Mgr
EMP: 120
SALES (corp-wide): 1.19B Privately Held
Web: www.hilton.com
SIC: 7011 Hotels and motels
HQ: Djont Operations, L.L.C.
125 E Houston St
San Antonio TX

(P-9750)
DJONT/CMB SSF LEASING LLC
Also Called: Embassy Sites-So San Francisco
250 Gateway Blvd (94080-7018)
PHONE..................650 589-3400
Rudy Ortiz, Genl Mgr
Dee Bradford, Ofcr
EMP: 60 EST: 1989
SALES (est): 22.73MM
SALES (corp-wide): 1.19B Privately Held
Web: www.hilton.com
SIC: 7011 Hotels and motels
HQ: Rangers Sub I, Llc
3 Bethesda Metro Ctr # 1000
Bethesda MD

(P-9751)
DJONT/JPM HSPTLITY LSG SPE LLC
Also Called: Embassy Stes - Mndlay Bch Rsor
2101 Mandalay Beach Rd (93035-3638)
PHONE..................805 984-2500
Colleen Huther, Genl Mgr
EMP: 112
SALES (corp-wide): 1.19B Privately Held
Web: www.hilton.com
SIC: 7011 Hotels
HQ: Djont/Jpm Hospitality Leasing (Spe), L.L.C.
400 Arch St
Philadelphia PA

(P-9752)
DK HOTELS LLC
501 N Cherokee Ln (95240-2402)
PHONE..................925 640-3616
EMP: 107
SALES (corp-wide): 131.43K Privately Held
SIC: 7011 Hotels
PA: Dk Hotels Llc
7662 Cottonwood Ln
Pleasanton CA

(P-9753)
DKN HOTEL LLC (PA)
42 Corporate Park Ste 200 (92606-5105)
PHONE..................714 427-4320
Nilesh Patel, *
John Jorgensen, *
Dahya Lal, *
EMP: 290 EST: 2002
SQ FT: 4,000
SALES (est): 38.6MM
SALES (corp-wide): 38.6MM Privately Held
Web: www.dknhotels.com
SIC: 7011 Hotels and motels

(P-9754)
DNC PARKS & RESORTS AT SEQUOIA
64740 Wuksachi Way Ofc C (93262-9607)
PHONE..................559 565-4070
Jeremy Jacobs, Ch
EMP: 106 EST: 2008
SALES (est): 238.33K
SALES (corp-wide): 400.8K Privately Held
Web: www.visitsequoia.com
SIC: 7011 Resort hotel
PA: Dnc Parks & Resorts At St Mary
40 Fountain Plz
Buffalo NY
406 646-7365

(P-9755)
DNC PRKS RESORTS AT TENAYA INC (DH)
Also Called: Tenaya Lodge
1122 Highway 41 (93623-9600)
P.O. Box 159 (93623-0159)
PHONE..................559 683-6555
Kevin T Kelly, Pr
Thomas Barney, VP
EMP: 132 EST: 2001
SALES (est): 24.62MM
SALES (corp-wide): 2.9B Privately Held
Web: www.visittenaya.com
SIC: 7011 Resort hotel
HQ: Delaware North Companies Parks & Resorts, Inc.
250 Delaware Ave Ste 3
Buffalo NY

(P-9756)
DNC PRKS RSORTS AT SEQUOIA INC
Also Called: Sequoia National Park
64740 Wuksachi Way (93262-9604)
PHONE..................559 565-4070
Joe St Laurent, CEO
Andy Grinsfelder, CEO
Dennis J Szefel, Pr
Thomas M Barney Junior, Dir
Christopher J Feeney, Dir
EMP: 69 EST: 1998
SALES (est): 4.97MM
SALES (corp-wide): 2.9B Privately Held
SIC: 7011 Resort hotel
HQ: Delaware North Companies Parks & Resorts, Inc.

(PA)=Parent Co (HQ)=Headquarters
✪ = New Business established in last 2 years

7011 - Hotels And Motels (P-9757)

250 Delaware Ave Ste 3
Buffalo NY

(P-9757)
DNC PRKS RSRTS AT YOSEMITE INC
Also Called: Yosemite Concession Services
9001 Village Dr (95389)
PHONE..................209 372-1001
Dan Jensen, *Pr*
Paul Jensen, *
Dan Lyle, *
Paul Jeppson, *
EMP: 1100 **EST:** 1911
SALES (est): 49.08MM
SALES (corp-wide): 2.9B **Privately Held**
Web: www.travelyosemite.com
SIC: 7011 5399 5812 5947 Resort hotel; Country general stores; Eating places; Gift shop
HQ: Delaware North Companies Parks & Resorts, Inc.
250 Delaware Ave Ste 3
Buffalo NY

(P-9758)
DODGE RIDGE CORPORATION
Also Called: Dodge Ridge Winter Sports Area
1 Dodge Ridge Rd (95364)
P.O. Box 1188 (95364-0188)
PHONE..................209 536-5300
EMP: 350 **EST:** 1960
SQ FT: 10,000
SALES (est): 26.31MM **Privately Held**
Web: www.dodgeridge.com
SIC: 7011 7033 Ski lodge; Campgrounds

(P-9759)
DODGE RIDGE MTN RESORT LLC
1 Dodge Ridge Rd (95364)
PHONE..................209 965-3474
Karl Kapuscinski, *Pr*
Michele Roy, *
EMP: 200 **EST:** 2021
SALES (est): 10.83MM **Privately Held**
Web: summer.dodgeridge.com
SIC: 7011 Resort hotel

(P-9760)
DOLCE INTERNATIONAL / NAPA LLC
1600 Atlas Peak Rd (94558-1425)
PHONE..................707 257-0200
Steven A Rudnitsky, *Pr*
Deborah W, *
EMP: 85 **EST:** 2014
SALES (est): 991.17K
SALES (corp-wide): 1.5B **Publicly Held**
SIC: 7011 Hotels and motels
HQ: Dolce International Holdings, Inc.
22 Sylvan Way
Parsippany NJ
201 307-8700

(P-9761)
DOLPHIN BAY HT & RESIDENCE INC
Also Called: Dolphin Bay Hotel & Residences
2727 Shell Beach Rd (93449-1602)
PHONE..................805 773-4300
Richard J Loughead Junior, *CEO*
EMP: 90 **EST:** 2005
SALES (est): 9.07MM **Privately Held**
Web: www.thedolphinbay.com
SIC: 7011 Resort hotel

(P-9762)
DONALD T STERLING CORPORATION
Also Called: Beverly Hills Plaza Hotel
10300 Wilshire Blvd (90024-4772)
PHONE..................310 275-5575
EMP: 80
SALES (corp-wide): 2.1MM **Privately Held**
Web: www.beverlyhillsplazahotel.com
SIC: 7011 Hotels
PA: Donald T. Sterling Corporation
9441 Wlshire Blvd Pnthuse Penthouse
Beverly Hills CA
310 278-8000

(P-9763)
DOUBLTREE BY HLTON HT CAMPBELL
Also Called: Doubletree
1995 S Bascom Ave (95008-2201)
PHONE..................408 559-4300
EMP: 60 **EST:** 2013
SALES (est): 2.24MM **Privately Held**
Web: www.hilton.com
SIC: 7011 Hotels and motels

(P-9764)
DOUBLTREE BY HLTON HT MONROVIA
Also Called: Doubletree By Hilton
924 W Huntington Dr (91016-3112)
PHONE..................626 357-1900
Jessi Willis, *Prin*
EMP: 123 **EST:** 2010
SALES (est): 12.42MM **Privately Held**
Web: www.hilton.com
SIC: 7011 Hotels

(P-9765)
DRD HOSPITALITY INC
Also Called: Holiday Inn Express Manteca
179 Commerce Ave (95336-5063)
PHONE..................916 952-6552
EMP: 160
SALES (corp-wide): 1.07MM **Privately Held**
Web: www.hiexpress.com
SIC: 7011 Hotels and motels
PA: Drd Hospitality, Inc.
9950 Koa Ln
Elk Grove CA
916 952-6552

(P-9766)
DT ONTRIO HT PRTNERS LSSEE LLC
Also Called: Doubltree By Hlton Ontrio Arpr
222 N Vineyard Ave (91764-4428)
PHONE..................909 937-0900
Bassam Shahin, *Pr*
EMP: 76 **EST:** 2016
SALES (est): 4.02MM
SALES (corp-wide): 2.5B **Publicly Held**
Web: www.hilton.com
SIC: 7011 Hotels and motels
PA: Park Hotels & Resorts Inc.
1775 Tysons Blvd Fl 7
Tysons VA
571 302-5757

(P-9767)
DTRS SANTA MONICA LLC
Also Called: Loews Santa Monica Beach Hotel
1700 Ocean Ave (90401-3214)
PHONE..................310 458-6700
Younes Atolah, *Genl Mgr*
Andrei Zotoff, *Managing Member*
EMP: 300 **EST:** 1989
SQ FT: 300,000
SALES (est): 15MM **Privately Held**
Web: www.loewshotels.com
SIC: 7011 Resort hotel

(P-9768)
DTRS ST FRANCIS LLC
Also Called: Westin St. Francis, The
335 Powell St (94102-1804)
PHONE..................415 397-7000
Marc Swerdlow, *Pr*
Mark Zettl, *
EMP: 147 **EST:** 1902
SALES (est): 25.76MM
SALES (corp-wide): 97.62MM **Privately Held**
Web: modules.marriott.com
SIC: 7011 Hotels
HQ: Ultima Hospitality, L.L.C.
30 S Wacker Dr Ste 3600
Chicago IL
312 948-4500

(P-9769)
E H SUMMIT INC (PA)
Also Called: Luxe Sunset Boulevard Hotel
11461 W Sunset Blvd (90049-2031)
PHONE..................310 476-6571
Efrem Harkhan, *CEO*
EMP: 60 **EST:** 1945
SALES (est): 18.77MM **Privately Held**
SIC: 7011 Hotels

(P-9770)
EAGLE MOUNTAIN CASINO
681 South Tule Reservation Road (93258)
P.O. Box 1659 (93258-1659)
PHONE..................559 788-6220
Tom Stewart, *Prin*
EMP: 196 **EST:** 2007
SALES (est): 11.34MM **Privately Held**
Web: www.eaglemtncasino.com
SIC: 7011 Casino hotel

(P-9771)
EAST PALO ALTO HOTEL DEV INC
Also Called: Four Seasons Hotel Silicon Vly
2050 University Ave (94303-2248)
PHONE..................650 566-1200
Tracy Mercer, *Genl Mgr*
EMP: 210 **EST:** 2005
SALES (est): 24.28MM **Privately Held**
SIC: 7011 7389 Resort hotel; Office facilities and secretarial service rental

(P-9772)
EDWARD THOMAS COMPANIES
Also Called: Jolly Roger Inn
640 W Katella Ave (92802-3411)
PHONE..................714 782-7500
Fred Kokash, *Brnch Mgr*
EMP: 110
SALES (corp-wide): 4.63MM **Privately Held**
Web: www.edwardthomasco.com
SIC: 7011 5812 Motels; Eating places
PA: The Edward Thomas Companies
9950 Santa Monica Blvd
Beverly Hills CA
310 859-9366

(P-9773)
EDWARD THOMAS HOSPITALITY CORP
Also Called: Shutters On The Beach
1 Pico Blvd (90405-1063)
PHONE..................310 458-0030
Klaus Mennekes, *Brnch Mgr*
EMP: 349
SALES (corp-wide): 9.7MM **Privately Held**
Web: www.shuttersonthebeach.com
SIC: 7011 5812 7991 5813 Hotels; Eating places; Physical fitness facilities; Drinking places
PA: The Edward Thomas Hospitality Corp
9950 Santa Monica Blvd
Beverly Hills CA
310 859-9366

(P-9774)
EL CENTRO HOSPITALITY LLC
Also Called: Fairfield Inn
503 E Danenberg Dr (92243-8507)
PHONE..................760 353-2600
Clarissa Clark, *Prin*
EMP: 223
SALES (corp-wide): 590.12K **Privately Held**
Web: fairfield.marriott.com
SIC: 7011 Hotels and motels
PA: El Centro Hospitality, L.L.C.
2300 Tower Dr
Monroe LA
318 325-5561

(P-9775)
EL CENTRO HOSPITALITY 2 LLC
Also Called: TownePlace Suites El Centro
3003 S Dogwood Rd (92243-9160)
PHONE..................760 370-3800
Dewey F Weaver Junior, *Brnch Mgr*
EMP: 247
SALES (corp-wide): 1.14MM **Privately Held**
Web: www.marriott.com
SIC: 7011 Hotel, franchised
PA: El Centro Hospitality 2, L.L.C.
2390 Tower Dr
Monroe LA
318 325-5561

(P-9776)
EL DORADO ENTERPRISES INC
Also Called: Hustler Casino
1000 W Redondo Beach Blvd (90247-4192)
PHONE..................310 719-9800
Larry C Flynt, *CEO*
EMP: 760 **EST:** 2000
SALES (est): 48.29MM **Privately Held**
Web: www.hustlercasino.com
SIC: 7011 Casino hotel

(P-9777)
EL ENCANTO INC
Also Called: Belmond El Encanto
800 Alvarado Pl (93103-2176)
PHONE..................805 845-5800
Richard M Levine, *CEO*
Martin O'grady, *CFO*
EMP: 61 **EST:** 2013
SALES (est): 9.63MM **Privately Held**
Web: www.belmond.com
SIC: 7011 Resort hotel

(P-9778)
ELK VALLEY CASINO INC
Also Called: Elk Valley Rancheria Cal
2021 Elk Ranch Rd (95531-9164)
PHONE..................707 464-1020
Dale Miller, *Ch Bd*
EMP: 82 **EST:** 1995
SALES (est): 10.95MM **Privately Held**
Web: www.elkvalleycasino.com
SIC: 7011 Casino hotel

(P-9779)
EMBASSY INVESTMENTS LLC
Also Called: Courtyard Marriott

PRODUCTS & SERVICES SECTION 7011 - Hotels And Motels (P-9801)

1350 Holiday Ln (94534-3449)
PHONE...................707 422-4111
Sushil Patel, *Managing Member*
Edward Deloumr, *Managing Member**
EMP: 77 EST: 1998
SALES (est): 2.25MM **Privately Held**
Web: courtyard.marriott.com
SIC: **7011** 5813 5812 Hotels and motels;
  Drinking places; Eating places

(P-9780)
EMBASSY SUITES & HOTEL
Also Called: Embassy Suites
11767 Harbor Blvd (92840-2701)
PHONE...................714 539-3300
Charlene Garcia, *OF ROOMS*
Tracy Stephens, *OF ROOMS*
Dominic Acolino, *Genl Mgr*
Charlene Garcia French, *Div Mgr*
EMP: 155 EST: 2002
SALES (est): 19.45MM
SALES (corp-wide): 2.5B **Publicly Held**
Web: www.hilton.com
SIC: **7011** Hotels and motels
PA: Park Hotels & Resorts Inc.
  1775 Tysons Blvd Fl 7
  Tysons VA
  571 302-5757

(P-9781)
EMERIK HOTEL CORP
Also Called: Luxe City Center
1020 S Figueroa St (90015-1305)
PHONE...................213 748-1291
Emerson Glazer, *Pr*
James Jones, *
Art Malmgren, *
John Kelly, *
EMP: 96 EST: 1987
SALES (est): 1.48MM **Privately Held**
SIC: **7011** 5813 5812 Hotels; Bar (drinking
  places); American restaurant

(P-9782)
ENCINA PEPPER TREE JOINT VENTR (PA)
Also Called: Best Western
3850 State St (93105-3112)
PHONE...................805 687-5511
Jeanette Webber, *Mng Pt*
Pamela Webber, *Pt*
Camille Shaar, *Pt*
David Potter, *Pt*
EMP: 70 EST: 1951
SQ FT: 100,000
SALES (est): 4.89MM
SALES (corp-wide): 4.89MM **Privately Held**
Web: www.bestwestern.com
SIC: **7011** Hotels and motels

(P-9783)
ENCINA PEPPER TREE JOINT VENTR
Also Called: Best Western
2220 Bath St (93105-4322)
PHONE...................805 682-7277
Pam Webber, *Owner*
EMP: 80
SALES (corp-wide): 4.89MM **Privately Held**
Web: www.bestwestern.com
SIC: **7011** Motels
PA: Pepper Encina Tree Joint Venture
  3850 State St
  Santa Barbara CA
  805 687-5511

(P-9784)
ENTERPRISE DEVELOPMENT AUTH
Also Called: Hard Rock Ht Csino Scrmnto At
3317 Forty Mile Rd (95692-8803)
PHONE...................833 337-3473
EMP: 918 EST: 2019
SALES (est): 9.88MM **Privately Held**
SIC: **7011** Casino hotel

(P-9785)
EQUINOX HOTEL MANAGEMENT INC
Also Called: Aloha Beach Resort
2422 Lake St (94121-1117)
PHONE...................415 668-6887
Abdul Suleman, *Pr*
EMP: 100 EST: 1995
SALES (est): 2.41MM **Privately Held**
Web: www.equinoxhotels.com
SIC: **7011** 6531 Hotels and motels; Real
  estate managers

(P-9786)
ESTANCIA HOTEL LLC
Also Called: Estancia La Jolla Hotel & Spa
9700 N Torrey Pines Rd (92037-1102)
PHONE...................949 474-7368
Timothy Busch, *CEO*
Brittany Enos, *Prin*
EMP: 111 EST: 2012
SALES (est): 13.74MM **Privately Held**
Web: www.estanciajolla.com
SIC: **7011** Resort hotel

(P-9787)
ET WHITEHALL SEASCAPE LLC
Also Called: Hotel Casa Del Mar
1910 Ocean Way (90405-1083)
PHONE...................310 581-5533
◆ EMP: 202 EST: 1998
SQ FT: 200,000
SALES (est): 11.89MM **Privately Held**
Web: www.hotelcasadelmar.com
SIC: **7011** 5812 Hotels; Eating places

(P-9788)
EUROPEAN HT INVSTORS I I A CAL
Also Called: O H I
2532 Dupont Dr (92612-1524)
PHONE...................949 474-7368
Timothy R Busch, *Genl Pt*
EMP: 80 EST: 1987
SQ FT: 9,000
SALES (est): 5.69MM **Privately Held**
Web: www.thebuschfirm.com
SIC: **7011** Hotels

(P-9789)
EVEREST SONOMA MANAGEMENT LLC
520 Newport Center Dr Fl 2 (92660-7020)
PHONE...................213 272-0088
Marshall Young, *Managing Member*
EMP: 60 EST: 2018
SQ FT: 10,000
SALES (est): 1.9MM
SALES (corp-wide): 6.23MM **Privately Held**
SIC: **7011** Hotels
PA: Everest Hotel Group, Llc
  2140 S Dupont Hwy
  Camden DE
  213 272-0088

(P-9790)
EVERGREEN DSTNTION HLDINGS LLC
Also Called: Evergreen Lodge
33160 Evergreen Rd (95321-9772)
PHONE...................209 379-2606
Lee Zimmerman, *
Dan Braun, *
EMP: 75 EST: 1975
SQ FT: 6,000
SALES (est): 7.46MM **Privately Held**
Web: www.evergreenlodge.com
SIC: **7011** 5812 Resort hotel; Eating places

(P-9791)
EXECUTIVE INN INC
Also Called: Ramada Inn Silicon Valley
1217 Wildwood Ave (94089-2701)
PHONE...................408 245-5330
Roger Chang, *Pr*
Roger Chang, *Ch Bd*
Jeffry S C Chang, *
David C M Chang, *
EMP: 97 EST: 1971
SQ FT: 15,400
SALES (est): 4.68MM **Privately Held**
Web: www.wyndhamhotels.com
SIC: **7011** Motels

(P-9792)
FAIRFELD INN BY MRROTT LTD PRT
Also Called: Marriott
1460 S Harbor Blvd (92802-2311)
PHONE...................714 772-6777
Helen Forbs, *Mgr*
EMP: 117 EST: 1989
SALES (est): 9.43MM **Privately Held**
Web: www.marriott.com
SIC: **7011** Hotels and motels

(P-9793)
FARGO COLONIAL LLC
Also Called: Grande Colonial
910 Prospect St (92037-4144)
PHONE...................858 454-2181
EMP: 63 EST: 1913
SQ FT: 46,480
SALES (est): 9.34MM **Privately Held**
Web: www.thegrandecolonial.com
SIC: **7011** 5812 Hotels; Eating places

(P-9794)
FARMHOUSE INN & RESTAURANT LLC
7871 River Rd (95436-9494)
PHONE...................707 887-3300
Catheryn Bartllomei, *Pr*
Stanley Mazor, *Pt*
EMP: 70 EST: 1991
SALES (est): 5.35MM **Privately Held**
Web: www.farmhouseinn.com
SIC: **7011** 5812 Bed and breakfast inn;
  Restaurant, family: independent

(P-9795)
FEDERTED INDANS GRTON RNCHERIA
Graton Resort & Casino
630 Park Ct (94928-7906)
PHONE...................707 588-7100
Greg Sarris, *Brnch Mgr*
EMP: 776
Web: www.gratonrancheria.com
SIC: **7011** Casino hotel
PA: Federated Indians Of Graton Rancheria
  6400 Redwood Dr Ste 300
  Rohnert Park CA
  619 917-9566

(P-9796)
FESS PRKER-RED LION GEN PARTNR
Also Called: Doubletree Hotel
633 E Cabrillo Blvd (93103-3611)
PHONE...................805 564-4333
Fess Parker, *Pt*
EMP: 138 EST: 1981
SALES (est): 2.72MM **Privately Held**
Web: www.hilton.com
SIC: **7011** Hotels and motels

(P-9797)
FIRST ORLEANS HOTEL ASSOC LP
222 Kearny St Ste 200 (94108-4503)
PHONE...................415 397-5572
Michael Tepatie, *CEO*
Thomas Latour, *Pt*
J Kirke Wrench, *Pt*
Alan Baer, *Contrlr*
EMP: 200 EST: 1999
SALES (est): 4.09MM **Privately Held**
Web: www.kimptonhotels.com
SIC: **7011** Hotels

(P-9798)
FJS INC
Also Called: Anabella Hotel The
888 S Disneyland Dr Ste 400 (92802-1847)
PHONE...................714 905-1050
EMP: 118 EST: 1989
SALES (est): 8.38MM **Privately Held**
SIC: **7011** Resort hotel

(P-9799)
FLORENCE VILLA HOTEL
Also Called: The Villa Florence Hotel
225 Powell St (94102-2205)
PHONE...................415 397-7700
Steve Miller, *Genl Mgr*
EMP: 200 EST: 1985
SALES (est): 9.08MM **Publicly Held**
Web: www.thebarnessf.com
SIC: **7011** 5812 Hotels; Eating places
PA: Pebblebrook Hotel Trust
  4747 Bethesda Ave # 1100
  Bethesda MD

(P-9800)
FORTUNA ENTERPRISES LP
Also Called: Hilton
5711 W Century Blvd (90045-5672)
PHONE...................310 410-4000
Henry H Hsu, *Pt*
David Hsu, *Pt*
Christine Hsu, *Pt*
EMP: 450 EST: 1992
SQ FT: 2,700
SALES (est): 45.04MM **Privately Held**
Web: www.hilton.com
SIC: **7011** 5812 5813 Hotels and motels;
  Eating places; Bar (drinking places)
HQ: Universal Fortuna Investment, Inc.
  5711 W Century Blvd # 16
  Los Angeles CA

(P-9801)
FOUNDERS MANAGEMENT II CORP
Also Called: Crowne Plaza Hotel
1221 Chess Dr (94404-1173)
PHONE...................650 570-5700
▲ EMP: 275 EST: 1986
SQ FT: 280,000
SALES (est): 24.87MM **Privately Held**
Web: www.eventscp.com
SIC: **7011** 5812 5813 Hotels; Eating places;
  Bar (drinking places)

(PA)=Parent Co (HQ)=Headquarters
✿ = New Business established in last 2 years

7011 - Hotels And Motels (P-9802)

(P-9802)
FOUR SEASONS HOTEL INC
Also Called: Four Ssons Hotel-San Francisco
735 Market St Fl 6 (94103-2034)
PHONE.............................415 633-3441
Stan Bromley, *Brnch Mgr*
EMP: 147
SALES (corp-wide): 414.66MM **Privately Held**
Web: www.fourseasons.com
SIC: **7011** Resort hotel
HQ: Four Seasons Hotels Limited
   1165 Leslie St
   North York ON
   416 449-1750

(P-9803)
FOUR SISTERS INNS
Also Called: Inns At Sonoma
630 Broadway (95476-7002)
PHONE.............................707 939-1340
Chapman Retterer, *Brnch Mgr*
EMP: 69
SALES (corp-wide): 24.21MM **Privately Held**
Web: www.innatsonoma.com
SIC: **7011** Bed and breakfast inn
PA: Four Sisters Inns
   460 Alma St Ste 100
   Monterey CA
   831 649-0908

(P-9804)
FRESNO AIRPORT HOTELS LLC
Also Called: Wyndham Garden Fresno Airport
5090 E Clinton Way (93727-1506)
PHONE.............................559 252-3611
Rohit Kumar, *Pr*
Leslie Beninga, *
EMP: 65 EST: 2016
SALES (est): 1.94MM **Privately Held**
Web: www.visitfresnocounty.org
SIC: **7011** Hotels

(P-9805)
G B COMMERCIAL LLC
Also Called: Four Pnts By Shrton Scrmnto In
4900 Duckhorn Dr (95834-2595)
PHONE.............................916 263-9000
Bobby Gosa Ceol, *Prin*
EMP: 60 EST: 2004
SQ FT: 83,000
SALES (est): 2.43MM **Privately Held**
Web: www.fourpointssacramentoairport.com
SIC: **7011** 6552 Hotels and motels;
   Subdividers and developers, nec

(P-9806)
GALLERIA PARK ASSOCIATES LLC
Also Called: Galleria Park Hotel
191 Sutter St (94104-4501)
PHONE.............................415 781-3060
James Lim, *Genl Mgr*
Paul Frentsos, *Managing Member**
EMP: 88 EST: 1984
SQ FT: 109,673
SALES (est): 12.37MM **Privately Held**
Web: www.galleriapark.com
SIC: **7011** 6512 5813 5812 Hotels;
   Nonresidential building operators; Drinking
   places; Eating places

(P-9807)
GARDEN CITY INC
Also Called: Garden City Casino & Rest
1887 Matrix Blvd (95110-2309)
PHONE.............................408 244-3333
Pete V Lunardi Iii, *CEO*
Eli Reinhard, *
Frederick Wyle, *
Llene Brandon, *
Kathy Reiner, *
EMP: 569 EST: 1974
SQ FT: 22,000
SALES (est): 29.19MM **Privately Held**
Web: www.gardencitycasino.com
SIC: **7011** Casino hotel

(P-9808)
GEARY DARLING LESSEE INC
Also Called: Marker Hotel, The
501 Geary St (94102-1640)
PHONE.............................415 292-0100
Alfred L Young, *CEO*
EMP: 150 EST: 2010
SQ FT: 20,000
SALES (est): 9.65MM **Publicly Held**
Web: www.themarkersf.com
SIC: **7011** 7991 5813 5812 Hotels; Physical
   fitness facilities; Drinking places; Eating
   places
PA: Pebblebrook Hotel Trust
   4747 Bethesda Ave # 1100
   Bethesda MD

(P-9809)
GENTRY ASSOCIATES LLC
Also Called: Park Manor Suites
525 Spruce St (92103-5814)
PHONE.............................619 291-0999
Elizabeth Willis, *Managing Member*
EMP: 65 EST: 1926
SALES (est): 4.84MM **Privately Held**
Web: www.shellvacationsclub.com
SIC: **7011** 5812 6531 Resort hotel; Eating
   places; Time-sharing real estate sales,
   leasing and rentals

(P-9810)
GOLDEN DOOR PROPERTIES LLC
Also Called: Golden Door
777 Deer Springs Rd (92069-9757)
PHONE.............................760 744-5777
Joanne Conway, *Managing Member*
Kathy Van Ness, *COO*
▲ EMP: 173 EST: 1958
SQ FT: 50,000
SALES (est): 21.93MM **Privately Held**
Web: www.goldendoor.com
SIC: **7011** Hotels and motels

(P-9811)
GOLDEN HOTELS LTD PARTNERSHIP
Also Called: Atrium Hotel
18700 Macarthur Blvd (92612-1409)
PHONE.............................949 833-2770
Mike Wang, *Pt*
John Wang, *
EMP: 140 EST: 1960
SQ FT: 120,000
SALES (est): 9.03MM **Privately Held**
Web: www.atriumhotel.com
SIC: **7011** Resort hotel

(P-9812)
GOLDEN WEST PARTNERS INC
Also Called: Golden West Casino
1001 S Union Ave (93307-3641)
PHONE.............................661 324-6936
Jaussauds Maison, *Brnch Mgr*
EMP: 218
Web: www.goldenwestcasino.com
SIC: **7011** Casino hotel
PA: Golden West Partners, Inc.
   200 Spectrum Center Dr # 1250
   Irvine CA

(P-9813)
GRAND DEL MAR RESORT LP
Also Called: Grand Del Mar
5300 Grand Del Mar Ct (92130-4901)
PHONE.............................858 314-2000
Tom Voss, *Pt*
EMP: 570 EST: 2005
SALES (est): 49.06MM **Privately Held**
Web: www.thegranddelmar.com
SIC: **7011** Resort hotel

(P-9814)
GRAND PACIFIC CARLSBAD HT LP
Also Called: Sheraton Carlsbad Resort & Spa
5480 Grand Pacific Dr (92008-4723)
PHONE.............................760 827-2400
Tim Shinkle, *CFO*
Janina Kershaw, *Contrlr*
EMP: 272 EST: 2008
SALES (est): 23.86MM **Privately Held**
Web: www.sheratoncarlsbad.com
SIC: **7011** Resort hotel

(P-9815)
GRAND PACIFIC RESORTS INC
Also Called: Resortime.com
5900 Pasteur Ct Ste 200 (92008-7336)
PHONE.............................760 431-8500
Sherri Weks, *Mgr*
EMP: 513
Web: www.grandpacificresorts.com
SIC: **7011** Resort hotel
PA: Grand Pacific Resorts, Inc.
   5900 Pasteur Ct Ste 200
   Carlsbad CA

(P-9816)
GRAND PACIFIC RESORTS SVCS LP
5900 Pasteur Ct Ste 200 (92008-7336)
PHONE.............................760 431-8500
Timothy Stripe, *Pt*
David Brown, *Pt*
EMP: 120 EST: 1992
SQ FT: 22,000
SALES (est): 4.55MM **Privately Held**
Web: www.grandpacificresorts.com
SIC: **7011** Resort hotel

(P-9817)
GRANLIBAKKEN MANAGEMENT CO LTD
Also Called: Granlbakken Ski Racquet Resort
725 Granlibakken Rd (96145-2370)
P.O. Box 6329 (96145-6329)
PHONE.............................800 543-3221
Willem G C Parson, *Pr*
Norma Parson, *
EMP: 60 EST: 1978
SALES (est): 9.74MM **Privately Held**
Web: www.granlibakken.com
SIC: **7011** Resort hotel

(P-9818)
GRCLT CONDOMINIUM INC
Also Called: Marriott Grnd Rsdnce CLB - Lk
1001 Heavenly Village Way (96150-7068)
PHONE.............................530 542-8400
Steve Weitz, *Pr*
EMP: 68 EST: 2001
SALES (est): 2.32MM **Privately Held**
Web: www.marriott.com
SIC: **7011** Resort hotel

(P-9819)
GREENLEAF HOTEL INC
515 S Figueroa St # 1850 (90071-3301)
EMP: 73 EST: 1995
SQ FT: 143,475
SALES (est): 1.06MM **Privately Held**
SIC: **7011** 5812 7299 Hotels; Eating places;
   Banquet hall facilities

(P-9820)
GREENS GROUP INC
16530 Bake Pkwy Ste 200 (92618-4685)
PHONE.............................949 829-4902
Ashutosh Kadakia, *CFO*
EMP: 145 EST: 2004
SALES (est): 6.48MM **Privately Held**
SIC: **7011** Resort hotel, franchised

(P-9821)
GREENWOOD HOLDINGS LLC
Also Called: Four Points San Diego-Seaworld
3888 Greenwood St (92110-4412)
PHONE.............................619 299-6633
EMP: 69 EST: 2002
SALES (est): 2.38MM **Privately Held**
SIC: **7011** Hotels and motels

(P-9822)
GRINGTEAM INC
Also Called: Doubletree Golf Resort
800 W Ivy St Ste D (92101-1771)
PHONE.............................858 485-4145
Russ Tanakaya, *Genl Mgr*
EMP: 80
SALES (corp-wide): 2.5B **Publicly Held**
Web: www.hilton.com
SIC: **7011** Hotels and motels
HQ: Gringteam Inc
   21725 Gateway Center Dr
   Diamond Bar CA

(P-9823)
GRINGTEAM INC
Also Called: Doubletree Hotel
1150 9th St Frnt (95354-0823)
PHONE.............................209 526-6000
Cindy Power, *Mgr*
EMP: 73
SALES (corp-wide): 2.5B **Publicly Held**
Web: www.hilton.com
SIC: **7011** 5813 Hotels and motels; Drinking
   places
HQ: Gringteam Inc
   21725 Gateway Center Dr
   Diamond Bar CA

(P-9824)
GRINGTEAM INC
Also Called: Doubletree By Hilton
7450 Hazard Center Dr (92108-4539)
PHONE.............................619 297-5466
Karima Zaki, *Mgr*
EMP: 300
SALES (corp-wide): 2.5B **Publicly Held**
Web: www.hilton.com
SIC: **7011** 5812 Hotels and motels; Eating
   places
HQ: Gringteam Inc
   21725 Gateway Center Dr
   Diamond Bar CA

(P-9825)
GRINGTEAM INC
Also Called: Doubletree Hotel
835 Airport Blvd (94010-1922)
PHONE.............................650 344-5500
Liza Normandy, *Brnch Mgr*
EMP: 73
SALES (corp-wide): 2.5B **Publicly Held**
Web: www.hilton.com
SIC: **7011** 6512 5813 5812 Hotels and motels
   ; Nonresidential building operators; Drinking
   places; Eating places

PRODUCTS & SERVICES SECTION

7011 - Hotels And Motels (P-9848)

HQ: Gringteam Inc
21725 Gateway Center Dr
Diamond Bar CA

(P-9826)
GRINGTEAM INC
Also Called: Doubletree Hotel
34402 Pacific Coast Hwy (92624-1211)
PHONE.................949 661-1100
EMP: 61
SALES (corp-wide): 2.5B Publicly Held
Web: www.hilton.com
SIC: 7011 Hotels and motels
HQ: Gringteam Inc
21725 Gateway Center Dr
Diamond Bar CA

(P-9827)
GRINGTEAM INC
Also Called: Doubltree By Hlton Ht Bkrsfeld
3100 Camino Del Rio Ct (93308-6245)
PHONE.................661 426-7919
Robert Balmer, Mgr
EMP: 63
SALES (corp-wide): 2.5B Publicly Held
Web: www.hilton.com
SIC: 7011 7299 Hotels; Banquet hall facilities
HQ: Gringteam Inc
21725 Gateway Center Dr
Diamond Bar CA

(P-9828)
GROSVENOR PROPERTIES LTD
Also Called: Best Western
380 S Airport Blvd (94080-6704)
PHONE.................650 873-3200
Jim Mcguire, Mgr
EMP: 160
SALES (corp-wide): 29.62MM Privately Held
Web: www.bestwestern.com
SIC: 7011 5813 5812 7299 Hotels and motels; Drinking places; Eating places; Banquet hall facilities
PA: Grosvenor Properties Ltd.
222 Front St Fl 7
San Francisco CA
415 421-5940

(P-9829)
GUESTY INC (PA)
340 S Lemon Ave (91789-2706)
PHONE.................415 244-0277
Amiad Soto, CEO
EMP: 77 EST: 2013
SALES (est): 9.3MM
SALES (corp-wide): 9.3MM Privately Held
Web: www.guesty.com
SIC: 7011 7371 Vacation lodges; Computer software development and applications

(P-9830)
H D G ASSOCIATES
Also Called: Hotel Marmonte
1111 E Cabrillo Blvd (93103-3701)
PHONE.................805 963-0744
Ruth Grande, Pr
EMP: 242 EST: 1979
SQ FT: 150,000
SALES (est): 8.1MM Publicly Held
Web: www.marmontehotel.com
SIC: 7011 Hotels
HQ: Hyatt Corporation
250 Vesey St Fl 15
New York NY
312 750-1234

(P-9831)
HAMPSTEAD LAFAYETTE HOTEL LLC
Also Called: Innsuites Hotels
2223 El Cajon Blvd (92104-1103)
PHONE.................619 296-2101
James Green, Mgr
EMP: 217
SALES (corp-wide): 4.92MM Privately Held
SIC: 7011 Resort hotel
PA: Lafayette Hampstead Hotel Llc
2223 El Cajon Blvd
San Diego CA
619 296-2101

(P-9832)
HANDLERY HOTELS INC
Also Called: Handlery Union Square Hotel
351 Geary St (94102-1801)
PHONE.................415 781-7800
John Handlery, Mgr
EMP: 238
SALES (corp-wide): 18.71MM Privately Held
Web: sf.handlery.com
SIC: 7011 Resort hotel
PA: Handlery Hotels, Inc.
180 Geary St Ste 700
San Francisco CA
415 781-4550

(P-9833)
HANDLERY HOTELS INC
Also Called: Handlery Hotels
950 Hotel Cir N (92108-2995)
PHONE.................415 781-4550
John Martin, Mgr
EMP: 150
SALES (corp-wide): 18.71MM Privately Held
Web: sd.handlery.com
SIC: 7011 5941 5812 5947 Resort hotel; Golf goods and equipment; Eating places; Gift, novelty, and souvenir shop
PA: Handlery Hotels, Inc.
180 Geary St Ste 700
San Francisco CA
415 781-4550

(P-9834)
HANFORD HOTELS INC
Also Called: Hotel Hanford, The
3131 Bristol St (92626-3037)
PHONE.................714 557-3000
Tony Eccher, Ex Dir
EMP: 239
SQ FT: 65,311
Web: www.hanfordhotels.com
SIC: 7011 Hotels
PA: Hanford Hotels, Inc.
17542 17th St Ste 450
Tustin CA

(P-9835)
HARBOR ISLAND HOTEL GROUP LP
Also Called: Holiday Inn
1080 Navigator Dr (93001-4365)
PHONE.................805 650-7770
EMP: 95
SALES (corp-wide): 1.27MM Privately Held
Web: www.hiexpress.com
SIC: 7011 Hotels and motels
PA: Harbor Island Hotel Group, Lp
21725 Gateway Center Dr
Diamond Bar CA
909 860-6255

(P-9836)
HARBOR VIEW HOTEL VENTURES LLC
Also Called: Doubletree Ht San Diego Dwntwn
1646 Front St (92101-2920)
PHONE.................619 239-6800
Michael Gallegos, Managing Member
EMP: 100 EST: 1997
SALES (est): 4.07MM Privately Held
Web: www.hilton.com
SIC: 7011 Hotels

(P-9837)
HARD ROCK CAFE INTL INC
Also Called: Hard Rock Ht Csino Scrmnto At
3317 Forty Mile Rd (95692-8803)
PHONE.................530 633-6938
EMP: 629
SALES (corp-wide): 47.3MM Privately Held
Web: www.hardrockhotels.com
SIC: 7011 5812 Casino hotel; Eating places
PA: Hard Rock Cafe International, Inc.
1 Seminole Way
Fort Lauderdale FL
228 437-6968

(P-9838)
HARVARD GRAND LP
Also Called: TownePlace Stes Anaheim Mingate
1730 S State College Blvd (92806-6022)
PHONE.................714 939-9700
EMP: 72
SALES (corp-wide): 856.87K Privately Held
Web: www.marriott.com
SIC: 7011 Hotel, franchised
PA: Harvard Grand, Lp
227 S Muirfield Rd
Los Angeles CA

(P-9839)
HAVASU LANDING CASINO (PA)
1 Main St (92363-9216)
PHONE.................760 858-5380
EMP: 71 EST: 2010
SALES (est): 9.63MM Privately Held
Web: www.havasulanding.com
SIC: 7011 Resort hotel

(P-9840)
HAWAIIAN GARDENS CASINO
11871 Carson St (90716-1127)
PHONE.................562 860-5887
David Moskowitz, CEO
Irving Moskowitz, *
▲ EMP: 1000 EST: 1998
SALES (est): 47.26MM Privately Held
Web: www.thegardenscasino.com
SIC: 7011 Casino hotel

(P-9841)
HAWAIIAN HOTELS & RESORTS INC
2830 Borchard Rd (91320-3810)
PHONE.................805 480-0052
Edward J Hogan, Pr
Glenn Hogan, *
EMP: 235 EST: 2001
SALES (est): 5.28MM
SALES (corp-wide): 1.08B Privately Held
Web: www.hawaiihotels.com
SIC: 7011 Resort hotel
HQ: Pleasant Holidays, Llc
2404 Townsgate Rd
Westlake Village CA

(P-9842)
HAYES MANSION CONFERENCE CTR
200 Edenvale Ave (95136-3309)
PHONE.................408 226-3200
Vickie Leong, Prin
EMP: 140 EST: 1994
SALES (est): 4.22MM Privately Held
Web: www.hayesmansion.com
SIC: 7011 Hotels

(P-9843)
HAZENS INVESTMENT LLC
Also Called: Sheraton
6101 W Century Blvd (90045-5310)
PHONE.................310 642-1111
Henry Pekun, Contrlr
EMP: 395 EST: 2002
SALES (est): 44.17MM Privately Held
Web: four-points.marriott.com
SIC: 7011 Hotels

(P-9844)
HCAL LLC
Also Called: Harrahs Resort Southern Cal
777 S Resort Dr (92082)
PHONE.................760 751-3100
EMP: 371 EST: 2005
SALES (est): 10.73MM
SALES (corp-wide): 10.82B Publicly Held
SIC: 7011 Casino hotel
HQ: Caesars Holdings, Inc.
1 Caesars Palace Dr
Las Vegas NV

(P-9845)
HEI HOSPITALITY LLC
Also Called: Marriott
21850 Oxnard St (91367-3631)
PHONE.................818 887-4800
Clay Andrews, Mgr
EMP: 167
SALES (corp-wide): 447.39MM Privately Held
Web: www.starbucks.com
SIC: 7011 Hotels and motels
PA: Hei Hospitality, Llc
101 Merritt 7
Norwalk CT
203 849-8844

(P-9846)
HEI LONG BEACH LLC
Also Called: Hilton Hotels
701 W Ocean Blvd (90831-3100)
PHONE.................562 983-3400
Clark Christopher, Prin
EMP: 125 EST: 2004
SALES (est): 10.6MM
SALES (corp-wide): 447.39MM Privately Held
Web: www.hilton.com
SIC: 7011 Hotels
PA: Hei Hospitality, Llc
101 Merritt 7
Norwalk CT
203 849-8844

(P-9847)
HI ANAHEIM LLC
100 W Katella Ave (92802-3602)
PHONE.................714 533-1500
EMP: 60 EST: 2018
SALES (est): 1.27MM Privately Held
SIC: 7011 Hotels

(P-9848)
HIGHLANDS INN INC
Also Called: Hyatt Carmel Highlands
120 Highland Dr (93923-9607)
P.O. Box 1700 (93921-1700)
PHONE.................831 620-1234
Mel Bettcher, Prin

7011 - Hotels And Motels (P-9849)

Paul C Reed, *
EMP: 225 **EST:** 1946
SALES (est): 3.37MM **Privately Held**
SIC: 7011 7389 Hotels and motels; Time-share condominium exchange

(P-9849)
HIGHLANDS INN INVESTORS II LP
Also Called: Hyatt Hotel
120 Highland Dr (93923-9607)
PHONE.................................831 624-3801
TOLL FREE: 800
Ulrich Samietz, *Genl Mgr*
Highlands Inn Investors, *Ltd Pt*
EMP: 184 **EST:** 1916
SALES (est): 1.94MM **Privately Held**
Web: www.hyatt.com
SIC: 7011 5812 5813 5947 Hotels; American restaurant; Drinking places; Gift, novelty, and souvenir shop

(P-9850)
HILTON DBLTREE SAN DEGO RGNAL
Also Called: Hilton
404 Camino Del Rio S (92108-3503)
PHONE.................................619 270-2600
Kelsi Dart, *Prin*
EMP: 75 **EST:** 2011
SALES (est): 2.39MM
SALES (corp-wide): 2.5B **Publicly Held**
Web: www.hilton.com
SIC: 7011 Resort hotel
HQ: Gringteam Inc
21725 Gateway Center Dr
Diamond Bar CA

(P-9851)
HILTON GARDEN INNS MGT LLC
Also Called: Hilton
6070 Monterey Rd (95020-9502)
PHONE.................................408 840-7000
TOLL FREE: 866
Paula Hutchison, *Brnch Mgr*
EMP: 249
SALES (corp-wide): 8.77B **Publicly Held**
Web: www.hilton.com
SIC: 7011 Resort hotel
HQ: Hilton Garden Inns Management Llc
7930 Jones Branch Dr
Mc Lean VA
703 883-1000

(P-9852)
HILTON GARDEN INNS MGT LLC
Also Called: Hilton
6450 Carlsbad Blvd (92011-1058)
PHONE.................................760 476-0800
Robert Moore, *Genl Mgr*
EMP: 477
SALES (corp-wide): 8.77B **Publicly Held**
Web: www.hiltongrandvacations.com
SIC: 7011 Resort hotel
HQ: Hilton Garden Inns Management Llc
7930 Jones Branch Dr
Mc Lean VA
703 883-1000

(P-9853)
HILTON GARDEN INNS MGT LLC
Also Called: Hilton Garden Inn Livermore
2801 Constitution Dr 2nd Fl (94551-7613)
PHONE.................................925 292-2000
Joan Baldon, *Mgr*
EMP: 366
SALES (corp-wide): 8.77B **Publicly Held**
Web: www.hilton.com
SIC: 7011 Resort hotel
HQ: Hilton Garden Inns Management Llc
7930 Jones Branch Dr
Mc Lean VA
703 883-1000

(P-9854)
HILTON LOS ANGLES UNIVERSAL CY
555 Universal Hollywood Dr (91608-1001)
PHONE.................................818 506-2500
Juan Aquinde, *Managing Member*
Matthew La Vine, *
▲ **EMP:** 184 **EST:** 2003
SALES (est): 9.04MM **Privately Held**
Web: www.hiltonuniversal.com
SIC: 7011 Hotels

(P-9855)
HILTON SAN FRANCISCO FINCL DST
Also Called: Hilton
750 Kearny St (94108-1860)
PHONE.................................415 433-6600
Randall King, *Prin*
EMP: 63 **EST:** 2006
SALES (est): 12.94MM **Privately Held**
Web: www.hilton.com
SIC: 7011 Hotels

(P-9856)
HILTON WOODLAND HILLS & TOWERS
6360 Canoga Ave (91367-2501)
PHONE.................................818 595-1000
Ed Debries, *Genl Mgr*
▲ **EMP:** 95 **EST:** 1989
SALES (est): 2.48MM **Privately Held**
Web: www.woodlandhillshotel.com
SIC: 7011 5813 5812 Hotels and motels; Drinking places; Eating places

(P-9857)
HISTORIC MISSION INN CORP
Also Called: Mission Inn Hotel and Spa, The
3649 Mission Inn Ave (92501-3364)
P.O. Box 1433 (92502-1433)
PHONE.................................951 784-0300
Duane R Roberts, *Pr*
Diana Rosure, *General Vice President**
Richard Shippee, *
Cliff Day, *
EMP: 460 **EST:** 1992
SALES (est): 33.22MM
SALES (corp-wide): 33.22MM **Privately Held**
Web: www.missioninn.com
SIC: 7011 7991 Resort hotel; Spas
PA: Entrepreneurial Capital Corporation
4100 Newport Place Dr # 400
Newport Beach CA
949 809-3900

(P-9858)
HISTORICAL PROPERTIES INC (PA)
Also Called: Horton Grand Hotel
311 Island Ave (92101-6923)
PHONE.................................619 230-8417
Doris J Rose, *Pr*
Santiago Ojeda, *
EMP: 96 **EST:** 1995
SQ FT: 60,000
SALES (est): 4.79MM **Privately Held**
Web: www.hortongrand.com
SIC: 7011 Hotels

(P-9859)
HIT PORTFOLIO II TRS LLC
Also Called: Hilton
400 N State College Blvd (92868-1708)
PHONE.................................714 938-1111
John Ault, *Mgr*
EMP: 60
SALES (corp-wide): 2.5B **Publicly Held**
Web: www.hilton.com
SIC: 7011 5812 Hotels and motels; Eating places
HQ: Hit Portfolio Ii Trs, Llc
7930 Jones Branch Dr
Mc Lean VA
703 883-1000

(P-9860)
HMB INVESTORS LLC
Also Called: Wrc Huntington
1075 California St (94108-2251)
PHONE.................................415 474-5400
EMP: 90 **EST:** 1941
SALES (est): 1.66MM **Privately Held**
SIC: 7011 Hotels

(P-9861)
HOLIDAY INN EXPRESS
Also Called: Holiday Inn
2550 Erringer Rd (93065-2353)
PHONE.................................805 584-6006
Ashok Israni, *Pr*
EMP: 166 **EST:** 1987
SALES (est): 952.46K
SALES (corp-wide): 96.92MM **Privately Held**
Web: www.hiexpress.com
SIC: 7011 Hotels and motels
PA: Pacifica Hosts, Inc.
1775 Hancock St Ste 200
San Diego CA
619 296-9000

(P-9862)
HOLIDAY INN EXPRESS MERCED
Also Called: Holiday Inn
730 Motel Dr (95341-5151)
PHONE.................................209 383-0333
Kainth Brothers, *Prin*
EMP: 100 **EST:** 1992
SALES (est): 4.84MM **Privately Held**
Web: www.hiexpress.com
SIC: 7011 Hotels and motels

(P-9863)
HOLLYWOOD PARK CASINO CO INC
3883 W Century Blvd (90303-1003)
PHONE.................................310 330-2800
Terrence E Fancher, *Pr*
EMP: 179 **EST:** 2007
SALES (est): 25.31MM **Privately Held**
Web: www.playhpc.com
SIC: 7011 Casino hotel

(P-9864)
HOLLYWOOD PARTNERSHIP
Also Called: Days Inn
5410 Hollywood Blvd (90027-3406)
PHONE.................................323 463-7171
Mohan Patel, *Pt*
Ratilal Patel, *Pt*
Matthew Solis, *Genl Mgr*
EMP: 64 **EST:** 1989
SQ FT: 20,000
SALES (est): 2.84MM **Privately Held**
Web: www.wyndhamhotels.com
SIC: 7011 Hotels and motels

(P-9865)
HOME AWAY INC
54432 Road 432 (93604-9762)
P.O. Box 149 (93604-0149)
PHONE.................................559 642-3121
EMP: 65 **EST:** 2004
SALES (est): 2.44MM **Privately Held**
Web: www.homeaway.com
SIC: 7011 Hotels and motels

(P-9866)
HOMEWOOD SUITES MANAGEMENT LLC
Also Called: Homewood Suites
1103 Embarcadero (94606-5122)
PHONE.................................510 663-2700
Jason Oliveras, *Mgr*
EMP: 71
SALES (corp-wide): 8.77B **Publicly Held**
Web: www.hilton.com
SIC: 7011 Hotels and motels
HQ: Homewood Suites Management Llc
7930 Jones Branch Dr
Mc Lean VA
703 883-1000

(P-9867)
HONEYMOON REAL ESTATE LP
Also Called: Avalon Hotel
9400 W Olympic Blvd (90212-4552)
PHONE.................................310 277-5221
Brad Korzen, *Pt*
EMP: 90 **EST:** 1997
SQ FT: 400,000
SALES (est): 8.09MM **Privately Held**
Web: www.avalon-hotel.com
SIC: 7011 Resort hotel

(P-9868)
HOST HOTELS & RESORTS LP
Also Called: JW Marriott Dsert Sprng Rsort S
74855 Country Club Dr (92260-1961)
PHONE.................................760 341-2211
Ken Forths, *Mgr*
EMP: 64
SALES (corp-wide): 4.91B **Publicly Held**
Web: www.hosthotels.com
SIC: 7011 Hotels and motels
HQ: Host Hotels & Resorts, L.P.
6903 Rockledge Dr # 1500
Bethesda MD
240 744-1000

(P-9869)
HOTEL BEL-AIR
701 Stone Canyon Rd (90077-2909)
PHONE.................................310 472-1211
EMP: 265 **EST:** 1994
SQ FT: 30,000
SALES (est): 9.58MM **Privately Held**
Web: www.dorchestercollection.com
SIC: 7011 Hotels
HQ: Kava Holdings, Inc.
701 Stone Canyon Rd
Los Angeles CA
310 472-1211

(P-9870)
HOTEL CIRCLE PROPERTY LLC
Also Called: Town and Country Hotel
500 Hotel Cir N (92108-3005)
PHONE.................................619 291-7131
April Shute, *Managing Member*
EMP: 500 **EST:** 2014
SQ FT: 1,132,560
SALES (est): 38.03MM **Privately Held**
Web: www.towncountry.com
SIC: 7011 Resort hotel

(P-9871)
HOTEL DURANT A LTD PARTNERSHIP
Also Called: Henry's Pub

PRODUCTS & SERVICES SECTION

7011 - Hotels And Motels (P-9893)

2600 Durant Ave (94704-1711)
PHONE...................510 845-8981
Stephen Wahrlich, *Genl Pt*
Thunderbird Investors, *Genl Pt*
Tracy W Wahrlich Junior, *Genl Pt*
EMP: 203 **EST:** 1928
SQ FT: 57,730
SALES (est): 3.28MM **Privately Held**
Web: www.hoteldurantberkeley.com
SIC: 7011 5812 5813 6512 Hotels; American restaurant; Bar (drinking places); Nonresidential building operators

(P-9872)
HOTEL HEALDSBURG LLC
317 Healdsburg Ave (95448-4105)
PHONE...................707 922-5399
Charlie Palmer, *Brnch Mgr*
EMP: 64
SALES (corp-wide): 9.21MM **Privately Held**
Web: www.drycreekkitchen.com
SIC: 7011 Inns
PA: Hotel Healdsburg, Llc
   25 Matheson St
   Healdsburg CA
   707 431-2800

(P-9873)
HOTEL MCINNIS MARIN LLC
Also Called: Embassy Suites
101 Mcinnis Pkwy (94903-2773)
PHONE...................415 499-9222
Shawn Milburn, *Managing Member*
Hope Fuerniss, *
EMP: 90 **EST:** 1990
SALES (est): 4.94MM **Privately Held**
Web: www.hilton.com
SIC: 7011 6512 4729 5812 Hotels and motels; Commercial and industrial building operation; Passenger transportation arrangement; Caterers

(P-9874)
HOTEL NIKKO SAN FRANCISCO INC
222 Mason St (94102-2115)
PHONE...................415 394-1111
TOLL FREE: 800
Anna Marie Presutti, *VP*
EMP: 260 **EST:** 1984
SQ FT: 540,000
SALES (est): 38.57MM **Privately Held**
Web: www.hotelnikkosf.com
SIC: 7011 5812 5813 7991 Resort hotel; Eating places; Bar (drinking places); Health club
HQ: Okura Nikko Hotel Management Co., Ltd.
   2-10-4, Toranomon
   Minato-Ku TKY

(P-9875)
HOTEL WHITCOMB
1231 Market St (94103-1405)
PHONE...................415 626-8000
Thomas Chan, *Contrlr*
EMP: 99 **EST:** 1988
SALES (est): 8.4MM **Privately Held**
Web: www.hotelwhitcomb.com
SIC: 7011 Hotels

(P-9876)
HP LQ INVESTMENT LP
Also Called: La Quinta Resort & Club
49499 Eisenhower Dr (92253-2722)
PHONE...................760 564-4111
EMP: 230 **EST:** 2021
SALES (est): 15.64MM
SALES (corp-wide): 8.77B **Publicly Held**
Web: www.laquintaresort.com
SIC: 7011 Resort hotel
PA: Hilton Worldwide Holdings Inc.
   7930 Jones Branch Dr # 100
   Mc Lean VA
   703 883-1000

(P-9877)
HST LESSEE BOSTON LLC
Also Called: Sheraton
1380 Harbor Island Dr (92101-1007)
PHONE...................619 692-2255
Joe Tursey, *Genl Mgr*
EMP: 75
SALES (corp-wide): 4.91B **Publicly Held**
Web: four-points.marriott.com
SIC: 7011 Hotels
HQ: Hst Lessee Boston Llc
   39 Dalton St
   Boston MA
   617 236-2000

(P-9878)
HST LESSEE MISSION HILLS LP
Also Called: Westin Rncho Mrage Golf Rsort
71333 Dinah Shore Dr (92270-1501)
PHONE...................760 328-5955
Hst Gp Mission Hills, *Genl Pt*
EMP: 100 **EST:** 2006
SALES (est): 15.4MM **Privately Held**
Web: www.westinmissionhills.com
SIC: 7011 Resort hotel

(P-9879)
HUMNIT HOTEL AT LAX LLC
Also Called: Concorse Ht At Los Angeles Arpr
6225 W Century Blvd (90045-5311)
PHONE...................424 702-1234
Jina Luman, *Prin*
Jina Luman, *Asst Tr*
EMP: 99 **EST:** 2013
SQ FT: 49,500
SALES (est): 7.7MM
SALES (corp-wide): 500.9MM **Publicly Held**
SIC: 7011 Hotels
PA: Amalgamated Financial Corp.
   275 7th Ave
   New York NY
   212 255-6200

(P-9880)
HUNTINGTON HOTEL COMPANY
5951 Linea Del Cielo (92067)
PHONE...................858 756-1131
Scott Jenkins, *CEO*
EMP: 88 **EST:** 1921
SQ FT: 5,000
SALES (est): 8.27MM **Privately Held**
Web: www.theinnatrsf.com
SIC: 7011 5812 Resort hotel; Eating places

(P-9881)
HUOYEN INTERNATIONAL INC
Also Called: Hotel Fullerton Anaheim, The
1500 S Raymond Ave (92831-5236)
P.O. Box 1071 (92822-1071)
PHONE...................714 635-9000
EMP: 90 **EST:** 1995
SQ FT: 144,698
SALES (est): 2.21MM **Privately Held**
SIC: 7011 Hotel, franchised

(P-9882)
HYATT CORP AS AGT BRCP HEF HT
Also Called: Hyatt Hotel
7100 Aviara Resort Dr (92011-4908)
PHONE...................760 603-6851
EMP: 134 **EST:** 2010
SALES (est): 8.1MM **Privately Held**
Web: www.parkhyattaviara.com
SIC: 7011 Resort hotel

(P-9883)
HYATT CORPORATION
Also Called: Hyatt Hotel
8401 W Sunset Blvd (90069-1909)
PHONE...................323 656-1234
Tim Flodin, *Mgr*
EMP: 233
Web: www.hyatt.com
SIC: 7011 5812 5813 Hotels and motels; Restaurant, family: independent; Bar (drinking places)
HQ: Hyatt Corporation
   250 Vesey St Fl 15
   New York NY
   312 750-1234

(P-9884)
HYATT CORPORATION
Also Called: Hyatt Rgncy San Frncisco Arprt
1333 Bayshore Hwy (94010-1804)
PHONE...................650 347-1234
Keith Butz, *Mgr*
EMP: 91
Web: www.hyatt.com
SIC: 7011 Hotels and motels
HQ: Hyatt Corporation
   250 Vesey St Fl 15
   New York NY
   312 750-1234

(P-9885)
HYATT CORPORATION
Also Called: Grand Hyatt San Francisco
345 Stockton St (94108-4606)
PHONE...................415 848-6050
Steve Trent, *Mgr*
EMP: 477
Web: www.hyatt.com
SIC: 7011 5813 5812 6512 Hotels and motels; Drinking places; Eating places; Nonresidential building operators
HQ: Hyatt Corporation
   250 Vesey St Fl 15
   New York NY
   312 750-1234

(P-9886)
HYATT CORPORATION
Also Called: Hyatt Hotel
50 Drumm Street (94111)
PHONE...................415 788-1234
Matthew Adams, *Mgr*
EMP: 872
Web: www.hyatt.com
SIC: 7011 5812 5813 Hotels and motels; Eating places; Bar (drinking places)
HQ: Hyatt Corporation
   250 Vesey St Fl 15
   New York NY
   312 750-1234

(P-9887)
HYATT CORPORATION
Also Called: Hyatt Hotel
200 S Pine Ave (90802-4537)
PHONE...................562 432-0161
Steve Smith, *Mgr*
EMP: 463
Web: www.hyatt.com
SIC: 7011 7299 Hotels and motels; Banquet hall facilities
HQ: Hyatt Corporation
   250 Vesey St Fl 15
   New York NY
   312 750-1234

(P-9888)
HYATT CORPORATION
Also Called: Hyatt Hotel
55 S Mcdonnell Rd (94128-3102)
PHONE...................650 454-1234
Shun Matsumoto, *Brnch Mgr*
EMP: 192
Web: www.hyatt.com
SIC: 7011 Hotels and motels
HQ: Hyatt Corporation
   250 Vesey St Fl 15
   New York NY
   312 750-1234

(P-9889)
HYATT CORPORATION
Also Called: Hyatt Regency Monterey
1 Old Golf Course Rd (93940-4908)
PHONE...................831 372-1234
Michael Koffler, *Mgr*
EMP: 87
Web: www.hyatt.com
SIC: 7011 Hotels and motels
HQ: Hyatt Corporation
   250 Vesey St Fl 15
   New York NY
   312 750-1234

(P-9890)
HYATT CORPORATION
Also Called: Hyatt Hotel
17900 Jamboree Rd (92614-6211)
PHONE...................949 975-1234
Rod T Schinnerer, *Genl Mgr*
EMP: 83
Web: www.hyatt.com
SIC: 7011 7992 7991 5813 Hotels and motels; Public golf courses; Physical fitness facilities; Drinking places
HQ: Hyatt Corporation
   250 Vesey St Fl 15
   New York NY
   312 750-1234

(P-9891)
HYATT CORPORATION
Also Called: Hyatt Hotel
1107 Jamboree Rd (92660-6219)
PHONE...................949 729-1234
Ruth Benjamin, *Genl Mgr*
EMP: 300
Web: www.hyatt.com
SIC: 7011 5813 5812 Hotels and motels; Drinking places; Eating places
HQ: Hyatt Corporation
   250 Vesey St Fl 15
   New York NY
   312 750-1234

(P-9892)
HYATT CORPORATION
Also Called: Hyatt Regency San Francisco Ht
5 Embarcadero Ctr (94111-4800)
PHONE...................415 788-1234
Jerry Simmons, *Genl Mgr*
EMP: 581
Web: www.hyatt.com
SIC: 7011 5812 5813 Hotels and motels; Eating places; Drinking places
HQ: Hyatt Corporation
   250 Vesey St Fl 15
   New York NY
   312 750-1234

(P-9893)
HYATT CORPORATION
Also Called: Hyatt Los Angeles Airport
6225 W Century Blvd (90045-5311)
PHONE...................312 750-1234
Donald J Henderson, *Mgr*

7011 - Hotels And Motels (P-9894)

EMP: 500
Web: www.hyattdevelopment.com
SIC: 7011 5812 5813 Hotels; Restaurant, family: chain; Bar (drinking places)
HQ: Hyatt Corporation
250 Vesey St Fl 15
New York NY
312 750-1234

(P-9894)
HYATT CORPORATION
Also Called: Hyatt House San Ramon
2323 San Ramon Valley Blvd (94583-1607)
PHONE..........................925 743-1882
Pam Callahan, Brnch Mgr
EMP: 316
Web: www.hyattdevelopment.com
SIC: 7011 Hotels
HQ: Hyatt Corporation
250 Vesey St Fl 15
New York NY
312 750-1234

(P-9895)
HYATT CORPORATION
Also Called: Hyatt Regency Lajolla
3777 La Jolla Village Dr (92122-1080)
PHONE..........................858 453-0018
Benjie Barin, Owner
EMP: 122 EST: 2000
SALES (est): 21.8MM Privately Held
Web: www.hyatt.com
SIC: 7011 Hotels

(P-9896)
HYATT CORPORATION
Also Called: Hyatt Grand Champion Resort
44600 Indian Wells Ln (92210-8707)
PHONE..........................760 341-1000
Allan Farwell, Mgr
EMP: 579
Web: www.hyatt.com
SIC: 7011 5813 5812 Hotels; Drinking places; Eating places
HQ: Hyatt Corporation
250 Vesey St Fl 15
New York NY
312 750-1234

(P-9897)
HYATT CORPORATION
Also Called: Manchester Grnd Hyatt San Diego
1 Market Pl (92101-7714)
PHONE..........................619 232-1234
Ted Kanatas, Mgr
EMP: 222
Web: www.hosthotels.com
SIC: 7011 Hotels
HQ: Hyatt Corporation
250 Vesey St Fl 15
New York NY
312 750-1234

(P-9898)
HYATT CORPORATION
Also Called: Andaz Sandiego
600 F St (92101-6310)
PHONE..........................619 849-1234
Rusty Middleton, Brnch Mgr
EMP: 105
Web: www.hyattdevelopment.com
SIC: 7011 Resort hotel
HQ: Hyatt Corporation
250 Vesey St Fl 15
New York NY
312 750-1234

(P-9899)
HYATT EQUITIES LLC
Also Called: Hyatt Hotel
285 Bay St (90802-8178)
PHONE..........................562 436-1047
Tracey Pool, Brnch Mgr
EMP: 77
Web: www.hyatt.com
SIC: 7011 Hotels and motels
HQ: Hyatt Equities, L.L.C.
71 S Wacker Dr Fl 14
Chicago IL
312 750-1234

(P-9900)
HYATT HOTELS MANAGEMENT CORP
Also Called: Hyatt Hotel
285 N Palm Canyon Dr (92262-5525)
PHONE..........................760 322-9000
Dania Duke, Mgr
EMP: 62
Web: www.hyatt.com
SIC: 7011 7299 7213 Hotels; Banquet hall facilities; Caterers
HQ: Hyatt Hotels Management Corporation
71 S Wacker Dr Ste 900
Chicago IL
312 750-1234

(P-9901)
HYATT REGENCY CENTURY PLAZA
2025 Avenue Of The Stars (90067-4741)
PHONE..........................310 228-1234
Rakesh Sarna, CEO
Ken Cruse, *
EMP: 650 EST: 2005
SALES (est): 9.39MM Privately Held
Web: centuryplaza.hyatt.com
SIC: 7011 Hotels

(P-9902)
HYATT REGENCY SANTA CLARA
Also Called: Hyatt Hotel
5101 Great America Pkwy (95054-1118)
PHONE..........................408 200-1234
Peter Reice, Genl Mgr
EMP: 74 EST: 2006
SALES (est): 13.29MM Privately Held
Web: www.hyatt.com
SIC: 7011 Hotels

(P-9903)
I CYPRESS COMPANY (PA)
Also Called: Pebble Beach Company
1700 17-Mile Dr (93953)
P.O. Box 1418 (93953-1418)
PHONE..........................831 647-7500
Bill Perocchi, CEO
Cody Plott, *
David Heuck, *
▲ EMP: 174 EST: 1992
SALES (est): 84.97MM
SALES (corp-wide): 84.97MM Privately Held
Web: www.pebblebeach.com
SIC: 7011 Resort hotel

(P-9904)
IA LODGING NAPA SOLANO TRS LLC
Also Called: NAPA Valley Marriott
3425 Solano Ave (94558-2709)
PHONE..........................707 253-8600
Amanda Hawkins-vogel, Genl Mgr
EMP: 210 EST: 2011
SQ FT: 200,000
SALES (est): 21.34MM Publicly Held
Web: www.napavalleymarriott.com
SIC: 7011 Resort hotel, franchised
PA: Xenia Hotels & Resorts, Inc.

200 S Orange Ave Ste 2700
Orlando FL

(P-9905)
IHG MANAGEMENT (MARYLAND) LLC
Also Called: Crown Plaza Los Angeles
5985 W Century Blvd (90045-5477)
PHONE..........................310 642-7500
William Block, Dir Fin
EMP: 86 EST: 2004
SQ FT: 14,000
SALES (est): 2.65MM Privately Held
Web: www.crowneplaza.com
SIC: 7011 Hotels

(P-9906)
IHG MANAGEMENT (MARYLAND) LLC
Also Called: Intercntnntal Los Angles Dwntw
900 Wilshire Blvd (90017-4701)
PHONE..........................213 688-7777
EMP: 87 EST: 2017
SALES (est): 4.99MM Privately Held
Web: dtla.intercontinental.com
SIC: 7011 Hotels

(P-9907)
IHMS (SF) LLC
Also Called: Campton Place, A Taj Hotel
340 Stockton St (94108-4609)
PHONE..........................415 781-5555
EMP: 150 EST: 2007
SALES (est): 20.91MM Privately Held
SIC: 7011 Hotels
PA: International Hotel Management Services Inc.
2 E 61st St
New York NY

(P-9908)
INDIAN WELLS PROPERTY LLC
45000 Indian Wells Ln (92210-8790)
PHONE..........................442 305-4500
Chris Currie, Managing Member
EMP: 65 EST: 2021
SALES (est): 2.66MM Privately Held
SIC: 7011 Hotels

(P-9909)
INN HAMPTON & SUITES
Also Called: Hampton Inn
6248 Redwood Dr (94928-2019)
PHONE..........................707 586-8700
J A Nordman, Genl Mgr
EMP: 82 EST: 2009
SALES (est): 563.27K Privately Held
Web: www.hilton.com
SIC: 7011 Hotels and motels

(P-9910)
INN VENTURES INC
Also Called: Hilton Garden Inn Roseville
1951 Taylor Rd (95661-3008)
PHONE..........................916 773-7171
Greg Juceam, CFO
Greg Juceam, COO
EMP: 72 EST: 2005
SALES (est): 4.01MM Privately Held
Web: www.hilton.com
SIC: 7011 Hotels and motels

(P-9911)
INTERCNTNNTAL HTELS SAN FRNCSC
Also Called: Intercntinental Hotels Resorts
888 Howard St (94103)
PHONE..........................770 604-5000

Thomas Murray, Pr
EMP: 92 EST: 1983
SALES (est): 3.05MM Privately Held
Web: www.ihg.com
SIC: 7011 Hotels
HQ: Six Continents Hotels, Inc
35016 Avenue D
Yucaipa CA
770 604-5000

(P-9912)
INTERCNTNNTAL HTELS SAN FRNCSC
Also Called: Intercntinental Hotels Resorts
888 Howard St (94103-3011)
PHONE..........................415 616-6500
EMP: 150
Web: www.icsanfrancisco.com
SIC: 7011 Hotels
HQ: Intercontinental Hotels Of San Francisco, Inc.
35016 Avenue D
Yucaipa CA

(P-9913)
INTERSTATE HOTELS RESORTS INC
Also Called: Santa Barbara Inn
901 E Cabrillo Blvd (93103-3642)
P.O. Box 5634 (93150-5634)
PHONE..........................805 966-2285
Clark Sarchet, Brnch Mgr
EMP: 75
Web: www.santabarbarainn.com
SIC: 7011 Hotels
HQ: Interstate Hotels & Resorts, Inc.
5301 Headquarters Dr
Plano TX
703 387-3100

(P-9914)
IRP LAX HOTEL LLC
Also Called: Four Pnts By Shrton La Intl Ar
9750 Airport Blvd (90045-5404)
PHONE..........................310 645-4600
EMP: 240 EST: 1994
SQ FT: 337,720
SALES (est): 8.32MM
SALES (corp-wide): 13.15B Publicly Held
Web: four-points.marriott.com
SIC: 7011 Resort hotel
HQ: Tishman Hotel Corporation
100 Park Ave Fl 18
New York NY

(P-9915)
ISLAND HOSPITALITY MGT LLC
Also Called: Residence Inn By Marriott
2000 Winward Way (94404-2472)
PHONE..........................650 574-4700
Omar Paredes, Brnch Mgr
EMP: 67
SALES (corp-wide): 442.84MM Privately Held
Web: www.islandhospitality.com
SIC: 7011 Hotels and motels
PA: Island Hospitality Management, Llc
222 Lakeview Ave Ste 200
West Palm Beach FL
561 832-6132

(P-9916)
ISLAND HOSPITALITY MGT LLC
Residence Inn By Marriott
1080 Stewart Dr (94085-3917)
PHONE..........................408 720-8893
Kort Gursu, Mgr
EMP: 64
SALES (corp-wide): 442.84MM Privately Held

PRODUCTS & SERVICES SECTION 7011 - Hotels And Motels (P-9938)

Web: www.islandhospitality.com
SIC: 7011 Hotels and motels
PA: Island Hospitality Management, Llc
222 Lakeview Ave Ste 200
West Palm Beach FL
561 832-6132

(P-9917)
J W MRROTT LOS ANGLES L A LIVE
900 W Olympic Blvd (90015-1338)
PHONE.................................213 765-8600
EMP: 62 **EST:** 2008
SALES (est): 5.47MM **Privately Held**
SIC: 7011 Hotels

(P-9918)
JAME HOTEL CORPORATION
Also Called: Hotel California
405 Taylor St (94102-1701)
PHONE.................................415 885-2500
Jack Schleifer, *Pr*
Jack Scheifer, *
EMP: 65 **EST:** 1972
SQ FT: 40,000
SALES (est): 2.81MM **Privately Held**
SIC: 7011 Hotels

(P-9919)
JHC INVESTMENT INC
Also Called: Dt Club Hotel Santa Ana
7 Hutton Centre Dr (92707-5753)
PHONE.................................714 751-2400
Jung-hsiung Chiu, *Pr*
EMP: 70 **EST:** 1993
SQ FT: 85,000
SALES (est): 2.06MM **Privately Held**
SIC: 7011 Hotels

(P-9920)
JIN YI ENTERPRISES INC
Also Called: Super 8 Anaheim Disneyland Drv
915 S Disneyland Dr (92802-1842)
PHONE.................................714 778-0350
Kevin Chen, *Genl Mgr*
Roger Chen, *
EMP: 65 **EST:** 1999
SQ FT: 42,752
SALES (est): 472.42K **Privately Held**
Web: www.wyndhamhotels.com
SIC: 7011 Motels

(P-9921)
JOIE DE VIVRE HOSPITALITY LLC
210 E Main St (95030-6107)
PHONE.................................408 335-1700
EMP: 66
SALES (corp-wide): 83.61MM **Privately Held**
Web: www.jdvhotels.com
SIC: 7011 Hotels
PA: Joie De Vivre Hospitality, Llc
1750 Geary Blvd
San Francisco CA
415 922-6000

(P-9922)
JOIE DE VIVRE HOSPITALITY LLC
Also Called: Hotel Vitale
8 Mission St (94105-1227)
PHONE.................................415 278-3700
Chip Conley, *Brnch Mgr*
EMP: 117
SALES (corp-wide): 83.61MM **Privately Held**
Web: www.jdvhotels.com
SIC: 7011 Hotels

PA: Joie De Vivre Hospitality, Llc
1750 Geary Blvd
San Francisco CA
415 922-6000

(P-9923)
JOIE DE VIVRE HOSPITALITY LLC
Also Called: Laurel Inn
444 Presidio Ave (94115-2004)
PHONE.................................415 567-8467
TOLL FREE: 800
Chip Conley, *Pr*
EMP: 130
SQ FT: 25,448
SALES (corp-wide): 83.61MM **Privately Held**
Web: www.jdvhotels.com
SIC: 7011 Hotels
PA: Joie De Vivre Hospitality, Llc
1750 Geary Blvd
San Francisco CA
415 922-6000

(P-9924)
JOIE DE VIVRE HOSPITALITY LLC
Also Called: Açqua Hotel
555 Redwood Hwy Frontage Rd (94941-3007)
PHONE.................................415 380-0400
Steve Conley, *Pr*
EMP: 84
SALES (corp-wide): 83.61MM **Privately Held**
Web: www.jdvhotels.com
SIC: 7011 Hotels
PA: Joie De Vivre Hospitality, Llc
1750 Geary Blvd
San Francisco CA
415 922-6000

(P-9925)
JOIE DE VIVRE HOSPITALITY LLC
580 Geary St (94102-1650)
PHONE.................................415 441-2700
Frank Okun, *Genl Mgr*
EMP: 65
SALES (corp-wide): 83.61MM **Privately Held**
Web: www.jdvhotels.com
SIC: 7011 8741 Hotels; Hotel or motel management
PA: Joie De Vivre Hospitality, Llc
1750 Geary Blvd
San Francisco CA
415 922-6000

(P-9926)
JOIE DE VIVRE HOSPITALITY LLC
Also Called: Hotel Del Sol
3100 Webster St (94123-3411)
PHONE.................................415 921-5520
Steve Conley, *Pr*
EMP: 98
SALES (corp-wide): 83.61MM **Privately Held**
Web: www.hoteldelsol.com
SIC: 7011 Hotels
PA: Joie De Vivre Hospitality, Llc
1750 Geary Blvd
San Francisco CA
415 922-6000

(P-9927)
JOIE DE VIVRE HOSPITALITY LLC

Also Called: Phoenix Hotel
601 Eddy St (94109-7904)
PHONE.................................415 776-1380
Steven Conley, *Prin*
EMP: 79
SALES (corp-wide): 83.61MM **Privately Held**
Web: www.jdvhotels.com
SIC: 7011 Hotels
PA: Joie De Vivre Hospitality, Llc
1750 Geary Blvd
San Francisco CA
415 922-6000

(P-9928)
JOIE DE VIVRE HOSPITALITY LLC
Also Called: Hotel Avante
860 E El Camino Real (94040-2808)
PHONE.................................650 940-1000
Fred Deftesano, *VP*
EMP: 121
SALES (corp-wide): 83.61MM **Privately Held**
Web: www.jdvhotels.com
SIC: 7011 Hotels
PA: Joie De Vivre Hospitality, Llc
1750 Geary Blvd
San Francisco CA
415 922-6000

(P-9929)
JOIE DE VIVRE HOSPITALITY LLC
Also Called: White Swan Inn, The
845 Bush St (94108-3312)
PHONE.................................415 775-1755
EMP: 107
SALES (corp-wide): 83.61MM **Privately Held**
Web: www.whiteswaninnsf.com
SIC: 7011 8741 Hotels; Management services
PA: Joie De Vivre Hospitality, Llc
1750 Geary Blvd
San Francisco CA
415 922-6000

(P-9930)
JP ALLEN EXTENDED STAY (PA)
Also Called: Days Inn
450 Pioneer Dr (91203-1713)
PHONE.................................818 956-0202
Joe Perry, *Owner*
EMP: 76 **EST:** 1945
SQ FT: 4,000
SALES: 7.43MM
SALES (corp-wide): 7.43MM **Privately Held**
Web: www.wyndhamhotels.com
SIC: 7011 Hotels and motels

(P-9931)
K3 DEV LLC
Also Called: AC Hotel San Jose Snnyvale Cpr
725 S Fair Oaks Ave (94086-7915)
PHONE.................................408 733-7950
Mayur Patel, *Prin*
Mona Rigdon, *
EMP: 80 **EST:** 2018
SALES (est): 2.08MM **Privately Held**
Web: ac-hotels.marriott.com
SIC: 7011 Hotels

(P-9932)
K3 DEV LLC
Also Called: AC Hotel Sunnyvale
597 E El Camino Real (94087-1942)
PHONE.................................408 733-7950
Mona Rigdon, *Prin*

Mayur Patel, *
EMP: 65 **EST:** 2019
SALES (est): 2.01MM **Privately Held**
Web: ac-hotels.marriott.com
SIC: 7011 Hotels

(P-9933)
KAIDAN HOSPITALITY LP
Also Called: Red Lion Hotel Redding
1830 Hilltop Dr (96002-0212)
PHONE.................................530 221-8700
EMP: 66 **EST:** 2014
SALES (est): 4.6MM **Privately Held**
Web: www.redlion.com
SIC: 7011 Hotels and motels

(P-9934)
KAM SANG COMPANY INC
Also Called: New Age Lamirada Inn
14419 Firestone Blvd (90638-5912)
PHONE.................................714 523-2800
Grace Tanji, *Genl Mgr*
EMP: 70
SALES (corp-wide): 20.56MM **Privately Held**
Web: www.kamsangcompany.com
SIC: 7011 Hotel, franchised
PA: Kam Sang Company, Inc.
411 E Huntington Dr # 305
Arcadia CA
626 446-2988

(P-9935)
KANG FAMILY PARTNERS LLC
Also Called: Santa Ynez Valley Marriott
555 Mcmurray Rd (93427-9559)
PHONE.................................805 688-1000
Daphne Kang, *Managing Member*
EMP: 110 **EST:** 1995
SALES (est): 9.54MM **Privately Held**
Web: www.syvmarriott.com
SIC: 7011 Hotel, franchised

(P-9936)
KAVA HOLDINGS INC (DH)
Also Called: Hotel Bel-Air
701 Stone Canyon Rd (90077-2909)
PHONE.................................310 472-1211
Hj Suharafadzil, *Pr*
Christopher Cowdary, *
Helen Smith, *
Eugenio Pirri, *
Franois Delahaye, *
EMP: 200 **EST:** 1994
SQ FT: 30,000
SALES (est): 62.94MM **Privately Held**
Web: www.dorchestercollection.com
SIC: 7011 Resort hotel
HQ: Dorchester Group Limited
3 Tilney Street
London
207 629-4848

(P-9937)
KEN REAL ESTATE LEASE LTD
Also Called: Anaheim Majestic Garden Hotel
900 S Disneyland Dr (92802-1844)
PHONE.................................714 778-1700
Shigeru Sato, *Pr*
EMP: 99 **EST:** 2005
SALES (est): 9.58MM **Privately Held**
Web: www.ken-realestate.jp
SIC: 7011 Resort hotel

(P-9938)
KHP V CARMEL TRS LLC
Also Called: Carmel Mission Inn
3665 Rio Rd (93923-8609)
PHONE.................................831 624-1841
Benjamin Rowe, *Prin*

7011 - Hotels And Motels (P-9939)

PRODUCTS & SERVICES SECTION

EMP: 80 EST: 2020
SALES (est): 5.36MM **Privately Held**
Web: www.carmelmissioninn.com
SIC: 7011 Hotels

(P-9939)
KIMPTON HOTEL & REST GROUP LLC
Also Called: Serrano Hotel
405 Taylor St (94102-1701)
PHONE.....................415 885-2500
John Turner, *Genl Mgr*
EMP: 470
Web: www.kimptonhotels.com
SIC: 7011 7299 Hotels; Banquet hall facilities
HQ: Kimpton Hotel & Restaurant Group Llc
222 Kearny St Ste 200
San Francisco CA
415 397-5572

(P-9940)
KIMPTON HOTEL & REST GROUP LLC
6317 Wilshire Blvd (90048-5600)
PHONE.....................323 852-6000
Ashley Gochnauer, *Mgr*
EMP: 225
Web: www.kimptonhotels.com
SIC: 7011 Hotels
HQ: Kimpton Hotel & Restaurant Group Llc
222 Kearny St Ste 200
San Francisco CA
415 397-5572

(P-9941)
KIMPTON HOTEL & REST GROUP LLC (HQ)
Also Called: Kimpton Hotel
222 Kearny St Ste 200 (94108-4503)
PHONE.....................415 397-5572
Mike Depatie, *CEO*
Niki Leondakis, *
Joe Long, *Executive Development Vice President**
Ben Rowe, *
Judy Miles, *
EMP: 100 EST: 1982
SALES (est): 606.51MM **Privately Held**
Web: www.kimptonhotels.com
SIC: 7011 8741 6794 Hotels; Hotel or motel management; Franchises, selling or licensing
PA: Intercontinental Hotels Group Plc
1 Windsor Dials
Windsor BERKS

(P-9942)
KIMPTON HOTEL & REST GROUP LLC
Also Called: Tuscan Inn
425 N Point St (94133-1405)
PHONE.....................415 561-1100
Jan Misch, *Mgr*
EMP: 225
Web: www.kimptonhotels.com
SIC: 7011 7299 5813 Hotels; Banquet hall facilities; Drinking places
HQ: Kimpton Hotel & Restaurant Group Llc
222 Kearny St Ste 200
San Francisco CA
415 397-5572

(P-9943)
KIMPTON HOTEL & REST GROUP LLC
Also Called: Monticello Inn
127 Ellis St (94102-2109)
PHONE.....................415 392-8800
Chris Holbrook, *Genl Mgr*
EMP: 169
Web: www.kimptonhotels.com
SIC: 7011 Hotels
HQ: Kimpton Hotel & Restaurant Group Llc
222 Kearny St Ste 200
San Francisco CA
415 397-5572

(P-9944)
KIMPTON HOTEL & REST GROUP LLC
Also Called: Pescatore
2455 Mason St (94133-1401)
PHONE.....................415 561-1111
Leon Calahan, *Mgr*
EMP: 197
Web: www.kimptonhotels.com
SIC: 7011 Hotels
HQ: Kimpton Hotel & Restaurant Group Llc
222 Kearny St Ste 200
San Francisco CA
415 397-5572

(P-9945)
KIMPTON HOTEL & REST GROUP LLC
Also Called: Hotel Moneco
501 Geary St (94102-1640)
PHONE.....................415 292-0100
Jimmy Hord, *Mgr*
EMP: 122
Web: www.kimptonhotels.com
SIC: 7011 5812 Hotels; Eating places
HQ: Kimpton Hotel & Restaurant Group Llc
222 Kearny St Ste 200
San Francisco CA
415 397-5572

(P-9946)
KINTETSU ENTERPRISES CO AMER (HQ)
Also Called: Kintetsu Enterprises Co Amer
21241 S Western Ave Ste 100 (90501)
PHONE.....................310 782-9300
Hisao Hiro, *Pr*
EMP: 200 EST: 1961
SALES (est): 22.87MM **Privately Held**
Web: www.miyakohybridhotel.com
SIC: 7011 6512 Hotel, franchised; Nonresidential building operators
PA: Kintetsu Group Holdings Co.,Ltd.
6-1-55, Uehonmachi, Tennoji-Ku
Osaka OSK

(P-9947)
KIRKWOOD COLLECTION INC
Also Called: Kirkwood Collection
301 N Canon Dr Ste 302 (90210-4724)
PHONE.....................424 532-1160
Alex Kirkwood, *CEO*
EMP: 76 EST: 2016
SALES (est): 2.7MM **Privately Held**
Web: www.kirkwoodcollection.com
SIC: 7011 7389 Hotels; Business Activities at Non-Commercial Site

(P-9948)
KIRKWOOD MOUNTAIN RESORTS LLC
Also Called: Kirkwood Resort Company
1501 Kirkwood Meadows Dr (95646)
P.O. Box 1 (95646-0001)
PHONE.....................209 258-6000
EMP: 100
Web: www.kirkwood.com
SIC: 7011 Ski lodge

(P-9949)
KITTRIDGE HOTELS & RESORTS LLC
Also Called: Hard Rock Hotel Palm Springs
150 S Indian Canyon Dr (92262-6604)
PHONE.....................760 325-9676
Andre Carpiac, *
EMP: 64 EST: 2004
SALES (est): 8.47MM **Privately Held**
Web: www.hardrockhotels.com
SIC: 7011 Resort hotel

(P-9950)
KNOTTS BERRY FARM LLC
Also Called: Knott's Berry Farm Hotel
7675 Crescent Ave (90620-3947)
PHONE.....................714 995-1111
Stan Dlander, *Mgr*
EMP: 99
SALES (corp-wide): 1.82B **Publicly Held**
Web: www.knotts.com
SIC: 7011 Resort hotel
HQ: Berry Knott's Farm Llc
8039 Beach Blvd
Buena Park CA
714 827-1776

(P-9951)
KSL RANCHO MIRAGE OPERATING CO INC
Also Called: Rancho Las Palmas Resort & Spa
41000 Bob Hope Dr (92270-4416)
PHONE.....................760 568-2727
EMP: 500
Web: www.omnihotels.com
SIC: 7011 Hotels and motels

(P-9952)
KSL RESORTS HOTEL DEL CORONADO
Also Called: Hotel Del Coronado
1500 Orange Ave (92118-2918)
PHONE.....................619 435-6611
Bob Antes, *Prin*
EMP: 212 EST: 1888
SALES (est): 4.96MM
SALES (corp-wide): 8.77B **Publicly Held**
Web: www.hoteldel.com
SIC: 7011 Resort hotel
HQ: Hilton Supply Management Llc
7926 Jones Branch Dr Fl 4
Mc Lean VA
703 883-1000

(P-9953)
KSSF ENTERPRISES LTD
181 3rd St (94103-3107)
PHONE.....................415 817-7840
Peter Wong, *Pr*
▲ EMP: 103 EST: 2009
SALES (est): 4.73MM **Privately Held**
Web: www.wsanfrancisco.com
SIC: 7011 Hotels and motels
HQ: Ocean Place Joint Venture Company Ltd
80 Dong Du And 88 Dong Khoi Street, Ho Chi Minh

(P-9954)
KT HOTELS LLC
Also Called: Pendry, The
3 Ada Ste 100 (92618-2322)
PHONE.....................949 715-5000
EMP: 136 EST: 2017
SALES (est): 3.06MM **Privately Held**
SIC: 7011 Hotels

(P-9955)
KUMAR HOTELS INC (PA)
Also Called: Holiday Inn
545 N Humboldt Ave (95988-3502)
PHONE.....................530 934-8900
Pawan Kumar, *Pr*
EMP: 125 EST: 2005
SALES (est): 4.58MM **Privately Held**
Web: www.holidayinn.com
SIC: 7011 Hotels and motels

(P-9956)
L & O ALISO VIEJO LLC
Also Called: Renaissance Hotel Clubsport
50 Enterprise (92656-6026)
PHONE.....................949 643-6700
Ed Tomlin, *Genl Mgr*
EMP: 102 EST: 2008
SALES (est): 16.5MM **Privately Held**
Web: www.evolutionswim.com
SIC: 7011 Hotels and motels

(P-9957)
L-O BEDFORD OPERATING LLC
Also Called: Doubletree Hotel Boston
11755 Wilshire Blvd Ste 1350 (90025-1506)
PHONE.....................781 275-5500
EMP: 200 EST: 2011
SALES (est): 4.8MM **Privately Held**
Web: www.hilton.com
SIC: 7011 Hotels and motels

(P-9958)
L-O CORONADO HOTEL INC
1500 Orange Ave (92118-2918)
PHONE.....................619 435-6611
Tod Shallon, *Pr*
EMP: 73 EST: 1886
SALES (est): 309.43K **Privately Held**
Web: www.hoteldel.com
SIC: 7011 5812 5813 5941 Resort hotel; Eating places; Cocktail lounge; Tennis goods and equipment

(P-9959)
L-O SOMA HOTEL INC
Also Called: Argent Hotel, The
50 3rd St (94103-3106)
PHONE.....................415 974-6400
Charles S Peck, *Pr*
Peter A Del Franco, *
Ronald A Silva, *
EMP: 1948 EST: 1998
SALES (est): 9.74MM
SALES (corp-wide): 367.25MM **Privately Held**
Web: www.argentwork.com
SIC: 7011 5812 Hotels; Eating places
HQ: Destination Residences Llc
10333 E Dry Creek Rd
Englewood CO
303 799-3830

(P-9960)
LA JOLLA BCH & TENNIS CLB INC
Also Called: Shores Restaurant
8110 Camino Del Oro (92037-3108)
PHONE.....................858 459-8271
John Cambel, *Mgr*
EMP: 285
SALES (corp-wide): 47.87MM **Privately Held**
Web: www.theshoresrestaurant.com
SIC: 7011 5812 5813 7299 Resort hotel; Restaurant, family: independent; Cocktail lounge; Banquet hall facilities
PA: La Jolla Beach & Tennis Club, Inc.
2000 Spindrift Dr
La Jolla CA
858 454-7126

PRODUCTS & SERVICES SECTION

7011 - Hotels And Motels (P-9984)

(P-9961)
LA JOLLA COVE HT MTL APRTMNTS
Also Called: La Jolla Cove Motel
1155 Coast Blvd (92037-3627)
P.O. Box 1067 (92038-1067)
PHONE.................................858 459-2621
Helen Jackman, VP
EMP: 78 **EST:** 1959
SQ FT: 78,000
SALES (est): 5.01MM **Privately Held**
Web: www.lajollacove.com
SIC: 7011 Hotels

(P-9962)
LA QUINTA INN
Also Called: La Quinta Inn
8465 Enterprise Way (94621-1317)
PHONE.................................510 632-8900
Shailandra Devdhara, Pr
Nitin Shah, *
Balwantsinh Thakor, *
Dilip Patel, *
EMP: 81 **EST:** 2001
SQ FT: 76,000
SALES (est): 1.54MM **Privately Held**
Web: www.lq.com
SIC: 7011 Hotels and motels

(P-9963)
LAKE ARRWHEAD RSORT OPRTOR INC (HQ)
Also Called: Marriott
27984 Hwy 189 (92352)
PHONE.................................909 336-1511
TOLL FREE: 800
Carmen Rodriguez, CEO
Veronique Williams, *
EMP: 115 **EST:** 1982
SALES (est): 13.59MM
SALES (corp-wide): 20.77B **Publicly Held**
Web: www.lakearrowheadresort.com
SIC: 7011 5813 5812 Resort hotel; Drinking places; Eating places
PA: Marriott International, Inc.
7750 Wisconsin Ave
Bethesda MD
301 380-3000

(P-9964)
LAKE NATOMA LODGING LP
Also Called: Lake Natoma Inn
702 Gold Lake Dr (95630-2559)
PHONE.................................916 351-1500
Robert Leach, Pt
Rick Fenstermaker, Genl Pt
EMP: 80 **EST:** 1992
SQ FT: 82,000
SALES (est): 10.74MM **Privately Held**
Web: www.lakenatomainn.com
SIC: 7011 Hotel, franchised

(P-9965)
LANGHAM HOTELS PACIFIC CORP
Also Called: Langham Hotels International
1401 S Oak Knoll Ave (91106-4508)
PHONE.................................617 451-1900
Ka Shui Lo, Pr
Brett Butcher, *
EMP: 117 **EST:** 2007
SALES (est): 11.49MM **Privately Held**
SIC: 7011 Hotels

(P-9966)
LARKSPUR GROUP LLC
Also Called: Hampton Inn & Suites By Hilton
2160 Larkspur Ln (96002-0628)
PHONE.................................530 223-9344
David Grabal, Brnch Mgr
EMP: 151
SALES (corp-wide): 1.39MM **Privately Held**
Web: www.hilton.com
SIC: 7011 Hotels
PA: Larkspur Group Llc
2160 Larkspur Ln
Redding CA
530 224-1001

(P-9967)
LARKSPUR HSPTALITY DEV MGT LLC
Also Called: Larkspur Landing Home Sweet Ht
690 Gateway Blvd (94080-7014)
PHONE.................................650 827-1515
EMP: 61
Web: www.larkspurhotels.com
SIC: 7011 Hotels
PA: Larkspur Hospitality Development And Management Company, Llc
125 E Sir Frncis Drake Bl
Larkspur CA

(P-9968)
LARKSPUR HSPTALITY DEV MGT LLC
Also Called: Hilton Grdn Inn San Frncsco Ar
670 Gateway Blvd (94080-7014)
PHONE.................................650 872-1515
EMP: 61
EST: 2017
Web: www.larkspurhotels.com
SIC: 7011 Resort hotel
PA: Larkspur Hospitality Development And Management Company, Llc
125 E Sir Frncis Drake Bl
Larkspur CA

(P-9969)
LAUBERGE DE SONOMA LLC
29 E Macarthur St (95476-7615)
PHONE.................................707 938-2929
Chad Parson, Managing Member
EMP: 180 **EST:** 2017
SALES (est): 17MM **Privately Held**
SIC: 7011 Hotels

(P-9970)
LAV HOTEL CORP
Also Called: Whaling Bar & Grill
1132 Prospect St (92037-4533)
PHONE.................................858 454-0771
Harry Collins, Pr
W M Allen Senior, Bd of Dir
W M Allen Junior, VP
EMP: 250 **EST:** 1928
SQ FT: 1,000
SALES (est): 17.75MM **Privately Held**
Web: www.lavalencia.com
SIC: 7011 Hotels

(P-9971)
LC TRS INC
Also Called: La Costa Resort & Spa
2100 Costa Del Mar Rd (92009-6823)
PHONE.................................760 438-9111
EMP: 872
SIC: 7011 5812 Resort hotel; Eating places

(P-9972)
LE MONTROSE HOTEL
Also Called: Le Montrose Suite Hotel
900 Hammond St Apt 534 (90069-4443)
PHONE.................................310 855-1115
John Douponce, Mng Pt
EMP: 69 **EST:** 1987
SQ FT: 1,000
SALES (est): 1.86MM **Privately Held**
SIC: 7011 Hotels

(P-9973)
LFS DEVELOPMENT LLC
Also Called: Intercontinental San Diego
901 Bayfront Ct Ste 1 (92101-3050)
PHONE.................................619 501-5400
EMP: 200 **EST:** 1946
SALES (est): 8.37MM **Privately Held**
SIC: 7011 Hotels

(P-9974)
LH INDIAN WELLS OPERATING LLC
4500 Indian Wells Ln (92210)
PHONE.................................760 341-2200
Bob Low, Prin
EMP: 220 **EST:** 2004
SALES (est): 399.11K **Privately Held**
SIC: 7011 7991 Resort hotel; Spas
PA: Lh Indian Wells Holding, Llc
11777 San Vicente Blvd
Los Angeles CA

(P-9975)
LH UNIVERSAL OPERATING LLC
Also Called: Sheraton
333 Universal Hollywood Dr (91608-1001)
PHONE.................................818 980-1212
EMP: 280 **EST:** 1969
SALES (est): 24.75MM **Privately Held**
Web: www.sheratonuniversal.com
SIC: 7011 Hotels

(P-9976)
LHO MSSION BAY RSIE LESSEE INC
Also Called: Hilton
1775 E Mission Bay Dr (92109-6801)
PHONE.................................619 276-4010
Greg Fracassa, Managing Member
EMP: 360 **EST:** 2005
SALES (est): 23.79MM **Privately Held**
Web: www.hilton.com
SIC: 7011 5812 5947 Resort hotel; Eating places; Gift, novelty, and souvenir shop

(P-9977)
LHOBERGE LESSEE INC
Also Called: L'Auberge Del Mar
1540 Camino Del Mar (92014-2411)
PHONE.................................858 259-1515
Jamie Sabatier, CEO
Charles Peck, *
Dennis Fischer, *
EMP: 250 **EST:** 1989
SQ FT: 84,312
SALES (est): 18.25MM **Privately Held**
Web: www.laubergedelmar.com
SIC: 7011 Resort hotel

(P-9978)
LIGHTSTONE DT LA LLC ⊙
Also Called: Moxy AC Ht Dwntwn Los Angeles
1260 S Figueron St (90015)
PHONE.................................310 669-9252
EMP: 300 **EST:** 2022
SALES (est): 9.64MM **Privately Held**
SIC: 7011 7389 Hotels; Business Activities at Non-Commercial Site

(P-9979)
LIONSGATE HT & CONFERENCE CTR
3410 Westover St (95652-1005)
PHONE.................................916 643-6222
Lary Kelly, Pr
EMP: 90 **EST:** 2001
SALES (est): 7.96MM **Privately Held**
Web: www.lionsgatehotel.com
SIC: 7011 Hotels

(P-9980)
LITTLE RIVER INN INC
Also Called: Little River Inn and Golf Crse
7901 N Highway 1 (95456-9527)
P.O. Box B (95456-0430)
PHONE.................................707 937-5942
Charles D Hervilla, CEO
Susan Mc Kinney, *
EMP: 176 **EST:** 1939
SQ FT: 3,000
SALES (est): 10MM **Privately Held**
Web: www.littleriverinn.com
SIC: 7011 5812 Bed and breakfast inn; American restaurant

(P-9981)
LODGEWORKS LP
1230 1st St (94559-2930)
PHONE.................................707 690-9800
Michael Collins, Brnch Mgr
EMP: 60
SALES (corp-wide): 46.64MM **Privately Held**
Web: www.lodgeworks.com
SIC: 7011 Hotels and motels
PA: Lodgeworks, L.P.
8100 E 22nd St N Bldg 500
Wichita KS
316 681-5100

(P-9982)
LOEWS HOLLYWOOD HOTEL LLC
1755 N Highland Ave (90028-4403)
PHONE.................................323 450-2235
Jonathan Tisch, Ch Bd
Reggie Dominique, *
EMP: 375 **EST:** 2012
SALES (est): 67.38MM
SALES (corp-wide): 14.04B **Publicly Held**
Web: www.loewshotels.com
SIC: 7011 Hotels
PA: Loews Corporation
667 Madison Ave Fl 7
New York NY
212 521-2000

(P-9983)
LONE CYPRESS COMPANY LLC
Also Called: Spyglass Hill Golf Shop
Stevenston & Spyglass Rd (93953)
P.O. Box 658 (93953-0658)
PHONE.................................831 625-8563
Jin Park, Mgr
EMP: 78
SALES (corp-wide): 302.53MM **Privately Held**
Web: www.pebblebeach.com
SIC: 7011 Resort hotel
PA: Lone Cypress Company Llc
2700 17 Mile Dr
Pebble Beach CA
831 647-7500

(P-9984)
LONG BEACH GOLDEN SAILS INC
Also Called: Best Western Golden Sails Ht
23545 Crenshaw Blvd Ste 100 (90505-5218)
PHONE.................................562 596-1631
TOLL FREE: 800
Luis Vasquez, Pr

7011 - Hotels And Motels (P-9985)

Ruben Garza, *
Vicki Arreguin, *
▲ EMP: 100 EST: 1964
SQ FT: 150,000
SALES (est): 9.28MM
SALES (corp-wide): 9.28MM Privately Held
Web: www.goldensailshotel.com
SIC: 7011 5812 5813 Hotels and motels; Restaurant, family: independent; Bar (drinking places)
PA: Abp Hotel, Llc
2200 W Valley Blvd
Alhambra CA
562 596-1631

(P-9985)
LONG POINT DEVELOPMENT LLC
Also Called: Terranea Resort
100 Terranea Way (90275-1013)
PHONE.................310 265-2800
Terri Haack, *Managing Member*
Jennifer Yang, *
EMP: 1000 EST: 2004
SALES (est): 138.42MM Privately Held
Web: www.terranea.com
SIC: 7011 Resort hotel

(P-9986)
LOTUS HOTELS - UNION CITY LLC
Also Called: Holiday Inn
31140 Alvarado Niles Rd (94587-2701)
PHONE.................510 475-0600
EMP: 65 EST: 2000
SQ FT: 50,000
SALES (est): 1.17MM Privately Held
Web: www.hiexpress.com
SIC: 7011 Hotels and motels

(P-9987)
LOWE ENTERPRISES
Also Called: Squaw Creek Transportation
400 Squaw Creek Rd (96146-9778)
P.O. Box 3333 (96146-3333)
PHONE.................530 581-6628
EMP: 71 EST: 1992
SALES (est): 789.4K Privately Held
Web: www.lowe-re.com
SIC: 7011 Resort hotel

(P-9988)
LOWE ENTERPRISES INC (PA)
Also Called: Lei AG Seattle
11777 San Vicente Blvd Ste 900 (90049-5084)
PHONE.................310 820-6661
Robert J Lowe Senior, *Ch*
Robert M Weekley, *Sr VP*
Peter O'keeffe, *Ex VP*
Linda Leonard, *Corporate Secretary*
EMP: 125 EST: 1972
SQ FT: 20,000
SALES (est): 367.25MM
SALES (corp-wide): 367.25MM Privately Held
Web: www.lowe-re.com
SIC: 7011 6552 Hotels and motels; Subdividers and developers, nec

(P-9989)
LQ MANAGEMENT LLC
Also Called: La Quinta Inn
5249 W Century Blvd (90045-5917)
PHONE.................310 645-2200
Ryan Thayer, *Brnch Mgr*
EMP: 60
SALES (corp-wide): 1.5B Publicly Held
Web: www.lq.com

SIC: 7011 Hotels and motels
HQ: Lq Management L.L.C.
909 Hidden Rdg Ste 600
Irving TX
214 492-6600

(P-9990)
LQR PROPERTY LLC
Also Called: La Quinta Resort & Club
49499 Eisenhower Dr (92253-2722)
PHONE.................760 564-4111
EMP: 121 EST: 2012
SALES (est): 21.67MM Privately Held
Web: www.lq.com
SIC: 7011 7999 Resort hotel; Golf driving range

(P-9991)
LUCKY CHANCES INC
Also Called: Lucky Chances Casino
1700 Hillside Blvd (94014-2801)
PHONE.................650 758-2237
Rommel R Medina, *CEO*
Ruell Medina, *
EMP: 650 EST: 1998
SALES (est): 25.03MM Privately Held
Web: www.luckychances.com
SIC: 7011 Casino hotel

(P-9992)
LYTTON RANCHERIA
Also Called: Casino San Pablo
13255 San Pablo Ave (94806-3907)
PHONE.................510 215-7888
Michael Gorczysnski, *Genl Mgr*
Cathi Hamel, *Prin*
EMP: 547 EST: 1995
SALES (est): 39.81MM Privately Held
Web: www.sanpablolytton.com
SIC: 7011 Casino hotel

(P-9993)
M&C HOTEL INTERESTS INC
530 Pico Blvd (90405-1223)
PHONE.................310 399-9344
Lisa Nagahori, *Brnch Mgr*
EMP: 263
Web: www.richfield.com
SIC: 7011 Hotels
HQ: M&C Hotel Interests, Inc.
6560 Greenwood Plaza Blvd
Greenwood Village CO

(P-9994)
M10 DEV LLC
Also Called: AC By Marriott Palo Alto
744 San Antonio Rd (94303-4632)
PHONE.................650 565-8100
Michael Lerman, *Genl Mgr*
EMP: 96
SALES (corp-wide): 816.15K Privately Held
Web: ac-hotels.marriott.com
SIC: 7011 Hotels
PA: M10 Dev, Llc
750 San Antonio Rd
Palo Alto CA
650 424-8991

(P-9995)
M4DEV LLC
Also Called: Hilton Grdn Inn San Dego Dwntw
2137 Pacific Hwy Ste A (92101-8472)
PHONE.................619 696-6300
EMP: 100 EST: 2016
SALES (est): 2.35MM Privately Held
Web: www.hilton.com
SIC: 7011 Resort hotel

(P-9996)
MAJESTIC INDUSTRY HILLS LLC
Also Called: Pacific Plms Conference Resort
1 Industry Hills Pkwy (91744-5160)
PHONE.................626 810-4455
Scott Huntsman, *Brnch Mgr*
EMP: 547
SALES (corp-wide): 42.1MM Privately Held
Web: www.pacificpalmsresort.com
SIC: 7011 7999 7389 7299 Resort hotel; Tennis courts, outdoor/indoor: non-membership; Convention and show services ; Banquet hall facilities
PA: Majestic Industry Hills, Llc
1 Industry Hills Pkwy
City Of Industry CA
562 692-9581

(P-9997)
MAKAR ANAHEIM LLC
Also Called: Hilton
777 W Convention Way (92802-3425)
PHONE.................714 740-4431
EMP: 1200 EST: 1984
SQ FT: 1,000,000
SALES (est): 52.04MM Privately Held
Web: www.hilton.com
SIC: 7011 Resort hotel

(P-9998)
MAMMOTH MOUNTAIN SKI AREA LLC (DH)
Also Called: Mammoth Mountain Inn
10001 Minaret Rd (93546)
P.O. Box 24 (93546-0024)
PHONE.................760 934-2571
Ron Cohen, *Pr*
▲ EMP: 347 EST: 1951
SQ FT: 140,000
SALES (est): 97.46MM
SALES (corp-wide): 1.3B Privately Held
Web: www.mammothmountain.com
SIC: 7011 5812 Ski lodge; Eating places
HQ: Alterra Mountain Company
3501 Wazee St Ste 400
Denver CO
303 749-8200

(P-9999)
MANCHESTER GRAND RESORTS LP
Also Called: Manchster Grnd Hyatt San Diego
1 Market Pl Fl 33 (92101-7714)
PHONE.................619 232-1234
Mark S Hoplamazian, *CEO*
Douglas F Manchester, *Pt*
Richard V Gibbons, *Pt*
H Charles Floyd, *Ex VP*
Peter Fulton, *Ex VP*
EMP: 245 EST: 1984
SALES (est): 44.38MM
SALES (corp-wide): 4.91B Publicly Held
Web: www.manchestergrandhyattsandiego.com
SIC: 7011 Hotel, franchised
PA: Host Hotels & Resorts, Inc.
4747 Bethesda Ave # 1300
Bethesda MD
240 744-1000

(P-10000)
MARCUS HOTELS INC
Also Called: Holiday Inn
4222 Vineland Ave (91602-3318)
PHONE.................818 980-8000
Kroy Walter, *Dir*
EMP: 155
SALES (corp-wide): 677.39MM Publicly Held

Web: www.holidayinn.com
SIC: 7011 Hotels and motels
HQ: Marcus Hotels Inc
100 E Wscnsin Ave Ste 190
Milwaukee WI

(P-10001)
MARGARTVLLE RSORT ORLNDO RSORT
Also Called: Margaritaville Resort Palm Sprng
1600 N Indian Canyon Dr (92262-4602)
PHONE.................760 327-8311
EMP: 235
SALES (corp-wide): 13.3MM Privately Held
Web: www.margaritavilleresorts.com
SIC: 7011 Resort hotel
PA: Margaritaville Resort Orlando Resort Services, Llc
8000 Fins Up Cir
Kissimmee FL
855 995-9099

(P-10002)
MARRIOTT HOTEL SERVICES INC
Also Called: Marriott
301 S Market St (95113-2832)
PHONE.................408 280-1300
Luke Massar, *Owner*
Kevin Fergason, *Dir*
EMP: 472 EST: 2007
SALES (est): 21.95MM
SALES (corp-wide): 21.95MM Privately Held
Web: www.marriott.com
SIC: 7011 7389 Hotels and motels; Office facilities and secretarial service rental
PA: Walton San Jose Investors Iii, L.L.C.
301 S Market St
San Jose CA
408 280-1300

(P-10003)
MARRIOTT INTERNATIONAL INC
Also Called: Marriott
5855 W Century Blvd (90045-5614)
PHONE.................310 641-5700
Jim Burns, *Genl Mgr*
EMP: 900
SALES (corp-wide): 20.77B Publicly Held
Web: www.marriott.com
SIC: 7011 7389 6513 Hotels and motels; Office facilities and secretarial service rental ; Residential hotel operation
PA: Marriott International, Inc.
7750 Wisconsin Ave
Bethesda MD
301 380-3000

(P-10004)
MARRIOTT INTERNATIONAL INC
Also Called: Marriott
18000 Von Karman Ave (92612-1004)
PHONE.................949 724-3606
Satinder Palpa, *Brnch Mgr*
EMP: 258
SALES (corp-wide): 20.77B Publicly Held
Web: www.marriott.com
SIC: 7011 7389 Hotels and motels; Office facilities and secretarial service rental
PA: Marriott International, Inc.
7750 Wisconsin Ave
Bethesda MD
301 380-3000

(P-10005)
MARRIOTT INTERNATIONAL INC
Also Called: Inn At Mssion San Juan Cpstran
31692 El Camino Real (92675-3221)

PRODUCTS & SERVICES SECTION
7011 - Hotels And Motels (P-10028)

PHONE.................................949 503-5700
Arne Sorenson, *CEO*
Kristi Kaib, *
EMP: 90 EST: 1997
SALES (est): 2.39MM **Privately Held**
Web: www.marriott.com
SIC: 7011 Hotels and motels

(P-10006)
MARRIOTT INTERNATIONAL INC
Also Called: Marriott
4240 La Jolla Village Dr (92037-1407)
PHONE.................................858 587-1414
Paul Corsinita, *Mgr*
EMP: 337
SALES (corp-wide): 20.77B **Publicly Held**
Web: www.marriott.com
SIC: 7011 Hotels and motels
PA: Marriott International, Inc.
   7750 Wisconsin Ave
   Bethesda MD
   301 380-3000

(P-10007)
MARRIOTT INTL HOTELS INC
Also Called: Courtyard Santa Barbara Dwntwn
1601 State St (93101-2519)
PHONE.................................805 975-0660
EMP: 67
SALES (corp-wide): 20.77B **Publicly Held**
Web: www.marriott.com
SIC: 7011 Hotels and motels
HQ: Marriott International Hotels, Inc.
   10400 Fernwood Rd
   Bethesda MD

(P-10008)
MARRIOTT VACATION CLUB INTL
Also Called: Marriott
9001 Shadow Ridge Rd (92211-2057)
PHONE.................................760 674-2927
Catalina Saldivar, *Prin*
EMP: 79 EST: 2012
SALES (est): 527.25K **Privately Held**
Web: www.marriott.com
SIC: 7011 Hotels and motels

(P-10009)
MASON STREET OPCO LLC
Also Called: Fairmont San Francisco
950 Mason St (94108-6000)
PHONE.................................415 772-5000
Seung Geon Kim, *Pr*
EMP: 850 EST: 2015
SQ FT: 750,000
SALES (est): 100.36MM
SALES (corp-wide): 713.02MM **Privately Held**
Web: www.fairmont.com
SIC: 7011 Hotels
HQ: Accor Services Us Llc
   950 Mason St
   San Francisco CA
   415 772-5000

(P-10010)
MAVERICK HOSPITALITY INC
17662 Irvine Blvd Ste 4 (92780-3132)
PHONE.................................714 730-7717
Brad Perrin, *Prin*
EMP: 97 EST: 2004
SALES (est): 1.01MM **Privately Held**
SIC: 7011 Hotels and motels

(P-10011)
MBP LAND LLC
Also Called: Courtyard Marriott Mission Vly
595 Hotel Cir S (92108-3403)
PHONE.................................619 291-5720
John Blem, *Managing Member*
EMP: 2494 EST: 2000
SALES (est): 1.09MM
SALES (corp-wide): 819.71MM **Privately Held**
Web: courtyard.marriott.com
SIC: 7011 Hotels
HQ: Evolution Hospitality, Llc
   1211 Puerta Del Sol # 170
   San Clemente CA
   949 325-1350

(P-10012)
MENDOCINO HOTEL & RESORT CORP
Also Called: Mendocino Hotel & Grdn Suites
45080 Main St (95460-9203)
PHONE.................................707 937-0511
Thomas Clark Kravis, *Owner*
EMP: 80 EST: 1881
SQ FT: 12,500
SALES (est): 2.18MM **Privately Held**
Web: www.mendocinohotel.com
SIC: 7011 5812 5813 7299 Hotels; Eating places; Bars and lounges; Banquet hall facilities

(P-10013)
MERISTAR SAN PEDRO HILTON LLC
Also Called: Hilton Port Los Angls-San Pdro
2800 Via Cabrillo Marina (90731-7223)
PHONE.................................310 514-3344
Paul Whetsell, *Managing Member*
John Emery, *
Jeff Milnes, *
EMP: 97 EST: 1986
SALES (est): 2.14MM **Privately Held**
SIC: 7011 Hotels and motels
HQ: Interstate Hotels & Resorts, Inc.
   5301 Headquarters Dr
   Plano TX
   703 387-3100

(P-10014)
MERITAGE RESORT LLC
Also Called: Meritage Resort and Spa, The
875 Bordeaux Way (94558-7524)
PHONE.................................707 251-1900
Timothy R Busch, *Pr*
Timothy R Busch, *Prin*
EMP: 350 EST: 2006
SALES (est): 40.18MM **Privately Held**
Web: www.meritageresort.com
SIC: 7011 Resort hotel

(P-10015)
MERRITT HOSPITALITY LLC
Also Called: Hilton
701 W Ocean Blvd (90831-3100)
PHONE.................................562 983-3400
Grace Sun, *Sls Mgr*
EMP: 123
SALES (corp-wide): 447.39MM **Privately Held**
Web: www.hilton.com
SIC: 7011 7991 5813 5812 Resort hotel; Physical fitness facilities; Drinking places; Eating places
HQ: Merritt Hospitality, Llc
   101 Merritt 7 Ste 14
   Norwalk CT
   203 849-8844

(P-10016)
MERRITT HOSPITALITY LLC
Also Called: Marriott
2701 Nutwood Ave (92831-5400)
PHONE.................................714 738-7800
Tom Beebon, *Mgr*
EMP: 171
SALES (corp-wide): 447.39MM **Privately Held**
Web: www.marriott.com
SIC: 7011 7991 5813 5812 Resort hotel; Physical fitness facilities; Drinking places; Eating places
HQ: Merritt Hospitality, Llc
   101 Merritt 7 Ste 14
   Norwalk CT
   203 849-8844

(P-10017)
METROPOLIS HOTEL MGT LLC
Also Called: Hotel Indigo Los Angeles Dwntwn
899 Francisco St (90017-2534)
PHONE.................................213 683-4855
Raymond Vermolen, *Genl Mgr*
EMP: 120 EST: 2016
SALES (est): 21.73MM **Privately Held**
Web: www.hotelindigo.com
SIC: 7011 Hotels
HQ: Inter-Continental Hotels Corporation
   35016 Avenue D
   Yucaipa CA
   770 604-5000

(P-10018)
MHF MV OPERATING VI LLC
Also Called: Courtyard San Dego Mssion Vlly
595 Hotel Cir S (92108-3403)
PHONE.................................619 481-5881
Robert A Indeglia Junior, *Pr*
EMP: 100 EST: 2019
SALES (est): 3.6MM **Privately Held**
SIC: 7011 Hotels

(P-10019)
MHRP RESORT INC
Also Called: Mountain High Ski Resort
24510 Highway 2 (92397)
P.O. Box 3010 (92397-3010)
PHONE.................................760 249-5808
Russel S Bernard, *Pr*
Kenneth Liang, *
Marc Porosoff, *
W Gregory Geiger, *
EMP: 100 EST: 1997
SALES (est): 5.54MM **Privately Held**
Web: www.mthigh.com
SIC: 7011 Resort hotel

(P-10020)
MILE POST PROPERTIES LLC
Also Called: La Quinta Inn
1050 Van Ness Ave (94109-6934)
PHONE.................................415 673-4711
Fred Reed, *Genl Mgr*
EMP: 96 EST: 1994
SQ FT: 100,000
SALES (est): 954.12K **Privately Held**
Web: www.lq.com
SIC: 7011 Hotels and motels

(P-10021)
MODESTO HOSPITALITY LLC
Also Called: Doubltree By Hilton Ht Modesto
1150 9th St (95354-0823)
PHONE.................................209 526-6000
EMP: 180 EST: 2006
SALES (est): 9.98MM **Privately Held**
Web: www.hilton.com
SIC: 7011 Hotels and motels

(P-10022)
MONDRIAN HOLDINGS LLC
8440 W Sunset Blvd (90069-1912)
PHONE.................................323 848-6004
Steve Del Rosario, *
EMP: 400 EST: 1999
SQ FT: 500,000
SALES (est): 8.62MM **Privately Held**
Web: book.ennismore.com
SIC: 7011 Hotels

(P-10023)
MONO WIND CASINO
Also Called: Big Sandy Rancheria
37302 Rancheria Ln (93602-9423)
P.O. Box 1060 (93602-1060)
PHONE.................................559 855-4350
EMP: 80 EST: 1996
SALES (est): 11.17MM **Privately Held**
Web: www.monowind.com
SIC: 7011 5812 Casino hotel; Restaurant, family: independent

(P-10024)
MONTAGE HOTELS & RESORTS LLC (PA)
Also Called: Montage Laguna Beach
3 Ada Ste 100 (92618-2322)
P.O. Box 52031 (85072-2031)
PHONE.................................949 715-5002
Alan Fuerstman, *Managing Member*
Jason Herthel, *
Iqbal Bashir, *
James D Bermingham, *
Bill Claypool, *
EMP: 640 EST: 2002
SQ FT: 586,000
SALES (est): 110.64MM
SALES (corp-wide): 110.64MM **Privately Held**
Web: www.montage.com
SIC: 7011 Resort hotel

(P-10025)
MONTCLAIR HOTELS MB LLC
Also Called: Holiday Inn
1050 Burnett Ave (94520-5713)
PHONE.................................925 687-5500
Stephanie Mullen, *Genl Mgr*
EMP: 306
Web: www.holidayinn.com
SIC: 7011 Hotels and motels
PA: Montclair Hotels Mb, Llc
   6600 Mannheim Rd
   Rosemont IL

(P-10026)
MONTEREY PLAZA HT LTD PARTNR
Also Called: Monterey Plaza Hotel & Spa
400 Cannery Row (93940-7501)
PHONE.................................800 334-3999
John V Narigi, *Genl Pt*
EMP: 360 EST: 1993
SALES (est): 48.98MM **Privately Held**
Web: www.montereyplazahotel.com
SIC: 7011 Resort hotel

(P-10027)
MOONRIDER LLC
Also Called: Moonrider Inn
18559 Colima Rd Apt H (91748-2815)
PHONE.................................318 828-1375
EMP: 67 EST: 2002
SALES (est): 366.11K **Privately Held**
SIC: 7011 Hotels
PA: Dalian Xinshun Trade Co., Ltd.
   317a-2, Market Building, Free Trade Zone
   Dalian LN

(P-10028)
MOONSTONE BCH INNVSTORS A CAL

7011 - Hotels And Motels (P-10029)

Also Called: Best Wstn Fireside Inn By Sea
6700 Moonstone Beach Dr (93428-1814)
PHONE..........................805 927-8661
Karen Fyse, Mgr
EMP: 199
Web: www.firesideinncambria.com
SIC: 7011 Hotels
PA: Moonstone Beach Innvestors, A
   California Limited Partnership
   170 Nwport Ctr Dr Ste 245
   Newport Beach CA

(P-10029)
MORGANS HOTEL GROUP MGT LLC
Also Called: Miramar Hotel
1555 S Jameson Ln (93108-2918)
PHONE..........................805 969-2203
Philip Dailey, Genl Mgr
EMP: 127
SALES (corp-wide): 713.02MM Privately Held
Web: www.sbe.com
SIC: 7011 Hotels
HQ: Morgans Hotel Group Management Llc
   475 10th Ave Fl 11
   New York NY

(P-10030)
MORGANS HOTEL GROUP MGT LLC
Also Called: Mondrian Hotel
8440 W Sunset Blvd (90069-1912)
PHONE..........................323 650-8999
David Weidlich, Genl Mgr
EMP: 200
SALES (corp-wide): 713.02MM Privately Held
Web: www.sbe.com
SIC: 7011 5813 5812 Hotels; Drinking places; Eating places
HQ: Morgans Hotel Group Management Llc
   475 10th Ave Fl 11
   New York NY

(P-10031)
MORGANS HOTEL GROUP MGT LLC
Also Called: Clift Hotel Four Season
495 Geary St (94102-1222)
PHONE..........................415 775-4700
Alexandra Walterstiel, Genl Mgr
EMP: 396
SQ FT: 271,387
SALES (corp-wide): 713.02MM Privately Held
Web: www.sbe.com
SIC: 7011 5812 7991 5813 Hotels; Eating places; Physical fitness facilities; Drinking places
HQ: Morgans Hotel Group Management Llc
   475 10th Ave Fl 11
   New York NY

(P-10032)
MOSSER COMPANIES INC
308 Jessie St (94103-3002)
PHONE..........................415 284-9000
Neveo Mosser, CEO
EMP: 99 EST: 2004
SALES (est): 16.47MM Privately Held
Web: www.mosserliving.com
SIC: 7011 5812 Hotels; American restaurant

(P-10033)
MSR HOTELS & RESORTS INC
Also Called: Residence Inn By Marriott
3701 Torrance Blvd (90503-4805)
PHONE..........................310 543-4566
David Zimmerman, Mgr
EMP: 125
SALES (corp-wide): 53.67B Publicly Held
Web: residence-inn.marriott.com
SIC: 7011 Hotels and motels
HQ: Msr Hotels & Resorts, Inc.
   450 S Orange Ave
   Orlando FL
   407 650-1000

(P-10034)
MSR HOTELS & RESORTS INC
Also Called: Sheraton
1100 N Mathilda Ave (94089-1206)
PHONE..........................408 745-6000
Randy Langley, Mgr
EMP: 125
SALES (corp-wide): 53.67B Publicly Held
Web: four-points.marriott.com
SIC: 7011 Hotels
HQ: Msr Hotels & Resorts, Inc.
   450 S Orange Ave
   Orlando FL
   407 650-1000

(P-10035)
MSR RESORT LODGING TENANT LLC
Also Called: Pga West By Wldorf Astoria MGT
49499 Eisenhower Dr (92253-2722)
P.O. Box 659 (92247-0659)
PHONE..........................760 564-4111
▲ EMP: 900
SIC: 7011 Hotels and motels

(P-10036)
NANA ENTERPRISES
Also Called: Travelodge
707 Redwood Hwy Frontage Rd (94941-2538)
PHONE..........................415 383-0340
Ebrahim Nana, Pr
Ilias Nana, Pr
Ebrahim M Nana, VP
Ilyas Nana, Treas
▲ EMP: 128 EST: 1977
SQ FT: 40,000
SALES (est): 2.02MM Privately Held
Web: www.wyndhamhotels.com
SIC: 7011 Hotels and motels

(P-10037)
NAPA VALLEY LODGE LP
Also Called: Bodega Bay Lodge
103 Coast Highway 1 (94923-9723)
PHONE..........................707 875-3525
Ellis Alden, Owner
EMP: 65
SALES (corp-wide): 6.19MM Privately Held
Web: www.napavalleylodge.com
SIC: 7011 Vacation lodges
PA: Napa Valley Lodge L.P.
   2230 Madison St
   Yountville CA
   707 944-2468

(P-10038)
NARVEN ENTERPRISES INC
Also Called: Rodeway Inn
1430 7th Ave Ste B (92101-2815)
PHONE..........................619 239-2261
Behram Baxter, Pr
EMP: 75 EST: 1982
SQ FT: 6,000
SALES (est): 8.88MM Privately Held
Web: www.narveninc.com
SIC: 7011 Hotels and motels

(P-10039)
NATIONAL 9 MOTELS INC
1500 Broadway (95667-5905)
PHONE..........................530 622-3884
Patel Vinot, Brnch Mgr
EMP: 78
SQ FT: 7,616
SALES (corp-wide): 951.54K Privately Held
Web: www.national9inns.com
SIC: 7011 Motels
PA: National 9 Motels Inc
   9571 S 700 E Ste 202
   Sandy UT
   801 208-0537

(P-10040)
NEW ASTER ENTERPRISES INC
Also Called: Silverlake Motel
2901 S Flower St (90007-3713)
PHONE..........................213 747-7566
Sam Tsutsumi, Mgr
EMP: 110
SALES (corp-wide): 156.85K Privately Held
SIC: 7011 Motels
PA: New Aster Enterprises, Inc.
   1549 Feliz St
   Monterey Park CA
   626 281-8714

(P-10041)
NEW COLUSA INDIAN BINGO
Also Called: Colusa Casino Resort
3770 State Highway 45 (95932-4021)
PHONE..........................530 458-8844
Steve Gonzales, Prin
EMP: 450 EST: 1986
SALES (est): 22.11MM Privately Held
Web: www.colusacasino.com
SIC: 7011 Casino hotel

(P-10042)
NEW FIGUEROA HOTEL INC
Also Called: Figueroa Hotel
1000 S Hope St Apt 201 (90015-1492)
PHONE..........................213 627-8971
Uno Thimansson, Pr
Elyse Omori, *
EMP: 70 EST: 1977
SQ FT: 200,000
SALES (est): 2.74MM Privately Held
Web: www.hotelfigueroa.com
SIC: 7011 5812 5813 Resort hotel; Eating places; Bars and lounges

(P-10043)
NEWPORT HOSPITALITY GROUP INC
Also Called: Holiday Inn
801 Truxtun Ave (93301-4726)
PHONE..........................661 323-1900
Eric Iokal, Mgr
EMP: 100
SALES (corp-wide): 9.58MM Privately Held
Web: www.holidayinn.com
SIC: 7011 Hotels and motels
PA: Newport Hospitality Group Inc
   1048 Irvine Ave Ste 365
   Newport Beach CA
   949 706-7002

(P-10044)
NEWPORT MESA INN LLC
Also Called: Best Western
2642 Newport Blvd (92627-4626)
PHONE..........................949 650-3020
James Hsuan, Managing Member
S P Lee, Pt
EMP: 67 EST: 1984
SQ FT: 60,000
SALES (est): 780.25K Privately Held
Web: www.bestwestern.com
SIC: 7011 Hotels and motels

(P-10045)
NHCA INC
Also Called: Crowne Plz Los Angeles Hbr Ht
2330 Grand Ave (90815-1761)
PHONE..........................310 519-8200
EMP: 151 EST: 1997
SALES (est): 4.84MM Privately Held
SIC: 7011 Hotels

(P-10046)
NICKS COVE INC
Also Called: Nick's Cove
23240 Ca-1 (94940)
PHONE..........................415 663-1033
Ruth Gibson, Owner
EMP: 70 EST: 1973
SQ FT: 1,000
SALES (est): 3.41MM Privately Held
Web: www.nickscove.com
SIC: 7011 Hotels

(P-10047)
NOB HILL PROPERTIES INC
Also Called: Big Four Restaurant
1075 California St (94108-2281)
PHONE..........................415 474-5400
John Cope, Pr
Newton Cope Senior, Ch Bd
Newton Cope Junior, VP
EMP: 280 EST: 1940
SALES (est): 14.25MM Privately Held
Web: www.huntingtonhotel.com
SIC: 7011 5812 Hotels; Eating places

(P-10048)
NOBLE INVESTMENT GROUP LLC
Also Called: Westin Long Beach Hotel, The
333 E Ocean Blvd (90802-4827)
PHONE..........................562 436-3000
Bharat Shah, Managing Member
EMP: 117 EST: 2003
SQ FT: 60,000
SALES (est): 976.12K Privately Held
Web: westin.marriott.com
SIC: 7011 Hotels

(P-10049)
NOBLE/UTAH LONG BEACH LLC
Also Called: Westin Long Beach Hotel, The
333 E Ocean Blvd (90802-4827)
PHONE..........................562 436-3000
Mitesh B Shah, Managing Member
EMP: 250 EST: 2005
SQ FT: 51,000
SALES (est): 21.7MM Privately Held
Web: westin.marriott.com
SIC: 7011 Hotels and motels
PA: Noble Investment Group, Llc
   3424 Peachtree Rd Ne
   Atlanta GA

(P-10050)
NOIRO WEST LLC
Also Called: Sheraton
701 A St (92101-4611)
PHONE..........................619 819-6620
EMP: 78 EST: 1990
SQ FT: 99,999
SALES (est): 2.25MM Privately Held
Web: four-points.marriott.com
SIC: 7011 Hotels

7011 - Hotels And Motels (P-10075)

(P-10051)
NORTHWEST HOTEL CORPORATION (PA)
Also Called: Howard Johnson
1380 S Harbor Blvd (92802-2310)
PHONE.....................714 776-6120
James P Edmondson, Pr
EMP: 75 EST: 1965
SQ FT: 50,000
SALES (est): 4.6MM
SALES (corp-wide): 4.6MM Privately Held
Web: www.wyndhamhotels.com
SIC: 7011 Hotels and motels

(P-10052)
NREA-TRC 711 LLC
Also Called: Sheraton
711 S Hope St (90017-3803)
PHONE.....................213 488-3500
EMP: 200 EST: 2013
SQ FT: 470,000
SALES (est): 8.57MM Privately Held
Web: four-points.marriott.com
SIC: 7011 Hotels

(P-10053)
OAK VALLEY HOTEL LLC
2270 Hotel Cir N (92108-2810)
PHONE.....................619 297-1101
EMP: 99 EST: 2016
SALES (est): 1.45MM Privately Held
SIC: 7011 Hotels

(P-10054)
OAKLAND RENAISSANCE ASSOCIATES
Also Called: Oakland Mrriott Hotels Resorts
1001 Broadway (94607-4019)
PHONE.....................510 451-4000
EMP: 375
Web: www.marriott.com
SIC: 7011 Hotels and motels
PA: Oakland Renaissance Associates
    388 9th St Ste 222
    Oakland CA

(P-10055)
OASIS WEST REALTY LLC
Also Called: Waldorf Astoria Beverly Hills
9850 Wilshire Blvd (90210-3115)
PHONE.....................310 860-6666
Damian Cabotaje, Managing Member
EMP: 161 EST: 2017
SALES (est): 5.11MM Privately Held
Web: waldorfastoria3.hilton.com
SIC: 7011 Hotels

(P-10056)
OCEAN AVENUE LLC
Also Called: Fairmont Miramar Hotel
101 Wilshire Blvd (90401-1106)
PHONE.....................310 576-7777
Ellis O'connor, Managing Member
EMP: 275 EST: 1973
SQ FT: 209,000
SALES (est): 25.87MM
SALES (corp-wide): 713.02MM Privately Held
Web: www.fairmont.com
SIC: 7011 Hotels
HQ: Accor Services Us Llc
    950 Mason St
    San Francisco CA
    415 772-5000

(P-10057)
OCEAN PARK HOTELS-HIT INC
9777 Blue Larkspur Ln Ste 102 (93940-6584)
PHONE.....................805 544-0812
EMP: 350
SIC: 7011 Hotels and motels

(P-10058)
OCEANS ELEVEN CASINO
Also Called: Ocean's Eleven
121 Brooks St (92054-3424)
PHONE.....................760 439-6988
Mark Kelegian, Mng Pt
EMP: 367 EST: 1996
SQ FT: 30,000
SALES (est): 22.62MM Privately Held
Web: www.oceans11.com
SIC: 7011 Casino hotel

(P-10059)
OH SO ORIGINAL INC
150 E Angeleno Ave (91502-1911)
PHONE.....................818 841-4770
Mark Crigler, Pr
Rich Reid,   *
EMP: 300 EST: 2015
SQ FT: 100,000
SALES (est): 11.31MM Privately Held
Web: www.jpallenapartments.com
SIC: 7011 6513 8741 Hotel, franchised; Apartment building operators; Hotel or motel management

(P-10060)
OHI RESORT HOTELS LLC
Also Called: Wyndham Anaheim Garden Grove
12021 Harbor Blvd (92840-4001)
PHONE.....................714 867-5555
Jeremy Yujuico, Prin
EMP: 98 EST: 1998
SALES (est): 6.26MM Privately Held
Web: anaheim.crowneplaza.com
SIC: 7011 Hotels

(P-10061)
OKA & OKA HAWAII LLC
Also Called: Kona Bay Hotel
1756 Ruhland Ave (90266-7132)
PHONE.....................808 329-1393
Tracey Kimi, Mgr
EMP: 196
SALES (corp-wide): 2.69MM Privately Held
SIC: 7011 Hotels
PA: Oka & Oka Hawaii, Llc
    75 5744 Alii Dr
    Hilo HI
    808 329-1393

(P-10062)
OLD TOWN FMLY HOSPITALITY CORP
Also Called: Fiesta De Reyes
2754 Calhoun St (92110-2706)
PHONE.....................619 246-8010
Chuck Ross, Pr
EMP: 240 EST: 2009
SQ FT: 1,600
SALES (est): 16MM Privately Held
Web: www.fiestadereyes.com
SIC: 7011 5812 Hotels; Eating places

(P-10063)
OLS HOTELS & RESORTS LLC
Also Called: Marriott
14635 Baldwin Park Towne Ctr (91706-5548)
PHONE.....................626 962-6000
Peter Ehienberg, Mgr
EMP: 509
SALES (corp-wide): 87.68MM Privately Held
Web: www.springboardhospitality.com
SIC: 7011 Hotels and motels
PA: Ols Hotels & Resorts, Llc
    16000 Ventura Blvd # 101
    Encino CA
    818 905-8280

(P-10064)
OLS HOTELS & RESORTS LLC
Also Called: Le Parc Suite Hotel
733 N West Knoll Dr (90069-5207)
PHONE.....................310 855-1115
Sam Ebeid, CEO
EMP: 508
SALES (corp-wide): 87.68MM Privately Held
Web: www.leparcsuites.com
SIC: 7011 8741 Hotels; Hotel or motel management
PA: Ols Hotels & Resorts, Llc
    16000 Ventura Blvd # 101
    Encino CA
    818 905-8280

(P-10065)
OMNI HOTELS CORPORATION
Also Called: Omni Hotels
41000 Bob Hope Dr (92270-4416)
PHONE.....................760 568-2727
EMP: 474
Web: www.omnihotels.com
SIC: 7011 Hotels and motels
HQ: Omni Hotels Corporation
    4001 Maple Ave Ste 500
    Dallas TX
    972 871-5600

(P-10066)
OMNI LA COSTA RESORT & SPA LLC
Also Called: Audrey's Boutique
2100 Costa Del Mar Rd (92009-6823)
PHONE.....................760 438-9111
Cydney Bruno, Mgr
EMP: 137
Web: www.omnihotels.com
SIC: 7011 Hotels and motels
HQ: Omni La Costa Resort & Spa, Llc
    2100 Costa Del Mar Rd
    Carlsbad CA
    760 438-9111

(P-10067)
OMNI LA COSTA RESORT & SPA LLC (DH)
2100 Costa Del Mar Rd (92009-6823)
PHONE.....................760 438-9111
Randy Zupanski, *
EMP: 104 EST: 2013
SALES (est): 24.47MM Privately Held
Web: www.omnihotels.com
SIC: 7011 Resort hotel
HQ: Omni Hotels Corporation
    4001 Maple Ave Ste 500
    Dallas TX
    972 871-5600

(P-10068)
ONE NOB HILL ASSOCIATES LLC
Also Called: Intercontinental Mark Hopkins
999 California St (94108-2250)
PHONE.....................415 392-3434
EMP: 86 EST: 2014
SALES (est): 5.37MM Privately Held
Web: www.sfmarkhopkins.com
SIC: 7011 Hotels

(P-10069)
ONTARIO AIRPORT HOTEL CORP
Also Called: Hilton
4949 Great America Pkwy (95054-1216)
PHONE.....................408 562-6709
James Evans, CFO
▲ EMP: 127 EST: 2004
SQ FT: 169,768
SALES (est): 13.87MM Privately Held
Web: www.hilton.com
SIC: 7011 Hotels

(P-10070)
ORANGEWOOD LLC
Also Called: Doubltree Stes By Hlton Anheim
2085 S Harbor Blvd (92802-3513)
PHONE.....................714 750-3000
Shirish H Patel, *
EMP: 175 EST: 2000
SALES (est): 8.88MM Privately Held
Web: www.doubletreeanaheim.com
SIC: 7011 5812 Hotels and motels; American restaurant

(P-10071)
ORLANDO WILSHIRE INVESTMENTS
Also Called: Orlando, The
8384 W 3rd St (90048-4311)
PHONE.....................323 658-6600
Kenneth Pressberg, Pt
Sidney Pressberg, *
EMP: 88 EST: 1981
SQ FT: 45,000
SALES (est): 863.38K Privately Held
SIC: 7011 Hotels

(P-10072)
OTAY HOSPITALITY INC
Also Called: Holiday Inn
4450 Main St (91910-6508)
PHONE.....................619 422-2600
Suresh Patel, Pr
Ashok Israni, Sec
EMP: 96 EST: 1994
SALES (est): 824.82K Privately Held
Web: www.holidayinn.com
SIC: 7011 Hotels and motels

(P-10073)
OTB ACQUISITION LLC
Also Called: Sierra Vista Extended Stay
770 S Brea Blvd Ste 227 (92821-5399)
PHONE.....................520 458-0540
EMP: 158
Web: www.ontheborder.com
SIC: 7011 Hotels and motels
PA: Otb Acquisition Llc
    2201 W Royal Ln Ste 170
    Irving TX

(P-10074)
OVIS LLC
Also Called: Ojai Valley Inn & Spa
905 Country Club Rd (93023-3734)
PHONE.....................805 646-5511
TOLL FREE: 888
Stephen Crown, Managing Member
EMP: 600 EST: 1923
SALES (est): 49.55MM Privately Held
Web: www.ojaivalleyinn.com
SIC: 7011 5813 5812 Resort hotel; Drinking places; Eating places

(P-10075)
OXFORD PALACE HOTEL LLC
745 S Oxford Ave (90005-2909)
PHONE.....................213 382-7756

7011 - Hotels And Motels (P-10076)

Bowhan Kim, *Prin*
Don W Chang, *
EMP: 96 **EST:** 1992
SALES (est): 4.75MM **Privately Held**
Web: www.oxfordhotel.com
SIC: 7011 5812 Resort hotel; Korean restaurant

(P-10076)
PAAR HOSPITALITY INC
500 W A St (94541-4843)
PHONE..................510 828-3585
EMP: 80
SIC: 7011 Hotels and motels
PA: Paar Hospitality Inc
25569 Gold Ridge Dr
Castro Valley CA

(P-10077)
PACIFIC CAMBRIA INC
Also Called: Cambria Pines Lodge
2905 Burton Dr (93428-4001)
PHONE..................805 927-6114
Dirk Winter, *Pr*
EMP: 90 **EST:** 1975
SQ FT: 70,000
SALES (est): 9.74MM **Privately Held**
Web: www.cambriapineslodge.com
SIC: 7011 5812 5813 Hotels; Restaurant, family: independent; Bar (drinking places)

(P-10078)
PACIFIC CATALINA HOTEL INC
Also Called: Catalina Canyon Resort
888 Country Club Dr (90704-2956)
P.O. Box 736 (90704-0736)
PHONE..................310 510-9255
Gonzalo Rodriguez, *Genl Mgr*
EMP: 305 **EST:** 1977
SALES (est): 1.16MM
SALES (corp-wide): 96.92MM **Privately Held**
Web: www.bestwestern.com
SIC: 7011 7389 Hotels; Hotel and motel reservation service
PA: Pacifica Hosts, Inc.
1775 Hancock St Ste 200
San Diego CA
619 296-9000

(P-10079)
PACIFIC CITY HOTEL LLC
Also Called: Pasea Hotel & Spa
21080 Pacific Coast Hwy (92648-5305)
PHONE..................714 698-6100
EMP: 300 **EST:** 2015
SALES (est): 2.8MM **Privately Held**
Web: www.meritagecollection.com
SIC: 7011 Resort hotel

(P-10080)
PACIFIC HOTEL DEV VENTR LP
Also Called: Sheraton Palo Alto
625 El Camino Real (94301-2301)
PHONE..................650 347-8260
Clement Chen, *VP*
EMP: 200 **EST:** 1998
SALES (est): 9.04MM **Privately Held**
Web: www.phmhotels.com
SIC: 7011 Hotels

(P-10081)
PACIFIC HOTEL MANAGEMENT LLC
Also Called: Sheraton
1603 Powell St (94608-2436)
PHONE..................510 547-7888
Michelle Sims, *Owner*
EMP: 141
SALES (corp-wide): 47.84MM **Privately Held**
Web: www.phmhotels.com
SIC: 7011 Hotels and motels
PA: Pacific Hotel Management, Llc
400 S El Cmino Real Ste 2
San Mateo CA
650 347-8260

(P-10082)
PACIFIC HOTEL MANAGEMENT LLC
Also Called: Hawthorn Suites Fremont Newark
39270 Cedar Blvd (94560-5024)
PHONE..................510 791-7700
EMP: 141
SALES (corp-wide): 47.84MM **Privately Held**
Web: www.wyndhamhotels.com
SIC: 7011 Hotels
PA: Pacific Hotel Management, Llc
400 S El Cmino Real Ste 2
San Mateo CA
650 347-8260

(P-10083)
PACIFIC HOTEL MANAGEMENT LLC
Also Called: Courtyard By Marriott
3150 Garrity Way (94806-1983)
PHONE..................510 262-0700
Curt Newport, *Brnch Mgr*
EMP: 141
SALES (corp-wide): 47.84MM **Privately Held**
Web: courtyard.marriott.com
SIC: 7011 7389 Hotels; Office facilities and secretarial service rental
PA: Pacific Hotel Management, Llc
400 S El Cmino Real Ste 2
San Mateo CA
650 347-8260

(P-10084)
PACIFIC HOTEL MANAGEMENT LLC
Also Called: Sheraton
625 El Camino Real (94301-2301)
PHONE..................650 328-2800
EMP: 141
SALES (corp-wide): 47.84MM **Privately Held**
Web: www.phmhotels.com
SIC: 7011 Hotels
PA: Pacific Hotel Management, Llc
400 S El Cmino Real Ste 2
San Mateo CA
650 347-8260

(P-10085)
PACIFIC HOTEL MANAGEMENT INC
Also Called: Radison Hotel Newport Beach
4545 Macarthur Blvd (92660-2022)
PHONE..................949 608-1091
EMP: 140 **EST:** 2003
SALES (est): 4.55MM **Privately Held**
Web: www.phmhotels.com
SIC: 7011 Hotels

(P-10086)
PACIFIC HUNTINGTON HOTEL CORP
Also Called: Langham Huntington Hotel & Spa
1401 S Oak Knoll Ave (91106-4508)
PHONE..................626 568-3900
Ying Shek Lo, *Pr*
EMP: 600 **EST:** 2000
SQ FT: 21,193
SALES (est): 49.28MM **Privately Held**
Web: www.langhamhotels.com
SIC: 7011 Resort hotel
HQ: Langham Hotels International Limited
33/F Great Eagle Ctr
Wan Chai HK

(P-10087)
PACIFIC MONARCH RESORTS INC
Also Called: Riviera Shores
34630 Pacific Coast Hwy (92624-1301)
PHONE..................949 248-2944
EMP: 91
SALES (corp-wide): 79.14MM **Privately Held**
Web: www.pacificmonarchresorts.com
SIC: 7011 6531 Resort hotel; Time-sharing real estate sales, leasing and rentals
PA: Pacific Monarch Resorts, Inc.
4000 Macarthur Blvd # 600
Newport Beach CA
949 609-2400

(P-10088)
PACIFIC SNOW VALLEY RESORT LLC
Also Called: Holiday Inn Resort At Lodge
40650 Village Dr (92315-2164)
PHONE..................909 866-3121
Dennis Montes, *Genl Mgr*
EMP: 60
Web: www.holidayinnresorts.com
SIC: 7011 7299 5812 5813 Vacation lodges; Banquet hall facilities; Eating places; Drinking places
PA: Pacific Snow Valley Resort Llc
704 Mira Monte Pl
Pasadena CA

(P-10089)
PACIFICA HOSTS INC
Also Called: Radisson Inn
6225 W Century Blvd (90045-5311)
PHONE..................310 670-9000
Ashok Israni, *Pr*
EMP: 68
SALES (corp-wide): 96.92MM **Privately Held**
Web: www.pacificacompanies.com
SIC: 7011 6552 5813 5812 Hotels; Subdividers and developers, nec; Drinking places; Eating places
PA: Pacifica Hosts, Inc.
1775 Hancock St Ste 200
San Diego CA
619 296-9000

(P-10090)
PACIFICA HOSTS INC
700 16th St (95814-2002)
PHONE..................619 296-9000
EMP: 104
SALES (corp-wide): 96.92MM **Privately Held**
Web: www.pacificahost.com
SIC: 7011 Hotels
PA: Pacifica Hosts, Inc.
1775 Hancock St Ste 200
San Diego CA
619 296-9000

(P-10091)
PACIFICA HOSTS INC
Also Called: Hotel Indigo Del Mar
710 Camino Del Mar (92014-3008)
PHONE..................858 755-1501
Susan Knapp, *Mgr*
EMP: 120
SALES (corp-wide): 96.92MM **Privately Held**
Web: www.hotelindigo.com
SIC: 7011 Hotels
PA: Pacifica Hosts, Inc.
1775 Hancock St Ste 200
San Diego CA
619 296-9000

(P-10092)
PACIFICA HOSTS INC
717 S Highway 101 (92075-2606)
PHONE..................858 792-8200
Julio Ongpin, *Genl Mgr*
EMP: 97
SALES (corp-wide): 96.92MM **Privately Held**
Web: www.pacificahost.com
SIC: 7011 Hotels
PA: Pacifica Hosts, Inc.
1775 Hancock St Ste 200
San Diego CA
619 296-9000

(P-10093)
PALA CASINO SPA & RESORT
Also Called: Pala Casino
11154 Highway 76 (92059-2904)
PHONE..................760 510-5100
TOLL FREE: 877
Robert Smith, *Ch Bd*
Bill Bembenek, *
Shauna Anton, *
Stacy Hoover, *
EMP: 1800 **EST:** 2000
SQ FT: 140,000
SALES (est): 206.9MM **Privately Held**
Web: www.palacasino.com
SIC: 7011 Casino hotel

(P-10094)
PALA MESA LIMITED PARTNERSHIP
Also Called: Pala Mesa Resort
2001 Old Highway 395 (92028-9771)
PHONE..................760 728-5881
Kevin Poorbaugh, *Mng Pt*
Bob Emch, *Contrlr*
Tray Crayton, *Pr*
Anil Y, *CEO*
EMP: 199 **EST:** 1983
SALES (est): 15.43MM **Privately Held**
Web: www.palamesa.com
SIC: 7011 7992 Resort hotel; Public golf courses

(P-10095)
PALM DESERT HOSPITALITY LLC
Also Called: Homewood Suites
36999 Cook St (92211-6066)
PHONE..................760 568-1600
Maria Banning, *Brnch Mgr*
EMP: 309
SALES (corp-wide): 1.94MM **Privately Held**
Web: www.hospitalitydental.com
SIC: 7011 Hotels and motels
PA: Palm Desert Hospitality, L.L.C.
2390 Tower Dr
Monroe LA
760 568-1600

(P-10096)
PAN PCFIC HTELS RSRTS AMER INC
Also Called: Pan Pacific San Diego
400 W Broadway (92101-3504)
PHONE..................619 239-4500
Jim Hollister, *Genl Mgr*
EMP: 238

PRODUCTS & SERVICES SECTION

7011 - Hotels And Motels (P-10118)

SALES (corp-wide): 22.68MM **Privately Held**
Web: www.wyndhamhotels.com
SIC: **7011** 5812 Hotels; Eating places
PA: Pan Pacific Hotels And Resorts America Inc.
500 Post St Ste 800
San Francisco CA
415 732-7747

(P-10097)
PARADIGM HOTELS GROUP LLC
Also Called: Canopy By Hltn San Frncsco So
250 4th St (94103-3109)
PHONE.............................415 534-6500
Jerome Serack, *Brnch Mgr*
EMP: 91
SALES (corp-wide): 4.85MM **Privately Held**
Web: www.paradigmhotelsgroup.com
SIC: **7011** Hotels
PA: Paradigm Hotels Group Llc
1001 Broadway Ste 300
Millbrae CA
650 333-7754

(P-10098)
PARADISE HOTEL INC
Also Called: Crocodile Restaurant
2819 State St (93105-3415)
PHONE.............................805 687-6444
Scott Perry, *Mgr*
EMP: 96
SALES (corp-wide): 743.39K **Privately Held**
Web: www.orangetreeinn.com
SIC: **7011** 5813 Hotels; Drinking places
PA: Paradise Hotel Inc
1920 State St
Santa Barbara CA
805 569-1521

(P-10099)
PARADISE LESSEE INC
Also Called: Paradise Point Resort & Spa
1404 Vacation Rd (92109-7905)
PHONE.............................858 274-4630
Alfred L Young, *CEO*
EMP: 328 EST: 1962
SALES (est): 24.8MM **Publicly Held**
Web: www.paradisepoint.com
SIC: **7011** Resort hotel
PA: Pebblebrook Hotel Trust
4747 Bethesda Ave # 1100
Bethesda MD

(P-10100)
PARC 55 LESSEE LLC
Also Called: Hilton
55 Cyril Magnin St (94102-2812)
PHONE.............................415 392-8000
EMP: 86 EST: 2014
SALES (est): 27.58MM
SALES (corp-wide): 2.5B **Publicly Held**
Web: www.hilton.com
SIC: **7011** Hotels
PA: Park Hotels & Resorts Inc.
1775 Tysons Blvd Fl 7
Tysons VA
571 302-5757

(P-10101)
PARK HOTELS & RESORTS INC
Also Called: Embassy Suites Brea
900 E Birch St (92821-5812)
PHONE.............................714 990-6000
Jay Badillo, *Brnch Mgr*
EMP: 60
SALES (corp-wide): 2.5B **Publicly Held**
Web: www.hilton.com

SIC: **7011** Hotels and motels
PA: Park Hotels & Resorts Inc.
1775 Tysons Blvd Fl 7
Tysons VA
571 302-5757

(P-10102)
PARK HOTELS & RESORTS INC
Also Called: Hilton
1 Hegenberger Rd (94621-1405)
P.O. Box 2549 (94614-0549)
PHONE.............................510 635-5000
Mark Clement, *Genl Mgr*
EMP: 114
SALES (corp-wide): 2.5B **Publicly Held**
Web: www.hilton.com
SIC: **7011** 5813 5812 Hotels and motels; Drinking places; Eating places
PA: Park Hotels & Resorts Inc.
1775 Tysons Blvd Fl 7
Tysons VA
571 302-5757

(P-10103)
PARK HOTELS & RESORTS INC
Also Called: San Francisco Hilton & Towers
333 Ofarrell St (94102-2116)
PHONE.............................415 771-1400
Holger B Gantz, *Mgr*
EMP: 97
SALES (corp-wide): 2.5B **Publicly Held**
Web: www.hilton.com
SIC: **7011** 5812 7299 Hotels; Eating places; Banquet hall facilities
PA: Park Hotels & Resorts Inc.
1775 Tysons Blvd Fl 7
Tysons VA
571 302-5757

(P-10104)
PARK HOTELS & RESORTS INC
Also Called: Hilton
9876 Wilshire Blvd (90210-3115)
PHONE.............................310 415-3340
Beverly Hilton, *Prin*
EMP: 113
SALES (corp-wide): 2.5B **Publicly Held**
Web: www.hiltongrandvacations.com
SIC: **7011** Resort hotel
PA: Park Hotels & Resorts Inc.
1775 Tysons Blvd Fl 7
Tysons VA
571 302-5757

(P-10105)
PARK MANAGEMENT GROUP LLC
Also Called: Jameson Inn
1825 Gillespie Wy Ste 101 (91601)
PHONE.............................404 350-9990
▲ EMP: 3500
SIC: **7011** Hotels and motels

(P-10106)
PARK US LESSEE HOLDINGS LLC
Also Called: Doubltree By Hlton Ht Snoma Wi
1 Doubletree Dr (94928-1336)
PHONE.............................707 887-7838
EMP: 90 EST: 2017
SALES (est): 2.16MM **Privately Held**
SIC: **7011** Hotels and motels

(P-10107)
PARKER PALM SPRINGS LLC
4200 E Palm Canyon Dr (92264-5230)
PHONE.............................760 770-5000
Adam Glick, *Prin*
EMP: 95 EST: 2003

SALES (est): 8.86MM **Privately Held**
Web: www.parkerpalmsprings.com
SIC: **7011** Resort hotel

(P-10108)
PASADENA HOTEL DEV VENTR LP
Also Called: Sheraton Pasadena
303 Cordova St (91101-2426)
PHONE.............................626 449-4000
Ray Serafin, *Prin*
EMP: 99 EST: 2008
SALES (est): 3.57MM **Privately Held**
Web: www.sheratonpasadena.com
SIC: **7011** Resort hotel

(P-10109)
PAUMA BAND OF MISSION INDIANS
Casino Pauma
777 Pauma Reservation Rd (92061)
P.O. Box 1067 (92061-1067)
PHONE.............................760 742-2177
Richard Darder, *CEO*
EMP: 500
Web: www.casinopauma.com
SIC: **7011** Casino hotel
PA: Pauma Band Of Mission Indians
1010 Pauma Reservation Rd
Pauma Valley CA

(P-10110)
PEBBLE BCH RSORT DBA LONE CYPR
US Open At Pebble Beach
17 Mile Dr (93953)
P.O. Box 567 (93953-0567)
PHONE.............................831 624-3811
Robert Lapso, *Brnch Mgr*
EMP: 235
SALES (corp-wide): 302.53MM **Privately Held**
Web: www.pebblebeach.com
SIC: **7011** 7992 5813 5812 Resort hotel; Public golf courses; Drinking places; Eating places
PA: Lone Cypress Company Llc
2700 17 Mile Dr
Pebble Beach CA
831 647-7500

(P-10111)
PEBBLE BCH RSORT DBA LONE CYPR
Also Called: Pebble Beach Co / Rdc Whse
2136 Sunset Dr (93950-3730)
P.O. Box 711 (93953-0711)
PHONE.............................831 625-8480
Mark Stilwell, *Brnch Mgr*
EMP: 254
SQ FT: 16,294
SALES (corp-wide): 302.53MM **Privately Held**
Web: www.pebblebeach.com
SIC: **7011** Resort hotel
PA: Lone Cypress Company Llc
2700 17 Mile Dr
Pebble Beach CA
831 647-7500

(P-10112)
PEBBLE BEACH CO A LTD PARTNR
Also Called: Spa At Pebble Beach, The
1518 Cypress Dr (93953)
PHONE.............................800 877-0597
David Stivers, *CEO*
EMP: 272
Web: www.pebblebeach.com

SIC: **7011** 7991 Resort hotel; Spas
PA: Pebble Beach Company, A Limited Partnership
2700 17 Mile Dr
Pebble Beach CA

(P-10113)
PECHANGA DEVELOPMENT CORP
Also Called: Pechanga Resort & Casino
45000 Pechanga Pkwy (92592-5810)
P.O. Box 9041 (92589-9041)
PHONE.............................951 695-4655
Patrick Murphy, *CEO*
Jerry Konchar, *
Randall Bardwell, *
Edith Atwood, *
Jared Munoa, *
◆ EMP: 4000 EST: 1995
SALES (est): 206.14MM **Privately Held**
Web: www.pechanga.com
SIC: **7011** 7929 7999 Casino hotel; Entertainment service; Gambling establishment

(P-10114)
PEPPER TREE INN
645 N Lake Blvd (96145-2274)
PHONE.............................530 583-3711
Thomas Brown, *Mgr*
EMP: 61
SQ FT: 18,609
SALES (corp-wide): 2.48MM **Privately Held**
Web: www.peppertreetahoe.com
SIC: **7011** Motels
PA: Pepper Tree Inn
106 Bluebonnet Ln Unit 13
Scotts Valley CA

(P-10115)
PERSONALITY HOTELS INC
Also Called: Diva Hotel
440 Geary St (94102-1223)
PHONE.............................415 885-0200
EMP: 126
Web: www.personalityhotels.com
SIC: **7011** Hotels and motels

(P-10116)
PHF II BURBANK LLC
Also Called: Burbank Airport Mariott Hotel
2500 N Hollywood Way (91505-1019)
PHONE.............................818 843-6000
Linda Davey, *Managing Member*
EMP: 220 EST: 2006
SALES (est): 4.61MM **Privately Held**
SIC: **7011** Hotels and motels

(P-10117)
PHF RUBY LLC
Also Called: Marriott Vacatlon Club Pulse
2620 Jones St (94133-1306)
PHONE.............................415 885-4700
EMP: 125 EST: 1988
SALES (est): 6.8MM **Privately Held**
Web: www.pier2620hotel.com
SIC: **7011** Hotel, franchised

(P-10118)
PICCADILLY HOSPITALITY LLC
Also Called: Piccadilly Inn Shaw
2305 W Shaw Ave (93711-3411)
PHONE.............................559 348-5520
Gene Chien, *Pt*
EMP: 60 EST: 2012
SALES (est): 1.94MM **Privately Held**
Web: www.hotel-piccadilly.com
SIC: **7011** Resort hotel

7011 - Hotels And Motels (P-10119)

PRODUCTS & SERVICES SECTION

(P-10119)
PINE & POWELL PARTNERS LLC
Also Called: Stanford Court Hotel
905 California St (94108-2201)
PHONE...............................415 989-3500
Michael Baier, *
Rosanna Harrison, *
EMP: 99 **EST:** 2014
SQ FT: 287,000
SALES (est): 9.5MM **Privately Held**
Web: www.stanfordcourt.com
SIC: 7011 Hotels and motels

(P-10120)
PINNACLE HOTELS USA INC
8369 Vickers St Ste 101 (92111-2113)
PHONE...............................858 974-8201
Bharat Lall, CEO
Hema Lall, *
EMP: 84 **EST:** 1999
SALES (est): 7.33MM **Privately Held**
Web: www.pinnacleholdings.com
SIC: 7011 Resort hotel

(P-10121)
PINNACLE RVRSIDE HSPITALITY LP
Also Called: Riverside Marriott
3400 Market St (92501-2826)
PHONE...............................951 784-8000
Doctor Bharat Lall, Genl Pt
EMP: 190 **EST:** 2007
SALES (est): 9.67MM **Privately Held**
Web: www.marriott.com
SIC: 7011 Hotels

(P-10122)
PISMO COAST VILLAGE INC
165 S Dolliver St (93449-2999)
PHONE...............................805 773-1811
Jay Jamison, Genl Mgr
Jay Jamison, CEO
Ronald Nunlist, *
Terris Hughes, *
Wayne Hardesty, *
EMP: 60 **EST:** 1975
SALES (est): 10.34MM **Privately Held**
Web: www.pismocoastvillage.com
SIC: 7011 Resort hotel

(P-10123)
PLAYA PROPER JV LLC
Also Called: Custom Hotel
8639 Lincoln Blvd (90045-3503)
PHONE...............................310 645-0400
Brad Korzen, CEO
Bryan De Lowe, *
Jeffrey Cruz, *
EMP: 80 **EST:** 2017
SALES (est): 2.45MM **Privately Held**
Web: www.thehoteljune.com
SIC: 7011 Hotels

(P-10124)
PORTOFINO HOTEL PARTNERS LP
Also Called: Hotel Portofino
260 Portofino Way (90277-2033)
PHONE...............................310 379-8481
Glenn Bishop, Prin
EMP: 151 **EST:** 1980
SALES (est): 10.06MM **Privately Held**
Web: www.hotelportofino.com
SIC: 7011 Resort hotel

(P-10125)
PORTOFINO INN & SUITES ANAHEIM
1831 S Harbor Blvd (92802-3509)
PHONE...............................714 782-7600
Jennifer Reihl, Dir
EMP: 310 **EST:** 2008
SALES (est): 1.98MM
SALES (corp-wide): 369.62MM **Privately Held**
Web: www.portofinoinnanaheim.com
SIC: 7011 Inns
HQ: Tarsadia Hotels
620 Nwport Ctr Dr Ste 140
Newport Beach CA

(P-10126)
POST ST RNSSNCE PRTNERS A CAL
Also Called: Prescott Hotel, The
545 Post St (94102-1228)
PHONE...............................415 563-0303
John Dern, Pr
EMP: 338 **EST:** 1987
SALES (est): 3.48MM **Privately Held**
Web: www.viceroyhotelsandresorts.com
SIC: 7011 Resort hotel
HQ: Kimpton Hotel & Restaurant Group Llc
222 Kearny St Ste 200
San Francisco CA
415 397-5572

(P-10127)
PRESIDIO HOTEL GROUP LLC
Also Called: Fairfield Inn
10713 White Rock Rd (95670-6031)
PHONE...............................916 631-7500
Sushil Patel, Brnch Mgr
EMP: 107
SALES (corp-wide): 7.16MM **Privately Held**
Web: fairfield.marriott.com
SIC: 7011 Hotels and motels
PA: Presidio Hotel Group, Llc
1011 10th St
Sacramento CA
707 429-6000

(P-10128)
PRIME HOSPITALITY LLC
Also Called: Radisson Hotel
2200 E Holt Blvd (91761-7671)
PHONE...............................909 975-5000
EMP: 90
Web: www.radissonhotels.com
SIC: 7011 Hotels and motels
PA: Prime Hospitality, Llc
2155 E Convention Ctr Way
Ontario CA

(P-10129)
PROPER HOSPITALITY LLC
73 Market St (90291-3603)
PHONE...............................310 277-5221
EMP: 229 **EST:** 2019
SALES (est): 8.44MM **Privately Held**
Web: www.properhotel.com
SIC: 7011 Hotels

(P-10130)
PRUTEL JOINT VENTURE
Also Called: Ritz-Carlton Laguna Niguel
1 Ritz Carlton Dr (92629-4205)
PHONE...............................949 240-5064
W B Johnson, Pt
Prudential Realty San Francisc o Ca, Pt
Paul Patterson, CFO
Kelly Steward, Genl Mgr
EMP: 700 **EST:** 1984
SALES (est): 31.03MM **Privately Held**
Web: www.ritzcarlton.com
SIC: 7011 Hotels

(P-10131)
PT GAMING LLC
235 Oregon St (90245-4215)
PHONE...............................323 260-5060
Patrick Tierney, Managing Member
EMP: 700 **EST:** 2012
SQ FT: 7,000
SALES (est): 35.86MM **Privately Held**
Web: www.ptgaming.com
SIC: 7011 Casino hotel

(P-10132)
QUAIL LODGE INC
Also Called: Covey, The
8205 Valley Greens Dr (93923-9513)
PHONE...............................831 624-1581
Clement Kwok, CEO
William Lawson Little, *
▲ **EMP:** 250 **EST:** 1962
SQ FT: 20,000
SALES (est): 24.53MM **Privately Held**
Web: www.quaillodge.com
SIC: 7011 7997 7389 5941 Resort hotel; Golf club, membership; Convention and show services; Golf goods and equipment

(P-10133)
QUEENSBAY HOTEL LLC
Also Called: Hotel Maya
700 Queensway Dr (90802-6343)
PHONE...............................562 481-3910
Cherie Davis, Mgr
EMP: 100
SALES (corp-wide): 8.77MM **Privately Held**
Web: www.hotelmayalongbeach.com
SIC: 7011 Hotels
PA: Queensbay Hotel, Llc
444 W Ocean Blvd
Long Beach CA
562 628-0625

(P-10134)
R & J HOSPITALITY LLC
101 N Virgil Ave (90004-4811)
PHONE...............................213 388-0301
EMP: 68
SALES (corp-wide): 42.44K **Privately Held**
SIC: 7011 Hotels and motels
PA: R & J Hospitality, Llc
5809 E Olympic Blvd
Los Angeles CA

(P-10135)
R P S RESORT CORP
1600 N Indian Canyon Dr (92262-4602)
PHONE...............................760 327-8311
Douglas Mccarron, Pr
EMP: 425 **EST:** 1990
SALES (est): 967.61K
SALES (corp-wide): 45.94MM **Privately Held**
SIC: 7011 Resort hotel
HQ: The San Bernardino Hilton
285 E Hospitality Ln
San Bernardino CA

(P-10136)
RADLAX GATEWAY HOTEL LLC
Also Called: Radisson Inn
6225 W Century Blvd (90045-5311)
PHONE...............................310 670-9000
Peter Dumon, Managing Member
EMP: 1474 **EST:** 2007
SALES (est): 2.04MM **Privately Held**
Web: www.radissonhotels.com

SIC: 7011 Hotels and motels
PA: Portfolio Hotels & Resorts, Llc
1211 W 22nd St Ste 1002
Oak Brook IL

(P-10137)
RAFFLES LRMITAGE BEVERLY HILLS
Also Called: L'Ermitage Hotel
9291 Burton Way (90210-3709)
PHONE...............................310 278-3344
Jack Naderkhani, Genl Mgr
▲ **EMP:** 249 **EST:** 1993
SALES (est): 11.74MM
SALES (corp-wide): 713.02MM **Privately Held**
Web: www.lermitagebeverlyhills.com
SIC: 7011 5813 5812 Hotels; Drinking places ; Eating places
HQ: Raffles International Limited
1 Wallich Street
Singapore

(P-10138)
RALEIGH ENTERPRISES INC (PA)
Also Called: Raleigh Holdings
5300 Melrose Ave (90038-5114)
PHONE...............................310 899-8900
Kristen J Raleigh, CEO
George I Rosenthal, Ch Bd
Mark Rosenthal, Pr
EMP: 130 **EST:** 1955
SQ FT: 20,000
SALES (est): 36.91MM
SALES (corp-wide): 36.91MM **Privately Held**
Web: www.raleighenterprises.com
SIC: 7011 Hotels

(P-10139)
RANCHO VLNCIA RSORT PRTNERS LL
5921 Valencia Cir (92067-9520)
P.O. Box 9126 (92067-4126)
PHONE...............................858 756-1123
Jeffrey Essakow, Managing Member
Hal Jacobs, *
EMP: 300 **EST:** 1989
SALES (est): 21.98MM **Privately Held**
Web: www.ranchovalencia.com
SIC: 7011 Resort hotel

(P-10140)
RAPS HOSPITALITY GROUP
Also Called: Holiday Inn
5977 Mowry Ave (94560-5005)
PHONE...............................510 795-7995
Gary Ghandi, Mgr
EMP: 122
SQ FT: 59,499
SALES (corp-wide): 2.45MM **Privately Held**
Web: www.rapshotels.com
SIC: 7011 Hotels and motels
PA: Raps Hospitality Group
229 Kings Ct
San Carlos CA
650 596-8820

(P-10141)
RBD HOTEL PALM SPRINGS LLC
Also Called: Hyatt Rgency Suites Palm Sprng
285 N Palm Canyon Dr (92262-5525)
PHONE...............................760 322-9000
Larry Mills, Sr VP
EMP: 75 **EST:** 2009
SALES (est): 950K **Privately Held**
Web: www.hyatt.com

PRODUCTS & SERVICES SECTION
7011 - Hotels And Motels (P-10163)

SIC: **7011** Resort hotel

(P-10142)
RECP/WNDSOR SCRAMENTO VENTR LP
Also Called: Windsor Capital Holet Group
4422 Y St (95817-2220)
PHONE.............................916 455-6800
Mike Cryan, *CEO*
Recp Windsor Rim Sacramento, *LLC*
EMP: 61 EST: 2005
SALES (est): 949.16K **Privately Held**
Web: courtyard.marriott.com
SIC: **7011** Hotels

(P-10143)
RED EARTH CASINO
3089 Norm Niver Rd (92274-6550)
PHONE.............................760 395-1200
Larry Drouse, *Genl Mgr*
EMP: 150 EST: 2007
SQ FT: 15,000
SALES (est): 16.26MM **Privately Held**
Web: www.redearthcasino.com
SIC: **7011** 7993 Casino hotel; Gambling establishments operating coin-operated machines

(P-10144)
REDDING RANCHERIA (PA)
Also Called: Win River Mini Mart
2000 Redding Rancheria Rd (96001-5528)
PHONE.............................530 225-8979
Tracy Edward, *CEO*
Christi Hines, *
Tamra Olson, *
EMP: 60 EST: 1922
SQ FT: 16,360
SALES (est): 36.58MM **Privately Held**
Web: www.reddingrancheria-nsn.gov
SIC: **7011** Hotels and motels

(P-10145)
REDDING RNCHRIA ECNMIC DEV COR
Also Called: Win-River Casino
2100 Redding Rancheria Rd (96001-5530)
PHONE.............................530 243-3377
Redding Rancheria Tribe, *Prin*
Redding Rancheria Tribe Prrin, *Prin*
Gary Hayward, *
EMP: 310 EST: 1993
SQ FT: 3,000
SALES (est): 22.21MM **Privately Held**
Web: www.winriver.com
SIC: **7011** Casino hotel

(P-10146)
REH COMPANY
Also Called: Westgate Hotel
1055 2nd Ave (92101-4811)
PHONE.............................619 238-1818
Richard Cox, *Brnch Mgr*
EMP: 197
SALES (corp-wide): 4.43B **Privately Held**
Web: www.westgatehotel.com
SIC: **7011** Hotels
PA: Reh Company
550 E South Temple
Salt Lake City UT
801 524-2700

(P-10147)
REMINGTON HOTEL CORPORATION
Also Called: Holiday Inn
1150 S Beverly Dr (90035-1120)
PHONE.............................310 553-6561
EMP: 69

Web: www.remingtonhospitality.com
SIC: **7011** Hotels and motels
PA: Remington Hotel Corporation
14185 Dallas Pkwy # 1150
Dallas TX

(P-10148)
REMINGTON HOTEL CORPORATION
Also Called: Palm Springs Renaissance
888 E Tahquitz Canyon Way (92262-6708)
PHONE.............................760 322-6000
EMP: 75
Web: www.remingtonhospitality.com
SIC: **7011** Hotels
PA: Remington Hotel Corporation
14185 Dallas Pkwy # 1150
Dallas TX

(P-10149)
RENAISSANCE HOTEL OPERATING CO
Also Called: Marriott
9620 Airport Blvd (90045-5402)
PHONE.............................310 337-2800
Gregory Lehman, *Mgr*
EMP: 300
SALES (corp-wide): 20.77B **Publicly Held**
Web: www.marriott.com
SIC: **7011** 5813 5812 7389 Hotels and motels; Drinking places; Eating places; Office facilities and secretarial service rental
HQ: Renaissance Hotel Operating Company
10400 Fernwood Rd
Bethesda MD

(P-10150)
RENAISSANCE HOTEL OPERATING CO
Also Called: Renaissance Indian Wells
44400 Indian Wells Ln (92210-8708)
PHONE.............................760 773-4444
Tom Tabler, *Prin*
EMP: 600
SALES (corp-wide): 20.77B **Publicly Held**
Web: renaissance-hotels.marriott.com
SIC: **7011** Hotels and motels
HQ: Renaissance Hotel Operating Company
10400 Fernwood Rd
Bethesda MD

(P-10151)
RENAISSANCE HOTEL OPERATING CO
Also Called: Marriott
905 California St (94108-2201)
PHONE.............................415 989-3500
Bill Love, *Brnch Mgr*
EMP: 401
SALES (corp-wide): 20.77B **Publicly Held**
Web: www.stanfordcourt.com
SIC: **7011** Hotels and motels
HQ: Renaissance Hotel Operating Company
10400 Fernwood Rd
Bethesda MD

(P-10152)
RENAISSNCE ESMRALDA RESORT SPA
Also Called: Renaissance
44400 Indian Wells Ln (92210-8708)
PHONE.............................760 773-4444
John Kalinski, *Prin*
EMP: 93 EST: 2011
SALES (est): 8.94MM **Privately Held**
Web: www.marriott.com

SIC: **7011** Resort hotel

(P-10153)
RENESON HOTELS INC (PA)
Also Called: Carriage Inn
2700 Junipero Serra Blvd (94015-1634)
PHONE.............................650 449-5353
Alrene Flynn, *Ch*
Garrett Grialou, *
Diane Grialou, *
Doug Sherer, *
▲ EMP: 100 EST: 1957
SALES (est): 22.6MM
SALES (corp-wide): 22.6MM **Privately Held**
Web: www.renesonhotels.com
SIC: **7011** Hotels and motels

(P-10154)
RENESON HOTELS INC
Also Called: Hotel Britton
112 7th St (94103-2809)
PHONE.............................415 621-7001
Norman Onaga, *Genl Mgr*
EMP: 202
SALES (corp-wide): 22.6MM **Privately Held**
Web: www.renesonhotels.com
SIC: **7011** Resort hotel
PA: Reneson Hotels, Inc.
2700 Junipero Serra Blvd
Daly City CA
650 449-5353

(P-10155)
RESIDENCE INN BY MARRIOTT LLC
Also Called: Residence Inn By Marriott
12011 Scripps Highlands Dr (92131-5156)
PHONE.............................858 740-2200
Trent Sclbrede, *Mgr*
EMP: 61
SALES (corp-wide): 20.77B **Publicly Held**
Web: residence-inn.marriott.com
SIC: **7011** Hotels and motels
HQ: Residence Inn By Marriott, Llc
10400 Fernwood Rd
Bethesda MD

(P-10156)
RESORT AT INDIAN SPRINGS LLC
Also Called: Indian Springs Resort & Spa
1712 Lincoln Ave (94515-1113)
PHONE.............................707 709-2434
Patricia Merchant, *Managing Member*
John Merchant, *Managing Member*
Pat Merchant, *
EMP: 150 EST: 1861
SALES (est): 13.69MM **Privately Held**
Web: www.indianspringscalistoga.com
SIC: **7011** 5812 Resort hotel; Restaurant, family: independent

(P-10157)
RESORT AT PELICAN HILL LLC
22701 Pelican Hill Rd S (92657-2008)
PHONE.............................949 467-6800
Elia Gutierrez, *Dir*
EMP: 439 EST: 2006
SALES (est): 14.08MM **Privately Held**
Web: www.pelicanhill.com
SIC: **7011** Resort hotel

(P-10158)
RESORTCOMM INTERNATIONAL
404 Camino Del Rio S Fl 4 (92108-3501)
PHONE.............................619 683-2470
EMP: 78 EST: 2016

SALES (est): 998.8K **Privately Held**
SIC: **7011** Resort hotel

(P-10159)
RGC GASLAMP LLC
Also Called: Pendry San Diego
550 J St (92101-7020)
PHONE.............................619 738-7000
Michael Odonohue, *Prin*
EMP: 136 EST: 2016
SALES (est): 13.53MM **Privately Held**
Web: www.pendry.com
SIC: **7011** Resort hotel

(P-10160)
RIO VISTA DEVELOPMENT CO INC (PA)
Also Called: Holiday Inn
4222 Vineland Ave (91602-3318)
PHONE.............................818 980-8000
Scott A Mills, *Prin*
Scott Mills, *
EMP: 133 EST: 1971
SQ FT: 100,000
SALES (est): 12.33MM
SALES (corp-wide): 12.33MM **Privately Held**
Web: www.thegarland.com
SIC: **7011** Hotels and motels

(P-10161)
RITZ-CARLTON HOTEL COMPANY LLC
Also Called: Ritz-Carlton
1 Ritz Carlton Dr (92629-4206)
PHONE.............................949 240-5020
Janinie Vanderoy, *Brnch Mgr*
EMP: 348
SALES (corp-wide): 20.77B **Publicly Held**
Web: www.ritzcarlton.com
SIC: **7011** Hotels
HQ: The Ritz-Carlton Hotel Company Llc
7750 Wisconsin Ave
Bethesda MD
301 380-3000

(P-10162)
RITZ-CARLTON HOTEL COMPANY LLC
Also Called: Ritz-Carlton
8301 Hollister Ave (93117-2474)
PHONE.............................805 968-0100
EMP: 650
SALES (corp-wide): 20.77B **Publicly Held**
Web: www.ritzcarlton.com
SIC: **7011** Hotels
HQ: The Ritz-Carlton Hotel Company Llc
7750 Wisconsin Ave
Bethesda MD
301 380-3000

(P-10163)
RITZ-CARLTON HOTEL COMPANY LLC
Also Called: Ritz-Carlton San Francisco
600 Stockton St (94108-2386)
PHONE.............................415 773-6168
Edward Madey, *Mgr*
EMP: 500
SALES (corp-wide): 20.77B **Publicly Held**
Web: www.ritzcarlton.com
SIC: **7011** Hotels
HQ: The Ritz-Carlton Hotel Company Llc
7750 Wisconsin Ave
Bethesda MD
301 380-3000

7011 - Hotels And Motels (P-10164)

(P-10164)
RITZ-CARLTON HOTEL COMPANY LLC
Also Called: Ritz Carlton Rancho Mirage
68900 Frank Sinatra Dr (92270-5300)
PHONE.................................760 321-8282
James H Palllin Junior, *Mgr*
EMP: 313
SALES (corp-wide): 20.77B **Publicly Held**
Web: www.ritzcarlton.com
SIC: 7011 Hotels
HQ: The Ritz-Carlton Hotel Company Llc
7750 Wisconsin Ave
Bethesda MD
301 380-3000

(P-10165)
RIVER ROCK ENTERTAINMENT AUTH
Also Called: River Rock Casino
3250 Highway 128 (95441-8908)
P.O. Box 607 (95441-0607)
PHONE.................................707 857-2777
David Fendrick, *CEO*
Joseph R Callahan, *CFO*
Yola Bawlec, *Ex Sec*
EMP: 616 **EST:** 2002
SALES (est): 20.77MM **Privately Held**
Web: www.riverrockcasino.com
SIC: 7011 Casino hotel

(P-10166)
RIVIERA PALM SPRNG A TRBUTE PR
Also Called: Tribute Portfolio Hotels
1600 N Indian Canyon Dr (92262-4602)
PHONE.................................760 327-8311
EMP: 149 **EST:** 2015
SALES (est): 569.39K
SALES (corp-wide): 569.39K **Privately Held**
Web: www.margaritavilleresorts.com
SIC: 7011 Resort hotel
PA: Agre Dcp Palm Springs Tenant Llc
1600 N Palm Spgs
Palm Springs CA
760 327-8311

(P-10167)
RMS FOUNDATION INC
Also Called: Queen Mary Hotel
1126 Queens Hwy (90802-6331)
PHONE.................................562 435-3511
Joseph F Prevratil, *Pr*
EMP: 650 **EST:** 1993
SQ FT: 750,000
SALES (est): 51.05MM **Privately Held**
Web: www.queenmary.com
SIC: 7011 Hotels and motels
PA: City Of Long Beach
1800 E Wardlow Rd
Long Beach CA
562 570-6450

(P-10168)
ROBRAY HOTEL PARTNERSHIP LLP
Also Called: Las Brisas Hotel
222 S Indian Canyon Dr (92262-6618)
PHONE.................................760 325-4372
Raymond Johnston, *Pr*
EMP: 61 **EST:** 1988
SALES (est): 974.01K **Privately Held**
SIC: 7011 Resort hotel

(P-10169)
ROLLING HILLS CASINO
2655 Everett Freeman Way (96021-9000)
PHONE.................................530 528-3500
EMP: 203
SALES (est): 13.92MM **Privately Held**
Web: www.rollinghillscasino.com
SIC: 7011 Casino hotel

(P-10170)
ROOSEVELT HOTEL LLC
Also Called: Hollywood Roosevelt Hotel
7000 Hollywood Blvd (90028-6003)
PHONE.................................323 466-7000
Goodwin Gaw, *Managing Member*
David Chan, *
EMP: 200 **EST:** 1995
SALES (est): 34.06MM **Privately Held**
Web: www.thehollywoodroosevelt.com
SIC: 7011 5813 5812 Hotels; Drinking places; Eating places

(P-10171)
ROPPONG-THOE LP A CAL LTD PRTN
Also Called: Lake Tahoe Resort Hotel
4130 Lake Tahoe Blvd (96150-6965)
PHONE.................................530 544-5400
Kunihiro Nakayabu, *Mng Pt*
Masaru Saito, *Mng Pt*
EMP: 200 **EST:** 2000
SALES (est): 16.94MM **Privately Held**
Web: www.tahoeresorthotel.com
SIC: 7011 Resort hotel

(P-10172)
ROSANNA INC
Also Called: Avenue of Arts Wyndham Hotel
3350 Avenue Of The Arts (92626-1913)
PHONE.................................714 751-5100
Nick Price, *Genl Mgr*
Paul Sanford, *
Rachael Moorhead, *
Rosanna Chan, *
Robin Reid, *OF AUDIT*
EMP: 151 **EST:** 2009
SALES (est): 19.08MM **Privately Held**
Web: www.wyndhamhotels.com
SIC: 7011 5812 Hotels; Food bars

(P-10173)
ROSCOE REAL ESTATE LTD PARTNR
Also Called: Elkor Properties
1819 Ocean Ave (90401-3215)
PHONE.................................310 260-7500
Vincent Piro, *Genl Mgr*
EMP: 74 **EST:** 2000
SALES (est): 3.72MM **Privately Held**
Web: www.viceroyhotelsandresorts.com
SIC: 7011 7389 Hotels; Hotel and motel reservation service

(P-10174)
ROSEWOOD HOTELS & RESORTS LLC
Also Called: Sense Spa
2825 Sand Hill Rd (94025-7022)
PHONE.................................650 561-1580
EMP: 229
SALES (corp-wide): 26.01MM **Privately Held**
Web: www.rosewoodhotels.com
SIC: 7011 Hotels
PA: Rosewood Hotels And Resorts Llc
2825 Sand Hill Rd
Menlo Park CA
650 561-1500

(P-10175)
ROSEWOOD HOTELS & RESORTS LLC (PA)
Also Called: Rosewood Sand Hill Hotel
2825 Sand Hill Rd (94025-7022)
PHONE.................................650 561-1500
Radha Arora, *Managing Member*
Radha Arora, *Prin*
EMP: 71 **EST:** 1997
SALES (est): 26.01MM
SALES (corp-wide): 26.01MM **Privately Held**
Web: www.rosewoodhotels.com
SIC: 7011 Resort hotel

(P-10176)
ROYAL GORGE NORDIC SKI RESORT (PA)
Also Called: Royal Grge Cross Cntry Ski Rso
9411 Hillside Rd (95728)
P.O. Box 1100 (95728-1100)
PHONE.................................530 426-3871
John Slouber, *Pr*
Frances Wiesel, *
EMP: 120 **EST:** 1971
SQ FT: 50,000
SALES (est): 4.99MM
SALES (corp-wide): 4.99MM **Privately Held**
Web: www.royalgorge.com
SIC: 7011 Resort hotel

(P-10177)
ROYAL HOSPITALITY INC
Also Called: Ramada Inn
5550 Kearny Mesa Rd (92111-1304)
PHONE.................................858 278-0800
Maurice Coreia, *Pr*
EMP: 60 **EST:** 1988
SQ FT: 63,000
SALES (est): 5.82MM **Privately Held**
Web: www.wyndhamhotels.com
SIC: 7011 Hotels and motels

(P-10178)
RP SCS WSD HOTEL LLC
Also Called: Hotel Republic San Diego
421 W B St (92101-3501)
PHONE.................................619 398-3020
Michael O'donohue, *Genl Mgr*
Maria Veronica Rodriguez, *
Melissa Silvers, *
EMP: 60 **EST:** 2006
SALES (est): 9.42MM **Privately Held**
Web: www.hotelrepublicsd.com
SIC: 7011 Hotel, franchised

(P-10179)
RP/KINETIC PARC 55 OWNER LLC
Also Called: Parc 55 Hotel
55 Cyril Magnin St (94102-2812)
PHONE.................................415 392-8000
Peter Beheda, *Sr VP*
Gary Gutierrez, *VP*
Rob Gauthier, *Genl Mgr*
Carolyn Endy, *Contrlr*
EMP: 101 **EST:** 2006
SALES (est): 162.9MM
SALES (corp-wide): 8.52B **Publicly Held**
Web: www.parc55hotel.com
SIC: 7011 Hotels
PA: Blackstone Inc.
345 Park Ave
New York NY
212 583-5000

(P-10180)
RPC OLD TOWN JFFRSON OWNER LLC
Also Called: Courtyard By Marriott
2435 Jefferson St (92110-3026)
PHONE.................................619 725-4221
Budd Barmeyer, *Genl Mgr*
Evan Hitter, *
EMP: 67 **EST:** 1987
SQ FT: 5,000
SALES (est): 9.19MM **Privately Held**
Web: www.courtyardoldtown.com
SIC: 7011 Hotels and motels

(P-10181)
RPD HOTELS 18 LLC (PA)
Also Called: Vagabond Inns
1801 S La Cienega Blvd Ste 301 (90035-4641)
PHONE.................................213 746-1531
Juan Sanchez Llaca, *Pr*
Don Johnson, *
Stewart Rubin, *
EMP: 800 **EST:** 1998
SALES (est): 23.05MM
SALES (corp-wide): 23.05MM **Privately Held**
Web: www.vagabondinn.com
SIC: 7011 Motels

(P-10182)
RUFFIN HOTEL CORP OF CAL
Also Called: Long Beach Marriott
4700 Airport Plaza Dr (90815-1252)
PHONE.................................562 425-5210
Phillip G Ruffin, *Pr*
EMP: 260 **EST:** 1993
SALES (est): 16.03MM **Privately Held**
Web: www.marriott.com
SIC: 7011 5812 5813 Hotels; Eating places; Drinking places

(P-10183)
RUNNING CREEK CASINO
635 E State Highway 20 (95485-8793)
P.O. Box 788 (95485-0788)
PHONE.................................707 275-9209
Mike Caryl, *Dir Fin*
EMP: 170 **EST:** 2011
SALES (est): 14.8MM **Privately Held**
Web: www.runningcreekcasino.com
SIC: 7011 5812 Casino hotel; Eating places

(P-10184)
S B H HOTEL CORPORATION
285 E Hospitality Ln (92408-3411)
PHONE.................................909 889-0133
Douglas Mccarron, *Brnch Mgr*
EMP: 570
SALES (corp-wide): 45.94MM **Privately Held**
SIC: 7011 Hotels
HQ: S B H Hotel Corporation
520 S Virgil Ave Fl 4
Los Angeles CA

(P-10185)
S W K PROPERTIES LLC
Also Called: Holiday Inn
2726 S Grand Ave Lbby (92705-5404)
PHONE.................................714 481-6300
Rod Hurt, *Mgr*
EMP: 129
SALES (corp-wide): 4.74MM **Privately Held**
Web: www.holidayinn.com
SIC: 7011 Hotels and motels
PA: S W K Properties Llc
3807 Wilshire Blvd # 122
Los Angeles CA
213 383-9204

(P-10186)
S W K PROPERTIES LLC (PA)
Also Called: Sheraton
3807 Wilshire Blvd Ste 1226 (90010-3101)

PRODUCTS & SERVICES SECTION
7011 - Hotels And Motels (P-10207)

PHONE..............................213 383-9204
EMP: 70 EST: 1998
SQ FT: 3,000
SALES (est): 4.74MM
SALES (corp-wide): 4.74MM **Privately Held**
Web: four-points.marriott.com
SIC: **7011** Hotels

(P-10187)
SACRAMENTO 49ER TRAVEL PLAZA
Also Called: Sacramento 49er
2828 El Centro Rd (95833-9602)
PHONE..............................916 927-4774
Tristen Griffith, *Pr*
Terrace Rust, *
EMP: 125 EST: 1976
SQ FT: 27,000
SALES (est): 11.52MM **Privately Held**
Web: www.sacramento49er.com
SIC: **7011** 5331 5812 5541 Motels; Variety stores; Restaurant, family: independent; Truck stops

(P-10188)
SAGE HOSPITALITY RESOURCES LLC
Also Called: Courtyard By Mrrott Los Angles
700 W Huntington Dr (91016-3104)
PHONE..............................626 357-5211
Dennis Hollingdrake, *Mgr*
EMP: 222
SALES (corp-wide): 286.23MM **Privately Held**
Web: courtyard.marriott.com
SIC: **7011** Hotels and motels
PA: Sage Hospitality Resources L.L.C.
 1575 Welton St Ste 300
 Denver CO
 303 595-7200

(P-10189)
SAGE HOSPITALITY RESOURCES LLC
Also Called: Homewood Stes Hlton Sfo Arprt
2000 Shoreline Ct (94005-1802)
PHONE..............................650 589-1600
Gina Merz, *Brnch Mgr*
EMP: 171
SALES (corp-wide): 286.23MM **Privately Held**
Web: homewoodsuites3.hilton.com
SIC: **7011** Hotels
PA: Sage Hospitality Resources L.L.C.
 1575 Welton St Ste 300
 Denver CO
 303 595-7200

(P-10190)
SAI MANAGEMENT CO INC
Also Called: Desert Inn & Suites
1600 S Harbor Blvd (92802-2314)
PHONE..............................714 772-5050
Priti Hansji, *Mgr*
EMP: 80
SALES (corp-wide): 4.91MM **Privately Held**
Web: www.anaheimdesertinn.com
SIC: **7011** Resort hotel
PA: Sai Management Co., Inc.
 631 W Katella Ave
 Anaheim CA
 714 776-8604

(P-10191)
SAJAHTERA INC
Also Called: Beverly Hills Hotel
9641 Sunset Blvd (90210-2938)
PHONE..............................310 276-2251
Junaidi Masri, *Pr*
Edward Mady, *OF WEST COAST USA* *
EMP: 600 EST: 1912
SQ FT: 10,758
SALES (est): 57.56MM **Privately Held**
Web: www.dorchestercollection.com
SIC: **7011** Resort hotel
HQ: Dorchester Group Limited
 3 Tilney Street
 London
 207 629-4848

(P-10192)
SALT LAKE HOTEL ASSOCIATES LP (PA)
222 Kearny St Ste 200 (94108-4537)
PHONE..............................415 397-5572
Tom Lataur, *Pr*
EMP: 111 EST: 1997
SALES (est): 9.75MM
SALES (corp-wide): 9.75MM **Privately Held**
SIC: **7011** Hotels

(P-10193)
SAN BERNARDINO HILTON (HQ)
Also Called: Hilton
285 E Hospitality Ln (92408-3411)
PHONE..............................909 889-0133
Douglas Mccarron, *Pr*
Morgan Mcpherson, *Ex Dir*
Ronald Schoen, *
EMP: 152 EST: 1984
SALES (est): 24.63MM
SALES (corp-wide): 45.94MM **Privately Held**
Web: www.hiltongrandvacations.com
SIC: **7011** 6512 5812 Hotels and motels; Commercial and industrial building operation; Eating places
PA: Carpenters Southwest Administrative Corporation
 533 S Fremont Ave
 Los Angeles CA
 213 386-8590

(P-10194)
SAN DIEGO FARAH PARTNERS LP
Also Called: Holiday Inn
1430 7th Ave Ste B (92101-2815)
PHONE..............................619 239-2261
Berham Baxter, *Genl Pt*
EMP: 63 EST: 1988
SQ FT: 99,999
SALES (est): 925.72K **Privately Held**
Web: www.holidayinn.com
SIC: **7011** Hotels and motels

(P-10195)
SAN DIEGO HOTEL COMPANY LLC
Also Called: Marriott San Dego Gslamp Qrter
660 K St (92101-7036)
PHONE..............................619 696-0234
James Evans, *CFO*
▲ EMP: 135 EST: 1999
SALES (est): 6.85MM **Privately Held**
Web: www.westerninn.com
SIC: **7011** Hotels

(P-10196)
SAN DIEGO LESSEE LLC
Also Called: Doubletree By Hilton
7450 Hazard Center Dr (92108-4539)
PHONE..............................619 297-5466
Owen Wilcox, *Sec*
Deanne Brand, *

Justin Ray Healey, *
Alexandra Neely, *
Joseph Berger, *
EMP: 100 EST: 2013
SALES (est): 7.66MM
SALES (corp-wide): 2.5B **Publicly Held**
Web: www.hilton.com
SIC: **7011** Hotels and motels
PA: Park Hotels & Resorts Inc.
 1775 Tysons Blvd Fl 7
 Tysons VA
 571 302-5757

(P-10197)
SAN DIEGO MISSION BAY RESORTS ✪
1775 E Mission Bay Dr (92109-6801)
PHONE..............................619 677-1161
EMP: 88 EST: 2022
SALES (est): 5.04MM **Privately Held**
Web: www.missionbayresort.com
SIC: **7011** Resort hotel

(P-10198)
SAN DIEGO SHERATON CORPORATION
Also Called: Starwood Hotels & Resorts
1590 Harbor Island Dr (92101-1009)
PHONE..............................619 291-6400
Robert Cartwright, *Genl Mgr*
EMP: 146 EST: 1998
SALES (est): 7.94MM
SALES (corp-wide): 20.77B **Publicly Held**
Web: sheraton.marriott.com
SIC: **7011** 5813 5812 4493 Hotels; Drinking places; Eating places; Marinas
HQ: Starwood Hotels & Resorts Worldwide, Llc
 7750 Wisconsin Ave
 Bethesda MD
 203 964-6000

(P-10199)
SAN FRANCISCO HOTEL GROUP LLC
Also Called: Loews Regency San Francisco
222 Sansome St (94104-2703)
PHONE..............................415 276-9888
Yue-tin Chang, *Pr*
Tracy Lee, *
Jonathan Tisch, *
▲ EMP: 99 EST: 1989
SALES (est): 7.73MM
SALES (corp-wide): 14.04B **Publicly Held**
Web: www.loewshotels.com
SIC: **7011** Resort hotel
HQ: Loews Hotels Holding Corporation
 9 W 57th St
 New York NY
 212 521-2000

(P-10200)
SAN JOSE FAIRMONT LESSEE LLC
170 S Market St Lbby (95113-2361)
PHONE..............................408 998-1900
EMP: 500
SIC: **7011** 5812 5813 Resort hotel; Ethnic food restaurants; Cocktail lounge

(P-10201)
SAN JOSE LESSEE LLC
Also Called: Doubletree By Hilton San Jose
2050 Gateway Pl (95110-1011)
PHONE..............................408 453-4000
Missoon Kong, *Genl Mgr*
Rowan Tejada, *
EMP: 99 EST: 2017
SALES (est): 9.7MM

SALES (corp-wide): 2.5B **Publicly Held**
Web: www.hilton.com
SIC: **7011** Hotels and motels
HQ: Park Us Lessee Holdings Inc.
 1600 Tysons Blvd Ste 1000
 Mclean VA
 703 883-1052

(P-10202)
SAN PSQUAL BAND MSSION INDIANS
Also Called: Valley View Casino
16300 Nyemii Pass Rd (92082-6769)
P.O. Box 2379 (92082-2379)
PHONE..............................760 291-5500
TOLL FREE: 866
Bruce Howards, *Genl Mgr*
EMP: 248
Web: www.sanpasqualbandofmissionindians.org
SIC: **7011** Casino hotel
PA: San Pasqual Band Of Mission Indians
 16400 Kumeyaay Way
 Valley Center CA

(P-10203)
SAN YSIDRO BB PROPERTY LLC
Also Called: Stonehouse Restaurant
900 San Ysidro Ln (93108-1325)
PHONE..............................805 368-6788
Seamus Mcmanus, *Managing Member*
EMP: 140 EST: 2000
SQ FT: 4,415
SALES (est): 13.76MM **Privately Held**
Web: www.sanysidroranch.com
SIC: **7011** 5812 Hotels; Eating places

(P-10204)
SANCI MARRIOTT HOTELS
Also Called: Marriott International
2000 2nd St (92118-1551)
PHONE..............................619 435-3000
EMP: 93 EST: 2012
SALES (est): 5.29MM **Privately Held**
Web: www.marriott.com
SIC: **7011** Hotels and motels

(P-10205)
SANDM SAN DEGO MRRIOTT DEL MAR
11966 El Camino Real (92130-2592)
PHONE..............................858 523-1700
Jenessa Schaniel, *Prin*
EMP: 1000 EST: 2009
SALES (est): 18.97MM **Privately Held**
Web: www.marriott.com
SIC: **7011** Hotels

(P-10206)
SANTA CLARA TRAVELODGE
Also Called: Travelodge
3477 El Camino Real (95051-2860)
PHONE..............................408 984-3364
Vikas G Patel, *Pt*
Rovindra G Patel, *Pt*
Natu Patel, *Pt*
Vanita Patel, *Pt*
Surekha Patel, *Pt*
EMP: 66 EST: 1973
SQ FT: 24,000
SALES (est): 522.07K **Privately Held**
Web: www.wyndhamhotels.com
SIC: **7011** Hotels and motels

(P-10207)
SANTA CRUZ SEASIDE COMPANY
Also Called: Sea & Sand Inn

7011 - Hotels And Motels (P-10208)

201 W Cliff Dr (95060-6144)
PHONE.................................831 427-3400
Lisa Morley, Mgr
EMP: 507
SALES (corp-wide): 51.32MM **Privately Held**
Web: www.seaandsandinn.com
SIC: **7011** Motels
PA: Santa Cruz Seaside Company Inc
400 Beach St
Santa Cruz CA
831 423-5590

(P-10208)
SANTA MONICA HOTEL OWNER LLC
Also Called: Doubltree Stes By Hlton Snta M
1707 4th St (90401-3301)
PHONE.................................310 395-3332
EMP: 135 EST: 2005
SALES (est): 3.88MM **Privately Held**
SIC: **7011** Hotels

(P-10209)
SANTA MONICA PROPER JV LLC
Also Called: Santa Monica Proper Hotel
700 Wilshire Blvd (90401-1708)
PHONE.................................310 620-9990
Brad Korzen, CEO
EMP: 250 EST: 2016
SALES (est): 36.5MM **Privately Held**
Web: www.properhotel.com
SIC: **7011** Hotels

(P-10210)
SANTANA ROW HOTEL PARTNERS LP
355 Santana Row Ste 1010 (95128-2049)
PHONE.................................408 551-0010
Bonnie Best, Genl Mgr
EMP: 200
Web: www.ozumosantanarow.com
SIC: **7011** Hotels
PA: Santana Row Hotel Partners Lp
4400 Post Oak Pkwy Ste 16
Houston TX

(P-10211)
SBE HOTEL GROUP LLC
8000 Beverly Blvd (90048-4547)
PHONE.................................323 655-8000
EMP: 65 EST: 2004
SQ FT: 11,000
SALES (est): 8.83MM
SALES (corp-wide): 713.02MM **Privately Held**
Web: www.sbe.com
SIC: **7011** Hotels
HQ: Sbe Entertainment Group, Llc
2535 Las Vegas Blvd S
Los Angeles CA
323 655-8000

(P-10212)
SD HOTEL CIRCLE LLC
Also Called: Homewood Suites
2201 Hotel Cir S (92108-3315)
PHONE.................................619 881-6800
Mayur Patel, *
Louisa Yeung, *
EMP: 75 EST: 2017
SALES (est): 4.31MM **Privately Held**
Web: homewoodsuites3.hilton.com
SIC: **7011** Hotels and motels

(P-10213)
SEACLIFF INN INC
Also Called: Best Western

7500 Old Dominion Ct (95003-3807)
PHONE.................................831 661-4671
Frank Giuliani, Pr
Coleen Giuliani, *
Norm Bei, VP
T J Scott, *
EMP: 90 EST: 1985
SQ FT: 60,000
SALES (est): 4.22MM
SALES (corp-wide): 98.27MM **Privately Held**
Web: www.bestwestern.com
SIC: **7011** Hotels and motels
HQ: Pacifica Hotel Company
39 Argonaut
Aliso Viejo CA
805 957-0095

(P-10214)
SEASCAPE RESORT OWNERS ASSN
1 Seascape Resort Dr (95003-5854)
PHONE.................................831 688-6800
Bob Perasso, CEO
EMP: 68 EST: 2008
SALES (est): 11.52MM **Privately Held**
Web: www.seascaperesort.com
SIC: **7011** Resort hotel

(P-10215)
SEASCAPE RSORT LTD A CAL LTD P
Also Called: Sanderlings
19 Seascape Vlg (95003-6102)
PHONE.................................831 662-7120
Mark Holcomb, Genl Pt
EMP: 86 EST: 1989
SQ FT: 45,000
SALES (est): 1.01MM **Privately Held**
Web: www.sanderlingsrestaurant.com
SIC: **7011** Resort hotel

(P-10216)
SEASIDE HOSPITALITY LP
1400 Del Monte Blvd (93955-4234)
PHONE.................................831 394-5335
EMP: 101
SIC: **7011** Hotels and motels
PA: Seaside Hospitality Lp
1775 Hancock St Ste 100
San Diego CA

(P-10217)
SEATTLE ARPRT HOSPITALITY LLC
Also Called: Holiday Inn
170 N Church Ln (90049-2044)
PHONE.................................310 476-6411
Robert Buescher, Genl Mgr
EMP: 99
Web: www.holidayinn.com
SIC: **7011 5813 5812** Hotels and motels; Drinking places; Eating places
PA: Seattle Airport Hospitality, Llc
5847 San Felipe St # 4650
Houston TX

(P-10218)
SECOND STREET CORPORATION
Also Called: Huntley Hotel Santa Monica Bch
1111 2nd St (90403-5003)
PHONE.................................310 394-5454
Sohrab Sassounian, Pr
Dora Levy, Stockholder*
Helal M El-sherif, CFO
Shiva Aghaipour, *
EMP: 250 EST: 1964
SQ FT: 185,000

SALES (est): 21.66MM **Privately Held**
Web: www.thehuntleyhotel.com
SIC: **7011 5812** Hotels; Eating places

(P-10219)
SELECT HOTELS GROUP LLC
Also Called: Hyatt Hse Emryvll/San Frncsco
5800 Shellmound St (94608-1966)
PHONE.................................510 601-5880
Alan Mass, Genl Mgr
EMP: 81
SQ FT: 16,424
Web: www.hyatt.com
SIC: **7011** Hotels
HQ: Select Hotels Group, L.L.C.
71 S Wacker Dr Ste 2500
Chicago IL
312 750-1234

(P-10220)
SELECT HOTELS GROUP LLC
Also Called: Hyatt Hse San Dg/Sorrento Mesa
10044 Pacific Mesa Blvd (92121-4386)
PHONE.................................858 597-0500
Shelley Dean Carroll, Genl Mgr
EMP: 74
Web: www.hyatt.com
SIC: **7011** Hotel, franchised
HQ: Select Hotels Group, L.L.C.
71 S Wacker Dr Ste 2500
Chicago IL
312 750-1234

(P-10221)
SERVICE HOSPITALITY LLC
1050 Burnett Ave (94520-5713)
PHONE.................................925 566-8820
EMP: 70 EST: 2017
SALES (est): 1.49MM **Privately Held**
SIC: **7011** Seasonal hotel

(P-10222)
SF MARRIOTT MARQUIS
780 Mission St (94103-3113)
PHONE.................................415 896-1600
EMP: 149 EST: 2015
SALES (est): 10.13MM **Privately Held**
Web: www.marriott.com
SIC: **7011** Hotels

(P-10223)
SFD PARTNERS LLC
Also Called: Sir Francis Drake Hotel
450 Powell St (94102-1504)
PHONE.................................415 392-7755
John Price, Genl Mgr
EMP: 148 EST: 1928
SALES (est): 902.62K **Privately Held**
SIC: **7011 5812 5813 7389** Hotels; Eating places; Drinking places; Hotel and motel reservation service

(P-10224)
SHADE HOTEL EMPLOYS 7
1221 N Valley Dr (90266-4778)
PHONE.................................310 546-4995
Michael Zislis, Owner
▲ EMP: 60 EST: 2005
SALES (est): 6.21MM **Privately Held**
Web: www.shadehotel.com
SIC: **7011** Hotels

(P-10225)
SHEN ZHEN NEW WORLD II LLC
Also Called: Sheraton
333 Universal Hollywood Dr (91608-1001)
PHONE.................................818 980-1212
EMP: 99 EST: 2011
SALES (est): 3.67MM **Privately Held**

Web: sheraton.marriott.com
SIC: **7011** Hotels

(P-10226)
SHERATON HT SAN DEGO MSSION VL
Also Called: Sheraton San Diego Mission Vly
1433 Camino Del Rio S (92108-3521)
PHONE.................................619 321-4602
Admiral Cynthia Adams Carlin, Prin
Cynthia Adams Carlin, Admn
Brooke Vandenbrink, Contrlr
EMP: 100 EST: 2007
SALES (est): 2.32MM **Privately Held**
Web: www.sheratonmissionvalley.com
SIC: **7011** Hotels

(P-10227)
SHERATON LLC
Also Called: Sheraton
6101 W Century Blvd (90045-5310)
PHONE.................................310 642-1111
Michael Washington, Genl Mgr
EMP: 75
SALES (corp-wide): 20.77B **Publicly Held**
Web: www.sheratonnewyork.com
SIC: **7011 5813 5812** Hotels; Drinking places; Eating places
HQ: The Sheraton Llc
1111 Westchester Ave
White Plains NY
800 328-6242

(P-10228)
SHERATON RDDING HT AT SNDIAL B
Also Called: Sheraton
820 Sundial Bridge Dr (96001-0978)
PHONE.................................530 364-2800
Marjorie Culley, Genl Mgr
EMP: 100 EST: 2018
SALES (est): 2.5MM **Privately Held**
Web: www.turtlebay.org
SIC: **7011** Resort hotel

(P-10229)
SHERWOOD VALLEY RANCHERIA
Also Called: Sherwood Vlley Rnchria Casino
100 Kawi Pl (95490-4674)
PHONE.................................707 459-7330
Kani Neves, Mgr
EMP: 75
Web: www.svrcasino.com
SIC: **7011** Casino hotel
PA: Sherwood Valley Rancheria
190 Sherwood Hill Dr
Willits CA
707 459-9690

(P-10230)
SHINGLE SPRNG TRBAL GMING AUTH
Also Called: Red Hawk Casino
1 Red Hawk Pkwy (95667-8639)
PHONE.................................530 677-7000
EMP: 1200 EST: 2008
SQ FT: 278,000
SALES (est): 57.34MM **Privately Held**
Web: www.redhawkcasino.com
SIC: **7011** Casino hotel
PA: Shingle Springs Rancheria
5168 Honpie Rd
Placerville CA

(P-10231)
SHIVA ENTERPRISES INC
Also Called: Holiday Inn
2834 El Camino Real (94061-4002)

PRODUCTS & SERVICES SECTION
7011 - Hotels And Motels (P-10254)

PHONE...................650 366-2000
Vijay Patel, *Pr*
Tina Patel, *VP*
H L Patel, *Treas*
EMP: 108 EST: 1975
SQ FT: 20,000
SALES (est): 1.39MM **Privately Held**
Web: www.holidayinn.com
SIC: **7011** Hotels and motels

(P-10232)
SHIVAY HOSPITALITY INC
1738 N Las Palmas Ave (90028-4805)
PHONE...................323 702-7103
Pankaj Naik, *Brnch Mgr*
EMP: 94
SALES (corp-wide): 412.88K **Privately Held**
SIC: **7011** Hotels and motels
PA: Shivay Hospitality Inc
    1427 Wilcox Ave
    Hollywood CA

(P-10233)
SIERRA AT TAHO SKI RESORTS
1111 Sierra At Tahoe Rd (95735-9505)
PHONE...................530 659-7519
John Rice, *Pr*
George Gillette, *
EMP: 110 EST: 1996
SALES (est): 1.69MM **Privately Held**
Web: www.sierraattahoe.com
SIC: **7011** Resort hotel

(P-10234)
SIERRA LODGINGS INC
Also Called: Plaza Suites, The
3100 Lakeside Dr (95054-2804)
PHONE...................408 748-9800
Daniel Freeberg, *CEO*
Scott Seymore, *Prin*
EMP: 83 EST: 2004
SALES (est): 4.46MM **Privately Held**
SIC: **7011** Resort hotel

(P-10235)
SIERRA SUMMIT INC
59265 Hwy 168 (93634)
P.O. Box 236 (93634-0236)
PHONE...................559 233-2500
Richard C Kun, *Pr*
Robert Law Exex, *VP*
Ken Wood, *
Alan Macquoid, *
EMP: 811 EST: 1977
SQ FT: 5,000
SALES (est): 961.06K
SALES (corp-wide): 59.84MM **Privately Held**
Web: www.skichinapeak.com
SIC: **7011** Ski lodge
PA: Snow Summit Ski Corporation
    880 Summit Blvd
    Big Bear Lake CA
    909 866-5766

(P-10236)
SILENT VALLEY CLUB INC
46305 Poppet Flats Rd (92220-9636)
PHONE...................951 849-4501
Patrick Buhrer, *Park Director*
EMP: 70 EST: 1973
SQ FT: 2,200
SALES (est): 3.79MM **Privately Held**
Web: www.silentvalleyclub.com
SIC: **7011** Resort hotel

(P-10237)
SILICON VALLEY CLUB LLC (PA)

Also Called: Hotel
579 Clyde Ave Ste 340 (94043-2271)
PHONE...................408 202-9424
EMP: 74 EST: 2012
SALES (est): 4.66MM
SALES (corp-wide): 4.66MM **Privately Held**
Web: residence-inn.marriott.com
SIC: **7011** Hotel, franchised

(P-10238)
SILICON VALLEY INNS INC
Also Called: Quality Inn
940 W Weddell Dr (94089-1537)
PHONE...................408 734-3742
EMP: 80 EST: 2010
SALES (est): 2.04MM **Privately Held**
Web: www.choicehotels.com
SIC: **7011** Hotels and motels

(P-10239)
SILVERADO RSORT SVCS GROUP LLC
Also Called: Silverado Resort
1600 Atlas Peak Rd (94558-1425)
PHONE...................707 257-0200
EMP: 450 EST: 2010
SALES (est): 49.79MM **Privately Held**
Web: www.silveradoresort.com
SIC: **7011** Resort hotel

(P-10240)
SIMI WEST INC
Also Called: Grand Vista Hotel
999 Enchanted Way (93065-1998)
PHONE...................760 346-5502
Leo Cook, *Ch Bd*
EMP: 120 EST: 1993
SALES (est): 9.18MM **Privately Held**
Web: www.grandvistasimi.com
SIC: **7011** Hotels and motels

(P-10241)
SISKIYOU DEVELOPMENT COMPANY
Also Called: HI Lo Motel
88 S Weed Blvd (96094-2607)
PHONE...................530 938-2731
Shawn Zanni, *Mgr*
EMP: 65
SALES (corp-wide): 30.87MM **Privately Held**
Web: www.hilomotel.com
SIC: **7011** Motels
PA: Siskiyou Development Company, Inc.
    130 S Weed Blvd
    Weed CA
    530 938-2904

(P-10242)
SITA RAM LLC
Also Called: Best Western Amador Inn
200 S State Highway 49 (95642-2548)
PHONE...................209 223-0211
EMP: 79 EST: 1983
SQ FT: 8,000
SALES (est): 835.67K **Privately Held**
Web: www.bestwestern.com
SIC: **7011** 5812 5813 7991 Hotels and motels; Eating places; Bar (drinking places); Physical fitness facilities

(P-10243)
SIX CONTINENTS HOTELS INC
Also Called: Holiday Inn
612 Wainwright Ct (93243)
PHONE...................661 343-3316
EMP: 122
Web: www.holidayinn.com

SIC: **7011** Hotels and motels
HQ: Six Continents Hotels, Inc
    35016 Avenue D
    Yucaipa CA
    770 604-5000

(P-10244)
SIX CONTINENTS HOTELS INC
Also Called: Inter Continental
2819 E Hamilton Ave (93721-3208)
PHONE...................559 272-7840
EMP: 74
Web: www.ihg.com
SIC: **7011** Hotels
HQ: Six Continents Hotels, Inc
    35016 Avenue D
    Yucaipa CA
    770 604-5000

(P-10245)
SIX CONTINENTS HOTELS INC
Also Called: Holiday Inn
50 8th St (94103-1409)
PHONE...................415 626-6103
Gino Lazzara, *Genl Mgr*
EMP: 160
Web: www.holidayinn.com
SIC: **7011** 5813 5812 6512 Hotels; Drinking places; Eating places; Nonresidential building operators
HQ: Six Continents Hotels, Inc
    35016 Avenue D
    Yucaipa CA
    770 604-5000

(P-10246)
SIX CONTINENTS HOTELS INC
Also Called: Holiday Inn
495 Bay St (94133-1860)
PHONE...................415 771-9000
Sheila Martin, *Genl Mgr*
EMP: 90
Web: www.holidayinn.com
SIC: **7011** 8741 Hotels; Hotel or motel management
HQ: Six Continents Hotels, Inc
    35016 Avenue D
    Yucaipa CA
    770 604-5000

(P-10247)
SKY COURT USA INC
Also Called: Hyatt Hotel
880 S Westlake Blvd (91361-2905)
PHONE...................805 497-9991
Tetsuo Nishida, *Pr*
EMP: 144 EST: 1990
SALES (est): 710.52K **Privately Held**
Web: www.hyatt.com
SIC: **7011** Hotels and motels

(P-10248)
SLS HOTEL AT BEVERLY HILLS
465 S La Cienega Blvd (90048-4001)
PHONE...................310 247-0400
Robert Leck, *Genl Mgr*
EMP: 101 EST: 2015
SALES (est): 10.41MM
SALES (corp-wide): 67.98MM **Privately Held**
Web: book.ennismore.com
SIC: **7011** Hotels
PA: The Sunrider Corporation
    1625 Abalone Ave
    Torrance CA
    310 781-3808

(P-10249)
SMITH RIVER LUCKY 7 CASINO
Also Called: Lucky 7 Casino

350 N Indian Rd (95567-9474)
PHONE...................707 487-7777
Terry Westrick, *Pt*
EMP: 100 EST: 1997
SALES (est): 10.14MM **Privately Held**
Web: www.lucky7casino.com
SIC: **7011** Casino hotel

(P-10250)
SMOKE TREE INC
Also Called: Smoke Tree Ranch
1850 Smoke Tree Ln (92264-1602)
PHONE...................760 327-1221
Lisa Bell, *Mgr*
Brad Poncher, *
EMP: 85 EST: 1945
SALES (est): 4.66MM **Privately Held**
Web: www.smoketreeranch.com
SIC: **7011** Resort hotel

(P-10251)
SNOW SUMMIT SKI CORPORATION (PA)
Also Called: Snow Summit
880 Summit Blvd (92315)
P.O. Box 77 (92315-0077)
PHONE...................909 866-5766
Richard C Kun, *Pr*
Robert Law, *
Alan Macquoid, *
Paula Lowery, *
Robert Tarras, *
EMP: 150 EST: 1960
SQ FT: 10,000
SALES (est): 59.84MM
SALES (corp-wide): 59.84MM **Privately Held**
Web: www.bigbearmountainresort.com
SIC: **7011** 5812 Ski lodge; American restaurant

(P-10252)
SONESTA INTL HOTELS CORP
Also Called: Clift Royal Sonesta Hotel, The
495 Geary St (94102-1222)
PHONE...................415 929-2393
EMP: 305
SALES (corp-wide): 449.18MM **Privately Held**
Web: www.sonesta.com
SIC: **7011** Hotels
PA: Sonesta International Hotels Corporation
    400 Centre St Ste 100
    Newton MA
    770 923-1775

(P-10253)
SONOMA HOTEL OPERATOR INC
Also Called: Fairmont Snoma Mission Inn Spa
100 Boyes Blvd (95476-3678)
P.O. Box 1447 (95476-1447)
PHONE...................707 938-9000
Rick Corcoran, *Genl Mgr*
EMP: 176
SALES (corp-wide): 713.02MM **Privately Held**
Web: www.fairmont.com
SIC: **7011** Hotels
HQ: Sonoma Hotel Operator, Llc
    50 Rockefeller Plz
    New York NY

(P-10254)
SONOMA HOTEL PARTNERS LP
Also Called: Sheraton Sonoma Cnty Petaluma
745 Baywood Dr (94954-5388)
PHONE...................707 283-2888
Scott Satterfield, *Genl Mgr*

7011 - Hotels And Motels (P-10255)

PRODUCTS & SERVICES SECTION

EMP: 95 EST: 1999
SQ FT: 134,732
SALES (est): 9.32MM **Privately Held**
Web: www.sheratonsonoma.com
SIC: **7011** Hotels

(P-10255)
SOULDRIVER LESSEE INC
Also Called: Hotel Solamar
435 6th Ave (92101-7007)
PHONE.............................619 819-9500
Maria Streedy, *Pr*
EMP: 80 EST: 2006
SALES (est): 10.19MM **Privately Held**
Web: www.margaritavilleresorts.com
SIC: **7011** Hotels

(P-10256)
SOUTH COAST WESTIN HOTEL CO
Also Called: Starwood Hotels & Resorts
686 Anton Blvd (92626-1920)
PHONE.............................714 540-2500
Steve Heyer, *CEO*
Mike Hall, *
Bob Jenness, *
EMP: 99 EST: 1970
SALES (est): 8.44MM
SALES (corp-wide): 20.77B **Publicly Held**
Web: www.westinsouthcoastplaza.com
SIC: **7011** 5812 Hotels; Eating places
HQ: Starwood Hotels & Resorts Worldwide, Llc
7750 Wisconsin Ave
Bethesda MD
203 964-6000

(P-10257)
SOUTHBOURNE INC
Also Called: Campton Place Hotel
340 Stockton St (94108-4609)
PHONE.............................415 781-5555
Reymond Dixon, *Dir*
EMP: 166 EST: 1983
SALES (est): 3.88MM **Privately Held**
Web: www.tajcamptonplace.com
SIC: **7011** Hotels
PA: Taj Hotels
Nandafata Aral Korpana
Wardha MH

(P-10258)
SPA RESORT CASINO
100 N Indian Canyon Dr (92262-6414)
PHONE.............................760 883-1034
Max Ross, *CFO*
EMP: 926
SALES (corp-wide): 23.57MM **Privately Held**
Web: www.aguacalientecasinos.com
SIC: **7011** Casino hotel
PA: Spa Resort Casino
401 E Amado Rd
Palm Springs CA
888 999-1995

(P-10259)
SPA RESORT CASINO (PA)
401 E Amado Rd (92262-6403)
PHONE.............................888 999-1995
Kato Moy, *Genl Mgr*
Agvahgue Eahilla Indian, *Owner*
EMP: 74 EST: 2004
SALES (est): 23.57MM
SALES (corp-wide): 23.57MM **Privately Held**
Web: www.aguacalientecasinos.com
SIC: **7011** Resort hotel

(P-10260)
SPECTRUM HOTEL GROUP LLC
Also Called: Doubletree Hotel
90 Pacifica (92618-3312)
PHONE.............................949 471-8888
Timothy R Busch, *General Member*
EMP: 106 EST: 1997
SALES (est): 1.98MM **Privately Held**
Web: www.hilton.com
SIC: **7011** 7991 5812 Hotels and motels; Physical fitness facilities; Eating places

(P-10261)
SPF CAPITAL REAL ESTATE LLC
Also Called: Crown Plaza La Harbor Hotel
601 S Palos Verdes St (90731-3329)
PHONE.............................310 519-8200
Tiegang Yin, *Prin*
Tim Yin, *Prin*
EMP: 99 EST: 2017
SALES (est): 4.62MM **Privately Held**
Web: www.ihg.com
SIC: **7011** Hotels

(P-10262)
SPORTSMENS LODGE HOTEL LLC
12825 Ventura Blvd (91604-2397)
PHONE.............................818 769-4700
EMP: 87 EST: 1962
SQ FT: 100,000
SALES (est): 7.93MM **Privately Held**
Web: www.shopsatsportsmenslodge.com
SIC: **7011** 5812 5813 Hotels; American restaurant; Cocktail lounge

(P-10263)
SPRING MOUNTAIN HOTEL LLC
2850 Birkham Ct (94534-8328)
PHONE.............................530 304-5619
EMP: 71
SALES (corp-wide): 446.68K **Privately Held**
SIC: **7011** Hotels
PA: Spring Mountain Hotel Llc
1485 Main St Ste 201
Saint Helena CA
530 304-5619

(P-10264)
SQUAW CREEK ASSOCIATES LLC
Also Called: Resort At Squaw Creek
400 Squaw Creek Rd (96146-9778)
P.O. Box 3333 (96146-3333)
PHONE.............................530 581-6624
EMP: 600 EST: 1990
SALES (est): 48.75MM **Privately Held**
Web: www.destinationhotels.com
SIC: **7011** Resort hotel

(P-10265)
SQUAW VALLEY SKI HOLDINGS LLC
1960 Squaw Valley Rd (96146-1030)
P.O. Box 2007 (96146-2007)
PHONE.............................800 403-0206
EMP: 293 EST: 2011
SALES (est): 3.01MM **Privately Held**
Web: www.palisadestahoe.com
SIC: **7011** Resort hotel

(P-10266)
SS HERITAGE INN ONTARIO LLC
3595 E Guasti Rd (91761-3705)
PHONE.............................909 937-5000

Aimee Fyke, *Managing Member*
EMP: 99 EST: 2018
SALES (est): 2.23MM **Privately Held**
SIC: **7011** Inns

(P-10267)
STANFORD HOTELS CORPORATION
Also Called: Hilton Santa Clara
4949 Great America Pkwy (95054-1216)
PHONE.............................408 330-0001
Peter Dolton, *Mgr*
EMP: 75
Web: www.stanfordhotels.com
SIC: **7011** Hotels
PA: Stanford Hotels Corporation
433 California St Ste 700
San Francisco CA

(P-10268)
STANFORD PARK HOTEL
100 El Camino Real (94025-5292)
PHONE.............................650 322-1234
Ellis Alden, *Pt*
EMP: 212 EST: 1984
SQ FT: 122,000
SALES (est): 9.7MM **Privately Held**
Web: www.stanfordparkhotel.com
SIC: **7011** 5813 5812 Resort hotel; Drinking places; Eating places

(P-10269)
STARWOOD INC
402 W Broadway Ste 400 (92101-3554)
PHONE.............................888 559-1749
Deborah Pippins, *Prin*
Mark Litz, *Prin*
▲ EMP: 156 EST: 1993
SQ FT: 1,800
SALES (est): 7.16MM **Privately Held**
SIC: **7011** 4731 4729 4724 Hotels and motels; Freight forwarding; Airline ticket offices; Travel agencies
PA: Peake & Company Limited, Thomas
177 Western Main Road Cocorite
Port-Of-Spain

(P-10270)
STARWOOD HOTEL
Also Called: Starwood Hotels & Resorts
5990 Green Valley Cir (90230-6907)
PHONE.............................310 641-7740
Ian Gee, *Managing Member*
EMP: 156 EST: 1999
SALES (est): 3.86MM
SALES (corp-wide): 20.77B **Publicly Held**
Web: sheraton.marriott.com
SIC: **7011** Hotels and motels
HQ: Starwood Hotels & Resorts Worldwide, Llc
7750 Wisconsin Ave
Bethesda MD
203 964-6000

(P-10271)
STARWOOD HTELS RSRTS WRLDWIDE
Also Called: Starwood Hotels & Resorts
335 Powell St (94102-1804)
PHONE.............................415 397-7000
Joe Burger, *Mgr*
EMP: 300
SALES (corp-wide): 20.77B **Publicly Held**
Web: westin.marriott.com
SIC: **7011** 5812 Hotels and motels; Eating places
HQ: Starwood Hotels & Resorts Worldwide, Llc
7750 Wisconsin Ave
Bethesda MD
203 964-6000

(P-10272)
STARWOOD HTELS RSRTS WRLDWIDE
Also Called: Starwood Hotels & Resorts
4 N Points By Sheraton 3737 Blac Ave (93726)
PHONE.............................559 230-8470
EMP: 195
SALES (corp-wide): 20.77B **Publicly Held**
Web: www.starwoodhotels.com
SIC: **7011** Hotels and motels
HQ: Starwood Hotels & Resorts Worldwide, Llc
7750 Wisconsin Ave
Bethesda MD
203 964-6000

(P-10273)
STARWOOD HTELS RSRTS WRLDWIDE
Also Called: Starwood Hotels & Resorts
2 New Montgomery St (94105-3402)
PHONE.............................415 512-1111
T Staramelino, *Mgr*
EMP: 195
SALES (corp-wide): 20.77B **Publicly Held**
Web: www.marriott.com
SIC: **7011** Hotels and motels
HQ: Starwood Hotels & Resorts Worldwide, Llc
7750 Wisconsin Ave
Bethesda MD
203 964-6000

(P-10274)
STARWOOD HTELS RSRTS WRLDWIDE
Also Called: Starwood Hotels & Resorts
910 Broadway Cir (92101-6114)
PHONE.............................619 239-2200
Doug Korn, *Genl Mgr*
EMP: 250
SALES (corp-wide): 20.77B **Publicly Held**
Web: westin.marriott.com
SIC: **7011** 7991 6512 5812 Hotels and motels; Physical fitness facilities; Nonresidential building operators; Eating places
HQ: Starwood Hotels & Resorts Worldwide, Llc
7750 Wisconsin Ave
Bethesda MD
203 964-6000

(P-10275)
STARWOOD HTELS RSRTS WRLDWIDE
Also Called: Sheraton
601 W Mckinley Ave (91768-1635)
PHONE.............................909 622-2220
John Gilbert, *Genl Mgr*
EMP: 195
SALES (corp-wide): 20.77B **Publicly Held**
Web: www.starwoodhotels.com
SIC: **7011** Hotels and motels
HQ: Starwood Hotels & Resorts Worldwide, Llc
7750 Wisconsin Ave
Bethesda MD
203 964-6000

(P-10276)
STATELINE TRAVELODGE INC
Also Called: Travelodge
4011 Lake Tahoe Blvd (96150-6930)
PHONE.............................530 544-6000
Manfred C Lohr, *Pr*
K Lohr, *Owner*
EMP: 83 EST: 1974
SQ FT: 80,000

PRODUCTS & SERVICES SECTION

7011 - Hotels And Motels (P-10299)

SALES (est): 124.17K **Privately Held**
Web: www.wyndhamhotels.com
SIC: **7011** Hotels and motels

(P-10277)
STAY CAL SAN JOSE LLC
Also Called: Row Hotel, The
2404 Stevens Creek Blvd (95128-1652)
PHONE.................................408 275-2147
EMP: 105
SALES (corp-wide): 575.12K **Privately Held**
SIC: **7011** Hotels
PA: Stay Cal San Jose, Llc
2110 S El Camino Real
San Mateo CA
408 293-5000

(P-10278)
STOCKBRIDGE/SBE HOLDINGS LLC
Also Called: SBE
5900 Wilshire Blvd Ste 3100 (90036-5013)
PHONE.................................323 655-8000
EMP: 3000 EST: 2007
SALES (est): 73.44MM **Privately Held**
SIC: **7011** Hotels

(P-10279)
STONEBRIDGE RLTY ADVISORS INC
Also Called: Hampton Inn
27102 Towne Centre Dr (92610-2801)
PHONE.................................949 597-8700
John Matthews, *Mgr*
EMP: 586
Web: www.hilton.com
SIC: **7011** Hotels and motels
PA: Stonebridge Realty Advisors, Inc.
9100 E Panorama Dr # 300
Englewood CO

(P-10280)
SUGAR BOWL CORPORATION
Also Called: Sugar Bowl Resort
629 Sugar Bowl Rd (95724)
P.O. Box 5 (95724-0005)
PHONE.................................530 426-9000
Nancy Bechtle, *Ch Bd*
Robert H Kautz, *
Dan Kingsley, *
Nicole Liberman, *
Bonny Bavetta, *
▲ EMP: 100 EST: 1937
SQ FT: 30,000
SALES (est): 25.08MM **Privately Held**
Web: www.sugarbowl.com
SIC: **7011** Resort hotel

(P-10281)
SUMMIT HOTEL TRS 115 LLC
Four Pnts By Shrton Ht Stes Sa
264 S Airport Blvd (94080-6701)
PHONE.................................650 624-3700
Jay Singh, *Brnch Mgr*
EMP: 71
SALES (corp-wide): 1.09MM **Privately Held**
Web: sheraton.marriott.com
SIC: **7011** Hotels
PA: Summit Hotel Trs 115, Llc
264 S Airport Blvd
South San Francisco CA
650 624-3700

(P-10282)
SUN HILL PROPERTIES INC
Also Called: Hilton Los Angls/Nversal Cy Ht
555 Universal Hollywood Dr (91608-1001)
PHONE.................................818 506-2500
Denn Hu, *Ch Bd*
▲ EMP: 350 EST: 1989
SALES (est): 26.29MM **Privately Held**
Web: www.sunhillprop.com
SIC: **7011** Hotels and motels
PA: Universal Paragon Corporation
150 Executive Park Blvd # 4
San Francisco CA

(P-10283)
SUNRISE HOSPITALITY INC
Also Called: Hampton Inn
2060 Freeway Dr (95776-9504)
PHONE.................................916 419-4440
EMP: 130
SALES (corp-wide): 32.59K **Privately Held**
Web: www.hilton.com
SIC: **7011** Hotels and motels
PA: Sunrise Hospitality, Inc.
5546 Kalispell Way
Sacramento CA

(P-10284)
SUNSET TOWER HOTEL LLC
8358 W Sunset Blvd (90069-1516)
PHONE.................................323 654-7100
E Peter Krulewitch, *Managing Member*
Jeffrey Klein, *Managing Member*
EMP: 68 EST: 2004
SALES (est): 17.89MM **Privately Held**
Web: www.sunsettowerhotel.com
SIC: **7011** Resort hotel

(P-10285)
SUNSHINE INN A CAL LTD PARTNR
Also Called: Doubletree Rosemead Hotel
888 Montebello Blvd (91770-4303)
PHONE.................................323 722-8800
Ying Ming Huang, *Pt*
EMP: 64 EST: 1985
SQ FT: 110,000
SALES (est): 3.61MM **Privately Held**
Web: murfreesboro.doubletree.com
SIC: **7011** Hotels

(P-10286)
SUNSTONE DURANTE LLC
Also Called: Hilton San Diego/Del Mar
15575 Jimmy Durante Blvd (92014-1901)
PHONE.................................858 792-5200
Scott Sloan, *Managing Member*
Damien Proctor, *Prin*
EMP: 250 EST: 2005
SALES (est): 9.79MM **Privately Held**
SIC: **7011** Hotels and motels

(P-10287)
SUNSTONE HOTEL PROPERTIES INC
Also Called: Residence Inn By Marriott
1177 S Beverly Dr (90035-1119)
PHONE.................................310 228-4100
Tom Beedon, *Genl Mgr*
EMP: 137
Web: residence-inn.marriott.com
SIC: **7011** Hotels and motels
HQ: Sunstone Hotel Properties Inc
120 Vantis Dr Ste 350
Aliso Viejo CA

(P-10288)
SUNSTONE HOTEL PROPERTIES INC
Also Called: Residence Inn By Marriott
1700 N Sepulveda Blvd (90266-5015)
PHONE.................................310 546-7627
Sandi Rae Kraft, *Brnch Mgr*
EMP: 250
Web: residence-inn.marriott.com
SIC: **7011** Hotels and motels
HQ: Sunstone Hotel Properties Inc
120 Vantis Dr Ste 350
Aliso Viejo CA

(P-10289)
SUNSTONE HOTEL PROPERTIES INC (DH)
Also Called: Residence Inn By Marriott
120 Vantis Dr Ste 350 (92656-2686)
PHONE.................................949 330-4000
Arthur Buser, *Pr*
EMP: 120 EST: 1994
SALES (est): 62.7MM **Privately Held**
Web: www.hilton.com
SIC: **7011** Hotels and motels
HQ: Interstate Hotels & Resorts, Inc.
5301 Headquarters Dr
Plano TX
703 387-3100

(P-10290)
SUNSTONE HOTEL PROPERTIES INC
3805 Murphy Canyon Rd (92123-4404)
PHONE.................................858 277-1199
Linda Dimeglio, *Mgr*
EMP: 63
Web: residence-inn.marriott.com
SIC: **7011** Hotels
HQ: Sunstone Hotel Properties Inc
120 Vantis Dr Ste 350
Aliso Viejo CA

(P-10291)
SUNSTONE TOP GUN LESSEE INC
Also Called: Embassy Suites
4550 La Jolla Village Dr (92122-1248)
PHONE.................................949 330-4000
Kenneth E Cruse, *CEO*
John V Arabia, *
Lindsay Monge, *
EMP: 150 EST: 2006
SALES (est): 9.27MM **Publicly Held**
Web: www.hilton.com
SIC: **7011** Hotels and motels
HQ: Sunstone Hotel Trs Lessee, Inc.
15 Enterprise Ste 200
Aliso Viejo CA

(P-10292)
SUPER 8 MOTEL GOLETA
Also Called: Super 8 Motel
6021 Hollister Ave, Us Hwy 101 (93117-3217)
PHONE.................................805 967-5591
Oliver Dixon, *Owner*
Van Bivans, *Mgr*
EMP: 63 EST: 1960
SQ FT: 12,000
SALES (est): 185.11K **Privately Held**
Web: www.wyndhamhotels.com
SIC: **7011** Hotels and motels

(P-10293)
SVI LAX LLC
Also Called: Residnce Inn By Mrriot Lx/Cntu
5933 W Century Blvd (90045-5471)
PHONE.................................310 281-0300
EMP: 60 EST: 2013
SQ FT: 213,000
SALES (est): 4.51MM **Privately Held**
Web: www.residenceinnlax.com
SIC: **7011** Hotels

(P-10294)
SWVP DEL MAR HOTEL LLC
Also Called: Doubletree San Diego Del Mar
11915 El Camino Real (92130-2539)
PHONE.................................858 481-5900
Tom Donahue, *Mgr*
EMP: 84 EST: 2015
SALES (est): 1.6MM **Privately Held**
SIC: **7011** Hotel, franchised

(P-10295)
SWVP WESTLAKE LLC
Also Called: Hyatt Westlake
880 S Westlake Blvd (91361-2905)
PHONE.................................805 557-1234
David Coonan, *Genl Mgr*
EMP: 250
SALES (corp-wide): 2.29MM **Privately Held**
Web: www.swvp.com
SIC: **7011** Motels
PA: Swvp Westlake Llc
12790 El Camino Real
San Diego CA
858 480-2900

(P-10296)
SYCAMORE MINERAL SPRING RESORT
1215 Avila Beach Dr (93405-8048)
PHONE.................................805 595-7302
Russell Kiessig, *Pr*
John King, *
Steve Gregory, *
Charles Yates, *
EMP: 65 EST: 1975
SQ FT: 36,150
SALES (est): 4.17MM **Privately Held**
Web: www.sycamoresprings.com
SIC: **7011** 7991 Resort hotel; Spas

(P-10297)
SYCUAN CASINO
5469 Casino Way (92019-1823)
PHONE.................................619 445-6002
EMP: 1844
SALES (corp-wide): 93.96MM **Privately Held**
Web: www.sycuan.com
SIC: **7011** Casino hotel
PA: Sycuan Casino
5459 Casino Way
El Cajon CA
619 445-6002

(P-10298)
SYDELL HOTELS LLC
Also Called: Line Hotel, The
3515 Wilshire Blvd (90010-2301)
PHONE.................................213 381-7411
Gary J Thomas, *
EMP: 130 EST: 2011
SALES (est): 29.01MM
SALES (corp-wide): 29.01MM **Privately Held**
Web: www.thelinehotel.com
SIC: **7011** Resort hotel
PA: Sydell Group Llc
276 5th Ave Rm 704
New York NY
646 810-0208

(P-10299)
SYDELL PALM SPRINGS LLC
Also Called: Saguaro Palm Springs, The
1800 E Palm Canyon Dr (92264-1617)
PHONE.................................760 323-1711
Curtis Pandes, *Genl Mgr*
EMP: 60 EST: 2011
SALES (est): 2.63MM **Privately Held**

7011 - Hotels And Motels (P-10300)

(P-10300)
T M MIAN & ASSOCIATES INC
Also Called: Hilton Garden Inn Calabasas
24150 Park Sorrento (91302-4101)
PHONE..............................818 591-2300
Shawn Nicoles, Genl Mgr
EMP: 67
SALES (corp-wide): 9.4MM Privately Held
Web: www.hilton.com
SIC: 7011 Resort hotel
PA: T. M. Mian & Associates, Inc.
1055 Regal Row
Dallas TX
972 960-2024

(P-10301)
T-12 THREE LLC
Also Called: Hard Rock Hotel
207 5th Ave (92101-6908)
PHONE..............................619 702-3000
EMP: 356 EST: 2007
SALES (est): 40.92MM Privately Held
Web: www.hardrockhotels.com
SIC: 7011 Hotels

(P-10302)
TABLE MOUNTAIN CASINO
Also Called: Table Mountain
8184 Table Mountain Rd (93626)
P.O. Box 777 (93626-0777)
PHONE..............................559 822-7777
Frances Dandy, Sr VP
▲ EMP: 1000 EST: 1987
SQ FT: 30,000
SALES (est): 51.41MM Privately Held
Web: www.tmcasino.com
SIC: 7011 Casino hotel

(P-10303)
TACHI PALACE CASINO RESORT
17225 Jersey Ave (93245-9760)
PHONE..............................559 924-7751
Tachi Yokut, Prin
Santa Yokut, *
◆ EMP: 1500 EST: 2006
SALES (est): 99.14MM Privately Held
Web: www.tachipalace.com
SIC: 7011 Casino hotel

(P-10304)
TAHOE BEACH & SKI CLUB
3601 Lake Tahoe Blvd (96150-8915)
PHONE..............................530 541-6220
EMP: 60 EST: 1970
SALES (est): 2.35MM Privately Held
Web: www.tahoebeachandski.com
SIC: 7011 6513 Resort hotel; Apartment hotel operation

(P-10305)
TAP ROOM AT LODGE
Also Called: Pebble Beach Company, The
Seventeen Mile Dr (93953)
P.O. Box 1767 (93953-1767)
PHONE..............................831 624-3811
Phil Jones, Mgr
Tim Yan, *
Eric Frey, *
EMP: 218 EST: 1919
SALES (est): 11.39MM Privately Held
Web: www.pebblebeach.com
SIC: 7011 Resort hotel

(P-10306)
TARSADIA HOTELS (DH)
620 Newport Center Dr Ste 1400 (92660)
PHONE..............................949 610-8000
▲ EMP: 63 EST: 1987
SALES (est): 43.93MM
SALES (corp-wide): 369.62MM Privately Held
Web: www.tarsadia.com
SIC: 7011 Hotels
HQ: Tarsadia Investments, Llc
520 Newport Center Dr # 2100
Newport Beach CA
949 610-8000

(P-10307)
TEMECULA HHG HOTEL DEV LP
Also Called: Home2 Sites By Hilton Temecula
28400 Rancho California Rd (92590-3617)
PHONE..............................951 331-3622
EMP: 96
SALES (corp-wide): 1.79MM Privately Held
Web: home2suites3.hilton.com
SIC: 7011 Hotels
PA: Temecula Hhg Hotel Development, Lp
105 Decker Ct Ste 500
Irving TX
972 510-1200

(P-10308)
TERRE DU SOLEIL LTD
Also Called: Auberge Du Soleil Resort
180 Rutherford Hill Road (94573)
P.O. Box B (94573-0902)
PHONE..............................707 963-1211
George Goeggel, Genl Pt
Robert Harmon, *
Claude Rouas, *
Bradley Reynolds, *
EMP: 280 EST: 1981
SQ FT: 20,000
SALES (est): 24.98MM Privately Held
Web: www.aubergeresorts.com
SIC: 7011 5812 Resort hotel; French restaurant

(P-10309)
THE LODGE AT TORREY PINES PARTNERSHIP L P
998 W Mission Bay Dr (92109-7803)
EMP: 275 EST: 1961
SALES (est): 17.04MM Privately Held
Web: www.lodgetorreypines.com
SIC: 7011 5812 Resort hotel; Coffee shop

(P-10310)
TIBURON HOSPITALITY LLC
Also Called: Super 8 Motel
901 Real Rd (93309-1003)
PHONE..............................661 322-1012
Mark Grotewohl, Pt
▲ EMP: 150 EST: 1980
SQ FT: 1,600
SALES (est): 4.32MM Privately Held
Web: www.wyndhamhotels.com
SIC: 7011 Hotels and motels

(P-10311)
TIC HOTELS INC
Also Called: Shorecliff Properties
2555 Price St (93449-2111)
PHONE..............................805 773-4671
Edward Brown, Mgr
EMP: 78
Web: www.shorecliff.com
SIC: 7011 5812 5813 Motels; Eating places; Bar (drinking places)
HQ: Tic Hotels, Inc.
1811 State St Ste C
Santa Barbara CA
805 898-0855

(P-10312)
TIC HOTELS INC
Also Called: Best Western Bayside Inn
555 W Ash St (92101-3414)
PHONE..............................619 238-7577
Tracey Wicken, Genl Mgr
EMP: 78
Web: www.bestwestern.com
SIC: 7011 Hotels
HQ: Tic Hotels, Inc.
1811 State St Ste C
Santa Barbara CA
805 898-0855

(P-10313)
TIDES CENTER
124 Turk St (94102-3926)
PHONE..............................415 359-9401
EMP: 179
Web: www.tides.org
SIC: 7011 Hotels and motels
PA: The Tides Center
The Prsdio 1014 Trney Ave The Presidio
San Francisco CA

(P-10314)
TODAYS IV
Also Called: Westin Bonaventure Ht & Suites
404 S Figueroa St Ste 516 (90071-1798)
PHONE..............................213 835-4016
Tee Fong Zen, CEO
Peter Zen, *
Ming Nin Zen, *
EMP: 693 EST: 1989
SQ FT: 1,200,000
SALES (est): 40.79MM Privately Held
Web: westin.marriott.com
SIC: 7011 5813 5812 Hotels; Drinking places; Eating places
PA: Today's Hotel Corporation
1500 Van Ness Ave
San Francisco CA

(P-10315)
TORREY SUITES LP
3939 Ocean Bluff Ave (92130-8654)
PHONE..............................858 720-9500
Robert Rauch, Genl Pt
EMP: 84 EST: 2008
SALES (est): 3.85MM Privately Held
SIC: 7011 Hotels

(P-10316)
TORREYANA GRILLE
Also Called: Hilton
10950 N Torrey Pines Rd (92037-1006)
PHONE..............................858 558-1500
Patrick Duffy, Pr
EMP: 60 EST: 2002
SALES (est): 9.14MM Privately Held
Web: www.hiltonlajollatorreypines.com
SIC: 7011 5812 Hotels and motels; Grills (eating places)

(P-10317)
TRADEWINDS LODGE (PA)
Also Called: Cliff House Restaurant
400 S Main St (95437-4806)
PHONE..............................707 964-4761
Dominic Affinito, Pt
EMP: 65 EST: 1965
SQ FT: 19,000
SALES (est): 1.5MM
SALES (corp-wide): 1.5MM Privately Held
SIC: 7011 5812 5813 6512 Motels; Restaurant, family: independent; Bars and lounges; Commercial and industrial building operation

(P-10318)
TRAVELODGE DOWNTOWN
Also Called: Budget Motel
345 Marsh St (93401-3820)
PHONE..............................805 543-6443
John Figone, Pt
Falko Forbrich, Pt
EMP: 76 EST: 1975
SALES (est): 248.79K Privately Held
Web: www.wyndhamhotels.com
SIC: 7011 Hotels and motels

(P-10319)
TRAVELODGE HOTELS INC
3327 Del Mar Ave (91770-2329)
PHONE..............................800 257-2297
EMP: 121
SALES (corp-wide): 1.5B Publicly Held
Web: www.wyndhamhotels.com
SIC: 7011 Hotels and motels
HQ: Travelodge Hotels, Inc.
1 Sylvan Way
Parsippany NJ
973 567-3708

(P-10320)
TREVI PARTNERS A CALIF LP
Also Called: Holiday Inn
1250 Bayshore Hwy (94010-1805)
PHONE..............................650 347-2381
Steven Dodaro, Mgr
EMP: 75
Web: www.holidayinn.com
SIC: 7011 Hotels and motels
HQ: Trevi Partners, A Calif. L.P.
6680 Regional St
Dublin CA
925 828-7750

(P-10321)
TREVI PARTNERS A CALIF LP
Also Called: Best Wstn Carmel Mission Inn
3665 Rio Rd (93923-8609)
PHONE..............................831 624-1841
Jose Cortega, Mgr
EMP: 60
Web: www.bestwestern.com
SIC: 7011 Hotels and motels
HQ: Trevi Partners, A Calif. L.P.
6680 Regional St
Dublin CA
925 828-7750

(P-10322)
TREVI PARTNERS A CALIF LP (PA)
5955 Coronado Ln (94588-8518)
PHONE..............................925 225-4000
Michael Madden, Pt
EMP: 120 EST: 2002
SALES (est): 29.42MM Privately Held
Web: www.holidayinn.com
SIC: 7011 Hotels and motels

(P-10323)
TREVI PARTNERS A CALIF LP
Also Called: Holiday Inn
160 Shoreline Hwy (94941-3610)
PHONE..............................415 332-5700
Jeffery Perry, Mgr
EMP: 75
Web: www.holidayinn.com
SIC: 7011 Hotels and motels
HQ: Trevi Partners, A Calif. L.P.
6680 Regional St
Dublin CA
925 828-7750

PRODUCTS & SERVICES SECTION

7011 - Hotels And Motels (P-10347)

(P-10324)
TREVI PARTNERS A CALIF LP
Also Called: Tollhouse Hotel
140 S Santa Cruz Ave (95030-6782)
PHONE..................................408 395-7070
Marie Tallman, *Mgr*
EMP: 90
Web: www.tollhousehotel.com
SIC: **7011** 5812 Hotels; Eating places
HQ: Trevi Partners, A Calif. L.P.
6680 Regional St
Dublin CA
925 828-7750

(P-10325)
TRIGILD INTERNATIONAL INC
Also Called: Ramada Inn
1680 Superior Ave (92627-3652)
PHONE..................................949 645-2221
Vince Andres, *Brnch Mgr*
EMP: 96
SALES (corp-wide): 20.67MM **Privately Held**
Web: www.wyndhamhotels.com
SIC: **7011** Hotels and motels
PA: Trigild International, Inc.
3323 Carmel Mountain Rd # 2
San Diego CA
858 720-6700

(P-10326)
TRIGILD INTERNATIONAL INC
Also Called: Days Inn
133 Encinitas Blvd (92024-3641)
PHONE..................................760 944-0260
Maria Rebollar, *Brnch Mgr*
EMP: 65
SALES (corp-wide): 20.67MM **Privately Held**
Web: www.wyndhamhotels.com
SIC: **7011** Hotels and motels
PA: Trigild International, Inc.
3323 Carmel Mountain Rd # 2
San Diego CA
858 720-6700

(P-10327)
TRIGILD INTERNATIONAL INC
Also Called: Howard Johnson
521 Roosevelt Ave (91950-1133)
PHONE..................................619 474-6517
EMP: 65
SALES (corp-wide): 20.67MM **Privately Held**
Web: www.wyndhamhotels.com
SIC: **7011** Hotels and motels
PA: Trigild International, Inc.
3323 Carmel Mountain Rd # 2
San Diego CA
858 720-6700

(P-10328)
TULARE LODGING ASSOCIATES LLC
Also Called: Fairfield Inn and Suites
1225 Hillman St (93274-8057)
PHONE..................................559 686-4700
Monica Sherburne, *Genl Mgr*
EMP: 93 EST: 2012
SALES (est): 12.69MM **Privately Held**
Web: fairfield.marriott.com
SIC: **7011** Hotels and motels

(P-10329)
TURLOCK HOSPITALITY LLC
Also Called: Candlewood Suites
1000 Powers Ct (95380-8455)
PHONE..................................209 250-1501
EMP: 86
Web: www.ihg.com

SIC: **7011** Hotels
PA: Turlock Hospitality, Llc
9500 Aquafina Ct
Elk Grove CA

(P-10330)
TYME MAIDU TRIBE-BERRY CREEK
Also Called: Gold Country Casino
4020 Olive Hwy (95966-5527)
PHONE..................................530 538-4560
EMP: 519 EST: 1996
SALES (est): 49.74MM **Privately Held**
Web: www.goldcountrycasino.com
SIC: **7011** Casino hotel

(P-10331)
UHG LAX PROP LLC
Also Called: Hotel Company
1985 E Grand Ave (90245-5015)
PHONE..................................310 322-0999
Charu Goyal, *Managing Member*
Jordan Austin, *
Mark Lewis, *
EMP: 125 EST: 2017
SALES (est): 3.9MM **Privately Held**
SIC: **7011** 5812 Hotels; Restaurant, family: independent

(P-10332)
UKA LLC
Also Called: Tarsadia Hotels
620 Newport Center Dr Ste 1400 (92660)
PHONE..................................949 610-8000
B U Patel, *Mgr*
EMP: 495 EST: 1997
SQ FT: 12,000
SALES (est): 532.58K
SALES (corp-wide): 369.62MM **Privately Held**
SIC: **7011** Hotels
HQ: Tarsadia Investments, Llc
520 Newport Center Dr # 2100
Newport Beach CA
949 610-8000

(P-10333)
UNITED PACIFIC HOTEL GROUP LP
1221 Chess Dr (94404-1173)
PHONE..................................650 295-6103
Solomon Tsai, *Pt*
Steve Tsai, *Pt*
Tina Tsai, *Pt*
Tenny Tsai, *Pt*
Elizabeth Tsai, *Pt*
EMP: 200 EST: 1990
SALES (est): 8.92MM **Privately Held**
Web: www.uphg.biz
SIC: **7011** Hotels

(P-10334)
UNIWELL CORPORATION
Also Called: Holiday Inn
7000 Beach Blvd (90620-1832)
PHONE..................................714 522-7000
Tracy Myer, *Brnch Mgr*
EMP: 150
SALES (corp-wide): 17.64MM **Privately Held**
Web: www.hibuenapark.com
SIC: **7011** 5813 5812 Hotels and motels; Drinking places; Eating places
PA: Uniwell Corporation
21172 Figueroa St
Carson CA
310 782-8888

(P-10335)
URBAN COMMONS QUEENSWAY LLC
Also Called: Queen Mary, The
1126 Queens Hwy (90802-6331)
PHONE..................................562 499-1611
EMP: 900 EST: 2016
SALES (est): 24.24MM **Privately Held**
SIC: **7011** Hotels

(P-10336)
US GRANT HOTEL VENTURES LLC
326 Broadway (92101-4800)
PHONE..................................619 744-2007
EMP: 80 EST: 2003
SQ FT: 99,999
SALES (est): 2.48MM **Privately Held**
Web: www.grantgrill.com
SIC: **7011** Resort hotel

(P-10337)
US HOTEL AND RESORT MGT INC
Also Called: Regency Inn
2544 Newport Blvd (92627-1331)
PHONE..................................949 650-2988
Peggy Chen, *Mgr*
EMP: 227
SALES (corp-wide): 17.94MM **Privately Held**
Web: www.ramkotacompanies.com
SIC: **7011** Resort hotel
HQ: U.S. Hotel And Resort Management, Inc.
3211 W Sencore Dr
Sioux Falls SD
605 334-2371

(P-10338)
V TODAYS INC
Also Called: Holiday Inn
19800 S Vermont Ave (90502-1126)
PHONE..................................310 781-9100
Belinda Zen, *CEO*
David Britton, *
EMP: 110 EST: 1986
SQ FT: 95,000
SALES (est): 9.05MM **Privately Held**
Web: www.holidayinn.com
SIC: **7011** Hotels and motels

(P-10339)
VACATION BAY HOTEL PRPTS INC
Also Called: Vacation Village Hotel
647 S Coast Hwy (92651-2415)
PHONE..................................949 494-8566
TOLL FREE: 800
Loren W Haneline, *Pr*
Linda K Haneline, *
Russell Haneline, *
Jeff Haneline, *
Christine Haneline, *
EMP: 73 EST: 1960
SQ FT: 74,000
SALES (est): 589.32K **Privately Held**
Web: www.pacificedgehotel.com
SIC: **7011** Resort hotel

(P-10340)
VALADON HOTEL LLC
Also Called: Petit Ermitage
8822 Cynthia St (90069-4502)
PHONE..................................310 854-1114
Adrian Ashkenazy, *
EMP: 80 EST: 1997
SQ FT: 40,000
SALES (est): 15.16MM **Privately Held**

Web: www.petitermitage.com
SIC: **7011** Hotels

(P-10341)
VALENCIA GROUP LLC
94 Mayfair (92620-2149)
PHONE..................................949 379-6489
EMP: 109
SALES (corp-wide): 59.42K **Privately Held**
Web: www.valenciahotelgroup.com
SIC: **7011** Hotels
PA: Valencia Group Llc
3495 Cabrillo Ave
Santa Clara CA

(P-10342)
VAN NESS HOTEL INC
1050 Van Ness Ave (94109-6934)
PHONE..................................415 673-4711
John M Scheurer, *Pr*
EMP: 100 EST: 2003
SALES (est): 892K **Privately Held**
SIC: **7011** Hotels

(P-10343)
VENTURA HSPTALITY PARTNERS LLC
Also Called: Crowne Plaza Ventura Beach
450 Harbor Blvd (93001-2708)
PHONE..................................805 648-2100
EMP: 140 EST: 2006
SQ FT: 143,000
SALES (est): 8.77MM **Privately Held**
Web: www.ihg.com
SIC: **7011** Hotels

(P-10344)
VICTORVLLE TRSURE HOLDINGS LLC
Also Called: Holiday Inn
15494 Palmdale Rd (92392-2408)
PHONE..................................760 245-6565
Benjamin Gonzales, *Genl Mgr*
EMP: 75 EST: 2011
SALES (est): 2.28MM **Privately Held**
Web: www.hivictorville.com
SIC: **7011** 5812 Hotels and motels; American restaurant

(P-10345)
VINTNERS INN
4350 Barnes Rd (95403-1514)
PHONE..................................707 575-7350
EMP: 100 EST: 2000
SQ FT: 30,670
SALES (est): 12.88MM **Privately Held**
Web: www.vintnersresort.com
SIC: **7011** Motels

(P-10346)
VPB OPERATING CO LLC
147 Stimson Ave (93449-2643)
PHONE..................................805 773-1011
EMP: 84
SALES (est): 1.66MM **Privately Held**
SIC: **7011** Resort hotel, franchised

(P-10347)
VWI CONCORD LLC
Also Called: Hilton Concord
1970 Diamond Blvd (94520-5718)
PHONE..................................925 827-2000
Jack Hlavac, *Genl Mgr*
Jim Dunbar, *Ofcr*
EMP: 130 EST: 2008
SALES (est): 9.24MM **Privately Held**
Web: www.hiltonconcord.com
SIC: **7011** Hotels and motels

7011 - Hotels And Motels (P-10348)

(P-10348)
W LODGING INC
Also Called: Ramada Inn
1825 Gillespie Way Ste 10 (92020-0501)
PHONE.....................619 258-6565
EMP: 800
SIC: 7011 5812 8741 Hotels and motels;
  Eating places; Hotel or motel management

(P-10349)
W LOS ANGELES
Also Called: Westwood Marquis Hotel & Grdns
930 Hilgard Ave (90024-3009)
P.O. Box 14029 (85267-4029)
PHONE.....................310 208-8765
George I Rosenthal, *Pr*
Anil Sharma, *
Mark Rosenthal, *
Damien Hirsch, *
EMP: 330 **EST:** 1977
SALES (est): 21.51MM
SALES (corp-wide): 36.91MM **Privately Held**
Web: www.wlosangeles.com
SIC: 7011 Resort hotel
PA: Raleigh Enterprises, Inc.
  5300 Melrose Ave Fl 4
  Los Angeles CA
  310 899-8900

(P-10350)
W&J BUSINESS VENTURES LLC
Also Called: Holiday Inn
8620 Airport Blvd (90045-4246)
PHONE.....................310 645-7700
Hsiu Lan Lee, *
EMP: 95 **EST:** 1960
SQ FT: 700,000
SALES (est): 1.35MM **Privately Held**
Web: www.holidayinn.com
SIC: 7011 Hotels and motels

(P-10351)
W2005 WYN HOTELS LP
Also Called: Doubletree Hotel
5757 Telegraph Rd (90040-1513)
PHONE.....................323 887-8100
Steve Barick, *COO*
EMP: 71 **EST:** 1991
SALES (est): 4.66MM **Privately Held**
Web: www.hilton.com
SIC: 7011 Hotels and motels

(P-10352)
WALTERS FAMILY PARTNERSHIP
Also Called: Hilton Resort In Palm Spring
400 E Tahquitz Canyon Way (92262-6605)
PHONE.....................760 320-6868
Lance Walters, *Pt*
EMP: 150 **EST:** 1981
SQ FT: 200,000
SALES (est): 4.92MM **Privately Held**
SIC: 7011 5813 5812 Hotels and motels;
  Drinking places; Eating places

(P-10353)
WARWICK CALIFORNIA CORPORATION
Also Called: Warwick Hotel San Francisco
490 Geary St (94102-1223)
PHONE.....................415 992-3809
Richard Chiu, *Pr*
Joseph Tung, *VP*
EMP: 86 **EST:** 1912
SQ FT: 23,386
SALES (est): 1.9MM **Privately Held**
Web: www.warwickhotels.com

SIC: 7011 7299 Hotels; Banquet hall facilities

(P-10354)
WATERFRONT HOTEL LLC
Also Called: Hilton
21100 Pacific Coast Hwy (92648-5307)
PHONE.....................714 845-8000
John Gilbert, *Mgr*
EMP: 298
Web: www.hilton.com
SIC: 7011 5813 5812 7299 Hotels and motels
  ; Drinking places; Eating places; Banquet
  hall facilities
PA: The Waterfront Hotel Llc
  660 Nwport Ctr Dr Ste 105
  Newport Beach CA

(P-10355)
WCO HOTELS INC
Also Called: Disneys Grnd Clifornian Ht Spa
1600 S Disneyland Dr (92802-2317)
PHONE.....................714 635-2300
Dorothy Stratton, *Brnch Mgr*
EMP: 824
SALES (corp-wide): 82.72B **Publicly Held**
SIC: 7011 Resort hotel
HQ: Wco Hotels, Inc.
  1150 W Magic Way
  Anaheim CA
  323 636-3251

(P-10356)
WELCOME GROUP INC
Also Called: Fairfield Inn By Mrrott Scrmnto
1780 Tribute Rd (95815-4402)
PHONE.....................916 920-5300
EMP: 171
SALES (corp-wide): 6.95MM **Privately Held**
Web: fairfield.marriott.com
SIC: 7011 Hotels and motels
PA: Welcome Group, Inc.
  5901 W Century Blvd # 1210
  Los Angeles CA
  860 741-2211

(P-10357)
WELCOME GROUP MANAGEMENT LLC
Also Called: Marriott
300 S Court St (93291-6214)
PHONE.....................310 378-6666
EMP: 97 **EST:** 2011
SQ FT: 3,224
SALES (est): 8.48MM **Privately Held**
Web: www.marriott.com
SIC: 7011 Hotels and motels

(P-10358)
WELK GROUP INC
Also Called: Welk Resort Center
8860 Lawrence Welk Dr (92026-6403)
PHONE.....................760 749-3000
Mario Trejo, *Mgr*
EMP: 400
SALES (corp-wide): 47.43MM **Privately Held**
Web: www.welkresorts.com
SIC: 7011 5812 Motels; Eating places
PA: The Welk Group Inc
  11400 W Olympic Blvd # 1450
  Los Angeles CA
  760 749-3000

(P-10359)
WELK GROUP INC (PA)
Also Called: Welk Music Group
11400 W Olympic Blvd Ste 760
(90064-1649)
PHONE.....................760 749-3000

Jon Fredricks, *Pr*
Marc L Luzzatto, *
EMP: 345 **EST:** 1955
SQ FT: 6,200
SALES (est): 47.43MM
SALES (corp-wide): 47.43MM **Privately Held**
Web: www.welkresorts.com
SIC: 7011 5099 Resort hotel; Compact discs

(P-10360)
WEST HOLLYWOOD EDITION
9040 W Sunset Blvd (90069-1851)
PHONE.....................310 795-7103
EMP: 89 **EST:** 2018
SALES (est): 9.18MM **Privately Held**
Web: www.editionhotels.com
SIC: 7011 Hotels

(P-10361)
WEST HOTEL PARTNERS LP
Also Called: Hilton
300 Almaden Blvd (95110-2703)
PHONE.....................408 947-4450
John Southwell, *Brnch Mgr*
EMP: 231
Web: www.hiltongrandvacations.com
SIC: 7011 7371 6512 5813 Hotels and motels
  ; Custom computer programming services;
  Nonresidential building operators; Drinking
  places
PA: West Hotel Partners, L.P.
  11828 La Grange Ave # 20
  Los Angeles CA

(P-10362)
WEST SAN CRLOS HT PARTNERS LLC
Also Called: Hyatt Place San Jose/Downtown
282 Almaden Blvd (95113-2003)
PHONE.....................408 998-0400
Tina Castaneda, *
EMP: 60 **EST:** 2010
SALES (est): 4.6MM **Privately Held**
Web: sanjose.place.hyatt.com
SIC: 7011 Hotels

(P-10363)
WESTGROUP SAN DIEGO ASSOCIATES
Also Called: Paradise Point Resort
1404 Vacation Rd (92109-7905)
PHONE.....................858 274-4630
David Feeney, *Pt*
EMP: 232 **EST:** 1998
SALES (est): 12.47MM **Privately Held**
Web: www.paradisepoint.com
SIC: 7011 Resort hotel

(P-10364)
WESTIN ANAHEIM RESORT
Also Called: Westin
1030 W Katella Ave (92802-3419)
PHONE.....................657 279-9786
EMP: 62 **EST:** 2018
SALES (est): 5.47MM **Privately Held**
Web: www.westinanaheim.com
SIC: 7011 Hotels

(P-10365)
WESTLAKE PROPERTIES INC
Also Called: Westlake Village Inn
31943 Agoura Rd (91361-4427)
PHONE.....................818 889-0230
John Notter, *Prin*
EMP: 150 **EST:** 1974
SALES (est): 14.22MM **Privately Held**
Web: www.westlakevillageinn.com
SIC: 7011 Resort hotel

(P-10366)
WHATEVER IT TAKES INC
Also Called: Desert Hot Springs Spa Hotel
10805 Palm Dr (92240-2511)
PHONE.....................760 329-6000
Michael Bickford, *Pr*
EMP: 68 **EST:** 1970
SQ FT: 50,000
SALES (est): 563.31K **Privately Held**
Web: www.whateverittakes.org
SIC: 7011 5812 Resort hotel; Eating places

(P-10367)
WHB CORPORATION
Also Called: Millennium Biltmore Hotel
506 S Grand Ave (90071-2602)
PHONE.....................213 624-1011
John Demola, *Brnch Mgr*
EMP: 630
SIC: 7011 5812 5813 Hotels; Eating places;
  Drinking places
HQ: Whb Corporation
  7600 E Orchard Rd 230s
  Greenwood Village CO
  303 779-2000

(P-10368)
WHV RESORT GROUP INC
Also Called: Lawrence Welk Desert Oasis
34567 Cathedral Canyon Dr (92234-6637)
PHONE.....................760 770-9755
Bill Palmer, *Mgr*
EMP: 902
Web: www.welkresorts.com
SIC: 7011 Resort hotel
HQ: Whv Resort Group, Inc.
  300 Rancheros Dr Ste 310
  San Marcos CA
  760 652-4913

(P-10369)
WHV RESORT PROPERTIES INC
300 Rancheros Dr Ste 310 (92069-2969)
PHONE.....................760 481-7739
Jon Fredricks, *Prin*
EMP: 60 **EST:** 2011
SALES (est): 5.11MM **Privately Held**
Web: www.welkresorts.com
SIC: 7011 Resort hotel

(P-10370)
WIN RIVER HOTEL CORPORATION
Also Called: Hilton
5050 Bechelli Ln (96002-3539)
PHONE.....................530 226-5111
Glen Howard, *Pr*
EMP: 527 **EST:** 2004
SALES (est): 3.95MM **Privately Held**
Web: www.hilton.com
SIC: 7011 Resort hotel
PA: Redding Rancheria
  2000 Redding Rancheria Rd
  Redding CA

(P-10371)
WIN TIME LTD (PA)
Also Called: Holiday Inn Express
9335 Kearny Mesa Rd (92126-4502)
PHONE.....................858 695-2300
Herman Lin, *Genl Pt*
Chue-huang Chiu, *Pt*
Yi-ho Huang, *Pt*
EMP: 166 **EST:** 1982
SQ FT: 100,000
SALES (est): 9.44MM
SALES (corp-wide): 9.44MM **Privately Held**
Web: www.holidayinn.com

PRODUCTS & SERVICES SECTION

7021 - Rooming And Boarding Houses (P-10393)

SIC: 7011 Hotels and motels

(P-10372)
WINDSOR CAPITAL GROUP INC
Also Called: Embassy Suites
1117 N H St (93436-8115)
PHONE..................805 735-8311
Toby Simmons, Mgr
EMP: 155
SALES (corp-wide): 149.18MM Privately Held
Web: www.hilton.com
SIC: 7011 Hotels and motels
PA: Windsor Capital Group, Inc.
2800 28th St Ste 385
Santa Monica CA
310 566-1100

(P-10373)
WINDSOR CAPITAL GROUP INC
Also Called: Embassy Suites
900 E Birch St (92821-5812)
PHONE..................714 990-6000
Regina Samy, Mgr
EMP: 116
SQ FT: 48,164
SALES (corp-wide): 149.18MM Privately Held
Web: www.hilton.com
SIC: 7011 Hotels and motels
PA: Windsor Capital Group, Inc.
2800 28th St Ste 385
Santa Monica CA
310 566-1100

(P-10374)
WINDSOR CAPITAL GROUP INC
Also Called: Embassy Suites
29345 Rancho California Rd (92591-5201)
PHONE..................951 676-5656
Tom Demott, Genl Mgr
EMP: 518
SALES (corp-wide): 149.18MM Privately Held
Web: www.hilton.com
SIC: 7011 Hotels and motels
PA: Windsor Capital Group, Inc.
2800 28th St Ste 385
Santa Monica CA
310 566-1100

(P-10375)
WINDSOR CAPITAL GROUP INC
Also Called: Embassy Suites
1325 E Dyer Rd (92705-5615)
PHONE..................714 241-3800
EMP: 183
SALES (corp-wide): 149.18MM Privately Held
Web: www.hilton.com
SIC: 7011 5813 5812 Hotels and motels; Drinking places; Eating places
PA: Windsor Capital Group, Inc.
2800 28th St Ste 385
Santa Monica CA
310 566-1100

(P-10376)
WINDSOR CAPITAL GROUP INC
Also Called: Pacific Suites Hotel
2800 28th St Ste 385 (90405-6211)
PHONE..................310 566-1100
Michael D Cryan, Mgr
EMP: 116
SALES (corp-wide): 149.18MM Privately Held
Web: www.windsorhospitality.com
SIC: 7011 Hotels
PA: Windsor Capital Group, Inc.
2800 28th St Ste 385
Santa Monica CA
310 566-1100

(P-10377)
WJ NEWPORT LLC
Also Called: Marriott
4500 Macarthur Blvd (92660-2010)
PHONE..................949 476-2001
EMP: 190 EST: 2016
SALES (est): 21.45MM Privately Held
Web: www.marriott.com
SIC: 7011 5812 Resort hotel; Family restaurants

(P-10378)
WOODBINE LGACY/PLAYA OWNER LLC
Also Called: Hilton Los Angeles Culver City
6161 W Centinela Ave (90230-6306)
PHONE..................678 292-4962
Lakeisha Walker, *
EMP: 75 EST: 2018
SALES (est): 3.07MM Privately Held
Web: www.hilton.com
SIC: 7011 Hotels and motels

(P-10379)
WORLD TRADE CTR HT ASSOC LTD
Also Called: Long Beach Hilton, The
701 W Ocean Blvd (90831-3100)
PHONE..................562 983-3400
Steve Holloway, Corporate Controller
Greater Los Angeles Trade Cent er, Genl Pt
EMP: 82 EST: 1990
SALES (est): 1.18MM Privately Held
SIC: 7011 7991 5813 5812 Hotels and motels; Physical fitness facilities; Drinking places; Eating places

(P-10380)
WORLDMARK CLUB
3927 E State Hwy 20 (95464-8647)
PHONE..................707 274-0118
Bennet Posman, Brnch Mgr
EMP: 69
SALES (corp-wide): 1.5B Publicly Held
Web: worldmark.wyndhamdestinations.com
SIC: 7011 Resort hotel
HQ: Worldmark, The Club
9805 Willows Rd Ne
Redmond WA

(P-10381)
WORLDMARK CLUB
Also Called: Worldmark At Palm Springs
1177 N Palm Canyon Dr (92262-4401)
PHONE..................760 416-4428
Al Hippe, Mgr
EMP: 61
SALES (corp-wide): 1.5B Publicly Held
Web: worldmark.wyndhamdestinations.com
SIC: 7011 6531 Resort hotel; Time-sharing real estate sales, leasing and rentals
HQ: Worldmark, The Club
9805 Willows Rd Ne
Redmond WA

(P-10382)
WS MMV HOTEL LLC
Also Called: San Diego Marriott Mission Vly
8757 Rio San Diego Dr (92108-1620)
PHONE..................619 692-3800
EMP: 99 EST: 2016
SALES (est): 2.45MM Privately Held
Web: www.marriott.com
SIC: 7011 Hotels

(P-10383)
WW SAN DIEGO HARBOR ISLAND LLC
Also Called: Hilton
1960 Harbor Island Dr (92101-1013)
PHONE..................619 291-6700
Shahid Kayani, Genl Mgr
EMP: 120 EST: 1980
SALES (est): 18.05MM
SALES (corp-wide): 50.61MM Privately Held
Web: www.hilton.com
SIC: 7011 Resort hotel
PA: Ww Lbv Inc.
2000 Hotel Plaza Blvd
Lake Buena Vista FL
407 828-2424

(P-10384)
WYNDHAM RESORT DEV CORP
Also Called: Wyndham Indio
42151 Worldmark Way (92203-9720)
PHONE..................760 342-1040
Stephen Arent, Brnch Mgr
EMP: 64
SALES (corp-wide): 1.5B Publicly Held
Web: www.wyndhamhotels.com
SIC: 7011 6531 Resort hotel; Time-sharing real estate sales, leasing and rentals
HQ: Wyndham Resort Development Corporation
6277 Sea Harbor Dr
Orlando FL

(P-10385)
XANTERRA PARKS & RESORTS INC
Also Called: Furnace Creek Ranch & Inn
Hwy 190 (92328)
P.O. Box 187 (92328-0187)
PHONE..................760 786-2345
Dominie Lenz, Brnch Mgr
EMP: 215
SALES (corp-wide): 373.61MM Privately Held
Web: www.xanterra.com
SIC: 7011 Resort hotel
HQ: Parks Xanterra & Resorts Inc
6312 S Fiddlers Green Cir
Greenwood Village CO
303 600-3400

(P-10386)
XLD GROUP LLC
Also Called: Torrance Marriott Hotel
3635 Fashion Way (90503-4809)
PHONE..................310 316-3636
Pam Ryan, Genl Mgr
EMP: 66
SALES (corp-wide): 9.6MM Privately Held
Web: www.starbucks.com
SIC: 7011 7389 Hotels; Office facilities and secretarial service rental
PA: Xld Group, Llc
500 Sansome St Ste 502
San Francisco CA

(P-10387)
YHB LONG BEACH LLC
Also Called: Holiday Inn
2640 N Lakewood Blvd (90815-1715)
PHONE..................562 597-4401
Traycee Mayer, Prin
EMP: 90 EST: 2003
SALES (est): 6.65MM Privately Held
Web: www.holidayinn.com
SIC: 7011 Hotels and motels

(P-10388)
YHB SAN FRANCISCO LLC
Also Called: Pickwick Hotel The
85 5th St (94103-1812)
PHONE..................415 421-7500
Fred Kleisner, CEO
EMP: 86 EST: 1926
SALES (est): 5.16MM Privately Held
Web: www.pickwickhotel.com
SIC: 7011 Hotels

(P-10389)
ZHG INC
Also Called: Monterey Beach Hotel
2600 Sand Dunes Dr (93940-3838)
PHONE..................831 394-3321
Theodore Richter, Pr
EMP: 67 EST: 1999
SQ FT: 4,996
SALES (est): 971.68K Privately Held
Web: www.ilasnet.org
SIC: 7011 Hotels

7021 Rooming And Boarding Houses

(P-10390)
AISHA ACADEMY
706 S Pershing Ave (95203-3243)
P.O. Box 4638 (90309-4638)
PHONE..................310 908-1962
Kelvin Williams, Ex Dir
Krystal Williams, *
EMP: 99 EST: 2014
SQ FT: 139,800
SALES (est): 16.7K Privately Held
Web: www.aishaacademy23.org
SIC: 7021 Rooming and boarding houses

(P-10391)
AMERICAN CMPUS COMMUNITIES INC
Also Called: Vista Del Campo
62600 Arroyo Dr (92617-4387)
PHONE..................949 854-0900
EMP: 91
SALES (corp-wide): 942.41MM Privately Held
Web: www.americancampus.com
SIC: 7021 Rooming and boarding houses
PA: American Campus Communities Llc
12700 Hill Country Blvd T-200
Austin TX
512 732-1000

(P-10392)
HOPE HOSPICE INC
6377 Clark Ave Ste 100 (94568-3001)
PHONE..................925 829-8770
Jennifer Hansen, Prin
EMP: 396
SALES (corp-wide): 14.78MM Privately Held
Web: www.hopehospice.com
SIC: 7021 5943 Rooming and boarding houses; Stationery stores
PA: Hope Hospice, Inc.
6377 Clark Ave Ste 100
Dublin CA
925 829-8770

(P-10393)
INTERNATIONAL HOUSE
Also Called: Interntnal Hse At U C Berkeley
2299 Piedmont Ave Ste 535 (94720-2392)
PHONE..................510 642-9490
Robert M Berdahl, Ch Bd
Joseph Lurie, *

7021 - Rooming And Boarding Houses (P-10394)

EMP: 162 EST: 1928
SQ FT: 100,000
SALES (est): 2.97MM **Privately Held**
Web: ihouse.berkeley.edu
SIC: **7021** Rooming and boarding houses

(P-10394)
M-AURORA WORLDWIDE (US) LP (PA)
2222 Corinth Ave (90064-1602)
PHONE.....................800 888-0808
▲ EMP: 200 EST: 1960
SALES (est): 74MM
SALES (corp-wide): 74MM **Privately Held**
SIC: **7021** 6531 Furnished room rental; Real estate brokers and agents

(P-10395)
OAKWOOD CORPORATE HOUSING INC
7922 Day Creek Blvd (91739-8584)
PHONE.....................909 922-8272
EMP: 119
SIC: **7021** Furnished room rental
PA: Oakwood Corporate Housing, Inc.
1 World Trade Ctr # 2400
Long Beach CA

(P-10396)
WORLDWIDE CORPORATE HOUSING LP
Also Called: Oakwood Temporary Housing
1 World Trade Ctr Ste 2400 (90831-2400)
PHONE.....................972 392-4747
Howard Ruby, *Pt*
EMP: 493
SALES (corp-wide): 74MM **Privately Held**
Web: www.discoverasr.com
SIC: **7021** Furnished room rental
HQ: Worldwide Corporate Housing, Lp
1 World Trade Ctr # 2400
Long Beach CA
562 473-7371

7032 Sporting And Recreational Camps

(P-10397)
ALISAL PROPERTIES (PA)
Also Called: Alisal Guest Ranch
1054 Alisal Rd (93463-3033)
PHONE.....................805 688-6411
Palmer Jackson, *Pr*
Joan Y Jackson, *VP*
Susanne Powell, *Sec*
EMP: 243 EST: 1946
SQ FT: 10,000
SALES (est): 26.51MM
SALES (corp-wide): 26.51MM **Privately Held**
Web: www.alisalranch.com
SIC: **7032** 7997 Sporting camps; Golf club, membership

(P-10398)
ALLIANCE RDWODS CNFRNCE GRUNDS
Also Called: Sonoma Canopy Tours
6250 Bohemian Hwy (95465-9105)
PHONE.....................707 874-3507
TOLL FREE: 800
Jim Blake, *CEO*
James Blake, *
EMP: 115 EST: 1979
SQ FT: 1,392
SALES (est): 9.43MM **Privately Held**
Web: www.allianceredwoods.com

SIC: **7032** Recreational camps

(P-10399)
BIG LGUE DREAMS CONSULTING LLC
33700 Date Palm Dr (92234-4731)
PHONE.....................760 324-5600
Steve Navarro, *VP*
EMP: 107
SALES (corp-wide): 49.84MM **Privately Held**
Web: www.bigleaguedreams.com
SIC: **7032** Recreational camps
PA: Big League Dreams Consulting, Llc
16333 Fairfield Ranch Rd
Chino Hills CA
909 287-1700

(P-10400)
COUNTY OF LOS ANGELES
Also Called: Parks & Recreation Dept
7326 Jordan Ave (91303-1237)
PHONE.....................818 340-2633
Sharon Haseltine, *Mgr*
EMP: 63
SALES (corp-wide): 31.7B **Privately Held**
Web: www.laparks.org
SIC: **7032** Recreational camps
PA: County Of Los Angeles
500 W Temple St Ste 437
Los Angeles CA
213 974-1101

(P-10401)
FOREST HOME INC
Also Called: Forest Home Ministries
40000 Valley Of The Falls Dr (92339-9674)
PHONE.....................909 389-2300
EMP: 250 EST: 1938
SALES (est): 22.64MM **Privately Held**
Web: www.foresthome.org
SIC: **7032** Cabin camp

(P-10402)
GUIDED DISCOVERIES INC
Also Called: Desert Sun Science Center, The
26800 Saunders Meadows Rd (92549-2546)
P.O. Box 3399 (92549-3399)
PHONE.....................951 659-6062
Allen Tiso, *Dir*
EMP: 64
SALES (corp-wide): 15.43MM **Privately Held**
Web: www.guideddiscoveries.org
SIC: **7032** 8299 Sporting and recreational camps; Educational services
PA: Guided Discoveries, Inc.
27282 Calle Arroyo
San Juan Capistrano CA
800 645-1423

(P-10403)
GUIDED DISCOVERIES INC
Also Called: Fox Landing
1 Toyon Bay Rd (90704)
P.O. Box 1920 (90704-1920)
PHONE.....................310 510-1622
Erica Felins, *Mgr*
EMP: 60
SALES (corp-wide): 15.43MM **Privately Held**
Web: www.cimi.org
SIC: **7032** Sporting and recreational camps
PA: Guided Discoveries, Inc.
27282 Calle Arroyo
San Juan Capistrano CA
800 645-1423

(P-10404)
INTERNAL DRIVE
Also Called: ID Tech Camps
910 E Hamilton Ave Ste 300 (95008-0645)
P.O. Box 111720 (95011-1720)
PHONE.....................408 871-2227
Pete Ingram Cauchi, *Pr*
EMP: 644 EST: 1999
SQ FT: 10,000
SALES (est): 19.61MM **Privately Held**
Web: www.idtech.com
SIC: **7032** Youth camps

(P-10405)
INTERVRSITY CHRSTN FLLWSHP/USA
Also Called: Campus By The Sea
Gallager'S Cove (90704)
P.O. Box 466 (90704-0466)
PHONE.....................310 510-0015
Susan Veon, *Dir*
EMP: 644
SALES (corp-wide): 119.41MM **Privately Held**
Web: www.intervarsity.org
SIC: **7032** 5942 Bible camp; Book stores
PA: Intervarsity Christian Fellowship/Usa
635 Science Dr
Madison WI
608 274-9001

(P-10406)
KIDZTOPROS INC
1584 Fulton Pl (94539-7936)
PHONE.....................408 421-0584
Pooja Shah, *CEO*
Shane Fernandes, *
EMP: 177 EST: 2015
SALES (est): 12.21MM **Privately Held**
Web: www.kidztopros.com
SIC: **7032** 8351 Sporting camps; Child day care services

(P-10407)
LLC WOODWARD WEST
28400 Stallion Springs Dr (93561-5266)
PHONE.....................661 822-7900
EMP: 143 EST: 2002
SALES (est): 9.64MM **Privately Held**
Web: www.woodwardwest.com
SIC: **7032** Sporting and recreational camps

(P-10408)
MOUNT HERMON ASSOCIATION INC (PA)
Also Called: Christian Conference Grounds
37 Conference Dr (95041-3002)
PHONE.....................831 335-4466
Roger E Williams, *Ex Dir*
Roger Williams, *
EMP: 87 EST: 1906
SQ FT: 10,000
SALES (est): 10.23MM
SALES (corp-wide): 10.23MM **Privately Held**
Web: www.mounthermon.org
SIC: **7032** 5942 Bible camp; Books, religious

(P-10409)
OLD CONNECTED CAMPS
3913 Spad Pl (90232-3613)
PHONE.....................323 287-5580
Mizuko Ito, *Prin*
EMP: 61 EST: 2015
SALES (est): 470.67K **Privately Held**
SIC: **7032** Sporting and recreational camps

(P-10410)
PALI CAMP
Also Called: Pali Adventures
30778 Hwy 18 (92382)
PHONE.....................909 867-5743
Andrew Wexler, *CEO*
EMP: 150 EST: 1990
SALES (est): 1.83MM **Privately Held**
Web: www.paliadventures.com
SIC: **7032** Summer camp, except day and sports instructional

(P-10411)
ROMAN CATHOLIC BISHP OF FRESNO
Also Called: Saint Anthony Retreat
43816 Sierra Dr (93271-9708)
P.O. Box 249 (93271-0249)
PHONE.....................559 561-4499
John Griesbach, *Brnch Mgr*
EMP: 80
SIC: **7032** Bible camp
PA: The Roman Catholic Bishop Of Fresno
1550 N Fresno St
Fresno CA

(P-10412)
SNOW VALLEY MTN RESORT LLC
Also Called: Snow Valley Mountain Sports Pk
Hwy 18 (92382)
P.O. Box 2337 (92382-2337)
PHONE.....................909 867-2751
Kevin Somes, *Genl Mgr*
EMP: 80 EST: 1948
SQ FT: 81,000
SALES (est): 7.32MM
SALES (corp-wide): 1.3B **Privately Held**
Web: www.bigbearmountainresort.com
SIC: **7032** 7999 5812 Sporting and recreational camps; Ski rental concession; Eating places
HQ: Alterra Mountain Company
3501 Wazee St Ste 400
Denver CO
303 749-8200

(P-10413)
WILSHIRE BOULEVARD TEMPLE
11495 Pacific Coast Hwy (90265-2006)
PHONE.....................310 457-7861
EMP: 75
SALES (corp-wide): 36.21MM **Privately Held**
Web: www.wbtcamps.org
SIC: **7032** Sporting and recreational camps
PA: Wilshire Boulevard Temple
3663 Wilshire Blvd
Los Angeles CA
213 388-2401

7033 Trailer Parks And Campsites

(P-10414)
BURLINGAME INDUSTRIES INC (PA)
Also Called: Eagle Roofing Products
3546 N Riverside Ave (92377-3878)
PHONE.....................909 355-7000
Robert C Burlingame, *Ch Bd*
Roger D Thompson, *Vice Chairman**
Kevin C Burlingame, *
Seamus P Burlingame, *
William L Robinson, *
▲ EMP: 100 EST: 1969
SQ FT: 100,000
SALES (est): 120.4MM

PRODUCTS & SERVICES SECTION
7213 - Linen Supply (P-10434)

SALES (corp-wide): 120.4MM **Privately Held**
Web: www.eagleroofing.com
SIC: **7033** 0971 3559 3259 Campgrounds; Hunting preserve; Tile making machines; Roofing tile, clay

(P-10415)
BURLINGAME INDUSTRIES INC
Also Called: Resort Campground Intl
277 Lytle Creek Rd (92358-9751)
PHONE.................................909 887-7038
Bob Boyter, *Mgr*
EMP: 108
SALES (corp-wide): 120.4MM **Privately Held**
Web: www.mountainlakesca.com
SIC: **7033** Campgrounds
PA: Burlingame Industries, Incorporated
    3546 N Riverside Ave
    Rialto CA
    909 355-7000

(P-10416)
COLORADO RIVER ADVENTURES INC (PA)
Also Called: Yuma Lakes Resort
2715 Parker Dam Rd (92242-9712)
P.O. Box 1088 (85344-1088)
PHONE.................................760 663-3737
Phil Younis, *Pr*
EMP: 112 EST: 1982
SQ FT: 6,500
SALES (est): 8.37MM
SALES (corp-wide): 8.37MM **Privately Held**
Web: www.coloradoriveradventures.com
SIC: **7033** 8641 7032 Campgrounds; Social club, membership; Recreational camps

(P-10417)
EL CAPITAN CANYON LLC
Also Called: El Capitan Canyon
11560 Calle Real (93117-9789)
PHONE.................................805 685-3887
Roger Himovitz, *Managing Member*
EMP: 62 EST: 1998
SALES (est): 8.46MM
SALES (corp-wide): 2.97B **Publicly Held**
Web: www.elcapitancanyon.com
SIC: **7033** Campgrounds
PA: Sun Communities, Inc.
    27777 Franklin Rd Ste 200
    Southfield MI
    248 208-2500

7041 Membership-basis Organization Hotels

(P-10418)
BERKELEY STUDENT COOP INC
2424 Ridge Rd (94709-1212)
PHONE.................................510 848-1936
Janette E Stokley, *Ex Dir*
Palmer Buchholz, *
Marjorie Greene, *
EMP: 100 EST: 1934
SQ FT: 18,000
SALES (est): 10.59MM **Privately Held**
Web: www.bsc.coop
SIC: **7041** Boarding house, organization

(P-10419)
CLUB QUARTERS MGT CO LLC
424 Clay St (94111-3207)
PHONE.................................415 392-7400
EMP: 74
SALES (corp-wide): 4.85MM **Privately Held**
SIC: **7041** Membership-basis organization hotels
PA: Club Quarters Management Company, L.L.C.
    333 Ludlow St Ste 3
    Stamford CT
    203 905-2100

(P-10420)
HEART CONSCIOUSNESS CHURCH INC (PA)
Also Called: Harbin Hot Springs
18424 Harbin Springs Rd (95461-9687)
P.O. Box 782 (95461-0782)
PHONE.................................707 987-2477
Robert F Hartley, *Pr*
Sajjad Mahmud, *
Julie Adams, *
Suzie Lecavalier, *
EMP: 110 EST: 1975
SQ FT: 4,000
SALES (est): 19.35MM
SALES (corp-wide): 19.35MM **Privately Held**
Web: www.harbin.org
SIC: **7041** Membership-basis organization hotels

(P-10421)
MEDIEVAL TIMES ENTRMT INC (HQ)
7662 Beach Blvd (90620-1838)
PHONE.................................714 523-1100
Kenneth H Kim, *Pr*
EMP: 1754 EST: 2001
SALES (est): 23.25MM **Privately Held**
Web: www.medievaltimes.com
SIC: **7041** 7996 Membership-basis organization hotels; Theme park, amusement
PA: Medieval Times Entertainment, Inc.
    5020 Riverside Dr Bldg 3
    Irving TX

7211 Power Laundries, Family And Commercial

(P-10422)
AMERICAN ETC INC
Also Called: Royal Laundry
1140 San Mateo Ave (94080-6602)
PHONE.................................650 873-5353
Kenn T Edwards, *CEO*
Don Luckenbach, *
▲ EMP: 325 EST: 1964
SQ FT: 70,000
SALES (est): 14.17MM **Privately Held**
SIC: **7211** Power laundries, family and commercial

(P-10423)
ANITSA INC
Also Called: Valet Services
6032 Shull St (90201-6237)
PHONE.................................213 237-0533
Margo Minisiam, *Pr*
Gary Von, *Corporate Accountant**
EMP: 135 EST: 1988
SQ FT: 65,000
SALES (est): 9.32MM **Privately Held**
SIC: **7211** 8742 Power laundries, family and commercial; Industry specialist consultants

(P-10424)
MISSION LINEN SUPPLY
520 E Mineral King Ave (93292-6921)
PHONE.................................559 625-5423
Paul Romer, *Mgr*
EMP: 77
SALES (corp-wide): 99.93MM **Privately Held**
Web: www.missionlinen.com
SIC: **7211** 7213 Power laundries, family and commercial; Uniform supply
PA: Mission Linen Supply
    717 E Yanonali St
    Santa Barbara CA
    805 730-3620

(P-10425)
RADIANT SERVICES CORP (PA)
651 W Knox St (90248-4409)
PHONE.................................310 327-6300
EMP: 235 EST: 1994
SALES (corp-wide): 8.8MM **Privately Held**
Web: www.radiantservices.com
SIC: **7211** 7216 Power laundries, family and commercial; Drycleaning plants, except rugs

7213 Linen Supply

(P-10426)
AMERICAN TEXTILE MAINT CO
Also Called: Republic Uniform
3001 E Anaheim St (90804-3810)
PHONE.................................562 438-7656
Lawrence Pallan, *Mgr*
EMP: 67
SALES (corp-wide): 88.21MM **Privately Held**
Web: www.republicmasterchefs.com
SIC: **7213** Linen supply
PA: American Textile Maintenance Company
    1667 W Washington Blvd
    Los Angeles CA
    323 731-3132

(P-10427)
AMERICAN TEXTILE MAINT CO
Also Called: Republic Master Chefs Textile
3001 E Anaheim St (90804-3810)
PHONE.................................562 438-1126
Lawrence Pallan, *Brnch Mgr*
EMP: 66
SALES (corp-wide): 88.21MM **Privately Held**
Web: www.republicmasterchefs.com
SIC: **7213** Linen supply
PA: American Textile Maintenance Company
    1667 W Washington Blvd
    Los Angeles CA
    323 731-3132

(P-10428)
AMERICAN TEXTILE MAINT CO
Also Called: Master-Chef's Linen Rental
1664 W Washington Blvd (90007-1115)
PHONE.................................323 735-1661
Bob Brill, *Brnch Mgr*
EMP: 155
SALES (corp-wide): 88.21MM **Privately Held**
Web: www.republicmasterchefs.com
SIC: **7213** Towel supply
PA: American Textile Maintenance Company
    1667 W Washington Blvd
    Los Angeles CA
    323 731-3132

(P-10429)
AMERICAN TEXTILE MAINT CO
Also Called: Medico Professional Linen Svc
1705 Hooper Ave (90021-3111)
P.O. Box 516564 (90051-0596)
PHONE.................................213 749-4433
Kenny Immazumi, *Mgr*
EMP: 89
SALES (corp-wide): 88.21MM **Privately Held**
Web: www.republicmasterchefs.com
SIC: **7213** Uniform supply
PA: American Textile Maintenance Company
    1667 W Washington Blvd
    Los Angeles CA
    323 731-3132

(P-10430)
AMERIPRIDE SERVICES INC
Also Called: AMERIPRIDE SERVICES, INC.
5950 Alcoa Ave (90058-3925)
PHONE.................................323 587-3941
TOLL FREE: 800
Ampett Easemero, *Brnch Mgr*
EMP: 103
SALES (corp-wide): 1.45B **Publicly Held**
Web: www.ameripride.com
SIC: **7213** Uniform supply
HQ: Ameripride Services, Llc
    10801 Wayzata Blvd # 100
    Minnetonka MN
    800 750-4628

(P-10431)
AMERIPRIDE SERVICES INC
Also Called: AMERIPRIDE SERVICES, INC.
7620 Wilbur Way (95828-4928)
P.O. Box 232150 (95823-0419)
PHONE.................................916 689-1111
Jay Luck, *Genl Mgr*
EMP: 133
SALES (corp-wide): 1.45B **Publicly Held**
Web: www.ameripride.com
SIC: **7213** 7218 Uniform supply; Industrial launderers
HQ: Ameripride Services, Llc
    10801 Wayzata Blvd # 100
    Minnetonka MN
    800 750-4628

(P-10432)
BRAUN LINEN SERVICE (PA)
Also Called: A-1 Pomona Linen
16514 Garfield Ave (90723-5304)
P.O. Box 348 (90723-0348)
PHONE.................................909 623-2678
Richard A Cornwell, *CEO*
William S Cornwell, *
▲ EMP: 125 EST: 1985
SQ FT: 28,000
SALES (est): 10.61MM
SALES (corp-wide): 10.61MM **Privately Held**
Web: www.braunlinen.com
SIC: **7213** Towel supply

(P-10433)
CINTAS SALES CORPORATION
Also Called: Cintas
2618 Oak St (92707-3720)
PHONE.................................714 957-2852
EMP: 100
SALES (corp-wide): 8.82B **Publicly Held**
SIC: **7213** 5999 5912 5699 Uniform supply; Alarm and safety equipment stores; Drug stores and proprietary stores; Uniforms and work clothing
HQ: Cintas Sales Corporation
    6800 Cintas Blvd
    Cincinnati OH

(P-10434)
FOASBERG LAUNDRY AND CLRS INC (PA)

(PA)=Parent Co (HQ)=Headquarters
✪ = New Business established in last 2 years

7213 - Linen Supply (P-10435)

Also Called: Crdn of Southern La County
640 E Wardlow Rd (90807-4624)
P.O. Box 17965 (90807-7965)
PHONE.....................562 426-7345
James W Foasberg, CEO
Richard Foasberg, *
EMP: 70 EST: 1937
SQ FT: 40,000
SALES (est): 2.77MM
SALES (corp-wide): 2.77MM Privately Held
Web: www.foasberg.com
SIC: 7213 7216 7211 7218 Uniform supply; Drycleaning collecting and distributing agency; Laundry collecting and distributing outlet; Industrial launderers

(P-10435)
GBS LINENS INC (PA)
Also Called: GBS Party Linens
305 N Muller St (92801-5445)
PHONE.....................714 778-6448
Pravin Mody, Pr
Sujata Mody, *
Ameer P Mody, *
Sudha Mody, *
▲ EMP: 100 EST: 1962
SQ FT: 57,000
SALES (est): 10.6MM
SALES (corp-wide): 10.6MM Privately Held
Web: www.gbslinens.com
SIC: 7213 2392 7211 5023 Linen supply; Household furnishings, nec; Power laundries, family and commercial; Homefurnishings

(P-10436)
KAHN RENNAISSANCE LLC
640 Bailey Rd Ste 509 (94565-4306)
PHONE.....................510 260-3161
Julius Chulu Junior, Prin
Julius Chulu Junior, Pr
David Chulu, *
Ophelia Chulu, *
EMP: 112 EST: 2015
SALES (est): 73.21K Privately Held
SIC: 7213 6798 Linen supply, clothing; Real estate investment trusts

(P-10437)
MEDICAL LINEN SERVICE INC
Also Called: Complete Linen Services
290 S Maple Ave (94080-6304)
PHONE.....................650 873-1221
TOLL FREE: 800
Steve Bruni, Pr
Colin Morf, *
Patrice Bruni, *
EMP: 100 EST: 1986
SQ FT: 14,000
SALES (est): 4.58MM Privately Held
Web: www.completelinen.com
SIC: 7213 Linen supply

(P-10438)
MISSION LINEN SUPPLY
Also Called: Mission Linen & Unf Svc 178
1260 N Jefferson St (92807-1612)
PHONE.....................909 364-8752
Jake Kungl, Genl Mgr
EMP: 69
SQ FT: 3,500
SALES (corp-wide): 99.93MM Privately Held
Web: www.missionlinen.com
SIC: 7213 7218 Towel supply; Industrial launderers
PA: Mission Linen Supply
    717 E Yanonali St
    Santa Barbara CA
    805 730-3620

(P-10439)
MISSION LINEN SUPPLY
619 W Avenue I (93534-2585)
PHONE.....................661 948-5052
Dick Grever, Mgr
EMP: 92
SALES (corp-wide): 99.93MM Privately Held
Web: www.missionlinen.com
SIC: 7213 Uniform supply
PA: Mission Linen Supply
    717 E Yanonali St
    Santa Barbara CA
    805 730-3620

(P-10440)
MISSION LINEN SUPPLY
Also Called: Mission Linen
435 W Market St (93901-1498)
PHONE.....................831 423-1630
Jim Stragalinos, Brnch Mgr
EMP: 63
SALES (corp-wide): 99.93MM Privately Held
Web: www.missionlinen.com
SIC: 7213 Uniform supply
PA: Mission Linen Supply
    717 E Yanonali St
    Santa Barbara CA
    805 730-3620

(P-10441)
MISSION LINEN SUPPLY
Also Called: Mission Linen & Uniform Svc
2727 Industry St (92054 4810)
PHONE.....................760 757-9099
Graig Rogers, Prin
EMP: 146
SALES (corp-wide): 99.93MM Privately Held
Web: www.missionlinen.com
SIC: 7213 7218 Uniform supply; Industrial launderers
PA: Mission Linen Supply
    717 E Yanonali St
    Santa Barbara CA
    805 730-3620

(P-10442)
MISSION LINEN SUPPLY
Also Called: Mission Linen & Uniform Svc
7520 Reese Rd (95828-3707)
PHONE.....................916 423-3179
Peppy Secaile, Mgr
EMP: 116
SALES (corp-wide): 99.93MM Privately Held
Web: www.missionlinen.com
SIC: 7213 7218 Uniform supply; Industrial launderers
PA: Mission Linen Supply
    717 E Yanonali St
    Santa Barbara CA
    805 730-3620

(P-10443)
MISSION LINEN SUPPLY
Also Called: Mission Linen & Uniform Svc
315 Kern St (93905-2595)
PHONE.....................831 424-1707
Mark Rogers, Mgr
EMP: 77
SALES (corp-wide): 99.93MM Privately Held
Web: www.missionlinen.com
SIC: 7213 Uniform supply
PA: Mission Linen Supply
    717 E Yanonali St
    Santa Barbara CA
    805 730-3620

(P-10444)
MISSION LINEN SUPPLY
Also Called: Mission Linen Supply & Svcs
1401 Summer St (95501-2246)
PHONE.....................707 443-8681
Jack Anderson, Genl Mgr
EMP: 62
SALES (corp-wide): 99.93MM Privately Held
Web: www.missionlinen.com
SIC: 7213 Uniform supply
PA: Mission Linen Supply
    717 E Yanonali St
    Santa Barbara CA
    805 730-3620

(P-10445)
MISSION LINEN SUPPLY
Also Called: Mission Linen & Uniform Svc
2555 S Orange Ave (93725-1398)
PHONE.....................559 268-0647
Allen Gregory, Mgr
EMP: 77
SALES (corp-wide): 99.93MM Privately Held
Web: www.missionlinen.com
SIC: 7213 Uniform supply
PA: Mission Linen Supply
    717 E Yanonali St
    Santa Barbara CA
    805 730-3620

(P-10446)
MISSION LINEN SUPPLY
Also Called: Mission Linen & Uniform Svc
505 Maulhardt Ave (93030-7925)
PHONE.....................805 485-6794
Matthew Aguelli, Mgr
EMP: 85
SALES (corp-wide): 99.93MM Privately Held
Web: www.missionlinen.com
SIC: 7213 Uniform supply
PA: Mission Linen Supply
    717 E Yanonali St
    Santa Barbara CA
    805 730-3620

(P-10447)
MISSION LINEN SUPPLY
Also Called: Mission Linen & Uniform Svc
5400 Alton Way (91710-7601)
PHONE.....................909 393-6857
Louis Filveria, Mgr
EMP: 123
SALES (corp-wide): 99.93MM Privately Held
Web: www.missionlinen.com
SIC: 7213 Uniform supply
PA: Mission Linen Supply
    717 E Yanonali St
    Santa Barbara CA
    805 730-3620

(P-10448)
MISSION LINEN SUPPLY
Also Called: Mission Linen & Uniform Svc 4
725 E Montecito St (93103-3237)
PHONE.....................805 963-0414
Paul Nicholson, Brnch Mgr
EMP: 62
SALES (corp-wide): 99.93MM Privately Held
Web: www.missionlinen.com
SIC: 7213 Uniform supply
PA: Mission Linen Supply
    717 E Yanonali St
    Santa Barbara CA
    805 730-3620

(P-10449)
MISSION LINEN SUPPLY
Also Called: Mission Linen & Uniform Svc
712 E Montecito St (93103-3295)
PHONE.....................805 962-7687
Curtos Lopez, Mgr
EMP: 139
SALES (corp-wide): 99.93MM Privately Held
Web: www.missionlinen.com
SIC: 7213 Uniform supply
PA: Mission Linen Supply
    717 E Yanonali St
    Santa Barbara CA
    805 730-3620

(P-10450)
MISSION LINEN SUPPLY
Also Called: Mission Linen & Uniform Svc
1340 W 7th St (95928-4907)
PHONE.....................530 342-4110
Nick Katzenstein, Mgr
EMP: 108
SALES (corp-wide): 99.93MM Privately Held
Web: www.missionlinen.com
SIC: 7213 5699 Uniform supply; Uniforms and work clothing
PA: Mission Linen Supply
    717 E Yanonali St
    Santa Barbara CA
    805 730-3620

(P-10451)
MISSION LINEN SUPPLY
Also Called: Mission Linen & Uniform Svc
721 Washington Blvd (90640-6222)
PHONE.....................323 888-8971
George Hernandez, Mgr
EMP: 62
SQ FT: 49,424
SALES (corp-wide): 99.93MM Privately Held
Web: www.missionlinen.com
SIC: 7213 Uniform supply
PA: Mission Linen Supply
    717 E Yanonali St
    Santa Barbara CA
    805 730-3620

(P-10452)
MISSION LINEN SUPPLY
Also Called: Mission Linen & Uniform Svc
602 S Western Ave (93458-5496)
PHONE.....................805 922-3579
Bill Bently, Genl Mgr
EMP: 85
SALES (corp-wide): 99.93MM Privately Held
Web: www.missionlinen.com
SIC: 7213 Uniform supply
PA: Mission Linen Supply
    717 E Yanonali St
    Santa Barbara CA
    805 730-3620

(P-10453)
MORGAN SERVICES INC
Also Called: Morgan Linen Service
905 Yale St (90012-1724)
PHONE.....................213 485-9666
Mark Smith, Brnch Mgr
EMP: 95
SQ FT: 51,339
SALES (corp-wide): 72.96MM Privately Held
Web: www.morganservices.com
SIC: 7213 7218 Linen supply; Industrial launderers
PA: Morgan Services, Inc.

323 N Michigan Ave
Chicago IL
312 346-3181

(P-10454)
PARK CLEANERS INC (PA)
Also Called: Park Uniform Rentals
419 Mcgroarty St (91776-2302)
PHONE..................................626 281-5942
James L Brittain, *Pr*
Ted Doll, *
EMP: 75 **EST:** 1946
SQ FT: 7,000
SALES (est): 3.81MM
SALES (corp-wide): 3.81MM **Privately Held**
SIC: 7213 7216 Uniform supply; Cleaning and dyeing, except rugs

(P-10455)
RFID CORPORATION
701 Willow Pass Rd Ste 10 (94565-1803)
PHONE..................................925 473-9978
John Burskens, *Manager*
EMP: 190
Web: www.angelica.com
SIC: 7213 Uniform supply
HQ: Rfid Corporation
1901 S Meyers Rd Ste 630
Oakbrook Terrace IL
678 823-4100

(P-10456)
SPS HOLDINGS INC
1702 W 134th St (90249-2016)
P.O. Box 1368 (90249-0368)
PHONE..................................310 532-7550
Saul Shrager, *Pr*
Nelson Shrager, *
Stephen Shrager, *
EMP: 80 **EST:** 1957
SQ FT: 40,000
SALES (est): 9.45MM **Privately Held**
Web: www.unifirst.com
SIC: 7213 Uniform supply

(P-10457)
VESTIS CORPORATION
Aramark
115 N First St (91502-1856)
P.O. Box 7891 (91510-7891)
PHONE..................................818 973-3700
EMP: 62
SALES (corp-wide): 1.45B **Publicly Held**
Web: www.vestis.com
SIC: 7213 Uniform supply
PA: Vestis Corporation
500 Colonial Center Pkwy # 1
Roswell GA
470 226-3655

(P-10458)
VESTIS CORPORATION
Also Called: Aramark
3333 N Sabre Dr (93727-7816)
P.O. Box 1289 (93613-1289)
PHONE..................................559 291-6631
Anthony Mollica, *Mgr*
EMP: 200
SQ FT: 130,449
SALES (corp-wide): 1.45B **Publicly Held**
Web: www.vestis.com
SIC: 7213 Uniform supply
PA: Vestis Corporation
500 Colonial Center Pkwy # 1
Roswell GA
470 226-3655

(P-10459)
YEE YUEN LAUNDRY AND CLRS INC
Also Called: Yee Yuen Linen Service
2575 S Normandie Ave (90007-1598)
PHONE..................................323 734-7205
Deborah Morikawa, *Pr*
Cynthia Louie, *
Luis Lee, *
EMP: 80 **EST:** 1928
SQ FT: 20,000
SALES (est): 2.02MM **Privately Held**
Web: www.yeeyuenlinen.com
SIC: 7213 Linen supply

7215 Coin-operated Laundries And Cleaning

(P-10460)
ALL VALLEY WASHER SERVICE INC
15008 Delano St (91411-2016)
PHONE..................................818 787-1100
TOLL FREE: 800
Ron Feinstein, *Pr*
Robert Feinstein, *
Billy Feinstein, *
EMP: 70 **EST:** 1961
SQ FT: 11,000
SALES (est): 12.95MM **Privately Held**
Web: www.allvalleywasher.com
SIC: 7215 6531 7359 5087 Laundry, coin-operated; Real estate agents and managers; Appliance rental; Laundry equipment and supplies

(P-10461)
AUTOMATIC LEASING INC
Also Called: Master Rent
260 Fulton St (93721-3127)
PHONE..................................559 233-2444
Peter Pierre Iii, *Pr*
EMP: 373
SALES (corp-wide): 22.17MM **Privately Held**
SIC: 7215 7514 Coin-operated laundries and cleaning; Passenger car rental
PA: Automatic Leasing, Inc.
445 S Figueroa St
Los Angeles CA
213 746-4117

(P-10462)
CROTHALL SERVICES GROUP
8190 Murray Ave (95020-4630)
PHONE..................................909 991-4887
EMP: 544
SALES (corp-wide): 29.97B **Privately Held**
Web: www.crothall.com
SIC: 7215 Coin-operated laundries and cleaning
HQ: Crothall Services Group
1500 Liberty Ridge Dr # 210
Chesterbrook PA

(P-10463)
CSC SERVICEWORKS INC
14426 Bonelli St (91746-3020)
PHONE..................................626 389-0169
Hal Sazzmann, *Pr*
EMP: 65
SALES (corp-wide): 1.97B **Privately Held**
Web: www.cscsw.com
SIC: 7215 Laundry, coin-operated
HQ: Csc Serviceworks, Inc.
35 Pinelawn Rd Ste 120w
Melville NY
516 349-8555

(P-10464)
PRO-WASH INC
9117 S Main St (90003-3722)
PHONE..................................323 756-6000
Steve Koo, *Pr*
EMP: 70 **EST:** 1991
SQ FT: 20,000
SALES (est): 2.34MM **Privately Held**
Web: www.pro-wash.org
SIC: 7215 Laundry, coin-operated

(P-10465)
WASH MLTFMILY LDRY SYSTEMS LLC (PA)
2200 195th St (90501-1120)
PHONE..................................800 421-6897
TOLL FREE: 800
Jim Gimeson, *CEO*
Arthur J Long, *
Andres De Armas, *CRO**
EMP: 150 **EST:** 2007
SQ FT: 130,000
SALES (est): 84.49MM
SALES (corp-wide): 84.49MM **Privately Held**
Web: www.wash.com
SIC: 7215 Laundry, coin-operated

7216 Drycleaning Plants, Except Rugs

(P-10466)
COIT SERVICES INC (PA)
Also Called: Coit
897 Hinckley Rd (94010-1502)
PHONE..................................650 697-5471
EMP: 174 **EST:** 1935
SALES (est): 16.43MM
SALES (corp-wide): 16.43MM **Privately Held**
Web: www.coit.com
SIC: 7216 7217 6794 Drapery, curtain drycleaning; Carpet and upholstery cleaning; Franchises, selling or licensing

(P-10467)
INTER-CITY CLEANERS LLC
Also Called: Boomerang Ex Dry Clg & Dlvry
438 S Airport Blvd (94080-6908)
PHONE..................................650 875-9200
Vera Gelfand, *
EMP: 68 **EST:** 1962
SQ FT: 9,000
SALES (est): 2.06MM **Privately Held**
Web: www.intercitymetrocleaners.com
SIC: 7216 7219 Cleaning and dyeing, except rugs; Laundry, except power and coin-operated

(P-10468)
PICO CLEANERS INC (PA)
9150 W Pico Blvd (90035-1320)
PHONE..................................310 274-2431
Sharam Jahanbani, *CEO*
Simon Djahanbani, *
EMP: 80 **EST:** 1963
SQ FT: 10,000
SALES (est): 4.47MM
SALES (corp-wide): 4.47MM **Privately Held**
Web: www.picocleaners.com
SIC: 7216 Cleaning and dyeing, except rugs

7217 Carpet And Upholstery Cleaning

(P-10469)
BONDED INC (PA)
Also Called: Bonded Carpet
7590 Carroll Rd (92121-2415)
P.O. Box 23910 (92193-3910)
PHONE..................................858 576-8400
Mitch Adler, *Pr*
Sherri Adler, *
EMP: 80 **EST:** 1975
SALES (est): 10MM
SALES (corp-wide): 10MM **Privately Held**
Web: www.bondedinc.com
SIC: 7217 5023 Carpet and furniture cleaning on location; Homefurnishings

(P-10470)
C & S DRAPERIES INC
Also Called: Coit Restoration Services
4210 Kiernan Ave (95356-9758)
PHONE..................................209 466-5371
Pete Bakker, *CEO*
Helen Bakker, *
EMP: 150 **EST:** 1975
SQ FT: 50,000
SALES (est): 9.19MM **Privately Held**
Web: www.coit.com
SIC: 7217 Carpet and furniture cleaning on location

(P-10471)
CLEANRITE INC
5601 Cedars Rd Ste I (96001-4467)
PHONE..................................530 246-4886
EMP: 64
SALES (corp-wide): 30.81MM **Privately Held**
Web: www.cleanrite-buildrite.com
SIC: 7217 Carpet and upholstery cleaning
PA: Cleanrite, Inc.
2684 Highway 32 Ste 100
Chico CA
530 891-0333

(P-10472)
COIT SERVICES INC
Also Called: Coit
1755 Helena Ave Ste C (95815-1968)
PHONE..................................916 731-7006
Obert L Kearn, *Pr*
EMP: 72
SALES (corp-wide): 16.43MM **Privately Held**
Web: www.coit.com
SIC: 7217 7216 Upholstery cleaning on customer premises; Drapery, curtain drycleaning
PA: Coit Services, Inc.
897 Hinckley Rd
Burlingame CA
650 697-5471

(P-10473)
COLT SERVICES INC
Also Called: Stanley Steemer Carpet Cleaner
9655 Via Excelencia (92126-4555)
PHONE..................................858 271-9910
TOLL FREE: 888
Steven R Thompson, *Pr*
EMP: 100 **EST:** 1979
SQ FT: 33,000
SALES (est): 7.68MM **Privately Held**
Web: www.stanleysteemer.com
SIC: 7217 Carpet and furniture cleaning on location

7217 - Carpet And Upholstery Cleaning (P-10474)

(P-10474)
EXPRESS CONTRACTORS INC
3810 Wacker Dr (91752-1142)
P.O. Box 310279 (92331-0279)
PHONE.................................951 360-6500
Amaer Alhamwi, *CEO*
EMP: 100 **EST:** 1992
SQ FT: 10,000
SALES (est): 10.67MM **Privately Held**
Web: www.expresscontractorsinc.com
SIC: 7217 1752 1721 1743 Carpet and rug cleaning and repairing plant; Carpet laying; Painting and paper hanging; Terrazzo, tile, marble and mosaic work

7218 Industrial Launderers

(P-10475)
1ST CLASS LAUNDRY
Also Called: 1st Class Laundry Services
33485 Western Ave (94587-3201)
PHONE.................................510 487-8297
Jefferey Lee Schlagel, *CEO*
EMP: 165 **EST:** 2006
SQ FT: 24,000
SALES (est): 13.58MM **Privately Held**
Web: www.1stclasslaundry.net
SIC: 7218 Industrial launderers

(P-10476)
AMERICAN TEXTILE MAINT CO
2201 E Carson St (90807-3043)
PHONE.................................562 424-1607
Steve Jones, *Mgr*
EMP: 66
SALES (corp-wide): 88.21MM **Privately Held**
Web: www.republicmasterchefs.com
SIC: 7218 7213 Industrial launderers; Uniform supply
PA: American Textile Maintenance Company
1667 W Washington Blvd
Los Angeles CA
323 731-3132

(P-10477)
AMERIPRIDE SERVICES INC
Also Called: Ameripride Uniform Services
1050 W Whites Bridge Ave (93706-1328)
P.O. Box 11884 (93775-1884)
PHONE.................................559 266-0627
Matt Wencel, *Mgr*
EMP: 139
SALES (corp-wide): 1.45B **Publicly Held**
Web: www.ameripride.com
SIC: 7218 7213 Radiation protective garment supply; Linen supply
HQ: Ameripride Services, Llc
10801 Wayzata Blvd # 100
Minnetonka MN
800 750-4628

(P-10478)
ARAMARK UNF & CAREER AP LLC
Also Called: Aramark
115 N First St Ste 203 (91502-1857)
P.O. Box 101179 (91189-0005)
PHONE.................................818 973-3700
John Zillmer, *CEO*
Brad Drummond, *
Robert N Deitz, *
EMP: 4180 **EST:** 1976
SQ FT: 63,000
SALES (est): 375MM
SALES (corp-wide): 1.45B **Publicly Held**
Web: www.vestis.com
SIC: 7218 Industrial uniform supply
HQ: Aramark Uniform & Career Apparel Group, Inc.
1101 Market St Ste 45
Philadelphia PA
215 238-3000

(P-10479)
MISSION LINEN SUPPLY
Also Called: Mission Linen & Uniform Svc
435 W Market St (93901-1498)
PHONE.................................831 424-1753
Bill Mccreary, *Mgr*
EMP: 92
SALES (corp-wide): 99.93MM **Privately Held**
Web: www.missionlinen.com
SIC: 7218 7213 Industrial uniform supply; Linen supply
PA: Mission Linen Supply
717 E Yanonali St
Santa Barbara CA
805 730-3620

(P-10480)
PRUDENTIAL OVERALL SUPPLY (PA)
Also Called: Prudential Cleanroom Services
1661 Alton Pkwy (92606-4801)
P.O. Box 11210 (92711-1210)
PHONE.................................949 250-4855
Dan Clark, *CEO*
Thomas C Watts, *
Donald C Lahn, *
▲ **EMP:** 95 **EST:** 1947
SQ FT: 20,000
SALES (est): 158.2M
SALES (corp-wide): 158.2MM **Privately Held**
Web: www.prudentialuniforms.com
SIC: 7218 Wiping towel supply

(P-10481)
RFID TEXTILE SERVICES INC
8190 Murray Ave (95020-4605)
PHONE.................................408 840-7504
John Beurskens, *Mgr*
EMP: 71
SIC: 7218 7213 Industrial launderers; Linen supply
HQ: Rfid Textile Services, Inc.
1105 Lakewood Pkwy # 210
Alpharetta GA
678 823-4100

(P-10482)
UNIFIRST CORPORATION
Also Called: Unifirst
700 Etiwanda Ave Ste C (91761-8608)
PHONE.................................909 390-8670
Jeff Martin, *Mgr*
EMP: 130
SALES (corp-wide): 2.23B **Publicly Held**
Web: www.unifirst.com
SIC: 7218 7213 Industrial uniform supply; Uniform supply
PA: Unifirst Corporation
68 Jonspin Rd
Wilmington MA
978 658-8888

(P-10483)
WORKRITE UNIFORM COMPANY INC (DH)
1701 Lombard St Ste 200 (93030-8235)
PHONE.................................805 483-0175
Philip C Williamson, *CEO*
Keith Suddaby, *
Mark Adler, *
EMP: 385 **EST:** 1968
SALES (est): 23.07MM
SALES (corp-wide): 11.61B **Publicly Held**
SIC: 7218 Flame and heat resistant clothing supply
HQ: Vf Outdoor, Llc
1551 Wewatta St
Denver CO
855 500-8639

7219 Laundry And Garment Services, Nec

(P-10484)
CM LAUNDRY LLC
14919 S Figueroa St (90248-1720)
PHONE.................................310 436-6170
Ernesto Munoz, *Managing Member*
EMP: 100 **EST:** 2007
SQ FT: 26,500
SALES (est): 2.27MM **Privately Held**
Web: www.cmlaundry.com
SIC: 7219 Laundry, except power and coin-operated

(P-10485)
DY-DEE SERVICE PASADENA INC
Also Called: California Linen Service
40 E California Blvd (91105-3203)
PHONE.................................626 792-6183
TOLL FREE: 800
Brian O'neil, *Pr*
EMP: 60 **EST:** 1938
SQ FT: 15,000
SALES (est): 2.51MM **Privately Held**
Web: www.dy-dee.com
SIC: 7219 7213 Diaper service; Linen supply, non-clothing

(P-10486)
JOB OPTIONS INCORPORATED
1110 S Washington Ave (92408-2244)
PHONE.................................909 890-4612
EMP: 820
SQ FT: 35,800
SIC: 7219 Fur garment cleaning, repairing, and storage
PA: Job Options, Incorporated
3465 Cmino Del Rio S Ste
San Diego CA

(P-10487)
PENINOU FRENCH LDRY & CLRS INC (PA)
101 S Maple Ave (94080-6303)
PHONE.................................800 392-2532
Todd Edwards, *CEO*
EMP: 90 **EST:** 1903
SQ FT: 25,000
SALES (est): 8.68MM
SALES (corp-wide): 8.68MM **Privately Held**
Web: www.peninou.com
SIC: 7219 7216 French hand laundry; Drycleaning collecting and distributing agency

(P-10488)
STAR LAUNDRY SERVICES INC
Also Called: Star Services
3410 Main St (92113-3803)
PHONE.................................619 572-1009
Abraham Yang, *Pr*
EMP: 80 **EST:** 2006
SALES (est): 2.21MM **Privately Held**
Web: www.starls.com
SIC: 7219 Laundry, except power and coin-operated

7221 Photographic Studios, Portrait

(P-10489)
BAY PHOTO INC
Also Called: BAY PHOTO, INC
2959 Park Ave Ste A (95073-2863)
PHONE.................................831 475-6090
Larry Abitbol, *Prin*
EMP: 137
SALES (corp-wide): 516MM **Privately Held**
Web: www.bayphoto.com
SIC: 7221 Photographer, still or video
HQ: Bay Photo, Inc.
920 Disc Dr
Scotts Valley CA
831 475-6686

(P-10490)
MARVEL STUDIOS LLC (HQ)
500 S Buena Vista St (91521-0001)
PHONE.................................310 727-2700
David Maisel, *Pr*
Tim Connors, *
Kevin Feige, *CCO**
EMP: 77 **EST:** 1998
SALES (est): 30.72MM
SALES (corp-wide): 82.72B **Publicly Held**
Web: www.marvel.com
SIC: 7221 Photographic studios, portrait
PA: The Walt Disney Company
500 S Buena Vista St
Burbank CA
818 560-1000

7231 Beauty Shops

(P-10491)
BEAUTY BARRAGE LLC
4340 Von Karman Ave Ste 240 (92660-2084)
PHONE.................................949 771-3399
Sonia Summers, *CEO*
Brady Heyborne, *
Alissa Spencer, *
EMP: 220 **EST:** 2015
SALES (est): 14.41MM **Privately Held**
Web: www.beautybarrage.com
SIC: 7231 8742 Beauty shops; Marketing consulting services

(P-10492)
BEAUTY BAZAR INC
Also Called: La Belle Days Spas and Salons
36 Stanford Shopping Ctr (94304-1423)
PHONE.................................650 326-8522
Vella Schner, *Owner*
EMP: 90
SALES (corp-wide): 2.3MM **Privately Held**
Web: www.labelledayspas.com
SIC: 7231 5999 Cosmetology and personal hygiene salons; Toiletries, cosmetics, and perfumes
PA: Beauty Bazar, Inc.
36 Stanford Shopping Ctr
Palo Alto CA
415 699-3575

(P-10493)
BEAUTY BOUTIQUE INC
Also Called: Bellus Academy
1073 E Main St (92021-6247)
PHONE.................................619 442-3407
William Lynch, *Pr*
Lynelll Lynch, *VP*
EMP: 183 **EST:** 1960
SQ FT: 6,500

PRODUCTS & SERVICES SECTION

7261 - Funeral Service And Crematories (P-10515)

SALES (est): 5.32MM **Privately Held**
Web: www.bellusacademy.edu
SIC: **7231** Beauty culture school

(P-10494)
BELLAMI HAIR LLC
Also Called: Bellami Hair
21123 Nordhoff St (91311-5816)
PHONE.................................844 235-5264
Julius Salerno, *Managing Member*
EMP: 100 EST: 2013
SALES (est): 24.76MM
SALES (corp-wide): 26.4MM **Privately Held**
Web: www.bellamihair.com
SIC: **7231** Hairdressers
PA: Beauty Industry Group Opco Llc
    1250 N Flyer Way Ste 100
    Salt Lake City UT
    801 206-4781

(P-10495)
BUENA VISTA BUSINESS SVCS LP (PA)
Also Called: Great Clips
1276 Lincoln Ave Ste 107 (95125-3008)
PHONE.................................908 452-9002
Ray Solnik, *Genl Pt*
EMP: 71 EST: 2008
SALES (est): 2.02MM
SALES (corp-wide): 2.02MM **Privately Held**
Web: www.greatclips.com
SIC: **7231** Unisex hair salons

(P-10496)
ESALONCOM LLC
1910 E Maple Ave (90245-3411)
PHONE.................................866 550-2424
EMP: 100 EST: 2008
SALES (est): 43.07MM **Privately Held**
Web: www.esalon.com
SIC: **7231** Hairdressers

(P-10497)
HAIR PERFECT INTERNATIONAL
Also Called: Hair Perfect
135 W California Blvd (91105-3005)
PHONE.................................626 304-9286
Ali Movasaghi, *Mgr*
EMP: 63
SALES (corp-wide): 975.18K **Privately Held**
SIC: **7231** Hairdressers
PA: Hair Perfect International Inc
    1405 San Marino Ave # 117
    San Marino CA

(P-10498)
HEADWAY TECHNOLOGIES INC
39639 Leslie St Apt 135 (94538-2245)
PHONE.................................425 503-2131
Hemlata Bhandari, *Brnch Mgr*
EMP: 735
Web: headway.tdk.com
SIC: **7231** Beauty shops
HQ: Headway Technologies, Inc.
    682 S Hillview Dr
    Milpitas CA
    408 934-5300

(P-10499)
HEAVENLY HANDS
21071 Foothill Blvd (94541-1513)
PHONE.................................510 881-0480
EMP: 69 EST: 2007
SALES (est): 46.89K **Privately Held**
SIC: **7231** Beauty shops

(P-10500)
J M D ENTERPRISES (PA)
Also Called: Supercuts
1434 N Main St (94596-4651)
PHONE.................................925 935-4780
Dianne Chavannes, *Pr*
EMP: 90 EST: 1989
SQ FT: 1,200
SALES (est): 1.44MM **Privately Held**
Web: www.supercuts.com
SIC: **7231** Unisex hair salons

(P-10501)
JLM & MAG ASSOCIATES INC
Also Called: Supercuts
9204 Lakewood Blvd (90240-2909)
PHONE.................................562 869-3343
James Miller, *Pr*
EMP: 71
SALES (corp-wide): 2.36MM **Privately Held**
Web: www.supercuts.com
SIC: **7231** Unisex hair salons
PA: Jlm & Mag Associates, Inc.
    22311 Ventura Blvd # 111
    Woodland Hills CA
    818 346-2667

(P-10502)
MINILUXE INC
Also Called: Miniluxe
11965 San Vicente Blvd (90049-5003)
PHONE.................................424 442-1630
EMP: 93
SALES (corp-wide): 15MM **Privately Held**
Web: www.miniluxe.com
SIC: **7231** Manicurist, pedicurist
PA: Miniluxe, Inc.
    1 Faneuil Hall Sq Fl 7
    Boston MA
    617 684-2731

(P-10503)
MURAD LLC
Also Called: Murad Spa
2141 Rosecrans Ave Ste 1151 (90245-4709)
PHONE.................................310 726-0470
Howard Murad, *Brnch Mgr*
▲ EMP: 104
SALES (corp-wide): 62.39B **Privately Held**
Web: www.murad.com
SIC: **7231** Facial salons
HQ: Murad, Llc
    2121 Park Pl Fl 1
    El Segundo CA

(P-10504)
NAIL ALLIANCE - NORTH AMER INC
4100 Bonita Pl (92835-1066)
PHONE.................................714 449-1568
EMP: 100
Web: www.gelish.com
SIC: **7231** Manicurist, pedicurist
PA: Nail Alliance - North America, Inc.
    1545 Moonstone
    Brea CA

(P-10505)
OPAL CONCEPTS INC (PA)
Also Called: Pro-Cuts
6401 E Nohl Ranch Rd Apt 10 (92807-4890)
PHONE.................................714 779-0545
Cameron Mcconnell, *Pr*
Ted Nelson, *
Charles W Stevens, *CAO**
EMP: 60 EST: 1992
SALES (est): 9.82MM **Privately Held**
Web: www.pro-cuts.com
SIC: **7231** Unisex hair salons

(P-10506)
PETROSIAN ESTHETIC ENTPS LLC
Also Called: Sev Lasers
2919 W Burbank Blvd (91505-2310)
PHONE.................................818 391-8231
Angineh Petrosian, *COO*
EMP: 180 EST: 2013
SALES (est): 2.11MM **Privately Held**
SIC: **7231** 7371 Beauty shops; Computer software development and applications

(P-10507)
SPORT CLIPS INC
Also Called: Sport Clips
4839 Clairemont Dr Ste E (92117-2727)
PHONE.................................858 273-9993
Milan Lidia, *Mgr*
EMP: 590
Web: www.sportclips.com
SIC: **7231** Beauty shops
PA: Sport Clips, Inc.
    110 Sport Clips Way
    Georgetown TX

(P-10508)
STYLESEAT INC
218a Clara St (94107-1004)
PHONE.................................415 638-6658
Melody Mccloskey, *Pr*
EMP: 66 EST: 2015
SALES (est): 4.81MM **Privately Held**
Web: www.styleseat.com
SIC: **7231** Beauty shops

(P-10509)
SUN DEEP INC
1900 Peters Ranch Rd (94526-5633)
PHONE.................................510 206-7405
EMP: 118
SALES (corp-wide): 19.68MM **Privately Held**
Web: www.sundeepinc.com
SIC: **7231** Beauty shops
PA: Sun Deep Inc.
    31285 San Clemente St
    Hayward CA
    510 441-2525

(P-10510)
SUPERBROWARD LLC
Also Called: Supercuts
1222 Broadway (94010-3424)
PHONE.................................650 348-4881
Rachel Hara, *Mgr*
EMP: 154
SALES (corp-wide): 2.16MM **Privately Held**
Web: www.supercuts.com
SIC: **7231** Unisex hair salons
PA: Superbroward Llc
    9000 Main Ave Ste B4
    Bakersfield CA
    661 664-8790

7241 Barber Shops

(P-10511)
GINO MORENA ENTERPRISES LLC
Also Called: Barber Beale
Bldg 2434 (95903)
PHONE.................................530 788-0053
Marilia Asaco, *Brnch Mgr*
EMP: 471
SALES (corp-wide): 66.69MM **Privately Held**
Web: www.ginomorena.com
SIC: **7241** 7231 Barber shops; Beauty shops
PA: Gino Morena Enterprises, Llc
    111 Starlite St
    South San Francisco CA
    800 227-6905

7261 Funeral Service And Crematories

(P-10512)
FOREST LAWN MORTUARY
66272 Pierson Blvd (92240-3658)
PHONE.................................760 329-8737
David Wenzil, *Genl Mgr*
EMP: 482
SALES (corp-wide): 214.25MM **Privately Held**
Web: www.forestlawn.com
SIC: **7261** Funeral home
HQ: Forest Lawn Mortuary
    1712 S Glendale Ave
    Glendale CA

(P-10513)
INGLEWOOD CMTRY MORTUARY INC
3801 W Manchester Blvd (90305-2106)
PHONE.................................310 412-6811
William J Mc Kinley, *Pr*
EMP: 62 EST: 1962
SQ FT: 10,000
SALES (est): 975.67K
SALES (corp-wide): 9.38MM **Privately Held**
Web: www.inglewoodcemeterymortuary.com
SIC: **7261** 6553 Funeral director; Cemeteries, real estate operation
PA: The Lafayette Corporation
    1525 State St Ste 203
    Santa Barbara CA
    805 965-2009

(P-10514)
NORTHSTAR MEMORIAL GROUP LLC
2562 State St (92008-1663)
P.O. Box 616 (90660-0616)
PHONE.................................800 323-1342
EMP: 103
Web: www.nsmg.com
SIC: **7261** Funeral home
PA: Northstar Memorial Group, Llc
    1900 Saint James Pl # 300
    Houston TX

(P-10515)
PIERCE BROTHERS (DH)
Also Called: SCI
10621 Victory Blvd (91606-3918)
PHONE.................................818 763-9121
Oliver Yeo, *Mgr*
R L Waltrip, *
David Anderson, *
Ray Gipson, *
Curtis Briggs, *
EMP: 80 EST: 1902
SQ FT: 10,000
SALES (est): 9.53MM
SALES (corp-wide): 4.11B **Publicly Held**
Web: www.portalofthefoldedwings.net
SIC: **7261** 6553 Crematory; Cemeteries, real estate operation
HQ: Sci Funeral Services Of New York, Inc.
    1929 Allen Pkwy
    Houston TX

7261 - Funeral Service And Crematories (P-10516)

(P-10516)
SINAI TEMPLE
Also Called: Mt Sinai Mem Pk & Mortuary
5950 Forest Lawn Dr (90068-1010)
PHONE...................................323 469-6000
TOLL FREE: 800
Len Lawrence, Mgr
EMP: 125
SQ FT: 22,633
SALES (corp-wide): 53.77MM Privately Held
Web: www.mountsinaiparks.org
SIC: **7261** 6553 Funeral home; Cemeteries, real estate operation
PA: Temple Sinai
    10400 Wilshire Blvd
    Los Angeles CA
    310 474-1518

(P-10517)
TEMPLE ISRAEL OF HOLLYWOOD (PA)
Also Called: Jewish Synagogue
7300 Hollywood Blvd (90046-2904)
PHONE...................................323 876-8330
Steve Sloan, Pr
Jane Zuckerman, *
Renee Mochkatel, *
David Cremin, *
Nancy Ortenberg, *
EMP: 83 EST: 1926
SQ FT: 15,000
SALES (est): 24.87MM
SALES (corp-wide): 24.87MM Privately Held
Web: www.tioh.org
SIC: **7261** 8299 8661 Funeral service and crematories; Religious school; Synagogue

7291 Tax Return Preparation Services

(P-10518)
AHG INC
340 S Lemon Ave 6633 (91789-2706)
PHONE...................................703 596-0111
Sanzar Kakar, Ofcr
EMP: 300 EST: 2018
SALES (est): 761.83K Privately Held
SIC: **7291** 8721 Tax return preparation services; Accounting, auditing, and bookkeeping

(P-10519)
ANDERSEN TAX LLC
400 S Hope St Ste 2000 (90071)
PHONE...................................213 593-2300
EMP: 135
SALES (corp-wide): 112.31MM Privately Held
Web: www.andersen.com
SIC: **7291** Tax return preparation services
PA: Andersen Tax Llc
    333 Bush St Ste 1700
    San Francisco CA
    415 764-2700

(P-10520)
CERIDIAN TAX SERVICE INC
Also Called: Ceridian
17390 Brookhurst St (92708-3720)
P.O. Box 20805 (92728-0805)
PHONE...................................714 963-1311
Webster Hill, Genl Mgr
EMP: 300 EST: 1998
SQ FT: 130,000
SALES (est): 24.68MM
SALES (corp-wide): 1.25B Publicly Held
Web: www.ceridian.com

SIC: **7291** Tax return preparation services
PA: Ceridian Hcm Holding Inc.
    3311 E Old Shakopee Rd
    Minneapolis MN
    952 853-8100

(P-10521)
EXACTAX INC (PA)
1100 E Orangethorpe Ave Ste 100 (92801-5168)
PHONE...................................714 284-4802
Kevin Love, Pr
Michael Leonetti, *
Bob Lynch, *
Richard Johnson, *
Franklin Pang, Stockholder*
EMP: 74 EST: 1989
SALES (est): 1.01MM Privately Held
Web: www.perfectdomain.com
SIC: **7291** 7371 Tax return preparation services; Computer software development

(P-10522)
H G GROUP INC
4225 Saviers Rd (93033-7158)
PHONE...................................805 486-6463
EMP: 382
SALES (corp-wide): 185.25MM Privately Held
Web: www.hyatt.com
SIC: **7291** Tax return preparation services
HQ: H G Group Inc
    71 S Wacker Dr Ste 1000
    Chicago IL

(P-10523)
INTERNAL REVENUE SERVICE
2400 E Katella Ave Ste 800 (92806-5901)
PHONE...................................714 512-2818
EMP: 73
Web: www.irs.gov
SIC: **7291** Tax return preparation services
HQ: Internal Revenue Service
    1111 Constitution Ave, Nw
    Washington DC
    202 803-9000

(P-10524)
OPTIMA TAX RELIEF LLC
Also Called: Optima Protection Plan
3100 S Harbor Blvd Ste 250 (92704-6823)
PHONE...................................714 361-4636
EMP: 180 EST: 2010
SQ FT: 30,000
SALES (est): 26.2MM Privately Held
Web: www.optimataxrelief.com
SIC: **7291** Tax return preparation services

(P-10525)
TAXES DECODED INC
4060 Glencoe Ave Apt 322 (90292-5886)
P.O. Box 504 (91365-0504)
PHONE...................................626 780-7076
Tina Su, Brnch Mgr
EMP: 61
Web: www.taxesdecoded.net
SIC: **7291** Tax return preparation services
PA: Taxes Decoded, Inc.
    148 E Fthill Blvd Ste 101
    Arcadia CA
    626 780-7076

(P-10526)
TAXRESOURCES INC (PA)
Also Called: Taxaudit.com
600 Coolidge Dr Ste 300 (95630-4211)
PHONE...................................877 369-7827
Mark D Olander, CEO
Nancy K Farwell, *
Jane T Smith, *

Dave E Du Val, *
EMP: 120 EST: 1988
SQ FT: 3,000
SALES (est): 13.95MM Privately Held
Web: www.taxaudit.com
SIC: **7291** Tax return preparation services

7299 Miscellaneous Personal Services

(P-10527)
3-DOWNTOWN BARS INC
Also Called: Panamas Bar & Cafe
191 E 2nd St (95928-5467)
PHONE...................................530 898-9898
Robert Mowry, Prin
Joshua Coker, *
EMP: 65 EST: 2006
SALES (est): 817.09K Privately Held
Web: www.chicoeventcenter.com
SIC: **7299** Banquet hall facilities

(P-10528)
AMERICAN FRUITS & FLAVORS LLC ◆
510 Park Ave (91340-2527)
PHONE...................................818 899-9574
William Haddad, Pr
EMP: 300 EST: 2023
SALES (est): 3.07MM
SALES (corp-wide): 6.31B Publicly Held
SIC: **7299** House sitting
PA: Monster Beverage Corporation
    1 Monster Way
    Corona CA
    951 739-6200

(P-10529)
AMERICOR FUNDING INC
18200 Von Karman Ave Ste 600 (92612-1023)
PHONE...................................866 333-8686
Banir Ganatra, CEO
EMP: 170 EST: 2008
SALES (est): 11MM Privately Held
Web: www.americor.com
SIC: **7299** Debt counseling or adjustment service, individuals

(P-10530)
BEYOND FINANCE LLC
Also Called: Accredited Debt Relief
9525 Towne Centre Dr Ste 100 (92121-1995)
PHONE...................................800 282-7186
Tim Ho, CEO
EMP: 558
SALES (corp-wide): 36.73MM Privately Held
Web: www.beyondfinance.com
SIC: **7299** Debt counseling or adjustment service, individuals
PA: Beyond Finance, Llc
    7322 Southwest Fwy # 1200
    Houston TX
    800 282-7186

(P-10531)
BUCKINGHAM PROPERTY MANAGEMENT
Also Called: Coventry Cove Apartments
12609 Moffatt Ln (93730-9704)
PHONE...................................559 322-1105
Cher Cha, Prin
EMP: 82
SALES (corp-wide): 21.33MM Privately Held
Web: www.buckinghampm.com

SIC: **7299** Apartment locating service
PA: Buckingham Property Management Inc
    601 Pollasky Ave Ste 201
    Clovis CA
    559 452-8250

(P-10532)
CALIFORNIA SUN INC
8265 Sierra College Blvd (95661-9403)
PHONE...................................916 789-1034
Michael Blore, Brnch Mgr
EMP: 80
Web: www.californiasun.com
SIC: **7299** Tanning salon
PA: California Sun, Inc.
    2630 Sierra Meadows Dr
    Rocklin CA

(P-10533)
CATTLEMENS
Also Called: Cattlemens Restaurant
2882 Kitty Hawk Rd (94551-7666)
PHONE...................................925 447-1224
Jackie Gibson, Genl Mgr
EMP: 84
SALES (corp-wide): 49.29MM Privately Held
Web: www.cattlemens.com
SIC: **7299** 5812 Banquet hall facilities; American restaurant
PA: Cattlemens
    250 Dutton Ave
    Santa Rosa CA
    707 528-1040

(P-10534)
CHOURA VENUE SERVICES
Also Called: Choura Vnue Svcs At Carson Ctr
4101 E Willow St (90815-1740)
PHONE...................................562 426-0555
James Choura, CEO
EMP: 99 EST: 2012
SALES (est): 3.63MM Privately Held
Web: www.thegrandlb.com
SIC: **7299** 5812 Information services, consumer; Caterers

(P-10535)
CIRI - STROUP INC
Also Called: Mile High Valet
25135 Park Lantern (92629-2878)
PHONE...................................949 488-3104
Rob Stroup, Owner
EMP: 103
SIC: **7299** 7521 Valet parking; Automobile parking
PA: Ciri - Stroup, Inc.
    1 Park Pl Ste 200
    Annapolis MD

(P-10536)
CLOUDSTAFF LLC
26895 Aliso Creek Rd # B-209 (92656-5301)
PHONE...................................888 551-5339
EMP: 471
SALES (corp-wide): 12.5MM Privately Held
Web: www.cloudstaffllc.com
SIC: **7299** Personal appearance services
PA: Cloudstaff Llc
    1165 E San Antonio Dr
    Long Beach CA
    888 551-5339

(P-10537)
CLUTTER INC (PA)
3526 Hayden Ave (90232-2413)
PHONE...................................800 805-4023
Ari Mir, CEO

PRODUCTS & SERVICES SECTION
7299 - Miscellaneous Personal Services (P-10558)

EMP: 121 EST: 2013
SALES (est): 44.73MM
SALES (corp-wide): 44.73MM **Privately Held**
Web: www.clutter.com
SIC: 7299 4212 Personal item care and storage services; Moving services

(P-10538)
CONDUIT LNGAGE SPECIALISTS INC
22720 Ventura Blvd Ste 100 (91364-1305)
PHONE.................................859 299-3178
Art Mathews, *Brnch Mgr*
EMP: 93
SALES (corp-wide): 4.11MM **Privately Held**
Web: www.conduitlanguage.com
SIC: 7299 Personal appearance services
PA: Conduit Language Specialists, Inc.
110 Augusta Way
Paris KY
818 389-4333

(P-10539)
CONSUMER CR CNSLING SVC SAN FR (PA)
Also Called: Balance
1655 Grant St Ste 1300 (94520-2789)
PHONE.................................888 456-2227
Rico Delgadillo, *CEO*
EMP: 60 EST: 1969
SQ FT: 14,000
SALES (est): 8.83MM
SALES (corp-wide): 8.83MM **Privately Held**
Web: www.balancepro.org
SIC: 7299 Debt counseling or adjustment service, individuals

(P-10540)
DEBTMERICA LLC
Also Called: Debtmerica Relief
3100 S Harbor Blvd Ste 250 (92704-6823)
PHONE.................................714 389-4200
Harry Langenberg, *
EMP: 65 EST: 2006
SQ FT: 15,000
SALES (est): 5.15MM **Privately Held**
Web: www.debtmerica.com
SIC: 7299 Debt counseling or adjustment service, individuals

(P-10541)
DEL MAR FAIRGROUNDS
2260 Jimmy Durante Blvd (92014-2216)
PHONE.................................858 792-4288
EMP: 95 EST: 2007
SALES (est): 8.26MM **Privately Held**
Web: www.delmarfairgrounds.com
SIC: 7299 Banquet hall facilities

(P-10542)
DESTINATION RESIDENCES LLC
Also Called: Tesancia La Jlla Ht Spa Resort
9700 N Torrey Pines Rd (92037-1102)
PHONE.................................858 550-1000
Charlie Peck, *Pr*
EMP: 487
SALES (corp-wide): 367.25MM **Privately Held**
Web: www.destinationhotels.com
SIC: 7299 7389 7991 7011 Banquet hall facilities; Convention and show services; Spas; Hotels
HQ: Destination Residences Llc
10333 E Dry Creek Rd
Englewood CO
303 799-3830

(P-10543)
EHARMONY INC (HQ)
Also Called: Eharmony.com
10900 Wilshire Blvd Fl 17 (90024-6522)
P.O. Box 241810 (90024-9610)
PHONE.................................424 258-1199
EMP: 119 EST: 2000
SQ FT: 6,000
SALES (est): 38.97MM
SALES (corp-wide): 4.32B **Privately Held**
Web: www.eharmony.com
SIC: 7299 Dating service
PA: Prosiebensat.1 Media Se
Medienallee 7
Unterfohring BY
89950710

(P-10544)
EMPYR INCORPORATED
Also Called: Figg
8910 University Center Ln Ste 400 (92122-1029)
PHONE.................................888 664-5669
Bryon Cook, *Pr*
Ryan Mcdonald, *CFO*
EMP: 65 EST: 2011
SALES (est): 15.86MM
SALES (corp-wide): 210.35MM **Privately Held**
Web: www.gofigg.com
SIC: 7299 Tax refund discounting
PA: Augeo Affinity Marketing, Inc.
2561 Territorial Rd
Saint Paul MN
651 917-9143

(P-10545)
EVEREST WTRPRFING RSTRTION INC
1270 Missouri St (94107-3310)
PHONE.................................415 282-9800
Keith Goldstein, *Pr*
Mark Murray, *
EMP: 64 EST: 1999
SQ FT: 5,000
SALES (est): 4.62MM **Privately Held**
Web: www.everestsf.com
SIC: 7299 Home improvement and renovation contractor agency

(P-10546)
FREEDOM FINANCIAL NETWORK LLC (PA)
Also Called: Freedom Debt Relief
1875 S Grant St Ste 400 (94402-2676)
PHONE.................................650 393-6619
Andrew Housser, *
Ralph L Leung, *
EMP: 117 EST: 2002
SQ FT: 20,000
SALES (est): 85.29MM
SALES (corp-wide): 85.29MM **Privately Held**
Web: www.freedomfinancialnetwork.com
SIC: 7299 Debt counseling or adjustment service, individuals

(P-10547)
GALKOS CONSTRUCTION INC (PA)
Also Called: GCI Energy Products
15262 Pipeline Ln (92649-1136)
PHONE.................................714 373-8545
Frank E Gialketsis, *Pr*
Lonnie Gailketsis, *
EMP: 60 EST: 1986
SALES (est): 18.05MM
SALES (corp-wide): 18.05MM **Privately Held**
Web: www.galkos.com
SIC: 7299 Home improvement and renovation contractor agency

(P-10548)
GLEN IVY HOT SPRINGS (PA)
25000 Glen Ivy Rd (92883-5103)
PHONE.................................951 277-3529
EMP: 60 EST: 1890
SALES (est): 12.11MM
SALES (corp-wide): 12.11MM **Privately Held**
Web: www.glenivy.com
SIC: 7299 7991 5812 5699 Massage parlor; Spas; Cafe; Bathing suits

(P-10549)
GLEN IVY HOT SPRINGS
1001 Brea Mall (92821-5721)
PHONE.................................714 990-2090
Jen Breakey, *Mgr*
EMP: 190
SALES (corp-wide): 12.11MM **Privately Held**
Web: www.glenivy.com
SIC: 7299 7991 5812 5699 Massage parlor; Spas; Cafe; Bathing suits
PA: Glen Ivy Hot Springs
25000 Glen Ivy Rd
Temescal Valley CA
951 277-3529

(P-10550)
HIGH MOON STUDIOS LLC
2051 Palomar Airport Rd Ste 250 (92011-1461)
PHONE.................................760 448-3000
Peter Della Penna, *Prin*
EMP: 114 EST: 2006
SALES (est): 8.64MM **Privately Held**
Web: www.highmoonstudios.com
SIC: 7299 Apartment locating service

(P-10551)
HOMEBOUND TECHNOLOGIES INC
1 Letterman Dr Ste 3500 (94129-1517)
PHONE.................................415 854-3296
Johnny Chen, *Prin*
EMP: 288 EST: 2018
SALES (est): 9.62MM **Privately Held**
Web: www.homebound.com
SIC: 7299 Miscellaneous personal service

(P-10552)
INFORMTION RFRRAL FDRTION OF L
Also Called: 211 La County
526 W Las Tunas Dr (91776-1111)
P.O. Box 726 (91778-0726)
PHONE.................................626 350-1841
Maribel Marin, *Ex Dir*
Amy Latzer, *
EMP: 100 EST: 1980
SQ FT: 23,000
SALES (est): 15.52MM **Privately Held**
Web: www.211la.org
SIC: 7299 Information services, consumer

(P-10553)
INSTANT CHECKMATE LLC
Also Called: Instant Checkmate
375 Camino De La Reina Ste 400 (92108-3083)
PHONE.................................800 222-8985
Steven Gray, *CEO*
EMP: 214
SALES (est): 740.91K
SALES (corp-wide): 30.81MM **Privately Held**
Web: www.peopleconnect.us
SIC: 7299 Information services, consumer
HQ: Pubrec Llc
375 Camino De La Reina # 400
San Diego CA

(P-10554)
INTELICARE DIRECT LLC
8885 Rio San Diego Dr (92108-1626)
PHONE.................................858 299-3636
Steven Gray, *CEO*
EMP: 94 EST: 2014
SALES (est): 9.93MM
SALES (corp-wide): 30.81MM **Privately Held**
Web: www.desertcallconnection.com
SIC: 7299 Information services, consumer
HQ: Pubrec Llc
375 Camino De La Reina # 400
San Diego CA

(P-10555)
INTELIUS LLC
Also Called: Intelius
375 Camino De La Reina (92108-3083)
PHONE.................................888 245-1655
Steven Gray, *CEO*
EMP: 184
SALES (est): 288.08K
SALES (corp-wide): 30.81MM **Privately Held**
SIC: 7299 Information services, consumer
HQ: Pubrec Llc
375 Camino De La Reina # 400
San Diego CA

(P-10556)
JASPER HALL LLC
Also Called: August Hall & Fifth Arrow
420 Mason St (94102-1706)
PHONE.................................415 872-5745
Nathan Valentine, *Mgr*
Scott Murphy, *
Chad Donnelly, *
EMP: 75 EST: 2018
SALES (est): 1.28MM **Privately Held**
SIC: 7299 Banquet hall facilities

(P-10557)
JC WEIGHT LOSS CENTRES INC (PA)
Also Called: Jenny Craig
5770 Fleet St (92008-4700)
PHONE.................................760 696-4000
Kent Kreh, *Ch Bd*
Jenny Craig, *
Dana Fiser, *
Patti Larchet, *
Jenice Lara, *
EMP: 130 EST: 1985
SQ FT: 50,000
SALES (est): 25.64MM **Privately Held**
Web: www.jennycraig.com
SIC: 7299 7991 6794 Diet center, without medical staff; Weight reducing clubs; Franchises, selling or licensing

(P-10558)
JN PROJECTS INC
Also Called: Hellosign
333 Brannan St (94107-1810)
PHONE.................................415 766-0273
Joseph H Walla, *CEO*
EMP: 100 EST: 2010
SALES (est): 12.42MM **Publicly Held**
Web: www.hellofax.com
SIC: 7299 Personal document and information services
PA: Dropbox, Inc.
1800 Owens St Ste 200

7299 - Miscellaneous Personal Services (P-10559)

San Francisco CA

(P-10559)
LIBERTY DEBT RELIEF LLC
Also Called: Liberty ADM Support Svcs
333 City Blvd W Fl 17 (92868-5905)
PHONE..............................800 756-8447
Omar Chouche, *CEO*
Aaron Bauer, *Managing Member**
EMP: 65 EST: 2017
SALES (est): 2.24MM **Privately Held**
Web: www.libertydebtrelief.com
SIC: 7299 Debt counseling or adjustment service, individuals

(P-10560)
MASSAGE ENVY
39016 Paseo Padre Pkwy (94538-1610)
PHONE..............................510 456-3689
Judith Nelson, *Owner*
EMP: 62 EST: 2008
SALES (est): 199.69K **Privately Held**
Web: www.massageenvy.com
SIC: 7299 Massage parlor

(P-10561)
MASTROIANNI FAMILY ENTPS LTD
Also Called: Jay's Catering
10581 Garden Grove Blvd (92843-1128)
PHONE..............................310 952-1700
Jay Mastroiannis, *Pr*
EMP: 360
SALES (corp-wide): 23.04MM **Privately Held**
Web: www.jayscatering.com
SIC: 7299 Banquet hall facilities
PA: Mastroianni Family Enterprises Ltd.
10581 Garden Grove Blvd
Garden Grove CA
714 636-6045

(P-10562)
MICHAAEL S HENSLEY
Also Called: Hensly Event Resources
180 W Hill Pl (94005-1216)
PHONE..............................650 692-7007
Michael Hensley, *Pr*
EMP: 120 EST: 1992
SALES (est): 4.2MM **Privately Held**
Web: www.hensleyeventresources.com
SIC: 7299 5947 Party planning service; Party favors

(P-10563)
MYHEALTHTEAMS INC
1 Post St Ste 2250 (94104-5228)
PHONE..............................415 860-7878
Eric Peacock, *CEO*
EMP: 86 EST: 2012
SALES (est): 5.79MM **Privately Held**
Web: www.myhealthteam.com
SIC: 7299 Information services, consumer

(P-10564)
OCBANG INC
2550 N 1st St Ste 100 (95131-1019)
PHONE..............................650 625-7908
EMP: 91 EST: 2018
SALES (est): 293.97K **Privately Held**
Web: www.ocbang.com
SIC: 7299 Miscellaneous personal service

(P-10565)
ONE CALL PLUMBER GOLETA
140 Nectarine Ave Apt 4 (93117-3359)
PHONE..............................805 284-0441
One Call Plumber Goleta, *Owner*
EMP: 99 EST: 2001
SALES (est): 236.06K **Privately Held**
Web: www.plumbersgoleta.com
SIC: 7299 Handyman service

(P-10566)
ONE EVENTS INC
8581 Santa Monica Blvd (90069-4120)
PHONE..............................310 498-5471
Nickolas William Potocic, *CEO*
EMP: 90 EST: 2012
SALES (est): 734.94K **Privately Held**
Web: www.oneevents.biz
SIC: 7299 Banquet hall facilities

(P-10567)
PACIFIC EVENT PRODUCTIONS INC (PA)
Also Called: Pep Creations
6989 Corte Santa Fe (92121-3260)
PHONE..............................858 458-9908
Lawrence J Toll, *CEO*
George Duff, *
Joanne Mera, *
EMP: 247 EST: 1990
SQ FT: 30,000
SALES (est): 12.57MM **Privately Held**
Web: www.pacificevents.com
SIC: 7299 Party planning service

(P-10568)
PALO ALTO HLLS GOLF CNTRY CLB
3000 Alexis Dr (94304-1303)
PHONE..............................650 948-1800
Padmanabhan Srinagesh, *CEO*
EMP: 75 EST: 1958
SQ FT: 25,000
SALES (est): 10.36MM **Privately Held**
Web: www.pahgcc.com
SIC: 7299 7997 Banquet hall facilities; Golf club, membership

(P-10569)
PENINSULA PARKING INC
541 Taylor Way Ste 12 (94070-6254)
PHONE..............................650 596-5728
Rae Ann Reichmuth, *CEO*
EMP: 60 EST: 2006
SALES (est): 3.02MM **Privately Held**
Web: www.peninsulaparking.com
SIC: 7299 7521 Valet parking; Parking garage

(P-10570)
PPS PARKING INC
1800 E Garry Ave Ste 107 (92705-5803)
P.O. Box 16635 (92623-6635)
PHONE..............................949 223-8707
Steve Paliska, *Pr*
EMP: 506 EST: 1982
SQ FT: 5,000
SALES (est): 14.12MM **Privately Held**
Web: www.ppsparkinginc.com
SIC: 7299 8748 Valet parking; Business consulting, nec

(P-10571)
PREMIER RESIDENTIAL SVCS LLC
43100 Cook St Ste 101 (92211-3124)
P.O. Box 13250 (92255-3250)
PHONE..............................760 773-4081
Daniel Loera, *Managing Member*
EMP: 60 EST: 1999
SALES (est): 2.31MM **Privately Held**
Web: www.premier-residential-services.com
SIC: 7299 Miscellaneous personal service

(P-10572)
REUNIFY LLC
12121 Wilshire Blvd Ste 214 (90025-1176)
PHONE..............................310 893-1736
EMP: 68 EST: 2011
SALES (est): 436.07K **Privately Held**
Web: www.reunify.com
SIC: 7299 Information services, consumer
PA: Njk Holding Corporation
411 S County Rd Ste 200
Palm Beach FL

(P-10573)
ROUSE SERVICES LLC
8383 Wilshire Blvd Ste 900 (90211-2444)
PHONE..............................310 360-9200
Darren Watt, *Mgr*
EMP: 77 EST: 2013
SALES (est): 5.53MM **Privately Held**
Web: www.rouseservices.com
SIC: 7299 Miscellaneous personal service

(P-10574)
SERVIZ INC
15303 Ventura Blvd Ste 1600 (91403-3133)
PHONE..............................818 381-4826
Zorik Gordon, *CEO*
Michael Klien, *
EMP: 70 EST: 2014
SQ FT: 8,000
SALES (est): 8.47MM
SALES (corp-wide): 2.95B **Publicly Held**
Web: pro.frontdoor.com
SIC: 7299 Home improvement and renovation contractor agency
PA: Gannett Co., Inc.
7950 Jones Branch Dr Fl 8
Mc Lean VA
703 854-6000

(P-10575)
SIGNATURE PARKING LLC
924 Chapala St Ste B (93101-8220)
PHONE..............................805 969-7275
EMP: 100 EST: 2000
SQ FT: 900
SALES (est): 2.36MM **Privately Held**
Web: www.signatureparking.com
SIC: 7299 Valet parking

(P-10576)
SKYWOOD EVENTS CORPORATION
Also Called: Mountain Terrace, The
17285 Skyline Blvd (94062-3780)
PHONE..............................650 851-1606
Terri Shearer, *Pr*
Katia Chanin, *CFO*
John B Squire, *Sec*
EMP: 65 EST: 2009
SALES (est): 578.23K **Privately Held**
SIC: 7299 5812 Facility rental and party planning services; Eating places

(P-10577)
SOIREE VALET PARKING SERVICE
1470 Howard St (94103-2523)
PHONE..............................415 284-9700
Jamie Dyos, *Pr*
EMP: 76 EST: 1989
SQ FT: 3,000
SALES (est): 2.2MM **Privately Held**
Web: www.soireevalet.com
SIC: 7299 7521 Valet parking; Automobile parking

(P-10578)
TINY PICTURES INC
454 Natoma St (94103-2909)
PHONE..............................415 513-5998
John Poisson, *CEO*
Sylvio Drouin, *
EMP: 98 EST: 2005
SALES (est): 843.83K
SALES (corp-wide): 2.37B **Privately Held**
Web: www.shutterfly.com
SIC: 7299 Personal document and information services
HQ: Shutterfly, Llc
2800 Bridge Pkwy
Redwood City CA
650 610-5200

(P-10579)
U P C INC
Also Called: Watercourse Way
165 Channing Ave (94301-2409)
PHONE..............................650 462-2010
Susan Nightingale, *Pr*
EMP: 102 EST: 1989
SALES (est): 7MM **Privately Held**
SIC: 7299 Massage parlor and steam bath services

(P-10580)
UCERTIFY LLC
1684 Decoto Rd (94587-3544)
PHONE..............................800 796-3062
David Jackson, *Prin*
EMP: 84 EST: 2010
SALES (est): 1.14MM **Privately Held**
Web: www.ucertify.com
SIC: 7299 Personal shopping service

(P-10581)
VIBIANA EVENTS LLC
Also Called: Vibiana
214 S Main St (90012-3708)
PHONE..............................213 626-1507
Amy Knoll Fraser, *Managing Member*
EMP: 88 EST: 2011
SALES (est): 2.36MM **Privately Held**
Web: www.vibiana.com
SIC: 7299 Facility rental and party planning services

(P-10582)
VISA INC
1 Market St Ste 600 (94105-1307)
PHONE..............................415 805-4000
Charles W Scharf, *CEO*
EMP: 67 EST: 2007
SALES (est): 15.05MM **Privately Held**
Web: usa.visa.com
SIC: 7299 Visa procurement service

(P-10583)
VISAGE IMAGING INC
12625 High Bluff Dr Ste 205 (92130-2052)
PHONE..............................858 345-4410
Sam Hupert, *CEO*
EMP: 75 EST: 2007
SQ FT: 1,200
SALES (est): 10.45MM **Privately Held**
Web: www.visageimaging.com
SIC: 7299 7379 Personal document and information services; Computer related consulting services
PA: Pro Medicus Limited
450 Swan St
Richmond VIC

PRODUCTS & SERVICES SECTION

7311 - Advertising Agencies (P-10605)

7311 Advertising Agencies

(P-10584)
180LA LLC
12555 W Jefferson Blvd Ste 200 (90066-7032)
PHONE...............................310 382-1400
Michael Allen, *Managing Member*
Michael Alllen, *Managing Member*
EMP: 110 EST: 2006
SQ FT: 13,000
SALES (est): 18.21MM
SALES (corp-wide): 14.29B **Publicly Held**
Web: www.180la.com
SIC: 7311 Advertising consultant
HQ: Tbwa Worldwide Inc.
220 E 42nd St Fl 14
New York NY

(P-10585)
AD POPULUM LLC (PA)
1234 6th St Apt 410 (90401-1602)
P.O. Box 212 (90406-0212)
PHONE...............................619 818-7644
EMP: 90 EST: 2016
SALES (est): 480.06MM
SALES (corp-wide): 480.06MM **Privately Held**
SIC: 7311 Advertising agencies

(P-10586)
ADCONION MEDIA INC (PA)
Also Called: Adconion Media Group
3301 Exposition Blvd Fl 1 (90404-5082)
PHONE...............................310 382-5521
Kristian Wilson, *Pr*
Scott Sullivan, *Global Chief Technology Officer*
EMP: 119 EST: 2007
SALES (est): 10.47MM
SALES (corp-wide): 10.47MM **Privately Held**
SIC: 7311 Advertising consultant

(P-10587)
ADVERTISE PURPLE
1431 7th St Ste 302 (90401-2751)
PHONE...............................424 272-7400
EMP: 90 EST: 2018
SALES (est): 870.91K **Privately Held**
Web: www.advertisepurple.com
SIC: 7311 Advertising agencies

(P-10588)
ALCONE MARKETING GROUP INC (HQ)
Also Called: Jeep Gear
4 Studebaker (92618-2012)
PHONE...............................949 595-5322
William Hahn, *CEO*
Bill Hahn, *
Sean Conciatore, *CCO*
▲ EMP: 100 EST: 1983
SQ FT: 90,000
SALES (est): 29.72MM
SALES (corp-wide): 14.29B **Publicly Held**
Web: www.alcone.com
SIC: 7311 Advertising consultant
PA: Omnicom Group Inc.
280 Park Ave Fl 31w
New York NY
212 415-3600

(P-10589)
AYZENBERG GROUP INC
49 E Walnut St (91103-3832)
PHONE...............................626 584-4070
Eric Ayzenberg, *Pr*
▲ EMP: 65 EST: 1993
SQ FT: 10,000
SALES (est): 24.81MM **Privately Held**
Web: www.ayzenberg.com
SIC: 7311 7336 Advertising consultant; Commercial art and graphic design

(P-10590)
BBDO WORLDWIDE INC
Also Called: BBDO
600 California St Fl 8 (94108-2726)
PHONE...............................415 808-6200
Linda D Merrick, *Sr VP*
EMP: 240
SALES (corp-wide): 14.29B **Publicly Held**
Web: www.bbdo.com
SIC: 7311 Advertising consultant
HQ: Bbdo Worldwide Inc.
1285 Ave Of The Amrcas Fl
New York NY
212 459-5000

(P-10591)
BERNARD HODES GROUP INC
720 Market St (94102-2512)
PHONE...............................212 999-9000
◆ EMP: 350
SIC: 7311 Advertising agencies

(P-10592)
BIG TOKEN INC
456 Seaton St (90013-2235)
PHONE...............................310 569-6553
Daina Middleton, *Prin*
Yin Woon Rani, *Prin*
EMP: 61 EST: 2019
SALES (est): 492.61K
SALES (corp-wide): 26.71MM **Publicly Held**
SIC: 7311 Advertising agencies
PA: Srax, Inc.
1014 S Westlake Blvd 14-2
Westlake Village CA
323 205-6109

(P-10593)
BRANDVIA ALLIANCE INC (HQ)
Also Called: Brandvia Powered By Halo
2901 Tasman Dr Ste 110 (95054-1137)
PHONE...............................408 955-0500
James Childers, *Pr*
James David Childers, *
Ted Greenwood, *
◆ EMP: 92 EST: 2003
SALES (est): 35.04MM
SALES (corp-wide): 526.77MM **Privately Held**
Web: www.brandvia.com
SIC: 7311 Advertising agencies
PA: Halo Branded Solutions, Inc.
1500 Halo Way
Sterling IL
815 625-0980

(P-10594)
BRIGHTROLL INC
343 Sansome St Ste 600 (94104-5603)
PHONE...............................415 677-9222
EMP: 421
Web: adtech.yahooinc.com
SIC: 7311 Advertising agencies

(P-10595)
BUTLER SHINE STERN PRTNERS LLC
Also Called: Bssp
20 Liberty Ship Way (94965-3312)
PHONE...............................415 331-6049
John Butler, *
Mike Shine, *
Dennis Moore, *
Matthew Curry, *Chief Creative Officer*
EMP: 139 EST: 2003
SALES (est): 28.94MM **Privately Held**
Web: www.bssp.com
SIC: 7311 Advertising consultant

(P-10596)
CAMPBELL-EWALD COMPANY
Also Called: Campbell-Ewald-West
1840 Century Park E Ste 1600 (90067-2116)
PHONE...............................310 358-4800
Jeffrey Fisher, *Mgr*
EMP: 149
SALES (corp-wide): 10.93B **Publicly Held**
Web: www.c-e.com
SIC: 7311 Advertising consultant
HQ: Campbell-Ewald Company
2000 Brush St Ste 601
Detroit MI
586 574-3400

(P-10597)
CASANOVA PUBLICIDAD LLC
Also Called: Casanova//Mccann
3337 Susan St Ste 200 (92626-1695)
PHONE...............................949 271-6344
Ingrid Smart, *Prin*
Enrily Levy, *
Elias Weinstock, *
Karla Acevedo, *
Will Pierce, *
EMP: 60 EST: 2020
SALES (est): 4.96MM **Privately Held**
Web: www.casanova.com
SIC: 7311 Advertising agencies

(P-10598)
CIMARRON PARTNER ASSOCIATES LLC
Also Called: Cimarron Group, The
6855 Santa Monica Blvd (90038-1119)
PHONE...............................323 337-0300
EMP: 150
Web: www.perfectdomain.com
SIC: 7311 Advertising agencies

(P-10599)
COLLAB INC (PA)
155 W Washington Blvd Ste 417 (90015-3581)
PHONE...............................310 991-0062
Tyler Mcfadden, *CEO*
James Mcfadden, *CEO*
Song Kang, *
EMP: 60 EST: 2011
SALES (est): 50MM
SALES (corp-wide): 50MM **Privately Held**
Web: www.collab.inc
SIC: 7311 Advertising agencies

(P-10600)
CONTROL GROUP MEDIA CO LLC
Also Called: People Connect
375 Camino De La Reina Ste 400 (92101)
PHONE...............................858 242-1350
Steven Gray, *CEO*
Rick Sutton, *CFO*
Shiem Edelbrock, *Prin*
EMP: 80 EST: 2012
SALES (est): 5.34MM **Privately Held**
Web: www.peopleconnect.us
SIC: 7311 8743 Advertising agencies; Public relations services

(P-10601)
DAILEY & ASSOCIATES
8687 Melrose Ave Ste G300 (90069-5076)
P.O. Box 931629 (90093-1629)
PHONE...............................323 490-3847
Jean Grabow, *CEO*
Michelle Wong, *
Bridget Johnson, *
Bradley Johnson, *
Steven Mitchell, *
EMP: 82 EST: 1964
SALES (est): 10.23MM **Privately Held**
Web: www.daileyla.com
SIC: 7311 Advertising consultant

(P-10602)
DAVID & GOLIATH LLC
909 N Pacific Coast Hwy Ste 700 (90245-2724)
PHONE...............................310 445-5200
Yumi Prentice, *Pr*
Wells Davis, *Chief Strategy Officer*
Bobby Pearce, *Chief Creative Officer*
EMP: 200 EST: 1999
SQ FT: 1,000
SALES (est): 33.55MM **Privately Held**
Web: www.dng.com
SIC: 7311 Advertising consultant
PA: Innocean Worldwide Inc.
308 Gangnam-Daero, Gangnam-Gu
Seoul

(P-10603)
DAVISELEN ADVERTISING INC (PA)
865 S Figueroa St Ste 1200 (90017-2543)
PHONE...............................213 688-7000
Mark Davis, *CEO*
Robert Elen, *
Thomas Saltarelli, *
Terry Sullivan, *
EMP: 172 EST: 1915
SQ FT: 32,000
SALES (est): 42.44MM
SALES (corp-wide): 42.44MM **Privately Held**
Web: www.daviselen.com
SIC: 7311 Advertising consultant

(P-10604)
DDB WORLDWIDE
Also Called: DDB WORLDWIDE COMMUNICATIONS GROUP, INC.
600 California St Fl 7 (94108-2731)
PHONE...............................415 732-3600
EMP: 160
SALES (corp-wide): 14.29B **Publicly Held**
Web: www.ddb.com
SIC: 7311 Advertising consultant
HQ: Ddb Worldwide Communications Group Llc
195 Broadway Fl 7
New York NY
212 415-2000

(P-10605)
DDB WRLDWIDE CMMNCTONS GROUP L
340 Main St (90291-2524)
PHONE...............................310 907-1500
Nick Bishop, *Mgr*
EMP: 71
SALES (corp-wide): 14.29B **Publicly Held**
Web: www.ddb.com
SIC: 7311 Advertising consultant
HQ: Ddb Worldwide Communications Group Llc
195 Broadway Fl 7
New York NY
212 415-2000

7311 - Advertising Agencies (P-10606)

PRODUCTS & SERVICES SECTION

(P-10606)
DEUTSCH LA INC
Also Called: Steelhead
12901 W Jefferson Blvd (90066-7023)
PHONE..................310 862-3000
Mike Sheldon, *CEO*
EMP: 100 **EST:** 1995
SALES (est): 23.89MM
SALES (corp-wide): 10.93B **Publicly Held**
Web: www.deutschla.com
SIC: 7311 Advertising agencies
PA: The Interpublic Group Of Companies Inc
909 3rd Ave
New York NY
212 704-1200

(P-10607)
DGWB INC
Also Called: Dgwb Advg & Communications
217 N Main St Ste 200 (92701-4843)
PHONE..................714 881-2300
Mike Wiseman, *CEO*
John Gothold, *
Cindy Melton, *
EMP: 70 **EST:** 1987
SALES (est): 21.28MM **Privately Held**
SIC: 7311 Advertising consultant

(P-10608)
DIGITAS INC
Also Called: Digitaslbi
13031 W Jefferson Blvd Ste 800 (90094-7002)
PHONE..................617 867-1000
EMP: 104
SALES (corp-wide): 25.29MM **Privately Held**
Web: www.digitas.com
SIC: 7311 Advertising agencies
HQ: Digitas, Inc.
40 Water St
Boston MA
617 369-8000

(P-10609)
DIGITAS INC
Also Called: Publicis Collective
350 Bush St Fl 18 (94104-2876)
PHONE..................617 867-1000
EMP: 86
SALES (corp-wide): 25.29MM **Privately Held**
Web: www.digitas.com
SIC: 7311 Advertising agencies
HQ: Digitas, Inc.
40 Water St
Boston MA
617 369-8000

(P-10610)
DOREAN ENTERPRISES INC
Also Called: AMR
212 Catalina Rd (92835-2506)
PHONE..................714 992-2900
Robert Charles Ressegue, *CEO*
EMP: 74 **EST:** 1976
SQ FT: 4,600
SALES (est): 2.4MM **Privately Held**
SIC: 7311 Advertising consultant

(P-10611)
DOREMUS & COMPANY
720 California St Fl 6 (94108-2478)
PHONE..................415 273-7800
Garrett Lawrence, *Mgr*
EMP: 84
SALES (corp-wide): 14.29B **Publicly Held**
Web: www.doremus.com
SIC: 7311 7319 Advertising consultant; Sky writing
HQ: Doremus & Company
1285 Ave Of The Amrcas 4t
New York NY
212 366-3076

(P-10612)
ELEVEN INC
Also Called: Eleven
394 Pacific Ave (94111-1721)
PHONE..................415 707-1111
Courtney Buechert, *CEO*
Ken Kula, *
Michael Borosky, *
Mike Mckay, *Pt*
Rob Price, *
EMP: 120 **EST:** 1999
SALES (est): 23.32MM **Privately Held**
Web: www.eleveninc.com
SIC: 7311 Advertising consultant

(P-10613)
FIRSTHIVE TECH CORPORATION
333 W San Carlos St Ste 600 (95110-2726)
PHONE..................408 368-3424
Aditya Bhamidipaty, *CEO*
EMP: 87 **EST:** 2020
SALES (est): 2.64MM **Privately Held**
Web: www.firsthive.com
SIC: 7311 7374 Advertising agencies; Data processing and preparation

(P-10614)
FORMERLY KNOWN AS LLC
40 E Verdugo Ave (91502-1931)
PHONE..................310 551-3500
Justin Archer, *Prin*
EMP: 78
SALES (corp-wide): 25.29MM **Privately Held**
Web: www.warefka.com
SIC: 7311 Advertising agencies
HQ: Formerly Known As, Llc
1230 Peachtree St Ne
Atlanta GA

(P-10615)
GIANT CREATIVE STRATEGY LLC
Also Called: Giant
1700 Montgomery St Ste 485 (94111-1025)
PHONE..................415 655-5200
Steven Gold, *CEO*
Adam Gelling, *
Jeff Nemy, *
Jodi Allen, *OF GLOBAL STRATEGY**
Kristina Ellis, *Executive Creative Director**
EMP: 150 **EST:** 2002
SQ FT: 24,000
SALES (est): 36.09MM
SALES (corp-wide): 5.57MM **Privately Held**
Web: www.evokegroup.com
SIC: 7311 Advertising agencies
PA: Huntsworth Limited
Holborn Gate
London

(P-10616)
GIANT MEDIA CORPORATION
5792 W Jefferson Blvd (90016-3107)
PHONE..................310 526-6739
David Segura, *CEO*
Huan Le, *CSO*
EMP: 78 **EST:** 2009
SALES (est): 2.63MM
SALES (corp-wide): 28.34MM **Privately Held**
Web: www.giantmedia.com
SIC: 7311 Advertising agencies
PA: Adknowledge, Inc.
420 Nichols Rd Fl 2
Kansas City MO
816 931-1771

(P-10617)
GIDDYUP GROUP INC
20 N Oak St Ste B (93001-2631)
PHONE..................800 828-2785
Christopher Grant, *CEO*
Chris Grant, *
Justin Grant, *
EMP: 60 **EST:** 2013
SALES (est): 6.96MM **Privately Held**
Web: www.giddyup.io
SIC: 7311 Advertising agencies

(P-10618)
GL NEMIROW INC
Also Called: Terry Hines & Assoc
2550 N Hollywood Way Ste 502 (91505-5023)
PHONE..................818 562-9433
Grant W Nemirow, *Pr*
Ralph Terraciano, *
EMP: 97 **EST:** 1989
SALES (est): 9.5MM **Privately Held**
SIC: 7311 Advertising agencies

(P-10619)
GODFREY DADICH PARTNERS LLC
564 Pacific Ave (94133-4608)
PHONE..................415 217-2800
Gary Cole, *Managing Member*
EMP: 63 **EST:** 2003
SALES (est): 7.81MM **Privately Held**
Web: www.godfreydadich.com
SIC: 7311 Advertising consultant

(P-10620)
GOODBY SLVERSTEIN PARTNERS INC
Also Called: Goodby Silverstein & Partners
720 California St (94108-2440)
PHONE..................415 392-0669
Rich Silverstein, *CEO*
Jeff Goodby, *
Leslie Barrett, *
Gareth Kay, *CSO**
Rob Smith, *
EMP: 200 **EST:** 1983
SQ FT: 60,000
SALES (est): 42.41MM
SALES (corp-wide): 14.29B **Publicly Held**
Web: www.goodbysilverstein.com
SIC: 7311 Advertising consultant
PA: Omnicom Group Inc.
280 Park Ave Fl 31w
New York NY
212 415-3600

(P-10621)
GRUPO GALLEGOS
Also Called: Gallegos United
300 Pacific Coast Hwy Ste 200 (92648-5109)
PHONE..................562 256-3600
John Gallegos, *CEO*
Jennifer Mull, *
EMP: 90 **EST:** 2004
SALES (est): 14MM **Privately Held**
Web: www.gallegosunited.com
SIC: 7311 Advertising consultant

(P-10622)
HAGGIN MARKETING LLC
Also Called: Stereomax
100 Shoreline Hwy A200 (94941-3650)
PHONE..................415 289-1110
EMP: 430
SIC: 7311 Advertising consultant

(P-10623)
HAVAS EDGE LLC (DH)
1525 Faraday Ave Ste 250 (92008-7373)
PHONE..................760 929-0041
Steve Netzley, *CEO*
Jennifer Peabody, *
Greg Johnson, *
Eric Bush, *
EMP: 98 **EST:** 1988
SALES (est): 50.97MM **Privately Held**
Web: www.havasedge.com
SIC: 7311 Advertising agencies
HQ: Havas
29 30
Puteaux
158478000

(P-10624)
HOMES MEDIA SOLUTIONS LLC
5510 Morehouse Dr Ste 100 (92121-3721)
PHONE..................888 510-8795
EMP: 72
Web: www.agentadvantage.com
SIC: 7311 8742 Advertising consultant; Marketing consulting services
HQ: Homes Media Solutions, Llc
325 John Knox Rd Bldg 200
Tallahassee FL
850 350-7800

(P-10625)
HORIZON MEDIA INC
Also Called: HORIZON MEDIA, INC.
1888 Century Park E Ste 700 (90067-1702)
PHONE..................310 282-0909
Zach Rosenberg, *Brnch Mgr*
EMP: 300
Web: www.horizonmedia.com
SIC: 7311 Advertising agencies
PA: Horizon Media, Llc
75 Varick St Ste 1404
New York NY

(P-10626)
HVSF TRANSITION LLC
Also Called: Heat
555 Mission St Ste 1400 (94105-0942)
PHONE..................415 477-1999
EMP: 108 **EST:** 1996
SALES (est): 4.42MM
SALES (corp-wide): 677.45K **Privately Held**
SIC: 7311 Advertising consultant
HQ: Deloitte Consulting Llp
30 Rockefeller Plz
New York NY
212 492-4000

(P-10627)
ICON MEDIA DIRECT INC (PA)
5910 Lemona Ave (91411-3006)
P.O. Box 55818 (91413-0818)
PHONE..................818 995-6400
Nancy Lazkani, *CEO*
Seth Klein, *
EMP: 81 **EST:** 1999
SQ FT: 16,445
SALES (est): 22.03MM
SALES (corp-wide): 22.03MM **Privately Held**
Web: www.iconmediadirect.com
SIC: 7311 Advertising consultant

PRODUCTS & SERVICES SECTION 7311 - Advertising Agencies (P-10650)

(P-10628)
IGNITE HEALTH LLC (PA)
7535 Irvine Center Dr Ste 200
(92618-2962)
PHONE...................................949 861-3200
Matt Brown, *Pr*
Richard E Fair, *
Timothy J Riley, *
Fabio Gratton, *
Brian Lefkowitz, *Chief Creative Officer**
EMP: 99 **EST:** 2000
SQ FT: 15,000
SALES (est): 9.32MM
SALES (corp-wide): 9.32MM **Privately Held**
Web: www.ignitehealth.com
SIC: 7311 Advertising consultant

(P-10629)
IGNITE VISIBILITY LLC
5060 Shoreham Pl Ste 260 (92122-5977)
PHONE...................................619 752-1955
Krish Coughran, *Pr*
EMP: 73 **EST:** 2013
SALES (est): 678.55K **Privately Held**
Web: www.ignitevisibility.com
SIC: 7311 Advertising agencies

(P-10630)
IGNITED LLC (PA)
111 Penn St (90245-3908)
PHONE...................................310 773-3100
William Rosenthal, *
Eric Springer, *Chief Creative Officer**
EMP: 115 **EST:** 1999
SQ FT: 55,000
SALES (est): 180MM
SALES (corp-wide): 180MM **Privately Held**
Web: www.ignitedusa.com
SIC: 7311 Advertising consultant

(P-10631)
INNOCEAN WRLDWIDE AMERICAS LLC (HQ)
Also Called: Innocean USA
180 5th St Ste 200 (92648-7107)
PHONE...................................714 861-5200
Ilsoo Jun, *Prin*
Tim Murphy, *COO*
EMP: 216 **EST:** 2002
SALES (est): 78.34MM **Privately Held**
Web: www.innoceanusa.com
SIC: 7311 Advertising consultant
PA: Innocean Worldwide Inc.
     308 Gangnam-Daero, Gangnam-Gu
     Seoul

(P-10632)
INTERACTIVE MEDIA HOLDINGS INC
Also Called: Viant
2722 Michelson Dr Ste 100 (92612-8905)
PHONE...................................949 861-8888
Timothy C Vanderhook, *Pr*
Roy E Luna, *
Chris Vanderhook, *
Larry Madden, *
EMP: 110 **EST:** 2004
SALES (est): 20.53MM
SALES (corp-wide): 197.17MM **Publicly Held**
SIC: 7311 7313 Advertising consultant; Newspaper advertising representative
HQ: Viant Technology Llc
     2722 Michelson Dr Ste 100
     Irvine CA
     949 861-8888

(P-10633)
INTERTREND COMMUNICATIONS INC
228 E Broadway (90802-4840)
PHONE...................................562 733-1888
Julia Huang, *CEO*
▲ **EMP:** 70 **EST:** 1991
SQ FT: 10,000
SALES (est): 18.34MM **Privately Held**
Web: www.intertrend.com
SIC: 7311 Advertising consultant

(P-10634)
ISEARCH MEDIA LLC
1710 S Amphlett Blvd Ste 320 (94402-2703)
PHONE...................................415 358-0882
EMP: 90 **EST:** 2007
SALES (est): 339.65K **Privately Held**
Web: www.3qdept.com
SIC: 7311 Advertising agencies
HQ: 3q Digital, Inc.
     155 Bovet Rd Ste 480
     San Mateo CA
     650 539-4124

(P-10635)
KANE & FINKEL LLC
Also Called: Kane Fnkle Hlthcare Cmmnctions
534 4th St (94107-1621)
P.O. Box 128 (94976-0128)
PHONE...................................415 777-4990
EMP: 70
Web: www.kaneandfinkel.com
SIC: 7311 Advertising agencies

(P-10636)
KATCH LLC
2381 Rosecrans Ave Ste 400 (90245-4920)
PHONE...................................310 219-6200
EMP: 70
Web: www.katch.com
SIC: 7311 Advertising agencies

(P-10637)
KERN ORGANIZATION INC
Also Called: Kern Direct Marketing
20955 Warner Center Ln (91367-6511)
PHONE...................................818 703-8775
Russell Kern, *Pr*
David Azulay, *
Tom Mackendrick, *
Zeke Ibarbia, *
Steven Orenstein, *
EMP: 80 **EST:** 2008
SQ FT: 11,350
SALES (est): 25.43MM
SALES (corp-wide): 14.29B **Publicly Held**
Web: www.thekernorg.com
SIC: 7311 Advertising consultant
PA: Omnicom Group Inc.
     280 Park Ave Fl 31w
     New York NY
     212 415-3600

(P-10638)
KINESSO LLC
600 Battery St (94111-1817)
PHONE...................................415 262-5900
Ian Johnson, *Genl Mgr*
EMP: 120
SALES (corp-wide): 10.93B **Publicly Held**
Web: www.matterkind.com
SIC: 7311 Advertising consultant
HQ: Kinesso, Llc
     100 W 33rd St Fl 8
     New York NY

(P-10639)
KLIENTBOOST LLC
2787 Bristol St Ste 100 (92626-5956)
PHONE...................................657 203-7866
J Dane Schuesler, *Managing Member*
Johnathan Dane Schuesler, *Managing Member*
EMP: 122 **EST:** 2015
SALES (est): 2.67MM **Privately Held**
Web: www.klientboost.com
SIC: 7311 Advertising consultant

(P-10640)
LEAD GENIUS
2054 University Ave (94704-2687)
PHONE...................................415 969-2915
Austin Brewin, *Ex Dir*
Santosh Sharan, *COO*
EMP: 64 **EST:** 2015
SALES (est): 5.41MM **Privately Held**
Web: www.leadgenius.com
SIC: 7311 Advertising agencies

(P-10641)
LEGENDARY PICTURES FILMS LLC
2900 W Alameda Ave (91505-4220)
PHONE...................................818 688-7003
Thomas Tull, *CEO*
Marlon Prager, *CFO*
EMP: 102 **EST:** 2006
SALES (est): 23.08MM **Privately Held**
Web: www.legendary.com
SIC: 7311 Advertising agencies
PA: Legend Pictures, Llc
     2900 W Alameda Ave Fl 15
     Burbank CA

(P-10642)
LIQUID ADVERTISING INC
138 Eucalyptus Dr (90245-3819)
PHONE...................................310 450-2653
William Akerlof, *CEO*
Marlo Huang, *
Alison Hamon, *
Alison Binetti, *
Shuly Millstein, *
EMP: 91 **EST:** 2000
SQ FT: 2,000
SALES (est): 14.09MM **Privately Held**
Web: www.liquidadvertising.com
SIC: 7311 Advertising consultant

(P-10643)
LOCAL CORPORATION (PA)
Also Called: Local.com
7555 Irvine Center Dr (92618-2912)
P.O. Box 50700 (92619-0700)
PHONE...................................949 784-0800
Frederick G Thiel, *CEO*
Kenneth S Cragun, *CFO*
Erick Herring, *Senior Vice President Technology*
EMP: 80 **EST:** 1999
SQ FT: 34,612
SALES (est): 12.93MM
SALES (corp-wide): 12.93MM **Publicly Held**
Web: www.localcorporation.com
SIC: 7311 Advertising agencies

(P-10644)
MANY LLC
17575 Pacific Coast Hwy (90272-4148)
PHONE...................................310 399-1515
Jens Stoelken, *Pt*
EMP: 71 **EST:** 2009
SALES (est): 5.55MM **Privately Held**
Web: www.themany.com

(P-10645)
MCCANN-ERICKSON CORPORATION (HQ)
Also Called: Interpublic Group of Companies
135 Main St 21st Fl (94105-1812)
PHONE...................................415 348-5600
Don Hov, *Treas*
EMP: 100 **EST:** 1982
SQ FT: 37,000
SALES (est): 28.99MM
SALES (corp-wide): 10.93B **Publicly Held**
SIC: 7311 Advertising agencies
PA: The Interpublic Group Of Companies Inc
     909 3rd Ave
     New York NY
     212 704-1200

(P-10646)
MEDIABRANDS WORLDWIDE INC
Also Called: Initiative Media North America
1840 Century Park E (90067-2101)
PHONE...................................323 370-8000
EMP: 300
SALES (corp-wide): 10.93B **Publicly Held**
Web: www.ipgmediabrands.com
SIC: 7311 Advertising consultant
HQ: Mediabrands Worldwide, Inc.
     100 W 33rd St Fl 3
     New York NY
     646 808-1282

(P-10647)
MERING HOLDINGS (PA)
1700 I St Ste 210 (95811-3018)
PHONE...................................916 441-0571
David Mering, *CEO*
Lori Bartle, *Pr*
Greg Carson, *CCO*
Lorie Brewster, *CFO*
Cori Boone, *Sec*
EMP: 79 **EST:** 1984
SQ FT: 11,000
SALES (est): 24.6MM
SALES (corp-wide): 24.6MM **Privately Held**
Web: www.theshipyard.com
SIC: 7311 Advertising consultant

(P-10648)
MH SUB I LLC (PA)
Also Called: Internet Brands
909 N Pacific Coast Hwy Fl 11 (90245-2724)
PHONE...................................310 280-4000
EMP: 286 **EST:** 2013
SALES (est): 1.01B
SALES (corp-wide): 1.01B **Privately Held**
Web: www.edoctors.com
SIC: 7311 Advertising agencies

(P-10649)
MINDGRUVE HOLDINGS INC
627 8th Ave Ste 300 (92101-6453)
PHONE...................................619 757-1325
Chad Robley, *CEO*
Dan Helleusch, *
EMP: 102 **EST:** 2017
SALES (est): 55.36MM **Privately Held**
Web: www.mindgruve.com
SIC: 7311 Advertising agencies

(P-10650)
MOB SCENE LLC (PA)
Also Called: Mob Scene Creative Productions
8447 Wilshire Blvd Ste 100 (90211-3228)

7311 - Advertising Agencies (P-10651)

PHONE.....................323 648-7200
EMP: 121 EST: 2005
SALES (est): 14.24MM Privately Held
Web: www.mobscene.com
SIC: 7311 7929 3993 7812 Advertising consultant; Entertainment service; Advertising artwork; Television film production

(P-10651)
MOVERS AND SHAKERS LLC
1217 Wilshire Blvd (90403-5466)
P.O. Box 3327 (90408-3327)
PHONE.....................310 893-7051
EMP: 100 EST: 2016
SALES (est): 5.22MM Privately Held
Web: www.moversshakers.co
SIC: 7311 Advertising agencies

(P-10652)
MULLENLOWE US INC
2121 Park Pl Ste 150 (90245-4843)
PHONE.....................424 738-6500
Jennifer Diodonet, Prin
EMP: 106
SALES (corp-wide): 10.93B Publicly Held
Web: us.mullenlowe.com
SIC: 7311 8743 8742 8732 Advertising agencies; Public relations and publicity; Marketing consulting services; Commercial nonphysical research
HQ: Mullenlowe U.S., Inc.
    2 Drydock Ave Fl 8
    Boston MA
    617 226-9000

(P-10653)
MULLENLOWE US INC
12130 Millennium (90094-2945)
PHONE.....................424 738-6600
EMP: 106
SALES (corp-wide): 10.93B Publicly Held
Web: us.mullenlowe.com
SIC: 7311 Advertising consultant
HQ: Mullenlowe U.S., Inc.
    2 Drydock Ave Fl 8
    Boston MA
    617 226-9000

(P-10654)
MUTESIX GROUP INC
Also Called: Mutesix, An Iprospect Company
5800 Bristol Pkwy Ste 500 (90230-6899)
PHONE.....................800 935-6856
Steve Weiss, CEO
Daniel Rutberg, *
EMP: 120 EST: 2018
SALES (est): 10.6MM Privately Held
SIC: 7311 Advertising agencies
HQ: Dentsu Uk Limited
    10 Triton Street
    London
    207 070-7700

(P-10655)
MYPOINTSCOM LLC (HQ)
Also Called: My Points.com
44 Montgomery St Ste 1050 (94104-4621)
PHONE.....................415 615-1100
EMP: 60 EST: 1996
SALES (est): 14.31MM
SALES (corp-wide): 26.88MM Privately Held
SIC: 7311 Advertising agencies
PA: Prodege, Llc
    2030 E Maple Ave Ste 200
    El Segundo CA
    310 294-9599

(P-10656)
NEXSTAR DIGITAL LLC
12777 W Jefferson Blvd Ste B100 (90066-7048)
PHONE.....................310 971-9300
Morgan Harris, Brnch Mgr
EMP: 100
SALES (corp-wide): 5.21MM Publicly Held
Web: www.nexstardigital.com
SIC: 7311 Advertising agencies
HQ: Nexstar Digital, Llc
    545 E John Carpenter Fwy
    Irving TX
    972 373-8800

(P-10657)
OGILVY GROUP LLC
2425 Olympic Blvd Ste 2200w (90404-4095)
PHONE.....................310 280-2200
Hugh Branigan, Brnch Mgr
EMP: 73
SALES (corp-wide): 17.37B Privately Held
Web: www.ogilvy.com
SIC: 7311 Advertising consultant
HQ: The Ogilvy Group Llc
    200 5th Ave
    New York NY
    212 237-4000

(P-10658)
ONE & ALL INC (HQ)
Also Called: Regency Group
2 N Lake Ave Ste 600 (91101-1868)
EMP: 215 EST: 1966
SALES (est): 45.57MM
SALES (corp-wide): 14.29B Publicly Held
Web: www.truesense.com
SIC: 7311 Advertising agencies
PA: Omnicom Group Inc.
    280 Park Ave Fl 31w
    New York NY
    212 415-3600

(P-10659)
ONE PLANET OPS INC (PA)
Also Called: Buyerlink
1820 Bonanza St Ste 200 (94596-4318)
PHONE.....................925 983-2800
Payam Zamani, CEO
EMP: 121 EST: 2001
SALES (est): 899.82K
SALES (corp-wide): 899.82K Privately Held
Web: www.oneplanetgroup.com
SIC: 7311 Advertising agencies

(P-10660)
PERCEPTIONEERING INC
Also Called: Davies Public Affairs
808 State St (93101-3200)
PHONE.....................805 962-4550
John Davies, CEO
EMP: 71 EST: 1989
SQ FT: 5,200
SALES (est): 5.66MM Privately Held
Web: www.daviespublicaffairs.com
SIC: 7311 8743 8651 Advertising agencies; Public relations services; Political campaign organization

(P-10661)
PETROL ADVERTISING INC
443 N Varney St (91502-1733)
PHONE.....................323 644-3720
EMP: 70
Web: www.petrolad.com
SIC: 7311 Advertising consultant

(P-10662)
POSTAER RUBIN AND ASSOCIATES
2525 Colorado Ave Ste 100 (90404-5576)
PHONE.....................312 644-3636
Bill Marks, Owner
EMP: 216
SALES (corp-wide): 91.73MM Privately Held
SIC: 7311 Advertising consultant
PA: Rubin Postaer And Associates
    2525 Colorado Ave Ste 100
    Santa Monica CA
    310 394-4000

(P-10663)
PRECISION EFFECT INC
Also Called: PRECISION EFFECT INC.
3 Macarthur Pl Ste 700 (92707-6078)
PHONE.....................800 634-5315
EMP: 63
SALES (corp-wide): 287.25MM Privately Held
Web: www.precisioneffect.com
SIC: 7311 Advertising agencies
HQ: Precision Effect, Inc.
    101 Tremont St Fl 2-3
    Boston MA
    800 634-5315

(P-10664)
PROMOVEO HEALTH LLC
701 Palomar Airport Rd (92011-1027)
PHONE.....................760 931-4794
Rolando Collado, *
EMP: 700 EST: 2014
SALES (est): 24.14MM Privately Held
Web: www.promoveohealth.com
SIC: 7311 Advertising agencies

(P-10665)
PSB
26012 Atlantic Ocean Dr (92630-8843)
PHONE.....................949 465-0772
EMP: 70
Web: www.psblitho.com
SIC: 7311 Advertising agencies

(P-10666)
QUIGLY-SIMPSON HEPPELWHITE INC
Also Called: Quigley-Simpson & Hepplewhite
11601 Wilshire Blvd Ste 710 (90025-0509)
PHONE.....................310 996-5800
Kathryn Browne, CFO
Gerald Bagg, *
Renee Hill Young, *
Alissa Stakgold, *
Duryea Ruffins, *
EMP: 150 EST: 2002
SQ FT: 10,500
SALES (est): 41.13MM Privately Held
Web: www.quigleysimpson.com
SIC: 7311 7319 Advertising agencies; Media buying service

(P-10667)
RAPP WORLDWIDE CALIFORNIA INC
55 Union St Fl 1 (94102-1227)
PHONE.....................415 248-7983
Anne Marie Neal, Pr
EMP: 122
Web: www.rapp.com
SIC: 7311 Advertising consultant
PA: Rapp Worldwide California Inc.
    12777 W Jefferson Blvd
    Los Angeles CA

(P-10668)
RAPP WORLDWIDE INC
Also Called: Rapp
12777 W Jefferson Blvd Bldg C (90066-7048)
PHONE.....................310 563-7200
Collins Rapp, Brnch Mgr
EMP: 110
SALES (corp-wide): 14.29B Publicly Held
Web: www.rapp.com
SIC: 7311 Advertising consultant
HQ: Rapp Worldwide Inc.
    220 E 42nd St Fl 12
    New York NY

(P-10669)
REACHLOCAL INC (DH)
Also Called: Reachlocal
21700 Oxnard St Ste 1600 (91367-7586)
PHONE.....................818 274-0260
Sharon T Rowlands, CEO
Ross G Landsbaum, *
Kris Barton, CPO*
Paras Maniar, CSO*
EMP: 142 EST: 2004
SQ FT: 38,592
SALES (est): 276.78MM
SALES (corp-wide): 2.95B Publicly Held
Web: www.localiq.com
SIC: 7311 7375 Advertising consultant; On-line data base information retrieval
HQ: Gannett Media Corp.
    7950 Jones Branch Dr Fl 8
    Mc Lean VA
    703 854-6000

(P-10670)
RESCUE AGENCY PUB BENEFT LLC (PA)
2437 Morena Blvd (92110-4152)
PHONE.....................619 231-7555
Kristin Carroll, CEO
Jeffrey Jordan, Pr
Connor Lynch, VP
Steven Andrews, Dir Fin
Dennis Triplett, COO
EMP: 70 EST: 2017
SALES (est): 10.16MM
SALES (corp-wide): 10.16MM Privately Held
Web: www.rescueagency.com
SIC: 7311 8732 Advertising agencies; Sociological research

(P-10671)
RUBIN POSTAER AND ASSOCIATES (PA)
Also Called: R P Direct
2525 Colorado Ave Ste 100 (90404-5576)
PHONE.....................310 394-4000
Willam C Hagelstein, CEO
Gerrold R Rubin, *
Vincent Mancuso, *
Larry Postaer, *
Tom Kirk, *
EMP: 201 EST: 1986
SQ FT: 130,000
SALES (est): 91.73MM
SALES (corp-wide): 91.73MM Privately Held
Web: www.rpa.com
SIC: 7311 Advertising consultant

(P-10672)
RUNYON SALTZMAN INC
Also Called: Rse
2020 L St Ste 100 (95811-4219)
PHONE.....................916 446-9900
Christopher Holben, Pr
Estelle Saltzman, *

PRODUCTS & SERVICES SECTION
7311 - Advertising Agencies (P-10694)

Scott Rose, *
Paul Mcclure, *VP*
EMP: 65 **EST:** 1960
SQ FT: 14,000
SALES (est): 16.58MM **Privately Held**
Web: www.rs-e.com
SIC: 7311 8743 Advertising consultant;
   Public relations and publicity

(P-10673)
SAATCHI & SAATCHI N AMER LLC
Team One
3501 Sepulveda Blvd (90505-2540)
PHONE..............................310 437-2500
EMP: 250
SALES (corp-wide): 25.29MM **Privately Held**
Web: www.teamone-usa.com
SIC: 7311 Advertising agencies
HQ: Saatchi & Saatchi North America, Llc.
   375 Hudson St
   New York NY
   212 463-2000

(P-10674)
SCDRG INC
473 S Carnegie Dr (92408-4207)
PHONE..............................818 874-0830
Richard Seiglery, *Pr*
Richard Seigler, *Pr*
EMP: 66 **EST:** 1997
SQ FT: 10,000
SALES (est): 7MM **Privately Held**
SIC: 7311 Advertising consultant

(P-10675)
SIZMEK DSP INC
Also Called: Rocket Fuel
1455 Market St Ste 2100 (94103-1331)
PHONE..............................415 757-2300
Devon Morehead, *Brnch Mgr*
EMP: 139
SIC: 7311 Advertising agencies
PA: Sizmek Dsp, Inc.
   2000 Seaport Blvd Ste 400
   Redwood City CA

(P-10676)
STN DIGITAL LLC
Also Called: Digital Marketing
3033 Bunker Hill St (92109-5705)
PHONE..............................619 292-8683
David Brickley, *Managing Member*
EMP: 81 **EST:** 2013
SALES (est): 15MM **Privately Held**
Web: www.stndigital.com
SIC: 7311 Advertising agencies

(P-10677)
SUISSA MILLER ADVERTISING LLC
8687 Melrose Ave (90069-5701)
PHONE..............................310 392-9666
EMP: 100 **EST:** 1985
SQ FT: 40,000
SALES (est): 3.57MM **Privately Held**
SIC: 7311 Advertising agencies

(P-10678)
SWIRL INC
Also Called: Swirl McGarrybowen
650 California St Fl 30 (94108-2611)
PHONE..............................415 276-8300
Martin Lauber, *Ch*
Ryan Lindholm, *
Wayne Esplana, *
Kevin Mccarthy, *Ex VP*
Greg Fischer, *

EMP: 60 **EST:** 1997
SALES (est): 22.76MM
SALES (corp-wide): 23.7MM **Privately Held**
Web: www.swirl.net
SIC: 7311 Advertising agencies
PA: Dentsu Mcgarry Bowen Llc
   150 E 42nd St Fl 13
   New York NY
   212 598-2900

(P-10679)
TEAM GARAGE LLC
Also Called: Garage Team Mazda
3200 Bristol St Ste 300 (92626-1838)
PHONE..............................714 913-9900
Michael Buttlar, *CEO*
Brian Rogers, *
Tom Nickerson, *
EMP: 70 **EST:** 2012
SALES (est): 10.16MM **Privately Held**
Web: www.garageteammazda.com
SIC: 7311 Advertising agencies

(P-10680)
THUNDER INDUSTRIES
313 Sheridan Ave (94306-2014)
PHONE..............................415 228-0861
EMP: 64 **EST:** 2017
SALES (est): 976.51K **Privately Held**
Web: www.makethunder.com
SIC: 7311 Advertising consultant

(P-10681)
TM SLEEVES LLC
475 14th St Ste 200 (94612-1936)
PHONE..............................415 374-8210
Bruce Friedman, *Managing Member*
EMP: 209 **EST:** 2000
SQ FT: 2,000
SALES (est): 802.86K
SALES (corp-wide): 33.63MM **Privately Held**
SIC: 7311 Advertising agencies
PA: Brite Media Llc
   350 Frank Ogawa Plz Ste 3
   Oakland CA
   877 479-7777

(P-10682)
TRAILER PARK INC (PA)
6922 Hollywood Blvd Fl 12 (90028-6104)
P.O. Box 2950 (90078-2950)
PHONE..............................310 845-3000
Rick Eiserman, *Pr*
Tim Nett, *Executive Creative Director**
Benedict Coulter, *
James Hale, *Stockholder**
EMP: 100 **EST:** 2005
SQ FT: 8,000
SALES (est): 46.39MM **Privately Held**
Web: www.trailerpark.com
SIC: 7311 Advertising agencies

(P-10683)
UE AUTHORITY CO
Also Called: DMS Insurance
225 Broadway Ste 2200 (92101-5011)
PHONE..............................800 466-4178
Joe Marinucci, *CEO*
EMP: 100 **EST:** 2008
SALES (est): 22.51MM
SALES (corp-wide): 391.15MM **Publicly Held**
SIC: 7311 7371 Advertising consultant;
   Computer software development
HQ: Digital Media Solutions, Llc
   4800 140th Ave N Ste 101
   Clearwater FL
   877 236-8632

(P-10684)
UNFOLD AGENCY INC
4841 Cherryvale Ave (95073-9762)
PHONE..............................818 679-4837
Brick Rucker, *Brnch Mgr*
EMP: 82
SALES (corp-wide): 5.66MM **Privately Held**
Web: www.unfoldagency.com
SIC: 7311 Advertising agencies
PA: Unfold Agency, Inc.
   11801 Teale St
   Culver City CA
   323 963-3108

(P-10685)
UNITED ONLINE ADVG NETWRK INC
21301 Burbank Blvd (91367-6679)
PHONE..............................818 287-3000
Mark Goldston, *Pr*
EMP: 62 **EST:** 2005
SALES (est): 1.78MM **Publicly Held**
SIC: 7311 Advertising agencies
PA: B. Riley Financial, Inc.
   11100 Santa Monica Blvd
   Los Angeles CA

(P-10686)
US INTERACTIVE DELAWARE
1270 Oakmead Pkwy Ste 318
(94085-4044)
PHONE..............................408 863-7500
Sunil Mathur, *Brnch Mgr*
EMP: 127
Web: www.usinteractive.com
SIC: 7311 Advertising consultant
PA: U.S. Interactive Corp Delaware
   1270 Oakmead Pkwy Ste 318
   Sunnyvale CA

(P-10687)
VENABLES/BELL & PARTNERS LLC
Also Called: Vbp Orange
201 Post St Fl 2 (94108-5012)
PHONE..............................415 288-3300
Kate Jeffers, *Pr*
Paul Venables, *Managing Member**
EMP: 190 **EST:** 2001
SQ FT: 30,000
SALES (est): 42.49MM **Privately Held**
Web: www.venablesbell.com
SIC: 7311 Advertising consultant

(P-10688)
VITROROBERTSON LLC
Also Called: Vitro
225 Broadway (92101-5005)
PHONE..............................619 234-0408
Tom Sullivan, *
Alan Bonine, *
EMP: 89 **EST:** 2004
SALES (est): 38.95MM
SALES (corp-wide): 2.69B **Publicly Held**
Web: www.vitroagency.com
SIC: 7311 Advertising consultant
HQ: A + N Real Estate & Business
   Management Corporation
   1 World Trade Ctr
   New York NY

(P-10689)
VUNGLE INC (PA)
Also Called: Vungle
1255 Battery St Ste 500 (94111-1167)
PHONE..............................415 800-1400
Jeremy Bond, *CEO*
EMP: 77 **EST:** 2011

SALES (est): 20.85MM
SALES (corp-wide): 20.85MM **Privately Held**
Web: www.liftoff.io
SIC: 7311 7319 7313 Advertising consultant;
   Display advertising service; Electronic
   media advertising representatives

(P-10690)
WONDERFUL AGENCY
11444 W Olympic Blvd Ste 210
(90064-1559)
PHONE..............................310 966-8600
Stewart A Resnick, *CEO*
Margaret Keene, *Chief Creative Officer*
EMP: 1745 **EST:** 2016
SALES (est): 10.09MM
SALES (corp-wide): 2.04B **Privately Held**
Web: www.wonderful.com
SIC: 7311 Advertising consultant
PA: The Wonderful Company Llc
   11444 W Olympic Blvd # 210
   Los Angeles CA
   310 966-5700

(P-10691)
YOUNG & RUBICAM LLC
Also Called: Landor Associates
7535 Irvine Center Dr (92618-2962)
PHONE..............................949 754-2100
Rick Eisermas, *Mgr*
EMP: 250
SALES (corp-wide): 17.37B **Privately Held**
Web: www.vmlyr.com
SIC: 7311 Advertising agencies
HQ: Young & Rubicam Llc
   3 Columbus Cir Fl 3 # 3
   New York NY
   212 210-3017

(P-10692)
YOUNG & RUBICAM LLC
Also Called: Y&R-Wcj Spectrum
7535 Irvine Center Dr (92618-2962)
PHONE..............................949 754-2000
David Murphy, *Pr*
EMP: 300
SALES (corp-wide): 17.37B **Privately Held**
Web: www.vmlyr.com
SIC: 7311 Advertising consultant
HQ: Young & Rubicam Llc
   3 Columbus Cir Fl 3 # 3
   New York NY
   212 210-3017

(P-10693)
YOUNG & RUBICAM LLC
Wunderman Cato Jhnsn-Los Angle
4751 Wilshire Blvd Ste 201 (90010-3827)
PHONE..............................213 930-5000
EMP: 135
SALES (corp-wide): 17.37B **Privately Held**
Web: www.vmlyr.com
SIC: 7311 Advertising consultant
HQ: Young & Rubicam Llc
   3 Columbus Cir Fl 3 # 3
   New York NY
   212 210-3017

(P-10694)
YUME INC (HQ)
Also Called: Yume
601 Montgomery St Ste 1600 (94111-2602)
PHONE..............................650 591-9400
Ted Hastings, *Pr*
Ed Reginelli, *
Dan Slivjanovski, *
Michael Hudes, *
Frank Barbieri, *Chief Product Officer**
EMP: 496 **EST:** 2004

7312 - Outdoor Advertising Services (P-10695)

SQ FT: 20,400
SALES (est): 54.47MM **Privately Held**
SIC: 7311 Advertising consultant
PA: Tremor International Ltd
    82 Alon Yigal
    Tel Aviv-Jaffa

7312 Outdoor Advertising Services

(P-10695)
BAMKO INC
Also Called: Bamko
11620 Wilshire Blvd Ste 610 (90025-1706)
PHONE..................................310 470-5859
EMP: 150
Web: www.bamko.net
SIC: 7312 7311 Outdoor advertising services; Advertising agencies

(P-10696)
PIXAR
Also Called: Pixar Animation Studios
1215 45th St (94608-2910)
PHONE..................................707 364-7854
EMP: 208
SALES (corp-wide): 82.72B **Publicly Held**
Web: www.pixar.com
SIC: 7312 Outdoor advertising services
HQ: Pixar
    1200 Park Ave
    Emeryville CA
    510 922-3000

(P-10697)
VOLTA CHARGING LLC
155 De Haro St (94103-5121)
PHONE..................................415 735-5169
Brandt Hastings, *Pr*
EMP: 70 EST: 2015
SQ FT: 8,250
SALES (est): 11.86MM
SALES (corp-wide): 381.31B **Privately Held**
Web: www.voltacharging.com
SIC: 7312 7694 Outdoor advertising services; Electric motor repair
HQ: Volta Industries, Inc.
    155 De Haro St
    San Francisco CA
    415 583-3805

7313 Radio, Television, Publisher Representatives

(P-10698)
101COMMUNICATIONS LLC (HQ)
Also Called: 1105 Government Group
9201 Oakdale Ave Ste 101 (91311-6546)
PHONE..................................818 734-1520
Neal Vitale, *Pr*
Jeffrey S Klein, *
Michael Valenti, *
Richard Vitale, *
EMP: 64 EST: 1998
SQ FT: 21,000
SALES (est): 25.99MM **Privately Held**
Web: www.1105media.com
SIC: 7313 7389 Printed media advertising representatives; Convention and show services
PA: 1105 Media, Inc.
    6300 Canoga Ave Ste 1150
    Woodland Hills CA

(P-10699)
ADACTIVE MEDIA CA INC
Also Called: Thoughtful Asia Limited
14724 Ventura Blvd Ste 1110 (91403-3501)
PHONE..................................818 465-7500
Bien Kiat Tan, *CEO*
EMP: 70 EST: 2010
SALES (est): 10.98MM
SALES (corp-wide): 5.64MM **Publicly Held**
Web: www.thoughtfulmedia.com
SIC: 7313 Electronic media advertising representatives
HQ: Thoughtful Media Group Incorporated
    701 S Carson St Ste 200
    Carson City NV

(P-10700)
APARTMENT SEO LLC
111 W Ocean Blvd Ste 1040 (90802-4687)
PHONE..................................877 309-7363
Ronn Ruiz, *CEO*
Martin Canthola, *
EMP: 60 EST: 2013
SALES (est): 5.65MM **Privately Held**
Web: www.apartmentseo.com
SIC: 7313 Electronic media advertising representatives

(P-10701)
APPSFLYER LTD
111 New Montgomery St Ste 400 (94105-3612)
PHONE..................................415 636-9430
Armando Osuna, *Pt*
EMP: 80 EST: 2015
SALES (est): 10.27MM **Privately Held**
Web: www.appsflyer.com
SIC: 7313 Electronic media advertising representatives

(P-10702)
ATTN INC
5700 Wilshire Blvd Ste 375 (90036-7212)
PHONE..................................323 413-2878
Jarrett Moreno, *CEO*
Matthew Segel, *
EMP: 200 EST: 2014
SQ FT: 100,000
SALES (est): 11.86MM **Privately Held**
Web: www.attn.com
SIC: 7313 Electronic media advertising representatives

(P-10703)
BEACHBODY LLC
Also Called: Team Beachbody
400 Continental Blvd Ste 400 (90245-5089)
PHONE..................................310 883-9000
Carl Daikeler, *Brnch Mgr*
EMP: 70
SALES (corp-wide): 692.2MM **Publicly Held**
Web: www.beachbody.com
SIC: 7313 Electronic media advertising representatives
HQ: Beachbody, Llc
    400 Continental Blvd # 400
    El Segundo CA
    310 883-9000

(P-10704)
BEACHBODY LLC (HQ)
Also Called: Beachbody
400 Continental Blvd Ste 400 (90245-5089)
P.O. Box 1227 (90660-5227)
PHONE..................................310 883-9000
Carl Daikeler, *Ch*
Jon Congdon, *CMO*
Brad Ramberg, *
Sue Collyns, *
Bryan Muehlberger, *CIO*
▲ EMP: 500 EST: 1998
SALES (est): 663.54MM
SALES (corp-wide): 692.2MM **Publicly Held**
Web: www.beachbody.com
SIC: 7313 7999 Electronic media advertising representatives; Physical fitness instruction
PA: The Beachbody Company Inc
    3301 Exposition Blvd
    Santa Monica CA
    310 883-9000

(P-10705)
BEACHBODY COMPANY INC (PA)
3301 Exposition Blvd (90404-5045)
PHONE..................................310 883-9000
Carl Daikeler, *Ch Bd*
Carl Daikeler, *CEO*
Mark R Goldston, *Ex Ch Bd*
Robert Gifford, *Pr*
Jonathan Gelfand, *Senior Vice President Business Development*
EMP: 208 EST: 2020
SQ FT: 133,000
SALES (est): 692.2MM
SALES (corp-wide): 692.2MM **Publicly Held**
SIC: 7313 7999 Electronic media advertising representatives; Physical fitness instruction

(P-10706)
BLT CMMNCTIONS LLC A LTD LBLTY
6430 W Sunset Blvd Ste 800 (90028-7901)
PHONE..................................323 860-4000
EMP: 182 EST: 2007
SALES (est): 4.62MM **Privately Held**
Web: www.bltomato.com
SIC: 7313 Electronic media advertising representatives

(P-10707)
BREITBART NEWS NETWORK LLC
Also Called: Bnn
149 S Barrington Ste 735 (90049)
PHONE..................................424 371-0585
Laurence Solov, *Managing Member*
Laurence Solov, *CEO*
EMP: 60 EST: 2011
SALES (est): 4.49MM **Privately Held**
Web: www.breitbart.com
SIC: 7313 Electronic media advertising representatives

(P-10708)
CANVAS WORLDWIDE LLC
12015 Bluff Creek Dr (90094-2930)
PHONE..................................424 303-4300
Paul Woolmington, *CEO*
Madhavi Tadikonda, *CIO*
EMP: 250 EST: 2015
SALES (est): 79.91MM **Privately Held**
Web: www.canvasworldwide.com
SIC: 7313 Electronic media advertising representatives
PA: Innocean Worldwide Inc.
    308 Gangnam-Daero, Gangnam-Gu
    Seoul

(P-10709)
DAVID WOOD AND ASSOCIATES INC
Also Called: Dwa Media
1160 Battery St Ste 400 (94111-1213)
PHONE..................................415 296-8050
David Wood, *Ch Bd*
Bob Ray, *CEO*
Patrick Knight, *COO*
EMP: 150 EST: 2009
SQ FT: 6,600
SALES (est): 38.81MM **Privately Held**
SIC: 7313 Electronic media advertising representatives
HQ: David Wood & Associates Limited
    10 Triton Street
    London

(P-10710)
EDMUNDSCOM INC (HQ)
2401 Colorado Ave Ste P1 (90404-3175)
PHONE..................................310 309-6300
Seth Berkowitz, *Pr*
Scott Fanelli, *VP*
Katti Fields, *VP*
Xiao Sun, *VP*
▲ EMP: 550 EST: 1966
SALES (est): 156.39MM **Privately Held**
Web: www.edmunds.com
SIC: 7313 Electronic media advertising representatives
PA: Edmunds Holding Company
    2401 Colorado Ave
    Santa Monica CA

(P-10711)
EREPUBLIC LLC ✪
100 Blue Ravine Rd (95630-4509)
PHONE..................................916 932-1300
Paul Harney, *
EMP: 199 EST: 2022
SALES (est): 11.18MM **Privately Held**
Web: www.erepublic.com
SIC: 7313 8742 Electronic media advertising representatives; Marketing consulting services

(P-10712)
GHOST MANAGEMENT GROUP LLC
41 Discovery (92618-3150)
PHONE..................................949 870-1400
Doug Francis, *
Albert Lopez, *
Chris Beals, *
Hendrik Davel, *Senior Controller*
EMP: 175 EST: 2012
SQ FT: 44,820
SALES (est): 20.79MM **Privately Held**
SIC: 7313 7371 Electronic media advertising representatives; Computer software development and applications

(P-10713)
KARGO GLOBAL INC
1437 4th St Ste 200 (90401-2377)
PHONE..................................212 979-9000
Natalie Nelson, *Brnch Mgr*
EMP: 139
Web: www.kargo.com
SIC: 7313 7372 7374 Electronic media advertising representatives; Application computer software; Computer graphics service
PA: Kargo Global, Inc.
    826 Broadway Fl 4
    New York NY

(P-10714)
LIVEUNIVERSE INC
9255 W Sunset Blvd Ste 1010 (90069-3309)
PHONE..................................310 492-2200
Bradley D Greenspan, *CEO*
Toan Nguyen, *
EMP: 60 EST: 2005

PRODUCTS & SERVICES SECTION
7322 - Adjustment And Collection Services (P-10735)

SQ FT: 10,137
SALES (est): 4.24MM **Privately Held**
Web: www.liveuniverse.com
SIC: **7313** Electronic media advertising representatives

(P-10715)
MEDIAALPHA INC (PA)
700 S Flower St Ste 640 (90017-4122)
PHONE.................................213 316-6256
Steven Yi, *Pr*
Tigran Sinanyan, *CFO*
EMP: 81 EST: 2020
SALES (est): 459.07MM
SALES (corp-wide): 459.07MM **Publicly Held**
Web: www.mediaalpha.com
SIC: **7313** Electronic media advertising representatives

(P-10716)
MODE MEDIA CORPORATION
Also Called: Project Y
1100 La Avenida St (94043-1452)
PHONE................................650 244-4000
EMP: 240
SIC: **7313 7311** Electronic media advertising representatives; Advertising agencies

(P-10717)
PAC-12 ENTEPRISES LLC
Also Called: PAC-12
12647 Alcosta Blvd (94583-9026)
PHONE................................415 580-4200
Lydia Murphy Stevens, *Pr*
Larry Scott, *
Jamie Zaninovich, *
Ron Mcquate, *CFO*
Woodie Dixon, *
EMP: 120 EST: 1915
SALES (est): 580.9MM **Privately Held**
Web: www.pac-12.com
SIC: **7313** Electronic media advertising representatives

(P-10718)
ROI DNA INC
156 Cascade Dr (94930-2106)
PHONE................................831 238-2514
Matt Quirie, *Prin*
EMP: 97 EST: 2012
SALES (est): 4.84MM **Privately Held**
Web: www.roidna.com
SIC: **7313** Electronic media advertising representatives

(P-10719)
SHED MEDIA US INC
3800 Barham Blvd Ste 410 (90068-1042)
PHONE................................323 904-4680
Nick Emmerson, *Pr*
Josh Mills, *
EMP: 101 EST: 2009
SALES (est): 5.55MM **Privately Held**
Web: www.shedmedia.com
SIC: **7313** Electronic media advertising representatives

(P-10720)
STUDIO 71 LP
Also Called: Collective Digital Studio, LLC
8383 Wilshire Blvd Ste 1050 (90211-2425)
PHONE................................323 370-1500
Michael Green, *
Dan Weinstein, *
Scott Weller, *
Jordan Toplitzky, *
EMP: 150 EST: 2011
SQ FT: 15,000
SALES (est): 42.61MM

SALES (corp-wide): 4.32B **Privately Held**
Web: www.studio71.com
SIC: **7313** Electronic media advertising representatives
PA: Prosiebensat.1 Media Se
Medienallee 7
Unterfohring BY
89950710

(P-10721)
TM HOLDCO LLC (PA)
Also Called: Gsa Media
50 1st St Ste 600 (94105-2429)
EMP: 112 EST: 2004
SALES (est): 8.21MM
SALES (corp-wide): 8.21MM **Privately Held**
SIC: **7313** Electronic media advertising representatives

(P-10722)
TRAVELZOO INC
800 W El Camino Real (94040-2688)
P.O. Box 612710 (95161-2710)
PHONE................................650 316-6956
Chris Loughlin, *CEO*
Ralph Bartel, *
Wayne Lee, *
EMP: 81 EST: 2005
SALES (est): 20.25MM
SALES (corp-wide): 70.6MM **Publicly Held**
Web: www.travelzoo.com
SIC: **7313** Electronic media advertising representatives
PA: Travelzoo
590 Madison Ave Fl 35
New York NY
212 484-4900

(P-10723)
WALDBERG INC
Also Called: Refinery, The
15301 Ventura Blvd Ste 300 (91403-5813)
PHONE................................818 843-0004
Adam Waldman, *CEO*
Brad Hochberg, *
EMP: 100 EST: 2006
SALES (est): 12.25MM **Privately Held**
Web: www.therefinerycreative.com
SIC: **7313** Electronic media advertising representatives

(P-10724)
ZAMBEZI LLC
3522 Hayden Ave (90232-2413)
PHONE................................310 450-6800
Jean Freeman, *Managing Member*
Christopher Raih, *Managing Member*
Alex Cohn, *Managing Member*
Gavin Lester, *
James Freeman, *
EMP: 65 EST: 2015
SALES (est): 10.12MM **Privately Held**
Web: www.zmbz.com
SIC: **7313** Electronic media advertising representatives

7319 Advertising, Nec

(P-10725)
AFFILIATE TRACTION
2125 Delaware Ave Ste E (95060-5752)
PHONE................................831 464-1441
Greg J Shepard, *Pr*
EMP: 166 EST: 2004
SQ FT: 7,500
SALES (est): 2.3MM
SALES (corp-wide): 70.73MM **Privately Held**

Web: www.partnerize.com
SIC: **7319** Display advertising service
HQ: Pepperjam Llc
7 S Main St Ste 301
Wilkes Barre PA
877 796-5700

(P-10726)
CARAT N AMER DNTSU AGEIS NTWRK
5800 Bristol Pkwy 5th Fl (90230-6696)
PHONE................................310 255-1000
John Barnes, *Brnch Mgr*
EMP: 82
SIC: **7319 7313** Media buying service; Printed media advertising representatives
HQ: Carat North America Dentsu Aegeis Network
150 E 42nd St Fl 14
New York NY
212 591-9100

(P-10727)
CBS INTERACTIVE INC (HQ)
Also Called: Cbsi
680 Folsom St (94107-2153)
PHONE................................415 344-2000
Jarl Mohn, *Ch Bd*
Jim Lanzone, *Pr*
Joseph Gillespie, *Ex VP*
EMP: 600 EST: 1992
SALES (est): 538.35MM
SALES (corp-wide): 30.15B **Publicly Held**
Web: www.paramount.com
SIC: **7319 7375 4832** Distribution of advertising material or sample services; On-line data base information retrieval; Radio broadcasting stations
PA: Paramount Global
1515 Broadway
New York NY
212 258-6000

(P-10728)
CHECKOUT HOLDING CORP
1 Maritime Plz Ste 1200 (94111-3502)
PHONE................................415 788-5111
Andrew Ballard, *Pr*
EMP: 1233 EST: 2007
SALES (est): 16.87MM **Privately Held**
SIC: **7319** Coupon distribution

(P-10729)
DIVERSFIED MRCURY CMMNCTONS LL
Also Called: Mercury Media
11620 Wilshire Blvd (90025-1706)
P.O. Box 57499 (91413-2499)
PHONE................................508 598-3569
Janet Campbell, *Brnch Mgr*
EMP: 64
SALES (corp-wide): 20.58MM **Privately Held**
SIC: **7319 7313** Media buying service; Television and radio time sales
HQ: Diversified Mercury Communications, Llc
3 Speen St Ste 140
Framingham MA

(P-10730)
FASTCLICK INC
Also Called: Fastclick.com
530 E Montecito St (93103-3245)
PHONE................................805 689-9839
EMP: 522 EST: 2000
SQ FT: 14,900
SALES (est): 7.48MM
SALES (corp-wide): 29.15MM **Privately Held**

Web: www.epsilon.com
SIC: **7319** Circular and handbill distribution
HQ: Conversant, Llc
101 N Wacker Dr
Chicago IL

(P-10731)
GILS DISTRIBUTING SERVICE
Also Called: Great Western Distributing Svc
718 E 8th St (90021-1802)
PHONE................................213 627-0539
Feleciano Gil, *Pr*
Fidel Gil, *
Gloria Gil, *
EMP: 112 EST: 1967
SQ FT: 5,000
SALES (est): 1.98MM **Privately Held**
SIC: **7319 4215** Circular and handbill distribution; Courier services, except by air

(P-10732)
IMAGE OPTIONS (PA)
Also Called: Image Options Painting & Dctg
80 Icon (92610-3000)
PHONE................................949 586-7665
Tim Bennett, *Ch Bd*
Dave Bales, *CEO*
Brian Hite, *Pr*
Dave Brewer, *VP*
Barry Polan, *CRO*
EMP: 63 EST: 1999
SQ FT: 22,000
SALES (est): 24.71MM
SALES (corp-wide): 24.71MM **Privately Held**
Web: www.imageoptions.net
SIC: **7319 7336 2759** Display advertising service; Commercial art and graphic design; Commercial printing, nec

(P-10733)
WILLIAMS SCOTSMAN INC
14015 Kirkham Way (92064-7146)
PHONE................................619 710-8468
EMP: 107
SALES (corp-wide): 2.14B **Publicly Held**
Web: www.willscot.com
SIC: **7319** Poster advertising service, except outdoor
HQ: Williams Scotsman, Inc.
4646 E Van Buren St # 40
Phoenix AZ
480 894-6311

7322 Adjustment And Collection Services

(P-10734)
AMERICAN RECOVERY SERVICE INC (DH)
Also Called: Arsi of California
555 Saint Charles Dr Ste 100 (91360)
P.O. Box 1025 (91358-0025)
PHONE................................805 379-8500
EMP: 200 EST: 1986
SALES (est): 24.24MM **Privately Held**
Web: www.arsigroup.com
SIC: **7322** Collection agency, except real estate
HQ: Firstsource Solutions Limited
5th Floor, Paradigm, B Wing, Mindspace
Mumbai MH

(P-10735)
ARS NATIONAL SERVICES INC (PA)
201 W Grand Ave (92025-2603)

7322 - Adjustment And Collection Services (P-10736)

P.O. Box 463023 (92046-3023)
PHONE..................................800 456-5053
Jason Howerton, *Pr*
John Howerton, *
Kathy Howerton, *
John Watson, *
Jim Beck, *
EMP: 150 **EST:** 1987
SQ FT: 33,000
SALES (est): 29.52MM **Privately Held**
Web: www.arsnational.com
SIC: 7322 Collection agency, except real estate

(P-10736)
ATTORNEY RECOVERY SYSTEMS INC (PA)
18757 Burbank Blvd Ste 300 (91356-3375)
PHONE..................................818 774-1420
Gene Bloom, *Pr*
EMP: 70 **EST:** 1989
SALES (est): 2.37MM **Privately Held**
Web: www.legalcollection.com
SIC: 7322 8111 Collection agency, except real estate; Legal services

(P-10737)
CAINE & WEINER COMPANY INC (PA)
Also Called: Caine & Weiner
5805 Sepulveda Blvd Fl 4 (91411-2508)
P.O. Box 55848 (91413-0848)
PHONE..................................818 226-6000
Greg A Cohen, *Pr*
Rick Luther, *
Brad Schaffer, *Senior Vice President Client Services*
Tony Albanesi, *CA**
Steve Simon, *SERVICES**
EMP: 90 **EST:** 1930
SQ FT: 14,400
SALES (est): 22.44MM
SALES (corp-wide): 22.44MM **Privately Held**
Web: www.caine-weiner.com
SIC: 7322 Collection agency, except real estate

(P-10738)
CMRE FINANCIAL SERVICES INC
3075 E Imperial Hwy Ste 200 (92821-6753)
PHONE..................................714 528-3200
Jeffrey Nieman, *Pr*
EMP: 450 **EST:** 2000
SQ FT: 35,000
SALES (est): 27.08MM **Privately Held**
Web: www.cmrefsi.com
SIC: 7322 Collection agency, except real estate

(P-10739)
COLLECTION TECHNOLOGY INC
Also Called: C T I
10801 6th St Ste 200 (91730-5904)
P.O. Box 2200 (91729-2200)
PHONE..................................800 743-4284
Chris Van Dellen, *CEO*
Paul Van Dellen, *
EMP: 100 **EST:** 1953
SALES (est): 10.88MM **Privately Held**
Web: www.collectiontechnology.com
SIC: 7322 Collection agency, except real estate

(P-10740)
EGS FINANCIAL CARE INC (DH)
Also Called: Total Debt Management
5 Park Plz Ste 1100 (92614-8502)
PHONE..................................877 217-4423
Jay King, *Pr*
Steven Winokur, *
Joshua Gindin, *
John R Schwab Treeas, *Prin*
▲ **EMP:** 300 **EST:** 1966
SALES (est): 138.11MM
SALES (corp-wide): 845.12MM **Privately Held**
SIC: 7322 Collection agency, except real estate
HQ: Alorica Global Solutions, Inc.
6652 Pinecrest Dr Ste 300
Plano TX

(P-10741)
FCI LENDER SERVICES INC
Also Called: F C I
8180 E Kaiser Blvd (92808-2277)
PHONE..................................800 931-2424
Michael W Griffith, *Pr*
EMP: 190 **EST:** 1982
SQ FT: 19,000
SALES (est): 33.31MM **Privately Held**
Web: www.trustfci.com
SIC: 7322 Adjustment and collection services

(P-10742)
GRANT & WEBER (PA)
Also Called: Grant & Weber Travel
26610 Agoura Rd Ste 209 (91302-2975)
P.O. Box 8669 (91372-8669)
PHONE..................................818 878-7700
Jimi Bingham, *CEO*
Ron Grossblatt, *CDO**
Spencer Weinerman, *
David Weinerman, *
Mary Kempski, *CIO**
▲ **EMP:** 85 **EST:** 1976
SQ FT: 30,000
SALES (est): 24.42MM
SALES (corp-wide): 24.42MM **Privately Held**
Web: www.grantweber.com
SIC: 7322 Collection agency, except real estate

(P-10743)
H&H RESOLUTION LLC
151 Bernal Rd Ste 6 (95119-1306)
PHONE..................................408 362-2293
Daniel Oditt, *Managing Member*
EMP: 100 **EST:** 2008
SALES (est): 2.07MM **Privately Held**
SIC: 7322 Collection agency, except real estate

(P-10744)
J & L COLLECTIONS SERVICES INC
Also Called: J&L Teamworks
8220 Longleaf Dr # 400 (95758-1322)
PHONE..................................800 481-6006
Donald R Johnsen, *Pr*
Kenneth M Lamont, *
EMP: 85 **EST:** 1990
SALES (est): 3.89MM
SALES (corp-wide): 41.54MM **Privately Held**
SIC: 7322 Collection agency, except real estate
PA: Uscb, Inc.
355 S Grand Ave Ste 3200
Los Angeles CA
213 985-2111

(P-10745)
JJ MAC INTYRE CO INC (PA)
4160 Temescal Canyon Rd Ste 601 (92883-4625)
P.O. Box 78150 (92877-0138)
PHONE..................................951 898-4300
Scott M Hall, *CEO*
Kenneth A Lee, *
EMP: 115 **EST:** 1959
SQ FT: 28,254
SALES (est): 2.15MM
SALES (corp-wide): 2.15MM **Privately Held**
SIC: 7322 Collection agency, except real estate

(P-10746)
OPTIO SOLUTIONS LLC
Also Called: Qualia Collection Services
1444 N Mcdowell Blvd (94954-6515)
PHONE..................................800 360-2827
Chris Schumacher, *CEO*
EMP: 263 **EST:** 2007
SALES (est): 11.7MM **Privately Held**
Web: www.optiosolutions.com
SIC: 7322 Collection agency, except real estate

(P-10747)
PERFORMANT RECOVERY INC
Also Called: DCS
17080 S Harlan Rd (95330-8739)
PHONE..................................209 858-3500
James Tracey, *Prin*
EMP: 184
Web: www.performantcorp.com
SIC: 7322 Collection agency, except real estate
HQ: Performant Recovery, Inc.
333 N Canyons Pkwy # 100
Livermore CA
209 858-3994

(P-10748)
PERFORMANT RECOVERY INC (HQ)
333 N Canyons Pkwy Ste 100 (94551-9478)
PHONE..................................209 858-3994
Simeon Kohl, *CEO*
Harold T Leach, *Pr*
Ian A Johnston, *CAO*
Rohit Ramchandani, *CFO*
EMP: 165 **EST:** 1976
SQ FT: 31,000
SALES (est): 45.36MM **Publicly Held**
Web: www.performantpayments.com
SIC: 7322 8742 7371 Collection agency, except real estate; Financial consultant; Custom computer programming services
PA: Performant Financial Corporation
333 N Canyons Pkwy # 100
Livermore CA

(P-10749)
PREMIERE CREDIT NORTH AMER LLC
17054 S Harlan Rd (95330-8739)
PHONE..................................844 897-2901
EMP: 120
Web: www.premierecredit.com
SIC: 7322 Collection agency, except real estate
HQ: Premiere Credit Of North America Llc
2002 Wellesley Blvd # 100
Indianapolis IN

(P-10750)
PROFESSIONAL BUREAU OF COLLECT
9675 Elk Grove Florin Rd (95624-2225)
PHONE..................................916 685-3399
Travis Justus, *Brnch Mgr*
EMP: 115
Web: www.pbccorp.com
SIC: 7322 Collection agency, except real estate
PA: Professional Bureau Of Collections Of Maryland, Inc.
5295 Dtc Pkwy Ste 145
Greenwood Village CO

(P-10751)
RM GALICIA INC
Also Called: Progressive Management Systems
1521 W Cameron Ave Ste 100 (91790-2738)
P.O. Box 2220 (91793-2220)
PHONE..................................626 813-6200
Timothy Chase Banta, *CEO*
William Gutierrez, *Sr VP*
EMP: 125 **EST:** 1978
SQ FT: 20,000
SALES (est): 9.12MM **Privately Held**
Web: www.pmscollects.com
SIC: 7322 Collection agency, except real estate

(P-10752)
SEQUOIA CONCEPTS INC
Also Called: Sequoia Financial Services
28632 Roadside Dr Ste 110 (91301-6074)
PHONE..................................818 409-6000
Roy Duplessis, *Pr*
Denise Duplessis, *
Roy Deplessis Ii, *Sec*
EMP: 75 **EST:** 1992
SQ FT: 9,100
SALES (est): 8.42MM **Privately Held**
Web: www.sequoiafinancial.com
SIC: 7322 Collection agency, except real estate

(P-10753)
USCB INC (PA)
Also Called: Uscb America
355 S Grand Ave Ste 3200 (90071-1591)
PHONE..................................213 985-2111
Albert Cadena, *CEO*
Melvin F Shaw, *
Thomas Isgrigg, *
Albert Cadena, *Prin*
Pat Esquivel, *
EMP: 213 **EST:** 1915
SQ FT: 34,000
SALES (est): 41.54MM
SALES (corp-wide): 41.54MM **Privately Held**
Web: www.uscbamerica.com
SIC: 7322 8741 Collection agency, except real estate; Management services

(P-10754)
VENGROFF WILLIAMS & ASSOC INC
2099 S State College Blvd Ste 600 (92806-6149)
PHONE..................................714 889-6200
Robert Sherman, *Brnch Mgr*
EMP: 102
SALES (corp-wide): 43.72MM **Privately Held**
Web: www.vengroffwilliams.com
SIC: 7322 Collection agency, except real estate
PA: Vengroff, Williams & Associates, Inc.
2211 Fruitville Rd
Sarasota FL
941 363-5200

PRODUCTS & SERVICES SECTION

7331 - Direct Mail Advertising Services (P-10776)

7323 Credit Reporting Services

(P-10755)
A-CHECK AMERICA LLC (HQ)
Also Called: A-Check America, Member Act 1
1501 Research Park Dr (92507-2114)
P.O. Box 29048 (91209-9048)
PHONE..................951 750-1501
Michael Hoyal, *Pr*
Gregg Hassler, *
▲ **EMP:** 170 **EST:** 1978
SQ FT: 30,000
SALES (est): 48.3MM
SALES (corp-wide): 766.78MM **Publicly Held**
Web: www.acheckglobal.com
SIC: 7323 7375 Credit reporting services; Information retrieval services
PA: Sterling Check Corp.
6150 Oak Tree Blvd Ste 49
Independence OH
212 736-5100

(P-10756)
BASEPOINT ANALYTICS LLC
703 Palomar Airport Rd Ste 350 (92011-1040)
PHONE..................760 602-4971
EMP: 408 **EST:** 2004
SALES (est): 230.63K
SALES (corp-wide): 1.64B **Privately Held**
SIC: 7323 Credit reporting services
HQ: Corelogic Systems, Inc.
40 Pacifica Ste 900
Irvine CA
714 250-6400

(P-10757)
CLARITY SERVICES INC
475 Anton Blvd (92626-7037)
P.O. Box 16 (75013-0001)
PHONE..................727 489-7266
EMP: 60 **EST:** 2008
SALES (est): 5.8MM **Privately Held**
Web: www.clarityservices.com
SIC: 7323 Consumer credit reporting bureau

(P-10758)
CORELOGIC INC
Also Called: Corelogic Info Solutions
11010 White Rock Rd Ste 200 (95670-6362)
PHONE..................916 431-2146
Christine Christian, *Brnch Mgr*
EMP: 95
SALES (corp-wide): 1.64B **Privately Held**
Web: www.corelogic.com
SIC: 7323 Credit reporting services
HQ: Corelogic, Inc.
40 Pacifica Ste 900
Irvine CA
866 873-3651

(P-10759)
CORELOGIC CREDCO LLC (DH)
Also Called: Corelogic Credco
40 Pacifica Ste 900 (92618-3375)
PHONE..................800 255-0792
Jim Balas, *CFO*
EMP: 220 **EST:** 2005
SALES (est): 54.06MM
SALES (corp-wide): 1.64B **Privately Held**
Web: www.corelogic.com
SIC: 7323 8748 Consumer credit reporting bureau; Business consulting, nec
HQ: Corelogic, Inc.
40 Pacifica Ste 900
Irvine CA
866 873-3651

(P-10760)
CORELOGIC CREDCO LLC
9645 Granite Ridge Dr Ste 300 (92123)
PHONE..................619 938-7028
Kathleen Manzione, *Brnch Mgr*
EMP: 280
SALES (corp-wide): 1.64B **Privately Held**
Web: www.corelogic.com
SIC: 7323 Consumer credit reporting bureau
HQ: Corelogic Credco, Llc
40 Pacifica Ste 900
Irvine CA
800 255-0792

(P-10761)
EXPERIAN CORPORATION
475 Anton Blvd (92704)
PHONE..................714 830-7000
EMP: 97 **EST:** 1996
SQ FT: 323,000
SALES (est): 6.75MM
SALES (corp-wide): 6.62B **Privately Held**
Web: www.experian.com
SIC: 7323 Consumer credit reporting bureau
HQ: Gus Holdings Unlimited
Landmark House
Nottingham NOTTS

(P-10762)
EXPERIAN INFO SOLUTIONS INC (DH)
Also Called: Experian
475 Anton Blvd (92626-7037)
P.O. Box 5001 (92628-5001)
PHONE..................714 830-7000
Chris Callero, *CEO*
Stephen Burnside, *Sr VP*
EMP: 3700 **EST:** 1996
SQ FT: 323,000
SALES (est): 973.87MM
SALES (corp-wide): 6.62B **Privately Held**
Web: www.experian.com
SIC: 7323 Consumer credit reporting bureau
HQ: Experian Holdings, Inc.
475 Anton Blvd
Costa Mesa CA
714 830-7000

(P-10763)
EXPERIAN MKTG SOLUTIONS LLC
Also Called: Experian Marketing
475 Anton Blvd (92626-7037)
PHONE..................714 830-7000
Kevin Dean, *Pr*
EMP: 501 **EST:** 2016
SQ FT: 4,000
SALES (est): 47.63MM
SALES (corp-wide): 912.58MM **Privately Held**
Web: www.experian.com
SIC: 7323 Consumer credit reporting bureau
PA: Vector Capital Management, L.P.
1 Market St Ste 2300
San Francisco CA
415 293-5000

(P-10764)
KEYPOINT CREDIT SERVICES LLC
378 W Calaveras Blvd (95035-5131)
PHONE..................800 745-7400
Priyesh Patel, *Managing Member*
EMP: 500 **EST:** 2020
SALES (est): 7.21MM **Privately Held**
Web: www.keypointcreditservices.com
SIC: 7323 Credit reporting services

(P-10765)
THE TAX CREDIT COMPANY
Also Called: Tax Credit Co, The
6464 W Sunset Blvd # 1150 (90028-8021)
PHONE..................323 927-0750
EMP: 100
SIC: 7323 8721 7291 Credit reporting services; Auditing services; Tax return preparation services

7331 Direct Mail Advertising Services

(P-10766)
ADVANTAGE MAILING LLC (PA)
Also Called: Advantage Mailing Service
1600 N Kraemer Blvd (92806-1410)
P.O. Box 66013 (92816-6013)
PHONE..................714 538-3881
Tom Ling, *Pr*
Brett Noss, *CFO*
EMP: 125 **EST:** 1994
SQ FT: 60,000
SALES (est): 91.39MM
SALES (corp-wide): 91.39MM **Privately Held**
Web: www.advantageinc.com
SIC: 7331 Mailing service

(P-10767)
AST SPORTSWEAR INC
P.O. Box 17219 (92817-7219)
PHONE..................714 223-2030
EMP: 395
Web: www.astsportswear.com
SIC: 7331 Mailing service
PA: Ast Sportswear, Inc.
2701 E Imperial Hwy
Brea CA

(P-10768)
BUSINESS SERVICES NETWORK CORP
1275 Fairfax Ave Ste 103 (94124-1759)
PHONE..................415 282-8161
Harry Yue, *Pr*
Cindy Yue, *
▲ **EMP:** 72 **EST:** 1984
SQ FT: 31,120
SALES (est): 4.28MM **Privately Held**
Web: www.bsnc.com
SIC: 7331 2752 7374 Mailing service; Offset printing; Data processing service

(P-10769)
CENTRAL VALLEY PRESORT INC
Also Called: Presort Center, The
4215 S Dans St (93277-7913)
PHONE..................559 906-2003
EMP: 85
Web: www.thepresort.com
SIC: 7331 2752 Mailing service; Promotional printing, lithographic

(P-10770)
DATABASE MARKETING GROUP INC
300 Commerce Ste 200 (92602-1305)
PHONE..................714 727-0800
John A Engstrom, *Pr*
Sharon M Engstrom, *VP*
EMP: 79 **EST:** 1991
SALES (est): 12.9MM **Privately Held**
Web: www.dbmgroup.com
SIC: 7331 8742 Mailing service; Marketing consulting services

(P-10771)
DIVERSIFIED MAILING INCORPORATED
Also Called: Diversified Direct
14407 S Alondra Blvd (90638-5504)
P.O. Box 2270777 (75222)
PHONE..................714 994-6245
TOLL FREE: 800
EMP: 157
SIC: 7331 Direct mail advertising services

(P-10772)
FINANCIAL STATEMENT SVCS INC (PA)
Also Called: Fssi
3300 S Fairview St (92704-7004)
PHONE..................714 436-3326
Jennifer Dietz, *CEO*
Jon Dietz, *
Karen Elsbury, *
Henry Perez, *
Dan Palmquist, *
EMP: 144 **EST:** 1984
SQ FT: 167,000
SALES (est): 31.62MM
SALES (corp-wide): 31.62MM **Privately Held**
Web: www.fssi-ca.com
SIC: 7331 7374 2759 Mailing service; Data processing and preparation; Laser printing

(P-10773)
LOMITA LOGISTICS LLC
Also Called: Xpo
3541 Lomita Blvd (90505-5016)
PHONE..................310 784-8485
EMP: 100
Web: internationalservices.rrd.com
SIC: 7331 Mailing service

(P-10774)
REAL ESTATE IMAGE INC (PA)
Also Called: Advanced Image Direct
1415 S Acacia Ave (92831-5317)
PHONE..................714 502-3900
Ty Mcmillin, *Pr*
Perry Wilson, *
Hugo Solorio, *Product Vice President*
EMP: 150 **EST:** 1981
SQ FT: 136,000
SALES (est): 29MM
SALES (corp-wide): 29MM **Privately Held**
Web: www.advancedimagedirect.com
SIC: 7331 2752 Mailing service; Commercial printing, lithographic

(P-10775)
RECALL MASTERS INC
740 Tunbridge Rd (94526-4338)
PHONE..................650 434-5211
Christopher J Miller, *Brnch Mgr*
EMP: 65
SALES (corp-wide): 2.47MM **Privately Held**
Web: www.recallmasters.com
SIC: 7331 Direct mail advertising services
PA: Recall Masters Inc.
23131 Verdugo Dr
Laguna Hills CA

(P-10776)
SPECTRUM INFORMATION SVCS LLC (PA)
3323 Spectrum (92618-3374)
PHONE..................949 752-7070
Curtis Pilon, *Pr*
Jim Bradford, *
EMP: 70 **EST:** 1991
SALES (est): 10.51MM **Privately Held**

7331 - Direct Mail Advertising Services (P-10777)

Web: www.spectruminformation.com
SIC: **7331** 7375 4813 Mailing service; Information retrieval services; Shipping documents preparation

(P-10777)
STAMPSCOM INC (PA)
Also Called: Stamps.com
1990 E Grand Ave (90245-5013)
PHONE..............................310 482-5800
Nathan Jones, *CEO*
Kyle Huebner, *Pr*
Jeff Carberry, *CFO*
Sebastian Buerba, *CMO*
EMP: 145 **EST:** 1996
SQ FT: 99,600
SALES (est): 757.98MM
SALES (corp-wide): 757.98MM **Privately Held**
Web: www.auctane.com
SIC: **7331** 5961 4813 Mailing service; Catalog and mail-order houses; Online service providers

(P-10778)
TRANSAMERICAN DIRECT INC
Also Called: Transamerican
355 State Pl (92029-1359)
PHONE..............................760 745-5343
Paul Barron, *CEO*
Eleanor Monica, *
▲ **EMP:** 100 **EST:** 1987
SALES (est): 9.45MM **Privately Held**
Web: www.transdirect.com
SIC: **7331** Mailing service

(P-10779)
UNIVERSAL MAIL DELIVERY SVC (PA)
Also Called: Universal Custom Courier
501 S Brand Blvd # 104 (91340-4000)
PHONE..............................818 365-3144
Robert M Reznick, *CEO*
Bernard Reznick, *
Barbara Reznick, *Stockholder*
Saddie Reznick, *Stockholder*
EMP: 95 **EST:** 1953
SQ FT: 1,000
SALES (est): 4.62MM
SALES (corp-wide): 4.62MM **Privately Held**
SIC: **7331** Mailing service

(P-10780)
VALASSIS DIRECT MAIL INC
1601 Response Rd Ste 100 (95815-5257)
PHONE..............................916 923-2398
Joseph Nix, *Brnch Mgr*
EMP: 68
Web: www.vericast.com
SIC: **7331** Mailing service
HQ: Valassis Direct Mail, Inc.
235 Great Pond Dr
Windsor CT
800 437-0479

7334 Photocopying And Duplicating Services

(P-10781)
ABI ATTORNEYS SERVICE INC (PA)
Also Called: ABI VIP Attorney Service
2015 W Park Ave (92373-6271)
P.O. Box 9240 (92375-2440)
PHONE..............................909 793-0613
Alice J Benge, *Pr*
Chuck Benge, *

EMP: 80 **EST:** 1985
SQ FT: 7,500
SALES (est): 4.69MM
SALES (corp-wide): 4.69MM **Privately Held**
SIC: **7334** Photocopying and duplicating services

(P-10782)
AMERICAN LEGAL COPY - OC LLC
655 W Broadway Ste 200 (92101-8476)
PHONE..............................415 777-4449
Joe Motz, *Prin*
EMP: 94 **EST:** 2003
SALES (est): 311.64K **Privately Held**
SIC: **7334** Photocopying and duplicating services
PA: American Legal Copy-Or, Llc
1001 4th Ave Ste 300
Seattle WA

(P-10783)
ARC DOCUMENT SOLUTIONS LLC
41521 Date St Apt 101 (92562-7088)
PHONE..............................951 445-4480
EMP: 689
SALES (corp-wide): 42.08MM **Privately Held**
Web: www.e-arc.com
SIC: **7334** Blueprinting service
PA: Arc Document Solutions, Llc
12657 Alcosta Blvd # 200
San Ramon CA
925 949-5100

(P-10784)
ARVATO USA LLC
Also Called: Arvato Digital Services
750 University Ave (95032-7695)
PHONE..............................408 402-3469
Dominik Dittrich, *Brnch Mgr*
EMP: 60
SALES (corp-wide): 54.57MM **Privately Held**
SIC: **7334** Photocopying and duplicating services
HQ: Arvato Usa Llc
51 Sawyer Rd Ste 620
Waltham MA
661 702-2700

(P-10785)
BPS REPROGRAPHICS SERVICES
Also Called: Blue Print Service
945 Bryant St (94103-4523)
PHONE..............................415 495-8700
EMP: 200
SIC: **7334** 7389 8744 7376 Photocopying and duplicating services; Printed circuitry graphic layout; Facilities support services; Computer facilities management

(P-10786)
COMPEX LEGAL SERVICES LLC
1225 Pear Ave # 110 (94043-1431)
PHONE..............................650 833-0460
EMP: 172
Web: www.compexlegal.com
SIC: **7334** 7389 Photocopying and duplicating services; Document embossing
PA: Compex Legal Services Llc
920 Main St Ste 115
Kansas City MO

(P-10787)
CRISP ENTERPRISES INC (PA)
Also Called: C2 Imaging
3180 Pullman St (92626-3323)
PHONE..............................714 668-5955
Gary Crisp, *CEO*
Julie Crisp, *
Arthur Gregory Lundeen Iii, *Stockholder*
William Govaars Ii, *Stockholder*
Barry Malkin, *
EMP: 60 **EST:** 2000
SQ FT: 28,000
SALES (est): 21.52MM
SALES (corp-wide): 21.52MM **Privately Held**
Web: www.crispimg.com
SIC: **7334** Blueprinting service

(P-10788)
FAR WESTERN GRAPHICS INC
Also Called: Denevi Digital
2642 Heritage Park Cir (95132-2211)
PHONE..............................408 481-9777
EMP: 65
Web: www.farwesterngraphics.com
SIC: **7334** 2752 Photocopying and duplicating services; Offset printing

(P-10789)
KNOX ATTORNEY SERVICE INC (PA)
Also Called: Knox Services
1550 Hotel Cir N Ste 440 (92108-2904)
PHONE..............................619 233-9700
Stephen Knox, *Pr*
Steve Knox, *
Robert Porambo, *
James Nemec, *
EMP: 165 **EST:** 1972
SQ FT: 165,929
SALES (est): 20.55MM
SALES (corp-wide): 20.55MM **Privately Held**
Web: www.knoxservices.com
SIC: **7334** 7389 7381 Photocopying and duplicating services; Process serving service; Private investigator

(P-10790)
LASR INC
Also Called: First Reprographic
1517 Beverly Blvd (90026-5704)
P.O. Box 749469 (90074-9469)
PHONE..............................877 591-9979
Martin Kayondo, *Pr*
Rick Matsumoto, *
EMP: 120 **EST:** 2002
SALES (est): 2.42MM **Privately Held**
SIC: **7334** Photocopying and duplicating services

(P-10791)
OFFICEMAX NORTH AMERICA INC
Also Called: OfficeMax
1465 Shaw Ave (93611-4056)
PHONE..............................559 298-0164
Armando Alvarez, *Admn*
EMP: 135
SALES (corp-wide): 8.49B **Publicly Held**
Web: www.officedepot.com
SIC: **7334** 5112 Photocopying and duplicating services; Office supplies, nec
HQ: Officemax North America, Inc.
263 Shuman Blvd Ste 145
Naperville IL
630 717-0791

(P-10792)
OFFICEMAX NORTH AMERICA INC
Also Called: OfficeMax
7075 Firestone Blvd (90241-4102)
PHONE..............................562 927-6444
Earl Dadis, *Brnch Mgr*
EMP: 144
SALES (corp-wide): 8.49B **Publicly Held**
SIC: **7334** Photocopying and duplicating services
HQ: Officemax North America, Inc.
263 Shuman Blvd Ste 145
Naperville IL
630 717-0791

(P-10793)
RIOT CREATIVE IMAGING
934 Venice Blvd (90015-3230)
PHONE..............................213 516-3160
EMP: 86 **EST:** 2010
SALES (est): 1.71MM **Privately Held**
Web: www.riotcolor.com
SIC: **7334** Blueprinting service

(P-10794)
SECOND IMAGE NATIONAL LLC (PA)
170 E Arrow Hwy (91773-3336)
P.O. Box 52969 (77052-2969)
PHONE..............................800 229-7477
Norman Fogwell, *CEO*
EMP: 145 **EST:** 1982
SQ FT: 25,500
SALES (est): 23.74MM
SALES (corp-wide): 23.74MM **Privately Held**
Web: www.ontellus.com
SIC: **7334** Photocopying and duplicating services

7335 Commercial Photography

(P-10795)
BRANDED ENTRMT NETWRK INC (PA)
14724 Ventura Blvd Ste 1200 (91403-3501)
PHONE..............................310 342-1500
Richard R Butler, *Pr*
Gary Shenk, *CEO*
Joe Schick, *CFO*
Jim Mitchell, *Senior Vice President Corporate Development*
EMP: 233 **EST:** 1989
SALES (est): 96.36MM **Privately Held**
Web: www.bengroup.com
SIC: **7335** Photographic studio, commercial

(P-10796)
DRONEBASE INC (PA)
2800 Olympic Blvd Fl 2 (90404-4101)
PHONE..............................310 684-3076
Daniel Burton, *CEO*
EMP: 70 **EST:** 2014
SALES (est): 10.92MM
SALES (corp-wide): 10.92MM **Privately Held**
Web: www.zeitview.com
SIC: **7335** Commercial photography

7336 Commercial Art And Graphic Design

(P-10797)
99DESIGNS INC (PA)

PRODUCTS & SERVICES SECTION
7336 - Commercial Art And Graphic Design (P-10817)

2201 Broadway Ste 815 (94612-3000)
P.O. Box 3330 (94609-0330)
PHONE..............................415 539-1088
Patrick Llewellyn, *CEO*
David Kaplan, *
EMP: 108 EST: 2011
SQ FT: 14,000
SALES (est): 14.97MM
SALES (corp-wide): 14.97MM **Privately Held**
Web: www.99designs.com
SIC: 7336 Graphic arts and related design

(P-10798)
BLT & ASSOCIATES INC
Also Called: BLT
6430 W Sunset Blvd Ste 800 (90028-7901)
PHONE..............................323 860-4000
Clive Baillie, *Pr*
Rick Lynch, *
Dawn Baillie, *
EMP: 170 EST: 1992
SQ FT: 15,000
SALES (est): 39.04MM **Privately Held**
SIC: 7336 Graphic arts and related design

(P-10799)
CINNABAR
4571 Electronics Pl (90039-1007)
PHONE..............................818 842-8190
EMP: 200 EST: 1982
SQ FT: 60,000
SALES (est): 21.6MM **Privately Held**
Web: www.cinnabar.com
SIC: 7336 3999 7819 Graphic arts and related design; Theatrical scenery; Sound effects and music production, motion picture

(P-10800)
CINNABAR CALIFORNIA INC
Also Called: Cinnabar
4571 Electronics Pl (90039-1007)
PHONE..............................818 842-8190
Leslie Crawford, *CFO*
Jonathan Katz, *
Basil Katz, *
Jeannie Lomma, *
EMP: 60 EST: 1982
SQ FT: 55,271
SALES (est): 9.25MM **Privately Held**
Web: www.cinnabar.com
SIC: 7336 8712 1796 Art design services; Architectural services; Installing building equipment

(P-10801)
CONTINENTAL GRAPHICS CORP (HQ)
Also Called: Continental Data Graphics
4060 N Lakewood Blvd Bldg 801 (90808-1700)
PHONE..............................714 503-4200
David Malmo, *CEO*
Michael Parven, *
James Mills, *
EMP: 200 EST: 1986
SQ FT: 45,000
SALES (est): 92.01MM
SALES (corp-wide): 66.61B **Publicly Held**
Web: services.boeing.com
SIC: 7336 8741 8711 8999 Commercial art and graphic design; Management services; Engineering services; Technical writing
PA: The Boeing Company
929 Long Bridge Dr
Arlington VA
703 414-6138

(P-10802)
COUNTY OF LOS ANGELES
Also Called: Gateway
1 Gateway Plz (90012-3745)
P.O. Box 90012 (90009-0012)
PHONE..............................213 922-6210
Roger Snoball, *Owner*
EMP: 245
SALES (corp-wide): 31.7B **Privately Held**
Web: www.lacounty.gov
SIC: 7336 9621 Commercial art and graphic design; Transportation department: government, nonoperating
PA: County Of Los Angeles
500 W Temple St Ste 437
Los Angeles CA
213 974-1101

(P-10803)
DANDREA GRAPHIC CORPORTION
Also Called: D'Andrea Graphics
6100 Gateway Dr (90630-4840)
PHONE..............................310 642-0260
David D'andrea, *CEO*
▲ EMP: 80 EST: 2005
SQ FT: 25,000
SALES (est): 17.81MM **Privately Held**
Web: www.dandreavisual.com
SIC: 7336 Graphic arts and related design

(P-10804)
DESIGNORY INC (HQ)
Also Called: Designory
211 E Ocean Blvd Ste 100 (90802-4808)
PHONE..............................562 624-0200
Paul Hosea, *CEO*
Janet M Thompson, *
Joel Fuller, *
Christine Ferguson, *
Matt Radigan, *
EMP: 115 EST: 1970
SALES (est): 26.4MM
SALES (corp-wide): 14.29B **Publicly Held**
Web: www.designory.com
SIC: 7336 Graphic arts and related design
PA: Omnicom Group Inc.
280 Park Ave Fl 31w
New York NY
212 415-3600

(P-10805)
DESTINATION MOON LP
Also Called: Turner Dockworth
615 Battery St Fl 6 (94111-1808)
PHONE..............................415 675-7777
David Turner, *CEO*
Bruce Duckworth, *
EMP: 70 EST: 1996
SQ FT: 5,600
SALES (est): 4.46MM **Privately Held**
SIC: 7336 Graphic arts and related design

(P-10806)
DIGITAL DOMAIN MEDIA GROUP INC
Also Called: Wyndcrest Dd Florida
12641 Beatrice St (90066-7003)
EMP: 813
SIC: 7336 7812 7371 7372 Commercial art and graphic design; Non-theatrical motion picture production; Custom computer programming services; Business oriented computer software

(P-10807)
FINAL FILM
Also Called: Flash Point Graphix
3620 W Valhalla Dr (91505-1127)
PHONE..............................323 467-0700
Thomas L Saliba, *Ch Bd*
Gregory D Davidiian, *
Gabe Lakatosh, *
Guy S Claudy, *
EMP: 62 EST: 1986
SQ FT: 20,000
SALES (est): 10.04MM **Privately Held**
Web: www.sandyalexander.com
SIC: 7336 Graphic arts and related design

(P-10808)
G3 ENTERPRISES INC
Also Called: Label Division
2612 Crows Landing Rd (95358-9400)
PHONE..............................209 341-5265
Tom Gallow, *Brnch Mgr*
EMP: 63
SALES (corp-wide): 116.51MM **Privately Held**
Web: www.g3enterprises.com
SIC: 7336 2752 Commercial art and graphic design; Commercial printing, lithographic
PA: G3 Enterprises, Inc.
502 E Whitmore Ave
Modesto CA
209 341-7515

(P-10809)
GEL-PAK LLC
31398 Huntwood Ave (94544-7818)
PHONE..............................510 576-2220
▲ EMP: 75 EST: 1997
SALES (est): 12.92MM
SALES (corp-wide): 50.07MM **Privately Held**
Web: www.gelpak.com
SIC: 7336 Package design
PA: Delphon Industries, Llc
31398 Huntwood Ave
Hayward CA
510 576-2220

(P-10810)
HARDING MKTG CMMUNICATIONS INC (PA)
Also Called: Harding & Associates
377 S Daniel Way (95128-5120)
PHONE..............................408 345-4545
James F Harding, *CEO*
Maria Richard, *
EMP: 70 EST: 1981
SQ FT: 10,000
SALES (est): 8.53MM
SALES (corp-wide): 8.53MM **Privately Held**
Web: www.hardingmarketing.com
SIC: 7336 Graphic arts and related design

(P-10811)
IDEO LP (PA)
2525 16th St Ste 200 (94103-4243)
PHONE..............................415 615-5000
Sandy Speicher, *CEO*
EMP: 135 EST: 1978
SALES (est): 46.48MM
SALES (corp-wide): 46.48MM **Privately Held**
Web: cantwait.ideo.com
SIC: 7336 7389 8711 Commercial art and graphic design; Design, commercial and industrial; Engineering services

(P-10812)
KIXEYE
333 Bush St Fl 19 (94104-2860)
PHONE..............................415 400-8280
EMP: 69 EST: 2019
SALES (est): 925.28K **Privately Held**
Web: corp.kixeye.com
SIC: 7336 Commercial art and graphic design

(P-10813)
LANDOR ASSOCIATES INTL LTD (HQ)
360 3rd St # 5 (94107-1213)
PHONE..............................415 365-1700
Lois Jacobs, *CEO*
Peter Law-gisiko, *Prin*
Cheryl Giovannoni, *
Craig Branigan, *
Ran Wadleigh, *
EMP: 200 EST: 1942
SALES (est): 50.26MM
SALES (corp-wide): 17.37B **Privately Held**
SIC: 7336 Graphic arts and related design
PA: Wpp Plc
22 Grenville Street
Jersey
370 707-1411

(P-10814)
MIRUM INC
Also Called: Digitaria
350 10th Ave Ste 1200 (92101-7433)
PHONE..............................619 237-5552
Daniel Khabie, *CEO*
Doug Hecht, *
Gary Correia, *
EMP: 200 EST: 1997
SQ FT: 4,000
SALES (est): 26.78MM
SALES (corp-wide): 17.37B **Privately Held**
SIC: 7336 Graphic arts and related design
HQ: Wunderman Thompson Llc
175 Greenwich St Fl 16
New York NY
212 210-7000

(P-10815)
MOTION THEORY INC
Also Called: Mirada
444 W Ocean Blvd Ste 1400 (90802-4522)
PHONE..............................310 396-9433
Andrew Merkin, *Dir*
Matthew Cullen, *
Janell Perez, *
EMP: 110 EST: 2000
SQ FT: 25,000
SALES (est): 4.81MM **Privately Held**
Web: www.motiontheory.com
SIC: 7336 7371 7812 Graphic arts and related design; Computer software development and applications; Motion picture production

(P-10816)
MOTIVATIONAL SYSTEMS INC (PA)
2200 Cleveland Ave (91950-6412)
PHONE..............................619 474-8246
Robert D Yound, *CEO*
David Cowan, *
Joe Jordan, *
Anthony Young, *
EMP: 100 EST: 1975
SQ FT: 50,000
SALES (est): 31.24MM
SALES (corp-wide): 31.24MM **Privately Held**
Web: www.motivational.com
SIC: 7336 3993 Graphic arts and related design; Signs and advertising specialties

(P-10817)
PULP STUDIO INCORPORATED
Also Called: CGB
2100 W 139th St (90249-2412)
P.O. Box 16231 (90209-2231)

7336 - Commercial Art And Graphic Design (P-10818)

PRODUCTS & SERVICES SECTION

PHONE.................................310 815-4999
Bernard Lax, *CEO*
Lynda N Lax, *
▲ **EMP**: 60 **EST**: 1940
SQ FT: 36,000
SALES (est): 12MM **Privately Held**
Web: www.pulpstudio.com
SIC: **7336** 3229 Commercial art and graphic design; Glass furnishings and accessories

(P-10818)
SCREENWORKS LLC
Also Called: Screenworks Nep
1900 Compton Ave Ste 101 (92881-7261)
PHONE.................................951 279-8877
Kevin Rabbitt, *CEO*
▲ **EMP**: 1306 **EST**: 2012
SALES (est): 9.68MM
SALES (corp-wide): 421.16MM **Privately Held**
Web: www.screenworksnep.com
SIC: **7336** Graphic arts and related design
HQ: Nep Supershooters, Lp
   2 Beta Dr
   Pittsburgh PA
   412 826-1414

(P-10819)
THINKBASIC INC
Also Called: Basic Agency
350 10th Ave (92101-7433)
PHONE.................................858 755-6922
Matthew Faulk, *CEO*
Ashley Reichel, *
Alisa Kuno, *
EMP: 120 **EST**: 2011
SALES (est): 6.31MM **Privately Held**
Web: www.basicagency.com
SIC: **7336** Graphic arts and related design

(P-10820)
TWENTIETH CNTURY FOX JAPAN INC
Also Called: News Corp - Fox
10201 W Pico Blvd (90064-2606)
PHONE.................................310 369-4636
Robert B Cohen, *CEO*
EMP: 4000 **EST**: 1981
SALES (est): 38.11MM
SALES (corp-wide): 82.72B **Publicly Held**
SIC: **7336** Film strip and slide producer
HQ: Tfcf Corporation
   1211 Ave Of The Americas
   New York NY
   212 852-7000

(P-10821)
UNIVERSITY CAL SAN DIEGO
Also Called: Graphics Department
9500 Gilman Dr Dept 908 (92093-0908)
PHONE.................................858 534-2377
Larry Fox, *Dir*
EMP: 367
SALES (corp-wide): 534.4MM **Privately Held**
Web: www.ucsd.edu
SIC: **7336** 8221 9411 Commercial art and graphic design; University; Administration of educational programs
HQ: University Of California, San Diego
   9500 Gilman Dr
   La Jolla CA
   858 534-2230

(P-10822)
XX ARTISTS LLC
12045 Waterfront Dr Ste 460 (90094-2999)
PHONE.................................503 871-5298
EMP: 70 **EST**: 2017
SALES (est): 2.69MM **Privately Held**

Web: www.xxartists.com
SIC: **7336** Graphic arts and related design

(P-10823)
YOUNG & RUBICAM LLC
Landor Associates
1001 Front St (94111-1424)
PHONE.................................415 365-1700
Courtney Reseer, *Dir*
EMP: 170
SALES (corp-wide): 17.37B **Privately Held**
Web: www.vmlyr.com
SIC: **7336** 8742 Commercial art and graphic design; Marketing consulting services
HQ: Young & Rubicam Llc
   3 Columbus Cir Fl 3 # 3
   New York NY
   212 210-3017

7338 Secretarial And Court Reporting

(P-10824)
ASAB INC (DH)
500 N Brand Blvd Fl 3 (91203-4725)
P.O. Box 29054 (91209-9054)
PHONE.................................818 551-7300
Alan Atkinson Baker, *CEO*
Sheila Atkinson-baker, *Pr*
EMP: 150 **EST**: 1987
SQ FT: 23,000
SALES (est): 36.07MM
SALES (corp-wide): 192.17MM **Privately Held**
Web: www.depo.com
SIC: **7338** Court reporting service
HQ: Veritext, Llc
   290 W Mount Pleasant Ave # 3
   Livingston NJ
   973 410-4040

(P-10825)
SOFTSCRIPT INC
2215 Campus Dr (90245-0001)
PHONE.................................310 451-2110
Howard Wisnicki, *CEO*
Yuriy Kotlyar, *
EMP: 1200 **EST**: 1996
SALES (est): 24.32MM **Privately Held**
Web: www.softscript.com
SIC: **7338** Court reporting service

7342 Disinfecting And Pest Control Services

(P-10826)
A-ABLE INC (PA)
Also Called: Fume-A-Pest & Termite Control
17801 Ventura Blvd (91316-3616)
PHONE.................................323 658-5779
Michael Herson, *Pr*
Jack Herson, *
EMP: 65 **EST**: 1971
SQ FT: 9,026
SALES (est): 4.58MM
SALES (corp-wide): 4.58MM **Privately Held**
Web: www.fumeapest.com
SIC: **7342** 1799 Pest control in structures; Steam cleaning of building exteriors

(P-10827)
ADVANCED INTEGRATED PEST MANAGEMENT
Also Called: Advanced Integrated Pest MGT
205 Kenroy Ln (95678-4201)
P.O. Box 1168 (95678-8168)

PHONE.................................916 786-2404
EMP: 215 **EST**: 1982
SALES (est): 10.82MM **Privately Held**
Web: www.advancedipm.com
SIC: **7342** Termite control

(P-10828)
AGURTO CORPORATION
888 N 1st St (95112-6345)
PHONE.................................408 564-6196
EMP: 119
Web: www.pestec.com
SIC: **7342** Pest control in structures
PA: Agurto Corporation
   3450 3rd St Ste 3f
   San Francisco CA

(P-10829)
BANKS PEST CONTROL
7440 District Blvd Ste A (93313-4821)
P.O. Box 113 (93302-0113)
PHONE.................................661 323-7858
Don Banks, *Pr*
Orland Banks, *
Janet Banks, *
EMP: 357 **EST**: 1969
SALES (est): 3.29MM
SALES (corp-wide): 2.7B **Publicly Held**
Web: www.bankspest.com
SIC: **7342** Pest control in structures
PA: Rollins, Inc.
   2170 Piedmont Rd Ne
   Atlanta GA
   404 888-2000

(P-10830)
BUSY BEE LLC
36798 Pictor Ave (92563-4202)
PHONE.................................951 404-9900
EMP: 80
SALES (corp-wide): 185.07K **Privately Held**
SIC: **7342** Disinfecting and pest control services
PA: Busy Bee Llc
   27100 Sunnyridge Rd
   Pls Vrds Pnsl CA

(P-10831)
CATS USA INC
Also Called: Cats U S A Pest Control
5683 Whitnall Hwy (91601-2213)
P.O. Box 151 (91603-0151)
PHONE.................................818 506-1000
Hirotaka Otomo, *Ch Bd*
EMP: 100 **EST**: 1971
SQ FT: 3,900
SALES (est): 9.76MM **Privately Held**
Web: www.catspestcontrol.com
SIC: **7342** Pest control in structures
HQ: Cats, Inc.
   15-13, Nampeidaicho
   Shibuya-Ku TKY

(P-10832)
CLARK PEST CTRL STOCKTON INC (HQ)
555 N Guild Ave (95240-0809)
P.O. Box 1480 (95241-1480)
PHONE.................................209 368-7152
Gary Rollins, *CEO*
EMP: 70 **EST**: 1950
SQ FT: 2,500
SALES (est): 85.47MM
SALES (corp-wide): 2.7B **Publicly Held**
Web: www.clarkpest.com
SIC: **7342** Pest control in structures
PA: Rollins, Inc.
   2170 Piedmont Rd Ne
   Atlanta GA
   404 888-2000

(P-10833)
CLARK PEST CTRL STOCKTON INC
480 E Service Rd (95358-9491)
PHONE.................................209 524-6384
Ron Fair, *Mgr*
EMP: 61
SALES (corp-wide): 2.7B **Publicly Held**
Web: www.clarkpest.com
SIC: **7342** Pest control in structures
HQ: Clark Pest Control Of Stockton, Inc.
   555 N Guild Ave
   Lodi CA
   209 368-7152

(P-10834)
CLEANRITE INC
814 Striker Ave Ste B (95834-2475)
PHONE.................................916 381-1321
Eric Martin, *Brnch Mgr*
EMP: 64
SALES (corp-wide): 30.81MM **Privately Held**
Web: www.cleanrite-buildrite.com
SIC: **7342** 7217 Disinfecting services; Carpet and upholstery cleaning
PA: Cleanrite, Inc.
   2684 Highway 32 Ste 100
   Chico CA
   530 891-0333

(P-10835)
CORKYS PEST CONTROL INC
909 Rancheros Dr (92069-3028)
PHONE.................................760 432-8801
Corky Mizer, *Pr*
▲ **EMP**: 60 **EST**: 1967
SQ FT: 5,000
SALES (est): 9.84MM **Privately Held**
Web: www.corkyspest.com
SIC: **7342** 0782 2879 5211 Pest control in structures; Lawn and garden services; Insecticides and pesticides; Insulation material, building
HQ: Anticimex Inc.
   106 Allen Rd Ste 310
   Basking Ridge NJ
   800 618-2847

(P-10836)
CRANE ACQUISITION INC
Also Called: Crane Pest Control
2700 Geary Blvd (94118-3406)
PHONE.................................415 922-1666
Harold Stein, *Pr*
Eugene Iarocci, *
Harry J Cynkus, *
EMP: 916 **EST**: 1930
SQ FT: 6,000
SALES (est): 11.73MM
SALES (corp-wide): 2.7B **Publicly Held**
Web: www.cranepestcontrol.com
SIC: **7342** Exterminating and fumigating
PA: Rollins, Inc.
   2170 Piedmont Rd Ne
   Atlanta GA
   404 888-2000

(P-10837)
HOMEGUARD INCORPORATED (PA)
Also Called: Redrocks Fumigation
510 Madera Ave (95112-2918)
PHONE.................................855 331-1900
James Steffenson Junior, *Pr*
Jim Hessling, *
▲ **EMP**: 75 **EST**: 1988
SQ FT: 6,000
SALES (est): 11.63MM
SALES (corp-wide): 11.63MM **Privately Held**

PRODUCTS & SERVICES SECTION

7349 - Building Maintenance Services, Nec (P-10859)

Web: www.homeguard.com
SIC: 7342 Pest control in structures

(P-10838)
NATURAL ORANGE INC
Also Called: Planet Orange
434 Park Ave (95110-2614)
PHONE..................408 963-6868
Nathan Cocozza, *Pr*
Mathew Warwick, *VP*
EMP: 68 **EST:** 2008
SQ FT: 17,000
SALES (est): 12.31MM **Privately Held**
Web: www.planetorange.com
SIC: 7342 Pest control in structures

(P-10839)
RENTOKIL NORTH AMERICA INC
1160 Sandhill Ave (90746-1315)
PHONE..................714 517-9000
EMP: 64
SALES (corp-wide): 4.47B **Privately Held**
Web: www.westernexterminator.com
SIC: 7342 Pest control in structures
HQ: Rentokil North America, Inc.
1125 Berkshire Blvd # 15
Wyomissing PA
470 643-3300

(P-10840)
RENTOKIL NORTH AMERICA INC
Also Called: Target Specialty Products
1155 Mabury Rd (95133-1029)
PHONE..................408 293-6032
Casey Brierley, *Mgr*
EMP: 70
SQ FT: 5,000
SALES (corp-wide): 4.47B **Privately Held**
Web: www.westernexterminator.com
SIC: 7342 5191 5169 Pest control in structures; Farm supplies; Chemicals and allied products, nec
HQ: Rentokil North America, Inc.
1125 Berkshire Blvd # 15
Wyomissing PA
470 643-3300

(P-10841)
RENTOKIL NORTH AMERICA INC
311 N Crescent Way (92801-6709)
PHONE..................714 563-2450
Julius C Ehrlich, *Brnch Mgr*
EMP: 70
SALES (corp-wide): 4.47B **Privately Held**
SIC: 7342 Pest control in structures
HQ: Rentokil North America, Inc.
1125 Berkshire Blvd # 15
Wyomissing PA
470 643-3300

(P-10842)
RENTOKIL NORTH AMERICA INC
3481 Arden Rd (94545-3905)
PHONE..................650 579-6565
Larry Newman, *Mgr*
EMP: 74
SALES (corp-wide): 4.47B **Privately Held**
Web: www.westernexterminator.com
SIC: 7342 Pest control in structures
HQ: Rentokil North America, Inc.
1125 Berkshire Blvd # 15
Wyomissing PA
470 643-3300

(P-10843)
RENTOKIL NORTH AMERICA INC
Also Called: Target Specialty Products
15415 Marquardt Ave (90670-5711)
P.O. Box 3408 (90670-1408)
PHONE..................562 802-2238
Rich Records, *Mgr*
EMP: 100
SALES (corp-wide): 4.47B **Privately Held**
SIC: 7342 Pest control in structures
HQ: Rentokil North America, Inc.
1125 Berkshire Blvd # 15
Wyomissing PA
470 643-3300

(P-10844)
YOUR WAY FUMIGATION INC
1660 Chicago Ave Ste N9 (92507-2053)
PHONE..................951 699-9116
Jose Manuel Aguilar, *Pr*
EMP: 90 **EST:** 2006
SALES (est): 2.36MM **Privately Held**
Web: www.ywfumigation.com
SIC: 7342 Pest control in structures

7349 Building Maintenance Services, Nec

(P-10845)
911 RESTORATION ENTPS INC
6932 Gross Ave (91307-2432)
PHONE..................832 887-2582
Ofer Kedem, *Brnch Mgr*
EMP: 283
SALES (corp-wide): 19.32MM **Privately Held**
Web: www.911restorationlosangeles.com
SIC: 7349 Building maintenance services, nec
PA: 911 Restoration Enterprises, Inc.
7721 Densmore Ave
Van Nuys CA
818 373-4880

(P-10846)
ABM ELCTRCAL LTG SOLUTIONS INC
6940 Koll Center Pkwy Ste 100 (94566-3100)
PHONE..................408 399-3030
EMP: 65
SALES (corp-wide): 7.81B **Publicly Held**
SIC: 7349 Lighting maintenance service
HQ: Abm Electrical & Lighting Solutions, Inc.
14201 Franklin Ave
Tustin CA
866 226-2838

(P-10847)
ABM JANITORIAL SERVICES INC
1335 N Plaza Dr Ste C (93291-8838)
PHONE..................559 651-1612
Tony Bautista, *Brnch Mgr*
EMP: 90
SALES (corp-wide): 7.81B **Publicly Held**
Web: www.abm.com
SIC: 7349 Janitorial service, contract basis
HQ: Abm Janitorial Services, Inc.
1111 Fannin St Ste 1500
Houston TX
866 624-1520

(P-10848)
ACME BUILDING MAINT CO INC (DH)
941 Catherine St (95002)
PHONE..................408 263-5911
Richard Sanchez, *Pr*
Henry Sanchez, *
Solomon Wong, *
EMP: 80 **EST:** 1970
SQ FT: 8,000
SALES (est): 66.8MM
SALES (corp-wide): 7.81B **Publicly Held**
SIC: 7349 Janitorial service, contract basis
HQ: Gca Services Group, Inc.
1350 Euclid Ave Ste 1500
Cleveland OH
800 422-8760

(P-10849)
ADVANCED CLNROOM MCRCLEAN CORP
Also Called: A C M
3250 S Susan St Ste A (92704-6807)
PHONE..................714 751-1152
Janet Ford, *CEO*
▲ **EMP:** 200 **EST:** 1982
SQ FT: 3,500
SALES (est): 19.65MM **Privately Held**
Web: www.advancedcleanroom.com
SIC: 7349 8734 Cleaning service, industrial or commercial; Testing laboratories

(P-10850)
AHTNA FACILITY SERVICES INC
3100 Beacon Blvd (95691-3483)
PHONE..................916 375-0199
EMP: 150
SALES (corp-wide): 517.44MM **Privately Held**
Web: www.ahtna.com
SIC: 7349 Janitorial service, contract basis
HQ: Ahtna Facility Services, Incorporated
110 W 38th Ave Ste 200e
Anchorage AK

(P-10851)
ALL-RITE LEASING COMPANY INC
950 S Coast Dr Ste 110 (92626-1778)
PHONE..................714 957-1822
Chris Schran, *Pr*
Pauline Rosenberg, *
EMP: 269 **EST:** 1991
SALES (est): 2.44MM **Privately Held**
SIC: 7349 Building maintenance services, nec

(P-10852)
AMERI-KLEEN
Also Called: Ameri-Kleen Building Services
313 W Beach St (95076-4508)
P.O. Box 2167 (95077-2167)
PHONE..................831 722-8888
Marisol Tavera, *Brnch Mgr*
EMP: 219
Web: www.ameri-kleen.com
SIC: 7349 Building maintenance services, nec
PA: Ameri-Kleen
119 W Beach St
Watsonville CA

(P-10853)
AMERI-KLEEN
Also Called: Ameri-Kleen Building Services
1023 E Grand Ave (93420-2504)
PHONE..................805 546-0706
Dan Erpenbach, *Brnch Mgr*
EMP: 220

Web: www.ameri-kleen.com
SIC: 7349 Janitorial service, contract basis
PA: Ameri-Kleen
119 W Beach St
Watsonville CA

(P-10854)
AMERICAN BLDG MAINT CO OF ILL
44870 Osgood Rd (94539-6101)
PHONE..................510 573-1618
EMP: 310
SALES (corp-wide): 7.81B **Publicly Held**
SIC: 7349 Janitorial service, contract basis
HQ: American Building Maintenance Co Of Illinois, Inc
420 Taylor St 200
San Francisco CA
415 351-4386

(P-10855)
AMERICAN BLDG MAINT CO-WEST (HQ)
Also Called: American Building Maintenance
75 Broadway Ste 111 (94111-1423)
PHONE..................415 733-4000
Henrik Slipsager, *Pr*
Douglas Bowlus, *
Harry H Kahn, *
EMP: 150 **EST:** 1986
SALES (est): 9.27MM
SALES (corp-wide): 7.81B **Publicly Held**
SIC: 7349 Janitorial service, contract basis
PA: Abm Industries Incorporated
1 Liberty Plz Fl 7
New York NY
212 297-0200

(P-10856)
AMERICAN BUILDING SERVICE INC
4578 Crow Canyon Pl (94552-4804)
P.O. Box 32 (94577-0003)
PHONE..................510 483-5120
Rui Donaldo Teixeira Canha, *Pr*
EMP: 100 **EST:** 1988
SALES (est): 977.22K **Privately Held**
Web: www.absbayarea.com
SIC: 7349 Janitorial service, contract basis

(P-10857)
AQUACLEAN JANITORIAL
9403 Compass Point Dr S (92126-5536)
P.O. Box 722557 (92172-2557)
PHONE..................858 537-9090
Amir B Chaudri, *Pr*
EMP: 65 **EST:** 1996
SALES (est): 1.02MM **Privately Held**
SIC: 7349 Janitorial service, contract basis

(P-10858)
ARAMARK FACILITY SERVICES LLC
Also Called: Aramark
941 W 35th St (90007-4002)
PHONE..................213 740-8968
Ron Cote, *Mgr*
EMP: 100
Web: www.aramark.es
SIC: 7349 Janitorial service, contract basis
HQ: Aramark Facility Services, Llc
2400 Market St Ste 209
Philadelphia PA
215 238-3000

(P-10859)
AVALON BUILDING MAINT INC
1832 Commercenter Cir (92408-3430)
PHONE..................714 693-2407

7349 - Building Maintenance Services, Nec (P-10860)

Steve J Healis, *CEO*
Tom Devlin, *
Tom Poston, *
EMP: 400 **EST:** 1988
SQ FT: 5,000
SALES (est): 4.5MM **Privately Held**
Web:
www.avalonbuildingmaintenance-ie.com
SIC: 7349 Janitorial service, contract basis

(P-10860)
BERGENSONS PROPERTY SVCS INC
Also Called: Solve All Facility Services
3605 Ocean Ranch Blvd Ste 200 (92056-2695)
PHONE..................760 631-5111
Mark M Minasian, *CEO*
Aram Minasian, *
EMP: 2000 **EST:** 1984
SQ FT: 2,000
SALES (est): 15.03MM **Privately Held**
Web: www.kbs-services.com
SIC: 7349 Building maintenance, except repairs

(P-10861)
BERKELEY UNIFIED SCHOOL DST
Also Called: Maintenance Department
1707 Russell St (94703-2119)
PHONE..................510 644-6250
Rhonda Bacot, *Dir*
EMP: 61
SALES (corp-wide): 249.87MM **Privately Held**
Web: www.berkeleyschools.net
SIC: 7349 Building maintenance services, nec
PA: Berkeley Unified School District
2020 Bonar St Rm 202
Berkeley CA
510 644-6150

(P-10862)
BILLING SVCS PLUS DBA APEX JNT
Also Called: Apex Janitorial Solutions
70 Dorman Ave (94124-1809)
PHONE..................415 604-3515
Gina Gregori, *Prin*
EMP: 99 **EST:** 2016
SQ FT: 300
SALES (est): 4.06MM **Privately Held**
SIC: 7349 Building and office cleaning services

(P-10863)
BISSELL BROTHERS JANITORIAL
Also Called: Bissell Bros Bldg Maint Servic
3207 Luyung Dr (95742-6862)
PHONE..................916 635-1852
David Bissell, *CEO*
EMP: 80 **EST:** 1980
SQ FT: 2,400
SALES (est): 1.03MM **Privately Held**
Web: www.cleaningcrew.com
SIC: 7349 Janitorial service, contract basis

(P-10864)
BMS CATASTROPHE INC
Also Called: BMS CATASTROPHE, INC.
30964 San Benito St (94544-7935)
PHONE..................877 730-1948
Kirk A Blackmon, *Brnch Mgr*
EMP: 87
SALES (corp-wide): 286.08MM **Privately Held**
Web: www.bmscat.com
SIC: 7349 Building maintenance services, nec
HQ: Bms Catastrophe, Llc
5718 Airport Fwy
Haltom City TX
817 332-2770

(P-10865)
BRILLIANT GENERAL MAINT INC (PA)
Also Called: Bgm
954 Chestnut St (95110-1504)
PHONE..................408 287-6708
Daniel Montes, *CEO*
EMP: 60 **EST:** 1983
SQ FT: 6,000
SALES (est): 10.2MM **Privately Held**
Web: www.rcc-bgm.com
SIC: 7349 Building maintenance, except repairs

(P-10866)
BRITEWORKS INC
Also Called: Briteworks
620 N Commercial Ave (91723-1309)
PHONE..................626 337-0099
Anita Ron, *Pr*
EMP: 75 **EST:** 2001
SQ FT: 4,800
SALES (est): 4.16MM **Privately Held**
Web: www.briteworks.com
SIC: 7349 Janitorial service, contract basis

(P-10867)
BZYA CORPORATION
100 Spectrum Center Dr Ste 900 (92618-4962)
PHONE..................949 656-3220
Susan Luo, *CEO*
EMP: 325 **EST:** 2017
SALES (est): 7.22MM **Privately Held**
SIC: 7349 Janitorial service, contract basis

(P-10868)
C&W FACILITY SERVICES INC
Also Called: Dtz
3011 Townsgate Rd Ste 410 (91361-5882)
PHONE..................805 267-7123
EMP: 1961
SALES (corp-wide): 10.11B **Privately Held**
Web: www.cwservices.com
SIC: 7349 Janitorial service, contract basis
HQ: C&W Facility Services Inc.
117 Kendrick St Ste 250
Needham MA
888 751-9100

(P-10869)
C&W FACILITY SERVICES INC
10 Almaden Blvd Ste 400 (95113-2226)
PHONE..................408 600-4169
EMP: 1961
SALES (corp-wide): 10.11B **Privately Held**
Web: www.cwservices.com
SIC: 7349 Janitorial service, contract basis
HQ: C&W Facility Services Inc.
117 Kendrick St Ste 250
Needham MA
888 751-9100

(P-10870)
CALICO BUILDING SERVICES INC
Also Called: Calico
15550 Rockfield Blvd Ste C (92618-2712)
PHONE..................949 380-8707
Ron Strand, *Pr*
Christopher Guidry, *
Thomas Miquelon, *
Orlando Fernandez, *
EMP: 185 **EST:** 1986
SQ FT: 1,700
SALES (est): 18.18MM **Privately Held**
Web: www.calicoweb.com
SIC: 7349 Janitorial service, contract basis

(P-10871)
CALIDAD INDUSTRIES INC
1700 Park St Ste 220 (94501-1571)
PHONE..................510 698-7200
Mathew Hoffman, *CEO*
Patrick Schmalz, *
Robert Taylor, *
James Caponigro, *
Virginia Robbins, *Pr*
EMP: 301 **EST:** 1989
SQ FT: 35,000
SALES (est): 2.31MM
SALES (corp-wide): 43.78MM **Privately Held**
Web: www.calidadindustries.org
SIC: 7349 8742 Building maintenance services, nec; Management consulting services
PA: Goodwill Industries Of The Greater East Bay, Inc.
1301 30th Ave
Oakland CA
510 698-7200

(P-10872)
CAPPSTONE INC
1699 Valencia St (94110-5012)
PHONE..................415 821-6757
EMP: 150 **EST:** 2012
SALES (est): 6.53MM **Privately Held**
Web: www.nomoredirt.com
SIC: 7349 Janitorial service, contract basis

(P-10873)
CITY OF SACRAMENTO
Also Called: Department of Public Works
5730 24th St Bldg 9 (95822-3604)
PHONE..................916 808-4044
Juan Montanez, *Mgr*
EMP: 256
Web: www.cityofsacramento.gov
SIC: 7349 9631 Building maintenance services, nec; Regulation, administration of utilities, Local government
PA: City Of Sacramento
915 I St Fl 5
Sacramento CA
916 808-5300

(P-10874)
CITY OF SAN MATEO
Also Called: Corporate Yard
1949 Pacific Blvd (94403-1430)
PHONE..................650 522-7300
Vernon Ficklind, *Mgr*
EMP: 60
SALES (corp-wide): 194.84MM **Privately Held**
Web: www.cityofsanmateo.org
SIC: 7349 9111 Building maintenance services, nec; Mayors' office
PA: City Of San Mateo
330 W 20th Ave
San Mateo CA
650 522-7000

(P-10875)
CJS MODEL HOME MAINT INC
240 Spring St (94566-6626)
P.O. Box 5547 (94566-1547)
PHONE..................925 485-3280
Carrie Wevill, *Pr*
Richard Wevill, *
EMP: 70 **EST:** 1990
SQ FT: 2,200
SALES (est): 2.03MM **Privately Held**
Web: www.cjsmodelhome.com
SIC: 7349 Building component cleaning service

(P-10876)
COASTAL BUILDING SERVICES INC
1433 W Central Park Ave N (92802-1417)
PHONE..................714 775-2855
Hipolito G Arias, *CEO*
Brett Dunstan, *
EMP: 300 **EST:** 1998
SALES (est): 9.27MM **Privately Held**
Web: www.cbsinc.us
SIC: 7349 Janitorial service, contract basis

(P-10877)
COME LAND MAINT SVC CO INC
1419 N San Fernando Blvd Ste 250 (91504-4185)
PHONE..................818 567-2455
Grace H Lee, *Pr*
William Lee, *
EMP: 513 **EST:** 1992
SQ FT: 12,750
SALES (est): 5.34MM **Privately Held**
SIC: 7349 Janitorial service, contract basis
PA: Come Land, Inc.
1419 N San Fernando Blvd # 250
Burbank CA

(P-10878)
CONTRACT SERVICES GROUP INC
Also Called: Celex Solutions
480 Capricorn St (92821-3203)
P.O. Box 8815 (92822-5815)
PHONE..................714 582-1800
John Pearce, *CEO*
Casey Pearce, *
EMP: 250 **EST:** 2003
SALES (est): 24.57MM **Privately Held**
Web: www.csgcares.com
SIC: 7349 Janitorial service, contract basis

(P-10879)
COUNTY OF BUTTE
Also Called: Butte County Facillities Svcs
2081 2nd St (95965-3413)
PHONE..................530 538-7407
Grant Hutchiker, *Mgr*
EMP: 61
Web: www.buttecounty.net
SIC: 7349 9111 Building maintenance services, nec; County supervisors' and executives' office
PA: County Of Butte
25 County Center Dr # 125
Oroville CA
530 538-7701

(P-10880)
CREATIVE MAINTENANCE SYSTEMS
1340 Reynolds Ave Ste 111 (92614-5503)
PHONE..................949 852-2871
Bill Koop, *Pr*
Christina Alexander, *
EMP: 100 **EST:** 2000
SQ FT: 2,000
SALES (est): 2.13MM **Privately Held**
SIC: 7349 Janitorial service, contract basis

7349 - Building Maintenance Services, Nec (P-10903)

(P-10881)
CROWN BUILDING MAINTENANCE CO
1832 Tribute Rd Ste H (95815-4309)
PHONE..................916 920-9556
Jeff Marquis, *Prin*
EMP: 280
SALES (corp-wide): 7.81B **Publicly Held**
SIC: 7349 1623 Janitorial service, contract basis; Water, sewer, and utility lines
HQ: Crown Building Maintenance Co.
  600 Harrison St Ste 600 # 600
  San Francisco CA
  415 981-8070

(P-10882)
CROWN BUILDING MAINTENANCE CO
Also Called: Able Building Maintenance
14201 Franklin Ave (92780-7008)
PHONE..................714 434-9494
Robert Hughes, *CEO*
EMP: 373
SALES (corp-wide): 7.81B **Publicly Held**
SIC: 7349 Janitorial service, contract basis
HQ: Crown Building Maintenance Co.
  600 Harrison St Ste 600 # 600
  San Francisco CA
  415 981-8070

(P-10883)
CROWN BUILDING MAINTENANCE CO
600 Harrison St Ste 600 (94107-1390)
PHONE..................303 680-3713
EMP: 280
SALES (corp-wide): 7.81B **Publicly Held**
SIC: 7349 8711 Janitorial service, contract basis; Engineering services
HQ: Crown Building Maintenance Co.
  600 Harrison St Ste 600 # 600
  San Francisco CA
  415 981-8070

(P-10884)
CROWN BUILDING MAINTENANCE CO
5482 Complex St Ste 108 (92123-1125)
PHONE..................858 560-5785
EMP: 280
SALES (corp-wide): 7.81B **Publicly Held**
SIC: 7349 8711 Janitorial service, contract basis; Engineering services
HQ: Crown Building Maintenance Co.
  600 Harrison St Ste 600 # 600
  San Francisco CA
  415 981-8070

(P-10885)
CROWN BUILDING MAINTENANCE CO
Also Called: Able Building Maintenance
1143 N Market Blvd Ste 3 (95834-1913)
PHONE..................415 546-6534
EMP: 280
SALES (corp-wide): 7.81B **Publicly Held**
SIC: 7349 Janitorial service, contract basis
HQ: Crown Building Maintenance Co.
  600 Harrison St Ste 600 # 600
  San Francisco CA
  415 981-8070

(P-10886)
CROWN ENERGY SERVICES INC
Also Called: Able Engineering Services
2601 S Figueroa St Bldg 1 (90007)
PHONE..................213 765-7800
Ed Figueroa, *Mgr*
EMP: 977
SALES (corp-wide): 7.81B **Publicly Held**
SIC: 7349 Janitorial service, contract basis
HQ: Crown Energy Services, Inc.
  600 Harrison St Ste 600 # 600
  San Francisco CA

(P-10887)
CUSTOMIZED PERFORMANCE INC
780 Montague Expy Ste 201 (95131-1322)
PHONE..................408 437-1720
EMP: 200
Web: www.custgroup.com
SIC: 7349 Janitorial service, contract basis

(P-10888)
DAVE CALHOUN AND ASSOC LLC
2575 Stanwell Dr Ste 100 (94520-4838)
PHONE..................925 688-1234
Sam Martinovich, *CEO*
Dave Calhoun, *
EMP: 195 EST: 1985
SALES (est): 4.4MM **Privately Held**
SIC: 7349 Janitorial service, contract basis

(P-10889)
DIAMOND CONTRACT SERVICES INC
11432 Vanowen St (91605-6220)
PHONE..................818 565-3554
EMP: 350
Web: www.diamondcontract.com
SIC: 7349 8748 Building maintenance, except repairs; Business consulting, nec

(P-10890)
DIMAR ENTERPRISES INC
Also Called: Drymaster
26021 Pala Ste 150 (92691-2718)
PHONE..................949 492-1100
Diane Combs, *CEO*
EMP: 182 EST: 2014
SALES (est): 9.44MM **Privately Held**
Web: www.drymaster.com
SIC: 7349 Building maintenance services, nec

(P-10891)
DMS FACILITY SERVICES INC
Also Called: D M S
3137 Skyway Ct (94539-5910)
PHONE..................510 656-9400
Loren Dotts, *Mgr*
EMP: 1165
SALES (corp-wide): 42.01MM **Privately Held**
Web: www.dmsfacilityservices.com
SIC: 7349 0782 Building maintenance, except repairs; Lawn and garden services
PA: Dms Facility Services, Inc.
  1040 Arroyo Dr
  South Pasadena CA
  626 305-8500

(P-10892)
DMS FACILITY SERVICES INC
Also Called: DMS
2861 E Coronado St (92806-2504)
PHONE..................949 975-1366
Douglas Gregory, *Prin*
EMP: 1325
SALES (corp-wide): 42.01MM **Privately Held**
Web: www.dmsfacilityservices.com
SIC: 7349 Janitorial service, contract basis
PA: Dms Facility Services, Inc.
  1040 Arroyo Dr
  South Pasadena CA
  626 305-8500

(P-10893)
ELITE CRAFTSMAN (PA)
Also Called: Stockmar Industrial
2763 Saint Louis Ave (90755-2025)
P.O. Box 90458 (90809-0458)
PHONE..................562 989-3511
William C Stockmar, *Pr*
Linda Pierson, *Sec*
George N Negrete, *VP*
EMP: 130 EST: 1972
SQ FT: 10,000
SALES (est): 7.89MM
SALES (corp-wide): 7.89MM **Privately Held**
SIC: 7349 Janitorial service, contract basis

(P-10894)
EXCEL BUILDING SERVICES LLC
Also Called: Ebs New Mexico
1061 Serpentine Ln Ste H (94566-4793)
PHONE..................925 474-1080
Jennifer Fabrique, *CEO*
Jack Fabrique, *
Scott Henley, *
Steve Sui, *
EMP: 1300 EST: 1998
SQ FT: 5,000
SALES (est): 39.4MM **Privately Held**
Web: www.excelbuildingservices.com
SIC: 7349 Janitorial service, contract basis

(P-10895)
FACILITY MASTERS INC (PA)
1604 Kerley Dr (95112-4815)
PHONE..................408 436-9090
Ramsin Bitmansour, *CEO*
James Machado, *
Osvaldo Almeida, *
EMP: 230 EST: 1980
SQ FT: 7,000
SALES (est): 14.03MM
SALES (corp-wide): 14.03MM **Privately Held**
Web: www.facilitymasters.com
SIC: 7349 Janitorial service, contract basis

(P-10896)
FLAGSHIP AIRPORT SERVICES INC (HQ)
Also Called: Flagship Airport Services
1050 N 5th St Ste E (95112-4400)
PHONE..................408 977-0155
David Pasek, *Prin*
Mark Cornish, *
Todd Jacobs, *Prin*
Jim Mikacich, *Prin*
Rick Olesek, *
EMP: 240 EST: 2003
SQ FT: 40,000
SALES (est): 22.6MM **Privately Held**
Web: www.flagshipinc.com
SIC: 7349 Janitorial service, contract basis
PA: Flagship Enterprises Holding, Inc.
  405 S Kimball Ave
  Southlake TX

(P-10897)
FLAGSHIP AIRPORT SERVICES INC
1830 W 208th St (90501-1807)
PHONE..................310 328-8221
EMP: 72
Web: www.flagshipinc.com
SIC: 7349 Janitorial service, contract basis
HQ: Flagship Airport Services, Inc.
  1050 N 5th St Ste E
  San Jose CA
  408 977-0155

(P-10898)
FLAGSHIP FACILITY SERVICES INC (HQ)
Also Called: Flagship
1050 N 5th St Ste E (95112-4400)
P.O. Box 612140 (95161-2140)
PHONE..................408 977-0155
EMP: 500 EST: 1988
SALES (est): 132.06MM **Privately Held**
Web: www.flagshipinc.com
SIC: 7349 Building and office cleaning services
PA: Flagship Enterprises Holding, Inc.
  405 S Kimball Ave
  Southlake TX

(P-10899)
FLAGSHIP FACILITY SERVICES INC
1050 N 5th St Ste E (95112-4400)
PHONE..................408 977-0155
Dave M Pasek, *CEO*
EMP: 323
Web: www.flagshipinc.com
SIC: 7349 Janitorial service, contract basis
HQ: Flagship Facility Services, Inc.
  1050 N 5th St Ste E
  San Jose CA
  408 977-0155

(P-10900)
FLAIR BUILDING SERVICES
Also Called: Flair Building Maintanance
3470 Edward Ave (95054-2130)
PHONE..................408 987-4040
Oscar Pena, *Pr*
John Mcevoy, *CEO*
Shirely Mcevoy, *Sec*
EMP: 90 EST: 1976
SQ FT: 2,400
SALES (est): 2.5MM **Privately Held**
Web: www.flairbuildingsvcs.com
SIC: 7349 Janitorial service, contract basis

(P-10901)
FLUOR FACILITY & PLANT SVCS
124 Blossom Hill Rd Ste H # 1524 (95123-2397)
PHONE..................408 256-1333
Brett Heckel, *Fin Mgr*
EMP: 125
SALES (corp-wide): 13.74B **Publicly Held**
SIC: 7349 Building maintenance services, nec
HQ: Fluor Facility & Plant Services, Inc
  3 Polaris Way
  Aliso Viejo CA

(P-10902)
GAMBRELL BONDIE
Also Called: Ladera-Fox Hills Self Storage
5855 W Centinela Ave (90045-1503)
P.O. Box 8896 (90008-0896)
PHONE..................310 641-8408
Bondie Gambrell, *Prin*
EMP: 60 EST: 1999
SALES (est): 1.24MM **Privately Held**
SIC: 7349 8741 7319 Cleaning service, industrial or commercial; Management services; Media buying service

(P-10903)
GLOBAL BUILDING SERVICES INC (PA)
27433 Tourney Rd Ste 280 (91355-5619)
PHONE..................800 675-6643
Julio Belloso, *Pr*
EMP: 61 EST: 1986
SALES (est): 29.17MM

7349 - Building Maintenance Services, Nec (P-10904)

SALES (corp-wide): 29.17MM **Privately Held**
Web: www.globalbuildingservices.com
SIC: 7349 Janitorial service, contract basis

(P-10904)
GMI BUILDING SERVICES INC
8001 Vickers St (92111-1917)
PHONE..............................858 279-6262
Larry Abrams, *Pr*
EMP: 225 **EST:** 1966
SQ FT: 15,000
SALES (est): 9.75MM **Privately Held**
SIC: 7349 5087 Janitorial service, contract basis; Janitors' supplies

(P-10905)
GREEN LIVING PLANET LLC
Also Called: Shine Facility Services
687 20th Ave (94121-3831)
PHONE..............................415 715-4718
Luis Ramirez, *Managing Member*
EMP: 75 **EST:** 2011
SALES (est): 2.46MM **Privately Held**
Web: www.shinefacilityservices.com
SIC: 7349 Janitorial service, contract basis

(P-10906)
H U S D MAINTENANCE OPERATION
24400 Amador St (94544-1302)
PHONE..............................510 784-2666
Joseph Zanini, *Dir*
EMP: 78 **EST:** 2005
SALES (est): 546.06K **Privately Held**
Web: www.husd.us
SIC: 7349 Building maintenance services, nec

(P-10907)
HAYNES BUILDING SERVICE LLC
16027 Arrow Hwy Ste I (91706-2064)
PHONE..............................626 359-6100
TOLL FREE: 800
John P Scharler, *Pr*
Michael Franco, *
EMP: 175 **EST:** 1982
SQ FT: 20,000
SALES (est): 2.39MM **Privately Held**
Web: www.haynesservices.com
SIC: 7349 Janitorial service, contract basis

(P-10908)
HUNTER EASTERDAY CORPORATION
1475 N Hundley St (92806-1323)
PHONE..............................714 238-3400
Sam Easterday, *CEO*
Manny Jones, *
Gilbert Anzaldua, *
Joanne Easterday, *
EMP: 135 **EST:** 1976
SQ FT: 4,400
SALES (est): 6.18MM **Privately Held**
Web: www.ebmcorp.com
SIC: 7349 5087 Janitorial service, contract basis; Janitors' supplies

(P-10909)
IMPEC GROUP INC (PA)
3350 Scott Blvd Bldg 8 (95054-3108)
PHONE..............................408 330-9350
Raffy Espiritu, *Pr*
Christine Chen, *
Jason Fang, *
EMP: 218 **EST:** 1991
SQ FT: 5,000
SALES (est): 15.99MM

SALES (corp-wide): 15.99MM **Privately Held**
Web: www.impecgroup.com
SIC: 7349 Janitorial service, contract basis

(P-10910)
INDUSTRIAL JANITOR SERVICE
Also Called: I J S
221 N San Dimas Ave Ste 217 (91773-2649)
PHONE..............................818 782-5658
Darla Drendel, *CEO*
Darla Artura, *
EMP: 100 **EST:** 1965
SQ FT: 7,500
SALES (est): 891.41K **Privately Held**
Web: www.ijsclean.com
SIC: 7349 Janitorial service, contract basis

(P-10911)
INNOVATIONS BUILDING SVCS LLC
402 S Orange Ave Apt D (91755-7554)
PHONE..............................323 787-6068
Helbert Daniel Torres, *Prin*
EMP: 100 **EST:** 2016
SALES (est): 2.09MM **Privately Held**
Web: www.innovationsbuildingservices.com
SIC: 7349 Janitorial service, contract basis

(P-10912)
INNOVATIVE CLEANING SVCS LLC
44 Waterworks Way (92618-3107)
PHONE..............................949 251-9188
Jennifer Corbett-shramo, *CEO*
John Gambino, *
Jaime Aburto, *
EMP: 500 **EST:** 2000
SALES (est): 8.73MM **Privately Held**
Web: www.ics-oc.com
SIC: 7349 Cleaning service, industrial or commercial

(P-10913)
JANPRO INC
Also Called: Pro-Clean Enterprises
92 N Bascom Ave (95128-1801)
PHONE..............................408 293-7679
Jose Mendoza, *Pr*
EMP: 107 **EST:** 1981
SQ FT: 4,000
SALES (est): 1.36MM **Privately Held**
Web: www.jan-pro.com
SIC: 7349 Janitorial service, contract basis

(P-10914)
K & P JANITORIAL SERVICES
412 S Pacific Coast Hwy Ste 200 (90277)
PHONE..............................310 540-8878
EMP: 100 **EST:** 1991
SALES (est): 4.82MM **Privately Held**
Web: www.kandpjanitorial.com
SIC: 7349 Janitorial service, contract basis

(P-10915)
KBM FCLITY SLTONS HOLDINGS LLC
Also Called: Kbm Building Services
7976 Engineer Rd Ste 200 (92111-1935)
PHONE..............................858 467-0202
Brian Snow, *CEO*
Rene Tuthscher, *
Susan Cologna, *
Shaun Gordon, *
Robert Kennedy Iii, *Dir*
EMP: 500 **EST:** 1981
SQ FT: 10,000

SALES (est): 27.13MM
SALES (corp-wide): 51.04MM **Privately Held**
Web: www.expiredwixdomain.com
SIC: 7349 Janitorial service, contract basis
PA: Pristine Environments Inc
3605 Ocean Ranch Blvd # 200
Oceanside CA
703 245-4751

(P-10916)
LANDMARK SERVICES INC
410 N Fairview St (92703-3412)
PHONE..............................714 240-7913
Dan Rogers, *Pr*
EMP: 60 **EST:** 2000
SQ FT: 130,000
SALES (est): 4.7MM **Privately Held**
Web: www.ocgoodwill.org
SIC: 7349 Janitorial service, contract basis

(P-10917)
LEES MAINTENANCE SERVICE INC
14740 Keswick St (91405-1205)
PHONE..............................818 988-6644
Tyrone P Ingram, *Pr*
EMP: 275 **EST:** 1961
SQ FT: 3,000
SALES (est): 2.79MM **Privately Held**
Web: www.leesmaint.com
SIC: 7349 5087 Janitorial service, contract basis; Laundry and dry cleaning equipment and supplies

(P-10918)
LEWIS & TAYLOR LLC
Also Called: Lewis & Taylor Bldg Svc Contrs
440 Bryant St (94107-1303)
PHONE..............................415 781-3496
Michael L Milstein, *CEO*
EMP: 150 **EST:** 1945
SQ FT: 4,000
SALES (est): 6.32MM **Privately Held**
Web: www.lewistaylor.com
SIC: 7349 Janitorial service, contract basis

(P-10919)
LIFE CYCLE ENGINEERING INC
7510 Airway Rd Ste 2 (92154-8303)
PHONE..............................619 785-5990
John Spencer, *Mgr*
EMP: 195
SALES (corp-wide): 73.8MM **Privately Held**
Web: www.lce.com
SIC: 7349 Building maintenance, except repairs
PA: Life Cycle Engineering, Inc.
4360 Corporate Rd Ste 100
North Charleston SC
843 744-7110

(P-10920)
LITTLE GIANT BLDG MAINT INC (PA)
Also Called: Lg
1485 Bay Shore Blvd Ste 117 (94124-4008)
PHONE..............................415 508-0282
David Dellanini, *Pr*
EMP: 80 **EST:** 1962
SQ FT: 1,000
SALES (est): 2.3MM
SALES (corp-wide): 2.3MM **Privately Held**
SIC: 7349 Janitorial service, contract basis

(P-10921)
LITTLE GIANT BLDG MAINT INC
15 Brooks Pl (94044-4403)

PHONE..............................415 508-0282
David Dellanini, *Brnch Mgr*
EMP: 170
SALES (corp-wide): 2.3MM **Privately Held**
SIC: 7349 7217 Window cleaning; Carpet and upholstery cleaning
PA: Little Giant Building Maintenance, Inc.
1485 Bay Shore Blvd # 117
San Francisco CA
415 508-0282

(P-10922)
LOS ANGELES UNIFIED SCHOOL DST
Also Called: Maintenance Dept
17729 S Figueroa St (90248-4237)
PHONE..............................310 808-1500
Roger Finstad, *Dir*
EMP: 89
SALES (corp-wide): 9.38B **Privately Held**
Web: www.laallcityband.com
SIC: 7349 School custodian, contract basis
PA: Los Angeles Unified School District
333 S Beaudry Ave Ste 209
Los Angeles CA
213 241-1000

(P-10923)
M-N-Z JANITORIAL SERVICES INC
2109 W Burbank Blvd (91506-1231)
PHONE..............................323 851-4115
Marc De Mauregne, *Ex VP*
Zorina Russell Kroop, *
Dennis Krebs, *Stockholder*
EMP: 110 **EST:** 1979
SQ FT: 1,000
SALES (est): 2.83MM **Privately Held**
Web: www.mnz.com
SIC: 7349 1799 Building maintenance, except repairs; Construction site cleanup

(P-10924)
MC-40 (PA)
Also Called: Mintie Technologies
777 N Georgia Ave (91702-2207)
PHONE..............................323 225-4111
Kevin J Mintie, *CEO*
James M Mintie, *
EMP: 122 **EST:** 1940
SALES (est): 12.68MM
SALES (corp-wide): 12.68MM **Privately Held**
Web: www.alliance-enviro.com
SIC: 7349 Building cleaning service

(P-10925)
MELIN ENTERPRISES INC
Also Called: ServiceMaster
812 W 18th St (95340-4605)
P.O. Box 2192 (95344-0192)
PHONE..............................209 726-9182
David Melin, *Pr*
EMP: 70 **EST:** 2006
SALES (est): 4.89MM **Privately Held**
Web: www.servicemasterbymelin.com
SIC: 7349 Building maintenance services, nec

(P-10926)
MERCHANTS BUILDING MAINT CO
Also Called: Merchants Building Maintenance
1639 E Edinger Ave Ste C (92705-5013)
PHONE..............................714 973-9272
George Rodriguez, *Brnch Mgr*
EMP: 438
SALES (corp-wide): 90.51MM **Privately Held**

PRODUCTS & SERVICES SECTION
7349 - Building Maintenance Services, Nec (P-10948)

Web: www.mbmonline.com
SIC: 7349 Janitorial service, contract basis
PA: Merchants Building Maintenance Company
1190 Monterey Pass Rd
Monterey Park CA
323 881-6701

(P-10927)
MERCHANTS BUILDING MAINT CO
9555 Distribution Ave Ste 102 (92121)
PHONE.................................858 455-0163
Eric Ruiz, *Mgr*
EMP: 350
SALES (corp-wide): 90.51MM **Privately Held**
Web: www.mbmonline.com
SIC: 7349 Janitorial service, contract basis
PA: Merchants Building Maintenance Company
1190 Monterey Pass Rd
Monterey Park CA
323 881-6701

(P-10928)
MERCHANTS BUILDING MAINT CO
Also Called: Merchants Building Maintenance
1995 W Holt Ave (91768-3352)
PHONE.................................909 622-8260
Angel Meza, *Brnch Mgr*
EMP: 526
SALES (corp-wide): 90.51MM **Privately Held**
Web: www.mbmonline.com
SIC: 7349 7381 Janitorial service, contract basis; Security guard service
PA: Merchants Building Maintenance Company
1190 Monterey Pass Rd
Monterey Park CA
323 881-6701

(P-10929)
MERCHANTS BUILDING MAINT CO
606 Monterey Pass Rd Ste 202 (91754)
PHONE.................................323 881-8902
Michael Anthony Palma, *Bd of Dir*
EMP: 130
SALES (corp-wide): 90.51MM **Privately Held**
Web: www.mbmonline.com
SIC: 7349 7381 Janitorial service, contract basis; Detective and armored car services
PA: Merchants Building Maintenance Company
1190 Monterey Pass Rd
Monterey Park CA
323 881-6701

(P-10930)
MIDA INDUSTRIES INC
6101 Obispo Ave (90805-3799)
PHONE.................................562 616-1020
Michael T Drake, *Pr*
John Valencia, *
Dawit Kidane, *
EMP: 250 EST: 1989
SQ FT: 10,000
SALES (est): 8.84MM **Privately Held**
Web: www.midaindustries.com
SIC: 7349 1799 Janitorial service, contract basis; Asbestos removal and encapsulation

(P-10931)
MILLARD GROUP INC
1950 E 20th St (95928-6369)
PHONE.................................530 899-7299
EMP: 119
SALES (corp-wide): 8.78B **Privately Held**
Web: www.aus.com
SIC: 7349 Janitorial service, contract basis
HQ: The Millard Group Inc
8140 River Dr
Morton Grove IL
847 674-4100

(P-10932)
MONTEBELLO UNIFIED SCHOOL DST
Also Called: Maintenance & Operation Dept
500 Hendricks St 2nd Fl (90640-1566)
PHONE.................................323 887-2140
Virgil Downs, *Prin*
EMP: 90
SALES (corp-wide): 539.05MM **Privately Held**
Web: www.montebello.k12.ca.us
SIC: 7349 Building maintenance services, nec
PA: Montebello Unified School District
123 S Montebello Blvd
Montebello CA
323 887-7900

(P-10933)
MORENO & ASSOCIATES INC
782 Auzerais Ave (95126-3503)
PHONE.................................408 924-0353
Ernie Moreno, *Pr*
EMP: 60 EST: 1993
SALES (est): 6.09MM **Privately Held**
Web: www.morenoclean.com
SIC: 7349 Janitorial service, contract basis

(P-10934)
NMS MANAGEMENT INC
155 W 35th St Ste A (91950-7922)
PHONE.................................619 425-0440
David Guaderrama, *Pr*
Sophia Guaderrama, *
EMP: 75 EST: 1985
SQ FT: 8,300
SALES (est): 3.44MM **Privately Held**
Web: www.nms-management.com
SIC: 7349 0781 Building maintenance, except repairs; Landscape services

(P-10935)
NOVA COMMERCIAL COMPANY INC (PA)
24683 Oneil Ave (94544-1627)
P.O. Box 759 (94543-0759)
PHONE.................................510 728-7000
Janice Slade, *VP*
Sophia Silva, *
EMP: 68 EST: 1968
SQ FT: 8,544
SALES (est): 4.52MM
SALES (corp-wide): 4.52MM **Privately Held**
Web: www.novacommercial.us
SIC: 7349 Janitorial service, contract basis

(P-10936)
ONE SILVER SERVE LLC
Also Called: SERVPRO Encino/Sherman Oaks
16601 Ventura Blvd Fl 4 (91436-1921)
PHONE.................................818 995-6444
Alan Reed, *CEO*
EMP: 80 EST: 2005
SALES (est): 9.53MM **Privately Held**
Web: www.servproencinoshermanoaks.com
SIC: 7349 Building maintenance services, nec

(P-10937)
OPEN AMERICA INC
Also Called: Openworks
4300 Long Beach Blvd Ste 450 (90807-2011)
PHONE.................................562 428-9210
John Palmer, *Brnch Mgr*
EMP: 188
SALES (corp-wide): 28.74MM **Privately Held**
Web: www.openworksweb.com
SIC: 7349 Janitorial service, contract basis
PA: O.P.E.N. America, Inc.
4742 N 24th St Ste 450
Phoenix AZ
602 224-0440

(P-10938)
OPTIMA BUILDING SERVICES INC
Also Called: Optima Building Services
210 Mountain View Ave (95407-8203)
PHONE.................................707 586-6640
Adolfo Mendoza, *Pr*
EMP: 100 EST: 2000
SALES (est): 2.4MM **Privately Held**
Web: www.optimabuildingservices.com
SIC: 7349 Janitorial service, contract basis

(P-10939)
PE FACILITY SOLUTIONS LLC (PA)
4217 Ponderosa Ave Ste A (92123-1536)
PHONE.................................858 467-0202
Shaun Gordon, *CEO*
EMP: 95 EST: 2017
SQ FT: 18,000
SALES (est): 2.09MM
SALES (corp-wide): 2.09MM **Privately Held**
SIC: 7349 Janitorial service, contract basis

(P-10940)
PEERLESS MAINTENANCE SVC INC
1100 S Euclid St (90631-6807)
P.O. Box 3900 (90632-3900)
PHONE.................................714 871-3380
Linda Gabriel, *Pr*
David Gabriel, *
EMP: 300 EST: 1979
SQ FT: 2,000
SALES (est): 8.88MM **Privately Held**
Web: www.peerlesssvc.com
SIC: 7349 Janitorial service, contract basis

(P-10941)
PEGASUS BUILDING SVCS CO INC
7966 Arjons Dr Ste A (92126-6361)
PHONE.................................858 444-2290
Judith Becker, *Pr*
Mark Tarin, *VP Opers*
Barry Becker, *Dir*
EMP: 350 EST: 1983
SQ FT: 12,800
SALES (est): 24.33MM **Privately Held**
Web: www.pegasusclean.com
SIC: 7349 Janitorial service, contract basis

(P-10942)
PERFORMANCE BUILDING SERVICES
Also Called: Performance Cleanroom Services
22642 Lambert St Ste 409 (92630-1645)
PHONE.................................949 364-4364
James Chriss, *Pr*
Ron Matthews, *
Robert Lynch, *
EMP: 104 EST: 2001
SALES (est): 4.43MM **Privately Held**
Web: www.performance-now.com
SIC: 7349 7699 Janitorial service, contract basis; Cleaning services

(P-10943)
PLATINUM CLG INDIANAPOLIS LLC
1522 2nd St (90401-2303)
PHONE.................................310 584-8000
EMP: 460 EST: 2008
SALES (est): 4.99MM **Privately Held**
SIC: 7349 Building and office cleaning services

(P-10944)
POLARIS BUILDING MAINT INC
2580 Wyandotte St Ste E (94043-2366)
PHONE.................................650 964-9400
Frank Schwarb, *Pr*
Roger Gomez, *
EMP: 80 EST: 1983
SQ FT: 2,700
SALES (est): 2.22MM **Privately Held**
Web: www.polarisbuildingmaintenance.net
SIC: 7349 Janitorial service, contract basis

(P-10945)
PRIORITY BUILDING SERVICES LLC
7313 Carroll Rd Ste G (92121-2319)
PHONE.................................858 695-1326
Simon Rocha, *Brnch Mgr*
EMP: 304
Web: www.priorityservices.net
SIC: 7349 Janitorial service, contract basis
PA: Priority Building Services Llc
1524 W Mable St
Anaheim CA

(P-10946)
PRIORITY BUILDING SERVICES LLC (PA)
Also Called: Priority Landscape Services
1524 W Mable St (92802-1022)
PHONE.................................714 255-2963
Simon Rocha, *Pr*
EMP: 71 EST: 2004
SQ FT: 6,000
SALES (est): 26.02MM **Privately Held**
Web: www.priorityservices.net
SIC: 7349 Janitorial service, contract basis

(P-10947)
PRO BUILDING MAINTENANCE INC (PA)
149 N Maple St Ste H (92878-3273)
PHONE.................................951 279-3386
EMP: 120 EST: 2006
SQ FT: 1,600
SALES (est): 1.73MM **Privately Held**
Web: www.probuildingmaintenance.com
SIC: 7349 Janitorial service, contract basis

(P-10948)
PROFESSIONAL MAINT SYSTEMS INC
Also Called: Professional Maint Systems
4912 Naples St (92110-3820)
P.O. Box 80038 (92138-0038)
PHONE.................................619 276-1150
Karen Berry, *CEO*
EMP: 925 EST: 1983
SQ FT: 9,000
SALES (est): 34.04MM **Privately Held**

7349 - Building Maintenance Services, Nec (P-10949)

Web: www.pmsjanitorial.com
SIC: 7349 Janitorial service, contract basis

(P-10949)
PRONTO JANITORIAL SVCS INC
12561 Persing Dr (90606-2713)
PHONE..................562 273-5997
Edgar Rodas, *Pr*
EMP: 80 EST: 2019
SALES (est): 1.01MM **Privately Held**
SIC: 7349 Janitorial service, contract basis

(P-10950)
PROPERTY MAINTENANCE COMPANY (PA)
Also Called: Dkd Property Management
2025 Gateway Pl (95110-1014)
PHONE..................408 297-7849
Sue Williams, *Pr*
EMP: 113 EST: 1979
SALES (est): 2.45MM
SALES (corp-wide): 2.45MM **Privately Held**
Web: www.propertymaintenancecompany.com
SIC: 7349 Building maintenance, except repairs

(P-10951)
PROTEC ASSOCIATION SERVICES (PA)
Also Called: Protec Building Services
10180 Willow Creek Rd (92131-1636)
PHONE..................858 569-1080
EMP: 140 EST: 1996
SQ FT: 12,500
SALES (est): 32.38MM **Privately Held**
Web: www.protec.com
SIC: 7349 Building maintenance services, nec

(P-10952)
RAINBOW - BRITE INDUS SVCS LLC
Also Called: Santa Rosa Indian Cmnty of Snt
463 E Salmon River Dr (93730-0860)
PHONE..................559 925-2580
Diana Tutson-snowden, *CEO*
EMP: 1243 EST: 2000
SALES (est): 494.81K **Privately Held**
Web: www.rainbowbriteservices.com
SIC: 7349 Janitorial service, contract basis
PA: Santa Rosa Indian Community Of The
    Santa Rosa Rancheria
    16835 Alkali Dr
    Lemoore CA
    559 924-1278

(P-10953)
RECOLOGY KING COUNTY INC
Also Called: Cleanscapessf
250 Executive Park Blvd Ste 2100 (94134-3394)
PHONE..................415 348-9700
Chris Husband, *Pr*
EMP: 124
SALES (corp-wide): 1.41B **Privately Held**
Web: www.recology.com
SIC: 7349 Office cleaning or charring
HQ: Recology King County Inc.
    801 S Fidalgo St Ste 100
    Seattle WA
    206 224-9513

(P-10954)
RHINO BUILDING SERVICES INC
6650 Flanders Dr Ste K (92121-3908)
PHONE..................858 455-1440
Cody Sears, *Pr*
EMP: 120 EST: 1985
SQ FT: 110
SALES (est): 2.37MM **Privately Held**
Web: www.rhinoinc.com
SIC: 7349 Janitorial service, contract basis

(P-10955)
RNA ANN ARBOR INCORPORATED
508 S Smith Ave Ste A202 (92882-7605)
PHONE..................877 762-7511
EMP: 107
SALES (corp-wide): 8.85MM **Privately Held**
Web: www.rnafacilitiesmanagement.com
SIC: 7349 Janitorial service, contract basis
PA: R.N.A. Of Ann Arbor, Incorporated
    717 W Ellsworth Rd
    Ann Arbor MI
    877 762-7511

(P-10956)
RUBICON PROGRAMS INCORPORATED (PA)
2500 Bissell Ave (94804-1815)
PHONE..................510 235-1516
Jane Fischberg, *Pr*
Adrienne Kimball, *
EMP: 66 EST: 1973
SQ FT: 14,500
SALES (est): 16.81MM
SALES (corp-wide): 16.81MM **Privately Held**
Web: www.rubiconprograms.org
SIC: 7349 8322 8331 Building maintenance services, nec; Social service center; Job training and related services

(P-10957)
SAN JOSE UNIFIED SCHOOL DST
Also Called: Maintenance Office
2222 Unified Way (95125-2060)
PHONE..................408 535-6200
Pat Bay, *Dir*
EMP: 72
SALES (corp-wide): 501.3MM **Privately Held**
Web: www.sjusd.org
SIC: 7349 Building maintenance services, nec
PA: San Jose Unified School District
    855 Lenzen Ave
    San Jose CA
    408 535-6000

(P-10958)
SANTA CLARA VALLEY CORPORATION
Also Called: Swenson Developers and Contrs
715 N 1st St Ste 27 (95112-6309)
PHONE..................408 947-1100
Case Swenson, *Pr*
Lisa Swenson, *
EMP: 85 EST: 1974
SQ FT: 1,200
SALES (est): 4.78MM **Privately Held**
Web: www.wewillrentforyou.com
SIC: 7349 0782 7623 7699 Building maintenance, except repairs; Lawn services; Refrigeration service and repair; Elevators: inspection, service, and repair

(P-10959)
SBM MANAGEMENT SERVICES LP
Also Called: Sbm Management Services
5241 Arnold Ave (95652-1025)
PHONE..................866 855-2211
Charles Somers, *CEO*
Donald Tracy, *Ex VP*
Ronald Alvarado, *Admn*
Ken Silva, *CFO*
Don Tracy, *Prin*
EMP: 300 EST: 2007
SALES (est): 71.76MM **Privately Held**
Web: www.sbmmanagement.com
SIC: 7349 Janitorial service, contract basis

(P-10960)
SBM SITE SERVICES LLC (PA)
Also Called: S B M
5241 Arnold Ave (95652-1025)
PHONE..................916 922-7600
Charles Somers, *Managing Member*
Ken Silva, *
Donald Tracy, *
Ron Alvardo, *Prin*
Mike Parker, *
EMP: 100 EST: 1994
SQ FT: 25,000
SALES (est): 89.2MM **Privately Held**
Web: www.sbmmanagement.com
SIC: 7349 Janitorial service, contract basis

(P-10961)
SBRM INC (PA)
Also Called: Servicmster Cmplete Rstoration
2342 Meyers Ave (92029-1008)
PHONE..................760 480-0208
TOLL FREE: 800
Barbara Robert, *Pr*
Mike Gamez, *
EMP: 70 EST: 1986
SQ FT: 20,000
SALES (est): 3.16MM **Privately Held**
Web: www.servicemaster.com
SIC: 7349 1521 Building maintenance services, nec; Repairing fire damage, single-family houses

(P-10962)
SCV FACILITIES SERVICES INC
1907 W 75th St (90047-2325)
PHONE..................310 803-4588
Samuel Valdez, *Owner*
EMP: 72 EST: 2013
SALES (est): 1.02MM **Privately Held**
Web: www.scvfs.com
SIC: 7349 7389 Janitorial service, contract basis; Business services, nec

(P-10963)
SERVI-TEK INC
Also Called: Servi-Tek Janitorial Services
8765 Sparren Way (92129-4437)
PHONE..................858 638-7735
Kurt G Lester, *
Eric S Friz, *
EMP: 300 EST: 2006
SALES (est): 14.26MM **Privately Held**
Web: www.servi-tek.net
SIC: 7349 Janitorial service, contract basis

(P-10964)
SERVICE BY MEDALLION
Also Called: Medallion Cnstr Clean-Up
455 National Ave (94043-2219)
PHONE..................650 625-1010
Roland H Strick, *CEO*
Roland F Strick, *
Maria Strick, *
Ben Strick, *
EMP: 620 EST: 1978
SALES (est): 45.94MM **Privately Held**
Web: www.servicebymedallion.com
SIC: 7349 Janitorial service, contract basis

(P-10965)
SERVICEMASTER BY BEST PROS INC
6474 Western Ave (92505-2130)
PHONE..................951 515-9051
Filip Busuioc, *CEO*
EMP: 99 EST: 2018
SALES (est): 1.28MM **Privately Held**
Web: www.servicemaster.com
SIC: 7349 1799 Building maintenance services, nec; Construction site cleanup

(P-10966)
SIGNATURE BUILDING MAINT INC
Also Called: Signature Facilities Services
4005 Clipper Ct (94538-6540)
P.O. Box 110340 (95011-0340)
PHONE..................408 377-8066
Anna Murphy, *Pr*
Tony Reyes, *
Patrick Murphy, *
Jeff Loyld, *
EMP: 80 EST: 1999
SALES (est): 8.91MM **Privately Held**
Web: www.signaturefacilities.com
SIC: 7349 Janitorial service, contract basis

(P-10967)
SIGNIFICANT CLEANING SVCS LLC
148 E Virginia St Ste 1 (95112-5881)
PHONE..................408 559-5959
EMP: 105 EST: 1988
SALES (est): 4.94MM **Privately Held**
Web: www.significantcleaning.com
SIC: 7349 Cleaning service, industrial or commercial

(P-10968)
SITE CREW INC
3185 Airway Ave Ste G (92626-4601)
PHONE..................714 668-0100
Tina Manavi, *CEO*
EMP: 300 EST: 2005
SQ FT: 2,160
SALES (est): 8.3MM **Privately Held**
Web: www.sitecrewinc.com
SIC: 7349 Janitorial service, contract basis

(P-10969)
SO CAL LAND MAINTENANCE INC
3121 E La Palma Ave Ste K (92806-2804)
PHONE..................714 231-1454
Stephen Guise, *Prin*
EMP: 72 EST: 2011
SALES (est): 2.16MM **Privately Held**
SIC: 7349 Building maintenance services, nec

(P-10970)
SOUTHERN MANAGEMENT CORP
808 S Olive St (90014-3006)
PHONE..................213 312-2268
EMP: 87
SALES (corp-wide): 7.81B **Publicly Held**
SIC: 7349 Building maintenance services, nec
HQ: Southern Management Corp.
    6478e Highway 90
    Milton FL

(P-10971)
SPENCER BUILDING MAINTENANCE
Also Called: Spencer Building Maintenance

PRODUCTS & SERVICES SECTION
7353 - Heavy Construction Equipment Rental (P-10992)

10457 Old Placerville Rd # 100 (95827-2508)
PHONE..................916 922-1900
Aaron D Spencer, *Pr*
EMP: 307 EST: 1997
SQ FT: 5,000
SALES (est): 10.2MM Privately Held
Web: www.spencerservices.com
SIC: 7349 Janitorial service, contract basis

(P-10972)
SUMMIT BUILDING SERVICES INC
1128 Willow Pass Ct (94520-1006)
PHONE..................925 827-9500
Matt Colchico, *CEO*
EMP: 100 EST: 1996
SALES (est): 4.95MM Privately Held
Web: www.summitbs.com
SIC: 7349 Janitorial service, contract basis

(P-10973)
TIM HOFER INC
Also Called: Environment Control
148 N Akers St (93291-5121)
P.O. Box 6445 (93290-6445)
PHONE..................559 732-6676
Timothy Hofer, *Pr*
Suzanne Hofer, *
EMP: 103 EST: 1984
SQ FT: 5,700
SALES (est): 1.61MM Privately Held
Web: www.environmentcontrol.com
SIC: 7349 Janitorial service, contract basis

(P-10974)
TOTAL QUALITY MAINTENANCE INC
895 Commercial St (94303-4906)
PHONE..................650 846-4700
Peter Vesanovic, *Pr*
Dee Vesanovic, *
EMP: 180 EST: 1997
SQ FT: 2,000
SALES (est): 4.63MM Privately Held
Web: www.tqm.bz
SIC: 7349 Janitorial service, contract basis

(P-10975)
TUTTLE FAMILY ENTERPRISES INC
Also Called: Peerless Building Maint Co
9510 Topanga Canyon Blvd (91311-4011)
PHONE..................818 534-2566
Tim Tuttle, *CEO*
EMP: 350 EST: 1948
SALES (est): 3.95MM Privately Held
SIC: 7349 Building maintenance, except repairs

(P-10976)
UNISERVE FACILITIES SVCS CORP (PA)
Also Called: Union Building Maintenance
2363 S Atlantic Blvd (90040-1256)
PHONE..................213 533-1000
Sam M Hwang, *Ch Bd*
EMP: 500 EST: 1966
SQ FT: 5,000
SALES (est): 16.38MM
SALES (corp-wide): 16.38MM Privately Held
Web: www.uniservecorp.com
SIC: 7349 Janitorial service, contract basis

(P-10977)
UNISERVE FACILITIES SVCS CORP
1200 Getty Center Dr (90049-1657)
PHONE..................310 440-6747
F Jackson, *Operations Staff*
EMP: 325
SALES (corp-wide): 16.38MM Privately Held
Web: www.uniservecorp.com
SIC: 7349 Janitorial service, contract basis
PA: Uniserve Facilities Services Corporation
2363 S Atlantic Blvd
Commerce CA
213 533-1000

(P-10978)
UNITED BUILDING MAINT INC
Also Called: United Building Maintenance
1143 N Market Blvd Ste 3 (95834-1913)
PHONE..................916 772-8101
Valerie Lynne Sherman, *CEO*
EMP: 225 EST: 2007
SALES (est): 11.94MM Privately Held
Web: www.unitedfullservice.com
SIC: 7349 Janitorial service, contract basis

(P-10979)
UNIVERSAL BLDG SVCS & SUP CO
Also Called: Universal Building Svc & Sup
1318 Ross St (94954-6526)
PHONE..................707 781-7434
Leonard Bruso, *Owner*
EMP: 113
SALES (corp-wide): 26.22MM Privately Held
Web: www.ubsco.com
SIC: 7349 Janitorial service, contract basis
PA: Universal Building Services And Supply Co.
3120 Pierce St
Richmond CA
510 527-1078

(P-10980)
UNIVERSAL BLDG SVCS & SUP CO (PA)
Also Called: Universal
3120 Pierce St (94804-5909)
PHONE..................510 527-1078
Grace Brusseau, *CEO*
Leonard Brusseau, *
EMP: 250 EST: 1963
SQ FT: 20,000
SALES: 26.22MM
SALES (corp-wide): 26.22MM Privately Held
Web: www.ubsco.com
SIC: 7349 5087 5169 Janitorial service, contract basis; Janitors' supplies; Chemicals and allied products, nec

(P-10981)
UNIVERSAL BLDG SVCS & SUP CO
421 N Buchanan Cir Ste 3 (94553-5142)
PHONE..................925 934-5533
Frank Batra, *Contrlr*
EMP: 81
SALES (corp-wide): 26.22MM Privately Held
Web: www.ubsco.com
SIC: 7349 Janitorial service, contract basis
PA: Universal Building Services And Supply Co.
3120 Pierce St
Richmond CA
510 527-1078

(P-10982)
UNIVERSAL BLDG SVCS & SUP CO
430 Roberson Ln (95112-1125)
PHONE..................408 995-5111
Su Miles, *Brnch Mgr*
EMP: 81
SALES (corp-wide): 26.22MM Privately Held
Web: www.ubsco.com
SIC: 7349 Janitorial service, contract basis
PA: Universal Building Services And Supply Co.
3120 Pierce St
Richmond CA
510 527-1078

(P-10983)
UNIVERSAL SERVICES AMERICA LP
1815 E Wilshire Ave Ste 912 (92705-4646)
PHONE..................714 923-3700
Mark Olivas, *Brnch Mgr*
EMP: 2876
SALES (corp-wide): 12.86B Privately Held
Web: www.aus.com
SIC: 7349 Janitorial service, contract basis
HQ: Universal Services Of America, Lp
450 Exchange
Irvine CA
866 877-1965

(P-10984)
UNIVERSAL SITE SERVICES INC (PA)
760 E Capitol Ave (95035-6812)
PHONE..................800 647-9337
Gina Vella, *Pr*
Joseph Vella, *
EMP: 82 EST: 1958
SQ FT: 20,000
SALES (est): 14MM
SALES (corp-wide): 14MM Privately Held
Web: www.universalsiteservices.com
SIC: 7349 4959 0782 Building maintenance, except repairs; Road, airport, and parking lot maintenance services; Lawn services

(P-10985)
VARSITY CONTRACTORS INC
24155 Laguna Hills Mall (92653-3667)
PHONE..................949 586-8283
EMP: 128
SALES (corp-wide): 620.83MM Privately Held
Web: www.kbs-services.com
SIC: 7349 Janitorial service, contract basis
HQ: Varsity Contractors, Inc.
1055 S 3600 W Ste 101
Salt Lake City UT
208 232-8598

(P-10986)
VNH ENTERPRISES INC
Also Called: Service Mstr Rcvery By C2c Rst
2636 Vista Pacific Dr (92056-3514)
PHONE..................877 468-3566
Steve Franco, *Genl Mgr*
EMP: 78
SALES (corp-wide): 1.58MM Privately Held
Web: www.servicemasterrestore.com
SIC: 7349 1799 Building maintenance services, nec; Post disaster renovations
PA: Vnh Enterprises, Inc.
10881 La Tuna Canyon Rd
Sun Valley CA
877 468-3566

(P-10987)
WTMG INC
Also Called: Janitek Cleaning Solutions
3225 Tomahawk Dr (95205-2450)
PHONE..................209 888-6600
EMP: 250 EST: 2007
SALES (est): 10.5MM Privately Held
SIC: 7349 Cleaning service, industrial or commercial

(P-10988)
WURMS JANITORIAL SERVICE INC
601 S Milliken Ave (91761-7898)
PHONE..................951 582-0003
Larry Stewart, *Pr*
Pam Costa, *
EMP: 80 EST: 1986
SALES (est): 2.17MM Privately Held
Web: www.ultrashine.com
SIC: 7349 Janitorial service, contract basis

7352 Medical Equipment Rental

(P-10989)
APRIA HEALTHCARE LLC
1450 Expo Pkwy Ste D (95815-5120)
PHONE..................530 677-2713
Nichola Denney, *Brnch Mgr*
EMP: 62
Web: www.apria.com
SIC: 7352 Medical equipment rental
HQ: Apria Healthcare Llc
7353 Company Dr
Indianapolis IN
949 639-2000

(P-10990)
DIGIRAD IMAGING SOLUTIONS INC
13100 Gregg St Ste A (92064-7150)
PHONE..................800 947-6134
EMP: 159
SALES (corp-wide): 112.15MM Publicly Held
Web: www.digirad.com
SIC: 7352 Medical equipment rental
HQ: Digirad Imaging Solutions Inc
1048 Industrial Ct Ste E
Poway CA
800 947-6134

(P-10991)
RAC & ASSOCIATES
Also Called: Special Care
9541 Ridgehaven Ct (92123-1624)
PHONE..................858 694-5800
Terry Racciato, *Pr*
Joseph Racciato, *
EMP: 60 EST: 2000
SQ FT: 15,000
SALES (est): 4.35MM Privately Held
Web: www.specialcaredme.com
SIC: 7352 Medical equipment rental

7353 Heavy Construction Equipment Rental

(P-10992)
AMERICAN CRANE RENTAL INC
17800 Comconex Rd (95336-8121)
P.O. Box 308 (95320-0308)
PHONE..................209 838-8815
Keith Powell, *CEO*
Denise Powell,
Everett Powell, *

7353 - Heavy Construction Equipment Rental (P-10993)

EMP: 65 EST: 2002
SALES (est): 13.99MM **Privately Held**
Web: www.americancranerental.net
SIC: 7353 Cranes and aerial lift equipment, rental or leasing

(P-10993)
BIGGE GROUP
14511 Industry Cir (90638-5814)
PHONE.................714 523-4092
EMP: 172
Web: www.bigge.com
SIC: 7353 Cranes and aerial lift equipment, rental or leasing
PA: Bigge Group
10700 Bigge St
San Leandro CA

(P-10994)
BRAGG INVESTMENT COMPANY INC
Also Called: Bragg Crane
13188 Dahlia St (92337-6903)
PHONE.................909 350-3738
Dyke Leonard, *Mgr*
EMP: 117
SALES (corp-wide): 489.53MM **Privately Held**
Web: www.braggcompanies.com
SIC: 7353 Cranes and aerial lift equipment, rental or leasing
PA: Bragg Investment Company, Inc.
6251 N Paramount Blvd
Long Beach CA
562 984-2400

(P-10995)
BRAGG INVESTMENT COMPANY INC (PA)
Also Called: Bragg Crane & Rigging
6251 N Paramount Blvd (90805-3713)
P.O. Box 727 (90801-0727)
PHONE.................562 984-2400
TOLL FREE: 800
M Scott Bragg, *Pr*
Mike Roy, *
Marilynn Bragg, *VP*
Dennis Ferguson, *
Kathleen Pool-ferrin, *Sec*
◆ EMP: 300 EST: 1946
SQ FT: 50,000
SALES (est): 489.53MM
SALES (corp-wide): 489.53MM **Privately Held**
Web: www.braggcompanies.com
SIC: 7353 4213 7389 1791 Cranes and aerial lift equipment, rental or leasing; Heavy hauling, nec; Crane and aerial lift service; Structural steel erection

(P-10996)
COUNTY OF ORANGE
Also Called: All Access Rental
1631 E Wilshire Ave (92705-4504)
PHONE.................714 647-1552
Kevin Aylesworth, *CEO*
EMP: 72
SALES (corp-wide): 5.2B **Privately Held**
Web: www.ocgov.com
SIC: 7353 5599 Cranes and aerial lift equipment, rental or leasing; Aircraft instruments, equipment or parts
PA: County Of Orange
400 W Civic Center Dr G36
Santa Ana CA
714 834-6200

(P-10997)
GLOBAL RENTAL CO INC
1253 Price Ave (91767-5839)
PHONE.................909 469-5160
James Dixon, *Brnch Mgr*
EMP: 120
SALES (corp-wide): 1.21B **Privately Held**
Web: www.altec.com
SIC: 7353 5082 Heavy construction equipment rental; Contractor's materials
HQ: Global Rental Co., Inc.
33 Inverness Center Pkwy # 250
Hoover AL

(P-10998)
HARBOR INDUSTRIAL SVCS CORP
Also Called: Harbor Industrial
211 N Marine Ave (90744-5724)
P.O. Box 1487 (90733-1487)
PHONE.................310 522-1193
W Michael Hawk, *Pr*
Maria Gray, *
▲ EMP: 80 EST: 1993
SALES (est): 10.74MM **Privately Held**
Web: www.harborindustrial.com
SIC: 7353 Cranes and aerial lift equipment, rental or leasing

(P-10999)
HAWTHORNE MACHINERY CO (PA)
Also Called: Hawthorne Cat
16945 Camino San Bernardo (92127-2405)
PHONE.................858 674-7000
TOLL FREE: 800
Tee K Ness, *Pr*
David Ness, *
◆ EMP: 200 EST: 1941
SQ FT: 130,000
SALES (est): 176.69MM
SALES (corp-wide): 176.69MM **Privately Held**
Web: www.hawthornecat.com
SIC: 7353 7699 5082 7359 Heavy construction equipment rental; Construction equipment repair; Construction and mining machinery; Equipment rental and leasing, nec

(P-11000)
HAWTHORNE RENT-IT SERVICE (HQ)
Also Called: Caterpillar Authorized Dealer
16945 Camino San Bernardo (92127-2405)
PHONE.................858 674-7000
Tee K Ness, *CEO*
Bob Price, *
Paul Hawthorne, *
Mike Johnson, *Product Vice President*
Steve Sager, *
EMP: 100 EST: 1974
SQ FT: 130,000
SALES (est): 33.17MM
SALES (corp-wide): 176.69MM **Privately Held**
Web: www.hawthornecat.com
SIC: 7353 5084 Heavy construction equipment rental; Industrial machinery and equipment
PA: Hawthorne Machinery Co.
16945 Camino San Bernardo
San Diego CA
858 674-7000

(P-11001)
KING EQUIPMENT LLC
1690 Ashley Way (92324-4000)
PHONE.................909 986-5300

Diane Quijada, *
EMP: 73 EST: 2007
SALES (est): 9.07MM **Privately Held**
Web: www.sunbeltrentals.com
SIC: 7353 Heavy construction equipment rental

(P-11002)
LLC BREWER CRANE
Also Called: Brewer Crane & Rigging
12570 Highway 67 (92040-1159)
PHONE.................619 390-8252
Brent S Brewer, *Pr*
Brent K Garcia, *
EMP: 72 EST: 1997
SQ FT: 2,500
SALES (est): 24MM **Privately Held**
Web: www.brewercrane.com
SIC: 7353 Cranes and aerial lift equipment, rental or leasing

(P-11003)
NOBLE RENTS INC
8314 Slauson Ave (90660-4323)
PHONE.................855 767-4424
Nabil Kassam, *CEO*
Suzy Taherian, *
EMP: 65 EST: 2011
SQ FT: 62,766
SALES (est): 6.25MM **Privately Held**
SIC: 7353 Heavy construction equipment rental

(P-11004)
NORTHWEST EXCAVATING INC
18201 Napa St (91325-3374)
PHONE.................818 349-5861
Susan Groff, *CEO*
Robbie Groff, *
EMP: 72 EST: 1959
SQ FT: 2,500
SALES (est): 11.3MM **Privately Held**
Web: www.nwexc.com
SIC: 7353 1794 Heavy construction equipment rental; Excavation and grading, building construction

(P-11005)
RDO CONSTRUCTION EQUIPMENT CO
Also Called: John Deere Authorized Dealer
10108 Riverford Rd (92040-2740)
PHONE.................619 443-3758
Ron Offets, *Pr*
EMP: 60 EST: 1978
SQ FT: 2,200
SALES (est): 8.99MM **Privately Held**
Web: www.rdoequipment.com
SIC: 7353 5082 Heavy construction equipment rental; General construction machinery and equipment

(P-11006)
RJ ALLEN INC
10392 Stanford Ave (92840-6301)
PHONE.................714 539-1022
Andrew Allen, *Pr*
Ron Markham, *
EMP: 65 EST: 1969
SQ FT: 20,000
SALES (est): 9.52MM **Privately Held**
Web: www.rjalleninc.com
SIC: 7353 Heavy construction equipment rental

(P-11007)
SHEEDY DRAYAGE CO (PA)
1215 Michigan St (94107-3518)
P.O. Box 77004 (94107-0004)
PHONE.................415 648-7171

Don Russell, *Ch*
Michael A Battaini, *
Richard Battaini, *
Peter Hogan, *
▲ EMP: 80 EST: 1925
SQ FT: 25,000
SALES (est): 25.41MM
SALES (corp-wide): 25.41MM **Privately Held**
Web: www.sheedycrane.com
SIC: 7353 Cranes and aerial lift equipment, rental or leasing

(P-11008)
THE NATIONAL BUS GROUP INC (PA)
Also Called: National Tube & Steel
15319 Chatsworth St (91345-2040)
PHONE.................818 221-6000
James Mooneyham, *Pr*
◆ EMP: 85 EST: 1985
SQ FT: 24,000
SALES (est): 123.15MM
SALES (corp-wide): 123.15MM **Privately Held**
Web: www.rentnational.com
SIC: 7353 5039 7359 3496 Earth moving equipment, rental or leasing; Wire fence, gates, and accessories; Garage facility and tool rental; Fencing, made from purchased wire

(P-11009)
WESTERN ENERGY SERVICES CORP
3430 Getty St (93308-5248)
PHONE.................403 984-5916
Alex R N Macausland, *CEO*
Jeffrey K Bowers, *VP*
EMP: 200 EST: 2005
SALES (est): 6.01MM **Privately Held**
SIC: 7353 Oil well drilling equipment, rental or leasing

(P-11010)
WHITES CRANE SERVICE INC
Also Called: White Crane
45524 Towne St (92201-4446)
PHONE.................760 347-3401
Edwin Neumeyer, *Pr*
EMP: 70 EST: 1999
SALES (est): 980.99K
SALES (corp-wide): 10.06MM **Privately Held**
Web: www.whitescraneservice.com
SIC: 7353 Cranes and aerial lift equipment, rental or leasing
PA: White's Steel, Inc.
45524 Towne St
Indio CA
760 347-3401

7359 Equipment Rental And Leasing, Nec

(P-11011)
AAA QUALITY SERVICES INC (PA)
Also Called: AAA Services
321 Noble Ave (93223-2503)
P.O. Box 535 (93223-0535)
PHONE.................559 594-1128
EMP: 111 EST: 1958
SALES (est): 10.85MM **Privately Held**
Web: www.aaaqsinc.com

PRODUCTS & SERVICES SECTION
7359 - Equipment Rental And Leasing, Nec (P-11035)

SIC: **7359** 1731 7382 1799 Portable toilet rental; Fire detection and burglar alarm systems specialization; Burglar alarm maintenance and monitoring; Sign installation and maintenance

(P-11012)
ADVANCED TEST EQUIPMENT CORP
Also Called: Advanced Test Eqp Rentals
10401 Roselle St (92121-1523)
PHONE................................858 558-6500
James P Berg, *CEO*
Jill E Berg, *
▲ **EMP:** 60 **EST:** 1984
SQ FT: 25,000
SALES (est): 14.08MM **Privately Held**
Web: www.atecorp.com
SIC: **7359** Equipment rental and leasing, nec

(P-11013)
AERCAP GLOBAL AVIATION TRUST (HQ)
10250 Constellation Blvd Ste 3400 (90067-6200)
PHONE................................310 788-1999
Sean Sullivan, *Pr*
Keith Helming, *
EMP: 109 **EST:** 2014
SALES (est): 2.25MM
SALES (corp-wide): 1.01B **Privately Held**
Web: www.aercap.com
SIC: **7359** 6159 Aircraft rental; Equipment and vehicle finance leasing companies
PA: Aercap Holdings N.V.
Onbekend Nederlands Adres
Onbekend
35316360650

(P-11014)
AFTER-PARTY2 INC
22674 Broadway # A (95476-8217)
PHONE................................408 457-1187
EMP: 74
SALES (corp-wide): 10.97B **Publicly Held**
SIC: **7359** Party supplies rental services
HQ: After-Party2, Inc.
901 W Hillcrest Blvd
Inglewood CA
310 202-0011

(P-11015)
AFTER-PARTY2 INC (DH)
Also Called: Classic Party Rentals
901 W Hillcrest Blvd (90301-2100)
PHONE................................310 202-0011
Jeff Black, *Pr*
▲ **EMP:** 200 **EST:** 1996
SALES (est): 65.61MM
SALES (corp-wide): 10.97B **Publicly Held**
SIC: **7359** Party supplies rental services
HQ: Apollo Asset Management, Inc.
9 W 57th St Fl 42
New York NY

(P-11016)
AFTER-PARTY6 INC
Also Called: Classic Party Rentals
901 W Hillcrest Blvd (90301-2100)
PHONE................................310 966-4900
EMP: 130
SIC: **7359** Party supplies rental services

(P-11017)
AIR LEASE CORPORATION (PA)
2000 Avenue Of The Stars Ste 1000n (90067-4734)
PHONE................................310 553-0555
EMP: 94 **EST:** 2010
SALES (est): 2.32B **Publicly Held**
Web: www.airleasecorp.com
SIC: **7359** 7389 Aircraft rental; Financial services

(P-11018)
ALL-IN PRDCTONS CSINO RNTALS L
Also Called: Casino Table Rentals
7222 Garden Grove Blvd (92683-2225)
PHONE................................866 875-8628
Andrew Litwin, *CEO*
EMP: 63 **EST:** 2009
SALES (est): 2.52MM **Privately Held**
Web: www.all-inproductions.net
SIC: **7359** Equipment rental and leasing, nec

(P-11019)
AMADA CAPITAL CORPORATION
7025 Firestone Blvd (90621-1869)
PHONE................................714 739-2111
Mike Guerin, *Pr*
David Kehrli, *
EMP: 62 **EST:** 1981
SQ FT: 103,000
SALES (est): 2.46MM **Privately Held**
Web: www.amadacapital.com
SIC: **7359** Equipment rental and leasing, nec
HQ: Amada North America, Inc
7025 Firestone Blvd
Buena Park CA

(P-11020)
ARENA EVENT SERVICES INC
Also Called: Stuart Event Rentals
454 S Abbott Ave (95035-5258)
PHONE................................408 856-3232
EMP: 67
SALES (corp-wide): 49.72MM **Privately Held**
Web: www.arenaamericas.com
SIC: **7359** Party supplies rental services
PA: Arena Event Services, Inc.
10861 S Howell Ave
Oak Creek WI
414 831-7000

(P-11021)
BA LEASING & CAPITAL CORP (DH)
555 California St Fl 4 (94104-1506)
PHONE................................415 765-1804
Richard Harris, *Pr*
K Thomas Rose, *
Oliver James Jim Warner, *VP*
Rod Hurd, *
EMP: 130 **EST:** 1955
SALES (est): 30.46MM
SALES (corp-wide): 94.95B **Publicly Held**
SIC: **7359** Equipment rental and leasing, nec
HQ: Banc Of America Leasing & Capital, Llc
555 California St Fl 4
San Francisco CA
415 765-7349

(P-11022)
BRIGHT EVENT RENTALS LLC (PA)
Also Called: Wine Country Party & Events
1640 W 190th St Ste A (90501-1122)
PHONE................................310 202-0011
Michael Bjornstad, *Managing Member*
▲ **EMP:** 240 **EST:** 2013
SALES (est): 49.33MM
SALES (corp-wide): 49.33MM **Privately Held**
Web: www.bright.com
SIC: **7359** Party supplies rental services

(P-11023)
CELTIC LEASING CORP
Also Called: Celtic Commercial Finance
4 Park Plz Ste 300 (92614-8511)
PHONE................................949 263-3880
EMP: 80
SIC: **7359** Equipment rental and leasing, nec

(P-11024)
CHOURA EVENTS
540 Hawaii Ave (90503-5148)
PHONE................................310 320-6200
James Ryan Choura, *CEO*
EMP: 80 **EST:** 2014
SALES (est): 10.57MM **Privately Held**
Web: www.choura.co
SIC: **7359** Party supplies rental services

(P-11025)
CLASSIC PARTY RENTALS INC
Also Called: Classic Party Rentals
901 W Hillcrest Blvd A (90301-2101)
PHONE................................310 966-4900
▲ **EMP:** 2500
SIC: **7359** Party supplies rental services

(P-11026)
CLASSIC/PRIME INC
Also Called: Classic Tents
540 Hawaii Ave (90503-5148)
PHONE................................310 328-5060
EMP: 100
SIC: **7359** Tent and tarpaulin rental

(P-11027)
COMPASS GROUP USA INC
Also Called: Canteen Vending
12640 Knott St (92841-3902)
PHONE................................714 899-2520
Ron Wanamaker, *VP*
EMP: 125
SALES (corp-wide): 29.97B **Privately Held**
Web: www.canteen.com
SIC: **7359** 7699 5962 Vending machine rental; Vending machine repair; Merchandising machine operators
HQ: Compass Group Usa, Inc.
2400 Yorkmont Rd
Charlotte NC

(P-11028)
DIAMOND ENVIRONMENTAL SVCS LP
Also Called: Diamond Environmental Services
807 E Mission Rd (92069-3002)
PHONE................................760 744-7191
EMP: 100 **EST:** 1997
SQ FT: 2,000
SALES (est): 19.45MM **Privately Held**
Web: www.diamondprovides.com
SIC: **7359** Portable toilet rental

(P-11029)
DIRECT CHASSISLINK INC
Also Called: Dcli
7777 Center Ave Ste 325 (92647-9132)
PHONE................................657 216-5846
Don Peltier, *Mgr*
EMP: 592
SALES (corp-wide): 116.43MM **Privately Held**
Web: www.dcli.com
SIC: **7359** Equipment rental and leasing, nec
PA: Direct Chassislink, Inc.
3525 Whthall Pk Dr Ste 40
Charlotte NC
704 594-3800

(P-11030)
ENCORE EVENTS RENTALS INC
1001 American Way (95492-7760)
PHONE................................707 431-3500
Bridget Doherty, *CEO*
EMP: 100 **EST:** 2010
SALES (est): 8.51MM **Privately Held**
Web: www.encoreeventsrentals.com
SIC: **7359** Party supplies rental services

(P-11031)
EPIC PRODUCTION TECHNOLOGIES (US SALES) INC
1401 Maulhardt Ave Ste A (93030-7960)
P.O. Box 454 (97034-0049)
EMP: 65 **EST:** 2008
SALES (est): 4.9MM **Privately Held**
Web: www.epicpt.com
SIC: **7359** Sound and lighting equipment rental
PA: Epic Holding Company Inc.
1401 Maulhardt Ave Ste A
Oxnard CA

(P-11032)
FENIX MARINE SERVICES LTD (DH)
614 Terminal Way (90731-7453)
PHONE................................310 548-8877
Sean Pierce, *Pr*
◆ **EMP:** 62 **EST:** 1978
SQ FT: 2,500
SALES (est): 34.73MM
SALES (corp-wide): 31.16K **Privately Held**
Web: www.fenixmarineservices.com
SIC: **7359** Shipping container leasing
HQ: Cma Cgm
4 Boulevard J Saade
Marseille
488919000

(P-11033)
GLOBAL TREND PRODUCTIONS INC
Also Called: Global Trend Productions
10537 Glenoaks Blvd Ste A (91331-1688)
PHONE................................818 768-4950
Isaac Campos, *CEO*
◆ **EMP:** 65 **EST:** 2002
SALES (est): 4.6MM **Privately Held**
Web: www.globaltrendpro.com
SIC: **7359** 5999 Audio-visual equipment and supply rental; Audio-visual equipment and supplies

(P-11034)
GUZMAN GRADING AND PAVING CORP
14030 Rose Ave (92337-7047)
PHONE................................909 428-5960
Jesus Guzman, *CEO*
EMP: 95 **EST:** 2003
SQ FT: 76,000
SALES (est): 4.7MM **Privately Held**
SIC: **7359** 1771 1611 Equipment rental and leasing, nec; Blacktop (asphalt) work; Highway and street construction

(P-11035)
HANA FINANCIAL INC (PA)
1000 Wilshire Blvd Ste 2000 (90017-2457)
PHONE................................213 240-1234
Sunnie S Kim, *CEO*
Young Shim, *
▲ **EMP:** 85 **EST:** 1994
SQ FT: 24,000
SALES (est): 13.65MM **Privately Held**
Web: www.hanafinancial.com

7359 - Equipment Rental And Leasing, Nec (P-11036)

SIC: 7359 6153 6159 Equipment rental and leasing, nec; Factoring services; Small business investment companies

(P-11036)
HARRY MCCUNE SOUND SERVICE INC (PA)
Also Called: McCune Audio Visual Video Ltg
101 Utah Ave (94080-6711)
PHONE..................650 873-1111
TOLL FREE: 800
EMP: 108 EST: 1931
SALES (est): 9.89MM
SALES (corp-wide): 9.89MM **Privately Held**
Web: www.mccune.com
SIC: 7359 7812 7389 Audio-visual equipment and supply rental; Audio-visual program production; Recording studio, noncommercial records

(P-11037)
J L FISHER INC
1000 W Isabel St (91506-1404)
PHONE..................818 846-8366
James L Fisher, *Pr*
Cary Clayton, *
▲ EMP: 60 EST: 1951
SALES (est): 5.28MM **Privately Held**
Web: www.jlfisher.com
SIC: 7359 3861 3663 Equipment rental and leasing, nec; Motion picture apparatus and equipment; Radio and t.v. communications equipment

(P-11038)
J M EQUIPMENT COMPANY INC (PA)
Also Called: John Deere Authorized Dealer
321 Spreckels Ave (95336-6007)
PHONE..................209 522-3271
Ray Azevedo, *CEO*
Ed Henriquez, *
Audie Burgan, *Sales Operations Vice President*
Brian Wagoner, *
Vincent C Victorine, *
▲ EMP: 80 EST: 1936
SQ FT: 7,000
SALES (est): 44.56MM
SALES (corp-wide): 44.56MM **Privately Held**
Web: www.jmequipment.com
SIC: 7359 5084 5999 Equipment rental and leasing, nec; Materials handling machinery; Farm equipment and supplies

(P-11039)
L A PARTY RENTS INC
13520 Saticoy St (91402-6428)
PHONE..................818 989-4300
Gerome Nehus, *Pr*
EMP: 100 EST: 1987
SALES (est): 3.83MM **Privately Held**
Web: www.lapartyrents.com
SIC: 7359 Party supplies rental services

(P-11040)
MACQUIRE ARCFT LSG SVCS US INC
2 Embarcadero Ctr Ste 200 (94111-3801)
PHONE..................415 829-6600
John R Willingham, *CEO*
Bruce Hogarth, *
Harry Forsythe, *
Timothy Jaeger, *
EMP: 60 EST: 2006
SALES (est): 32.91MM
SALES (corp-wide): 560.17MM **Privately Held**

Web: www.macquarie.aero
SIC: 7359 Aircraft rental
HQ: Macquarie Airfinance (No 2) Limited
Level 1, South Bank House
Dublin

(P-11041)
MEETING SERVICES INC
Also Called: MSI Production Services
1125 Joshua Way (92081-7840)
PHONE..................858 348-0100
EMP: 90
Web: www.msiprod.com
SIC: 7359 7629 5049 Audio-visual equipment and supply rental; Electrical equipment repair, high voltage; Theatrical equipment and supplies

(P-11042)
MICROFINANCIAL INCORPORATED
2801 Townsgate Rd (91361-3003)
PHONE..................805 367-8900
Richard Latour, *CEO*
EMP: 106
SALES (corp-wide): 99.27MM **Privately Held**
Web: www.timepayment.com
SIC: 7359 Business machine and electronic equipment rental services
HQ: Microfinancial Incorporated
200 Summit Dr Ste 100
Burlington MA
781 994-4800

(P-11043)
MICROLEASE INC (DH)
6060 Sepulveda Blvd (91411-2501)
PHONE..................866 520-0200
Gordon Curwen, *VP*
EMP: 85 EST: 2001
SQ FT: 20,000
SALES (est): 45.48MM
SALES (corp-wide): 254.4MM **Privately Held**
SIC: 7359 Rental store, general
HQ: Electro Rent Uk Limited
Unit 1
Harrow MIDDX
208 420-0200

(P-11044)
MUFG AMERICAS LEASING CORP (DH)
445 S Figueroa St Ste 2700 (90071-1602)
PHONE..................213 488-3700
Hideya Takaishi, *CEO*
Mark Helman, *General*
Paul Nolan, *
Rory Laughna, *
David A Meehan, *
EMP: 100 EST: 1973
SALES (est): 47.47MM **Privately Held**
Web: www.mufgamericas.com
SIC: 7359 Equipment rental and leasing, nec
HQ: Mufg Americas Holdings Corporation
1251 Ave Of The Americas
New York NY
212 782-6800

(P-11045)
NATIONAL CNSTR RENTALS INC (HQ)
Also Called: National Rent A Fence Co.
15319 Chatsworth St (91345-2040)
PHONE..................818 221-6000
James R Mooneyham, *Pr*
W Robert Mooneyham, *Executive President*

◆ EMP: 85 EST: 1961
SQ FT: 23,000
SALES (est): 89.73MM
SALES (corp-wide): 123.15MM **Privately Held**
Web: www.rentnational.com
SIC: 7359 Equipment rental and leasing, nec
PA: The National Business Group, Inc.
15319 Chatsworth St
Mission Hills CA
818 221-6000

(P-11046)
NATIONAL TRENCH SAFETY LLC
Also Called: Trench Plate Rental
13217 Laureldale Ave (90242-5140)
PHONE..................562 602-1642
Dexter Poston, *Brnch Mgr*
EMP: 185
SALES (corp-wide): 104.07MM **Privately Held**
Web: www.ntsafety.com
SIC: 7359 Equipment rental and leasing, nec
PA: National Trench Safety, Llc
260 N Sam Houston Pkwy E
Houston TX
832 200-0988

(P-11047)
OHANA PARTNERS INC (PA)
Also Called: Stuart Rental Company
454 S Abbott Ave (95035-5258)
PHONE..................408 856-3232
Michael Berman, *CEO*
R Andrew Sutton, *
▲ EMP: 95 EST: 2002
SALES (est): 15.07MM
SALES (corp-wide): 15.07MM **Privately Held**
Web: www.stuartrental.com
SIC: 7359 5947 Party supplies rental services; Gifts and novelties

(P-11048)
P J J ENTERPRISES INC
1250 Delevan Dr (92102-2437)
PHONE..................619 232-6136
John Lenore, *Pr*
Roger Carey, *
Dorothy Lenore, *
EMP: 78 EST: 1966
SQ FT: 20,000
SALES (est): 1.26MM
SALES (corp-wide): 45.4MM **Privately Held**
SIC: 7359 Rental store, general
PA: Lenore John & Co
1250 Delevan Dr
San Diego CA
619 232-6136

(P-11049)
PANAVISION INC (PA)
Also Called: Panavision Group
6101 Variel Ave (91367-3722)
PHONE..................818 316-1000
▲ EMP: 550 EST: 1990
SQ FT: 150,000
SALES (est): 160.24MM **Privately Held**
Web: www.panavision.com
SIC: 7359 3861 3648 5063 Equipment rental and leasing, nec; Cameras and related equipment; Stage lighting equipment; Lighting fixtures

(P-11050)
PICO RENTS INC
Also Called: Pico Party Rents
4646 E Los Angeles Ave (93063-3407)

PHONE..................310 275-9431
TOLL FREE: 800
William Edwards Junior, *Pr*
Darren G Edwards, *
EMP: 60 EST: 1926
SALES (est): 4.98MM **Privately Held**
Web: www.picopartyrents.com
SIC: 7359 Party supplies rental services

(P-11051)
PSAV HOLDINGS LLC (PA)
111 W Ocean Blvd Ste 1110 (90802-4688)
PHONE..................562 366-0138
J Michael Mcilwain, *CEO*
Ben Erwin, *
Michael Leone, *CCO*
Cathie Kozik, *CIO*
Charlie Young, *Chief Human Resource Officer*
EMP: 122 EST: 2013
SALES (est): 460.08MM
SALES (corp-wide): 460.08MM **Privately Held**
Web: www.encoreglobal.com
SIC: 7359 Audio-visual equipment and supply rental

(P-11052)
RAPHAELS PARTY RENTALS INC (PA)
8606 Miramar Rd (92126-4326)
PHONE..................858 444-1692
Raphael Silverman, *Pr*
Phillip Silverman, *
Kitty Silverman, *
▲ EMP: 175 EST: 1981
SQ FT: 60,000
SALES (est): 13.6MM
SALES (corp-wide): 13.6MM **Privately Held**
Web: www.raphaels.com
SIC: 7359 Party supplies rental services

(P-11053)
RSI LEASING LLC
1314 E Puente Ave (91790-1361)
PHONE..................626 966-6129
Ronadl Chaplen, *Prin*
EMP: 99 EST: 2010
SALES (est): 207.25K
SALES (corp-wide): 1B **Publicly Held**
SIC: 7359 Equipment rental and leasing, nec
PA: Sotera Health Company
9100 S Hills Blvd Ste 300
Broadview Heights OH
440 262-1410

(P-11054)
SHOWROOM INTERIORS LLC
Also Called: Vesta Luxury Home Staging
8905 Rex Rd (90660-3799)
PHONE..................323 348-1551
Julianne Buckner, *Managing Member*
EMP: 105 EST: 2016
SALES (est): 5MM
SALES (corp-wide): 5MM **Privately Held**
SIC: 7359 Furniture rental
PA: Showroom, Inc
8905 Rex Rd
Pico Rivera CA
323 348-1551

(P-11055)
SRG HOLDINGS LLC (HQ)
500 Stevens Ave Ste 100 (92075-2055)
PHONE..................858 792-9300
J Wickliffe Peterson, *CFO*
Michael Grust, *Pr*
EMP: 532 EST: 1998
SQ FT: 12,300

PRODUCTS & SERVICES SECTION

7361 - Employment Agencies (P-11076)

SALES (est): 26.69MM
SALES (corp-wide): 189.7MM Privately Held
SIC: 7359 Business machine and electronic equipment rental services
PA: Senior Resource Group, Llc
500 Stevens Ave Ste 100
Solana Beach CA
858 792-9300

(P-11056)
TOWN & CNTRY EVENT RENTALS INC (PA)
Also Called: Tacer
7725 Airport Business Pkwy (91406)
PHONE..................818 908-4211
Richard Loguercio, CEO
Chris Mackey, *
Christopher Keesler, *
Wayne Tay, *
▲ **EMP:** 400 **EST:** 1998
SQ FT: 1,100
SALES (est): 64.1MM
SALES (corp-wide): 64.1MM Privately Held
Web: www.tacer.biz
SIC: 7359 Party supplies rental services

(P-11057)
TOWN & CNTRY EVENT RENTALS INC
1 N Calle Cesar Chavez (93103-3662)
PHONE..................805 770-5729
EMP: 398
SALES (corp-wide): 64.1MM Privately Held
Web: www.tacer.biz
SIC: 7359 Party supplies rental services
PA: Town & Country Event Rentals, Inc.
7725 Airport Bus Pkwy
Van Nuys CA
818 908-4211

(P-11058)
TRAFFIC CONTROL SERVICE INC
Also Called: Allied Trench Shoring Service
4695 Macarthur Ct Ste 1100 (92660-1866)
TOLL FREE: 800
EMP: 207
SIC: 7359 5099 1799 Sign rental; Signs, except electric; Flag pole erection

(P-11059)
UNITED SITE SERVICES CAL INC
Also Called: Acme
3408 Hillcap Ave (95136-1306)
PHONE..................408 295-2263
Frank Youngblood, Pr
Dan Youngblood, *
Jim Youngblood, *
Terence P Moriarty, *
EMP: 200 **EST:** 2004
SALES (est): 22.16MM
SALES (corp-wide): 703MM Privately Held
Web: www.unitedsiteservices.com
SIC: 7359 Portable toilet rental
PA: United Site Services, Inc.
118 Flanders Rd
Westborough MA
508 594-2655

(P-11060)
UNITED SITE SERVICES CAL INC
411 S Beckwith Rd (93060-3047)
PHONE..................805 933-2793
Dave Parker, Brnch Mgr
EMP: 61

SALES (corp-wide): 703MM Privately Held
Web: www.unitedsiteservices.com
SIC: 7359 Portable toilet rental
HQ: United Site Services Of California, Inc.
4511 Rowland Ave
El Monte CA

(P-11061)
UNITED TERMINAL LEASING LLC
3 Embarcadero Ctr Ste 550 (94111-4048)
PHONE..................510 302-3900
Gail Parris, Managing Member
EMP: 360 **EST:** 2002
SALES (est): 10.59MM Privately Held
SIC: 7359 Equipment rental and leasing, nec

(P-11062)
VCI EVENT TECHNOLOGY INC
Also Called: Videocam
25172 Arctic Ocean Dr Ste 102 (92630-8851)
PHONE..................714 772-2002
TOLL FREE: 888
Kirk Rhinehart, CEO
Evan H Goldschlag, *
Kirk Rhinehart, VP
▲ **EMP:** 166 **EST:** 1993
SALES (est): 18.39MM Privately Held
Web: www.vcievents.com
SIC: 7359 Audio-visual equipment and supply rental

(P-11063)
WESTERN OILFIELDS SUPPLY CO
Also Called: Rain For Rent
5101 Office Park Dr Ste 100 (93309-0615)
P.O. Box File 52541 (90074-0001)
PHONE..................480 895-9225
EMP: 76
SALES (corp-wide): 250.88MM Privately Held
Web: www.rainforrent.com
SIC: 7359 Equipment rental and leasing, nec
PA: Western Oilfields Supply Co Inc
3404 State Rd
Bakersfield CA
661 399-9124

(P-11064)
WESTERN OILFIELDS SUPPLY CO (PA)
Also Called: Rain For Rent
3404 State Rd (93308-4538)
P.O. Box 2248 (93303-2248)
PHONE..................661 399-9124
Robert Lake, CEO
Maston Cunningham, CFO
▲ **EMP:** 150 **EST:** 1934
SQ FT: 57,000
SALES (est): 250.88MM
SALES (corp-wide): 250.88MM Privately Held
Web: www.rainforrent.com
SIC: 7359 3523 5083 Equipment rental and leasing, nec; Farm machinery and equipment; Irrigation equipment

(P-11065)
WRIGHT CELEBRATIONS INC
Also Called: Celebrtions Pty Rentals Tents
8845 Washington Blvd Ste 140 (95678-6205)
PHONE..................916 773-2133
Susan Wright, Pr
Michael Wright, *
EMP: 99 **EST:** 2000

SQ FT: 7,000
SALES (est): 15.47MM Privately Held
Web: www.celebrationspartyrentals.com
SIC: 7359 5947 Party supplies rental services; Gift, novelty, and souvenir shop

7361 Employment Agencies

(P-11066)
24-HOUR MED STAFFING SVCS LLC
1370 Valley Vista Dr Ste 280 (91765-3911)
PHONE..................909 895-8960
EMP: 110 **EST:** 2000
SALES (est): 8.71MM Privately Held
Web: www.24-hrmed.com
SIC: 7361 Employment agencies

(P-11067)
40 HRS INC
Also Called: 40 Hours Staffing
1669 Flanigan Dr (95121-1682)
PHONE..................408 414-0158
Bryan Phan, Pr
EMP: 1000 **EST:** 2006
SQ FT: 3,000
SALES (est): 22.98MM Privately Held
Web: www.40hrs.us
SIC: 7361 Executive placement

(P-11068)
5 STAR JOB SOURCE
12025 Garfield Ave (90280-7822)
PHONE..................562 788-7391
Fernando Carrillo Morales, CEO
EMP: 70 **EST:** 2018
SALES (est): 3.44MM Privately Held
SIC: 7361 Employment agencies

(P-11069)
80 TWENTY LLC
369 Pine St Ste 208 (94104-3306)
PHONE..................415 592-7773
EMP: 86 **EST:** 2011
SALES (est): 986.41K Privately Held
Web: www.80twenty.com
SIC: 7361 Executive placement

(P-11070)
A OSEGUERA COMPANY INC
1099 Rogge Rd (93906-1305)
P.O. Box 5195 (93915-5195)
PHONE..................831 443-4155
Antonio Oseguera, Pr
Connie Oseguera, *
EMP: 500 **EST:** 1985
SALES (est): 15.7MM Privately Held
Web: www.aoseguera.com
SIC: 7361 Labor contractors (employment agency)

(P-11071)
ABSO
101 Creekside Ridge Ct Fl 2 (95678-3595)
PHONE..................800 943-2589
William Greenblatt, CEO
Bradley Landin, *
EMP: 135 **EST:** 2000
SQ FT: 19,000
SALES (est): 20.24MM
SALES (corp-wide): 766.78MM Publicly Held
Web: www.absolutelyproductions.com
SIC: 7361 Executive placement
HQ: Sterling Infosystems, Inc.
6150 Oak Tree Blvd # 490
Independence OH
212 736-5100

(P-11072)
ACCESS NURSES INC
5935 Cornerstone Ct W Ste 300 (92121-3737)
PHONE..................858 458-4400
Alan Braynin, CEO
EMP: 91 **EST:** 2001
SQ FT: 20,000
SALES (est): 7.99MM Privately Held
Web: www.accessnurses.com
SIC: 7361 Nurses' registry

(P-11073)
ACCOUNTBLE HLTHCARE STFFING IN
Also Called: Hrn Services
7777 Greenback Ln Ste 205 (95610-5800)
PHONE..................916 286-7667
Tina Wilson, Brnch Mgr
EMP: 161
SALES (corp-wide): 117.95MM Privately Held
Web: www.ahcstaff.com
SIC: 7361 Nurses' registry
PA: Accountable Healthcare Staffing, Inc.
999 W Yamato Rd Ste 210
Boca Raton FL
561 235-7810

(P-11074)
ACCOUNTBLE HLTHCARE STFFING IN
Also Called: Hrn Services
1999 S Bascom Ave Ste 590 (95008-2236)
PHONE..................408 377-9960
Mary Begin, Brnch Mgr
EMP: 368
SALES (corp-wide): 117.95MM Privately Held
Web: www.ahcstaff.com
SIC: 7361 Nurses' registry
PA: Accountable Healthcare Staffing, Inc.
999 W Yamato Rd Ste 210
Boca Raton FL
561 235-7810

(P-11075)
ACT 1 GROUP INC (PA)
Also Called: Agileone
1999 W 190th St (90504-6202)
P.O. Box 2886 (90509-2886)
PHONE..................310 750-3400
Janice B Howroyd, CEO
Bernard Howroyd, *
Michael Hoyal, *
Carlton Bryant, *
Tina B Robinson, *
EMP: 90 **EST:** 1978
SQ FT: 18,026
SALES (est): 508.88MM Privately Held
Web: www.actonegroup.com
SIC: 7361 8741 Employment agencies; Administrative management

(P-11076)
ADECCO EMPLOYMENT SERVICES
25301 Cabot Rd Ste 214 (92653-5505)
PHONE..................949 586-2342
Tina Robinson, Brnch Mgr
EMP: 150
Web: www.adeccona.com
SIC: 7361 Employment agencies
HQ: Adecco Employment Services, Inc
4800 Deerwood Campus Pkwy # 800
Jacksonville FL
631 844-7100

7361 - Employment Agencies (P-11077)

(P-11077)
ADVANCE STAFFING INC
2060 Walsh Ave Ste 101 (95050-2568)
P.O. Box 391447 (94039-1447)
PHONE............................408 205-6154
Jose Badillo, Pr
EMP: 300 EST: 2007
SALES (est): 9.82MM **Privately Held**
Web: www.advance-staffing.com
SIC: 7361 Employment agencies

(P-11078)
ADVANCED MED PRSONNEL SVCS INC
12400 High Bluff Dr Ste 100 (92130-3077)
PHONE............................386 756-4395
Jennfier Fuicelli, CEO
EMP: 100 EST: 1989
SALES (est): 9.01MM
SALES (corp-wide): 5.24B **Publicly Held**
Web: www.amnhealthcare.com
SIC: 7361 7363 Nurses' registry; Medical help service
HQ: Amn Healthcare, Inc.
12400 High Bluff Dr # 100
San Diego CA

(P-11079)
ALL HEALTH SERVICES CORP (PA)
11104 Bonneyview Ln (93230-6308)
PHONE............................559 583-9101
Dave Matthews, Pr
Michael Ross, *
Jeremy Matthews, *
Robert Garcia, *
EMP: 65 EST: 2004
SALES (est): 8.23MM
SALES (corp-wide): 8.23MM **Privately Held**
Web: www.allhs.net
SIC: 7361 Employment agencies

(P-11080)
ALOIS LLC
Also Called: Alois Staffing
548 Market St Ste 47970 (94104-5401)
PHONE............................215 297-4492
Farhad Wadia, CEO
John Thomas, *
Kinjal Desai, *
EMP: 150 EST: 2016
SALES (est): 20MM **Privately Held**
Web: www.aloissolutions.com
SIC: 7361 7389 Employment agencies; Business Activities at Non-Commercial Site

(P-11081)
AMN HEALTHCARE INC
Also Called: American Mobile Healthcare
12235 El Camino Real Ste 200 (92130)
PHONE............................800 282-0300
EMP: 92 EST: 2017
SALES (est): 2MM **Privately Held**
Web: www.amnhealthcare.com
SIC: 7361 Employment agencies

(P-11082)
APPLEONE INC (HQ)
Also Called: Appleone Employment Services
327 W Broadway (91204-1301)
PHONE............................818 240-8688
Janice Bryant Howroyd, CEO
Bernard Howroyd, *
Michael Hoyal, *
Brett Howroyd, *
♦ EMP: 175 EST: 1964
SQ FT: 27,000
SALES (est): 145.38MM **Privately Held**
Web: www.appleone.com
SIC: 7361 Labor contractors (employment agency)
PA: The Act 1 Group Inc
1999 W 190th St
Torrance CA

(P-11083)
APPLEONE INC
Also Called: Appleone Employment Services
325 W Broadway (91204-1301)
PHONE............................818 240-8688
Marie Rounsavell, Mgr
EMP: 120
Web: www.appleone.com
SIC: 7361 Labor contractors (employment agency)
HQ: Appleone, Inc.
327 W Broadway
Glendale CA
818 240-8688

(P-11084)
AROSE RECRUITING CO INC
2429 W Coast Hwy Ste 208 (92663-4745)
PHONE............................949 642-2696
Deborah Brooks, Pr
Pamela Dempsey, *
EMP: 77 EST: 1989
SQ FT: 2,150
SALES (est): 2.96MM **Privately Held**
SIC: 7361 Executive placement

(P-11085)
ASSISTED HOME RECOVERY INC (PA)
Also Called: Assisted Home Care
8550 Balboa Blvd Lbby (91325-5808)
PHONE............................818 894-8117
Elaine S Donley, Adm/Dir
Bill Donley, *
EMP: 110 EST: 1979
SQ FT: 4,000
SALES (est): 11.42MM
SALES (corp-wide): 11.42MM **Privately Held**
SIC: 7361 Nurses' registry

(P-11086)
ATTORNEY NETWORK SERVICES INC
Also Called: Attorney Network Services
725 S Figueroa St Ste 3065 (90017-5524)
PHONE............................213 430-0440
Nick Karapetian, Pr
Gavin Rubin, VP
EMP: 90 EST: 1997
SQ FT: 4,000
SALES (est): 5.53MM **Privately Held**
Web: www.karapetianrubin.com
SIC: 7361 Executive placement

(P-11087)
B2 SERVICES LLC
Also Called: At Work
17291 Irvine Blvd Ste 258 (92780-2949)
PHONE............................714 363-3481
Lori Brower, Pr
EMP: 100 EST: 2017
SALES (est): 2.25MM **Privately Held**
Web: www.atwork.com
SIC: 7361 Employment agencies

(P-11088)
BARONHR LLC
13085 Central Ave Ste 4 (91710-4184)
PHONE............................909 517-3800
EMP: 92
SALES (corp-wide): 50.76MM **Privately Held**
Web: www.baronhr.com
SIC: 7361 Employment agencies
PA: Baronhr, Llc
8101 E Kaiser Blvd
Anaheim CA
714 860-7800

(P-11089)
BARRETT BUSINESS SERVICES INC
Also Called: B B S I
8880 Rio San Diego Dr Ste 800 (92108-1634)
PHONE............................858 314-1100
Milan Todorovic, Brnch Mgr
EMP: 3056
SALES (corp-wide): 1.05B **Publicly Held**
Web: www.bbsi.com
SIC: 7361 Employment agencies
PA: Barrett Business Services Inc
8100 Ne Parkway Dr # 200
Vancouver WA
360 828-0700

(P-11090)
BARRETT BUSINESS SERVICES INC
862 E Hospitality Ln (92408-3530)
PHONE............................909 890-3633
EMP: 3056
SALES (corp-wide): 1.05B **Publicly Held**
Web: www.bbsi.com
SIC: 7361 Employment agencies
PA: Barrett Business Services Inc
8100 Ne Parkway Dr # 200
Vancouver WA
360 828-0700

(P-11091)
BARRETT BUSINESS SERVICES INC
Also Called: Barrett Business Services
1840 Gateway Dr (94404-4027)
PHONE............................650 653-7588
EMP: 3056
SALES (corp-wide): 1.05B **Publicly Held**
Web: www.bbsi.com
SIC: 7361 Employment agencies
PA: Barrett Business Services Inc
8100 Ne Parkway Dr # 200
Vancouver WA
360 828-0700

(P-11092)
BARRETT BUSINESS SERVICES INC
Also Called: Bbsi Camarillo
815 Camarillo Springs Rd Ste C (93012-9457)
PHONE............................805 987-0331
Dee Levy, Brnch Mgr
EMP: 4584
SALES (corp-wide): 1.05B **Publicly Held**
Web: www.bbsi.com
SIC: 7361 8742 Employment agencies; Human resource consulting services
PA: Barrett Business Services Inc
8100 Ne Parkway Dr # 200
Vancouver WA
360 828-0700

(P-11093)
BAY AREA TECHWORKERS (PA)
Also Called: Techworkers
2000 Crow Canyon Pl Ste 150 Ste (94596)
PHONE............................925 359-2200
Don Peed, CEO
Rob Olsen, *
Steve Powers, *
H B Drake, VP
Kelly Scott, *
EMP: 65 EST: 1998
SALES (est): 70.86MM
SALES (corp-wide): 70.86MM **Privately Held**
Web: www.techworkers.com
SIC: 7361 Placement agencies

(P-11094)
BC LABOR CONTRACTORS
2272 Alisal Rd (93908-9701)
PHONE............................831 751-6000
Bulmaro Castro, Pr
EMP: 200 EST: 2001
SALES (est): 8.09MM **Privately Held**
SIC: 7361 Labor contractors (employment agency)

(P-11095)
BLUECREW LLC
821 Folsom St Ste 102 (94107-6100)
PHONE............................510 684-7362
Gino Rooney, Prin
EMP: 85 EST: 2016
SALES (est): 2.47MM **Privately Held**
Web: www.bluecrewjobs.com
SIC: 7361 Employment agencies

(P-11096)
BODY FIT PLUS INC
Also Called: Healthcare
440 N Wolfe Rd (94085-3869)
PHONE............................925 226-7744
Siva Konatham, CEO
EMP: 207 EST: 2007
SALES (est): 20MM **Privately Held**
Web: www.bodyfitplusinc.com
SIC: 7361 Nurses' registry

(P-11097)
BOILING POINT REST S CA INC
13668 Valley Blvd Unit C2 (91746-2572)
PHONE............................626 551-5181
Chi How Chou, Ch
Michael Lin, *
EMP: 300 EST: 2012
SALES (est): 21.31MM **Privately Held**
SIC: 7361 5812 Employment agencies; Chinese restaurant

(P-11098)
BUTLER AMERICA HOLDINGS INC
12625 Frederick St Ste E2 (92553-5253)
PHONE............................951 563-0020
EMP: 293
SALES (corp-wide): 79.52MM **Privately Held**
SIC: 7361 Employment agencies
PA: Butler America Holdings, Inc.
3820 State St Ste B
Santa Barbara CA
805 880-1978

(P-11099)
BUTLER AMERICA HOLDINGS INC
8647 Haven Ave Ste 100 (91730-4887)
PHONE............................909 417-3660
Cecilia La Tour, Brnch Mgr
EMP: 293
SALES (corp-wide): 79.52MM **Privately Held**
SIC: 7361 Employment agencies
PA: Butler America Holdings, Inc.
3820 State St Ste B
Santa Barbara CA
805 880-1978

PRODUCTS & SERVICES SECTION

7361 - Employment Agencies (P-11122)

(P-11100)
BUTLER INTERNATIONAL INC (PA)
3820 State St Ste A (93105-3182)
PHONE..................805 882-2200
Edward M Kopko, *Ch Bd*
Edward M Kopko, *Ch Bd*
James J Beckley, *
Mark Koscinski, *
EMP: 200 **EST:** 1985
SALES (est): 242.14MM
SALES (corp-wide): 242.14MM **Privately Held**
Web: www.butleritresources.com
SIC: 7361 8742 Employment agencies; Management consulting services

(P-11101)
CALABRIA GROUP INC (PA)
Also Called: Dynamic Staffing
920 Reserve Dr Ste 150 (95678-1382)
PHONE..................916 773-3900
EMP: 148 **EST:** 1996
SQ FT: 2,768
SALES (est): 13.79MM **Privately Held**
SIC: 7361 Executive placement

(P-11102)
CAREER GROUP INC (PA)
Also Called: Fourthfloor Fashion Talent
10100 Santa Monica Blvd Ste 900 (90067-4002)
PHONE..................310 277-8188
Michael B Levine, *CEO*
Susan Levine, *
Scott H Pick, *
▲ **EMP:** 2100 **EST:** 1980
SQ FT: 11,986
SALES (est): 55.71MM
SALES (corp-wide): 55.71MM **Privately Held**
Web: www.careergroupcompanies.com
SIC: 7361 Executive placement

(P-11103)
CAREER GROUP INC
345 California St Ste 1650 (94104-2652)
PHONE..................415 781-8188
EMP: 150
SALES (corp-wide): 55.71MM **Privately Held**
Web: www.careergroupcompanies.com
SIC: 7361 Executive placement
PA: Career Group, Inc.
   10100 Santa Monica Blvd # 900
   Los Angeles CA
   310 277-8188

(P-11104)
CAREER STRATEGIES TMPRY INC
9267 Haven Ave Ste 225 (91730-5458)
PHONE..................909 230-4504
Darin Rado, *Prin*
EMP: 104
Web: www.csi4jobs.com
SIC: 7361 Placement agencies
PA: Career Strategies Temporary, Inc.
   1 Chisholm Trail Rd # 210
   Round Rock TX

(P-11105)
CAREER STRATEGIES TMPRY INC
21031 Ventura Blvd Ste 1005 (91364-2255)
PHONE..................818 883-0440
EMP: 104
Web: www.csi4jobs.com
SIC: 7361 Placement agencies
PA: Career Strategies Temporary, Inc.
   1 Chisholm Trail Rd # 210
   Round Rock TX

(P-11106)
CAREER STRATEGIES TMPRY INC
1990 N California Blvd # 8 (94596-3742)
PHONE..................925 296-9600
EMP: 104
Web: www.csipropertymanagement.com
SIC: 7361 Executive placement
PA: Career Strategies Temporary, Inc.
   1 Chisholm Trail Rd # 210
   Round Rock TX

(P-11107)
CAREER STRATEGIES TMPRY INC
78060 Calle Estado (92253-2960)
PHONE..................760 564-5959
EMP: 104
Web: www.csi4jobs.com
SIC: 7361 Executive placement
PA: Career Strategies Temporary, Inc.
   1 Chisholm Trail Rd # 210
   Round Rock TX

(P-11108)
CAREER STRATEGIES TMPRY INC
1755 Locust St (94596-4120)
PHONE..................925 296-9600
Jacquee Landry, *Prin*
EMP: 104
Web: www.csi4jobs.com
SIC: 7361 Executive placement
PA: Career Strategies Temporary, Inc.
   1 Chisholm Trail Rd # 210
   Round Rock TX

(P-11109)
CAREER STRATEGIES TMPRY INC
575 Anton Blvd Ste 630 (92626-1948)
PHONE..................714 824-6840
Mat Mcgowen, *Mgr*
EMP: 104
Web: www.csi4jobs.com
SIC: 7361 Executive placement
PA: Career Strategies Temporary, Inc.
   1 Chisholm Trail Rd # 210
   Round Rock TX

(P-11110)
CARTER ASTON INC
1601 Response Rd Ste 100 (95815-5257)
PHONE..................916 431-3922
EMP: 120
SALES (corp-wide): 15.88B **Privately Held**
Web: www.astoncarter.com
SIC: 7361 Executive placement
HQ: Aston Carter, Inc.
   7317 Parkway Dr
   Hanover MD

(P-11111)
CENTURY HLTH STAFFING SVCS INC
1701 Westwind Dr Ste 101 (93301-3045)
PHONE..................661 322-0606
Richard Ochieng, *Pr*
Lissa Harris-soto, *VP*
EMP: 213 **EST:** 2006
SQ FT: 2,000
SALES (est): 4.49MM **Privately Held**
Web: www.centurynurse.com
SIC: 7361 Nurses' registry

(P-11112)
CONTINUING LF COMMUNITIES LLC (PA)
Also Called: La Costa Glen
1940 Levante St (92009-5174)
PHONE..................760 704-6400
Richard D Aschenbrenner, *Managing Member*
Richard D Aschenbrenner, *Mgr*
E Justin Wilson Iii, *CEO*
Warren E Spieker Junior, *Mgr*
EMP: 97 **EST:** 1991
SALES (est): 47.09MM
SALES (corp-wide): 47.09MM **Privately Held**
Web: www.continuinglife.com
SIC: 7361 Employment agencies

(P-11113)
CREATIVE SOLUTIONS SVCS LLC
Also Called: Higher Talent
1745 N Vista St (90046-2234)
PHONE..................646 495-1558
Ashish Kaushal, *Managing Member*
EMP: 212 **EST:** 2016
SALES (est): 7.67MM **Privately Held**
Web: www.css-llc.net
SIC: 7361 Executive placement

(P-11114)
CROSSCIRCLES INC
Also Called: Robin.ly
627 E Calaveras Blvd Pmb 1005 (95035-7705)
PHONE..................626 341-8469
EMP: 65 **EST:** 2018
SALES (est): 645.2K **Privately Held**
SIC: 7361 Executive placement

(P-11115)
CROSSROADS DIVERSFD SVCS INC
7011 Sylvan Rd Ste A (95610-3800)
PHONE..................916 676-2540
Danny Marquez, *Prin*
EMP: 69
SALES (corp-wide): 12.42MM **Privately Held**
Web: www.prideindustries.com
SIC: 7361 Executive placement
PA: Crossroads Diversified Services, Inc.
   10030 Foothills Blvd
   Roseville CA
   916 457-1900

(P-11116)
CROWDSTAFFING
6030 Hellyer Ave Ste 100 (95138-1018)
PHONE..................844 467-2300
EMP: 99 **EST:** 2019
SALES (est): 1.7MM **Privately Held**
Web: www.prosperix.com
SIC: 7361 Employment agencies

(P-11117)
CTPARTNERS EXEC SEARCH INC
8001 Irvine Center Dr (92618-2938)
PHONE..................949 754-2821
Robin Caldwell, *Brnch Mgr*
EMP: 62
SALES (corp-wide): 71.96MM **Privately Held**
Web: www.ctnet.com
SIC: 7361 Executive placement
PA: Ctpartners Executive Search Inc.
   1166 Ave Of The Amrcas Fl
   New York NY
   212 588-3500

(P-11118)
CULVER PERSONNEL AGENCIES INC
Also Called: Culver Personnel Services
445 Marine View Ave Ste 101 (92014-3969)
P.O. Box 910569 (92191-0569)
PHONE..................888 600-5733
Timothy J Culver, *Pr*
John Weaver, *
EMP: 120 **EST:** 1979
SQ FT: 7,500
SALES (est): 4.9MM **Privately Held**
SIC: 7361 Executive placement

(P-11119)
CVPARTNERS INC (HQ)
655 Montgomery St Ste 1200 (94111-2601)
PHONE..................415 543-8600
Kent Gray, *Pr*
EMP: 161 **EST:** 2001
SALES (est): 28.16MM
SALES (corp-wide): 166.95MM **Privately Held**
Web: www.addisongroup.com
SIC: 7361 Executive placement
PA: Addison Professional Financial Search Llc
   125 S Wacker Dr Fl 27
   Chicago IL
   312 424-0300

(P-11120)
CYBERCODERS INC
Also Called: Cyberscientific
6591 Irvine Center Dr Ste 200 (92618-2118)
PHONE..................949 885-5151
Heidi Golledge, *CEO*
Matt Miller, *
EMP: 140 **EST:** 1999
SALES (est): 41.06MM
SALES (corp-wide): 4.58B **Publicly Held**
Web: www.cybercoders.com
SIC: 7361 Executive placement
PA: Asgn Incorporated
   4400 Cox Rd Ste 110
   Glen Allen VA
   888 482-8068

(P-11121)
CYBERCODERS STAFFING SVCS LLC
6591 Irvine Center Dr Ste 200 (92618-2129)
PHONE..................949 885-5151
EMP: 68 **EST:** 2017
SALES (est): 721.43K **Privately Held**
Web: www.cybercoders.com
SIC: 7361 Employment agencies

(P-11122)
DECTON INC
555 W Redondo Beach Blvd Ste 205 (90248-1612)
PHONE..................310 838-7246
EMP: 64
SALES (corp-wide): 23.27MM **Privately Held**
Web: www.dectoninc.com
SIC: 7361 Employment agencies
PA: Decton, Inc.
   15635 Alton Pkwy Ste 475
   Irvine CA
   949 851-0111

7361 - Employment Agencies (P-11123)

(P-11123)
DELTA-T GROUP INC
4420 Hotel Circle Ct Ste 205 (92108-3423)
PHONE................................619 543-0556
EMP: 102
Web: www.delta-tgroup.com
SIC: 7361 Employment agencies
PA: Delta-T Group, Inc.
  950 E Haverford Rd # 200
  Bryn Mawr PA

(P-11124)
DIAMOND PEO LLC
27442 Calle Arroyo Ste A (92675-6753)
PHONE................................714 728-5186
EMP: 180 EST: 2016
SALES (est): 9.1MM Privately Held
Web: www.diamondpeo.com
SIC: 7361 Employment agencies

(P-11125)
DIVERSITY BUS SOLUTIONS INC
3532 Old Archibald Ranch Rd (91761-9160)
PHONE................................909 395-0243
Sandy Tribby, CEO
EMP: 200 EST: 2011
SALES (est): 4.93MM Privately Held
Web: www.dbsinc.org
SIC: 7361 Employment agencies

(P-11126)
E Z STAFFING INC (PA)
200 N Maryland Ave Ste 303 (91206-4276)
PHONE................................818 845-2500
Abraham F Abirafeh, Pr
EMP: 298 EST: 1994
SALES (est): 9.99MM Privately Held
Web: www.ezstaffing.com
SIC: 7361 Nurses' registry

(P-11127)
EASTERN STAFFING LLC
Also Called: Select Staffing
301 Mentor Dr # 210 (93111-3339)
PHONE................................805 882-2200
Stephen Sorensen, Managing Member
EMP: 469 EST: 2004
SALES (est): 1.82MM
SALES (corp-wide): 242.14MM Privately Held
Web: www.select.com
SIC: 7361 Employment agencies
PA: Butler International, Inc.
  3820 State St Ste A
  Santa Barbara CA
  805 882-2200

(P-11128)
ELITECARE MEDICAL STAFFING LLC
761 E Locust Ave Ste 103 (93720-3023)
PHONE................................559 438-7700
EMP: 60 EST: 2002
SALES (est): 3.03MM Privately Held
Web: www.elitecare.net
SIC: 7361 Nurses' registry

(P-11129)
EMPLOYNET INC
838 S Main St Ste B (93901-2408)
PHONE................................831 233-9999
EMP: 1327
SALES (corp-wide): 104.23MM Privately Held
Web: www.employnet.com
SIC: 7361 Employment agencies
PA: Employnet, Inc.
  2555 Garden Rd Ste H
  Monterey CA
  866 527-4473

(P-11130)
EMPLOYNET INC
123 E 9th St Ste 103 (91786-6033)
PHONE................................909 458-0961
EMP: 1327
SALES (corp-wide): 104.23MM Privately Held
Web: www.employnet.com
SIC: 7361 Employment agencies
PA: Employnet, Inc.
  2555 Garden Rd Ste H
  Monterey CA
  866 527-4473

(P-11131)
EPLICA INC
17785 Center Court Dr N (90703-8573)
PHONE................................562 977-4300
Jade Jenkins, Brnch Mgr
EMP: 94
SALES (corp-wide): 139MM Privately Held
Web: www.eplicaservices.com
SIC: 7361 Employment agencies
PA: Eplica, Inc.
  2385 Northside Dr Ste 250
  San Diego CA
  619 260-2000

(P-11132)
EPLICA CORPORATE SERVICES INC
Also Called: Eastridge Workforce Solutions
2385 Northside Dr Ste 250 (92108-2716)
PHONE................................619 282-1400
Seth Stein, CEO
EMP: 1770 EST: 2010
SALES (est): 3.9MM
SALES (corp-wide): 139MM Privately Held
SIC: 7361 Employment agencies
PA: Eplica, Inc.
  2385 Northside Dr Ste 250
  San Diego CA
  619 260-2000

(P-11133)
ESPARZA ENTERPRISES INC
51335 Cesar Chavez St Ste 112 (92236-1528)
PHONE................................760 398-0349
Manuel Padilla, Mgr
EMP: 792
SALES (corp-wide): 135MM Privately Held
Web: www.esparzainc.com
SIC: 7361 Labor contractors (employment agency)
PA: Esparza Enterprises, Inc.
  3851 Fruitvale Ave
  Bakersfield CA
  661 831-0002

(P-11134)
ESPARZA ENTERPRISES INC
222 S Union Ave (93307-3325)
PHONE................................661 631-0347
EMP: 792
SALES (corp-wide): 135MM Privately Held
Web: www.esparzainc.com
SIC: 7361 Labor contractors (employment agency)
PA: Esparza Enterprises, Inc.
  3851 Fruitvale Ave
  Bakersfield CA
  661 831-0002

(P-11135)
EXECUTIVE PERSONNEL SERVICES
1526 Brookhollow Dr Ste 83 (92705-5421)
PHONE................................714 310-9506
Mario Mendoza, Pr
Alinne Espinoza, *
EMP: 300 EST: 2013
SALES (est): 6.68MM Privately Held
SIC: 7361 Executive placement

(P-11136)
EXPRESS PERSONNEL SERVICES
Also Called: Express Personnel Services
870 W Onstott Frontage Rd Ste E (95991-3500)
PHONE................................530 671-9202
Tina Williams, Pr
Tom Williams, VP
EMP: 96 EST: 1985
SALES (est): 985.12K Privately Held
Web: www.expresspros.com
SIC: 7361 Employment agencies

(P-11137)
FANEUIL INC
Also Called: Faneuil, Inc.
5012 Dudley Blvd (95652-1029)
PHONE................................757 722-4095
EMP: 271
SALES (corp-wide): 149.31MM Privately Held
Web: www.faneuil.com
SIC: 7361 Employment agencies
HQ: Faneuil, Llc
  2 Eaton St Ste 1002
  Hampton VA

(P-11138)
FIRST CALL STAFFING INC
401 Wilshire Blvd Ste 1050 (90401-1450)
PHONE................................310 264-9914
Richard R Stolz, CEO
Marcia Allen, Prin
Marie Dwight, Contrlr
EMP: 61 EST: 2011
SALES (est): 972.86K Privately Held
Web: www.firstcallstaff.com
SIC: 7361 Placement agencies

(P-11139)
FLEXCARE LLC
Also Called: Flexcare Medical Staffing
532 Gibson Dr Ste 100 (95678-5878)
PHONE................................866 564-3589
Nate Porter, Managing Member
EMP: 1000 EST: 2007
SALES (est): 48.71MM Privately Held
Web: www.flexcarestaff.com
SIC: 7361 Employment agencies

(P-11140)
G2 SECURE STAFF
5757 W Century Blvd Ste 518 (90045-6456)
PHONE................................310 486-8155
EMP: 111 EST: 2018
SALES (est): 2.12MM Privately Held
Web: www.g2securestaff.com
SIC: 7361 Employment agencies

(P-11141)
GARICH INC (PA)
Also Called: The Tristaff Group
6050 Santo Rd Ste 200 (92124-1194)
PHONE................................858 453-1331
Gary O Van Eik, Pr
Richard N Papike, *
EMP: 295 EST: 1971
SALES (est): 23.07MM
SALES (corp-wide): 23.07MM Privately Held
Web: www.tristaff.com
SIC: 7361 8742 Executive placement; Management consulting services

(P-11142)
GARICH INC
Also Called: Tristaff Group
504 E Alvarado St Ste 201 (92028-2364)
PHONE................................951 302-4750
EMP: 365
SALES (corp-wide): 23.07MM Privately Held
SIC: 7361 Employment agencies
PA: Garich, Inc.
  6050 Santo Rd Ste 200
  San Diego CA
  858 453-1331

(P-11143)
GLASSDOOR INC (HQ)
Also Called: Glassdoor.com
50 Beale St Fl 16 (94105-1825)
PHONE................................415 275-7411
Robert Hohman, CEO
Christian Sutherland-wong, COO
Moody Glasgow, *
Brad Mirkovich, CRO*
Heather Friedland, Chief Product Officer*
EMP: 74 EST: 2007
SQ FT: 2,000
SALES (est): 166.69MM Privately Held
Web: www.glassdoor.com
SIC: 7361 7375 7371 Employment agencies; On-line data base information retrieval; Computer software development and applications
PA: Recruit Holdings Co., Ltd.
  1-9-2, Marunouchi
  Chiyoda-Ku TKY

(P-11144)
GO-STAFF INC
9878 Complex Dr (92054)
PHONE................................760 730-8520
EMP: 1234
SALES (corp-wide): 27.11MM Privately Held
Web: www.go-staff.com
SIC: 7361 Executive placement
PA: Go-Staff, Inc.
  8798 Complex Dr
  San Diego CA
  858 292-8562

(P-11145)
GO-STAFF INC
240 W Lincoln Ave (92805-2903)
PHONE................................657 242-9350
EMP: 1234
SALES (corp-wide): 27.11MM Privately Held
Web: www.go-staff.com
SIC: 7361 Executive placement
PA: Go-Staff, Inc.
  8798 Complex Dr
  San Diego CA
  858 292-8562

(P-11146)
GRANITE SOLUTIONS GROUPE INC (PA)
235 Montgomery St Ste 430 (94104-2907)
P.O. Box 3399 (95619-3399)
PHONE................................415 963-3999
Daniel Hector L'abbe, CEO
Ann Bauer, *

PRODUCTS & SERVICES SECTION
7361 - Employment Agencies (P-11169)

John Henning, *
EMP: 207 **EST:** 1998
SQ FT: 3,582
SALES (est): 19.14MM
SALES (corp-wide): 19.14MM **Privately Held**
Web: www.granitesolutionsgroupe.com
SIC: 7361 8742 Executive placement; Management consulting services

(P-11147)
GROWERS COMPANY INC
Also Called: THE GROWERS COMPANY, INC
21570 Potter Rd (93908-9727)
P.O. Box 6217 (93912-6217)
PHONE.................................831 424-3850
EMP: 100
SALES (corp-wide): 24.64MM **Privately Held**
Web: www.thegrowerscompany.com
SIC: 7361 Labor contractors (employment agency)
PA: The Growers Company Inc
   15834 S Avenue G
   Somerton AZ
   928 627-8080

(P-11148)
HARVEST TECHNICAL SERVICE INC
1839 Ygnacio Valley Rd Ste 390 (94598-3214)
PHONE.................................925 937-4874
Judy Fick, *Pr*
Chris Fick, *
EMP: 150 **EST:** 1997
SQ FT: 1,000
SALES (est): 7.82MM **Privately Held**
Web: www.harvtech.com
SIC: 7361 Executive placement

(P-11149)
HIRE UP STAFFING SERVICE
575 E Locust Ave Ste 203 (93720-2928)
PHONE.................................559 579-1331
Rebecca Abell, *Pr*
EMP: 450 **EST:** 2010
SALES (est): 15.76MM **Privately Held**
Web: www.hireupss.com
SIC: 7361 Executive placement

(P-11150)
HIRETEAMMATE INC
Also Called: Hiretual
2513 Charleston Rd Ste 200 (94043-1634)
PHONE.................................650 386-5017
Haiqing Jiang, *CEO*
EMP: 241 **EST:** 2015
SALES (est): 5.05MM **Privately Held**
Web: www.hireez.com
SIC: 7361 Executive placement

(P-11151)
HRN SERVICES INC
520 N Brand Blvd Ste 200 (91203-4734)
PHONE.................................323 951-1450
EMP: 95
Web: www.hrnservices.com
SIC: 7361 Nurses' registry

(P-11152)
HUNTINGTON BEACH UNION HIGH
7180 Yorktown Ave (92648-2680)
P.O. Box 787 (92648-0787)
PHONE.................................714 478-7684
EMP: 103
SALES (corp-wide): 301.2MM **Privately Held**
Web: www.hbuhsd.edu
SIC: 7361 Placement agencies
PA: Huntington Beach Union High School District
   5832 Bolsa Ave
   Huntington Beach CA
   714 903-7000

(P-11153)
IBFTECH INC
Also Called: Image Business Forms
343 Main St (90245-3814)
PHONE.................................424 217-8010
John Koch, *Pr*
EMP: 100 **EST:** 1979
SQ FT: 4,000
SALES (est): 5.6MM **Privately Held**
Web: www.chiptonross.com
SIC: 7361 Executive placement

(P-11154)
IDC TECHNOLOGIES INC (PA)
920 Hillview Ct Ste 250 (95035-4560)
PHONE.................................408 376-0212
Prateek Gattani, *CEO*
Yogen Malvia, *
EMP: 209 **EST:** 2003
SQ FT: 4,000
SALES (est): 97.72MM **Privately Held**
Web: www.idctechnologies.com
SIC: 7361 Placement agencies

(P-11155)
IDEAL PROGRAM SERVICES INC
3970 W Martin Luther King Jr Blvd (90008-1732)
PHONE.................................323 296-2255
Omolara Okunubi, *CEO*
EMP: 71 **EST:** 1989
SQ FT: 8,880
SALES (est): 4.58MM **Privately Held**
Web: www.idealprogramsservices.org
SIC: 7361 5999 8322 Employment agencies; Technical aids for the handicapped; Social services for the handicapped

(P-11156)
INNOVATIVE PLACEMENTS INC
Also Called: Ipi Travel
12400 High Bluff Dr Ste 100 (92130-3077)
PHONE.................................800 322-9796
Letha Engelman, *Pr*
Retha Clark, *
John Engelman, *
EMP: 150 **EST:** 1999
SALES (est): 5.87MM **Privately Held**
SIC: 7361 Placement agencies

(P-11157)
INSIGHT GLOBAL INC
725 S Figueroa St Ste 2800 (90017-5467)
PHONE.................................213 404-4140
Robert Bernatz, *Mgr*
EMP: 184 **EST:** 2011
SALES (est): 1.18MM **Privately Held**
Web: www.insightglobal.com
SIC: 7361 Executive placement

(P-11158)
INTEGRATED ASSOCIATES INC
4010 Morena Blvd Ste 222 (92117-4547)
P.O. Box 420818 (92142-0818)
PHONE.................................858 412-6189
Anthony Moser, *Prin*
Ethan Gillespie, *Stockholder*
EMP: 231 **EST:** 2012
SALES (est): 4.8MM **Privately Held**
Web: www.integratedassociatesinc.com

SIC: 7361 8748 Executive placement; Business consulting, nec

(P-11159)
JOSEPHINES PROF STAFFING INC (PA)
Also Called: Josephine's Personnel Services
2158 Ringwood Ave (95131-1720)
PHONE.................................408 943-0111
Josephine Hughes, *Pr*
Victoria Picard, *
EMP: 225 **EST:** 1988
SQ FT: 4,000
SALES (est): 9.58MM **Privately Held**
Web: www.jps-inc.com
SIC: 7361 8742 8721 7363 Placement agencies; Management consulting services; Accounting, auditing, and bookkeeping; Help supply services

(P-11160)
JT RESOURCES INC
26372 Ruether Ave (91350-2990)
PHONE.................................661 367-6827
Darren Jackson, *Prin*
EMP: 110 **EST:** 2015
SALES (est): 9MM **Privately Held**
Web: www.jtresources.com
SIC: 7361 Labor contractors (employment agency)

(P-11161)
KIMCO STAFFING SERVICES INC
Also Called: Kimco Staffing Solutions
1770 Iowa Ave Ste 160 (92507-7400)
P.O. Box 25190 (92799-5190)
PHONE.................................951 686-3800
Silvia Roberts, *Mgr*
EMP: 1039
SALES (corp-wide): 96.64MM **Privately Held**
Web: www.kimco.com
SIC: 7361 Employment agencies
PA: Kimco Staffing Services, Inc.
   17872 Cowan
   Irvine CA
   949 331-1199

(P-11162)
KIMCO STAFFING SERVICES INC
3415 S Sepulveda Blvd Ste 1100 (90034-7090)
PHONE.................................310 622-1616
EMP: 520
SALES (corp-wide): 96.64MM **Privately Held**
Web: www.kimco.com
SIC: 7361 Placement agencies
PA: Kimco Staffing Services, Inc.
   17872 Cowan
   Irvine CA
   949 331-1199

(P-11163)
KIMCO STAFFING SERVICES INC
Also Called: Kimco Services
4295 Jurupa St Ste 107 (91761-1429)
PHONE.................................909 390-9881
Pammy Burton, *Mgr*
EMP: 1039
SALES (corp-wide): 96.64MM **Privately Held**
Web: www.kimco.com
SIC: 7361 Labor contractors (employment agency)
PA: Kimco Staffing Services, Inc.
   17872 Cowan
   Irvine CA
   949 331-1199

(P-11164)
KINETICOM INC (PA)
333 H St (91910-5561)
PHONE.................................619 330-3100
Michael Wager, *CEO*
William Coyman, *
Casey Marquand, *
Blair Bode, *
Michael Steadman, *
EMP: 80 **EST:** 1999
SALES (est): 25.83MM
SALES (corp-wide): 25.83MM **Privately Held**
Web: www.kineticom.com
SIC: 7361 Executive placement

(P-11165)
KORE1 LLC
530 Technology Dr Ste 150 (92618-1368)
PHONE.................................949 706-6990
Steven Quarles, *Managing Member*
EMP: 153 **EST:** 2017
SALES (est): 35.75MM **Privately Held**
Web: www.kore1.com
SIC: 7361 Executive placement

(P-11166)
KORN FERRY (PA)
Also Called: Korn Ferry
1900 Avenue Of The Stars Ste 1500 (90067-4507)
PHONE.................................310 552-1834
Gary D Burnison, *Pr*
Robert P Rozek, *CCO*
EMP: 209 **EST:** 1969
SALES (est): 2.86B
SALES (corp-wide): 2.86B **Publicly Held**
Web: www.kornferry.com
SIC: 7361 8742 Employment agencies; Management consulting services

(P-11167)
L&T STAFFING INC
Also Called: Staffing Solutions
2122 W Whittier Blvd (90640-4013)
PHONE.................................323 727-9056
Fortino Rivera, *Brnch Mgr*
EMP: 313
SALES (corp-wide): 17.43MM **Privately Held**
Web: www.staffingsolutions.us
SIC: 7361 Employment agencies
PA: L&T Staffing, Inc.
   950 W 17th St Ste E
   Santa Ana CA
   714 558-1821

(P-11168)
L&T STAFFING INC (PA)
Also Called: Staffing Solutions
950 W 17th St Ste E (92706-3573)
PHONE.................................714 558-1821
Fortino Rivera, *CEO*
Lucia Montellano, *CFO*
EMP: 67 **EST:** 2004
SQ FT: 1,500
SALES (est): 17.43MM
SALES (corp-wide): 17.43MM **Privately Held**
Web: www.staffingsolutions.us
SIC: 7361 Executive placement

(P-11169)
LATERAL LINK GROUP INC
940 E 2nd St Apt 2 (90012-4348)
PHONE.................................310 405-0092

7361 - Employment Agencies (P-11170)

EMP: 75 EST: 2018
SALES (est): 2.95MM **Privately Held**
SIC: 7361 Executive placement

(P-11170)
LEADSTACK INC
611 Gateway Blvd Ste 120 (94080-7066)
PHONE....................................628 200-3063
Kazi Ahmed, *CEO*
EMP: 64 EST: 2016
SALES (est): 7.21MM **Privately Held**
Web: www.leadstackinc.com
SIC: 7361 Employment agencies

(P-11171)
LEGACY PERSONNEL INC
1680 Civic Center Dr Ste 230 (95050-4110)
PHONE....................................877 850-5132
Anthony Alabaster, *CEO*
Anthony Alabaster, *Pr*
EMP: 365 EST: 2015
SALES (est): 45.55MM **Privately Held**
Web: www.legacypersonnel.com
SIC: 7361 Labor contractors (employment agency)

(P-11172)
LOAN ADMINISTRATION NETWRK INC
Also Called: Lani
2082 Business Center Dr Ste 250 (92612)
PHONE....................................949 752-5246
Charlene Nichols, *Pr*
EMP: 100 EST: 1992
SALES (est): 5.76MM **Privately Held**
Web: www.lani.com
SIC: 7361 8742 Employment agencies; Financial consultant

(P-11173)
LUMICITY LLC
7901 Santa Monica Blvd Ste 205 (90046-5177)
PHONE....................................213 262-2064
James Gorfin, *CEO*
EMP: 69 EST: 2015
SALES (est): 3.41MM **Privately Held**
SIC: 7361 Executive placement

(P-11174)
MALEKO PERSONNEL INC
24301 Southland Dr Ste 400 (94545)
PHONE....................................480 405-2905
EMP: 92 EST: 2019
SALES (est): 235.94K **Privately Held**
Web: www.malekopersonnel.com
SIC: 7361 Employment agencies

(P-11175)
MARATHON STAFFING SOLUTIONS
2950 Beacon Blvd Ste 45 (95691-5031)
PHONE....................................978 649-6230
Chris Panagiotopoulos, *Prin*
Athena Panagiotakos, *
Suzanne Deshler, *
EMP: 99 EST: 2016
SALES (est): 2.4MM **Privately Held**
SIC: 7361 Employment agencies

(P-11176)
MCM HARVESTERS INC
1585 Lirio Ave (93004-3227)
P.O. Box 4731 (93007-0731)
PHONE....................................805 659-6833
EMP: 300
SQ FT: 4,000
SALES (est): 11.48MM **Privately Held**

(P-11177)
SIC: 7361 Labor contractors (employment agency)

(P-11177)
MEDISCAN DIAGNOSTIC SVCS LLC
Also Called: Mediscan Staffing Services
21050 Califa St Ste 100 (91367-5103)
PHONE....................................818 758-4224
Val Serebryany, *Pr*
EMP: 100 EST: 1995
SALES (est): 19.69MM
SALES (corp-wide): 2.81B **Publicly Held**
Web: www.crosscountry.com
SIC: 7361 Employment agencies
HQ: Mediscan Nursing Staffing, Llc
    21050 Califa St Ste 100
    Woodland Hills CA
    818 758-8680

(P-11178)
MHS CUSTOMER SERVICES INC
7586 Trade St Ste C (92121-2427)
PHONE....................................858 695-2151
Don T Fryer, *Pr*
Theresa Phebes, *
EMP: 75 EST: 1985
SQ FT: 8,600
SALES (est): 5.72MM **Privately Held**
Web: www.callmhs.com
SIC: 7361 1542 1531 7299 Labor contractors (employment agency); Nonresidential construction, nec; Operative builders; Handyman service

(P-11179)
MODUS LLC
Also Called: Modus Making It Move
240 Stockton St Fl 3 (94108-5315)
PHONE....................................415 989-1102
Chad Abbott, *Managing Member*
EMP: 108 EST: 2016
SALES (est): 10.78MM **Privately Held**
Web: www.nextedgenetworks.com
SIC: 7361 Employment agencies

(P-11180)
NEATLY TECHNOLOGIES INC
Also Called: Rocket
3397 Silver Springs Ct (94549-5249)
PHONE....................................415 509-1274
Abhinav Agrawal, *CEO*
Arjun Lall, *
Anant Chaudhary, *
EMP: 65 EST: 2017
SALES (est): 2.34MM **Privately Held**
SIC: 7361 Employment agencies

(P-11181)
NETPACE INC
5000 Executive Pkwy Ste 530 (94583-4210)
PHONE....................................925 543-7760
Omar Khan, *Pr*
EMP: 123 EST: 1996
SQ FT: 4,000
SALES (est): 9.39MM **Privately Held**
Web: www.netpace.com
SIC: 7361 7363 7371 Employment agencies; Temporary help service; Custom computer programming services

(P-11182)
NETPOLARITY INC
Also Called: Netpolarity
16301 Lavender Ln (95032-3606)
PHONE....................................408 971-1100
Haixia Zhang, *CEO*
David Chuang, *
EMP: 150 EST: 2000

SALES (est): 24.04MM **Privately Held**
Web: www.netpolarity.com
SIC: 7361 Executive placement

(P-11183)
NORTH AMRCN STAFFING GROUP INC
3 Pointe Dr Ste 100 (92821-7623)
PHONE....................................714 599-8399
Fred Flores, *Pr*
Cesar Hindu, *VP*
EMP: 69 EST: 2014
SALES (est): 2.87MM **Privately Held**
Web: www.nasg.com
SIC: 7361 8742 Employment agencies; Management consulting services

(P-11184)
NORTHWEST STFFING RSOURCES INC
Also Called: Resource Staffing Group
100 Howe Ave (95825-8202)
PHONE....................................916 960-2668
Windy Richard, *Mgr*
EMP: 2824
SALES (corp-wide): 25.31MM **Privately Held**
Web: www.resourcestaff.com
SIC: 7361 7363 Labor contractors (employment agency); Temporary help service
PA: Northwest Staffing Resources, Inc.
    851 Sw 6th Ave Ste 300
    Portland OR
    503 323-9190

(P-11185)
NOVATIME TECHNOLOGY INC (DH)
9680 Haven Ave Ste 200 (91730-5899)
PHONE....................................909 895-8100
Frank Su, *Pr*
▲ EMP: 60 EST: 1999
SQ FT: 6,000
SALES (est): 10.26MM
SALES (corp-wide): 1.14B **Privately Held**
Web: www.novatime.com
SIC: 7361 Executive placement
HQ: Ascentis Corporation
    11995 Singletree Ln # 400
    Eden Prairie MN
    866 382-6229

(P-11186)
NURSECHOICE
12400 High Bluff Dr (92130-3077)
PHONE....................................866 557-6050
EMP: 88 EST: 2019
SALES (est): 1MM **Privately Held**
Web: www.nursechoice.com
SIC: 7361 Employment agencies

(P-11187)
NURSEFINDERS INC
Also Called: Nursefinders
5120 W Goldleaf Cir Ste 100 (90056-1292)
PHONE....................................925 660-1153
EMP: 82
SALES (corp-wide): 995.64K **Privately Held**
Web: www.nursefinders.com
SIC: 7361 Employment agencies
PA: Nursefinders, Inc.
    12400 High Bluff Dr
    San Diego CA
    800 445-0459

(P-11188)
NURSEFINDERS LLC
Also Called: Nursefinders
1832 Commercenter Cir B (92408-3430)
PHONE....................................909 890-2286
TOLL FREE: 877
FAX: 909 890-2346
EMP: 150
SALES (corp-wide): 1.9B **Publicly Held**
SIC: 7361 7363 Employment agencies; Temporary help service
HQ: Nursefinders, Llc
    12400 High Bluff Dr
    San Diego CA
    858 314-7427

(P-11189)
NURSEFINDERS LLC (HQ)
Also Called: Nursefinders
12400 High Bluff Dr (92130-3077)
P.O. Box 919024 (92191-9024)
PHONE....................................858 314-7427
Susan Salka, *CEO*
Ralph S Henderson, *Pr*
Denise L Jackson, *Sr VP*
Chad W, *Reg Dir*
Meredith M, *Brnch Mgr*
EMP: 110 EST: 1975
SQ FT: 22,000
SALES (est): 91.25MM
SALES (corp-wide): 5.24B **Publicly Held**
Web: www.nursefinders.com
SIC: 7361 8082 7363 8049 Placement agencies; Home health care services; Help supply services; Nurses, registered and practical
PA: Amn Healthcare Services, Inc.
    2999 Olympus Blvd Ste 500
    Coppell TX
    866 871-8519

(P-11190)
OFFICEWORKS INC
300 Frank H Ste 269 (94612)
PHONE....................................510 444-2161
EMP: 85
SALES (corp-wide): 22.84MM **Privately Held**
Web: www.officeworksrx.com
SIC: 7361 Employment agencies
PA: Officeworks, Inc.
    3200 E Guasti Rd Ste 100
    Ontario CA
    909 606-4100

(P-11191)
OFFICEWORKS INC
11801 Pierce St Fl 2 (92505-4400)
PHONE....................................951 784-2534
EMP: 85
SALES (corp-wide): 22.84MM **Privately Held**
Web: www.officeworksrx.com
SIC: 7361 Employment agencies
PA: Officeworks, Inc.
    3200 E Guasti Rd Ste 100
    Ontario CA
    909 606-4100

(P-11192)
OS4LABOR LLC
120 N Fairway Ln Ste A (91791-1729)
PHONE....................................626 838-6745
EMP: 117 EST: 2008
SALES (est): 9.68MM **Privately Held**
Web: www.os4labor.com
SIC: 7361 Employment agencies

PRODUCTS & SERVICES SECTION
7361 - Employment Agencies (P-11216)

(P-11193)
OSI STAFFING INC
10913 La Reina Ave Ste B (90241-3654)
PHONE.................................562 261-5753
Jose Vazquez, *CEO*
Sid Dakoria, *
EMP: 100 EST: 2018
SALES (est): 4MM **Privately Held**
Web: www.osistaff.net
SIC: 7361 Placement agencies

(P-11194)
PACIFIC GTWY WRKFRCE PRTNR INC
4811 Airport Plaza Dr Ste 200 (90815)
PHONE.................................562 570-3700
Nick Schultz, *Ex Dir*
EMP: 60 EST: 2010
SALES (est): 722.77K **Privately Held**
Web: www.pacific-gateway.org
SIC: 7361 Labor contractors (employment agency)

(P-11195)
PARTNERS PRSNNEL - MGT SVCS LL
Also Called: Nexem Staffing
3820 State St Ste B (93105-3182)
PHONE.................................805 689-8191
EMP: 16932 EST: 2017
SALES (est): 184.95MM
SALES (corp-wide): 184.95MM **Privately Held**
Web: www.partnerspersonnel.com
SIC: 7361 Employment agencies
PA: Staffing Partners Holdings Inc.
   3820 State St Ste B
   Santa Barbara CA
   805 880-1900

(P-11196)
PARTNERSHIP STAFFING SVCS INC
Also Called: Partnership Staffing Solutions
19431 Soledad Canyon Rd A3 (91351-2632)
PHONE.................................661 542-7074
Judith Robledo, *CEO*
Richard Schonfeld, *CFO*
EMP: 710 EST: 2020
SALES (est): 38MM **Privately Held**
Web: www.partnershipstaffing.net
SIC: 7361 Employment agencies

(P-11197)
PDS DEFENSE INC
Also Called: Pds Tech
1798 Technology Dr Ste 130 (95110)
PHONE.................................408 916-4848
EMP: 222
Web: www.pdstech.com
SIC: 7361 Employment agencies
HQ: Pds Defense, Inc.
   300 E John Carpenter Fwy
   Irving TX
   214 647-9600

(P-11198)
PDS DEFENSE INC
3100 S Harbor Blvd Ste 135 (92704-6823)
PHONE.................................214 647-9600
Dj Englert, *Mgr*
EMP: 222
Web: www.pdstech.com
SIC: 7361 Employment agencies
HQ: Pds Defense, Inc.
   300 E John Carpenter Fwy
   Irving TX
   214 647-9600

(P-11199)
PEAK TECHNICAL SERVICES INC
2150 Trade Zone Blvd Ste 100 (95131-1730)
PHONE.................................855 650-7325
EMP: 291
SALES (corp-wide): 47.71MM **Privately Held**
Web: www.peaktechnical.com
SIC: 7361 Employment agencies
PA: Peak Technical Services, Inc.
   583 Epsilon Dr
   Pittsburgh PA
   412 696-1080

(P-11200)
PERSONAL ENERGY FINANCE INC
Also Called: Renovate America Financing
16870 W Bernardo Dr Ste 408 (92127-1677)
P.O. Box 270469 (92198-2469)
PHONE.................................877 858-3855
Shawn Stone, *CEO*
EMP: 64 EST: 2018
SALES (est): 2.07MM **Privately Held**
SIC: 7361 Employment agencies
PA: Renovate America, Inc.
   16870 W Bernardo Dr # 408
   San Diego CA

(P-11201)
PIONEER HEALTHCARE SVCS LLC
6255 Ferris Sq # F (92121-3232)
PHONE.................................800 683-1209
Daniel Rietti, *CEO*
Daniel Rietti, *Managing Member*
EMP: 300 EST: 2012
SALES (est): 20.14MM **Privately Held**
Web: www.pioneer-healthcare.com
SIC: 7361 8049 8099 Employment agencies; Physical therapist; Blood related health services

(P-11202)
PRE-EMPLOYCOM INC
Also Called: The Pr-Mplycom Fmly Cmpnies In
3615 Meadow View Dr (96002-9715)
P.O. Box 491570 (96049-1570)
PHONE.................................800 300-1821
Robert V Mather, *Pr*
EMP: 100 EST: 1993
SALES (est): 10.46MM **Privately Held**
Web: www.pre-employ.com
SIC: 7361 Employment agencies

(P-11203)
PRECISE FIT LIMITED ONE LLC
Also Called: Pfitech
17011 Beach Blvd Ste 900 (92647-5998)
PHONE.................................310 824-1800
EMP: 380 EST: 2001
SQ FT: 10,000
SALES (est): 37.54MM **Privately Held**
SIC: 7361 Employment agencies

(P-11204)
PREFERRED HLTHCARE RGISTRY INC
4909 Murphy Canyon Rd Ste 310 (92123-4349)
P.O. Box 17860 (92177-7860)
PHONE.................................800 787-6787
Melanie Reiten, *Pr*
Rebecca Edwards Diata, *
EMP: 170 EST: 1994
SQ FT: 2,100
SALES (est): 22.04MM **Privately Held**
Web: www.mypreferred.com
SIC: 7361 7363 Employment agencies; Temporary help service

(P-11205)
PREMIER STAFFING INC
Also Called: Premier Talent Partners
3595 Mt Diablo Blvd Ste 340 (94549-3849)
PHONE.................................415 362-2211
Sara Menke, *CEO*
EMP: 67 EST: 1998
SQ FT: 5,400
SALES (est): 16.06MM **Privately Held**
Web: www.premiertalentpartners.com
SIC: 7361 Executive placement

(P-11206)
PRIME ONE INC
22410 Hawthorne Blvd Ste 4 (90505-2539)
PHONE.................................310 378-1944
Elvira Musell, *Pr*
EMP: 156 EST: 2001
SQ FT: 1,000
SALES (est): 5.83MM **Privately Held**
SIC: 7361 Employment agencies

(P-11207)
PROFESSNL RGISTRY NETWRK CORP
Also Called: Gem Medical Management
17592 17th St Ste 225 (92780-7917)
PHONE.................................714 832-5776
George Makridis, *Pr*
EMP: 77 EST: 2004
SALES (est): 3.41MM **Privately Held**
SIC: 7361 Employment agencies

(P-11208)
PSG GLOBAL SOLUTIONS LLC (HQ)
4551 Glencoe Ave Ste 150 (90292-7921)
PHONE.................................310 405-0340
Brian Cotter, *Pr*
Maureen Maranca, *VP Fin*
EMP: 78 EST: 2008
SALES (est): 99.8MM
SALES (corp-wide): 226.27MM **Privately Held**
Web: www.psgglobalsolutions.com
SIC: 7361 Executive placement
PA: Teleperformance Se
   Du Na 21 Au 25
   Paris

(P-11209)
PTS ADVANCE
Also Called: Pts
1775 Flight Way Ste 100 (92782-1845)
PHONE.................................949 268-4000
EMP: 220 EST: 1995
SALES (est): 10.54MM **Privately Held**
Web: www.ptsadvance.com
SIC: 7361 Employment agencies

(P-11210)
QUANTUM WORLD TECHNOLOGIES INC
4281 Katella Ave Ste 102 (90720-3592)
PHONE.................................805 834-0532
Rakesh Srivastava, *CFO*
EMP: 450 EST: 2016
SALES (est): 50MM **Privately Held**
Web: www.quantumworldit.com
SIC: 7361 Placement agencies

(P-11211)
R&D CONSULTING GROUP INC
Also Called: R & D Partners
8910 University Center Ln Ste 400 (92122-1025)
PHONE.................................415 697-2585
Nancy Baltzer, *CEO*
EMP: 125 EST: 2012
SALES (est): 12.01MM **Privately Held**
Web: www.r-dpartners.com
SIC: 7361 Labor contractors (employment agency)

(P-11212)
RAMCO ENTERPRISES LP
585 Auto Center Dr (95076-3764)
PHONE.................................831 722-3370
EMP: 372
SALES (corp-wide): 125.53MM **Privately Held**
Web: www.ramcoenterpriseslp.com
SIC: 7361 Employment agencies
PA: Ramco Enterprises, L.P.
   710 La Guardia St
   Salinas CA
   831 758-5272

(P-11213)
RAMCO ENTERPRISES LP
325 Plaza Dr Ste 1 (93454-6929)
PHONE.................................805 922-9888
EMP: 371
SALES (corp-wide): 125.53MM **Privately Held**
Web: www.ramcoenterpriseslp.com
SIC: 7361 Executive placement
PA: Ramco Enterprises, L.P.
   710 La Guardia St
   Salinas CA
   831 758-5272

(P-11214)
RANDSTAD PROFESSIONALS US LLC
Also Called: Randstad Finance & Accounting
111 Anza Blvd Ste 202 (94010-1910)
PHONE.................................650 343-5111
Shannon Guzzetta, *Brnch Mgr*
EMP: 132
SALES (corp-wide): 24.5B **Privately Held**
Web: www.randstadusa.com
SIC: 7361 Executive placement
HQ: Randstad Professionals Us, Llc
   150 Presidential Way Fl 4
   Woburn MA

(P-11215)
RANDSTAD PROFESSIONALS US LLC
Also Called: Accountants International
2033 Gateway Pl Ste 120 (95110-3713)
PHONE.................................408 573-1111
Rona Patroni, *Brnch Mgr*
EMP: 88
SALES (corp-wide): 24.5B **Privately Held**
Web: www.randstadusa.com
SIC: 7361 Executive placement
HQ: Randstad Professionals Us, Llc
   150 Presidential Way Fl 4
   Woburn MA

(P-11216)
RANDSTAD PROFESSIONALS US LLC
Also Called: Randstad Finance & Accounting
17777 Center Court Dr N Ste 225 (90703-9320)
PHONE.................................562 468-0111
EMP: 66

7361 - Employment Agencies (P-11217)

SALES (corp-wide): 24.5B **Privately Held**
Web: www.randstadusa.com
SIC: **7361** Executive placement
HQ: Randstad Professionals Us, Llc
150 Presidential Way Fl 4
Woburn MA

(P-11217)
READYLINK INC
72030 Metroplex Dr (92276)
PHONE..................................760 343-7000
Daniel Caliendo, *Prin*
EMP: 99 EST: 2017
SALES (est): 9.85MM **Privately Held**
Web: www.readylinkstaffing.com
SIC: **7361** Employment agencies

(P-11218)
READYLINK HEALTHCARE
72030 Metroplex Dr (92276)
P.O. Box 1047 (92276-1047)
PHONE..................................760 343-7000
Barry L Treash, *Pr*
EMP: 85 EST: 2002
SALES (est): 17.62MM **Privately Held**
Web: www.readylinkstaffing.com
SIC: **7361** Nurses' registry

(P-11219)
RECRUIT 360
457 Ogle St (92627-3243)
PHONE..................................949 250-4420
Greg Kennedy, *Pr*
EMP: 115 EST: 2007
SALES (est): 3.32MM **Privately Held**
Web: www.recruit360.net
SIC: **7361** Executive placement

(P-11220)
REDLANDS EMPLOYMENT SERVICES
Also Called: Redlands Staffing Services
4295 Jurupa St Ste 110 (91761-1429)
PHONE..................................951 688-0083
Matt Tahlmeyer, *Pr*
EMP: 344
Web: www.arrowstaffing.com
SIC: **7361** Placement agencies
PA: Redlands Employment Services Inc
499 W State St
Redlands CA

(P-11221)
REHABABILITIES INC
Also Called: Social Service Professionals
11835 W Olympic Blvd Ste 1090e (90064-5001)
PHONE..................................310 473-4448
Ms. Meryl Stern, *Brnch Mgr*
EMP: 235
SALES (corp-wide): 8.82MM **Privately Held**
Web: www.rehababilities.com
SIC: **7361** Registries
PA: Rehababilities, Inc.
3401 Centre Lake Dr # 480
Ontario CA
909 989-5699

(P-11222)
RESOURCES CONNECTION LLC (HQ)
Also Called: Resources Global Professionals
17101 Armstrong Ave Ste 100 (92614-5717)
PHONE..................................714 430-6400
Donald B Murray, *Ch Bd*
Kate W Duchene, *
Herbert M Mueller, *

John D Bower, *CAO**
Tanja Cebula, *
EMP: 60 EST: 1999
SQ FT: 16,366
SALES (est): 583.41MM **Publicly Held**
Web: www.rgp.com
SIC: **7361** 8742 Executive placement; Management consulting services
PA: Resources Connection, Inc.
17101 Armstrong Ave # 100
Irvine CA

(P-11223)
RIVER CITY STAFFING INC
7777 Greenback Ln (95610-5800)
PHONE..................................916 485-1588
Cindy Bunker, *Pr*
Doug Bunker, *VP*
EMP: 114 EST: 1998
SALES (est): 3.41MM **Privately Held**
Web: www.rivercitystaffing.com
SIC: **7361** Executive placement

(P-11224)
SAGE GROUP
33 Falmouth St (94107-1046)
PHONE..................................415 512-8200
Cara France, *CEO*
Chris Yelton, *Pr*
EMP: 100 EST: 2016
SALES (est): 9.53MM
SALES (corp-wide): 26.17MM **Privately Held**
Web: www.thesagegroup.com
SIC: **7361** Employment agencies
PA: 24 Seven, Llc
41 Madison Ave Fl 37
New York NY
212 966-4426

(P-11225)
SAMUEL HALE LLC
Also Called: Samuel Hale
2365 Iron Point Rd Ste 190 (95630-8713)
PHONE..................................916 235-1477
Michael Dimanno, *CEO*
George Knowles, *
EMP: 2500 EST: 2016
SALES (est): 25.65MM **Privately Held**
Web: www.samuelhale.com
SIC: **7361** Employment agencies

(P-11226)
SE SCHER CORPORATION
Also Called: Acrobat Staffing
6731 Five Star Blvd Ste C (95677-2680)
PHONE..................................916 632-1363
EMP: 663
SALES (corp-wide): 61.69MM **Privately Held**
SIC: **7361** Employment agencies
PA: S.E. Scher Corporation
303 Hegenberger Rd # 300
Oakland CA
415 431-8826

(P-11227)
SE SCHER CORPORATION
Also Called: Acrobat Staffing
2525 Camino Del Rio S Ste 200 (92108-3717)
PHONE..................................858 546-8300
EMP: 663
SALES (corp-wide): 61.69MM **Privately Held**
SIC: **7361** Executive placement
PA: S.E. Scher Corporation
303 Hegenberger Rd # 300
Oakland CA
415 431-8826

(P-11228)
SELECT TEMPORARIES LLC (DH)
Also Called: Select Personnel Services
3820 State St (93105-3112)
PHONE..................................805 882-2200
Thomas A Bickes, *Pr*
Paul Galleberg, *
Shawn W Poole, *
▲ EMP: 90 EST: 1985
SQ FT: 30,000
SALES (est): 19.66MM
SALES (corp-wide): 10.97B **Publicly Held**
Web: www.select.com
SIC: **7361** Employment agencies
HQ: Employment Solutions Management, Inc.
1845 Satellite Blvd # 300
Duluth GA
770 671-1900

(P-11229)
SIGNATURE SELECT PERSONNEL LLC
138 W Bonita Ave Ste 207 (91773-3083)
PHONE..................................626 940-3351
Kenji Morinaga, *Managing Member*
Robert Morinaga, *
EMP: 500 EST: 2019
SALES (est): 14.18MM **Privately Held**
SIC: **7361** Employment agencies

(P-11230)
SIRACUSA ENTERPRISES INC
Also Called: Quality Temp Staffing
17737 Chatsworth St Ste 200 (91344-5628)
PHONE..................................818 831-1130
Joe Alas, *Pr*
Marie Alas, *
EMP: 70 EST: 1988
SALES (est): 3.11MM **Privately Held**
Web: www.qualitytempstaffing.com
SIC: **7361** Employment agencies

(P-11231)
SLINGSHOT CONNECTIONS LLC
840 The Alameda (95126-3145)
PHONE..................................408 247-8233
Jan Sonneman, *Prin*
Kelly Sheahan, *CFO*
Maritess Sagon, *Dir*
EMP: 79 EST: 2012
SALES (est): 4.15MM **Privately Held**
Web: www.slingshotconnections.com
SIC: **7361** Executive placement

(P-11232)
SOLID PERSONNEL INC
5175 Johnson Dr (94588-3343)
PHONE..................................510 370-3550
Cameron Mcnabb, *Pr*
EMP: 99 EST: 2014
SALES (est): 4.96MM **Privately Held**
Web: www.solidpersonnel.com
SIC: **7361** Labor contractors (employment agency)

(P-11233)
SOURCE ONE STAFFING LLC
5312 Irwindale Ave Ste 1h (91706-2076)
PHONE..................................626 337-0560
EMP: 9500
Web: www.s1staffing.com
SIC: **7361** Employment agencies

(P-11234)
SPEC PERSONNEL LLC
Also Called: Spec. Personnel
433 Airport Blvd Ste 310 (94010-2010)
PHONE..................................408 727-8000
EMP: 85
SALES (corp-wide): 26.44MM **Privately Held**
Web: www.speconthejob.com
SIC: **7361** Employment agencies
PA: Spec Personnel, Llc
4625 Creekstone Dr # 130
Durham NC
203 254-9935

(P-11235)
SPEC PERSONNEL LLC
Also Called: Spectra
1900 Lafayette St Ste 125 (95050)
PHONE..................................408 727-8000
Andrew Bergen, *Brnch Mgr*
EMP: 86
SALES (corp-wide): 26.44MM **Privately Held**
Web: www.speconthejob.com
SIC: **7361** Employment agencies
PA: Spec Personnel, Llc
4625 Creekstone Dr # 130
Durham NC
203 254-9935

(P-11236)
STAFF ASSISTANCE INC
Also Called: Assisted Home Care
72 Moody Ct Ste 100 (91360-7426)
PHONE..................................805 371-9980
Elaine Thinney, *Brnch Mgr*
EMP: 300
SIC: **7361** 8082 Nurses' registry; Home health care services
PA: Staff Assistance, Inc.
72 Moody Ct Ste 100
Thousand Oaks CA

(P-11237)
STAFFING SOLUTIONS INC
Also Called: Balance Staffing
2142 Bering Dr (95131-2013)
PHONE..................................408 980-9000
John Moss, *CEO*
Robert Feinstein, *
EMP: 80 EST: 1997
SQ FT: 4,000
SALES (est): 8.78MM **Privately Held**
Web: www.balancestaffing.com
SIC: **7361** 7363 Employment agencies; Help supply services

(P-11238)
STAR H-R
105 E 1st St (95425-3701)
PHONE..................................707 894-4404
EMP: 1008
SALES (corp-wide): 30.18MM **Privately Held**
Web: www.starhr.com
SIC: **7361** Employment agencies
PA: Star H-R
3820 Cypress Dr Ste 2
Petaluma CA
707 762-4447

(P-11239)
STAR H-R
1822 Jefferson St (94559-1618)
PHONE..................................707 265-9911
EMP: 1008
SALES (corp-wide): 30.18MM **Privately Held**
Web: www.starhr.com

PRODUCTS & SERVICES SECTION

7361 - Employment Agencies (P-11262)

SIC: **7361** Executive placement
PA: Star H-R
3820 Cypress Dr Ste 2
Petaluma CA
707 762-4447

(P-11240)
STAT NURSING SERVICES INC (PA)
2740 Van Ness Ave Ste 210 (94109-0216)
PHONE..................................415 673-9791
Kathleen Cleary, *Pr*
Charles Duck, *CEO*
EMP: 63 EST: 1979
SQ FT: 3,600
SALES (est): 9.59MM
SALES (corp-wide): 9.59MM **Privately Held**
Web: www.statrn.com
SIC: **7361** Nurses' registry

(P-11241)
T & R BANGIS ARGRICULTURE SVCS
375 Rd 200 (93261)
P.O. Box 724 (93216-0724)
PHONE..................................661 725-1948
Terry Bangi, *Pr*
Ted Bangi, *
EMP: 800 EST: 1943
SQ FT: 2,400
SALES (est): 11.7MM **Privately Held**
SIC: **7361** Labor contractors (employment agency)

(P-11242)
TALENT SPACE INC
1650 The Alameda (95126-2307)
PHONE..................................408 330-1900
Lisa Flores, *Pr*
EMP: 80 EST: 2004
SALES (est): 6.15MM **Privately Held**
Web: www.svtalentspace.com
SIC: **7361** Placement agencies

(P-11243)
TEAM-ONE STAFFING SERVICES INC
Also Called: Teamone Employment
16030 Ventura Blvd Ste 430 (91436-4457)
PHONE..................................951 616-3515
EMP: 1753
SIC: **7361** Placement agencies
PA: Team-One Staffing Services, Inc.
24318 Hemlock Ave Ste C1
Moreno Valley CA

(P-11244)
TEG STAFFING INC
Also Called: Eastridge Workforce Solutions
2385 Northside Dr Ste 250 (92108-2716)
PHONE..................................800 918-1678
Seth Stein, *CEO*
Brandon Stanford, *
Erin Medina, *CLO**
Kasey Hadjis, *CAO**
Jairo Carrion, *
EMP: 1600 EST: 1971
SALES (est): 61.11MM
SALES (corp-wide): 139MM **Privately Held**
SIC: **7361** Employment agencies
PA: Eplica, Inc.
2385 Northside Dr Ste 250
San Diego CA
619 260-2000

(P-11245)
TEKBERRY INC
3763 Shillingford Pl (95404-7666)
P.O. Box 9222 (95405-1222)
PHONE..................................707 313-5345
Ed Hamilton, *CEO*
EMP: 400 EST: 2005
SALES (est): 25MM **Privately Held**
Web: www.tekberry.com
SIC: **7361** Placement agencies

(P-11246)
TEMPS PLUS INC
Also Called: Sales Advantage Group
268 N Lincoln Ave Ste 12 (92882-7103)
PHONE..................................951 549-8309
EMP: 234 EST: 1996
SALES (est): 9MM **Privately Held**
Web: www.s3staffing.com
SIC: **7361** Executive placement

(P-11247)
TEMPUS LLC
Also Called: Emerald Health Services
2041 Rosecrans Ave Ste 245 (90245-4707)
PHONE..................................800 917-5055
Mark Siegel, *CEO*
Mark Stagen, *
EMP: 70 EST: 2002
SALES (est): 20.97MM **Privately Held**
Web: www.epictravelstaffing.com
SIC: **7361** Nurses' registry

(P-11248)
TETRA TECH EXECUTIVE SVCS INC
3475 E Foothill Blvd (91107-6024)
PHONE..................................626 470-2400
Sam Box, *Prin*
EMP: 162 EST: 2013
SALES (est): 22.93MM
SALES (corp-wide): 3.5B **Publicly Held**
Web: www.tetratech.com
SIC: **7361** Employment agencies
PA: Tetra Tech, Inc.
3475 E Foothill Blvd
Pasadena CA
626 351-4664

(P-11249)
TWOMAGNETS INC
Also Called: Clipboard Health
440 N Barranca Ave Ste 5028 (91723-1722)
PHONE..................................408 837-0116
Wei Deng, *CEO*
EMP: 650 EST: 2016
SALES (est): 51.12MM **Privately Held**
Web: www.clipboardhealth.com
SIC: **7361** Employment agencies

(P-11250)
UPWORK INC (PA)
2625 Augustine Dr Ste 601 (95054-2956)
PHONE..................................650 316-7500
Thomas Layton, *Non-Executive Chairman of the Board*
Stephane Kasriel, *
Brian Kinion, *CFO*
Brian Levey, *Business AFFAIRS Legal*
Hayden Brown, *Chief Marketing*
EMP: 237 EST: 2013
SQ FT: 32,000
SALES (est): 618.32MM
SALES (corp-wide): 618.32MM **Publicly Held**
Web: www.upwork.com
SIC: **7361** Executive placement

(P-11251)
URSUS IT STAFFING AND SERVICES
600 California St (94108-2701)
PHONE..................................877 668-7787
Cheryle Peikert, *CFO*
EMP: 78 EST: 2017
SALES (est): 773.32K **Privately Held**
SIC: **7361** Employment agencies

(P-11252)
VALLEY HEALTH CARE SYSTEMS INC
Also Called: Valley Healthcare Staffing
1300 National Dr Ste 140 (95834-1981)
PHONE..................................916 505-4112
Sejal Shah, *CEO*
Jason Beck, *Pr*
EMP: 150 EST: 2002
SQ FT: 5,000
SALES (est): 24.35MM
SALES (corp-wide): 49.54MM **Privately Held**
Web: www.totalmed.com
SIC: **7361** Nurses' registry
PA: Totalmed Llc
221 W College Ave Fl 2
Appleton WI
866 288-8001

(P-11253)
VISH CONSULTING SERVICES INC
9655 Granite Ridge Dr Ste 200 (92123)
PHONE..................................916 800-3762
Dhruv Bindra, *Pr*
EMP: 80 EST: 2011
SALES (est): 40.57MM **Privately Held**
Web: www.vishusa.com
SIC: **7361** 7363 Employment agencies; Temporary help service

(P-11254)
VOLT MANAGEMENT CORP
Also Called: Volt Workforce Solutions
3700 Old Redwood Hwy Ste 105 (95403-5738)
PHONE..................................707 547-1660
EMP: 67
SALES (corp-wide): 885.39MM **Privately Held**
Web: www.volt.com
SIC: **7361** Employment agencies
HQ: Volt Management Corp.
2400 Meadowbrook Pkwy
Duluth GA

(P-11255)
WELCOMETECH LLC
105 Serra Way # 145 (95035-5206)
PHONE..................................408 582-7998
Dev Nisar, *CEO*
EMP: 65 EST: 2006
SALES (est): 522.27K **Privately Held**
Web: www.welcometech.com
SIC: **7361** Executive placement

(P-11256)
WILLIAM MRRIS ENDVOR ENTRMT LL (DH)
Also Called: Wme
9601 Wilshire Blvd (90210-5213)
PHONE..................................212 586-5100
Walter Zifkin, *CEO*
Norman Brokaw, *
Jerry Katzman, *
Leonard Hirshan, *
Owen Laster, *
EMP: 200 EST: 1898
SQ FT: 46,000
SALES (est): 471.07MM
SALES (corp-wide): 5.27B **Publicly Held**
Web: www.wmeagency.com
SIC: **7361** Employment agencies
HQ: Endeavor Operating Company, Llc
11 Madison Ave
New York NY
212 586-5100

(P-11257)
WISE SKULLS LLC
1812 W Burbank Blvd (91506-1315)
PHONE..................................669 260-9005
EMP: 60
SALES (est): 1.16MM **Privately Held**
Web: www.wiseskulls.com
SIC: **7361** Employment agencies

(P-11258)
WMBE PAYROLLING INC
Also Called: Tcwglobal
3545 Aero Ct (92123-5700)
PHONE..................................858 810-3000
Samer Khouli, *CEO*
EMP: 130 EST: 2009
SALES (est): 349.34MM **Privately Held**
Web: www.tcwglobal.com
SIC: **7361** Placement agencies

(P-11259)
WONOLO INC
535 Mission St (94105-2903)
PHONE..................................415 766-7692
Yong Kim, *CEO*
Asher Brustein, *
Jeremy Burton, *
Beatrice Pang, *
Margot Moellenberg, *
EMP: 85 EST: 2014
SQ FT: 7,500
SALES (est): 15.83MM **Privately Held**
Web: www.wonolo.com
SIC: **7361** Labor contractors (employment agency)

(P-11260)
WORKWAY INC
3111 Camino Del Rio N Ste 400 (92108)
PHONE..................................619 278-0012
Bea Ogle, *Mgr*
EMP: 226
Web: www.workway.com
SIC: **7361** Executive placement
PA: Workway, Inc.
5151 Belt Line Rd
Dallas TX

(P-11261)
WORKWAY INC
19742 Macarthur Blvd Ste 235 (92612-2446)
PHONE..................................949 553-8700
Jill Burdock, *Brnch Mgr*
EMP: 227
Web: www.workway.com
SIC: **7361** Labor contractors (employment agency)
PA: Workway, Inc.
5151 Belt Line Rd
Dallas TX

(P-11262)
WORLDBRIDGE PARTNERS
25000 Avenue Stanford Ste 250 (91355)
PHONE..................................661 775-9999
John Broderick, *Brnch Mgr*
EMP: 152
Web: www.worldbridgepartners.com

7361 - Employment Agencies (P-11263)

SIC: **7361** Executive placement
PA: Worldbridge Partners
3721 Douglas Blvd
Roseville CA

(P-11263)
XL STAFFING INC
Also Called: Excell Staffing & SEC Svcs
826 Jackman St (92020-3053)
PHONE.................................619 579-0442
EMP: 200 **EST:** 1996
SALES (est): 9.87MM **Privately Held**
Web: www.xlstaffing.com
SIC: **7361** 7381 Executive placement;
Security guard service

(P-11264)
ZIONS BANCORPORATION
Also Called: Zions Bank
200 N Pacific Coast Hwy Ste 1850 (90245)
PHONE.................................424 290-5123
EMP: 5182
SALES (corp-wide): 3.34B **Publicly Held**
Web: careers.zionsbancorp.com
SIC: **7361** Employment agencies
HQ: Zions Bancorporation
1 S Main St Fl 15
Salt Lake City UT
801 844-7637

7363 Help Supply Services

(P-11265)
A P R INC
Also Called: Alpha Professional Resources
100 E Thousand Oaks Blvd Ste 240 (91360)
PHONE.................................805 379-3400
Salvador Ramirez, *Pr*
Cliff Goodwin, *
EMP: 125 **EST:** 1993
SQ FT: 1,100
SALES (est): 9.86MM **Privately Held**
Web: www.alphaprotemps.com
SIC: **7363** 7361 Temporary help service;
Employment agencies

(P-11266)
ADECCO EMPLOYMENT SERVICES
1231 W Robinhood Dr (95207-5655)
PHONE.................................209 474-0443
Alice Prouty, *Brnch Mgr*
EMP: 73
Web: www.adeccona.com
SIC: **7363** Temporary help service
HQ: Adecco Employment Services, Inc
4800 Deerwood Campus Pkwy # 800
Jacksonville FL
631 844-7100

(P-11267)
ADO STAFFING INC
Also Called: Adecco Staffing
850 Lagoon Dr Bldg 99a (91910-2001)
PHONE.................................619 691-3659
Susannah Wright, *Mgr*
EMP: 200
Web: www.olsten.com
SIC: **7363** Temporary help service
HQ: Ado Staffing, Inc.
4800 Deerwood Campus Pkwy # 800
Jacksonville FL
631 844-7800

(P-11268)
ADVANCED MEDICAL REVIEWS LLC
Also Called: Advanced Medical Reviews
600 Corporate Pointe Ste 300 (90230)
PHONE.................................310 575-0900
Barak Mevorak, *CEO*
EMP: 61 **EST:** 2005
SQ FT: 10,000
SALES (est): 17MM **Privately Held**
Web: www.admere.com
SIC: **7363** Medical help service
PA: Examworks Group, Inc.
3280 Peachtree Rd Ne # 26
Atlanta GA

(P-11269)
ADVANTAGE WORKFORCE SVCS LLC
55 Hawthorne St (94105-3991)
PHONE.................................415 212-6464
EMP: 125 **EST:** 2019
SALES (est): 4.04MM **Privately Held**
SIC: **7363** Temporary help service

(P-11270)
ALL STARZ STFFING CNSLTING INC
9375 Archibald Ave Ste 202 (91730-5729)
PHONE.................................909 870-9559
EMP: 61
SALES (corp-wide): 5.18MM **Privately Held**
Web: www.allstarzstaffing.com
SIC: **7363** Temporary help service
PA: All Starz Staffing & Consulting, Inc.
15215 52nd Ave S Ste 200
Tukwila WA
253 277-4000

(P-11271)
ALTECH SERVICES INC
400 Continental Blvd Fl 6 (90245-5074)
PHONE.................................888 725-8324
EMP: 296
Web: www.altechts.com
SIC: **7363** 7361 Help supply services; Labor contractors (employment agency)
PA: Altech Services, Inc.
695 Rte 46 W Ste 301b
Fairfield NJ

(P-11272)
ANDERSON ASSOC STAFFING CORP (PA)
8200 Wilshire Blvd Ste 200 (90211-2328)
PHONE.................................323 930-3170
Tom Anderson, *Pr*
EMP: 200 **EST:** 1997
SALES (est): 11.82MM
SALES (corp-wide): 11.82MM **Privately Held**
SIC: **7363** Temporary help service

(P-11273)
AYA HEALTHCARE INC (PA)
5930 Cornerstone Ct W Ste 300 (92121-3741)
PHONE.................................858 458-4410
Alan Braynin, *Pr*
EMP: 335 **EST:** 2009
SQ FT: 20,000
SALES (est): 6B **Privately Held**
Web: www.ayahealthcare.com
SIC: **7363** 8049 Temporary help service; Nurses, registered and practical

(P-11274)
B2B STAFFING SERVICES INC
Also Called: B2b Payroll Services
4501 Cerritos Ave Ste 201 (90630-4215)
PHONE.................................714 243-4104
Brian Wigdor, *Pr*
Bruce Underwood, *
EMP: 350 **EST:** 2006
SALES (est): 12MM **Privately Held**
Web: www.b2bstaffingservices.com
SIC: **7363** Temporary help service

(P-11275)
BANYAN SOLUTIONS INC
Also Called: Banyon Transcription
2809 Blue Oak Ct (94513-4617)
PHONE.................................650 766-9338
Jyoti Challi, *Pr*
EMP: 65 **EST:** 2000
SALES (est): 2.18MM **Privately Held**
Web: www.banyansolutionsinc.com
SIC: **7363** 7389 Medical help service; Business Activities at Non-Commercial Site

(P-11276)
BUTLER SERVICE GROUP INC (HQ)
3820 State St Ste A (93105-3182)
PHONE.................................201 891-5312
EMP: 100 **EST:** 1965
SQ FT: 82,000
SALES (est): 146.12MM
SALES (corp-wide): 242.14MM **Privately Held**
SIC: **7363** 8711 8748 3661 Engineering help service; Engineering services; Communications consulting; Telephone and telegraph apparatus
PA: Butler International, Inc.
3820 State St Ste A
Santa Barbara CA
805 882-2200

(P-11277)
CANON RECRUITING GROUP LLC
27651 Lincoln Pl Ste 250 (91387-8818)
PHONE.................................661 252-7400
Laurie Grayem, *CEO*
Laurie Grayem, *Managing Member*
Tim Grayem, *
EMP: 500 **EST:** 1980
SQ FT: 7,500
SALES (est): 23.82MM **Privately Held**
Web: www.canonrecruiting.com
SIC: **7363** 7361 Office help supply service; Executive placement

(P-11278)
CARE STFFING PROFESSIONALS INC
2151 E Convention Center Way Ste 204 (91764-5429)
PHONE.................................909 906-2060
D'andre Lampkin, *CEO*
EMP: 80 **EST:** 2016
SALES (est): 4.65MM **Privately Held**
Web: www.carestaffingprofessionals.com
SIC: **7363** 7361 8049 8082 Medical help service; Nurses' registry; Nurses and other medical assistants; Visiting nurse service

(P-11279)
CEDAR SINAI
9090 Wilshire Blvd Ste 200 (90211-1848)
PHONE.................................310 285-7268
EMP: 67 **EST:** 2015
SALES (est): 2.19MM **Privately Held**
Web: www.cedars-sinai.org
SIC: **7363** Medical help service

(P-11280)
CHILDCARE CAREERS LLC
2000 Sierra Point Pkwy Ste 702 (94005-1845)
PHONE.................................650 372-0211
EMP: 1000 **EST:** 2010
SQ FT: 6,300
SALES (est): 52.2MM **Privately Held**
Web: www.childcarecareers.com
SIC: **7363** 7361 Temporary help service; Teachers' agency

(P-11281)
CLEARPATH WORKFORCE MGT INC
1215 W Center St Ste 102 (95337-4280)
P.O. Box 1930 (95336-1156)
PHONE.................................209 239-8700
Renee Fink, *CEO*
Jason Posel, *
Judy Gnade, *
Sue Ortiz, *Compliance Vice President*
Sandi Silva, *
EMP: 224 **EST:** 2001
SQ FT: 3,171
SALES (est): 2.66MM
SALES (corp-wide): 23.69MM **Privately Held**
Web: www.1099oremployee.com
SIC: **7363** Temporary help service
PA: Clearpath Management Group, Inc.
1215 W Center St Ste 102
Manteca CA
209 239-8700

(P-11282)
COAST PERSONNEL SERVICES INC (PA)
2295 De La Cruz Blvd (95050-3020)
P.O. Box 328 (95052-0328)
PHONE.................................408 653-2100
Larry K Bunker, *CEO*
Larry Broun, *
EMP: 1895 **EST:** 1987
SQ FT: 7,500
SALES (est): 38.45MM
SALES (corp-wide): 38.45MM **Privately Held**
Web: www.coastjobs.com
SIC: **7363** Temporary help service

(P-11283)
EMERGNCY MDCINE SPCLIST ORNGE
Also Called: Emsoc
1310 W Stewart Dr Ste 212 (92868-3837)
PHONE.................................714 543-8911
Matthey Mallarky, *Managing Member*
Mark Falcone Parnter, *Prin*
Jonathen Blair, *Pt*
Courtney Aldama, *Mgr*
EMP: 96 **EST:** 1976
SALES (est): 3.41MM **Privately Held**
Web: www.emsoc.net
SIC: **7363** Medical help service

(P-11284)
EPLICA INC (PA)
Also Called: Eastridge Workforce Solutions
2385 Northside Dr Ste 250 (92108-2703)
PHONE.................................619 260-2000
Robert Svet, *Pr*
EMP: 175 **EST:** 1971
SQ FT: 15,000
SALES (est): 139MM
SALES (corp-wide): 139MM **Privately Held**
Web: www.eplicaservices.com

PRODUCTS & SERVICES SECTION
7363 - Help Supply Services (P-11306)

SIC: **7363** 7361 Temporary help service;
Employment agencies

(P-11285)
EPN ENTERPRISES INC
Also Called: 24/7 Medstaff
1900 Point West Way Ste 171
(95815-4705)
PHONE..............................888 788-5424
Edward Navales, *Pr*
EMP: 70 EST: 2008
SALES (est): 5.4MM **Privately Held**
Web: www.247medstaff.com
SIC: **7363** 8099 Temporary help service;
Medical services organization

(P-11286)
FELTON INSTITUTE (PA)
Also Called: Family Svc Agcy San Francisco
1500 Franklin St (94109-4523)
PHONE..............................415 474-7310
Albert Gilbert Iii, *Pr*
Marvin L Davis, *CFO*
Robert W Bennet, *Prin*
Michael Hofman, *Prin*
EMP: 70 EST: 1898
SQ FT: 14,000
SALES (est): 31.92MM
SALES (corp-wide): 31.92MM **Privately Held**
Web: www.felton.org
SIC: **7363** Help supply services

(P-11287)
GET HEAL INC
Also Called: Heal
528 Palisades Dr Ste 176 (90272-2844)
PHONE..............................310 528-4957
EMP: 63
SALES (corp-wide): 23.27MM **Privately Held**
Web: www.heal.com
SIC: **7363** Medical help service
PA: Get Heal, Inc.
4553 Glencoe Ave Ste 320
Marina Del Rey CA
310 528-4957

(P-11288)
GOODWILL OF SILICON VALLEY (PA)
Also Called: INSTITUTE FOR CAREER DEVELOPME
1080 N 7th St (95112-4425)
PHONE..............................408 998-5774
Michael E Fox, *CEO*
Frank Kent, *
Christopher King, *
Santi Varaceros, *
Dale Achabal, *
▲ EMP: 100 EST: 1937
SQ FT: 180,000
SALES (est): 57.89MM
SALES (corp-wide): 57.89MM **Privately Held**
Web: www.goodwillsv.org
SIC: **7363** 5932 Help supply services; Used merchandise stores

(P-11289)
HEALTHCARE RESOURCE GROUP
6571 Altura Blvd Ste 200 (90620-1020)
PHONE..............................562 945-7224
EMP: 192
SALES (corp-wide): 326.65MM **Publicly Held**
Web: www.hrgpros.com
SIC: **7363** Medical help service
HQ: Healthcare Resource Group, Inc

12610 E Mirabeau Pkwy # 900
Spokane Valley WA

(P-11290)
HOST HEALTHCARE INC
4225 Executive Sq Ste 1500 (92037-1466)
P.O. Box 927190 (92192-7190)
PHONE..............................858 999-3579
Adam Francis, *CEO*
William Bulger, *
EMP: 525 EST: 2012
SQ FT: 1,400
SALES (est): 51.02MM **Privately Held**
Web: www.hosthealthcare.com
SIC: **7363** Help supply services

(P-11291)
I N C BUILDERS INC
Also Called: Acme Staffing
1560 Ocotillo Dr Ste L (92243-4237)
PHONE..............................760 352-4200
EMP: 350
SALES (corp-wide): 11.06MM **Privately Held**
Web: www.acmestaffing.com
SIC: **7363** Temporary help service
PA: I N C Builders, Inc.
550 E 32nd St Ste 5a
Yuma AZ
928 344-8367

(P-11292)
ICONMA LLC
4701 Patrick Henry Dr Bldg 6 (95054-1819)
PHONE..............................888 451-2519
EMP: 170
SALES (corp-wide): 72.77MM **Privately Held**
Web: www.iconma.com
SIC: **7363** Temporary help service
PA: Iconma, L.L.C.
850 Stephenson Hwy # 612
Troy MI
248 583-1930

(P-11293)
INTERCTIVE MED SPECIALISTS INC
252 Waterside Cir (94903-2795)
PHONE..............................415 472-4204
EMP: 70 EST: 1994
SALES (est): 2.8MM **Privately Held**
Web: www.imsspecialists.com
SIC: **7363** Medical help service

(P-11294)
INTERIM INC
Also Called: Interim Services
200 Casentini St (93907-2299)
P.O. Box 3222 (93912-3222)
PHONE..............................831 758-9457
Helen Childres, *Dir*
EMP: 75
SALES (corp-wide): 24.17MM **Privately Held**
Web: www.interiminc.org
SIC: **7363** 8399 Temporary help service; Health and welfare council
PA: Interim, Inc.
604 Pearl St Frnt
Monterey CA
831 649-4399

(P-11295)
INTERIM HEALTHCARE INC
Also Called: Interim Services
1521 N Carpenter Rd Ste D3 (95351-1147)
PHONE..............................209 577-5936
Ron Murphy, *Pr*
EMP: 105

Web: www.interimhealthcare.com
SIC: **7363** 8082 Temporary help service; Home health care services
PA: Interim Healthcare Inc.
1551 Sawgrs Corp Pkwy # 230
Sunrise FL

(P-11296)
JUNE GROUP LLC
Also Called: Qualstaff Resources
9909 Mira Mesa Blvd Ste 240 (92131-3003)
PHONE..............................858 450-4290
R Scott Silver-hill, *Managing Member*
EMP: 100 EST: 2003
SALES (est): 8.44MM **Privately Held**
SIC: **7363** Temporary help service

(P-11297)
KAMPS COMPANY
1915 Moffat Blvd (95336-8945)
PHONE..............................209 823-8924
EMP: 160 EST: 1997
SALES (est): 14.76MM **Privately Held**
Web: www.kampspropane.com
SIC: **7363** Employee leasing service
PA: Services Group, Inc.
1870 Winton Rd S Ste 200
Rochester NY

(P-11298)
LLOYD STAFFING INC
18000 Studebaker Rd Ste 700 (90703-2679)
PHONE..............................631 777-7600
Luly Santana, *Pr*
EMP: 562
SALES (corp-wide): 48.53MM **Privately Held**
Web: www.lloydstaffing.com
SIC: **7363** Temporary help service
PA: Lloyd Staffing, Inc.
445 Broadhollow Rd # 119
Melville NY
631 777-7600

(P-11299)
MAGNIT RS INC
Also Called: Rightsourcing, Inc.
9 Executive Cir Ste 290 (92614-4704)
PHONE..............................800 660-9544
EMP: 77 EST: 2003
SALES (est): 64.4MM **Privately Held**
Web: www.rightsourcingusa.com
SIC: **7363** Help supply services
PA: Magnit, Llc
2635 Iron Pt Rd Ste 270
Folsom CA

(P-11300)
MAXIM HEALTHCARE SERVICES INC
28470 Avenue Stanford Ste 250 (91355)
PHONE..............................661 964-6350
Kowalczyk David, *Mgr*
EMP: 87
Web: www.maximhealthcare.com
SIC: **7363** 8099 8748 Medical help service; Blood related health services; Testing services
PA: Maxim Healthcare Services, Inc.
7227 Lee Deforest Dr
Columbia MD

(P-11301)
MAXIM HEALTHCARE SERVICES INC
1515 W 190th St (90248-4319)
PHONE..............................310 329-9115
EMP: 107

Web: www.maximhealthcare.com
SIC: **7363** Medical help service
PA: Maxim Healthcare Services, Inc.
7227 Lee Deforest Dr
Columbia MD

(P-11302)
MAXIM HEALTHCARE SERVICES INC
Also Called: Sacramento Staffing
1651 Response Rd Ste 200 (95815-5255)
PHONE..............................916 614-9539
Manpreet Singh, *Brnch Mgr*
EMP: 86
Web: www.maximhealthcare.com
SIC: **7363** Medical help service
PA: Maxim Healthcare Services, Inc.
7227 Lee Deforest Dr
Columbia MD

(P-11303)
MAXIM HEALTHCARE SERVICES INC
Also Called: San Frncisco Staffing Staffing
2100 Powell St (94608-1826)
PHONE..............................510 873-0700
J Cronte, *Mgr*
EMP: 87
Web: www.maximhealthcare.com
SIC: **7363** 7361 Medical help service; Nurses' registry
PA: Maxim Healthcare Services, Inc.
7227 Lee Deforest Dr
Columbia MD

(P-11304)
MAXIM HEALTHCARE SERVICES INC
Also Called: Fresno Staffing
5066 N Fresno St Ste 103 (93710-7615)
PHONE..............................559 224-0299
Tina Roberts, *Mgr*
EMP: 108
Web: www.maximhealthcare.com
SIC: **7363** 8082 Medical help service; Home health care services
PA: Maxim Healthcare Services, Inc.
7227 Lee Deforest Dr
Columbia MD

(P-11305)
MAXIM HEALTHCARE SERVICES INC
Also Called: Roseville Home Healthcare
151 N Sunrise Ave Ste 905 (95661-2929)
PHONE..............................916 771-7444
Andrew Brusaschetti, *Mgr*
EMP: 108
Web: www.maximhealthcare.com
SIC: **7363** 8082 Medical help service; Home health care services
PA: Maxim Healthcare Services, Inc.
7227 Lee Deforest Dr
Columbia MD

(P-11306)
MAXIM HEALTHCARE SERVICES INC
Also Called: San Mateo Staffing
1101 S Winchester Blvd Ste F164 (94403)
PHONE..............................410 910-1500
Jeff Nugent, *Mgr*
EMP: 87
Web: www.maximhealthcare.com
SIC: **7363** Medical help service
PA: Maxim Healthcare Services, Inc.
7227 Lee Deforest Dr
Columbia MD

(PA)=Parent Co (HQ)=Headquarters
✧ = New Business established in last 2 years

7363 - Help Supply Services (P-11307)

(P-11307)
MAXIM HEALTHCARE SERVICES INC
Also Called: Temecula Homecare
27555 Ynez Rd (92591-4678)
PHONE.................................951 694-0100
Jeff Abbott, *Mgr*
EMP: 108
Web: www.maximhealthcare.com
SIC: 7363 Medical help service
PA: Maxim Healthcare Services, Inc.
7227 Lee Deforest Dr
Columbia MD

(P-11308)
MAXIM HEALTHCARE SERVICES INC
Also Called: Riverside Companion Services
1845 Business Center Dr Ste 112 (92408)
PHONE.................................951 684-4148
Elijah Hall, *Mgr*
EMP: 87
Web: www.maximhealthcare.com
SIC: 7363 Medical help service
PA: Maxim Healthcare Services, Inc.
7227 Lee Deforest Dr
Columbia MD

(P-11309)
MAXIM HEALTHCARE SERVICES INC
Also Called: Bakersfield Respite Homecare
5201 California Ave Ste 200 (93309-1674)
PHONE.................................661 322-3039
Reyes Robles, *Brnch Mgr*
EMP: 87
Web: www.maximhealthcare.com
SIC: 7363 Medical help service
PA: Maxim Healthcare Services, Inc.
7227 Lee Deforest Dr
Columbia MD

(P-11310)
MAXIM HEALTHCARE SERVICES INC
801 Corporate Center Dr Ste 210 (91768-2627)
PHONE.................................626 962-6453
Kirk Grant, *Mgr*
EMP: 87
Web: www.maximhealthcare.com
SIC: 7363 7361 Medical help service; Nurses' registry
PA: Maxim Healthcare Services, Inc.
7227 Lee Deforest Dr
Columbia MD

(P-11311)
MEK INDUSTRIES INC
3517 Camino Del Rio S Ste 215 (92108)
PHONE.................................858 610-9601
Marc Kranz, *CEO*
EMP: 200 **EST:** 2019
SALES (est): 11.65MM **Privately Held**
SIC: 7363 Manpower pools

(P-11312)
MERITAGE MEDICAL NETWORK
4 Hamilton Landing Ste 100 (94949-8256)
PHONE.................................415 884-1840
Joel Criste, *CEO*
EMP: 101 **EST:** 1993
SALES (est): 6.41MM **Privately Held**
Web: www.meritagemed.com
SIC: 7363 Pilot service, aviation

(P-11313)
MERRITT HAWKINS & ASSOC LLC (HQ)
12400 High Bluff Dr Ste 100 (92130-3077)
PHONE.................................858 792-0711
Susan Salka Fka Nowakowski, *CEO*
Brian Scott, *
Denise Jackson, *
John Dillon, *
Maria Creps, *
EMP: 120 **EST:** 1987
SQ FT: 96,000
SALES (est): 23.57MM
SALES (corp-wide): 5.24B **Publicly Held**
Web: www.merritthawkins.com
SIC: 7363 Medical help service
PA: Amn Healthcare Services, Inc.
2999 Olympus Blvd Ste 500
Coppell TX
866 871-8519

(P-11314)
OPERATIONAL TECHNICAL SVCS LLC
10250 Constellation Blvd Ste 3-115 (90067-6200)
PHONE.................................424 203-6352
David Sibelman, *CEO*
Shahnaz Levyim, *
EMP: 61 **EST:** 2020
SALES (est): 3.24MM **Privately Held**
Web: www.getots.com
SIC: 7363 8748 Temporary help service; Environmental consultant

(P-11315)
PERSONNEL PLUS INC
12052 Imperial Hwy Ste 200 (90650-3090)
P.O. Box 817 (90651-0817)
PHONE.................................562 712-5490
EMP: 155
Web: www.ppitemps.com
SIC: 7363 7361 Temporary help service; Employment agencies

(P-11316)
PHOENIX ENGINEERING CO INC
Also Called: Phoenix Personnel
2480 Armacost Ave (90064-2714)
P.O. Box 66395 (90066-0395)
PHONE.................................310 532-1134
Silvia Maron, *Pr*
Silvia Lugo, *
EMP: 100 **EST:** 1974
SQ FT: 1,700
SALES (est): 4.86MM **Privately Held**
Web: www.artschangeleaders.org
SIC: 7363 7361 Office help supply service; Employment agencies

(P-11317)
PLANT MAINTENANCE INC
Also Called: Temporary Plant Cleaners
1330 Arnold Dr Ste 147 (94553-6538)
P.O. Box 6124 (94524-1124)
PHONE.................................925 228-3285
Tim Hollz, *Pr*
Kenneth B Johnson, *
EMP: 90 **EST:** 1996
SQ FT: 2,800
SALES (est): 1.72MM
SALES (corp-wide): 37.78MM **Privately Held**
Web: www.apmsteam.com
SIC: 7363 Industrial help service
PA: Monterey Mechanical Co.
8275 San Leandro St
Oakland CA
510 632-3173

(P-11318)
PLATINUM EMPIRE GROUP INC
Also Called: Platinum Healthcare Staffing
2430 Amsler St Ste B (90505-5302)
P.O. Box 10338 (90505-1238)
PHONE.................................310 821-5888
Arun Mahtani, *Pr*
Maluh Silvano, *
Aaron Quiboloy, *
EMP: 120 **EST:** 2005
SALES (est): 13.1MM **Privately Held**
Web: www.platinumhealthcarestaffing.com
SIC: 7363 Temporary help service

(P-11319)
PLUS GROUP INC
3300 Tully Rd Ste B1 (95350-0848)
PHONE.................................209 342-9022
Knowledge Hardy, *Mgr*
EMP: 610
Web: www.theplusgroup.com
SIC: 7363 7361 Temporary help service; Employment agencies
PA: The Plus Group Inc
7425 Janes Ave Ste 201
Woodridge IL

(P-11320)
PLUS GROUP INC
Also Called: Jobs Plus
2551 San Ramon Valley Blvd Ste 201 (94583-1661)
PHONE.................................925 831-8551
Patrick O'donnell, *Brnch Mgr*
EMP: 215
Web: www.theplusgroup.com
SIC: 7363 7361 Temporary help service; Executive placement
PA: The Plus Group Inc
7425 Janes Ave Ste 201
Woodridge IL

(P-11321)
RANDSTAD PROFESSIONALS US LLC
Also Called: Mergis Group, The
3333 Michelson Dr Ste 210 (92612-1682)
PHONE.................................781 213-1500
EMP: 66
SALES (corp-wide): 24.5B **Privately Held**
Web: www.spherion.com
SIC: 7363 Temporary help service
HQ: Randstad Professionals Us, Llc
150 Presidential Way Fl 4
Woburn MA

(P-11322)
RANDSTAD PROFESSIONALS US LLC
Also Called: Randstad Engineering
2321 Rosecrans Ave Ste 2215 (90245-4903)
PHONE.................................424 246-4400
Joe Davis, *Brnch Mgr*
EMP: 66
SALES (corp-wide): 24.5B **Privately Held**
Web: www.randstadusa.com
SIC: 7363 Temporary help service
HQ: Randstad Professionals Us, Llc
150 Presidential Way Fl 4
Woburn MA

(P-11323)
REMEDYTEMP INC (DH)
Also Called: Remedy Intelligent Staffing
101 Enterprise Ste 100 (92656-2604)
PHONE.................................949 425-7600
David Stephen Sorensen, *CEO*
Richard Hulme, *Ex VP*
Jeff R Mitchell, *CFO*
EMP: 143 **EST:** 1974
SQ FT: 51,000
SALES (est): 42.08MM
SALES (corp-wide): 10.97B **Publicly Held**
Web: www.remedystaffing.com
SIC: 7363 7361 Temporary help service; Employment agencies
HQ: Employbridge, Llc
301 Mentor Dr Ste 210
Santa Barbara CA

(P-11324)
ROBERT HALF INC (PA)
2884 Sand Hill Rd Ste 200 (94025-7059)
PHONE.................................650 234-6000
M Keith Waddell, *V Ch Bd*
Harold M Messmer Junior, *Ex Ch Bd*
Michael C Buckley, *Ex VP*
Robert W Glass, *Executive Corporate Development Vice President*
▲ **EMP:** 100 **EST:** 1948
SALES (est): 7.24B
SALES (corp-wide): 7.24B **Publicly Held**
Web: www.roberthalf.com
SIC: 7363 7361 8748 8721 Temporary help service; Placement agencies; Business consulting, nec; Auditing services

(P-11325)
ROTH STAFFING COMPANIES LP (PA)
Also Called: Ultimate Staffing Services
450 N State College Blvd (92868-1708)
PHONE.................................714 939-8600
Adam Roth, *CEO*
Ben Roth, *
Pam Sexauer, *
◆ **EMP:** 80 **EST:** 1994
SALES (est): 88.3MM **Privately Held**
Web: www.rothstaffing.com
SIC: 7363 Help supply services

(P-11326)
RX PRO HEALTH LLC
12400 High Bluff Dr Ste 100 (92130-3077)
PHONE.................................858 369-4050
Susan R Salka, *CEO*
EMP: 1800 **EST:** 2003
SQ FT: 175,000
SALES (est): 41.9MM
SALES (corp-wide): 5.24B **Publicly Held**
SIC: 7363 Medical help service
PA: Amn Healthcare Services, Inc.
2999 Olympus Blvd Ste 500
Coppell TX
866 871-8519

(P-11327)
SAGE STAFFING CONSULTANTS INC (PA)
Also Called: Sage Staffing
27441 Tourney Rd Ste 150 (91355-5312)
PHONE.................................661 254-4026
Laura Kincaid, *CEO*
Greg Kincaid, *Pr*
EMP: 190 **EST:** 1987
SQ FT: 5,000
SALES (est): 4.82MM **Privately Held**
Web: www.sagestaffing.com
SIC: 7363 Temporary help service

(P-11328)
SAN DIEGO PRO STAFFING
591 Camino De La Reina Ste 1020 (92108)
PHONE.................................858 731-3116
Innesa Zavulunova, *CEO*
EMP: 63 **EST:** 2014
SALES (est): 5.85MM **Privately Held**

PRODUCTS & SERVICES SECTION

7363 - Help Supply Services (P-11352)

Web: www.boutiquerecruiting.com
SIC: **7363** Temporary help service

(P-11329)
SE SCHER CORPORATION
1585 The Alameda (95126-2310)
PHONE.................................408 844-0772
EMP: 664
SALES (corp-wide): 61.69MM **Privately Held**
SIC: **7363** Help supply services
PA: S.E. Scher Corporation
    303 Hegenberger Rd # 300
    Oakland CA
    415 431-8826

(P-11330)
SFN GROUP INC
Also Called: Spherion Prof Recruiting Group
4660 La Jolla Village Dr Ste 910 (92122-4601)
PHONE.................................858 458-9200
Bobby Nerini, *Mgr*
EMP: 955
SALES (corp-wide): 24.5B **Privately Held**
Web: www.spherion.com
SIC: **7363** Temporary help service
HQ: Sfn Group, Inc.
    2050 Spectrum Blvd
    Fort Lauderdale FL
    954 308-7600

(P-11331)
SFN GROUP INC
114 Pacifica Ste 210 (92618-3320)
PHONE.................................949 727-8500
Tammy Hawkins, *Mgr*
EMP: 716
SALES (corp-wide): 24.5B **Privately Held**
Web: www.spherion.com
SIC: **7363** Temporary help service
HQ: Sfn Group, Inc.
    2050 Spectrum Blvd
    Fort Lauderdale FL
    954 308-7600

(P-11332)
SFN GROUP INC
919 E Hillsdale Blvd (94404-2112)
PHONE.................................650 348-4967
Dayna Miller, *Brnch Mgr*
EMP: 716
SALES (corp-wide): 24.5B **Privately Held**
Web: www.spherion.com
SIC: **7363** Temporary help service
HQ: Sfn Group, Inc.
    2050 Spectrum Blvd
    Fort Lauderdale FL
    954 308-7600

(P-11333)
SFN GROUP INC
401 River Oaks Pkwy (95134-1916)
PHONE.................................408 526-0115
Chris Van Groningen, *Brnch Mgr*
EMP: 716
SALES (corp-wide): 24.5B **Privately Held**
Web: www.spherion.com
SIC: **7363** Temporary help service
HQ: Sfn Group, Inc.
    2050 Spectrum Blvd
    Fort Lauderdale FL
    954 308-7600

(P-11334)
SFN GROUP INC
Also Called: Spherion Staffing Group
3050 Victor Ave Ste A (96002)
PHONE.................................530 222-3434
Sheryl Lakowski, *Brnch Mgr*
EMP: 716
SALES (corp-wide): 24.5B **Privately Held**
Web: www.spherion.com
SIC: **7363** Temporary help service
HQ: Sfn Group, Inc.
    2050 Spectrum Blvd
    Fort Lauderdale FL
    954 308-7600

(P-11335)
SFN GROUP INC
Also Called: Spherion Technology Svcs Group
3825 Hopyard Rd Ste 270 (94588-2958)
PHONE.................................925 847-8500
EMP: 716
SALES (corp-wide): 24.5B **Privately Held**
Web: www.spherion.com
SIC: **7363** Temporary help service
HQ: Sfn Group, Inc.
    2050 Spectrum Blvd
    Fort Lauderdale FL
    954 308-7600

(P-11336)
SFN GROUP INC
Also Called: Spherion Hr Consulting
2150 N 1st St Ste 230 (95131-2020)
PHONE.................................408 452-4845
EMP: 716
SALES (corp-wide): 24.5B **Privately Held**
Web: www.spherion.com
SIC: **7363** Temporary help service
HQ: Sfn Group, Inc.
    2050 Spectrum Blvd
    Fort Lauderdale FL
    954 308-7600

(P-11337)
SFN GROUP INC
1 Meyer Plz (94590-5925)
PHONE.................................707 551-2719
EMP: 716
SALES (corp-wide): 24.5B **Privately Held**
Web: www.spherion.com
SIC: **7363** Temporary help service
HQ: Sfn Group, Inc.
    2050 Spectrum Blvd
    Fort Lauderdale FL
    954 308-7600

(P-11338)
SOUTHERN HOME CARE SVCS INC
Also Called: Kelly Services
2900 Bristol St Ste D107 (92626-5914)
PHONE.................................714 979-7413
Vicki Demirozu, *Dir*
EMP: 85
SALES (corp-wide): 5.27B **Privately Held**
Web: www.kellyservices.com
SIC: **7363** 8082 Temporary help service; Home health care services
HQ: Southern Home Care Services, Inc.
    805 N Whittington Pkwy
    Louisville KY

(P-11339)
TAD PGS INC
12062 Valley View St Ste 108 (92845-1773)
PHONE.................................800 261-3779
Latonya Walker, *Dir*
EMP: 797
Web: www.tadpgs.com
SIC: **7363** Temporary help service
HQ: Tad Pgs, Inc.
    1001 3rd Ave W Ste 460
    Bradenton FL
    941 746-4434

(P-11340)
TAD PGS INC
10805 Holder St Ste 250 (90630-5142)
PHONE.................................571 451-2428
EMP: 797
Web: www.tadpgs.com
SIC: **7363** Temporary help service
HQ: Tad Pgs, Inc.
    1001 3rd Ave W Ste 460
    Bradenton FL
    941 746-4434

(P-11341)
TAOS MOUNTAIN LLC
1 Market St 36th Fl (94105-1420)
PHONE.................................888 826-7686
EMP: 72
SALES (corp-wide): 60.53B **Publicly Held**
Web: www.taos.com
SIC: **7363** Temporary help service
HQ: Taos Mountain, Llc
    1307 S Eagle Flight Way
    Boise ID

(P-11342)
THE MORNING STAR COMPANY (PA)
724 Main St Ste 202 (95695-3491)
PHONE.................................530 666-6600
◆ EMP: 70 **EST:** 1970
SALES (est): 481.12K
SALES (corp-wide): 481.12K **Privately Held**
Web: www.morningstarco.com
SIC: **7363** 8741 4212 2033 Employee leasing service; Management services; Local trucking, without storage; Canned fruits and specialties

(P-11343)
TRIPOD INC
Also Called: Brightstar Care Oxnard Cmrllo
1545 W 5th St Ste 200 (93030-6510)
PHONE.................................805 585-2273
EMP: 74
SALES (corp-wide): 1.76MM **Privately Held**
SIC: **7363** Medical help service
PA: Tripod Inc.
    148 N Brent St Ste 201
    Ventura CA

(P-11344)
USA STAFFING INC
505 Higuera St (93401-6107)
PHONE.................................805 269-2677
Susan Elson, *Mgr*
EMP: 75 **EST:** 2010
SALES (est): 2.11MM **Privately Held**
Web: www.unitedwestaff.com
SIC: **7363** Temporary help service

(P-11345)
VACAVILLE HEALTHCARE INC
585 Nut Tree Ct (95687-3353)
PHONE.................................707 449-8000
Joseph M Niccoli Junior, *Pr*
EMP: 150 **EST:** 2003
SALES (est): 7.92MM **Privately Held**
SIC: **7363** Medical help service

(P-11346)
VANPIKE INC (PA)
6336 Greenwich Dr Ste 100 (92122-5918)
PHONE.................................858 453-1331
Gary Van Eik, *Pr*
Richard Papike, *
EMP: 60 **EST:** 1971
SQ FT: 9,000
SALES (est): 29.16MM
SALES (corp-wide): 29.16MM **Privately Held**
Web: www.tristaff.com
SIC: **7363** 7361 Temporary help service; Executive placement

(P-11347)
VASINDA INVESTMENTS INC
Also Called: Around The Clock Care
5353 Truckston Ave (93309)
PHONE.................................661 324-4277
EMP: 75 **EST:** 1994
SALES (est): 2.48MM **Privately Held**
Web: www.bakersfieldcare.com
SIC: **7363** Domestic help service

(P-11348)
VAYA WORKFORCE SOLUTIONS LLC
5930 Cornerstone Ct W Ste 300 (92121-3741)
PHONE.................................866 687-7390
Alan Braynin, *Pr*
EMP: 150 **EST:** 2021
SALES (est): 11.09MM **Privately Held**
Web: www.vayaworkforce.com
SIC: **7363** Temporary help service
PA: Aya Healthcare, Inc.
    5930 Cornerstone Ct W # 3
    San Diego CA

(P-11349)
VOLT MANAGEMENT CORP
Also Called: Volt Workforce Solutions
715 6th St (93446-2871)
PHONE.................................805 237-0882
EMP: 67
SALES (corp-wide): 885.39MM **Privately Held**
Web: www.volt.com
SIC: **7363** Help supply services
HQ: Volt Management Corp.
    2400 Meadowbrook Pkwy
    Duluth GA

(P-11350)
VOLT MANAGEMENT CORP
Also Called: Volt Workforce Solutions
635 Sanborn Pl (93901-4533)
PHONE.................................831 975-4374
Abegail Nunez, *Brnch Mgr*
EMP: 67
SALES (corp-wide): 885.39MM **Privately Held**
Web: www.volt.com
SIC: **7363** Help supply services
HQ: Volt Management Corp.
    2400 Meadowbrook Pkwy
    Duluth GA

(P-11351)
VOLT MANAGEMENT CORP
Also Called: Volt Workforce Solutions
1650 Iowa Ave Ste 140 (92507-2432)
PHONE.................................951 789-8133
Scott Giroux, *Brnch Mgr*
EMP: 67
SALES (corp-wide): 885.39MM **Privately Held**
Web: www.volt.com
SIC: **7363** Help supply services
HQ: Volt Management Corp.
    2400 Meadowbrook Pkwy
    Duluth GA

(P-11352)
VOLT MANAGEMENT CORP
Also Called: Volt Workforce Solutions
1701 Solar Dr Ste 145 (93030-0137)

7363 - Help Supply Services (P-11353)

PHONE..................805 485-0506
EMP: 67
SALES (corp-wide): 885.39MM **Privately Held**
Web: www.volt.com
SIC: **7363** Help supply services
HQ: Volt Management Corp.
2400 Meadowbrook Pkwy
Duluth GA

(P-11353)
VOLT MANAGEMENT CORP
Also Called: Volt Workforce Solutions
19191 S Vermont Ave Ste 950 (90502-1098)
PHONE..................310 316-8523
Rhona Driggs, *Brnch Mgr*
EMP: 67
SALES (corp-wide): 885.39MM **Privately Held**
Web: www.volt.com
SIC: **7363** Temporary help service
HQ: Volt Management Corp.
2400 Meadowbrook Pkwy
Duluth GA

(P-11354)
VOLT MANAGEMENT CORP
Also Called: Volt Temporary Services
2411 N Glassell St (92865-2717)
PHONE..................800 654-2624
Rhona Driggs, *Brnch Mgr*
EMP: 300
SALES (corp-wide): 885.39MM **Privately Held**
Web: www.volt.com
SIC: **7363** **7373** Temporary help service; Computer integrated systems design
HQ: Volt Management corp.
2400 Meadowbrook Pkwy
Duluth GA

(P-11355)
VOLT MANAGEMENT CORP
Also Called: Volt Workforce Solutions
100 N Citrus St Ste 150 (91791-1656)
PHONE..................626 931-1437
Rhona Driggs, *Brnch Mgr*
EMP: 67
SALES (corp-wide): 885.39MM **Privately Held**
Web: www.volt.com
SIC: **7363** Temporary help service
HQ: Volt Management Corp.
2400 Meadowbrook Pkwy
Duluth GA

(P-11356)
VOLT MANAGEMENT CORP
Also Called: Volt Workforce Solutions
1400 N Harbor Blvd Ste 103 (92835-4107)
PHONE..................714 879-9330
Scott Giroux, *Brnch Mgr*
EMP: 67
SQ FT: 11,000
SALES (corp-wide): 885.39MM **Privately Held**
Web: www.volt.com
SIC: **7363** Temporary help service
HQ: Volt Management Corp.
2400 Meadowbrook Pkwy
Duluth GA

(P-11357)
VOLT MANAGEMENT CORP
Also Called: Volt Workforce Solutions
7676 Hazard Center Dr Ste 1000 (92108-4503)
PHONE..................858 576-3140
Rhona Driggs, *Brnch Mgr*

EMP: 89
SALES (corp-wide): 885.39MM **Privately Held**
Web: www.volt.com
SIC: **7363** Temporary help service
HQ: Volt Management Corp.
2400 Meadowbrook Pkwy
Duluth GA

(P-11358)
VOLT MANAGEMENT CORP
Also Called: Volt Workforce Solutions
1300 Santa Barbara St Ste A (93101-6041)
PHONE..................805 560-8658
Scott Giroux, *Brnch Mgr*
EMP: 78
SALES (corp-wide): 885.39MM **Privately Held**
Web: www.volt.com
SIC: **7363** Temporary help service
HQ: Volt Management Corp.
2400 Meadowbrook Pkwy
Duluth GA

(P-11359)
VOLT MANAGEMENT CORP
Also Called: Volt Workforce Solutions
7330 N Palm Ave Ste 105 (93711-5768)
PHONE..................559 435-1255
Scott Giroux, *Brnch Mgr*
EMP: 67
SALES (corp-wide): 885.39MM **Privately Held**
Web: www.volt.com
SIC: **7363** **7361** Temporary help service; Employment agencies
HQ: Volt Management Corp.
2400 Meadowbrook Pkwy
Duluth GA

(P-11360)
VOLT MANAGEMENT CORP
Also Called: Volt Workforce Solutions
1544 Eureka Rd Ste 100 (95661-3092)
PHONE..................916 923-0454
Tim Chapman, *Brnch Mgr*
EMP: 78
SALES (corp-wide): 885.39MM **Privately Held**
Web: www.volt.com
SIC: **7363** Temporary help service
HQ: Volt Management Corp.
2400 Meadowbrook Pkwy
Duluth GA

(P-11361)
VOLT MANAGEMENT CORP
Also Called: Volt Workforce Solutions
3558 Deer Park Dr # 2 (95219-2350)
PHONE..................209 952-5627
Scott Giroux, *Brnch Mgr*
EMP: 89
SALES (corp-wide): 885.39MM **Privately Held**
Web: www.volt.com
SIC: **7363** Temporary help service
HQ: Volt Management Corp.
2400 Meadowbrook Pkwy
Duluth GA

(P-11362)
WEAVE INC (PA)
1900 K St Ste 200 (95811-4187)
PHONE..................916 448-2321
Beth Hassett, *Ex Dir*
Garry Maisel, *
Neil Forester, *
Bryan Merica, *
Priya Batra, *
EMP: 95 EST: 1977

SALES (est): 14.89MM
SALES (corp-wide): 14.89MM **Privately Held**
Web: www.weaveinc.org
SIC: **7363** **8322** Domestic help service; Individual and family services

(P-11363)
WEST VALLEY ENGINEERING INC (PA)
Also Called: West Valley Staffing Group
390 Potrero Ave (94085-4116)
PHONE..................408 735-1420
Michael F Williams, *Pr*
Teresa Kossayian, *
EMP: 1230 EST: 1969
SALES (est): 46.85MM
SALES (corp-wide): 46.85MM **Privately Held**
Web: www.westvalley.com
SIC: **7363** Temporary help service

(P-11364)
WORK FORCE SERVICES INC
Also Called: Work Force Staffing
1811 Oak St (93301-3062)
PHONE..................661 327-5019
Brooks Whitehead, *Pr*
EMP: 250 EST: 1981
SALES (est): 9.86MM **Privately Held**
Web: www.wfskern.com
SIC: **7363** Temporary help service

7371 Custom Computer Programming Services

(P-11365)
22ND CENTURY TECHNOLOGIES INC
6203 San Ignacio Ave Ste 110 (95119-1371)
PHONE..................866 537-9191
Satvinder Singh, *Pr*
EMP: 437
SALES (corp-wide): 100.85MM **Privately Held**
Web: www.tscti.com
SIC: **7371** Computer software systems analysis and design, custom
PA: 22nd Century Technologies Inc.
8251 Greensboro Dr # 900
Mc Lean VA
732 537-9191

(P-11366)
314E CORPORATION (PA)
6701 Koll Center Pkwy Ste 340 (94566-8061)
PHONE..................510 371-6736
Abhishek Begerhotta, *Pr*
EMP: 157 EST: 2004
SQ FT: 10,078
SALES (est): 13.28MM **Privately Held**
Web: www.314e.com
SIC: **7371** Computer software development

(P-11367)
3DNA CORP (PA)
Also Called: Nationbuilder
750 W 7th St Ste 201 (90017-3710)
P.O. Box 811428 (90081-0008)
PHONE..................213 992-4809
Lea Endres, *CEO*
EMP: 127 EST: 2007
SALES (est): 21.72MM
SALES (corp-wide): 21.72MM **Privately Held**
Web: www.nationbuilder.com

SIC: **7371** Computer software development

(P-11368)
3K TECHNOLOGIES LLC
1114 Cadillac Ct (95035-3058)
PHONE..................408 716-5900
Krishna Chittabbathini, *
EMP: 105 EST: 2002
SQ FT: 2,000
SALES (est): 6.32MM **Privately Held**
Web: www.3ktechnologies.com
SIC: **7371** Custom computer programming services

(P-11369)
4D INC
95 S Market St Ste 240 (95113-2311)
PHONE..................408 557-4600
Laurent Ribardiere, *CEO*
Doris Beaulieu, *
Phillipe Berthault, *
EMP: 101 EST: 2000
SALES (est): 10.67MM
SALES (corp-wide): 937.39K **Privately Held**
Web: us.4d.com
SIC: **7371** **7372** Computer software development; Prepackaged software
HQ: 4d
Entree 4 Parc Des Erables
Le Pecq
130539200

(P-11370)
6WIND USA INC
2445 Augustine Dr Ste 150 (95054-3032)
PHONE..................408 816-1366
Eric Carmes, *Pr*
Charlie Ashton, *
EMP: 88 EST: 2008
SALES (est): 4.76MM **Privately Held**
SIC: **7371** Computer software development

(P-11371)
ABACUS DATA SYSTEMS INC (PA)
Also Called: Abacusnext
9171 Towne Centre Dr Ste 200 (92122)
PHONE..................858 452-4280
Keri Gohman, *CEO*
Jerome Fodor, *
Eric Cutler, *Chief Sales & Marketing Officer**
Tomas Suros, *SOLN'S**
Chris Cardinal, *OF Software ENG'G**
EMP: 158 EST: 1983
SQ FT: 10,000
SALES (est): 67.08MM
SALES (corp-wide): 67.08MM **Privately Held**
Web: www.getcaret.com
SIC: **7371** **7374** Computer software systems analysis and design, custom; Data processing and preparation

(P-11372)
ABACUS DATA SYSTEMS INC
Also Called: Abacusnext
3262 Holiday Ct Ste 101 (92037-1804)
PHONE..................858 529-0020
EMP: 98 EST: 2018
SALES (est): 6.11MM **Privately Held**
Web: www.getcaret.com
SIC: **7371** Computer software development

(P-11373)
ABACUS SERVICE CORPORATION
1725 23rd St (95816-5964)
PHONE..................916 288-8948

PRODUCTS & SERVICES SECTION
7371 - Custom Computer Programming Services (P-11395)

Michelle Reuter, *Brnch Mgr*
EMP: 300
SALES (corp-wide): 24.38MM **Privately Held**
Web: www.abacusservice.com
SIC: 7371 Custom computer programming services
PA: Abacus Service Corporation
   25925 Telg Rd Ste 206
   Southfield MI
   248 324-9200

(P-11374)
ABBYY USA SOFTWARE HOUSE INC (HQ)
Also Called: Abbyy USA
860 Hillview Ct Ste 330 (95035-4569)
PHONE.................................408 457-9777
Ding Yuan Tang, *CEO*
Arthur Whipple, *Pr*
Sheryl Lodolce, *CFO*
Anthony Macciola, *CIO*
EMP: 105 EST: 2000
SQ FT: 31,000
SALES (est): 26.96MM **Privately Held**
Web: www.abbyy.com
SIC: 7371 Computer software development
PA: Abbyy Software Limited
   61 Kyriakou Matsi Avenue
   Nicosia

(P-11375)
ABJAYON INC
42808 Christy St Ste 228 (94538-3116)
PHONE.................................510 824-3260
Anita Bolinjkar, *CEO*
Neeraj Datta, *
EMP: 250 EST: 2007
SALES (est): 10MM **Privately Held**
Web: www.abjayon.com
SIC: 7371 Computer software development

(P-11376)
ACCESS SYSTEMS AMERICAS INC
3965 Freedom Cir Ste 200 (95054-1293)
PHONE.................................408 400-3000
Kiyo Oishi, *CEO*
Michael Kelley, *
Jeanne Seeley, *
EMP: 60 EST: 2001
SQ FT: 71,000
SALES (est): 5.02MM **Privately Held**
Web: www.ipinfusion.com
SIC: 7371 7372 Computer software development; Prepackaged software
PA: Access Co., Ltd.
   3, Kandaneribeicho
   Chiyoda-Ku TKY

(P-11377)
ACTIVIDENTITY INC
6623 Dumbarton Cir (94555-3603)
PHONE.................................510 574-0100
EMP: 284
SIC: 7371 Computer software systems analysis and design, custom

(P-11378)
ACTUATE CORPORATION (HQ)
951 Mariners Island Blvd Ste 600 (94404-1558)
PHONE.................................650 645-3000
Mark J Barrenechea, *Pr*
Gordon A Davies, *Corporate Secretary**
John Doolittle, *
Adam Howatson, *CMO**
Jonathan Hunter, *Executive Worldwide Field Operations Vice President**
EMP: 64 EST: 1993

SQ FT: 58,000
SALES (est): 109.24MM
SALES (corp-wide): 832.31MM **Privately Held**
Web: www.opentext.com
SIC: 7371 Computer software development
PA: Open Text Corporation
   275 Frank Tompa Dr
   Waterloo ON
   519 888-7111

(P-11379)
ADAPTAMED LLC
6699 Alvarado Rd Ste 2301 (92120-5241)
PHONE.................................877 478-7773
EMP: 120 EST: 2011
SALES (est): 4.74MM **Privately Held**
Web: www.ehryourway.com
SIC: 7371 Computer software development

(P-11380)
ADCOLONY INC
11400 W Olympic Blvd # 1200 (90064-1583)
PHONE.................................650 625-1262
EMP: 100 EST: 2008
SALES (est): 20.51MM **Publicly Held**
Web: www.digitalturbine.com
SIC: 7371 Computer software development
HQ: Adcolony Holdings Us, Inc.
   901 Mariners Blvd Ste 250
   San Mateo CA
   650 625-1262

(P-11381)
ADLER DEV LLC
Also Called: Software Dev Technical Support
2554 Front St Apt 3 (92103-6532)
PHONE.................................707 229-3162
Anthony Thomas, *Managing Member*
EMP: 60 EST: 2018
SALES (est): 7MM **Privately Held**
SIC: 7371 Computer software development and applications

(P-11382)
ADVANTECH CORPORATION (HQ)
Also Called: Advantech
380 Fairview Way (95035-3062)
P.O. Box 45895 (94145-0895)
PHONE.................................408 519-3800
▲ EMP: 300 EST: 1987
SALES (est): 512.81MM **Privately Held**
Web: www.advantech.com
SIC: 7371 Computer software systems analysis and design, custom
PA: Advantech Co., Ltd.
   No. 1, Alley 20, Lane 26, Rueiguang Rd.
   Taipei City TAP

(P-11383)
ADVENT RESOURCES INC
235 W 7th St (90731-3321)
PHONE.................................310 241-1500
Ysidro Salinas, *Ch Bd*
Timothy Gill, *
EMP: 80 EST: 1984
SQ FT: 22,000
SALES (est): 13.68MM **Privately Held**
Web: www.adventresources.com
SIC: 7371 Computer software development

(P-11384)
ADVENT SOFTWARE INC (HQ)
Also Called: SS&c Advent
600 Townsend St Fl 4 (94103-4945)
PHONE.................................415 543-7696
David Peter Hess Junior, *Pr*

Stephanie Dimarco, *
James Cox, *
Todd Gottula, *Global Vice President**
Chris Momsen, *Global Vice President**
EMP: 248 EST: 1995
SQ FT: 158,264
SALES (est): 130.04MM
SALES (corp-wide): 5.28B **Publicly Held**
Web: www.advent.com
SIC: 7371 7373 7372 6722 Custom computer programming services; Computer integrated systems design; Prepackaged software; Management investment, open-end
PA: Ss&C Technologies Holdings, Inc.
   80 Lamberton Rd Fl 1
   Windsor CT
   860 298-4500

(P-11385)
AECHELON TECHNOLOGY INC (PA)
611 Gateway Blvd Ste 300 (94080-7015)
PHONE.................................415 255-0120
Nacho Sanz-pastor, *CEO*
Luis Barcena, *
Chris Blumenthal, *
Bruce Johnson, *
▲ EMP: 147 EST: 1998
SALES (est): 26.82MM
SALES (corp-wide): 26.82MM **Privately Held**
Web: www.aechelon.com
SIC: 7371 3571 Computer software development and applications; Electronic computers

(P-11386)
AERA TECHNOLOGY INC (PA)
707 California St (94041-2005)
PHONE.................................408 524-2222
Frederic Laluyaux, *CEO*
Tony Wessels, *CMO**
Travis Adlman, *
EMP: 99 EST: 1999
SALES (est): 15.74MM **Privately Held**
Web: www.aeratechnology.com
SIC: 7371 Computer software development

(P-11387)
AFTERSHOCK LA STUDIOS INC
3633 Lenawee Ave Ste 100 (90016-4319)
PHONE.................................650 450-9660
Kent Wakeford, *CEO*
EMP: 60 EST: 2016
SALES (est): 1.33MM **Privately Held**
SIC: 7371 Computer software development and applications

(P-11388)
AGENT IMAGE INC
1700 E Walnut Ave (90245-2629)
PHONE.................................310 577-9222
EMP: 400 EST: 1999
SALES (est): 23.52MM **Privately Held**
Web: www.agentimage.com
SIC: 7371 Computer software systems analysis and design, custom

(P-11389)
AIDASH INC (PA)
3031 Tisch Way Ste 110pw (95128-2584)
PHONE.................................408 703-1099
Abhishek Singh, *CEO*
Rahul Saxena, *
EMP: 207 EST: 2019
SALES (est): 24.18MM
SALES (corp-wide): 24.18MM **Privately Held**
Web: www.aidash.com

SIC: 7371 Computer software development

(P-11390)
AIRBYTE INC
2261 Market St Pmb 4381 (94114-1612)
PHONE.................................415 307-4864
Michel Tricot, *CEO*
Jean Lafleur, *
EMP: 96 EST: 2020
SALES (est): 10K **Privately Held**
Web: www.airbyte.com
SIC: 7371 Computer software development

(P-11391)
AISERA INC
1121 San Antonio Rd Ste C202 (94303-4325)
PHONE.................................650 667-4308
Sudhakar Muddu, *Pr*
EMP: 165 EST: 2018
SALES (est): 6.67MM **Privately Held**
Web: www.aisera.com
SIC: 7371 Computer software development

(P-11392)
AKKODIS INC
Also Called: Modis
135 Main St Ste 1040 (94105-1818)
PHONE.................................415 896-5566
Michael Terozzi, *Brnch Mgr*
EMP: 209
Web: www.modis.com
SIC: 7371 Computer software systems analysis and design, custom
HQ: Akkodis, Inc.
   4800 Deerwood Campus Pkwy
   Jacksonville FL
   904 360-2300

(P-11393)
AKKODIS INC
Also Called: Modis
2055 Gateway Pl Ste 300 (95110-1015)
PHONE.................................408 441-7144
Steven Ranson, *Mng Dir*
EMP: 313
Web: www.modis.com
SIC: 7371 Computer software systems analysis and design, custom
HQ: Akkodis, Inc.
   4800 Deerwood Campus Pkwy
   Jacksonville FL
   904 360-2300

(P-11394)
AKKODIS INC
Also Called: Modis
801 N Brand Blvd Ste 250 (91203-3251)
PHONE.................................818 546-2848
Lisa Bertram, *Brnch Mgr*
EMP: 108
Web: www.modis.com
SIC: 7371 Computer software systems analysis and design, custom
HQ: Akkodis, Inc.
   4800 Deerwood Campus Pkwy
   Jacksonville FL
   904 360-2300

(P-11395)
ALFRESCO SOFTWARE AMERICAS INC
428 University Ave (94301-1812)
PHONE.................................888 317-3395
EMP: 194
SALES (corp-wide): 1.2B **Privately Held**
Web: www.alfresco.com
SIC: 7371 Computer software systems analysis and design, custom
HQ: Alfresco Software Americas, Inc.

(PA)=Parent Co (HQ)=Headquarters
✪ = New Business established in last 2 years

7371 - Custom Computer Programming Services (P-11396)

2849 Paces Ferry Rd Se
Atlanta GA

(P-11396)
ALINOR HOLDINGS INC
Also Called: Onriva Travel
4 W 4th Ave Fl 6 (94402-1619)
PHONE.................................650 393-4865
Vajid Hussein Jafri, *Pr*
Steve Dunn, *CFO*
EMP: 75 **EST:** 2015
SALES (est): 1.24MM **Privately Held**
SIC: 7371 Custom computer programming services

(P-11397)
ALOGENT HOLDINGS INC
Also Called: Alogent
5868 Owens Ave Ste 200 (92008-6541)
PHONE.................................760 410-9000
EMP: 80
SALES (corp-wide): 26.1MM **Privately Held**
Web: www.alogent.com
SIC: 7371 Computer software development
PA: Alogent Holdings, Inc.
    35 Technology Pkwy S # 200
    Peachtree Corners GA
    770 752-6400

(P-11398)
ALPHA NET CONSULTING LLC (PA)
3211 Scott Blvd Ste 203 (95054-3010)
PHONE.................................408 550-5686
Surjit Bedi, *Pt*
EMP: 142 **EST:** 1999
SALES (est): 41.01MM
SALES (corp-wide): 41.01MM **Privately Held**
Web: www.anetcorp.com
SIC: 7371 Custom computer programming services

(P-11399)
ALPHABET INC (PA)
Also Called: Alphabet
1600 Amphitheatre Pkwy (94043-1351)
PHONE.................................650 253-0000
Sundar Pichai, *CEO*
John L Hennessy, *Non-Executive Chairman of the Board*
Kent Walker, *CLO*
Ruth M Porat, *Sr VP*
Amie Thuener O'toole, *CAO*
EMP: 283 **EST:** 1998
SALES (est): 282.84B
SALES (corp-wide): 282.84B **Publicly Held**
Web: www.abc.xyz
SIC: 7371 Computer software development and applications

(P-11400)
ALTIUM INC (HQ)
4225 Executive Sq Ste 800 (92037-9150)
PHONE.................................858 864-1500
Aram Mirkazemi, *CEO*
Ted Pawela, *
Joe Bedewi, *
EMP: 70 **EST:** 1988
SQ FT: 11,000
SALES (est): 28.09MM **Privately Held**
Web: www.altium-na.com
SIC: 7371 Computer software development
PA: Altium Limited
    Tower B The Zenith L 6 821 Pacific Hwy
    Chatswood NSW

(P-11401)
AMAZON STUDIOS LLC
9336 Washington Blvd (90232-2628)
PHONE.................................818 804-0884
Jen Salke, *CEO*
EMP: 132
Web: press.amazonstudios.com
SIC: 7371 Computer software development and applications
HQ: Amazon Studios Llc
    410 Terry Ave N
    Seattle WA
    310 573-2305

(P-11402)
AMBER HOLDINGS INC
Also Called: Vista Equity Partners Fund III
150 California St (94111-4500)
PHONE.................................415 765-6500
Robert F Smith, *Pr*
Brian N Sheth, *
EMP: 1014 **EST:** 1995
SALES (est): 2MM
SALES (corp-wide): 1.65B **Privately Held**
SIC: 7371 Computer software development
HQ: Vista Equity Partners Fund Iii, L.P.
    4 Embarcadero Ctr # 2000
    San Francisco CA

(P-11403)
AMP TECHNOLOGIES LLC
445 Melrose Ct (94582-5103)
PHONE.................................877 442-2824
Neel Naicker, *CEO*
Arvind Sathyamoorthy, *
EMP: 140 **EST:** 2011
SALES (est): 5.37MM **Privately Held**
Web: www.theampwebsite.com
SIC: 7371 Computer software development and applications

(P-11404)
AMPLITUDE INC (PA)
Also Called: Amplitude Analytics
201 3rd St Ste 200 (94103-3143)
PHONE.................................650 988-5131
Spenser Skates, *CEO*
Thomas Hansen, *Pr*
Hoang Vuong, *CFO*
Matt Heinz, *CRO*
Jennifer Johnson, *Chief Marketing*
EMP: 82 **EST:** 2012
SALES (est): 238.07MM
SALES (corp-wide): 238.07MM **Publicly Held**
Web: www.amplitude.com
SIC: 7371 Computer software development

(P-11405)
ANGAZA DESIGN INC (PA)
315 Montgomery St Fl 10 (94104-1823)
PHONE.................................415 993-5595
Lesley Marincola, *CEO*
EMP: 70 **EST:** 2010
SALES (est): 5.1MM
SALES (corp-wide): 5.1MM **Privately Held**
Web: www.angaza.com
SIC: 7371 Computer software development

(P-11406)
ANIMOTO LLC
333 Kearny St Fl 6 (94108-3269)
P.O. Box 320428 (94132-0428)
PHONE.................................415 987-3139
EMP: 60 **EST:** 2006
SQ FT: 15,000
SALES (est): 5.02MM **Privately Held**
Web: www.animoto.com
SIC: 7371 Computer software development

(P-11407)
ANJANA SOFTWARE SOLUTIONS INC
1445 E Los Angeles Ave Ste 305 (93065-2807)
PHONE.................................805 583-0121
Saravana Kumarasamy, *Pr*
Muthu Palanisamy, *Sr VP*
Venkatesh Ramachandran, *
Kritik A Govindan, *
▲ **EMP:** 75 **EST:** 2000
SQ FT: 3,000
SALES (est): 4.92MM **Privately Held**
Web: www.anjanasoft.com
SIC: 7371 Computer software development
PA: Anjana Software Solutions Private Limited
    Module No. 306, Nsic Software Technology Park
    Chennai TN

(P-11408)
ANRE TECHNOLOGIES INC
Also Called: Anre Tech
741 W Woodbury Rd (91001-5310)
PHONE.................................818 627-5433
EMP: 150 **EST:** 2010
SQ FT: 600
SALES (est): 9.95MM **Privately Held**
Web: www.anretech.com
SIC: 7371 7376 7379 Computer software development and applications; Computer facilities management; Computer related maintenance services

(P-11409)
ANVILOGIC INC
644 Emerson St Ste 100 (94301-1611)
PHONE.................................650 665-7707
Karthik Kannan, *CEO*
EMP: 65 **EST:** 2019
SALES (est): 6.75MM **Privately Held**
Web: www.anvilogic.com
SIC: 7371 Computer software development

(P-11410)
ANYSCALE INC
55 Hawthorne St Fl 9 (94105-3967)
PHONE.................................650 248-8086
Robert Nishihara, *CEO*
Matthew Burns, *
EMP: 90 **EST:** 2019
SALES (est): 4.88MM **Privately Held**
Web: www.anyscale.com
SIC: 7371 Computer software development

(P-11411)
AOA TECHNOLOGY PARTNERS
342 Linda Way (94941-3805)
PHONE.................................888 828-6426
Aaron De Zafra, *CEO*
EMP: 90 **EST:** 2020
SALES (est): 2.24MM **Privately Held**
SIC: 7371 7389 Computer software development and applications; Business Activities at Non-Commercial Site

(P-11412)
APIGEE CORPORATION
1600 Amphitheatre Pkwy (94043-1351)
PHONE.................................408 343-7300
Chet Kapoor, *CEO*
Tim Wan, *
Anant Jhingran, *
Stacey Giamalis, *Chief Counsel*
EMP: 374 **EST:** 2004
SQ FT: 41,000
SALES (est): 51.04MM
SALES (corp-wide): 282.84B **Publicly Held**
Web: cloud.google.com
SIC: 7371 Computer software development and applications
HQ: Google Llc
    1600 Amphitheatre Pkwy
    Mountain View CA
    650 253-0000

(P-11413)
APPDYNAMICS LLC (HQ)
Also Called: Appdynamics
500 Terry A Francois Blvd Fl 3 (94158-2354)
PHONE.................................408 526-4000
EMP: 309 **EST:** 2008
SQ FT: 83,500
SALES (est): 278MM
SALES (corp-wide): 57B **Publicly Held**
Web: www.appdynamics.com
SIC: 7371 Computer software development
PA: Cisco Systems, Inc.
    170 W Tasman Dr
    San Jose CA
    408 526-4000

(P-11414)
APPLIED COMPUTER SOLUTIONS (DH)
110 Progress (92618-0333)
PHONE.................................714 861-2200
Elaine Bellock, *Pr*
Michael Davis, *
Warren Barnes, *
EMP: 70 **EST:** 1989
SALES (est): 51.51MM **Privately Held**
Web: www.acsacs.com
SIC: 7371 Custom computer programming services
HQ: Pivot Technology Solutions, Inc
    55 Renfrew Dr Suite 200
    Markham ON
    416 360-4777

(P-11415)
APPLIED ENGINEERING MGT CORP
Also Called: Aem Corporation
760 Paseo Camarillo Ste 101 (93010-6000)
P.O. Box 1263 (93011-1263)
PHONE.................................805 484-1909
Anne Morgan, *Brnch Mgr*
EMP: 250
SALES (corp-wide): 35.31MM **Privately Held**
Web: www.aemcorp.com
SIC: 7371 Computer software development
PA: Applied Enterprise Management Corporation
    13880 Dulles Corner Ln # 300
    Herndon VA
    703 464-7030

(P-11416)
APPLIED INTUITION INC (PA)
145 E Dana St (94041-1507)
PHONE.................................630 935-8986
Qasar Younis, *CEO*
Marc Andreessen, *Bd of Dir*
EMP: 73 **EST:** 2017
SALES (est): 2MM
SALES (corp-wide): 2MM **Privately Held**
Web: www.appliedintuition.com
SIC: 7371 Computer software development

(P-11417)
APPSFLYER INC
100 1st St Ste 2500 (94105-3082)
PHONE.................................408 367-9938
EMP: 241 **EST:** 2018
SALES (est): 5.82MM **Privately Held**

▲ = Import ▼ = Export
◆ = Import/Export

PRODUCTS & SERVICES SECTION
7371 - Custom Computer Programming Services (P-11440)

Web: www.appsflyer.com
SIC: 7371 Computer software development

(P-11418)
APTELIGENT INC
1100 La Avenida St Ste A (94043-1453)
PHONE..................................415 371-1402
Zane Rowe, *CFO*
Sanjay Poonen, *
Raghu Raghuram, *
Rajiv Ramaswami, *
EMP: 60 **EST:** 2011
SALES (est): 4.46MM
SALES (corp-wide): 13.35B **Privately Held**
Web: www.vmware.com
SIC: 7371 Computer software development
PA: Vmware, Inc.
3401 Hillview Ave
Palo Alto CA
650 427-5000

(P-11419)
ARCTOUCH LLC
1001 Front St (94111-1424)
PHONE..................................415 944-2000
Eric Shapiro, *CEO*
Adam Fingerman, *Chief Experience Officer*
EMP: 200 **EST:** 2009
SALES (est): 27.46MM
SALES (corp-wide): 17.37B **Privately Held**
Web: www.arctouch.com
SIC: 7371 Computer software development and applications
HQ: Grey Global Group Llc
200 5th Ave Fl 5
New York NY
212 546-2000

(P-11420)
ARCULES INC
17875 Von Karman Ave Ste 450 (92614-6212)
PHONE..................................949 439-0053
Andreas Pettersson, *CEO*
Nigel Waterton, *CRO*
EMP: 70 **EST:** 2017
SALES (est): 6.57MM **Privately Held**
Web: www.arcules.com
SIC: 7371 Software programming applications

(P-11421)
ARIA SYSTEMS INC (PA)
Also Called: Aria
575 Market St Fl 4 (94105-5818)
PHONE..................................415 852-7250
Tom Dibble, *Pr*
Brendan O'brien, *Prin*
Arun Thakur, *
Rick Lund, *
Cary Platkin, *
▼ **EMP:** 196 **EST:** 2003
SALES (est): 47.53MM
SALES (corp-wide): 47.53MM **Privately Held**
Web: www.ariasystems.com
SIC: 7371 Computer software development

(P-11422)
ARICENT INC
303 Twin Dolphin Dr # 600 (94065-1422)
PHONE..................................650 632-4310
EMP: 1014
SIC: 7371 Computer software development

(P-11423)
ARICENT US INC
303 Twin Dolphin Dr Ste 600 (94065-1497)
PHONE..................................650 632-4310
EMP: 123

SIC: 7371 Computer software development
PA: Aricent Us Inc.
3979 Freedom Cir Ste 950
Santa Clara CA

(P-11424)
ARMORBLOX INC
100 S Murphy Ave Ste 200 (94086-6112)
PHONE..................................831 428-2124
Dhananjay Sampath, *CEO*
EMP: 70 **EST:** 2017
SALES (est): 5.33MM **Privately Held**
Web: www.armorblox.com
SIC: 7371 Computer software development

(P-11425)
ARRCUS INC
2077 Gateway Pl Ste 400 (95110-1085)
PHONE..................................408 884-1965
Shekar Ayyar, *Ch Bd*
EMP: 91 **EST:** 2016
SALES (est): 5.7MM **Privately Held**
Web: www.arrcus.com
SIC: 7371 Computer software development

(P-11426)
ARRIS COMPOSITES INC
745 Heinz Ave (94710-2732)
PHONE..................................510 730-0067
Ethan Escowitz, *Owner*
EMP: 117
SALES (corp-wide): 4.68MM **Privately Held**
Web: www.arriscomposites.com
SIC: 7371 Computer software development and applications
PA: Arris Composites, Inc.
710 Bancroft Way
Berkeley CA
510 730-0067

(P-11427)
ARTIC SENTINEL INC
1700 E Walnut Ave Ste 200 (90245-2648)
PHONE..................................310 227-8230
EMP: 85
SIC: 7371 7379 Computer software development and applications; Online services technology consultants

(P-11428)
ASHUNYA INC
642 N Eckhoff St (92868-1004)
PHONE..................................714 385-1900
Melanie Merchant, *Prin*
EMP: 88 **EST:** 2001
SALES (est): 9.78MM **Privately Held**
Web: www.ashunya.com
SIC: 7371 7372 7373 Computer software development and applications; Application computer software; Office computer automation systems integration

(P-11429)
ASPECT DEVELOPMENT INC (DH)
1395 Charleston Rd (94043-1332)
PHONE..................................650 428-2700
Sanjiv S Sidhu, *CEO*
EMP: 303 **EST:** 1990
SQ FT: 28,000
SALES (est): 28.8MM **Privately Held**
SIC: 7371 Computer software development
HQ: I2 Technologies, Inc.
11701 Luna Rd
Dallas TX

(P-11430)
ASPIREZ INC
Also Called: Pegasus One
1440 N Harbor Blvd Ste 900 (92835-4127)
PHONE..................................714 485-8104
Tushar Puri, *CEO*
EMP: 87 **EST:** 2010
SALES (est): 2.97MM **Privately Held**
SIC: 7371 7373 7379 7372 Custom computer programming services; Computer integrated systems design; Computer related maintenance services; Prepackaged software

(P-11431)
ASTUTE BUSINESS SOLUTIONS
11501 Dublin Blvd Ste 200 (94568-2827)
PHONE..................................925 997-3267
Sudhir Mehandru, *Ex Dir*
Arvind Rajan, *
Sudhir Mehandru, *VP Sls*
Joe Finlinson, *
EMP: 152 **EST:** 2006
SQ FT: 2,530
SALES (est): 12.24MM **Privately Held**
Web: www.beastute.com
SIC: 7371 Computer software development

(P-11432)
ATRENTA INC (HQ)
690 E Middlefield Rd (94043-4010)
PHONE..................................408 453-3333
Ajoy K Bose, *Pr*
Bert Clement, *
EMP: 70 **EST:** 1995
SQ FT: 8,000
SALES (est): 46.33MM
SALES (corp-wide): 5.08B **Publicly Held**
SIC: 7371 Computer software development
PA: Synopsys, Inc.
675 Almanor Ave
Sunnyvale CA
650 584-5000

(P-11433)
AUDITBOARD INC (PA)
12900 Park Plaza Dr Ste 200 (90703-8564)
PHONE..................................877 769-5444
Scott Arnold, *CEO*
EMP: 100 **EST:** 2014
SQ FT: 10,000
SALES (est): 26.54MM
SALES (corp-wide): 26.54MM **Privately Held**
Web: www.auditboard.com
SIC: 7371 Computer software development

(P-11434)
AUGUSTINE GAMING MGT CORP
Also Called: Augustine Casino
84001 Avenue 54 (92236-9780)
PHONE..................................760 391-9500
Jeff Bauer, *Genl Mgr*
John Corrigan, *Finance*
EMP: 99
SALES (est): 7.4MM **Privately Held**
Web: www.augustinecasino.com
SIC: 7371 Computer software development and applications

(P-11435)
AUTOMATION ANYWHERE INC (PA)
633 River Oaks Pkwy (95134-1907)
P.O. Box 640007 (95164-0007)
PHONE..................................888 484-3535
Mihir Shukla, *CEO*
James Budge, *
Mike Mirucci, *
Rob Ferguson, *CRO*

Prince Kohli, *
EMP: 500 **EST:** 2003
SQ FT: 14,000
SALES (est): 100.39MM **Privately Held**
Web: www.automationanywhere.com
SIC: 7371 5045 Computer software writing services; Computer software

(P-11436)
AUTOMOTIVEMASTERMIND INC
201 Mission St Fl 10 (94105-1805)
PHONE..................................646 679-3441
Marco G Schnabl, *Pr*
Eric Daniels, *CFO*
Mohamed Al-daqa, *CIO*
Pam Perry, *CPO*
Firati Kozkopar, *Dir Fin*
EMP: 80 **EST:** 2012
SALES (est): 4.68MM
SALES (corp-wide): 11.18B **Publicly Held**
Web: www.automotivemastermind.com
SIC: 7371 Software programming applications
HQ: Markit North America, Inc.
55 Water St Fl 39
New York NY
212 931-4900

(P-11437)
AUTOMOTUS INC
3415 S Sepulveda Blvd Ste 1166 (90034-6060)
PHONE..................................805 504-5750
Jordan Justus, *CEO*
EMP: 90 **EST:** 2017
SALES (est): 4.85MM **Privately Held**
Web: www.automotus.co
SIC: 7371 Computer software development and applications

(P-11438)
AUTONOMIC LLC (PA)
3251 Hillview Ave # 200 (94304-1202)
PHONE..................................650 823-1806
Julie Davies, *
Amy Wengler, *
EMP: 66 **EST:** 2016
SQ FT: 8,700
SALES (est): 14.52MM
SALES (corp-wide): 14.52MM **Privately Held**
Web: www.autonomic.com
SIC: 7371 Software programming applications

(P-11439)
AVAMAR TECHNOLOGIES INC
135 Technology Dr (92618-2402)
PHONE..................................949 743-5100
EMP: 100
SIC: 7371 Computer software development

(P-11440)
AVANQUEST NORTH AMERICA LLC (HQ)
Also Called: Nova Development
23801 Calabasas Rd Ste 2005 (91302-1547)
PHONE..................................818 591-9600
Roger Bloxberg, *CEO*
Todd Helfstein, *
Sharon Chiu, *
▲ **EMP:** 80 **EST:** 1984
SQ FT: 12,000
SALES (est): 83.58MM
SALES (corp-wide): 4.02MM **Privately Held**
Web: www.avanquest.com
SIC: 7371 Computer software development
PA: Claranova S.E.

7371 - Custom Computer Programming Services (P-11441)

Avanquest Blue Squad Bvrp Software
Cs8 Immeuble Adamas
Courbevoie

(P-11441)
AVEVA SOFTWARE LLC
5850 El Camino Real (92008-8816)
PHONE.................................760 268-7700
Chris Porter, *Brnch Mgr*
EMP: 192
SALES (corp-wide): 82.05K **Privately Held**
Web: www.aveva.com
SIC: **7371** 5045 Computer software development; Computer software
HQ: Aveva Software, Llc
26561 Rancho Pkwy S
Lake Forest CA

(P-11442)
AZUMIO INC (PA)
255 Shoreline Dr Ste 130 (94065-1495)
PHONE.................................719 310-3774
Bojan Bostjancic, *Pr*
EMP: 100 EST: 2011
SALES (est): 5.85MM
SALES (corp-wide): 5.85MM **Privately Held**
Web: www.azumio.com
SIC: **7371** Computer software development

(P-11443)
AZUMO LLC
Also Called: Azumo
3130 Alpine Rd Ste 288 # 485 (94028-7541)
PHONE.................................415 610-7002
Chike Agbai, *CEO*
EMP: 125 EST: 2016
SALES (est): 6.3MM **Privately Held**
Web: www.azumo.com
SIC: **7371** Custom computer programming services

(P-11444)
BABYFIRST AMERICAS LLC
10390 Santa Monica Blvd Ste 310 (90025-5058)
PHONE.................................310 442-9853
Guy Oranim, *CEO*
Sharon Rechter, *Pr*
Karl Knipliy, *CFO*
EMP: 75 EST: 2010
SALES (est): 3.65MM
SALES (corp-wide): 3.65MM **Privately Held**
SIC: **7371** Computer software development and applications
PA: Bftv, Llc
10390 Santa Monica Blvd # 310
Los Angeles CA
310 442-9853

(P-11445)
BAHARE
11769 W Sunset Blvd (90049-6903)
PHONE.................................516 472-1457
Bahareh Saleh Nia, *CEO*
EMP: 105 EST: 2021
SALES (est): 2.12MM **Privately Held**
SIC: **7371** 7389 Computer software development and applications; Business Activities at Non-Commercial Site

(P-11446)
BAIRESDEV LLC
1999 S Bascom Ave (95008-2216)
PHONE.................................847 796-1636
Ignacio De Marco, *CEO*
Fernando Horacio Galano, *
Pablo Sebastian Azorin, *

EMP: 3500 EST: 2012
SALES (est): 300MM **Privately Held**
Web: www.bairesdev.com
SIC: **7371** Computer software development

(P-11447)
BAKBONE SOFTWARE INC (HQ)
9540 Towne Centre Dr Ste 100 (92121-1988)
PHONE.................................858 450-9009
Michael S Dell, *CEO*
Stephen J Felice, *
Brian Tgladden, *
Kenneth Horner, *Senior Vice President Corporate Development & Strategy*
Roy Hogsed, *Senior Vice President Worldwide Sales*
EMP: 72 EST: 1999
SQ FT: 22,600
SALES (est): 36.67MM
SALES (corp-wide): 647.68MM **Privately Held**
Web: www.quest.com
SIC: **7371** 7375 Computer software systems analysis and design, custom; Information retrieval services
PA: Quest Software Inc.
20 Enterprise Ste 100
Aliso Viejo CA
949 754-8000

(P-11448)
BALBIX INC
3031 Tisch Way Ste 800 (95128-2532)
PHONE.................................866 936-3180
Gaurav Banga, *Pr*
Rich Campagna, *CMO*
EMP: 85 EST: 2015
SALES (est): 6.41MM **Privately Held**
Web: www.balbix.com
SIC: **7371** Computer software development

(P-11449)
BALBOA INTRMDIATE HOLDINGS LLC (PA)
3307 Hillview Ave (94304-1204)
PHONE.................................650 846-1000
Dan Streetman, *CEO*
EMP: 878 EST: 2014
SQ FT: 292,000
SALES (est): 4.38B
SALES (corp-wide): 4.38B **Privately Held**
SIC: **7371** 7373 Custom computer programming services; Systems integration services

(P-11450)
BAYONE SOLUTIONS
4637 Chabot Dr Ste 250 (94588-2752)
PHONE.................................408 930-1600
Yogesh Virmani, *CEO*
Rahul Sharma, *
EMP: 130 EST: 2012
SALES (est): 10MM **Privately Held**
Web: www.bayonesolutions.com
SIC: **7371** 7379 Custom computer programming services; Computer related consulting services

(P-11451)
BEA SYSTEMS INC (HQ)
2315 N 1st St (95131-1010)
PHONE.................................650 506-7000
Alfred S Chuang, *Ch Bd*
Alfred S Chuang, *Ch Bd*
William Klein, *Executive Corporate Development Vice President*
Wai M Wong, *Product Vice President*
Mark T Carges, *Vice President Business*
EMP: 1000 EST: 1995

SQ FT: 236,000
SALES (est): 99.95MM
SALES (corp-wide): 49.95B **Publicly Held**
Web: www.bea.gov
SIC: **7371** 7372 Computer software development; Prepackaged software
PA: Oracle Corporation
2300 Oracle Way
Austin TX
737 867-1000

(P-11452)
BEHAVIOSEC INC
160 W Santa Clara St Ste 1100 (95113-1732)
PHONE.................................833 248-6732
Neil Costigan, *CEO*
EMP: 290 EST: 2011
SALES (est): 2.43MM
SALES (corp-wide): 10.3B **Privately Held**
Web: risk.lexisnexis.com
SIC: **7371** Computer software development
HQ: Lexisnexis Risk Solutions Inc.
1000 Alderman Dr
Alpharetta GA
678 694-6000

(P-11453)
BEN GROUP INC
14724 Ventura Blvd Ste 1200 (91403-3512)
PHONE.................................310 342-1500
Richard Ray Butler, *CEO*
Keith Moffatt, *
Ted Sheffield, *
EMP: 420 EST: 2017
SALES (est): 100MM **Privately Held**
SIC: **7371** 7311 Custom computer programming services; Advertising agencies

(P-11454)
BETA SOFT SYSTEMS INC
2570 N 1st St 2nd Fl (95131-1035)
PHONE.................................408 766-0000
EMP: 250
Web: www.betasoftsystems.com
SIC: **7371** Computer software development

(P-11455)
BETTERWORKS SYSTEMS INC
Also Called: Betterworks
101 Jefferson Dr 1st Fl (94025-1114)
PHONE.................................650 656-9013
Doug Dennerline, *Ofcr*
EMP: 75 EST: 2013
SALES (est): 8MM **Privately Held**
Web: www.betterworks.com
SIC: **7371** Computer software development

(P-11456)
BIONIC STORK INC
2345 Yale St (94306-1448)
PHONE.................................650 600-1494
Idan Ninyo, *CEO*
EMP: 110 EST: 2020
SALES (est): 10MM **Privately Held**
Web: www.bionic.ai
SIC: **7371** Computer software development

(P-11457)
BIRD RIDES INC
2501 Colorado Ave (90404-3500)
PHONE.................................866 205-2442
Evan Conroy, *Mgr*
EMP: 100
SALES (corp-wide): 244.66MM **Publicly Held**
Web: www.bird.co
SIC: **7371** Computer software development and applications
HQ: Bird Rides, Inc.

8605 Santa Monica Blvd # 203
West Hollywood CA
866 205-2442

(P-11458)
BIRST INC
45 Fremont St Ste 1800 (94105-2228)
PHONE.................................415 766-4800
Jay Larson, *CEO*
Brad Peters, *Chief Product Officer**
Rick Spickelmier, *
Paul Staelin, *Chief Customer Officer**
Carl Tsukahara, *
EMP: 300 EST: 2005
SQ FT: 36,171
SALES (est): 43.63MM
SALES (corp-wide): 36.93B **Privately Held**
Web: www.birst.com
SIC: **7371** Computer software development
HQ: Infor, Inc.
641 Ave Of The Americas # 4
New York NY
646 336-1700

(P-11459)
BISTA SOLUTIONS INC (PA)
39180 Liberty St Ste 101 (94538-1522)
PHONE.................................858 401-2332
Faisal Basar, *Pr*
Shahid Bandarkar, *Sec*
Saifal Basar, *Prin*
EMP: 195 EST: 2010
SALES (est): 12.63MM
SALES (corp-wide): 12.63MM **Privately Held**
Web: www.bistasolutions.com
SIC: **7371** Computer software development

(P-11460)
BITALIGN INC
Also Called: Grio
95 Minna St Fl 4 (94105-3029)
PHONE.................................415 395-9525
Douglas Kadlecek, *CEO*
Bradley Johnson, *
EMP: 60 EST: 2006
SALES (est): 10.2MM **Privately Held**
SIC: **7371** Computer software development

(P-11461)
BITGLASS INC
675 Campbell Technology Pkwy Ste 225 (95008-5059)
PHONE.................................408 337-0190
Nat Kausik, *CEO*
Andrew Urushima, *VP*
Anoop Bhattacharjya, *Sec*
EMP: 113 EST: 2013
SQ FT: 10,000
SALES (est): 13.27MM **Privately Held**
Web: www.forcepoint.com
SIC: **7371** Computer software development

(P-11462)
BITWARDEN INC
1 N Calle Cesar Chavez Ste 102 (93103-3662)
PHONE.................................904 664-9194
EMP: 79 EST: 2020
SALES (est): 5.51MM **Privately Held**
Web: www.bitwarden.com
SIC: **7371** Computer software development

(P-11463)
BLAST MOTION INC
Also Called: Blast Motion
1780 La Costa Meadows Dr Ste 101 (92078-5106)
PHONE.................................760 803-2724
Michael J Fitzpatrick, *CEO*

Tyler Terrien, *
EMP: 77 EST: 2010
SALES (est): 11.04MM Privately Held
Web: www.blastmotion.com
SIC: 7371 Software programming applications

(P-11464)
BLAZE SOLUTIONS INC
155 N Riverview Dr (92808-1225)
PHONE..................415 964-5689
Chris Violas, CEO
Justin Kirk, CPO*
EMP: 75 EST: 2018
SALES (est): 700K Privately Held
Web: www.blaze.me
SIC: 7371 Computer software development

(P-11465)
BLU DIGITAL GROUP INC (PA)
Also Called: Blufocus
2233 N Ontario St # 130 (91504-4503)
PHONE..................818 527-2763
Paulette E Pantoja, CEO
EMP: 162 EST: 2007
SQ FT: 7,000
SALES (est): 12.28MM Privately Held
Web: www.bludigitalgroup.com
SIC: 7371 8748 7379 Software programming applications; Systems analysis and engineering consulting services; Computer related consulting services

(P-11466)
BLUEBEAM INC (PA)
443 S Raymond Ave (91105-2630)
PHONE..................626 788-4100
Usman Shuja, CEO
Richard Lee, *
Jim Atkinson, *
Miekie Liebenberg, *
EMP: 200 EST: 2002
SALES (est): 47.98MM
SALES (corp-wide): 47.98MM Privately Held
Web: www.bluebeam.com
SIC: 7371 Computer software development

(P-11467)
BLUR STUDIO INC
3960 Ince Blvd (90232-2635)
PHONE..................424 258-3145
Tim Miller, Pr
David Stinnett, *
EMP: 70 EST: 1995
SQ FT: 20,000
SALES (est): 10.25MM Privately Held
Web: www.blur.com
SIC: 7371 Custom computer programming services

(P-11468)
BOKU INC (PA)
Also Called: Mobillcash
660 Market St Ste 400 (94104-5004)
P.O. Box 190725 (94119-0725)
PHONE..................415 375-3160
Mark J Britto, Ch
Ron Hirson, *
Dave Arnold, *
Stuart Neal, Chief Business Officer*
Christian Hinrichs, *
EMP: 104 EST: 2008
SALES (est): 23.94MM Privately Held
Web: www.boku.com
SIC: 7371 7322 Computer software development and applications; Collection agency, except real estate

(P-11469)
BOLT
1235 Howard St Ste D (94103-2711)
PHONE..................650 804-0633
EMP: 63 EST: 2016
SALES (est): 2.14MM Privately Held
Web: www.bolt.com
SIC: 7371 Computer software development

(P-11470)
BOOMR LLC
660 Menlo Oaks Dr (94025-2350)
PHONE..................877 687-6228
Matthew Bowersox, CEO
Noah Lively, *
EMP: 696 EST: 2011
SALES (est): 242.2K
SALES (corp-wide): 982.7MM Privately Held
SIC: 7371 Computer software development
PA: Justworks, Inc.
 55 Water St Fl 29
 New York NY
 888 534-1711

(P-11471)
BPO MANAGEMENT SERVICES INC (PA)
8175 E Kaiser Blvd # 100 (92808-2214)
PHONE..................714 972-2670
Patrick A Dolan, Ch Bd
James Cortens, Pr
Donald W Rutherford, CFO
EMP: 73 EST: 1982
SQ FT: 5,871
SALES (est): 36.61MM
SALES (corp-wide): 36.61MM Privately Held
SIC: 7371 Computer software development

(P-11472)
BRAIN CORPORATION
10182 Telesis Ct Ste 100 (92121-4777)
PHONE..................858 689-7600
Eugene Izhikevich, CEO
David Pinn, CFO
EMP: 220 EST: 2009
SALES (est): 40MM Privately Held
Web: www.braincorp.com
SIC: 7371 Computer software development

(P-11473)
BRAIN TECHNOLOGIES INC
400 S El Camino Real Ste 250 (94402)
P.O. Box 938 (94403-0538)
PHONE..................650 918-2245
Sheng Yue, CEO
EMP: 315 EST: 2015
SALES (est): 21.6MM Privately Held
SIC: 7371 Computer software development and applications
PA: Xi'an Huateng Photoelectricity Co., Ltd.
 Incubation Zone, Floor 3,
 Comprehensive Office Building, Interne
 Xi'an SN

(P-11474)
BRIENCE INC (DH)
Also Called: A Development Stage Company
128 Spear St Fl 3 (94105-5147)
PHONE..................415 974-5300
Roderick Mcgeary, Ch Bd
Stephen E Recht, CFO
Keyur Patel, Chief Strategy Officer*
James Drumright, COO
EMP: 90 EST: 2000
SQ FT: 15,000
SALES (est): 21.7MM Privately Held
Web: www.brience.com

SIC: 7371 Computer software development and applications
HQ: Syniverse Technologies, Llc
 8125 Highwoods Palm Way
 Tampa FL

(P-11475)
BRIGHTERION INC
123 Mission St Ste 1700 (94105-5133)
PHONE..................415 986-5600
Akli Adjaoute, CEO
EMP: 62 EST: 1999
SALES (est): 7.35MM
SALES (corp-wide): 22.24B Publicly Held
Web: www.brighterion.com
SIC: 7371 Computer software development
PA: Mastercard Incorporated
 2000 Purchase St
 Purchase NY
 914 249-2000

(P-11476)
BRISTLECONE INCORPORATED
Also Called: Mahindra Bristlecone
10 Almaden Blvd Ste 600 (95113-2226)
PHONE..................650 386-4000
Nirav Patel, Pr
Naresh Hingorani, *
Ramesh Sivakaminathan, *
Kulashekar Raghavan, *
Bhaskar Ramanasundaram, *
EMP: 1300 EST: 1998
SQ FT: 10,000
SALES (est): 81.5MM Privately Held
Web: www.bristlecone.com
SIC: 7371 8742 Software programming applications; Management consulting services
PA: Mahindra And Mahindra Limited
 Mahindra Towers, 3rd Floor, Dr. G M Bosale Marg,
 Mumbai MH

(P-11477)
BRITIVE INC
450 N Brand Blvd Ste 600 (91203-2349)
PHONE..................213 915-4142
Artyom Poghosyan, CEO
Armen Poghosyan, *
EMP: 60 EST: 2018
SALES (est): 5.2MM Privately Held
Web: www.britive.com
SIC: 7371 Computer software development

(P-11478)
BUDDY GROUP INC
7 Studebaker (92618-2013)
P.O. Box 1021 (92609-1021)
PHONE..................949 468-0042
Peter R Deutschman, Pr
EMP: 99 EST: 2007
SALES (est): 3.41MM Privately Held
Web: www.thebuddygroup.com
SIC: 7371 Computer software development and applications

(P-11479)
BYND LLC
100 Montgomery St Ste 1102 (94104-4301)
PHONE..................415 944-2293
Nicholas Rappolt, CEO
Matthew Iliffe, *
James Williams, Head OF Finance*
EMP: 100 EST: 2004
SALES (est): 15.06MM
SALES (corp-wide): 866.9MM Privately Held
Web: www.bynd.com
SIC: 7371 Computer software development and applications

PA: Next 15 Group Plc
 60 Great Portland Street
 London
 203 128-8000

(P-11480)
BYNDER
734 El Camino Real (94070-3106)
PHONE..................415 227-4886
EMP: 93 EST: 2019
SALES (est): 879.19K Privately Held
Web: www.bynder.com
SIC: 7371 Computer software development

(P-11481)
CALLFIRE INC
Also Called: EZ Texting
548 Market St Ste 44523 (94104-5401)
PHONE..................213 221-2289
Vijesh Mehta, CEO
Greg Wookey, *
EMP: 61 EST: 2004
SALES (est): 13.34MM Privately Held
Web: www.eztexting.com
SIC: 7371 Computer software development

(P-11482)
CAPTIVATEIQ INC
480 2nd St Ste 100 (94107-1429)
PHONE..................650 930-0619
Teng Conway, CEO
Hubert Wong Engineering, Prin
Mark Schopmeyer, *
EMP: 95 EST: 2017
SALES (est): 5.62MM Privately Held
Web: www.captivateiq.com
SIC: 7371 Computer software systems analysis and design, custom

(P-11483)
CARBONFIVE INCORPORATED
Also Called: Carbon Five
201 Mission St Ste 1800 (94105-1805)
PHONE..................415 546-0500
Don Thompson, COO
Don Thompson, Prin
Mike Wynholds, *
EMP: 62 EST: 2001
SALES (est): 7.47MM Privately Held
Web: www.carbonfive.com
SIC: 7371 Computer software development

(P-11484)
CASETEXT INC
330 Townsend St Ste 100 (94107-1655)
PHONE..................317 407-0790
Jacob Heller, CEO
EMP: 110 EST: 2015
SALES (est): 6.46MM Privately Held
Web: www.casetext.com
SIC: 7371 7379 Computer software development and applications; Computer related services, nec

(P-11485)
CASTLE GLOBAL INC
Also Called: Hive, The
575 Market St Fl 15 (94105-5815)
PHONE..................401 523-9531
Kevin Guo, CEO
EMP: 120 EST: 2013
SALES (est): 9.68MM Privately Held
Web: www.castleglobal.com
SIC: 7371 Computer software development

(P-11486)
CATAMORPHIC CO (PA)
Also Called: Launchdarkly
1999 Harrison St Ste 1100 (94612-3515)

7371 - Custom Computer Programming Services (P-11487)

PHONE 415 579-3275
Edith Ellen Harbaugh, *CEO*
EMP: 194 **EST:** 2014
SQ FT: 5,000
SALES (est): 12.83MM
SALES (corp-wide): 12.83MM **Privately Held**
Web: www.launchdarkly.com
SIC: 7371 Software programming applications

(P-11487)
CATAPHORA INC (PA)
3425 Edison Way (94025-1813)
P.O. Box 2007 (94026-2007)
PHONE 650 622-9840
Elizabeth B Charnock, *Pr*
EMP: 60 **EST:** 2002
SQ FT: 25,000
SALES (est): 7.94MM
SALES (corp-wide): 7.94MM **Privately Held**
Web: www.cataphora.com
SIC: 7371 Computer software development

(P-11488)
CHIPPER CASH INC
Also Called: Chipper
180 Montgomery St Ste 1860 (94104-4233)
PHONE 844 386-3753
EMP: 85 **EST:** 2021
SALES (est): 4.46MM **Privately Held**
Web: www.chippercash.com
SIC: 7371 Computer software development and applications

(P-11489)
CIGNEX HOLDING CORP
2350 Mission College Blvd Ste 490 (95054-1532)
PHONE 408 327-9900
Jeff Colvin, *CEO*
EMP: 218 **EST:** 2000
SALES (est): 1.05MM **Privately Held**
Web: www.cignex.com
SIC: 7371 Computer software development

(P-11490)
CIMATRON GIBBS LLC
Also Called: Gibbs & Associates
2545 W Hillcrest Dr Ste 210 (91320-2296)
PHONE 805 523-0004
Bill Gibbs, *Owner*
William F Gibbs, *
EMP: 61 **EST:** 1982
SALES (est): 12.08MM **Publicly Held**
SIC: 7371 Computer software development
PA: 3d Systems Corporation
333 Three D Systems Cir
Rock Hill SC

(P-11491)
CITRIX ONLINE LLC
Also Called: Citrix Online Group
7414 Hollister Ave (93117-2583)
PHONE 805 690-6400
EMP: 500
SIC: 7371 Computer software development

(P-11492)
CLARI INC (PA)
1154 Sonora Ct (94086-5308)
PHONE 650 265-2111
Andrew Byrne, *CEO*
David Karel, *CMO*
Kevin Knieriem, *CRO*
EMP: 540 **EST:** 2012
SALES (est): 55.74MM
SALES (corp-wide): 55.74MM **Privately Held**
Web: www.clari.com
SIC: 7371 Computer software development

(P-11493)
CLARIS INTERNATIONAL INC (HQ)
1 Apple Park Way (95014-0642)
PHONE 800 725-2747
Dominique Philippe Goupil, *Pr*
Bill Epling, *Senior Vice President Finance Operations*
John F Pinheiro, *VP Legal*
EMP: 230 **EST:** 1987
SQ FT: 128,000
SALES (est): 65.74MM
SALES (corp-wide): 383.29B **Publicly Held**
Web: www.claris.com
SIC: 7371 Computer software development and applications
PA: Apple Inc.
1 Apple Park Way
Cupertino CA
408 996-1010

(P-11494)
CLEO LABS INC
85 2nd St Ste 710 (94105-3465)
PHONE 415 234-3437
Chitra Akileswaran, *Prin*
EMP: 148 **EST:** 2016
SALES (est): 4.72MM **Privately Held**
Web: www.hicleo.com
SIC: 7371 Computer software development and applications

(P-11495)
CLOCK SHARK LLC
900 Fortress St Ste 100 (95973-9547)
PHONE 530 433-0981
Cliff Mitchell, *Prin*
EMP: 65 **EST:** 2014
SALES (est): 5.88MM **Privately Held**
Web: www.clockshark.com
SIC: 7371 Computer software development

(P-11496)
CLOUDERA INC (HQ)
5470 Great America Pkwy (95054-3644)
PHONE 650 362-0488
Robert Bearden, *Pr*
Mick Hollison, *
Kevin Cook, *
EMP: 79 **EST:** 2008
SQ FT: 92,000
SALES (est): 1.26B
SALES (corp-wide): 1.26B **Privately Held**
Web: www.cloudera.com
SIC: 7371 Computer software development
PA: Sky Parent Inc.
5470 Great America Pkwy
Santa Clara CA
650 362-0488

(P-11497)
CLUMIO INC
4555 Great America Pkwy Ste 101 (95054-1243)
PHONE 603 321-2495
Chadd Kenney, *Co-Vice President*
Chadd Vp-chief Technologist Ke nney, *Prin*
EMP: 93 **EST:** 2017
SALES (est): 4.54MM **Privately Held**
Web: www.clumio.com
SIC: 7371 Computer software development

(P-11498)
CODAZEN INC
Also Called: Codazen
60 Bunsen (92618-4210)
PHONE 949 916-6266
Michael Merchant, *Pr*
Michael H Merchant, *
Angela Merchant, *
EMP: 85 **EST:** 2007
SALES (est): 5.2MM **Privately Held**
Web: www.codazen.com
SIC: 7371 Computer software development

(P-11499)
CODESIGNAL INC
201 California St (94111-5002)
PHONE 669 200-9704
Tigran Sloyan, *CEO*
Sophia Baik, *
EMP: 150 **EST:** 2015
SALES (est): 13.14MM **Privately Held**
Web: www.codesignal.com
SIC: 7371 Computer software development and applications

(P-11500)
CODILITY US INC
575 Market St Fl 4 (94105-5818)
PHONE 415 568-5055
Rachel Whitehead, *Prin*
EMP: 150 **EST:** 2015
SALES (est): 8.57MM **Privately Held**
Web: www.codility.com
SIC: 7371 Computer software development and applications

(P-11501)
COGNITIVE MEDICAL SYSTEMS INC (PA)
Also Called: Computer Software Development
9920 Pacific Heights Blvd Ste 150 # 5604 (92121)
PHONE 858 509-4949
EMP: 62 **EST:** 2010
SALES (est): 10.49MM **Privately Held**
Web: www.cognitivemedicalsystems.com
SIC: 7371 Computer software development

(P-11502)
COGNITIVECLOUDS SOFTWARE INC
5433 Ontario Cmn (94555-2930)
PHONE 415 234-3611
Prasanna Gopinath, *Prin*
EMP: 70 **EST:** 2017
SALES (est): 2.98MM **Privately Held**
Web: www.cognitiveclouds.com
SIC: 7371 Computer software development

(P-11503)
COHESITY INC (PA)
300 Park Ave Ste 1700 (95110-2774)
PHONE 855 926-4374
Sanjay Poonen, *Pr*
Lynn Lucas, *CMO*
Robert Salmon, *
Michael Cremen, *CRO*
Marcus Loh, *
EMP: 500 **EST:** 2013
SQ FT: 98,000
SALES (est): 221.15MM
SALES (corp-wide): 221.15MM **Privately Held**
Web: www.cohesity.com
SIC: 7371 Custom computer programming services

(P-11504)
COLSA CORPORATION
Digital Wizards Division
2727 Cmino Del Rio S Ste (92108)
PHONE 619 553-0031
Patricia Hodges, *Prin*
EMP: 68
SALES (corp-wide): 362.72MM **Privately Held**
Web: www.colsa.com
SIC: 7371 8711 Computer software development; Engineering services
PA: Colsa Corporation
6728 Odyssey Dr Nw
Huntsville AL
256 964-5361

(P-11505)
COM2US USA INC
Also Called: Gamevil Com2us USA
999 N Pacific Coast Hwy Ste 450 (90245)
PHONE 310 416-1100
Kayla Rech, *Prin*
EMP: 61 **EST:** 2006
SALES (est): 5.56MM **Privately Held**
Web: www.com2us.com
SIC: 7371 Computer software development and applications

(P-11506)
COMMERCIAL RE EXCH INC
Also Called: Crexi
5510 Lincoln Blvd (90094-2034)
PHONE 888 273-0423
Michael Degiorgio, *CEO*
Erek Benz, *
Ben Widhelm, *
Hans Ku, *CPO*
Courtney Ettus, *CMO*
EMP: 250 **EST:** 2015
SQ FT: 2,000
SALES (est): 23.31MM **Privately Held**
Web: www.crexi.com
SIC: 7371 Computer software development and applications

(P-11507)
COMMURE INC (PA)
2261 Market St # 4072 (94114-1612)
PHONE 888 994-2443
Brent Dover, *CEO*
EMP: 60 **EST:** 2017
SQ FT: 11,500
SALES (est): 33.29MM
SALES (corp-wide): 33.29MM **Privately Held**
Web: www.commure.com
SIC: 7371 Computer software development

(P-11508)
COMPONENT CONTROLCOM INC
Also Called: Component Control Systems
1731 Kettner Blvd (92101-2523)
PHONE 619 696-5400
Zvi Baron, *CEO*
Todd Lewis, *
EMP: 60 **EST:** 1985
SALES (est): 7.7MM **Privately Held**
Web: www.componentcontrol.com
SIC: 7371 Computer software development

(P-11509)
COMPULINK MANAGEMENT CTR INC (PA)
Also Called: Laserfiche Document Imaging
3443 Long Beach Blvd (90807-4432)
PHONE 562 988-1688
Nien-ling Wacker, *Pr*
Christopher Wacker, *
Jim Haney, *
▲ **EMP:** 197 **EST:** 1976
SALES (est): 45.38MM
SALES (corp-wide): 45.38MM **Privately Held**

PRODUCTS & SERVICES SECTION
7371 - Custom Computer Programming Services (P-11529)

Web: www.laserfiche.com
SIC: 7371 Computer software development

(P-11510)
COMPUTER PROC UNLIMITED INC
Also Called: Cpu Medical Management Systems
9235 Activity Rd Ste 104 (92126-4440)
PHONE..........................858 530-0875
Michael Stringer, *Pr*
Douglas C Pence, *
Brian Castle, *
Jean Campbell, *
Duane Findling, *
EMP: 128 EST: 1982
SQ FT: 11,250
SALES (est): 10.18MM
SALES (corp-wide): 276.71B **Publicly Held**
SIC: 7371 5045 Computer software systems analysis and design, custom; Computer peripheral equipment
PA: Mckesson Corporation
6555 State Highway 161
Irving TX
972 446-4800

(P-11511)
COMPUTRITION INC (HQ)
Also Called: Dfm Dietary Food Management
8521 Fallbrook Ave Ste 100 (91304)
PHONE..........................818 961-3999
Scott Saklad, *Pr*
Kim C Goldberg, *Marketing*
EMP: 60 EST: 1981
SQ FT: 16,763
SALES (est): 13.33MM
SALES (corp-wide): 6.62B **Privately Held**
Web: www.computrition.com
SIC: 7371 7372 Computer software development; Prepackaged software
PA: Constellation Software Inc
20 Adelaide St E Suite 1200
Toronto ON
416 861-9677

(P-11512)
CONCORD WORLDWIDE INC
177 Post St Ste 910 (94108-4712)
PHONE..........................415 689-5488
Mathieu Lhoumeau, *CEO*
Florian Parain, *
EMP: 65 EST: 2014
SQ FT: 2,700
SALES (est): 5.54MM **Privately Held**
Web: www.concordnow.com
SIC: 7371 Computer software development

(P-11513)
CONSERVIS CORP
Also Called: Conservis
352 W Spruce Ave (93611-8705)
PHONE..........................612 424-6300
Sherman Black, *CEO*
Charles Faison, *Chief Technician*
EMP: 82 EST: 2009
SALES (est): 3.62MM **Privately Held**
Web: www.conservis.ag
SIC: 7371 Computer software development and applications

(P-11514)
CONVEX LABS INC
703 Market St Ste 17 (94103-2102)
P.O. Box 7775 (94120-7775)
PHONE..........................408 692-0852
Charlie Warren, *CEO*
Blake Meulmester, *
EMP: 100 EST: 2017
SALES (est): 11.47MM **Privately Held**
Web: www.convex.com
SIC: 7371 Computer software development and applications

(P-11515)
CORDIAL EXPERIENCE INC
402 W Broadway Ste 700 (92101-8572)
P.O. Box 307 (92040-0307)
PHONE..........................619 793-9787
Jeremy Swift, *CEO*
Stephanie Robotham, *CMO*
EMP: 70 EST: 2014
SALES (est): 3.41MM **Privately Held**
Web: www.cordial.com
SIC: 7371 Computer software systems analysis and design, custom

(P-11516)
CORELATION INC
2305 Historic Decatur Rd Ste 300 (92106-6052)
PHONE..........................619 876-5074
John F Landis, *CEO*
Theresa Benavidez, *
Harold Barnabas, *
Lori Paige, *
Dwayne Jacobs, *
EMP: 200 EST: 2007
SALES (est): 24.28MM **Privately Held**
Web: www.corelationinc.com
SIC: 7371 Computer software development

(P-11517)
CORPTAX LLC
21550 Oxnard St Ste 700 (91367-7170)
PHONE..........................818 316-2400
EMP: 133
Web: www.corptax.com
SIC: 7371 Computer software development
PA: Corptax, Llc
2100 E Lake Cook Rd # 800
Buffalo Grove IL

(P-11518)
COUCHBASE INC (PA)
Also Called: COUCHBASE
3250 Olcott St (95054-3005)
PHONE..........................650 417-7500
Matthew M Cain, *Pr*
Gregory N Henry, *Sr VP*
Margaret Chow, *CLO*
Huw Owen, *CRO*
EMP: 152 EST: 2008
SQ FT: 46,000
SALES (est): 154.82MM
SALES (corp-wide): 154.82MM **Publicly Held**
Web: www.couchbase.com
SIC: 7371 7372 Computer software development; Business oriented computer software

(P-11519)
COUNTY OF LOS ANGELES
Also Called: Internal Services
1100 N Eastern Ave (90063-3200)
PHONE..........................562 940-4324
David Wesolik, *Genl Mgr*
EMP: 2000
SALES (corp-wide): 31.7B **Privately Held**
Web: www.lacounty.gov
SIC: 7371 Computer software development and applications
PA: County Of Los Angeles
500 W Temple St Ste 437
Los Angeles CA
213 974-1101

(P-11520)
COVEO SOFTWARE CORP
44 Montgomery St (94104-4602)
PHONE..........................800 635-5476
Louis Tetu, *CEO*
Benoit Hogue, *
Mark Floisand, *
Laurent Simoneau, *
John Lavigueur, *
EMP: 64 EST: 2005
SQ FT: 2,000
SALES (est): 25.42MM
SALES (corp-wide): 14.42MM **Privately Held**
Web: www.coveo.com
SIC: 7371 8748 Computer software development; Business consulting, nec
PA: Coveo Solutions Inc.
3175 Ch Des Quatre-Bourgeois
Bureau 200
Quebec QC
418 263-1111

(P-11521)
CRAFT MACHINE INC (PA)
Also Called: Craft
564 Market St Ste 150 (94104-5430)
PHONE..........................650 862-9580
Ilya Levtov, *CEO*
EMP: 95 EST: 2016
SQ FT: 1,100
SALES (est): 5.76MM
SALES (corp-wide): 5.76MM **Privately Held**
Web: www.craft.co
SIC: 7371 Computer software development

(P-11522)
CRESCENTONE INC (HQ)
Also Called: Fujitsu Glovia, Inc.
200 Continental Blvd Fl 3 (90245-4526)
PHONE..........................310 563-7000
Chikara Ono, *CEO*
Jim Errington, *Ex VP*
Masahiro Cho, *CFO*
EMP: 150 EST: 1970
SQ FT: 53,000
SALES (est): 46.73MM **Privately Held**
Web: www.crescentone.com
SIC: 7371 7372 Computer software development; Prepackaged software
PA: Fujitsu Limited
1-5-2, Higashishimbashi
Minato-Ku TKY

(P-11523)
CROSS MATCH INC
6607 Kaiser Dr (94555-3608)
PHONE..........................650 474-4000
EMP: 228
SALES (corp-wide): 11.51B **Privately Held**
SIC: 7371 Computer software development
HQ: Cross Match, Inc.
3950 Rca Blvd Ste 5001
Palm Beach Gardens FL
561 622-1650

(P-11524)
CSRA LLC
524 Logue Ave (94043-4048)
PHONE..........................703 641-2000
Lawrence Prior, *CEO*
Helaine Elderkin, *
EMP: 1000 EST: 2015
Web: www.gdit.com
SIC: 7371 8733 7376 7374 Custom computer programming services; Scientific research agency; Computer facilities management; Data processing and preparation

(P-11525)
CU DIRECT CORPORATION (PA)
Also Called: Cudc
2855 E Guasti Rd Ste 500 (91761-1253)
P.O. Box 51482 (91761-0082)
PHONE..........................833 908-0121
Antony Boutelle, *Pr*
Keith Sultemeier, *
Jim Laffoon, *Vice Chairman*
Jerry Neemann, *
Craig S Montesanti, *
EMP: 175 EST: 1994
SQ FT: 30,000
SALES (est): 88.92MM
SALES (corp-wide): 88.92MM **Privately Held**
Web: www.cudirect.com
SIC: 7371 Computer software development

(P-11526)
CUBIC TRNSP SYSTEMS INC (DH)
Also Called: Cubic
9233 Balboa Ave (92123-1513)
P.O. Box 85587 (92186-5587)
PHONE..........................858 268-3100
Stephen O Shewmaker, *CEO*
Walter C Zable, *
Raymond De Kozan, *
Steve Purcell, *
◆ EMP: 550 EST: 1950
SALES (est): 244.67MM
SALES (corp-wide): 1.48B **Privately Held**
Web: www.cubic.com
SIC: 7371 1731 3829 Custom computer programming services; Telephone and telephone equipment installation; Fare registers, for street cars, buses, etc.
HQ: Cubic Corporation
9233 Balboa Ave
San Diego CA
858 277-6780

(P-11527)
DAILY CO
548 Market St Unit 39113 (94104-5401)
PHONE..........................855 660-1224
Kwindla Hultman Kramer, *CEO*
Meghann Wu, *Chief of Staff*
EMP: 60 EST: 2015
SALES (est): 3.8MM **Privately Held**
SIC: 7371 Computer software development and applications

(P-11528)
DATADIRECT NETWORKS INC (PA)
Also Called: D D N
9351 Deering Ave (91311-5858)
PHONE..........................818 700-7600
Alex Bouzari, *CEO*
Paul Bloch, *
Ian Angelo, *
Robert Triendl, *
Bret Weber, *
▲ EMP: 120 EST: 1988
SQ FT: 50,000
SALES (est): 149.51MM
SALES (corp-wide): 149.51MM **Privately Held**
Web: www.ddn.com
SIC: 7371 7374 Custom computer programming services; Data processing service

(P-11529)
DATASTAX INC (PA)
2755 Augustine Dr 8th Fl (95054-2919)
PHONE..........................650 389-6000
Chet Kapoor, *CEO*

7371 - Custom Computer Programming Services (P-11530)

Don Dixon, *
Robin Schumacher, *
Debbie Murray, *
Martin Van Ryswyk, *
EMP: 418 **EST:** 2010
SALES (est): 174.23MM
SALES (corp-wide): 174.23MM **Privately Held**
Web: www.datastax.com
SIC: 7371 Computer software development

(P-11530)
DATAVANT INC (PA)
44 Montgomery St Ste 300 (94104-4624)
PHONE..............................415 520-1171
Pete Mccabe, *CEO*
Travis May, *
Jose Garcia, *
EMP: 112 **EST:** 2018
SALES (est): 647.13MM
SALES (corp-wide): 647.13MM **Privately Held**
Web: www.datavant.com
SIC: 7371 Computer software development and applications

(P-11531)
DAYBREAK GAME COMPANY LLC
Also Called: Daybreak
13500 Evening Creek Dr N Ste 300 (92128-8125)
PHONE..............................858 239-0500
▲ **EMP:** 450 **EST:** 2006
SALES (est): 49.21MM
SALES (corp-wide): 182.44MM **Privately Held**
Web: maintenance.daybreakgames.com
SIC: 7371 Computer software development
PA: Enad Global 7 Ab (Publ)
Ringvagen 100, 6tr
Stockholm
738204439

(P-11532)
DAZ SYSTEMS LLC
Also Called: Daz
1003 E 4th Pl Ste 800 (90013-2775)
PHONE..............................310 640-1300
EMP: 375 **EST:** 1995
SALES (est): 38.43MM **Privately Held**
SIC: 7371 7372 Computer software development; Prepackaged software
HQ: Accenture Llp
500 W Madison St
Chicago IL
312 693-0161

(P-11533)
DEADLINE HOLLYWOOD MEDIA LLC
11175 Santa Monica Blvd (90025-3330)
PHONE..............................310 321-5000
EMP: 66 **EST:** 2018
SALES (est): 3.52MM **Privately Held**
Web: www.deadline.com
SIC: 7371 Computer software development and applications

(P-11534)
DEALERTRACK CLLTRAL MGT SVCS I
Also Called: Fdi Collateral Management
9750 Goethe Rd (95827-3500)
PHONE..............................916 368-5300
Mark O'neil, *CEO*
Mark O Neil, *Prin*
Daniel L Wollenberg, *Pr*
Beverly Devine, *Ex VP*
Tony Panganiban, *VP Fin*
EMP: 220 **EST:** 1992
SQ FT: 84,900
SALES (est): 31.06MM
SALES (corp-wide): 16.61B **Privately Held**
Web: us.dealertrack.com
SIC: 7371 Computer software development
HQ: Trivin, Inc.
115 Pohegarut Dr Ste 201
Groton CT
860 448-3177

(P-11535)
DEEPGRAM INC
548 Market St Ste 25104 (94104-5401)
PHONE..............................415 302-7624
Noah John Shutty, *Prin*
EMP: 100 **EST:** 2015
SALES (est): 10.03MM **Privately Held**
Web: www.deepgram.com
SIC: 7371 Computer software development and applications

(P-11536)
DELINEA INC (HQ)
221 Main St Ste 1300 (94105-1903)
P.O. Box 60428 (94088-0428)
PHONE..............................669 444-5200
Art Gilliland, *CEO*
EMP: 112 **EST:** 2004
SQ FT: 8,300
SALES (est): 108.03MM
SALES (corp-wide): 122MM **Privately Held**
Web: www.delinea.com
SIC: 7371 Computer software development
PA: Thycoticcentrify Holdings, Inc.
201 Rdwood Shres Pkwy St3
Redwood City CA
669 444-5200

(P-11537)
DELPHIX CORP (PA)
1450 Veterans Blvd Ste 120 (94063-2619)
PHONE..............................650 494-1645
Jedidiah Yueh, *CEO*
Jedidiah Yueh, *Ch Bd*
Chris Cook, *
John Kemmerer, *VP*
Hilary Ahern, *Dir. Fin*
EMP: 572 **EST:** 2008
SALES (est): 82.17MM
SALES (corp-wide): 82.17MM **Privately Held**
Web: www.delphix.com
SIC: 7371 Computer software development

(P-11538)
DEMANDTEC LLC
1 Franklin Pkwy Bldg 910 (94403-1906)
PHONE..............................914 499-1900
Daniel R Fishback, *Pr*
Mark A Culhane, *
William R Phelps, *
Michael A Bromme Senior, *Retail Vice President*
EMP: 340 **EST:** 1999
SQ FT: 82,000
SALES (est): 28.77MM
SALES (corp-wide): 60.53B **Publicly Held**
Web: www.demandtec.com
SIC: 7371 Computer software development
PA: International Business Machines Corporation
1 New Orchard Rd Ste 1 # 1
Armonk NY
914 499-1900

(P-11539)
DEVIATION GAMES LLC
12100 Wilshire Blvd Ste 1150 (90025-7120)
PHONE..............................310 873-5225
EMP: 98 **EST:** 2020
SALES (est): 1.58MM **Privately Held**
Web: www.deviationgames.com
SIC: 7371 Computer software development and applications

(P-11540)
DGN TECHNOLOGIES INC (PA)
46500 Fremont Blvd Ste 708 (94538-6467)
PHONE..............................510 252-0346
Ranvir Singh, *Pr*
Manpreet Bajaj, *VP*
EMP: 60 **EST:** 2003
SQ FT: 1,863
SALES (est): 20.37MM
SALES (corp-wide): 20.37MM **Privately Held**
Web: www.dgntechnologies.com
SIC: 7371 8748 Computer software development; Systems engineering consultant, ex. computer or professional

(P-11541)
DIGITE INC
21060 Homestead Rd Ste 220 (95014-0204)
PHONE..............................408 418-3834
Suhas S Patil, *Ch Bd*
Sridhar Auynam, *
Raghunath Basavanahalli, *
Sudipta Lahiri, *
Ram Subramanian, *
EMP: 150 **EST:** 1998
SQ FT: 1,400
SALES (est): 13.86MM **Privately Held**
Web: www.nimblework.com
SIC: 7371 Computer software development

(P-11542)
DIRECTLY INC
333 Bryant St Ste 250 (94107-1443)
PHONE..............................650 714-7334
Michael De La Cruz, *CEO*
EMP: 68 **EST:** 2015
SALES (est): 722.48K **Privately Held**
Web: www.directly.com
SIC: 7371 Computer software development and applications

(P-11543)
DISCORD INC
444 De Haro St Ste 200 (94107-2578)
PHONE..............................650 389-2453
Jason Citron, *CEO*
EMP: 150 **EST:** 2014
SALES (est): 27.68MM **Privately Held**
Web: www.discord.com
SIC: 7371 Computer software development and applications

(P-11544)
DISNEY CNSMR PDTS INTRCTIVE MD
Also Called: Dcpi
1201 Flower St (91201-2417)
PHONE..............................818 263-1374
James Pitaro, *Ch*
Michael White, *Sr VP*
EMP: 115 **EST:** 2016
SALES (est): 3.99MM
SALES (corp-wide): 82.72B **Publicly Held**
Web: www.disneyconnect.com
SIC: 7371 Software programming applications
PA: The Walt Disney Company
500 S Buena Vista St
Burbank CA
818 560-1000

(P-11545)
DISNEY INTERACTIVE STUDIOS INC
601 Circle Seven Dr (91201-2332)
PHONE..............................818 560-1000
Peter Casciani, *Mgr*
EMP: 270
SALES (corp-wide): 82.72B **Publicly Held**
SIC: 7371 Computer software development
HQ: Disney Interactive Studios, Inc.
500 S Buena Vista St
Burbank CA
818 560-1000

(P-11546)
DISNEY INTERACTIVE STUDIOS INC
Also Called: Disney Interactive Studios
681 W Buena Vista St (91521-0001)
PHONE..............................818 553-5000
EMP: 270
SALES (corp-wide): 82.72B **Publicly Held**
SIC: 7371 Computer software development
HQ: Disney Interactive Studios, Inc.
500 S Buena Vista St
Burbank CA
818 560-1000

(P-11547)
DISTILLERY TECH INC
Also Called: Distillery
1500 Rosecrans Ave Ste 500 (90266-3707)
PHONE..............................310 776-6234
Andrey Kudievskiy, *Pr*
EMP: 220 **EST:** 2012
SALES (est): 13.7MM **Privately Held**
Web: www.distillery.com
SIC: 7371 7372 7373 Computer software development; Application computer software ; Computer systems analysis and design

(P-11548)
DOCKER INC (PA)
3790 El Camino Real Ste 1052 (94303-4504)
P.O. Box 61180 (94306-6180)
PHONE..............................415 941-0376
Scott Johnston, *CEO*
Edwin Scott Baumgartner, *
Lisa Catherine Berry, *
EMP: 347 **EST:** 2010
SALES (est): 44.65MM
SALES (corp-wide): 44.65MM **Privately Held**
Web: www.docker.com
SIC: 7371 Computer software development

(P-11549)
DOCUPACE TECHNOLOGIES LLC (PA)
400 Corporate Pointe Ste 300 (90230)
P.O. Box 92117 (89193-2117)
PHONE..............................310 445-7722
Michael Pinsker, *Managing Member*
John Cunningham, *CIO*
James Caulkins, *CRO*
EMP: 200 **EST:** 2002
SQ FT: 1,500
SALES (est): 18.78MM
SALES (corp-wide): 18.78MM **Privately Held**
Web: www.docupace.com
SIC: 7371 Computer software development

PRODUCTS & SERVICES SECTION
7371 - Custom Computer Programming Services (P-11572)

(P-11550)
DOMINO DATA LAB INC (PA)
135 Townsend St (94107-2017)
P.O. Box 78062 (94107-8062)
PHONE...............................415 570-2425
Nick Elprin, *CEO*
Dennis Sevilla, *
Shaun Seah, *
EMP: 209 **EST:** 2012
SALES (est): 37.79MM
SALES (corp-wide): 37.79MM **Privately Held**
Web: www.dominodatalab.com
SIC: 7371 Custom computer programming services

(P-11551)
DORADO SOFTWARE INC
Also Called: Visiworks Software
4805 Golden Foothill Pkwy (95762-9651)
PHONE...............................916 673-1100
Timothy Sebring, *Pr*
EMP: 80 **EST:** 1997
SALES (est): 10.41MM **Privately Held**
Web: www.doradosoftware.com
SIC: 7371 Computer software development

(P-11552)
DOTSOLVED SYSTEMS INC
4900 Hopyard Rd (94588-7100)
PHONE...............................925 218-6903
Pushpanjali Ashok, *CEO*
Pushpanjali Ashok, *Pr*
Geethanjali Gnaneswaran, *Prin*
EMP: 200 **EST:** 2002
SQ FT: 635
SALES (est): 9.57MM **Privately Held**
Web: www.dotsolved.com
SIC: 7371 8748 Computer software writing services; Systems analysis or design

(P-11553)
DOXIMITY INC (PA)
500 3rd St Ste 510 (94107-6803)
PHONE...............................650 549-4330
Jeffrey Tangney, *CEO*
Anna Bryson, *CFO*
Joseph Kleine, *CCO*
EMP: 548 **EST:** 2010
SQ FT: 23,000
SALES (est): 419.05MM
SALES (corp-wide): 419.05MM **Publicly Held**
Web: www.doximity.com
SIC: 7371 Custom computer programming services

(P-11554)
DRISHTI TECHNOLOGIES INC
800 W El Camino Real Ste 180 (94040)
PHONE...............................214 748-3647
Gary Jackson, *CEO*
Prasad Akell, *
Srida Joisa, *
EMP: 155 **EST:** 2017
SALES (est): 11.73MM **Privately Held**
Web: www.drishti.com
SIC: 7371 Computer software development

(P-11555)
DRIVENBI LLC
1606 Camino Lindo (91030-4130)
PHONE...............................626 795-2088
EMP: 60 **EST:** 2006
SALES (est): 4.99MM **Privately Held**
Web: www.drivenbi.com
SIC: 7371 Computer software development

(P-11556)
DUETTO RESEARCH INC
333 Bush St Ste 1200 (94104-2815)
PHONE...............................415 968-9389
Patrick Bosworth, *Ch Bd*
David Woolenberg, *Pr*
Marco Benvenuti, *Prin*
Greg Stanger, *CFO*
EMP: 115 **EST:** 2012
SALES (est): 5.63MM **Privately Held**
Web: www.duettocloud.com
SIC: 7371 Computer software development

(P-11557)
DYNASTY MARKETPLACE INC
716 Hampton Dr (90291-3019)
PHONE...............................804 837-0119
Elliot Burris, *CEO*
EMP: 325 **EST:** 2016
SALES (est): 213.52K
SALES (corp-wide): 471.88MM **Publicly Held**
SIC: 7371 Computer software development and applications
PA: Appfolio, Inc.
70 Castilian Dr
Santa Barbara CA
805 364-6093

(P-11558)
DZKICORP INC
762 Higuera St Ste 216 (93401-3573)
P.O. Box 1465 (93406-1465)
PHONE...............................805 464-0573
Eric Doster, *CEO*
EMP: 75 **EST:** 2019
SALES (est): 3.34MM **Privately Held**
SIC: 7371 Computer software development

(P-11559)
E2OPEN INC
4100 E 3rd Ave Ste 400 (94404-4819)
PHONE...............................866 432-6736
EMP: 61 **EST:** 2019
SALES (est): 915.03K **Privately Held**
Web: www.e2open.com
SIC: 7371 Computer software development

(P-11560)
EACOM INC
209 Redwood Shores Pkwy (94065-1175)
PHONE...............................650 628-1500
E Stanton Mc Kee, *Co-Vice President*
E Stanton Mc Kee, *CAO*
Ruth A Kennedy, *
Bryan Neider, *
EMP: 140 **EST:** 1999
SALES (est): 23.03MM
SALES (corp-wide): 7.43B **Publicly Held**
Web: www.ea.com
SIC: 7371 Computer software development
PA: Electronic Arts Inc.
209 Redwood Shores Pkwy
Redwood City CA
650 628-1500

(P-11561)
ECONOSOFT INC
2375 Zanker Rd Ste 250 (95131-1143)
PHONE...............................408 442-3663
Chander Shaiker, *Pr*
EMP: 72 **EST:** 2000
SALES (est): 1.18MM
SALES (corp-wide): 18.3MM **Privately Held**
Web: www.econosoftinc.com
SIC: 7371 Computer software systems analysis and design, custom
PA: Ace Technologies, Inc.
2375 Zanker Rd Ste 250
San Jose CA
408 324-1203

(P-11562)
EFRONT FINANCIAL SOLUTIONS INC
135 Main St Ste 1330 (94105-1843)
PHONE...............................415 653-3239
Tarek Chouman, *CEO*
Thibaut De Laval, *CSO CMO*
Tom Gardner, *CSO*
Dave Cox Csso, *Prin*
Michael Bischoff, *
EMP: 88 **EST:** 2008
SALES (est): 1.58MM **Privately Held**
Web: www.efrontlearning.com
SIC: 7371 Computer software development

(P-11563)
EHEALTHINSURANCE SERVICES INC
Also Called: Ehealth Insurance.com
11919 Foundation Pl Ste 100 (95670-4537)
PHONE...............................916 608-6101
Robert Hurley, *Brnch Mgr*
EMP: 200
SIC: 7371 Computer software development
HQ: Ehealthinsurance Services, Inc.
2625 Augustine Dr Ste 201
Santa Clara CA
650 584-2700

(P-11564)
EIGHTEENTH MERIDIAN INC
Also Called: Secure-Dmz
200 Spectrum Center Dr Ste 300 (92618-5003)
PHONE...............................714 706-3643
Erol Karabeg, *Pr*
Dino Beslic, *
EMP: 500 **EST:** 1998
SALES (est): 18.56MM **Privately Held**
SIC: 7371 Custom computer programming services

(P-11565)
EINFOCHIPS INC
2361 Campus Dr Ste 105 (92612-1465)
PHONE...............................949 527-6459
Pratul Shroff, *Brnch Mgr*
EMP: 86
SALES (corp-wide): 37.12B **Publicly Held**
Web: www.einfochips.com
SIC: 7371 Computer software development
HQ: Einfochips Inc.
2025 Gateway Pl Ste 238
San Jose CA
408 496-1882

(P-11566)
EINFOCHIPS INC (HQ)
2025 Gateway Pl Ste 238 (95110-1000)
PHONE...............................408 496-1882
Pratul Shroff, *CEO*
Raj Sirohi, *
Sribash Dey, *
Parag Mehta, *Business*
Shashank Waman Khare, *
EMP: 63 **EST:** 1998
SALES (est): 23.53MM
SALES (corp-wide): 37.12B **Publicly Held**
Web: www.einfochips.com
SIC: 7371 7373 Computer software development; Systems software development services
PA: Arrow Electronics, Inc.
9201 E Dry Creek Rd
Centennial CO
303 824-4000

(P-11567)
EINSTEIN INDUSTRIES INC
Also Called: Einstein Dental
6825 Flanders Dr (92121-2905)
P.O. Box 27149 (92198-1149)
PHONE...............................858 459-1182
EMP: 180 **EST:** 1995
SALES (est): 27.09MM **Privately Held**
Web: www.einsteinlaw.com
SIC: 7371 8742 8322 Computer software development; Marketing consulting services; Referral service for personal and social problems

(P-11568)
EITACIES INC
4701 Patrick Henry Dr Bldg 25 (95054-1819)
PHONE...............................805 500-4366
Nirmal Gorla, *Ex Dir*
Rajani Penubothu, *
EMP: 100 **EST:** 2008
SALES (est): 5.07MM **Privately Held**
Web: www.eitacies.com
SIC: 7371 8243 Computer software development; Software training, computer

(P-11569)
ELLATION LLC (DH)
Also Called: Crunchyroll
835 Market St Ste 700 (94103-1906)
PHONE...............................415 796-3560
Tom Pickett, *CEO*
EMP: 156 **EST:** 2015
SALES (est): 27.03MM **Privately Held**
Web: www.crunchyroll.com
SIC: 7371 5932 Computer software development and applications; Used merchandise stores
HQ: Sony Corporation Of America
25 Madison Ave Fl 27
New York NY

(P-11570)
ELLIE MAE INC
Also Called: ELLIE MAE, INC.
24025 Park Sorrento Ste 210 (91302-4018)
PHONE...............................818 223-2000
EMP: 327
SALES (corp-wide): 7.29B **Publicly Held**
Web: www.icemortgagetechnology.com
SIC: 7371 Computer software systems analysis and design, custom
HQ: Ice Mortgage Technology, Inc.
4420 Rosewood Dr Ste 500
Pleasanton CA
855 224-8572

(P-11571)
EMIDS TECH PRIVATE LTD CORP
6320 Canoga Ave (91367-2526)
PHONE...............................805 304-5986
EMP: 2157
Web: www.emids.com
SIC: 7371 Computer software development
PA: Emids Technologies Private Limited Corp.
318 Seaboard Ln Ste 110
Franklin TN

(P-11572)
EPIC CREATIONS INC
702 Marshall St Ste 280 (94063-1823)
PHONE...............................650 918-7327
Suren Markosian, *CEO*
EMP: 112 **EST:** 2012
SALES (est): 9.57MM **Privately Held**
Web: www.getepic.com
SIC: 7371 Computer software development and applications

7371 - Custom Computer Programming Services (P-11573)

PA: Think & Learn Private Limited
Ibc Knowledge Park, 4/1, 2nd Floor,
Tower D
Bengaluru KA

(P-11573)
EPITEC INC
515 Olive Ave (92083-3439)
PHONE...................760 650-2515
William Grivas, *Pr*
EMP: 900
SALES (corp-wide): 79.55MM **Privately Held**
Web: www.epitec.com
SIC: 7371 Computer software systems analysis and design, custom
PA: Epitec, Inc.
26555 Evergreen Rd # 1700
Southfield MI
248 353-6800

(P-11574)
EPR RECRUITING INC
4000 Calle Tecate Ste 213 (93012-5288)
PHONE...................213 607-2001
EMP: 61 EST: 2015
SALES (est): 1.06MM **Privately Held**
Web: www.eprrecruiting.com
SIC: 7371 Custom computer programming services

(P-11575)
EQUATOR LLC (HQ)
Also Called: Equator Business Solutions
6060 Center Dr Ste 500 (90045-8857)
PHONE...................310 469-9500
EMP: 200 EST: 2003
SALES (est): 41.28MM
SALES (corp-wide): 2.67MM **Privately Held**
Web: www.equator.com
SIC: 7371 Computer software development and applications
PA: Altisource Portfolio Solutions S.A.
Boulevard Prince Henri 33
Luxembourg

(P-11576)
ERGOMOTION INC
6790 Navigator Way (93117-3656)
P.O. Box 8330 (93118-8330)
PHONE...................888 550-3746
Guohai Tang, *CEO*
Zhifan Yang, *
▲ EMP: 70 EST: 2006
SALES (est): 22.44MM **Privately Held**
Web: www.ergomotion.com
SIC: 7371 Computer software development and applications

(P-11577)
ERP INTEGRATED SOLUTIONS LLC
Also Called: Shiperp
5000 Airport Plaza Dr Ste 230 (90815)
PHONE...................562 425-7800
Joseph Cabrera, *Pr*
Doug Cole, *
Anthony Raimo, *
EMP: 100 EST: 2008
SALES (est): 9.86MM **Privately Held**
Web: www.shiperp.com
SIC: 7371 Computer software development

(P-11578)
ERT OPERATING COMPANY
5615 Scotts Valley Dr Ste 150 (95066-3492)
PHONE...................412 390-3000
Douglas Engfer, *Pr*
EMP: 667
SALES (corp-wide): 1.37MM **Privately Held**
Web: www.clario.com
SIC: 7371 Computer software development
HQ: Ert Operating Company
1818 Market St Ste 1000
Philadelphia PA
215 972-0420

(P-11579)
ESSENTIAL PRODUCTS INC
380 Portage Ave (94306-2244)
PHONE...................650 300-0000
Andrew E Rubin, *CEO*
Matt Hershenson, *
Niccolo De Masi, *
Meena Srinivasan, *
EMP: 82 EST: 2015
SALES (est): 9.76MM **Privately Held**
Web: www.essential.com
SIC: 7371 Computer software systems analysis and design, custom

(P-11580)
ESTUATE INC
830 Hillview Ct Ste 280 (95035-4564)
PHONE...................408 946-0002
Prakash Balebail, *Pr*
Nagaraja Kini, *
EMP: 67 EST: 2005
SQ FT: 2,558
SALES (est): 11.12MM **Privately Held**
Web: www.estuate.com
SIC: 7371 Computer software development

(P-11581)
ETCH MOBILE INC
Also Called: Goodtime.io
835 Howard St # 3 (94103-3009)
PHONE...................512 299-3514
EMP: 60 EST: 2015
SALES (est): 586.13K **Privately Held**
Web: www.goodtime.io
SIC: 7371 Custom computer programming services

(P-11582)
EVERGENT TECHNOLOGIES INC
Also Called: Evergent
1250 Borregas Ave (94089-1309)
PHONE...................877 897-1240
Vijay Sajja, *CEO*
Bill Woods, *Executive Global Sales Vice President*
Jennifer Overbaugh, *Head OF GLOBAL Marketing*
EMP: 325 EST: 2003
SQ FT: 2,000
SALES (est): 20.16MM **Privately Held**
Web: www.evergent.com
SIC: 7371 Computer software development

(P-11583)
EVERNOTE CORPORATION (PA)
12671 High Bluff Dr (92130-2014)
PHONE...................650 216-7700
Chris O'neill, *CEO*
Phil Libin, *
Stepan Pachikov Fundr, *Prin*
Jeff Shotts, *
Dave Engberg, *
▲ EMP: 308 EST: 2004
SALES (est): 97.23MM
SALES (corp-wide): 97.23MM **Privately Held**
Web: www.evernote.com
SIC: 7371 Computer software development

(P-11584)
EVERYONE COUNTS INC
3945 Freedom Cir Ste 560 (95054-1269)
EMP: 70 EST: 2005
SALES (est): 9.72MM
SALES (corp-wide): 9.72MM **Privately Held**
Web: www.votem.com
SIC: 7371 Computer software development
PA: Votem Corp.
2515 Jay Ave Fl 1
Cleveland OH
216 930-4300

(P-11585)
EVIDATION HEALTH INC
11 N Ellsworth Ave (94401-2819)
PHONE...................650 389-2494
EMP: 237
SALES (corp-wide): 22.34MM **Privately Held**
Web: www.evidation.com
SIC: 7371 Computer software development and applications
PA: Evidation Health, Inc.
101 S Ellsworth Ave # 20
San Mateo CA
650 727-5557

(P-11586)
EVIDENTIO INC (HQ)
7901 Stoneridge Dr Ste 150 (94588-3677)
PHONE...................855 933-1337
Mark Mclaughlin, *CEO*
EMP: 85 EST: 2013
SQ FT: 5,000
SALES (est): 15.78MM
SALES (corp-wide): 6.89B **Publicly Held**
SIC: 7371 Computer software systems analysis and design, custom
PA: Palo Alto Networks Inc.
3000 Tannery Way
Santa Clara CA
408 753-4000

(P-11587)
EVOLVEWARE INC
4677 Old Ironsides Dr Ste 240 (95054-1825)
P.O. Box 2297 (94087-0297)
PHONE...................408 748-8301
Miten Marfatia, *Pr*
EMP: 78 EST: 2000
SQ FT: 1,200
SALES (est): 5.36MM **Privately Held**
Web: www.evolveware.com
SIC: 7371 Computer software development

(P-11588)
EXIGEN (USA) INC (PA)
Also Called: Exigen Group
345 California St Fl 22 (94104-2606)
PHONE...................415 402-2600
Greg Shenkman, *CEO*
Alec Miloslavsky, *
Sam Kvitko, *
EMP: 320 EST: 1993
SQ FT: 26,000
SALES (est): 47.72MM **Privately Held**
Web: www.eisgroup.com
SIC: 7371 Computer software development

(P-11589)
EXPANSE LLC
425 Market St Fl 8 (94105-2465)
PHONE...................415 590-0129
Timothy Junio, *CEO*
Matt Kraning, *
Daniel Quinlan, *
EMP: 180 EST: 2012
SALES (est): 19.27MM
SALES (corp-wide): 6.89B **Publicly Held**
Web: www.paloaltonetworks.com
SIC: 7371 Computer software development and applications
PA: Palo Alto Networks Inc.
3000 Tannery Way
Santa Clara CA
408 753-4000

(P-11590)
EXPLODING KITTENS INC
101 S La Brea Ave # A (90036-2998)
PHONE...................919 738-8440
Ashley Mitchell, *Prin*
EMP: 62 EST: 2017
SALES (est): 1.63MM **Privately Held**
Web: www.explodingkittens.com
SIC: 7371 Computer software development and applications

(P-11591)
FAIR FINANCIAL CORP (PA)
1540 2nd St Ste 200 (90401-3513)
P.O. Box 409 (10523-0409)
PHONE...................800 584-5000
Bradley Stewart, *CEO*
Georg Bauer, *
Craig Nehamen, *
EMP: 82 EST: 2015
SALES (est): 23.37MM
SALES (corp-wide): 23.37MM **Privately Held**
SIC: 7371 Computer software development and applications

(P-11592)
FAMOUS SOFTWARE LLC
8080 N Palm Ave Ste 210 (93711-5797)
PHONE...................559 431-8100
Heather Hammack, *
EMP: 65 EST: 2000
SALES (est): 2.64MM **Privately Held**
SIC: 7371 Computer software development

(P-11593)
FASTLY INC (PA)
475 Brannan St Ste 300 (94107-5420)
P.O. Box 78266 (94107-8266)
PHONE...................844 432-7859
Joshua Bixby, *CEO*
Artur Bergman, *
Ronald W Kisling, *CFO*
Brett Shirk, *CRO*
Paul Luongo, *Sr VP*
EMP: 432 EST: 2011
SQ FT: 71,343
SALES (est): 432.73MM
SALES (corp-wide): 432.73MM **Publicly Held**
Web: www.fastly.com
SIC: 7371 Computer software development

(P-11594)
FCS SOFTWARE SOLUTIONS LIMITED
2375 Zanker Rd Ste 250 (95131-1143)
PHONE...................408 324-1203
Dalip Kumar, *Pr*
Janak Sharma, *
EMP: 97 EST: 2001
SALES (est): 3MM **Privately Held**
Web: www.fcsltd.com
SIC: 7371 Computer software development
PA: Fcs Software Solutions Limited
Plot No 83 Fcs House
Noida UP

PRODUCTS & SERVICES SECTION
7371 - Custom Computer Programming Services (P-11616)

(P-11595)
FEEDZAI INC
1875 S Grant St Ste 950 (94402-7015)
PHONE....................650 649-9486
Nuno Sebastiao, *CEO*
Paulo Marques, *
EMP: 500 **EST:** 2012
SALES (est): 30.2MM **Privately Held**
Web: www.feedzai.com
SIC: 7371 Computer software development

(P-11596)
FENDER DIGITAL LLC
1575 N Gower St Ste 170 (90028-6421)
PHONE....................323 462-2198
EMP: 75 **EST:** 2015
SQ FT: 25,000
SALES (est): 9.8MM
SALES (corp-wide): 1.87B **Privately Held**
Web: www.fenderdigital.com
SIC: 7371 Computer software development and applications
HQ: Fender Musical Instruments Corporation
17600 N Perimeter Dr # 100
Scottsdale AZ
480 596-9690

(P-11597)
FICTIV INC
168 Welsh St (94107-5513)
PHONE....................415 580-2509
David Evans, *CEO*
Nathan Evans, *
EMP: 120 **EST:** 2013
SQ FT: 1,000
SALES (est): 14.94MM **Privately Held**
Web: www.fictiv.com
SIC: 7371.3089 Computer software development; Air mattresses, plastics

(P-11598)
FIGMA INC (PA)
760 Market St Fl 10 (94102-2300)
PHONE....................888 236-4310
Dylan Field, *CEO*
Praveer Melwani, *
EMP: 69 **EST:** 2012
SALES (est): 24.02MM
SALES (corp-wide): 24.02MM **Privately Held**
Web: www.figma.com
SIC: 7371 Computer software development

(P-11599)
FINANCIALFORCECOM INC (PA)
Also Called: Certinia
60 S Market St Ste 750 (95113-2362)
PHONE....................866 743-2220
Donald J Paoni, *CEO*
Jeremy Roche, *
Gordy Brooks, *
John Moss, *
Fred Studer, *CMO**
EMP: 622 **EST:** 2009
SALES (est): 87.16MM
SALES (corp-wide): 87.16MM **Privately Held**
Web: www.certinia.com
SIC: 7371 Computer software development

(P-11600)
FINDEM INC
1991 Broadway St (94063-1956)
PHONE....................925 212-7277
Hariharan Govindarajan, *CEO*
EMP: 115 **EST:** 2019
SALES (est): 5.94MM **Privately Held**
Web: www.findem.ai

SIC: 7371 Computer software development and applications

(P-11601)
FINLINK INC (PA)
Also Called: Mbanq
241 Center St Ste B (95448-4401)
PHONE....................888 999-5467
Vlad Lounegov, *CEO*
EMP: 126 **EST:** 2016
SQ FT: 1,000
SALES (est): 8.34MM
SALES (corp-wide): 8.34MM **Privately Held**
Web: www.mbanq.com
SIC: 7371 Computer software development

(P-11602)
FLEXON TECHNOLOGIES INC
7901 Stoneridge Dr Ste 390 (94588-3677)
PHONE....................925 398-8280
Sanjay Madhwal, *Pr*
EMP: 121 **EST:** 2015
SQ FT: 75,000
SALES (est): 9.48MM **Privately Held**
Web: www.flexontechnologies.com
SIC: 7371 Computer software development

(P-11603)
FLUXX LABS INC
Also Called: Fluxx
2261 Market St Pmb 4060 (94114-1612)
PHONE....................415 851-2453
Kristy Gannon, *CEO*
Kerrin Mitchell, *COO*
EMP: 66 **EST:** 2010
SALES (est): 10.22MM **Privately Held**
Web: www.fluxx.io
SIC: 7371 Computer software development

(P-11604)
FORESCOUT TECHNOLOGIES INC (PA)
Also Called: Forescout
300 Santana Row Ste 400 (95128-2424)
PHONE....................408 213-3191
Wael Mohamed, *CEO*
Theresia Gouw, *
David G Dewalt, *
Christopher Harms, *CFO*
EMP: 864 **EST:** 2000
SQ FT: 95,950
SALES (est): 336.8MM
SALES (corp-wide): 336.8MM **Privately Held**
Web: www.forescout.com
SIC: 7371 Computer software development

(P-11605)
FORGEROCK INC (PA)
Also Called: Forgerock
201 Mission St Ste 2900 (94105-1858)
PHONE....................415 599-1100
Francis Rosch, *Pr*
Bruce Golden, *
John Fernandez, *Ex VP*
Peter Barker, *CPO*
Pete Angstadt, *CRO*
EMP: 120 **EST:** 2009
SQ FT: 16,000
SALES (est): 217.51MM
SALES (corp-wide): 217.51MM **Privately Held**
Web: www.forgerock.com
SIC: 7371 Computer software systems analysis and design, custom

(P-11606)
FORWARD ADVANTAGE INC
7255 N 1st St Ste 106 (93720-2972)
PHONE....................559 447-1777
Chris Roggenstein, *CEO*
Chris Roggenstein, *Pr*
Mike Knebel, *
EMP: 80 **EST:** 1992
SQ FT: 5,000
SALES (est): 23.99MM **Privately Held**
Web: www.forwardadvantagefoundation.org
SIC: 7371 Computer software development

(P-11607)
FRONT PORCH INC (PA)
Also Called: Get More Math
27 S Shepherd St (95370-4768)
P.O. Box 5045 (95370-2045)
PHONE....................209 288-5500
Zach Britton, *Pr*
Zachary Britton, *
Robert Hohne Junior, *CFO*
Cheri Oteri, *
▼ **EMP:** 60 **EST:** 1998
SQ FT: 1,022
SALES (est): 10.19MM
SALES (corp-wide): 10.19MM **Privately Held**
Web: www.frontporch.com
SIC: 7371 Computer software development

(P-11608)
FUEL50 INC
30025 Alicia Pkwy # 20-23 (92677-2090)
PHONE....................833 844-1103
Ron Shah, *Admn*
Ron Shah, *CFO*
EMP: 72 **EST:** 2020
SALES (est): 4.59MM **Privately Held**
Web: www.fuel50.com
SIC: 7371 Computer software development

(P-11609)
FUNCTIONAL SOFTWARE INC (PA)
Also Called: Sentry
132 Hawthorne St (94107-1308)
PHONE....................415 823-8009
David Cramer, *Managing Member*
EMP: 93 **EST:** 2012
SQ FT: 15,000
SALES (est): 9.42MM
SALES (corp-wide): 9.42MM **Privately Held**
Web: www.sentry.io
SIC: 7371 Custom computer programming services

(P-11610)
FUTURE DIAL INCORPORATED (PA)
Also Called: Futuredial K.K.
392 Potrero Ave (94085-4116)
PHONE....................408 245-8880
George C Huang Ph.d., *CEO*
Steve Chan, *Acting Senior Vice President**
Thomas Rayas, *
Stephen Manning, *
Jason Li, *VP Engg*
▲ **EMP:** 66 **EST:** 1999
SQ FT: 8,000
SALES (est): 8MM
SALES (corp-wide): 8MM **Privately Held**
Web: www.futuredial.com
SIC: 7371 Computer software development

(P-11611)
G2 SOFTWARE SYSTEMS INC
4025 Hancock St Ste 105 (92110-5167)
PHONE....................619 222-8025
EMP: 140 **EST:** 1898
SQ FT: 4,000
SALES (est): 12.56MM **Privately Held**
Web: www.g2ss.com
SIC: 7371 Computer software development

(P-11612)
GAME PLAY NETWORK INC
Also Called: B Spot
10866 Wilshire Blvd Ste 700 (90024-4303)
PHONE....................844 462-7768
David Marshall, *CEO*
Aaron Fischer, *CSO*
Sam Kiki, *Chief Commercial Officer*
Tod Lower, *COO*
EMP: 69 **EST:** 2012
SALES (est): 5.85MM **Privately Held**
Web: www.bspot.com
SIC: 7371 Computer software development and applications

(P-11613)
GAN LIMITED
400 Spectrum Center Dr Ste 1900 (92618-5025)
PHONE....................702 964-5777
Seamus Mcgill, *Interim Chief Executive Officer*
Simon Knock, *CIO*
Sylvia Tiscareno, *CLO*
Brian Chang, *Interim Chief Financial Officer*
EMP: 288 **EST:** 2002
SALES (est): 141.53MM **Privately Held**
Web: www.gan.com
SIC: 7371 7374 Custom computer programming services; Data processing and preparation

(P-11614)
GEHRY TECHNOLOGIES INC
12181 Bluff Creek Dr (90094-2992)
PHONE....................310 862-1200
Meaghan Lloyd, *CEO*
Michael Lin, *CFO*
Dhruba Kalita, *CIO*
EMP: 95 **EST:** 2002
SQ FT: 2,000
SALES (est): 14.36MM
SALES (corp-wide): 3.68B **Publicly Held**
Web: www.gehrytechnologies.com
SIC: 7371 Computer software development and applications
PA: Trimble Inc.
10368 Westmoor Dr
Westminster CO
720 887-6100

(P-11615)
GEM SOFTWARE INC
1 Post St Fl 18 (94104-5222)
PHONE....................650 924-1622
Steven Bartel, *CEO*
Nicolas Andrij Bushak, *Sec*
EMP: 175 **EST:** 2017
SALES (est): 5.22MM **Privately Held**
Web: www.gem.com
SIC: 7371 Computer software development and applications

(P-11616)
GENEX (DH)
800 Corporate Pointe Ste 100 (90230-7667)
PHONE....................424 672-9500
EMP: 130 **EST:** 1995
SQ FT: 12,000

7371 - Custom Computer Programming Services (P-11617)

SALES (est): 11.15MM
SALES (corp-wide): 3.68B **Publicly Held**
Web: www.genex.com
SIC: 7371 7379 4813 Computer software development and applications; Computer related consulting services; Online service providers
HQ: Hawkeye Acquisition, Inc.
1716 Locust St
Des Moines IA
515 284-3000

(P-11617)
GENIUM INC
4 W 4th Ave Ste 600 (94402-1615)
PHONE................................415 935-3593
Alexander Ledovskiy, *CEO*
Alex Iceman, *
EMP: 150 EST: 2013
SALES (est): 5.27MM **Privately Held**
Web: www.genium.com
SIC: 7371 8742 Computer software development; Human resource consulting services

(P-11618)
GETFEEDBACK INC
1 Curiosity Way (94403-2396)
PHONE................................888 684-8821
Kraig Swensrud, *CEO*
EMP: 60 EST: 2013
SALES (est): 7.58MM
SALES (corp-wide): 694.97MM **Privately Held**
Web: www.getfeedback.com
SIC: 7371 Computer software development and applications
HQ: Surveymonkey Inc.
1 Curiosity Way
San Mateo CA
650 543-8400

(P-11619)
GIGSTER INC
301 Howard St Ste 1800 (94105-2241)
PHONE................................941 888-4447
Andy Tryba, *CEO*
EMP: 200 EST: 2013
SALES (est): 25.26MM
SALES (corp-wide): 25.26MM **Privately Held**
Web: www.gigster.com
SIC: 7371 Computer software development
PA: Ionic Partners, Llc
500 W 5th St Ste 1010
Austin TX

(P-11620)
GINGERIO INC
116 New Montgomery St Ste 500 (94105-3603)
PHONE................................408 455-0574
Russell Gla, *CEO*
Michelle Patruno, *
EMP: 62 EST: 2011
SALES (est): 6.18MM
SALES (corp-wide): 115.97MM **Privately Held**
Web: www.ginger.com
SIC: 7371 Computer software development and applications
PA: Orangedot, Inc.
2415 Michigan Ave
Santa Monica CA
310 526-4194

(P-11621)
GLADLY SOFTWARE INC
423 Broadway # 503 (94030-1905)
PHONE................................650 387-8485

Yolanda Ruiz, *VP Fin*
EMP: 60 EST: 2014
SALES (est): 5.22MM **Privately Held**
Web: www.sagansystems.com
SIC: 7371 Computer software development

(P-11622)
GLASSBEAM INC
2033 Gateway Pl Ste 658 (95110-3709)
P.O. Box 610 (95002-0610)
PHONE................................408 740-4600
Richard Jones, *CEO*
Rhonda Longmore-grund, *Ch Bd*
EMP: 93 EST: 2004
SALES (est): 5.48MM **Privately Held**
Web: www.glassbeam.com
SIC: 7371 Computer software development

(P-11623)
GLOBAL SERVICE RESOURCES INC
Also Called: Computerworks Technologies
711 S Victory Blvd (91502-2426)
P.O. Box 4057 (91503-4057)
PHONE................................800 679-7658
Nick Sefayan, *Pr*
▲ EMP: 80 EST: 1991
SQ FT: 7,000
SALES (est): 5.9MM **Privately Held**
Web: www.globalserviceresources.com
SIC: 7371 7363 Computer software development; Labor resource services

(P-11624)
GLOBAL TOUCHPOINTS INC
3017 Douglas Blvd Ste 300 (95661-3850)
PHONE................................916 878-5954
Naren Kini, *CEO*
Udayan Chanda, *
Seema Chanda, *
Sandhya Shenoy, *
EMP: 94 EST: 2004
SALES (est): 24.2MM **Privately Held**
Web: www.touchpointsinc.com
SIC: 7371 7373 Computer software development; Computer systems analysis and design

(P-11625)
GLOBALLOGIC INC (HQ)
Also Called: Skookum
2535 Augustine Dr Fl 5 (95054-3003)
PHONE................................408 273-8900
Shashank Samant, *CEO*
Betsy Atkins, *
Charles Wayne Grubbs, *
Jim Dellamore, *
Jim Walsh, *
EMP: 213 EST: 2000
SALES (est): 406.51MM **Privately Held**
Web: www.globallogic.com
SIC: 7371 7373 7379 Computer software development; Systems engineering, computer related; Computer related consulting services
PA: Hitachi, Ltd.
1-6-6, Marunouchi
Chiyoda-Ku TKY

(P-11626)
GLORY GLOBAL SOLUTIONS INC
11135 Knott Ave Ste C (90630-5139)
PHONE................................714 897-7545
Gari Sithamaraju, *Brnch Mgr*
EMP: 78
Web: www.glory-global.com
SIC: 7371 Computer software development
HQ: Glory Global Solutions Inc.
3333 Warrenville Rd # 310

Lisle IL
920 262-3300

(P-11627)
GLU MOBILE INC (HQ)
209 Redwood Shores Pkwy (94065-1175)
PHONE................................415 800-6100
Nick Earl, *Pr*
Eric R Ludwig, *
Chris Akhavan, *CRO**
Scott J Leichtner, *Corporate Secretary**
EMP: 82 EST: 2001
SALES (est): 540.52MM
SALES (corp-wide): 7.43B **Publicly Held**
Web: www.glu.com
SIC: 7371 Computer software development and applications
PA: Electronic Arts Inc.
209 Redwood Shores Pkwy
Redwood City CA
650 628-1500

(P-11628)
GOOD SPORTS PLUS LTD
Also Called: ARC
370 Amapola Ave Ste 208 (90501-7241)
PHONE................................310 671-4400
Gary Lipsky, *
Kitty Cohen, *
EMP: 300 EST: 2002
SQ FT: 3,500
SALES (est): 30.47MM **Privately Held**
Web: www.arc-experience.com
SIC: 7371 7997 Computer software development and applications; Outdoor field clubs

(P-11629)
GOOD TECHNOLOGY CORPORATION (HQ)
3001 Bishop Dr Ste 400 (94583-5005)
PHONE................................408 352-9102
Christy Wyatt, *Pr*
Ronald J Fior, *
Chet Mandair, *CIO**
EMP: 160 EST: 2014
SQ FT: 80,000
SALES (est): 86.45MM
SALES (corp-wide): 656MM **Privately Held**
SIC: 7371 7382 Computer software development; Protective devices, security
PA: Blackberry Limited
2200 University Ave E
Waterloo ON
519 888-7465

(P-11630)
GORGIAS INC
180 Sansome St (94104-3724)
PHONE................................917 859-5689
Romain Lapeyre, *CEO*
Alex Plugaru, *
EMP: 240 EST: 2015
SALES (est): 250K **Privately Held**
Web: www.gorgias.com
SIC: 7371 Computer software development

(P-11631)
GREE INTERNATIONAL INC
275 Battery St Ste 1700 (94111-3369)
PHONE................................415 409-5200
Naoki Aoyagi, *CEO*
Shanti Bergel, *
Andrew Sheppard, *
EMP: 250 EST: 2011
SALES (est): 28.04MM **Privately Held**
Web: www.gree-corp.com
SIC: 7371 Computer software development and applications

HQ: Gree, Inc.
6-11-1, Roppongi
Minato-Ku TKY

(P-11632)
GREE INTERNATIONAL ENTRMT INC
185 Berry St Ste 590 (94107-9105)
PHONE................................415 409-5200
Andrew Sheppard, *CEO*
Ryotaro Shima, *
Shanti Bergel, *
Yoshikazu Tanaka, *
EMP: 220 EST: 2016
SALES (est): 9.83MM **Privately Held**
SIC: 7371 Computer software development and applications
HQ: Gree, Inc.
6-11-1, Roppongi
Minato-Ku TKY

(P-11633)
GRIDIRON SYSTEMS INC
4555 Great America Pkwy # 150 (95054-1243)
PHONE................................201 502-0512
EMP: 179
SIC: 7371 Computer software development and applications

(P-11634)
GRINDR LLC
750 N San Vicente Blvd (90069-5788)
P.O. Box 69176 (90069-0176)
PHONE................................310 776-6680
George Arison, *CEO*
EMP: 206 EST: 2010
SALES (est): 31.61MM
SALES (corp-wide): 195.01MM **Publicly Held**
Web: www.grindr.com
SIC: 7371 Computer software development
PA: Grindr Inc.
750 N San Vicnte Blvd
West Hollywood CA

(P-11635)
GROQ INC
400 Castro St Ste 600 (94041-2008)
PHONE................................650 521-9007
Jonathan Ross, *CEO*
EMP: 186 EST: 2016
SQ FT: 3,900
SALES (est): 16.02MM **Privately Held**
Web: www.groq.com
SIC: 7371 Computer software development

(P-11636)
H & R ACCOUNTS INC
Also Called: Avadyne Health
3131 Camino Del Rio N Ste 1500 (92108)
PHONE................................619 819-8844
Linda Hevern, *Brnch Mgr*
EMP: 150
SALES (corp-wide): 50.81MM **Privately Held**
Web: www.avadynehealth.com
SIC: 7371 Computer software development
HQ: H & R Accounts, Inc.
5320 22nd Ave
Moline IL
309 736-2255

(P-11637)
H2OAI INC
Also Called: H2o.ai
2307 Leghorn St (94043-1609)
PHONE................................650 429-8337
Srisatish Ambati, *CEO*
Allison Washburn, *Assistant Chief Executive Officer**

PRODUCTS & SERVICES SECTION
7371 - Custom Computer Programming Services (P-11660)

Bill Gallmeister, *
Ingrid Burton, *CMO**
Raman Kapur, *
EMP: 103 **EST:** 2011
SALES (est): 14.5MM **Privately Held**
Web: www.h2o.ai
SIC: 7371 Computer software development

(P-11638)
HAPPYCO INC (PA)
5857 Owens Ave Ste 300 (92008-5507)
PHONE...............................415 230-9832
Jindou Lee, *CEO*
EMP: 195 **EST:** 2011
SALES (est): 18.03MM
SALES (corp-wide): 18.03MM **Privately Held**
Web: www.happy.co
SIC: 7371 Computer software development

(P-11639)
HASHICORP INC (PA)
Also Called: Hashi
101 2nd St Ste 700 (94105-3648)
PHONE...............................415 301-3250
David Mcjannet, *Ch Bd*
Armon Dadgar, *
Navam Welihinda, *CFO*
Marc Holmes, *CMO*
Brandon Sweeney, *CRO*
EMP: 535 **EST:** 2013
SQ FT: 37,000
SALES (est): 475.89MM
SALES (corp-wide): 475.89MM **Publicly Held**
Web: www.hashicorp.com
SIC: 7371 Custom computer programming services

(P-11640)
HCL AMERICA SOLUTIONS INC
2600 Great America Way (95054-1169)
PHONE...............................408 733-0480
Manish Anand, *CEO*
Raj Walia, *
EMP: 1038 **EST:** 2012
SALES (est): 1.84MM **Privately Held**
SIC: 7371 Computer software development
HQ: Hcl America Inc.
2600 Great America Way # 1
Santa Clara CA
408 733-0480

(P-11641)
HEAT WAVES LLC
Also Called: Heat Software
4201 Jamboree Rd Unit 518 (92660-3066)
PHONE...............................719 651-4942
EMP: 135 **EST:** 2018
SALES (est): 1.25MM **Privately Held**
Web: www.heatwaves.co
SIC: 7371 Computer software development and applications

(P-11642)
HITACHI VANTARA LLC (HQ)
2535 Augustine Dr (95054-3003)
PHONE...............................858 225-2095
Minoru Kosuge, *CEO*
EMP: 117 **EST:** 2019
SALES (est): 57.28MM **Privately Held**
Web: www.hitachivantara.com
SIC: 7371 Computer software development
PA: Hitachi, Ltd.
1-6-6, Marunouchi
Chiyoda-Ku TKY

(P-11643)
HOME JUNCTION INC
1 Venture Ste 300 (92618-7416)
PHONE...............................858 777-9533
John Perkins, *CEO*
EMP: 88 **EST:** 2013
SALES (est): 10.6MM
SALES (corp-wide): 17.24MM **Privately Held**
Web: www.homejunction.com
SIC: 7371 Computer software development
PA: Attom Data Solutions, Llc
530 Technology Dr Ste 100
Irvine CA
949 502-8300

(P-11644)
HONEY SCIENCE LLC
Also Called: Honey
963 E 4th St Ste 100 (90013-2645)
PHONE...............................949 795-1695
George Ruan, *Managing Member*
Ryan Hudson, *
EMP: 112 **EST:** 2012
SALES (est): 11.83MM
SALES (corp-wide): 27.52B **Publicly Held**
Web: www.joinhoney.com
SIC: 7371 Software programming applications
PA: Paypal Holdings, Inc.
2211 N 1st St
San Jose CA
408 967-1000

(P-11645)
HONOR TECHNOLOGY INC (PA)
400 S El Camino Real Ste 800 (94402)
PHONE...............................512 762-2195
Seth Sternberg, *CEO*
EMP: 67 **EST:** 2014
SALES (est): 102.53MM
SALES (corp-wide): 102.53MM **Privately Held**
Web: www.honorcare.com
SIC: 7371 Computer software development

(P-11646)
HORIZON 3 AI INC
683 Spruce St (94118-2609)
PHONE...............................304 677-4102
EMP: 94 **EST:** 2020
SALES (est): 1.39MM **Privately Held**
Web: www.horizon3.ai
SIC: 7371 Computer software development and applications

(P-11647)
HTEC GROUP INC (PA)
535 Mission St Fl 14 (94105-2903)
P.O. Box 5545 (94063-0545)
PHONE...............................213 785-7824
Aleksandar Cabrilo, *Pr*
Timothy Gens, *
EMP: 823 **EST:** 2015
SALES (est): 27.04MM
SALES (corp-wide): 27.04MM **Privately Held**
Web: www.htecgroup.com
SIC: 7371 Computer software development

(P-11648)
HUMANAPI INC
951 Mariners Island Blvd Ste 300 (94404-1558)
PHONE...............................650 542-9800
Andrei Pop, *CEO*
Cecilia Hewett, *Managing Member**
EMP: 60 **EST:** 2013
SALES (est): 8.31MM **Privately Held**
Web: www.humanapi.co
SIC: 7371 Computer software development

(P-11649)
HUSTLE INC
548 Market St Pmb 19841 (94104-5401)
PHONE...............................415 851-4878
Steve Pease, *CEO*
EMP: 159 **EST:** 2014
SALES (est): 6.1MM **Privately Held**
Web: www.hustle.com
SIC: 7371 Computer software development and applications

(P-11650)
HVANTAGE TECHNOLOGIES INC (PA)
22048 Sherman Way Ste 306 (91303-3011)
PHONE...............................818 661-6301
Krishna Baderia, *CEO*
EMP: 79 **EST:** 2011
SALES (est): 4.62MM
SALES (corp-wide): 4.62MM **Privately Held**
Web: www.hvantagetechnologies.com
SIC: 7371 8748 7372 7373 Computer software development; Systems engineering consultant, ex. computer or professional; Application computer software ; Systems engineering, computer related

(P-11651)
HYPERGRID INC
425 Tasso St (94301-1545)
PHONE...............................650 316-5524
Manoj Nair, *CEO*
John Kim, *
EMP: 64 **EST:** 2009
SALES (est): 7.54MM **Privately Held**
Web: www.cloudsphere.com
SIC: 7371 5045 Computer software development; Computers, peripherals, and software

(P-11652)
HYRO AI INC
440 N Barranca Ave (91723-1722)
PHONE...............................313 942-4560
Israel Krush, *CEO*
EMP: 60
SALES (est): 3.01MM **Privately Held**
SIC: 7371 Software programming applications

(P-11653)
IBASET FEDERAL SERVICES LLC (PA)
27442 Portola Pkwy Ste 300 (92610-2823)
PHONE...............................949 598-5200
Ladeira Poonian, *Ch*
Vic Sial, *
Naveen Poonian, *
EMP: 75 **EST:** 1986
SQ FT: 30,000
SALES (est): 24.48MM **Privately Held**
Web: www.ibaset.com
SIC: 7371 Computer software development

(P-11654)
ICANN INC
Also Called: Icann Pharmaceutical
933 Berryessa Rd Ste 10 (95133-1006)
PHONE...............................408 432-8818
Phuc Ngo, *Prin*
EMP: 70 **EST:** 2015
SALES (est): 168.74K **Privately Held**
Web: www.icann.org
SIC: 7371 Computer software development and applications

(P-11655)
ID ANALYTICS LLC
10089 Willow Creek Rd Ste 120 (92131-1698)
PHONE...............................858 312-6200
Rick Trainor, *CEO*
EMP: 140 **EST:** 2002
SALES (est): 23.72MM
SALES (corp-wide): 10.3B **Privately Held**
Web: risk.lexisnexis.com
SIC: 7371 Computer software development
HQ: Lexisnexis Risk Solutions Inc.
1000 Alderman Dr
Alpharetta GA
678 694-6000

(P-11656)
ILLUMIO INC (PA)
920 De Guigne Dr (94085-3900)
PHONE...............................669 800-5000
Andrew Rubin, *CEO*
Emily Couey Vp People, *Prin*
Scott Downie, *OK Vice President*
Matthew Glenn, *MGMT*
EMP: 465 **EST:** 2012
SALES (est): 60.99MM
SALES (corp-wide): 60.99MM **Privately Held**
Web: www.illumio.com
SIC: 7371 Computer software development

(P-11657)
IMPERVA INC (HQ)
1 Curiosity Way Ste 203 (94403-2396)
PHONE...............................650 345-9000
Pam Murphy, *CEO*
Ron Bennatan, *DATA SECURITY*
Moshe Lipsker, *Senior Vice President Product Development*
Steven Schoenfeld, *Senior Vice President Product Management*
EMP: 116 **EST:** 2002
SALES (est): 679.94MM
SALES (corp-wide): 277.29MM **Privately Held**
Web: www.imperva.com
SIC: 7371 6799 Computer software development; Venture capital companies
PA: Thales
4 Rue De La Verrerie
Meudon

(P-11658)
INFINITE TECHNOLOGIES LLC
1667 N Batavia St (92867-3508)
PHONE...............................786 408-7995
EMP: 147 **EST:** 2017
SALES (est): 2.54MM **Privately Held**
Web: www.infinitetechs.com
SIC: 7371 Computer software development and applications

(P-11659)
INFLUXDATA INC
548 Market St Pmb 77953 (94104-5401)
PHONE...............................415 295-1901
Evan Kaplan, *CEO*
Paul Dix, *
Winnie Cheng, *
Brian Mullen, *
Arwa Kaddoura, *
EMP: 105 **EST:** 2012
SALES (est): 10.4MM **Privately Held**
Web: www.influxdata.com
SIC: 7371 Computer software development

(P-11660)
INFOBLOX INC (HQ)
2390 Mission College Blvd Ste 501 (95054-1554)

7371 - Custom Computer Programming Services (P-11661)

PHONE..................408 986-4000
Hoke Horne, *
Mitch Breen, CRO*
▲ EMP: 306 EST: 1999
SQ FT: 42,000
SALES (est): 281.58MM
SALES (corp-wide): 281.58MM Privately Held
Web: www.infoblox.com
SIC: 7371 7379 7374 Custom computer programming services; Computer related consulting services; Data processing service
PA: Delta Holdco, Llc
4 Embarcadero Ctr Fl 20
San Francisco CA
415 765-6500

(P-11661)
INFOMAGNUS LLC
5882 Bolsa Ave Ste 210 (92649-5700)
PHONE..................714 810-3430
Sal Manzo, Managing Member
Kaveh Mahjoob, *
EMP: 90 EST: 2013
SALES (est): 5.96MM Privately Held
Web: www.infomagnus.com
SIC: 7371 7379 Software programming applications; Computer related consulting services

(P-11662)
INFOWAY SOLUTIONS LLC
46520 Fremont Blvd Ste 614 (94538-6478)
PHONE..................925 435-9672
Kismat Kathrani, CEO
Kismat Kathrani, Managing Member
EMP: 190 EST: 2012
SQ FT: 4,100
SALES (est): 8.35MM Privately Held
Web: www.infowaygroup.com
SIC: 7371 Computer software development

(P-11663)
INFOWORKSIO INC
490 California Ave Ste 200 (94306-1900)
PHONE..................408 899-4687
Buno Pati, CEO
David Dorman, *
Amar Arsikere, CPO*
EMP: 108 EST: 2014
SALES (est): 5.25MM Privately Held
Web: www.infoworks.io
SIC: 7371 Computer software development

(P-11664)
INNOPATH SOFTWARE INC
Also Called: Innopath
333 W El Camino Real Ste 230 (94087)
P.O. Box 2454 (95015-2454)
PHONE..................408 962-9200
EMP: 210
Web: www.innopath.com
SIC: 7371 Computer software development

(P-11665)
INNOVACCER INC (PA)
101 Mission St Ste 1950 (94105-1727)
PHONE..................510 327-8900
Deepak Murthy, Chief Business Officer
David K Nace, CMO
Mike Sutten, CDO
Inder Sidhu, Chief Customer Officer
EMP: 390 EST: 2014
SALES (est): 26.13MM
SALES (corp-wide): 26.13MM Privately Held
Web: www.innovaccer.com
SIC: 7371 Computer software development

(P-11666)
INNOVASYSTEMS INTL LLC
850 Beech St Unit 1006 (92101-2895)
PHONE..................619 955-5890
EMP: 198
SALES (corp-wide): 46.49MM Privately Held
Web: www.innovasi.com
SIC: 7371 Computer software development
HQ: Innovasystems International Llc
2385 Northside Dr Ste 300
San Diego CA
619 955-5800

(P-11667)
INSEEGO CORP (PA)
Also Called: Inseego
9710 Scranton Rd Ste 200 (92121-1744)
PHONE..................858 812-3400
Ashish Sharma, Pr
Dan Mondor, *
Robert G Barbieri, CFO
Doug Kahn, Ofcr
EMP: 72 EST: 1996
SQ FT: 25,000
SALES (est): 245.32MM
SALES (corp-wide): 245.32MM Publicly Held
Web: www.inseego.com
SIC: 7371 Software programming applications

(P-11668)
INSPIRA INC
4125 Blackford Ave Ste 255 (95117-1837)
PHONE..................408 247-9500
Ravindra Gudapati, Pr
EMP: 111 EST: 1997
SQ FT: 2,908
SALES (est): 3.23MM Privately Held
Web: www.inspira.com
SIC: 7371 Software programming applications

(P-11669)
INSTABUG INC
855 El Camino Real Ste 13a-111 (94301)
PHONE..................650 422-9555
EMP: 65 EST: 2013
SALES (est): 9.73MM Privately Held
Web: www.instabug.com
SIC: 7371 Computer software development

(P-11670)
INSTANT SYSTEMS INC
Also Called: Instantsys
447 King Ave (94536-1516)
PHONE..................510 657-8100
Vipin K Chawla, Pr
Uzay Takaoglu, *
Mamta Chawla, *
▲ EMP: 90 EST: 2004
SALES (est): 4.69MM Privately Held
Web: www.instantsys.com
SIC: 7371 7372 Custom computer programming services; Business oriented computer software

(P-11671)
INTAPP US INC (HQ)
Also Called: Intapp
3101 Park Blvd (94306-2233)
PHONE..................650 852-0400
John Hall, CEO
Dan Tacone, *
Sanjeev Gandhi, *
Pat Archbold, *
Steve Robertson, *
EMP: 200 EST: 2005
SALES (est): 186.85MM
SALES (corp-wide): 350.87MM Publicly Held
Web: www.intapp.com
SIC: 7371 7372 Computer software development and applications; Business oriented computer software
PA: Intapp, Inc.
3101 Park Blvd
Palo Alto CA
650 852-0400

(P-11672)
INTELEX SYSTEMS INC
21900 Burbank Blvd Ste 3087 (91367-6469)
PHONE..................818 992-2969
Saritha Myadam, CEO
Sarith Myadam, CFO
EMP: 84 EST: 2009
SALES (est): 4.38MM Privately Held
Web: www.intelexsystemsinc.com
SIC: 7371 Computer software development

(P-11673)
INTELLICUS TECH PVT LTD
Also Called: Intellicus
720 University Ave Ste 130 (95032-7609)
PHONE..................408 213-3314
Praveen Kankiria, CEO
Jerry Malec, Pr
Rajesh Murthy, VP Engg
EMP: 60 EST: 2003
SQ FT: 1,000
SALES (est): 811.75K Privately Held
Web: www.intellicus.com
SIC: 7371 Computer software development

(P-11674)
INTELLISWIFT SOFTWARE INC (PA)
Also Called: Magagnini
39600 Balentine Dr Ste 200 (94560-5304)
PHONE..................510 370-2600
Parag Patel, CEO
Bob Patel, *
EMP: 225 EST: 2001
SQ FT: 5,200
SALES (est): 53.13MM
SALES (corp-wide): 53.13MM Privately Held
Web: www.intelliswift.com
SIC: 7371 Computer software development

(P-11675)
INTELLISYNC CORPORATION
313 Fairchild Dr (94043-2215)
PHONE..................650 625-2185
Woodson Hobbs, Pr
Clyde Foster, COO
David Eichler, CFO
Robert Gerber, CMO
EMP: 456 EST: 1993
SQ FT: 33,821
SALES (est): 21.8MM
SALES (corp-wide): 25.87B Privately Held
SIC: 7371 7372 Computer software development; Prepackaged software
PA: Nokia Oyj
Karakaari 7
Espoo
104488000

(P-11676)
INTERCOM INC
55 2nd St Fl 4 (94105-3441)
PHONE..................831 920-7088
Eoghan Mccabe, CEO
Des Traynor, CSO*
Ciaran Lee, *
Leslie Chung, *
EMP: 300 EST: 1983
SALES (est): 29.5MM Privately Held
Web: www.intercom.com
SIC: 7371 Computer software development

(P-11677)
INTERNATIONAL BUS MCHS CORP
Also Called: IBM
555 Bailey Ave (95141-1003)
PHONE..................408 463-2000
Lou Gerstner, Mgr
EMP: 1500
SALES (corp-wide): 60.53B Publicly Held
Web: www.ibm.com
SIC: 7371 7372 5961 Computer software development; Prepackaged software; Catalog and mail-order houses
PA: International Business Machines Corporation
1 New Orchard Rd Ste 1 # 1
Armonk NY
914 499-1900

(P-11678)
IPTOR SUPPLY CHAIN SYSTEMS USA (DH)
Also Called: I B S
915 Highland Pointe Dr (95678-5419)
PHONE..................916 542-2820
Doug Braun, CEO
Christian Paulsson, *
Fredrik Sandelin, *
David Rode, *
Hiten Varia, *
EMP: 153 EST: 1978
SQ FT: 55,000
SALES (est): 34.73MM Privately Held
Web: www.ibs.net
SIC: 7371 5045 Computer software development; Computer software
HQ: Iptor Supply Chain Systems Ab
Hemvarnsgatan 11
Solna
86272300

(P-11679)
IRISE (PA)
2381 Rosecrans Ave Ste 100 (90245-4920)
PHONE..................800 556-0399
Emmet B Keeffe Iii, CEO
Maurice Martin, *
Jacques Marine, *
Stephen Brickley, *
Dean Terry, *
▲ EMP: 94 EST: 1997
SALES (est): 21.52MM
SALES (corp-wide): 21.52MM Privately Held
Web: www.irise.com
SIC: 7371 Computer software development

(P-11680)
ISAAC FAIR CORPORATION
Also Called: Mindwave Software
3661 Valley Centre Dr (92130-3321)
PHONE..................858 369-8000
Steve Gutschow, Prin
EMP: 88
SALES (corp-wide): 1.51B Publicly Held
Web: www.fico.com
SIC: 7371 Computer software development
PA: Fair Isaac Corporation
5 W Mendenhall St Ste 105
Bozeman MT
406 982-7276

7371 - Custom Computer Programming Services (P-11704)

(P-11681)
ISCS INC
100 Great Oaks Blvd Ste 100 (95119-1462)
PHONE....................408 362-3000
Andy J Scurto, *Pr*
Andy Scurto, *Pr*
Tim Shelton, *Ex VP*
EMP: 201 EST: 1994
SQ FT: 11,000
SALES (est): 27.52MM
SALES (corp-wide): 905.34MM **Publicly Held**
SIC: 7371 Software programming applications
PA: Guidewire Software, Inc.
  970 Park Pl Ste 200
  San Mateo CA
  650 357-9100

(P-11682)
ISHERIFF INC
555 Twin Dolphin Dr (94065-2129)
PHONE....................650 412-4300
Paul Lipman, *CEO*
Oscar Marquez, *CPO**
James Socas, *
Marcus Smith, *
Luis Curet, *
EMP: 235 EST: 2011
SALES (est): 21.49MM **Privately Held**
Web: www.isheriff.com
SIC: 7371 Software programming applications
PA: Mimecast Uk Limited
  Floor 4
  London

(P-11683)
ITREX GROUP USA CORPORATION
120 Vantis Dr Ste 545 (92656-2679)
PHONE....................213 436-7785
EMP: 275
SALES (corp-wide): 12.84MM **Privately Held**
Web: www.itrexgroup.com
SIC: 7371 Computer software development
PA: Itrex Group Usa Corporation
  1120 Vantis Dr Ste 545
  Aliso Viejo CA
  213 436-7785

(P-11684)
IXSYSTEMS INC (PA)
Also Called: Ix Systems
2490 Kruse Dr (95131-1234)
PHONE....................408 943-4100
Mike Lauth, *CEO*
Valerie Burniece, *CFO*
EMP: 125 EST: 1991
SQ FT: 20,000
SALES (est): 80.66MM
SALES (corp-wide): 80.66MM **Privately Held**
Web: www.ixsystems.com
SIC: 7371 Computer software development

(P-11685)
JIFF INC (DH)
150 Spear St Ste 400 (94105-1500)
PHONE....................415 829-1400
EMP: 400 EST: 2011
SALES (est): 56.06MM
SALES (corp-wide): 147.46MM **Privately Held**
Web: www.castlighthealth.com
SIC: 7371 Computer software development
HQ: Castlight Health, Inc.
  150 Spear St Ste 400
  San Francisco CA

(P-11686)
JOTFORM INC
4 Embarcadero Ctr Ste 780 (94111-4102)
PHONE....................347 624-5569
Aytekin Tank, *CEO*
EMP: 64 EST: 2014
SALES (est): 6.25MM **Privately Held**
Web: www.jotform.com
SIC: 7371 Computer software development

(P-11687)
JOYABLE INC
11770 Snowpeak Way (96161-7090)
PHONE....................914 552-6753
Peter Shalek, *CEO*
Jill Isenstadt, *
EMP: 598 EST: 2014
SALES (est): 648.9K
SALES (corp-wide): 324.16B **Publicly Held**
SIC: 7371 Computer software development and applications
HQ: Ableto, Inc.
  320 W 37th St Fl 7
  New York NY
  646 757-3031

(P-11688)
JUMPSHOT INC (PA)
333 Bryant St Ste 240 (94107-1421)
P.O. Box 78071 (94107-8071)
PHONE....................415 212-9250
Deren Baker, *CEO*
Michael Perlman, *CRO**
EMP: 85 EST: 2015
SALES (est): 6.1MM
SALES (corp-wide): 6.1MM **Privately Held**
SIC: 7371 Computer software development

(P-11689)
JUPITER INTELLIGENCE INC
181 2nd Ave Ste 300 (94401-3815)
PHONE....................650 477-2117
Rich Sorkin, *CEO*
Eric Wun, *
EMP: 82 EST: 2017
SALES (est): 9.15MM **Privately Held**
Web: www.jupiterintel.com
SIC: 7371 Computer software development and applications

(P-11690)
KABAM INC (HQ)
575 Market St Ste 2450 (94105-2896)
PHONE....................604 256-0054
Seungwon Lee, *Pr*
Jangwon Seo, *
EMP: 699 EST: 2006
SALES (est): 84.61MM **Privately Held**
Web: www.kabam.com
SIC: 7371 Computer software development and applications
PA: Netmarble Corporation
  G-Tower
  Seoul

(P-11691)
KALLIDUS INC
Also Called: Skava
555 Mission St Ste 1950 (94105-2933)
PHONE....................877 554-2176
Arish Ali, *Pr*
Khurram Khan, *
EMP: 100 EST: 2002
SALES (est): 10.93MM **Privately Held**
Web: www.kallidus.com
SIC: 7371 Computer software development
PA: Infosys Limited
  Plot No. 44 & 97a, Electronics City,
  Bengaluru KA

(P-11692)
KIKA TECH INC
211 Westhill Dr (95032-5022)
P.O. Box 24336 (95154-4336)
PHONE....................650 229-3673
Bill Hu, *CEO*
EMP: 101 EST: 2015
SALES (est): 4.27MM **Privately Held**
Web: www.kikatech.com
SIC: 7371 Computer software development

(P-11693)
KINSTA INC
8605 Santa Monica Blvd # 92581 (90069-4109)
PHONE....................310 736-9306
Mark Gavalda, *CEO*
EMP: 73
SALES (est): 3.64MM **Privately Held**
Web: www.kinsta.com
SIC: 7371 Computer software development

(P-11694)
KIXIE ONLINE INC
Also Called: Kixie
406 Wilshire Blvd (90401-1410)
PHONE....................424 800-3330
Jeff Kuei, *Managing Member*
Keith Muenze, *
EMP: 60 EST: 2013
SALES (est): 6.19MM **Privately Held**
Web: www.kixie.com
SIC: 7371 Computer software development and applications

(P-11695)
KOFAX INC (PA)
15211 Laguna Canyon Rd (92618-3146)
PHONE....................949 783-1000
Reynolds Bish, *CEO*
Cort Townsend, *
Howard Dratler, *
Anthony Macciola, *
Grant Johnson, *
▼ EMP: 500 EST: 1985
SQ FT: 100,000
SALES (est): 449.47MM
SALES (corp-wide): 449.47MM **Privately Held**
Web: www.kofax.com
SIC: 7371 3577 Computer software development; Input/output equipment, computer

(P-11696)
KONSUS INC
470 Ramona St (94301-1707)
PHONE....................415 659-9852
EMP: 181 EST: 2016
SALES (est): 4.74MM **Privately Held**
Web: www.superside.com
SIC: 7371 Computer software development

(P-11697)
KPIT INFOSYSTEMS INC
111 Woodmere Rd Ste 200 (95630-4750)
PHONE....................916 985-0300
EMP: 79 EST: 2016
SALES (est): 943.35K **Privately Held**
Web: www.kpit.com
SIC: 7371 Computer software development

(P-11698)
KRG TECHNOLOGIES INC (PA)
25000 Avenue Stanford Ste 243 (91355)
PHONE....................661 257-9967
Balamurugan Subbiah, *Pr*
Hemalatha Rajagopala, *CEO*
EMP: 490 EST: 2003
SQ FT: 780
SALES (est): 42.74MM
SALES (corp-wide): 42.74MM **Privately Held**
Web: www.krgtech.com
SIC: 7371 Computer software development and applications

(P-11699)
KTB SOFTWARE LLC ✪
11101 W Olympic Blvd (90064-1805)
PHONE....................213 935-0902
Diop Mckenzie, *Managing Member*
EMP: 84 EST: 2023
SALES (est): 2.35MM **Privately Held**
SIC: 7371 Computer software development and applications

(P-11700)
KUGGA INC
1841 Sunnyvale Ave (94597-1811)
PHONE....................925 639-0721
Yifan Ren, *CEO*
EMP: 60 EST: 2017
SALES (est): 1.27MM **Privately Held**
SIC: 7371 Computer software development and applications

(P-11701)
LAMBDA INC
Also Called: Lambda
2510 Zanker Rd (95131-1127)
PHONE....................650 741-0738
Steven Balaban, *Pr*
Mitesh Agrawal, *
EMP: 130 EST: 2012
SALES (est): 150MM **Privately Held**
Web: www.lambdalabs.com
SIC: 7371 3571 7373 7377 Computer software development; Computers, digital, analog or hybrid; Computer systems analysis and design; Computer hardware rental or leasing, except finance leasing

(P-11702)
LAND GORILLA LLC
1241 Johnson Ave Ste 154 (93401-3306)
PHONE....................805 242-5847
Sean Faries, *Prin*
EMP: 74 EST: 2011
SALES (est): 4.7MM **Privately Held**
Web: www.landgorilla.com
SIC: 7371 Computer software development

(P-11703)
LAYLINE AUTOMATION
1005 Northgate Dr (94903-2500)
PHONE....................415 758-0044
Hal Mccormack, *Pr*
EMP: 68 EST: 2013
SALES (est): 2.15MM **Privately Held**
Web: www.laylineautomation.com
SIC: 7371 8748 7372 Computer software systems analysis and design, custom; Telecommunications consultant; Utility computer software

(P-11704)
LEADIQ INC
548 Market St Pmb 20317 (94104-5401)
PHONE....................888 653-2347
Mei Siauw, *Prin*
EMP: 84 EST: 2018
SALES (est): 3.94MM **Privately Held**
Web: www.leadiq.com
SIC: 7371 Computer software development

7371 - Custom Computer Programming Services (P-11705)

(P-11705)
LEENA AI INC
3260 Hillview Ave (94304-1220)
PHONE.................................332 232-9740
Adit Jain, *CEO*
EMP: 150 **EST:** 2018
SALES (est): 12.64MM **Privately Held**
Web: www.leena.ai
SIC: 7371 Computer software development

(P-11706)
LEVER INC
939 Noe St (94114-3368)
PHONE.................................415 458-2731
Nathaniel Smith, *CEO*
EMP: 100 **EST:** 2014
SALES (est): 10.19MM **Privately Held**
Web: www.lever.co
SIC: 7371 Computer software development and applications

(P-11707)
LIGHTBEND INC
580 California St Ste 1231 (94104-1000)
PHONE.................................877 989-7372
Jonas Bonr, *Pr*
Brad Murdoch, *Ex VP*
Enno Runne, *VP Engg*
Mike Nash, *Operations*
Kimberly Falk, *VP Mktg*
EMP: 72 **EST:** 2010
SALES (est): 12.6MM **Privately Held**
Web: www.lightbend.com
SIC: 7371 Computer software development

(P-11708)
LIGHTYEAR CORPORATION
365 Fulton St Apt 225 (94102-4492)
PHONE.................................415 605-9050
Marc Siino, *Pr*
EMP: 60 **EST:** 2017
SALES (est): 1.07MM **Privately Held**
SIC: 7371 Computer software development

(P-11709)
LILT INC (PA)
2200 Powell St Ste 900 (94608-1983)
P.O. Box 20391 (94309-0391)
PHONE.................................415 992-5088
William Green, *CEO*
Zack Kass, *VP*
EMP: 102 **EST:** 2015
SALES (est): 8.1MM
SALES (corp-wide): 8.1MM **Privately Held**
Web: www.lilt.com
SIC: 7371 Custom computer software development

(P-11710)
LIMINEX INC (PA)
Also Called: Goguardian
2030 E Maple Ave Ste 100 (90245-5008)
PHONE.................................888 310-0410
Advait Shinde, *CEO*
Michael Jonas, *CFO*
Dionna Smith, *DIVERSITY*
EMP: 219 **EST:** 2014
SQ FT: 30,000
SALES (est): 58.73MM
SALES (corp-wide): 58.73MM **Privately Held**
Web: www.goguardian.com
SIC: 7371 7389 Computer software development; Business services, nec

(P-11711)
LINDEN RESEARCH INC
Also Called: Linden Lab
945 Battery St (94111-1305)
P.O. Box 2374 (94126-2374)
PHONE.................................415 243-9000
Ebbe Altberg, *CEO*
Lori Medeiros, *
Jeff Peterson, *
Lee Senderov, *
John Zdanowski, *
EMP: 330 **EST:** 1999
SALES (est): 39.99MM **Privately Held**
Web: www.lindenlab.com
SIC: 7371 Computer software development

(P-11712)
LIVEFYRE INC
Also Called: Livefyre
360 3rd St Ste 700 (94107-2164)
PHONE.................................415 800-0900
EMP: 105
SIC: 7371 Computer software development

(P-11713)
LMI INC (PA)
Also Called: Liftoff
900 Middlefield Rd Fl 2 (94063-1681)
PHONE.................................650 453-8305
Mark Ellis, *Pr*
EMP: 65 **EST:** 2012
SALES (est): 21.88MM
SALES (corp-wide): 21.88MM **Privately Held**
Web: www.liftoff.io
SIC: 7371 Computer software development

(P-11714)
LMNTRIX LLC
333 City Blvd W Ste 1700 (92868-5905)
PHONE.................................888 388-1879
Hamlet Khodaverdian, *Pr*
Tam Nguyen, *
EMP: 65 **EST:** 2017
SALES (est): 2.73MM **Privately Held**
Web: www.lmntrix.com
SIC: 7371 Computer software development

(P-11715)
LOGIGEAR CORPORATION (PA)
Also Called: Softgear Technologies
1730 S Amphlett Blvd Ste 110 (94402-2707)
PHONE.................................650 572-1400
EMP: 544 **EST:** 1996
SALES (est): 24.89MM **Privately Held**
Web: www.logigear.com
SIC: 7371 Computer software development

(P-11716)
LOGLOGIC INC
110 Rose Orchard Way Ste 200 (95134-1358)
PHONE.................................408 215-5900
EMP: 170
SIC: 7371 Computer software development

(P-11717)
LOHIKA SYSTEMS INC
1825 S Grant St Ste 400 (94402-7039)
PHONE.................................216 904-9751
Daniel Dargham, *Pr*
Michael Makishima, *CFO*
EMP: 202 **EST:** 2001
SALES (est): 5.11MM
SALES (corp-wide): 415.14MM **Privately Held**
Web: www.lohika.com
SIC: 7371 Computer software development
HQ: Altran Technologies
    76 Avenue Kleber
    Paris

(P-11718)
LUCIDLINK CORP
58 West Portal Ave # 256 (94127-1304)
PHONE.................................650 517-0855
George Dochev, *Ch*
Peter Thompson, *CEO*
EMP: 84 **EST:** 2016
SALES (est): 3.45MM **Privately Held**
SIC: 7371 Computer software development and applications

(P-11719)
LUMIN DIGITAL LLC
3001 Bishop Dr Ste 110 (94583-5005)
PHONE.................................727 561-2227
Brian Caldarelli, *
Jeff Chambers, *
EMP: 95 **EST:** 2019
SALES (est): 7.67MM **Privately Held**
Web: www.lumindigital.com
SIC: 7371 Computer software development

(P-11720)
LUMINARY CLOUD INC
500 Arguello St Ste 105 (94305-6101)
PHONE.................................650 279-9579
Jason Lango, *Pr*
EMP: 62 **EST:** 2019
SALES (est): 582.56K **Privately Held**
Web: www.luminarycloud.com
SIC: 7371 Computer software development and applications

(P-11721)
LUMIRADX INC
444 S Cedros Ave Ste 101 (92075-1966)
PHONE.................................951 201-9384
Jarrod Provins, *Prin*
EMP: 137
SALES (corp-wide): 421.43MM **Privately Held**
Web: www.lumiradx.com
SIC: 7371 Custom computer programming services
HQ: Lumiradx, Inc.
    221 Crescent St Ste 502
    Waltham MA
    617 621-9775

(P-11722)
MACHINE ZONE INC
Also Called: Epic War
1050 Page Mill Rd (94304-1019)
PHONE.................................650 320-1678
Kristen Dumont, *CEO*
Halbert Nakagawa, *
Eric Brown, *
Dan Nash, *
EMP: 74 **EST:** 2008
SALES (est): 20.17MM **Publicly Held**
Web: www.mz.com
SIC: 7371 Computer software development
PA: Applovin Corporation
    1100 Page Mill Rd
    Palo Alto CA

(P-11723)
MACHINIFY INC
635 High St (94301-1626)
PHONE.................................650 313-2932
Prasanna Ganesan, *CEO*
Tony Miranz, *
Edward Lichty, *
EMP: 71 **EST:** 2016
SALES (est): 7.99MM **Privately Held**
Web: www.machinify.com
SIC: 7371 Software programming applications

(P-11724)
MAGIC LABS INC
548 Market St (94104-5401)
PHONE.................................707 653-5739
Shang Li, *CEO*
Mengfei He, *Head OF Operations*
Lars Christian Anders, *Chief of Staff*
EMP: 61 **EST:** 2018
SALES (est): 2.61MM **Privately Held**
Web: www.magic.link
SIC: 7371 Computer software development and applications

(P-11725)
MAGMA DESIGN AUTOMATION INC (HQ)
1650 Technology Dr Ste 100 (95110)
PHONE.................................408 565-7500
Rajeev Madhavan, *CEO*
Peter S Teshima, *Corporate Vice President*
Roy E Jewell, *
▲ **EMP:** 410 **EST:** 1997
SQ FT: 106,854
SALES (est): 66.85MM
SALES (corp-wide): 5.08B **Publicly Held**
SIC: 7371 7373 Computer software development; Computer integrated systems design
PA: Synopsys, Inc.
    675 Almanor Ave
    Sunnyvale CA
    650 584-5000

(P-11726)
MAGMA DESIGN AUTOMATION INC
2880 Zanker Rd Ste 203 (95134-2122)
PHONE.................................408 432-7288
Andy Huang, *Prin*
EMP: 67
SALES (corp-wide): 5.08B **Publicly Held**
SIC: 7371 7361 Computer software development; Employment agencies
HQ: Magma Design Automation, Inc.
    1650 Tech Dr Ste 100
    San Jose CA
    408 565-7500

(P-11727)
MAINTECH INCORPORATED
2401 N Glassell St (92865-2705)
P.O. Box 13500 (92857-8500)
PHONE.................................714 921-8000
Tony Donato, *VP*
EMP: 200
SQ FT: 1,200
SALES (corp-wide): 25.9MM **Privately Held**
Web: www.maintech.com
SIC: 7371 3577 Computer software systems analysis and design, custom; Computer peripheral equipment, nec
PA: Maintech, Incorporated
    14 Commerce Dr Ste 200
    Cranford NJ
    973 330-3200

(P-11728)
MAKING SENSE LLC
228 Hamilton Ave Ste 300 (94301-2583)
PHONE.................................210 364-0050
EMP: 60
Web: www.makingsense.com
SIC: 7371 Computer software development
PA: Making Sense, Llc
    17806 Ih 10 W Ste 300
    San Antonio TX

7371 - Custom Computer Programming Services (P-11751)

(P-11729)
MANGO TECHNOLOGIES INC (PA)
Also Called: Clickup
350 10th Ave Ste 500 (92101-7497)
PHONE..............................888 625-4258
Brian Evans, *CEO*
EMP: 694 **EST:** 2016
SALES (est): 99.03MM
SALES (corp-wide): 99.03MM **Privately Held**
Web: www.clickup.com
SIC: 7371 Computer software development and applications

(P-11730)
MANTICORE GAMES INC (PA)
1800 Gateway Dr Ste 250 (94404-4072)
PHONE..............................650 257-8177
Frederic Descamps, *CEO*
EMP: 87 **EST:** 2016
SALES (est): 4.63MM
SALES (corp-wide): 4.63MM **Privately Held**
Web: www.manticoregames.com
SIC: 7371 Computer software development and applications

(P-11731)
MAPLELABS INC
1248 Reamwood Ave (94089-2225)
PHONE..............................408 743-4414
Pramod Murthy, *Pr*
EMP: 190 **EST:** 2014
SALES (est): 6MM **Privately Held**
Web: www.maplelabs.com
SIC: 7371 Custom computer programming services
PA: Xoriant Corporation
1248 Reamwood Ave
Sunnyvale CA

(P-11732)
MARIGOLD
Also Called: Campaign Monitor
631 Howard St Fl 5 (94105-3934)
PHONE..............................888 533-8098
EMP: 1576
Web: www.campaignmonitor.com
SIC: 7371 8742 Computer software development; Marketing consulting services
HQ: Marigold
9 Lea Ave
Nashville TN
888 533-8098

(P-11733)
MARIGOLD USA INC
Also Called: Experian Qas
475 Anton Blvd (92626-7037)
PHONE..............................617 385-6786
Thomas Schutz, *Genl Mgr*
EMP: 166
SALES (corp-wide): 72.21MM **Privately Held**
Web: www.cheetahdigital.com
SIC: 7371 Computer software development
HQ: Marigold Usa, Inc.
72 W Adams St Fl 8
Chicago IL

(P-11734)
MARKET SCAN INFO SYSTEMS INC
Also Called: Market Scan
815 Camarillo Springs Rd (93012-9457)
PHONE..............................800 658-7226
Russell West, *Pr*
Carsten Preisz, *Chief Business Officer*
Mathew Hermann, *
EMP: 85 **EST:** 1987
SQ FT: 10,500
SALES (est): 10.84MM
SALES (corp-wide): 11.18B **Publicly Held**
Web: www.marketscan.com
SIC: 7371 Computer software development
PA: S&P Global Inc.
55 Water St
New York NY
212 438-1000

(P-11735)
MARKETO INC (HQ)
901 Mariners Island Blvd Ste 200 (94404-1592)
PHONE..............................650 376-2303
Allison Blais, *CEO*
Keith San Felipe, *
Jonathan Vaas, *
EMP: 329 **EST:** 2006
SQ FT: 102,670
SALES (est): 112.1MM
SALES (corp-wide): 17.61B **Publicly Held**
SIC: 7371 7372 Computer software development; Prepackaged software
PA: Adobe Inc.
345 Park Ave
San Jose CA
408 536-6000

(P-11736)
MARKLOGIC CORPORATION (HQ)
333 Twin Dolphin Dr Ste 380 (94065-1453)
PHONE..............................650 655-2300
Jeffrey Casale, *CEO*
Peter Norman, *
EMP: 108 **EST:** 2003
SALES (est): 102.86MM
SALES (corp-wide): 602.01MM **Publicly Held**
Web: www.marklogic.com
SIC: 7371 Computer software development
PA: Progress Software Corporation
15 Wayside Rd Ste 4
Burlington MA
781 280-4000

(P-11737)
MATTERMOST INC (PA)
530 Lytton Ave (94301-1541)
PHONE..............................650 667-8512
Ian Tien, *CEO*
Tim Quock, *
EMP: 120 **EST:** 2011
SALES (est): 16.88MM
SALES (corp-wide): 16.88MM **Privately Held**
Web: www.mattermost.com
SIC: 7371 Computer software development

(P-11738)
MAVENIR INTERNATIONAL HOLDINGS INC
Also Called: Stoke
2890 Zanker Rd Ste 207 (95134-2118)
PHONE..............................408 855-2900
EMP: 60
SIC: 7371 Computer software development and applications

(P-11739)
MAXPLORE TECHNOLOGIES INC
4450 Rosewood Dr Ste 200 (94588-3061)
PHONE..............................925 621-1400
Sam Mukherjee, *Prin*
EMP: 100 **EST:** 2011
SALES (est): 1.76MM **Privately Held**

SIC: 7371 Computer software development

(P-11740)
MELISSA DATA CORPORATION (PA)
Also Called: Mailers Software
22382 Avenida Empresa (92688-2112)
PHONE..............................949 858-3000
EMP: 90 **EST:** 1985
SALES (est): 7.57MM
SALES (corp-wide): 7.57MM **Privately Held**
Web: www.melissa.com
SIC: 7371 Computer software development

(P-11741)
MELLMO INC
Also Called: Roambi
131 Aberdeen Dr (92007-1821)
PHONE..............................858 847-3272
EMP: 140
SIC: 7371 Custom computer programming services

(P-11742)
MEMVERGE INC
1525 Mccarthy Blvd Ste 218 (95035-7451)
PHONE..............................408 605-0841
Charles Fan, *CEO*
EMP: 60 **EST:** 2017
SALES (est): 4.72MM **Privately Held**
Web: www.memverge.com
SIC: 7371 Computer software development

(P-11743)
MERAKI INC
500 Terry A Francois Blvd (94158-2354)
PHONE..............................415 632-5800
▲ **EMP:** 109 **EST:** 2015
SALES (est): 13.74MM **Privately Held**
SIC: 7371 8731 Computer software development and applications; Computer (hardware) development

(P-11744)
MERCARI INC
Also Called: Mercari App
1530 Page Mill Rd Ste 100 (94304-1125)
P.O. Box 60178 (94306-0178)
PHONE..............................855 464-7482
Ryo Ishizuka, *Pr*
EMP: 464 **EST:** 2014
SALES (est): 10.32MM **Privately Held**
Web: www.mercari.com
SIC: 7371 Computer software development and applications
PA: Mercari, Inc.
6-10-1, Roppongi
Minato-Ku TKY

(P-11745)
MERIT INTERNATIONAL INC
100 S Murphy Ave (94086-6118)
PHONE..............................833 463-7487
Tomer Kagan, *CEO*
Jacob Orrin, *
Viral Kadakia, *Chief Product Officer*
Daniel Yun, *
EMP: 120 **EST:** 2015
SQ FT: 6,000
SALES (est): 11MM **Privately Held**
Web: www.merits.com
SIC: 7371 Computer software development

(P-11746)
MICRO FOCUS LLC
Also Called: Micro Focus
6701 Koll Center Pkwy # 300 (94566-8061)
PHONE..............................925 784-3242
EMP: 99
SALES (corp-wide): 555.38K **Privately Held**
Web: www.microfocus.com
SIC: 7371 Computer software development
HQ: Micro Focus, Llc
1800 Novell Pl
Provo UT
801 861-7000

(P-11747)
MIDDESK INC
85 2nd St Ste 710 (94105-3465)
PHONE..............................408 306-2663
EMP: 76 **EST:** 2018
SALES (est): 2.47MM **Privately Held**
Web: www.middesk.com
SIC: 7371 Computer software development

(P-11748)
MIGHTYHIVE INC (HQ)
311 California St Ste 200 (94104-2600)
PHONE..............................888 727-9742
Peter Kim, *CEO*
Christopher S Martin, *
Lexi Viripaeff, *
Leah Kim, *CMO*
EMP: 69 **EST:** 2012
SALES (est): 26.48MM
SALES (corp-wide): 1.29B **Privately Held**
Web: www.mightyhive.com
SIC: 7371 8742 7311 Computer software development; Marketing consulting services; Advertising agencies
PA: S4 Capital Plc
12 St. James's Place
London
203 793-0003

(P-11749)
MINDSPARK INC
21021 Ventura Blvd Ste 220 (91364-2214)
PHONE..............................310 390 9292
David Aspinall, *CEO*
Gray Benoist, *
EMP: 68 **EST:** 2013
SQ FT: 1,700
SALES (est): 1.84MM **Privately Held**
Web: www.mindsparktech.com
SIC: 7371 Computer software development and applications

(P-11750)
MINERVA NETWORKS INC (PA)
Also Called: Minerva
100 Century Center Ct Ste 800 (95112-4537)
PHONE..............................800 806-9594
Mauro Bonomi, *Pr*
Doctor Jean-georges Fritsch, *COO*
Jean-georges Fritsch, *VP*
Randy Osborne, *
Todd Clayton, *
EMP: 95 **EST:** 1992
SQ FT: 25,600
SALES (est): 15.87MM **Privately Held**
Web: www.minervanetworks.com
SIC: 7371 Software programming applications

(P-11751)
MINIO INC
275 Shoreline Dr Ste 100 (94065-1412)
PHONE..............................833 696-6342
Anand Babu Periasamy, *CEO*
Garima Kapoor, *
EMP: 62 **EST:** 2014
SALES (est): 7.05MM **Privately Held**
Web: www.min.io

7371 - Custom Computer Programming Services (P-11752)

SIC: 7371 Computer software development

(P-11752)
MIR3 INC
3398 Carmel Mountain Rd # 100
(92121-1044)
PHONE..................................858 724-1200
EMP: 90
SIC: 7371 Computer software development
and applications

(P-11753)
MITCHELL INTERNATIONAL INC (PA)
Also Called: Enlyte
9771 Clairemont Mesa Blvd Ste A
(92124-1300)
P.O. Box 229001 (92192-9001)
PHONE..................................858 368-7000
Alex Sun, CEO
Nina Smith, *
Debbie Day, *
Dave Torrence, *
Erez Nir, *
EMP: 229 EST: 1977
SQ FT: 141,000
SALES (est): 3.1B
SALES (corp-wide): 3.1B Privately Held
Web: www.mitchell.com
SIC: 7371 Computer software development

(P-11754)
MODERN CAMPUS USA INC (PA)
1320 Flynn Rd Ste 100 (93012-8745)
PHONE..................................805 484-9400
Brian Kibby, CEO
Tom Nalevanko, *
EMP: 60 EST: 1982
SQ FT: 6,600
SALES (est): 12.37MM
SALES (corp-wide): 12.37MM Privately Held
Web: www.moderncampus.com
SIC: 7371 7372 Computer software development; Prepackaged software

(P-11755)
MODULAR INC ◊
228 Hamilton Ave Fl 3 (94301-2583)
PHONE..................................408 508-4539
Chris Lattner, CEO
EMP: 62 EST: 2022
SALES (est): 2.96MM Privately Held
SIC: 7371 Computer software development
and applications

(P-11756)
MOLOCO INC (PA)
Also Called: Moloco
601 Marshall St Fl 5 (94063-1621)
PHONE..................................858 531-6550
Ikkjin Ahn, CEO
Brandon Maultasch, CFO
David Shin, Sec
EMP: 542 EST: 2013
SALES (est): 40.62MM
SALES (corp-wide): 40.62MM Privately Held
Web: www.moloco.com
SIC: 7371 Custom computer programming services

(P-11757)
MONKEYBRAINS
1611 17th St (94607-1641)
PHONE..................................415 974-1313
EMP: 60 EST: 2020
SALES (est): 1.73MM Privately Held
Web: www.monkeybrains.net

SIC: 7371 Custom computer programming services

(P-11758)
MOOMOO TECHNOLOGIES INC
550 California Ave Ste 201 (94306-1441)
PHONE..................................650 798-5700
Keith Chan, CEO
William Floyd, CIO*
EMP: 3000 EST: 2018
SALES (est): 15.23MM Privately Held
Web: www.moomoo.com
SIC: 7371 Computer software development

(P-11759)
MOTION MATH INC
Also Called: Motion Math
582 Market St Ste 511 (94104-5322)
PHONE..................................415 590-2961
Jacob Klein, CEO
EMP: 815 EST: 2010
SALES (est): 1.02MM
SALES (corp-wide): 519.28MM Privately Held
Web: www.curriculumassociates.com
SIC: 7371 Computer software development and applications
PA: Curriculum Associates, Llc
153 Rangeway Rd
North Billerica MA
978 667-8000

(P-11760)
MOZILLA FOUNDATION (PA)
149 New Montgomery St (94105-3740)
PHONE..................................650 903-0800
Mark Surman, CEO
EMP: 288 EST: 2003
SALES (est): 30.69MM
SALES (corp-wide): 30.69MM Privately Held
Web: www.mozilla.org
SIC: 7371 Computer software development

(P-11761)
MUDFLAP INC
400 Hamilton Ave Ste 410 (94301-1834)
PHONE..................................888 885-3835
Sanjay Desai, CEO
Sanjay Desai, Prin
EMP: 99 EST: 2016
SALES (est): 15.02MM Privately Held
Web: www.mudflapinc.com
SIC: 7371 Computer software development and applications

(P-11762)
N MODEL INC (PA)
Also Called: Model N
777 Mariners Island Blvd Ste 300 (94404-5008)
PHONE..................................650 610-4600
Jason Blessing, CEO
Baljit Dail, Non-Executive Chairman of the Board*
John Ederer, CFO
Chris Lyon, CRO
Suresh Kannan, CPO
EMP: 337 EST: 1999
SQ FT: 35,000
SALES (est): 219.16MM
SALES (corp-wide): 219.16MM Publicly Held
Web: www.modeln.com
SIC: 7371 Computer software development

(P-11763)
NARUS INC
329 Bernardo Ave (94043-5225)
P.O. Box 3707 (98124-2207)

PHONE..................................408 215-4300
EMP: 150
SIC: 7371 Computer software development

(P-11764)
NAVAGIS INC (PA)
50 California St Ste 1500 (94111-4612)
PHONE..................................800 819-7872
David Moore, CEO
EMP: 80 EST: 2012
SALES (est): 11.12MM
SALES (corp-wide): 11.12MM Privately Held
Web: www.navagis.com
SIC: 7371 Computer software systems analysis and design, custom

(P-11765)
NCIRCLE NETWORK SECURITY INC
Also Called: Ncircle
101 2nd St Ste 400 (94105-3645)
PHONE..................................415 625-5900
EMP: 86
SIC: 7371 Computer software development and applications

(P-11766)
NEONROOTS LLC
8560 W Sunset Blvd Ste 500 (90069-2311)
PHONE..................................310 907-9210
Benjamin C Lee, CEO
EMP: 125 EST: 2012
SALES (est): 4.27MM Privately Held
Web: www.neonroots.com
SIC: 7371 Computer software development and applications

(P-11767)
NETBASE SOLUTIONS INC (PA)
Also Called: Netbase Quid
3945 Freedom Cir Ste 730 (95054-1203)
PHONE..................................650 810-2100
Peter M Caswell, CEO
Bob Goodson, *
Bob Ciccone, *
David Pefley, *
Paige Leidig, CMO*
EMP: 117 EST: 2004
SALES (est): 29MM
SALES (corp-wide): 29MM Privately Held
Web: www.netbasequid.com
SIC: 7371 Computer software development

(P-11768)
NETEASE INFORMATION TECH CORP
790 E Colorado Blvd Ste 280 (91101)
PHONE..................................919 579-3051
Zhuo Huang, CEO
EMP: 60 EST: 2014
SALES (est): 4.47MM Privately Held
Web: www.jazzhr.com
SIC: 7371 Computer software development

(P-11769)
NEUBLOC LLC (PA)
10803 Thornmint Rd Ste 200 (92127-2406)
PHONE..................................858 674-8701
Alexander Nawrocki, Pt
EMP: 71 EST: 2005
SALES (est): 5.22MM Privately Held
Web: www.neubloc.com
SIC: 7371 Computer software development

(P-11770)
NEUDESIC LLC (HQ)
Also Called: Neuron Esb
200 Spectrum Center Dr Ste 2000 (92618-5013)

PHONE..................................949 754-4500
Parsa Rohani, CEO
Tim Marshall, *
EMP: 125 EST: 2001
SQ FT: 15,150
SALES (est): 50.74MM
SALES (corp-wide): 60.53B Publicly Held
Web: www.neudesic.com
SIC: 7371 Computer software development
PA: International Business Machines Corporation
1 New Orchard Rd Ste 1 # 1
Armonk NY
914 499-1900

(P-11771)
NEUINTEL LLC (PA)
Also Called: Pricespider
20 Pacifica Ste 1000 (92618-3307)
PHONE..................................949 625-6117
Anthony Ferry, CEO
Jon Pfortmiller, Pr
Lucas Baerg, CFO
EMP: 80 EST: 2004
SQ FT: 17,000
SALES (est): 26.97MM
SALES (corp-wide): 26.97MM Privately Held
Web: www.pricespider.com
SIC: 7371 Computer software development

(P-11772)
NEUTRON HOLDINGS INC (PA)
Also Called: Limebike
85 2nd St Ste 100 (94105-3400)
PHONE..................................888 546-3345
Wayne Ting, CEO
Andrea Ellis, *
Joe Kraus, *
EMP: 1005 EST: 2017
SALES (est): 100MM
SALES (corp-wide): 100MM Privately Held
Web: www.li.me
SIC: 7371 Computer software development and applications

(P-11773)
NEW CAM COMMERCE SOLUTIONS LLC
5555 Garden Grove Blvd Ste 100 (92683-8227)
PHONE..................................714 338-0200
EMP: 77 EST: 2010
SQ FT: 26,000
SALES (est): 10.86MM
SALES (corp-wide): 19.7MM Privately Held
SIC: 7371 Computer software development
PA: Celerant Technology, Corp.
4830 Arthur Kill Rd Ste 3
Staten Island NY
718 351-2000

(P-11774)
NEXGENIX INC (PA)
2 Peters Canyon Rd # 200 (92606-1798)
PHONE..................................714 665-6240
Rick Dutta, CEO
Don Ganguly, Ch Bd
Mark Iwanowski, COO
Ravi Renduchintala, VP
EMP: 258 EST: 1990
SQ FT: 14,264
SALES (est): 19.94MM Privately Held
SIC: 7371 8748 4813 Computer software development; Systems analysis or design; Online service providers

PRODUCTS & SERVICES SECTION
7371 - Custom Computer Programming Services (P-11796)

(P-11775)
NEXTGEN HLTHCARE INFO SYSTEMS (HQ)
Also Called: Nextgen Healthcare
18111 Von Karman Ave Ste 700 (92612-1007)
PHONE.....................949 255-2600
John Frantz, *Pr*
Steve Plochocki, *
Paul Holt, *
Michael Lovett, *
Daniel J Morefield, *
EMP: 65 **EST:** 1996
SALES (est): 248.72MM
SALES (corp-wide): 653.17MM **Privately Held**
Web: www.nextgen.com
SIC: 7371 5072 Computer software systems analysis and design, custom; Hardware
PA: Nextgen Healthcare, Inc.
 18111 Von Karman Ave # 6
 Irvine CA
 949 255-2600

(P-11776)
NGA 911 LLC
Also Called: Telecommunication
8383 Wilshire Blvd Ste 800 (90211-2425)
PHONE.....................877 899-8337
Don Ferguson, *CEO*
Jackie Barnes, *
EMP: 80 **EST:** 2016
SALES (est): 20MM **Privately Held**
Web: www.nga911.com
SIC: 7371 Computer software development and applications

(P-11777)
NIANTIC INC (PA)
1 Ferry Building Ste 200 (94111-4213)
PHONE.....................415 570-8871
John Hanke, *CEO*
Phillip Keslin, *
EMP: 81 **EST:** 1995
SALES (est): 107.99MM
SALES (corp-wide): 107.99MM **Privately Held**
Web: www.nianticlabs.com
SIC: 7371 Computer software development and applications

(P-11778)
NIMBLE ROBOTICS INC
488 8th St (94103-4428)
PHONE.....................267 864-6879
Simon Kalouche, *CEO*
Amelia Stemke, *
EMP: 90 **EST:** 2019
SALES (est): 9.71MM **Privately Held**
Web: www.nimble.ai
SIC: 7371 Computer software development and applications

(P-11779)
NINTHDECIMAL INC (PA)
Also Called: Ninthdecimal
150 Post St Ste 500 (94108-4720)
PHONE.....................415 264-1849
Michael Fordyce, *CEO*
Amy Caplan, *Sr VP*
David Staas, *Pr*
Greg Archibald, *CRO*
Jeff Stephens, *CFO*
EMP: 94 **EST:** 2003
SQ FT: 7,487
SALES (est): 16.5MM **Privately Held**
Web: www.inmarket.com
SIC: 7371 Computer software development

(P-11780)
NISUM TECHNOLOGIES INC
71 Stevenson St Ste 446 (94105-2934)
PHONE.....................714 619-7989
EMP: 602
SALES (corp-wide): 15.72MM **Privately Held**
Web: www.nisum.com
SIC: 7371 Computer software development
PA: Nisum Technologies, Inc.
 500 S Kraemer Blvd # 301
 Brea CA
 714 579-7979

(P-11781)
NISUM TECHNOLOGIES INC
46231 Landing Pkwy (94538-6407)
PHONE.....................714 579-7979
EMP: 603
SALES (corp-wide): 15.72MM **Privately Held**
Web: www.nisum.com
SIC: 7371 Computer software development
PA: Nisum Technologies, Inc.
 500 S Kraemer Blvd # 301
 Brea CA
 714 579-7979

(P-11782)
NITRO SOFTWARE INC (HQ)
Also Called: Nitro
447 Sutter St (94108-4618)
PHONE.....................415 632-4894
Cormac Whelan, *CEO*
Peter Bardwick, *CFO*
Gina O Reilly, *COO*
Richard Wenzel, *Treas*
▼ **EMP:** 125 **EST:** 2007
SALES (est): 26.03MM **Privately Held**
Web: www.gonitro.com
SIC: 7371 Computer software development
PA: Nitro Software Limited
 Level 7 330 Collins Street
 Melbourne VIC

(P-11783)
NLYTE SOFTWARE AMERICAS LTD
1380 El Cajon Blvd Ste 220 (92020-5703)
PHONE.....................866 386-5983
Bernard Liautaud, *Ch*
EMP: 85
SALES (corp-wide): 20.42B **Publicly Held**
Web: www.nlyte.com
SIC: 7371 Computer software development
HQ: Nlyte Software Americas Limited
 275 Raritan Center Pkwy
 Edison NJ

(P-11784)
NOODLE ANALYTICS INC
Also Called: Noodle.ai
115 Sansome St Fl 8 (94104-3609)
PHONE.....................415 412-2139
Stephen Pratt, *CEO*
Stephen Pratt, *Owner*
Deepinder Dhingra, *CPO*
Gail Moody-byrd, *CMO*
EMP: 100 **EST:** 2016
SALES (est): 6.67MM **Privately Held**
Web: www.noodle.ai
SIC: 7371 Computer software development and applications

(P-11785)
NOREDINK CORP
442 N Barranca Ave Ste 153 (91723-1722)
PHONE.....................844 667-3346
Jeff Scheur, *CEO*
EMP: 76 **EST:** 2013
SALES (est): 6.76MM **Privately Held**
Web: www.noredink.com
SIC: 7371 Computer software development

(P-11786)
NOVALOGIC INC (PA)
27489 Agoura Rd Ste 300 (91301-2419)
PHONE.....................818 880-1997
John Garcia, *CEO*
David Seeholzer, *VP*
John Butrovich, *VP*
Kyle Freeman, *VP*
EMP: 95 **EST:** 1985
SALES (est): 7.14MM
SALES (corp-wide): 7.14MM **Privately Held**
Web: www.novalogic.com
SIC: 7371 5734 7372 Computer software development; Software, business and non-game; Prepackaged software

(P-11787)
NTT CLOUD INFRASTRUCTURE INC (HQ)
Also Called: Dimension Data Cloud
5201 Great America Pkwy Ste 122 (95054-1122)
PHONE.....................408 567-2000
Graham Mcneill Jefferson, *CEO*
Ray Solnik, *Pr*
Don Green, *Sr VP*
Bryan Tolls, *CFO*
Richard Dym, *CMO*
EMP: 75 **EST:** 2002
SALES (est): 45.02MM **Privately Held**
SIC: 7371 Computer software development
PA: Dimension Data (Pty) Ltd
 Wanderers Bldg, 57 Sloane St
 Gauteng GP

(P-11788)
NUCLEUSHEALTH LLC
Also Called: Statrad - Radconnect
13280 Evening Creek Dr S Ste 110 (92128-4101)
PHONE.....................858 251-3400
EMP: 98 **EST:** 2008
SQ FT: 8,413
SALES (est): 20.19MM
SALES (corp-wide): 324.16B **Publicly Held**
Web: www.statrad.com
SIC: 7371 8748 Computer software development; Business consulting, nec
HQ: Change Healthcare Inc.
 424 Church St Ste 1400
 Nashville TN
 615 932-3000

(P-11789)
NUNA INCORPORATED
Also Called: Nuna Health
370 Townsend St (94107-1607)
PHONE.....................415 942-5200
EMP: 100 **EST:** 2010
SQ FT: 25,000
SALES (est): 11.73MM **Privately Held**
Web: www.nuna.com
SIC: 7371 Computer software development

(P-11790)
OBERON MEDIA INC (PA)
1100 La Avenida St Ste A (94043-1453)
PHONE.....................646 367-2020
David Lebow, *CEO*
Tal Kerret, *
Ofer Leidner, *CSO**
Don Ryan, *
Bob Hayes, *
EMP: 467 **EST:** 2003
SQ FT: 24,000
SALES (est): 24.22MM
SALES (corp-wide): 24.22MM **Privately Held**
Web: www.iwin.com
SIC: 7371 Computer software development

(P-11791)
OC ACQUISITION LLC (HQ)
500 Oracle Pkwy (94065-1677)
PHONE.....................650 506-7000
Dorian Daley, *Pr*
Eric Ball, *Treas*
EMP: 241 **EST:** 2011
SALES (est): 7.17B
SALES (corp-wide): 49.95B **Publicly Held**
SIC: 7371 7372 Computer software development; Business oriented computer software
PA: Oracle Corporation
 2300 Oracle Way
 Austin TX
 737 867-1000

(P-11792)
OMNICELL INC
1201 Charleston Rd (94043-1337)
PHONE.....................650 251-6100
Randall Lipps, *Pr*
EMP: 165 **EST:** 2018
SALES (est): 13.45MM **Privately Held**
Web: www.omnicell.com
SIC: 7371 Computer software development

(P-11793)
ONE INC SOFTWARE CORPORATION (PA)
620 Coolidge Dr Ste 200 (95630-3183)
PHONE.....................866 343-6940
Christopher W Ewing, *Pr*
Tim Tyannikov, *
Steve Hall, *
Tom Temple, *
Elizabeth Hoemeke, *CIO**
EMP: 279 **EST:** 2009
SALES (est): 28.54MM **Privately Held**
Web: www.oneinc.com
SIC: 7371 Custom computer programming services

(P-11794)
ONE CONVERGENCE INC
Also Called: One Convergence
99 Almaden Blvd Ste 600 (95113-1605)
PHONE.....................669 292-5251
Prasad Vellanki, *CEO*
Hemanth Ravi, *
EMP: 77 **EST:** 2006
SQ FT: 3,000
SALES (est): 4MM **Privately Held**
Web: www.dkube.io
SIC: 7371 Computer software development

(P-11795)
ONFLEET INC
703 Market St Fl 20 (94103-2102)
PHONE.....................650 283-7547
Khaled Naim, *CEO*
Mikel Carmenes, *
EMP: 71 **EST:** 2012
SALES (est): 7MM **Privately Held**
Web: www.onfleet.com
SIC: 7371 Computer software development

(P-11796)
OPEN TEXT INC (HQ)
Also Called: Hightail
2440 Sand Hill Rd Ste 302 (94025-6900)
PHONE.....................650 645-3000
Mark J Barrenechea, *Vice Chairman*

7371 - Custom Computer Programming Services (P-11797)

Gordon Davies, *CORP Development*
EMP: 109 **EST:** 1989
SALES (est): 469.43MM
SALES (corp-wide): 832.31MM **Privately Held**
Web: www.opentext.com
SIC: 7371 Computer software development
PA: Open Text Corporation
275 Frank Tompa Dr
Waterloo ON
519 888-7111

(P-11797)
OPEN TEXT INC
8717 Research Dr Ste 100 (92618-4273)
PHONE 949 784-8000
Mark Smith, *Mgr*
EMP: 63
SALES (corp-wide): 832.31MM **Privately Held**
Web: www.opentext.com
SIC: 7371 Computer software development
HQ: Open Text Inc.
2440 Sand Hill Rd Ste 302
Menlo Park CA
650 645-3000

(P-11798)
OPENAI INC (PA)
3180 18th St Ste 100 (94110-2042)
PHONE 650 387-6701
Samuel Altman, *CEO*
Chris Clark, *CFO*
EMP: 109 **EST:** 2015
SALES (est): 11.73K
SALES (corp-wide): 11.73K **Privately Held**
Web: www.openai.com
SIC: 7371 Computer software development

(P-11799)
OPERATION TECHNOLOGY INC
Also Called: Etap
17 Goodyear Ste 100 (92618-1812)
PHONE 949 462-0100
Farrokh Shokooh, *Pr*
Nikta Nikzad Shokooh, *Corporate Secretary*
EMP: 90 **EST:** 1986
SQ FT: 32,000
SALES (est): 20.14MM **Privately Held**
Web: www.etap.com
SIC: 7371 8732 8249 Computer software development; Research services, except laboratory; Business training services

(P-11800)
ORACLE CORPORATION
Also Called: Oracle
75 Hawthorne St Ste 2000 (94105-3919)
PHONE 415 541-9462
Julian J Brandes, *Prin*
EMP: 200
SALES (corp-wide): 49.95B **Publicly Held**
Web: www.oracle.com
SIC: 7371 8748 Custom computer programming services; Business consulting, nec
PA: Oracle Corporation
2300 Oracle Way
Austin TX
737 867-1000

(P-11801)
ORACLE SYSTEMS CORPORATION
Also Called: Oracle
17527 Via Sereno (95030-3201)
PHONE 650 506-4060
EMP: 92
SALES (corp-wide): 37.73B **Publicly Held**
SIC: 7371 Computer software development
HQ: Oracle Systems Corporation
500 Oracle Pkwy
Redwood City CA
650 506-7000

(P-11802)
ORION SOLIDIFIED INC (PA)
10232 Arroyo Ave (92345-2800)
PHONE 818 483-0100
Kla Arachchige, *CEO*
EMP: 68 **EST:** 2022
SALES (est): 1.19MM
SALES (corp-wide): 1.19MM **Privately Held**
SIC: 7371 7379 Computer software development and applications; Computer related consulting services

(P-11803)
OSHYN INC
100 W Broadway Ste 330 (90802-4431)
PHONE 213 483-1770
Diego Rebosio, *CEO*
EMP: 75 **EST:** 2001
SALES (est): 9.96MM **Privately Held**
Web: www.oshyn.com
SIC: 7371 Computer software development

(P-11804)
OSISOFT LLC (DH)
Also Called: OSI Software
1600 Alvarado St (94577-2600)
PHONE 510 297-5800
Andrew Mccloskey, *CEO*
J Kennedy, *Prin*
▲ **EMP:** 418 **EST:** 1980
SQ FT: 55,000
SALES (est): 78.46MM
SALES (corp-wide): 82.05K **Privately Held**
Web: www.aveva.com
SIC: 7371 7372 7373 Computer software development; Application computer software; Computer integrated systems design
HQ: Aveva Group Limited
High Cross
Cambridge CAMBS

(P-11805)
OSSO VR INC
2806 San Ardo Way (94002-1342)
PHONE 310 709-8289
Justin Barad, *Prin*
EMP: 158 **EST:** 2016
SALES (est): 5.16MM **Privately Held**
Web: www.ossovr.com
SIC: 7371 Computer software development and applications

(P-11806)
OUTRIGHT INC
100 Mathilda Pl Ste 100 (94086-6019)
PHONE 918 926-6578
EMP: 96 **EST:** 2008
SALES (est): 535.43K
SALES (corp-wide): 9.76MM **Privately Held**
Web: www.outright.com
SIC: 7371 Computer software development
PA: Yam Special Holdings, Inc.
15475 N 84th St
Scottsdale AZ
480 505-8800

(P-11807)
OUTWARD INC
10444 Berkshire Dr (94024-6502)
PHONE 408 828-5492
EMP: 70
SALES (corp-wide): 2.14MM **Privately Held**
SIC: 7371 Software programming applications
PA: Outward, Inc.
675 N 1st St Ste 1250
San Jose CA
415 572-8683

(P-11808)
P MURPHY & ASSOCIATES INC
39600 Balentine Dr (94560-5376)
PHONE 818 841-2002
Phyliss Murphy, *Pr*
EMP: 121 **EST:** 1981
SALES (est): 11.76MM
SALES (corp-wide): 53.13MM **Privately Held**
Web: www.pmurphy.com
SIC: 7371 7361 Computer software development; Employment agencies
PA: Intelliswift Software, Inc.
39600 Balentine Dr # 200
Newark CA
510 370-2600

(P-11809)
PACIFIC TECH SOLUTIONS LLC
15530 Rockfield Blvd Ste B4 (92618)
PHONE 949 830-1623
Frederick Minturn, *Managing Member*
EMP: 108 **EST:** 1987
SQ FT: 3,000
SALES (est): 4.97MM **Privately Held**
Web: www.pts1.com
SIC: 7371 Computer software development
HQ: Msx International Rns Llc
26555 Evergreen Rd # 1300
Southfield MI
248 829-6300

(P-11810)
PANASAS INC (PA)
2680 N 1st St Ste 150 (95134-2042)
PHONE 408 215-6800
Faye Pairman, *Pr*
Barbara Murphy, *CMO*
Stephanie Vinella, *CFO*
Bill Ribera, *VP*
▲ **EMP:** 100 **EST:** 2000
SQ FT: 20,000
SALES (est): 24.27MM
SALES (corp-wide): 24.27MM **Privately Held**
Web: www.panasas.com
SIC: 7371 Computer software development

(P-11811)
PANDEMIC STUDIOS LLC
5510 Lincoln Blvd (90094-2034)
PHONE 310 450-5199
Joshua Resnick, *VP*
Andrew Goldman, *
Greg Borrud, *
EMP: 260 **EST:** 1998
SQ FT: 50,000
SALES (est): 22.19MM
SALES (corp-wide): 7.43B **Publicly Held**
SIC: 7371 Computer software development
HQ: Electronic Arts Redwood Llc
209 Redwood Shores Pkwy
Redwood City CA
650 628-1500

(P-11812)
PANTHEON SYSTEMS INC (PA)
717 California St (94108-2455)
PHONE 855 927-9387
Zachary Rosen, *Pr*
Christine Park, *
Meredith Brown, *Chief Product Officer*
John Gardiner, *
EMP: 93 **EST:** 2010
SALES (est): 40.81MM
SALES (corp-wide): 40.81MM **Privately Held**
Web: www.pantheon.io
SIC: 7371 Computer software development

(P-11813)
PARACCEL INC
500 Arguello St Ste 200 (94063-1567)
PHONE 858 309-4733
EMP: 88
SIC: 7371 Computer software development

(P-11814)
PARACOSMA INC
2081 Norris Rd (94596-5446)
PHONE 650 924-9896
Kenneth Ehrhart, *Pr*
EMP: 75 **EST:** 2016
SALES (est): 1.5MM **Privately Held**
Web: www.paracosma.com
SIC: 7371 7379 Computer software development and applications; Computer related consulting services

(P-11815)
PARAFIN INC
301 Howard St Ste 1500 (94105-6611)
PHONE 646 919-0669
Ralph Furman, *Pr*
EMP: 80 **EST:** 2020
SALES (est): 8.08MM **Privately Held**
Web: www.parafin.com
SIC: 7371 Computer software development and applications

(P-11816)
PARALLEL DOMAIN INC
44 Montgomery St Ste 300 (94104-4624)
P.O. Box 720 (94104-0720)
PHONE 585 943-8571
Kevin Mcnamara, *CEO*
Kevin Mcnamara, *Pr*
James Grieve, *
Robert Newell, *
EMP: 85 **EST:** 2017
SALES (est): 5.38MM **Privately Held**
Web: www.paralleldomain.com
SIC: 7371 Computer software development

(P-11817)
PARTNERSTACK INC
1049 El Monte Ave Ste C # 512 (94040-2399)
PHONE 619 648-4388
Bryn Jones, *CEO*
Margaret Jones, *CFO*
EMP: 220 **EST:** 2015
SALES (est): 15MM **Privately Held**
Web: www.partnerstack.com
SIC: 7371 Computer software development

(P-11818)
PATREON INC (PA)
600 Townsend St Ste 500 (94103-5696)
PHONE 415 967-2735
Jack Conte, *CEO*
EMP: 181 **EST:** 2013
SALES (est): 16.46MM
SALES (corp-wide): 16.46MM **Privately Held**
Web: www.patreon.com
SIC: 7371 Computer software development and applications

(P-11819)
PENCIL AND PIXEL INC
Also Called: Modsy

340 Brannan St Ste 500 (94107-1892)
PHONE.............................510 422-5036
Shanna Tellerman, *CEO*
EMP: 120 EST: 2015
SALES (est): 11.36MM **Privately Held**
Web: www.modsy.com
SIC: 7371 Computer software development

(P-11820)
PEOPLEAI INC
303 Twin Dolphin Dr Fl 6 (94065-1409)
P.O. Box 1366 (94070-7366)
PHONE.............................888 997-3675
Oleg Rogynskyy, *CEO*
Andrey Akselrod, *
John Gilman, *CRO*
Thomas Wyatt, *CPO*
Art Harding, *
EMP: 92 EST: 2016
SQ FT: 14,794
SALES (est): 11.64MM **Privately Held**
Web: www.people.ai
SIC: 7371 Computer software development and applications

(P-11821)
PERFECT WORLD ENTRMT INC
100 Redwood Shores Pkwy # 200 (94065-1155)
PHONE.............................650 590-7700
Alan Chen, *CEO*
Bill Wang, *
EMP: 150 EST: 2007
SQ FT: 10,000
SALES (est): 22.61MM **Privately Held**
SIC: 7371 Computer software development and applications
HQ: Perfect World Co., Ltd.
    701-20, Floor 7, Building 5, No.1 Courtyard, Shangdi E. Road, Ha Beijing BJ

(P-11822)
PERNIXDATA INC
1740 Technology Dr Ste 150 (95110)
PHONE.............................408 724-8413
Poojan Kumar, *CEO*
Mike Munoz, *CRO*
EMP: 75 EST: 2012
SALES (est): 10.46MM **Publicly Held**
Web: www.nutanix.com
SIC: 7371 Computer software development
PA: Nutanix, Inc.
    1740 Tech Dr Ste 150
    San Jose CA

(P-11823)
PERSISTENT SYSTEMS INC (HQ)
2055 Laurelwood Rd Ste 210 (95054-2727)
PHONE.............................408 216-7010
Anand Deshpande, *CEO*
Sudhir Kulkarni, *DIGITAL**
Thomas Klein, *
Narasinha Upadhye, *
Sunil Sapre, *
EMP: 65 EST: 2001
SQ FT: 25,500
SALES (est): 172.06MM **Privately Held**
Web: www.persistent.com
SIC: 7371 Computer software development
PA: Persistent Systems Limited
    Bhageerath, 402 Senapati Bapat Road, Pune MH

(P-11824)
PERSPECTIUM CORP
10301 Meanley Dr Ste 250 (92131-3011)
PHONE.............................858 530-8093
Emily Wilson, *VP*
David W Loo, *

Sarah Loo, *
EMP: 65 EST: 2013
SALES (est): 7.36MM **Privately Held**
Web: www.perspectium.com
SIC: 7371 Computer software development

(P-11825)
PETDESK
2044 1st Ave Ste 200 (92101-2089)
PHONE.............................202 431-3045
Abraham Hanono, *Prin*
EMP: 98 EST: 2017
SALES (est): 5.03MM **Privately Held**
Web: www.petdesk.com
SIC: 7371 Computer software development and applications

(P-11826)
PHOENIX TECHNOLOGIES INC
2105 S Bascom Ave Ste 316 (95008-3295)
PHONE.............................408 570-1000
Gerard Moore, *CEO*
Jonathan O'connell, *CFO*
Michelle Lu, *
Terry Chen, *
James Mortensen, *
EMP: 177 EST: 2020
SALES (est): 15MM **Privately Held**
Web: www.phoenix.com
SIC: 7371 Computer software systems analysis and design, custom

(P-11827)
PHONE CHECK SOLUTIONS LLC
Also Called: Software
16027 Ventura Blvd Ste 605 (91436)
PHONE.............................310 365-1855
Chris Sabeti, *CEO*
EMP: 358 EST: 2016
SALES (est): 10.75MM **Privately Held**
Web: www.phonecheck.com
SIC: 7371 Software programming applications

(P-11828)
PINGCAP (US) INC
1250 Borregas Ave (94089-1309)
PHONE.............................650 382-9973
Qiu Cui, *CFO*
EMP: 64 EST: 2017
SALES (est): 4.12MM **Privately Held**
Web: www.pingcap.com
SIC: 7371 Computer software development

(P-11829)
PIVOT HEALTH TECHNOLOGIES INC
Also Called: Carrot Behavioral Health
1010 Commercial St Ste C (94070-4026)
PHONE.............................650 216-9680
David Utley, *CEO*
EMP: 70 EST: 2015
SQ FT: 4,000
SALES (est): 5.18MM **Privately Held**
Web: www.pivot.co
SIC: 7371 Computer software development and applications

(P-11830)
PIVOTAL SOFTWARE INC (HQ)
Also Called: Pivotal Labs
875 Howard St Fl 5 (94103-3009)
PHONE.............................415 777-4868
Paul Maritz, *Ch Bd*
Robert Mee, *CEO*
William Cook, *Pr*
Cynthia Gaylor, *Sr VP*
Andrew Cohen, *Sr VP*

EMP: 242 EST: 2013
SQ FT: 66,510
SALES (est): 657.49MM
SALES (corp-wide): 13.35B **Privately Held**
Web: tanzu.vmware.com
SIC: 7371 Computer software development
PA: Vmware, Inc.
    3401 Hillview Ave
    Palo Alto CA
    650 427-5000

(P-11831)
PIXLEE TURNTO INC
2443 Fillmore St (94115-1814)
PHONE.............................718 753-5307
Kyle Wong, *CEO*
EMP: 101 EST: 2012
SALES (est): 10.76MM **Privately Held**
Web: www.pixlee.com
SIC: 7371 Computer software development and applications
PA: Emplifi, Inc.
    4400 Easton Cmns
    Columbus OH

(P-11832)
PLACER LABS INC
Also Called: Placer.ai
440 N Barranca Ave Pmb 1277 (91723-1722)
PHONE.............................415 228-2444
Noam Ben-zvi, *CEO*
EMP: 500 EST: 2014
SALES (est): 23.01MM **Privately Held**
Web: www.placer.ai
SIC: 7371 Computer software development

(P-11833)
PLANETSCALE INC
535 Mission St Fl 14 (94105-3253)
PHONE.............................415 706-2184
EMP: 73 EST: 2018
SALES (est): 4.24MM **Privately Held**
Web: www.planetscale.com
SIC: 7371 Computer software development

(P-11834)
PLATFORM SCIENCE INC
9560 Towne Centre Dr # 200 (92121-1972)
PHONE.............................844 475-8724
John C Kennedy Iii, *CEO*
Chris Sultemeier, *
Greg Ivancich, *
Gerald Choung, *CRO*
EMP: 140 EST: 2015
SALES (est): 18.46MM **Privately Held**
Web: www.platformscience.com
SIC: 7371 7372 Custom computer programming services; Business oriented computer software

(P-11835)
PLATFORM9 SYSTEMS INC
800 W El Camino Real Ste 180 (94040)
PHONE.............................650 898-7369
Bhaskar Gorti, *CEO*
Ravi Jacob, *CFO*
Sirish Raghuram, *CGO*
EMP: 100 EST: 2014
SALES (est): 15.93MM **Privately Held**
Web: www.platform9.com
SIC: 7371 Computer software development

(P-11836)
PLAYHAVEN LLC
1447 2nd St Ste 200 (90401-2301)
PHONE.............................310 308-9668
Mike Jones, *Pr*
Greg Gilman, *
Tom Dare, *

EMP: 115 EST: 2014
SQ FT: 15,000
SALES (est): 426.1K **Privately Held**
SIC: 7371 7311 Computer software development and applications; Advertising agencies
PA: Rockyou, Inc.
    3305 Jerusalem Ave # 201
    Wantagh NY

(P-11837)
PLAYPHONE INC
3031 Tisch Way Ste 110pw (95128-2584)
PHONE.............................408 261-6200
Takahito Yasuki, *Ch*
Ron Czerny, *
Bhaskar Roy, *CPO*
Dean Takahashi, *
EMP: 61 EST: 2005
SALES (est): 13.38MM **Privately Held**
Web: www.playphone.com
SIC: 7371 Computer software development

(P-11838)
POLARIS NETWORKS INCORPORATED
Also Called: Polaris Networks
14856 Holden Way (95124-4515)
PHONE.............................408 625-7273
Buddhadeb Biswas, *CEO*
EMP: 100 EST: 2003
SQ FT: 2,000
SALES (est): 6.56MM **Privately Held**
Web: www.polarisnetworks.net
SIC: 7371 7373 Computer software development; Computer integrated systems design

(P-11839)
PONYAI INC
3501 Gateway Blvd (94538-6585)
PHONE.............................510 906-8868
Jun Peng, *CEO*
Tiancheng Lou, *
Philip Mao, *
EMP: 333 EST: 2016
SQ FT: 50,000
SALES (est): 34.53MM
SALES (corp-wide): 1.23MM **Privately Held**
Web: www.pony.ai
SIC: 7371 Computer software development
PA: Guangzhou Pony.Ai Technology Co., Ltd.
    Room 1201, No.1 Mingzhu Street, Hengli Town, Nansha District (Of Guangzhou GD

(P-11840)
PORTWORX INC
Also Called: Portworx
650 Castro St Ste 400 (94041-2081)
PHONE.............................650 386-0766
Murli Thirumale, *CEO*
Vinod Jayaraman, *
Goutham Rao, *Engr*
EMP: 90 EST: 2015
SALES (est): 5.84MM **Publicly Held**
Web: www.portworx.com
SIC: 7371 Software programming applications
PA: Pure Storage, Inc.
    2555 Augustine Dr
    Santa Clara CA

(P-11841)
POSTMAN INC (PA)
Also Called: Postman
201 Mission St Ste 2375 (94105-1839)
PHONE.............................415 796-6470

7371 - Custom Computer Programming Services (P-11842)

Abhinav Asthana, *CEO*
Abhinav Asthana, *Pr*
Yatin Mody, *Head OF Finance*
Dane So Ctrl, *Prin*
EMP: 60 **EST:** 2015
SALES (est): 8.35MM
SALES (corp-wide): 8.35MM **Privately Held**
Web: www.postman.com
SIC: 7371 Computer software development

(P-11842)
PREVEDERE INC
440 N Wolfe Rd (94085-3869)
PHONE.................................888 686-7746
EMP: 84
SALES (corp-wide): 3.87MM **Privately Held**
Web: www.prevedere.com
SIC: 7371 Software programming applications
PA: Prevedere, Inc.
580 N 4th St Ste 240
Columbus OH
888 686-7746

(P-11843)
PRIMARY DIAGNOSTICS INC
595 Pacific Ave Fl 4 (94133-4685)
PHONE.................................619 356-3701
Andrew Kobylinski, *CEO*
Jessica Perkowitz, *CAO*
Tucker Warner, *COO*
EMP: 119 **EST:** 2020
SALES (est): 13.19MM **Privately Held**
Web: www.primary.health
SIC: 7371 Software programming applications

(P-11844)
PRIMERO SYSTEMS INCORPORATED
14123 Rasmussen Way (92129-3825)
P.O. Box 720490 (92172-0490)
PHONE.................................866 426-0779
Gary Saner, *Pr*
Melissa Saner, *
EMP: 60 **EST:** 2001
SALES (est): 4.73MM **Privately Held**
Web: www.primerosystems.com
SIC: 7371 7389 Computer software development; Business Activities at Non-Commercial Site

(P-11845)
PRIVACERA INC
Also Called: Privacera
39300 Civic Center Dr Ste 140 (94538-2338)
PHONE.................................510 413-7300
Balaji Ganesan, *CEO*
Don Bosco Durai, *
EMP: 67 **EST:** 2016
SALES (est): 6.48MM **Privately Held**
Web: www.privacera.com
SIC: 7371 Computer software development

(P-11846)
PROCORE TECHNOLOGIES INC (PA)
6309 Carpinteria Ave (93013-2924)
PHONE.................................866 477-6267
Craig F Courtemanche Junior, *Pr*
Craig F Courtemanche Junior, *Ch Bd*
Howard Fu, *CFO*
Benjamin C Singer, *CLO*
Joy D Durling, *CDO*
EMP: 3304 **EST:** 2002
SQ FT: 200,000
SALES (est): 720.2MM
SALES (corp-wide): 720.2MM **Publicly Held**
Web: www.procore.com
SIC: 7371 Computer software development

(P-11847)
PRODEGE LLC (PA)
Also Called: Swagbucks
2030 E Maple Ave Ste 200 (90245-5008)
PHONE.................................310 294-9599
EMP: 77 **EST:** 2005
SALES (est): 26.88MM
SALES (corp-wide): 26.88MM **Privately Held**
Web: www.prodege.com
SIC: 7371 8742 Computer software development and applications; Marketing consulting services

(P-11848)
PROPEL SOFTWARE SOLUTIONS
451 El Camino Real (95050-4376)
PHONE.................................408 755-3780
Ross Meyercord, *CEO*
Raymond Hein, *
Carmine Napolitano, *
EMP: 75 **EST:** 2015
SALES (est): 5.2MM **Privately Held**
Web: www.propelsoftware.com
SIC: 7371 Computer software development

(P-11849)
PSI SYSTEMS INC
Also Called: Endicia
323 N Mathilda Ave (94085-4207)
PHONE.................................650 321-2640
EMP: 200 **EST:** 1993
SALES (est): 20.84MM
SALES (corp-wide): 757.98MM **Privately Held**
Web: www.endicia.com
SIC: 7371 Custom computer programming services
PA: Stamps.Com Inc.
1990 E Grand Ave
El Segundo CA
310 482-5800

(P-11850)
PSYONIX LLC
Also Called: Rocket League
401 W A St Ste 2400 (92101-3524)
PHONE.................................619 622-8772
David F Hagewood, *CEO*
Jessica Hagewood, *Sec*
EMP: 83 **EST:** 2012
SQ FT: 40,000
SALES (est): 11.26MM **Privately Held**
Web: www.psyonix.com
SIC: 7371 Computer software development
PA: Epic Games, Inc.
620 Crossroads Blvd
Cary NC

(P-11851)
PUBMATIC INC (PA)
Also Called: Pubmatic
601 Marshall St (94063-1621)
PHONE.................................650 331-3485
Rajeev K Goel, *CEO*
Amar K Goel, *CIO*
Steven Pantelick, *CFO*
Paulina Klimenko, *CGO*
Andrew Woods, *Corporate Secretary*
EMP: 266 **EST:** 2006
SALES (est): 256.38MM **Publicly Held**
Web: www.pubmatic.com
SIC: 7371 Custom computer programming services

(P-11852)
PULSE SECURE LLC (DH)
2700 Zanker Rd Ste 200 (95134-2140)
PHONE.................................408 372-9600
Sudhakar Ramakrishna, *CEO*
Jeffrey C Key, *CFO*
Rick Barr, *AR Vice President*
David Goldschlag, *Sr VP*
Jeff Green, *Sr VP*
EMP: 85 **EST:** 2014
SALES (est): 22.93MM
SALES (corp-wide): 29.07MM **Privately Held**
Web: www.ivanti.com
SIC: 7371 4899 Computer software development; Communication signal enhancement network services
HQ: Ivanti, Inc.
10377 S Jordan Gtwy # 110
South Jordan UT
801 208-1500

(P-11853)
PULSE SYSTEMS INC (DH)
438 Listowe Dr (95630-6204)
PHONE.................................316 636-5900
Charles Walls, *CEO*
Charles Walls, *Pr*
Elias Hourani, *COO*
Tana Goering, *CMO*
Samuel Ambrose, *CMO*
EMP: 70 **EST:** 1982
SALES (est): 16.07MM
SALES (corp-wide): 8.5MM **Privately Held**
Web: www.pulseinc.com
SIC: 7371 Computer software development
HQ: Cegedim
Cegedim Dendrite Pharma Crm
Division 129 137
Boulogne Billancourt

(P-11854)
PULSORA INC
3321 Octavia St (94123-2212)
PHONE.................................650 575-5255
Murat Sonmez, *CEO*
Inderjeet Singh, *
EMP: 107 **EST:** 2021
SALES (est): 676.72K **Privately Held**
Web: www.pulsora.com
SIC: 7371 7389 Software programming applications; Business Activities at Non-Commercial Site

(P-11855)
QRS CORPORATION (DH)
1400 Marina Way S (94804-3747)
PHONE.................................510 215-5000
Elizabeth Fetter, *Pr*
David B Cooper Junior, *Sr VP*
James G Rowley, *
Ray Rike, *Senior Vice President Worldwide Sales*
EMP: 70 **EST:** 1984
SQ FT: 63,000
SALES (est): 49.91MM
SALES (corp-wide): 832.31MM **Privately Held**
Web: www.qrs.com
SIC: 7371 8742 7375 Custom computer programming services; Management consulting services; Information retrieval services
HQ: Inovis Usa, Inc.
11720 Amberpark Dr # 400
Alpharetta GA
770 521-2284

(P-11856)
QUADRIGA INC
Also Called: Taller Technologies
1 Sansome St Ste 3500 (94104-4436)
PHONE.................................650 270-6326
Lucas E Fuller, *CEO*
EMP: 70 **EST:** 2008
SALES (est): 6.05MM **Privately Held**
SIC: 7371 Custom computer programming services

(P-11857)
QUALYS INC (PA)
Also Called: Qualys
919 E Hillsdale Blvd Ste 400 (94404-2112)
PHONE.................................650 801-6100
Sumedh S Thakar, *CPO*
Sumedh S Thakar, *CPO*
Sandra E Bergeron, *
Joo Mi Kim, *CFO*
Bruce K Posey, *Corporate Secretary*
EMP: 1413 **EST:** 1999
SQ FT: 76,922
SALES (est): 489.72MM
SALES (corp-wide): 489.72MM **Publicly Held**
Web: www.qualys.com
SIC: 7371 7372 Custom computer programming services; Prepackaged software

(P-11858)
QUICKEN INC
3760 Haven Ave Ste C (94025-1012)
PHONE.................................650 564-3399
Eric Dunn, *CEO*
Gary Hornbeek, *CFO*
Linda Itskovitz, *CMO*
EMP: 104 **EST:** 2015
SQ FT: 10,000
SALES (est): 15.71MM **Privately Held**
Web: www.quicken.com
SIC: 7371 Computer software development and applications

(P-11859)
QUID LLC (PA)
3960 Freedom Cir Ste 200 (95054-1204)
PHONE.................................415 813-5300
Bob Goodson, *CEO*
Dan Buczaczer, *CMO*
Sinohe Terrero, *
Saravanan Subbiah, *
Angela Bakker-lee, *CSO*
EMP: 123 **EST:** 2006
SALES (est): 24.83MM
SALES (corp-wide): 24.83MM **Privately Held**
Web: www.netbasequid.com
SIC: 7371 7372 Computer software development; Prepackaged software

(P-11860)
QXV SOFTWARE LLC ◆
215 N Marengo Ave (91101-1503)
PHONE.................................626 219-0522
Diop Mckenzie, *Managing Member*
EMP: 74 **EST:** 2023
SALES (est): 2.04MM **Privately Held**
SIC: 7371 Computer software development

(P-11861)
R SOFTWARE INC (PA)
Also Called: Rapidapi
85 2nd St Ste 400 (94105-3462)
PHONE.................................650 575-7633
Iddo Gino, *CEO*
EMP: 74 **EST:** 2016
SALES (est): 5.22MM
SALES (corp-wide): 5.22MM **Privately Held**

PRODUCTS & SERVICES SECTION
7371 - Custom Computer Programming Services (P-11885)

Web: www.rapidapi.com
SIC: 7371 Custom computer programming services

(P-11862)
RAINTREE SYSTEMS INC
30650 Rancho California Rd Ste 406 (92591-3279)
PHONE...................................951 252-9400
Richard V Welty, CEO
Vu Nguyen, CPO*
Scott Rongo, *
EMP: 190 EST: 1982
SALES (est): 25.24MM Privately Held
Web: www.raintreeinc.com
SIC: 7371 5045 5734 Computer software development; Computer software; Computer and software stores

(P-11863)
RAMY INFOTECH INC
5201 Great America Pkwy Ste 320 (95054-1122)
PHONE...................................408 317-9256
Jyoti Gill, Pr
EMP: 128 EST: 2010
SALES (est): 3.24MM Privately Held
Web: www.ramyinfotechinc.com
SIC: 7371 7379 Computer software development; Computer related consulting services

(P-11864)
READY PRICE LLC
5671 Santa Teresa Blvd (95123-6515)
PHONE...................................408 357-0931
Richard Soukoulis, CEO
EMP: 950 EST: 2005
SALES (est): 523.31K
SALES (corp-wide): 499.71MM Privately Held
Web: www.readyprice.com
SIC: 7371 6162 Computer software development and applications; Mortgage bankers and loan correspondents
PA: Situsamc Holdings Corporation
5065 Westheimer Rd # 700
Houston TX
713 328-4400

(P-11865)
REAL-TIME INNOVATIONS INC (PA)
Also Called: R T I
232 E Java Dr (94089-1318)
PHONE...................................408 990-7400
Stanley Schneider, CEO
Mekler Catherine, VP
Douglas C Schmidt, Prin
Jody Schneider, CFO
EMP: 60 EST: 1986
SQ FT: 1,000
SALES (est): 24.68MM Privately Held
Web: www.rti.com
SIC: 7371 7379 Computer software development; Computer related consulting services

(P-11866)
REAPPLICATIONS INC
8910 University Center Ln Ste 300 (92122-1029)
PHONE...................................619 230-0209
Richard Boyle, CEO
EMP: 171 EST: 1996
SALES (est): 962K
SALES (corp-wide): 2.18B Publicly Held
Web: www.reapplications.com
SIC: 7371 Computer software development
HQ: Loopnet, Inc.
101 California St # 4300
San Francisco CA

(P-11867)
RECIPROCAL LABS CORP
Also Called: Propeller Health
9001 Spectrum Center Blvd (92123-1438)
PHONE...................................608 251-0470
EMP: 72 EST: 2013
SALES (est): 9.06MM Publicly Held
SIC: 7371 Software programming applications
PA: Resmed Inc.
9001 Spectrum Center Blvd
San Diego CA

(P-11868)
RED CONDOR INC
1300 Valley House Dr Ste 115 (94928-4927)
PHONE...................................707 569-7419
Ron Longo, Pr
EMP: 114 EST: 2003
SALES (est): 1.08MM Privately Held
Web: www.gosecure.net
SIC: 7371 Computer software development

(P-11869)
REDIS INC
700 E El Camino Real Ste 250 (94040-2813)
PHONE...................................415 930-9666
Ofer Bengal, CEO
Jason Forget, CRO
Manish Gupta, CMO
Regev Yativ, VP Sls
EMP: 439 EST: 2013
SALES (est): 49.3MM Privately Held
Web: www.redis.com
SIC: 7371 Computer software development
PA: Redis Ltd
94 Alon Yigal
Tel Aviv-Jaffa

(P-11870)
REDTAIL TECHNOLOGY INC
3131 Fite Cir (95827-1801)
PHONE...................................800 206-5030
Brian T Mclaughlin, CEO
Gary Curry, *
Kathi Jacoway, *
Susan Curry, *
EMP: 80 EST: 2003
SALES (est): 18.9MM Privately Held
Web: corporate.redtailtechnology.com
SIC: 7371 Computer software development

(P-11871)
REFLEKTIVE INC (DH)
123 Townsend St Ste 300 (94107-1938)
PHONE...................................203 886-9240
David Laszewski, Interim Chief Executive Officer
Rachel Ernst, Chief Human Resource Officer*
Jaisimha Muthegere, *
Marc Caltabiano, CPO*
Travis Wentling, *
EMP: 199 EST: 2013
SALES (est): 925.05K
SALES (corp-wide): 718.65MM Privately Held
Web: www.reflektive.com
SIC: 7371 Computer software development
HQ: Learning Technologies Group Inc.
300 5th Ave
Waltham MA
781 530-2000

(P-11872)
RELTIO INC (PA)
100 Marine Pkwy Ste 275 (94065-5234)
PHONE...................................855 360-3282
EMP: 381 EST: 2011
SQ FT: 6,242
SALES (est): 113MM Privately Held
Web: www.reltio.com
SIC: 7371 Custom computer programming services

(P-11873)
RELYANCE INC
Also Called: Relyance Ai
1900 S Norfolk St Ste 350 (94403-1171)
PHONE...................................866 735-9623
Leila Golchehreh, Prin
Abhi Sharma, *
Michelle Dempsey Senior, Dir Fin
EMP: 70 EST: 2020
SALES (est): 2.1MM Privately Held
Web: www.relyance.ai
SIC: 7371 Computer software development

(P-11874)
REMIX SOFTWARE INC
Also Called: Remix Software
1128 Howard St (94103-3914)
PHONE...................................415 900-4332
EMP: 85 EST: 2014
Web: www.remix.com
SIC: 7371 Computer software development and applications

(P-11875)
REPLICATED INC
8605 Santa Monica Blvd # 66909 (90069-4109)
PHONE...................................424 672-6624
EMP: 66 EST: 2017
SALES (est): 3.6MM Privately Held
Web: www.replicated.com
SIC: 7371 Computer software development

(P-11876)
RESOLVE SYSTEMS LLC (PA)
300 Orchard City Dr Ste 110 (95008)
PHONE...................................949 325-0120
Martin B Savitt, CEO
EMP: 65 EST: 2000
SALES (est): 20.76MM Privately Held
Web: www.resolve.io
SIC: 7371 Computer software development

(P-11877)
RESONATE I INC (PA)
90 Great Oaks Blvd Ste 205 (95119-1314)
PHONE...................................408 545-5500
EMP: 160 EST: 1995
SQ FT: 38,000
SALES (est): 13.88MM Privately Held
Web: www.resonatenetworks.com
SIC: 7371 7372 Computer software development; Business oriented computer software

(P-11878)
RETAILNEXT INC (PA)
60 S Market St Ste 310 (95113-2336)
PHONE...................................408 884-2162
Alexei Agratchev, CEO
Marlie Liu, VP
Diego Aragon, VP
Bridget Johns, VP
David Woods, VP
EMP: 129 EST: 2007
SALES (est): 41.9MM
SALES (corp-wide): 41.9MM Privately Held
Web: www.retailnext.net
SIC: 7371 Computer software development

(P-11879)
REVINATE LLC
2345 Yale St Fl 1 (94306-1429)
PHONE...................................415 671-4703
Marc Heyneker, CEO
Steve Chiu, *
Dan Hang, *
Gary Lawrence, *
EMP: 177 EST: 2010
SALES (est): 10.02MM Privately Held
Web: www.revinate.com
SIC: 7371 Computer software development

(P-11880)
RHOMBUS SYSTEMS INC
1920 20th St (95811-6830)
PHONE...................................877 746-6797
Garrett Larsson, CEO
Sue Ellen Ash, *
EMP: 150 EST: 2016
SALES (est): 11.94MM Privately Held
Web: www.rhombus.com
SIC: 7371 Computer software development

(P-11881)
RHYTHM NEWMEDIA INC
800 W El Camino Real Ste 100 (94040-2587)
PHONE...................................650 961-9024
EMP: 70
Web: www.rhythmnewmedia.com
SIC: 7371 Computer software development

(P-11882)
RIGETTI & CO LLC (PA)
Also Called: Rigetti Quantum Computing
775 Heinz Ave (94710-2732)
PHONE...................................510 210-5550
Chad Rigetti, CEO
Brian Sereda, *
EMP: 163 EST: 2013
SALES (est): 22.12MM
SALES (corp-wide): 22.12MM Privately Held
Web: www.rigetti.com
SIC: 7371 Computer software development

(P-11883)
RISKOPTICS INC
Also Called: Recipro
548 Market St 73905 (94104-5401)
PHONE...................................415 851-8667
Michael Maggio, CEO
Kenneth Lynch, *
EMP: 125 EST: 2009
SQ FT: 5,300
SALES (est): 16.39MM Privately Held
Web: www.reciprocity.com
SIC: 7371 Computer software systems analysis and design, custom

(P-11884)
RMD GROUP LLC
614 5th Ave Ste A (92101-6964)
PHONE...................................619 955-5750
EMP: 67 EST: 2008
SALES (est): 5.06MM Privately Held
Web: www.rmdgroupsd.com
SIC: 7371 Computer software development and applications

(P-11885)
ROADSTER INC
250 Holger Way (95134-1300)
PHONE...................................833 568-5968
Andrew Moss, CEO

7371 - Custom Computer Programming Services (P-11886)

EMP: 566 EST: 2013
SALES (est): 13.86MM
SALES (corp-wide): 1.67B Privately Held
Web: www.roadster.com
SIC: 7371 Computer software development
HQ: Cdk Global, Inc.
    1950 Hassell Rd
    Hoffman Estates IL
    847 397-1700

(P-11886)
ROBERT BOSCH HEALTHCARE SYSTEMS INC
2400 Geng Rd Ste 200 (94303-3350)
PHONE.................................650 690-9100
EMP: 138
SIC: 7371 Computer software development

(P-11887)
ROO VETERINARY INC
595 Pacific Ave Fl 4 (94133-4685)
PHONE.................................917 805-5220
EMP: 85 EST: 2018
SALES (est): 5.72MM Privately Held
Web: www.roo.vet
SIC: 7371 Computer software development and applications

(P-11888)
ROOTSTRAP INC
8306 Wilshire Blvd Ste 249 (90211-2304)
PHONE.................................310 907-9210
David Jarrett, *CEO*
Fernando Colman, *
Anthony Figueroa, *
EMP: 134 EST: 2015
SALES (est): 4.31MM Privately Held
Web: www.rootstrap.com
SIC: 7371 Computer software development

(P-11889)
RYSUN LABS INC
1525 Mccarthy Blvd Ste 212 (95035-7451)
PHONE.................................855 527-7890
Parthive Zaveri, *CEO*
Vishal Shukla, *
EMP: 200 EST: 2012
SQ FT: 550
SALES (est): 10.97MM Privately Held
Web: www.rysun.com
SIC: 7371 7379 Computer software development; Computer related consulting services
PA: Rysun Labs Private Limited
    04th Floor, Atal Kalam Buildingopp
    Gusec
    Ahmedabad GJ

(P-11890)
RYZLINK CORP
Also Called: Chuwa American
2855 Kifer Rd Ste 135 (95051-0835)
PHONE.................................510 296-5433
Hang Zhang, *CEO*
Hang Zhang, *Pr*
Ming Xu, *Stockholder**
EMP: 66 EST: 2010
SALES (est): 2.13MM Privately Held
Web: www.ryzlink.com
SIC: 7371 Computer software development

(P-11891)
SAALEX CORP
27525 Enterprise Cir W Ste 101a (92590)
PHONE.................................951 543-9259
EMP: 567
SALES (corp-wide): 96.07MM Privately Held
Web: www.saalex.com

SIC: 7371 Custom computer programming services
PA: Saalex Corp.
    811 Camarillo Springs Rd A
    Camarillo CA
    805 482-1070

(P-11892)
SAAMA TECHNOLOGIES INC (PA)
Also Called: Saama
900 E Hamilton Ave Ste 200 (95008-0664)
PHONE.................................408 371-1900
Vivek Sharma, *CEO*
Ken Coleman, *
Suresh Katta, *
Sandip Dadkar, *
Vasant Shetty, *
EMP: 237 EST: 1997
SQ FT: 10,000
SALES (est): 57.6MM
SALES (corp-wide): 57.6MM Privately Held
Web: www.saama.com
SIC: 7371 Computer software development

(P-11893)
SAFE SECURITIES INC (PA)
3000 El Camino Real Bldg 4 (94306)
PHONE.................................650 398-3669
Saket Modi, *CEO*
EMP: 200 EST: 2018
SALES (est): 13.76MM
SALES (corp-wide): 13.76MM Privately Held
Web: www.safe.security
SIC: 7371 Computer software development

(P-11894)
SAFRAN PASS INNOVATIONS LLC (HQ)
Also Called: Zodiac Inflight Innovations US
3151 E Imperial Hwy (92821-6720)
PHONE.................................714 854-8600
EMP: 73 EST: 1996
SALES (est): 55.16MM
SALES (corp-wide): 650.78MM Privately Held
Web: www.safran-group.com
SIC: 7371 Computer software systems analysis and design, custom
PA: Safran
    2 Bd Du General Martial Valin
    Paris

(P-11895)
SAGO MINI INC
5880 W Jefferson Blvd Ste A (90016-3160)
PHONE.................................416 731-8586
Anne-sophie Brieger, *Admn*
EMP: 76 EST: 2021
SALES (est): 1.29MM Privately Held
SIC: 7371 Custom computer programming services

(P-11896)
SALT SECURITY INC
3921 Fabian Way (94303-4640)
PHONE.................................650 254-6580
Roey Eliyahu, *CEO*
Michael Nicosia, *
EMP: 65 EST: 2019
SALES (est): 4.86MM Privately Held
Web: www.salt.security
SIC: 7371 Computer software development

(P-11897)
SAMBANOVA SYSTEMS INC (PA)

2200 Geng Rd Ste 100 (94303-3358)
PHONE.................................650 263-1153
Rodrigo Liang, *CEO*
Jonathan Chang, *
EMP: 431 EST: 2017
SALES (est): 51.22MM
SALES (corp-wide): 51.22MM Privately Held
Web: www.sambanova.ai
SIC: 7371 Computer software systems analysis and design, custom

(P-11898)
SAMEDAY TECHNOLOGIES INC
Also Called: Sameday Health
523 Victoria Ave (90291-4832)
PHONE.................................310 697-8126
Felix Huettenbach, *Pr*
EMP: 238 EST: 2021
SALES (est): 4.64MM Privately Held
Web: www.samedayhealth.com
SIC: 7371 Computer software development and applications

(P-11899)
SAMEPAGE LABS INC
307 Orchard City Dr (95008-2931)
PHONE.................................408 628-0393
Scott Schreiman, *CEO*
EMP: 449 EST: 2015
SALES (est): 461.57K
SALES (corp-wide): 1.17B Publicly Held
SIC: 7371 Computer software development and applications
PA: Paylocity Holding Corporation
    1400 American Ln
    Schaumburg IL
    847 463-3200

(P-11900)
SAN DIEGO HOME SELLER INC
Also Called: Porchlight
4304 Ridgeway Dr (92116-2051)
PHONE.................................619 909-6345
EMP: 62 EST: 2019
SALES (est): 1.16MM Privately Held
Web: www.porchlightsocal.com
SIC: 7371 7389 Computer software development and applications; Business Activities at Non-Commercial Site

(P-11901)
SANDBOX VR MISSION VALLEY LLC
4695 Chabot Dr Ste 200 (94588-2756)
PHONE.................................323 207-0840
EMP: 87 EST: 2019
SALES (est): 1.09MM
SALES (corp-wide): 36.98MM Privately Held
SIC: 7371 Computer software development and applications
PA: Glostation Core Usa, Inc.
    548 Market St
    San Francisco CA

(P-11902)
SANO INTELLIGENCE INC
Also Called: Sano
1155 Bryant St (94103-4336)
PHONE.................................408 483-6518
Ashwin Pushpala, *CEO*
EMP: 175 EST: 2011
SALES (est): 891.61K
SALES (corp-wide): 9.18MM Privately Held
Web: www.onedrop.today
SIC: 7371 Computer software systems analysis and design, custom
PA: Informed Data Systems Inc.

166 Mercer St Apt 2
New York NY
917 442-8626

(P-11903)
SATMETRIX SYSTEMS INC
555 Twin Dolphin Dr Ste 365 (94065-2129)
PHONE.................................650 227-8300
Richard Owen, *Pr*
Raymond Yue, *
Brian Curry, *
EMP: 250 EST: 1996
SALES (est): 28.07MM Privately Held
Web: www.satmetrix.com
SIC: 7371 Software programming applications

(P-11904)
SCHOOL-LINK TECHNOLOGIES INC
1437 6th St (90401-2509)
P.O. Box 2410 (90407-2410)
PHONE.................................310 434-2700
EMP: 90
Web: www.heartlandschoolsolutions.com
SIC: 7371 Computer software development

(P-11905)
SCIENCE 37 INC
12121 Bluff Creek Dr Ste 100 (90094-2994)
PHONE.................................984 377-3737
EMP: 61
SALES (est): 224.94K Privately Held
Web: www.science37.com
SIC: 7371 Computer software development

(P-11906)
SECOND SPECTRUM INC
312 E 1st St (90012-3902)
PHONE.................................213 995-6860
Yu-han Chang, *Owner*
EMP: 122 EST: 2013
SALES (est): 6.54MM Privately Held
Web: www.secondspectrum.com
SIC: 7371 Software programming applications

(P-11907)
SECUREAUTH CORPORATION (PA)
49 Discovery (92618-6713)
PHONE.................................949 777-6959
Paul Trulove, *CEO*
Jeff Lo, *
Darin Pendergraft, *
Nick Mansour, *Executive Worldwide Sales Vice-President**
Keith Graham, *
EMP: 186 EST: 2005
SALES (est): 33.75MM Privately Held
Web: www.secureauth.com
SIC: 7371 Computer software development

(P-11908)
SECURITI INC (PA)
3031 Tisch Way Ste 502 (95128-2531)
PHONE.................................408 401-1160
Rehan Jalil, *CEO*
EMP: 191 EST: 2018
SALES (est): 30.06MM
SALES (corp-wide): 30.06MM Privately Held
Web: www.securiti.ai
SIC: 7371 Computer software development

(P-11909)
SELECT DATA INC
Also Called: Select Data
4175 E La Palma Ave Ste 205 (92807-1842)

PRODUCTS & SERVICES SECTION   **7371 - Custom Computer Programming Services (P-11931)**

PHONE..................714 577-1000
Edward A Buckley, *CEO*
Pam Hernandez, *
Tawny Nichols, *
Ted A Schulte, *
Pete Poulis, *
EMP: 151 **EST:** 1991
SALES (est): 25.6MM **Privately Held**
Web: www.selectdata.com
SIC: 7371 7372 Computer code authors; Prepackaged software

(P-11910)
SERVICEMAX INC (HQ)
4450 Rosewood Dr Ste 200 (94588-3061)
PHONE..................800 756-4960
Neil Barua, *CEO*
Simon Edwards, *CFO*
Stacey Epstein, *Chief Marketing CUSTOMER EXPERIENCE*
Tony Zingale, *Ch Bd*
EMP: 120 **EST:** 1999
SALES (est): 53.36MM
SALES (corp-wide): 1.93B **Publicly Held**
Web: resources.servicemax.com
SIC: 7371 Computer software development
PA: Ptc Inc.
    121 Seaport Blvd
    Boston MA
    781 370-5000

(P-11911)
SERVICETITAN INC (PA)
801 N Brand Blvd Ste 700 (91203-1215)
PHONE..................855 899-0970
Ara Mahdessian, *CEO*
Vahe Kuzoyan, *Pr*
Guy Longworth, *CMO*
Ross Biestman, *CRO*
Chris Trombetta, *CPO*
EMP: 69 **EST:** 2015
SALES (est): 45.95MM
SALES (corp-wide): 45.95MM **Privately Held**
Web: www.servicetitan.com
SIC: 7371 Computer software development

(P-11912)
SETSCHEDULE LLC
100 Spectrum Center Dr Fl 9 (92618-4972)
PHONE..................888 222-0011
Udi Dorner, *Managing Member*
EMP: 112 **EST:** 2014
SALES (est): 9.72MM **Privately Held**
Web: www.setschedule.com
SIC: 7371 Computer software development

(P-11913)
SHIPHAWK
3463 State St Ste 245 (93105-2662)
PHONE..................805 335-2432
Aaron Freeman, *CFO*
EMP: 64
SALES (corp-wide): 11.44MM **Privately Held**
Web: www.shiphawk.com
SIC: 7371 Computer software development
PA: Shiphawk
    925 De La Vina St Ste 300
    Santa Barbara CA
    805 335-2432

(P-11914)
SIFT SCIENCE INC (PA)
Also Called: Sift
525 Market St Fl 6 (94105-2714)
PHONE..................415 882-7709
Jason Tan, *CEO*
Marc Olesen, *
EMP: 197 **EST:** 2011

SALES (est): 22.52MM
SALES (corp-wide): 22.52MM **Privately Held**
Web: www.sift.com
SIC: 7371 Computer software development

(P-11915)
SIGNALWIRE INC
228 Hamilton Ave Fl 3 (94301-2583)
P.O. Box 516 (53589-0516)
PHONE..................650 382-0000
Anthony Minessale, *CEO*
Sean Heiney, *
Brian West, *
Michael Jerris, *
EMP: 100 **EST:** 2017
SALES (est): 5.32MM **Privately Held**
Web: www.signalwire.com
SIC: 7371 Computer software development

(P-11916)
SILICON VALLEY COMMERCE LLC
16 Jessie St (94105-2782)
PHONE..................888 507-8266
EMP: 81
SALES (corp-wide): 23.87MM **Privately Held**
Web: www.siliconvalleycommerce.com
SIC: 7371 Custom computer programming services
PA: Silicon Valley Commerce Llc
    1466 Us Highway 395 N # 200
    Gardnerville NV
    888 507-8266

(P-11917)
SISU DATA INC
548 Market St (94104-5401)
PHONE..................415 795-8250
EMP: 60
SALES (est): 4.91MM **Privately Held**
Web: www.sisudata.com
SIC: 7371 Computer software development

(P-11918)
SKILLZ INC (PA)
1061 Market St Fl 6 (94103-1667)
P.O. Box 445 (94104-0445)
PHONE..................415 762-0511
Andrew Paradise, *Ch Bd*
Jason Roswig, *Pr*
Casey Chafkin, *CRO*
Stanley Mbugua, *CAO*
Charlotte Edelman, *Corporate Secretary*
EMP: 635 **EST:** 2020
SALES (est): 269.71MM
SALES (corp-wide): 269.71MM **Publicly Held**
Web: games.skillz.com
SIC: 7371 Computer software development and applications

(P-11919)
SKYBOX SECURITY INC (PA)
2077 Gateway Pl Ste 200 (95110-1016)
PHONE..................408 441-8060
Gideon Cohen, *CEO*
Charlie Velasquez, *CFO*
EMP: 64 **EST:** 2002
SALES (est): 22.24MM
SALES (corp-wide): 22.24MM **Privately Held**
Web: www.skyboxsecurity.com
SIC: 7371 Computer software development

(P-11920)
SKYLITE NETWORKS
761 Mabury Rd Ste 75 (95133-1018)
PHONE..................408 934-9349

Idress M Munir, *CEO*
EMP: 70 **EST:** 2015
SALES (est): 4.83MM **Privately Held**
Web: www.skylite.com
SIC: 7371 Computer software development

(P-11921)
SLI SYSTEMS INC
333 W San Carlos St Ste 1250 (95110-2728)
PHONE..................408 255-2487
Michael Grantham, *Brnch Mgr*
EMP: 63
Web: www.sli-systems.com
SIC: 7371 Computer software development
PA: S.L.I. Systems, Inc.
    268 Bush St Ste 3900
    San Francisco CA

(P-11922)
SLIDERULE LABS INC (PA)
Also Called: Springboard
22 Battery St Ste 1100 (94111-5502)
PHONE..................646 748-0378
Parul Gupta, *Mgr*
EMP: 137 **EST:** 2013
SALES (est): 10.47MM
SALES (corp-wide): 10.47MM **Privately Held**
Web: www.springboard.com
SIC: 7371 Computer software development and applications

(P-11923)
SMART ENERGY SYSTEMS INC
Michelson Dr Ste 3370 (92612)
PHONE..................909 703-9609
EMP: 119
SALES (corp-wide): 10.19MM **Privately Held**
Web: www.sew.ai
SIC: 7371 Computer software development
PA: Smart Energy Systems, Inc.
    15495 Sand Canyon Ave # 100
    Irvine CA
    909 703-9609

(P-11924)
SMART UTILITY SYSTEMS INC
Also Called: Smart Energy Water
19900 Macarthur Blvd Ste 370 (92612-2445)
PHONE..................909 217-3344
Kurt Sweetser, *Prin*
EMP: 100 **EST:** 2014
SALES (est): 10.54MM **Privately Held**
SIC: 7371 7373 8741 Computer software development; Systems software development services; Management services

(P-11925)
SMARTDRIVE SYSTEMS INC (PA)
9515 Towne Centre Dr (92121-1973)
PHONE..................858 225-5550
Steve Mitgang, *CEO*
Jason Palmer, *
Michael J Baker, *
Dan Lehman, *CORP Development*
▲ **EMP:** 97 **EST:** 2005
SALES (est): 47.27MM **Privately Held**
Web: www.smartdrive.net
SIC: 7371 Computer software development and applications

(P-11926)
SMARTRECRUITERS INC (PA)
166 Geary St (94108-5602)
PHONE..................415 659-9130

Jerome Ternynck, *CEO*
Jeremy Johnson, *
Mark Jewett, *CMO*
EMP: 375 **EST:** 2010
SALES (est): 49.02MM
SALES (corp-wide): 49.02MM **Privately Held**
Web: www.smartrecruiters.com
SIC: 7371 Computer software development and applications

(P-11927)
SNACKPASS LLC
26 Ofarrell St Fl 8 (94108-5825)
PHONE..................203 684-5156
Jamie Marshall, *Managing Member*
EMP: 89 **EST:** 2020
SALES (est): 2.51MM **Privately Held**
SIC: 7371 Software programming applications

(P-11928)
SNAP INC (PA)
Also Called: Snapchat
3000 31st St Ste C (90405-3059)
PHONE..................310 399-3339
Evan Spiegel, *CEO*
Michael Lynton, *
Derek Andersen, *CFO*
Jerry Hunter, *COO*
Robert Murphy, *
EMP: 545 **EST:** 2010
SQ FT: 720,000
SALES (est): 4.6B
SALES (corp-wide): 4.6B **Publicly Held**
Web: www.snap.com
SIC: 7371 7372 Computer software development and applications; Application computer software

(P-11929)
SNAPCOMMS INC
155 N Lake Ave Fl 9 (91101-1849)
PHONE..................805 715-0300
Chris Leonard, *CEO*
EMP: 80 **EST:** 2012
SALES (est): 4.59MM
SALES (corp-wide): 431.89MM **Publicly Held**
Web: www.snapcomms.com
SIC: 7371 Computer software development
PA: Everbridge, Inc.
    155 N Lake Ave Ste 100
    Pasadena CA
    818 230-9700

(P-11930)
SOFTSOL RESOURCES INC (HQ)
Also Called: Softsol
42840 Christy St Ste 231 (94538-3194)
PHONE..................510 824-2000
Srini Madala, *Pr*
Kris Yalavarthy, *
▲ **EMP:** 100 **EST:** 1993
SALES (est): 12.23MM **Privately Held**
Web: www.softsol.com
SIC: 7371 Computer software development
PA: Softsol India Limited
    Plot No-4
    Hyderabad TG

(P-11931)
SOFTWARE MANAGEMENT CONS LLC
Also Called: Smci
959 S Coast Dr Ste 415 (92626-7839)
PHONE..................714 662-1841
Cesar Sanchez, *Prin*
EMP: 142

7371 - Custom Computer Programming Services (P-11932)

SALES (corp-wide): 253.48MM **Privately Held**
Web: www.milestone.tech
SIC: **7371** Computer software development
HQ: Software Management Consultants, Llc
500 N Brand Blvd
Glendale CA
818 240-3177

(P-11932)
SOLANA LABS INC
530 Divisadero St Pmb 722 (94117-2213)
PHONE.............................628 629-3265
Anatoly Yakovenko, CEO
EMP: 60 **EST:** 2018
SALES (est): 9.82MM **Privately Held**
Web: www.solana.com
SIC: **7371** Computer software development and applications

(P-11933)
SOLIX TECHNOLOGIES INC (PA)
4701 Patrick Henry Dr Ste 2001 (95054-1819)
PHONE.............................408 654-6405
Sai Gundavelli, CEO
▼ **EMP:** 60 **EST:** 2002
SQ FT: 17,000
SALES (est): 19.25MM
SALES (corp-wide): 19.25MM **Privately Held**
Web: www.solix.com
SIC: **7371** Computer software development

(P-11934)
SONATA SOFTWARE NORTH AMER INC (HQ)
Also Called: Sonata
39300 Civic Center Dr Ste 270 (94538-2337)
PHONE.............................510 791-7220
Amit Kumar, Pr
EMP: 66 **EST:** 1992
SALES (est): 40.79MM **Privately Held**
Web: www.sonata-software.com
SIC: **7371** Computer software development
PA: Sonata Software Limited
1/4, A.P.S Trust Building,
Bengaluru KA

(P-11935)
SONATUS INC (PA)
330 Gibraltar Dr (94089-1326)
PHONE.............................650 488-8500
Jeffrey P Chou, CEO
Simon Wu, *
EMP: 120 **EST:** 2018
SALES (est): 5.6MM
SALES (corp-wide): 5.6MM **Privately Held**
Web: www.sonatus.com
SIC: **7371** Computer software development

(P-11936)
SONY CORPORATION OF AMERICA
Sony Interactive Studios Amer
2207 Bridgepointe Pkwy (94404-5060)
PHONE.............................650 655-8000
Kelly Flock, Mgr
EMP: 200
Web: www.sony.com
SIC: **7371** Computer software development
HQ: Sony Corporation Of America
25 Madison Ave Fl 27
New York NY

(P-11937)
SPARK UNLIMITED INC
40 E Verdugo Ave # 2 (91502-1931)

EMP: 68 **EST:** 2002
SALES (est): 6.13MM **Privately Held**
Web: www.sparkunlimited.com
SIC: **7371** Computer software development

(P-11938)
SPECTRUM LABS INC
1990 N California Blvd Ste 800 (94596-7261)
PHONE.............................415 295-2752
Justin Davis, Prin
Justin Davis, Prin
EMP: 61 **EST:** 2019
SALES (est): 4.28MM **Privately Held**
SIC: **7371** Custom computer programming services

(P-11939)
SPERASOFT INC
2033 Gateway Pl Ste 500 (95110-3712)
PHONE.............................408 715-6615
Igor Efremov, CEO
Alexei Kudriashov, *
EMP: 375 **EST:** 2005
SQ FT: 15,000
SALES (est): 31.03MM
SALES (corp-wide): 717.37MM **Privately Held**
Web: www.sperasoft.com
SIC: **7371** Software programming applications
HQ: Keywords International Limited
Whelan House
Dublin

(P-11940)
SPIREON INC (PA)
Also Called: Goldstar
18881 Von Karman Ave Ste 1500 (92612-1582)
PHONE.............................800 557-1449
Kevin Weiss, CEO
Brian Skutta, *
Tim Welch, *
Rita Parvaneh, *
Carla Fitzgerald, CMO*
EMP: 175 **EST:** 2002
SALES (est): 172.39MM
SALES (corp-wide): 172.39MM **Privately Held**
Web: www.spireon.com
SIC: **7371 8741** Computer software development; Business management

(P-11941)
SPRUCE TECHNOLOGY INC
3516 Browntail Way (94582-5245)
PHONE.............................925 415-8160
Muttu Nagubandi, Brnch Mgr
EMP: 145
SALES (corp-wide): 48.57MM **Privately Held**
Web: www.sprucetech.com
SIC: **7371** Computer software development and applications
PA: Spruce Technology Inc
1149 Bloomfield Ave Ste G
Clifton NJ
201 693-8843

(P-11942)
SRS CONSULTING INC (PA)
39465 Paseo Padre Pkwy Ste 3200 (94538-5349)
PHONE.............................510 252-0625
Sangeetha Chowhan, CEO
Shankar Chowhan, *
EMP: 258 **EST:** 2002
SQ FT: 1,250
SALES (est): 14.62MM

SALES (corp-wide): 14.62MM **Privately Held**
Web: www.srsconsultinginc.com
SIC: **7371 7379** Computer software development; Computer related consulting services

(P-11943)
STARSHIP TECHNOLOGIES INC
535 Mission St 19fl (94105-2997)
PHONE.............................844 445-5333
EMP: 180 **EST:** 2018
SALES (est): 2.68MM **Privately Held**
Web: www.starship.xyz
SIC: **7371** Computer software development and applications

(P-11944)
STARTEL CORPORATION (PA)
16 Goodyear B-125 (92618-3743)
PHONE.............................949 863-8700
William Lane, Pr
EMP: 60 **EST:** 1980
SQ FT: 27,000
SALES (est): 11.28MM
SALES (corp-wide): 11.28MM **Privately Held**
Web: www.startel.com
SIC: **7371 3661** Computer software development; Communication headgear, telephone

(P-11945)
STARTUP FARMS INTL LLC
Also Called: Sufi
45690 Northport Loop E (94538-6477)
PHONE.............................510 440-0110
EMP: 350 **EST:** 2006
SALES (est): 10.6MM **Privately Held**
Web: www.startupfarms.com
SIC: **7371** Computer software development

(P-11946)
STEADY PLATFORM INC
5636 Fallsgrove St (90016-5027)
PHONE.............................678 792-8364
Adam Roseman, CEO
Nancy Bush, *
Adam Roseman, Sec
EMP: 70 **EST:** 2017
SALES (est): 4.42MM **Privately Held**
Web: www.steadyapp.com
SIC: **7371** Custom computer programming services

(P-11947)
STEPPECHANGE LLC
900 Uccelli Dr Apt 9301 (94063-3051)
PHONE.............................415 279-7638
Igor Neyman, Managing Member
EMP: 70 **EST:** 2010
SALES (est): 2.17MM **Privately Held**
Web: www.steppechange.com
SIC: **7371** Computer software development

(P-11948)
STONERIVER INC
770 The City Dr S Ste 5000 (92868)
PHONE.............................714 705-8227
John Grundman, Prin
EMP: 97
Web: www.sapiens.com
SIC: **7371** Computer software development
HQ: Stoneriver, Inc.
20 Horseneck Ln Ste 1
Greenwich CT
303 729-7500

(P-11949)
STRATACARE LLC
Also Called: Stratacare
17838 Gillette Ave Ste D (92614-6502)
P.O. Box 19600 (92623-9600)
PHONE.............................949 743-1200
Scott R Green, CEO
John Zavoli, Chief Compliance Officer*
Dave Perbix, *
Michael Josephs, *
Robert Mccaffrey, SALES
▲ **EMP:** 250 **EST:** 1998
SALES (est): 30.52MM
SALES (corp-wide): 3.86B **Publicly Held**
Web: www.conduent.com
SIC: **7371** Computer software development and applications
HQ: Conduent Workers Compensation Holdings, Inc.
17838 Gillette Ave
Irvine CA

(P-11950)
STRATGIC HLTHCARE PROGRAMS LLC
6500 Hollister Ave Ste 210 (93117-3011)
PHONE.............................805 963-9446
Barbara Rosenblum, CEO
EMP: 94 **EST:** 2012
SALES (est): 5.85MM
SALES (corp-wide): 5.37B **Publicly Held**
Web: www.shpdata.com
SIC: **7371** Computer software development
PA: Roper Technologies, Inc.
6901 Prof Pkwy E Ste 200
Sarasota FL
941 556-2601

(P-11951)
STREAMLABS LLC
565 Commercial St Fl 3 (94111-3031)
P.O. Box 318188 (94131-8188)
PHONE.............................415 990-9187
EMP: 84 **EST:** 2017
SALES (est): 194.7K **Privately Held**
SIC: **7371** Computer software development and applications
HQ: General Workings Inc.
565 Commercial St Fl 3
San Francisco CA
415 990-9187

(P-11952)
STRIVR LABS INC
3520 Thomas Rd Ste C (95054-2048)
PHONE.............................650 656-9987
Derek Belch, CEO
EMP: 140 **EST:** 2015
SALES (est): 20.72MM **Privately Held**
Web: www.strivr.com
SIC: **7371** Computer software development and applications

(P-11953)
STYRA INC
548 Market St (94104-5401)
PHONE.............................650 980-4280
Mark Pundsack, CEO
EMP: 62 **EST:** 2015
SALES (est): 5.08MM **Privately Held**
Web: www.styra.com
SIC: **7371** Custom computer programming services

(P-11954)
SUGARCRM INC (PA)
10050 N Wolfe Rd Ste Sw2130 (95014-2528)
PHONE.............................877 842-7276
Larry Augustin, Ch Bd

PRODUCTS & SERVICES SECTION
7371 - Custom Computer Programming Services (P-11974)

Craig Charlton, *
Jennifer Stagnaro, *
Glenn Cross, *
David Gearhart, *
EMP: 110 EST: 2004
SQ FT: 40,000
SALES (est): 49.43MM
SALES (corp-wide): 49.43MM Privately Held
Web: www.sugarcrm.com
SIC: 7371 Computer software development

(P-11955)
SUMO LOGIC INC (PA)
Also Called: Sumo Logic
305 Main St (94063-1729)
PHONE..................650 810-8700
Joe Kim, Pr
Christian Beedgen, *
Stewart Grierson, CFO
Suku Krishnaraj Chettiar, CMO
EMP: 889 EST: 2010
SQ FT: 56,000
SALES (est): 300.67MM
SALES (corp-wide): 300.67MM Privately Held
Web: www.sumologic.com
SIC: 7371 Computer software development

(P-11956)
SUPER EVIL MEGA CORP (PA)
119a S B St (94401-3908)
PHONE..................650 696-0608
Kristian Segerstrale, CEO
Robert Daly, CEO
Kristian Federstrale, COO
EMP: 67 EST: 2012
SALES (est): 10.33MM
SALES (corp-wide): 10.33MM Privately Held
Web: www.superevilmegacorp.com
SIC: 7371 Computer software development and applications

(P-11957)
SYBASE 365 LLC
1 Sybase Dr (94568-7976)
PHONE..................925 236-5000
EMP: 78 EST: 2000
SALES (est): 4.69MM
SALES (corp-wide): 32.06B Privately Held
Web: www.sybase.com
SIC: 7371 Computer software development
HQ: Sap America, Inc.
   3999 West Chester Pike
   Newtown Square PA
   610 661-1000

(P-11958)
SYMITAR SYSTEMS INC
8985 Balboa Ave (92123-1507)
PHONE..................619 542-6700
EMP: 220 EST: 1984
SALES (est): 36.66MM
SALES (corp-wide): 2.08B Publicly Held
Web: www.jackhenry.com
SIC: 7371 Computer software development
PA: Jack Henry & Associates, Inc.
   663 W Highway 60
   Monett MO
   417 235-6652

(P-11959)
SYNACK INC (PA)
Also Called: SYNACK
303 Twin Dolphin Dr Fl 6 (94065-1497)
PHONE..................855 796-2251
Jay Kaplan, CEO
Jim Roll Ctrl, Prin
EMP: 248 EST: 2013

SALES (est): 55.12MM
SALES (corp-wide): 55.12MM Privately Held
Web: www.synack.com
SIC: 7371 Software programming applications

(P-11960)
SYNARC INC (DH)
Also Called: Bioclinica
777 Mariners Island Blvd Ste 550 (94404-1562)
PHONE..................415 817-8900
Claus Christiansen, CEO
Harry K Genant, *
David Buhler, *
Aaron Timm, *
Ralf Reyes, *
EMP: 153 EST: 1998
SALES (est): 35.46MM
SALES (corp-wide): 1.37MM Privately Held
SIC: 7371 Computer software development and applications
HQ: Bioclinica, Inc.
   1818 Market St
   Philadelphia PA

(P-11961)
SYNOPHIC SYSTEMS INC
19925 Stevens Creek Blvd (95014-2305)
PHONE..................408 459-7676
Kondal Balusu, CEO
EMP: 500 EST: 2010
SALES (est): 25MM Privately Held
Web: www.prodapt.com
SIC: 7371 7373 4899 Computer software systems analysis and design, custom; Systems engineering, computer related; Communication signal enhancement network services

(P-11962)
SYRINX CONSULTING CORP
1919 S Bascom Ave (95008-2242)
P.O. Box 920201 (02492-0003)
PHONE..................781 487-7800
Andrew Gelina, CEO
Colin Reposa, Pr
Patricia Gelina, *
EMP: 65 EST: 1998
SALES (est): 8.69MM
SALES (corp-wide): 9.33MM Privately Held
Web: www.syrinx.com
SIC: 7371 Computer software development
PA: Dewinter Group, Llc
   1919 S Bascom Ave Ste 250
   Campbell CA
   408 297-7500

(P-11963)
SYSDIG INC (PA)
135 Main St 21st Fl (94105-1812)
PHONE..................415 872-9473
Suresh Vasudevan, CEO
Bryce Hein, CMO*
Karen Walker, *
EMP: 207 EST: 2013
SALES (est): 27.97MM
SALES (corp-wide): 27.97MM Privately Held
Web: www.sysdig.com
SIC: 7371 Computer software development

(P-11964)
SYSTECH SOLUTIONS INC (PA)
500 N Brand Blvd Ste 1900 (91203-3308)
PHONE..................818 550-9690
Arun Gollapudi, Pr

Srinivasan Ramaswamy, *
Ashish Parikh, *
EMP: 81 EST: 1993
SQ FT: 1,500
SALES (est): 23.82MM
SALES (corp-wide): 23.82MM Privately Held
Web: www.systechusa.com
SIC: 7371 Computer software systems analysis and design, custom

(P-11965)
TALENT & ACQUISITION LLC
Also Called: Stand 8 Technology Services
3020 Old Ranch Pkwy Ste 300 (90740-2751)
PHONE..................888 970-9575
Quinn Fillmon, Managing Member
EMP: 150 EST: 2009
SALES (est): 10.43MM Privately Held
Web: www.stand8.io
SIC: 7371 7379 7363 7361 Computer software development and applications; Computer related consulting services; Help supply services; Employment agencies

(P-11966)
TANGIBLE PLAY INC (HQ)
Also Called: Tangible Play
195 Page Mill Rd Ste 105 (94306-2073)
PHONE..................650 667-1693
Pramod Sharma, CEO
Jerome Scholler, *
EMP: 100 EST: 2013
SALES (est): 14.48MM Privately Held
SIC: 7371 3944 Software programming applications; Board games, children's and adults'
PA: Think & Learn Private Limited
   Ibc Knowledge Park, 4/1, 2nd Floor, Tower D
   Bengaluru KA

(P-11967)
TAO DIGITAL SOLUTIONS INC ✪
4699 Old Ironsides Dr Ste 430 (95054-1824)
PHONE..................408 391-0930
Rajkumar Velagapudi, Prin
EMP: 200 EST: 2022
SALES (est): 6.98MM Privately Held
SIC: 7371 Software programming applications

(P-11968)
TAPESTRY SOLUTIONS INC (HQ)
6910 Carroll Rd (92121-2211)
PHONE..................858 503-1990
Geoff Evans, Pr
Vince Montepare, *
Mark Young, *
Mary Ann Wagner, *
EMP: 125 EST: 1993
SQ FT: 36,073
SALES (est): 48.95MM
SALES (corp-wide): 66.61B Publicly Held
Web: www.tapestrysolutions.com
SIC: 7371 5045 Custom computer programming services; Computer software
PA: The Boeing Company
   929 Long Bridge Dr
   Arlington VA
   703 414-6338

(P-11969)
TASK HELP LLC
1390 Market St Ste 200 (94102-5404)
PHONE..................833 229-0726
EMP: 68 EST: 2019

SALES (est): 9.66MM Privately Held
Web: www.task.help
SIC: 7371 Software programming applications

(P-11970)
TAULIA LLC (HQ)
Also Called: Taulia
95 3rd St Ste 284 (94103-3103)
PHONE..................415 376-8280
Cedric Bru, Pr
Rene Ho, *
EMP: 199 EST: 2009
SALES (est): 33.31MM
SALES (corp-wide): 32.06B Privately Held
Web: www.taulia.com
SIC: 7371 Computer software development
PA: Sap Se
   Dietmar-Hopp-Allee 16
   Walldorf BW
   622 774-7474

(P-11971)
TAVANT TECHNOLOGIES INC (PA)
3965 Freedom Cir Ste 750 (95054-1285)
PHONE..................408 519-5400
Sarvesh Mahesh, CEO
Manish Arya, *
Venkata Devana, *
Rajiv Ranjan, *
Jerome Marr, *
EMP: 167 EST: 2000
SALES (est): 94.96MM
SALES (corp-wide): 94.96MM Privately Held
Web: www.tavant.com
SIC: 7371 Computer software development

(P-11972)
TCG SOFTWARE SERVICES INC
320 Commerce Ste 200 (92602-1363)
PHONE..................714 665-6200
Greg Blevins, Brnch Mgr
EMP: 278
SIC: 7371 Custom computer programming services
PA: Tcg Software Services, Inc.
   265 Davidson Ave Ste 220
   Somerset NJ

(P-11973)
TEBRA TECHNOLOGIES INC (PA)
Also Called: Kareo PM
1111 Bayside Dr Ste 150 (92625-1762)
P.O. Box 1922 (92616)
PHONE..................888 775-2736
Daniel Rodrigues, CEO
Tom Giannulli, CMO*
Tom Patterson, *
James Armijo, *
Jason Leu, *
EMP: 232 EST: 2004
SALES (est): 95.22MM Privately Held
Web: www.kareo.com
SIC: 7371 Computer software development

(P-11974)
TELESTREAM LLC (PA)
848 Gold Flat Rd (95959-3208)
PHONE..................530 470-1300
Daniel Castles, CEO
Scott Puopolo, CEO
Mark Cuny, CFO
Dan Castles, *
▲ EMP: 100 EST: 1998
SALES (est): 122.84MM
SALES (corp-wide): 122.84MM Privately Held

7371 - Custom Computer Programming Services (P-11975)

Web: www.telestream.net
SIC: 7371 Computer software development and applications

(P-11975)
THISMOMENT INC
690 Market St Unit 1101 (94104-5123)
PHONE...................................415 200-4730
EMP: 135 EST: 2008
SQ FT: 15,000
SALES (est): 12.69MM Privately Held
Web: www.thismoment.com
SIC: 7371 Computer software development

(P-11976)
THOMAS GALLAWAY CORPORATION (PA)
Also Called: Technologent
100 Spectrum Center Dr Ste 700 (92618-4962)
PHONE...................................949 517-9500
Lezlie Gallaway, CEO
Thomas Gallaway, *
Marco Mohajer, *
Mike Mclaughlin, VP
Jim Bevis, *
EMP: 70 EST: 2002
SQ FT: 4,500
SALES (est): 471.27MM
SALES (corp-wide): 471.27MM Privately Held
Web: www.technologent.com
SIC: 7371 Computer software development

(P-11977)
THREATMETRIX INC (DH)
160 W Santa Clara St Ste 1400 (95113-1732)
PHONE...................................408 200-5700
Reed Taussig, Pr
Alisdair Faulkner, Chief Products Officer
Frank Teruel, CFO
EMP: 165 EST: 2008
SQ FT: 10,000
SALES (est): 31.37MM
SALES (corp-wide): 10.3B Privately Held
Web: risk.lexisnexis.com
SIC: 7371 7374 7382 Computer software development and applications; Computer processing services; Security systems services
HQ: Lexisnexis Risk Solutions Inc.
1000 Alderman Dr
Alpharetta GA
678 694-6000

(P-11978)
THUNKABLE INC
605 Market St Ste 700 (94105-3217)
P.O. Box 22162 (94122-0162)
PHONE...................................415 200-3736
Arun Karthik Saigal, CEO
EMP: 113 EST: 2015
SALES (est): 7.95MM Privately Held
Web: www.thunkable.com
SIC: 7371 Computer software development and applications

(P-11979)
TICKETMANAGER
26635 Agoura Rd Ste 200 (91302-3810)
PHONE...................................818 698-3616
EMP: 69 EST: 2016
SALES (est): 2.65MM Privately Held
Web: www.ticketmanager.com
SIC: 7371 Computer software development and applications

(P-11980)
TIGHTDB INC
Also Called: Realm
100 Forest Ave (94301-1612)
PHONE...................................415 766-2020
Alexander Stigsen, CEO
Bjarne Christiansen, *
EMP: 60 EST: 2011
SALES (est): 3.26MM Privately Held
Web: www.tightdb.com
SIC: 7371 Computer software development and applications

(P-11981)
TONOMI INC
4600 Bohannon Dr Ste 220 (94025-1044)
PHONE...................................650 523-5000
Victoria Livschitz, CEO
EMP: 258 EST: 2010
SALES (est): 501.16K
SALES (corp-wide): 310.48MM Publicly Held
SIC: 7371 Computer software development
HQ: Ririo.Com, Inc.
5000 Executive Pkwy # 520
San Ramon CA

(P-11982)
TORREY POINT GROUP LLC
Also Called: Torreypoint
1350 Dell Ave Ste 206 (95008-6619)
PHONE...................................408 734-1500
▼ EMP: 80
SIC: 7371 Custom computer programming services

(P-11983)
TOUCHPINT REST INNOVATIONS INC
Also Called: Touchpoint Rest Innovations
263 California Ave (94306-1912)
PHONE...................................800 992-9540
Israel L'heureux, Pr
EMP: 119 EST: 2012
SALES (est): 6.2MM Privately Held
Web: www.touchpoint.io
SIC: 7371 Computer software development

(P-11984)
TRACKR INC
7410 Hollister Ave (93117-2583)
PHONE...................................855 981-1690
Christopher G Herbert, CEO
Christian J Smith, *
Nathan Kelly, *
Matthew Pigeon, *
EMP: 100 EST: 2009
SQ FT: 40,000
SALES (est): 8.78MM Privately Held
Web: www.thetrackr.com
SIC: 7371 Computer software development

(P-11985)
TRADE DESK INC (PA)
Also Called: THETRADEDESK
42 N Chestnut St (93001-2662)
PHONE...................................805 585-3434
Jeff T Green, Ch Bd
Blake J Grayson, CFO
David R Pickles, *
Jay R Grant, CLO
EMP: 271 EST: 2009
SALES (est): 1.58B
SALES (corp-wide): 1.58B Publicly Held
Web: www.thetradedesk.com
SIC: 7371 7372 Software programming applications; Prepackaged software

(P-11986)
TRANTOR INC
Also Called: Trantor
3723 Haven Ave (94025-1011)
PHONE...................................650 777-5480
Sriram Iyer, CEO
Pradeep Bakshi, *
EMP: 1100 EST: 2012
SALES (est): 25MM Privately Held
Web: www.trantorinc.com
SIC: 7371 Computer software development

(P-11987)
TREASURE DATA INC (HQ)
800 W El Camino Real Ste 180 (94040)
PHONE...................................866 899-5386
Kazuki Ohta, CEO
Dan Weirich, *
Hiroshi Nakamura, *
Kim Bronstein, CPO*
EMP: 72 EST: 2011
SALES (est): 24.25MM Privately Held
Web: www.treasuredata.com
SIC: 7371 7374 Custom computer programming services; Optical scanning data service
PA: Svf Holdco (Uk) Limited
69 Grosvenor Street
London

(P-11988)
TRIBRIDGE HOLDINGS LLC
523 W 6th St Ste 830 (90014-1243)
PHONE...................................813 287-8887
Criatritinia Valentin, Brnch Mgr
EMP: 512
SALES (corp-wide): 14.43B Publicly Held
SIC: 7371 Computer software development
HQ: Tribridge Holdings, Llc
20408 Bashan Dr Ste 231
Ashburn VA

(P-11989)
TROVATA INC (PA)
Also Called: Trovata
312 S Cedros Ave Ste 312 (92075-1943)
PHONE...................................312 914-8106
Brett Turner, CEO
Scott Harrington, *
Joseph Drambarean, *
EMP: 88 EST: 2016
SALES (est): 9.19MM
SALES (corp-wide): 9.19MM Privately Held
Web: www.trovata.io
SIC: 7371 Computer software development

(P-11990)
TROVE INFORMATION TECH INC (PA)
Also Called: Pave
1 Montgomery St Ste 700 (94104-4536)
PHONE...................................610 945-6533
Matthew Schulman, CEO
EMP: 135 EST: 2019
SALES (est): 16MM
SALES (corp-wide): 16MM Privately Held
Web: www.pave.com
SIC: 7371 Computer software development

(P-11991)
TRUCKING JOBS TECHNOLOGIES INC
19925 Stevns Crk Blvd # 100 (95014-2384)
PHONE...................................202 918-2404
EMP: 209 EST: 2019
SALES (est): 7.06MM Privately Held
SIC: 7371 Custom computer programming services

(P-11992)
TRUE NORTH AMERICA INC
Also Called: Truenorth
8 Cadiz Cir (94065-1333)
PHONE...................................877 525-8783
Alexander Gonikman, CEO
EMP: 65 EST: 2018
SALES (est): 2.52MM Privately Held
SIC: 7371 Computer software development

(P-11993)
TRUEWORK
325 Pacific Ave Fl 2 (94111-1714)
PHONE...................................833 878-3967
EMP: 170 EST: 2019
SALES (est): 15.58MM Privately Held
Web: www.truework.com
SIC: 7371 Custom computer programming services

(P-11994)
TRUSSWORKS INC
Also Called: Truss
548 Market St # 97444 (94104-5401)
PHONE...................................415 891-0828
Everett Harper, CEO
Jennifer Leech, *
EMP: 145 EST: 2012
SALES (est): 20.5MM Privately Held
Web: www.truss.works
SIC: 7371 Custom computer programming services

(P-11995)
TRYFACTA INC
Also Called: Systems America Public Sector
4637 Chabot Dr Ste 100 (94588-2753)
PHONE...................................408 419-9200
Ratika Tyagi, CEO
EMP: 351 EST: 1996
SALES (est): 42.79MM Privately Held
Web: www.tryfacta.com
SIC: 7371 7361 7373 8748 Computer software systems analysis and design, custom; Labor contractors (employment agency); Systems software development services; Systems engineering consultant, ex. computer or professional

(P-11996)
TURING VIDEO
1730 S El Camino Real Ste 480 (94402)
PHONE...................................877 730-8222
Song Cao, CEO
Ron Rothman, *
Christopher Zenalty, *
Daisy Li Cos, Prin
Qing Li, CFO
EMP: 70 EST: 2017
SALES (est): 6.23MM Privately Held
Web: www.turing.ai
SIC: 7371 Computer software development and applications

(P-11997)
TWILIO SEGMENT
100 California St Ste 700 (94111-4512)
PHONE...................................415 603-6900
EMP: 244 EST: 2017
SALES (est): 7.37MM Privately Held
Web: www.segment.com
SIC: 7371 Computer software development

(P-11998)
UBICS INC
1050 Bridgeway (94965-2173)
PHONE...................................415 289-1400
Vijay Mallya, Brnch Mgr
EMP: 140

PRODUCTS & SERVICES SECTION
7371 - Custom Computer Programming Services (P-12020)

Web: www.ubics.com
SIC: 7371 Custom computer programming services
PA: Ubics, Inc.
400 Sthpinte Blvd Ste 425
Canonsburg PA

(P-11999)
UBISOFT HOLDINGS INC
Also Called: Red Storm
625 3rd St Fl 3 (94107-1918)
PHONE.................................415 547-4000
EMP: 192
SIC: 7371 Computer software writing services

(P-12000)
UJWAL INC
Also Called: Level Ai
148 Castro St Unit 2a (94041-2811)
PHONE.................................503 708-4410
Ashish Nagar, CEO
EMP: 60 EST: 2018
SALES (est): 2.98MM Privately Held
SIC: 7371 Software programming applications

(P-12001)
ULTIMO SOFTWARE SOLUTIONS INC
33268 Central Ave # 2 (94587-2010)
PHONE.................................408 943-1490
Venkatasubhash Pasumarthy, Pr
Venkatasubhash Pasumarthy, Pr
Smita Pasumarthi, *
EMP: 127 EST: 2002
SQ FT: 4,000
SALES (est): 7.16MM Privately Held
Web: www.ultimosoft.com
SIC: 7371 Computer software development

(P-12002)
UNISYS CORPORATION
9701 Jeronimo Rd Ste 100 (92618-2076)
PHONE.................................949 380-5000
Carmen Lynch, Mgr
EMP: 142
SALES (corp-wide): 1.98B Publicly Held
Web: www.unisys.com
SIC: 7371 Computer software development
PA: Unisys Corporation
801 Lakeview Dr Ste 100
Blue Bell PA
215 986-4011

(P-12003)
UNITED SUPPORT SERVICES INC
3252 Holiday Ct Ste 110 (92037-1807)
PHONE.................................858 373-9500
Michael Fernandez, Pr
EMP: 190 EST: 2003
SQ FT: 2,600
SALES (est): 15MM Privately Held
Web: www.usscompany.com
SIC: 7371 8711 Custom computer programming services; Consulting engineer

(P-12004)
UNITY SOFTWARE INC (PA)
30 3rd St (94103-3104)
PHONE.................................415 539-3162
John Riccitiello, Ex Ch Bd
John Riccitiello, Ex Ch Bd
Luis Visoso, Ex VP
Carol Carpenter, CMO
Anirma Gupta, Corporate Secretary
EMP: 267 EST: 2004
SQ FT: 86,000
SALES (est): 1.39B
SALES (corp-wide): 1.39B Publicly Held
Web: www.unity.com
SIC: 7371 7372 Computer software development; Prepackaged software

(P-12005)
UNRAVEL DATA SYSTEMS INC
801 High St (94301-2421)
PHONE.................................650 741-3442
EMP: 75 EST: 2013
SALES (est): 2.29MM Privately Held
SIC: 7371 Custom computer programming services

(P-12006)
USERTESTING TECHNOLOGIES INC
1484 Pollard Rd # 271 (95032-1031)
PHONE.................................888 877-1882
Andy Macmillan, CEO
Alfonso De La Nuez, *
Xavier Mestres, *
Arthur Moan, OF CUST SUCCESS & EUROPE*
Matt Paulus, Senior Account Executive*
EMP: 80 EST: 2007
SALES (est): 11.2MM Privately Held
Web: www.usertesting.com
SIC: 7371 Computer software development

(P-12007)
USHUR INC (PA)
3975 Freedom Cir (95054-1241)
PHONE.................................408 744-6802
Simha Sadasiva, CEO
EMP: 148 EST: 2014
SALES (est): 10.66MM
SALES (corp-wide): 10.66MM Privately Held
Web: www.ushur.com
SIC: 7371 Computer software development

(P-12008)
UST GLOBAL INC (HQ)
Also Called: UST
5 Polaris Way (92656-5374)
PHONE.................................949 716-8757
Krishna Sudheendra, CEO
Paras Chandaria, *
Arun Narayanan, *
Sunil Kanchi, CIO*
Murali Gopalan, CCO*
EMP: 100 EST: 2007
SQ FT: 20,000
SALES (est): 511.43MM Privately Held
SIC: 7371 Computer software development
PA: Ust Holdings Ltd
C/O R&H Services Limited
Hamilton

(P-12009)
V2SOLUTIONS INC
7150 Rainbow Dr Apt 18 (95129-4546)
PHONE.................................408 981-3075
Vijay G Shah, Brnch Mgr
EMP: 79
Web: www.v2solutions.com
SIC: 7371 Computer software development
PA: V2solutions, Inc.
2340 Walsh Ave Ste D
Santa Clara CA

(P-12010)
VAGARO INC
Also Called: Vagaro
4430 Rosewood Dr # 500 (94588-3050)
PHONE.................................800 919-0157
Fred Helou, CEO
EMP: 194 EST: 2009
SALES (est): 17.66MM Privately Held
Web: www.vagaro.com
SIC: 7371 Custom computer programming services

(P-12011)
VALGENESIS INC (PA)
5201 Great America Pkwy Ste 354 (95054-1127)
PHONE.................................510 445-0505
Siva Samy, CEO
Kevin O'donnell, CFO
Steve Reynolds, CRO*
Narayan Raj, *
Mike Hicks, *
▼ EMP: 85 EST: 2005
SALES (est): 10.54MM
SALES (corp-wide): 10.54MM Privately Held
Web: www.valgenesis.com
SIC: 7371 5045 Computer software development and applications; Computer software

(P-12012)
VALLEY AGRICULTURAL SFTWR INC
220 S Akers St Ste E (93291-5185)
PHONE.................................559 686-9496
Connor Jameson, Pr
Steve Eicker, *
William Avila, *
Manuel Soares, *
John Mitchell, *
EMP: 311 EST: 1986
SALES (est): 21.23MM Privately Held
Web: www.vas.com
SIC: 7371 Software programming applications

(P-12013)
VCOMPLY TECHNOLOGIES INC
75 E Santa Clara St Fl 6 (95113-1827)
PHONE.................................650 319-8842
Harsh Kariwala, CEO
EMP: 100 EST: 2016
SALES (est): 5.31MM Privately Held
Web: www.v-comply.com
SIC: 7371 Computer software development

(P-12014)
VEGATEK CORPORATION
Also Called: Intellective
470 Wald (92618-4638)
P.O. Box 436057 (40253-6057)
PHONE.................................949 502-0090
Matthew Barnickle, CEO
Boris Zhilin, *
EMP: 70 EST: 2005
SQ FT: 6,000
SALES (est): 8.56MM Privately Held
Web: www.intellective.com
SIC: 7371 7379 6411 Computer software development; Computer related consulting services; Insurance information and consulting services

(P-12015)
VENDOR DIRECT SOLUTIONS LLC (PA)
515 S Figueroa St Ste 1900 (90071-3336)
PHONE.................................213 362-5622
Jules Buenabenta, Managing Member
Jim Young, *
Ron Mcelhaney, Dir Opers
Angel E Nevarez, *
Stephanie Simmons, *
EMP: 247 EST: 2006
SQ FT: 1,200
SALES (est): 25.02MM Privately Held

Web: www.teamvds.com
SIC: 7371 Computer software development

(P-12016)
VERITAS TECHNOLOGIES LLC (DH)
Also Called: Veritas
2625 Augustine Dr (95054-2956)
PHONE.................................866 837-4827
Greg Hughes, CEO
John Gannon, Ex VP
Matt Cain, CPO
Brett Shirk, Ex VP
Mick Lopez, CFO
EMP: 200 EST: 2014
SALES (est): 191.9MM
SALES (corp-wide): 4.44B Publicly Held
Web: www.veritas.com
SIC: 7371 7375 Computer software development and applications; Information retrieval services
HQ: Veritas Holdings Ltd.
C/O Ocorian Services (Bermuda) Limited
Hamilton

(P-12017)
VERITAS TECHNOLOGIES LLC
16501 Ventura Blvd Ste 400 (91436-2007)
PHONE.................................310 202-0757
EMP: 200
SALES (corp-wide): 4.44B Publicly Held
Web: www.veritas.com
SIC: 7371 7375 Computer software development and applications; Data base information retrieval
HQ: Veritas Technologies Llc
2625 Augustine Dr
Santa Clara CA
866 837-4827

(P-12018)
VERITAS US INC
2625 Augustine Dr (95054-2956)
PHONE.................................650 933-1000
Greg Huges, CEO
EMP: 200 EST: 2014
SALES (est): 62.75MM Privately Held
Web: www.veritas.com
SIC: 7371 Computer software development and applications

(P-12019)
VERSA NETWORKS INC (PA)
2550 Great America Way Ste 350 (95054-1165)
PHONE.................................408 385-7660
Kulvinder Ahuja, CEO
Kelly Ahuja, CEO
Kumar Mehta, Chief Development Officer
Pankaj Patel, Prin
EMP: 101 EST: 2012
SQ FT: 37,000
SALES (est): 100.32MM
SALES (corp-wide): 100.32MM Privately Held
Web: www.versa-networks.com
SIC: 7371 Computer software development

(P-12020)
VERSEIO INC
Also Called: Short Sale Agent Finder
550 W B St Fl 4 (92101-3581)
PHONE.................................888 373-9942
Tal David, CEO
EMP: 90 EST: 2012
SALES (est): 8.44MM Privately Held
Web: www.verse.io
SIC: 7371 Software programming applications

7371 - Custom Computer Programming Services (P-12021)

(P-12021)
VIDA HEALTH INC
100 Montgomery St Ste 750 (94104-4301)
PHONE............................415 989-1017
Stephanie Tilenius, CEO
Cynthia Mark, CCO*
EMP: 100 EST: 2013
SALES (est): 7.82MM Privately Held
Web: www.vida.com
SIC: 7371 Computer software development and applications

(P-12022)
VIDEOJEEVES INC
45333 Fremont Blvd Ste 5 (94538-6317)
PHONE............................877 958-8129
Kenneth Perks, Pr
EMP: 250 EST: 2017
SALES (est): 5.91MM Privately Held
Web: www.videojeeves.com
SIC: 7371 8742 Computer software development and applications; Marketing consulting services

(P-12023)
VIM INC
548 Market St Pmb 84904 (94104-5401)
PHONE............................910 727-1834
Oron Afek, CEO
EMP: 120 EST: 2015
SALES (est): 9.15MM Privately Held
Web: www.getvim.com
SIC: 7371 Computer software development

(P-12024)
VIRTUNET LLC
Also Called: Virtunet Systems
1900 S Norfolk St Ste 300 (94403-1165)
PHONE............................650 847-8633
EMP: 64 EST: 2010
SQ FT: 1,000
SALES (est): 2.54MM Privately Held
Web: www.virtunetsystems.com
SIC: 7371 Computer software development

(P-12025)
VISION SOLUTIONS INC (HQ)
15300 Barranca Pkwy (92618-2200)
PHONE............................949 253-6500
Nicolaas Vlok, Pr
Alan Arnold, *
Don Scott, *
Robert Johnson, *
Wm Edward Vesely, CMO*
▲ EMP: 90 EST: 1989
SQ FT: 25,000
SALES (est): 51.14MM
SALES (corp-wide): 446.91MM Privately Held
SIC: 7371 7373 Computer software development; Systems integration services
PA: Precisely Software Incorporated
1700 District Ave Ste 300
Burlington MA
978 436-8900

(P-12026)
VISIQUATE INC
520 3rd St Ste 300 (95401-6414)
PHONE............................707 546-4377
Brian Robertson, CEO
EMP: 129 EST: 2009
SALES (est): 10.16MM Privately Held
Web: www.visiquate.com
SIC: 7371 Computer software development

(P-12027)
VISUAL CONCEPTS ENTERTAINMENT
10 Hamilton Landing (94949-8207)
PHONE............................415 479-3634
Gregory Thomas, Pr
Scott Patterson, VP
EMP: 301 EST: 1988
SALES (est): 5.4MM Publicly Held
Web: www.vcentertainment.com
SIC: 7371 Computer software development
PA: Take-Two Interactive Software, Inc.
110 W 44th St
New York NY

(P-12028)
VISUAL SUPPLY COMPANY (PA)
Also Called: Vsco
1500 Broadway Ste 300 (94612-2002)
PHONE............................847 721-9285
Joel Flory, CEO
Bryan Mason, *
EMP: 93 EST: 2011
SQ FT: 50,000
SALES (est): 22.44MM
SALES (corp-wide): 22.44MM Privately Held
Web: www.vsco.co
SIC: 7371 Computer software development

(P-12029)
VIVID DIGITAL
Also Called: Vivid Interactive
1933 N Bronson Ave Apt 209 (90068-5603)
PHONE............................818 908-0481
EMP: 60 EST: 1993
SALES (est): 2.01MM Privately Held
Web: www.vividtv.com
SIC: 7371 7812 Computer software development and applications; Motion picture and video production

(P-12030)
VM SERVICES INC (DH)
1621 Barber Ln (95035-7455)
PHONE............................510 744-3720
Chin Tong Wong, CEO
▲ EMP: 120 EST: 1996
SALES (est): 63.35MM Privately Held
Web: www.venturemfg-usa.com
SIC: 7371 Computer software development
HQ: Cebelian Holdings Pte Ltd
5006 Ang Mo Kio Avenue 5
Singapore

(P-12031)
VM SERVICES INC
6723 Mowry Ave (94560-4927)
PHONE............................510 744-3720
EMP: 90
Web: www.venturemfg-usa.com
SIC: 7371 Computer software development
HQ: Vm Services, Inc.
1621 Barber Ln
Milpitas CA
510 744-3720

(P-12032)
VRP CONSULTING INC
268 Bush St 3836 (94104-3503)
PHONE............................415 225-6466
Roman Medvedev, Pr
Niels Andersen, *
EMP: 572 EST: 1998
SQ FT: 1,000
SALES (est): 36.12MM Privately Held
Web: www.vrpconsulting.com
SIC: 7371 8742 Computer software development; Industry specialist consultants

(P-12033)
VWISE INC
85 Enterprise Ste 320 (92656-2504)
PHONE............................949 716-1276
Tony F Mingo, CEO
Dave Ferrigno, *
EMP: 60 EST: 2007
SALES (est): 4.16MM Privately Held
Web: www.vwise.com
SIC: 7371 Computer software development

(P-12034)
WANCLOUDS INC
2811 Mission College Blvd Fl 7 (95054-1884)
PHONE............................408 663-6753
Faiz Khan, CEO
Amir Gohar, *
EMP: 60 EST: 2013
SALES (est): 3.87MM Privately Held
Web: www.wanclouds.net
SIC: 7371 Computer software development

(P-12035)
WATERWISEONE
23411 Aliso Viejo Pkwy (92656-1532)
PHONE............................866 758-4393
Chris Mathews, Ex Dir
Shama Niazo, Ch Bd
EMP: 89 EST: 2008
SALES (est): 18.9MM Privately Held
SIC: 7371 8748 Software programming applications; Energy conservation consultant

(P-12036)
WATT INC
Also Called: Northstar
8605 Santa Monica Blvd Pmb 65044 (90069-4109)
PHONE............................310 896-8197
William Peng, CEO
Matthew Mattison, Pr
EMP: 70 EST: 2016
SALES (est): 4.88MM Privately Held
Web: www.northstarmoney.com
SIC: 7371 Computer software development and applications

(P-12037)
WAYVE TECHNOLOGIES INC
709 N Shoreline Blvd (94043-3208)
PHONE............................832 651-4438
Alex Kendall, CEO
EMP: 150 EST: 2021
SALES (est): 5.34MM Privately Held
Web: www.wayve.ai
SIC: 7371 Computer software development and applications

(P-12038)
WERIDE CORP
2630 Orchard Pkwy (95134-2020)
PHONE............................408 645-7118
Qing Lu, CEO
EMP: 106 EST: 2017
SALES (est): 3.01MM Privately Held
Web: www.weride.ai
SIC: 7371 Computer software development

(P-12039)
WHI SOLUTIONS INC (HQ)
2145 Hamilton Ave (95125-5905)
PHONE............................914 697-9301
Bryan Murphy, Pr
Dan Grace, *
EMP: 60 EST: 1998
SALES (est): 15.17MM Publicly Held
Web: www.whisolutions.com
SIC: 7371 Computer software development
PA: Ebay Inc.
2025 Hamilton Ave
San Jose CA

(P-12040)
WHITERABBITAI INC
3930 Freedom Cir Ste 101 (95054-1246)
P.O. Box 6465 (95056-6465)
PHONE............................408 215-8876
Rakesh Mathur, Pr
Maureen O'connor, Pr
Jason Su, *
EMP: 60 EST: 2018
SALES (est): 5.48MM Privately Held
Web: www.whiterabbit.ai
SIC: 7371 Computer software development and applications

(P-12041)
WIDEORBIT LLC (PA)
Also Called: Wideorbit
1160 Battery St Ste 300 (94111-1212)
PHONE............................415 675-6700
Eric Mathewson, CEO
Kathy Crawford Past, Pr
Brian Lilly, Owner
Nathan Gans, *
Mike Zinsmeister, *
EMP: 85 EST: 1999
SQ FT: 9,000
SALES (est): 24.64MM Privately Held
Web: www.wideorbit.com
SIC: 7371 Computer software development

(P-12042)
WISE COMMERCE INC
1730 S El Camino Real Ste 500 (94402)
PHONE............................855 469-4737
Arie Shpanya, CEO
EMP: 105 EST: 2013
SALES (est): 761.87K Privately Held
Web: www.wiser.com
SIC: 7371 Computer software development

(P-12043)
WISETACK INC
460 Brannan St Unit 78384 (94107-7622)
PHONE............................415 918-2380
EMP: 129
SALES (est): 2.05MM Privately Held
Web: www.wisetack.com
SIC: 7371 Computer software development and applications

(P-12044)
WOOCOMMERCE INC
60 29th St (94110-4929)
PHONE............................650 388-0901
Matt Mullenweg, CEO
EMP: 400 EST: 2020
SALES (est): 26.57MM Privately Held
Web: www.automattic.com
SIC: 7371 Software programming applications

(P-12045)
WORKATO INC (PA)
215 Castro St Fl 3 (94041-2821)
PHONE............................844 469-6752
Vijay Tella, CEO
EMP: 746 EST: 2013
SALES (est): 59.86MM
SALES (corp-wide): 59.86MM Privately Held
Web: www.workato.com
SIC: 7371 Software programming applications

(P-12046)
WORKDAY INC (PA)
Also Called: Workday
6110 Stoneridge Mall Rd (94588-3211)
PHONE............................925 951-9000

PRODUCTS & SERVICES SECTION
7371 - Custom Computer Programming Services (P-12069)

Aneel Bhusri, *Ch Bd*
Carl M Eschenbach, *
George J Still Junior, *V Ch Bd*
EMP: 1334 **EST:** 2005
SQ FT: 1,200,000
SALES (est): 6.22B **Publicly Held**
Web: www.workday.com
SIC: 7371 7374 Custom computer programming services; Data processing and preparation

(P-12047)
WORKFORCELOGIC
425 California St (94104-2102)
PHONE.................707 939-4300
Catherine Candland, *CEO*
Catherine Wingate, *Senior Vice President Global Service*
Stuart Thompto, *Senior Vice President Product Development*
Glen Tolleson, *Client Services Vice President*
Steve Furtado, *CFO*
EMP: 90 **EST:** 2000
SALES (est): 7.21MM **Privately Held**
SIC: 7371 7361 Computer software development; Executive placement
HQ: Workforcelogic Llc
999 Stewart Ave Ste 100
Bethpage NY
877 937-6242

(P-12048)
WORKSPAN
3 Twin Dolphin Dr Ste 350 (94065-1027)
PHONE.................650 223-4243
Amit Sina, *Prin*
EMP: 70 **EST:** 2017
SALES (est): 1.8MM **Privately Held**
Web: www.workspan.com
SIC: 7371 Computer software development

(P-12049)
WORKSTREAM TECHNOLOGIES INC
521 7th St (94103-4709)
PHONE.................415 767-1006
Huang Hui Lim, *CEO*
EMP: 76 **EST:** 2016
SALES (est): 7.4MM **Privately Held**
Web: www.workstream.us
SIC: 7371 Computer software development and applications

(P-12050)
WOVEN BY TOYOTA US INC
Also Called: Woven Planet North America Inc
900 Arastradero Rd (94304-1332)
PHONE.................808 221-7117
Luc Vincent, *Pr*
EMP: 300 **EST:** 2021
SALES (est): 46.82MM **Privately Held**
SIC: 7371 Custom computer programming services
PA: Toyota Motor Corporation
1, Toyotacho
Toyota AIC

(P-12051)
XACTLY CORPORATION (HQ)
221 Los Gatos Saratoga Rd (95030-5308)
PHONE.................408 977-3132
Christopher W Cabrera, *CEO*
L Evan Ellis Junior, *Pr*
Joseph C Consul, *
Elizabeth Salomon, *
Marc Gemassmer, *CSO*
EMP: 75 **EST:** 2005
SALES (est): 90.1MM
SALES (corp-wide): 140.98MM **Privately Held**
Web: www.xactlycorp.com
SIC: 7371 7372 Software programming applications; Prepackaged software
PA: Excalibur Parent, Llc
300 Park Ave Ste 1700
San Jose CA
408 977-3132

(P-12052)
XBP INC
Also Called: Voipment
333 El Camino Real Ste 201 (92780)
PHONE.................888 895-7116
John Lloyd Davis, *CEO*
Moe Navid, *
Kevin Moshayedi, *CMO*
EMP: 91 **EST:** 2015
SQ FT: 2,500
SALES (est): 360.69K
SALES (corp-wide): 41.22MM **Privately Held**
Web: www.xbp.io
SIC: 7371 Computer software development
PA: Quality Speaks Llc
9221 Corbin Ave Ste 260
Northridge CA
818 264-4400

(P-12053)
XGRID INC
6598 Alleghany Ct (95120-3001)
PHONE.................408 242-7937
Syed Abdullah Shah, *CEO*
EMP: 120 **EST:** 2017
SALES (est): 2.75MM **Privately Held**
SIC: 7371 7389 Custom computer programming services; Business Activities at Non-Commercial Site

(P-12054)
YARDI SYSTEMS INC (PA)
430 S Fairview Ave (93117-3637)
PHONE.................805 699-2040
Anant Yardi, *CEO*
Gordon Morrell, *
Fritz Schindelbeck, *
John Pendergast, *
Robert Teel, *
EMP: 380 **EST:** 1982
SQ FT: 160,000
SALES (est): 856.64MM
SALES (corp-wide): 856.64MM **Privately Held**
Web: www.yardi.com
SIC: 7371 Computer software development

(P-12055)
YOSEMITE TECHNOLOGIES INC
7435 N Ingram Ave (93711-6101)
PHONE.................559 449-8181
George Symons, *Prin*
George Symons, *CEO*
Sue Staicer, *
Dennis Hagobian, *
EMP: 60 **EST:** 1996
SQ FT: 10,000
SALES (est): 1.99MM **Privately Held**
SIC: 7371 Computer software development

(P-12056)
YUGABYTEDB INC (PA)
771 Vaqueros Ave (94085-3527)
PHONE.................408 663-6632
Bill Cook, *CEO*
Kannan Muthukkaruppan, *Pr*
EMP: 382 **EST:** 2016
SALES (est): 23.88MM
SALES (corp-wide): 23.88MM **Privately Held**
Web: www.yugabyte.com
SIC: 7371 Computer software development and applications

(P-12057)
YVAAI INC
Also Called: Yva.ai
2445 Augustine Dr Ste 150 (95054-3032)
PHONE.................650 704-5503
David Yan, *CEO*
EMP: 66 **EST:** 2016
SALES (est): 1.98MM **Privately Held**
SIC: 7371 Computer software development

(P-12058)
ZANTAZ INC
5758 W Las Positas Blvd (94588-4083)
PHONE.................925 598-3000
▲ **EMP:** 300
SIC: 7371 Computer software systems analysis and design, custom

(P-12059)
ZAPPOS IP INC
121 2nd St Fl 3 (94105-3611)
PHONE.................702 943-7725
EMP: 664
Web: www.zappos.com
SIC: 7371 Custom computer programming services
HQ: Zappos Ip, Inc.
400 Stewart Ave
Las Vegas NV
702 943-7777

(P-12060)
ZAZMIC INC (PA)
156 2nd St (94105-3724)
PHONE.................415 728-1621
Yann Kronberg, *CEO*
EMP: 235 **EST:** 2012
SALES (est): 9.6MM
SALES (corp-wide): 9.6MM **Privately Held**
Web: www.zazmic.com
SIC: 7371 7389 Computer software development; Business services, nec

(P-12061)
ZENNIFY LLC
1755 Creekside Oaks Dr (95833-3645)
PHONE.................208 739-2118
EMP: 70 **EST:** 2018
SALES (est): 842.8K **Privately Held**
Web: www.zennify.com
SIC: 7371 Computer software development

(P-12062)
ZENPUT INC
548 Market St (94104-5401)
PHONE.................800 537-0227
Vladislav Rikhter, *CEO*
David Karel, *CMO*
EMP: 66 **EST:** 2014
SALES (est): 5.65MM **Privately Held**
Web: www.zenput.com
SIC: 7371 Computer software development

(P-12063)
ZERO COGNITIVE SYSTEMS INC
Also Called: Zero
1475 S Bascom Ave Ste 204 (95008-0629)
PHONE.................650 720-2324
Alex Babin, *CEO*
Alexander Volkov, *
Gevorg Karapetyan, *
EMP: 80 **EST:** 2014
SALES (est): 5.47MM **Privately Held**
Web: www.zerosystems.com
SIC: 7371 Computer software development

(P-12064)
ZESTFINANCE INC
Also Called: Zest.ai
3900 W Alameda Ave Ste 1600 (91505-4333)
PHONE.................323 450-3000
Mike De Vere, *CEO*
Douglas Merrill, *
EMP: 85 **EST:** 2012
SALES (est): 9.65MM **Privately Held**
Web: www.zest.ai
SIC: 7371 Computer software development

(P-12065)
ZIGNAL LABS INC
600 California St Fl 11 (94108-2727)
PHONE.................415 683-7871
Guy Chuchward, *CEO*
Adam Beaugh, *
Bob Deppisch, *
Josh Ginsberg, *
Chris Krook, *
EMP: 72 **EST:** 2011
SALES (est): 10.53MM **Privately Held**
Web: www.zignallabs.com
SIC: 7371 Computer software development and applications

(P-12066)
ZIPLINE INTERNATIONAL INC
333 Corey Way (94080-6706)
PHONE.................508 340-3291
Peter Winn, *CEO*
William Hemsworth, *Operations*
EMP: 114 **EST:** 2006
SALES (est): 6.35MM **Privately Held**
Web: www.flyzipline.com
SIC: 7371 Computer software development and applications

(P-12067)
ZL TECHNOLOGIES INC (PA)
860 N Mccarthy Blvd Ste 100 (95035-5110)
PHONE.................408 240-8989
Kon Leong, *Pr*
EMP: 63 **EST:** 1999
SQ FT: 1,860
SALES (est): 13.43MM
SALES (corp-wide): 13.43MM **Privately Held**
Web: www.zlti.com
SIC: 7371 5045 Computer software systems analysis and design, custom; Computer software

(P-12068)
ZOOM VIDEO COMMUNICATIONS INC (PA)
Also Called: Zoom
55 Almaden Blvd Ste 600 (95113-1612)
PHONE.................888 799-9666
Eric S Yuan, *Ch Bd*
Kelly Steckelberg, *CFO*
Aparna Bawa, *Interim CAO*
EMP: 7342 **EST:** 2011
SQ FT: 103,000
SALES (est): 4.39B
SALES (corp-wide): 4.39B **Publicly Held**
Web: www.zoom.us
SIC: 7371 Computer software development

(P-12069)
ZSCALER INC (PA)
Also Called: Zscaler
120 Holger Way (95134-1376)
PHONE.................408 533-0288
Jagtar S Chaudhry, *Ch Bd*
Remo Canessa, *CFO*
Dali Rajic, *COO*
Robert Schlossman, *CLO*

7371 - Custom Computer Programming Services (P-12070)

PRODUCTS & SERVICES SECTION

EMP: 534 EST: 2007
SQ FT: 172,000
SALES (est): 1.62B **Publicly Held**
Web: www.zscaler.com
SIC: 7371 7372 Computer software development; Prepackaged software

(P-12070)
ZUUM TRANSPORTATION INC
131 Innovation Dr Ste 100 (92617-3072)
PHONE..............................909 667-7478
Mustafa Azizi, *CEO*
Victor Manuel, *
Elliot Sobel, *
EMP: 62 EST: 2016
SALES (est): 12.25MM **Privately Held**
Web: www.zuumapp.com
SIC: 7371 Computer software development and applications

7372 Prepackaged Software

(P-12071)
ACCELA INC (PA)
2633 Camino Ramon Ste 500 (94583-9149)
PHONE..............................925 659-3200
Gary Kovacs, *CEO*
Ed Daihl, *
Maury Blackman, *
John Alves, *
Jeffrey Toung, *
EMP: 150 EST: 1979
SALES (est): 95.11MM **Privately Held**
Web: www.accela.com
SIC: 7372 Business oriented computer software

(P-12072)
ACTIANCE INC
900 Veterans Blvd Ste 500 (94063-1715)
PHONE..............................650 631-6300
EMP: 150
Web: www.smarsh.com
SIC: 7372 8742 Prepackaged software; Management consulting services

(P-12073)
ACTIVISION BLIZZARD INC (HQ)
Also Called: Activision Blizzard
2701 Olympic Blvd Bldg B (90404-4183)
PHONE..............................310 255-2000
Robert A Kotick, *CEO*
Brian G Kelly, *
Armin Zerza, *CFO*
Brian Bulatao, *Chief*
Julie Hodges, *CPO*
EMP: 333 EST: 1979
SALES (est): 7.53B
SALES (corp-wide): 211.91B **Publicly Held**
Web: www.activisionblizzard.com
SIC: 7372 Prepackaged software
PA: Microsoft Corporation
   1 Microsoft Way
   Redmond WA
   425 882-8080

(P-12074)
ACTIVISION BLIZZARD INC
Blizzard Entertainment
3 Blizzard (92618-3628)
P.O. Box 18979 (92623-8979)
PHONE..............................949 955-1380
EMP: 85
SALES (corp-wide): 211.91B **Publicly Held**
Web: www.activisionblizzard.com

SIC: 7372 Prepackaged software
HQ: Activision Blizzard, Inc.
   2701 Olympic Blvd Bldg B
   Santa Monica CA
   310 255-2000

(P-12075)
ADAPTIVE INSIGHTS LLC (HQ)
2300 Geng Rd Ste 100 (94303-3352)
PHONE..............................650 528-7500
Thomas F Bogan, *CEO*
Bhaskar Himatsingka, *Chief Product Officer*
Frederick M Gewant, *
Connie Dewitt, *
James D Johnson, *
EMP: 200 EST: 2003
SALES (est): 79.2MM **Publicly Held**
Web: www.workday.com
SIC: 7372 Business oriented computer software
PA: Workday, Inc.
   6110 Stoneridge Mall Rd
   Pleasanton CA

(P-12076)
ADARA INC (PA)
2625 Middlefield Rd Ste 827 (94306-2516)
PHONE..............................408 876-6360
Layton Han, *CEO*
Frank Teruel, *
Elizabeth Harz, *
Melissa Stein, *
Ellen Lee, *
EMP: 60 EST: 2005
SALES (est): 35.93MM
SALES (corp-wide): 35.93MM **Privately Held**
Web: www.adara.com
SIC: 7372 Business oriented computer software

(P-12077)
ADOBE INC (PA)
345 Park Ave (95110-2704)
PHONE..............................408 536-6000
Shantanu Narayen, *Ch Bd*
Daniel Durn, *Ex VP*
Scott Belsky, *Chief Product Officer*
Ann Lewnes, *CMO*
Dana Rao, *Corporate Secretary*
EMP: 600 EST: 1982
SQ FT: 1,100,000
SALES (est): 17.61B
SALES (corp-wide): 17.61B **Publicly Held**
Web: www.adobe.com
SIC: 7372 Prepackaged software

(P-12078)
AFRESH TECHNOLOGIES INC
33 New Montgomery St Ste 1100 (94105-4506)
PHONE..............................415 651-5068
Matthew Schwartz, *CEO*
Nathan Fenner, *
Volodymyr Kuleshov, *
EMP: 100 EST: 2017
SQ FT: 1,400
SALES (est): 8.35MM **Privately Held**
Web: www.afresh.com
SIC: 7372 Business oriented computer software

(P-12079)
AGENCYCOM LLC
5353 Grosvenor Blvd (90066-6913)
PHONE..............................415 817-3800
Chan Suh, *CEO*
Rob Elliott, *CFO*
EMP: 400 EST: 1995
SQ FT: 130,000

SALES (est): 49.16MM
SALES (corp-wide): 14.29B **Publicly Held**
SIC: 7372 Application computer software
PA: Omnicom Group Inc.
   280 Park Ave Fl 31w
   New York NY
   212 415-3600

(P-12080)
AGILEPOINT INC (PA)
1916 Old Middlefield Way Ste B (94043-2555)
PHONE..............................650 968-6789
Jesse Shiah, *Pr*
EMP: 85 EST: 2003
SQ FT: 2,000
SALES (est): 12.02MM
SALES (corp-wide): 12.02MM **Privately Held**
Web: www.agilepoint.com
SIC: 7372 Business oriented computer software

(P-12081)
AGILOFT INC (PA)
303 Twin Dolphin Dr Fl 6 (94065-1497)
P.O. Box 2574 (94546-0574)
PHONE..............................650 459-5637
Eric Laughlin, *CEO*
EMP: 275 EST: 1990
SQ FT: 3,200
SALES (est): 33.28MM **Privately Held**
Web: www.agiloft.com
SIC: 7372 Business oriented computer software

(P-12082)
AHA LABS INC
20 Gloria Cir (94025-3556)
PHONE..............................650 575-1425
Brian De Haaff, *CEO*
Christopher Waters, *
EMP: 100 EST: 2013
SALES (est): 5.74MM **Privately Held**
Web: www.aha.io
SIC: 7372 Business oriented computer software

(P-12083)
AIRA TECH CORP
Also Called: Aira Tech
3451 Via Montebello Ste 192 Pmb 214 (92009-8492)
PHONE..............................800 835-1934
Troy Otillio, *CEO*
EMP: 65 EST: 2015
SALES (est): 10.18MM **Privately Held**
Web: www.aira.io
SIC: 7372 Application computer software

(P-12084)
AIRBASE INC
548 Market St Ste 93249 (94104-5401)
PHONE..............................415 625-6222
Thejo Kote, *CEO*
EMP: 300 EST: 2016
SALES (est): 43.05MM **Privately Held**
Web: www.airbase.com
SIC: 7372 Application computer software

(P-12085)
AKTANA INC (PA)
207 Powell St Ste 800 (94102-2205)
PHONE..............................888 707-3125
David Ehrlich, *CEO*
EMP: 374 EST: 2008
SALES (est): 52MM **Privately Held**
Web: www.aktana.com
SIC: 7372 Prepackaged software

(P-12086)
ALATION INC (PA)
3 Lagoon Dr Ste 300 (94065-1567)
P.O. Box 1216 (94064-1216)
PHONE..............................650 779-4440
Satyen Sangani, *CEO*
Max Ochoa, *
Paul Sieben, *
Steve Kennedy, *CRO*
Bob Block Ccso, *Prin*
EMP: 484 EST: 2012
SALES (est): 68.82MM
SALES (corp-wide): 68.82MM **Privately Held**
Web: www.alation.com
SIC: 7372 Application computer software

(P-12087)
ALERTENTERPRISE INC (PA)
4350 Starboard Dr (94538-6434)
PHONE..............................510 440-0840
Jasvir Gill, *CEO*
Kaval Kaur, *COO*
Mark Weatherford Ciso, *Prin*
EMP: 140 EST: 2007
SQ FT: 24,000
SALES (est): 14.67MM **Privately Held**
Web: www.alertenterprise.com
SIC: 7372 Prepackaged software

(P-12088)
ALLDATA LLC
9650 W Taron Dr Ste 100 (95757-8197)
PHONE..............................916 684-5200
Harry L Goldsmith, *
Bob Olsen, *
EMP: 400 EST: 1986
SQ FT: 35,000
SALES (est): 86.69MM
SALES (corp-wide): 17.46B **Publicly Held**
Web: www.alldata.com
SIC: 7372 Business oriented computer software
PA: Autozone, Inc.
   123 S Front St
   Memphis TN
   901 495-6500

(P-12089)
AMBER HOLDING INC
1601 Cloverfield Blvd (90404-4087)
PHONE..............................603 324-3000
Charles E Moran, *Pr*
Tom Mcdonald, *CFO*
Jerry Nine, *
EMP: 96 EST: 2009
SALES (est): 23.45MM
SALES (corp-wide): 555.12MM **Publicly Held**
SIC: 7372 Prepackaged software
HQ: Skillsoft (Us) Llc
   300 Innovative Way # 201
   Nashua NH
   603 324-3000

(P-12090)
APPETIZE TECHNOLOGIES INC
100 California St (94111-4505)
PHONE..............................877 559-4225
Max Roper, *CEO*
Jason Pratts, *
Kevin Anderson, *
Dan Machock, *
Mark Eastwood, *Chief Product Officer*
EMP: 110 EST: 2011
SALES (est): 27.03MM **Privately Held**
Web: www.spoton.com
SIC: 7372 Application computer software

PRODUCTS & SERVICES SECTION
7372 - Prepackaged Software (P-12111)

(P-12091)
APPFOLIO INC
Also Called: Mycase
9201 Spectrum Center Blvd Ste 100 (92123-1407)
PHONE..............................866 648-1536
Troy Alford, *Eng/Dir*
EMP: 81
SALES (corp-wide): 471.88MM **Publicly Held**
Web: www.appfolio.com
SIC: 7372   Prepackaged software
PA: Appfolio, Inc.
   70 Castilian Dr
   Santa Barbara CA
   805 364-6093

(P-12092)
APPFOLIO INC (PA)
Also Called: APPFOLIO
70 Castilian Dr   (93117-3027)
PHONE..............................805 364-6093
Jason Randall, *Pr*
Andreas Von Blottnitz, *
Jonathan Walker, *
Fay Sien Goon, *
Matt Mazza, *CLO*
EMP: 340 EST: 2006
SALES (est): 471.88MM
SALES (corp-wide): 471.88MM **Publicly Held**
Web: www.appfolio.com
SIC: 7372   Business oriented computer software

(P-12093)
APPLIED BIOSYSTEMS LLC (DH)
Also Called: Applied Biosystems
5791 Van Allen Way   (92008-7321)
▲ EMP: 120 EST: 1937
SQ FT: 51,000
SALES (est): 739.54MM
SALES (corp-wide): 44.91B **Publicly Held**
Web: www.thermofisher.com
SIC: 7372 3826   Prepackaged software; Gas chromatographic instruments
HQ: Life Technologies Corporation
   5781 Van Allen Way
   Carlsbad CA
   760 603-7200

(P-12094)
APPLIED STATISTICS & MGT INC
Also Called: Md-Staff
32848 Wolf Store Rd Ste A (92592-8277)
P.O. Box 2738 (92593-2738)
PHONE..............................951 699-4600
Trung Phan, *Pr*
Nickolaus Phan, *
EMP: 95 EST: 1982
SQ FT: 4,000
SALES (est): 12.05MM **Privately Held**
Web: www.mdstaff.com
SIC: 7372 7371 Prepackaged software; Computer software systems analysis and design, custom

(P-12095)
APPLOVIN CORPORATION (PA)
1100 Page Mill Rd   (94304-1047)
PHONE..............................800 839-9646
Adam Foroughi, *Ch Bd*
Herald Chen, *
Katie Jansen, *CMO*
Victoria Valenzuela, *CLO*
EMP: 122 EST: 2011
SQ FT: 72,812
SALES (est): 2.82B **Publicly Held**
Web: www.applovin.com

SIC: 7372   Prepackaged software

(P-12096)
APTIV DIGITAL LLC
2160 Gold St   (95002-3700)
PHONE..............................818 295-6789
Neil Jones, *Pr*
EMP: 85 EST: 1996
SALES (est): 12.34MM
SALES (corp-wide): 438.93MM **Publicly Held**
SIC: 7372   Home entertainment computer software
HQ: Rovi Guides, Inc.
   2233 N Ontario St Ste 100
   Burbank CA

(P-12097)
ARCARIS INC (PA)
Also Called: Playvox
530 Lawrence Expy   (94085-4014)
PHONE..............................415 854-3801
Louis Bucciarelli, *CEO*
Oscar Giraldo, *
EMP: 243 EST: 2012
SALES (est): 23.74MM
SALES (corp-wide): 23.74MM **Privately Held**
Web: www.playvox.com
SIC: 7372   Prepackaged software

(P-12098)
ARCORO HOLDINGS CORP
9452 Telephone Rd Pmb 227 (93004-2600)
PHONE..............................818 222-1836
John Herr, *CEO*
Karen Williams, *Sr VP*
EMP: 196 EST: 2018
SALES (est): 20.36MM **Privately Held**
SIC: 7372   Business oriented computer software

(P-12099)
ARCTIC WOLF NETWORKS INC
111 W Evelyn Ave Ste 115 (94086-6131)
PHONE..............................888 272-8429
EMP: 115 EST: 2012
SALES (est): 5MM **Privately Held**
Web: www.arcticwolf.com
SIC: 7372   Business oriented computer software

(P-12100)
AREA 1 SECURITY INC
101 Townsend St   (94107-1934)
PHONE..............................650 924-1637
Patrick Sweeney, *CEO*
Oren Falkowitz, *
Steve Pataky, *CRO*
EMP: 65 EST: 2014
SALES (est): 8.56MM **Privately Held**
Web: www.area1security.com
SIC: 7372   Prepackaged software

(P-12101)
ARIBA INC (DH)
3420 Hillview Ave   (94304-1355)
PHONE..............................650 849-4000
EMP: 105 EST: 1996
SQ FT: 86,000
SALES (est): 204.35MM
SALES (corp-wide): 32.06B **Privately Held**
Web: www.ariba.com
SIC: 7372   Business oriented computer software
HQ: Sap America, Inc.
   3999 West Chester Pike
   Newtown Square PA
   610 661-1000

(P-12102)
ASCENDER SOFTWARE INC
8885 Rio San Diego Dr Ste 270 (92108-1624)
PHONE..............................877 561-7501
Theodore Kye, *Prin*
EMP: 242 EST: 2006
SALES (est): 875.69K
SALES (corp-wide): 309.28MM **Privately Held**
Web: www.matrixmedicalnetwork.com
SIC: 7372   Prepackaged software
PA: Community Care Health Network, Llc
   9201 E Mtn Vw Rd Ste 22
   Scottsdale AZ
   877 564-3627

(P-12103)
ATOB ASSET VEHICLE I LLC
4 Embarcadero Ctr Ste 140 (94111-4106)
PHONE..............................703 663-0658
EMP: 76 EST: 2021
SALES (est): 351.6K
SALES (corp-wide): 8.51MM **Privately Held**
SIC: 7372   Prepackaged software
PA: Celegans Labs, Inc.
   4 Embarcadero Ctr # 1400
   San Francisco CA
   650 283-4882

(P-12104)
AUGMEDIX INC (PA)
111 Sutter St Fl.13 (94104-4541)
PHONE..............................888 669-4885
Emmanuel Krakaris, *Pr*
Gerard Van Hamel Platerink, *Ch Bd*
Sandra Breber, *COO*
Paul Ginocchio, *CFO*
EMP: 526 EST: 2020
SALES (est): 30.93MM
SALES (corp-wide): 30.93MM **Publicly Held**
Web: www.augmedix.com
SIC: 7372   Prepackaged software

(P-12105)
AURORA INNOVATION INC
Also Called: AURORA INNOVATION, INC.
77 Stillman St   (94107-1309)
PHONE..............................646 725-4999
Christopher Paul Urmson, *CEO*
EMP: 305
SALES (corp-wide): 68MM **Publicly Held**
Web: www.aurora.tech
SIC: 7372   Utility computer software
HQ: Aurora Operations, Inc.
   50 33rd St
   Pittsburgh PA
   888 583-9506

(P-12106)
AUTODESK INC (PA)
Also Called: Autodesk
1 Market St Ste 400 (94105-1336)
PHONE..............................415 507-5000
Andrew Anagnost, *Pr*
Stacy J Smith, *Non-Executive Chairman of the Board*
Steve M Blum, *COO*
Deborah L Clifford, *Ex VP*
Pascal W Di Fronzo, *CLO*
◆ EMP: 400 EST: 1982
SALES (est): 4.39B
SALES (corp-wide): 4.39B **Publicly Held**
Web: www.autodesk.com
SIC: 7372   Prepackaged software

(P-12107)
AUTODESK INC
1 Market St   (94105-1336)
PHONE..............................415 356-0700
Chris Bradshaw, *Brnch Mgr*
EMP: 61
SALES (corp-wide): 4.39B **Publicly Held**
Web: www.autodesk.com
SIC: 7372   Application computer software
PA: Autodesk, Inc.
   1 Market St Ste 400
   San Francisco CA
   415 507-5000

(P-12108)
AVAST SOFTWARE INC (PA)
501 E Middlefield Rd   (94043-4042)
PHONE..............................844 340-9251
Vincent Wayne Steckler, *CEO*
EMP: 76 EST: 2011
SALES (est): 93.2MM
SALES (corp-wide): 93.2MM **Privately Held**
Web: www.avast.com
SIC: 7372   Application computer software

(P-12109)
AZUL SYSTEMS INC (PA)
385 Moffett Park Dr Ste 115 (94089-1217)
PHONE..............................650 230-6500
Scott Sellers, *Pr*
Gil Tene, *
Peter Maloney, *
Ian Whiting, *CRO*
Andrew Savitz, *CMO*
EMP: 66 EST: 2002
SALES (est): 30.03MM
SALES (corp-wide): 30.03MM **Privately Held**
Web: www.azul.com
SIC: 7372   Operating systems computer software

(P-12110)
BARRA LLC (HQ)
Also Called: Msci Barra
2100 Milvia St   (94704-1861)
PHONE..............................510 548-5442
Kamal Duggirala, *CEO*
Andrew Rudd, *Ch Bd*
Greg Stockett, *CFO*
Aamir Sheikh, *Pr*
▲ EMP: 280 EST: 1975
SQ FT: 35,000
SALES (est): 97.48MM **Publicly Held**
Web: www.msci.com
SIC: 7372 8741 6282   Business oriented computer software; Financial management for business; Investment advisory service
PA: Msci Inc.
   250 Greenwich St Fl 49
   New York NY

(P-12111)
BARRACUDA NETWORKS INC (PA)
Also Called: Barracuda
3175 Winchester Blvd (95008-6557)
PHONE..............................408 342-5400
Hatem Naguib, *Pr*
William D Jenkins Junior, *Pr*
Joe Billante, *
Siroui Mushegian, *CIO*
EMP: 225 EST: 2003
SQ FT: 61,400
SALES (est): 418MM
SALES (corp-wide): 418MM **Privately Held**
Web: www.barracuda.com

7372 - Prepackaged Software (P-12112)

PRODUCTS & SERVICES SECTION

SIC: 7372 7373 Prepackaged software; Computer integrated systems design

(P-12112)
BEATS MUSIC LLC
235 2nd St (94105-3124)
PHONE..............................415 590-5104
Timothy Cook, CEO
EMP: 95 EST: 2012
SALES (est): 21.21MM
SALES (corp-wide): 383.29B Publicly Held
SIC: 7372 Prepackaged software
PA: Apple Inc.
   1 Apple Park Way
   Cupertino CA
   408 996-1010

(P-12113)
BIG SWITCH NETWORKS LLC
5453 Great America Pkwy (95054-3645)
PHONE..............................650 322-6510
Douglas Murray, Pr
Kyle Forster, *
Prashant Gandhi, MGT AND STRAT*
Gregg Holzrichter, CMO*
Shaun Page, Worldwide Sales Vice President*
EMP: 180 EST: 2010
SALES (est): 27.37MM Publicly Held
Web: www.arista.com
SIC: 7372 Prepackaged software
PA: Arista Networks, Inc.
   5453 Great America Pkwy
   Santa Clara CA

(P-12114)
BIGFIX INC
1480 64th St Ste 200 (94608-1292)
PHONE..............................510 652-6700
EMP: 200
SIC: 7372 Prepackaged software

(P-12115)
BILL HOLDINGS INC (PA)
Also Called: Bill.com
6220 America Center Dr Ste 100 (95002-2563)
P.O. Box 370 (95002-0370)
PHONE..............................650 621-7700
Rene Lacerte, Ch Bd
John Rettig, Pr
Loren Padelford, Chief Commercial Officer
Raj Aji, Chief Compliance Officer
EMP: 259 EST: 2006
SQ FT: 138,000
SALES (est): 1.06B
SALES (corp-wide): 1.06B Publicly Held
Web: www.bill.com
SIC: 7372 Prepackaged software

(P-12116)
BILLCOM LLC (HQ)
6220 America Center Dr Ste 100 (95002-2563)
P.O. Box 370 (95002-0370)
PHONE..............................650 353-3301
Rene Lacerte, CEO
Mark Orttung, COO
John Rettig, CFO
Irana Wasti, CPO
EMP: 140 EST: 2006
SALES (est): 129.43MM
SALES (corp-wide): 1.06B Publicly Held
Web: www.bill.com
SIC: 7372 Application computer software
PA: Bill Holdings, Inc.
   6220 America Center Dr # 100
   San Jose CA
   650 621-7700

(P-12117)
BLACKBERRY CORPORATION
331 Fairchild Dr (94043-2200)
PHONE..............................650 564-0016
EMP: 1568
SALES (corp-wide): 656MM Privately Held
Web: www.blackberry.com
SIC: 7372 Prepackaged software
HQ: Blackberry Corporation
   3001 Bishop Dr
   San Ramon CA
   972 650-6126

(P-12118)
BLACKBERRY CORPORATION (HQ)
Also Called: Rim
3001 Bishop Dr (94583-5005)
PHONE..............................972 650-6126
John Chen, CEO
▲ EMP: 67 EST: 1999
SALES (est): 500.44MM
SALES (corp-wide): 656MM Privately Held
Web: www.blackberry.com
SIC: 7372 Prepackaged software
PA: Blackberry Limited
   2200 University Ave E
   Waterloo ON
   519 888-7465

(P-12119)
BLACKLINE INC (PA)
Also Called: Blackline
21300 Victory Blvd Fl 12 (91367-7734)
PHONE..............................818 223-9008
Owen Ryan, Ch Bd
Mark Partin, CFO
Karole Morgan-prager, Legal
EMP: 135 EST: 2001
SQ FT: 89,000
SALES (est): 522.94MM
SALES (corp-wide): 522.94MM Publicly Held
Web: www.blackline.com
SIC: 7372 Business oriented computer software

(P-12120)
BLIZZARD ENTERTAINMENT INC (DH)
1 Blizzard (92618-3628)
P.O. Box 18979 (92623-8979)
PHONE..............................949 955-1380
Mike Morhaime, CEO
J Allen Brack, Pr
Paul Sams, Pr
Chris Metzen, Sr VP
Todd Pawlowski, VP
▲ EMP: 85 EST: 2004
SALES (est): 155.37MM
SALES (corp-wide): 211.91B Publicly Held
Web: careers.blizzard.com
SIC: 7372 5734 7819 Prepackaged software ; Software, computer games; Reproduction services, motion picture production
HQ: Activision Blizzard, Inc.
   2701 Olympic Blvd Bldg B
   Santa Monica CA
   310 255-2000

(P-12121)
BLUE COAT LLC
350 Ellis St (94043-2202)
PHONE..............................408 220-2200
Michael Fey, Pr
Stephen Trilling, *
Thomas Seifert, *
Scott Taylor, *
Amy Cappellanti-wolf, Chief Human Resource Officer
EMP: 1583 EST: 2015
SALES (est): 207.87MM
SALES (corp-wide): 3.34B Publicly Held
Web: www.broadcom.com
SIC: 7372 Prepackaged software
PA: Gen Digital Inc.
   60 E Rio Salado Pkwy # 1
   Tempe AZ
   650 527-8000

(P-12122)
BLUESHIFT LABS INC
433 California St Ste 600 (94130-1709)
PHONE..............................844 258-3735
Vijay Chittoor, Pr
Subramanyam Mallela, *
Mehul Shah, *
Tae Hea Nahm, *
Josh Francia, CGO*
EMP: 176 EST: 2014
SQ FT: 5,000
SALES (est): 9.21MM Privately Held
Web: www.blueshift.com
SIC: 7372 Business oriented computer software

(P-12123)
BOOMERANG COMMERCE INC (PA)
2100 Geng Rd Ste 210 (94303-3307)
PHONE..............................602 459-2578
Gurushyam Hariharan, CEO
Abhimanyu Maheswari, VP
Jaya Jaware, CFO
EMP: 169 EST: 2012
SALES (est): 21MM
SALES (corp-wide): 21MM Privately Held
Web: www.commerceiq.ai
SIC: 7372 Publisher's computer software

(P-12124)
BOX INC (PA)
900 Jefferson Ave (94063-1837)
PHONE..............................877 729-4269
Aaron Levie, CEO
Bethany Mayer, *
Dylan Smith, CFO
Stephanie Carullo, COO
Eliahu Berkovitch, CAO
EMP: 623 EST: 2005
SQ FT: 340,000
SALES (est): 990.87MM
SALES (corp-wide): 990.87MM Publicly Held
Web: www.box.com
SIC: 7372 Application computer software

(P-12125)
BPOMS/HRO INC (HQ)
8175 E Kaiser Blvd # 100 (92808-2214)
PHONE..............................714 974-2670
Patrick Dolan, Ch Bd
James Cortens, COO
Don Rutherford, CFO
EMP: 62 EST: 2008
SQ FT: 3,500
SALES (est): 6.74MM
SALES (corp-wide): 36.61MM Privately Held
SIC: 7372 7371 Prepackaged software; Custom computer programming services
PA: Bpo Management Services, Inc.
   8175 E Kaiser Blvd 100
   Anaheim CA
   714 972-2670

(P-12126)
BQE SOFTWARE INC
3825 Del Amo Blvd (90503)
PHONE..............................310 602-4020
EMP: 95 EST: 1995
SQ FT: 20,000
SALES (est): 12.55MM Privately Held
Web: www.bqe.com
SIC: 7372 5734 Application computer software; Software, business and non-game

(P-12127)
C3AI INC (PA)
1400 Seaport Blvd Ste 100 (94063-5594)
PHONE..............................650 503-2200
Thomas M Siebel, Ch Bd
Edward Y Abbo, Pr
Juho Parkkinen, Sr VP
Guy Wanger, CAO
EMP: 894 EST: 2009
SALES (est): 266.8MM Publicly Held
Web: www.c3.ai
SIC: 7372 Prepackaged software

(P-12128)
CA INC
Also Called: CA
3965 Freedom Cir Fl 6 (95054-1286)
PHONE..............................800 225-5224
EMP: 166
SALES (corp-wide): 33.2B Publicly Held
Web: www.broadcom.com
SIC: 7372 Business oriented computer software
HQ: Ca, Inc.
   520 Madison Ave
   New York NY
   800 225-5224

(P-12129)
CADENCE DESIGN SYSTEMS INC (PA)
Also Called: Cadence
2655 Seely Ave Bldg 5 (95134-1931)
PHONE..............................408 943-1234
Anirudh Devgan, Pr
John M Wall, Sr VP
Karna Nisewaner, Corporate Vice President
Neil Zaman, CRO
Thomas P Beckley, Sr VP
▲ EMP: 700 EST: 1982
SALES (est): 3.56B
SALES (corp-wide): 3.56B Publicly Held
Web: www.cadence.com
SIC: 7372 Prepackaged software

(P-12130)
CALAMP CORP (PA)
Also Called: CALAMP
15635 Alton Pkwy Ste 250 (92618-7328)
PHONE..............................949 600-5600
Jason Cohenour, Interim Chief Executive Officer
Henry J Maier, *
Jikun Kim, Sr VP
Richard Scott, CLO
Jeffrey Clark, CPO
◆ EMP: 96 EST: 1981
SQ FT: 23,000
SALES (est): 294.95MM
SALES (corp-wide): 294.95MM Publicly Held
Web: www.calamp.com
SIC: 7372 Application computer software

(P-12131)
CATO NETWORKS INC
3031 Tisch Way 110 Plz W (95128-2561)
PHONE..............................646 975-9243
Shlomo Kramer, CEO

PRODUCTS & SERVICES SECTION — 7372 - Prepackaged Software (P-12150)

Steven Krausz, *VP*
Tomer Wald, *CFO*
EMP: 78 **EST:** 2015
SALES (est): 11.68MM **Privately Held**
Web: www.catonetworks.com
SIC: 7372 Application computer software

(P-12132)
CHATMETER INC
225 Broadway Ste 2200 (92101-5011)
PHONE...................619 300-1050
EMP: 80 **EST:** 2009
SALES (est): 9.81MM **Privately Held**
Web: www.chatmeter.com
SIC: 7372 Prepackaged software

(P-12133)
CHECK POINT SOFTWARE TECH INC (HQ)
Also Called: Check Point Software
959 Skyway Rd Ste 300 (94070-2723)
PHONE...................650 628-2000
Gil Shwed, *CEO*
Tal Payne, *CFO*
Doctor Dorit Dor, *CPO*
Dan Yerushalmi, *CCO*
Peter Alexander, *CMO*
▲ **EMP:** 120 **EST:** 1996
SALES (est): 250.29MM **Privately Held**
Web: www.checkpoint.com
SIC: 7372 Operating systems computer software
PA: Check Point Software Technologies Ltd.
5 Shlomo Kaplan
Tel Aviv-Jaffa

(P-12134)
CHOWNOW INC
12181 Bluff Creek Dr Ste W200 (90094-2627)
PHONE...................888 707-2469
Eric Jaffe, *Pr*
Stuart Hathaway, *
Andre Mancl, *
EMP: 100 **EST:** 2010
SQ FT: 25,000
SALES (est): 16.12MM **Privately Held**
Web: www.chownow.com
SIC: 7372 Business oriented computer software

(P-12135)
CHROME RIVER TECHNOLOGIES INC
5757 Wilshire Blvd Ste 270 (90036-5814)
PHONE...................888 781-0088
Eric Friedrichsen, *CEO*
Nord Samuelson, *Pr*
Adriana Carpenter, *CFO*
Courtney Ryan, *CPO*
EMP: 148 **EST:** 2007
SALES (est): 1.81MM **Privately Held**
Web: www.chromeriver.com
SIC: 7372 Prepackaged software

(P-12136)
CIPHERCLOUD INC (HQ)
2581 Junction Ave Ste 200 (95134-1923)
PHONE...................408 687-4350
EMP: 90 **EST:** 2010
SQ FT: 21,800
SALES (est): 69.57MM **Privately Held**
Web: www.lookout.com
SIC: 7372 Business oriented computer software
PA: Lookout, Inc.
275 Battery St Ste 200
San Francisco CA

(P-12137)
CISCO SYSTEMS LLC (HQ)
Also Called: Cisco Systems
170 W Tasman Dr (95134-1706)
PHONE...................650 989-6500
Scott Weiss, *CEO*
Bob Kavner, *Ch*
Craig Collins, *CFO*
Kelly Bodnar Battles, *VP*
EMP: 260 **EST:** 2000
SALES (est): 100.26MM
SALES (corp-wide): 57B **Publicly Held**
Web: www.cisco.com
SIC: 7372 5045 Prepackaged software; Computers, peripherals, and software
PA: Cisco Systems, Inc.
170 W Tasman Dr
San Jose CA
408 526-4000

(P-12138)
CLASSY INC
Also Called: Classy
350 10th Ave Ste 1300 (92101-8703)
PHONE...................619 961-1892
Chris Himes, *CEO*
EMP: 156 **EST:** 2006
SALES (est): 22.34MM
SALES (corp-wide): 23MM **Privately Held**
Web: www.classy.org
SIC: 7372 Prepackaged software
PA: Gofundme Inc.
1010 Doyle St Ste 250
Menlo Park CA
650 260-3436

(P-12139)
CLEARLAKE CAPITAL PARTNERS
233 Wilshire Blvd Ste 800 (90401-1207)
PHONE...................310 400-8800
John A Mckenna Junior, *Pr*
EMP: 1832 **EST:** 2012
SALES (est): 28.77MM **Privately Held**
SIC: 7372 Prepackaged software

(P-12140)
CLIMATE CORPORATION (DH)
Also Called: Climate Fieldview
201 3rd St Ste 1010 (94103-3129)
PHONE...................415 363-0500
Mike Stern, *CEO*
Greg Smirin, *
Ranjeeta Singh, *CPO**
EMP: 64 **EST:** 2006
SALES (est): 27.9MM
SALES (corp-wide): 52.7B **Privately Held**
Web: www.climate.com
SIC: 7372 5045 Prepackaged software; Computer software
HQ: Bayer Northern Production Co., Llc
800 N Lindbergh Blvd
Saint Louis MO
314 694-1000

(P-12141)
CLOUDFLARE INC (PA)
Also Called: Cloudflare
101 Townsend St (94107-1912)
PHONE...................888 993-5273
Matthew Prince, *Ch Bd*
Michelle Zatlyn, *
Thomas Seifert, *CFO*
EMP: 2082 **EST:** 2009
SQ FT: 81,000
SALES (est): 975.24MM **Publicly Held**
Web: www.cloudflare.com
SIC: 7372 2741 7371 Prepackaged software; Internet publishing and broadcasting; Computer software development

(P-12142)
CLOUDSHIELD TECHNOLOGIES LLC
212 Gibraltar Dr (94089-1324)
PHONE...................408 331-6640
Randy Brumfield, *Sr VP*
Todd Beine, *
Timothy Laehy, *
EMP: 115 **EST:** 2000
SQ FT: 35,000
SALES (est): 15.01MM
SALES (corp-wide): 43.71MM **Privately Held**
SIC: 7372 8741 8742 Prepackaged software; Business management; Business management consultant
HQ: Lookingglass Cyber Solution, Inc.
1834 S Charles St
Baltimore MD
703 351-1000

(P-12143)
CLOUDSIMPLE INC
1600 Amphitheatre Pkwy (94043-1351)
PHONE...................412 568-3487
Gururaj Pangal, *CEO*
EMP: 78 **EST:** 2016
SALES (est): 22.06MM
SALES (corp-wide): 282.84B **Publicly Held**
SIC: 7372 Application computer software
HQ: Google Llc
1600 Amphitheatre Pkwy
Mountain View CA
650 253-0000

(P-12144)
COMPOSITE SOFTWARE LLC (DH)
755 Sycamore Dr (95035-7411)
PHONE...................800 553-6387
Jim Green, *CEO*
David Besemer, *
Jon Bode, *
EMP: 74 **EST:** 2002
SQ FT: 14,000
SALES (est): 31.25MM
SALES (corp-wide): 4.38B **Privately Held**
SIC: 7372 Prepackaged software
HQ: Cloud Software Group, Inc.
851 W Cypress Creek Rd
Fort Lauderdale FL

(P-12145)
COMPULINK BUSINESS SYSTEMS INC (PA)
Also Called: Compulink Healthcare Solutions
1100 Business Center Cir (91320-1124)
PHONE...................805 446-2050
Link Wilson, *Pr*
EMP: 117 **EST:** 1985
SQ FT: 15,000
SALES (est): 23.14MM
SALES (corp-wide): 23.14MM **Privately Held**
Web: www.compulinkadvantage.com
SIC: 7372 Business oriented computer software

(P-12146)
CONFLUENT INC (PA)
899 W Evelyn Ave (94041-1225)
PHONE...................800 439-3207
Edward Kreps, *CEO*
Jay Kreps, *
Steffan Tomlinson, *CFO*
Stephanie Buscemi, *CMO*
EMP: 2350 **EST:** 2014
SQ FT: 75,475
SALES (est): 585.94MM
SALES (corp-wide): 585.94MM **Publicly Held**
Web: www.confluent.io
SIC: 7372 Application computer software

(P-12147)
CONSENSUS CLOUD SOLUTIONS INC (PA)
700 S Flower St Fl 15 (90017-4101)
PHONE...................323 860-9200
Scott Turicchi, *CEO*
John Nebergall, *COO*
Steve Emberland, *Contrlr*
James Malone, *CFO*
EMP: 65 **EST:** 2021
SALES (est): 352.66MM
SALES (corp-wide): 352.66MM **Publicly Held**
Web: www.consensus.com
SIC: 7372 Prepackaged software

(P-12148)
CONVERSIONPOINT HOLDINGS INC
840 Newport Center Dr Ste 450 (92660)
PHONE...................888 706-6764
Robert Tallack, *Pr*
Don Walker Barrett Iii, *COO*
Raghu Kilambi, *CFO*
EMP: 85 **EST:** 2018
SALES (est): 2.22MM **Privately Held**
SIC: 7372 Prepackaged software

(P-12149)
CORNERSTONE ONDEMAND INC (HQ)
Also Called: Cornerstone
1601 Cloverfield Blvd Ste 620s (90404-4178)
PHONE...................310 752-0200
Himanshu Palsule, *CEO*
Chirag Shah, *
Heidi Spirgi, *CSO CGO**
Adam Weiss, *CAO**
Srinivasa Ogireddy, *
EMP: 269 **EST:** 1999
SQ FT: 94,000
SALES (est): 740.92MM
SALES (corp-wide): 740.92MM **Privately Held**
Web: www.cornerstoneondemand.com
SIC: 7372 Business oriented computer software
PA: Sunshine Software Holdings, Inc.
1601 Cloverf Blvd Ste 62
Santa Monica CA

(P-12150)
COUPA SOFTWARE INCORPORATED (HQ) ✪
Also Called: Coupa
1855 S Grant St (94402-7016)
PHONE...................650 931-3200
Robert Bernshteyn, *CEO*
Anthony Tiscornia, *CFO*
Mark Riggs, *CCO*
Robert Glenn, *Executive Global Sales Vice President*
EMP: 128 **EST:** 2022
SQ FT: 69,220
SALES (est): 725.29MM
SALES (corp-wide): 725.29MM **Privately Held**
Web: www.coupa.com
SIC: 7372 Business oriented computer software
PA: Coupa Holdings, Llc
1855 S Grant St
San Mateo CA
650 931-3200

7372 - Prepackaged Software (P-12151)

(P-12151)
COURSERA INC (PA)
Also Called: COURSERA
381 E Evelyn Ave (94041-1530)
PHONE.....................650 963-9884
Jeffrey N Maggioncalda, Pr
Andrew Y Ng, Non-Executive Chairman of the Board*
Kenneth R Hahn, Sr VP
Anne T Cappel, Sr VP
Michele M Meyers, CAO
EMP: 1017 EST: 2011
SALES (est): 523.76MM
SALES (corp-wide): 523.76MM Publicly Held
Web: www.coursera.org
SIC: 7372 Prepackaged software

(P-12152)
CUMULUS NETWORKS INC (PA)
Also Called: Cumulus Networks
185 E Dana St (94041-1507)
PHONE.....................650 383-6700
Jame Rivers, CEO
Reza Malekzadeh, *
Nolan Leake, *
Edward Leake, *
EMP: 124 EST: 2010
SALES (est): 22.71MM
SALES (corp-wide): 22.71MM Privately Held
Web: www.nvidia.com
SIC: 7372 7371 Publisher's computer software; Computer software development

(P-12153)
CXAPP INC ◊
4 Palo Alto Sq Ste 200 (94306-2122)
PHONE.....................650 575-4456
Khurram P Sheikh, Interim Chief Financial Officer
Khurram P Sheikh, Interim Chief Financial Officer
Leon Papkoff, CPO
EMP: 87 EST: 2023
SALES (est): 8.63MM
SALES (corp-wide): 8.63MM Publicly Held
Web: www.kins-tech.com
SIC: 7372 Prepackaged software
PA: Kins Capital Llc
4 Palo Alto Sq Ste 200
Palo Alto CA
650 575-4456

(P-12154)
CYARA INC (PA)
Also Called: Cyara
805 Veterans Blvd Ste 105 (94063-1712)
PHONE.....................650 549-8522
Alok Kulkarni, CEO
Mark Verbeck, *
James Isaacs, *
Matt Melymuka, *
Bonny Malik, *
EMP: 142 EST: 2016
SALES (est): 17.68MM
SALES (corp-wide): 17.68MM Privately Held
Web: www.cyara.com
SIC: 7372 Application computer software

(P-12155)
CYLANCE INC (DH)
3001 Bishop Dr Ste 400 (94583-5005)
PHONE.....................949 375-3380
Stuart Mcclure, CEO
Daniel Doimo, *
Gregory Fitzgerald, CMO*
Shane Shook, Chief Knowledge*
Brady Berg, *
EMP: 87 EST: 2012
SALES (est): 200MM
SALES (corp-wide): 656MM Privately Held
Web: www.blackberry.com
SIC: 7372 Application computer software
HQ: Blackberry Corporation
3001 Bishop Dr
San Ramon CA
972 650-6126

(P-12156)
D-WAVE QUANTUM INC
2650 E Bayshore Rd (94303-3211)
PHONE.....................604 630-1428
Alan Baratz, Pr
Steven M West, *
John M Markovich, CFO
Victoria Brydon, PEOPLE & OPERATIONAL EXCELLENCE
EMP: 190 EST: 1999
SQ FT: 6,000
SALES (est): 12.79MM Privately Held
SIC: 7372 Prepackaged software

(P-12157)
D3PUBLISHER OF AMERICA INC
Also Called: D3 Go
15910 Ventura Blvd Ste 800 (91436-2802)
PHONE.....................310 268-0820
Yoji Takenaka, Pr
Yuji Itoh, Non-Executive Chairman of the Board
Hidetaka Tachibana, CFO
EMP: 63 EST: 2004
SQ FT: 6,129
SALES (est): 18.5MM Privately Held
Web: www.d3go.com
SIC: 7372 Home entertainment computer software
HQ: D3 Publisher Inc.
3-5-2, Kandakajicho
Chiyoda-Ku TKY

(P-12158)
DATAVISOR INC
967 N Shoreline Blvd (94043-1932)
PHONE.....................408 331-9886
Yinglian Xie, CEO
Jon Sakoda, *
Fang Yu, *
Ron Bernal, *
EMP: 75 EST: 2014
SALES (est): 563.77K Privately Held
Web: www.datavisor.com
SIC: 7372 Business oriented computer software

(P-12159)
DAVE INC (PA)
1265 S Cochran Ave (90019-2846)
PHONE.....................844 857-3283
Jason Wilk, Pr
Kyle Beilman, CFO
EMP: 219 EST: 2015
SQ FT: 36,000
SALES (est): 204.84MM
SALES (corp-wide): 204.84MM Publicly Held
Web: www.dave.com
SIC: 7372 7389 Prepackaged software; Financial services

(P-12160)
DEEM INC (DH)
1330 Broadway Fl 7 (94612-2537)
PHONE.....................415 590-8300
John F Rizzo, Pr
Eddie Bridgers, CRO
Hoshedar Mana, INFO SECURITY OCFR
Neil Markey, CIO
David Shiba, Sr VP
▲ EMP: 65 EST: 2001
SQ FT: 133,000
SALES (est): 90.41MM
SALES (corp-wide): 7.04B Privately Held
Web: www.deem.com
SIC: 7372 Prepackaged software
HQ: Enterprise Holdings, Inc.
600 Corporate Park Dr
Saint Louis MO
314 512-5000

(P-12161)
DEMANDWHIZ LLC
4079 Middle Park Dr (95135-1022)
PHONE.....................408 600-2720
Manish S, Managing Member
EMP: 100 EST: 2015
SALES (est): 2.79MM Privately Held
Web: www.demandwhiz.com
SIC: 7372 Prepackaged software

(P-12162)
DOCUSIGN INC (PA)
221 Main St Ste 1550 (94105-1947)
PHONE.....................415 489-4940
Allan Thygesen, Pr
Mary Agnes Wilderotter, *
Cynthia Gaylor, CFO
James P Shaughnessy, CLO
EMP: 300 EST: 2003
SQ FT: 93,000
SALES (est): 2.52B
SALES (corp-wide): 2.52B Publicly Held
Web: www.docusign.com
SIC: 7372 Prepackaged software

(P-12163)
DORADO NETWORK SYSTEMS CORP
Also Called: Corelogic Dorado
40 Pacifica (92618-7471)
PHONE.....................650 227-7300
Dain Ehring, CEO
Karen Camp, *
EMP: 140 EST: 1998
SALES (est): 25.34MM
SALES (corp-wide): 1.64B Privately Held
Web: www.corelogic.com
SIC: 7372 Application computer software
HQ: Corelogic, Inc.
40 Pacifica Ste 900
Irvine CA
866 873-3651

(P-12164)
DOUBLEDUTCH INC (DH)
44 Tehama St Ste 504 (94105-3110)
PHONE.....................800 748-9024
Lawrence Coburn, CEO
Brad Roberts, CFO
EMP: 94 EST: 1984
SALES (est): 30.15MM
SALES (corp-wide): 1.2B Privately Held
Web: www.thedoubledutch.com
SIC: 7372 Application computer software
HQ: Cvent, Inc.
1765 Grnsboro Stn Pl Fl 7
Tysons Corner VA
703 226-3500

(P-12165)
DOZUKI
1105 Higuera St Ste 100 (93401-3293)
P.O. Box 1465 (93406-1465)
PHONE.....................805 464-0573
EMP: 72 EST: 2015
SALES (est): 8.67MM Privately Held
Web: www.dozuki.com
SIC: 7372 Prepackaged software

(P-12166)
DRIVEAI INC
365 Ravendale Dr (94043-5217)
P.O. Box 57 (94023-0057)
PHONE.....................408 693-0765
Sameep Tandon, CEO
EMP: 150 EST: 2015
SALES (est): 11.29MM Privately Held
SIC: 7372 Prepackaged software

(P-12167)
DRIVER INC
438 Shotwell St (94110-1914)
PHONE.....................415 999-4960
EMP: 85 EST: 2011
SALES (est): 9.4MM Privately Held
Web: www.drivergrp.com
SIC: 7372 Educational computer software

(P-12168)
DROPBOX INC (PA)
Also Called: Dropbox
1800 Owens St Ste 200 (94158-2533)
PHONE.....................415 857-6800
Andrew W Houston, Ch Bd
Timothy Young, Pr
Timothy Regan, CFO
Bart E Volkmer, CLO
EMP: 2219 EST: 2007
SALES (est): 2.32B Publicly Held
Web: www.dropbox.com
SIC: 7372 Prepackaged software

(P-12169)
DUDA MOBILE INC
577 College Ave (94306-1433)
P.O. Box 60432 (94306-0432)
PHONE.....................855 790-0003
Itia Sadan, CEO
Sarah Carpenter, CFO
EMP: 67 EST: 2011
SALES (est): 4.68MM Privately Held
Web: www.duda.co
SIC: 7372 Application computer software

(P-12170)
EAGLE TOPCO LP
18200 Von Karman Ave (92612-1023)
PHONE.....................949 585-4329
EMP: 4000
SIC: 7372 Business oriented computer software

(P-12171)
ECRIO INC
19925 Stevens Creek Blvd Ste 100 (95014-2300)
PHONE.....................408 973-7290
Randy Granovetter, CEO
Nagesh Challa, Chief Strategy Officer
Tad Bogdan, Ex VP
Lina Martin, VP Fin
Ted Goldstein, Chief Strategy Officer
EMP: 90 EST: 1998
SALES (est): 7.13MM Privately Held
Web: www.ecrio.com
SIC: 7372 Prepackaged software

(P-12172)
EDGEWAVE INC
4225 Executive Sq # 1600 (92037-1487)
PHONE.....................800 782-3762
EMP: 100
SIC: 7372 Operating systems computer software

PRODUCTS & SERVICES SECTION
7372 - Prepackaged Software (P-12194)

(P-12173)
EDUCATION ELEMENTS INC
101 Hickey Blvd Ste A # 526 (94080-1177)
PHONE..................................650 440-7860
Anthony Kim, *CEO*
Victoria Bernholz, *
EMP: 68 **EST:** 2010
SALES (est): 6.79MM **Privately Held**
Web: www.edelements.com
SIC: 7372 Educational computer software

(P-12174)
EFINIX INC (PA)
20400 Stevens Creek Blvd Ste 200 (95014-2290)
PHONE..................................408 789-6917
Sammy Cheung, *CEO*
EMP: 113 **EST:** 2012
SALES (est): 10.41MM
SALES (corp-wide): 10.41MM **Privately Held**
Web: www.efinixinc.com
SIC: 7372 Business oriented computer software

(P-12175)
EGAIN CORPORATION (PA)
Also Called: Egain
1252 Borregas Ave (94089-1309)
PHONE..................................408 636-4500
Ashutosh Roy, *Ch Bd*
Eric Smit, *CFO*
Promod Narang, *Sr VP*
EMP: 405 **EST:** 1997
SQ FT: 42,541
SALES (est): 98.01MM
SALES (corp-wide): 98.01MM **Publicly Held**
Web: www.egain.com
SIC: 7372 7371 Prepackaged software; Custom computer programming services

(P-12176)
EGL HOLDCO INC
18200 Von Karman Ave # 1000 (92612-1023)
PHONE..................................800 678-7423
EMP: 4000
SALES (est): 98.44MM **Privately Held**
SIC: 7372 Prepackaged software

(P-12177)
EIGHTFOLD AI INC (PA)
2625 Augustine Dr 6th Fl (95054-2956)
PHONE..................................650 265-7380
Eightfold Garg, *CEO*
Ashutosh Garg, *
Rupa Veerapuneni, *
EMP: 114 **EST:** 2016
SALES (est): 8.44MM
SALES (corp-wide): 8.44MM **Privately Held**
Web: www.eightfold.ai
SIC: 7372 Prepackaged software

(P-12178)
EIS GROUP INC
4 Embarcadero Ctr (94111-4187)
PHONE..................................415 402-2622
EMP: 128 **EST:** 2008
SALES (est): 31.45MM **Privately Held**
Web: www.eisgroup.com
SIC: 7372 Business oriented computer software

(P-12179)
ELECTRONIC ARTS INC (PA)
Also Called: Ea
209 Redwood Shores Pkwy (94065-1175)
PHONE..................................650 628-1500
Andrew Wilson, *Ch Bd*
Laura Miele, *COO*
Mala Singh, *CPO*
Jacob J Schatz, *CLO*
Stuart Canfield, *Ex VP*
▲ **EMP:** 475 **EST:** 1982
SALES (est): 7.43B
SALES (corp-wide): 7.43B **Publicly Held**
Web: www.ea.com
SIC: 7372 Home entertainment computer software

(P-12180)
ELECTRONIC CLEARING HOUSE INC (HQ)
730 Paseo Camarillo (93010-6064)
PHONE..................................805 419-8700
Charles J Harris, *Pr*
Alice L Cheung, *
Rick Slater, *
William Wied, *CIO**
Karl Asplund, *
EMP: 100 **EST:** 1981
SQ FT: 32,669
SALES (est): 49.29MM
SALES (corp-wide): 14.37B **Publicly Held**
Web: www.echo-inc.com
SIC: 7372 Business oriented computer software
PA: Intuit Inc.
2700 Coast Ave
Mountain View CA
650 944-6000

(P-12181)
ENTCO LLC
Also Called: Autonomy Interwoven
1140 Enterprise Way (94089-1412)
PHONE..................................312 580-9100
EMP: 916
SIC: 7372 Business oriented computer software

(P-12182)
ESPRESSIVE INC
5201 Great America Pkwy Ste 110 (95054-1122)
PHONE..................................408 753-8766
EMP: 66 **EST:** 2016
SALES (est): 4.74MM **Privately Held**
Web: www.espressive.com
SIC: 7372 Application computer software

(P-12183)
ETECH-360 INC (PA)
Also Called: 360s2g
555 California St (94104-1503)
P.O. Box 7491 (92624-7491)
PHONE..................................714 900-3486
Isabelle Hughes, *CEO*
Douglas Carver, *
Amanda Gutierrez, *Senior Vice President Client Management**
Devon Knittle, *
Pat Kyomoto, *
EMP: 551 **EST:** 2010
SQ FT: 8,000
SALES (est): 43.23MM
SALES (corp-wide): 43.23MM **Privately Held**
Web: www.360s2g.com
SIC: 7372 5045 7371 8243 Prepackaged software; Computers, peripherals, and software; Custom computer programming services; Data processing schools

(P-12184)
EVERBRIDGE INC (PA)
155 N Lake Ave Ste 900 (91101-1857)
PHONE..................................818 230-9700
David Wagner, *Pr*
Jaime Ellertson, *
David Henshall, *Vice Chairman**
Robert Hughes, *
Patrick Brickley, *
EMP: 111 **EST:** 2002
SQ FT: 45,000
SALES (est): 431.89MM
SALES (corp-wide): 431.89MM **Publicly Held**
Web: www.everbridge.com
SIC: 7372 4899 Prepackaged software; Data communication services

(P-12185)
EVOCATIVE INC
600 W 7th St Ste 510 (90017-3864)
PHONE..................................888 365-2656
EMP: 75 **EST:** 1996
SQ FT: 15,000
SALES (est): 13.94MM
SALES (corp-wide): 39.94MM **Privately Held**
Web: www.evocative.com
SIC: 7372 Application computer software
PA: Evodc, Llc
600 W 7th St Ste 510
Los Angeles CA
888 365-2656

(P-12186)
EVOLUTION ROBOTICS INC
1055 E Colorado Blvd Ste 320 (91106)
PHONE..................................626 993-3300
Paolo Pirjanian, *CEO*
Bill Gross, *
Doug Mcpherson, *Sec*
EMP: 146 **EST:** 2001
SALES (est): 11.68MM **Publicly Held**
Web: careers.evolution.com
SIC: 7372 Application computer software
PA: Irobot Corporation
8 Crosby Dr
Bedford MA

(P-12187)
EXADEL INC (PA)
1340 Treat Blvd Ste 375 (94597-7590)
PHONE..................................925 363-9510
Fima Katz, *CEO*
Alex Kreymer, *
EMP: 2656 **EST:** 1995
SALES (est): 99.03MM **Privately Held**
Web: www.exadel.com
SIC: 7372 Application computer software

(P-12188)
FAIR ISAAC INTERNATIONAL CORP (HQ)
200 Smith Ranch Rd (94903-5551)
PHONE..................................415 446-6000
EMP: 600 **EST:** 1979
SALES (est): 151.18MM
SALES (corp-wide): 1.51B **Publicly Held**
Web: www.fico.com
SIC: 7372 Business oriented computer software
PA: Fair Isaac Corporation
5 W Mendenhall St Ste 105
Bozeman MT
406 982-7276

(P-12189)
FIRSTUP INC (PA)
1 Montgomery St Ste 2150 (94104-5505)
PHONE..................................844 975-2533
Nicole Alvino, *CEO*
Gary Nakamura, *
Gregory Shove, *
Peter C Horan, *
Valerie Johnson, *
EMP: 392 **EST:** 2010
SALES (est): 39.13MM
SALES (corp-wide): 39.13MM **Privately Held**
Web: www.firstup.io
SIC: 7372 Business oriented computer software

(P-12190)
FITSTAR INC
80 Langton St (94103-3916)
PHONE..................................415 409-8348
Mike Maser, *CEO*
EMP: 1323 **EST:** 2004
SALES (est): 3.12MM
SALES (corp-wide): 282.84B **Publicly Held**
Web: www.fitstar.com
SIC: 7372 Application computer software
HQ: Fitbit Llc
199 Fremont St Fl 14
San Francisco CA

(P-12191)
FIVE9 INC (PA)
3001 Bishop Dr Ste 350 (94583-5005)
PHONE..................................925 201-2000
Rowan Trollope, *CEO*
Michael Burkland, *
Barry Zwarenstein, *CFO*
Daniel Burkland, *Pr*
Scott Welch, *CLOUD OPRS & PLATFORM ENGINEERING*
EMP: 691 **EST:** 2001
SQ FT: 104,000
SALES (est): 778.85MM
SALES (corp-wide): 778.85MM **Publicly Held**
Web: www.five9.com
SIC: 7372 7374 Prepackaged software; Data processing and preparation

(P-12192)
FIVETRAN INC (PA)
405 14th St Ste 1100 (94612-2707)
PHONE..................................415 805-2799
George Fraser, *CEO*
Taylor Brown, *Prin*
Rachel Thornton, *CMO*
EMP: 1198 **EST:** 2014
SALES (est): 200MM
SALES (corp-wide): 200MM **Privately Held**
Web: www.fivetran.com
SIC: 7372 Business oriented computer software

(P-12193)
FORGEROCK US INC (HQ)
201 Mission St Ste 2900 (94105-1858)
PHONE..................................415 599-1100
EMP: 73 **EST:** 2010
SQ FT: 15,744
SALES (est): 26.38MM
SALES (corp-wide): 217.51MM **Privately Held**
Web: www.forgerock.com
SIC: 7372 5045 Prepackaged software; Computer software
PA: Forgerock, Inc.
201 Mission St Ste 2900
San Francisco CA
415 599-1100

(P-12194)
FORMER NT CORP
1054 S De Anza Blvd # 202 (95129-3553)
PHONE..................................330 702-3070

7372 - Prepackaged Software (P-12195)

EMP: 60
SIC: 7372 Business oriented computer software

(P-12195)
FORTEZZA IRIDIUM HOLDINGS INC
150 California St (94111-4500)
PHONE..........................415 765-6500
Robert F Smith, *Pr*
EMP: 836 **EST:** 2006
SALES (est): 59.3MM **Privately Held**
SIC: 7372 Business oriented computer software
PA: Vista Equity Fund Ii Lp
150 California St Fl 19
San Francisco CA

(P-12196)
FORWARD NETWORKS INC
2390 Mission College Blvd # 401 (95054-1530)
PHONE..........................844 393-6389
David Erickson, *CEO*
Brandon Heller, *
Nikhil Ashok Handigol, *
Denis Maynard, *CRO*
EMP: 75 **EST:** 2013
SALES (est): 4.02MM **Privately Held**
Web: www.forwardnetworks.com
SIC: 7372 8748 Application computer software; Systems engineering consultant, ex. computer or professional

(P-12197)
FOUNDATION 9 ENTERTAINMENT INC (PA)
30211 Avenida De Las Bandera Ste 200 (92688)
PHONE..........................949 698-1500
James N Hearn, *CEO*
John Goldman, *
David Mann, *
EMP: 200 **EST:** 2005
SALES (est): 59.5MM **Privately Held**
SIC: 7372 Home entertainment computer software

(P-12198)
FRESHWORKS INC (PA)
Also Called: Freshworks
2950 S Delaware St Ste 201 (94403)
PHONE..........................650 513-0514
Rathna Girish Mathrubootham, *Ch Bd*
Rathna Girish Mathrubootham, *Ch Bd*
Dennis M Woodside, *Pr*
Tyler Sloat, *CFO*
Stacey Epstein, *CMO*
EMP: 122 **EST:** 2010
SQ FT: 20,000
SALES (est): 498MM
SALES (corp-wide): 498MM **Publicly Held**
Web: www.freshworks.com
SIC: 7372 Prepackaged software

(P-12199)
FRONTAPP INC
Also Called: Front
300 Montgomery St (94104-1916)
PHONE..........................415 680-3048
Mathilde Collin, *CEO*
Laurent Perrin, *
EMP: 71 **EST:** 2014
SALES (est): 5MM **Privately Held**
Web: www.front.com
SIC: 7372 Application computer software

(P-12200)
GAINSIGHT INC (PA)
350 Bay St Ste 100 (94133-1902)
PHONE..........................888 623-8562
Nick Mehta, *CEO*
Alka Tandan, *
Kellie Capote, *CCO*
Monika Saha, *CMO*
Jeff Depa, *CRO*
EMP: 409 **EST:** 2013
SALES (est): 153.28MM
SALES (corp-wide): 153.28MM **Privately Held**
Web: www.gainsight.com
SIC: 7372 7371 Prepackaged software; Custom computer programming services

(P-12201)
GAZILLION INC
Also Called: Slipgatte Ironworks
475 Concar Dr (94402-2650)
PHONE..........................650 393-6500
EMP: 300
SIC: 7372 Publisher's computer software

(P-12202)
GE DIGITAL LLC
2700 Camino Ramon (94583-5004)
PHONE..........................925 242-6200
EMP: 278
SALES (corp-wide): 76.56B **Publicly Held**
Web: www.ge.com
SIC: 7372 Prepackaged software
HQ: Ge Digital Llc
58 Charles St
Cambridge MA
925 242-6200

(P-12203)
GEARBOX PUBG SAN FRANCISCO INC ✪
100 Redwood Shores Pkwy Fl 2 (94065)
PHONE..........................650 590-7700
Yoon Im, *CEO*
EMP: 71 **EST:** 2022
SALES (est): 1.1MM **Privately Held**
Web: sf.gearboxpublishing.com
SIC: 7372 Publisher's computer software

(P-12204)
GENESYS CLOUD SERVICES INC (HQ)
Also Called: Genesys Telecom Labs
1302 El Camino Real Ste 300 (94025)
PHONE..........................650 466-1100
Paul Segre, *Ch Bd*
Tony Bates, *
Tom Eggemeier, *
EMP: 450 **EST:** 1990
SQ FT: 156,000
SALES (est): 930.03MM
SALES (corp-wide): 220.02MM **Privately Held**
Web: www.genesys.com
SIC: 7372 Business oriented computer software
PA: Permira Advisers Llp
80 Pall Mall
London
207 632-1000

(P-12205)
GINSBERG HOLDCO INC
3300 Olcott St (95054-3005)
PHONE..........................408 831-4000
Paul A Hooper, *CEO*
Rex S Jackson, *CFO*
Kim Decarlis, *CMO*
EMP: 500 **EST:** 2017

SQ FT: 105,600
SALES (est): 25.86MM **Privately Held**
Web: www.gigamon.com
SIC: 7372 3577 Prepackaged software; Computer peripheral equipment, nec

(P-12206)
GLADIATOR CORPORATION
2882 Sand Hill Rd Ste 280 (94025-7057)
PHONE..........................650 233-2900
EMP: 338
SIC: 7372 Prepackaged software

(P-12207)
GLOBAL CASH CARD INC
3972 Barranca Pkwy Ste J610 (92606-1204)
PHONE..........................949 751-0360
EMP: 165
SIC: 7372 Business oriented computer software

(P-12208)
GOLINKS ENTERPRISES INC
Also Called: Go/Links
2558 Forest Ave (95117-1117)
PHONE..........................562 715-4848
Jorge Zamora, *CEO*
George Samora, *
EMP: 75 **EST:** 2016
SALES (est): 6.28MM **Privately Held**
Web: www.golinks.io
SIC: 7372 Application computer software

(P-12209)
GOOD TECHNOLOGY SOFTWARE INC
430 N Mary Ave Ste 200 (94085-2923)
PHONE..........................408 212-7500
EMP: 600
SIC: 7372 3661 Prepackaged software; Telephones and telephone apparatus

(P-12210)
GOVERNMENTJOBSCOM INC
Also Called: Neogov
2120 Park Pl Ste 100 (90245-4741)
PHONE..........................310 426-6304
Damir Davidovic, *CEO*
Scott Letourneau, *
EMP: 130 **EST:** 2000
SQ FT: 5,000
SALES (est): 29.72MM **Privately Held**
Web: www.neogov.com
SIC: 7372 Prepackaged software

(P-12211)
GREEN HILLS SOFTWARE LLC (HQ)
Also Called: Green Hills Software
30 W Sola St (93101-2599)
PHONE..........................805 965-6044
Daniel O Dowd, *CEO*
Daniel O'dowd, *CEO*
Jeffrey Hazarian, *
EMP: 105 **EST:** 1986
SALES (est): 89.29MM
SALES (corp-wide): 124.94MM **Privately Held**
Web: www.ghs.com
SIC: 7372 Prepackaged software
PA: Ghs Holding Company
30 W Sola St
Santa Barbara CA
805 965-6044

(P-12212)
GREMLIN INC
440 N Barranca Ave Ste 3101 (91789)

PHONE..........................408 214-9885
Josh Leslie, *CEO*
Kolton Andrus, *
EMP: 80 **EST:** 2016
SALES (est): 12.16MM **Privately Held**
Web: www.gremlin.com
SIC: 7372 8742 Prepackaged software; Management consulting services

(P-12213)
GRIDGAIN SYSTEMS INC (PA)
1065 E Hillsdale Blvd Ste 410 (94404-1615)
PHONE..........................650 241-2281
Eoin O' Connor, *CEO*
Elena Schtein, *
Sarah Jadidi, *
EMP: 126 **EST:** 2010
SALES (est): 17.14MM
SALES (corp-wide): 17.14MM **Privately Held**
Web: www.gridgain.com
SIC: 7372 Prepackaged software

(P-12214)
GROOVE LABS INC
660 4th St # 684 (94107-1618)
PHONE..........................650 999-0200
Chris Rothstein, *CEO*
Michael Sutherland, *VP*
EMP: 68 **EST:** 2014
SALES (est): 5.66MM
SALES (corp-wide): 55.74MM **Privately Held**
Web: www.groove.co
SIC: 7372 Application computer software
PA: Clari Inc.
1154 Sonora Ct
Sunnyvale CA
650 265-2111

(P-12215)
GUIDANCE SOFTWARE INC (HQ)
1055 E Colorado Blvd Ste 400 (91106)
PHONE..........................626 229-9191
Patrick Dennis, *Pr*
Barry Plaga, *
Michael Harris, *CMO*
Alfredo Gomez, *Corporate Secretary*
EMP: 215 **EST:** 2006
SQ FT: 90,000
SALES (est): 51.33MM
SALES (corp-wide): 832.31MM **Privately Held**
Web: www.opentext.com
SIC: 7372 3572 Business oriented computer software; Computer storage devices
PA: Open Text Corporation
275 Frank Tompa Dr
Waterloo ON
519 888-7111

(P-12216)
GUIDEWIRE SOFTWARE INC (PA)
Also Called: Guidewire
970 Park Pl Ste 200 (94403-1907)
PHONE..........................650 357-9100
Michael Rosenbaum, *CEO*
Marcus S Ryu, *
Priscilla Hung, *Pr*
Jeff Cooper, *CFO*
Winston King, *CAO*
EMP: 538 **EST:** 2001
SQ FT: 78,911
SALES (est): 905.34MM
SALES (corp-wide): 905.34MM **Publicly Held**
Web: www.guidewire.com

PRODUCTS & SERVICES SECTION
7372 - Prepackaged Software (P-12237)

SIC: 7372 Business oriented computer software

(P-12217)
GUSTO INC (PA)
525 20th St (94107-4345)
PHONE..................800 936-0383
Joshua D Reeves, *CEO*
Tomer London, *CPO*
Mike Dinsdale, *CFO*
Lexi Reese, *COO*
EMP: 250 EST: 2011
SALES (est): 103.63MM
SALES (corp-wide): 103.63MM **Privately Held**
Web: www.gusto.com
SIC: 7372 Business oriented computer software

(P-12218)
HEALTH GORILLA INC
800 W El Camino Real Ste 100 (94040)
PHONE..................844 446-7455
Steven Yaskin, *CEO*
Sergio Wagner, *
EMP: 120 EST: 2014
SALES (est): 10.52MM **Privately Held**
Web: www.healthgorilla.com
SIC: 7372 8011 Application computer software; Health maintenance organization

(P-12219)
HEARSAY SYSTEMS INC (PA)
Also Called: Hearsay Social
600 Harrison St Ste 120 (94107-1307)
PHONE..................888 399-2280
Clara Shih, *CEO*
Michael H Lock, *
Caitlin Haberberger, *
William Salisbury, *
Mark Gilbert, *
EMP: 182 EST: 2009
SALES (est): 57.23MM
SALES (corp-wide): 57.23MM **Privately Held**
Web: www.hearsaysystems.com
SIC: 7372 Publisher's computer software

(P-12220)
HEAT SOFTWARE USA INC
490 N Mccarthy Blvd Ste 100 (95035-5118)
PHONE..................408 601-2800
EMP: 258
SIC: 7372 Prepackaged software

(P-12221)
HEAVYAI INC
100 Montgomery St 5th Fl (94104-4301)
PHONE..................415 997-2814
Jon Kondo, *CEO*
EMP: 90 EST: 2013
SQ FT: 2,000
SALES (est): 7.96MM **Privately Held**
Web: www.heavy.ai
SIC: 7372 Business oriented computer software

(P-12222)
HIGHER ONE PAYMENTS INC
Also Called: Cashnet
80 Swan Way Ste 200 (94621-1439)
PHONE..................510 769-9888
Dan Peterson, *Pr*
Greg Schuster, *Sr VP*
Chuck Haddock, *
EMP: 397 EST: 1983
SQ FT: 4,500
SALES (est): 3.37MM
SALES (corp-wide): 90.41MM **Privately Held**
Web: www.transactcampus.com
SIC: 7372 Business oriented computer software
HQ: Higher One, Inc.
18700 N Hayden Rd Ste 230
Scottsdale AZ

(P-12223)
HITACHI ENERGY USA INC
60 Spear St (94105-1506)
PHONE..................415 527-2850
Greg Dukat, *Brnch Mgr*
EMP: 99
SIC: 7372 Business oriented computer software
HQ: Hitachi Energy Usa Inc
901 Main Campus Dr
Raleigh NC
919 856-2360

(P-12224)
HORTONWORKS INC (DH)
Also Called: Hortonworks
5470 Great America Pkwy (95054-3644)
PHONE..................408 916-4121
EMP: 725 EST: 2011
SQ FT: 92,000
SALES (est): 229.59MM
SALES (corp-wide): 1.26B **Privately Held**
Web: www.cloudera.com
SIC: 7372 Application computer software
HQ: Cloudera, Inc.
5470 Great America Pkwy
Santa Clara CA
650 362-0488

(P-12225)
HPE ENTERPRISES LLC (HQ)
6280 America Center Dr (95002-2563)
PHONE..................650 857-5817
EMP: 120 EST: 2015
SALES (est): 84.79MM
SALES (corp-wide): 28.5B **Publicly Held**
Web: www.hpe.com
SIC: 7372 7379 3572 Prepackaged software; Computer related maintenance services; Computer storage devices
PA: Hewlett Packard Enterprise Company
1701 E Mossy Oaks Rd
Spring TX
678 259-9860

(P-12226)
HVR SOFTWARE USA INC
44 Montgomery St Ste 3 (94104-4618)
PHONE..................415 489-3427
Anthony Brooks Williams, *CEO*
Kyle Klopfer, *CFO*
EMP: 62 EST: 2014
SALES (est): 6.32MM **Privately Held**
SIC: 7372 Business oriented computer software

(P-12227)
ICE MORTGAGE TECHNOLOGY INC (HQ)
Also Called: Ellie Mae
4420 Rosewood Dr Ste 500 (94588-3059)
PHONE..................855 224-8572
Jonathan Corr, *Pr*
Dan Madden, *
Brian Brown, *
Joe Tyrrell, *
Cathleen Schreiner Gates, *
EMP: 468 EST: 1997
SQ FT: 280,680
SALES (est): 480.27MM
SALES (corp-wide): 7.29B **Publicly Held**
Web: www.icemortgagetechnology.com
SIC: 7372 7371 Prepackaged software; Computer software systems analysis and design, custom
PA: Intercontinental Exchange, Inc.
5660 New Northside Dr # 3
Atlanta GA
770 857-4700

(P-12228)
IMPLY DATA INC (PA)
Also Called: Imply
1633 Bayshore Hwy Ste 232 (94010)
PHONE..................415 685-8187
Fang Jin Yang, *CEO*
Gian Merlino, *
Anthony Russo, *
Juleen Konkel, *
EMP: 126 EST: 2015
SQ FT: 1,000
SALES (est): 10MM
SALES (corp-wide): 10MM **Privately Held**
Web: www.imply.io
SIC: 7372 Business oriented computer software

(P-12229)
INDIUM SOFTWARE INC
19925 Stevens Creek Blvd Ste 100 (95014-2300)
PHONE..................408 501-8844
Harsha Nutalapati, *CEO*
Vijay Shankar Balaji, *
EMP: 89 EST: 2006
SALES (est): 11.63MM **Privately Held**
Web: www.indiumsoftware.com
SIC: 7372 Prepackaged software
HQ: Indium Software (India) Private Limited
2nd Floor Vds House
Chennai TN

(P-12230)
INFOR PUBLIC SECTOR INC (DH)
11092 Sun Center Dr (95670-6109)
PHONE..................916 921-0883
Charles Hansen, *CEO*
Mark Watts, *
Bob Benstead, *
EMP: 160 EST: 1983
SQ FT: 28,000
SALES (est): 49.57MM
SALES (corp-wide): 36.93B **Privately Held**
Web: www.infor.com
SIC: 7372 Application computer software
HQ: Infor (Us), Llc
641 Ave Of The Americas
New York NY
866 244-5479

(P-12231)
INFORMATICA HOLDCO INC
2100 Seaport Blvd (94063-5596)
PHONE..................650 385-5000
Amit Walia, *CEO*
EMP: 4897 EST: 2015
SALES (est): 480.33MM **Privately Held**
Web: www.informatica.com
SIC: 7372 Prepackaged software

(P-12232)
INFORMATICA INC
Also Called: Informatica
2100 Seaport Blvd (94063-5596)
PHONE..................650 385-5000
Amit Walia, *CEO*
Bruce Chizen, *
Eric Brown, *Ex VP*
Jitesh Ghai, *CPO*
John Schweitzer, *CRO*
EMP: 5249 EST: 1993
SQ FT: 290,000
SALES (est): 1.51B **Privately Held**
Web: www.informatica.com
SIC: 7372 Prepackaged software

(P-12233)
INFORMATICA LLC (DH)
Also Called: Informatica LLC of Delaware
2100 Seaport Blvd (94063-5596)
PHONE..................650 385-5000
Amit Walia, *CEO*
Bradford Lewis, *CLO**
Graeme Thompson, *CIO**
Erin Andre, *Chief Human Resource Officer**
Ansa Sekharan, *
EMP: 347 EST: 1999
SQ FT: 290,000
SALES (est): 1.51B
SALES (corp-wide): 220.02MM **Privately Held**
Web: www.informatica.com
SIC: 7372 Prepackaged software
HQ: Permira Advisers Llc
320 Park Ave Fl 28
New York NY
212 386-7480

(P-12234)
INMAGE SYSTEMS INC
1065 La Avenida St (94043-1421)
PHONE..................408 200-3840
Debbie Button, *CEO*
John Ferraro, *
Marty Bradford, *
EMP: 99 EST: 2001
SALES (est): 22.21MM
SALES (corp-wide): 211.91B **Publicly Held**
SIC: 7372 Business oriented computer software
PA: Microsoft Corporation
1 Microsoft Way
Redmond WA
425 882-8080

(P-12235)
INTELLECTYX INC
Also Called: Intellectyx
680 E Colorado Blvd Ste 180 (91101)
PHONE..................720 256-7540
Raj Joseph, *CEO*
EMP: 70 EST: 2010
SALES (est): 3.9MM **Privately Held**
Web: www.intellectyx.com
SIC: 7372 Business oriented computer software

(P-12236)
INTERACTIVE SOLUTIONS INC (DH)
Also Called: Web Traffic School
283 4th St Ste 301 (94607-4320)
P.O. Box 209 (94604-0209)
PHONE..................510 214-9002
Isaak Tsifrin, *CEO*
Gary Golduber, *
Gary Tsifrin, *
EMP: 67 EST: 1987
SQ FT: 14,000
SALES (est): 13.35MM
SALES (corp-wide): 1.21B **Privately Held**
SIC: 7372 Prepackaged software
HQ: Edriving Llc
1255 Treat Blvd Ste 300
Walnut Creek CA
800 243-4008

(P-12237)
INTERMDIA CLOUD CMMNCTIONS INC

7372 - Prepackaged Software (P-12238)

100 Mathilda Pl Ste 600 (94086-6081)
PHONE..................................650 641-4000
Michael J Gold, *Pr*
Jason H Veldhuis, *CFO*
Jonathan S Mccormick, *CRO*
EMP: 1088 **EST:** 1993
SQ FT: 19,600
SALES (est): 310.27MM
SALES (corp-wide): 310.27MM **Privately Held**
Web: www.intermedia.com
SIC: 7372 Prepackaged software
PA: Ivy Parent Holdings, Llc
70 W Madison St Ste 4600
Chicago IL
312 895-1000

(P-12238)
INTUIT INC (PA)
Also Called: Intuit
2700 Coast Ave (94043-1140)
P.O. Box 7850 (94039-7850)
PHONE..................................650 944-6000
Sasan K Goodarzi, *Pr*
Scott Cook, *
Michelle M Clatterbuck, *Ex VP*
Kerry J Mclean, *Corporate Secretary*
Lara Balazs, *CMO*
EMP: 70 **EST:** 1983
SALES (est): 14.37B
SALES (corp-wide): 14.37B **Publicly Held**
Web: www.intuit.com
SIC: 7372 Prepackaged software

(P-12239)
INTUIT INC
21650 Oxnard St Ste 2200 (91367-7824)
PHONE..................................818 436-7800
Michael Ermi, *Brnch Mgr*
EMP: 105
SALES (corp-wide): 14.37B **Publicly Held**
Web: quickbooks.intuit.com
SIC: 7372 Business oriented computer software
PA: Intuit Inc.
2700 Coast Ave
Mountain View CA
650 944-6000

(P-12240)
INTUIT INC
2535 Garcia Ave (94043-1111)
PHONE..................................650 944-6000
Connie Berg, *Brnch Mgr*
EMP: 128
SALES (corp-wide): 14.37B **Publicly Held**
Web: www.intuit.com
SIC: 7372 Business oriented computer software
PA: Intuit Inc.
2700 Coast Ave
Mountain View CA
650 944-6000

(P-12241)
INTUIT INC
7535 Torrey Santa Fe Rd (92129-5704)
PHONE..................................858 780-2846
Brian Bequette, *Prin*
EMP: 182
SALES (corp-wide): 14.37B **Publicly Held**
Web: www.intuit.com
SIC: 7372 Business oriented computer software
PA: Intuit Inc.
2700 Coast Ave
Mountain View CA
650 944-6000

(P-12242)
INTUIT INC
Also Called: Turbotax
7545 Torrey Santa Fe Rd (92129-5704)
PHONE..................................858 215-8000
Jason Jackson, *Brnch Mgr*
EMP: 300
SALES (corp-wide): 14.37B **Publicly Held**
Web: www.intuit.com
SIC: 7372 Business oriented computer software
PA: Intuit Inc.
2700 Coast Ave
Mountain View CA
650 944-6000

(P-12243)
INVESTOPEDIA LLC
555 12th St Ste 500 (94607-3699)
PHONE..................................510 985-7400
David Siegel, *CEO*
EMP: 113 **EST:** 2013
SALES (est): 1.62MM
SALES (corp-wide): 5.24B **Publicly Held**
Web: www.iac.com
SIC: 7372 Educational computer software
HQ: Iac Search, Llc
555 W 18th St
New York NY
212 314-7300

(P-12244)
INVOICE2GO LLC (DH)
2317 Broadway St Fl 2 (94063-1674)
PHONE..................................650 300-5180
Mark Lenhard, *CEO*
Sean Deorsey, *
EMP: 140 **EST:** 2014
SALES (est): 25.91MM
SALES (corp-wide): 1.06B **Publicly Held**
Web: invoice.2go.com
SIC: 7372 Prepackaged software
HQ: Bill.Com, Llc
6220 America Center Dr # 100
San Jose CA
650 353-3301

(P-12245)
IPOLIPO INC
Also Called: Jifflenow
440 N Wolfe Rd (94085-3869)
PHONE..................................408 916-5290
Hari Shetty, *Pr*
Shekhar Kirani, *
Rajesh Setty, *
EMP: 75 **EST:** 2006
SALES (est): 6.61MM **Privately Held**
Web: www.jifflenow.com
SIC: 7372 Application computer software

(P-12246)
IQMS LLC (DH)
2231 Wisteria Ln (93446-9820)
PHONE..................................805 227-1122
Gary Nemmers, *Pr*
Matt Ouska, *
Steve Bieszczat, *CMO**
Dan Vertachnik, *CRO**
Dan Radunz, *
EMP: 130 **EST:** 1989
SQ FT: 60,000
SALES (est): 49.15MM **Privately Held**
SIC: 7372 Prepackaged software
HQ: Dassault Systemes
10 Rue Marcel Dassault
Velizy Villacoublay
161626162

(P-12247)
JACADA INC
Also Called: Jacada Autonomous Cx
1001 Page Mill Rd Ste 100 (94304-1073)
PHONE..................................770 352-1300
Gideon Hollander, *CEO*
Tzvia Broida, *
Guy Yair, *
Caroline Cronin, *
Dan Weil, *
EMP: 85 **EST:** 1991
SALES (est): 9.2MM
SALES (corp-wide): 15.19MM **Privately Held**
Web: www.uniphore.com
SIC: 7372 Business oriented computer software
PA: Uniphore Technologies Inc.
1001 Page Mill Rd Bldg 4
Palo Alto CA
650 352-5500

(P-12248)
JAM CITY INC
2255 N Ontario St (91504-3187)
PHONE..................................804 920-8760
Tiffany Van Decker, *Prin*
EMP: 76
SALES (corp-wide): 59.07MM **Privately Held**
Web: www.jamcity.com
SIC: 7372 Prepackaged software
PA: Jam City, Inc.
3562 Eastham Dr
Culver City CA
310 205-4800

(P-12249)
KHAN ACADEMY INC
1200 Villa St Ste 200 (94041-2922)
P.O. Box 1630 (94042-1630)
PHONE..................................650 336-5426
Salman Khan, *Ex Dir*
Shantanu Sinha, *
EMP: 85 **EST:** 2009
SALES (est): 59.26MM **Privately Held**
Web: www.khanacademy.org
SIC: 7372 Educational computer software

(P-12250)
KLOUDGIN INC
Also Called: Kloudgin
440 N Wolfe Rd (94085-3869)
PHONE..................................877 256-8303
Vikram Takru, *CEO*
Dharmesh Sethi, *CFO*
EMP: 175 **EST:** 2010
SALES (est): 13.17MM **Privately Held**
Web: www.kloudgin.com
SIC: 7372 Business oriented computer software

(P-12251)
KLOUDSPOT INC
1285 Oakmead Pkwy (94085-4040)
PHONE..................................800 709-2211
Ravi Akireddy, *CEO*
EMP: 80 **EST:** 2017
SALES (est): 2.61MM **Privately Held**
Web: www.kloudspot.com
SIC: 7372 Prepackaged software

(P-12252)
KNO INC
2200 Mission College Blvd (95054-1537)
PHONE..................................408 844-8120
Ronald D Dickel, *CEO*
Babur Habib, *
EMP: 70 **EST:** 1998
SQ FT: 35,000
SALES (est): 22.7MM
SALES (corp-wide): 63.05B **Publicly Held**
Web: www.kno.com
SIC: 7372 Educational computer software
PA: Intel Corporation
2200 Mission College Blvd
Santa Clara CA
408 765-8080

(P-12253)
KRANEM CORPORATION
Also Called: Kranem
560 S Winchester Blvd Ste 500 (95128-2536)
PHONE..................................650 319-6743
Ajay Batheja, *Ch Bd*
Edward Miller, *CFO*
Luigi Caramico, *Corporate Strategy Vice President*
EMP: 190 **EST:** 2002
SALES (est): 17.44MM **Privately Held**
SIC: 7372 Business oriented computer software

(P-12254)
LABELBOX INC
510 Treat Ave (94110-2014)
PHONE..................................415 294-0791
Manu Sharma, *CEO*
EMP: 175 **EST:** 2018
SALES (est): 6.9MM **Privately Held**
SIC: 7372 Prepackaged software

(P-12255)
LASTLINE INC (PA)
3401 Hillview Ave (94304-1320)
PHONE..................................877 671-3239
John Dilullo, *CEO*
Brian Laing, *
Bert Rankin, *
Ananth Avva, *
EMP: 191 **EST:** 2009
SALES (est): 44.94MM **Privately Held**
SIC: 7372 Prepackaged software

(P-12256)
LIVEOFFICE LLC
Also Called: Advisorsquare
900 Corporate Pointe (90230-7609)
PHONE..................................877 253-2793
Matt Smith, *
Nikhil Menta, *
Jeffrey W Hausman, *
Matt Hardy, *
EMP: 73 **EST:** 2007
SQ FT: 15,000
SALES (est): 10MM
SALES (corp-wide): 3.34B **Publicly Held**
Web: www.liveoffice.com
SIC: 7372 Prepackaged software
PA: Gen Digital Inc.
60 E Rio Salado Pkwy # 1
Tempe AZ
650 527-8000

(P-12257)
LOGINEXT SOLUTIONS INC
Also Called: Loginext
5002 Spring Crest Ter (94536-6525)
PHONE..................................510 894-6225
Dhruvil Sanghvi, *CEO*
Manisha Raisinghani, *
EMP: 200 **EST:** 2017
SALES (est): 12.84MM **Privately Held**
Web: www.loginextsolutions.com
SIC: 7372 7371 7379 8243 Prepackaged software; Computer software systems analysis and design, custom; Computer related consulting services; Software training, computer

PRODUCTS & SERVICES SECTION
7372 - Prepackaged Software (P-12278)

(P-12258)
LPA INSURANCE AGENCY INC
Also Called: Sat
3800 Watt Ave Ste 147 (95821-2676)
PHONE..................916 286-7850
Michael Winkel, *Pr*
EMP: 115 EST: 1983
SALES (est): 3.51MM
SALES (corp-wide): 14.53B **Publicly Held**
SIC: 7372 Application computer software
HQ: Fis Capital Markets Us Llc
   347 Riverside Ave
   Jacksonville FL
   877 776-3706

(P-12259)
MAGNIT LLC (PA)
2635 Iron Point Rd Ste 270 (95630)
PHONE..................516 437-3300
EMP: 146 EST: 1992
SALES (est): 420.51MM **Privately Held**
Web: www.magnitglobal.com
SIC: 7372 8741 Application computer software; Personnel management

(P-12260)
MALWAREBYTES INC (PA)
Also Called: Malwarebytes
3979 Freedom Cir Fl 12 (95054-1256)
PHONE..................408 852-4336
Marcin Kleczynski, *CEO*
Mark Harris, *
Bruce Harrison, *
Justin Dolly Ciso, *Prin*
Thomas R Fox, *
EMP: 600 EST: 2009
SALES (est): 103.51MM
SALES (corp-wide): 103.51MM **Privately Held**
Web: www.malwarebytes.com
SIC: 7372 Prepackaged software

(P-12261)
MARQETA INC (PA)
180 Grand Ave Ste 600 (94612-3746)
PHONE..................888 462-7738
Jason Gardner, *Ch Bd*
Philip Faix, *CFO*
Darren Mowry, *CRO*
Seth Weissman, *CLO*
EMP: 479 EST: 2010
SQ FT: 63,284
SALES (est): 748.21MM
SALES (corp-wide): 748.21MM **Publicly Held**
Web: www.marqeta.com
SIC: 7372 Prepackaged software

(P-12262)
MATERIAL SECURITY INC
1003 Main St (94063-1910)
PHONE..................408 649-9882
Ryan Noon, *CEO*
Ryan Seu, *Prin*
EMP: 65 EST: 2017
SALES (est): 4.58MM **Privately Held**
Web: www.material.security
SIC: 7372 Business oriented computer software

(P-12263)
MATTERPORT INC (PA)
Also Called: MATTERPORT
352 E Java Dr (94089-1328)
PHONE..................650 641-2241
Raymond J Pittman, *Ch Bd*
James D Fay, *CFO*
Matthew Zinn, *CLO*
Peter Presunka, *CAO*
EMP: 190 EST: 2011
SQ FT: 28,322
SALES (est): 136.13MM
SALES (corp-wide): 136.13MM **Publicly Held**
Web: www.matterport.com
SIC: 7372 Prepackaged software

(P-12264)
MCAFEE LLC (DH)
6220 America Ctr Dr (95002-2563)
PHONE..................888 847-8766
Peter Leav, *Pr*
Michael Berry, *
Terry Hicks, *
Sarah Decker, *CLO CCO**
▲ EMP: 149 EST: 1992
SQ FT: 208,000
SALES (est): 808.44MM
SALES (corp-wide): 1.92B **Privately Held**
Web: www.mcafee.com
SIC: 7372 Application computer software
HQ: Mcafee Corp.
   6220 America Center Dr
   San Jose CA
   866 622-3911

(P-12265)
MCAFEE CORP (HQ)
Also Called: McAfee
6220 America Center Dr (95002-2563)
PHONE..................866 622-3911
Peter Leav, *Pr*
Jennifer Biry, *Ex VP*
Gagan Singh, *PRODUCT*
EMP: 110 EST: 2017
SQ FT: 85,000
SALES (est): 1.92B
SALES (corp-wide): 1.92B **Privately Held**
Web: www.mcafee.com
SIC: 7372 7382 Prepackaged software; Security systems services
PA: Condor Bidco, Inc.
   320 Park Ave Fl 28
   New York NY
   866 622-3911

(P-12266)
MCAFEE FINANCE 2 LLC
2821 Mission College Blvd (95054-1838)
P.O. Box 3128 (95002-3128)
PHONE..................888 847-8766
EMP: 1955 EST: 2016
SALES (est): 2.11MM
SALES (corp-wide): 333.48MM **Privately Held**
SIC: 7372 Prepackaged software
HQ: Mcafee Finance 1, Llc
   2821 Mission College Blvd
   Santa Clara CA
   888 847-8766

(P-12267)
MEDALLIA INC (HQ)
6220 Stoneridge Mall Rd Fl 2 (94588)
PHONE..................650 321-3000
Joe Tyrrell, *CEO*
Borge Hald, *CSO*
Roxanne M Oulman, *Ex VP*
Jimmy C Duan, *CCO*
Mikael J Ottosson, *Ex VP*
EMP: 145 EST: 2000
SALES (est): 477.22MM
SALES (corp-wide): 477.22MM **Privately Held**
Web: www.medallia.com
SIC: 7372 8732 Business oriented computer software; Market analysis, business, and economic research
PA: Medallia Parent, Lp
   6220 Stnrdge Mall Rd Fl 2
   Pleasanton CA
   650 321-3000

(P-12268)
MEDITAB SOFTWARE INC
8795 Folsom Blvd Ste 205 (95826-3721)
P.O. Box 255687 (95865-5687)
PHONE..................510 201-0130
Paragi Patel, *CEO*
Kunal Shah, *Pr*
Paragi Patel, *CFO*
EMP: 79 EST: 2002
SALES (est): 16.1MM **Privately Held**
Web: www.meditab.com
SIC: 7372 Business oriented computer software
PA: Meditab Software (India) Private Limited
   Officeno. 219/A, 2nd Floor
   Ahmedabad GJ

(P-12269)
MEDRIO INC (PA)
345 California St Ste 325 (94104-2658)
PHONE..................415 963-3700
Nicole Latimer, *CEO*
Richard H Scheller, *
Nathan Weems, *
EMP: 100 EST: 2006
SALES (est): 20.24MM
SALES (corp-wide): 20.24MM **Privately Held**
Web: www.medrio.com
SIC: 7372 Business oriented computer software

(P-12270)
MERIDIAN PROJECT SYSTEMS INC
Also Called: Meridian Systems
1720 Prairie City Rd Ste 120 (95630)
PHONE..................916 294-2000
EMP: 120
SIC: 7372 Business oriented computer software

(P-12271)
METRICSTREAM INC (PA)
Also Called: Complianceonline
6201 America Center Dr Ste 240 (95002-2563)
P.O. Box 246 (95002-0246)
PHONE..................650 620-2955
Gaurav Kapoor, *
Prasad Sabbineni, *
Tony Caroll, *
EMP: 150 EST: 1999
SALES (est): 169.87MM **Privately Held**
Web: www.metricstream.com
SIC: 7372 Application computer software

(P-12272)
MITRATECH HOLDINGS INC
5900 Wilshire Blvd Ste 1500 (90036-5031)
PHONE..................323 964-0000
Jason Parkman, *CEO*
EMP: 125
SALES (corp-wide): 98.42MM **Privately Held**
Web: www.mitratech.com
SIC: 7372 Business oriented computer software
PA: Mitratech Holdings, Inc.
   5001 Plz On The Lk Ste 11
   Austin TX
   512 382-7322

(P-12273)
MOJO NETWORKS INC (HQ)
5453 Great America Pkwy (95054-3645)
PHONE..................650 961-1111
Rick Wilmer, *CEO*
Freddy Mangum, *CMO**
Faysal A Sohail, *
Mike Anthofer, *
EMP: 66 EST: 2003
SALES (est): 32.45MM **Publicly Held**
Web: www.arista.com
SIC: 7372 Prepackaged software
PA: Arista Networks, Inc.
   5453 Great America Pkwy
   Santa Clara CA

(P-12274)
MONTAVISTA SOFTWARE LLC (DH)
2315 N 1st St 4th Fl (95131-1010)
PHONE..................408 572-8000
Art Landro, *Pr*
Sanjay Uppal, *
James Ready, *
Jason B Wacha, *
EMP: 100 EST: 1999
SALES (est): 14.38MM
SALES (corp-wide): 5.92B **Publicly Held**
Web: www.mvista.com
SIC: 7372 Prepackaged software
HQ: Cavium, Llc
   5488 Marvell Ln
   Santa Clara CA

(P-12275)
MOVEWORKS INC (PA)
1277 Terra Bella Ave (94043-1843)
PHONE..................408 435-5100
Bhavin Shah, *CEO*
Vaibhav Nivargi, *Engr*
EMP: 110 EST: 2016
SQ FT: 818
SALES (est): 14.16MM
SALES (corp-wide): 14.16MM **Privately Held**
Web: www.moveworks.com
SIC: 7372 7371 Business oriented computer software; Custom computer programming services

(P-12276)
MSCSOFTWARE CORPORATION (HQ)
5161 California Ave Ste 200 (92617-8002)
PHONE..................714 540-8900
Roger Assaker, *CEO*
Alex Montgomery, *
EMP: 245 EST: 1963
SALES (est): 125.34MM
SALES (corp-wide): 5.09MM **Privately Held**
Web: www.hexagon.com
SIC: 7372 Business oriented computer software
PA: Hexagon Ab
   Lilla Bantorget 15
   Stockholm
   86012620

(P-12277)
MURSION INC
2443 Fillmore St Pmb 515 (94115-1814)
PHONE..................415 746-9631
Mark Atkinson, *CEO*
Chris Laidley, *
EMP: 200 EST: 2014
SQ FT: 3,600
SALES (est): 24.5MM **Privately Held**
Web: www.mursion.com
SIC: 7372 Educational computer software

(P-12278)
MUSICMATCH INC
16935 W Bernardo Dr Ste 270 (92127-1634)
PHONE..................858 485-4300

7372 - Prepackaged Software (P-12279)

Dennis Mudd, *CEO*
Peter Csathy, *
Gary Acord, *
Don Leigh, *
Chris Allen Senior Vp Mkting S tragic Planning, *Prin*
EMP: 140 **EST:** 1997
SQ FT: 20,000
SALES (est): 22.01MM **Privately Held**
SIC: 7372 5734 Prepackaged software; Software, business and non-game
PA: Altaba Inc.
140 E 45th St Fl 15
New York NY

(P-12279)
MY EYE MEDIA LLC
2211 N Hollywood Way (91505-1113)
PHONE................................818 559-7200
Michael Kadenacy, *Pr*
Rodd Feingold, *CFO*
EMP: 80 **EST:** 2004
SQ FT: 20,000
SALES (est): 10.27MM
SALES (corp-wide): 20.42MM **Privately Held**
Web: www.resillion.com
SIC: 7372 Business oriented computer software
HQ: Eurofins Product Testing Us Holdings, Inc.
11720 N Creek Pkwy N
Bothell WA
800 383-0085

(P-12280)
NAVIS LP (PA)
55 Harrison St Ste 600 (94607-3776)
PHONE................................510 267-5000
EMP: 133 **EST:** 1998
SALES (est): 23.56MM **Privately Held**
Web: www.kaleris.com
SIC: 7372 Prepackaged software

(P-12281)
NC4 SOLTRA LLC
21515 Hawthorne Blvd # 52 (90503-6501)
PHONE................................408 489-5579
Tommy Mcdowell, *Managing Member*
EMP: 67 **EST:** 2016
SALES (est): 4.6MM
SALES (corp-wide): 9.82MM **Privately Held**
SIC: 7372 Prepackaged software
PA: Celerium Inc.
21515 Hawthorne Blvd # 520
Torrance CA
408 489-5579

(P-12282)
NET OPTICS INC
Also Called: Ixia
5301 Stevens Creek Blvd (95051-7201)
PHONE................................408 737-7777
EMP: 85 **EST:** 1997
SQ FT: 39,000
SALES (est): 35.99MM
SALES (corp-wide): 5.42B **Publicly Held**
SIC: 7372 Operating systems computer software
HQ: Ixia
26601 Agoura Rd
Calabasas CA
818 871-1200

(P-12283)
NETSKOPE INC (PA)
2445 Augustine Dr 3rd Fl (95054-3032)
PHONE................................800 979-6988
Sanjay Beri, *CEO*
Jason Clark, *CSO**
Lamont Orange Ciso, *Prin*
Andrew Del Matto, *
Jenefer Chin, *
EMP: 630 **EST:** 2012
SQ FT: 62,086
SALES (est): 450.09MM
SALES (corp-wide): 450.09MM **Privately Held**
Web: www.netskope.com
SIC: 7372 7371 Application computer software; Computer software development

(P-12284)
NETSOL TECHNOLOGIES INC (PA)
Also Called: Netsol
16000 Ventura Blvd Ste 770 (91436-2758)
PHONE................................818 222-9197
Najeeb Ghauri, *Ch Bd*
Naeem Ghauri, *Pr*
Roger Almond, *CFO*
Malea Farsai, *Corporate Counsel*
Patti L W Mcglasson, *Sr VP*
EMP: 60 **EST:** 1997
SQ FT: 5,000
SALES (est): 52.39MM
SALES (corp-wide): 52.39MM **Publicly Held**
Web: www.netsoltech.com
SIC: 7372 7373 7299 Business oriented computer software; Computer integrated systems design; Personal document and information services

(P-12285)
NETSUITE INC (DH)
Also Called: Oracle
2955 Campus Dr Ste 100 (94403-2539)
PHONE................................650 627-1000
Dorian Daley, *Pr*
Jim Mcgeever, *Ex VP*
Evan Goldberg, *
Jason Maynard, *
David Rodman, *
EMP: 892 **EST:** 1998
SQ FT: 165,000
SALES (est): 403.23MM
SALES (corp-wide): 49.95B **Publicly Held**
Web: www.netsuite.com
SIC: 7372 Business oriented computer software
HQ: Oc Acquisition Llc
500 Oracle Pkwy
Redwood City CA
650 506-7000

(P-12286)
NEW BI US GAMING LLC
10920 Via Frontera Ste 420 (92127-1729)
PHONE................................858 592-2472
Ian Bonner, *CEO*
Russell Schechter, *
Kimberly Armstrong, *
EMP: 92 **EST:** 2012
SALES (est): 4.97MM **Privately Held**
Web: www.vizexplorer.com
SIC: 7372 Prepackaged software

(P-12287)
NEW RELIC INC (PA)
188 Spear St Fl 11 (94105-1752)
PHONE................................650 777-7600
William Staples, *CEO*
Lewis Cirne, *Non-Executive Chairman of the Board**
David Barter, *CFO*
Kristy Friedrichs, *COO*
Mark Dodds, *CRO*
EMP: 2527 **EST:** 2007
SQ FT: 73,000
SALES (est): 925.63MM **Privately Held**
Web: www.newrelic.com
SIC: 7372 Prepackaged software

(P-12288)
NEXTGEN HEALTHCARE INC (PA)
18111 Von Karman Ave Ste 600 (92612-0199)
PHONE................................949 255-2600
David Sides, *Pr*
Jeffrey H Margolis, *
James R Arnold Junior, *Ex VP*
Srinivas S Velamoor, *Chief Growth Vice President*
Mitchell L Waters, *Executive Commercial Vice President*
EMP: 252 **EST:** 1974
SALES (est): 653.17MM
SALES (corp-wide): 653.17MM **Privately Held**
Web: www.nextgen.com
SIC: 7372 7373 Prepackaged software; Computer integrated systems design

(P-12289)
NEXTRACKER LLC (HQ)
6200 Paseo Padre Pkwy (94555-3601)
PHONE................................510 270-2500
Daniel Shugar, *CEO*
Bruce Ledesma, *
Dave Bennett, *
Alex Au, *
Leah Schlesinger, *
◆ **EMP:** 489 **EST:** 2013
SQ FT: 30,000
SALES (est): 151.72MM
SALES (corp-wide): 1.9B **Publicly Held**
Web: www.nextracker.com
SIC: 7372 1711 Prepackaged software; Solar energy contractor
PA: Nextracker Inc.
6200 Paseo Padre Pkwy
Fremont CA
510 270-2500

(P-12290)
NEXTROLL INC (PA)
Also Called: Adroll
201 California St Ste 500 (94111)
PHONE................................415 236-3956
Robin Bordoli, *CEO*
Aaron Bell, *CPO**
Peter Krivkovich, *
EMP: 703 **EST:** 2006
SALES (est): 203.95MM
SALES (corp-wide): 203.95MM **Privately Held**
Web: www.nextroll.com
SIC: 7372 Prepackaged software

(P-12291)
NGROK INC
548 Market St Pmb 26741 (94104-5401)
PHONE................................415 323-4184
Alan Shreve, *CEO*
Alan Shreve, *Mgr*
EMP: 80 **EST:** 2015
SALES (est): 5.16MM **Privately Held**
Web: www.ngrok.com
SIC: 7372 Application computer software

(P-12292)
NOMINUM INC
3355 Scott Blvd Fl 3 (95054-3127)
PHONE................................650 381-6000
Garry Messiana, *CEO*
Pete Wisowaty, *
Bob Verheecke, *
EMP: 126 **EST:** 1999
SQ FT: 15,000
SALES (est): 24.79MM
SALES (corp-wide): 3.62B **Publicly Held**
SIC: 7372 Prepackaged software
PA: Akamai Technologies, Inc.
145 Broadway
Cambridge MA
617 444-3000

(P-12293)
NREACH ONLINE SERVICES INC
303 Twin Dolphin Dr Ste 6080 (94065-1497)
PHONE................................425 301-9168
Mayank Singh, *Sr VP*
EMP: 400 **EST:** 2019
SALES (est): 40MM **Privately Held**
SIC: 7372 Prepackaged software

(P-12294)
NTRUST INFOTECH INC
230 Commerce Ste 180 (92602-1336)
PHONE................................562 207-1600
Srikanth Ramachandran, *CEO*
EMP: 65 **EST:** 2003
SALES (est): 5.59MM **Privately Held**
Web: www.ntrustinfotech.com
SIC: 7372 7371 Business oriented computer software; Computer software development and applications

(P-12295)
NUMERICAL TECHNOLOGIES INC
70 W Plumeria Dr (95134-2134)
PHONE................................408 919-1910
EMP: 215 **EST:** 1995
SQ FT: 39,300
SALES (est): 35.78MM
SALES (corp-wide): 5.08B **Publicly Held**
SIC: 7372 7374 Business oriented computer software; Data processing and preparation
PA: Synopsys, Inc.
675 Almanor Ave
Sunnyvale CA
650 584-5000

(P-12296)
NURSEFLY INC
645 Harrison St Ste 200 (94107-3624)
PHONE................................760 641-5940
Parth Bhakta, *CEO*
EMP: 97 **EST:** 2017
SALES (est): 18.86MM
SALES (corp-wide): 3.19B **Publicly Held**
SIC: 7372 Prepackaged software
PA: Match Group, Inc.
8750 N Cntl Expy Ste 1400
Dallas TX
214 576-9352

(P-12297)
NUTANIX INC (PA)
Also Called: Nutanix
1740 Technology Dr Ste 150 (95110)
PHONE................................408 216-8360
EMP: 623 **EST:** 2009
SQ FT: 333,000
SALES (est): 1.86B **Publicly Held**
Web: www.nutanix.com
SIC: 7372 7371 Prepackaged software; Computer software development

(P-12298)
NWP SERVICES CORPORATION (DH)
535 Anton Blvd Ste 1100 (92626-7699)
P.O. Box 19661 (92623-9661)

7372 - Prepackaged Software (P-12319)

PHONE..................949 253-2500
EMP: 141 EST: 1995
SQ FT: 21,171
SALES (est): 48.94MM Privately Held
Web: www.mynwpsc.com
SIC: 7372 8721 Utility computer software; Billing and bookkeeping service
HQ: Realpage, Inc.
2201 Lakeside Blvd
Richardson TX
972 820-3000

(P-12299)
OKTA INC (PA)
Also Called: Okta
100 1st St Ste 600 (94105-3513)
PHONE..................888 722-7871
Todd Mckinnon, Ch Bd
J Frederic Kerrest, Executive Vice Chairman of the Board*
Brett Tighe, CFO
Shibu Ninan, CAO
Larissa Schwartz, CLO
EMP: 5137 EST: 2009
SQ FT: 285,996
SALES (est): 1.86B
SALES (corp-wide): 1.86B Publicly Held
Web: www.okta.com
SIC: 7372 7371 Prepackaged software; Software programming applications

(P-12300)
ON24 INC (PA)
50 Beale St Fl 8 (94105-1863)
PHONE..................415 369-8000
Sharat Sharan, Pr
Steven Vattuone, CFO
James Blackie, CRO
Jayesh Sahasi, Ex VP
EMP: 487 EST: 1998
SQ FT: 31,182
SALES (est): 190.87MM
SALES (corp-wide): 190.87MM Publicly Held
Web: www.on24.com
SIC: 7372 Business oriented computer software

(P-12301)
ONELOGIN INC (DH)
848 Battery St (94111)
PHONE..................415 645-6830
EMP: 175 EST: 2009
SQ FT: 44,461
SALES (est): 98.2MM
SALES (corp-wide): 647.68MM Privately Held
Web: www.onelogin.com
SIC: 7372 Prepackaged software
HQ: One Identity Llc
20 Enterprise Ste 100
Aliso Viejo CA
949 754-8000

(P-12302)
ONESIGNAL INC (PA)
Also Called: Onesignal
201 S B St Ste 200 (94401-4283)
PHONE..................408 506-0701
George Deglin, CEO
George Deglin, Pr
Long Vo, *
EMP: 147 EST: 2011
SALES (est): 10.01MM
SALES (corp-wide): 10.01MM Privately Held
Web: www.onesignal.com
SIC: 7372 Business oriented computer software

(P-12303)
ONVANTAGE INC
3290 Freedom Cir 200 (95054)
PHONE..................408 562-3388
John Chang, CEO
David K Hunt, *
Edward J Tromczynski, DIV*
Stanley Chin, Corporate President*
Paul S Nestvold, *
EMP: 100 EST: 1991
SQ FT: 22,000
SALES (est): 5.35MM Privately Held
SIC: 7372 Prepackaged software

(P-12304)
OPENTV INC
Also Called: Nagra
275 Sacramento St (94111-3810)
PHONE..................415 962-5000
EMP: 325
SIC: 7372 Prepackaged software

(P-12305)
ORACLE AMERICA INC
4120 Network Cir (95054-1778)
PHONE..................408 276-3331
EMP: 150 EST: 1986
SALES (est): 16.99MM Privately Held
Web: www.jcp.org
SIC: 7372 Prepackaged software

(P-12306)
ORACLE CORPORATION
Also Called: Oracle
1 Bolero (92692-5164)
PHONE..................626 315-7513
Hemesh Surana, Brnch Mgr
EMP: 302
SALES (corp-wide): 49.95B Publicly Held
Web: www.oracle.com
SIC: 7372 Prepackaged software
PA: Oracle Corporation
2300 Oracle Way
Austin TX
737 867-1000

(P-12307)
ORACLE CORPORATION
Also Called: Oracle
1001 Sunset Blvd (95765-3702)
PHONE..................916 315-3500
Chris Wilson, Brnch Mgr
EMP: 500
SALES (corp-wide): 49.95B Publicly Held
Web: www.oracle.com
SIC: 7372 7371 Business oriented computer software; Custom computer programming services
PA: Oracle Corporation
2300 Oracle Way
Austin TX
737 867-1000

(P-12308)
ORACLE TALEO LLC (HQ)
4140 Dublin Blvd Ste 400 (94568-7757)
PHONE..................925 452-3000
Dorian Daley, Pr
Eric Ball, *
Neil Hudspith, Executive Worldwide Field Operations Vice President*
Guy Gauvin, Executive Global Services Vice President*
Jason Blessing, Senior Vice President Products*
EMP: 400 EST: 1999
SQ FT: 47,500
SALES (est): 101.27MM
SALES (corp-wide): 49.95B Publicly Held
Web: www.oracle.com

SIC: 7372 Business oriented computer software
PA: Oracle Corporation
2300 Oracle Way
Austin TX
737 867-1000

(P-12309)
ORACLE USA INC
500 Oracle Pkwy (94065-1677)
PHONE..................650 506-7000
EMP: 526
SIC: 7372 Prepackaged software

(P-12310)
OUTREACH CORPORATION
Also Called: Sales & Marketing
600 California St Fl 7 (94108-2731)
PHONE..................888 938-7356
EMP: 269
SALES (corp-wide): 101.15MM Privately Held
Web: www.outreach.io
SIC: 7372 Business oriented computer software
PA: Outreach Corporation
333 Elliott Ave W Ste 500
Seattle WA
206 235-3672

(P-12311)
PAGERDUTY INC (PA)
Also Called: Pagerduty
600 Townsend St Ste 200 (94103-4959)
PHONE..................844 800-3889
Jennifer Tejada, Ch Bd
Howard Wilson, CFO
Jeremy Kmet Senior, Global Vice President
Shelley Webb, Senior Vice President Legal
Eric Johnson, CIO
EMP: 1099 EST: 2010
SQ FT: 59,000
SALES (est): 370.79MM
SALES (corp-wide): 370.79MM Publicly Held
Web: www.pagerduty.com
SIC: 7372 Prepackaged software

(P-12312)
PAKEDGE DEVICE & SOFTWARE INC
17011 Beach Blvd Ste 600 (92647-5962)
PHONE..................714 880-4511
Dusan Jankov, Brnch Mgr
EMP: 144
SALES (corp-wide): 1.12B Publicly Held
Web: www.pakedge.com
SIC: 7372 Application computer software
HQ: Pakedge Device & Software Inc.
11734 S Election Rd
Draper UT
650 385-8700

(P-12313)
PARENTSQUARE INC
6144 Calle Real Ste 200a (93117-2012)
PHONE..................888 496-3168
Sohit Wadhwa, CEO
Anupama Vaid, Prin
EMP: 65 EST: 2011
SALES (est): 5.71MM Privately Held
Web: www.parentsquare.com
SIC: 7372 Educational computer software

(P-12314)
PATRON SOLUTIONS LLC
5171 California Ave Ste 200 (92617-3066)
PHONE..................949 823-1700
Steve Shaw, Owner
EMP: 245 EST: 2015
SALES (est): 4.88MM Privately Held
SIC: 7372 Application computer software

(P-12315)
PAXATA INC
1800 Seaport Blvd # 1 (94063-5543)
PHONE..................650 542-7897
Prakasa Nanduri, CEO
David Brewster, *
Christopher Maddox, *
Nenshad Bardoliwalla, *
EMP: 90 EST: 2012
SALES (est): 20.46K
SALES (corp-wide): 183.94K Privately Held
Web: www.datarobot.com
SIC: 7372 Business oriented computer software
PA: Datarobot, Inc.
225 Franklin St Ste 1300
Boston MA
617 765-4500

(P-12316)
PAYLOCITY HOLDING CORPORATION
2107 Livingston St (94606-5218)
PHONE..................847 956-4850
EMP: 718
SALES (corp-wide): 1.17B Publicly Held
Web: www.paylocity.com
SIC: 7372 Prepackaged software
PA: Paylocity Holding Corporation
1400 American Ln
Schaumburg IL
847 463-3200

(P-12317)
PDF SOLUTIONS INC (PA)
Also Called: Pdf Solutions
2858 De La Cruz Blvd (95050-2619)
PHONE..................408 280-7900
John K Kibarian, Pr
Adnan Raza, Ex VP
Kimon Michaels, Ex VP
EMP: 143 EST: 1992
SQ FT: 20,800
SALES (est): 148.55MM Publicly Held
Web: www.pdf.com
SIC: 7372 7371 Prepackaged software; Computer software development

(P-12318)
PIVOT3 INC
614 Lighthouse Ave Ste C (93950-2680)
PHONE..................512 807-2666
Bill Stover, CEO
Bill Galloway, *
Rance Poehler, Global Sales Vice President*
John Spires, OF STRATEGIES*
Carlo Garbagnati, *
EMP: 205 EST: 2002
SALES (est): 77MM Privately Held
SIC: 7372 Business oriented computer software

(P-12319)
PLANFUL INC (HQ)
555 Twin Dolphin Dr Ste 400 (94065-2100)
PHONE..................650 249-7100
Grant Halloran, CEO
Ron Baden, CRO*
Richard Ratkowski, *
Aravind Balakrishnan, *
John Perkins, *
EMP: 120 EST: 2000
SALES (est): 47.8MM Privately Held
Web: www.planful.com

7372 - Prepackaged Software (P-12320)

SIC: 7372 Application computer software
PA: Planful Software India Private Limited
503 Model House
Hyderabad TG

(P-12320)
PLANGRID INC (HQ)
Also Called: Loupe
2111 Mission St Ste 400 (94110-1219)
P.O. Box 194087 (94119-4087)
PHONE..............................800 646-0796
Tracy Young, CEO
Linda Keala, Chief Human Resource Officer
Michael Galvin, CFO
EMP: 85 EST: 2011
SQ FT: 16,000
SALES (est): 16.07MM
SALES (corp-wide): 4.39B Publicly Held
Web: construction.autodesk.com
SIC: 7372 Application computer software
PA: Autodesk, Inc.
1 Market St Ste 400
San Francisco CA
415 507-5000

(P-12321)
PLUSAI INC
3315 Scott Blvd. (95054-3103)
PHONE..............................408 508-4758
David Wanqian Liu, CEO
EMP: 100 EST: 2016
SALES (est): 12.27MM Privately Held
Web: www.plus.ai
SIC: 7372 Application computer software

(P-12322)
PLX TECHNOLOGY INC (DH)
Also Called: Plx Technology
1320 Ridder Park Dr (95131-2313)
▲ EMP: 115 EST: 1986
SQ FT: 55,000
SALES (est): 6.19MM
SALES (corp-wide): 33.2B Publicly Held
SIC: 7372 3674 Business oriented computer software; Integrated circuits, semiconductor networks, etc.
HQ: Avago Technologies Wireless (U.S.A.) Manufacturing Llc
4380 Ziegler Rd
Fort Collins CO

(P-12323)
POLARION SOFTWARE INC
1001 Marina Village Pkwy Ste 403 (94501-6401)
PHONE..............................877 572-4005
Frank Schrder, CEO
George Briner, *
Stefano Rizzo, *
Nikolay Entin, *
Jiri Walek, *
EMP: 90 EST: 2005
SALES (est): 6.8MM Privately Held
Web: polarion.plm.automation.siemens.com
SIC: 7372 Prepackaged software

(P-12324)
POPOUT INC (PA)
Also Called: Shippo
731 Market St Ste 200 (94103-2005)
PHONE..............................415 691-7447
Laura Behrens Wu, CEO
EMP: 81 EST: 2013
SALES (est): 9.2MM
SALES (corp-wide): 9.2MM Privately Held
Web: www.goshippo.com
SIC: 7372 Business oriented computer software

(P-12325)
POSHMARK INC (HQ)
203 Redwood Shores Pkwy Fl 8 (94065)
PHONE..............................650 262-4771
Manish Chandra, Pr
Rodrigo Brumana, *
John Mcdonald, COO
EMP: 729 EST: 2011
SQ FT: 75,876
SALES (est): 326.01MM Privately Held
Web: www.poshmark.com
SIC: 7372 5611 5621 Application computer software; Men's and boys' clothing stores; Women's clothing stores
PA: Naver Corporation
95 Jeongjail-Ro, Bundang-Gu
Seongnam

(P-12326)
POWERSCHOOL GROUP LLC (HQ)
150 Parkshore Dr (95630-4710)
PHONE..............................916 288-1588
Hardeep Gulati, CEO
Mark Oldemeyer, *
Bryan Macdonald Csto, Prin
EMP: 107 EST: 2015
SALES (est): 265.14MM
SALES (corp-wide): 1.65B Privately Held
Web: www.powerschool.com
SIC: 7372 Prepackaged software
PA: Vista Equity Partners Management, Llc
401 Congress Ave Ste 3100
Austin TX
512 730-2400

(P-12327)
POWERSCHOOL HOLDINGS INC
150 Parkshore Dr (95630-4710)
PHONE..............................877 873-1550
Hardeep Gulati, CEO
Eric Shander, CFO
Maulik Datanwala, COO
Marcy Daniel, CPO
EMP: 2905 EST: 2020
SQ FT: 61,338
SALES (est): 630.68MM Privately Held
SIC: 7372 Prepackaged software

(P-12328)
PROGRESS SOFTWARE CORPORATION
800 W El Camino Real (94040-2567)
PHONE..............................650 341-7733
EMP: 68
SALES (corp-wide): 602.01MM Publicly Held
Web: www.progress.com
SIC: 7372 Application computer software
PA: Progress Software Corporation
15 Wayside Rd Ste 4
Burlington MA
781 280-4000

(P-12329)
PURE STORAGE INC (PA)
Also Called: PURE STORAGE
2555 Augustine Dr (95054-3003)
PHONE..............................800 379-7873
Charles Giancarlo, Ch Bd
Scott Dietzen, *
Kevan Krysler, CFO
John Colgrove Cvo, Prin
Ajay Singh, CPO
▲ EMP: 598 EST: 2009
SALES (est): 2.75B Publicly Held
Web: www.purestorage.com
SIC: 7372 3572 Prepackaged software; Computer storage devices

(P-12330)
QAD INC (HQ)
Also Called: Qad
101 Innovation Pl (93108-2268)
PHONE..............................805 566-6000
Anton Chilton, CEO
Peter R Van Cuylenburg, *
Pamela M Lopker, *
Daniel Lender, Ex VP
Kara Bellamy, CAO
EMP: 219 EST: 1979
SALES (est): 307.87MM
SALES (corp-wide): 474.06MM Privately Held
Web: www.qad.com
SIC: 7372 Prepackaged software
PA: Qad Parent, Llc
101 Innovation Pl
Santa Barbara CA
805 566-6000

(P-12331)
QUEST SOFTWARE INC
Also Called: Cloud Automation Division
20 Enterprise (92656-7104)
PHONE..............................949 754-8000
EMP: 80
SALES (corp-wide): 647.68MM Privately Held
Web: www.quest.com
SIC: 7372 Prepackaged software
PA: Quest Software Inc.
20 Enterprise Ste 100
Aliso Viejo CA
949 754-8000

(P-12332)
REDSEAL INC
1300 El Camino Real Ste 300 (94025)
PHONE..............................408 641-2200
Gregory Enriquez, CEO
Bryan Barney, *
Bill Gadala, *
EMP: 145 EST: 2004
SQ FT: 6,500
SALES (est): 43.35MM Privately Held
Web: www.redseal.net
SIC: 7372 Prepackaged software

(P-12333)
RELATIONALAI INC
2120 University Ave (94704-1026)
PHONE..............................650 307-8776
Molham Aref, Pr
EMP: 74 EST: 2018
SALES (est): 5.18MM Privately Held
Web: www.relational.ai
SIC: 7372 Prepackaged software

(P-12334)
REPLICANT SOLUTIONS INC
1 Letterman Dr # 3500 (94129-1517)
PHONE..............................415 854-3296
Gadi Shamia, CEO
EMP: 120 EST: 2017
SALES (est): 15.51MM Privately Held
Web: www.replicant.com
SIC: 7372 Application computer software

(P-12335)
REPUTATIONCOM INC (PA)
6111 Bollinger Canyon Rd Ste 580 (94583-5186)
PHONE..............................800 888-0924
Joe Fuca, CEO
Jason Grier, CCO*
Amir Jafari, *
Manish Balsara, *
Rebecca Biestman, CMO*
EMP: 460 EST: 2006
SQ FT: 21,454
SALES (est): 100MM Privately Held
Web: www.reputation.com
SIC: 7372 7371 Business oriented computer software; Computer software development and applications

(P-12336)
RETAIL ZIPLINE INC (PA)
2370 Market St Ste 436 (94114-1696)
PHONE..............................510 390-4904
Melissa Wong, CEO
EMP: 82 EST: 2014
SALES (est): 7.43MM
SALES (corp-wide): 7.43MM Privately Held
Web: www.getzipline.com
SIC: 7372 Business oriented computer software

(P-12337)
REVJET CORPORATION
981 Industrial Rd Ste D (94070-4150)
PHONE..............................650 508-2215
Patrick Mcnenny, VP
David Mackay, CRO*
EMP: 110 EST: 2017
SALES (est): 10.03MM Privately Held
Web: www.revjet.com
SIC: 7372 Application computer software

(P-12338)
ROADZEN INC
111 Anza Blvd Ste 109 (94010-1918)
PHONE..............................347 745-6448
Rohan Malhotra, CEO
Steven Carlson, *
Mohit Pasricha, CFO
Ankur Kamboj, COO
EMP: 400 EST: 2015
Web: www.vahannatech.com
SIC: 7372 Prepackaged software

(P-12339)
ROBLOX CORPORATION (PA)
Also Called: Roblox
970 Park Pl (94403-1907)
PHONE..............................888 858-2569
David Baszucki, Ch Bd
Michael Guthrie, CFO
Craig Donato, Chief Business Officer
EMP: 878 EST: 1989
SQ FT: 300,000
SALES (est): 434.97MM
SALES (corp-wide): 434.97MM Publicly Held
Web: www.roblox.com
SIC: 7372 Prepackaged software

(P-12340)
SABA SOFTWARE INC (DH)
4120 Dublin Blvd Ste 200 (94568-7759)
PHONE..............................877 722-2101
Phil Saunders, Pr
Jeff Lautenbach, *
Chirag Shah, *
Theresa Damato, CMO*
Adam Weiss, CAO*
EMP: 100 EST: 1997
SQ FT: 36,000
SALES (est): 122.57MM
SALES (corp-wide): 740.92MM Privately Held
Web: www.cornerstoneondemand.com
SIC: 7372 7371 Application computer software; Computer software development and applications
HQ: Cornerstone Ondemand, Inc.
1601 Cloverf Blvd 620s
Santa Monica CA
310 752-0200

PRODUCTS & SERVICES SECTION
7372 - Prepackaged Software (P-12360)

(P-12341)
SAGE SOFTWARE HOLDINGS INC (HQ)
6561 Irvine Center Dr (92618-2118)
PHONE...........................866 530-7243
Stev Swenson, *CEO*
Doug Meyer, *
Mack Lout, *
Stephen Kelly, *Prin*
Steve Hare, *Prin*
EMP: 400 EST: 2000
SALES (est): 870.22MM
SALES (corp-wide): 2.29B **Privately Held**
SIC: 7372 7371 Business oriented computer software; Custom computer programming services
PA: The Sage Group Plc.
C23 - 5 & 6 Cobalt Park Way
Newcastle-Upon-Tyne
800 923-0344

(P-12342)
SALESFORCE
117 University Ave (94301-1629)
PHONE...........................650 327-0110
EMP: 98 EST: 2019
SALES (est): 209.06K **Privately Held**
Web: www.salesforce.com
SIC: 7372 Business oriented computer software

(P-12343)
SALESFORCE INC (PA)
Also Called: Salesforce
415 Mission St Fl 3 (94105-2504)
PHONE...........................415 901-7000
Marc Benioff, *Ch Bd*
Brian Millham, *Pr*
Amy Weaver, *Pr*
Brent Hyder, *CPO*
Sabastian Niles, *CLO*
EMP: 600 EST: 1999
SQ FT: 1,600,000
SALES (est): 31.35B
SALES (corp-wide): 31.35B **Publicly Held**
Web: www.salesforce.com
SIC: 7372 7375 7371 7374 Business oriented computer software; Information retrieval services; Custom computer programming services; Data processing and preparation

(P-12344)
SALESFORCEORG LLC
1 Market St (94105-1420)
PHONE...........................415 901-7000
EMP: 588 EST: 2008
SALES (est): 9.94MM **Privately Held**
Web: www.salesforce.org
SIC: 7372 Business oriented computer software

(P-12345)
SAP LABS LLC (DH)
3410 Hillview Ave (94304-1395)
PHONE...........................650 849-4000
◆ EMP: 300 EST: 1996
SQ FT: 200,000
SALES (est): 100.03MM
SALES (corp-wide): 32.06B **Privately Held**
Web: www.sap.com
SIC: 7372 Prepackaged software
HQ: Sap America, Inc.
3999 West Chester Pike
Newtown Square PA
610 661-1000

(P-12346)
SCOPELY INC (DH)
3530 Hayden Ave Ste A (90232-2413)
PHONE...........................323 400-6618
EMP: 200 EST: 2011
SALES (est): 128.36MM **Privately Held**
Web: www.scopely.com
SIC: 7372 Home entertainment computer software
HQ: Savvy Games Group
Office 2.14 B, 6th Floor, Kafd, King Fahad Road
Riyadh

(P-12347)
SENTINELONE INC (PA)
Also Called: Sentinelone
444 Castro St Ste 400 (94041-2053)
PHONE...........................855 868-3733
Tomer Weingarten, *Ch Bd*
David Bernhardt, *CFO*
Srivatsan Narayanan, *COO*
Keenan Conder, *CLO*
EMP: 1839 EST: 2013
SQ FT: 10,000
SALES (est): 422.18MM
SALES (corp-wide): 422.18MM **Publicly Held**
Web: www.sentinelone.com
SIC: 7372 7382 Prepackaged software; Protective devices, security

(P-12348)
SIGHT MACHINE INC
243 Vallejo St (94111-1511)
PHONE...........................888 461-5739
Jon Sobel, *CEO*
Nathan Oostendorp, *
Keith Hartley, *CRO*
Kurt Demaagd, *Analytics Vice President*
Adam Taisch, *Vice-President Customer Development*
EMP: 60 EST: 2013
SQ FT: 6,500
SALES (est): 6.71MM **Privately Held**
Web: www.sightmachine.com
SIC: 7372 Business oriented computer software

(P-12349)
SIGNIFYD INC
99 Almaden Blvd Ste 400 (95113-1604)
PHONE...........................866 220-1415
Rajesh Ramanand, *CEO*
Dan Strong, *
Danny Lorenzo, *CSO*
Indy Guha, *CMO*
Emily Mikailli, *People Operations*
EMP: 350 EST: 2011
SALES (est): 28.54MM **Privately Held**
Web: www.signifyd.com
SIC: 7372 Prepackaged software

(P-12350)
SIMPPLR INC (PA)
3 Twin Dolphin Dr Ste 160 (94065-1027)
PHONE...........................650 396-2646
Dhiraj Sharma, *CEO*
EMP: 130 EST: 2014
SALES (est): 12.11MM
SALES (corp-wide): 12.11MM **Privately Held**
Web: www.simpplr.com
SIC: 7372 Business oriented computer software

(P-12351)
SITECORE USA INC (DH)
Also Called: Parent Is Sitecore USA Holding
101 California St Fl 16 (94111-6100)
PHONE...........................415 380-0600
EMP: 150 EST: 2009
SALES (est): 90.12MM
SALES (corp-wide): 2.67MM **Privately Held**
Web: www.sitecore.com
SIC: 7372 Business oriented computer software
HQ: Sitecore Corporation A/S
Vester Farimagsgade 3, Sal 5
Kobenhavn V
70236660

(P-12352)
SLACK TECHNOLOGIES INC (HQ)
Also Called: Slack
500 Howard St Ste 100 (94105-3002)
PHONE...........................970 299-4848
Stewart Butterfield, *
Allen Shim, *CFO*
Tamar Yehoshua, *CPO*
Robert Frati, *SLS & CUSTOMER SUCCESS*
EMP: 192 EST: 2009
SQ FT: 228,998
SALES (est): 902.61MM
SALES (corp-wide): 31.35B **Publicly Held**
Web: www.slack.com
SIC: 7372 Business oriented computer software
PA: Salesforce, Inc.
415 Mission St Fl 3
San Francisco CA
415 901-7000

(P-12353)
SMARSH INC
Also Called: Actiance
900 Veterans Blvd Ste 500 (94063-1715)
PHONE...........................650 631-6300
EMP: 150
SALES (corp-wide): 346.27MM **Privately Held**
Web: www.smarsh.com
SIC: 7372 8742 Prepackaged software; Management consulting services
HQ: Smarsh Inc.
851 Sw 6th Ave Ste 800
Portland OR
866 762-7741

(P-12354)
SMARTLOGIC SEMAPHORE INC
Also Called: Smartlogic
111 N Market St Ste 365 (95113-1101)
PHONE...........................408 213-9500
Rupert Bentley, *Pr*
EMP: 150 EST: 2010
SALES (est): 30.17MM
SALES (corp-wide): 602.01MM **Publicly Held**
Web: www.progress.com
SIC: 7372 Business oriented computer software
HQ: Marklogic Corporation
333 Twin Dolphin Dr # 380
Redwood City CA
650 655-2300

(P-12355)
SNAPLOGIC INC (PA)
1825 S Grant St Ste 550 (94402-2719)
PHONE...........................888 494-1570
Gaurav Dhillon, *CEO*
Ahsan Malik, *
James Markarian, *
David Downing, *CMO*
Dayle Hall, *CMO*
EMP: 136 EST: 2006
SALES (est): 25.7MM **Privately Held**
Web: www.snaplogic.com
SIC: 7372 Business oriented computer software

(P-12356)
SNAPWIZ INC
Also Called: Edulastic
39300 Civic Center Dr Ste 310 (94538-2338)
PHONE...........................510 328-3277
Madhu Narasa, *CEO*
Jeff Bork, *
Satish Kumar, *
EMP: 120 EST: 2010
SALES (est): 8.35MM **Privately Held**
Web: www.edulastic.com
SIC: 7372 Educational computer software

(P-12357)
SOLIDCORE SYSTEMS INC (DH)
3965 Freedom Cir (95054-1206)
PHONE...........................408 387-8400
Anne Bonaparte, *Pr*
Rosen Sharma, *
Jay Vaishnav, *
David Walker Senior, *Worldwide Operations Vice President*
Bob Vieraitis, *
EMP: 100 EST: 2003
SQ FT: 2,000
SALES (est): 36.2MM
SALES (corp-wide): 1.92B **Privately Held**
SIC: 7372 Prepackaged software
HQ: Mcafee, Llc
6220 America Center Dr
San Jose CA

(P-12358)
SOLV ENERGY LLC
Also Called: Swinerton Builders
16798 W Bernardo Dr (92128-2850)
PHONE...........................858 622-4040
Danielle Hammersmith, *Mgr*
EMP: 446
Web: www.solvenergy.com
SIC: 7372 Prepackaged software
HQ: Solv Energy, Llc
16680 W Bernardo Dr
San Diego CA
858 251-4888

(P-12359)
SONY BIOTECHNOLOGY INC
1730 N 1st St 2nd Fl (95112-4642)
PHONE...........................800 275-5963
James Graziadei, *Pr*
Narayan Prabhu, *
Peter Kim, *
EMP: 65 EST: 2003
SALES (est): 19.92MM **Privately Held**
Web: www.sonybiotechnology.com
SIC: 7372 3699 Prepackaged software; Laser systems and equipment
HQ: Sony Corporation Of America
25 Madison Ave Fl 27
New York NY

(P-12360)
SPLUNK INC (PA)
Also Called: Splunk
270 Brannan St (94107-2007)
PHONE...........................415 848-8400
Gary Steele, *Pr*
Gary Steele, *Pr*
Graham V Smith, *
Scott Morgan, *CLO*
Sharyl Givens, *CPO*
EMP: 160 EST: 2003
SQ FT: 182,000

7372 - Prepackaged Software (P-12361)

SALES (est): 3.65B
SALES (corp-wide): 3.65B **Publicly Held**
Web: www.splunk.com
SIC: 7372 Prepackaged software

(P-12361)
STACKLA INC
548 Market St (94104-5401)
PHONE.............................415 789-3304
Damien Mahoney, *CEO*
Peter Cassaidy, *CPO**
EMP: 65 EST: 2014
SALES (est): 9.04MM **Privately Held**
Web: www.nosto.com
SIC: 7372 Application computer software

(P-12362)
STANDARD COGNITION CORP (PA)
548 Market St # 96346 (94104-5401)
PHONE.............................415 324-4156
Prena Patel, *Admn*
Jordan Fisher, *
Michael Suswal, *
Anthony Lutz, *
EMP: 71 EST: 2017
SALES (est): 9.79MM
SALES (corp-wide): 9.79MM **Privately Held**
Web: www.standard.ai
SIC: 7372 Business oriented computer software

(P-12363)
STEELWEDGE SOFTWARE INC
3875 Hopyard Rd Ste 300 (94588-8527)
PHONE.............................925 460-1700
EMP: 70
Web: www.e2open.com
SIC: 7372 Prepackaged software

(P-12364)
STELLAR CYBER INC
2590 N 1st St Ste 360 (95131-1057)
PHONE.............................408 548-0860
Changming Liu, *CEO*
Aimei Wei, *VP*
EMP: 100 EST: 2015
SALES (est): 13.46MM **Privately Held**
Web: www.stellarcyber.ai
SIC: 7372 Business oriented computer software

(P-12365)
STRATEGY COMPANION CORP
100 Pacifica (92618-7441)
PHONE.............................714 460-8398
Robert Sterling, *Pr*
EMP: 70 EST: 2006
SALES (est): 10.99MM **Privately Held**
Web: www.strategycompanion.com
SIC: 7372 Prepackaged software
PA: Strategy Companion Corp.
   Scotia Centre 4th Floor
   George Town GR CAYMAN

(P-12366)
STROMASYS INC
871 Marlborough Ave (92507-2133)
PHONE.............................919 239-8450
George Koukis, *Ch Bd*
John Prot, *
Chris Pavlou, *
Serge Pavoncello, *
EMP: 78 EST: 2008
SALES (est): 9.9MM
SALES (corp-wide): 600K **Privately Held**
Web: www.stromasys.com

SIC: 7372 5734 Operating systems computer software; Software, business and non-game
HQ: Stromasys Sa
   Avenue Louis-Casai 84
   Cointrin GE

(P-12367)
STRYDER CORP (PA)
Also Called: Handshake
225 Bush St Fl 12 (94104-4201)
P.O. Box 40770 (94140-0770)
PHONE.............................415 981-8400
Garrett Lord, *Ch Bd*
Scott Ringwelski, *
Ben Christensen, *
Asif Makhani, *
EMP: 91 EST: 2014
SALES (est): 16.12MM
SALES (corp-wide): 16.12MM **Privately Held**
Web: www.joinhandshake.com
SIC: 7372 7371 7379 Educational computer software; Computer software development and applications; Computer related consulting services

(P-12368)
SUCCESSFACTORS INC (DH)
Also Called: Sap America Inc Newtown Sq PA
1500 Fashion Island Blvd (94404-1597)
EMP: 85 EST: 2001
SALES (est): 202.38MM
SALES (corp-wide): 32.06B **Privately Held**
Web: www.successfactors.com
SIC: 7372 Prepackaged software
HQ: Sap America, Inc.
   3999 West Chester Pike
   Newtown Square PA
   610 661-1000

(P-12369)
SUNGARD TREASURY SYSTEMS INC
Also Called: Sungard
23975 Park Sorrento Ste 100 (91302-4010)
PHONE.............................818 223-2300
EMP: 250
SIC: 7372 Prepackaged software

(P-12370)
SUPPLYSHIFT (PA)
217 River St (95060-2770)
PHONE.............................831 824-4326
Supplyshift Gershenson, *CEO*
EMP: 62 EST: 2012
SALES (est): 5.4MM
SALES (corp-wide): 5.4MM **Privately Held**
Web: www.supplyshift.net
SIC: 7372 Business oriented computer software

(P-12371)
SYMANTEC
Also Called: Symantec
1200 W 7th St (90017-2310)
PHONE.............................213 489-3262
EMP: 65 EST: 2019
SALES (est): 1.53MM **Privately Held**
SIC: 7372 Prepackaged software

(P-12372)
SYNOPSYS INC (PA)
Also Called: Synopsys
675 Almanor Ave (94085-2925)
PHONE.............................650 584-5000
Aart J De Geus, *Ch Bd*
Sassine Ghazi, *Pr*
Shelagh Glaser, *CFO*
Richard Mahoney, *CRO*

John F Runkel Junior, *Corporate Secretary*
EMP: 500 EST: 1986
SALES (est): 5.08B
SALES (corp-wide): 5.08B **Publicly Held**
Web: www.synopsys.com
SIC: 7372 7371 Prepackaged software; Computer software development

(P-12373)
SYNPLICITY INC (HQ)
690 E Middlefield Rd (94043-4010)
PHONE.............................650 584-5000
Gary Meyers, *Pr*
Alisa Yaffa, *SEC VP INTELLECTUAL PROPERTY*
John J Hanlon, *VP Fin*
Andrew Haines, *VP Mktg*
EMP: 160 EST: 1994
SQ FT: 66,212
SALES (est): 52.1MM
SALES (corp-wide): 5.08B **Publicly Held**
Web: www.synopsys.com
SIC: 7372 Prepackaged software
PA: Synopsys, Inc.
   675 Almanor Ave
   Sunnyvale CA
   650 584-5000

(P-12374)
SYSTEM1 INC (PA)
4235 Redwood Ave (90066-5605)
PHONE.............................310 924-6037
Michael Blend, *Ch Bd*
Paul Filsinger, *Pr*
Tridivesh Kidambi, *CFO*
Brian Coppola, *Chief Product Officer*
EMP: 288 EST: 2020
SALES (est): 773.94MM
SALES (corp-wide): 773.94MM **Publicly Held**
Web: www.couponfollow.com
SIC: 7372 Business oriented computer software

(P-12375)
TANIUM INC
2100 Powell St 3rd Fl (94608-1826)
PHONE.............................510 704-0202
EMP: 706
SALES (corp-wide): 272.04MM **Privately Held**
Web: www.tanium.com
SIC: 7372 Application computer software
PA: Tanium, Inc.
   3550 Carillon Pt
   Kirkland WA
   510 704-0202

(P-12376)
TERADATA CORPORATION (PA)
Also Called: Teradata
17095 Via Del Campo (92127-1711)
PHONE.............................866 548-8348
Stephen Mcmillan, *Pr*
Claire Bramley, *CFO*
Suzanne Zoumaras, *Chief Human Resources Officer*
Kathy Cullen-cote, *Chief Human Resource Officer*
EMP: 1081 EST: 1979
SALES (est): 1.79B **Publicly Held**
Web: www.teradata.com
SIC: 7372 3572 7371 3571 Prepackaged software; Computer storage devices; Software programming applications; Mainframe computers

(P-12377)
TESSITURA NETWORK INC
2295 Fletcher Pkwy Ste 101 (92020-2145)

PHONE.............................888 643-5778
Jack B Rubin, *Pr*
Jack B Rubin, *CEO*
Andrew Recinos, *
Laura Bowden, *
Ivan Medanic, *OF**
EMP: 198 EST: 2002
SALES (est): 29.16MM **Privately Held**
Web: www.tessituranetwork.com
SIC: 7372 Prepackaged software

(P-12378)
THOUGHTSPOT INC (PA)
444 Castro St Ste 1000 (94041-2070)
PHONE.............................800 508-7008
Sudheesh Nair, *CEO*
Ajeet Singh, *
Amit Prakash, *
EMP: 370 EST: 2012
SALES (est): 105.57MM
SALES (corp-wide): 105.57MM **Privately Held**
Web: www.thoughtspot.com
SIC: 7372 Business oriented computer software

(P-12379)
THOUSANDEYES LLC (HQ)
500 Terry A Francois Blvd (94158-2355)
PHONE.............................415 513-4526
Mohit Lad, *CEO*
Ricardo Oliviera, *
EMP: 73 EST: 2010
SALES (est): 20.49MM
SALES (corp-wide): 57B **Publicly Held**
Web: www.thousandeyes.com
SIC: 7372 Business oriented computer software
PA: Cisco Systems, Inc.
   170 W Tasman Dr
   San Jose CA
   408 526-4000

(P-12380)
THQ INC
Also Called: Thq San Diego
21900 Burbank Blvd (91367-6469)
PHONE.............................818 591-1310
EMP: 1088
Web: www.thqnordic.com
SIC: 7372 Prepackaged software

(P-12381)
TOTAL CMMNICATOR SOLUTIONS INC
Also Called: Spark Compass
11150 Sta Monica Ste 600 (90025-3314)
PHONE.............................619 277-1488
Brent Erik Bjojegard, *CEO*
EMP: 95 EST: 2012
SALES (est): 5MM **Privately Held**
Web: www.mobicontext.com
SIC: 7372 Application computer software

(P-12382)
TRACKONOMY SYSTEMS INC (PA)
214 Devcon Dr (95112-4210)
PHONE.............................833 872-2566
Erik Volkerink, *CEO*
Ajay Khoche, *
Steve Roeser, *
Jake Medwell, *
Troy Ford, *
EMP: 275 EST: 2017
SALES (est): 19.26MM
SALES (corp-wide): 19.26MM **Privately Held**
Web: www.trackonomysystems.com

PRODUCTS & SERVICES SECTION

7372 - Prepackaged Software (P-12406)

SIC: 7372 7371 7377 3663 Prepackaged software; Computer software development and applications; Computer hardware rental or leasing, except finance leasing; Radio and t.v. communications equipment

(P-12383)
TRAFFIC MANAGEMENT PDTS INC
Also Called: Fivesixtwo Inc
4900 Airport Plaza Dr Ste 300 (90815)
PHONE.................................800 763-3999
Jonathan E Spano, *CEO*
Ed Barrera, *
Christopher H Spano, *
EMP: 1269 EST: 2015
SALES (est): 1.19MM **Privately Held**
SIC: 7372 Prepackaged software
PA: Traffic Management, Inc.
 4900 Arprt Plz Dr Ste 300
 Long Beach CA

(P-12384)
TRAXERO NORTH AMERICA LLC
1730 E Holly Ave Ste 740 (90245-4404)
PHONE.................................423 497-1164
Mark Sedgley, *Managing Member*
EMP: 90 EST: 2020
SALES (est): 5.1MM **Privately Held**
SIC: 7372 Business oriented computer software

(P-12385)
TRION WORLDS INC
2400 Bridge Pkwy 100 (94065-1166)
PHONE.................................650 631-9800
EMP: 294
SIC: 7372 Home entertainment computer software

(P-12386)
TUBEMOGUL INC
1250 53rd St Ste 1 (94608-2965)
PHONE.................................510 653-0126
EMP: 577 EST: 2007
SQ FT: 49,000
SALES (est): 119.14MM
SALES (corp-wide): 17.61B **Publicly Held**
SIC: 7372 Application computer software
PA: Adobe Inc.
 345 Park Ave
 San Jose CA
 408 536-6000

(P-12387)
UNBROKEN STUDIOS LLC
2120 Park Pl Ste 110 (90245-4741)
PHONE.................................310 741-2670
Paul Ohanian, *CEO*
Anthony Scott, *
EMP: 80 EST: 2018
SALES (est): 8.99MM
SALES (corp-wide): 13.85MM **Privately Held**
Web: www.unbrokenstudios.com
SIC: 7372 Prepackaged software
PA: Pound Sand, Llc
 2120 Park Pl Ste 110
 El Segundo CA
 310 741-2670

(P-12388)
UPSTANDING LLC
Also Called: Mobilityware
440 Exchange Ste 100 (92602-1390)
PHONE.................................949 788-9900
John Libby, *
EMP: 180 EST: 1990
SQ FT: 48,000
SALES (est): 8.96MM **Privately Held**

Web: www.mobilityware.com
SIC: 7372 Business oriented computer software

(P-12389)
VEEVA SYSTEMS INC (PA)
Also Called: Veeva
4280 Hacienda Dr (94588-2719)
PHONE.................................925 452-6500
Peter P Gassner, *CEO*
Gordon Ritter, *Non-Executive Chairman of the Board*
Thomas D Schwenger, *Pr*
Gordon Heneweer, *CFO*
E Nitsa Zuppas, *CMO*
EMP: 443 EST: 2007
SALES (est): 2.16B **Publicly Held**
Web: www.veeva.com
SIC: 7372 7371 7379 Prepackaged software ; Software programming applications; Computer related consulting services

(P-12390)
VERANA HEALTH INC
360 3rd St Ste 425 (94107-2164)
PHONE.................................888 774-0077
Sujay Jadhav, *CEO*
Miki Kapoor, *
Marie-eve Piche, *CFO*
Matthew Roe, *Chief Medical Officer*
EMP: 200 EST: 2008
SALES (est): 18.19MM **Privately Held**
Web: www.veranahealth.com
SIC: 7372 Prepackaged software

(P-12391)
VIDEOAMP INC (PA)
2229 S Carmelina Ave (90064-1001)
PHONE.................................424 272-7774
Ross Mccray, *CEO*
EMP: 86 EST: 2014
SALES (est): 10.46MM
SALES (corp-wide): 10.46MM **Privately Held**
Web: www.videoamp.com
SIC: 7372 Prepackaged software

(P-12392)
VINDICIA INC
1000 Sansome St Ste 200 (94111-1346)
PHONE.................................650 264-4700
Kris Nagel, *CEO*
Mark Elrod, *
Brett Thomas, *
EMP: 135 EST: 2003
SALES (est): 42.05MM
SALES (corp-wide): 4.58B **Privately Held**
Web: www.vindicia.com
SIC: 7372 Business oriented computer software
HQ: Amdocs, Inc.
 625 Mryvlle Cntre Dr Ste
 Saint Louis MO
 314 212-7000

(P-12393)
VMWARE INC (PA)
Also Called: Vmware
3401 Hillview Ave (94304-1383)
PHONE.................................650 427-5000
Raghu Raghuram, *CEO*
Michael Dell, *Ch Bd*
Sumit Dhawan, *Pr*
Karen E Dykstra, *CFO*
Jean-pierre Brulard, *Executive Worldwide Sales Vice-President*
▲ EMP: 1704 EST: 1998
SQ FT: 1,603,237
SALES (est): 13.35B
SALES (corp-wide): 13.35B **Privately Held**

Web: www.vmware.com
SIC: 7372 Prepackaged software

(P-12394)
WAGGL INC (PA)
1750 Bridgeway Ste B103 (94965-1900)
PHONE.................................415 399-9949
Michael Papay, *CEO*
EMP: 60 EST: 2014
SALES (est): 4.63MM
SALES (corp-wide): 4.63MM **Privately Held**
Web: go.perceptyx.com
SIC: 7372 Application computer software

(P-12395)
WEBMETRO
Also Called: Multivest
160 Via Verde Ste 1 (91773-3901)
PHONE.................................909 599-8885
EMP: 85
SIC: 7372 7311 Prepackaged software; Advertising agencies

(P-12396)
WEST COAST CONSULTING LLC
9233 Research Dr Ste 200 (92618-4294)
PHONE.................................949 250-4102
EMP: 125 EST: 1997
SALES (est): 9.17MM **Privately Held**
Web: www.westcoastllc.com
SIC: 7372 Prepackaged software

(P-12397)
WILDFIRE INTERACTIVE INC
1600 Amphitheatre Pkwy (94043-1351)
PHONE.................................650 253-0000
EMP: 250
Web: marketingplatform.google.com
SIC: 7372 Prepackaged software

(P-12398)
WIND RIVER SYSTEMS INC (HQ)
Also Called: Wind River
500 Wind River Way (94501-1162)
PHONE.................................510 748-4100
Bryan Leblanc, *CEO*
Sean Lamb, *
EMP: 600 EST: 1981
SQ FT: 273,000
SALES (est): 397.95MM
SALES (corp-wide): 17.49B **Privately Held**
Web: www.windriver.com
SIC: 7372 7373 Application computer software; Systems software development services
PA: Aptiv Plc
 13 Castle Street
 Jersey
 163 422-4000

(P-12399)
WM TECHNOLOGY INC
Also Called: Wm Technology
41 Discovery (92618-3150)
PHONE.................................844 933-3627
Christopher Beals, *CEO*
Scott Gordon, *
Juanjo Feijoo, *COO*
Arden Lee, *CFO*
Justin Dean, *CIO*
EMP: 434 EST: 2008
SALES (est): 215.53MM **Privately Held**
Web: www.weedmaps.com
SIC: 7372 Prepackaged software

(P-12400)
WME BI LLC
17075 Camino (92127)

PHONE.................................877 592-2472
EMP: 60 EST: 2012
SALES (est): 2.54MM **Privately Held**
SIC: 7372 Operating systems computer software

(P-12401)
WONDERWARE CORPORATION (DH)
26561 Rancho Pkwy S (92630-8301)
PHONE.................................949 727-3200
Rick Bullotta, *VP*
Brian Dibenedetto, *
Karen Hamilton, *
Peter Kent, *
Dave Pickett, *
EMP: 300 EST: 1993
SQ FT: 32,000
SALES (est): 40.76MM
SALES (corp-wide): 82.05K **Privately Held**
Web: www.aveva.com
SIC: 7372 Prepackaged software
HQ: Aveva Software, Llc
 26561 Rancho Pkwy S
 Lake Forest CA

(P-12402)
WORDSMART CORPORATION
10025 Mesa Rim Rd (92121-2913)
P.O. Box 366 (92038-0366)
EMP: 70 EST: 1990
SQ FT: 12,375
SALES (est): 2.12MM **Privately Held**
SIC: 7372 Educational computer software

(P-12403)
WORKBOARD INC (PA)
487 Seaport Ct Ste 100 (94063-2730)
PHONE.................................650 294-4480
Deidre Paknad, *CEO*
Diedre Paknad, *
Karim Damji, *
David Ginsburg, *Chief Customer Officer*
Stuart Crabb, *
EMP: 222 EST: 2013
SALES (est): 18.39MM
SALES (corp-wide): 18.39MM **Privately Held**
Web: www.workboard.com
SIC: 7372 Business oriented computer software

(P-12404)
XCELMOBILITY INC
Also Called: XCEL
2225 E Bayshore Rd Ste 200 (94303)
PHONE.................................650 320-1728
Zhixiong Wei, *Ch Bd*
Li Ouyang, *CFO*
Ying Yang, *Corporate Secretary*
EMP: 98 EST: 2007
SALES (est): 5.98MM **Privately Held**
Web: www.xcelmobility.com
SIC: 7372 7999 Business oriented computer software; Gambling and lottery services

(P-12405)
YARDI KUBE INC
Also Called: Wun
430 S Fairview Ave (93117-3637)
PHONE.................................805 699-2040
EMP: 61 EST: 2018
SALES (est): 4.54MM **Privately Held**
Web: www.yardi.com
SIC: 7372 Prepackaged software

(P-12406)
YOURPEOPLE INC
Also Called: Trinet Zenefits
50 Beale St Ste 1000 (94105-1808)

7372 - Prepackaged Software

PHONE..................................888 249-3263
Jay Fulcher, *CEO*
Shaun Wiley, *Sr VP*
EMP: 700 **EST:** 2012
SALES (est): 158.44MM **Publicly Held**
Web: www.zenefits.com
SIC: 7372 8741 6411 Business oriented computer software; Administrative management; Insurance brokers, nec
PA: Trinet Group, Inc.
   1 Park Pl Ste 600
   Dublin CA

(P-12407)
YUJA INC
84 W Santa Clara St Ste 400 (95113-1820)
PHONE..................................888 257-2278
Ajit Singh, *Pr*
Nathan Arora, *Chief Business Officer**
EMP: 125 **EST:** 2013
SALES (est): 9.82MM **Privately Held**
Web: www.yuja.com
SIC: 7372 Prepackaged software

(P-12408)
ZENDESK INC (HQ)
Also Called: Zendesk
989 Market St (94103-1708)
PHONE..................................415 418-7506
EMP: 204 **EST:** 2007
SQ FT: 108,000
SALES (est): 1.56B
SALES (corp-wide): 1.77B **Privately Held**
Web: www.zendesk.com
SIC: 7372 Business oriented computer software
PA: Zoro Bidco, Inc.
   3000 Sand Hill Rd Bldg 1
   Menlo Park CA
   650 681-4701

(P-12409)
ZINIO SYSTEMS INC
114 Sansome St 4th Fl (94104-3803)
PHONE..................................415 494-2700
Rusty Lewis, *CEO*
Richard A Maggiotto, **
Jeanniey Mullen, *CMO**
Tom Nofziger, **
Michelle Bottomley, **
EMP: 75 **EST:** 2000
SALES (est): 11.64MM **Privately Held**
Web: www.zinio.com
SIC: 7372 Publisher's computer software

(P-12410)
ZUORA INC (PA)
Also Called: ZUORA
101 Redwood Shores Pkwy Ste 100 (94065-6131)
PHONE..................................800 425-1281
Tien Tzuo, *Ch Bd*
Todd E Mcelhatton, *CFO*
Jennifer W Pileggi, *Sr VP*
Robert J E Traube, *CRO*
Sridhar N Srinivasan, *PRODUCT*
EMP: 300 **EST:** 2007
SQ FT: 100,000
SALES (est): 396.09MM **Publicly Held**
Web: www.zuora.com
SIC: 7372 Business oriented computer software

(P-12411)
ZWIFT INC (PA)
111 W Ocean Blvd Ste 1800 (90802-7936)
PHONE..................................855 469-9438
Eric Min, *CEO*
Kurt Beilder, **
EMP: 280 **EST:** 2014
SALES (est): 26.57MM
SALES (corp-wide): 26.57MM **Privately Held**
Web: us.zwift.com
SIC: 7372 5961 Publisher's computer software; Fitness and sporting goods, mail order

7373 Computer Integrated Systems Design

(P-12412)
10UP INC (PA)
Also Called: 10up.com
2765 Carradale Dr (95661-4089)
PHONE..................................888 571-7130
Jake Goldman, *Pr*
John Eckman, *CEO*
EMP: 91 **EST:** 2012
SQ FT: 1,300
SALES (est): 6.33MM
SALES (corp-wide): 6.33MM **Privately Held**
Web: www.10up.com
SIC: 7373 Systems software development services

(P-12413)
AARKI INC (PA)
530 Lakeside Dr Ste 260 (94085-4064)
PHONE..................................408 382-1180
EMP: 101 **EST:** 2007
SALES (est): 23.14MM **Privately Held**
Web: www.aarki.com
SIC: 7373 7372 8742 7313 Systems software development services; Business oriented computer software; Marketing consulting services; Electronic media advertising representatives

(P-12414)
ACTIVEVIDEO NETWORKS LLC (DH)
333 W San Carlos St Ste 900 (95110-2715)
PHONE..................................408 931-9200
Jeff Miller, *Pr*
Chris Linden, *COO*
Matt Andrade, *CFO*
EMP: 73 **EST:** 1988
SALES (est): 10.02MM **Publicly Held**
Web: www.activevideo.com
SIC: 7373 Computer integrated systems design
HQ: Ruckus Wireless, Inc.
   350 W Java Dr
   Sunnyvale CA

(P-12415)
ACUMEN LLC
Also Called: Medric
500 Airport Blvd Ste 100 (94010-1980)
PHONE..................................650 558-8882
Thomas Macurdy, *Managing Member*
EMP: 166 **EST:** 1996
SALES (est): 24.38MM **Privately Held**
Web: www.acumenllc.com
SIC: 7373 7379 8742 Systems software development services; Computer related consulting services; Management consulting services

(P-12416)
AIZON LLC
44 Montgomery St Ste 3 (94104-4618)
PHONE..................................312 285-4605
EMP: 109 **EST:** 2019
SALES (est): 2.1MM **Privately Held**

SIC: 7373 7375 Computer systems analysis and design; Information retrieval services

(P-12417)
APTTUS CORPORATION (PA)
3001 Bishop Dr (94583-5005)
PHONE..................................650 445-7700
Frank Holland, *CEO*
David Murphy, **
Neehar Giri, *SOLN'S**
Gregg Hampton, **
Ben Allen, **
EMP: 566 **EST:** 2012
SALES (est): 172.49MM **Privately Held**
Web: www.conga.com
SIC: 7373 Systems software development services

(P-12418)
ARYAKA NETWORKS INC (PA)
1850 Gateway Dr Ste 500 (94404-4064)
PHONE..................................888 692-7925
Matthew Carter, *CEO*
Shailesh Shukla, **
Ashwath Nagaraj, **
Brad Kinnish, **
EMP: 337 **EST:** 2008
SALES (est): 78.1MM **Privately Held**
Web: www.aryaka.com
SIC: 7373 8748 Systems software development services; Telecommunications consultant

(P-12419)
ASHTON-TATE LLC
403 Main St (94105-2067)
PHONE..................................415 639-5873
Ray Jeter, *Managing Member*
EMP: 141 **EST:** 2021
SALES (est): 5.02MM **Privately Held**
Web: www.ashton-tate.com
SIC: 7373 Computer system selling services

(P-12420)
AT ROAD INC
888 Tasman Dr (95035-7439)
PHONE..................................510 668-1638
EMP: 582
SIC: 7373 7372 Systems integration services; Prepackaged software

(P-12421)
ATAC (PA)
2770 De La Cruz Blvd (95050-2624)
PHONE..................................408 736-2822
Mark Cochran, *Ch*
Scott Simcox, **
Charles Winkleman, **
EMP: 65 **EST:** 1979
SQ FT: 31,000
SALES (est): 23.42MM
SALES (corp-wide): 23.42MM **Privately Held**
Web: www.atac.com
SIC: 7373 7376 7379 8711 Computer integrated systems design; Computer facilities management; Computer related maintenance services; Engineering services

(P-12422)
AURORA OPERATIONS INC
280 Bernardo Ave (94043-5238)
PHONE..................................888 583-9506
Chris Urmson, *CEO*
Richard Tame, *CFO*
William Mouat, *Sec*
EMP: 100 **EST:** 2000
SALES (est): 5.42MM **Privately Held**
Web: www.aurora.tech

SIC: 7373 Computer integrated systems design

(P-12423)
AUTOMATION HOLDCO INC
10815 Rancho Bernardo Rd Ste 102 (92127)
PHONE..................................858 967-8650
Leo Castaneda, *Pr*
EMP: 80 **EST:** 2013
SALES (est): 4.55MM **Privately Held**
SIC: 7373 Systems integration services

(P-12424)
AVEVA SOFTWARE LLC (DH)
Also Called: Wonderware
26561 Rancho Pkwy S (92630-8301)
PHONE..................................949 727-3200
EMP: 350 **EST:** 2014
SALES (est): 220.34MM
SALES (corp-wide): 82.05K **Privately Held**
Web: www.aveva.com
SIC: 7373 Computer integrated systems design
HQ: Aveva Inc.
   11044 Res Blvd Ste A100
   Austin TX
   713 977-1225

(P-12425)
AVI-SPL LLC
44911 Industrial Dr (94538-6486)
PHONE..................................510 344-5618
EMP: 612
SALES (corp-wide): 509.35MM **Privately Held**
Web: www.avispl.com
SIC: 7373 Systems integration services
PA: Avi-Spl Llc
   6301 Benjamin Rd Ste 101
   Tampa FL
   813 884-7168

(P-12426)
AZUGA INC (DH)
Also Called: Azuga
42840 Christy St Ste 205 (94538-3118)
PHONE..................................866 497-2512
Anan Rani, *CEO*
Subash Gopalkrishnan, **
▲ **EMP:** 306 **EST:** 2012
SQ FT: 1,800
SALES (est): 38.05MM **Privately Held**
Web: www.azuga.com
SIC: 7373 Computer integrated systems design
HQ: Bridgestone Americas, Inc.
   200 4th Ave S Ste 100
   Nashville TN
   615 937-1000

(P-12427)
BRILLIUS TECHNOLOGIES INC
4305 Hacienda Dr (94588-2743)
PHONE..................................510 379-9027
Ram Danda, *Pr*
Prasha Ganga, **
EMP: 148 **EST:** 2013
SQ FT: 1,500
SALES (est): 16.32MM **Privately Held**
Web: www.brillius.com
SIC: 7373 7372 Systems engineering, computer related; Business oriented computer software

(P-12428)
CACI ENTERPRISE SOLUTIONS LLC
1455 Frazee Rd Ste 700 (92108-4308)
PHONE..................................619 881-6000

PRODUCTS & SERVICES SECTION

7373 - Computer Integrated Systems Design (P-12448)

J P London, *CEO*
EMP: 252
SALES (corp-wide): 6.7B **Publicly Held**
Web: www.caci.com
SIC: **7373** Computer integrated systems design
HQ: Caci Enterprise Solutions, Llc
 1100 N Glebe Rd Ste 200
 Arlington VA
 703 841-7800

(P-12429)
CADENT INC
Also Called: Orthocad
2560 Orchard Pkwy (95131-1033)
PHONE..................................408 470-1000
Timothy Mack, *Pr*
Roger Blanchette, *
▲ EMP: 130 EST: 1999
SQ FT: 24,000
SALES (est): 9.03MM
SALES (corp-wide): 3.73B **Publicly Held**
Web: www.cadent.tv
SIC: **7373** Computer systems analysis and design
HQ: Cadent Holdings, Inc.
 2560 Orchard Pkwy
 San Jose CA

(P-12430)
CAPTIVA SOFTWARE CORPORATION (DH)
10145 Pacific Heights Blvd (92121-4234)
PHONE..................................858 320-1000
Reynolds C Bish, *Pr*
Patrick L Edsell, *
Rick E Russo, *CFO*
Jim Nicol, *Executive Product Development Vice President*
Howard Dratler, *OK Vice President*
EMP: 80 EST: 1986
SQ FT: 25,000
SALES (est): 25.91MM **Publicly Held**
SIC: **7373** 7372 Office computer automation systems integration; Prepackaged software
HQ: Emc Corporation
 176 South St
 Hopkinton MA
 508 435-1000

(P-12431)
CAST IRON SYSTEMS INC
4400 N 1st St (95134-1257)
PHONE..................................914 499-1900
EMP: 77
Web: www.castiron.com
SIC: **7373** Systems software development services

(P-12432)
CELESTIX NETWORKS INC
4125 Hopyard Rd Ste 225 (94588-8534)
P.O. Box 255 (94583-0255)
PHONE..................................510 668-0700
Yong Thye Lin, *CEO*
Yong Ping Lin, *
Bobby Chen, *
▲ EMP: 70 EST: 1999
SQ FT: 9,000
SALES (est): 10.87MM **Privately Held**
Web: www.celestix.com
SIC: **7373** Systems software development services
PA: Celestix Networks Pte Ltd
 62 Ubi Road 1
 Singapore

(P-12433)
CEREBRAS SYSTEMS INC
1237 E Arques Ave (94085-4701)
PHONE..................................650 933-4980
Andrew Feldman, *CEO*
Michael James, *
Gary Lauterbach, *
Rebecca Boyden, *
EMP: 150 EST: 2016
SALES (est): 25.14MM **Privately Held**
Web: www.cerebras.net
SIC: **7373** 7389 Systems software development services; Business Activities at Non-Commercial Site

(P-12434)
CLINICOMP INTERNATIONAL INC (PA)
9655 Towne Centre Dr (92121-1964)
PHONE..................................858 546-8202
Chris Haudenschild, *CEO*
Eloisa Haudenschild, *CFO*
William Mcdonald, *Contrlr*
Jiao Fan Ph.d., *VP*
Kelley Malott, *VP*
EMP: 99 EST: 1983
SQ FT: 42,000
SALES (est): 28.97MM
SALES (corp-wide): 28.97MM **Privately Held**
Web: www.clinicomp.com
SIC: **7373** 7371 3571 Systems software development services; Custom computer programming services; Electronic computers

(P-12435)
CNET NETWORKS INC
235 2nd St (94105-3100)
PHONE..................................415 344-2000
EMP: 1242
SALES (est): 29.78MM
SALES (corp-wide): 30.15B **Publicly Held**
Web: www.cnet.com
SIC: **7373** 7371 Systems software development services; Computer software development and applications
HQ: Cbs Interactive Inc.
 680 Folsom St
 San Francisco CA

(P-12436)
COGNIZANT TRZTTO SFTWR GROUP I
3631 S Harbor Blvd Ste 200 (92704-6951)
PHONE..................................714 481-0396
Kathy Kantocello, *Contrlr*
EMP: 221
SIC: **7373** 4813 Systems software development services; Internet connectivity services
HQ: Cognizant Trizetto Software Group, Inc.
 9655 Maroon Cir
 Englewood CO

(P-12437)
COMPUTER TECH RESOURCES INC
16 Technology Dr Ste 202 (92618-2329)
PHONE..................................714 665-6507
Alok Mundra, *Brnch Mgr*
EMP: 192
SALES (corp-wide): 95.63MM **Privately Held**
Web: www.astcorporation.com
SIC: **7373** Computer integrated systems design
HQ: Computer Technology Resources, Inc.
 8333 Clairemont Mesa Blvd
 San Diego CA
 858 492-1400

(P-12438)
CONDUENT STATE LCAL SLTONS INC
455 The Embarcadero Ste 103 (94111-2023)
PHONE..................................415 486-2409
Marilyn Malakowsky, *Mgr*
EMP: 1685
SALES (corp-wide): 3.86B **Publicly Held**
SIC: **7373** 7379 Computer integrated systems design; Online services technology consultants
HQ: Conduent State & Local Solutions, Inc.
 100 Campus Dr Ste 200
 Florham Park NJ
 301 820-4200

(P-12439)
CONTENT GURU INC
900 E Hamilton Ave Ste 510 (95008-0664)
PHONE..................................408 559-3988
Sean Taylor, *Pr*
EMP: 300 EST: 2005
SALES (est): 23.3MM
SALES (corp-wide): 68.32MM **Privately Held**
Web: www.contentguru.com
SIC: **7373** Computer integrated systems design
PA: Redwood Technologies Group Ltd
 Radius Court
 Bracknell BERKS
 134 485-2350

(P-12440)
CORDOBA CORPORATION
1401 N Broadway (90012-1410)
PHONE..................................213 895-0224
George Pla, *Pr*
Maria Mehranian, *COO*
EMP: 93 EST: 1993
SALES (est): 1.4MM **Privately Held**
Web: www.cordobacorp.com
SIC: **7373** Computer integrated systems design

(P-12441)
CORE BTS INC
5250 Lankershim Blvd Ste 620 (91601-3112)
PHONE..................................818 766-2400
EMP: 106
Web: www.corebts.com
SIC: **7373** Systems integration services
HQ: Core Bts, Inc.
 5875 Castle Creek Parkway
 Indianapolis IN
 317 566-6200

(P-12442)
CUBIC CORPORATION
Also Called: Cubic Defense Systems
9233 Balboa Ave (92123-1513)
PHONE..................................858 277-6780
Brigitte Jen, *Brnch Mgr*
EMP: 2000
SALES (corp-wide): 1.48B **Privately Held**
Web: www.cubic.com
SIC: **7373** Computer integrated systems design
HQ: Cubic Corporation
 9233 Balboa Ave
 San Diego CA
 858 277-6780

(P-12443)
DATA DOMAIN LLC
2421 Mission College Blvd (95054-1214)
PHONE..................................408 980-4800
Frank Slootman, *Pr*
Nick Bacica, *
Daniel R Mcgee, *Sr VP*
Michael P Scarpelli, *
David L Schneider, *
EMP: 777 EST: 2001
SQ FT: 200,000
SALES (est): 102.79MM **Publicly Held**
Web: www.datadomain.com
SIC: **7373** Computer integrated systems design
HQ: Emc Corporation
 176 South St
 Hopkinton MA
 508 435-1000

(P-12444)
DEALPATH INC
300 California St Ste 200 (94104-1410)
PHONE..................................415 876-8441
Miichael Sroka, *CEO*
EMP: 99 EST: 2014
SALES (est): 4.97MM **Privately Held**
Web: www.dealpath.com
SIC: **7373** Systems software development services

(P-12445)
DELART TECHNOLOGY SERVICES LLC
312 Arizona Ave (90401-1306)
PHONE..................................949 229-2786
Alireza Tarighat, *Pt*
EMP: 60 EST: 2007
SALES (est): 15MM **Privately Held**
SIC: **7373** Systems engineering, computer related

(P-12446)
DELEGATA CORPORATION
2450 Venture Oaks Way Ste 400 (95833-3292)
PHONE..................................916 609-5400
Kais Menoufy, *Pr*
Barbara Halsey, *
Jacquelyn Silver, *Senior Program Manager*
EMP: 100 EST: 2000
SQ FT: 5,000
SALES (est): 6.32MM **Privately Held**
Web: www.delegata.com
SIC: **7373** Computer integrated systems design

(P-12447)
DIGITALIST USA LTD
611 Gateway Blvd Ste 120 (94080-7066)
PHONE..................................949 278-1354
Jo Javier, *VP*
EMP: 1000 EST: 2010
SALES (est): 45.83MM **Privately Held**
SIC: **7373** 8731 Systems software development services; Computer (hardware) development
PA: Digitalist Group Oyj
 Siltasaarenkatu 18c
 Helsinki

(P-12448)
DILIGENTE TECHNOLOGIES LLC
226 Airport Pkwy (95110-1099)
PHONE..................................510 304-0852
Rohita Joshi, *Managing Member*
EMP: 500 EST: 2010
SALES (est): 23.49MM **Privately Held**
Web: www.diligentetechnologies.com
SIC: **7373** 7379 Computer integrated systems design; Computer related maintenance services

7373 - Computer Integrated Systems Design (P-12449)

(P-12449)
DROISYS INC (PA)
Also Called: Ebsavvy
46540 Fremont Blvd Ste 516 (94538-6487)
PHONE...................................408 874-8333
Amit Goel, *CEO*
Sanjiv Goyal, *Pr*
Amit Kumar, *Sec*
Douglas Blizel, *Prin*
EMP: 63 **EST:** 2003
SQ FT: 3,374
SALES (est): 15.57MM
SALES (corp-wide): 15.57MM **Privately Held**
Web: www.droisys.com
SIC: 7373 7371 7379 Systems software development services; Custom computer programming services; Computer related consulting services

(P-12450)
ECIFM SOLUTIONS INC
3160 Crow Canyon Rd Ste 240 (94583-1331)
PHONE...................................925 830-1925
Vimaljit Uberoi, *Pr*
EMP: 135 **EST:** 2000
SQ FT: 3,750
SALES (est): 9MM **Privately Held**
Web: www.ecifm.com
SIC: 7373 7376 Computer integrated systems design; Computer facilities management

(P-12451)
ELECTRONIC ONLINE SYSTEMS INTERNATIONAL
Also Called: E O S International
2292 Faraday Ave Frnt (92008-7237)
PHONE...................................760 431-8400
EMP: 64 **EST:** 1981
SALES (est): 4.99MM **Privately Held**
SIC: 7373 7371 7372 Turnkey vendors, computer systems; Computer software development; Prepackaged software

(P-12452)
ELSA CORP
139 Old Orchard Dr (95032-5029)
PHONE...................................408 431-6735
Vu Van, *CEO*
Tu Ngo, *
EMP: 159 **EST:** 2015
SALES (est): 16.91MM **Privately Held**
Web: www.elsapeak.com
SIC: 7373 Computer integrated systems design

(P-12453)
EMR CPR LLC
32970 Alvarado Niles Rd Ste 736 (94587-3194)
PHONE...................................408 471-6804
Edward Ohara, *CEO*
David Ohara, *
EMP: 412 **EST:** 2012
SALES (est): 25.58MM **Privately Held**
Web: www.emrcpr.com
SIC: 7373 7374 Systems engineering, computer related; Data entry service

(P-12454)
EXPERIAN HEALTH INC
2233 Watt Ave Ste 275 (95825-0570)
PHONE...................................415 716-6633
Milton Boyd, *Brnch Mgr*
EMP: 116
SALES (corp-wide): 6.62B **Privately Held**
Web: www.experian.com
SIC: 7373 Computer integrated systems design
HQ: Experian Health, Inc.
720 Cool Springs Blvd # 200
Franklin TN

(P-12455)
FILENET CORPORATION
3565 Harbor Blvd (92626-1405)
PHONE...................................800 345-3638
EMP: 1695
SIC: 7373 7372 Computer integrated systems design; Business oriented computer software

(P-12456)
FORCE10 NETWORKS GLOBAL INC
Also Called: Dell
350 Holger Way (95134-1362)
PHONE...................................800 289-3355
Michael Dell, *CEO*
James Hanley, *Field Operator*
Bruce Miller, *Technology Vice President*
Ebrahim Abbasi, *Executive Corporate Development Vice President*
William Zerella, *CFO*
▲ **EMP:** 582 **EST:** 1999
SQ FT: 97,000
SALES (est): 65.14MM **Publicly Held**
Web: www.force10networks.com
SIC: 7373 Computer integrated systems design
HQ: Dell Inc.
1 Dell Way
Round Rock TX
800 289-3355

(P-12457)
FRANCISCO PARTNERS GP III LP (HQ)
Also Called: FP
1 Letterman Dr Bldg C (94129-2402)
PHONE...................................415 418-2900
Dipanjan Deb, *Mng Pt*
Chris Adams, *Pt*
Ben Ball, *Pt*
Neil Garfinkel, *Pt*
Peter Christodoulo, *Pt*
EMP: 60 **EST:** 2000
SALES (est): 115.53MM
SALES (corp-wide): 2.68B **Privately Held**
Web: www.franciscopartners.com
SIC: 7373 7372 Systems integration services; Prepackaged software
PA: Francisco Partners Management, L.P.
1 Letterman Dr Ste 410
San Francisco CA
415 418-2900

(P-12458)
FUJITSU NORTH AMERICA INC (HQ)
350 Cobalt Way (94085-5426)
PHONE...................................408 746-6000
Masashige Nagoshi, *CEO*
John Lanius, *Sec*
EMP: 74 **EST:** 2013
SALES (est): 9.53MM **Privately Held**
SIC: 7373 Computer integrated systems design
PA: Fujitsu Limited
1-5-2, Higashishimbashi
Minato-Ku TKY

(P-12459)
GEMALTO COGENT INC (HQ)
2964 Bradley St (91107-1560)
PHONE...................................626 325-9600
Alan Pelligrini, *Pr*
Antonio Lo Brutto, *
Daniel Asraf, *
Ramsey Billups, *
Alex Woods, *
▲ **EMP:** 95 **EST:** 2004
SQ FT: 151,000
SALES (est): 47.81MM
SALES (corp-wide): 277.29MM **Privately Held**
SIC: 7373 Computer-aided system services
PA: Thales
4 Rue De La Verrerie
Meudon

(P-12460)
GENEA ENERGY PARTNERS INC
19100 Von Karman Ave Ste 550 (92612-6571)
PHONE...................................714 694-0536
Michal Pasula, *Admn*
Jon Haahr, *
Keith Voysey, *
David Balkin, *
EMP: 120 **EST:** 2006
SQ FT: 10,000
SALES (est): 10.4MM **Privately Held**
Web: www.getgenea.com
SIC: 7373 Systems software development services

(P-12461)
GRAMMARLY INC (PA)
548 Market St Ste 35410 (94104-5401)
PHONE...................................888 318-6146
Brad Hoover, *CEO*
Andy Chen, *
EMP: 233 **EST:** 2009
SQ FT: 9,000
SALES (est): 116.49MM
SALES (corp-wide): 116.49MM **Privately Held**
Web: www.grammarly.com
SIC: 7373 8299 Systems software development services; Educational services

(P-12462)
HARMAN CNNCTED SVCS HOLDG CORP (DH)
636 Ellis St (94043-2207)
PHONE...................................650 623-9400
Sanjay Dhawan, *Pr*
Pradeep Chaudhry, *CFO*
Subash A K Rao, *Chief Human Resource Officer*
EMP: 226 **EST:** 2012
SALES (est): 83.01MM **Privately Held**
Web: www.harman.com
SIC: 7373 Systems software development services
HQ: Harman International Industries Incorporated
400 Atlantic St Ste 15
Stamford CT
203 328-3500

(P-12463)
HASURA INC
576 Folsom St Fl 3 (94105-3183)
PHONE...................................415 861-9195
Tanmai Gopal, *CEO*
EMP: 188 **EST:** 2018
SALES (est): 14.24MM **Privately Held**
Web: www.hasura.io
SIC: 7373 Systems software development services

(P-12464)
HEARTFLOW INC (PA)
331 E Evelyn Ave Ste 100 (94041-1550)
PHONE...................................650 241-1221
John Farquhar, *Pr*
John Stevens, *
Charles Taylor, *
Campbell Rogers, *CMO*
Yoshiki Kawabata, *
EMP: 133 **EST:** 2007
SQ FT: 3,400
SALES (est): 45.72MM **Privately Held**
Web: www.heartflow.com
SIC: 7373 Systems software development services

(P-12465)
HUBB SYSTEMS LLC
Also Called: Data 911
12305 Crosthwaite Cir (92064-6817)
PHONE...................................510 865-9100
Abigail Baker, *CEO*
Donald R Hubbard, *
Brian Mccown, *CFO*
EMP: 75 **EST:** 1982
SALES (est): 12.38MM
SALES (corp-wide): 23.63MM **Privately Held**
SIC: 7373 7379 Turnkey vendors, computer systems; Computer related consulting services
PA: Broadcast Microwave Services, Llc
13475 Danielson St # 130
Poway CA
858 391-3050

(P-12466)
HUMANE INC
969 Folsom St (94107-1020)
PHONE...................................415 891-1900
Imran Chaudhri, *Ch Bd*
Bethany Bongiorno, *
EMP: 200 **EST:** 2019
SALES (est): 16.65MM **Privately Held**
Web: hu.ma.ne
SIC: 7373 Computer integrated systems design

(P-12467)
ICTV
Also Called: Active Video
333 W San Carlos St Ste 900 (95110-2715)
PHONE...................................408 931-9200
EMP: 66 **EST:** 2011
SALES (est): 2.27MM **Privately Held**
Web: www.ithaca.edu
SIC: 7373 Computer integrated systems design

(P-12468)
INFORMATION MGT RESOURCES INC (PA)
Also Called: Imri
85 Argonaut Ste 215 (92656-4105)
PHONE...................................949 215-8889
Martha Daniel, *CEO*
EMP: 132 **EST:** 1986
SQ FT: 5,000
SALES (est): 16.61MM **Privately Held**
Web: www.imri.com
SIC: 7373 8742 7371 Computer integrated systems design; Management consulting services; Computer software systems analysis and design, custom

(P-12469)
INSEEGO NORTH AMERICA LLC (HQ)
Also Called: 1-Carasight Surveillance
9605 Scranton Rd Ste 300 (92121-1789)
PHONE...................................541 685-9045
Michael Newman, *Sec*
EMP: 65 **EST:** 2007

PRODUCTS & SERVICES SECTION
7373 - Computer Integrated Systems Design (P-12490)

SQ FT: 36,000
SALES (est): 9.2MM
SALES (corp-wide): 245.32MM Publicly Held
Web: www.inseego.com
SIC: 7373 Computer integrated systems design
PA: Inseego Corp.
 9710 Scranton Rd Ste 200
 San Diego CA
 858 812-3400

(P-12470)
INTELLIMIZE INC
341 Dwight Rd (94010-2814)
PHONE..................................415 760-5710
Guy Yalif, *Prin*
EMP: 60 EST: 2016
SALES (est): 1.61MM Privately Held
Web: www.intellimize.com
SIC: 7373 Computer integrated systems design

(P-12471)
INTERNET CORP FOR ASSGNED NMES (PA)
Also Called: Icann
12025 Waterfront Dr Ste 300 (90094-2536)
PHONE..................................310 823-9358
Cherine Chalaby, *Ch*
Chris Disspain, *Vice Chairman**
EMP: 146 EST: 1998
SALES (est): 84.27MM
SALES (corp-wide): 84.27MM Privately Held
Web: www.icann.org
SIC: 7373 Systems software development services

(P-12472)
JUNIPER NETWORKS INC
Also Called: Proof of Concept Poc Lab
1137 Innovation Way Bldg B (94089-1228)
PHONE..................................408 745-2000
Florin A Oprescu, *Prin*
EMP: 2000
Web: www.juniper.net
SIC: 7373 7372 Computer integrated systems design; Prepackaged software
PA: Juniper Networks, Inc.
 1133 Innovation Way
 Sunnyvale CA

(P-12473)
JUNIPER NETWORKS INC
Aurrion
6868 Cortona Dr Ste C (93117-1363)
PHONE..................................805 880-2000
EMP: 60
Web: www.juniper.net
SIC: 7373 Computer integrated systems design
PA: Juniper Networks, Inc.
 1133 Innovation Way
 Sunnyvale CA

(P-12474)
JUNIPER NETWORKS (US) INC (HQ)
1133 Innovation Way (94089-1228)
PHONE..................................408 745-2000
Rami Rahim, *CEO*
Scott Kriens, *Ch Bd*
Faye Fingles, *Ex Sec*
EMP: 96 EST: 2000
SALES (est): 23.64MM Publicly Held
Web: www.juniper.net
SIC: 7373 Computer integrated systems design
PA: Juniper Networks, Inc.

1133 Innovation Way
Sunnyvale CA

(P-12475)
KOAM ENGINEERING SYSTEMS INC
Also Called: K E S
7807 Convoy Ct Ste 200 (92111-1213)
PHONE..................................858 292-0922
John S Yi, *Pr*
Richard Comber, *
Erica Tofson, *
John Schiltz, *
Jim Meadows, *
EMP: 105 EST: 1994
SQ FT: 5,700
SALES (est): 22.05MM Privately Held
Web: www.kes.com
SIC: 7373 Computer integrated systems design

(P-12476)
KOREA TRADE AND INV PROM AGCY
Also Called: Kotra
3003 N 1st St (95134-2004)
PHONE..................................408 432-5000
Jack Dorsey, *CEO*
EMP: 190 EST: 2011
SALES (est): 3.34MM Privately Held
Web: www.kotrasv.org
SIC: 7373 6726 Systems software development services; Investment offices, nec

(P-12477)
LAMBDATEST INC
1390 Market St Ste 200 (94102-5404)
PHONE..................................866 430-7087
Asad Khan, *CEO*
Jay Singh, *
Ss Rahman, *Head OF INTEGRATIONS**
Alekh Agarawal Fd, *Prin*
Mudit Singh Digital, *Mktg Dir*
EMP: 250 EST: 2017
SALES (est): 27.04MM Privately Held
Web: www.lambdatest.com
SIC: 7373 Computer systems analysis and design

(P-12478)
LATTICE ENGINES INC (DH)
1820 Gateway Dr Ste 200 (94404-4059)
PHONE..................................877 460-0010
Bryan T Hipsher, *CEO*
Colleen Haley, *Sec*
EMP: 105 EST: 2010
SALES (est): 22.86MM
SALES (corp-wide): 2.22B Publicly Held
SIC: 7373 7372 Computer system selling services; Business oriented computer software
HQ: The Dun & Bradstreet Corporation
 5335 Gate Pkwy Ste 100
 Jacksonville FL

(P-12479)
LIFERAY INC (PA)
Also Called: LIFERAY
1400 Montefino Ave Ste 100 (91765-5501)
PHONE..................................877 543-3729
Bryan Cheung, *
Paul Hinz, *CMO*
Jc Choi, *CFO*
Caris Chan, *CAO*
Brian Kim, *COO*
EMP: 1222 EST: 2006
SALES (est): 120K
SALES (corp-wide): 120K Privately Held
Web: www.liferay.com

SIC: 7373 Systems software development services

(P-12480)
LOCKHEED MARTIN UNMANNED
125 Venture Dr Ste 110 (93401-9103)
PHONE..................................805 503-4340
Jesse May, *CEO*
EMP: 80
Web: www.gyrocamsystems.com
SIC: 7373 Computer systems analysis and design
HQ: Lockheed Martin Unmanned Integrated Systems, Inc.
 133 W Park Loop Nw
 Huntsville AL

(P-12481)
LOOKOUT INC (PA)
Also Called: Flexilis
275 Battery St Ste 200 (94111-3379)
PHONE..................................650 241-2358
James Dolce, *CEO*
Mark Nasiff, *COO*
EMP: 172 EST: 2005
SALES (est): 258.26MM Privately Held
Web: www.lookout.com
SIC: 7373 Systems software development services

(P-12482)
LUCID DESIGN GROUP INC
55 Harrison St Ste 200 (94607-3772)
PHONE..................................510 907-0400
Will Coleman, *CEO*
Vladisoav Shunturov, *
EMP: 80 EST: 2004
SALES (est): 13.94MM
SALES (corp-wide): 3.95B Publicly Held
Web: www.atrius.com
SIC: 7373 Systems software development services
PA: Acuity Brands, Inc.
 1170 Peachtree St Ne # 23
 Atlanta GA
 404 853-1400

(P-12483)
LUCIDWORKS INC (PA)
235 Montgomery St Ste 500 (94104-2908)
PHONE..................................415 329-6515
Michael Sinoway, *CEO*
Will Hayes, *CEO*
Reade Frank, *CFO*
EMP: 148 EST: 2007
SALES (est): 39.82MM Privately Held
Web: www.lucidworks.com
SIC: 7373 Systems software development services

(P-12484)
LUXURY PRESENCE INC
2805 W 233rd St (90505-3113)
PHONE..................................310 955-1077
Malte Kramer, *Managing Member*
EMP: 156 EST: 2015
SALES (est): 3.66MM Privately Held
Web: www.luxurypresence.com
SIC: 7373 7371 Computer integrated systems design; Computer software systems analysis and design, custom

(P-12485)
MACKEVISION LLC
1255 Treat Blvd Ste 250 (94597-7997)
PHONE..................................248 656-6566
Armin Pohl, *CEO*
Lindy Brodeur, *
EMP: 120 EST: 2007
SQ FT: 8,000

SALES (est): 21.68MM Privately Held
SIC: 7373 Computer-aided design (CAD) systems service
HQ: Accenture Song Content Germany Gmbh
 Forststr. 7
 Stuttgart BW
 7114906039000

(P-12486)
MATRIXX SOFTWARE INC (PA)
Also Called: Matrixx Software
1098 Foster City Blvd Ste 106 # 836 (94404)
PHONE..................................669 267-6333
Glo Gordon, *CEO*
Luther Kitahata, *
Jennifer Kyriakakis, *
Milan Parikh, *
EMP: 77 EST: 2008
SALES (est): 27.52MM
SALES (corp-wide): 27.52MM Privately Held
Web: www.matrixx.com
SIC: 7373 Systems software development services

(P-12487)
MERGE HEALTHCARE SOLUTIONS INC
Also Called: IBM Watson Health
10140 Mesa Rim Rd (92121-2914)
PHONE..................................858 625-3344
Anne Le Grand, *Genl Mgr*
EMP: 65
SALES (corp-wide): 547.95MM Privately Held
Web: www.merative.com
SIC: 7373 7375 Computer integrated systems design; Data base information retrieval
HQ: Merge Healthcare Solutions Inc.
 900 Walnut Ridge Dr
 Hartland WI
 262 367-0700

(P-12488)
MESFIN ENTERPRISES
Also Called: Transnational Computer Tech
222 N Pacific Coast Hwy Ste 1570 (90245)
PHONE..................................310 615-0881
Wond Wossen Mesfin, *Pr*
EMP: 376 EST: 1978
SQ FT: 11,250
SALES (est): 35.33MM Privately Held
SIC: 7373 7376 5734 Systems integration services; Computer facilities management; Software, business and non-game

(P-12489)
MILESTONE TECHNOLOGIES INC (PA)
3101 Skyway Ct (94539-5910)
PHONE..................................510 651-2454
Sameer Kishore, *Pr*
EMP: 1788 EST: 1997
SQ FT: 6,500
SALES (est): 253.48MM
SALES (corp-wide): 253.48MM Privately Held
Web: www.milestone.tech
SIC: 7373 7374 Computer integrated systems design; Data processing and preparation

(P-12490)
MIRO TECHNOLOGIES INC
5643 Copley Dr (92111-7903)
P.O. Box 3707 (98124-2207)
PHONE..................................858 677-2100

7373 - Computer Integrated Systems Design (P-12491)

EMP: 150
SIC: 7373 Turnkey vendors, computer systems

(P-12491)
MIST SYSTEMS INC
Also Called: Mist
1601 S De Anza Blvd Ste 248 (95014-5301)
PHONE.................................408 326-0346
Sujai Hajela, *CEO*
Brett Galloway, *Ch Bd*
Laura Perrone, *CFO*
EMP: 125 EST: 2014
SALES (est): 18.07MM **Publicly Held**
Web: www.mist.com
SIC: 7373 Local area network (LAN) systems integrator
PA: Juniper Networks, Inc.
1133 Innovation Way
Sunnyvale CA

(P-12492)
MIVA INC
Also Called: Miva Merchant
16870 W Bernardo Dr Ste 100 (92127-1604)
PHONE.................................858 490-2570
Rick Wilson, *CEO*
Nathan Osborne, *
David Hubbard, *
EMP: 120 EST: 2007
SALES (est): 17.84MM **Privately Held**
Web: www.miva.com
SIC: 7373 5961 Systems software development services; Catalog and mail-order houses

(P-12493)
MOBICA US INC
2570 N 1st St 2nd Fl (95131-1035)
PHONE.................................650 450-6654
Marcin Kloda, *CEO*
Rafael Janczyk, *
EMP: 900 EST: 2012
SALES (est): 54.08MM **Publicly Held**
Web: www.mobica.com
SIC: 7373 Systems software development services
HQ: Mobica Limited
Crown House
Wilmslow

(P-12494)
MOBISYSTEMS INC
4501 Mission Bay Dr Ste 3a (92109)
PHONE.................................858 350-0315
Stanislav Minchev, *CEO*
Stoyan Gogov, *
EMP: 150 EST: 2001
SQ FT: 1,200
SALES (est): 11.33MM **Privately Held**
Web: www.mobisystems.com
SIC: 7373 Systems software development services

(P-12495)
MORPHOTRAK LLC (DH)
Also Called: Safran
5515 E La Palma Ave Ste 100 (92807-2127)
PHONE.................................714 238-2000
Celeste Thomasson, *Managing Member*
Clark Nelson, *VP*
Katie Murphy, *Sec*
Florian Hebras, *CFO*
EMP: 175 EST: 1985
SQ FT: 32,000
SALES (est): 38.45MM
SALES (corp-wide): 2.44B **Privately Held**
Web: www.morphotrak.com
SIC: 7373 Computer integrated systems design
HQ: Idemia Identity & Security France
2 Place Samuel De Champlain
Courbevoie

(P-12496)
MOZILLA CORP
149 New Montgomery St (94105-3740)
PHONE.................................650 903-0800
EMP: 117 EST: 2013
SALES (est): 4.63MM **Privately Held**
Web: www.mozilla.org
SIC: 7373 Systems software development services

(P-12497)
MY ALLY INC
1000 Elwell Ct Ste 105 (94303-4306)
PHONE.................................650 387-9118
Deepti Yenireddy, *CEO*
Carter Perez, *
EMP: 70 EST: 2015
SALES (est): 4.1MM **Privately Held**
Web: www.myally.ai
SIC: 7373 Systems software development services

(P-12498)
NANTWORKS LLC (PA)
9920 Jefferson Blvd (90232-3506)
PHONE.................................310 883-1300
Charles N Kenworthy, *Managing Member*
EMP: 79 EST: 2011
SALES (est): 158.26K
SALES (corp-wide): 158.26K **Publicly Held**
Web: www.nantworks.com
SIC: 7373 Computer-aided system services

(P-12499)
NETAPP INC
6320 Canoga Ave Ste 1500 (91367-2517)
PHONE.................................818 227-5025
James Mccormick Iii, *Mgr*
EMP: 209
Web: www.netapp.com
SIC: 7373 Computer integrated systems design
PA: Netapp, Inc.
3060 Olsen Dr
San Jose CA

(P-12500)
NETWORK INTGRTION PARTNERS INC
Also Called: Nic Partners
11981 Jack Benny Dr Ste 103 (91739-9232)
PHONE.................................909 919-2800
Franklin P Spaeth, *Pr*
EMP: 80 EST: 2007
SQ FT: 6,000
SALES (est): 21.82MM **Privately Held**
Web: nic.clients.zebrakick.com
SIC: 7373 Local area network (LAN) systems integrator

(P-12501)
NEW DIRECTIONS TECH INC (PA)
Also Called: Ndti
137 W Drummond Ave Ste A (93555-3583)
PHONE.................................760 384-2444
EMP: 65 EST: 1992
SQ FT: 6,000
SALES (est): 24.25MM **Privately Held**
Web: www.ndti.net

SIC: 7373 7374 8711 7371 Systems software development services; Data processing and preparation; Engineering services; Computer software development and applications

(P-12502)
NORTHROP GRUMMAN SPACE & MISSION SYSTEMS CORP
6379 San Ignacio Ave (95119-1200)
PHONE.................................703 280-2900
◆ EMP: 12000
SIC: 7373 3663 3661 3812 Computer integrated systems design; Radio and t.v. communications equipment; Telephone and telegraph apparatus; Defense systems and equipment

(P-12503)
NOYO TECHNOLOGIES INC
735 Montgomery St Ste 250 (94111-2137)
PHONE.................................347 721-2816
Shannon Goggin, *Pr*
EMP: 83 EST: 2018
SALES (est): 3.14MM **Privately Held**
Web: www.noyo.com
SIC: 7373 Computer integrated systems design

(P-12504)
NUAGE NETWORKS
200 S Mathilda Ave Ste 5 (94086-6135)
PHONE.................................415 439-9420
Sunil Khandekar, *Owner*
EMP: 86 EST: 2014
SALES (est): 671.48K **Privately Held**
Web: www.nuagenetworks.net
SIC: 7373 Local area network (LAN) systems integrator

(P-12505)
NURLOGIC DESIGN INC (DH)
5580 Morehouse Dr (92121-1755)
PHONE.................................858 455-7570
EMP: 60 EST: 1997
SQ FT: 34,000
SALES (est): 12.73MM **Privately Held**
SIC: 7373 Computer integrated systems design
HQ: Arm, Inc.
120 Rose Orchard Way
San Jose CA

(P-12506)
O2 MICRO INC
3118 Patrick Henry Dr (95054-1850)
PHONE.................................408 987-5920
EMP: 100 EST: 1995
SQ FT: 37,000
SALES (est): 25.1MM **Privately Held**
Web: ir.o2micro.com
SIC: 7373 Computer integrated systems design
PA: O2micro International Limited
The Grand Pavillion
George Town GR CAYMAN

(P-12507)
OBERMAN TIVOLI & PICKERT INC
Also Called: Media Services
500 S Sepulveda Blvd Ste 500 (90049-3551)
PHONE.................................310 440-9600
Robert Oberman, *Pr*
Barry Oberman, *
Alan Tivoli, *VP*
Sanaa Wadsworth, *
EMP: 230 EST: 1989

SALES (est): 23.63MM **Privately Held**
Web: www.mediaservices.com
SIC: 7373 8721 8741 Systems software development services; Payroll accounting service; Business management

(P-12508)
OTO ANALYTICS INC
Also Called: Womply
548 Market St Ste 73871 (94104-5401)
PHONE.................................310 683-0000
Toby Scammell, *CEO*
EMP: 454 EST: 2011
SALES (est): 37.92MM **Privately Held**
Web: www.womply.com
SIC: 7373 Computer integrated systems design

(P-12509)
PACKETEER INC
420 N Mary Ave (94085-4121)
PHONE.................................408 220-2200
▲ EMP: 428
SIC: 7373 Computer integrated systems design

(P-12510)
PFU AMERICA INC (HQ)
Also Called: Fujitsu Computer Pdts Amer Inc
1250 E Arques Ave (94085-5401)
PHONE.................................800 626-4686
Etsuro Sato, *Pr*
Victor Kan, *V PRESS**
Motoyasu Matsuzaki, *
▲ EMP: 340 EST: 1991
SQ FT: 75,335
SALES (est): 68.48MM **Privately Held**
Web: pfu-us.ricoh.com
SIC: 7373 Computer integrated systems design
PA: Fujitsu Limited
1-5-2, Higashishimbashi
Minato-Ku TKY

(P-12511)
PLURIS INC
10455 Bandley Dr (95014-1900)
PHONE.................................408 863-9920
Joseph S Kennedy, *Pr*
Bulent Erbilgin, *VP Engg*
Diana Everett, *VP Fin*
Warren Roddy, *Senior Vice President Worldwide Sales*
David Cox, *VP Opers*
EMP: 220 EST: 1996
SQ FT: 38,000
SALES (est): 4.3MM **Privately Held**
SIC: 7373 Computer integrated systems design

(P-12512)
QOLSYS INC (HQ)
Also Called: Qolsys
1919 S Bascom Ave Ste 600 (95008-2237)
PHONE.................................855 476-5797
David Lewis Pulling, *CEO*
Prasad Vindla, *
EMP: 139 EST: 2010
SALES (est): 16.31MM **Privately Held**
Web: www.qolsys.com
SIC: 7373 Systems software development services
PA: Johnson Controls International Public Limited Company
1 Albert Quay
Cork

(P-12513)
QSOLV INC
440 N Wolfe Rd Ste 26 (94085-3869)

PRODUCTS & SERVICES SECTION
7373 - Computer Integrated Systems Design (P-12533)

PHONE.................408 429-0918
Sujaya Viswanathan, CEO
Shyam Gopal, *
EMP: 112 EST: 1997
SALES (est): 4.76MM Privately Held
Web: www.qsolv-inc.com
SIC: 7373 7379 7371 Computer systems analysis and design; Computer related consulting services; Software programming applications

(P-12514)
QUEST SOFTWARE INC (PA)
20 Enterprise Ste 100 (92656-7104)
PHONE.................949 754-8000
Patrick Nichols, CEO
Carolyn Mccarthy, CFO
EMP: 600 EST: 1987
SQ FT: 170,000
SALES (est): 647.68MM
SALES (corp-wide): 647.68MM Privately Held
Web: www.quest.com
SIC: 7373 7379 7372 Computer integrated systems design; Computer related consulting services; Business oriented computer software

(P-12515)
QUOTIT CORPORATION
721 S Parker St Ste 330 (92868-4739)
PHONE.................714 564-5000
Chad Hogan, Sr VP
EMP: 102 EST: 1999
SQ FT: 2,400
SALES (est): 4.77MM Publicly Held
Web: www.quotit.com
SIC: 7373 Systems software development services
HQ: National General Holdings Corp.
59 Maiden Ln Fl 38
New York NY

(P-12516)
R SYSTEMS INC
5000 Windplay Dr Ste 5 (95762-9319)
PHONE.................916 939-9696
Satinder S Rekhi, CEO
Harpreet Rekhi, *
Sartaj Singh Rekhi, *
EMP: 120 EST: 1993
SQ FT: 7,000
SALES (est): 23.54MM Privately Held
Web: www.rsystems.com
SIC: 7373 Systems software development services
PA: R Systems International Limited
C 40, Sector 59
Noida UP

(P-12517)
RAVENSWOOD SOLUTIONS INC (HQ)
48371 Fremont Blvd Ste 105 (94538-6580)
PHONE.................650 241-3661
Kipp Peppel, CEO
Kipp Peppel, Pr
John Prausa, *
Ernesto Lozano Junior, Prin
Peter Kuebler, *
EMP: 96 EST: 2015
SALES (est): 10.12MM
SALES (corp-wide): 249.22MM Privately Held
Web: www.ravenswoodsolutions.com
SIC: 7373 7379 3679 8711 Systems engineering, computer related; Computer related maintenance services; Antennas, receiving; Engineering services
PA: Sri International

333 Ravenswood Ave
Menlo Park CA
650 859-2000

(P-12518)
RESULT GROUP INC
2603 Main St Ste 710 (92614-4263)
PHONE.................480 777-7130
William Derick Robson, Pr
David Griffiths, *
EMP: 83 EST: 2003
SALES (est): 389.73K
SALES (corp-wide): 6.62B Privately Held
SIC: 7373 7372 Systems software development services; Business oriented computer software
HQ: Wynne Systems, Inc.
2601 Main St Ste 270
Irvine CA

(P-12519)
REVIEW WAVE
16531 Scientific (92618-4356)
PHONE.................800 563-0469
EMP: 72 EST: 2020
SALES (est): 3.61MM Privately Held
Web: www.reviewwave.com
SIC: 7373 Systems software development services

(P-12520)
SAFELYYOU INC
Also Called: Safelyyou
36 Clyde St (94107-1718)
PHONE.................713 822-6924
George Netscher, CEO
Shirley Nickels, *
Tom Bang, Chief Strategy Officer*
Glen Xiong, Chief Medical Officer*
Russell Burt, *
EMP: 86 EST: 2015
SALES (est): 5.52MM Privately Held
Web: www.safely-you.com
SIC: 7373 Computer-aided system services

(P-12521)
SAMSARA INC (PA)
1 De Haro St (94103-5205)
PHONE.................415 985-2400
Sanjit Biswas, Ch Bd
Dominic Phillips, Ex VP
John Bicket, *
Adam Eltoukhy, CLO
EMP: 2183 EST: 2015
SQ FT: 133,000
SALES (est): 652.54MM
SALES (corp-wide): 652.54MM Publicly Held
Web: www.samsara.com
SIC: 7373 Computer systems analysis and design

(P-12522)
SCALEFLUX INC
900 N Mccarthy Blvd Ste 200 (95035-5135)
PHONE.................408 628-2291
Hao Zhong, CEO
EMP: 60 EST: 2014
SALES (est): 6.76MM Privately Held
Web: www.scaleflux.com
SIC: 7373 Systems engineering, computer related

(P-12523)
SCIENCE APPLICATIONS INTL CORP
Also Called: Saic
4015 Hancock St (92110-5121)
PHONE.................858 826-3061
Gordon Saakamodo, Mgr

EMP: 600
SALES (corp-wide): 7.7B Publicly Held
Web: www.saic.com
SIC: 7373 Systems engineering, computer related
PA: Science Applications International Corporation
12010 Sunset Hills Rd
Reston VA
703 676-4300

(P-12524)
SOFT MACHINES INC
Also Called: Smachines
3920 Freedom Cir (95054-1240)
PHONE.................408 969-0215
Mahesh Lingareddy, CEO
Mohammad Abdallah, *
EMP: 65 EST: 2006
SQ FT: 5,000
SALES (est): 9.39MM Privately Held
SIC: 7373 Systems software development services

(P-12525)
SOFTWARE DYNAMICS INCORPORATED
8501 Fallbrook Ave Ste 200 (91304)
PHONE.................818 992-3299
Matthew Hale, Pr
Christopher J Stein, *
Richard Dobb, *
Geoffrey Gill, *
EMP: 67 EST: 1982
SQ FT: 40,000
SALES (est): 949.59K Publicly Held
SIC: 7373 7371 Computer systems analysis and design; Computer software development
HQ: S1 Corporation
705 Westech Dr
Norcross GA
678 966-9499

(P-12526)
SOLUGENIX CORPORATION (PA)
Also Called: Solugenix
601 Valencia Ave Ste 260 (92823-6357)
PHONE.................866 749-7658
Shashi Jasthi, CEO
Damola Akinola, *
EMP: 138 EST: 2004
SQ FT: 1,600
SALES (est): 35.59MM
SALES (corp-wide): 35.59MM Privately Held
Web: www.solugenix.com
SIC: 7373 Computer integrated systems design

(P-12527)
SONICWALL INC (PA)
1033 Mccarthy Blvd (95035-7920)
PHONE.................888 557-6642
Robert Vankirk, Pr
John Gmuender, *
Jeff Dolce, *
Michelle Ragusa-mcbain, VP
▲ EMP: 1685 EST: 1991
SQ FT: 86,000
SALES (est): 153.96MM Privately Held
Web: www.sonicwall.com
SIC: 7373 Systems software development services

(P-12528)
SOUL MACHINES INC
44 Tehama St Ste 411 (94105-3110)
PHONE.................649 283-0863
Mark Sagar, Dir

Greg Cross, Dir
Chris Liu, Dir
EMP: 75 EST: 2017
SALES (est): 4.98MM Privately Held
SIC: 7373 Systems software development services

(P-12529)
STRIPE HEAVY INDUSTRIES INC (HQ)
Also Called: Stripe
354 Oyster Point Blvd (94080-1912)
PHONE.................877 887-7815
EMP: 238 EST: 2015
SALES (est): 2.09MM Privately Held
SIC: 7373 Systems software development services
PA: Stripe, Inc.
354 Oyster Point Blvd
South San Francisco CA

(P-12530)
SYNAPSE DESIGN AUTOMATION INC (DH)
Also Called: Synapse Design
2200 Laurelwood Rd (95054-1515)
PHONE.................408 850-9527
Satish Bagalkotkar, CEO
EMP: 64 EST: 2015
SALES (est): 13.58MM Privately Held
Web: www.synapse-da.com
SIC: 7373 Computer integrated systems design
HQ: Quest Global Services-Na, Inc.
175 Addison Rd
Windsor CT

(P-12531)
SYSTEM INTEGRATORS INC
Also Called: Netlinx Publishing Solutions
1740 N Market Blvd (95834-1997)
PHONE.................916 830-2400
Paul Donlan, Pr
Allan Katzen, *
EMP: 180 EST: 1973
SQ FT: 70,000
SALES (est): 14.43MM
SALES (corp-wide): 355.83K Privately Held
SIC: 7373 7372 7371 Computer integrated systems design; Prepackaged software; Custom computer programming services
PA: Net-Linx Ag
Kathe-Kollwitz-Ufer 76-79
Dresden SN
351318750

(P-12532)
TECHNET PARTNERS INC
Also Called: Technet Partners
6116 Innovation Way (92009-1728)
PHONE.................760 683-8393
Brian Schumann, CEO
Floyd Auten, *
Ryan Hardesty, *
EMP: 72 EST: 2011
SALES (est): 9.32MM Privately Held
Web: www.technetpartners.com
SIC: 7373 1731 8748 Local area network (LAN) systems integrator; Fiber optic cable installation; Systems engineering consultant, ex. computer or professional

(P-12533)
TRACE3 LLC (HQ)
Also Called: Trace3
7505 Irvine Center Dr Ste 100 (92618-3078)
PHONE.................949 333-2300
Rich Fennessy, CEO

7373 - Computer Integrated Systems Design (P-12534)

Tyler Beecher, *
Kevin Manzo, *
EMP: 113 **EST:** 2001
SALES (est): 583.64MM
SALES (corp-wide): 583.64MM **Privately Held**
Web: www.trace3.com
SIC: 7373 Computer systems analysis and design
PA: Escape Velocity Holdings, Inc.
7505 Irvine Center Dr # 10
Irvine CA
949 333-2381

(P-12534)
TRAMS INC (DH)
7 Lower Blackwater Cyn Rd (90274-4053)
PHONE....................310 641-8726
Lee B Rosen, Pr
EMP: 65 **EST:** 1984
SALES (est): 8.41MM **Publicly Held**
Web: www.trams.com
SIC: 7373 Systems software development services
HQ: Sabre Glbl Inc.
3150 Sabre Dr
Southlake TX
682 605-1000

(P-12535)
TRANSCENTRA INC
20500 Belshaw Ave (90746-3506)
PHONE....................310 603-0105
Dwayne Moore, Brnch Mgr
EMP: 517
SALES (corp-wide): 1.08B **Publicly Held**
Web: www.exelatech.com
SIC: 7373 Systems software development services
HQ: Transcentra, Inc.
4145 Shackleford Rd # 330
Norcross GA
678 728-2500

(P-12536)
TRAPEZE NETWORKS INC
Also Called: Juniper Networks
5753 W Las Positas Blvd (94588-4084)
PHONE....................925 474-2200
▲ **EMP:** 112
SIC: 7373 Local area network (LAN) systems integrator

(P-12537)
TRINITY TECHNOLOGY GROUP INC
2015 J St Ste 105 (95811-3124)
PHONE....................916 779-0201
Randall E Duart, CEO
Jane Duart, *
Timothy Purdy, *
Stephen Williamson, *
EMP: 67 **EST:** 1999
SQ FT: 2,800
SALES (est): 14.86MM **Privately Held**
Web: www.trinitytg.com
SIC: 7373 Systems software development services

(P-12538)
TUSIMPLE HOLDINGS INC (PA)
Also Called: Tusimple
9191 Towne Centre Dr Ste 600 (92122)
PHONE....................619 916-3144
Cheng Lu, CEO
Eric Tapia, CAO
Susan Marsch, Interim General Counsel
EMP: 486 **EST:** 2015
SQ FT: 80,000
SALES (est): 9.37MM
SALES (corp-wide): 9.37MM **Publicly Held**
Web: www.tusimple.com
SIC: 7373 Computer integrated systems design

(P-12539)
UBIQUITI NETWORKS INC
91 E Tasman Dr (95134-1620)
PHONE....................408 942-3085
Robert J Pera, Ch
EMP: 120 **EST:** 2014
SALES (est): 5.07MM **Publicly Held**
SIC: 7373 5045 7372 Local area network (LAN) systems integrator; Computer software; Prepackaged software
PA: Ubiquiti Inc.
685 3rd Ave Fl 27
New York NY

(P-12540)
ULTISAT INC
Also Called: A Speedcast Co
11839 Sorrento Valley Rd (92121-1040)
PHONE....................240 243-5107
EMP: 1238
SALES (corp-wide): 423MM **Privately Held**
Web: www.ultisat.com
SIC: 7373 Systems integration services
PA: Ultisat, Inc.
14399 Penrose Pl Ste 410
Chantilly VA
240 243-5100

(P-12541)
VCORE TECHNOLOGY PARTNERS LLC (PA)
5185 Foxglove Dr (92649-4091)
PHONE....................877 348-7714
Steven Leavitt, CEO
EMP: 63 **EST:** 2010
SALES (est): 48.58MM
SALES (corp-wide): 48.58MM **Privately Held**
SIC: 7373 Value-added resellers, computer systems

(P-12542)
VERTISYSTEM INC
39300 Civic Center Dr Ste 160 (94538-2338)
PHONE....................510 794-8099
Shaloo Jeswani, CEO
Rakesh Sadhwani, *
Deebali Syed, *
Shaloo Jeswani, Owner
Chavi Vijay, *
EMP: 200 **EST:** 2008
SQ FT: 2,744
SALES (est): 11.09MM **Privately Held**
Web: www.vertisystem.com
SIC: 7373 Systems software development services

(P-12543)
WAVESTRONG INC
2000 Crow Canyon Pl Ste 150 (94583-1383)
PHONE....................844 299-8264
Harpreet Walia, CEO
Mandeet Dhoat, *
Raj Khanna, *
EMP: 94 **EST:** 2001
SALES (est): 9.61MM **Privately Held**
Web: www.wavestrong.com
SIC: 7373 7379 Computer integrated systems design; Computer related consulting services

(P-12544)
WEST PUBLISHING CORPORATION
Also Called: Elite
800 Crprate Pinte Ste 150 (90230)
P.O. Box 51606 (90051-5906)
PHONE....................424 243-2100
Salim Sunderji, VP
EMP: 663
SALES (corp-wide): 10.66B **Publicly Held**
Web: home.westacademic.com
SIC: 7373 7371 Computer integrated systems design; Custom computer programming services
HQ: West Publishing Corporation
610 Opperman Dr
Eagan MN
651 687-7000

(P-12545)
ZELAR SOFT LLC
595 Pacific Ave Fl 4 (94133-4685)
PHONE....................510 262-2801
Jagdish Medarametla, Managing Member
EMP: 175 **EST:** 2017
SALES (est): 2.5MM **Privately Held**
SIC: 7373 Systems software development services

7374 Data Processing And Preparation

(P-12546)
6 SENSE INSIGHTS INC (PA)
Also Called: 6sense
450 Mission St Ste 201 (94105-2513)
PHONE....................415 212-9225
Jason Zintak, CEO
Rob Goldenberg, CFO
Sanjay Kini, Chief Customer Officer
Samuel Lam, Mgr
EMP: 74 **EST:** 2013
SALES (est): 271.66MM
SALES (corp-wide): 271.66MM **Privately Held**
Web: www.6sense.com
SIC: 7374 7389 Computer graphics service; Business Activities at Non-Commercial Site

(P-12547)
ACTIVIDENTITY CORPORATION
6623 Dumbarton Cir (94555-3603)
PHONE....................510 574-0100
▲ **EMP:** 218
Web: www.hidglobal.com
SIC: 7374 Data verification service

(P-12548)
ALIGNED COMPANY
Also Called: Extra
360 E 2nd St Ste 809 (90012-4238)
PHONE....................917 558-4565
Cyrus Summerlin, Pr
EMP: 68 **EST:** 2018
SALES (est): 4.94MM **Privately Held**
SIC: 7374 5961 6141 Computer graphics service; Electronic shopping; Consumer finance companies

(P-12549)
AMAZON PROCESSING LLC
Also Called: Appstar Financial
4619 Viewridge Ave Ste C (92123-5611)
PHONE....................858 565-1135
EMP: 193 **EST:** 2002
SALES (est): 12.08MM **Privately Held**
Web: www.appstar.net

SIC: 7374 Data processing service

(P-12550)
AMG DATA SERVICES
5440 Ericson Way Ste B (95521-9293)
P.O. Box 1085 (95518-1085)
PHONE....................707 822-4888
Robert Adler, Owner
EMP: 100 **EST:** 1991
SALES (est): 1.3MM **Privately Held**
SIC: 7374 Data processing service

(P-12551)
AUTOMATIC DATA PROCESSING INC
Also Called: ADP
3972 Barranca Pkwy Ste J610 (92606-1204)
PHONE....................949 751-0360
EMP: 165
SALES (corp-wide): 16.5B **Publicly Held**
Web: www.adp.com
SIC: 7374 Data processing service
PA: Automatic Data Processing, Inc.
1 Adp Blvd Ste 1 # 1
Roseland NJ
973 974-5000

(P-12552)
AUTOMATIC DATA PROCESSING INC
Also Called: ADP
400 W Covina Blvd (91773-2954)
PHONE....................800 225-5237
Rodney Hroblak, Prin
EMP: 117
SALES (corp-wide): 16.5B **Publicly Held**
Web: www.adp.com
SIC: 7374 8721 Data processing service; Accounting, auditing, and bookkeeping
PA: Automatic Data Processing, Inc.
1 Adp Blvd Ste 1 # 1
Roseland NJ
973 974-5000

(P-12553)
BLACK KNIGHT INFOSERV LLC
2500 Redhill Ave Ste 100 (92705-5518)
PHONE....................904 854-5100
Miriam Moore, Brnch Mgr
EMP: 163
SALES (corp-wide): 7.29B **Publicly Held**
Web: www.blackknightinc.com
SIC: 7374 Data processing and preparation
HQ: Black Knight Infoserv, Llc
601 Riverside Ave
Jacksonville FL

(P-12554)
BRANCH METRICS INC (PA)
195 Page Mill Rd Ste 101 (94306-2073)
PHONE....................650 209-6461
Alexander John Austin, CEO
Michael Charles Molinet, *
EMP: 305 **EST:** 2013
SALES (est): 42.12MM
SALES (corp-wide): 42.12MM **Privately Held**
Web: www.branch.io
SIC: 7374 Data processing service

(P-12555)
CASTLIGHT HEALTH INC (HQ)
150 Spear St Ste 400 (94105-1500)
PHONE....................415 829-1400
EMP: 93 **EST:** 2008
SQ FT: 31,000
SALES (est): 146.71MM
SALES (corp-wide): 147.46MM **Privately Held**

PRODUCTS & SERVICES SECTION

7374 - Data Processing And Preparation (P-12577)

Web: www.mycastlighthealth.com
SIC: 7374 7372 Data processing and preparation; Prepackaged software
PA: Vera Whole Health, Inc
    1201 2nd Ave Ste 1400
    Seattle WA
    206 395-7870

(P-12556)
CCH INCORPORATED
2050 W 190th St (90504-6228)
PHONE......................310 800-9800
EMP: 1221
SQ FT: 280,000
SALES (corp-wide): 5.4B Privately Held
Web: www.wolterskluwer.com
SIC: 7374 7372 7371 Data processing and preparation; Prepackaged software; Custom computer programming services
HQ: Cch Incorporated
    2700 Lake Cook Rd
    Riverwoods IL
    847 267-7000

(P-12557)
CELESTIAL-SATURN PARENT INC (PA)
40 Pacifica (92618-7471)
PHONE......................949 214-1000
EMP: 139 EST: 2021
SALES (est): 1.64B
SALES (corp-wide): 1.64B Privately Held
Web: www.corelogic.com
SIC: 7374 Data processing and preparation

(P-12558)
COFA MEDIA GROUP LLC
5650 El Camino Real Ste 100a (92008)
PHONE......................877 293-2007
EMP: 88 EST: 2009
SALES (est): 2.35MM
SALES (corp-wide): 44.98MM Privately Held
Web: www.cofamedia.com
SIC: 7374 Computer graphics service
PA: Geary Lsf Group, Inc.
    332 Pine St Fl 6
    San Francisco CA
    877 616-8226

(P-12559)
COMPUSHARE INC
3 Hutton Centre Dr Ste 700 (92707)
PHONE......................714 427-1000
EMP: 141
Web: www.compushare.com
SIC: 7374 Data processing and preparation

(P-12560)
COUNTY OF LOS ANGELES
Also Called: Voter Prcnct Vter Rgstrtion Of
12400 Imperial Hwy (90650-3134)
PHONE......................562 462-2094
Connie Mccormack, Brnch Mgr
EMP: 73
SALES (corp-wide): 31.7B Privately Held
Web: www.lacounty.gov
SIC: 7374 9111 Data entry service; Executive offices
PA: County Of Los Angeles
    500 W Temple St Ste 437
    Los Angeles CA
    213 974-1101

(P-12561)
CYBER INFRASTRUCTURE INC
2880 Zanker Rd Ste 20 (95134-2117)
PHONE......................408 364-6849
Khizer Hayat, CEO
EMP: 74 EST: 2017
SALES (est): 801.92K Privately Held
Web: www.cisin.com
SIC: 7374 Calculating service (computer)

(P-12562)
CYBER-PRO SYSTEMS INC
Also Called: Medical Data Exchange
2121 S Towne Centre Pl Ste 200 (92806)
PHONE......................562 256-3800
Gerry Ibanez, CEO
Scott H Kramer, *
EMP: 162 EST: 1985
SALES (est): 8.88MM
SALES (corp-wide): 2.71B Publicly Held
Web: www.mdxnet.com
SIC: 7374 Data processing service
PA: Agilon Health, Inc.
    6210 E Hwy 290 Ste 450
    Austin TX
    562 256-3800

(P-12563)
CYBERSOURCE CORPORATION (HQ)
900 Metro Center Blvd (94404-2172)
P.O. Box 8999 (94128-8999)
PHONE......................650 432-7350
Alfred F Kelly Junior, Pr
Scott R Cruickshank, *
Steven D Pellizzer, *
Robert J Ford, Executive Product Development Vice President*
John Bodine, *
EMP: 135 EST: 1998
SALES (est): 90.92MM Publicly Held
Web: www.cybersource.com
SIC: 7374 Data processing service
PA: Visa Inc.
    900 Metro Center Blvd
    Foster City CA

(P-12564)
D E M ENTERPRISES INC
Also Called: Webtyme Design & Hosting
15 S Bayshore Blvd (94401-2045)
PHONE......................650 401-6200
Don Mahnke, Pr
▲ EMP: 100 EST: 1998
SALES (est): 6.13MM Privately Held
Web: www.abctrans.com
SIC: 7374 4119 6512 Computer graphics service; Limousine rental, with driver; Commercial and industrial building operation

(P-12565)
DESIGN PEOPLE INC
1700 E Walnut Ave Ste 400 (90245-2609)
PHONE......................800 969-5799
Jon Krabbe, Pr
Tiger Bitanga, *
Jon Krabbe, CFO
Luigi Amante, *
EMP: 160 EST: 1998
SQ FT: 9,200
SALES (est): 9.69MM Privately Held
Web: www.thedesignpeople.com
SIC: 7374 Computer graphics service

(P-12566)
EDATA SOLUTIONS INC
2450 Peralta Blvd Ste 202 (94536-3826)
PHONE......................510 574-5380
Manan Kothari, CEO
EMP: 1000 EST: 2014
SALES (est): 4.77MM Privately Held
Web: www.edataweb.com
SIC: 7374 7371 Data processing service; Computer software development and applications

(P-12567)
ELEVATED RESOURCES INC (PA)
3990 Westerly Pl Ste 270 (92660-2348)
PHONE......................949 419-6632
EMP: 225 EST: 2007
SQ FT: 1,900
SALES (est): 18.22MM Privately Held
Web: www.elevatedresources.com
SIC: 7374 Data processing and preparation

(P-12568)
EMERALD CONNECT LLC (HQ)
15050 Avenue Of Science Ste 200 (92128-3419)
PHONE......................800 233-2834
Adam D Amsterdam, Managing Member
Sharon Greener, *
Heather Hinkle, *
Heidi Saucier, OF DIGITAL STRAT*
EMP: 100 EST: 1986
SQ FT: 35,000
SALES (est): 17.26MM Publicly Held
Web: www.broadridge.com
SIC: 7374 7331 Data processing service; Mailing service
PA: Broadridge Financial Solutions, Inc.
    5 Dakota Dr Ste 300
    New Hyde Park NY

(P-12569)
ENCLARITY INC
16815 Von Karman Ave Ste 125 (92606-2404)
PHONE......................949 797-7160
Sean Downs, CEO
Thomas Suk, *
Warren Gouk Andrea, *
Paul Perleberg, *
Scott Marber, *
EMP: 348 EST: 2005
SQ FT: 3,500
SALES (est): 5.39MM
SALES (corp-wide): 10.3B Privately Held
Web: risk.lexisnexis.com
SIC: 7374 Data processing service
HQ: Lexisnexis Risk Solutions Inc.
    1000 Alderman Dr
    Alpharetta GA
    678 694-6000

(P-12570)
ENERVEE CORPORATION
11845 W Olympic Blvd Ste 1100w (90064-1149)
PHONE......................844 363-7833
Matthias Kurwig, CEO
Donald Epperson, *
EMP: 102 EST: 2009
SALES (est): 11.28MM Privately Held
Web: www.enervee.com
SIC: 7374 Computer processing services

(P-12571)
EPOCHCOM LLC
Also Called: Epoch.com
3110 Main St Ste 220 (90405-5353)
PHONE......................310 664-5700
Joel Hall, Managing Member
Esther Martinez, *
EMP: 150 EST: 2004
SQ FT: 22,000
SALES (est): 14.69MM Privately Held
Web: www.epoch.com
SIC: 7374 Data processing service

(P-12572)
EVERYPATH INC
101 University Ave # 100 (94301-1638)
PHONE......................408 562-8000
Mark Tapling, Pr
Prakash Iyer, *
Stuart Finn, *
Matt Dimaria, *
Toshi Otani, *
EMP: 87 EST: 1998
SQ FT: 14,417
SALES (est): 3.18MM Privately Held
SIC: 7374 Computer graphics service

(P-12573)
FICO
3661 Valley Centre Dr (92130-3337)
PHONE......................858 369-8000
EMP: 64 EST: 2017
SALES (est): 7.25MM Privately Held
Web: www.fico.com
SIC: 7374 Data processing service

(P-12574)
FLYR INC (PA)
3205 Pico Blvd (90405-2113)
PHONE......................415 841-3597
Alexander Mans, CEO
EMP: 62 EST: 2013
SQ FT: 4,838
SALES (est): 12.89MM
SALES (corp-wide): 12.89MM Privately Held
Web: www.flyrlabs.com
SIC: 7374 Data processing and preparation

(P-12575)
GLINT INC
1000 W Maude Ave (94085-2810)
PHONE......................650 817-7240
Jim Barnett, CEO
Dennis Jang, CFO
Mary Poppen, CCO
Marc Maloy, CRO
EMP: 100 EST: 2013
SALES (est): 12.68MM
SALES (corp-wide): 211.91B Publicly Held
Web: www.glintinc.com
SIC: 7374 Data processing and preparation
HQ: Linkedin Corporation
    1000 W Maude Ave
    Sunnyvale CA
    650 687-3600

(P-12576)
GOODRX HOLDINGS INC (PA)
Also Called: GOODRX
2701 Olympic Blvd (90404-4183)
PHONE......................855 268-2822
Scott Wagner, Interim Chief Executive Officer
Trevor Bezdek, *
Douglas Hirsch, CMO*
Karsten Voermann, CFO
Raj Beri, COO
EMP: 300 EST: 2011
SQ FT: 132,000
SALES (est): 766.55MM
SALES (corp-wide): 766.55MM Publicly Held
Web: www.goodrx.com
SIC: 7374 Computer processing services

(P-12577)
GREENSOFT TECHNOLOGY INC
155 S El Molino Ave Ste 100 (91101-2563)
PHONE......................323 254-5961
Larry Yen, Pr
Jon Wu, *
EMP: 121 EST: 2002
SALES (est): 5.94MM Privately Held
Web: www.greensofttech.com

7374 - Data Processing And Preparation (P-12578)

PRODUCTS & SERVICES SECTION

SIC: 7374 Data processing service

(P-12578)
HEWLETT PACKARD ENTERPRISE CO
4555 Great America Pkwy Ste 201 (95054-1243)
PHONE.............................408 914-2390
EMP: 600
SALES (corp-wide): 28.5B Publicly Held
Web: www.hpe.com
SIC: 7374 Data processing service
PA: Hewlett Packard Enterprise Company
  1701 E Mossy Oaks Rd
  Spring TX
  678 259-9860

(P-12579)
HONK TECHNOLOGIES INC
2251 Barry Ave (90064-1401)
P.O. Box 910 (90078-0910)
PHONE.............................800 979-3162
Corey Brundage, CEO
Dan Rosenthal, *
EMP: 151 EST: 2014
SQ FT: 8,000
SALES (est): 75MM Privately Held
Web: www.honkforhelp.com
SIC: 7374 7372 7371 Data processing and preparation; Business oriented computer software; Custom computer programming services

(P-12580)
HYVE SOLUTIONS CORPORATION (HQ)
44201 Nobel Dr (94538-3178)
PHONE.............................855 869-6873
Dennis John Polk, CEO
Marshall Willaim Wit, CFO
Simon Y Leung, Sec
▲ EMP: 142 EST: 2012
SALES (est): 66.13MM
SALES (corp-wide): 62.34B Publicly Held
Web: www.hyvesolutions.com
SIC: 7374 5734 Data processing and preparation; Computer and software stores
PA: Td Synnex Corporation
  44201 Nobel Dr
  Fremont CA
  510 656-3333

(P-12581)
IKANO COMMUNICATIONS INC (PA)
Also Called: A & S Technologies
9221 Corbin Ave Ste 260 (91324-1625)
PHONE.............................801 924-0900
EMP: 91 EST: 1991
SQ FT: 50,000
SALES (est): 17.46MM Privately Held
Web: www.ikano.com
SIC: 7374 Data processing and preparation

(P-12582)
INFLECTION RISK SOLUTIONS LLC
Also Called: Trust Safety
555 Twin Dolphin Dr Ste 600 (94065-2129)
PHONE.............................650 618-9910
Max Wesman, VP
Max Wesman, COO
Ellen Perelman, CMO*
EMP: 169 EST: 2011
SQ FT: 7,095
SALES (est): 13.48MM
SALES (corp-wide): 473.9MM Privately Held
Web: www.goodhire.com

SIC: 7374 Data processing and preparation
PA: Checkr, Inc.
  1 Montgomery St Ste 2400
  San Francisco CA
  844 824-3257

(P-12583)
INKO INDUSTRIAL CORPORATION
695 Vaqueros Ave (94085-3524)
PHONE.............................408 830-1040
George Kuo, Pr
▲ EMP: 100 EST: 1983
SQ FT: 80,000
SALES (est): 11.17MM Privately Held
Web: www.pellicle-inko.com
SIC: 7374 Computer graphics service

(P-12584)
JASPERSOFT CORPORATION
350 Rhode Island St # 250 (94103-5187)
P.O. Box 77648 (94107-0648)
PHONE.............................415 348-2300
EMP: 175
SIC: 7374 7372 7379 Computer graphics service; Business oriented computer software; Computer related consulting services

(P-12585)
KEYNOTE LLC
Also Called: Keynote Systems
777 Mariners Island Blvd (94404-5083)
PHONE.............................650 376-3033
EMP: 495
SIC: 7374 7373 Data processing and preparation; Computer system selling services

(P-12586)
LEAF GROUP LTD (HQ)
Also Called: Leaf Group
1655 26th St (90404-4016)
PHONE.............................310 394-6400
EMP: 133 EST: 2006
SALES (est): 62.96MM
SALES (corp-wide): 3.92B Publicly Held
Web: www.leafgroup.com
SIC: 7374 Data processing and preparation
PA: Graham Holdings Company
  1300 17th St N Fl 17
  Arlington VA
  703 345-6362

(P-12587)
LEANPLUM INC
Also Called: Leanplum
1550 Bryant St Ste 525 (94103-4808)
PHONE.............................844 532-6758
George Garrick, Pr
EMP: 191 EST: 2012
SALES (est): 23.81MM
SALES (corp-wide): 23.81MM Privately Held
Web: www.leanplum.com
SIC: 7374 Data processing service
PA: Wizrocket Inc.
  607 W Dana St Ste A
  Mountain View CA
  860 422-5443

(P-12588)
LEGALZOOMCOM INC (PA)
Also Called: LEGALZOOM
101 N Brand Blvd Fl 11 (91203-2638)
PHONE.............................323 962-8600
Dan Wernikoff, CEO
Jeffrey Stibel, Ch Bd
Noel Watson, CFO
Rich Preece, CPO

EMP: 300 EST: 2000
SQ FT: 56,000
SALES (est): 619.98MM Publicly Held
Web: www.legalzoom.com
SIC: 7374 8111 Data processing and preparation; Legal services

(P-12589)
LIVERAMP HOLDINGS INC (PA)
Also Called: LIVERAMP
225 Bush St Fl 17 (94104-4248)
PHONE.............................888 987-6764
Scott E Howe, CEO
Clark M Kokich, Non-Executive Chairman of the Board
Lauren R Dillard, Interim Chief Financial Officer
Jerry C Jones, ETHICS Legal
Mohsin Hussain, Ex VP
EMP: 416 EST: 1969
SALES (est): 596.58MM
SALES (corp-wide): 596.58MM Publicly Held
Web: www.liveramp.com
SIC: 7374 Data processing and preparation

(P-12590)
MAINTENANCENET LLC
170 W Tasman Dr (95134-1700)
PHONE.............................408 526-4000
EMP: 169 EST: 2003
SALES (est): 15.83MM
SALES (corp-wide): 57B Publicly Held
Web: www.cisco.com
SIC: 7374 Computer graphics service
PA: Cisco Systems, Inc.
  170 W Tasman Dr
  San Jose CA
  408 526-4000

(P-12591)
MANAGEMENT APPLIED PRGRM INC (PA)
Also Called: Benefit Programs ADM
13191 Crossroads Pkwy N Ste 205 (91746)
PHONE.............................562 463-5000
Phiroze Dalal, CEO
Hormazd Dalal, *
EMP: 95 EST: 1964
SALES (est): 9.95MM
SALES (corp-wide): 9.95MM Privately Held
Web: www.mapinc.com
SIC: 7374 Data processing service

(P-12592)
MAPLEBEAR INC (PA)
Also Called: INSTACART
50 Beale St Ste 600 (94105-1871)
PHONE.............................888 246-7822
Fidji Simo, CEO
Apoorva Mehta, Ch Bd
Carolyn Everson, Pr
Nick Giovanni, CFO
EMP: 245 EST: 2012
SALES (est): 950.5MM
SALES (corp-wide): 950.5MM Publicly Held
Web: www.instacart.com
SIC: 7374 7372 7389 Data processing service; Publisher's computer software

(P-12593)
MARIN SOFTWARE INCORPORATED (PA)
Also Called: MARIN SOFTWARE
149 New Montgomery St Fl 4 (94105-3740)
PHONE.............................415 399-2580
Christopher Lien, Ch Bd
Robert Bertz, CFO

Wister Walcott, Ex VP
EMP: 87 EST: 2006
SQ FT: 43,000
SALES (est): 20.02MM Publicly Held
Web: www.marinsoftware.com
SIC: 7374 7372 Data processing and preparation; Prepackaged software

(P-12594)
MERCHANT SERVICES INC (PA)
1 S Van Ness Ave Fl 5 (94103-5416)
PHONE.............................817 725-0900
Lorraine Stimmell, CEO
Le Tran-ti, Sr VP
EMP: 400 EST: 1996
SQ FT: 58,336
SALES (est): 39.69MM
SALES (corp-wide): 39.69MM Privately Held
Web: www.merchantsvcs.com
SIC: 7374 Data processing service

(P-12595)
MERCURY DEFENSE SYSTEMS INC
Also Called: Mercury Systems
10855 Business Center Dr Ste A (90630)
PHONE.............................714 898-8200
EMP: 85
Web: www.mrcy.com
SIC: 7374 Data processing service

(P-12596)
MERCURY SYSTEMS INC
10855 Business Center Dr Ste A (90630)
PHONE.............................714 898-8200
EMP: 85
SALES (corp-wide): 973.88MM Publicly Held
Web: www.mrcy.com
SIC: 7374 Data processing service
PA: Mercury Systems, Inc.
  50 Minuteman Rd
  Andover MA
  978 256-1300

(P-12597)
MERCURY TECHNOLOGY GROUP INC
6430 Oak Cyn Ste 100 (92618-5227)
PHONE.............................949 417-0260
EMP: 70
Web: www.mercurytechnology.com
SIC: 7374 Data processing and preparation

(P-12598)
METABASE INC
9740 Campo Rd Pmb 1029 (91977-1415)
PHONE.............................415 767-0490
Sameer Al-nakran, CEO
EMP: 60 EST: 2014
SALES (est): 3.8MM Privately Held
Web: www.metabase.com
SIC: 7374 Data processing service

(P-12599)
MINDBODY INC (PA)
Also Called: Mindbody
651 Tank Farm Rd (93401-7062)
PHONE.............................877 755-4279
Richard Stollmeyer, Ch Bd
Josh Mccarter, Pr
Michael Mansbach, *
Brett White, *
Kimberly Lytikainen, CLO*
EMP: 109 EST: 2001
SALES (est): 456.62MM Privately Held
Web: www.mindbodyonline.com

PRODUCTS & SERVICES SECTION

7374 - Data Processing And Preparation (P-12621)

SIC: 7374 7372 8741 Data processing and preparation; Business oriented computer software; Business management

(P-12600) MOCEAN LLC
Also Called: Mocean
2440 S Sepulveda Blvd Ste 150 (90064-1712)
PHONE..............................310 481-0808
Craig R Murray, *Managing Member*
Michael Mcintyre, *Pr*
EMP: 200 EST: 2000
SALES (est): 24.18MM **Privately Held**
Web: www.moceanla.com
SIC: 7374 7822 Computer graphics service; Motion picture distribution

(P-12601) NEAR INTELLIGENCE INC
100 W Walnut St Ste A-4 (91124-0001)
PHONE..............................628 889-7680
Anil Mathews, *Ch Bd*
Shobhit Shukla, *Pr*
Rahul Agarwal, *CFO*
Gladys Kong, *COO*
EMP: 261 EST: 2012
SQ FT: 26,752
SALES (est): 12.49MM **Privately Held**
SIC: 7374 Data processing and preparation

(P-12602) OOMA INC (PA)
Also Called: Ooma
525 Almanor Ave Ste 200 (94085-3542)
PHONE..............................650 566-6600
Eric B Stang, *Ch Bd*
Shig Hamamatsu, *CFO*
James A Gustke, *VP Mktg*
Jenny C Yeh, *
Namrata Sabharwal, *CAO*
▲ EMP: 91 EST: 2003
SQ FT: 33,400
SALES (est): 216.16MM **Publicly Held**
Web: www.ooma.com
SIC: 7374 4813 Data processing and preparation; Internet connectivity services

(P-12603) ORDERMARK INC
12045 Waterfront Dr Ste 400 # 3 (90094-3226)
P.O. Box 260206 (91426-0206)
PHONE..............................833 673-3762
Alex Canter, *CEO*
Mike Jacobs, *COO*
Paul Allen, *Ofcr*
EMP: 105 EST: 2017
SALES (est): 5.64MM **Privately Held**
Web: www.ordermark.com
SIC: 7374 Data processing and preparation

(P-12604) PAYMENT CLOUD LLC
Also Called: Paymentcloud
16501 Ventura Blvd Ste 300 (91436-2007)
PHONE..............................800 988-2215
Shawnn Silver, *CEO*
Shawn Silver, *CEO*
EMP: 81 EST: 2017
SALES (est): 4.61MM **Privately Held**
Web: www.paymentcloudinc.com
SIC: 7374 Data processing and preparation

(P-12605) PAYPAL GLOBAL HOLDINGS INC
303 Bryant St (94041-1552)
PHONE..............................408 967-1000
Chen Christopher, *Pr*
EMP: 87 EST: 2003
SALES (est): 2.88MM
SALES (corp-wide): 27.52B **Publicly Held**
SIC: 7374 4813 Data processing and preparation; Telephone communication, except radio
PA: Paypal Holdings, Inc.
2211 N 1st St
San Jose CA
408 967-1000

(P-12606) PEOPLE DATA LABS INC
455 Market St Ste 1670 (94105-2472)
PHONE..............................415 568-8415
Sean Thorne, *CEO*
Henry Nevue, *
Daniel Amaya, *
EMP: 80 EST: 2015
SALES (est): 10.02MM **Privately Held**
Web: www.peopledatalabs.com
SIC: 7374 Data processing and preparation

(P-12607) PINTEREST INC (PA)
Also Called: Pinterest
651 Brannan St (94107-1532)
PHONE..............................415 762-7100
Bill Ready, *CEO*
Benjamin Silbermann, *
Evan Sharp, *DESIGN CREATIVE*
Todd Morgenfeld, *CFO*
Christine Flores, *Corporate Secretary*
EMP: 405 EST: 2008
SQ FT: 339,000
SALES (est): 2.8B
SALES (corp-wide): 2.8B **Publicly Held**
Web: www.pinterestcareers.com
SIC: 7374 Data processing and preparation

(P-12608) PLANET LABS INC (HQ)
Also Called: Planet
645 Harrison St Fl 4 (94107-3624)
PHONE..............................415 829-3313
William Marshall, *CEO*
Christopher Boshuizen, *
Tom Barton, *
Eric Heurtaux, *
EMP: 267 EST: 2010
SQ FT: 25,000
SALES (est): 111.44MM
SALES (corp-wide): 191.26MM **Publicly Held**
Web: www.planet.com
SIC: 7374 Data processing service
PA: Planet Labs Pbc
645 Harrison St Fl 4
San Francisco CA
415 829-3313

(P-12609) PROBUSINESS HOLDINGS INC
Also Called: Pbs Paymaster Sales & Service
3785 Brickway Blvd Ste 200 (95403-9033)
PHONE..............................845 354-5372
Jay Levine, *Pr*
EMP: 90 EST: 1978
SALES (est): 5.82MM **Privately Held**
Web: www.shorelineoralsurgerysb.com
SIC: 7374 8742 Computer graphics service; Marketing consulting services

(P-12610) PROOFPOINT INC (HQ)
Also Called: Proofpoint
925 W Maude Ave (94085-2802)
PHONE..............................408 517-4710
Remi Thomas, *Interim Chief Executive Officer*
EMP: 159 EST: 2002
SQ FT: 242,400
SALES (est): 1.05B
SALES (corp-wide): 1.05B **Privately Held**
Web: www.proofpoint.com
SIC: 7374 Data processing and preparation
PA: Proofpoint Holdings, Lp
925 W Maude Ave
Sunnyvale CA
408 517-4710

(P-12611) R/GA MEDIA GROUP INC
45 Fremont St (94105-2230)
PHONE..............................415 624-2000
EMP: 70
SALES (corp-wide): 10.93B **Publicly Held**
SIC: 7374 Computer graphics service
HQ: R/Ga Media Group, Inc.
450 W 33rd St Fl 12
New York NY
212 946-4000

(P-12612) RACKSPACE HOSTING INC
Also Called: Datapipe
650 Castro St Ste 270 (94041-2057)
PHONE..............................201 792-1918
EMP: 174
SALES (corp-wide): 3.12B **Publicly Held**
Web: www.rackspace.com
SIC: 7374 7371 Data processing and preparation; Custom computer programming services
HQ: Rackspace Technology Global, Inc.
1 Fanatical Pl
San Antonio TX

(P-12613) RACKSPACE HOSTING INC
Also Called: Datapipe
150 S 1st St Ste 289 (95113-2611)
PHONE..............................201 792-1918
EMP: 436
SALES (corp-wide): 3.12B **Publicly Held**
Web: www.rackspace.com
SIC: 7374 Data entry service
HQ: Rackspace Technology Global, Inc.
1 Fanatical Pl
San Antonio TX

(P-12614) REDICA SYSTEMS INC
6700 Koll Center Pkwy Ste 140 (94566-7032)
PHONE..............................844 332-3320
Michael De La Torre, *CEO*
Anthony S Chen, *
Oliver Yu, *
EMP: 75 EST: 2010
SQ FT: 1,700
SALES (est): 5.93MM **Privately Held**
Web: www.redica.com
SIC: 7374 Data processing service

(P-12615) RESEARCH AMERICA INC
1232 Q St Ste 100 (95811-5801)
PHONE..............................916 443-4722
Robert Porter, *CEO*
EMP: 135 EST: 1990
SQ FT: 7,300
SALES (est): 2.2MM **Privately Held**
Web: www.researchamericainc.com
SIC: 7374 Data verification service

(P-12616) REVENUE SOLUTIONS INC
2990 Lava Ridge Ct Ste 200 (95661-3076)
PHONE..............................916 780-8741
Chris Marakas, *Prin*
EMP: 285
SALES (corp-wide): 51.04MM **Privately Held**
Web: www.rsidelivers.com
SIC: 7374 Data processing service
PA: Revenue Solutions, Inc.
42 Winter St Ste 36
Pembroke MA
781 826-1546

(P-12617) RINGCENTRAL INC (PA)
Also Called: Ringcentral
20 Davis Dr (94002-3002)
PHONE..............................650 472-4100
Vladimir Shmunis, *Ch Bd*
Mo Katibeh, *Pr*
David Sipes, *COO*
Mitesh Dhruv, *CFO*
Praful Shah, *CSO*
▲ EMP: 80 EST: 1999
SQ FT: 110,000
SALES (est): 1.99B
SALES (corp-wide): 1.99B **Publicly Held**
Web: www.ringcentral.com
SIC: 7374 4899 Data processing and preparation; Data communication services

(P-12618) ROCKSTAR SAN DIEGO INC
2200 Faraday Ave Ste 200 (92008-7233)
PHONE..............................760 929-0700
Allan Wasserman, *Pr*
EMP: 70 EST: 1984
SQ FT: 24,000
SALES (est): 9.43MM **Publicly Held**
SIC: 7374 7372 Computer graphics service; Prepackaged software
PA: Take-Two Interactive Software, Inc.
110 W 44th St
New York NY

(P-12619) RUBRIK INC (PA)
3495 Deer Creek Rd (94304-1316)
PHONE..............................650 300-5862
Bipul Sinha, *CEO*
Peter Mcgoff, *CLO*
Jeff Vijungco, *CPO*
EMP: 1377 EST: 2014
SALES (est): 178.95MM
SALES (corp-wide): 178.95MM **Privately Held**
Web: www.rubrik.com
SIC: 7374 7371 7372 Data processing and preparation; Computer software development and applications; Application computer software

(P-12620) RUITENG INTERNET TECHNOLOGY CO
1344 W Foothill Blvd D (91702-2846)
PHONE..............................302 597-7438
Canzhi Zhen, *Prin*
Chris Zhang, *
Wendy Huang, *
◆ EMP: 220 EST: 2018
SQ FT: 500
SALES (est): 3.53MM **Privately Held**
SIC: 7374 Computer graphics service

(P-12621) SAN DIEGO DATA PROCESSING CORPORATION INC
202 C St 3rd Fl (92101-4806)
PHONE..............................858 581-9600
EMP: 11130
Web: www.sddpc.org

7374 - Data Processing And Preparation (P-12622)

(P-12622)
SARITASA LLC (PA)
Also Called: Clickbrand
20411 Sw Birch St Ste 330 (92660-1771)
PHONE.................................949 200-6839
Nik Froehlich, *CEO*
Melinda Mccartney, *VP*
Dmitry Semenov, *
EMP: 61 **EST:** 2005
SQ FT: 12,000
SALES (est): 8.75MM **Privately Held**
Web: www.saritasa.com
SIC: 7374 8742 7336 7371 Computer graphics service; Marketing consulting services; Graphic arts and related design; Custom computer programming services

(P-12623)
SECURE ONE DATA SOLUTIONS LLC
11090 Artesia Blvd Ste D (90703-2545)
PHONE.................................562 924-7056
David Sandobal, *Pr*
EMP: 90
Web: www.secure1outsource.com
SIC: 7374 Keypunch service
PA: Secure One Data Solutions, Llc
2801 N 33rd Ave Ste 1
Phoenix AZ

(P-12624)
SHIPT
701 Pine St Apt 43 (94108-3150)
PHONE.................................408 592-1029
David E Toomey, *Owner*
EMP: 1180 **EST:** 2017
SALES (est): 60.11MM **Privately Held**
Web: www.shipt.com
SIC: 7374 Data processing and preparation

(P-12625)
SHOPPINGCOM INC
199 Fremont St Fl 4 (94105-6634)
PHONE.................................650 616-6500
Gautam Thakar, *CEO*
Amir Ashkenazi, *
Robert J Krolik, *
Hendrik Krampe, *
EMP: 230 **EST:** 1997
SALES (est): 8.84MM **Publicly Held**
SIC: 7374 Data processing and preparation
PA: Ebay Inc.
2025 Hamilton Ave
San Jose CA

(P-12626)
SKAEL INC
535 Mission St Fl 14 (94105-3253)
PHONE.................................415 653-9433
Baba Nadimpalli, *CEO*
Baba Nadimpalli, *Pr*
Ragu Mantatikar, *
EMP: 71 **EST:** 2016
SALES (est): 4.99MM **Privately Held**
Web: www.skael.com
SIC: 7374 Data processing service

(P-12627)
SOCIETY6 LLC
Also Called: Society6
1655 26th St (90404-4016)
PHONE.................................310 394-6400
EMP: 71 **EST:** 2011
SQ FT: 25,000
SALES (est): 29.35MM
SALES (corp-wide): 3.92B **Publicly Held**
Web: www.society6.com
SIC: 7374 Computer graphics service
HQ: Leaf Group Ltd.
1655 26th St
Santa Monica CA

(P-12628)
SONY PICTURES IMAGEWORKS INC
9050 Washington Blvd (90232-2518)
PHONE.................................310 840-8000
Michelle Grady, *Pr*
Ken Ralston, *
EMP: 1000 **EST:** 1992
SALES (est): 56.2MM **Privately Held**
Web: www.imageworks.com
SIC: 7374 Computer graphics service
HQ: Sony Pictures Entertainment, Inc.
10202 Washington Blvd
Culver City CA
310 244-4000

(P-12629)
SPLIT SOFTWARE INC (PA)
2317 Broadway St Fl 3 (94063-1659)
PHONE.................................650 399-0005
Brian Bell, *CEO*
Adil Aijaz, *
Trevor Stuart, *
EMP: 127 **EST:** 2015
SALES (est): 9MM
SALES (corp-wide): 9MM **Privately Held**
Web: www.split.io
SIC: 7374 Data processing service

(P-12630)
SPOUTABLE LLC
4150 Mission Blvd Ste 220 (92109-5054)
PHONE.................................609 743-7491
EMP: 165 **EST:** 2015
SALES (est): 355.89K
SALES (corp-wide): 87.06MM **Privately Held**
Web: www.sovrn.com
SIC: 7374 Computer graphics service
PA: Proper Media, Llc
4150 Mission Blvd Ste 220
San Diego CA
702 427-7949

(P-12631)
STARK SERVICES
12444 Victory Blvd Ste 300 (91606-3173)
PHONE.................................818 985-2003
Maricel Zabel, *Pr*
Steve Pugh, *
EMP: 75 **EST:** 1975
SALES (est): 2.4MM **Privately Held**
Web: www.starkservices.com
SIC: 7374 Data processing service

(P-12632)
SWEETRUSH INC
363 Valencia St Apt 4 (94103-3570)
PHONE.................................415 647-1956
Arthur Schwartzberg, *Pr*
Andrei Hedstrom, *Sec*
EMP: 118 **EST:** 2001
SALES (est): 5.29MM **Privately Held**
Web: www.sweetrush.com
SIC: 7374 8243 Computer graphics service; Operator training, computer

(P-12633)
TALKWALKER INC
600 California St Fl 14 (94108-2701)
PHONE.................................415 805-7240
John Zhao, *Mgr*
EMP: 178
SALES (corp-wide): 2.67MM **Privately Held**
Web: www.talkwalker.com
SIC: 7374 Data processing service
HQ: Talkwalker Inc.
3616 Far West Blvd 117p
Austin TX
646 712-9441

(P-12634)
TEALIUM INC (PA)
11095 Torreyana Rd Fl 2 (92121-1104)
PHONE.................................858 779-1344
Jeffrey W Lunsford, *CEO*
Ali Behnam, *
Doug Lindroth, *
Peter Ching, *
Ted Purcell, *CRO*
EMP: 558 **EST:** 2008
SQ FT: 40,864
SALES (est): 69.06MM **Privately Held**
Web: www.tealium.com
SIC: 7374 7371 Computer graphics service; Computer software development

(P-12635)
TECHNOSOCIALWORKCOM LLC
Also Called: Stria
4300 Resnik Ct Unit 103 (93313-4836)
P.O. Box 21660 (93390-1660)
PHONE.................................661 617-6601
Jim Damian, *Managing Member*
EMP: 75 **EST:** 2002
SQ FT: 10,000
SALES (est): 9.55MM **Privately Held**
Web: www.stria.com
SIC: 7374 Computer graphics service

(P-12636)
TEGRA118 WEALTH SOLUTIONS INC (HQ)
700 N San Vicente Blvd Ste G605 (90069-5060)
PHONE.................................888 800-0188
Cheryl Nash, *Pr*
Andrew Schwartz, *
EMP: 139 **EST:** 2011
SALES (est): 24.06MM
SALES (corp-wide): 95.29MM **Privately Held**
SIC: 7374 7371 Data processing service; Computer software development and applications
PA: Investcloud, Inc.
700 N San Vicnte Blvd
West Hollywood CA
310 385-7394

(P-12637)
TRUELITE TRACE INC
Also Called: Fleetup
675 N 1st St Ste 1100 (95112-5156)
PHONE.................................833 663-5338
Soon Beom Lee, *Pr*
Sung Bok Kwak, *
EMP: 60 **EST:** 2014
SQ FT: 200
SALES (est): 6.56MM **Privately Held**
Web: www.fleetup.com
SIC: 7374 Data processing service

(P-12638)
TRULIA INC (HQ)
535 Mission St Ste 700 (94105-3223)
PHONE.................................415 648-4358
Peter Flint, *CEO*
Prashant Aggarwal, *CFO*
Paul Levine, *COO*
Lloyd Frink, *Pr*
EMP: 357 **EST:** 2014
SQ FT: 32,000
SALES (est): 312.83MM
SALES (corp-wide): 1.96B **Publicly Held**
Web: www.trulia.com
SIC: 7374 Data processing and preparation
PA: Zillow Group, Inc.
1301 2nd Ave Fl 31
Seattle WA
206 470-7000

(P-12639)
UNIVERSITY CAL SAN DIEGO
Also Called: San Diego Supercomputer Center
10100 Hopkins Dr (92093-0001)
P.O. Box 85608 (92186-5608)
PHONE.................................858 534-5000
Michael Norman, *Dir*
EMP: 289
SALES (corp-wide): 534.4MM **Privately Held**
Web: www.sdsc.edu
SIC: 7374 8731 8221 9411 Data processing and preparation; Commercial physical research; University; Administration of educational programs
HQ: University Of California, San Diego
9500 Gilman Dr
La Jolla CA
858 534-2230

(P-12640)
VERIZON CONNECT TELO INC (DH)
15505 Sand Canyon Ave (92618-3114)
PHONE.................................844 617-1100
Ralph Mason, *CEO*
A Newth Morris Iv, *TELOGIS ROUTE & TELOGIS NAV*
Jason Koch, *TELOGIS FLEET*
Susan Heystee, *
Ted Serentelos, *
▼ **EMP:** 150 **EST:** 2001
SALES (est): 64.88MM
SALES (corp-wide): 136.84B **Publicly Held**
Web: www.verizonconnect.com
SIC: 7374 Data processing and preparation
HQ: Verizon Connect Inc.
5055 N Point Pkwy
Alpharetta GA
404 573-5800

(P-12641)
VITESSE LLC
1601 Willow Rd (94025-1452)
PHONE.................................650 543-4800
Christopher R Gardner, *CEO*
EMP: 3000 **EST:** 2010
SALES (est): 47.46MM
SALES (corp-wide): 116.61B **Publicly Held**
SIC: 7374 Data processing service
PA: Meta Platforms, Inc.
1601 Willow Rd
Menlo Park CA
650 543-4800

(P-12642)
WEBFLOW INC (PA)
398 11th St Fl 2 (94103-4393)
PHONE.................................916 607-8280
Vladimir Magdalin, *CEO*
EMP: 397 **EST:** 2012
SALES (est): 22.65MM
SALES (corp-wide): 22.65MM **Privately Held**
Web: www.webflow.com
SIC: 7374 Computer graphics service

7375 - Information Retrieval Services

(P-12643)
YAHOO CV LLC (HQ)
701 First Ave (94089-1019)
PHONE..................408 349-3300
Terry Semel, *Managing Member*
EMP: 64 EST: 2006
SALES (est): 10.79MM Privately Held
SIC: 7374 Data processing and preparation
PA: Yahoo Inc.
   770 Broadway Fl 4
   New York NY

(P-12644)
YAHOO CV LLC
11985 Bluff Creek Dr (90094-2929)
PHONE..................408 349-3300
EMP: 188
SIC: 7374 Data processing and preparation
HQ: Yahoo Cv, Llc
   701 First Ave
   Sunnyvale CA

(P-12645)
YELLOWBRICK DATA INC (PA)
660 W Dana St (94041-1302)
PHONE..................877 492-3282
Neil Carson, *CEO*
David Lawler, *
Brian Bulkowski, *
EMP: 153 EST: 2015
SALES (est): 21.33MM
SALES (corp-wide): 21.33MM Privately Held
Web: www.yellowbrick.com
SIC: 7374 Data processing service

(P-12646)
Z57 INC
2443 Impala Dr Ste B (92010-7227)
PHONE..................858 623-5577
EMP: 105
SALES (corp-wide): 6.62B Privately Held
Web: www.z57.com
SIC: 7374 Computer graphics service
HQ: Z57, Inc.
   11350 Mccormick Ep 3 Rd # 200
   Hunt Valley MD
   858 623-5577

(P-12647)
ZYNGA INC (HQ)
Also Called: Zynga
1200 Park Pl Ste 100 (94403-1591)
PHONE..................855 449-9642
Frank Gibeau, *CEO*
Gerard Griffin, *CFO*
Jeff Ryan, *CPO*
Phuong Y Phillips, *CLO*
Amy M Rawlings, *CAO*
EMP: 242 EST: 2007
SQ FT: 185,000
SALES (est): 2.8B Publicly Held
Web: www.zynga.com
SIC: 7374 7372 Data processing and preparation; Application computer software
PA: Take-Two Interactive Software, Inc.
   110 W 44th St
   New York NY

7375 Information Retrieval Services

(P-12648)
23ANDME INC (HQ)
349 Oyster Point Blvd (94080-1947)
PHONE..................650 961-7152
Anne Wojcicki, *CEO*
Andy Page, *Pr*
Dean Schorno, *CFO*
Daniel Chu, *Chief Product Officer*
EMP: 706 EST: 2006
SALES (est): 106.63MM
SALES (corp-wide): 299.49MM Publicly Held
Web: www.23andme.com
SIC: 7375 Information retrieval services
PA: 23andme Holding Co.
   349 Oyster Point Blvd
   South San Francisco CA
   650 938-6300

(P-12649)
ACCURATE BACKGROUND LLC (PA)
Also Called: Selectforce
200 Spectrum Center Dr Ste 1100 (92618-5003)
PHONE..................800 784-3911
Tim Dowd, *CEO*
David C Dickerson, *
Brian Fujioka, *
Rashid Ismail, *
Aaron Hayes, *
EMP: 315 EST: 1998
SQ FT: 98,024
SALES (est): 117.65MM
SALES (corp-wide): 117.65MM Privately Held
Web: www.accurate.com
SIC: 7375 Information retrieval services

(P-12650)
AERIAL TOPCO LP
1 Embarcadero Ctr Ste 3900 (94111-3753)
PHONE..................415 983-2700
EMP: 1988 EST: 2015
SALES (est): 18.78MM Privately Held
SIC: 7375 4899 Information retrieval services; Data communication services

(P-12651)
ANCESTRYCOM LLC
Also Called: Ancestry.com
153 Townsend St Ste 800 (94107-1957)
PHONE..................415 795-6000
Jim Porzak, *Prin*
EMP: 304
SALES (corp-wide): 477.52MM Privately Held
Web: www.ancestry.com
SIC: 7375 Information retrieval services
HQ: Ancestry.Com Llc
   1300 W Traverse Pkwy
   Lehi UT
   801 705-7000

(P-12652)
BACKBLAZE INC
201 Baldwin Ave (94401-3914)
PHONE..................650 352-3738
Gleb Budman, *Ch Bd*
Frank Patchel, *CFO*
Tim Nufire, *CCO**
Kevin Gavin, *CMO*
EMP: 228 EST: 2007
SALES (est): 85.16MM Privately Held
Web: www.backblaze.com
SIC: 7375 Information retrieval services

(P-12653)
BETTERDOCTOR INC
945 Bryant St Ste 350 (94103-4523)
PHONE..................844 668-2543
Ari Tulla, *CEO*
EMP: 160 EST: 2011
SALES (est): 2.52MM
SALES (corp-wide): 18.78MM Privately Held
Web: www.questanalytics.com
SIC: 7375 Data base information retrieval
PA: Quest Analytics, L.L.C.
   9225 Indian Creek Pkwy # 200
   Overland Park KS
   920 739-4552

(P-12654)
CHANGEORG INC (PA)
383 Rhode Island St Ste 300 (94103-5178)
PHONE..................415 817-1840
EMP: 114 EST: 2006
SQ FT: 10,000
SALES (est): 17.4MM Privately Held
Web: www.change.org
SIC: 7375 On-line data base information retrieval

(P-12655)
CORVENTIS INC
2033 Gateway Pl Ste 100 (95110-3713)
PHONE..................408 790-9300
EMP: 102
Web: www.corventis.com
SIC: 7375 Information retrieval services

(P-12656)
COUNTY OF LOS ANGELES
Also Called: Department of Mental Health
320 W Temple St Fl 9 (90012-3217)
PHONE..................213 974-0515
Jacqueline Criddell, *Mgr*
EMP: 150
SALES (corp-wide): 31.7B Privately Held
Web: www.lacounty.gov
SIC: 7375 9131 Information retrieval services; Executive and legislative combined, level of government
PA: County Of Los Angeles
   500 W Temple St Ste 437
   Los Angeles CA
   213 974-1101

(P-12657)
DIGITAL INSIGHT CORPORATION
5601 Lindero Canyon Rd Ste 100 (91362-6494)
PHONE..................818 879-1010
Paul Nieman, *Prin*
EMP: 72
SALES (corp-wide): 7.84B Publicly Held
Web: www.ncr.com
SIC: 7375 Information retrieval services
HQ: Digital Insight Corporation
   1300 Seaport Blvd Ste 300
   Redwood City CA

(P-12658)
DIGITAL INSIGHT CORPORATION (HQ)
Also Called: Intuit Financial Services
1300 Seaport Blvd Ste 300 (94063-5591)
PHONE..................818 879-1010
Jeffrey E Stiefler, *Pr*
Joseph M Mcdoniel, *Ex VP*
Robert R Surridge, *
Tom Shen, *
▲ EMP: 200 EST: 1997
SQ FT: 46,000
SALES (est): 92.66MM
SALES (corp-wide): 7.84B Publicly Held
Web: www.ncr.com
SIC: 7375 7372 7371 Information retrieval services; Prepackaged software; Custom computer programming services
PA: Ncr Voyix Corporation
   864 Spring St Nw
   Atlanta GA
   937 445-1936

(P-12659)
DRIVESAVERS INC
Also Called: Drivesavers Data Recovery
400 Bel Marin Keys Blvd (94949-5642)
PHONE..................415 382-2000
Jay Hagan, *CEO*
Scott Moyer, *
EMP: 90 EST: 1990
SQ FT: 4,400
SALES (est): 14.32MM Privately Held
Web: www.drivesaversdatarecovery.com
SIC: 7375 Information retrieval services

(P-12660)
E-TIMES CORPORATION (PA)
601 S Figueroa St Ste 5000 (90017-3883)
PHONE..................213 452-6720
Chiharu Nakahara, *Pr*
EMP: 300 EST: 2003
SALES (est): 9.6MM
SALES (corp-wide): 9.6MM Privately Held
Web: www.etimesltd.com
SIC: 7375 7374 8742 Information retrieval services; Computer graphics service; Administrative services consultant

(P-12661)
EDMUNDS HOLDING COMPANY (PA)
Also Called: Edmunds.com
2401 Colorado Ave (90404-3585)
PHONE..................310 309-6300
Avi Steinlauf, *CEO*
Seth Berkowitz, *Pr*
Charles Farrell, *CFO*
EMP: 650 EST: 1962
SALES (est): 156.39MM Privately Held
Web: www.edmunds.com
SIC: 7375 Information retrieval services

(P-12662)
ELAVON INC
700 S Western Ave (90005-5113)
PHONE..................865 403-7000
John Macht, *Brnch Mgr*
EMP: 400
SALES (corp-wide): 27.4B Publicly Held
Web: www.elavon.com
SIC: 7375 Information retrieval services
HQ: Elavon, Inc.
   2 Concourse Pkwy Ste 800
   Atlanta GA

(P-12663)
FACEBOOK PARK TOWER
250 Howard St (94105-1803)
PHONE..................949 725-8637
EMP: 4000 EST: 2019
SALES (est): 75.69MM
SALES (corp-wide): 116.61B Publicly Held
SIC: 7375 Information retrieval services
PA: Meta Platforms, Inc.
   1601 Willow Rd
   Menlo Park CA
   650 543-4800

(P-12664)
GOOGLE LLC (HQ)
Also Called: Google
1600 Amphitheatre Pkwy (94043-1351)
P.O. Box 2050 (94042-2050)
PHONE..................650 253-0000
Sundar Pichai, *CEO*
Ruth Porat, *
David Drummond, *
Nikesh Arora, *
Jade Raymond, *
▲ EMP: 250 EST: 1998
SQ FT: 4,800,000

7375 - Information Retrieval Services (P-12665)

SALES (est): 2.49B
SALES (corp-wide): 282.84B **Publicly Held**
Web: www.google.com
SIC: **7375 7371** Data base information retrieval; Computer software development
PA: Alphabet Inc.
1600 Amphitheatre Pkwy
Mountain View CA
650 253-0000

(P-12665)
GROUNDWORK OPEN SOURCE INC
23332 Mill Creek Dr Ste 155 (92653-7911)
PHONE.................................415 992-4500
Dave Lilly, *CEO*
EMP: 100 EST: 2004
SALES (est): 10.82MM
SALES (corp-wide): 609.02MM **Privately Held**
Web: www.gwos.com
SIC: **7375 7371** On-line data base information retrieval; Custom computer programming services
HQ: Fox Technologies, Inc.
6455 City West Pkwy
Eden Prairie MN
800 328-1000

(P-12666)
IAC SEARCH & MEDIA INC (HQ)
Also Called: Ask.com
555 12th St Ste 500 (94607-4022)
PHONE.................................510 985-7400
Doug Leeds, *CEO*
Shane Mcgilloway, *COO*
Steven J Sordello, *
Brett M Robertson, *
Tuoc Luong, *Executive Technology Vice President*
EMP: 200 EST: 1996
SQ FT: 76,000
SALES (est): 79.44MM
SALES (corp-wide): 5.24B **Publicly Held**
Web: www.iac.com
SIC: **7375** On-line data base information retrieval
PA: Iac Inc.
555 W 18th St
New York NY
212 314-7300

(P-12667)
INSTAGRAM LLC
Also Called: Instagram
1601 Willow Rd (94025-1452)
PHONE.................................650 543-4800
Adam Mosseri, *CEO*
EMP: 130 EST: 2010
SALES (est): 20.38MM
SALES (corp-wide): 116.61B **Publicly Held**
Web: www.instagram.com
SIC: **7375** On-line data base information retrieval
PA: Meta Platforms, Inc.
1601 Willow Rd
Menlo Park CA
650 543-4800

(P-12668)
INTERNET ARCHIVE
300 Funston Ave (94118-2116)
PHONE.................................415 561-6767
Brewster Kahle, *Dir*
Bruce Gilliat, *
Kathleen Burch, *
Rick Prelinger, *
EMP: 173 EST: 1996

SALES (est): 3MM **Privately Held**
Web: www.archive.org
SIC: **7375** On-line data base information retrieval

(P-12669)
JEPPESEN DATAPLAN INC
225 W Santa Clara St Ste 1600 (95113-1752)
PHONE.................................408 961-2825
Mark Van Tine, *Pr*
Jepson Fuller, *
EMP: 1699 EST: 1974
SQ FT: 20,000
SALES (est): 7.83MM
SALES (corp-wide): 66.61B **Publicly Held**
SIC: **7375** Information retrieval services
HQ: Boeing Digital Solutions, Inc.
55 Inverness Way E
Englewood CO
303 799-9090

(P-12670)
JIFF INC
1999 Harrison St Ste 2070 (94612-3583)
PHONE.................................510 844-4139
EMP: 127
SALES (corp-wide): 147.46MM **Privately Held**
Web: www.castlighthealth.com
SIC: **7375** On-line data base information retrieval
HQ: Jiff, Inc.
150 Spear St Ste 400
San Francisco CA
415 829-1400

(P-12671)
LIFESCRIPT INC
Also Called: Lifescript
4000 Macarthur Blvd Ste 800 (92660-2544)
PHONE.................................949 454-0422
EMP: 110
Web: www.everydayhealth.com
SIC: **7375** Information retrieval services

(P-12672)
LINKEDIN CORPORATION (HQ)
1000 W Maude Ave (94085-2810)
PHONE.................................650 687-3600
Ryan Roslansky, *CEO*
Jeff Weiner, *
James Chuong, *
Dan Shapero, *
EMP: 252 EST: 2003
SQ FT: 373,000
SALES (est): 15.14B
SALES (corp-wide): 211.91B **Publicly Held**
Web: www.linkedin.com
SIC: **7375** On-line data base information retrieval
PA: Microsoft Corporation
1 Microsoft Way
Redmond WA
425 882-8080

(P-12673)
LOGICMONITOR INC (PA)
820 State St Fl 5 (93101-3271)
PHONE.................................805 394-8632
Christina Kosmowski, *CEO*
Kevin Mcgibben, *Ofcr*
Steven Francis, *CPO*
Jie Song, *
Andrew Arrastia, *
EMP: 152 EST: 2007
SALES (est): 86.84MM **Privately Held**
Web: www.logicmonitor.com

SIC: **7375** Information retrieval services

(P-12674)
LOGIK SYSTEMS INC (HQ)
Also Called: Logikcull
111 Sutter St (94104-4545)
PHONE.................................844 363-3347
Andy Wilson, *CEO*
Sheng Yang, *
EMP: 82 EST: 2007
SALES (est): 10.75MM
SALES (corp-wide): 5.71MM **Privately Held**
Web: www.logikcull.com
SIC: **7375** Information retrieval services
PA: Reveal Data Corporation
145 S Wells St Ste 600
Chicago IL
844 319-9909

(P-12675)
LOON LLC (DH)
1600 Amphitheatre Pkwy (94043-1351)
EMP: 65 EST: 2006
SALES (est): 44.81MM
SALES (corp-wide): 282.84B **Publicly Held**
Web: www.x.company
SIC: **7375** On-line data base information retrieval
HQ: Google Llc
1600 Amphitheatre Pkwy
Mountain View CA
650 253-0000

(P-12676)
LOWERMYBILLS INC
Also Called: Lowermybills.com
12181 Bluff Creek Dr Ste 250 (90094-2992)
PHONE.................................310 348-6800
EMP: 200
SIC: **7375** Information retrieval services

(P-12677)
META PLATFORMS INC (PA)
Also Called: Meta
1601 Willow Rd (94025-1452)
PHONE.................................650 543-4800
Mark Zuckerberg, *Ch Bd*
Susan Li, *CFO*
Javier Olivan, *COO*
Jennifer G Newstead, *CLO*
EMP: 800 EST: 2004
SALES (est): 116.61B
SALES (corp-wide): 116.61B **Publicly Held**
Web: www.facebook.com
SIC: **7375** On-line data base information retrieval

(P-12678)
NEEVA INC
450 Concar Dr (94402-2681)
PHONE.................................408 220-9086
Sridhar Ramaswamy, *CEO*
Vivek Raghunathan, *
Cosmos Nicolaou, *
Lara Moore, *
EMP: 65 EST: 2018
SALES (est): 6.89MM **Privately Held**
Web: www.neeva.com
SIC: **7375** Information retrieval services

(P-12679)
NEXTDOORCOM INC (PA)
Also Called: Nextdoor
875 Stevenson St Ste 100 (94103-0906)
PHONE.................................415 236-0000
Nirav Tolia, *CEO*
Prakash Janakiraman, *

Sarah Leary, *
EMP: 100 EST: 2011
SALES (est): 16.11MM
SALES (corp-wide): 16.11MM **Privately Held**
Web: www.nextdoor.com
SIC: **7375** On-line data base information retrieval

(P-12680)
PERFORMANT FINANCIAL CORP (PA)
333 N Canyons Pkwy Ste 100 (94551-9480)
PHONE.................................925 960-4800
Simeon M Kohl, *CEO*
Lisa C Im, *Ex Ch Bd*
Rohit Ramchandani, *CFO*
Ian A Johnston, *CAO*
EMP: 489 EST: 1976
SQ FT: 50,000
SALES (est): 109.18MM **Publicly Held**
Web: www.performantcorp.com
SIC: **7375 7374 8099** Information retrieval services; Data entry service; Medical services organization

(P-12681)
PLAID INC (PA)
1098 Harrison St (94103-4521)
PHONE.................................415 799-1354
George Zachary Perret, *Pr*
William Hockey, *
Eric Hart, *
EMP: 96 EST: 2012
SALES (est): 29.64MM
SALES (corp-wide): 29.64MM **Privately Held**
Web: www.plaid.com
SIC: **7375** Information retrieval services

(P-12682)
PROCTORU INC
3687 Old Santa Rita Rd Ste 203 (94588-3469)
PHONE.................................205 870-8122
EMP: 301
SALES (corp-wide): 29.94MM **Privately Held**
Web: www.proctoru.com
SIC: **7375** Information retrieval services
PA: Proctoru, Inc.
7901 Jones Branch Dr
Mc Lean VA
925 273-7588

(P-12683)
RELATIONEDGE LLC
10120 Pacific Heights Blvd Ste 110 (92121-4205)
PHONE.................................858 451-4665
Matthew Stoyka, *CEO*
EMP: 125 EST: 2013
SALES (est): 23.43MM
SALES (corp-wide): 3.12B **Publicly Held**
SIC: **7375** On-line data base information retrieval
HQ: Rackspace Us, Inc.
1 Fanatical Pl
Windcrest TX
210 728-4549

(P-12684)
REPRINTS DESK INC
15821 Ventura Blvd Ste 165 (91436-2915)
PHONE.................................310 477-0354
Alan Urban, *CFO*
EMP: 92 EST: 2006
SQ FT: 2,500
SALES (est): 10.41MM **Publicly Held**

PRODUCTS & SERVICES SECTION
7378 - Computer Maintenance And Repair (P-12704)

Web: www.researchsolutions.com
SIC: 7375 Information retrieval services
PA: Research Solutions, Inc.
  16350 Ventura Blvd Ste D
  Encino CA

(P-12685)
TINTRI INC
Also Called: Tintri
303 Ravendale Dr (94043-5329)
PHONE.................................650 810-8200
EMP: 445 EST: 2008
SQ FT: 127,000
SALES (est): 66.67MM
SALES (corp-wide): 149.51MM **Privately Held**
Web: www.tintri.com
SIC: 7375 7374 Data base information retrieval; Data processing and preparation
PA: Datadirect Networks, Inc.
  9351 Deering Ave
  Chatsworth CA
  818 700-7600

(P-12686)
TROJAN PROFESSIONAL SVCS INC
11075 Knott Ave Ste A (90630-5135)
P.O. Box 1270 (90720-1270)
PHONE.................................714 816-7169
Mark Dunn, CEO
Ingrid M Kidd, *
Chris Iseri, *
EMP: 99 EST: 1976
SALES (est): 10.12MM **Privately Held**
Web: www.trojanonline.com
SIC: 7375 Data base information retrieval

(P-12687)
WESTERN FELD INVSTIGATIONS INC (PA)
Also Called: Releasepoint
405 W Foothill Blvd Ste 204 (91711-2786)
P.O. Box 246 (91740-0246)
PHONE.................................800 999-9589
Gerard F Halvey, Pr
Clair Halvey, VP
Derrick Halvey, VP
EMP: 94 EST: 1972
SALES (est): 8.1MM
SALES (corp-wide): 8.1MM **Privately Held**
Web: www.wfi-inc.com
SIC: 7375 Information retrieval services

(P-12688)
X CORP
1355 Market St Ste 900 (94103-1337)
PHONE.................................415 222-9670
Elon Musk, Brnch Mgr
EMP: 1500
SALES (corp-wide): 176.56MM **Privately Held**
SIC: 7375 7313 On-line data base information retrieval; Electronic media advertising representatives
HQ: X Corp.
  2533 N Carson St
  Carson City NV

(P-12689)
YELP INC (PA)
350 Mission St Fl 10 (94105-2275)
PHONE.................................415 908-3801
Jeremy Stoppelman, CEO
Diane M Irvine, *
David Schwarzbach, CFO
Joseph R Nachman, COO
Laurence Wilson, Chief
EMP: 93 EST: 2004
SALES (est): 1.19B

SALES (corp-wide): 1.19B **Publicly Held**
Web: www.yelp.com
SIC: 7375 On-line data base information retrieval

(P-12690)
ZOOMINFO TECHNOLOGIES LLC
Dept La 24789 (91185-0001)
PHONE.................................360 783-6924
Henry Schuck, Managing Member
EMP: 592
SALES (corp-wide): 1.1B **Publicly Held**
Web: www.zoominfo.com
SIC: 7375 Information retrieval services
HQ: Zoominfo Technologies Llc
  805 Broadway St Ste 900
  Vancouver WA
  360 783-6800

(P-12691)
ZYME SOLUTIONS INC (PA)
240 Twin Dolphin Dr Ste D (94065-1403)
PHONE.................................650 585-2258
Chandran Sankaran, Pr
Edward Dimbero, *
Adam Brenner, *
EMP: 100 EST: 2004
SALES (est): 19.61MM **Privately Held**
Web: www.e2open.com
SIC: 7375 Information retrieval services

7376 Computer Facilities Management

(P-12692)
ALLIED DIGITAL SERVICES LLC
1075 Mt Vernon Ave (92507-1828)
PHONE.................................310 431-2361
Paresh Shah, CEO
EMP: 115
Web: www.allieddigital.net
SIC: 7376 Computer facilities management
HQ: Allied Digital Services, Llc
  680 Knox St Ste 200
  Torrance CA

(P-12693)
COMPUTER SCIENCES CORPORATION
1520 Railroad Ave (94595)
PHONE.................................702 558-8092
Paul Branske, CEO
EMP: 145
SALES (corp-wide): 14.43B **Publicly Held**
Web: www.dxc.com
SIC: 7376 Computer facilities management
HQ: Computer Sciences Corporation
  20408 Bashan Dr Ste 231
  Ashburn VA
  855 716-0853

(P-12694)
COUNTY OF SACRAMENTO
Also Called: Communication & Info Tech
799 G St (95814-1212)
PHONE.................................916 874-7752
Rami Zakaria, Brnch Mgr
EMP: 429
SALES (corp-wide): 3.56B **Privately Held**
Web: www.saccounty.net
SIC: 7376 9631 Computer facilities management; Communications commission, government
PA: County Of Sacramento
  700 H St Ste 7650
  Sacramento CA
  916 874-8515

(P-12695)
GLOBAL BLUE DVBE INC
4470 Yankee Hill Rd Ste 160 (95677-1631)
PHONE.................................916 632-2583
Dave Hornbeck, Pr
Michael Terpstra, *
Mark Eckert, Business Development*
EMP: 75 EST: 2011
SALES (est): 5.39MM **Privately Held**
Web: www.gbdvbe.com
SIC: 7376 7379 7371 Computer facilities management; Computer related consulting services; Computer software development and applications

(P-12696)
HCL AMERICA INC (DH)
2600 Great America Way Ste 101& (95054-1169)
PHONE.................................408 733-0480
C Vijayakumar, CEO
Raj Walia Kumar, CFO
Raghu Raman Lakshmanan, Sec
Shiv Nadar, Dir
Anoop Tiwari, Dir
EMP: 200 EST: 1988
SQ FT: 31,000
SALES (est): 3.28B **Privately Held**
Web: www.hcl.com
SIC: 7376 7371 8741 Computer facilities management; Computer software development; Management services
HQ: Hcl Bermuda Limited
  C/O Ocorian Services (Bermuda) Limited
  Hamilton

(P-12697)
NEW DREAM NETWORK LLC (PA)
Also Called: Dreamhost.com
417 S Associated Rd Pmb 257 (92821)
PHONE.................................626 644-9466
EMP: 60 EST: 1997
SALES (est): 7.07MM
SALES (corp-wide): 7.07MM **Privately Held**
Web: www.dreamhost.com
SIC: 7376 Computer facilities management

(P-12698)
NTT GLBAL DATA CTRS AMRCAS INC (DH)
Also Called: Raging Wire
1625 National Dr (95834-2901)
P.O. Box 348060 (95834-8060)
PHONE.................................916 286-3000
Douglas S Adams, Pr
Joel Stone, *
Joe Goldsmith, CRO*
Judi A Lee, Senior Vice President Human Resources*
▲ EMP: 275 EST: 2000
SALES (est): 106.7MM **Privately Held**
Web: services.global.ntt
SIC: 7376 8748 Computer facilities management; Telecommunications consultant
HQ: Ntt Communications Corporation
  2-3-1, Otemachi
  Chiyoda-Ku TKY

(P-12699)
TPUSA - FHCS INC (DH)
Also Called: Teleperformance
215 N Marengo Ave Ste 160 (91101-1525)
PHONE.................................213 873-5100
Jeff Balagna, Pr
Dean Duncan, *
Peter Phan, *

EMP: 200 EST: 1998
SQ FT: 1,029,146
SALES (est): 22.42MM
SALES (corp-wide): 226.27MM **Privately Held**
Web: www.teleperformance.com
SIC: 7376 7373 Computer facilities management; Systems integration services
HQ: Tpusa, Inc.
  5295 S Commerce Dr # 600
  Murray UT
  801 257-5800

7377 Computer Rental And Leasing

(P-12700)
RENTEX INCORPORATED
2915 Whipple Rd (94587-1207)
PHONE.................................833 737-6839
EMP: 80
SALES (corp-wide): 54.94MM **Privately Held**
Web: www.rentex.com
SIC: 7377 Computer rental and leasing
PA: Rentex Incorporated
  110 Shawmut Rd Ste 8
  Canton MA
  781 232-4485

7378 Computer Maintenance And Repair

(P-12701)
ALQUEST TECHNOLOGIES INC
1760 Yeager Ave (91750-5850)
PHONE.................................909 592-8708
EMP: 70 EST: 2000
SALES (est): 10.01MM **Privately Held**
Web: www.alquestonline.com
SIC: 7378 Computer maintenance and repair

(P-12702)
AMKOTRON INC (PA)
16220 Bloomfield Ave (90703-2113)
PHONE.................................562 921-3330
▲ EMP: 60 EST: 1989
SALES (est): 8.5MM **Privately Held**
Web: www.amkotron.com
SIC: 7378 5065 Computer peripheral equipment repair and maintenance; Electronic parts and equipment, nec

(P-12703)
APEX COMPUTER SYSTEMS INC
13875 Cerritos Corporate Dr Ste A (90703-2470)
P.O. Box 4859 (90703-4859)
PHONE.................................562 926-6820
Philip C Chen, CEO
Dennis Rice, *
Jessica C Chow, *
EMP: 60 EST: 1983
SQ FT: 18,146
SALES (est): 19.43MM **Privately Held**
Web: www.acsi2000.com
SIC: 7378 5734 Computer maintenance and repair; Computer and software stores

(P-12704)
BCP SYSTEMS INC
1560 S Sinclair St (92806-5933)
PHONE.................................714 202-3900
Carlos P Torres, CEO
William W Price, *
EMP: 60 EST: 1994

7378 - Computer Maintenance And Repair (P-12705)

SALES (est): 10.09MM **Privately Held**
Web: www.bcpsystems.com
SIC: 7378 3571 5063 Computer and data processing equipment repair/maintenance; Electronic computers; Electrical apparatus and equipment

(P-12705)
COKEVA INC
Also Called: Applied Materials
9000 Foothills Blvd (95747-4412)
PHONE..................................916 462-6001
Ann D Nguyen, *CEO*
Qui Nguyen, *
Dominick Derosa, *
▲ **EMP**: 181 **EST**: 1990
SQ FT: 175,000
SALES (est): 28.94MM **Privately Held**
Web: www.cokeva.com
SIC: 7378 Computer maintenance and repair

(P-12706)
ESL TECHNOLOGIES INC
8875 Washington Blvd B (95678-6214)
PHONE..................................916 677-4500
▲ **EMP**: 350 **EST**: 1996
SQ FT: 100,000
SALES (est): 23.47MM **Privately Held**
SIC: 7378 Computer peripheral equipment repair and maintenance
HQ: Teleplan Holding Usa, Inc.
  8875 Washington Blvd B
  Roseville CA
  916 677-4500

(P-12707)
FAKOURI ELECTRICAL ENGRG INC
Also Called: F E E
30001 Comercio (92688-2106)
PHONE..................................949 888-2400
Maryam Ewalt, *Pr*
Charles Ewalt, *
John Oveisi, *
▲ **EMP**: 79 **EST**: 1979
SQ FT: 15,000
SALES (est): 11.59MM **Privately Held**
Web: www.fee-ups.com
SIC: 7378 8742 Computer maintenance and repair; Maintenance management consultant

(P-12708)
HYUNDAI AUTOEVER AMERICA LLC
Also Called: Haea
10550 Talbert Ave 3rd Fl (92708-6032)
PHONE..................................714 965-3000
EMP: 284 **EST**: 2004
SQ FT: 20,000
SALES (est): 60.01MM **Privately Held**
Web: www.haeaus.com
SIC: 7378 Computer and data processing equipment repair/maintenance
HQ: Hyundai Motor America
  10550 Talbert Ave
  Fountain Valley CA
  714 965-3000

(P-12709)
INHOUSEIT INC
400 Exchange Ste 100 (92602-1340)
PHONE..................................949 660-5655
Glen Ackerman, *CEO*
Steve Bender, *
EMP: 70 **EST**: 1998
SALES (est): 8.6MM **Privately Held**
Web: www.inhouse-it.de

SIC: 7378 Computer and data processing equipment repair/maintenance

(P-12710)
QUEST INTL MONITOR SVC INC (PA)
Also Called: Quest International
60 Parker 65 (92618)
PHONE..................................949 581-9900
Shahnam Arshadi, *Pr*
Kamyar Katouzian, *
▲ **EMP**: 60 **EST**: 1985
SALES (est): 31.55MM
SALES (corp-wide): 31.55MM **Privately Held**
Web: www.questinc.com
SIC: 7378 7379 7371 7373 Computer maintenance and repair; Computer related maintenance services; Custom computer programming services; Systems integration services

(P-12711)
RAKWORX INC
1 Mason (92618-2514)
PHONE..................................949 215-1362
Yue Cong, *VP*
Zhiyong Ding, *
EMP: 150 **EST**: 2016
SALES (est): 4.09MM **Privately Held**
Web: www.rakworx.com
SIC: 7378 3577 Computer and data processing equipment repair/maintenance; Data conversion equipment, media-to-media: computer

(P-12712)
TELEPLAN SERVICE SOLUTIONS INC
151 N Sunrise Ave Ste 1008 (95661-2900)
PHONE..................................916 677-4500
Russell Sproull, *CEO*
Jack Rockwood, *
Donna Kwidzinski, *
Pk Bala, *
Jan Piet Valk, *
▲ **EMP**: 75 **EST**: 2000
SALES (est): 5.14MM **Privately Held**
Web: www.reconext.com
SIC: 7378 Computer maintenance and repair
HQ: Teleplan Holding Usa, Inc.
  8875 Washington Blvd B
  Roseville CA
  916 677-4500

(P-12713)
TUSA INC (PA)
Also Called: Terix Computer Service
986 Walsh Ave (95050-2649)
PHONE..................................888 848-3749
Bernd Appleby, *CEO*
EMP: 105 **EST**: 2016
SALES (est): 6.82MM
SALES (corp-wide): 6.82MM **Privately Held**
SIC: 7378 Computer maintenance and repair

(P-12714)
VALTRON TECHNOLOGIES INC
28309 Avenue Crocker (91355-1251)
PHONE..................................805 257-0333
Andrew Hart, *Pr*
Steve Nober, *
EMP: 95 **EST**: 1988
SQ FT: 48,000
SALES (est): 1.7MM **Privately Held**
SIC: 7378 5734 Computer and data processing equipment repair/maintenance; Modems, monitors, terminals, and disk drives: computers

7379 Computer Related Services, Nec

(P-12715)
24 7AI INC (PA)
2105 S Bascom Ave Ste 195 (95008-3291)
PHONE..................................650 385-2247
P V Kannan, *Ch Bd*
Lawrence Vertin, *
Rohan Ganeson, *
William Bose, *
EMP: 242 **EST**: 2000
SQ FT: 5,000
SALES (est): 470.77MM **Privately Held**
Web: www.247.ai
SIC: 7379 Online services technology consultants

(P-12716)
A P R CONSULTING INC
17852 17th St Ste 206 (92780-2143)
PHONE..................................714 544-3696
Darryl Stone, *Brnch Mgr*
EMP: 787
Web: www.aprconsulting.com
SIC: 7379 7371 Computer related maintenance services; Custom computer programming services
PA: A P R Consulting, Inc.
  1370 Valley Vista Dr # 280
  Diamond Bar CA

(P-12717)
A10 NETWORKS INC (PA)
Also Called: A10
2300 Orchard Pkwy (95131-1017)
PHONE..................................408 325-8668
Dhrupad Trivedi, *Ch Bd*
Brian Becker, *CFO*
Matthew Bruening, *Ex VP*
Robert Cochran, *RISK*
▲ **EMP**: 536 **EST**: 2004
SQ FT: 116,381
SALES (est): 280.34MM **Publicly Held**
Web: www.a10networks.com
SIC: 7379 7372 Computer related maintenance services; Prepackaged software

(P-12718)
ACCELLION INC
Also Called: Accellion
1510 Fashion Island Blvd (94404-1545)
PHONE..................................650 485-4300
Rebecca Soler, *VP*
Glen Segal, *VP*
Yaron Galant, *CPO*
Laureen Smith, *VP*
EMP: 150 **EST**: 1997
SALES (est): 24.76MM **Privately Held**
Web: www.kiteworks.com
SIC: 7379 Computer related maintenance services

(P-12719)
ACCRETE SOLUTIONS LLC
1027 Calaveras Ridge Dr (95035-3459)
PHONE..................................877 849-5838
Sanjay Minocha, *CEO*
EMP: 290 **EST**: 2008
SALES (est): 10.47MM **Privately Held**
Web: www.acnsol.com
SIC: 7379 8742 7373 Computer related consulting services; Management consulting services; Systems integration services

(P-12720)
ACER AMERICA CORPORATION (DH)
1730 N 1st St Ste 400 (95112-4642)
PHONE..................................408 533-7700
Greg Prendergast, *CEO*
Ming Wang, *
◆ **EMP**: 100 **EST**: 1976
SALES (est): 58.7MM **Privately Held**
Web: www.acer.com
SIC: 7379 Online services technology consultants
HQ: Gateway, Inc.
  7565 Irvine Center Dr # 150
  Irvine CA
  949 471-7000

(P-12721)
ADAMS COMM & ENGRG TECH INC
1875 Century Park E Ste 1130 (90067-2253)
PHONE..................................301 861-5000
Charles Adams, *Pr*
EMP: 125
SALES (corp-wide): 27.37MM **Privately Held**
Web: www.adamscomm.com
SIC: 7379 Online services technology consultants
PA: Adams Communication & Engineering Technology, Inc.
  10740 Parkridge Blvd # 700
  Reston VA
  443 345-5285

(P-12722)
ADCOM INTERACTIVE MEDIA INC
Also Called: Admedia
21200 Oxnard St # 429 (91367-5014)
PHONE..................................800 296-7104
EMP: 100 **EST**: 2009
SALES (est): 6.9MM **Privately Held**
Web: www.admedia.com
SIC: 7379 Online services technology consultants

(P-12723)
ADVANTIS GLOBAL INC (PA)
Also Called: Advantis
20 Sunnyside Ave Ste E (94941-1938)
PHONE..................................415 612-3338
Bryan Barber, *CEO*
Jeff Taylor, *
Randi Haaker, *
EMP: 110 **EST**: 2007
SALES (est): 40MM
SALES (corp-wide): 40MM **Privately Held**
Web: www.advantisglobal.com
SIC: 7379 Computer related consulting services

(P-12724)
AICENT INC
900 E Hamilton Ave # 600 (95008-0664)
PHONE..................................408 324-1316
EMP: 106
SIC: 7379 Data processing consultant

(P-12725)
AJILON LLC
4590 Macarthur Blvd (92660-2030)
PHONE..................................949 955-0100
EMP: 233
Web: www.lhh.com
SIC: 7379 Diskette duplicating service
HQ: Ajilon Llc
  4800 Deerwood Campus Pkwy # 800

PRODUCTS & SERVICES SECTION
7379 - Computer Related Services, Nec (P-12749)

Jacksonville FL
631 844-7800

(P-12726)
AKSHAYA INC (PA)
415 Boulder Ct Ste 100 (94566-8321)
PHONE..........................925 914-7395
Swaroop Antoo, *CEO*
EMP: 128 **EST:** 2012
SQ FT: 3,145
SALES (est): 7.51MM
SALES (corp-wide): 7.51MM **Privately Held**
Web: www.akshaya-inc.com
SIC: 7379 Computer related consulting services

(P-12727)
ALL COVERED INC
1051 E Hillsdale Blvd Ste 510 (94404-1603)
PHONE..........................650 486-5000
EMP: 435
Web: kmbs.konicaminolta.us
SIC: 7379 7378 Computer related consulting services; Computer maintenance and repair

(P-12728)
ALLCLOUD USA LLC
155 Montgomery St Ste 810 (94104-4113)
PHONE..........................510 717-3785
EMP: 68 **EST:** 2012
SALES (est): 823.77K **Privately Held**
SIC: 7379 Online services technology consultants

(P-12729)
ALPHABOLD
2011 Palomar Airport Rd Ste 305 (92011-1432)
PHONE..........................949 637-7148
EMP: 84 **EST:** 2017
SALES (est): 2.59MM **Privately Held**
Web: www.alphabold.com
SIC: 7379 Computer related consulting services

(P-12730)
ALTEXSOFT INC
6590 Lockheed Dr (96002-9013)
PHONE..........................877 777-9097
Oleksandr Medovoi, *Pr*
EMP: 146
SALES (corp-wide): 5.83MM **Privately Held**
Web: www.altexsoft.com
SIC: 7379 Computer related consulting services
PA: Altexsoft Inc.
    41829 Albrae St 111
    Fremont CA
    877 777-9097

(P-12731)
ANAPLAN INC (PA)
Also Called: Anaplan
50 Hawthorne St (94105-3902)
PHONE..........................415 742-8199
Frank Calderoni, *Pr*
Frank Calderoni, *Ch Bd*
Vikas Mehta, *CAO*
Ana Pinczuk, *CDO*
Vivie Lee, *CSO*
EMP: 368 **EST:** 2008
SQ FT: 55,000
SALES (est): 592.18MM
SALES (corp-wide): 592.18MM **Privately Held**
Web: www.anaplan.com

SIC: 7379 Online services technology consultants

(P-12732)
APSTRA INC (HQ)
1137 Innovation Way (94089-1228)
PHONE..........................650 307-3245
EMP: 70 **EST:** 2014
SALES (est): 8.62MM **Publicly Held**
Web: www.juniper.net
SIC: 7379 Computer related consulting services
PA: Juniper Networks, Inc.
    1133 Innovation Way
    Sunnyvale CA

(P-12733)
ASANA INC (PA)
Also Called: Asana
633 Folsom St Ste 100 (94107-3600)
PHONE..........................415 525-3888
Dustin Moskovitz, *Ch Bd*
Tim Wan, *CFO*
Anne Raimondi, *COO*
Eleanor Lacey, *Corporate Secretary*
EMP: 1008 **EST:** 2008
SQ FT: 88,000
SALES (est): 547.21MM
SALES (corp-wide): 547.21MM **Publicly Held**
Web: www.asana.com
SIC: 7379 7372 Computer related consulting services; Prepackaged software

(P-12734)
ASSIGN CORPORATION
200 N Maryland Ave Ste 204 (91206-4262)
PHONE..........................818 247-7100
Umesh Lalwani, *CEO*
EMP: 120 **EST:** 1997
SQ FT: 1,300
SALES (est): 2.36MM **Privately Held**
SIC: 7379 Online services technology consultants

(P-12735)
AUTOVITALS INC
4141 Jutland Dr Ste 300 (92117-3658)
PHONE..........................866 949-2848
Jon Belmonte, *CEO*
EMP: 70 **EST:** 2009
SALES (est): 5.86MM **Privately Held**
Web: www.autovitals.com
SIC: 7379 Computer related services, nec

(P-12736)
AUXILIO INC
27271 Las Ramblas Ste 200 (92691-8042)
PHONE..........................949 614-0731
EMP: 74 **EST:** 2019
SALES (est): 1.01MM **Privately Held**
Web: www.auxilioinc.com
SIC: 7379 Computer related consulting services

(P-12737)
AVIDEX INDUSTRIES LLC
20382 Hermana Cir (92630-8701)
PHONE..........................949 428-6333
Mike Stammire, *Brnch Mgr*
EMP: 100
Web: www.avidex.com
SIC: 7379 1731 Computer related consulting services; Electrical work
HQ: Avidex Industries, L.L.C.
    1100 Crescent Green # 200
    Cary NC
    919 772-8604

(P-12738)
BAIDU USA LLC
1195 Bordeaux Dr (94089-1210)
PHONE..........................669 224-6400
Lydia Liu, *Managing Member*
EMP: 187 **EST:** 2010
SALES (est): 38.5MM **Privately Held**
Web: usa.baidu.com
SIC: 7379 Online services technology consultants
HQ: Baidu Japan Inc.
    6-10-1, Roppongi
    Minato-Ku TKY

(P-12739)
BASIC SOLUTIONS CORP
46724 Fremont Blvd (94538-6538)
PHONE..........................510 573-3658
Jang Badhesha, *CEO*
EMP: 108 **EST:** 2005
SALES (est): 21.86MM **Privately Held**
Web: www.basicsolutions.com
SIC: 7379 Computer related maintenance services

(P-12740)
BE SCHOOL INC
Also Called: Sv Academy
12 Grace St Fl 3 (94103-2676)
PHONE..........................650 576-5263
EMP: 151 **EST:** 2016
SALES (est): 2.82MM **Privately Held**
Web: www.sv.academy
SIC: 7379 Computer related services, nec

(P-12741)
BESTITCOM INC (PA)
Also Called: Bestit
1464 Madera Rd (93065-3077)
PHONE..........................602 667-5613
Harry Curtin, *CEO*
Susan Silberstein, *
Rich Hybner, *
Fred Chen, *
EMP: 65 **EST:** 2004
SQ FT: 20,000
SALES (est): 5.27MM **Privately Held**
SIC: 7379 Computer related consulting services

(P-12742)
BEYONDID INC
535 Mission St Fl 14 (94105-3253)
PHONE..........................415 878-6210
Arun Shrestha, *CEO*
Charles Fortune, *
Sasi Kelam Engineering, *Prin*
Sanjay Shah, *
Neeraj Methi, *
EMP: 65 **EST:** 2018
SALES (est): 5.3MM **Privately Held**
Web: www.beyondid.com
SIC: 7379 Computer related consulting services

(P-12743)
BIARCA INC (PA)
333 W San Carlos St Ste 600 (95110-2731)
PHONE..........................408 564-4465
Subhashini Rajana, *CEO*
Kris Rajana, *
EMP: 74 **EST:** 2016
SALES (est): 4.55MM
SALES (corp-wide): 4.55MM **Privately Held**
Web: www.biarca.io
SIC: 7379 7371 Computer related consulting services; Custom computer programming services

(P-12744)
BODHTREE SOLUTIONS INC
74 W Neal St Ste 100 (94566-6632)
PHONE..........................844 409-0510
EMP: 235
Web: www.bodhtree.com
SIC: 7379 Computer related consulting services

(P-12745)
BT INS INC
1600 Memorex Dr Ste 200 (95050-2842)
PHONE..........................408 330-2700
EMP: 900
SIC: 7379 Computer related consulting services

(P-12746)
CALIFORNIA DEPARTMENT TECH
Also Called: Office of Technology
3101 Gold Camp Dr (95670-6099)
PHONE..........................916 464-3747
Amy Tom, *Brnch Mgr*
EMP: 200
SALES (corp-wide): 534.4MM **Privately Held**
Web: www.ca.gov
SIC: 7379 Online services technology consultants
HQ: California Department Of Technology
    1325 J St Ste 1600
    Sacramento CA

(P-12747)
CALIFORNIA DEPARTMENT TECH (DH)
Also Called: Dts
1325 J St Ste 1600 (95814-2941)
P.O. Box 1810 (95741-1810)
PHONE..........................916 319-9223
Marybel Batjer, *Sec*
EMP: 147 **EST:** 1978
SALES (est): 55.61MM
SALES (corp-wide): 534.4MM **Privately Held**
Web: www.ca.gov
SIC: 7379 Online services technology consultants
HQ: California Government Operations Agency
    915 Capitol Mall Ste 200
    Sacramento CA

(P-12748)
CALIFRNIA CRTIVE SOLUTIONS INC (PA)
Also Called: CCS Global Tech
13475 Danielson St Ste 230 (92064-8855)
PHONE..........................458 208-4131
Raminder Singh, *CEO*
EMP: 72 **EST:** 1997
SALES (est): 27.45MM
SALES (corp-wide): 27.45MM **Privately Held**
Web: www.ccsglobaltech.com
SIC: 7379 Computer related consulting services

(P-12749)
CAPGEMINI AMERICA INC
427 Brannan St (94107-1715)
PHONE..........................415 796-6777
EMP: 100
SALES (corp-wide): 415.14MM **Privately Held**
Web: www.capgemini.com
SIC: 7379 Online services technology consultants

7379 - Computer Related Services, Nec (P-12750)

PRODUCTS & SERVICES SECTION

HQ: Capgemini America, Inc.
79 5th Ave Fl 3
New York NY
212 314-8000

(P-12750)
CAPIOT SOFTWARE INC
2055 Laurelwood Rd Ste 210 (95054-2727)
PHONE.............................408 216-7010
Anil Kshirsagar, *Dir*
EMP: 180 **EST:** 2014
SALES (est): 16.44MM **Privately Held**
Web: www.persistent.com
SIC: 7379 7371 Computer related consulting services; Computer software development
HQ: Persistent Systems Inc.
2055 Laurelwood Rd # 210
Santa Clara CA
408 216-7010

(P-12751)
CAYLENT INC
4521 Campus Dr Ste 344 (92612-2621)
PHONE.............................800 215-9124
Lori Williams, *CEO*
Valerie Henderson, *Pr*
Jacob Hill, *CFO*
Ginger Siedschlag, *COO*
EMP: 176 **EST:** 2015
SQ FT: 450
SALES (est): 10.79MM **Privately Held**
Web: www.caylent.com
SIC: 7379 Computer related consulting services

(P-12752)
CENTERBEAM INC
710 Lakeway Dr Ste 195 (94085-4048)
EMP: 175
SIC: 7379 7374 Data processing consultant; Data processing and preparation

(P-12753)
CENTRAL BUSINESS SOLUTIONS INC (PA)
37600 Central Ct Ste 214 (94560-3456)
PHONE.............................510 573-5500
Anjul Katare, *Pr*
EMP: 70 **EST:** 2000
SALES (est): 6.73MM
SALES (corp-wide): 6.73MM **Privately Held**
Web: www.cbsinfosys.com
SIC: 7379 Online services technology consultants

(P-12754)
CGI FEDERAL INC
7480 Mission Valley Rd Ste 100 (92108)
PHONE.............................619 260-0602
Amy Agviluro, *Brnch Mgr*
EMP: 76
SALES (corp-wide): 9.87B **Privately Held**
Web: www.cgi.com
SIC: 7379 Computer related consulting services
HQ: Cgi Federal Inc.
12601 Fair Lakes Cir
Fairfax VA
703 227-6000

(P-12755)
CGI TECHNOLOGIES SOLUTIONS INC
621 Capitol Mall Ste 2025 (95814-4733)
PHONE.............................916 830-1100
Jerri Magers, *Brnch Mgr*
EMP: 103
SALES (corp-wide): 9.87B **Privately Held**
SIC: 7379 Computer related consulting services
HQ: Cgi Technologies And Solutions Inc.
11325 Rndom Hills Rd Fl 8 Flr 8
Fairfax VA
703 267-5111

(P-12756)
CIPHERTRACE INC
140 Victory Ln (95030-5922)
PHONE.............................650 996-2142
David Jevans, *CEO*
Stephen Ryan, *COO*
EMP: 75 **EST:** 2015
SALES (est): 8.89MM
SALES (corp-wide): 22.24B **Publicly Held**
Web: www.ciphertrace.com
SIC: 7379 8748 7372 7371 Computer related consulting services; Systems engineering consultant, ex. computer or professional; Application computer software ; Custom computer programming services
PA: Mastercard Incorporated
2000 Purchase St
Purchase NY
914 249-2000

(P-12757)
CIVICACTIONS INC
3527 Mt Diablo Blvd Ste 269 (94549-3815)
PHONE.............................510 408-7510
Henry Poole, *Pr*
EMP: 70 **EST:** 2009
SALES (est): 15MM **Privately Held**
Web: www.civicactions.com
SIC: 7379 Computer related consulting services

(P-12758)
CLOSINGCORP INC
9645 Granite Ridge Dr Ste 300 (92123-2660)
PHONE.............................858 551-1500
Bob Jennings, *CEO*
Michael D Reynolds, *
Pat Carney, *CIO*
Dan Mugge, *
EMP: 63 **EST:** 2005
SALES (est): 10.38MM
SALES (corp-wide): 1.64B **Privately Held**
Web: www.closing.com
SIC: 7379 7375 4813 Online services technology consultants; Information retrieval services; Proprietary online service networks
HQ: Corelogic, Inc.
40 Pacifica Ste 900
Irvine CA
866 873-3651

(P-12759)
CLOUD CREATIONS INC
301 N Lake Ave Ste 600 (91101-5129)
PHONE.............................800 951-7651
Justin Davis, *CEO*
Justin Paul Davis, *
EMP: 74 **EST:** 2015
SQ FT: 5,000
SALES (est): 4.46MM **Privately Held**
Web: www.cloudcreations.com
SIC: 7379 Computer related consulting services

(P-12760)
CLOUDINARY INC
3400 Central Expy Ste 110 (95051-0703)
PHONE.............................650 772-1833
Itai Lahan, *CEO*
EMP: 288 **EST:** 2015
SALES (est): 10.05MM **Privately Held**
Web: www.cloudinary.com
SIC: 7379 Online services technology consultants
PA: Cloudinary Ltd
20 Bart Aharon
Petah Tikva

(P-12761)
CLOUDWICK TECHNOLOGIES INC (PA)
39899 Balentine Dr Ste 345 (94560-5355)
PHONE.............................650 346-5788
Maninder Chhabra, *CEO*
EMP: 87 **EST:** 2012
SQ FT: 6,000
SALES (est): 20.34MM
SALES (corp-wide): 20.34MM **Privately Held**
Web: www.cloudwick.com
SIC: 7379 Computer related consulting services

(P-12762)
COGNIZANT TRIZETTO
567 San Nicolas Dr Ste 360 (92660-6513)
PHONE.............................949 719-2200
Jeffrey Margolis, *Mgr*
EMP: 72
SIC: 7379 Computer related consulting services
HQ: Cognizant Trizetto Software Group, Inc.
9655 Maroon Cir
Englewood CO

(P-12763)
COMITY DESIGNS INC
41 Marvin Ave (94022-3709)
PHONE.............................415 967-1530
Dushyant Pandya, *CEO*
Piyush Pandya, *
EMP: 100 **EST:** 2005
SALES (est): 14.37MM **Privately Held**
Web: www.comitydesigns.com
SIC: 7379 Computer related consulting services
HQ: Brillio, Llc
399 Thornall St Ste 68
Edison NJ
800 317-0575

(P-12764)
COMPUTACENTER US INC (HQ)
Also Called: Fusionstorm
2 Bryant St Ste 150 (94105-1641)
PHONE.............................714 861-2200
Mike Norris, *CEO*
Amy Morrissey, *
EMP: 765 **EST:** 2006
SQ FT: 6,500
SALES (est): 2.3B **Privately Held**
Web: www.computacenter.com
SIC: 7379 7371 7374 7376 Computer related maintenance services; Computer software systems analysis and design, custom; Data processing service; Computer facilities management
PA: Computacenter Plc
Administration Centre
Hatfield HERTS

(P-12765)
CONTROLTEC INC
101 State Pl Ste Q (92029-1365)
PHONE.............................760 975-9750
Norbert Haupt, *Pr*
EMP: 70 **EST:** 1996
SALES (est): 8.93MM **Privately Held**
Web: www.kindersystems.com
SIC: 7379 7371 Computer related consulting services; Computer software systems analysis and design, custom

(P-12766)
COVESTIC LLC
3101 Skyway Ct (94539-5910)
PHONE.............................425 803-9889
John Schaffer, *Pr*
EMP: 92 **EST:** 2001
SALES (est): 9.1MM **Privately Held**
Web: www.covestic.com
SIC: 7379 Online services technology consultants

(P-12767)
COYOTE CREEK CONSULTING LLC
Also Called: Coyote Creek Consulting
1057 Cochrane Rd Ste 160 Pmb 1017 (95037)
PHONE.............................408 383-9200
Michael R Faster, *CEO*
EMP: 78 **EST:** 1998
SALES (est): 14.15MM
SALES (corp-wide): 14.15MM **Privately Held**
Web: www.praecipio.com
SIC: 7379 Online services technology consultants
PA: Praecipio Consulting Llc
501 Congress Ave Ste 150
Austin TX
512 266-8271

(P-12768)
CPACKET NETWORKS INC
2130 Gold St Ste 200 (95002-3700)
PHONE.............................650 969-9500
EMP: 77 **EST:** 2020
SALES (est): 898.03K **Privately Held**
Web: www.cpacket.com
SIC: 7379 Computer related consulting services

(P-12769)
CPUTER INC
Also Called: Ground Force One
2110 Artesia Blvd (90278-3073)
PHONE.............................844 394-1538
Nikolai Nedovodin, *CEO*
EMP: 84 **EST:** 2013
SALES (est): 2.83MM **Privately Held**
Web: www.cputer.com
SIC: 7379 4119 Computer related consulting services; Limousine rental, with driver

(P-12770)
CROWDSTRIKE INC
15440 Laguna Canyon Rd Ste 250 (92618-2138)
PHONE.............................888 512-8906
EMP: 104
SALES (corp-wide): 2.24B **Publicly Held**
Web: www.crowdstrikeracing.com
SIC: 7379 Computer related maintenance services
HQ: Crowdstrike, Inc.
206 E 9th St Ste 1400
Austin TX

(P-12771)
CROWDSTRIKE INC
15441 Laguna Canyon Rd, Ste 260 (92618)
PHONE.............................888 512-8906
EMP: 104
SALES (corp-wide): 2.24B **Publicly Held**
Web: www.crowdstrikeracing.com

PRODUCTS & SERVICES SECTION
7379 - Computer Related Services, Nec (P-12793)

SIC: 7379 Computer related maintenance services
HQ: Crowdstrike, Inc.
206 E 9th St Ste 1400
Austin TX

(P-12772)
CROWDSTRIKE INC
400 Continental Blvd Ste 275 (90245-5076)
PHONE..................................888 512-8906
EMP: 104
SALES (corp-wide): 2.24B Publicly Held
Web: www.crowdstrikeracing.com
SIC: 7379 Computer related maintenance services
HQ: Crowdstrike, Inc.
206 E 9th St Ste 1400
Austin TX

(P-12773)
CULTURA TECHNOLOGIES INC
1810 Mesquite Ct (95376-9293)
PHONE..................................209 923-6278
James Baker, Brnch Mgr
EMP: 61
SALES (corp-wide): 6.62B Privately Held
Web: www.culturatech.com
SIC: 7379 Computer related maintenance services
HQ: Cultura Technologies Inc.
3820 Mansell Rd Ste 350
Alpharetta GA
678 249-3200

(P-12774)
DATAGRAIL
164 Townsend St Unit 12 (94107-1991)
PHONE..................................650 781-3680
EMP: 89 EST: 2019
SALES (est): 2.52MM Privately Held
Web: www.datagrail.io
SIC: 7379 Computer related services, nec

(P-12775)
DECLARA INC
977 Commercial St (94303-4908)
PHONE..................................877 216-0604
Ramona Pierson, CEO
Nelson Gonzalez, CSO*
EMP: 68 EST: 2012
SQ FT: 3,000
SALES (est): 6.56MM Privately Held
SIC: 7379 Data processing consultant

(P-12776)
DEFENSEWEB TECHNOLOGIES INC
Also Called: Nliven
10188 Telesis Ct Ste 300 (92121-4779)
P.O. Box 14601 (40214-0601)
PHONE..................................858 272-8505
EMP: 90
Web: www.transcendinsights.com
SIC: 7379 7371 Computer related consulting services; Computer software development

(P-12777)
DELTA COMPUTER CONSULTING
25550 Hawthorne Blvd Ste 106 (90505-6831)
PHONE..................................310 541-9440
Marzieh Daneshvar, Pr
Masih Hakimpour, *
EMP: 180 EST: 1987
SQ FT: 2,000
SALES (est): 10.86MM Privately Held
Web: www.deltacci.com
SIC: 7379 Computer related consulting services

(P-12778)
DEPLABS INC
Also Called: Deplabs
2872 Ygnacio Valley Rd Ste 241 (94598-3534)
PHONE..................................415 456-5600
Sergii Ostapenko, CEO
EMP: 65 EST: 2005
SALES (est): 5.23MM Privately Held
Web: www.miracommerce.com
SIC: 7379 8748 7371 Computer related consulting services; Systems analysis and engineering consulting services; Software programming applications

(P-12779)
DIRECTAPPS INC (PA)
Also Called: Direct Technology
3009 Douglas Blvd Ste 300 (95661-3895)
PHONE..................................916 787-2200
Rick Nelson, CEO
Federico Michanie, *
Casey Stenzel, *
John Sercu, *
EMP: 125 EST: 1995
SQ FT: 19,000
SALES (est): 24.81MM
SALES (corp-wide): 24.81MM Privately Held
Web: www.directtechnology.com
SIC: 7379 Online services technology consultants

(P-12780)
DROISYS INC
4657 Hedgewick Ave (94538-3327)
PHONE..................................408 329-1761
Sanjiv Goyal, Brnch Mgr
EMP: 144
SALES (corp-wide): 15.57MM Privately Held
Web: www.droisys.com
SIC: 7379 Computer related consulting services
PA: Droisys Inc.
46540 Fremont Blvd # 516
Fremont CA
408 874-8333

(P-12781)
DTI SERVICES INC (PA)
601 S Figueroa St Ste 4300 (90017-5757)
PHONE..................................213 670-1100
Satoru Amano, Pr
Ken Yasuda, *
Chad D Harmon, *
EMP: 60 EST: 1996
SALES (est): 9.01MM
SALES (corp-wide): 9.01MM Privately Held
Web: www.dtiservices.com
SIC: 7379 4813 7374 7389 Online services technology consultants; Internet host services; Computer graphics service; Business services, nec

(P-12782)
DYNTEK INC (PA)
5241 California Ave Ste 150 (92617-3215)
PHONE..................................949 271-6700
Ron Ben-iyshay, Dir
Michael Gullard, Ch
Karen S Rosenberger, CFO
EMP: 105 EST: 1989
SQ FT: 10,250
SALES (est): 108.89MM Privately Held
Web: www.dyntek.com
SIC: 7379 Online services technology consultants

(P-12783)
EDGECAST INC (HQ)
13031 W Jefferson Blvd Ste 900 (90094-7000)
PHONE..................................310 396-7400
Monica Mijaleski, CEO
Julie Jacobs, *
Scott Garner, *
EMP: 68 EST: 2006
SQ FT: 50,000
SALES (est): 57.18MM
SALES (corp-wide): 338.6MM Publicly Held
Web: www.yahooinc.com
SIC: 7379 Online services technology consultants
PA: Edgio, Inc.
2222 W 14th St
Tempe AZ
602 850-5000

(P-12784)
ELATION HEALTH INC (PA)
530 Divisadero St # 872 (94117-2213)
PHONE..................................415 213-5164
Kyna Fong, CEO
Lennart Lepner, CFO
Paul Bussi, CRO
EMP: 67 EST: 2008
SQ FT: 5,000
SALES (est): 12.53MM
SALES (corp-wide): 12.53MM Privately Held
Web: www.elationhealth.com
SIC: 7379 Computer related consulting services

(P-12785)
ENEXUS GLOBAL INC
39510 Paseo Padre Pkwy Ste 390 (94538-4707)
PHONE..................................510 936-4044
Dinesh Puri, Pr
Ridhima Puri, *
EMP: 74 EST: 2015
SALES (est): 4.91MM Privately Held
Web: www.enexusglobal.com
SIC: 7379 Computer related services, nec

(P-12786)
ENTERPRISE NTWRKING SLTONS INC
2860 Gold Tailings Ct (95670-6106)
P.O. Box 123 (95628-0123)
EMP: 108 EST: 1999
SALES (est): 27.14MM Privately Held
Web: www.optm.com
SIC: 7379 Computer related consulting services

(P-12787)
ETHERWAN SYSTEMS INC
2301 E Winston Rd (92806-5542)
PHONE..................................714 779-3800
Mitch Yang, Pr
▲ EMP: 100 EST: 1996
SQ FT: 5,000
SALES (est): 18.46MM
SALES (corp-wide): 3.37B Privately Held
Web: www.etherwan.com
SIC: 7379 3577 Computer related maintenance services; Computer peripheral equipment, nec
HQ: Etherwan Systems, Inc.
8f, No. 2, Alley 6, Lane 235, Baoqiao Rd.
New Taipei City TAP

(P-12788)
ETOUCH SYSTEMS CORP
Also Called: Etouch
39899 Balentine Dr Ste 200 (94560-5361)
PHONE..................................510 795-4800
Aniruddha Gadre, CEO
EMP: 600 EST: 1996
SQ FT: 12,800
SALES (est): 52.55MM
SALES (corp-wide): 1.31B Privately Held
SIC: 7379 Online services technology consultants
HQ: Virtusa Corporation
132 Turnpike Rd Ste 300b
Southborough MA
508 389-7300

(P-12789)
EVAULT INC
6001 Shellmound St (94608-2448)
PHONE..................................415 432-2200
EMP: 160
SIC: 7379 Computer related consulting services

(P-12790)
EVENTBRITE INC (PA)
Also Called: Eventbrite
535 Mission St Fl 8 (94105-3223)
PHONE..................................415 692-7779
Julia Hartz, CEO
Kevin Hartz, *
Charles Baker, CFO
Shane Crehan, CAO
John Adcock, CPO
EMP: 331 EST: 2003
SQ FT: 48,812
SALES (est): 260.93MM
SALES (corp-wide): 260.93MM Publicly Held
Web: www.eventbrite.com
SIC: 7379 Online services technology consultants

(P-12791)
EXOIS INC
Also Called: Datadivider
2567 Ingleton Ave (92009-3060)
PHONE..................................408 777-6630
Jonathan Clark, CEO
John D Clark, *
EMP: 249 EST: 2004
SQ FT: 2,000
SALES (est): 2.49MM
SALES (corp-wide): 44.89MM Privately Held
Web: www.exois.com
SIC: 7379 Computer related consulting services
PA: Sharedlabs, Inc.
6 E Bay St Fl 4
Jacksonville FL
800 960-0149

(P-12792)
FLIPBOARD INC (PA)
811 Hamilton St (94063-1652)
PHONE..................................650 323-6547
EMP: 119 EST: 2010
SALES (est): 25.15MM Privately Held
Web: www.flipboard.com
SIC: 7379 Online services technology consultants

(P-12793)
FUTURE STATE
Also Called: Techprose
415 Mission St Ste 3300 (94105-5422)
PHONE..................................925 956-4200
Julie Sweet, Pr

7379 - Computer Related Services, Nec (P-12794)

EMP: 126 EST: 1988
SALES (est): 21.99MM **Privately Held**
Web: www.accenture.com
SIC: **7379** 8742 Data processing consultant; Management consulting services
HQ: Accenture Inc.
161 N Clark St Ste 1100
Chicago IL
312 693-0161

(P-12794)
GDR GROUP INC
3 Park Plz Ste 1700 (92614-8540)
PHONE..............................949 453-8818
Ellen Dorse, *Prin*
Bruce Greenburg, *
Robert Redwitz, *
Tony S, *
Karen S, *
EMP: 76 EST: 1997
SALES (est): 18.19MM **Privately Held**
Web: www.gdrgroup.com
SIC: **7379** Online services technology consultants

(P-12795)
GEBBS SOFTWARE INTL INC
4640 Admiralty Way Fl 9 (90292-6630)
PHONE..............................201 227-0088
Nitin Thakor, *CEO*
EMP: 70 EST: 1997
SQ FT: 2,500
SALES (est): 5.58MM **Privately Held**
SIC: **7379** Computer related consulting services
PA: Gebbs Software International Private Limited
Gebbs House
Mumbai MH

(P-12796)
GEEK SQUAD INC
Also Called: Geek Squad
12989 Park Plaza Dr (90703-8565)
PHONE..............................562 402-1555
EMP: 88
SALES (corp-wide): 46.3B **Publicly Held**
Web: www.bestbuy.com
SIC: **7379** Computer related consulting services
HQ: Geek Squad, Inc.
1213 Washington Ave N
Minneapolis MN

(P-12797)
GEMINI SOLUTIONS LLC
814 Mission St Fl 5 (94280)
PHONE..............................650 329-8194
EMP: 170 EST: 2005
SALES (est): 4.71MM **Privately Held**
Web: www.geminisols.com
SIC: **7379** Computer related consulting services

(P-12798)
GENERAL DYNAMICS INFO TECH INC
1615 Murray Canyon Rd Ste 600 (92108-4314)
PHONE..............................619 881-8989
Dan Morrissey, *Brnch Mgr*
EMP: 66
SALES (corp-wide): 39.41B **Publicly Held**
Web: www.gdit.com
SIC: **7379** Computer related maintenance services
HQ: General Dynamics Information Technology, Inc.
3150 Fairview Park Dr
Falls Church VA
703 995-8700

(P-12799)
GENERAL NETWORKS CORPORATION
3524 Ocean View Blvd (91208-1212)
PHONE..............................818 249-1962
Robert Todd Withers, *Pr*
Todd Withers, *
David Horwatt, *
Randall C Wise, *
Cort Baker, *
EMP: 60 EST: 1986
SQ FT: 3,600
SALES (est): 12.57MM **Privately Held**
Web: www.gennet.com
SIC: **7379** 5045 7372 Computer related consulting services; Terminals, computer; Prepackaged software

(P-12800)
GRID DYNAMICS INTL LLC (HQ)
5000 Executive Pkwy Ste 520 (94583-4210)
PHONE..............................650 523-5000
Leonard Livschitz, *CEO*
Anil Doradla, *CFO*
EMP: 191 EST: 2006
SQ FT: 1,700
SALES (est): 2.5MM
SALES (corp-wide): 310.48MM **Publicly Held**
Web: www.griddynamics.com
SIC: **7379** Computer related consulting services
PA: Grid Dynamics Holdings, Inc.
5000 Executive Pkwy # 520
San Ramon CA
650 523-5000

(P-12801)
HACKERONE INC (PA)
22 4th St Fl 5 (94103-3173)
PHONE..............................415 891-0777
Marten Mickos, *CEO*
John Hering, *Dir*
Jon Sakoda, *Dir*
Bill Gurley, *Dir*
EMP: 195 EST: 2013
SQ FT: 16,374
SALES (est): 32.17MM
SALES (corp-wide): 32.17MM **Privately Held**
Web: www.hackerone.com
SIC: **7379** Computer related maintenance services

(P-12802)
HEADSTRONG CORPORATION
150 Mathilda Pl Ste 200 (94086-6011)
PHONE..............................408 732-8700
Sandip Sahai, *Mgr*
EMP: 152
SIC: **7379** 8711 1731 Computer related consulting services; Engineering services; Electrical work
HQ: Headstrong Corporation
11921 Freedom Dr Ste 550
Reston VA
703 272-6761

(P-12803)
HOMESTAR SYSTEMS INC
Also Called: Izmocars
251 Post St Ste 302 (94108-5020)
PHONE..............................415 323-4008
Tej Soni, *CEO*
Layton Judd, *
EMP: 85 EST: 2003
SALES (est): 7.54MM **Privately Held**
Web: www.izmocars.com

SIC: **7379** Computer related consulting services

(P-12804)
IDEA SOLUTIONS INC
2099 Gateway Pl Ste 340 (95110-1017)
PHONE..............................408 436-3800
EMP: 375
Web: www.ideasolutionsinc.com
SIC: **7379** Computer related maintenance services

(P-12805)
IDRIVE INC
Also Called: Ibackup.com
26115 Mureau Rd Ste A (91302-3179)
PHONE..............................818 594-5972
EMP: 70 EST: 1995
SALES (est): 9.62MM **Privately Held**
Web: www.idrive.com
SIC: **7379** Computer related maintenance services

(P-12806)
INCEDO INC
2350 Mission College Blvd Ste 246 (95054-1532)
PHONE..............................408 531-6040
EMP: 133 EST: 2019
SALES (est): 1MM **Privately Held**
Web: www.incedoinc.com
SIC: **7379** Computer related consulting services

(P-12807)
INCODE TECHNOLOGIES INC (PA)
221 Main St Ste 520 (94105-1983)
PHONE..............................650 446-3444
Ricardo Amper, *CEO*
Marianna Amper, *
EMP: 247 EST: 2015
SALES (est): 24.86MM
SALES (corp-wide): 24.86MM **Privately Held**
Web: www.incode.com
SIC: **7379** 7371 Computer related consulting services; Computer software development

(P-12808)
INFOGAIN CORPORATION (PA)
485 Alberto Way Ste 100 (95032-5476)
PHONE..............................408 355-6000
Sunil Bhatia, *CEO*
Kapil K Nanda, *
Ayan Mukerji, *
Phil Johnson, *
Kulesh Bansal, *
▲ EMP: 186 EST: 1990
SQ FT: 14,487
SALES (est): 212.66MM **Privately Held**
Web: www.infogain.com
SIC: **7379** 7373 8742 8748 Computer related consulting services; Computer integrated systems design; Management information systems consultant; Systems engineering consultant, ex. computer or professional

(P-12809)
INFOGEN LABS INC
25350 Magic Mountain Pkwy Ste 300 (91355-1151)
PHONE..............................323 816-4810
Sanjeev Kuwadeker, *Pr*
Sid Patti, *
EMP: 70 EST: 2017
SALES (est): 2.27MM **Privately Held**

SIC: **7379** Computer related consulting services

(P-12810)
INFORMATION TECH PARTNERS INC
Also Called: I T P
3003 N San Fernando Blvd (91504-2525)
PHONE..............................800 789-7487
Michael Thompson, *Pr*
Christian Thompson, *
EMP: 60 EST: 1991
SQ FT: 10,000
SALES (est): 20.59MM **Privately Held**
Web: www.itpnet.com
SIC: **7379** Computer related consulting services

(P-12811)
INFOSTRIDE INC
3031 Tisch Way Ste 110 (95128-2561)
PHONE..............................415 360-1700
Ritu Mangla, *CEO*
Ritu Mangla, *Dir*
EMP: 60 EST: 2014
SQ FT: 150
SALES (est): 7.81MM **Privately Held**
Web: www.infostride.com
SIC: **7379** 7371 Computer related consulting services; Custom computer programming services

(P-12812)
INNOVA SOLUTIONS INC
3211 Scott Blvd Ste 202 (95054-3009)
PHONE..............................408 889-2020
Rajiv Sardana, *Brnch Mgr*
EMP: 1100
SALES (corp-wide): 1.65MM **Privately Held**
Web: www.innovasolutions.com
SIC: **7379** Computer related consulting services
HQ: Innova Solutions, Inc.
2400 Meadowbrook Pkwy
Duluth GA
770 493-5588

(P-12813)
INTEGRATED INTERMODAL SVCS INC
8600 Banana Ave (92335-3033)
PHONE..............................909 355-4100
Greg Philip Stefflre, *Pr*
EMP: 100 EST: 1991
SALES (est): 2.23MM **Privately Held**
SIC: **7379** Computer related maintenance services

(P-12814)
INTEGRATED MEDIA TECH INC (PA)
Also Called: I M T
832 N Victory Blvd (91502-1630)
PHONE..............................818 761-9770
Bruce Lyon, *CEO*
Jackson Fluor, *CFO*
Mike Braico, *Ex VP*
EMP: 91 EST: 2007
SALES (est): 21.34MM **Privately Held**
Web: www.imtglobalinc.com
SIC: **7379** Online services technology consultants

(P-12815)
INTELLIPRO GROUP INC (PA)
3120 Scott Blvd # 301 (95054-3326)
PHONE..............................408 200-9891
Grace Ma, *CEO*

▲ = Import ▼ = Export
◆ = Import/Export

PRODUCTS & SERVICES SECTION
7379 - Computer Related Services, Nec (P-12839)

Luoyin Zhao, *
EMP: 368 **EST:** 2009
SALES (est): 16.24MM **Privately Held**
Web: www.intelliprogroup.com
SIC: 7379 Computer related consulting services

(P-12816)
INVISION NETWORKING LLC
333 City Blvd W Ste 1700 (92868-5905)
PHONE.................................949 309-3441
Justin Johnson, CEO
EMP: 135 **EST:** 2006
SALES (est): 3.71MM **Privately Held**
Web: www.invisionnetworking.com
SIC: 7379 Computer related consulting services

(P-12817)
INXEPTION CORPORATION
20450 Stevens Creek Blvd Ste 150 (95014-6817)
PHONE.................................888 852-4783
Farzad Dibachi, Pr
Josh Allen, CMO*
Jay Hanson, *
Amir Ameri, *
EMP: 220 **EST:** 2017
SALES (est): 220MM **Privately Held**
Web: www.inxeption.com
SIC: 7379 4213 5961 Online services technology consultants; Automobiles, transport and delivery; Electronic shopping

(P-12818)
ISPACE INC
840 Apollo St Ste 100 (90245-4641)
PHONE.................................310 563-3800
Suresh Kothapalli, CEO
EMP: 139 **EST:** 2000
SALES (est): 38.96MM **Privately Held**
Web: www.ispace.com
SIC: 7379 Online services technology consultants

(P-12819)
ITCO SOLUTIONS INC
1003 Whitehall Ln (94061-3687)
P.O. Box 610090 (94061-0090)
PHONE.................................650 367-0514
Ryan Edwards, Mng Dir
Chris Middleton, *
Tom Kramer, *
EMP: 295 **EST:** 1997
SALES (est): 10.55MM **Privately Held**
Web: www.itcosolutions.com
SIC: 7379 Online services technology consultants

(P-12820)
ITEK SERVICES INC
25501 Arctic Ocean Dr (92630-8827)
PHONE.................................949 770-4835
Donald W Rowley, CEO
John Curl, *
EMP: 100 **EST:** 2004
SQ FT: 12,000
SALES (est): 12.39MM **Privately Held**
Web: www.itekservices.com
SIC: 7379 Computer related maintenance services

(P-12821)
JOYENT INC
645 Clyde Ave Ste 502 (94043-2213)
PHONE.................................415 400-0600
EMP: 120 **EST:** 2005
SQ FT: 11,408
SALES (est): 25.14MM **Privately Held**
Web: www.joyent.com
SIC: 7379 Computer related consulting services
HQ: Samsung Semiconductor, Inc.
3655 N 1st St
San Jose CA
408 544-4000

(P-12822)
KAIZEN SYNDICATE LLC
10413 Magical Waters Ct (91978-2037)
PHONE.................................858 309-2028
EMP: 103 **EST:** 2019
SALES (est): 1.52MM **Privately Held**
Web: www.kaizensecurity.life
SIC: 7379 5047 Online services technology consultants; Medical equipment and supplies

(P-12823)
KENNA SECURITY INC
170 W Tasman Dr (95134-1700)
PHONE.................................855 474-7546
Karim Toubba, CEO
Ed Bellis, *
Jeff Heuer, CDO*
EMP: 130 **EST:** 2009
SALES (est): 15.49MM
SALES (corp-wide): 57B **Publicly Held**
Web: www.cisco.com
SIC: 7379 Online services technology consultants
PA: Cisco Systems, Inc.
170 W Tasman Dr
San Jose CA
408 526-4000

(P-12824)
KODELLA LLC
17922 Fitch Ste 200 (92614-1611)
PHONE.................................844 563-3552
Chris Heath, CEO
EMP: 104 **EST:** 2016
SALES (est): 10.48MM **Privately Held**
Web: www.kodella.com
SIC: 7379 8243 Computer related consulting services; Software training, computer

(P-12825)
KORE1 INC
530 Technology Dr Ste 150 (92618-1368)
PHONE.................................949 706-6990
Brian Hunt, CEO
Steven Quarles, *
EMP: 100 **EST:** 2005
SALES (est): 35.75MM **Privately Held**
Web: www.kore1.com
SIC: 7379 Online services technology consultants

(P-12826)
LEIDOS GOVERNMENT SERVICES INC
500 N Via Val Verde (90640-2358)
PHONE.................................323 721-6979
Nate Sadorian, Brnch Mgr
EMP: 157
SIC: 7379 7372 Computer related consulting services; Prepackaged software
HQ: Leidos Government Services, Inc.
9737 Washingtonian Blvd
Gaithersburg MD
856 486-5156

(P-12827)
LEXISNEXIS EXAMEN INC
3831 N Freeway Blvd Ste 200 (95834-1933)
P.O. Box 7247-6182 (19170-0001)
PHONE.................................916 921-4300
EMP: 200
SIC: 7379 Computer related consulting services

(P-12828)
LIQUID THINKING INC
548 4th St (94107-1621)
PHONE.................................415 869-3300
Keith Schaefer, CEO
Sal Fuentes, *
John Lucena, *
Christina Munson, *
Gail Yoshimoto, *
EMP: 99 **EST:** 2000
SQ FT: 3,000
SALES (est): 3.31MM **Privately Held**
SIC: 7379 Online services technology consultants

(P-12829)
LITTLETHINGS INC
642 Harrison St Fl 3 (94107-1323)
PHONE.................................917 364-9277
EMP: 95 **EST:** 2011
SALES (est): 3.87MM **Privately Held**
SIC: 7379 Online services technology consultants

(P-12830)
LOGIN CONSULTING SERVICES INC
300 Continental Blvd Ste 405 (90245-5042)
PHONE.................................310 607-9091
EMP: 75 **EST:** 1996
SQ FT: 3,200
SALES (est): 5.31MM **Privately Held**
Web: www.loginconsult.com
SIC: 7379 Online services technology consultants

(P-12831)
LUMINOUS COMPUTING INC
4750 Patrick Henry Dr (95054-1851)
PHONE.................................650 275-5950
Marcus Vincent Gomez, CEO
Michael Hochberg, *
EMP: 100 **EST:** 2018
SALES (est): 10.02MM **Privately Held**
Web: www.luminous.com
SIC: 7379 Computer hardware requirements analysis

(P-12832)
MAGICOM INC
Also Called: Pixverse
1375 55th St (94608-2609)
PHONE.................................415 404-6094
EMP: 75
SIC: 7379 Online services technology consultants

(P-12833)
MAGMA CONSULTING GROUP LLC
Also Called: Magmalabs
830 Traction Ave 3a (90013-1816)
PHONE.................................415 315-9364
Carlos Rocha, CEO
EMP: 60 **EST:** 2015
SALES (est): 2.38MM **Privately Held**
SIC: 7379 Computer related consulting services

(P-12834)
MAXONIC INC
2542 S Bascom Ave Ste 190 (95008-5542)
PHONE.................................408 739-4900
Ajay Narain, CEO
Nitin Khanna, *
EMP: 65 **EST:** 2002
SQ FT: 3,499
SALES (est): 8MM **Privately Held**
Web: www.maxonic.com
SIC: 7379 7371 Computer related consulting services; Computer software development and applications

(P-12835)
MCLAREN STRATEGIC SOLUTIONS
1 Park Plz Ste 600 (92614-5987)
PHONE.................................310 564-6754
John Vilina, CFO
EMP: 100 **EST:** 2020
SALES (est): 25MM **Privately Held**
Web: www.mclarensv.com
SIC: 7379 Online services technology consultants

(P-12836)
MERAKI LLC (HQ)
Also Called: Cisco Meraki
500 Terry A Francois Blvd Ste 400 (94158-2354)
PHONE.................................415 632-5800
John Bicket, *
Hans Robertson, *
Dan Atler, *
▲ **EMP:** 216 **EST:** 2006
SQ FT: 1,500
SALES (est): 128.33MM
SALES (corp-wide): 57B **Publicly Held**
Web: meraki.cisco.com
SIC: 7379 Computer related consulting services
PA: Cisco Systems, Inc.
170 W Tasman Dr
San Jose CA
408 526-4000

(P-12837)
METABYTE INC
Also Called: Hotdoodle.com
43238 Christy St (94538-3171)
PHONE.................................510 494-9700
Manu Mehta, CEO
EMP: 100 **EST:** 1993
SALES (est): 14.04MM **Privately Held**
Web: www.metabyte.com
SIC: 7379 Online services technology consultants

(P-12838)
MEZMO INC
2059 Camden Ave # 297 (95124-2024)
PHONE.................................408 471-9997
Tucker Callaway, CEO
EMP: 200 **EST:** 2013
SALES (est): 24.72MM **Privately Held**
Web: www.mezmo.com
SIC: 7379 Online services technology consultants

(P-12839)
MIPS TECH LLC
780 Montague Expy Ste 308 (95131-1317)
PHONE.................................408 530-5000
EMP: 78 **EST:** 1992
SALES (est): 7.96MM
SALES (corp-wide): 22.77MM **Privately Held**
Web: www.mips.com
SIC: 7379 Computer data escrow service
PA: Wave Computing, Inc.
780 Montague Expy Ste 308
San Jose CA
408 412-8645

7379 - Computer Related Services, Nec (P-12840)

(P-12840)
MISSION CLOUD SERVICES INC (PA)
9350 Wilshire Blvd Ste 203 (90212-3214)
PHONE..................................855 647-7466
Simon Anderson, CEO
EMP: 104 EST: 2017
SALES (est): 15.52MM
SALES (corp-wide): 15.52MM Privately Held
Web: www.missioncloud.com
SIC: 7379 Computer related consulting services

(P-12841)
MONSOON COMMERCE INC
Also Called: MONSOON COMMERCE, INC.
1250 45th St Ste 100 (94608-2924)
PHONE..................................510 594-4500
Kanth Gopalpur, CEO
EMP: 102
Web: www.monsooninc.com
SIC: 7379 Online services technology consultants
HQ: Monsoon, Inc.
    733 Sw 2nd Ave Ste 215
    Portland OR
    503 239-1055

(P-12842)
NAGARRO INC (PA)
Also Called: Projistics
1737 N 1st St Ste 590 (95112-4619)
PHONE..................................408 436-6170
Vikram Sehgal, Pr
EMP: 163 EST: 1999
SALES (est): 260.52MM
SALES (corp-wide): 260.52MM Privately Held
Web: www.nagarro.com
SIC: 7379 Computer related consulting services

(P-12843)
NC INTERACTIVE LLC
Also Called: Ncsoft
660 Newport Center Dr Ste 800 (92660)
PHONE..................................512 623-8700
Songyee Yoon, Prin
EMP: 100
SIC: 7379 Computer related consulting services
HQ: Nc Interactive Llc
    3180 139th Ave Se Ste 500
    Bellevue WA
    206 588-7200

(P-12844)
NCC GROUP INC (HQ)
123 Mission St Ste 1020 (94105-5126)
PHONE..................................415 268-9300
Rob Cotton, Pr
Craig Motta, *
Craig Foster, *
EMP: 90 EST: 2005
SQ FT: 12,000
SALES (est): 44.09MM Privately Held
Web: www.nccgroup.com
SIC: 7379 Computer data escrow service
PA: Ncc Group Plc
    Xyz Building
    Manchester

(P-12845)
NEUTONAI INC
6200 Stoneridge Mall Rd Ste 300 (94588)
PHONE..................................925 399-6400
Andrey Korobitsyn, CEO
EMP: 105 EST: 2021
SALES (est): 4.62MM Privately Held
Web: www.neuton.ai
SIC: 7379 7389 Online services technology consultants; Business services, nec

(P-12846)
NORLAND GROUP INC
3350 Scott Blvd Ste 6501 (95054-3125)
PHONE..................................408 855-8255
Mayling Liang, Pr
▲ EMP: 105 EST: 1996
SQ FT: 2,200
SALES (est): 4.55MM Privately Held
Web: www.norlandgroup.com
SIC: 7379 7361 Computer related consulting services; Employment agencies

(P-12847)
NOWCOM LLC
Also Called: Hankey Group
4751 Wilshire Blvd Ste 205 (90010-3860)
PHONE..................................323 746-6888
EMP: 165 EST: 1996
SQ FT: 4,800
SALES (est): 20.29MM
SALES (corp-wide): 352.68MM Privately Held
Web: www.nowcom.com
SIC: 7379 Online services technology consultants
PA: Hankey Investment Company, Lp
    4751 Wilshire Blvd # 110
    Los Angeles CA
    323 692-4008

(P-12848)
NZXT INC (PA)
15736 E Valley Blvd (91744-3927)
PHONE..................................800 228-9395
Johnny Chun Ju Hou, CEO
▲ EMP: 326 EST: 2015
SALES (est): 80.55MM
SALES (corp-wide): 80.55MM Privately Held
Web: www.nzxt.com
SIC: 7379 3571 5045 Computer hardware requirements analysis; Computers, digital, analog or hybrid; Computers, peripherals, and software

(P-12849)
ONEHEALTH SOLUTIONS INC
420 Stevens Ave Ste 200 (92075-2078)
PHONE..................................858 947-6333
Bruce Springer, Pr
John Shade, *
Jeff Goe, *
Chuck Mitchell, *
EMP: 133 EST: 2011
SALES (est): 911.58K Privately Held
SIC: 7379 Online services technology consultants
HQ: Simplywell, Inc.
    10670 N Cntl Expy Ste 700
    Dallas TX
    214 827-4400

(P-12850)
ORACLE SYSTEMS CORPORATION (HQ)
500 Oracle Pkwy (94065-1677)
PHONE..................................650 506-7000
Safra A Catz, CEO
Mark Hurd, *
Jeffrey O Henley, *
Mark V Hurd, *
Dorian Daley, *
EMP: 2300 EST: 1987
SQ FT: 2,200,000
SALES (est): 1.44B
SALES (corp-wide): 49.95B Publicly Held
SIC: 7379 8243 7372 Data processing consultant; Software training, computer; Business oriented computer software
PA: Oracle Corporation
    2300 Oracle Way
    Austin TX
    737 867-1000

(P-12851)
OUTLOOK AMUSEMENTS INC
3746 Foothill Blvd (91214-1740)
PHONE..................................818 433-3800
Jason Freeland, CEO
Tim Youd, *
Thomas Wszalek, *
Tom Wszalek, *
EMP: 150 EST: 2003
SALES (est): 26.22MM Privately Held
Web: www.outlookamusements.com
SIC: 7379 Online services technology consultants

(P-12852)
OVATION TECH INC
Also Called: L M S
17551 Von Karman Ave (92614-6207)
PHONE..................................949 271-0054
Stacey Powell, CEO
Jon Schmidt, *
Jeff Greene, *
Steve Youngblood, *
Minh Vu, *
EMP: 110 EST: 2000
SQ FT: 20,000
SALES (est): 15.52MM Privately Held
Web: www.lmsservice.com
SIC: 7379 Computer related consulting services

(P-12853)
PARTNERS INFORMATION TECH (HQ)
Also Called: Calance
888 S Disneyland Dr Ste 500 (92802-1847)
PHONE..................................714 736-4487
Amit Govil, Ch
Bill Darden, *
Asit Govil, *
EMP: 100 EST: 2011
SALES (est): 48.96MM Privately Held
SIC: 7379 Online services technology consultants
PA: Calance Software Private Limited
    Suite No. 201, Greenwood Plaza
    Gurugram HR

(P-12854)
PCG TECHNOLOGY SOLUTIONS LLC
2150 River Plaza Dr Ste 380 (95833-3883)
PHONE..................................916 565-8090
William Mosakowski, Pr
Daniel Heaney, *
EMP: 112 EST: 1996
SALES (est): 4.15MM
SALES (corp-wide): 501.56MM Privately Held
SIC: 7379 8748 8742 8322 Computer related consulting services; Business consulting, nec; Management consulting services; Disaster service
PA: Public Consulting Group Holdings, Inc.
    148 State St Fl 10
    Boston MA
    617 426-2026

(P-12855)
PEGASUS SQUIRE INC
12021 Wilshire Blvd Ste 770 (90025-1206)
PHONE..................................866 208-6837
Scott Cooper, CEO
EMP: 100 EST: 2002
SALES (est): 3.47MM Privately Held
Web: www.pegasussquire.com
SIC: 7379 Computer related consulting services

(P-12856)
PERFICT GLOBAL INC
1800 Sutter St Ste 870 (94520-2540)
PHONE..................................949 945-8956
Vishal Sethi, CEO
Kim Sethi, *
EMP: 105 EST: 2012
SALES (est): 3.93MM Privately Held
Web: www.perfictglobal.com
SIC: 7379 Online services technology consultants

(P-12857)
PERFORMANCE TECH PARTNERS LLC
500 Capitol Mall Ste 2350 (95814-4760)
PHONE..................................800 787-4143
EMP: 106 EST: 2004
SALES (est): 14.16MM Privately Held
Web: www.ptpinc.com
SIC: 7379 Online services technology consultants

(P-12858)
POSITIONING UNIVERSAL INC
7071 Convoy Ct Ste 300 (92111-1023)
PHONE..................................619 639-0235
Mark Wells, CEO
Mark Levey, *
Greg Gower, *
EMP: 76 EST: 2013
SALES (est): 9.56MM Privately Held
Web: www.positioninguniversal.com
SIC: 7379 Computer hardware requirements analysis

(P-12859)
PRAMIRA INC
404 N Berry St (92821-3104)
PHONE..................................800 678-1169
Omar Houari, CEO
EMP: 125 EST: 2014
SALES (est): 15.53MM Privately Held
Web: www.pramira.com
SIC: 7379 8711 Computer related consulting services; Engineering services

(P-12860)
PRECISEQ INC
11601 Wilshire Blvd Fl 5 (90025-0509)
PHONE..................................310 709-6094
Mark Dorner, Mng Pt
Guy Livneh, *
EMP: 80 EST: 2015
SQ FT: 1,200
SALES (est): 2.46MM Privately Held
SIC: 7379 Computer related consulting services

(P-12861)
PRECISION NETWRK SOLUTIONS LLC
4259 Deeboyar Ave (90712-3901)
PHONE..................................562 318-4242
Amanda Hunt, Pr
Korey Ornelas, *
Steven Hunt, *
Fernando Ornelas, *
EMP: 60 EST: 2018
SALES (est): 1.72MM Privately Held
SIC: 7379 Computer related consulting services

PRODUCTS & SERVICES SECTION
7379 - Computer Related Services, Nec (P-12882)

(P-12862)
PRIMITIVE LOGIC INC
130 Battery St Fl 3 (94111-4905)
PHONE.................................415 391-8080
Jill P Reber, *CEO*
Kevin Moos, *
Mike Mcdermott, *Sr VP*
Andy Lin, *
Anisha Weber, *
EMP: 63 **EST:** 1996
SALES (est): 12.04MM **Privately Held**
Web: www.primitivelogic.com
SIC: 7379 Computer related consulting services

(P-12863)
PRO-TEK CONSULTING (PA)
21300 Victory Blvd Ste 240 (91367-2525)
PHONE.................................805 807-5571
Raj Kessireddy, *CEO*
Divya Reddy Pyreddy, *
EMP: 110 **EST:** 2010
SQ FT: 2,400
SALES (est): 9.49MM
SALES (corp-wide): 9.49MM **Privately Held**
Web: www.pro-tekconsulting.com
SIC: 7379 Online services technology consultants

(P-12864)
PROSITES INC
38977 Sky Canyon Dr Ste 200 (92563-2682)
PHONE.................................888 932-3644
Jeffry Tobin, *Pr*
EMP: 139 **EST:** 2003
SALES (est): 15.59MM **Privately Held**
Web: www.prosites.com
SIC: 7379 Computer related maintenance services

(P-12865)
QUEST MEDIA & SUPPLIES INC (PA)
Also Called: Quest
9000 Foothills Blvd Ste 100 (95131)
P.O. Box 910 (95678-0910)
PHONE.................................916 338-7070
Timothy Burke, *CEO*
Cindy P Burke, *
Francine Walrath, *
Kathy Campbell, *
EMP: 92 **EST:** 1979
SQ FT: 9,500
SALES (est): 118.38MM
SALES (corp-wide): 118.38MM **Privately Held**
Web: www.questsys.com
SIC: 7379 Computer related consulting services

(P-12866)
R S SOFTWARE INDIA LIMITED
1900 Mccarthy Blvd Ste 103 (95035-7436)
PHONE.................................408 382-1200
Rajnit Jain, *Pr*
Bibek Das, *
EMP: 96 **EST:** 1992
SQ FT: 3,100
SALES (est): 11.08MM **Privately Held**
Web: www.rssoftware.com
SIC: 7379 7371 Computer related consulting services; Computer software development
PA: R S Software (India) Limited
A - 2, Fmc Fortuna, 234 3a,
Kolkata WB

(P-12867)
RAHI SYSTEMS INC (HQ)
Also Called: Rahi Systems Holdings
48303 Fremont Blvd (94538-6580)
PHONE.................................510 651-2205
Tarun Raisoni, *CEO*
Rashi Mehta, *
Sushil Goyal, *
EMP: 92 **EST:** 2013
SALES (est): 165.65MM **Publicly Held**
Web: www.rahisystems.com
SIC: 7379 7374 Online services technology consultants; Data processing and preparation
PA: Wesco International, Inc.
225 W Station Square Dr # 700
Pittsburgh PA

(P-12868)
REDFISH LABS INC
Also Called: Torch Leadership Labs
548 Market St Pmb 24776 (94104-5401)
PHONE.................................415 935-4249
Cameron Yarbrough, *CEO*
Melanie Steger, *VP Fin*
EMP: 130 **EST:** 2017
SALES (est): 14.39MM **Privately Held**
Web: www.torch.io
SIC: 7379 Online services technology consultants

(P-12869)
RELATED TECHNOLOGIES INC
81 Blue Ravine Rd Ste 230 (95630-4766)
P.O. Box 6975 (95763-6975)
PHONE.................................916 357-5900
Cheryl A Borgonah, *Pr*
EMP: 85 **EST:** 2001
SALES (est): 5.17MM **Privately Held**
Web: www.relatedtechnologies.com
SIC: 7379 Computer related consulting services

(P-12870)
SACA TECHNOLOGIES INC
5101 E La Palma Ave Ste 200 (92807-2056)
PHONE.................................888 603-9030
Alexander Saca, *CEO*
EMP: 66 **EST:** 2008
SALES (est): 10.63MM **Privately Held**
Web: www.ironorbit.com
SIC: 7379 Online services technology consultants

(P-12871)
SADA SYSTEMS INC (PA)
Also Called: Sada
5250 Lankershim Blvd Ste 720 (91601-3188)
PHONE.................................818 766-2400
Tony Safoian, *CEO*
Annie Safoian, *
Hovig Safoian, *
Matt Lawrence, *
Dana Berg, *
EMP: 106 **EST:** 2000
SQ FT: 10,503
SALES (est): 42.54MM
SALES (corp-wide): 42.54MM **Privately Held**
Web: www.sada.com
SIC: 7379 Computer related consulting services

(P-12872)
SAPPHIRE SOFTECH SOLUTIONS LLC
123 E 9th St Ste 323 (91786-6050)
P.O. Box 6220 (92878-6220)
PHONE.................................888 357-5222
Rajdeep Singh Oberoi, *
Jasmeer Oberoi, *
EMP: 60 **EST:** 2015
SALES (est): 2.19MM **Privately Held**
Web: www.sapphiresoftech.com
SIC: 7379 Computer related maintenance services

(P-12873)
SCIENCE APPLICATIONS INTL CORP
Also Called: Saic Government Solutions
4065 Hancock St (92110-5151)
PHONE.................................703 676-4300
EMP: 99
SALES (corp-wide): 7.7B **Publicly Held**
Web: www.saic.com
SIC: 7379 Computer related consulting services
PA: Science Applications International Corporation
12010 Sunset Hills Rd
Reston VA
703 676-4300

(P-12874)
SENSATA TECHNOLOGIES INC
Also Called: BEI Industrial Encoders
1461 Lawrence Dr (91320-1303)
PHONE.................................805 716-0322
Glenn Avolio, *Division Head*
EMP: 70
SALES (corp-wide): 4.03B **Privately Held**
Web: www.sensata.com
SIC: 7379 3827 3663 Computer related maintenance services; Optical instruments and lenses; Radio and t.v. communications equipment
HQ: Sensata Technologies, Inc.
529 Pleasant St
Attleboro MA

(P-12875)
SENTEK CONSULTING INC
Also Called: Sentek Global
2811 Nimitz Blvd Ste G (92106-4311)
PHONE.................................619 543-9550
Eric Basu, *CEO*
Jason Galetti, *
Peter Kuebler, *
EMP: 129 **EST:** 2001
SALES (est): 25.33MM
SALES (corp-wide): 677.45K **Privately Held**
Web: www.sentekglobal.com
SIC: 7379 Online services technology consultants
HQ: Deloitte Consulting Llp
30 Rockefeller Plz
New York NY
212 492-4000

(P-12876)
SIMILITY LLC
2211 N 1st St (95131-2021)
PHONE.................................650 351-7592
Rahul Pangam, *CEO*
EMP: 80 **EST:** 2014
SALES (est): 14.02MM
SALES (corp-wide): 27.52B **Publicly Held**
Web: www.simility.com
SIC: 7379 Online services technology consultants
PA: Paypal Holdings, Inc.
2211 N 1st St
San Jose CA
408 967-1000

(P-12877)
SIMULSTAT INCORPORATED
440 Stevens Ave Ste 200 (92075-2059)
PHONE.................................858 546-4337
C Adam Sharp, *Pr*
EMP: 86 **EST:** 2001
SALES (est): 5.6MM **Privately Held**
Web: www.simulstat.com
SIC: 7379 Computer related consulting services

(P-12878)
SIZMEK DSP INC (PA)
2000 Seaport Blvd Ste 400 (94063-5584)
PHONE.................................650 595-1300
Mark Grether, *CEO*
Stephen Snyder, *
Richard Song, *CRO*
Mark Torrance, *
Eric Duerr, *CMO*
EMP: 111 **EST:** 2008
SALES (est): 77.77MM **Privately Held**
SIC: 7379 7371 Computer related consulting services; Computer software development and applications

(P-12879)
SMARTEK21 LLC
530 Lytton Ave Fl 2 (94301-1541)
PHONE.................................650 617-3221
EMP: 437
Web: www.smartek21.com
SIC: 7379 Computer related consulting services
PA: Smartek21, Llc
300 Carnegie Ctr Ste 150
Princeton NJ

(P-12880)
SOFTWARE MANAGEMENT CONS LLC (HQ)
Also Called: Smci
500 N Brand Blvd (91203-1923)
PHONE.................................818 240-3177
Spencer L Karpf, *CEO*
EMP: 320 **EST:** 1976
SALES (est): 54.97MM
SALES (corp-wide): 253.48MM **Privately Held**
Web: www.milestone.tech
SIC: 7379 7361 Computer related consulting services; Placement agencies
PA: Milestone Technologies Inc.
3101 Skyway Ct
Fremont CA
510 651-2454

(P-12881)
SPRINGML INC
Also Called: Springml
6200 Stoneridge Mall Rd Ste 300 (94588)
PHONE.................................916 316-1566
Charles Landry, *CEO*
Prabu Palanisamy, *CSO*
Girish Reddy, *
EMP: 80 **EST:** 2015
SQ FT: 1,200
SALES (est): 8.56MM **Privately Held**
Web: www.springml.com
SIC: 7379 7371 Computer related consulting services; Computer software development and applications

(P-12882)
STELLA TECHNOLOGY INCORPORATED
450 S Abel St Unit 360832 (95035-5211)
PHONE.................................402 350-1681
Christopher Henkenius, *CEO*

7379 - Computer Related Services, Nec (P-12883)

Sandra Sarnoff, COO
Lin Wan, Engr
Salim Kizaraly, CFO
EMP: 90 **EST:** 2012
SALES (est): 5.22MM **Privately Held**
Web: www.stellatechnology.com
SIC: 7379 Online services technology consultants

(P-12883)
STEMCONNECTOR LLC
Also Called: STEMCONNECTOR LLC
1500 Rosecrans Ave Ste 500 (90266-3763)
PHONE..................................424 543-4074
Joanne Webber, Prin
EMP: 93
SALES (corp-wide): 662.32K **Privately Held**
Web: www.stemconnector.com
SIC: 7379 Computer related consulting services
PA: Stemconnector, Llc
  2005 Market St Ste 3300
  Philadelphia PA
  215 656-3552

(P-12884)
STRATA INFORMATION GROUP INC
3935 Harney St Ste 203 (92110-2849)
PHONE..................................619 296-0170
Henry A Eimstad, Pr
Frank Vaskelis, *
Tiffany Palacz, *
Jon Poole, *
EMP: 93 **EST:** 1988
SQ FT: 2,000
SALES (est): 11.81MM **Privately Held**
Web: www.sigcorp.com
SIC: 7379 Online services technology consultants

(P-12885)
SUTHERLAND DIGITAL SVCS INC
691 S Milpitas Blvd (95035-5476)
PHONE..................................510 474-2616
EMP: 493
SALES (corp-wide): 1.63B **Privately Held**
Web: www.suneratech.com
SIC: 7379 Computer related consulting services
HQ: Sutherland Digital Services Inc.
  631 E Big Beaver Rd # 109
  Troy MI

(P-12886)
SYNECTIC SOLUTIONS INC (PA)
Also Called: S S I
771 E Daily Dr Ste 200 (93010-6044)
PHONE..................................805 483-4800
Lynn Dines, Pr
Toby Doane, *
Joel Dines, *
EMP: 78 **EST:** 1997
SALES (est): 9.9MM
SALES (corp-wide): 9.9MM **Privately Held**
Web: www.synecticsolutions.com
SIC: 7379 8331 Online services technology consultants; Job training services

(P-12887)
SYNOPTEK LLC (PA)
19520 Jamboree Rd Ste 110 (92612-2429)
PHONE..................................949 241-8600
Tim Britt, CEO
Jeremy Daum, *
EMP: 67 **EST:** 1988
SALES (est): 104.47MM **Privately Held**
Web: www.synoptek.com

SIC: 7379 Computer related consulting services

(P-12888)
SYSTECH INTEGRATORS INC
2050 Gateway Pl (95110-1011)
PHONE..................................408 441-2700
Sam Tyagi, CEO
Rajeev Tyagi, *
EMP: 124 **EST:** 2001
SALES (est): 2.79MM **Privately Held**
Web: www.softtek.com
SIC: 7379 Computer related consulting services
HQ: Valores Corporativos Softtek, S.A. De C.V.
  Jaime Balmes No. 8, Piso 8, Oficina 801
  Ciudad De Mexico CMX

(P-12889)
TACTICAL ENGRG & ANALIS INC (PA)
6050 Santo Rd Ste 250 (92124-1194)
P.O. Box 421425 (92142-1425)
PHONE..................................858 573-9869
Lawrence Massaro, Pr
Lawrence Massaro, VP
Robert Rosado, *
EMP: 82 **EST:** 1998
SQ FT: 14,000
SALES (est): 35.23MM
SALES (corp-wide): 35.23MM **Privately Held**
Web: www.tac-eng.com
SIC: 7379 8711 Computer related consulting services; Engineering services

(P-12890)
TAHEEM JOHNSON INC
1237 S Victoria Ave (93035-1292)
PHONE..................................818 835-3785
Taheem M Johnson, CEO
EMP: 80 **EST:** 2021
SALES (est): 1.48MM **Privately Held**
Web: corp.taheemjohnson.com
SIC: 7379 Online services technology consultants

(P-12891)
TATA AMERICA INTL CORP
Also Called: Tata Consulting Services
5201 Great America Pkwy Ste 522 (95054-1143)
PHONE..................................408 569-5845
S K Bhattacharjee, Mgr
EMP: 71
Web: www.tata.com
SIC: 7379 Computer related consulting services
HQ: Tata America International Corporation
  101 Park Ave Fl 2603
  New York NY
  212 557-8038

(P-12892)
TATA AMERICA INTL CORP
Also Called: Tata Consultancy Services
500 N Brand Blvd (91203-1923)
PHONE..................................818 333-1650
Devashis Senapati, Brnch Mgr
EMP: 65
Web: www.tata.com
SIC: 7379 Online services technology consultants
HQ: Tata America International Corporation
  101 Park Ave Fl 2603
  New York NY
  212 557-8038

(P-12893)
TECH MAHINDRA CERIUM SYSTEMS
Also Called: Cerium Systems Inc
1735 Technology Dr Ste 575 (95110)
PHONE..................................408 623-0787
Venkat Arunarthi, Dir
EMP: 79 **EST:** 2014
SALES (est): 12.17MM **Privately Held**
SIC: 7379 Online services technology consultants
HQ: Tech Mahindra Cerium Private Limited
  157/A, 3rd Floor Sector-5,
  Bengaluru KA

(P-12894)
TENSORIOT INC
625 The City Dr S Ste 485 (92868-4924)
PHONE..................................909 342-2459
Ravikumar Raghunathan, CEO
EMP: 87 **EST:** 2017
SALES (est): 1.82MM **Privately Held**
Web: www.tensoriot.com
SIC: 7379 7371 Computer related consulting services; Computer software development and applications

(P-12895)
THALES ESECURITY INC (HQ)
Also Called: AES Networks
2125 Zanker Rd (95131-2109)
PHONE..................................408 433-6000
Alan Kessler, Pr
Greg Paulsen, *
Sol Cates, CSO*
▼ **EMP:** 79 **EST:** 2001
SALES (est): 25.44MM
SALES (corp-wide): 277.29MM **Privately Held**
Web: cpl.thalesgroup.com
SIC: 7379 Computer related maintenance services
PA: Thales
  4 Rue De La Verrerie
  Meudon

(P-12896)
TIGERCONNECT INC (PA)
2054 Broadway (90404-2910)
PHONE..................................310 401-1820
Jeffrey Evans, CEO
Sean Whiteley, COO
John Friedman, Dir
Herbert Madan, Dir
EMP: 61 **EST:** 2010
SALES (est): 20.92MM
SALES (corp-wide): 20.92MM **Privately Held**
Web: www.tigerconnect.com
SIC: 7379 7372 7373 Computer related maintenance services; Publisher's computer software; Computer systems analysis and design

(P-12897)
TOPTAL LLC
548 Market St Ste 36879 (94104-5401)
PHONE..................................888 604-3188
EMP: 407
SALES (corp-wide): 25.88MM **Privately Held**
Web: www.toptal.com
SIC: 7379 Computer related consulting services
PA: Toptal, Llc
  2810 N Church St # 36879
  Wilmington DE
  414 550-3054

(P-12898)
TREERING CORPORATION
217 S B St Ste 5 (94401-4039)
PHONE..................................650 385-8733
Aaron Greco, CEO
Kevin Zerber, Sec
▼ **EMP:** 82 **EST:** 2009
SALES (est): 3.05MM **Privately Held**
Web: www.treering.com
SIC: 7379 Online services technology consultants

(P-12899)
TRUU INC
2350 Mission College Blvd Ste 380 (95054-1550)
PHONE..................................888 498-0107
Lucas Budman, CEO
EMP: 60 **EST:** 2017
SALES (est): 5.86MM **Privately Held**
Web: www.truu.ai
SIC: 7379 Online services technology consultants

(P-12900)
UC INNOVATION INC
2855 Michelle Ste 190 (92606-1026)
PHONE..................................949 415-8246
Christine C Chen, CEO
Ken Tang, VP
EMP: 68 **EST:** 2014
SALES (est): 1.8MM **Privately Held**
Web: www.ucinnovation.com
SIC: 7379 Computer related consulting services

(P-12901)
UNITED STATES TECHNICAL SVCS
Also Called: Usts
16541 Gothard St Ste 214 (92647-4436)
PHONE..................................714 374-6300
Bob Polk, Pr
John Courtney, *
Cynthia Dugger, *
EMP: 122 **EST:** 1998
SQ FT: 2,500
SALES (est): 10.81MM **Privately Held**
Web: www.usts.com
SIC: 7379 Online services technology consultants

(P-12902)
UNIVERSITY CALIFORNIA BERKELEY
Also Called: Uc Berkeley Comm Network Svcs
2195 Hearst Ave Ste 250 (94720-1083)
PHONE..................................510 642-6000
Diane Perez, Mgr
EMP: 63
SALES (corp-wide): 534.4MM **Privately Held**
Web: www.berkeley.edu
SIC: 7379 8221 9411 Computer related maintenance services; University; Administration of educational programs
HQ: The University California Berkeley
  200 Clfrnia Hall Spc 1500
  Berkeley CA
  510 642-6000

(P-12903)
US DATA MANAGEMENT LLC (PA)
Also Called: Usdm Life Science
535 Chapala St (93101-3411)
PHONE..................................888 231-0816
Kevin Brown, CEO

PRODUCTS & SERVICES SECTION 7381 - Detective And Armored Car Services (P-12925)

Kevin Brown, *Managing Member*
Vega Finucan, *
EMP: 100 **EST:** 2000
SQ FT: 4,000
SALES (est): 17.75MM
SALES (corp-wide): 17.75MM **Privately Held**
Web: www.akanewmedia.com
SIC: 7379 Computer related consulting services

(P-12904)
VERYS LLC
Also Called: Verys
1251 E Dyer Rd Ste 210 (92705-5660)
PHONE..............................949 423-3295
Christopher B Antonius, *CEO*
Mike Alan Zerkel, *Pr*
EMP: 125 **EST:** 2012
SQ FT: 15,500
SALES (est): 13.48MM
SALES (corp-wide): 332.34MM **Privately Held**
Web: www.verys.com
SIC: 7379 7371 7372 Online services technology consultants; Computer software development and applications; Application computer software
PA: West Monroe Partners, Llc
  311 W Monroe St Ste 1400
  Chicago IL
  312 602-4000

(P-12905)
VISIONARY INTGRTION PRFSSNALS (HQ)
Also Called: Visionary Intgrtion Prfssonals
80 Iron Point Cir Ste 100 (95630-8592)
PHONE..............................916 985-9625
Jonna Ward, *CEO*
Patti Bennion, *
Steve Carpenter, *
EMP: 80 **EST:** 2005
SQ FT: 9,000
SALES (est): 53.66MM **Privately Held**
Web: www.trustvip.com
SIC: 7379 8742 Computer related maintenance services; Management consulting services
PA: Visionary Integration Professionals, Inc.
  80 Iron Point Cir Ste 100
  Folsom CA

(P-12906)
WAZUH INC (PA)
1021 Lenor Way (95128-4111)
PHONE..............................844 349-2984
Santiago Gonzalez-bassett, *CEO*
EMP: 145 **EST:** 2015
SALES (est): 4.82MM
SALES (corp-wide): 4.82MM **Privately Held**
Web: www.wazuh.com
SIC: 7379 Computer related consulting services

(P-12907)
WE SEE DRAGONS LLC
1100 Glendon Ave Ste 1700 (90024-3588)
PHONE..............................310 361-5700
Zack Zalon, *Mng Pt*
EMP: 105 **EST:** 2014
SALES (est): 3.74MM **Privately Held**
Web: www.weseedragons.com
SIC: 7379 Computer related maintenance services

(P-12908)
WORK TRUCK SOLUTIONS INC
2485 Notre Dame Blvd Ste 370e (95928-7161)
PHONE..............................855 987-4544
Kathryn Schifferle, *CEO*
EMP: 80 **EST:** 2011
SALES (est): 5.32MM **Privately Held**
Web: www.worktrucksolutions.com
SIC: 7379 Computer related services, nec

(P-12909)
XCOMMERCE INC (HQ)
Also Called: Magento
345 Park Ave (95110-2704)
PHONE..............................310 954-8012
Mark Lavelle, *Pr*
Phillip Depaul, *
▼ **EMP:** 93 **EST:** 2010
SQ FT: 4,000
SALES (est): 95.83MM
SALES (corp-wide): 17.61B **Publicly Held**
SIC: 7379 5961 Online services technology consultants; Catalog sales
PA: Adobe Inc.
  345 Park Ave
  San Jose CA
  408 536-6000

(P-12910)
XORIANT CORPORATION (PA)
Also Called: Xoriant
1248 Reamwood Ave (94089-2225)
PHONE..............................408 743-4400
Sukamal Banerjee, *CEO*
Subu Subramanian; *
Mahesh Nalavade; *
Hari Haran, *CRO*
Nithin V Jaganmohan, *
EMP: 120 **EST:** 1990
SALES (est): 236.48MM **Privately Held**
Web: www.xoriant.com
SIC: 7379 7371 Computer related consulting services; Computer software development

(P-12911)
YAMMER INC
410 Townsend St (94107-1537)
PHONE..............................415 796-7400
EMP: 160 **EST:** 2008
SALES (est): 33.46MM
SALES (corp-wide): 211.91B **Publicly Held**
Web: www.yammer.com
SIC: 7379 Computer related maintenance services
PA: Microsoft Corporation
  1 Microsoft Way
  Redmond WA
  425 882-8080

(P-12912)
ZINIER INC
3182 Campus Dr Ste 333 (94403-3123)
PHONE..............................787 504-4826
Prateek Chakravarty, *CEO*
EMP: 150 **EST:** 2018
SALES (est): 15.38MM **Privately Held**
Web: www.zinier.com
SIC: 7379 Computer related maintenance services

(P-12913)
ZULTYS INC
785 Lucerne Dr (94085-3848)
PHONE..............................408 328-0450
Vladimir Movshovich, *CEO*
David Termondt, *
▲ **EMP:** 60 **EST:** 2006
SQ FT: 20,000
SALES (est): 11.23MM **Privately Held**
Web: www.zultys.com
SIC: 7379 Online services technology consultants

7381 Detective And Armored Car Services

(P-12914)
A1 PROTECTIVE SERVICES INC
5 Thomas Mellon Cir (94134-2501)
PHONE..............................415 467-7200
Paula Jones, *Pr*
EMP: 84 **EST:** 1998
SQ FT: 900
SALES (est): 6.22MM **Privately Held**
Web: www.a1prosecurity.com
SIC: 7381 Security guard service

(P-12915)
A3 SMART HOME LP
Also Called: AAA Smart Home
1277 Treat Blvd Ste 1000 (94597-8863)
PHONE..............................800 669-7779
Dustin Cramer, *Pt*
EMP: 138 **EST:** 1998
SALES (est): 10.5MM **Privately Held**
Web: www.a3smarthome.com
SIC: 7381 Guard services

(P-12916)
ABC SECURITY SERVICE INC
1840 Embarcadero (94606-5220)
P.O. Box 1709 (94604-1709)
PHONE..............................510 436-0666
Ana Chretien, *Pr*
Roger Chretien, *
EMP: 226 **EST:** 1968
SQ FT: 17,000
SALES (est): 11.95MM **Privately Held**
Web: www.abcsecurityservice.us
SIC: 7381 Security guard service

(P-12917)
ABM ONSITE SERVICES INC
3337 Michelson Dr Ste Cn7 (92612-1699)
PHONE..............................949 863-9100
EMP: 914
SALES (corp-wide): 7.81B **Publicly Held**
Web: www.abm.com
SIC: 7381 7521 8711 7349 Security guard service; Automobile parking; Engineering services; Janitorial service, contract basis
HQ: Abm Onsite Services, Inc.
  1 Liberty Plz Fl 7
  New York NY

(P-12918)
ACCESS CONTROL SECURITY INC
2622 W Lincoln Ave Ste 108 (92801-6370)
PHONE..............................714 826-3800
Reza Jalala, *Brnch Mgr*
EMP: 73
Web: www.accesscontrolsecurity.com
SIC: 7381 Security guard service
PA: Access Control Security, Inc.
  21049 Devonshire St # 211
  Chatsworth CA

(P-12919)
AEGIS SEC & INVESTIGATIONS INC
10866 Washington Blvd Ste 308 (90232-3610)
PHONE..............................310 838-2787
Jeffrey Nathaniel Zisner, *CEO*
EMP: 102 **EST:** 2010
SALES (est): 9.3MM **Privately Held**
Web: www.aegis.com
SIC: 7381 Security guard service

(P-12920)
AIRBORNE SECURITY PATROL INC
9462 Rush Creek Ct (95624-6077)
PHONE..............................916 599-8120
Kathleen Mccown, *Brnch Mgr*
EMP: 71
SALES (corp-wide): 1.57MM **Privately Held**
Web: www.airbornesecuritypatrol.com
SIC: 7381 Security guard service
PA: Airborne Security Patrol, Inc.
  10481 Grant Line Rd # 175
  Elk Grove CA
  916 394-2400

(P-12921)
ALL PHASE SECURITY INC
Also Called: Sj Lighting
2959 Promenade St Ste 200 (95691-6400)
P.O. Box 980363 (95798-0363)
PHONE..............................916 919-3859
EMP: 88 **EST:** 1994
SQ FT: 8,000
SALES (est): 3.81MM
SALES (corp-wide): 12.86B **Privately Held**
Web: www.allphasesecurity.com
SIC: 7381 Security guard service
HQ: Universal Protection Service, Lp
  545 Sansome St
  San Francisco CA
  866 877-1965

(P-12922)
ALLIED PROTECTION SERVICES INC
Also Called: Armed/Xctive Prtction Armed Un
24303 Berendo Ave (90710-1839)
PHONE..............................310 330-8314
Leon Brooks, *Pr*
EMP: 178 **EST:** 1999
SALES (est): 7.13MM **Privately Held**
Web: www.alliedprotection.com
SIC: 7381 Security guard service

(P-12923)
ALLIED UNIVERSAL
533 Airport Blvd Ste 303 (94010-2040)
PHONE..............................650 223-3221
Peter Daskalakis, *Prin*
EMP: 76 **EST:** 2018
SALES (est): 155.65K **Privately Held**
Web: www.aus.com
SIC: 7381 Security guard service

(P-12924)
ALLIED UNIVERSAL TOPCO LLC
5308 Pacific Ave (95207-5613)
PHONE..............................209 472-0455
EMP: 5002
SALES (corp-wide): 8.78B **Privately Held**
SIC: 7381 Security guard service
HQ: Allied Universal Topco Llc
  450 Exchange Ste 100
  Irvine CA
  714 619-9700

(P-12925)
AMERICAN EGLE PRTCTIVE SVCS IN
Also Called: American Eagle Protective Svcs
425 W Kelso St (90301-2539)
PHONE..............................310 412-0019
Joelle Fopoussi Epoh, *CEO*
Alma Serrano, *
EMP: 90 **EST:** 2011
SALES (est): 2.33MM **Privately Held**
Web: www.aeprotectiveservices.com

7381 - Detective And Armored Car Services (P-12926)

SIC: 7381 Security guard service

(P-12926)
AMERICAN GUARD SERVICES INC (PA)
1125 W 190th St (90248-4303)
PHONE...............................310 645-6200
Sherine Assal, Pr
EMP: 400 EST: 1997
SQ FT: 28,000
SALES (est): 97.91MM
SALES (corp-wide): 97.91MM Privately Held
Web: www.americanguardservices.com
SIC: 7381 Security guard service

(P-12927)
AMERICAN POWER SEC SVC INC
1451 Rimpau Ave Ste 207 (92879-7522)
PHONE...............................866 974-9994
Mohamed Faty, Pr
EMP: 85 EST: 2015
SALES (est): 550K Privately Held
Web: www.americanpowersecurity.com
SIC: 7381 Security guard service

(P-12928)
AMERICAN PROTECTION GROUP INC (PA)
Also Called: Apg
8741 Van Nuys Blvd Ste 202 (91402-2440)
PHONE...............................818 279-2433
Anthony Brown, Pr
EMP: 107 EST: 2012
SALES (est): 5.4MM
SALES (corp-wide): 5.4MM Privately Held
Web: www.apg-svcs.com
SIC: 7381 5063 7382 Security guard service; Alarm systems, nec; Burglar alarm maintenance and monitoring

(P-12929)
AMERICAN PRTCTIVE SVCS INVSTGT
12471 Balsam Rd (92395-9474)
P.O. Box 4640 (91765-0640)
PHONE...............................626 705-8600
Allan Bailey, Pr
EMP: 225 EST: 1998
SALES (est): 2.43MM Privately Held
SIC: 7381 Security guard service

(P-12930)
ANDREWS INTERNATIONAL INC
Also Called: Vance Executive Protection
11601 Wilshire Blvd Ste 500 (90025-0509)
PHONE...............................310 575-4844
Rocco Barnes, Dir
EMP: 371
SALES (corp-wide): 251B Privately Held
SIC: 7381 Security guard service
HQ: Andrews International, Inc.
5870 Trinity Pkwy Ste 300
Centreville VA
703 592-1400

(P-12931)
ANDREWS INTERNATIONAL INC (DH)
455 N Moss St (91502-1727)
PHONE...............................818 487-4060
Randy Andrews, Pr
Roger Andrews, VP
Michael Topf, CFO
Ty Richmond, COO
James Wood, COO
EMP: 1700 EST: 1986

SQ FT: 5,000
SALES (est): 108.53MM
SALES (corp-wide): 251B Privately Held
Web: www.andrewsinternational.com
SIC: 7381 Security guard service
HQ: Allied Security Holdings Llc
161 Washington St Ste 600
Conshohocken PA
484 351-1300

(P-12932)
ARMED GUARD PRIVATE SEC INC
50 Landing Cir (95973-7873)
PHONE...............................530 751-3218
Adam Stricker, CEO
EMP: 60 EST: 2018
SALES (est): 2.22MM Privately Held
Web: www.armedguard.net
SIC: 7381 Security guard service

(P-12933)
ARMOROUS
3550 Round Barn Blvd Ste 313 (95403-0922)
PHONE...............................707 387-4400
Eric Hanson, Pr
EMP: 96 EST: 2018
SALES (est): 6MM Privately Held
Web: www.armorous.com
SIC: 7381 Security guard service

(P-12934)
ASSET PRIVATE SECURITY INC
36 Quail Run Cir Unit 100 (93907-2351)
PHONE...............................831 809-9779
Jay A Agamao, CEO
Jorge Sareli, CFO
Allan Tucker, COO
EMP: 65 EST: 2013
SALES (est): 2.39MM
SALES (corp-wide): 2.48MM Privately Held
Web: www.assetsecinc.com
SIC: 7381 Security guard service
PA: Jpt Group Inc.
1735 Tech Dr Ste 720
San Jose CA

(P-12935)
ATI SYSTEMS INTERNATIONAL INC
8807 Complex Dr (92123-1403)
PHONE...............................858 715-8484
Tony Vasquez, Brnch Mgr
EMP: 5038
SALES (corp-wide): 175.11MM Privately Held
Web: www.garda.com
SIC: 7381 Detective and armored car services
HQ: Ati Systems International, Inc.
2000 Nw Corp Blvd Ste 101
Boca Raton FL
561 939-7000

(P-12936)
ATLAS OPERATIONS GROUP ◆
240 N Main St Ste 388 (96101-4047)
PHONE...............................844 414-2857
Justin Quinn, CEO
EMP: 85 EST: 2022
SALES (est): 2.18MM Privately Held
Web: www.atlasoperationsgroup.com
SIC: 7381 Security guard service

(P-12937)
BABYLON SECURITY SERVICES INC

6032 One Half Vineland Ave (91606)
PHONE...............................818 766-8122
Arvin Younan, Prin
EMP: 85 EST: 1997
SALES (est): 2MM Privately Held
SIC: 7381 Security guard service

(P-12938)
BARBIER SECURITY GROUP
20 Galli Dr # 9-10 (94949-5735)
PHONE...............................415 747-8473
Harry Evan Barbier, Pr
EMP: 150 EST: 2011
SALES (est): 10.82MM Privately Held
Web: www.barbiersecuritygroup.com
SIC: 7381 Security guard service

(P-12939)
BARRYS SECURITY SERVICES INC (PA)
16739 Van Buren Blvd (92504-5744)
PHONE...............................951 789-7575
Michelle Barry, CEO
Martin Morales, *
EMP: 188 EST: 1999
SQ FT: 5,000
SALES (est): 9.82MM
SALES (corp-wide): 9.82MM Privately Held
Web: www.weguard.biz
SIC: 7381 Security guard service

(P-12940)
BOYD AND ASSOCIATES
445 E Esplanade Dr Ste 210 (93036-2126)
PHONE...............................805 988-8298
Kathy Correll, Mgr
EMP: 80
SALES (corp-wide): 14.27MM Privately Held
Web: www.boydsecurity.com
SIC: 7381 Security guard service
PA: Boyd And Associates
2191 E Thompson Blvd
Ventura CA
818 752-1888

(P-12941)
BOYD AND ASSOCIATES (PA)
2191 E Thompson Blvd (93001-3538)
PHONE...............................818 752-1888
Raymond G Boyd Senior, Ch Bd
Barbara K Boyd, *
Daniel Boyd, *
EMP: 160 EST: 1967
SQ FT: 8,000
SALES (est): 14.27MM
SALES (corp-wide): 14.27MM Privately Held
Web: www.boydsecurity.com
SIC: 7381 7382 Security guard service; Security systems services

(P-12942)
BRINKS INCORPORATED
Also Called: Brink's
7191 Patterson Dr (92841-1415)
PHONE...............................714 903-9272
Al Kent, Mgr
EMP: 120
SALES (corp-wide): 4.54B Publicly Held
Web: us.brinks.com
SIC: 7381 Armored car services
HQ: Brink's, Incorporated
1801 Bayberry Ct Ste 400
Richmond VA
804 289-9600

(P-12943)
CALIFRNIA SUTHLAND PRIVATE SEC
1818 S State College Blvd (92806-6053)
PHONE...............................714 367-4005
Alessandro Hickey, CEO
Alessandro Hickey, Managing Member
Juan Arevalo, *
Joesph Fasano, *
EMP: 200 EST: 2019
SALES (est): 3.45MM Privately Held
Web: www.californiasouthlandinc.com
SIC: 7381 Security guard service

(P-12944)
CITIGUARD INC
22736 Vanowen St Ste 300 (91307-2656)
PHONE...............................800 613-5903
Sammy Nomir, Pr
EMP: 475 EST: 2015
SALES (est): 18.32MM Privately Held
Web: www.mysecurityguards.com
SIC: 7381 Security guard service

(P-12945)
COMMERCIAL PROTECTIVE SVCS INC
Also Called: CPS Security
17215 Studebaker Rd Ste 205 (90703-2523)
PHONE...............................310 515-5290
Christopher Coffey, Pr
William R Babcock, *
EMP: 1800 EST: 1997
SALES (est): 46.16MM Privately Held
SIC: 7381 Security guard service

(P-12946)
COMMUNITY PATROL INC
1420 E Edinger Ave Ste 213 (92705-4816)
PHONE...............................657 247-4744
Alicia Ledesma, Owner
EMP: 90 EST: 2019
SALES (est): 2.29MM Privately Held
SIC: 7381 Security guard service

(P-12947)
COMPREHENSIVE SEC SVCS INC (PA)
10535 E Stockton Blvd Ste G (95624-9758)
P.O. Box 246719 (95824-6719)
PHONE...............................916 683-3605
Bashir A Choudry, Pr
Jamal-eddine Kabbaj, Ex VP
EMP: 75 EST: 1989
SQ FT: 3,300
SALES (est): 15.85MM Privately Held
Web: www.comprehensivesecurity.net
SIC: 7381 7382 Security guard service; Security systems services

(P-12948)
CONSTRUCTION PROTECTIVE SERVICES INC (PA)
Also Called: Commercial Protective Services
436 W Walnut St (90248-3137)
PHONE...............................800 257-5512
EMP: 700 EST: 1992
SALES (est): 51.88MM Privately Held
Web: www.garda.com
SIC: 7381 7382 Security guard service; Confinement surveillance systems maintenance and monitoring

(P-12949)
CONTEMPORARY SERVICES CORP (PA)
Also Called: C S C

PRODUCTS & SERVICES SECTION
7381 - Detective And Armored Car Services (P-12972)

17101 Superior St (91325-1961)
PHONE.....................818 885-5150
Damon Zumwalt, CEO
Jim Granger, *
▲ EMP: 514 EST: 1972
SQ FT: 20,000
SALES (est): 297.45MM
SALES (corp-wide): 297.45MM Privately Held
Web: www.csc-usa.com
SIC: 7381 Security guard service

(P-12950)
COOKE & ASSOCIATES INC
4101 Dublin Blvd Ste F Pmb 337 (94568-4603)
PHONE.....................408 842-0602
Harry Arruda, CEO
EMP: 450 EST: 2003
SALES (est): 6.72MM Privately Held
Web: www.cookepi.com
SIC: 7381 6211 Protective services, guard; Securities flotation companies

(P-12951)
CORNERSTONE PROTECTIVE SVCS
400 Continental Blvd Ste 6056 (90245-5076)
PHONE.....................888 848-4791
Maxwell Okoh, CEO
EMP: 200 EST: 2020
SALES (est): 2.49MM Privately Held
SIC: 7381 Detective and armored car services

(P-12952)
CORPORATE SECURITY SERVICE INC
901 Mission St Ste 80b (94103-3168)
PHONE.....................415 626-9271
Joseph Mc Reynolds, CEO
Judy Mc Reynolds, *
Ave Seltsam, *
EMP: 150 EST: 1976
SALES (est): 3.56MM Privately Held
Web: www.csssecurity.com
SIC: 7381 Security guard service

(P-12953)
COTTRELL PAUL ENTERPRISES LLC (PA)
Also Called: Unique Protective Services
16654 Soledad Canyon Rd Ste 233 (91387-3217)
PHONE.....................661 212-2357
Paul Cottrell, Managing Member
EMP: 120 EST: 1997
SQ FT: 400
SALES (est): 3.02MM Privately Held
SIC: 7381 Security guard service

(P-12954)
COURTESY SECURITY INC
Also Called: Securelion Security
2252 Erie Ct (95304-5803)
PHONE.....................888 572-5545
Ajmal Boomwal, Prin
EMP: 60 EST: 2016
SALES (est): 1.2MM Privately Held
Web: www.securelionsecurity.com
SIC: 7381 Security guard service

(P-12955)
COVENANT AVIATION SECURITY LLC
1000 Marina Blvd Ste 100 (94005-1839)
P.O. Box 280440 (94128-0440)
PHONE.....................650 219-3473
EMP: 635
SALES (corp-wide): 49.39MM Privately Held
Web: www.covenantsecurity.com
SIC: 7381 Security guard service
HQ: Covenant Aviation Security, Llc
156 Tamarack Ave
Naperville IL
630 771-0800

(P-12956)
CPS SECURITY SOLUTIONS INC
799 Fletcher Ln Ste 201 (94544-1057)
PHONE.....................510 806-7227
EMP: 288
SIC: 7381 Security guard service
PA: Cps Security Solutions, Inc.
17215 Studebaker Rd # 205
Cerritos CA

(P-12957)
CREATIVE SECURITY COMPANY INC
150 Barack Obama Blvd Ste B (95110-2516)
PHONE.....................408 295-2600
Charles Wall, Pr
Brian Wall, *
Mike Mattocks, INVESTIGATIONS*
EMP: 350 EST: 1999
SQ FT: 12,000
SALES (est): 22.28MM Privately Held
Web: www.creativesecurity.com
SIC: 7381 Security guard service

(P-12958)
CRIMETEK SECURITY INC
Also Called: Crimetek
3448 N Golden State Blvd Ste G (95382-9709)
P.O. Box 845 (95381-0845)
PHONE.....................209 668-6208
Edward Esmaili, Pr
Ed Esmaili, Pt
Rosy Esmaili, Pt
EMP: 160 EST: 1999
SQ FT: 2,200
SALES (est): 10.55MM Privately Held
Web: www.crimetek.com
SIC: 7381 Security guard service

(P-12959)
CROSSING GUARD COMPANY
10440 Pioneer Blvd Ste 5 (90670-8238)
PHONE.....................310 202-8284
EMP: 1762 EST: 2011
SALES (est): 170.58K
SALES (corp-wide): 47.91MM Privately Held
Web: www.thecrossingguardcompany.com
SIC: 7381 Guard services
PA: All-City Management Services, Inc.
10440 Pioneer Blvd Ste 5
Santa Fe Springs CA
310 202-8284

(P-12960)
CYPRESS PRIVATE SECURITY LP (DH)
478 Tehama St (94103-4141)
P.O. Box 1322 (94957-1322)
PHONE.....................866 345-1277
Kes Narbutas, CEO
EMP: 100 EST: 1996
SQ FT: 3,500
SALES (est): 32.35MM
SALES (corp-wide): 12.86B Privately Held
Web: www.cypress-security.com
SIC: 7381 Security guard service
HQ: Universal Services Of America, Lp
450 Exchange
Irvine CA
866 877-1965

(P-12961)
CYPRESS PRIVATE SECURITY LP
9926 Pioneer Blvd Ste 106 (90670-6243)
PHONE.....................562 222-4197
Kes Narbutas, CEO
EMP: 75
SALES (corp-wide): 12.86B Privately Held
Web: www.cypress-security.com
SIC: 7381 Security guard service
HQ: Cypress Private Security, Lp
478 Tehama St
San Francisco CA
866 345-1277

(P-12962)
CYPRESS SECURITY LLC
Also Called: Cypress Private Security
1762 Tech Dr Ste 122 (95110)
PHONE.....................408 217-6063
Jason Berckart, Managing Member
EMP: 75
SALES (corp-wide): 12.86B Privately Held
Web: www.cypress-security.com
SIC: 7381 Security guard service
HQ: Cypress Private Security, Lp
478 Tehama St
San Francisco CA
866 345-1277

(P-12963)
DAVID SHIELD SECURITY INC
Also Called: Dss
23945 Calabasas Rd Ste 102 (91302-1503)
PHONE.....................310 849-4950
Athan Bazaz, Pr
Snir Warshaziak, *
EMP: 100 EST: 2015
SALES (est): 5MM Privately Held
Web: www.davidshieldsecurity.com
SIC: 7381 Security guard service

(P-12964)
DELTA PERSONNEL SERVICES INC
Also Called: Guardian Security Agency
1820 Galindo St Ste 3 (94520-2416)
PHONE.....................925 356-3034
Judith Travers, CEO
Heather Travers, *
EMP: 80 EST: 1983
SQ FT: 4,300
SALES (est): 8.79MM Privately Held
Web: www.guardiansecurityagency.com
SIC: 7381 Security guard service

(P-12965)
DIPLOMATIC SECURITY SVCS LLC
7581 Etiwanda Ave (91739)
PHONE.....................909 463-8409
EMP: 99 EST: 2014
SQ FT: 1,500
SALES (est): 784.5K Privately Held
SIC: 7381 Security guard service

(P-12966)
DREW CHAIN SECURITY CORP
55 S Raymond Ave Ste 303 (91801-7100)
PHONE.....................626 457-8626
Kenneth Y Lee, Pr
EMP: 71 EST: 2004
SQ FT: 800
SALES (est): 4.4MM Privately Held
Web: www.drewchain.com
SIC: 7381 Security guard service

(P-12967)
EAGLE SECURITY SERVICES INC
12903 S Normandie Ave (90249-2123)
PHONE.....................310 642-0656
Mohsen Kamel, Pr
EMP: 150 EST: 2003
SQ FT: 5,000
SALES (est): 6.22MM Privately Held
Web: www.eagless.com
SIC: 7381 Security guard service

(P-12968)
ELITE ENFRCMENT SEC SLTONS INC
29970 Technology Dr Ste 117d (92563-2645)
PHONE.....................866 354-8308
Kevin Roncevich, Brnch Mgr
EMP: 112
SALES (corp-wide): 4.62MM Privately Held
SIC: 7381 Security guard service
PA: Elite Enforcement Security Solutions, Inc.
1290 N Hancock St Ste 101
Anaheim CA
866 354-8308

(P-12969)
ELITE SHOW SERVICES INC
2878 Camino Del Rio S Ste 260 (92108)
PHONE.....................619 574-1589
John Kontopuls, CEO
John Kontopuls, Pr
Gus Kontopuls, *
EMP: 3123 EST: 1995
SALES (est): 91.02MM Privately Held
Web: www.elitesecuritystaffing.com
SIC: 7381 Security guard service

(P-12970)
FIRST ALARM SEC & PATROL INC
1240 Briggs Ave (95401-4760)
PHONE.....................707 584-1110
EMP: 319
Web: www.firstalarm.com
SIC: 7381 Security guard service
PA: First Alarm Security & Patrol, Inc.
1731 Tech Dr Ste 800
San Jose CA

(P-12971)
FIRST TEAM SECURITY INC
1038 Harrison Ave (90291-5023)
PHONE.....................310 709-4921
Clarence Julius Carter, Brnch Mgr
EMP: 66
SALES (corp-wide): 396.66K Privately Held
Web: www.firstteamsecurity.com
SIC: 7381 Security guard service
PA: First Team Security Inc.
171 Pier Ave Ste 385
Santa Monica CA
310 714-6632

(P-12972)
FIRSTCALL (PA)
Also Called: Steele Corp SEC Advisory Svcs
1 Salmon St Ste 3500 (94104-4436)
PHONE.....................415 781-4300
▼ EMP: 138 EST: 1989
SQ FT: 5,000

7381 - Detective And Armored Car Services (P-12973)

SALES (est): 49.08MM **Privately Held**
Web: www.firstcallcss.com
SIC: **7381** 8742 8748 Security guard service; Management consulting services; Agricultural consultant

(P-12973)
FPK SECURITY INC
Also Called: Fpk Investigaions
28348 Constellation Rd Ste 880 (91355-5097)
P.O. Box 55597 (91385-0597)
PHONE..................661 702-9091
Mark David, *CEO*
Robert Esquivel, *
EMP: 365 EST: 2005
SQ FT: 1,200
SALES (est): 10.87MM **Privately Held**
Web: www.fpksecurity.com
SIC: **7381** Security guard service

(P-12974)
FRASCO INC (PA)
Also Called: Frasco Investigative Services
215 W Alameda Ave (91502-2555)
PHONE..................818 848-3888
John C Simmers, *Pr*
Richard Smith, *
Noelle Harling, *
Mary Elterman, *Corporate Secretary**
Jason Simmers, *
EMP: 65 EST: 1964
SQ FT: 10,000
SALES (est): 23.88MM
SALES (corp-wide): 23.88MM **Privately Held**
Web: www.frasco.com
SIC: **7381** Private investigator

(P-12975)
GARDA CL WEST INC (HQ)
Also Called: Gcl W
1612 W Pico Blvd (90015-2410)
PHONE..................213 383-3611
Stephan Cretier, *Pr*
Chris W Jamroz, *
▲ EMP: 375 EST: 2015
SQ FT: 25,000
SALES (est): 290.58MM
SALES (corp-wide): 726.35MM **Privately Held**
SIC: **7381** Security guard service
PA: Gardaworld Cash Services, Inc.
2000 Nw Corporate Blvd
Boca Raton FL
561 939-7000

(P-12976)
GARDA WORLD SECURITY CORP
Also Called: GARDA WORLD SECURITY CORP
20325 E Walnut Dr N (91789-2916)
PHONE..................909 468-2229
EMP: 102
SALES (corp-wide): 11.59MM **Privately Held**
Web: www.garda.com
SIC: **7381** Armored car services
PA: Gardaworld
2000 Nw Corporate Blvd
Boca Raton FL
561 939-7000

(P-12977)
GEIL ENTERPRISES INC
Also Called: CIS Security
1945 N Helm Ave Ste 102 (93727-1670)
PHONE..................559 495-3000
Sam Geil, *Ch*
Ryan Geil, *
EMP: 540 EST: 1986
SQ FT: 10,000
SALES (est): 28.15MM **Privately Held**
Web: www.geilenterprises.com
SIC: **7381** 7349 Protective services, guard; Janitorial service, contract basis

(P-12978)
GLOBAL RISK SOLUTIONS INC
2100 Geng Rd Ste 210 (94303-3307)
P.O. Box 1787 (94505-7787)
PHONE..................888 981-9484
Mena Ghali, *CEO*
Jessica Ghali, *
EMP: 85 EST: 2018
SALES (est): 3.46MM **Privately Held**
Web: www.grsprotection.com
SIC: **7381** Security guard service

(P-12979)
GOLDEN WEST SECURITY
Also Called: Golden West K-9
12502 Van Nuys Blvd Ste 215 (91331-1321)
PHONE..................818 897-5965
Chris Monica, *CEO*
Ralf Santarelli, *Pr*
EMP: 120 EST: 1971
SALES (est): 2.49MM **Privately Held**
Web: www.goldenwestsecurityinc.com
SIC: **7381** Security guard service

(P-12980)
GSG PROTECTIVE SERVICES CA INC
15901 Hawthorne Blvd Ste 324 (90278)
PHONE..................310 371-5300
Marks Victor, *Prin*
EMP: 182 EST: 2014
SALES (est): 2.57MM **Privately Held**
SIC: **7381** Security guard service

(P-12981)
GUARD MANAGEMENT INC
Also Called: G M I
8001 Vickers St (92111-1917)
PHONE..................858 279-8282
Larry Abrams, *Pr*
EMP: 154 EST: 1992
SALES (est): 8.38MM **Privately Held**
Web: www.aus.com
SIC: **7381** Security guard service

(P-12982)
GUARD-SYSTEMS INC
1910 S Archibald Ave Ste M2 (91761-8502)
PHONE..................909 947-5400
Patrick Crawford, *Mgr*
EMP: 567
SALES (corp-wide): 15.51MM **Privately Held**
Web: www.guardsystemsinc.com
SIC: **7381** Protective services, guard
PA: Guard-Systems, Inc.
1190 Monterey Pass Rd
Monterey Park CA
626 443-0031

(P-12983)
GUARD-SYSTEMS INC
Also Called: Guard Systems District 1
1190 Monterey Pass Rd (91754-3615)
PHONE..................323 881-6715
Theodore Haas, *Owner*
EMP: 568
SALES (corp-wide): 15.51MM **Privately Held**
Web: www.guardsystemsinc.com
SIC: **7381** Security guard service
PA: Guard-Systems, Inc.
1190 Monterey Pass Rd
Monterey Park CA
626 443-0031

(P-12984)
GUARDIAN INTL SOLUTIONS
Also Called: Patrol and Security Services
3415 S Sepulveda Blvd Ste 1100 (90034-6060)
PHONE..................323 528-6555
Rodney Finnell, *CEO*
EMP: 95 EST: 2017
SALES (est): 2.7MM **Privately Held**
SIC: **7381** Security guard service

(P-12985)
GUARDSMARK LLC (DH)
1551 N Tustin Ave Ste 650 (92705-8664)
PHONE..................714 619-9700
Steven S Jones, *CEO*
EMP: 98 EST: 2002
SQ FT: 32,107
SALES (est): 195.15MM
SALES (corp-wide): 12.86B **Privately Held**
SIC: **7381** 8742 2721 Security guard service; Industry specialist consultants; Periodicals, publishing only
HQ: Universal Protection Service, Lp
545 Sansome St
San Francisco CA
866 877-1965

(P-12986)
HAYES PROTECTIVE SERVICES INC
2930 W Imperial Hwy 200b (90303-3143)
P.O. Box 4684 (90749-4684)
PHONE..................323 755-2282
Berlin Hayes, *Pr*
EMP: 210 EST: 1986
SALES (est): 4.09MM **Privately Held**
SIC: **7381** Security guard service

(P-12987)
HIGHCOM SECURITY SERVICES
1900 Webster St Ste B (94612-2946)
PHONE..................510 893-7600
Sammy Joselewitz, *Pr*
EMP: 60 EST: 2005
SALES (est): 4.37MM **Privately Held**
Web: www.highcomsecurityservices.com
SIC: **7381** 8742 Security guard service; Management consulting services

(P-12988)
HORSEMEN INC
16911 Algonquin St (92649-3812)
PHONE..................714 847-4243
Patrick Carroll, *Pr*
EMP: 100 EST: 1995
SALES (est): 7.16MM **Privately Held**
Web: www.horsemeninc.com
SIC: **7381** Private investigator

(P-12989)
INTER-CON SECURITY SYSTEMS INC (PA)
210 S De Lacey Ave (91105-2048)
PHONE..................626 535-2200
Enrique Hernandez Junior, *Ch Bd*
Roland A Hernandez, *
EMP: 19885 EST: 1973
SQ FT: 17,000
SALES (est): 362.19MM
SALES (corp-wide): 362.19MM **Privately Held**
Web: www.icsecurity.com

(P-12990)
IUNLIMITED INCORPORATED
7801 Folsom Blvd Ste 203 (95826-2620)
P.O. Box 276390 (95827-6390)
PHONE..................916 218-6198
Todd M Tano, *CEO*
Keith Jacobs, *
Jeff Walters, *Chief Business Officer**
EMP: 115 EST: 2006
SALES (est): 12.78MM
SALES (corp-wide): 31.64MM **Privately Held**
Web: www.registrar-transfers.com
SIC: **7381** Private investigator
PA: Insight Service Group, Inc.
55 Ferncroft Rd Ste 300
Danvers MA
800 278-0550

(P-12991)
J WATERS INC
Also Called: Achates Security
75 San Miguel Ave Ste 5 (93901-3059)
PHONE..................866 424-1946
Kristine Waters, *Brnch Mgr*
EMP: 65
SALES (corp-wide): 4.65MM **Privately Held**
SIC: **7381** Armored car services
PA: J. Waters, Inc.
10000 Ne 7th St
Vancouver WA
831 424-1946

(P-12992)
J&E PRIVATE SECURITY CORP
3227 Producer Way Ste 110 (91768-3919)
PHONE..................909 594-1111
Megan Hsu, *Sec*
Edwin Inocencio, *CFO*
EMP: 60 EST: 2016
SALES (est): 1.7MM **Privately Held**
Web: www.jeprivatesecurity.com
SIC: **7381** Security guard service

(P-12993)
LANDMARK EVENT STAFFING
4790 Irvine Blvd Ste 105 (92620-1998)
PHONE..................714 293-4248
Peter Kranske, *Pr*
EMP: 1259
Web: www.aus.com
SIC: **7381** Security guard service
PA: Landmark Event Staffing Services, Inc.
4131 Harbor Walk Dr
Fort Collins CO

(P-12994)
LANTZ SECURITY SYSTEMS INC
101 N Westlake Blvd Ste 200 (91362-3753)
PHONE..................805 496-5775
Terry Oestreich, *Mgr*
EMP: 147
Web: www.lantzsecurity.com
SIC: **7381** 7382 Security guard service; Security systems services
PA: Lantz Security Systems, Inc.
43440 Sahuayo St
Lancaster CA

(P-12995)
LANTZ SECURITY SYSTEMS INC (PA)
Also Called: Lantz Security
43440 Sahuayo St (93535-4659)
PHONE..................661 949-3565
Jack E Lantz, *Pr*
Jose Reyes, *

PRODUCTS & SERVICES SECTION
7381 - Detective And Armored Car Services (P-13019)

EMP: 60 EST: 1994
SQ FT: 2,100
SALES (est): 22.09MM Privately Held
Web: www.lantzsecurity.com
SIC: 7381 Security guard service

(P-12996)
LAO-HMONG SECURITY AGENCY INC
10682 Trask Ave (92843-2407)
PHONE..................714 533-6776
Mouasu Bliaya, Pr
George Moua, *
EMP: 100 EST: 1981
SALES (est): 2.41MM Privately Held
Web: www.l-hsa.com
SIC: 7381 Security guard service

(P-12997)
LEAD STAR SECURITY INC
937 Enterprise Dr (95825-3901)
PHONE..................916 971-6218
Brian Clay, CEO
EMP: 100 EST: 2018
SALES (est): 5.4MM Privately Held
Web: www.leadstarsecurity.com
SIC: 7381 Security guard service

(P-12998)
LOCATOR SERVICES INC
Also Called: Able Patrol & Guard
4616 Mission Gorge Pl (92120-4133)
PHONE..................619 229-6100
George Grauer, Pr
Diane G Edwards, *
George Grauer Junior, VP
Deborah L Kopki, *
EMP: 120 EST: 1964
SQ FT: 4,500
SALES (est): 7.92MM Privately Held
Web: www.ablepatrolandguard.com
SIC: 7381 Security guard service

(P-12999)
M & S SECURITY SERVICES INC
Also Called: Westside Security Patrol
2900 L St (93301-2351)
PHONE..................661 397-9616
Marvin Fuller Senior, CEO
Steve Fuller, *
Darlene Fuller, *
EMP: 100 EST: 1972
SQ FT: 3,000
SALES (est): 5MM Privately Held
Web: www.mssecurityservices.com
SIC: 7381 7382 1731 Protective services, guard; Security systems services; Fire detection and burglar alarm systems specialization

(P-13000)
MARINA SECURITY SERVICES INC
465 California St Ste 626 (94104-1816)
PHONE..................415 773-2300
Sam Tadesse, CEO
EMP: 275 EST: 1997
SALES (est): 7.69MM Privately Held
Web: www.marinasecurityservices.com
SIC: 7381 Security guard service

(P-13001)
MASTER LIGHTNING SEC SOLUTIONS
Also Called: Master Lightning SEC Solutions
545 N Mountain Ave Ste 207 (91786-5073)
PHONE..................626 337-2915
Peter Suaez, Prin
EMP: 70 EST: 2011

SALES (est): 4.84MM Privately Held
Web: www.mlsscorp.com
SIC: 7381 Security guard service

(P-13002)
MULHOLLAND SEC & PATROL INC
Also Called: Centurion Group, The
11454 San Vicente Blvd (90049-6208)
PHONE..................818 755-0202
David Rosenberg, Pr
Steven Lemmer, *
Daniel Campbell, *
EMP: 350 EST: 1992
SQ FT: 2,500
SALES (est): 15.72MM Privately Held
Web: www.centuriongroup.com
SIC: 7381 Protective services, guard

(P-13003)
MULHOLLAND SECURITY CTRS LLC
Also Called: Mulholland Brand
21260 Deering Ct (91304-5015)
PHONE..................818 983-9206
EMP: 65 EST: 2018
SALES (est): 3.61MM Privately Held
Web: www.mulhollandbrand.com
SIC: 7381 Detective and armored car services

(P-13004)
NAFEES MEMON
Also Called: Nafees Mmon Cmmand Intl SEC Sv
6819 Sepulveda Blvd Ste 312 (91405-4463)
PHONE..................818 997-1666
Nafees Memon, Owner
EMP: 90 EST: 2008
SQ FT: 700
SALES (est): 3MM Privately Held
Web: www.commandinternational.com
SIC: 7381 Security guard service

(P-13005)
NASTEC INTERNATIONAL INC
23875 Ventura Blvd Ste 204 (91302-1420)
PHONE..................818 222-0355
Shiraya Ben-menahem, Ex Dir
Shiraya Honig, *
▼ EMP: 100 EST: 1994
SQ FT: 3,109
SALES (est): 5.99MM Privately Held
Web: www.nastec.com
SIC: 7381 1731 6411 Detective services; Safety and security specialization; Inspection and investigation services, insurance

(P-13006)
NATIONAL SECURITY INDUSTRIES
Also Called: National Security Santa Cruz
501 Mission St Ste 1a (95060-3661)
PHONE..................831 425-2052
James Clarke, Brnch Mgr
EMP: 253
Web: www.registrar-transfers.com
SIC: 7381 Security guard service
PA: National Security Industries
940 Park Ave Frnt Frnt
San Jose CA

(P-13007)
NATIONWIDE GUARD SERVICES INC
9327 Fairway View Pl Ste 200 (91730)
PHONE..................909 608-1112

EMP: 325 EST: 1984
SALES (est): 10.54MM Privately Held
Web: www.nwguards.com
SIC: 7381 Security guard service

(P-13008)
NORTH AMRCN SEC INVESTIGATIONS
550 E Carson Plaza Dr Ste 222 (90746-3229)
PHONE..................323 634-1911
Kenny Hillman, Pr
Arthur Lopez, *
EMP: 100 EST: 2004
SQ FT: 6,000
SALES (est): 2.22MM Privately Held
Web: www.nasi-pi.com
SIC: 7381 Security guard service

(P-13009)
OFF DUTY OFFICERS INC
2365 La Mirada Dr (92081-7863)
PHONE..................888 408-5900
EMP: 1300 EST: 1993
SQ FT: 4,000
SALES (est): 38.84MM Privately Held
Web: www.offdutyofficers.com
SIC: 7381 8742 Security guard service; Management consulting services

(P-13010)
OLINN SECURITY INCORPORATED
1027 S Palm Canyon Dr (92264-8378)
PHONE..................760 320-5303
Kimberly Olinn, CEO
Kimberly S Olinn, *
EMP: 130 EST: 1985
SALES (est): 4.1MM Privately Held
Web: www.olinnsecurityinc.com
SIC: 7381 Security guard service

(P-13011)
ONTEL SECURITY SERVICES INC
2125 Wylie Dr Ste 11 (95355-3847)
P.O. Box 579730 (95357-9730)
PHONE..................209 521-0200
David Ackerman, CEO
Roberta Gray, *
Michael Ackerman, *
David Mccann, COO
EMP: 71 EST: 2006
SQ FT: 2,500
SALES (est): 3.44MM Privately Held
Web: www.ontelsecurity.com
SIC: 7381 Security guard service

(P-13012)
OPSEC SPECIALIZED PROTECTION
44262 Division St Ste A (93535-3548)
PHONE..................661 942-3999
Fred Porras, Owner
Jeannie Groff, *
EMP: 99 EST: 2001
SALES (est): 2.43MM Privately Held
Web: www.opsecpro.com
SIC: 7381 Security guard service

(P-13013)
ORION SECURITY PATROL INC
Also Called: Orion Security Patrol
675 E Gish Rd (95112-2708)
PHONE..................408 287-4411
Yooshieh Gahramani, Pr
Ed Trumbull, *
Harry L Stice, *
EMP: 450 EST: 1997

SALES (est): 10.63MM Privately Held
Web: www.orionsecurity.com
SIC: 7381 Security guard service
PA: Yosh Enterprises, Inc.
675 E Gish Rd
San Jose CA

(P-13014)
OVERTON SECURITY SERVICES INC
39300 Civic Center Dr Ste 370 (94538-2397)
P.O. Box 8020 (94537-8020)
PHONE..................510 791-7380
Andrew Overton, Pr
Sandra Overton, *
EMP: 215 EST: 2007
SALES (est): 15.66MM Privately Held
Web: www.overtonsecurity.com
SIC: 7381 Security guard service

(P-13015)
PACIFIC NATIONAL SECURITY INC
3719 Robertson Blvd (90232-2304)
PHONE..................310 842-7073
EMP: 225
Web: www.pacificnationalsecurity.com
SIC: 7381 Security guard service

(P-13016)
PACWEST SECURITY SERVICES
Also Called: PACWEST SECURITY SERVICES
2990 Inland Empire Blvd (91764-4899)
PHONE..................909 948-0279
Jery Winkfield, Brnch Mgr
EMP: 104
Web: www.pacwestsecurity.com
SIC: 7381 Security guard service
PA: Silvino Nieto
3303 Harbor Blvd Ste A103
Costa Mesa CA

(P-13017)
PACWEST SECURITY SERVICES
Also Called: PACWEST SECURITY SERVICES
1545 Wilshire Blvd Ste 302 (90017-4501)
PHONE..................213 413-3500
Salvador Crespo, Brnch Mgr
EMP: 155
Web: www.pacwestsecurity.com
SIC: 7381 Security guard service
PA: Silvino Nieto
3303 Harbor Blvd Ste A103
Costa Mesa CA

(P-13018)
PALADIN PRTCTION SPCALISTS INC
Also Called: Paladin Private Security
320 Commerce Cir (95815-4213)
PHONE..................916 331-3175
Louis G Aljens, CEO
Matthew Carroll, *
M Scott Johnson, *
EMP: 135 EST: 2003
SALES (est): 4.71MM Privately Held
SIC: 7381 Security guard service

(P-13019)
PATROL BLACK KNIGHT INC
505 S Pacific Ave Unit 201 (90731)
PHONE..................213 985-6499
Manuel Jimenez, CEO
EMP: 70 EST: 2015
SALES (est): 6.4MM Privately Held
Web: www.blackknightpatrol.com

7381 - Detective And Armored Car Services (P-13020)

SIC: **7381** Security guard service

(P-13020)
PATROL SOLUTIONS LLC
6060 Sunrise Vista Dr Ste 1500
(95610-7053)
PHONE..................916 919-6079
Klinton Kehoe, *CEO*
Clinton Kehoe, *Managing Member*
EMP: 135 EST: 2011
SALES (est): 3.3MM **Privately Held**
Web: www.patrolsolutions.com
SIC: **7381** Protective services, guard

(P-13021)
PERSONAL PROTECTIVE SVCS INC (PA)
398 Beach Rd 2nd Fl (94010-2004)
P.O. Box 14007 (94614-2007)
PHONE..................650 344-3302
EMP: 88 EST: 1993
SQ FT: 1,500
SALES (est): 4.86MM **Privately Held**
Web: www.personalprotective.com
SIC: **7381** Security guard service

(P-13022)
PICORE BRISTAIN INITIATIVE INC
Also Called: Pbi
23679 Calabasas Rd # 215 (91302-1502)
PHONE..................818 888-3659
EMP: 100 EST: 2010
SQ FT: 3,000
SALES (est): 1.96MM **Privately Held**
SIC: **7381** Security guard service

(P-13023)
PROBE INFORMATION SERVICES INC
3835 N Freeway Blvd Ste 228
(95834-1955)
P.O. Box 418429 (95841-8429)
PHONE..................916 676-1826
Ross O Stewart, *Pr*
EMP: 101 EST: 1992
SALES (est): 4.98MM **Privately Held**
Web: probeinfo.vrcinvestigations.com
SIC: **7381** Private investigator

(P-13024)
PROFESSIONAL SECURITY CONS (PA)
Also Called: Professional Security Cons
11454 San Vicente Blvd 2nd Fl
(90049-6208)
PHONE..................310 207-7729
Moshe Alon, *Pr*
Ilene Alon, *
EMP: 100 EST: 1985
SALES (est): 59.1MM **Privately Held**
Web: www.pscsite.com
SIC: **7381** 7382 Security guard service; Security systems services

(P-13025)
PROFESSNAL TCHNCAL SEC SVCS IN
1970 Broadway Ste 840 (94612-2299)
PHONE..................510 645-9200
EMP: 359
SALES (corp-wide): 9.17MM **Privately Held**
Web: www.palamerican.com
SIC: **7381** Security guard service
PA: Professional Technical Security Services, Inc.
625 Market St Fl 9
San Francisco CA
415 243-2100

(P-13026)
PROTECT-US
3505 Cadillac Ave (92626-1448)
PHONE..................714 721-8127
Nadiya Aziz, *Prin*
EMP: 180 EST: 2018
SALES (est): 1.96MM **Privately Held**
Web: www.protect.us
SIC: **7381** Security guard service

(P-13027)
REEL SECURITY CALIFORNIA INC
15303 Ventura Blvd Ste 1080 (91403-3110)
PHONE..................818 928-4737
Mario Inez Ramirez, *CEO*
Bradley Bush, *
EMP: 99 EST: 2017
SALES (est): 1.54MM **Privately Held**
Web: www.reelsecurity.com
SIC: **7381** Security guard service

(P-13028)
RICHMAN MANAGEMENT CORPORATION
35400 Bob Hope Dr Ste 107 (92270-1772)
PHONE..................760 832-8520
EMP: 358
SALES (corp-wide): 168.49K **Privately Held**
Web: www.therichmangroup.com
SIC: **7381** Security guard service
HQ: Richman Management Corporation
7840 Mssion Ctr Ct Ste 10
San Diego CA
619 275-7007

(P-13029)
RICHMAN MANAGEMENT CORPORATION
Also Called: Heritage Security Services
41743 Entp Cir N Ste 209 (92590)
PHONE..................909 296-6189
EMP: 287
SALES (corp-wide): 168.49K **Privately Held**
Web: www.therichmangroup.com
SIC: **7381** Security guard service
HQ: Richman Management Corporation
7840 Mssion Ctr Ct Ste 10
San Diego CA
619 275-7007

(P-13030)
RJN INVESTIGATIONS INC
360 E 1st St Ste 696 (92780-3211)
P.O. Box 55451 (92517-0451)
PHONE..................951 686-7638
Robert Nagle, *Pr*
Fred Martino, *
EMP: 80 EST: 1992
SALES (est): 4.48MM **Privately Held**
Web: www.rjninv.com
SIC: **7381** Detective agency

(P-13031)
SAFEGUARD ON DEMAND INC
Also Called: Security and Patrol Services
11037 Warner Ave # 297 (92708-4007)
PHONE..................800 640-2327
Ahmad B Nawabi, *CEO*
Ahmad Nawabi, *
EMP: 125 EST: 2015
SALES (est): 2.43MM **Privately Held**
Web: www.safeguardondemand.com

SIC: **7381** Security guard service

(P-13032)
SCIS AIR SECURITY CORPORATION
1006 W Hillcrest Blvd (90301-2020)
PHONE..................310 645-1216
EMP: 67
SALES (corp-wide): 34.03B **Privately Held**
Web: www.scisairsecurity.com
SIC: **7381** Security guard service
HQ: Scis Air Security Corporation
1521 N Cooper St Ste 300
Arlington TX
817 792-4500

(P-13033)
SECTRAN SECURITY INCORPORATED (PA)
Also Called: Sectran Armored Truck Service
7633 Industry Ave (90660-4301)
P.O. Box 7267 (90022-0967)
PHONE..................562 948-1446
Fred Kunik, *Pr*
Irving Barr, *
EMP: 141 EST: 1982
SQ FT: 19,736
SALES (est): 17.38MM
SALES (corp-wide): 17.38MM **Privately Held**
Web: www.sectransecurity.com
SIC: **7381** Armored car services

(P-13034)
SECURE NET ALLIANCE
Also Called: Security Company
601 S Glenoaks Blvd Ste 409 (91502-1474)
PHONE..................818 848-4900
Jonathan Kraut, *CEO*
Jonathan Kraut, *Pt*
Levi Quintana, *CEO*
EMP: 85 EST: 2007
SALES (est): 3.16MM **Privately Held**
Web: www.securenetprotect.com
SIC: **7381** Security guard service

(P-13035)
SECURITAS SEC SVCS USA INC
Also Called: Western Operations Center
4330 Park Terrace Dr (91361-4630)
PHONE..................818 706-6800
Edie Stafford, *Mgr*
EMP: 350
SALES (corp-wide): 12.7B **Privately Held**
Web: www.securitasinc.com
SIC: **7381** Security guard service
HQ: Securitas Security Services Usa, Inc.
9 Campus Dr Ste 25
Parsippany NJ
973 267-5300

(P-13036)
SECURITECH SECURITY SVCS INC
2733 N San Fernando Rd (90065-1318)
P.O. Box 65097 (90065-0097)
PHONE..................213 387-5050
Serge Tachdjian, *Pr*
Adriana Alvarez, *
EMP: 110 EST: 1999
SALES (est): 4.87MM **Privately Held**
Web: www.securitechguards.com
SIC: **7381** Security guard service

(P-13037)
SECURITY INDUST SPCIALISTS INC
2880 Stevens Creek Blvd (95128-4622)
PHONE..................408 247-0100

EMP: 978
SALES (corp-wide): 143.82MM **Privately Held**
Web: www.sis.us
SIC: **7381** 5065 Guard services; Security control equipment and systems
PA: Security Industry Specialists, Inc.
6071 Bristol Pkwy
Culver City CA
310 215-5100

(P-13038)
SECURITY INDUST SPCIALISTS INC (PA)
Also Called: SIS
6071 Bristol Pkwy (90230-6601)
PHONE..................310 215-5100
John Spesak, *CEO*
Tom Seltz, *
Kit Knudsen, *
EMP: 132 EST: 1999
SQ FT: 9,000
SALES (est): 143.82MM
SALES (corp-wide): 143.82MM **Privately Held**
Web: www.sis.us
SIC: **7381** 5065 Security guard service; Security control equipment and systems

(P-13039)
SECURITY INDUST SPCIALISTS INC
477 N Oak St (90302-3314)
PHONE..................323 924-9147
EMP: 978
SALES (corp-wide): 143.82MM **Privately Held**
Web: www.sis.us
SIC: **7381** Detective services
PA: Security Industry Specialists, Inc.
6071 Bristol Pkwy
Culver City CA
310 215-5100

(P-13040)
SERVEXO
Also Called: Servexo Protective Service
1411 W 190th St Ste 475 (90248-4323)
P.O. Box 9017 (90734-9017)
PHONE..................323 527-9994
John Palmer, *CEO*
EMP: 500 EST: 2012
SALES (est): 5.33MM **Privately Held**
Web: www.servexousa.com
SIC: **7381** Protective services, guard

(P-13041)
SHIELD SECURITY INC (DH)
1551 N Tustin Ave Ste 650 (92705-8664)
PHONE..................714 210-1501
Ed Klosterman Junior, *Pr*
Kenneth Klosterman, *
EMP: 300 EST: 1964
SQ FT: 5,500
SALES (est): 84.15MM
SALES (corp-wide): 12.86B **Privately Held**
Web: www.clementshieldsecurity.com
SIC: **7381** Security guard service
HQ: Universal Protection Service, Lp
545 Sansome St
San Francisco CA
866 877-1965

(P-13042)
SHIELD SECURITY INC
21110 Vanowen St (91303-2821)
PHONE..................818 239-5800
Kenneth Klosterman, *Brnch Mgr*
EMP: 220
SALES (corp-wide): 12.86B **Privately Held**

PRODUCTS & SERVICES SECTION

7381 - Detective And Armored Car Services (P-13065)

Web: www.clementshieldsecurity.com
SIC: 7381 Security guard service
HQ: Shield Security, Inc.
    1551 N Tustin Ave Ste 650
    Santa Ana CA
    714 210-1501

(P-13043)
SHIELD SECURITY INC
150 E Wardlow Rd (90807-4417)
PHONE..................................562 283-1100
Leo Green, *Mgr*
EMP: 457
SALES (corp-wide): 12.86B **Privately Held**
Web: www.clementshieldsecurity.com
SIC: 7381 Security guard service
HQ: Shield Security, Inc.
    1551 N Tustin Ave Ste 650
    Santa Ana CA
    714 210-1501

(P-13044)
SHIELD SECURITY INC
265 N Euclid Ave (91786-6038)
PHONE..................................909 920-1173
Paul Srankowski, *Mgr*
EMP: 324
SALES (corp-wide): 12.86B **Privately Held**
Web: www.clementshieldsecurity.com
SIC: 7381 Security guard service
HQ: Shield Security, Inc.
    1551 N Tustin Ave Ste 650
    Santa Ana CA
    714 210-1501

(P-13045)
SIGNAL 88 LLC
Also Called: Signal 88
821 S Rockefeller Ave (91761-8119)
PHONE..................................714 713-5306
Mark Anderson, *Brnch Mgr*
EMP: 874
SALES (corp-wide): 30.1MM **Privately Held**
Web: www.teamsignal.com
SIC: 7381 Guard services
PA: Signal 88, Llc
    3880 S 149th St Ste 102
    Omaha NE
    877 498-8494

(P-13046)
SILICON VLY SEC & PATROL INC (PA)
1131 Luchessi Dr Ste 2 (95118-3770)
PHONE..................................408 267-1539
Ray Higdon, *CEO*
Lisa Higdon, *
EMP: 150 EST: 1994
SQ FT: 4,000
SALES (est): 10.04MM
SALES (corp-wide): 10.04MM **Privately Held**
Web: www.bastionsecurityservices.com
SIC: 7381 Security guard service

(P-13047)
SINTEX SECURITY SERVICES INC
501 Bangs Ave Ste D (95356-8978)
PHONE..................................209 543-9044
Jerry Sterner, *Pr*
EMP: 75 EST: 1993
SQ FT: 2,500
SALES (est): 2.21MM **Privately Held**
Web: www.sintexsecurity.com
SIC: 7381 Security guard service

(P-13048)
SOS SECURITY INCORPORATED
3000 S Robertson Blvd Ste 100 (90034-3145)
PHONE..................................310 392-9600
Doug Hamilton, *Mgr*
EMP: 118
SALES (corp-wide): 51.62MM **Privately Held**
Web: www.sossecurity.com
SIC: 7381 Security guard service
PA: Sos Security Incorporated
    1915 Us Highway 46 Ste 1
    Parsippany NJ
    973 402-6600

(P-13049)
SOUTHWEST PATROL INC
1800 E Lambert Rd Ste 155 (92821-4396)
PHONE..................................909 861-1884
TOLL FREE: 800
EMP: 86 EST: 1992
SALES (est): 4.27MM **Privately Held**
Web: www.southwestpatrol.com
SIC: 7381 Security guard service

(P-13050)
SOUTHWEST PROTECTIVE SVCS INC
Also Called: Southwest Security
404 W Heil Ave (92243-3328)
P.O. Box 2915 (92244-2915)
PHONE..................................760 996-1285
Jason Jackson, *CEO*
EMP: 250 EST: 2015
SALES (est): 4.35MM **Privately Held**
Web: www.southwestsecurity.net
SIC: 7381 Guard services

(P-13051)
STAFF PRO INC
675 Convention Way (92101-7805)
PHONE..................................619 544-1774
Mike Hernandez, *Mgr*
EMP: 1498
Web: www.staffpro.com
SIC: 7381 Security guard service
PA: Staff Pro Inc.
    5455 Garden Grove Blvd
    Westminster CA

(P-13052)
STAR PRO SECURITY PATROL INC
3303 Harbor Blvd Ste B3 (92626-1517)
PHONE..................................714 617-5056
Sally Covington, *Pr*
EMP: 124 EST: 2016
SALES (est): 2.29MM **Privately Held**
Web: www.starprosecurity.com
SIC: 7381 Security guard service

(P-13053)
STAR PROTECTION AGENCY LLC
Also Called: Star Protection Agency CA
7901 Oakport St Ste 2000 (94621-2058)
PHONE..................................510 635-1732
Edward Lynd, *Brnch Mgr*
EMP: 61
SALES (corp-wide): 8.78B **Privately Held**
Web: www.starprotectionagency.com
SIC: 7381 7389 Security guard service;
    Personal investigation service
HQ: Star Protection Agency Llc
    846 S Hotel St Ste 309
    Honolulu HI
    808 532-3911

(P-13054)
SUPREME SECURITY SERVICES INC
3517 Cameo Dr Unit 84 (92056-6372)
PHONE..................................760 415-7399
Lorenzo Middlebrook, *Pr*
Sharon Middlebrook, *
EMP: 60 EST: 2005
SALES (est): 2.08MM **Privately Held**
Web: www.supremesecurityservicesinc.com
SIC: 7381 7389 Security guard service;
    Business Activities at Non-Commercial Site

(P-13055)
TRANS-WEST SERVICES INC
8503 Crippen St (93311-8993)
PHONE..................................661 381-2900
Brooke L Antonioni, *Pr*
Duane Williams, *
Katy Williams, *
EMP: 300 EST: 1973
SQ FT: 8,500
SALES (est): 22.58MM **Privately Held**
Web: www.trans-west.net
SIC: 7381 Security guard service

(P-13056)
TRINE INTEGRATED SERVICES INC
241 E 10th St Ste A (95376-4076)
PHONE..................................209 521-1590
Conrad Levoit, *CEO*
EMP: 80 EST: 2017
SALES (est): 1.04MM **Privately Held**
Web: www.trineinc.com
SIC: 7381 Security guard service

(P-13057)
TRIUMPH PROTECTION GROUP INC
853 Cotting Ct Ste D (95688-8701)
P.O. Box 852 (95696-0852)
PHONE..................................800 224-0286
Jeffrey Fields, *CEO*
EMP: 350 EST: 2013
SQ FT: 2,200
SALES (est): 22MM **Privately Held**
Web: www.triumphprotection.com
SIC: 7381 Security guard service

(P-13058)
UNIFIED PROTECTIVE SVCS INC
4431 W Rosecrans Ave Ste 300 (90250-1502)
P.O. Box 66487 (90066-0487)
PHONE..................................310 350-1755
Sherif Antoon, *CEO*
EMP: 64 EST: 2013
SALES (est): 3.69MM **Privately Held**
Web: www.unifiedprotectiveservices.com
SIC: 7381 Security guard service

(P-13059)
UNITED FACILITY SOLUTIONS INC
Also Called: Command Gard Srvces Wsa Srvces
19208 S Vermont Ave Ste 200 (90248-4414)
PHONE..................................310 743-3000
Martin Benom, *CEO*
Mark Myers, *Pr*
EMP: 400 EST: 2015
SALES (est): 8.15MM **Privately Held**
Web: www.commandguards.com
SIC: 7381 7349 Security guard service;
    Janitorial service, contract basis

(P-13060)
UNITED GUARD SECURITY INC
1100 W Town And Country Rd Ste 1250 (92868-4633)
PHONE..................................714 242-4051
Ismael Zita, *CEO*
EMP: 128
SALES (corp-wide): 9.5MM **Privately Held**
Web: www.unitedguardsecurity.net
SIC: 7381 Security guard service
PA: United Guard Security Inc.
    879 W 190th St Ste 280
    Gardena CA
    800 228-2505

(P-13061)
UNITED GUARD SECURITY INC
473 E Carnegie Dr Ste 200 (92408)
PHONE..................................909 402-0754
Ismael Zita, *CEO*
EMP: 128
SALES (corp-wide): 9.5MM **Privately Held**
Web: www.unitedguardsecurity.net
SIC: 7381 Security guard service
PA: United Guard Security Inc.
    879 W 190th St Ste 280
    Gardena CA
    800 228-2505

(P-13062)
UNITED SEC SPECIALISTS INC
2010 El Camino Real (95050-4051)
PHONE..................................408 878-5120
Henry Sierra, *Brnch Mgr*
EMP: 237
SALES (corp-wide): 24.34MM **Privately Held**
Web: www.usselite.com
SIC: 7381 Security guard service
HQ: United Security Specialists, Inc.
    275 Saratoga Ave Ste 200
    Santa Clara CA
    408 431-0691

(P-13063)
UNIVERSAL PROTECTION SVC LP (HQ)
Also Called: Allied Universal Security Svcs
545 Sansome St (94111-2908)
PHONE..................................866 877-1965
Brian Cescolini, *Pt*
Steve Jones, *Pt*
EMP: 88 EST: 2009
SALES (est): 695.68MM
SALES (corp-wide): 12.86B **Privately Held**
Web: www.aus.com
SIC: 7381 Security guard service
PA: Atlas Ontario Lp
    199 Bay St Suite 4000
    Toronto ON
    484 351-1586

(P-13064)
UNIVERSAL PRTCTION SEC SYSTEMS (DH)
1815 E Wilshire Ave Ste 910 (92705-4646)
PHONE..................................714 923-3700
EMP: 100 EST: 2009
SALES (est): 13.91MM
SALES (corp-wide): 12.86B **Privately Held**
SIC: 7381 Security guard service
HQ: Universal Services Of America, Lp
    450 Exchange
    Irvine CA
    866 877-1965

(P-13065)
UNIVERSAL SERVICES AMERICA LP

7381 - Detective And Armored Car Services (P-13066)

77725 Enfield Ln (92211-0468)
PHONE..................................760 200-2865
EMP: 5044
SALES (corp-wide): 12.86B Privately Held
Web: www.aus.com
SIC: 7381 Security guard service
HQ: Universal Services Of America, Lp
    450 Exchange
    Irvine CA
    866 877-1965

(P-13066)
UNIVERSAL SERVICES AMERICA LP (HQ)
Also Called: Allied Universal
450 Exchange (92602-5002)
PHONE..................................866 877-1965
Steve Jones, *CEO*
EMP: 100 EST: 2001
SALES (est): 1.22B
SALES (corp-wide): 12.86B Privately Held
Web: www.aus.com
SIC: 7381 7349 Security guard service;
    Janitorial service, contract basis
PA: Atlas Ontario Lp
    199 Bay St Suite 4000
    Toronto ON
    484 351-1586

(P-13067)
UNIVERSAL SERVICES AMERICA LP
777 N 1st St Ste 150 (95112-6347)
PHONE..................................408 993-1965
Darryl Coleman, *Brnch Mgr*
EMP: 4853
SALES (corp-wide): 12.86B Privately Held
Web: www.aus.com
SIC: 7381 Security guard service
HQ: Universal Services Of America, Lp
    450 Exchange
    Irvine CA
    866 877-1965

(P-13068)
US SECURITY ASSOCIATES INC
Also Called: US Security Associates
455 N Moss St (91502-1727)
PHONE..................................818 697-1809
EMP: 302
SALES (corp-wide): 251B Privately Held
Web: www.ussecurityassociates.com
SIC: 7381 Security guard service
HQ: U.S. Security Associates, Inc.
    200 Mansell Ct E Fl 5
    Roswell GA

(P-13069)
US SECURITY ASSOCIATES INC
2275 W 190th St Ste 100 (90504-6007)
PHONE..................................714 352-0773
Richard L Wyckoff, *Brnch Mgr*
EMP: 431
SALES (corp-wide): 251B Privately Held
Web: www.ussecurityassociates.com
SIC: 7381 Security guard service
HQ: U.S. Security Associates, Inc.
    200 Mansell Ct E Fl 5
    Roswell GA

(P-13070)
VENUE MANAGEMENT SYSTEMS INC
Also Called: V M S
2041 E Gladstone St Ste A (91740-5385)
P.O. Box 25 (91773-0025)
PHONE..................................626 445-6000
Charles E Mcintyre, *Pr*
EMP: 6000 EST: 2001

SQ FT: 35,000
SALES (est): 10.95MM Privately Held
Web: www.venueservices.com
SIC: 7381 7363 8742 Detective and armored
    car services; Employee leasing service;
    Human resource consulting services

(P-13071)
VESCOM CORPORATION (PA)
1125 W 190th St (90248-4303)
PHONE..................................207 945-5051
Sherif Assal, *Pr*
Pamela J Treadwell, *
EMP: 622 EST: 1986
SALES (est): 9.08MM Privately Held
Web: www.vescom.com
SIC: 7381 Security guard service

(P-13072)
VETS SECURING AMERICA INC
1125 W 190th St (90248-4303)
PHONE..................................310 645-6200
Gerald A Gregory, *Pr*
EMP: 4000 EST: 2008
SALES (est): 17.51MM Privately Held
Web: www.vetssecuringamerica.com
SIC: 7381 Security guard service

(P-13073)
VIGILANT PRIVATE SECURITY
Also Called: Vigilant Private Security
2100 N Winery Ave Ste 102 (93703-4813)
PHONE..................................559 800-7233
Alena Trybunalava, *CEO*
EMP: 70 EST: 2013
SALES (est): 2.41MM Privately Held
Web: www.vigilantprivatesecurity.com
SIC: 7381 Security guard service

(P-13074)
WADE CASEY
Also Called: Crime Prevention Patrol
1648 Kathleen Ave Ste A (95815-1815)
P.O. Box 245982 (95824-5982)
PHONE..................................916 395-9996
Wade Casey, *Owner*
Wade Casey, *Pt*
Elizabeth Casey, *
EMP: 92 EST: 1985
SQ FT: 1,500
SALES (est): 1.12MM Privately Held
SIC: 7381 Protective services, guard

(P-13075)
WHELAN SECURITY CO
400 Continental Blvd (90245-5033)
PHONE..................................310 343-8628
Gregory Twardowski, *Brnch Mgr*
EMP: 196
SALES (corp-wide): 175.11MM Privately Held
Web: www.garda.com
SIC: 7381 Security guard service
HQ: Whelan Security Co.
    1699 S Hanley Rd Ste 350
    Saint Louis MO
    314 644-3227

(P-13076)
WORLD PRIVATE SECURITY INC
16921 Parthenia St Ste 201 (91343-4568)
PHONE..................................818 894-1800
Fred Youssif, *Pr*
Jeannette Youssif, *
EMP: 200 EST: 1997
SALES (est): 2.11MM Privately Held
Web: www.worldsecurityinc.com
SIC: 7381 Security guard service

(P-13077)
WORLDWIDE SECURITY ASSOC INC (HQ)
10311 S La Cienega Blvd (90045-6109)
PHONE..................................310 743-3000
EMP: 300 EST: 1991
SQ FT: 5,000
SALES (est): 55.12MM Privately Held
SIC: 7381 Security guard service
PA: Wsa Group Inc
    19208 S Vermont Ave 200
    Gardena CA

(P-13078)
WSA GROUP INC
19208 S Vermont Ave # 200 (90248-4414)
PHONE..................................310 743-3000
Andres Martinez, *Pr*
James E Bush, *
EMP: 2000 EST: 1991
SQ FT: 10,000
SALES (est): 13.23MM Privately Held
SIC: 7381 7349 Security guard service;
    Janitorial service, contract basis

(P-13079)
WSB & ASSOCIATES INC
150 Executive Park Blvd Ste 4700
(94134-3303)
PHONE..................................415 864-3510
Bobby Sisk, *CEO*
EMP: 177 EST: 1994
SALES (est): 7.88MM Privately Held
Web: www.wsbassociates.net
SIC: 7381 Security guard service

(P-13080)
YOSH ENTERPRISES INC (PA)
Also Called: Paramount Investigations
675 E Gish Rd (95112-2708)
PHONE..................................408 287-4411
Yosh Gahramani, *Pr*
EMP: 187 EST: 1983
SQ FT: 6,800
SALES (est): 14.64MM Privately Held
Web: www.orionsecurity.com
SIC: 7381 6531 8742 0782 Security guard
    service; Real estate managers; Industrial
    and labor consulting services; Lawn and
    garden services

7382 Security Systems Services

(P-13081)
313 ACQUISITION LLC
1111 Citrus St Ste 1 (92507-1735)
PHONE..................................801 234-6374
Jakob Imig, *Brnch Mgr*
EMP: 4888
SALES (corp-wide): 493.76MM Privately Held
SIC: 7382 Security systems services
PA: 313 Acquisition Llc
    4931 N 300 W
    Provo UT
    877 404-4129

(P-13082)
3VR SECURITY INC
1 Kaiser Plz Ste 1030 (94612-3601)
PHONE..................................415 513-4577
Robert A Shipp, *CEO*
Charles F Ryan Iii, *CFO*
EMP: 90 EST: 2002
SALES (est): 12.95MM Publicly Held
Web: www.identiv.com

SIC: 7382 Protective devices, security
PA: Identiv, Inc.
    2201 Walnut Ave Ste 100
    Fremont CA

(P-13083)
ABM SECURITY SERVICES INC
830 Riverside Pkwy Ste 30 (95605-1505)
PHONE..................................916 614-9571
Steve Cader, *Mgr*
EMP: 72
SALES (corp-wide): 7.81B Publicly Held
SIC: 7382 7381 5063 Security systems
    services; Guard services; Alarm systems,
    nec
HQ: Abm Security Services, Inc.
    3800 Buffalo Spdwy Ste 32
    Houston TX
    713 928-5344

(P-13084)
ADMIRAL SECURITY SERVICES INC
2151 Salvio St Ste 260 (94520-2436)
PHONE..................................888 471-1128
Mohamed S Ahmed, *CEO*
Youssef Abdallah, *
EMP: 400 EST: 2004
SQ FT: 3,500
SALES (est): 24.34MM Privately Held
Web: www.admiralsecurityservices.com
SIC: 7382 7381 Security systems services;
    Protective services, guard

(P-13085)
ADT LLC
731 E Ball Rd (92805-5950)
PHONE..................................714 450-6461
EMP: 113
SALES (corp-wide): 6.4B Publicly Held
Web: www.adt.com
SIC: 7382 Security systems services
HQ: Adt Llc
    1501 W Yamato Rd
    Boca Raton FL
    561 988-3600

(P-13086)
ADT LLC
9201 Oakdale Ave Ste 100 (91311-6543)
PHONE..................................818 464-5001
EMP: 113
SALES (corp-wide): 6.4B Publicly Held
Web: www.adt.com
SIC: 7382 Security systems services
HQ: Adt Llc
    1501 W Yamato Rd
    Boca Raton FL
    561 988-3600

(P-13087)
ADT LLC
Also Called: Home Security and HM Ctrl Svcs
475 N Muller St (92801-5452)
PHONE..................................626 593-1020
EMP: 131
SALES (corp-wide): 6.4B Publicly Held
Web: www.adt.com
SIC: 7382 Burglar alarm maintenance and
    monitoring
HQ: Adt Llc
    1501 W Yamato Rd
    Boca Raton FL
    561 988-3600

(P-13088)
ADT LLC
Also Called: ADT Security Services
9555 Owensmouth Ave (91311-4811)
PHONE..................................818 574-3809

PRODUCTS & SERVICES SECTION **7382 - Security Systems Services (P-13109)**

EMP: 71
SALES (corp-wide): 6.4B **Publicly Held**
Web: www.adt.com
SIC: **7382** Burglar alarm maintenance and monitoring
HQ: Adt Llc
1501 W Yamato Rd
Boca Raton FL
561 988-3600

(P-13089)
ADT LLC
Also Called: ADT Security Services
1808 Commercenter W Ste E (92408-3302)
PHONE.................................951 824-7205
EMP: 107
SALES (corp-wide): 6.4B **Publicly Held**
Web: www.adt.com
SIC: **7382** Burglar alarm maintenance and monitoring
HQ: Adt Llc
1501 W Yamato Rd
Boca Raton FL
561 988-3600

(P-13090)
ADT LLC
4071 Port Chicago Hwy Ste 150 (94520-1197)
PHONE.................................925 602-0500
Pete Fitch, *Brnch Mgr*
EMP: 71
SALES (corp-wide): 6.4B **Publicly Held**
Web: www.adt.com
SIC: **7382** 5999 Burglar alarm maintenance and monitoring; Alarm and safety equipment stores
HQ: Adt Llc
1501 W Yamato Rd
Boca Raton FL
561 988-3600

(P-13091)
ADT LLC
26074 Avenue Hall Ste 1 (91355-3444)
PHONE.................................818 373-6200
Ron Bogen, *Brnch Mgr*
EMP: 113
SALES (corp-wide): 6.4B **Publicly Held**
Web: www.adt.com
SIC: **7382** 5999 Burglar alarm maintenance and monitoring; Alarm and safety equipment stores
HQ: Adt Llc
1501 W Yamato Rd
Boca Raton FL
561 988-3600

(P-13092)
ADT LLC
Also Called: Protection One
1120 Palmyrita Ave Ste 280 (92507-1709)
PHONE.................................951 782-6900
EMP: 184
SALES (corp-wide): 6.4B **Publicly Held**
Web: www.adt.com
SIC: **7382** 5999 5063 1731 Burglar alarm maintenance and monitoring; Alarm signal systems; Burglar alarm systems; Safety and security specialization
HQ: Adt Llc
1501 W Yamato Rd
Boca Raton FL
561 988-3600

(P-13093)
ADVANCED PROTECTION INDS LLC
Also Called: National Monitoring Center
25341 Commercentre Dr (92630-8856)

PHONE.................................800 662-1711
Woodie Andrawos, *Pr*
Todd Shuff, *
Frank Farag, *
EMP: 120 EST: 2018
SALES (est): 18.46MM **Privately Held**
Web: www.nmccentral.com
SIC: **7382** Burglar alarm maintenance and monitoring

(P-13094)
AERO PORT SERVICES INC (PA)
216 W Florence Ave (90301-1213)
PHONE.................................310 623-8230
Chris Paik, *Pr*
Robert Yim, *
Julie Hong, *
Stephan Park, *
▲ EMP: 848 EST: 2002
SALES (est): 51.25MM
SALES (corp-wide): 51.25MM **Privately Held**
Web: www.aeroportservices.com
SIC: **7382** Security systems services

(P-13095)
ANOMALI INCORPORATED
808 Winslow St (94063-1608)
PHONE.................................844 484-7328
Ahmed Rubaie, *CEO*
Hugh Njemanze, *Pr*
EMP: 225 EST: 2013
SALES (est): 26.78MM **Privately Held**
Web: www.anomali.com
SIC: **7382** Security systems services

(P-13096)
ARECONT VISION COSTAR LLC
1801 Highland Ave (91010-2808)
PHONE.................................818 937-0700
EMP: 64
Web: www.arecontvision.com
SIC: **7382** Security systems services
HQ: Arecont Vision Costar, Llc
7330 Trade St
San Diego CA
818 937-0700

(P-13097)
ARKOSE LABS HOLDINGS INC (PA)
400 Concar Dr (94402-2681)
PHONE.................................415 917-8701
Kevin Gosschalk, *CEO*
Mark Resnick, *COO*
EMP: 121 EST: 2017
SALES (est): 10.9MM
SALES (corp-wide): 10.9MM **Privately Held**
Web: www.arkoselabs.com
SIC: **7382** Security systems services

(P-13098)
ARMIS FEDERAL LLC
300 Hamilton Ave Fl 5 (94301-2581)
PHONE.................................888 452-4011
Jonathan Carr, *Managing Member*
EMP: 500 EST: 2019
SALES (est): 5MM **Privately Held**
SIC: **7382** Protective devices, security

(P-13099)
BOLIDE TECHNOLOGY GROUP INC
Also Called: Bolide International
468 S San Dimas Ave (91773-4045)
PHONE.................................909 305-8889
TOLL FREE: 800
David Liu, *Pr*

◆ EMP: 70 EST: 1994
SQ FT: 16,000
SALES (est): 6.39MM **Privately Held**
Web: www.bolideco.com
SIC: **7382** Security systems services

(P-13100)
BRIGHTCLOUD INC
4370 La Jolla Village Dr Ste 820 (92122-1277)
PHONE.................................858 652-4803
Quinn Curtis, *Pr*
EMP: 280 EST: 2005
SALES (est): 445.92K
SALES (corp-wide): 832.31MM **Privately Held**
Web: www.brightcloud.com
SIC: **7382** Security systems services
HQ: Webroot Inc.
385 Interlocken Blvd # 800
Broomfield CO
303 442-3813

(P-13101)
CHRONICLE LLC
250 Mayfield Ave (94043-4124)
PHONE.................................650 214-5199
Ben Heben, *CFO*
Jan Kang, *CLO**
EMP: 65 EST: 2018
SALES (est): 9.21MM
SALES (corp-wide): 282.84B **Publicly Held**
Web: www.chronicle.security
SIC: **7382** Security systems services
PA: Alphabet Inc.
1600 Amphitheatre Pkwy
Mountain View CA
650 253-0000

(P-13102)
CONTEMPORARY SERVICES CORP
369 Van Ness Way Ste 702 (90501-6245)
PHONE.................................310 320-8418
Roy Sukimoto, *Brnch Mgr*
EMP: 109
SALES (corp-wide): 297.45MM **Privately Held**
Web: www.csc-usa.com
SIC: **7382** 7381 7299 Security systems services; Guard services; Party planning service
PA: Contemporary Services Corporation
17101 Superior St
Northridge CA
818 885-5150

(P-13103)
CORINTHIAN INTL PRKG SVCS INC (PA)
Also Called: Corinthian Parking Services
19925 Stevens Creek Blvd Ste 126 (95014-2300)
PHONE.................................408 867-7275
Todd Fedde, *CEO*
EMP: 500 EST: 1997
SQ FT: 6,000
SALES (est): 32.69MM **Privately Held**
Web: www.corinthiantransportation.com
SIC: **7382** Security systems services

(P-13104)
CORPORATE ALNCE STRATEGIES INC
3410 La Sierra Ave Ste F244 (92503-5270)
PHONE.................................877 777-7487
Leah L Pinto, *Dir*
Leah Pinto, *

EMP: 115 EST: 2015
SALES (est): 3.6MM **Privately Held**
Web: www.corporatealliancestrategies.com
SIC: **7382** Security systems services

(P-13105)
DELTA SCIENTIFIC CORPORATION (PA)
40355 Delta Ln (93551-3616)
PHONE.................................661 575-1100
Harry D Dickinson, *CEO*
David Dickinson, *
Richard I Winger, *
Keith Bobrosky, *
◆ EMP: 188 EST: 1974
SQ FT: 200,000
SALES (est): 24.6MM
SALES (corp-wide): 24.6MM **Privately Held**
Web: www.deltascientific.com
SIC: **7382** Security systems services

(P-13106)
DIAL SECURITY INC (PA)
Also Called: Dial Communications
760 W Ventura Blvd (93010-8382)
P.O. Box 34781 (20827-0781)
PHONE.................................805 389-6700
William H Dundas, *Pr*
EMP: 250 EST: 1974
SQ FT: 12,000
SALES (est): 17.39MM
SALES (corp-wide): 17.39MM **Privately Held**
Web: www.dialcomm.com
SIC: **7382** 7381 Protective devices, security; Detective and armored car services

(P-13107)
DTIQ HOLDINGS INC
Also Called: Dtt
1755 N Main St (90031-2516)
PHONE.................................323 576-1400
Sam Naficy, *CEO*
Jeffrey Moran, *
Thomas M Moran, *
Michael Sutton, *
Adam Watson, *
EMP: 119 EST: 2009
SALES (est): 1.11MM **Privately Held**
Web: www.dtiq.com
SIC: **7382** Confinement surveillance systems maintenance and monitoring

(P-13108)
EASTERNCCTV (USA) LLC
Also Called: Ens Security
525 Parriott Pl W (91745-1033)
PHONE.................................626 961-8999
Xianjie Xiong, *Pr*
EMP: 171
SALES (corp-wide): 23.24MM **Privately Held**
Web: www.enssecurity.com
SIC: **7382** Security systems services
PA: Easterncctv (Usa), Llc
50 Commercial St
Plainview NY
516 870-3779

(P-13109)
ECAMSECURE (DH)
Also Called: Ecamsecure
3400 E Airport Way (90806-2412)
PHONE.................................888 246-0556
Christopher Coffey, *Pr*
William R Babcock, *CFO*
EMP: 66 EST: 1985
SQ FT: 3,500

7382 - Security Systems Services (P-13110)

SALES (est): 11.1MM
SALES (corp-wide): 175.11MM **Privately Held**
Web: ecamsecure.garda.com
SIC: **7382** 5065 Security systems services; Electronic parts and equipment, nec
HQ: Whelan Security Co.
1699 S Hanley Rd Ste 350
Saint Louis MO
314 644-3227

(P-13110)
EDGEWORTH INTEGRATION LLC
2360 Shasta Way Ste F (93065-1800)
PHONE.................................805 915-0211
EMP: 85
SALES (corp-wide): 2.09MM **Privately Held**
Web: www.edgeworthsecurity.com
SIC: **7382** Security systems services
PA: Edgeworth Integration, Llc
1000 Commerce Dr Fl 2
Pittsburgh PA
800 421-9130

(P-13111)
ELITE SECURITY GROUP INC
Also Called: Elite Security Group
640 Bailey Rd 124 (94565-4306)
PHONE..............................925 597-8852
Robert Shane Taylor, *CEO*
EMP: 78 EST: 2016
SQ FT: 1,000
SALES (est): 2.16MM **Privately Held**
SIC: **7382** Security systems services

(P-13112)
EMERGENCY TECHNOLOGIES INC
Also Called: American Two-Way
7345 Varna Ave (91605-4009)
PHONE.................................818 765-4421
Christopher Baskin, *CEO*
EMP: 72 EST: 1995
SQ FT: 13,000
SALES (est): 2.19MM **Privately Held**
SIC: **7382** Security systems services

(P-13113)
ENTERPRISE SECURITY INC (PA)
Also Called: Enterprise Security Solutions
22860 Savi Ranch Pkwy (92887-4610)
PHONE.................................714 630-9100
Samuel Troy Laughlin, *CEO*
Troy Laughlin, *
Daniel Steiner, *
Joseph Emens, *
EMP: 74 EST: 2000
SALES (est): 10.73MM **Privately Held**
Web: www.entersecurity.com
SIC: **7382** 3699 3429 6211 Protective devices, security; Security devices; Security cable locking systems; Dealers, security

(P-13114)
EVENT INTELLIGENCE GROUP
4140 Jackson Ave (90232-3234)
PHONE...............................310 237-5375
Allen Cook, *CEO*
EMP: 96 EST: 2014
SALES (est): 384.3K **Privately Held**
SIC: **7382** Security systems services
PA: Tourtechsupport, Inc.
1723 Round Rock Dr
Raleigh NC

(P-13115)
EZVIZ INC
18639 Railroad St (91748-1317)
PHONE...............................855 693-9849
Shengyang Jin, *CEO*
Jeffrey He, *
Hsin Lin, *
Yuying Wang, *
EMP: 200 EST: 2015
SQ FT: 32,000
SALES (est): 6.13MM **Privately Held**
Web: www.ezviz.com
SIC: **7382** Confinement surveillance systems maintenance and monitoring
HQ: Hikvision Usa Inc.
18639 Railroad St
City Of Industry CA
909 895-0400

(P-13116)
FIRST ALARM (PA)
1111 Estates Dr (95003-3572)
PHONE.................................831 476-1111
Jarl E Saal, *Ch*
Jim Norkoli, *
EMP: 120 EST: 1982
SQ FT: 14,000
SALES (est): 36.99MM
SALES (corp-wide): 36.99MM **Privately Held**
Web: www.firstalarm.com
SIC: **7382** Burglar alarm maintenance and monitoring

(P-13117)
FIRST ALARM SEC & PATROL INC
5250 Claremont Ave (95207-5700)
PHONE................................209 473-1110
EMP: 355
Web: www.firstalarm.com
SIC: **7382** 5063 Security systems services; Transformers and transmission equipment
PA: First Alarm Security & Patrol, Inc.
1731 Tech Dr Ste 800
San Jose CA

(P-13118)
FIRST ALARM SEC & PATROL INC
1801 Oakland Blvd Ste 315 (94596-7017)
PHONE................................925 295-1260
EMP: 355
Web: www.firstalarm.com
SIC: **7382** Security systems services
PA: First Alarm Security & Patrol, Inc.
1731 Tech Dr Ste 800
San Jose CA

(P-13119)
FIRST ALARM SEC & PATROL INC (PA)
Also Called: First Security Services
1731 Technology Dr Ste 800 (95110)
PHONE................................408 866-1111
Cal Horton, *Pr*
Jarl E Saal, *
EMP: 250 EST: 1989
SALES (est): 39.5MM **Privately Held**
Web: www.firstalarm.com
SIC: **7382** Security systems services

(P-13120)
GLARE TECHNOLOGY USA INC
30898 Wealth St (92563-2534)
PHONE................................909 437-6999
Laith Salih, *CEO*
EMP: 120 EST: 2015
SALES (est): 1.71MM **Privately Held**
Web: www.rideglarewheel.com
SIC: **7382** Security systems services

(P-13121)
GO GET EM INC
45248 Trevor Ave (93534-1614)
PHONE...............................702 985-5637
Michael Sprague, *Pr*
EMP: 60 EST: 2017
SALES (est): 1.38MM **Privately Held**
SIC: **7382** Security systems services

(P-13122)
GREATER ALARM COMPANY INC (DH)
3750 Schaufele Ave Ste 200 (90808-1779)
PHONE................................949 474-0555
TOLL FREE: 800
George De Marco, *Pr*
James De Marco, *
EMP: 71 EST: 1981
SQ FT: 11,500
SALES (est): 4.17MM
SALES (corp-wide): 170.75MM **Privately Held**
SIC: **7382** Security systems services
HQ: Interface Security Systems, Llc
3773 Corporate Centre Dr
Earth City MO
314 595-0100

(P-13123)
HARRISON IYKE
Also Called: Diplomatic Security Services
7611 Etiwanda Ave (91739-9715)
PHONE................................909 463-8409
EMP: 99
SALES (est): 4.7MM **Privately Held**
SIC: **7382** Security systems services

(P-13124)
HIKVISION USA INC (HQ)
18639 Railroad St (91748-1317)
PHONE................................909 895-0400
Jeffrey He, *CEO*
Ning Tang, *
Tony Yang, *
▲ EMP: 120 EST: 2007
SALES (est): 44.12MM **Privately Held**
Web: www.hikvision.com
SIC: **7382** Confinement surveillance systems maintenance and monitoring
PA: Hangzhou Hikvision Digital Technology Co., Ltd.
No.518, Wulianwang Street, Binjiang District
Hangzhou ZJ

(P-13125)
IDENTITY INTLLIGENCE GROUP LLC
Also Called: Idiq
43454 Business Park Dr (92590-5530)
PHONE................................626 522-7993
Scott Hermann, *Managing Member*
EMP: 232 EST: 2010
SALES (est): 12.55MM **Privately Held**
Web: www.idiq.com
SIC: **7382** Security systems services

(P-13126)
IRAJE INC
Also Called: Iraje
6200 Stnrdge Mall Rd Ste (94588)
PHONE................................925 400-6558
Samir Jaipuriyar, *CEO*
EMP: 125 EST: 2016
SALES (est): 2.7MM **Privately Held**
SIC: **7382** Security systems services

(P-13127)
JOHNSON CNTRLS SEC SLTIONS LLC
3870 Murphy Canyon Rd Ste 140 (92123-4446)
PHONE...............................561 988-3600
Greg Pavlicek, *Mgr*
EMP: 64
Web: datasource.johnsoncontrols.com
SIC: **7382** Burglar alarm maintenance and monitoring
HQ: Johnson Controls Security Solutions Llc
6600 Congress Ave
Boca Raton FL
561 264-2071

(P-13128)
JOHNSON CONTROLS
12728 Shoemaker Ave (90670-6345)
PHONE...............................562 405-3817
Andy Bernot, *Mgr*
EMP: 150
SIC: **7382** 1731 1711 Security systems services; Fire detection and burglar alarm systems specialization; Plumbing, heating, air-conditioning
HQ: Johnson Controls Fire Protection Lp
6600 Congress Ave
Boca Raton FL
561 988-7200

(P-13129)
KERN SECURITY CORPORATION
Also Called: Kern Security Systems
2701 Fruitvale Ave (93308-5905)
PHONE...............................661 363-6874
John Affeld, *Pr*
Ronald C Mcvicar, *CFO*
EMP: 76 EST: 1982
SQ FT: 4,000
SALES (est): 2.2MM
SALES (corp-wide): 26.85MM **Privately Held**
Web: www.ssdalarm.com
SIC: **7382** 5999 1731 Burglar alarm maintenance and monitoring; Alarm signal systems; Closed circuit television installation
PA: Security Signal Devices, Inc.
1740 N Lemon St
Anaheim CA
800 888-0444

(P-13130)
KRATOS PUBLIC SAFETY & SECURITY SOLUTIONS INC
4820 Eastgate Mall Ste 200 (92121)
PHONE...............................858 812-7300
EMP: 99
SIC: **7382** Security systems services

(P-13131)
LAWRENCE LIVERMORE NAT SEC LLC
2300 1st St Ste 204 (94550-3141)
PHONE...............................925 453-3584
Penrose C Albright, *Managing Member*
George Miller, *
EMP: 256 EST: 2006
SALES (est): 49.91MM **Privately Held**
Web: www.llnl.gov
SIC: **7382** 1629 8711 Security systems services; Industrial plant construction; Civil engineering

PRODUCTS & SERVICES SECTION
7382 - Security Systems Services (P-13154)

(P-13132)
LIFE ALERT EMRGNCY RSPONSE INC (PA)
Also Called: Life Alert
16027 Ventura Blvd Ste 400 (91436-2728)
PHONE..................800 247-0000
Isaac Shepher, *Pr*
Miriam Shepher, *
Felix Leung, *
▲ **EMP:** 175 **EST:** 1987
SQ FT: 29,489
SALES (est): 51.34MM
SALES (corp-wide): 51.34MM **Privately Held**
Web: www.lifealert.com
SIC: 7382 5731 Confinement surveillance systems maintenance and monitoring; Consumer electronic equipment, nec

(P-13133)
MATSON ALARM CO INC
2005 W Ashland Ave Ste A (93277-6244)
PHONE..................559 438-8000
Larry Matson, *Owner*
EMP: 67
SALES (corp-wide): 416.15MM **Privately Held**
Web: www.matsonalarm.com
SIC: 7382 Security systems services
HQ: Matson Alarm Co., Inc.
581 W Fllbrook Ave Ste 10
Fresno CA
559 438-8000

(P-13134)
NAVTRAK LLC
20 Enterprise Ste 100 (92656-7104)
PHONE..................410 548-2337
EMP: 97
SIC: 7382 Security systems services

(P-13135)
NOZOMI NETWORKS INC (HQ)
575 Market St Ste 3650 (94105-5823)
PHONE..................800 314-6114
Edgard Capdevielle, *Pr*
Andrea Carcano, *CPO**
Moreno Carullo, *
Michael Plante, *CMO**
EMP: 71 **EST:** 2016
SALES (est): 8.97MM **Privately Held**
Web: www.nozominetworks.com
SIC: 7382 Security systems services
PA: Nozomi Holding Sagl
Via Maria Ghioldi-Schweizer 2
Mendrisio TI

(P-13136)
PACIFIC WEST SECURITY INC
Also Called: Sonitrol
1587 Schallenberger Rd (95131-2434)
PHONE..................801 748-1034
Paul Schumate, *Pr*
Sandra Oswalt, *
EMP: 60 **EST:** 1986
SQ FT: 8,000
SALES (est): 9.43MM **Privately Held**
Web: www.sonitrolsv.com
SIC: 7382 1731 Burglar alarm maintenance and monitoring; Fire detection and burglar alarm systems specialization

(P-13137)
PELCO INC (HQ)
Also Called: Pelco
625 W Alluvial Ave (93711-5762)
PHONE..................559 292-1981
◆ **EMP:** 2100 **EST:** 1957
SALES (est): 115MM
SALES (corp-wide): 9.11B **Publicly Held**
Web: www.pelco.com
SIC: 7382 3663 Security systems services; Television closed circuit equipment
PA: Motorola Solutions, Inc.
500 W Monroe St Ste 4400
Chicago IL
847 576-5000

(P-13138)
POST ALARM SYSTEMS (PA)
Also Called: Post Alarm Systems Patrol Svcs
47 E Saint Joseph St (91006-2861)
PHONE..................626 446-7159
William Post, *Pr*
Bill Post, *
Lois Post, *
EMP: 98 **EST:** 1956
SQ FT: 10,500
SALES (est): 12.46MM
SALES (corp-wide): 12.46MM **Privately Held**
Web: www.postalarm.com
SIC: 7382 1731 5063 Burglar alarm maintenance and monitoring; Fire detection and burglar alarm systems specialization; Electrical apparatus and equipment

(P-13139)
PROGUARD SECURITY SERVICES INC
300 Montgomery St (94104-1918)
PHONE..................415 672-0786
EMP: 79 **EST:** 2016
SALES (est): 7.67MM **Privately Held**
Web: www.proguardsecurityservices.com
SIC: 7382 Security systems services

(P-13140)
REDWOOD SUPPORT GROUP INC
50 Woodside Plz (94061-2500)
PHONE..................650 815-8933
Jared Stahl, *CEO*
EMP: 73
SALES (est): 1.26MM **Privately Held**
SIC: 7382 Security systems services

(P-13141)
RTI SYSTEMS INC
7635 N San Fernando Rd (91505-1073)
PHONE..................213 599-8470
Paul Thompson, *Pr*
EMP: 76 **EST:** 2017
SALES (est): 4MM **Privately Held**
Web: www.rtisystems.com
SIC: 7382 Protective devices, security

(P-13142)
SAFE & SOUND SECURITY
2125 Oak Grove Rd Ste 128 (94598-2534)
PHONE..................925 942-0795
Patrick A Chown, *CEO*
EMP: 69 **EST:** 2008
SALES (est): 15.29MM **Privately Held**
Web: www.getsafeandsound.com
SIC: 7382 Security systems services

(P-13143)
SECURITAS TECHNOLOGY CORP
7002 Convoy Ct (92111-1017)
PHONE..................858 812-7349
EMP: 99
SALES (corp-wide): 12.7B **Privately Held**
Web: www.securitastechnology.com
SIC: 7382 Security systems services
HQ: Securitas Technology Corporation
3800 Tabs Dr
Uniontown OH
800 548-4478

(P-13144)
SENTINEL MONITORING CORP (HQ)
220 Technology Dr Ste 200 (92618-2424)
PHONE..................949 453-1550
Robert Contestabile, *Pr*
EMP: 100 **EST:** 1993
SALES (est): 10.3MM
SALES (corp-wide): 94.13MM **Privately Held**
Web: www.sentineladvantage.com
SIC: 7382 Confinement surveillance systems maintenance and monitoring
PA: Sentinel Offender Services Llc
1290 N Hancock St Ste 103
Anaheim CA
949 453-1550

(P-13145)
SENTINEL OFFENDER SERVICES LLC (PA)
1290 N Hancock St Ste 103 (92807-1925)
PHONE..................949 453-1550
EMP: 85 **EST:** 1993
SALES (est): 94.13MM
SALES (corp-wide): 94.13MM **Privately Held**
Web: www.sentineladvantage.com
SIC: 7382 Confinement surveillance systems maintenance and monitoring

(P-13146)
SKYHIGH NETWORKS INC (DH)
900 E Hamilton Ave Ste 400 (95008-0670)
PHONE..................408 564-0278
Christopher D Young, *CEO*
Michael Berry, *CFO*
John Giamatteo, *CONSUMER BUS GROUP*
Scott Lovett, *Global Vice President*
Dawn Smith, *CLO*
EMP: 76 **EST:** 2011
SALES (est): 23.73MM
SALES (corp-wide): 1.92B **Privately Held**
Web: www.mcafee.com
SIC: 7382 Security systems services
HQ: Mcafee, Llc
6220 America Center Dr
San Jose CA

(P-13147)
SPECTRUM SECURITY SERVICES INC (PA)
13967 Campo Rd Ste 101 (91935-3232)
P.O. Box 744 (91935-0744)
PHONE..................619 669-6660
Sam Ersan, *Pr*
Porter Erent, *
EMP: 212 **EST:** 1989
SQ FT: 1,200
SALES (est): 14.29MM **Privately Held**
Web: www.spectrumdetentionservices.com
SIC: 7382 Security systems services

(P-13148)
STAFF PRO INC (PA)
Also Called: Allied Universal Event Svcs
5455 Garden Grove Blvd (92683-1891)
PHONE..................714 230-7200
Cory Meredith, *CEO*
EMP: 700 **EST:** 1987
SALES (est): 37.53MM **Privately Held**
Web: www.staffpro.com
SIC: 7382 8741 Security systems services; Management services

(P-13149)
SYMONS FIRE PROTECTION INC
Also Called: Fire Sprnklr Fire Alarm Dsign
9475 Chesapeake Dr Ste A (92123-1337)
PHONE..................619 588-6364
Jamil Shamoon, *Pr*
David Symons, *
EMP: 110 **EST:** 1993
SALES (est): 8.39MM **Privately Held**
Web: www.symonsfp.com
SIC: 7382 1731 8711 7389 Fire alarm maintenance and monitoring; Fire detection and burglar alarm systems specialization; Building construction consultant; Inspection and testing services

(P-13150)
SYSTEMS TECH UNLIMITED LLC
7409 West Blv (90305-1222)
PHONE..................310 341-5169
Caryron Oard, *CEO*
EMP: 60 **EST:** 2021
SALES (est): 1.58MM **Privately Held**
SIC: 7382 Security systems services

(P-13151)
TAD GROUP LLC
5000 Birch St Ste 3000 (92660-2140)
PHONE..................949 476-3601
EMP: 150 **EST:** 2007
SALES (est): 2.87MM **Privately Held**
Web: www.sunsnow.com
SIC: 7382 7373 Security systems services; Computer integrated systems design

(P-13152)
TURNER CAMERA SEC SYSTEMS INC
Also Called: Don Turner and Associates
120 W Shields Ave (93705-4101)
PHONE..................559 486-3466
Donald A Turner, *Pr*
EMP: 190 **EST:** 1972
SQ FT: 3,700
SALES (est): 17.59MM **Privately Held**
Web: www.turnersecurityfresno.com
SIC: 7382 Security systems services

(P-13153)
VERKADA INC (PA)
406 E 3rd Ave (94401-3480)
PHONE..................650 514-2500
Filip Kaliszan, *CEO*
Hans Robertson, *
Benjamin Bercovitz, *
James Ren Swe, *Prin*
EMP: 1692 **EST:** 2016
SALES (est): 104.2MM
SALES (corp-wide): 104.2MM **Privately Held**
Web: www.verkada.com
SIC: 7382 Security systems services

(P-13154)
VOLTAGE SECURITY LLC
20400 Stevens Creek Blvd Ste 500 (95014-2217)
PHONE..................408 886-3200
EMP: 95
SIC: 7382 7373 Protective devices, security; Systems engineering, computer related

7383 News Syndicates

(P-13155)
BUENA VISTA TELEVISION (DH)
Also Called: Buena Vista TV Advg Sls
500 S Buena Vista St (91521-0001)
PHONE..................818 560-1878
Janice Marinelli, CEO
Mort Marcus, *
Marsha Reed, *
Jed Cohen, *
Anne L Buettner, *
▲ EMP: 129 EST: 1985
SALES (est): 20.81MM
SALES (corp-wide): 82.72B Publicly Held
Web: www.thewaltdisneycompany.com
SIC: 7383 News feature syndicate
HQ: Disney Enterprises, Inc.
500 S Buena Vista St
Burbank CA
818 560-1000

(P-13156)
BUSINESS WIRE INC (HQ)
Also Called: Business Wire
101 California St Fl 20 (94111-5852)
PHONE..................415 986-4422
EMP: 145 EST: 1961
SALES (est): 47.5MM
SALES (corp-wide): 302.09B Publicly Held
Web: www.businesswire.com
SIC: 7383 News syndicates
PA: Berkshire Hathaway Inc.
3555 Farnam St Ste 1440
Omaha NE
402 346-1400

(P-13157)
GIGA OMNI MEDIA INC
1613a Lyon St (94115-2414)
PHONE..................415 974-6355
Paul Walborsky, CEO
EMP: 75 EST: 2010
SALES (est): 9.5MM Privately Held
SIC: 7383 News pictures, gathering and distributing

(P-13158)
THE COPLEY PRESS INC
Also Called: Copley Newspapers
7776 Ivanhoe Ave (92037-4572)
P.O. Box 1530 (92038-1530)
PHONE..................858 454-0411
EMP: 4170
SIC: 7383 2711 7011 News syndicates; Newspapers, publishing and printing; Resort hotel

7384 Photofinish Laboratories

(P-13159)
COLOREDGE
3520 W Valhalla Dr (91505-1126)
PHONE..................818 842-1121
Mike Lannin, CEO
EMP: 189 EST: 1957
SQ FT: 60,000
SALES (est): 3.68MM Privately Held
Web: www.coloredge.com
SIC: 7384 Photofinish laboratories
HQ: Coloredge, Inc.
190 Jony Dr
Carlstadt NJ
212 594-4800

(P-13160)
JAKE HEY INCORPORATED
Also Called: A & I Color Laboratory
257 S Lake St (91502-2111)
PHONE..................323 856-5280
David Alexander, Pr
James Ishihara, *
EMP: 144 EST: 1978
SQ FT: 16,000
SALES (est): 4.01MM Privately Held
Web: www.aandibooks.com
SIC: 7384 Photofinishing laboratory

(P-13161)
PILGRIM STUDIOS INC
12020 Chandler Blvd Ste 200 (91607)
PHONE..................818 728-8800
Craig M Piligian, CEO
EMP: 82 EST: 2013
SALES (est): 3.23MM Privately Held
Web: www.pilgrimmediagroup.com
SIC: 7384 Home movies, developing and processing

(P-13162)
SHUTTERFLY LLC (HQ)
2800 Bridge Pkwy Ste 100 (94065-1192)
PHONE..................650 610-5200
Hilary Schneider, CEO
Dwayne Black, Sr VP
Mike Eklund, Sr VP
EMP: 105 EST: 1999
SQ FT: 100,000
SALES (est): 2.37B
SALES (corp-wide): 2.37B Privately Held
Web: www.shutterflyinc.com
SIC: 7384 5946 Photofinishing laboratory; Camera and photographic supply stores
PA: Photo Holdings, Llc
2800 Bridge Pkwy
Redwood City CA
650 610-5200

(P-13163)
TECHNICOLOR INC
Also Called: Technicolor Lab
2255 N Ontario St Ste 180 (91504-4509)
PHONE..................818 260-4577
Joe Berchtold, Pr
EMP: 400 EST: 1966
SALES (est): 39.42MM Privately Held
SIC: 7384 Photofinish laboratories

7389 Business Services, Nec

(P-13164)
1111 6TH AVE LLC
1111 6th Ave Ste 102 (92101-5214)
PHONE..................312 283-3683
William Bennett, Managing Member
Kayley Dicicco, Managing Member
EMP: 75 EST: 2019
SALES (est): 1.32MM Privately Held
SIC: 7389 Office facilities and secretarial service rental

(P-13165)
2310 CATALINA LLC
1507 Western Ave (91201-1215)
PHONE..................818 696-2040
Ararat Yesayan, Brnch Mgr
EMP: 67
SALES (corp-wide): 721.73K Privately Held
SIC: 7389 Personal service agents, brokers, and bureaus
PA: 2310 Catalina Llc
635 W Colorado St Ste 109
Glendale CA
818 824-6304

(P-13166)
5 PALMS LLC
800 S B St Fl 1 (94401-4271)
PHONE..................650 457-0539
EMP: 212 EST: 2014
SALES (est): 2.38MM Privately Held
SIC: 7389 5083 3523
; Agricultural machinery and equipment; Farm machinery and equipment

(P-13167)
A F EVANS COMPANY INC
Also Called: Byron Park
1700 Tice Valley Blvd Ofc (94595-1654)
PHONE..................925 937-1700
Kirsten Korhsege, Mgr
EMP: 76
SALES (corp-wide): 41.99MM Privately Held
SIC: 7389 Personal service agents, brokers, and bureaus
PA: A. F. Evans Company, Inc.
2033 N Main St Ste 340
Walnut Creek CA
510 891-9400

(P-13168)
A J PARENT COMPANY INC (PA)
Also Called: Americas Printer.com
6910 Aragon Cir Ste 6 (90620-8103)
PHONE..................714 521-1100
Arthur Parent, CEO
EMP: 88 EST: 1997
SALES (est): 18.16MM
SALES (corp-wide): 18.16MM Privately Held
Web: www.americasprinter.com
SIC: 7389 2752 Printers' services: folding, collating, etc.; Commercial printing, lithographic

(P-13169)
AAA RESTAURANT FIRE CTRL INC
Also Called: AAA Fire Protection Service
30113 Union City Blvd (94587-1511)
P.O. Box 3626 (94540-3626)
PHONE..................510 786-9555
Brent Patterson, Pr
Brian Patterson, *
Jeanne Patterson, *
Karen Patterson, *
EMP: 90 EST: 1974
SQ FT: 10,000
SALES (est): 11.02MM Privately Held
Web: www.aaafireprotection.com
SIC: 7389 Fire extinguisher servicing

(P-13170)
AARON THOMAS COMPANY INC (PA)
Also Called: Aaron Thomas
7421 Chapman Ave (92841-2115)
PHONE..................714 894-4468
Aerick Bacon, Pr
James T Chang, *
Thomas Bacon, *
Jean Chang, *
Linda Bacon, *
▲ EMP: 125 EST: 1973
SQ FT: 207,000
SALES (est): 44.17MM
SALES (corp-wide): 44.17MM Privately Held
Web: www.packaging.com
SIC: 7389 Packaging and labeling services

(P-13171)
ABI DOCUMENT SUPPORT SVCS LLC
Also Called: ABI Document Support Service
11010 White Rock Rd Ste 1 (95670-6361)
PHONE..................909 793-0613
Maggie Dragna, Brnch Mgr
EMP: 71
Web: www.abidss.com
SIC: 7389 5044 Microfilm recording and developing service; Office equipment
HQ: Abi Document Support Services, Llc
3534 E Sunshine St Ste L
Springfield MO

(P-13172)
ABI DOCUMENT SUPPORT SVCS LLC
Also Called: ABI Document Support Services
10459 Mountain View Ave Ste E (92354-2033)
PHONE..................909 793-0613
David Benge, Brnch Mgr
EMP: 86
Web: www.abidss.com
SIC: 7389 5044 Microfilm recording and developing service; Office equipment
HQ: Abi Document Support Services, Llc
3534 E Sunshine St Ste L
Springfield MO

(P-13173)
ABSOLUTDATA TECHNOLOGIES INC
1320 Harbor Bay Pkwy Ste 170 (94502-6578)
PHONE..................510 748-9922
Anil Kaul, Pr
Suhale Kapoor, *
Sudeshna Datta, *
EMP: 75 EST: 2000
SQ FT: 1,600
SALES (est): 9.68MM Privately Held
Web: absolutdata.infogain.com
SIC: 7389 7374 Personal service agents, brokers, and bureaus; Data processing service

(P-13174)
ACACIA PHARMA INC
Also Called: ACACIA PHARMA, INC.
440 Stevens Ave Ste 200 (92075-2059)
PHONE..................317 941-9576
EMP: 67
Web: www.acaciapharma.com
SIC: 7389 Personal service agents, brokers, and bureaus
HQ: Acacia Pharma Inc.
8440 Allison Pointe Blvd # 100
Indianapolis IN
317 505-1280

(P-13175)
ACCT HOLDINGS LLC
5949 Fair Oaks Blvd (95608-5221)
PHONE..................916 971-1981
EMP: 594
SALES (corp-wide): 395.07MM Privately Held
Web: www.juliprun.com
SIC: 7389 Telemarketing services
PA: Acct Holdings Llc
1235 Westlakes Dr Ste 160
Berwyn PA
610 695-0500

(P-13176)
ACCURATE FIRESTOP INC
Also Called: Accurate Firestop & Insulation

7389 - Business Services, Nec (P-13196)

PRODUCTS & SERVICES SECTION

1057 Serpentine Ln Ste A (94566-8465)
PHONE..................925 701-8600
Gabrielle Lucatero, *Managing Member*
Gabrielle Lucatero, *Prin*
Javier Lucatero, *
EMP: 150 EST: 1995
SALES (est): 8.96MM **Privately Held**
Web: www.accuratefirestop.com
SIC: 7389 Fire protection service other than forestry or public

(P-13177)
AD ART INC (PA)
Also Called: Ad Art Sign Company
150 Executive Park Blvd Ste 2100 (94134-3364)
PHONE..................415 869-6460
Terry J Long, *CEO*
Robert Kiereczyk, *
Duane Contento, *
Doug Head, *
David Esajian, *
▲ EMP: 70 EST: 2003
SQ FT: 4,000
SALES (est): 28.96MM
SALES (corp-wide): 28.96MM **Privately Held**
Web: www.adart.com
SIC: 7389 7532 7812 3648 Interior design services; Exterior repair services; Video production; Decorative area lighting fixtures

(P-13178)
ADMINISTRATIVE SYSTEMS INC
1651 Response Rd Ste 350 (95815-5255)
P.O. Box 15437 (95851-0437)
PHONE..................916 563-1121
Donald J Robinson, *Pr*
James R Powell, *
Geraldine M Fong, *
Keith Crane, *
EMP: 75 EST: 1972
SALES (est): 12.34MM **Privately Held**
Web: www.asipay.com
SIC: 7389 Personal service agents, brokers, and bureaus

(P-13179)
ADVANSTAR COMMUNICATIONS INC (DH)
Also Called: Advanstar Global
2501 Colorado Ave Ste 280 (90404-3754)
PHONE..................310 857-7500
◆ EMP: 177 EST: 1987
SALES (est): 40.29MM
SALES (corp-wide): 2.72B **Privately Held**
Web: epay.advanstar.com
SIC: 7389 2721 7331 Trade show arrangement; Magazines: publishing only, not printed on site; Direct mail advertising services
HQ: Ubm Limited
    240 Blackfriars Road
    London
    207 921-5000

(P-13180)
AFFINITY AUTO PROGRAMS INC
Also Called: Costco Auto Program
10251 Vista Sorrento Pkwy Ste 300 (92121)
PHONE..................858 643-9324
Jeff Skeen, *Pr*
Gary Drean, *
EMP: 266 EST: 1988
SQ FT: 34,000
SALES (est): 90.16MM **Privately Held**
Web: www.costcoauto.com

SIC: 7389 Advertising, promotional, and trade show services

(P-13181)
AFM & SG-FTRA INTLLCTUAL PRPRT
4705 Laurel Canyon Blvd Ste 400 (91607-3911)
PHONE..................818 255-7980
Dennis Dreith, *Ex Dir*
Shari Hoffman, *
Jennifer Leblanc, *
EMP: 70 EST: 2011
SQ FT: 21,600
SALES (est): 10.9MM **Privately Held**
Web: www.afmsagaftrafund.org
SIC: 7389 Fund raising organizations

(P-13182)
AIRBNB INC (PA)
Also Called: Airbnb
888 Brannan St Fl 4 (94103-5070)
PHONE..................415 510-4027
Brian Chesky, *Ch Bd*
Dave Stephenson, *CFO*
Nathan Blecharczyk, *CSO*
Catherine Powell Global Health Hosting, *Prin*
EMP: 1032 EST: 2008
SQ FT: 941,000
SALES (est): 8.4B
SALES (corp-wide): 8.4B **Publicly Held**
Web: www.airbnb.com
SIC: 7389 Reservation services

(P-13183)
ALL-PRO BAIL BONDS INC
530 Hacienda Dr Ste 104d (92081-6640)
PHONE..................760 512-1969
Steffan Gibbs, *Brnch Mgr*
EMP: 100
SALES (corp-wide): 10.07MM **Privately Held**
Web: www.allprobailbond.com
SIC: 7389 Bail bonding
PA: All-Pro Bail Bonds Inc.
    512 Via De La Vlle Ste 30 Valle
    Solana Beach CA
    858 481-1200

(P-13184)
ALORICA CUSTOMER CARE INC
8885 Rio San Diego Dr Ste 107 (92108-1624)
PHONE..................619 298-7103
EMP: 100
SALES (corp-wide): 845.12MM **Privately Held**
SIC: 7389 Telemarketing services
HQ: Alorica Customer Care, Inc.
    5085 W Park Blvd Ste 300
    Plano TX

(P-13185)
ALORICA CUSTOMER CARE INC
5161 California Ave Ste 100 (92617-8002)
PHONE..................941 906-9000
EMP: 175
SALES (corp-wide): 845.12MM **Privately Held**
Web: www.alorica.com
SIC: 7389 Telemarketing services
HQ: Alorica Customer Care, Inc.
    5085 W Park Blvd Ste 300
    Plano TX

(P-13186)
ALORICA INC (PA)
5161 California Ave Ste 100 (92617-8002)
PHONE..................866 256-7422

Greg Haller, *CEO*
Chris Crowley, *Chief Commercial Officer*
Steve Phillips, *CIO*
Max Schwendner, *CFO*
▲ EMP: 100 EST: 1999
SALES (est): 845.12MM
SALES (corp-wide): 845.12MM **Privately Held**
Web: www.alorica.com
SIC: 7389 Telephone answering service

(P-13187)
ALTEC PRODUCTS INC (PA)
23422 Mill Creek Dr Ste 225 (92653-7910)
PHONE..................949 727-1248
Mark Ford, *CEO*
Brandt Morell, *
Mark Tague, *
Frank Sansone, *
Bill Brown, *
EMP: 79 EST: 1985
SQ FT: 12,500
SALES (est): 12.96MM
SALES (corp-wide): 12.96MM **Privately Held**
Web: www.altecproductsinc.com
SIC: 7389 Telemarketing services

(P-13188)
ALTERNATIVE IRA SERVICES LLC
Also Called: Bitcoin Ira
15303 Ventura Blvd Ste 1060 (91403-3110)
PHONE..................877 936-7175
EMP: 201 EST: 2016
SALES (est): 2.53MM **Privately Held**
Web: www.bitcoinira.com
SIC: 7389 Financial services

(P-13189)
AMERICAN COPAK CORPORATION
9175 Eton Ave (91311-5806)
PHONE..................818 576-1000
Steven A Brooker, *Pr*
EMP: 150 EST: 1987
SQ FT: 150,000
SALES (est): 4.28MM **Privately Held**
Web: www.americancopak.com
SIC: 7389 Packaging and labeling services

(P-13190)
AMERICAN HEALTH CONNECTION
8484 Wilshire Blvd Ste 501 (90211-3243)
PHONE..................424 226-0420
Yuriy Koltyar, *CEO*
Azabeh Williamson, *
EMP: 850 EST: 2011
SQ FT: 3,500
SALES (est): 13.61MM **Privately Held**
Web: www.americanhealthconnection.com
SIC: 7389 Telemarketing services

(P-13191)
AMPLE INC (PA)
100 Hooper St Ste 25 (94107-2204)
PHONE..................617 504-3557
Khaled Hassounah, *CEO*
Marianella Cateriano, *
EMP: 64 EST: 2014
SALES (est): 12.25MM
SALES (corp-wide): 12.25MM **Privately Held**
Web: www.ample.com
SIC: 7389 Business Activities at Non-Commercial Site

(P-13192)
ANDPAK INC
Also Called: Zip-Chem Products
400 Jarvis Dr Ste A (95037-2809)
PHONE..................408 776-1072
Dick Varien, *CEO*
Jack Douglass, *
Dennis Wagner, *
Chuck Pottier, *
EMP: 70 EST: 1978
SQ FT: 50,000
SALES (est): 19.91MM **Privately Held**
Web: www.andpak.com
SIC: 7389 Packaging and labeling services

(P-13193)
ANDREW LAUREN COMPANY INC
15225 Alton Pkwy Unit 300 (92618-2345)
PHONE..................949 861-4222
Mark Noonan, *Prin*
EMP: 117
Web: int.andrewlauren.com
SIC: 7389 5713 Interior design services; Carpets
PA: The Andrew Lauren Company Inc
    8909 Kenamar Dr Ste 101
    San Diego CA

(P-13194)
ANHEUSER-BUSCH LLC
Also Called: Anheuser-Busch
15800 Roscoe Blvd (91406-1350)
PHONE..................805 381-4700
Charles Cindric, *Mgr*
EMP: 255
SALES (corp-wide): 1.31B **Privately Held**
Web: www.anheuser-busch.com
SIC: 7389 Office facilities and secretarial service rental
HQ: Anheuser-Busch, Llc
    1 Busch Pl
    Saint Louis MO
    800 342-5283

(P-13195)
ANSWER FINANCIAL INC (HQ)
15910 Ventura Blvd Fl 6 (91436-2803)
PHONE..................818 644-4000
Robert J Slingerland, *CEO*
Daniel John Bryce, *
Peter Foley, *
John E Galaviz, *
Craig Lozofsky, *
EMP: 200 EST: 2006
SQ FT: 45,000
SALES (est): 66.55MM **Publicly Held**
Web: www.answerfinancial.com
SIC: 7389 6411 Brokers, business: buying and selling business enterprises; Property and casualty insurance agent
PA: The Allstate Corporation
    3100 Sanders Rd
    Northbrook IL

(P-13196)
ARRIVAL COMMUNICATIONS INC (DH)
1800 19th St (93301-4315)
PHONE..................661 716-2100
Richard Jalkut, *CEO*
Tony Distefano, *
Warren Heffelfinger, *
Geoffrey Whynot, *
David Riordan, *
EMP: 75 EST: 1991
SQ FT: 4,000
SALES (est): 10.26MM **Privately Held**
Web: www.arrivalcommunications.com
SIC: 7389 Design services

7389 - Business Services, Nec (P-13197)

HQ: U.S. Telepacific Corp.
303 Colorado St Ste 2075
Austin TX
877 487-8722

(P-13197)
ARVATO USA LLC
2053 E Jay St (91764-1847)
PHONE..................502 356-8063
Dominik Dittrich, *Brnch Mgr*
EMP: 106
SALES (corp-wide): 54.57MM **Privately Held**
SIC: 7389 Telephone answering service
HQ: Arvato Usa Llc
51 Sawyer Rd Ste 620
Waltham MA
661 702-2700

(P-13198)
ASSOCTED LDSCP DSPLAY GROUP IN
Also Called: Associated Group
1005 Mateo St (90021-1715)
PHONE..................714 558-6100
Laurie Resnick, *Pr*
Greg Salmeri, *
Angelica Arreola *Seasonal Disp lay*, *Dir*
Angela Hicks, *
EMP: 90 **EST:** 1986
SALES (est): 9MM **Privately Held**
Web: www.ag-ca.com
SIC: 7389 0781 Plant care service; Landscape services

(P-13199)
ASSURED RELOCATION INC
50 Woodside Plz Ste 441 (94061-2500)
PHONE..................888 670-9700
Janette Macdonell, *Pr*
EMP: 125 **EST:** 2003
SALES (est): 15.59MM **Privately Held**
Web: www.assuredrelocation.com
SIC: 7389 Relocation service
PA: Temporary Housing, Inc.
10851 N Black Canyon Hwy # 700
Phoenix AZ

(P-13200)
ATEL CORPORATION
600 Montgomery St Fl 9 (94111-2711)
PHONE..................415 989-8800
Dean L Cash, *Pr*
Vasco Morais, *
EMP: 61 **EST:** 2018
SQ FT: 2,000
SALES (est): 9.4MM **Privately Held**
Web: www.atel.com
SIC: 7389 Office facilities and secretarial service rental
PA: Atel Capital Group
505 Montgomery St Fl 11
San Francisco CA

(P-13201)
AUGMEDIX OPERATING CORPORATION
111 Sutter St Fl 13 (94104-4541)
PHONE..................855 720-2929
Manny Krakaris, *CEO*
EMP: 92 **EST:** 2013
SALES (est): 11.16MM
SALES (corp-wide): 30.93MM **Publicly Held**
Web: www.augmedix.com
SIC: 7389 Handwriting analysis
PA: Augmedix, Inc.
111 Sutter St Ste 1300
San Francisco CA
888 669-4885

(P-13202)
AUTOCRIB INC
2882 Dow Ave (92780-7258)
PHONE..................714 274-0400
Stephen Pixley, *CEO*
▲ **EMP:** 150 **EST:** 1999
SQ FT: 58,000
SALES (est): 43.82MM
SALES (corp-wide): 4.49B **Publicly Held**
Web: www.autocrib.com
SIC: 7389 3581 Inventory computing service; Automatic vending machines
PA: Snap-On Incorporated
2801 80th St
Kenosha WI
262 656-5200

(P-13203)
AXIM GEOSPATIAL LLC
2701 Loker Ave W (92010-6638)
PHONE..................608 352-4180
EMP: 67
SALES (corp-wide): 786.78MM **Publicly Held**
Web: www.aximgeo.com
SIC: 7389 Mapmaking or drafting, including aerial
HQ: Axim Geospatial, Llc
100 Qbe Way Ste 1225
Sun Prairie WI
608 352-4180

(P-13204)
AZTECS TELECOM INC
1353 Walker Ln (92879-1775)
PHONE..................714 373-1560
Robert Lopez, *CEO*
EMP: 80 **EST:** 2000
SALES (est): 5.17MM **Privately Held**
Web: www.aztecs.net
SIC: 7389 1731 Telephone services; Communications specialization

(P-13205)
B RILEY SECURITIES INC
11100 Santa Monica Blvd (90025-3384)
PHONE..................310 966-1444
Bryant Riley, *CEO*
EMP: 126 **EST:** 1989
SALES (est): 15.96MM **Publicly Held**
Web: www.brileyfin.com
SIC: 7389 Financial services
PA: B. Riley Financial, Inc.
11100 Santa Monica Blvd
Los Angeles CA

(P-13206)
BACK OF HOUSE INC
2020 Union St (94123-4103)
PHONE..................415 550-8626
Adriano Paganini, *CEO*
EMP: 84 **EST:** 2015
SALES (est): 4.84MM **Privately Held**
Web: www.backofthehouseinc.com
SIC: 7389 Design services

(P-13207)
BAD BOYS BAIL BONDS INC (PA)
595 Park Ave Ste 200 (95110-2641)
PHONE..................408 298-3333
Clifford J Stanley, *Pr*
Craig A Stanley, *
▲ **EMP:** 75 **EST:** 1998
SQ FT: 3,000
SALES (est): 8.57MM
SALES (corp-wide): 8.57MM **Privately Held**
Web: www.badboysbailbonds.com
SIC: 7389 Bail bonding

(P-13208)
BANCOLMBIA PR INTRNACIONAL INC
2625 E Florence Ave Ste E (90255-4756)
PHONE..................323 582-2255
Julio Melara Junior, *Mgr*
EMP: 162
Web: www.bancolombiamiami.com
SIC: 7389 Financial services
HQ: Bancolombia Puerto Rico Internacional Inc.
270 Munoz Rivera Ste 502
San Juan PR

(P-13209)
BANKCARD SERVICES (PA)
21281 S Western Ave (90501-2958)
PHONE..................213 365-1122
EMP: 110 **EST:** 2012
SALES (est): 24.85MM
SALES (corp-wide): 24.85MM **Privately Held**
Web: www.navyz.com
SIC: 7389 Credit card service

(P-13210)
BANKCARD USA MERCHANT SRVC
5701 Lindero Canyon Rd (91362-4060)
PHONE..................818 597-7000
EMP: 85 **EST:** 1993
SQ FT: 20,000
SALES (est): 146.14K **Privately Held**
Web: www.bankcardusa.com
SIC: 7389 Credit card service

(P-13211)
BART MANUFACTURING INC
1300 E Victor Rd (95240-0800)
PHONE..................408 250-4975
EMP: 114
SALES (corp-wide): 9.55MM **Privately Held**
Web: www.bartmanufacturing.com
SIC: 7389 Personal service agents, brokers, and bureaus
PA: Bart Manufacturing, Inc.
1043 Di Giulio Ave
Santa Clara CA
408 320-4373

(P-13212)
BAXALTA US INC
17511 Armstrong Ave (92614-5725)
PHONE..................949 474-6301
EMP: 191
SIC: 7389 Personal service agents, brokers, and bureaus
HQ: Baxalta Us Inc.
1200 Lakeside Dr
Bannockburn IL
224 948-2000

(P-13213)
BEST CHOICE LLC
22568 Mission Blvd Ste 344 (94541)
PHONE..................510 862-4989
EMP: 101
SALES (corp-wide): 418.73K **Privately Held**
SIC: 7389 Personal service agents, brokers, and bureaus
PA: Best Choice Llc
750 El Camino Real
Tustin CA

(P-13214)
BIU INC
9268 1/2 Hall Rd (90241-5308)
PHONE..................909 556-1311
EMP: 91
SALES (corp-wide): 295.56K **Privately Held**
SIC: 7389 Personal service agents, brokers, and bureaus
PA: Biu Inc.
3100 Airway Ave
Costa Mesa CA
714 785-4751

(P-13215)
BLACK KNIGHT INFOSERV LLC
601 California St Ste 980 (94108-2800)
PHONE..................415 989-9800
EMP: 109
SALES (corp-wide): 7.29B **Publicly Held**
Web: www.blackknightinc.com
SIC: 7389 7374 Financial services; Data processing and preparation
HQ: Black Knight Infoserv, Llc
601 Riverside Ave
Jacksonville FL

(P-13216)
BOOST MOBILE LLC
6316 Irvine Blvd (92620-2102)
PHONE..................949 451-1563
EMP: 1290
SIC: 7389 Telephone services

(P-13217)
BRADFORD MESSENGER SERVICE
4955 E Andersen Ave # 118 (93727-1543)
PHONE..................559 252-0775
EMP: 60
SQ FT: 1,500
SALES (est): 1.62MM **Privately Held**
SIC: 7389 Courier or messenger service

(P-13218)
BREX INC (PA)
Also Called: Brex Technologies
115 Sansome St Ste 1200 (94104-3630)
PHONE..................844 725-9569
Henrique Dubugras, *CEO*
Pedro Franceschi, *
Michael Tannenbaum, *
EMP: 962 **EST:** 2017
SALES (est): 84.32MM
SALES (corp-wide): 84.32MM **Privately Held**
Web: www.brex.com
SIC: 7389 Credit card service

(P-13219)
C P SHADES INC
2633 Ashby Ave (94705-2229)
PHONE..................510 647-9605
EMP: 385
SALES (corp-wide): 25.46MM **Privately Held**
Web: www.cpshades.com
SIC: 7389 Design services
PA: C P Shades, Inc.
403 Coloma St
Sausalito CA
415 331-4581

(P-13220)
CALI BEACH BEARS LLC
335 E Betteravia Rd (93454-7805)
PHONE..................805 361-0260
EMP: 74
SALES (corp-wide): 497.25K **Privately Held**
SIC: 7389 Personal service agents, brokers, and bureaus
PA: Cali Beach Bears, Llc

PRODUCTS & SERVICES SECTION

7389 - Business Services, Nec (P-13242)

599 Higuera St Ste B
San Luis Obispo CA

(P-13221)
CALIFORNIA HLTH COLLABORATIVE (PA)
1680 W Shaw Ave (93711-3504)
P.O. Box 25609 (93729-5609)
PHONE.................559 221-6315
Gary Erickson, *Ch*
Stephen Ramirez, *
Rueben Cuadrof, *
EMP: 68 **EST:** 1982
SQ FT: 11,400
SALES (est): 13.02MM
SALES (corp-wide): 13.02MM **Privately Held**
Web: www.healthcollaborative.org
SIC: 7389 Fund raising organizations

(P-13222)
CALIFORNIA TRAFFIC CONTROL
Also Called: California Traffic Ctrl Svcs
3333 Cherry Ave (90807-4901)
PHONE.................562 595-7575
Delores Kepl, *CFO*
EMP: 70 **EST:** 2010
SALES (est): 4.49MM **Privately Held**
Web: www.californiatrafficcontrol.com
SIC: 7389 Flagging service (traffic control)

(P-13223)
CALIFRNIA CLNIC PLSTIC SURGERY
73180 El Paseo (92260-4218)
PHONE.................760 346-0611
EMP: 184
SALES (corp-wide): 3.97MM **Privately Held**
SIC: 7389 Personal service agents, brokers, and bureaus
PA: California Clinic Plastic Surgery
    100 E California Blvd
    Pasadena CA
    626 817-0818

(P-13224)
CALIFRNIA GRNHSE FRM II LTD PR
17712 Adobe Rd (93307-9756)
PHONE.................949 715-3987
Li Hui Lo, *Pr*
EMP: 78 **EST:** 2012
SALES (est): 1.09MM **Privately Held**
SIC: 7389 Business Activities at Non-Commercial Site

(P-13225)
CANYON SPRINGS PKWY QSR LLC
6231 Valley Springs Pkwy (92507-0957)
PHONE.................951 413-6081
EMP: 72
SALES (corp-wide): 450.07K **Privately Held**
SIC: 7389 Personal service agents, brokers, and bureaus
PA: Canyon Springs Pkwy Qsr, Llc
    683 Cliffside Dr
    San Dimas CA
    909 293-7588

(P-13226)
CARDSERVICE INTERNATIONAL INC (DH)
5898 Condor Dr # 220 (93021-2603)
EMP: 450 **EST:** 2002
SQ FT: 34,000
SALES (est): 49.55MM
SALES (corp-wide): 17.74B **Publicly Held**
SIC: 7389 6153 Credit card service; Short-term business credit institutions, except agricultural
HQ: First Data Corporation
    255 Fiserv Dr
    Brookfield WI

(P-13227)
CARECREDIT LLC
555 Anton Blvd Ste 700 (92626-7659)
PHONE.................800 300-3046
EMP: 120 **EST:** 1996
SALES (est): 12.63MM
SALES (corp-wide): 17.53B **Publicly Held**
Web: www.carecredit.com
SIC: 7389 8742 Financial services; Banking and finance consultant
PA: Synchrony Financial
    777 Long Ridge Rd Ste 2
    Stamford CT
    203 585-2400

(P-13228)
CASECENTRAL INC (DH)
Also Called: Casecentral.com
1055 E Colorado Blvd Ste 400 (91106)
PHONE.................415 989-2300
EMP: 60 **EST:** 1993
SALES (est): 27.87MM
SALES (corp-wide): 832.31MM **Privately Held**
Web: www.casecentral.com
SIC: 7389 4813 4226 Legal and tax services; Online service providers; Document and office records storage
HQ: Guidance Software, Inc.
    1055 E Colo Blvd Ste 400
    Pasadena CA
    626 229-9191

(P-13229)
CASHEDGE INC
525 Almanor Ave Ste 150 (94085-3545)
PHONE.................408 541-3900
Mckenzie Lyons, *Prin*
EMP: 100
SALES (corp-wide): 17.74B **Publicly Held**
Web: www.fiserv.com
SIC: 7389 Financial services
HQ: Cashedge Inc.
    255 Fiserv Dr
    Brookfield WI
    262 879-5000

(P-13230)
CETERA FINANCIAL GROUP INC (PA)
655 W Broadway Ste 1680 (92101-8495)
PHONE.................866 489-3100
EMP: 238 **EST:** 2009
SQ FT: 70,000
SALES (est): 315.75K **Privately Held**
Web: www.cetera.com
SIC: 7389 6282 Financial services; Investment advisory service

(P-13231)
CHECKR INC (PA)
1 Montgomery St Ste 2400 (94104-5524)
PHONE.................844 824-3257
Daniel Yanisse, *CEO*
EMP: 169 **EST:** 2014
SALES (est): 473.9MM
SALES (corp-wide): 473.9MM **Privately Held**
Web: www.checkr.com
SIC: 7389 Personal investigation service

(P-13232)
CISCO SYSTEMS CAPITAL CORP (HQ)
Also Called: Cisco
170 W Tasman Dr (95134-1706)
PHONE.................610 386-5870
Kristine A Snow, *Pr*
David A Rogan, *
Frank Calderoni, *
John T Chambers, *
David K Holland, *
EMP: 111 **EST:** 1996
SALES (est): 465.58MM
SALES (corp-wide): 57B **Publicly Held**
Web: www.cisco.com
SIC: 7389 Financial services
PA: Cisco Systems, Inc.
    170 W Tasman Dr
    San Jose CA
    408 526-4000

(P-13233)
CISCO WEBEX LLC (HQ)
Also Called: Webex.com
170 W Tasman Dr (95134-1700)
PHONE.................408 526-4000
Charles Robbins, *CEO*
Aruna Ravichandran, *CMO*
Snorre Kjesbu, *
EMP: 1108 **EST:** 1995
SQ FT: 160,000
SALES (est): 149.38MM
SALES (corp-wide): 57B **Publicly Held**
Web: www.webex.com
SIC: 7389 4813 Teleconferencing services; Data telephone communications
PA: Cisco Systems, Inc.
    170 W Tasman Dr
    San Jose CA
    408 526-4000

(P-13234)
CITY OF LODI (PA)
221 W Pine St (95240-2019)
P.O. Box 3006 (95241-1910)
PHONE.................209 333-6700
Bob Johnson, *Mayor*
Phil Katvakian, *
Blair King, *
EMP: 60 **EST:** 1906
SQ FT: 6,320
SALES (est): 98.03MM
SALES (corp-wide): 98.03MM **Privately Held**
Web: www.lodi.gov
SIC: 7389 Business Activities at Non-Commercial Site

(P-13235)
CITY OF SACRAMENTO
Also Called: Convention & Cultural Services
1401 K St (95814-3915)
PHONE.................916 808-5291
Michael W Ross, *Genl Mgr*
EMP: 163
Web: www.cityofsacramento.gov
SIC: 7389 9199 Convention and show services; General government administration, Local government
PA: City Of Sacramento
    915 I St Fl 5
    Sacramento CA
    916 808-5300

(P-13236)
CITY RISE LLC
18826 N Lower Sacramento Rd (95258)
PHONE.................209 334-2703
Nicole Beadles, *Mgr*
EMP: 100

SALES (corp-wide): 10.4MM **Privately Held**
Web: www.cityrisesafety.com
SIC: 7389 Flagging service (traffic control)
PA: City Rise, Llc
    1225 S Sacramento St
    Lodi CA
    209 333-0807

(P-13237)
CLEARXCHANGE LLC
275 Sacramento St # 400 (94111-3810)
PHONE.................415 813-4801
EMP: 99 **EST:** 2011
SALES (est): 235.58K **Privately Held**
Web: www.zellepay.com
SIC: 7389 Financial services
PA: Early Warning Services, Llc
    5801 N Pima Rd
    Scottsdale AZ

(P-13238)
CLIQ INC
2900 Bristol St Ste F (92626-5914)
PHONE.................714 361-1900
Andrew M Phillips, *Pr*
EMP: 75 **EST:** 2008
SALES (est): 15.9MM **Privately Held**
Web: www.cliq.com
SIC: 7389 Credit card service

(P-13239)
COASTAL INTL HOLDINGS LLC
Also Called: Coastal International
2832 Walnut Ave Ste B (92780-7002)
PHONE.................714 635-1200
EMP: 285
SALES (corp-wide): 33.79MM **Privately Held**
Web: www.coastalintl.com
SIC: 7389 Trade show arrangement
PA: Coastal International Holdings, Llc
    3 Harbor Dr
    Sausalito CA
    415 339-1700

(P-13240)
COMPASS GROUP USA INC
Also Called: Canteen Refreshment Services
20929 Cabot Blvd (94545-1155)
PHONE.................510 259-0416
Larry Rich, *Brnch Mgr*
EMP: 395
SALES (corp-wide): 29.97B **Privately Held**
Web: www.compass-usa.com
SIC: 7389 Coffee service
HQ: Compass Group Usa, Inc.
    2400 Yorkmont Rd
    Charlotte NC

(P-13241)
COMPUMAIL INFORMATION SVCS INC
4057 Port Chicago Hwy Ste 300 (94520-1160)
P.O. Box 6756 (94524-1756)
PHONE.................925 689-7100
▲ **EMP:** 75 **EST:** 1992
SQ FT: 22,000
SALES (est): 20.46MM **Privately Held**
Web: www.compumailinc.com
SIC: 7389 Printers' services: folding, collating, etc.

(P-13242)
CONCENTRIX CORPORATION (PA)
Also Called: CONCENTRIX
44111 Nobel Dr (94538-3173)

7389 - Business Services, Nec (P-13243)

PHONE.................................800 747-0583
Christopher Caldwell, *Pr*
Kathryn Hayley, *
Andre Valentine, *CFO*
Steve Richie, *Ex VP*
Cormac Twomey, *Ex VP*
EMP: 693 EST: 2004
SALES (est): 6.32B
SALES (corp-wide): 6.32B **Publicly Held**
Web: www.concentrix.com
SIC: 7389 8748 7374
; Business consulting, nec; Data processing service

(P-13243)
CONSOLDTED FIRE PROTECTION LLC (HQ)
153 Technology Dr Ste 200 (92618-2402)
PHONE.................................949 727-3277
Keith Fielding, *
Steve Shaffer, *
EMP: 800 EST: 1999
SALES (est): 52.85MM **Privately Held**
Web: www.cfpfire.com
SIC: 7389 Fire protection service other than forestry or public
PA: Mx Holdings Us, Inc.
153 Technology Dr Ste 200
Irvine CA

(P-13244)
CONTINENTAL EXCH SOLUTIONS INC
Also Called: Ria Financial Services
7001 Village Dr Ste 200 (90621-2232)
PHONE.................................562 345-2100
EMP: 70
Web: us.riafinancial.com
SIC: 7389 Financial services
HQ: Continental Exchange Solutions Inc.
6565 Knott Ave
Buena Park CA

(P-13245)
CONTINENTAL EXCH SOLUTIONS INC
506 N Milpas St (93103-3137)
PHONE.................................805 965-0663
EMP: 61
Web: us.riafinancial.com
SIC: 7389 Financial services
HQ: Continental Exchange Solutions Inc.
6565 Knott Ave
Buena Park CA

(P-13246)
COUNTRY VILLA SERVICE CORP
39950 Vista Del Sol (92270-3206)
PHONE.................................760 340-0053
Georgeanne Slapper, *Brnch Mgr*
EMP: 102
SALES (corp-wide): 88.5MM **Privately Held**
Web: www.evictionlawyer.com
SIC: 7389 Personal service agents, brokers, and bureaus
PA: Country Villa Service Corp.
2400 E Katella Ave # 800
Anaheim CA
310 574-3733

(P-13247)
COUNTY OF LOS ANGELES
Also Called: Internal Services Dept
1100 N Eastern Ave (90063-3200)
PHONE.................................323 267-2771
Linnette Bookman, *Superintnt*
EMP: 81
SALES (corp-wide): 31.7B **Privately Held**

Web: www.lacounty.gov
SIC: 7389 9631 Telephone services; Communications commission, government
PA: County Of Los Angeles
500 W Temple St Ste 437
Los Angeles CA
213 974-1101

(P-13248)
COUNTY OF SAN DIEGO
Also Called: Public Works
5510 Overland Ave Ste 410 (92123-1239)
PHONE.................................858 694-2960
Wayne Williams, *Mgr*
EMP: 192
Web: www.sdcda.org
SIC: 7389 Personal service agents, brokers, and bureaus
PA: County Of San Diego
1600 Pacific Hwy Ste 209
San Diego CA
619 531-5880

(P-13249)
CREATIVE DESIGN CONSULTANTS (PA)
Also Called: C D C
2915 Red Hill Ave Ste G201 (92626-5923)
PHONE.................................714 641-4868
Dana Eggerts, *Prin*
Christie Pettus, *Prin*
Julie Ann Stark, *Prin*
Lisa Kells, *Prin*
Cassie Nguyen, *Prin*
EMP: 95 EST: 1994
SQ FT: 9,988
SALES (est): 11.24MM
SALES (corp-wide): 11.24MM **Privately Held**
Web: www.cdcdesigns.com
SIC: 7389 Interior designer

(P-13250)
CREDIBILITY CORP
22761 Pacific Coast Hwy (90265-5064)
PHONE.................................310 456-8271
EMP: 732
Web: www.credibility.com
SIC: 7389 Financial services

(P-13251)
CREDIT CARD SERVICES INC (PA)
Also Called: Bankcard Services
21281 S Western Ave (90501-2958)
PHONE.................................213 365-1122
Patrick S Hong, *CEO*
EMP: 95 EST: 1996
SQ FT: 17,000
SALES (est): 20.26MM **Privately Held**
Web: www.navyz.com
SIC: 7389 Credit card service

(P-13252)
CREDIT KARMA LLC (HQ)
1100 Broadway Ste 1800 (94607-4192)
PHONE.................................415 510-5059
Kenneth Lin, *CEO*
EMP: 149 EST: 2020
SALES (est): 237.65MM
SALES (corp-wide): 14.37B **Publicly Held**
Web: www.creditkarma.com
SIC: 7389 Credit card service
PA: Intuit Inc.
2700 Coast Ave
Mountain View CA
650 944-6000

(P-13253)
CREDIT KARMA INC
760 Market St Fl 2 (94102-2402)
PHONE.................................415 510-5059
EMP: 750
Web: www.creditkarma.com
SIC: 7389 Credit card service

(P-13254)
CURRENT TV LLC
118 King St (94107-1905)
PHONE.................................415 995-8328
Joel Hyatt, *
Guy Barbaro, *
Mark Golmon, *
Paul Hollerbach, *
EMP: 200 EST: 2004
SQ FT: 27,000
SALES (est): 52.63MM **Privately Held**
Web: www.current.com
SIC: 7389 Field audits, cable television
HQ: Al Jazeera Media Network
Qatar Television Building Khalifa Street
Doha

(P-13255)
D & D CAHILL INC
Also Called: Titan Tank Lines
2626 Terrace Ave (93657-9195)
PHONE.................................559 708-7601
Dennis Cahill, *Admn*
EMP: 65 EST: 2010
SALES (est): 1.89MM **Privately Held**
SIC: 7389 Business Activities at Non-Commercial Site

(P-13256)
DA VINCI SCHOOLS FUND
201 N Douglas St (90245-4637)
PHONE.................................310 725-5800
Matthew Wunder, *Admn*
EMP: 190 EST: 2017
SALES (est): 35.36MM **Privately Held**
Web: www.davincischools.org
SIC: 7389 Design services

(P-13257)
DANE KARNO INC
1798 Larkhaven Gln (92026-1091)
PHONE.................................619 813-8585
Dane Karno, *Brnch Mgr*
EMP: 75
SALES (corp-wide): 460.04K **Privately Held**
SIC: 7389 Personal service agents, brokers, and bureaus
PA: Dane Karno Inc
3861 Mission Ave Ste B4
Oceanside CA

(P-13258)
DATA COUNCIL LLC
Also Called: Logix3
15310 Barranca Pkwy Ste 100 (92618-2215)
PHONE.................................904 512-3200
John Kocher, *Pr*
Lloyd Kammerer, *Prin*
EMP: 100 EST: 2014
SALES (est): 9.86MM
SALES (corp-wide): 4.71B **Publicly Held**
Web: www.thedatacouncil.com
SIC: 7389 Commodity inspection
HQ: Advantage Sales & Marketing Llc
15310 Barranca Pkwy # 100
Irvine CA
949 797-2900

(P-13259)
DECIMAL INC
Also Called: Ubiquity
1160 Battery St Ste 350 (94111-1238)
PHONE.................................855 980-6612
Chad Parks, *Pr*
Mary Torgerson, *
EMP: 82 EST: 2000
SQ FT: 5,000
SALES (est): 11.04MM **Privately Held**
Web: www.myubiquity.com
SIC: 7389 Financial services

(P-13260)
DEKRA-LITE INDUSTRIES INC
Also Called: DI Imaging
3102 W Alton Ave (92704-6817)
PHONE.................................714 436-0705
Jeffrey Lopez, *CEO*
▲ EMP: 80 EST: 1987
SQ FT: 30,000
SALES (est): 12.82MM **Privately Held**
Web: www.dekra-lite.com
SIC: 7389 5999 3999 Decoration service for special events; Art, picture frames, and decorations; Advertising curtains

(P-13261)
DELPHI PRODUCTIONS INC
Also Called: Group Delphi
950 W Tower Ave (94501-5049)
PHONE.................................510 748-7494
Justin Hersh, *Pr*
Pete Bowes, *CFO*
Debbie Parrott, *Development*
EMP: 142 EST: 1987
SALES (est): 35.65MM **Privately Held**
SIC: 7389 Trade show arrangement

(P-13262)
DENIOS RSVLLE FRMRS MKT ACTN I
2013 Opportunity Dr (95678-3023)
PHONE.................................916 782-2704
Jeff Ronten, *CEO*
Ken Denio, *
Marilee Denio, *
EMP: 120 EST: 1947
SQ FT: 18,212
SALES (est): 10.33MM **Privately Held**
Web: www.deniosmarket.com
SIC: 7389 Flea market

(P-13263)
DERIVATIVE PATH INC
2001 N Main St Ste 250 (94596-7262)
PHONE.................................415 992-8200
Pradeep Bhatia, *CEO*
Pradeeb Bhatia, *
Zack Nagelberg, *
John Fleming, *
Kristin Kelly, *Chief Product Officer**
EMP: 70 EST: 2013
SALES (est): 6.15MM **Privately Held**
Web: www.derivativepath.com
SIC: 7389 Financial services

(P-13264)
DEROUEN ENTERPRISES LLC
1547 Palos Verdes Mall (94597-2228)
PHONE.................................925 360-5743
EMP: 77
SALES (corp-wide): 243.76K **Privately Held**
SIC: 7389 Personal service agents, brokers, and bureaus
PA: Derouen Enterprises Llc
4337 Machado Dr
Concord CA
925 360-5743

PRODUCTS & SERVICES SECTION
7389 - Business Services, Nec (P-13289)

(P-13265)
DESERVE INC
Also Called: Deserve
195 Page Mill Rd Ste 109 (94306-2073)
P.O. Box 1286 (94026-1286)
PHONE...............................800 418-7353
Kalpesh Kapadia, CEO
Cameron Gray, Engr
John Collins, Development
EMP: 117 EST: 2012
SALES (est): 5.01MM Privately Held
Web: www.deserve.com
SIC: 7389 Financial services

(P-13266)
DF ONE OPERATOR LLC
11 Via Santanella (92270-5817)
PHONE...............................310 961-9739
EMP: 84
SALES (corp-wide): 2.61MM Privately Held
SIC: 7389 Personal service agents, brokers, and bureaus
PA: Df One Operator Llc
65441 Two Bunch Palms Trl
Desert Hot Springs CA
605 472-5422

(P-13267)
DIABLO VLY COLLEGE FOUNDATION (PA)
321 Golf Club Rd (94523-1544)
PHONE...............................925 685-1230
Mark G Edelstein, Pr
Katherine Guptill, *
EMP: 350 EST: 1975
SQ FT: 1,000
SALES (est): 862.85K
SALES (corp-wide): 862.85K Privately Held
Web: www.dvc.edu
SIC: 7389 8221 Fund raising organizations; Colleges and universities

(P-13268)
DIBA FASHIONS INC
472 N Bowling Green Way (90049-2820)
PHONE...............................323 232-3775
John Gir Daneshrad, Pr
Shahin Daneshrad, *
EMP: 70 EST: 1980
SQ FT: 22,400
SALES (est): 1.75MM Privately Held
SIC: 7389 2339 Sewing contractor; Women's and misses' outerwear, nec

(P-13269)
DIGITAL WIRELESS TELECOM INC
482 Alvarado St (93940-2729)
PHONE...............................650 472-7064
Brahim Boumakh, CEO
EMP: 85 EST: 1998
SALES (est): 1.29MM Privately Held
SIC: 7389 Telephone services

(P-13270)
DISTINCTIVE CORPORATION
14413 Big Basin Way (95070-6008)
PHONE...............................408 568-5598
EMP: 88
SALES (corp-wide): 991.41K Privately Held
SIC: 7389 Personal service agents, brokers, and bureaus
PA: Distinctive Corporation
707 1st St
Gilroy CA
408 219-1922

(P-13271)
DIVIDEND FINANCE
3661 Valley Centre Dr Ste 250 (92130)
PHONE...............................858 880-7710
EMP: 64 EST: 2018
SALES (est): 1.57MM Privately Held
Web: www.dividendfinance.com
SIC: 7389 Financial services

(P-13272)
DOCMAGIC INC
Also Called: Document Systems
1800 W 213th St (90501-2832)
PHONE...............................800 649-1362
Dominic Iannitti, Pr
Alan Brisbane, Chief of Staff*
Mike Zarrilli, Operations*
Michael Morford, OF INTEGRATION SVCS*
Gavin Ales, Chief Compliance Officer*
EMP: 79 EST: 1987
SQ FT: 20,000
SALES (est): 23.12MM Privately Held
Web: www.docmagic.com
SIC: 7389 Legal and tax services

(P-13273)
E & C FASHION INC
Also Called: Pacific Concept Laundry
1420 Esperanza St (90023-3914)
PHONE...............................323 262-0099
William Moo Han Bae, CEO
Maria Bae, *
Elizabeth Bae, *
Claudia Kye, *
▲ EMP: 300 EST: 1989
SALES (est): 9.96MM Privately Held
Web: www.atomicdenim.com
SIC: 7389 Sewing contractor

(P-13274)
EAGLERIDER FINANCE LLC
11860 S La Cienega Blvd (90250-3461)
P.O. Box 2346 (90251-2346)
PHONE...............................310 321-3191
EMP: 70 EST: 2008
SALES (est): 878.49K Privately Held
SIC: 7389 Financial services
PA: J.C. Bromac Corporation
11860 S La Cienega Blvd
Hawthorne CA

(P-13275)
EAST BAY INNOVATIONS
2450 Washington Ave Ste 240 (94577-5921)
PHONE...............................510 618-1580
Tom Heinz, Dir
EMP: 60 EST: 1993
SALES (est): 11.38MM Privately Held
Web: www.eastbayinnovations.org
SIC: 7389 Personal service agents, brokers, and bureaus

(P-13276)
EAST BAY REGIONAL PARK DST
Also Called: Tilden Park
10 Golf Course Dr (94708-1160)
P.O. Box 5381 (94605-0381)
PHONE...............................510 848-7373
Stephen Garett, Mgr
EMP: 92
SALES (corp-wide): 239.05MM Privately Held
Web: www.ebparks.org
SIC: 7389 Fire protection service other than forestry or public
PA: East Bay Regional Park District
2950 Peralta Oaks Ct
Oakland CA
888 327-2757

(P-13277)
ECONTACTLIVE INC
Also Called: Telecontact Resource Services
6436 Oakdale Rd (95367-9648)
PHONE...............................209 548-4300
Julie Hutchings, CEO
EMP: 62 EST: 1993
SQ FT: 42,000
SALES (est): 8.5MM Privately Held
Web: www.econtactlive.com
SIC: 7389 Telemarketing services

(P-13278)
EDISON ENERGY LLC
2 Park Plz Ste 200 (92614-8569)
PHONE...............................949 491-1633
EMP: 189 EST: 2012
SALES (est): 2.76MM Privately Held
SIC: 7389 Business services, nec

(P-13279)
EDRIVING FLEET LLC (DH)
5760 Fleet St Ste 210 (92008-4700)
PHONE...............................877 566-6323
Celia Stokes, CEO
Tony Gentile, CPO
Peter Gregovich, CFO
Lowel Orelup, CMO
EMP: 66 EST: 2016
SALES (est): 10.33MM
SALES (corp-wide): 1.21B Privately Held
Web: www.edriving.com
SIC: 7389 Drive-a-way automobile service
HQ: Edriving Llc
1255 Treat Blvd Ste 300
Walnut Creek CA
800 243-4008

(P-13280)
EQUILAR INC
1100 Marshall St (94063-2595)
PHONE...............................877 441-6090
David Chun, CEO
Timothy Ranzetta, *
EMP: 217 EST: 2000
SALES (est): 9.54MM Privately Held
Web: www.equilar.com
SIC: 7389 Financial services

(P-13281)
EREPUBLIC INC (PA)
Also Called: Government Technology
100 Blue Ravine Rd (95630-4509)
PHONE...............................916 932-1300
Dennis Mckenna, CEO
Dee Pearson, VP
Randall Mott, CIO
John Flynn, VP
EMP: 120 EST: 1984
SQ FT: 36,000
SALES (est): 26.48MM
SALES (corp-wide): 26.48MM Privately Held
Web: www.erepublic.com
SIC: 7389 2759 2721 Convention and show services; Publication printing; Periodicals

(P-13282)
EVEN RESPONSIBLE FINANCE INC
1440 Bdwy Fl 5 (94612-2025)
PHONE...............................360 977-2475
David Baga, CEO
Stephen Taylor, *
EMP: 63 EST: 2014
SALES (est): 3.99MM Privately Held
Web: www.even.com
SIC: 7389 Financial services

(P-13283)
EZCARETECH USA INC
21081 S Western Ave Ste 130 (90501)
PHONE...............................424 558-3191
Justin Chung, CEO
Kyungho Min, *
Justin Park, *
EMP: 350 EST: 2019
SALES (est): 5.83MM Privately Held
Web: www.ezcaretech.com
SIC: 7389 Business services, nec

(P-13284)
FACTER DIRECT LTD
4751 Wilshire Blvd Ste 140 (90010-3827)
PHONE...............................323 634-1999
Larry Keefer, Contrlr
EMP: 252
SALES (corp-wide): 9.8MM Privately Held
SIC: 7389 8742 Telemarketing services; Marketing consulting services
PA: Facter Direct Ltd
11500 W Olympic Blvd
Los Angeles CA
310 788-9000

(P-13285)
FEDEX SERVICES
5391 Rickenbacker Rd (90201-6439)
PHONE...............................323 881-3400
EMP: 73 EST: 2014
SALES (est): 162.97K Privately Held
SIC: 7389 4215 Courier or messenger service; Courier services, except by air

(P-13286)
FIGURE TECHNOLOGIES INC
650 California St Fl 2700 (94108-2608)
PHONE...............................888 819-6388
Michael Cagney, CEO
Jakub Jurek, CDO
Asiff Hirji, Pr
EMP: 281 EST: 2018
SALES (est): 23.72MM Privately Held
SIC: 7389 Financial services

(P-13287)
FINANCIAL SVC CTRS COOP INC
924 Overland Ct (91773-1742)
PHONE...............................909 753-1213
EMP: 98
SALES (corp-wide): 1.38MM Privately Held
Web: www.fscc.com
SIC: 7389 Financial services
PA: Financial Service Centers Cooperative, Inc.
2855 E Guasti Rd Ste 202
Ontario CA
888 372-2669

(P-13288)
FIRST PAGE SAGE LLC
2930 Domingo Ave (94705-2454)
PHONE...............................206 369-6516
EMP: 61
SALES (corp-wide): 500.21K Privately Held
Web: www.firstpagesage.com
SIC: 7389 Personal service agents, brokers, and bureaus
PA: First Page Sage Llc
2690 Filbert St
San Francisco CA
206 369-6516

(P-13289)
FLAGSHIP CREDIT ACCEPTANCE LLC

7389 - Business Services, Nec (P-13290)

7525 Irvine Center Dr (92618-3066)
PHONE..................949 748-7172
EMP: 120
Web: www.flagshipcredit.com
SIC: 7389 Financial services
PA: Flagship Credit Acceptance Llc
3 Christy Dr Ste 203
Chadds Ford PA

(P-13290)
FNTECH
3000 W Segerstrom Ave (92704-6526)
PHONE..................714 429-7833
Jeremy Muir, *CEO*
EMP: 91 EST: 2010
SALES (est): 9.56MM **Privately Held**
Web: www.fntech.com
SIC: 7389 Decoration service for special events

(P-13291)
FOREVER 21 LOGISTICS LLC
110 E 9th St Ste C910 (90079-5804)
PHONE..................888 494-3837
◆ EMP: 401 EST: 2002
SALES (est): 9.35MM
SALES (corp-wide): 100.19K **Privately Held**
SIC: 7389 Purchasing service
HQ: Forever 21 Retail, Inc.
110 E 9th St Ste C500
Los Angeles CA
323 343-9368

(P-13292)
FORMA LLC
Also Called: Development Design Mgmt
201 Filbert St (94133-3237)
PHONE..................415 477-0700
EMP: 85 EST: 2002
SALES (est): 321.71K **Privately Held**
Web: www.formasf.com
SIC: 7389 Design services

(P-13293)
FORMERRA LLC
Also Called: FORMERRA, LLC
11400 Newport Dr Ste B (91730-5511)
PHONE..................888 502-0951
EMP: 71
SALES (corp-wide): 36.53MM **Privately Held**
SIC: 7389 Business Activities at Non-Commercial Site
PA: Formerra Llc
1250 Windham Pkwy
Romeoville IL
888 502-0951

(P-13294)
FORUSALL INC
665 3rd St Ste 400 (94107-1968)
P.O. Box 1328 (94070-7268)
PHONE..................844 401-2253
EMP: 63 EST: 2013
SALES (est): 2.74MM **Privately Held**
Web: www.forusall.com
SIC: 7389 Financial services

(P-13295)
FRASER YACHTS FLORIDA INC
Also Called: Fraser Yachts
4960 N Harbor Dr Ste 100 (92106-2369)
PHONE..................619 225-0588
EMP: 65
SALES (corp-wide): 2.31B **Publicly Held**
Web: www.fraseryachts.com
SIC: 7389 Yacht brokers
HQ: Fraser Yachts Florida, Inc.
1800 Se 10th Ave Ste 400
Fort Lauderdale FL
954 463-0600

(P-13296)
FREEMAN EXPOSITIONS LLC
Also Called: Freeman
2170 S Towne Centre Pl Ste 100 (92806-6127)
PHONE..................714 254-3400
Pattie Balding, *Mgr*
EMP: 200
SALES (corp-wide): 1.56B **Privately Held**
Web: www.freeman.com
SIC: 7389 Trade show arrangement
HQ: Freeman Expositions, Llc
1600 Viceroy Dr Ste 100
Dallas TX
214 445-1000

(P-13297)
FRESH GRILL LLC
111 E Garry Ave (92707-4201)
PHONE..................714 444-2126
Jeff Heavirland, *Managing Member*
▲ EMP: 200 EST: 1996
SQ FT: 27,000
SALES (est): 22.45MM
SALES (corp-wide): 22.45MM **Privately Held**
Web: www.freshgrillfoods.com
SIC: 7389 Packaging and labeling services
PA: Fb Holding Company, Llc
111 E Garry Ave
Santa Ana CA
714 444-2126

(P-13298)
FRESNO METRO FLOOD CTRL DST
5469 E Olive Ave (93727-2541)
PHONE..................559 456-3292
Bob Van Wyk, *Genl Mgr*
Jerry Lakeman, *
EMP: 75 EST: 1955
SQ FT: 12,965
SALES (est): 10.79MM **Privately Held**
Web: www.fresnofloodcontrol.org
SIC: 7389 Personal service agents, brokers, and bureaus

(P-13299)
FUTURE FAST INC
5081 W Brown Ave (93722-0439)
PHONE..................559 813-0113
EMP: 68
SALES (corp-wide): 83.13K **Privately Held**
SIC: 7389 Business Activities at Non-Commercial Site
PA: Future Fast, Inc
5928 E Grove Ave
Fresno CA
559 813-0113

(P-13300)
GBR HOLDINGS LLC
6414 Cayenne Ln (92009-4301)
PHONE..................702 283-6519
EMP: 69
SALES (corp-wide): 324.38K **Privately Held**
SIC: 7389 Personal service agents, brokers, and bureaus
PA: Gbr Holdings Llc
13465 Cmino Cnada Ste 106
El Cajon CA

(P-13301)
GELFAND RENNERT & FELDMAN LLP (PA)
1880 Century Park E Ste 1600 (90067-1661)
PHONE..................310 553-1707
Marshall M Gelfand, *Mng Pt*
Tyson Beem, *Pt*
Todd Gelfand, *Pt*
EMP: 200 EST: 1967
SALES (est): 67.85K
SALES (corp-wide): 67.85K **Privately Held**
Web: www.grfllp.com
SIC: 7389 8721 8741 Legal and tax services ; Accounting, auditing, and bookkeeping; Business management

(P-13302)
GLOBAL CUSTOMER SERVICES INC
17373 Lilac St (92345-5162)
PHONE..................760 995-7949
David Syfrig, *CEO*
Kevin Senart, *
Ernie Bernard, *
Alejandro Joffroy, *
EMP: 100 EST: 2021
SALES (est): 15MM
SALES (corp-wide): 214.75MM **Privately Held**
Web: www.go-gcs.com
SIC: 7389 Flagging service (traffic control)
PA: Arizona Pipeline Company
17372 Lilac St
Hesperia CA
760 244-8212

(P-13303)
GLOBAL EXPRNCE SPECIALISTS INC
Also Called: Ges
18504 Beach Blvd Unit 511 (92648-0915)
PHONE..................619 498-6300
Tom Robins, *Mgr*
EMP: 166
Web: www.ges.com
SIC: 7389 Convention and show services
HQ: Global Experience Specialists, Inc.
7000 Lindell Rd
Las Vegas NV
702 515-5500

(P-13304)
GLOBAL LANGUAGE SOLUTIONS LLC
19800 Macarthur Blvd (92612-2402)
PHONE..................949 798-1400
EMP: 100 EST: 1994
SQ FT: 7,500
SALES (est): 7.74MM **Privately Held**
SIC: 7389 Translation services
PA: Welocalize, Inc.
15 W 37th St Fl 4
New York NY

(P-13305)
GOODWILL SRVING THE PPLE STHER (PA)
Also Called: Links Sign Lngage Intrprting S
800 W Pacific Coast Hwy (90806-5243)
PHONE..................562 435-3411
Janet Mccarthy, *CEO*
EMP: 100 EST: 1939
SQ FT: 80,000
SALES (est): 32.29MM
SALES (corp-wide): 32.29MM **Privately Held**
Web: www.linksinterpreting.com
SIC: 7389 8331 5932 Translation services; Job training and related services; Used merchandise stores

(P-13306)
GOOGLE PAYMENT CORP
Also Called: Google Checkout
1600 Amphitheatre Pkwy (94043-1351)
PHONE..................888 986-7944
EMP: 153 EST: 2005
SALES (est): 6.54MM
SALES (corp-wide): 282.84B **Publicly Held**
SIC: 7389 Charge account service
HQ: Google Llc
1600 Amphitheatre Pkwy
Mountain View CA
650 253-0000

(P-13307)
GORDON AND SCHWENKMEYER INC
1860 Howe Ave Ste 300 (95825-1098)
PHONE..................916 569-1740
Brett Carter, *Ex VP*
EMP: 170
SALES (corp-wide): 4.42MM **Privately Held**
Web: www.gsitel.com
SIC: 7389 Personal service agents, brokers, and bureaus
PA: Gordon And Schwenkmeyer, Inc.
20300 S Vt Ave Ste 210
Torrance CA
310 615-2300

(P-13308)
HARINGA INC (PA)
Also Called: Premier Packaging/Assembly
14422 Best Ave (90670-5133)
P.O. Box 4707 (90703-4707)
PHONE..................800 499-9991
Victoria Haringa, *CEO*
Vicki Haringa, *
Randy Haringa, *
▲ EMP: 77 EST: 1991
SQ FT: 200,000
SALES (est): 8.51MM
SALES (corp-wide): 8.51MM **Privately Held**
SIC: 7389 Packaging and labeling services

(P-13309)
HARTMANN STUDIOS INC
1150 Brickyard Cove Rd Ste 202 (94801-4181)
PHONE..................510 232-5030
Thomas J Mahoney, *CEO*
EMP: 150 EST: 2018
SALES (est): 11.46MM
SALES (corp-wide): 107.45MM **Privately Held**
Web: www.hartmannstudios.com
SIC: 7389 Convention and show services
PA: Ita Group, Inc
4600 Westown Pkwy Ste 100
West Des Moines IA
515 326-3400

(P-13310)
HCT PACKAGING INC (PA)
Also Called: Hct Group
2800 28th St Ste 240 (90405-6214)
PHONE..................310 260-7680
Tim Thorpe, *Pr*
◆ EMP: 125 EST: 1996
SQ FT: 1,500
SALES (est): 17.17MM
SALES (corp-wide): 17.17MM **Privately Held**
Web: www.hctgroup.com
SIC: 7389 Packaging and labeling services

PRODUCTS & SERVICES SECTION

7389 - Business Services, Nec (P-13335)

(P-13311)
HELLO DIGIT LLC
Also Called: Digit
2 Circle Star Way (94070-6200)
PHONE.................................415 260-2684
Ethan Mark Bloch, *CEO*
Michael Murray, *
EMP: 100 **EST:** 2012
SALES (est): 10.31MM **Publicly Held**
Web: www.digit.co
SIC: 7389 Financial services
PA: Oportun Financial Corporation
2 Circle Star Way
San Carlos CA

(P-13312)
HENKEL CORPORATION
405 Industrial Way (95620-9764)
PHONE.................................707 731-4964
EMP: 135
SALES (corp-wide): 23.26B **Privately Held**
Web: www.henkel-northamerica.com
SIC: 7389 Automobile recovery service
HQ: Henkel Corporation
1 Henkel Way
Rocky Hill CT
860 571-5100

(P-13313)
HERITAGE AUCTIONS INC
9478 W Olympic Blvd (90212-4246)
PHONE.................................310 300-8390
Greg Rohan, *Pr*
EMP: 100 **EST:** 2010
SALES (est): 4.57MM **Privately Held**
SIC: 7389 Auctioneers, fee basis

(P-13314)
HH GLOBAL LIMITED
Also Called: Hh Global
14 Geary St 2nd Fl (94108-5702)
PHONE.................................847 984-2448
EMP: 329
Web: www.hhglobal.com
SIC: 7389 Packaging and labeling services
HQ: Hh Global Limited
Grove House
Leatherhead

(P-13315)
HIGH TIMES PRODUCTIONS INC
10990 Wilshire Blvd (90024-3913)
PHONE.................................844 933-3287
EMP: 204 **EST:** 1991
SALES (est): 1.02MM **Privately Held**
Web: ir.hightimes.com
SIC: 7389 Advertising, promotional, and trade show services

(P-13316)
HIRSCH/BEDNER INTL INC (PA)
Also Called: Hba International
3216 Nebraska Ave (90404-4214)
PHONE.................................310 829-9087
Rene G Kaerskov, *CEO*
Michael J Bedner, *
Howard Pharr, *
Bruce Jones, *
EMP: 70 **EST:** 1964
SQ FT: 14,000
SALES (est): 21.04MM
SALES (corp-wide): 21.04MM **Privately Held**
Web: www.hba.com
SIC: 7389 Interior designer

(P-13317)
HOLLYWOOD SPORTS PARK LLC
Also Called: Giant Sportz Paintball Park
9030 Somerset Blvd (90706-3402)
PHONE.................................562 867-9600
Dennis Bukowski, *Managing Member*
▲ **EMP:** 100 **EST:** 1999
SQ FT: 20,000
SALES (est): 7.28MM **Privately Held**
Web: www.hollywoodsports.com
SIC: 7389 Personal service agents, brokers, and bureaus

(P-13318)
HOOVER INSTITUTION
434 Galvez Mall (94305-6003)
PHONE.................................650 723-1754
John Raisian, *Dir*
EMP: 200 **EST:** 1920
SALES (est): 12.81MM **Privately Held**
Web: www.hoover.org
SIC: 7389 Personal service agents, brokers, and bureaus

(P-13319)
HYDROPROCESSING ASSOCIATES LLC
Also Called: Hpa-USA
19122 S Santa Fe Ave (90221-5910)
PHONE.................................310 667-6456
Kees Ooms, *Brnch Mgr*
EMP: 81
SALES (corp-wide): 94.66MM **Privately Held**
Web: www.swatservice.com
SIC: 7389 Petroleum refinery inspection service
HQ: Hydroprocessing Associates, Llc
40492 Cannon Rd
Gonzales LA

(P-13320)
ICON DESIGN AND DISPLAY INC
645 4th St Ste 212 (95404-4435)
PHONE.................................707 284-3400
▲ **EMP:** 90
Web: www.goldenwestpackaging.com
SIC: 7389 Personal service agents, brokers, and bureaus

(P-13321)
INCIRCLE LLC
44000 Winchester Rd (92590-2578)
PHONE.................................800 843-7477
EMP: 597 **EST:** 2018
SALES (est): 468.79K
SALES (corp-wide): 539.81MM **Privately Held**
SIC: 7389 Business Activities at Non-Commercial Site
PA: Fff Enterprises, Inc.
44000 Winchester Rd
Temecula CA
951 296-2500

(P-13322)
INDUSTRIAL STITCHTECH INC
520 Library St (91340-2524)
PHONE.................................818 361-6319
Ed Perez, *Pr*
EMP: 150 **EST:** 1996
SQ FT: 35,000
SALES (est): 3.52MM **Privately Held**
Web: www.industrialstitchtech.com
SIC: 7389 Sewing contractor

(P-13323)
INGENUITY STUDIOS INTL INC
941 N Highland Ave 2nd Fl (90038-2412)
PHONE.................................323 460-6096
David Lebensfeld, *CEO*
EMP: 165 **EST:** 2004
SALES (est): 6.9MM **Privately Held**
Web: www.ingenuitystudios.com
SIC: 7389 Recording studio, noncommercial records

(P-13324)
INNOVATION SPECIALTIES
Also Called: Clockparts
11869 Teale St Ste 302 (90230-7701)
PHONE.................................888 827-2387
EMP: 198
SALES (corp-wide): 28.37MM **Privately Held**
Web: www.clockparts.com
SIC: 7389 Product endorsement service
PA: Innovation Specialties
11869 Teale St
Culver City CA
310 398-8116

(P-13325)
INNOVATIVE SILICON INC
4800 Great America Pkwy # 500 (95054-1221)
P.O. Box 391657 (94039-1657)
PHONE.................................408 572-8700
EMP: 80
SQ FT: 11,000
SALES (est): 3.41MM **Privately Held**
Web: www.innovativesilicon.com
SIC: 7389 Personal service agents, brokers, and bureaus

(P-13326)
INSPECTORATE AMERICA CORP
Also Called: INSPECTORATE AMERICA CORPORATION
3401 Jack Northrop Ave (90250-4428)
PHONE.................................800 424-0099
EMP: 148
SALES (corp-wide): 247.19MM **Privately Held**
SIC: 7389 Petroleum refinery inspection service
HQ: Bureau Veritas Commodities And Trade, Inc.
1300 Hercules Ave Ste 105
Houston TX
713 944-2000

(P-13327)
INTERIOR SPECIALISTS INC
15822 Bernardo Center Dr Ste 1 (92127-2362)
PHONE.................................909 983-5386
EMP: 300
SALES (corp-wide): 499.75MM **Privately Held**
Web: www.interiorlogicgroup.com
SIC: 7389 Interior designer
HQ: Interior Specialists, Inc.
1630 Faraday Ave
Carlsbad CA
760 929-6700

(P-13328)
INTERPAC TECHNOLOGIES INC
Also Called: Interpac Distribution Center
260 N Pioneer Ave (95776-5934)
PHONE.................................530 662-6363
Roderick W Miner, *Pr*
Corinne Christenson, *
▲ **EMP:** 75 **EST:** 2000
SALES (est): 8.22MM **Privately Held**
Web: www.interpactechnologies.com
SIC: 7389 Packaging and labeling services

(P-13329)
INTERPRETING SERVICES INTL LLC
700 N Brand Blvd Ste 950 (91203-1207)
PHONE.................................818 753-9181
Isi Solutions, *Admn*
EMP: 60 **EST:** 1982
SALES (est): 2.53MM **Privately Held**
Web: www.isilanguagesolutions.com
SIC: 7389 Translation services

(P-13330)
IPAYMENT INC
3325 Wilshire Blvd Ste 535 (90010-1703)
PHONE.................................213 387-1353
Guillermo Ramirez, *Brnch Mgr*
EMP: 285
SALES (corp-wide): 232.73MM **Privately Held**
Web: www.paysafe.com
SIC: 7389 Credit card service
HQ: Ipayment, Inc.
30721 Russell Ranch Rd # 200
Westlake Village CA
212 802-7200

(P-13331)
ISI INSPECTION SERVICES INC (PA)
Also Called: Inspection Services
1798 University Ave (94703-1514)
PHONE.................................510 900-2101
EMP: 70 **EST:** 1995
SQ FT: 9,700
SALES (est): 9.88MM **Privately Held**
Web: www.inspectionservices.net
SIC: 7389 Inspection and testing services

(P-13332)
JENCO PRODUCTIONS INC (PA)
401 S J St (92410-2605)
PHONE.................................909 381-9453
Jennifer Imbriani, *Pr*
◆ **EMP:** 160 **EST:** 1995
SQ FT: 50,000
SALES (est): 25.39MM
SALES (corp-wide): 25.39MM **Privately Held**
Web: www.jencoproductions.com
SIC: 7389 2789 2653 7331 Packaging and labeling services; Bookbinding and related work; Boxes, corrugated: made from purchased materials; Mailing service

(P-13333)
JMS INTERIORS INC
10735 Prospect Ave (92071-4536)
PHONE.................................619 749-5098
James Michael Snyder, *Prin*
EMP: 75 **EST:** 2016
SALES (est): 1.89MM **Privately Held**
Web: www.jmsinteriorsinc.com
SIC: 7389 Interior design services

(P-13334)
JOPARI SOLUTIONS INC
1850 Gateway Blvd (94520-8400)
PHONE.................................925 459-5200
John Stevens Ii, *CEO*
John Gilmartin, *
Tom Turi, *CSO CMO*
EMP: 65 **EST:** 2003
SALES (est): 8.81MM **Privately Held**
Web: www.jopari.com
SIC: 7389 Financial services

(P-13335)
KENNETH BRDWICK INTR DSGNS INC
Also Called: Beverly Hills Luxury Interiors
1615 Westwood Blvd Ste 202 (90024-5653)
PHONE.................................310 274-9999

7389 - Business Services, Nec (P-13336)

Kenneth Bordewick, *CEO*
EMP: 73 **EST:** 2004
SALES (est): 1.35MM **Privately Held**
SIC: 7389 Interior designer

(P-13336)
KEWEIER NANO TECHNOLOGIES INC
41222 Malcolmson St Apt 20 (94538-4863)
PHONE.................................415 948-4335
Jin Ye, *Brnch Mgr*
EMP: 135
SALES (corp-wide): 78.76K **Privately Held**
SIC: 7389 Personal service agents, brokers, and bureaus
PA: Keweier Nano Technologies, Inc.
1135 Sonora Ct
Sunnyvale CA
408 656-3779

(P-13337)
KING-REYNOLDS VENTURES LLC
Also Called: Costanoa
2001 Rossi Rd (94060-9732)
PHONE.................................650 879-2136
EMP: 81 **EST:** 2003
SALES (est): 8.75MM **Privately Held**
Web: www.costanoa.com
SIC: 7389 Financial services

(P-13338)
KIRSCHENMAN ENTERPRISES SLS LP
12826 Edison Hwy (93220)
P.O. Box 27 (93220-0027)
PHONE.................................661 366-5736
EMP: 120 **EST:** 2009
SQ FT: 5,000
SALES (est): 100MM **Privately Held**
Web: www.kirschenman.com
SIC: 7389 Brokers, business: buying and selling business enterprises

(P-13339)
KMS FINANCIAL SERVICES INC
251 Coon Heights Rd (95005-9727)
PHONE.................................360 770-5117
EMP: 100
SALES (corp-wide): 2.31B **Privately Held**
SIC: 7389 Financial services
HQ: Kms Financial Services, Inc
12325 Port Grace Blvd
La Vista NE
206 441-2885

(P-13340)
KOOS MANUFACTURING INC
Also Called: Big Star
2741 Seminole Ave (90280-5550)
PHONE.................................323 249-1000
U Yul Ku, *CEO*
John Hur, *
Nathan Aroonprapun, *
▲ **EMP:** 639 **EST:** 1985
SQ FT: 180,000
SALES (est): 39.61MM **Privately Held**
Web: www.koos.com
SIC: 7389 2325 2339 2369 Sewing contractor; Jeans: men's, youths', and boys'; Jeans: women's, misses', and juniors'; Jeans: girls', children's, and infants'

(P-13341)
KORVALABS INC
Also Called: Coddingtontown
1000 Coddingtown Ctr (95401-3513)
PHONE.................................888 702-9042
EMP: 182

SALES (corp-wide): 2.71MM **Privately Held**
SIC: 7389 Personal service agents, brokers, and bureaus
PA: Korvalabs, Inc.
430 S Cataract Ave
San Dimas CA
424 645-7575

(P-13342)
KPWR RADIO LLC
9550 Firestone Blvd Ste 105 (90241-5560)
PHONE.................................562 745-2300
Alex Meruelo, *Managing Member*
EMP: 150 **EST:** 2017
SALES (est): 9.51MM
SALES (corp-wide): 10.68MM **Privately Held**
SIC: 7389 Music and broadcasting services
PA: Meruelo Group Llc
9550 Firestone Blvd # 105
Downey CA
562 745-2300

(P-13343)
LA JOLLA GROUP INC (PA)
Also Called: Ljg
14350 Myford Rd (92606-1002)
PHONE.................................949 428-2800
Michael Pratt, *CEO*
▲ **EMP:** 426 **EST:** 2007
SALES (est): 50.18MM
SALES (corp-wide): 50.18MM **Privately Held**
Web: www.lajollagroup.com
SIC: 7389 6794 2326 Apparel designers, commercial; Copyright buying and licensing; Men's and boy's work clothing

(P-13344)
LAG AND ASSOCIATES LLC
1514 E Adams Park Dr (91724-3101)
PHONE.................................909 242-4394
Roland Irvin, *Managing Member*
EMP: 62 **EST:** 2019
SALES (est): 1.11MM **Privately Held**
SIC: 7389 Financial services

(P-13345)
LAKESIDE TAX & FINANCIAL SVCS
9748 Los Coches Rd Ste 3 (92040-4215)
PHONE.................................619 561-2681
Jodie Herzig, *Pr*
EMP: 68 **EST:** 2012
SALES (est): 955.33K **Privately Held**
Web: www.lakesidetfs.com
SIC: 7389 Financial services

(P-13346)
LAKEWOOD PARK HEALTH CTR INC (PA)
12023 Lakewood Blvd (90242-2699)
PHONE.................................562 869-0978
Daniel Zilafro, *Pr*
EMP: 285 **EST:** 1985
SALES (est): 4.94MM **Privately Held**
Web: www.lwhealthcare.com
SIC: 7389 Personal service agents, brokers, and bureaus

(P-13347)
LANDOR & FITCH LLC (HQ)
Also Called: Landor Associates
360 3rd St (94107-2165)
PHONE.................................415 365-1700
Lois Jacobs, *CEO*
James Bruce, *CFO*
Peter Harleman, *Vice Chairman*

EMP: 215 **EST:** 2002
SALES (est): 10.11MM
SALES (corp-wide): 17.37B **Privately Held**
SIC: 7389 8742 Financial services; Management consulting services
PA: Wpp Plc
22 Grenville Street
Jersey
370 707-1411

(P-13348)
LANGUAGE LINE HOLDINGS INC (HQ)
Also Called: Languageline Solutions
1 Lower Ragsdale Dr Bldg 2 (93940-5747)
PHONE.................................831 648-5800
Dennis Dracup, *CEO*
Matthew Gibbs, *
EMP: 255 **EST:** 2004
SALES (est): 206.88MM
SALES (corp-wide): 226.27MM **Privately Held**
Web: www.languageline.com
SIC: 7389 Translation services
PA: Teleperformance Se
Du Na 21 Au 25
Paris

(P-13349)
LARK INDUSTRIES INC (DH)
Also Called: Residential Design Services
18565 Jamboree Rd Ste 125 (92612-2543)
PHONE.................................714 701-4200
Kendall Hoyd, *Pr*
Kip Cruze, *
EMP: 61 **EST:** 1988
SALES (est): 98.53MM
SALES (corp-wide): 499.77MM **Privately Held**
Web: www.interiorlogicgroup.com
SIC: 7389 3281 Interior design services; Cut stone and stone products
HQ: Interior Logic Group, Inc.
18565 Jamboree Rd Ste 125
Irvine CA
800 959-8333

(P-13350)
LAUNDRY DESIGN LLC
4079 Redwood Ave Ste A (90066-5143)
PHONE.................................323 933-2800
Troy Moore, *Managing Member*
EMP: 145 **EST:** 2005
SALES (est): 988.21K **Privately Held**
Web: www.laundry.studio
SIC: 7389 Design, commercial and industrial

(P-13351)
LAUREN ANDREW SURFACES INC
Also Called: Granite Fabrication Facility
13220 Cambridge St (90670)
PHONE.................................562 921-9549
David Dominguez, *CEO*
EMP: 64
SALES (corp-wide): 4.97MM **Privately Held**
SIC: 7389 Interior decorating
PA: Lauren Andrew Surfaces Inc
8909 Kenamar Dr Ste 101
San Diego CA
858 793-5319

(P-13352)
LENDINGUSA LLC
15303 Ventura Blvd Ste 850 (91403-3110)
PHONE.................................800 994-6177
Camilo Concha, *CEO*
Manoj Mathew, *
Johannes Haze, *CMO**

Vale Gardi, *
EMP: 78 **EST:** 2015
SALES (est): 6.5MM **Privately Held**
Web: www.lendingusa.com
SIC: 7389 Financial services

(P-13353)
LFP ECOMMERCE LLC
210 N Sunset Ave (91790-2257)
PHONE.................................314 428-5069
EMP: 73
SALES (corp-wide): 1.91MM **Privately Held**
SIC: 7389 Personal service agents, brokers, and bureaus
PA: Lfp Ecommerce, Llc
8484 Wilshire Blvd # 900
Beverly Hills CA
323 651-5400

(P-13354)
LINDSEY & SONS
Also Called: Flo-CHI
1226 E 76th St (90001-2416)
PHONE.................................657 306-5369
Andre Lindsey Senior, *Pr*
EMP: 100 **EST:** 2021
SALES (est): 1.11MM **Privately Held**
SIC: 7389 Business Activities at Non-Commercial Site

(P-13355)
LITIGTION RSRCES OF AMERICA-CA (PA)
Also Called: Legal Enterprise
4232-1 Las Virgenes Rd Ste 100 (91302-3589)
PHONE.................................818 878-9227
Tony Maddocks, *Pr*
Rick Matsumoto, *
EMP: 75 **EST:** 1993
SALES (est): 3.52MM **Privately Held**
SIC: 7389 8111 Document storage service; General practice attorney, lawyer

(P-13356)
LIVE NATION ENTERTAINMENT INC (PA)
Also Called: Live Nation
9348 Civic Center Dr Lbby (90210-3642)
PHONE.................................310 867-7000
Michael Rapino, *Pr*
Greg Maffei, *Non-Executive Chairman of the Board**
Joe Berchtold, *Pr*
Brian Capo, *CAO*
▲ **EMP:** 200 **EST:** 2005
SALES (est): 16.68B **Publicly Held**
Web: www.livenation.com
SIC: 7389 7922 7941 Promoters of shows and exhibitions; Entertainment promotion; Sports clubs, managers, and promoters

(P-13357)
LOON LLC
100 Mayfield Ave (94043-4122)
PHONE.................................310 625-3449
Westgrath Eleister, *CEO*
EMP: 200 **EST:** 2000
SALES (est): 10.34MM **Privately Held**
Web: www.x.company
SIC: 7389 Business Activities at Non-Commercial Site

(P-13358)
LOS ANGELES UNIFIED SCHOOL DST
Also Called: L A U S D
8525 Rex Rd (90660-6702)

PRODUCTS & SERVICES SECTION   7389 - Business Services, Nec (P-13380)

PHONE..................562 654-9007
Marc Monforte, Brnch Mgr
EMP: 105
SALES (corp-wide): 9.38B Privately Held
Web: www.laallcityband.com
SIC: 7389 Purchasing service
PA: Los Angeles Unified School District
    333 S Beaudry Ave Ste 209
    Los Angeles CA
    213 241-1000

(P-13359)
LOYAL3 HOLDINGS INC
Also Called: Loyal3
150 California St Ste 400 (94111-4566)
P.O. Box 26027 (94126-6027)
PHONE..................415 981-0700
Barry L Schneider, CEO
Stephen Klein, *
Jeff Modisett, *
Peter Coleman, *
Bill Blais, *
EMP: 80 EST: 2008
SQ FT: 8,900
SALES (est): 6.88MM Privately Held
Web: www.loyal3.com
SIC: 7389 Financial services

(P-13360)
MABIE MARKETING GROUP INC
Also Called: California Marketing
8352 Clairemont Mesa Blvd (92111-1302)
P.O. Box 33708 (92163-3708)
PHONE..................858 279-5585
John Mabie, Pr
Ramyar Ravansari, *
EMP: 200 EST: 1984
SALES (est): 15.5MM Privately Held
Web: www.calmarketinggroup.com
SIC: 7389 Telemarketing services

(P-13361)
MACRO-PRO INC (PA)
Also Called: Micro-Pro Microfilming Svcs
2400 Grand Ave (90815-1762)
P.O. Box 90459 (90809-0459)
PHONE..................562 595-0900
Patty Waldeck, Pr
EMP: 140 EST: 1988
SQ FT: 24,000
SALES (est): 8.35MM
SALES (corp-wide): 8.35MM Privately Held
Web: www.macropro.com
SIC: 7389 7334 Legal and tax services; Photocopying and duplicating services

(P-13362)
MARIA ALEEN VILLARIN BALCE INC
2897 Forbes Ave (95051-5665)
PHONE..................408 320-2684
Maria Aileen Balce, Brnch Mgr
EMP: 73
SALES (corp-wide): 279.3K Privately Held
Web: www.aileenvbalcedds.com
SIC: 7389 Personal service agents, brokers, and bureaus
PA: Maria Aileen Villarin Balce, Inc.
    1680 Civic Center Dr # 230
    Santa Clara CA

(P-13363)
MARINE TECHNICAL SERVICES INC
Also Called: Dockside Machine & Ship Repair
211 N Marine Ave (90744-5724)
P.O. Box 1301 (90733-1301)
PHONE..................310 549-8030
Dianne Marie Hawke, Pr

▼ EMP: 75 EST: 1989
SQ FT: 20,000
SALES (est): 9.35MM Privately Held
Web: www.marinetechserv.com
SIC: 7389 7699 Crane and aerial lift service; Nautical repair services

(P-13364)
MASERGY CLOUD CMMNICATIONS INC
3663 Greve Dr (90275-6281)
PHONE..................310 921-7000
Chris Macfarland, CEO
EMP: 61 EST: 2005
SALES (est): 18.55MM
SALES (corp-wide): 121.43B Publicly Held
Web: www.masergy.com
SIC: 7389 Telephone services
HQ: Masergy Communications, Inc.
    2740 Dallas Pkwy Ste 100
    Plano TX
    214 442-5700

(P-13365)
MATH HOLDINGS INC (PA)
Also Called: Motivtnal Flfilment Lgstics Sv
15820 Euclid Ave (91708-9162)
PHONE..................909 517-2200
▲ EMP: 229 EST: 1977
SQ FT: 300,000
SALES (est): 47.01MM Privately Held
Web: www.mfals.com
SIC: 7389 8748 4225 Telemarketing services; Business consulting, nec; General warehousing and storage

(P-13366)
MB COATINGS INC
1540 S Lewis St (92805-6423)
PHONE..................714 625-2118
Michael Bartle, Pr
Amanda Bartle, *
EMP: 80 EST: 1996
SALES (est): 4.85MM Privately Held
Web: www.mbcoatings.com
SIC: 7389 Hand painting, textile

(P-13367)
MEDHOLDINGS OF NEWNAN LLC
Also Called: Capitol Records
1750 Vine St (90028-5209)
PHONE..................213 462-6252
EMP: 1500
SIC: 7389 8999 Music and broadcasting services; Music arranging and composing

(P-13368)
MEDUSIND SOLUTIONS INC (PA)
31103 Rancho Viejo Rd Ste 2150 (92675-1759)
PHONE..................949 240-8895
Rajiv Sahney, Ch
Vipul Bansal, *
Robert Beck, *
Dhiren Kapadia, *
Kranti Munje, *
EMP: 80 EST: 2002
SALES (est): 7.26MM
SALES (corp-wide): 7.26MM Privately Held
Web: www.medusind.com
SIC: 7389 Personal service agents, brokers, and bureaus

(P-13369)
MEGA APPRAISERS INC
14724 Ventura Blvd Ste 800 (91403-3501)

PHONE..................818 246-7370
Levon Hairapetian, Pr
EMP: 600 EST: 2003
SALES (est): 7.68MM Privately Held
Web: www.megaappraisers.com
SIC: 7389 Appraisers, except real estate

(P-13370)
MERCHANT OF TENNIS INC
1625 Proforma Ave (91761-7607)
PHONE..................909 923-3388
Larry Khemlani, Prin
EMP: 663
SALES (corp-wide): 491.1MM Privately Held
Web: www.merchant-of-tennis.com
SIC: 7389 Packaging and labeling services
HQ: The Merchant Of Tennis Inc
    8737 Wilshire Blvd
    Beverly Hills CA
    310 228-4000

(P-13371)
MERIBEAR PRODUCTIONS INC
Also Called: Meredith Baer & Associates
4100 Ardmore Ave (90280-3246)
PHONE..................310 204-5353
Meridith Baer, Pr
▲ EMP: 90 EST: 1980
SQ FT: 55,000
SALES (est): 14.97MM Privately Held
Web: www.meridithbaer.com
SIC: 7389 Interior design services

(P-13372)
MERICAL LLC
447 W Freedom Ave (92865-2644)
PHONE..................714 685-0977
Jeffrey Stallings, Brnch Mgr
EMP: 153
SALES (corp-wide): 200.29MM Privately Held
Web: www.merical.com
SIC: 7389 Packaging and labeling services
HQ: Merical, Llc
    2995 E Miraloma Ave
    Anaheim CA
    714 238-7225

(P-13373)
MERICAL LLC
Also Called: Merical/Vita-Pak
233 E Bristol Ln (92865-2715)
PHONE..................714 283-9551
EMP: 259
SALES (corp-wide): 200.29MM Privately Held
Web: www.merical.com
SIC: 7389 Packaging and labeling services
HQ: Merical, Llc
    2995 E Miraloma Ave
    Anaheim CA
    714 238-7225

(P-13374)
MERICAL LLC
445 W Freedom Ave (92865-2644)
PHONE..................714 238-7225
Roshni Patel, Mgr
EMP: 139
SALES (corp-wide): 200.29MM Privately Held
Web: www.merical.com
SIC: 7389 Packaging and labeling services
HQ: Merical, Llc
    2995 E Miraloma Ave
    Anaheim CA
    714 238-7225

(P-13375)
METROPOLITAN IMPORTS LLC
16311 Ventura Blvd (91436-2124)
PHONE..................646 980-5343
Starr King Williams Iii, Managing Member
EMP: 144 EST: 2014
SALES (est): 52MM Privately Held
Web: www.metropolitanimports.com
SIC: 7389 7999 Yacht brokers; Pleasure boat rental

(P-13376)
MIGO MONEY INC
3739 Balboa St Ste 1101 (94121-2605)
PHONE..................415 906-4040
Ekechi Nwokah, CEO
Derek White, Prin
EMP: 61 EST: 2013
SALES (est): 14MM Privately Held
Web: us.migo.money
SIC: 7389 Financial services

(P-13377)
MKTG INC
Also Called: MKTG, INC.
5800 Bristol Pkwy Ste 500 (90230-6899)
PHONE..................310 972-7900
Patty Hubbard, Brnch Mgr
EMP: 458
Web: www.mktgse.com
SIC: 7389 Advertising, promotional, and trade show services
HQ: 'mktg, Inc.'
    32 Avenue Of The Americas # 1
    New York NY

(P-13378)
MODERA LLC
137 Ranch Dr (95035-5105)
PHONE..................408 946-2161
EMP: 64
SALES (corp-wide): 491.56K Privately Held
SIC: 7389 Personal service agents, brokers, and bureaus
PA: Modera Llc
    12929 Pierce Rd
    Saratoga CA
    408 218-2548

(P-13379)
MODERN DEV CO A LTD PARTNR
Also Called: Paramount Swap Meet
7900 All America City Way (90723-3400)
PHONE..................949 646-6400
Darren Kurkowski, Brnch Mgr
EMP: 84
SALES (corp-wide): 9.58MM Privately Held
Web: www.paramountswap.com
SIC: 7389 Flea market
PA: Modern Development Co, A Limited Partnership
    496 N Coast Hwy Ste A
    Laguna Beach CA
    949 646-6400

(P-13380)
MONEX INC
8383 Wilshire Blvd Ste 340 (90211-2626)
PHONE..................310 695-3059
EMP: 60
Web: www.monexusa.com
SIC: 7389 Financial services
HQ: Monex Inc.
    1101 K St Nw Ste 600
    Washington DC
    202 785-5534

7389 - Business Services, Nec (P-13381)

(P-13381)
MONTEBELLO UNIFIED SCHOOL DST
831 Perry Ave (90640-2429)
PHONE.................323 440-2899
EMP: 90
SALES (corp-wide): 539.05MM Privately Held
Web: www.montebello.k12.ca.us
SIC: 7389 Business Activities at Non-Commercial Site
PA: Montebello Unified School District
123 S Montebello Blvd
Montebello CA
323 887-7900

(P-13382)
MOOD MEDIA NORTH AMERICA LLC
3860 Calle Fortunada Ste 100 (92123-4800)
PHONE.................858 362-2323
◆ EMP: 73 EST: 2003
SQ FT: 4,800
SALES (est): 2.96MM
SALES (corp-wide): 282.28MM Privately Held
Web: www.moodmedia.com
SIC: 7389 Recording studio, noncommercial records
PA: Mood Media Llc
2100 S Ih 35 Frntage Rd S
Austin TX
800 345-5000

(P-13383)
MORENO VALLEY SNF LLC
Also Called: Rancho Bellagio Post Acute
26940 E Hospital Rd (92555-3923)
PHONE.................951 363-5434
EMP: 78 EST: 2020
SALES (est): 1.07MM
SALES (corp-wide): 1.53B Privately Held
Web: www.ranchobellagiopa.com
SIC: 7389 Business Activities at Non-Commercial Site
PA: Providence Group, Inc.
262 N University Ave
Farmington UT
801 447-9829

(P-13384)
MSCI INC
2100 Milvia St (94704-1863)
PHONE.................510 548-5442
Kamal Duggirala, *CEO*
EMP: 88
Web: www.msci.com
SIC: 7389 7371 6282 8742 Financial services; Software programming applications; Investment advice; Management consulting services
PA: Msci Inc.
250 Greenwich St Fl 49
New York NY

(P-13385)
MULTI-PAK CORPORATION
Also Called: Multipak
20131 Bahama St (91311-6202)
PHONE.................818 709-0508
Randall B Unthank, *Pr*
EMP: 60 EST: 1955
SQ FT: 20,000
SALES (est): 4.69MM Privately Held
Web: www.multi-pak.com
SIC: 7389 Packaging and labeling services

(P-13386)
MULTIVISION INC (DH)
Also Called: Bacon's Multivision
66 Franklin St 3rd Fl (94607-3728)
PHONE.................510 740-5600
Babak Farahi, *Pr*
EMP: 70 EST: 2002
SALES (est): 9.89MM
SALES (corp-wide): 934.8MM Privately Held
SIC: 7389 Press clipping service
HQ: Cision Us Inc.
300 S Riverside Plz
Chicago IL
312 922-2400

(P-13387)
MVENTIX INC (PA)
Also Called: Mventix
21600 Oxnard St Ste 1700 (91367-4972)
PHONE.................818 337-3747
Kristian Beloff, *CEO*
Vesselin Kavrakov, *Research & Development*
Pavel Monev, *
EMP: 70 EST: 2004
SQ FT: 6,606
SALES (est): 8.91MM
SALES (corp-wide): 8.91MM Privately Held
Web: www.mventix.com
SIC: 7389 8732 7372 Advertising, promotional, and trade show services; Survey service: marketing, location, etc.; Business oriented computer software

(P-13388)
NABIEKIM ENTERPRISES INC
Also Called: Bulldoc Korean Fusion
3039 E Campus Pointe Dr (93710-7525)
PHONE.................646 645-1958
EMP: 90
SALES (corp-wide): 556.64K Privately Held
SIC: 7389 Personal service agents, brokers, and bureaus
PA: Nabiekim Enterprises, Inc.
3039 E Campus Pointe Dr
Fresno CA
559 207-3717

(P-13389)
NATIONAL BUS INVSTIGATIONS INC
Also Called: MPS Security
25020 Las Brisas Rd Ste A (92562-4064)
PHONE.................951 677-3500
Michael D Julian, *Pr*
EMP: 60 EST: 1967
SQ FT: 2,000
SALES (est): 7.01MM Privately Held
Web: www.investigations-nbi.com
SIC: 7389 7381 Personal investigation service; Private investigator

(P-13390)
NEFAB PACKAGING WEST LLC
Also Called: Nefab
8477 Central Ave (94560-3431)
PHONE.................408 678-2516
EMP: 60 EST: 2014
SALES (est): 3.79MM
SALES (corp-wide): 903.19MM Privately Held
SIC: 7389 Packaging and labeling services
HQ: Nefab Companies, Inc.
204 Airline Dr Ste 100
Coppell TX
866 332-4425

(P-13391)
NETWORK TELEPHONE SERVICES INC (PA)
Also Called: N T S
21135 Erwin St (91367-3713)
PHONE.................800 742-5687
Joseph Preston, *CEO*
Daniel Coleman, *
EMP: 87 EST: 1988
SQ FT: 70,000
SALES (est): 21.82MM
SALES (corp-wide): 21.82MM Privately Held
Web: www.nts.net
SIC: 7389 4813 7374 Telephone services; Internet connectivity services; Data processing and preparation

(P-13392)
NEW AMERICA FUNDING LLC
Also Called: NEW AMERICA FUNDING, LLC
11820 Pierce St (92505-4403)
PHONE.................951 637-2300
Neil Wachsberger, *Mgr*
EMP: 71
Web: www.newamericanfunding.com
SIC: 7389 Personal service agents, brokers, and bureaus
PA: New American Funding, Llc
14511 Myford Rd Ste 100
Tustin CA

(P-13393)
NEW CREW PRODUCTION CORP
1100 W 135th St (90247-1919)
PHONE.................323 234-8880
Kris Park, *Pr*
Joseph Park, *
▲ EMP: 110 EST: 2002
SALES (est): 3.45MM Privately Held
Web: www.newcrewproductioncorp.com
SIC: 7389 Sewing contractor

(P-13394)
NEW SCHOOLS VENTURE FUND
1616 Franklin St # 2 (94612-2806)
PHONE.................415 615-6860
Stacey Childress, *CEO*
Kim Smith, *Ex Ch Bd*
EMP: 63 EST: 1998
SQ FT: 4,000
SALES (est): 41.22MM Privately Held
Web: www.newschools.org
SIC: 7389 8742 Fund raising organizations; Management consulting services

(P-13395)
NEWPORT DIVERSIFIED INC
Also Called: Parkway Bowl
1286 Fletcher Pkwy (92020-1826)
PHONE.................619 448-4111
Tony Casarrubia, *Mgr*
EMP: 101
SALES (corp-wide): 14.72MM Privately Held
Web: www.nd-inc.com
SIC: 7389 7933 7996 Flea market; Bowling centers; Amusement parks
PA: Newport Diversified, Inc.
4695 Macarthur Ct # 1420
Newport Beach CA
949 851-1355

(P-13396)
NEWPORT DIVERSIFIED INC
Santa Fe Springs Swap Meet
13963 Alondra Blvd (90670-5814)
PHONE.................562 921-4359
EMP: 101
SQ FT: 10,846
SALES (corp-wide): 14.72MM Privately Held
Web: www.sfsswapmeet.com
SIC: 7389 5932 Flea market; Used merchandise stores
PA: Newport Diversified, Inc.
4695 Macarthur Ct # 1420
Newport Beach CA
949 851-1355

(P-13397)
NEXT ISSUE MEDIA LLC
1 Apple Park Way (95014-0642)
PHONE.................650 521-5151
EMP: 90
Web: www.nextissuemedia.com
SIC: 7389 Subscription fulfillment services: magazine, newspaper, etc.

(P-13398)
NIRVANA TECH INC
595 Market St Fl 10 (94105-2809)
PHONE.................617 800-6650
Rushil Goel, *CEO*
EMP: 80 EST: 2021
SALES (est): 2.84MM Privately Held
Web: www.nirvanatech.com
SIC: 7389 Business services, nec

(P-13399)
NITTO AVECIA PHARMA SVCS INC
6 Vanderbilt (92618-2010)
PHONE.................949 951-4425
EMP: 60
Web: www.aveciapharma.com
SIC: 7389 Automobile recovery service
HQ: Nitto Avecia Pharma Services, Inc.
10 Vanderbilt
Irvine CA
949 951-4425

(P-13400)
NOR-CAL BEVERAGE CO INC
Also Called: Norcal Beverage Co
1226 N Olive St (92801-2543)
PHONE.................714 526-8600
William Mcfarland, *Mgr*
EMP: 68
SALES (corp-wide): 231.77MM Privately Held
Web: www.ncbev.com
SIC: 7389 2033 Packaging and labeling services; Canned fruits and specialties
PA: Nor-Cal Beverage Co., Inc.
2150 Stone Blvd
West Sacramento CA
916 372-0600

(P-13401)
NOVATO FIRE PROTECTION DST
95 Rowland Way (94945-5001)
PHONE.................415 878-2690
Daniel Hom, *Dir Fin*
Marc Revere, *
EMP: 90 EST: 1926
SALES (est): 4.8MM Privately Held
Web: www.novatofire.org
SIC: 7389 Fire protection service other than forestry or public

(P-13402)
NUCOR BLDG SYSTEMS UTAH LLC
1100 Pinot Noir Dr (95240-7410)
PHONE.................209 608-7701
EMP: 86
SALES (corp-wide): 41.51B Publicly Held
Web: www.nucorbuildingsystems.com

7389 - Business Services, Nec (P-13422)

SIC: 7389 Automobile recovery service
HQ: Nucor Building Systems Utah Llc
    1050 N Watery Ln
    Brigham City UT

(P-13403)
NUVIA WATER TECHNOLOGIES INC
108 Business Center Dr (92878-3218)
PHONE..................951 734-7400
Kellie Johnson, *Pr*
EMP: 60 EST: 2011
SALES (est): 6.95MM **Privately Held**
Web: www.nuviawater.com
SIC: 7389 Personal service agents, brokers, and bureaus

(P-13404)
OCEANX LLC (PA)
100 N Pacific Coast Hwy Ste 1500 (90245)
PHONE..................310 774-4088
Steve Adams, *Managing Member*
EMP: 98 EST: 2015
SALES (est): 39.85MM
SALES (corp-wide): 39.85MM **Privately Held**
Web: www.oceanx.com
SIC: 7389 4731 Subscription fulfillment services: magazine, newspaper, etc.; Freight transportation arrangement

(P-13405)
OEOE CORP
927 S Grand View St # 10 (90006-2176)
PHONE..................213 387-0933
Young Hawk Oh, *Brnch Mgr*
EMP: 122
SALES (corp-wide): 342.2K **Privately Held**
SIC: 7389 Personal service agents, brokers, and bureaus
PA: Oeoe Corp
    1740 S Los Angeles St
    Los Angeles CA

(P-13406)
ONEIL DIGITAL SOLUTIONS LLC
12655 Beatrice St (90066-7300)
PHONE..................310 448-6407
David Woodley, *Contrlr*
EMP: 201
SALES (corp-wide): 335.64MM **Privately Held**
Web: www.oneildigitalsolutions.com
SIC: 7389 2752 5045 Mailbox rental and related service; Commercial printing, lithographic; Computer software
HQ: O'neil Digital Solutions, Llc
    3100 E Plano Pkwy
    Plano TX
    972 881-1282

(P-13407)
ONTARIO CONVENTION CENTER CORP
Also Called: Smg Management Facility
2000 E Convention Center Way (91764-5633)
PHONE..................909 937-3000
Dick Walsh, *Mayor*
Michael K Krouse, *CEO*
EMP: 334 EST: 1995
SQ FT: 225,000
SALES (est): 3.3MM
SALES (corp-wide): 461.59MM **Privately Held**
Web: www.gocvb.org
SIC: 7389 Convention and show services
PA: City Of Ontario
    303 E B St
    Ontario CA
    909 395-2012

(P-13408)
OPENTABLE INC (HQ)
1 Montgomery St Ste 500 (94104-4535)
PHONE..................415 344-4200
Debby Soo, *CEO*
Matthew Roberts, *
I Duncan Robertson, *
Joseph Essas, *
Jeff Mccombs, *CFO*
EMP: 125 EST: 1998
SALES (est): 166.18MM
SALES (corp-wide): 17.09B **Publicly Held**
Web: www.opentable.com
SIC: 7389 Restaurant reservation service
PA: Booking Holdings Inc.
    800 Connecticut Ave
    Norwalk CT
    203 299-8000

(P-13409)
ORANGE COAST TITLE COMPANY (PA)
1551 N Tustin Ave Ste 300 (92705-8638)
P.O. Box 11825 (92711-1825)
PHONE..................714 558-2836
Mike Kaluger, *Pr*
EMP: 100 EST: 1973
SQ FT: 24,000
SALES (est): 106.01MM **Privately Held**
Web: www.octitle.com
SIC: 7389 6361 6541 Personal service agents, brokers, and bureaus; Title insurance; Title and trust companies

(P-13410)
ORANGE COURIER INC
Also Called: Asbury
15300 Desman Rd (90638-5762)
P.O. Box 5308 (92704-0308)
PHONE..................714 384-3600
Evell T Stanley, *Pr*
▲ EMP: 300 EST: 1992
SALES (est): 28.43MM **Privately Held**
Web: www.orangecourier.com
SIC: 7389 4213 4225 Courier or messenger service; Trucking, except local; General warehousing and storage

(P-13411)
ORCHID COURT INC
650 Camino Real Cir (92543-2608)
PHONE..................951 766-7840
Elisa R Gosuico, *Brnch Mgr*
EMP: 74
SALES (corp-wide): 985.43K **Privately Held**
Web: www.orchidcourt.com
SIC: 7389 Personal service agents, brokers, and bureaus
PA: Orchid Court, Inc.
    307 S Arrowhead Ave
    San Bernardino CA
    909 884-3044

(P-13412)
ORION GROUP WORLD LLC
143 Seminary Dr Apt Q (94941-6212)
PHONE..................415 602-5233
Ace Stojanovski, *Pr*
Monika Szczuka, *
EMP: 120 EST: 2017
SALES (est): 1.43MM **Privately Held**
SIC: 7389 3812 3482 3489 Business Activities at Non-Commercial Site; Defense systems and equipment; Cartridges, 30 mm. and below; Rocket launchers

(P-13413)
OST TRUCKS AND CRANES INC
Also Called: Ost Crane Service
2951 N Ventura Ave (93001-1210)
P.O. Box 237 (93002-0237)
PHONE..................805 643-9963
TOLL FREE: 800
L Dennis Zermeno, *Pr*
Don D Zermeno, *
Ron J Zermeno, *
EMP: 73 EST: 1962
SQ FT: 3,000
SALES (est): 12.92MM **Privately Held**
Web: www.ostcranes.com
SIC: 7389 4212 4225 Crane and aerial lift service; Local trucking, without storage; General warehousing and storage

(P-13414)
PACIFIC COAST COMPANIES INC
10811 International Dr (95670-7319)
P.O. Box 419074 (95741-9074)
PHONE..................916 631-6500
David J Lucchetti, *Pr*
Daniel Yanagihara, *General Vice President*
Dale Waldschmitt, *
Joshua Kimerer, *
Ken Kerrick, *CIO*
EMP: 125 EST: 2003
SALES (est): 49.7MM
SALES (corp-wide): 1.19B **Privately Held**
Web: www.paccoast.com
SIC: 7389 8742 Legal and tax services; Human resource consulting services
PA: Pacific Coast Building Products, Inc.
    10600 White Rock Rd # 100
    Rancho Cordova CA
    916 631-6500

(P-13415)
PACIFIC COAST PRODUCERS
650 S Guild Ave (95240-3114)
PHONE..................209 365-9982
Jim Farmer, *Brnch Mgr*
EMP: 139
SALES (corp-wide): 510.52MM **Privately Held**
Web: www.pacificcoastproducers.com
SIC: 7389 5141 Packaging and labeling services; Groceries, general line
PA: Pacific Coast Producers
    631 N Cluff Ave
    Lodi CA
    209 367-8800

(P-13416)
PACIFIC MEDICAL INC (PA)
Also Called: Pacific Med Prsthtics Orthtics
1700 N Chrisman Rd (95304-9314)
P.O. Box 149 (95378-0149)
PHONE..................800 726-9180
John M Petlansky, *CEO*
Jeffrey Leonard, *
Mark Weaver, *
EMP: 69 EST: 1988
SQ FT: 18,000
SALES (est): 90.62MM **Privately Held**
Web: www.pacmedical.com
SIC: 7389 7352 Brokers, contract services; Medical equipment rental

(P-13417)
PAR WESTERN LINE CONTRS LLC
11276 5th St Ste 100 (91730-0922)
PHONE..................760 737-0925
Jim Stapp, *Pr*
Irene Anderson, *CTRL**
Travis Walser, *
Kody Kilshaw, *
EMP: 550 EST: 2000
SQ FT: 800
SALES (est): 41.48MM
SALES (corp-wide): 17.07B **Publicly Held**
Web: www.parwlc.com
SIC: 7389 8711 1731 1623 Mapmaking services; Engineering services; General electrical contractor; Oil and gas line and compressor station construction
PA: Quanta Services, Inc.
    2727 North Loop W Ste 100
    Houston TX
    713 629-7600

(P-13418)
PARADIGM INDUSTRIES INC
2522 E 37th St (90058-1725)
PHONE..................310 965-1900
William Jun, *CEO*
Chu Kim, *
▲ EMP: 80 EST: 2000
SALES (est): 2.49MM **Privately Held**
Web: www.paradigmindustries.net
SIC: 7389 Textile and apparel services

(P-13419)
PARTNERS CAPITAL GROUP INC (PA)
Also Called: Partners Capital Group
201 Sandpointe Ave Ste 500 (92707-5778)
PHONE..................949 916-3900
Mark Davin, *CEO*
EMP: 80 EST: 2005
SQ FT: 25,000
SALES (est): 24.72MM **Privately Held**
Web: www.partnerscapitalgrp.com
SIC: 7389 Financial services

(P-13420)
PASADENA CENTER OPERATING CO
Also Called: Pasadena Convention Center
300 E Green St (91101-2399)
PHONE..................626 795-9311
Michael Ross, *CEO*
EMP: 116 EST: 1973
SQ FT: 32,000
SALES (est): 24.24MM **Privately Held**
Web: www.visitpasadena.com
SIC: 7389 Convention and show services

(P-13421)
PATRICK K WILLIS AND CO INC
Also Called: American Recovery Service
5118 Robert J Mathews Pkwy (95762-5703)
PHONE..................800 398-6480
David Baker, *Sr VP*
Christian Beyer, *
EMP: 300 EST: 1984
SQ FT: 10,000
SALES (est): 27.87MM **Privately Held**
Web: www.americanrecoveryservice.com
SIC: 7389 Repossession service

(P-13422)
PAYPAL INC (HQ)
Also Called: Paypal
2211 N 1st St (95131-2021)
P.O. Box 7397 (92375-0397)
PHONE..................877 981-2163
Jonathan Auerbach, *VP*
Tomer Barelm, *Prin*
Patrick Dupuis, *
Rupert Keeley, *
Archana Deskus, *CIO**
◆ EMP: 282 EST: 1998
SALES (est): 2.59B
SALES (corp-wide): 27.52B **Publicly Held**

7389 - Business Services, Nec (P-13423)

Web: www.paypal.com
SIC: 7389 Credit card service
PA: Paypal Holdings, Inc.
2211 N 1st St
San Jose CA
408 967-1000

(P-13423)
PAYPAL HOLDINGS INC (PA)
Also Called: Paypal
2211 N 1st St (95131-2021)
PHONE.................408 967-1000
Alex Chriss, CEO
John J Donahoe, Non-Executive Chairman of the Board
Jonathan Auerbach, STRAT GROWTH DATA
Sripada Shivananda, Ex VP
Gabrielle Rabinovitch, Sr VP
EMP: 1242 EST: 2015
SQ FT: 700,000
SALES (est): 27.52B
SALES (corp-wide): 27.52B Publicly Held
Web: www.paypal.com
SIC: 7389 6099 7374 Financial services; Electronic funds transfer network, including switching; Data processing and preparation

(P-13424)
PAYSAFE PARTNERS LP
2600 Michelson Dr Ste 1600 (92612-1550)
PHONE.................949 788-1010
EMP: 64 EST: 2017
SALES (est): 21.15MM
SALES (corp-wide): 232.73MM Privately Held
Web: www.paysafe.com
SIC: 7389 Credit card service
PA: Paysafe Group Limited
3rd Floor
Isle Of Man
207 608-8460

(P-13425)
PHONE WARE INC
8902 Activity Rd Ste A (92126-4471)
PHONE.................858 530-8550
William J Nassir, Pr
Hazel Nassir, *
EMP: 366 EST: 1974
SQ FT: 20,000
SALES (est): 23.72MM Privately Held
Web: www.phonewareinc.com
SIC: 7389 8742 Telemarketing services; Marketing consulting services

(P-13426)
PIONEER THEATRES INC
Also Called: Roadium Open Air Market
2500 Redondo Beach Blvd (90504-1529)
PHONE.................310 532-8183
William Fleischman, Pr
William Warnick, *
EMP: 110 EST: 1949
SQ FT: 3,000
SALES (est): 4.58MM Privately Held
Web: www.roadium.com
SIC: 7389 5431 Flea market; Fruit and vegetable markets

(P-13427)
PIXAR
500 N Buena Vista St (91505-3209)
PHONE.................510 922-4075
Jody B Silverman, Brnch Mgr
EMP: 208
SALES (corp-wide): 82.72B Publicly Held
Web: www.pixar.com
SIC: 7389 Business Activities at Non-Commercial Site
HQ: Pixar
1200 Park Ave
Emeryville CA
510 922-3000

(P-13428)
PRECISION IDEO INC
Also Called: Ideo
2525 16th St (94103-4234)
PHONE.................650 688-3400
Tim Brown, Pr
EMP: 400 EST: 1992
SALES (est): 29.22MM Privately Held
Web: cantwait.ideo.com
SIC: 7389 Design services

(P-13429)
PRIMERICA FINANCIAL SERVICES
Also Called: Primerica
1620 N Carpenter Rd Ste D47 (95351)
PHONE.................209 545-5887
Joseph Pedres, Prin
EMP: 100 EST: 2010
SALES (est): 189.47K Privately Held
Web: www.primerica.com
SIC: 7389 Financial services

(P-13430)
PRO-TECH DESIGN & MFG INC (PA)
Also Called: Pro-Tech
14561 Marquardt Ave (90670-5137)
PHONE.................562 207-1680
Pamela Mc Master, CEO
Aaron Swanson, Pr
Jeff Swanson, VP
David Mc Master, CFO
▲ EMP: 60 EST: 1979
SALES (est): 14.04MM
SALES (corp-wide): 14.04MM Privately Held
Web: www.protechdesign.com
SIC: 7389 8711 Packaging and labeling services; Industrial engineers

(P-13431)
PRODUCT DEVELOPMENT CORP
30 Ragsdale Dr Ste 101 (93940-5772)
P.O. Box 3736 (93912-3736)
PHONE.................831 333-1100
EMP: 832
Web: www.deliverphonebooks.com
SIC: 7389 Telephone directory distribution, contract or fee basis

(P-13432)
PRODUCTIVE PLAYHOUSE INC (PA)
25231 Paseo De Alicia Ste 205 (92653-4645)
PHONE.................323 250-3445
Harry Ralston, CEO
EMP: 268 EST: 2009
SALES (est): 9.62MM
SALES (corp-wide): 9.62MM Privately Held
Web: www.productiveplayhouse.com
SIC: 7389 Translation services

(P-13433)
PROGRAM PLG PROFESSIONALS INC
71 Stevenson St Ste 825 (94105-2942)
PHONE.................415 692-5870
Beverly Barnett, Brnch Mgr
EMP: 123

Web: www.migso-pcubed.com
SIC: 7389 Interior design services
HQ: Program Planning Professionals, Inc.
1340 Eisenhower Pl
Ann Arbor MI
734 741-7770

(P-13434)
PROLOGIC RDMPTION SLUTIONS INC (PA)
2121 Rosecrans Ave (90245-4743)
PHONE.................310 322-7774
William Atkinson, CEO
Paul Cooley, Pr
John Mccurry, Ex VP
Robb Warwick, CFO
Kelly Fuller, CCO
EMP: 700 EST: 2008
SALES (est): 36.8MM
SALES (corp-wide): 36.8MM Privately Held
SIC: 7389 Coupon redemption service

(P-13435)
PROMPT DELIVERY INC
Also Called: Southern California Messenger
5757 Wilshire Blvd Ph 3 (90036-3681)
PHONE.................858 549-8000
Mike Dysland, Mgr
EMP: 100
SIC: 7389 4212 Courier or messenger service; Delivery service, vehicular
PA: Prompt Delivery, Inc.
5757 Wilshire Blvd # 210
Los Angeles CA

(P-13436)
PROPLUS DESIGN SOLUTIONS INC (PA)
2025 Gateway Pl Ste 130 (95110-1005)
PHONE.................408 459-6128
Lianfeng Yang, VP Mktg
Zhijian Ma, CEO
EMP: 119 EST: 2007
SALES (est): 4.35MM Privately Held
Web: www.proplussolutions.com
SIC: 7389 Design services

(P-13437)
PSYCHROM INC
Also Called: PSYCHROM INC
56310 Pima Trl Ste C (92284-7516)
PHONE.................760 366-9811
EMP: 69
SALES (corp-wide): 876.99K Privately Held
SIC: 7389 Personal service agents, brokers, and bureaus
PA: Psychrom Inc.
23365 Continental Dr
Canyon Lake CA
951 244-7201

(P-13438)
PTW AMERICA INC
1042 Princeton Dr Ste B (90292-5497)
PHONE.................424 289-0347
Deborah Kirkham, CEO
EMP: 60 EST: 2009
SALES (est): 4.91MM Privately Held
SIC: 7389 Translation services

(P-13439)
PUFF GLOBAL INC
Also Called: Puff Candy,
402 W Broadway Ste 400 (92101-3554)
PHONE.................619 520-3499
David Soria, CEO
▲ EMP: 80 EST: 2013

SALES (est): 2.72MM Privately Held
SIC: 7389 Business Activities at Non-Commercial Site

(P-13440)
QOLOGY DIRECT LLC
Also Called: Centerfield Media
12130 Millennium Ste 600 (90094-2819)
PHONE.................310 341-4420
Brett Cravatt, Pr
Jason Cohen, Pr
EMP: 170 EST: 2012
SQ FT: 90,000
SALES (est): 10.08MM
SALES (corp-wide): 60.59MM Privately Held
Web: www.centerfield.com
SIC: 7389 Telephone services
HQ: Qology Direct Holdings, Inc.
12130 Millennium Ste 600
Los Angeles CA

(P-13441)
QUIDEL CARDIOVASCULAR INC
9975 Summers Ridge Rd (92121-2997)
PHONE.................858 552-1100
Douglas C Bryant, CEO
Randall Steward, *
EMP: 74 EST: 2017
SALES (est): 22.29MM
SALES (corp-wide): 3.27B Publicly Held
Web: www.quidel.com
SIC: 7389 Inspection and testing services
HQ: Quidel Corporation
9975 Summers Ridge Rd
San Diego CA
858 552-1100

(P-13442)
R G CANNING ENTERPRISES INC
4515 E 59th Pl (90270-3201)
PHONE.................323 560-7469
Richard G Canning, Pr
Charles R Canning, *
EMP: 215 EST: 1955
SQ FT: 50,000
SALES (est): 4.96MM Privately Held
Web: www.rgcshows.com
SIC: 7389 Promoters of shows and exhibitions

(P-13443)
REGUS BUSINESS CENTRE LLC
Also Called: Plaza Tower 1
600 Anton Blvd Ste 1100 (92626-7100)
PHONE.................714 371-4000
Karen Barbeau, Mgr
EMP: 212
SALES (corp-wide): 3.31B Privately Held
Web: www.regus.com
SIC: 7389 Office facilities and secretarial service rental
HQ: Regus Business Centre Llc
15455 Dallas Pkwy Ste 600
Addison TX
972 361-8100

(P-13444)
REGUS EQUITY BUSINESS CTRS LLC
Also Called: Spear Tower
One Market 35th And 36th Floors (94105-1596)
PHONE.................415 293-8000
Vertie Mentzer, Brnch Mgr
EMP: 88
SALES (corp-wide): 3.31B Privately Held
SIC: 7389 Office facilities and secretarial service rental

PRODUCTS & SERVICES SECTION

7389 - Business Services, Nec (P-13467)

HQ: Regus Equity Business Centers, L.L.C.
  15305 Dallas Pkwy Ste 40
  Addison TX
  972 361-8100

(P-13445)
RGIS LLC
Also Called: Rgis, Llc
1937 W Chapman Ave (92868-2632)
PHONE.................714 938-0663
EMP: 133
SALES (corp-wide): 156.24MM **Privately Held**
Web: www.rgis.com
SIC: 7389 Inventory computing service
PA: Wis Ivs, Llc
  2000 Taylor Rd
  Auburn Hills MI
  248 221-4000

(P-13446)
RGIS LLC
Also Called: Rgis, Llc
6529 Riverside Ave Ste 215 (92506)
PHONE.................951 369-7131
Katherine Barton, *Mgr*
EMP: 65
SALES (corp-wide): 156.24MM **Privately Held**
Web: www.rgis.com
SIC: 7389 Inventory computing service
PA: Wis Ivs, Llc
  2000 Taylor Rd
  Auburn Hills MI
  248 221-4000

(P-13447)
RGIS LLC
Also Called: Rgis, Llc
365 S Rancho Santa Fe Rd Ste 103 (92078-2338)
PHONE.................760 736-9241
EMP: 165
SALES (corp-wide): 156.24MM **Privately Held**
Web: www.rgis.com
SIC: 7389 Inventory computing service
PA: Wis Ivs, Llc
  2000 Taylor Rd
  Auburn Hills MI
  248 221-4000

(P-13448)
RGN-SAN DIEGO I LLC
350 10th Ave Ste 1000 (92101-8705)
PHONE.................619 344-2500
EMP: 207
SALES (corp-wide): 3.31B **Privately Held**
SIC: 7389 Office facilities and secretarial service rental
HQ: Diego I Rgn-San Llc
  15305 Dallas Pkwy Ste 400
  Addison TX
  972 361-8100

(P-13449)
RGN-SAN FRANCISCO IV LLC
75 Broadway Ste 202 (94111-1423)
PHONE.................415 882-6300
EMP: 69
SALES (corp-wide): 3.31B **Privately Held**
SIC: 7389 Office facilities and secretarial service rental
HQ: Rgn-San Francisco Iv, Llc
  15305 Dallas Pkwy Ste 400
  Addison TX
  972 361-8100

(P-13450)
RIVER CITY AUTO RECOVERY INC
3401 Fitzgerald Rd (95742-6815)
PHONE.................916 851-1100
EMP: 71
SQ FT: 15,000
SALES (est): 2.23MM
SALES (corp-wide): 577.01MM **Privately Held**
SIC: 7389 Repossession service
PA: United Road Services, Inc.
  10701 Middlebelt Rd
  Romulus MI
  734 946-3232

(P-13451)
ROAD SAFETY INC
4335 Pacific St Ste A (95677-2104)
PHONE.................916 543-4600
Jason Bamberg, *Pr*
Melissa L Bamberg, *
Jason Bamberg, *CEO*
EMP: 120 EST: 2008
SQ FT: 6,000
SALES (est): 22.6MM **Privately Held**
Web: www.roadsafetyinc.net
SIC: 7389 Flagging service (traffic control)

(P-13452)
RONSIN LTGTION SPPORT SVCS INC (PA)
215 Lemon Creek Dr (91789-2643)
PHONE.................909 594-5995
Dennis Grant, *Pr*
Robert Alkema, *
Cheryl Alkema, *
EMP: 60 EST: 1976
SQ FT: 12,000
SALES (est): 4.9MM
SALES (corp-wide): 4.9MM **Privately Held**
Web: www.ronsinphotocopy.com
SIC: 7389 Microfilm recording and developing service

(P-13453)
ROSE & SHORE INC
5151 Alcoa Ave (90058-3715)
P.O. Box 58225 (90058-0225)
PHONE.................323 826-2144
Irwin Miller, *Pr*
Carol Miller, *
EMP: 320 EST: 1968
SQ FT: 60,000
SALES (est): 25.22MM **Privately Held**
Web: www.roseandshore.com
SIC: 7389 5147 Packaging and labeling services; Meats, cured or smoked

(P-13454)
RTI SERVICES INC
2836 Vail Ave (90040-2697)
PHONE.................323 725-6370
Kelly Mcleland, *Mgr*
EMP: 62
SALES (corp-wide): 5.06MM **Privately Held**
SIC: 7389 Salvaging of damaged merchandise, service only
PA: Rti Services, Inc.
  800 Berkshire Ln N
  Plymouth MN
  952 475-0242

(P-13455)
RVL PACKAGING INC
31330 Oak Crest Dr (91361-4632)
PHONE.................818 735-5000
▼ EMP: 200
SIC: 7389 2396 2241 Packaging and labeling services; Automotive and apparel trimmings; Narrow fabric mills

(P-13456)
SACRAMENTO MUNICPL UTILITY DST
Also Called: Smud Financing Authority
14295 Clay East Rd (95638-9770)
PHONE.................916 732-5743
EMP: 150
SALES (corp-wide): 2.15B **Privately Held**
Web: www.smud.org
SIC: 7389 Financial services
PA: Sacramento Municipal Utility District
  6201 S St
  Sacramento CA
  916 452-3211

(P-13457)
SAMESKY HEALTH INC
5250 Lankershim Blvd (91601-3187)
PHONE.................855 735-6726
Abner Mason, *CEO*
Vikram Bakhru, *CFO*
EMP: 60 EST: 2009
SALES (est): 5.67MM **Privately Held**
Web: www.sameskyhealth.com
SIC: 7389 Business services, nec

(P-13458)
SAMSUNG PAY INC
Also Called: Loop
665 Clyde Ave (94043-2235)
PHONE.................617 279-0520
William Graylin, *Ch*
EMP: 78 EST: 2007
SALES (est): 4.43MM **Privately Held**
Web: www.samsung.com
SIC: 7389 3577 7372 Credit card service; Computer peripheral equipment, nec; Prepackaged software

(P-13459)
SAN DEGO CNVNTION CTR CORP INC (PA)
Also Called: Convention Center
111 W Harbor Dr (92101-7822)
PHONE.................619 782-4388
Clifford R Rippetoe, *CEO*
Mardeen Mattix, *
▲ EMP: 281 EST: 1984
SALES (est): 50.5MM
SALES (corp-wide): 50.5MM **Privately Held**
Web: www.visitsandiego.com
SIC: 7389 Convention and show services

(P-13460)
SAN DIEGO OF SAN DIEGO
2251 Las Palmas Dr (92011-1527)
PHONE.................760 710-2242
EMP: 72 EST: 2014
SALES (est): 3MM **Privately Held**
Web: www.sandiegotechhub.com
SIC: 7389 Convention and show services

(P-13461)
SAN FRANCISCO FOUNDATION
1 Embarcadero Ctr Ste 1400 (94111-3703)
PHONE.................415 733-8500
Sandra Hernandez Md, *Dir*
Galen Maness, *
Ophelia B Basgal, *
Robert Friedman, *Vice Chairman**
EMP: 60 EST: 1948
SQ FT: 22,000
SALES (est): 297.44MM **Privately Held**
Web: www.sff.org
SIC: 7389 Fund raising organizations

(P-13462)
SAN FRANCISCO TRAVEL ASSN
Also Called: Ss Travel
1 Front St Ste 2900 (94111-5333)
PHONE.................415 974-6900
Joe D'alessandro, *Pr*
Matt Stiker, *
Bill Poland, *
Tina Wu, *
Paul Frentsos, *
EMP: 70 EST: 1909
SQ FT: 15,000
SALES (est): 15.74MM **Privately Held**
Web: www.sftravel.com
SIC: 7389 Convention and show services

(P-13463)
SAN MNUEL BAND MISSION INDIANS
Also Called: San Manuel Fire Dept
26540 Indian Service Rd (92346-1714)
PHONE.................909 864-6928
EMP: 118
Web: www.sanmanuel-nsn.gov
SIC: 7389 Fire protection service other than forestry or public
PA: San Manuel Band Of Mission Indians
  26569 Community Center Dr
  Highland CA
  909 864-8933

(P-13464)
SANTA CLARA COUNTY OF
Also Called: SANTA CLARA, COUNTY OF
2325 Enborg Ln (95128-2659)
PHONE.................408 793-6410
Edward Garner, *Prin*
EMP: 94
Web: home.sccgov.org
SIC: 7389 Personal service agents, brokers, and bureaus
PA: County Of Santa Clara
  70 W Hedding St
  San Jose CA
  408 299-5200

(P-13465)
SANTA CLARA CONVENTION CENTER
5001 Great America Pkwy (95054-1119)
PHONE.................408 748-7000
Donald C Riccardi, *Genl Mgr*
▲ EMP: 67 EST: 1986
SQ FT: 238,000
SALES (est): 10.49MM **Privately Held**
Web: www.santaclara.org
SIC: 7389 Convention and show services

(P-13466)
SCA ENTERPRISES INC (PA)
Also Called: Southern Cal Appraisal Co
3817 W Magnolia Blvd (91505-2820)
P.O. Box 1455 (91507-1455)
PHONE.................818 845-7621
Timothy S Davis, *CEO*
Paula Davis, *
▲ EMP: 65 EST: 1979
SQ FT: 1,200
SALES (est): 14.38MM **Privately Held**
Web: www.sca-appraisal.com
SIC: 7389 Appraisers, except real estate

(P-13467)
SCHERZER INTERNATIONAL CORP (PA)
21650 Oxnard St Ste 300 (91367-4989)
PHONE.................818 227-2770

7389 - Business Services, Nec (P-13468)

PRODUCTS & SERVICES SECTION

Larry S Scherzer, *Pr*
Carol Scherzer, *
EMP: 60 **EST:** 1991
SQ FT: 11,400
SALES (est): 10.11MM **Privately Held**
Web: www.scherzer.com
SIC: 7389 Financial services

(P-13468)
SCRATCH FINANCIAL INC
Also Called: Scratchpay
225 S Lake Ave Ste 250 (91101-4895)
PHONE..................................855 727-2395
John Keatley, *CEO*
Caleb Morse, *
EMP: 66 **EST:** 2016
SQ FT: 3,000
SALES (est): 4.56MM **Privately Held**
Web: www.scratchpay.com
SIC: 7389 Financial services

(P-13469)
SD&A TELESERVICES INC (HQ)
5757 W Century Blvd Ste 300 (90045-6432)
EMP: 300 **EST:** 2004
SALES (est): 22.02MM
SALES (corp-wide): 54.58MM **Privately Held**
Web: www.sdats.com
SIC: 7389 Telemarketing services
PA: Robert W. Woodruff Arts Center, Inc.
1280 Peachtree St Ne
Atlanta GA
404 733-4200

(P-13470)
SERVICING SOLUTIONS LLC
1 City Blvd W Ste 200 (92868-3689)
PHONE..................................844 907-6583
EMP: 61
SALES (corp-wide): 5.37MM **Privately Held**
Web: www.servicingsolutions.com
SIC: 7389 Process serving service
PA: Servicing Solutions, Llc
3660 Regent Blvd Ste 200
Irving TX
844 907-6583

(P-13471)
SEVEN ONE INC (PA)
Also Called: Professional Tele Answering Svc
21540 Prairie St Ste E (91311-5814)
PHONE..................................818 904-3435
James Thompson, *Pr*
EMP: 83 **EST:** 1983
SQ FT: 4,000
SALES (est): 2.43MM **Privately Held**
Web: www.answer24live.com
SIC: 7389 Telephone answering service

(P-13472)
SHERPA CLINICAL PACKAGING LLC
6920 Carroll Rd (92121-2211)
PHONE..................................858 997-1493
EMP: 63
SALES (corp-wide): 16.81MM **Privately Held**
Web: www.pci.com
SIC: 7389 Packaging and labeling services
PA: Sherpa Clinical Packaging, Llc
6166 Nancy Ridge Dr
San Diego CA
858 997-1490

(P-13473)
SHINWOO P&C USA INC (HQ)
2177 Britannia Blvd Ste 203 (92154-8307)
PHONE..................................619 407-7164
Il Kim, *CEO*
▲ **EMP:** 348 **EST:** 2007
SQ FT: 300
SALES (est): 26.35MM **Privately Held**
SIC: 7389 Packaging and labeling services
PA: Shinan Packaging Co.,Ltd.
19b-5l, Banwol Industrial Complex
Ansan

(P-13474)
SIGNET TESTING LABS INC
498 N 3rd St (95811-0215)
PHONE..................................916 374-0754
EMP: 75
SALES (corp-wide): 24.71MM **Privately Held**
Web: www.signettesting.com
SIC: 7389 Inspection and testing services
HQ: Signet Testing Laboratories, Inc.
3526 Breakwater Ct
Hayward CA

(P-13475)
SIGUE CORPORATION (PA)
Also Called: Sigue
13190 Telfair Ave (91342-3573)
PHONE..................................818 837-5939
Guillermo Dela Vina, *CEO*
Christina M Pappas, *
Alfredo Dela Vina, *
EMP: 100 **EST:** 1996
SQ FT: 3,000
SALES (est): 109.03MM
SALES (corp-wide): 109.03MM **Privately Held**
Web: www.sigue.com
SIC: 7389 4822 Financial services; Telegraph and other communications

(P-13476)
SIMPLICONTRACT TECH INC
6387 Alvord Way (94588-3965)
PHONE..................................403 833-5556
Guru Venkatesan, *CEO*
Makesh Kumar, *CPO*
EMP: 80 **EST:** 2020
SALES (est): 1.33MM **Privately Held**
SIC: 7389 Business Activities at Non-Commercial Site

(P-13477)
SINECERA INC
Also Called: Crown Vly Precision Machining
5397 3rd St (91706-2085)
PHONE..................................626 962-1087
Donald Brown, *CEO*
Dale B Mikus, *CFO*
EMP: 80 **EST:** 1984
SQ FT: 10,500
SALES (est): 24.79MM
SALES (corp-wide): 101.1MM **Privately Held**
Web: www.crownprecision.com
SIC: 7389 3492 Grinding, precision: commercial or industrial; Control valves, aircraft; hydraulic and pneumatic
PA: H-D Advanced Manufacturing Company
2418 Greens Rd
Houston TX
346 219-0320

(P-13478)
SMG HOLDINGS LLC
Also Called: Moscone Center
747 Howard St (94103-3118)
PHONE..................................415 974-4040
Richard Shaff, *Genl Mgr*
EMP: 69
SALES (corp-wide): 422MM **Privately Held**
Web: www.moscone.com
SIC: 7389 8611 6512 Convention and show services; Business associations; Nonresidential building operators
HQ: Smg Holdings, Llc
300 Cnshohckn State Rd # 450
Conshohocken PA

(P-13479)
SOBOBA BAND LUISENO INDIANS
Also Called: Soboba Casino
22777 Soboba Rd (92583-2935)
PHONE..................................951 665-1000
TOLL FREE: 888
EMP: 900
Web: www.soboba.com
SIC: 7389 7011 Personal service agents, brokers, and bureaus; Casino hotel
PA: Soboba Band Of Luiseno Indians
23906 Soboba Rd
San Jacinto CA
951 654-2765

(P-13480)
SONOVA USA INC
47257 Fremont Blvd (94538-6502)
PHONE..................................510 743-3900
EMP: 79
Web: www.phonak.com
SIC: 7389 Business Activities at Non-Commercial Site
HQ: Sonova Usa Inc.
444 Commerce St Ste 112
Aurora IL
763 744-3300

(P-13481)
SONY INTERACTIVE ENTRMT LLC
Also Called: Sony Interactive Entertainment
919 E Hillsdale Blvd (94404-2112)
PHONE..................................858 824-5501
Sangita Patel, *VP*
EMP: 71
Web: www.playstation.com
SIC: 7389 Music distribution systems
HQ: Sony Interactive Entertainment Llc
2207 Bridgepointe Pkwy
Foster City CA
310 981-1500

(P-13482)
SOUTHWEST DEALER SERVICES INC
1001 G St Ste 113 (95814-0834)
PHONE..................................925 753-0696
EMP: 119
Web: www.acrisurepg.com
SIC: 7389 Brokers, contract services
PA: Southwest Dealer Services, Inc.
8659 Research Dr Ste 100
Irvine CA

(P-13483)
STACCATO COMMUNICATIONS INC
6195 Lusk Blvd Ste 200 (92121-3723)
PHONE..................................858 812-1000
Rick Kornfeld, *Pr*
Roberto Aiello, *
Mark Bowles, *
Marty Colombatto, *
Colin Macnab, *
EMP: 65 **EST:** 2002
SALES (est): 4.87MM **Privately Held**
Web: www.staccatocommunications.com
SIC: 7389 Personal service agents, brokers, and bureaus

(P-13484)
STANFORD LAW SCHL OFF FNCL AID
559 Nathan Abbott Way Rm 107 (94305)
PHONE..................................650 723-9247
EMP: 238 **EST:** 2010
SALES (est): 2.41MM **Privately Held**
Web: www.stanford.edu
SIC: 7389 Financial services

(P-13485)
STANTEC ARCHITECTURE INC
Also Called: Rnl Design
801 S Figueroa St Ste 300 (90017-3007)
PHONE..................................213 955-9775
Patrick Mckelvey, *Brnch Mgr*
EMP: 388
SALES (corp-wide): 4.23B **Privately Held**
Web: www.stantec.com
SIC: 7389 8712 Interior designer; Architectural engineering
HQ: Stantec Architecture Inc.
224 S Michigan Ave # 1400
Chicago IL
336 714-7413

(P-13486)
STARCO GROUP INC (PA)
9160 Hyssop Dr (91730-6100)
PHONE..................................909 989-9898
Ross Sklar, *CEO*
▲ **EMP:** 60 **EST:** 2013
SALES (est): 38.95MM
SALES (corp-wide): 38.95MM **Privately Held**
Web: www.starcogp.com
SIC: 7389 Design services

(P-13487)
STRATEGIC OPERATIONS INC
4705 Ruffin Rd (92123-1611)
PHONE..................................858 244-0559
Stuart Segall, *CEO*
EMP: 250 **EST:** 2002
SQ FT: 12,000
SALES (est): 24.34MM **Privately Held**
Web: www.strategic-operations.com
SIC: 7389 Personal service agents, brokers, and bureaus

(P-13488)
STRATHMOORE PRESS INC
Also Called: Warwick, Mal & Associates
2550 9th St Ste 103 (94710-2551)
PHONE..................................510 843-8888
EMP: 80 **EST:** 1996
SALES (est): 1.47MM **Privately Held**
SIC: 7389 Brokers, business: buying and selling business enterprises

(P-13489)
STRIPE INC (PA)
Also Called: Stripe Payments Company
354 Oyster Point Blvd (94080-1912)
PHONE..................................888 963-8955
EMP: 153 **EST:** 2009
SALES (est): 450.39MM **Privately Held**
Web: www.stripe.com
SIC: 7389 Financial services

(P-13490)
SUGAR FOODS CORPORATION
Also Called: Sygma Network, The

▲ = Import ▼ = Export
◆ = Import/Export

PRODUCTS & SERVICES SECTION

7389 - Business Services, Nec (P-13513)

9500 El Dorado Ave (91352-1339)
PHONE.................818 768-7900
Stephen Odell, Pt
EMP: 200
SALES (corp-wide): 286.33MM Privately Held
Web: www.sugarfoods.com
SIC: 7389 2099 2062 Packaging and labeling services; Food preparations, nec; Cane sugar refining
PA: Sugar Foods Corporation
950 3rd Ave Fl 21
New York NY
212 753-6900

(P-13491)
SUN LIGHT & POWER
1035 Folger Ave (94710-2819)
PHONE.................510 845-2997
Gary Gerber, Pr
Eric Nyman, *
Blake Gleason, *
Patch Garcia, *
Troy Tyler, *
EMP: 70 EST: 1975
SQ FT: 10,000
SALES (est): 17MM Privately Held
Web: www.sunlightandpower.com
SIC: 7389 1796 3433 Design services; Power generating equipment installation; Solar heaters and collectors

(P-13492)
SUPER CENTER CONCEPTS INC
1130 W 6th St (92882-3133)
PHONE.................951 372-9485
EMP: 82
Web: www.superiorgrocers.com
SIC: 7389 Design services
PA: Super Center Concepts, Inc.
15510 Carmenita Rd
Santa Fe Springs CA

(P-13493)
SUPER CENTER CONCEPTS INC
Also Called: Superior Grocers
133 W Avenue 45 (90065-3022)
PHONE.................323 223-3878
Chris Gonzalez, Dist Mgr
EMP: 123
Web: www.superiorgrocers.com
SIC: 7389 Design services
PA: Super Center Concepts, Inc.
15510 Carmenita Rd
Santa Fe Springs CA

(P-13494)
SUTTER CONNECT LLC
Also Called: SUTTER CONNECT, LLC
2000 Powell St Ste 100 (94608-1774)
PHONE.................510 596-4700
Tom Bacci, Mgr
EMP: 333
SALES (corp-wide): 14.77B Privately Held
Web: www.sutterhealth.org
SIC: 7389 Personal service agents, brokers, and bureaus
HQ: Sutter Physician Services
10470 Old Placerville Rd
Sacramento CA

(P-13495)
SWIFT MEDIA ENTERTAINMENT INC
5340 Alla Rd Ste 101 (90066-7036)
PHONE.................310 308-3694
Andy Dinh, CEO
EMP: 75 EST: 2017
SALES (est): 3.24MM Privately Held
SIC: 7389 Advertising, promotional, and trade show services

(P-13496)
SWISSTEX CALIFORNIA INC (PA)
13660 S Figueroa St (90061-1023)
PHONE.................310 516-6800
▲ EMP: 104 EST: 1995
SALES (est): 21.72MM Privately Held
Web: www.swisstex-ca.com
SIC: 7389 Textile and apparel services

(P-13497)
SYNC BROKERAGE INC
22020 Clarendon St Ste 200 (91367-6335)
PHONE.................818 770-3663
Wael Khalafawi, Prin
EMP: 88 EST: 2017
SALES (est): 5.2MM Privately Held
Web: www.syncbrokerage.com
SIC: 7389 Brokers' services

(P-13498)
TACTICAL TELESOLUTIONS INC
2121 N California Blvd Ste 290 (94596-7351)
PHONE.................415 788-8808
TOLL FREE: 800
Laura Hylton, Pr
Kurt Stenzel, *
EMP: 130 EST: 1991
SALES (est): 10.43MM Privately Held
Web: www.ttstechnique.com
SIC: 7389 Telemarketing services

(P-13499)
TALENTBURST INC
575 Market St Ste 3025 (94105-5840)
PHONE.................415 813-4011
EMP: 65
SALES (corp-wide): 21.19MM Privately Held
Web: www.talentburst.com
SIC: 7389 7375 Check validation service; Information retrieval services
PA: Talentburst, Inc.
679 Worcester St Ste 1
Natick MA
508 628-7516

(P-13500)
TBWA CHIAT/DAY INC
5353 Grosvenor Blvd (90066-6913)
PHONE.................310 305-5000
Lee Clow, Mgr
EMP: 374
SALES (corp-wide): 14.29B Publicly Held
Web: www.tbwachiatdayla.com
SIC: 7389 Interior design services
HQ: Tbwa Chiat/Day Inc.
220 E 42nd St
New York NY
212 804-1000

(P-13501)
TD SYNNEX CORPORATION
44131 Nobel Dr. (94538-3173)
PHONE.................510 688-3507
EMP: 71
SALES (corp-wide): 62.34B Publicly Held
Web: www.tdsynnex.com
SIC: 7389 Telemarketing services
PA: Td Synnex Corporation
44201 Nobel Dr
Fremont CA
510 656-3333

(P-13502)
TEAM SAN JOSE
408 Almaden Blvd (95110-2709)
PHONE.................408 295-9600
Janette Divol, *
Dave Costain, *
Janette Sutton, *
Ihab Sabry, *
Simone Harms, *
EMP: 900 EST: 2003
SQ FT: 300,000
SALES (est): 2.54MM Privately Held
Web: www.sanjose.org
SIC: 7389 Convention and show services

(P-13503)
TECHNICON DESIGN CORPORATION
30011 Ivy Glenn Dr Ste 115 (92677-5016)
PHONE.................949 218-1300
Frank Goodchild, Pr
Danton Fitch, *
Helen Carstens, *
EMP: 120 EST: 1989
SALES (est): 20.36MM
SALES (corp-wide): 1.17MM Privately Held
Web: www.technicondesign.com
SIC: 7389 Design services
PA: Technicon Design Limited
Technicon House
Luton BEDS
158 250-6600

(P-13504)
TECMA GROUP LLC
6020 Progressive Ave (92154-6633)
PHONE.................619 918-7371
EMP: 968
Web: www.tecma.com
SIC: 7389 Brokers' services
PA: The Tecma Group L L C
2000 Wyoming Ave Ste A
El Paso TX

(P-13505)
TEEKO LLC
500 Hazel Ave (94030-2318)
PHONE.................415 652-3380
EMP: 64
SALES (corp-wide): 75.65K Privately Held
SIC: 7389 Personal service agents, brokers, and bureaus
PA: Teeko Llc
432 Richmond Dr Apt 2
Millbrae CA

(P-13506)
TELE-DIRECT COMMUNICATIONS INC
4741 Madison Ave Ste 200 (95841-2516)
PHONE.................916 348-2170
A James Puff, Ch
Sandra Coggeshall, *
Celia Puff, *
Thomas Coshow, *
Jamei Puff, *
EMP: 73 EST: 1961
SQ FT: 6,000
SALES (est): 5.18MM Privately Held
Web: www.teledirect.com
SIC: 7389 5999 Telemarketing services; Telephone and communication equipment

(P-13507)
TELECOM INC
2201 Broadway Ste 103 (94612-3028)
PHONE.................510 873-8283
Jon Martin, Pr
EMP: 100 EST: 1993
SALES (est): 8.4MM Privately Held
Web: www.telecominc.com
SIC: 7389 4813 8742 Telemarketing services; Data telephone communications; Marketing consulting services

(P-13508)
THATS NO MOON ENTRMT INC
5419 Mcconnell Ave (90066-7027)
PHONE.................310 795-8282
Taylor Kurosaki, CEO
Tina Kowalewski, CSO*
George Allison, *
EMP: 68 EST: 2020
SALES (est): 2.14MM Privately Held
SIC: 7389 Design services

(P-13509)
THOUSAND OAKS PRTG & SPC INC
Also Called: T/O Printing
5334 Sterling Center Dr (91361-4612)
PHONE.................818 706-8330
Steve Mahr, Pr
▲ EMP: 140 EST: 1981
SQ FT: 60,000
SALES (est): 21.05MM
SALES (corp-wide): 15B Privately Held
Web: www.rrd.com
SIC: 7389 2752 Printing broker; Offset printing
HQ: Consolidated Graphics, Inc.
5858 Westheimer Rd # 200
Houston TX

(P-13510)
THYDE INC (PA)
300 El Sobrante Rd (92879-5757)
PHONE.................951 817-2300
Tim Hyde, Pr
EMP: 200 EST: 1984
SQ FT: 70,000
SALES (est): 29.83MM
SALES (corp-wide): 29.83MM Privately Held
SIC: 7389 Packaging and labeling services

(P-13511)
TMC FINANCING
1611 Telegraph Ave (94612-2253)
PHONE.................415 989-8855
Barbara Morrison, Pr
Barbara Morrison, Pr
Linda Lee, *
EMP: 65 EST: 2012
SALES (est): 6.06MM Privately Held
Web: www.tmcfinancing.com
SIC: 7389 6141 Financial services; Personal credit institutions

(P-13512)
TOUCHOFMODERN INC
30063 Ahern Ave (94587-1234)
PHONE.................888 868-1232
EMP: 155
SALES (corp-wide): 59.74MM Privately Held
Web: www.touchofmodern.com
SIC: 7389 Interior design services
PA: Touchofmodern, Inc.
1025 Sansome St
San Francisco CA
415 230-0750

(P-13513)
TRAFFIC MANAGEMENT INC (PA)
4900 Airport Plaza Dr Ste 300 (90815)

7389 - Business Services, Nec (P-13514)

PHONE..................562 595-4278
▲ EMP: 144 EST: 1992
SALES (est): 105.24MM Privately Held
Web: www.trafficmanagement.com
SIC: 7389 8741 Flagging service (traffic control); Business management

(P-13514)
TRANS-PAK INCORPORATED
Also Called: Transpak Los Angeles
2601 S Garnsey St (92707-3338)
PHONE..................310 618-6937
Charles Frasier, Prin
EMP: 108
SALES (corp-wide): 130.93MM Privately Held
Web: www.transpak.com
SIC: 7389 Packaging and labeling services
PA: Transpak, Inc.
520 Marburg Way
San Jose CA
408 254-0500

(P-13515)
TRANSLATIONS LLC
3255 Broderick St (94123-1865)
PHONE..................415 373-7396
EMP: 60 EST: 2016
SALES (est): 698.15K Privately Held
Web: www.translationsllc.com
SIC: 7389 Translation services

(P-13516)
TRANSPRTTION OPRTION MGT SLTON ◯
1917 Palomar Oaks Way Ste 110 (92008-5512)
PHONE..................858 391-0260
Lee Wilcox, Pr
Steve Haddix, *
Brad White, *
Cindy Adamos, *
EMP: 250 EST: 2023
SALES (est): 45MM Privately Held
SIC: 7389 Personal service agents, brokers, and bureaus

(P-13517)
TREASURY PRIME INC
2261 Market St # 4037 (94114-1612)
PHONE..................415 439-0241
Chris Dean, CEO
James Ethan Brusstar, Sec
EMP: 82 EST: 2017
SALES (est): 3.97MM Privately Held
Web: www.treasuryprime.com
SIC: 7389 7371 Financial services; Computer software development and applications

(P-13518)
TRILLIANT NETWORKS INC (PA)
1100 Island Dr Ste 201 (94065-5187)
PHONE..................650 204-5050
Andy White, Prin
Andy White, Pr
Mike Mortimer, *
Dave Kranzler, *
Ryan Gerbrandt, *
EMP: 65 EST: 2004
SALES (est): 23.42MM Privately Held
Web: www.trilliant.com
SIC: 7389 Meter readers, remote

(P-13519)
TRINITY PACKING COMPANY INC (PA)
18700 E South Ave (93654-9711)
P.O. Box 28905 (93729-8905)
PHONE..................559 433-3785
David E White, CEO
Lance Shebelut, *
▲ EMP: 300 EST: 2009
SALES (est): 22.96MM
SALES (corp-wide): 22.96MM Privately Held
Web: www.trinityfruit.com
SIC: 7389 Packaging and labeling services

(P-13520)
TRINITY PACKING COMPANY INC
7612 S Reed Ave (93654-9712)
PHONE..................559 743-3913
Sam Gomez, Brnch Mgr
EMP: 300
SALES (corp-wide): 22.96MM Privately Held
SIC: 7389 Packaging and labeling services
PA: Trinity Packing Company, Inc.
18700 E South Ave
Reedley CA
559 433-3785

(P-13521)
TRUEPIC INC
402 W Broadway Ste 400 Pmb 5021 (92101)
PHONE..................619 848-3632
Jeffrey Mcgregor, CEO
Carl Mack, *
EMP: 66 EST: 2016
SALES (est): 58.41K Privately Held
SIC: 7389 Business Activities at Non-Commercial Site

(P-13522)
TWO JINN INC (PA)
Also Called: Aladdin Bail Bonds
1000 Aviara Dr Ste 300 (92011-4218)
PHONE..................760 431-9911
Robert H Hayes, Ch Bd
Leah Taniguchi, *
EMP: 75 EST: 2004
SALES (est): 21.21MM
SALES (corp-wide): 21.21MM Privately Held
Web: www.aladdinbailbonds.com
SIC: 7389 Bail bonding

(P-13523)
UBER TECHNOLOGIES INC (PA)
Also Called: Uber
1515 3rd St (94158-2211)
PHONE..................415 612-8582
Dara Khosrowshahi, CEO
Ronald Sugar, *
Nelson Chai, CFO
Jill Hazelbaker, PUBLIC AFFAIRS
Nikki Krishnamurthy, CPO
EMP: 9000 EST: 2009
SQ FT: 2,300,000
SALES (est): 31.88B
SALES (corp-wide): 31.88B Publicly Held
Web: www.uber.com
SIC: 7389 4119 Drive-a-way automobile service; Local passenger transportation, nec

(P-13524)
UNITED TALENT AGENCY LLC
Also Called: United Talent Agency, LLC
9336 Civic Center Dr (90210-3604)
PHONE..................310 776-8160
EMP: 102
SALES (corp-wide): 231.9MM Privately Held
Web: www.unitedtalent.com
SIC: 7389 Personal service agents, brokers, and bureaus
PA: United Talent Agency Holdings, Inc.
888 7th Ave Ste 922
New York NY
310 273-6700

(P-13525)
UNITED TEXTILE INC
1025 98th Ave Bldg A (94603-2356)
PHONE..................510 276-2288
◆ EMP: 60 EST: 1931
SALES (est): 4.75MM Privately Held
SIC: 7389 Textiles, sponging or shrinking

(P-13526)
UNITY COURIER SERVICE INC
955 W Center St (95337-7300)
PHONE..................209 239-5400
EMP: 125
SALES (corp-wide): 2.89B Privately Held
SIC: 7389 4215 Courier or messenger service; Courier services, except by air
HQ: Unity Courier Service, Inc.
3231 Fletcher Dr
Los Angeles CA
323 255-9800

(P-13527)
UNITY COURIER SERVICE INC
1645 Parkway Blvd Ste A (95691-5052)
PHONE..................916 246-0390
Terry Ragsdale, Mgr
EMP: 125
SALES (corp-wide): 2.89B Privately Held
SIC: 7389 Courier or messenger service
HQ: Unity Courier Service, Inc.
3231 Fletcher Dr
Los Angeles CA
323 255-9800

(P-13528)
UNIVERSAL CARD INC
Also Called: Merchant Services
9012 Research Dr Ste 200 (92618-4254)
PHONE..................949 861-4000
Jason Moore, Pr
Jason W Moore, *
Robert Parisi, *
EMP: 400 EST: 2000
SQ FT: 40,000
SALES (est): 26.65MM Privately Held
Web: www.merchantsvcs.com
SIC: 7389 Credit card service

(P-13529)
UNIVERSAL MUS GROUP DIST CORP
111 Universal Hollywood Dr Ste 1420 (91608-1054)
PHONE..................818 508-9550
Clarence Mcdonald, Brnch Mgr
EMP: 93
Web: www.universalmusic.com
SIC: 7389 Music recording producer
HQ: Universal Music Group Distribution, Corp.
2220 Colorado Ave
Santa Monica CA
310 235-4700

(P-13530)
UNIVERSAL MUS INVESTMENTS INC (HQ)
2220 Colorado Ave (90404-3506)
PHONE..................888 583-7176
Lucian C Grainge, CEO
Joe Arambula, *
▲ EMP: 80 EST: 1996
SALES (est): 100.67MM Privately Held
Web: www.universalmusic.com

SIC: 7389 7929 Music recording producer; Musical entertainers
PA: Vivendi Se
42 Avenue De Friedland
Paris

(P-13531)
UNIVERSAL MUSIC GROUP INC (HQ)
2220 Colorado Ave (90404-3506)
PHONE..................310 865-0770
Lucian Grainge, CEO
Jeffrey Harleston, *
Philippe Flageul, *
Boyd Muir, *
▲ EMP: 100 EST: 1998
SALES (est): 509.22MM Privately Held
Web: www.universalmusic.com
SIC: 7389 2741 Music recording producer; Miscellaneous publishing
PA: Universal Music Group N.V.
's-Gravelandseweg 80
Hilversum NH

(P-13532)
UNIVERSITY CALIFORNIA IRVINE
1001 Health Sciences Rd (92617-3054)
PHONE..................949 824-6483
EMP: 114
SALES (corp-wide): 534.4MM Privately Held
Web: www.uci.edu
SIC: 7389 Automobile recovery service
HQ: University Of California, Irvine
510 Aldrich Hall
Irvine CA
949 824-5011

(P-13533)
UNSPOKEN LANGUAGE SERVICES INC
1370 Valley Vista Dr Ste 200 (91765-3911)
PHONE..................626 532-8096
Amanda Martin, *
EMP: 498 EST: 2019
SALES (est): 9.3MM Privately Held
Web: www.unspokenasl.com
SIC: 7389 Translation services

(P-13534)
UPLIFT INC
Also Called: Uplift Travel Services
440 N Wolfe Rd (94085-3869)
PHONE..................408 396-3374
Brian Barth, CEO
Kelly Campbell, *
EMP: 180 EST: 2014
SALES (est): 640MM Privately Held
Web: www.uplift.com
SIC: 7389 Financial services

(P-13535)
UPS STORE INC (HQ)
Also Called: Mail Boxes Etc
6060 Cornerstone Ct W (92121-3712)
PHONE..................858 455-8800
Walter T Davis, CEO
Michelle Van Slyke, *
EMP: 313 EST: 1980
SQ FT: 66,000
SALES (est): 154.51MM
SALES (corp-wide): 100.34B Publicly Held
Web: www.theupsstore.com
SIC: 7389 8742 4783 Mailbox rental and related service; Business management consultant; Packing goods for shipping
PA: United Parcel Service, Inc.

PRODUCTS & SERVICES SECTION

7389 - Business Services, Nec (P-13556)

55 Glenlake Pkwy
Atlanta GA
404 828-6000

(P-13536)
US BANKCARD SERVICES INC
17171 Gale Ave Ste 110 (91745-1822)
PHONE..................................888 888-8872
Christopher J Chang, *Pr*
▲ **EMP:** 75 **EST:** 1996
SQ FT: 3,000
SALES (est): 15.8MM **Privately Held**
Web: www.usbsi.com
SIC: 7389 Credit card service

(P-13537)
V A ANDERSON ENTERPRISES INC (PA)
Also Called: Kopy Kat Attorney Service
400 Atlas St (92821-3117)
P.O. Box 1029 (92822-1029)
PHONE..................................714 990-6100
Pat Flynn, *Pr*
Bob Flynn, *
▲ **EMP:** 62 **EST:** 1973
SQ FT: 10,000
SALES (est): 2.43MM
SALES (corp-wide): 2.43MM **Privately Held**
SIC: 7389 Microfilm recording and developing service

(P-13538)
VASTEK INC
1230 Columbia St Ste 1180 (92101-8520)
PHONE..................................925 948-5701
Vikash Mishra, *CEO*
EMP: 171 **EST:** 2015
SQ FT: 1,600
SALES (est): 17.73MM **Privately Held**
Web: www.vastekgroup.com
SIC: 7389 7371 Air pollution measuring service; Custom computer programming services

(P-13539)
VENTURE DESIGN SERVICES INC
451 Aviation Blvd Ste 215 (95403-1055)
PHONE..................................707 524-8368
Robert Eves, *Brnch Mgr*
EMP: 69
SALES (corp-wide): 10MM **Privately Held**
SIC: 7389 Design services
PA: Venture Design Services Inc.
1051 S East St
Anaheim CA
714 765-3740

(P-13540)
VIBRANT PLANET PBC
Also Called: Vibrant Planet
11025 Pioneer Trl (96161-0281)
P.O. Box 1118 (94023-1118)
PHONE..................................530 208-9839
Allison Wolff, *CEO*
Allison Wolff, *Prin*
Scott Conway, *
Guy Bayes, *
Maria Tran, *
EMP: 60 **EST:** 2020
SALES (est): 1.66MM **Privately Held**
SIC: 7389 Business Activities at Non-Commercial Site

(P-13541)
VICTOR RANE GROUP INC
2337 Buckingham Ln (90077-1339)
PHONE..................................424 248-3623
Richard A Lazenby, *Brnch Mgr*
EMP: 70
SALES (corp-wide): 2.61MM **Privately Held**
Web: www.victorrane.com
SIC: 7389 Personal service agents, brokers, and bureaus
PA: Victor Rane Group, Inc.
9350 Wilshire Blvd # 308
Beverly Hills CA
310 388-4849

(P-13542)
VINTAGE DESIGN LLC
8310 Juniper Creek Ln (92126-1072)
PHONE..................................858 695-9544
Elizabeth Casey, *Brnch Mgr*
EMP: 94
SALES (corp-wide): 321MM **Privately Held**
Web: www.vintagedesigninc.com
SIC: 7389 Interior decorating
HQ: Vintage Design, Llc
25200 Commercentre Dr
Lake Forest CA
949 900-5400

(P-13543)
VISA INC (PA)
Also Called: Visa
900 Metro Center Blvd (94404-2775)
P.O. Box 8999 (94128-8999)
PHONE..................................650 432-3200
Alfred F Kelly Junior, *Ch Bd*
Vasant M Prabhu, *Vice Chairman*
Kelly Mahon Tullier, *Vice Chairman*
Ryan Mcinerney, *Pr*
Paul Fabara, *CRO*
EMP: 2000 **EST:** 1958
SALES (est): 29.31B **Publicly Held**
Web: usa.visa.com
SIC: 7389 Credit card service

(P-13544)
VISA INTERNATIONAL SVC ASSN (HQ)
Also Called: Visa
900 Metro Center Blvd (94404-2172)
P.O. Box 8999 (94128-8999)
PHONE..................................650 432-3200
Alfred F Kelly Junior, *Pr*
William I Campbell, *
John Elkins, *Global Vice President**
Terence Milholland, *
Thomas M'guinness, *Ex VP*
EMP: 248 **EST:** 1974
SQ FT: 200,000
SALES (est): 61.86MM **Publicly Held**
Web: usa.visa.com
SIC: 7389 Credit card service
PA: Visa Inc.
900 Metro Center Blvd
Foster City CA

(P-13545)
VISA USA INC (HQ)
900 Metro Center Blvd (94404-2172)
P.O. Box 8999 (94128-8999)
PHONE..................................650 432-3200
Alfred F Kelly Junior, *Pr*
Victor W Dahir, *
Joshua R Floum, *
Kevin J Schultz, *INTEGRATED SOLUTIONS**
Douglas Michelman, *Corporate Vice President**
EMP: 62 **EST:** 1970
SALES (est): 83MM **Publicly Held**
Web: usa.visa.com

SIC: 7389 Credit card service
PA: Visa Inc.
900 Metro Center Blvd
Foster City CA

(P-13546)
VISUAL PAK SAN DIEGO LLC
2320 Paseo De Las Americas Ste 201 (92154)
PHONE..................................847 689-1000
David Waldron, *Managing Member*
▲ **EMP:** 250 **EST:** 2012
SALES (est): 16.49MM **Privately Held**
Web: www.visualpak.com
SIC: 7389 Packaging and labeling services

(P-13547)
VOLCOM LLC (HQ)
Also Called: Stone Entertainment
1740 Monrovia Ave (92627-4407)
PHONE..................................949 646-2175
Todd Hymel, *CEO*
EMP: 200 **EST:** 1991
SQ FT: 104,000
SALES (est): 103.81MM **Privately Held**
Web: www.volcom.com
SIC: 7389 2253 7822 5136 Design services; Bathing suits and swimwear, knit; Motion picture and tape distribution; Men's and boy's clothing
PA: Authentic Brands Group Llc
1411 Broadway Fl 4
New York NY

(P-13548)
VXI GLOBAL SOLUTIONS LLC (PA)
Also Called: Vxi Global Solutions
220 W 1st St Fl 3 (90012-4105)
PHONE..................................213 739-4720
Eva Yi Hui Wang, *Pr*
Kit Wan, *VP*
Steven Wang, *CFO*
David Zhou, *COO*
Jared Morrison, *COO*
EMP: 1200 **EST:** 1998
SALES (est): 342.05MM
SALES (corp-wide): 342.05MM **Privately Held**
Web: www.vxi.com
SIC: 7389 Telemarketing services

(P-13549)
WARNER BROS RECORDS INC (DH)
777 S Santa Fe Ave (90021-1750)
PHONE..................................818 846-9090
Livia Tortella, *
Rob Cavallo, *
Lenny Warnoker, *
Murray Gitlin, *
EMP: 460 **EST:** 1958
SALES (est): 198.94MM **Publicly Held**
Web: www.warnerrecords.com
SIC: 7389 Music recording producer
HQ: Warner Music Inc.
1633 Broadway
New York NY

(P-13550)
WASHINGTON INVENTORY SERVICE
Also Called: Wis
9265 Sky Park Ct Ste 100 (92123-4303)
PHONE..................................858 565-8111
Jim Rose, *CEO*
Howard L Madden, *
Tom Compogiannis, *
EMP: 1000 **EST:** 1960
SQ FT: 30,000
SALES (est): 64.08MM **Publicly Held**
SIC: 7389 Inventory computing service
HQ: Western Inventory Service Ltd.
335 Britannia Rd E Suite 102
Mississauga ON
905 677-1947

(P-13551)
WAVELABS TECHNOLOGIES INC
691 S Milpitas Blvd Ste 217 (95035-5476)
PHONE..................................408 203-7670
Mansoor Ali Khan, *CEO*
Vineel Nalla, *
EMP: 99 **EST:** 2018
SALES (est): 3.68MM **Privately Held**
Web: www.wavelabs.ai
SIC: 7389 Personal service agents, brokers, and bureaus

(P-13552)
WE PACK IT ALL LLC
2745 Huntington Dr (91010-2302)
PHONE..................................626 301-9214
George Gellert, *
Robert Gellert, *
Sharon Bershtel, *
Mark Lebovitz, *
EMP: 155 **EST:** 1972
SQ FT: 50,000
SALES (est): 28.15MM **Privately Held**
Web: www.wepackitall.com
SIC: 7389 Packaging and labeling services

(P-13553)
WELLS FARGO CAPITAL FINANCE INC
Also Called: Wfcf Technology E2040-030
2450 Colo Ave 3000w 3rd Fl (90404)
PHONE..................................310 453-7300
▲ **EMP:** 195
SIC: 7389 Financial services

(P-13554)
WET (PA)
Also Called: Wet Design
10847 Sherman Way (91352-4829)
PHONE..................................818 769-6200
Mark W Fuller, *CEO*
Shemi Hart, *
Tania Avedissian, *
Helen Park, *
Maria Villamil, *
▲ **EMP:** 185 **EST:** 1983
SQ FT: 112,000
SALES (est): 47.15MM
SALES (corp-wide): 47.15MM **Privately Held**
Web: www.wetdesign.com
SIC: 7389 8711 3443 Design services; Engineering services; Metal parts

(P-13555)
WISE BUYS LIQUIDATORS INC
Also Called: Wise Buys 9.98 or Less
1159 Roseville Sq (95678-2810)
P.O. Box 430 (95661-0430)
PHONE..................................916 773-3998
EMP: 75
Web: www.wisebuysliquidators.net
SIC: 7389 Merchandise liquidators

(P-13556)
WOODLAND MEMORIAL HOSPITAL
3400 Data Dr (95670-7956)
PHONE..................................916 851-2150
EMP: 126

7389 - Business Services, Nec (P-13557)

SALES (corp-wide): 911.59K **Privately Held**
Web: www.woodlandchamber.org
SIC: 7389 Personal service agents, brokers, and bureaus
PA: Woodland Memorial Hospital
1325 Cottonwood St
Woodland CA
530 669-5323

(P-13557)
WORLDLINK LLC (PA)
Also Called: Worldlink East
6100 Wilshire Blvd Ste 1400 (90048-5111)
PHONE...............................323 866-5900
Toni E Knight, *Managing Member*
EMP: 60 EST: 1997
SQ FT: 20,000
SALES (est): 9.71MM
SALES (corp-wide): 9.71MM **Privately Held**
Web: www.worldlinkmedia.com
SIC: 7389 Personal service agents, brokers, and bureaus

(P-13558)
YAHOO INC
950 Teal Dr (95051-4209)
PHONE...............................408 248-3589
John L Mobley, *Prin*
EMP: 80 EST: 2011
SALES (est): 226.42K **Privately Held**
Web: www.yahooinc.com
SIC: 7389 Business Activities at Non-Commercial Site

(P-13559)
YAPSTONE INC (PA)
Also Called: Rentpayment.com
2121 N California Blvd Ste 400 (94596-7305)
PHONE...............................866 289-5977
Tom Villante, *CEO*
Bryan Murphy, *
Kelly Kay, *
Mary Hentges, *
John Malnar, *
EMP: 92 EST: 1999
SALES (est): 47.29MM
SALES (corp-wide): 47.29MM **Privately Held**
Web: www.yapstone.com
SIC: 7389 Credit card service

(P-13560)
YC CABLE USA INC (HQ)
48010 Fremont Blvd (94538-6500)
PHONE...............................510 824-2788
Gary Hsu, *Pr*
Kao Y Fang, *Stockholder*
▲ EMP: 70 EST: 1991
SQ FT: 45,000
SALES (est): 26.48MM **Privately Held**
Web: www.yccable.com
SIC: 7389 3643 Field audits, cable television ; Power line cable
PA: Y.C. Cable Co., Ltd.
5f, No. 12, Lane 270, Beishen Rd., Sec. 3
New Taipei City TAP

(P-13561)
YELLOWPAGESCOM LLC (DH)
Also Called: Dexyp
611 N Brand Blvd Ste 500 (91203-3293)
PHONE...............................818 937-5500
Williams Clenney, *
Brad Mohs, *
EMP: 260 EST: 2004
SALES (est): 62.72MM

SALES (corp-wide): 1.2B **Publicly Held**
SIC: 7389 Telephone directory distribution, contract or fee basis
HQ: Thryv, Inc.
2200 W Airfield Dr
Dfw Airport TX
972 453-7000

7513 Truck Rental And Leasing, Without Drivers

(P-13562)
NATIONAL FREIGHT INC
Also Called: Nfi Transportation
179 Grand Ave (91789-5205)
PHONE...............................909 348-5464
Susan Nolte, *Brnch Mgr*
EMP: 60
SALES (corp-wide): 1.26B **Privately Held**
Web: www.nfiindustries.com
SIC: 7513 4213 Truck rental and leasing, no drivers; Trucking, except local
HQ: National Freight, Inc.
2 Cooper St
Camden NJ
856 691-7000

(P-13563)
PENSKE CORPORATION
6551 Ventura Blvd (93003-7229)
PHONE...............................805 983-3788
Owen Donahue, *Prin*
EMP: 159
SALES (corp-wide): 5.16B **Privately Held**
Web: www.pensketruckrental.com
SIC: 7513 Truck rental and leasing, no drivers
PA: Penske Corporation
2555 S Telegraph Rd
Bloomfield Hills MI
248 648-2000

(P-13564)
PENSKE MOTOR GROUP LLC
Also Called: Penske
2010 E Garvey Ave S (91791-1911)
PHONE...............................626 859-1200
Glen Hightman, *Brnch Mgr*
EMP: 277
SALES (corp-wide): 5.16B **Privately Held**
Web: www.pensketruckrental.com
SIC: 7513 7538 Truck rental and leasing, no drivers; General automotive repair shops
HQ: Penske Motor Group, Llc
3534 Peck Rd
El Monte CA

(P-13565)
PENSKE TRANSPORTATION MGT LLC
2280 Wardlow Cir (92878-9078)
PHONE...............................844 847-9518
EMP: 82
SALES (corp-wide): 2.11B **Privately Held**
Web: www.penskelogistics.com
SIC: 7513 Truck rental and leasing, no drivers
HQ: Penske Transportation Management Llc
2675 Morgantown Rd
Reading PA
800 529-6531

(P-13566)
ROLLINS LEASING LLC
Also Called: Rollins Truck Rental-Leasing
18305 Arenth Ave (91748-1226)
PHONE...............................626 913-7186
Dave Bettson, *Mgr*

EMP: 88
SQ FT: 10,370
SALES (corp-wide): 2.11B **Privately Held**
Web: www.pensketruckrental.com
SIC: 7513 Truck rental and leasing, no drivers
HQ: Rollins Leasing Llc
2200 Concord Pike
Wilmington DE
302 426-2700

(P-13567)
RP AUTOMOTIVE II INC
Also Called: Penske Ford Chula Vista
560 Auto Park Dr (91911-6026)
PHONE...............................619 656-2500
Roger S Penske Junior, *Brnch Mgr*
EMP: 90
SALES (corp-wide): 48.07MM **Privately Held**
Web: www.pensketruckrental.com
SIC: 7513 Truck rental and leasing, no drivers
PA: Rp Automotive Ii, Inc.
9136 Firestone Blvd
Downey CA
626 430-9011

(P-13568)
U-HAUL BUSINESS CONSULTANTS
Also Called: U-Haul
5220 Auburn Blvd (95841-2707)
PHONE...............................916 331-7601
Aaron Anderson, *Mgr*
EMP: 249
SALES (corp-wide): 5.86B **Publicly Held**
Web: www.uhaul.com
SIC: 7513 Truck rental and leasing, no drivers
HQ: U-Haul Business Consultants, Inc
2727 N Central Ave
Phoenix AZ
602 263-6011

(P-13569)
U-HAUL BUSINESS CONSULTANTS
Also Called: U-Haul
314 E 6th St (92879-1520)
PHONE...............................951 736-7811
EMP: 249
SALES (corp-wide): 5.86B **Publicly Held**
Web: www.uhaul.com
SIC: 7513 Truck rental and leasing, no drivers
HQ: U-Haul Business Consultants, Inc
2727 N Central Ave
Phoenix AZ
602 263-6011

(P-13570)
U-HAUL CO OF CALIFORNIA (DH)
Also Called: U-Haul
44511 S Grimmer Blvd (94538-6309)
PHONE...............................602 287-7830
Dave Adams, *Pr*
EMP: 150 EST: 1971
SALES (est): 152.15MM
SALES (corp-wide): 5.86B **Publicly Held**
Web: www.uhaul.com
SIC: 7513 7519 4226 Truck rental and leasing, no drivers; Trailer rental; Special warehousing and storage, nec
HQ: U-Haul International, Inc.
2727 N Central Ave
Phoenix AZ
602 263-6011

(P-13571)
U-HAUL LEASING & SALES CO
Also Called: U-Haul
23730 Sunnymead Blvd (92553-3022)
PHONE...............................951 485-2003
Timothy Faust, *Mgr*
EMP: 371
SALES (corp-wide): 5.86B **Publicly Held**
Web: www.uhaul.com
SIC: 7513 7519 5984 5531 Truck rental and leasing, no drivers; Trailer rental; Propane gas, bottled; Trailer hitches, automotive
HQ: U-Haul Leasing & Sales Co.
2727 N Central Ave
Phoenix AZ
602 263-6011

7514 Passenger Car Rental

(P-13572)
ALAMO RENTAL (US) INC
Also Called: Alamo Rent A Car
711 W Katella Ave (92802-3412)
PHONE...............................714 748-7368
William R Smith, *S*
EMP: 82
SALES (corp-wide): 7.04B **Privately Held**
Web: www.alamo.com
SIC: 7514 Rent-a-car service
HQ: Alamo Rental (Us) Inc.
600 Corporate Park Dr
Saint Louis MO

(P-13573)
ALAMO RENTAL (US) INC
Also Called: Alamo Rent A Car
9020 Aviation Blvd (90301-2907)
PHONE...............................310 649-2242
Cesar Saurez, *Mgr*
EMP: 109
SALES (corp-wide): 7.04B **Privately Held**
Web: www.alamo.com
SIC: 7514 Rent-a-car service
HQ: Alamo Rental (Us) Inc.
600 Corporate Park Dr
Saint Louis MO

(P-13574)
ALAMO RENTAL (US) INC
Also Called: Alamo Rent A Car
2627 N Hollywood Way Unit 9 (91505-1062)
PHONE...............................818 953-5438
James Botsch, *Mgr*
EMP: 63
SALES (corp-wide): 7.04B **Privately Held**
Web: www.alamo.com
SIC: 7514 Rent-a-car service
HQ: Alamo Rental (Us) Inc.
600 Corporate Park Dr
Saint Louis MO

(P-13575)
ALAMO RENTAL (US) INC
Also Called: Alamo Rent A Car
3450 E Airport Dr Ste 300 (91761-7669)
PHONE...............................888 826-6893
Michael Stephens, *Mgr*
EMP: 100
SALES (corp-wide): 7.04B **Privately Held**
Web: www.alamo.com
SIC: 7514 Rent-a-car service
HQ: Alamo Rental (Us) Inc.
600 Corporate Park Dr
Saint Louis MO

(P-13576)
ALAMO RENTAL (US) INC
Also Called: Alamo Rent A Car

PRODUCTS & SERVICES SECTION

7515 - Passenger Car Leasing (P-13597)

617 S Highway 101 (92075-2215)
PHONE..................858 792-2522
Ati P Deans, *Prin*
EMP: 63
SALES (corp-wide): 7.04B **Privately Held**
Web: www.alamo.com
SIC: 7514 Rent-a-car service
HQ: Alamo Rental (Us) Inc.
600 Corporate Park Dr
Saint Louis MO

(P-13577)
ALAMO RENTAL (US) INC
Also Called: Alamo Rent A Car
750 Bush St (94108-3403)
PHONE..................415 693-0191
Alfred Husary, *Mgr*
EMP: 63
SALES (corp-wide): 7.04B **Privately Held**
Web: www.alamo.com
SIC: 7514 Rent-a-car service
HQ: Alamo Rental (Us) Inc.
600 Corporate Park Dr
Saint Louis MO

(P-13578)
ALAMO RENTAL (US) INC
Also Called: Alamo Rent A Car
3400 E Tahquitz Canyon Way Ste 5
(92262-6966)
PHONE..................760 778-6271
Robin Killingdeck, *Mgr*
EMP: 91
SALES (corp-wide): 7.04B **Privately Held**
Web: www.alamo.com
SIC: 7514 Rent-a-car service
HQ: Alamo Rental (Us) Inc.
600 Corporate Park Dr
Saint Louis MO

(P-13579)
ENTERPRISE RENT-A-CAR CO OF SAN FRANCISCO LLC (DH)
Also Called: Enterprise Rent-A-Car
2633 Camino Ramon Ste 400
(94583-2176)
PHONE..................925 464-5100
EMP: 100 **EST:** 1980
SALES (est): 50.63MM
SALES (corp-wide): 7.04B **Privately Held**
SIC: 7514 Rent-a-car service
HQ: Enterprise Holdings, Inc.
600 Corporate Park Dr
Saint Louis MO
314 512-5000

(P-13580)
ENTERPRISE RNT--CAR BOSTON LLC
Also Called: Enterprise Rent-A-Car
17541 Beach Blvd (92647-6801)
PHONE..................714 841-4141
EMP: 79
SALES (corp-wide): 7.04B **Privately Held**
Web: www.enterprise.com
SIC: 7514 Rent-a-car service
HQ: Enterprise Rent-A-Car Company Of
Boston, Llc
10 2nd Ave
Burlington MA
781 935-5858

(P-13581)
ENTERPRISE RNT--CAR LOS ANGLES (DH)
Also Called: Enterprise Rent-A-Car
333 City Blvd W Ste 1000 (92868-2921)
PHONE..................657 221-4400
Andrew C Taylor, *
Pamela Nicholson, *
Greg Stubblefield, *
William W Snyder, *
▲ **EMP:** 90 **EST:** 1957
SQ FT: 30,000
SALES (est): 755.11MM
SALES (corp-wide): 7.04B **Privately Held**
Web: www.enterprise.com
SIC: 7514 7513 5511 Rent-a-car service;
Truck rental and leasing, no drivers; Trucks,
tractors, and trailers: new and used
HQ: Enterprise Holdings, Inc.
600 Corporate Park Dr
Saint Louis MO
314 512-5000

(P-13582)
ENTERPRISE RNT--CAR SCRMNTO LL
Also Called: Enterprise Rent-A-Car
6320 Mcnair Cir (95837-1118)
PHONE..................916 576-3164
Alfred Husary, *Mgr*
EMP: 118
SALES (corp-wide): 7.04B **Privately Held**
Web: www.enterprise.com
SIC: 7514 Rent-a-car service
HQ: Enterprise Rent-A-Car Company Of
Sacramento, Llc
150 N Sunrise Ave
Roseville CA

(P-13583)
ENTERPRISE RNT--CAR SCRMNTO LL
Also Called: Enterprise Rent-A-Car
7034 Rossmore Ln (95762-7126)
PHONE..................916 934-0783
EMP: 118
SALES (corp-wide): 7.04B **Privately Held**
Web: www.enterprise.com
SIC: 7514 Rent-a-car service
HQ: Enterprise Rent-A-Car Company Of
Sacramento, Llc
150 N Sunrise Ave
Roseville CA

(P-13584)
ENTERPRISE RNT--CAR SCRMNTO LL
Also Called: Enterprise Rent-A-Car
3216 Palm St (95652-2510)
PHONE..................916 648-1725
Susan M Irwin, *VP*
EMP: 118
SALES (corp-wide): 7.04B **Privately Held**
Web: www.enterprise.com
SIC: 7514 Rent-a-car service
HQ: Enterprise Rent-A-Car Company Of
Sacramento, Llc
150 N Sunrise Ave
Roseville CA

(P-13585)
ENTERPRISE RNT--CAR SCRMNTO LL
Also Called: Enterprise Rent-A-Car
217 E Cypress Ave (96002-0111)
PHONE..................530 223-0700
Daniel Patrie, *Mgr*
EMP: 118
SALES (corp-wide): 7.04B **Privately Held**
Web: www.enterprise.com
SIC: 7514 Rent-a-car service
HQ: Enterprise Rent-A-Car Company Of
Sacramento, Llc
150 N Sunrise Ave
Roseville CA

(P-13586)
EUGENE HARRIS
3351 Duckhorn Dr (95834-2625)
PHONE..................916 776-3393
Eugene Harris, *Owner*
EMP: 71
SALES (est): 1.53MM **Privately Held**
SIC: 7514 7389 Passenger car rental;
Business services, nec

(P-13587)
FOX RENT A CAR INC
325 Baker St (92626-4518)
PHONE..................310 342-5155
Trent Dennis, *Brnch Mgr*
EMP: 68
SALES (corp-wide): 290.01B **Privately Held**
Web: www.foxrentacar.com
SIC: 7514 Passenger car rental
HQ: Fox Rent A Car, Inc.
4135 S 100th East Ave
Tulsa OK

(P-13588)
FOX RENT A CAR INC
Also Called: Europcar
5500 W Century Blvd (90045-5914)
PHONE..................310 342-5155
Allen Rezapour, *Pr*
EMP: 105
SALES (corp-wide): 290.01B **Privately Held**
Web: www.foxrentacar.com
SIC: 7514 Passenger car rental
HQ: Fox Rent A Car, Inc.
4135 S 100th East Ave
Tulsa OK

(P-13589)
FOX RENT A CAR INC
1776 E Holt Blvd (91761-2110)
PHONE..................909 635-6390
Syed Mahdi, *Brnch Mgr*
EMP: 86
SALES (corp-wide): 290.01B **Privately Held**
Web: www.foxrentacar.com
SIC: 7514 Rent-a-car service
HQ: Fox Rent A Car, Inc.
4135 S 100th East Ave
Tulsa OK

(P-13590)
FOX RENT A CAR INC
Also Called: Fox Rent-A-Car & Truck
7600 Earhart Rd Ste 9 # O (94621-4558)
PHONE..................408 210-2208
Greta Randev, *Mgr*
EMP: 91
SALES (corp-wide): 290.01B **Privately Held**
Web: www.foxrentacar.com
SIC: 7514 Rent-a-car service
HQ: Fox Rent A Car, Inc.
4135 S 100th East Ave
Tulsa OK

(P-13591)
GALPIN MOTORS INC
Galpin Studio Rentals
1763 Ivar Ave (90028-5105)
PHONE..................323 957-3333
EMP: 76
SALES (corp-wide): 372.23MM **Privately Held**
Web: www.galpinstudiorentals.com
SIC: 7514 Rent-a-car service
PA: Galpin Motors, Inc.
15505 Roscoe Blvd
North Hills CA
818 787-3800

(P-13592)
MIDWAY RENT A CAR INC
2263 Pacific Hwy (92101-1744)
PHONE..................619 238-9600
EMP: 68
Web: www.midwaycarrental.com
SIC: 7514 Rent-a-car service
PA: Midway Rent A Car, Inc.
4751 Wilshire Blvd # 120
Los Angeles CA

(P-13593)
SANTA BARBARA AIRBUS
750 Technology Dr (93117-3839)
PHONE..................805 964-7759
Eric Onnen, *Pr*
Mark Klopstein, *
Kelly Onnen, *
EMP: 60 **EST:** 1983
SQ FT: 4,000
SALES (est): 4.37MM **Privately Held**
Web: www.sbairbus.com
SIC: 7514 4119 Rent-a-car service;
Limousine rental, with driver

(P-13594)
TURO INC (PA)
111 Sutter St Ste 600 (94104-4512)
PHONE..................866 735-2901
EMP: 216 **EST:** 2011
SALES (est): 43.3MM **Privately Held**
Web: www.turo.com
SIC: 7514 Rent-a-car service

7515 Passenger Car Leasing

(P-13595)
EL CAJON MOTORS (PA)
Also Called: El Cajon Ford
1595 E Main St (92021-5902)
P.O. Box 1236 (92022-1236)
PHONE..................619 579-8888
Paul F Leader, *Pr*
Andrew Breech, *
John Blake, *
▲ **EMP:** 100 **EST:** 1946
SQ FT: 311,226
SALES (est): 9.23MM
SALES (corp-wide): 9.23MM **Privately Held**
Web: www.quicklane.com
SIC: 7515 5511 7538 Passenger car leasing;
Automobiles, new and used; General
automotive repair shops

(P-13596)
EXECUTIVE CAR LEASING COMPANY (PA)
Also Called: Newco Auto Leasing
7807 Santa Monica Blvd (90046-5398)
P.O. Box 933009 (90093-3009)
PHONE..................800 800-3932
EMP: 100 **EST:** 1953
SALES (est): 13.78MM
SALES (corp-wide): 13.78MM **Privately Held**
Web: www.executivecarleasing.com
SIC: 7515 7513 Passenger car leasing;
Truck leasing, without drivers

(P-13597)
MIDWAY RENT A CAR INC
Also Called: Midway Car Rental
4201 Lankershim Blvd (91602-2856)
PHONE..................818 985-9770
Jeff Riesenberg, *Brnch Mgr*

7519 - Utility Trailer Rental (P-13598)

EMP: 67
Web: www.midwaycarrental.com
SIC: 7515 7514 Passenger car leasing; Passenger car rental
PA: Midway Rent A Car, Inc.
4751 Wilshire Blvd # 120
Los Angeles CA

7519 Utility Trailer Rental

(P-13598)
EL MONTE RENTS INC (HQ)
Also Called: El Monte Rv
12818 Firestone Blvd (90670-5404)
PHONE..................................562 404-9300
Kenneth Schork, *CEO*
EMP: 110 **EST:** 1970
SALES (est): 48.03MM **Privately Held**
Web: www.elmonterv.com
SIC: 7519 5561 Motor home rental; Motor homes
PA: Tourism Holdings Limited
L 1, 83 Beach Road
Auckland AUK

(P-13599)
U-HAUL NEIGHBORHOOD DEALER
Also Called: U-Haul
300 Mowry Ave (94536-4107)
PHONE..................................510 371-0122
EMP: 63 **EST:** 2016
SALES (est): 915.22K **Privately Held**
Web: www.uhaul.com
SIC: 7519 7513 7359 Utility trailer rental; Truck rental and leasing, no drivers; Equipment rental and leasing, nec

7521 Automobile Parking

(P-13600)
ABM PARKING SERVICES INC
Also Called: Ampco Airport Parking
1150 S Olive St Fl 19 (90015-2479)
PHONE..................................213 284-7600
▲ **EMP:** 9469
SIC: 7521 7349 Parking lots; Janitorial service, contract basis

(P-13601)
ALL ABOUT PARKING
100 S Ellsworth Ave Ste 203 (94401-3939)
PHONE..................................650 508-8886
Roy Nickolai, *Admn*
EMP: 71 **EST:** 2010
SALES (est): 975.53K **Privately Held**
Web: www.allaboutparking.com
SIC: 7521 Parking lots

(P-13602)
ALL STAR PARKING
Also Called: Wally Parking
9700 Bellanca Ave (90045-5510)
PHONE..................................310 337-1944
Sohal Islam, *Genl Mgr*
Charles Bassett, *Genl Mgr*
Carl Calhoun, *Mgr*
EMP: 102 **EST:** 2001
SALES (est): 3.87MM **Privately Held**
Web: www.wallypark.com
SIC: 7521 Parking lots

(P-13603)
AMERIPARK LLC
17165 Von Karman Ave Ste 110 (92614-0905)
PHONE..................................949 279-7525
Josh Hess, *Brnch Mgr*

EMP: 300
SALES (corp-wide): 1.71B **Privately Held**
Web: www.ameripark.com
SIC: 7521 Parking lots
HQ: Ameripark, Llc
233 Peachtree St Ne # 2600
Atlanta GA

(P-13604)
CLASSIC PARKING INC
34 S Autumn St (95110-2513)
P.O. Box 720781 (95172-0781)
PHONE..................................408 278-1444
Richard Flores, *CFO*
EMP: 690
Web: www.classicparking.com
SIC: 7521 Parking garage
PA: Classic Parking, Inc.
3208 Royal St
Los Angeles CA

(P-13605)
EVERPARK INC
3470 Wilshire Blvd Ste 940 (90010-2207)
PHONE..................................310 987-6922
Alazar Asmamaw, *CEO*
Abiy Wouldgerema, *
Abbi Abebe, *
EMP: 200 **EST:** 2007
SALES (est): 2.89MM **Privately Held**
Web: www.everpark.com
SIC: 7521 Automobile parking

(P-13606)
IMPERIAL PARKING (US) LLC
Also Called: City Park
1740 Cesar Chavez Fl 2 (94124-1134)
PHONE..................................415 495-3909
Tim Leonoudakis, *Brnch Mgr*
EMP: 650
SALES (corp-wide): 1.71B **Privately Held**
Web: www.impark.com
SIC: 7521 Parking lots
HQ: Imperial Parking (U.S.), Llc
216 Haddon Ave Ste 400
Haddon Township NJ

(P-13607)
IMPERIAL PARKING INDS INC
9454 Wilshire Blvd Ste P1a (90212-2903)
PHONE..................................310 276-9766
Yagini Ali, *Brnch Mgr*
EMP: 63
SALES (corp-wide): 4.27MM **Privately Held**
Web: www.ipicorp.net
SIC: 7521 Parking lots
PA: Imperial Parking Industries, Inc.
6404 Wilshire Blvd B
Los Angeles CA
323 651-5588

(P-13608)
L AND R AUTO PARKS INC
Also Called: Joe's Auto Parks
707 Wilshire Blvd Ste 4300 (90017-3601)
PHONE..................................213 784-3018
Charles Bassett, *Pr*
Mark Funk, *
Jeff Matsuno, *
Gabriel Rubin, *
Stuart Rubin Board, *Prin*
EMP: 250 **EST:** 1951
SQ FT: 5,000
SALES (est): 19.79MM **Privately Held**
Web: www.joesautoparks.com
SIC: 7521 7542 7371 Parking lots; Carwashes; Computer software development and applications

(P-13609)
LAZ KARP ASSOCIATES LLC
1400 Ivar Ave (90028-8122)
PHONE..................................323 464-4190
EMP: 169
Web: www.lazparking.com
SIC: 7521 Parking lots
PA: Laz Karp Associates, Llc
1 Financial Plz
Hartford CT

(P-13610)
MODERN PARKING INC
4955 Van Nuys Blvd Frnt (91403-1813)
PHONE..................................818 783-3143
EMP: 167
Web: www.modernparking.com
SIC: 7521 Parking lots
PA: Modern Parking, Inc.
303 S Union Ave Fl 1
Los Angeles CA

(P-13611)
MODERN PARKING INC
415 N Bedford Dr (90210-4302)
PHONE..................................310 271-1125
EMP: 167
Web: www.modernparking.com
SIC: 7521 Parking garage
PA: Modern Parking, Inc.
303 S Union Ave Fl 1
Los Angeles CA

(P-13612)
MODERN PARKING INC
14110 Palawan Way (90292-6231)
PHONE..................................310 821-1081
Arisur Rahnan, *Prin*
EMP: 167
Web: www.modernparking.com
SIC: 7521 Parking garage
PA: Modern Parking, Inc.
303 S Union Ave Fl 1
Los Angeles CA

(P-13613)
MODERN PARKING INC
1025 W Laurel St Ste 105 (92101-1254)
PHONE..................................619 233-0412
Richard Viera, *Brnch Mgr*
EMP: 167
Web: www.modernparking.com
SIC: 7521 Parking garage
PA: Modern Parking, Inc.
303 S Union Ave Fl 1
Los Angeles CA

(P-13614)
PACIFIC PARK MANAGEMENT INC
989 Franklin St (94607-4470)
PHONE..................................510 836-7730
EMP: 85
Web: www.pacificparkonline.com
SIC: 7521 Parking lots
PA: Pacific Park Management Inc
311 California St Ste 310
San Francisco CA

(P-13615)
PARKING COMPANY OF AMERICA
Also Called: Pcamp
3165 Garfield Ave (90040-3217)
PHONE..................................562 862-2118
Alex Martin Chaves Junior, *Pr*
Eric Chaves, *
EMP: 100 **EST:** 1990
SALES (est): 9.34MM **Privately Held**

Web: www.parkpca.com
SIC: 7521 Parking lots

(P-13616)
PARKING CONCEPTS INC
33 E Green St (91105-2022)
PHONE..................................626 577-8963
EMP: 96
SALES (corp-wide): 51.57MM **Privately Held**
Web: www.parkingconcepts.com
SIC: 7521 Parking lots
PA: Parking Concepts, Inc.
12 Mauchly Ste I
Irvine CA
949 753-7525

(P-13617)
PARKING CONCEPTS INC
1020 W Civic Center Dr (92703-2303)
PHONE..................................714 543-5725
Gilbert Bernick, *Brnch Mgr*
EMP: 96
SALES (corp-wide): 51.57MM **Privately Held**
Web: www.parkingconcepts.com
SIC: 7521 Parking lots
PA: Parking Concepts, Inc.
12 Mauchly Ste I
Irvine CA
949 753-7525

(P-13618)
PARKING CONCEPTS INC
2999 Oak Rd (94597-2066)
PHONE..................................925 944-1964
EMP: 97
SALES (corp-wide): 51.57MM **Privately Held**
Web: www.parkingconcepts.com
SIC: 7521 Parking lots
PA: Parking Concepts, Inc.
12 Mauchly Ste I
Irvine CA
949 753-7525

(P-13619)
PARKING CONCEPTS INC
25 Division St Ste 107 (94103-5234)
PHONE..................................415 553-6883
EMP: 97
SALES (corp-wide): 51.57MM **Privately Held**
Web: www.parkingconcepts.com
SIC: 7521 Parking lots
PA: Parking Concepts, Inc.
12 Mauchly Ste I
Irvine CA
949 753-7525

(P-13620)
PARKING CONCEPTS INC
1036 Broxton Ave (90024-2824)
PHONE..................................310 208-1611
Jorge Lopez, *Mgr*
EMP: 97
SALES (corp-wide): 51.57MM **Privately Held**
Web: www.parkingconcepts.com
SIC: 7521 Parking lots
PA: Parking Concepts, Inc.
12 Mauchly Ste I
Irvine CA
949 753-7525

(P-13621)
PARKING CONCEPTS INC
1801 Georgia St (90015-3477)
PHONE..................................213 746-5764
Bob Hindle, *Mgr*

EMP: 242
SALES (corp-wide): 51.57MM **Privately Held**
Web: www.parkingconcepts.com
SIC: 7521 8748 Parking lots; Traffic consultant
PA: Parking Concepts, Inc.
12 Mauchly Ste I
Irvine CA
949 753-7525

(P-13622)
PARKING CONCEPTS INC
14110 Palawan Way (90292-6231)
PHONE..................310 821-1081
Frank Vargas, *Genl Mgr*
EMP: 97
SALES (corp-wide): 51.57MM **Privately Held**
Web: www.parkingconcepts.com
SIC: 7521 8741 Parking lots; Management services
PA: Parking Concepts, Inc.
12 Mauchly Ste I
Irvine CA
949 753-7525

(P-13623)
PARKING CONCEPTS INC
800 Wilshire Blvd (90017-2604)
PHONE..................213 623-2661
Juan Cortes, *Brnch Mgr*
EMP: 97
SALES (corp-wide): 51.57MM **Privately Held**
Web: www.parkingconcepts.com
SIC: 7521 Parking lots
PA: Parking Concepts, Inc.
12 Mauchly Ste I
Irvine CA
949 753-7525

(P-13624)
PARKING CONCEPTS INC
12001 Vista Del Mar (90293-8518)
PHONE..................310 322-5008
Zahid Hossian, *Brnch Mgr*
EMP: 97
SALES (corp-wide): 51.57MM **Privately Held**
Web: www.parkingconcepts.com
SIC: 7521 Parking lots
PA: Parking Concepts, Inc.
12 Mauchly Ste I
Irvine CA
949 753-7525

(P-13625)
PCAM LLC
3165 Garfield Ave (90040-3217)
PHONE..................562 862-2118
EMP: 80 EST: 2011
SALES (est): 12.77MM **Privately Held**
Web: www.parkpca.com
SIC: 7521 Parking lots

(P-13626)
PROFESSIONAL PARKING
309 Palm St (92661-1200)
PHONE..................949 723-4027
Ralph Caldin, *Brnch Mgr*
EMP: 115
SIC: 7521 Parking garage
HQ: Professional Parking
2799 E 21st St
Signal Hill CA

(P-13627)
RESORT PARKING SERVICES INC
39755 Berkey Dr # B (92211-1106)
PHONE..................760 328-4041
Mario Gardner, *Pr*
EMP: 120 EST: 1973
SQ FT: 1,100
SALES (est): 4.84MM **Privately Held**
Web: www.resortparkingservices.com
SIC: 7521 7299 Parking lots; Personal item care and storage services

(P-13628)
SAN FRANCISCO PARKING INC
Also Called: Sfo Shuttle Bus Company
325 5th St (94107-1040)
PHONE..................415 495-3909
EMP: 650
Web: www.californiaparking.com
SIC: 7521 Parking lots

(P-13629)
TPS PARKING MANAGEMENT LLC
Also Called: Parking Spot, The
9101 S Sepulveda Blvd (90045-4803)
PHONE..................310 846-4747
Chris Fincutter, *Mgr*
EMP: 67
SALES (corp-wide): 49.98MM **Privately Held**
Web: www.theparkingspot.com
SIC: 7521 Parking lots
PA: Tps Parking Management, Llc
200 W Monroe St Ste 1500
Chicago IL
312 781-9396

(P-13630)
VALET PARKING SVC A CAL PARTNR (PA)
Also Called: Valet Parking Service
6933 Hollywood Blvd (90028-6146)
PHONE..................323 465-5873
Anthony Policella, *CEO*
EMP: 1268 EST: 1946
SQ FT: 10,000
SALES (est): 24.42MM
SALES (corp-wide): 24.42MM **Privately Held**
Web: www.lazparking.com
SIC: 7521 7299 Parking lots; Valet parking

7532 Top And Body Repair And Paint Shops

(P-13631)
ANAHEIM HILLS AUTO BODY INC
3500 E La Palma Ave (92806-2116)
PHONE..................714 632-8266
TOLL FREE: 800
Robert Smith, *Pr*
EMP: 60 EST: 1978
SQ FT: 33,000
SALES (est): 4.4MM **Privately Held**
Web: www.anaheimhillsautobody.com
SIC: 7532 Body shop, automotive

(P-13632)
CALIBER BODYWORKS TEXAS INC
Also Called: CALIBER BODYWORKS OF TEXAS, INC.
11182 I Ave (92345-5214)
PHONE..................760 949-6269
Jim Bates, *Mgr*
EMP: 61
SALES (corp-wide): 1.07MM **Privately Held**
Web: www.caliber.com
SIC: 7532 Body shop, automotive
PA: Caliber Bodyworks Of Texas Llc
2941 Lake Vista Dr
Lewisville TX
469 794-5653

(P-13633)
CALIBER BODYWORKS TEXAS INC
Also Called: Caliber Collision Centers
5 Auto Center Dr (92782-8402)
PHONE..................714 665-3905
David Adams, *Brnch Mgr*
EMP: 100
SALES (corp-wide): 1.07MM **Privately Held**
Web: www.caliber.com
SIC: 7532 Body shop, automotive
PA: Caliber Bodyworks Of Texas Llc
2941 Lake Vista Dr
Lewisville TX
469 794-5653

(P-13634)
CALIBER BODYWORKS TEXAS INC
Also Called: Caliber Collision Centers
3517 Hillcap Ave (95136-1391)
PHONE..................408 972-0300
Abel Silva, *Brnch Mgr*
EMP: 100
SALES (corp-wide): 1.07MM **Privately Held**
Web: www.caliber.com
SIC: 7532 Body shop, automotive
PA: Caliber Bodyworks Of Texas Llc
2941 Lake Vista Dr
Lewisville TX
469 794-5653

(P-13635)
CALIBER HOLDINGS CORPORATION
Also Called: Classic Collision Center 2
3020 Riverside Dr (90039-2014)
P.O. Box 39827 (90039-0437)
PHONE..................323 913-4000
Madjid Berenji, *Pr*
EMP: 60
Web: www.abraauto.com
SIC: 7532 Body shop, automotive
PA: Caliber Holdings Of Georgia Llc
2941 Lake Vista Dr
Lewisville TX

(P-13636)
FAITH QUALITY AUTO BODY INC
41130 Nick Ln (92562-7012)
PHONE..................951 698-8215
Lee Amaradio, *Pr*
EMP: 60 EST: 1979
SALES (est): 3.41MM **Privately Held**
Web: www.faithqualityautobody.com
SIC: 7532 Body shop, automotive

(P-13637)
GREENWLDS ATBODY FRMEWORKS INC
2850 Erie St (92117-6143)
PHONE..................619 477-2600
Daniel Greenwald, *Prin*
EMP: 70 EST: 1986
SALES (est): 1.73MM **Privately Held**
Web: www.greenwaldsautobody.com
SIC: 7532 Body shop, automotive

(P-13638)
HARRYS AUTO BODY INC
Also Called: Harry's Auto Collision
1013 S La Brea Ave (90019-6902)
PHONE..................323 933-4600
Harry Barseghian, *Pr*
▲ EMP: 65 EST: 1979
SQ FT: 5,000
SALES (est): 4.48MM **Privately Held**
Web: www.harryscollision.com
SIC: 7532 Body shop, automotive

(P-13639)
HOLMES BODY SHOP-ALHAMBRA
1130 E Main St (91801-4111)
PHONE..................626 282-6173
EMP: 111 EST: 1992
SALES (est): 238.23K
SALES (corp-wide): 4.84MM **Privately Held**
SIC: 7532 Body shop, automotive
PA: Holmes Body Shop-Alhambra, Inc.
466 Foothill Blvd
La Canada Flintridge CA
626 795-6447

(P-13640)
HOLMES BODY SHOP-ALHAMBRA INC (PA)
466 Foothill Blvd (91011-3518)
PHONE..................626 795-6447
Thomas V Holmes, *Pr*
EMP: 64 EST: 1970
SQ FT: 300,000
SALES (est): 4.84MM
SALES (corp-wide): 4.84MM **Privately Held**
Web: www.holmesbodyshop.com
SIC: 7532 Body shop, automotive

(P-13641)
M2 AUTOMOTIVE
1100 Colorado Ave 2nd Fl (90401-3010)
PHONE..................310 399-3887
D Hunt Ramsbottom Junior, *CEO*
EMP: 750 EST: 1996
SALES (est): 3.94MM **Privately Held**
SIC: 7532 Collision shops, automotive

(P-13642)
MAIMONE LIQUIDATING CORP (PA)
Also Called: Marco's Auto Body
1390 E Palm St (91001-2042)
PHONE..................626 286-5691
Marco G Maimone, *Pr*
Carl Canzano, *
Lillian Maimone, *
EMP: 100 EST: 1974
SQ FT: 14,000
SALES (est): 2.69MM
SALES (corp-wide): 2.69MM **Privately Held**
Web: www.caliber.com
SIC: 7532 7539 Body shop, automotive; Frame and front end repair services

(P-13643)
PLATINUM PERFORMANCE INC
760 Mcmurray Rd (93427-2510)
PHONE..................800 553-2400
Kristin Peck, *CEO*
Kate Russo, *
EMP: 80 EST: 1997
SALES (est): 590.6K **Privately Held**
Web: www.platinumperformance.com
SIC: 7532 Body shop, automotive

7532 - Top And Body Repair And Paint Shops (P-13644)

PRODUCTS & SERVICES SECTION

(P-13644)
PRESTIGE AUTO COLLISION INC
23726 Via Fabricante (92691-3145)
PHONE.................................949 470-6031
Bernie Gates, *Pr*
Laurie Gates, *
EMP: 65 **EST:** 1984
SQ FT: 10,000
SALES (est): 2.39MM **Privately Held**
Web: www.prestigeac.co
SIC: 7532 Body shop, automotive

(P-13645)
PRIDE COLLISION CENTERS INC (HQ)
Also Called: Pride Auto Body
7950 Haskell Ave (91406-1923)
PHONE.................................818 909-0660
Randy Stabler, *Pr*
Robert Turchan, *
EMP: 65 **EST:** 1982
SQ FT: 44,000
SALES (est): 10.69MM **Privately Held**
SIC: 7532 Body shop, automotive
PA: Classic Collision, Llc
375 Northridge Rd Ste 450
Sandy Springs GA

(P-13646)
RAY GASKIN SERVICE
8553 Weyand Ave (95828-2662)
PHONE.................................916 682-5155
Tom Snider, *Prin*
EMP: 63
SALES (corp-wide): 1.11MM **Privately Held**
Web: www.raygaskinservice.com
SIC: 7532 Top and body repair and paint shops
PA: Ray Gaskin Service
14572 Rancho Vista Dr
Fontana CA
909 574-7000

(P-13647)
REDLANDS FORD INC
1121 W Colton Ave (92374-2935)
PHONE.................................909 793-3211
Steve Rojas, *CEO*
Steve Rojas, *Pr*
Tracey Hooper, *
EMP: 85 **EST:** 2002
SALES (est): 10.56MM **Privately Held**
Web: www.redlandsford.com
SIC: 7532 5511 Body shop, automotive; Automobiles, new and used

(P-13648)
SAN DIEGO SATURN RETAILERS INC
Miramar Collision Center
9985 Huennekens St (92121-2918)
PHONE.................................858 373-3001
Gary Leger, *Mgr*
EMP: 94
SQ FT: 24,766
Web: www.teamkiaofelcajon.com
SIC: 7532 Collision shops, automotive
PA: San Diego Saturn Retailers, Inc.
541 N Johnson Ave
El Cajon CA

(P-13649)
STERLING COLLISION LLC (PA)
Also Called: Sea Breeze Collision
1111 Bell Ave Ste A (92780-6463)
PHONE.................................714 259-1111
Ray Shaai, *Genl Pt*
EMP: 65 **EST:** 1999
SALES (est): 3.76MM
SALES (corp-wide): 3.76MM **Privately Held**
Web: www.sterlingcollisioncenter.com
SIC: 7532 Body shop, automotive

(P-13650)
WAND TOPCO INC
4774 W Adams Blvd (90016-2949)
PHONE.................................323 734-3333
EMP: 2234
SALES (corp-wide): 423.12MM **Privately Held**
SIC: 7532 Body shop, automotive
PA: Wand Topco Inc
2941 Lake Vista Dr
Lewisville TX
469 948-9500

(P-13651)
WAND TOPCO INC
Also Called: Caliber Collision
123 California Dr (94010-4322)
PHONE.................................650 375-0600
EMP: 1779
SALES (corp-wide): 423.12MM **Privately Held**
SIC: 7532 Body shop, automotive
PA: Wand Topco Inc
2941 Lake Vista Dr
Lewisville TX
469 948-9500

(P-13652)
WAND TOPCO INC
Also Called: Caliber Cllsion - 1127 Mdesto
331 Bangs Ave (95356-8900)
PHONE.................................209 524-6824
EMP: 3635
SALES (corp-wide): 423.12MM **Privately Held**
SIC: 7532 Collision shops, automotive
PA: Wand Topco Inc
2941 Lake Vista Dr
Lewisville TX
469 948-9500

7537 Automotive Transmission Repair Shops

(P-13653)
PDQ AUTOMATIC TRANSM PARTS INC
8380 Tiogawoods Dr (95828-5048)
PHONE.................................916 681-7701
John G Hicks Junior, *Pr*
Tracy Hicks, *
John Hicks Senior, *Treas*
Amy Hicks, *
▲ **EMP:** 62 **EST:** 1971
SQ FT: 33,600
SALES (est): 8.7MM **Privately Held**
Web: www.pdqparts.com
SIC: 7537 Automotive transmission repair shops

7538 General Automotive Repair Shops

(P-13654)
ADVANCED INNOVATIVE TECH CORP
1675 W Park Ave (92373-8072)
PHONE.................................417 831-9444
EMP: 87
Web: www.trakmotive.com
SIC: 7538 General automotive repair shops
PA: Advanced Innovative Technology Corporation
350 Nevada St
Redlands CA

(P-13655)
ALIGNTECH
2820 Orchard Pkwy (95134-2019)
PHONE.................................714 605-7114
EMP: 93 **EST:** 2004
SALES (est): 12.64MM **Privately Held**
Web: www.aligntech.com
SIC: 7538 General truck repair

(P-13656)
ALLIED LUBE INC
Also Called: Jiffy Lube
3087 Edinger Ave (92780-7240)
PHONE.................................949 651-8814
Lillian Kline, *Acctnt*
EMP: 84
Web: www.jiffylube.com
SIC: 7538 7549 General automotive repair shops; Lubrication service, automotive
PA: Allied Lube, Inc.
27240 La Paz Rd
Mission Viejo CA

(P-13657)
BAE SYSTEMS SRRA DTROIT DESL A (HQ)
1755 Adams Ave (94577-1001)
PHONE.................................510 635-8991
Cindy Bergstrom, *Pr*
Wade Sperry, *MFG DIVISION*
EMP: 95 **EST:** 1982
SQ FT: 45,000
SALES (est): 14.74MM
SALES (corp-wide): 152.81MM **Privately Held**
SIC: 7538 5084 5085 Diesel engine repair: automotive; Engines and parts, diesel; Industrial supplies
PA: Bae Systems Resolution Inc.
1000 La St Ste 4950
Houston TX
713 868-7700

(P-13658)
BRAKE DEPOT SYSTEMS INC
1205 E 1st St (92701-6324)
PHONE.................................714 623-9030
EMP: 258
Web: www.tiredepotcompany.com
SIC: 7538 General automotive repair shops
PA: Brake Depot Systems Inc
8901 Sw Canyon Rd
Portland OR

(P-13659)
CITY CHEVROLET OF SAN DIEGO
Also Called: City Chevrolet of Volkswagen
2111 Morena Blvd (92110-3440)
P.O. Box 85345 (92186-5345)
PHONE.................................619 276-6171
EMP: 148 **EST:** 2016
SALES (est): 14.57MM **Privately Held**
SIC: 7538 5511 7515 5015 General automotive repair shops; Automobiles, new and used; Passenger car leasing; Automotive supplies, used: wholesale and retail

(P-13660)
CITY OF BURBANK
Also Called: Public Works Equipment
124 S Lake St (91502-2108)
P.O. Box 6459 (91510-6459)
PHONE.................................818 238-3838
Ari Omessi, *Mgr*
EMP: 75
SALES (corp-wide): 259.01MM **Privately Held**
Web: www.burbankca.gov
SIC: 7538 9111 General automotive repair shops; Executive offices
PA: City Of Burbank
275 E Olive Ave
Burbank CA
818 238-5800

(P-13661)
COUNTY OF CONTRA COSTA
Also Called: General Services
2467 Waterbird Way (94553-1457)
PHONE.................................510 313-7077
Richard Batterstick, *Prin*
EMP: 70
SQ FT: 4,095
SALES (corp-wide): 2.51B **Privately Held**
Web: contracosta.ca.gov
SIC: 7538 9199 General automotive repair shops; General government administration
PA: County Of Contra Costa
625 Court St Ste 100
Martinez CA
925 957-5280

(P-13662)
FLT INC
Also Called: Folsom Lake Toyota
12747 Folsom Blvd (95630-8097)
PHONE.................................916 355-1500
Charles G Peterson, *Pr*
Pam Peterson, *
EMP: 125 **EST:** 1990
SALES (est): 9.75MM **Publicly Held**
Web: www.toyota.com
SIC: 7538 5511 7532 5531 General automotive repair shops; Automobiles, new and used; Body shop, automotive; Automotive parts
PA: Group 1 Automotive, Inc.
800 Gessner Rd Ste 500
Houston TX

(P-13663)
HAMBLINS BDY PNT FRAME SP INC
Also Called: Hamblin's Auto & Body Shop
7590 Cypress Ave (92503-1904)
PHONE.................................951 689-8440
Rod Perry, *Pr*
EMP: 70 **EST:** 1965
SALES (est): 4.9MM **Privately Held**
Web: www.kaizenautocare.com
SIC: 7538 7532 General automotive repair shops; Body shop, automotive

(P-13664)
IRONMAN RENEWAL LLC
2535 Anselmo Dr (92879-8092)
PHONE.................................951 735-3710
EMP: 87
SIC: 7538 Truck engine repair, except industrial

(P-13665)
LANCASTER CMNTY SVCS FNDTION I
Also Called: Development Services
46008 7th St W (93534-7602)
PHONE.................................661 723-6230
Randy Williams, *Mgr*
EMP: 200
Web: www.lancastercommunityhospital.net

PRODUCTS & SERVICES SECTION

7542 - Carwashes (P-13685)

SIC: 7538 9111 General automotive repair shops; Mayors' office
PA: The Lancaster Community Services Foundation Inc
44933 Fern Ave
Lancaster CA
661 723-6000

(P-13666)
LOS ANGELES TRUCK CENTERS LLC (PA)
Also Called: Velocity Vehicle Group
2429 Peck Rd (90601-1605)
P.O. Box 101284 (91189-0005)
PHONE.................................562 447-1200
EMP: 90 EST: 1998
SALES (est): 233.56MM
SALES (corp-wide): 233.56MM Privately Held
Web: www.velocityvehiclegroup.com
SIC: 7538 5012 5013 7532 Truck engine repair, except industrial; Trucks, commercial; Truck parts and accessories; Body shop, trucks

(P-13667)
MARTIN AUTOMOTIVE INC
Also Called: Glendora Chevrolet
1959 Auto Centre Dr (91740-6714)
PHONE.................................909 394-9899
Michael W Martin, CEO
Melissa Alvarez Ctrl, Prin
EMP: 65 EST: 2014
SALES (est): 2.11MM Privately Held
Web: www.chevrolet.com
SIC: 7538 General automotive repair shops

(P-13668)
MISSION SERVICE INC
1800 Avenue Of The Stars Ste 1400 (90067-4216)
PHONE.................................323 266-2593
John E Anderson, Pr
John E Anderson Junior, Treas
EMP: 1160 EST: 1976
SALES (est): 996.26K
SALES (corp-wide): 251.02MM Privately Held
SIC: 7538 Truck engine repair, except industrial
PA: Topa Equities, Ltd.
1900 Avenue Of The Stars # 1050
Los Angeles CA
310 203-9199

(P-13669)
PAPE TRUCKS INC
Also Called: Pape' Kenworth
2892 E Jensen Ave (93706-5111)
P.O. Box 407 (97440-0407)
PHONE.................................559 268-4344
Charles Davis, Genl Mgr
EMP: 77
Web: www.papekenworth.com
SIC: 7538 5511 5531 General truck repair; Trucks, tractors, and trailers; new and used; Truck equipment and parts
HQ: Pape' Trucks, Inc.
355 Goodpasture Island Rd
Eugene OR

(P-13670)
PLEASANTON TRUCK & EQP RPS INC
8844 Elder Creek Rd Ste A (95828-1819)
PHONE.................................916 387-5288
EMP: 105
SALES (corp-wide): 864.78K Privately Held
Web: www.a-1enterprisesbayarea.com

SIC: 7538 General truck repair
PA: Pleasanton Truck & Equipment Repairs, Inc.
3110 Busch Rd
Pleasanton CA
925 846-9222

(P-13671)
PRICE-SIMMS INC (PA)
898 W El Camino Real (94087-1153)
PHONE.................................408 245-6640
Adam Simms, Pr
Tom Price, *
EMP: 70 EST: 1959
SQ FT: 35,000
SALES (est): 74.39K
SALES (corp-wide): 74.39K Privately Held
Web: www.toyotasunnyvale.com
SIC: 7538 5511 5521 5531 General automotive repair shops; Automobiles, new and used; Used car dealers; Auto and home supply stores

(P-13672)
QUALIS AUTOMOTIVE LLC
21046 Figueroa St (90745-1906)
PHONE.................................859 689-7772
EMP: 100
SALES (corp-wide): 70.48MM Privately Held
Web: www.centricparts.com
SIC: 7538 General automotive repair shops
PA: Qualis Automotive, L.L.C.
14528 Bonelli St
City Of Industry CA
310 218-1082

(P-13673)
R&C MOTOR CORPORATION
Also Called: Claremont Toyota
601 Auto Center Dr (91711-5470)
PHONE.................................909 625-1500
EMP: 200 EST: 1992
SALES (est): 19.24MM Privately Held
Web: www.claremonttoyota.com
SIC: 7538 5511 General automotive repair shops; Automobiles, new and used

(P-13674)
SANGERA BUICK INC
Also Called: Mercedes Benz of Bakersfield
5600 Gasoline Alley Dr (93313-3737)
PHONE.................................661 833-5200
Damon Culbertson, Pr
Mehnga Sangera, *
Hardev Sangera, *
EMP: 85 EST: 1969
SQ FT: 20,000
SALES (est): 10.63MM Privately Held
Web: www.sangera.com
SIC: 7538 5531 5511 General automotive repair shops; Automotive parts; Automobiles, new and used

(P-13675)
SANTA ROSA CITY OF
Also Called: Public Works-Garage
55 Stony Point Rd (95401-4446)
PHONE.................................707 543-3882
George Marion, Brnch Mgr
EMP: 74
SALES (corp-wide): 237.84MM Privately Held
Web: www.srcity.org
SIC: 7538 7699 General automotive repair shops; Aircraft and heavy equipment repair services
PA: Santa Rosa, City Of
100 Santa Rosa Ave Ste 6
Santa Rosa CA
707 543-3010

(P-13676)
SIEMENS MOBILITY INC
5301 Price Ave (95652-2401)
PHONE.................................916 621-2700
Christopher Maynard, Dist Vice President
EMP: 100
SALES (corp-wide): 71.74B Privately Held
SIC: 7538 3743 General truck repair; Train cars and equipment, freight or passenger
HQ: Siemens Mobility, Inc.
1 Penn Plz Ste 1100
New York NY
212 672-4000

(P-13677)
TED FORD JONES INC (PA)
Also Called: Ken Grody Ford
6211 Beach Blvd (90621-2307)
P.O. Box 2154 (90621-0654)
PHONE.................................714 521-3110
Kenneth B Grody, Pr
Ken Grody, *
Curt Maletych, *
▼ EMP: 110 EST: 1995
SQ FT: 4,500
SALES (est): 45.03MM
SALES (corp-wide): 45.03MM Privately Held
Web: www.quicklane.com
SIC: 7538 5511 General automotive repair shops; Automobiles, new and used

(P-13678)
VROOM AUTOMOTIVE FINANCE CORP (HQ)
1071 Camelback St Ste 100 (92660-3046)
PHONE.................................949 224-1226
James Vagim, Pr
Guillermo Bron, Ch Bd
Ravi R Gandhi, Credit RISK
Steve Singh, COO
EMP: 382 EST: 1998
SQ FT: 31,214
SALES (est): 96.49MM
SALES (corp-wide): 1.95B Publicly Held
SIC: 7538 General automotive repair shops
PA: Vroom, Inc.
1375 Broadway Fl 11
New York NY
855 524-1300

(P-13679)
YOURMECHANIC INC
Also Called: Yourmechanic
20 Park Rd Ste H (94010-4443)
PHONE.................................800 701-6230
Maddy Martin, Genl Mgr
EMP: 95 EST: 2015
SALES (est): 7.65MM Privately Held
Web: www.yourmechanic.com
SIC: 7538 6794 General automotive repair shops; Franchises, selling or licensing

7539 Automotive Repair Shops, Nec

(P-13680)
AKH COMPANY INC
Also Called: Discount Tire Center 025
7120 Laurel Canyon Blvd (91605-5740)
PHONE.................................818 691-1978
Leo Gonzalez, Mgr
EMP: 66
SALES (corp-wide): 31.08MM Privately Held
Web: www.discounttires.com
SIC: 7539 5014 5531 Wheel alignment, automotive; Automobile tires and tubes; Automotive tires

PA: Akh Company, Inc.
1160 N Anaheim Blvd
Anaheim CA
800 999-2878

(P-13681)
EDF RENEWABLES SERVICES INC (HQ)
Also Called: Enxco
15445 Innovation Dr (92128-3432)
PHONE.................................858 521-3575
Tristan Grimbert, Pr
Ryan Pfaff, *
Luis Silva, *
EMP: 65 EST: 1988
SQ FT: 70,000
SALES (est): 104.01MM Privately Held
Web: www.edf-re.com
SIC: 7539 Alternators and generators, rebuilding and repair
PA: Edf Renewables, Inc.
15445 Innovation Dr
San Diego CA

(P-13682)
PEBBLE BEACH CO A LTD PARTNR
4005 Sunridge Rd (93953-3003)
PHONE.................................831 624-0348
Mike Wato, Genl Mgr
EMP: 272
Web: www.pebblebeach.com
SIC: 7539 Automotive repair shops, nec
PA: Pebble Beach Company, A Limited Partnership
2700 17 Mile Dr
Pebble Beach CA

(P-13683)
ST GEORGE AUTO CENTER INC
Also Called: Stg Auto Group
13861 Harbor Blvd (92843-4043)
P.O. Box 2129 (91763-0629)
PHONE.................................657 212-5042
EMP: 85
SALES (corp-wide): 8.3MM Privately Held
SIC: 7539 Automotive repair shops, nec
PA: St. George Auto Center, Inc.
10325 Central Ave
Montclair CA
909 341-1189

7542 Carwashes

(P-13684)
BLUE BEACON USA LP
Also Called: Blue Beacon of Wheeler Ridge
5831 Santa Elena Dr (93203-9705)
PHONE.................................661 858-2090
Jose Gonzalez, Mgr
EMP: 107
SALES (corp-wide): 38MM Privately Held
Web: www.bluebeacon.com
SIC: 7542 Truck wash
PA: Blue Beacon U.S.A., L.P.
500 Graves Blvd
Salina KS
785 825-2221

(P-13685)
BLUE BEACON USA LP II
1630 Mcgarry St (90021-3117)
PHONE.................................213 477-1060
Jerry Anno, Off Mgr
EMP: 72
SALES (corp-wide): 88.72MM Privately Held
Web: www.bluebeacon.com
SIC: 7542 Truck wash

7542 - Carwashes (P-13686)

PA: Blue Beacon U.S.A., L.P. li
500 Graves Blvd
Salina KS
785 825-2221

(P-13686)
BODY BEAUTIFUL CAR WASH INC
13236 Poway Rd (92064-4614)
PHONE.................................858 748-4400
Dennis Mcknight, VP
EMP: 65
SALES (corp-wide): 49.85MM **Privately Held**
Web: www.bodybeautiful.com
SIC: 7542 Washing and polishing, automotive
PA: Body Beautiful Car Wash, Inc.
4282 Camino Del Rio N
San Diego CA
619 563-5566

(P-13687)
BOWIE ENTERPRISES (PA)
Also Called: Chevron
4411 N Blackstone Ave (93726-1904)
PHONE.................................559 227-6221
David Bowie, Pr
James M Bowie, *
Kathryn Bowie, *
Karen Bowie, *
EMP: 60 **EST:** 1966
SQ FT: 7,700
SALES (est): 14.84MM
SALES (corp-wide): 14.84MM **Privately Held**
Web: www.redcarpetcarwash.com
SIC: 7542 5541 Carwash, automatic; Filling stations, gasoline

(P-13688)
BOWIE ENTERPRISES
Also Called: Red Carpet Car Wash
801 W Shaw Ave (93612-3218)
PHONE.................................559 292-6565
EMP: 95
SALES (corp-wide): 14.84MM **Privately Held**
Web: www.redcarpetcarwash.com
SIC: 7542 Washing and polishing, automotive
PA: Bowie Enterprises
4411 N Blackstone Ave
Fresno CA
559 227-6221

(P-13689)
CANEPAS CAR WASH
Also Called: Chevron
642 N Hunter St (95202-2022)
PHONE.................................209 951-9772
Remo J Canepa, Pr
Steven Canepa, *
Marion Canepa, *
EMP: 60 **EST:** 1959
SQ FT: 30,000
SALES (est): 4.64MM **Privately Held**
Web: www.chevron.com
SIC: 7542 5541 5947 Washing and polishing, automotive; Filling stations, gasoline; Gift shop

(P-13690)
CAR WASH PARTNERS INC
Also Called: CAR WASH PARTNERS, INC.
2619 Mount Vernon Ave (93306-2900)
PHONE.................................661 377-1020
EMP: 172
SALES (corp-wide): 876.51MM **Publicly Held**

Web: www.mistercarwash.com
SIC: 7542 Washing and polishing, automotive
HQ: Car Wash Partners, Llc
222 E 5th St
Tucson AZ
520 615-4000

(P-13691)
CAR WASH PARTNERS INC
Also Called: CAR WASH PARTNERS INC.
5375 Olive Dr (93308-2921)
PHONE.................................661 231-3689
EMP: 76
SALES (corp-wide): 422MM **Privately Held**
Web: www.mistercarwash.com
SIC: 7542 Washing and polishing, automotive
HQ: Car Wash Partners, Inc.
1503 S Collins St
Plant City FL

(P-13692)
DYNAMIC AUTO IMAGES INC
Also Called: Dynamic Detail
2860 Michelle Ste 140 (92606-1007)
PHONE.................................714 771-3400
Tom Miller, Pr
EMP: 300 **EST:** 2004
SALES (est): 8.95MM **Privately Held**
Web: www.dynamicautoimages.com
SIC: 7542 7532 Washing and polishing, automotive; Collision shops, automotive

(P-13693)
GREEN-N-CLEAN EX CAR WASH INC
Also Called: H2go Car Wash
28622 Oso Pkwy Pmb C (92688-5540)
PHONE.................................949 749-4977
Ryan Blanchard, CEO
EMP: 75 **EST:** 2010
SALES (est): 8MM **Privately Held**
Web: www.h2gocarwash.com
SIC: 7542 Carwashes

(P-13694)
JACKS CAR WASH 3
6745 N West Ave (93711-4304)
PHONE.................................559 438-8201
EMP: 60 **EST:** 2003
SALES (est): 638.9K **Privately Held**
SIC: 7542 5947 5812 Carwash, self-service; Gift shop; Coffee shop

(P-13695)
JKF AUTO SERVICE INC
Also Called: Five Star Auto Repair and Wash
6818 Five Star Blvd (95677-2660)
PHONE.................................916 315-0555
Jeff Finerman, Pr
Karen W Finerman, *
EMP: 60 **EST:** 1993
SALES (est): 2.01MM **Privately Held**
Web: www.fivestarrocklin.com
SIC: 7542 7549 7539 Washing and polishing, automotive; Lubrication service, automotive; Automotive repair shops, nec

(P-13696)
LARK AVENUE CAR WASH
Also Called: Lark Ave Classic Car Wash
16500 Lark Ave (95032-2505)
PHONE.................................408 356-2525
Brett Kott, Mgr
EMP: 72
SALES (corp-wide): 42.95MM **Privately Held**
Web: www.classiccarwash.com

SIC: 7542 Washing and polishing, automotive
PA: Lark Avenue Car Wash
871 E Hamilton Ave
Campbell CA
408 371-2414

(P-13697)
LARK AVENUE CAR WASH
Also Called: Chevron
5005 Almaden Expy (95118-2049)
P.O. Box 5993 (95150-5993)
PHONE.................................408 371-2565
Chuck Mina, Mgr
EMP: 72
SQ FT: 7,859
SALES (corp-wide): 42.95MM **Privately Held**
Web: www.classiccarwash.com
SIC: 7542 Washing and polishing, automotive
PA: Lark Avenue Car Wash
871 E Hamilton Ave
Campbell CA
408 371-2414

(P-13698)
LARK AVENUE CAR WASH
Also Called: Chevron
981 E Hamilton Ave (95008-0648)
PHONE.................................408 377-2525
Mike Davis, Prin
EMP: 72
SALES (corp-wide): 42.95MM **Privately Held**
Web: www.classiccarwash.com
SIC: 7542 Washing and polishing, automotive
PA: Lark Avenue Car Wash
871 E Hamilton Ave
Campbell CA
408 371-2414

(P-13699)
LITTLE SISTERS TRUCK WASH INC (PA)
Also Called: Little Sister's Truck Wash
25 Rolling View Ln (92028-9234)
P.O. Box 333 (92003-0333)
PHONE.................................760 731-3170
EMP: 69 **EST:** 1991
SALES (est): 9.51MM **Privately Held**
Web: www.littlesisterstruckwash.com
SIC: 7542 Washing and polishing, automotive

(P-13700)
LOZANO INC
Also Called: Lozano Car Wash
2690 W El Camino Real (94040-1117)
PHONE.................................650 941-0590
Manuel J Lozano, Pr
Claudia Rozriduez, *
EMP: 107 **EST:** 1961
SQ FT: 500
SALES (est): 4.91MM **Privately Held**
Web: www.yessicalozano.com
SIC: 7542 Carwash, automatic

(P-13701)
PETROLEUM SALES INC (PA)
1475 2nd St (94901-2754)
PHONE.................................415 256-1600
Ben Shimek, Pr
EMP: 120 **EST:** 1969
SALES (est): 13.55MM
SALES (corp-wide): 13.55MM **Privately Held**
Web: www.shineology.com

SIC: 7542 5541 Carwashes; Gasoline service stations

(P-13702)
TEAM DYKSPRA (PA)
2315 California Ave (92881-6655)
PHONE.................................951 898-6482
Lenny Dykstra, Pr
EMP: 60 **EST:** 1992
SALES (est): 4.85MM **Privately Held**
Web: www.cracked-screens.com
SIC: 7542 7549 Washing and polishing, automotive; Automotive maintenance services

(P-13703)
VICTORVILLE SPEEDWASH INC
13311 Main St (92345-9132)
PHONE.................................760 998-2482
EMP: 73
SALES (corp-wide): 876.51MM **Publicly Held**
Web: www.mistercarwash.com
SIC: 7542 Washing and polishing, automotive
HQ: Victorville Speedwash Inc.
12147 Industrial Blvd
Victorville CA
760 962-9700

(P-13704)
VICTORVILLE SPEEDWASH INC
15200 Palmdale Rd (92392-2502)
PHONE.................................760 388-0112
EMP: 73
SALES (corp-wide): 876.51MM **Publicly Held**
Web: www.mistercarwash.com
SIC: 7542 Washing and polishing, automotive
HQ: Victorville Speedwash Inc.
12147 Industrial Blvd
Victorville CA
760 962-9700

(P-13705)
VICTORVILLE SPEEDWASH INC
12875 Bear Valley Rd (92392-9786)
PHONE.................................760 388-0113
EMP: 73
SALES (corp-wide): 876.51MM **Publicly Held**
Web: www.mistercarwash.com
SIC: 7542 Washing and polishing, automotive
HQ: Victorville Speedwash Inc.
12147 Industrial Blvd
Victorville CA
760 962-9700

7549 Automotive Services, Nec

(P-13706)
ALLIED GARDENS TOWING INC (PA)
9150 Chesapeake Dr Ste 240 (92123-1061)
PHONE.................................619 563-4060
Edward S Bischop, Pr
EMP: 60 **EST:** 1970
SQ FT: 1,500
SALES (est): 2.2MM
SALES (corp-wide): 2.2MM **Privately Held**
SIC: 7549 Towing service, automotive

7623 - Refrigeration Service And Repair (P-13727)

(P-13707)
ALLIED LUBE INC
Also Called: Jiffy Lube
17010 Walnut Grove Dr (95037-4437)
PHONE.................408 779-8969
Paul Delacruz, *Brnch Mgr*
EMP: 95
Web: www.jiffylube.com
SIC: 7549 Lubrication service, automotive
PA: Allied Lube, Inc.
27240 La Paz Rd
Mission Viejo CA

(P-13708)
AMERIT FLEET SOLUTIONS INC
15325 Manila St (92337-7261)
PHONE.................909 357-0100
David Kristy, *Mgr*
EMP: 887
Web: www.ameritfleetsolutions.com
SIC: 7549 Inspection and diagnostic service, automotive
HQ: Amerit Fleet Solutions Inc.
1333 N California Blvd # 345
Walnut Creek CA
877 512-6374

(P-13709)
AMERIT FLEET SOLUTIONS INC (HQ)
1333 N California Blvd (94596-4502)
PHONE.................877 512-6374
Dan Williams, *CEO*
Nick Healing, *
Amein Punjani, *
EMP: 100 EST: 2010
SALES (est): 132.34MM **Privately Held**
Web: www.ameritfleetsolutions.com
SIC: 7549 4785 Inspection and diagnostic service, automotive; Transportation inspection services
PA: Kelleyamerit Holdings, Inc.
1331 N Calif Blvd Ste 150
Walnut Creek CA

(P-13710)
AUTOMOTIVE TSTG & DEV SVCS INC (PA)
400 Etiwanda Ave (91761-8637)
PHONE.................909 390-1100
Devon Larry Smith, *CEO*
Kay Smith, *
▲ EMP: 185 EST: 1989
SQ FT: 24,000
SALES (est): 16.41MM **Privately Held**
Web: www.automotivetesting.com
SIC: 7549 8734 8711 Emissions testing without repairs, automotive; Testing laboratories; Engineering services

(P-13711)
COMPLETE COACH WORKS
42882 Ivy St (92562-7218)
PHONE.................800 300-3751
EMP: 227
SALES (corp-wide): 54.62MM **Privately Held**
Web: www.completecoach.com
SIC: 7549 Trailer maintenance
HQ: Complete Coach Works
1863 Service Ct
Riverside CA

(P-13712)
COVEY AUTO EXPRESS INC (PA)
Also Called: Pacific Towing
1444 El Pinal Dr (95205-2642)
PHONE.................253 826-0461
Michael D Covey, *Pr*
Kathy Covey, *
EMP: 66 EST: 1986
SQ FT: 19,000
SALES (est): 8.99MM
SALES (corp-wide): 8.99MM **Privately Held**
Web: www.coveyautoinc.com
SIC: 7549 Towing service, automotive

(P-13713)
EZ LUBE LLC
Also Called: EZ Lube- Costco
13421 Washington Blvd (90292-5658)
PHONE.................310 821-2517
Doug Paysse, *Mgr*
EMP: 130
SALES (corp-wide): 21.83MM **Privately Held**
Web: www.ezlube.com
SIC: 7549 Lubrication service, automotive
PA: Ez Lube, Llc
3540 Howard Way Ste 200
Costa Mesa CA

(P-13714)
EZ LUBE LLC
Also Called: Valvoline Instant Oil Change
3599 Harbor Blvd (92626-1405)
PHONE.................714 966-1647
EMP: 126
SALES (corp-wide): 21.83MM **Privately Held**
Web: www.expresscare.com
SIC: 7549 Lubrication service, automotive
PA: Ez Lube, Llc
3540 Howard Way Ste 200
Costa Mesa CA

(P-13715)
HORIZON GLOBAL AMERICAS INC
Also Called: Cequent Towing Products
3181 S Willow Ave Ste 104 (93725-9460)
PHONE.................559 266-9000
Sam Weissman, *Mgr*
EMP: 85
SALES (corp-wide): 8.02B **Privately Held**
Web: www.horizonglobal.com
SIC: 7549 Towing services
HQ: Horizon Global Americas Inc.
47912 Halyard Dr Ste 100
Plymouth MI

(P-13716)
JANS TOWING INC
134 N Valencia Ave (91741-2477)
PHONE.................909 596-9060
Jan Qualkenbush, *Brnch Mgr*
EMP: 157
Web: www.janstowing.com
SIC: 7549 Towing service, automotive
PA: Jan's Towing Inc.
1045 W Kirkwall Rd
Azusa CA

(P-13717)
METROPRO ROAD SERVICES INC
Also Called: A & P Towing-Metropro Rd Svcs
957 W 17th St (92627-4402)
PHONE.................714 556-7600
TOLL FREE: 800
Bradley T Humphreys, *CEO*
Jody Campbell, *
EMP: 100 EST: 1998
SALES (est): 1.92MM **Privately Held**
Web: www.metro-pro.com
SIC: 7549 Towing service, automotive

(P-13718)
ROSS BAKER TOWING INC
Also Called: Ross Baker Towing Service
8750 Vanalden Ave (91324-3656)
PHONE.................818 886-7411
Greg Baker, *Pr*
EMP: 64 EST: 1960
SQ FT: 2,000
SALES (est): 2.39MM
SALES (corp-wide): 94.77MM **Privately Held**
Web: www.rossbakertowing.com
SIC: 7549 Towing service, automotive
HQ: United Road Towing, Inc.
16325 Crawford Ave
Markham IL

(P-13719)
SINGER VEHICLE DESIGN LLC (PA)
19500 S Vermont Ave (90502-1120)
PHONE.................213 592-2728
Mazen Fawaz, *CEO*
Robert Peter Dickinson, *CPO*
Jason Grant, *CFO*
Jason Franklin, *COO*
EMP: 250 EST: 2009
SALES (est): 25.24MM
SALES (corp-wide): 25.24MM **Privately Held**
Web: www.singervehicledesign.com
SIC: 7549 3714 Automotive customizing services, nonfactory basis; Acceleration equipment, motor vehicle

(P-13720)
SUNBELT TOWING INC (PA)
Also Called: Western Towing
4370 Pacific Hwy (92110-3106)
PHONE.................619 297-8697
Steven Hendrickson, *Pr*
EMP: 70 EST: 1978
SALES (est): 4.98MM
SALES (corp-wide): 4.98MM **Privately Held**
Web: www.westerntowing.com
SIC: 7549 7532 Towing service, automotive; Top and body repair and paint shops

(P-13721)
VALVOLINE INSTANT OIL CHNGE FR
Also Called: Valvoline Instant Oil Change
9520 John St (90670-2904)
PHONE.................562 906-6200
Brian Nichols, *Brnch Mgr*
EMP: 75
Web: www.valvoline.com
SIC: 7549 Lubrication service, automotive
HQ: Valvoline Instant Oil Change Franchising, Inc.
100 Valvoline Way
Lexington KY

(P-13722)
YOURMECHANIC INC
520 San Antonio Rd Ste 110 (94040-1217)
PHONE.................215 253-7941
Anthony Rodio, *Pr*
Paul Bruso, *
EMP: 107 EST: 2011
SALES (est): 12.38MM
SALES (corp-wide): 21.72MM **Privately Held**
Web: www.yourmechanic.com
SIC: 7549 High performance auto repair and service
PA: Wrench, Inc.
701 5th Ave Ste 7250
Seattle WA
844 997-3624

7623 Refrigeration Service And Repair

(P-13723)
ARCTICOM GROUP RFRGN LLC
Also Called: PMC Southwest LLC
3675 De Forest Cir (91752-1139)
PHONE.................916 484-3190
Sean Patrick, *Pr*
EMP: 406 EST: 2017
SALES (est): 9.67MM
SALES (corp-wide): 71.46MM **Privately Held**
Web: www.pmc-southwest.com
SIC: 7623 Refrigeration service and repair
PA: The Arcticom Group Llc
1676 N California Blvd # 420
Walnut Creek CA
925 334-7222

(P-13724)
CITY MECHANICAL INC
724 Alfred Nobel Dr (94547-1805)
PHONE.................510 724-9088
Russell Will Junior, *CEO*
Ronald Tinkey, *
EMP: 70 EST: 1989
SALES (est): 13.62MM **Privately Held**
Web: www.citymechanical.com
SIC: 7623 1711 Refrigeration service and repair; Heating systems repair and maintenance

(P-13725)
CLIMA-TECH INC
1820 Town And Country Dr (92860-3616)
PHONE.................909 613-5513
William C Valenzuela, *CEO*
Husein Aziz, *
Ada Roberts, *
EMP: 89 EST: 2004
SALES (est): 9.96MM **Privately Held**
Web: www.climatechref.com
SIC: 7623 1711 Refrigeration service and repair; Refrigeration contractor

(P-13726)
CONTROL AIR ENTERPRISES LLC
1390 Armorlite Dr (92069-1342)
PHONE.................760 744-2727
Mike Eepn, *Brnch Mgr*
EMP: 475
SALES (corp-wide): 277.7MM **Privately Held**
Web: www.controlac.com
SIC: 7623 1711 Refrigeration service and repair; Heating systems repair and maintenance
PA: Control Air Enterprises Llc
5200 E La Palma Ave
Anaheim CA
714 777-8600

(P-13727)
MERCY AIR TRI-COUNTY LLC
1670 Miro Way (92376-8629)
P.O. Box 2532 (92334-2532)
PHONE.................909 829-1051
David Dolstein, *Managing Member*
EMP: 250 EST: 1989
SQ FT: 11,288
SALES (est): 3.39MM
SALES (corp-wide): 1.71B **Privately Held**
SIC: 7623 4119 3721 7359 Air conditioning repair; Local passenger transportation, nec; Helicopters; Aircraft and industrial truck rental services
HQ: Air Methods Corporation

7623 - Refrigeration Service And Repair (P-13728)

5500 S Quebec St Ste 300
Greenwood Village CO
855 896-9067

(P-13728)
PACIFIC COAST SALES & SERVICE INC (PA)
Also Called: Pacific Coast Trane Service Co
310 Soquel Way (94085-4101)
PHONE.....................408 481-3600
EMP: 80 EST: 1930
SALES (est): 15.42MM
SALES (corp-wide): 15.42MM Privately Held
Web: www.pacificcoasttrane.com
SIC: 7623 5075 5074 Air conditioning repair; Warm air heating equipment and supplies; Plumbing and hydronic heating supplies

(P-13729)
PRIBUSS ENGINEERING INC
523 Mayfair Ave (94080-4509)
PHONE.....................650 588-0447
Bayardo Chamorro, CEO
Bayardo Chamorro, Pr
John Pribuss, *
EMP: 70 EST: 1968
SQ FT: 16,000
SALES (est): 17.94MM Privately Held
Web: www.pribuss.com
SIC: 7623 1711 Refrigeration service and repair; Plumbing, heating, air-conditioning

(P-13730)
VLY AIR COND & RPR
825 S Topeka Ave (93721-2406)
PHONE.....................559 237-2123
Tobbie Viglion, CEO
EMP: 70 EST: 2015
SALES (est): 1.25MM Privately Held
Web: www.valleyairrepair.com
SIC: 7623 Air conditioning repair

7629 Electrical Repair Shops

(P-13731)
ABLE CABLE INC (PA)
Also Called: A C I Communications
5115 Douglas Fir Rd Ste A (91302-2588)
PHONE.....................818 223-3600
Russell Ramas, Pr
Russell Ramas, CEO
Michael Collette, *
David Gardner, *
EMP: 175 EST: 1983
SQ FT: 3,500
SALES (est): 9.72MM
SALES (corp-wide): 9.72MM Privately Held
Web: www.acicommunications.com
SIC: 7629 1731 4813 Telephone set repair; Telephone and telephone equipment installation; Telephone communication, except radio

(P-13732)
AUTHORIZED CELLULAR SERVICE
Also Called: ACS
8808 S Sepulveda Blvd (90045-4810)
PHONE.....................310 466-4144
EMP: 100 EST: 1993
SQ FT: 10,000
SALES (est): 1.71MM Privately Held
SIC: 7629 5999 Telephone set repair; Telephone equipment and systems

(P-13733)
BSH HOME APPLIANCES CORP (DH)
1901 Main St Ste 600 (92614-0521)
PHONE.....................949 440-7100
TOLL FREE: 800
◆ EMP: 220 EST: 1996
SQ FT: 52,000
SALES (est): 529.92MM
SALES (corp-wide): 230.19MM Privately Held
Web: www.bsh-group.com
SIC: 7629 Electrical household appliance repair
HQ: Bsh Hausgerate Gmbh
    Carl-Wery-Str. 34
    Munchen BY
    89459001

(P-13734)
CABLECOM LLC
Also Called: Cable Com
5745 E Fountain Way (93727-7815)
PHONE.....................559 412-8720
EMP: 77
SALES (corp-wide): 3.81B Publicly Held
Web: www.cablecomllc.us
SIC: 7629 1731 Electrical repair shops; Electrical work
HQ: Cablecom Llc
    8602 Maltby Rd
    Woodinville WA
    360 668-1300

(P-13735)
CABLECOM LLC
1251 N Jefferson St (92807-1611)
PHONE.....................714 666-2400
EMP: 77
SALES (corp-wide): 3.81B Publicly Held
Web: www.cablecomllc.us
SIC: 7629 1731 Telecommunication equipment repair (except telephones); Telephone and telephone equipment installation
HQ: Cablecom Llc
    8602 Maltby Rd
    Woodinville WA
    360 668-1300

(P-13736)
CABLECOM LLC
Also Called: Cablecom
5337 Luce Ave (95652-2440)
PHONE.....................916 891-2400
EMP: 77
SALES (corp-wide): 3.81B Publicly Held
Web: www.cablecomllc.us
SIC: 7629 1731 Telecommunication equipment repair (except telephones); Telephone and telephone equipment installation
HQ: Cablecom Llc
    8602 Maltby Rd
    Woodinville WA
    360 668-1300

(P-13737)
COMMUNICATIONS & PWR INDS LLC
Microwave Pwr Pdts Div - Ecnco
1318 Commerce Ave (95776-5908)
PHONE.....................530 662-7553
EMP: 73
Web: www.cpii.com
SIC: 7629 3671 Electrical repair shops; Vacuum tubes
HQ: Communications & Power Industries Llc
    811 Hansen Way
    Palo Alto CA

(P-13738)
CPI ECONCO DIVISION
Also Called: Econco Broadcast Service
1318 Commerce Ave (95776-5908)
PHONE.....................530 662-7553
◆ EMP: 73
Web: www.cpii.com
SIC: 7629 3671 Electrical repair shops; Vacuum tubes

(P-13739)
DACOR
14525 Clark Ave (91745-1236)
PHONE.....................626 961-2256
EMP: 74
Web: www.dacor.com
SIC: 7629 Electrical household appliance repair
HQ: Dacor
    14425 Clark Ave
    City Of Industry CA
    626 799-1000

(P-13740)
FOLSOM LAKE APPLIANCE INC
8146 Greenback Ln Ste 102 (95628-2536)
PHONE.....................916 985-3426
Scott Mcconnell, CEO
Krystle Mcconnell, Prin
EMP: 70 EST: 2005
SQ FT: 3,300
SALES (est): 9.42MM Privately Held
Web: www.lakeappliancerepair.com
SIC: 7629 Electrical household appliance repair

(P-13741)
JJR ENTERPRISES INC (HQ)
Also Called: Caltronics Business Systems
2431 Mercantile Dr (95742-6218)
PHONE.....................916 363-2666
Frank Gaspari, CEO
Daniel Reilly, *
Karen Roscher, *
Jamie Paro, *
EMP: 95 EST: 1975
SALES (est): 48.46MM Privately Held
Web: www.caltronics.net
SIC: 7629 5044 7359 Business machine repair, electric; Office equipment; Equipment rental and leasing, nec
PA: Flexprint, Llc
    2845 N Omaha
    Mesa AZ

(P-13742)
NSG TECHNOLOGY INC
Also Called: Hon Hai Precision Industry
1705 Junction Ct Ste 200 (95112-1019)
PHONE.....................408 547-8770
Ted Dubbs, CEO
▲ EMP: 353 EST: 1995
SALES (est): 99.93MM Privately Held
Web: www.nsgtechnology.com
SIC: 7629 Electronic equipment repair
HQ: Maxwell Holdings Limited
    C/O Vistra (Cayman) Limited
    George Town GR CAYMAN

(P-13743)
SCHROFF INC
Also Called: Pentair Equipment Protection
7328 Trade St (92121-3435)
PHONE.....................858 740-2400
Robert Bradley, Brnch Mgr
EMP: 120
Web: schroff.nvent.com
SIC: 7629 3469 Telecommunication equipment repair (except telephones); Electronic enclosures, stamped or pressed metal
HQ: Schroff, Inc.
    170 Commerce Dr
    Warwick RI
    763 204-7700

(P-13744)
SCOTTEL VOICE & DATA INC
Also Called: Black Box Network Services
6100 Center Dr Ste 720 (90045-9228)
PHONE.....................310 737-7300
George Robertson, Genl Mgr
EMP: 130 EST: 1984
SQ FT: 5,200
SALES (est): 9.7MM Privately Held
SIC: 7629 1731 Telecommunication equipment repair (except telephones); Telephone and telephone equipment installation
HQ: Black Box Corporation
    1000 Park Dr
    Lawrence PA
    724 746-5500

(P-13745)
SIMCO ELECTRONICS (PA)
Also Called: Simco Electronics
3131 Jay St Ste 100 (95054-3336)
PHONE.....................408 734-9750
Brian Kenna, CEO
EMP: 75 EST: 1962
SQ FT: 24,222
SALES (est): 44.38MM
SALES (corp-wide): 44.38MM Privately Held
Web: www.simco.com
SIC: 7629 8734 5045 7379 Electrical repair shops; Calibration and certification; Computer software; Computer related consulting services

(P-13746)
STANDARD CALIBRATIONS INC
681 Anita St Ste 103 (91911-4663)
PHONE.....................619 477-1668
Victor Lewis, Brnch Mgr
EMP: 72
Web: www.standardcal.com
SIC: 7629 Electrical measuring instrument repair and calibration
PA: Standard Calibrations, Inc.
    501 Resource Row
    Chesapeake VA

(P-13747)
TELENET VOIP INC
Also Called: Telenet
850 N Park View Dr (90245-4914)
PHONE.....................310 253-9000
TOLL FREE: 800
Asghar Ghassemy, Pr
Nicol Payab, *
EMP: 65 EST: 1977
SQ FT: 11,000
SALES (est): 11.94MM Privately Held
Web: www.telenetvoip.com
SIC: 7629 7379 7382 3612 Telephone set repair; Computer related consulting services; Security systems services; Transmission and distribution voltage regulators

(P-13748)
TESTEQUITY LLC (PA)
Also Called: Techni-Tools
6100 Condor Dr (93021-2608)
PHONE.....................805 498-9933
Ruzz Frazee, Pr

PRODUCTS & SERVICES SECTION

7699 - Repair Services, Nec (P-13768)

Nick Hawtrey, *
▲ EMP: 166 EST: 1971
SQ FT: 75,000
SALES (est): 163.89MM Privately Held
Web: www.testequity.com
SIC: 7629 3825 Electrical equipment repair services; Test equipment for electronic and electrical circuits

(P-13749)
TOTAL TELCO SPECIALISTS INC
Also Called: Tts
602 W Southern Ave (92865-3219)
PHONE.....................................805 541-2232
Earl J Darway, Pr
Phil Calkins, *
Eric Larson, *
EMP: 60 EST: 1995
SQ FT: 14,000
SALES (est): 8.49MM Privately Held
Web: www.totaltelco.net
SIC: 7629 Telecommunication equipment repair (except telephones)

7631 Watch, Clock, And Jewelry Repair

(P-13750)
ADVANCE SERVICES INC
8021 Kern Ave (95020-4051)
PHONE.....................................408 767-2797
Vanessa Valencia, Mgr
EMP: 1042
Web: www.advanceservices.com
SIC: 7631 Watch, clock, and jewelry repair
PA: Advance Services, Inc.
12702 Wsport Pkwy Ste 201
La Vista NE

7692 Welding Repair

(P-13751)
HAYES WELDING INC (PA)
Also Called: Valew Welding & Fabrication
12522 Violet Rd (92301-2704)
P.O. Box 310 (92301-0310)
PHONE.....................................760 246-4878
Roger L Hayes, CEO
Velma D Hayes, Pr
Vernon L Hayes, VP
▲ EMP: 91 EST: 1954
SQ FT: 45,000
SALES (est): 14.27MM
SALES (corp-wide): 14.27MM Privately Held
Web: www.valew.com
SIC: 7692 3465 3714 3713 Welding repair; Automotive stampings; Fuel systems and parts, motor vehicle; Truck and bus bodies

(P-13752)
JABIL SILVER CREEK INC (HQ)
4050 Technology Pl (94538-6362)
PHONE.....................................669 255-2900
John P Wolfe, CEO
Rita Wolfe, *
▲ EMP: 101 EST: 1992
SALES (est): 24.1MM
SALES (corp-wide): 34.7B Publicly Held
Web: www.jabil.com
SIC: 7692 8711 3674 3317 Welding repair; Engineering services; Semiconductors and related devices; Steel pipe and tubes
PA: Jabil, Inc.
10800 Roosevelt Blvd N
Saint Petersburg FL
727 577-9749

(P-13753)
SOUTHCOAST WELDING & MFG LLC
2591 Faivre St Ste 1 (91911-7146)
PHONE.....................................619 429-1337
Patrick Shoup, Pr
Jay Parast, *
Leo Mathieu, *
EMP: 270 EST: 2004
SQ FT: 82,000
SALES (est): 44.01MM Privately Held
Web: www.southcoastwelding.net
SIC: 7692 Welding repair

(P-13754)
T L FABRICATIONS LP
2921 E Coronado St (92806-2502)
PHONE.....................................562 802-3980
Ryan Kerrigan, Pr
Michael Hsu, *
▲ EMP: 60 EST: 1980
SQ FT: 30,000
SALES (est): 6.5MM Privately Held
SIC: 7692 Welding repair

(P-13755)
WELDLOGIC INC
Also Called: Weldlogic Gas & Supply
2651 Lavery Ct (91320-1502)
PHONE.....................................805 375-1670
Robert Elizarraz, Pr
Jack Froschauer, *
▲ EMP: 65 EST: 1980
SQ FT: 25,000
SALES (est): 9.44MM Privately Held
Web: www.weldlogic.com
SIC: 7692 Welding repair

(P-13756)
WEST COAST WLDG & PIPING INC
Also Called: Pipline
750 W Hueneme Rd (93033-9013)
PHONE.....................................805 246-5841
Gabriel Nunez, Managing Member
Jose Vargas, *
Mike Barbey, *
EMP: 80 EST: 2018
SALES (est): 1.21MM Privately Held
Web: www.wcwpiping.com
SIC: 7692 Welding repair

7694 Armature Rewinding Shops

(P-13757)
AUL CORP (DH)
1250 Main St Ste 300 (94559-2622)
P.O. Box 830029 (35283-0029)
PHONE.....................................707 257-9700
Luis Nieves, Pr
EMP: 118 EST: 1989
SQ FT: 8,500
SALES (est): 2.29MM Privately Held
Web: www.aulcorp.com
SIC: 7694 7549 Motor repair services; Automotive maintenance services
HQ: Protective Life Corporation
2801 Highway 280 S Ofc
Birmingham AL
205 268-1000

(P-13758)
EANDM
126 Mill St (95448-4438)
PHONE.....................................707 473-3137
Stephanie Clark, Prin
EMP: 60 EST: 2017
SALES (est): 2.05MM Privately Held
Web: www.eandm.com
SIC: 7694 Electric motor repair

(P-13759)
WRIGHTS SUPPLY INC
Also Called: Foothill Electric Motors
25838 Springbrook Ave (91350-2565)
PHONE.....................................661 254-8400
Steve Dalton, Genl Mgr
EMP: 97
SALES (corp-wide): 9.97MM Privately Held
Web: www.wrightssupply.com
SIC: 7694 7699 5999 5084 Electric motor repair; Pumps and pumping equipment repair; Engine and motor equipment and supplies; Water pumps (industrial)
PA: Wright's Supply, Inc.
640 Allen Ave
Glendale CA
818 242-1418

7699 Repair Services, Nec

(P-13760)
AER TECHNOLOGIES INC
Also Called: Aer Logistics
650 Columbia St (92821-2912)
PHONE.....................................714 871-7357
Kim Quick, CEO
Michael Mcgroarty, Pr
Ingrid Osborne, *
EMP: 320 EST: 1953
SQ FT: 50,000
SALES (est): 24.98MM Privately Held
Web: www.aertech.com
SIC: 7699 Precision instrument repair

(P-13761)
ALPHATECH GENERAL INC
Also Called: Ametek-Ameron
4750 Littlejohn St (91706-2274)
PHONE.....................................626 337-4640
EMP: 90
SIC: 7699 3812 Aircraft and heavy equipment repair services; Aircraft/aerospace flight instruments and guidance systems

(P-13762)
AMERICAN VISION WINDOWS INC
Also Called: American Vision Baths
2125 N Madera Rd Ste A (93065-7709)
PHONE.....................................805 582-1833
William Herren, CEO
Monica Estrada, *
Al Alfieri, *
EMP: 215 EST: 1999
SALES (est): 39.98MM Privately Held
Web: www.americanvisionwindows.com
SIC: 7699 1799 5031 Door and window repair; Home/office interiors finishing, furnishing and remodeling; Metal doors, sash and trim

(P-13763)
AMKO SERVICE COMPANY
17909 Adelanto Rd (92301-1745)
PHONE.....................................760 246-3600
Michael Medsker, Mgr
EMP: 70
Web: www.amkotech.com
SIC: 7699 Tank repair and cleaning services
HQ: Amko Service Company
3211 Brightwood Rd
Midvale OH
330 364-8857

(P-13764)
APPLIED FUSION LLC
1915 Republic Ave (94577-4220)
PHONE.....................................510 351-8314
EMP: 60 EST: 1972
SALES (est): 6.46MM Privately Held
Web: www.imgcompaniesllc.com
SIC: 7699 3599 Metal reshaping and replating services; Machine and other job shop work

(P-13765)
ARCLINE ELVTION SVCS HLDNGS LL
4 Embarcadero Ctr Ste 3460 (94111-4106)
PHONE.....................................860 805-2025
Mark Boelhouwer, Managing Member
Angelo Messina, CFO
EMP: 1000 EST: 2020
SALES (est): 2.65MM
SALES (corp-wide): 653.43MM Privately Held
SIC: 7699 Elevators: inspection, service, and repair
PA: Arcline Investment Management Lp
4 Embarcadero Ctr # 2660
San Francisco CA
415 801-4570

(P-13766)
CHROMALLOY SAN DIEGO CORP
7007 Consolidated Way (92121-2604)
PHONE.....................................858 877-2800
Armand F Lauzon Junior, CEO
Carlo Luzzatto, *
David G Albert, *
Michael Beffel, *
John Mckirdy, VP
EMP: 120 EST: 1986
SQ FT: 120,000
SALES (est): 16.69MM
SALES (corp-wide): 1.2B Privately Held
Web: www.chromalloy.com
SIC: 7699 3724 Aircraft and heavy equipment repair services; Aircraft engines and engine parts
HQ: Chromalloy American Llc
330 Blaisdell Rd
Orangeburg NY
845 230-7355

(P-13767)
CLEAN POWER FINANCE INC
50 Osgood Pl Ste 400 (94133-4644)
EMP: 102 EST: 2006
SALES (est): 3.72MM
SALES (corp-wide): 998.42MM Privately Held
Web: www.sprucepower.com
SIC: 7699 7389 Cleaning services; Financial services
HQ: Spruce Finance Inc.
50 Osgood Pl Ste 400
San Francisco CA
866 525-2123

(P-13768)
COLLECTORS UNIVERSE INC (PA)
Also Called: Collectors Universe
1610 E Saint Andrew Pl (92705-4931)
P.O. Box 6280 (92658-6280)
PHONE.....................................949 567-1234
Joseph J Orlando, CEO
Bruce A Stevens, *
Joseph J Wallace, CFO
EMP: 231 EST: 1986
SQ FT: 62,755

7699 - Repair Services, Nec (P-13769)

PRODUCTS & SERVICES SECTION

SALES (est): 78.89MM
SALES (corp-wide): 78.89MM Privately Held
Web: www.collectors.com
SIC: 7699 Hobby and collectors services

(P-13769)
CROTHALL SERVICES GROUP
14710 Northam St (90638-5620)
PHONE..............................714 562-9275
Frank Arcos, Brnch Mgr
EMP: 1208
SALES (corp-wide): 29.97B Privately Held
Web: www.crothall.com
SIC: 7699 Hospital equipment repair services
HQ: Crothall Services Group
   1500 Liberty Ridge Dr # 210
   Chesterbrook PA

(P-13770)
FLEETWOOD MOTOR HOMES-CALIFINC
Also Called: Fleetwood Homes
2350 Fleetwood Dr (92509-2409)
PHONE..............................951 274-2000
David Lewis, Brnch Mgr
EMP: 185
SIC: 7699 5271 Mobile home repair; Mobile home dealers
HQ: Fleetwood Motor Homes-Calif.Inc
   3125 Myers St
   Riverside CA
   951 354-3000

(P-13771)
FRESH WATER SYSTEMS INC
9265 Dowdy Dr Ste 202 (92126-6374)
PHONE..............................619 933-8275
Brian Folk, Brnch Mgr
EMP: 65
Web: www.freshwatersystems.com
SIC: 7699 5999 5074 Household appliance repair services; Water purification equipment; Water purification equipment
PA: Fresh Water Systems, Inc.
   2299 Ridge Rd
   Greenville SC

(P-13772)
GENESIS TECH PARTNERS LLC
21540 Plummer St Ste A (91311-4143)
PHONE..............................800 950-2647
EMP: 240 EST: 1998
SQ FT: 3,000
SALES (est): 319K
SALES (corp-wide): 3.7B Privately Held
SIC: 7699 Medical equipment repair, non-electric
HQ: Cohr, Inc.
   10510 Twin Lakes Pkwy
   Charlotte NC
   704 948-5700

(P-13773)
HAWKER PACIFIC AEROSPACE
11240 Sherman Way (91352-4942)
PHONE..............................818 765-6201
Bernd Riggers, CEO
Brian Carr, *
Troy Trower, *
◆ EMP: 355 EST: 1980
SQ FT: 193,000
SALES (est): 49.57MM
SALES (corp-wide): 34.03B Privately Held
Web: www.lufthansa-technik.com
SIC: 7699 5088 3728 Hydraulic equipment repair; Aircraft parts, nec; Aircraft parts and equipment, nec
HQ: Lufthansa Technik Ag
   Weg Beim Jager 193
   Hamburg HH
   4050700

(P-13774)
HRD AERO SYSTEMS INC (PA)
25555 Avenue Stanford (91355-1101)
PHONE..............................661 295-0670
Tom Salamone, Pr
Tim Mcbride, CFO
◆ EMP: 101 EST: 1986
SQ FT: 70,000
SALES (est): 12.22MM Privately Held
Web: www.hrd-aerosystems.com
SIC: 7699 8711 Aircraft and heavy equipment repair services; Aviation and/or aeronautical engineering

(P-13775)
HYDRATECH LLC (HQ)
453 Pollasky Ave Ste 106 (93612-1178)
PHONE..............................559 233-0876
Dave Ogden, *
▲ EMP: 84 EST: 1987
SALES (est): 9.26MM
SALES (corp-wide): 467.96MM Privately Held
Web: www.hydratechcylinders.com
SIC: 7699 3593 Hydraulic equipment repair; Fluid power cylinders, hydraulic or pneumatic
PA: Ligon Industries, Llc
   1927 1st Ave N Fl 5
   Birmingham AL
   205 322-3302

(P-13776)
INLAND BUSINESS MACHINES INC (DH)
Also Called: Inland Business Machines
1326 N Market Blvd (95834-1912)
PHONE..............................916 928-0770
EMP: 67 EST: 1977
SALES (est): 10.06MM
SALES (corp-wide): 7.11B Publicly Held
Web: www.inlandbusiness.us
SIC: 7699 5044 5999 Printing trades machinery and equipment repair; Office equipment; Photocopy machines
HQ: Xerox Business Solutions Inc
   8701 Florida Mining Blvd
   Tampa FL

(P-13777)
KETTMANN MACHINING INC
3590 Snell Ave Ste 10 (95136-1379)
PHONE..............................408 727-5538
EMP: 170
SALES (corp-wide): 3.38MM Privately Held
Web: www.kettmannmachining.com
SIC: 7699 Industrial machinery and equipment repair
PA: Kettmann Machining, Inc.
   5464 Skylane Blvd Ste A
   Santa Rosa CA

(P-13778)
KONE INC
15021 Wicks Blvd (94577-6621)
PHONE..............................510 351-5141
Drew Furman, Brnch Mgr
EMP: 92
Web: www.kone.us
SIC: 7699 3534 1796 Elevators: inspection, service, and repair; Elevators and moving stairways; Installing building equipment
HQ: Kone Inc.
   3333 Warrenville Rd
   Lisle IL
   630 577-1650

(P-13779)
LA HYDRO-JET ROOTER SVC INC
Also Called: La Hydrojet
10639 Wixom St (91352-4603)
PHONE..............................818 768-4225
Daniel Baldwin, Pr
Lori Baldwin, *
EMP: 68 EST: 1991
SALES (est): 9.61MM Privately Held
Web: www.lahydrojet.com
SIC: 7699 Sewer cleaning and rodding

(P-13780)
LEATHER FACTORY LP
Also Called: Tandy Leather 05
788 W Shaw Ave (93612-3216)
PHONE..............................559 297-7375
Delight Knight, Mgr
EMP: 88
SALES (corp-wide): 80.33MM Publicly Held
SIC: 7699 Leather goods, cleaning and repair
HQ: The Leather Factory L P
   3835 Union Deposit Rd
   Harrisburg PA

(P-13781)
MACH49 LLC
130 Solana Rd (94028-7329)
PHONE..............................415 939-1943
Russell Mark Lampert, Prin
EMP: 74 EST: 2014
SALES (est): 1.55MM Privately Held
Web: www.mach49.com
SIC: 7699 Industrial machinery and equipment repair

(P-13782)
MACS EQUIPMENT INC
187 S Madera Ave (93630-1101)
PHONE..............................559 846-6668
EMP: 78
SALES (corp-wide): 3.28MM Privately Held
SIC: 7699 5999 Farm machinery repair; Farm machinery, nec
PA: Mac's Equipment Inc.
   3690 S Madera Ave
   Kerman CA
   559 846-6534

(P-13783)
MARINE GROUP BOAT WORKS LLC
Also Called: Marine Group Boat Works
997 G St (91910-3414)
PHONE..............................619 427-6767
Herb Engel, Managing Member
Arthur E Engel, *
Todd Roberts, *
▲ EMP: 115 EST: 2008
SALES (est): 32.96MM Privately Held
Web: www.marinegroupbw.com
SIC: 7699 Boat repair

(P-13784)
MELAN INC
13700 Alton Pkwy Ste 154-2 (92618-1628)
PHONE..............................818 489-1745
Mickaiel H Kamran, Brnch Mgr
EMP: 85
SALES (corp-wide): 504.69K Privately Held
SIC: 7699 Industrial machinery and equipment repair
PA: Melan, Inc.
   23151 Verdugo Dr Ste 103
   Laguna Hills CA
   818 489-1745

(P-13785)
N & S TRACTOR CO (PA)
600 S Highway 59 (95341-6543)
P.O. Box 910 (95341-0910)
PHONE..............................209 383-5888
Arthur R Nutcher, CEO
Stephanie Nutcher, *
Mary Wallace, *
▲ EMP: 60 EST: 1954
SQ FT: 8,700
SALES (est): 27.66MM
SALES (corp-wide): 27.66MM Privately Held
Web: www.nstractor.com
SIC: 7699 5083 Farm machinery repair; Agricultural machinery and equipment

(P-13786)
NAVY UNITED STATES DEPARTMENT
Also Called: Maintenance Dept
311 Navy Base Ventura County (93042-0001)
PHONE..............................805 989-1328
Art Baulyut, Mgr
EMP: 250
Web: www.navy.mil
SIC: 7699 9711 Aircraft and heavy equipment repair services; Navy
HQ: United States Department Of The Navy
   1200 Navy Pentagon
   Washington DC

(P-13787)
NIACC-AVITECH TECHNOLOGIES INC (PA)
245 W Dakota Ave (93612-5608)
PHONE..............................559 291-2500
Jeff Andrews, CEO
Thomas S Irwin, *
Elizabeth R Letendre, *
EMP: 80 EST: 1983
SALES (est): 13.76MM
SALES (corp-wide): 13.76MM Privately Held
Web: www.heico.com
SIC: 7699 3471 Aircraft flight instrument repair; Plating of metals or formed products

(P-13788)
NORTHFIELD MEDICAL INC
13631 Pawnee Rd (92308-5880)
PHONE..............................248 268-2500
EMP: 78
SALES (corp-wide): 1.12B Publicly Held
Web: www.agilitihealth.com
SIC: 7699 Hospital equipment repair services
HQ: Northfield Medical, Inc.
   30275 Hudson Dr
   Novi MI

(P-13789)
OXYHEAL HEALTH GROUP INC
3224 Hoover Ave (91950-7224)
PHONE..............................619 336-2022
EMP: 250
SIC: 7699 Industrial equipment services

(P-13790)
PACIFIC COAST ELEVATOR CORP
Also Called: Amtech Elevator Services
3041 Roswell St (90065-2213)
PHONE..............................323 345-2550
Tom Bertsch, Brnch Mgr
EMP: 85
SALES (corp-wide): 13.69B Publicly Held
Web: www.amtechelevator.com

PRODUCTS & SERVICES SECTION

7699 - Repair Services, Nec (P-13809)

SIC: 7699 1796 Elevators: inspection, service, and repair; Elevator installation and conversion
HQ: Pacific Coast Elevator Corporation
1 Farm Springs Rd
Farmington CT
860 676-6000

(P-13791)
PEGGS COMPANY INC (PA)
4851 Felspar St (92509-3024)
P.O. Box 907 (91752-0907)
PHONE.................253 584-9548
Brett Nelson, *Pr*
Chresten Revelle Nelson, *
John L Peggs, *
◆ **EMP:** 100 **EST:** 1964
SQ FT: 80,000
SALES (est): 32.15MM
SALES (corp-wide): 32.15MM **Privately Held**
Web: www.thepeggscompany.com
SIC: 7699 3496 5046 7359 Shopping cart repair; Miscellaneous fabricated wire products; Commercial equipment, nec; Equipment rental and leasing, nec

(P-13792)
PKL SERVICES INC
14265 Danielson St (92064-8818)
PHONE.................858 679-1755
Samuel Flores Junior, *Pr*
Linda Young, *
David K Howell, *
Michael Nisley, *
Paul Callan, *
EMP: 160 **EST:** 2003
SQ FT: 6,000
SALES (est): 29.42MM **Privately Held**
Web: www.pklservices.com
SIC: 7699 Aircraft and heavy equipment repair services

(P-13793)
PROPULSION CONTROLS ENGRG (PA)
1620 Rigel St (92113-3832)
P.O. Box 13606 (92170-3606)
PHONE.................619 235-0961
David P Clapp, *CEO*
John P Reilly Iii, *Sec*
EMP: 70 **EST:** 1974
SQ FT: 22,000
SALES (est): 23.33MM
SALES (corp-wide): 23.33MM **Privately Held**
Web: www.pcesandiego.com
SIC: 7699 Boiler repair shop

(P-13794)
RAYMOND HANDLING CONCEPTS CORP (DH)
Also Called: Rhcc
41400 Boyce Rd (94538-3113)
PHONE.................510 745-7500
TOLL FREE: 800
James Wilcox, *Pr*
EMP: 60 **EST:** 1987
SQ FT: 32,000
SALES (est): 61.65MM **Privately Held**
Web: www.raymondwest.com
SIC: 7699 5084 7359 7629 Industrial machinery and equipment repair; Materials handling machinery; Equipment rental and leasing, nec; Electrical repair shops
HQ: The Raymond Corporation
22 S Canal St
Greene NY
607 656-2311

(P-13795)
RICHMOND SANITARY SERVICE INC (HQ)
Also Called: Crockett Garbage Service
3260 Blume Dr Ste 100 (94806-1960)
P.O. Box 4100 (94804-0100)
PHONE.................510 262-7100
Richard Granzella, *Pr*
Joe Della Zoppa, *
Dennis Varni, *
Caesar Nuti, *
Loyd Bonfante, *
▲ **EMP:** 200 **EST:** 1924
SALES (est): 9.49MM
SALES (corp-wide): 13.51B **Publicly Held**
Web: www.richmondsanitaryservices.com
SIC: 7699 Septic tank cleaning service
PA: Republic Services, Inc.
18500 N Allied Way # 100
Phoenix AZ
480 627-2700

(P-13796)
RUSSELL-WARNER INC
Also Called: Roto-Rooter
24971 Avenue Stanford (91355-1278)
P.O. Box 74 (89411-0074)
PHONE.................661 257-9200
EMP: 240
SIC: 7699 6794 1711 Sewer cleaning and rodding; Patent owners and lessors; Plumbing, heating, air-conditioning

(P-13797)
SA CAMP PUMP COMPANY
Also Called: SA Camp Pump and Drilling Co
17876 Zerker Rd (93308-9221)
P.O. Box 82575 (93380-2575)
PHONE.................661 399-2976
James S Camp, *Pr*
EMP: 60 **EST:** 1952
SQ FT: 10,000
SALES (est): 18.46MM
SALES (corp-wide): 22.14MM **Privately Held**
Web: www.sacampcompanies.com
SIC: 7699 3561 Agricultural equipment repair services; Pumps and pumping equipment
PA: S A Camp Companies
17876 Zerker Rd
Bakersfield CA
661 399-4451

(P-13798)
SCHINDLER ELEVATOR CORPORATION
16450 Foothill Blvd Ste 200 (91342)
PHONE.................818 336-3000
Lance Howard, *Mgr*
EMP: 240
Web: us.schindler.com
SIC: 7699 Elevators: inspection, service, and repair
HQ: Schindler Elevator Corporation
20 Whippany Rd
Morristown NJ
973 397-6500

(P-13799)
SNOW WELL SERVICE INC
1150 Black Gold Rd (93308-8800)
P.O. Box 1125 (93268-1125)
PHONE.................661 765-7980
Candi Snow, *Pr*
Jerry Snow, *
EMP: 65 **EST:** 2001
SALES (est): 7.38MM **Privately Held**
Web: www.snowwellservice.com
SIC: 7699 Pumps and pumping equipment repair

(P-13800)
SOUTH BAY SAND BLSTG TANK CLG
Also Called: Sbsbtc
326 W 30th St (91950-7206)
P.O. Box 13009 (92170-3009)
PHONE.................619 238-8338
Canuto Lopez, *CEO*
EMP: 100 **EST:** 1991
SQ FT: 60,000
SALES (est): 11.96MM **Privately Held**
Web: www.sobaysandblast.com
SIC: 7699 4212 Ship boiler and tank cleaning and repair, contractors; Hazardous waste transport

(P-13801)
SUNVAIR AEROSPACE GROUP INC (PA)
29145 The Old Rd (91355-1015)
PHONE.................661 294-3777
Udo Reider, *CEO*
Glenn Miller, *
EMP: 80 **EST:** 2014
SQ FT: 77,000
SALES (est): 30.27MM
SALES (corp-wide): 30.27MM **Privately Held**
Web: www.sunvair.com
SIC: 7699 Aircraft and heavy equipment repair services

(P-13802)
SURVIVAL SYSTEMS INTL INC (PA)
Also Called: Ssi
34140 Valley Center Rd (92082-6017)
P.O. Box 1855 (92082-1855)
PHONE.................760 749-6800
George Beatty, *CEO*
Mark Beatty, *
Colin Hooper, *
▲ **EMP:** 95 **EST:** 1968
SQ FT: 100,000
SALES (est): 20.08MM
SALES (corp-wide): 20.08MM **Privately Held**
Web: www.survivalsystemsinternational.com
SIC: 7699 3531 3086 Industrial equipment services; Winches; Plastics foam products

(P-13803)
TARSCO HOLDINGS LLC
11905 Regentview Ave (90241-5515)
PHONE.................562 869-0200
Terry S Warren, *Managing Member*
EMP: 121 **EST:** 2007
SALES (est): 2.91MM
SALES (corp-wide): 164.48MM **Privately Held**
Web: www.tfwarren.com
SIC: 7699 Tank repair
PA: T.F. Warren Group Inc
57 Old Onondaga Rd W
Brantford ON
519 756-8222

(P-13804)
TECH KNOWLEDGE ASSOCIATES LLC
Also Called: Tka
1 Centerpointe Dr Ste 200 (90623-1050)
PHONE.................714 735-3810
Joe Randolph, *CEO*
Ed Wong, *
Steve Gilbert, *
EMP: 80 **EST:** 2011
SALES (est): 24.98MM
SALES (corp-wide): 32.76MM **Privately Held**
Web: www.ii-techknow.com
SIC: 7699 Medical equipment repair, non-electric
HQ: St. Joseph Health System
3345 Michelson Dr Ste 100
Irvine CA
949 381-4000

(P-13805)
TED LEVINE DRUM CO (PA)
1817 Chico Ave (91733-2943)
P.O. Box 3246 (91733-0246)
PHONE.................626 579-1084
TOLL FREE: 800
Ozzie Levine, *Pr*
EMP: 80 **EST:** 1983
SQ FT: 200,000
SALES (est): 9.41MM
SALES (corp-wide): 9.41MM **Privately Held**
Web: www.tldrumco.com
SIC: 7699 4959 3412 Industrial equipment services; Sanitary services, nec; Metal barrels, drums, and pails

(P-13806)
TODD PLUMBING INC
Also Called: Todd Plumbing
1701 Clancy Ct (93291-5256)
P.O. Box 7629 (93290-7629)
PHONE.................559 651-5820
EMP: 120
Web: www.toddplumbing.com
SIC: 7699 Septic tank cleaning service

(P-13807)
UNITED CALIFORNIA GLASS & DOOR
Also Called: California Glass
745 Cesar Chavez (94124-1211)
PHONE.................415 824-8500
Judith Ticktin, *Pr*
▲ **EMP:** 70 **EST:** 1991
SQ FT: 31,000
SALES (est): 17.09MM **Privately Held**
Web: www.ucgd.com
SIC: 7699 1793 Door and window repair; Glass and glazing work

(P-13808)
UPWIND BLADE SOLUTIONS INC
2869 Historic Decatur Rd Ste 100, (92106-6176)
PHONE.................866 927-3142
Marty Crotty, *CEO*
Bo Thisted, *Pr*
Bryan Coggins, *CFO*
EMP: 288 **EST:** 2011
SALES (est): 4.58MM
SALES (corp-wide): 15.08B **Privately Held**
SIC: 7699 Pumps and pumping equipment repair
HQ: Upwind Solutions, Inc.
1417 Nw Everett St
Portland OR

(P-13809)
WARDLOW 2 LP (PA)
333 S Grand Ave Ste 4070 (90071-1544)
PHONE.................562 432-8066
Steven B Mcleod, *Pt*
Joe Gregorio, *Pt*
EMP: 99 **EST:** 2007
SALES (est): 20.38MM **Privately Held**

7699 - Repair Services, Nec (P-13810)

SIC: 7699 Construction equipment repair

(P-13810)
WHITE HOUSE SANITATION INC
18916 Seaton Ave (92570-8720)
P.O. Box 3038 (90605-0038)
PHONE.................................951 943-1550
Karen A Blackburn, *CEO*
Tim Blackburn, *
EMP: 63 **EST:** 1985
SQ FT: 6,000
SALES (est): 806.6K
SALES (corp-wide): 39.23MM **Privately Held**
Web: www.whitehousesanitation.com
SIC: 7699 7359 Septic tank cleaning service; Portable toilet rental
PA: Universal Waste Systems, Inc.
    9016 Norwalk Blvd
    Santa Fe Springs CA
    562 695-8236

(P-13811)
WHITING DOOR MFG CORP
301 S Milliken Ave (91761-7800)
PHONE.................................909 877-0120
Abdullah Eren, *Brnch Mgr*
EMP: 92
SQ FT: 5,400
SALES (corp-wide): 101.87MM **Privately Held**
Web: www.whitingdoor.com
SIC: 7699 3713 5531 5211 Door and window repair; Truck and bus bodies; Truck equipment and parts; Garage doors, sale and installation
PA: Whiting Door Mfg Corp
    113 Cedar St
    Akron NY
    716 542-5427

(P-13812)
WOODSIDE ELECTRONICS CORP
Also Called: Weco
1311 Blue Grass Pl (95776-5918)
PHONE.................................530 666-9190
▲ **EMP:** 92 **EST:** 1982
SALES (est): 21.55MM
SALES (corp-wide): 1.84B **Privately Held**
Web: www.wecotek.com
SIC: 7699 3523 Farm machinery repair; Farm machinery and equipment
HQ: Duravant Llc
    3500 Lacey Rd Ste 290
    Downers Grove IL

(P-13813)
ZEF SCIENTIFIC INC (PA)
Also Called: Zef SCI
9920 Pacific Heights Blvd Ste 150 (92121)
PHONE.................................781 791-5799
Mohammed El Fallah, *Pr*
Squad Sobhy, *
▲ **EMP:** 63 **EST:** 2005
SALES (est): 17MM **Privately Held**
Web: www.zefsci.com
SIC: 7699 Laboratory instrument repair

7812 Motion Picture And Video Production

(P-13814)
ABC FAMILY WORLDWIDE INC (HQ)
Also Called: ABC Family
500 S Buena Vista St (91521-0001)
PHONE.................................818 560-1000
EMP: 500 **EST:** 1996
SALES (est): 268.48MM
SALES (corp-wide): 82.72B **Publicly Held**
Web: www.thewaltdisneycompany.com
SIC: 7812 4841 Cartoon production, television; Cable and other pay television services
PA: The Walt Disney Company
    500 S Buena Vista St
    Burbank CA
    818 560-1000

(P-13815)
ADVANCED DIGITAL SERVICES INC (PA)
Also Called: A D S
948 N Cahuenga Blvd (90038-2615)
PHONE.................................323 962-8585
Thomas Engdahl, *Pr*
Andrew Mcintyre, *Ch Bd*
Brad Weyl, *
▲ **EMP:** 87 **EST:** 1989
SQ FT: 33,000
SALES (est): 9.51MM **Privately Held**
Web: www.adshollywood.com
SIC: 7812 7819 Video tape production; Film processing, editing, and titling: motion picture

(P-13816)
ALLIED ENTERTAINMENT GROUP INC (PA)
Also Called: Allied Artists International
273 W Allen Ave (91746)
PHONE.................................626 330-0600
Greg Hammond, *Pr*
John Mason, *
Ashley D Posner, *
Kim Richards, *
Robert Fitzpatrick, *
♦ **EMP:** 325 **EST:** 1999
SQ FT: 60,000
SALES (est): 7.53MM
SALES (corp-wide): 7.53MM **Privately Held**
Web: www.alliedentertainment.com
SIC: 7812 Video production

(P-13817)
AMBLIN PARTNERS
100 Universal City Plz (91608-1002)
PHONE.................................818 733-9665
EMP: 71 **EST:** 2019
SALES (est): 2.52MM **Privately Held**
Web: www.amblin.com
SIC: 7812 Motion picture and video production

(P-13818)
ANONYMOUS CONTENT LLC (PA)
8501 Washington Blvd (90232-7443)
PHONE.................................310 558-6000
▲ **EMP:** 60 **EST:** 1999
SALES (est): 250MM
SALES (corp-wide): 250MM **Privately Held**
Web: www.anonymouscontent.com
SIC: 7812 Video production

(P-13819)
ARTISAN ENTERTAINMENT INC
2700 Colorado Ave Ste 200 (90404-5502)
PHONE.................................310 449-9200
Wayne Levin, *Pr*
James W Barge, *
Brian James Gladstone, *
Kristine Klimczak, *
EMP: 1000 **EST:** 1988
SALES (est): 21.01MM
SALES (corp-wide): 3.6B **Privately Held**
SIC: 7812 Motion picture production
HQ: Lions Gate Entertainment Inc.
    2700 Colorado Ave Ste 200
    Santa Monica CA
    310 449-9200

(P-13820)
BARNSTORM VFX INC
2860 N Naomi St (91504-2023)
PHONE.................................818 792-1899
Bharti Sattar, *Managing Member*
EMP: 91 **EST:** 2015
SALES (est): 9.8MM **Privately Held**
Web: www.barnstormvfx.com
SIC: 7812 Video production

(P-13821)
BENTO BOX ENTERTAINMENT LLC
5161 Lankershim Blvd Ste 120 (91601-3718)
PHONE.................................818 333-7700
Scott Greenberg, *CEO*
Brett Coker, *COO*
EMP: 300 **EST:** 2009
SALES (est): 40.55MM
SALES (corp-wide): 14.91B **Publicly Held**
Web: www.bentoboxent.com
SIC: 7812 Motion picture production and distribution
HQ: Fox Television Stations, Inc.
    1999 S Bundy Dr
    Los Angeles CA
    310 584-2000

(P-13822)
BLIND DECKER PRODUCTIONS INC
3000 Olympic Blvd (90404-5073)
PHONE.................................310 264-4247
EMP: 67
SIC: 7812 Motion picture production
PA: Blind Decker Productions Inc
    8621 Hayden Pl
    Culver City CA

(P-13823)
BRILLSTEIN ENTRMT PARTNERS LLC (HQ)
Also Called: Brillstein Grey Entertainment
9150 Wilshire Blvd Ste 350 (90212-3453)
PHONE.................................310 205-5100
Brad Grey, *Pr*
EMP: 90 **EST:** 1980
SALES (est): 16.29MM
SALES (corp-wide): 116.26MM **Privately Held**
Web: www.bepmedia.com
SIC: 7812 Television film production
PA: Wasserman Media Group, Llc
    10900 Wilshire Blvd Fl 12
    Los Angeles CA
    310 407-0200

(P-13824)
BUDDY STOOPID STOODIOS LLC
220 S Flower St (91502-2101)
PHONE.................................818 333-8600
EMP: 106 **EST:** 2011
SALES (est): 6.2MM **Privately Held**
Web: www.leagueofbuddies.com
SIC: 7812 Cartoon motion picture production

(P-13825)
BUENA VISTA INTERNATIONAL INC
350 S Buena Vista St (91521-0004)
PHONE.................................818 295-5200
EMP: 115
SALES (corp-wide): 82.72B **Publicly Held**
SIC: 7812 7822 3695 Video tape production; Video tapes, recorded: wholesale; Video recording tape, blank
HQ: Buena Vista International Inc
    500 S Buena Vista St
    Burbank CA
    818 560-1000

(P-13826)
BUNIM-MURRAY PRODUCTIONS
Also Called: Bmp
1015 Grandview Ave (91201-2205)
PHONE.................................818 756-5100
Jon Murray, *
Gil Goldschein, *
Mark Lebowitz, *
Julie Pizzi, *
▲ **EMP:** 150 **EST:** 1989
SQ FT: 20,000
SALES (est): 31.14MM
SALES (corp-wide): 12.61MM **Privately Held**
Web: www.bunim-murray.com
SIC: 7812 Television film production
HQ: Banijay Entertainment
    5 Rue Francois 1er
    Paris
    143189191

(P-13827)
CBS STUDIOS INC
4024 Radford Ave (91604-2190)
PHONE.................................818 655-5160
David Stapf, *CEO*
Eris Gray, *CFO*
Christa A D'alimonte, *Sec*
EMP: 150 **EST:** 2005
SALES (est): 12.4MM **Privately Held**
Web: www.radfordsc.com
SIC: 7812 Motion picture and video production

(P-13828)
CHM PRODUCTIONS INC
Also Called: Tmz TV
8033 W Sunset Blvd Ste 875 (90046-2401)
PHONE.................................818 972-8433
Pamela Russo, *Prin*
EMP: 82 **EST:** 2009
SALES (est): 692.47K **Privately Held**
SIC: 7812 Television film production

(P-13829)
COLUMBIA PICTURES INDS INC
4024 Radford Ave (91604-2101)
PHONE.................................818 655-5820
Cynthia Phillips, *Prin*
EMP: 85
SIC: 7812 Motion picture and video production
HQ: Columbia Pictures Industries, Inc.
    10202 Washington Blvd
    Culver City CA
    310 244-4000

(P-13830)
COLUMBIA PICTURES INDS INC (DH)
Also Called: Columbia Pictures
10202 Washington Blvd (90232-3119)
PHONE.................................310 244-4000
Michael Lynton, *CEO*

PRODUCTS & SERVICES SECTION
7812 - Motion Picture And Video Production (P-13852)

Ronald Jacobi, *Ex VP*
Doug Belgrad, *Pr*
Edgar Howells, *CFO*
EMP: 200 **EST:** 1987
SALES (est): 69.43MM **Privately Held**
SIC: 7812 Motion picture production and distribution
HQ: Sony Pictures Entertainment, Inc.
10202 Washington Blvd
Culver City CA
310 244-4000

(P-13831)
CONCORD VERANDA CINEMA LLC
Also Called: Veranda Luxe Cinema
2035 Diamond Blvd Ste 150 (94520-5701)
P.O. Box 750595 (94975-0595)
PHONE.................................707 762-0990
EMP: 142 **EST:** 2016
SALES (est): 3.98MM **Privately Held**
SIC: 7812 7832 Motion picture production; Motion picture theaters, except drive-in

(P-13832)
CRAFTY APES LLC (PA)
127 Lomita St (90245-4114)
PHONE.................................310 837-3900
EMP: 542 **EST:** 2011
SALES (est): 18.63MM
SALES (corp-wide): 18.63MM **Privately Held**
Web: www.craftyapes.com
SIC: 7812 Video production

(P-13833)
CREATIVE PARK PRODUCTIONS LLC
Also Called: Universal Studios
100 Universal City Plz (91608-1002)
PHONE.................................818 622-3702
EMP: 157 **EST:** 2002
SALES (est): 19.77MM **Privately Held**
SIC: 7812 Motion picture and video production

(P-13834)
CRUNCHYROLL LLC (DH)
Also Called: Funimation Entertainment
10202 Washington Blvd (90232-3119)
PHONE.................................972 355-7300
General Fukunaga, *Pr*
Greg Stevenson, *CFO*
▲ **EMP:** 82 **EST:** 1994
SALES (est): 23.78MM **Privately Held**
Web: www.funimation.com
SIC: 7812 4813 7822 Cartoon production, television; Internet host services; Video tapes, recorded: wholesale
HQ: Sony Pictures Entertainment, Inc.
10202 Washington Blvd
Culver City CA
310 244-4000

(P-13835)
CYBERNET ENTERTAINMENT LLC
1800 Mission St (94103-3502)
PHONE.................................415 865-0230
Peter Ackworth, *Managing Member*
EMP: 115 **EST:** 1998
SALES (est): 9.01MM **Privately Held**
Web: www.cybernetentertainment.com
SIC: 7812 Video production

(P-13836)
DARK BURN CREATIVE LLC
21122 Erwin St (91367-3712)
PHONE.................................818 471-4948

Chase Boyajian, *Prin*
EMP: 76 **EST:** 2017
SALES (est): 2.09MM **Privately Held**
Web: www.darkburn.com
SIC: 7812 Video production

(P-13837)
DELUXE MEDIA SERVICES LLC
1377 N Serrano Ave (90027-5623)
PHONE.................................323 462-6171
John Suh, *Prin*
EMP: 60 **EST:** 2012
SALES (est): 1.8MM **Privately Held**
SIC: 7812 Video production

(P-13838)
DIGITAL DOMAIN 30 INC (PA)
12641 Beatrice St (90066-7003)
PHONE.................................213 797-3100
Daniel Seah, *CEO*
Od Welch, *
Amit Chopra, *
Rich Flier Md, *Prin*
John Lagerling, *
EMP: 300 **EST:** 2012
SALES (est): 72.99MM
SALES (corp-wide): 72.99MM **Privately Held**
Web: www.digitaldomain.com
SIC: 7812 Video production

(P-13839)
DISNEY ENTERPRISES INC
Also Called: Disney
700 W Ball Rd (92802-1843)
P.O. Box 3232 (92803-3232)
PHONE.................................714 781-1651
Matt Ouimet, *Brnch Mgr*
EMP: 213
SALES (corp-wide): 82.72B **Publicly Held**
Web: www.disney.com
SIC: 7812 Motion picture production and distribution
HQ: Disney Enterprises, Inc.
500 S Buena Vista St
Burbank CA
818 560-1000

(P-13840)
DISNEY ENTERPRISES INC
Also Called: Disney
1101 Flower St (91201-2415)
PHONE.................................818 553-4103
EMP: 103
SALES (corp-wide): 82.72B **Publicly Held**
Web: www.disney.com
SIC: 7812 Motion picture production and distribution, television
HQ: Disney Enterprises, Inc.
500 S Buena Vista St
Burbank CA
818 560-1000

(P-13841)
DISNEY ENTERPRISES INC
Also Called: Disney
1313 S Harbor Blvd (92802-2309)
PHONE.................................407 397-6000
Marlene Madrid, *Mgr*
EMP: 100
SALES (corp-wide): 82.72B **Publicly Held**
Web: www.thewaltdisneycompany.com
SIC: 7812 Motion picture production and distribution, television
HQ: Disney Enterprises, Inc.
500 S Buena Vista St
Burbank CA
818 560-1000

(P-13842)
DISNEY INCORPORATED (DH)
Also Called: Disney
500 S Buena Vista St (91521-0001)
PHONE.................................818 560-1000
Matthew L Mcginnis, *CEO*
Sanford M Litvack, *
▲ **EMP:** 150 **EST:** 1952
SALES (est): 411.73MM
SALES (corp-wide): 82.72B **Publicly Held**
Web: www.disney.com
SIC: 7812 Motion picture production and distribution
HQ: Disney Enterprises, Inc.
500 S Buena Vista St
Burbank CA
818 560-1000

(P-13843)
DREAMWORKS ANIMATION PUBG LLC
1000 Flower St (91201-3007)
PHONE.................................818 695-5000
EMP: 975 **EST:** 2014
SALES (est): 948.34K
SALES (corp-wide): 121.43B **Publicly Held**
SIC: 7812 Motion picture and video production
HQ: Dwa Holdings, Llc
1000 Flower St
Glendale CA
818 695-5000

(P-13844)
DWA HOLDINGS LLC (DH)
1000 Flower St (91201-3007)
PHONE.................................818 695-5000
Mellody Hobson, *Prin*
Jeffrey Katzenberg, *
Ann Daly, *
Fazal Merchant, *
Steven A Adams, *CAO*
EMP: 97 **EST:** 1994
SQ FT: 500,000
SALES (est): 501.05MM
SALES (corp-wide): 121.43B **Publicly Held**
Web: research.dreamworks.com
SIC: 7812 Cartoon motion picture production
HQ: Nbcuniversal Media, Llc
30 Rockefeller Plz Fl 2
New York NY

(P-13845)
EFILM LLC
Also Called: E Film Digital Labratories
1144 N Las Palmas Ave (90038-1209)
PHONE.................................323 463-7041
Dominik J Schmidt, *
EMP: 150 **EST:** 2002
SALES (est): 22.96MM **Privately Held**
Web: www.company3.com
SIC: 7812 Video production

(P-13846)
ENDEMOL SHINE NORTH AMERICA
5161 Lankershim Blvd Ste 400 (91601-4962)
PHONE.................................747 529-8000
Sharon Levy, *CEO*
EMP: 84 **EST:** 2015
SALES (est): 1.76MM **Privately Held**
Web: www.endemolshine.us
SIC: 7812 Motion picture production

(P-13847)
EVOLUTION FILM & TAPE INC
Also Called: Evolution Media
3310 W Vanowen St (91505-1239)
PHONE.................................818 260-0300
Douglas A Ross, *CEO*
Alex Baskin, *
Greg B Stewart, *
EMP: 67 **EST:** 1987
SQ FT: 25,000
SALES (est): 7.48MM **Privately Held**
Web: www.evolutionusa.com
SIC: 7812 Video production

(P-13848)
FANCY LIFE ENTERPRISES LLC (PA) ✪
Also Called: Fancy Life Studios
8030 La Mesa Blvd Pmb 3039 (91942-0335)
PHONE.................................619 560-9890
Seana Earls, *Managing Member*
EMP: 125 **EST:** 2022
SALES (est): 12MM
SALES (corp-wide): 12MM **Privately Held**
Web: fancy-life-studios.business.site
SIC: 7812 Television film production

(P-13849)
FILM ROMAN LLC
6320 Canoga Ave Ste 450 (91367-2526)
PHONE.................................818 748-4000
Dana Booton, *Mgr*
EMP: 214
SQ FT: 87,000
SALES (corp-wide): 3.6B **Privately Held**
Web: www.filmroman.com
SIC: 7812 Cartoon motion picture production
HQ: Film Roman, Llc.
8900 Liberty Cir
Englewood CO
720 852-6327

(P-13850)
FOCUS FEATURES LLC (DH)
1540 2nd St Ste 200 (90401-3513)
EMP: 89 **EST:** 1999
SQ FT: 30,000
SALES (est): 22.81MM
SALES (corp-wide): 121.43B **Publicly Held**
Web: www.focusfeatures.com
SIC: 7812 Motion picture production and distribution
HQ: Nbcuniversal Media, Llc
30 Rockefeller Plz Fl 2
New York NY

(P-13851)
FOX NET INC
Also Called: 20th Century Fox Studio
10201 W Pico Blvd (90064-2606)
PHONE.................................310 369-1000
Chase Carey, *Pr*
EMP: 1426 **EST:** 1992
SALES (est): 30.76MM
SALES (corp-wide): 82.72B **Publicly Held**
SIC: 7812 Motion picture and video production
HQ: Twentieth Television, Inc.
10201 W Pico Blvd
Los Angeles CA

(P-13852)
HARPO PRODUCTIONS INC
Also Called: Harpo Entertainment Group
7619 N Patriot Way (91405-5648)
PHONE.................................312 633-1000
Oprah Winfrey, *Ch Bd*
Tim Bennett, *

7812 - Motion Picture And Video Production (P-13853)

Doug Pattison, *
Bill Becker, *General Vice President**
EMP: 200 EST: 1988
SALES (est): 9.09MM Privately Held
SIC: 7812 Television film production

(P-13853)
HERZOG & COMPANY
4640 Lankershim Blvd Ste 400
(91602-1841)
PHONE..................818 762-4640
Jonathan Buss, *Dir*
EMP: 74 EST: 2015
SALES (est): 4.28MM Privately Held
Web: www.herzogcompany.com
SIC: 7812 Television film production

(P-13854)
HIGH TECHNOLOGY VIDEO INC
Also Called: H T V
10900 Ventura Blvd (91604-3340)
PHONE..................323 969-8822
Jim Hardy, *CEO*
Steve Weiner, *
EMP: 73 EST: 1995
SQ FT: 30,000
SALES (est): 11.04MM Privately Held
Web: www.illuminatehollywood.com
SIC: 7812 Video production

(P-13855)
HUNGRY HEART MEDIA INC
Also Called: Wondros
5450 W Washington Blvd (90016-1135)
PHONE..................323 951-0010
Jesse Dylan, *CEO*
EMP: 140 EST: 2011
SALES (est): 21.16MM Privately Held
Web: www.wondros.com
SIC: 7812 8742 Motion picture and video production; Marketing consulting services

(P-13856)
IF LIVE LLC (PA)
2254 S Sepulveda Blvd (90064-1812)
PHONE..................323 957-6868
EMP: 69 EST: 2001
SALES (est): 1.59MM
SALES (corp-wide): 1.59MM Privately Held
Web: www.lalive.com
SIC: 7812 Motion picture and video production

(P-13857)
IGNITION CREATIVE LLC
1201 W 5th St Ste T1100 (90017-5158)
PHONE..................310 315-6300
EMP: 82 EST: 2003
SALES (est): 10.13MM Privately Held
Web: www.ignitioncreative.com
SIC: 7812 Video production

(P-13858)
JERRY BRUCKHEIMER INC
Also Called: Bruckheimer, Jerry Films
1631 10th St (90404-3705)
PHONE..................310 664-6260
Jerry Bruckheimer, *Pr*
EMP: 70 EST: 1987
SALES (est): 10.27MM Privately Held
Web: www.jbfilms.com
SIC: 7812 Television film production

(P-13859)
LEGENDARY ENTERTAINMENT LLC
2900 W Alameda Ave Unit 1500
(91505-4220)
PHONE..................818 688-7003
Thomas Tull, *CEO*
EMP: 60 EST: 2009
SALES (est): 10.09MM Privately Held
Web: www.legendary.com
SIC: 7812 Motion picture production

(P-13860)
LEMONLIGHT MEDIA INC
226 S Glasgow Ave (90301-2106)
PHONE..................310 402-0275
Hope Horner, *CEO*
EMP: 67 EST: 2018
SALES (est): 3.03MM Privately Held
Web: www.lemonlight.com
SIC: 7812 Video tape production

(P-13861)
LIONS GATE FILMS INC
2700 Colorado Ave (90404-3553)
PHONE..................310 449-9200
Jon Feltheimer, *Pr*
James Keegan, *
Steve Beeks, *
EMP: 147 EST: 1998
SQ FT: 30,000
SALES (est): 43.79MM
SALES (corp-wide): 3.6B Privately Held
Web: www.lionsgate.com
SIC: 7812 Motion picture production
HQ: Lions Gate Entertainment Inc.
2700 Colorado Ave Ste 200
Santa Monica CA
310 449-9200

(P-13862)
LUCASFILM LTD LLC (DH)
Also Called: Lucasfilm Coml Productions
1110 Gorgas Ave Bldg C (94129-1406)
P.O. Box 29901 (94129-0901)
PHONE..................415 623-1000
▲ EMP: 250 EST: 1971
SALES (est): 81.35MM
SALES (corp-wide): 82.72B Publicly Held
Web: www.lucasfilm.com
SIC: 7812 6794 Motion picture production and distribution; Patent owners and lessors
HQ: Disney Enterprises, Inc.
500 S Buena Vista St
Burbank CA
818 560-1000

(P-13863)
LUMA PICTURES INC
1453 3rd Street Promenade Ste 400
(90401-3428)
PHONE..................310 888-8738
Payam Shohadai, *Pr*
John Betdul, *
EMP: 171 EST: 2002
SALES (est): 14.74MM Privately Held
Web: www.luma.inc
SIC: 7812 Motion picture and video production

(P-13864)
MERLOT FILM PRODUCTIONS INC
Also Called: CBS Network News
7800 Beverly Blvd (90036-2112)
PHONE..................323 575-2906
EMP: 164 EST: 1996
SALES (est): 14.15MM
SALES (corp-wide): 30.15B Publicly Held
SIC: 7812 4833 Motion picture and video production; Television broadcasting stations
HQ: Cbs Broadcasting Inc.
524 W 57th St
New York NY
212 975-4321

(P-13865)
METRO-GOLDWYN-MAYER INC (DH)
Also Called: MGM
245 N Beverly Dr (90210-5319)
PHONE..................310 449-3000
EMP: 300 EST: 1996
SQ FT: 131,400
SALES (est): 1.04B Publicly Held
Web: www.mgm.com
SIC: 7812 Motion picture production and distribution
HQ: Mgm Holdings Ii, Inc.
245 N Beverly Dr
Beverly Hills CA
310 449-3000

(P-13866)
MIRAMAX LLC
1901 Avenue Of The Stars Ste 2000
(90067-6021)
PHONE..................310 409-4321
Bill Block, *CEO*
EMP: 71 EST: 2011
SALES (est): 8.54MM Privately Held
Web: www.miramax.com
SIC: 7812 Motion picture production and distribution
PA: Bein Media Group Wll
Behind Ahli Hospital, Al Asmakh
Tower No. 864, Zone 63
Doha

(P-13867)
MOVELLA TECHNOLOGIES NA INC
Also Called: Xsens North America Inc.
101 N Pacific Coast Hwy Ste 306 (90245)
PHONE..................310 481-1800
Casper Peeters, *Pr*
EMP: 77 EST: 2009
SALES (est): 4.89MM Publicly Held
SIC: 7812 Motion picture production
HQ: Movella Technologies B.V.
Pantheon 6 A + 8a
Enschede OV

(P-13868)
NBC UNIVERSAL INC
100 Universal City Plz (91608-1002)
◆ EMP: 532
SIC: 7812 Motion picture production and distribution

(P-13869)
NEW PARADIGM PRODUCTIONS INC (PA)
Also Called: Edelman Productions
39 Mesa St Ste 212 (94129-1019)
PHONE..................415 924-8000
Steve Edelman, *Pr*
EMP: 100 EST: 1981
SQ FT: 8,500
SALES (est): 2.43MM
SALES (corp-wide): 2.43MM Privately Held
Web: www.edelmanproductions.com
SIC: 7812 Video production

(P-13870)
NEW REGENCY PRODUCTIONS INC (PA)
Also Called: Regency Enterprises
10201 W Pico Blvd Bldg 12 (90064-2606)
PHONE..................424 446-4092
Arnon Milchan, *Pr*
Mimi Mtseng, *
Yariv Milchan, *
Brad Weston, *
Yariv Milchan, *
▼ EMP: 60 EST: 1991
SQ FT: 13,000
SALES (est): 17.17MM Privately Held
Web: www.newregency.com
SIC: 7812 Video production

(P-13871)
NW ENTERTAINMENT INC (PA)
Also Called: New Wave Entertainment
2660 W Olive Ave (91505-4525)
PHONE..................818 295-5000
Paul Apel, *CEO*
Alan Duke, *
Greg Woertz, *
Brian Volk-weiss, *Pr*
Matt Sample, *
▲ EMP: 110 EST: 1986
SQ FT: 40,000
SALES (est): 37.24MM
SALES (corp-wide): 37.24MM Privately Held
SIC: 7812 Motion picture production

(P-13872)
ORION PICTURES CORPORATION
245 N Beverly Dr (90210-5319)
PHONE..................310 449-3000
Alex Yemenidjian, *Ch Bd*
Daniel J Taylor, *
EMP: 1000 EST: 1995
SALES (est): 20.77MM Publicly Held
SIC: 7812 Motion picture production and distribution
HQ: Metro-Goldwyn-Mayer, Inc.
245 N Beverly Dr
Beverly Hills CA

(P-13873)
PARAMOUNT PICTURES CORPORATION (HQ)
Also Called: Paramount Studios
5555 Melrose Ave (90038-3197)
PHONE..................323 956-5000
Brian Robbins, *Pr*
Jim Gianopulos, *Ch Bd*
Rob Moore, *V Ch Bd*
Frederick Huntsberry, *COO*
Mark Badagliacca, *Ex VP*
◆ EMP: 1700 EST: 1912
SALES (est): 648.72MM
SALES (corp-wide): 30.15B Publicly Held
Web: www.paramountstudiotour.com
SIC: 7812 4833 7829 5099 Motion picture production and distribution, television; Television broadcasting stations; Motion picture distribution services; Video cassettes, accessories and supplies
PA: Paramount Global
1515 Broadway
New York NY
212 258-6000

(P-13874)
PARAMOUNT TELEVISION SERVICE
Also Called: Paramount Pictures
5555 Melrose Ave Rm 204 (90038-3989)
PHONE..................323 956-5000
Brad Grey, *CEO*
EMP: 73 EST: 1977
SALES (est): 9.95MM
SALES (corp-wide): 30.15B Publicly Held
Web: www.paramount.com
SIC: 7812 Motion picture production and distribution, television
HQ: Paramount Pictures Corporation
5555 Melrose Ave
Los Angeles CA
323 956-5000

PRODUCTS & SERVICES SECTION
7812 - Motion Picture And Video Production (P-13897)

(P-13875)
PARAMUNT OVRSEAS PRDCTIONS INC
5515 Melrose Ave (90038-3149)
PHONE..................323 956-5225
▲ EMP: 683 EST: 1980
SALES (est): 12.22MM
SALES (corp-wide): 30.15B **Publicly Held**
Web: www.paramount.com
SIC: **7812** Motion picture and video production
PA: Paramount Global
1515 Broadway
New York NY
212 258-6000

(P-13876)
PICTURE SHOP LLC
1017 N Las Palmas Ave Fl 3 (90038-2408)
PHONE..................323 785-1550
EMP: 65
SALES (corp-wide): 12.66MM **Privately Held**
Web: www.pictureshop.com
SIC: **7812** Video production
PA: Picture Shop, Llc
1132 Vine St
Los Angeles CA
818 855-7467

(P-13877)
PIE TOWN PRODUCTIONS INC
5433 Laurel Canyon Blvd (91607-2114)
PHONE..................818 255-9300
EMP: 160 EST: 1994
SALES (est): 5.04MM **Privately Held**
Web: www.pietown.tv
SIC: **7812** Video production

(P-13878)
PIXAR (DH)
Also Called: Pixar Animation Studios
1200 Park Ave (94608-3677)
PHONE..................510 922-3000
James W Morris, *CEO*
John Lasseter, *Creative Vice President**
▲ EMP: 434 EST: 1985
SQ FT: 247,000
SALES (est): 122.62MM
SALES (corp-wide): 82.72B **Publicly Held**
Web: www.pixar.com
SIC: **7812** 7372 7371 Cartoon motion picture production; Prepackaged software; Computer software development
HQ: Twdc Enterprises 18 Corp.
500 S Buena Vista St
Burbank CA

(P-13879)
PLAYBOY ENTRMT GROUP INC (DH)
2300 W Empire Ave (91504-3341)
PHONE..................323 276-4000
Brinda Viloa, *Dir*
James Griffiths, *
EMP: 139 EST: 1984
SALES (est): 22.09MM
SALES (corp-wide): 266.93MM **Publicly Held**
Web: www.criticalcontent.com
SIC: **7812** Video tape production
HQ: Playboy Enterprises, Inc.
10960 Wilshire Blvd Fl 22
Los Angeles CA
310 424-1800

(P-13880)
POINT360
1133 N Hollywood Way (91505-2528)
PHONE..................818 556-5700
Brian Ehrlich, *Mgr*
EMP: 96
Web: www.point360.com
SIC: **7812** Video production
PA: Point.360
2701 Media Center Dr
Los Angeles CA

(P-13881)
POWER STUDIOS INC
Also Called: Digital Domain
300 Rose Ave (90291-2628)
PHONE..................310 314-2800
EMP: 200
SIC: **7812** 7819 Motion picture production; Services allied to motion pictures

(P-13882)
PRAGER UNIVERSITY FOUNDATION
15021 Ventura Blvd Ste 552 (91403-2442)
PHONE..................833 772-4378
Marissa Streit, *CEO*
EMP: 92 EST: 2011
SALES (est): 56.63MM **Privately Held**
Web: www.prageru.com
SIC: **7812** Motion picture and video production

(P-13883)
PURPLE LANGUAGE SERVICES CO
595 Menlo Dr (95765-3708)
PHONE..................916 435-8216
EMP: 140
Web: www.purplelanguageservices.us
SIC: **7812** Video production

(P-13884)
RESPAWN ENTERTAINMENT LLC
20131 Prairie St (91311-6106)
PHONE..................818 960-4400
Jason West, *Managing Member*
▲ EMP: 165 EST: 2010
SALES (est): 15.23MM
SALES (corp-wide): 7.43B **Publicly Held**
Web: www.respawn.com
SIC: **7812** Video production
PA: Electronic Arts Inc.
209 Redwood Shores Pkwy
Redwood City CA
650 628-1500

(P-13885)
RHYTHM AND HUES INC (PA)
Also Called: Rhythm & Hues Studios
2100 E Grand Ave Ste A (90245-5055)
PHONE..................310 448-7500
John Hughes, *Pr*
Pauline Tso, *Sec*
Keith Goldfarb, *Stockholder**
EMP: 207 EST: 1987
SALES (est): 13.58MM
SALES (corp-wide): 13.58MM **Privately Held**
SIC: **7812** Cartoon production, television

(P-13886)
RIPE DIGITAL ENTERTAINMENT INC
729 Seward St (90038-3503)
PHONE..................323 463-7070
Ryan R Magnussen, *CEO*
Timothy Wesley, *
EMP: 75 EST: 2005
SALES (est): 1.38MM **Privately Held**
Web: www.ripedigital.com
SIC: **7812** Motion picture and video production

(P-13887)
RODAX DISTRIBUTORS
7230 Coldwater Canyon Ave (91605-4203)
P.O. Box 16539 (91615-6539)
PHONE..................818 765-6400
Daniel Mamane, *Pr*
Tom Yofee, *
EMP: 78 EST: 1995
SALES (est): 1.28MM **Privately Held**
SIC: **7812** Video tape production

(P-13888)
ROUNDABOUT ENTERTAINMENT INC
Also Called: Secuto Music
217 S Lake St (91502-2111)
PHONE..................818 842-9300
Craig S Clark, *CEO*
EMP: 84 EST: 1992
SQ FT: 6,000
SALES (est): 10.8MM **Privately Held**
Web: www.roundabout.com
SIC: **7812** Video production

(P-13889)
SCANLINE VFX INC
6087 W Sunset Blvd (90028-6434)
PHONE..................310 827-1555
EMP: 1200 EST: 2019
SALES (est): 37.44MM **Privately Held**
Web: www.scanlinevfx.com
SIC: **7812** Video production

(P-13890)
SCANLINEVFX LA LLC
Also Called: Eyeline Studios
6087 W Sunset Blvd (90028-6434)
PHONE..................310 827-1555
EMP: 179 EST: 2007
SALES (est): 12.94MM **Publicly Held**
Web: www.scanlinevfx.com
SIC: **7812** Video production
PA: Netflix, Inc.
121 Albright Way
Los Gatos CA

(P-13891)
SDI MEDIA USA INC (HQ)
Also Called: Iyuno-Sdi Group
6060 Center Dr Ste 100 (90045-1574)
PHONE..................310 388-8800
Mark Howorth, *Pr*
EMP: 95 EST: 1974
SQ FT: 13,000
SALES (est): 48.85MM
SALES (corp-wide): 48.85MM **Privately Held**
Web: www.iyuno.com
SIC: **7812** Video production
PA: Iyuno Media Group
3601 W Olive Ave Ste 650
Burbank CA
818 812-1213

(P-13892)
SENIOR PRDCRS IN RTRMNT TV
Also Called: Senior TV
75895 Altamira Dr (92210-8768)
PHONE..................760 773-9525
EMP: 68
SALES (est): 1.6MM **Privately Held**
Web: www.seniortv.com
SIC: **7812** Television film production

(P-13893)
SONY PCTRES WRLDWIDE ACQSTONS
10202 Washington Blvd (90232-3119)
PHONE..................310 244-4000
Rory Bruer, *Pr*
EMP: 101 EST: 1988
SALES (est): 6MM **Privately Held**
Web: www.sonypictures.com
SIC: **7812** Video production
PA: Sony Group Corporation
1-7-1, Konan
Minato-Ku TKY

(P-13894)
SONY PICTURES ENTRMT INC (DH)
Also Called: Sony Pictures Studios
10202 Washington Blvd (90232-3119)
PHONE..................310 244-4000
Tony Vinciquerra, *Ch*
Robert Lawson, *Ex VP*
George Rose, *WORLDWIDE PEOPLE & ORGANIZATION*
▲ EMP: 3000 EST: 1982
SALES (est): 1.55B **Privately Held**
Web: www.sonypictures.com
SIC: **7812** 7822 7832 Motion picture production and distribution; Distribution, exclusive of production: motion picture; Motion picture theaters, except drive-in
HQ: Sony Corporation Of America
25 Madison Ave Fl 27
New York NY

(P-13895)
SONY PICTURES STUDIOS INC
10202 Washington Blvd (90232-3195)
PHONE..................310 244-4000
Jack Kindberg, *Pr*
Jared Jussim, *
EMP: 222 EST: 1989
SALES (est): 9.77MM **Privately Held**
Web: www.sonypicturesstudios.com
SIC: **7812** Motion picture production
HQ: Sony Pictures Entertainment, Inc.
10202 Washington Blvd
Culver City CA
310 244-4000

(P-13896)
SONY PICTURES TELEVISION INC (DH)
10202 Washington Blvd (90232-3119)
PHONE..................310 244-7625
Ravi Ahuja, *Ch*
Keith Le Goy, *
Jeff Frost, *
Jason Clodfelter, *
Wayne Garvie, *
▲ EMP: 300 EST: 1982
SALES (est): 22.16MM **Privately Held**
Web: www.sonypictures.com
SIC: **7812** Motion picture production and distribution, television
HQ: Sony Pictures Entertainment, Inc.
10202 Washington Blvd
Culver City CA
310 244-4000

(P-13897)
SPS WEST LLC
1642 17th St (90404-3820)
PHONE..................818 845-8050
Joseph Melody, *Prin*
EMP: 73 EST: 2016
SALES (est): 1.3MM **Privately Held**
Web: www.smartpostsound.com

7812 - Motion Picture And Video Production (P-13898)

(P-13898)
STARGATE FILMS INC
Also Called: Stargate Digital
1001 El Centro St (91030-5206)
PHONE................................626 403-8403
Samuel Nicholson, *CEO*
Pete Ware, *
EMP: 65 EST: 1989
SQ FT: 50,000
SALES (est): 8.92MM **Privately Held**
Web: www.stargatestudios.net
SIC: 7812 Video production

(P-13899)
STUDIO CITY
5161 Lankershim Blvd # 200 (91601-4962)
PHONE................................818 557-7777
Stuart Weiss, *Prin*
EMP: 95 EST: 2008
SALES (est): 5.24MM **Privately Held**
Web: www.scpxl.com
SIC: 7812 5049 Motion picture and video production; Professional equipment, nec

(P-13900)
STUDIO DISTRIBUTION SVCS LLC
4000 Warner Blvd (91522-0001)
PHONE................................818 954-6000
Eddie Cunningham, *Managing Member*
EMP: 140 EST: 2020
SALES (est): 3.99MM **Privately Held**
SIC: 7812 Motion picture production and distribution

(P-13901)
STX FINANCING LLC
Also Called: Stx Entertainment
3900 W Alameda Ave Fl 32 (91505-4316)
PHONE................................310 742-2300
Robert Simonds, *Ch*
Noah Fogelson, *CEO*
Andrew Warren, *CFO*
EMP: 98 EST: 2014
SALES (est): 29.98MM **Privately Held**
Web: www.erosstx.com
SIC: 7812 Motion picture production and distribution, television
PA: Najafi Companies, Llc
    2525 E Camelback Rd Ste 8
    Phoenix AZ

(P-13902)
TRIAGE ENTERTAINMENT LLC
6701 Center Dr W Ste 300 (90045-2482)
PHONE................................310 417-4800
EMP: 60 EST: 1995
SQ FT: 15,000
SALES (est): 8.74MM **Privately Held**
Web: www.triageinc.com
SIC: 7812 Motion picture and video production

(P-13903)
TWENTETH CNTURY FOX HM ENTRMT (PA)
10201 W Pico Blvd (90064-2606)
PHONE................................310 369-1000
EMP: 1000 EST: 1953
SQ FT: 25,000
SALES (est): 43.19MM **Privately Held**
SIC: 7812 Television film production

(P-13904)
TWENTIETH CNTURY FOX FILM CORP (DH)
Also Called: Fox Films Entertainment
10201 W Pico Blvd (90064-2606)
P.O. Box 900 (90213-0900)
◆ EMP: 75 EST: 1915
SQ FT: 25,000
SALES (est): 164.25MM
SALES (corp-wide): 82.72B **Publicly Held**
SIC: 7812 Motion picture production and distribution
HQ: Fox Entertainment Group, Llc
    1211 Ave Of The Americas
    New York NY
    212 852-7000

(P-13905)
TWENTIETH TELEVISION INC (DH)
Also Called: My Network TV
10201 W Pico Blvd (90064-2606)
P.O. Box 900 (90213-0900)
PHONE................................310 369-1000
Rick Jacobson, *Pr*
Paul Franklin, *General Vice President*
Bob Cesa, *VP Sls*
Cheri Vincent, *VP Fin*
Greg Meidel, *Pr*
EMP: 62 EST: 1995
SALES (est): 59.1MM
SALES (corp-wide): 82.72B **Publicly Held**
Web: www.mynetworktv.com
SIC: 7812 Television film production
HQ: Fox Entertainment Group, Llc
    1211 Ave Of The Americas
    New York NY
    212 852-7000

(P-13906)
UNIVERSAL CITY STUDIOS LLLP
Also Called: Universal Studios
100 Universal City Plz (91608-1085)
PHONE................................818 622-8477
▲ EMP: 7400
SIC: 7812 7996 Motion picture production and distribution; Theme park, amusement

(P-13907)
UNIVERSAL PCTRES HM ENTRMT LLC (DH)
100 Universal City Plz Bldg 1440/7 (91608)
PHONE................................818 777-1000
EMP: 76 EST: 1965
SALES (est): 22.29MM
SALES (corp-wide): 121.43B **Publicly Held**
Web: www.nbcuniversal.com
SIC: 7812 Motion picture and video production
HQ: Nbcuniversal, Llc
    1221 Ave Of The Amrcas St
    New York NY
    212 664-4444

(P-13908)
UNIVERSAL STUDIOS COMPANY LLC (DH)
100 Universal City Plz (91608-1002)
PHONE................................818 777-1000
Adam Fogelson, *Ch*
Donna Langley, *
Ron Meyer, *
Sean Gamble, *
▲ EMP: 605 EST: 1958
SQ FT: 100,000
SALES (est): 986.31MM
SALES (corp-wide): 121.43B **Publicly Held**
Web: www.universalstudioshollywood.com

SIC: 7812 3652 2741 5947 Motion picture production and distribution; Phonograph records, prerecorded; Music, sheet: publishing and printing; Gift shop
HQ: Nbcuniversal Media, Llc
    30 Rockefeller Plz Fl 2
    New York NY

(P-13909)
VIACOM NETWORKS
Also Called: Mtv Networks
1575 N Gower St Ste 100 (90028-6488)
PHONE................................310 752-8000
EMP: 73 EST: 2010
SALES (est): 3.07MM **Privately Held**
SIC: 7812 7822 Television film production; Motion picture and tape distribution

(P-13910)
VILLAGE ROAD SHOW PICTURES USA
10100 Santa Monica Blvd Ste 200 (90067-4003)
PHONE................................310 385-4300
Greg Basser, *Ch*
Bruce Berman, *CEO*
Simon Phillipson, *Pr*
▲ EMP: 71 EST: 1988
SQ FT: 9,000
SALES (est): 20.93MM **Privately Held**
Web: www.vreg.com
SIC: 7812 Motion picture production and distribution
HQ: Village Roadshow Pty Ltd
    Level 4 650 Chapel Street
    South Yarra VIC

(P-13911)
VUMEDI INC (PA)
Also Called: Vumedi
555 12th St Ste 1775 (94607-4664)
PHONE................................650 450-2603
Roman Giverts, *CEO*
EMP: 63 EST: 2008
SALES (est): 5.95MM
SALES (corp-wide): 5.95MM **Privately Held**
Web: www.vumedi.com
SIC: 7812 8299 Video production; Educational services

(P-13912)
VYOND
204 2nd Ave Ste 638 (94401-3904)
PHONE................................888 360-9639
EMP: 62 EST: 2021
SALES (est): 1.1MM **Privately Held**
Web: www.vyond.com
SIC: 7812 Video production

(P-13913)
WALT DISNEY MUSIC COMPANY (DH)
Also Called: Disney
500 S Buena Vista St (91521-0007)
P.O. Box 3232 (92803-3232)
PHONE................................818 560-1000
Tom Macdougall, *Pr*
Robert Cavallo, *Ch Bd*
Cathleen Tass, *Treas*
Cathleen M Taff, *CEO*
▲ EMP: 148 EST: 1947
SALES (est): 51.25MM
SALES (corp-wide): 82.72B **Publicly Held**
Web: www.thewaltdisneycompany.com
SIC: 7812 Motion picture and video production
HQ: Disney Enterprises, Inc.
    500 S Buena Vista St
    Burbank CA
    818 560-1000

(P-13914)
WALT DISNEY PICTURES
Also Called: Disney
811 Sonora Ave (91201-2433)
PHONE................................818 409-2200
Meredith Roberts, *Sr VP*
EMP: 300 EST: 1983
SQ FT: 461,000
SALES (est): 43.33MM
SALES (corp-wide): 82.72B **Publicly Held**
Web: movies.disney.com
SIC: 7812 Motion picture and video production
PA: The Walt Disney Company
    500 S Buena Vista St
    Burbank CA
    818 560-1000

(P-13915)
WALT DISNEY RECORDS DIRECT (DH)
Also Called: Disney
500 S Buena Vista St (91521-0007)
PHONE................................818 560-1000
Alan H Bergman, *Sr VP*
Rob Moore, *
Nick Franklin, *
Marsha Reed, *
◆ EMP: 2990 EST: 1996
SQ FT: 600,000
SALES (est): 112.36MM
SALES (corp-wide): 82.72B **Publicly Held**
Web: www.thewaltdisneycompany.com
SIC: 7812 Motion picture production and distribution
HQ: Disney Enterprises, Inc.
    500 S Buena Vista St
    Burbank CA
    818 560-1000

(P-13916)
WARNER BROS ENTERTAINMENT INC (DH)
Also Called: Victory Studio
4000 Warner Blvd (91522-0002)
P.O. Box 29113 (71903-9113)
PHONE................................818 954-6000
Ann Sarnoff, *CEO*
Alan Horn, *
John Schulman, *
Barry M Meyer, *
◆ EMP: 132 EST: 2001
SALES (est): 542.49MM **Publicly Held**
Web: www.warnerbros.com
SIC: 7812 Television film production
HQ: Warner Media, Llc
    30 Hudson Yards
    New York NY

(P-13917)
WARNER BROS ENTERTAINMENT INC
Also Called: Warner Bros Studio Facilities
3500 W Olive Ave Ste 200 (91505-4644)
PHONE................................818 954-2209
Steven Singer, *Brnch Mgr*
EMP: 168
Web: www.warnerbros.com
SIC: 7812 Television film production
HQ: Warner Bros. Entertainment Inc.
    4000 Warner Blvd
    Burbank CA
    818 954-6000

(P-13918)
WARNER BROS HOME ENTRMT INC (DH)
4000 Warner Blvd Bldg 160 (91522-0002)
P.O. Box 9153 (02021-9153)

PRODUCTS & SERVICES SECTION

7819 - Services Allied To Motion Pictures (P-13938)

PHONE.................818 954-6000
James Cardwell, *Pr*
Edward Byrnes, *
Frank Walsh, *
Timmy Treu, *
Ronald J Sanders, *
▲ **EMP:** 80 **EST:** 1978
SQ FT: 12,000
SALES (est): 48.08MM **Publicly Held**
SIC: 7812 Television film production
HQ: Warner Bros. Entertainment Inc.
  4000 Warner Blvd
  Burbank CA
  818 954-6000

(P-13919)
WARNER BROS INTL TV DIST INC
4000 Warner Blvd (91522-0002)
PHONE.................818 954-6000
Robert Blair, *Pr*
Margee Schubert, *
EMP: 99 **EST:** 2003
SALES (est): 5.38MM **Publicly Held**
SIC: 7812 Television film production
HQ: Warner Bros. Entertainment Inc.
  4000 Warner Blvd
  Burbank CA
  818 954-6000

(P-13920)
WESTBROOK OPS LLC
24151 Ventura Blvd Ste 200 (91302-1277)
PHONE.................818 832-2300
EMP: 78 **EST:** 2019
SALES (est): 344.03K **Privately Held**
SIC: 7812 Motion picture and video production

(P-13921)
YES VIDEOCOM INC (PA)
2805 Bowers Ave Ste 230 (95051-0971)
PHONE.................408 907-7600
Michael Chang, *CEO*
▲ **EMP:** 68 **EST:** 1999
SQ FT: 36,000
SALES (est): 21.06MM
SALES (corp-wide): 21.06MM **Privately Held**
Web: www.yesvideo.com
SIC: 7812 Motion picture production

(P-13922)
ZOIC INC
Also Called: Zoic Studios
3582 Eastham Dr (90232-2409)
PHONE.................310 838-0770
Loni Peristere, *CEO*
Chris Jones, *
Tim Mcbride, *Treas*
EMP: 125 **EST:** 2002
SQ FT: 15,000
SALES (est): 12.94MM **Privately Held**
Web: www.zoicstudios.com
SIC: 7812 Video production

(P-13923)
ZOO DIGITAL PRODUCTION LLC
Also Called: Zoo
2201 Park Pl Ste 100 (90245-4909)
PHONE.................310 220-3939
Laura Herbers, *Adm/Asst*
EMP: 169 **EST:** 2010
SALES (est): 23.18MM **Privately Held**
Web: www.zoodigital.com
SIC: 7812 Video production

7819 Services Allied To Motion Pictures

(P-13924)
A FILML INC
Also Called: Filml.a
737 N Western Ave # 101 (90029-3725)
PHONE.................213 977-8600
Paul Audley, *Pr*
Paul Audley, *Pr*
Denise Gutches, *
EMP: 95 **EST:** 1995
SALES (est): 12.36MM **Privately Held**
Web: www.filmla.com
SIC: 7819 Services allied to motion pictures

(P-13925)
ANNAPURNA PICTURES LLC
817 Hilldale Ave (90069-4906)
PHONE.................310 385-7701
EMP: 88 **EST:** 2017
SALES (est): 3.61MM **Privately Held**
Web: www.annapurna.com
SIC: 7819 Film processing, editing, and titling: motion picture

(P-13926)
ASPECT RATIO INC (HQ)
5161 Lankershim Blvd Ste 300 (91601-4962)
PHONE.................323 467-2121
Robert Israel, *CEO*
Mark Trugman, *
Dennis Hamilton, *
EMP: 60 **EST:** 1978
SQ FT: 11,000
SALES (est): 6.16MM
SALES (corp-wide): 9.94MM **Privately Held**
Web: www.teamaspect.com
SIC: 7819 Film processing, editing, and titling: motion picture
PA: Aspect Group Llc
  1347 N Cahuenga Blvd
  Los Angeles CA
  323 467-2121

(P-13927)
BEAR NASH PRODUCTIONS
521 E Sycamore Ave (90245-2406)
PHONE.................310 428-5167
Albert Chi, *Prin*
EMP: 65 **EST:** 2019
SALES (est): 415.02K **Privately Held**
SIC: 7819 Developing and laboratory services, motion picture

(P-13928)
CARA COMMUNICATIONS LLC
Also Called: Vin Di Bona Productions
12233 W Olympic Blvd Ste 170 (90064-1034)
PHONE.................310 442-5600
Vincent Dibona, *Pr*
EMP: 78 **EST:** 1989
SALES (est): 10.22MM
SALES (corp-wide): 10.84MM **Privately Held**
Web: www.vindibonaproductions.com
SIC: 7819 7812 7922 Directors, independent: motion picture; Television film production; Television program, including commercial producers
PA: V10 Entertainment Holdings Lp
  12233 W Olympic Blvd
  Los Angeles CA
  310 442-5600

(P-13929)
CHAPMN/LNARD STDIO EQP CNADA I (PA)
12950 Raymer St (91605-4211)
PHONE.................323 877-5309
Leonard Chapman, *Pr*
Michael Chapman, *
▲ **EMP:** 145 **EST:** 1945
SQ FT: 300,000
SALES (est): 20.97MM
SALES (corp-wide): 20.97MM **Privately Held**
Web: www.chapman-leonard.com
SIC: 7819 Studio property rental, motion picture

(P-13930)
CONDOR PRODUCTIONS LLC
245 N Beverly Dr (90210-5319)
PHONE.................310 449-3000
EMP: 99 **EST:** 2016
SQ FT: 5,000
SALES (est): 293.23K **Privately Held**
SIC: 7819 TV tape services: editing, transfers, etc.

(P-13931)
DELUXE MEDIA INC (PA)
Also Called: Deluxe Digital Studios
2130 N Hollywood Way (91505-1522)
PHONE.................818 565-3697
Cyril Drabinsky, *CEO*
Michael Gunter, *CFO*
Warren Stein, *COO*
EMP: 62 **EST:** 2013
SALES (est): 94.02MM
SALES (corp-wide): 94.02MM **Privately Held**
Web: www.bydeluxe.com
SIC: 7819 Sound effects and music production, motion picture

(P-13932)
DIRECTORS GUILD AMERICA INC (PA)
Also Called: D G A
7920 W Sunset Blvd (90046-3300)
PHONE.................310 289-2000
Jay D Roth, *Ex Dir*
Lesli Linka Glatter, *
Ed Sherin, *
Martha Coolidge, *
Max Schindler, *
EMP: 110 **EST:** 1936
SQ FT: 100,000
SALES (est): 40.88MM
SALES (corp-wide): 40.88MM **Privately Held**
Web: www.dga.org
SIC: 7819 8631 Directors, independent: motion picture; Labor organizations

(P-13933)
DNEG NORTH AMERICA INC (PA)
Also Called: Prime Focus World
5750 Hannum Ave Ste 100 (90230-6666)
PHONE.................323 461-7887
Namit Malhotra, *CEO*
Robert Hummel, *
Sue Murphree, *
Oliver Welch, *
Anshul Doshi, *Prin*
EMP: 85 **EST:** 1985
SQ FT: 50,000
SALES (est): 12.83MM
SALES (corp-wide): 12.83MM **Privately Held**

(P-13934)
DTS INC (DH)
5220 Las Virgenes Rd (91302-1064)
PHONE.................818 436-1000
Jon E Kirchner, *CEO*
Melvin L Flanigan, *
Blake A Welcher, *
Kevin Doohan, *CMO*
Kris M Graves, *
▲ **EMP:** 150 **EST:** 1990
SQ FT: 89,000
SALES (est): 52.35MM
SALES (corp-wide): 438.93MM **Publicly Held**
Web: www.dts.com
SIC: 7819 3651 Services allied to motion pictures; Household audio and video equipment
HQ: Adeia Holdings Inc.
  3025 Orchard Pkwy
  San Jose CA
  408 473-2500

(P-13935)
FOR CALI PRODUCTIONS LLC
5555 Melrose Ave Bldg 213 (90038-3996)
PHONE.................323 956-9500
EMP: 287
SIC: 7819 Services allied to motion pictures
HQ: For Cali Productions, Llc
  5808 W Sunset Blvd
  Los Angeles CA
  323 956-9508

(P-13936)
FOTO-KEM INDUSTRIES INC (PA)
Also Called: Foto Kem Film & Video
2801 W Alameda Ave (91505-4405)
P.O. Box 7755 (91510-7755)
PHONE.................818 846-3102
William F Brodersen, *CEO*
Christine M Burdick, *
Gerald D Brodersen Junior, *VP*
▲ **EMP:** 249 **EST:** 1963
SQ FT: 43,000
SALES (est): 44.05MM
SALES (corp-wide): 44.05MM **Privately Held**
Web: www.fotokem.com
SIC: 7819 Laboratory service, motion picture

(P-13937)
FULL THROTTLE FILMS LLC (DH)
Also Called: Ver
757 W California Ave (91203-1591)
PHONE.................818 956-1444
TOLL FREE: 800
Bob Krakauer, *CEO*
▲ **EMP:** 65 **EST:** 1982
SQ FT: 2,000
SALES (est): 29.28MM
SALES (corp-wide): 1.59B **Privately Held**
Web: www.prggear.com
SIC: 7819 Equipment and prop rental, motion picture production
HQ: Production Resource Group Llc
  630 9th Ave Ste 610
  New York NY

(P-13938)
FUSEFX LLC
Also Called: Fusefx
14823 Califa St (91411-3108)
PHONE.................818 237-5052
David Altenau, *CEO*

7819 - Services Allied To Motion Pictures (P-13939)

Tim Jacobsen, *Chief Development Officer*
EMP: 300 **EST:** 2006
SQ FT: 12,500
SALES (est): 26.49MM **Privately Held**
Web: www.fusefx.com
SIC: 7819 Visual effects production

(P-13939)
HOLLYWOOD RNTALS PROD SVCS LLC (PA)
5300 Melrose Ave (90038-5111)
PHONE.................................818 407-7800
Mark A Rosenthal, *Managing Member*
▲ **EMP:** 100 **EST:** 2000
SQ FT: 100,000
SALES (est): 9.55MM
SALES (corp-wide): 9.55MM **Privately Held**
Web: www.the-mbsgroup.com
SIC: 7819 Equipment rental, motion picture

(P-13940)
JACKSON SHRUB SUPPLY INC
11505 Vanowen St (91605-6232)
PHONE.................................818 982-0100
Gary Jackson, *Pr*
EMP: 60 **EST:** 1936
SQ FT: 16,000
SALES (est): 2.35MM **Privately Held**
Web: www.jacksonshrub.com
SIC: 7819 Services allied to motion pictures

(P-13941)
LEGEND FILMS
2200 Faraday Ave Ste 100 (92008-7233)
PHONE.................................858 793-4420
EMP: 350 **EST:** 2013
SALES (est): 1.26MM **Privately Held**
Web: www.legendfilms.com
SIC: 7819 Services allied to motion pictures

(P-13942)
MOTOR TREND GROUP LLC (HQ)
Also Called: Extreme Ventures
831 S Douglas St (90245-4902)
PHONE.................................630 353-2505
Alex Wellen, *Managing Member*
EMP: 67 **EST:** 2017
SALES (est): 16.05MM **Publicly Held**
Web: www.motortrendgroup.com
SIC: 7819 Visual effects production
PA: Warner Bros. Discovery, Inc.
 230 Park Ave S Lbby 1
 New York NY

(P-13943)
NEP BEXEL INC (HQ)
Also Called: Bexel
7850 Ruffner Ave Ste B (91406-1619)
PHONE.................................818 565-4399
EMP: 80 **EST:** 1980
SALES (est): 24.93MM
SALES (corp-wide): 421.16MM **Privately Held**
Web: www.bexel.com
SIC: 7819 5731 5065 Equipment rental, motion picture; Video cameras and accessories; Electronic parts and equipment, nec
PA: Nep Group, Inc.
 2 Beta Dr
 Pittsburgh PA
 412 826-1414

(P-13944)
OLIVE AVENUE PRODUCTIONS LLC
4000 Warner Blvd (91522-0001)
PHONE.................................770 214-7052
EMP: 500 **EST:** 2018
SALES (est): 4.62MM **Privately Held**
SIC: 7819 Developing and laboratory services, motion picture

(P-13945)
OMEGA/CINEMA PROPS INC
1515 E 15th St (90021-2711)
PHONE.................................323 466-8201
E Jay Krause, *Pr*
Cheryl Jordan, *
▲ **EMP:** 90 **EST:** 1967
SQ FT: 300,000
SALES (est): 9.39MM **Privately Held**
Web: www.omegacinemaprops.com
SIC: 7819 Equipment rental, motion picture

(P-13946)
PIXOMONDO LLC
2055 S Barrington Ave (90025-1276)
PHONE.................................310 394-0555
Jonny Slow, *CEO*
EMP: 662 **EST:** 2008
SALES (est): 79.07MM **Privately Held**
Web: www.pixomondo.com
SIC: 7819 Visual effects production
HQ: Sony Pictures Entertainment, Inc.
 10202 Washington Blvd
 Culver City CA
 310 244-4000

(P-13947)
POINT360 (PA)
Also Called: Digital Film Labs
2701 Media Center Dr (90065-1700)
PHONE.................................818 565-1400
Haig S Bagerdjian, *Ch Bd*
Alan R Steel, *Executive Vice President Finance & Administration*
EMP: 82 **EST:** 1997
SQ FT: 64,600
SALES (est): 20.63MM **Privately Held**
Web: www.point360.com
SIC: 7819 7822 7829 Video tape or disk reproduction; Motion picture and tape distribution; Motion picture distribution services

(P-13948)
POST GROUP INC (PA)
1415 N Cahuenga Blvd (90028-8125)
P.O. Box 3870 (91617-3870)
PHONE.................................323 462-2300
Frederic Rheinstein, *Ch*
Vincent Lyons, *
Duke Gallagher, *
EMP: 110 **EST:** 1974
SQ FT: 40,000
SALES (est): 9.26MM
SALES (corp-wide): 9.26MM **Privately Held**
Web: www.postgroup.com
SIC: 7819 7812 Editing services, motion picture production; Motion picture and video production

(P-13949)
RUNWAY INC
1330 Vine St (90028-8140)
P.O. Box 1536 (90078-1536)
PHONE.................................310 636-2000
Roberta Margolis, *Pr*
EMP: 80 **EST:** 1974
SQ FT: 17,500
SALES (est): 4.48MM **Privately Held**
Web: www.runway.com
SIC: 7819 Video tape or disk reproduction

(P-13950)
STAR WAGGONS LLC
13334 Ralston Ave (91342-7608)
PHONE.................................818 367-5946
EMP: 87 **EST:** 1979
SALES (est): 8.25MM **Publicly Held**
Web: www.ziostudioservices.com
SIC: 7819 Studio property rental, motion picture
PA: Hudson Pacific Properties, Inc.
 11601 Wilshire Blvd # 16
 Los Angeles CA

(P-13951)
STEREO D LLC
Also Called: Stereo
3355 W Empire Ave 1st Fl (91504-3160)
P.O. Box 892164 (92589-2164)
PHONE.................................818 861-3100
William Sherak, *Pr*
Milton Adamou, *
Prafull Gade, *
Aaron Parry, *
EMP: 88 **EST:** 2009
SQ FT: 55,000
SALES (est): 2.1MM **Privately Held**
Web: www.sdfxstudios.com
SIC: 7819 Editing services, motion picture production

(P-13952)
TECHNCLOR CRATIVE SVCS USA INC
Also Called: Technicolor Creative Studios
8921 Lindblade St (90232-2438)
PHONE.................................818 260-1214
Timothy Sarnoff, *CEO*
Richard Andrews, *
John Hancock, *
Claude Gagnon, *
EMP: 450 **EST:** 1980
SQ FT: 25,000
SALES (est): 43.9MM **Privately Held**
Web: www.technicolor.com
SIC: 7819 Video tape or disk reproduction
PA: Vantiva
 10 Boulevard De Grenelle
 Paris

(P-13953)
TECHNCLOR VDOCASSETTE MICH INC (DH)
Also Called: Technicolor Video Service
3601 Calle Tecate Ste 120 (93012-5057)
PHONE.................................805 445-1122
Lanni Ormonvo, *Pr*
John H Oliphant, *
▲ **EMP:** 500 **EST:** 1987
SALES (est): 93.72MM **Privately Held**
SIC: 7819 Video tape or disk reproduction
HQ: Technicolor Thomson Group, Inc
 2233 N Ontario St Ste 300
 Burbank CA

(P-13954)
TECHNICOLOR THOMSON GROUP INC (HQ)
Also Called: Technicolor Entertainment Svcs
2233 N Ontario St Ste 300 (91504-4500)
◆ **EMP:** 291 **EST:** 1922
SALES (est): 212.92MM **Privately Held**
SIC: 7819 7384 Video tape or disk reproduction; Photofinish laboratories
PA: Vantiva
 10 Boulevard De Grenelle
 Paris

(P-13955)
TEN PUBLISHING MEDIA LLC (PA)
831 S Douglas St (90245-4956)
PHONE.................................310 531-9900
Scott P Dickey, *CEO*
Peter H Englehart, *Ch Bd*
Chris Argentieri, *Pr*
John B Bode, *Ex VP*
Stephanie S Justice, *Ex VP*
EMP: 230 **EST:** 1991
SALES (est): 24.68MM **Privately Held**
SIC: 7819 Visual effects production

(P-13956)
TESTRONIC INC
Also Called: Testronic Labs
111 N First St Ste 204 (91502-1851)
PHONE.................................818 845-3223
Dominic Wheatley, *CEO*
▲ **EMP:** 140 **EST:** 1996
SALES (est): 9.33MM **Privately Held**
Web: www.testroniclabs.com
SIC: 7819 Video tape or disk reproduction

(P-13957)
VANTIVA SUP CHAIN SLUTIONS INC
Also Called: Accounts Payable Department
5491 E Philadelphia St (91761-2807)
P.O. Box 2459 (91729-2459)
PHONE.................................909 974-2016
EMP: 106
SIC: 7819 Video tape or disk reproduction
HQ: Vantiva Supply Chain Solutions, Inc.
 3601 Calle Tecate Ste 120
 Camarillo CA

(P-13958)
VANTIVA SUP CHAIN SLUTIONS INC
Also Called: Technicolor
461 Rood Rd Ste A (92231-9768)
PHONE.................................760 357-3372
EMP: 79
SIC: 7819 Video tape or disk reproduction
HQ: Vantiva Supply Chain Solutions, Inc.
 3601 Calle Tecate Ste 120
 Camarillo CA

(P-13959)
VANTIVA SUP CHAIN SLUTIONS INC (HQ)
Also Called: Technicolor Video Services
3601 Calle Tecate Ste 120 (93012-5057)
PHONE.................................805 445-1122
Lanny Raimondo, *CEO*
Orlando F Raimondo, *
Patricia Dave, *
◆ **EMP:** 500 **EST:** 1983
SALES (est): 480.55MM **Privately Held**
SIC: 7819 Video tape or disk reproduction
PA: Vantiva
 10 Boulevard De Grenelle
 Paris

(P-13960)
WALT DSNEY IMGNRING RES DEV IN (DH)
Also Called: Disney
1401 Flower St (91201-2421)
P.O. Box 25020 (91221-5020)
PHONE.................................818 544-6500
Thomas O Staggs, *CEO*
Craig Russell, *DESIGN DELIVERY**
Bruce Vaughn, *CREATIVE**
Martin A Sklar, *
Jessica Hodgins, *

PRODUCTS & SERVICES SECTION
7832 - Motion Picture Theaters, Except Drive-in (P-13980)

◆ EMP: 1011 EST: 1986
SQ FT: 100,000
SALES (est): 88.5MM
SALES (corp-wide): 82.72B Publicly Held
Web: www.disneyimaginations.com
SIC: 7819 8712 1542 8741 Visual effects production; Architectural services; Custom builders, non-residential; Management services
HQ: Disney Enterprises, Inc.
    500 S Buena Vista St
    Burbank CA
    818 560-1000

7822 Motion Picture And Tape Distribution

(P-13961)
BAD ROBOT PRODUCTIONS INC
1221 Olympic Blvd (90404-3721)
PHONE..................310 664-3456
Mike Silver, Mgr
EMP: 71
SALES (corp-wide): 2.63MM Privately Held
SIC: 7822 Motion picture and tape distribution
PA: Bad Robot Productions, Inc.
    1925 Century Park E Fl 22
    Los Angeles CA
    310 664-3456

(P-13962)
CHP
11338 Walnut St (92374-7611)
PHONE..................909 213-3788
Glen Brian Copeland, Prin
EMP: 97 EST: 2011
SALES (est): 450.42K Privately Held
Web: chp.ca.gov
SIC: 7822 Motion picture and tape distribution

(P-13963)
DELUXE NMS INC
4499 Glencoe Ave (90292-6357)
PHONE..................310 760-8500
Cyril Drabinsky, CEO
EMP: 200 EST: 2010
SQ FT: 20,000
SALES (est): 17.2MM
SALES (corp-wide): 2.24B Publicly Held
Web: www.dadcdigital.com
SIC: 7822 7374 Motion picture and tape distribution; Data processing and preparation
PA: Deluxe Corporation
    801 Marquette Ave
    Minneapolis MN
    651 483-7111

(P-13964)
GRAMERCY PRODUCTIONS LLC
100 Universal City Plz Bldg 2150 (91608)
PHONE..................818 777-1677
John Alfred, Ofcr
EMP: 86 EST: 2010
SALES (est): 522.12K
SALES (corp-wide): 121.43B Publicly Held
SIC: 7822 Motion picture and tape distribution
HQ: Focus Features Productions Llc
    100 Unvrsl Cy Plz Bldg 2
    Universal City CA
    818 777-1677

(P-13965)
LFP BROADCASTING LLC (PA)
8484 Wilshire Blvd Ste 900 (90211-3227)
PHONE..................323 852-5020
EMP: 78 EST: 2004
SALES (est): 40MM
SALES (corp-wide): 40MM Privately Held
SIC: 7822 Distribution, for television: motion picture

(P-13966)
LIONSGATE PRODUCTIONS INC
2700 Colorado Ave Ste 200 (90404-5502)
PHONE..................310 255-3937
Jon Feltheimer, CEO
Steve Beeks, *
Wayne Levin, *
Michael Burns, Vice Chairman
Wayne Levin, Chief Strategic Officer*
EMP: 283 EST: 2010
SALES (est): 55.62MM
SALES (corp-wide): 3.6B Privately Held
SIC: 7822 Motion picture and tape distribution
HQ: Lions Gate Entertainment Inc.
    2700 Colorado Ave Ste 200
    Santa Monica CA
    310 449-9200

(P-13967)
SONAR ENTERTAINMENT INC (PA)
2834 Colorado Ave Ste 300 (90404-3644)
PHONE..................424 230-7140
Thomas F Lesinski, CEO
Henry S Hoberman, *
William J Aliber, *
Joel E Denton, Distributor*
EMP: 80 EST: 2007
SALES (est): 53.07MM
SALES (corp-wide): 53.07MM Privately Held
Web: www.halcyonstudios.tv
SIC: 7822 Motion picture and tape distribution

(P-13968)
TWENTIETH CNTURY FOX INTL CORP (HQ)
Also Called: Fox
10201 W Pico Blvd Bldg 1 (90064-2606)
Rural Route 900 (90213)
PHONE..................310 369-1000
Robert A Iger, CEO
◆ EMP: 233 EST: 1972
SQ FT: 115,000
SALES (est): 1.31MM
SALES (corp-wide): 82.72B Publicly Held
Web: www.fox.com
SIC: 7822 7922 Motion picture distribution; Television program, including commercial producers
PA: The Walt Disney Company
    500 S Buena Vista St
    Burbank CA
    818 560-1000

(P-13969)
UNITED ARTISTS CORPORATION
10250 Constellation Blvd Fl 19 (90067-6200)
PHONE..................310 449-3000
Danny Rosett, Pr
EMP: 115 EST: 1986
SALES (est): 6.96MM Publicly Held
SIC: 7822 Distribution, exclusive of production: motion picture
HQ: Metro-Goldwyn-Mayer Studios Inc.
    245 N Beverly Dr
    Beverly Hills CA
    310 449-3000

(P-13970)
UNITED ARTISTS FILMS COMPANY (DH)
Also Called: United Artist Releasing
245 N Beverly Dr (90210-5319)
PHONE..................310 449-3000
Alex Yemenidjian, Pr
EMP: 195 EST: 1987
SALES (est): 5.55MM Publicly Held
SIC: 7822 Distribution, exclusive of production: motion picture
HQ: Mgm Holdings Ii, Inc.
    245 N Beverly Dr
    Beverly Hills CA
    310 449-3000

(P-13971)
UNITED ARTISTS PRODUCTIONS INC
10250 Constellation Blvd Fl 19 (90067-6200)
PHONE..................310 449-3000
Christopher Mcgurk, Pr
EMP: 227 EST: 1995
SALES (est): 1.45MM Publicly Held
SIC: 7822 Distribution, exclusive of production: motion picture
HQ: United Artists Pictures Inc.
    10250 Constellation Blvd
    Los Angeles CA

(P-13972)
UNITED ARTISTS TELEVISION CORP
10250 Constellation Blvd Fl 27 (90067-6200)
PHONE..................310 449-3000
EMP: 263 EST: 1931
SALES (est): 802.07K Publicly Held
SIC: 7822 Distribution, exclusive of production: motion picture
HQ: United Artists Pictures Inc.
    10250 Constellation Blvd
    Los Angeles CA

(P-13973)
VPD IV INC
Also Called: Video Products Distributors
150 Parkshore Dr (95630-4710)
PHONE..................916 605-1500
▲ EMP: 366
SIC: 7822 5092 Video tapes, recorded: wholesale; Video games

(P-13974)
WARNER BROS TRANSATLANTIC INC
Warner Bros
4001 W Olive Ave (91505-4272)
PHONE..................818 954-5990
Dan Romanelli, Brnch Mgr
EMP: 317
Web: property.warnerbros.com
SIC: 7822 Distribution, exclusive of production: motion picture
HQ: Warner Bros. (Transatlantic), Inc.
    4000 Warner Blvd
    Burbank CA

(P-13975)
WARNER BROS TRANSATLANTIC INC
Also Called: Warner Bros
3300 W Olive Ave Ste 200 (91505-4658)
PHONE..................818 977-6384
EMP: 262
Web: property.warnerbros.com
SIC: 7822 Distribution, exclusive of production: motion picture
HQ: Warner Bros. (Transatlantic), Inc.
    4000 Warner Blvd
    Burbank CA

7829 Motion Picture Distribution Services

(P-13976)
OUR ALCHEMY LLC
Also Called: Alchemy
5900 Wilshire Blvd Fl 18 (90036-5013)
PHONE..................310 893-6289
EMP: 80 EST: 2010
SQ FT: 30,000
SALES (est): 5.6MM Privately Held
Web: www.ouralchemy.com
SIC: 7829 Motion picture distribution services

7832 Motion Picture Theaters, Except Drive-in

(P-13977)
BRENDEN THEATRE CORPORATION (PA)
1985 Willow Pass Rd Ste C (94520-2533)
PHONE..................925 677-0462
John Brenden, Pr
EMP: 189 EST: 1989
SQ FT: 70,000
SALES (est): 25.17MM Privately Held
Web: www.brendentheatres.com
SIC: 7832 Motion picture theaters, except drive-in

(P-13978)
BRENDEN THEATRE CORPORATION
531 Davis St (95688-4632)
PHONE..................707 469-0180
Tim Kruse, Brnch Mgr
EMP: 105
Web: www.brendentheatres.com
SIC: 7832 Exhibitors, itinerant: motion picture
PA: Brenden Theatre Corporation
    1985 Willow Pass Rd Ste C
    Concord CA

(P-13979)
BRENDEN THEATRE CORPORATION
1021 10th St Frnt (95354-0888)
PHONE..................209 491-7770
Saul Trujllo, Genl Mgr
EMP: 93
Web: www.brendentheatres.com
SIC: 7832 Exhibitors, itinerant: motion picture
PA: Brenden Theatre Corporation
    1985 Willow Pass Rd Ste C
    Concord CA

(P-13980)
CARMIKE CINEMAS LLC
Also Called: Carmike Cinemas
166 W Hillcrest Dr (91360-4209)
PHONE..................805 494-4702
EMP: 86
Web: www.amctheatres.com
SIC: 7832 Exhibitors, itinerant: motion picture
HQ: Carmike Cinemas, Llc
    11500 Ash St
    Leawood KS
    913 213-2000

7832 - Motion Picture Theaters, Except Drive-in (P-13981)

(P-13981)
CENTURY THEATRES INC
Also Called: Century 14
109 Plaza Dr (94591-3703)
PHONE........................707 648-3456
EMP: 232
Web: www.cinemark.com
SIC: 7832 Motion picture theaters, except drive-in
HQ: Century Theatres, Inc
  3900 Dallas Pkwy Ste 500
  Plano TX
  972 665-1000

(P-13982)
CENTURY THEATRES INC
Also Called: CENTURY THEATRES, INC
7777 Edinger Ave Ste 170 (92647-8690)
PHONE........................714 373-4573
EMP: 174
Web: www.cinemark.com
SIC: 7832 Motion picture theaters, except drive-in
HQ: Century Theatres, Inc
  3900 Dallas Pkwy Ste 500
  Plano TX
  972 665-1000

(P-13983)
CENTURY THEATRES INC
Also Called: Capitol Drive-In
3630 Hillcap Ave (95136-1344)
PHONE........................408 226-2251
Teresa Dinh, Mgr
EMP: 174
Web: www.westwinddi.com
SIC: 7832 Motion picture theaters, except drive-in
HQ: Century Theatres, Inc
  3900 Dallas Pkwy Ste 500
  Plano TX
  972 665-1000

(P-13984)
CENTURY THEATRES INC
Also Called: Century Theatres Anchorage
150 Pelican Way (94901-5550)
PHONE........................415 448-8400
EMP: 5000 EST: 2003
SQ FT: 30,000
SALES (est): 17.79MM Publicly Held
SIC: 7832 Motion picture theaters, except drive-in
HQ: Cinemark Usa, Inc.
  3900 Dallas Pkwy Ste 500
  Plano TX
  972 665-1000

(P-13985)
DECURION CORPORATION (PA)
120 N Robertson Blvd Fl 3 (90048-3115)
PHONE........................310 659-9432
Michael R Forman, Pr
Jerome Forman, *
James Cotter, *
EMP: 100 EST: 1966
SQ FT: 31,000
SALES (est): 175.87MM
SALES (corp-wide): 175.87MM Privately Held
Web: www.decurion.com
SIC: 7832 7833 Motion picture theaters, except drive-in; Drive-in motion picture theaters

(P-13986)
EDWARDS THEATRES INC
Also Called: Kaleidoscope Stadium Cinema
27741 Crown Valley Pkwy Ste 301 (92691-6532)
PHONE........................949 582-4078
EMP: 173
SIC: 7832 Motion picture theaters, except drive-in
HQ: Edwards Theatres, Inc.
  300 Newport Center Dr
  Newport Beach CA
  949 640-4600

(P-13987)
EDWARDS THEATRES INC (DH)
Also Called: Edwards Theatres Circuit, Inc.
300 Newport Center Dr (92660-7529)
PHONE........................949 640-4600
James Edwards Iii, Ch Bd
Steve Coffey, *
Joan Randolph, *
Marcella Sheldon, *
EMP: 118 EST: 1930
SQ FT: 30,000
SALES (est): 106.22MM Privately Held
SIC: 7832 Motion picture theaters, except drive-in
HQ: Regal Cinemas, Inc.
  101 E Blount Ave
  Knoxville TN

(P-13988)
EDWARDS THEATRES INC
Also Called: Calabasas Stadium 6
4767 Commons Way (91302-3362)
PHONE........................844 462-7342
Corey J Coggin, Mgr
EMP: 62
SIC: 7832 Motion picture theaters, except drive-in
HQ: Edwards Theatres, Inc.
  300 Newport Center Dr
  Newport Beach CA
  949 640-4600

(P-13989)
EDWARDS THEATRES INC
Also Called: La Verne Cinema 12
1950 Foothill Blvd (91750-3557)
PHONE........................844 462-7342
EMP: 173
SIC: 7832 Motion picture theaters, except drive-in
HQ: Edwards Theatres, Inc.
  300 Newport Center Dr
  Newport Beach CA
  949 640-4600

(P-13990)
EDWARDS THEATRES CIRCUIT INC
Also Called: Aliso Viejo Stadium Cinemas 10
26701 Aliso Creek Rd (92656-2887)
PHONE........................949 425-3838
EMP: 62
SIC: 7832 Motion picture theaters, except drive-in
HQ: Edwards Theatres, Inc.
  300 Newport Center Dr
  Newport Beach CA
  949 640-4600

(P-13991)
EDWARDS THEATRES CIRCUIT INC
Also Called: Mesa Pointe Stadium 12
901 S Coast Dr (92626-1747)
PHONE........................714 428-0962
Minh Duong, Brnch Mgr
EMP: 178
SIC: 7832 Motion picture theaters, except drive-in
HQ: Edwards Theatres, Inc.
  300 Newport Center Dr
  Newport Beach CA
  949 640-4600

(P-13992)
EDWARDS THEATRES CIRCUIT INC
Also Called: Rancho San Diego Cinema 16
2951 Jamacha Rd (92019-4342)
PHONE........................619 660-3460
EMP: 160
SIC: 7832 Motion picture theaters, except drive-in
HQ: Edwards Theatres, Inc.
  300 Newport Center Dr
  Newport Beach CA
  949 640-4600

(P-13993)
EDWARDS THEATRES CIRCUIT INC
Also Called: Mira Mesa Stadium 18
10733 Westview Pkwy (92126-2963)
PHONE........................858 635-7716
Peter Brandon Pt, Brnch Mgr
EMP: 160
SIC: 7832 Motion picture theaters, except drive-in
HQ: Edwards Theatres, Inc.
  300 Newport Center Dr
  Newport Beach CA
  949 640-4600

(P-13994)
EDWARDS THEATRES CIRCUIT INC
Also Called: Fairfield Stadium Cinema
1549 Gateway Blvd (94533-6902)
PHONE........................707 432-2121
EMP: 62
SIC: 7832 Motion picture theaters, except drive-in
HQ: Edwards Theatres, Inc.
  300 Newport Center Dr
  Newport Beach CA
  949 640-4600

(P-13995)
EDWARDS THEATRES CIRCUIT INC
Also Called: Temecula Stadium Cinemas 15
40750 Winchester Rd (92591-5524)
PHONE........................951 296-0144
EMP: 169
SIC: 7832 Motion picture theaters, except drive-in
HQ: Edwards Theatres, Inc.
  300 Newport Center Dr
  Newport Beach CA
  949 640-4600

(P-13996)
EDWARDS THEATRES CIRCUIT INC
Also Called: Edwards Cinemas University
4245 Campus Dr (92612-2752)
PHONE........................949 854-8811
Mike Peterson, Brnch Mgr
EMP: 169
SIC: 7832 Motion picture theaters, except drive-in
HQ: Edwards Theatres, Inc.
  300 Newport Center Dr
  Newport Beach CA
  949 640-4600

(P-13997)
HARKINS THEATRES INC
3100 Chino Ave (91709-3518)
PHONE........................909 627-8010
Sarah Yeats, Prin
EMP: 99
Web: www.harkins.com
SIC: 7832 Motion picture theaters, except drive-in
PA: Harkins Theatres, Inc.
  8901 E Mcdonald Dr
  Scottsdale AZ

(P-13998)
HARKINS THEATRES INC
27481 San Bernardino Ave (92374-5032)
PHONE........................909 793-7993
EMP: 86
Web: www.harkins.com
SIC: 7832 Motion picture theaters, except drive-in
PA: Harkins Theatres, Inc.
  8901 E Mcdonald Dr
  Scottsdale AZ

(P-13999)
IMAX CORPORATION
Also Called: Hackworth Imax Dome
201 S Market St (95113-2008)
PHONE........................408 294-8324
EMP: 60
SALES (corp-wide): 137MM Privately Held
Web: www.thetech.org
SIC: 7832 Motion picture theaters, except drive-in
HQ: Imax Corporation
  12582 Millennium
  Los Angeles CA

(P-14000)
KRIKORIAN PREMIERE THEATRE LLC
8290 La Palma Ave (90620)
PHONE........................714 826-7469
Ted Goldbeck, Brnch Mgr
EMP: 94
SALES (corp-wide): 25.61MM Privately Held
SIC: 7832 Motion picture theaters, except drive-in
PA: Krikorian Premiere Theatre Llc
  2275 W 190th St
  Torrance CA
  310 856-1270

(P-14001)
KRIKORIAN PREMIERE THEATRE LLC
25 Main St (92083-5800)
PHONE........................760 945-7469
EMP: 93
SALES (corp-wide): 25.61MM Privately Held
SIC: 7832 Motion picture theaters, except drive-in
PA: Krikorian Premiere Theatre Llc
  2275 W 190th St
  Torrance CA
  310 856-1270

(P-14002)
KRIKORIAN PREMIERE THEATRE LLC
8540 Whittier Blvd (90660-2520)
PHONE........................562 205-3456
EMP: 93
SALES (corp-wide): 25.61MM Privately Held
SIC: 7832 Motion picture theaters, except drive-in
PA: Krikorian Premiere Theatre Llc

PRODUCTS & SERVICES SECTION

7833 - Drive-in Motion Picture Theaters (P-14022)

2275 W 190th St
Torrance CA
310 856-1270

(P-14003)
METROPOLITAN THEATRES CORP
Also Called: Camelot Theatres
789 E Tahquitz Canyon Way (92262-6705)
PHONE..................760 323-3221
Carl Kilebrew, Genl Mgr
EMP: 66
SALES (corp-wide): 140.61K Privately Held
Web: www.metrotheatres.com
SIC: 7832 7833 Motion picture theaters, except drive-in; Drive-in motion picture theaters
PA: Metropolitan Theatres Corporation
8727 W 3rd St Ste 301
Los Angeles CA
310 858-2800

(P-14004)
NORTH AMERICAN CINEMAS INC
Also Called: Airport Cinemas 12
409 Aviation Blvd (95403-1069)
PHONE..................707 571-1412
Nicholas Mann, Genl Mgr
EMP: 192
Web: www.santarosacinemas.com
SIC: 7832 Motion picture theaters, except drive-in
PA: North American Cinemas, Inc.
816 4th St
Santa Rosa CA

(P-14005)
NORTH AMERICAN CINEMAS INC
551 Summerfield Rd (95405-5239)
PHONE..................707 539-6773
EMP: 164
Web: www.santarosacinemas.com
SIC: 7832 Exhibitors, itinerant: motion picture
PA: North American Cinemas, Inc.
816 4th St
Santa Rosa CA

(P-14006)
READING ENTERTAINMENT INC (HQ)
500 Citadel Dr Ste 300 (90040-1575)
PHONE..................213 235-2226
▲ EMP: 78 EST: 1996
SQ FT: 3,300
SALES (est): 6.69MM
SALES (corp-wide): 203.12MM Publicly Held
SIC: 7832 Motion picture theaters, except drive-in
PA: Reading International, Inc.
189 2nd Ave Apt 2s
New York NY
213 235-2240

(P-14007)
REGAL CINEMAS INC
Also Called: Natomas Marketplace 16
3561 Truxel Rd (95834-3641)
PHONE..................916 419-0205
Ricks Hescock, Mgr
EMP: 64
Web: www.regmovies.com
SIC: 7832 Motion picture theaters, except drive-in
HQ: Regal Cinemas, Inc.
101 E Blount Ave
Knoxville TN

(P-14008)
WESTSTAR CINEMAS INC
Also Called: Plant 16
7876 Van Nuys Blvd (91402-6069)
PHONE..................818 779-0323
Randy Dingwall, Brnch Mgr
EMP: 71
SALES (corp-wide): 22.59MM Privately Held
SIC: 7832 Motion picture theaters, except drive-in
PA: Weststar Cinemas, Inc.
16530 Ventura Blvd # 500
Encino CA
818 784-6266

(P-14009)
WESTSTAR CINEMAS INC
Also Called: Man Theateres
180 Promenade Way Ste R (91362-3826)
PHONE..................805 379-8966
Joseph Leptore, Mgr
EMP: 117
SALES (corp-wide): 22.59MM Privately Held
SIC: 7832 Motion picture theaters, except drive-in
PA: Weststar Cinemas, Inc.
16530 Ventura Blvd # 500
Encino CA
818 784-6266

(P-14010)
WESTSTAR CINEMAS INC
Also Called: Buenaventura 6
1440 Eastman Ave (93003-7784)
PHONE..................805 658-6544
Lyndon Golin, Brnch Mgr
EMP: 63
SALES (corp-wide): 22.59MM Privately Held
SIC: 7832 Motion picture theaters, except drive-in
PA: Weststar Cinemas, Inc.
16530 Ventura Blvd # 500
Encino CA
818 784-6266

(P-14011)
WESTSTAR CINEMAS INC
Also Called: Augora Hills 8 Cinema Center
29045 Agoura Rd (91301-2572)
PHONE..................818 707-9987
Raymond Cornelio, Genl Mgr
EMP: 72
SALES (corp-wide): 22.59MM Privately Held
SIC: 7832 Motion picture theaters, except drive-in
PA: Weststar Cinemas, Inc.
16530 Ventura Blvd # 500
Encino CA
818 784-6266

7833 Drive-in Motion Picture Theaters

(P-14012)
CENTURY THEATRES INC
Also Called: Century Laguna 16
9349 Big Horn Blvd (95758-7934)
PHONE..................916 683-5290
EMP: 261
Web: www.cinemark.com
SIC: 7833 7832 Drive-in motion picture theaters; Motion picture theaters, except drive-in
HQ: Century Theatres, Inc
3900 Dallas Pkwy Ste 500
Plano TX
972 665-1000

(P-14013)
CENTURY THEATRES INC
Also Called: Century 20
1010 Great Mall Dr (95035-8034)
PHONE..................408 942-7441
EMP: 261
Web: www.cinemark.com
SIC: 7833 7832 Drive-in motion picture theaters; Motion picture theaters, except drive-in
HQ: Century Theatres, Inc
3900 Dallas Pkwy Ste 500
Plano TX
972 665-1000

(P-14014)
CENTURY THEATRES INC
Also Called: CENTURY THEATRES, INC
825 Middlefield Rd (94063-1627)
PHONE..................866 322-4547
EMP: 165
Web: www.cinemark.com
SIC: 7833 Drive-in motion picture theaters
HQ: Century Theatres, Inc
3900 Dallas Pkwy Ste 500
Plano TX
972 665-1000

(P-14015)
CENTURY THEATRES INC
Also Called: CENTURY THEATRES, INC
3200 Klose Way (94806-5792)
PHONE..................510 758-9626
Makisha Jones, Mgr
EMP: 252
Web: www.cinemark.com
SIC: 7833 7832 Drive-in motion picture theaters; Motion picture theaters, except drive-in
HQ: Century Theatres, Inc
3900 Dallas Pkwy Ste 500
Plano TX
972 665-1000

(P-14016)
CENTURY THEATRES INC
Also Called: Century Downtown 10
555 E Main St (93001-2628)
PHONE..................805 641-6555
EMP: 252
Web: www.cinemark.com
SIC: 7833 7832 Drive-in motion picture theaters; Motion picture theaters, except drive-in
HQ: Century Theatres, Inc
3900 Dallas Pkwy Ste 500
Plano TX
972 665-1000

(P-14017)
CENTURY THEATRES INC
Also Called: Century Presidio
2340 Chestnut St (94123-2610)
PHONE..................415 776-2388
Pamela Knopp, Mgr
EMP: 194
Web: www.lntsf.com
SIC: 7833 7832 Drive-in motion picture theaters; Motion picture theaters, except drive-in
HQ: Century Theatres, Inc
3900 Dallas Pkwy Ste 500
Plano TX
972 665-1000

(P-14018)
CENTURY THEATRES INC
Also Called: Century 8
12827 Victory Blvd (91606-3012)
PHONE..................818 508-1943
Terrell Hammack, Brnch Mgr
EMP: 252
Web: www.cinemark.com
SIC: 7833 7832 Drive-in motion picture theaters; Motion picture theaters, except drive-in
HQ: Century Theatres, Inc
3900 Dallas Pkwy Ste 500
Plano TX
972 665-1000

(P-14019)
CENTURY THEATRES INC
Also Called: Century Cinema
1500 N Shoreline Blvd (94043-1314)
PHONE..................650 961-3828
Luis Alvarez, Asst Mgr
EMP: 291
Web: www.cinemark.com
SIC: 7833 7832 Drive-in motion picture theaters; Motion picture theaters, except drive-in
HQ: Century Theatres, Inc
3900 Dallas Pkwy Ste 500
Plano TX
972 665-1000

(P-14020)
CENTURY THEATRES INC
Also Called: Cinedome 9
6233 Garfield Ave (95841-2010)
PHONE..................916 332-2622
Sayward Gray, Brnch Mgr
EMP: 252
Web: www.cinemark.com
SIC: 7833 7832 Drive-in motion picture theaters; Motion picture theaters, except drive-in
HQ: Century Theatres, Inc
3900 Dallas Pkwy Ste 500
Plano TX
972 665-1000

(P-14021)
CENTURY THEATRES INC
Also Called: Empire Cinema
85 West Portal Ave (94127-1303)
PHONE..................415 661-2539
Robert Morgan, Mgr
EMP: 261
Web: www.cinemark.com
SIC: 7833 7832 Drive-in motion picture theaters; Motion picture theaters, except drive-in
HQ: Century Theatres, Inc
3900 Dallas Pkwy Ste 500
Plano TX
972 665-1000

(P-14022)
CENTURY THEATRES INC
Also Called: Sacramento Drive In
9616 Oates Dr (95827-1607)
PHONE..................916 363-6572
Raymond Syufy, Brnch Mgr
EMP: 194
Web: www.westwinddi.com
SIC: 7833 7832 Drive-in motion picture theaters; Motion picture theaters, except drive-in
HQ: Century Theatres, Inc
3900 Dallas Pkwy Ste 500
Plano TX
972 665-1000

7833 - Drive-in Motion Picture Theaters (P-14023)

(P-14023)
NATIONWIDE THEATRES CORP (HQ)
120 N Robertson Blvd Fl 3 (90048-3115)
PHONE.................................310 657-8420
Christopher Forman, *Pr*
Nora Dashwood, *
EMP: 75 **EST:** 1956
SQ FT: 25,000
SALES (est): 50.16MM
SALES (corp-wide): 175.87MM **Privately Held**
SIC: 7833 7832 Drive-in motion picture theaters; Motion picture theaters, except drive-in
PA: The Decurion Corporation
   120 N Robertson Blvd Fl 3
   Los Angeles CA
   310 659-9432

7841 Video Tape Rental

(P-14024)
EROS STX GLOBAL CORPORATION
3900 W Alameda Ave Fl 32 (91505-4316)
PHONE.................................818 524-7000
Kishore Lulla, *C Executive**
Rishika Lulla Singh, *
Andrew Warren, *CFO*
EMP: 502 **EST:** 1977
SALES (est): 434.26MM **Privately Held**
Web: www.erosstx.com
SIC: 7841 Video disk/tape rental to the general public

7922 Theatrical Producers And Services

(P-14025)
ADVENTIST MEDIA CENTER INC (PA)
Also Called: It Is Written
11291 Pierce St (92505-2705)
P.O. Box 101 (93062-0101)
PHONE.................................805 955-7777
Daniel R Jackson, *CEO*
Marshall Chase, *
Warren Judd, *
Daniel Jackson, *
▲ **EMP:** 183 **EST:** 1972
SQ FT: 76,000
SALES (est): 566.81K
SALES (corp-wide): 566.81K **Privately Held**
Web: www.adventistmediaministries.com
SIC: 7922 Television program, including commercial producers

(P-14026)
AEG PRESENTS LLC (DH)
Also Called: AEG Presents
425 W 11th St (90015-3459)
PHONE.................................323 930-5700
Jay Marciano, *Ch*
Jorge Melendez, *
John Meglen, *
Paul Gongaware, *
Shawn A Trell, *
▲ **EMP:** 140 **EST:** 2002
SQ FT: 16,400
SALES (est): 21.64MM **Privately Held**
Web: www.aegpresents.com
SIC: 7922 Entertainment promotion
HQ: Anschutz Entertainment Group, Inc.
   800 W Olympic Blvd # 305
   Los Angeles CA
   213 763-7700

(P-14027)
AGENCY FOR PERFORMING ARTS INC (PA)
405 S Beverly Dr Ste 500 (90212-4401)
PHONE.................................310 557-9049
James Gosnell, *
EMP: 100 **EST:** 1962
SALES (est): 39.99MM
SALES (corp-wide): 39.99MM **Privately Held**
Web: www.apa-agency.com
SIC: 7922 Theatrical producers and services

(P-14028)
BISCUIT FILMWORKS LLC
7026 Santa Monica Blvd (90038-1012)
PHONE.................................323 856-9200
EMP: 62 **EST:** 2014
SALES (est): 1.73MM **Privately Held**
Web: www.biscuitfilmworks.com
SIC: 7922 Television program, including commercial producers

(P-14029)
BROADWAY BY BAY
1972 2nd Ave (94597-2563)
P.O. Box 728 (94070-0728)
PHONE.................................650 579-5565
Waren Doan, *Pr*
EMP: 140 **EST:** 1967
SQ FT: 1,600
SALES (est): 466.87K **Privately Held**
Web: www.bbbay.org
SIC: 7922 Ticket agency, theatrical

(P-14030)
BROADWAY SACRAMENTO (PA)
Also Called: Music Circus
1510 J St Ste 200 (95814-2099)
PHONE.................................916 446-5880
Richard Lewis, *Pr*
▲ **EMP:** 150 **EST:** 1951
SQ FT: 7,000
SALES (est): 19.6MM **Privately Held**
Web: www.broadwaysacramento.com
SIC: 7922 Theatrical companies

(P-14031)
CALIFORNIA SHAKESPEARE THEATER (PA)
Also Called: Cal Shakes
100 California Shakespear Theater Way (94563)
PHONE.................................510 548-3422
Eric Ting, *Ex Dir*
Megan Barton, *Point of Contact**
EMP: 89 **EST:** 1974
SALES (est): 4.36MM
SALES (corp-wide): 4.36MM **Privately Held**
Web: www.calshakes.org
SIC: 7922 Plays, road and stock companies

(P-14032)
CENTER THTRE GROUP LOS ANGELES (PA)
601 W Temple St (90012-2621)
PHONE.................................213 972-7344
Meghan Pressman, *CEO*
Stephen Rountree, *
William Ahmanson, *
Kiki Gindler, *
Brindell Gottlieb, *
▲ **EMP:** 130 **EST:** 1966
SQ FT: 20,000
SALES (est): 15.78MM
SALES (corp-wide): 15.78MM **Privately Held**
Web: www.centertheatregroup.org
SIC: 7922 Theatrical companies

(P-14033)
CIRCLE TALENT AGENCY LLC
8383 Wilshire Blvd (90211-2425)
PHONE.................................323 424-4970
Steve Gordon, *Owner*
EMP: 74 **EST:** 2012
SALES (est): 1.2MM **Privately Held**
Web: www.unitedtalent.com
SIC: 7922 Talent agent, theatrical

(P-14034)
CITY OF DOWNEY
Also Called: Downey Civic Theatre
8435 Firestone Blvd (90241-3843)
P.O. Box 607 (90241-0607)
PHONE.................................562 861-8211
Gerald Caton, *Mgr*
EMP: 108
SALES (corp-wide): 148.39MM **Privately Held**
Web: www.downeyca.org
SIC: 7922 Legitimate live theater producers
PA: City Of Downey
   11111 Brookshire Ave
   Downey CA
   562 869-7331

(P-14035)
CREATIVE ARTSTS AGCY HLDNGS LL (PA)
Also Called: C A A
2000 Avenue Of The Stars Ste 100 (90067-4700)
PHONE.................................424 288-2000
Steve Hasker, *CEO*
Rick Nicita, *
Lee Gabler, *
Richard Lovett, *
Bruce King, *Finance**
EMP: 800 **EST:** 1975
SALES (est): 524.81MM
SALES (corp-wide): 524.81MM **Privately Held**
Web: www.caa.com
SIC: 7922 Agent or manager for entertainers

(P-14036)
DELICATE PRODUCTIONS INC (PA)
874 Verdulera St (93010-8371)
PHONE.................................415 484-1174
James Steve Dabbs, *CEO*
Steven I Gilbard, *
Angus Thomson, *
Christopher Smyth, *
Brian Boy, *
EMP: 62 **EST:** 1978
SQ FT: 19,937
SALES (est): 9.51MM
SALES (corp-wide): 9.51MM **Privately Held**
Web: www.delicate.com
SIC: 7922 7359 Equipment rental, theatrical; Sound and lighting equipment rental

(P-14037)
FANDANGO INC (HQ)
Also Called: Fandangonow
12200 W Olympic Blvd Ste 400 (90064-1047)
PHONE.................................310 954-0278
Chuck Davis, *CEO*
Paul Yanover, *
Arthur Levitt Iii, *Pr*
Walter Williams, *
Daniel V Murray, *
EMP: 71 **EST:** 1996
SQ FT: 10,000
SALES (est): 49.84MM
SALES (corp-wide): 121.43B **Publicly Held**
Web: www.fandango.com
SIC: 7922 Ticket agency, theatrical
PA: Comcast Corporation
   1 Comcast Ctr
   Philadelphia PA
   215 286-1700

(P-14038)
FIGUREPLANT LLC
2122 Bryant St (94110-2128)
PHONE.................................503 289-2070
David Fredrickson, *Brnch Mgr*
EMP: 69
SALES (corp-wide): 8.93MM **Privately Held**
Web: www.figureplant.com
SIC: 7922 Scenery design, theatrical
PA: Figureplant Llc
   8411 N Denver Ave
   Portland OR
   415 206-0407

(P-14039)
FRIENDS OF CULTURAL CENTER INC
Also Called: McCallum Theatre
73000 Fred Waring Dr (92260-2800)
PHONE.................................760 346-6505
Jamie Grant, *Pr*
William Towers, *
Harold Matzner, *Vice Chairman**
Ron Gregroire, *
Robert Mcconnaughey, *CFO*
EMP: 100 **EST:** 1973
SQ FT: 66,000
SALES (est): 20.41MM **Privately Held**
Web: www.mccallumtheatre.com
SIC: 7922 Legitimate live theater producers

(P-14040)
INNOVTIVE ARTSTS TLENT LTRARY (PA)
1505 10th St (90401-2805)
PHONE.................................310 656-0400
Scott Harris, *Pr*
EMP: 75 **EST:** 1982
SALES (est): 10.59MM
SALES (corp-wide): 10.59MM **Privately Held**
Web: www.innovativeartists.com
SIC: 7922 7819 Talent agent, theatrical; Casting bureau, motion picture

(P-14041)
J C ENTERTAINMENT LTG SVCS INC
Also Called: E L S
5435 W San Fernando Rd (90039-1014)
PHONE.................................818 252-7481
John Allen Chuck, *CEO*
Kevin Dowling, *
Derek Smith, *
Todd Richards, *
EMP: 106 **EST:** 1991
SQ FT: 69,000
SALES (est): 4.74MM **Privately Held**
Web: www.4wall.com
SIC: 7922 5719 Equipment rental, theatrical; Lighting, lamps, and accessories

(P-14042)
LAGUNA PLAYHOUSE (PA)
606 Laguna Canyon Rd (92651-1837)
P.O. Box 1747 (92652-1747)
PHONE.................................949 497-2787
Karen Wood, *CEO*

PRODUCTS & SERVICES SECTION
7922 - Theatrical Producers And Services (P-14062)

Richard Stein, *
Bob Crowson, *
EMP: 225 **EST:** 1920
SQ FT: 19,000
SALES (est): 2.83MM
SALES (corp-wide): 2.83MM Privately Held
Web: www.lagunaplayhouse.com
SIC: 7922 Legitimate live theater producers

(P-14043)
LOS ANGELES OPERA COMPANY
135 N Grand Ave Ste 327 (90012-3018)
PHONE.................213 972-7219
▲ **EMP:** 500 **EST:** 1966
SALES (est): 46.17MM Privately Held
Web: www.laopera.org
SIC: 7922 Theatrical producers and services

(P-14044)
LUCAS DIGITAL LTD (DH)
3155 Kerner Blvd (94901-5410)
P.O. Box 3000 (94912-3000)
PHONE.................415 258-2000
James Morris, *Pr*
EMP: 500 **EST:** 1993
SALES (est): 9.49MM
SALES (corp-wide): 82.72B Publicly Held
SIC: 7922 7819 Theatrical producers and services; Sound effects and music production, motion picture
HQ: Lucasfilm Ltd. Llc
1110 Gorgas Ave Bldg C
San Francisco CA
415 623-1000

(P-14045)
LUTHER BURBANK MEM FOUNDATION
50 Mark West Springs Rd (95403-1436)
PHONE.................707 546-3600
Richard Nowlin, *Ex Dir*
EMP: 74 **EST:** 1978
SQ FT: 120,000
SALES (est): 3.61MM Privately Held
Web: www.lutherburbankcenter.org
SIC: 7922 8299 6519 Performing arts center production; Music and drama schools; Real property lessors, nec

(P-14046)
MAGIC MOUNTAIN LLC
Also Called: Six Flags Magic Mountain
26101 Magic Mountain Pkwy (91355-1052)
P.O. Box 5500 (91380-5500)
PHONE.................661 255-4100
▲ **EMP:** 216 **EST:** 2006
SALES (est): 8.89MM
SALES (corp-wide): 1.36B Publicly Held
Web: www.sixflags.com
SIC: 7922 7996 Entertainment promotion; Theme park, amusement
PA: Six Flags Entertainment Corp
1000 Ballpark Way Ste 400
Arlington TX
972 595-5000

(P-14047)
MANAGEMENT 360
9111 Wilshire Blvd (90210-5508)
P.O. Box A (90213-3087)
PHONE.................310 272-7000
Evelyn O Neill, *Prin*
EMP: 68 **EST:** 1992
SALES (est): 5.45MM Privately Held
Web: www.management360.com
SIC: 7922 Agent or manager for entertainers

(P-14048)
NBC STUDIOS INC
Also Called: NBC
100 Universal City Plz Fl 3 (91608-1002)
PHONE.................818 777-1000
EMP: 1000
SIC: 7922 Television program, including commercial producers

(P-14049)
NEWPORT TELEVISION LLC
4880 N 1st St (93726-0514)
PHONE.................559 761-0243
EMP: 327
SALES (corp-wide): 20.65MM Privately Held
Web: www.newporttv.com
SIC: 7922 Television program, including commercial producers
PA: Newport Television Llc
460 Nichols Rd Ste 250
Kansas City MO
816 751-0200

(P-14050)
OLD GLOBE THEATRE
Also Called: Old Globe
1363 Old Globe Way (92101-1696)
P.O. Box 122171 (92112-2171)
PHONE.................619 234-5623
Michael G Murphy, *CEO*
Louis Spisto, *
Mark Somers, *
▲ **EMP:** 500 **EST:** 1937
SALES (est): 29.92MM Privately Held
Web: www.theoldglobe.org
SIC: 7922 Performing arts center production

(P-14051)
PARADIGM MUSIC LLC (PA)
Also Called: Paradigm
360 N Crescent Dr (90210-4874)
PHONE.................310 288-8000
EMP: 70 **EST:** 1993
SALES (est): 24.9MM Privately Held
SIC: 7922 Talent agent, theatrical

(P-14052)
PARADIGM TALENT AGENCY LLC
6725 W Sunset Blvd (90028-7119)
PHONE.................310 288-8000
Sam Gores, *Brnch Mgr*
EMP: 72
SALES (corp-wide): 11.05MM Privately Held
Web: www.paradigmagency.com
SIC: 7922 Talent agent, theatrical
PA: Paradigm Talent Agency, Llc
700 N San Vicnte Blvd
West Hollywood CA
310 288-8000

(P-14053)
PARAMOUNT THEATRE OF ARTS INC
2025 Broadway (94612-2303)
PHONE.................510 893-2300
Leslee Stewart, *Dir*
EMP: 60 **EST:** 1986
SQ FT: 37,000
SALES (est): 5.04MM Privately Held
Web: www.paramountoakland.org
SIC: 7922 Legitimate live theater producers

(P-14054)
PERFORMING ARTS CTR LOS ANGLES
Also Called: Music Center
135 N Grand Ave Ste 314 (90012-3004)
PHONE.................213 972-7512
John Emerson, *Ch Bd*
Stephen Rountree, *
William Taylor, *
Lisa Whitney, *Prin*
Lisa Specht, *
▲ **EMP:** 250 **EST:** 1961
SQ FT: 24,000
SALES (est): 37.37MM
SALES (corp-wide): 37.37MM Privately Held
Web: www.musiccenter.org
SIC: 7922 Theatrical production services
PA: The Music Center Of Los Angeles County Inc
135 N Grand Ave Ste 201
Los Angeles CA
213 972-8007

(P-14055)
PLAYWRIGHTS FOUNDATION INC
1616 16th St Ste 350 (94103-5164)
PHONE.................415 626-2176
Amy Mueller, *Dir*
Linda Brewer, *
EMP: 73 **EST:** 1978
SQ FT: 1,200
SALES (est): 378.35K Privately Held
Web: www.playwrightsfoundation.org
SIC: 7922 Legitimate live theater producers

(P-14056)
PRDCTIONS N FREMANTLE AMER INC (DH)
Also Called: Fremantle Media
2900 W Alameda Ave Unit 800 (91505-4216)
PHONE.................818 748-1100
Thom Beers, *CEO*
Dan Goldberg, *
Donna Redier Linsk, *
Ellen Goldstein, *
EMP: 100 **EST:** 1995
SALES (est): 39.03MM
SALES (corp-wide): 54.57MM Privately Held
Web: www.fremantle.com
SIC: 7922 Television program, including commercial producers
HQ: Fremantlemedia Group Limited
1 Stephen Street
London
207 691-6000

(P-14057)
PREMIERE RADIO NETWORK INC (DH)
Also Called: Prn Radio Networks
15260 Ventura Blvd Ste 400 (91403-5349)
PHONE.................818 377-5300
Stephen C Lehman, *CEO*
Kraig T Kitchin, *
Timothy M Kelly, *
EMP: 200 **EST:** 1987
SQ FT: 15,000
SALES (est): 21.93MM Publicly Held
Web: www.premierenetworks.com
SIC: 7922 7389 4832 Radio producers; Advertising, promotional, and trade show services; Radio broadcasting stations
HQ: Jacor Communications Company
200 E Basse Rd
San Antonio TX
210 822-2828

(P-14058)
PROFESSNAL INTRCTIVE ENTRMT IN
Also Called: Global Gaming League
6080 Center Dr Ste 600 (90045-1540)
PHONE.................310 823-4445
Brett W Hawkins Junior, *CEO*
Ted Owen, *
Greg Johnson, *CMO*
EMP: 75 **EST:** 2002
SALES (est): 5.05MM Privately Held
SIC: 7922 Entertainment promotion

(P-14059)
RADFORD STUDIO CENTER LLC
Also Called: CBS Studio Center
4024 Radford Ave (91604-2101)
PHONE.................818 655-5000
Michael Klausman, *Pr*
Nina Tassler, *
EMP: 300 **EST:** 1927
SALES (est): 49.7MM
SALES (corp-wide): 30.15B Publicly Held
Web: www.radfordsc.com
SIC: 7922 6512 7999 Television program, including commercial producers; Nonresidential building operators; Martial arts school, nec
HQ: Cbs Broadcasting Inc.
524 W 57th St
New York NY
212 975-4321

(P-14060)
ROSE BRAND WIPERS INC
11440 Sheldon St (91352-1121)
PHONE.................818 505-6290
Tina Carlin, *Prin*
EMP: 72
SALES (corp-wide): 81.51MM Privately Held
Web: www.rosebrand.com
SIC: 7922 Costume and scenery design services
PA: Rose Brand Wipers, Inc.
4 Emerson Ln
Secaucus NJ
201 809-1730

(P-14061)
SACRAMENTO THEATRE COMPANY
1419 H St (95814-1901)
PHONE.................916 446-7501
Daniel Brunner, *Ch Bd*
Kendra Lewis Md, *Prin*
EMP: 76 **EST:** 1942
SALES (est): 881.3K Privately Held
Web: www.sactheatre.org
SIC: 7922 Legitimate live theater producers

(P-14062)
SACRAMENTO THEATRICAL LTG LTD
Also Called: S T L
410 N 10th St (95811-0333)
PHONE.................916 447-3258
TOLL FREE: 800
John W Cox, *CEO*
Kaye Newton, *
Bobbie Odehnal Theatrical, *Mgr*
EMP: 65 **EST:** 1947
SALES (est): 4.96MM Privately Held
Web: www.stlltd.com
SIC: 7922 5063 Equipment rental, theatrical; Lighting fixtures

7922 - Theatrical Producers And Services (P-14063)

(P-14063)
SAN DEGO REPERTORY THEATRE INC
79 Horton Plz (92101-6144)
PHONE..................619 231-3586
Samuel Woodhouse, *Dir*
EMP: 99 EST: 1976
SQ FT: 40,000
SALES (est): 6.02MM **Privately Held**
Web: www.sdrep.org
SIC: **7922** Legitimate live theater producers

(P-14064)
SAN DIEGO OPERA ASSOCIATION
3074 Commercial St (92113-1413)
PHONE..................619 232-5911
EMP: 225
SALES (corp-wide): 9.59MM **Privately Held**
Web: www.sdopera.org
SIC: **7922** Opera company
PA: San Diego Opera Association Inc
  233 A St Ste 500
  San Diego CA
  619 232-7636

(P-14065)
SAN DIEGO OPERA ASSOCIATION
Also Called: Scenic Studio
3064 Commercial St (92113-1413)
PHONE..................619 232-5911
Ron Allen, *Mgr*
EMP: 225
SQ FT: 35,000
SALES (corp-wide): 9.59MM **Privately Held**
Web: www.sdopera.org
SIC: **7922** Legitimate live theater producers
PA: San Diego Opera Association Inc
  233 A St Ste 500
  San Diego CA
  619 232-7636

(P-14066)
SAN FRANCISCO BALLET ASSN
Also Called: San Francisco Ballet
455 Franklin St (94102-4471)
PHONE..................415 865-2000
Glenn Mccoy, *Ex Dir*
Donald B Paterson, *
J Stuart Francis, *
Jennifer J Mccall, *Sec*
▲ EMP: 250 EST: 1933
SQ FT: 70,000
SALES (est): 3.7MM **Privately Held**
Web: www.sfballet.org
SIC: **7922** **7911** Ballet production; Dance studio and school

(P-14067)
SAN FRANCISCO OPERA ASSN
301 Van Ness Ave (94102-4509)
PHONE..................415 861-4008
John A Gunn, *Ch*
Karl O Mills, *Vice Chairman**
David Gockley, *
Keith B Geeslin, *
Paul Crane Dorfman, *
▲ EMP: 1050 EST: 1932
SALES (est): 27.25MM **Privately Held**
Web: www.sfopera.com
SIC: **7922** Legitimate live theater producers

(P-14068)
SENCLUB LLC
788 Mountain Shadows Dr (92881-3554)
PHONE..................626 317-8073
EMP: 75
SALES (est): 780.08K **Privately Held**
SIC: **7922** **7389** Entertainment promotion; Business Activities at Non-Commercial Site

(P-14069)
SOUTH COAST REPERTORY INC
Also Called: S C R
655 Town Center Dr (92626-1918)
P.O. Box 2197 (92628-2197)
PHONE..................714 708-5500
Martin Benson, *Dir*
David Emmes, *
EMP: 60 EST: 1964
SQ FT: 40,000
SALES (est): 10.89MM **Privately Held**
Web: cart.scr.org
SIC: **7922** Legitimate live theater producers

(P-14070)
TENNIS CHANNEL INC (HQ)
3003 Exposition Blvd (90404-5026)
PHONE..................310 392-1920
Ken Solomon, *CEO*
William Simon, *
EMP: 70 EST: 2001
SALES (est): 25.68MM
SALES (corp-wide): 3.93B **Publicly Held**
Web: www.thetennischannel.com
SIC: **7922** Television program, including commercial producers
PA: Sinclair Broadcast Group, Inc.
  10706 Beaver Dam Rd
  Hunt Valley MD
  410 568-1500

(P-14071)
THE GERSH AGENCY LLC (PA)
9465 Wilshire Blvd Fl 6 (90212-2605)
PHONE..................310 274-6611
Robert Gersh, *Pr*
David Gersh, *VP*
Beatrice Gersh, *VP*
EMP: 100 EST: 1949
SQ FT: 15,000
SALES (est): 20.5MM
SALES (corp-wide): 20.5MM **Privately Held**
Web: www.gersh.com
SIC: **7922** Talent agent, theatrical

(P-14072)
WESTSTAR CINEMAS INC
742 W Lancaster Blvd (93534-3130)
PHONE..................661 723-9392
EMP: 215
SALES (corp-wide): 22.59MM **Privately Held**
SIC: **7922** Theatrical companies
PA: Weststar Cinemas, Inc.
  16530 Ventura Blvd # 500
  Encino CA
  818 784-6266

(P-14073)
WILLIAM MRRIS ENDVOR ENTRMT FN (DH)
9601 Wilshire Blvd Fl 3 (90210-5219)
PHONE..................310 285-9000
Tom Strickler, *Pr*
Richard Rosen, *
Adam Venit, *
Phillip Raskind, *
EMP: 180 EST: 2000
SALES (est): 47.24MM
SALES (corp-wide): 5.27B **Publicly Held**
Web: www.wmeagency.com
SIC: **7922** **7829** Talent agent, theatrical; Motion picture distribution services
HQ: William Morris Endeavor Entertainment, Llc
  9601 Wilshire Blvd
  Beverly Hills CA
  212 586-5100

(P-14074)
WILLIAM MRRIS ENDVOR ENTRMT LL
Also Called: William Morris Consulting
9601 Wilshire Blvd Fl 3 (90210-5219)
PHONE..................310 285-9000
Chris Newman, *Brnch Mgr*
EMP: 393
SALES (corp-wide): 5.27B **Publicly Held**
Web: www.wmeagency.com
SIC: **7922** Talent agent, theatrical
HQ: William Morris Endeavor Entertainment, Llc
  9601 Wilshire Blvd
  Beverly Hills CA
  212 586-5100

7929 Entertainers And Entertainment Groups

(P-14075)
51 MINDS ENTERTAINMENT LLC
Also Called: Mindless Entertainment
5200 Lankershim Blvd Ste 200 (91601-3155)
PHONE..................818 643-8200
Julie Pizzi, *Pr*
▼ EMP: 60 EST: 2004
SALES (est): 10.07MM
SALES (corp-wide): 27.72MM **Privately Held**
Web: www.51minds.com
SIC: **7929** **7812** Entertainers; Television film production
PA: Endemol Usa Holding, Inc.
  5161 Lankershim Blvd # 40
  North Hollywood CA
  747 529-8000

(P-14076)
ANSCHUTZ ENTRMT GROUP INC (HQ)
Also Called: AEG Worldwide
800 W Olympic Blvd Ste 305 (90015-1366)
PHONE..................213 763-7700
Tim Leiweke, *Pr*
Dan Beckerman, *
Tracy Hartman, *
Dennis Dennehy, *CCO**
EMP: 154 EST: 1994
SALES (est): 431.33K **Privately Held**
Web: www.aegworldwide.com
SIC: **7929** Entertainment service
PA: The Anschutz Corporation
  555 17th St Ste 2400
  Denver CO

(P-14077)
ARAMARK SPT & ENTRMT GROUP LLC
Also Called: Aramark
525 W Santa Clara St (95113-1520)
PHONE..................408 999-5735
John Heberden, *Prin*
EMP: 65
Web: www.aramark.com
SIC: **7929** Entertainers and entertainment groups
HQ: Aramark Sports And Entertainment Group, Llc
  2400 Market St
  Philadelphia PA
  215 238-3000

(P-14078)
ARTISTIC ENTRMT SVCS LLC
120 N Aspan Ave (91702-4224)
PHONE..................626 334-9388
Craig Bugajski, *Managing Member*
EMP: 60 EST: 2003
SALES (est): 12.22MM **Privately Held**
Web: www.aescreative.com
SIC: **7929** Entertainment service

(P-14079)
BANG ZOOM ENTERTAINMENT INC
1100 N Hollywood Way Ste A (91505-2538)
PHONE..................818 295-3939
Eric Sherman, *Owner*
EMP: 70 EST: 1994
SALES (est): 7.51MM **Privately Held**
Web: www.bangzoomstudios.com
SIC: **7929** Entertainment service

(P-14080)
CZND INC
8444 Wilshire Blvd Fl 5 (90211-3200)
PHONE..................323 378-6505
Luigi Picarazzi, *Pr*
EMP: 68 EST: 2015
SALES (est): 1.25MM **Privately Held**
Web: www.cznd.co
SIC: **7929** Entertainment service

(P-14081)
EASE ENTERTAINMENT SERVICES LP
8383 Wilshire Blvd Ste 90 (90211-2430)
PHONE..................310 469-7300
EMP: 75
SIC: **7929** Entertainers and entertainment groups

(P-14082)
ENTERTINMENT STUDIOS MEDIA INC (PA)
1925 Century Park E Ste 1025 (90067-2701)
PHONE..................310 277-3500
Byron Allen Folks, *CEO*
Eric Gould Evp, *Finance**
Nora Zimmett, *CCO**
EMP: 65 EST: 1993
SQ FT: 5,000
SALES (est): 204.87MM **Privately Held**
SIC: **7929** Entertainers and entertainment groups

(P-14083)
ESL GAMING AMERICA INC
Also Called: Esl
1212 Chestnut St (91506-1627)
PHONE..................818 861-7315
Ralf Reichert, *CEO*
EMP: 99 EST: 2014
SALES (est): 8.57MM **Privately Held**
Web: www.esl.com
SIC: **7929** Entertainment service
HQ: Savvy Games Group
  Office 2.14 B, 6th Floor, Kafd, King Fahad Road
  Riyadh

(P-14084)
HOB ENTERTAINMENT LLC
Also Called: House of Blues Anaheim
400 W Disney Way Ste 337 (92802-2912)
PHONE..................714 520-2310
Darryl Taketa, *Brnch Mgr*
EMP: 181
Web: www.houseofblues.com

PRODUCTS & SERVICES SECTION
7929 - Entertainers And Entertainment Groups (P-14107)

SIC: 7929 Entertainment service
HQ: Hob Entertainment, Llc
   7060 Hollywood Blvd
   Los Angeles CA

(P-14085)
HOB ENTERTAINMENT LLC
1055 5th Ave (92101-5101)
PHONE..................................619 299-2583
Jim Biasore, *Mgr*
EMP: 79
Web: www.houseofblues.com
SIC: 7929 Entertainment service
HQ: Hob Entertainment; Llc
   7060 Hollywood Blvd
   Los Angeles CA

(P-14086)
HOB ENTERTAINMENT LLC (DH)
Also Called: House of Blues
7060 Hollywood Blvd (90028-6014)
PHONE..................................323 769-4600
Michael Rapino, *CEO*
Joseph C Kaczorowski, *
Peter Cyffka, *
EMP: 172 EST: 1993
SQ FT: 53,000
SALES (est): 305.78MM **Publicly Held**
Web: www.houseofblues.com
SIC: 7929 Entertainment service
HQ: Live Nation Worldwide, Inc.
   430 W 15th St
   New York NY
   917 421-5100

(P-14087)
HOUSE OF BLUES CONCERTS INC (DH)
6255 W Sunset Blvd Fl 16 (90028-7403)
PHONE..................................323 769-4977
Joe Kazoworski, *Pr*
EMP: 150 EST: 1978
SALES (est): 19.21MM **Publicly Held**
Web: www.houseofblues.com
SIC: 7929 Entertainers and entertainment groups
HQ: Hob Entertainment, Llc
   7060 Hollywood Blvd
   Los Angeles CA

(P-14088)
ILLUMINATION ENTERTAINMENT
2043 Colorado Ave (90404-3415)
PHONE..................................626 298-1879
Chris Meledandri, *CEO*
EMP: 141 EST: 2007
SALES (est): 31.1MM
SALES (corp-wide): 121.43B **Publicly Held**
Web: www.illuminationentertainment.com
SIC: 7929 Entertainment service
HQ: Universal Studios Limited
   1 Central St. Giles
   London
   203 618-8000

(P-14089)
INMOTION ENTRMT GROUP LLC
3225 N Harbor Dr (92101-1024)
PHONE..................................904 332-0459
EMP: 135
Web: www.inmotionstores.com
SIC: 7929 Entertainers
HQ: Inmotion Entertainment Group, Llc
   3755 W Sunset Rd Ste A
   Las Vegas NV
   904 332-0450

(P-14090)
INSOMNIAC INC
Also Called: Insomniac
5023 Parkway Calabasas (91302-1421)
PHONE..................................323 874-7020
Pasquale Rotella, *CEO*
Simon Rust Lamb, *
John Boyle, *Interim Chief Financial Officer*
▲ EMP: 195 EST: 1998
SALES (est): 48.35MM **Privately Held**
Web: www.insomniac.com
SIC: 7929 Entertainment service

(P-14091)
KATCH ENTERTAINMENT LLC
170 Wildwood Way (94062-2352)
PHONE..................................650 380-0607
EMP: 97 EST: 2018
SALES (est): 164.9K **Privately Held**
SIC: 7929 Entertainment service

(P-14092)
LIVE NATION WORLDWIDE INC (HQ)
Also Called: Observatory, The
9348 Civic Center Dr Lbby (90210-3642)
PHONE..................................310 867-7000
Kathy Willard, *CEO*
EMP: 8800 EST: 1997
SALES (est): 116.81MM **Publicly Held**
Web: www.livenationentertainment.com
SIC: 7929 Entertainers and entertainment groups
PA: Live Nation Entertainment, Inc.
   9348 Civic Center Dr Lbby
   Beverly Hills CA

(P-14093)
LOS ANGELES PHILHARMONIC ASSN (PA)
Also Called: L A PHILHARMONIC
151 S Grand Ave (90012-3034)
P.O. Box 1951 (90078-1951)
PHONE..................................213 972-7300
Chad Smith, *CEO*
Thomas L Beckman, *
Alan Wayte, *
Ben Cadwallader, *
Gail Samuel, *HOLLYWOOD BOWL*
EMP: 200 EST: 1934
SQ FT: 13,467
SALES (est): 158.2MM
SALES (corp-wide): 158.2MM **Privately Held**
Web: www.laphil.com
SIC: 7929 Symphony orchestra

(P-14094)
LOS ANGELES PHILHARMONIC ASSN
Also Called: Hollywood Bowl
2301 N Highland Ave (90068-2742)
PHONE..................................323 850-2060
Ed Tom, *Dir*
EMP: 899
SALES (corp-wide): 158.2MM **Privately Held**
Web: www.hollywoodbowl.com
SIC: 7929 Entertainment group
PA: Los Angeles Philharmonic Association
   151 S Grand Ave
   Los Angeles CA
   213 972-7300

(P-14095)
MAKER STUDIOS LLC (DH)
3515 Eastham Dr (90232-2440)
PHONE..................................310 606-2182
Courtney Holt, *CEO*

Lisa Donovan, *
EMP: 250 EST: 2009
SQ FT: 20,000
SALES (est): 49.51MM
SALES (corp-wide): 82.72B **Publicly Held**
SIC: 7929 Entertainment service
HQ: Twdc Enterprises 18 Corp.
   500 S Buena Vista St
   Burbank CA

(P-14096)
MING ENTERTAINMENT GROUP LLC
2082 Business Center Dr Ste 292 (92612)
PHONE..................................949 679-2089
EMP: 65 EST: 2007
SALES (est): 1.24MM **Privately Held**
Web: www.mingentertainment.com
SIC: 7929 Entertainers and entertainment groups

(P-14097)
MPC PRODUCTIONS LLC
12035 Killion St (91401)
PHONE..................................310 418-8115
EMP: 75 EST: 2016
SALES (est): 152.02K **Privately Held**
SIC: 7929 Entertainment service

(P-14098)
NOW CASTING INC
211 N Victory Blvd (91502-1839)
PHONE..................................818 588-3732
Robert Stewart, *CEO*
Melody Stewart, *Sec*
Richard La Fond, *COO*
EMP: 110 EST: 1997
SALES (est): 975.91K **Privately Held**
Web: www.nowcasting.com
SIC: 7929 Entertainment service

(P-14099)
PACIFIC SYMPHONY
17620 Fitch Ave Ste 100 (92614-6081)
PHONE..................................714 755-5788
Jjohn Forsyte, *Pr*
John E Forsyte, *
Rhonda Halverson, *
Arthur Ong, *
EMP: 60 EST: 1980
SQ FT: 5,750
SALES (est): 30.87MM **Privately Held**
Web: www.pacificsymphony.org
SIC: 7929 Symphony orchestra

(P-14100)
RED BULL NORTH AMERICA INC (HQ)
Also Called: Red Bull TV
1630 Stewart St (90404-4020)
PHONE..................................310 460-5356
▲ EMP: 100 EST: 1995
SALES (est): 412.82MM
SALES (corp-wide): 10.06B **Privately Held**
Web: www.redbull.com
SIC: 7929 Entertainment service
PA: Red Bull Gmbh
   Am Brunnen 1
   Fuschl Am See
   66265820

(P-14101)
ROC NATION LLC (HQ)
9348 Civic Center Dr (90210-3624)
PHONE..................................310 975-6854
EMP: 71 EST: 2008
SALES (est): 23.28MM **Publicly Held**
Web: www.rocnation.com

SIC: 7929 Entertainment service
PA: Live Nation Entertainment, Inc.
   9348 Civic Center Dr Lbby
   Beverly Hills CA

(P-14102)
SAN DEGO SYMPHONY ORCHESTRA ASS
1245 7th Ave (92101-4302)
PHONE..................................619 235-0800
Edward B Gill, *Ex Dir*
EMP: 110 EST: 1928
SALES (est): 89.36MM **Privately Held**
Web: www.sandiegosymphony.org
SIC: 7929 Symphony orchestra

(P-14103)
SAN DIEGO SYMPHONY FOUNDATION
1245 7th Ave (92101-4398)
PHONE..................................619 235-0800
EMP: 135 EST: 2011
SALES (est): 925.95K **Privately Held**
Web: www.sandiegosymphony.org
SIC: 7929 Symphony orchestra

(P-14104)
SAN FRANCISCO SYMPHONY (PA)
201 Van Ness Ave (94103-3713)
PHONE..................................415 552-8000
Brent Assink, *CEO*
Mark Koenig, *
Liz Pesch, *
▲ EMP: 178 EST: 1911
SALES (est): 66.43MM
SALES (corp-wide): 66.43MM **Privately Held**
Web: www.sfsymphony.org
SIC: 7929 Symphony orchestra

(P-14105)
SONY INTERACTIVE ENTRMT LLC
2207 Bridgepointe Pkwy (94404)
PHONE..................................650 655-8000
Fumihiko Kanagawa, *Mgr*
EMP: 192
Web: www.playstation.com
SIC: 7929 Entertainment service
HQ: Sony Interactive Entertainment Llc
   2207 Bridgepointe Pkwy
   Foster City CA
   310 981-1500

(P-14106)
SPSV ENTERTAINMENT LLC
Also Called: Skypark At Santa's Village
28950 State Highway 18 (92385-0460)
P.O. Box 369 (92385-0369)
PHONE..................................909 744-9373
William Johnson, *Managing Member*
EMP: 99 EST: 2016
SALES (est): 5.21MM **Privately Held**
Web: www.skyparksantasvillage.com
SIC: 7929 Entertainers and entertainment groups

(P-14107)
TRI STAR SPT ENTRMT GROUP INC
9255 W Sunset Blvd Fl 2 (90069-3309)
PHONE..................................615 309-0969
Lou Taylor, *CEO*
EMP: 100 EST: 2016
SALES (est): 1.11MM **Privately Held**
SIC: 7929 Entertainers and entertainment groups

7929 - Entertainers And Entertainment Groups (P-14108)

PRODUCTS & SERVICES SECTION

(P-14108)
TWENTY MILE PRODUCTIONS LLC
11833 Mississippi Ave Ste 101 (90025-6135)
PHONE.................................412 251-0767
Margaret Ellison, *
EMP: 150 **EST:** 2013
SALES (est): 1.13MM **Privately Held**
SIC: 7929 Entertainment group

(P-14109)
TWO BIT CIRCUS DTLA LLC
Also Called: Two Bit Circus
634 Mateo St (90021-1312)
PHONE.................................323 438-9808
Brent Bushnell, *Prin*
Eric Co Gradam, *Prin*
Kimberly Schaefer, *
Christopher Ogilvie, *
EMP: 80 **EST:** 2018
SALES (est): 1.4MM **Privately Held**
Web: www.twobitcircus.com
SIC: 7929 Entertainment service

(P-14110)
UBICOM INC
625 3rd St Fl 3 (94107-1901)
PHONE.................................415 547-4000
Yves Guillemot, *Pr*
EMP: 94 **EST:** 2011
SALES (est): 8.37MM
SALES (corp-wide): 2.51B **Privately Held**
Web: www.ubisoft.com
SIC: 7929 Entertainers and entertainment groups
PA: Ubisoft Entertainment
  2 Rue Du Chene Heleuc
  Carentoir

(P-14111)
WARNER BROS HOME ENTRMT GROUP (DH)
4000 Warner Blvd (91522-0002)
PHONE.................................818 954-6000
EMP: 62 **EST:** 2005
SALES (est): 62.15MM **Publicly Held**
SIC: 7929 Entertainment service
HQ: Warner Bros. (Transatlantic), Inc.
  4000 Warner Blvd
  Burbank CA

(P-14112)
YANKA INDUSTRIES INC
Also Called: Masterclass
660 4th St Ste 443 (94107-1618)
PHONE.................................855 981-8208
David Jeremy Rogier, *CEO*
Paul Bankhead, *Chief Product Officer*
EMP: 314 **EST:** 2012
SALES (est): 8.67MM **Privately Held**
Web: www.masterclass.com
SIC: 7929 7812 2721 Entertainment service; Video production; Periodicals

(P-14113)
YOU ME AND SCIENCES INC ✪
202 W Manchester Ave (90293-7710)
P.O. Box 90307 (90009-0307)
PHONE.................................310 406-7350
Jessica Lesley, *CEO*
EMP: 85 **EST:** 2022
SALES (est): 1.61MM **Privately Held**
Web: www.youmeandsciences.com
SIC: 7929 Entertainment service

(P-14114)
ZEUS NETWORKS LLC
Also Called: Zeus
11713 Riverside Dr (91607-4020)
PHONE.................................323 910-4420
EMP: 75 **EST:** 2018
SALES (est): 20MM **Privately Held**
SIC: 7929 Entertainment service

7933 Bowling Centers

(P-14115)
GABLE HOUSE INC
Also Called: Gable House Bowl
1611 S Pacific Coast Hwy (90277-5605)
PHONE.................................310 378-2265
Michael Mickey Cogan, *Pr*
EMP: 100 **EST:** 1959
SALES (est): 5.14MM **Privately Held**
Web: www.gablehousebowl.com
SIC: 7933 5813 5812 Ten pin center; Bar (drinking places); Snack bar

(P-14116)
LUCKY STRIKE ENTERTAINMENT INC
800 W Olympic Blvd Ste 250 (90015-1366)
PHONE.................................213 542-4880
Bobby Braydoy, *Brnch Mgr*
EMP: 297
Web: www.luckystrikeent.com
SIC: 7933 5813 5812 Ten pin center; Tavern (drinking places); American restaurant
PA: Lucky Strike Entertainment, Inc.
  15260 Ventura Blvd # 1110
  Sherman Oaks CA

(P-14117)
LUCKY STRIKE ENTERTAINMENT LLC
6801 Hollywood Blvd Ste 143 (90028-6138)
PHONE.................................818 933-3752
David Bradley, *Genl Mgr*
EMP: 60
SALES (corp-wide): 1.06B **Publicly Held**
Web: www.luckystrikeent.com
SIC: 7933 Ten pin center
HQ: Lucky Strike Entertainment, Llc
  16350 Ventura Blvd Ste D
  Encino CA
  818 933-3752

(P-14118)
LUCKY STRIKE ENTERTAINMENT LLC
Also Called: Lucky Strike Novi
15260 Ventura Blvd Ste 1110 (91403-5346)
PHONE.................................248 374-3420
Eddie Bourque, *Brnch Mgr*
EMP: 62
SALES (corp-wide): 1.06B **Publicly Held**
Web: www.luckystrikeent.com
SIC: 7933 Ten pin center
HQ: Lucky Strike Entertainment, Llc
  16350 Ventura Blvd Ste D
  Encino CA
  818 933-3752

(P-14119)
LUCKY STRIKE ENTERTAINMENT LLC
20 City Blvd W Ste G2 (92868-3131)
PHONE.................................248 374-3420
Ismail Saleem, *Brnch Mgr*
EMP: 99
SALES (corp-wide): 1.06B **Publicly Held**
Web: www.luckystrikeent.com
SIC: 7933 Ten pin center
HQ: Lucky Strike Entertainment, Llc
  16350 Ventura Blvd Ste D
  Encino CA
  818 933-3752

(P-14120)
NATIONWIDE THEATRES CORP
Also Called: Cal Coffee Shop
2500 Carson St (90712-4107)
PHONE.................................562 421-8448
Tom Moeller, *Mgr*
EMP: 2720
SALES (corp-wide): 175.87MM **Privately Held**
Web: www.calbowl.com
SIC: 7933 5813 5812 Ten pin center; Cocktail lounge; Coffee shop
HQ: Nationwide Theatres Corp.
  120 N Robertson Blvd Fl 3
  Los Angeles CA
  310 657-8420

(P-14121)
PINSETTERS INC
Also Called: Country Club Lanes
2600 Watt Ave (95821-6296)
PHONE.................................916 488-7545
Greg Kassis, *Ch Bd*
Dave Haness, *
Dave Kassis, *
Kerry Kassis, *
Jim Kassis, *
EMP: 75 **EST:** 1958
SQ FT: 70,000
SALES (est): 3.72MM **Privately Held**
Web: www.countryclublanes.com
SIC: 7933 5812 5813 Ten pin center; Snack bar; Bar (drinking places)

(P-14122)
STRIKES UNLIMITED INC
5681 Lonetree Blvd (95765-3735)
PHONE.................................916 626-3600
Kari Pegram, *CEO*
EMP: 90 **EST:** 2011
SQ FT: 54,000
SALES (est): 5.08MM **Privately Held**
Web: www.bowlero.com
SIC: 7933 5812 Ten pin center; Eating places

7941 Sports Clubs, Managers, And Promoters

(P-14123)
ANAHEIM ARENA MANAGEMENT LLC
Also Called: AAM
2695 E Katella Ave (92806-5904)
PHONE.................................714 704-2400
Michael Schulman, *
Angela Wergechik, *
James Pearson, *
EMP: 600 **EST:** 2001
SQ FT: 106,000
SALES (est): 81.4MM **Privately Held**
Web: www.hondacenter.com
SIC: 7941 Sports field or stadium operator, promoting sports events

(P-14124)
ANAHEIM DUCKS HOCKEY CLUB LLC
Also Called: Anaheim Ducks
2101 E Coast Hwy Fl 3 (92625-1900)
PHONE.................................714 940-2900
Michel Schulman, *Managing Member*
EMP: 69
Web: www.nhl.com
SIC: 7941 Sports clubs, managers, and promoters
PA: Anaheim Ducks Hockey Club, Llc
  2695 E Katella Ave
  Anaheim CA

(P-14125)
ANAHEIM DUCKS HOCKEY CLUB LLC (PA)
2695 E Katella Ave (92806-5904)
PHONE.................................714 940-2900
Michel Schulman, *Managing Member*
Doug Heller, *
Bob Murray, *
Tim Ryan, *
David Mcnab, *Sr VP*
EMP: 81 **EST:** 2005
SALES (est): 30.81MM **Privately Held**
Web: www.nhl.com
SIC: 7941 Sports clubs, managers, and promoters

(P-14126)
ANGELS BASEBALL LP (PA)
Also Called: Los Angeles Angels of Anaheim
2000 E Gene Autry Way (92806-6143)
PHONE.................................714 940-2000
Dennis Kuhl, *Genl Pt*
Bill Beverage, *Pt*
Molly Jolly, *Pt*
Tim Mead, *Pt*
Richard Mcclemmy, *Pt*
EMP: 790 **EST:** 1996
SALES (est): 113.58MM
SALES (corp-wide): 113.58MM **Privately Held**
Web: www.mlb.com
SIC: 7941 Baseball club, professional and semi-professional

(P-14127)
ATHLETICS INVESTMENT GROUP LLC (PA)
Also Called: Oakland Athletics
7000 Coliseum Way Ste 3 (94621-1945)
P.O. Box 2220 (94621-0120)
PHONE.................................510 638-4900
Lewis N Wolff, *Managing Member*
EMP: 177 **EST:** 1901
SALES (est): 45.04MM
SALES (corp-wide): 45.04MM **Privately Held**
Web: www.mlb.com
SIC: 7941 Baseball club, professional and semi-professional

(P-14128)
BIG LGUE DREAMS CONSULTING LLC
2155 Trumble Rd (92571-9211)
PHONE.................................619 846-8855
EMP: 107
SALES (corp-wide): 49.84MM **Privately Held**
Web: www.bigleaguedreams.com
SIC: 7941 Sports field or stadium operator, promoting sports events
PA: Big League Dreams Consulting, Llc
  16333 Fairfield Ranch Rd
  Chino Hills CA
  909 287-1700

(P-14129)
BIG LGUE DREAMS CONSULTING LLC
2100 S Azusa Ave (91792-1507)
PHONE.................................626 839-1100
Jeffrey Odekirk, *Prin*
EMP: 107
SALES (corp-wide): 49.84MM **Privately Held**
Web: www.bigleaguedreams.com
SIC: 7941 Sports field or stadium operator, promoting sports events
PA: Big League Dreams Consulting, Llc

PRODUCTS & SERVICES SECTION
7941 - Sports Clubs, Managers, And Promoters (P-14151)

16333 Fairfield Ranch Rd
Chino Hills CA
909 287-1700

(P-14130)
BIG3 BASKETBALL LLC
13351 Riverside Dr (91423-2542)
PHONE..................213 417-2013
Jeff Kwatinetz, *CEO*
O'shea Jackson Senior, *Prin*
EMP: 67 **EST:** 2016
SALES (est): 4.15MM **Privately Held**
Web: www.big3.com
SIC: 7941 Basketball club

(P-14131)
CALIFORNIA SPORTSERVICE INC
Also Called: San Diego Padres
100 Park Blvd (92101-7405)
PHONE..................619 795-5000
Jeremy M Jacobs, *Pr*
EMP: 380 **EST:** 1940
SALES (est): 24.28MM
SALES (corp-wide): 2.9B **Privately Held**
Web: www.mlb.com
SIC: 7941 Baseball club, professional and semi-professional
HQ: Delaware North Companies Sportservice, Inc.
250 Delaware Ave
Buffalo NY
716 858-5000

(P-14132)
CHARGERS FOOTBALL COMPANY LLC (PA)
Also Called: Los Angeles Chargers
3333 Susan St (92626-1632)
PHONE..................619 280-2121
Dean A Spanos, *Pr*
Dean A Spanos, *Managing Member*
Jim Steeg, *
Alex Spanos, *
Jeanne M Bonk, *
EMP: 70 **EST:** 1959
SALES (est): 691.7K
SALES (corp-wide): 691.7K **Privately Held**
Web: www.chargers.com
SIC: 7941 Football club

(P-14133)
CITY OF SAN DIEGO
Also Called: Petco Park
100 Park Blvd (92101-7405)
PHONE..................619 795-5000
John Morris, *Pr*
EMP: 263
SALES (corp-wide): 2.67B **Privately Held**
Web: www.petcoparkinsider.com
SIC: 7941 Sports field or stadium operator, promoting sports events
PA: City Of San Diego
202 C St
San Diego CA
619 236-6330

(P-14134)
CITY VIEW AT METREON
135 4th St Ste 4000 (94103-3060)
PHONE..................415 369-6142
EMP: 209 **EST:** 2014
SALES (est): 504.4K **Privately Held**
Web: www.cityviewmetreon.com
SIC: 7941 Stadium event operator services
HQ: Starwood Retail Partners, Llc
1 E Wacker Dr Ste 3600
Chicago IL
312 242-3200

(P-14135)
EARTHQUAKES SOCCER LLC
Also Called: Earthquakes
1123 Coleman Ave (95110-1104)
PHONE..................408 556-7700
EMP: 93 **EST:** 2006
SQ FT: 5,200
SALES (est): 20.34MM **Privately Held**
Web: www.sjearthquakes.com
SIC: 7941 Soccer club

(P-14136)
ENDEAVOR GROUP HOLDINGS INC (PA)
9601 Wilshire Blvd Fl 3 (90210-5219)
PHONE..................310 285-9000
Ariel Emanuel, *CEO*
Patrick Whitesell, *Ex Ch Bd*
Egon Durban, *Ch Bd*
Mark Shapiro, *Pr*
Jason Lublin, *CFO*
EMP: 90 **EST:** 2019
SALES (est): 5.27B
SALES (corp-wide): 5.27B **Publicly Held**
Web: www.mainconcept.com
SIC: 7941 Sports field or stadium operator, promoting sports events

(P-14137)
FORTY NINERS FOOTBALL CO LLC
Also Called: San Francisco 49ers
4949 Marie P Debartolo Way (95054-1156)
PHONE..................408 562-4949
Denise Debartolo York, *Prin*
Jed York, *Prin*
Al Guido, *Prin*
EMP: 99 **EST:** 1971
SALES (est): 37.41MM **Privately Held**
Web: www.49ers.com
SIC: 7941 Football club

(P-14138)
FOX BASEBALL HOLDINGS INC
1000 Vin Scully Ave (90012-2112)
PHONE..................323 224-1500
Frank Mccourt, *Pr*
EMP: 226 **EST:** 2000
SALES (est): 2.31MM
SALES (corp-wide): 82.72B **Publicly Held**
SIC: 7941 Baseball club, professional and semi-professional
HQ: Fox Entertainment Group, Llc
1211 Ave Of The Americas
New York NY
212 852-7000

(P-14139)
FOX BSB HOLDCO INC (HQ)
Also Called: GUGGENHEIM INVESTMENTS
1000 Vin Scully Ave (90012-2112)
PHONE..................323 224-1500
Steve Soboroff, *Vice Chairman*
Ron Wheeler, *
Santiago Fernandez, *
Dannis Mannion, *
Peter Wilhelm, *CFO*
EMP: 367 **EST:** 1971
SQ FT: 20,000
SALES (est): 126.17MM
SALES (corp-wide): 1.8B **Privately Held**
Web: www.mlb.com
SIC: 7941 Baseball club, professional and semi-professional
PA: Guggenheim Partners, Llc
330 Madison Ave Rm 201
New York NY
212 739-0700

(P-14140)
GEMINI BASKETBALL LLC
Also Called: Los Angeles Sparks
9100 Wilshire Blvd Ste 700e (90212-3415)
PHONE..................213 929-1300
Paula Williams Madison, *CEO*
EMP: 83 **EST:** 2006
SALES (est): 2.33MM **Privately Held**
Web: sparks.wnba.com
SIC: 7941 Basketball club

(P-14141)
GOLDEN STATE WARRIORS LLC
1 Warriors Way (94158-2250)
PHONE..................415 388-0100
Christopher Cohan, *Managing Member*
Robert Rowell, *
Dwayne Redman, *
Brandon Schneider, *
Jeff Barnett, *
EMP: 100 **EST:** 1962
SALES (est): 3.08MM **Privately Held**
Web: www.warriors.com
SIC: 7941 Basketball club

(P-14142)
IMMORTALS LLC
11460 W Washington Blvd (90066-6030)
P.O. Box 641729 (90064-6729)
PHONE..................310 554-8267
Noah Whinston, *CEO*
Ari Segal, *COO*
Jonathan Stein, *VP*
EMP: 85 **EST:** 2015
SQ FT: 30,000
SALES (est): 1.55MM **Privately Held**
Web: www.cityofimmortals.com
SIC: 7941 Professional and semi-professional sports clubs

(P-14143)
INLAND EMPIRE 66ERS BSBAL CLB
280 Se St (92401-2009)
PHONE..................909 888-9922
David Elmore, *Ch*
Donna Tuttle, *
Jhon Fonsaker, *
EMP: 110 **EST:** 1993
SQ FT: 600
SALES (est): 37.76K
SALES (corp-wide): 34.1MM **Privately Held**
Web: inlandempire.66ers.milb.com
SIC: 7941 Baseball club, professional and semi-professional
PA: The Elmore Group Ltd
19 N Grant St Ste 2
Hinsdale IL
630 325-6228

(P-14144)
KINGS ARENA LTD PARTNERSHIP
Also Called: Maloof Sport Entertainment
1 Sports Pkwy (95834-2300)
PHONE..................916 928-0000
Gavin Maloof, *Mng Pt*
John Thomas, *
John Rinehart, *
EMP: 60 **EST:** 1992
SALES (est): 4.9MM **Privately Held**
SIC: 7941 Boxing and wrestling arena

(P-14145)
LA CLIPPERS LLC
1212 S Flower St Fl 5 (90015-2117)
PHONE..................213 742-7500
Steven A Ballmer, *Managing Member*
EMP: 226 **EST:** 2014
SALES (est): 12.13MM **Privately Held**
Web: www.clippers.com
SIC: 7941 Basketball club

(P-14146)
LA SPORTS PROPERTIES INC
Also Called: Los Angeles Clippers
1212 S Flower St Fl 5 (90015-2123)
PHONE..................213 742-7500
Dick Parsons, *Interim Chief Executive Officer*
Andrew Roeser, *Ex VP*
EMP: 195 **EST:** 1946
SQ FT: 5,000
SALES (est): 24.44MM **Privately Held**
SIC: 7941 Basketball club

(P-14147)
LAFC SPORTS LLC
4751 Wilshire Blvd Fl 3 (90010-3827)
PHONE..................323 549-4350
EMP: 60 **EST:** 2014
SALES (est): 11.96MM **Privately Held**
Web: www.lafc.com
SIC: 7941 7371 Soccer club; Computer software development

(P-14148)
LIVE NATION WORLDWIDE INC
Also Called: Clear Channel Entertainment
325 N Maple Dr (90210-3429)
PHONE..................310 867-7000
Jennifer Scott, *Mgr*
EMP: 300
SIC: 7941 Sports clubs, managers, and promoters
HQ: Live Nation Worldwide, Inc.
430 W 15th St
New York NY
917 421-5100

(P-14149)
LIVERMORE VALLEY ATHC CLB INC ✪
2000 Arroyo Rd (94550-6027)
PHONE..................925 443-7700
Ankit Arora, *CEO*
EMP: 60 **EST:** 2022
SALES (est): 268.57K **Privately Held**
SIC: 7941 Sports clubs, managers, and promoters

(P-14150)
LOS ANGELES RAMS LLC (PA)
Also Called: ST LOUIS RAMS
29899 Agoura Rd (91301-2511)
PHONE..................314 982-7267
E Stanley Kroenke, *Managing Member*
Kevin Demoff, *Managing Member**
Les Snead, *Managing Member**
Tony Pastoors, *Managing Member**
EMP: 100 **EST:** 1939
SALES (est): 1.23MM
SALES (corp-wide): 1.23MM **Privately Held**
Web: www.therams.com
SIC: 7941 Football club

(P-14151)
NFL PROPERTIES LLC
Also Called: Nfl Network
10950 Washington Blvd Ste 100 (90232-4032)
PHONE..................310 840-4635
Steve Bernstein, *Prin*
EMP: 100
SALES (corp-wide): 603.28MM **Privately Held**
Web: www.nfl.com

7941 - Sports Clubs, Managers, And Promoters (P-14152)

SIC: **7941** Football club
PA: Nfl Properties Llc
345 Park Ave
New York NY
212 450-2000

(P-14152)
NIKE USA INC
222 E Redondo Beach Blvd Ste C
(90248-2302)
PHONE..................310 670-6770
EMP: 4981
SALES (corp-wide): 51.22B **Publicly Held**
SIC: **7941** Sports clubs, managers, and promoters
HQ: Nike Usa, Inc.
1 Sw Bowerman Dr
Beaverton OR

(P-14153)
PADRES LP
Also Called: San Diego Padres
100 Park Blvd Petco Park (92101)
P.O. Box 122000 (92112-2000)
PHONE..................619 795-5000
EMP: 1100 EST: 1969
SQ FT: 3,000
SALES (est): 265.26MM **Privately Held**
Web: www.mlb.com
SIC: **7941** Baseball club, professional and semi-professional

(P-14154)
PSE HOLDING LLC (DH)
Also Called: The Palace of Auburn Hills
360 N Crescent Dr (90210-4874)
PHONE..................248 377-0165
EMP: 300 EST: 1985
SALES (est): 115.27MM **Privately Held**
SIC: **7941 7922** Stadium event operator services; Summer theater
HQ: Pistons Palace Holdings, Llc
360 N Crescent Dr
Beverly Hills CA
310 228-9521

(P-14155)
SACRAMNTO RPUB FOTBALL CLB LLC
Also Called: Sacramento Republic Fc
2421 117th St (95818)
PHONE..................916 307-6100
Kevin Nagle, *Mng Pt*
▲ EMP: 74 EST: 2012
SALES (est): 737.23K **Privately Held**
Web: www.sacrepublicfc.com
SIC: **7941** Football club

(P-14156)
SAN FRANCISCO BASEBALL ASSOCIATES LLC (PA)
Also Called: San Francisco Giants
24 Willie Mays Plz (94107-2134)
PHONE..................415 972-2000
EMP: 1240 EST: 1891
SALES (est): 129.33MM
SALES (corp-wide): 129.33MM **Privately Held**
Web: www.mlb.com
SIC: **7941** 5947 Baseball club, professional and semi-professional; Souvenirs

(P-14157)
SAN FRANCISCO FORTY NINERS (PA)
4949 Marie P Debartolo Way (95054-1156)
PHONE..................408 562-4949
Denise Debartolo York, *Ch Bd*
Peter Harris, *

Larry Macneil, *
EMP: 120 EST: 1948
SQ FT: 50,000
SALES (est): 5.03MM
SALES (corp-wide): 5.03MM **Privately Held**
Web: www.49ers.com
SIC: **7941** Football club

(P-14158)
SAN JOSE SHARKS LLC (PA)
Also Called: HP Pavillion At San Jose
525 W Santa Clara St (95113-1500)
PHONE..................408 999-6810
Greg Jamison, *Pr*
EMP: 169 EST: 1990
SALES (est): 29.38MM **Privately Held**
Web: www.nhl.com
SIC: **7941** Ice hockey club

(P-14159)
SANTA CRUZ WARRIORS
903 Pacific Ave Ste 101 (95060-4460)
PHONE..................831 466-3200
EMP: 61 EST: 2013
SALES (est): 6.22MM **Privately Held**
Web: santacruz.gleague.nba.com
SIC: **7941** Soccer club

(P-14160)
SHARKS SPORTS & ENTRMT LLC
Also Called: SSE Merchandise
525 W Santa Clara St (95113-1520)
PHONE..................408 287-7070
Hasso Plattner, *Managing Member*
Greg Jamison, *
Tricia Sullivan, *
John Tortora, *
EMP: 800 EST: 1999
SALES (est): 83.9MM **Privately Held**
Web: www.nhl.com
SIC: **7941** Sports field or stadium operator, promoting sports events

(P-14161)
SOCAL SPORTSNET LLC
100 Park Blvd (92101-7405)
PHONE..................619 795-5000
EMP: 588 EST: 2012
SALES (est): 591.9K
SALES (corp-wide): 12.1MM **Privately Held**
Web: www.mlb.com
SIC: **7941** Baseball club, professional and semi-professional
PA: Padre Time, Llc
100 Park Blvd
San Diego CA
619 795-5000

(P-14162)
WME IMG LLC (DH)
Also Called: International Merchandising
9601 Wilshire Blvd (90210-5213)
PHONE..................212 586-5100
Ari Emanuel, *CEO*
Patrick Whitesell, *
Richard Miao, *
Neil Graff, *
Jason Lublin, *
EMP: 202 EST: 1961
SALES (est): 113.75MM
SALES (corp-wide): 5.27B **Publicly Held**
Web: www.endeavorco.com
SIC: **7941** 8742 Sports promotion; Business planning and organizing services
HQ: William Morris Endeavor Entertainment, Llc
9601 Wilshire Blvd

Beverly Hills CA
212 586-5100

7948 Racing, Including Track Operation

(P-14163)
DEL MAR THOROUGHBRED CLUB
Also Called: SURFSIDE RACE PLACE AT DEL MAR
2260 Jimmy Durante Blvd (92014-2216)
P.O. Box 700 (92014-0700)
PHONE..................858 755-1141
Joe Harper, *Pr*
Craig Fravel, *
Mike Ernst, *
Tom Robbins, *
Craig Dado, *
▲ EMP: 400 EST: 1970
SALES (est): 40.31MM **Privately Held**
Web: www.dmtc.com
SIC: **7948** Thoroughbred horse racing

(P-14164)
LOS ANGELES TURF CLUB INC (DH)
Also Called: Santa Anita Park
285 W Huntington Dr (91007-3439)
P.O. Box 60014 (91066-6014)
PHONE..................626 574-6330
Gregory C Avioli, *CEO*
Frank Stronach, *Ch Bd*
George Haines Ii, *Pr*
Frank Demarco Junior, *VP*
▲ EMP: 109 EST: 1964
SALES (est): 71.29MM
SALES (corp-wide): 37.84B **Privately Held**
Web: www.santaanita.com
SIC: **7948** Horse race track operation
HQ: Magna Car Top Systems Of America, Inc.
456 Wimpole Dr
Rochester Hills MI
248 836-4500

(P-14165)
NATIONAL HOT ROD ASSOCIATION (PA)
Also Called: Nhra
140 Via Verde Ste 100 (91773-5117)
P.O. Box 5555 (91740-0950)
PHONE..................626 914-4761
Wally Parks, *Dir*
Richard Wells, *
EMP: 200 EST: 1951
SQ FT: 30,000
SALES (est): 84.07MM
SALES (corp-wide): 84.07MM **Privately Held**
Web: www.nhra.com
SIC: **7948** 2711 2741 Auto race track operation; Newspapers: publishing only, not printed on site; Miscellaneous publishing

(P-14166)
PACIFIC RACING ASSOCIATION
Also Called: Golden Gate Fields
1100 Eastshore Hwy (94710-1002)
P.O. Box 6027 (94706-0027)
PHONE..................510 559-7300
Frank Stronach, *Pr*
EMP: 140 EST: 1941
SALES (est): 13.64MM **Privately Held**
Web: www.goldengatefields.com
SIC: **7948** Horses, racing

(P-14167)
SPEEDWAY SONOMA LLC
Also Called: Infineon Raceway
Hwy 37 N (95476)
PHONE..................707 938-8448
Sarah Grasal, *
▲ EMP: 60 EST: 2000
SALES (est): 8.31MM
SALES (corp-wide): 522.79MM **Privately Held**
Web: www.sonomaraceway.com
SIC: **7948** Auto race track operation
HQ: Speedway Motorsports, Llc
5555 Concord Pkwy S
Concord NC

7991 Physical Fitness Facilities

(P-14168)
24 HOUR FITNESS USA LLC (HQ)
Also Called: 24 Hour Fitness
1265 Laurel Tree Ln Ste 200 (92011-4221)
PHONE..................925 543-3100
Karl Sanft, *CEO*
Tony Ueber, *
Frank Napolitano, *
Patrick Flanagan, *
▲ EMP: 183 EST: 1983
SALES (est): 815.88MM
SALES (corp-wide): 815.88MM **Privately Held**
Web: www.24hourfitness.com
SIC: **7991** Health club
PA: All Day Holdings Llc
1265 Laurel Tree Ln # 200
Carlsbad CA
925 543-3100

(P-14169)
24 HOUR FITNESS WORLDWIDE INC
1265 Laurel Tree Ln Ste 200 (92011-4221)
PHONE..................925 543-3100
EMP: 7184
Web: www.24hourfit.com
SIC: **7991** Health club

(P-14170)
ADDISN-PNZAK JWISH CMNTY CTR S
Also Called: JEWISH COMMUNITY CENTER
14855 Oka Rd Ste 201 (95032-1956)
PHONE..................408 358-3636
Nate Stein, *CEO*
Stuart Phillips, *CFO*
EMP: 236 EST: 1973
SALES (est): 8.22MM **Privately Held**
Web: www.apjcc.org
SIC: **7991** 8299 Physical fitness facilities; Educational services

(P-14171)
ALMADEN VALLEY ATHLETIC CLUB
Also Called: Avac
5400 Camden Ave (95124-5897)
PHONE..................408 445-4900
Joseph Shank, *Genl Pt*
EMP: 70 EST: 1974
SQ FT: 20,000
SALES (est): 6.98MM **Privately Held**
Web: www.avac.us
SIC: **7991** Health club

PRODUCTS & SERVICES SECTION
7991 - Physical Fitness Facilities (P-14195)

(P-14172)
BA SPORTS NUTRITION LLC
630 Clinton Pl (90210-1917)
PHONE.................................718 357-7402
EMP: 80 EST: 2019
SALES (est): 1.38MM Privately Held
Web: www.drinkbodyarmor.com
SIC: 7991 Physical fitness facilities

(P-14173)
BALLY TOTAL FITNESS CORPORATION
Also Called: Bally Total Fitness
12440 Imperial Hwy # 300 (90650-3178)
P.O. Box 739 (60039-0739)
PHONE.................................562 484-2000
▲ EMP: 12340
SIC: 7991 Health club

(P-14174)
BARRYS BOOTCAMP LLC (PA)
Also Called: Barry's Boot Camp
7373 Beverly Blvd (90036-2502)
PHONE.................................323 452-0037
Joey Consolis, CEO
John Mumford, *
Rachel Mumford, *
EMP: 67 EST: 2015
SALES (est): 28.92MM
SALES (corp-wide): 28.92MM Privately Held
SIC: 7991 Physical fitness facilities

(P-14175)
BAY CLUBS COMPANY LLC (HQ)
1 Lombard St (94111-1132)
PHONE.................................415 781-1874
Matthew Stevens, Pr
Victor Woo, *
Lisa Graf, *
Annie Appel, *
EMP: 82 EST: 2009
SALES (est): 4.91MM
SALES (corp-wide): 5.09MM Privately Held
Web: www.bayclubs.com
SIC: 7991 7997 Physical fitness facilities; Swimming club, membership
PA: York Capital Management (Us) Advisors, L.P.
1330 Ave Of The Amrcas Fl
New York NY
212 300-1300

(P-14176)
BAY CLUBS COMPANY LLC
Also Called: Decathlon Club
3250 Central Expy (95051-0828)
PHONE.................................408 738-2582
Erin Rucker, Mgr
EMP: 294
SALES (corp-wide): 5.09MM Privately Held
Web: www.bayclubs.com
SIC: 7991 7997 5813 5812 Athletic club and gymnasiums, membership; Membership sports and recreation clubs; Drinking places ; Eating places
HQ: The Bay Clubs Company Llc
1 Lombard St
San Francisco CA
415 781-1874

(P-14177)
BAY CLUBS COMPANY LLC
Also Called: Spectrum Club Thousand Oaks
19867 Prairie St Ste 200 (91311-6533)
PHONE.................................805 778-0888
Adam Kinaan, Mgr
EMP: 294

SALES (corp-wide): 5.09MM Privately Held
Web: www.bayclubs.com
SIC: 7991 8049 Health club; Physical therapist
HQ: The Bay Clubs Company Llc
1 Lombard St
San Francisco CA
415 781-1874

(P-14178)
BAY CLUBS COMPANY LLC
Also Called: Spectrum Club
6833 Park Ter (90045-1539)
PHONE.................................310 216-3060
Thomas Broks, Genl Mgr
EMP: 294
SALES (corp-wide): 5.09MM Privately Held
Web: www.bayclubs.com
SIC: 7991 Health club
HQ: The Bay Clubs Company Llc
1 Lombard St
San Francisco CA
415 781-1874

(P-14179)
BAY CLUBS COMPANY LLC
Also Called: Sanctuary, The
200 Redwood Shores Pkwy (94065-1100)
PHONE.................................650 593-1112
Erin Cker, Mgr
EMP: 294
SALES (corp-wide): 5.09MM Privately Held
Web: www.bayclubs.com
SIC: 7991 7997 5812 5699 Health club; Swimming club, membership; Eating places ; Sports apparel
HQ: The Bay Clubs Company Llc
1 Lombard St
San Francisco CA
415 781-1874

(P-14180)
BLADIUM INC (PA)
Also Called: Bladium Sports Clubs
800 W Tower Ave Bldg 40 (94501-5048)
PHONE.................................510 814-4999
Brad C Shook, Pr
David Walsh, *
EMP: 60 EST: 1994
SQ FT: 115,000
SALES (est): 8.53MM Privately Held
Web: www.bladiumalameda.com
SIC: 7991 Health club

(P-14181)
BLISS WORLD LLC
6250 Hollywood Blvd Fl 4 (90028-5325)
PHONE.................................323 500-0921
EMP: 70
Web: www.blissworld.com
SIC: 7991 Spas
HQ: Bliss World Llc
42 W 39th St Fl 9
New York NY
212 931-6383

(P-14182)
BOXUNION SANTA MONICA LLC (PA)
Also Called: Boxunion
1755 Ocean Ave (90401-3615)
PHONE.................................310 882-5508
EMP: 248 EST: 2016
SALES (est): 19.52MM
SALES (corp-wide): 19.52MM Privately Held
Web: www.boxunion.com

SIC: 7991 Physical fitness facilities

(P-14183)
CALIFORNIA FAMILY HEALTH LLC (PA)
Also Called: California Family Fitness
8680 Greenback Ln Ste 108 (95662-3970)
P.O. Box 2350 (95662-7416)
PHONE.................................916 987-2030
EMP: 150 EST: 1991
SALES (est): 24.17MM Privately Held
Web: www.californiafamilyfitness.com
SIC: 7991 Health club

(P-14184)
CALISTOGA SPA INC
Also Called: Calistoga Spa Hot Springs
1006 Washington St (94515-1499)
PHONE.................................707 942-6269
Bradley L Barrett, Pr
Diane Barrett, *
EMP: 65 EST: 1967
SQ FT: 50,000
SALES (est): 4.6MM Privately Held
Web: www.calistogaspa.com
SIC: 7991 Spas

(P-14185)
CHOPRA GLOBAL LLC
6451 El Camino Real Ste A (92009-2800)
P.O. Box 1944 (10156-1944)
PHONE.................................760 494-1604
Tonia O'connor, Managing Member
Richard Wallach, *
EMP: 72 EST: 2004
SALES (est): 17MM Privately Held
Web: www.chopra.com
SIC: 7991 Spas

(P-14186)
CLUB AT LOS GATOS INC
285 E Main St (95030-6106)
PHONE.................................408 354-4808
David S Wilson, CEO
EMP: 60 EST: 2015
SALES (est): 2.79MM Privately Held
Web: www.theclublg.com
SIC: 7991 Physical fitness clubs with training equipment

(P-14187)
CLUB CORP INCORPORATED
Also Called: Delta Valley Athletic Club
120 Guthrie Ln (94513-4037)
PHONE.................................925 240-2990
Matthew Ellison, Pr
Vicky Zakoian, Mgr
EMP: 100 EST: 2003
SALES (est): 3.98MM Privately Held
Web: www.deltavac.com
SIC: 7991 Physical fitness facilities

(P-14188)
CLUB ONE INC
Also Called: Club One Fitness
555 Market St Fl 13 (94105-2860)
PHONE.................................415 477-3000
EMP: 2000
SIC: 7991 Physical fitness facilities

(P-14189)
CLUBSPORT SAN RAMON LLC
Also Called: Oakwood Athletic Club
4000 Mt Diablo Blvd (94549-3498)
PHONE.................................925 283-4000
Michael Reardon, Mgr
EMP: 90
SQ FT: 63,749
Web: www.clubsportsr.com

SIC: 7991 7997 Athletic club and gymnasiums, membership; Membership sports and recreation clubs
PA: Clubsport San Ramon, Llc
350 Bollinger Canyon Ln
San Ramon CA

(P-14190)
CLUBSPORT SAN RAMON LLC (PA)
Also Called: Spa At Club Sport
350 Bollinger Canyon Ln (94582-4592)
PHONE.................................925 735-1182
Al Schaffer, Pt
John Moore, Pt
Mike Reardon, Genl Mgr
EMP: 170 EST: 1989
SQ FT: 70,000
SALES (est): 12.49MM Privately Held
Web: www.clubsportsr.com
SIC: 7991 Health club

(P-14191)
CROSSFIT LLC
1101 Pacific Ave Ste 230 (95060-4418)
PHONE.................................619 540-5017
Don Faul, CEO
Eric Roza, *
EMP: 125 EST: 2020
SALES (est): 6.8K Privately Held
Web: www.crossfit.com
SIC: 7991 Physical fitness facilities

(P-14192)
CRUNCH LLC
Also Called: Crunch Fitness
61 New Montgomery St (94105-3438)
PHONE.................................415 543-1110
Ben Vadi, Brnch Mgr
EMP: 207
Web: www.crunch.com
SIC: 7991 Physical fitness facilities
PA: Crunch, Llc
220 W 19th St
New York NY

(P-14193)
CRUNCH LLC
Also Called: Embarcadero, The
345 Spear St Ste 104 (94105-1659)
PHONE.................................415 495-1939
Mahogany Lenard, Brnch Mgr
EMP: 65
Web: www.crunch.com
SIC: 7991 Health club
PA: Crunch, Llc
220 W 19th St
New York NY

(P-14194)
CRUNCH FITNESS
19867 Prairie St Ste 200 (91311-6533)
PHONE.................................805 522-5454
Teresa Frost, Genl Mgr
EMP: 65 EST: 1980
SALES (est): 2.82MM Privately Held
Web: www.crunch.com
SIC: 7991 Athletic club and gymnasiums, membership

(P-14195)
DELTA VALLEY HEALTH CLUB
120 Guthrie Ln (94513-4037)
PHONE.................................925 240-2990
Matt Ellison, Pr
Vicky Zakoian, *
EMP: 100 EST: 2018
SALES (est): 1.66MM Privately Held
Web: www.deltavac.com

7991 - Physical Fitness Facilities (P-14196)

SIC: 7991 Physical fitness facilities

(P-14196)
ENCINO LIVING LLC
16710 Magnolia Blvd (91436-1012)
PHONE.................818 907-1343
Danny Petrasek, *Brnch Mgr*
EMP: 120
SALES (corp-wide): 790.77K **Privately Held**
Web: www.encinoseniorliving.com
SIC: 7991 Health club
PA: Encino Living Llc
  7515 Woodley Ave
  Van Nuys CA
  818 781-9119

(P-14197)
EQUINOX HOLDINGS INC
Also Called: Equinox Fitness Club
747 Market St (94103-2001)
PHONE.................415 243-0492
Amie Skidmore, *Genl Mgr*
EMP: 89
SALES (corp-wide): 2.05B **Privately Held**
Web: www.equinox.com
SIC: 7991 Health club
HQ: Equinox Holdings, Inc.
  32 Hudson Yards
  New York NY
  212 677-0180

(P-14198)
EQUINOX-76TH STREET INC
5400 W Rosecrans Ave Ste Uppr (90250-6609)
PHONE.................310 727-9543
Larry Schneider, *Brnch Mgr*
EMP: 77
SALES (corp-wide): 2.05B **Privately Held**
SIC: 7991 Health club
HQ: Equinox-76th Street, Inc.
  895 Broadway Fl 3
  New York NY

(P-14199)
EQUINOX-76TH STREET INC
112 S Lakeview Canyon Rd (91362-3925)
PHONE.................805 367-3925
EMP: 67
SALES (corp-wide): 2.05B **Privately Held**
SIC: 7991 Health club
HQ: Equinox-76th Street, Inc.
  895 Broadway Fl 3
  New York NY

(P-14200)
EQUINOX-76TH STREET INC
1835 S Sepulveda Blvd (90025-6941)
PHONE.................310 479-5200
Tonya Jacobs, *Mgr*
EMP: 96
SALES (corp-wide): 2.05B **Privately Held**
SIC: 7991 Health club
HQ: Equinox-76th Street, Inc.
  895 Broadway Fl 3
  New York NY

(P-14201)
EQUINOX-76TH STREET INC
Also Called: Equinox
301 Pine St (94104-3301)
PHONE.................415 398-0747
Patrick Ahern, *Mgr*
EMP: 115
SALES (corp-wide): 2.05B **Privately Held**
Web: www.equinox.com
SIC: 7991 Health club
HQ: Equinox-76th Street, Inc.
  895 Broadway Fl 3
  New York NY

(P-14202)
EQUINOX-76TH STREET INC
Also Called: Equinox Fitness Club
19540 Jamboree Rd (92612-8448)
PHONE.................949 296-1700
Herb Umphreyville, *Genl Mgr*
EMP: 90
SALES (corp-wide): 2.05B **Privately Held**
SIC: 7991 Health club
HQ: Equinox-76th Street, Inc.
  895 Broadway Fl 3
  New York NY

(P-14203)
EQUINOX-76TH STREET INC
Also Called: Equinox Fitness Club
10250 Santa Monica Blvd (90067-6404)
PHONE.................310 552-0420
Mathew Herbert, *Brnch Mgr*
EMP: 86
SALES (corp-wide): 2.05B **Privately Held**
SIC: 7991 Health club
HQ: Equinox-76th Street, Inc.
  895 Broadway Fl 3
  New York NY

(P-14204)
GRIT MANAGEMENT LLC
Also Called: Gritcycle
234 E 17th St Ste 212 (92627-3855)
PHONE.................949 220-7765
Gail Gray, *Managing Member*
Jonathan Gray, *Managing Member*
EMP: 69 EST: 2020
SALES (est): 584.07K **Privately Held**
SIC: 7991 Physical fitness facilities

(P-14205)
HARBOR BAY CLUB INC
200 Packet Landing Rd (94502-6599)
P.O. Box 1450 (94501-0158)
PHONE.................510 521-5414
C Timothy Hoppen, *Pr*
Timothy Hoppen, *
EMP: 90 EST: 1978
SQ FT: 30,000
SALES (est): 3.91MM **Privately Held**
Web: www.harborbayclub.com
SIC: 7991 5813 5941 5812 Athletic club and gymnasiums, membership; Bar (drinking places); Golf goods and equipment; Eating places
PA: Harbor Bay Club Associates, A California Limited Partnership
  1141 Harbor Bay Pkwy # 221
  Alameda CA

(P-14206)
HEALTHSPORT LTD A LTD PARTNR (PA)
Also Called: Healthsport-Arcata
300 Dr Martin Luther King Jr Pkwy (95521)
PHONE.................707 822-3488
Susan Johnson, *Pt*
EMP: 110 EST: 1991
SQ FT: 24,560
SALES (est): 7.62MM **Privately Held**
Web: www.healthsport.com
SIC: 7991 Health club

(P-14207)
IBAM INC
Also Called: 24 Hour In Motion Fitness
1293 E 1st Ave (95926-1548)
PHONE.................530 343-5678
Carleton J Sommer, *Pr*
EMP: 82 EST: 1987
SQ FT: 19,400
SALES (est): 7.03MM **Privately Held**
Web: www.inmotionfitness.com
SIC: 7991 Health club

(P-14208)
IN SHAPE MANAGEMENT COMPANY
Also Called: In Shape Health Clubs
6 S El Dorado St (95202-2962)
PHONE.................209 472-2231
Morton Rothbard, *Pr*
Paul Rothbard, *
Rob Farrens, *
EMP: 300 EST: 1993
SQ FT: 60,000
SALES (est): 4.63MM **Privately Held**
Web: www.inshape.com
SIC: 7991 Health club

(P-14209)
JAZZERCISE INC (PA)
Also Called: Jazzercise
2460 Impala Dr (92010-7226)
PHONE.................760 476-1750
Judi Sheppard Missett, *CEO*
Sally Baldridge, *
Shanna Missett Nelson, *
EMP: 100 EST: 1972
SQ FT: 24,228
SALES (est): 12.2MM
SALES (corp-wide): 12.2MM **Privately Held**
Web: www.jazzercise.com
SIC: 7991 6794 5961 Aerobic dance and exercise classes; Franchises, selling or licensing; Fitness and sporting goods, mail order

(P-14210)
LA BONNE VIE INC
2723 Shell Beach Rd (93449-1629)
PHONE.................805 773-5003
Maureen Raynaud-loughead, *Pr*
EMP: 100 EST: 2005
SALES (est): 225.48K **Privately Held**
SIC: 7991 Spas

(P-14211)
LA BOXING FRANCHISE CORP
1241 E Dyer Rd Ste 100 (92705-5611)
PHONE.................714 668-0911
Anthony Geisler, *Pr*
▲ EMP: 346 EST: 1992
SALES (est): 3.85MM
SALES (corp-wide): 89.52MM **Privately Held**
SIC: 7991 Physical fitness facilities
PA: U Gym, Llc
  1501 Quail St Ste 100
  Newport Beach CA
  714 668-0911

(P-14212)
LA WORKOUT INC
Also Called: La Workout Camarillo West
500 Paseo Camarillo (93010-5900)
PHONE.................805 482-8884
Steve Rivera, *Brnch Mgr*
EMP: 115
Web: www.perfectdomain.com
SIC: 7991 Health club
PA: La Workout, Inc.
  2510g Las Posas Rd Ste 44
  Camarillo CA

(P-14213)
LIFE TIME INC
Also Called: Life Time Fitness
111 Avenida Vista Montana (92672-6094)
PHONE.................949 492-1515
Steve Johnson, *Pr*
EMP: 95
SALES (corp-wide): 1.82B **Publicly Held**
Web: www.lifetime.life
SIC: 7991 Health club
HQ: Life Time, Inc.
  2902 Corporate Pl
  Chanhassen MN

(P-14214)
LIFE TIME INC
1435 E Roseville Pkwy (95661-3066)
PHONE.................916 472-2000
Jennifer Hallahan, *Brnch Mgr*
EMP: 132
SALES (corp-wide): 1.82B **Publicly Held**
Web: www.lifetime.life
SIC: 7991 Health club
HQ: Life Time, Inc.
  2902 Corporate Pl
  Chanhassen MN

(P-14215)
LIFE TIME INC
1055 Wall St (92037-4400)
PHONE.................858 459-0281
EMP: 95
SALES (corp-wide): 1.82B **Publicly Held**
Web: www.lifetime.life
SIC: 7991 Health club
HQ: Life Time, Inc.
  2902 Corporate Pl
  Chanhassen MN

(P-14216)
LOS ANGELES ATHLETIC CLUB INC
431 W 7th St (90014-1691)
PHONE.................213 625-2211
Karen Hathaway, *Pr*
Bryan Cusworth, *
EMP: 182 EST: 1986
SALES (est): 6.3MM **Publicly Held**
Web: www.laac.com
SIC: 7991 Athletic club and gymnasiums, membership
HQ: Laaco, Ltd.
  4469 Admiralty Way
  Marina Del Rey CA
  213 622-1254

(P-14217)
LOS GATOS SWIM AND RACQUET CLB
Also Called: Lgsrc
14700 Oka Rd (95032-1998)
PHONE.................408 356-2136
S Denevi, *Treas*
Ron Denevi, *
Shelli Denevi, *
EMP: 61 EST: 1955
SQ FT: 14,000
SALES (est): 5.08MM **Privately Held**
Web: www.lgsrc.com
SIC: 7991 7997 Health club; Tennis club, membership

(P-14218)
LOUNGE SPA INC
4016 East Blvd (90066-4608)
PHONE.................310 745-1646
Alice Koskas, *Brnch Mgr*
EMP: 60
SALES (corp-wide): 55.21K **Privately Held**
Web: www.theloungespa.com
SIC: 7991 Spas
PA: Lounge Spa Inc
  3830 Vly Cntre Dr Ste 70
  San Diego CA

PRODUCTS & SERVICES SECTION — 7991 - Physical Fitness Facilities (P-14242)

(P-14219)
MONIQUE SURACI
Also Called: Murrieta Day Spa
41885 Ivy St (92562-8607)
PHONE.................................951 677-8111
Monique Suraci, *Owner*
EMP: 60 **EST:** 1989
SALES (est): 4.8MM **Privately Held**
Web: www.mdayspa.com
SIC: 7991 Spas

(P-14220)
MUSCLEBOUND INC
Also Called: Golds Gym
19835 Nordhoff St (91324-3331)
PHONE.................................818 349-0123
EMP: 350 **EST:** 1990
SQ FT: 8,625
SALES (est): 16.26MM **Privately Held**
Web: www.goldsgym.com
SIC: 7991 Physical fitness facilities

(P-14221)
NRG HEALTH & FITNESS LLC
79 Promesa Ave (92694-1592)
PHONE.................................310 570-5436
EMP: 63
SALES (est): 251.72K **Privately Held**
SIC: 7991 7389 Physical fitness clubs with training equipment; Business services, nec

(P-14222)
NUZUNA CORPORATION
Also Called: Nuzuna Fitness
1451 Quail St Ste 104 (92660-2747)
P.O. Box 8807 (92658-8807)
PHONE.................................949 335-7790
Charlie Laverty, *CEO*
Aileen Pham, *
Raymond Godeke, *
EMP: 90 **EST:** 2019
SALES (est): 3.63MM **Privately Held**
Web: www.nuzunafit.com
SIC: 7991 Physical fitness facilities

(P-14223)
OLYMPIX FITNESS LLC
4101 E Olympic Plz (90803-2807)
PHONE.................................562 366-4600
EMP: 91 **EST:** 2016
SALES (est): 212K **Privately Held**
SIC: 7991 Physical fitness facilities

(P-14224)
RACHAS INC
Also Called: Chuze Fitness
135 N Beach Blvd (92801-6135)
PHONE.................................714 290-0636
Cory Brightwell, *Brnch Mgr*
EMP: 67
SALES (corp-wide): 109.4MM **Privately Held**
Web: www.chuzefitness.com
SIC: 7991 Physical fitness facilities
PA: Rachas, Inc.
1011 Cmino Del Rio S Ste
San Diego CA
619 780-0141

(P-14225)
RANCHO LA PUERTA INC
11722 Sorrento Valley Rd Ste G
(92121-1021)
PHONE.................................858 764-5500
Deborah Szekely, *Mgr*
EMP: 67
SALES (corp-wide): 8.46MM **Privately Held**
Web: www.rancholapuerta.com
SIC: 7991 7011 Spas; Resort hotel
PA: Rancho La Puerta, Inc.
5090 Shoreham Pl
San Diego CA
858 764-5500

(P-14226)
REDWOOD HEALTH CLUB (PA)
3101 S State St (95482-6938)
PHONE.................................707 468-0441
Rob Marthe Deomont, *Pt*
EMP: 70 **EST:** 1979
SQ FT: 20,000
SALES (est): 998.66K
SALES (corp-wide): 998.66K **Privately Held**
Web: www.redwoodhealthclubofukiah.com
SIC: 7991 7997 5812 5813 Health club; Racquetball club, membership; Snack bar; Drinking places

(P-14227)
RIEKES CTR FOR HUMN ENHNCEMENT
3455 Edison Way (94025-1813)
PHONE.................................650 364-2509
EMP: 68 **EST:** 2010
SALES (est): 3.53MM **Privately Held**
Web: www.riekes.org
SIC: 7991 Physical fitness facilities

(P-14228)
ROW HOUSE FRANCHISE LLC
Also Called: Row House
17877 Von Karman Ave Ste 100
(92614-4201)
PHONE.................................949 341-5585
Eric Von Frohlich, *CEO*
EMP: 146 **EST:** 2017
SALES (est): 9.96MM
SALES (corp-wide): 244.95MM **Publicly Held**
Web: www.therowhouse.com
SIC: 7991 6794 Physical fitness clubs with training equipment; Franchises, selling or licensing
HQ: Xponential Fitness Llc
17877 Von Karman Ave # 1
Irvine CA
949 346-3000

(P-14229)
RSG GROUP NORTH AMERICA LP
7007 Romaine St Ste 101 (90038-2439)
PHONE.................................714 609-0572
Sebastian Schoepe, *CEO*
EMP: 220 **EST:** 2016
SALES (est): 4.04MM **Privately Held**
SIC: 7991 Physical fitness facilities

(P-14230)
SALVATION ARMY RAY & JOAN
Also Called: Salvation Army
6845 University Ave (92115-5829)
PHONE.................................619 287-5762
James Knaggs, *Pr*
David Hudson, *
EMP: 300 **EST:** 1998
SALES (est): 22.58MM
SALES (corp-wide): 2.41B **Privately Held**
Web: sd.kroccenter.org
SIC: 7991 8661 7032 7922 Physical fitness clubs with training equipment; Miscellaneous denomination church; Sporting and recreational camps; Community theater production
PA: The Salvation Army National Corporation
615 Slaters Ln
Alexandria VA
703 684-5500

(P-14231)
SPA FITNESS CENTER INC
Also Called: Spa Fitness Center
25 Penny Ln (95076-3058)
PHONE.................................831 722-3895
Harry Jennings, *Owner*
EMP: 99
SALES (corp-wide): 2.47MM **Privately Held**
Web: www.spafitness.com
SIC: 7991 Health club
PA: Spa Fitness Center, Inc
1200 41st Ave Ste C
Capitola CA
831 462-2004

(P-14232)
SPA HAVENS LP
Also Called: Cal-A-Vie
29402 Spa Haven Way (92084-2234)
PHONE.................................760 945-2055
John Havens, *Owner*
▲ **EMP:** 105 **EST:** 1984
SALES (est): 12.49MM **Privately Held**
Web: www.cal-a-vie.com
SIC: 7991 Spas

(P-14233)
SPARE-TIME INC
Also Called: Natomas Racquet Club
2450 Natomas Park Dr (95833-2938)
PHONE.................................916 649-0909
Joe Rose, *Mgr*
EMP: 104
SALES (corp-wide): 52.26MM **Privately Held**
Web: www.sparetimeinc.com
SIC: 7991 Health club
PA: Spare-Time, Inc.
11344 Coloma Rd Ste 350
Gold River CA
916 859-5910

(P-14234)
SPARE-TIME INC
Also Called: Rio Del Oro Racquet Club
119 Scripps Dr (95825-6305)
PHONE.................................916 488-8100
Dana Rose, *Mgr*
EMP: 74
SALES (corp-wide): 52.26MM **Privately Held**
Web: www.sparetimesportsclubs.com
SIC: 7991 7999 7997 Health club; Tennis services and professionals; Tennis club, membership
PA: Spare-Time, Inc.
11344 Coloma Rd Ste 350
Gold River CA
916 859-5910

(P-14235)
SPECTRUM CLUBS INC
840 Apollo St Ste 100 (90245-4701)
PHONE.................................310 727-9300
EMP: 1600
SIC: 7991 Health club

(P-14236)
SWEATHEORY LLC
1503 N Cahuenga Blvd (90028-7312)
PHONE.................................310 956-2307
EMP: 64 **EST:** 2016
SALES (est): 800.78K **Privately Held**
Web: www.sweatheory.com
SIC: 7991 Health club

(P-14237)
THINK TOGETHER
12016 Telegraph Rd (90670-3784)
PHONE.................................562 236-3835
EMP: 344
SALES (corp-wide): 75.71MM **Privately Held**
Web: www.thinktogether.org
SIC: 7991 Physical fitness facilities
PA: Think Together
2101 E 4th St Ste 200b
Santa Ana CA
714 543-3807

(P-14238)
TRI-CITY HOSPITAL DISTRICT
Also Called: Tri-City Wellness Center
6250 El Camino Real (92009-1603)
PHONE.................................760 93 , 3171
EMP: 374
SALES (corp-wide): 319.28MM **Privately Held**
Web: www.tricitywellness.com
SIC: 7991 Health club
PA: Tri-City Hospital District (Inc)
4002 Vista Way
Oceanside CA
760 724-8411

(P-14239)
TW HOLDINGS INC
10805 Rancho Bernardo Rd Ste 120
(92127)
PHONE.................................858 217-8750
Gene Lamott, *CEO*
Karen Wischmann, *
Rob Zielinski, *
EMP: 600 **EST:** 2007
SALES (est): 24.67MM **Privately Held**
SIC: 7991 Physical fitness clubs with training equipment

(P-14240)
U GYM LLC (PA)
Also Called: Ufc Gym
1501 Quail St Ste 100 (92660-2797)
PHONE.................................714 668-0911
Adam Sedlack, *CEO*
Brent Leffel, *
Mark Mastrov, *
Michael Pilatos, *
EMP: 70 **EST:** 2008
SALES (est): 89.52MM
SALES (corp-wide): 89.52MM **Privately Held**
Web: www.ufcgym.com
SIC: 7991 5699 6794 Health club; Shirts, custom made; Franchises, selling or licensing

(P-14241)
WALSH GROUP INC
Also Called: Sun Oaks Tennis & Fitness
3135 Agassi Ln (96002-9548)
PHONE.................................530 221-4405
Jo Campbell, *Prin*
Jo Campbell, *Genl Mgr*
Jeremiah Walsh, *
EMP: 95 **EST:** 2016
SQ FT: 217,800
SALES (est): 2.41MM **Privately Held**
Web: www.sunoaks.com
SIC: 7991 Health club

(P-14242)
WESTERN ATHLETIC CLUBS INC
1 Lombard St (94111-1127)
PHONE.................................415 781-1874
▲ **EMP:** 431
Web: www.bayclubs.com

7991 - Physical Fitness Facilities (P-14243)

SIC: 7991 7997 5812 5699 Health club; Swimming club, membership; Eating places ; Sports apparel

(P-14243)
WORLD GYM INTERNATIONAL LLC
Also Called: World Gym Fitness Centers
1901 Avenue Of The Stars Ste 1100 (90067-6001)
PHONE.................................310 557-8804
EMP: 108 EST: 2008
SALES (est): 2.33MM **Privately Held**
Web: www.worldgym.com
SIC: 7991 6794 Health club; Franchises, selling or licensing

(P-14244)
XI ENTERPRISE INC
2140 E Palmdale Blvd (93550-1202)
PHONE.................................661 266-3200
Shah Roshan, *CEO*
EMP: 74 EST: 2011
SALES (est): 2.29MM **Privately Held**
SIC: 7991 Physical fitness facilities

(P-14245)
XPONENTIAL FITNESS INC (PA)
17877 Von Karman Ave Ste 100 (92614-4201)
PHONE.................................949 346-3000
Anthony Geisler, *CEO*
Mark Grabowski, *Non-Executive Chairman of the Board**
Sarah Luna, *Pr*
Ryan Junk, *COO*
John Meloun, *CFO*
EMP: 270 EST: 2017
SALES (est): 244.95MM
SALES (corp-wide): 244.95MM **Publicly Held**
Web: www.xponential.com
SIC: 7991 Athletic club and gymnasiums, membership

7992 Public Golf Courses

(P-14246)
BRIDGES AT GALE RANCH LLC
Also Called: Bridges Golf Club, The
9000 S Gale Ridge Rd (94582-9174)
PHONE.................................925 735-4253
Joey Pickavance, *Mgr*
EMP: 90 EST: 1999
SALES (est): 4.99MM **Privately Held**
Web: www.thebridgesgolf.com
SIC: 7992 Public golf courses

(P-14247)
BSL GOLF CORP
Also Called: Bayonet/Blackhorse Golf Course
1 Mcclure Way (93955-7100)
PHONE.................................831 899-7271
Joe Priddy, *Mgr*
EMP: 101
SALES (corp-wide): 19.36MM **Privately Held**
Web: www.bayonetblackhorse.com
SIC: 7992 Public golf courses
PA: Bsl Golf Corp.
  402 Heights Blvd
  Houston TX
  713 522-4547

(P-14248)
CHAPMAN GOLF DEVELOPMENT LLC
Also Called: Tradition Golf Club
78505 Avenue 52 (92253-2802)
PHONE.................................760 564-8723
David Chapman, *Managing Member*
EMP: 100 EST: 1999
SALES (est): 1.9MM **Privately Held**
SIC: 7992 Public golf courses

(P-14249)
CITY OF DELANO
Also Called: City Corporation Yard
725 S Lexington St (93215-3617)
PHONE.................................661 721-3350
Phil Newhouse, *Brnch Mgr*
EMP: 63
SALES (corp-wide): 39.7MM **Privately Held**
Web: www.cityofdelano.org
SIC: 7992 Public golf courses
PA: City Of Delano
  1015 11th Ave
  Delano CA
  661 721-3300

(P-14250)
CITY OF HUNTINGTON BEACH
Also Called: Meadowlark Golf Course
16782 Graham St (92649-3754)
PHONE.................................714 846-4450
Nick Beck, *Mgr*
EMP: 74
SALES (corp-wide): 308.41MM **Privately Held**
Web: www.huntingtonbeachca.gov
SIC: 7992 Public golf courses
PA: City Of Huntington Beach
  2000 Main St
  Huntington Beach CA
  714 536-5202

(P-14251)
CITY OF OAKLAND
Also Called: Lake Chabot Golf Course
11450 Golf Links Rd (94605-5720)
PHONE.................................510 351-5812
Raymond Chester, *Genl Mgr*
EMP: 67
SALES (corp-wide): 1.47B **Privately Held**
Web: www.lakechabotgolf.com
SIC: 7992 Public golf courses
PA: City Of Oakland
  1 Frank H Ogawa Plz 2nd
  Oakland CA
  510 238-3280

(P-14252)
CITY OF SAN JOSE
Also Called: San Jose Mini Golf Course
1560 Oakland Rd (95131-2430)
PHONE.................................408 441-4653
Bob Mcgrath, *Mgr*
EMP: 66
SQ FT: 300
SALES (corp-wide): 2.14B **Privately Held**
Web: www.sanjoseca.gov
SIC: 7992 9512 Public golf courses; Recreational program administration, government
PA: City Of San Jose
  200 E Santa Clara St 13th
  San Jose CA
  408 535-3500

(P-14253)
COUNTY OF LOS ANGELES
Also Called: Parks and Recreation Dept
1875 Fairplex Dr (91768-1240)
PHONE.................................909 231-0549
Chad Hackman, *Genl Mgr*
EMP: 181
SALES (corp-wide): 31.7B **Privately Held**
Web: www.mountainmeadowsgc.com
SIC: 7992 9512 7299 Public golf courses; Recreational program administration, government; Wedding chapel, privately operated
PA: County Of Los Angeles
  500 W Temple St Ste 437
  Los Angeles CA
  213 974-1101

(P-14254)
COURSECO INC
Also Called: NAPA Golf Course At Kennedy Pk
2295 Streblow Dr (94558-6211)
PHONE.................................707 255-4333
Tom Sims, *Brnch Mgr*
EMP: 501
Web: www.courseco.com
SIC: 7992 Public golf courses
PA: Courseco, Inc.
  5341 Old Redwood Hwy # 202
  Petaluma CA

(P-14255)
CROCKETT & COINC
Also Called: Bonita Golf Club
5540 Sweetwater Rd (91902-2137)
PHONE.................................619 267-1103
Clayton Crockett, *Prin*
EMP: 80
SALES (corp-wide): 4.72MM **Privately Held**
Web: www.bonitagolf.net
SIC: 7992 5812 Public golf courses; Eating places
PA: Crockett & Co.Inc.
  5120 Robinwood Rd Ste A22
  Bonita CA
  619 267-6410

(P-14256)
DESERT WILLOW GOLF RESORT
Also Called: Marriott
38500 Portola Ave (92260-0613)
PHONE.................................760 346-7060
Paul Bucy, *Dir*
EMP: 65 EST: 2011
SALES (est): 751.21K **Privately Held**
Web: www.desertwillow.com
SIC: 7992 Public golf courses

(P-14257)
DESERT WILLOW GOLF RESORT INC
Also Called: Desert Willow Golf Course
38995 Desert Willow Dr (92260-1674)
PHONE.................................760 346-0015
Richard Mogensen, *Genl Mgr*
EMP: 150 EST: 1997
SQ FT: 33,000
SALES (est): 2.51MM **Privately Held**
Web: www.desertwillow.com
SIC: 7992 Public golf courses

(P-14258)
EAGLE GLEN COUNTRY CLUB LLC
Also Called: Eagle Glen Golf Club
1800 Eagle Glen Pkwy (92883-0620)
PHONE.................................951 272-4653
Jim Previty, *Ch*
EMP: 60 EST: 1999
SQ FT: 26,000
SALES (est): 5.72MM **Privately Held**
Web: www.eagleglengc.com
SIC: 7992 Public golf courses

(P-14259)
EAGLE VNES VNYRDS GOLF CLB LLC
1733 S Anaheim Blvd (92805-6518)
P.O. Box 2398 (94558-0239)
PHONE.................................707 257-4470
Nobu Mizuhara, *General Vice President*
EMP: 70 EST: 2010
SALES (est): 4.96MM **Privately Held**
Web: www.eaglevinesgolfclub.com
SIC: 7992 Public golf courses

(P-14260)
EL PRADO GOLF COURSE LP
6555 Pine Ave (91708-9192)
PHONE.................................909 597-1751
Bruce Jenke, *Genl Pt*
G Barton Heuler, *Pt*
Anthony Foo, *Pt*
Walter Heuler, *Pt*
EMP: 80 EST: 1975
SQ FT: 5,000
SALES (est): 4.67MM **Privately Held**
Web: www.elpradogolfcourses.com
SIC: 7992 Public golf courses

(P-14261)
ESTATES AT TRUMP NAT GOLF CLB
Also Called: Trump Nat Golf CLB Los Angeles
1 Trump National Dr (90275-6173)
PHONE.................................310 265-5000
Jill Martin, *CEO*
Mike Vandergles, *Prin*
EMP: 212 EST: 2002
SALES (est): 10.88MM
SALES (corp-wide): 2.37MM **Privately Held**
Web: www.trumpnationallosangeles.com
SIC: 7992 Public golf courses
HQ: Trump Golf Management Llc
  725 5th Ave Bsmt A
  New York NY
  212 832-2000

(P-14262)
FOUNTAINGROVE GOLF & ATHC CLB
Also Called: FOUNTAINGROVE CLUB, THE
1525 Fountaingrove Pkwy (95403-1778)
PHONE.................................707 701-3050
Greg Sabens, *Mgr*
EMP: 75 EST: 1996
SQ FT: 33,000
SALES (est): 9.95MM **Privately Held**
Web: www.thefountaingroveclub.com
SIC: 7992 7299 5941 7997 Public golf courses; Banquet hall facilities; Golf goods and equipment; Golf club, membership

(P-14263)
GLEN ANNIE GOLF CLUB
Also Called: Annie Golf Club
405 Glen Annie Rd (93117-1427)
PHONE.................................805 968-6400
Richard Nahas, *Genl Mgr*
EMP: 80 EST: 1997
SALES (est): 2.47MM **Privately Held**
Web: www.glenanniegolf.com
SIC: 7992 Public golf courses

(P-14264)
GOLF MANAGEMENT OPERATING LLC ◆
50200 Avnida Vista Bonita (92253)
PHONE.................................760 777-4839
Jim Hinckley, *Pr*
Doug Howe, *
Greg Adair, *

PRODUCTS & SERVICES SECTION

7992 - Public Golf Courses (P-14285)

Jack Marquardt, *
Melissa Mckibben, *Prin*
EMP: 2800 **EST:** 2022
SALES (est): 4.42MM **Privately Held**
SIC: 7992 Public golf courses

(P-14265)
GREEN RIVER GOLF CORPORATION
Also Called: Green River Golf Course
5215 Green River Rd (92878-9404)
PHONE.................................714 970-8411
Judy Saguchi, *Pr*
EMP: 100 **EST:** 1977
SQ FT: 30,000
SALES (est): 9.56MM **Privately Held**
Web: weddings.playgreenriver.com
SIC: 7992 5941 5813 5812 Public golf courses; Sporting goods and bicycle shops; Drinking places; Eating places
PA: Courseco, Inc.
5341 Old Redwood Hwy # 202
Petaluma CA

(P-14266)
HERITAGE GOLF GROUP LLC
Also Called: Talega Golf Club
990 Avenida Talega (92673-6849)
PHONE.................................949 369-6226
David Foster, *Brnch Mgr*
EMP: 90
SALES (corp-wide): 97.99MM **Privately Held**
SIC: 7992 Public golf courses
PA: Heritage Golf Group, Llc
12750 High Bluff Dr Fl 4
San Diego CA
858 720-0694

(P-14267)
HERITAGE GOLF GROUP LLC
Also Called: Valencia Country Club
27330 Tourney Rd (91355-1806)
PHONE.................................661 254-4401
Jim Fitzsimmons, *Mgr*
EMP: 117
SALES (corp-wide): 97.99MM **Privately Held**
SIC: 7992 Public golf courses
PA: Heritage Golf Group, Llc
12750 High Bluff Dr Fl 4
San Diego CA
858 720-0694

(P-14268)
KSL RECREATION MANAGEMENT OPERATIONS LLC
50905 Avenida Bermudas (92253-8910)
PHONE.................................760 564-8000
EMP: 8000
SIC: 7992 7011 Public golf courses; Hotels and motels

(P-14269)
LAKESIDE GOLF CLUB
4500 W Lakeside Dr (91505-4088)
P.O. Box 2386 (91610-0386)
PHONE.................................818 984-0601
Jerry Fard, *Mgr*
Michael E Henry, *CEO*
EMP: 98 **EST:** 1924
SQ FT: 25,000
SALES (est): 11.57MM **Privately Held**
Web: www.lakesidegolfclub.com
SIC: 7992 Public golf courses

(P-14270)
LONE CYPRESS COMPANY LLC (PA)
2700 17 Mile Dr (93953-2668)
P.O. Box 567 (93953-0567)
PHONE.................................831 647-7500
Bill Perocchi, *CEO*
Cody Plott, *
Dave Heuck, *
Paul Spengler, *
Mark Stilwell, *
▲ **EMP:** 150 **EST:** 1919
SQ FT: 2,197
SALES (est): 302.53MM
SALES (corp-wide): 302.53MM **Privately Held**
Web: www.pebblebeach.com
SIC: 7992 7997 Public golf courses; Country club, membership

(P-14271)
LOS SERRANOS GOLF CLUB
Also Called: Los Serranos Golf & Cntry CLB
15656 Yorba Ave (91709-3129)
PHONE.................................909 597-1769
John A Kramer Junior, *CEO*
John A Kramer Senior, *Pr*
Ronald Kramer, *
Gloria Kramer, *Stockholder**
Kevin Sullivan, *
EMP: 135 **EST:** 1953
SQ FT: 41,896
SALES (est): 6.66MM **Privately Held**
Web: www.losserranoscountryclub.com
SIC: 7992 5812 5813 Public golf courses; American restaurant; Cocktail lounge

(P-14272)
MADERAS GOLF CLUB
17750 Old Coach Rd (92064-6621)
PHONE.................................858 451-8100
Bill O'brien, *Genl Mgr*
EMP: 78 **EST:** 2007
SALES (est): 5.1MM **Privately Held**
Web: www.maderasgolf.com
SIC: 7992 Public golf courses

(P-14273)
MADISON CLUB OWNERS ASSN
Also Called: Madison Club, The
53035 Meriwether Way (92253-5535)
P.O. Box 1558 (92247-1558)
PHONE.................................760 777-9320
Douglas Siebold, *CEO*
Brian Ellis, *
EMP: 125 **EST:** 2006
SQ FT: 70,000
SALES (est): 10.61MM
SALES (corp-wide): 435.04MM **Privately Held**
Web: www.madisonclubca.com
SIC: 7992 Public golf courses
PA: Discovery Land Company, Llc
14605 N 73rd St
Scottsdale AZ

(P-14274)
MCMILLIN COMMUNITIES INC
Also Called: Temeku Hills
41687 Temeku Dr (92591-3909)
PHONE.................................951 506-3303
Sonia Howard, *Brnch Mgr*
EMP: 940
SALES (corp-wide): 46.31MM **Privately Held**
Web: www.mcmillin.com
SIC: 7992 Public golf courses
PA: Mcmillin Communities, Inc.
2750 Womble Rd Ste 102
San Diego CA
619 477-4117

(P-14275)
MESA VERDE PARTNERS
Also Called: Costa Mesa Country Club
1701 Golf Course Dr (92626-5049)
PHONE.................................714 540-7500
Scott Henderson, *Pt*
EMP: 120 **EST:** 1992
SQ FT: 12,000
SALES (est): 4.56MM
SALES (corp-wide): 8.81MM **Privately Held**
Web: www.costamesacountryclub.com
SIC: 7992 7997 5813 5812 Public golf courses; Membership sports and recreation clubs; Drinking places; Eating places
PA: Santa Anita Associates
405 S Santa Anita Ave
Arcadia CA
626 447-2764

(P-14276)
MILE SQUARE GOLF COURSE
10401 Warner Ave (92708-1604)
PHONE.................................714 962-5541
David A Rainville, *Pt*
EMP: 109 **EST:** 1969
SQ FT: 12,000
SALES (est): 4.45MM **Privately Held**
Web: www.milesquaregolfcourse.com
SIC: 7992 7999 5812 Public golf courses; Golf driving range; American restaurant

(P-14277)
MONARCH BEACH GOLF LINKS (HQ)
50 Monarch Beach Resort N (92629-4084)
PHONE.................................949 240-8247
Hale Kelly, *Dir*
EMP: 80 **EST:** 1983
SALES (est): 9.95MM **Privately Held**
Web: www.monarchbeachgolf.com
SIC: 7992 Public golf courses
PA: Troon Golf, L.L.C.
15044 N Scottsdale Rd # 300
Scottsdale AZ

(P-14278)
MORTON GOLF MANAGEMENT LLC
Also Called: Haggin Oaks Golf Shop
3645 Fulton Ave (95821-1808)
PHONE.................................916 481-4653
Terry Daubert, *Mgr*
Terry Daubert, *Prin*
EMP: 100 **EST:** 1932
SQ FT: 13,800
SALES (est): 9.49MM **Privately Held**
Web: www.hagginoaks.com
SIC: 7992 5941 5813 5812 Public golf courses; Golf goods and equipment; Drinking places; Eating places

(P-14279)
OAKMONT GOLF CLUB INC
7025 Oakmont Dr (95409-6301)
PHONE.................................707 538-2454
John Yacobellis, *Dir*
EMP: 80 **EST:** 1963
SQ FT: 4,000
SALES (est): 1.46MM **Privately Held**
Web: www.valleyofthemoonclub.com
SIC: 7992 7997 5941 Public golf courses; Golf club, membership; Golf goods and equipment

(P-14280)
PALM DSERT RCRTL FCLITIES CORP
Also Called: Pdrfc
38995 Desert Willow Dr (92260-1674)
P.O. Box 14290 (92255-4290)
PHONE.................................760 346-0015
Richard Mogensen, *Genl Mgr*
Kathy Anderson, *
EMP: 72 **EST:** 1997
SQ FT: 10,000
SALES (est): 10.53MM
SALES (corp-wide): 123.69MM **Privately Held**
Web: www.desertwillow.com
SIC: 7992 Public golf courses
PA: City Of Palm Desert
73510 Fred Waring Dr
Palm Desert CA
760 346-0611

(P-14281)
POPPY RIDGE INC
Also Called: Poppy Ridge Golf Course
4280 Greenville Rd (94550-9720)
PHONE.................................925 456-8229
EMP: 73 **EST:** 1992
SALES (est): 12.02MM **Privately Held**
Web: poppyridgegolf.ncga.org
SIC: 7992 Public golf courses
PA: Poppy Holding, Inc.
3200 Lopez Rd
Pebble Beach CA

(P-14282)
PRESERVE GOLF CLUB INC
1 Rancho San Carlos Rd (93923-7999)
PHONE.................................831 620-6871
Thomas Gray, *Pr*
EMP: 78 **EST:** 1999
SQ FT: 20,000
SALES (est): 7.52MM **Privately Held**
Web: www.santaluciapreserve.com
SIC: 7992 Public golf courses

(P-14283)
QUARRY AT LA QUINTA INC (PA)
41865 Boardwalk Ste 214 (92211-9033)
PHONE.................................760 777-1100
William Morrow, *Pr*
EMP: 60 **EST:** 1993
SALES (est): 4.4MM **Privately Held**
Web: www.thequarrygc.com
SIC: 7992 Public golf courses

(P-14284)
RANCHO VISTA DEVELOPMENT CO
Also Called: Rancho Vista Golf Course
3905 Club Rancho Dr (93551-5334)
PHONE.................................661 272-9082
Mark Frugal, *Brnch Mgr*
EMP: 60
SALES (corp-wide): 4.63MM **Privately Held**
Web: www.ranchovistagolfclub.com
SIC: 7992 5941 Public golf courses; Golf goods and equipment
PA: Rancho Vista Development Co
3011 Rancho Vista Blvd
Palmdale CA
661 266-9785

(P-14285)
RUBY HILL GOLF CLUB LLC
3400 W Ruby Hill Dr (94566-3604)
PHONE.................................925 417-5840
Michael Rood, *
Anne Fay, *

7992 - Public Golf Courses (P-14286)

EMP: 67 EST: 1994
SALES (est): 7.07MM **Privately Held**
Web: www.rubyhill.com
SIC: 7992 Public golf courses

(P-14286)
SAN JUAN OAKS LLC
Also Called: San Juan Oaks Golf Club
3825 Union Rd (95023-9135)
PHONE..................................831 636-6113
TOLL FREE: 800
EMP: 80 EST: 1994
SQ FT: 1,800
SALES (est): 6.25MM **Privately Held**
Web: www.sanjuanoaks.com
SIC: 7992 5941 5812 5813 Public golf courses; Golf goods and equipment; Eating places; Bar (drinking places)

(P-14287)
SANTA ANITA ASSOCIATES (PA)
Also Called: Santa Anita Golf Course
405 S Santa Anita Ave (91006-3509)
PHONE..................................626 447-2764
Scott L Henderson, *Mng Pt*
Mike Donavan, *Pt*
EMP: 60 EST: 1986
SQ FT: 16,000
SALES (est): 8.81MM
SALES (corp-wide): 8.81MM **Privately Held**
Web: www.santaanitagc.com
SIC: 7992 5812 7999 7299 Public golf courses; American restaurant; Golf cart, power, rental; Banquet hall facilities

(P-14288)
SILVER ROCK RESORT GOLF CLUB
79179 Ahmanson Ln (92253-5715)
PHONE..................................760 777-8884
EMP: 100 EST: 2005
SALES (est): 4.6MM
SALES (corp-wide): 91.88MM **Privately Held**
Web: www.silverrock.org
SIC: 7992 Public golf courses
PA: City Of La Quinta
78495 Calle Tampico
La Quinta CA
760 777-7000

(P-14289)
SISKIYOU LAKE GOLF RESORT INC
Also Called: Mount Shasta Resort
1000 Siskiyou Lake Blvd (96067-9482)
PHONE..................................530 926-3030
John Cullison, *Pr*
John Fryer, *
EMP: 80 EST: 1991
SALES (est): 4.71MM **Privately Held**
Web: www.mountshastaresort.com
SIC: 7992 5941 7011 5812 Public golf courses; Golf goods and equipment; Tourist camps, cabins, cottages, and courts; American restaurant

(P-14290)
SPE GO HOLDINGS INC
Also Called: Mount Woodson Country Club
16422 N Woodson Dr (92065-6800)
PHONE..................................858 638-0672
Steve Dawe, *Ex VP*
EMP: 60
SALES (corp-wide): 12.87B **Publicly Held**
Web: www.mtwoodsongolfclub.com
SIC: 7992 Public golf courses
HQ: Spe Go Holdings, Inc.
11575 Great Oaks Way # 210
Alpharetta GA
401 621-4200

(P-14291)
STERLING HILLS LLC
Also Called: Sterling Hills Golf Club
901 Sterling Hills Dr (93010-9101)
PHONE..................................805 604-1234
EMP: 60 EST: 2000
SALES (est): 1.2MM **Privately Held**
Web: www.sterlinghillsgolf.com
SIC: 7992 Public golf courses

(P-14292)
SUN CITY RSVLLE CMNTY ASSN INC (PA)
Also Called: TIMBER CREEK GOLF COURSE
7050 Del Webb Blvd (95747-8040)
PHONE..................................916 774-3880
Dewolfe Emory, *CEO*
EMP: 180 EST: 1994
SALES (est): 14.19MM
SALES (corp-wide): 14.19MM **Privately Held**
Web: www.suncityroseville.org
SIC: 7992 5812 Public golf courses; Eating places

(P-14293)
SYCAMORE CC INC
Also Called: The Golf Club of California
39500 Robert Trent Jones Pkwy (92563-5849)
PHONE..................................760 451-3700
William Lyon, *Pr*
EMP: 60 EST: 2001
SALES (est): 4.25MM
SALES (corp-wide): 8.22B **Publicly Held**
Web: www.thegolfclubatfallbrook.com
SIC: 7992 Public golf courses
HQ: William Lyon Homes
4695 Macarthur Ct Ste 800
Newport Beach CA

(P-14294)
TRADITIONS GOLF LLC
Also Called: Cinnabar Hills Golf Club
23600 Mckean Rd (95141-1001)
PHONE..................................408 323-5200
Lee Brandenburg, *
Paul Pugh, *
EMP: 100 EST: 1998
SQ FT: 25,000
SALES (est): 9.98MM **Privately Held**
Web: www.cinnabarhills.com
SIC: 7992 Public golf courses

(P-14295)
TRILOGY GOLF AT LA QUINTA
60151 Trilogy Pkwy (92253-7640)
PHONE..................................760 771-0707
Tom Williams Pga, *Genl Mgr*
Marge Deschaak, *
Ralph Bernhisel, *
EMP: 320 EST: 2004
SALES (est): 2.36MM
SALES (corp-wide): 2.1B **Privately Held**
Web: www.thegolfclubatlaquinta.com
SIC: 7992 Public golf courses
HQ: J.F. Shea Construction, Inc.
655 Brea Canyon Rd
Walnut CA
909 594-9500

(P-14296)
WELK GROUP INC
Also Called: Foutains Executive Course
8860 Lawrence Welk Dr (92026-6403)
PHONE..................................760 749-3225
Larry Welk Junior, *VP*
EMP: 143
SALES (corp-wide): 47.43MM **Privately Held**
Web: www.welkresorts.com
SIC: 7992 7011 Public golf courses; Resort hotel
PA: The Welk Group Inc
11400 W Olympic Blvd # 1450
Los Angeles CA
760 749-3000

7993 Coin-operated Amusement Devices

(P-14297)
CAMPO BAND MISSIONS INDIANS
Also Called: Golden Acorn Casino & Trvl Ctr
1800 Golden Acorn Way (91906-2301)
P.O. Box 310 (91906-0310)
PHONE..................................619 938-6000
Don Trimble, *Mgr*
EMP: 330
Web: www.goldenacorncasino.com
SIC: 7993 5812 Gambling establishments operating coin-operated machines; American restaurant
PA: Campo Band Of Missions Indians
36190 Church Rd
Campo CA

(P-14298)
MOORETOWN RANCHERIA
Also Called: Feather Falls Casino
3 Alverda Dr (95966-9379)
PHONE..................................530 533-3885
Tom Yarbrough, *Genl Mgr*
EMP: 340
Web: www.featherfallscasino.com
SIC: 7993 7999 Gambling establishments operating coin-operated machines; Gambling establishment
PA: Mooretown Rancheria
1 Alverda Dr
Oroville CA

(P-14299)
SEGA ENTERTAINMENT USA INC
600 N Brand Blvd 5th Fl (91203-4207)
PHONE..................................310 217-9500
▲ EMP: 1550
SIC: 7993 Coin-operated amusement devices

7996 Amusement Parks

(P-14300)
CEDAR FAIR LP
Auntie Anne's
4701 Great America Pkwy (95054-1287)
P.O. Box 1776 (95052-1776)
PHONE..................................408 988-1776
David Mannix, *Brnch Mgr*
EMP: 120
SALES (corp-wide): 1.82B **Publicly Held**
Web: www.cagreatamerica.com
SIC: 7996 5461 Theme park, amusement; Pretzels
PA: Cedar Fair, L.P.
1 Cedar Point Dr
Sandusky OH
419 627-2344

(P-14301)
CITY OF LANCASTER
Also Called: Big Eight
43011 N 10th St W (93534-6012)
PHONE..................................661 723-6071
Jeff Campbell, *Brnch Mgr*
EMP: 153
Web: www.cityoflancasterca.org
SIC: 7996 Amusement parks
PA: City Of Lancaster
44933 Fern Ave
Lancaster CA

(P-14302)
DISNEYLAND INTERNATIONAL (DH)
Also Called: Disneyland
1313 S Harbor Blvd (92802-2309)
PHONE..................................714 781-4565
James Thomas, *Pr*
James Cora, *Ch Bd*
Michael Eisner, *Dir*
Richard Nunis, *Dir*
Doris Smith, *Sec*
EMP: 200 EST: 1961
SALES (est): 260.45MM
SALES (corp-wide): 82.72B **Publicly Held**
Web: disneyland.disney.go.com
SIC: 7996 Theme park, amusement
HQ: Disney Enterprises, Inc.
500 S Buena Vista St
Burbank CA
818 560-1000

(P-14303)
FESTIVAL FUN PARKS LLC
Also Called: Raging Waters San Jose 704
2333 S White Rd (95148-1518)
PHONE..................................408 238-9900
James Judy, *Mgr*
EMP: 101
SALES (corp-wide): 355.83K **Privately Held**
Web: www.rwsplash.com
SIC: 7996 Theme park, amusement
HQ: Festival Fun Parks Llc
285 E Waterfront Dr # 150
West Homestead PA
949 261-0404

(P-14304)
GILROY GARDENS FAMILY THEME PK
3050 Hecker Pass Rd (95020-9411)
PHONE..................................408 840-7100
Michael Bonfante, *Dir*
EMP: 204 EST: 1998
SALES (est): 14.25MM **Privately Held**
Web: www.gilroygardens.org
SIC: 7996 Theme park, amusement

(P-14305)
KNOTTS BERRY FARM LLC (HQ)
Also Called: Knott's Berry Farm
8039 Beach Blvd (90620-3200)
P.O. Box 5002 (90622-5002)
PHONE..................................714 827-1776
Jack Falfas, *Pt*
▲ EMP: 500 EST: 1920
SQ FT: 5,000
SALES (est): 170.68MM
SALES (corp-wide): 1.82B **Publicly Held**
Web: www.knotts.com
SIC: 7996 Theme park, amusement
PA: Cedar Fair, L.P.
1 Cedar Point Dr
Sandusky OH
419 627-2344

(P-14306)
LEGOLAND CALIFORNIA LLC
Also Called: Legoland California Resort
1 Legoland Dr (92008-4610)
PHONE..................................760 450-3661

PRODUCTS & SERVICES SECTION
7997 - Membership Sports And Recreation Clubs (P-14327)

▲ EMP: 400 EST: 1994
SALES (est): 89.5MM
SALES (corp-wide): 2.42B **Privately Held**
Web: www.legoland.com
SIC: 7996 Theme park, amusement
HQ: Merlin Entertainments Group Limited
   Link House
   Poole

(P-14307)
MARINE WORLD FOUNDATION
Also Called: Marine World/Africa USA
   Marine World Pkwy (94589)
   PHONE..........................707 644-4000
Phil Ensor, *Prin*
EMP: 350 EST: 1978
SALES (est): 1.87MM **Privately Held**
SIC: 7996 Theme park, amusement

(P-14308)
PARC WATERWORLD LLC
Also Called: Waterworld California
   1950 Waterworld Pkwy (94520-2602)
   PHONE..........................925 609-1364
EMP: 222 EST: 2007
SALES (est): 896.84K
SALES (corp-wide): 99.55MM **Privately Held**
Web: www.waterworldcalifornia.com
SIC: 7996 Theme park, amusement
PA: Parc Management, Llc
   1545 Parkway
   Sevierville TN
   904 732-7272

(P-14309)
PARK MANAGEMENT CORP
Also Called: Cold Stone Creamery
   1001 Fairgrounds Dr (94589-4001)
   PHONE..........................707 643-6722
Dale Kaetzel, *Pr*
Don Mccoy, *Pr*
▲ EMP: 196 EST: 1997
SALES (est): 59.25MM
SALES (corp-wide): 1.36B **Publicly Held**
Web: www.sixflags.com
SIC: 7996 Theme park, amusement
PA: Six Flags Entertainment Corp
   1000 Ballpark Way Ste 400
   Arlington TX
   972 595-5000

(P-14310)
RAGING WATERS GROUP INC
Also Called: Raging Waters
   111 Raging Waters Dr (91773-3998)
   PHONE..........................909 802-2200
EMP: 1092 EST: 2000
SALES (est): 9.97MM
SALES (corp-wide): 53.97MM **Privately Held**
Web: www.ragingwaters.com
SIC: 7996 Theme park, amusement
PA: Alfa Smartparks, Inc
   1 W Adams St Ste 200
   Jacksonville FL
   904 358-1027

(P-14311)
RAVINE WATERPARK LLC
Also Called: Ravine Waterpark, The
   2301 Airport Rd (93446-8549)
   PHONE..........................805 237-8500
James Walsh, *Prin*
EMP: 205 EST: 2004
SALES (est): 4.94MM **Privately Held**
Web: www.ravinewaterpark.com
SIC: 7996 Theme park, amusement

(P-14312)
SANTA CRUZ SEASIDE COMPANY (PA)
Also Called: Santa Cruz Beach Boardwalk
   400 Beach St (95060-5416)
   PHONE..........................831 423-5590
Charles L Canfield, *Pr*
Karl Jeffrey Rice, *Prin*
▲ EMP: 299 EST: 1915
SQ FT: 8,000
SALES (est): 51.32MM
SALES (corp-wide): 51.32MM **Privately Held**
Web: www.scseaside.com
SIC: 7996 7011 7933 6531 Pier, amusement
   ; Motels; Bowling centers; Real estate
   agents and managers

(P-14313)
SANTA MONICA AMUSEMENTS LLC
Also Called: Pacific Park
   380 Santa Monica Pier (90401-3128)
   PHONE..........................310 451-9641
Mary Ann Powell, *CEO*
Jeff Klocke, *
David Gillam, *
Dana Wyatt, *
EMP: 325 EST: 1992
SQ FT: 70,000
SALES (est): 24.91MM **Privately Held**
Web: www.pacpark.com
SIC: 7996 Theme park, amusement

(P-14314)
SEAWORLD PARKS & ENTRMT LLC
   1660 S Shores Rd (92109-7906)
   PHONE..........................619 226-3910
Sam Munoz, *Brnch Mgr*
EMP: 81
Web: www.seaworld.com
SIC: 7996 Theme park, amusement
PA: Seaworld Parks & Entertainment Llc
   500 Sea World Dr
   San Diego CA

(P-14315)
SIX FLAGS MAGIC MOUNTAIN INC
   26101 Magic Mountain Pkwy (91355-1095)
   P.O. Box 5500 (91380-5500)
   PHONE..........................661 255-4100
Larry B Cochran, *CEO*
EMP: 85 EST: 1979
SALES (est): 26.27MM
SALES (corp-wide): 1.36B **Publicly Held**
Web: www.sixflags.com
SIC: 7996 Theme park, amusement
PA: Six Flags Entertainment Corp
   1000 Ballpark Way Ste 400
   Arlington TX
   972 595-5000

(P-14316)
WALT DISNEY COMPANY (PA)
Also Called: Disney
   500 S Buena Vista St (91521-0007)
   PHONE..........................818 560-1000
Robert A Iger, *CEO*
Alan N Braverman, *
Horacio E Gutierrez, *
Zenia B Mucha, *
EMP: 1381 EST: 1923
SALES (est): 82.72B
SALES (corp-wide): 82.72B **Publicly Held**
Web: www.thewaltdisneycompany.com
SIC: 7996 4841 Amusement parks; Cable
   television services

(P-14317)
YANACO INC
Also Called: Waterworks Park
   151 N Boulder Dr (96003-4607)
   PHONE..........................530 246-9550
Joe Murphy, *Pr*
EMP: 176 EST: 2005
SQ FT: 1,000
SALES (est): 4.76MM **Privately Held**
Web: www.waterworkspark.com
SIC: 7996 Amusement parks

7997 Membership Sports And Recreation Clubs

(P-14318)
1334 PARTNERS LP
Also Called: Manhattan Country Club
   1330 Park View Ave (90266-3704)
   PHONE..........................310 546-5656
Keith Brackpool, *Pt*
EMP: 100 EST: 1982
SQ FT: 80,000
SALES (est): 8.22MM **Privately Held**
SIC: 7997 6512 7991 5813 Country club,
   membership; Commercial and industrial
   building operation; Physical fitness facilities
   ; Drinking places

(P-14319)
ALMADEN GOLF & COUNTRY CLUB
   6663 Hampton Dr (95120-5536)
   PHONE..........................408 323-4812
Robert Osshalem, *Genl Mgr*
EMP: 60 EST: 1954
SQ FT: 26,000
SALES (est): 9.03MM **Privately Held**
Web: www.almadengcc.org
SIC: 7997 Country club, membership

(P-14320)
ALTA VISTA COUNTRY CLUB LLC
   777 Alta Vista St (92870-5101)
   PHONE..........................714 524-1591
Karl Reul, *Managing Member*
EMP: 60 EST: 1998
SQ FT: 6,751,800
SALES (est): 2.3MM **Privately Held**
Web: www.altavistacc.com
SIC: 7997 Country club, membership

(P-14321)
ALTADENA TOWN AND COUNTRY CLUB
   2290 Country Club Dr (91001-3202)
   PHONE..........................626 345-9088
David Edens, *Pr*
EMP: 80 EST: 1946
SQ FT: 50,000
SALES (est): 5.98MM **Privately Held**
Web: www.altaclub.com
SIC: 7997 Country club, membership

(P-14322)
AMERICAN GOLF CORPORATION
Also Called: Oakhurst Country Club
   1001 Peacock Creek Dr (94517-2201)
   PHONE..........................925 672-9737
Craig Wong, *Genl Mgr*
EMP: 100
Web: www.oakhurstcc.com
SIC: 7997 Country club, membership
HQ: American Golf Corporation
   909 N Pacific Coast Hwy # 650
   El Segundo CA
   310 664-4000

(P-14323)
AMERICAN GOLF CORPORATION (HQ)
   909 N Pacific Coast Hwy Ste 650 (90245-2715)
   PHONE..........................310 664-4000
Meng Lai, *CFO*
Kim Wong, *
Keith Brown, *
Jim Allison, *
Craig Kniffen, *
EMP: 150 EST: 1973
SALES (est): 281.77MM **Privately Held**
Web: www.americangolf.com
SIC: 7997 7999 5812 5941 Golf club,
   membership; Golf services and
   professionals; Eating places; Golf goods
   and equipment
PA: Drive Shack Inc.
   10670 N Cntl Expy Ste 700
   Dallas TX

(P-14324)
ANNANDALE GOLF CLUB
   1 N San Rafael Ave (91105-1299)
   PHONE..........................626 796-6125
Christoff Granger, *Genl Mgr*
EMP: 125 EST: 1905
SQ FT: 10,000
SALES (est): 11.75MM **Privately Held**
Web: www.annandalegolf.com
SIC: 7997 Golf club, membership

(P-14325)
ANTELOPE VLY CNTRY CLB IMPRV
   39800 Country Club Dr (93551-2970)
   PHONE..........................661 947-3142
Mark Range, *
EMP: 150 EST: 1952
SQ FT: 22,000
SALES (est): 3.76MM **Privately Held**
Web: www.antelopevalleycountryclub.com
SIC: 7997 Country club, membership

(P-14326)
BAKERSFIELD COUNTRY CLUB
   4200 Country Club Dr (93306-3700)
   P.O. Box 6007 (93386-6007)
   PHONE..........................661 871-4000
Jon Van Boening, *Pr*
EMP: 75 EST: 1948
SQ FT: 30,000
SALES (est): 4.98MM **Privately Held**
Web: www.bakersfieldcountryclub.com
SIC: 7997 5812 5813 Country club,
   membership; Eating places; Bar (drinking
   places)

(P-14327)
BALBOA BAY CLUB INC (HQ)
   1221 W Coast Hwy (92663-5092)
   PHONE..........................949 645-5000
David Wooten, *Pr*
W D Ray, *
EMP: 260 EST: 1948
SALES (est): 24.76MM
SALES (corp-wide): 46.07MM **Privately Held**
Web: www.balboabayclub.com
SIC: 7997 7011 Country club, membership;
   Resort hotel
PA: International Bay Clubs, Llc
   1221 W Coast Hwy Ste 145
   Newport Beach CA
   949 645-5000

7997 - Membership Sports And Recreation Clubs (P-14328)

(P-14328)
BAY CLUB AMERICA INC
Also Called: Pacific Athletic Club
1 Lombard St Ste 201 (94111-1128)
PHONE....................415 781-1874
James Gerber, *Pr*
EMP: 108 **EST:** 1990
SQ FT: 10,000
SALES (est): 2.18MM **Privately Held**
Web: www.bayclubs.com
SIC: 7997 Membership sports and recreation clubs
PA: Bay Club Holdings Iii, Llc
  1 Lombard St Lbby
  San Francisco CA

(P-14329)
BAY CLUBS COMPANY LLC
6144 Calle Real (93117-2012)
PHONE....................805 964-0556
Jody Moon, *Brnch Mgr*
EMP: 294
SALES (corp-wide): 5.09MM **Privately Held**
Web: www.bayclubs.com
SIC: 7997 Membership sports and recreation clubs
HQ: The Bay Clubs Company Llc
  1 Lombard St
  San Francisco CA
  415 781-1874

(P-14330)
BAY CLUBS COMPANY LLC
21 W Carrillo St (93101-3212)
PHONE....................805 965-0999
Ramone Adams, *Mgr*
EMP: 294
SALES (corp-wide): 5.09MM **Privately Held**
Web: www.bayclubs.com
SIC: 7997 Membership sports and recreation clubs
HQ: The Bay Clubs Company Llc
  1 Lombard St
  San Francisco CA
  415 781-1874

(P-14331)
BAY CLUBS COMPANY LLC
2250 Park Pl (91362-1717)
PHONE....................310 643-6878
Alyce Jones, *Brnch Mgr*
EMP: 294
SALES (corp-wide): 5.09MM **Privately Held**
Web: www.bayclubs.com
SIC: 7997 Membership sports and recreation clubs
HQ: The Bay Clubs Company Llc
  1 Lombard St
  San Francisco CA
  415 781-1874

(P-14332)
BAY CLUBS COMPANY LLC
3908 State St (93105-3114)
PHONE....................805 563-8700
Cindy Capra, *Mgr*
EMP: 294
SALES (corp-wide): 5.09MM **Privately Held**
Web: www.bayclubs.com
SIC: 7997 Membership sports and recreation clubs
HQ: The Bay Clubs Company Llc
  1 Lombard St
  San Francisco CA
  415 781-1874

(P-14333)
BAY CLUBS COMPANY LLC
Also Called: Bay Club Marin
220 Corte Madera Town Ctr (94925-1208)
PHONE....................415 945-3000
Maegan Devlin, *Mgr*
EMP: 294
SALES (corp-wide): 5.09MM **Privately Held**
Web: www.bayclubs.com
SIC: 7997 Membership sports and recreation clubs
HQ: The Bay Clubs Company Llc
  1 Lombard St
  San Francisco CA
  415 781-1874

(P-14334)
BAY CLUBS COMPANY LLC
Also Called: Sanctuary Spa
12000 Carmel Country Rd (92130-6101)
PHONE....................858 509-9933
EMP: 294
SALES (corp-wide): 5.09MM **Privately Held**
Web: www.bayclubs.com
SIC: 7997 Membership sports and recreation clubs
HQ: The Bay Clubs Company Llc
  1 Lombard St
  San Francisco CA
  415 781-1874

(P-14335)
BAY CLUBS COMPANY LLC
Also Called: Bay Club Financial District
555 California St (94104-1503)
PHONE....................415 362-7800
Janna Uddyback, *Prin*
EMP: 294
SALES (corp-wide): 5.09MM **Privately Held**
Web: www.bayclubs.com
SIC: 7997 Membership sports and recreation clubs
HQ: The Bay Clubs Company Llc
  1 Lombard St
  San Francisco CA
  415 781-1874

(P-14336)
BAY CLUBS COMPANY LLC
51 Peninsula Ctr Ste 51d (90275)
PHONE....................310 541-2582
Eric Rogers, *Genl Mgr*
EMP: 294
SALES (corp-wide): 5.09MM **Privately Held**
Web: www.bayclubs.com
SIC: 7997 Membership sports and recreation clubs
HQ: The Bay Clubs Company Llc
  1 Lombard St
  San Francisco CA
  415 781-1874

(P-14337)
BAY CLUBS COMPANY LLC
2425 Olympic Blvd Ste 100 (90404-4030)
PHONE....................310 829-4995
Andy Gillen, *COO*
EMP: 294
SALES (corp-wide): 5.09MM **Privately Held**
Web: www.bayclubs.com
SIC: 7997 Membership sports and recreation clubs
HQ: The Bay Clubs Company Llc
  1 Lombard St
  San Francisco CA
  415 781-1874

(P-14338)
BEACH CLUB
201 Palisades Beach Rd (90402-1401)
PHONE....................310 395-3254
Gregg Patterson, *Ex Dir*
EMP: 60 **EST:** 1923
SQ FT: 35,000
SALES (est): 10.51MM **Privately Held**
Web: www.thebc.org
SIC: 7997 5812 5813 Beach club, membership; Eating places; Bar (drinking places)

(P-14339)
BEL-AIR BAY CLUB LTD
16801 Pacific Coast Hwy (90272-3350)
PHONE....................310 230-4700
William Howard, *CEO*
EMP: 200 **EST:** 1927
SQ FT: 7,500
SALES (est): 12.04MM **Privately Held**
Web: www.belairbayclub.com
SIC: 7997 Membership sports and recreation clubs

(P-14340)
BEL-AIR COUNTRY CLUB
10768 Bellagio Rd (90077-3799)
PHONE....................310 472-9563
Joseph Wagner, *Genl Mgr*
Peter Best, *
EMP: 140 **EST:** 1924
SQ FT: 10,000
SALES (est): 14.61MM **Privately Held**
Web: www.bel-aircc.golf
SIC: 7997 5941 Country club, membership; Golf goods and equipment

(P-14341)
BELLA COLLINA SAN CLEMENTE
200 Avenida La Pata (92673-6301)
PHONE....................949 498-6604
EMP: 80 **EST:** 2009
SALES (est): 2.27MM **Privately Held**
Web: www.bellacollinasanclemente.com
SIC: 7997 Golf club, membership

(P-14342)
BERKELEY COUNTRY CLUB
7901 Cutting Blvd (94530-1877)
P.O. Box 2636 (94530-5636)
PHONE....................510 233-7550
Richard Pettler, *Pr*
Charles Ibbotson, *
Bob Langbein, *
Ken Kipp, *
EMP: 92 **EST:** 1920
SQ FT: 12,000
SALES (est): 5.45MM **Privately Held**
Web: www.berkeleycountryclub.com
SIC: 7997 Country club, membership

(P-14343)
BIG CANYON COUNTRY CLUB
1 Big Canyon Dr (92660-5299)
PHONE....................949 644-5404
Donald Tippett, *CEO*
William Stamply, *
EMP: 180 **EST:** 1971
SQ FT: 50,000
SALES (est): 24.83MM **Privately Held**
Web: www.bigcanyoncc.org
SIC: 7997 Country club, membership

(P-14344)
BIG LGUE DREAMS CONSULTING LLC
20155 Viking Way (96003-8293)
PHONE....................530 223-1177
Brandi Merkel, *Prin*
EMP: 107
SALES (corp-wide): 49.84MM **Privately Held**
Web: www.bigleaguedreams.com
SIC: 7997 Baseball club, except professional and semi-professional
PA: Big League Dreams Consulting, Llc
  16333 Fairfield Ranch Rd
  Chino Hills CA
  909 287-1700

(P-14345)
BIGHORN GOLF CLUB CHARITIES
255 Palowet Dr (92260-7311)
PHONE....................760 773-2468
Carl T Cardinalli, *Pr*
Joe Curtis, *
EMP: 190 **EST:** 1990
SALES (est): 1.66MM **Privately Held**
Web: www.bighorngolf.com
SIC: 7997 7992 Country club, membership; Public golf courses

(P-14346)
BIRNAM WOOD GOLF CLUB (PA)
1941 E Valley Rd (93108-1427)
PHONE....................805 969-2223
Robert Thornburgh, *Pr*
Michael-m C Gardner, *COO*
Robert Trent Jones, *
EMP: 61 **EST:** 1967
SQ FT: 45,000
SALES (est): 13.14MM
SALES (corp-wide): 13.14MM **Privately Held**
Web: www.bwgc.net
SIC: 7997 7992 5812 Golf club, membership; Public golf courses; Eating places

(P-14347)
BLACKHAWK COUNTRY CLUB
599 Blackhawk Club Dr (94506-4522)
PHONE....................925 736-6500
Michael G Burton, *CEO*
Larry Marx, *
Kevin Dunne, *General MNG**
EMP: 230 **EST:** 1987
SQ FT: 35,743
SALES (est): 25.82MM **Privately Held**
Web: www.blackhawkcc.org
SIC: 7997 7992 5812 Golf club, membership; Public golf courses; Eating places

(P-14348)
BOYS GIRLS CLUBS OF PENINSULA
401 Pierce Rd (94025-1240)
PHONE....................650 322-6255
Peter Fortenbaugh, *Dir*
EMP: 60 **EST:** 1975
SQ FT: 2,000
SALES (est): 26.97MM **Privately Held**
Web: www.bgcp.org
SIC: 7997 Membership sports and recreation clubs

(P-14349)
BRAEMAR COUNTRY CLUB INC
Also Called: Braemar Country Club
4001 Reseda Blvd (91356-5330)
P.O. Box 570217 (91357-0217)
PHONE....................323 873-6880
Steven Held, *Mgr*
EMP: 199 **EST:** 1959
SQ FT: 20,000
SALES (est): 9.13MM
SALES (corp-wide): 2.44B **Privately Held**

PRODUCTS & SERVICES SECTION
7997 - Membership Sports And Recreation Clubs (P-14371)

Web: www.invitedclubs.com
SIC: **7997** Country club, membership
HQ: Clubcorp Usa, Inc.
 5215 N O Connor Blvd # 2
 Irving TX
 972 243-6191

(P-14350)
BRENTWOOD COUNTRY CLUB LOS ANGELES
Also Called: BRENTWOOD COUNTRY CLUB
590 S Burlingame Ave (90049-4826)
PHONE..............................310 451-8011
EMP: 100 **EST:** 1948
SALES (est): 17.68MM **Privately Held**
Web: www.brentwoodcc.net
SIC: **7997** Country club, membership

(P-14351)
BROOKSIDE COUNTRY CLUB
3603 Saint Andrews Dr (95219-1868)
PHONE..............................209 956-6200
Barney Kramer, *CEO*
New England Life, *
EMP: 70 **EST:** 1991
SQ FT: 5,000
SALES (est): 4.94MM **Privately Held**
Web: www.brooksidegolf.net
SIC: **7997** 7999 5941 5812 Country club, membership; Golf driving range; Golf goods and equipment; Eating places

(P-14352)
BURLINGAME COUNTRY CLUB
80 New Place Rd (94010-6499)
PHONE..............................650 696-8100
Ralston P Roberts, *CEO*
EMP: 97 **EST:** 1893
SALES (est): 11.97MM **Privately Held**
Web: www.burlingamecc.org
SIC: **7997** Country club, membership

(P-14353)
CALIFRNIA GOLF CLB SAN FRNCSCO
844 W Orange Ave (94080-3125)
PHONE..............................650 588-9021
Jon Mcgovern, *CEO*
Gregory Spencer, *
Henry Bullock, *
Junaid Sheikh, *
Steven Ruwe, *
EMP: 74 **EST:** 1918
SQ FT: 30,000
SALES (est): 9.75MM **Privately Held**
Web: www.calclub.org
SIC: **7997** Country club, membership

(P-14354)
CAMERON PARK COUNTRY CLUB INC
Also Called: CAMERON PARK COUNTRY CLUB
3201 Royal Dr (95682-8559)
PHONE..............................530 672-9840
J Poindexter, *Genl Mgr*
Jack Mehl, *
Michael Fleig, *Club Manager*
Don Seese, *
Joe William, *
EMP: 60 **EST:** 1979
SQ FT: 50,000
SALES (est): 5.42MM **Privately Held**
Web: www.cameronparkcc.com
SIC: **7997** Country club, membership

(P-14355)
CANYON CREST COUNTRY CLUB INC
Also Called: Golf Pro Shop
975 Country Club Dr (92506-3699)
PHONE..............................951 274-7900
Robert H Dedman, *Ch Bd*
Frank Gore, *
Richard S Poole, *
Murray Page, *
James Maser, *
EMP: 67 **EST:** 1967
SQ FT: 4,000
SALES (est): 9MM
SALES (corp-wide): 2.44B **Privately Held**
Web: www.canyoncrestcc.com
SIC: **7997** 5812 5813 Golf club, membership; American restaurant; Bar (drinking places)
HQ: Clubcorp Usa, Inc.
 5215 N O Connor Blvd # 2
 Irving TX
 972 243-6191

(P-14356)
CASTLE CREEK COUNTRY CLUB INC
8797 Circle R Dr (92026-5802)
PHONE..............................760 749-2877
Yoshimichi Umeda, *Pr*
EMP: 60 **EST:** 1980
SQ FT: 15,000
SALES (est): 1.61MM **Privately Held**
Web: www.castlecreekcountryclub.com
SIC: **7997** 5941 5812 Golf club, membership; Golf goods and equipment; Eating places

(P-14357)
CASTLEWOOD COUNTRY CLUB
707 Country Club Cir (94566-9743)
PHONE..............................925 846-2871
Jerry Olson, *CEO*
Jerry Olsen, *
Rick Hankins, *
Tom Rutherford, *
EMP: 167 **EST:** 1954
SQ FT: 55,000
SALES (est): 16.12MM **Privately Held**
Web: www.castlewoodcc.org
SIC: **7997** Country club, membership

(P-14358)
CATTA VERDERA COUNTRY CLUB LLC
1111 Catta Verdera (95648-9649)
PHONE..............................916 645-7200
Christopher R Steele, *Managing Member*
EMP: 90 **EST:** 2004
SQ FT: 196,020
SALES (est): 9.41MM **Privately Held**
Web: www.cattaverdera.com
SIC: **7997** Golf club, membership

(P-14359)
CLAREMONT COUNTRY CLUB
5295 Broadway Ter (94618-1498)
PHONE..............................510 653-6789
Harold Peter Smith, *CEO*
Alec Churchward, *
Warren Chip Brown, *
Thomas C Crosby, *
Richard W Kraber, *
EMP: 85 **EST:** 1903
SQ FT: 479,160
SALES (est): 15.51MM **Privately Held**
Web: www.claremontcountryclub.com
SIC: **7997** Country club, membership

(P-14360)
CLAREMONT TENNIS CLUB
Also Called: Claremont Club, The
1777 Monte Vista Ave (91711-2916)
P.O. Box 157 (91785-0157)
PHONE..............................909 625-9515
Michael G Alpert, *Pr*
Geoffrey Clark, *
EMP: 200 **EST:** 1973
SQ FT: 40,000
SALES (est): 21.08MM **Privately Held**
Web: www.claremontclub.com
SIC: **7997** 7991 5812 Membership sports and recreation clubs; Health club; Eating places

(P-14361)
COMEDY CLUB OXNARD LLC
Also Called: Levity Live
591 Collection Blvd (93036-5454)
PHONE..............................805 535-5400
Alireza Ghaemian, *Prin*
EMP: 88 **EST:** 2015
SALES (est): 991.77K **Privately Held**
SIC: **7997** Membership sports and recreation clubs

(P-14362)
CONTRA COSTA COUNTRY CLUB
801 Golf Club Rd (94523-1101)
PHONE..............................925 798-7135
Bill Wampler, *Club Manager*
EMP: 69 **EST:** 1925
SQ FT: 20,000
SALES (est): 8.57MM **Privately Held**
Web: www.contracostacc.org
SIC: **7997** 5812 5813 Golf club, membership; American restaurant; Drinking places

(P-14363)
CORDEVALLE GOLF CLUB LLC
1 Cordevalle Club Dr (95046-9472)
PHONE..............................408 695-4500
EMP: 1258 **EST:** 1999
SALES (est): 3.82MM
SALES (corp-wide): 435.04MM **Privately Held**
SIC: **7997** Golf club, membership
PA: Discovery Land Company, Llc
 14605 N 73rd St
 Scottsdale AZ
 480 624-5200

(P-14364)
CORRAL DE TIERRA COUNTRY CLUB
81 Corral De Tierra Rd (93908-9477)
PHONE..............................831 484-1325
Mike Oprish, *Pr*
Dominic Guzzo, *
EMP: 100 **EST:** 1959
SQ FT: 15,000
SALES (est): 8.54MM **Privately Held**
Web: www.corraldetierracc.com
SIC: **7997** Golf club, membership

(P-14365)
COURTSIDE TENNIS CLUB
Also Called: Courtside Club
14675 Winchester Blvd (95032-1890)
PHONE..............................408 395-7111
James Hinckley, *Pr*
Jim Gerber, *Pr*
EMP: 77 **EST:** 1982
SQ FT: 100,000
SALES (est): 10.61MM
SALES (corp-wide): 2.44B **Privately Held**
Web: www.bayclubs.com
SIC: **7997** 7991 5812 Tennis club, membership; Physical fitness facilities; Eating places
HQ: Clubcorp Usa, Inc.
 5215 N O Connor Blvd # 2
 Irving TX
 972 243-6191

(P-14366)
CS-PLEASANTON LLC
Also Called: Clubsport of Pleasanton
7090 Johnson Dr (94588-3328)
PHONE..............................925 463-2822
Steve Gilmour, *Pr*
EMP: 1122 **EST:** 2002
SALES (est): 3.83MM
SALES (corp-wide): 46.12MM **Privately Held**
Web: www.bayclubs.com
SIC: **7997** Membership sports and recreation clubs
PA: Leisure Sports, Inc.
 225 Spring St
 Pleasanton CA
 925 600-1966

(P-14367)
DEL MAR COUNTRY CLUB INC
6001 Clubhouse Dr (92067-9589)
P.O. Box 9866 (92067-4866)
PHONE..............................858 759-5500
Madeleine Pickens, *Pr*
EMP: 90 **EST:** 1993
SQ FT: 18,000
SALES (est): 10.12MM **Privately Held**
Web: www.delmarcountryclub.com
SIC: **7997** Country club, membership

(P-14368)
DEL PASO COUNTRY CLUB
3333 Marconi Ave (95821-6231)
PHONE..............................916 489-3681
Chris Shanks, *Contrlr*
Eric Hatzenbiler, *
EMP: 105 **EST:** 1916
SALES (est): 9.76MM **Privately Held**
Web: www.delpasocc.org
SIC: **7997** 5941 5812 Country club, membership; Sporting goods and bicycle shops; Eating places

(P-14369)
DEL RIO GOLF & COUNTRY CLUB
Also Called: Brighton
801 Stewart Rd (95356-9639)
PHONE..............................209 341-2414
John Bellizzi, *Prin*
Duncan Reno, *
Jay Ward, *
Ken Dieker, *Prin*
Eric Tobias, *Prin*
EMP: 112 **EST:** 1946
SQ FT: 48,000
SALES (est): 11.27MM **Privately Held**
Web: www.delriocountryclub.com
SIC: **7997** 5941 Country club, membership; Sporting goods and bicycle shops

(P-14370)
DHCCNP
Also Called: DESERT HORIZONS COUNTRY CLUB
44900 Desert Horizons Dr (92210-7401)
PHONE..............................760 340-4646
Jurgen Gross, *Mgr*
EMP: 86 **EST:** 1979
SQ FT: 30,000
SALES (est): 5.47MM **Privately Held**
Web: www.deserthorizons.org
SIC: **7997** 7992 5812 Country club, membership; Public golf courses; Eating places

(P-14371)
EL CABALLERO COUNTRY CLUB

7997 - Membership Sports And Recreation Clubs (P-14372)

18300 Tarzana Dr (91356-4216)
PHONE..............................818 654-3000
Bary West, *Pr*
Gary Diamond, *
Peter Jimenez, *
EMP: 125 **EST:** 1956
SQ FT: 20,000
SALES (est): 11.28MM **Privately Held**
Web: www.elcaballerocc.com
SIC: 7997 7992 5812 Country club, membership; Public golf courses; Eating places

(P-14372)
EL MACERO COUNTRY CLUB INC
44571 Clubhouse Dr (95618-1073)
PHONE..............................530 753-3363
Steven Backman, *Genl Mgr*
EMP: 60 **EST:** 1962
SQ FT: 21,000
SALES (est): 5.76MM **Privately Held**
Web: www.elmaceroCC.org
SIC: 7997 5941 5812 5813 Golf club, membership; Golf goods and equipment; American restaurant; Bar (drinking places)

(P-14373)
ELDORADO COUNTRY CLUB
46000 E Eldorado Dr (92210-8631)
PHONE..............................760 346-8081
Geoff Hasley, *Pr*
EMP: 200 **EST:** 1959
SQ FT: 50,000
SALES (est): 18.17MM **Privately Held**
Web: www.eldoradocc.org
SIC: 7997 5812 Golf club, membership; Eating places

(P-14374)
EVERGREEN ALLIANCE GOLF LTD LP
Also Called: Shandin Hills Golf Club
3380 Little Mountain Dr (92405-0900)
PHONE..............................909 886-0669
Tony Chavez, *Mgr*
EMP: 67
SQ FT: 12,000
SALES (corp-wide): 120.96MM **Privately Held**
Web: www.arcisgolf.com
SIC: 7997 7992 Golf club, membership; Public golf courses
PA: Evergreen Alliance Golf Limited, L.P.
8343 Douglas Ave Ste 200
Dallas TX
214 722-6000

(P-14375)
FAIRBANKS RANCH CNTRY CLB INC
15150 San Dieguito Rd (92067)
P.O. Box 8586 (92067-8586)
PHONE..............................858 259-8811
Mike Kendall, *CEO*
Brad Forrester, *
Stan Kinsey, *
Robert Macier, *
EMP: 180 **EST:** 1983
SQ FT: 35,000
SALES (est): 13.41MM **Privately Held**
Web: www.bayclubs.com
SIC: 7997 Country club, membership

(P-14376)
FORT WASH GOLF & CNTRY CLB
Also Called: FORT, THE
10272 N Millbrook Ave (93730-3400)
PHONE..............................559 434-1702
Dean Pryor, *Pr*
Alan Ehnes Club Pro, *Prin*
Bruce Waltz, *
Dean Pryor, *CFO*
EMP: 95 **EST:** 1923
SQ FT:
SALES (est): 5.62MM **Privately Held**
Web: www.fortwashingtoncc.org
SIC: 7997 5813 5812 Golf club, membership; Cocktail lounge; American restaurant

(P-14377)
FRIENDLY HLLS CNTRY CLB FNDTIO
8500 Villaverde Dr (90605-1342)
PHONE..............................562 698-0331
Dave Goodrich, *COO*
Chris Banner, *
EMP: 110 **EST:** 1969
SQ FT: 42,000
SALES (est): 5.4MM **Privately Held**
Web: www.friendlyhillscc.com
SIC: 7997 Country club, membership

(P-14378)
GLENDORA COUNTRY CLUB
2400 Country Club Drive (91741)
PHONE..............................626 335-4051
Jack Stoughton, *CEO*
Jim Leahy, *
Mike Kerstetter, *
Bill Mckinley, *Treas*
Susan Taylor, *
EMP: 90 **EST:** 1954
SQ FT: 10,000
SALES (est): 5.98MM **Privately Held**
Web: www.glendoracountryclub.com
SIC: 7997 5812 5813 Country club, membership; Eating places; Drinking places

(P-14379)
GREEN VALLEY COUNTRY CLUB
35 Country Club Dr (94534-1305)
PHONE..............................707 864-1101
Tom Snell, *Pr*
EMP: 75 **EST:** 1950
SALES (est): 5.96MM **Privately Held**
Web: www.greenvalleycc.com
SIC: 7997 Country club, membership

(P-14380)
HACIENDA GOLF CLUB
718 East Rd (90631-8155)
PHONE..............................562 694-1081
Frank Cordeiro, *Genl Mgr*
EMP: 95 **EST:** 1919
SQ FT: 30,000
SALES (est): 7.73MM **Privately Held**
Web: www.haciendagolfclub.com
SIC: 7997 5812 5813 Golf club, membership; American restaurant; Bar (drinking places)

(P-14381)
HIDEAWAY CLUB
Also Called: Hideaway
80440 Hideaway Club Ct (92253-7867)
P.O. Box 1540 (92247-1540)
PHONE..............................760 777-7400
Brian J Ellis, *CEO*
EMP: 450 **EST:** 2015
SALES (est): 8.91MM
SALES (corp-wide): 435.04MM **Privately Held**
Web: www.hideawaygolfclub.com
SIC: 7997 6531 Membership sports and recreation clubs; Real estate agents and managers
PA: Discovery Land Company, Llc
14605 N 73rd St
Scottsdale AZ
480 624-5200

(P-14382)
HILLCREST COUNTRY CLUB
10000 W Pico Blvd (90064-3417)
PHONE..............................310 553-8911
John Jameson, *Pr*
John Goldsmith, *CEO*
Tom Driefus, *CFO*
Richard Powell, *Prin*
Leonard Fisher, *Prin*
EMP: 180 **EST:** 1920
SQ FT: 69,081
SALES (est): 25.59MM **Privately Held**
Web: www.hcc-la.com
SIC: 7997 Country club, membership

(P-14383)
INDIAN WELLS COUNTRY CLUB INC
46000 Club Dr (92210-8870)
PHONE..............................760 345-2561
Gabe Codding, *Genl Mgr*
James Hinckley, *
Douglas Howe, *
Jack Lupton, *
Terry Taylor, *
EMP: 60 **EST:** 1956
SQ FT: 65,000
SALES (est): 2.93MM
SALES (corp-wide): 2.44B **Privately Held**
Web: www.invitedclubs.com
SIC: 7997 Country club, membership
HQ: Clubcorp Usa, Inc.
5215 N O Connor Blvd # 2
Irving TX
972 243-6191

(P-14384)
INTERNATIONAL BAY CLUBS LLC (PA)
Also Called: Balboa Bay Club and Resort
1221 W Coast Hwy Ste 145 (92663-5001)
PHONE..............................949 645-5000
Todd M Pickup, *CEO*
David Wooten, *Pr*
EMP: 105 **EST:** 1948
SQ FT: 330,000
SALES (est): 46.07MM
SALES (corp-wide): 46.07MM **Privately Held**
Web: www.balboabayclub.com
SIC: 7997 4493 6552 7011 Country club, membership; Marinas; Land subdividers and developers, residential; Hotels and motels

(P-14385)
JONATHAN CLUB
Also Called: Jonathan Beach Club
850 Palisades Beach Rd (90403-1008)
PHONE..............................310 393-9245
Ernie Dunn, *Mgr*
EMP: 100
SQ FT: 12,784
SALES (corp-wide): 30.26MM **Privately Held**
Web: www.jc.org
SIC: 7997 5812 8641 Beach club, membership; Grills (eating places); Civic and social associations
PA: Jonathan Club
545 S Figueroa St
Los Angeles CA
213 624-0881

(P-14386)
LA CANADA FLINTRIDGE CNTRY CLB
5500 Godbey Dr (91011-1836)
PHONE..............................818 790-0611
Gilbert Dreyfus, *Pr*
Evelyn Dreyfus, *
EMP: 80 **EST:** 1977
SQ FT: 24,000
SALES (est): 6.01MM **Privately Held**
Web: www.lcfcountryclub.com
SIC: 7997 Country club, membership

(P-14387)
LA CUMBRE COUNTRY CLUB
4015 Via Laguna (93110-2298)
PHONE..............................805 687-2421
Brian Bahman, *Genl Mgr*
EMP: 100 **EST:** 1956
SQ FT: 8,000
SALES (est): 13.16MM **Privately Held**
Web: www.lacumbrecc.org
SIC: 7997 Country club, membership

(P-14388)
LA JOLLA BCH & TENNIS CLB INC (PA)
Also Called: Marine Room Restaurant
2000 Spindrift Dr (92037-3237)
PHONE..............................858 454-7126
William J Kellogg, *CEO*
Jeannie Porter, *
▲ **EMP:** 165 **EST:** 1940
SQ FT: 3,500
SALES (est): 47.87MM
SALES (corp-wide): 47.87MM **Privately Held**
Web: www.ljbtc.com
SIC: 7997 8742 Membership sports and recreation clubs; Food and beverage consultant

(P-14389)
LA JOLLA COUNTRY CLUB INC
7301 High Ave (92037-5210)
PHONE..............................858 454-9601
Andrew Gorton, *Genl Mgr*
EMP: 91 **EST:** 1928
SQ FT: 39,000
SALES (est): 14.02MM **Privately Held**
Web: www.lajollacountryclub.com
SIC: 7997 5812 5941 5813 Golf club, membership; Eating places; Golf goods and equipment; Bar (drinking places)

(P-14390)
LA RINCONADA COUNTRY CLUB INC
17405 Zena Ave (95030-2256)
PHONE..............................408 395-4181
Rick Forney, *Managing Member*
EMP: 162
SALES (corp-wide): 13.45MM **Privately Held**
Web: www.larinconadacc.com
SIC: 7997 Golf club, membership
PA: La Rinconada Country Club, Inc.
14595 Clearview Dr
Los Gatos CA
408 395-4181

(P-14391)
LAFC PARTNERS LLLP
818 W 7th St Ste 1200 (90017-3435)
PHONE..............................213 334-4239
EMP: 260
SALES (corp-wide): 10.95MM **Privately Held**
Web: www.lafc.com
SIC: 7997 Membership sports and recreation clubs
PA: Lafc Partners, Lllp
4751 Wilshire Blvd
Los Angeles CA
323 648-6000

PRODUCTS & SERVICES SECTION
7997 - Membership Sports And Recreation Clubs (P-14412)

(P-14392)
LAHONTAN GOLF CLUB
12700 Lodgetrail Dr (96161-5125)
PHONE..................................530 550-2400
Jon Madonna, *Pr*
Steve Harris, *
EMP: 150 **EST:** 1996
SQ FT: 500,000
SALES (est): 8.91MM **Privately Held**
Web: www.lahontangolf.com
SIC: 7997 Golf club, membership

(P-14393)
LAKE MERCED GOLF CLUB
2300 Junipero Serra Blvd (94015-1630)
PHONE..................................650 755-2233
Dale Holub, *CEO*
Nick Bailey, *
Sara Krishnamachari, *
EMP: 75 **EST:** 1922
SQ FT: 38,000
SALES (est): 11.36MM **Privately Held**
Web: www.lmgc.org
SIC: 7997 5813 Country club, membership; Bars and lounges

(P-14394)
LAKES COUNTRY CLUB ASSN INC (PA)
Also Called: Lakes Country Club, The
161 Old Ranch Rd (92211-3211)
PHONE..................................760 568-4321
Gerald Lee Hagood, *Pr*
Ron Phipps, *
Sandy Seddon, *
Frank Melon, *
EMP: 125 **EST:** 1982
SQ FT: 3,600
SALES (est): 14.35MM
SALES (corp-wide): 14.35MM **Privately Held**
Web: www.thelakescc.com
SIC: 7997 5941 5812 Country club, membership; Sporting goods and bicycle shops; Eating places

(P-14395)
LAS POSAS COUNTRY CLUB
Also Called: Lpcc
955 Fairway Dr (93010-8499)
PHONE..................................805 482-4518
Todd Keefer, *Genl Mgr*
EMP: 146 **EST:** 1957
SALES (est): 2.29MM
SALES (corp-wide): 45.8MM **Privately Held**
Web: www.lasposascc.com
SIC: 7997 7992 5812 0781 Country club, membership; Public golf courses; Eating places; Landscape counseling and planning
PA: Century Golf Partners Management Lp
5430 Lyndon B Johnson Fwy
Dallas TX
972 419-1400

(P-14396)
LONE CYPRESS COMPANY LLC
Also Called: Beach & Tennis Club
1567 Cypress Dr (93953)
P.O. Box 1128 (93953-1128)
PHONE..................................831 625-8507
Steve Hurst, *Brnch Mgr*
EMP: 78
SALES (corp-wide): 302.53MM **Privately Held**
Web: www.pebblebeach.com
SIC: 7997 7999 5812 7991 Beach club, membership; Tennis services and professionals; Caterers; Physical fitness facilities
PA: Lone Cypress Company Llc
2700 17 Mile Dr
Pebble Beach CA
831 647-7500

(P-14397)
LONG BEACH YACHT CLUB
6201 E Appian Way (90803-4199)
PHONE..................................562 598-9401
Louis Izurieta, *Genl Mgr*
Louis Izureita, *
Robert Frazer, *
EMP: 63 **EST:** 1929
SQ FT: 25,000
SALES (est): 5.34MM **Privately Held**
Web: www.lbyc.org
SIC: 7997 Yacht club, membership

(P-14398)
LOS ALTOS GOLF AND COUNTRY CLB
1560 Country Club Dr (94024-5907)
PHONE..................................650 947-3100
Bill Schneider, *Pr*
EMP: 70 **EST:** 1921
SALES (est): 15.7MM **Privately Held**
Web: www.lagcc.com
SIC: 7997 Country club, membership

(P-14399)
LOS ANGELES COUNTRY CLUB
10101 Wilshire Blvd (90024-4703)
PHONE..................................310 276-6104
Kirk O Reese, *Prin*
EMP: 250 **EST:** 1898
SQ FT: 75,000
SALES (est): 24.95MM **Privately Held**
Web: www.thelacc.org
SIC: 7997 Country club, membership

(P-14400)
LOS ANGLES RYAL VSTA GOLF CRSE
Also Called: Los Angles Ryal Vsta Golf Crse
20055 Colima Rd (91789-3502)
PHONE..................................909 595-7441
TOLL FREE: 800
Don Crooker, *Mgr*
EMP: 74
SALES (corp-wide): 2.34MM **Privately Held**
Web: www.larv.com
SIC: 7997 5941 Golf club, membership; Golf goods and equipment
HQ: Los Angeles Royal Vista Golf Courses, Inc.
770 Kapiolani Blvd # 506
Honolulu HI
808 592-4800

(P-14401)
MARIN COUNTRY CLUB INC
500 Country Club Dr (94949-5896)
PHONE..................................415 382-6700
Ryan Wilson, *CEO*
EMP: 75 **EST:** 1976
SQ FT: 5,000
SALES (est): 11.4MM **Privately Held**
Web: www.marincountryclub.com
SIC: 7997 5812 Country club, membership; Eating places

(P-14402)
MAYACAMA GOLF CLUB LLC
Also Called: Mayacama
1240 Mayacama Club Dr (95403-8251)
PHONE..................................707 569-2900
Johnathan Wilhelm, *Mng Pt*
Greg Brown, *
EMP: 120 **EST:** 1999
SQ FT: 5,000
SALES (est): 21.72MM **Privately Held**
Web: www.mayacama.com
SIC: 7997 Golf club, membership

(P-14403)
MEADOW CLUB
1001 Bolinas Rd (94930-2200)
P.O. Box 129 (94978-0129)
PHONE..................................415 453-3274
John Grehan, *Genl Mgr*
EMP: 81 **EST:** 1927
SQ FT: 3,000
SALES (est): 11.77MM **Privately Held**
Web: www.meadowclub.com
SIC: 7997 Country club, membership

(P-14404)
MENLO CIRCUS CLUB
190 Park Ln (94027-4121)
PHONE..................................650 322-4616
Steve De Laet, *CEO*
Nora B Stent, *Pr*
Susie Frimel, *Sec*
Matt Quinlan, *CFO*
EMP: 70 **EST:** 1923
SQ FT: 14,000
SALES (est): 10.72MM **Privately Held**
Web: www.menlocircusclub.com
SIC: 7997 Country club, membership

(P-14405)
MESA VERDE COUNTRY CLUB
3000 Club House Rd (92626-3599)
PHONE..................................714 549-0377
John Hayhoe, *CEO*
Robert Heflin, *
Diane Burnes, *
EMP: 125 **EST:** 1959
SQ FT: 34,000
SALES (est): 11.86MM **Privately Held**
Web: www.mesaverdecc.com
SIC: 7997 Country club, membership

(P-14406)
METROPOLITAN CLUB
640 Sutter St (94102-1097)
PHONE..................................415 673-0600
Clint Prescott, *Genl Mgr*
Gibbs Freeman, *
Kayne Maynard, *
Margaret Handelman, *
EMP: 65 **EST:** 1915
SQ FT: 101,662
SALES (est): 4.81MM **Privately Held**
Web: www.metropolitanclubsf.org
SIC: 7997 Membership sports and recreation clubs

(P-14407)
MISSION HILLS COUNTRY CLUB INC
34600 Mission Hills Dr (92270-1300)
PHONE..................................760 324-9000
Josh Tanner, *Genl Mgr*
Doug Howe, *
EMP: 130 **EST:** 1983
SQ FT: 75,000
SALES (est): 9.9MM
SALES (corp-wide): 2.44B **Privately Held**
Web: www.invitedclubs.com
SIC: 7997 7992 5812 Country club, membership; Public golf courses; Eating places
HQ: Clubcorp Usa, Inc.
5215 N O Connor Blvd # 2
Irving TX
972 243-6191

(P-14408)
MISSION VIEJO COUNTRY CLUB
26200 Country Club Dr (92691-5905)
PHONE..................................949 582-1550
Michael Lance Kennedy, *Managing Member*
Chad Pettit, *
Enrique Martinez, *
Scot Dey, *
Veronica Alva Roman, *
EMP: 103 **EST:** 1969
SALES (est): 9.05MM **Privately Held**
Web: www.missionviejocc.com
SIC: 7997 7991 5812 7299 Country club, membership; Physical fitness facilities; Eating places; Banquet hall facilities

(P-14409)
MONTECITO COUNTRY CLUB INC
920 Summit Rd (93108-2326)
PHONE..................................805 969-0800
Tai Warner, *Pr*
Hiro Suzuki, *
EMP: 100 **EST:** 1921
SQ FT: 10,000
SALES (est): 10.49MM **Privately Held**
Web: www.montecitoclub1918.com
SIC: 7997 5812 5813 Country club, membership; Eating places; Bar (drinking places)
PA: Tsukamoto Corporation Co., Ltd.
1-6-5, Nihombashihoncho
Chuo-Ku TKY

(P-14410)
MONTEREY PENINSULA COUNTRY CLB
Also Called: Mpcc
3000 Club Rd (93953-2542)
PHONE..................................831 373-1556
Robert Perry Smith, *CEO*
Michael Bowhay, *
EMP: 130 **EST:** 1925
SQ FT: 70,000
SALES (est): 29.2MM **Privately Held**
Web: www.mpccpb.org
SIC: 7997 Country club, membership

(P-14411)
MORAGA CNTRY CLB HMOWNERS ASSN
Also Called: Moraga Country Club
1600 Saint Andrews Dr (94556-1194)
PHONE..................................925 376-2200
Frank Meln, *Genl Mgr*
EMP: 100 **EST:** 1973
SQ FT: 10,000
SALES (est): 13.51MM **Privately Held**
Web: www.moragacc.com
SIC: 7997 Country club, membership

(P-14412)
NAPA GOLF ASSOCIATES LLC
Also Called: Chardnnay Golf CLB Vnyrds - NA
2555 Jameson Canyon Rd (94558)
P.O. Box 3779 (94558-0377)
PHONE..................................707 257-1900
Jim Gianulias, *
Gus Gianulias, *
EMP: 84 **EST:** 2005
SQ FT: 24,000
SALES (est): 8.79MM
SALES (corp-wide): 2.44B **Privately Held**
Web: www.chardonnaygolfclub.com
SIC: 7997 Golf club, membership
HQ: Clubcorp Usa, Inc.
5215 N O Connor Blvd # 2
Irving TX
972 243-6191

7997 - Membership Sports And Recreation Clubs (P-14413)

(P-14413)
NAPA VALLEY COUNTRY CLUB
3385 Hagen Rd (94558-3849)
PHONE.....................707 252-1111
Todd Jeffrey Meginness, *CEO*
Mike Wilson, *
Patrick Smorra, *
Jeorge Hise, *
Todd Meginness, *
▲ **EMP:** 92 **EST:** 1923
SQ FT: 8,000
SALES (est): 8.48MM **Privately Held**
Web: www.napavalleycc.com
SIC: **7997** 5813 5812 Country club, membership; Bar (drinking places); Eating places

(P-14414)
NEW PVCC INC
15835 Pauma Valley Dr (92061-1612)
PHONE.....................760 742-1230
Butt Suze, *Pr*
EMP: 76 **EST:** 1961
SQ FT: 3,000
SALES (est): 5.03MM **Privately Held**
Web: www.paumavalleycc.com
SIC: **7997** Country club, membership

(P-14415)
NEWPORT BEACH COUNTRY CLUB INC
Also Called: Newport Beach Country Club
1 Clubhouse Dr (92660-7107)
PHONE.....................949 644-9550
David Wooten, *Pr*
Jerry Anderson, *General Vice President*
Gerald Johnson, *
EMP: 90 **EST:** 1985
SALES (est): 10.36MM
SALES (corp-wide): 46.07MM **Privately Held**
Web: www.newportbeachcc.com
SIC: **7997** 7991 5941 5813 Country club, membership; Physical fitness facilities; Sporting goods and bicycle shops; Drinking places
PA: International Bay Clubs, Llc
1221 W Coast Hwy Ste 145
Newport Beach CA
949 645-5000

(P-14416)
NORTH RANCH COUNTRY CLUB
4761 Valley Spring Dr (91362-4399)
PHONE.....................818 889-3531
Mark Bagaaso, *CEO*
Scott London, *
EMP: 160 **EST:** 1976
SQ FT: 53,000
SALES (est): 14.71MM **Privately Held**
Web: www.northranchcc.org
SIC: **7997** 5812 5941 Country club, membership; Eating places; Sporting goods and bicycle shops

(P-14417)
NORTH RIDGE COUNTRY CLUB
7600 Madison Ave (95628-3400)
PHONE.....................916 967-5717
Dennis Tootelian, *CEO*
Rink Sanford, *
EMP: 75 **EST:** 1952
SQ FT: 5,000
SALES (est): 8.15MM **Privately Held**
Web: www.northridgegolf.com
SIC: **7997** Country club, membership

(P-14418)
OAKMONT COUNTRY CLUB
3100 Country Club Dr (91208-1799)
PHONE.....................818 542-4260
Pat Dahlson, *CEO*
John Schiller, *
Michael Hyler, *
EMP: 125 **EST:** 1955
SQ FT: 37,000
SALES (est): 13.7MM **Privately Held**
Web: www.oakmontcc.com
SIC: **7997** Country club, membership

(P-14419)
OLYMPIC CLUB
665 Sutter St (94102-1017)
PHONE.....................415 676-1412
EMP: 84
SALES (corp-wide): 49.42MM **Privately Held**
Web: www.olyclub.com
SIC: **7997** Golf club, membership
PA: The Olympic Club
524 Post St
San Francisco CA
415 345-5100

(P-14420)
ORINDA COUNTRY CLUB
315 Camino Sobrante (94563-1899)
PHONE.....................925 254-4313
Jeff Bause, *Pr*
EMP: 90 **EST:** 1924
SALES (est): 14.41MM **Privately Held**
Web: www.orindacc.org
SIC: **7997** Country club, membership

(P-14421)
PACIFIC GOLF & COUNTRY CLUB
200 Avenida La Pata (92673-6301)
PHONE.....................949 498-6604
Tom Frost, *Cnslt*
EMP: 77 **EST:** 1986
SQ FT: 27,000
SALES (est): 520.53K
SALES (corp-wide): 2.19MM **Privately Held**
Web: www.bellacollinasanclemente.com
SIC: **7997** 7992 Golf club, membership; Public golf courses
PA: Golf Investment Llc
200 Avenida La Pata
San Clemente CA
949 498-6604

(P-14422)
PASADERA CLUB OC LLC
Also Called: Club At Pasadera The
100 Pasadera Dr (93940-7637)
PHONE.....................831 647-2400
Kurt Burmeister, *COO*
Chancey Calhoon, *
Chris Laver, *
EMP: 90 **EST:** 2018
SALES (est): 1.27MM **Privately Held**
Web: www.theclubatpasadera.com
SIC: **7997** Country club, membership

(P-14423)
PENINSULA GOLF & COUNTRY CLUB
701 Madera Dr (94403-1287)
PHONE.....................650 638-2200
EMP: 100 **EST:** 1911
SALES (est): 17.19MM **Privately Held**
Web: www.thepgcc.org

SIC: **7997** 5813 5812 Country club, membership; Bar (drinking places); Eating places

(P-14424)
PORTER VALLEY COUNTRY CLUB INC
Also Called: Porter Valley Catering
19216 Singing Hills Dr (91326-1799)
PHONE.....................818 360-1071
Robert H Dedman, *Ch Bd*
John Beckett, *
Doug Howe, *
EMP: 110 **EST:** 1966
SQ FT: 18,000
SALES (est): 8.28MM
SALES (corp-wide): 2.44B **Privately Held**
Web: www.invitedclubs.com
SIC: **7997** 5812 5941 Golf club, membership; Steak restaurant; Sporting goods and bicycle shops
HQ: Clubcorp Usa, Inc.
5215 N O Connor Blvd # 2
Irving TX
972 243-6191

(P-14425)
RANCHO MURIETA COUNTRY CLUB
7000 Alameda Dr (95683-9148)
PHONE.....................916 354-2400
Robert Wright, *CEO*
Vince Lepera, *
Dick Stenstrom, *
Buzz Breedlove, *
Chris Pasek, *
EMP: 90 **EST:** 1973
SQ FT: 40,000
SALES (est): 9.9MM **Privately Held**
Web: www.ranchomurietacc.com
SIC: **7997** Country club, membership

(P-14426)
RANCHO SANTA FE ASSOCIATION
Also Called: Rancho Sante Fe Golf Club
5827 Viadelacumere (92067)
P.O. Box A (92067-0359)
PHONE.....................858 756-1182
Stephen Nordstrom, *Mgr*
EMP: 100
SALES (corp-wide): 26.07MM **Privately Held**
Web: www.rsfgolfclub.com
SIC: **7997** Golf club, membership
PA: Rancho Santa Fe Association
17022 Avenida De Acacias
Rancho Santa Fe CA
858 756-1174

(P-14427)
RED HILL COUNTRY CLUB
8358 Red Hill Country Club Dr (91730-1899)
PHONE.....................909 982-1358
Rob Mocskley, *Pr*
EMP: 92 **EST:** 1921
SQ FT: 20,000
SALES (est): 7.44MM **Privately Held**
Web: www.redhillcc.com
SIC: **7997** 5812 Country club, membership; Eating places

(P-14428)
REDLANDS COUNTRY CLUB
1749 Garden St (92373-7248)
PHONE.....................909 793-2661
Scott Reding, *Pr*
Jason Murphy, *

EMP: 80 **EST:** 1946
SQ FT: 22,000
SALES (est): 6.67MM **Privately Held**
Web: www.redlandscountryclub.com
SIC: **7997** 5812 5813 Country club, membership; Snack shop; Bar (drinking places)

(P-14429)
RESERVE CLUB
49400 Desert Butte Trl (92210-7075)
PHONE.....................760 674-2222
Kenneth Novack, *Pr*
C Ted Mccarter, *Treas*
EMP: 80 **EST:** 1998
SQ FT: 10,000
SALES (est): 8.82MM **Privately Held**
Web: www.thereserveclub.com
SIC: **7997** Country club, membership

(P-14430)
RIVERVIEW GOLF AND COUNTRY CLB
4200 Bechelli Ln (96002-3533)
PHONE.....................530 224-2254
Ralph Stroch, *Pr*
Ralph Storch, *
EMP: 72 **EST:** 1947
SQ FT: 30,000
SALES (est): 3.27MM **Privately Held**
Web: www.riverviewgolf.net
SIC: **7997** 5812 5813 Country club, membership; Eating places; Bar (drinking places)

(P-14431)
ROLLING HILLS COUNTRY CLUB
Also Called: Rolling Hlls Cntry CLB Golf Sp
1 Chandler Ranch Rd (90274-3301)
PHONE.....................424 903-0000
EMP: 82 **EST:** 1965
SALES (est): 16.91MM **Privately Held**
Web: www.rollinghillscc.com
SIC: **7997** 5941 Country club, membership; Golf goods and equipment

(P-14432)
ROSE BOWL AQUATICS CENTER
360 N Arroyo Blvd (91103-3201)
PHONE.....................626 564-0330
Judy Biggs, *Ex Dir*
Kurt Knop, *
Robert Kamins, *
Alison Laster, *
Lyn Beckett Cacciatore, *
EMP: 80 **EST:** 1992
SALES (est): 7.85MM **Privately Held**
Web: www.rosebowlaquatics.org
SIC: **7997** Swimming club, membership

(P-14433)
ROUND HILL COUNTRY CLUB
3169 Roundhill Rd (94507-1735)
PHONE.....................925 934-8211
Bruce Rarter, *Pr*
Michael Mcdonald, *VP*
Greg Gonsalves, *
Brian Plopner, *
EMP: 89 **EST:** 1959
SQ FT: 20,000
SALES (est): 7.84MM **Privately Held**
Web: www.rhcountryclub.com
SIC: **7997** 5813 5812 7371 Country club, membership; Bar (drinking places); American restaurant; Computer software development and applications

PRODUCTS & SERVICES SECTION

7997 - Membership Sports And Recreation Clubs (P-14458)

(P-14434)
SADDLEBACK VLY
25631 Peter A Hartman Way (92691-3142)
PHONE..................................949 586-1234
Don Cuzick, *Prin*
EMP: 82 **EST:** 2008
SALES (est): 7.24MM **Privately Held**
Web: www.svusd.org
SIC: 7997 Membership sports and recreation clubs

(P-14435)
SALINAS GOLF AND CNTRY CLB INC
475 San Juan Grade Rd (93906-1110)
P.O. Box 4277 (93912-4277)
PHONE..................................831 449-6617
Ed Winnaki, *Genl Mgr*
EMP: 76 **EST:** 1939
SQ FT: 8,500
SALES (est): 1.38MM **Privately Held**
Web: www.clubatcrazyhorse.com
SIC: 7997 Country club, membership

(P-14436)
SAN DIEGO COUNTRY CLUB INC
88 L St (91911-1499)
PHONE..................................619 422-8895
David Morris, *Genl Mgr*
EMP: 125 **EST:** 1896
SQ FT: 36,140
SALES (est): 7.76MM **Privately Held**
Web: www.sandiegocountryclub.org
SIC: 7997 Country club, membership

(P-14437)
SAN DIEGO STATE UNIVERSITY
Also Called: San Diego State Aztecs
5302 55th St (92182-0001)
PHONE..................................619 594-4263
John Jentz, *CEO*
EMP: 200
SALES (corp-wide): 534.4MM **Privately Held**
Web: www.sdsu.edu
SIC: 7997 7922 4832 Membership sports and recreation clubs; Theatrical producers and services; Sports
HQ: San Diego State University
5500 Campanile Dr
San Diego CA

(P-14438)
SAN GABRIEL COUNTRY CLUB
350 E Hermosa Dr (91775-2346)
PHONE..................................626 287-9671
Tom Dukes, *Pr*
EMP: 80 **EST:** 1904
SQ FT: 48,000
SALES (est): 8.76MM **Privately Held**
Web: www.sangabrielcc.com
SIC: 7997 Country club, membership

(P-14439)
SAN JOAQUIN COUNTRY CLUB
3484 W Bluff Ave (93711-0199)
PHONE..................................559 439-3483
Jeffrey Newman, *Pr*
Melissa Allen, *Business Office Manager*
EMP: 63 **EST:** 1961
SQ FT: 39,615
SALES (est): 5.02MM **Privately Held**
Web: www.sjcc.cc
SIC: 7997 5812 5813 Country club, membership; American restaurant; Bar (drinking places)

(P-14440)
SAN JOSE COUNTRY CLUB
15571 Alum Rock Ave (95127-2799)
PHONE..................................408 258-4901
Chris Simpson, *Genl Mgr*
Jason Green, *
Kevin Sullivan, *
EMP: 70 **EST:** 1898
SQ FT: 24,000
SALES (est): 6.29MM **Privately Held**
Web: www.sanjosecountryclub.org
SIC: 7997 7299 Ice sports; Color consultant

(P-14441)
SAN LUIS OBISPO GOLF CNTRY CLB
Also Called: Slogcc
255 Country Club Dr (93401-8939)
PHONE..................................805 543-3400
David Cole, *Pr*
Carol Kerwin, *
Christopher Simpson, *
EMP: 110 **EST:** 1958
SQ FT: 10,000
SALES (est): 11.82MM **Privately Held**
Web: www.slocountryclub.com
SIC: 7997 Country club, membership

(P-14442)
SANTA ANA COUNTRY CLUB
20382 Newport Blvd (92707-5396)
PHONE..................................714 556-3000
Joseph Jj Wagner, *Prin*
Joseph J Wagner, *CEO*
EMP: 100 **EST:** 1914
SALES (est): 12.21MM **Privately Held**
Web: www.santaanacc.org
SIC: 7997 Country club, membership

(P-14443)
SANTA LUCIA PRESERVE COMPANY
1 Rancho San Carlos Rd (93923-7999)
PHONE..................................831 620-6760
Tom Gray, *Prin*
EMP: 65 **EST:** 2011
SALES (est): 12.55MM **Privately Held**
Web: www.santaluciapreserve.com
SIC: 7997 Country club, membership

(P-14444)
SANTALUZ CLUB INC
8170 Caminito Santaluz E (92127-2577)
PHONE..................................858 759-3120
Steve Cowell, *CEO*
James Hoselton, *
Michael Forsum, *
Timothy A Kaehr, *
Terry D Randall, *
EMP: 120 **EST:** 2000
SQ FT: 19,000
SALES (est): 16.77MM **Privately Held**
Web: www.thesantaluzclub.com
SIC: 7997 Country club, membership

(P-14445)
SARATOGA COUNTRY CLUB INC
21990 Prospect Rd (95070-6541)
PHONE..................................408 253-0340
Joe Callan, *Genl Mgr*
EMP: 70 **EST:** 1958
SQ FT: 12,000
SALES (est): 8.6MM **Privately Held**
Web: www.saratogacc.com
SIC: 7997 Country club, membership

(P-14446)
SATICOY COUNTRY CLUB
4450 Clubhouse Dr (93066-9798)
PHONE..................................805 647-1153
Douglas Taxton, *Pr*
Kathy Sube, *
James R Van Wyck, *
EMP: 80 **EST:** 1921
SALES (est): 34.18K **Privately Held**
Web: www.thesaticoyclub.com
SIC: 7997 Country club, membership

(P-14447)
SCCR PROPERTIES INC
Also Called: SILVERADO RESORT AND SPA
1600 Atlas Peak Rd (94558-1425)
PHONE..................................707 257-0200
EMP: 600 **EST:** 1968
SQ FT: 2,000
SALES (est): 136.81K **Privately Held**
Web: www.silveradoresort.com
SIC: 7997 Country club, membership

(P-14448)
SERRANO ASSOCIATES LLC
Also Called: Serrano Country Club
5005 Serrano Pkwy (95762-7511)
PHONE..................................916 939-3333
Kevitt Sale, *Mgr*
EMP: 113
Web: www.parkerdevco.com
SIC: 7997 5941 5813 5812 Golf club, membership; Sporting goods and bicycle shops; Drinking places; Eating places
PA: Serrano Associates, Llc
4525 Serrano Pkwy Ste 100
El Dorado Hills CA

(P-14449)
SERRANO COUNTRY CLUB
5005 Serrano Pkwy # P (95762-7511)
PHONE..................................916 933-5005
Dean Cummings, *Pr*
EMP: 105 **EST:** 1995
SALES (est): 9.59MM **Privately Held**
Web: www.serranocountryclub.org
SIC: 7997 Country club, membership

(P-14450)
SEVEN OAKS COUNTRY CLUB
2000 Grand Lakes Ave (93311-2931)
P.O. Box 11165 (93389-1165)
PHONE..................................661 664-6404
David H Murdock, *CEO*
Bruce Freeman, *
Don Ciota, *
EMP: 125 **EST:** 1991
SQ FT: 39,000
SALES (est): 14.72MM **Privately Held**
Web: www.sevenoakscountryclub.com
SIC: 7997 Country club, membership

(P-14451)
SHADY CANYON GOLF CLUB INC
100 Shady Canyon Dr (92603-0301)
PHONE..................................949 856-7000
James T Wood, *CEO*
Thomas Heggi, *
Robert Leenhouts, *
EMP: 157 **EST:** 2003
SALES (est): 269.42K **Privately Held**
Web: www.shadycanyongolfclub.com
SIC: 7997 Country club, membership

(P-14452)
SHERWOOD COUNTRY CLUB
320 W Stafford Rd (91361-5000)
PHONE..................................805 496-3036
Lance Fisher, *Genl Mgr*
EMP: 133 **EST:** 1989
SALES (est): 14.91MM **Privately Held**
Web: www.sherwoodcc.com

(P-14453)
SIERRA VIEW COUNTRY CLUB
Also Called: SIERRA VIEW
105 Alta Vista Ave (95678-1647)
P.O. Box 676 (95678-0676)
PHONE..................................916 782-3741
Barry Macdonald, *CEO*
Steve Rainwater, *
EMP: 75 **EST:** 1958
SQ FT: 5,000
SALES (est): 8.16MM **Privately Held**
Web: www.sierraviewcc.org
SIC: 7997 5812 5813 Golf club, membership; American restaurant; Bar (drinking places)

(P-14454)
SILVER CREEK VLY CNTRY CLB INC
Also Called: Silicon Valley Country Club
5460 Country Club Pkwy (95138-2215)
PHONE..................................408 239-5775
Rene Devos, *Genl Mgr*
Robert E Lee, *
EMP: 95 **EST:** 1992
SALES (est): 20.16MM **Privately Held**
Web: www.scvcc.com
SIC: 7997 5941 Country club, membership; Sporting goods and bicycle shops

(P-14455)
SOUTH HILLS COUNTRY CLUB
2655 S Citrus St (91791-3405)
PHONE..................................626 339-1231
James Wendoll, *CEO*
EMP: 78 **EST:** 1852
SQ FT: 34,000
SALES (est): 5.09MM **Privately Held**
Web: www.southhillscountryclub.org
SIC: 7997 5813 5812 Country club, membership; Bar (drinking places); American restaurant

(P-14456)
SOUTH PARK COMMONS LLC
27 S Park St Ste 101 (94107-5805)
PHONE..................................978 815-7723
EMP: 81 **EST:** 2018
SALES (est): 1.13MM **Privately Held**
Web: www.southparkcommons.com
SIC: 7997 Membership sports and recreation clubs

(P-14457)
SPANISH HILLS CLUB LLC
999 Crestview Ave (93010-7429)
PHONE..................................805 388-5000
Alain O'connor, *Managing Member*
EMP: 99 **EST:** 2019
SALES (est): 835.84K **Privately Held**
Web: www.thespanishhillsclub.com
SIC: 7997 Country club, membership

(P-14458)
SPANISH HILLS COUNTRY CLUB (PA)
999 Crestview Ave (93010-8493)
PHONE..................................805 389-1644
Joe Topper, *Pr*
Steve Thomas, *
EMP: 150 **EST:** 1989
SQ FT: 42,000
SALES (est): 9.15MM **Privately Held**
Web: www.thespanishhillsclub.com
SIC: 7997 Country club, membership

7997 - Membership Sports And Recreation Clubs (P-14459)

(P-14459)
SPARE-TIME INC
Also Called: Broadstone Raquet Club
820 Halidon Way (95630-8406)
PHONE..............................916 983-9180
Gavin Russo, Genl Mgr
EMP: 117
SALES (corp-wide): 52.26MM Privately Held
Web: www.sparetimesportsclubs.com
SIC: 7997 7991 Racquetball club, membership; Health club
PA: Spare-Time, Inc.
 11344 Coloma Rd Ste 350
 Gold River CA
 916 859-5910

(P-14460)
SPARE-TIME INC
Also Called: Twin Arbors Athletic Club
1900 S Hutchins St (95240-6116)
PHONE..............................209 334-4897
Dennis Kaufman, Mgr
EMP: 114
SALES (corp-wide): 52.26MM Privately Held
Web: www.sparetimesportsclubs.com
SIC: 7997 7991 Racquetball club, membership; Health club
PA: Spare-Time, Inc.
 11344 Coloma Rd Ste 350
 Gold River CA
 916 859-5910

(P-14461)
SPARE-TIME INC
Also Called: Johnson Ranch Racquet Club
2501 Eureka Rd (95661-6400)
PHONE..............................916 782-2600
Tim Munson, Genl Mgr
EMP: 128
SQ FT: 21,584
SALES (corp-wide): 52.26MM Privately Held
Web: www.sparetimesportsclubs.com
SIC: 7997 Racquetball club, membership
PA: Spare-Time, Inc.
 11344 Coloma Rd Ste 350
 Gold River CA
 916 859-5910

(P-14462)
SPARE-TIME INC
Also Called: Gold River Racquet Club
2201 Gold Rush Dr (95670-4466)
PHONE..............................916 638-7001
Mike Burchett, Genl Mgr
EMP: 104
SALES (corp-wide): 52.26MM Privately Held
Web: www.sparetimesportsclubs.com
SIC: 7997 Racquetball club, membership
PA: Spare-Time, Inc.
 11344 Coloma Rd Ste 350
 Gold River CA
 916 859-5910

(P-14463)
SPARE-TIME INC
Also Called: Laguna Creek Racquet Club
9570 Racquet Ct (95758-4349)
PHONE..............................916 859-5910
Kimberley Miller, Mgr
EMP: 84
SALES (corp-wide): 52.26MM Privately Held
Web: www.sparetimesportsclubs.com
SIC: 7997 7999 7991 Racquetball club, membership; Racquetball club, non-membership; Health club

PA: Spare-Time, Inc.
 11344 Coloma Rd Ste 350
 Gold River CA
 916 859-5910

(P-14464)
SPRINGS CLUB INC
Also Called: SPRINGS COUNTRY CLUB, THE
1 Duke Dr (92270-3647)
PHONE..............................760 328-0254
Robert Middlemas, CEO
Daniel Cooper, COO
Douglas R Hart, Prin
Doug Lober, Prin
Ronda Allen, Prin
EMP: 65 EST: 1973
SQ FT: 36,000
SALES (est): 5.03MM Privately Held
Web: club.thespringsrm.com
SIC: 7997 5812 5813 Golf club, membership; American restaurant; Cocktail lounge

(P-14465)
ST FRANCIS YACHT CLUB
700 Marina Blvd (94123-1040)
PHONE..............................415 563-6363
Jim Diepenbrock, CEO
Robert Hanelt, *
◆ EMP: 110 EST: 1922
SQ FT: 20,000
SALES (est): 14.15MM Privately Held
Web: www.stfyc.com
SIC: 7997 4493 Yacht club, membership; Marinas

(P-14466)
STOCKDALE COUNTRY CLUB
7001 Stockdale Hwy (93309-1313)
P.O. Box 9727 (93389-9727)
PHONE..............................661 832-0310
Sam Monroe, Pr
Linda Voiland, *
Michael Davis, *
EMP: 100 EST: 1925
SQ FT: 12,000
SALES (est): 7.24MM Privately Held
Web: www.stockdalecc.com
SIC: 7997 Country club, membership

(P-14467)
STOCKTON GOLF AND COUNTRY CLUB
3800 Country Club Blvd (95204-3800)
PHONE..............................209 466-4313
EMP: 100 EST: 1914
SALES (est): 4.47MM Privately Held
Web: www.stocktongolfcc.com
SIC: 7997 Golf club, membership

(P-14468)
TEAM BRUIN LLC
1 Ironsides St Apt 4 (90292-5960)
PHONE..............................310 206-6784
C L Gallagher, Prin
EMP: 67 EST: 2011
SALES (est): 115.21K Privately Held
Web: www.bruinbiometrics.com
SIC: 7997 Membership sports and recreation clubs

(P-14469)
TGA FRANCHISE SPT HOLDINGS LLC
Also Called: Tga Premier Sports
1960 E Grand Ave Ste 811 (90245-5156)
PHONE..............................310 333-0622
EMP: 81 EST: 2019
SALES (est): 1.11MM Privately Held
Web: www.playtga.com
SIC: 7997 6794 Membership sports and recreation clubs; Franchises, selling or licensing

(P-14470)
THE SAN DIEGO YACHT CLUB
1011 Anchorage Ln (92106-3005)
PHONE..............................619 221-8400
EMP: 120 EST: 1886
SALES (est): 9.55MM Privately Held
Web: www.sdyc.org
SIC: 7997 Yacht club, membership

(P-14471)
THE WOODBRIDGE GOLF CNTRY CLB
800 E Woodbridge Rd (95258-9628)
P.O. Box 806 (95258-0806)
PHONE..............................209 369-2371
Jerry Leonard, CEO
EMP: 79 EST: 1924
SQ FT: 20,000
SALES (est): 3.96MM Privately Held
Web: www.woodbridgegcc.com
SIC: 7997 Country club, membership

(P-14472)
THUNDERBIRD COUNTRY CLUB
70737 Country Club Dr (92270-3500)
P.O. Box 5005 (92270-1065)
PHONE..............................760 328-2161
Brian Rice, CEO
Michaell Crandall, *
EMP: 60 EST: 1954
SQ FT: 30,000
SALES (est): 10.98MM Privately Held
Web: www.thunderbirdcc.org
SIC: 7997 5812 7011 Country club, membership; Eating places; Hotels and motels

(P-14473)
TOSCANA COUNTRY CLUB INC
76009 Via Club Villa (92210-7851)
PHONE..............................760 404-1444
Paul K Levy, CEO
EMP: 150 EST: 2004
SALES (est): 15.74MM Privately Held
Web: www.toscanacc.com
SIC: 7997 Country club, membership

(P-14474)
TRADITION GOLF CLUB ASSOCIATES
78505 Avenue 52 (92253-2802)
PHONE..............................760 564-3355
EMP: 68 EST: 1997
SALES (est): 642.05K Privately Held
Web: www.traditiongc.com
SIC: 7997 Golf club, membership

(P-14475)
VALLEY-HI COUNTRY CLUB
9595 Franklin Blvd (95758-9532)
PHONE..............................916 684-2120
Edgar Gill, CEO
Nick West, *
EMP: 100 EST: 1958
SQ FT: 20,000
SALES (est): 4.35MM Privately Held
Web: members.valleyhicc.com
SIC: 7997 Country club, membership

(P-14476)
VICTORIA CLUB
2521 Arroyo Dr (92506-1598)
PHONE..............................951 683-5323
EMP: 105 EST: 1903

SALES (est): 4.98MM Privately Held
Web: www.victoriaclub.com
SIC: 7997 Country club, membership

(P-14477)
VILLAGES GOLF AND COUNTRY CLUB
Also Called: Villages, The
5000 Cribari Ln (95135-1397)
PHONE..............................408 274-4400
Virginia Fanelli, CEO
Jim White, *
EMP: 170 EST: 1967
SALES (est): 15.12MM Privately Held
Web: www.thevillagesgcc.com
SIC: 7997 Country club, membership

(P-14478)
VINTAGE CLUB
75001 Vintage Dr W (92210-7304)
PHONE..............................760 340-0500
John Buttemiller Broker Sales E, Prin
Marc D Ray, *
John Buttemiller Broker, Sls Dir
Carmen Wolfe, Marketing TRANSACTION*
Jamie Shelton, PGA Professional*
EMP: 90 EST: 1979
SQ FT: 86,000
SALES (est): 22.42MM Privately Held
Web: www.thevintageclub.com
SIC: 7997 5813 5812 5941 Country club, membership; Bar (drinking places); American restaurant; Golf goods and equipment

(P-14479)
VIRGINIA CNTRY CLB OF LONG BCH
4602 N Virginia Rd (90807-1916)
PHONE..............................562 427-0924
Jamie Mulligan, CEO
EMP: 110 EST: 1909
SQ FT: 15,000
SALES (est): 9.12MM Privately Held
Web: www.vcc1909.org
SIC: 7997 Country club, membership

(P-14480)
VISALIA COUNTRY CLUB
625 N Ranch St (93291-4317)
P.O. Box 3410 (93278-3410)
PHONE..............................559 734-3733
Steve Beargeon, Prin
Tom Ringer, Prin
EMP: 80 EST: 1921
SQ FT: 60,000
SALES (est): 6.67MM Privately Held
Web: www.visaliacc.net
SIC: 7997 Country club, membership

(P-14481)
VISTA VALLEY COUNTRY CLUB
Also Called: V Vcc Havens
29354 Vista Valley Dr (92084-2209)
PHONE..............................760 758-2800
John Havens, Pr
EMP: 79 EST: 1976
SQ FT: 15,000
SALES (est): 9.44MM Privately Held
Web: www.vistavalley.com
SIC: 7997 5812 7999 Country club, membership; Eating places; Golf cart, power, rental

(P-14482)
WELK GROUP INC
Also Called: Meadow Lake Country Club
10333 Meadow Glen Way E (92026-6918)
PHONE..............................760 749-0983

PRODUCTS & SERVICES SECTION

7999 - Amusement And Recreation, Nec (P-14504)

Brad Van Horn, *Mgr*
EMP: 210
SQ FT: 5,000
SALES (corp-wide): 47.43MM **Privately Held**
Web: www.welkresorts.com
SIC: 7997 Country club, membership
PA: The Welk Group Inc
 11400 W Olympic Blvd # 1450
 Los Angeles CA
 760 749-3000

(P-14483)
WESTGROUP KONA KAI LLC
Also Called: Kona Kai Resort Hotel
1551 Shelter Island Dr (92106-3102)
PHONE.................................619 221-8000
EMP: 99 **EST:** 2011
SALES (est): 9.21MM **Privately Held**
Web: www.resortkonakai.com
SIC: 7997 7011 Membership sports and recreation clubs; Resort hotel

(P-14484)
WILSHIRE COUNTRY CLUB
301 N Rossmore Ave (90004-2403)
PHONE.................................323 934-6050
Jeffrey Ornstein, *CEO*
Norman Branchflower, *
Doctor Mirion Bowers Md, *VP*
EMP: 94 **EST:** 1919
SQ FT: 50,000
SALES (est): 11.22MM **Privately Held**
Web: www.wilshirecountryclub.com
SIC: 7997 5941 5812 Country club, membership; Sporting goods and bicycle shops; Eating places

(P-14485)
YOUNG MNS CHRSTN ASSN ORNGE CN
Also Called: South Coast YMCA
29831 Crown Valley Pkwy (92677-1944)
PHONE.................................949 495-9622
Jennifer Heinen, *Brnch Mgr*
EMP: 77
SALES (corp-wide): 33.29MM **Privately Held**
Web: www.ymcaoc.org
SIC: 7997 8641 Membership sports and recreation clubs; Civic and social associations
PA: Young Men's Christian Association Of Orange County
 13821 Newport Ave Ste 200
 Tustin CA
 714 549-9622

7999 Amusement And Recreation, Nec

(P-14486)
29 PALMS ENTERPRISES CORP
Also Called: Spotlight 29 Casino
46200 Harrison Pl (92236-2087)
PHONE.................................760 775-5566
Darrel Mike, *Pr*
EMP: 600 **EST:** 1995
SQ FT: 70,000
SALES (est): 71.39MM **Privately Held**
Web: www.spotlight29.com
SIC: 7999 5812 Gambling establishment; Eating places

(P-14487)
ADVENTURE CITY INC
1238 S Beach Blvd (92804-4828)
PHONE.................................714 821-3311
Allan Ansdell Junior, *Pr*

Yvonne Ansdell, *
EMP: 100 **EST:** 1992
SALES (est): 5.97MM **Privately Held**
Web: www.adventurecity.com
SIC: 7999 7996 Tourist attractions, amusement park concessions and rides; Amusement parks

(P-14488)
ALAMEDA COUNTY AG FAIR ASSN
Also Called: Alameda County Fair
4501 Pleasanton Ave (94566-7001)
PHONE.................................925 426-7600
Jerome Hoban, *CEO*
Randy Maggie, *
EMP: 75 **EST:** 1939
SQ FT: 125,000
SALES (est): 22.27MM **Privately Held**
Web: www.alamedacountyfair.com
SIC: 7999 Agricultural fair

(P-14489)
ANAHEIM ICE
Also Called: Rinks Anaheim Ice, The
300 W Lincoln Ave (92805-2947)
PHONE.................................714 535-7465
Eddie Hawkins, *Genl Mgr*
Art Trottier, *VP*
Jill Herzogge, *Genl Mgr*
EMP: 72 **EST:** 1996
SALES (est): 3.76MM **Privately Held**
Web: anaheimice.therinks.com
SIC: 7999 Ice skating rink operation

(P-14490)
ANSCHUTZ STHERN CAL SPT CMPLEX
Also Called: Stop Hop Center
18400 Avalon Blvd Ste 100 (90746-2180)
PHONE.................................310 630-2000
Katherine Pandolfo, *Genl Mgr*
Anschutz Grp, *
Kedie Pendolfo, *
EMP: 160 **EST:** 2000
SALES (est): 346.8K **Privately Held**
SIC: 7999 7941 Exhibition and carnival operation services; Sports field or stadium operator, promoting sports events
HQ: Anschutz Entertainment Group, Inc.
 800 W Olympic Blvd # 305
 Los Angeles CA
 213 763-7700

(P-14491)
ARIZONA CHANNEL ISLA
300 W 9th St (93030-7060)
PHONE.................................480 788-0755
EMP: 75
SQ FT: 60,000
SALES (est): 282.99K **Privately Held**
SIC: 7999 Amusement and recreation, nec

(P-14492)
AROMA SPA & SPORTS LLC
Also Called: Aroma Wilshire Center
3680 Wilshire Blvd Ste 301 (90010-2708)
PHONE.................................213 387-2111
EMP: 60 **EST:** 2000
SALES (est): 932.76K **Privately Held**
Web: www.aromaresort.com
SIC: 7999 7991 Recreation center; Health club

(P-14493)
ARTICHOKE JOES
Also Called: Artichoke Joe's Casino
659 Huntington Ave (94066-3608)
PHONE.................................650 589-8812

Dennis J Sammut, *CEO*
Helen Sammut, *
EMP: 330 **EST:** 1916
SALES (est): 24.96MM **Privately Held**
Web: www.artichokejoes.com
SIC: 7999 5812 5813 Game parlor; Eating places; Tavern (drinking places)

(P-14494)
AUBURN AREA RECREATION PK DST
471 Maidu Dr Ste 200 (95603-5774)
PHONE.................................530 537-2185
Veona Galbraith, *Admn*
EMP: 60 **EST:** 2018
SALES (est): 824.72K **Privately Held**
Web: www.auburnrec.com
SIC: 7999 Tourist attractions, amusement park concessions and rides

(P-14495)
BAY AREA SEATING SERVICE INC
Also Called: Bass Tickets
1855 Gateway Blvd Ste 630 (94520-3200)
PHONE.................................925 671-4000
W Thomas Gimple, *Pr*
Doug Levenson, *
EMP: 300 **EST:** 1974
SQ FT: 18,000
SALES (est): 3.73MM
SALES (corp-wide): 4.71MM **Privately Held**
SIC: 7999 Ticket sales office for sporting events, contract
HQ: California Tickets.Com Inc.
 555 Anton Blvd Fl 11
 Costa Mesa CA
 714 327-5400

(P-14496)
BEACON PARK SCHOOL
200 Cultivate (92618-1029)
PHONE.................................949 936-8400
Bob Curley, *Prin*
EMP: 66 **EST:** 2016
SALES (est): 179.89K **Privately Held**
Web: beaconpark.iusd.org
SIC: 7999 Instruction schools, camps, and services

(P-14497)
BEAR VALLEY SKI CO
Also Called: Bear Valley Mountain Resort
2280 State Rte 207 (95223)
P.O. Box 5038 (95223-5038)
PHONE.................................209 753-2301
Tim Bottomley, *CEO*
EMP: 325 **EST:** 1991
SQ FT: 70,000
SALES (est): 26.08MM
SALES (corp-wide): 99.53MM **Privately Held**
Web: www.bearvalley.com
SIC: 7999 5941 Recreation services; Skiing equipment
PA: Skyline Investments Inc
 36 King St E Suite 700
 Toronto ON
 416 368-2565

(P-14498)
BELL GARDENS BICYCLE CLUB INC
Also Called: Bicycle Club Casino
888 Bicycle Casino Dr (90201-7617)
PHONE.................................562 806-4646
George Hardie, *Pr*
George G Hardie, *

EMP: 1300 **EST:** 1984
SQ FT: 110,000
SALES (est): 42.37MM **Privately Held**
Web: www.thebike.com
SIC: 7999 5812 Card rooms; Coffee shop

(P-14499)
BLACK OAK CASINO
19400 Tuolumne Rd N (95379-9696)
PHONE.................................209 928-9300
Ron Patel, *Genl Mgr*
EMP: 99 **EST:** 2000
SQ FT: 168,000
SALES (est): 24.63MM **Privately Held**
Web: www.blackoakcasino.com
SIC: 7999 Gambling establishment
PA: Tuolumne Me-Wuk Tribal Council
 19595 Mi Wu St
 Tuolumne CA

(P-14500)
BVK GAMING INC
3466 Broadway St (94503-1263)
P.O. Box 10078 (94503-0078)
PHONE.................................707 644-8853
Brian Altizer, *Sec*
Von Altizer, *
EMP: 90 **EST:** 2005
SALES (est): 2.69MM **Privately Held**
SIC: 7999 Card rooms

(P-14501)
CAESARS ENTRTNMENT OPRTING INC
Also Called: Harrah's
777 Harrahs Rincon Way (92082-5343)
PHONE.................................760 751-3100
Janet Deronio, *Brnch Mgr*
EMP: 1400
SALES (corp-wide): 10.82B **Publicly Held**
Web: www.harrahssocal.com
SIC: 7999 7011 Gambling establishment; Casino hotel
HQ: Caesars Entertainment Operating Company, Inc.
 1 Caesars Palace Dr
 Las Vegas NV
 702 407-6000

(P-14502)
CAHUILLA CREEK REST & CASINO
Also Called: Cahuilla Creek Casino
52702 Us Highway 371 (92539-8707)
PHONE.................................951 763-1200
Leonardo Pasquarelli, *Genl Mgr*
Jon Gregory, *
EMP: 103 **EST:** 1996
SQ FT: 14,000
SALES (est): 18.88MM **Privately Held**
Web: www.cahuillacasinohotel.com
SIC: 7999 5812 5813 Gambling establishment; American restaurant; Bar (drinking places)

(P-14503)
CAPITOL CASINO
411 N 16th St (95811-0516)
PHONE.................................916 446-0700
Clarke Rosa, *Pr*
EMP: 107 **EST:** 1991
SQ FT: 7,500
SALES (est): 4.12MM **Privately Held**
Web: www.capitol-casino.com
SIC: 7999 5813 Card rooms; Cocktail lounge

(P-14504)
CARMICHAEL RCRTION PK DST FNDT

7999 - Amusement And Recreation, Nec (P-14505)

PRODUCTS & SERVICES SECTION

5750 Grant Ave (95608-3779)
PHONE..................................916 485-5322
Ronald D Cuppy, *Admn*
EMP: 60 EST: 1946
SALES (est): 123.01K **Privately Held**
Web: www.carmichaelpark.com
SIC: 7999 Recreation center

(P-14505)
CHER-AE HEIGHTS INDIAN CMNTY
Also Called: Cher Ae Heights Casino
27 Scenic Dr (95570-9767)
P.O. Box 610 (95570-0610)
PHONE..................................707 677-3611
TOLL FREE: 800
Ron Dadouin, *Mgr*
EMP: 196
Web: www.funattheheights.com
SIC: 7999 7011 Card rooms; Casino hotel
PA: Cher-Ae Heights Indian Community
     1 Cher Ae Ln
     Trinidad CA
     707 677-0211

(P-14506)
CHICO AREA RECREATION & PK DST (PA)
Also Called: Dorothy Johnson Center
545 Vallombrosa Ave (95926-4037)
PHONE..................................530 895-4711
Mary Cahill, *Genl Mgr*
Steve Zisconti, *
Scott Dowel, *
EMP: 131 EST: 1947
SQ FT: 27,000
SALES (est): 10.01MM
SALES (corp-wide): 10.01MM **Privately Held**
Web: www.chicorec.com
SIC: 7999 8322 Recreation services; Individual and family services

(P-14507)
CONCESSIONAIRES URBAN PARK (PA)
Also Called: Angel Island Co
2150 Main St Ste 5 (96080-2334)
PHONE..................................530 529-1512
John W Koeberer, *CEO*
Pamela Koeberrer Pitts, *
Kris Koeberer, *
EMP: 300 EST: 1981
SQ FT: 2,800
SALES (est): 25.85MM
SALES (corp-wide): 25.85MM **Privately Held**
Web: www.basecamphospitality.com
SIC: 7999 5941 5812 Beach and water sports equipment rental and services; Fishing equipment; Snack bar

(P-14508)
CONCESSIONAIRES URBAN PARK
Also Called: Camanche Recreation-North
2000 Camanche Rd Ofc Ofc (95640-9420)
PHONE..................................209 763-5121
Chris Cantwell, *Brnch Mgr*
EMP: 159
SALES (corp-wide): 25.85MM **Privately Held**
Web: www.golakecamanche.com
SIC: 7999 7032 Beach and water sports equipment rental and services; Recreational camps
PA: Urban Park Concessionaires
     2150 Main St Ste 5
     Red Bluff CA
     530 529-1512

(P-14509)
CONCESSIONAIRES URBAN PARK
Also Called: Ranch At Little Hills, The
2150 Main St (96080-2372)
PHONE..................................530 529-1513
Michele Silva Lane, *Mgr*
EMP: 68
SALES (corp-wide): 25.85MM **Privately Held**
Web: www.basecamphospitality.com
SIC: 7999 5941 5812 Beach and water sports equipment rental and services; Fishing equipment; Snack bar
PA: Urban Park Concessionaires
     2150 Main St Ste 5
     Red Bluff CA
     530 529-1512

(P-14510)
COSUMNES COMMUNITY SVCS DST
9355 E Stockton Blvd Ste 185 (95624-9476)
PHONE..................................916 405-7150
Rod Brewer, *Brand President*
Rich Lozano, *VP*
EMP: 387 EST: 1985
SQ FT: 10,000
SALES (est): 7.65MM **Privately Held**
Web: www.cosumnescsd.gov
SIC: 7999 Recreation services

(P-14511)
COUNTY OF SANTA CLARA
Parks & Recreation Dept
298 Garden Hill Dr (95032-7669)
PHONE..................................408 355-2200
Lisa Killough, *Brnch Mgr*
EMP: 240
Web: www.sccfd.org
SIC: 7999 9512 Recreation services; Land, mineral, and wildlife conservation
PA: County Of Santa Clara
     70 W Hedding St
     San Jose CA
     408 299-5200

(P-14512)
CTOUR HOLIDAY LLC
222 E Huntington Dr Ste 105 (91016-8014)
PHONE..................................323 261-8811
Charlie Lu, *Managing Member*
EMP: 300 EST: 2016
SALES (est): 4.17MM **Privately Held**
Web: www.seagullholiday.com.cn
SIC: 7999 Tour and guide services

(P-14513)
DISNEY REGIONAL ENTRMT INC (DH)
Also Called: Disney
500 S Buena Vista St (91521-0001)
PHONE..................................818 560-1000
EMP: 200 EST: 1996
SALES (est): 80.4MM
SALES (corp-wide): 82.72B **Publicly Held**
Web: www.thewaltdisneycompany.com
SIC: 7999 5812 5813 Recreation center; Eating places; Drinking places
HQ: Twdc Enterprises 18 Corp.
     500 S Buena Vista St
     Burbank CA

(P-14514)
DROPZONE WATERPARK
2165 Trumble Rd (92571-9211)
PHONE..................................951 210-1600
Erica Bice, *Dir*
EMP: 150 EST: 2014
SALES (est): 443.58K **Privately Held**
Web: www.dropzonewaterpark.com
SIC: 7999 Recreation services

(P-14515)
EAST BAY REGIONAL PARK DISTRICT (PA)
2950 Peralta Oaks Ct (94605-5320)
P.O. Box 5381 (94605-0381)
PHONE..................................888 327-2757
EMP: 106 EST: 1934
SALES (est): 239.05MM
SALES (corp-wide): 239.05MM **Privately Held**
Web: www.ebparks.org
SIC: 7999 Recreation services

(P-14516)
EAST BAY REGIONAL PARK DST
Also Called: East Bay Rgnal Pk Pub Sfety De
17930 Lake Chabot Rd (94546-1950)
PHONE..................................510 881-1833
Timothy Anderson, *Chief*
EMP: 171
SALES (corp-wide): 239.05MM **Privately Held**
Web: www.ebparks.org
SIC: 7999 Recreation services
PA: East Bay Regional Park District
     2950 Peralta Oaks Ct
     Oakland CA
     888 327-2757

(P-14517)
EAST VALLEY TOURIST DEV AUTH
Also Called: Fantasy Springs Resort Casino
84245 Indio Springs Dr (92203-3405)
PHONE..................................760 342-5000
John James, *Ch Bd*
Mark Benitez, *
Brenda Soulliere, *
Angela Roosevelt, *
EMP: 1200 EST: 1983
SQ FT: 94,000
SALES (est): 79.1MM **Privately Held**
Web: www.starbucks.com
SIC: 7999 Gambling establishment

(P-14518)
EASTBIZ CORPORATION
3501 Jack Northrop Ave (90250-4444)
PHONE..................................310 212-7134
EMP: 114
SIC: 7999 5091 Sporting goods rental, nec; Sporting and recreation goods

(P-14519)
EL DORADO HILLS CMNTY SVCS DST
1021 Harvard Way (95762-4353)
PHONE..................................916 933-6624
Kevin Loewen, *CEO*
Wayne Lowery, *
EMP: 83 EST: 1962
SQ FT: 18,500
SALES (est): 994.46K **Privately Held**
Web: www.eldoradohillscsd.org
SIC: 7999 Recreation center

(P-14520)
FAIRPLEX ENTERPRISES INC
1101 W Mckinley Ave (91768-1650)
PHONE..................................909 623-3111
James Henwood, *Pr*
▲ EMP: 128 EST: 2011
SALES (est): 25.06MM
SALES (corp-wide): 57.69MM **Privately Held**
Web: www.fairplex.com
SIC: 7999 Fair, nsk
PA: Los Angeles County Fair Association
     1101 W Mckinley Ave
     Pomona CA
     909 623-3111

(P-14521)
FAZE CLAN INC
720 N Cahuenga Blvd (90038-3702)
PHONE..................................818 688-6373
Lee Trink, *CEO*
Erik Anderson, *
EMP: 496 EST: 2016
SALES (est): 45.5MM
SALES (corp-wide): 70.02MM **Publicly Held**
Web: www.fazeclan.com
SIC: 7999 5961 Games, instruction; Electronic shopping
PA: Faze Holdings Inc.
     720 N Cahuenga Blvd
     Los Angeles CA
     818 688-6373

(P-14522)
FAZE HOLDINGS INC (PA)
720 N Cahuenga Blvd (90038-3702)
PHONE..................................818 688-6373
Lee Trink, *Ch Bd*
Zach Katz, *Pr*
Tamara Brandt, *CLO*
Kainoa Henry, *CLO*
Christoph Pachler, *CFO*
EMP: 106 EST: 2010
SALES (est): 70.02MM
SALES (corp-wide): 70.02MM **Publicly Held**
SIC: 7999 5961 Games, instruction; Electronic shopping

(P-14523)
FEATHER RVER RECREATION PK DST
1875 Feather River Blvd (95965-5701)
PHONE..................................530 533-2011
Vicky Smith, *Ch*
EMP: 76 EST: 1953
SQ FT: 3,000
SALES (est): 2.93MM **Privately Held**
Web: www.frrpd.com
SIC: 7999 Recreation center

(P-14524)
FIT ATHLETIC CLUB
12171 World Trade Dr (92128-3709)
PHONE..................................858 592-2440
Robin Brumley, *Dir*
EMP: 82 EST: 2016
SALES (est): 5.13MM **Privately Held**
Web: www.fitathletic.com
SIC: 7999 7991 Yoga instruction; Physical fitness clubs with training equipment

(P-14525)
FLOATIES SWIM SCHOOL LLC
Also Called: Floaties Swim School
13180 Poway Rd (92064-4612)
PHONE..................................877 277-7946
Kira La Forgia, *Dir Opers*
EMP: 75 EST: 2006
SALES (est): 1.17MM **Privately Held**
Web: www.floatiesswimschool.com
SIC: 7999 Swimming instruction

(P-14526)
FORTISS LLC
1100 S Flower St Ste 3100 (90015-2127)
PHONE..................................323 415-4900
John Park, *Managing Member*

PRODUCTS & SERVICES SECTION
7999 - Amusement And Recreation, Nec (P-14549)

Michael Vasey, *
EMP: 80 **EST:** 2004
SALES (est): 11.87MM **Privately Held**
Web: www.fortiss.com
SIC: 7999 Card and game services

(P-14527)
FUNTOPIA INC
3700 Brookstone Dr (95382-9290)
PHONE................510 246-3098
Sukhdeep Garcha, *Admn*
EMP: 60 **EST:** 2019
SALES (est): 618.04K **Privately Held**
SIC: 7999 Tourist attractions, amusement park concessions and rides

(P-14528)
GLAD ENTERTAINMENT INC (PA)
Also Called: Blackbeard's Family Fun Center
4055 N Chestnut Ave (93726-4701)
PHONE................559 292-9000
Greg Florer, *Pr*
Don Jackley, *
EMP: 70 **EST:** 1977
SQ FT: 12,000
SALES (est): 2.48MM
SALES (corp-wide): 2.48MM **Privately Held**
Web: www.blackbeards.com
SIC: 7999 Miniature golf course operation

(P-14529)
GLO YOGA
18041 Blue Sail Dr (90272-2902)
PHONE................310 801-9031
EMP: 65 **EST:** 2019
SALES (est): 1.97MM **Privately Held**
Web: www.glo.com
SIC: 7999 Yoga instruction

(P-14530)
GOLFLAND ENTRMT CTRS INC
Also Called: Milpitas Golfland
1199 Jacklin Rd (95035-3421)
PHONE................408 263-6855
Maracio Ceron, *Mgr*
EMP: 163
SALES (corp-wide): 14.11MM **Privately Held**
Web: www.golfland.com
SIC: 7999 7993 5812 Miniature golf course operation; Video game arcade; Pizzeria, independent
PA: Golfland Entertainment Centers, Inc.
155 W Hampton Ave
Mesa AZ
480 834-8319

(P-14531)
GRATON RESORT & CASINO
288 Golf Course Dr (94928-1756)
PHONE................707 588-7100
EMP: 248 **EST:** 2015
SALES (est): 9.17MM **Privately Held**
Web: www.gratonresortcasino.com
SIC: 7999 Gambling establishment

(P-14532)
GREATER VALLEJO RECREATION DST
395 Amador St (94590-6320)
PHONE................707 648-4600
William Pendergast Iii, *Ch Bd*
EMP: 66 **EST:** 1944
SQ FT: 5,000
SALES (est): 9.85MM **Privately Held**
Web: www.gvrd.org
SIC: 7999 Recreation services

(P-14533)
HAWAIIAN GARDENS CASINO
11871 Carson St (90716-1127)
PHONE................562 860-5887
FAX: 562 860-5823
EMP: 840
SALES (corp-wide): 63.26MM **Privately Held**
SIC: 7999 Card and game services
PA: Hawaiian Gardens Casino
21520 Pioneer Blvd # 305
Hawaiian Gardens CA
562 860-5887

(P-14534)
HOPLAND BAND POMO INDIANS INC
Also Called: Casino
13101 Nokomis Rd (95449-9793)
PHONE................707 744-1395
John O'neil, *Mgr*
EMP: 122
SALES (corp-wide): 17.41MM **Privately Held**
Web: www.hoplandtribe.com
SIC: 7999 7011 5813 5812 Gambling establishment; Casino hotel; Drinking places; Eating places
PA: Hopland Band Of Pomo Indians Inc.
3000 Shanel Rd
Hopland CA
707 472-2100

(P-14535)
HOUSE OF AIR LLC (PA)
926 Mason St (94129-1602)
PHONE................415 345-9675
EMP: 61 **EST:** 2009
SALES (est): 2.16MM
SALES (corp-wide): 2.16MM **Privately Held**
Web: www.houseofair.com
SIC: 7999 Recreation center

(P-14536)
KIDS EMPIRE USA LLC
8605 Santa Monica Blvd (90069-4109)
PHONE................424 527-1039
Haim Elbaz, *CEO*
EMP: 93 **EST:** 2017
SALES (est): 1.28MM **Privately Held**
SIC: 7999 Recreation services

(P-14537)
KINEMA FITNESS INC
11601 Wilshire Blvd Ste 500 (90025-0509)
PHONE................610 909-9331
Joshua Love, *Pr*
EMP: 68 **EST:** 2009
SALES (est): 3.43MM **Privately Held**
Web: www.kinemafitness.com
SIC: 7999 7991 7389 Physical fitness instruction; Physical fitness facilities; Business Activities at Non-Commercial Site

(P-14538)
KINGS CARD CLUB
6111 West Ln (95210-3389)
PHONE................209 267-4567
Jordan Conner, *Genl Mgr*
Gregory Valdivia, *Contrlr*
EMP: 188 **EST:** 2014
SALES (est): 20MM **Privately Held**
Web: www.kingscardclub.com
SIC: 7999 Gambling establishment

(P-14539)
KONOCTI VISTA CASINO (PA)
2755 Mission Rancheria Rd (95453-9612)
P.O. Box 57 (95435-0057)
PHONE................707 262-1900
Sam Dornham, *Genl Mgr*
EMP: 221 **EST:** 1994
SALES (est): 10.71MM **Privately Held**
Web: www.konocti-vista-casino.com
SIC: 7999 Gambling establishment

(P-14540)
LIFETIME TENNIS INC
6715 Corte Santa Maria (94566-8612)
PHONE................925 931-3449
Dana Gill, *Ex Dir*
EMP: 61 **EST:** 2012
SALES (est): 1.88MM **Privately Held**
Web: www.lifetimeactivities.com
SIC: 7999 Tennis services and professionals

(P-14541)
LIME
1 Sansome St (94104-4448)
PHONE................650 762-9697
EMP: 214 **EST:** 2018
SALES (est): 4.96MM **Privately Held**
Web: www.li.me
SIC: 7999 Bicycle rental

(P-14542)
LIVERMORE AREA RCRATION PK DST (PA)
4444 East Ave (94550-5053)
PHONE................925 373-5700
Tim Barry, *Genl Mgr*
Maryalice Faltings, *
Scott Kamena, *
Dale Turner, *
Steve Goodman, *
EMP: 253 **EST:** 1947
SQ FT: 71,000
SALES (est): 23.13MM
SALES (corp-wide): 23.13MM **Privately Held**
Web: www.larpd.org
SIC: 7999 Recreation services

(P-14543)
LOS ANGELES COUNTY FAIR ASSN (PA)
Also Called: Fairplex Rv Park
1101 W Mckinley Ave (91768-1639)
PHONE................909 623-3111
Ronald Bolding, *Dir*
Micheal Seder, *
EMP: 100 **EST:** 1922
SALES (est): 57.69MM
SALES (corp-wide): 57.69MM **Privately Held**
Web: www.fairplex.com
SIC: 7999 8412 Fair, nsk; Museums and art galleries

(P-14544)
MARINE CORPS COMMUNITY SVCS
Also Called: Marine Corps Cmnty Svcs Dept
2273 Elrod Ave (92145-0001)
P.O. Box 452008 (92145-2008)
PHONE................858 577-1061
Mary Bradford, *Dir*
EMP: 259
Web: www.usmc-mccs.org
SIC: 7999 9711 Recreation center; Marine Corps
HQ: Marine Corps Community Services
3044 Catlin Ave
Quantico VA
703 432-0109

(P-14545)
MARINE CORPS COMMUNITY SVCS
Also Called: Moral Welfare and Recreation
Acs Mccs Attn Semper Fi Box 555020
Marine Corp Base (92055)
PHONE................760 725-6195
Mike Wilkinson, *Department Director*
EMP: 179
SQ FT: 1,152
Web: www.usmc-mccs.org
SIC: 7999 9711 Recreation services; Marine Corps
HQ: Marine Corps Community Services
3044 Catlin Ave
Quantico VA
703 432-0109

(P-14546)
MORONGO BAND MISSION INDIANS
Also Called: Morongo Casino Resort Spa
49500 Seminole Dr (92230-2202)
P.O. Box 366 (92230-0366)
PHONE................951 849-3080
Dual Cooper, *Brnch Mgr*
EMP: 133
Web: www.morongocasinoresort.com
SIC: 7999 9131 Gambling establishment; Indian Reservation
PA: Morongo Band Of Mission Indians
12700 Pumarra Rd
Banning CA
951 849-4697

(P-14547)
MOUNT SAN JCNTO WINTER PK CORP
1 Tramway Rd (92262-1827)
PHONE................760 325-1449
Nancy Nichols, *Pr*
Rob Parkins, *
Marjorie Dela Cruz, *
Tara Meinkey, *
▲ **EMP:** 73 **EST:** 1945
SQ FT: 50,000
SALES (est): 16.94MM **Privately Held**
Web: www.pstramway.com
SIC: 7999 Aerial tramway or ski lift, amusement or scenic

(P-14548)
MOUNTAIN VISTA GOLF COURSE AT
38180 Del Webb Blvd (92211-1256)
PHONE................760 200-2200
Andrea Goodwin, *Pr*
John Celli, *
Ron Delgado, *
Bill Wirian, *
Chuck Carpenter, *
EMP: 85 **EST:** 1992
SQ FT: 300
SALES (est): 30MM **Privately Held**
Web: www.mountainvistagolfclub.com
SIC: 7999 Golf services and professionals

(P-14549)
NAPA VALLEY WINE TRAIN LLC (HQ)
Also Called: NAPA Valley Railroad Co
1275 Mckinstry St (94559-1925)
PHONE................707 253-2160
TOLL FREE: 800
Vincent M De Deminico Junior, *VP Opers*
▲ **EMP:** 125 **EST:** 1984
SQ FT: 20,000
SALES (est): 24.34MM **Privately Held**
Web: www.winetrain.com

(PA)=Parent Co (HQ)=Headquarters
✪ = New Business established in last 2 years

2024 Directory of California
WholeSalers and Service Companies

7999 - Amusement And Recreation, Nec (P-14550)

SIC: 7999 5812 4011 4119 Scenic railroads for amusement; Eating places; Railroads, line-haul operating; Local passenger transportation, nec
PA: Noble House Hotels & Resorts, Ltd.
600 6th St S
Kirkland WA

(P-14550)
PARC MANAGEMENT LLC
Also Called: Waterworld USA
1950 Waterworld Pkwy (94520-2602)
PHONE...................925 609-1364
Steve Mayer, *Mgr*
EMP: 155
SALES (corp-wide): 99.55MM **Privately Held**
Web: www.parcentertainment.com
SIC: 7999 Picnic ground operation
PA: Parc Management, Llc
1545 Parkway
Sevierville TN
904 732-7272

(P-14551)
QUECHAN INDIAN TRIBE
Also Called: Quechan Gaming Commission
450 Quechan Rd (92283-9676)
P.O. Box 2737 (85366-2573)
PHONE...................760 572-2413
EMP: 106
Web: www.paradise-casinos.com
SIC: 7999 5812 Gambling establishment; Eating places
PA: Quechan Indian Tribe
350 Picacho Rd
Winterhaven CA
760 572-0213

(P-14552)
RANCHO BERNARDO GOLF CLUB
Also Called: COUNTRY CLUB OF RANCHO BERNARD
17550 Bernardo Oaks Dr (92128-2112)
PHONE...................858 487-1134
Jeff Grace, *Pr*
Mary Campbell, *
Sandy Douglass, *
Mike Curry, *
David Mrachek, *
EMP: 62 EST: 1976
SQ FT: 23,000
SALES (est): 4.81MM **Privately Held**
Web: www.ranchobernardoinn.com
SIC: 7999 7371 Golf services and professionals; Computer software development and applications

(P-14553)
REDWOOD EMPIRE ICE OPRTONS LLC (PA)
Also Called: Snoopy's Galary and Gift Shop
1667 W Steele Ln (95403-2625)
PHONE...................707 546-7147
▲ EMP: 70 EST: 1968
SQ FT: 40,000
SALES (est): 5.65MM
SALES (corp-wide): 5.65MM **Privately Held**
Web: www.snoopyshomeice.com
SIC: 7999 5947 5812 Ice skating rink operation; Gift shop; Coffee shop

(P-14554)
RIVIERA COUNTRY CLUB INC
Also Called: Grand Slam Tennis Program
1250 Capri Dr (90272-4001)
PHONE...................310 454-6591
Noboru Watanabe, *CEO*

EMP: 118 EST: 1989
SALES (est): 13.29MM **Privately Held**
Web: www.therivieracountryclub.com
SIC: 7999 7997 Tennis club, non-membership; Membership sports and recreation clubs

(P-14555)
ROCKIN JUMP HOLDINGS LLC
Also Called: Rockin' Jump Trampoline
1301 W Rancho Vista Blvd Ste B (93551-3101)
PHONE...................661 233-9907
EMP: 301
SALES (corp-wide): 51.07MM **Privately Held**
Web: www.rockinjump.com
SIC: 7999 Trampoline operation
HQ: Rockin' Jump Holdings, Llc
18 Crow Canyon Ct Ste 350
San Ramon CA
925 401-7200

(P-14556)
ROSEVILLE GOLFLAND LTD PARTNR
Also Called: Golfland-Sunsplash
1893 Taylor Rd (95661-3008)
PHONE...................916 784-1273
Fred Kenney, *Pt*
EMP: 81 EST: 2000
SALES (est): 4.76MM **Privately Held**
Web: www.golfland.com
SIC: 7999 Tourist attractions, amusement park concessions and rides

(P-14557)
S J S ENTERPRISE INC
Also Called: S C Village
9030 Somerset Blvd (90706-3402)
PHONE...................949 489-9000
EMP: 150 EST: 1987
SALES (est): 2.7MM **Privately Held**
Web: www.hollywoodsports.com
SIC: 7999 Indoor court clubs

(P-14558)
SAN BRNRDINO CNTY RGONAL PARKS
777 E Rialto Ave (92415-1005)
PHONE...................909 387-2583
EMP: 99 EST: 2020
SALES (est): 522.95K **Privately Held**
Web: parks.sbcounty.gov
SIC: 7999 Recreation center

(P-14559)
SAN DIEGO GULLS HOCKEY CLB LLC
7676 Hazard Center Dr Ste 1075 (92108-4503)
PHONE...................619 359-4700
Michael Schulman, *Board Director*
Michael Schulman, *Bd of Dir*
EMP: 65 EST: 2013
SQ FT: 2,000
SALES (est): 7.96MM **Privately Held**
Web: www.sandiegogulls.com
SIC: 7999 Sports professionals, nec

(P-14560)
SAN FRANCISCO ZOOLOGICAL SOC
Also Called: San Francisco Zoo
1 Zoo Rd (94132-1098)
PHONE...................415 753-7080
Tanya Peterson, *CEO*
Robert Pedrero, *
EMP: 222 EST: 1954

SQ FT: 2,000
SALES (est): 25.87MM **Privately Held**
Web: www.sfzoo.org
SIC: 7999 7389 Concession operator; Fund raising organizations

(P-14561)
SAN JOSE ARENA MANAGEMENT LLC
Also Called: Ice Center of San Jose
1500 S 10th St (95112-6410)
PHONE...................408 279-6000
John Gustasson, *Mgr*
EMP: 81
SALES (corp-wide): 21.61MM **Privately Held**
Web: www.sapcenter.com
SIC: 7999 Ice skating rink operation
PA: San Jose Arena Management, Llc
525 W Santa Clara St
San Jose CA
408 287-7070

(P-14562)
SAN MANUEL ENTERTAINMENT AUTH (PA)
Also Called: Yaamava Rsort Csino At San Mnu
777 San Manuel Blvd (92346-6713)
PHONE...................909 864-5050
TOLL FREE: 800
James Ramos, *Ch*
Rebecca Spalding, *CFO*
Jimmy Starcher, *Ex Dir*
Steve Lengeo, *Ex Dir*
Rikki Tanenbaum, *COO*
▲ EMP: 2950 EST: 1987
SALES (est): 154.97MM
SALES (corp-wide): 154.97MM **Privately Held**
Web: www.yaamava.com
SIC: 7999 Bingo hall

(P-14563)
SANTA CLARA CNTY FRGRNDS MGT C
Also Called: SANTA CLARA COUNTY FMC
344 Tully Rd (95111-1913)
PHONE...................408 494-3100
Delana Romero, *Ex Dir*
Howard Thomas, *CFO*
EMP: 91 EST: 1995
SQ FT: 125,000
SALES (est): 8.65MM **Privately Held**
Web: www.thefairgrounds.org
SIC: 7999 Fair, nsk

(P-14564)
SELF-HELP FOR ELDERLY
Also Called: Lady Shaw Activity Center
1483 Mason St (94133-4283)
PHONE...................415 677-7581
Karon Ho, *Mgr*
EMP: 94
SALES (corp-wide): 30.97MM **Privately Held**
Web: www.selfhelpelderly.org
SIC: 7999 8322 Recreation services; Senior citizens' center or association
PA: Self-Help For The Elderly
731 Sansome St Ste 100
San Francisco CA
415 677-7600

(P-14565)
SENOR SISIG
2277 Shafter Ave (94124-1918)
P.O. Box 883094 (94188-3094)
PHONE...................415 608-5048

Evan Kidera, *CEO*
EMP: 60 EST: 2009
SALES (est): 2.3MM **Privately Held**
Web: www.senorsisig.com
SIC: 7999 Concession operator

(P-14566)
SYCUAN CASINO (PA)
Also Called: Sycuan Resort and Casino
5459 Casino Way (92019)
PHONE...................619 445-6002
John Denius, *Genl Mgr*
Angela Scantling, *
EMP: 156 EST: 1983
SQ FT: 236,000
SALES (est): 93.96MM
SALES (corp-wide): 93.96MM **Privately Held**
Web: www.sycuan.com
SIC: 7999 7997 Gambling establishment; Membership sports and recreation clubs

(P-14567)
T ALLANCE ONE - PALM SPRNG LLC
Also Called: Doubltree Palm Sprng Golf Rsor
67967 Vista Chino (92234-7408)
PHONE...................760 322-7000
EMP: 99 EST: 2013
SALES (est): 2.46MM **Privately Held**
Web: www.doubletreepalmsprings.com
SIC: 7999 Golf professionals

(P-14568)
TAC AIR CALIFORNIA INC
Also Called: Skydive San Diego
13531 Otay Lakes Rd (91935-7003)
PHONE...................619 216-8416
Jeffery Bramstedt, *Prin*
Brian Tucker, *
Tony Goodman, *
Catherine Bedell, *
EMP: 65 EST: 2015
SALES (est): 2.17MM **Privately Held**
Web: www.skydivesandiego.com
SIC: 7999 Parachute training, for pleasure

(P-14569)
TG ART INC
1109 Washington Ave (94706-1676)
PHONE...................510 525-0070
Daesoo Min, *Brnch Mgr*
EMP: 84
SIC: 7999 Art gallery, commercial
PA: T.G Art, Inc.
250 El Cerrito Plz
El Cerrito CA

(P-14570)
TICKETMASTER CORPORATION
Also Called: Ticketmaster
7060 Hollywood Blvd Ste 2 (90028-6030)
PHONE...................323 769-4600
EMP: 4390
SIC: 7999 7922 Ticket sales office for sporting events, contract; Theatrical producers and services

(P-14571)
TICKETMASTER ENTERTAINMENT LLC
8800 W Sunset Blvd (90069-2105)
PHONE...................800 653-8000
Ron Bension, *Managing Member*
EMP: 4390 EST: 2010
SALES (est): 103.99MM **Publicly Held**
SIC: 7999 Ticket sales office for sporting events, contract
PA: Live Nation Entertainment, Inc.

PRODUCTS & SERVICES SECTION

8011 - Offices And Clinics Of Medical Doctors (P-14593)

9348 Civic Center Dr Lbby
Beverly Hills CA

(P-14572)
TICKETMASTER GROUP INC
Also Called: Ticketmaster
3701 Wilshire Blvd Fl 9 (90010-2804)
PHONE.................................800 745-3000
EMP: 4390
SIC: 7999   Ticket sales office for sporting events, contract

(P-14573)
TICKETMSTER NEW VNTRES HLDNGS (HQ)
Also Called: Ticketmaster
325 N Maple Dr (90210-3428)
PHONE.................................800 653-8000
Irving Azoff, *CEO*
EMP: 104 **EST:** 1996
SALES (est): 59.47MM **Publicly Held**
SIC: 7999   Ticket sales office for sporting events, contract
PA: Live Nation Entertainment, Inc.
9348 Civic Center Dr Lbby
Beverly Hills CA

(P-14574)
TIERRA DEL SOL FOUNDATION
Also Called: Tierra Del Soul
250 W 1st St Ste 120 (91711-4741)
PHONE.................................909 626-8301
Rebecca Hamm, *Brnch Mgr*
EMP: 85
SALES (corp-wide): 21.23MM **Privately Held**
Web: www.tierradelsol.org
SIC: 7999 5999   Art gallery, commercial; Art dealers
PA: Tierra Del Sol Foundation
9919 Sunland Blvd
Sunland CA
818 352-1419

(P-14575)
TONAL SYSTEMS INC
617 Bryant St (94107-1612)
PHONE.................................855 698-6625
Aly Orady, *CEO*
EMP: 65 **EST:** 2015
SALES (est): 16.78MM **Privately Held**
Web: www.tonal.com
SIC: 7999   Physical fitness instruction

(P-14576)
TOWN OF DANVILLE
420 Front St (94526-3404)
PHONE.................................925 314-3400
Craig Bowen, *Brnch Mgr*
EMP: 99
SALES (corp-wide): 42.47MM **Privately Held**
Web: danville.ca.gov
SIC: 7999   Recreation center
PA: Town Of Danville
510 La Gonda Way
Danville CA
925 314-3171

(P-14577)
TOYOTA ARENA
4000 E Ontario Center Pkwy (91764-7966)
PHONE.................................909 244-5500
EMP: 92 **EST:** 2019
SALES (est): 5.82MM **Privately Held**
Web: www.toyota-arena.com
SIC: 7999   Ice skating rink operation

(P-14578)
TRUCKEE DNNER RCREATION PK DST
10981 Truckee Way (96161-2904)
PHONE.................................530 582-7720
Steve Randall, *Genl Mgr*
Janet Brady, *
Peter Werbel, *
Kevin Murphy, *
EMP: 100 **EST:** 1962
SQ FT: 10,000
SALES (est): 12.4MM **Privately Held**
Web: www.tdrpd.org
SIC: 7999   Recreation services

(P-14579)
TUMBLEWEED EDUCTL ENTPS INC
Also Called: Tumbleweed Day Camp
1024 Hanley Ave (90049-1306)
P.O. Box 49291 (90049-0291)
PHONE.................................310 444-3232
Erin Benfield, *Pr*
EMP: 160 **EST:** 1954
SQ FT: 6,500
SALES (est): 12.04MM **Privately Held**
Web: www.tumbleweedtransportation.com
SIC: 7999 4151   Day camp; School buses

(P-14580)
UNITED STUDIOS SELF DEF INC
13331 Poway Rd (92064-4625)
PHONE.................................858 486-8773
Zachary Cummings Smith, *Pr*
EMP: 137
Web: www.ussd.com
SIC: 7999   Martial arts school, nec
PA: United Studios Of Self Defense, Inc.
23402 S Pointe Dr
Laguna Hills CA

(P-14581)
UNITED STUDIOS SELF DEF INC
28251 Marguerite Pkwy Ste J (92692-3721)
PHONE.................................949 293-1391
EMP: 137
Web: www.ussd.com
SIC: 7999   Martial arts school, nec
PA: United Studios Of Self Defense, Inc.
23402 S Pointe Dr
Laguna Hills CA

(P-14582)
VOLUME SERVICES INC
Also Called: Centerplate
24 Willie Mays Plz (94107-2134)
PHONE.................................415 972-1500
Angie Perrilliat, *Genl Mgr*
EMP: 394
SALES (corp-wide): 206.19MM **Privately Held**
Web: us.sodexo.com
SIC: 7999   Concession operator
HQ: Volume Services, Inc.
2187 Atlantic St Ste 6
Stamford CT

(P-14583)
VOLUME SERVICES INC
5333 Zoo Dr (90027-1451)
PHONE.................................323 644-6038
Greg Edgar, *Mgr*
EMP: 260
SALES (corp-wide): 206.19MM **Privately Held**
Web: us.sodexo.com
SIC: 7999   Concession operator
HQ: Volume Services, Inc.
2187 Atlantic St Ste 6
Stamford CT

(P-14584)
VOLUME SERVICES INC
111 W Harbor Dr (92101-7822)
PHONE.................................619 525-5800
EMP: 260
SALES (corp-wide): 206.19MM **Privately Held**
Web: us.sodexo.com
SIC: 7999   Concession operator
HQ: Volume Services, Inc.
2187 Atlantic St Ste 6
Stamford CT

(P-14585)
WATERSAFE SWIM SCHOOL INC
Also Called: Watersafe Swim School
3686 Cerritos Ave (90720-2417)
PHONE.................................562 596-8608
Nathanael Najarian, *CEO*
EMP: 64
Web: www.watersafe.com
SIC: 7999   Swimming instruction
PA: Watersafe Swim School, Inc.
345 10th St
Seal Beach CA

(P-14586)
WINCHESTER MYSTERY HOUSE LLC
Also Called: Winchester Mystery House
525 S Winchester Blvd (95128-2588)
PHONE.................................408 247-2101
Vakerue Bovone, *
EMP: 90 **EST:** 1923
SQ FT: 44,000
SALES (est): 9.87MM **Privately Held**
Web: www.winchestermysteryhouse.com
SIC: 7999   Tourist attraction, commercial

(P-14587)
YOGA SHELTER LLC
Also Called: Yoga Shelter
12408 Ventura Blvd (91604-2406)
PHONE.................................818 691-3000
Eric Paskel, *Owner*
EMP: 64
SALES (corp-wide): 895.78K **Privately Held**
Web: www.boldflowyoga.com
SIC: 7999   Yoga instruction
PA: Yoga Shelter Llc
6363 Orchard Lake Rd
West Bloomfield MI
248 538-0200

(P-14588)
YOGA SOURCE PARTNERS LLC
Also Called: Yogasource
16185 Los Gatos Blvd (95032-4568)
PHONE.................................408 402-9642
Linda Mcgrath, *Managing Member*
Steve Mcgrath, *Managing Member*
EMP: 100 **EST:** 2002
SALES (est): 1.42MM **Privately Held**
Web: www.oneyogasource.com
SIC: 7999   Yoga instruction

(P-14589)
YOGAWORKS INC (HQ)
Also Called: Myyogaworks
5780 Uplander Way (90230-6906)
PHONE.................................310 664-6470
Rosanna C Mccollough, *Pr*
Peter L Garran, *
Vance Y Chang, *
EMP: 60 **EST:** 1987
SQ FT: 6,800
SALES (est): 59.59MM
SALES (corp-wide): 391.31MM **Privately Held**
Web: www.yogaworks.com
SIC: 7999 5961 7991   Yoga instruction; Mail order house, nec; Exercise salon
PA: Great Hill Equity Partners V, L.P.
200 Clarendon St Ste 2901
Boston MA
617 790-9400

(P-14590)
YOUNG MNS CHRSTN ASSN STHAST V
Also Called: Simi Valley Family YMCA
3200 Cochran St (93065-2769)
PHONE.................................805 583-5338
Dan Jaeger, *Dir*
EMP: 62
SALES (corp-wide): 8.13MM **Privately Held**
Web: www.sevymca.org
SIC: 7999 8351 8641 7997   Recreation center ; Child day care services; Civic and social associations; Membership sports and recreation clubs
PA: Young Men's Christian Association Of Southeast Ventura County
31105 E Thusand Oaks Blvd
Thousand Oaks CA
805 497-3081

8011 Offices And Clinics Of Medical Doctors

(P-14591)
1LIFE HEALTHCARE INC (HQ)
Also Called: One Medical
1 Embarcadero Ctr Ste 1900 (94111-3723)
PHONE.................................415 814-0927
Amir Dan Rubin, *Ch Bd*
Bjorn B Thaler, *CFO*
Andrew S Diamond, *CMO*
Lisa A Mango, *Corporate Secretary*
EMP: 81 **EST:** 2002
SQ FT: 60,874
SALES (est): 1.05B **Publicly Held**
Web: www.onemedical.com
SIC: 8011   Primary care medical clinic
PA: Amazon.Com, Inc.
410 Terry Ave N
Seattle WA

(P-14592)
A B C PEDIATRICS
50 S San Mateo Dr Ste 260 (94401-3859)
PHONE.................................650 579-6500
Patricia Soong, *Pt*
Alger Chapmin, *Pt*
Jeanne Beymer, *Pt*
EMP: 127 **EST:** 1958
SQ FT: 4,000
SALES (est): 3.15MM **Privately Held**
Web: www.abcped.com
SIC: 8011   Pediatrician

(P-14593)
ADVANCED PROF IMGING MED GROUP
Also Called: Seven California Med Diagnstc
1109 S Central Ave (91204-2212)
PHONE.................................818 244-4646
EMP: 133
SALES (corp-wide): 2.31MM **Privately Held**
SIC: 8011   Radiologist
PA: Advanced Professional Imaging Medical Group

8011 - Offices And Clinics Of Medical Doctors (P-14594)

6905 Oslo Cir Ste F
Buena Park CA
714 995-5400

(P-14594)
ADVENTIST HEALTH SYSTEM
Also Called: Adventist Health Cmnty. Care
250 W El Monte Way (93618-1554)
PHONE.................................559 595-9890
Wayne Ferch, *Brnch Mgr*
EMP: 259
Web: www.adventhealth.com
SIC: 8011 Offices and clinics of medical doctors
PA: Adventist Health System Sunbelt Healthcare Corporation
900 Hope Way
Altamonte Springs FL

(P-14595)
AGILE OCCUPATIONAL MEDICINE PC
710 N Euclid St Ste 107 (92801-4132)
PHONE.................................949 464-4036
EMP: 83
SALES (corp-wide): 12.75MM **Privately Held**
Web: www.agileoccmed.com
SIC: 8011 Pediatrician
PA: Agile Occupational Medicine, Pc
3200 Bristol St Ste 600
Costa Mesa CA
407 413-5350

(P-14596)
AHMC INC
100 S Raymond Ave (91801-3166)
PHONE.................................626 570-1606
Jonathan Wu, *Pr*
EMP: 77 **EST:** 1998
SALES (est): 2.91MM **Privately Held**
Web: www.alhambrahospital.com
SIC: 8011 General and family practice, physician/surgeon

(P-14597)
ALL CARE MEDICAL GROUP INC
Also Called: Professional Svcs Med Group
31 Crescent St (90255)
PHONE.................................408 278-3550
Samuel Rotenberg Md, *Dir*
EMP: 85 **EST:** 1946
SQ FT: 33,000
SALES (est): 9.15MM **Privately Held**
Web: www.allcaremg.com
SIC: 8011 Physicians' office, including specialists

(P-14598)
ALLIANCE MEDICAL CENTER INC
1381 University St (95448-3314)
PHONE.................................707 431-8234
Beatrice Bostick, *CEO*
Jack Neureuter, *
EMP: 99 **EST:** 1975
SALES (est): 21.22MM **Privately Held**
Web: www.alliancemed.org
SIC: 8011 Clinic, operated by physicians

(P-14599)
ALPINE ALLRGY ASTHMA ASSOC INC
Also Called: Auburn Dermatology Center
3254 Professional Dr (95602-2412)
PHONE.................................530 888-1016
Michael Mccormick, *Prin*
EMP: 69

Web: www.alpineallergy.com
SIC: 8011 Allergist
PA: Alpine Allergy And Asthma Associates, Inc.
300 Sierra College Dr # 235
Grass Valley CA

(P-14600)
ALTAMED HEALTH SERVICES CORP
5427 Whittier Blvd (90022-4101)
PHONE.................................323 980-4466
Irene Avilar, *Prin*
EMP: 132
SALES (corp-wide): 1.05B **Privately Held**
Web: www.altamedfoundation.org
SIC: 8011 Clinic, operated by physicians
PA: Altamed Health Services Corporation
2040 Camfield Ave
Commerce CA
323 725-8751

(P-14601)
ALTAMED HEALTH SERVICES CORP
Also Called: Ultimate
1500 Hughes Way Ste A150 (90810-1883)
PHONE.................................562 923-9414
Chikita Emel, *Dir*
EMP: 149
SALES (corp-wide): 1.05B **Privately Held**
Web: www.altamed.org
SIC: 8011 Gynecologist
PA: Altamed Health Services Corporation
2040 Camfield Ave
Commerce CA
323 725-8751

(P-14602)
ALTAMED HEALTH SERVICES CORP
Also Called: Altamed Adhc Golden Age
3820 Martin Luther King Jr Blvd (90262-3625)
PHONE.................................310 632-0415
Peter M Feldman, *Prin*
EMP: 133
SALES (corp-wide): 1.05B **Privately Held**
Web: www.altamed.org
SIC: 8011 8099 Gynecologist; Medical services organization
PA: Altamed Health Services Corporation
2040 Camfield Ave
Commerce CA
323 725-8751

(P-14603)
ALTAMED HEALTH SERVICES CORP
1325 N Anaheim Blvd # 101 (92801-1202)
PHONE.................................714 635-0593
EMP: 73
SALES (corp-wide): 1.05B **Privately Held**
Web: www.altamed.org
SIC: 8011 Gynecologist
PA: Altamed Health Services Corporation
2040 Camfield Ave
Commerce CA
323 725-8751

(P-14604)
ALTAMED HEALTH SERVICES CORP
6330 Rugby Ave Ste 200 (90255-6938)
PHONE.................................323 277-7678
Yorka Rodriguez, *Mgr*
EMP: 81
SALES (corp-wide): 1.05B **Privately Held**
Web: www.altamed.org

SIC: 8011 8322 Gynecologist; Individual and family services
PA: Altamed Health Services Corporation
2040 Camfield Ave
Commerce CA
323 725-8751

(P-14605)
ALTAMED HEALTH SERVICES CORP
2720 S Bristol St (92704-6207)
PHONE.................................714 426-5400
EMP: 72
SALES (corp-wide): 1.05B **Privately Held**
Web: www.altamed.org
SIC: 8011 Gynecologist
PA: Altamed Health Services Corporation
2040 Camfield Ave
Commerce CA
323 725-8751

(P-14606)
ALTAMED HEALTH SERVICES CORP (PA)
2040 Camfield Ave (90040-1574)
PHONE.................................323 725-8751
Castulo De La Rocha, *CEO*
Zoila D Escobar, *
Marie S Torres, *
Jose U Esparza, *
EMP: 135 **EST:** 1970
SQ FT: 27,345
SALES (est): 1.05B
SALES (corp-wide): 1.05B **Privately Held**
Web: www.altamed.org
SIC: 8011 8099 Gynecologist; Medical services organization

(P-14607)
ALTAMED HEALTH SERVICES CORP
Also Called: Senior Health and Activity Ctr
5425 Pomona Blvd (90022-1716)
PHONE.................................323 728-0411
Mariela Bauer, *Brnch Mgr*
EMP: 176
SQ FT: 24,369
SALES (corp-wide): 1.05B **Privately Held**
Web: www.altamedfoundation.org
SIC: 8011 8099 Gynecologist; Medical services organization
PA: Altamed Health Services Corporation
2040 Camfield Ave
Commerce CA
323 725-8751

(P-14608)
ALTAMED HEALTH SERVICES CORP
2219 E 1st St (90033-3901)
PHONE.................................323 269-0421
Shi Y Wong, *Brnch Mgr*
EMP: 144
SALES (corp-wide): 1.05B **Privately Held**
Web: www.altamedfoundation.org
SIC: 8011 8099 Gynecologist; Medical services organization
PA: Altamed Health Services Corporation
2040 Camfield Ave
Commerce CA
323 725-8751

(P-14609)
ALTURA CENTERS FOR HEALTH
1201 N Cherry St (93274-2233)
PHONE.................................559 686-9097
Graciela Soto-perez, *Pr*
Dennis Jungwirth, *
EMP: 83 **EST:** 1996

SQ FT: 18,000
SALES (est): 36.78MM **Privately Held**
Web: www.altura.org
SIC: 8011 8021 Clinic, operated by physicians; Offices and clinics of dentists

(P-14610)
AMEN CLINICS INC A MED CORP (PA)
3150 Bristol St Ste 400 (92626-3054)
PHONE.................................888 564-2700
Daniel Amen, *Pr*
▲ **EMP:** 75 **EST:** 2000
SALES (est): 45.94MM
SALES (corp-wide): 45.94MM **Privately Held**
Web: www.amenclinics.com
SIC: 8011 Psychiatric clinic

(P-14611)
AMN HEALTHCARE INC (HQ)
12400 High Bluff Dr Ste 100 (92130-3077)
PHONE.................................858 792-0711
Susan R Nowakowski, *CEO*
Susan R Salka, *Pr*
Julie Fletcher, *VP*
Marcia Faller, *VP*
Denise L Jackson, *VP*
EMP: 253 **EST:** 1985
SALES (est): 643.21MM
SALES (corp-wide): 5.24B **Publicly Held**
Web: www.amnhealthcare.com
SIC: 8011 Primary care medical clinic
PA: Amn Healthcare Services, Inc.
2999 Olympus Blvd Ste 500
Coppell TX
866 871-8519

(P-14612)
ANAHEIM URGENT CARE INC
831 S State College Blvd (92806-4613)
PHONE.................................714 533-2273
Pejman Bolourian, *Pr*
EMP: 64 **EST:** 2007
SALES (est): 3.82MM **Privately Held**
Web: www.exerurgentcare.com
SIC: 8011 Clinic, operated by physicians

(P-14613)
ANESTHSIA MED GROUP SNTA BRBAR
Also Called: Anesthsia Med Group Snta Brbar
514 W Pueblo St Fl 2 (93105-6219)
PHONE.................................805 682-7751
Eric Amador, *Dir*
Douglas Etsel, *
John King, *
Clinton Lagrange, *
Derrick Willsey, *
EMP: 89 **EST:** 1970
SALES (est): 9.91MM **Privately Held**
Web: www.amgsb.com
SIC: 8011 Anesthesiologist

(P-14614)
ANTELOPE VALLEY HOSPITAL INC
Ob Clinic
1600 W Avenue J (93534-2894)
PHONE.................................661 726-6180
Vikki Haley, *Prin*
EMP: 336
SALES (corp-wide): 494.78MM **Privately Held**
Web: www.avmc.org
SIC: 8011 Offices and clinics of medical doctors
PA: Antelope Valley Health Care District
1600 W Avenue J

PRODUCTS & SERVICES SECTION

8011 - Offices And Clinics Of Medical Doctors (P-14635)

Lancaster CA
661 949-5000

(P-14615)
ARCADIA EYE CTR
Also Called: Arcadia Eye Center
622 W Duarte Rd Ste 103 (91007-9268)
PHONE..............................626 445-4873
John Beauclair Md, *Pr*
Catherine Beauclair, *
Maria Montanez, *
EMP: 75 EST: 1972
SALES (est): 1.85MM
SALES (corp-wide): 20.91MM **Privately Held**
SIC: **8011** Opthalmologist
PA: Doheny Eye Institute
150 N Orange Grove Blvd
Pasadena CA
323 342-7120

(P-14616)
ARROYO SECO MEDICAL GROUP (PA)
301 S Fair Oaks Ave Ste 300 (91105-2561)
PHONE..............................626 795-7556
Henry Sideropoulos, *Pr*
Henry Sideropoulos Md Pers, *Prin*
Andrew Muller Md, *VP*
EMP: 65 EST: 1978
SQ FT: 9,145
SALES (est): 4.72MM
SALES (corp-wide): 4.72MM **Privately Held**
Web: www.arroyoseco.net
SIC: **8011** Internal medicine, physician/surgeon

(P-14617)
ARROYO VSTA FMLY HLTH FNDATION
Also Called: Arroyo Vista Family Health Ctr
2411 N Broadway (90031-2218)
PHONE..............................323 224-2188
Line Fernandez, *Mgr*
EMP: 100
SQ FT: 13,435
Web: www.arroyovista.org
SIC: **8011** Clinic, operated by physicians
PA: Arroyo Vista Family Health Foundation
6000 N Figueroa St
Los Angeles CA

(P-14618)
ASIAN HEALTH SERVICES (PA)
101 8th St (94607-4707)
PHONE..............................510 986-6800
Sherry Hirota, *CEO*
EMP: 147 EST: 1973
SQ FT: 30,000
SALES (est): 89.67MM
SALES (corp-wide): 89.67MM **Privately Held**
Web: www.asianhealthservices.org
SIC: **8011** Clinic, operated by physicians

(P-14619)
ASSOCIATED FMLY PHYSICIANS INC
8110 Timberlake Way (95823-5401)
PHONE..............................916 689-4111
David Kosh Md, *Pr*
Hope Kosh, *VP*
Tamie Forester, *Admn*
EMP: 68 EST: 1990
SALES (est): 12.02MM **Privately Held**
Web: www.familymd.com
SIC: **8011** General and family practice, physician/surgeon

(P-14620)
ASSOCIATED STUDENTS UCLA
Also Called: Ucla Mdcn SC Phrmclgy
650 Charles Young Dr S Rm 23120 (90095-0001)
PHONE..............................310 825-9451
Michael Phelps, *Prin*
EMP: 74
SALES (corp-wide): 47.49MM **Privately Held**
Web: asucla.ucla.edu
SIC: **8011** General and family practice, physician/surgeon
PA: Associated Students U.C.L.A.
308 Westwood Plz
Los Angeles CA
310 794-8836

(P-14621)
BAKERSFIELD FAMILY MEDICAL GROUP INC (PA)
Also Called: Bakersfield Family Medical Ctr
4580 California Ave (93309-7013)
P.O. Box 12022 (93389-2022)
PHONE..............................661 327-4411
EMP: 94 EST: 1984
SALES (est): 26.9MM
SALES (corp-wide): 26.9MM **Privately Held**
Web: www.bfmc.com
SIC: **8011** Medical centers

(P-14622)
BALBOA NPHROLOGY MED GROUP INC
4225 Executive Sq Ste 450 (92037-8411)
PHONE..............................858 810-8000
EMP: 222
SALES (est): 11.24MM **Privately Held**
Web: www.balboacare.com
SIC: **8011** Nephrologist

(P-14623)
BAY AREA COMMUNITY HEALTH (PA)
40910 Fremont Blvd (94538-4375)
PHONE..............................510 770-8040
Zettie Page Iii, *CEO*
Olivia Dear, *
Cheryl Petersen Pine, *
EMP: 119 EST: 1972
SALES (est): 110.22MM
SALES (corp-wide): 110.22MM **Privately Held**
Web: www.bach.health
SIC: **8011** Clinic, operated by physicians

(P-14624)
BAY AREA SRGCAL SPCLSTS INC A
2637 Shadelands Dr (94598-2512)
PHONE..............................925 350-4044
EMP: 171 EST: 2006
SALES (est): 32.47MM **Privately Held**
Web: www.bassmedicalgroup.com
SIC: **8011** General and family practice, physician/surgeon

(P-14625)
BAY IMAGING CONS MED GROUP INC (PA)
2125 Oak Grove Rd Ste 200 (94598-2520)
PHONE..............................925 296-7150
Anton C Pogany, *Dir*
EMP: 80 EST: 1985
SQ FT: 4,500
SALES (est): 17.12MM
SALES (corp-wide): 17.12MM **Privately Held**
Web: www.bicrad.com
SIC: **8011** Radiologist

(P-14626)
BAY MEDICAL MANAGEMENT LLC
2125 Oak Grove Rd Ste 200 (94598-2520)
PHONE..............................925 296-7150
Mary Gerard, *Managing Member*
Barry Engelstad, *Managing Member*
EMP: 160 EST: 1992
SALES (est): 45.59MM **Privately Held**
Web: www.bicrad.com
SIC: **8011** Radiologist

(P-14627)
BAY VALLEY MEDICAL GROUP INC (PA)
319 Diablo Rd Ste 105 (94526-3428)
PHONE..............................510 785-5000
Shelley A Horwitz, *CEO*
Roland J Wong, *
Juliana Wong, *
Misha Roitshteyn, *
Eric S Kohleriter, *
EMP: 93 EST: 1954
SALES (est): 12.72MM
SALES (corp-wide): 12.72MM **Privately Held**
Web: www.stanfordhealthcare.org
SIC: **8011** Physicians' office, including specialists

(P-14628)
BAYSPORT INC
Also Called: Baysport Physical Therapy
200 Redwood Shores Pkwy (94065-1100)
PHONE..............................650 593-2800
EMP: 157
Web: www.baysport.com
SIC: **8011** **8741** Sports medicine specialist, physician; Management services
PA: Baysport, Inc.
14830 Los Gatos Blvd # 101
Los Gatos CA

(P-14629)
BEAVER MEDICAL CLINIC INC (PA)
1615 Orange Tree Ln (92374-2804)
P.O. Box 10069 (92423-0069)
PHONE..............................909 793-3311
Robert Klein, *Pr*
EMP: 190 EST: 1945
SQ FT: 79,212
SALES (est): 342.5K
SALES (corp-wide): 342.5K **Privately Held**
Web: www.beavermedicalgroup.com
SIC: **8011** Clinic, operated by physicians

(P-14630)
BEAVER MEDICAL GROUP LP (HQ)
Also Called: Beaver Medical Clinic
7000 Boulder Ave (92346-3348)
PHONE..............................909 425-3321
John Goodman, *CEO*
Robert Rentschler, *
James Watson Md, *Ltd Pt*
Robert Bourne Md, *Ltd Pt*
EMP: 155 EST: 1995
SALES (est): 34.46MM **Privately Held**
Web: www.beavermedicalgroup.com
SIC: **8011** General and family practice, physician/surgeon
PA: Epic Management, L.P.
1615 Orange Tree Ln
Redlands CA

(P-14631)
BECKMAN RES INST OF THE CY HOP
1500 Duarte Rd (91010-3012)
PHONE..............................626 359-8111
Michael A Friedman, *CEO*
Harlan Levine, *
Robert Stone, *
Terry Blackwood, *
Ric Magnuson, *
EMP: 250 EST: 1979
SALES (est): 288.28MM
SALES (corp-wide): 334.97MM **Privately Held**
Web: www.cityofhope.org
SIC: **8011** Offices and clinics of medical doctors
PA: City Of Hope
1500 Duarte Rd
Duarte CA
626 256-4673

(P-14632)
BELVILLE ENTERPRISES INC
Also Called: Ron's Pharmacy Services
6225 Nancy Ridge Dr (92121-2245)
PHONE..............................858 652-6960
Ronald W Belville, *CEO*
EMP: 75 EST: 1996
SQ FT: 27,000
SALES (est): 3.94MM **Privately Held**
Web: www.ronspharmacyservices.com
SIC: **8011** **5912** Offices and clinics of medical doctors; Drug stores and proprietary stores

(P-14633)
BORREGO CMNTY HLTH FOUNDATION (PA)
Also Called: Borrego Medical Center
587 Palm Canyon Dr Ste 208 (92004-4000)
P.O. Box 2369 (92004-2369)
PHONE..............................855 436-1234
Isaac Lee, *CRO*
Bruce E Smith, *
Dianna Troncoso, *
EMP: 140 EST: 1990
SQ FT: 8,054
SALES (est): 235.82MM
SALES (corp-wide): 235.82MM **Privately Held**
Web: www.borregohealth.org
SIC: **8011** Offices and clinics of medical doctors

(P-14634)
BORREGO CMNTY HLTH FOUNDATION
1121 E Washington Ave (92025-2214)
PHONE..............................760 466-1080
EMP: 139
SALES (corp-wide): 235.82MM **Privately Held**
Web: www.borregohealth.org
SIC: **8011** Clinic, operated by physicians
PA: Borrego Community Health Foundation
587 Palm Canyon Dr # 208
Borrego Springs CA
855 436-1234

(P-14635)
BORREGO CMNTY HLTH FOUNDATION
Also Called: Borrego Health
651 N State St Ste 5 (92583-6574)
PHONE..............................951 487-8506
Michael D Dew, *Brnch Mgr*
EMP: 140
SALES (corp-wide): 235.82MM **Privately Held**

8011 - Offices And Clinics Of Medical Doctors (P-14636)

Web: www.borregohealth.org
SIC: 8011 Clinic, operated by physicians
PA: Borrego Community Health Foundation
587 Palm Canyon Dr # 208
Borrego Springs CA
855 436-1234

(P-14636)
BORREGO CMNTY HLTH FOUNDATION
11750 Cholla Dr Ste B (92240-3066)
PHONE..............................760 251-0044
EMP: 140
SALES (corp-wide): 235.82MM Privately Held
Web: www.borregohealth.org
SIC: 8011 Clinic, operated by physicians
PA: Borrego Community Health Foundation
587 Palm Canyon Dr # 208
Borrego Springs CA
855 436-1234

(P-14637)
BRETT V CRTIS MD A PROF CORP I
Also Called: Medical Center of Marin
101 Casa Buena Dr (94925-1762)
PHONE..............................415 924-4525
Brett V Curtis, CEO
Brett Cuirtis Md, CEO
Warren L Cipa D.c., COO
EMP: 71 EST: 1981
SQ FT: 2,400
SALES (est): 5.07MM Privately Held
Web: www.mcomarin.com
SIC: 8011 Specialized medical practitioners, except internal

(P-14638)
BRIGHT HEALTH PHYSICIANS (PA)
15725 Whittier Blvd Ste 500 (90603-2350)
PHONE..............................562 947-8478
William H Stimmler Md, Ch Bd
Keith Miyamoto Md, VP
Berent Gray Md, Sec
EMP: 140 EST: 1991
SQ FT: 50,000
SALES (est): 38.79MM Privately Held
Web: www.pihhealth.org
SIC: 8011 Physicians' office, including specialists

(P-14639)
BROWN & TOLAND MEDICAL GROUP
Also Called: BROWN & TOLAND MEDICAL GROUP INC
2100 Webster St Ste 117 (94115-2374)
PHONE..............................415 923-3015
Carol Louie, Off Mgr
EMP: 120
SALES (corp-wide): 8.08B Privately Held
Web: www.brownandtoland.com
SIC: 8011 Orthopedic physician
HQ: Brown & Toland Physician Services Organization, Inc.
1221 Broadway Ste 700
Oakland CA
415 972-4162

(P-14640)
BROWN & TOLAND MEDICAL GROUP
Also Called: BROWN & TOLAND MEDICAL GROUP INC
3905 Sacramento St Ste 301 (94118-1636)
PHONE..............................415 752-8038
EMP: 120
SALES (corp-wide): 8.08B Privately Held
Web: www.brownandtoland.com
SIC: 8011 Physicians' office, including specialists
HQ: Brown & Toland Physician Services Organization, Inc.
1221 Broadway Ste 700
Oakland CA
415 972-4162

(P-14641)
BROWN TLAND PHYSCN SVCS ORGNZT (DH)
1221 Broadway Ste 700 (94612-1898)
P.O. Box 72710 (94612-8910)
PHONE..............................415 972-4162
Kelly Robison, CEO
EMP: 240 EST: 1997
SQ FT: 8,000
SALES (est): 98.57MM
SALES (corp-wide): 8.08B Privately Held
Web: www.brownandtoland.com
SIC: 8011 Medical centers
HQ: Altais Clinical Services
601 12th St Fl 16
Oakland CA
510 607-4000

(P-14642)
CABRILLO CRDOLGY MED GROUP INC
2241 Wankel Way Ste C (93030-0191)
PHONE..............................805 983-0922
David Schmidt Md, Pr
David E Schmidt, *
Richard Rothchild Md, Treas
Scott Zager, *
Esam Obed, *
EMP: 81 EST: 1971
SALES (est): 9.22MM Privately Held
SIC: 8011 Cardiologist and cardio-vascular specialist

(P-14643)
CALIFORNIA DEPT OF PUB HLTH
Also Called: Genetic Dsase Screening Program
850 Marina Bay Pkwy F175 (94804-6403)
PHONE..............................510 231-7408
James Harmon, Brnch Mgr
EMP: 412
SALES (corp-wide): 534.4MM Privately Held
Web: cdph.ca.gov
SIC: 8011 9431 Offices and clinics of medical doctors; Administration of public health programs
HQ: The California Department Of Public Health
1615 Capitol Ave
Sacramento CA
916 558-1784

(P-14644)
CALIFORNIA EYE INSTITUTE
1360 E Herndon Ave Ste 230 (93720)
PHONE..............................559 449-5000
Kathy Ploszaj, Admn
Gary R Fogg Md, Stockholder
Andrew Maxwell Md, Stockholder
EMP: 180 EST: 1984
SQ FT: 59,000
SALES (est): 1.5K Privately Held
Web: www.caleyeinstitute.com
SIC: 8011 Opthalmologist

(P-14645)
CALIFORNIA SCHOOLS VEBA
1843 Hotel Cir S (92108-3320)
PHONE..............................888 276-0250
George Mcgregor, Managing Member
EMP: 60 EST: 2019
SALES (est): 500K Privately Held
Web: www.vebaonline.com
SIC: 8011 Health maintenance organization

(P-14646)
CALIFORNIA SKIN INSTITUTE
603 S Knickerbocker Dr (94087-1034)
PHONE..............................408 736-0441
Greg S Morganroth Md, Prin
EMP: 78
SALES (corp-wide): 18.97MM Privately Held
Web: www.californiaskininstitute.com
SIC: 8011 7231 Dermatologist; Cosmetology and personal hygiene salons
PA: California Skin Institute
6399 San Ignacio Ave
San Jose CA
650 969-5600

(P-14647)
CALIFORNIA SKIN INSTITUTE
20400 Lake Chabot Rd Ste 202 (94546-5311)
PHONE..............................510 881-7822
EMP: 78
SALES (corp-wide): 18.97MM Privately Held
Web: www.californiaskininstitute.com
SIC: 8011 Dermatologist
PA: California Skin Institute
6399 San Ignacio Ave
San Jose CA
650 969-5600

(P-14648)
CALIFRNIA CNCER CARE A MED GRO
1350 S Eliseo Dr Ste 200 (94904-2018)
PHONE..............................415 925-5000
Kent Adler, Pr
Myron Turbow, Pr
EMP: 64 EST: 1978
SQ FT: 5,000
SALES (est): 9.44MM Privately Held
SIC: 8011 Oncologist

(P-14649)
CAMARENA HEALTH (PA)
344 E 6th St (93638-3631)
P.O. Box 299 (93639-0299)
PHONE..............................559 664-4000
Paulo A Soares, CEO
EMP: 73 EST: 1980
SQ FT: 25,311
SALES (est): 64.44MM
SALES (corp-wide): 64.44MM Privately Held
Web: www.camarenahealth.org
SIC: 8011 Health maintenance organization

(P-14650)
CANCER CENTER OF SANTA BARBARA
Also Called: THE CANCER CENTER OF SANTA BARBARA
2410 Fletcher Ave Ste 104 (93105-4875)
PHONE..............................805 898-2182
EMP: 76
SALES (corp-wide): 7.3MM Privately Held
Web: cancer.ridleytreecc.com
SIC: 8011 Clinic, operated by physicians
PA: Cancer Foundation Of Santa Barbara
300 W Pueblo St
Santa Barbara CA
805 682-7300

(P-14651)
CAPITAL EYE MEDICAL GROUP
6620 Coyle Ave Ste 408 (95608-6338)
P.O. Box 279 (95661-0279)
PHONE..............................916 241-9378
Mitra Ayazifar, Pr
EMP: 131 EST: 2011
SALES (est): 2.3MM
SALES (corp-wide): 110.02MM Privately Held
Web: www.capeyemed.com
SIC: 8011 Surgeon
PA: Nvision Laser Eye Centers Inc.
75 Enterprise Ste 200
Aliso Viejo CA
877 455-9942

(P-14652)
CARBON HEALTH TECHNOLOGIES INC
500 First St (93446-3742)
PHONE..............................805 226-4222
EMP: 101
SALES (corp-wide): 104.49MM Privately Held
Web: www.carbonhealth.com
SIC: 8011 Freestanding emergency medical center
PA: Carbon Health Technologies, Inc.
2100 Franklin St Ste 355
Oakland CA
415 223-2858

(P-14653)
CARBON HEALTH TECHNOLOGIES INC
500 E Remington Dr Ste 20 (94087-2612)
PHONE..............................650 318-3384
Inna Yaskin, Prin
EMP: 101
SALES (corp-wide): 104.49MM Privately Held
Web: www.carbonhealth.com
SIC: 8011 Primary care medical clinic
PA: Carbon Health Technologies, Inc.
2100 Franklin St Ste 355
Oakland CA
415 223-2858

(P-14654)
CARBON HEALTH TECHNOLOGIES INC
1421 W Macarthur Blvd Ste E (92704-7318)
PHONE..............................714 710-3030
Tom Long Le, Prin
EMP: 101
SALES (corp-wide): 104.49MM Privately Held
Web: www.carbonhealth.com
SIC: 8011 Physicians' office, including specialists
PA: Carbon Health Technologies, Inc.
2100 Franklin St Ste 355
Oakland CA
415 223-2858

(P-14655)
CARDIO VASCULAR ASSOCIATES
Also Called: Heart Group, The
1313 E Herndon Ave Ste 203 (93720-3306)
PHONE..............................559 439-6808
Robert Chambers Md, Pt
Delpinder Sandhu Md, Pt
John Telles, Pt
Dale Merrill, Pt
James Lee, Pt
EMP: 80 EST: 1994

PRODUCTS & SERVICES SECTION

8011 - Offices And Clinics Of Medical Doctors (P-14676)

SALES (est): 11.12MM **Privately Held**
SIC: **8011** Cardiologist and cardio-vascular specialist

(P-14656)
CARDIONET INC
Also Called: CARDIONET, INC.
750 B St Ste 1400 (92101-8190)
PHONE.................................619 243-7500
Jim Sweeney, *Prin*
EMP: 88
SALES (corp-wide): 133.64MM **Privately Held**
Web: www.gobio.com
SIC: **8011** Cardiologist and cardio-vascular specialist
HQ: Cardionet, Llc
  1000 Cedar Hollow Rd # 10
  Malvern PA
  610 729-7000

(P-14657)
CARDIOVASCULAR CONSULTANTS HEA
1207 E Herndon Ave (93720-3235)
PHONE.................................559 432-4303
Kevin J Boran, *Pr*
Donald Gregory Md, *Sec*
William Edward Hanks Md, *Treas*
EMP: 67 EST: 1980
SQ FT: 17,000
SALES (est): 11.57MM **Privately Held**
Web: www.cvcfresno.com
SIC: **8011** Cardiologist and cardio-vascular specialist

(P-14658)
CAREONSITE INC
1805 Arnold Dr (94553-4182)
PHONE.................................562 437-0381
EMP: 500
SALES (corp-wide): 50MM **Privately Held**
Web: www.tangandcompany.com
SIC: **8011** Occupational and industrial specialist, physician/surgeon
PA: Careonsite, Inc.
  20300 S Vermont Ave # 265
  Torrance CA
  562 437-0831

(P-14659)
CARES COMMUNITY HEALTH
Also Called: Pharmacy At Cares, The
1500 21st St (95811-5216)
PHONE.................................916 443-3299
Christy Ward, *CEO*
Bob Styron, *
Mark Thomas, *
Kathleen Marshall, *
Richard Soohoo, *
EMP: 105 EST: 1989
SALES (est): 22.63MM **Privately Held**
Web: www.onecommunityhealth.com
SIC: **8011** 8299 Offices and clinics of medical doctors; Educational services

(P-14660)
CB TANG MD INCORPORATED
Also Called: Long Beach Medical Clinic
1250 Pacific Ave (90813-3026)
PHONE.................................562 437-0831
EMP: 96
Web: www.tangandcompany.com
SIC: **8011** Occupational and industrial specialist, physician/surgeon

(P-14661)
CC CO HEALTH CNTR INFORMATION
Also Called: Pittsburgh Health Center
2311 Loveridge Rd (94565-5117)
P.O. Box 2523 (94553-0317)
PHONE.................................925 431-2300
Waynette Mason, *Genl Mgr*
EMP: 143 EST: 2002
SALES (est): 8.67MM **Privately Held**
Web: www.cchealth.org
SIC: **8011** Offices and clinics of medical doctors

(P-14662)
CEDARS-SINAI MEDICAL CENTER
Also Called: Cardiac Noninvasive Laboratory
127 S San Vicente Blvd Rm 3417 (90048-3311)
PHONE.................................310 423-3849
Timothy Henry, *Dir*
EMP: 346
SALES (corp-wide): 4.7B **Privately Held**
Web: www.cedars-sinai.org
SIC: **8011** Cardiologist and cardio-vascular specialist
PA: Cedars-Sinai Medical Center
  8700 Beverly Blvd
  West Hollywood CA
  310 423-3277

(P-14663)
CEDARS-SINAI MEDICAL CENTER
8631 W 3rd St # 800-E (90048-5901)
PHONE.................................310 423-7900
Carla Wesley, *Brnch Mgr*
EMP: 80
SALES (corp-wide): 4.7B **Privately Held**
Web: www.cedars-sinai.org
SIC: **8011** Neurologist
PA: Cedars-Sinai Medical Center
  8700 Beverly Blvd
  West Hollywood CA
  310 423-3277

(P-14664)
CEDARS-SINAI MEDICAL CENTER
Also Called: Radiation Onclogy - Cdrs-Snai
8720 Beverly Blvd Lower Level Ste Ac1010 (90048)
PHONE.................................310 423-4208
Palmer Burnison Hakami, *Prin*
EMP: 80
SALES (corp-wide): 4.7B **Privately Held**
Web: www.cedars-sinai.org
SIC: **8011** Physicians' office, including specialists
PA: Cedars-Sinai Medical Center
  8700 Beverly Blvd
  West Hollywood CA
  310 423-3277

(P-14665)
CENTRAL ANSTHSIA SVC EXCH MED
Also Called: Case Medical Group
3315 Watt Ave (95821-3600)
P.O. Box 660910 (95866-0910)
PHONE.................................916 481-6800
David Downs Md, *Pr*
EMP: 80 EST: 1986
SALES (est): 11.19MM **Privately Held**
Web: www.casemedgroup.com
SIC: **8011** Group health association

(P-14666)
CENTRAL CAL EAR NOSE THROAT ME
Also Called: Physicians Hearing Services

1351 E Spruce Ave (93720-3342)
PHONE.................................559 432-3724
Marvin Beil Md, *Pt*
Richard Weinberg Md, *Pt*
Brent Lanier Md, *Pt*
Allan Evans Md, *Pt*
Jerry Moore Md, *Pt*
EMP: 66 EST: 1977
SQ FT: 24,000
SALES (est): 22.83MM **Privately Held**
Web: www.ccent.com
SIC: **8011** 8049 5999 Eyes, ears, nose, and throat specialist: physician/surgeon; Audiologist; Hearing aids

(P-14667)
CENTRAL CAL FCLTY MED GROUP IN
Also Called: University Surgical Associates
2335 E Kashian Ln Ste 220 (93701-2211)
PHONE.................................559 435-6600
Jenny Eastman, *Brnch Mgr*
EMP: 83
SALES (corp-wide): 54.75MM **Privately Held**
Web: www.universitymds.com
SIC: **8011** Internal medicine, physician/surgeon
PA: Central California Faculty Medical Group, Inc.
  2625 E Divisadero St
  Fresno CA
  559 453-5200

(P-14668)
CENTRAL CAL FCLTY MED GROUP IN
Also Called: Pulmonary Sleep Disorders Ctr
6311 N Fresno St (93710-5290)
PHONE.................................559 435-4700
Lois Ceja, *Mgr*
EMP: 97
SALES (corp-wide): 54.75MM **Privately Held**
Web: www.universitymds.com
SIC: **8011** Pulmonary specialist, physician/surgeon
PA: Central California Faculty Medical Group, Inc.
  2625 E Divisadero St
  Fresno CA
  559 453-5200

(P-14669)
CENTRAL CAL FCLTY MED GROUP IN (PA)
Also Called: Medical Group
2625 E Divisadero St (93721-1431)
PHONE.................................559 453-5200
Karl Van Gundy, *CEO*
Karl Van Gundy, *Pr*
Gene W Kallsen, *Vice Chairman**
Michael Peterson, *
Randall Stern, *
EMP: 100 EST: 1979
SQ FT: 19,053
SALES (est): 54.75MM
SALES (corp-wide): 54.75MM **Privately Held**
Web: www.universitymds.com
SIC: **8011** Medical centers

(P-14670)
CENTRAL CAL FCLTY MED GROUP IN
2828 Fresno St Ste 203 (93721-1306)
PHONE.................................559 320-1090
EMP: 82
SALES (corp-wide): 54.75MM **Privately Held**

Web: www.universitymds.com
SIC: **8011** General and family practice, physician/surgeon
PA: Central California Faculty Medical Group, Inc.
  2625 E Divisadero St
  Fresno CA
  559 453-5200

(P-14671)
CENTRAL CARDIOLOGY MED CLINIC
2901 Sillect Ave Ste 100 (93308-6370)
P.O. Box 1139 (93302-1139)
PHONE.................................661 395-0000
Brijesh Bahmbi, *Pt*
William Nyitray Md, *Pt*
Peter Nalos Md, *Pt*
EMP: 120 EST: 1974
SALES (est): 21.49MM **Privately Held**
Web: www.heart24.com
SIC: **8011** Cardiologist and cardio-vascular specialist

(P-14672)
CENTRAL CAST CRDLGY A MED CORP
Also Called: Zetterlund, Patrik MD
230 San Jose St (93901-3901)
PHONE.................................831 758-2100
Anthony Sintetos Md, *Pr*
EMP: 118 EST: 1993
SQ FT: 5,000
SALES (est): 10.57MM **Privately Held**
SIC: **8011** Surgeon

(P-14673)
CENTRAL VALLEY INDIAN HLTH INC (PA)
2740 Herndon Ave (93611-6813)
PHONE.................................559 299-2578
Chuck Fowler, *Ex Dir*
Gurpal S Bains, *
EMP: 74 EST: 1974
SQ FT: 14,000
SALES (est): 35.87MM
SALES (corp-wide): 35.87MM **Privately Held**
Web: www.cvih.org
SIC: **8011** 8021 8042 8093 Clinic, operated by physicians; Dental clinic; Offices and clinics of optometrists; Substance abuse clinics (outpatient)

(P-14674)
CEP AMERICA - ILLINOIS LLP
2100 Powell St Ste 400 (94608-1872)
PHONE.................................510 350-2777
Philip Piccinini, *Pt*
EMP: 60 EST: 2021
SALES (est): 1.18MM **Privately Held**
SIC: **8011** Physicians' office, including specialists

(P-14675)
CEP AMERICA LLC
Also Called: Vituity
2100 Powell St # 400 (94608-1803)
PHONE.................................510 350-2691
EMP: 90 EST: 2011
SALES (est): 4.1MM **Privately Held**
Web: www.cepamerica.com
SIC: **8011** Offices and clinics of medical doctors

(P-14676)
CHA HEALTH SYSTEMS INC (PA)
Also Called: Cha Renetative Medicine
3731 Wilshire Blvd Ste 850 (90010-2851)

8011 - Offices And Clinics Of Medical Doctors (P-14677)

PHONE..................213 487-3211
Doctor K Cha, *CEO*
Jean Yi, *COO*
Thomas J May, *CAO*
EMP: 1250 **EST:** 2004
SALES (est): 81.88MM **Privately Held**
Web: www.hollywoodpresbyterian.com
SIC: 8011 Clinic, operated by physicians

(P-14677)
CHAPA-DE INDIAN HLTH PRGRAM IN (PA)
11670 Atwood Rd (95603-9522)
PHONE..................530 887-2800
Lisa Davies, *Pr*
Sierk Haitsma, *
EMP: 85 **EST:** 1970
SQ FT: 65,000
SALES (est): 65.02MM
SALES (corp-wide): 65.02MM **Privately Held**
Web: www.chapa-de.org
SIC: 8011 8322 8021 8042 Clinic, operated by physicians; Outreach program; Dentists' office; Offices and clinics of optometrists

(P-14678)
CHATTOPADHYAY RUNI MD
Also Called: Palo Alto Medical Foundation
795 El Camino Real (94301-2302)
PHONE..................650 853-2946
Runi Chattopadhyay, *Prin*
EMP: 79 **EST:** 2007
SALES (est): 4.46MM **Privately Held**
SIC: 8011 General and family practice, physician/surgeon

(P-14679)
CHEN DVID MD DGNSTC MED GROUP
Also Called: Diagnostic Medical Group
208 N Garfield Ave (91754-1705)
PHONE..................626 288-8029
Anthony Tsun, *CEO*
EMP: 76
Web: www.airqualityremediation.com
SIC: 8011 Radiologist
PA: Chen, David Md Diagnostic Medical Group Inc
1129 S San Gabriel Blvd
San Gabriel CA

(P-14680)
CHILDRENS CLNIC SRVING CHLDREN
701 E 28th St Ste 200 (90806-2784)
PHONE..................562 264-4638
Elisa A Nicholas, *Ex Dir*
Maria Y Chandler, *
Jina Lee Lawler, *
Knut P Thune, *
Albert P Ocampo, *
EMP: 320 **EST:** 1939
SQ FT: 24,000
SALES (est): 50.37MM **Privately Held**
Web: www.thechildrensclinic.org
SIC: 8011 Clinic, operated by physicians

(P-14681)
CHILDRENS HEALTHCARE CAL
Also Called: Pediatric Cancer Research
455 S Main St (92868-3835)
P.O. Box 5700 (92863-5700)
PHONE..................714 997-3000
Kimberly Crite, *CEO*
EMP: 300
Web: www.choc.org
SIC: 8011 Pediatrician
PA: Children's Healthcare Of California
1201 W La Veta Ave
Orange CA

(P-14682)
CHILDRENS ONCOLOGY GROUP
800 Royal Oaks Dr Ste 101 (91016-6364)
PHONE..................626 447-0064
Joseph Woelkers, *CEO*
EMP: 119 **EST:** 2013
SALES (est): 2.96MM **Privately Held**
Web: www.childrensoncologygroup.org
SIC: 8011 Oncologist

(P-14683)
CHILDRENS SPCLSTS OF SAN DEGO (PA)
Also Called: Childrens Associated Med Group
3020 Childrens Way (92123-4223)
PHONE..................858 576-1700
Michael Segall Md, *Pr*
Robin Steinhorn, *
EMP: 350 **EST:** 1978
SALES (est): 17.87MM
SALES (corp-wide): 17.87MM **Privately Held**
Web: www.rchsd.org
SIC: 8011 Physicians' office, including specialists

(P-14684)
CHINO MEDICAL GROUP INC
5475 Walnut Ave (91710-2699)
PHONE..................909 591-6446
J Alex Lira Md, *Pr*
Fidel F Pinzon Md, *VP*
Jeffrey R Unger Md, *VP*
Steven Pulverman, *
EMP: 100 **EST:** 1977
SQ FT: 36,000
SALES (est): 9.87MM **Privately Held**
Web: www.myfamilymg.com
SIC: 8011 8031 Clinic, operated by physicians; Offices and clinics of osteopathic physicians

(P-14685)
CHME INC
780 Montague Expy Ste 704 (95131-1321)
PHONE..................650 931-8713
EMP: 64
SALES (corp-wide): 6.79MM **Privately Held**
Web: www.chme.org
SIC: 8011 Offices and clinics of medical doctors
PA: Chme, Inc.
180 N Pennsylvania Ave
Glendora CA

(P-14686)
CIRRUS HEALTH II LP
Also Called: Laguna Hills Surgery Center
24331 El Toro Rd Ste 150 (92637-8818)
PHONE..................949 855-0562
Kim Wood, *Prin*
EMP: 113
SALES (corp-wide): 22.62MM **Privately Held**
SIC: 8011 Clinic, operated by physicians
PA: Cirrus Health Ii, L.P.
2800 E Highway 114 # 300
Trophy Club TX
214 217-0100

(P-14687)
CITY OF HOPE
Also Called: City of Hope Medical Group
209 Fair Oaks Ave (91030-1814)
PHONE..................626 396-2900
Melinda Lane, *Dir*
EMP: 106
SALES (corp-wide): 334.97MM **Privately Held**
Web: www.cityofhope.org
SIC: 8011 Medical centers
PA: City Of Hope
1500 Duarte Rd
Duarte CA
626 256-4673

(P-14688)
CLINIC INC
Also Called: TO HELP EVERYONE HEALTH AND WE
3834 S Western Ave (90062-1104)
PHONE..................323 730-1920
Jamesina E Henderson, *Ex Dir*
EMP: 85 **EST:** 1974
SQ FT: 26,000
SALES (est): 18.5MM **Privately Held**
Web: www.tohelpeveryone.org
SIC: 8011 Clinic, operated by physicians

(P-14689)
CLINICA SIERRA VISTA (PA)
Also Called: KERN RIVER HEALTH CENTER
1430 Truxtun Ave Ste 400 (93301-5216)
P.O. Box 1559 (93302-1559)
PHONE..................661 635-3050
Stacy Ferreira, *CEO*
Stacy Ferreira, *Chief Human Resource Officer*
Matthew Clark, *
EMP: 90 **EST:** 1971
SQ FT: 14,599
SALES (est): 165.74MM
SALES (corp-wide): 165.74MM **Privately Held**
Web: www.clinicasierravista.org
SIC: 8011 Clinic, operated by physicians

(P-14690)
CLINICA SIERRA VISTA
Also Called: Clinica Srra Vsta Adult Mntal
8787 Hall Rd (93241-1953)
P.O. Box 457 (93241-0457)
PHONE..................661 845-3717
Mercedes Macias, *Brnch Mgr*
EMP: 86
SALES (corp-wide): 165.74MM **Privately Held**
Web: www.clinicasierravista.org
SIC: 8011 Clinic, operated by physicians
PA: Clinica Sierra Vista
1430 Truxtun Ave Ste 400
Bakersfield CA
661 635-3050

(P-14691)
CLINICAS DE SLUD DEL PEBLO INC (PA)
Also Called: Innercare
852 E Danenberg Dr (92243-8517)
P.O. Box 1279 (92227-1279)
PHONE..................760 344-9951
Yvonne Bell, *CEO*
Gloria Santillan, *
EMP: 62 **EST:** 1970
SQ FT: 15,251
SALES (est): 80.86MM
SALES (corp-wide): 80.86MM **Privately Held**
Web: www.innercare.org
SIC: 8011 8049 Clinic, operated by physicians; Nutrition specialist

(P-14692)
CNS INC
5215 Ashe Rd (93313-2069)
PHONE..................661 872-3408
Dennis R Hays, *Prin*
EMP: 92 **EST:** 2009
SALES (est): 4.72MM **Privately Held**
Web: www.neuroskills.com
SIC: 8011 Internal medicine, physician/surgeon

(P-14693)
COASTAL RDTION ONCLOGY MED GRO
1240 S Westlake Blvd Ste 103 (91361-1929)
PHONE..................805 494-4483
Kimberly Commins, *Dir*
Lauren Lovett, *Dir*
EMP: 99 **EST:** 2018
SALES (est): 2.15MM **Privately Held**
SIC: 8011 Oncologist

(P-14694)
COLUSA INDIAN CMNTY COUNCIL
3720 State Highway 45 (95932-4027)
PHONE..................530 458-5787
EMP: 72
Web: www.syix.com
SIC: 8011 Medical centers
PA: Colusa Indian Community Council
3730 State Highway 45 B
Colusa CA

(P-14695)
COLUSA INDIAN CMNTY COUNCIL
3710 State Highway 45 Ste A (95932-4026)
PHONE..................530 458-5501
Mark Burg, *Admn*
EMP: 185
Web: www.syix.com
SIC: 8011 Medical centers
PA: Colusa Indian Community Council
3730 State Highway 45 B
Colusa CA

(P-14696)
COMMUNICARE HEALTH CENTERS (PA)
2051 John Jones Rd (95616-9701)
P.O. Box 1260 (95617-1260)
PHONE..................530 758-2060
Melissa Marshall, *CEO*
Carolina Apicella, *
EMP: 98 **EST:** 1973
SALES (est): 40.98MM
SALES (corp-wide): 40.98MM **Privately Held**
Web: www.communicarehc.org
SIC: 8011 Clinic, operated by physicians

(P-14697)
COMMUNICARE HEALTH CENTERS
215 W Beamer St (95695-2510)
PHONE..................530 753-3498
EMP: 124
SALES (corp-wide): 40.98MM **Privately Held**
Web: www.communicarehc.org
SIC: 8011 Clinic, operated by physicians
PA: Communicare Health Centers
2051 John Jones Rd
Davis CA
530 758-2060

(P-14698)
COMMUNICARE HEALTH CENTERS
Also Called: John H Jones Community Clinic

PRODUCTS & SERVICES SECTION
8011 - Offices And Clinics Of Medical Doctors (P-14720)

2051 John Jones Rd (95616-9701)
PHONE..................530 758-2060
EMP: 71
SALES (corp-wide): 40.98MM Privately Held
Web: www.communicarehc.org
SIC: 8011 Clinic, operated by physicians
PA: Communicare Health Centers
2051 John Jones Rd
Davis CA
530 758-2060

(P-14699)
COMMUNICARE HEALTH CENTERS
Also Called: Davis Cmmnity Clnic Dntl Prgra
2040 Sutter Pl (95616-6201)
PHONE..................530 758-2060
EMP: 100
SALES (corp-wide): 40.98MM Privately Held
Web: www.communicarehc.org
SIC: 8011 Clinic, operated by physicians
PA: Communicare Health Centers
2051 John Jones Rd
Davis CA
530 758-2060

(P-14700)
COMMUNITY HEALTH GROUP
2420 Fenton St Ste 100 (91914-3516)
PHONE..................800 224-7766
Norma A Diaz, CEO
William Rice, *
EMP: 140 EST: 1982
SQ FT: 26,000
SALES (est): 59.17MM Privately Held
Web: www.chgsd.com
SIC: 8011 Health maintenance organization

(P-14701)
COMMUNITY HEALTH SYSTEMS INC
Also Called: MORENO VALLEY FAMILY HEALTH CE
21801 Alessandro Blvd (92553-8202)
PHONE..................951 571-2300
Lori Holeman, CEO
Yolanda Gomez, *
EMP: 130 EST: 1984
SALES (est): 40.4MM Privately Held
Web: www.chsica.org
SIC: 8011 Primary care medical clinic

(P-14702)
COMMUNITY HLTHCARE PARTNER INC
Also Called: COLORADO RIVER MEDICAL CENTER
1401 Bailey Ave (92363-3103)
PHONE..................760 326-4531
Bing Lum, Ex VP
Knaya Tabora, Prin
EMP: 100 EST: 1999
SQ FT: 46,000
SALES (est): 10.4MM Privately Held
Web: www.crmccares.com
SIC: 8011 8062 Clinic, operated by physicians; General medical and surgical hospitals

(P-14703)
COMMUNITY ORTHPD MED GROUP PRT
26401 Crown Valley Pkwy Ste 101 (92691-6302)
PHONE..................949 348-4000
Kent Adamson, Pr
EMP: 76 EST: 1973

SALES (est): 10.74MM Privately Held
Web: www.comg.com
SIC: 8011 Orthopedic physician

(P-14704)
COMMUNITY REGIONAL MEDICAL CTR
1560 E Shaw Ave (93710-8004)
PHONE..................559 459-2415
Myleene Turner, Prin
EMP: 70 EST: 2016
SALES (est): 1.9MM Privately Held
Web: www.universitymds.com
SIC: 8011 Medical centers

(P-14705)
COMMUNITY TRNSTIONAL RESOURCES
1209 Woodrow Ave Ste B10 (95350-1284)
PHONE..................209 529-2200
Doctor Doyle Edson, Ex Dir
EMP: 70 EST: 1980
SQ FT: 10,600
SALES (est): 1.51MM Privately Held
SIC: 8011 Health maintenance organization

(P-14706)
CONTRA CSTA RGONAL MED CTR AUX
2500 Alhambra Ave (94553-3156)
PHONE..................925 370-5000
Jo-ann Lee, CEO
EMP: 275 EST: 1969
SALES (est): 17.4K Privately Held
Web: www.cchealth.org
SIC: 8011 Medical centers

(P-14707)
CORE MED STAFF
3946 Wilshire Blvd (90010-3303)
PHONE..................213 382-5550
Therece Nery, Pr
EMP: 66 EST: 2005
SALES (est): 10.31MM Privately Held
Web: www.core.la
SIC: 8011 General and family practice, physician/surgeon

(P-14708)
CORONA REGIONAL MED CTR LLC
800 S Main St (92882-3420)
PHONE..................951 737-4343
EMP: 219 EST: 2009
SALES (est): 10.7MM Privately Held
SIC: 8011 Medical centers

(P-14709)
COUNTY OF LOS ANGELES
Also Called: Health Services, Dept of
1900 Zonal Ave (90033-1033)
P.O. Box 866001 (90086-6001)
PHONE..................323 226-7131
Linda Guerra, Mgr
EMP: 529
SALES (corp-wide): 31.7B Privately Held
Web: www.lacounty.gov
SIC: 8011 9431 Offices and clinics of medical doctors; Administration of public health programs
PA: County Of Los Angeles
500 W Temple St Ste 437
Los Angeles CA
213 974-1101

(P-14710)
COUNTY OF LOS ANGELES
Also Called: Hudson H Clude Cmplete Hlth Ct

2829 S Grand Ave (90007-3304)
PHONE..................213 744-3919
Michael Mills, Admn
EMP: 82
SALES (corp-wide): 31.7B Privately Held
Web: dhs.lacounty.gov
SIC: 8011 9431 8093 Medical centers; Administration of public health programs; Specialty outpatient clinics, nec
PA: County Of Los Angeles
500 W Temple St Ste 437
Los Angeles CA
213 974-1101

(P-14711)
COUNTY OF LOS ANGELES
Also Called: Health Services, Dept of
15930 Central Ave Ste 100 (91744-5410)
PHONE..................626 968-3711
Mary Anne Moreno, Mgr
EMP: 73
SALES (corp-wide): 31.7B Privately Held
Web: www.lacounty.gov
SIC: 8011 9431 Medical centers; Administration of public health programs
PA: County Of Los Angeles
500 W Temple St Ste 437
Los Angeles CA
213 974-1101

(P-14712)
COUNTY OF LOS ANGELES
Also Called: Health Services, Dept of
10005 Flower St (90706)
PHONE..................562 804-8111
Earnst Espinoza, Dir
EMP: 73
SALES (corp-wide): 31.7B Privately Held
Web: www.lacounty.gov
SIC: 8011 9431 Medical centers; Administration of public health programs
PA: County Of Los Angeles
500 W Temple St Ste 437
Los Angeles CA
213 974-1101

(P-14713)
COUNTY OF LOS ANGELES
Also Called: Health Services, Dept of
150 N Azusa Ave (91702-3521)
PHONE..................626 969-7885
Carmelida Ruffles, Mgr
EMP: 63
SALES (corp-wide): 31.7B Privately Held
Web: www.lacounty.gov
SIC: 8011 9431 Clinic, operated by physicians; Administration of public health programs
PA: County Of Los Angeles
500 W Temple St Ste 437
Los Angeles CA
213 974-1101

(P-14714)
COUNTY OF RIVERSIDE
Also Called: Public Social Services
26520 Cactus Ave (92555-3927)
PHONE..................951 486-4000
Donna Matney, Admn
EMP: 552
SALES (corp-wide): 4.58B Privately Held
Web: www.countyofriverside.us
SIC: 8011 9431 Medical centers; Mental health agency administration, government
PA: County Of Riverside
4080 Lemon St Fl 11
Riverside CA
951 955-1110

(P-14715)
COUNTY OF RIVERSIDE
Also Called: Community Health Agency
26520 Cactus Ave (92555-3927)
PHONE..................951 486-4000
TOLL FREE: 800
Jim Watkins, Prin
EMP: 452
SALES (corp-wide): 4.58B Privately Held
Web: www.countyofriverside.us
SIC: 8011 9431 Medical centers; Public health agency administration, government
PA: County Of Riverside
4080 Lemon St Fl 11
Riverside CA
951 955-1110

(P-14716)
COUNTY OF RIVERSIDE
Also Called: Rubidoux Family Care Center
5256 Mission Blvd (92509-4624)
PHONE..................951 955-0840
Koen Brown, Ex Dir
EMP: 157
SALES (corp-wide): 4.58B Privately Held
Web: www.ruhealth.org
SIC: 8011 Clinic, operated by physicians
PA: County Of Riverside
4080 Lemon St Fl 11
Riverside CA
951 955-1110

(P-14717)
COUNTY OF SAN MATEO
Also Called: San Mateo Medical Center
222 W 39th Ave (94403-4364)
PHONE..................650 208-3480
David Mcgrew, Brnch Mgr
EMP: 1265
Web: www.smchealth.org
SIC: 8011 Clinic, operated by physicians
PA: County Of San Mateo
555 County Ctr Fl 4
Redwood City CA
650 363-4123

(P-14718)
COUNTY OF SAN MATEO
Also Called: Health System
222 W 39th Ave (94403-4364)
PHONE..................650 573-2662
Lynn Marshall, Dir
EMP: 126
Web: www.smchealth.org
SIC: 8011 9431 Psychiatric clinic; Administration of public health programs, County government
PA: County Of San Mateo
555 County Ctr Fl 4
Redwood City CA
650 363-4123

(P-14719)
COUNTY OF SANTA CLARA
751 S Bascom Ave (95128-2604)
PHONE..................408 885-5000
EMP: 888
Web: www.scscourt.org
SIC: 8011 Internal medicine, physician/surgeon
PA: County Of Santa Clara
70 W Hedding St
San Jose CA
408 299-5200

(P-14720)
COVID CLINIC INC
16541 Gothard St (92647-4473)
PHONE..................877 219 8378
Matthew Collins, CEO

8011 - Offices And Clinics Of Medical Doctors (P-14721)

Matthew Abinante, *CFO*
EMP: 340 **EST:** 2020
SALES (est): 198.82MM **Privately Held**
Web: www.covidclinic.org
SIC: 8011 Offices and clinics of medical doctors

(P-14721)
CUROLOGY INC
5717 Pacific Center Blvd Ste 200 (92121)
PHONE..................617 959-2480
EMP: 436
SALES (corp-wide): 49.59MM **Privately Held**
Web: www.curology.com
SIC: 8011 Dermatologist
PA: Curology, Inc
  353 Sacramento St # 2000
  San Francisco CA
  858 859-1188

(P-14722)
DAVITA MAGAN MANAGEMENT INC (DH)
Also Called: M M C
420 W Rowland St (91723-2943)
PHONE..................626 331-6411
Bradley J Rosenberg, *Prin*
Howard Ort Md, *Ex VP*
EMP: 250 **EST:** 1975
SQ FT: 66,000
SALES (est): 54.95MM **Publicly Held**
Web: www.optum.com
SIC: 8011 Clinic, operated by physicians
HQ: Optumcare Management, Llc
  2175 Park Pl
  El Segundo CA

(P-14723)
DELTA RADIOLOGY MEDICAL GROUP
1031 S Fairmont Ave (95240-5165)
PHONE..................209 334-4416
Frank Michael Hartwick, *CEO*
Frank Michael Hartwick, *Pr*
Walter C Tim Md, *Sec*
EMP: 60 **EST:** 1948
SQ FT: 3,420
SALES (est): 4.89MM **Privately Held**
Web: www.deltarad.com
SIC: 8011 Radiologist

(P-14724)
DEPARTMENT OF PUBLIC HEALTH
Also Called: Radiologic Health Branch
1500 Capitol Ave 5 Fl Ms 7610 (92101)
P.O. Box 997414 (92101)
PHONE..................619 338-2493
Michael Dorsey, *Mgr*
EMP: 262
SALES (corp-wide): 534.4MM **Privately Held**
Web: main.sbcounty.gov
SIC: 8011 Radiologist
HQ: Department Of Public Health
  1615 Capitol Ave
  Sacramento CA
  916 449-5560

(P-14725)
DESERT CRDLGY CONS MED GROUP I
Also Called: Desert Cardiology Cons Med G
39000 Bob Hope Dr (92270-3221)
PHONE..................760 346-0642
Keenan F Barber Md, *VP*
Charles W Shaeffer Junior, *Sec*
Merle R Bolton, *

Barry Hackshaw, *
EMP: 141 **EST:** 1974
SALES (est): 11.35MM **Privately Held**
Web: www.desertcard.com
SIC: 8011 Cardiologist and cardio-vascular specialist

(P-14726)
DESERT MEDICAL GROUP INC (PA)
Also Called: Desert Oasis Healthcare
275 N El Cielo Rd Ste D-402 (92262-6972)
PHONE..................760 320-8814
Richard E Merkin Md, *Pr*
EMP: 240 **EST:** 1981
SQ FT: 13,000
SALES (est): 49.93MM
SALES (corp-wide): 49.93MM **Privately Held**
SIC: 8011 General and family practice, physician/surgeon

(P-14727)
DESERT ORTHPD CTR A MED GROUP (PA)
39000 Bob Hope Dr Ste W301 (92270-3221)
PHONE..................760 568-2684
Ronald Lamb Md, *Pr*
Robert Murphy Md, *Ch Bd*
Stephen O'connell Md, *CFO*
Adrian Graff-radford Md, *Sec*
David Friscia, *
EMP: 78 **EST:** 1990
SQ FT: 23,000
SALES (est): 8.99MM **Privately Held**
Web: www.desertortho.com
SIC: 8011 Orthopedic physician

(P-14728)
DESERT VALLEY MED GROUP INC (PA)
Also Called: Desert Valley Medical Group
16850 Bear Valley Rd (92395-5794)
PHONE..................760 241-8000
Prem Reddy Md, *CEO*
Lex Reddy, *
M Mansukhani, *
EMP: 300 **EST:** 1981
SQ FT: 15,000
SALES (est): 49.04MM
SALES (corp-wide): 49.04MM **Privately Held**
Web: www.desertvalleymedicalgroup.com
SIC: 8011 Physicians' office, including specialists

(P-14729)
DEVRON H CHAR MD
Also Called: U C S F Medical Center
45 Castro St Ste 309 (94114-1032)
PHONE..................415 522-0700
Devron H Char Md, *Owner*
EMP: 66 **EST:** 2002
SALES (est): 24.86MM **Privately Held**
Web: www.tumori.org
SIC: 8011 Physicians' office, including specialists

(P-14730)
DIAGNSTIC INTRVNTNAL SRGCAL CT
13160 Mindanao Way Ste 150 (90292-6358)
PHONE..................310 574-0400
Robert S Bray Junior, *Pr*
Keren Reiter, *
EMP: 100 **EST:** 2006

SALES (est): 8MM **Privately Held**
SIC: 8011 Orthopedic physician

(P-14731)
EBSC LP
Also Called: Surgery Center of Health South
3875 Telegraph Ave (94609-2428)
PHONE..................510 547-2244
Judy Rich, *Admn*
EMP: 98 **EST:** 1986
SQ FT: 12,500
SALES (est): 4.25MM **Privately Held**
Web: www.thesurgerycenter.net
SIC: 8011 Surgeon

(P-14732)
EDINGER MEDICAL GROUP INC
Also Called: Willis, Burton F MD
18682 Beach Blvd Ste 150 (92648-2050)
PHONE..................714 965-2500
Burton Willis, *Mgr*
EMP: 61
SALES (corp-wide): 14.55MM **Privately Held**
Web: www.edingermedicalgroup.com
SIC: 8011 General and family practice, physician/surgeon
PA: Edinger Medical Group, Inc.
  9900 Talbert Ave 302
  Fountain Valley CA
  714 965-2500

(P-14733)
EISENHOWER MEDICAL CENTER
Also Called: Eisenhower-Memory-Care-center
34450 Gateway Dr (92211-0843)
PHONE..................760 836-0232
EMP: 206
SALES (corp-wide): 3.81MM **Privately Held**
Web: www.eisenhowerhealth.org
SIC: 8011 Medical centers
PA: Eisenhower Medical Center
  39000 Bob Hope Dr
  Rancho Mirage CA
  760 340-3911

(P-14734)
EISENHOWER MEDICAL CENTER
Also Called: Dessert Cancer Care
57475 29 Palms Hwy Ste 104 (92284-2906)
PHONE..................760 228-9900
EMP: 83
SALES (corp-wide): 3.81MM **Privately Held**
Web: www.eisenhowerhealth.org
SIC: 8011 Medical centers
PA: Eisenhower Medical Center
  39000 Bob Hope Dr
  Rancho Mirage CA
  760 340-3911

(P-14735)
EL CAMINO HOSPITAL DISTRICT RE
2660 Grant Rd (94040-4308)
PHONE..................650 962-4360
EMP: 239
Web: www.elcaminohealthcaredistrict.org
SIC: 8011 Offices and clinics of medical doctors
PA: El Camino Hospital District Retirees Medical Trust
  2500 Grant Rd
  Mountain View CA

(P-14736)
EL DORADO COUNTY HEALTH DEPT
Also Called: County of El Dorado
931 Spring St (95667-4543)
PHONE..................530 621-6100
Lori Walker, *CFO*
EMP: 94 **EST:** 1998
SALES (est): 9.75MM **Privately Held**
Web: www.edcgov.us
SIC: 8011 Primary care medical clinic

(P-14737)
EMANATE HEALTH
Also Called: Emanate Health
1722 Desire Ave Ste 206 (91748-2970)
PHONE..................626 912-5282
EMP: 160
SALES (corp-wide): 515.46MM **Privately Held**
Web: www.emanatehealth.org
SIC: 8011 Physicians' office, including specialists
PA: Emanate Health Medical Center
  1115 S Sunset Ave
  West Covina CA
  626 962-4011

(P-14738)
EMERGENT MEDICAL ASSOCIATES
Also Called: Pacifica Emergency Med Assoc
16237 Ventura Blvd (91436-2201)
PHONE..................818 995-5350
Irv E Edwards, *Prin*
EMP: 81
SALES (corp-wide): 5.59MM **Privately Held**
Web: www.ema.us
SIC: 8011 Medical centers
PA: Emergent Medical Associates
  111 N Sepulveda Blvd # 210
  Manhattan Beach CA
  310 379-2134

(P-14739)
ENCOMPASS FMLY PHYSCANS MED GR
10225 Austin Dr Ste 103 (91978-1521)
PHONE..................619 660-6212
John Dailey, *Ex Dir*
Terry Winegar, *
Joseph Aiello D.o.s., *Treas*
EMP: 60 **EST:** 1991
SQ FT: 700
SALES (est): 3.39MM **Privately Held**
SIC: 8011 General and family practice, physician/surgeon

(P-14740)
ENKI HEALTH AND RES SYSTEMS
Also Called: Enki Health Care
160 S 7th Ave (91746-3211)
PHONE..................626 961-8971
Maria M Carmichael, *Dir*
EMP: 88
SALES (corp-wide): 22.76MM **Privately Held**
Web: www.enkihealth.org
SIC: 8011 8733 Psychiatric clinic; Medical research
PA: Enki Health And Research Systems
  150 E Olive Ave Ste 203
  Burbank CA
  818 973-4899

PRODUCTS & SERVICES SECTION

8011 - Offices And Clinics Of Medical Doctors (P-14762)

(P-14741)
ENLOE CARDIOLOGY SVCS CLINIC
185 E 7th Ave Ste A (95926-3356)
PHONE.................530 332-4400
EMP: 86 EST: 2017
SALES (est): 241.66K **Privately Held**
SIC: **8011** Offices and clinics of medical doctors

(P-14742)
EXER HOLDING COMPANY LLC
15503 Ventura Blvd (91436-3114)
PHONE.................818 287-0894
EMP: 195 EST: 2014
SALES (est): 24.45MM **Privately Held**
Web: www.exerurgentcare.com
SIC: **8011** Clinic, operated by physicians

(P-14743)
EYE CARE INSTITUTE
1017 2nd St (95404-6608)
PHONE.................707 546-9800
Gary A Barth Md, *Pr*
Daniel Barth Md, *Pr*
Bruce Abramson O.d., *VP*
Gary Barth Md, *Sec*
EMP: 61 EST: 1955
SQ FT: 5,000
SALES (est): 2.13MM **Privately Held**
Web: www.see-eci.com
SIC: **8011** Opthalmologist

(P-14744)
EYE Q VISION CARE (PA)
7075 N Sharon Ave (93720-3329)
PHONE.................559 486-2000
Scott Bridgeman, *CEO*
EMP: 175 EST: 2007
SALES (est): 23.67MM **Privately Held**
Web: www.eyeqvc.com
SIC: **8011** 8042 8031 Opthalmologist; Offices and clinics of optometrists; Offices and clinics of osteopathic physicians

(P-14745)
FAMILY HLTH CTRS SAN DIEGO INC
1845 Logan Ave (92113-2111)
PHONE.................619 515-2526
Gracie Duran, *Brnch Mgr*
EMP: 347
SALES (corp-wide): 147.12MM **Privately Held**
Web: www.fhcsd.org
SIC: **8011** Clinic, operated by physicians
PA: Family Health Centers Of San Diego, Inc.
823 Gateway Center Way
San Diego CA
619 515-2303

(P-14746)
FAMILY HLTH CTRS SAN DIEGO INC
2391 Island Ave (92102-2941)
PHONE.................619 515-2435
Martha Barba, *Mgr*
EMP: 348
SALES (corp-wide): 147.12MM **Privately Held**
Web: www.fhcsd.org
SIC: **8011** Clinic, operated by physicians
PA: Family Health Centers Of San Diego, Inc.
823 Gateway Center Way
San Diego CA
619 515-2303

(P-14747)
FAMILY HLTH CTRS SAN DIEGO INC
5379 El Cajon Blvd (92115-4730)
PHONE.................619 515-2400
Tom Murray, *Owner*
EMP: 348
SALES (corp-wide): 147.12MM **Privately Held**
Web: www.fhcsd.org
SIC: **8011** Clinic, operated by physicians
PA: Family Health Centers Of San Diego, Inc.
823 Gateway Center Way
San Diego CA
619 515-2303

(P-14748)
FAMILY HLTH CTRS SAN DIEGO INC
Also Called: Family Health Center San Diego
8788 Jamacha Rd (91977-4035)
PHONE.................619 515-2555
EMP: 348
SQ FT: 10,970
SALES (corp-wide): 147.12MM **Privately Held**
Web: www.fhcsd.org
SIC: **8011** Clinic, operated by physicians
PA: Family Health Centers Of San Diego, Inc.
823 Gateway Center Way
San Diego CA
619 515-2303

(P-14749)
FAMILY HLTH CTRS SAN DIEGO INC
Also Called: Beach Area Family Health Ctr
3705 Mission Blvd (92109-7104)
PHONE.................619 515-2444
Gracie Duram, *Dir*
EMP: 348
SALES (corp-wide): 147.12MM **Privately Held**
Web: www.fhcsd.org
SIC: **8011** Clinic, operated by physicians
PA: Family Health Centers Of San Diego, Inc.
823 Gateway Center Way
San Diego CA
619 515-2303

(P-14750)
FLORENCE WSTN MED CLINIC INC
13500 Van Nuys Blvd (91331-3028)
PHONE.................818 896-2999
EMP: 104
SALES (corp-wide): 914.05K **Privately Held**
Web: www.florencewesternmc.com
SIC: **8011** Clinic, operated by physicians
PA: Florence Western Medical Clinic, Inc.
7301 S Western Ave
Los Angeles CA
323 778-2131

(P-14751)
FOLSOM SURGERY CENTER INC
Also Called: Folsom Outpatient Surgery Ctr
1651 Creekside Dr Ste 100 (95630-3833)
PHONE.................916 673-1990
Guy Guilfoy, *Pr*
Jay Hendrickson, *VP*
Ellie Marek, *Sec*
EMP: 66 EST: 2000
SALES (est): 10.37MM **Privately Held**
Web: www.folsom-sc.com
SIC: **8011** Surgeon

(P-14752)
FOOTHILL HEALTH CENTER INC
Also Called: San Jose Fthill Fmly Cmnty Cln
2670 S White Rd Ste 200 (95148-2073)
PHONE.................408 729-4290
EMP: 170
Web: www.sjffcc.org
SIC: **8011** Primary care medical clinic

(P-14753)
FRED FINCH YOUTH CENTER (PA)
3800 Coolidge Ave (94602-3311)
PHONE.................510 773-6669
EMP: 170 EST: 1891
SALES (est): 33.56MM
SALES (corp-wide): 33.56MM **Privately Held**
Web: www.fredfinch.org
SIC: **8011** 8211 Psychiatric clinic; Private special education school

(P-14754)
FREMONT AMBLTORY SRGERY CTR LP
Also Called: Fremont Surgery Center
39350 Civic Center Dr Ste 350 (94538-2343)
PHONE.................510 456-4600
John Mazoros, *Genl Pt*
EMP: 80 EST: 1986
SQ FT: 19,000
SALES (est): 19.92MM **Privately Held**
Web: www.fremontsurgerycenter.com
SIC: **8011** Surgeon

(P-14755)
FRESNO CMNTY HOSP & MED CTR
Also Called: Clovis Community Medical Ctr
2755 Herndon Ave (93611-6800)
PHONE.................559 324-4000
Phyllis Baltz, *Mgr*
EMP: 95
SQ FT: 36,000
SALES (corp-wide): 2.17B **Privately Held**
Web: www.communitymedical.org
SIC: **8011** Clinic, operated by physicians
HQ: Fresno Community Hospital And Medical Center
2823 Fresno St
Fresno CA

(P-14756)
GARDEN GROVE ADVANCED IMAGING
1510 Cotner Ave (90025-3303)
PHONE.................310 445-2800
EMP: 159 EST: 2015
SALES (est): 9.83MM **Publicly Held**
Web: www.radnet.com
SIC: **8011** Radiologist
HQ: Radnet Management Iii, Inc.
1510 Cotner Ave
Los Angeles CA
310 445-2800

(P-14757)
GARDNER FAMILY HLTH NETWRK INC
Also Called: Wic
3030 Alum Rock Ave (95127-2807)
PHONE.................408 254-5197
Kim Potter, *Dir*
EMP: 140

SALES (corp-wide): 81.8MM **Privately Held**
Web: www.gfhn.org
SIC: **8011** Clinic, operated by physicians
PA: Gardner Family Health Network, Inc.
160 E Virginia St Ste 100
San Jose CA
408 457-7100

(P-14758)
GARDNER FAMILY HLTH NETWRK INC
Also Called: Alviso Health Center
1621 Gold St (95002-3530)
PHONE.................408 457-7100
EMP: 141
SALES (corp-wide): 81.8MM **Privately Held**
Web: www.gardnerhealthservices.org
SIC: **8011** Clinic, operated by physicians
PA: Gardner Family Health Network, Inc.
160 E Virginia St Ste 100
San Jose CA
408 457-7100

(P-14759)
GARFIELD IMAGING CENTER INC
555 N Garfield Ave (91754-1202)
PHONE.................626 572-0912
Clark Gardner Md, *Pr*
EMP: 107 EST: 1980
SQ FT: 3,000
SALES (est): 2.54MM
SALES (corp-wide): 359.96MM **Privately Held**
Web: www.garfieldimaging.com
SIC: **8011** Radiologist
HQ: Insight Health Services Corp.
5775 Wayzata Blvd Ste 400
Minneapolis MN

(P-14760)
GARRISON FAMILY MED GROUP INC
Also Called: Garrison Family Medical Group
41210 11th St W Ste K (93551-1447)
PHONE.................661 947-7100
EMP: 60 EST: 1980
SALES (est): 4.97MM **Privately Held**
Web: www.garrisonfamilymedicalgroup.com
SIC: **8011** General and family practice, physician/surgeon

(P-14761)
GASTROENTEROLOGY DIVISION
Also Called: San Francisco General Hospital
1001 Potrero Ave Ste 1e21 (94110-3518)
PHONE.................415 206-8823
Amy Akbarian, *Admn*
EMP: 101 EST: 1998
SALES (est): 19.81MM **Privately Held**
SIC: **8011** Gastronomist

(P-14762)
GLENDALE EYE MEDICAL GROUP (PA)
Also Called: Amsurg
607 N Central Ave Ste 203 (91203-1845)
PHONE.................818 956-1010
Richard Weise, *Pt*
Stephen Chang, *Pt*
EMP: 63 EST: 1981
SALES (est): 5.77MM
SALES (corp-wide): 5.77MM **Privately Held**
Web: www.glendaleeye.com

8011 - Offices And Clinics Of Medical Doctors (P-14763)

SIC: **8011** Physicians' office, including specialists

(P-14763)
GOLDEN VALLEY HEALTH CENTERS (PA)
737 W Childs Ave (95341-6805)
PHONE.................................209 383-1848
Tony Weber, *CEO*
EMP: 250 EST: 1972
SQ FT: 23,000
SALES (est): 150.33MM
SALES (corp-wide): 150.33MM **Privately Held**
Web: www.gvhc.org
SIC: **8011** Clinic, operated by physicians

(P-14764)
GOLDEN VALLEY HEALTH CENTERS
Also Called: Planada Family Health Center
1910 Customer Care Way (95301-5167)
PHONE.................................209 382-0253
Lina Lua, *Supervisor*
EMP: 82
SALES (corp-wide): 150.33MM **Privately Held**
Web: www.gvhc.org
SIC: **8011** Clinic, operated by physicians
PA: Golden Valley Health Centers
   737 W Childs Ave
   Merced CA
   209 383-1848

(P-14765)
GOOD SAMARITAN HOSPITAL AUX
1225 Wilshire Blvd (90017-1901)
PHONE.................................213 977-2121
Andrew Leeka, *CEO*
EMP: 290 EST: 2001
SALES (est): 44.66K **Privately Held**
SIC: **8011** Medical centers

(P-14766)
GRAYBILL MEDICAL GROUP INC (PA)
225 E 2nd Ave (92025-4249)
PHONE.................................866 228-2236
Floyd Farley, *CEO*
David Borecky, *
Marvin V Beddoe, *
George A Pleitez, *
EMP: 180 EST: 1932
SALES (est): 50MM
SALES (corp-wide): 50MM **Privately Held**
Web: www.graybill.org
SIC: **8011** General and family practice, physician/surgeon

(P-14767)
GRAYBILL MEDICAL GROUP INC
1035 S Main Ave (92028-3338)
PHONE.................................760 728-2777
Brenda Patterson, *Mgr*
EMP: 60
SALES (corp-wide): 50MM **Privately Held**
Web: www.graybill.org
SIC: **8011** General and family practice, physician/surgeon
PA: Graybill Medical Group, Inc.
   225 E 2nd Ave Ste 203
   Escondido CA
   866 228-2236

(P-14768)
GROVE DIAGNSTC IMAGING CTR INC
8805 Haven Ave Ste 120 (91730-5149)
PHONE.................................909 982-8638
Broc Larouche, *Genl Mgr*
EMP: 447
Web: www.radnet.com
SIC: **8011** Radiologist
HQ: Grove Diagnostic Imaging Center, Inc.
   8283 Grove Ave Ste 101
   Rancho Cucamonga CA

(P-14769)
HEALTHSMART PACIFIC INC
Also Called: Health Smart Clinic
2683 Pacific Ave (90806-2610)
PHONE.................................562 595-1911
Mike Drobot, *CEO*
EMP: 294
SALES (corp-wide): 42.31MM **Privately Held**
SIC: **8011** Clinic, operated by physicians
PA: Healthsmart Pacific, Inc.
   5150 E Pacific Cst Hwy # 200
   Long Beach CA
   562 595-1911

(P-14770)
HEALTHTAP INC
Also Called: Docphin
209 E Java Dr Unit 61987 (94088-8020)
PHONE.................................650 268-9806
Bill Gossman, *CEO*
Jay Wohlgemuth, *CHO*
EMP: 66 EST: 2010
SQ FT: 16,000
SALES (est): 1.61MM **Privately Held**
Web: www.healthtap.com
SIC: **8011** 7372 Group health association; Application computer software

(P-14771)
HERALD CHRISTIAN HEALTH CENTER (PA)
3401 Aero Jet Ave (91731-2801)
PHONE.................................626 286-8700
David Lee, *CEO*
Emily Szeto, *
Carolin Eng, *
EMP: 80 EST: 2005
SALES (est): 15.14MM **Privately Held**
Web: www.hchcla.org
SIC: **8011** 8021 Primary care medical clinic; Dental clinics and offices

(P-14772)
HIGH DSERT MED CORP A MED GROU (PA)
Also Called: Heritage Health Care
43839 15th St W (93534-4756)
P.O. Box 7007 (93539-7007)
PHONE.................................661 945-5984
Richard N Merkin, *CEO*
Charles M Lim, *Dir*
Rafael Gonzalez, *Admn*
Don V Parazo, *Dir*
Anthony J Dulgeroff, *Dir*
EMP: 120 EST: 1984
SQ FT: 25,000
SALES (est): 43.89MM
SALES (corp-wide): 43.89MM **Privately Held**
Web: www.hdmg.net
SIC: **8011** Clinic, operated by physicians

(P-14773)
HILL PHYSICIANS MED GROUP INC (PA)
2409 Camino Ramon (94583-4285)
P.O. Box 5080 (94583-0980)
PHONE.................................800 445-5747
David Joyner, *CEO*
Elisabeth H Renner Md, *Prin*
Alvin M Sockolov Md, *Prin*
Gregory Coe Md, *Prin*
EMP: 412 EST: 1984
SQ FT: 36,000
SALES (est): 79.61MM **Privately Held**
Web: www.hillphysicians.com
SIC: **8011** 8031 General and family practice, physician/surgeon; Offices and clinics of osteopathic physicians

(P-14774)
HIV NEURAL BEHAVIORAL CENTER
150 W Washington St (92093-0001)
PHONE.................................619 543-5000
Igor Grant, *Dir*
EMP: 70
SALES (est): 969.6K **Privately Held**
SIC: **8011** Medical centers

(P-14775)
HOUSE EAR CLINIC INC (PA)
Also Called: House Ear
1245 Wilshire Blvd Ste 812 (90017-4808)
P.O. Box 52001 (85072-2001)
PHONE.................................213 483-9930
Derald E Brackmann Md, *Pr*
John W House Md, *Treas*
Antonio De La Cruz Md, *Sec*
EMP: 87 EST: 1969
SALES (est): 11.02MM
SALES (corp-wide): 11.02MM **Privately Held**
Web: www.houseinstitute.com
SIC: **8011** 5999 Ears, nose, and throat specialist: physician/surgeon; Hearing aids

(P-14776)
HUNTINGTON MEDICAL FOUNDATION
10 Congress St Ste 208 (91105-3027)
PHONE.................................626 795-4210
Donna Ellis, *Mgr*
EMP: 91
Web: www.huntingtonhealth.org
SIC: **8011** Internal medicine, physician/surgeon
PA: The Huntington Medical Foundation
   100 W California Blvd
   Pasadena CA

(P-14777)
HUNTINGTON RADIOLOGY
11525 Brookshire Ave # 11 (90241-4985)
PHONE.................................562 904-1111
Eugene Tsimerinov, *Brnch Mgr*
EMP: 73
SIC: **8011** Radiologist
PA: Huntington Radiology
   2679 Zoe Ave
   Huntington Park CA

(P-14778)
HUTCHINS HEALTHCARE INC
27101 Puerta Real Ste 450 (92691-8566)
PHONE.................................949 487-9500
Kevin Reese, *Pr*
Beverly Wittekind, *Sec*
EMP: 83 EST: 2016
SALES (est): 2.49MM
SALES (corp-wide): 3.03B **Publicly Held**
SIC: **8011** Offices and clinics of medical doctors
PA: The Ensign Group Inc
   29222 Rncho Vejo Rd Ste 1
   San Juan Capistrano CA
   949 487-9500

(P-14779)
IGO MEDICAL GROUP A MED CORP (PA)
Also Called: Infertlity Gynclogy Obstetrics
9339 Genesee Ave Ste 220 (92121-2196)
PHONE.................................858 455-7520
Benito Villanueva, *Pr*
Doctor Stephen Herbert, *Physician*
Doctor Dianne Rosenberg, *Physician*
Doctor Philip E Young, *Physician*
Doctor M E Ted Quigley, *Physician*
EMP: 68 EST: 1994
SQ FT: 11,500
SALES (est): 11.73MM
SALES (corp-wide): 11.73MM **Privately Held**
Web: www.igomed.com
SIC: **8011** Gynecologist

(P-14780)
IMAGING HLTHCARE SPCALISTS LLC
6386 Alvarado Ct (92120-4905)
PHONE.................................619 229-2299
EMP: 108
Web: www.imaginghealthcare.com
SIC: **8011** Radiologist
PA: Imaging Healthcare Specialists, Llc
   150 W Washington St
   San Diego CA

(P-14781)
INDIAN HEALTH COUNCIL INC (PA)
50100 Golsh Rd (92082-5338)
P.O. Box 406 (92061-0406)
PHONE.................................760 749-1410
EMP: 96 EST: 1970
SALES (est): 18.68MM **Privately Held**
Web: www.indianhealth.com
SIC: **8011** Clinic, operated by physicians

(P-14782)
INDIAN HLTH CTR SNTA CLARA VLY
1333 Meridian Ave (95125-5212)
PHONE.................................408 445-3400
Sonya M Tetnowski, *CEO*
EMP: 200 EST: 1977
SQ FT: 10,000
SALES (est): 38.53MM **Privately Held**
Web: www.indianhealthcenter.org
SIC: **8011** 8322 Clinic, operated by physicians; Individual and family services

(P-14783)
INDUSTRIAL MEDICAL GROUP
2501 G St (93301-2811)
PHONE.................................661 327-2225
Larry M Cho, *Owner*
EMP: 60 EST: 1984
SQ FT: 4,000
SALES (est): 8.22MM **Privately Held**
Web: industrial-group.edan.io
SIC: **8011** Occupational and industrial specialist, physician/surgeon

(P-14784)
INLAND EYE INST MED GROUP INC (PA)
1900 E Washington St (92324-4698)
P.O. Box 1427 (92324-0836)
PHONE.................................909 825-3425
TOLL FREE: 800
Loren Denler Md, *Pr*

PRODUCTS & SERVICES SECTION
8011 - Offices And Clinics Of Medical Doctors (P-14804)

Wayne B Isaeff, *
Harold P Wallar, *
EMP: 70 **EST:** 1976
SQ FT: 12,500
SALES (est): 9.78MM
SALES (corp-wide): 9.78MM **Privately Held**
Web: www.inlandeye.com
SIC: 8011 Opthalmologist

(P-14785)
INPATIENT CONSULTANTS ALA INC
8511 Fallbrook Ave Ste 120 (91304)
PHONE..................888 447-2362
EMP: 67 **EST:** 2011
SALES (est): 10.07MM
SALES (corp-wide): 3.6B **Privately Held**
SIC: 8011 Physicians' office, including specialists
HQ: Ipc Healthcare, Inc.
4605 Lankershim Blvd # 617
North Hollywood CA
888 447-2362

(P-14786)
INTERNAL REVENUE SERVICE
2469 Arf Ave (94545-4107)
PHONE..................510 576-7589
EMP: 88
Web: www.irs.gov
SIC: 8011 Internal medicine, physician/surgeon
HQ: Internal Revenue Service
1111 Constitution Ave, Nw
Washington DC
202 803-9000

(P-14787)
INTERNAL REVENUE SERVICE
9006 Morganfield Pl (95624-3608)
PHONE..................916 974-5678
EMP: 88
Web: www.irs.gov
SIC: 8011 Internal medicine, physician/surgeon
HQ: Internal Revenue Service
1111 Constitution Ave, Nw
Washington DC
202 803-9000

(P-14788)
IPC HEALTHCARE INC (DH)
4605 Lankershim Blvd Ste 617 (91602-1856)
PHONE..................888 447-2362
Adam D Singer, *CEO*
R Jeffrey Taylor, *Pr*
Richard H Kline Iii, *CFO*
Kerry E Weiner, *CMO*
Richard G Russell, *CDO*
EMP: 173 **EST:** 1995
SALES (est): 408.74MM
SALES (corp-wide): 3.6B **Privately Held**
SIC: 8011 Physicians' office, including specialists
HQ: Team Health Holdings, Inc.
265 Brkview Cntre Way Ste
Knoxville TN
865 693-1000

(P-14789)
KAISER FOUNDATION HOSPITALS
10800 Magnolia Ave (92505-3000)
PHONE..................951 353-7790
Laura Estrada, *Brnch Mgr*
EMP: 85
SALES (corp-wide): 68.1B **Privately Held**
Web: www.kaisercenter.com
SIC: 8011 Offices and clinics of medical doctors
HQ: Kaiser Foundation Hospitals Inc
1 Kaiser Plz
Oakland CA
510 271-6611

(P-14790)
KAISER FOUNDATION HOSPITALS
9521 Dalen St (90242-4847)
PHONE..................817 372-8201
EMP: 70
SALES (corp-wide): 68.1B **Privately Held**
Web: www.kaisercenter.com
SIC: 8011 Offices and clinics of medical doctors
HQ: Kaiser Foundation Hospitals Inc
1 Kaiser Plz
Oakland CA
510 271-6611

(P-14791)
KAISER FOUNDATION HOSPITALS
1550 N Edgemont St (90027-5210)
PHONE..................323 783-7955
EMP: 181
SALES (corp-wide): 68.1B **Privately Held**
Web: www.kaisercenter.com
SIC: 8011 Offices and clinics of medical doctors
HQ: Kaiser Foundation Hospitals Inc
1 Kaiser Plz
Oakland CA
510 271-6611

(P-14792)
KAISER FOUNDATION HOSPITALS
Also Called: La Palma Medical Offices
5 Centerpointe Dr (90623-1050)
PHONE..................714 562-3420
Josefina Guzman-inouye, *Mgr*
EMP: 117
SALES (corp-wide): 68.1B **Privately Held**
Web: www.kaisercenter.com
SIC: 8011 Offices and clinics of medical doctors
HQ: Kaiser Foundation Hospitals Inc
1 Kaiser Plz
Oakland CA
510 271-6611

(P-14793)
KAISER FOUNDATION HOSPITALS
Also Called: Kaiser Prmnnte Antioch Med Ctr
4501 Sand Creek Rd (94531-8687)
PHONE..................925 813-6500
Albert L Carver, *Brnch Mgr*
EMP: 453
SALES (corp-wide): 68.1B **Privately Held**
Web: www.kaisercenter.com
SIC: 8011 Internal medicine practitioners
HQ: Kaiser Foundation Hospitals Inc
1 Kaiser Plz
Oakland CA
510 271-6611

(P-14794)
KAISER FOUNDATION HOSPITALS
13652 Cantara St (91402-5423)
PHONE..................818 375-4023
Andrea D Mason O T R, *Brnch Mgr*
EMP: 166
SALES (corp-wide): 68.1B **Privately Held**
Web: www.kaisercenter.com
SIC: 8011 Internal medicine practitioners
HQ: Kaiser Foundation Hospitals Inc
1 Kaiser Plz
Oakland CA
510 271-6611

(P-14795)
KAISER FOUNDATION HOSPITALS
Also Called: Lakeview Medical Offices
411 N Lakeview Ave (92807-3028)
PHONE..................714 279-4675
Suzie Characky, *Mgr*
EMP: 105
SALES (corp-wide): 68.1B **Privately Held**
Web: www.kaisercenter.com
SIC: 8011 Medical centers
HQ: Kaiser Foundation Hospitals Inc
1 Kaiser Plz
Oakland CA
510 271-6611

(P-14796)
KAISER FOUNDATION HOSPITALS
Also Called: Aliso Viejo Medical Offices
24502 Pacific Park Dr (92656-3033)
PHONE..................949 425-3150
Bruce Sogioka, *Brnch Mgr*
EMP: 70
SALES (corp-wide): 68.1B **Privately Held**
Web: aliso-viejo-air-duct-cleaning.my-free.website
SIC: 8011 Medical centers
HQ: Kaiser Foundation Hospitals Inc
1 Kaiser Plz
Oakland CA
510 271-6611

(P-14797)
KAISER FOUNDATION HOSPITALS
Also Called: Kaiser Prmnnte Snta Rosa Med C
401 Bicentennial Way (95403-2149)
PHONE..................707 393-4000
Susan Janvirin, *Brnch Mgr*
EMP: 2014
SALES (corp-wide): 68.1B **Privately Held**
Web: www.kaisercenter.com
SIC: 8011 Medical centers
HQ: Kaiser Foundation Hospitals Inc
1 Kaiser Plz
Oakland CA
510 271-6611

(P-14798)
KAISER FOUNDATION HOSPITALS
Also Called: Kaiser Permanente
780 Shadowridge Dr (92083-7986)
PHONE..................619 528-5000
TOLL FREE: 800
Leslei Oliver, *Mgr*
EMP: 94
SALES (corp-wide): 68.1B **Privately Held**
Web: www.kaisercenter.com
SIC: 8011 Medical centers
HQ: Kaiser Foundation Hospitals Inc
1 Kaiser Plz
Oakland CA
510 271-6611

(P-14799)
KAISER FOUNDATION HOSPITALS
Also Called: Kaiser Permanente
12100 Euclid St (92840-3304)
PHONE..................714 741-3448
Betty Bohner, *Admn*
EMP: 120
SALES (corp-wide): 68.1B **Privately Held**
Web: www.kaisercenter.com
SIC: 8011 Medical centers
HQ: Kaiser Foundation Hospitals Inc
1 Kaiser Plz
Oakland CA
510 271-6611

(P-14800)
KAISER FOUNDATION HOSPITALS
Also Called: Kaiser Foundation Health Plan
2350 Geary Blvd Fl 2 (94115-3305)
PHONE..................415 833-2616
EMP: 108
SALES (corp-wide): 68.1B **Privately Held**
Web: www.kaisercenter.com
SIC: 8011 Medical centers
HQ: Kaiser Foundation Hospitals Inc
1 Kaiser Plz
Oakland CA
510 271-6611

(P-14801)
KAISER FOUNDATION HOSPITALS
Also Called: Kaiser Permanente
710 S Broadway (94596-5294)
PHONE..................925 295-4145
Vikki Antonelli, *Mgr*
EMP: 76
SALES (corp-wide): 68.1B **Privately Held**
Web: www.kaisercenter.com
SIC: 8011 Medical centers
HQ: Kaiser Foundation Hospitals Inc
1 Kaiser Plz
Oakland CA
510 271-6611

(P-14802)
KAISER FOUNDATION HOSPITALS
Also Called: Oakland Medical Center
3600 Broadway (94611-5730)
P.O. Box 12929 (94604-3010)
PHONE..................510 752-1000
David J Artenburn, *Mgr*
EMP: 2200
SALES (corp-wide): 68.1B **Privately Held**
Web: www.kaisercenter.com
SIC: 8011 8062 Medical centers; General medical and surgical hospitals
HQ: Kaiser Foundation Hospitals Inc
1 Kaiser Plz
Oakland CA
510 271-6611

(P-14803)
KAISER FOUNDATION HOSPITALS
Also Called: Kaiser Permanente San
2425 Geary Blvd (94115-3358)
PHONE..................415 833-2000
Harry Chima, *Brnch Mgr*
EMP: 750
SALES (corp-wide): 68.1B **Privately Held**
Web: www.kaisercenter.com
SIC: 8011 8062 Medical centers; General medical and surgical hospitals
HQ: Kaiser Foundation Hospitals Inc
1 Kaiser Plz
Oakland CA
510 271-6611

(P-14804)
KAISER FOUNDATION HOSPITALS

8011 - Offices And Clinics Of Medical Doctors (P-14805)

PRODUCTS & SERVICES SECTION

Also Called: Kaiser Permanente
2200 Ofarrell St (94115-3357)
PHONE..............................415 833-2200
Dee Marie Munoz, *Prin*
EMP: 283
SQ FT: 14,712
SALES (corp-wide): 68.1B **Privately Held**
Web: www.kaisercenter.com
SIC: 8011 Medical centers
HQ: Kaiser Foundation Hospitals Inc
1 Kaiser Plz
Oakland CA
510 271-6611

(P-14805)
KAISER FOUNDATION HOSPITALS
Also Called: Kaiser Permanente
1301 California St (92374-2910)
PHONE..............................888 750-0036
Cindy Wong, *Dir*
EMP: 126
SALES (corp-wide): 68.1B **Privately Held**
Web: www.kaisercenter.com
SIC: 8011 Medical centers
HQ: Kaiser Foundation Hospitals Inc
1 Kaiser Plz
Oakland CA
510 271-6611

(P-14806)
KAISER FOUNDATION HOSPITALS
Also Called: Kaiser Permanente
1900 E Lambert Rd (92821-4371)
PHONE..............................714 672-5100
David Jeng, *Prin*
EMP: 67
SQ FT: 9,240
SALES (corp-wide): 68.1B **Privately Held**
Web: www.kaisercenter.com
SIC: 8011 Medical centers
HQ: Kaiser Foundation Hospitals Inc
1 Kaiser Plz
Oakland CA
510 271-6611

(P-14807)
KAISER FOUNDATION HOSPITALS
Also Called: Kaiser Permanente
99 Montecillo Rd (94903-3308)
PHONE..............................415 444-2000
Patricia Kendall, *Admn*
EMP: 1500
SALES (corp-wide): 68.1B **Privately Held**
Web: www.kaisercenter.com
SIC: 8011 8062 Medical centers; General medical and surgical hospitals
HQ: Kaiser Foundation Hospitals Inc
1 Kaiser Plz
Oakland CA
510 271-6611

(P-14808)
KAISER FOUNDATION HOSPITALS
Also Called: Kaiser Permanente
901 Nevin Ave (94801-3143)
PHONE..............................510 307-1500
Debbie Vachau, *Mgr*
EMP: 2459
SALES (corp-wide): 68.1B **Privately Held**
Web: www.kaisercenter.com
SIC: 8011 8062 Medical centers; General medical and surgical hospitals
HQ: Kaiser Foundation Hospitals Inc
1 Kaiser Plz
Oakland CA
510 271-6611

(P-14809)
KAISER FOUNDATION HOSPITALS
Also Called: Kaiser Prmnnte W Los Angles Me
6041 Cadillac Ave (90034-1700)
PHONE..............................323 857-2000
Howard Fullman, *Dir*
EMP: 2368
SALES (corp-wide): 68.1B **Privately Held**
Web: www.kaisercenter.com
SIC: 8011 Medical centers
HQ: Kaiser Foundation Hospitals Inc
1 Kaiser Plz
Oakland CA
510 271-6611

(P-14810)
KAISER FOUNDATION HOSPITALS
Also Called: Kaiser Permanente
13651 Willard St (91402)
PHONE..............................818 375-2000
Dev Mahadevan, *Prin*
EMP: 2380
SALES (corp-wide): 68.1B **Privately Held**
Web: www.kaisercenter.com
SIC: 8011 Medical centers
HQ: Kaiser Foundation Hospitals Inc
1 Kaiser Plz
Oakland CA
510 271-6611

(P-14811)
KAISER FOUNDATION HOSPITALS
Also Called: Kaiser Foundation Health Plan
14011 Park Ave (92392-2413)
PHONE..............................888 750-0036
EMP: 70
SALES (corp-wide): 68.1B **Privately Held**
Web: www.kaisercenter.com
SIC: 8011 Medical centers
HQ: Kaiser Foundation Hospitals Inc
1 Kaiser Plz
Oakland CA
510 271-6611

(P-14812)
KAISER FOUNDATION HOSPITALS
Also Called: Carson Medical Offices
18600 S Figueroa St (90248-4505)
PHONE..............................800 780-1230
EMP: 70
SALES (corp-wide): 68.1B **Privately Held**
Web: www.kaisercenter.com
SIC: 8011 Medical centers
HQ: Kaiser Foundation Hospitals Inc
1 Kaiser Plz
Oakland CA
510 271-6611

(P-14813)
KAISER FOUNDATION HOSPITALS
Also Called: Modesto Medical Offices
4601 Dale Rd (95356-9718)
PHONE..............................209 735-5000
EMP: 99
SALES (corp-wide): 68.1B **Privately Held**
Web: www.kaisercenter.com
SIC: 8011 Medical centers
HQ: Kaiser Foundation Hospitals Inc
1 Kaiser Plz
Oakland CA
510 271-6611

(P-14814)
KAISER FOUNDATION HOSPITALS
Also Called: Ontario Vineyard Medical Offs
2295 S Vineyard Ave (91761-7925)
PHONE..............................909 724-5000
EMP: 114
SALES (corp-wide): 68.1B **Privately Held**
Web: www.kaisercenter.com
SIC: 8011 Medical centers
HQ: Kaiser Foundation Hospitals Inc
1 Kaiser Plz
Oakland CA
510 271-6611

(P-14815)
KAISER FOUNDATION HOSPITALS
Also Called: Kaiser Prmnnte San Lndro Med C
2500 Merced St (94577-4201)
PHONE..............................510 454-1000
Thomas S Hanenburg, *Sr VP*
EMP: 243
SALES (corp-wide): 68.1B **Privately Held**
Web: www.kaisercenter.com
SIC: 8011 8062 Medical centers; General medical and surgical hospitals
HQ: Kaiser Foundation Hospitals Inc
1 Kaiser Plz
Oakland CA
510 271-6611

(P-14816)
KAISER FOUNDATION HOSPITALS
Also Called: Kaiser Prmnnte Oakland Med Ctr
280 W Macarthur Blvd (94611-5642)
PHONE..............................510 752-1000
Barbara Stumpf, *Dir*
EMP: 88
SALES (corp-wide): 68.1B **Privately Held**
Web: www.kaisercenter.com
SIC: 8011 Medical centers
HQ: Kaiser Foundation Hospitals Inc
1 Kaiser Plz
Oakland CA
510 271-6611

(P-14817)
KAISER FOUNDATION HOSPITALS
Also Called: Kaiser Permanente
250 Hospital Pkwy (95119-1103)
PHONE..............................408 972-7000
Joann Zimmerman, *Brnch Mgr*
EMP: 1047
SALES (corp-wide): 68.1B **Privately Held**
Web: www.kaisercenter.com
SIC: 8011 Medical centers
HQ: Kaiser Foundation Hospitals Inc
1 Kaiser Plz
Oakland CA
510 271-6611

(P-14818)
KAISER FOUNDATION HOSPITALS
Also Called: Kaiser Permanente
3401 S Harbor Blvd (92704-7933)
PHONE..............................714 830-6500
Kip Taylor, *Brnch Mgr*
EMP: 79
SALES (corp-wide): 68.1B **Privately Held**
Web: www.kaisercenter.com
SIC: 8011 Medical centers
HQ: Kaiser Foundation Hospitals Inc
1 Kaiser Plz
Oakland CA
510 271-6611

(P-14819)
KAISER FOUNDATION HOSPITALS
Also Called: Kaiser Permanente
12001 W Washington Blvd (90066-5801)
PHONE..............................310 915-5000
James Corb, *Ex Dir*
EMP: 82
SQ FT: 46,281
SALES (corp-wide): 68.1B **Privately Held**
Web: www.kaisercenter.com
SIC: 8011 Medical centers
HQ: Kaiser Foundation Hospitals Inc
1 Kaiser Plz
Oakland CA
510 271-6611

(P-14820)
KAISER FOUNDATION HOSPITALS
Also Called: Kaiser Permanente
1100 Veterans Blvd (94063-2037)
PHONE..............................650 299-2000
Eric Rasmussen, *Mgr*
EMP: 1228
SALES (corp-wide): 68.1B **Privately Held**
Web: www.kaisercenter.com
SIC: 8011 8062 Medical centers; General medical and surgical hospitals
HQ: Kaiser Foundation Hospitals Inc
1 Kaiser Plz
Oakland CA
510 271-6611

(P-14821)
KAISER FOUNDATION HOSPITALS
Also Called: Kaiser Permanente
1425 S Main St (94596-5318)
PHONE..............................925 295-4000
Michael Tully-cintron, *Brnch Mgr*
EMP: 1088
SQ FT: 11,840
SALES (corp-wide): 68.1B **Privately Held**
Web: www.kaisercenter.com
SIC: 8011 Medical centers
HQ: Kaiser Foundation Hospitals Inc
1 Kaiser Plz
Oakland CA
510 271-6611

(P-14822)
KAISER FOUNDATION HOSPITALS
Also Called: Kaiser Permanente
25825 Vermont Ave (90710-3518)
PHONE..............................310 325-5111
Mary Ann Barnes, *Brnch Mgr*
EMP: 892
SALES (corp-wide): 68.1B **Privately Held**
Web: www.kaisercenter.com
SIC: 8011 Medical centers
HQ: Kaiser Foundation Hospitals Inc
1 Kaiser Plz
Oakland CA
510 271-6611

(P-14823)
KAISER FOUNDATION HOSPITALS
Also Called: Kaiser Permanente
9961 Sierra Ave (92335-6720)
PHONE..............................909 427-5000
William Meyer, *Prin*
EMP: 1582
SALES (corp-wide): 68.1B **Privately Held**
Web: www.kaisercenter.com
SIC: 8011 Medical centers
HQ: Kaiser Foundation Hospitals Inc

PRODUCTS & SERVICES SECTION
8011 - Offices And Clinics Of Medical Doctors (P-14842)

1 Kaiser Plz
Oakland CA
510 271-6611

(P-14824)
KAISER FOUNDATION HOSPITALS
Also Called: Stockdale Medical Offices
3501 Stockdale Hwy (93309-2150)
PHONE.................................661 398-5011
Ky P Ho, *Prin*
EMP: 143
SALES (corp-wide): 68.1B **Privately Held**
Web: www.kaisercenter.com
SIC: 8011 Medical centers
HQ: Kaiser Foundation Hospitals Inc
  1 Kaiser Plz
  Oakland CA
  510 271-6611

(P-14825)
KAISER FOUNDATION HOSPITALS
Also Called: Milpitas Medical Offices
770 E Calaveras Blvd (95035-5491)
PHONE.................................408 945-2900
Ellen Sinclair, *Mgr*
EMP: 360
SALES (corp-wide): 68.1B **Privately Held**
Web: www.kaisercenter.com
SIC: 8011 8062 Medical centers; General medical and surgical hospitals
HQ: Kaiser Foundation Hospitals Inc
  1 Kaiser Plz
  Oakland CA
  510 271-6611

(P-14826)
KAISER FOUNDATION HOSPITALS
Also Called: Kaiser Permanente
3951 Van Buren Blvd (92503-3620)
PHONE.................................951 352-0292
Nancy Kingson, *Brnch Mgr*
EMP: 67
SALES (corp-wide): 68.1B **Privately Held**
Web: www.kaisercenter.com
SIC: 8011 Medical centers
HQ: Kaiser Foundation Hospitals Inc
  1 Kaiser Plz
  Oakland CA
  510 271-6611

(P-14827)
KAISER FOUNDATION HOSPITALS
Also Called: Glendale Medical Offices
444 W Glenoaks Blvd (91202-2917)
PHONE.................................818 552-3000
Avetis Tashyan, *Brnch Mgr*
EMP: 143
SALES (corp-wide): 68.1B **Privately Held**
Web: www.kaisercenter.com
SIC: 8011 Medical centers
HQ: Kaiser Foundation Hospitals Inc
  1 Kaiser Plz
  Oakland CA
  510 271-6611

(P-14828)
KAISER FOUNDATION HOSPITALS
Also Called: Kaiser Prmnnte Psadena Med Off
3280 E Foothill Blvd (91107-3148)
P.O. Box 7005 (91109-7005)
PHONE.................................626 440-5639
EMP: 128
SALES (corp-wide): 68.1B **Privately Held**
Web: www.kaisercenter.com

SIC: 8011 Medical centers
HQ: Kaiser Foundation Hospitals Inc
  1 Kaiser Plz
  Oakland CA
  510 271-6611

(P-14829)
KAISER FOUNDATION HOSPITALS
Also Called: El Cajon Medical Offices
250 Travelodge Dr (92020-4126)
PHONE.................................619 528-5000
Carolyn Bonner, *Admn*
EMP: 85
SQ FT: 47,486
SALES (corp-wide): 68.1B **Privately Held**
Web: www.kaisercenter.com
SIC: 8011 Medical centers
HQ: Kaiser Foundation Hospitals Inc
  1 Kaiser Plz
  Oakland CA
  510 271-6611

(P-14830)
KAISER FOUNDATION HOSPITALS
Also Called: Escondido Medical Offices
732 N Broadway (92025-1897)
PHONE.................................619 528-5000
Han Kim, *Mgr*
EMP: 108
SALES (corp-wide): 68.1B **Privately Held**
Web: www.kaisercenter.com
SIC: 8011 Medical centers
HQ: Kaiser Foundation Hospitals Inc
  1 Kaiser Plz
  Oakland CA
  510 271-6611

(P-14831)
KAISER FOUNDATION HOSPITALS
Also Called: Davis Medical Offices
1955 Cowell Blvd (95618-6325)
PHONE.................................530 757-7100
Robert Talkington, *Mgr*
EMP: 99
SALES (corp-wide): 68.1B **Privately Held**
Web: www.kaisercenter.com
SIC: 8011 Medical centers
HQ: Kaiser Foundation Hospitals Inc
  1 Kaiser Plz
  Oakland CA
  510 271-6611

(P-14832)
KAISER FOUNDATION HOSPITALS
Also Called: Petaluma Medical Offices
3900 Lakeville Hwy (94954-5698)
PHONE.................................707 765-3900
Claudia Renate Viazzoli, *Prin*
EMP: 316
SQ FT: 39,000
SALES (corp-wide): 68.1B **Privately Held**
Web: www.kp2020.org
SIC: 8011 Medical centers
HQ: Kaiser Foundation Hospitals Inc
  1 Kaiser Plz
  Oakland CA
  510 271-6611

(P-14833)
KAISER FOUNDATION HOSPITALS
Also Called: Kaiser Prmnnte Hayward Med Ctr
27400 Hesperian Blvd (94545-4235)
PHONE.................................510 678-4000

SIC: 8011 Medical centers
HQ: Kaiser Foundation Hospitals Inc
  1 Kaiser Plz
  Oakland CA
  510 271-6611

(P-14834)
KAISER FOUNDATION HOSPITALS
Also Called: Permanentee Medical Group
1001 Riverside Ave (95678-5134)
PHONE.................................916 784-4000
Deb Royer, *Mgr*
EMP: 91
SALES (corp-wide): 68.1B **Privately Held**
Web: www.kaisercenter.com
SIC: 8011 Medical centers
HQ: Kaiser Foundation Hospitals Inc
  1 Kaiser Plz
  Oakland CA
  510 271-6611

(P-14835)
KAISER FOUNDATION HOSPITALS
Also Called: Kaiser Permanente
2241 Geary Blvd Ste 118 (94115-3415)
PHONE.................................415 833-3450
Lee Hemmingway, *Mgr*
EMP: 132
SALES (corp-wide): 68.1B **Privately Held**
Web: www.kaisercenter.com
SIC: 8011 Medical centers
HQ: Kaiser Foundation Hospitals Inc
  1 Kaiser Plz
  Oakland CA
  510 271-6611

(P-14836)
KAISER FOUNDATION HOSPITALS
Also Called: Kaiser Permanente
5055 California Ave Ste 110 (93309-0701)
P.O. Box 12099 (93389-2099)
PHONE.................................661 334-2020
EMP: 94
SALES (corp-wide): 68.1B **Privately Held**
Web: www.kaisercenter.com
SIC: 8011 Medical centers
HQ: Kaiser Foundation Hospitals Inc
  1 Kaiser Plz
  Oakland CA
  510 271-6611

(P-14837)
KAISER FOUNDATION HOSPITALS
Also Called: Kaiser Permanente
1200 El Camino Real (94080-3208)
PHONE.................................650 742-2000
Evelyn Chan, *Brnch Mgr*
EMP: 3049
SALES (corp-wide): 68.1B **Privately Held**
Web: www.kaisercenter.com
SIC: 8011 8062 Medical centers; General medical and surgical hospitals
HQ: Kaiser Foundation Hospitals Inc
  1 Kaiser Plz
  Oakland CA
  510 271-6611

(P-14838)
KAISER FOUNDATION HOSPITALS
Also Called: Kaiser Permanente

Cynthia Seay, *Mgr*
EMP: 2846
SALES (corp-wide): 68.1B **Privately Held**
Web: www.kaisercenter.com
SIC: 8011 Medical centers
HQ: Kaiser Foundation Hospitals Inc
  1 Kaiser Plz
  Oakland CA
  510 271-6611

39400 Paseo Padre Pkwy (94538-2310)
PHONE.................................510 248-3000
Calvin Wheeler, *Mgr*
EMP: 3023
SQ FT: 86,710
SALES (corp-wide): 68.1B **Privately Held**
Web: www.kaisercenter.com
SIC: 8011 8062 Medical centers; General medical and surgical hospitals
HQ: Kaiser Foundation Hospitals Inc
  1 Kaiser Plz
  Oakland CA
  510 271-6611

(P-14839)
KAISER FOUNDATION HOSPITALS
Also Called: Kaiser Permanente
27107 Tourney Rd (91355-1860)
PHONE.................................661 222-2323
Pat Kenney, *Prin*
EMP: 64
SQ FT: 70,835
SALES (corp-wide): 68.1B **Privately Held**
Web: www.kaisercenter.com
SIC: 8011 Medical centers
HQ: Kaiser Foundation Hospitals Inc
  1 Kaiser Plz
  Oakland CA
  510 271-6611

(P-14840)
KAISER FOUNDATION HOSPITALS
Also Called: Riverside Medical Center
10800 Magnolia Ave (92505-3000)
PHONE.................................951 353-2000
Vita Willett, *Dir*
EMP: 699
SALES (corp-wide): 68.1B **Privately Held**
Web: www.kaisercenter.com
SIC: 8011 8062 Medical centers; General medical and surgical hospitals
HQ: Kaiser Foundation Hospitals Inc
  1 Kaiser Plz
  Oakland CA
  510 271-6611

(P-14841)
KAISER FOUNDATION HOSPITALS
Also Called: Kaiser Prmnnte Manteca Med Ctr
1777 W Yosemite Ave (95337-5187)
PHONE.................................209 825-3700
Anita Kennedy, *COO*
EMP: 1479
SALES (corp-wide): 68.1B **Privately Held**
Web: www.kaisercenter.com
SIC: 8011 Medical centers
HQ: Kaiser Foundation Hospitals Inc
  1 Kaiser Plz
  Oakland CA
  510 271-6611

(P-14842)
KAISER FOUNDATION HOSPITALS
Also Called: Kaiser Permanente
2425 Geary Blvd (94115-3358)
PHONE.................................415 833-2000
Mike Alexander, *Sr VP*
EMP: 720
SALES (corp-wide): 68.1B **Privately Held**
Web: www.kaisercenter.com
SIC: 8011 Medical centers
HQ: Kaiser Foundation Hospitals Inc
  1 Kaiser Plz
  Oakland CA
  510 271-6611

8011 - Offices And Clinics Of Medical Doctors (P-14843)

(P-14843)
KAISER FOUNDATION HOSPITALS
Also Called: Kaiser Prmnnte Mreno Vly Med C
27300 Iris Ave (92555-4802)
PHONE..................951 243-0811
Tom Mc Ciltock, Mgr
EMP: 1494
SALES (corp-wide): 68.1B Privately Held
Web: www.kaisercenter.com
SIC: 8011 Medical centers
HQ: Kaiser Foundation Hospitals Inc
1 Kaiser Plz
Oakland CA
510 271-6611

(P-14844)
KAISER FOUNDATION HOSPITALS
Also Called: Kaiser Permanente
110 N La Brea Ave (90301-1708)
PHONE..................310 419-3303
Victor Ahaiwe, Pr
EMP: 82
SALES (corp-wide): 68.1B Privately Held
Web: www.kaisercenter.com
SIC: 8011 Medical centers
HQ: Kaiser Foundation Hospitals Inc
1 Kaiser Plz
Oakland CA
510 271-6611

(P-14845)
KAISER FOUNDATION HOSPITALS
Also Called: Kaiser Prmnnte Lvrmore Med Ctr
3000 Las Positas Rd (94551-9627)
PHONE..................925 432-6000
EMP: 120
SALES (corp-wide): 68.1B Privately Held
Web: www.kaisercenter.com
SIC: 8011 8062 Medical centers; General medical and surgical hospitals
HQ: Kaiser Foundation Hospitals Inc
1 Kaiser Plz
Oakland CA
510 271-6611

(P-14846)
KAISER FOUNDATION HOSPITALS
Also Called: Kaiser Permanente
7300 N Fresno St (93720-2941)
PHONE..................559 448-4500
Susan Ryan, Sr VP
EMP: 892
SALES (corp-wide): 68.1B Privately Held
Web: www.kaisercenter.com
SIC: 8011 Medical centers
HQ: Kaiser Foundation Hospitals Inc
1 Kaiser Plz
Oakland CA
510 271-6611

(P-14847)
KAISER FOUNDATION HOSPITALS
Also Called: Kaiser Permanente
1900 E 4th St (92705-3910)
PHONE..................714 967-4700
EMP: 190
SALES (corp-wide): 68.1B Privately Held
Web: www.kaisercenter.com
SIC: 8011 Medical centers
HQ: Kaiser Foundation Hospitals Inc
1 Kaiser Plz
Oakland CA
510 271-6611

(P-14848)
KAISER FOUNDATION HOSPITALS
Also Called: Folsom Ambulatory Surgery Ctr
285 Palladio Pkwy (95630-8741)
PHONE..................916 986-4178
EMP: 61
SALES (corp-wide): 68.1B Privately Held
Web: www.kaisercenter.com
SIC: 8011 Ambulatory surgical center
HQ: Kaiser Foundation Hospitals Inc
1 Kaiser Plz
Oakland CA
510 271-6611

(P-14849)
KAISER FOUNDATION HOSPITALS
Kaiser Permanente
1950 Franklin St (94612-5190)
PHONE..................510 987-1000
Maryanne Williams, Mgr
EMP: 793
SALES (corp-wide): 68.1B Privately Held
Web: www.kaisercenter.com
SIC: 8011 Health maintenance organization
HQ: Kaiser Foundation Hospitals Inc
1 Kaiser Plz
Oakland CA
510 271-6611

(P-14850)
KAISER FOUNDATION HOSPITALS
Also Called: Kaiser Perminente
2155 Iron Point Rd (95630-8707)
PHONE..................916 817-5200
Larry Marini, Mgr
EMP: 90
SALES (corp-wide): 68.1B Privately Held
Web: www.kaisercenter.com
SIC: 8011 Health maintenance organization
HQ: Kaiser Foundation Hospitals Inc
1 Kaiser Plz
Oakland CA
510 271-6611

(P-14851)
KAISER FOUNDATION HOSPITALS
Also Called: Kaiser Permanente
1515 N Vermont Ave Fl 3 (90027-5337)
PHONE..................323 783-8306
Cecilia Militante, Prin
EMP: 263
SALES (corp-wide): 68.1B Privately Held
Web: www.kaisercenter.com
SIC: 8011 Dermatologist
HQ: Kaiser Foundation Hospitals Inc
1 Kaiser Plz
Oakland CA
510 271-6611

(P-14852)
KAISER FOUNDATION HOSPITALS
Also Called: Kaiser Prmnnte San Jose Med Ct
250 Hospital Pkwy Bldg D (95119-1103)
PHONE..................408 972-3000
Thomas Hau, Brnch Mgr
EMP: 105
SQ FT: 5,976
SALES (corp-wide): 68.1B Privately Held
Web: www.kaisercenter.com
SIC: 8011 8062 General and family practice, physician/surgeon; General medical and surgical hospitals
HQ: Kaiser Foundation Hospitals Inc
1 Kaiser Plz
Oakland CA
510 271-6611

(P-14853)
KAISER FOUNDATION HOSPITALS
1011 Baldwin Park Blvd (91706-5806)
PHONE..................310 922-8916
Abdalla Mallouk, Brnch Mgr
EMP: 64
SALES (corp-wide): 68.1B Privately Held
Web: www.kaisercenter.com
SIC: 8011 Physicians' office, including specialists
HQ: Kaiser Foundation Hospitals Inc
1 Kaiser Plz
Oakland CA
510 271-6611

(P-14854)
KAISER FOUNDATION HOSPITALS
6041 Cadillac Ave (90034-1700)
PHONE..................323 857-2000
Kenneth Nudelman, Brnch Mgr
EMP: 132
SALES (corp-wide): 68.1B Privately Held
Web: www.kaisercenter.com
SIC: 8011 Physicians' office, including specialists
HQ: Kaiser Foundation Hospitals Inc
1 Kaiser Plz
Oakland CA
510 271-6611

(P-14855)
KAISER FUNDATION HLTH PLAN INC (PA)
Also Called: Kaiser Foundation Health Plan
1 Kaiser Plz (94612-3610)
PHONE..................510 271-5800
Greg Adams, Ch Bd
Anthony Barrueta, *
Yazdi Bagli, *
Patrick Courneya, CMO*
Raymond Baxter, Prin
EMP: 450 EST: 1955
SQ FT: 90,000
SALES (est): 68.1B
SALES (corp-wide): 68.1B Privately Held
Web: healthy.kaiserpermanente.org
SIC: 8011 Health maintenance organization

(P-14856)
KAISER PRMANENTE UN CY LANDING
30116 Eigenbrodt Way (94587-1225)
PHONE..................408 235-4005
EMP: 60 EST: 2019
SALES (est): 726.81K Privately Held
SIC: 8011 Medical centers

(P-14857)
KAISER PRMNNTE SCHL ANESTHESIA
100 S Los Robles Ste 501 (91101-2453)
PHONE..................626 564-3016
Kaiser Permanente, Owner
EMP: 137 EST: 2009
SALES (est): 24.14MM Privately Held
Web: www.kpsan.org
SIC: 8011 Anesthesiologist

(P-14858)
KARTHIKEYA DEVIREDDY M D INC
311 W I St (93635-3479)
PHONE..................209 826-2222
Karthikeya Devireddy, Prin
EMP: 85 EST: 1980
SALES (est): 2.13MM Privately Held
SIC: 8011 Offices and clinics of medical doctors

(P-14859)
KECK MEDICAL CENTER OF USC
1520 San Pablo St (90033-5310)
PHONE..................323 371-9535
Melina Thaxton, Mgr
EMP: 91
SALES (corp-wide): 861.65MM Privately Held
Web: www.keckmedicine.org
SIC: 8011 General and family practice, physician/surgeon
PA: Keck Medical Center Of Usc
1510 San Pablo St
Los Angeles CA
800 872-2273

(P-14860)
KERLAN-JOBE ORTHOPEDIC CLINIC (PA)
6801 Park Ter Ste 500 (90045-1539)
PHONE..................310 665-7200
Ralph A Gambardella, CEO
Stephen Lombardo, *
EMP: 78 EST: 1973
SQ FT: 37,000
SALES (est): 13.81MM
SALES (corp-wide): 13.81MM Privately Held
Web: www.kerlanjobe.org
SIC: 8011 Orthopedic physician

(P-14861)
KERN HEALTH SYSTEMS INC
Also Called: Kern Family Helathcare
2900 Buck Owens Blvd (93308-6316)
P.O. Box 85000 (93380-5000)
PHONE..................661 664-5000
Carol L Sorrell, CEO
EMP: 98 EST: 1995
SQ FT: 16,000
SALES (est): 26.74MM Privately Held
Web: www.kernfamilyhealthcare.com
SIC: 8011 Clinic, operated by physicians

(P-14862)
KERN RDLGY IMAGING SYSTEMS INC (PA)
2301 Bahamas Dr (93309-0663)
PHONE..................661 326-9600
David P Schale, CEO
John Gundzik Md, VP
Jeff Child Md, Treas
EMP: 65 EST: 1968
SQ FT: 20,000
SALES (est): 29.68MM
SALES (corp-wide): 29.68MM Privately Held
Web: www.radnet.com
SIC: 8011 Radiologist

(P-14863)
KERN RDLGY IMAGING SYSTEMS INC
4100 Truxtun Ave Ste 306 (93309-0657)
PHONE..................661 322-9958
John M Gundzik, Prin
EMP: 70
SALES (corp-wide): 29.68MM Privately Held
Web: www.radnet.com
SIC: 8011 Radiologist
PA: Kern Radiology Imaging Systems, Inc.

PRODUCTS & SERVICES SECTION

8011 - Offices And Clinics Of Medical Doctors (P-14884)

2301 Bahamas Dr
Bakersfield CA
661 326-9600

(P-14864)
LA CLINICA DE LA RAZA INC
1515 Fruitvale Ave (94601-2355)
PHONE.................510 535-6300
Jim Eitel, Pt
EMP: 266
SALES (corp-wide): 144.12MM Privately Held
Web: www.laclinica.org
SIC: 8011 8699 Clinic, operated by physicians; Charitable organization
PA: La Clinica De La Raza, Inc.
    1450 Fruitvale Ave Fl 3
    Oakland CA
    510 535-4000

(P-14865)
LA CLINICA DE LA RAZA INC
243 Georgia St (94590-5905)
PHONE.................707 556-8100
Jane Garcia, Brnch Mgr
EMP: 128
SALES (corp-wide): 144.12MM Privately Held
Web: www.laclinica.org
SIC: 8011 Clinic, operated by physicians
PA: La Clinica De La Raza, Inc.
    1450 Fruitvale Ave Fl 3
    Oakland CA
    510 535-4000

(P-14866)
LA CLINICA DE LA RAZA INC
Also Called: Wic
1450 Fruitvale Ave # B (94601-2313)
PHONE.................510 535-4110
Ana Dorman, Brnch Mgr
EMP: 332
SALES (corp-wide): 144.12MM Privately Held
Web: www.laclinica.org
SIC: 8011 Clinic, operated by physicians
PA: La Clinica De La Raza, Inc.
    1450 Fruitvale Ave Fl 3
    Oakland CA
    510 535-4000

(P-14867)
LA CLINICA DE LA RAZA INC
3050 E 16th St (94601-2319)
PHONE.................510 535-4700
Magnolia Rios, Off Mgr
EMP: 100
SQ FT: 5,208
SALES (corp-wide): 144.12MM Privately Held
Web: www.laclinica.org
SIC: 8011 Clinic, operated by physicians
PA: La Clinica De La Raza, Inc.
    1450 Fruitvale Ave Fl 3
    Oakland CA
    510 535-4000

(P-14868)
LA CLINICA DE LA RAZA INC
Also Called: Mental Health Department
1601 Fruitvale Ave (94601-2418)
PHONE.................510 535-6200
Jane Garcia, CEO
EMP: 200
SALES (corp-wide): 144.12MM Privately Held
Web: www.laclinica.org
SIC: 8011 Clinic, operated by physicians
PA: La Clinica De La Raza, Inc.
    1450 Fruitvale Ave Fl 3
    Oakland CA
    510 535-4000

(P-14869)
LA CLINICA DE LA RAZA INC
Also Called: Laclinica
337 E Leland Rd (94565-4911)
PHONE.................925 431-1250
Viola Lujan, Brnch Mgr
EMP: 129
SALES (corp-wide): 144.12MM Privately Held
Web: www.laclinica.org
SIC: 8011 Clinic, operated by physicians
PA: La Clinica De La Raza, Inc.
    1450 Fruitvale Ave Fl 3
    Oakland CA
    510 535-4000

(P-14870)
LA JOLLA ORTHPDIC SRGERY CTR L
4120 La Jolla Village Dr (92037-1406)
PHONE.................858 657-0055
Scott Leggett, Managing Member
EMP: 98 EST: 2000
SALES (est): 11.11MM Privately Held
Web: www.osclajolla.com
SIC: 8011 Orthopedic physician

(P-14871)
LA MAESTRA FAMILY CLINIC INC (PA)
Also Called: LA MAESTRA COMMUNITY HEALTH CE
4060 Fairmount Ave (92105-1608)
PHONE.................619 584-1612
Zara Marselian, CEO
Samuel Mirelles, *
Carlos Hanessian, *
Alex Pantoja, *
Alejandrina Areizaga, *
EMP: 197 EST: 1991
SQ FT: 5,000
SALES (est): 78.1MM Privately Held
Web: www.lamaestra.org
SIC: 8011 Clinic, operated by physicians

(P-14872)
LA PEER SURGERY CENTER LLC
Also Called: La Peer Health Systems
8920 Wilshire Blvd Ste 101 (90211-2007)
PHONE.................310 360-9119
Doctor Siamak Tabib, Managing Member
EMP: 78 EST: 2000
SQ FT: 2,300
SALES (est): 23.69MM
SALES (corp-wide): 2.54B Publicly Held
Web: www.lapeerhealth.com
SIC: 8011 Surgeon
PA: Surgery Partners, Inc.
    340 Sven Sprng Way Ste 60
    Brentwood TN
    615 234-5900

(P-14873)
LAC & USC MEDICAL CENTER
2051 Marengo St (90033-1352)
P.O. Box 861749 (90086-1749)
PHONE.................323 409-2345
Marisa Danbee, Prin
EMP: 85 EST: 2009
SALES (est): 40.23MM Privately Held
Web: dhs.lacounty.gov
SIC: 8011 Primary care medical clinic

(P-14874)
LANCASTER CRDLGY MED GROUP INC (PA)
Also Called: Physicians Referral Service
43847 Heaton Ave Ste B (93534-4922)
PHONE.................661 726-3058
Shun K Sunder Md, Pr
E Ekong Md, VP
Kanagaratham Sivalingam Md, Sec
EMP: 80 EST: 1976
SQ FT: 30,000
SALES (est): 4.5MM
SALES (corp-wide): 4.5MM Privately Held
SIC: 8011 Cardiologist and cardio-vascular specialist

(P-14875)
LINDA LOMA UNIV HLTH CARE (PA)
11175 Campus St A-1108 (92350-1700)
PHONE.................909 558-4729
Trevor Wright, CEO
Roger Hadley, *
David B Hinshaw Junior Md, V Ch Bd
Brian Bull Md, Sec
EMP: 850 EST: 1989
SQ FT: 70,000
SALES (est): 208.25MM Privately Held
Web: home.llu.edu
SIC: 8011 Clinic, operated by physicians

(P-14876)
LIVINGSTON COMMUNITY HEALTH (PA)
Also Called: Livingston Health Center
600 B St Bldg A (95334-9593)
PHONE.................209 394-7913
Leslie Mcgowan, CEO
Selina Montoya, *
EMP: 97 EST: 1970
SALES (est): 18.92MM
SALES (corp-wide): 18.92MM Privately Held
Web: www.visitlch.org
SIC: 8011 Primary care medical clinic

(P-14877)
LODI MEMORIAL HOSPITAL
801 S Ham Ln Ste S (95242-7503)
PHONE.................209 204-5004
EMP: 134 EST: 2019
SALES (est): 1.11MM Privately Held
SIC: 8011 Offices and clinics of medical doctors

(P-14878)
LOMA LNDA UNIV FMLY MED GROUP
25455 Barton Rd Ste 204b (92354-3130)
PHONE.................909 558-6600
John Testerman, Pr
EMP: 83 EST: 1980
SALES (est): 3.08MM Privately Held
Web: www.lluh.org
SIC: 8011 Clinic, operated by physicians

(P-14879)
LOS ANGELES CARDIOLOGY ASSOC (HQ)
1245 Wilshire Blvd Ste 703 (90017-4810)
PHONE.................213 977-0419
Guy Mayeda, CEO
EMP: 65 EST: 1989
SQ FT: 12,000
SALES (est): 24.66MM
SALES (corp-wide): 923.01K Privately Held
Web: www.cedars-sinai.org

SIC: 8011 Physicians' office, including specialists
PA: Pih Health, Inc.
    12401 Washington Blvd
    Whittier CA
    562 698-0811

(P-14880)
LOS ANGELES FREE CLINIC
5205 Melrose Ave (90038-3144)
PHONE.................323 653-1990
EMP: 110
SALES (corp-wide): 39.22MM Privately Held
Web: www.sabancommunityclinic.org
SIC: 8011 Clinic, operated by physicians
PA: The Los Angeles Free Clinic
    8405 Beverly Blvd
    Los Angeles CA
    323 653-8622

(P-14881)
LOS ANGELES FREE CLINIC (PA)
Also Called: Saban Community Clinic
8405 Beverly Blvd (90048-3401)
PHONE.................323 653-8622
Jeffrey Bujer, CEO
EMP: 79 EST: 1967
SQ FT: 26,615
SALES (est): 39.22MM
SALES (corp-wide): 39.22MM Privately Held
Web: www.sabancommunityclinic.org
SIC: 8011 Clinic, operated by physicians

(P-14882)
LOS ROBLES REGIONAL MED CTR
Also Called: Neuroscience Gamma Knife Ctr
2200 Lynn Rd (91360-2071)
PHONE.................805 494-0880
Cherrie De La La Cruz, Prin
EMP: 261
Web: www.californiagammaknife.com
SIC: 8011 Neurologist
HQ: Los Robles Regional Medical Center
    215 W Janss Rd
    Thousand Oaks CA

(P-14883)
LOS ROBLES REGIONAL MED CTR
150 Via Merida (91362-3816)
PHONE.................805 370-4531
Simin Shandiz, Prin
EMP: 261
Web: www.losrobleshospital.com
SIC: 8011 Medical centers
HQ: Los Robles Regional Medical Center
    215 W Janss Rd
    Thousand Oaks CA

(P-14884)
LYRA HEALTH INC
Also Called: Lyra Administrative Services
270 East Ln (94010-2881)
PHONE.................800 505-5972
David Ebersman, CEO
Bob Kocher, *
Bryan Roberts, *
Giovanni Colella, *
Dena Bravata, *
EMP: 145 EST: 2015
SALES (est): 26.3MM Privately Held
Web: www.lyrahealth.com
SIC: 8011 Clinic, operated by physicians

8011 - Offices And Clinics Of Medical Doctors (P-14885)

(P-14885)
MAINSTAY MEDICAL LIMITED
2159 India St Ste 200 (92101-1766)
PHONE..................................619 261-9144
Jason Hannon, *CEO*
EMP: 80 **EST:** 2008
SALES (est): 516.01K **Privately Held**
SIC: 8011 Primary care medical clinic

(P-14886)
MARIN COMMUNITY CLINIC
Also Called: MARIN COMMUNITY CLINICS
9 Commercial Blvd Ste 100 (94949-6137)
PHONE..................................415 448-1500
Linda Tavaszi, *CEO*
Peggy Dracker, *
David Klinetobe, *
John Shen, *
EMP: 99 **EST:** 1974
SQ FT: 9,000
SALES (est): 74.12MM **Privately Held**
Web: www.marinclinic.org
SIC: 8011 Clinic, operated by physicians

(P-14887)
MARK E JACOBSON M D
1260 N Dutton Ave Ste 230 (95401-7161)
PHONE..................................707 571-4022
EMP: 60
SALES (est): 658.37K **Privately Held**
SIC: 8011 Offices and clinics of medical doctors

(P-14888)
MCHENRY MEDICAL GROUP INC
1541 Florida Ave Ste 200 (95350-4438)
PHONE..................................209 577-3388
John Porteous, *Pr*
Harris M Goodman, *
EMP: 62 **EST:** 1969
SQ FT: 22,000
SALES (est): 4.99MM **Privately Held**
Web: www.fcppcentralvalley.com
SIC: 8011 Internal medicine, physician/surgeon

(P-14889)
MD IMAGING INC A PROF MED CORP
Also Called: Women's Imaging Center
2020 Court St (96001-1822)
PHONE..................................530 243-1249
Michael G Davis, *CEO*
Richard J Slepicka, *
EMP: 100 **EST:** 1994
SALES (est): 21.7MM **Privately Held**
Web: www.mdimaging.net
SIC: 8011 Radiologist

(P-14890)
MEDICAL ANESTHESIA CONS LLC
100 N Wiget Ln Ste 160 (94598-5917)
PHONE..................................925 287-1505
David Fitzgerald, *Brnch Mgr*
EMP: 102
Web: www.macmgi.com
SIC: 8011 Anesthesiologist
HQ: Medical Anesthesia Consultants Llc
1525 Nw 62nd St
Fort Lauderdale FL
925 543-0140

(P-14891)
MEDICAL IMGING CTR STHERN CAL
2811 Wilshire Blvd Ste 100 (90403-4803)
PHONE..................................310 829-9788
Bradley Jabour Md, *Pr*
Nicole Pelissier, *
EMP: 65 **EST:** 1985
SQ FT: 22,000
SALES (est): 7.4MM **Privately Held**
Web: www.micsc.com
SIC: 8011 Radiologist

(P-14892)
MEDICAL INSURANCE EXCHANGE CAL
6250 Claremont Ave (94618-1324)
PHONE..................................510 596-4935
Doctor Bradford Cohn, *Pr*
Doctor Bradford Cohn, *Ch*
Doctor William Donald, *V Ch Bd*
Doctor Conrad Anderson, *Sec*
EMP: 74 **EST:** 1975
SQ FT: 13,000
SALES (est): 9.12MM **Privately Held**
Web: www.miec.com
SIC: 8011 Medical insurance plan

(P-14893)
MEMORIAL CRDOLGY MED GROUP INC
Also Called: Cardiology
2898 Linden Ave (90806-1627)
PHONE..................................562 988-2995
Serge Pobias, *Pr*
Winfried Waider Md, *Prin*
Serge Tobias, *
EMP: 71 **EST:** 1979
SALES (est): 4.72MM **Privately Held**
Web: www.memorialcardiologylb.com
SIC: 8011 Cardiologist and cardio-vascular specialist

(P-14894)
MEMORIAL ORTHPDIC SRGCAL GROUP
Also Called: Southern Cal Ctr For Spt Mdcin
2760 Atlantic Ave (90806-2755)
PHONE..................................562 424-6666
Peter R Kurzweil, *CEO*
Douglas W Jackson Md, *Pr*
Curtis W Spencer Iii Md, *VP*
David Morrison Md, *Mgr*
David S Morrison Md, *Sec*
▲ **EMP:** 70 **EST:** 1977
SQ FT: 12,000
SALES (est): 14.07MM **Privately Held**
Web: www.memorialorthopaedic.com
SIC: 8011 Orthopedic physician

(P-14895)
MENDOCINO CMNTY HLTH CLNIC INC (PA)
Also Called: MCHC
333 Laws Ave (95482-6540)
PHONE..................................707 468-1010
John Pavoni, *CEO*
EMP: 130 **EST:** 1992
SQ FT: 24,000
SALES (est): 45.92MM
SALES (corp-wide): 45.92MM **Privately Held**
Web: www.mchcinc.org
SIC: 8011 Primary care medical clinic

(P-14896)
MENDOCINO CMNTY HLTH CLNIC INC
45 Hazel St (95490-4222)
PHONE..................................707 456-9600
Deborah Frank, *Mgr*
EMP: 105
SALES (corp-wide): 45.92MM **Privately Held**
Web: www.mchcinc.org
SIC: 8011 Primary care medical clinic
PA: Mendocino Community Health Clinic, Inc.
333 Laws Ave
Ukiah CA
707 468-1010

(P-14897)
MENLO MED CLINIC A MED CORP
1300 Crane St (94025-4260)
PHONE..................................650 498-6500
Ed Kelly, *Admn*
Charles R Tucker Md, *Mng Pt*
David L Gregg Md, *Pt*
George L Paris Md, *Pt*
George F Waltuch Md, *Pt*
EMP: 150 **EST:** 1946
SQ FT: 40,000
SALES (est): 24.19MM **Privately Held**
SIC: 8011 Clinic, operated by physicians

(P-14898)
MERCY SAN JUAN MEDICAL CENTER
Also Called: Nicholas W Rotas, D.D.S.
9241 Sierra College Blvd # 150 (95661-5919)
PHONE..................................916 773-1188
Nicholas W Rotas, *Brnch Mgr*
EMP: 101
Web: www.placeromfs.com
SIC: 8011 Medical centers
HQ: Mercy San Juan Medical Center
3808 Auburn Blvd Ste 54
Sacramento CA
916 979-0347

(P-14899)
MICHA-RETTENMAIER PARTNERSHIP
Also Called: Gynecologic Oncology Assoc
351 Hospital Rd Ste 507 (92663-3500)
PHONE..................................714 280-1645
John Paul Micha Md, *Pt*
Mark A Rettenmaier Md, *Pt*
EMP: 88 **EST:** 1989
SQ FT: 3,500
SALES (est): 9.77MM **Privately Held**
Web: www.hoag.org
SIC: 8011 Gynecologist

(P-14900)
MING TSUANG DR
Also Called: Ucsd
9500 Gillman Dr Mc 0603 (92093-5004)
PHONE..................................858 822-2464
Doctor Ming Tsuang, *Owner*
▲ **EMP:** 69 **EST:** 2004
SALES (est): 31.44MM **Privately Held**
SIC: 8011 8299 Psychiatrist; Educational services

(P-14901)
MISSION INTERNAL MED GROUP INC
Also Called: West Coast Physical Therapy
27882 Forbes Rd Ste 110 (92677-1267)
PHONE..................................949 364-3605
Joan Shrum-brown, *Prin*
EMP: 91
SALES (corp-wide): 19.19MM **Privately Held**
SIC: 8011 8049 Cardiologist and cardio-vascular specialist; Physical therapist
PA: Mission Internal Medical Group, Inc.
26732 Crown Valley Pkwy # 351
Mission Viejo CA
949 282-1600

(P-14902)
MISSION INTERNAL MED GROUP INC
Also Called: Arthur Loussararian MD
26800 Crown Valley Pkwy Ste 103 (92691-6389)
PHONE..................................949 364-3570
Arthur Loussararian, *Prin*
EMP: 90
SALES (corp-wide): 19.19MM **Privately Held**
SIC: 8011 Primary care medical clinic
PA: Mission Internal Medical Group, Inc.
26732 Crown Valley Pkwy # 351
Mission Viejo CA
949 282-1600

(P-14903)
MISSION NEIGHBORHOOD HLTH CTR (PA)
Also Called: Mission Neighborhood Hlth Ctr
240 Shotwell St (94110-1323)
PHONE..................................415 552-3870
Brenda Storey, *CEO*
Amelia Martinez, *
Luisa Eztouerro, *
Nora Abaunza, *
Ricardo Alvarezm, *
EMP: 110 **EST:** 1968
SQ FT: 21,000
SALES (est): 22.45MM
SALES (corp-wide): 22.45MM **Privately Held**
Web: www.mnhc.org
SIC: 8011 Primary care medical clinic

(P-14904)
MISSION PEAK ORTHOPEDICS
5924 Stoneridge Dr Ste 200 (94588-2887)
PHONE..................................510 797-3933
Co V Banh, *Prin*
EMP: 65 **EST:** 2010
SALES (est): 2.48MM **Privately Held**
Web: www.mportho.com
SIC: 8011 Orthopedic physician

(P-14905)
MOHAWK MEDICAL GROUP INC
9500 Stockdale Hwy Ste 200 (93311-3621)
PHONE..................................661 324-4747
Jorge Deltoro, *Pr*
Luis Cousin, *
EMP: 80 **EST:** 1985
SQ FT: 18,500
SALES (est): 5.63MM **Privately Held**
SIC: 8011 General and family practice, physician/surgeon

(P-14906)
MOLINA HEALTHCARE INC (PA)
Also Called: Molina Healthcare
200 Oceangate Ste 100 (90802-4317)
P.O. Box 22813 (90801-5813)
PHONE..................................562 435-3666
Joseph M Zubretsky, *Pr*
Dale B Wolf, *Non-Executive Chairman of the Board*
Ronna E Romney, *
EMP: 2800 **EST:** 1980
SALES (est): 31.97B
SALES (corp-wide): 31.97B **Publicly Held**
Web: www.molinahealthcare.com
SIC: 8011 6324 Health maintenance organization; Hospital and medical service plans

(P-14907)
MOLINA HEALTHCARE CALIFORNIA

PRODUCTS & SERVICES SECTION
8011 - Offices And Clinics Of Medical Doctors (P-14927)

200 Oceangate Ste 100 (90802-4303)
PHONE.................................800 526-8196
EMP: 1835 EST: 2016
SALES (est): 4.6MM
SALES (corp-wide): 31.97B Publicly Held
Web: www.molinahealthcare.com
SIC: 8011 Offices and clinics of medical doctors
PA: Molina Healthcare, Inc.
200 Oceangate Ste 100
Long Beach CA
562 435-3666

(P-14908)
MOLINA HEALTHCARE NEW YORK INC
200 Oceangate Ste 100 (90802-4317)
PHONE.................................888 562-5442
EMP: 75 EST: 2019
SALES (est): 2.22MM
SALES (corp-wide): 31.97B Publicly Held
SIC: 8011 Health maintenance organization
PA: Molina Healthcare, Inc.
200 Oceangate Ste 100
Long Beach CA
562 435-3666

(P-14909)
MOLINA PATHWAYS LLC
200 Oceangate Ste 100 (90802-4317)
PHONE.................................562 491-5773
Craig Bass, CEO
EMP: 493 EST: 2011
SALES (est): 2.36MM
SALES (corp-wide): 31.97B Publicly Held
SIC: 8011 Health maintenance organization
PA: Molina Healthcare, Inc.
200 Oceangate Ste 100
Long Beach CA
562 435-3666

(P-14910)
MONARCH HEALTHCARE A MEDICAL
675 Camino De Los Mares Ste 300 (92673)
PHONE.................................949 489-1960
Adam Crawford D.o.s., Brnch Mgr
EMP: 159
SALES (corp-wide): 324.16B Publicly Held
Web: www.monarchhealthcare.com
SIC: 8011 Group health association
HQ: Monarch Healthcare, A Medical Group, Inc.
11 Technology Dr
Irvine CA

(P-14911)
MONARCH HEALTHCARE A MEDICAL (HQ)
11 Technology Dr (92618-2302)
PHONE.................................949 923-3200
Bartley Asner, CEO
Jay J Cohen Md, VP
Steven Rudy Md, VP
James Selevan Md, Mgr
Marvin Gordon Md, CFO
EMP: 98 EST: 1986
SQ FT: 75,000
SALES (est): 95.06MM
SALES (corp-wide): 324.16B Publicly Held
Web: www.monarchhealthcare.com
SIC: 8011 Group health association
PA: Unitedhealth Group Incorporated
9900 Bren Rd E Ste 300w
Minnetonka MN
952 936-1300

(P-14912)
MONTAGE MEDICAL GROUP
23845 Holman Hwy Ste 203 (93940-5901)
PHONE.................................831 241-9155
EMP: 184
SIC: 8011 Offices and clinics of medical doctors
PA: Montage Medical Group
505 Montgomery St Ste 800
San Francisco CA

(P-14913)
MUIR ORTHOPEDIC SPECIALISTS
2405 Shadelands Dr Ste 210 (94598-5905)
PHONE.................................925 939-8585
K C Campion, CEO
Ramiro Miranda Md, Pr
EMP: 177 EST: 1982
SALES (est): 23.07MM Privately Held
Web: www.muirortho.com
SIC: 8011 Orthopedic physician

(P-14914)
N S C CHANNEL ISLANDS INC
Also Called: HealthSouth
2300 Wankel Way (93030-2665)
PHONE.................................805 485-1908
Susan Clark, Admn
EMP: 477 EST: 1995
SQ FT: 14,000
SALES (est): 18.71MM
SALES (corp-wide): 4.35B Publicly Held
SIC: 8011 Surgeon
HQ: Healthsouth Rehabilitation Hospital Of Cypress, Llc
9001 Liberty Pkwy
Birmingham AL

(P-14915)
NATIVE AMERICAN HEALTH CTR INC (PA)
2950 International Blvd (94601-2228)
PHONE.................................510 535-4400
Martin Waukazoo, CEO
Ana M Oconnor, *
Doctor Joseph Marquis, CMO
Alan Wong, *
Natalie Aguilera, *
EMP: 80 EST: 1971
SQ FT: 16,000
SALES (est): 36.09MM
SALES (corp-wide): 36.09MM Privately Held
Web: www.nativehealth.org
SIC: 8011 8021 8093 Clinic, operated by physicians; Dentists' office; Mental health clinic, outpatient

(P-14916)
NAVY UNITED STATES DEPARTMENT
Also Called: Branch Medical Center
19871 Mitscher Way (92145-5103)
P.O. Box 452002 (92145-2002)
PHONE.................................858 577-9849
EMP: 300
Web: www.navy.mil
SIC: 8011 9711 Medical centers; Navy
HQ: United States Department Of The Navy
1200 Navy Pentagon
Washington DC

(P-14917)
NEIGHBORHOOD HEALTHCARE
855 E Madison Ave (92020-3819)
PHONE.................................619 440-2751
Alex Nunez, Dir Opers
EMP: 79

SQ FT: 9,198
SALES (corp-wide): 101.79MM Privately Held
Web: www.nhcare.org
SIC: 8011 Clinic, operated by physicians
PA: Neighborhood Healthcare
425 N Date St Ste 203
Escondido CA
760 520-8372

(P-14918)
NEIGHBORHOOD HEALTHCARE
460 N Elm St (92025-3002)
PHONE.................................760 737-2000
Gail Thomsky, Mgr
EMP: 136
SQ FT: 9,288
SALES (corp-wide): 101.79MM Privately Held
Web: www.nhcare.org
SIC: 8011 Clinic, operated by physicians
PA: Neighborhood Healthcare
425 N Date St Ste 203
Escondido CA
760 520-8372

(P-14919)
NES HEALTH CARE GROUP
39 Main St (94920-2507)
P.O. Box 156 (94920-0156)
PHONE.................................415 435-4591
Thomas Zguris, Brnch Mgr
EMP: 84
Web: www.neshealth-care.com
SIC: 8011 Offices and clinics of medical doctors
HQ: Nes Health Care Group
4250 Veterans Memorial
Holbrook NY

(P-14920)
NEWPORT BEACH SURGERY CTR LLC
361 Hospital Rd Ste 124 (92663-3521)
PHONE.................................949 631-0988
Perter Broekelschen, Managing Member*
Harvey Heinrichs, Managing Member*
Bruce Albert, *
Robert Anderson, *
EMP: 120 EST: 1992
SQ FT: 10,000
SALES (est): 15.69MM Privately Held
Web: www.newportbeachsurgerycenter.com
SIC: 8011 Surgeon

(P-14921)
NORTH CAST SRGERY CTR LTD A CA
3903 Waring Rd (92056-4405)
PHONE.................................760 940-0997
Doctor Bruce Hochman, Pt
Doctor Bruce Hochman, Mng Pt
EMP: 79 EST: 1985
SQ FT: 11,000
SALES (est): 24.71MM
SALES (corp-wide): 324.16B Publicly Held
Web: www.northcoastsurgerycenter.com
SIC: 8011 Surgeon
PA: Unitedhealth Group Incorporated
9900 Bren Rd E Ste 300w
Minnetonka MN
952 936-1300

(P-14922)
NORTH COAST FMLY MED GROUP INC
477 N El Camino Real Ste A306 (92024)
PHONE.................................760 942-0118

James Hay Md, Pr
EMP: 64 EST: 1978
SQ FT: 2,400
SALES (est): 8.77MM Privately Held
Web: www.ncfmg.com
SIC: 8011 General and family practice, physician/surgeon

(P-14923)
NORTH COUNTY HEALTH PRJ INC (PA)
Also Called: North County Services
150 Valpreda Rd Frnt (92069-2944)
PHONE.................................760 736-6755
Irma Cota, CEO
Kathy Martinez, *
EMP: 221 EST: 1973
SQ FT: 69,880
SALES (est): 82.7MM
SALES (corp-wide): 82.7MM Privately Held
Web: www.nchs-health.org
SIC: 8011 Clinic, operated by physicians

(P-14924)
NORTH COUNTY HEALTH PRJ INC
1130 2nd St (92024-5008)
PHONE.................................760 736-6767
Patricia Cheu, Prin
EMP: 125
SQ FT: 7,513
SALES (corp-wide): 82.7MM Privately Held
Web: www.nchs-health.org
SIC: 8011 Clinic, operated by physicians
PA: North County Health Project Incorporated
150 Valpreda Rd Frnt
San Marcos CA
760 736-6755

(P-14925)
NORTH COUNTY HEALTH PRJ INC
605 Crouch St Bldg C (92054-4415)
PHONE.................................760 757-4566
Alicia Santos, Mgr
EMP: 68
SALES (corp-wide): 82.7MM Privately Held
Web: www.nchs-health.org
SIC: 8011 8093 Clinic, operated by physicians; Family planning and birth control clinics
PA: North County Health Project Incorporated
150 Valpreda Rd Frnt
San Marcos CA
760 736-6755

(P-14926)
NORTH EAST MEDICAL SERVICES (PA)
1520 Stockton St (94133-3354)
PHONE.................................415 391-9686
EMP: 100 EST: 1968
SALES (est): 154.39MM
SALES (corp-wide): 154.39MM Privately Held
Web: www.nems.org
SIC: 8011 Primary care medical clinic

(P-14927)
NORTHEAST VALLEY HEALTH CORP
12756 Van Nuys Blvd (91331-1696)
PHONE.................................818 896-0531
Kathreen Dayanim, Mgr

8011 - Offices And Clinics Of Medical Doctors (P-14928)

EMP: 73
SQ FT: 11,645
SALES (corp-wide): 119.71MM **Privately Held**
SIC: **8011** 8071 Clinic, operated by physicians; Medical laboratories
PA: Northeast Valley Health Corp
1172 N Maclay Ave
San Fernando CA
818 898-1388

(P-14928)
NORTHEASTERN RUR HLTH CLINICS (PA)
Also Called: WESTWOOD FAMILY PRACTICE
1850 Spring Ridge Dr (96130-6100)
PHONE.............................530 251-5000
Phil Nowak, *CEO*
Pamela Robbins, *
Richard Hrezo, *
Naomi Rea, *Dir*
Charles Giddings, *
EMP: 65 EST: 1977
SQ FT: 27,000
SALES (est): 17.35MM
SALES (corp-wide): 17.35MM **Privately Held**
Web: www.northeasternhealth.org
SIC: **8011** Clinic, operated by physicians

(P-14929)
OAK GROVE INST FOUNDATION INC (PA)
Also Called: Oak Grove Center
24275 Jefferson Ave (92562-7285)
PHONE.............................951 677-5599
Tamara L Wilson, *CEO*
Barry Soper, *
Fe Santiago, *
EMP: 148 EST: 1986
SQ FT: 39,000
SALES (est): 23.08MM **Privately Held**
Web: www.oakgrovecenter.org
SIC: **8011** 8211 8361 Psychiatric clinic; Specialty education; Residential care

(P-14930)
OAKS DIAGNOSTICS INC (PA)
Also Called: California Imaging Nework
6310 San Vicente Blvd (90048-5426)
P.O. Box 5355 (90209-5355)
PHONE.............................310 855-0035
Ronald Grusd Md, *CEO*
EMP: 60 EST: 1989
SQ FT: 9,000
SALES (est): 11.72MM **Privately Held**
SIC: **8011** Radiologist

(P-14931)
OCONNOR HOSPITAL
Also Called: O'Conner Wound Care Clinic
2105 Forest Ave 125 (95128-1471)
PHONE.............................408 947-2804
TOLL FREE: 800
Jena Eibschun, *Mgr*
EMP: 148
Web: och.sccgov.org
SIC: **8011** Medical centers
HQ: O'connor Hospital
2105 Forest Ave
San Jose CA
408 947-2500

(P-14932)
OJAI VLY FMLY MEDICINE GROUP
117 Pirie Rd Ste D (93023-3166)
PHONE.............................805 646-7246

James R Halverson Md, *Pt*
Carl Gross Md, *Pt*
Mary Dial Md, *Pt*
James Halverson Md, *Pt*
EMP: 65 EST: 1979
SALES (est): 9.71MM **Privately Held**
SIC: **8011** General and family practice, physician/surgeon

(P-14933)
OLE HEALTH
1141 Pear Tree Ln Ste 100 (94558-6485)
PHONE.............................707 254-1770
Alicia Hardy, *CEO*
Molly Nelson, *
EMP: 99 EST: 1972
SALES (est): 2.47MM **Privately Held**
Web: www.olehealth.org
SIC: **8011** General and family practice, physician/surgeon

(P-14934)
OLIVE VIEW-UCLA MEDICAL CENTER (PA)
Also Called: Valley Care Olive View Med Ctr
14445 Olive View Dr (91342-1437)
PHONE.............................818 364-1555
Carolyn Rhee, *CEO*
EMP: 85 EST: 2001
SALES (est): 80.94MM
SALES (corp-wide): 80.94MM **Privately Held**
Web: www.uclaoliveview.org
SIC: **8011** Medical centers

(P-14935)
OMNI FAMILY HEALTH (PA)
Also Called: COMMUNITY HEALTH CENTER
4900 California Ave Ste 400b (93309-7081)
P.O. Box 1060 (93263-1060)
PHONE.............................661 459-1900
Francisco L Castillon, *CEO*
Novira Irawan, *
Petrus Tjandra, *
Aurora Cooper, *
EMP: 80 EST: 1978
SQ FT: 14,000
SALES (est): 129.62MM
SALES (corp-wide): 129.62MM **Privately Held**
Web: www.omnifamilyhealth.org
SIC: **8011** Clinic, operated by physicians

(P-14936)
ON LOK INC
1333 Bush St (94109-5691)
PHONE.............................415 292-8888
Grace Li, *CEO*
Kelly Walsh, *
Grace Li, *COO*
EMP: 99 EST: 1989
SALES (est): 17.38MM **Privately Held**
Web: www.onlok.org
SIC: **8011** Offices and clinics of medical doctors

(P-14937)
ONE MEDICAL GROUP INC (HQ)
Also Called: One Medical
1 Embarcadero Ctr Ste 1900 (94111-3723)
PHONE.............................415 578-3100
Andrew Diamond, *CEO*
EMP: 96 EST: 2009
SALES (est): 102.73MM **Publicly Held**
Web: www.onemedical.com
SIC: **8011** General and family practice, physician/surgeon
PA: Amazon.Com, Inc.
410 Terry Ave N
Seattle WA

(P-14938)
ONRAD INC
Also Called: Onrad Medical Group
1770 Iowa Ave Ste 280 (92507-7401)
PHONE.............................800 848-5876
David Engert, *Pr*
Samuel Salen, *
Scott Castle, *CFO*
EMP: 79 EST: 2008
SQ FT: 1,500
SALES (est): 19.14MM **Privately Held**
Web: www.onradinc.com
SIC: **8011** Radiologist

(P-14939)
OPERATION SAMAHAN INC
Also Called: Camino Ruiz Suite 235
10737 Camino Ruiz Ste 235138 (92126-2375)
PHONE.............................619 477-4451
Dirk Virbel, *CEO*
EMP: 128
SALES (corp-wide): 15.49MM **Privately Held**
Web: www.operationsamahan.org
SIC: **8011** 8021 Clinic, operated by physicians; Offices and clinics of dentists
PA: Operation Samahan, Inc.
1428 Highland Ave
National City CA
619 477-4451

(P-14940)
OPTUMCARE MANAGEMENT LLC
Harriman Jones Medical
2600 Redondo Ave Ste 405 (90806-2330)
PHONE.............................562 988-7000
Jill R Cortese, *Prin*
EMP: 146
SIC: **8011** Clinic, operated by physicians
HQ: Optumcare Management, Llc
2175 Park Pl
El Segundo CA

(P-14941)
OPTUMCARE MANAGEMENT LLC (HQ)
Also Called: Healthcare Partners Med Group
2175 Park Pl (90245-4705)
PHONE.............................310 354-4200
EMP: 600 EST: 1994
SQ FT: 38,000
SALES (est): 596.22MM **Publicly Held**
SIC: **8011** Group health association
PA: Davita Inc.
2000 16th St
Denver CO

(P-14942)
OPTUMCARE MANAGEMENT LLC
502 Torrance Blvd (90277-3413)
PHONE.............................310 316-0811
Mark Moser, *Brnch Mgr*
EMP: 73
SQ FT: 23,000
SIC: **8011** General and family practice, physician/surgeon
HQ: Optumcare Management, Llc
2175 Park Pl
El Segundo CA

(P-14943)
ORANGE COAST WNS MED GROUP INC
1031 Avenida Pico Ste 204 (92673-6352)
PHONE.............................949 829-5522
EMP: 85

SALES (corp-wide): 16.1MM **Privately Held**
Web: www.ocwmg.com
SIC: **8011** Gynecologist
PA: Orange Coast Women's Medical Group, Inc.
24411 Health Center Dr # 200
Laguna Hills CA
949 829-5500

(P-14944)
OROHEALTH CORPORATION
Also Called: Oroville Hospital
900 Oro Dam Blvd E (95965-5832)
PHONE.............................530 534-9183
Mark Heinrich, *Dir*
EMP: 1127
SALES (corp-wide): 5.03MM **Privately Held**
SIC: **8011** 8062 Internal medicine, physician/surgeon; General medical and surgical hospitals
PA: Orohealth Corporation A Nonprofit Healthcare System
2767 Olive Hwy
Oroville CA
530 533-8500

(P-14945)
PACIFIC HMTLOGY ONCOLOGY ASSOC
2100 Webster St Ste 225 (94115-2376)
PHONE.............................415 923-3012
Kathleen Grant, *Owner*
Doctor Bertrand Y Tuan, *Pt*
Doctor Ari Baron, *Pt*
EMP: 63 EST: 1979
SQ FT: 1,856
SALES (est): 9.15MM **Privately Held**
Web: www.phoamd.com
SIC: **8011** Hematologist

(P-14946)
PACIFIC SHORES MED GROUP INC (HQ)
1043 Elm Ave Ste 104 (90813-3244)
PHONE.............................562 590-0345
Simon Tchekmedyian, *CEO*
EMP: 60 EST: 1995
SQ FT: 3,300
SALES (est): 19.42MM
SALES (corp-wide): 334.97MM **Privately Held**
Web: www.cityofhope.org
SIC: **8011** Medical centers
PA: City Of Hope
1500 Duarte Rd
Duarte CA
626 256-4673

(P-14947)
PACKARD CHILDRENS HLTH ALIANCE
Also Called: LUCILE PACKARD CHILDREN'S HOSP
725 Welch Rd (94304-1601)
PHONE.............................650 497-8000
Kim Robert, *CEO*
Lisa Holbrook, *COO*
EMP: 100 EST: 2012
SALES (est): 124.69MM
SALES (corp-wide): 15.13B **Privately Held**
Web: www.packardnetwork.org
SIC: **8011** Pediatrician
HQ: Lucile Salter Packard Children's Hospital At Stanford
725 Welch Rd
Palo Alto CA
650 497-8000

(P-14948)
PALO ALTO MED FNDTION STA CRUZ
2025 Soquel Ave (95062-1323)
PHONE..................831 458-5670
Larry Beghttaldi, *Pr*
Howard Salvay Md, *Sec*
EMP: 74 **EST:** 2004
SALES (est): 5.29MM **Privately Held**
SIC: 8011 General and family practice, physician/surgeon

(P-14949)
PALO ALTO MEDICAL FOUNDATION
795 El Camino Real (94301-2302)
PHONE..................650 321-4121
Karen L Butterfield, *Prin*
▲ **EMP:** 2920 **EST:** 1992
SALES (est): 18.63MM
SALES (corp-wide): 14.77B **Privately Held**
Web: www.pamf.org
SIC: 8011 General and family practice, physician/surgeon
PA: Sutter Health
2200 River Plaza Dr
Sacramento CA
916 733-8800

(P-14950)
PAVILION SURGERY CENTER LLC
Also Called: Pavilion Surgery Center
1140 W La Veta Ave Ste 300 (92868-4225)
PHONE..................714 744-8850
David Yomtoob, *Ch Bd*
EMP: 70 **EST:** 2016
SQ FT: 49,000
SALES (est): 9.63MM **Privately Held**
Web: www.pavilionsurgery.com
SIC: 8011 Surgeon

(P-14951)
PEACH TREE HEALTHCARE
5730 Packard Ave Ste 500 (95901-7119)
PHONE..................530 749-3242
Thomas Walther, *Pr*
EMP: 97 **EST:** 2000
SALES (est): 33.05MM **Privately Held**
Web: www.pickpeach.org
SIC: 8011 Clinic, operated by physicians

(P-14952)
PEACHWOOD MED GROUP CLOVIS INC
275 W Herndon Ave (93612-0204)
PHONE..................559 324-6200
Lee Copeland Md, *Pr*
Sue Marino, *
Jeffrey Hubbard, *
EMP: 70 **EST:** 1995
SQ FT: 33,595
SALES (est): 23.01MM **Privately Held**
Web: www.peachwoodmedicalgroup.com
SIC: 8011 General and family practice, physician/surgeon

(P-14953)
PEDIATRIC & FAMILY MEDICAL CTR
Also Called: EISNER PEDIATRIC & FAMILY MEDI
1530 S Olive St (90015-3023)
PHONE..................213 342-3325
Carl Coan, *CEO*
Kevin Rossi, *
Edward Matthews Iii, *V Ch*
Irma Avila, *
Carl Edward Coan, *
EMP: 160 **EST:** 1920
SQ FT: 21,000
SALES (est): 65.8MM **Privately Held**
Web: www.eisnerhealth.org
SIC: 8011 Clinic, operated by physicians

(P-14954)
PEDIATRIC NROLOGY THERAPEUTICS
7090 Miratech Dr (92121-3109)
PHONE..................858 304-6440
Melissa D Knopp, *Dir*
EMP: 82 **EST:** 2017
SALES (est): 237.28K **Privately Held**
Web: www.corticacare.com
SIC: 8011 Neurologist

(P-14955)
PEOPLE CREATING SUCCESS INC
380 Arneill Rd (93010-6406)
PHONE..................805 644-9480
Marie Mcmanus, *Brnch Mgr*
EMP: 99
SALES (corp-wide): 14.09MM **Privately Held**
Web: www.pcs-services.org
SIC: 8011 Offices and clinics of medical doctors
PA: People Creating Success, Inc.
2585 Teller Rd
Newbury Park CA
805 375-9222

(P-14956)
PERLMAN CLINIC
3900 5th Ave Ste 110 (92103-3122)
PHONE..................858 554-1212
EMP: 149 **EST:** 2010
SALES (est): 5.51MM **Privately Held**
Web: www.perlmanclinic.com
SIC: 8011 General and family practice, physician/surgeon

(P-14957)
PERMANENTE MEDICAL GROUP INC
Also Called: Kaiser Prmnnte Modesto Med Ctr
4601 Dale Rd (95356-9718)
PHONE..................209 735-5000
EMP: 1670
SALES (corp-wide): 68.1B **Privately Held**
Web: www.permanente.org
SIC: 8011 Offices and clinics of medical doctors
HQ: The Permanente Medical Group Inc
1950 Franklin St Fl 7th
Oakland CA
866 858-2226

(P-14958)
PERMANENTE MEDICAL GROUP INC
97 San Marin Dr (94945-1100)
PHONE..................415 899-7400
Willa Jefferson-stokes, *Mgr*
EMP: 522
SALES (corp-wide): 68.1B **Privately Held**
Web: www.permanente.org
SIC: 8011 Internal medicine practitioners
HQ: The Permanente Medical Group Inc
1950 Franklin St Fl 7th
Oakland CA
866 858-2226

(P-14959)
PERMANENTE MEDICAL GROUP INC
395 Hickey Blvd Fl 2 (94015-2770)
PHONE..................650 301-5800
EMP: 626
SALES (corp-wide): 68.1B **Privately Held**
Web: www.permanente.org
SIC: 8011 Medical centers
HQ: The Permanente Medical Group Inc
1950 Franklin St Fl 7th
Oakland CA
866 858-2226

(P-14960)
PERMANENTE MEDICAL GROUP INC
1617 Broadway St (94590-2406)
PHONE..................707 765-3930
Robin E Bjorger, *Brnch Mgr*
EMP: 522
SALES (corp-wide): 68.1B **Privately Held**
Web: www.permanente.org
SIC: 8011 Medical centers
HQ: The Permanente Medical Group Inc
1950 Franklin St Fl 7th
Oakland CA
866 858-2226

(P-14961)
PERMANENTE MEDICAL GROUP INC
1800 Harrison St 7th Fl (94612-3467)
PHONE..................510 625-6262
Connie Wilson, *Brnch Mgr*
EMP: 835
SALES (corp-wide): 68.1B **Privately Held**
Web: www.permanente.org
SIC: 8011 Medical centers
HQ: The Permanente Medical Group Inc
1950 Franklin St Fl 7th
Oakland CA
866 858-2226

(P-14962)
PERMANENTE MEDICAL GROUP INC
7300 N Fresno St (93720-2941)
PHONE..................559 448-4500
Irene Ann Heetebry, *Prin*
EMP: 626
SALES (corp-wide): 68.1B **Privately Held**
Web: www.permanente.org
SIC: 8011 Medical centers
HQ: The Permanente Medical Group Inc
1950 Franklin St Fl 7th
Oakland CA
866 858-2226

(P-14963)
PERMANENTE MEDICAL GROUP INC
901 El Camino Real (94066-3009)
PHONE..................650 742-2100
Cheryl Halcovich, *Mgr*
EMP: 522
SALES (corp-wide): 68.1B **Privately Held**
Web: www.permanente.org
SIC: 8011 Medical centers
HQ: The Permanente Medical Group Inc
1950 Franklin St Fl 7th
Oakland CA
866 858-2226

(P-14964)
PERMANENTE MEDICAL GROUP INC
3558 Round Barn Blvd (95403-1780)
PHONE..................707 393-4000
Pat Henson, *Prin*
EMP: 731
SALES (corp-wide): 68.1B **Privately Held**
Web: www.permanente.org
SIC: 8011 Medical centers
HQ: The Permanente Medical Group Inc
1950 Franklin St Fl 7th
Oakland CA
866 858-2226

(P-14965)
PERMANENTE MEDICAL GROUP INC
Also Called: Labratory
2425 Geary Blvd (94115-3358)
PHONE..................415 833-2000
Harry Chima, *Mgr*
EMP: 626
SALES (corp-wide): 68.1B **Privately Held**
Web: www.permanente.org
SIC: 8011 Medical centers
HQ: The Permanente Medical Group Inc
1950 Franklin St Fl 7th
Oakland CA
866 858-2226

(P-14966)
PERMANENTE MEDICAL GROUP INC
275 Hospital Pkwy Ste 470 (95119-1104)
PHONE..................408 972-6883
Maurice Alfaro, *Dir*
EMP: 418
SALES (corp-wide): 68.1B **Privately Held**
Web: www.permanente.org
SIC: 8011 Medical centers
HQ: The Permanente Medical Group Inc
1950 Franklin St Fl 7th
Oakland CA
866 858-2226

(P-14967)
PERMANENTE MEDICAL GROUP INC
200 Muir Rd (94553-4614)
PHONE..................925 372-1000
EMP: 418
SALES (corp-wide): 68.1B **Privately Held**
Web: www.permanente.org
SIC: 8011 Medical centers
HQ: The Permanente Medical Group Inc
1950 Franklin St Fl 7th
Oakland CA
866 858-2226

(P-14968)
PERMANENTE MEDICAL GROUP INC
3779 Piedmont Ave (94611-5347)
PHONE..................510 752-1000
Ellen P Brennan, *Brnch Mgr*
EMP: 418
SALES (corp-wide): 68.1B **Privately Held**
Web: www.permanente.org
SIC: 8011 Medical centers
HQ: The Permanente Medical Group Inc
1950 Franklin St Fl 7th
Oakland CA
866 858-2226

(P-14969)
PERMANENTE MEDICAL GROUP INC
39400 Paseo Padre Pkwy (94538-2310)
PHONE..................510 248-3000
EMP: 522
SALES (corp-wide): 68.1B **Privately Held**
Web: www.permanente.org

8011 - Offices And Clinics Of Medical Doctors (P-14970)

PRODUCTS & SERVICES SECTION

SIC: 8011 Medical centers
HQ: The Permanente Medical Group Inc
1950 Franklin St Fl 7th
Oakland CA
866 858-2226

(P-14970)
PERMANENTE MEDICAL GROUP INC
235 W Macarthur Blvd (94611-5641)
PHONE.....................510 752-1190
Marta Perl, *Brnch Mgr*
EMP: 626
SALES (corp-wide): 68.1B **Privately Held**
Web: www.permanente.org
SIC: 8011 Medical centers
HQ: The Permanente Medical Group Inc
1950 Franklin St Fl 7th
Oakland CA
866 858-2226

(P-14971)
PERMANENTE MEDICAL GROUP INC
770 E Calaveras Blvd (95035-5491)
PHONE.....................408 945-2900
Bindu Israni, *Brnch Mgr*
EMP: 418
SALES (corp-wide): 68.1B **Privately Held**
Web: www.permanente.org
SIC: 8011 Medical centers
HQ: The Permanente Medical Group Inc
1950 Franklin St Fl 7th
Oakland CA
866 858-2226

(P-14972)
PERMANENTE MEDICAL GROUP INC
4501 Sand Creek Rd (94531-8687)
PHONE.....................925 813-6149
Kim Daily, *Brnch Mgr*
EMP: 522
SALES (corp-wide): 68.1B **Privately Held**
Web: www.permanente.org
SIC: 8011 Medical centers
HQ: The Permanente Medical Group Inc
1950 Franklin St Fl 7th
Oakland CA
866 858-2226

(P-14973)
PERMANENTE MEDICAL GROUP INC
1150 Veterans Blvd (94063-2037)
PHONE.....................650 299-2000
Arlene Mccarthy, *Prin*
EMP: 731
SALES (corp-wide): 68.1B **Privately Held**
Web: www.permanente.org
SIC: 8011 Medical centers
HQ: The Permanente Medical Group Inc
1950 Franklin St Fl 7th
Oakland CA
866 858-2226

(P-14974)
PERMANENTE MEDICAL GROUP INC
910 Marshall St (94063-2033)
PHONE.....................650 299-2015
Christina Apostolakos, *Dir*
EMP: 522
SALES (corp-wide): 68.1B **Privately Held**
Web: www.permanente.org
SIC: 8011 Medical centers
HQ: The Permanente Medical Group Inc
1950 Franklin St Fl 7th
Oakland CA
866 858-2226

(P-14975)
PERMANENTE MEDICAL GROUP INC
914 Marina Way S (94804-3739)
PHONE.....................510 231-5406
C J Bhalla, *VP*
EMP: 626
SALES (corp-wide): 68.1B **Privately Held**
Web: www.permanente.org
SIC: 8011 Medical centers
HQ: The Permanente Medical Group Inc
1950 Franklin St Fl 7th
Oakland CA
866 858-2226

(P-14976)
PERMANENTE MEDICAL GROUP INC
3184 Arden Way (95825-3701)
PHONE.....................916 486-5686
Greg Chappel, *Brnch Mgr*
EMP: 418
SALES (corp-wide): 68.1B **Privately Held**
Web: www.permanente.org
SIC: 8011 Medical centers
HQ: The Permanente Medical Group Inc
1950 Franklin St Fl 7th
Oakland CA
866 858-2226

(P-14977)
PERMANENTE MEDICAL GROUP INC
2500 Merced St (94577-4201)
PHONE.....................510 454-1000
EMP: 1670
SALES (corp-wide): 68.1B **Privately Held**
Web: www.permanente.org
SIC: 8011 Medical centers
HQ: The Permanente Medical Group Inc
1950 Franklin St Fl 7th
Oakland CA
866 858-2226

(P-14978)
PERMANENTE MEDICAL GROUP INC
99 Montecillo Rd (94903-3308)
PHONE.....................415 444-2000
EMP: 418
SALES (corp-wide): 68.1B **Privately Held**
Web: www.permanente.org
SIC: 8011 Medical centers
HQ: The Permanente Medical Group Inc
1950 Franklin St Fl 7th
Oakland CA
866 858-2226

(P-14979)
PERMANENTE MEDICAL GROUP INC
320 Lennon Ln (94598-2419)
PHONE.....................925 906-2000
EMP: 522
SALES (corp-wide): 68.1B **Privately Held**
Web: www.permanente.org
SIC: 8011 Medical centers
HQ: The Permanente Medical Group Inc
1950 Franklin St Fl 7th
Oakland CA
866 858-2226

(P-14980)
PERMANENTE MEDICAL GROUP INC
100 Rowland Way Ste 125 (94945-5040)
PHONE.....................415 209-2444
EMP: 418

SALES (corp-wide): 68.1B **Privately Held**
Web: www.permanente.org
SIC: 8011 Medical centers
HQ: The Permanente Medical Group Inc
1950 Franklin St Fl 7th
Oakland CA
866 858-2226

(P-14981)
PERMANENTE MEDICAL GROUP INC
1600 Eureka Rd (95661-3027)
PHONE.....................916 784-4000
Craig Green Md, *Dir*
EMP: 731
SALES (corp-wide): 68.1B **Privately Held**
Web: www.permanente.org
SIC: 8011 Medical centers
HQ: The Permanente Medical Group Inc
1950 Franklin St Fl 7th
Oakland CA
866 858-2226

(P-14982)
PERMANENTE MEDICAL GROUP INC
7373 West Ln (95210-3377)
PHONE.....................209 476-3737
Michael Coleman, *Prin*
EMP: 522
SALES (corp-wide): 68.1B **Privately Held**
Web: www.permanente.org
SIC: 8011 Medical centers
HQ: The Permanente Medical Group Inc
1950 Franklin St Fl 7th
Oakland CA
866 858-2226

(P-14983)
PERMANENTE MEDICAL GROUP INC
2238 Geary Blvd (94115-3416)
PHONE.....................415 833-2000
Philip R Madvig Md Physn, *Prin*
EMP: 626
SALES (corp-wide): 68.1B **Privately Held**
Web: www.permanente.org
SIC: 8011 Medical centers
HQ: The Permanente Medical Group Inc
1950 Franklin St Fl 7th
Oakland CA
866 858-2226

(P-14984)
PERMANENTE MEDICAL GROUP INC
1750 2nd St (94710-1705)
PHONE.....................510 559-5338
Dianne Easterwood, *Genl Mgr*
EMP: 522
SALES (corp-wide): 68.1B **Privately Held**
Web: www.permanente.org
SIC: 8011 Medical centers
HQ: The Permanente Medical Group Inc
1950 Franklin St Fl 7th
Oakland CA
866 858-2226

(P-14985)
PERMANENTE MEDICAL GROUP INC
1305 Tommydon St (95210-3364)
PHONE.....................209 476-2000
Jack Gillimand, *Brnch Mgr*
EMP: 626
SALES (corp-wide): 68.1B **Privately Held**
Web: www.permanente.org
SIC: 8011 Medical centers
HQ: The Permanente Medical Group Inc
1950 Franklin St Fl 7th
Oakland CA
866 858-2226

(P-14986)
PERMANENTE MEDICAL GROUP INC
Also Called: S C P M G
25825 Vermont Ave (90710-3518)
PHONE.....................310 325-5111
TOLL FREE: 800
Leroy Foster, *Mgr*
EMP: 522
SALES (corp-wide): 68.1B **Privately Held**
Web: www.permanente.org
SIC: 8011 Medical centers
HQ: The Permanente Medical Group Inc
1950 Franklin St Fl 7th
Oakland CA
866 858-2226

(P-14987)
PERMANENTE MEDICAL GROUP INC
3000 Las Positas Rd (94551-9627)
PHONE.....................925 243-2600
Stan Combs, *Mgr*
EMP: 522
SALES (corp-wide): 68.1B **Privately Held**
Web: www.permanente.org
SIC: 8011 Medical centers
HQ: The Permanente Medical Group Inc
1950 Franklin St Fl 7th
Oakland CA
866 858-2226

(P-14988)
PERMANENTE MEDICAL GROUP INC
1000 Franklin Pkwy (94403-1922)
PHONE.....................650 358-7000
EMP: 522
SALES (corp-wide): 68.1B **Privately Held**
Web: www.permanente.org
SIC: 8011 Medical centers
HQ: The Permanente Medical Group Inc
1950 Franklin St Fl 7th
Oakland CA
866 858-2226

(P-14989)
PERMANENTE MEDICAL GROUP INC
3900 Lakeville Hwy (94954-5698)
PHONE.....................707 765-3900
Willa Jefferson-stokes, *Mgr*
EMP: 522
SALES (corp-wide): 68.1B **Privately Held**
Web: www.permanente.org
SIC: 8011 Clinic, operated by physicians
HQ: The Permanente Medical Group Inc
1950 Franklin St Fl 7th
Oakland CA
866 858-2226

(P-14990)
PERMANENTE MEDICAL GROUP INC
10725 International Dr (95670-7967)
PHONE.....................916 631-3000
Donald Forrester, *Brnch Mgr*
EMP: 418
SALES (corp-wide): 68.1B **Privately Held**
Web: www.permanente.org
SIC: 8011 Clinic, operated by physicians
HQ: The Permanente Medical Group Inc
1950 Franklin St Fl 7th
Oakland CA
866 858-2226

PRODUCTS & SERVICES SECTION — 8011 - Offices And Clinics Of Medical Doctors (P-15011)

(P-14991)
PERMANENTE MEDICAL GROUP INC
6600 Bruceville Rd (95823-4671)
PHONE..................916 688-2055
Kevin L Smith, *Brnch Mgr*
EMP: 626
SALES (corp-wide): 68.1B **Privately Held**
Web: www.permanente.org
SIC: 8011 Gynecologist
HQ: The Permanente Medical Group Inc
1950 Franklin St Fl 7th
Oakland CA
866 858-2226

(P-14992)
PETALUMA HEALTH CENTER INC
Also Called: PETALUMA HEALTH CENTER
1179 N Mcdowell Blvd Ste A (94954-1171)
PHONE..................707 559-7500
Kathryn Powell, *CEO*
Brian Burns, *
Daymon Doss, *
Jane Read, *
EMP: 325 EST: 1999
SALES (est): 63.58MM **Privately Held**
Web: www.phealthcenter.org
SIC: 8011 Clinic, operated by physicians

(P-14993)
PETER CASTILLO MD PA
Also Called: Kaiser Prmnnte Snta Clara Med
15215 National Ave Ste 104 (95032-2425)
PHONE..................408 236-6400
Peter Castillo, *Owner*
EMP: 716 EST: 2007
SALES (est): 12.24MM **Privately Held**
SIC: 8011 General and family practice, physician/surgeon

(P-14994)
PINE PARK HEALTH INC
2144 65th Ave Ste F (94621-3818)
PHONE..................925 594-3533
George Kahfin, *CEO*
EMP: 68 EST: 2020
SALES (est): 2.91MM **Privately Held**
Web: www.pineparkhealth.com
SIC: 8011 General and family practice, physician/surgeon

(P-14995)
PLACER DRMTLOGY SKIN CARE CTR
9624 Wexford Cir (95746-7113)
PHONE..................916 797-6261
Artur Z Henke, *Brnch Mgr*
EMP: 60
Web: www.placerdermatology.com
SIC: 8011 Dermatologist
PA: Placer Dermatology & Skin Care Center Inc.
9285 Sierra College Blvd
Roseville CA

(P-14996)
PLUSHCARE INC
101 Mission St Ste 800 (94105-1744)
PHONE..................415 231-5333
Ryan Mcquaid, *Prin*
James Wantuck, *
EMP: 100 EST: 2013
SALES (est): 10.88MM **Publicly Held**
Web: www.plushcare.com
SIC: 8011 Offices and clinics of medical doctors
PA: Accolade, Inc.
1201 3rd Ave Ste 1700
Seattle WA

(P-14997)
PRECISION DERMATOLOGY INC
7064 Corline Ct Ste C (95472-4528)
PHONE..................415 202-1540
EMP: 66
SALES (corp-wide): 1.32MM **Privately Held**
SIC: 8011 Dermatologist
PA: Precision Dermatology, Inc.
1 Blackfield Dr
Belvedere Tiburon CA
415 887-8201

(P-14998)
PREMIER OTPTENT SRGERY CTR INC
Also Called: Amsurg
900 E Washington St Ste 155 (92324-7111)
PHONE..................909 370-2190
David Wood, *Pr*
EMP: 103 EST: 2000
SQ FT: 70,000
SALES (est): 3.52MM **Privately Held**
Web: www.premierosc.com
SIC: 8011 Surgeon

(P-14999)
PROGRESSIVE HEALTH CARE SYSTEM
Also Called: P H S
8510 Balboa Blvd Ste 150 (91325-5810)
PHONE..................818 707-9603
EMP: 100 EST: 1999
SQ FT: 10,000
SALES (est): 4.49MM **Privately Held**
Web: www.msophs.com
SIC: 8011 Offices and clinics of medical doctors

(P-15000)
PROSPECT MEDICAL HOLDINGS INC (PA)
3415 S Sepulveda Blvd Fl 9 (90034-6060)
PHONE..................310 943-4500
Samuel Lee, *Ch Bd*
Mike Heather, *
Donna Vigil, *
Linda Hodges, *
EMP: 211 EST: 1993
SQ FT: 7,154
SALES (est): 3.91B
SALES (corp-wide): 3.91B **Privately Held**
Web: www.pmh.com
SIC: 8011 Health maintenance organization

(P-15001)
PROVIDNCE FACEY MED FOUNDATION (PA)
15451 San Fernando Mission Blvd (91345-1301)
PHONE..................818 365-9531
Bill Gill, *CEO*
Jim Corwin, *
EMP: 170 EST: 1991
SQ FT: 306,000
SALES (est): 91.37MM
SALES (corp-wide): 91.37MM **Privately Held**
Web: www.facey.com
SIC: 8011 Physicians' office, including specialists

(P-15002)
PROVIDNCE FACEY MED FOUNDATION
27924 Seco Canyon Rd (91350-3870)
PHONE..................661 513-2100
Joan Rhee, *Mgr*
EMP: 91
SALES (corp-wide): 91.37MM **Privately Held**
Web: www.facey.com
SIC: 8011 Physicians' office, including specialists
PA: Providence Facey Medical Foundation
15451 San Frnndo Mssion B
Mission Hills CA
818 365-9531

(P-15003)
PROVIDNCE FACEY MED FOUNDATION
11165 Sepulveda Blvd (91345-1113)
PHONE..................818 365-9531
Judy Breen, *Brnch Mgr*
EMP: 122
SALES (corp-wide): 91.37MM **Privately Held**
Web: www.facey.com
SIC: 8011 Physicians' office, including specialists
PA: Providence Facey Medical Foundation
15451 San Frnndo Mssion B
Mission Hills CA
818 365-9531

(P-15004)
PSYCHTRIC CTRS AT SAN DEGO INC (HQ)
4542 Ruffner St Ste 200 (92111-2239)
P.O. Box 609001 (92160-9001)
PHONE..................619 528-4600
Christopher Morache, *Pr*
Fernando Kwiatkowski, *
Jada Brathwaite, *
▲ EMP: 68 EST: 1969
SQ FT: 2,000
SALES (est): 13.65MM
SALES (corp-wide): 70.44MM **Privately Held**
Web: www.mindpath.com
SIC: 8011 Psychiatrist
PA: Community Psychiatry Management, Llc
3835 N Freeway Blvd # 100
Sacramento CA
855 501-1004

(P-15005)
QUEENSCARE HEALTH CENTERS
Also Called: Queenscare Fmly Clnics - Estsi
4816 E 3rd St (90022-1602)
PHONE..................323 780-4510
Evelyn Moody, *Mgr*
EMP: 82
SALES (corp-wide): 36.05MM **Privately Held**
Web: www.queenscarehealthcenters.org
SIC: 8011 Clinic, operated by physicians
PA: Queenscare Health Centers
950 Suth Grnd Ave Fl 2
Los Angeles CA
323 669-4301

(P-15006)
QUEENSCARE HEALTH CENTERS
4618 Fountain Ave (90029-1830)
PHONE..................323 644-6180
Guillermo Diaz, *Brnch Mgr*
EMP: 83
SALES (corp-wide): 36.05MM **Privately Held**
Web: www.queenscarehealthcenters.org
SIC: 8011 Clinic, operated by physicians
PA: Queenscare Health Centers
950 Suth Grnd Ave Fl 2
Los Angeles CA
323 669-4301

(P-15007)
RADIOLOGY PARTNERS INC (HQ)
Also Called: Cirpa Radiology Management
2101 E El Segundo Blvd Ste 401 (90245-4518)
PHONE..................424 290-8004
Richard Whitney, *CEO*
EMP: 500 EST: 2012
SALES (est): 126.78MM
SALES (corp-wide): 137.27MM **Privately Held**
Web: www.radpartners.com
SIC: 8011 Radiologist
PA: Radiology Partners Holdings, Llc
2330 Utah Ave Ste 200
El Segundo CA
424 290-8004

(P-15008)
RADIOLOGY PRTNERS HOLDINGS LLC (PA)
2330 Utah Ave Ste 200 (90245-4817)
PHONE..................424 290-8004
Rich Whitney, *CEO*
Jay Bronner, *Pr*
Steve Tumbarello, *CFO*
Anthony Gabriel, *COO*
Krishna Nallamshetty, *CMO*
EMP: 118 EST: 2013
SALES (est): 137.27MM
SALES (corp-wide): 137.27MM **Privately Held**
SIC: 8011 Radiologist

(P-15009)
RADNET MANAGEMENT I INC
Also Called: Radnet Management
44725 10th St W Ste 150 (93534-3000)
PHONE..................661 945-5855
Mike Buxton, *Mgr*
EMP: 101 EST: 1982
SQ FT: 1,600
SALES (est): 9.48MM **Publicly Held**
SIC: 8011 Radiologist
PA: Radnet, Inc.
1510 Cotner Ave
Los Angeles CA

(P-15010)
RADY CHILDRENS SPECIALISTS
7920 Frost St Ste 200 (92123-4289)
PHONE..................858 966-8197
Kimberly Coly, *Off Mgr*
EMP: 60 EST: 2015
SALES (est): 995.91K **Privately Held**
Web: www.rchsd.org
SIC: 8011 Physicians' office, including specialists

(P-15011)
RAVI PATEL MD INC
Also Called: Comprehensive Blood Cancer Ctr
6501 Truxtun Ave (93309-0633)
PHONE..................661 862-7113
EMP: 250 EST: 1987
SALES (est): 30.27MM **Privately Held**
Web: www.cbccusa.com
SIC: 8011 Medical centers

8011 - Offices And Clinics Of Medical Doctors (P-15012)

(P-15012)
REDDING PATHOLOGISTS LAB (PA)
1725 Gold St (96001-1820)
PHONE..................530 225-8000
TOLL FREE: 800
Richard Severance Md, *Pt*
Richard O Boyd Md, *Pt*
John P Greaves Junior Md, *Pt*
Don Stanton Md, *Pt*
Tikoes Blankenberg Md, *Pt*
EMP: 115 EST: 1954
SQ FT: 8,000
SALES (est): 8.39MM
SALES (corp-wide): 8.39MM Privately Held
SIC: 8011 8071 Pathologist; Medical laboratories

(P-15013)
REDWOOD FAMILY CARE NETWRK INC
13920 City Center Dr (91709-5432)
PHONE..................909 942-0218
David Catrell, *Pr*
EMP: 2300 EST: 2021
SALES (est): 70.95MM Privately Held
Web: www.redwoodfcn.com
SIC: 8011 Medical centers

(P-15014)
REDWOOD RGNAL MED GROUP DRG LL
Also Called: Mirda, Daniel P MD
1100 Trancas St Ste 256 (94558-2921)
PHONE..................707 253-7161
Paul J Dugan, *Dir*
EMP: 68
SALES (corp-wide): 11.15MM Privately Held
SIC: 8011 Hematologist
PA: Redwood Regional Medical Group Drug Company, Llc
990 Sonoma Ave Ste 15
Santa Rosa CA
707 525-4080

(P-15015)
RENEW MEDICAL GROUP INC
1125 S Beverly Dr Ste 720 (90035-1180)
PHONE..................310 929-9790
EMP: 84
SALES (corp-wide): 899.19K Privately Held
SIC: 8011 Medical centers
PA: Renew Medical Group, Inc.
3142 Vista Way Ste 206
Oceanside CA
760 721-4000

(P-15016)
REPRODUCTIVE SCIENCE CENTER
Also Called: Reproductive Science Ctr Bay
100 Park Pl Ste 200 (94583-4416)
PHONE..................925 867-1800
Susan Willman, *CEO*
Susan Willman, *Prin*
Donald I Galen, *
Louis Weckstein, *
EMP: 75 EST: 1985
SALES (est): 17.17MM Privately Held
Web: www.rscbayarea.com
SIC: 8011 Physicians' office, including specialists

(P-15017)
RIVERSD-SAN BRNRDINO CNTY INDI (PA)
11980 Mount Vernon Ave (92313-5172)
PHONE..................909 864-1097
Jackie Wisespirit, *Pr*
Charles Castello, *
Faith Morreo, *
Brandie Miranda, *
Bill Thomsen, *
EMP: 113 EST: 1974
SQ FT: 38,000
SALES (est): 92.69MM
SALES (corp-wide): 92.69MM Privately Held
Web: www.rsbcihi.org
SIC: 8011 8093 Clinic, operated by physicians; Specialty outpatient clinics, nec

(P-15018)
RIVERSD-SAN BRNRDINO CNTY INDI
Also Called: Soboba Indian Health Clinic
607 Donna Way (92583-5517)
PHONE..................951 654-0803
Maria Adams, *Mgr*
EMP: 135
SALES (corp-wide): 92.69MM Privately Held
Web: www.rsbcihi.org
SIC: 8011 Clinic, operated by physicians
PA: Riverside-San Bernardino County Indian Health, Inc.
11980 Mount Vernon Ave
Grand Terrace CA
909 864-1097

(P-15019)
RIVERSIDE MEDICAL CLINIC INC
Also Called: Riverside Medical Clinic
7117 Brockton Ave (92506-3987)
PHONE..................951 683-6370
Judy Carpenter, *Mgr*
EMP: 65
SALES (corp-wide): 102.29MM Privately Held
Web: www.riversidemedicalclinic.com
SIC: 8011 Clinic, operated by physicians
PA: Riverside Medical Clinic, Inc.
3660 Arlington Ave
Riverside CA
951 683-6370

(P-15020)
RIVERSIDE MEDICAL CLINIC INC
6250 Clay St (92509-6005)
PHONE..................951 360-5250
Sandra Alvarez, *Mgr*
EMP: 65
SALES (corp-wide): 102.29MM Privately Held
Web: www.riversidemedicalclinic.com
SIC: 8011 Clinic, operated by physicians
PA: Riverside Medical Clinic, Inc.
3660 Arlington Ave
Riverside CA
951 683-6370

(P-15021)
RIVERSIDE MEDICAL CLINIC INC
Also Called: Albert Y Li MD Appintment Line
7117 Brockton Ave Fl 3 (92506-3987)
PHONE..................951 782-3614
Albert Li, *Prin*
EMP: 65
SALES (corp-wide): 102.29MM Privately Held

(P-15022)
RIVERSIDE MEDICAL CLINIC INC
Also Called: Riverside Med Clinic Cyn Sprng
6405 Day St (92507-0901)
PHONE..................951 683-6370
Mary Pat Gates, *Prin*
EMP: 65
SALES (corp-wide): 102.29MM Privately Held
Web: www.riversidemedicalclinic.com
SIC: 8011 Clinic, operated by physicians
PA: Riverside Medical Clinic, Inc.
3660 Arlington Ave
Riverside CA
951 683-6370

(P-15023)
RIVERSIDE MEDICAL CLINIC INC
12742 Limonite Ave (92880-9630)
PHONE..................626 388-2392
EMP: 65
SALES (corp-wide): 102.29MM Privately Held
Web: www.riversidemedicalclinic.com
SIC: 8011 Clinic, operated by physicians
PA: Riverside Medical Clinic, Inc.
3660 Arlington Ave
Riverside CA
951 683-6370

(P-15024)
RIVERSIDE MEDICAL CLINIC INC (PA)
Also Called: Riverside Med Clnic Ptient Ctr
3660 Arlington Ave (92506-3912)
PHONE..................951 683-6370
Steven E Larson, *Pr*
Judy Carpenter, *
Steven E Larson, *Pr*
EMP: 89 EST: 1993
SQ FT: 65,000
SALES (est): 102.29MM
SALES (corp-wide): 102.29MM Privately Held
Web: www.riversidemedicalclinic.com
SIC: 8011 Clinic, operated by physicians

(P-15025)
RIVERSIDE MEDICAL CLINIC INC
Also Called: Anil Garde M.D.
7117 Brockton Ave Fl 2 (92506-3987)
PHONE..................951 782-3615
Anil R Garde, *Prin*
EMP: 65
SQ FT: 672
SALES (corp-wide): 102.29MM Privately Held
Web: www.riversidemedicalclinic.com
SIC: 8011 Clinic, operated by physicians
PA: Riverside Medical Clinic, Inc.
3660 Arlington Ave
Riverside CA
951 683-6370

(P-15026)
RIVERSIDE MEDICAL CLINIC INC
Also Called: Lawrence D. Sharpe M.D.
7117 Brockton Ave (92506-3987)
PHONE..................951 782-3684
Lawrence D Sharpe, *Prin*
EMP: 65
SALES (corp-wide): 102.29MM Privately Held
Web: www.riversidemedicalclinic.com
SIC: 8011 Clinic, operated by physicians
PA: Riverside Medical Clinic, Inc.
3660 Arlington Ave
Riverside CA
951 683-6370

(P-15027)
RIVERSIDE MEDICAL CLINIC INC
7160 Brockton Ave (92506-2620)
PHONE..................951 782-3846
Shira L Young, *Mgr*
EMP: 65
SALES (corp-wide): 102.29MM Privately Held
Web: www.riversidemedicalclinic.com
SIC: 8011 Gynecologist
PA: Riverside Medical Clinic, Inc.
3660 Arlington Ave
Riverside CA
951 683-6370

(P-15028)
ROBERT K MALONEY MD INC
Also Called: Maloney Vision Institute
10921 Wilshire Blvd Ste 900 (90024-3906)
PHONE..................310 208-3937
Robert K Maloney, *Pr*
EMP: 61 EST: 1999
SALES (est): 10.4MM Privately Held
Web: www.maloneyshamievision.com
SIC: 8011 8062 Opthalmologist; General medical and surgical hospitals

(P-15029)
ROBIN RED BREAST INC
6616 Lexington Ave (90038-1306)
PHONE..................323 466-7800
Jesse Meoli, *Admn*
EMP: 76 EST: 2010
SALES (est): 1.23MM Privately Held
Web: www.titmouse.net
SIC: 8011 General and family practice, physician/surgeon

(P-15030)
ROLLING OAKS RADIOLOGY INC
Also Called: Westlake Diagnostic Center
415 Rolling Oaks Dr (91361-1029)
PHONE..................805 778-1513
Robert A Princethal Md, *Pr*
Roy Gottlieb, *
Josephine Lee, *
EMP: 73 EST: 1993
SQ FT: 2,500
SALES (est): 24.08MM Publicly Held
Web: www.radnet.com
SIC: 8011 Radiologist
PA: Radnet, Inc.
1510 Cotner Ave
Los Angeles CA

(P-15031)
SACRAMNTO BHVRAL HLTHCARE HOSP
1400 Expo Pkwy (95815-4230)
PHONE..................916 437-6410
Susan Rose, *Managing Member*
EMP: 150 EST: 2012
SALES (est): 7.63MM Privately Held
Web: www.norcalbehavioral.com
SIC: 8011 Psychiatric clinic

PRODUCTS & SERVICES SECTION
8011 - Offices And Clinics Of Medical Doctors (P-15053)

(P-15032)
SACRAMNTO NTIV AMERCN HLTH CTR
2020 J St (95811-3120)
PHONE....................916 341-0575
Ricardo Torres, *
Britta Guerrero, *
Ricardo Torres, *
EMP: 119 EST: 2005
SQ FT: 39,573
SALES (est): 20.11MM Privately Held
Web: www.snahc.org
SIC: 8011 Clinic, operated by physicians

(P-15033)
SAINT JHNS HLTH CTR FOUNDATION
Wayne, John Cancer Institute
2200 Santa Monica Blvd (90404-2312)
PHONE....................310 315-6111
Donald Mortan, Dir
EMP: 125
SQ FT: 7,100
SALES (corp-wide): 10.75B Privately Held
Web: www.pacificneuroscienceinstitute.org
SIC: 8011 8731 Primary care medical clinic; Commercial physical research
HQ: Saint John's Health Center Foundation.
2121 Santa Monica Blvd
Santa Monica CA
310 829-5511

(P-15034)
SALINAS VALLEY MEDICAL CLINIC
236 San Jose St (93901-3901)
PHONE....................831 424-7389
EMP: 94 EST: 2017
SALES (est): 5.19MM
SALES (corp-wide): 255.85K Privately Held
Web: www.salinasvalleyhealth.com
SIC: 8011 Cardiologist and cardio-vascular specialist
PA: Salinas Valley Health
450 E Romie Ln
Salinas CA
831 757-4333

(P-15035)
SALUD PARA LA GENTE
Also Called: SALUD PARA LA GENTE HEALTH CLI
195 Aviation Way Ste 200 (95076-2059)
PHONE....................831 728-0222
Dori Rose Inda, Interim Chief Executive Officer
Tony Balistreri, *
EMP: 125 EST: 1980
SALES (est): 43.04MM Privately Held
Web: www.splg.org
SIC: 8011 Clinic, operated by physicians

(P-15036)
SAN ANTNIO AMBLTORY SRGCAL CTR
901 San Bernardino Rd 2nd Fl (91786-4912)
PHONE....................909 579-1500
C Perry Chu, Pr
EMP: 76 EST: 1999
SALES (est): 9.93MM Privately Held
Web: www.sanantonioasc.com
SIC: 8011 Surgeon

(P-15037)
SAN DEGO PTHLGSTS MED GROUP IN
7592 Metropolitan Dr Ste 406 (92108)
PHONE....................619 297-4012
Carla Stayboldt Md, Pr
Bruce Robbins Md, Ex VP
Ralph Shishido Md, Sec
Slavek Niewiadomski Md, Treas
David Francis Md, VP
EMP: 120 EST: 1969
SQ FT: 3,500
SALES (est): 8.06MM Privately Held
Web: www.sdpath.com
SIC: 8011 Pathologist

(P-15038)
SAN DEGO SPT MDCINE FMLY HLTH
6699 Alvarado Rd Ste 2100 (92120-5238)
PHONE....................619 229-3909
Jo Baxter, Mgr
EMP: 63 EST: 2002
SALES (est): 10.3MM Privately Held
Web: www.sdsm.com
SIC: 8011 Clinic, operated by physicians

(P-15039)
SAN DIEGO FAMILY CARE
4388 Thorn St (92105-4238)
PHONE....................858 279-9676
Roberta L Feinberg, CEO
EMP: 68
SALES (corp-wide): 28.39MM Privately Held
Web: www.sdfamilycare.org
SIC: 8011 Clinic, operated by physicians
PA: San Diego Family Care
6973 Linda Vista Rd
San Diego CA
858 279-0925

(P-15040)
SAN DIEGO FAMILY CARE (PA)
Also Called: LINDA VISTA HEALTH CARE CENTER
6973 Linda Vista Rd (92111-6342)
PHONE....................858 279-0925
Roberta L Feinberg, CEO
Manuel Quintanar, *
EMP: 93 EST: 1972
SALES (est): 28.39MM
SALES (corp-wide): 28.39MM Privately Held
Web: www.sdfamilycare.org
SIC: 8011 Clinic, operated by physicians

(P-15041)
SAN DIEGO FAMILY CARE
4290 Polk Ave (92105-1524)
PHONE....................619 563-0250
EMP: 69
SALES (corp-wide): 28.39MM Privately Held
Web: www.sdfamilycare.org
SIC: 8011 Clinic, operated by physicians
PA: San Diego Family Care
6973 Linda Vista Rd
San Diego CA
858 279-0925

(P-15042)
SAN DIMAS MEDICAL GROUP INC
100 Old River Rd (93311-8823)
PHONE....................661 663-4800
Frank Ynostroza Md, Ch Bd
David Lewis Md, Sec
Philip H Davis Md, Prin
Wendy Crenshaw Md, Prin
Marietta M Tan Md, Prin
EMP: 60 EST: 1971
SQ FT: 20,000
SALES (est): 13.6MM Privately Held
Web: www.sandimasmedical.com
SIC: 8011 Gynecologist

(P-15043)
SAN GBRIEL AMBLTORY SRGERY CTR
207 S Santa Anita St Ste G16 (91776-1146)
PHONE....................626 300-5300
Brenda Durgin, Mgr
EMP: 155 EST: 2003
SALES (est): 23.33MM
SALES (corp-wide): 19.58B Publicly Held
SIC: 8011 Opthalmologist
HQ: United Surgical Partners International, Inc.
14201 Dallas Pkwy
Dallas TX
972 713-3500

(P-15044)
SANSUM CLINIC (PA)
470 S Patterson Ave (93111-2404)
P.O. Box 1200 (93102-1200)
PHONE....................805 681-7700
Kurt Ransohoff Md, Pr
Tom Colbert, CIO*
Chad Hine, *
Paul Jaconette, CAO*
EMP: 60 EST: 1921
SQ FT: 10,944
SALES (est): 365.94MM
SALES (corp-wide): 365.94MM Privately Held
Web: www.sansumclinic.org
SIC: 8011 Clinic, operated by physicians

(P-15045)
SANTA BRBARA CNTY PUB HLTH DEP
220 S Palisade Dr Ste 104 (93454-5931)
PHONE....................805 739-8718
Elizabeth A Snyder, Asstg
EMP: 62 EST: 2020
SALES (est): 1.66MM Privately Held
Web: www.sbcphd.org
SIC: 8011 Offices and clinics of medical doctors

(P-15046)
SANTA CLARA VALLEY MEDICAL CTR
2400 Moorpark Ave (95128-2631)
PHONE....................408 885-6300
EMP: 982
Web: www.jklbuild.com
SIC: 8011 Medical centers
PA: Santa Clara Valley Medical Center
751 S Bascom Ave
San Jose CA

(P-15047)
SANTA CLARA VALLEY MEDICAL CTR
976 Lenzen Ave (95126-2737)
PHONE....................408 792-5586
EMP: 982
SIC: 8011 Clinic, operated by physicians
PA: Santa Clara Valley Medical Center
751 S Bascom Ave
San Jose CA

(P-15048)
SANTA CRUZ MEDICAL FOUNDATION (HQ)
2025 Soquel Ave (95062-1323)
PHONE....................831 458-5537
Larry De Ghetaldi, Dir
EMP: 85 EST: 1953
SQ FT: 60,000
SALES (est): 23.46MM
SALES (corp-wide): 14.77B Privately Held
Web: www.sutterhealth.org
SIC: 8011 General and family practice, physician/surgeon
PA: Sutter Health
2200 River Plaza Dr
Sacramento CA
916 733-8800

(P-15049)
SANTA CRUZ MEDICAL FOUNDATION
2900 Chanticleer Ave (95065-1816)
PHONE....................831 477-2325
Vicki Wilson, Brnch Mgr
EMP: 1176
SALES (corp-wide): 14.77B Privately Held
Web: www.santacruzmedical.org
SIC: 8011 General and family practice, physician/surgeon
HQ: Santa Cruz Medical Foundation
2025 Soquel Ave
Santa Cruz CA
831 458-5537

(P-15050)
SANTA MONICA BAY PHYSICIANS HE (PA)
Also Called: Bay Area Community Med Group
5767 W Century Blvd (90045-5631)
PHONE....................310 417-5900
Eileen Mcgrath, Pr
Doctor Steven Seizer, VP
Doctor David Cutler, Sec
Doctor Richard Zachrich, Treas
EMP: 85 EST: 1985
SALES (est): 21.28MM
SALES (corp-wide): 21.28MM Privately Held
Web: www.uclahealth.org
SIC: 8011 Clinic, operated by physicians

(P-15051)
SB WATERMAN HOLDINGS INC (PA)
1700 N Waterman Ave (92404-5115)
PHONE....................909 883-8611
James Malin, CEO
James W Malin, *
Paul G Godfrey Md, VP
Thomas Hellwig, *
Louis Francisco Md, Treas
EMP: 150 EST: 1954
SQ FT: 55,000
SALES (est): 21.33MM
SALES (corp-wide): 21.33MM Privately Held
Web: www.sbmed.com
SIC: 8011 Clinic, operated by physicians

(P-15052)
SCRIBEMD LLC
1310 W Stewart Dr Ste 212 (92868-3837)
PHONE....................714 543-8911
Coutney Aldama, CEO
Matthew Mullarky, *
EMP: 90 EST: 2009
SALES (est): 1.23MM Privately Held
Web: www.scribemd.com
SIC: 8011 Offices and clinics of medical doctors

(P-15053)
SCRIPPS CLINIC MEDICAL GROUP

8011 - Offices And Clinics Of Medical Doctors (P-15054)

10666 N Torrey Pines Rd (92037-1092)
PHONE..............................858 554-9606
Thomas Waltz, CEO
James Collins, CFO
EMP: 64 EST: 1979
SALES (est): 12.87MM Privately Held
Web: www.scripps.org
SIC: 8011 Physicians' office, including specialists

(P-15054)
SERRA COMMUNITY MED CLINIC INC
Also Called: Serra Community Medical Clinic
9375 San Fernando Rd (91352-1428)
PHONE..............................818 768-3000
Sadayappa K Durairaj, CEO
Doctor Arnold Jacobs, Treas
Doctor Carlos Jimenez, Sec
Dan Bumgarner, *
Kumar Soundar, *
EMP: 163 EST: 1975
SQ FT: 60,000
SALES (est): 23.5MM Privately Held
Web: www.serramedicalgroup.com
SIC: 8011 Clinic, operated by physicians

(P-15055)
SHARP HEALTHCARE
8860 Center Dr Ste 450 (91942-7001)
PHONE..............................619 460-6200
Scott Musicant, Brnch Mgr
EMP: 83
SALES (corp-wide): 2.37B Privately Held
Web: www.vascularsandiego.com
SIC: 8011 General and family practice, physician/surgeon
PA: Sharp Healthcare
   8695 Spectrum Center Blvd
   San Diego CA
   858 499-4000

(P-15056)
SHARP HEALTHCARE
10670 Wexford St (92131-3940)
PHONE..............................858 621-4090
EMP: 79
SALES (corp-wide): 2.37B Privately Held
Web: www.sharp.com
SIC: 8011 Physicians' office, including specialists
PA: Sharp Healthcare
   8695 Spectrum Center Blvd
   San Diego CA
   858 499-4000

(P-15057)
SHARP RES-STEALY MED GROUP INC
7862 El Cajon Blvd Ste C (91942-6712)
PHONE..............................619 644-6405
Behrooz Akbarnia, Prin
EMP: 176
Web: www.sharp.com
SIC: 8011 Internal medicine practitioners
PA: Sharp Rees-Stealy Medical Group, Inc.
   300 Fir St
   San Diego CA

(P-15058)
SHARP RES-STEALY MED GROUP INC
3555 Kenyon St Ste 200 (92110-5341)
PHONE..............................619 221-9547
Betty Thompson, Mgr
EMP: 177
Web: www.sharp.com
SIC: 8011 Physicians' office, including specialists
PA: Sharp Rees-Stealy Medical Group, Inc.
   300 Fir St
   San Diego CA

(P-15059)
SIERRA INTRNAL MDCINE MED GROU
680 Guzzi Ln Ste 201 (95370-5288)
PHONE..............................209 536-3738
James D Mosson, Pr
Terrel Spitze, *
Lynn Austin, *
Terril Spitze, *
Henry Kao, VP
EMP: 62 EST: 1985
SALES (est): 2.47MM
SALES (corp-wide): 789.42MM Privately Held
Web: www.adventisthealth.org
SIC: 8011 Internal medicine, physician/surgeon
PA: Adventist Health System/West, Corporation
   1 Adventist Health Way
   Roseville CA
   844 574-5686

(P-15060)
SIERRA PCF ORTHPDIC CTR MED GR
1630 E Herndon Ave (93720-3305)
PHONE..............................559 256-5200
Joe Clark, CEO
Eric C Hanson, *
EMP: 200 EST: 2000
SALES (est): 20.41MM Privately Held
Web: www.spoc-ortho.com
SIC: 8011 Orthopedic physician

(P-15061)
SIERRA PRMRY CARE MED GROUP A
Also Called: Sierra Medical Group
38636 Medical Center Dr Ste C (93551)
PHONE..............................661 273-0100
Sherry Connelly, Mgr
EMP: 68
SALES (corp-wide): 13.73MM Privately Held
Web: www.heritagesmg.com
SIC: 8011 8049 Primary care medical clinic; Physical therapist
PA: Sierra Primary Care Medical Group, A Medical Corporation
   44469 10th St W
   Lancaster CA
   661 945-9411

(P-15062)
SIERRA VIEW DST HOSP LEAG INC (PA)
Also Called: Sierra View Medical Center
465 W Putnam Ave (93257-3320)
PHONE..............................559 784-1110
Donna Hefner, Pr
Douglas Dickson, CFO
◆ EMP: 417 EST: 1948
SQ FT: 135,000
SALES (est): 98.83MM
SALES (corp-wide): 98.83MM Privately Held
Web: www.sierra-view.com
SIC: 8011 8062 Offices and clinics of medical doctors; General medical and surgical hospitals

(P-15063)
SLEEP DATA SERVICES LLC
5471 Kearny Villa Rd Ste 200 (92123)
PHONE..............................619 299-6299
Gaston Sanchez, Prin
EMP: 90 EST: 2017
SALES (est): 9.62MM Privately Held
Web: www.sleepdata.com
SIC: 8011 Offices and clinics of medical doctors

(P-15064)
SONOMA CNTY INDIAN HLTH PRJ IN (PA)
Also Called: Scihp
144 Stony Point Rd (95401-4122)
PHONE..............................707 521-4545
Betty Arterverry, CEO
Molin T Malicay, *
EMP: 150 EST: 1971
SQ FT: 70,000
SALES (est): 34.62MM
SALES (corp-wide): 34.62MM Privately Held
Web: www.scihp.org
SIC: 8011 Clinic, operated by physicians

(P-15065)
SONORA COMMUNITY HOSPITAL
1000 Greenley Rd (95370-5200)
PHONE..............................209 536-5012
Michelle Fuentes, CEO
Greg Mcculloch, CFO
Meredith Jobe, Sec
EMP: 118 EST: 1958
SALES (est): 321.3MM Privately Held
SIC: 8011 General and family practice, physician/surgeon

(P-15066)
SOUTH CENTRAL FAMILY HLTH CTR
4425 S Central Ave (90011-3629)
PHONE..............................323 908-4200
Richard Veloz, Pr
Paul Ramos, *
Ruby Raya Morones, CMO*
Sandra Tatum Green, *
EMP: 92 EST: 1983
SQ FT: 13,000
SALES (est): 32.76MM Privately Held
Web: www.scfhc.org
SIC: 8011 Clinic, operated by physicians

(P-15067)
SOUTH CNTY CMNTY HLTH CTR INC (PA)
Also Called: RAVENSWOOD FAMILY HEALTH CENTE
1885 Bay Rd (94303-1312)
PHONE..............................650 330-7407
Wayne Yost, CFO
Luisa Buada, *
EMP: 70 EST: 2001
SALES (est): 52.55MM
SALES (corp-wide): 52.55MM Privately Held
Web: www.ravenswoodfhn.org
SIC: 8011 Clinic, operated by physicians

(P-15068)
SOUTH CNTY ORTHPD SPCLSTS A ME
Also Called: Orthowest
24331 El Toro Rd Ste 200 (92637-3116)
PHONE..............................949 586-3200
James Mullen, Pr
Lance J Wrobel, *
Larry M Gursten, *
Lonnie J Moskow, *
Kyle W Coker, *
EMP: 91 EST: 1994
SALES (est): 23.94MM Privately Held
Web: www.scosortho.com
SIC: 8011 Orthopedic physician

(P-15069)
SOUTH COAST GLOBAL MED CTR INC
2701 S Bristol St (92704-6201)
PHONE..............................714 754-5454
Jamie Yoo, CEO
EMP: 93 EST: 2004
SALES (est): 10.68MM Privately Held
Web: www.southcoastglobalmedicalcenter.com
SIC: 8011 Medical centers

(P-15070)
SOUTHERN CA GASTROENTEROLOGY
50 Alessandro Pl Ste A30 (91105-3141)
PHONE..............................818 425-9761
Mary Yebremian, Prin
EMP: 92 EST: 2016
SALES (est): 1.06MM Privately Held
Web: www.insitedigestive.com
SIC: 8011 Gastronomist

(P-15071)
SOUTHERN CA HLTH & RHBLTN PRG
2610 Industry Way Ste A (90262-4028)
PHONE..............................310 631-8004
Doctor Jack M Barbour, CFO
Rita Floyd, *
EMP: 165 EST: 1993
SQ FT: 6,000
SALES (est): 10.42MM Privately Held
Web: www.scharpca.com
SIC: 8011 Psychiatric clinic

(P-15072)
SOUTHERN CAL DGNSTC IMGING INC
1110 W La Palma Ave (92801-2821)
PHONE..............................714 991-3367
Elaine Tran, Brnch Mgr
EMP: 76
SALES (corp-wide): 2.05MM Privately Held
SIC: 8011 Radiologist
PA: Southern California Diagnostic Imaging, Inc.
   408 S Beach Blvd Ste 106
   Anaheim CA
   714 995-5471

(P-15073)
SOUTHERN CAL ORTHPD INST LP (PA)
6815 Noble Ave (91405-6516)
PHONE..............................818 901-6600
Marc J Friedman, Pt
EMP: 135 EST: 1992
SALES (est): 171.1K Privately Held
Web: www.scoi.com
SIC: 8011 8249 Orthopedic physician; Medical training services

(P-15074)
SOUTHERN CAL PRMNNTE MED GROUP
Also Called: S C P M G
411 N Lakeview Ave (92807-3028)
PHONE..............................714 279-4675
Ryan Williams, Mgr
EMP: 158
SALES (corp-wide): 68.1B Privately Held

PRODUCTS & SERVICES SECTION

8011 - Offices And Clinics Of Medical Doctors (P-15093)

Web: www.permanente.org
SIC: **8011** Offices and clinics of medical doctors
HQ: Southern California Permanente Medical Group
393 Walnut Dr
Pasadena CA
626 405-5704

(P-15075)
SOUTHERN CAL PRMNNTE MED GROUP
3501 Stockdale Hwy (93309-2150)
PHONE..................................661 398-5085
EMP: 158
SALES (corp-wide): 68.1B **Privately Held**
Web: www.permanente.org
SIC: **8011** Medical centers
HQ: Southern California Permanente Medical Group
393 Walnut Dr
Pasadena CA
626 405-5704

(P-15076)
SOUTHERN CAL PRMNNTE MED GROUP
Also Called: Kaiser Permanente
4647 Zion Ave (92120-2507)
PHONE..................................619 528-5000
Terry Belmont, *Prin*
EMP: 360
SALES (corp-wide): 68.1B **Privately Held**
Web: www.permanente.org
SIC: **8011** Medical centers
HQ: Southern California Permanente Medical Group
393 Walnut Dr
Pasadena CA
626 405-5704

(P-15077)
SOUTHERN CAL PRMNNTE MED GROUP
3830 Martin Luther King Jr Blvd (90262-3625)
PHONE..................................310 604-5700
EMP: 194
SALES (corp-wide): 68.1B **Privately Held**
Web: www.permanente.org
SIC: **8011** Medical centers
HQ: Southern California Permanente Medical Group
393 Walnut Dr
Pasadena CA
626 405-5704

(P-15078)
SOUTHERN CAL PRMNNTE MED GROUP
25825 Vermont Ave (90710-3518)
PHONE..................................800 780-1230
EMP: 180
SALES (corp-wide): 68.1B **Privately Held**
Web: www.permanente.org
SIC: **8011** Medical centers
HQ: Southern California Permanente Medical Group
393 Walnut Dr
Pasadena CA
626 405-5704

(P-15079)
SOUTHERN CAL PRMNNTE MED GROUP
4841 Hollywood Blvd (90027-5301)
PHONE..................................323 783-5455
EMP: 230
SALES (corp-wide): 68.1B **Privately Held**
Web: www.permanente.org
SIC: **8011** Medical centers
HQ: Southern California Permanente Medical Group
393 Walnut Dr
Pasadena CA
626 405-5704

(P-15080)
SOUTHERN CAL PRMNNTE MED GROUP
Also Called: S C P M G
789 E Cooley Dr (92324-4007)
PHONE..................................909 370-2501
EMP: 158
SALES (corp-wide): 68.1B **Privately Held**
Web: www.permanente.org
SIC: **8011** Medical centers
HQ: Southern California Permanente Medical Group
393 Walnut Dr
Pasadena CA
626 405-5704

(P-15081)
SOUTHERN CAL PRMNNTE MED GROUP
Also Called: S C P M G
5620 Mesmer Ave (90230-6315)
PHONE..................................310 737-4900
Olive Goldsmith, *Mgr*
EMP: 182
SALES (corp-wide): 68.1B **Privately Held**
Web: www.permanente.org
SIC: **8011** Medical centers
HQ: Southern California Permanente Medical Group
393 Walnut Dr
Pasadena CA
626 405-5704

(P-15082)
SOUTHERN CAL PRMNNTE MED GROUP
Also Called: S C P M G
110 N La Brea Ave (90301-1708)
PHONE..................................310 419-3306
Helen Jones, *Mgr*
EMP: 158
SALES (corp-wide): 68.1B **Privately Held**
Web: www.permanente.org
SIC: **8011** Medical centers
HQ: Southern California Permanente Medical Group
393 Walnut Dr
Pasadena CA
626 405-5704

(P-15083)
SOUTHERN CAL PRMNNTE MED GROUP
18081 Beach Blvd (92648-1304)
PHONE..................................714 841-7293
EMP: 158
SALES (corp-wide): 68.1B **Privately Held**
Web: www.permanente.org
SIC: **8011** Medical centers
HQ: Southern California Permanente Medical Group
393 Walnut Dr
Pasadena CA
626 405-5704

(P-15084)
SOUTHERN CAL PRMNNTE MED GROUP
Also Called: S C P M G
1630 E Main St (92021-5204)
PHONE..................................619 528-5000
Brenda Scott-mead, *Mgr*
EMP: 182
SALES (corp-wide): 68.1B **Privately Held**
Web: www.permanente.org
SIC: **8011** Medical centers
HQ: Southern California Permanente Medical Group
393 Walnut Dr
Pasadena CA
626 405-5704

(P-15085)
SOUTHERN CAL PRMNNTE MED GROUP
Also Called: S C P M G
30400 Camino Capistrano (92675-1300)
PHONE..................................949 234-2139
EMP: 158
SALES (corp-wide): 68.1B **Privately Held**
Web: www.permanente.org
SIC: **8011** Medical centers
HQ: Southern California Permanente Medical Group
393 Walnut Dr
Pasadena CA
626 405-5704

(P-15086)
SOUTHERN CAL PRMNNTE MED GROUP
Also Called: S C P M G
4405 Vandever Ave (92120-3315)
PHONE..................................619 516-6000
Thomas Volle, *Mgr*
EMP: 194
SALES (corp-wide): 68.1B **Privately Held**
Web: www.permanente.org
SIC: **8011** Medical centers
HQ: Southern California Permanente Medical Group
393 Walnut Dr
Pasadena CA
626 405-5704

(P-15087)
SOUTHERN CAL PRMNNTE MED GROUP
Also Called: S C P M G
732 N Broadway (92025-1870)
PHONE..................................760 839-7200
Alex Anderson, *Mgr*
EMP: 151
SALES (corp-wide): 68.1B **Privately Held**
Web: www.permanente.org
SIC: **8011** Medical centers
HQ: Southern California Permanente Medical Group
393 Walnut Dr
Pasadena CA
626 405-5704

(P-15088)
SOUTHERN CAL PRMNNTE MED GROUP
Also Called: S C P M G
7825 Atlantic Ave (90201-5022)
PHONE..................................323 562-6459
Maria Gonzalez, *Prin*
EMP: 182
SALES (corp-wide): 68.1B **Privately Held**
Web: www.permanente.org
SIC: **8011** Medical centers
HQ: Southern California Permanente Medical Group
393 Walnut Dr
Pasadena CA
626 405-5704

(P-15089)
SOUTHERN CAL PRMNNTE MED GROUP
Also Called: S C P M G
21263 Erwin St (91367-3715)
PHONE..................................818 592-3038
Cary Glass, *Brnch Mgr*
EMP: 187
SALES (corp-wide): 68.1B **Privately Held**
Web: www.permanente.org
SIC: **8011** Medical centers
HQ: Southern California Permanente Medical Group
393 Walnut Dr
Pasadena CA
626 405-5704

(P-15090)
SOUTHERN CAL PRMNNTE MED GROUP
Also Called: S C P M G
27107 Tourney Rd (91355-1860)
PHONE..................................661 222-2150
EMP: 180
SALES (corp-wide): 68.1B **Privately Held**
Web: www.permanente.org
SIC: **8011** Medical centers
HQ: Southern California Permanente Medical Group
393 Walnut Dr
Pasadena CA
626 405-5704

(P-15091)
SOUTHERN CAL PRMNNTE MED GROUP
5055 California Ave (93309-0701)
PHONE..................................661 334-2020
EMP: 187
SALES (corp-wide): 68.1B **Privately Held**
Web: www.permanente.org
SIC: **8011** Medical centers
HQ: Southern California Permanente Medical Group
393 Walnut Dr
Pasadena CA
626 405-5704

(P-15092)
SOUTHERN CAL PRMNNTE MED GROUP
6 Willard (92604-4694)
PHONE..................................949 262-5780
Debra Dannemeyer, *Admn*
EMP: 187
SALES (corp-wide): 68.1B **Privately Held**
Web: www.permanente.org
SIC: **8011** Clinic, operated by physicians
HQ: Southern California Permanente Medical Group
393 Walnut Dr
Pasadena CA
626 405-5704

(P-15093)
SOUTHERN CAL PRMNNTE MED GROUP
Also Called: S C P M G
1900 E 4th St (92705-3910)
PHONE..................................714 967-4760
Julie White-dahlgren, *Brnch Mgr*
EMP: 158
SALES (corp-wide): 68.1B **Privately Held**
Web: www.permanente.org
SIC: **8011** 8049 Obstetrician; Psychiatric social worker
HQ: Southern California Permanente Medical Group
393 Walnut Dr

8011 - Offices And Clinics Of Medical Doctors (P-15094)

Pasadena CA
626 405-5704

(P-15094)
SOUTHERN CAL PRMNNTE MED GROUP
Also Called: Orthopedics Department
4760 W Sunset Blvd (90027-6063)
PHONE.................323 783-4893
Dolores Cobbarrubias, *Off Mgr*
EMP: 182
SALES (corp-wide): 68.1B **Privately Held**
Web: www.permanente.org
SIC: 8011 Orthopedic physician
HQ: Southern California Permanente
Medical Group
393 Walnut Dr
Pasadena CA
626 405-5704

(P-15095)
SOUTHERN CAL PRMNNTE MED GROUP
6041 Cadillac Ave (90034-1702)
PHONE.................323 857-2000
Larry Poston, *Dir*
EMP: 230
SALES (corp-wide): 68.1B **Privately Held**
Web: www.permanente.org
SIC: 8011 Radiologist
HQ: Southern California Permanente
Medical Group
393 Walnut Dr
Pasadena CA
626 405-5704

(P-15096)
SPALDING SRGCAL CTR BVRLY HLLS
Also Called: S&B Surgery Center II
27520 Hawthorne Blvd Ste 176 (90274-3576)
PHONE.................949 863-0022
Theordore Goldstrein, *Pr*
Randy Rosen, *
EMP: 71 **EST:** 1998
SQ FT: 8,000
SALES (est): 4.92MM **Privately Held**
SIC: 8011 Plastic surgeon

(P-15097)
ST JOSEPHS SURGERY CENTER LP
1800 N California St Ste 1 (95204-6019)
PHONE.................209 467-6316
Don Wiley, *Pr*
EMP: 75 **EST:** 2004
SALES (est): 11.63MM
SALES (corp-wide): 19.58B **Publicly Held**
Web: www.stjosephs-sc.com
SIC: 8011 Surgeon
PA: Tenet Healthcare Corporation
14201 Dallas Pkwy
Dallas TX
469 893-2200

(P-15098)
ST JSEPH HERITG MED GROUP LLC (PA)
Also Called: Yorba Park Medical Group
2212 E 4th St Ste 201 (92705-3872)
PHONE.................714 633-1011
Charles Foster, *Pr*
Benjamin Harper Md, *Prin*
C R Burke, *
Ivan Nichols Md, *Prin*
Dennis Long Md, *Treas*
▲ **EMP:** 134 **EST:** 1964
SQ FT: 58,000
SALES (est): 24.53MM
SALES (corp-wide): 24.53MM **Privately Held**
Web: www.sjhmg.org
SIC: 8011 General and family practice, physician/surgeon

(P-15099)
STALLERGENES GREER
7203 Convoy Ct (92111-1020)
PHONE.................858 292-1060
EMP: 81 **EST:** 2016
SALES (est): 736.2K **Privately Held**
Web: www.stagrveterinaryallergy.com
SIC: 8011 Allergist

(P-15100)
STANFORD HEALTH CARE
801 Welch Rd (94304-1611)
PHONE.................650 723-5281
EMP: 228
SALES (corp-wide): 15.13B **Privately Held**
Web: www.stanfordhealthcare.org
SIC: 8011 Clinic, operated by physicians
HQ: Stanford Health Care
300 Pasteur Dr
Stanford CA
650 723-4000

(P-15101)
STANFORD HLTH CARE TRI-VALLEY
Also Called: Urgent Care Center
1111 E Stanley Blvd (94550-4115)
PHONE.................925 373-4018
Jeff Coigan, *Prin*
EMP: 137
SALES (corp-wide): 15.13B **Privately Held**
Web: www.stanfordhealthcare.org
SIC: 8011 Freestanding emergency medical center
HQ: Stanford Health Care Tri-Valley
5555 W Las Positas Blvd
Pleasanton CA
925 847-3000

(P-15102)
STEVEN P ABELOW MD
2311 Lake Tahoe Blvd (96150-7129)
PHONE.................530 544-8033
Steven Abelow Md, *Owner*
EMP: 100 **EST:** 1982
SALES (est): 2.16MM **Privately Held**
SIC: 8011 Orthopedic physician

(P-15103)
SUCCESS HEALTHCARE 1 LLC
Also Called: Acute Psychiatric Hospital
7500 Hellman Ave (91770-2216)
PHONE.................626 288-1160
EMP: 633
SALES (corp-wide): 87.5MM **Privately Held**
Web: www.silverlakemc.com
SIC: 8011 Offices and clinics of medical doctors
PA: Success Healthcare 1, Llc
1711 W Temple St
Los Angeles CA
213 989-6100

(P-15104)
SULPIZIO CARDIOVASCULAR CENTER
9434 Medical Center Dr (92037-1337)
PHONE.................858 657-7000
EMP: 144 **EST:** 2015
SALES (est): 2.34MM
SALES (corp-wide): 534.4MM **Privately Held**
Web: health.ucsd.edu
SIC: 8011 Cardiologist and cardio-vascular specialist
HQ: University Of California, San Diego
9500 Gilman Dr
La Jolla CA
858 534-2230

(P-15105)
SUN HEALTHCARE GROUP INC (DH)
27442 Portola Pkwy Ste 200 (92610-2822)
▲ **EMP:** 300 **EST:** 1993
SALES (est): 2.28B
SALES (corp-wide): 5.86B **Publicly Held**
Web: www.sunh.com
SIC: 8011 8322 Medical insurance plan; Referral service for personal and social problems
HQ: Genesis Hc Llc
101 E State St
Kennett Square PA
610 444-6350

(P-15106)
SUTTER BAY HOSPITALS
3698 California St (94118-1702)
P.O. Box 7999 (94120-7999)
PHONE.................415 600-2632
EMP: 71
SALES (corp-wide): 14.77B **Privately Held**
Web: www.cpmcri.org
SIC: 8011 8093 8062 General and family practice, physician/surgeon; Rehabilitation center, outpatient treatment; General medical and surgical hospitals
HQ: Sutter Bay Hospitals
475 Brannan St Ste 130
San Francisco CA
415 600-6000

(P-15107)
SUTTER BAY MEDICAL FOUNDATION
Also Called: Patient Accounting
535 Oakmead Pkwy (94085-4023)
PHONE.................408 730-4321
Lynn Murray, *Prin*
EMP: 120
SALES (corp-wide): 14.77B **Privately Held**
Web: www.sutterhealth.org
SIC: 8011 Medical centers
HQ: Sutter Bay Medical Foundation
795 El Camino Real
Palo Alto CA
650 321-4121

(P-15108)
SUTTER BAY MEDICAL FOUNDATION
Also Called: Pamf - PA Division
2951 Gordon Ave (95051-0709)
PHONE.................650 812-3751
Jessica Memosano, *Mgr*
EMP: 62
SALES (corp-wide): 14.77B **Privately Held**
Web: www.sutterhealth.org
SIC: 8011 Clinic, operated by physicians
HQ: Sutter Bay Medical Foundation
795 El Camino Real
Palo Alto CA
650 321-4121

(P-15109)
SUTTER BAY MEDICAL FOUNDATION
877 W Fremont Ave Ste N (94087-2332)
PHONE.................650 934-7956
Richard Slavin, *Prin*
EMP: 62
SALES (corp-wide): 14.77B **Privately Held**
Web: www.sutterhealth.org
SIC: 8011 Clinic, operated by physicians
HQ: Sutter Bay Medical Foundation
795 El Camino Real
Palo Alto CA
650 321-4121

(P-15110)
SUTTER BAY MEDICAL FOUNDATION (HQ)
Also Called: Palo Alto Clinic
795 El Camino Real (94301-2302)
P.O. Box 254738 (95865-4738)
PHONE.................650 321-4121
David Drucker, *Pr*
Jeff Gerard, *
EMP: 700 **EST:** 1948
SQ FT: 200,000
SALES (est): 3.23B
SALES (corp-wide): 14.77B **Privately Held**
Web: www.pamf.org
SIC: 8011 General and family practice, physician/surgeon
PA: Sutter Health
2200 River Plaza Dr
Sacramento CA
916 733-8800

(P-15111)
SUTTER HEALTH
Also Called: Vascular and Varicose Vein Ctr
1680 E Roseville Pkwy Ste 100 (95661)
PHONE.................916 783-8114
EMP: 231
SALES (corp-wide): 14.77B **Privately Held**
Web: www.sutterhealth.org
SIC: 8011 8071 Offices and clinics of medical doctors; Medical laboratories
PA: Sutter Health
2200 River Plaza Dr
Sacramento CA
916 733-8800

(P-15112)
SUTTER HEALTH
Also Called: Campus Commons Imaging
2 Scripps Dr Ste 110 (95825-6207)
PHONE.................916 929-3393
Jan Curry, *Brnch Mgr*
EMP: 62
SALES (corp-wide): 14.77B **Privately Held**
Web: www.checksutterfirst.org
SIC: 8011 8071 General and family practice, physician/surgeon; Medical laboratories
PA: Sutter Health
2200 River Plaza Dr
Sacramento CA
916 733-8800

(P-15113)
SUTTER HLTH SCRMNTO SIERRA REG
Also Called: Sutter Counseling Center
7700 Folsom Blvd (95826-2608)
PHONE.................916 386-3000
Diane Stewart, *Brnch Mgr*
EMP: 408
SALES (corp-wide): 14.77B **Privately Held**
Web: www.sutterhealth.org
SIC: 8011 8621 Psychiatrist; Professional organizations
HQ: Sutter Health Sacramento Sierra Region
2200 River Plaza Dr
Sacramento CA
916 733-8800

PRODUCTS & SERVICES SECTION

8011 - Offices And Clinics Of Medical Doctors (P-15134)

(P-15114)
SUTTER MED GROUP OF RDWODS INC
3883 Airway Dr Ste 202 (95403-1671)
PHONE.................707 546-2788
John Dervin Md, *Pr*
Steven Levenberg, *
Sean Gaskie Md, *Treas*
Romayne Farrell Fnp, *
EMP: 120 **EST:** 1992
SALES (est): 23.48MM
SALES (corp-wide): 14.77B **Privately Held**
Web: www.suttersantarosa.org
SIC: 8011 General and family practice, physician/surgeon
HQ: Sutter Santa Rosa Regional Hospital
30 Mark West Springs Rd
Santa Rosa CA
707 576-4000

(P-15115)
SUTTER NORTH MED FOUNDATION (PA)
Also Called: Multi Specialty Group Practice
969 Plumas St (95991-4011)
PHONE.................530 741-1300
Bruce Tigner, *CEO*
Kelly Danna, *
Tom Walther, *
EMP: 160 **EST:** 1947
SALES (est): 21.64MM
SALES (corp-wide): 21.64MM **Privately Held**
Web: www.sutternorth.com
SIC: 8011 General and family practice, physician/surgeon

(P-15116)
SUTTER REGIONAL MED FOUNDATION
2720 Low Ct (94534-9771)
PHONE.................707 631-9423
Carolyn Appenzeller, *Prin*
EMP: 187
SALES (corp-wide): 45.62MM **Privately Held**
SIC: 8011 Physicians' office, including specialists
PA: Sutter Regional Medical Foundation Inc
2702 Low Ct
Fairfield CA
707 427-4900

(P-15117)
SUTTER REGIONAL MED FOUNDATION
770 Mason St (95688-4646)
PHONE.................707 454-5800
EMP: 187
SALES (corp-wide): 45.62MM **Privately Held**
SIC: 8011 Physicians' office, including specialists
PA: Sutter Regional Medical Foundation Inc
2702 Low Ct
Fairfield CA
707 427-4900

(P-15118)
SUTTER VALLEY MED FOUNDATION
Also Called: Sutter Medical Plaza Roseville
3100 Douglas Blvd (95661-3866)
PHONE.................916 865-1140
EMP: 110
Web: www.suttermedicalfoundation.org
SIC: 8011 Physicians' office, including specialists
PA: Sutter Valley Medical Foundation
2700 Gateway Oaks Dr
Sacramento CA

(P-15119)
SUTTER VALLEY MED FOUNDATION
Also Called: Sutter Gould Med Foundation
600 Coffee Rd (95355-4201)
PHONE.................209 524-1211
Laurie Scott, *Prin*
EMP: 179
Web: www.suttergould.org
SIC: 8011 Physicians' office, including specialists
PA: Sutter Valley Medical Foundation
2700 Gateway Oaks Dr
Sacramento CA

(P-15120)
SYMBION INC
Also Called: Specialty Surgical of Westlake
696 Hampshire Rd Ste 100 (91361-4456)
PHONE.................805 413-7920
Kelly Kapp, *Brnch Mgr*
EMP: 128
Web: www.surgerypartners.com
SIC: 8011 Surgeon
HQ: Symbion, Inc.
340 Seven Springs Way
Brentwood TN
615 234-5900

(P-15121)
SYMBION INC
Also Called: Specialty Sugical Ctr Encino
16501 Ventura Blvd Ste 103 (91436-2007)
PHONE.................818 501-1080
Michael Roub, *Brnch Mgr*
EMP: 124
Web: www.surgerypartners.com
SIC: 8011 Surgeon
HQ: Symbion, Inc.
340 Seven Springs Way
Brentwood TN
615 234-5900

(P-15122)
TATCHA LLC
37 Estates Dr (94030-1564)
PHONE.................650 239-9000
Adeline Leong, *Brnch Mgr*
EMP: 121
SALES (corp-wide): 62.39B **Privately Held**
Web: www.tatcha.com
SIC: 8011 Dermatologist
HQ: Tatcha Llc
208 Utah St Ste 300
San Francisco CA
877 322-8633

(P-15123)
TENET HEALTHSYSTEM MEDICAL INC
Los Alamitos Med Ctr
3751 Katella Ave (90720-3113)
PHONE.................805 546-7698
Michelle Finney, *Prin*
EMP: 267
SALES (corp-wide): 19.58B **Publicly Held**
Web: validate.perfdrive.com
SIC: 8011 8062 Offices and clinics of medical doctors; General medical and surgical hospitals
HQ: Tenet Healthsystem Medical, Inc.
14201 Dallas Pkwy
Dallas TX
469 893-2000

(P-15124)
TENET HEALTHSYSTEM MEDICAL INC
Also Called: Leisure World Pharmacy
1661 Golden Rain Rd (90740-4907)
P.O. Box 2685 (90740-1685)
PHONE.................562 493-9581
Diana Doyle, *Mgr*
EMP: 148
SALES (corp-wide): 19.58B **Publicly Held**
Web: www.mygnp.com
SIC: 8011 5912 Offices and clinics of medical doctors; Drug stores
HQ: Tenet Healthsystem Medical, Inc.
14201 Dallas Pkwy
Dallas TX
469 893-2000

(P-15125)
TENET HEALTHSYSTEM MEDICAL INC
Also Called: Lakewood Regional Medical Ctr
3700 South St (90712-1419)
PHONE.................562 531-2550
Carol Mammolite, *Brnch Mgr*
EMP: 512
SALES (corp-wide): 19.58B **Publicly Held**
Web: validate.perfdrive.com
SIC: 8011 8062 Medical centers; General medical and surgical hospitals
HQ: Tenet Healthsystem Medical, Inc.
14201 Dallas Pkwy
Dallas TX
469 893-2000

(P-15126)
THE ORTHOPEDIC INSTITUTE OF
616 Witmer St (90017-2308)
PHONE.................213 977-2010
EMP: 5026 **EST:** 1990
SALES (est): 840.73K
SALES (corp-wide): 923.01K **Privately Held**
SIC: 8011 Orthopedic physician
HQ: Pih Health Good Samaritan Hospital
1225 Wilshire Blvd
Los Angeles CA
213 977-2121

(P-15127)
TOWER HMTLOGY ONCOLOGY MED GROU
9090 Wilshire Blvd Ste 200 (90211-1848)
P.O. Box 5624 (90209-5605)
PHONE.................310 888-8680
Robert W Decker Md, *Pt*
Leland M Green Md, *Pt*
EMP: 94 **EST:** 1992
SQ FT: 13,000
SALES (est): 9.61MM **Privately Held**
Web: www.cedars-sinai.org
SIC: 8011 Hematologist

(P-15128)
TRANSLTNAL PLMNARY IMMNLOGY RE
Also Called: Southern Cal Fd Allergy Inst
701 E 28th St Ste 419 (90806-2775)
PHONE.................562 490-9900
Doctor Inderpal Randhawa, *Prin*
EMP: 90 **EST:** 2016
SALES (est): 10.32MM **Privately Held**
Web: www.foodallergyinstitute.com
SIC: 8011 Allergist

(P-15129)
TRUXTUN RADIOLOGY MED GROUP LP
20960 Sage Ln Ste B (93561-6408)
PHONE.................661 822-6619
EMP: 99
Web: www.radnet.com
SIC: 8011 Radiologist
HQ: Truxtun Radiology Medical Group, Lp
1817 Truxtun Ave
Bakersfield CA

(P-15130)
TRUXTUN RADIOLOGY MED GROUP LP
3940 San Dimas St (93301-1458)
PHONE.................661 325-6200
Girish Patel, *Brnch Mgr*
EMP: 102
Web: www.radnet.com
SIC: 8011 Radiologist
HQ: Truxtun Radiology Medical Group, Lp
1817 Truxtun Ave
Bakersfield CA

(P-15131)
TRUXTUN RADIOLOGY MED GROUP LP
1917 Truxtun Ave (93301-5010)
PHONE.................661 616-1201
EMP: 99
Web: www.radnet.com
SIC: 8011 Radiologist
HQ: Truxtun Radiology Medical Group, Lp
1817 Truxtun Ave
Bakersfield CA

(P-15132)
TRUXTUN RADIOLOGY MED GROUP LP
11622 Harrington St (93311-9273)
PHONE.................661 205-6567
EMP: 99
Web: www.radnet.com
SIC: 8011 Radiologist
HQ: Truxtun Radiology Medical Group, Lp
1817 Truxtun Ave
Bakersfield CA

(P-15133)
TUOLUMNE M-WUK INDIAN HLTH CTR
Also Called: Tuolumne Mewuk Indian Health
18880 Cherry Valley Blvd (95379-9506)
PHONE.................209 928-5400
Frank Isele, *Admn*
Tammy Barker, *Finance*
Christopher Gorsky, *
Darla Merlin, *
EMP: 90 **EST:** 2003
SQ FT: 11,000
SALES (est): 19.55MM **Privately Held**
Web: www.tmwihc.org
SIC: 8011 8021 Offices and clinics of medical doctors; Dental clinics and offices

(P-15134)
TWIN CITIES COMMUNITY HOSP INC
1100 Las Tablas Rd (93465-9704)
PHONE.................805 434-3500
Mark P Lisa, *CEO*
Paul Posmosga, *
EMP: 450 **EST:** 1977
SQ FT: 120,000
SALES (est): 17.75K
SALES (corp-wide): 19.58B **Publicly Held**

8011 - Offices And Clinics Of Medical Doctors (P-15135)

SIC: **8011** 8062 Medical centers; General medical and surgical hospitals
PA: Tenet Healthcare Corporation
14201 Dallas Pkwy
Dallas TX
469 893-2200

(P-15135)
U C SAN FRANCISCO GYNECOLOGY
2356 Sutter St (94115-3006)
PHONE....................................415 885-7788
Kimberly Calvail, *Mgr*
EMP: 97 EST: 2011
SALES (est): 25.78MM
SALES (corp-wide): 104.63MM **Privately Held**
Web: www.ucsfhealth.org
SIC: **8011** Physicians' office, including specialists
PA: Uc San Francisco
1111 Franklin St Fl 12
Oakland CA
858 534-7323

(P-15136)
UCLA SNTA MNICA GSTRENTEROLOGY
1223 16th St Ste 3100 (90404-1275)
PHONE....................................310 582-6240
EMP: 65 EST: 2019
SALES (est): 900.3K **Privately Held**
Web: www.uclahealth.org
SIC: **8011** Offices and clinics of medical doctors

(P-15137)
UCSD NEUROSCIENCE CENTER
6645 Alvarado Rd (92120-5208)
PHONE....................................619 287-7661
David D Barba, *Prin*
EMP: 100 EST: 2010
SALES (est): 223.47K **Privately Held**
SIC: **8011** Primary care medical clinic

(P-15138)
UCSF BENIOFF CHILDRENS HOSP
2401 Shadelands Dr Ste 120 (94598-2494)
PHONE....................................925 979-4000
Kelly Tremmel-howell, *Owner*
EMP: 99 EST: 2018
SALES (est): 406.55K **Privately Held**
Web: www.ucsfbenioffchildrens.org
SIC: **8011** Physicians' office, including specialists

(P-15139)
UCSF BENIOFF CHLD PHYSICIANS
6425 Christie Ave Ste 220 (94608-1073)
PHONE....................................415 476-4977
Bertram Lubin, *Pr*
Richard Decarlo, *Ex VP*
Carolyn G Dossa, *VP*
David J Durand, *Sr VP*
Lisa Ozaeta, *Sr VP*
EMP: 67 EST: 2015
SALES (est): 10.48MM **Privately Held**
Web: www.ubcp.org
SIC: **8011** Physicians' office, including specialists

(P-15140)
UCSF MEDICAL CENTER
150 Executive Park Blvd Ste 150c (94134-3301)
PHONE....................................415 353-9229
Tom Mcmurtry, *Prin*
EMP: 195 EST: 2011
SALES (est): 23.69MM **Privately Held**
Web: www.ucsf.edu
SIC: **8011** Medical centers

(P-15141)
UNITED FMLY CARE INC A MED COR
8110 Mango Ave Ste 104 (92335-3603)
PHONE....................................909 874-1679
Keith Schauermann, *Pr*
EMP: 120 EST: 1999
SALES (est): 10.69MM **Privately Held**
Web: pmg.optum.com
SIC: **8011** General and family practice, physician/surgeon

(P-15142)
UNITED HLTH CTRS OF SAN JQUIN (PA)
3875 W Beechwood Ave (93711-0795)
P.O. Box 790 (93648-0790)
PHONE....................................559 646-6618
Colleen Curtis, *CEO*
Robert Shankerman, *Prin*
Justin Preas, *COO*
EMP: 70 EST: 1971
SQ FT: 7,500
SALES (est): 188.06MM
SALES (corp-wide): 188.06MM **Privately Held**
Web: www.unitedhealthcenters.org
SIC: **8011** Clinic, operated by physicians

(P-15143)
UNITED INDIAN HEALTH SVCS INC (PA)
Also Called: Potawot Health Clinic
1600 Weeot Way (95521-4734)
PHONE....................................707 825-5000
David Rosen, *CFO*
EMP: 150 EST: 1970
SQ FT: 46,304
SALES (est): 45.33MM
SALES (corp-wide): 45.33MM **Privately Held**
Web: www.unitedindianhealthservices.org
SIC: **8011** 8021 8031 5912 Clinic, operated by physicians; Dental clinics and offices; Offices and clinics of osteopathic physicians; Drug stores

(P-15144)
UNITED MEDICAL DOCTORS
Also Called: United Gastroenterologists
28078 Baxter Rd Ste 530 (92563-1405)
PHONE....................................951 566-5229
Samantha Cottrell, *Prin*
EMP: 70 EST: 2003
SALES (est): 14.46MM **Privately Held**
Web: www.unitedmd.com
SIC: **8011** Gastronomist

(P-15145)
UNITED MEDICAL IMAGING INC (PA)
1762 Westwood Blvd Ste 230 (90024-5648)
PHONE....................................310 943-8400
Nasser Hiekali, *CEO*
EMP: 78 EST: 2006
SALES (est): 26.91MM **Privately Held**
Web: www.umih.com
SIC: **8011** Radiologist

(P-15146)
UNIVERSITY CAL SAN DIEGO
Also Called: U.C.S.d Plastic Surgery
4520 Executive Dr Ste 101 (92121-3019)
PHONE....................................619 294-3746
Anne Wallace, *Dir*
EMP: 67
SALES (corp-wide): 534.4MM **Privately Held**
Web: www.ucsd.edu
SIC: **8011** 8221 9411 Primary care medical clinic; University; Administration of educational programs
HQ: University Of California, San Diego
9500 Gilman Dr
La Jolla CA
858 534-2230

(P-15147)
UNIVERSITY CAL SAN FRANCISCO
Also Called: UNIVERSITY CAL SAN FRANCISCO
311 California St Ste 410 (94104-2616)
PHONE....................................415 989-5339
EMP: 104
SALES (corp-wide): 534.4MM **Privately Held**
Web: www.ucsf.edu
SIC: **8011** Offices and clinics of medical doctors
HQ: University Cal San Francisco
513 Parnassus Ave 115f
San Francisco CA

(P-15148)
UNIVERSITY CAL SAN FRANCISCO
400 Parnassus Ave (94143-2202)
PHONE....................................415 353-2383
Michael Prados, *Brnch Mgr*
EMP: 62
SALES (corp-wide): 534.4MM **Privately Held**
Web: www.ucsf.edu
SIC: **8011** 8221 9411 Internal medicine practitioners; University; Administration of educational programs
HQ: University Cal San Francisco
513 Parnassus Ave 115f
San Francisco CA

(P-15149)
UNIVERSITY CAL SAN FRANCISCO
1545 Divisadero St (94143-3400)
PHONE....................................415 353-7900
EMP: 249
SALES (corp-wide): 534.4MM **Privately Held**
Web: www.ucsf.edu
SIC: **8011** 8221 9411 Medical centers; University; Administration of educational programs
HQ: University Cal San Francisco
513 Parnassus Ave 115f
San Francisco CA

(P-15150)
UNIVERSITY CAL SAN FRANCISCO
Also Called: Ucsf Orthpdic Srgery Fclty Prc
1500 Owens St (94158-2334)
PHONE....................................415 353-1915
Piere Leavell, *Prin*
EMP: 197
SALES (corp-wide): 534.4MM **Privately Held**
Web: orthosurgery.ucsf.edu
SIC: **8011** 8221 9411 Medical centers; University; Administration of educational programs
HQ: University Cal San Francisco
513 Parnassus Ave 115f
San Francisco CA

(P-15151)
UNIVERSITY CAL SAN FRANCISCO
Also Called: Ucsf Sports Medicine Center
1701 Divisadero St Ste 240 (94115-3011)
PHONE....................................415 353-7576
Bill Durmey, *Brnch Mgr*
EMP: 73
SALES (corp-wide): 534.4MM **Privately Held**
Web: www.ucsf.edu
SIC: **8011** 8221 9411 Medical centers; University; Administration of educational programs
HQ: University Cal San Francisco
513 Parnassus Ave 115f
San Francisco CA

(P-15152)
UNIVERSITY CAL SAN FRANCISCO
Also Called: Ucsf/Div Behv & Dev Pediatrics
400 Parnassus Ave Fl 2 (94143-2202)
PHONE....................................415 476-4575
W Thomas Voice, *Brnch Mgr*
EMP: 62
SALES (corp-wide): 534.4MM **Privately Held**
Web: www.ucsf.edu
SIC: **8011** 8221 9411 Medical centers; University; Administration of educational programs
HQ: University Cal San Francisco
513 Parnassus Ave 115f
San Francisco CA

(P-15153)
UNIVERSITY CALIFORNIA DAVIS
Also Called: Khamishon, Ilya MD
251 Turn Pike Dr (95630-8129)
PHONE....................................916 985-9300
Mary Simpson, *Brnch Mgr*
EMP: 73
SALES (corp-wide): 534.4MM **Privately Held**
Web: health.ucdavis.edu
SIC: **8011** 8221 9411 Offices and clinics of medical doctors; University; Administration of educational programs
HQ: University Of California, Davis
1 Shields Ave
Davis CA

(P-15154)
UNIVERSITY CALIFORNIA DAVIS
Also Called: Specialty Clinic
2660 W Covell Blvd (95616-5645)
PHONE....................................530 747-3000
EMP: 91
SALES (corp-wide): 534.4MM **Privately Held**
Web: health.ucdavis.edu
SIC: **8011** 8221 9411 Offices and clinics of medical doctors; University; Administration of educational programs
HQ: University Of California, Davis
1 Shields Ave
Davis CA

(P-15155)
UNIVERSITY CALIFORNIA DAVIS
3200 Bell Rd (95603-9244)
PHONE....................................530 885-5618
EMP: 73
SALES (corp-wide): 534.4MM **Privately Held**
Web: www.ucdavis.edu

PRODUCTS & SERVICES SECTION

8011 - Offices And Clinics Of Medical Doctors (P-15174)

SIC: **8011** 8221 9411 Offices and clinics of medical doctors; University; Administration of educational programs
HQ: University Of California, Davis
1 Shields Ave
Davis CA

(P-15156)
UNIVERSITY CALIFORNIA DAVIS
4150 V St (95817-1460)
PHONE..................916 734-8514
Dua Anderson, *Brnch Mgr*
EMP: 73
SALES (corp-wide): 534.4MM **Privately Held**
Web: www.ucdavis.edu
SIC: **8011** 8221 9411 Medical centers; University; Administration of educational programs
HQ: University Of California, Davis
1 Shields Ave
Davis CA

(P-15157)
UNIVERSITY CALIFORNIA DAVIS
Also Called: Wildlife Health Center
Rm Tb 128 Old Davis Rd (95616)
PHONE..................530 752-4167
Jonna Mazet, *Dir*
EMP: 109
SALES (corp-wide): 534.4MM **Privately Held**
Web: www.ucdavis.edu
SIC: **8011** 8221 9411 Medical centers; University; Administration of educational programs
HQ: University Of California, Davis
1 Shields Ave
Davis CA

(P-15158)
UNIVERSITY CALIFORNIA DAVIS
Also Called: Davis Medical Group
4860 Y St (95817-2307)
PHONE..................916 734-3588
Valerie Adame, *Brnch Mgr*
EMP: 73
SALES (corp-wide): 534.4MM **Privately Held**
Web: www.ucdavis.edu
SIC: **8011** 8221 9411 Primary care medical clinic; University; Administration of educational programs
HQ: University Of California, Davis
1 Shields Ave
Davis CA

(P-15159)
UNIVERSITY CALIFORNIA DAVIS
550 W Ranch View Dr Ste 2005 (95765-5396)
PHONE..................916 295-5700
EMP: 64
SALES (corp-wide): 534.4MM **Privately Held**
Web: www.ucdavis.edu
SIC: **8011** 8221 9411 General and family practice, physician/surgeon; University; Administration of educational programs
HQ: University Of California, Davis
1 Shields Ave
Davis CA

(P-15160)
UNIVERSITY CALIFORNIA DAVIS
Also Called: Zacharias, Don M MD
500 University Ave Ste 220 (95825-6504)
PHONE..................916 442-1011
EMP: 64
SALES (corp-wide): 534.4MM **Privately Held**
Web: health.ucdavis.edu
SIC: **8011** 8221 9411 General and family practice, physician/surgeon; University; Administration of educational programs
HQ: University Of California, Davis
1 Shields Ave
Davis CA

(P-15161)
UNIVERSITY CALIFORNIA DAVIS
Also Called: Uc Davis Children's Hospital
2315 Stockton Blvd Rm 6309 (95817-2201)
PHONE..................916 734-2846
Valerie Adame, *Brnch Mgr*
EMP: 128
SALES (corp-wide): 534.4MM **Privately Held**
Web: health.ucdavis.edu
SIC: **8011** 8221 9411 Surgeon; University; Administration of educational programs
HQ: University Of California, Davis
1 Shields Ave
Davis CA

(P-15162)
UNIVERSITY CALIFORNIA IRVINE
43 Cambria Dr (92625-1004)
PHONE..................949 644-5245
EMP: 68
SALES (corp-wide): 534.4MM **Privately Held**
Web: www.uci.edu
SIC: **8011** Offices and clinics of medical doctors
HQ: University Of California, Irvine
510 Aldrich Hall
Irvine CA
949 824-5011

(P-15163)
UNIVERSITY CALIFORNIA IRVINE
Also Called: Uc Irvine Hlth Rgonal Burn Ctr
101 The City Dr S Bldg 1a (92868-3201)
PHONE..................714 456-6170
EMP: 1757
SALES (corp-wide): 534.4MM **Privately Held**
Web: www.uci.edu
SIC: **8011** 8221 9411 Medical centers; University; Administration of educational programs
HQ: University Of California, Irvine
510 Aldrich Hall
Irvine CA
949 824-5011

(P-15164)
UNIVERSITY CALIFORNIA IRVINE
Also Called: UCI Family Health Center
800 N Main St (92701-3576)
PHONE..................714 480-2443
Nancy Downey Hurtado, *Mgr*
EMP: 262
SQ FT: 49,361
SALES (corp-wide): 534.4MM **Privately Held**
Web: www.uci.edu
SIC: **8011** 8221 9411 Medical centers; University; Administration of educational programs
HQ: University Of California, Irvine
510 Aldrich Hall
Irvine CA
949 824-5011

(P-15165)
UNIVERSITY CALIFORNIA IRVINE
Also Called: Barr, Ronald J MD /UCI Med Gro
101 The City Dr S (92868-3201)
PHONE..................714 456-7890
EMP: 114
SALES (corp-wide): 534.4MM **Privately Held**
Web: www.uci.edu
SIC: **8011** 8221 9411 Dermatologist; University; Administration of educational programs
HQ: University Of California, Irvine
510 Aldrich Hall
Irvine CA
949 824-5011

(P-15166)
UNIVERSITY CALIFORNIA IRVINE
1640 Newport Blvd Ste 340 (92627-7730)
PHONE..................949 646-2267
Olivia Reil, *Brnch Mgr*
EMP: 68
SALES (corp-wide): 534.4MM **Privately Held**
Web: www.uci.edu
SIC: **8011** 8221 9411 Gynecologist; University; Administration of educational programs
HQ: University Of California, Irvine
510 Aldrich Hall
Irvine CA
949 824-5011

(P-15167)
UNIVERSITY CALIFORNIA IRVINE
Also Called: UIC
101 The City Dr S Ste 313 (92868-3201)
PHONE..................714 456-6966
Sharon Mccarthy, *Mgr*
EMP: 80
SALES (corp-wide): 534.4MM **Privately Held**
Web: www.ucihealth.org
SIC: **8011** 8221 9411 Surgeon; University; Administration of educational programs
HQ: University Of California, Irvine
510 Aldrich Hall
Irvine CA
949 824-5011

(P-15168)
UNIVERSITY SOUTHERN CALIFORNIA
Also Called: Usc/Radiation Onocology
1441 Eastlake Ave (90089-1019)
PHONE..................323 865-3050
Parvesh Kumar, *Prin*
EMP: 62
SALES (corp-wide): 5.57B **Privately Held**
Web: www.keckmedicine.org
SIC: **8011** 8221 Radiologist; University
PA: University Of Southern California
3720 S Flower St Fl 3
Los Angeles CA
213 740-7762

(P-15169)
UPLIFT FAMILY SERVICES
Also Called: Asian Pacific Family Center
9353 E Valley Blvd Ste C (91770-1923)
PHONE..................626 287-2988
Terry Gock, *Dir*
EMP: 90
SALES (corp-wide): 147.1MM **Privately Held**
Web: www.pacificclinics.org
SIC: **8011** 8322 8093 Clinic, operated by physicians; Individual and family services; Mental health clinic, outpatient
PA: Uplift Family Services
251 Llewellyn Ave
Campbell CA
408 379-3790

(P-15170)
UROLOGY ASSOCIATES CENTRAL CAL
7014 N Whitney Ave Ste A (93720-0155)
PHONE..................559 321-2800
Gilbert Dale Md, *Pr*
Irwin S Barg Md, *VP*
William Schiff Md, *Sec*
Artin Jibilian Md, *Treas*
EMP: 90 EST: 1997
SQ FT: 28,074
SALES (est): 10.46MM **Privately Held**
Web: www.urologyassociates.net
SIC: **8011** Urologist

(P-15171)
US DERMATOLOGY MEDICAL MANAGEMENT INC
1401 N Batavia St Ste 204 (92867-3500)
P.O. Box 7587 (78683-7587)
PHONE..................817 962-2157
EMP: 92
SIC: **8011** Dermatologist

(P-15172)
US HEALTHWORKS INC (DH)
Also Called: U.S. Healthworks Medical Group
28035 Avenue Stanford (91355-1104)
PHONE..................661 678-2300
Keith Newton, *Pr*
John Anderson, *CMO**
John Delorimier, *
Jim Talalai, *CIO**
Su Zan Nelson, *
EMP: 60 EST: 1995
SALES (est): 156.93MM
SALES (corp-wide): 5.53B **Publicly Held**
SIC: **8011** Clinic, operated by physicians
HQ: Concentra Inc.
5080 Spectrum Dr Ste 500w
Addison TX
972 364-8000

(P-15173)
USC KECK SCHOOL OF MEDICINE
Also Called: Usc Oncology/Hematology
330 Old Newport Blvd (92663-4121)
PHONE..................949 474-5730
Louis Vandermolen, *Brnch Mgr*
EMP: 61
SALES (corp-wide): 5.57B **Privately Held**
Web: www.keckmedicine.org
SIC: **8011** General and family practice, physician/surgeon
HQ: Usc Keck School Of Medicine
1975 Zonal Ave Ste Kam500
Los Angeles CA
323 442-2830

(P-15174)
USC KECK SCHOOL OF MEDICINE
Also Called: Usc Oncology/Hematology
300 Old Newport Blvd (92663-4121)
PHONE..................949 474-5720
Jill Chiascione, *Pr*
EMP: 61
SALES (corp-wide): 5.57B **Privately Held**
Web: www.keckmedicine.org

8011 - Offices And Clinics Of Medical Doctors (P-15175)

SIC: **8011** General and family practice, physician/surgeon
HQ: Usc Keck School Of Medicine
1975 Zonal Ave Ste Kam500
Los Angeles CA
323 442-2830

(P-15175)
USC KECK SCHOOL OF MEDICINE
Also Called: Usc Onclgy/Hmtlogy Infsion Ctr
330 Old Newport Blvd (92663-4121)
PHONE.................................949 646-6441
EMP: 61
SALES (corp-wide): 5.57B **Privately Held**
Web: www.keckmedicine.org
SIC: **8011** General and family practice, physician/surgeon
HQ: Usc Keck School Of Medicine
1975 Zonal Ave Ste Kam500
Los Angeles CA
323 442-2830

(P-15176)
VALLEY CHLD HLTHCARE FUNDATION
9300 Valley Childrens Pl (93636-8761)
PHONE.................................559 353-3000
Todd Suntrapak, *CEO*
William Chaltraw, *
EMP: 2800 EST: 2013
SALES (est): 793.85MM **Privately Held**
Web: www.valleychildrens.org
SIC: **8011** 8069 Physical medicine, physician/surgeon; Childrens' hospital

(P-15177)
VALLEY COMMUNITY HEALTHCARE
6801 Coldwater Canyon Ave Ste 1b (91605-5164)
PHONE.................................818 763-8836
Paula Wilson, *CEO*
Lee Huey, *
EMP: 300 EST: 1970
SQ FT: 15,000
SALES (est): 32.36MM **Privately Held**
Web: www.valleycommunityhealthcare.org
SIC: **8011** Clinic, operated by physicians

(P-15178)
VANGUARD HEALTH SYSTEMS INC
Also Called: North Anaheim Surgery Center
1154 N Euclid St (92801-1955)
PHONE.................................714 635-6272
J Rasmussen, *Admn*
Jeanette Rasmussen, *Admn*
EMP: 411 EST: 1991
SQ FT: 12,000
SALES (est): 7.99MM
SALES (corp-wide): 19.58B **Publicly Held**
SIC: **8011** 5999 Ambulatory surgical center; Medical apparatus and supplies
HQ: Vanguard Health Systems, Inc.
20 Burton Hills Blvd # 100
Nashville TN
615 665-6000

(P-15179)
VENICE FAMILY CLINIC
Also Called: VENICE FAMILY CLINIC
2509 Pico Blvd (90405-1828)
PHONE.................................310 392-8636
Elizabeth B Forer, *Prin*
EMP: 78
SALES (corp-wide): 84.76MM **Privately Held**

Web: www.venicefamilyclinic.org
SIC: **8011** Clinic, operated by physicians
PA: Venice Family Clinic Foundation
604 Rose Ave
Venice CA
310 664-7703

(P-15180)
VENICE FMLY CLINIC FOUNDATION (PA)
604 Rose Ave (90291-2767)
PHONE.................................310 664-7703
Mitesh Popat, *CEO*
Lee Rosenberg, *
Karl Keener, *
Gordon Lee, *
William Flumenbaum, *Ch*
EMP: 84 EST: 2010
SALES (est): 84.76MM
SALES (corp-wide): 84.76MM **Privately Held**
Web: www.venicefamilyclinic.org
SIC: **8011** Clinic, operated by physicians

(P-15181)
VENTURA CNTY OBSTET GYNCLGIC M
2795 Loma Vista Rd (93003-1544)
PHONE.................................805 643-8695
Richard Reisman, *Pr*
Steven Coyle, *VP*
John C Gustafson, *Sec*
EMP: 92 EST: 1977
SALES (est): 5.72MM **Privately Held**
Web: www.vtaobgyn.com
SIC: **8011** Gynecologist

(P-15182)
VENTURA COUNTY MEDICAL CENTER
Also Called: Santa Paula Hospital
845 N 10th St Ste 3 (93060-1348)
PHONE.................................805 933-8600
EMP: 121
SALES (corp-wide): 77.09MM **Privately Held**
Web: www.vchca.org
SIC: **8011** Medical centers
PA: Ventura County Medical Center
3291 Loma Vista Rd
Ventura CA
805 652-6000

(P-15183)
VENTURA COUNTY MEDICAL CENTER
Also Called: Ana Nacapa Surgical Associates
3291 Loma Vista Rd Bldg 343 (93003-3099)
PHONE.................................805 652-6201
Scott Arnold, *Prin*
EMP: 112
SALES (corp-wide): 77.09MM **Privately Held**
Web: www.anacapasurgical.com
SIC: **8011** Medical centers
PA: Ventura County Medical Center
3291 Loma Vista Rd
Ventura CA
805 652-6000

(P-15184)
VEP HEALTHCARE INC
Also Called: Vep-Ohec
1001 Galaxy Way Ste 400 (94520-5725)
PHONE.................................925 482-2839
Steve Maron, *Pr*
EMP: 200 EST: 2015
SALES (est): 26.46MM **Privately Held**

Web: www.usacs.com
SIC: **8011** Specialized medical practitioners, except internal

(P-15185)
VERDUGO HLLS PSYCHTHRAPY CTR A (PA)
Also Called: Pacific Child and Family Assoc
410 Arden Ave Ste 201 (91203-4006)
PHONE.................................818 241-6780
Ira Heilveil, *Pr*
EMP: 115 EST: 1988
SALES (est): 13.31MM **Privately Held**
SIC: **8011** Psychoanalyst

(P-15186)
VERITY MEDICAL FOUNDATION (PA)
Also Called: San Jose Medical Group / MGT
6300 Canoga Ave Ste 1500 (91367-8015)
PHONE.................................408 278-3000
Ernest Wallerstein, *CEO*
Christine Hoskinson, *CFO*
EMP: 80 EST: 2011
SALES (est): 9.65MM
SALES (corp-wide): 9.65MM **Privately Held**
Web: medfoundation.verity.org
SIC: **8011** 8741 Medical centers; Management services

(P-15187)
VETERANS HEALTH ADMINISTRATION
Also Called: Central Cal Healthcare Sys
2615 E Clinton Ave (93703-2223)
PHONE.................................559 225-6100
Al Perry, *Brnch Mgr*
EMP: 541
Web: benefits.va.gov
SIC: **8011** 9451 Medical centers; Administration of veterans' affairs
HQ: Veterans Health Administration
810 Vermont Ave Nw
Washington DC

(P-15188)
VETERANS HEALTH ADMINISTRATION
Also Called: Palo Alto VA Medical Center
3801 Miranda Ave Bldg 101 (94304-1207)
PHONE.................................650 493-5000
Elizabeth Freeman, *Dir*
EMP: 1548
Web: benefits.va.gov
SIC: **8011** 9451 Medical centers; Administration of veterans' affairs, Federal government
HQ: Veterans Health Administration
810 Vermont Ave Nw
Washington DC

(P-15189)
VETERANS HEALTH ADMINISTRATION
Also Called: San Francisco Vamc
4150 Clement St Bldg 6 (94121-1563)
PHONE.................................415 750-2009
Brian J Kelly, *Mgr*
EMP: 778
Web: benefits.va.gov
SIC: **8011** 9451 Medical centers; Administration of veterans' affairs, Federal government
HQ: Veterans Health Administration
810 Vermont Ave Nw
Washington DC

(P-15190)
VETERANS HEALTH ADMINISTRATION
Also Called: Loma Linda Healthcare Sys 605
11201 Benton St (92357-1000)
PHONE.................................909 825-7084
Debbie Romero, *Brnch Mgr*
EMP: 1405
Web: benefits.va.gov
SIC: **8011** 9451 Medical centers; Administration of veterans' affairs, Federal government
HQ: Veterans Health Administration
810 Vermont Ave Nw
Washington DC

(P-15191)
VETERANS HEALTH ADMINISTRATION
Also Called: West Los Angeles V A Med Ctr
11301 Wilshire Blvd (90073-1003)
PHONE.................................310 478-3711
Donna Beiter, *Dir*
EMP: 1499
Web: benefits.va.gov
SIC: **8011** 9451 Clinic, operated by physicians; Administration of veterans' affairs, Federal government
HQ: Veterans Health Administration
810 Vermont Ave Nw
Washington DC

(P-15192)
VETERANS HEALTH ADMINISTRATION
Also Called: Martinez Outpatient Clinic
150 Muir Rd (94553-4668)
PHONE.................................925 372-2000
Dina Moore, *Dir*
EMP: 246
Web: benefits.va.gov
SIC: **8011** 9451 Clinic, operated by physicians; Administration of veterans' affairs, Federal government
HQ: Veterans Health Administration
810 Vermont Ave Nw
Washington DC

(P-15193)
VIA CARE CMNTY HLTH CTR INC
Also Called: BIENVENIDOS COMMUNITY HEALTH C
507 S Atlantic Blvd (90022-2621)
PHONE.................................323 268-9191
Deborah Villar, *CEO*
Joe Gotsill, *
EMP: 60 EST: 2010
SALES (est): 12.66MM **Privately Held**
Web: www.viacarela.org
SIC: **8011** Primary care medical clinic

(P-15194)
VISALIA MEDICAL CLINIC
839 Sequoia Ave (93247-1424)
PHONE.................................559 562-1361
Gerald Moore, *Brnch Mgr*
EMP: 68
SALES (corp-wide): 5.99MM **Privately Held**
Web: www.kaweahhealthmedicalgroup.org
SIC: **8011** Clinic, operated by physicians
PA: Visalia Medical Clinic
5448 W De Las Robles
Visalia CA
559 738-7500

PRODUCTS & SERVICES SECTION

8021 - Offices And Clinics Of Dentists (P-15215)

(P-15195)
VISALIA MEDICAL CLINIC INC (PA)
Also Called: Multi Specialty Medical Svc
5400 W Hillsdale Ave (93291-8222)
PHONE..................................559 733-5222
Richard E Strid, *CEO*
EMP: 289 **EST:** 1973
SQ FT: 70,000
SALES (est): 57.6MM
SALES (corp-wide): 57.6MM **Privately Held**
Web: www.kaweahhealthmedicalgroup.org
SIC: 8011 8071 Clinic, operated by physicians; Medical laboratories

(P-15196)
VISION CARE CTR A MED GROUP IN (PA)
Also Called: Vision Care Center Central Cal
7075 N Sharon Ave (93720-3329)
PHONE..................................559 486-2000
Julie Cleeland, *CEO*
Ralph Hadley O.d., *Pr*
Michael Herman, *
EMP: 82 **EST:** 1963
SQ FT: 18,000
SALES (est): 14.21MM
SALES (corp-wide): 14.21MM **Privately Held**
Web: www.eyeqvc.com
SIC: 8011 8042 Opthalmologist; Offices and clinics of optometrists

(P-15197)
WARBRITTON & ASSOC IMPAIRMENT
24301 Southland Dr (94545-1542)
PHONE..................................510 781-0211
EMP: 67
SIC: 8011 Gynecologist
PA: Warbritton & Associates Impairment Rating Specialists Medical Corp., Inc.
300 Frank H Ogawa Plz
Oakland CA

(P-15198)
WASHINGTON OTPTENT SRGERY CTR
Also Called: Washington Otpent Surgery Ctr
2299 Mowry Ave Fl 1 (94538-1621)
PHONE..................................510 791-5374
Gary Charland, *Pt*
EMP: 97 **EST:** 1986
SQ FT: 18,000
SALES (est): 17.2MM
SALES (corp-wide): 38.47MM **Privately Held**
Web: www.washosc.com
SIC: 8011 Surgeon
PA: Washington Township Hospital Development Corporation
2000 Mowry Ave
Fremont CA
510 797-1111

(P-15199)
WATTS HEALTHCARE CORPORATION (PA)
Also Called: WATTS HEALTH
10300 Compton Ave (90002-3628)
PHONE..................................323 564-4331
Roderick Seamster, *Pr*
Roderick Seamster, *Pr*
Carroll J Mcneely, *CFO*
EMP: 180 **EST:** 2002
SALES (est): 39.95MM
SALES (corp-wide): 39.95MM **Privately Held**
Web: www.wattshealth.org
SIC: 8011 Clinic, operated by physicians

(P-15200)
WAVE PLASTIC SURGERY CTR INC
18433 Colima Rd (91748-5815)
PHONE..................................626 964-7788
Peter Lee, *Pr*
EMP: 71
SALES (corp-wide): 21.31MM **Privately Held**
Web: www.waveplasticsurgery.com
SIC: 8011 Plastic surgeon
PA: Wave Plastic Surgery Center Inc.
3680 Wilshire Blvd Fl 2
Los Angeles CA
213 383-4800

(P-15201)
WELLSPACE WOMENS HEALTH CENTER
7601 Hospital Dr Ste 200 (95823-5408)
PHONE..................................916 313-8462
EMP: 60 **EST:** 2018
SALES (est): 2.1MM **Privately Held**
Web: www.wellspacehealth.org
SIC: 8011 Clinic, operated by physicians

(P-15202)
WEST COUNTY HEALTH CENTERS INC (PA)
16312 3rd St (95446)
P.O. Box 1449 (95446-1449)
PHONE..................................707 869-1594
Mary Szecsey, *Ex Dir*
John Kornfeld, *
Debra Johnson, *
Dwight Cary, *
EMP: 75 **EST:** 1974
SALES (est): 24.94MM
SALES (corp-wide): 24.94MM **Privately Held**
Web: www.wchealth.org
SIC: 8011 Primary care medical clinic

(P-15203)
WEST COVINA MEDICAL CLINIC INC (PA)
1500 W West Covina Pkwy Ste 100 (91790-2708)
PHONE..................................626 960-8614
Ziad Dabuni, *Pr*
Doctor Ziad Dabuni, *Pr*
Doctor Shivani Shah, *Ex VP*
Doctor Lucio Sanchez, *Sec*
Doctor Suntheetha Ali, *Treas*
EMP: 222 **EST:** 1950
SQ FT: 50,000
SALES (est): 9.18MM
SALES (corp-wide): 9.18MM **Privately Held**
SIC: 8011 Clinic, operated by physicians

(P-15204)
WEST DERMATOLOGY MED MGT INC (PA)
Also Called: West Dermatology
680 Newport Center Dr Ste 150 (92660)
PHONE..................................909 793-3000
J Robert West, *Pr*
EMP: 532 **EST:** 2004
SALES (est): 47.44MM
SALES (corp-wide): 47.44MM **Privately Held**
Web: www.westdermatology.com
SIC: 8011 Dermatologist

(P-15205)
WESTERN UNIV HLTH SCIENCES
Also Called: Mission Medical Clinic
360 E Mission Blvd (91766-1847)
PHONE..................................909 865-2565
Alan D Cundari, *Prin*
EMP: 78
SALES (corp-wide): 230.61MM **Privately Held**
Web: www.westernu.edu
SIC: 8011 8221 Clinic, operated by physicians; University
PA: Western University Of Health Sciences
309 E 2nd St
Pomona CA
909 623-6116

(P-15206)
WESTSIDE CRDVSCLAR MED GROUP I
99 N La Cienega Blvd Ste 203 (90211-2222)
PHONE..................................310 289-9955
Norman E Lepor, *Prin*
EMP: 162
SALES (corp-wide): 8.57MM **Privately Held**
SIC: 8011 Radiologist
PA: Westside Cardiovascular Medical Group, Inc.
99 N La Cienega Blvd # 10
Beverly Hills CA
310 623-1150

(P-15207)
WHITE MEM CMNTY HLTH CTR A CAL
1828 E Cesar E Chavez Ave Ste 6100 (90033-2400)
PHONE..................................323 987-1222
Carl Coan, *CEO*
EMP: 61 **EST:** 2016
SALES (est): 4.18MM **Privately Held**
Web: www.wmchealthcenter.org
SIC: 8011 Physical medicine, physician/surgeon

(P-15208)
WHITE MEMORIAL MED GROUP INC (PA)
1701 E Cesar E Chavez Ave Ste 510 (90033-2464)
P.O. Box 51741 (90051-6041)
PHONE..................................323 987-1300
Alan Lau, *Pr*
EMP: 71 **EST:** 1983
SQ FT: 20,000
SALES (est): 14.56MM
SALES (corp-wide): 14.56MM **Privately Held**
Web: www.adventisthealth.org
SIC: 8011 8742 Medical centers; Hospital and health services consultant

(P-15209)
WHITE MEMORIAL MEDICAL CENTER
1720 E Cesar E Chavez Ave (90033-2414)
PHONE..................................323 260-5739
Beth D Zachary, *Brnch Mgr*
EMP: 800
SALES (corp-wide): 789.42MM **Privately Held**
Web: www.adventisthealth.org
SIC: 8011 Medical centers
HQ: White Memorial Medical Center Inc
1720 E Cesar E Chavez Ave
Los Angeles CA
323 268-5000

(P-15210)
WILLOW SPRINGS LLC
Also Called: Sierra Vista Hospital
8001 Bruceville Rd (95823-2329)
PHONE..................................916 288-0300
Mike Zauner, *CEO*
EMP: 2612
SALES (corp-wide): 13.4B **Publicly Held**
Web: www.uhs.com
SIC: 8011 8063 Psychiatric clinic; Psychiatric hospitals
HQ: Willow Springs, Llc
6640 Carothers Pkwy # 400
Franklin TN
615 312-5700

(P-15211)
WILLOW SPRINGS LLC
Fremont Hospital
39001 Sundale Dr (94538-2005)
PHONE..................................510 796-1100
TOLL FREE: 888
Joan Bettencourt Newman, *Prin*
EMP: 876
SALES (corp-wide): 13.4B **Publicly Held**
Web: www.fremonthospital.com
SIC: 8011 8093 8361 8069 Psychiatric clinic; Specialty outpatient clinics, nec; Residential care; Specialty hospitals, except psychiatric
HQ: Willow Springs, Llc
6640 Carothers Pkwy # 400
Franklin TN
615 312-5700

(P-15212)
WOMENS CANCER CENTER
Also Called: Edraki, Babak MD
1455 Montego Ste 100 (94598-2952)
PHONE..................................925 627-3440
Nini Turner, *Mgr*
EMP: 60
SIC: 8011 Internal medicine practitioners
PA: Women's Cancer Center
170 Knowles Dr Ste 203
Los Gatos CA

(P-15213)
WOMENS HEALTH SPECIALISTS
2299 Mowry Ave Ste 3c (94538-1621)
PHONE..................................510 248-1470
Gary Charland, *Off Mgr*
Gary Charland, *Mgr*
EMP: 66 **EST:** 1987
SQ FT: 5,300
SALES (est): 4.87MM **Privately Held**
Web: www.mywtmf.com
SIC: 8011 Obstetrician

8021 Offices And Clinics Of Dentists

(P-15214)
ACCESS DENTAL PLAN (PA)
Also Called: Access Dental Centers
530 S Main St (92868-4555)
PHONE..................................916 922-5000
Reza M Abbaszadeh, *Pr*
Teri Abbaszadeh, *
▲ **EMP:** 70 **EST:** 1989
SALES (est): 22.98MM **Privately Held**
Web: www.westerndental.com
SIC: 8021 Dental clinic

(P-15215)
ADARSH KAUR DDS INC
3423 Ashbourne Cir (94583-6012)
PHONE..................................530 892-1218
EMP: 68

8021 - Offices And Clinics Of Dentists (P-15216)

SALES (corp-wide): 245.02K **Privately Held**
SIC: **8021** Offices and clinics of dentists
PA: Adarsh Kaur, D.D.S., Inc.
1430 East Ave Ste 5a
Chico CA
530 892-1218

(P-15216)
AMPLA HEALTH (PA)
935 Market St (95991-4210)
PHONE..................530 674-4261
Benjamin Flores, *CEO*
Hilton Perez, *
Dale Johnson, *
EMP: 245 EST: 1964
SQ FT: 10,200
SALES (est): 93.32MM
SALES (corp-wide): 93.32MM **Privately Held**
Web: www.amplahealth.org
SIC: **8021** 8011 Dental clinic; Health maintenance organization

(P-15217)
AZAD PROFESSIONAL DENTAL CORP
Also Called: Calidental
4221 S H St (93304-7205)
PHONE..................661 558-0022
EMP: 64
SALES (corp-wide): 524.01K **Privately Held**
SIC: **8021** Dentists' office
PA: Azad Professional Dental Corporation
1009 N H St Ste P
Lompoc CA
805 242-4044

(P-15218)
BOYD DENTAL CORPORATION
362 E Vanderbilt Way (92408-3593)
PHONE..................909 890-0421
EMP: 91
SALES (corp-wide): 897.96K **Privately Held**
Web: www.idcsanbernardino.com
SIC: **8021** Dentists' office
PA: Boyd Dental Corporation
599 Inland Center Dr # 110
San Bernardino CA
909 384-1111

(P-15219)
CHAPA-DE INDIAN HLTH PRGRAM IN
1350 E Main St (95945-5208)
PHONE..................530 477-8545
EMP: 60
SALES (corp-wide): 65.02MM **Privately Held**
Web: www.chapa-de.org
SIC: **8021** 8011 8322 Dentists' office; Clinic, operated by physicians; Outreach program
PA: Chapa-De Indian Health Program, Inc.
11670 Atwood Rd
Auburn CA
530 887-2800

(P-15220)
CHROMIUM DENTAL II LLC
Also Called: Labs.dental
1524 Brookhollow Dr (92705-5426)
PHONE..................949 733-3111
Charbel Louis Karam, *Managing Member*
EMP: 220 EST: 2018
SALES (est): 9.56MM **Privately Held**
SIC: **8021** Dentists' office

(P-15221)
CLEARCHOICE MGT SVCS LLC
9225 Sierra College Blvd (95661-5919)
PHONE..................916 742-6055
Tom Andrews, *Ofcr*
EMP: 65
SALES (corp-wide): 512.86MM **Privately Held**
Web: www.clearchoice.com
SIC: **8021** Dental clinic
HQ: Clearchoice Management Services, Llc
8350 E Crescent Pkwy # 300
Greenwood Village CO

(P-15222)
CLEARCHOICE MGT SVCS LLC
1655 The Alameda (95126-2203)
PHONE..................408 288-7710
EMP: 65
SALES (corp-wide): 512.86MM **Privately Held**
Web: www.clearchoice.com
SIC: **8021** Dental clinic
HQ: Clearchoice Management Services, Llc
8350 E Crescent Pkwy # 300
Greenwood Village CO

(P-15223)
CLEARCHOICE MGT SVCS LLC
21525 Hawthorne Blvd (90503-6605)
PHONE..................424 337-1178
EMP: 65
SALES (corp-wide): 512.86MM **Privately Held**
Web: www.clearchoice.com
SIC: **8021** Dental clinic
HQ: Clearchoice Management Services, Llc
8350 E Crescent Pkwy # 300
Greenwood Village CO

(P-15224)
DAVID TOMA DDS INC
645 Sweetwater Rd (91977-5628)
PHONE..................858 583-6147
EMP: 62
SIC: **8021** Offices and clinics of dentists
PA: David Toma, D.D.S., Inc.
8524 1/2 Rosecrans Ave
Paramount CA

(P-15225)
DEDICATED DENTAL SYSTEMS INC
9800 S La Cienega Blvd Ste 800 (90301-4440)
PHONE..................661 397-5513
Arthur Kaiser, *Pr*
EMP: 65 EST: 1987
SQ FT: 5,000
SALES (est): 4.61MM
SALES (corp-wide): 120.83MM **Privately Held**
Web: www.gentledentalplan.com
SIC: **8021** 6324 Dental clinic; Hospital and medical service plans
HQ: Interdent Service Corporation
9800 S La Cnga Blvd # 800
Inglewood CA

(P-15226)
FAMILY HLTH CTRS SAN DIEGO INC
1809 National Ave (92113-2113)
PHONE..................619 515-2300
Brian Woolford Md, *Dir*
EMP: 348
SALES (corp-wide): 147.12MM **Privately Held**
Web: www.fhcsd.org

SIC: **8021** Offices and clinics of dentists
PA: Family Health Centers Of San Diego, Inc.
823 Gateway Center Way
San Diego CA
619 515-2303

(P-15227)
GENTLE DENTAL
853 Middlefield Rd Ste 1 (94301-2900)
PHONE..................650 341-8008
EMP: 784 EST: 1990
SQ FT: 2,200
SALES (est): 1.49MM
SALES (corp-wide): 120.83MM **Privately Held**
Web: www.interdent.com
SIC: **8021** Dental clinic
HQ: Interdent Service Corporation
9800 S La Cnga Blvd # 800
Inglewood CA

(P-15228)
GENTLE DENTAL SERVICE CORP (DH)
9800 S La Cienega Blvd Ste 800 (90301-4408)
PHONE..................800 277-1112
Fred Vanerden, *CFO*
EMP: 64 EST: 2007
SALES (est): 79.45MM **Privately Held**
Web: www.interdent.com
SIC: **8021** Dental clinic
HQ: H.I.G. Capital, L.L.C.
1450 Brickell Ave Fl 31
Miami FL
305 379-2322

(P-15229)
INTERDENT SERVICE CORPORATION
3630 Central Ave (92506-5908)
PHONE..................951 682-1720
Carlos Espadas, *Brnch Mgr*
EMP: 64
SALES (corp-wide): 120.83MM **Privately Held**
Web: www.interdent.com
SIC: **8021** Dental clinic
HQ: Interdent Service Corporation
9800 S La Cnga Blvd # 800
Inglewood CA

(P-15230)
INTERDENT SERVICE CORPORATION
Also Called: Martin, Steve DDS
1421 Guerneville Rd Ste 102 (95403-7220)
PHONE..................707 528-7000
R Pranin, *Brnch Mgr*
EMP: 86
SALES (corp-wide): 120.83MM **Privately Held**
Web: www.interdent.com
SIC: **8021** Dental clinic
HQ: Interdent Service Corporation
9800 S La Cnga Blvd # 800
Inglewood CA

(P-15231)
JOSE C CASTILLO DDS INC
2918 5th Ave Ste 310 (92103-5910)
PHONE..................619 295-2288
EMP: 72
SALES (corp-wide): 866.28K **Privately Held**
SIC: **8021** Orthodontist
PA: Jose C Castillo Dds Inc
5050 Clairemont Mesa Blvd

San Diego CA

(P-15232)
LAKE CNTY TRBAL HLTH CNSRTIUM
925 Bevins Ct (95453-9754)
P.O. Box 1950 (95453-1950)
PHONE..................707 263-8382
Mike Icay, *Pr*
Crista Ray, *
Tina Ramos, *
Tanya Michel, *
EMP: 80 EST: 1983
SQ FT: 10,832
SALES (est): 43.37MM **Privately Held**
Web: www.lcthc.com
SIC: **8021** Dental clinic

(P-15233)
LANCE RYGG DENTAL CORP
10405 Tierrasanta Blvd (92124-2603)
PHONE..................858 492-9300
EMP: 162
SIC: **8021** Dentists' office
PA: Lance Rygg Dental Corp
2860 Michelle Fl 2
Irvine CA

(P-15234)
LEONID M GLSMAN DDS A DNTL COR
Also Called: Dentalville
5021 Florence Ave (90201-3802)
PHONE..................323 560-4514
EMP: 130
SALES (corp-wide): 4.66MM **Privately Held**
Web: www.panoramacitydentistca.com
SIC: **8021** Dentists' office
PA: Leonid M. Glosman, D.D.S., A Dental Corporation
7864 Van Nuys Blvd
Panorama City CA
323 266-1000

(P-15235)
LOUIS F MASCOLA DDS
Also Called: MASCOLA, LOUIS F DDS
3660 Lomita Blvd (90505-3938)
PHONE..................310 986-2930
Bartok Garcia, *Brnch Mgr*
EMP: 142
SALES (corp-wide): 874.34K **Privately Held**
Web: www.mascoladds.com
SIC: **8021** Dentists' office
PA: Louis F. Mascola, D.D.S., Inc.
770 W 9th St
San Pedro CA
310 831-2377

(P-15236)
LUCERO DENTAL CLINIC
2740 S Bristol St Ste 206 (92704-6233)
PHONE..................714 557-0201
Martha R Lucero Perez, *Brnch Mgr*
EMP: 65
Web: www.lucerodental.com
SIC: **8021** Dentists' office
PA: Lucero Dental Clinic
12833 Harbor Blvd Ste F3
Garden Grove CA

(P-15237)
M & M NOORI DENTAL CORP
4323 Mills Cir Ste 101 (91764-5251)
PHONE..................909 476-3000
EMP: 63
SALES (corp-wide): 120.62K **Privately Held**

PRODUCTS & SERVICES SECTION
8031 - Offices And Clinics Of Osteopathic Physicians (P-15258)

SIC: 8021 Dental clinic
PA: M & M Noori Dental Corp.
1838 N Euclid Ave
Upland CA

(P-15238)
MANSKE DENTAL CORPORATION
1418 7th St Apt 102 (90401-2694)
PHONE..................213 907-4027
EMP: 74
SALES (corp-wide): 198.02K Privately Held
SIC: 8021 Offices and clinics of dentists
PA: Manske Dental Corporation
1355 N Sierra Bonita Ave
West Hollywood CA
424 354-9336

(P-15239)
MARINE CORPS COMMUNITY SVCS
Camp Pendleton Marine Corps Base (92055)
P.O. Box 555221 (92055-5221)
PHONE..................760 725-5187
EMP: 160
Web: www.usmc-mccs.org
SIC: 8021 9711 Offices and clinics of dentists ; Marine Corps
HQ: Marine Corps Community Services
3044 Catlin Ave
Quantico VA
703 432-0109

(P-15240)
MICHAEL P BYKO DDS A PROF CORP (PA)
164 W Hospitality Ln Ste 14 (92408-3316)
PHONE..................909 888-7817
Michael Boyko, Pr
◆ EMP: 60 EST: 1980
SQ FT: 3,000
SALES (est): 8.82MM
SALES (corp-wide): 8.82MM Privately Held
SIC: 8021 Dental clinic

(P-15241)
MY KIDS DENTIST
24635 Madison Ave Ste E (92562-7556)
PHONE..................951 600-1062
Theresa Gomez, Brnch Mgr
EMP: 400
SALES (corp-wide): 13.98MM Privately Held
Web: www.mkdmurrieta.com
SIC: 8021 Dentists' office
PA: My Kid's Dentist
17000 Red Hill Ave
Irvine CA
909 854-1437

(P-15242)
NORTHERN VLY INDIAN HLTH INC
2500 Main St (96080-2336)
PHONE..................530 529-2567
Robin Brownfield, Mgr
EMP: 62
SALES (corp-wide): 71.48MM Privately Held
Web: www.nvih.org
SIC: 8021 Offices and clinics of dentists
PA: Northern Valley Indian Health, Inc.
207 N Butte St
Willows CA
530 934-9293

(P-15243)
NORTHERN VLY INDIAN HLTH INC
845 W East Ave (95926-2002)
PHONE..................530 896-9400
Maureen Self, Mgr
EMP: 63
SALES (corp-wide): 71.48MM Privately Held
Web: www.nvih.org
SIC: 8021 8011 Dental clinic; Primary care medical clinic
PA: Northern Valley Indian Health, Inc.
207 N Butte St
Willows CA
530 934-9293

(P-15244)
PACIFIC DENTAL SERVICES LLC (PA)
Also Called: Pds
17000 Red Hill Ave (92614-5626)
P.O. Box 19723 (92623-9723)
PHONE..................714 845-8500
▲ EMP: 300 EST: 1991
SQ FT: 40,000
SALES (est): 1.77MM Privately Held
Web: www.pacificdentalservices.com
SIC: 8021 6794 Dental clinic; Franchises, selling or licensing

(P-15245)
PACIFIC DENTAL SERVICES LLC
Also Called: P D S
17000 Red Hill Ave (92614-5626)
PHONE..................714 845-8500
EMP: 72 EST: 1997
SALES (est): 1.37MM Privately Held
Web: www.pacificdentalservices.com
SIC: 8021 Dentists' office

(P-15246)
PACIFIC DNTL SVCS HOLDG CO INC
17000 Red Hill Ave (92614-5626)
PHONE..................714 845-8500
Stephen E Thorne Iv, CEO
EMP: 114 EST: 2013
SALES (est): 9.05MM Privately Held
Web: www.pacificdentalservices.com
SIC: 8021 6794 Dental clinic; Franchises, selling or licensing

(P-15247)
PETER WYLAN DDS
Also Called: Bellflower Dental Group
10318 Rosecrans Ave (90706-2702)
PHONE..................562 925-3765
Peter Wylan D.d.s., Owner
EMP: 100 EST: 1955
SQ FT: 2,000
SALES (est): 4.64MM Privately Held
Web: www.bellflowerdentalgroup.com
SIC: 8021 8072 Dentists' office; Dental laboratories

(P-15248)
PREMIER DENTAL HOLDINGS INC (PA)
Also Called: Sonrava
530 S Main St Ste 600 (92868-4544)
P.O. Box 14227 (92863-1227)
PHONE..................714 480-3000
Daniel Crowley, CEO
EMP: 264 EST: 2010
SALES (est): 734.01MM
SALES (corp-wide): 734.01MM Privately Held
Web: www.westerndental.com
SIC: 8021 Dental clinic

(P-15249)
SCHNIEROW DENTAL CARE
Also Called: Piehl, Joel J DDS
13450 Hawthorne Blvd (90250-5806)
PHONE..................310 377-6453
Burton Schnierow D.d.s., Pr
EMP: 63 EST: 1948
SQ FT: 3,200
SALES (est): 7.25MM Privately Held
Web: www.hawthorne-dentist.com
SIC: 8021 Dentists' office

(P-15250)
SETAREHSHENAS DENTAL CORP
1197 E Los Angeles Ave (93065-2868)
PHONE..................805 583-5700
Katayoun Setarehshenas, Brnch Mgr
EMP: 161
SIC: 8021 Dentists' office
PA: Setarehshenas Dental Corp
2860 Michelle Fl 2
Irvine CA

(P-15251)
TOAN D NGUYEN DDS INC
Also Called: TOAN D NGUYEN DDS INC
213 N San Dimas Ave (91773-2649)
PHONE..................909 599-3398
EMP: 87
SALES (corp-wide): 280.72K Privately Held
Web: www.sandimasdentistry.com
SIC: 8021 Dentists' office
PA: Toan D. Nguyen, D.D.S., Inc.
511 E 1st St Ste C
Tustin CA
562 926-3354

(P-15252)
TOIYABE INDIAN HEALTH PRJ INC (PA)
250 N See Vee Ln (93514-8130)
PHONE..................760 873-8461
David Lent, Ex Dir
Monty Bengochia, *
Mary Daniel, *
EMP: 86 EST: 1971
SQ FT: 66,300
SALES (est): 18.71MM
SALES (corp-wide): 18.71MM Privately Held
Web: www.toiyabe.us
SIC: 8021 8011 Dental clinic; Clinic, operated by physicians

(P-15253)
UNIVERSITY CAL SAN FRANCISCO
Also Called: Ucsf Dental Center-Buchanan
100 Buchanan St (94102-6147)
PHONE..................415 476-5608
Mark Kirkland D.d.s., Admn
EMP: 93
SALES (corp-wide): 534.4MM Privately Held
Web: www.ucsf.edu
SIC: 8021 Dental clinics and offices
HQ: University Cal San Francisco
513 Parnassus Ave 115f
San Francisco CA

(P-15254)
WESTERN DENTAL SERVICES INC (HQ)
Also Called: Western Dental & Orthodontics
530 S Main St Ste 600 (92868-4544)
P.O. Box 14227 (92863-1227)
PHONE..................714 480-3000
TOLL FREE: 800
Daniel D Crowley, CEO
Jeffrey Miller, CLO*
John Luther, Chief Dental Officer*
Preet M Takkar, *
William Dembereckyj, *
EMP: 350 EST: 1984
SALES (est): 733.77MM
SALES (corp-wide): 734.01MM Privately Held
Web: www.westerndental.com
SIC: 8021 Dentists' office
PA: Premier Dental Holdings, Inc.
530 S Main St Ste 600
Orange CA
714 480-3000

8031 Offices And Clinics Of Osteopathic Physicians

(P-15255)
ARTEMIS INST FOR CLNCAL RES LL
770 Washington St Ste 300 (92103-2209)
PHONE..................858 278-3647
EMP: 73 EST: 2008
SALES (est): 11.06MM Privately Held
Web: www.artemis-research.com
SIC: 8031 8011 Offices and clinics of osteopathic physicians; Psychiatrist

(P-15256)
CARBON HEALTH TECHNOLOGIES INC
Also Called: La Costa Urgent Care
6971 El Camino Real Ste 101 (92009)
P.O. Box 355 (92067-0355)
PHONE..................760 603-3221
EMP: 135
SALES (corp-wide): 104.49MM Privately Held
Web: www.carbonhealth.com
SIC: 8031 8011 Offices and clinics of osteopathic physicians; Freestanding emergency medical center
PA: Carbon Health Technologies, Inc.
2100 Franklin St Ste 355
Oakland CA
415 223-2858

(P-15257)
PROVIDNCE FACEY MED FOUNDATION
Also Called: Exer
2655 1st St (93065-1547)
PHONE..................805 206-2000
EMP: 91
SALES (corp-wide): 91.37MM Privately Held
Web: www.facey.com
SIC: 8031 8011 Offices and clinics of osteopathic physicians; Offices and clinics of medical doctors
PA: Providence Facey Medical Foundation
15451 San Frnndo Mssion B
Mission Hills CA
818 365-9531

(P-15258)
PROVIDNCE FACEY MED FOUNDATION
191 S Buena Vista St (91505-4554)
PHONE..................818 861-7831
Jennifer Sung Md, Brnch Mgr
EMP: 91
SALES (corp-wide): 91.37MM Privately Held

8031 - Offices And Clinics Of Osteopathic Physicians (P-15259)

Web: www.facey.com
SIC: 8031 8011 Offices and clinics of osteopathic physicians; Offices and clinics of medical doctors
PA: Providence Facey Medical Foundation
15451 San Frnndo Mssion B
Mission Hills CA
818 365-9531

(P-15259)
TEACHORG WHICH WILL DO BUS IN
174 Hermann St (94102-6131)
PHONE..................................650 575-5277
Anne Mahle, Pr
EMP: 70 EST: 2016
SALES (est): 381.01K Privately Held
SIC: 8031 Offices and clinics of osteopathic physicians

(P-15260)
VISTA COMMUNITY CLINIC (PA)
1000 Vale Terrace Dr (92084-5218)
PHONE..................................760 631-5000
Fernando Sanudo, CEO
Michele Lambert, *
EMP: 280 EST: 1972
SQ FT: 60,000
SALES (est): 83.58MM
SALES (corp-wide): 83.58MM Privately Held
Web: www.vistacommunityclinic.org
SIC: 8031 8011 Offices and clinics of osteopathic physicians; Medical centers

8041 Offices And Clinics Of Chiropractors

(P-15261)
CHIROTECH INC
Also Called: Chirotouch
9265 Sky Park Ct Ste 200 (92123-4303)
PHONE..................................619 528-0040
Ron Nielle, Owner
EMP: 212 EST: 2007
SALES (est): 11.79MM Privately Held
Web: www.chirotouch.com
SIC: 8041 Offices and clinics of chiropractors

(P-15262)
LANDMARK HEALTHCARE SVCS INC (DH)
1610 Arden Way Ste 280 (95815-4050)
PHONE..................................800 638-4557
Adam Boehler, CEO
Christopher Goldsmith, *
Carol Devol, *
EMP: 120 EST: 1986
SQ FT: 330,215
SALES (est): 24.54MM
SALES (corp-wide): 180.52B Publicly Held
Web: www.lmhealthcare.com
SIC: 8041 8049 Offices and clinics of chiropractors; Acupuncturist
HQ: Carecore National, Llc
400 Buckwalter Place Blvd
Bluffton SC
800 918-8924

8042 Offices And Clinics Of Optometrists

(P-15263)
GOLDEN OPTICAL CORPORATION
2855 Stevens Creek Blvd Ste 1051 (95050-6709)
PHONE..................................408 246-4500
EMP: 88
SALES (corp-wide): 59.53MM Privately Held
SIC: 8042 Offices and clinics of optometrists
PA: Golden Optical Corporation
19800 W 8 Mile Rd
Southfield MI
248 483-0812

(P-15264)
OCEAN PARK OPTOMETRY
2605 Lincoln Blvd (90405-4619)
PHONE..................................310 452-1039
EMP: 75 EST: 2019
SALES (est): 3.62MM Privately Held
Web: www.opoptometry.com
SIC: 8042 Specialized optometrists

(P-15265)
SANTEN INCORPORATED
6401 Hollis St Ste 125 (94608-1462)
PHONE..................................415 268-9100
EMP: 100 EST: 1993
SALES (est): 22.84MM Privately Held
Web: www.santen.com
SIC: 8042 Specialized optometrists
PA: Santen Pharmaceutical Co., Ltd.
4-20, Ofukacho, Kita-Ku
Osaka OSK

(P-15266)
TOTAL VISION LLC
27271 Las Ramblas Ste 200a (92691-8041)
PHONE..................................949 652-7242
Scott Strachan, Pr
Doug Lattime, VP Fin
Broke Jakovich, VP Opers
EMP: 194 EST: 2014
SQ FT: 3,000
SALES (est): 19MM
SALES (corp-wide): 19MM Privately Held
Web: www.yourtotalvision.com
SIC: 8042 Group and corporate practice, optometrist
PA: Total Vision Holdings, Llc
277 Park Ave Fl 27
New York NY
212 704-5364

8049 Offices Of Health Practitioner

(P-15267)
A IS FOR APPLE INC
1420 Koll Cir (95112-4620)
PHONE..................................877 991-0009
Marilyn Freeman, Pr
John Freeman, *
EMP: 106 EST: 1999
SALES (est): 2.75MM Privately Held
Web: www.aisforapple.com
SIC: 8049 Speech pathologist

(P-15268)
ANDERSON PHYSICAL THERAPY INC
202 Providence Mine Rd Ste 206 (95959-2946)
PHONE..................................530 265-8100
Joni Anderson, Prin
EMP: 63 EST: 2008
SALES (est): 876.31K
SALES (corp-wide): 73.61MM Privately Held
Web: www.andersonptandsportsmedicine.com
SIC: 8049 Physiotherapist
PA: Therapeutic Associates, Inc.
20829 72nd Ave S Ste 710
Kent WA
253 872-6028

(P-15269)
BURGER PHYSCL THERAPY SVCS INC (HQ)
Also Called: Burger Physcl Thrapy Rhbltion
1301 E Bidwell St Ste 201 (95630-3565)
PHONE..................................916 983-5900
Carol Burger, Pr
EMP: 140 EST: 1985
SALES (est): 7.91MM Privately Held
Web: www.burgerrehab.com
SIC: 8049 Physical therapist
PA: Burger Rehabilitation Systems, Inc.
1301 E Bidwell St Ste 201
Folsom CA

(P-15270)
BURGER RHBLITATION SYSTEMS INC (PA)
1301 E Bidwell St Ste 201 (95630-3565)
PHONE..................................800 900-8491
Carol K Burger, Pr
EMP: 200 EST: 1978
SQ FT: 5,000
SALES (est): 24.54MM Privately Held
Web: www.burgerrehab.com
SIC: 8049 Occupational therapist

(P-15271)
CASA CLINA HOSP CTRS FOR HLTHC
910 E Alosta Ave (91702-2709)
PHONE..................................626 334-8735
EMP: 149
SALES (corp-wide): 136.57MM Privately Held
Web: www.casacolina.org
SIC: 8049 Physical therapist
HQ: Casa Colina Hospital And Centers For Healthcare
255 E Bonita Ave
Pomona CA
909 596-7733

(P-15272)
CBEM LLC CORPORATE OFFICE
1101 5th Ave (94901-2903)
PHONE..................................415 454-3700
Gloria Dal Poggetto, Prin
EMP: 71
SALES (corp-wide): 16.19MM Privately Held
Web: www.cbemllc.com
SIC: 8049 Acupuncturist
PA: Cbem Llc Corporate Office
270 Lafayette Cir
Lafayette CA
925 283-9000

(P-15273)
CENTER FOR SOCIAL DYNAMICS LLC
Also Called: Csd Autism Services
10390 Coloma Rd Ste A (95670-2152)
PHONE..................................916 382-4447
EMP: 77
SALES (corp-wide): 46.84MM Privately Held
Web: www.csdautismservices.com
SIC: 8049 Nutrition specialist
PA: Center For Social Dynamics, Llc
1200 Concord Ave Ste 100
Concord CA
510 268-8120

(P-15274)
CENTER FOR SOCIAL DYNAMICS LLC
Also Called: Csd Autism Services
9360 N Name Uno (95020-3540)
PHONE..................................408 843-9350
EMP: 77
SALES (corp-wide): 46.84MM Privately Held
Web: www.csdautismservices.com
SIC: 8049 Nutrition specialist
PA: Center For Social Dynamics, Llc
1200 Concord Ave Ste 100
Concord CA
510 268-8120

(P-15275)
CENTER FOR SOCIAL DYNAMICS LLC
Also Called: Csd Autism Services
3170 De La Cruz Blvd Ste 107 (95054-2411)
PHONE..................................408 320-2590
EMP: 77
SALES (corp-wide): 46.84MM Privately Held
Web: www.csdautismservices.com
SIC: 8049 Acupuncturist
PA: Center For Social Dynamics, Llc
1200 Concord Ave Ste 100
Concord CA
510 268-8120

(P-15276)
CENTER FOR SOCIAL DYNAMICS LLC
Also Called: Csd Autism Services
1001 Sneath Ln Ste 200 (94066-2349)
PHONE..................................650 243-9849
EMP: 77
SALES (corp-wide): 46.84MM Privately Held
Web: www.csdautismservices.com
SIC: 8049 Acupuncturist
PA: Center For Social Dynamics, Llc
1200 Concord Ave Ste 100
Concord CA
510 268-8120

(P-15277)
CHE SNIOR PSYCHLOGICAL SVCS PC
4929 Wilshire Blvd Ste 510 (90010-3808)
PHONE..................................888 307-0893
Joe Tritel, Brnch Mgr
EMP: 110
SALES (corp-wide): 22.32MM Privately Held
Web: www.cheservices.com
SIC: 8049 Clinical psychologist
PA: Che Senior Psychological Services, P.C.
3512 Quentin Rd
Brooklyn NY
718 854-8370

(P-15278)
COMMUNITY PSYCHIATRY MGT LLC (PA)
Also Called: Mindpath Health
3835 N Freeway Blvd Ste 100 (95834-1928)
PHONE..................................855 501-1004
J Christopher Brengard, CEO
Julie Mccarter, COO
Mark Brandow, CFO
Ernie Varvoutis, CGO
EMP: 100 EST: 2008
SALES (est): 70.44MM

PRODUCTS & SERVICES SECTION
8049 - Offices Of Health Practitioner (P-15300)

SALES (corp-wide): 70.44MM **Privately Held**
Web: www.mindpath.com
SIC: **8049** 8011 Clinical psychologist; Psychiatrist

(P-15279)
ED SPED SOLUTIONS INC
39159 Paseo Padre Pkwy Ste 205 (94538-1608)
PHONE..............................408 372-8280
Nadia Ramirez, *VP*
EMP: 73 EST: 2018
SALES (est): 2.06MM **Privately Held**
SIC: **8049** Offices of health practitioner

(P-15280)
ENLOE MEDICAL CENTER
Also Called: Enloe Rehabilitation Center
340 W East Ave (95926-7238)
PHONE..............................530 332-6138
Diane Jones, *Dir*
EMP: 267
SQ FT: 61,571
SALES (corp-wide): 814.04MM **Privately Held**
Web: www.enloe.org
SIC: **8049** Physical therapist
PA: Enloe Medical Center
1531 Esplanade
Chico CA
530 332-7300

(P-15281)
EQUINOX-76TH STREET INC
Also Called: Health Fitness America
1980 Main St Fl 4 (92614-7200)
PHONE..............................949 975-8400
Ian Mcfodden, *Mgr*
EMP: 77
SALES (corp-wide): 2.05B **Privately Held**
SIC: **8049** 7991 Physical therapist; Health club
HQ: Equinox-76th Street, Inc.
895 Broadway Fl 3
New York NY

(P-15282)
GOLDEN BEAR PHYSCL THRAPY SPT
210 W Pine St (95240-2020)
PHONE..............................209 622-1191
EMP: 66
SALES (corp-wide): 21.92MM **Privately Held**
Web: www.therapypartnersgroup.com
SIC: **8049** Physical therapist
PA: Golden Bear Physical Therapy Sports Injury Center, Inc.
305 Banner Ct
Modesto CA
209 576-1185

(P-15283)
GOLDEN BEAR PHYSCL THRAPY SPT
4318 Spyres Way (95356-9259)
PHONE..............................209 576-0888
Nicolas King, *Brnch Mgr*
EMP: 66
SALES (corp-wide): 21.92MM **Privately Held**
Web: www.therapypartnersgroup.com
SIC: **8049** Physical therapist
PA: Golden Bear Physical Therapy Sports Injury Center, Inc.
305 Banner Ct
Modesto CA
209 576-1185

(P-15284)
GOLDEN BEAR PHYSICAL THERAPY
1700 Keystone Pacific Pkwy Unit C2 (95363-8874)
PHONE..............................209 895-4206
EMP: 66
SALES (corp-wide): 21.92MM **Privately Held**
Web: www.therapypartnersgroup.com
SIC: **8049** 8011 Physical therapist; Offices and clinics of medical doctors
PA: Golden Bear Physical Therapy Sports Injury Center, Inc.
305 Banner Ct
Modesto CA
209 576-1185

(P-15285)
HOLMAN FAMILY COUNSELING INC (PA)
Also Called: Holman Group, The
8511 Fallbrook Ave Ste 400 (91304)
PHONE..............................818 704-1444
Ron Holman Ph.d., *Pr*
Elizabeth Holman, *
Jane Galvin, *
EMP: 66 EST: 1979
SALES (est): 9.43MM
SALES (corp-wide): 9.43MM **Privately Held**
SIC: **8049** Clinical psychologist

(P-15286)
IN STEPPS INC
Also Called: Support Trtmnt Edcatn For Prnt
10 Skypark Circle, Suite 110 (92614)
PHONE..............................949 474-1493
Y E M Bruinsma, *Ex Dir*
Yvonne E M Bruinsma, *Ex Dir*
Lindsey Lewis, *Reg Dir*
EMP: 99 EST: 2010
SALES (est): 9.83MM **Privately Held**
Web: www.instepps.com
SIC: **8049** Occupational therapist

(P-15287)
INLAND EMPIRE THERAPY PROVIDER (PA)
Also Called: Life Enchancing Therapies
1150 N Mountain Ave # 214 (91786-3668)
PHONE..............................909 985-7905
James W Milton, *Pr*
EMP: 65 EST: 1997
SALES (est): 3.11MM
SALES (corp-wide): 3.11MM **Privately Held**
SIC: **8049** Physical therapist

(P-15288)
INLAND VALLEY PARTNERS LLC
Also Called: Inland Valley Care & Rehab Ctr
250 W Artesia St (91768-1807)
PHONE..............................909 623-7100
EMP: 250 EST: 1998
SALES (est): 31.86MM **Privately Held**
Web: www.inlandvalleyhopepartners.org
SIC: **8049** Nurses and other medical assistants

(P-15289)
INSTITUTE FOR APPLIED BHVIOR A
9221 Corbin Ave (91324-2483)
PHONE..............................818 341-1933
EMP: 83
SALES (corp-wide): 25.84MM **Privately Held**
Web: www.iaba.com
SIC: **8049** Nutrition specialist
PA: Institute For Applied Behavior Analysis, A Psychological Corporation
5601 W Slauson Ave # 290
Culver City CA
310 649-0499

(P-15290)
INSTITUTE FOR APPLIED BHVIOR A (PA)
Also Called: Iaba
5601 W Slauson Ave (90230-6589)
PHONE..............................310 649-0499
Gary W Lavigna Ph.d., *Pr*
▲ EMP: 140 EST: 1982
SALES (est): 25.84MM
SALES (corp-wide): 25.84MM **Privately Held**
Web: www.iaba.com
SIC: **8049** 8741 8093 Clinical psychologist; Management services; Specialty outpatient clinics, nec

(P-15291)
INSTITUTE FOR APPLIED BHVIOR A
Also Called: Iaba
2310 E Ponderosa Dr Ste 1 (93010-4747)
PHONE..............................805 987-5886
Gary Lavigna, *Dir*
EMP: 84
SALES (corp-wide): 25.84MM **Privately Held**
Web: www.iaba.com
SIC: **8049** 8399 Clinical psychologist; Community development groups
PA: Institute For Applied Behavior Analysis, A Psychological Corporation
5601 W Slauson Ave # 290
Culver City CA
310 649-0499

(P-15292)
INTERCARE THERAPY INC
4221 Wilshire Blvd Ste 300a (90010-3537)
PHONE..............................323 866-1880
Naomi Heller, *Pr*
Eri Heller, *
EMP: 130 EST: 1979
SALES (est): 16.26MM **Privately Held**
Web: www.intercaretherapy.com
SIC: **8049** Psychologist, psychotherapist and hypnotist

(P-15293)
INTERFACE REHAB INC
774 S Placentia Ave Ste 200 (92870-6838)
PHONE..............................714 646-8300
Anant B Desai, *CEO*
Falguni Desai, *
EMP: 1000 EST: 1995
SQ FT: 10,000
SALES (est): 98.26MM **Privately Held**
Web: www.interfacerehab.com
SIC: **8049** Physical therapist

(P-15294)
INTERGRO REHAB SERVICE
13211 Foothill Blvd (92705-6203)
PHONE..............................714 901-4200
Sherrilyn Tong, *Pr*
EMP: 80 EST: 1990
SALES (est): 9.95MM **Privately Held**
Web: www.intergrorehab.com
SIC: **8049** Physical therapist

(P-15295)
LOCUMS UNLIMITED LLC
4141 Jutland Dr Ste 305 (92117-3657)
PHONE..............................619 550-3763
EMP: 851 EST: 2015
SALES (est): 1.75MM **Privately Held**
SIC: **8049** Nurses and other medical assistants
PA: Aya Healthcare, Inc.
5930 Cornerstone Ct W # 3
San Diego CA

(P-15296)
MICHAEL G FRTNSCE PHYSCL THRAP
Also Called: Fortanasce & Associates
24630 Washington Ave Ste 200 (92562-6131)
P.O. Box 661150 (91066-1150)
PHONE..............................626 446-7027
Michael Fortanasce, *Pr*
EMP: 120 EST: 1981
SALES (est): 3.72MM **Privately Held**
SIC: **8049** Physiotherapist

(P-15297)
OCCUPATIONAL THERAPY
19401 S Vermont Ave Ste A200 (90502-4418)
PHONE..............................310 323-6887
EMP: 67 EST: 2012
SALES (est): 1.01MM **Privately Held**
Web: www.ottp.org
SIC: **8049** Offices of health practitioner

(P-15298)
OROVILLE HOSPITAL
Also Called: Golden Vly Occpational Therapy
2353 Myers St Ste B (95966-5334)
PHONE..............................530 538-8700
Trish Hopps, *Brnch Mgr*
EMP: 280
SALES (corp-wide): 383.94MM **Privately Held**
Web: www.orovillehospital.com
SIC: **8049** Physical therapist
PA: Oroville Hospital
2767 Olive Hwy
Oroville CA
530 533-8500

(P-15299)
PHYSICAL RHBLTATION NETWRK LLC (PA)
Also Called: Cal Rehab
2035 Corte Del Nogal Ste 200 (92011-1459)
PHONE..............................760 931-8310
EMP: 75 EST: 1992
SALES (est): 84.16MM **Privately Held**
Web: www.prnpt.com
SIC: **8049** 8011 8093 Physiotherapist; Sports medicine specialist, physician; Rehabilitation center, outpatient treatment

(P-15300)
PROFESSIONAL ASSESSMENT &
9330 Baseline Rd Ste 108 (91701-5827)
PHONE..............................909 980-1000
Aurelio Enriquez Junior, *Prin*
EMP: 73 EST: 2014
SALES (est): 1.01MM **Privately Held**
Web: mail.magee.edu
SIC: **8049** Psychotherapist, except M.D.

8049 - Offices Of Health Practitioner (P-15301)

(P-15301)
QUANTUM BHVIORAL SOLUTIONS INC (PA)
445 S Figueroa St Ste 3100 (90071-1602)
PHONE..............................626 531-6999
Gevork Gevojanyan, *Prin*
EMP: 71 EST: 2012
SALES (est): 5.81MM
SALES (corp-wide): 5.81MM Privately Held
Web:
www.quantumbehavioralsolutions.com
SIC: **8049** Clinical psychologist

(P-15302)
QUANTUM BHVIORAL SOLUTIONS INC
2400 E Katella Ave Ste 800 (92806-5945)
PHONE..............................626 531-6999
EMP: 70
SALES (corp-wide): 5.81MM Privately Held
Web:
www.quantumbehavioralsolutions.com
SIC: **8049** Clinical psychologist
PA: Quantum Behavioral Solutions, Inc.
   445 S Figueroa St # 3100
   Los Angeles CA
   626 531-6999

(P-15303)
RANCHO PHYSICAL THERAPY INC
Also Called: Rancho Physical Therapy
277 Rancheros Dr (92069-2976)
PHONE..............................760 752-1011
James Lin, *Brnch Mgr*
EMP: 166
SALES (corp-wide): 19.16MM Privately Held
Web: www.ranchopt.com
SIC: **8049** 8011 Physical therapist; Offices and clinics of medical doctors
PA: Rancho Physical Therapy, Inc.
   24630 Washington Ave # 200
   Murrieta CA
   951 696-9353

(P-15304)
RANCHO PHYSICAL THERAPY INC (PA)
24630 Washington Ave Ste 200 (92562-6177)
PHONE..............................951 696-9353
John Waite, *CEO*
Bill Atkins, *
Greg Smith, *
EMP: 63 EST: 1984
SALES (est): 19.16MM
SALES (corp-wide): 19.16MM Privately Held
Web: www.ranchopt.com
SIC: **8049** 8093 Physical therapist; Respiratory therapy clinic

(P-15305)
ROBERT BALLARD REHAB HOSPITAL (HQ)
Also Called: Ballard Rehabilitation Hosp
1760 W 16th St (92411-1160)
PHONE..............................909 473-1200
Edward Palacios, *CEO*
Mary Hunt, *COO*
▲ EMP: 93 EST: 1993
SALES (est): 21.56MM
SALES (corp-wide): 690.44MM Privately Held
Web: www.ballardrehab.com

SIC: **8049** 8051 8069 Physical therapist; Skilled nursing care facilities; Specialty hospitals, except psychiatric
PA: Vibra Healthcare, Llc
   4600 Lena Dr
   Mechanicsburg PA
   717 591-5700

(P-15306)
SAN FRANCISCO SPORT AND SPINE
2191 Market St Ste C (94114-4314)
PHONE..............................415 861-1856
Lowen Cattolico, *Brnch Mgr*
EMP: 118
SALES (corp-wide): 2.98MM Privately Held
Web: www.agilept.com
SIC: **8049** Physical therapist
PA: San Francisco Sport And Spine Physical Therapy
   100 Bush St Ste 800
   San Francisco CA
   415 593-2532

(P-15307)
SAN JQUIN VLY RHBLTTION HOSP A
Also Called: SAN JOAQUIN VALLEY REHABILITATION HOSPITAL, A DELAWARE LIMITED PARTNERSHIP
40232 Junction Dr (93644-8719)
PHONE..............................559 658-6490
Susan Jackson, *Brnch Mgr*
EMP: 137
SALES (corp-wide): 690.44MM Privately Held
Web: www.sjvrehab.com
SIC: **8049** Physical therapist
HQ: San Joaquin Valley Rehabilitation Hospital, A Delaware Limited Partnership
   7173 N Sharon Ave
   Fresno CA
   559 436-3600

(P-15308)
SUTTER VALLEY MED FOUNDATION
1625 Stockton Blvd Ste 110 (95816-7097)
PHONE..............................916 924-7764
Judi Monday, *Brnch Mgr*
EMP: 68
Web: www.sutterhealth.org
SIC: **8049** 8011 Physical therapist; Offices and clinics of medical doctors
PA: Sutter Valley Medical Foundation
   2700 Gateway Oaks Dr
   Sacramento CA

(P-15309)
TAO OF WLLNESS SNTA MNICA A PR
171 S Los Robles Ave (91101-2417)
PHONE..............................626 397-1000
Emm Wang, *Brnch Mgr*
EMP: 87
SALES (corp-wide): 4.51MM Privately Held
Web: www.taoofwellness.com
SIC: **8049** Acupuncturist
PA: Tao Of Wellness Santa Monica, A Professional Acupuncture Corporation
   1240 6th St
   Santa Monica CA
   310 917-2200

(P-15310)
THERAPYTRAVELERS LLC
355 Redondo Ave (90814-2656)
PHONE..............................888 223-8002
EMP: 71 EST: 2017
SALES (est): 4.85MM Privately Held
Web: www.epicspecialeducationstaffing.com
SIC: **8049** Biofeedback therapist

(P-15311)
VENTURA COUNTY MEDICAL CENTER
300 Hillmont Ave (93003-1651)
PHONE..............................805 652-6729
Myung Ryang, *Prin*
EMP: 217
SALES (corp-wide): 77.09MM Privately Held
Web: www.vchca.org
SIC: **8049** Clinical psychologist
PA: Ventura County Medical Center
   3291 Loma Vista Rd
   Ventura CA
   805 652-6000

(P-15312)
VISTA JV PARTNERS LLC ◊
2035 Corte Del Nogal Ste 200 (92011-1459)
PHONE..............................214 738-2771
Ajay Gupta, *CEO*
Herschel Sharp, *Sr VP*
EMP: 300 EST: 2023
SALES (est): 4.84MM Privately Held
SIC: **8049** Physical therapist

8051 Skilled Nursing Care Facilities

(P-15313)
1000 EXECUTIVE PARKWAY LLC
Also Called: Oroville Hospital Post Acute Center
1000 Executive Pkwy (95966-5100)
PHONE..............................530 533-7335
Tina Nickolas, *Admn*
EMP: 161 EST: 2013
SALES (est): 17.15MM
SALES (corp-wide): 383.94MM Privately Held
Web: www.orovillepostacute.com
SIC: **8051** Mental retardation hospital
PA: Oroville Hospital
   2767 Olive Hwy
   Oroville CA
   530 533-8500

(P-15314)
1135 N LEISURE CT INC
Also Called: Leisure Court Nursing Center
1135 N Leisure Ct (92801-2939)
PHONE..............................714 772-1353
Patricia Smith, *Dir*
Aura Galindo, *
EMP: 68 EST: 1965
SQ FT: 15,000
SALES (est): 14.38MM Privately Held
Web: www.leisurecourtnc.com
SIC: **8051** Skilled nursing care facilities

(P-15315)
A B C D ASSOCIATES
Also Called: Casa Coloma Health Care Center
10410 Coloma Rd (95670-2108)
PHONE..............................916 363-4843
Deborah Portela, *Pt*

Arden Millermon, *Pt*
Betty Millermon, *Pt*
EMP: 106 EST: 1975
SQ FT: 37,000
SALES (est): 9.11MM Privately Held
Web: www.casacoloma.com
SIC: **8051** 8052 Convalescent home with continuous nursing care; Intermediate care facilities

(P-15316)
ACCREDITED NURSING SERVICES
Also Called: Accredited Nursing Care
80 S Lake Ave Ste 630 (91101-4971)
PHONE..............................626 573-1234
Teresa Salvino, *Mgr*
EMP: 230
SALES (corp-wide): 32.94MM Privately Held
SIC: **8051** Skilled nursing care facilities
PA: Accredited Nursing Services
   17141 Ventura Blvd # 201
   Encino CA
   818 986-6017

(P-15317)
ACCREDITED NURSING SERVICES
Also Called: Accredited Nursing Care
591 Camino De La Reina Ste 421 (92108)
PHONE..............................619 265-1234
Pam Saffire, *Mgr*
EMP: 61
SALES (corp-wide): 32.94MM Privately Held
SIC: **8051** 8082 Skilled nursing care facilities; Visiting nurse service
PA: Accredited Nursing Services
   17141 Ventura Blvd # 201
   Encino CA
   818 986-6017

(P-15318)
AHMC GARFIELD MEDICAL CTR LP
Also Called: Garfield Medical Center
525 N Garfield Ave (91754-1202)
PHONE..............................626 573-2222
Patrick Petre, *CEO*
Steve Maekewa, *Pt*
EMP: 150 EST: 1997
SALES (est): 87.61MM
SALES (corp-wide): 476.02MM Privately Held
Web: www.ahmchealth.com
SIC: **8051** 8062 Skilled nursing care facilities; General medical and surgical hospitals
PA: Ahmc Healthcare Inc.
   506 W Valley Blvd Ste 300
   San Gabriel CA
   626 943-7526

(P-15319)
AIR FORCE VILLAGE WEST INC
Also Called: Village West Health Center
17050 Arnold Dr (92518-2806)
PHONE..............................951 697-2000
Mary Carruthers, *CEO*
James L Melin, *Prin*
Charles Dalton, *
Ervin Reed, *
EMP: 350 EST: 1985
SQ FT: 494,000
SALES (est): 5.76MM Privately Held
Web: www.westmontliving.com
SIC: **8051** 8052 Convalescent home with continuous nursing care; Intermediate care facilities

PRODUCTS & SERVICES SECTION

8051 - Skilled Nursing Care Facilities (P-15340)

(P-15320)
ALAMEDA HLTHCARE & WELLNSS CTR
Also Called: Alameda Halthcare Wellness Ctr
430 Willow St (94501-6130)
PHONE.................................510 523-8857
Sol Majer, *
EMP: 99 EST: 2010
SALES (est): 9.1MM **Privately Held**
Web: www.alamedahc.com
SIC: 8051 Convalescent home with continuous nursing care

(P-15321)
ALAMITOS-BELMONT REHAB INC
Also Called: Alamitos Blmont Rhbltion Hosp
3901 E 4th St (90814-1632)
PHONE.................................562 434-8421
Shaun Dahl, Admn
Darian Dahl, *
EMP: 150 EST: 1969
SQ FT: 30,000
SALES (est): 11.7MM **Privately Held**
Web: www.alamitosbelmont.com
SIC: 8051 Skilled nursing care facilities

(P-15322)
ALL SAINTSIDENCE OPCO LLC
Also Called: All Snts Sbcute Trnstonal Care
1652 Mono Ave (94578-2020)
PHONE.................................510 481-3200
Jason Murray, Pr
EMP: 284 EST: 2015
SALES (est): 12.99MM
SALES (corp-wide): 1.53B **Privately Held**
Web: www.allsaintshc.com
SIC: 8051 Convalescent home with continuous nursing care
HQ: Providence Group North, Llc
    262 N University Ave
    Farmington UT
    801 447-9829

(P-15323)
AMADA ENTERPRISES INC
Also Called: View Heights Convalescent Hosp
12619 Avalon Blvd (90061-2727)
PHONE.................................323 757-1881
Shedrick D Jones, CEO
John Jones, *
EMP: 135 EST: 1968
SQ FT: 36,600
SALES (est): 13.61MM **Privately Held**
Web: www.viewheights.com
SIC: 8051 Convalescent home with continuous nursing care

(P-15324)
AMERICAN RETIREMENT CORP
2107 Ocean Ave (90405-2299)
PHONE.................................310 399-3227
EMP: 104
SALES (corp-wide): 2.83B **Publicly Held**
Web: www.brookdale.com
SIC: 8051 Skilled nursing care facilities
HQ: American Retirement Corporation
    111 Westwood Pl Ste 200
    Brentwood TN
    615 221-2250

(P-15325)
AMERICAN-WAY SERVICES CORP
Also Called: Immediate Nursing Services
110 N Bascom Ave (95128-1804)
PHONE.................................408 223-8912
George Dumlao, Mgr
EMP: 148
SQ FT: 680
SIC: 8051 Skilled nursing care facilities
PA: American-Way Services Corp
    393 E Hamilton Ave
    Campbell CA

(P-15326)
ANAHEIM HEALTHCARE CENTER LLC
Also Called: Anaheim Healthcare Center
501 S Beach Blvd (92804-1810)
PHONE.................................714 816-0540
EMP: 68 EST: 1995
SALES (est): 31.75MM **Privately Held**
Web: www.anaheimhealthcare.com
SIC: 8051 Convalescent home with continuous nursing care

(P-15327)
ANBERRY TRANSITIONAL CARE LLC
1000 W Yosemite Ave (95348-5111)
PHONE.................................209 357-3420
Donald Gormly Junior, Prin
Jerry Holloway, *
EMP: 110 EST: 2016
SALES (est): 11.47MM **Privately Held**
Web: www.anberrymerced.com
SIC: 8051 Skilled nursing care facilities

(P-15328)
ANTELOPE VLY RETIREMENT HM INC
Also Called: Antelope Vly Retirement Manor
44523 15th St W (93534-2847)
PHONE.................................661 949-5584
Mark Aronoss, Brnch Mgr
EMP: 179
SALES (corp-wide): 11.41MM **Privately Held**
SIC: 8051 8361 Skilled nursing care facilities; Residential care
PA: Antelope Valley Retirement Home, Inc.
    44523 15th St W
    Lancaster CA
    661 949-5584

(P-15329)
ANTIOCH DUNES HEALTHCARE LLC
Also Called: Delta View Post Acute
1210 A St (94509-2327)
PHONE.................................925 757-8787
Jason Murray, Prin
Mark Hancock, *
EMP: 89 EST: 2020
SALES (est): 6.29MM
SALES (corp-wide): 1.53B **Privately Held**
Web: www.deltaviewpa.com
SIC: 8051 Convalescent home with continuous nursing care
PA: Providence Group, Inc.
    262 N University Ave
    Farmington UT
    801 447-9829

(P-15330)
AQUINAS CORPORATION
Also Called: SAN TOMAS CONVALESCENT HOSPITA
3580 Payne Ave (95117-2925)
PHONE.................................408 248-7100
Ken Dunton, Ch Bd
Julita Javier, *
EMP: 135 EST: 1974
SQ FT: 15,000
SALES (est): 11.04MM **Privately Held**
Web: www.aquinashvac.com
SIC: 8051 8059 Convalescent home with continuous nursing care; Convalescent home

(P-15331)
ARBOR POST ACUTE LLC
Also Called: Arbor Post Acute
1200 Springfield Dr (95928-6340)
PHONE.................................530 342-4885
Jason Murray, Prin
Mark Hancock, *
EMP: 79 EST: 2018
SALES (est): 38.49MM
SALES (corp-wide): 1.53B **Privately Held**
Web: www.arborpa.com
SIC: 8051 Convalescent home with continuous nursing care
HQ: Lakeport Chico Master Tenant, Llc
    262 N University Ave
    Farmington UT
    801 447-9829

(P-15332)
ARCADIA CONVALESCENT HOSP INC
Also Called: Shadow Hills Convalescent Home
10158 Sunland Blvd (91040-1651)
PHONE.................................818 352-4438
Orlando Clarizio, Admn
EMP: 74
SALES (corp-wide): 18.4MM **Privately Held**
Web: www.arcadiahcc.com
SIC: 8051 Convalescent home with continuous nursing care
PA: Arcadia Convalescent Hospital, Inc.
    1601 S Baldwin Ave
    Arcadia CA
    626 445-2170

(P-15333)
ASBURY PK NRSING RHBLTTION CTR
Also Called: Asbury Park Nursing
2257 Fair Oaks Blvd (95825-5501)
PHONE.................................916 649-2000
John Lund, Pr
EMP: 130 EST: 1997
SQ FT: 30,000
SALES (est): 21.01MM **Privately Held**
SIC: 8051 Convalescent home with continuous nursing care

(P-15334)
ASH HOLDINGS LLC
Also Called: Redlands Healthcare Center
1620 W Fern Ave (92373-4918)
PHONE.................................909 793-2609
Novie Sitanggang, Managing Member
EMP: 85 EST: 1999
SALES (est): 9.03MM
SALES (corp-wide): 1.53B **Privately Held**
Web: www.redlandshealthcarecenter.com
SIC: 8051 Skilled nursing care facilities
HQ: California Opco, Llc
    100 E San Marcos Blvd
    San Marcos CA

(P-15335)
ASMB LLC
Also Called: Berkley East Healthcare Center
2021 Arizona Ave (90404-1335)
PHONE.................................949 347-7100
Ryan Case, CEO
Jeffrey Bradshaw, *
EMP: 99 EST: 2019
SALES (est): 1.79MM **Privately Held**
Web: www.berkleyeast.com
SIC: 8051 Convalescent home with continuous nursing care

(P-15336)
ATHERTON BAPTIST HOMES
214 S Atlantic Blvd (91801-3298)
PHONE.................................626 863-1710
Craig Statton, Pr
Dennis E Mcfadden, Pr
Jackie Pascual, *
Angela Paniagua, *
Dale Torry, *
EMP: 200 EST: 1914
SQ FT: 42,000
SALES (est): 24.63MM **Privately Held**
Web: www.abh.org
SIC: 8051 Convalescent home with continuous nursing care

(P-15337)
ATLANTIC MEM HLTHCARE ASSOC IN (HQ)
Also Called: Atlantic Mem Healthcare Ctr
2750 Atlantic Ave (90806-2713)
PHONE.................................562 424-8101
Jake Rothey, Pr
EMP: 75 EST: 2002
SALES (est): 12.36MM
SALES (corp-wide): 3.03B **Publicly Held**
Web: www.atlanticmemorial.com
SIC: 8051 Convalescent home with continuous nursing care
PA: The Ensign Group Inc
    29222 Rncho Vejo Rd Ste 1
    San Juan Capistrano CA
    949 487-9500

(P-15338)
AUBURN OAKS CARE CENTER
3400 Bell Rd (95603-9241)
PHONE.................................650 949-7777
Ellen Kuykendall, Pr
Kevin Hadfield, Admn
EMP: 99 EST: 2011
SALES (est): 11.49MM **Privately Held**
Web: www.auburnoakscarecenter.com
SIC: 8051 Convalescent home with continuous nursing care

(P-15339)
AVALON CARE CEN
Also Called: Hy-Lond Hlth Care Cnter-Merced
3170 M St (95348-2403)
PHONE.................................209 723-1056
EMP: 102 EST: 2003
SALES (est): 33.23MM
SALES (corp-wide): 1.09B **Privately Held**
Web: www.avalonhealthcare.com
SIC: 8051 Skilled nursing care facilities
PA: Avalon Health Care, Inc.
    206 N 2100 W Ste 300
    Salt Lake City UT
    801 596-8844

(P-15340)
AVALON CARE CENTER - MODESTO
Also Called: Hy-Lond Hlth Care Cntr-Modesto
1900 Coffee Rd (95355-2703)
PHONE.................................209 526-1775
Randy Kirton, CEO
EMP: 107 EST: 2003
SALES (est): 83.94MM
SALES (corp-wide): 1.09B **Privately Held**
Web: www.avalonhealthcare.com
SIC: 8051 Convalescent home with continuous nursing care
PA: Avalon Health Care, Inc.
    206 N 2100 W Ste 300
    Salt Lake City UT
    801 596-8844

8051 - Skilled Nursing Care Facilities (P-15341)

(P-15341)
AVALON CARE CTR - CHWCHLLA LLC
Also Called: Chowchilla Conv. Center
1010 Ventura Ave (93610-2368)
PHONE..................559 665-4826
EMP: 128 EST: 2003
SALES (est): 24.25MM
SALES (corp-wide): 1.09B Privately Held
SIC: 8051 Skilled nursing care facilities
PA: Avalon Health Care, Inc.
    206 N 2100 W Ste 300
    Salt Lake City UT
    801 596-8844

(P-15342)
AVALON CARE CTR - MRCED FRNCSC
Also Called: Franciscan Conv. Hospital
3169 M St (95348-2404)
PHONE..................209 722-6231
Larry Imperial, Admn
EMP: 74 EST: 2003
SALES (est): 32.69MM
SALES (corp-wide): 1.09B Privately Held
Web: www.avalonhealthcare.com
SIC: 8051 Skilled nursing care facilities
PA: Avalon Health Care, Inc.
    206 N 2100 W Ste 300
    Salt Lake City UT
    801 596-8844

(P-15343)
AVALON CARE CTR - NEWMAN LLC
Also Called: San Luis Care Center
709 N St (95360-1162)
PHONE..................209 862-2862
EMP: 64 EST: 2003
SALES (est): 19.01MM
SALES (corp-wide): 1.09B Privately Held
Web: www.avalonhealthcare.com
SIC: 8051 Convalescent home with continuous nursing care
PA: Avalon Health Care, Inc.
    206 N 2100 W Ste 300
    Salt Lake City UT
    801 596-8844

(P-15344)
AVALON CARE CTR - SAN ANDREAS
Also Called: AVALON HEALTH CARE GROUP
900 Mountain Ranch Rd (95249-9713)
PHONE..................209 754-3823
Larry Washington, *
EMP: 80 EST: 2003
SALES (est): 11.59MM
SALES (corp-wide): 1.09B Privately Held
Web: www.calaverasedc.org
SIC: 8051 Convalescent home with continuous nursing care
PA: Avalon Health Care, Inc.
    206 N 2100 W Ste 300
    Salt Lake City UT
    801 596-8844

(P-15345)
AVALON CARE CTR - SONORA LLC
Also Called: AVALON HEALTH CARE GROUP
19929 Greenley Rd (95370-5996)
PHONE..................209 533-2500
Faye Lincoln, VP
EMP: 114 EST: 2003
SALES (est): 20.76MM
SALES (corp-wide): 1.09B Privately Held
Web: www.avalonhealthcare.com
SIC: 8051 Convalescent home with continuous nursing care
PA: Avalon Health Care, Inc.
    206 N 2100 W Ste 300
    Salt Lake City UT
    801 596-8844

(P-15346)
B-SPRING VALLEY LLC
Also Called: Brighton Place Spring Valley
9009 Campo Rd (91977-1112)
PHONE..................619 797-3991
EMP: 91 EST: 2006
SALES (est): 9.5MM Privately Held
Web: www.brightonplacesv.com
SIC: 8051 Convalescent home with continuous nursing care

(P-15347)
BAKERSFELD HLTHCARE WLLNESS CN
Also Called: Rehabilitation Ctr Bakersfield
2211 Mount Vernon Ave (93306-3309)
PHONE..................661 872-2121
EMP: 99 EST: 2009
SALES (est): 8.75MM Privately Held
Web: www.bakersfieldrehabilitation.com
SIC: 8051 Convalescent home with continuous nursing care

(P-15348)
BAKERSFIELDIDENCE OPCO LLC
Also Called: Kern River Transitional Care
5151 Knudsen Dr (93308-7199)
PHONE..................661 399-2472
Jason Murray, Prin
Mark Hancock, *
EMP: 180 EST: 2016
SALES (est): 9.73MM
SALES (corp-wide): 1.53B Privately Held
Web: www.kernrivertc.com
SIC: 8051 Convalescent home with continuous nursing care
HQ: Providence Group North, Llc
    262 N University Ave
    Farmington UT
    801 447-9829

(P-15349)
BALBOA ENTERPRISES INC
Also Called: MOUNTAIN VIEW HEALTHCARE CENTE
2530 Solace Pl (94040-4309)
PHONE..................650 961-6161
Karl Vitt, Pr
EMP: 77 EST: 1964
SQ FT: 30,000
SALES (est): 12.36MM Privately Held
Web: www.mvhealthcare.com
SIC: 8051 Convalescent home with continuous nursing care

(P-15350)
BAY VIEW RHBILITATION HOSP LLC
516 Willow St (94501-6132)
PHONE..................510 521-5600
Thomas Chambers, Managing Member
Adrian Manesh, *
EMP: 99 EST: 2012
SALES (est): 31.42MM Privately Held
Web: www.bayviewnursing.com
SIC: 8051 8062 8361 Convalescent home with continuous nursing care; General medical and surgical hospitals; Rehabilitation center, residential: health care incidental

(P-15351)
BAYSHORE HEALTHCARE INC
Also Called: Bella Vsta Trnstional Care Ctr
3033 Augusta St (93401-5820)
PHONE..................805 544-5100
Benjamin Flinders, CEO
Johannah Tamba, *
Paul Mclean, Sec
EMP: 160 EST: 1975
SQ FT: 43,000
SALES (est): 8.59MM Privately Held
Web: www.compass-health.com
SIC: 8051 Convalescent home with continuous nursing care

(P-15352)
BAYSIDE HEALTHCARE INC
Also Called: South Bay Post Acute Care
553 F St (91910-3515)
PHONE..................619 426-8611
Glenn Matthews, Prin
Perris Bennett, *
EMP: 176 EST: 2014
SALES (est): 4.8MM Privately Held
SIC: 8051 Skilled nursing care facilities

(P-15353)
BEAVER DAM HEALTH CARE CENTER
Also Called: Beverly Healthcare
340 Victoria St (92627-1914)
P.O. Box 1933 (92079-1933)
PHONE..................949 642-0387
David Sedgwick, Ex Dir
EMP: 84
SALES (corp-wide): 831.2MM Privately Held
Web: www.victoriacares.com
SIC: 8051 Convalescent home with continuous nursing care
PA: Golden Living Llc
    5220 Tennyson Pkwy # 400
    Plano TX
    972 372-6300

(P-15354)
BEAVER DAM HEALTH CARE CENTER
Also Called: Golden Living Center - Chateau
1221 Rosemarie Ln (95207-6703)
PHONE..................707 546-0471
Susan Morgan, Mgr
EMP: 69
SALES (corp-wide): 831.2MM Privately Held
Web: www.beaverdamhcc.com
SIC: 8051 Convalescent home with continuous nursing care
PA: Golden Living Llc
    5220 Tennyson Pkwy # 400
    Plano TX
    972 372-6300

(P-15355)
BEAVER DAM HEALTH CARE CENTER
Also Called: Beverly Healthcare
950 S Fairmont Ave (95240-5131)
PHONE..................209 368-0693
Beverly Mannon, Prin
EMP: 116
SALES (corp-wide): 831.2MM Privately Held
Web: www.fairmontrehab.com
SIC: 8051 Convalescent home with continuous nursing care
PA: Golden Living Llc
    5220 Tennyson Pkwy # 400
    Plano TX
    972 372-6300

(P-15356)
BELL VILLA CARE ASSOCIATES LLC
Also Called: Rose Villa Healthcare Center
9028 Rose St (90706-6418)
PHONE..................562 925-4252
David Howell, Ex Dir
EMP: 95 EST: 2003
SALES (est): 1.72MM Privately Held
Web: www.rosevillahealthcare.com
SIC: 8051 Convalescent home with continuous nursing care

(P-15357)
BETHANY HM SOC SAN JQUIN CNTY
Also Called: Bethany Adult Day Care
368 S Wilma Ave (95366-2356)
PHONE..................209 599-7670
EMP: 114
SALES (corp-wide): 13.68MM Privately Held
Web: www.bethanyripon.org
SIC: 8051 8361 Convalescent home with continuous nursing care; Residential care
PA: Bethany Home Society Of San Joaquin County, Inc.
    930 W Main St
    Ripon CA
    209 599-4221

(P-15358)
BEVERLY WEST HEALTH CARE INC
1020 S Fairfax Ave (90019-4401)
PHONE..................323 938-2451
Louise Koss, Pr
Lydia Cruz, *
EMP: 85 EST: 1981
SQ FT: 23,848
SALES (est): 8.77MM Privately Held
SIC: 8051 Convalescent home with continuous nursing care

(P-15359)
BRIDGESTONE LIVING LLC
27101 Puerta Real Ste 450 (92691-8566)
PHONE..................949 487-9500
John Gurrieri, Pr
EMP: 69 EST: 2014
SALES (est): 7.44MM
SALES (corp-wide): 3.03B Publicly Held
SIC: 8051 Skilled nursing care facilities
PA: The Ensign Group Inc
    29222 Rncho Vejo Rd Ste 1
    San Juan Capistrano CA
    949 487-9500

(P-15360)
BURLINGTON CONVALESCENT HOSP (PA)
Also Called: View Park Convalescent Center
845 S Burlington Ave (90057-4296)
PHONE..................213 381-5585
Jacob Friedman, Pr
Ervin Friedman, *
Kathleen Becker, *
EMP: 100 EST: 1967
SQ FT: 5,000
SALES (est): 9.61MM
SALES (corp-wide): 9.61MM Privately Held
Web: www.alternativesforseniors.com
SIC: 8051 8059 8052 Convalescent home with continuous nursing care; Convalescent home; Intermediate care facilities

PRODUCTS & SERVICES SECTION
8051 - Skilled Nursing Care Facilities (P-15383)

(P-15361)
BURLINGTON CONVALESCENT HOSP
Also Called: View Park Convalescent Center
3737 Don Felipe Dr (90008-4210)
PHONE.................................323 295-7737
Joe Voltes, Mgr
EMP: 179
SQ FT: 40,000
SALES (corp-wide): 9.61MM Privately Held
Web: www.alternativesforseniors.com
SIC: 8051 Convalescent home with continuous nursing care
PA: Burlington Convalescent Hospital
845 S Burlington Ave
Los Angeles CA
213 381-5585

(P-15362)
CALIFRNIA DEPT DVLPMENTAL SVCS
Also Called: Porterville Developmental Ctr
26501 Avenue 140 (93257-9109)
P.O. Box 2000 (93258-2000)
PHONE.................................559 782-2222
Theresa Villeci, Prin
EMP: 1800
SALES (corp-wide): 534.4MM Privately Held
Web: dds.ca.gov
SIC: 8051 9431 Mental retardation hospital; Administration of public health programs
HQ: California Department Of Developmental Services
1215 O St
Sacramento CA

(P-15363)
CALIFRNIA NRSING RHBLTTION CTR
Also Called: CALIFORNIA NURSING & REHABILIT
2299 N Indian Ave (92262)
PHONE.................................760 325-2937
Kennon Shea, Admn
Victoria Shea, *
Linda Jackson, *
Shlomo Rechnitz, *
EMP: 75 EST: 1965
SQ FT: 22,000
SALES (est): 8.59MM Privately Held
Web: www.californianursingrc.com
SIC: 8051 Convalescent home with continuous nursing care

(P-15364)
CALIMESA OPERATIONS LLC
Also Called: CALIMESA POST ACUTE
13542 2nd St (92399-5396)
PHONE.................................909 795-2421
Covey Christensen, *
EMP: 105 EST: 2015
SALES (est): 9.66MM Privately Held
SIC: 8051 Skilled nursing care facilities

(P-15365)
CAMBRIDGE SIERRA HOLDINGS LLC
Also Called: RECHE CANYON REGIONAL REHAB CE
1350 Reche Canyon Rd (92324-9528)
PHONE.................................909 370-4411
Rb Bridges, CEO
EMP: 350 EST: 1991
SALES (est): 26.56MM Privately Held
SIC: 8051 Convalescent home with continuous nursing care

(P-15366)
CASTLE MANOR INC
Also Called: CASTLE MANOR CONVALESCENT CENT
541 S V Ave (91950-2828)
PHONE.................................619 791-7900
Ruth Cheneweth, Pr
J Edwin Cheneweth, *
EMP: 73 EST: 1986
SALES (est): 12.13MM Privately Held
Web: www.lifegen.net
SIC: 8051 Convalescent home with continuous nursing care

(P-15367)
CATHEDRAL PIONEER CHURCH HOMES (PA)
Also Called: Pioneer House
415 P St Ofc (95814-5300)
PHONE.................................916 442-4906
Calvin Hara, Admn
EMP: 96 EST: 1963
SQ FT: 52,000
SALES (est): 4.52MM
SALES (corp-wide): 4.52MM Privately Held
Web: www.pioneerhouseretirement.org
SIC: 8051 8699 Skilled nursing care facilities ; Charitable organization

(P-15368)
CEDAR HOLDINGS LLC
Also Called: Highland Palms Healthcare Ctr
7534 Palm Ave (92346-3736)
PHONE.................................909 862-0611
Ryan Mccook, Managing Member
EMP: 99 EST: 2001
SALES (est): 9.45MM
SALES (corp-wide): 1.53B Privately Held
Web: www.highlandpalmshc.com
SIC: 8051 Convalescent home with continuous nursing care
HQ: California Opco, Llc
100 E San Marcos Blvd
San Marcos CA

(P-15369)
CEDAR OPERATIONS LLC
Also Called: Cedar Mountain Post Acute
11970 4th St (92399-2720)
PHONE.................................909 790-2273
EMP: 140 EST: 2001
SALES (est): 13.56MM
SALES (corp-wide): 28.4MM Privately Held
SIC: 8051 Skilled nursing care facilities
PA: Madison Creek Partners, Llc
26522 La Alameda Ste 300
Mission Viejo CA
949 449-2500

(P-15370)
CENTINELA SKLLED NRSING WLLNES
950 S Flower St (90301-4111)
PHONE.................................310 674-3216
Nichole Tons, VP
EMP: 99 EST: 2008
SQ FT: 6,000
SALES (est): 8.81MM Privately Held
Web: www.centinelanursingwest.com
SIC: 8051 Skilled nursing care facilities

(P-15371)
CF MERCED LA SIERRA LLC
Also Called: La Sierra Care Center
2424 M St (95340-2808)
PHONE.................................209 723-4224
Carson Day, Pr
Bryan Tanner, *
EMP: 82 EST: 1966
SQ FT: 15,000
SALES (est): 5.7MM
SALES (corp-wide): 88.5MM Privately Held
Web: www.lasierracarecenter.com
SIC: 8051 Skilled nursing care facilities
PA: Country Villa Service Corp.
2400 E Katella Ave # 800
Anaheim CA
310 574-3733

(P-15372)
CF SUSANVILLE LLC
Also Called: Country Vlla Rvrview Rhab Hlth
2005 River St (96130-4524)
PHONE.................................530 257-5341
Admiral Antoine Goodie, Prin
EMP: 60 EST: 2004
SALES (est): 4.85MM Privately Held
SIC: 8051 Skilled nursing care facilities

(P-15373)
CHA HOLLYWOOD MEDICAL CTR LP
4636 Fountain Ave (90029-1830)
PHONE.................................213 413-3000
Annette Brunin, Brnch Mgr
EMP: 1487
Web: www.hollywoodpresbyterian.com
SIC: 8051 Skilled nursing care facilities
HQ: Cha Hollywood Medical Center Lp
1300 N Vermont Ave
Los Angeles CA
213 413-3000

(P-15374)
CHANCELLOR HLTH CARE OF CAL IV
Also Called: Chancellor Place of Lodi
2220 W Kettleman Ln Ofc (95242-4348)
PHONE.................................209 367-8870
Keith Payne, Dir
Edmond Peters, *
Roger Vitrano, *
Arline Delacruz, *
EMP: 276 EST: 1998
SALES (est): 3.49MM Privately Held
Web: www.chancellorhealthcare.com
SIC: 8051 Convalescent home with continuous nursing care
PA: Chancellor Health Care, Inc.
115 Johnson St
Windsor CA

(P-15375)
CHAPARRAL FOUNDATION
Also Called: Chaparral House
1309 Allston Way (94702-1920)
PHONE.................................510 848-8774
K J Paige, Admn
EMP: 90 EST: 1978
SQ FT: 21,000
SALES (est): 8.35MM Privately Held
Web: www.chaparralhouse.org
SIC: 8051 Convalescent home with continuous nursing care

(P-15376)
COASTAL HEALTH CARE INC
Also Called: BRENTWOOD HEALTH CARE CENTER
1321 Franklin St (90404-2603)
PHONE.................................310 828-5596
John Sorensen, Pr
Tim Paulsen, Ex VP
EMP: 75 EST: 1987
SALES (est): 10.48MM Privately Held
Web: www.brentwoodnursing.com
SIC: 8051 Convalescent home with continuous nursing care

(P-15377)
COASTAL VIEW HALTHCARE CTR LLC
Also Called: Coastal View Healthcare Center
4904 Telegraph Rd (93003-4109)
PHONE.................................805 642-4101
EMP: 96 EST: 2012
SALES (est): 10.96MM Privately Held
Web: www.coastalviewhcc.com
SIC: 8051 Convalescent home with continuous nursing care

(P-15378)
COLDWATER CARE CENTER LLC
Also Called: Sherman Village Hlth Care Ctr
12750 Riverside Dr (91607-3319)
PHONE.................................818 766-6105
EMP: 170 EST: 2010
SALES (est): 14.62MM Privately Held
Web: www.shermanvillagehc.com
SIC: 8051 Convalescent home with continuous nursing care

(P-15379)
COMMUNITY CARE CENTER
8665 La Mesa Blvd (91942-9503)
PHONE.................................619 465-0702
EMP: 85 EST: 2019
SALES (est): 19.44MM Privately Held
Web: www.communitycarectr.com
SIC: 8051 Convalescent home with continuous nursing care

(P-15380)
COMMUNITY CARE ON PALM RVRSIDE
4768 Palm Ave (92501-4012)
PHONE.................................951 686-9001
Ezequiel Bercovich, Prin
EMP: 85 EST: 2020
SALES (est): 1.1MM Privately Held
Web: www.cconpalm.com
SIC: 8051 Skilled nursing care facilities

(P-15381)
COMPASS HEALTH INC
Also Called: Mission View Health Center
1425 Woodside Dr (93401-5936)
PHONE.................................805 543-0210
Linda Lindsey, Mgr
EMP: 155
Web: www.compass-health.com
SIC: 8051 Skilled nursing care facilities
PA: Compass Health, Inc.
200 S 13th St Ste 208
Grover Beach CA

(P-15382)
COMPASS HEALTH INC
Also Called: Bayside Care Center
1405 Teresa Dr (93442-2457)
PHONE.................................805 772-7372
Harold Carder, Mgr
EMP: 155
Web: www.compass-health.com
SIC: 8051 Skilled nursing care facilities
PA: Compass Health, Inc.
200 S 13th St Ste 208
Grover Beach CA

(P-15383)
COMPASS HEALTH INC
Also Called: Arroyo Grande Care Center
1212 Farroll Ave (93420-3718)

8051 - Skilled Nursing Care Facilities (P-15384)

PHONE..................805 489-8137
Harold Carder, *Admn*
EMP: 155
Web: www.compass-health.com
SIC: 8051 Skilled nursing care facilities
PA: Compass Health, Inc.
200 S 13th St Ste 208
Grover Beach CA

(P-15384)
COMPASS HEALTH INC
Also Called: Danish Care Center
10805 El Camino Real (93422-8868)
PHONE..................805 466-9254
Mark Woolpert, *Pr*
EMP: 155
Web: www.compass-health.com
SIC: 8051 Skilled nursing care facilities
PA: Compass Health, Inc.
200 S 13th St Ste 208
Grover Beach CA

(P-15385)
COMPASS HEALTH INC
Also Called: Compas Health
290 Heather Ct (93465-9738)
PHONE..................805 434-3035
Mark Woolpert, *Pr*
EMP: 155
Web: www.compass-health.com
SIC: 8051 Convalescent home with continuous nursing care
PA: Compass Health, Inc.
200 S 13th St Ste 208
Grover Beach CA

(P-15386)
COMPASS HEALTH INC
Also Called: Alto Lucero Transitional Care
3880 Via Lucero (93110-1605)
PHONE..................805 687-6651
Kirk Klotthor, *Admn*
EMP: 155
Web: www.compass-health.com
SIC: 8051 Convalescent home with continuous nursing care
PA: Compass Health, Inc.
200 S 13th St Ste 208
Grover Beach CA

(P-15387)
CONGAREE HEALTH HOLDINGS LLC
29222 Rancho Viejo Rd Ste 127 (92675)
PHONE..................949 487-9500
EMP: 78 **EST:** 2015
SALES (est): 4.92MM
SALES (corp-wide): 3.03B **Publicly Held**
SIC: 8051 Skilled nursing care facilities
PA: The Ensign Group Inc
29222 Rncho Vejo Rd Ste 1
San Juan Capistrano CA
949 487-9500

(P-15388)
CORECARE V A CAL LTD PARTNR
Also Called: Park Vista At Morningside
2525 Brea Blvd (92835-2787)
PHONE..................714 256-1000
Gary R Stork, *Prin*
Melody Olmstead, *Contrlr*
EMP: 60 **EST:** 1992
SALES (est): 14.47MM **Privately Held**
Web: www.parkvista.net
SIC: 8051 Convalescent home with continuous nursing care

(P-15389)
COSTA MESA HEALTHCARE INC
Also Called: Milestone Health Care Center
2570 Newport Blvd (92627-1331)
PHONE..................949 631-4282
Tony Ricci, *Pr*
EMP: 71 **EST:** 1998
SQ FT: 22,000
SALES (est): 13.53MM **Privately Held**
SIC: 8051 Skilled nursing care facilities

(P-15390)
COUNTRY HILLS HEALTH CARE INC
Also Called: Country Hills Post Acute
1580 Broadway (92021-5124)
PHONE..................619 441-8745
Glen Larson, *Pr*
EMP: 247 **EST:** 1991
SALES (est): 34.85MM **Privately Held**
Web: www.countryhills.com
SIC: 8051 Convalescent home with continuous nursing care

(P-15391)
COUNTRY OAKS CARE CENTER INC
830 E Chapel St (93454-4699)
PHONE..................805 922-6657
John Henning, *Adm/Dir*
Sharon Henning, *
EMP: 70 **EST:** 1968
SQ FT: 14,000
SALES (est): 4.89MM **Privately Held**
Web: www.countryoakscarecenter.com
SIC: 8051 Convalescent home with continuous nursing care

(P-15392)
COUNTRY VILLA NURSING CTR INC
Also Called: COUNTRY VILLA NURSING & REHABI
340 S Alvarado St (90057-2915)
PHONE..................213 484-9730
Stephen Reissman, *CEO*
Steven Reissman, *CEO*
Diane Reissman, *Sr VP*
Eddie Rowles, *VP*
EMP: 125 **EST:** 1990
SQ FT: 18,000
SALES (est): 22.3MM **Privately Held**
Web: www.losangelesrehabwc.com
SIC: 8051 Convalescent home with continuous nursing care

(P-15393)
COUNTRY VILLA SERVICE CORP
1208 S Central Ave (91204-2504)
PHONE..................818 246-5516
Adam Mitchel, *Admn*
EMP: 102
SALES (corp-wide): 88.5MM **Privately Held**
Web: www.evictionlawyer.com
SIC: 8051 Skilled nursing care facilities
PA: Country Villa Service Corp.
2400 E Katella Ave # 800
Anaheim CA
310 574-3733

(P-15394)
COUNTRY VILLA SERVICE CORP
400 W Huntington Dr (91007-3470)
PHONE..................626 445-2421
Shelly Andresen, *Prin*
EMP: 102
SALES (corp-wide): 88.5MM **Privately Held**
Web: www.huntingtondrivehcc.com
SIC: 8051 Skilled nursing care facilities
PA: Country Villa Service Corp.
2400 E Katella Ave # 800
Anaheim CA
310 574-3733

(P-15395)
COUNTRY VILLA SERVICE CORP
3611 E Imperial Hwy (90262-2608)
PHONE..................310 537-2500
EMP: 102
SALES (corp-wide): 88.5MM **Privately Held**
Web: www.evictionlawyer.com
SIC: 8051 Convalescent home with continuous nursing care
PA: Country Villa Service Corp.
2400 E Katella Ave # 800
Anaheim CA
310 574-3733

(P-15396)
COUNTY OF SAN DIEGO
Also Called: Health & Human Services- Aging
9065 Edgemoor Dr (92071-6957)
PHONE..................619 956-2800
Gwen Marie Hilleary, *Mgr*
EMP: 84
Web: www.sandiegocounty.gov
SIC: 8051 9431 Skilled nursing care facilities ; Administration of public health programs, County government
PA: County Of San Diego
1600 Pacific Hwy Ste 209
San Diego CA
619 531-5880

(P-15397)
COVENANT CARE LLC
Also Called: Pacific Coast Manor
1935 Wharf Rd (95010-2606)
PHONE..................831 476-0770
Christine Sims, *Mgr*
EMP: 65 **EST:** 2006
SALES (est): 34.15MM **Privately Held**
SIC: 8051 Convalescent home with continuous nursing care
HQ: Covenant Care California, Llc
120 Vantis Dr Ste 200
Aliso Viejo CA

(P-15398)
COVENANT CARE CALIFORNIA LLC
Also Called: Capital Transitional Care
6821 24th St (95822-4037)
PHONE..................916 391-6011
Richard Thorp, *Brnch Mgr*
EMP: 62
Web: www.covenantcare.com
SIC: 8051 Skilled nursing care facilities
HQ: Covenant Care California, Llc
120 Vantis Dr Ste 200
Aliso Viejo CA

(P-15399)
COVENANT CARE CALIFORNIA LLC
Also Called: Wagner Hts Nrsing Rhbltion Ct
9289 Branstetter Pl (95209-1700)
PHONE..................209 477-5252
Janey Hargreaves, *Brnch Mgr*
EMP: 130
Web: www.covenantcare.com
SIC: 8051 Convalescent home with continuous nursing care
HQ: Covenant Care California, Llc
120 Vantis Dr Ste 200
Aliso Viejo CA

(P-15400)
COVENANT CARE CALIFORNIA LLC
Also Called: Palo Alto Nursing Center
911 Bryant St (94301-2711)
PHONE..................415 327-0511
Roland Gandy, *Brnch Mgr*
EMP: 75
Web: www.covenantcare.com
SIC: 8051 8059 Convalescent home with continuous nursing care; Personal care home, with health care
HQ: Covenant Care California, Llc
120 Vantis Dr Ste 200
Aliso Viejo CA

(P-15401)
COVENANT CARE CALIFORNIA LLC
Also Called: Mission Skilled Nursing Home
410 N Winchester Blvd (95050-6325)
PHONE..................408 248-3736
Kathleen Glass, *Mgr*
EMP: 75
Web: www.covenantcare.com
SIC: 8051 Convalescent home with continuous nursing care
HQ: Covenant Care California, Llc
120 Vantis Dr Ste 200
Aliso Viejo CA

(P-15402)
COVENANT CARE CALIFORNIA LLC
Also Called: Huntington Park Nursing Center
6425 Miles Ave (90255-4315)
PHONE..................323 589-5941
Toni Mazzeo, *Brnch Mgr*
EMP: 62
Web: www.covenantcare.com
SIC: 8051 Convalescent home with continuous nursing care
HQ: Covenant Care California, Llc
120 Vantis Dr Ste 200
Aliso Viejo CA

(P-15403)
COVENANT CARE CALIFORNIA LLC
Also Called: Pacific Grdns Nrsing Rhbltion
577 S Peach Ave (93727-3952)
PHONE..................559 251-8463
Bart Vanderwal, *Brnch Mgr*
EMP: 66
SQ FT: 40,000
Web: www.covenantcare.com
SIC: 8051 Convalescent home with continuous nursing care
HQ: Covenant Care California, Llc
120 Vantis Dr Ste 200
Aliso Viejo CA

(P-15404)
COVENANT CARE CALIFORNIA LLC
Also Called: Buena Vista Care Center
160 S Patterson Ave (93111-2006)
PHONE..................805 964-4871
David Hibarger, *Brnch Mgr*
EMP: 62
Web: www.covenantcare.com
SIC: 8051 Convalescent home with continuous nursing care
HQ: Covenant Care California, Llc
120 Vantis Dr Ste 200
Aliso Viejo CA

PRODUCTS & SERVICES SECTION
8051 - Skilled Nursing Care Facilities (P-15426)

(P-15405)
COVENANT CARE CALIFORNIA LLC
Also Called: Turlock Nrsing Rhabilation Ctr
1111 E Tuolumne Rd (95382-1541)
PHONE..................................209 632-3821
Loris Gielczyk, Prin
EMP: 92
Web: www.covenantcare.com
SIC: 8051 Convalescent home with continuous nursing care
HQ: Covenant Care California, Llc
120 Vantis Dr Ste 200
Aliso Viejo CA

(P-15406)
COVENANT CARE CALIFORNIA LLC
Also Called: Gilroy Health Care
8170 Murray Ave (95020-4605)
PHONE..................................408 842-9311
Doreen Mcgary, Dir
EMP: 62
Web: www.livinglegendshealth.com
SIC: 8051 Convalescent home with continuous nursing care
HQ: Covenant Care California, Llc
120 Vantis Dr Ste 200
Aliso Viejo CA

(P-15407)
COVENANT CARE CALIFORNIA LLC
Also Called: Los Altos Sb-Cute Rhbltion Ct
809 Fremont Ave (94024-5617)
PHONE..................................650 941-5255
EMP: 113
Web: www.covenantcare.com
SIC: 8051 8093 Convalescent home with continuous nursing care; Rehabilitation center, outpatient treatment
HQ: Covenant Care California, Llc
120 Vantis Dr Ste 200
Aliso Viejo CA

(P-15408)
COVENANT CARE LA JOLLA LLC
Also Called: La Jolla Nrsing Rhbltation Ctr
2552 Torrey Pines Rd Ste 1 (92037-3432)
PHONE..................................858 453-5810
Lisa Parker, Admn
Carol Tiaadwai, Admn
EMP: 200 EST: 2005
SALES (est): 30.77MM Privately Held
SIC: 8051 Convalescent home with continuous nursing care
HQ: Covenant Care California, Llc
120 Vantis Dr Ste 200
Aliso Viejo CA

(P-15409)
COVENANT CARE LLC (PA)
120 Vantis Dr Ste 200 (92656-2677)
PHONE..................................949 349-1200
EMP: 413 EST: 1994
SALES (est): 561.46MM Privately Held
SIC: 8051 Skilled nursing care facilities

(P-15410)
COVENANT RTIREMENT COMMUNITIES
Also Called: COVENANT RETIREMENT COMMUNITIES
2550 Treasure Dr (93105-4148)
PHONE..................................805 687-0701
EMP: 80
Web: www.covliving.org
SIC: 8051 Skilled nursing care facilities
HQ: Covenant Living West
5700 Old Orchard Rd # 10
Skokie IL

(P-15411)
COVENTRY COURT HEALTH CENTER
2040 S Euclid St (92802-3111)
PHONE..................................714 636-2800
Saun Dohl, CEO
EMP: 200 EST: 2000
SALES (est): 9.31MM Privately Held
Web: www.coventrycourt.org
SIC: 8051 Skilled nursing care facilities

(P-15412)
COVINA REHABILITATION CENTER
Also Called: REGENCY HEALTH SERVICES
261 W Badillo St (91723-1907)
PHONE..................................626 967-3874
Teresa Dearmond, Dir
Agnes Maron, *
EMP: 110 EST: 1971
SQ FT: 27,800
SALES (est): 11.96MM Privately Held
SIC: 8051 Skilled nursing care facilities

(P-15413)
CRESTWOOD BEHAVIORAL HLTH INC
Also Called: 1112 Modesto Snf/STP
1400 Celeste Dr (95355-5041)
PHONE..................................209 526-8050
Lauri Blaufus, Brnch Mgr
EMP: 343
SQ FT: 56,538
SALES (corp-wide): 278.96MM Privately Held
Web: www.crestwoodbehavioralhealth.com
SIC: 8051 Skilled nursing care facilities
PA: Crestwood Behavioral Health, Inc.
520 Capitol Mall Ste 800
Sacramento CA
209 955-2326

(P-15414)
CRESTWOOD BEHAVIORAL HLTH INC
Also Called: 1122 Redding IMD
3062 Churn Creek Rd (96002-2124)
PHONE..................................530 221-0976
Jacob Stevens, Admn
EMP: 104
SQ FT: 15,000
SALES (corp-wide): 278.96MM Privately Held
Web: www.crestwoodbehavioralhealth.com
SIC: 8051 Skilled nursing care facilities
PA: Crestwood Behavioral Health, Inc.
520 Capitol Mall Ste 800
Sacramento CA
209 955-2326

(P-15415)
CRESTWOOD BEHAVIORAL HLTH INC
Also Called: 1134 Alameda Snf/STP
4303 Stevenson Blvd (94538-2645)
PHONE..................................510 651-1244
Leeann Labrie, Admn
EMP: 257
SQ FT: 33,790
SALES (corp-wide): 278.96MM Privately Held
Web: www.crestwoodbehavioralhealth.com
SIC: 8051 Skilled nursing care facilities
PA: Crestwood Behavioral Health, Inc.
520 Capitol Mall Ste 800
Sacramento CA
209 955-2326

(P-15416)
CRESTWOOD BEHAVIORAL HLTH INC
Also Called: 1120 Fremont Snf
2171 Mowry Ave (94538-1717)
PHONE..................................510 793-8383
Kulbinder Hans, Admn
EMP: 142
SQ FT: 10,000
SALES (corp-wide): 278.96MM Privately Held
Web: www.crestwoodbehavioralhealth.com
SIC: 8051 Skilled nursing care facilities
PA: Crestwood Behavioral Health, Inc.
520 Capitol Mall Ste 800
Sacramento CA
209 955-2326

(P-15417)
CRESTWOOD BEHAVIORAL HLTH INC
Also Called: 1101 Stockton Accounting Off
7590 Shoreline Dr (95219-5455)
PHONE..................................209 478-5291
Margarita Rosero, Admn
EMP: 89
SALES (corp-wide): 278.96MM Privately Held
Web: www.crestwoodbehavioralhealth.com
SIC: 8051 Skilled nursing care facilities
PA: Crestwood Behavioral Health, Inc.
520 Capitol Mall Ste 800
Sacramento CA
209 955-2326

(P-15418)
CROCUS HOLDINGS LLC
Also Called: Roseville Care Center
1161 Cirby Way (95661-4421)
PHONE..................................916 782-1238
EMP: 99 EST: 2011
SALES (est): 23.12MM
SALES (corp-wide): 1.53B Privately Held
Web: www.rosevillecarecenter.com
SIC: 8051 Convalescent home with continuous nursing care
HQ: Hudson River Opco, Llc
262 N University Ave
Farmington UT
801 447-9829

(P-15419)
CULVER WEST HEALTH CENTER LLC
4035 Grand View Blvd (90066-5211)
PHONE..................................310 390-9506
EMP: 90 EST: 1996
SQ FT: 25,000
SALES (est): 9.4MM Privately Held
Web: www.culverwest.com
SIC: 8051 Convalescent home with continuous nursing care

(P-15420)
CUPERTINO HLTHCARE WLLNESS CTR
Also Called: Cupertino Hlthcare Wllness Ctr
22590 Voss Ave Fl 1 (95014-2627)
PHONE..................................408 253-9034
EMP: 99 EST: 2010
SALES (est): 15.91MM Privately Held
Web: www.cupertinohc.com
SIC: 8051 Convalescent home with continuous nursing care

(P-15421)
DEL AMO GRDNS CNVLSCENT HOSP S
Also Called: DEL AMO GARDENS CONVALESCENT H
22419 Kent Ave (90505-2303)
PHONE..................................310 378-4233
Morris Weiss, Pr
Barry Weiss, *
Harry Jacobs, *
Michael Gruenbaum, *
EMP: 61 EST: 1960
SQ FT: 21,298
SALES (est): 8.12MM Privately Held
Web: www.delamogardens.com
SIC: 8051 Convalescent home with continuous nursing care

(P-15422)
DEL RIO SANITARIUM INC
Also Called: Del Rio Convalescent
7002 Gage Ave (90201-2014)
PHONE..................................562 927-6586
Joy Thune, Pr
EMP: 150 EST: 1963
SALES (est): 11.37MM Privately Held
SIC: 8051 Skilled nursing care facilities

(P-15423)
DEL ROSA VILLA INC
2018 Del Rosa Ave (92404-5642)
PHONE..................................909 885-3261
Carol Wagner Nha, Admn
Thomas S Plott, *
Elizabeth Plott, *
EMP: 85 EST: 1965
SQ FT: 20,000
SALES (est): 4.66MM Privately Held
Web: www.delrosavillapostacute.com
SIC: 8051 Convalescent home with continuous nursing care

(P-15424)
DELANO DST SKLLED NRSING FCLTY
1509 Tokay St (93215-3603)
PHONE..................................661 720-2100
Dennis Karnowski, Admn
EMP: 113 EST: 1991
SQ FT: 30,000
SALES (est): 23.48MM Privately Held
Web: www.nksthd.org
SIC: 8051 Convalescent home with continuous nursing care

(P-15425)
DIAMOND VLY HLTH HOLDINGS LLC
29222 Rancho Viejo Rd Ste 127 (92675)
PHONE..................................949 487-9500
EMP: 78 EST: 2015
SALES (est): 4.15MM
SALES (corp-wide): 3.03B Publicly Held
SIC: 8051 Skilled nursing care facilities
PA: The Ensign Group Inc
29222 Rncho Vejo Rd Ste 1
San Juan Capistrano CA
949 487-9500

(P-15426)
DOUGLAS FIR HOLDINGS LLC
Also Called: Huntington Vly Healthcare Ctr
8382 Newman Ave (92647-7038)
PHONE..................................714 842-5551

8051 - Skilled Nursing Care Facilities (P-15427)

Brad Truhar, *Admn*
EMP: 145 **EST:** 2000
SALES (est): 18.28MM
SALES (corp-wide): 1.53B **Privately Held**
Web: www.hvhcc.com
SIC: 8051 Convalescent home with continuous nursing care
HQ: California Opco, Llc
100 E San Marcos Blvd
San Marcos CA

(P-15427)
DOWNEY COMMUNITY HEALTH CENTER
8425 Iowa St (90241-4929)
P.O. Box 340 (90241-0340)
PHONE....................562 862-6506
Rich Coberly, *Admn*
Stanley Diller, *
EMP: 175 **EST:** 1980
SQ FT: 60,000
SALES (est): 21.79MM **Privately Held**
Web: www.downeycommunityhealthcenter.com
SIC: 8051 Convalescent home with continuous nursing care

(P-15428)
EAST LOS ANGLES HEALTHCARE LLC (PA)
Also Called: Costa Del Sol Healthcare
1016 S Record Ave (90023-2533)
PHONE....................323 268-0106
EMP: 75 **EST:** 1971
SQ FT: 15,000
SALES (est): 8.37MM
SALES (corp-wide): 8.37MM **Privately Held**
SIC: 8051 Convalescent home with continuous nursing care

(P-15429)
EISENBERG VLG OF THE LOS ANGLE
18855 Victory Blvd (91335-6445)
PHONE....................818 774-3372
EMP: 83 **EST:** 2011
SALES (est): 32.73MM **Privately Held**
Web: www.lajhealth.org
SIC: 8051 Skilled nursing care facilities

(P-15430)
EL MONTE CONVALESCENT HOSPITAL
4096 Easy St (91731-1054)
PHONE....................626 442-1500
Jesse Telles, *CEO*
EMP: 69 **EST:** 1964
SQ FT: 21,208
SALES (est): 6.39MM **Privately Held**
Web: www.elmonteconvalescent.com
SIC: 8051 Convalescent home with continuous nursing care

(P-15431)
ELDER CARE ALLIANCE CAMARILLO
Also Called: ALMAVIA OF CAMARILLO
2500 Ponderosa Dr N (93010-2383)
PHONE....................510 769-2700
EMP: 75 **EST:** 1999
SALES (est): 6.7MM **Privately Held**
Web: www.eldercarealliance.org
SIC: 8051 Skilled nursing care facilities

(P-15432)
ELDER CARE ALLIANCE SAN MATEO
Also Called: Villa At San Mateo
4000 S El Camino Real (94403-4566)
PHONE....................650 212-4400
EMP: 121
SALES (corp-wide): 4.51MM **Privately Held**
Web: www.thevillaatsanmateo.com
SIC: 8051 Skilled nursing care facilities
HQ: Elder Care Alliance Of San Mateo
1301 Marina Vil Pkwy 21 # 210
Alameda CA
510 769-2700

(P-15433)
ELDORADO CARE CENTER LP
Also Called: Avocado Post Acute
510 E Washington Ave (92020-5324)
PHONE....................619 440-1211
Jacob Graff, *Owner*
EMP: 298 **EST:** 2008
SALES (est): 39.22MM **Privately Held**
Web: www.avocadopostacute.com
SIC: 8051 8322 Convalescent home with continuous nursing care; Adult day care center

(P-15434)
EMERITUS CORPORATION
290 Regency Cir (93906-5581)
PHONE....................831 443-6467
EMP: 141
SALES (corp-wide): 2.83B **Publicly Held**
Web: www.brookdaleliving.com
SIC: 8051 Skilled nursing care facilities
HQ: Emeritus Corporation
6737 W Wa St Ste 2300
Milwaukee WI

(P-15435)
EMERITUS CORPORATION
38035 Martha Ave (94536-3808)
PHONE....................510 797-4011
Trish Rosner, *Brnch Mgr*
EMP: 151
SALES (corp-wide): 2.83B **Publicly Held**
Web: www.brookdaleliving.com
SIC: 8051 Skilled nursing care facilities
HQ: Emeritus Corporation
6737 W Wa St Ste 2300
Milwaukee WI

(P-15436)
EMERITUS CORPORATION
Also Called: Emeritus At San Dimas
1740 S San Dimas Ave (91773-5108)
PHONE....................909 394-0304
George Dualan, *Brnch Mgr*
EMP: 141
SALES (corp-wide): 2.83B **Publicly Held**
Web: www.brookdaleliving.com
SIC: 8051 Skilled nursing care facilities
HQ: Emeritus Corporation
6737 W Wa St Ste 2300
Milwaukee WI

(P-15437)
EMERITUS CORPORATION
Also Called: Brookdale Clairemont
5219 Clairemont Mesa Blvd (92117-2206)
PHONE....................858 292-8044
S Wheeler, *Ex Dir*
EMP: 169
SALES (corp-wide): 2.83B **Publicly Held**
Web: www.brookdaleliving.com
SIC: 8051 Skilled nursing care facilities
HQ: Emeritus Corporation
6737 W Wa St Ste 2300
Milwaukee WI

(P-15438)
EMERITUS CORPORATION
1001 N Lyon Ave (92545-1753)
PHONE....................951 744-9861
EMP: 111
SALES (corp-wide): 2.83B **Publicly Held**
Web: www.brookdaleliving.com
SIC: 8051 Skilled nursing care facilities
HQ: Emeritus Corporation
6737 W Wa St Ste 2300
Milwaukee WI

(P-15439)
EMERITUS CORPORATION
2261 Tuolumne St (94589-2560)
PHONE....................707 552-3336
EMP: 121
SALES (corp-wide): 2.83B **Publicly Held**
Web: www.brookdaleliving.com
SIC: 8051 Skilled nursing care facilities
HQ: Emeritus Corporation
6737 W Wa St Ste 2300
Milwaukee WI

(P-15440)
EMERITUS CORPORATION
142 S Prospect St (92869-3842)
PHONE....................714 639-3590
Bernice Holmes, *Ex Dir*
EMP: 141
SALES (corp-wide): 2.83B **Publicly Held**
Web: www.brookdaleliving.com
SIC: 8051 Skilled nursing care facilities
HQ: Emeritus Corporation
6737 W Wa St Ste 2300
Milwaukee WI

(P-15441)
EMERITUS CORPORATION
Also Called: Villa Del Rey Retirement Inn
1351 E Washington Ave (92027-1934)
PHONE....................760 741-3055
Pam Judkins, *Brnch Mgr*
EMP: 141
SQ FT: 60,000
SALES (corp-wide): 2.83B **Publicly Held**
Web: www.brookdaleliving.com
SIC: 8051 Skilled nursing care facilities
HQ: Emeritus Corporation
6737 W Wa St Ste 2300
Milwaukee WI

(P-15442)
EMERITUS CORPORATION
Also Called: Emeritus At Casa Glendale
426 Piedmont Ave (91206-3448)
PHONE....................818 246-7457
David Wilkens, *Brnch Mgr*
EMP: 151
SALES (corp-wide): 2.83B **Publicly Held**
Web: www.emeritus.com
SIC: 8051 Skilled nursing care facilities
HQ: Emeritus Corporation
6737 W Wa St Ste 2300
Milwaukee WI

(P-15443)
EMERITUS CORPORATION
Also Called: Emeritus At Villa Colima
19850 Colima Rd (91789-3411)
PHONE....................909 595-5030
Wanda Reynolds, *Brnch Mgr*
EMP: 121
SALES (corp-wide): 2.83B **Publicly Held**
Web: www.brookdaleliving.com
SIC: 8051 Skilled nursing care facilities
HQ: Emeritus Corporation
6737 W Wa St Ste 2300
Milwaukee WI

(P-15444)
EMERITUS CORPORATION
Also Called: Rosewood Court
411 E Commonwealth Ave (92832-2018)
PHONE....................714 441-0644
Jane Kim, *Off Mgr*
EMP: 181
SALES (corp-wide): 2.83B **Publicly Held**
Web: www.emeritus.com
SIC: 8051 Skilled nursing care facilities
HQ: Emeritus Corporation
6737 W Wa St Ste 2300
Milwaukee WI

(P-15445)
EMERITUS CORPORATION
Also Called: Terrace, The
22325 Barton Rd (92313-5006)
PHONE....................909 420-0153
Larry Smith, *Dir*
EMP: 151
SALES (corp-wide): 2.83B **Publicly Held**
Web: www.brookdaleliving.com
SIC: 8051 Skilled nursing care facilities
HQ: Emeritus Corporation
6737 W Wa St Ste 2300
Milwaukee WI

(P-15446)
EMPRES FINANCIAL SERVICES LLC
Also Called: Living Centers
1527 Springs Rd (94591-5448)
PHONE....................707 643-2793
David Hicks, *Mgr*
EMP: 886
SALES (corp-wide): 900.43MM **Privately Held**
Web: www.empres.com
SIC: 8051 Skilled nursing care facilities
HQ: Empres Financial Services, Llc
4601 Ne 77th Ave Ste 300
Vancouver WA
360 892-6628

(P-15447)
ENCORE SENIOR LIVING III LLC
Also Called: Sierra Vista
13815 Rodeo Dr Ofc (92395-5648)
PHONE....................760 243-2271
Jana Herrera, *Admn*
EMP: 60
SIC: 8051 Skilled nursing care facilities
PA: Encore Senior Living Iii, Llc
400 Locust St Ste 820
Des Moines IA

(P-15448)
ENDURA HEALTHCARE INC
29222 Rancho Viejo Rd Ste 127 (92675)
PHONE....................949 487-9500
EMP: 115 **EST:** 2014
SALES (est): 6.37MM
SALES (corp-wide): 3.03B **Publicly Held**
SIC: 8051 Skilled nursing care facilities
PA: The Ensign Group Inc
29222 Rncho Vejo Rd Ste 1
San Juan Capistrano CA
949 487-9500

(P-15449)
ENGLISH OAKS CONVALESCENT
Also Called: ENGLISH OAKS CONVALESCENT & RE
2633 W Rumble Rd (95350-0154)
PHONE....................209 577-1001
Terry L Mundy, *CEO*
Pamela Mundy, *

PRODUCTS & SERVICES SECTION

8051 - Skilled Nursing Care Facilities (P-15469)

EMP: 74 EST: 1985
SQ FT: 57,000
SALES (est): 19.13MM Privately Held
Web: www.lifegen.net
SIC: 8051 Convalescent home with continuous nursing care

(P-15450)
ENSIGN CLOVERDALE LLC
Also Called: Cloverdale Healthcare Center
300 Cherry Creek Rd (95425-3811)
PHONE..................707 894-5201
Soon Burnam, Admn
Christopher Christensen, *
EMP: 391 EST: 2004
SALES (est): 9.35MM
SALES (corp-wide): 3.03B Publicly Held
SIC: 8051 Convalescent home with continuous nursing care
HQ: Northern Pioneer Healthcare, Inc.
   27101 Puerta Real
   Mission Viejo CA
   949 487-9500

(P-15451)
ENSIGN GROUP INC
Also Called: Downey Care Center
13007 Paramount Blvd (90242-4329)
PHONE..................562 923-9301
Marc Brian, Prin
EMP: 204
SALES (corp-wide): 3.03B Publicly Held
Web: www.ensigngroup.net
SIC: 8051 Convalescent home with continuous nursing care
PA: The Ensign Group Inc
   29222 Rncho Vejo Rd Ste 1
   San Juan Capistrano CA
   949 487-9500

(P-15452)
ENSIGN GROUP INC
Also Called: Panaroma Gardens
9541 Van Nuys Blvd (91402-1315)
PHONE..................818 893-6385
Alicia Gamero, Admn
EMP: 199
SALES (corp-wide): 3.03B Publicly Held
Web: www.ensigngroup.net
SIC: 8051 Convalescent home with continuous nursing care
PA: The Ensign Group Inc
   29222 Rncho Vejo Rd Ste 1
   San Juan Capistrano CA
   949 487-9500

(P-15453)
ENSIGN GROUP INC
Also Called: Whittier Hills Health Care Ctr
10426 Bogardus Ave (90603-2642)
PHONE..................562 947-7817
Lisa Matarazzo, Admn
EMP: 185
SQ FT: 36,316
SALES (corp-wide): 3.03B Publicly Held
Web: www.ensigngroup.net
SIC: 8051 8059 Convalescent home with continuous nursing care; Rest home, with health care
PA: The Ensign Group Inc
   29222 Rncho Vejo Rd Ste 1
   San Juan Capistrano CA
   949 487-9500

(P-15454)
ENSIGN GROUP INC
Also Called: Park View Gardens
3751 Montgomery Dr (95405-5214)
PHONE..................707 525-1250
Eric Moessing, Dir
EMP: 222
SALES (corp-wide): 3.03B Publicly Held
Web: www.ensigngroup.net
SIC: 8051 Convalescent home with continuous nursing care
PA: The Ensign Group Inc
   29222 Rncho Vejo Rd Ste 1
   San Juan Capistrano CA
   949 487-9500

(P-15455)
ENSIGN GROUP INC
Also Called: Mission Care Center
4800 Delta Ave (91770-1127)
PHONE..................626 607-2400
Tin Nelson, Dir
EMP: 88
SALES (corp-wide): 3.03B Publicly Held
Web: www.missioncareandrehab.com
SIC: 8051 Convalescent home with continuous nursing care
PA: The Ensign Group Inc
   29222 Rncho Vejo Rd Ste 1
   San Juan Capistrano CA
   949 487-9500

(P-15456)
ENSIGN PALM I LLC
Also Called: ENSIGN
2990 E Ramon Rd (92264-7931)
PHONE..................760 323-2638
Soon Burnam, Treas
Leeron Hever, Admn
EMP: 134 EST: 2001
SALES (est): 10.26MM
SALES (corp-wide): 3.03B Publicly Held
Web: www.premiercarecenter.net
SIC: 8051 Convalescent home with continuous nursing care
PA: The Ensign Group Inc
   29222 Rncho Vejo Rd Ste 1
   San Juan Capistrano CA
   949 487-9500

(P-15457)
ENSIGN PLEASANTON LLC
Also Called: ENSIGN
1349 S Dora St (95482-6512)
PHONE..................707 462-8864
Lowell Smith, CEO
Ferdinand Buot, Ex Dir
Soon Burnam, Treas
EMP: 138 EST: 2001
SALES (est): 6.38MM
SALES (corp-wide): 3.03B Publicly Held
Web: www.ukiahpostacute.com
SIC: 8051 Convalescent home with continuous nursing care
PA: The Ensign Group Inc
   29222 Rncho Vejo Rd Ste 1
   San Juan Capistrano CA
   949 487-9500

(P-15458)
ENSIGN SERVICES INC
29222 Rancho Viejo Rd Ste 127 (92675)
PHONE..................949 487-9500
EMP: 90 EST: 2002
SALES (est): 51.62MM
SALES (corp-wide): 3.03B Publicly Held
Web: www.ensigngroup.net
SIC: 8051 Convalescent home with continuous nursing care
PA: The Ensign Group Inc
   29222 Rncho Vejo Rd Ste 1
   San Juan Capistrano CA
   949 487-9500

(P-15459)
ENSIGN SONOMA LLC
Also Called: Broadway Villa Post Acute
1250 Broadway (95476-7500)
PHONE..................707 938-8406
Michael Empey, Ex Dir
EMP: 179 EST: 2001
SALES (est): 15.64MM
SALES (corp-wide): 3.03B Publicly Held
SIC: 8051 Convalescent home with continuous nursing care
HQ: Northern Pioneer Healthcare, Inc.
   27101 Puerta Real
   Mission Viejo CA
   949 487-9500

(P-15460)
ENSIGN SOUTHLAND LLC
Also Called: Southland Care
29222 Rancho Viejo Rd Ste 127 (92675)
PHONE..................949 487-9500
EMP: 241 EST: 2000
SALES (est): 9.43MM
SALES (corp-wide): 3.03B Publicly Held
SIC: 8051 Extended care facility
PA: The Ensign Group Inc
   29222 Rncho Vejo Rd Ste 1
   San Juan Capistrano CA
   949 487-9500

(P-15461)
ENSIGN WHITTIER EAST LLC
Also Called: ENSIGN
10426 Bogardus Ave (90603-2642)
PHONE..................562 947-7817
EMP: 139 EST: 2001
SALES (est): 19.32MM
SALES (corp-wide): 3.03B Publicly Held
Web: www.whittierhillshealthcare.com
SIC: 8051 Convalescent home with continuous nursing care
PA: The Ensign Group Inc
   29222 Rncho Vejo Rd Ste 1
   San Juan Capistrano CA
   949 487-9500

(P-15462)
ENSIGN WHITTIER WEST LLC
27101 Puerta Real Ste 450 (92691-8566)
PHONE..................949 487-9500
EMP: 101 EST: 2015
SALES (est): 5.83MM
SALES (corp-wide): 3.03B Publicly Held
SIC: 8051 Convalescent home with continuous nursing care
PA: The Ensign Group Inc
   29222 Rncho Vejo Rd Ste 1
   San Juan Capistrano CA
   949 487-9500

(P-15463)
ENSIGN WILLITS LLC
Also Called: Northbrook Healthcare Center
64 Northbrook Way (95490-3019)
PHONE..................707 459-5592
Shawndee Gamble, Ex Dir
EMP: 203 EST: 2001
SALES (est): 5.35MM
SALES (corp-wide): 3.03B Publicly Held
Web: www.northbrooknursing.com
SIC: 8051 Convalescent home with continuous nursing care
PA: The Ensign Group Inc
   29222 Rncho Vejo Rd Ste 1
   San Juan Capistrano CA
   949 487-9500

(P-15464)
EPISCOPAL COMMUNITIES & SERVIC
Also Called: Canterbury, The
5801 Crestridge Rd (90275-4961)
PHONE..................310 544-2204
Consuelo Haire, Brnch Mgr
EMP: 100
SALES (corp-wide): 86.44MM Privately Held
Web: www.ecsforseniors.org
SIC: 8051 8361 8059 Extended care facility; Aged home; Personal care home, with health care
PA: Episcopal Communities & Services For Seniors
   605 E Huntington Dr # 207
   Monrovia CA
   626 403-5880

(P-15465)
ESKATON PROPERTIES INC
Also Called: Eskaton Village Care Center
3847 Walnut Ave (95608-2148)
PHONE..................916 974-2060
Larry Bahr, Mgr
EMP: 122
SIC: 8051 Skilled nursing care facilities
PA: Eskaton Properties Incorporated
   5105 Manzanita Ave Ste A
   Carmichael CA

(P-15466)
ESKATON PROPERTIES INC
Eskaton Manzanita Manor
5318 Manzanita Ave (95608-0512)
PHONE..................916 331-8513
Denie Crum, Admn
EMP: 122
Web: www.eskaton.org
SIC: 8051 Convalescent home with continuous nursing care
PA: Eskaton Properties Incorporated
   5105 Manzanita Ave Ste A
   Carmichael CA

(P-15467)
ESTRELLA INC
Also Called: Woodruff Convalescent Center
1340 Highland Ave # 12 (91010-2520)
PHONE..................562 925-6418
Liberation De Leon Md, Pr
EMP: 110 EST: 1969
SALES (est): 6.25MM Privately Held
Web: www.estrella.com
SIC: 8051 Convalescent home with continuous nursing care

(P-15468)
EUREKA RHBLTTION WLLNESS CTR L
Also Called: EUREKA REHABILITATION & WELLNE
2353 23rd St (95501-3201)
PHONE..................707 445-3261
Sharrod Brooks, Pt
Shlomo Rechnitz, Pt
EMP: 98 EST: 2011
SALES (est): 9.79MM Privately Held
Web: www.eurekarehabwc.com
SIC: 8051 Skilled nursing care facilities

(P-15469)
EVERGREEN AT LAKEPORT LLC (PA)
Also Called: Evergreen Lkport Halthcare Ctr
1291 Craig Ave (95453-5704)
PHONE..................707 263-6382
EMP: 100 EST: 1986
SQ FT: 36,240
SALES (est): 17.02MM
SALES (corp-wide): 17.02MM Privately Held

8051 - Skilled Nursing Care Facilities (P-15470)

SIC: 8051 Convalescent home with continuous nursing care

(P-15470)
EVERGREEN AT LAKEPORT LLC
Also Called: Evergreen Healthcare Center
6212 Tudor Way (93306-7067)
PHONE..................................661 871-3133
Gloria Melliti, *Mgr*
EMP: 100
SALES (corp-wide): 17.02MM **Privately Held**
SIC: 8051 Convalescent home with continuous nursing care
PA: Evergreen At Lakeport, L.L.C.
1291 Craig Ave
Lakeport CA
707 263-6382

(P-15471)
EVERGREEN AT SPRINGS ROAD LLC
Also Called: SPRINGS ROAD HEALTHCARE
1527 Springs Rd (94591-5448)
PHONE..................................360 892-6628
EMP: 74
SALES (est): 6.24MM **Privately Held**
Web: www.empres.com
SIC: 8051 Convalescent home with continuous nursing care

(P-15472)
EVERGREEN HEALTH CARE LLC
323 Campus Dr (93203-1047)
PHONE..................................661 854-4475
Cody Rasmussen, *Ex Dir*
Rush Melliti, *
EMP: 1522 EST: 1985
SALES (est): 27.61MM
SALES (corp-wide): 900.43MM **Privately Held**
SIC: 8051 Convalescent home with continuous nursing care
HQ: Evergreen At Chico, L.L.C.
4601 Ne 77th Ave Ste 300
Vancouver WA
530 342-4885

(P-15473)
EXTENDED CARE HOSP WESTMINSTER
206 Hospital Cir (92683-3910)
PHONE..................................714 891-2769
George Rhodes, *Admn*
Fred Landry, *Pt*
Mark Landry, *Pt*
Connie Black, *Pt*
EMP: 71 EST: 1977
SALES (est): 12.17MM **Privately Held**
Web: www.westminsterec.com
SIC: 8051 8069 Convalescent home with continuous nursing care; Specialty hospitals, except psychiatric

(P-15474)
FAR WEST INC
Also Called: Linwood Grdns Convalescent Ctr
4444 W Meadow Ave (93277-1652)
PHONE..................................559 627-1241
Robert Barker, *Mgr*
EMP: 113
Web: www.farwest.org
SIC: 8051 8059 Convalescent home with continuous nursing care; Convalescent home
HQ: Far West, Inc.
4020 Sierra College Blvd
Rocklin CA

(P-15475)
FAR WEST INC
Also Called: Medical Center
467 E Gilbert St (92404-5318)
PHONE..................................909 884-4781
Frank De Leosa, *Mgr*
EMP: 63
Web: www.medcentercare.com
SIC: 8051 8059 Convalescent home with continuous nursing care; Rest home, with health care
HQ: Far West, Inc.
4020 Sierra College Blvd
Rocklin CA

(P-15476)
FH & HF-TORRANCE I LLC
Also Called: SUNNYSIDE NURSING CENTER
22617 S Vermont Ave (90502-2550)
PHONE..................................310 320-4130
Larry Bell, *Prin*
EMP: 73 EST: 1975
SQ FT: 35,000
SALES (est): 22.92MM **Privately Held**
Web: www.sunnysidenursing.com
SIC: 8051 8361 8069 8052 Convalescent home with continuous nursing care; Residential care; Specialty hospitals, except psychiatric; Intermediate care facilities

(P-15477)
FIG HOLDINGS LLC
Also Called: Garden City Healthcare Center
1310 W Granger Ave (95350-3911)
PHONE..................................209 524-4817
EMP: 100 EST: 2002
SQ FT: 23,000
SALES (est): 13.12MM
SALES (corp-wide): 1.53B **Privately Held**
Web: www.gardencityhealthcare.com
SIC: 8051 Convalescent home with continuous nursing care
HQ: Hudson River Opco, Llc
262 N University Ave
Farmington UT
801 447-9829

(P-15478)
FIVE STAR QULTY CARE-CA II LLC (DH)
Also Called: THOUSAND OAKS HEALTH CARE CENTER
93 W Avenida De Los Arboles (91360)
PHONE..................................805 492-2444
Eugene Tito, *Admn*
EMP: 70 EST: 2004
SALES (est): 14.71MM
SALES (corp-wide): 934.59MM **Privately Held**
SIC: 8051 Skilled nursing care facilities
HQ: Alerislife Inc.
255 Washington St Ste 300
Newton MA

(P-15479)
FIVE STAR QULTY CARE-CA II LLC
Also Called: Lasaltte Hlth Rhbilitation Ctr
537 E Fulton St (95204-2227)
PHONE..................................209 466-2066
Gus Ropalidis, *Admn*
EMP: 105
SALES (corp-wide): 934.59MM **Privately Held**
Web: www.fivestarseniorliving.com
SIC: 8051 Convalescent home with continuous nursing care
HQ: Five Star Quality Care-Ca Ii, Llc
93 W Avnida De Los Arbles
Thousand Oaks CA
805 492-2444

(P-15480)
FIVE STAR SENIOR LIVING INC
Also Called: Remington Club I & II
16925 Hierba Dr (92128-2688)
PHONE..................................858 673-6300
Kristen Crinigan, *Ex Dir*
EMP: 144
SALES (corp-wide): 934.59MM **Privately Held**
Web: www.theremingtonclub.com
SIC: 8051 Skilled nursing care facilities
HQ: Alerislife Inc.
255 Washington St Ste 300
Newton MA

(P-15481)
FREEDOM VILLAGE HEALTHCARE CTR
Also Called: REHABWORKS AT FREEDOM VILLAGE
23442 El Toro Rd Bldg 2 (92630-6992)
PHONE..................................949 472-4733
EMP: 89 EST: 1977
SALES (est): 23.54MM **Privately Held**
Web: www.freedomvillage.org
SIC: 8051 8052 Convalescent home with continuous nursing care; Intermediate care facilities

(P-15482)
FRESNO SKILLED NURSING
Also Called: Healthcare Centre of Fresno
1665 M St (93721-1121)
PHONE..................................559 268-5361
EMP: 99 EST: 2009
SALES (est): 4.43MM **Privately Held**
Web: www.hcfresno.com
SIC: 8051 Mental retardation hospital

(P-15483)
FRONT PORCH COMMUNITIES & SVCS
Also Called: Kingsley Manor
1055 N Kingsley Dr (90029-1207)
PHONE..................................323 661-1128
Cindy Gonzales, *Prin*
EMP: 172
SQ FT: 106,521
Web: www.frontporch.net
SIC: 8051 Skilled nursing care facilities
PA: Front Porch Communities And Services
800 N Brand Blvd Fl 19
Glendale CA

(P-15484)
FRONT PORCH COMMUNITIES & SVCS
Also Called: Fredericka Manor Care Center
111 Third Ave (91910-1822)
PHONE..................................619 427-2777
Loraine Wiencek, *Brnch Mgr*
EMP: 113
Web: www.frederickamanorcarecenter.org
SIC: 8051 Convalescent home with continuous nursing care
PA: Front Porch Communities And Services
800 N Brand Blvd Fl 19
Glendale CA

(P-15485)
FULLERTON HLTHCARE WLLNESS CNT
Also Called: Evergreen Fullerton Healthcare
2222 N Harbor Blvd (92835-2605)
PHONE..................................714 992-5701
Shlomo Rechnitz, *Pt*
Sharrod Brooks, *Pt*
EMP: 125 EST: 2013
SALES (est): 22.73MM **Privately Held**
Web: www.sunnyhillshc.com
SIC: 8051 Convalescent home with continuous nursing care

(P-15486)
GARDEN CREST CNVLSCENT HOSP IN
Also Called: GARDEN CREST RETIREMENT RESIDE
909 Lucile Ave (90026-1598)
PHONE..................................323 663-8281
Paul Barron, *CEO*
Vera Barron, *
EMP: 90 EST: 1954
SQ FT: 30,000
SALES (est): 6.95MM **Privately Held**
Web: www.gardencrestweb.com
SIC: 8051 8059 8322 Convalescent home with continuous nursing care; Convalescent home; Old age assistance

(P-15487)
GARDEN GROVE MEDICAL INVESTORS (HQ)
Also Called: Garden Grove Rehabilitation
12332 Garden Grove Blvd (92843-1804)
PHONE..................................714 534-1041
Nelia Yonzen, *Ex Dir*
EMP: 93 EST: 1976
SQ FT: 10,000
SALES (est): 130.3K
SALES (corp-wide): 139.21MM **Privately Held**
SIC: 8051 8069 Convalescent home with continuous nursing care; Specialty hospitals, except psychiatric
PA: Life Care Centers Of America, Inc.
3570 Keith St Nw
Cleveland TN
423 472-9585

(P-15488)
GARDENA RETIREMENT CENTER INC
14741 S Vermont Ave (90247-3098)
PHONE..................................310 327-4091
EMP: 104
SALES (corp-wide): 3.55MM **Privately Held**
Web: www.gardenaretirement.com
SIC: 8051 Skilled nursing care facilities
PA: Gardena Retirement Center, Inc.
11627 Telg Rd Ste 200
Santa Fe Springs CA
310 327-4091

(P-15489)
GARFIELD NURSING HOME INC
Also Called: Morton Bakar Center
1100 Marina Village Pkwy Ste 100 (94501-6461)
PHONE..................................510 582-7676
Ann Bakar, *CEO*
Marshall D Langfeld, *
Ross C Peterson, *
EMP: 66 EST: 1980
SALES (est): 7.32MM
SALES (corp-wide): 440.9MM **Privately Held**
SIC: 8051 Convalescent home with continuous nursing care
PA: Telecare Corporation
1080 Marina Village Pkwy # 100
Alameda CA
510 337-7950

PRODUCTS & SERVICES SECTION

8051 - Skilled Nursing Care Facilities (P-15512)

(P-15490)
GATE THREE HEALTHCARE LLC
Also Called: Palm Ter Hlthcare Rhblttion Ct
24962 Calle Aragon (92637-3883)
PHONE.............................949 587-9000
EMP: 172 **EST:** 2004
SALES (est): 14.43MM
SALES (corp-wide): 3.03B **Publicly Held**
Web: www.palmterracecares.com
SIC: 8051 Convalescent home with continuous nursing care
PA: The Ensign Group Inc
   29222 Rncho Vejo Rd Ste 1
   San Juan Capistrano CA
   949 487-9500

(P-15491)
GENESIS HEALTHCARE LLC
Also Called: Spring Senior Assisted Living
20900 Earl St Ste 100 (90503-4309)
PHONE.............................310 370-3594
EMP: 287
Web: www.genesishcc.com
SIC: 8051 Skilled nursing care facilities
HQ: Genesis Healthcare Llc
   101 E State St
   Kennett Square PA

(P-15492)
GENESIS HEALTHCARE LLC
Also Called: Creekside Center
9107 Davis Rd (95209-1807)
PHONE.............................209 478-6488
EMP: 383
Web: www.genesishcc.com
SIC: 8051 Convalescent home with continuous nursing care
HQ: Genesis Healthcare Llc
   101 E State St
   Kennett Square PA

(P-15493)
GENESIS HEALTHCARE LLC
425 Barcellus Ave (93454-6901)
PHONE.............................805 922-3558
EMP: 698
Web: www.villamariapostacute.com
SIC: 8051 Convalescent home with continuous nursing care
HQ: Genesis Healthcare Llc
   101 E State St
   Kennett Square PA

(P-15494)
GEORGIA ATKISON SNF LLC
Also Called: Alliance Nrsing Rhbltation Ctr
3825 Durfee Ave (91732-2505)
PHONE.............................626 444-2535
Eli Quinones, *Managing Member*
EMP: 81 **EST:** 1996
SQ FT: 30,000
SALES (est): 10.12MM **Privately Held**
SIC: 8051 Convalescent home with continuous nursing care

(P-15495)
GERI-CARE INC
Also Called: Harbor Post Acute Care Center
21521 S Vermont Ave (90502-1939)
PHONE.............................310 320-0961
Emmanuel David, *Pr*
EMP: 100 **EST:** 1975
SQ FT: 30,000
SALES (est): 10.81MM **Privately Held**
Web: www.harborpostacute.com
SIC: 8051 Convalescent home with continuous nursing care

(P-15496)
GHC OF PLEASANTON LLC
Also Called: Pleasanton Nursing & Rehab Ctr
300 Neal St (94566-7317)
PHONE.............................925 462-2400
EMP: 120 **EST:** 1971
SQ FT: 43,000
SALES (est): 20.85MM
SALES (corp-wide): 112.74MM **Privately Held**
SIC: 8051 Convalescent home with continuous nursing care
PA: Life Generations Healthcare Llc
   6 Hutton Cntre Dr Ste 400
   Santa Ana CA
   714 241-5600

(P-15497)
GHC OF SAN RAFAEL LLC
Also Called: Smith Ranch Nursing Center
1550 Silveira Pkwy (94903-4879)
PHONE.............................415 499-1000
Thomas Olds, *CEO*
EMP: 67 **EST:** 2017
SALES (est): 6.55MM
SALES (corp-wide): 112.74MM **Privately Held**
SIC: 8051 Skilled nursing care facilities
PA: Life Generations Healthcare Llc
   6 Hutton Cntre Dr Ste 400
   Santa Ana CA
   714 241-5600

(P-15498)
GOLD COUNTRY HEALTH CENTER INC (PA)
Also Called: Gold Country Health Center
4301 Golden Center Dr (95667-6260)
PHONE.............................530 621-1100
Suzanne Valoppi, *Admn*
EMP: 130 **EST:** 1984
SQ FT: 57,000
SALES (est): 8.46MM
SALES (corp-wide): 8.46MM **Privately Held**
SIC: 8051 Skilled nursing care facilities

(P-15499)
GOLDEN STATE HABILITATION CONV (PA)
Also Called: Golden State Care Center
1758 Big Dalton Ave (91706-5910)
PHONE.............................626 962-3274
Eden Salceda, *Pr*
Emmanual David, *
Claudio Hernandez, *
EMP: 175 **EST:** 1971
SALES (est): 9.1MM **Privately Held**
Web: www.gsccdd.com
SIC: 8051 8361 8052 Convalescent home with continuous nursing care; Residential care; Intermediate care facilities

(P-15500)
GPH MEDICAL & LEGAL SERVICES (PA)
Also Called: G P H Medical Services
468 N Camden Dr (90210-4507)
PHONE.............................213 207-2700
Summer Reed, *Pr*
Michael Mcbay Md, *VP*
Doctor Samuel Wesley, *Sec*
Olen Maxwell Ph.d., *Stockholder*
William Maxwell Ph.d., *Stockholder*
▲ **EMP:** 187 **EST:** 1986
SQ FT: 4,000
SALES (est): 12.12MM **Privately Held**
Web: www.nulegal.com

(P-15501)
GR8 CARE INC
14518 Los Angeles St (91706-2636)
PHONE.............................626 337-7229
Edwin Raquel, *CEO*
Napoleon Garcia, *
EMP: 73 **EST:** 2007
SQ FT: 9,710
SALES (est): 2.56MM **Privately Held**
SIC: 8051 Skilled nursing care facilities

(P-15502)
GRAND AVENUE HLTH HOLDINGS LLC
29222 Rancho Viejo Rd Ste 127 (92675)
PHONE.............................949 487-9500
EMP: 92 **EST:** 2018
SALES (est): 2.93MM
SALES (corp-wide): 3.03B **Publicly Held**
SIC: 8051 Convalescent home with continuous nursing care
PA: The Ensign Group Inc
   29222 Rncho Vejo Rd Ste 1
   San Juan Capistrano CA
   949 487-9500

(P-15503)
GRIFFITH PK RHBLTATION CTR LLC
Also Called: Griffith Park Healthcare Ctr
201 Allen Ave (91201-2803)
PHONE.............................818 845-8507
EMP: 75 **EST:** 2015
SALES (est): 13.19MM **Privately Held**
SIC: 8051 Convalescent home with continuous nursing care

(P-15504)
HACIENDA CARE CENTER INC
Also Called: Sierra Valley Rehab Center
301 W Putnam Ave (93257-3429)
PHONE.............................559 784-7375
Emmanuel B David, *Pr*
Emmanuel B David, *Pr*
Ramona Villaluz, *
EMP: 145 **EST:** 1984
SQ FT: 26,000
SALES (est): 11.07MM **Privately Held**
Web: www.svsnf.com
SIC: 8051 Skilled nursing care facilities

(P-15505)
HACIENDA POST ACUTE INC
Also Called: Hacienda Health Care
361 E Grangeville Blvd (93230-3054)
PHONE.............................559 582-9221
Rex Moore, *Brnch Mgr*
EMP: 120
SALES (corp-wide): 5.58MM **Privately Held**
Web: www.haciendacares.com
SIC: 8051 8069 Convalescent home with continuous nursing care; Specialty hospitals, except psychiatric
PA: Hacienda Post Acute, Inc.
   1440 S State College Blvd
   Anaheim CA
   714 778-0221

(P-15506)
HARBOR GLEN CARE CENTER
Also Called: Arbor Glen Care Center
1033 E Arrow Hwy (91740-6110)
PHONE.............................626 963-7531
Kevin Thomas, *Owner*
SIC: 8051 8059 7361 7812 Skilled nursing care facilities; Convalescent home; Nurses' registry; Television film production

(P-15507)
HCR MANORCARE MED SVCS FLA LLC
Also Called: Manorcare Health Services
24962 Calle Aragon (92653)
PHONE.............................949 587-9000
EMP: 150
SALES (corp-wide): 2.27B **Publicly Held**
SIC: 8051 Skilled nursing care facilities
HQ: Hcr Manorcare Medical Services Of Florida, Llc
   333 N Summit St Ste 100
   Toledo OH
   419 252-5500

(P-15508)
HEALTHCARE CTR OF DOWNEY LLC
Also Called: Lakewood Healthcare Center
12023 Lakewood Blvd (90242-2635)
PHONE.............................562 869-0978
Vince Hambright, *CEO*
EMP: 250 **EST:** 2011
SQ FT: 1,076,391
SALES (est): 19.44MM **Privately Held**
Web: www.lwhealthcare.com
SIC: 8051 Mental retardation hospital

(P-15509)
HEALTHCARE INVESTMENTS INC (PA)
Also Called: Rosecrans Care Center
1140 W Rosecrans Ave (90247-2664)
PHONE.............................310 323-3194
Pompeyo Rosales, *Pr*
Gonzalo Delrosario, *
EMP: 91 **EST:** 1991
SALES (est): 12.64MM **Privately Held**
SIC: 8051 Convalescent home with continuous nursing care

(P-15510)
HEALTHCARE MANAGEMENT SYSTEMS INC
Also Called: Bradley Court
900 Lane Ave Ste 190 (91914-3502)
PHONE.............................619 521-9641
EMP: 120
SIC: 8051 Skilled nursing care facilities

(P-15511)
HEBREW HOME FOR AGED DISABLED
Also Called: JEWISH HOME FOR THE AGED
302 Silver Ave (94112-1510)
PHONE.............................415 334-2500
Daniel Ruth, *Pr*
Kevin T Potter, *
EMP: 600 **EST:** 1889
SALES (est): 93.95MM **Privately Held**
Web: www.sfcjl.org
SIC: 8051 Skilled nursing care facilities

(P-15512)
HELIOS HEALTHCARE LLC
Also Called: 2733 Idylwood Care Center
1002 W Fremont Ave (94087-3031)

8051 - Skilled Nursing Care Facilities (P-15513)

PHONE..............................408 739-2383
EMP: 271
SALES (corp-wide): 27.25MM **Privately Held**
SIC: 8051 Skilled nursing care facilities
PA: Helios Healthcare, Llc
520 Capitol Mall Ste 800
Sacramento CA
916 471-2241

(P-15513)
HELIOS HEALTHCARE LLC
Also Called: Rosewood Care Center
1911 Oak Park Blvd (94523-4601)
PHONE..............................925 935-6630
EMP: 110
SALES (corp-wide): 24.17MM **Privately Held**
SIC: 8051 8093 Skilled nursing care facilities; Rehabilitation center, outpatient treatment
PA: Helios Healthcare, Llc
520 Capitol Mall Ste 800
Sacramento CA
916 471-2241

(P-15514)
HERITAGE HEALTH CARE INC
Also Called: Heritage Gardens Hlth Care Ctr
25271 Barton Rd (92354-3013)
PHONE..............................909 796-0216
Stephen Flood, *CEO*
Stephen Flood, *Dir*
Gregory S Goings, *
Jim Kilian, *
EMP: 150 EST: 1963
SALES (est): 10.93MM **Privately Held**
Web: www.progressivecarecenters.com
SIC: 8051 8059 Skilled nursing care facilities; Rest home, with health care

(P-15515)
HIGHLAND HLTHCARE CMLLIA GRDNS
Also Called: Camellia Gardens Care Center
1920 N Fair Oaks Ave (91103-1623)
PHONE..............................626 798-6777
Samuel Chazanow, *CEO*
Bernard Friedman, *
EMP: 130 EST: 2019
SALES (est): 9.34MM **Privately Held**
Web: www.camelliagardenscc.com
SIC: 8051 Convalescent home with continuous nursing care

(P-15516)
HIGHLAND PK SKLLED NRSING WLLN
5125 Monte Vista St (90042-3931)
PHONE..............................323 254-6125
EMP: 72 EST: 2008
SALES (est): 6.86MM **Privately Held**
Web: www.highlandparkwc.com
SIC: 8051 Convalescent home with continuous nursing care

(P-15517)
HORIZON WEST HEALTHCARE INC (HQ)
4020 Sierra College Blvd Ste 190 (95677-3906)
PHONE..............................916 624-6230
Martine D Harmon, *CEO*
Bernice Schrabeck, *
Dennis Roccaforte, *
EMP: 76 EST: 1973
SQ FT: 6,000
SALES (est): 143.47MM **Privately Held**
SIC: 8051 Convalescent home with continuous nursing care

PA: Horizon West, Inc.
4020 Sierra College Blvd
Rocklin CA

(P-15518)
HOSPICE OF SAN JOAQUIN
3888 Pacific Ave (95204-1953)
PHONE..............................209 957-3888
Stephen L Guasco, *CEO*
Barbara Tognoli, *
Gail Wigley, *
Kerrie Biddle, *
EMP: 90 EST: 1980
SQ FT: 5,000
SALES (est): 17.58MM **Privately Held**
Web: www.hospicesj.org
SIC: 8051 8641 Skilled nursing care facilities; Social associations

(P-15519)
HYDE PK REHABILITATION CTR LLC
6520 West Blvd (90043-4311)
PHONE..............................323 753-1354
EMP: 90
SALES (est): 1.01MM **Privately Held**
SIC: 8051 Skilled nursing care facilities

(P-15520)
ICARE PRIVATE DUTY INC
Also Called: Safe Harbor Home Care
5473 Kearny Villa Rd Ste 110b (92123)
PHONE..............................858 634-1012
Susan Graaff, *Prin*
Edwin Peterson, *Prin*
Soon Burnam, *Prin*
EMP: 68 EST: 2016
SALES (est): 1.63MM
SALES (corp-wide): 3.03B **Publicly Held**
SIC: 8051 Skilled nursing care facilities
PA: The Ensign Group Inc
29222 Rncho Vejo Rd Ste 1
San Juan Capistrano CA
949 487-9500

(P-15521)
IMAGINATIVE HORIZONS INC
Also Called: Hillcrest Manor Sanitarium
1889 National City Blvd (91950-5517)
PHONE..............................619 477-1176
Gary Byrnes, *Pr*
Rosella Byrnes, *
EMP: 84 EST: 1930
SQ FT: 30,000
SALES (est): 4.29MM **Privately Held**
Web: www.specialized-care.com
SIC: 8051 Skilled nursing care facilities

(P-15522)
IN GRANADA HLLS CNVLSCENT HOSP
Also Called: Granada Hills Care Center
16123 Chatsworth St (91344-7045)
PHONE..............................818 891-1745
Seid Sadat, *Pr*
Abraham Birnbaum, *
Kim Marconet, *
EMP: 64 EST: 1963
SQ FT: 96,680
SALES (est): 4.9MM **Privately Held**
Web: www.ghcarecenter.com
SIC: 8051 Convalescent home with continuous nursing care

(P-15523)
INLAND CHRSTN HM FUNDATION INC
1950 S Mountain Ave Ofc (91762-6709)
PHONE..............................909 395-9322

David Stienstra, *Pr*
Karen Miedema, *
EMP: 114 EST: 1973
SQ FT: 100,000
SALES (est): 112.96K **Privately Held**
Web: www.ichome.org
SIC: 8051 8052 6513 8361 Skilled nursing care facilities; Intermediate care facilities; Retirement hotel operation; Residential care

(P-15524)
INTERCOMMUNITY CARE CTRS INC
Also Called: Intercommunity Care Center
2626 Grand Ave (90815-1707)
PHONE..............................562 427-8915
Russel Boydston, *Brnch Mgr*
EMP: 141
SQ FT: 32,159
SALES (corp-wide): 8.8MM **Privately Held**
Web: www.iccare.org
SIC: 8051 Convalescent home with continuous nursing care
PA: Intercommunity Care Centers, Inc.
2660 Grand Ave
Long Beach CA
562 426-1368

(P-15525)
J P H CONSULTING INC
4515 Huntington Dr S (90032-1940)
PHONE..............................323 934-5660
EMP: 131
SALES (corp-wide): 52.03MM **Privately Held**
SIC: 8051 Skilled nursing care facilities
PA: J P H Consulting, Inc.
1101 Crenshaw Blvd
Los Angeles CA
323 934-5660

(P-15526)
JEWISH HM FOR THE AGING ORNGE
Also Called: HERITAGE POINTE
27356 Bellogente (92691-6341)
PHONE..............................949 364-9685
David Zarnow, *VP*
Rena Loveless, *
EMP: 120 EST: 1969
SQ FT: 88,928
SALES (est): 12.33MM **Privately Held**
Web: www.heritagepointe.org
SIC: 8051 Skilled nursing care facilities

(P-15527)
KARMA INC
Also Called: PAKSN MANAGEMENT SERVICES
410 Eastwood Ave (95336-3167)
PHONE..............................209 239-1222
Antony Thekkek, *Pr*
Prema Thekkek, *
EMP: 160 EST: 2003
SQ FT: 29,700
SALES (est): 11.64MM
SALES (corp-wide): 14.18MM **Privately Held**
SIC: 8051 Convalescent home with continuous nursing care
PA: Paksn, Inc.
540 W Monte Vista Ave
Vacaville CA
707 449-3400

(P-15528)
KATELLA PROPERTIES
Also Called: Alamitos W Convalescent Hosp
3902 Katella Ave (90720-3304)
PHONE..............................562 596-5561

Marilyn Gelgincolin, *Dir*
EMP: 85
SALES (corp-wide): 8.82MM **Privately Held**
Web: www.alamitoswest.com
SIC: 8051 Convalescent home with continuous nursing care
PA: Katella Properties
3952 Katella Ave
Los Alamitos CA
562 596-2773

(P-15529)
KENDAL AT SNOMA A ZEN INSPRED
1801 Boxheart Dr (95448-3255)
PHONE..............................707 756-5036
Rosemary Jordan, *CEO*
Susan O'connell, *Sec*
EMP: 75 EST: 2019
SALES (est): 4.68MM **Privately Held**
SIC: 8051 Extended care facility
PA: The Kendal Corporation
1109 E Baltimore Pike
Kennett Square PA

(P-15530)
KNOLLS CONVALESCENT HOSP INC (PA)
Also Called: Desert Knlls Convalescent Hosp
16890 Green Tree Blvd (92395-5618)
PHONE..............................760 245-5361
Gary L Bechtold, *Pr*
Larry Bechtold, *
Fred Bechtold, *
EMP: 130 EST: 1971
SQ FT: 5,421
SALES (est): 14.35MM
SALES (corp-wide): 14.35MM **Privately Held**
Web: www.knollswestpostacute.com
SIC: 8051 8052 Convalescent home with continuous nursing care; Intermediate care facilities

(P-15531)
KNOLLS WEST ENTERPRISE
Also Called: Knolls West Residential Care
16890 Green Tree Blvd (92395-5618)
PHONE..............................760 245-0107
Larry Bechtold, *Pt*
Gary Bechtold, *Pt*
Fred Bechtold, *Pt*
EMP: 161 EST: 1979
SQ FT: 44,000
SALES (est): 9.4MM
SALES (corp-wide): 14.35MM **Privately Held**
Web: www.knollswestpostacute.com
SIC: 8051 Convalescent home with continuous nursing care
PA: Knolls Convalescent Hospital, Inc.
16890 Green Tree Blvd
Victorville CA
760 245-5361

(P-15532)
KSM HEALTHCARE INC
Also Called: Dreier's Nursing Care Center
1400 W Glenoaks Blvd (91201-1911)
PHONE..............................818 242-1183
John Haedrich, *CEO*
EMP: 76 EST: 1947
SQ FT: 40,000
SALES (est): 7.74MM **Privately Held**
Web: www.nursing-care.com
SIC: 8051 Skilled nursing care facilities

8051 - Skilled Nursing Care Facilities (P-15551)

(P-15533)
KU KYOUNG
Also Called: Eden Villa
#unknown (96003)
P.O. Box 590428 (96003)
PHONE.................510 582-2765
Kyoung Ku, *Owner*
EMP: 170 EST: 1986
SQ FT: 37,157
SALES (est): 10.6MM **Privately Held**
SIC: 8051 1522 Convalescent home with continuous nursing care; Residential construction, nec

(P-15534)
LA JOLLA SKILLED INC
Also Called: ENSIGN
3884 Nobel Dr (92122-5700)
PHONE.................858 625-8700
Glenn Matthews, *CEO*
Craig Fitch, *
Soon Burnam, *
EMP: 124 EST: 2014
SALES (est): 9.59MM
SALES (corp-wide): 3.03B **Publicly Held**
Web: www.sprlj.com
SIC: 8051 Convalescent home with continuous nursing care
PA: The Ensign Group Inc
29222 Rncho Vejo Rd Ste 1
San Juan Capistrano CA
949 487-9500

(P-15535)
LEGACY AND NURSING REHAB
1790 Muir Rd (94553-4718)
PHONE.................925 228-8383
Dipa Gupta, *Owner*
Sherry Jansen, *
Thomas Joseph, *
Burnadett Joseph, *
EMP: 90 EST: 1998
SALES (est): 4.73MM **Privately Held**
SIC: 8051 Convalescent home with continuous nursing care

(P-15536)
LEMON GROVE HEALTH ASSOC LLC
Also Called: Lemon Grove Care Rhblttion Ctr
8351 Broadway (91945-2009)
PHONE.................619 463-0294
Preet Kambo, *Ex Dir*
Mason Hunter, *
EMP: 298 EST: 2004
SALES (est): 23.25MM
SALES (corp-wide): 3.03B **Publicly Held**
Web: www.lemongrovecare.com
SIC: 8051 Convalescent home with continuous nursing care
PA: The Ensign Group Inc
29222 Rncho Vejo Rd Ste 1
San Juan Capistrano CA
949 487-9500

(P-15537)
LIFE CARE CENTERS AMERICA INC
Also Called: Life Care Center of La Habra
1233 W La Habra Blvd (90631-5296)
PHONE.................562 690-0852
Daniel Husband, *Admn*
EMP: 237
SALES (corp-wide): 139.21MM **Privately Held**
Web: www.lcca.com
SIC: 8051 Convalescent home with continuous nursing care
PA: Life Care Centers Of America, Inc.
3570 Keith St Nw
Cleveland TN
423 472-9585

(P-15538)
LIFE CARE CENTERS AMERICA INC
Also Called: Mirada Hlls Rehb Cnvlscent Hos
12200 La Mirada Blvd (90638-1306)
PHONE.................562 947-8691
Selina Stewart, *Ex Dir*
EMP: 177
SALES (corp-wide): 139.21MM **Privately Held**
Web: www.lcca.com
SIC: 8051 Convalescent home with continuous nursing care
PA: Life Care Centers Of America, Inc.
3570 Keith St Nw
Cleveland TN
423 472-9585

(P-15539)
LIFE CARE CENTERS AMERICA INC
Also Called: Life Care Centers of Escondido
1980 Felicita Rd (92025-5922)
PHONE.................760 741-6109
Trent Weaver, *Admn*
EMP: 197
SALES (corp-wide): 139.21MM **Privately Held**
Web: www.lcca.com
SIC: 8051 Convalescent home with continuous nursing care
PA: Life Care Centers Of America, Inc.
3570 Keith St Nw
Cleveland TN
423 472-9585

(P-15540)
LIFE CARE CENTERS AMERICA INC
Also Called: Imperial Convalescent
11926 La Mirada Blvd (90638-1303)
PHONE.................562 943-7156
Ted Stultz, *Mgr*
EMP: 139
SALES (corp-wide): 139.21MM **Privately Held**
Web: www.lcca.com
SIC: 8051 8741 Convalescent home with continuous nursing care; Management services
PA: Life Care Centers Of America, Inc.
3570 Keith St Nw
Cleveland TN
423 472-9585

(P-15541)
LIFE CARE CENTERS AMERICA INC
Also Called: Bel Tren Vlla Cnvalescent Hosp
16910 Woodruff Ave (90706-6036)
PHONE.................562 867-1761
Tooren Bel, *Mgr*
EMP: 132
SALES (corp-wide): 139.21MM **Privately Held**
Web: www.lcca.com
SIC: 8051 Convalescent home with continuous nursing care
PA: Life Care Centers Of America, Inc.
3570 Keith St Nw
Cleveland TN
423 472-9585

(P-15542)
LIFE CARE CENTERS AMERICA INC
Also Called: Life Care Center of Norwalk
12350 Rosecrans Ave (90650-5064)
PHONE.................562 921-6624
Steve Ramsdel, *VP*
EMP: 80
SALES (corp-wide): 139.21MM **Privately Held**
Web: www.lcca.com
SIC: 8051 Convalescent home with continuous nursing care
PA: Life Care Centers Of America, Inc.
3570 Keith St Nw
Cleveland TN
423 472-9585

(P-15543)
LIFE CARE CENTERS AMERICA INC
27555 Rimrock Rd (92311-4230)
PHONE.................760 252-2515
EMP: 187
SALES (corp-wide): 139.21MM **Privately Held**
Web: www.lcca.com
SIC: 8051 Convalescent home with continuous nursing care
PA: Life Care Centers Of America, Inc.
3570 Keith St Nw
Cleveland TN
423 472-9585

(P-15544)
LIFE GNERATIONS HEALTHCARE LLC
Also Called: Arbor Hills Nursing Center
7800 Parkway Dr (91942-2001)
PHONE.................619 460-2330
EMP: 63
SALES (corp-wide): 112.74MM **Privately Held**
Web: www.lifegen.net
SIC: 8051 Convalescent home with continuous nursing care
PA: Life Generations Healthcare Llc
6 Hutton Cntre Dr Ste 400
Santa Ana CA
714 241-5600

(P-15545)
LIGHTHOUSE HEALTHCARE CTR LLC
2222 Santa Ana S (90059-1350)
PHONE.................323 564-4461
EMP: 99 EST: 2007
SALES (est): 16.01MM **Privately Held**
SIC: 8051 Skilled nursing care facilities

(P-15546)
LITTLE SSTERS OF THE POOR LOS
Also Called: Jeanne Jugan, A Residence
2100 S Western Ave (90732-4331)
PHONE.................310 548-0625
Margaret Mcarthy, *Pr*
Michael Mugan, *
Clotilde Jardim, *
EMP: 100 EST: 1905
SQ FT: 145,530
SALES (est): 8.34MM **Privately Held**
Web: www.littlesistersofthepoorsanpedro.org
SIC: 8051 8361 8052 Extended care facility; Residential care; Intermediate care facilities

(P-15547)
LONE TREE CNVALESCENT HOSP INC
4001 Lone Tree Way (94509-6232)
PHONE.................925 754-0470
Lowell Callaway, *Pr*
Velda C Pierce, *Executive Administrator*
Mark Callaway, *
EMP: 135 EST: 1968
SQ FT: 10,000
SALES (est): 9.3MM **Privately Held**
SIC: 8051 Convalescent home with continuous nursing care

(P-15548)
LONG BEACH CARE CENTER INC
2615 Grand Ave (90815-1708)
PHONE.................562 426-6141
William A Nelson, *Pr*
EMP: 108 EST: 2003
SQ FT: 43,962
SALES (est): 18.54MM **Privately Held**
Web: www.longbeach.gov
SIC: 8051 Convalescent home with continuous nursing care

(P-15549)
LONGWOOD MANAGEMENT CORP
Also Called: Imperial Crest Healthcare Ctr
11834 Inglewood Ave (90250-2731)
PHONE.................310 679-1461
Robert Villalub, *Admn*
EMP: 125
SALES (corp-wide): 79.33MM **Privately Held**
Web: www.longwoodmgmt.com
SIC: 8051 Convalescent home with continuous nursing care
PA: Longwood Management Corp.
4032 Wilshire Blvd Fl 6
Los Angeles CA
213 389-6900

(P-15550)
LONGWOOD MANAGEMENT CORP
Also Called: Magnolia Grdns Convalescent HM
17922 San Fernando Mission Blvd (91344-4043)
PHONE.................818 360-1864
Ojjjoji Gervacio, *Prin*
EMP: 97
SALES (corp-wide): 79.33MM **Privately Held**
Web: www.longwoodmgmt.com
SIC: 8051 Convalescent home with continuous nursing care
PA: Longwood Management Corp.
4032 Wilshire Blvd Fl 6
Los Angeles CA
213 389-6900

(P-15551)
LONGWOOD MANAGEMENT CORP
Also Called: Green Acres Lodge
8101 Hill Dr (91770-4169)
PHONE.................626 280-2293
Karen Fugate, *Admn*
EMP: 108
SALES (corp-wide): 79.33MM **Privately Held**
Web: www.longwoodmgmt.com
SIC: 8051 Convalescent home with continuous nursing care
PA: Longwood Management Corp.
4032 Wilshire Blvd Fl 6
Los Angeles CA
213 389-6900

8051 - Skilled Nursing Care Facilities (P-15552)

(P-15552)
LONGWOOD MANAGEMENT CORP
Also Called: San Gabriel Convalescent Ctr
8035 Hill Dr (91770-4116)
PHONE.....................626 280-4820
Gigi Garcia, Brnch Mgr
EMP: 122
SALES (corp-wide): 79.33MM **Privately Held**
Web: www.longwoodmgmt.com
SIC: **8051** Convalescent home with continuous nursing care
PA: Longwood Management Corp.
  4032 Wilshire Blvd Fl 6
  Los Angeles CA
  213 389-6900

(P-15553)
LONGWOOD MANAGEMENT CORP
Also Called: Crenshaw Nursing
1900 S Longwood Ave (90016-1408)
PHONE.....................323 933-1560
Gilbert Fimbres, Mgr
EMP: 117
SALES (corp-wide): 79.33MM **Privately Held**
Web: www.longwoodmgmt.com
SIC: **8051** **8052** Convalescent home with continuous nursing care; Intermediate care facilities
PA: Longwood Management Corp.
  4032 Wilshire Blvd Fl 6
  Los Angeles CA
  213 389-6900

(P-15554)
LOS ANGLES JEWISH HM FOR AGING (PA)
Also Called: Grancell Village
7150 Tampa Ave (91335-3700)
PHONE.....................818 774-3000
Andrew Berman, Ch Bd
Jeffrey Glassman, *
Molly Forrest, *
Sherri B Cunningham, *
Shelly J Ryan, *
EMP: 400 EST: 1912
SQ FT: 35,000
SALES (est): 32.41MM
SALES (corp-wide): 32.41MM **Privately Held**
Web: www.lajhealth.org
SIC: **8051** **8361** Skilled nursing care facilities ; Residential care

(P-15555)
LOS ANGLES JEWISH HM FOR AGING
Also Called: Eisenberg Village
18855 Victory Blvd (91335-6445)
PHONE.....................818 774-3000
Kathleen Glass, Mgr
EMP: 500
SALES (corp-wide): 32.41MM **Privately Held**
Web: www.lajhealth.org
SIC: **8051** Convalescent home with continuous nursing care
PA: Los Angeles Jewish Home For The Aging
  7150 Tampa Ave
  Reseda CA
  818 774-3000

(P-15556)
MADERA CONVALESCENT HOSP INC (PA)
517 S A St (93638-3896)
PHONE.....................559 673-9228
Arden Bennett, CEO
Emile Damia, *
Dennis Albers, *
Mathilde Albers, *
EMP: 160 EST: 1965
SQ FT: 1,500
SALES (est): 7.32MM
SALES (corp-wide): 7.32MM **Privately Held**
SIC: **8051** Convalescent home with continuous nursing care

(P-15557)
MAGNOLIA HOLDINGS LLC
Also Called: Oak River Rehabilitation
3300 Franklin St (96007-3279)
PHONE.....................530 365-0025
EMP: 150 EST: 2007
SQ FT: 3,000
SALES (est): 25.07MM
SALES (corp-wide): 1.53B **Privately Held**
Web: www.oakriver-rehab.com
SIC: **8051** Convalescent home with continuous nursing care
HQ: Hudson River Opco, Llc
  262 N University Ave
  Farmington UT
  801 447-9829

(P-15558)
MANCHSTER MNOR CNVLESCENT HOSP
837 W Manchester Ave (90044-4913)
PHONE.....................323 753-1789
Phadra Johnson-fenton, Admn
EMP: 65 EST: 1963
SQ FT: 10,000
SALES (est): 3.79MM **Privately Held**
Web: www.manchestermanorch.com
SIC: **8051** Convalescent home with continuous nursing care

(P-15559)
MANNING GARDENS CARE CTR INC
2113 E Manning Ave (93725-9681)
PHONE.....................559 834-2586
Ronald Kinnersley, Pr
EMP: 82 EST: 2011
SALES (est): 7.78MM **Privately Held**
Web: www.manninggardensnr.com
SIC: **8051** Skilled nursing care facilities

(P-15560)
MARINER HEALTH CARE INC
Also Called: Driftwood Health Care Ctr
4109 Emerald St (90503-3105)
PHONE.....................310 371-4628
Jennifer Torgrude, Mgr
EMP: 126
SALES (corp-wide): 1.02B **Privately Held**
Web: www.driftwoodhc.com
SIC: **8051** Convalescent home with continuous nursing care
PA: Mariner Health Care, Inc.
  3060 Mercer University Dr # 200
  Atlanta GA
  678 443-7000

(P-15561)
MARINER HEALTH CARE INC
Also Called: El Rancho Vista Hlth Care Ctr
8925 Mines Ave (90660-3006)
PHONE.....................562 942-7019
Richard Widerynski, Mgr
EMP: 98
SALES (corp-wide): 1.02B **Privately Held**
Web: www.elranchovista.com
SIC: **8051** Convalescent home with continuous nursing care
PA: Mariner Health Care, Inc.
  3060 Mercer University Dr # 200
  Atlanta GA
  678 443-7000

(P-15562)
MARINER HEALTH CARE INC
Also Called: Arden Health & Rehab Ctr
3400 Alta Arden Expy (95825-2103)
PHONE.....................916 481-5500
John Pritchard, Mgr
EMP: 75
SALES (corp-wide): 1.02B **Privately Held**
Web: www.marinerhealthcare.com
SIC: **8051** **8069** Extended care facility; Specialty hospitals, except psychiatric
PA: Mariner Health Care, Inc.
  3060 Mercer University Dr # 200
  Atlanta GA
  678 443-7000

(P-15563)
MARINER HEALTH CARE INC
Also Called: Freemont Health Care Center
39022 Presidio Way (94538-1221)
PHONE.....................510 792-3743
Carinagayle Gorospe, Admn
EMP: 166
SALES (corp-wide): 1.02B **Privately Held**
Web: www.marinerhealthcare.com
SIC: **8051** Extended care facility
PA: Mariner Health Care, Inc.
  3060 Mercer University Dr # 200
  Atlanta GA
  678 443-7000

(P-15564)
MARINER HEALTH CARE INC
Also Called: Gilroy Health & Rehab Ctr
8170 Murray Ave (95020-4605)
PHONE.....................408 842-9311
Gerald Hunter, Admn
EMP: 81
SALES (corp-wide): 1.02B **Privately Held**
Web: www.marinerhealthcare.com
SIC: **8051** Extended care facility
PA: Mariner Health Care, Inc.
  3060 Mercer University Dr # 200
  Atlanta GA
  678 443-7000

(P-15565)
MARINER HEALTH CARE INC
Also Called: Skyline Health Care Center
2065 Forest Ave (95128-4807)
PHONE.....................408 298-3950
Richard Park, Admn
EMP: 160
SALES (corp-wide): 1.02B **Privately Held**
Web: www.marinerhealthcare.com
SIC: **8051** Extended care facility
PA: Mariner Health Care, Inc.
  3060 Mercer University Dr # 200
  Atlanta GA
  678 443-7000

(P-15566)
MARINER HEALTH CARE INC
Also Called: Parkview Healthcare Center
27350 Tampa Ave (94544-4429)
PHONE.....................510 783-8150
Ada Lukban, Mgr
EMP: 130
SALES (corp-wide): 1.02B **Privately Held**
Web: www.marinerhealthcare.com
SIC: **8051** Extended care facility
PA: Mariner Health Care, Inc.
  3060 Mercer University Dr # 200
  Atlanta GA
  678 443-7000

(P-15567)
MARINER HEALTH CARE INC
Also Called: Vale Healthcare Center
13484 San Pablo Ave (94806-3904)
PHONE.....................510 232-5945
Remy Dise, Dir
EMP: 389
SALES (corp-wide): 1.02B **Privately Held**
Web: www.marinerhealthcare.com
SIC: **8051** Extended care facility
PA: Mariner Health Care, Inc.
  3060 Mercer University Dr # 200
  Atlanta GA
  678 443-7000

(P-15568)
MARINER HEALTH CARE INC
Also Called: Monterey Palms Health Care Ctr
44610 Monterey Ave (92260-3326)
PHONE.....................760 776-7700
J Simanjunt, Admn
EMP: 156
SALES (corp-wide): 1.02B **Privately Held**
Web: www.marinerhealthcare.com
SIC: **8051** Extended care facility
PA: Mariner Health Care, Inc.
  3060 Mercer University Dr # 200
  Atlanta GA
  678 443-7000

(P-15569)
MARINER HEALTH CARE INC
Also Called: Inglewood Health Care Center
100 S Hillcrest Blvd (90301-1313)
PHONE.....................310 677-9114
Amanda Arevalo, Admn
EMP: 68
SALES (corp-wide): 1.02B **Privately Held**
Web: www.marinerhealthcare.com
SIC: **8051** Extended care facility
PA: Mariner Health Care, Inc.
  3060 Mercer University Dr # 200
  Atlanta GA
  678 443-7000

(P-15570)
MARINER HEALTH CARE INC
Also Called: Skyline Health Care Ctr
3032 Rowena Ave (90039-2005)
PHONE.....................323 665-1185
Kathleen Glass, Admn
EMP: 68
SALES (corp-wide): 1.02B **Privately Held**
Web: www.marinerhealthcare.com
SIC: **8051** Extended care facility
PA: Mariner Health Care, Inc.
  3060 Mercer University Dr # 200
  Atlanta GA
  678 443-7000

(P-15571)
MARINER HEALTH CARE INC
Also Called: Autumn Hills Convalescent Home
430 N Glendale Ave (91206-3309)
PHONE.....................818 246-5677
Jenik Akopian, Prin
EMP: 94
SALES (corp-wide): 1.02B **Privately Held**
Web: www.marinerhealthcare.com
SIC: **8051** Extended care facility
PA: Mariner Health Care, Inc.
  3060 Mercer University Dr # 200
  Atlanta GA
  678 443-7000

PRODUCTS & SERVICES SECTION
8051 - Skilled Nursing Care Facilities (P-15593)

(P-15572)
MARINER HEALTH CARE INC
675 24th Ave (95062-4205)
PHONE 831 475-6323
EMP: 73
SALES (corp-wide): 1.02B **Privately Held**
Web: www.marinerhealthcare.com
SIC: 8051 Extended care facility
PA: Mariner Health Care, Inc.
3060 Mercer University Dr # 200
Atlanta GA
678 443-7000

(P-15573)
MARINER HEALTH CARE INC
Also Called: Hayward Hills Health Care Ctr
1768 B St (94541-3102)
PHONE 510 538-4424
Annamarie Magna, *Brnch Mgr*
EMP: 158
SALES (corp-wide): 1.02B **Privately Held**
Web: www.marinerhealthcare.com
SIC: 8051 Extended care facility
PA: Mariner Health Care, Inc.
3060 Mercer University Dr # 200
Atlanta GA
678 443-7000

(P-15574)
MARINER HEALTH CARE INC
Also Called: Driftwood Healthcare Center
19700 Hesperian Blvd (94541-4704)
PHONE 510 785-2880
Ellen Renner, *Admn*
EMP: 139
SALES (corp-wide): 1.02B **Privately Held**
Web: www.marinerhealthcare.com
SIC: 8051 Extended care facility
PA: Mariner Health Care, Inc.
3060 Mercer University Dr # 200
Atlanta GA
678 443-7000

(P-15575)
MARINER HEALTH CARE INC
Also Called: Pinedridge Care Ctr
45 Professional Center Pkwy (94903-2702)
PHONE 415 479-3610
Louise Kalchek, *Dir*
EMP: 105
SALES (corp-wide): 1.02B **Privately Held**
Web: www.marinerhealthcare.com
SIC: 8051 Extended care facility
PA: Mariner Health Care, Inc.
3060 Mercer University Dr # 200
Atlanta GA
678 443-7000

(P-15576)
MARINER HEALTH CARE INC
Also Called: Almaden Health & Rehab Ctr
2065 Los Gatos Almaden Rd (95124-5417)
PHONE 408 377-9275
Yvette Bonnet, *Brnch Mgr*
EMP: 92
SALES (corp-wide): 1.02B **Privately Held**
Web: www.marinerhealthcare.com
SIC: 8051 Extended care facility
PA: Mariner Health Care, Inc.
3060 Mercer University Dr # 200
Atlanta GA
678 443-7000

(P-15577)
MARINER HEALTH CARE INC
Also Called: Verdugo Vista Healthcare Ctr
3050 Montrose Ave (91214-3619)
PHONE 818 957-0850
Jeri-enn Shelton, *Admn*
EMP: 96
SALES (corp-wide): 1.02B **Privately Held**
Web: www.marinerhealthcare.com
SIC: 8051 Extended care facility
PA: Mariner Health Care, Inc.
3060 Mercer University Dr # 200
Atlanta GA
678 443-7000

(P-15578)
MARINIDENCE OPCO LLC
Also Called: Marin Post Acute
234 N San Pedro Rd (94903-2858)
PHONE 415 479-3450
Mark Hancock, *CFO*
EMP: 199 EST: 2017
SALES (est): 11.79MM
SALES (corp-wide): 1.53B **Privately Held**
SIC: 8051 Skilled nursing care facilities
HQ: Providence Group North, Llc
262 N University Ave
Farmington UT
801 447-9829

(P-15579)
MARK & FRED ENTERPRISES
Also Called: West Anaheim Care Center
645 S Beach Blvd (92804-3102)
PHONE 714 821-1993
Mark Landry, *Mng Pt*
Connie Black, *Pt*
EMP: 125 EST: 1989
SQ FT: 39,000
SALES (est): 14.2MM **Privately Held**
Web: www.beachcreekpostacute.com
SIC: 8051 Convalescent home with
continuous nursing care

(P-15580)
MARLORA INVESTMENTS LLC
Also Called: Marlora Post Accute Rhblttion
3801 E Anaheim St (90804-4004)
PHONE 562 494-3311
EMP: 100 EST: 1998
SQ FT: 22,118
SALES (est): 8.57MM **Privately Held**
Web: www.marlora.com
SIC: 8051 Convalescent home with
continuous nursing care

(P-15581)
MARY HLTH OF SICK CNVLSCENT NR
2929 Theresa Dr (91320-3136)
PHONE 805 498-3644
Jody Rupp, *Admn*
Sister Purificaion Fererro, *
Diane Zimanski, *
EMP: 92 EST: 1964
SQ FT: 5,000
SALES (est): 7.42MM **Privately Held**
Web: www.maryhealth.com
SIC: 8051 Convalescent home with
continuous nursing care

(P-15582)
MEK ESCONDIDO LLC
Also Called: Escondido Post Acute Rehab
421 E Mission Ave (92025-1909)
PHONE 760 747-0430
EMP: 180 EST: 2000
SALES (est): 13.94MM **Privately Held**
SIC: 8051 Convalescent home with
continuous nursing care

(P-15583)
MELON HOLDINGS LLC
Also Called: Marysville Post-Acute
1617 Ramirez St (95901-4334)
PHONE 530 742-7311
Joseph Cunliffe, *Admn*
Matt Jackson, *
Nicklas Anderson, *
EMP: 99 EST: 2016
SALES (est): 9.61MM
SALES (corp-wide): 1.53B **Privately Held**
Web: www.marysvillepostacute.com
SIC: 8051 Convalescent home with
continuous nursing care
HQ: California Opco, Llc
100 E San Marcos Blvd
San Marcos CA

(P-15584)
MERAKEY USA
3336 Bradshaw Rd Ste 175 (95827-2631)
PHONE 916 923-9823
EMP: 84
SALES (corp-wide): 60.74MM **Privately Held**
Web: www.merakey.org
SIC: 8051 Skilled nursing care facilities
PA: Merakey Usa
620 Germantown Pike
Lafayette Hill PA
610 260-4600

(P-15585)
MESA VRDE CNVALESCENT HOSP INC
Also Called: Mesa Verde Prosecute Care
661 Center St (92627-2708)
PHONE 949 548-5584
Rita Simms, *Admn*
Joseph Munoz, *
Joye Tsuchiyama, *
EMP: 200 EST: 1972
SALES (est): 22.73MM **Privately Held**
Web: www.mesaverdehealthcare.com
SIC: 8051 Convalescent home with
continuous nursing care

(P-15586)
MIRAMONTE ENTERPRISES LLC
Also Called: San Jacinto Healthcare
275 N San Jacinto St (92543-4453)
PHONE 951 658-9441
Emmanuel B David, *Pr*
EMP: 134 EST: 2005
SQ FT: 22,968
SALES (est): 8.3MM **Privately Held**
Web: www.sjsnf.com
SIC: 8051 Convalescent home with
continuous nursing care

(P-15587)
MISSION HILLS HEALTH CARE INC
Also Called: Mission Hills Healthcare Ctr
726 Torrance St (92103-3813)
PHONE 619 297-4086
Patrick Higgins, *Admn*
Leah Higgins, *
EMP: 92 EST: 1990
SALES (est): 10.56MM **Privately Held**
Web: www.missionhillshealthcare.com
SIC: 8051 Convalescent home with
continuous nursing care

(P-15588)
MODOC MEDIAL CENTER HOSP AUX
Also Called: Warnerview Skilled Nursing
225 W Mcdowell Ave (96101-3933)
P.O. Box 190 (96101-0190)
PHONE 530 233-3416
Paula Boissineau, *Prin*
EMP: 91
Web: www.modocmedicalcenter.org
SIC: 8051 Skilled nursing care facilities
PA: Modoc Medical Center Hospital
Auxiliary
1111 N Nagle St
Alturas CA

(P-15589)
MOMS PLACE
Also Called: Give ME Shelter
30 La Patera Ct (93010-8412)
PHONE 805 383-6855
Jackie Biederman, *Owner*
EMP: 73 EST: 2001
SALES (est): 704.38K **Privately Held**
Web: www.momsplaces.com
SIC: 8051 Skilled nursing care facilities

(P-15590)
MONTECITO RETIREMENT ASSN
Also Called: Casa Dorinda
300 Hot Springs Rd (93108-2037)
PHONE 805 969-8011
Robin Drew, *CFO*
EMP: 265 EST: 1973
SQ FT: 350,000
SALES (est): 24.99MM **Privately Held**
Web: www.casadorinda.org
SIC: 8051 8052 8361 Skilled nursing care
facilities; Personal care facility; Rest home,
with health care incidental

(P-15591)
MONTEREY PINES SKLLD NURSG FAC
Also Called: Horizon West
1501 Skyline Dr (93940-4110)
PHONE 831 373-3716
Gene Sajcich, *Admn*
EMP: 94 EST: 1980
SQ FT: 32,000
SALES (est): 8.49MM **Privately Held**
SIC: 8051 Convalescent home with
continuous nursing care
HQ: Horizon West Healthcare, Inc.
4020 Sierra College Blvd # 190
Rocklin CA
916 624-6230

(P-15592)
MT MIQUEL COVENANT VILLAGE
325 Kempton St (91977-5810)
PHONE 619 479-4790
Rich Miller, *Dir*
EMP: 151 EST: 1993
SQ FT: 316,465
SALES (est): 21.89MM **Privately Held**
Web: www.covlivingmountmiguel.org
SIC: 8051 Skilled nursing care facilities
PA: Covenant Living Communities And
Services
5700 Old Orchard Rd
Skokie IL

(P-15593)
MT RUBIDOUXIDENCE OPCO LLC
Also Called: Jurupa Hills Post Acute
6401 33rd St (92509-1404)
PHONE 951 681-2200
Jason Murray, *Prin*
Mark Hancock, *
Debra Gogerty, *
EMP: 199 EST: 2015
SALES (est): 31.59MM
SALES (corp-wide): 1.53B **Privately Held**
SIC: 8051 Skilled nursing care facilities
HQ: Providence Group Of Southern
California, Llc

8051 - Skilled Nursing Care Facilities (P-15594)

262 N University Ave
Farmington UT
801 447-9829

(P-15594)
NAPAIDENCE OPCO LLC
Also Called: NAPA Post Acute
705 Trancas St (94558-3014)
PHONE.................................707 255-6060
Jason Murray, Prin
Mark Hancock, *
EMP: 130 EST: 2016
SALES (est): 16.34MM
SALES (corp-wide): 1.53B Privately Held
Web: www.napapostacute.com
SIC: 8051 Skilled nursing care facilities
HQ: Providence Group Wine Country, Llc
262 N University Ave
Farmington UT
801 447-9829

(P-15595)
NAVIGAGE FOUNDATION (PA)
849 Foothill Blvd Ste 8 (91011-3368)
PHONE.................................818 790-2522
Judy Vallas, CEO
EMP: 100 EST: 1932
SQ FT: 90,000
SALES (est): 579.61K
SALES (corp-wide): 579.61K Privately Held
SIC: 8051 8059 8052 Skilled nursing care facilities; Rest home, with health care; Intermediate care facilities

(P-15596)
NORTH PT HLTH WELLNESS CTR LLC
Also Called: NORTHPOINTE HEALTHCARE CENTRE
668 E Bullard Ave (93710-5401)
PHONE.................................559 320-2200
EMP: 99 EST: 2011
SALES (est): 10.62MM Privately Held
Web: www.northpointhc.com
SIC: 8051 Convalescent home with continuous nursing care

(P-15597)
NORTH SHORE INVESTMENT INC
Also Called: Crescent Cy Convalescent Hosp
1280 Marshall St (95531-2217)
PHONE.................................707 464-6151
EMP: 100 EST: 1988
SQ FT: 35,000
SALES (est): 7.91MM Privately Held
SIC: 8051 Convalescent home with continuous nursing care

(P-15598)
NORTHERN CALIFORNIA PRESBYTERI
Also Called: Sequos-San Frncsco Residential
1400 Geary Blvd (94109-6561)
PHONE.................................415 922-9700
Michael Daugherty, Brnch Mgr
EMP: 153
SALES (corp-wide): 114.59MM Privately Held
Web: www.sequoialiving.org
SIC: 8051 Convalescent home with continuous nursing care
PA: Sequoia Living, Inc.
1525 Post St
San Francisco CA
415 202-7808

(P-15599)
NORWALK MEADOWS NURSING CTR LP
Also Called: Norwalk Meadows Nursing Center
10625 Leffingwell Rd (90650-3434)
PHONE.................................562 864-2541
Pnina Graff, Pt
Jacob Graff, *
EMP: 65 EST: 1997
SQ FT: 23,632
SALES (est): 32.73MM Privately Held
Web: www.norwalkmeadows.com
SIC: 8051 Convalescent home with continuous nursing care

(P-15600)
NOVATO HEALTHCARE CENTER LLC
Also Called: NOVATO HEALTHCARE CENTER
1565 Hill Rd (94947-4063)
PHONE.................................415 897-6161
EMP: 200 EST: 2007
SALES (est): 23.48MM Privately Held
Web: www.novatohealthcare.com
SIC: 8051 Convalescent home with continuous nursing care

(P-15601)
OAKHURST SKLLED NRSING WLLNESS
Also Called: Oakhurst Hlthcare Wllness Cntr
40131 Highway 49 (93644-9560)
PHONE.................................559 683-2244
Admiral Stepan Sarmazian, Prin
EMP: 99 EST: 2009
SALES (est): 8.04MM Privately Held
Web: www.oakhursthcllc.com
SIC: 8051 Convalescent home with continuous nursing care

(P-15602)
OAKLAND HEALTHCARE & WELLNESS
Also Called: Akland Healthcare Wellness Ctr
3030 Webster St (94609-3411)
PHONE.................................323 330-6572
Sol Majer, Managing Member
EMP: 131 EST: 2010
SQ FT: 20,000
SALES (est): 9.77MM Privately Held
Web: www.oaklandhc.com
SIC: 8051 Convalescent home with continuous nursing care

(P-15603)
OCADIAN CARE CENTERS LLC
Also Called: Alta Bates Medical Center
2450 Ashby Ave (94705-2067)
PHONE.................................510 204-5801
Cindy Cirdz, Brnch Mgr
EMP: 468
SALES (corp-wide): 68.77MM Privately Held
SIC: 8051 Skilled nursing care facilities
PA: Ocadian Care Centers, Llc
104 Main St
Belvedere Tiburon CA
415 789-5427

(P-15604)
OCADIAN CARE CENTERS LLC
Also Called: Greenbrea Care Center
1220 S Eliseo Dr (94904-2006)
PHONE.................................415 461-9700
Susan Weaver, Mgr
EMP: 279
SALES (corp-wide): 68.77MM Privately Held
SIC: 8051 8069 8052 Skilled nursing care facilities; Specialty hospitals, except psychiatric; Intermediate care facilities
PA: Ocadian Care Centers, Llc
104 Main St
Belvedere Tiburon CA
415 789-5427

(P-15605)
OCADIAN CARE CENTERS LLC
Also Called: Northern Cal Rehabilitation
2801 Eureka Way (96001-0222)
PHONE.................................530 246-9000
Chris Jones, Ex Dir
EMP: 851
SALES (corp-wide): 68.77MM Privately Held
SIC: 8051 5912 8069 Convalescent home with continuous nursing care; Drug stores and proprietary stores; Specialty hospitals, except psychiatric
PA: Ocadian Care Centers, Llc
104 Main St
Belvedere Tiburon CA
415 789-5427

(P-15606)
OCADIAN CARE CENTERS LLC
Also Called: Medical Hill Rehabilitation
475 29th St (94609-3510)
PHONE.................................510 832-3222
Robert G Peirce, Pr
EMP: 526
SALES (corp-wide): 68.77MM Privately Held
SIC: 8051 Convalescent home with continuous nursing care
PA: Ocadian Care Centers, Llc
104 Main St
Belvedere Tiburon CA
415 789-5427

(P-15607)
OCADIAN CARE CENTERS LLC
1550 Silveira Pkwy (94903-4879)
PHONE.................................415 499-1000
Linda Creekmoore, Mgr
EMP: 340
SALES (corp-wide): 68.77MM Privately Held
SIC: 8051 8361 Convalescent home with continuous nursing care; Residential care
PA: Ocadian Care Centers, Llc
104 Main St
Belvedere Tiburon CA
415 789-5427

(P-15608)
OCADIAN CARE CENTERS LLC
Also Called: Homewood Care Center
75 N 13th St (95112-3439)
PHONE.................................408 295-2665
David Martinez, Admn
EMP: 279
SALES (corp-wide): 68.77MM Privately Held
SIC: 8051 Convalescent home with continuous nursing care
PA: Ocadian Care Centers, Llc
104 Main St
Belvedere Tiburon CA
415 789-5427

(P-15609)
OCEANSIDE HARBOR HOLDINGS LLC ◆
Also Called: Beach Creek Post-Acute
645 S Beach Blvd (92804-3102)
PHONE.................................760 331-3177
Curt Rodriguez, *
EMP: 200 EST: 2022
SALES (est): 9.19MM Privately Held
SIC: 8051 Skilled nursing care facilities

(P-15610)
OLEANDER HOLDINGS LLC
Also Called: Sacramento Post-Acute
5255 Hemlock St (95841-3017)
PHONE.................................916 331-4590
EMP: 99 EST: 2011
SALES (est): 15.61MM
SALES (corp-wide): 1.53B Privately Held
Web: www.sacpostacute.com
SIC: 8051 Convalescent home with continuous nursing care
HQ: Hudson River Opco, Llc
262 N University Ave
Farmington UT
801 447-9829

(P-15611)
ORANGE COAST CARE INC
Also Called: New Orange Hills
5017 E Chapman Ave (92869-4211)
PHONE.................................714 997-7090
Darian Dahl, Pr
EMP: 73 EST: 2018
SALES (est): 20.77MM Privately Held
Web: www.orangecoastpa.com
SIC: 8051 Convalescent home with continuous nursing care

(P-15612)
ORANGE HLTHCARE WLLNESS CNTRE
920 W La Veta Ave (92868-4302)
PHONE.................................714 633-3568
EMP: 110 EST: 2009
SALES (est): 9.39MM Privately Held
Web: www.orangerehabilitation.com
SIC: 8051 Convalescent home with continuous nursing care

(P-15613)
ORCHARD - POST ACUTE CARE CTR
12385 Washington Blvd (90606-2502)
PHONE.................................562 693-7701
Rich Jorgensen, Prin
EMP: 97 EST: 2011
SALES (est): 13.91MM
SALES (corp-wide): 3.03B Publicly Held
Web: www.theorchardpostacute.com
SIC: 8051 Convalescent home with continuous nursing care
PA: The Ensign Group Inc
29222 Rncho Vejo Rd Ste 1
San Juan Capistrano CA
949 487-9500

(P-15614)
OUR LADY FATIMA VILLA INC
20400 Saratoga Los Gatos Rd (95070-5997)
PHONE.................................408 741-2950
Admiral Bella Mahoney, Prin
EMP: 90 EST: 1945
SQ FT: 45,123
SALES (est): 9.43MM Privately Held
Web: www.fatimavilla.org
SIC: 8051 Skilled nursing care facilities

(P-15615)
PACIFIC PALMS HEALTHCARE LLC
Empress Rehabilitation Center
1020 Termino Ave (90804-4123)
PHONE.................................562 433-6791
EMP: 88

PRODUCTS & SERVICES SECTION
8051 - Skilled Nursing Care Facilities (P-15637)

SALES (corp-wide): 9.04MM **Privately Held**
Web: www.ppsnf.com
SIC: **8051** Convalescent home with continuous nursing care
PA: Pacific Palms Healthcare, Llc
1020 Termino Ave
Long Beach CA
562 433-6791

(P-15616)
PALM HAVEN NURSING & REHAB LLC
Also Called: Palm Haven Care Center
4104 Fern Grove Ct (95356-9370)
PHONE.....................209 823-1788
EMP: 104 EST: 1962
SALES (est): 5.85MM **Privately Held**
SIC: **8051** Convalescent home with continuous nursing care

(P-15617)
PALMCREST GRAND CARE CTR INC
3501 Cedar Ave (90807-3809)
PHONE.....................562 595-4551
William Nelson, *Pr*
EMP: 99 EST: 2004
SALES (est): 4.05MM **Privately Held**
Web: www.palmcrestgrandretirement.com
SIC: **8051** Skilled nursing care facilities

(P-15618)
PALMCREST MEDALLION CONVALESC
3355 Pacific Pl (90806-1239)
PHONE.....................562 595-4336
FAX: 562 424-6499
EMP: 85
SQ FT: 30,000
SALES (est): 1.71MM **Privately Held**
SIC: **8051** Skilled nursing care facilities

(P-15619)
PARKVIEW JLIAN CNVLESCENT HOSP
1801 Julian Ave (93304-6419)
PHONE.....................661 831-9150
Ligia Denham, *VP*
Douglas Rice, *
EMP: 130 EST: 1971
SQ FT: 8,000
SALES (est): 8.35MM **Privately Held**
Web: www.parkviewjulian-snf.com
SIC: **8051** Convalescent home with continuous nursing care

(P-15620)
PARKVIEW JULIAN LLC
Also Called: Parkview Julian Healthcare Ctr
1801 Julian Ave (93304-6419)
PHONE.....................661 831-9150
David Levy, *Managing Member*
Moshe Frankel, *Managing Member*
EMP: 150 EST: 2017
SALES (est): 7.29MM **Privately Held**
SIC: **8051** Convalescent home with continuous nursing care

(P-15621)
PASADENA HOSPITAL ASSN LTD
Also Called: Huntington Extended Care Ctr
716 S Fair Oaks Ave (91105-2618)
PHONE.....................626 397-3322
Ken Hoff, *Mgr*
EMP: 386
SALES (corp-wide): 688.61MM **Privately Held**
Web: www.huntingtonhealth.org
SIC: **8051** Skilled nursing care facilities
PA: Pasadena Hospital Association, Ltd.
100 W California Blvd
Pasadena CA
626 397-5000

(P-15622)
PASADENA MADOWS NURSING CTR LP
150 Bellefontaine St (91105-3102)
PHONE.....................626 796-1103
Pnina Graff, *Pt*
EMP: 99 EST: 2012
SALES (est): 5.08MM **Privately Held**
Web: www.pasadenameadows.com
SIC: **8051** Skilled nursing care facilities

(P-15623)
PATER DIGNITAS INC
Also Called: Carmel Hills Care Center
23795 Holman Hwy (93940-5903)
PHONE.....................831 624-1875
Robert Bowersox, *Pr*
Kim Bowersox, *
EMP: 90 EST: 2004
SQ FT: 30,000
SALES (est): 11.03MM **Privately Held**
Web: www.carmelhillscarecenter.com
SIC: **8051** Convalescent home with continuous nursing care

(P-15624)
PCI CARE VENTURE I
Also Called: Prestige Asssted Lving At Lncs
43454 30th St W Ofc (93536-5307)
PHONE.....................661 949-2177
Pat Elliott, *Mgr*
EMP: 77
SALES (corp-wide): 381.63MM **Privately Held**
SIC: **8051** Skilled nursing care facilities
HQ: Pci Care Venture I
7700 Ne Parkway Dr # 300
Vancouver WA

(P-15625)
PCI CARE VENTURE I
Also Called: Prestige Asssted Lving At Vsli
3120 W Caldwell Ave (93277-7003)
PHONE.....................559 735-0828
Helen Hurley, *Mgr*
EMP: 65
SQ FT: 42,457
SALES (corp-wide): 381.63MM **Privately Held**
SIC: **8051** Skilled nursing care facilities
HQ: Pci Care Venture I
7700 Ne Parkway Dr # 300
Vancouver WA

(P-15626)
PENNANT GROUP INC
Also Called: Mainplace Senior Living
1800 W Culver Ave (92868-4127)
PHONE.....................714 978-2534
EMP: 442
SALES (corp-wide): 473.24MM **Publicly Held**
Web: www.pennantgroup.com
SIC: **8051** Convalescent home with continuous nursing care
PA: The Pennant Group Inc
1675 E Riverside Dr # 150
Eagle ID
208 506-6100

(P-15627)
PINERS NURSING HOME INC
Also Called: Piner's Medical Supply
1800 Pueblo Ave (94558-4751)
PHONE.....................707 224-7925
Gary Piner, *Pr*
Starr Piner, *
EMP: 65 EST: 1944
SQ FT: 20,000
SALES (est): 8.47MM **Privately Held**
Web: www.pinersnursinghome.com
SIC: **8051** 4119 5999 Convalescent home with continuous nursing care; Ambulance service; Medical apparatus and supplies

(P-15628)
PLEASANT HILLIDENCE OPCO LLC
Also Called: Pleasant Hill Post Acute
1625 Oak Park Blvd (94523-4487)
PHONE.....................925 935-5222
Jason Murray, *Prin*
Mark Hancock, *
EMP: 208 EST: 2016
SALES (est): 18.79MM
SALES (corp-wide): 1.53B **Privately Held**
Web: www.pleasanthillpa.com
SIC: **8051** Convalescent home with continuous nursing care
HQ: Providence Group North, Llc
262 N University Ave
Farmington UT
801 447-9829

(P-15629)
PLUM HEALTHCARE GROUP LLC
100 E San Marcos Blvd Ste 200 (92069-2986)
PHONE.....................760 471-0388
EMP: 223 EST: 1999
SALES (est): 45.68MM
SALES (corp-wide): 1.53B **Privately Held**
Web: www.plumhealthcaregroup.com
SIC: **8051** Skilled nursing care facilities
HQ: Bay Bridge Capital Partners, Llc
262 N University Ave
Farmington UT
801 447-9829

(P-15630)
POINT LOMA CONVALESCENT HOSP
3202 Duke St (92110-5401)
PHONE.....................619 224-4141
Samuel Horowitz, *Pt*
Reena Horowitz, *Genl Pt*
Joseph Fisch, *Genl Pt*
J Axelrod, *Ltd Pt*
B Crow, *Ltd Pt*
EMP: 61 EST: 1963
SQ FT: 25,402
SALES (est): 10.05MM **Privately Held**
SIC: **8051** Convalescent home with continuous nursing care

(P-15631)
POINT LOMA RHBLITATION CTR LLC
Also Called: Pavilion At Ocean Point, The
3202 Duke St (92110-5401)
PHONE.....................619 308-3200
EMP: 130 EST: 2006
SQ FT: 30,895
SALES (est): 10.02MM **Privately Held**
Web: www.pointlomarehab.com
SIC: **8051** Convalescent home with continuous nursing care

(P-15632)
POMERADO OPERATIONS LLC
Also Called: BOULDER CREEK POST ACUTE
12696 Monte Vista Rd (92064-2500)
PHONE.....................858 487-6242
Covey Christensen, *CEO*
Travis Greenwood, *
Leland Bruce, *
James Gamett, *
EMP: 99 EST: 2014
SALES (est): 18.52MM **Privately Held**
Web: www.bouldercreekpa.care
SIC: **8051** Convalescent home with continuous nursing care

(P-15633)
POWERS PARK HEALTHCARE INC
Also Called: Channel Islands Post Acute
3880 Via Lucero (93110-1605)
PHONE.....................805 687-6651
Cory Monette, *Ex Dir*
EMP: 99 EST: 2019
SALES (est): 17.3MM **Privately Held**
Web: www.channelislandspa.com
SIC: **8051** Convalescent home with continuous nursing care

(P-15634)
RAMONA CARE INC
Also Called: Ramona Nrsing Rhbilitation Ctr
11900 Ramona Blvd (91732-2314)
PHONE.....................626 442-5721
Michael Hyer, *Pr*
Victor Lundquist, *
Jeffrey Daly, *
EMP: 140 EST: 1990
SQ FT: 35,000
SALES (est): 9.14MM **Privately Held**
Web: www.ramonarehab.com
SIC: **8051** Convalescent home with continuous nursing care

(P-15635)
REHABLTION CNTRE OF BVRLY HLLS
580 S San Vicente Blvd (90048-4621)
PHONE.....................323 782-1500
Eldon Teper, *Pr*
EMP: 200 EST: 1998
SALES (est): 16.62MM **Privately Held**
Web: www.rehabcentre.com
SIC: **8051** Convalescent home with continuous nursing care

(P-15636)
REHABLTTION CTR OF ORNGE CNTY
9021 Knott Ave (90620-4138)
PHONE.....................714 826-2330
Peter Madigan, *Pr*
Robert Nelson, *
EMP: 125 EST: 1967
SALES (est): 11.8MM **Privately Held**
SIC: **8051** 8059 Convalescent home with continuous nursing care; Rest home, with health care

(P-15637)
RHF PLYMOUTH TOWER
Also Called: Plymouth Tower
3401 Lemon St Ofc (92501-2817)
PHONE.....................951 248-0456
Wes Jones, *Admn*
EMP: 65 EST: 2004
SALES (est): 2.28MM **Privately Held**
SIC: **8051** Convalescent home with continuous nursing care

8051 - Skilled Nursing Care Facilities (P-15638)

(P-15638)
RIDGECREST HEALTHCARE INC
5808 Monterey Rd (90042-4926)
PHONE....................760 446-3591
Kristine Parel, *Prin*
EMP: 98
Web: www.windsorridgecrest.com
SIC: 8051 Convalescent home with continuous nursing care
PA: Ridgecrest Healthcare, Inc.
1131 N China Lake Blvd
Ridgecrest CA

(P-15639)
RIVER BEND HOLDINGS LLC
Also Called: River Bend Nursing Center
2215 Oakmont Way (95691-3022)
PHONE....................916 371-1890
Bryan Boeher, *
Richard Martin, *
EMP: 153 **EST:** 1968
SQ FT: 34,000
SALES (est): 9.9MM **Privately Held**
Web: www.riverbendnursingcenter.com
SIC: 8051 Convalescent home with continuous nursing care

(P-15640)
RIVERA SANATARIUM INC
Also Called: Colonial Gardens Nursing Home
7246 Rosemead Blvd (90660-4010)
P.O. Box 2098 (90662-2098)
PHONE....................562 949-2591
Elizabeth Stephens, *Pr*
Kent Stephens, *
EMP: 86 **EST:** 1959
SQ FT: 30,000
SALES (est): 8.72MM **Privately Held**
SIC: 8051 Convalescent home with continuous nursing care

(P-15641)
RIVERSIDE CARE INC
Also Called: Valencia Gardens Health Care Center
4301 Caroline Ct (92506-2902)
PHONE....................951 683-7111
Ted Holt, *Pr*
Jenny Ortiz, *
Spencer E Olsen, *
EMP: 130 **EST:** 1971
SALES (est): 10.92MM **Privately Held**
Web: www.valenciagardenshealth.com
SIC: 8051 Convalescent home with continuous nursing care
PA: North American Client Services, Inc.
25910 Acero Ste 350
Mission Viejo CA

(P-15642)
RIVERSIDE EQUITIES LLC
Also Called: SUN MAR HEALTH CARE
8487 Magnolia Ave (92504-3222)
PHONE....................951 688-2222
Frank Johnson, *CEO*
Irving Bauman, *
EMP: 372 **EST:** 2008
SALES (est): 8.75MM **Privately Held**
Web: www.missioncarecenter.com
SIC: 8051 Convalescent home with continuous nursing care
PA: Sun Mar Management Services
3050 Saturn St Ste 201
Brea CA

(P-15643)
RIVIERA NURSING & CONVA
Also Called: Riviera Health Care Center
8203 Telegraph Rd (90660-4905)
PHONE....................562 806-2576
Morris Weiss, *Pr*
Bessie Weiss, *
EMP: 118 **EST:** 1966
SQ FT: 60,000
SALES (est): 9.14MM **Privately Held**
Web: www.rivierahealthcare.com
SIC: 8051 8059 Convalescent home with continuous nursing care; Convalescent home

(P-15644)
ROWLAND CONVALESCENT HOSP INC
Also Called: ROWLAND, THE
330 W Rowland St (91723-2941)
PHONE....................626 967-2741
Anthony Kalomas, *Pr*
EMP: 100 **EST:** 1979
SQ FT: 30,000
SALES (est): 6.92MM **Privately Held**
Web: www.rowlandconvalescent.com
SIC: 8051 Convalescent home with continuous nursing care

(P-15645)
ROYAL TERRACE HEALTHCARE LLC
1340 Highland Ave (91010-2520)
PHONE....................626 256-4654
EMP: 60 **EST:** 2003
SALES (est): 5.22MM **Privately Held**
Web: www.royalterracehealth.com
SIC: 8051 Convalescent home with continuous nursing care

(P-15646)
RRT ENTERPRISES LP (PA)
Also Called: Country Vlla Mar Vsta Nrsing C
3966 Marcasel Ave (90066-4616)
PHONE....................310 397-2372
Stephen Reissman, *Genl Pt*
Diane Reissman, *Genl Pt*
EMP: 125 **EST:** 1972
SQ FT: 18,000
SALES (est): 16.4MM
SALES (corp-wide): 16.4MM **Privately Held**
SIC: 8051 Skilled nursing care facilities

(P-15647)
RRT ENTERPRISES LP
Also Called: RRT ENTERPRISES LP
855 N Fairfax Ave (90046-7207)
PHONE....................323 653-1521
Stephen Reissman, *Brnch Mgr*
EMP: 225
SALES (corp-wide): 16.4MM **Privately Held**
SIC: 8051 Skilled nursing care facilities
PA: Rrt Enterprises L.P.
3966 Marcasel Ave
Los Angeles CA
310 397-2372

(P-15648)
SACRAMENTO OPERATING CO LP
Also Called: Double Tree Past Acute
7400 24th St (95822-5350)
PHONE....................916 422-4825
Kenneth Tabler, *Pt*
EMP: 120 **EST:** 2006
SALES (est): 7.6MM **Privately Held**
Web: www.doubletreepa.com
SIC: 8051 Extended care facility

(P-15649)
SAGEBRUSH HEALTHCARE INC
Also Called: Fairfield Post-Acute Rehab
1255 Travis Blvd (94533-4801)
PHONE....................707 425-0623
Steve Hendrickson, *Admn*
Joan Wandyke, *
EMP: 69 **EST:** 1971
SALES (est): 14.01MM **Privately Held**
Web: www.fairfieldrehab.net
SIC: 8051 Convalescent home with continuous nursing care

(P-15650)
SAINT CLAIRES NURSING CTR LLC
6248 66th Ave (95823-2733)
PHONE....................916 392-4440
Kathryn J Hill, *Pr*
Michael Maderas, *
EMP: 124 **EST:** 1983
SALES (est): 4.75MM **Privately Held**
SIC: 8051 Skilled nursing care facilities

(P-15651)
SAN DIEGO HEBREW HOMES (PA)
Also Called: LEICHTAG ASSISTED LIVING
211 Saxony Rd (92024-2721)
PHONE....................760 942-2695
Yehudi Gaffen, *Ch*
Betty Byrnes, *Vice Chairman**
Mitchell Berner, *Vice Chairman**
Pam Ferris, *
Robin P Israel, *
EMP: 180 **EST:** 1944
SQ FT: 219,000
SALES (est): 21.03MM
SALES (corp-wide): 21.03MM **Privately Held**
Web: www.seacrestvillage.org
SIC: 8051 8059 6513 Skilled nursing care facilities; Rest home, with health care; Retirement hotel operation

(P-15652)
SAN LEANDRO HLTH CARE CTR INC
Also Called: San Leandro Healthcare Center
368 Juana Ave (94577-4811)
PHONE....................510 357-4015
Pat Poddatoori, *Pr*
EMP: 70 **EST:** 2003
SALES (est): 8.56MM **Privately Held**
Web: www.sanleandro.org
SIC: 8051 Convalescent home with continuous nursing care

(P-15653)
SAN PEDRO CONVALESCENT HM INC
Also Called: Los Palos Convalescent Hosp
1430 W 6th St (90732-3503)
PHONE....................310 832-6431
Celia Valdomar, *Pr*
EMP: 90 **EST:** 1963
SQ FT: 10,000
SALES (est): 8.28MM **Privately Held**
Web: www.lpconv.com
SIC: 8051 Convalescent home with continuous nursing care

(P-15654)
SANTA ANITA CNVLSCENT HOSP RTR
5522 Gracewood Ave (91780)
PHONE....................626 579-0310
Martin J Weiss, *Pr*
Jacob Kasirer, *
Ronni J Mayer, *
EMP: 150 **EST:** 1968
SQ FT: 88,615
SALES (est): 24.63MM
SALES (corp-wide): 74.01MM **Privately Held**
Web: www.santaanita-convalescent.com
SIC: 8051 Convalescent home with continuous nursing care
PA: Golden State Health Centers, Inc.
13347 Ventura Blvd
Sherman Oaks CA
818 385-3200

(P-15655)
SANTA ROSAIDENCE OPCO LLC
Also Called: Santa Rosa Post Acute
4650 Hoen Ave (95405-9407)
PHONE....................707 546-0471
Jason Murray, *Prin*
Mark Hancock, *
EMP: 135 **EST:** 2016
SALES (est): 14.64MM
SALES (corp-wide): 1.53B **Privately Held**
Web: www.santarosapostacute.com
SIC: 8051 Skilled nursing care facilities
HQ: Providence Group Wine Country, Llc
262 N University Ave
Farmington UT
801 447-9829

(P-15656)
SCOTT ST SNIOR HSING CMPLEX IN
Also Called: RHODA GOLDMAN PLAZA
2180 Post St (94115-6013)
PHONE....................415 345-5083
Marrianne Nannesthad, *Dir*
Simeon Meyer, *
EMP: 105 **EST:** 2000
SQ FT: 195,000
SALES (est): 14.8MM **Privately Held**
Web: www.rgplaza.org
SIC: 8051 Skilled nursing care facilities

(P-15657)
SEA BREEZE HEALTH CARE INC
7781 Garfield Ave (92648-2026)
PHONE....................714 847-9671
Seth Braithwaite, *Pr*
Victor Lundquist, *
Jeffrey Daly, *
EMP: 132 **EST:** 2003
SQ FT: 14,895
SALES (est): 7.52MM **Privately Held**
Web: www.beachsidenursing.com
SIC: 8051 Convalescent home with continuous nursing care

(P-15658)
SEACREST CONVALESCENT HOSP INC
1416 W 6th St (90732-3550)
PHONE....................310 833-3526
Cecelia Valdomar, *Pr*
Cecelia D Valdomar, *
David B David, *
Joy Nacionales, *
Jose Valdomar, *
EMP: 70 **EST:** 1962
SALES (est): 5.83MM **Privately Held**
Web: www.scconv.com
SIC: 8051 Convalescent home with continuous nursing care

(P-15659)
SELA HEALTHCARE INC (PA)
Also Called: Holiday Manor Care Center
867 E 11th St (91786-4867)
PHONE....................909 985-1981

PRODUCTS & SERVICES SECTION

8051 - Skilled Nursing Care Facilities (P-15679)

Philip Weinberger, *CEO*
Marylynn Mahan, *
EMP: 140 **EST:** 2002
SQ FT: 60,000
SALES (est): 13.3MM
SALES (corp-wide): 13.3MM **Privately Held**
SIC: 8051 Skilled nursing care facilities

(P-15660)
SELA HEALTHCARE INC
Also Called: Holiday Manor Care Center
20554 Roscoe Blvd (91306-1746)
PHONE..................................818 341-9800
Victorio Ocbena Sosing, *Prin*
EMP: 310
SALES (corp-wide): 13.3MM **Privately Held**
SIC: 8051 Convalescent home with continuous nursing care
PA: Sela Healthcare, Inc.
867 E 11th St
Upland CA
909 985-1981

(P-15661)
SHADOW HLLS CNVLSCENT HOSP INC
10158 Sunland Blvd (91040-1651)
PHONE..................................818 352-4438
EMP: 67 **EST:** 1968
SQ FT: 13,000
SALES (est): 2.22MM **Privately Held**
SIC: 8051 Convalescent home with continuous nursing care

(P-15662)
SHARON CARE CENTER LLC
Also Called: GENESIS HEALTHCARE CORPORATION
8167 W 3rd St (90048-4314)
PHONE..................................323 655-2023
Isaac Shabat, *Ex Dir*
EMP: 94 **EST:** 2003
SALES (est): 12.06MM
SALES (corp-wide): 5.86B **Publicly Held**
Web: www.sharoncarecenter.com
SIC: 8051 8059 Skilled nursing care facilities ; Convalescent home
HQ: Genesis Hc Llc
101 E State St
Kennett Square PA
610 444-6350

(P-15663)
SHATTUCK HEALTH CARE INC
Also Called: ELMWOOD CARE CENTER
2829 Shattuck Ave (94705-1037)
PHONE..................................510 665-2800
Pat Podatorri, *Pr*
Terry Mcgregor, *VP*
EMP: 97 **EST:** 2005
SQ FT: 34,404
SALES (est): 11.07MM **Privately Held**
Web: www.elmwoodnursingrehab.com
SIC: 8051 Convalescent home with continuous nursing care

(P-15664)
SHERWOOD OAKS ENTERPRISES INC
Also Called: Sherwood Oaks Health Center
130 Dana St (95437-4506)
PHONE..................................707 964-6333
Melanie Reding, *Pr*
Joe Reding, *
EMP: 90 **EST:** 1975
SQ FT: 19,000
SALES (est): 9.79MM **Privately Held**
Web: www.sherwoodoakshealthcenter.com
SIC: 8051 Convalescent home with continuous nursing care

(P-15665)
SHIELDS NURSING CENTERS INC (PA)
Also Called: Shields
606 Alfred Nobel Dr (94547-1834)
EMP: 150 **EST:** 1978
SQ FT: 6,100
SALES (est): 12.76MM
SALES (corp-wide): 12.76MM **Privately Held**
Web: www.shieldsnursingcenters.com
SIC: 8051 Convalescent home with continuous nursing care

(P-15666)
SIERRA VIEW HOMES
Also Called: Sierra View Hmes Rsdntial Care
1155 E Springfield Ave (93654-3225)
PHONE..................................559 637-2256
Vito Genna, *Ex Dir*
EMP: 140 **EST:** 1960
SQ FT: 63,600
SALES (est): 8.82MM **Privately Held**
Web: www.sierraview.org
SIC: 8051 8059 6513 Skilled nursing care facilities; Personal care home, with health care; Apartment hotel operation

(P-15667)
SILVERADO SENIOR LIVING INC (PA)
6400 Oak Cyn Ste 200 (92618-5233)
PHONE..................................949 240-7200
George L Chapman, *CEO*
Loren B Shook, *
Stephen Winner, *
Thomas Croal, *
Kristina Hulsey, *CCO*
EMP: 65 **EST:** 1996
SQ FT: 65,000
SALES (est): 130.57K
SALES (corp-wide): 130.57K **Privately Held**
Web: www.silverado.com
SIC: 8051 Skilled nursing care facilities

(P-15668)
SILVERADO SENIOR LIVING INC
Also Called: Newport Mesa Memory Care Cmnty
350 W Bay St (92627-2020)
PHONE..................................949 945-0189
Michelle Egrer, *Prin*
EMP: 71
SQ FT: 20,331
SALES (corp-wide): 130.57K **Privately Held**
Web: www.silverado.com
SIC: 8051 Skilled nursing care facilities
PA: Senior Silverado Living Inc
6400 Oak Cyn Ste 200
Irvine CA
949 240-7200

(P-15669)
SILVERADO SENIOR LIVING INC
Also Called: Huntington Memory Care Cmnty
1118 N Stoneman Ave (91801-1007)
PHONE..................................626 872-3941
Vida Gwin, *Admn*
EMP: 90
SALES (corp-wide): 130.57K **Privately Held**
Web: www.silverado.com
SIC: 8051 Skilled nursing care facilities
PA: Senior Silverado Living Inc
6400 Oak Cyn Ste 200
Irvine CA
949 240-7200

(P-15670)
SILVERADO SENIOR LIVING INC
Also Called: Escondido Memory Care Cmnty
1500 Borden Rd (92026-2373)
PHONE..................................760 456-5137
Jean Busher, *Admn*
EMP: 76
SQ FT: 33,000
SALES (corp-wide): 130.57K **Privately Held**
Web: www.silverado.com
SIC: 8051 Skilled nursing care facilities
PA: Senior Silverado Living Inc
6400 Oak Cyn Ste 200
Irvine CA
949 240-7200

(P-15671)
SILVERADO SENIOR LIVING INC
Also Called: Encinitas Memory Care Cmnty
335 Saxony Rd (92024-2723)
PHONE..................................760 270-9917
Dina Trester, *Dir*
EMP: 62
SALES (corp-wide): 130.57K **Privately Held**
Web: www.silverado.com
SIC: 8051 Skilled nursing care facilities
PA: Senior Silverado Living Inc
6400 Oak Cyn Ste 200
Irvine CA
949 240-7200

(P-15672)
SILVERADO SENIOR LIVING INC
Also Called: Calabasas Memory Care Cmnty
25100 Calabasas Rd (91302-1435)
PHONE..................................818 746-2583
Rachel Dardeau, *Admn*
EMP: 76
SALES (corp-wide): 130.57K **Privately Held**
Web: www.silverado.com
SIC: 8051 Skilled nursing care facilities
PA: Senior Silverado Living Inc
6400 Oak Cyn Ste 200
Irvine CA
949 240-7200

(P-15673)
SILVERADO SENIOR LIVING INC
Also Called: Beverly Pl Memory Care Cmnty
330 N Hayworth Ave (90048-2702)
PHONE..................................323 984-7313
EMP: 62
SALES (corp-wide): 130.57K **Privately Held**
Web: www.silverado.com
SIC: 8051 Skilled nursing care facilities
PA: Senior Silverado Living Inc
6400 Oak Cyn Ste 200
Irvine CA
949 240-7200

(P-15674)
SKILLED HEALTHCARE LLC (DH)
27442 Portola Pkwy Ste 200 (92610-2822)
PHONE..................................949 282-5800
Richard Edwards, *
EMP: 131 **EST:** 1963
SQ FT: 22,000
SALES (est): 644.99MM **Privately Held**
Web: www.skilledhealthcare.com
SIC: 8051 6513 5122 Convalescent home with continuous nursing care; Retirement hotel operation; Drugs, proprietaries, and sundries
HQ: Genesis Healthcare Llc
101 E State St
Kennett Square PA

(P-15675)
SKYLINE HLTHCARE WLLNESS CTR L
Also Called: SKYLINE HEALTHCARE CENTER
3032 Rowena Ave (90039-2005)
PHONE..................................323 665-1185
Bernon Aguilar, *Admn*
Sharrod Brooks, *
EMP: 99 **EST:** 2010
SALES (est): 7.69MM **Privately Held**
Web: www.skylinehc.com
SIC: 8051 Convalescent home with continuous nursing care

(P-15676)
SOLEDAD CMNTY HLTH CARE DST FN
Also Called: Soledad Medical Group
612 Main St (93960-2533)
PHONE..................................831 678-2462
Steven Pritt, *CEO*
Ralph Sarmento, *
Jack Franscioni, *
Rosemary Guidotti, *
EMP: 80 **EST:** 1948
SALES (est): 21.45K **Privately Held**
Web: www.edenvalleycare.com
SIC: 8051 Skilled nursing care facilities

(P-15677)
SOLVANG LUTHERAN HOME INC
Also Called: Atterdag Village of Solvang
636 Atterdag Rd (93463-2687)
PHONE..................................805 688-3263
EMP: 120 **EST:** 1951
SALES (est): 14.12MM **Privately Held**
Web: www.peoplewhocare.com
SIC: 8051 8052 6513 Skilled nursing care facilities; Intermediate care facilities; Apartment building operators

(P-15678)
SPRING VALLEY POST ACUTE LLC
14973 Hesperia Rd (92395-3923)
PHONE..................................760 245-6477
David Johnson, *Managing Member*
Thomas Chambers, *Managing Member**
Matheson Chambers, *Managing Member**
EMP: 200 **EST:** 2013
SALES (est): 20.09MM **Privately Held**
Web: www.springvalleypostacute.com
SIC: 8051 Convalescent home with continuous nursing care

(P-15679)
SSC CARMICHAEL OPERATING CO LP
Also Called: Mission Crmchael Hlthcare Ctr
3630 Mission Ave (95608-2933)
PHONE..................................916 485-4793
Anne Gilles, *Admn*
Wayne M Sanner, *Pt*
EMP: 560 **EST:** 2004
SALES (est): 14.34MM
SALES (corp-wide): 1.33B **Privately Held**
Web: www.missioncarmichael.com
SIC: 8051 Convalescent home with continuous nursing care
HQ: Savaseniorcare, Llc

8051 - Skilled Nursing Care Facilities (P-15680)

300 Colonial Center Pkwy # 100
Roswell GA
770 829-5100

(P-15680)
SSC SAN JOSE OPERATING CO LP
Also Called: SAVA SENIOR CARE
340 Northlake Dr. (95117-1251)
　PHONE.............................408 249-0344
　EMP: 537 EST: 2005
　SALES (est): 9.18MM
　SALES (corp-wide): 1.33B Privately Held
　Web: www.courtyardcare.com
　SIC: 8051 Convalescent home with continuous nursing care
　HQ: Savaseniorcare, Llc
　　300 Colonial Center Pkwy # 100
　　Roswell GA
　　770 829-5100

(P-15681)
STERLING CARE INC
Also Called: Paradise Valley Manor
2575 E 8th St (91950-2913)
　PHONE.............................619 470-6700
　Kenneth M Funk, Prin
　EMP: 118
　SALES (est): 1.53MM
　SALES (corp-wide): 1.53B Privately Held
　SIC: 8051 Convalescent home with continuous nursing care
　PA: Providence Group, Inc.
　　262 N University Ave
　　Farmington UT
　　801 447-9829

(P-15682)
STJOHN GOD RTIREMENT CARE CTR
2468 S St Andrews Pl (90018-2042)
　PHONE.............................323 731-0641
　Admiral Michael Bessimer, Prin
　Michael Bessimer, Admn
　EMP: 200 EST: 1942
　SQ FT: 99,392
　SALES (est): 24.43MM Privately Held
　Web: www.stjogrcc.org
　SIC: 8051 8052 Skilled nursing care facilities ; Intermediate care facilities

(P-15683)
STONEBROOK CONVALESCENT CENTER
Also Called: Stonebrook Health Care Center
4367 Concord Blvd (94521-1100)
　PHONE.............................925 689-7457
　James D Hightower, Pr
　EMP: 117 EST: 1990
　SQ FT: 44,000
　SALES (est): 14.74MM Privately Held
　Web: www.stonebrookhc.com
　SIC: 8051 Convalescent home with continuous nursing care
　PA: Healthmark Services Inc
　　217 Lakewood Rd
　　Van Buren AR

(P-15684)
SUMMERVILLE AT HAZEL CREEK LLC
Also Called: Hazel Creek Assisted Living
6125 Hazel Ave (95662-4558)
　PHONE.............................916 988-7901
　Lonnie Irvine, Pr
　EMP: 211 EST: 2006
　SALES (est): 3.68MM
　SALES (corp-wide): 2.83B Publicly Held
　SIC: 8051 Skilled nursing care facilities
　HQ: Emeritus Corporation
　　6737 W Wa St Ste 2300
　　Milwaukee WI

(P-15685)
SUMMIT TRAIL HLTH HOLDINGS LLC
29222 Rancho Viejo Rd Ste 127 (92675)
　PHONE.............................949 487-9500
　EMP: 74 EST: 2019
　SALES (est): 3.78MM
　SALES (corp-wide): 3.03B Publicly Held
　SIC: 8051 Skilled nursing care facilities
　PA: The Ensign Group Inc
　　29222 Rncho Vejo Rd Ste 1
　　San Juan Capistrano CA
　　949 487-9500

(P-15686)
SUNBRDGE BRTTANY RHBLTTION CTR
Also Called: American Rver Care Rhblttion C
3900 Garfield Ave (95608-6647)
　PHONE.............................916 484-1393
　Andrew Turner, Pr
　Anne Butler, *
　EMP: 2884 EST: 1986
　SALES (est): 40.3MM
　SALES (corp-wide): 5.86B Publicly Held
　Web: www.americanrivercc.com
　SIC: 8051 8069 Skilled nursing care facilities ; Specialty hospitals, except psychiatric
　HQ: Regency Health Services, Inc.
　　5100 Sun Ave Ne
　　Albuquerque NM
　　505 821-3355

(P-15687)
SUNBRDGE PRDISE RHBLTTION CTR
Also Called: Pine View Center
8777 Skyway (95969-2110)
　PHONE.............................530 872-3200
　Annie Buerhaus, Brnch Mgr
　EMP: 5162
　SALES (corp-wide): 5.86B Publicly Held
　SIC: 8051 8049 Convalescent home with continuous nursing care; Speech therapist
　HQ: Sunbridge Paradise Rehabilitation Center, Llc
　　101 Sun Ave Ne
　　Albuquerque NM
　　530 872-3200

(P-15688)
SUNBRIDGE CARE ENTPS W LLC
Also Called: Kingsburg Center
1101 Stroud Ave (93631-1016)
　PHONE.............................559 897-5881
　Ron Kennersly, Mgr
　EMP: 160
　SALES (corp-wide): 5.86B Publicly Held
　SIC: 8051 Convalescent home with continuous nursing care
　HQ: Sunbridge Care Enterprises West, Llc
　　101 Sun Ave Ne
　　Albuquerque NM
　　530 938-4429

(P-15689)
SUNNYVALE HEALTHCARE CENTER
Also Called: Sunnyvale Health Care
1291 S Bernardo Ave (94087-2060)
　PHONE.............................408 245-8070
　Hermina Chavez, CEO
　Mario Chavez, *
　John Chavez, *
　Vanessa Chavez, *
　EMP: 66 EST: 1969
　SQ FT: 26,679
　SALES (est): 7.68MM Privately Held
　Web: www.sunnyvalepostacute.com
　SIC: 8051 Convalescent home with continuous nursing care

(P-15690)
SUNRISE SENIOR LIVING LLC
Also Called: Sunrise of Claremont
2053 N Towne Ave (91711-2427)
　PHONE.............................909 398-4688
　Jenny Ito, Dir
　EMP: 69
　SQ FT: 38,139
　SALES (corp-wide): 2.92B Privately Held
　Web: www.sunriseseniorliving.com
　SIC: 8051 8361 Skilled nursing care facilities ; Residential care
　HQ: Sunrise Senior Living, Llc
　　7902 Westpark Dr
　　Mc Lean VA

(P-15691)
SUNRISE SENIOR LIVING LLC
Also Called: Sunrise At Canyon Crest
5265 Chapala Dr (92507-5907)
P.O. Box 900 (37605-0900)
　PHONE.............................951 686-6075
　Kay Russell, Mgr
　EMP: 67
　SALES (corp-wide): 2.92B Privately Held
　Web: www.sunriseseniorliving.com
　SIC: 8051 Skilled nursing care facilities
　HQ: Sunrise Senior Living, Llc
　　7902 Westpark Dr
　　Mc Lean VA

(P-15692)
SUNRISE SENIOR LIVING LLC
Also Called: Sunrise of Mission Viejo
26151 Country Club Dr (92691-5907)
　PHONE.............................949 582-2010
　Lynn Piglao, Dir
　EMP: 61
　SALES (corp-wide): 2.92B Privately Held
　Web: www.sunriseseniorliving.com
　SIC: 8051 Skilled nursing care facilities
　HQ: Sunrise Senior Living, Llc
　　7902 Westpark Dr
　　Mc Lean VA

(P-15693)
SUNRISE SENIOR LIVING LLC
Also Called: Sunrise At Bonita
3302 Bonita Rd (91910-3207)
　PHONE.............................619 470-2220
　Gwen Krushensky, Mgr
　EMP: 60
　SALES (corp-wide): 2.92B Privately Held
　Web: www.sunriseseniorliving.com
　SIC: 8051 8361 Skilled nursing care facilities ; Residential care
　HQ: Sunrise Senior Living, Llc
　　7902 Westpark Dr
　　Mc Lean VA

(P-15694)
SUNRISE SENIOR LIVING LLC
Also Called: Sunrise of Woodland Hills
5501 Newcastle Ave Apt 130 (91316-2147)
　PHONE.............................818 346-9046
　Tom Colomaria, Mgr
　EMP: 67
　SALES (corp-wide): 2.92B Privately Held
　Web: www.sunriseseniorliving.com
　SIC: 8051 8361 Skilled nursing care facilities ; Residential care
　HQ: Sunrise Senior Living, Llc
　　7902 Westpark Dr
　　Mc Lean VA

(P-15695)
SUNRISE SENIOR LIVING LLC
Also Called: Sunrise of Sunnyvale
633 S Knickerbocker Dr Ste 263 (94087-1034)
　PHONE.............................408 749-8600
　Tina Bagheri, Mgr
　EMP: 61
　SALES (corp-wide): 2.92B Privately Held
　Web: www.sunriseseniorliving.com
　SIC: 8051 8361 Skilled nursing care facilities ; Aged home
　HQ: Sunrise Senior Living, Llc
　　7902 Westpark Dr
　　Mc Lean VA

(P-15696)
SUNRISE SENIOR LIVING LLC
Also Called: Sunrise of Fresno
7444 N Cedar Ave (93720-3636)
　PHONE.............................559 325-8170
　Jessica Lopez, Dir
　EMP: 60
　SALES (corp-wide): 2.92B Privately Held
　Web: www.sunriseseniorliving.com
　SIC: 8051 8361 Skilled nursing care facilities ; Residential care
　HQ: Sunrise Senior Living, Llc
　　7902 Westpark Dr
　　Mc Lean VA

(P-15697)
SUNRISE SENIOR LIVING LLC
Also Called: Sunrise At Tustin
12291 Newport Ave (92705-3205)
　PHONE.............................714 544-5959
　Kim Wiedman, Dir
　EMP: 62
　SALES (corp-wide): 2.92B Privately Held
　Web: www.sunriseseniorliving.com
　SIC: 8051 Skilled nursing care facilities
　HQ: Sunrise Senior Living, Llc
　　7902 Westpark Dr
　　Mc Lean VA

(P-15698)
SUNRISE SENIOR LIVING LLC
Also Called: Sunrise of Monterey
1110 Cass St (93940-4510)
　PHONE.............................831 643-2400
　Susan Sundell, Brnch Mgr
　EMP: 62
　SALES (corp-wide): 2.92B Privately Held
　Web: www.sunriseseniorliving.com
　SIC: 8051 8361 Skilled nursing care facilities ; Aged home
　HQ: Sunrise Senior Living, Llc
　　7902 Westpark Dr
　　Mc Lean VA

(P-15699)
SUNRISE SENIOR LIVING MGT INC
3140 El Camino Real (92008-2108)
　PHONE.............................760 720-9898
　Sylvia Segi, Prin
　EMP: 147
　SALES (corp-wide): 2.92B Privately Held
　Web: www.sunriseseniorliving.com
　SIC: 8051 Skilled nursing care facilities
　HQ: Sunrise Senior Living Management, Inc.
　　7902 Westpark Dr
　　Mc Lean VA
　　703 273-7500

PRODUCTS & SERVICES SECTION
8051 - Skilled Nursing Care Facilities (P-15720)

(P-15700)
SUTTER HEALTH
3707 Schriever Ave (95655-4202)
PHONE...............................916 454-8200
Sheila Black, *Brnch Mgr*
EMP: 60
SALES (corp-wide): 14.77B **Privately Held**
Web: www.sutterhealth.org
SIC: **8051** 8062 Skilled nursing care facilities ; General medical and surgical hospitals
PA: Sutter Health
2200 River Plaza Dr
Sacramento CA
916 733-8800

(P-15701)
SUTTER VSTING NRSE ASSN HSPICE
1651 Alvarado St (94577-2636)
PHONE...............................510 618-5277
Rosemarie Avery, *Mgr*
EMP: 147
SALES (corp-wide): 14.77B **Privately Held**
SIC: **8051** 8082 Skilled nursing care facilities ; Home health care services
HQ: Sutter Visiting Nurse Association & Hospice
1900 Powell St Ste 300
Emeryville CA
866 652-9178

(P-15702)
TETON HEALTHCARE INC
27101 Puerta Real Ste 450 (92691-8566)
PHONE...............................949 487-9500
EMP: 74 EST: 2014
SALES (est): 1.61MM
SALES (corp-wide): 3.03B **Publicly Held**
SIC: **8051** Skilled nursing care facilities
PA: The Ensign Group Inc
29222 Rncho Vejo Rd Ste 1
San Juan Capistrano CA
949 487-9500

(P-15703)
TIBURON COMMUNITY SNF LLC
Also Called: Tiburon Hills Care Center
30 Hacienda Dr (94920-1127)
PHONE...............................415 435-4554
EMP: 89 EST: 2021
SALES (est): 1.93MM
SALES (corp-wide): 1.53B **Privately Held**
SIC: **8051** Skilled nursing care facilities
PA: Providence Group, Inc.
262 N University Ave
Farmington UT
801 447-9829

(P-15704)
TLC OF BAY AREA INC
Also Called: Valley House Care Center
991 Clyde Ave (95054-1905)
P.O. Box 607 (15701-0607)
PHONE...............................408 988-7667
Marcy Colkitt, *Pr*
Merlin Davey, *
EMP: 82 EST: 1994
SALES (est): 29.71MM **Privately Held**
SIC: **8051** Convalescent home with continuous nursing care

(P-15705)
TORRANCE CARE CENTER WEST INC
4333 Torrance Blvd (90503-4401)
PHONE...............................310 370-4561
EMP: 180 EST: 1999
SALES (est): 21.96MM **Privately Held**
Web: www.torranceca.gov
SIC: **8051** Convalescent home with continuous nursing care

(P-15706)
TOWN CNTRY MNOR OF CHRSTN MSSN
555 E Memory Ln Side (92706-1753)
PHONE...............................714 547-7581
Dirk De Wolfe, *Admn*
EMP: 210 EST: 1975
SQ FT: 208,000
SALES (est): 24.69MM **Privately Held**
SIC: **8051** 8059 8052 Skilled nursing care facilities; Nursing home, except skilled and intermediate care facility; Intermediate care facilities

(P-15707)
TRINITY HEALTH SYSTEMS (PA)
Also Called: Villa Maria Care Center
14318 Ohio St (91706-2553)
PHONE...............................626 960-1971
Randal Kleis, *Pr*
EMP: 80 EST: 1989
SQ FT: 35,000
SALES (est): 11.47MM
SALES (corp-wide): 11.47MM **Privately Held**
Web: www.sierraviewcarecenter.com
SIC: **8051** Convalescent home with continuous nursing care

(P-15708)
TWILIGHT HVEN A CAL NN-PRFIT C
1717 S Winery Ave (93727-5011)
PHONE...............................559 251-8417
Gary A Karle, *CEO*
Admiral David Viancourt, *Prin*
Kenneth Karle, *
Robert Herman, *
Teresa Long, *
EMP: 95 EST: 1957
SQ FT: 70,000
SALES (est): 7.03MM **Privately Held**
Web: www.twilighthaven.com
SIC: **8051** 8052 8361 Convalescent home with continuous nursing care; Personal care facility; Rest home, with health care incidental

(P-15709)
UCSF BTTY IRENE MOORE WNS HOSP (HQ)
Also Called: Ucsf Medical Center
1855 4th St (94143-2350)
PHONE...............................415 476-1000
EMP: 63 EST: 2015
SALES (est): 166.54K
SALES (corp-wide): 534.4MM **Privately Held**
Web: womenshealth.ucsf.edu
SIC: **8051** Skilled nursing care facilities
PA: State Of California
State Capital
Sacramento CA
916 445-2841

(P-15710)
UNITED COM-SERVE
Also Called: Fountains, The
1260 Williams Way (95991-2400)
PHONE...............................530 790-3000
Ryan Dickerson, *Pr*
Chris Parker, *
EMP: 84 EST: 1990
SQ FT: 40,000
SALES (est): 25.25MM
SALES (corp-wide): 498.18MM **Privately Held**
Web: www.adventisthealth.org
SIC: **8051** Skilled nursing care facilities
PA: Freemont Rideout Health Group
989 Plumas St
Yuba City CA
530 751-4010

(P-15711)
UNITED HEALTH SYSTEMS INC
Also Called: Alderson Convalescent Hospital
124 Walnut St (95695-3137)
PHONE...............................530 662-9161
Santiago M S Miguel, *CEO*
Thomas E Mullen, *
Lynn Mullen, *
EMP: 154 EST: 1976
SQ FT: 40,000
SALES (est): 11.25MM **Privately Held**
Web: www.achwoodland.com
SIC: **8051** Convalescent home with continuous nursing care

(P-15712)
UPLAND COMMUNITY CARE INC
Also Called: ENSIGN
1221 E Arrow Hwy (91786-4911)
PHONE...............................909 985-1903
Owen Hammond, *CEO*
EMP: 162 EST: 2008
SALES (est): 28.05MM
SALES (corp-wide): 3.03B **Publicly Held**
Web: www.uplandcare.com
SIC: **8051** Convalescent home with continuous nursing care
PA: The Ensign Group Inc
29222 Rncho Vejo Rd Ste 1
San Juan Capistrano CA
949 487-9500

(P-15713)
US SKILLSERVE INC
Also Called: Community Cnvlscent Hosp Mntcl
9620 Fremont Ave (91763-2320)
PHONE...............................909 621-4751
Johannes Simanjuntak, *Brnch Mgr*
EMP: 987
SALES (corp-wide): 23.84MM **Privately Held**
Web: www.communityech.com
SIC: **8051** Convalescent home with continuous nursing care
PA: U.S. Skillserve Inc
4115 E Broadway Ste A
Long Beach CA
562 930-0777

(P-15714)
VALE OPERATING COMPANY LP
Also Called: Vale Healthcare Center
13484 San Pablo Ave (94806-3904)
PHONE...............................510 232-5945
Tim Neal, *Prin*
EMP: 13480
SALES (corp-wide): 1.02B **Privately Held**
SIC: **8051** Skilled nursing care facilities
HQ: Vale Operating Company, Lp
1 Ravinia Dr Ste 1400
Atlanta GA

(P-15715)
VALLEY CAREIDENCE OPCO LLC
Also Called: Gateway Post Acute
661 W Poplar Ave (93257-5926)
PHONE...............................559 784-8371
Jason Murray, *CEO*
Mark Hancock, *
EMP: 75 EST: 2014
SALES (est): 7.2MM
SALES (corp-wide): 1.53B **Privately Held**
Web: www.gatewaypostacute.com
SIC: **8051** Convalescent home with continuous nursing care
HQ: Providence Group Of California, Llc
262 N University Ave
Farmington UT
801 447-9829

(P-15716)
VALLEY HEALTHCARE CENTER LLC
Also Called: Valley Healthcare Center
4840 E Tulare Ave (93727-3062)
PHONE...............................559 251-7161
George V Hagaer Junior, *CEO*
EMP: 100 EST: 2003
SALES (est): 17.84MM **Privately Held**
SIC: **8051** Convalescent home with continuous nursing care
HQ: Genesis Healthcare Llc
101 E State St
Kennett Square PA

(P-15717)
VALLEY VSTA NRSING TRNSTNAL CA
Also Called: Valley Vsta Nrsing Trnstnal Ca
6120 Vineland Ave (91606-4914)
PHONE...............................818 763-6275
EMP: 170 EST: 2017
SALES (est): 7.48MM **Privately Held**
SIC: **8051** Convalescent home with continuous nursing care

(P-15718)
VICTORIA CARE CENTER
5445 Everglades St (93003-6523)
PHONE...............................805 642-1736
Scott Porter, *Ex Dir*
Jay Brady, *
EMP: 100 EST: 1987
SQ FT: 85,000
SALES (est): 18.73MM **Privately Held**
Web: www.victoriacarecenter.com
SIC: **8051** Convalescent home with continuous nursing care
PA: Beverly Health Care Corporation
5445 Everglades St
Ventura CA

(P-15719)
VICTORIA VNTURA ASSSTED LVING
27101 Puerta Real Ste 450 (92691-8566)
PHONE...............................805 642-1736
EMP: 88 EST: 2014
SALES (est): 24.74MM
SALES (corp-wide): 3.03B **Publicly Held**
SIC: **8051** Convalescent home with continuous nursing care
PA: The Ensign Group Inc
29222 Rncho Vejo Rd Ste 1
San Juan Capistrano CA
949 487-9500

(P-15720)
VICTORIA VNTURA HEALTHCARE LLC
Also Called: Victoria Care Center
5445 Everglades St (93003-6523)
PHONE...............................805 642-1736
Tim Cooley, *Ex Dir*
EMP: 262 EST: 2003
SALES (est): 13.41MM **Privately Held**
Web: www.victoriacarecenter.com
SIC: **8051** Convalescent home with continuous nursing care

8051 - Skilled Nursing Care Facilities (P-15721)

(P-15721)
VIENNA CONVALESCENT HOSP INC
Also Called: Vienna Nrsing Rhbilitation Ctr
800 S Ham Ln (95242-3543)
PHONE.............................209 368-7141
Kenneth Heffel, *Pr*
Diana Heffel, *
EMP: 131 EST: 1966
SQ FT: 25,000
SALES (est): 9.74MM **Privately Held**
Web: www.viennanursingrehab.com
SIC: **8051** Convalescent home with continuous nursing care

(P-15722)
VILLA CONVALESCENT HOSP INC
Also Called: VILLA CONVALESCENT HOSPITAL
8965 Magnolia Ave (92503-4432)
PHONE.............................951 689-5788
Admiral Jacob Paulson, *Prin*
EMP: 90 EST: 1971
SQ FT: 25,000
SALES (est): 9.4MM **Privately Held**
Web: www.villahealthcare.com
SIC: **8051** Convalescent home with continuous nursing care

(P-15723)
VILLA SERENA HEALTHCARE CENTER
723 E 9th St (90813-4611)
PHONE.............................562 437-2797
Matt Carp, *Pr*
EMP: 70 EST: 2014
SALES (est): 2.59MM **Privately Held**
Web: www.villaserenahealthcare.com
SIC: **8051** Skilled nursing care facilities

(P-15724)
VINDRA INC
Also Called: Meadowood Nursing Center
3805 Dexter Ln (95422-8850)
PHONE.............................707 994-7738
Calvin Baker Senior, *Pr*
Calvin Baker Junior, *Pr*
Hibarger David, *Admn*
Stewart Timothy, *Pr*
EMP: 100 EST: 1984
SQ FT: 30,250
SALES (est): 8.28MM **Privately Held**
SIC: **8051** **8069** Convalescent home with continuous nursing care; Specialty hospitals, except psychiatric

(P-15725)
VISTA PACIFICA ENTERPRISES INC (PA)
Also Called: Vista Pacifica Center
3674 Pacific Ave (92509-1948)
PHONE.............................951 682-4833
Cheryl Jumonville, *CEO*
A L Braswell Junior, *Pr*
Ruth Braswell, *Stockholder**
James Braswell, *Stockholder**
EMP: 180 EST: 1988
SALES (est): 19.68MM **Privately Held**
Web: www.vistapacificaent.com
SIC: **8051** **8059** Convalescent home with continuous nursing care; Domiciliary care

(P-15726)
VISTA WOODS HEALTH ASSOC LLC
Also Called: Vista Knoll Spclzed Care Fclty
2000 Westwood Rd (92083-5123)
PHONE.............................760 630-2273
Ron Cook, *Managing Member*
EMP: 162 EST: 2003
SALES (est): 28.3MM
SALES (corp-wide): 3.03B **Publicly Held**
Web: www.vistaknoll.com
SIC: **8051** Convalescent home with continuous nursing care
PA: The Ensign Group Inc
    29222 Rncho Vejo Rd Ste 1
    San Juan Capistrano CA
    949 487-9500

(P-15727)
WATERMAN CONVALESCENT HOSP INC (PA)
Also Called: Mt Rubidoux Convalescent Hosp
1850 N Waterman Ave (92404-4895)
PHONE.............................909 882-1215
Thomas Plott, *Pr*
Mister Terry Steege, *Acct Ex*
Elizabeth Plott, *
EMP: 109 EST: 1964
SQ FT: 13,000
SALES (est): 9.92MM
SALES (corp-wide): 9.92MM **Privately Held**
SIC: **8051** Convalescent home with continuous nursing care

(P-15728)
WATERMARK RTRMENT CMMNTIES INC
Also Called: Fountains At The Carlotta, The
41505 Carlotta Dr (92211-3279)
PHONE.............................760 346-5420
EMP: 95
Web: www.watermarkcommunities.com
SIC: **8051** **8052** Skilled nursing care facilities; Intermediate care facilities
HQ: Watermark Retirement Communities, Inc.
    2020 W Rudasill Rd
    Tucson AZ

(P-15729)
WESCORDON INCORPORATED
Also Called: Valley Care Center
661 W Poplar Ave (93257-5926)
P.O. Box 3566 (93258-3566)
PHONE.............................559 784-8371
Donald C Smith, *Pr*
EMP: 150 EST: 1948
SQ FT: 14,000
SALES (est): 4.64MM **Privately Held**
SIC: **8051** Convalescent home with continuous nursing care

(P-15730)
WEST CNTINELA VLY CARE CTR INC
Also Called: Centinela Skld Nrng Wlns Cntr
950 S Flower St (90301-4186)
PHONE.............................310 674-3216
EMP: 99
SALES (est): 5.7MM **Privately Held**
SIC: **8051** Skilled nursing care facilities

(P-15731)
WESTGATE GARDENS CARE CTR INC
4020 Sierra College Blvd Ste 190 (95677-3906)
PHONE.............................916 624-6230
Larry Bear, *Pr*
EMP: 127 EST: 1974
SQ FT: 2,700
SALES (est): 11.6MM **Privately Held**
Web: www.westgategardenscarecenter.com
SIC: **8051** Convalescent home with continuous nursing care
HQ: Far West, Inc.
    4020 Sierra College Blvd
    Rocklin CA

(P-15732)
WESTLAKE HEALTH CARE CENTER
1101 Crenshaw Blvd (90019-3112)
PHONE.............................805 494-1233
Jeoung Lee, *Pr*
EMP: 325 EST: 2001
SALES (est): 16.79MM
SALES (corp-wide): 52.03MM **Privately Held**
SIC: **8051** Skilled nursing care facilities
PA: J P H Consulting, Inc.
    1101 Crenshaw Blvd
    Los Angeles CA
    323 934-5660

(P-15733)
WESTVIEW SERVICES INC
Also Called: Westview Cmnty Arts Program
1701 S Euclid St Ste E (92802-2408)
PHONE.............................714 956-4199
Britain Semain, *Mgr*
EMP: 79
SALES (corp-wide): 14.51MM **Privately Held**
Web: www.westviewservices.org
SIC: **8051** **8322** Mental retardation hospital; Adult day care center
PA: Westview Services, Inc
    10522 Katella Ave
    Anaheim CA
    714 517-6606

(P-15734)
WESTWOOD HEALTHCARE CENTER LP
Also Called: COUNTRY VILLA WESTWOOD NURSING
12121 Santa Monica Blvd (90025-2515)
PHONE.............................310 826-0821
Stephen Reissman, *Genl Pt*
Hillard Torgan, *Pt*
EMP: 81 EST: 1970
SQ FT: 18,000
SALES (est): 10.96MM **Privately Held**
SIC: **8051** Skilled nursing care facilities

(P-15735)
WILD KARMA INC
Also Called: Divine Home Care
5275 Broadway (94618-1425)
PHONE.............................510 639-9088
Robbin R Beebe, *CEO*
Robin Beebe, *
EMP: 270 EST: 2007
SALES (est): 31.94MM **Privately Held**
Web: www.thekey.com
SIC: **8051** **8059** Convalescent home with continuous nursing care; Personal care home, with health care

(P-15736)
WILLOW CREEK HALTHCARE CTR LLC
Also Called: Willow Creek Healthcare Center
650 W Alluvial Ave (93611-6716)
PHONE.............................559 323-6200
George V Hager Junior, *CEO*
EMP: 233
SALES (est): 3.2MM **Privately Held**
SIC: **8051** Convalescent home with continuous nursing care
HQ: Genesis Healthcare Llc
    101 E State St
    Kennett Square PA

(P-15737)
WINDSOR ANAHEIM HEALTHCARE (PA)
Also Called: Windsor Grdns Cnvlescent Ctr A
3415 W Ball Rd (92804-3708)
PHONE.............................714 826-8950
Lee Samson, *Pr*
EMP: 164 EST: 1996
SQ FT: 37,245
SALES (est): 23.85MM **Privately Held**
Web: www.anaheimhealthcare.com
SIC: **8051** Convalescent home with continuous nursing care

(P-15738)
WINDSOR CNVLSCENT RHBLTTION CT
Also Called: Windsor Manor Rehabilitation Center of Co
3806 Clayton Rd (94521-2516)
PHONE.............................925 689-2266
Lee Samson, *Managing Member*
EMP: 100 EST: 1950
SALES (est): 22.72MM **Privately Held**
Web: www.windsorconcord.com
SIC: **8051** Convalescent home with continuous nursing care
PA: Lexington Group International, Inc
    9200 W Sunset Blvd # 950
    West Hollywood CA

(P-15739)
WINDSOR CNVLSCENT RHBLTTION CT
Also Called: Windsor Park Care Center of Fremont
2400 Parkside Dr (94536-5332)
PHONE.............................510 793-7222
Lee Samson, *Managing Member*
EMP: 92 EST: 2005
SALES (est): 9.83MM **Privately Held**
Web: www.windsorparkcare.com
SIC: **8051** Convalescent home with continuous nursing care
PA: Lexington Group International, Inc
    9200 W Sunset Blvd # 950
    West Hollywood CA

(P-15740)
WINDSOR CNVLSCENT RHBLTTION CT
Also Called: Windsor Gardens Rehabilitation Center of Salinas
637 E Romie Ln (93901-4205)
PHONE.............................831 424-0687
Lee Samson, *Managing Member*
EMP: 90 EST: 2005
SALES (est): 15.54MM **Privately Held**
Web: www.windsorgardenssalinas.com
SIC: **8051** Convalescent home with continuous nursing care
PA: Lexington Group International, Inc
    9200 W Sunset Blvd # 950
    West Hollywood CA

(P-15741)
WINDSOR REDDING CARE CTR LLC
2490 Court St (96001-2540)
PHONE.............................530 246-0600
EMP: 99 EST: 2007
SALES (est): 13.77MM **Privately Held**
Web: www.windsorreddingcc.com

PRODUCTS & SERVICES SECTION
8052 - Intermediate Care Facilities (P-15764)

SIC: 8051 Convalescent home with continuous nursing care

(P-15742)
WINDSOR TWIN PLMS HLTHCARE CTR
Also Called: Windsor Palms Care Ctr Artesia
11900 Artesia Blvd (90701-4039)
PHONE.................................562 865-0271
EMP: 133 EST: 2005
SALES (est): 28.44MM Privately Held
Web: www.windsorartesia.com
SIC: 8051 Convalescent home with continuous nursing care
PA: Lexington Group International, Inc
9200 W Sunset Blvd # 950
West Hollywood CA

(P-15743)
WOODWAY HEALTHCARE INC
27101 Puerta Real Ste 450 (92691-8566)
PHONE.................................254 420-0056
EMP: 69 EST: 2019
SALES (est): 8.04MM
SALES (corp-wide): 3.03B Publicly Held
SIC: 8051 Skilled nursing care facilities
PA: The Ensign Group Inc
29222 Rncho Vejo Rd Ste 1
San Juan Capistrano CA
949 487-9500

8052 Intermediate Care Facilities

(P-15744)
A-1 HOSPICE CARE INC
217 E Alameda Ave Ste 306 (91502-2621)
PHONE.................................818 237-2700
Femi Samuel, CFO
EMP: 65 EST: 2012
SQ FT: 2,800
SALES (est): 1.68MM Privately Held
Web: www.a-1hospice.com
SIC: 8052 Personal care facility

(P-15745)
ADVANCED HM HLTH & HOSPICE INC
Also Called: ADVANCED HOME HOUSE
4354 Auburn Blvd (95841-4107)
PHONE.................................916 978-0744
Angela Sehr, CEO
▲ EMP: 143 EST: 2011
SALES (est): 6.93MM Privately Held
Web: www.excelin.com
SIC: 8052 Personal care facility

(P-15746)
ARCADIA GARDENS MGT CORP
Also Called: Indepndnt Asstd Lvng & Memory
720 W Camino Real Ave (91007-7839)
PHONE.................................626 574-8571
Julie Chirikian, Pr
David Chirikian, *
EMP: 100 EST: 2004
SQ FT: 120,320
SALES (est): 10.08MM Privately Held
Web: www.arcadiagardensretirement.com
SIC: 8052 Intermediate care facilities

(P-15747)
BIG HEALTH INC
Also Called: Sleepio
461 Bush St Ste 200 (94108-3716)
PHONE.................................707 653-5570
Peter Hames, Pr
Peter Andrew, *

EMP: 200 EST: 2015
SALES (est): 20.26MM Privately Held
Web: www.bighealth.com
SIC: 8052 Home for the mentally retarded, with health care

(P-15748)
BLYTH/WNDSOR CNTRY PK HLTHCARE
3232 E Artesia Blvd (90805-2811)
PHONE.................................310 385-1090
Jon Peralez, Prin
EMP: 99 EST: 2013
SALES (est): 8.04MM Privately Held
SIC: 8052 Intermediate care facilities

(P-15749)
CHARTER HOSPICE COLTON LLC
1007 E Cooley Dr Ste 100 (92324-3901)
PHONE.................................909 825-2969
Fred Frank, Pr
EMP: 120 EST: 2008
SALES (est): 17.04MM Privately Held
Web: www.charterhcg.com
SIC: 8052 Personal care facility

(P-15750)
COMMUNITY HOME PARTNERS LLC
Also Called: Pacific Gardens
2384 Pacific Dr (95051-1458)
PHONE.................................408 985-5252
EMP: 85 EST: 1998
SQ FT: 56,300
SALES (est): 9.95MM Privately Held
Web: www.pacificgardens.org
SIC: 8052 Intermediate care facilities

(P-15751)
COMMUNITY HOSPICE INC (PA)
Also Called: C H I
4368 Spyres Way (95356-9259)
PHONE.................................209 578-6300
Charlotte Mcleod, CEO
Rick Dahlseid, CFO
EMP: 125 EST: 1979
SQ FT: 24,000
SALES (est): 26.18MM
SALES (corp-wide): 26.18MM Privately Held
Web: www.hospiceheart.org
SIC: 8052 8069 Personal care facility; Specialty hospitals, except psychiatric

(P-15752)
COUNTY OF ORANGE
405 W 5th St Ofc (92701-4519)
PHONE.................................714 834-6021
David L Riley, Dir
EMP: 72
SALES (corp-wide): 5.2B Privately Held
Web: www.ocgov.com
SIC: 8052 Intermediate care facilities
PA: County Of Orange
400 W Civic Center Dr G36
Santa Ana CA
714 834-6200

(P-15753)
DEL ROSA VILLAIDENCE OPCO LLC
Also Called: Del Rosa Villa
2018 Del Rosa Ave (92404-5642)
PHONE.................................909 885-3261
Jason Murray, Prin
Mark Hancock, *
EMP: 349 EST: 2014
SALES (est): 3.92MM

SALES (corp-wide): 1.53B Privately Held
Web: www.delrosavillapostacute.com
SIC: 8052 Intermediate care facilities
HQ: Providence Group Of Southern California, Llc
262 N University Ave
Farmington UT
801 447-9829

(P-15754)
EMERITUS CORPORATION
Also Called: Emerald Hlls Asssted Lving Fcl
11550 Education St Apt 212 (95602-2463)
PHONE.................................530 653-1974
Lisa Huntzinger, Mgr
EMP: 221
SALES (corp-wide): 2.83B Publicly Held
Web: www.brookdaleliving.com
SIC: 8052 8051 Personal care facility; Skilled nursing care facilities
HQ: Emeritus Corporation
6737 W Wa St Ste 2300
Milwaukee WI

(P-15755)
EMERITUS CORPORATION
800 Oregon St (95476-6445)
PHONE.................................707 996-7101
EMP: 159
SALES (corp-wide): 2.83B Publicly Held
Web: www.brookdaleliving.com
SIC: 8052 8361 Personal care facility; Geriatric residential care
HQ: Emeritus Corporation
6737 W Wa St Ste 2300
Milwaukee WI

(P-15756)
EMERITUS CORPORATION
300 Fountaingrove Pkwy (95403-5720)
PHONE.................................707 324-7087
Scott Bissey, Brnch Mgr
EMP: 129
SALES (corp-wide): 2.83B Publicly Held
Web: www.brookdaleliving.com
SIC: 8052 6513 Personal care facility; Retirement hotel operation
HQ: Emeritus Corporation
6737 W Wa St Ste 2300
Milwaukee WI

(P-15757)
FRONT ST INC
Also Called: Front St Residential Care
1201 Shaffer Rd Ste 1a (95060-5761)
PHONE.................................831 420-0120
Ann Butler, CEO
Anne Butler, *
Peggy Butler, *
EMP: 180 EST: 1989
SALES (est): 1.96MM Privately Held
Web: www.frontst.com
SIC: 8052 Personal care facility

(P-15758)
GOLDEN GATEIDENCE OPCO LLC
Also Called: Victorian Post Acute
2121 Pine St (94115-2829)
PHONE.................................415 922-5085
EMP: 122 EST: 2017
SALES (est): 16.8MM
SALES (corp-wide): 1.53B Privately Held
SIC: 8052 8051 Intermediate care facilities; Skilled nursing care facilities
HQ: Bay Area Master Tenant, Llc
262 N University Ave
Farmington UT
801 447-9829

(P-15759)
HANFORDIDENCE OPCO LLC
Also Called: Hanford Post Acute
1007 W Lacey Blvd (93230-4331)
PHONE.................................559 582-2871
Jason Murray, CEO
Mark Hancock, CFO
EMP: 161 EST: 2019
SALES (est): 9.78MM
SALES (corp-wide): 1.53B Privately Held
Web: www.hanfordpa.com
SIC: 8052 Intermediate care facilities
HQ: Providence Group North, Llc
262 N University Ave
Farmington UT
801 447-9829

(P-15760)
HEALTH HUMN SVCS AGCY NAPA CNT
2361 Elm St (94559)
PHONE.................................707 253-4306
Howard Himes, Dir
EMP: 63 EST: 2011
SALES (est): 419.51K Privately Held
Web: www.countyofnapa.org
SIC: 8052 Home for the mentally retarded, with health care

(P-15761)
HILLSIDE HOUSE
1235 Veronica Springs Rd (93105-4522)
PHONE.................................805 687-0788
Michael Rassler, Ex Dir
Pam Flynt, *
Craig Olson, *
Peter Troesch, *
Chuck Klein, *
EMP: 98 EST: 1945
SQ FT: 24,000
SALES (est): 7.45MM Privately Held
Web: www.hillsidesb.org
SIC: 8052 Home for the mentally retarded, with health care

(P-15762)
HINDS HOSPICE (PA)
2490 W Shaw Ave Ste 100a (93711-3305)
P.O. Box 1325 (93639-1325)
PHONE.................................559 674-0407
Nancy Hinds, Ex Dir
EMP: 170 EST: 1984
SALES (est): 27.71MM
SALES (corp-wide): 27.71MM Privately Held
Web: www.hindshospice.org
SIC: 8052 Personal care facility

(P-15763)
HOFFMANN HOSPICE OF VALLEY INC
Also Called: Hoffman Hospice
4325 Buena Vista Rd (93311-8701)
PHONE.................................661 410-1010
Beth Hosman, Pr
EMP: 67 EST: 1994
SALES (est): 21.99MM Privately Held
Web: www.hoffmannhospice.org
SIC: 8052 Personal care facility

(P-15764)
HOME STREET OPERATIONS LLC
114 Pacifica Ste 230 (92618-3317)
PHONE.................................949 449-2500
EMP: 82
SALES (corp-wide): 1.86MM Privately Held

(PA)=Parent Co (HQ)=Headquarters
✪ = New Business established in last 2 years

8052 - Intermediate Care Facilities (P-15765)

SIC: 8052 Intermediate care facilities
PA: Home Street Operations, Llc
4001 Home St
Castle Rock CO
303 688-3174

(P-15765)
HOSPICE AND PALLIATIVE CARE
Also Called: Hospice of The East Bay
2849 Miranda Ave (94507-1443)
PHONE..................925 945-8924
Laura Pakar, Brnch Mgr
EMP: 75
Web: www.hospiceeastbay.org
SIC: 8052 Personal care facility
PA: Hospice And Palliative Care
3470 Buskirk Ave
Concord CA

(P-15766)
INLAND VALLEY HOSPICE CO
19167 Us Highway 18 Ste 6 (92307-2561)
PHONE..................760 243-2501
EMP: 84
Web: www.inlandvalleyhospice.com
SIC: 8052 Personal care facility
PA: Inland Valley Hospice Co
3770 Myers St
Riverside CA

(P-15767)
KERN VALLEYIDENCE OPCO LLC
Also Called: San Jquin Nrsing Rhblttion Ctr
3601 San Dimas St (93301-1405)
PHONE..................661 323-2894
Jason Murray, CEO
Mark Hancock, CFO
EMP: 134 EST: 2017
SALES (est): 11.57MM
SALES (corp-wide): 1.53B Privately Held
SIC: 8052 Intermediate care facilities
HQ: Providence Group Wine Country, Llc
262 N University Ave
Farmington UT
801 447-9829

(P-15768)
L & A CARE CORPORATION
Also Called: Roze Room Hospice
5000 Overland Ave Ste 101 (90230-4969)
PHONE..................310 202-7693
Lena M Beker, Brnch Mgr
EMP: 112
SALES (corp-wide): 3.22MM Privately Held
Web: www.rozeroom.org
SIC: 8052 Personal care facility
PA: L & A Care Corporation
18107 Sherman Way Ste 100
Reseda CA
323 938-1155

(P-15769)
LAKEPORT POST ACUTE LLC
Also Called: Lakeport Post Acute
1291 Craig Ave (95453-5704)
PHONE..................707 263-6382
EMP: 81 EST: 2018
SALES (est): 11.57MM
SALES (corp-wide): 1.53B Privately Held
Web: www.lakeportpa.com
SIC: 8052 Intermediate care facilities
HQ: Lakeport Chico Master Tenant, Llc
262 N University Ave
Farmington UT
801 447-9829

(P-15770)
LEISURE CARE LLC
Also Called: Fairwinds-West Hills
8138 Woodlake Ave (91304-3500)
PHONE..................818 713-0900
Pat Luc, Genl Mgr
EMP: 117
SALES (corp-wide): 106.71MM Privately Held
Web: www.leisurecare.com
SIC: 8052 Intermediate care facilities
HQ: Leisure Care, Llc
999 3rd Ave Ste 4550
Seattle WA
206 436-7827

(P-15771)
LOS ANGLES CNTY RNCHO LOS AMGO
7601 Imperial Hwy (90242-3456)
PHONE..................562 385-7111
Jorge Orozco, CEO
EMP: 1400 EST: 2009
SALES (est): 108.38MM Privately Held
Web: dhs.lacounty.gov
SIC: 8052 Personal care facility
PA: Rancho Los Amigos National Rehabiliatation Center
7601 Imperial Hwy
Downey CA

(P-15772)
MARYMOUNT VILLA LLC
345 Davis St Ofc (94577-2795)
PHONE..................510 895-5007
EMP: 65 EST: 2004
SALES (est): 6.5MM Privately Held
Web: www.marymountvilla.com
SIC: 8052 8059 Personal care facility; Convalescent home

(P-15773)
MAUBERTIDENCE OPCO LLC
Also Called: All Saints Maubert
15731 Maubert Ave (94578-2014)
PHONE..................510 481-3200
Jason Murray, Prin
Mark Hancock, Prin
EMP: 170 EST: 2014
SALES (est): 8.57MM
SALES (corp-wide): 1.53B Privately Held
Web: www.allsaintshc.com
SIC: 8052 Intermediate care facilities
HQ: Providence Group North, Llc
262 N University Ave
Farmington UT
801 447-9829

(P-15774)
MISSION HOSPICE & HM CARE INC
66 Bovet Rd Ste 100 (94402-3126)
PHONE..................650 554-1000
Dwight Wilson, Ex Dir
EMP: 200 EST: 1979
SALES (est): 18.62MM Privately Held
Web: www.missionhospice.org
SIC: 8052 Personal care facility

(P-15775)
MOUNTAIN SHADOWS SUPPORT GROUP (PA)
Also Called: MOUNTAIN SHADOWS COMMUNITY HOM
2067 W El Norte Pkwy (92026-1899)
PHONE..................760 743-3714
Richard W Marrs, Pr
Wade Wilde, *
EMP: 61 EST: 1990
SQ FT: 3,000
SALES (est): 27.85MM Privately Held
Web: www.mtnshadows.org
SIC: 8052 8059 Personal care facility; Rest home, with health care

(P-15776)
MOUNTAIN VLY CHILD FMLY SVCS I
24077 St Hwy 49 (95959-8519)
PHONE..................530 265-9057
Daniel Petrie, CEO
Richard Milhous, *
EMP: 220 EST: 1972
SQ FT: 22,000
SALES (est): 8.67MM Privately Held
Web: www.mountainvalleyfamilyservices.net
SIC: 8052 8361 Intermediate care facilities; Residential care

(P-15777)
NEW VISTA BEHAVIORAL HLTH LLC
3 Park Plz Ste 550 (92614-2537)
PHONE..................949 284-0095
Jennifer Hale, Brnch Mgr
EMP: 99
SALES (corp-wide): 12.71MM Privately Held
Web: www.pristenhealth.com
SIC: 8052 Home for the mentally retarded, with health care
PA: New Vista Behavioral Health, Llc
1901 Newport Blvd Ste 204
Costa Mesa CA
888 316-3665

(P-15778)
OAKHURST HEALTHCARE CENTER LLC
Also Called: Skilled Nursing Facility
40131 Highway 49 (93644-9560)
PHONE..................559 683-2244
EMP: 93 EST: 2018
SALES (est): 6.42MM Privately Held
Web: www.oakhursthc.com
SIC: 8052 Intermediate care facilities

(P-15779)
OAKLANDIDENCE OPCO LLC
Also Called: Medical Hill Healthcare Center
475 29th St (94609-3510)
PHONE..................510 832-3222
Jason Murray, Prin
Debra Gogerty, Prin
EMP: 99 EST: 2017
SALES (est): 20.84MM
SALES (corp-wide): 1.53B Privately Held
Web: www.medicalhillhc.com
SIC: 8052 Intermediate care facilities
HQ: Bay Area Master Tenant, Llc
262 N University Ave
Farmington UT
801 447-9829

(P-15780)
OJAI HEALTHIDENCE OPCO LLC
Also Called: Ojai Health & Rehabilitation
601 N Montgomery St (93023-2751)
PHONE..................805 646-8124
EMP: 170 EST: 2014
SALES (est): 1.83MM
SALES (corp-wide): 1.53B Privately Held
SIC: 8052 Intermediate care facilities
HQ: Providence Group North, Llc
262 N University Ave
Farmington UT
801 447-9829

(P-15781)
ONTARIOIDENCE OPCO LLC
Also Called: Las Colinas Post Acute
800 E 5th St (91764-2432)
PHONE..................909 984-8629
Jason Murray, Prin
Mark Hancock, *
EMP: 436 EST: 2014
SALES (est): 7.97MM
SALES (corp-wide): 1.53B Privately Held
SIC: 8052 Intermediate care facilities
HQ: Providence Group Of Southern California, Llc
262 N University Ave
Farmington UT
801 447-9829

(P-15782)
ORANGE TREEIDENCE OPCO LLC
Also Called: Riverwalk Post Acute
4000 Harrison St (92503-3514)
PHONE..................951 785-6060
Jason Murray, Prin
Mark Hancock, *
EMP: 371 EST: 2014
SALES (est): 3.02MM
SALES (corp-wide): 1.53B Privately Held
SIC: 8052 Intermediate care facilities
HQ: Providence Group Of Southern California, Llc
262 N University Ave
Farmington UT
801 447-9829

(P-15783)
PARKSIDE HEALTHCARE INC
Also Called: Parkside Health & Wellness Ctr
444 W Lexington Ave (92020-4416)
PHONE..................619 442-7744
Matthew Oldroyd, Prin
EMP: 85 EST: 2014
SALES (est): 3.1MM Privately Held
Web: www.parksidehealth.net
SIC: 8052 Intermediate care facilities

(P-15784)
PRAIRIE CITY COMMONS LLC
Also Called: Prairie City Landing
645 Willard Dr (95630-4048)
PHONE..................916 458-0303
Eric Hostetter, Managing Member
EMP: 85 EST: 2016
SALES (est): 4.69MM Privately Held
Web: www.prairiecitylanding.com
SIC: 8052 Intermediate care facilities

(P-15785)
PROMEDICA HEALTH SYSTEM INC
Also Called: Heartland Hospice Services
1050 Northgate Dr Ste 400 (94903-2575)
PHONE..................415 472-2637
Jeff Govum, Brnch Mgr
EMP: 240
SALES (corp-wide): 187.07MM Privately Held
Web: www.gentivahs.com
SIC: 8052 Personal care facility
PA: Promedica Health System, Inc.
100 Madison Ave
Toledo OH
567 585-9600

(P-15786)
QUAIL PARK RETIREMENT VLG LLC
Also Called: Quail Park Retirement Village
4520 W Cypress Ave (93277-1577)

8052 - Intermediate Care Facilities (P-15806)

PHONE.............................559 624-3500
Denis Bryant, *Mgr*
EMP: 65 **EST:** 2001
SALES (est): 5.06MM **Privately Held**
Web: www.qpvisalia.com
SIC: 8052 6513 Intermediate care facilities; Apartment building operators

(P-15787)
RANCHO VISTA HEALTH CENTER
Also Called: Rancho Vista
200 Grapevine Rd Apt 15 (92083-4042)
PHONE.............................760 941-1480
Alan Shigley, *Ex Dir*
EMP: 178 **EST:** 1983
SALES (est): 11.27MM
SALES (corp-wide): 40.58MM **Privately Held**
SIC: 8052 8051 8361 Intermediate care facilities; Skilled nursing care facilities; Residential care
PA: Activcare Living, Inc.
   10603 Rancho Bernardo Rd
   San Diego CA
   858 565-4424

(P-15788)
RES-CARE INC
5250 Claremont Ave (95207-5700)
PHONE.............................209 473-1202
Gregory Kessinger, *CFO*
EMP: 75
SALES (corp-wide): 5.27B **Privately Held**
Web: www.rescare.com
SIC: 8052 Home for the mentally retarded, with health care
HQ: Res-Care, Inc.
   805 N Whittington Pkwy
   Louisville KY
   502 394-2100

(P-15789)
RES-CARE INC
1485 Response Rd (95815-4847)
PHONE.............................916 567-1244
Brenda Collins, *Brnch Mgr*
EMP: 82
SALES (corp-wide): 5.27B **Privately Held**
Web: www.rescare.com
SIC: 8052 Home for the mentally retarded, with health care
HQ: Res-Care, Inc.
   805 N Whittington Pkwy
   Louisville KY
   502 394-2100

(P-15790)
RES-CARE INC
45691 Monroe St Ste 6 (92201-3943)
PHONE.............................760 775-2887
EMP: 68
SALES (corp-wide): 5.27B **Privately Held**
Web: www.rescare.com
SIC: 8052 Home for the mentally retarded, with health care
HQ: Res-Care, Inc.
   805 N Whittington Pkwy
   Louisville KY
   502 394-2100

(P-15791)
RES-CARE INC
22635 Alessandro Blvd (92553-8550)
PHONE.............................951 653-1311
EMP: 82
SALES (corp-wide): 5.27B **Privately Held**
Web: www.rescare.com
SIC: 8052 Home for the mentally retarded, with health care

HQ: Res-Care, Inc.
   805 N Whittington Pkwy
   Louisville KY
   502 394-2100

(P-15792)
RES-CARE INC
2120 Foothill Blvd Ste 205 (91750-2941)
PHONE.............................909 596-5360
Jill Crowell, *Mgr*
EMP: 82
SALES (corp-wide): 5.27B **Privately Held**
Web: www.rescare.com
SIC: 8052 Home for the mentally retarded, with health care
HQ: Res-Care, Inc.
   805 N Whittington Pkwy
   Louisville KY
   502 394-2100

(P-15793)
SALINASIDENCE OPCO LLC
Also Called: Pacific Coast Post Acute
720 E Romie Ln (93901-4208)
PHONE.............................831 424-8072
EMP: 118 **EST:** 2019
SALES (est): 5.36MM
SALES (corp-wide): 1.53B **Privately Held**
SIC: 8052 Intermediate care facilities
HQ: Bay Area Master Tenant, Llc
   262 N University Ave
   Farmington UT
   801 447-9829

(P-15794)
SENIOR LIVING SOLUTIONS LLC
1725 S Bascom Ave Apt 105 (95008-0676)
PHONE.............................408 385-1835
EMP: 120
SALES (est): 1.9MM **Privately Held**
SIC: 8052 Personal care facility

(P-15795)
SNOWLINE HSPICE EL DORADO CNTY
Also Called: SNOWLINE HOSPICE
6520 Pleasant Valley Rd (95619-9512)
PHONE.............................530 621-7820
Michael Sehmidt, *Ex Dir*
Richard B Esposito, *
Jon Lehrman, *
William Fisher, *
Leah Hall, *
EMP: 140 **EST:** 2003
SQ FT: 8,900
SALES (est): 16.25MM **Privately Held**
Web: www.snowlinehospice.org
SIC: 8052 Personal care facility

(P-15796)
SONOMAIDENCE OPCO LLC
Also Called: Sonoma Post Acute
678 2nd St W (95476-6901)
PHONE.............................707 938-1096
Jason Murray, *Prin*
Mark Hancock, *
EMP: 86 **EST:** 2016
SALES (est): 9.98MM
SALES (corp-wide): 1.53B **Privately Held**
Web: www.sonomapostacute.com
SIC: 8052 8051 Intermediate care facilities; Skilled nursing care facilities
HQ: Providence Group Wine Country, Llc
   262 N University Ave
   Farmington UT
   801 447-9829

(P-15797)
STRATGIES TO EMPWER PEOPLE INC (PA)
Also Called: Step
2330 Glendale Ln (95825-2454)
PHONE.............................916 679-1555
Jacquine Difoss, *Pr*
EMP: 77 **EST:** 1994
SALES (est): 23.5MM
SALES (corp-wide): 23.5MM **Privately Held**
Web: www.stepagency.com
SIC: 8052 Personal care facility

(P-15798)
SUTTER HEALTH
1651 Alvarado St (94577-2636)
PHONE.............................510 618-5200
EMP: 71
SALES (corp-wide): 14.77B **Privately Held**
Web: www.sutterhealth.org
SIC: 8052 Personal care facility
PA: Sutter Health
   2200 River Plaza Dr
   Sacramento CA
   916 733-8800

(P-15799)
VALLEY POINTEIDENCE OPCO LLC
Also Called: Valley Pnte Nrsing Rhblttion C
20090 Stanton Ave (94546-5203)
PHONE.............................510 538-8464
Jason Murray, *Prin*
Mark Hancock, *
EMP: 72 **EST:** 2014
SALES (est): 4.9MM
SALES (corp-wide): 1.53B **Privately Held**
SIC: 8052 Intermediate care facilities
HQ: Providence Group North, Llc
   262 N University Ave
   Farmington UT
   801 447-9829

(P-15800)
VALLEY VILLAGE
8727 Fenwick St (91040-1952)
PHONE.............................818 446-0366
EMP: 113
SALES (corp-wide): 21.42MM **Privately Held**
Web: www.valleyvillage.org
SIC: 8052 Intermediate care facilities
PA: Valley Village
   20830 Sherman Way
   Winnetka CA
   818 587-9450

(P-15801)
VITAS HEALTHCARE CORPORATION
9106 Pulsar Ct Ste D (92883-4632)
PHONE.............................858 805-6254
EMP: 96
SALES (corp-wide): 2.13B **Publicly Held**
Web: www.vitas.com
SIC: 8052 Personal care facility
HQ: Vitas Healthcare Corporation
   201 S Biscayne Blvd # 400
   Miami FL
   305 374-4143

(P-15802)
VITAS HEALTHCARE CORPORATION
670 N Mccarthy Blvd Ste 220 (95035-5119)
PHONE.............................415 874-4400
EMP: 82
SALES (corp-wide): 2.13B **Publicly Held**

Web: www.vitas.com
SIC: 8052 Personal care facility
HQ: Vitas Healthcare Corporation
   201 S Biscayne Blvd # 400
   Miami FL
   305 374-4143

(P-15803)
VITAS HEALTHCARE CORPORATION
333 N Lantana St Ste 124 (93010-9007)
PHONE.............................805 437-2100
Rita Peddycoart, *Mgr*
EMP: 96
SALES (corp-wide): 2.13B **Publicly Held**
Web: www.vitas.com
SIC: 8052 Personal care facility
HQ: Vitas Healthcare Corporation
   201 S Biscayne Blvd # 400
   Miami FL
   305 374-4143

(P-15804)
WATERMANIDENCE OPCO LLC
Also Called: Waterman Canyon Post Acute
1850 N Waterman Ave (92404-4831)
PHONE.............................909 882-1215
Jason Murray, *Prin*
Mark Hancock, *
EMP: 327 **EST:** 2014
SALES (est): 4.4MM
SALES (corp-wide): 1.53B **Privately Held**
SIC: 8052 Intermediate care facilities
HQ: Providence Group Of Southern California, Llc
   262 N University Ave
   Farmington UT
   801 447-9829

(P-15805)
WATTS HEALTH FOUNDATION INC (HQ)
Also Called: Uhp Healthcare
3405 W Imperial Hwy Ste 304 (90303-2219)
PHONE.............................310 424-2220
Doctor Clyde W Oden, *Pr*
Jennifer Stapalding, *CEO*
Ron Bolding V Press, *Business Operations*
EMP: 400 **EST:** 1967
SALES (est): 69.59MM
SALES (corp-wide): 70.19MM **Privately Held**
Web: www.wattshealth.org
SIC: 8052 8011 8741 Intermediate care facilities; Health maintenance organization; Management services
PA: Watts Health Systems, Inc.
   3405 W Imperial Hwy
   Inglewood CA
   310 424-2220

(P-15806)
WEST VALLEYIDENCE OPCO LLC
Also Called: West Valley Post Acute
7057 Shoup Ave (91307-2335)
PHONE.............................818 348-8422
Jason Murray, *Prin*
Mark Hancock, *Prin*
EMP: 142 **EST:** 2015
SALES (est): 4.26MM
SALES (corp-wide): 1.53B **Privately Held**
SIC: 8052 Intermediate care facilities
HQ: Providence Group North, Llc
   262 N University Ave
   Farmington UT
   801 447-9829

8059 Nursing And Personal Care, Nec

(P-15807)
14766 WASH AVE OPERATIONS LLC
14766 Washington Ave (94578-4220)
PHONE..................510 352-2211
EMP: 84
SALES (est): 6.08MM
SALES (corp-wide): 5.86B Publicly Held
Web: www.washingtoncenter.com
SIC: 8059 Nursing home, except skilled and intermediate care facility
HQ: Sun Healthcare Group, Inc.
27442 Portola Pkwy # 200
Foothill Ranch CA

(P-15808)
AMBERWOOD CONVALESCENT HOSP
6071 York Blvd (90042-3503)
PHONE..................323 254-3407
Jeanie Barrett, Admn
Ben Garrett, *
EMP: 100 EST: 1967
SALES (est): 4.09MM
SALES (corp-wide): 4.51MM Privately Held
Web: www.yorkhealthcareandwellness.com
SIC: 8059 Convalescent home
PA: Casner Consolidated, Llc.
1020 Huntington Dr
San Marino CA
626 282-8443

(P-15809)
ANTELOPE VLY RETIREMENT HM INC
Also Called: Antelope Vly Convalecent Hosp
44445 15th St W (93534-2801)
PHONE..................661 948-7501
Marsha Weldon, Dir
EMP: 178
SALES (corp-wide): 11.41MM Privately Held
SIC: 8059 8051 Convalescent home; Skilled nursing care facilities
PA: Antelope Valley Retirement Home, Inc.
44523 15th St W
Lancaster CA
661 949-5584

(P-15810)
ANTELOPE VLY RETIREMENT HM INC
Also Called: A V Nursing Care Center
44567 15th St W (93534-2803)
PHONE..................661 949-5524
Alfred Jones, Mgr
EMP: 178
SALES (corp-wide): 11.41MM Privately Held
Web: www.yolocare2.com
SIC: 8059 8051 Convalescent home; Skilled nursing care facilities
PA: Antelope Valley Retirement Home, Inc.
44523 15th St W
Lancaster CA
661 949-5584

(P-15811)
ARARAT HOME LOS ANGELES INC
Also Called: Ararat Convalescent Hospital
2373 Colorado Blvd (90041-1157)
PHONE..................323 256-8012
Violette Alahaidoyan, Brnch Mgr
EMP: 131
SQ FT: 9,104
SALES (corp-wide): 37.97MM Privately Held
Web: www.ararathome.org
SIC: 8059 8051 Convalescent home; Skilled nursing care facilities
PA: Ararat Home Of Los Angeles, Inc.
15105 Mission Hills Rd
Mission Hills CA
818 365-3000

(P-15812)
ARARAT HOME LOS ANGELES INC
Also Called: Ararat Nursing Facility
15099 Mission Hills Rd (91345-1102)
PHONE..................818 837-1800
M Kebhichien, Admn
EMP: 109
SALES (corp-wide): 37.97MM Privately Held
Web: www.ararathome.org
SIC: 8059 8051 Nursing home, except skilled and intermediate care facility; Skilled nursing care facilities
PA: Ararat Home Of Los Angeles, Inc.
15105 Mission Hills Rd
Mission Hills CA
818 365-3000

(P-15813)
ARCADIA CONVALESCENT HOSP INC (PA)
Also Called: Arcadia Health Care Center
1601 S Baldwin Ave (91007-7930)
PHONE..................626 445-2170
Orlando Clarizio Junior, CEO
EMP: 117 EST: 1962
SQ FT: 21,342
SALES (est): 18.4MM
SALES (corp-wide): 18.4MM Privately Held
Web: www.arcadiahcc.com
SIC: 8059 8051 Convalescent home; Skilled nursing care facilities

(P-15814)
ARTESIA CHRISTIAN HOME INC
11614 183rd St (90701-5506)
PHONE..................562 865-5218
Elroy Van Derley, Ex Dir
EMP: 140 EST: 1947
SQ FT: 43,223
SALES (est): 11.87MM Privately Held
Web: www.achome.org
SIC: 8059 8052 8051 Convalescent home; Intermediate care facilities; Skilled nursing care facilities

(P-15815)
B & E CONVALESCENT CENTER INC (PA)
Also Called: Gardena Convalescent Center
11627 Telegraph Rd Ste 200 (90670)
PHONE..................562 923-9449
Barry J Weiss, Pr
Esther Weiss, *
EMP: 60 EST: 1968
SALES (est): 5.94MM
SALES (corp-wide): 5.94MM Privately Held
SIC: 8059 Convalescent home

(P-15816)
BEN BENNETT INC (PA)
Also Called: COMMUNITY CARE AND REHABILITAT
3419 Via Lido # 646 (92663-3908)
PHONE..................949 209-9712
Bruce Bennett, Pr
▲ EMP: 200 EST: 1965
SQ FT: 50,000
SALES (est): 16.46MM
SALES (corp-wide): 16.46MM Privately Held
SIC: 8059 8069 8051 Convalescent home; Specialty hospitals, except psychiatric; Skilled nursing care facilities

(P-15817)
BERKELEY E CONVALESCENT HOSP
Also Called: Berkeley E Convalescent Hosp
2021 Arizona Ave (90404-1335)
PHONE..................310 829-5377
Paul Bartolucce, Adm/Dir
Saul Galper, *
EMP: 150 EST: 1965
SQ FT: 10,000
SALES (est): 10.72MM Privately Held
SIC: 8059 Convalescent home

(P-15818)
BERNARDO HTS HEALTHCARE INC
Also Called: Carmel Mtn Rhab Healthcare Ctr
11895 Avenue Of Industry (92128-3423)
PHONE..................858 673-0101
Christopher R Christensen, CEO
Covey C Christensen, *
Matt Rutter, *
EMP: 171 EST: 2005
SALES (est): 21.34MM
SALES (corp-wide): 3.03B Publicly Held
Web: www.carmelmountain.net
SIC: 8059 8051 8011 Nursing home, except skilled and intermediate care facility; Skilled nursing care facilities; Clinic, operated by physicians
PA: The Ensign Group Inc
29222 Rncho Vejo Rd Ste 1
San Juan Capistrano CA
949 487-9500

(P-15819)
BETHEL LUTHERAN HOME INC
2280 Dockery Ave (93662-3898)
PHONE..................559 896-4900
C Kaylene Steele, Admn
EMP: 100 EST: 1928
SQ FT: 33,000
SALES (est): 9.33MM Privately Held
SIC: 8059 8051 Domiciliary care; Extended care facility

(P-15820)
BMB 1 LLC
Also Called: Ride At Home Care
495 E Rincon St Ste 211 (92879-1379)
PHONE..................951 741-0663
Michael Barboza, Managing Member
EMP: 65 EST: 2017
SALES (est): 562.7K Privately Held
SIC: 8059 8051 Nursing and personal care, nec; Convalescent home with continuous nursing care

(P-15821)
BONNIE BRAE CNVLSCENT HOSP INC (PA)
Also Called: California Convalescent Center
420 S Bonnie Brae St (90057-3010)
PHONE..................213 483-8144
Elma Cayton, CEO
Albert Ballo, *
EMP: 60 EST: 1960
SALES (est): 5.35MM
SALES (corp-wide): 5.35MM Privately Held
SIC: 8059 8051 Convalescent home; Skilled nursing care facilities

(P-15822)
BRADLEY COURT
675 E Bradley Ave (92021-3110)
PHONE..................619 448-6633
Erwin Cablayan, Pr
Rita Stewart, *
EMP: 60 EST: 1970
SQ FT: 13,000
SALES (est): 3.58MM Privately Held
SIC: 8059 Convalescent home

(P-15823)
BRIGHTON CONVALESCENT CENTER
1836 N Fair Oaks Ave (91103-1619)
PHONE..................626 798-9124
Alex Makabuhay, Admn
Pat Capello, *
Rose Wilson, Management Company*
EMP: 100 EST: 1992
SALES (est): 10.71MM Privately Held
Web: www.brighton1836.com
SIC: 8059 8051 Convalescent home; Skilled nursing care facilities

(P-15824)
BUENA VENTURA CARE CENTER INC
Also Called: Leisure Glen Convalescent Ctr
1505 Colby Dr (91205-3307)
PHONE..................818 247-4476
Yolanda Wise, Admn
EMP: 80
SALES (corp-wide): 8.37MM Privately Held
SIC: 8059 8051 Convalescent home; Skilled nursing care facilities
PA: East Los Angeles Healthcare, Llc
1016 S Record Ave
Los Angeles CA
323 268-0106

(P-15825)
CALIFORNIA HM FOR THE AGED INC
Also Called: California Armenian Home
6720 E Kings Canyon Rd (93727-3603)
PHONE..................559 251-8414
Admiral Ray Wark, Prin
EMP: 165 EST: 1950
SQ FT: 39,000
SALES (est): 26.01MM Privately Held
Web: www.lifeatthevineyards.org
SIC: 8059 Convalescent home

(P-15826)
CALIFORNIA VOCATIONS INC
Also Called: Arthur Schawlow Center
564 Rio Lindo Ave Ste 204 (95926-1852)
P.O. Box 538 (95967-0538)
PHONE..................530 877-0937
Bob Irvine, Ex Dir
Richard Welsh, *
George Dailey, *
Paul Johnson, *
EMP: 195 EST: 1984
SQ FT: 5,700
SALES (est): 6.04MM Privately Held
Web: www.calvoc.org
SIC: 8059 Home for the mentally retarded, ex. skilled or intermediate

8059 - Nursing And Personal Care, Nec (P-15846)

(P-15827)
CALIFRNIA-NEVADA METHDST HOMES
Also Called: Lake Park Retirement Residence
1850 Alice St Ofc (94612-4169)
PHONE.................510 835-5511
Steve Jacobson, *Brnch Mgr*
EMP: 105
SALES (corp-wide): 22.94MM **Privately Held**
Web: www.cnmh.org
SIC: 8059 Rest home, with health care
PA: California-Nevada Methodist Homes
201 19th St Ste 100
Oakland CA
510 893-8989

(P-15828)
CARE CHOICE HEALTH SYSTEMS INC
Also Called: Care Choice Home Care
2236 Lone Oak Ln (92084-7718)
PHONE.................760 798-4508
Tara Pardo, *CEO*
EMP: 60 EST: 2015
SALES (est): 6.34MM **Privately Held**
Web: www.carechoicehomecare.com
SIC: 8059 8082 Personal care home, with health care; Home health care services

(P-15829)
CHANNING HOUSE
850 Webster St Ofc (94301-2833)
PHONE.................650 327-0950
Melvin Matsumoto, *CEO*
Carl Braginsky, *
EMP: 100 EST: 1960
SQ FT: 300,000
SALES (est): 23.08MM **Privately Held**
Web: www.channinghouse.org
SIC: 8059 Rest home, with health care

(P-15830)
CHASE CARE CENTER INC
Also Called: Chase Care Center
1101 Crenshaw Blvd (90019-3112)
PHONE.................323 935-8490
Jeoung H Lee, *Pr*
John Yoo, *
EMP: 65 EST: 1996
SQ FT: 83,000
SALES (est): 16.48MM **Privately Held**
SIC: 8059 8051 Convalescent home; Skilled nursing care facilities

(P-15831)
CLEAR VIEW SANITARIUM INC
Also Called: Clear View Sanitarium
15823 S Western Ave (90247-3703)
PHONE.................310 538-2323
Mark D Towns, *CEO*
Jeffrey B Towns, *
EMP: 175 EST: 1937
SQ FT: 40,000
SALES (est): 7.08MM **Privately Held**
Web: www.clearviewcare.com
SIC: 8059 Home for the mentally retarded, ex. skilled or intermediate

(P-15832)
COUNTRY VILLA SERVICE CORP
112 E Broadway (91776-1805)
PHONE.................626 285-2165
J Caballero, *Admn*
EMP: 102
SALES (corp-wide): 88.5MM **Privately Held**
Web: www.evictionlawyer.com
SIC: 8059 Nursing home, except skilled and intermediate care facility
PA: Country Villa Service Corp.
2400 E Katella Ave # 800
Anaheim CA
310 574-3733

(P-15833)
COUNTRY VILLA TERRACE (PA)
Also Called: Country Vlla Convalescent Hosp
6050 W Pico Blvd (90035-2647)
PHONE.................323 653-3980
Steven Reissman, *Pr*
Diana Reissman, *
EMP: 75 EST: 1963
SQ FT: 6,000
SALES (est): 4.51MM
SALES (corp-wide): 4.51MM **Privately Held**
SIC: 8059 8361 Convalescent home; Residential care

(P-15834)
COVENANT CARE CALIFORNIA LLC
Also Called: Vintage Fire Nrsing Rhbltion C
3620 Dale Rd Ste B (95356-0598)
PHONE.................209 521-2094
Julie Abram, *Admn*
EMP: 108
Web: www.covenantcare.com
SIC: 8059 8051 Convalescent home; Skilled nursing care facilities
HQ: Covenant Care California, Llc
120 Vantis Dr Ste 200
Aliso Viejo CA

(P-15835)
CPCC INC
Also Called: CHATSWORTH PARK HEALTH CARE CE
10610 Owensmouth Ave (91311-2151)
PHONE.................818 882-3200
John Sorensen, *Pr*
Greg Ethington, *
EMP: 99 EST: 1982
SALES (est): 15.05MM **Privately Held**
Web: www.chatsworthparkcare.com
SIC: 8059 8051 Convalescent home; Skilled nursing care facilities

(P-15836)
CRESTWOOD BEHAVIORAL HLTH INC
Also Called: 1140 Kingsburg Mhrc
1200 Smith St (93631-2216)
PHONE.................559 238-6981
Martha Crawford, *Admn*
EMP: 65
SALES (corp-wide): 278.96MM **Privately Held**
Web: www.crestwoodbehavioralhealth.com
SIC: 8059 Home for the mentally retarded, ex. skilled or intermediate
PA: Crestwood Behavioral Health, Inc.
520 Capitol Mall Ste 800
Sacramento CA
209 955-2326

(P-15837)
CRESTWOOD BEHAVIORAL HLTH INC
Also Called: 1107 San Jose Mhrc
1425 Fruitdale Ave (95128-3234)
PHONE.................408 275-1067
Gail Mcdonald, *Admn*
EMP: 148
SALES (corp-wide): 278.96MM **Privately Held**
Web: www.crestwoodbehavioralhealth.com
SIC: 8059 Home for the mentally retarded, ex. skilled or intermediate
PA: Crestwood Behavioral Health, Inc.
520 Capitol Mall Ste 800
Sacramento CA
209 955-2326

(P-15838)
CRESTWOOD BEHAVIORAL HLTH INC
Also Called: 1106 Sacramento Mhrc
2600 Stockton Blvd (95817-2210)
PHONE.................916 452-1431
Adrain Smith, *CEO*
EMP: 66
SALES (corp-wide): 278.96MM **Privately Held**
Web: www.crestwoodbehavioralhealth.com
SIC: 8059 Home for the mentally retarded, ex. skilled or intermediate
PA: Crestwood Behavioral Health, Inc.
520 Capitol Mall Ste 800
Sacramento CA
209 955-2326

(P-15839)
CRESTWOOD BEHAVIORAL HLTH INC
Also Called: 1154 San Diego Mhrc
5550 University Ave Ste A (92105-2307)
PHONE.................619 481-6790
Robyn Ramsey, *Admn*
EMP: 155
SALES (corp-wide): 278.96MM **Privately Held**
Web: www.crestwoodbehavioralhealth.com
SIC: 8059 Home for the mentally retarded, ex. skilled or intermediate
PA: Crestwood Behavioral Health, Inc.
520 Capitol Mall Ste 800
Sacramento CA
209 955-2326

(P-15840)
CRESTWOOD BEHAVIORAL HLTH INC
Also Called: 1167 Fallbrook Mhrc
624 E Elder St (92028-3004)
PHONE.................760 451-4165
Corey Hise, *Admn*
EMP: 132
SALES (corp-wide): 278.96MM **Privately Held**
Web: www.crestwoodbehavioralhealth.com
SIC: 8059 Home for the mentally retarded, ex. skilled or intermediate
PA: Crestwood Behavioral Health, Inc.
520 Capitol Mall Ste 800
Sacramento CA
209 955-2326

(P-15841)
CRESTWOOD BEHAVIORAL HLTH INC
Also Called: 1116 Angwin Mhrc
295 Pine Breeze Dr (94508-9620)
PHONE.................707 965-2461
Lindsy Morrison, *Admn*
EMP: 66
SALES (corp-wide): 278.96MM **Privately Held**
Web: www.crestwoodbehavioralhealth.com
SIC: 8059 Home for the mentally retarded, ex. skilled or intermediate
PA: Crestwood Behavioral Health, Inc.
520 Capitol Mall Ste 800
Sacramento CA
209 955-2326

(P-15842)
CRESTWOOD BEHAVIORAL HLTH INC
Also Called: 1115 Bakersfield Mhrc
6700 Eucalyptus Dr Ste A (93306-6076)
PHONE.................661 363-8127
Sukhdeep Kaur, *Prin*
EMP: 82
SALES (corp-wide): 278.96MM **Privately Held**
Web: www.crestwoodbehavioralhealth.com
SIC: 8059 Home for the mentally retarded, ex. skilled or intermediate
PA: Crestwood Behavioral Health, Inc.
520 Capitol Mall Ste 800
Sacramento CA
209 955-2326

(P-15843)
ENSIGN SAN DIMAS LLC
Also Called: Arbor Glen Care Center
1033 E Arrow Hwy (91740-6110)
PHONE.................626 963-7531
Steve Powell, *Operations*
Don R Bybee, *Prin*
EMP: 102 EST: 2010
SALES (est): 10.65MM
SALES (corp-wide): 3.03B **Publicly Held**
Web: www.arborglencare.com
SIC: 8059 Convalescent home
PA: The Ensign Group Inc
29222 Rncho Vejo Rd Ste 1
San Juan Capistrano CA
949 487-9500

(P-15844)
FAR WEST INC
Also Called: Westgage Grdn Convalescent Ctr
4525 W Tulare Ave (93277-1560)
PHONE.................559 733-0901
Ellen Rioux, *Prin*
EMP: 68
SIC: 8059 8051 Convalescent home; Skilled nursing care facilities
HQ: Far West, Inc.
4020 Sierra College Blvd
Rocklin CA

(P-15845)
FRONT PORCH COMMUNITIES & SVCS
3775 Modoc Rd (93105-4474)
PHONE.................805 687-0793
Roberta Jacobsen, *Brnch Mgr*
EMP: 104
SQ FT: 68,000
Web: www.frontporch.net
SIC: 8059 8051 Rest home, with health care; Skilled nursing care facilities
PA: Front Porch Communities And Services
800 N Brand Blvd Fl 19
Glendale CA

(P-15846)
FRONT PRCH CMMNTIES OPRTING GR
Also Called: FREDERICKA MANOR CARE CENTER
800 N Brand Blvd Fl 19 (91203-1231)
PHONE.................800 233-3709
John Woodward, *CEO*
EMP: 190 EST: 2013
SALES (est): 80.38MM **Privately Held**
Web: www.frontporch.net

8059 - Nursing And Personal Care, Nec (P-15847)

SIC: 8059 Nursing and personal care, nec

(P-15847)
GENESIS HEALTHCARE LLC
Also Called: Fountain View Cnvalescent Hosp
5310 Fountain Ave (90029-1005)
PHONE.................................323 461-9961
EMP: 479
Web: www.genesishcc.com
SIC: 8059 8051 8069 Convalescent home; Skilled nursing care facilities; Specialty hospitals, except psychiatric
HQ: Genesis Healthcare Llc
 101 E State St
 Kennett Square PA

(P-15848)
GERI-CARE II INC
Also Called: Vermont Care Center
22035 S Vermont Ave (90502-2120)
P.O. Box 6069 (90504-0069)
PHONE.................................310 328-0812
Emmanuel David, Pr
Engelica Vivillanueva, *
EMP: 250 EST: 1989
SQ FT: 40,000
SALES (est): 13.17MM Privately Held
Web: www.vermonthc.com
SIC: 8059 8051 Convalescent home; Skilled nursing care facilities

(P-15849)
GIBRALTAR CNVALESCENT HOSP INC (PA)
Also Called: Del Mar Convalescent Hospital
3050 Saturn St Ste 201 (92821-6278)
PHONE.................................714 577-3880
Irving Bauman, CEO
Presnell William, CFO
EMP: 60 EST: 1972
SALES (est): 9.31MM
SALES (corp-wide): 9.31MM Privately Held
SIC: 8059 Convalescent home

(P-15850)
GIBRALTAR CNVALESCENT HOSP INC
Also Called: Sunset Manor Convalescent Hosp
2720 Nevada Ave (91733-2318)
PHONE.................................626 443-9425
Marcel Morales, Mgr
EMP: 100
SALES (corp-wide): 9.31MM Privately Held
Web: www.sunsetmanorcare.com
SIC: 8059 8051 Convalescent home; Skilled nursing care facilities
PA: Gibraltar Convalescent Hospital, Inc.
 3050 Saturn St Ste 201
 Brea CA
 714 577-3880

(P-15851)
GOLDEN CARE INC
Also Called: Valley Manor Convalescent Hosp
6120 Vineland Ave (91606-4914)
PHONE.................................818 763-6275
Evelyn Del Rosario, Pr
Gonzalo Del Rosario, *
EMP: 80 EST: 1963
SQ FT: 32,000
SALES (est): 4.56MM Privately Held
SIC: 8059 8361 Convalescent home; Residential care

(P-15852)
GOLDEN STATE HEALTH CTRS INC
Also Called: Ocean View Conveleesent Hosp
1340 15th St (90404-1802)
PHONE.................................310 451-9706
Dina Closas R.n., Dir
EMP: 200
SALES (corp-wide): 74.01MM Privately Held
Web: www.goldenstatehealth.com
SIC: 8059 8051 Convalescent home; Skilled nursing care facilities
PA: Golden State Health Centers, Inc.
 13347 Ventura Blvd
 Sherman Oaks CA
 818 385-3200

(P-15853)
HANK FISHER PROPERTIES INC
Also Called: Chateau At River's Edge
641 Feature Dr Apt 233 (95825-8331)
PHONE.................................916 921-1970
Jeff Hertzig, Dir
EMP: 192 EST: 1988
SALES (est): 1.65MM
SALES (corp-wide): 15.81MM Privately Held
SIC: 8059 8052 Convalescent home; Intermediate care facilities
PA: Hank Fisher Properties, Inc.
 641 Fulton Ave Ste 200
 Sacramento CA
 916 485-1441

(P-15854)
HILLSDALE GROUP LP
Also Called: Sherman Village Hlth Care Ctr
12750 Riverside Dr (91607-3319)
PHONE.................................818 623-2170
Rich Terrell, Prin
EMP: 249
SALES (corp-wide): 24.71MM Privately Held
SIC: 8059 8051 8093 8011 Convalescent home; Skilled nursing care facilities; Rehabilitation center, outpatient treatment; Clinic, operated by physicians
PA: The Hillsdale Group L P
 1199 Howard Ave Ste 200
 Burlingame CA

(P-15855)
HILLSDALE GROUP LP
Also Called: Green Hills Retirement Center
1201 Broadway Ofc (94030-1976)
PHONE.................................650 742-9150
Pooja Sadarangani, Mgr
EMP: 242
SALES (corp-wide): 24.71MM Privately Held
SIC: 8059 8051 Nursing home, except skilled and intermediate care facility; Skilled nursing care facilities
PA: The Hillsdale Group L P
 1199 Howard Ave Ste 200
 Burlingame CA

(P-15856)
HILLSDALE GROUP LP
Also Called: Hayward Convalescent Hospital
1832 B St (94541-3140)
PHONE.................................510 538-3866
Mark Bornta, Mgr
EMP: 97
SALES (corp-wide): 24.71MM Privately Held

SIC: 8059 8051 Nursing home, except skilled and intermediate care facility; Convalescent home with continuous nursing care
PA: The Hillsdale Group L P
 1199 Howard Ave Ste 200
 Burlingame CA

(P-15857)
HORIZON WEST HEALTHCARE INC
Also Called: Sierra Regency, The
1015 Madden Ln Ofc (95661-4462)
PHONE.................................916 786-3173
Natalie Lake, Brnch Mgr
EMP: 64
Web: www.sierraregency.com
SIC: 8059 8361 Convalescent home; Residential care
HQ: Horizon West Healthcare, Inc.
 4020 Sierra College Blvd # 190
 Rocklin CA
 916 624-6230

(P-15858)
HUMANGOOD (PA)
Also Called: Terraces At Squaw Peak
1900 Huntington Dr (91010-2694)
PHONE.................................602 906-4024
John Cochran, CEO
EMP: 110 EST: 1959
SALES (est): 27.02MM
SALES (corp-wide): 27.02MM Privately Held
Web: www.humangood.org
SIC: 8059 8051 8322 Rest home, with health care; Skilled nursing care facilities; Old age assistance

(P-15859)
HUMANGOOD NORCAL
Also Called: Pilgrim Haven
373 Pine Ln (94022-1694)
PHONE.................................650 948-8291
Rae Holt, Mgr
EMP: 104
SQ FT: 95,130
SALES (corp-wide): 27.02MM Privately Held
Web: www.humangood.org
SIC: 8059 8052 8051 Convalescent home; Intermediate care facilities; Skilled nursing care facilities
HQ: Humangood Norcal
 1900 Huntington Dr
 Duarte CA
 925 924-7100

(P-15860)
HUMANGOOD NORCAL
Also Called: Rosewood Retirement Community
1401 New Stine Rd (93309-3530)
PHONE.................................661 834-0620
Ellen Renner, Brnch Mgr
EMP: 121
SALES (corp-wide): 27.02MM Privately Held
Web: www.humangood.org
SIC: 8059 8052 8051 Rest home, with health care; Intermediate care facilities; Skilled nursing care facilities
HQ: Humangood Norcal
 1900 Huntington Dr
 Duarte CA
 925 924-7100

(P-15861)
HUMANGOOD NORCAL
Also Called: Plymouth Village

900 Salem Dr (92373-6147)
PHONE.................................909 793-1233
Keith Kasin, Brnch Mgr
EMP: 170
SQ FT: 8,000
SALES (corp-wide): 27.02MM Privately Held
SIC: 8059 8051 Rest home, with health care; Skilled nursing care facilities
HQ: Humangood Norcal
 1900 Huntington Dr
 Duarte CA
 925 924-7100

(P-15862)
HUMANGOOD NORCAL
Also Called: Terraces of Los Gatos Agei
800 Blossom Hill Rd Ofc (95032-3563)
PHONE.................................408 357-1100
A Candalla, Ex Dir
EMP: 113
SALES (corp-wide): 27.02MM Privately Held
Web: www.humangood.org
SIC: 8059 8052 8051 6513 Rest home, with health care; Intermediate care facilities; Skilled nursing care facilities; Apartment building operators
HQ: Humangood Norcal
 1900 Huntington Dr
 Duarte CA
 925 924-7100

(P-15863)
INSTITUTE ON AGING
2880 Zanker Rd (95134-2117)
PHONE.................................510 536-3377
EMP: 125
Web: www.ioaging.org
SIC: 8059 Convalescent home
PA: Institute On Aging
 3575 Geary Blvd
 San Francisco CA

(P-15864)
LEXINGTON GROUP INTERNATIONAL
260 E Market St (90805-5910)
PHONE.................................562 428-4681
EMP: 180
SIC: 8059 Convalescent home
PA: Lexington Group International, Inc
 9200 W Sunset Blvd # 950
 West Hollywood CA

(P-15865)
LIFE CARE CENTERS AMERICA INC
Also Called: Vista Del Mar Health Centers
304 N Melrose Dr (92083-4814)
PHONE.................................760 724-8222
Michael Ramstead, Brnch Mgr
EMP: 228
SALES (corp-wide): 139.21MM Privately Held
Web: www.lcca.com
SIC: 8059 8051 Convalescent home; Skilled nursing care facilities
PA: Life Care Centers Of America, Inc.
 3570 Keith St Nw
 Cleveland TN
 423 472-9585

(P-15866)
LOMITA VERDE INC
Also Called: LOMITA CARE CENTER
1955 Lomita Blvd (90717-1807)
PHONE.................................310 325-1970
Donald G Laws, Pr

David E Sorenson, *
EMP: 60 EST: 1986
SALES (est): 7.79MM **Privately Held**
Web: www.lomitacare.com
SIC: **8059** 8322 Convalescent home; Individual and family services

(P-15867)
LONGWOOD MANAGEMENT CORP
Also Called: Sunny View Care Center
2000 W Washington Blvd (90018-1637)
PHONE..................................323 735-5146
Amber Gooden, *Admn*
EMP: 100
SALES (corp-wide): 79.33MM **Privately Held**
Web: www.longwoodmgmt.com
SIC: **8059** Convalescent home
PA: Longwood Management Corp.
4032 Wilshire Blvd Fl 6
Los Angeles CA
213 389-6900

(P-15868)
LONGWOOD MANAGEMENT CORP
Also Called: Broadway Manor Care Center
605 W Broadway (91204-1007)
PHONE..................................818 246-7174
Dolly Piper, *Mgr*
EMP: 97
SQ FT: 7,000
SALES (corp-wide): 79.33MM **Privately Held**
Web: www.broadwaymanorhc.com
SIC: **8059** 8051 Convalescent home; Skilled nursing care facilities
PA: Longwood Management Corp.
4032 Wilshire Blvd Fl 6
Los Angeles CA
213 389-6900

(P-15869)
LONGWOOD MANAGEMENT CORP
Also Called: Western Convelescence
2190 W Adams Blvd (90018-2039)
PHONE..................................323 737-7778
Emma Camanag, *Admn*
EMP: 76
SALES (corp-wide): 79.33MM **Privately Held**
Web: www.longwoodmgmt.com
SIC: **8059** 6512 Convalescent home; Commercial and industrial building operation
PA: Longwood Management Corp.
4032 Wilshire Blvd Fl 6
Los Angeles CA
213 389-6900

(P-15870)
LONGWOOD MANAGEMENT CORP
Also Called: Aldon Ter Convalsent Hosptial
1240 S Hoover St (90006-3606)
PHONE..................................213 382-8461
John Sicat, *Prin*
EMP: 155
SALES (corp-wide): 79.33MM **Privately Held**
Web: www.longwoodmgmt.com
SIC: **8059** 8051 Convalescent home; Skilled nursing care facilities
PA: Longwood Management Corp.
4032 Wilshire Blvd Fl 6
Los Angeles CA
213 389-6900

(P-15871)
LONGWOOD MANAGEMENT CORP
Also Called: Imperial Care Center
11429 Ventura Blvd (91604-3143)
PHONE..................................818 980-8200
Emma Dellanuoni, *Mgr*
EMP: 153
SQ FT: 29,525
SALES (corp-wide): 79.33MM **Privately Held**
Web: www.studiocityrehab.com
SIC: **8059** 8051 Convalescent home; Skilled nursing care facilities
PA: Longwood Management Corp.
4032 Wilshire Blvd Fl 6
Los Angeles CA
213 389-6900

(P-15872)
LONGWOOD MANAGEMENT CORP
Also Called: Live Oak Rehab
537 W Live Oak St (91776-1149)
PHONE..................................626 289-3763
Ranita Phan, *Mgr*
EMP: 130
SALES (corp-wide): 79.33MM **Privately Held**
Web: www.liveoakrehab.com
SIC: **8059** 8051 Convalescent home; Skilled nursing care facilities
PA: Longwood Management Corp.
4032 Wilshire Blvd Fl 6
Los Angeles CA
213 389-6900

(P-15873)
LONGWOOD MANAGEMENT CORP
Also Called: Colonial Care Center
1913 E 5th St (90802-2024)
PHONE..................................562 432-5751
EMP: 128
SALES (corp-wide): 79.33MM **Privately Held**
Web: www.longwoodmgmt.com
SIC: **8059** 8051 Convalescent home; Skilled nursing care facilities
PA: Longwood Management Corp.
4032 Wilshire Blvd Fl 6
Los Angeles CA
213 389-6900

(P-15874)
MAGNOLIA RHBLTTION NURSING CTR
Also Called: Magnolia Convalescent Hospital
8133 Magnolia Ave (92504-3409)
PHONE..................................951 688-4321
Larry Mays, *Pr*
Bennie J Mays, *
Bobbie N Mays, *
Grant Edgeson, *
EMP: 140 EST: 1971
SQ FT: 25,000
SALES (est): 9.51MM **Privately Held**
Web: www.magnolia-rehab.com
SIC: **8059** 8051 Convalescent home; Skilled nursing care facilities

(P-15875)
MARK ONE CORPORATION
Also Called: Hale Aloha Convalescent
812 W Main St (95380-4645)
P.O. Box 1129 (95381-1129)
PHONE..................................209 667-2484
John C Sims, *CEO*
John C Sims-ceo, *Prin*
EMP: 190 EST: 1962
SQ FT: 33,000
SALES (est): 9.56MM **Privately Held**
SIC: **8059** 8051 Nursing home, except skilled and intermediate care facility; Skilled nursing care facilities

(P-15876)
MARLINDA MANAGEMENT INC (PA)
Also Called: Sherwood Guest Home
3351 E Imperial Hwy (90262-3305)
PHONE..................................310 631-6122
Martha Lang, *Pr*
Linda Gassoumis, *
EMP: 120 EST: 1961
SALES (est): 4.17MM
SALES (corp-wide): 4.17MM **Privately Held**
SIC: **8059** Convalescent home

(P-15877)
MARNA HEALTH SERVICES INC
Also Called: Sillcrest Nursing Home
4280 Cypress Dr (92407-2960)
PHONE..................................909 882-2965
Maria Barrios, *Pr*
Napoleon Garcia, *
EMP: 70 EST: 2013
SQ FT: 120
SALES (est): 8.18MM **Privately Held**
SIC: **8059** 7389 8049 Personal care home, with health care; Business Activities at Non-Commercial Site; Physical therapist

(P-15878)
MARYCREST MANOR
10664 Saint James Dr (90230-5498)
PHONE..................................310 838-2778
Sister V Del Carmen, *Admn*
Sister Veronica Del Carmen, *Admn*
EMP: 94 EST: 1961
SQ FT: 43,449
SALES (est): 7.79MM **Privately Held**
Web: www.marycrestculvercity.com
SIC: **8059** 8051 Convalescent home; Skilled nursing care facilities

(P-15879)
MOYLES HEALTH CARE INC
604 E Merritt Ave (93274-2135)
PHONE..................................559 686-1601
Kensett J Moyle Iii, *Pr*
Kensett J Moyle Iv, *VP*
Mark Harris, *
EMP: 550 EST: 1971
SALES (est): 11.87MM **Privately Held**
SIC: **8059** Convalescent home

(P-15880)
NEW VISTA HEALTH SERVICES
Also Called: New Vsta Post Acute Care Ctr W
1516 Sawtelle Blvd (90025-3207)
PHONE..................................310 477-5501
Eugene Tipo, *Admn*
EMP: 224
SALES (corp-wide): 9.28MM **Privately Held**
Web: www.newvista.us
SIC: **8059** 8051 Nursing home, except skilled and intermediate care facility; Skilled nursing care facilities
PA: New Vista Health Services, Inc
1987 Vartikian Ave
Clovis CA
559 298-3236

(P-15881)
NEW VISTA HEALTH SERVICES
Also Called: New Vsta Nrsing Rhbltation Ctr
8647 Fenwick St (91040-1957)
PHONE..................................818 352-1421
Robert Craig, *Pr*
EMP: 224
SALES (corp-wide): 9.28MM **Privately Held**
Web: www.newvista.us
SIC: **8059** 8361 Nursing home, except skilled and intermediate care facility; Rehabilitation center, residential: health care incidental
PA: New Vista Health Services, Inc
1987 Vartikian Ave
Clovis CA
559 298-3236

(P-15882)
NORCAL CARE CENTERS INC
Also Called: Antioch Convalescent Hospital
1210 A St (94509-2327)
PHONE..................................925 757-8787
Thaylene Sunga, *Mgr*
EMP: 80
SALES (corp-wide): 4.32MM **Privately Held**
Web: www.tranquilityinconline.com
SIC: **8059** Nursing home, except skilled and intermediate care facility
PA: Norcal Care Centers, Inc.
3788 Fairway Dr
Cameron Park CA
530 677-9477

(P-15883)
NORTHERN CAL CNGRGTNAL RTRMENT
Also Called: CARMEL VALLEY MANOR
8545 Carmel Valley Rd (93923-9556)
PHONE..................................831 624-1281
Roger D Bolgard, *Ch Bd*
Jane Ipsen, *
EMP: 162 EST: 1960
SQ FT: 196,800
SALES (est): 21.23MM **Privately Held**
Web: www.cvmanor.com
SIC: **8059** Convalescent home

(P-15884)
OLYMPIA CONVALESCENT HOSPITAL
1100 S Alvarado St (90006-4110)
PHONE..................................213 487-3000
Otto Schwartz, *Admn*
Sam Lidell, *
Andre Pollak, *
EMP: 115 EST: 1971
SQ FT: 25,000
SALES (est): 12.59MM **Privately Held**
Web: www.olympia.com
SIC: **8059** 8051 Convalescent home; Skilled nursing care facilities

(P-15885)
ON MY OWN COMMUNITY SERVICES
6060 Sunrise Vista Dr Ste 2400 (95610-7053)
PHONE..................................916 726-0792
EMP: 75
Web: www.onmyown-web.com
SIC: **8059** Domiciliary care
PA: On My Own Community Services
6060 Sunrise Vista Dr
Citrus Heights CA

8059 - Nursing And Personal Care, Nec (P-15886)

(P-15886)
ORANGE CNTY RYALE CNVLSCENT HO (PA)
Also Called: Royale Convalescent Hospital
1030 W Warner Ave (92707-3147)
PHONE..............................714 546-6450
Mitchell Kantor, *Pr*
Donald Connelly Admtr, *Prin*
EMP: 330 **EST:** 1965
SQ FT: 87,000
SALES (est): 17.01MM
SALES (corp-wide): 17.01MM **Privately Held**
Web: www.royalehealth.com
SIC: 8059 8051 Convalescent home; Skilled nursing care facilities

(P-15887)
PACIFIC HAVEN CONVALESCENT HM
12072 Trask Ave (92843-3881)
PHONE..............................714 534-1942
Mike Uranga, *Admn*
EMP: 100 **EST:** 1978
SALES (est): 11.36MM **Privately Held**
Web: www.pachaven.com
SIC: 8059 8051 Convalescent home; Skilled nursing care facilities

(P-15888)
PARK MARINO CONVALESCENT CTR
2585 E Washington Blvd (91107-1446)
PHONE..............................626 463-4105
Admiral William Kite, *Prin*
EMP: 182 **EST:** 1966
SALES (est): 4.89MM
SALES (corp-wide): 9.98MM **Privately Held**
Web: www.parkmarino.com
SIC: 8059 8051 Convalescent home; Skilled nursing care facilities
PA: Diversified Health Services (Del)
136 Washington Ave
Richmond CA
510 231-6200

(P-15889)
PILGRIM PLACE IN CLAREMONT (PA)
625 Mayflower Rd (91711-4240)
PHONE..............................909 399-5500
William R Cunitz, *Pr*
Joyce Yarborough, *
Sue Fairley, *
Bernard Valek, *
Mary Ann Macias, *
EMP: 175 **EST:** 1914
SQ FT: 2,000
SALES (est): 22.23MM
SALES (corp-wide): 22.23MM **Privately Held**
Web: www.pilgrimplace.org
SIC: 8059 8051 8052 Rest home, with health care; Skilled nursing care facilities; Intermediate care facilities

(P-15890)
RAFAEL CONVALESCENT HOSPITAL
234 N San Pedro Rd (94903-2858)
PHONE..............................415 479-3450
Timothy J Egan, *Pr*
Michael Egan, *
EMP: 72 **EST:** 1958
SQ FT: 9,000
SALES (est): 7.81MM **Privately Held**
Web: www.rafaelconvalescent.com
SIC: 8059 8051 Convalescent home; Skilled nursing care facilities

(P-15891)
RIVERSIDE CNVALESCENT HOSP INC
Also Called: RIVERSIDE CONVALESCENT HOSPIT
375 Cohasset Rd (95926-2211)
PHONE..............................530 343-5595
Gladys Jennings, *Pr*
EMP: 72 **EST:** 1963
SQ FT: 50,000
SALES (est): 12.3MM **Privately Held**
Web: www.riversideconvalescent.com
SIC: 8059 Convalescent home

(P-15892)
RIVERSIDE HEALTH CARE CORP (PA)
1469 Humboldt Rd Ste 175 (95928-9204)
PHONE..............................530 897-5100
Sharon Jennings Kearns, *CEO*
EMP: 60 **EST:** 1985
SQ FT: 9,000
SALES (est): 26.06MM
SALES (corp-wide): 26.06MM **Privately Held**
Web: www.riversidehealthca.com
SIC: 8059 Convalescent home

(P-15893)
SAN BERNARDINO CARE COMPANY
467 E Gilbert St (92404-5318)
PHONE..............................909 884-4781
Jenq Chen, *Pr*
EMP: 110 **EST:** 2004
SALES (est): 4.67MM **Privately Held**
SIC: 8059 Convalescent home

(P-15894)
SAN DEGO CTR FOR CHLDREN FNDTI (PA)
3002 Armstrong St (92111-5702)
PHONE..............................858 277-9550
Moises Baron, *CEO*
EMP: 90 **EST:** 1887
SQ FT: 38,000
SALES (est): 24.56MM
SALES (corp-wide): 24.56MM **Privately Held**
Web: www.centerforchildren.org
SIC: 8059 8361 Personal care home, with health care; Residential care

(P-15895)
SAN FRANCISCOIDENCE OPCO LLC
Also Called: San Francisco Post Acute
5767 Mission St (94112-4208)
PHONE..............................415 584-3294
Jason Murray, *Pr*
Mark Hancock, *
EMP: 95 **EST:** 2014
SALES (est): 10.57MM
SALES (corp-wide): 1.53B **Privately Held**
Web: www.sfpostacute.com
SIC: 8059 Nursing and personal care, nec
HQ: Providence Group North, Llc
262 N University Ave
Farmington UT
801 447-9829

(P-15896)
SANHYD INC
Also Called: Jones Rest HM Cnvalescent Hosp
524 Callan Ave (94577-4610)
PHONE..............................510 483-6200
Pratap Poddatoori, *Pr*
EMP: 84 **EST:** 1948
SQ FT: 25,000
SALES (est): 22.74MM **Privately Held**
Web: www.sanleandrobytes.com
SIC: 8059 Convalescent home

(P-15897)
SEQUOIA LIVING INC
Also Called: Tamal Pais
501 Via Casitas Ofc (94904-1958)
PHONE..............................415 464-1767
EMP: 114
SALES (corp-wide): 114.59MM **Privately Held**
Web: www.sequoialiving.org
SIC: 8059 8062 8051 8052 Rest home, with health care; General medical and surgical hospitals; Skilled nursing care facilities; Intermediate care facilities
PA: Sequoia Living, Inc.
1525 Post St
San Francisco CA
415 202-7808

(P-15898)
SSC OAKLAND FRUITVALE OPER LP
Also Called: FRUITVALE HEALTHCARE CENTER
3020 E 15th St (94601-2305)
PHONE..............................510 261-5613
Remy Tibayan, *Prin*
EMP: 99 **EST:** 2000
SALES (est): 16.77MM **Privately Held**
Web: www.marinerhealthcare.com
SIC: 8059 8051 Convalescent home; Skilled nursing care facilities

(P-15899)
SSC PITTSBURG OPERATING CO LP
Also Called: SAVA SENIOR CARE
2351 Loveridge Rd (94565-5117)
PHONE..............................925 427-4444
EMP: 427 **EST:** 2011
SALES (est): 13.45MM
SALES (corp-wide): 1.33B **Privately Held**
Web: www.diamondridgehealthcare.com
SIC: 8059 Nursing home, except skilled and intermediate care facility
HQ: Savaseniorcare, Llc
300 Colonial Center Pkwy # 100
Roswell GA
770 829-5100

(P-15900)
ST JOHNS RETIREMENT VILLAGE
Also Called: STOLLWOOD CONVALESCENT HOSPITA
135 Woodland Ave (95695-2759)
PHONE..............................530 662-9674
John Prichard, *Admn*
EMP: 142 **EST:** 1964
SALES (est): 5.41MM **Privately Held**
Web: www.thevillageatstjohn.com
SIC: 8059 8051 8361 Convalescent home; Convalescent home with continuous nursing care; Geriatric residential care

(P-15901)
STOCKTON EDSON HEALTHCARE CORP
Also Called: GOOD SAMARITAN REHAB AND CARE
1630 N Edison St (95204-5633)
PHONE..............................209 948-8762
Emanuel Bernabe, *Pr*
Sedy Demesa, *
Gilda Dizon, *
EMP: 100 **EST:** 1988
SQ FT: 4,000
SALES (est): 9.79MM **Privately Held**
SIC: 8059 8051 Nursing home, except skilled and intermediate care facility; Skilled nursing care facilities

(P-15902)
TEMPLE PK CNVALESCENT HOSP INC
2411 W Temple St (90026-4817)
PHONE..............................213 380-2035
Barry Kohn, *Pr*
Toby Kohn, *
EMP: 77 **EST:** 1976
SALES (est): 9.92MM **Privately Held**
SIC: 8059 Convalescent home

(P-15903)
TJD LLC
Also Called: ANBERRY REHABILITATION HOSPITA
1685 Shaffer Rd (95301-4456)
PHONE..............................209 357-3420
EMP: 140 **EST:** 2000
SQ FT: 40,000
SALES (est): 7.98MM **Privately Held**
Web: www.lifegen.net
SIC: 8059 8051 8093 Nursing home, except skilled and intermediate care facility; Convalescent home with continuous nursing care; Rehabilitation center, outpatient treatment

(P-15904)
TRANQUILITY INCORPORATED
Also Called: San Miguel Villa
1050 San Miguel Rd (94518-2094)
PHONE..............................925 825-4280
Velda Pierce, *CEO*
EMP: 180 **EST:** 1976
SQ FT: 20,000
SALES (est): 17.56MM **Privately Held**
SIC: 8059 8051 Convalescent home; Skilled nursing care facilities

(P-15905)
TWO PALMS NURSING CENTER INC
Also Called: Marlinda Imperial Hospital
150 Bellefontaine St (91105-3102)
PHONE..............................626 796-1103
EMP: 185
SQ FT: 28,955
SALES (corp-wide): 3.22MM **Privately Held**
Web: www.pasadenameadows.com
SIC: 8059 8051 Convalescent home; Skilled nursing care facilities
PA: Two Palms Nursing Center, Inc.
2637 E Washington Blvd
Pasadena CA
626 798-8991

(P-15906)
UNITED CONVALESCENT FACILITIES
Also Called: University Park Healthcare Ctr
230 E Adams Blvd (90011-1426)
PHONE..............................213 748-0491
Doug Easton, *Owner*
EMP: 80 **EST:** 1998
SQ FT: 1,300
SALES (est): 8.1MM **Privately Held**

PRODUCTS & SERVICES SECTION
8062 - General Medical And Surgical Hospitals (P-15924)

SIC: 8059 Nursing home, except skilled and intermediate care facility

(P-15907)
UNITED MEDICAL MANAGEMENT INC
Also Called: Valley Healthcare
1680 N Waterman Ave (92404-5113)
PHONE.................909 886-5291
Alan Hull, Admn
EMP: 125 EST: 1982
SQ FT: 30,000
SALES (est): 7.24MM Privately Held
Web: www.progressivecarecenters.com
SIC: 8059 8051 8322 Convalescent home; Skilled nursing care facilities; Rehabilitation services

(P-15908)
VACAVLLE CNVALESCENT REHAB CTR
585 Nut Tree Ct (95687-3353)
PHONE.................707 449-8000
Joe Nicolli, Pr
EMP: 111 EST: 1994
SQ FT: 38,000
SALES (est): 24.93MM Privately Held
SIC: 8059 Convalescent home

(P-15909)
VALLE VSTA CNVLESCENT HOSP INC
1025 W 2nd Ave (92025-3839)
PHONE.................760 745-1288
Kristina Kuivon, CEO
EMP: 85 EST: 1961
SQ FT: 19,000
SALES (est): 4.45MM Privately Held
SIC: 8059 Convalescent home
PA: Covenant Care, Llc
    120 Vantis Dr Ste 200
    Aliso Viejo CA

(P-15910)
VILLA DE LA MAR INC
Also Called: Bel Vista Healthcare Center
5001 E Anaheim St (90804-3214)
PHONE.................562 494-5001
Alan Anderson, Pr
Dorothy Erickson, *
EMP: 160 EST: 1983
SALES (est): 10.37MM
SALES (corp-wide): 1.53B Privately Held
Web: www.belvista.com
SIC: 8059 Convalescent home
PA: Providence Group, Inc.
    262 N University Ave
    Farmington UT
    801 447-9829

(P-15911)
WESTLAKE DEVELOPMENT GROUP LLC
Also Called: Leisure Gardens Retirement HM
799 Yellowstone Dr Ofc (95687-3470)
PHONE.................707 447-7496
EMP: 64
SALES (corp-wide): 17.8MM Privately Held
Web: www.westlake-realty.com
SIC: 8059 Convalescent home
PA: Westlake Development Group, Llc
    520 S El Camino Real # 900
    San Mateo CA
    650 579-1010

(P-15912)
WINDSOR CYPRESS GRDNS HLTHCARE
Also Called: Windsor Cypress Garden
9025 Colorado Ave (92503-2157)
PHONE.................951 688-3643
Lee Samson, CEO
Stanley Angermeir, *
Edward Erzen, *
EMP: 3179 EST: 1972
SALES (est): 28.39MM Privately Held
SIC: 8059 8051 Convalescent home; Skilled nursing care facilities
PA: S&F Management Company, Llc
    1901 Avenue Of The Stars # 1060
    Los Angeles CA

(P-15913)
WINDSOR GARDENS HEALTHCARE C
1628 B St (94541-3020)
PHONE.................510 582-4636
Lee Samson, CEO
EMP: 133 EST: 1968
SQ FT: 5,000
SALES (est): 19.91MM Privately Held
Web: www.windsorgardenshayward.com
SIC: 8059 Convalescent home
PA: Lexington Group International, Inc
    9200 W Sunset Blvd # 950
    West Hollywood CA

8062 General Medical And Surgical Hospitals

(P-15914)
1125 SIR FRNCIS DRAKE BLVD OPE
Also Called: Kentfield Rehabilitation Hosp
1125 Sir Francis Drake Blvd (94904-1418)
PHONE.................415 456-9680
EMP: 250 EST: 2003
SALES (est): 49.91MM
SALES (corp-wide): 690.44MM Privately Held
Web: www.kentfieldhospital.com
SIC: 8062 General medical and surgical hospitals
PA: Vibra Healthcare, Llc
    4600 Lena Dr
    Mechanicsburg PA
    717 591-5700

(P-15915)
ADVENTIST HEALTH DELANO (HQ)
Also Called: Delano Regional Medical Center
1401 Garces Hwy (93215-3699)
P.O. Box 460 (93216-0460)
PHONE.................661 725-4800
EMP: 523 EST: 1973
SALES (est): 98.9MM
SALES (corp-wide): 789.42MM Privately Held
Web: www.adventisthealth.org
SIC: 8062 General medical and surgical hospitals
PA: Adventist Health System/West, Corporation
    1 Adventist Health Way
    Roseville CA
    844 574-5686

(P-15916)
ADVENTIST HEALTH DELANO
Also Called: Delano Regional Medical Center
1205 Garces Hwy Ste 208 (93215-3658)
PHONE.................661 721-5337
Ester Bumabod, Mgr
EMP: 131
SALES (corp-wide): 789.42MM Privately Held
Web: www.adventisthealth.org
SIC: 8062 5047 General medical and surgical hospitals; Therapy equipment
HQ: Adventist Health Delano
    1401 Garces Hwy Bldg A
    Delano CA
    661 725-4800

(P-15917)
ADVENTIST HEALTH MED TEHACHAPI (PA)
305 S Robinson St (93561-1726)
P.O. Box 669 (93581-0669)
PHONE.................661 750-4848
Eugene Suksi, CEO
Allen Burgess, *
EMP: 108 EST: 1949
SQ FT: 18,000
SALES (est): 2.95MM
SALES (corp-wide): 2.95MM Privately Held
Web: www.tvhd.org
SIC: 8062 General medical and surgical hospitals

(P-15918)
ADVENTIST HEALTH SONORA (HQ)
1000 Greenley Rd (95370-5200)
PHONE.................209 532-5000
Michelle Fuentes, Pr
David Larsen, *
Julie Kline S, VP
Greg Mcculloch, CFO
Stephanie Stuart, CMO*
EMP: 712 EST: 1957
SQ FT: 60,000
SALES (est): 267MM
SALES (corp-wide): 789.42MM Privately Held
Web: www.adventisthealth.org
SIC: 8062 8051 General medical and surgical hospitals; Skilled nursing care facilities
PA: Adventist Health System/West, Corporation
    1 Adventist Health Way
    Roseville CA
    844 574-5686

(P-15919)
ADVENTIST HEALTH TULARE
Also Called: ADVENTIST HEALTH
869 N Cherry St (93274-2207)
P.O. Box 619002 (93274)
PHONE.................559 688-0821
Andrea Kofl, Pr
EMP: 500 EST: 2018
SALES (est): 35.42MM
SALES (corp-wide): 789.42MM Privately Held
Web: www.adventisthealth.org
SIC: 8062 General medical and surgical hospitals
PA: Adventist Health System/West, Corporation
    1 Adventist Health Way
    Roseville CA
    844 574-5686

(P-15920)
ADVENTIST HLTH CLRLAKE HOSP IN
15140 Lakeshore Dr (95422-8106)
PHONE.................707 994-6486
Nancy Bailey, Mgr
EMP: 199
SALES (corp-wide): 789.42MM Privately Held
Web: www.adventisthealth.org
SIC: 8062 8071 General medical and surgical hospitals; Medical laboratories
HQ: Adventist Health Clearlake Hospital, Inc.
    15630 18th Ave
    Clearlake CA
    707 994-6486

(P-15921)
ADVENTIST HLTH CLRLAKE HOSP IN (HQ)
Also Called: Adventist Health Clearlake
15630 18th Ave (95422-9336)
PHONE.................707 994-6486
David Santos, CEO
Terry Newmyer, *
Jeff Eller, *
Colleen Assavapisitkul, *
Carlton Jacobson, *
EMP: 287 EST: 1968
SQ FT: 41,750
SALES (est): 164.44MM
SALES (corp-wide): 789.42MM Privately Held
Web: www.adventisthealth.org
SIC: 8062 8011 Hospital, affiliated with AMA residency; Medical centers
PA: Adventist Health System/West, Corporation
    1 Adventist Health Way
    Roseville CA
    844 574-5686

(P-15922)
ADVENTIST HLTH SYSTM/WEST CORP (PA)
Also Called: Adventist Health
1 Adventist Health Way (95661-3266)
P.O. Box 619002 (95661-9002)
PHONE.................844 574-5686
Kerry Heinrich, CEO
Todd Hofheins, *
Joyce Newmyer, CCO*
Alex Bryan, CMO*
Jason Wells Ccio, Prin
EMP: 350 EST: 1973
SQ FT: 55,000
SALES (est): 789.42MM
SALES (corp-wide): 789.42MM Privately Held
Web: www.adventisthealth.org
SIC: 8062 General medical and surgical hospitals

(P-15923)
ADVENTIST HLTH SYSTM/WEST CORP
Also Called: Bakersfield Heart Hospital
3001 Sillect Ave (93308-6337)
PHONE.................661 316-6000
Kerry Heinrich, Brnch Mgr
EMP: 336
SALES (corp-wide): 789.42MM Privately Held
Web: www.adventisthealth.org
SIC: 8062 General medical and surgical hospitals
PA: Adventist Health System/West, Corporation
    1 Adventist Health Way
    Roseville CA
    844 574-5686

(P-15924)
ADVENTIST HLTH SYSTM/WEST CORP

8062 - General Medical And Surgical Hospitals (P-15925)

Also Called: St Helena Hospital Clearlake
18th Ave Hwy 53 (95422)
PHONE......................707 994-6486
Kendall Fults, *CEO*
EMP: 77
SALES (corp-wide): 789.42MM **Privately Held**
Web: www.adventisthealth.org
SIC: **8062** General medical and surgical hospitals
PA: Adventist Health System/West, Corporation
1 Adventist Health Way
Roseville CA
844 574-5686

(P-15925)
ADVENTIST MED CENTER-HANFORD (HQ)
Also Called: ADVENTIST HEALTH
115 Mall Dr (93230-5786)
P.O. Box 619002 (93230)
PHONE......................559 582-9000
Eric Martinson, *CFO*
EMP: 121 EST: 2010
SALES (est): 375.47MM
SALES (corp-wide): 789.42MM **Privately Held**
Web: www.adventisthealth.org
SIC: **8062** General medical and surgical hospitals
PA: Adventist Health System/West, Corporation
1 Adventist Health Way
Roseville CA
844 574-5686

(P-15926)
ADVENTIST MED CENTER-HANFORD
125 Mall Dr (93230-5787)
PHONE......................559 537-1377
EMP: 132
SALES (corp-wide): 789.42MM **Privately Held**
Web: www.adventisthealth.org
SIC: **8062** General medical and surgical hospitals
HQ: Adventist Medical Center-Hanford
115 Mall Dr
Hanford CA
559 582-9000

(P-15927)
ADVENTIST HLTH CLEARLAKE HOSP
Also Called: ST HELANA HOSPITAL CLEARLAKE
18th Ave & Hwy 53 (95422)
PHONE......................707 994-6486
Terry Newmeyer, *CEO*
Terry Newmeyer, *Pr*
Jeniffer Swenson, *
EMP: 114 EST: 1975
SQ FT: 62,000
SALES (est): 143.24MM **Privately Held**
SIC: **8062** General medical and surgical hospitals

(P-15928)
AHM GEMCH INC
Also Called: Greater El Monte Cmnty Hosp
1701 Santa Anita Ave (91733-3411)
PHONE......................626 579-7777
Jeffrey Flocken, *CEO*
Patrick Steinhauser, *COO*
Gary Louis, *CFO*
EMP: 180 EST: 1973
SQ FT: 71,500
SALES (est): 40.24MM
SALES (corp-wide): 476.02MM **Privately Held**
Web: www.ahmchealth.com
SIC: **8062** General medical and surgical hospitals
PA: Ahmc Healthcare Inc.
506 W Valley Blvd Ste 300
San Gabriel CA
626 943-7526

(P-15929)
AHMC ANHEIM RGIONAL MED CTR LP
1111 W La Palma Ave (92801-2804)
PHONE......................714 774-1450
Barry Arbuckle, *Prin*
Jane Cutler, *
Donald Lorack, *
Kathy Doi, *
▲ EMP: 4174 EST: 1959
SQ FT: 500
SALES (est): 23.89MM
SALES (corp-wide): 476.02MM **Privately Held**
Web: www.ahmchealth.com
SIC: **8062** General medical and surgical hospitals
PA: Ahmc Healthcare Inc.
506 W Valley Blvd Ste 300
San Gabriel CA
626 943-7526

(P-15930)
AHMC ANHEIM RGIONAL MED CTR LP (PA)
Also Called: Anaheim Regional Medical Ctr
1111 W La Palma Ave (92801-2804)
PHONE......................714 774-1450
Patrick Petre, *CEO*
Deborah Webber, *
Kathy Doi, *
Marie Trembath, *
EMP: 976 EST: 1958
SALES (est): 137.25MM
SALES (corp-wide): 137.25MM **Privately Held**
Web: www.ahmchealth.com
SIC: **8062** 8069 General medical and surgical hospitals; Childrens' hospital

(P-15931)
AHMC HEALTHCARE INC (PA)
506 W Valley Blvd Ste 300 (91776-5716)
PHONE......................626 943-7526
Jonathan Wu Md, *CEO*
EMP: 150 EST: 2004
SALES (est): 476.02MM
SALES (corp-wide): 476.02MM **Privately Held**
Web: www.ahmchealth.com
SIC: **8062** 8641 General medical and surgical hospitals; Civic and social associations

(P-15932)
AHMC HEALTHCARE INC
1701 Santa Anita Ave (91733-3411)
PHONE......................626 579-7777
EMP: 143
SALES (corp-wide): 476.02MM **Privately Held**
Web: www.ahmchealth.com
SIC: **8062** General medical and surgical hospitals
PA: Ahmc Healthcare Inc.
506 W Valley Blvd Ste 300
San Gabriel CA
626 943-7526

(P-15933)
AHMC SETON MEDICAL CENTER LLC
Also Called: Seton Medical Center Coastside
600 Marine Blvd (94038-9641)
PHONE......................650 563-7100
Judy Cook, *Brnch Mgr*
EMP: 411
SALES (corp-wide): 22.97MM **Privately Held**
Web: www.ahmchealth.com
SIC: **8062** 5812 8051 General medical and surgical hospitals; Eating places; Skilled nursing care facilities
PA: Ahmc Seton Medical Center Llc
1900 Sullivan Ave
Daly City CA
650 992-4000

(P-15934)
AHMC WHITTIER HOSP MED CTR LP
9080 Colima Rd (90605-1600)
PHONE......................562 945-3561
Richard Castro, *CEO*
EMP: 850 EST: 2001
SQ FT: 16,782
SALES (est): 183.04MM
SALES (corp-wide): 476.02MM **Privately Held**
Web: www.ahmchealth.com
SIC: **8062** General medical and surgical hospitals
PA: Ahmc Healthcare Inc.
506 W Valley Blvd Ste 300
San Gabriel CA
626 943-7526

(P-15935)
ALAKOR HEALTHCARE LLC
Also Called: MONROVIA MEMORIAL HOSPITAL
323 S Heliotrope Ave (91016-2914)
PHONE......................626 408-9800
Jon Woods, *
Ron Kupferstein, *
EMP: 126 EST: 2004
SQ FT: 10,000
SALES (est): 15.69MM **Privately Held**
Web: www.monroviamemorial.com
SIC: **8062** General medical and surgical hospitals

(P-15936)
ALHAMBRA HOSPITAL MED CTR LP
Also Called: Alhambra Hospital Medical Ctr
100 S Raymond Ave (91801-3166)
PHONE......................626 570-1606
Iris Lai, *Managing Member*
EMP: 160 EST: 1920
SQ FT: 200,000
SALES (est): 79.79MM
SALES (corp-wide): 476.02MM **Privately Held**
Web: www.alhambrahospital.com
SIC: **8062** General medical and surgical hospitals
PA: Ahmc Healthcare Inc.
506 W Valley Blvd Ste 300
San Gabriel CA
626 943-7526

(P-15937)
ALTA HEALTHCARE SYSTEM LLC (HQ)
4081 E Olympic Blvd (90023-3330)
PHONE......................323 267-0477
David Topper, *Managing Member*
Sam Lee, *
EMP: 250 EST: 1998
SALES (est): 108.98MM
SALES (corp-wide): 3.91B **Privately Held**
Web: www.sch-culvercity.com
SIC: **8062** General medical and surgical hospitals
PA: Prospect Medical Holdings, Inc.
3415 S Sepulveda Blvd # 9
Los Angeles CA
310 943-4500

(P-15938)
ALTA HOSPITALS SYSTEM LLC
Also Called: Foothill Regional Medical Ctr
14662 Newport Ave (92780-6064)
PHONE......................714 619-7700
EMP: 575
SALES (corp-wide): 3.91B **Privately Held**
Web: www.pmh.com
SIC: **8062** General medical and surgical hospitals
HQ: Alta Hospitals System, Llc
3415 S Sepulveda Blvd # 9
Los Angeles CA

(P-15939)
ALVARADO HOSPITAL LLC (DH)
6655 Alvarado Rd (92120-5208)
PHONE......................619 287-3270
Darlene Wetton, *
Gudrun Moll, *
EMP: 232 EST: 1989
SALES (est): 71.09MM
SALES (corp-wide): 534.4MM **Privately Held**
Web: www.alvaradohospital.com
SIC: **8062** General medical and surgical hospitals
HQ: University Of California, San Diego
9500 Gilman Dr
La Jolla CA
858 534-2230

(P-15940)
ALVARADO HOSPITAL MED CTR INC
6655 Alvarado Rd (92120-5208)
PHONE......................619 287-3270
Sharilee Smith, *Pr*
EMP: 791 EST: 2000
SALES (est): 122.61MM
SALES (corp-wide): 19.58B **Publicly Held**
Web: www.alvaradohospital.com
SIC: **8062** General medical and surgical hospitals
PA: Tenet Healthcare Corporation
14201 Dallas Pkwy
Dallas TX
469 893-2200

(P-15941)
AMERICAN HLTHCARE SYSTEMS CORP (PA)
505 N Brand Blvd Ste 1110 (91203-3932)
PHONE......................818 646-9933
Michael Sarian, *Dir*
Aimee Gill, *VP*
Aramais Paronyan, *CMO*
Jonathan Burket, *CCO*
EMP: 293 EST: 2021
SALES (est): 143.23MM
SALES (corp-wide): 143.23MM **Privately Held**
SIC: **8062** General medical and surgical hospitals

8062 - General Medical And Surgical Hospitals (P-15959)

(P-15942)
AMERICAN HOSPITAL MGT CORP (PA)
Also Called: Mad River Community Hospital
3800 Janes Rd (95521-4742)
P.O. Box 1115 (95518-1115)
PHONE...................707 822-3621
Allen E Shaw, *Pr*
Doug A Shaw, *
Charles F Forbes, *
Michael Young, *
EMP: 500 **EST:** 1955
SQ FT: 60,000
SALES (est): 117.42MM
SALES (corp-wide): 117.42MM **Privately Held**
Web: www.madriverhospital.com
SIC: 8062 General medical and surgical hospitals

(P-15943)
AMI-HTI TRZANA ENCINO JINT VNT
Also Called: A M I Encn-Trzana Rgnal Med Ce
18321 Clark St (91356-3501)
PHONE...................818 881-0800
Dale Surowitz, *Mng Pt*
EMP: 79 **EST:** 1993
SQ FT: 180,000
SALES (est): 4.09MM **Privately Held**
SIC: 8062 General medical and surgical hospitals

(P-15944)
AMISUB OF CALIFORNIA INC (DH)
Also Called: Amisub
18321 Clark St (91356-3501)
PHONE...................818 881-0800
Dale Surowitz, *CEO*
Don Kreitz, *
Nick Lymberopolous, *
EMP: 900 **EST:** 1979
SQ FT: 180,000
SALES (est): 98.79MM
SALES (corp-wide): 19.58B **Publicly Held**
SIC: 8062 General medical and surgical hospitals
HQ: Tenet Healthsystem Medical, Inc.
14201 Dallas Pkwy
Dallas TX
469 893-2000

(P-15945)
ANAHEIM GLOBAL MEDICAL CENTER
1025 S Anaheim Blvd (92805-5806)
PHONE...................714 533-6220
Jamie You, *CEO*
Marven E Howard, *
Jason Liu, *
EMP: 975 **EST:** 1981
SALES (est): 108.46MM **Privately Held**
Web: www.anaheimglobalmedicalcenter.com
SIC: 8062 General medical and surgical hospitals
HQ: Kpc Healthcare, Inc.
1301 N Tustin Ave
Santa Ana CA
714 953-3652

(P-15946)
ANAHEIM REGIONAL MEDICAL CTR
Also Called: Cardiac Unit
1111 W La Palma Ave (92801-2804)
PHONE...................714 774-1450
EMP: 112

SALES (corp-wide): 137.25MM **Privately Held**
Web: www.ahmchealth.com
SIC: 8062 General medical and surgical hospitals
PA: Ahmc Anaheim Regional Medical Center Lp
1111 W La Palma Ave
Anaheim CA
714 774-1450

(P-15947)
ANAHEIM REGIONAL MEDICAL CTR
Also Called: Ahmc
1211 W La Palma Ave (92801-2815)
PHONE...................714 999-3847
Patrick Petre, *Brnch Mgr*
EMP: 112
SALES (corp-wide): 137.25MM **Privately Held**
Web: www.ahmchealth.com
SIC: 8062 General medical and surgical hospitals
PA: Ahmc Anaheim Regional Medical Center Lp
1111 W La Palma Ave
Anaheim CA
714 774-1450

(P-15948)
ANTELOPE VALLEY HEALTH CARE DI (PA)
Also Called: Avmc
1600 W Avenue J (93534-2814)
P.O. Box 7001 (93539-7001)
PHONE...................661 949-5000
Edward Mirzabegian, *CEO*
Abdallah Farrukh, *
Dennis Empey, *
Slavka Rehacek, *
EMP: 1660 **EST:** 1955
SQ FT: 300,000
SALES (est): 494.78MM
SALES (corp-wide): 494.78MM **Privately Held**
Web: www.avmc.com
SIC: 8062 General medical and surgical hospitals

(P-15949)
ANTELOPE VALLEY HOSPITAL INC
Also Called: Antelope Valley Home Care
44335 Lowtree Ave (93534-4167)
PHONE...................661 949-5936
Patti Sheldon, *Mgr*
EMP: 168
SALES (corp-wide): 494.78MM **Privately Held**
Web: www.avmc.org
SIC: 8062 8082 General medical and surgical hospitals; Home health care services
PA: Antelope Valley Health Care District
1600 W Avenue J
Lancaster CA
661 949-5000

(P-15950)
ANTELOPE VALLEY HOSPITAL INC
Also Called: Antelope Valley Hlth Care Dst
44335 Lowtree Ave (93534-4167)
PHONE...................661 949-5000
Cheryl Akerly, *Brnch Mgr*
EMP: 216
SALES (corp-wide): 494.78MM **Privately Held**
Web: www.avmc.org

SIC: 8062 General medical and surgical hospitals
PA: Antelope Valley Health Care District
1600 W Avenue J
Lancaster CA
661 949-5000

(P-15951)
ANTELOPE VALLEY HOSPITAL INC
Antelope Otpatient Imaging Ctr
44105 15th St W Ste 100 (93534-4090)
PHONE...................661 726-6050
Veronica Munoz-rivera, *Brnch Mgr*
EMP: 168
SALES (corp-wide): 494.78MM **Privately Held**
Web: www.avmc.org
SIC: 8062 8099 General medical and surgical hospitals; Medical services organization
PA: Antelope Valley Health Care District
1600 W Avenue J
Lancaster CA
661 949-5000

(P-15952)
ARROWHEAD REGIONAL MEDICAL CTR
Also Called: Armc
400 N Pepper Ave (92324-1801)
PHONE...................909 580-1000
Patrick Petre, *Dir*
Sam Hessami, *CMO*
EMP: 2500 **EST:** 1952
SQ FT: 950,000
SALES (est): 595.65MM
SALES (corp-wide): 4.01B **Privately Held**
Web: www.arrowheadregional.org
SIC: 8062 General medical and surgical hospitals
PA: San Bernardino County
385 N Arrowhead Ave
San Bernardino CA
909 387-3841

(P-15953)
ARROYO GRANDE COMMUNITY HOSPITAL
Also Called: Emergency Dept Dignity Hlth
345 S Halcyon Rd (93420-3817)
PHONE...................805 473-7626
EMP: 400
SIC: 8062 General medical and surgical hospitals

(P-15954)
AUXILARY OF MSSION HOSP MSSION
Also Called: Mission Hospital
27700 Medical Center Rd (92691-6426)
PHONE...................949 364-1400
Eduardo Jordan, *Ch Bd*
Kenn Mcfarland, *Pr*
Vicki J Veal, *
EMP: 1242 **EST:** 2011
SALES (est): 156.11K
SALES (corp-wide): 765.86MM **Privately Held**
Web: www.mission4health.com
SIC: 8062 General medical and surgical hospitals
PA: Mission Hospital Regional Medical Center Inc
27700 Medical Center Rd
Mission Viejo CA
949 364-1400

(P-15955)
BAKERSFELD MEM HOSP FOUNDATION
420 34th St (93301-2237)
PHONE...................661 327-4647
Ken Keller, *Prin*
Ken Keller, *CEO*
Tracy Kiser, *1st*
David Morton Second, *Vice Chairman*
Andrew Paulden, *Treas*
EMP: 60 **EST:** 1980
SALES (est): 2.76MM **Privately Held**
Web: www.supportbakersfield.org
SIC: 8062 General medical and surgical hospitals

(P-15956)
BAKERSFIELD MEMORIAL HOSPITAL
Also Called: Memorial Center
420 34th St (93301-2237)
P.O. Box 2400 (85002-2400)
PHONE...................661 327-1792
Jon Van Boening, *CEO*
Gordon K Foster, *
EMP: 1100 **EST:** 1953
SQ FT: 364,000
SALES (est): 566.75MM **Privately Held**
Web: www.dignityhealth.org
SIC: 8062 Hospital, affiliated with AMA residency
HQ: Dignity Health
185 Berry St Ste 200
San Francisco CA
415 438-5500

(P-15957)
BANNER LSSEN MED CTR FNDTION I
Also Called: Banner Lassen Medical Center
1800 Spring Ridge Dr (96130-6100)
PHONE...................530 252-2000
Bob Edwards, *CEO*
Shelby Diede, *CFO*
EMP: 200 **EST:** 1996
SALES (est): 42.85MM **Privately Held**
Web: www.bannerhealth.com
SIC: 8062 8051 General medical and surgical hospitals; Skilled nursing care facilities

(P-15958)
BARTON MEMORIAL HOSPITAL
Also Called: Barton Home Health and Hospice
2092 Lake Tahoe Blvd Ste 500 (96150-6429)
PHONE...................530 543-5581
EMP: 544
SALES (corp-wide): 228.6MM **Privately Held**
Web: www.bartonhealth.org
SIC: 8062 General medical and surgical hospitals
HQ: Barton Memorial Hospital
2170 South Ave
South Lake Tahoe CA
530 541-3420

(P-15959)
BAYVIEW HOSP MNTAL HLTH SYSTEM
330 Moss St (91911-2005)
PHONE...................619 426-6310
Robert Bourseau, *Prin*
EMP: 135 **EST:** 1971
SALES (est): 26.36MM **Privately Held**
Web: www.paradisevalleyhospital.net
SIC: 8062 General medical and surgical hospitals

8062 - General Medical And Surgical Hospitals (P-15960)

PA: Prime Healthcare Paradise Valley, Llc
2400 E 4th St
National City CA

(P-15960)
BEAR VLY CMNTY HEALTHCARE DST (PA)
41870 Garstin Dr (92315-2088)
PHONE..................909 866-6501
Raymond Hino, *CEO*
Donna Nicely, *
Barbara Espinoza, *
Christopher Fagan, *
EMP: 150 EST: 1985
SQ FT: 25,000
SALES (est): 341.35K
SALES (corp-wide): 341.35K **Privately Held**
Web: www.bearvalleycommunityhospital.com
SIC: **8062** General medical and surgical hospitals

(P-15961)
BEVERLY COMMUNITY HOSP ASSN (PA)
Also Called: Beverly Hospital
309 W Beverly Blvd (90640-4308)
PHONE..................323 726-1222
Alice Cheng, *CEO*
Gary Kiff, *
Renee D Martinez, *
David I Chambers, *
Mohammad A, *
EMP: 937 EST: 1949
SQ FT: 274,000
SALES (est): 145.51MM
SALES (corp-wide): 145.51MM **Privately Held**
Web: www.beverly.org
SIC: **8062** General medical and surgical hospitals

(P-15962)
BIO-MED SERVICES INC
Also Called: Prime Healthcare Services
3300 E Guasti Rd (91761-8655)
PHONE..................909 235-4400
Prem Reddy, *CEO*
EMP: 85 EST: 2006
SALES (est): 29.17MM
SALES (corp-wide): 1.03B **Privately Held**
SIC: **8062** General medical and surgical hospitals
HQ: Prime Healthcare Services Inc
3480 E Guasti Rd
Ontario CA

(P-15963)
BROTMAN MEDICAL CENTER INC
Also Called: Southern Cal Hosp At Culver Cy
3828 Delmas Ter (90232-6806)
PHONE..................310 836-7000
TOLL FREE: 800
Michael Klepin, *CEO*
EMP: 300 EST: 1961
SQ FT: 183,000
SALES (est): 61.07MM
SALES (corp-wide): 3.91B **Privately Held**
Web: www.sch-culvercity.com
SIC: **8062** General medical and surgical hospitals
PA: Prospect Medical Holdings, Inc.
3415 S Sepulveda Blvd # 9
Los Angeles CA
310 943-4500

(P-15964)
CALIFRNIA HOSP MED CTR FNDTION
1401 S Grand Ave (90015-3010)
PHONE..................213 742-5867
Phillip C Hill, *Ch Bd*
Nathan R Nusbaum, *
Clark Underwood, *
David Milovich, *
Linda Bolor, *
▲ EMP: 1500 EST: 1926
SQ FT: 800,000
SALES (est): 249.47MM **Privately Held**
Web: www.supportcaliforniahospital.org
SIC: **8062** Hospital, med school affiliated with nursing and residency
HQ: Dignity Health
185 Berry St Ste 200
San Francisco CA
415 438-5500

(P-15965)
CALIFRNIA RHBLITATION INST LLC
Also Called: SELECT MEDICAL
2070 Century Park E (90067-1907)
P.O. Box 2034 (17055-0793)
PHONE..................424 363-1003
Michael Tarvin, *VP*
EMP: 72 EST: 2014
SALES (est): 143.99MM
SALES (corp-wide): 5.53B **Publicly Held**
Web: www.californiarehabinstitute.com
SIC: **8062** General medical and surgical hospitals
PA: Select Medical Holdings Corporation
4714 Gettysburg Rd
Mechanicsburg PA
717 972-1100

(P-15966)
CARBON HEALTH TECHNOLOGIES INC
411 Grand Ave (94610-5022)
PHONE..................510 844-4097
EMP: 135
SALES (corp-wide): 104.49MM **Privately Held**
Web: www.carbonhealth.com
SIC: **8062** General medical and surgical hospitals
PA: Carbon Health Technologies, Inc.
2100 Franklin St Ste 355
Oakland CA
415 223-2858

(P-15967)
CASA CLINA HOSP CTRS FOR HLTHC (HQ)
Also Called: Casa Clina Ctrs For Rhbltation
255 E Bonita Ave (91767-1923)
P.O. Box 6001 (91769-6001)
PHONE..................909 596-7733
Kelly Linden, *Pr*
Steve Norin, *
Randy Blackman, *Vice Chairman* *
Mary Lou Jensen, *
Stephen Graeber, *
▲ EMP: 500 EST: 1936
SQ FT: 90,000
SALES (est): 96.69MM
SALES (corp-wide): 136.57MM **Privately Held**
Web: www.casacolina.org
SIC: **8062** General medical and surgical hospitals
PA: Casa Colina, Inc.
255 E Bonita Ave
Pomona CA
909 596-7733

(P-15968)
CATHOLIC HEALTHCARE WEST
Also Called: St Mary's Medical Center
450 Stanyan St (94117-1019)
PHONE..................415 668-1000
EMP: 1100
Web: www.dignityhealth.org
SIC: **8062** General medical and surgical hospitals

(P-15969)
CATHOLIC HLTHCARE W STHERN CAL (HQ)
1050 Linden Ave (90813-3321)
PHONE..................562 491-9000
EMP: 125
SALES (est): 43.27MM
SALES (corp-wide): 7.06B **Privately Held**
SIC: **8062** General medical and surgical hospitals
PA: Dignity Health
185 Berry St Ste 300
San Francisco CA
415 438-5500

(P-15970)
CEDARS-SINAI MEDICAL CENTER
Also Called: Nephrology
8635 W 3rd St Ste 1195 (90048-6146)
P.O. Box 48956 (90048-0956)
PHONE..................310 824-3664
Larry Froch, *Prin*
EMP: 586
SALES (corp-wide): 4.7B **Privately Held**
Web: www.cedars-sinai.org
SIC: **8062** General medical and surgical hospitals
PA: Cedars-Sinai Medical Center
8700 Beverly Blvd
West Hollywood CA
310 423-3277

(P-15971)
CEDARS-SINAI MEDICAL CENTER
Also Called: Cedars Surgical Research Ctr
8700 Beverly Blvd # 4018 (90048-1804)
PHONE..................310 855-7701
Linda Protcor, *Div Mgr*
EMP: 293
SALES (corp-wide): 4.7B **Privately Held**
Web: www.cedars-sinai.org
SIC: **8062** 8733 General medical and surgical hospitals; Medical research
PA: Cedars-Sinai Medical Center
8700 Beverly Blvd
West Hollywood CA
310 423-3277

(P-15972)
CEDARS-SINAI MEDICAL CENTER
8797 Beverly Blvd Ste 220 (90048-1892)
PHONE..................310 423-5468
EMP: 107
SALES (corp-wide): 4.7B **Privately Held**
Web: www.cedars-sinai.org
SIC: **8062** General medical and surgical hospitals
PA: Cedars-Sinai Medical Center
8700 Beverly Blvd
West Hollywood CA
310 423-3277

(P-15973)
CEDARS-SINAI MEDICAL CENTER
8727 W 3rd St (90048-3843)
PHONE..................310 423-6451
Eric Fee, *Genl Mgr*
EMP: 107
SALES (corp-wide): 4.7B **Privately Held**
Web: www.cedars-sinai.org
SIC: **8062** General medical and surgical hospitals
PA: Cedars-Sinai Medical Center
8700 Beverly Blvd
West Hollywood CA
310 423-3277

(P-15974)
CEDARS-SINAI MEDICAL CENTER
8730 Alden Dr West 220 (90048-3690)
PHONE..................310 423-2587
EMP: 133
SALES (corp-wide): 4.7B **Privately Held**
Web: www.cedars-sinai.org
SIC: **8062** General medical and surgical hospitals
PA: Cedars-Sinai Medical Center
8700 Beverly Blvd
West Hollywood CA
310 423-3277

(P-15975)
CEDARS-SINAI MEDICAL CENTER
Also Called: Clinical Translational RES Ctr
8723 Alden Dr (90048-3692)
PHONE..................310 423-8965
EMP: 266
SALES (corp-wide): 4.7B **Privately Held**
Web: www.cedars-sinai.org
SIC: **8062** General medical and surgical hospitals
PA: Cedars-Sinai Medical Center
8700 Beverly Blvd
West Hollywood CA
310 423-3277

(P-15976)
CEDARS-SINAI MEDICAL CENTER
Anesthesiology Department
8700 Beverly Blvd Ste 8211 (90048-1804)
PHONE..................310 423-5841
Tom Pirscelac, *Admn*
EMP: 133
SALES (corp-wide): 4.7B **Privately Held**
Web: www.cedars-sinai.org
SIC: **8062** 3841 General medical and surgical hospitals; Anesthesia apparatus
PA: Cedars-Sinai Medical Center
8700 Beverly Blvd
West Hollywood CA
310 423-3277

(P-15977)
CEDARS-SINAI MEDICAL CENTER
8700 Beverly Blvd Ste 2216 (90048-1804)
PHONE..................310 423-5147
Thomas Priselac, *Pr*
EMP: 80
SALES (corp-wide): 4.7B **Privately Held**
Web: www.cedars-sinai.org
SIC: **8062** General medical and surgical hospitals
PA: Cedars-Sinai Medical Center
8700 Beverly Blvd
West Hollywood CA
310 423-3277

PRODUCTS & SERVICES SECTION
8062 - General Medical And Surgical Hospitals (P-15996)

(P-15978)
CEDARS-SINAI MEDICAL CENTER
310 N San Vicente Blvd (90048-1810)
PHONE...................310 423-9310
Sylvia Salgado Estrada, *Prin*
EMP: 133
SALES (corp-wide): 4.7B **Privately Held**
Web: www.cedars-sinai.org
SIC: 8062 General medical and surgical hospitals
PA: Cedars-Sinai Medical Center
 8700 Beverly Blvd
 West Hollywood CA
 310 423-3277

(P-15979)
CEDARS-SINAI MEDICAL CENTER
99 N La Cienega Blvd Ste Mezz (90211-2222)
PHONE...................310 967-1884
Lloyd Greig, *Brnch Mgr*
EMP: 133
SALES (corp-wide): 4.7B **Privately Held**
Web: www.cedars-sinai.org
SIC: 8062 General medical and surgical hospitals
PA: Cedars-Sinai Medical Center
 8700 Beverly Blvd
 West Hollywood CA
 310 423-3277

(P-15980)
CEDARS-SINAI MEDICAL CENTER
Also Called: Cedars-Sinai Home Care
8635 W 3rd St Ste 1165w (90048-6134)
PHONE...................310 423-3277
Sheldon King, *Pr*
EMP: 346
SALES (corp-wide): 4.7B **Privately Held**
Web: www.cedars-sinai.org
SIC: 8062 General medical and surgical hospitals
PA: Cedars-Sinai Medical Center
 8700 Beverly Blvd
 West Hollywood CA
 310 423-3277

(P-15981)
CEDARS-SINAI MEDICAL CENTER
Also Called: Medical Genetics
444 S San Vicente Blvd Ste 1001 (90048-4170)
PHONE...................310 423-9520
David Rimoin, *Mgr*
EMP: 453
SALES (corp-wide): 4.7B **Privately Held**
Web: www.cedars-sinai.org
SIC: 8062 8099 General medical and surgical hospitals; Health screening service
PA: Cedars-Sinai Medical Center
 8700 Beverly Blvd
 West Hollywood CA
 310 423-3277

(P-15982)
CEDARS-SINAI MEDICAL CENTER
4100 W 190th St (90504-5513)
PHONE...................310 967-1900
Clyde Goldman, *Prin*
EMP: 586
SALES (corp-wide): 4.7B **Privately Held**
Web: www.cedars-sinai.org
SIC: 8062 8011 General medical and surgical hospitals; Medical centers
PA: Cedars-Sinai Medical Center
 8700 Beverly Blvd
 West Hollywood CA
 310 423-3277

(P-15983)
CEDARS-SINAI MEDICAL CENTER
Also Called: Health System Medical Network
250 N Robertson Blvd # 101 (90211-1788)
PHONE...................310 385-3400
EMP: 719
SALES (corp-wide): 4.7B **Privately Held**
Web: www.cedars-sinai.org
SIC: 8062 8011 General medical and surgical hospitals; Offices and clinics of medical doctors
PA: Cedars-Sinai Medical Center
 8700 Beverly Blvd
 West Hollywood CA
 310 423-3277

(P-15984)
CEDARS-SINAI MEDICAL CENTER
Emergency Services
8700 Beverly Blvd Ste 1103 (90048-1804)
PHONE...................310 423-8780
EMP: 133
SALES (corp-wide): 4.7B **Privately Held**
Web: www.cedars-sinai.org
SIC: 8062 General medical and surgical hospitals
PA: Cedars-Sinai Medical Center
 8700 Beverly Blvd
 West Hollywood CA
 310 423-3277

(P-15985)
CEDARS-SNAI IMGING MED GROUP A
8700 Beverly Blvd (90048-1804)
P.O. Box 48750 (90048-0750)
PHONE...................310 423-8000
Barry D Pressman, *Ch Bd*
EMP: 61 **EST:** 1992
SALES (est): 3.93MM **Privately Held**
Web: www.cedars-sinai.org
SIC: 8062 General medical and surgical hospitals

(P-15986)
CENTRAL VALLEY GENERAL HOSP (HQ)
1025 N Douty St (93230-3722)
PHONE...................559 583-2100
Wayne Ferch, *CEO*
Douglas Lafferty, *
Kirby Mckague, *VP Fin*
EMP: 400 **EST:** 1992
SQ FT: 96,000
SALES (est): 77.28MM
SALES (corp-wide): 789.42MM **Privately Held**
Web: www.adventisthealth.org
SIC: 8062 General medical and surgical hospitals
PA: Adventist Health System/West, Corporation
 1 Adventist Health Way
 Roseville CA
 844 574-5686

(P-15987)
CENTRAL VLY SPECIALTY HOSP INC
730 17th St (95354-1209)
PHONE...................209 248-7700
Gia Smith, *CEO*
EMP: 139 **EST:** 2012
SALES (est): 51.69MM **Privately Held**
Web: www.centralvalleyspecialty.com
SIC: 8062 General medical and surgical hospitals

(P-15988)
CFHS HOLDINGS INC
Also Called: Centinela Frman Rgonal Med Ctr
4650 Lincoln Blvd (90292-6306)
PHONE...................310 823-8911
EMP: 906
SQ FT: 150,000
SALES (corp-wide): 4.7B **Privately Held**
Web: www.marinahospital.com
SIC: 8062 General medical and surgical hospitals
HQ: Cfhs Holdings, Inc.
 4650 Lincoln Blvd
 Marina Del Rey CA

(P-15989)
CFHS HOLDINGS INC
Also Called: Centinela Frman Rgonal Med Ctr
4640 Admiralty Way Ste 650 (90292-6667)
PHONE...................310 448-7800
Bob Bokern, *Prin*
EMP: 1036
SALES (corp-wide): 4.7B **Privately Held**
Web: www.marinahospital.com
SIC: 8062 General medical and surgical hospitals
HQ: Cfhs Holdings, Inc.
 4650 Lincoln Blvd
 Marina Del Rey CA

(P-15990)
CFHS HOLDINGS INC
Also Called: Centinela Frman Rgonal Med Ctr
555 E Hardy St (90301-4011)
PHONE...................310 673-4660
Michael Rembis, *Brnch Mgr*
EMP: 777
SALES (corp-wide): 4.7B **Privately Held**
Web: www.marinahospital.com
SIC: 8062 General medical and surgical hospitals
HQ: Cfhs Holdings, Inc.
 4650 Lincoln Blvd
 Marina Del Rey CA

(P-15991)
CHAPMAN GLOBAL MEDICAL CTR INC
Also Called: Chapman Family Health
2601 E Chapman Ave (92869-3206)
PHONE...................714 633-0011
TOLL FREE: 800
Matt Whaley, *CEO*
Robert Heinemeier, *
EMP: 425 **EST:** 1968
SQ FT: 96,000
SALES (est): 98.36K **Privately Held**
Web: www.chapmanglobalmedicalcenter.com
SIC: 8062 General medical and surgical hospitals
HQ: Kpc Healthcare, Inc.
 1301 N Tustin Ave
 Santa Ana CA
 714 953-3652

(P-15992)
CHILDRENS HOSP LOS ANGLES MED (PA)
Also Called: CHILDRENS HOSPITAL LOS ANGELES
6430 W Sunset Blvd Ste 600 (90028-7901)
PHONE...................323 361-2336
Robert Adler, *Pr*

Kelly M Johnson, *
EMP: 60 **EST:** 1977
SQ FT: 10,000
SALES (est): 229.93MM
SALES (corp-wide): 229.93MM **Privately Held**
Web: www.chla.org
SIC: 8062 General medical and surgical hospitals

(P-15993)
CHILDRENS HOSP OKLAND RES INST
Also Called: Childrens Hosp RES Ctr At Okla
5700 Martin Luther King Jr Way (94609-1673)
PHONE...................510 450-7600
Antonie H Paap, *Pr*
EMP: 73 **EST:** 1983
SALES (est): 31.93MM
SALES (corp-wide): 719.93MM **Privately Held**
Web: www.chori.org
SIC: 8062 General medical and surgical hospitals
PA: Children's Hospital & Research Center At Oakland
 747 52nd St
 Oakland CA
 510 428-3000

(P-15994)
CHILDRENS HOSP RES CTR AT OKLA (PA)
Also Called: Ucsf Benioff Chld Hosp Oakland
747 52nd St (94609-1809)
PHONE...................510 428-3000
TOLL FREE: 800
Matthew Cook, *Pr*
Harold Davis, *
Rina Smith, *
Betsy Biern, *
Kathleen Cain, *
EMP: 1900 **EST:** 1912
SQ FT: 160,000
SALES (est): 719.93MM
SALES (corp-wide): 719.93MM **Privately Held**
Web: www.ucsfbenioffchildrens.org
SIC: 8062 Hospital, AMA approved residency

(P-15995)
CHILDRENS HOSPITAL LOS ANGELES
Also Called: Saban Research Institute, The
4661 W Sunset Blvd (90027-6042)
PHONE...................323 361-2751
Cheryl Saban, *Brnch Mgr*
EMP: 450
SALES (corp-wide): 1.38B **Privately Held**
Web: www.chla.org
SIC: 8062 General medical and surgical hospitals
PA: The Childrens Hospital Los Angeles
 4650 W Sunset Blvd
 Los Angeles CA
 323 660-2450

(P-15996)
CHILDRENS HOSPITAL ORANGE CNTY
Also Called: Choc Childern's
10602 Chapman Ave Ste 200 (92840-3147)
PHONE...................714 638-5990
Gina Sue Cadogan, *Brnch Mgr*
EMP: 268
SALES (corp-wide): 1.11B **Privately Held**
Web: www.choc.org
SIC: 8062 General medical and surgical hospitals

8062 - General Medical And Surgical Hospitals (P-15997)

PA: Children's Hospital Of Orange County
1201 W La Veta Ave
Orange CA
714 509-8300

(P-15997)
CHILDRENS HOSPITAL ORANGE CNTY (PA)
Also Called: Choc
1201 W La Veta Ave (92868-4203)
PHONE..............................714 509-8300
Kimberly Cripe, *Pr*
L Kenneth Heuler D.d.s., *Ch Bd*
Jessica L Miley, *CDO*
Kim Milstien, *
EMP: 2019 **EST:** 1950
SQ FT: 328,200
SALES (est): 1.11B
SALES (corp-wide): 1.11B **Privately Held**
Web: www.choc.org
SIC: 8062 General medical and surgical hospitals

(P-15998)
CHILDRENS HOSPITAL ORANGE CNTY
Also Called: Choc Mission
455 S Main St (92868-3835)
PHONE..............................949 365-2416
Kerri Ruppert Schiller, *Prin*
EMP: 384
SALES (corp-wide): 1.11B **Privately Held**
Web: www.choc.org
SIC: 8062 General medical and surgical hospitals
PA: Children's Hospital Of Orange County
1201 W La Veta Ave
Orange CA
714 509-8300

(P-15999)
CHILDRENS HOSPITAL ORANGE CNTY
980 Roosevelt (92620-3672)
PHONE..............................949 387-2586
EMP: 137
SALES (corp-wide): 1.11B **Privately Held**
Web: www.choc.org
SIC: 8062 8099 8082 6321 General medical and surgical hospitals; Childbirth preparation clinic; Home health care services; Accident and health insurance
PA: Children's Hospital Of Orange County
1201 W La Veta Ave
Orange CA
714 509-8300

(P-16000)
CHINESE HOSPITAL ASSOCIATION (PA)
845 Jackson St (94133-4851)
PHONE..............................415 982-2400
Brenda Yee, *CEO*
Thomas Bolger, *
Linda Schumacher, *
EMP: 279 **EST:** 1923
SQ FT: 54,000
SALES (est): 83.9MM
SALES (corp-wide): 83.9MM **Privately Held**
Web: www.chinesehospital-sf.org
SIC: 8062 General medical and surgical hospitals

(P-16001)
CITRUS VLY HLTH PARTNERS INC
Also Called: Queen of The Valley Campus
1115 S Sunset Ave (91790-3940)
PHONE..............................626 962-4011
Debbie Segaram, *Brnch Mgr*
EMP: 916
Web: www.emanatehealth.org
SIC: 8062 General medical and surgical hospitals
PA: Emanate Health Medical Group
210 W San Bernardino Rd
Covina CA

(P-16002)
CITY & COUNTY SAN FRANCISCO
Also Called: San Francisco General Hospital
1001 Potrero Ave (94110-3518)
PHONE..............................415 206-8000
Susan Currin, *Prin*
EMP: 8000
SALES (corp-wide): 7.18B **Privately Held**
Web: www.sf.gov
SIC: 8062 General medical and surgical hospitals
PA: City & County Of San Francisco
1 Dr Carlton B Goodlett P
San Francisco CA
415 554-7500

(P-16003)
CITY ALAMEDA HEALTH CARE CORP
Also Called: Alameda Hospital
2070 Clinton Ave (94501-4399)
PHONE..............................510 522-3700
Deborah E Stebbins, *CEO*
EMP: 520 **EST:** 1894
SQ FT: 150,000
SALES (est): 83.76MM **Privately Held**
Web: www.alamedahealthsystem.org
SIC: 8062 8051 General medical and surgical hospitals; Skilled nursing care facilities

(P-16004)
CITY HOPE NATIONAL MEDICAL CTR (HQ)
Also Called: City of Hope Corona
1500 Duarte Rd (91010-3012)
PHONE..............................626 256-4673
Michael A Friedman, *CEO*
Robert Stone, *
EMP: 549 **EST:** 1948
SALES (est): 1.99B
SALES (corp-wide): 334.97MM **Privately Held**
Web: www.cityofhope.org
SIC: 8062 General medical and surgical hospitals
PA: City Of Hope
1500 Duarte Rd
Duarte CA
626 256-4673

(P-16005)
COALINGA REGIONAL MED CTR AUX
Also Called: Crmc
1191 Phelps Ave (93210-9609)
PHONE..............................559 935-6400
Sharon A Spurgen, *CEO*
Sandy Beach, *
Catherine Underwood, *
Mark Gritton, *
Sandra Earls, *
EMP: 230 **EST:** 1947
SQ FT: 60,000
SALES (est): 61.41MM
SALES (corp-wide): 789.42MM **Privately Held**
Web: www.coalingamedicalcenter.com

SIC: 8062 8051 Hospital, affiliated with AMA residency; Skilled nursing care facilities
PA: Adventist Health System/West, Corporation
1 Adventist Health Way
Roseville CA
844 574-5686

(P-16006)
COAST PLZ DCTORS HOSP A CAL LT (DH)
13100 Studebaker Rd (90650-2531)
PHONE..............................562 868-3751
John Ferrelli, *Ltd Pt*
Craig B Garner, *
Mihi Lee, *
EMP: 75 **EST:** 1968
SQ FT: 58,000
SALES (est): 48.17MM
SALES (corp-wide): 938.2MM **Privately Held**
SIC: 8062 Hospital, medical school affiliation
HQ: Avanti Hospitals, Llc
898 N Pcf Cast Hwy Ste 70
El Segundo CA

(P-16007)
COLLEGE HOSPITAL COSTA MESA MSO INC (HQ)
Also Called: COLLEGE HOSPITAL CERRITOS
301 Victoria St (92627-1995)
PHONE..............................949 642-2734
EMP: 100 **EST:** 1968
SALES (est): 39.57MM
SALES (corp-wide): 72.33MM **Privately Held**
Web: www.chc.la
SIC: 8062 General medical and surgical hospitals
PA: College Hospital, Inc.
10802 College Pl
Cerritos CA
562 924-9581

(P-16008)
COMMUNITY HLTH ALANCE PASADENA (PA)
Also Called: CHAP
1855 N Fair Oaks Ave Ste 200 (91103-1620)
P.O. Box 94873 (91109-4873)
PHONE..............................626 398-6300
Margaret Martinez, *CEO*
Marcy Chavez, *
Sergio Bautista, *
EMP: 68 **EST:** 1995
SALES (est): 28.28MM
SALES (corp-wide): 28.28MM **Privately Held**
Web: www.chapcare.org
SIC: 8062 General medical and surgical hospitals

(P-16009)
COMMUNITY HOSP MNTREY PNINSULA
Also Called: COMMUNITY HOSPITAL OF MONTEREY PENINSULA
23625 Holman Hwy (93940-5902)
PHONE..............................831 625-4500
Steven Packer, *Pr*
EMP: 221
SALES (corp-wide): 947.23MM **Privately Held**
SIC: 8062 8011 General medical and surgical hospitals; Offices and clinics of medical doctors
HQ: Community Hospital Of The Monterey Peninsula

23625 Holman Hwy
Monterey CA
831 624-5311

(P-16010)
COMMUNITY HOSP SAN BERNARDINO (DH)
1805 Medical Center Dr (92411-1217)
PHONE..............................909 887-6333
June Collisone, *Pr*
Ed Sorenson, *
Darryl Vanzenbosch, *CFO*
EMP: 350 **EST:** 1938
SALES (est): 266.28MM **Privately Held**
Web: www.dignityhealth.org
SIC: 8062 Hospital, affiliated with AMA residency
HQ: Dignity Health
185 Berry St Ste 200
San Francisco CA
415 438-5500

(P-16011)
COMMUNITY HOSPITAL LONG BEACH
Also Called: Community Hospital
1760 Termino Ave Ste 105 (90804-2104)
P.O. Box 92456 (90809-2456)
PHONE..............................562 494-0600
John Bishop, *CEO*
Krikor Jansian, *
Julie Shepard Resources, *Coordtr*
Kevin Peterson, *
EMP: 570 **EST:** 2000
SALES (est): 80.11MM **Privately Held**
Web: www.chlbfoundation.org
SIC: 8062 Hospital, affiliated with AMA residency
PA: Memorial Health Services
17360 Brookhurst St # 160
Fountain Valley CA

(P-16012)
COMMUNITY HOSPITAL MONTEREY
23625 Holman Hwy (93940-5902)
PHONE..............................831 625-4600
Michael S Lebowitz Md, *Prin*
EMP: 104 **EST:** 1972
SALES (est): 27.35MM **Privately Held**
SIC: 8062 General medical and surgical hospitals

(P-16013)
COMMUNITY HOSPITALS CENTL CAL (PA)
Also Called: Community Health System
2823 Fresno St (93721-1324)
P.O. Box 1232 (93715-1232)
PHONE..............................559 459-6000
Tim A Joslin, *CEO*
Joseph Nowicki, *Ex VP*
Craig S Castro, *Sr VP*
Robin Van Patton, *CLO*
EMP: 3400 **EST:** 1945
SQ FT: 200,000
SALES (est): 2.17B
SALES (corp-wide): 2.17B **Privately Held**
Web: www.communitymedical.org
SIC: 8062 8011 8051 General medical and surgical hospitals; Ambulatory surgical center; Extended care facility

(P-16014)
COMMUNITY HOSPITALS CENTL CAL
Also Called: Community Regional Medical Ctr
2823 Fresno St (93721-1324)
PHONE..............................559 459-6000

PRODUCTS & SERVICES SECTION

8062 - General Medical And Surgical Hospitals (P-16034)

EMP: 1000 EST: 1982
SALES (est): 85.16MM **Privately Held**
Web: www.communitymedical.org
SIC: **8062** General medical and surgical hospitals

(P-16015)
COMMUNITY MEM HOSP SAN BNVNTUR
Also Called: Purchasing Department
147 N Brent St (93003-2809)
PHONE.................................805 652-5072
▲ EMP: 96 EST: 1927
SALES (est): 16.18MM **Privately Held**
Web: www.mycmh.org
SIC: **8062** General medical and surgical hospitals

(P-16016)
COMMUNITY MEMORIAL HEALTH SYS (PA)
Also Called: Community Memorial Hospital
147 N Brent St (93003-2809)
PHONE.................................805 652-5011
Gary Wilde, *Pr*
Adam Thunell, *
David Glyar, *
▲ EMP: 1881 EST: 1933
SQ FT: 174,000
SALES (est): 526.61MM
SALES (corp-wide): 526.61MM **Privately Held**
Web: www.mycmh.org
SIC: **8062** General medical and surgical hospitals

(P-16017)
COMMUNITY MEMORIAL HEALTH SYS
Also Called: Ojai Valley Community Hospital
1306 Maricopa Hwy (93023-3131)
PHONE.................................805 646-1401
Gary Wilde, *Pr*
EMP: 120
SALES (corp-wide): 526.61MM **Privately Held**
Web: www.mycmh.org
SIC: **8062** General medical and surgical hospitals
PA: Community Memorial Health System
147 N Brent St
Ventura CA
805 652-5011

(P-16018)
COMMUNTY HSPTAL OF THE MNTREY
109 San Benancio Rd (93908-8506)
PHONE.................................831 596-8986
Timothy Knapp, *Prin*
EMP: 71 EST: 2010
SALES (est): 424.28K **Privately Held**
SIC: **8062** General medical and surgical hospitals

(P-16019)
CORCORAN DISTRICT HOSPITAL FOUNDATION
1310 Hanna Ave (93212-2314)
P.O. Box 758 (93212-0758)
PHONE.................................559 992-3300
EMP: 100
SIC: **8062** General medical and surgical hospitals

(P-16020)
COTTAGE HEALTH
2050 Viborg Rd (93463-2220)
PHONE.................................805 688-6432
EMP: 87
SALES (corp-wide): 152.81MM **Privately Held**
SIC: **8062** General medical and surgical hospitals
PA: Cottage Health
400 W Pueblo St
Santa Barbara CA
805 682-7111

(P-16021)
COUNTY OF ALAMEDA
Also Called: Fairmont Hsptal- Rgstrtion Dep
15400 Foothill Blvd (94578-1009)
PHONE.................................510 895-4200
Michael Wall, *Pr*
EMP: 460
Web: www.acgov.org
SIC: **8062** 9431 General medical and surgical hospitals; Administration of public health programs
PA: County Of Alameda
1221 Oak St Ste 555
Oakland CA
510 272-6691

(P-16022)
COUNTY OF CONTRA COSTA
Also Called: Department of Health Services
2500 Alhambra Ave (94553-3156)
PHONE.................................925 370-5000
Jeff Smith, *CEO*
EMP: 200
SALES (corp-wide): 2.51B **Privately Held**
Web: contracosta.ca.gov
SIC: **8062** 9431 General medical and surgical hospitals; Administration of public health programs
PA: County Of Contra Costa
625 Court St Ste 100
Martinez CA
925 957-5280

(P-16023)
COUNTY OF KERN
Public Health Dept
1700 Mount Vernon Ave (93306-4018)
P.O. Box 3519 (93385-3519)
PHONE.................................661 326-2054
Peter Bryan, *CEO*
EMP: 800
Web: www.kerncounty.com
SIC: **8062** 9431 General medical and surgical hospitals; Administration of public health programs
PA: County Of Kern
1115 Truxtun Ave Rm 505
Bakersfield CA
661 868-3690

(P-16024)
COUNTY OF LOS ANGELES
Also Called: Health Services Dept
1000 W Carson St 8th Fl (90274)
PHONE.................................310 222-2401
Miguel Ortiz Marroquin, *CEO*
EMP: 126
SALES (corp-wide): 31.7B **Privately Held**
Web: www.lacounty.gov
SIC: **8062** 9431 General medical and surgical hospitals; Administration of public health programs
PA: County Of Los Angeles
500 W Temple St Ste 437
Los Angeles CA
213 974-1101

(P-16025)
COUNTY OF LOS ANGELES
Also Called: Health Services, Dept of
12025 Wilmington Ave (90059-3019)
PHONE.................................310 668-4545
Willie T May, *Ex Dir*
EMP: 272
SALES (corp-wide): 31.7B **Privately Held**
Web: www.lacounty.gov
SIC: **8062** 9431 General medical and surgical hospitals; Administration of public health programs
PA: County Of Los Angeles
500 W Temple St Ste 437
Los Angeles CA
213 974-1101

(P-16026)
COUNTY OF LOS ANGELES
Also Called: Health Services Dept
1100 N Mission Rd Rm 236 (90033-1017)
PHONE.................................323 226-6021
Scott Drewgan, *Dir*
EMP: 117
SALES (corp-wide): 31.7B **Privately Held**
Web: www.lacounty.gov
SIC: **8062** 9431 General medical and surgical hospitals; Administration of public health programs
PA: County Of Los Angeles
500 W Temple St Ste 437
Los Angeles CA
213 974-1101

(P-16027)
COUNTY OF LOS ANGELES
Also Called: Los Angles Cnty Cntl Jail Hosp
450 Bauchet St (90012-2907)
PHONE.................................213 473-6100
Don Knable, *Ch Bd*
EMP: 126
SALES (corp-wide): 31.7B **Privately Held**
Web: www.lacounty.gov
SIC: **8062** 9431 General medical and surgical hospitals; Administration of public health programs, County government
PA: County Of Los Angeles
500 W Temple St Ste 437
Los Angeles CA
213 974-1101

(P-16028)
COUNTY OF MONTEREY
Also Called: Residncy Prgram Natividad Hosp
1441 Constitution Blvd Ste 100 (93906-3136)
P.O. Box 81611 (93912-1611)
PHONE.................................831 755-4201
Doctor Gary Gray, *Dir*
EMP: 118
SALES (corp-wide): 1.04B **Privately Held**
Web: co.monterey.ca.us
SIC: **8062** General medical and surgical hospitals
PA: County Of Monterey
168 W Alisal St Fl 3
Salinas CA
831 755-5040

(P-16029)
COUNTY OF SAN LUIS OBISPO
Also Called: County General Hospital
2180 Johnson Ave (93401-4558)
PHONE.................................805 781-4753
Nancy Rosen, *Mgr*
EMP: 85
SQ FT: 4,500
Web: slocounty.ca.gov
SIC: **8062** 8721 General medical and surgical hospitals; Accounting, auditing, and bookkeeping
PA: County of San Luis Obispo
Government Center Rm 300
San Luis Obispo CA
805 781-5040

(P-16030)
COUNTY OF SANTA CLARA
Also Called: Santa Clara Vly Hlth Hosp Syst
2325 Enborg Ln 2h260 (95128-2659)
PHONE.................................408 885-7470
Katelyn Hart, *Adm/Asst*
EMP: 66
Web: home.sccgov.org
SIC: **8062** General medical and surgical hospitals
PA: County Of Santa Clara
70 W Hedding St
San Jose CA
408 299-5200

(P-16031)
COUNTY OF SONOMA
Also Called: Palm Drive Healthcare District
501 Petaluma Ave (95472-4215)
PHONE.................................707 823-8511
Shawndra Nimtz, *CEO*
EMP: 200
SQ FT: 3,684
SALES (corp-wide): 1.24B **Privately Held**
Web: sonomacounty.ca.gov
SIC: **8062** 8051 General medical and surgical hospitals; Skilled nursing care facilities
PA: County Of Sonoma
585 Fiscal Dr 100
Santa Rosa CA
707 565-2431

(P-16032)
COUNTY OF STANISLAUS
Also Called: Stanislaus Medical Center
830 Scenic Dr (95350-6131)
P.O. Box 3271 (95353-3271)
PHONE.................................209 525-7000
Beverly M Finley, *Mgr*
EMP: 191
SQ FT: 1,866
Web: www.stancounty.com
SIC: **8062** General medical and surgical hospitals
PA: County Of Stanislaus
1010 10th St Ste 5100
Modesto CA
209 525-6398

(P-16033)
COVENANT CARE CALIFORNIA LLC
Also Called: Grant-Cuesta Nursing Center
1949 Grant Rd (94040-3217)
PHONE.................................650 964-0543
EMP: 111
Web: www.covenantcare.com
SIC: **8062** 8051 8069 General medical and surgical hospitals; Skilled nursing care facilities; Specialty hospitals, except psychiatric
HQ: Covenant Care California, Llc
120 Vantis Dr Ste 200
Aliso Viejo CA

(P-16034)
COVENANT LIVING WEST
Also Called: Brandel Manor
1801 N Olive Ave (95382-2568)
PHONE.................................209 667-5600
Dawn Sughruel, *Dir*

8062 - General Medical And Surgical Hospitals (P-16035)

EMP: 80
SQ FT: 58,282
Web: www.brandelmanor.org
SIC: 8062 8051 General medical and surgical hospitals; Convalescent home with continuous nursing care
HQ: Covenant Living West
5700 Old Orchard Rd # 10
Skokie IL

(P-16035)
DAMERON HOSPITAL ASSOCIATION (HQ)
525 W Acacia St (95203-2484)
PHONE.................................209 944-5550
Daniel Wolcott, *Pr*
EMP: 987 **EST:** 1943
SQ FT: 136,061
SALES (est): 138.7MM
SALES (corp-wide): 789.42MM **Privately Held**
Web: www.dameronhospital.org
SIC: 8062 General medical and surgical hospitals
PA: Adventist Health System/West, Corporation
1 Adventist Health Way
Roseville CA
844 574-5686

(P-16036)
DAVIS UC MEDICAL CENTER
Also Called: Care Management Services
4800 2nd Ave # 3010 (95817-2216)
PHONE.................................916 734-2011
Janet Heath, *Pr*
EMP: 203 **EST:** 2012
SALES (est): 269.57MM **Privately Held**
Web: health.ucdavis.edu
SIC: 8062 General medical and surgical hospitals

(P-16037)
DEANCO HEALTHCARE LLC
Also Called: MISSION COMMUNITY HOSPITAL
14850 Roscoe Blvd (91402-4618)
PHONE.................................818 787-2222
EMP: 700 **EST:** 2010
SALES (est): 156.97MM **Privately Held**
Web: www.mchonline.org
SIC: 8062 General medical and surgical hospitals

(P-16038)
DESERT REGIONAL MED CTR INC (HQ)
Also Called: Tenet
1150 N Indian Canyon Dr (92262-4872)
P.O. Box 2739 (92263-2739)
PHONE.................................760 323-6511
TOLL FREE: 888
Michele Finney, *Pr*
Frank Ercoli, *
Ralph M Steiger, *
EMP: 1200 **EST:** 1948
SQ FT: 400,000
SALES (est): 217MM
SALES (corp-wide): 19.58B **Publicly Held**
Web: www.desertfamilymed.com
SIC: 8062 General medical and surgical hospitals
PA: Tenet Healthcare Corporation
14201 Dallas Pkwy
Dallas TX
469 893-2200

(P-16039)
DESERT REGIONAL MED CTR INC
Also Called: Tenet
1180 N Indian Canyon Dr Ste W110 (92262-4800)
PHONE.................................760 416-4613
EMP: 63
SALES (corp-wide): 19.58B **Publicly Held**
Web: www.desertfamilymed.com
SIC: 8062 General medical and surgical hospitals
HQ: Desert Regional Medical Center, Inc.
1150 N Indian Canyon Dr
Palm Springs CA
760 323-6511

(P-16040)
DESERT VALLEY HOSPITAL INC (DH)
16850 Bear Valley Rd (92395-5794)
PHONE.................................760 241-8000
Margaret R Peterson, *CEO*
Roger Krissman, *
▲ **EMP:** 181 **EST:** 1985
SQ FT: 63,000
SALES (est): 208.51MM
SALES (corp-wide): 1.03B **Privately Held**
Web: www.dvmc.com
SIC: 8062 General medical and surgical hospitals
HQ: Prime Healthcare Services Inc
3480 E Guasti Rd
Ontario CA

(P-16041)
DIGNITY HEALTH
1650 Creekside Dr (95630-3400)
PHONE.................................916 983-7400
Karl L Silberstein, *Mgr*
EMP: 162
Web: www.dignityhealth.org
SIC: 8062 General medical and surgical hospitals
HQ: Dignity Health
185 Berry St Ste 200
San Francisco CA
415 438-5500

(P-16042)
DIGNITY HEALTH
Also Called: Marian Regional Medical Center
1400 E Church St (93454-5906)
PHONE.................................805 739-3000
Charles Cova, *Pr*
EMP: 400
Web: locations.dignityhealth.org
SIC: 8062 8011 General medical and surgical hospitals; Offices and clinics of medical doctors
HQ: Dignity Health
185 Berry St Ste 200
San Francisco CA
415 438-5500

(P-16043)
DIGNITY HEALTH
Also Called: Mercy San Juan Med Lvel II Tru
6501 Coyle Ave Fl 6 (95608-0306)
PHONE.................................916 537-5151
Donna Utley, *Dir*
EMP: 314
Web: www.dignityhealth.org
SIC: 8062 General medical and surgical hospitals
HQ: Dignity Health
185 Berry St Ste 200
San Francisco CA
415 438-5500

(P-16044)
DIGNITY HEALTH
3400 Data Dr (95670-7956)
PHONE.................................916 379-2996
Susan Carson, *Prin*
EMP: 105
Web: www.dignityhealth.org
SIC: 8062 General medical and surgical hospitals
HQ: Dignity Health
185 Berry St Ste 200
San Francisco CA
415 438-5500

(P-16045)
DIGNITY HEALTH
Also Called: Information Services
1800 N California St (95204-6019)
PHONE.................................209 467-6353
Glen Whipple, *Brnch Mgr*
EMP: 175
Web: www.dignityhealth.org
SIC: 8062 General medical and surgical hospitals
HQ: Dignity Health
185 Berry St Ste 200
San Francisco CA
415 438-5500

(P-16046)
DIGNITY HEALTH
Also Called: Saint John's Hospital X Ray
200 Oceangate (90802-4302)
PHONE.................................805 988-2868
Steve Higgs Managing, *Brnch Mgr*
EMP: 474
Web: www.dignityhealth.org
SIC: 8062 General medical and surgical hospitals
HQ: Dignity Health
185 Berry St Ste 200
San Francisco CA
415 438-5500

(P-16047)
DIGNITY HEALTH
Also Called: Northridge Hospital Med Ctr
18300 Roscoe Blvd (91325-4105)
PHONE.................................818 885-8500
Paul Watkins, *Pr*
EMP: 1750
Web: www.dignityhealth.org
SIC: 8062 General medical and surgical hospitals
HQ: Dignity Health
185 Berry St Ste 200
San Francisco CA
415 438-5500

(P-16048)
DIGNITY HEALTH
Also Called: Saint Mary Medical Center
1050 Linden Ave (90813-3321)
PHONE.................................562 491-9000
Chris Diccio, *Prin*
EMP: 397
Web: www.dignityhealth.org
SIC: 8062 General medical and surgical hospitals
HQ: Dignity Health
185 Berry St Ste 200
San Francisco CA
415 438-5500

(P-16049)
DIGNITY HEALTH (HQ)
185 Berry St Ste 200 (94107-1777)
PHONE.................................415 438-5500
Lloyd Dean, *Pr*
Kevin E Lofton, *
Marvin O'quinn, *VP*
Michael Blaszyk, *
Lisa Zuckerman, *
▲ **EMP:** 120 **EST:** 1954
SALES (est): 10.1B **Privately Held**
Web: www.dignityhealth.org
SIC: 8062 General medical and surgical hospitals
PA: Commonspirit Health
444 W Lake St Ste 2500
Chicago IL

(P-16050)
DIGNITY HEALTH
Also Called: Mercy San Juan Medical Center
6501 Coyle Ave (95608-0306)
PHONE.................................916 537-5000
Rian Ivie, *Dir*
EMP: 1500
Web: www.dignityhealth.org
SIC: 8062 8011 General medical and surgical hospitals; Offices and clinics of medical doctors
HQ: Dignity Health
185 Berry St Ste 200
San Francisco CA
415 438-5500

(P-16051)
DIGNITY HEALTH
Also Called: Methodist Hospital Sacramento
7500 Hospital Dr (95823-5403)
PHONE.................................916 423-5940
William J Hunt, *Prin*
EMP: 193
Web: www.dignityhealth.org
SIC: 8062 General medical and surgical hospitals
HQ: Dignity Health
185 Berry St Ste 200
San Francisco CA
415 438-5500

(P-16052)
DIGNITY HEALTH
Also Called: St. Johns Pleasant Valley Hosp
2309 Antonio Ave (93010-1414)
PHONE.................................805 389-5800
Daniel Herlinger, *Brnch Mgr*
EMP: 250
Web: locations.dignityhealth.org
SIC: 8062 General medical and surgical hospitals
HQ: Dignity Health
185 Berry St Ste 200
San Francisco CA
415 438-5500

(P-16053)
DIGNITY HEALTH
Also Called: St Johns Regional Medical Ctr
1600 N Rose Ave (93030-3722)
PHONE.................................805 988-2500
George West, *Brnch Mgr*
EMP: 1900
Web: www.dignityhealth.org
SIC: 8062 General medical and surgical hospitals
HQ: Dignity Health
185 Berry St Ste 200
San Francisco CA
415 438-5500

(P-16054)
DIGNITY HEALTH
Also Called: St. Mary's Medical Center
450 Stanyan St (94117-1019)
PHONE.................................415 668-1000
John Allen, *Pr*
EMP: 1100

PRODUCTS & SERVICES SECTION
8062 - General Medical And Surgical Hospitals (P-16073)

Web: www.dignityhealth.org
SIC: **8062** 8322 General medical and surgical hospitals; Adult day care center
HQ: Dignity Health
185 Berry St Ste 200
San Francisco CA
415 438-5500

(P-16055)
DIGNITY HEALTH
Also Called: Pedi Center
400 Old River Rd (93311-9781)
P.O. Box 119 (93302-0119)
PHONE.................................661 663-6000
Kirk Douglas, *Brnch Mgr*
EMP: 255
Web: locations.dignityhealth.org
SIC: **8062** 8099 8011 General medical and surgical hospitals; Childbirth preparation clinic; Offices and clinics of medical doctors
HQ: Dignity Health
185 Berry St Ste 200
San Francisco CA
415 438-5500

(P-16056)
DIGNITY HEALTH MED FOUNDATION (DH)
Also Called: Dignity Hlth Med Grp-Dominican
3400 Data Dr (95670-7956)
PHONE.................................916 851-2000
Laurie Schwarctz, *Pr*
Theresa Hylen, *
EMP: 200 EST: 1990
SQ FT: 45,000
SALES (est): 1.35B **Privately Held**
Web: www.dignityhealth.org
SIC: **8062** General medical and surgical hospitals
HQ: Dignity Health
185 Berry St Ste 200
San Francisco CA
415 438-5500

(P-16057)
DOCTORS HOSPITAL MANTECA INC
1205 E North St (95336-4932)
PHONE.................................209 823-3111
Nicholas Tejeda, *CEO*
Katherine Medeiros, *
Mark Lisa, *
Tracy Roman, *
Tina Burch, *
EMP: 400 EST: 2001
SALES (est): 62MM
SALES (corp-wide): 19.58B **Publicly Held**
SIC: **8062** General medical and surgical hospitals
PA: Tenet Healthcare Corporation
14201 Dallas Pkwy
Dallas TX
469 893-2200

(P-16058)
DOCTORS HOSPITAL W COVINA INC
Also Called: WEST COVINA PHYSICAL THERAPY
725 S Orange Ave (91790-2614)
PHONE.................................626 338-8481
Pareed Mohamed, *CEO*
Akbar Omar Md, *VP*
Jong Kim Md, *Treas*
Pareed Aliyar Md, *Sec*
EMP: 155 EST: 1958
SQ FT: 50,000
SALES (est): 25MM **Privately Held**

SIC: **8062** 8049 General medical and surgical hospitals; Physical therapist

(P-16059)
DOCTORS MED CTR MODESTO INC (HQ)
1441 Florida Ave (95350-4404)
PHONE.................................209 578-1211
Warren J Kirk, *CEO*
Greg Berry, *
Misty Oglesby, *
Dharati Trivedi, *
EMP: 310 EST: 1939
SALES (est): 587.92MM
SALES (corp-wide): 19.58B **Publicly Held**
Web: www.modestogi.com
SIC: **8062** General medical and surgical hospitals
PA: Tenet Healthcare Corporation
14201 Dallas Pkwy
Dallas TX
469 893-2200

(P-16060)
DOCTORS MEDICAL CENTER LLC
2000 Vale Rd (94806-3808)
P.O. Box 20760 (94820-0760)
PHONE.................................510 970-5000
EMP: 937
SIC: **8062** General medical and surgical hospitals

(P-16061)
DOMINICAN HOSPITAL FOUNDATION (DH)
1555 Soquel Dr (95065-1705)
P.O. Box 2400 (85002-2400)
PHONE.................................831 462-7700
Beverly Grova, *CEO*
Sam Leask, *
Chuck Maffia, *
Jon Sisk, *
Ted Burke, *
EMP: 111 EST: 1966
SQ FT: 110,000
SALES (est): 4.44MM **Privately Held**
Web: www.supportdominican.org
SIC: **8062** 8051 General medical and surgical hospitals; Skilled nursing care facilities
HQ: Dignity Health
185 Berry St Ste 200
San Francisco CA
415 438-5500

(P-16062)
EAST LOS ANGLES DCTORS HOSP IN
4060 Whittier Blvd (90023-2526)
EMP: 350 EST: 1978
SALES (est): 74.22MM
SALES (corp-wide): 218.29MM **Privately Held**
Web: www.eladoctorshospital.com
SIC: **8062** Hospital, affiliated with AMA residency
PA: Pipeline Health, Llc
898 N Pcf Cast Hwy Ste 70
El Segundo CA
310 379-2134

(P-16063)
EAST VALLEY GLENDORA HOSP LLC
Also Called: Glendora Oaks Bhvral Hlth Hosp
150 W Route 66 (91740-6207)
PHONE.................................626 852-5000
Robert Gordon, *

EMP: 448 EST: 1957
SQ FT: 60,592
SALES (est): 48.12MM **Privately Held**
Web: www.glendorahospital.com
SIC: **8062** General medical and surgical hospitals
PA: College Health Enterprises, Llc
11627 Telg Rd Ste 200
Santa Fe Springs CA

(P-16064)
EDEN LABS MED GROUP INC
20103 Lake Chabot Rd (94546-5305)
PHONE.................................510 537-1234
John Carney, *Pr*
Katherine Thomas, *
EMP: 173 EST: 1971
SQ FT: 9,000
SALES (est): 7.84MM **Privately Held**
Web: www.edenmedicalcenter.org
SIC: **8062** General medical and surgical hospitals

(P-16065)
EDEN TOWNSHIP HOSPITAL DISTRICT INC
Also Called: Eden Medical Center
20400 Lake Chabot Rd # 303 (94546-5311)
PHONE.................................510 538-2031
EMP: 968
SIC: **8062** 8011 General medical and surgical hospitals; Offices and clinics of medical doctors

(P-16066)
EISENHOWER MEDICAL CENTER
45280 Seeley Dr (92253-6834)
PHONE.................................760 610-7200
EMP: 248
SALES (corp-wide): 3.81MM **Privately Held**
Web: www.eisenhowerhealth.org
SIC: **8062** General medical and surgical hospitals
PA: Eisenhower Medical Center
39000 Bob Hope Dr
Rancho Mirage CA
760 340-3911

(P-16067)
EISENHOWER MEDICAL CENTER
555 E Tachevah Dr (92262-5750)
PHONE.................................760 325-6621
EMP: 124
SALES (corp-wide): 3.81MM **Privately Held**
Web: www.eisenhowerhealth.org
SIC: **8062** General medical and surgical hospitals
PA: Eisenhower Medical Center
39000 Bob Hope Dr
Rancho Mirage CA
760 340-3911

(P-16068)
EISENHOWER MEDICAL CENTER (PA)
Also Called: Eisenhower Health
39000 Bob Hope Dr (92270-3221)
PHONE.................................760 340-3911
G Aubrey Serfling, *CEO*
Martin Massiello, *
Kimberly Osborne, *
Liz Guignier, *
Joseph Scherger, *
▲ EMP: 2000 EST: 1971
SQ FT: 240,000

SALES (est): 3.81MM
SALES (corp-wide): 3.81MM **Privately Held**
Web: www.eisenhowerhealth.org
SIC: **8062** 8082 General medical and surgical hospitals; Home health care services

(P-16069)
EL CAMINO HOSPITAL (PA)
Also Called: EL CAMINO HEALTH
2500 Grant Rd (94040-4378)
P.O. Box 7025 (94039-7025)
PHONE.................................650 940-7000
EMP: 765 EST: 1961
SALES (est): 1.43B
SALES (corp-wide): 1.43B **Privately Held**
Web: www.elcaminohealth.org
SIC: **8062** General medical and surgical hospitals

(P-16070)
EL CAMINO HOSPITAL
Also Called: Willow Pavillion
2480 Grant Rd (94040-4336)
PHONE.................................650 940-7000
Michelle Zien, *Pr*
EMP: 140
SALES (corp-wide): 1.43B **Privately Held**
Web: www.elcaminohealth.org
SIC: **8062** General medical and surgical hospitals
PA: El Camino Hospital
2500 Grant Rd
Mountain View CA
650 940-7000

(P-16071)
EL CAMINO SURGERY CENTER LLC
15046 Karl Ave (95030-2211)
PHONE.................................650 961-1200
Lisa Cooper, *Managing Member*
Marla Marlow, *Managing Member**
EMP: 70 EST: 1987
SALES (est): 9.34MM **Privately Held**
SIC: **8062** General medical and surgical hospitals

(P-16072)
EL CENTRO RGNAL MED CTR FNDTIO (PA)
Also Called: E C R M C
1415 Ross Ave (92243-4306)
PHONE.................................760 339-7100
Pablo Velez, *CEO*
Robert R Frantz, *
Kathy Farmer, *CFO*
Barbara Blevins, *
Debra Drifkill, *
EMP: 603 EST: 2005
SQ FT: 187,044
SALES (est): 212.33K **Privately Held**
Web: www.ecrmc.org
SIC: **8062** General medical and surgical hospitals

(P-16073)
EMANATE HEALTH
Also Called: Citrus Vly Hlth Care Partners
427 W Carroll Ave (91741-4214)
PHONE.................................626 857-3477
Sue Benson, *Dir*
EMP: 495
SALES (corp-wide): 515.46MM **Privately Held**
Web: www.emanatehealth.org
SIC: **8062** General medical and surgical hospitals
PA: Emanate Health Medical Center

8062 - General Medical And Surgical Hospitals (P-16074)

PRODUCTS & SERVICES SECTION

1115 S Sunset Ave
West Covina CA
626 962-4011

(P-16074)
EMANATE HEALTH MEDICAL CENTER (PA)
Also Called: Emanate Health
1115 S Sunset Ave (91790-3940)
P.O. Box 6108 (91722-5108)
PHONE....................626 962-4011
Robert Curry, *Pr*
Elvia Foulke, *
Roger Sharma, *
EMP: 1229 EST: 1959
SQ FT: 285,000
SALES (est): 515.46MM
SALES (corp-wide): 515.46MM **Privately Held**
Web: www.emanatehealth.org
SIC: **8062** General medical and surgical hospitals

(P-16075)
EMANATE HEALTH MEDICAL CENTER
Also Called: Human Resources Department
140 W College St (91723-2007)
PHONE....................626 858-8515
Robert H Curry, *Admn*
EMP: 413
SALES (corp-wide): 515.46MM **Privately Held**
Web: www.emanatehealth.org
SIC: **8062** General medical and surgical hospitals
PA: Emanate Health Medical Center
1115 S Sunset Ave
West Covina CA
626 962-4011

(P-16076)
EMANATE HEALTH MEDICAL CENTER
Also Called: Queen of The Valley Hospital
1115 S Sunset Ave (91790-3940)
PHONE....................626 963-8411
Robert Curry, *Pr*
EMP: 329
SALES (corp-wide): 515.46MM **Privately Held**
Web: www.emanatehealth.org
SIC: **8062** General medical and surgical hospitals
PA: Emanate Health Medical Center
1115 S Sunset Ave
West Covina CA
626 962-4011

(P-16077)
EMANATE HEALTH MEDICAL CENTER
Also Called: Inter Community Hospital
210 W San Bernardino Rd (91723-1515)
PHONE....................626 331-7331
TOLL FREE: 877
Jim Yoshioka, *Pr*
EMP: 863
SALES (corp-wide): 515.46MM **Privately Held**
Web: www.emanatehealth.org
SIC: **8062** General medical and surgical hospitals
PA: Emanate Health Medical Center
1115 S Sunset Ave
West Covina CA
626 962-4011

(P-16078)
EMANATE HEALTH MEDICAL GROUP (PA)
Also Called: Emanate Hlth Intr-Cmmnity Hosp
210 W San Bernardino Rd (91723-1515)
P.O. Box 6108 (91722-5108)
PHONE....................626 331-7331
Robert Curry, *CEO*
James Yoshioka, *Pr*
Alvia Polk, *Ex VP*
Lois Conyers, *Sr VP*
Paveljit Bindra, *CMO*
EMP: 1200 EST: 1983
SQ FT: 237,000
SALES (est): 75.42MM **Privately Held**
Web: www.emanatehealth.org
SIC: **8062** General medical and surgical hospitals

(P-16079)
EMANATE HLTH FTHILL PRSBT HOSP (PA)
Also Called: Foothill Presbyterian Hospital
250 S Grand Ave (91741-4218)
PHONE....................626 857-3145
Robert Curry, *Pr*
Earl Washington Cmh, *Prin*
Admiral Diana Zenner, *Prin*
Ed Tronez, *
Melissa Howard, *Chief Nurse*
EMP: 97 EST: 1973
SQ FT: 104,371
SALES (est): 122MM
SALES (corp-wide): 122MM **Privately Held**
SIC: **8062** Hospital, affiliated with AMA residency

(P-16080)
EMC HEALTH INC (DH)
825 Delbon Ave (95382-2016)
PHONE....................209 667-4200
Linda Stuhmer, *CEO*
Lawrence Anderson, *
EMP: 850 EST: 1974
SQ FT: 200,000
SALES (est): 305.57MM
SALES (corp-wide): 19.58B **Publicly Held**
SIC: **8062** General medical and surgical hospitals
HQ: Doctors Medical Center Of Modesto, Inc.
1441 Florida Ave
Modesto CA
209 578-1211

(P-16081)
ENLOE HOSPT-PHYS THRPY
1444 Magnolia Ave (95926-3227)
PHONE....................530 891-7300
EMP: 254
SALES (corp-wide): 9.13MM **Privately Held**
SIC: **8062** General medical and surgical hospitals
PA: Enloe Hospital - Physical Therapy Dept
1600 Esplanade
Chico CA
530 891-7300

(P-16082)
ENLOE MEDICAL CENTER
Also Called: E E G and E P
560 Cohasset Rd (95926-2281)
PHONE....................530 332-4111
Joan Lilly, *Prin*
EMP: 214
SALES (corp-wide): 814.04MM **Privately Held**
Web: www.enloe.org

SIC: **8062** General medical and surgical hospitals
PA: Enloe Medical Center
1531 Esplanade
Chico CA
530 332-7300

(P-16083)
ENLOE MEDICAL CENTER
Also Called: Payroll Dept.
175 W 5th Ave (95926)
PHONE....................530 332-7522
Linda Irvine, *Brnch Mgr*
EMP: 136
SALES (corp-wide): 814.04MM **Privately Held**
Web: www.enloe.org
SIC: **8062** General medical and surgical hospitals
PA: Enloe Medical Center
1531 Esplanade
Chico CA
530 332-7300

(P-16084)
ENLOE MEDICAL CENTER (PA)
1531 Esplanade (95926-3310)
P.O. Box 742816 (90074-2816)
PHONE....................530 332-7300
EMP: 1500 EST: 1913
SALES (est): 814.04MM
SALES (corp-wide): 814.04MM **Privately Held**
Web: www.enloe.org
SIC: **8062** General medical and surgical hospitals

(P-16085)
ENLOE MEDICAL CENTER
Also Called: Enloe Hospice Program
1536 Arcadian Ave (95926-3217)
PHONE....................530 332-5520
Janet Miller, *Mgr*
EMP: 163
SQ FT: 1,283
SALES (corp-wide): 814.04MM **Privately Held**
Web: www.enloe.org
SIC: **8062** General medical and surgical hospitals
PA: Enloe Medical Center
1531 Esplanade
Chico CA
530 332-7300

(P-16086)
ENLOE MEDICAL CENTER
Also Called: Enloe Outpatient Center
888 Lakeside Vlg Cmns (95928-3979)
PHONE....................530 332-6400
Joleen Nixon, *Dir*
EMP: 217
SQ FT: 44,171
SALES (corp-wide): 814.04MM **Privately Held**
Web: www.enloe.org
SIC: **8062** 8093 General medical and surgical hospitals; Specialty outpatient clinics, nec
PA: Enloe Medical Center
1531 Esplanade
Chico CA
530 332-7300

(P-16087)
ENLOE MEDICAL CENTER
Also Called: Children's Health Center
1515 Springfield Dr Ste 175 (95928)
PHONE....................530 332-6000
Dorothy Chinnock, *Brnch Mgr*

EMP: 162
SALES (corp-wide): 814.04MM **Privately Held**
Web: www.enloe.org
SIC: **8062** General medical and surgical hospitals
PA: Enloe Medical Center
1531 Esplanade
Chico CA
530 332-7300

(P-16088)
ESSENCE HEALTHCARE CAL INC
Also Called: Stanford Health Care Advantage
300 Pasteur Dr (94305-2200)
PHONE....................650 723-4000
David Entwistle, *Pr*
Quinn Mckenna, *COO*
Linda Hoff, *
Niraj Sehgal, *CMO*
Dale Beatty, *
EMP: 13810 EST: 2013
SALES (est): 50.15MM **Privately Held**
Web: www.stanfordhealthcare.org
SIC: **8062** General medical and surgical hospitals
HQ: Essence Healthcare, Inc.
13900 Riverport Dr
Maryland Heights MO

(P-16089)
FEATHER RIVER HOSPITAL
5974 Pentz Rd (95969-5509)
PHONE....................530 877-9361
EMP: 925
SIC: **8062** 8051 General medical and surgical hospitals; Convalescent home with continuous nursing care

(P-16090)
FOOTHILL REGIONAL MEDICAL CTR
Also Called: NEWPORT SPECIALTY HOSPITAL
14662 Newport Ave (92780-6064)
PHONE....................310 943-4500
EMP: 115 EST: 2014
SALES (est): 78.64MM **Privately Held**
Web: www.foothillregionalmedicalcenter.com
SIC: **8062** General medical and surgical hospitals

(P-16091)
FOUNTAIN VLY RGNAL HOSP MED CT
17100 Euclid St (92708-4004)
P.O. Box 8010 (92728-8010)
PHONE....................714 966-7200
Clay Farell, *CEO*
Edward F Littlejohn, *
Ken Jordan, *
C J Lee, *Chief Strategy Officer*
EMP: 1200 EST: 1969
SALES (est): 239.53MM
SALES (corp-wide): 19.58B **Publicly Held**
Web: validate.perfdrive.com
SIC: **8062** Hospital, affiliated with AMA residency
HQ: Tenet Healthsystem Medical, Inc.
14201 Dallas Pkwy
Dallas TX
469 893-2000

(P-16092)
FREEMONT RIDEOUT HEALTH GROUP
Also Called: Fremont-Rideout Health Group

PRODUCTS & SERVICES SECTION
8062 - General Medical And Surgical Hospitals (P-16110)

726 4th St (95901-5656)
PHONE.................................530 751-4270
Gloria Lees, *Brnch Mgr*
EMP: 627
SALES (corp-wide): 498.18MM **Privately Held**
Web: www.adventisthealth.org
SIC: **8062** 8741 General medical and surgical hospitals; Management services
PA: Freemont Rideout Health Group
    989 Plumas St
    Yuba City CA
    530 751-4010

(P-16093)
FREMONT BHC HOSPITAL INC
39001 Sundale Dr (94538-2005)
PHONE.................................510 796-1100
EMP: 77 EST: 1996
SALES (est): 10.36MM **Privately Held**
Web: www.fremonthospital.com
SIC: **8062** General medical and surgical hospitals

(P-16094)
FREMONT HOSPITAL
Also Called: Fremont Medical Center
620 J St (95901-5413)
PHONE.................................530 751-4000
Thomas P Hayes, *CEO*
Jeanne Martin, *
EMP: 144 EST: 1985
SQ FT: 121,000
SALES (est): 15.99MM
SALES (corp-wide): 498.18MM **Privately Held**
SIC: **8062** General medical and surgical hospitals
PA: Freemont Rideout Health Group
    989 Plumas St
    Yuba City CA
    530 751-4010

(P-16095)
FRENCH HOSPITAL MEDICAL CENTER (DH)
1911 Johnson Ave (93401-4197)
PHONE.................................805 543-5353
Jim Copeland, *Ch*
Allan Iftiniuk, *
Sue Anderson, *
EMP: 480 EST: 1946
SQ FT: 80,000
SALES (est): 196.54MM **Privately Held**
Web: www.dignityhealth.org
SIC: **8062** Hospital, affiliated with AMA residency
HQ: Dignity Health
    185 Berry St Ste 200
    San Francisco CA
    415 438-5500

(P-16096)
FRESNO CMNTY HOSP & MED CTR (HQ)
Also Called: COMMUNITY HEALTH SYSTEM
2823 Fresno St (93721-1324)
P.O. Box 1232 (93715-1232)
PHONE.................................559 459-3948
Phillip Hinton, *Pr*
Tim A Joslin, *
William Grigg, *
Roger Fretwell, *
Mike Kingbury, *
EMP: 3000 EST: 1945
SQ FT: 2,469
SALES (est): 2.18B
SALES (corp-wide): 2.17B **Privately Held**
Web: www.communitymedical.org

SIC: **8062** General medical and surgical hospitals
PA: Community Hospitals Of Central California
    2823 Fresno St
    Fresno CA
    559 459-6000

(P-16097)
FRESNO CMNTY HOSP & MED CTR
Also Called: Hospital Loading Dock
2130 E Illinois Avenue (93701)
PHONE.................................559 459-6000
EMP: 1950
SALES (corp-wide): 2.17B **Privately Held**
Web: www.communitymedical.org
SIC: **8062** General medical and surgical hospitals
HQ: Fresno Community Hospital And Medical Center
    2823 Fresno St
    Fresno CA

(P-16098)
FRESNO HEART HOSPITAL LLC
15 E Audubon Dr (93720-1542)
PHONE.................................559 433-8000
Wanda Holderman, *Managing Member*
Tim A Joslin, *
Patrick Rafferty, *
Peg Breen, *
EMP: 330 EST: 1999
SQ FT: 140,000
SALES (est): 51.53MM
SALES (corp-wide): 2.17B **Privately Held**
Web: www.fresnoheartandsurgical.org
SIC: **8062** General medical and surgical hospitals
PA: Community Hospitals Of Central California
    2823 Fresno St
    Fresno CA
    559 459-6000

(P-16099)
FRESNO SURGERY CENTER LP (PA)
Also Called: Fresno Surgical Hospital
6125 N Fresno St (93710-5207)
PHONE.................................559 431-8000
Kristine Kassahn, *CEO*
Paramjeet Gill, *Ch*
Bruce Cecil, *CFO*
EMP: 212 EST: 1987
SQ FT: 32,000
SALES (est): 74.07MM
SALES (corp-wide): 74.07MM **Privately Held**
Web: www.fresnosurgicalhospital.com
SIC: **8062** 8011 General medical and surgical hospitals; Orthopedic physician

(P-16100)
GARDENA HOSPITAL LP
Also Called: Memorial Hospital of Gardena
1145 W Redondo Beach Blvd (90247-3511)
PHONE.................................310 532-4200
Kathy Wojno, *CEO*
John N Loizeaux-witte, *Pt*
David Lee, *CFO*
EMP: 760 EST: 1999
SALES (est): 141.92MM
SALES (corp-wide): 218.29MM **Privately Held**
Web: www.memorialhospitalgardena.com
SIC: **8062** General medical and surgical hospitals
PA: Pipeline Health, Llc

898 N Pcf Cast Hwy Ste 70
El Segundo CA
310 379-2134

(P-16101)
GARDENS REGIONAL HOSPITAL AND MEDICAL CENTER INCORPORATED
Also Called: Gardens Regional Hosp Med Ctr
21530 Pioneer Blvd (90716-2608)
PHONE.................................877 877-1104
EMP: 350
Web: www.tcrmc.org
SIC: **8062** General medical and surgical hospitals

(P-16102)
GLENDALE ADVENTIST MEDICAL CTR (HQ)
1509 Wilson Ter (91206-4007)
PHONE.................................818 409-8000
Kevin A Roberts, *Pr*
Irene Bourdon, *
Warren Tetz, *
Kelly Turner, *
Judy Blair, *
EMP: 2550 EST: 1905
SQ FT: 700,000
SALES (est): 486.07MM
SALES (corp-wide): 789.42MM **Privately Held**
Web: www.adventisthealth.org
SIC: **8062** 8093 8011 General medical and surgical hospitals; Mental health clinic, outpatient; Freestanding emergency medical center
PA: Adventist Health System/West, Corporation
    1 Adventist Health Way
    Roseville CA
    844 574-5686

(P-16103)
GLENDALE MEM HLTH FOUNDATION
1420 S Central Ave (91204-2508)
PHONE.................................818 502-2375
EMP: 251 EST: 1981
SALES (est): 213.36MM **Privately Held**
Web: www.supportglendale.org
SIC: **8062** General medical and surgical hospitals
HQ: Dignity Health
    185 Berry St Ste 200
    San Francisco CA
    415 438-5500

(P-16104)
GLENDALE MEMORIAL HEALTH CORP
Also Called: Glendale Memorial Breast Ctr
222 W Eulalia St (91204-2849)
PHONE.................................818 502-2323
FAX: 818 502-4747
EMP: 1000
SALES (corp-wide): 7.06B **Privately Held**
SIC: **8062** 8099 General medical and surgical hospitals; Medical services organization
HQ: Glendale Memorial Health Corporation
    1420 S Central Ave
    Glendale CA
    818 502-1900

(P-16105)
GLENDALE MEMORIAL HEALTH CORPORATION
Also Called: Glendale Memorial Center
1420 S Central Ave (91204-2508)

PHONE.................................818 502-1900
EMP: 1245
Web: www.supportglendale.org
SIC: **8062** General medical and surgical hospitals

(P-16106)
GLENN MEDICAL CENTER INC
1133 W Sycamore St (95988-2601)
PHONE.................................530 934-4681
William Casey, *CEO*
Gary Pea, *
EMP: 99 EST: 1898
SQ FT: 62,000
SALES (est): 13.76MM **Privately Held**
Web: www.gmcmed.org
SIC: **8062** General medical and surgical hospitals

(P-16107)
GLENOAKS CONVALESCENT HOSPITAL
409 W Glenoaks Blvd (91202-2916)
PHONE.................................818 240-4300
Elaine Levine, *Pt*
EMP: 85 EST: 1984
SQ FT: 22,306
SALES (est): 8.62MM **Privately Held**
Web: www.gshci.com
SIC: **8062** General medical and surgical hospitals

(P-16108)
GOLDEN EMPIRE CONVALESCENT HOS
121 Dorsey Dr (95945-5201)
PHONE.................................530 273-1316
Vicki Young, *Pt*
EMP: 180 EST: 1996
SALES (est): 12.97MM **Privately Held**
Web: www.goldenempiresnf.com
SIC: **8062** General medical and surgical hospitals

(P-16109)
GOLETA VALLEY COTTAGE HOSP AUX
Also Called: Cottage Health System
351 S Patterson Ave (93111-2403)
P.O. Box 689 (93102-0689)
PHONE.................................805 681-6468
Ronald C Werft, *Pr*
Robert Knight, *
Diane Wisby, *
Joan Bricher, *
Joanne Rapp, *
EMP: 300 EST: 1966
SQ FT: 92,273
SALES (est): 104.45MM
SALES (corp-wide): 152.81MM **Privately Held**
SIC: **8062** General medical and surgical hospitals
PA: Cottage Health
    400 W Pueblo St
    Santa Barbara CA
    805 682-7111

(P-16110)
GOOD SAMARITAN HOSPITAL LP (DH)
Also Called: Good Samaritan Hospital
2425 Samaritan Dr (95124-3985)
P.O. Box 240002 (95154-2402)
PHONE.................................408 559-2011
Frank Hirano, *VP*
Darrel Neuenschwander, *CFO*
Paul Deaupre, *Chief Medical Officer*
Lana Arad, *CFO*

8062 - General Medical And Surgical Hospitals (P-16111)

Jordan Herget, *COO*
EMP: 1200 **EST:** 1983
SALES (est): 610.75MM **Publicly Held**
Web: www.goodsamsanjose.com
SIC: 8062 General medical and surgical hospitals
HQ: Hca Inc.
1 Park Plz
Nashville TN
615 344-9551

(P-16111)
GOOD SAMARITAN HOSPITAL LP
Also Called: Good Samaritan Breastcare Ctr
15400 National Ave Ste 200 (95032-2433)
PHONE.................408 358-8414
Tricia Baker, *Mgr*
EMP: 178
Web: www.goodsamsanjose.com
SIC: 8062 8099 General medical and surgical hospitals; Health screening service
HQ: Good Samaritan Hospital, L.P.
2425 Samaritan Dr
San Jose CA
408 559-2011

(P-16112)
GOOD SAMARITAN HOSPITAL LP
Also Called: Mission Oaks Hospital
15891 Los Gatos Almaden Rd (95032-3742)
PHONE.................408 356-4111
Brian Knecht, *COO*
EMP: 181
Web: www.goodsamsanjose.com
SIC: 8062 General medical and surgical hospitals
HQ: Good Samaritan Hospital, L.P.
2425 Samaritan Dr
San Jose CA
408 559-2011

(P-16113)
GOOD SMRTAN HOSP A CAL LTD PRT
901 Olive Dr (93308-4137)
P.O. Box 85002 (93380-5002)
PHONE.................661 903-9555
Amandeep Basra, *Pr*
Andrew B Leeka, *
Anand Manohara, *
Sakrepatna Manohara, *
David Huff, *
EMP: 400 **EST:** 1965
SQ FT: 49,001
SALES (est): 23.75MM **Privately Held**
Web: www.goodsamhospital.com
SIC: 8062 8063 8069 General medical and surgical hospitals; Psychiatric hospitals; Specialty hospitals, except psychiatric

(P-16114)
GROSSMONT HOSPITAL CORPORATION (HQ)
5555 Grossmont Center Dr (91942-3077)
PHONE.................619 740-6000
Dan Gross, *CEO*
EMP: 1740 **EST:** 1953
SQ FT: 494,000
SALES (est): 959.59MM
SALES (corp-wide): 2.37B **Privately Held**
Web: www.sharp.com
SIC: 8062 General medical and surgical hospitals
PA: Sharp Healthcare
8695 Spectrum Center Blvd
San Diego CA
858 499-4000

(P-16115)
GROSSMONT HOSPITAL CORPORATION
Also Called: Grossmont Home Hlth & Hospice
8881 Fletcher Pkwy Ste 105 (91942-3134)
PHONE.................619 667-1900
Jean Cruise, *Mgr*
EMP: 353
SALES (corp-wide): 2.37B **Privately Held**
Web: www.sharp.com
SIC: 8062 8082 General medical and surgical hospitals; Home health care services
HQ: Grossmont Hospital Corporation
5555 Grossmont Center Dr
La Mesa CA
619 740-6000

(P-16116)
HALSEN HEALTHCARE LLC
Also Called: Watsonville Community Hospital
75 Neilson St (95076-2468)
PHONE.................831 724-4741
Sean Fowler, *Brnch Mgr*
EMP: 820
SALES (corp-wide): 102.4MM **Privately Held**
Web: www.watsonvillehospital.com
SIC: 8062 General medical and surgical hospitals
HQ: Halsen Healthcare, Llc
1872 Sharon Ln
Santa Ana CA
714 726-6189

(P-16117)
HANFORD COMMUNITY HOSPITAL (HQ)
Also Called: Hanford Community Medical Ctr
115 Mall Dr (93230-5786)
P.O. Box 240 (93232-0240)
PHONE.................559 582-9000
EMP: 640 **EST:** 1956
SQ FT: 52,060
SALES (est): 434.72MM
SALES (corp-wide): 789.42MM **Privately Held**
Web: www.adventisthealth.org
SIC: 8062 General medical and surgical hospitals
PA: Adventist Health System/West, Corporation
1 Adventist Health Way
Roseville CA
844 574-5686

(P-16118)
HANFORD COMMUNITY HOSPITAL
Also Called: Adventist Health Selma
1141 Rose Ave (93662-3241)
PHONE.................559 891-1000
Wayne Ferch, *Pr*
EMP: 339
SALES (corp-wide): 789.42MM **Privately Held**
Web: www.adventisthealth.org
SIC: 8062 8051 General medical and surgical hospitals; Skilled nursing care facilities
HQ: Hanford Community Hospital
115 Mall Dr
Hanford CA
559 582-9000

(P-16119)
HAYWARD SISTERS HOSPITAL (HQ)
27200 Calaroga Ave (94545-4339)
PHONE.................510 264-4000
Michael Mahoney, *Pr*
Sherman L Balch, *
Alexandra Budde D.v.m., *Dir*
Craig Bueno, *
Sandra D Davini, *
EMP: 842 **EST:** 1968
SQ FT: 173,000
SALES (est): 123.56MM **Privately Held**
Web: www.strosehospital.org
SIC: 8062 Hospital, affiliated with AMA residency
PA: Alecto Healthcare Services Llc
101 N Brand Blvd Ste 1920
Glendale CA

(P-16120)
HDMC HOLDINGS LLC
Also Called: Hi-Desert Medical Center
6601 White Feather Rd (92252-6607)
PHONE.................760 366-3711
Jeffrey Koury, *CEO*
EMP: 132 **EST:** 2015
SALES (est): 20.46MM
SALES (corp-wide): 19.58B **Publicly Held**
SIC: 8062 General medical and surgical hospitals
PA: Tenet Healthcare Corporation
14201 Dallas Pkwy
Dallas TX
469 893-2200

(P-16121)
HEALTH INVESTMENT CORPORATION
14642 Newport Ave Ste 388 (92780-6059)
PHONE.................714 669-2085
EMP: 1700
SIC: 8062 General medical and surgical hospitals

(P-16122)
HEALTH RESOURCES CORP
Also Called: Coastal Community Hospital
2701 S Bristol St (92704-6201)
PHONE.................714 754-5454
Trevor Fetter, *Pr*
EMP: 400 **EST:** 1984
SALES (est): 51.08MM **Privately Held**
SIC: 8062 General medical and surgical hospitals
HQ: Kpc Healthcare, Inc.
1301 N Tustin Ave
Santa Ana CA
714 953-3652

(P-16123)
HEALTHCARE BARTON SYSTEM (PA)
2170 South Ave (96150-7026)
P.O. Box 9578 (96158-9578)
PHONE.................530 541-3420
Clint Purvance, *CEO*
Kelly Neiger, *
Denise Earls, *
Carla Adams, *
EMP: 554 **EST:** 1960
SQ FT: 112,190
SALES (est): 228.6MM
SALES (corp-wide): 228.6MM **Privately Held**
Web: www.bartonhealth.org
SIC: 8062 General medical and surgical hospitals

(P-16124)
HEALTHSMART PACIFIC INC (PA)
Also Called: Long Beach Pain Center
5150 E Pacific Coast Hwy Ste 200 (90804-3312)
PHONE.................562 595-1911
TOLL FREE: 800
Michael D Drobot, *
G William Hammer, *Prin*
EMP: 610 **EST:** 1932
SALES (est): 42.31MM
SALES (corp-wide): 42.31MM **Privately Held**
SIC: 8062 General medical and surgical hospitals

(P-16125)
HEMET VALLEY MEDICAL CENTER-EDUCATION
Also Called: Hemet Valley Medical Center
1117 E Devonshire Ave (92543-3083)
PHONE.................951 652-2811
EMP: 1200
Web: www.hemetglobalmedcenter.com
SIC: 8062 General medical and surgical hospitals

(P-16126)
HENRY MAYO NEWHALL MEM HOSP (PA)
23845 Mcbean Pkwy (91355-2001)
PHONE.................661 253-8000
Roger E Seaver, *Pr*
Elizabeth Hopp, *Ch Bd*
Robert Pretzlaff, *CMO*
EMP: 1322 **EST:** 1972
SQ FT: 210,000
SALES (est): 458.62MM
SALES (corp-wide): 458.62MM **Privately Held**
Web: www.henrymayo.com
SIC: 8062 General medical and surgical hospitals

(P-16127)
HENRY MAYO NWHALL MEM HLTH FND
Also Called: Henrymayo Newhall Mem Hosp
23845 Mcbean Pkwy (91355-2001)
P.O. Box 55279 (91385-0279)
PHONE.................661 253-8000
Roger Seaver, *Pr*
EMP: 1500 **EST:** 1972
SALES (est): 411.3MM **Privately Held**
SIC: 8062 General medical and surgical hospitals

(P-16128)
HOAG CLINIC
Also Called: HOAG CORPORATE HEALTH
1 Hoag Dr (92663-4162)
P.O. Box 6100 (92658-6100)
PHONE.................949 764-1888
EMP: 349 **EST:** 1995
SALES (est): 211.63MM **Privately Held**
Web: www.hoag.org
SIC: 8062 General medical and surgical hospitals

(P-16129)
HOAG FAMILY CANCER INSTITUTE
1190 Baker St (92626-4108)
PHONE.................949 764-7777
Inga Barillas, *Brnch Mgr*
EMP: 189
Web: www.hoag.org
SIC: 8062 General medical and surgical hospitals
PA: Hoag Family Cancer Institute
1 Hoag Dr Bldg 41
Newport Beach CA

PRODUCTS & SERVICES SECTION
8062 - General Medical And Surgical Hospitals (P-16148)

(P-16130)
HOAG HOSPITAL FOUNDATION (HQ)
330 Placentia Ave Ste 100 (92663-3309)
P.O. Box 6100 (92658-6200)
PHONE.............................949 764-7217
TOLL FREE: 877
Karen Linden, *CEO*
Roger T Kirwan, *Ch*
James D Slavik, *Sr VP*
Greg Brakovich, *Sec*
Flynn A Andrizzi, *CEO*
▲ **EMP:** 60 **EST:** 1944
SQ FT: 500,000
SALES (est): 185.76MM **Privately Held**
Web: www.hoaghospitalfoundation.org
SIC: 8062 General medical and surgical hospitals
PA: Hoag Memorial Hospital Presbyterian
1 Hoag Dr
Newport Beach CA

(P-16131)
HOAG HOSPITAL IRVINE
16200 Sand Canyon Ave (92618-3714)
PHONE.............................949 764-4624
EMP: 99 **EST:** 2009
SALES (est): 26.16MM **Privately Held**
Web: www.hoag.org
SIC: 8062 General medical and surgical hospitals

(P-16132)
HOAG MEMORIAL HOSPITAL PRESBT (PA)
1 Hoag Dr (92663-4162)
P.O. Box 6100 (92658-6100)
PHONE.............................949 764-4624
Robert Braithwaite, *Pr*
Flynn A Andrizzi, *
Kathy Azeez-narain, *Chief Digital Officer*
EMP: 3600 **EST:** 1944
SALES (est): 1.28B **Privately Held**
Web: www.hoag.org
SIC: 8062 General medical and surgical hospitals

(P-16133)
HOAG ORTHOPEDIC INSTITUTE LLC
Also Called: Hoag Orthpd Inst Srgery Ctr -
22 Corporate Plaza Dr Ste 150 (92660-7999)
PHONE.............................949 515-0708
James Caillouette, *Ch Bd*
EMP: 346
SALES (corp-wide): 143.89MM **Privately Held**
Web: www.hoagorthopedicinstitute.com
SIC: 8062 General medical and surgical hospitals
PA: Hoag Orthopedic Institute, Llc
16250 Sand Canyon Ave
Irvine CA
949 764-8690

(P-16134)
HOLLYWOOD CMNTY HOSP MED CTR I
Also Called: Hollywood Cmnty Hosp Hollywood
6245 De Longpre Ave (90028-8253)
PHONE.............................323 462-2271
Robert Starling, *CEO*
Ron Messenger, *
Manfred Krukemeyer, *
EMP: 220 **EST:** 1982
SQ FT: 100,000
SALES (est): 26.98MM

SALES (corp-wide): 3.91B **Privately Held**
Web: www.sch-hollywood.com
SIC: 8062 Hospital, affiliated with AMA residency
HQ: Southern California Healthcare System, Inc.
3415 S Sepulveda Blvd 9thf
Los Angeles CA

(P-16135)
HOLLYWOOD MEDICAL CENTER LP
Also Called: Hollywood Presbyterian Med Ctr
1300 N Vermont Ave (90027-6098)
PHONE.............................213 413-3000
Jeff Nelson, *Pt*
EMP: 1250 **EST:** 1928
SALES (est): 81.88MM **Privately Held**
Web: www.hollywoodpresbyterian.com
SIC: 8062 General medical and surgical hospitals
PA: Cha Health Systems, Inc
3731 Wilshire Blvd # 850
Los Angeles CA

(P-16136)
HOSPITAL OF BARSTOW INC (DH)
Also Called: Barstow Community Hospital
820 E Mountain View St (92311-3004)
PHONE.............................760 256-1761
Justin Sheridan, *CEO*
Shawn Curtis, *
EMP: 91 **EST:** 1958
SQ FT: 54,000
SALES (est): 66.23MM
SALES (corp-wide): 1.69B **Privately Held**
Web: www.barstowhospital.com
SIC: 8062 Hospital, affiliated with AMA residency
HQ: Qhc California Holdings, Llc
1573 Mallory Ln
Brentwood TN

(P-16137)
HOSPITAL OF COMMUNITY
2 Upper Ragsdale Dr Ste D100 (93940-7838)
PHONE.............................831 649-7700
Alan H Rosen, *Prin*
EMP: 221
SALES (corp-wide): 947.23MM **Privately Held**
SIC: 8062 General medical and surgical hospitals
HQ: Community Hospital Of The Monterey Peninsula
23625 Holman Hwy
Monterey CA
831 624-5311

(P-16138)
HUNTINGTON MEDICAL FOUNDATION
65 N Madison Ave Ste 800 (91101-2038)
PHONE.............................626 792-3141
Laura Hernandez, *Mgr*
EMP: 121
Web: www.huntingtonhealth.org
SIC: 8062 General medical and surgical hospitals
PA: The Huntington Medical Foundation
100 W California Blvd
Pasadena CA

(P-16139)
INLAND VLY RGIONAL MED CTR INC
36485 Inland Valley Dr (92595-9681)

PHONE.............................951 677-1111
Alan B Miller, *CEO*
Barry Thorfinnson, *
EMP: 500 **EST:** 1983
SQ FT: 77,000
SALES (est): 98.03MM
SALES (corp-wide): 13.4B **Publicly Held**
Web: www.inlandvalleymedcenter.com
SIC: 8062 8011 General medical and surgical hospitals; Clinic, operated by physicians
PA: Universal Health Services, Inc.
367 S Gulph Rd
King Of Prussia PA
610 768-3300

(P-16140)
JFK MEMORIAL HOSPITAL INC
47111 Monroe St (92201-6739)
PHONE.............................760 347-6191
Gary Honts, *Pr*
EMP: 189 **EST:** 2001
SALES (est): 29.3MM
SALES (corp-wide): 19.58B **Publicly Held**
SIC: 8062 General medical and surgical hospitals
PA: Tenet Healthcare Corporation
14201 Dallas Pkwy
Dallas TX
469 893-2200

(P-16141)
JOHN C FREMONT HEALTHCARE DST
Also Called: Fremont Hospital
5189 Hospital Rd (95338-9524)
P.O. Box 216 (95338-0216)
PHONE.............................209 966-3631
Lynn Buskill, *Interim Chief Executive Officer*
Linda Pribyl, *
Andrew Smith, *
EMP: 265 **EST:** 1951
SQ FT: 59,112
SALES (est): 26.27MM **Privately Held**
Web: www.jcf-hospital.com
SIC: 8062 General medical and surgical hospitals

(P-16142)
JOHN F KENNEDY MEM HOSP AUX
Also Called: DES PERES HOSPITAL, INC.
47111 Monroe St (92201-6799)
PHONE.............................760 347-6191
TOLL FREE: 800
Gary Honts, *CEO*
EMP: 650 **EST:** 1986
SALES (est): 1.01MM
SALES (corp-wide): 72.97MM **Privately Held**
SIC: 8062 Hospital, affiliated with AMA residency
HQ: St. Luke's Des Peres Episcopal-Presbyterian Hospital
2345 Dougherty Ferry Rd
Saint Louis MO
314 966-9100

(P-16143)
JOHN MUIR HEALTH (HQ)
1601 Ygnacio Valley Rd (94598-3122)
P.O. Box 9023 (94596-9023)
PHONE.............................925 947-4449
Calvin Cal Knight, *CEO*
Ken Meehan, *
Michael S Thomas, *
Jane A Willemsen, *
EMP: 1600 **EST:** 1958
SQ FT: 5,500
SALES (est): 1.93B

SALES (corp-wide): 428.02MM **Privately Held**
Web: www.johnmuirhealth.com
SIC: 8062 General medical and surgical hospitals
PA: John Muir Physician Network
1450 Treat Blvd
Walnut Creek CA
925 296-9700

(P-16144)
JOHN MUIR HEALTH
Also Called: John Muir Medical Center
1601 Ygnacio Valley Rd (94598-3122)
PHONE.............................925 939-3000
Vicki C Lee, *Admn*
EMP: 775
SALES (corp-wide): 428.02MM **Privately Held**
Web: www.johnmuirhealth.com
SIC: 8062 General medical and surgical hospitals
HQ: John Muir Health
1601 Ygnacio Valley Rd
Walnut Creek CA
925 947-4449

(P-16145)
JOHN MUIR PHYSICIAN NETWORK (PA)
Also Called: John Muir Medical Center
1450 Treat Blvd (94597-2168)
PHONE.............................925 296-9700
Cal Knight, *Prin*
EMP: 1601 **EST:** 1997
SQ FT: 83,579
SALES (est): 428.02MM
SALES (corp-wide): 428.02MM **Privately Held**
Web: www.johnmuirhealth.com
SIC: 8062 8069 8093 7363 General medical and surgical hospitals; Substance abuse hospitals; Substance abuse clinics (outpatient); Medical help service

(P-16146)
JUPITER BELLFLOWER DOCTORS HOSPITAL
Also Called: Bellflower Medical Center
3699 Wilshire Blvd Ste 540 (90010-2718)
EMP: 500
SIC: 8062 General medical and surgical hospitals

(P-16147)
KAISER FOUNDATION HOSPITALS
1200 Discovery Dr (93309-7032)
PHONE.............................661 631-3045
EMP: 61
SALES (corp-wide): 68.1B **Privately Held**
Web: www.kaisercenter.com
SIC: 8062 General medical and surgical hospitals
HQ: Kaiser Foundation Hospitals Inc
1 Kaiser Plz
Oakland CA
510 271-6611

(P-16148)
KAISER FOUNDATION HOSPITALS
Also Called: Barranca Medical Offices
6 Willard (92604-4694)
PHONE.............................949 262-5780
George Disalvo, *Owner*
EMP: 181
SQ FT: 51,080
SALES (corp-wide): 68.1B **Privately Held**

8062 - General Medical And Surgical Hospitals (P-16149)

Web: www.kaisercenter.com
SIC: **8062** General medical and surgical hospitals
HQ: Kaiser Foundation Hospitals Inc
 1 Kaiser Plz
 Oakland CA
 510 271-6611

(P-16149)
KAISER FOUNDATION HOSPITALS
Also Called: Kaiser Foundation Health Plan
1 Quality Dr Fl A1 (95688-9494)
PHONE.....................707 624-4000
Kim Trumbull, *Brnch Mgr*
EMP: 1149
SALES (corp-wide): 68.1B **Privately Held**
Web: www.kaisercenter.com
SIC: **8062** General medical and surgical hospitals
HQ: Kaiser Foundation Hospitals Inc
 1 Kaiser Plz
 Oakland CA
 510 271-6611

(P-16150)
KAISER FOUNDATION HOSPITALS
Also Called: Kaiser Prmnnte Eye Svcs - Optm
1680 E Roseville Pkwy (95661-3988)
PHONE.....................916 746-3937
Daniel Rule, *Brnch Mgr*
EMP: 178
SALES (corp-wide): 68.1B **Privately Held**
Web: www.kaisercenter.com
SIC: **8062** General medical and surgical hospitals
HQ: Kaiser Foundation Hospitals Inc
 1 Kaiser Plz
 Oakland CA
 510 271-6611

(P-16151)
KAISER FOUNDATION HOSPITALS
3100 Dublin Blvd (94568-7213)
PHONE.....................925 556-4200
EMP: 158
SALES (corp-wide): 68.1B **Privately Held**
Web: www.kaisercenter.com
SIC: **8062** General medical and surgical hospitals
HQ: Kaiser Foundation Hospitals Inc
 1 Kaiser Plz
 Oakland CA
 510 271-6611

(P-16152)
KAISER FOUNDATION HOSPITALS
Also Called: Kaiser Permanente
5601 De Soto Ave (91367-6701)
PHONE.....................818 719-2000
Cathy Casas, *Admn*
EMP: 1200
SALES (corp-wide): 68.1B **Privately Held**
Web: www.kaisercenter.com
SIC: **8062** General medical and surgical hospitals
HQ: Kaiser Foundation Hospitals Inc
 1 Kaiser Plz
 Oakland CA
 510 271-6611

(P-16153)
KAISER FOUNDATION HOSPITALS
Also Called: Kaiser Permanente
12620 Prescott Ave (92782-1066)
PHONE.....................951 353-4000
Danh V Le, *Dir*
EMP: 137
SALES (corp-wide): 68.1B **Privately Held**
Web: www.kaisercenter.com
SIC: **8062** General medical and surgical hospitals
HQ: Kaiser Foundation Hospitals Inc
 1 Kaiser Plz
 Oakland CA
 510 271-6611

(P-16154)
KAISER FOUNDATION HOSPITALS
Also Called: Kaiser Permanente
8800 Ming Ave (93311-1308)
PHONE.....................661 412-6777
EMP: 143
SALES (corp-wide): 68.1B **Privately Held**
Web: www.kaisercenter.com
SIC: **8062** General medical and surgical hospitals
HQ: Kaiser Foundation Hospitals Inc
 1 Kaiser Plz
 Oakland CA
 510 271-6611

(P-16155)
KAISER FOUNDATION HOSPITALS
Also Called: Kaiser Permanente
4867 W Sunset Blvd (90027-5969)
PHONE.....................323 783-4011
Vicken Aharonian, *Dir*
EMP: 60
SALES (corp-wide): 68.1B **Privately Held**
Web: www.kaisercenter.com
SIC: **8062** 8099 6321 6324 General medical and surgical hospitals; Physical examination service, insurance; Health insurance carriers; Hospital and medical service plans
HQ: Kaiser Foundation Hospitals Inc
 1 Kaiser Plz
 Oakland CA
 510 271-6611

(P-16156)
KAISER FOUNDATION HOSPITALS
Also Called: Park Shadelands Medical Offs
320 Lennon Ln (94598-2419)
PHONE.....................925 906-2380
David Nievr, *Pr*
EMP: 193
SALES (corp-wide): 68.1B **Privately Held**
Web: www.kpcosmeticservices.com
SIC: **8062** 8011 General medical and surgical hospitals; General and family practice, physician/surgeon
HQ: Kaiser Foundation Hospitals Inc
 1 Kaiser Plz
 Oakland CA
 510 271-6611

(P-16157)
KAISER FOUNDATION HOSPITALS
5831 Cottle Rd (95123-3734)
PHONE.....................408 363-4801
EMP: 67
SALES (corp-wide): 68.1B **Privately Held**
Web: www.kphearingcenters.com
SIC: **8062** General medical and surgical hospitals
HQ: Kaiser Foundation Hospitals Inc
 1 Kaiser Plz
 Oakland CA
 510 271-6611

(P-16158)
KAISER FOUNDATION HOSPITALS
Also Called: Kaiser Prmnnte Ornge Cnty-Nhei
3440 E La Palma Ave (92806-2020)
PHONE.....................714 644-2000
Patrick Steinhauser, *Brnch Mgr*
EMP: 4046
SQ FT: 125,000
SALES (corp-wide): 68.1B **Privately Held**
Web: www.kaisercenter.com
SIC: **8062** 8011 General medical and surgical hospitals; General and family practice, physician/surgeon
HQ: Kaiser Foundation Hospitals Inc
 1 Kaiser Plz
 Oakland CA
 510 271-6611

(P-16159)
KAISER FOUNDATION HOSPITALS
400 S Sepulveda Blvd (90266-6814)
PHONE.....................310 937-4311
EMP: 152
SALES (corp-wide): 68.1B **Privately Held**
Web: www.kaisercenter.com
SIC: **8062** General medical and surgical hospitals
HQ: Kaiser Foundation Hospitals Inc
 1 Kaiser Plz
 Oakland CA
 510 271-6611

(P-16160)
KAISER FOUNDATION HOSPITALS (HQ)
Also Called: Kaiser Permanente
1 Kaiser Plz (94612-3610)
P.O. Box 12929 (94604-3010)
PHONE.....................510 271-6611
Gregory A Adams, *Ch*
Anthony Barreta, *
Kathy Lancaster, *
Janet Liang, *Group President**
Catherine Hernandez, *CCO**
▲ EMP: 250 **EST:** 1948
SQ FT: 90,000
SALES (est): 32.23B
SALES (corp-wide): 68.1B **Privately Held**
Web: www.kaisercenter.com
SIC: **8062** 8011 General medical and surgical hospitals; Medical centers
PA: Kaiser Foundation Health Plan, Inc.
 1 Kaiser Plz
 Oakland CA
 510 271-5800

(P-16161)
KAISER FOUNDATION HOSPITALS
4733 W Sunset Blvd Fl 2 (90027-6021)
PHONE.....................323 783-4011
EMP: 184
SALES (corp-wide): 68.1B **Privately Held**
Web: www.kaisercenter.com
SIC: **8062** General medical and surgical hospitals
HQ: Kaiser Foundation Hospitals Inc
 1 Kaiser Plz
 Oakland CA
 510 271-6611

(P-16162)
KAISER FOUNDATION HOSPITALS
Also Called: Kaiser Permanente
280 W Macarthur Blvd (94611-5642)
PHONE.....................510 752-1000
Bettie Coles, *Mgr*
EMP: 1161
SALES (corp-wide): 68.1B **Privately Held**
Web: www.kaisercenter.com
SIC: **8062** General medical and surgical hospitals
HQ: Kaiser Foundation Hospitals Inc
 1 Kaiser Plz
 Oakland CA
 510 271-6611

(P-16163)
KAISER FOUNDATION HOSPITALS
Also Called: Kaiser Permanente
501 J St (95814-2325)
PHONE.....................916 558-6520
EMP: 137
SALES (corp-wide): 68.1B **Privately Held**
Web: www.kaisercenter.com
SIC: **8062** 8011 General medical and surgical hospitals; Medical centers
HQ: Kaiser Foundation Hospitals Inc
 1 Kaiser Plz
 Oakland CA
 510 271-6611

(P-16164)
KAISER FOUNDATION HOSPITALS
Also Called: Kaiser Permanente
1255 W Arrow Hwy (91773-2340)
PHONE.....................909 394-2530
Will Tatum, *Mgr*
EMP: 172
SQ FT: 23,801
SALES (corp-wide): 68.1B **Privately Held**
Web: www.kaisercenter.com
SIC: **8062** 8011 General medical and surgical hospitals; General and family practice, physician/surgeon
HQ: Kaiser Foundation Hospitals Inc
 1 Kaiser Plz
 Oakland CA
 510 271-6611

(P-16165)
KAISER FOUNDATION HOSPITALS
Also Called: Kaiser Permanente
4405 Vandever Ave Fl 5 (92120-3315)
PHONE.....................619 528-2583
David Mandler, *Mgr*
EMP: 164
SALES (corp-wide): 68.1B **Privately Held**
Web: www.kaisercenter.com
SIC: **8062** General medical and surgical hospitals
HQ: Kaiser Foundation Hospitals Inc
 1 Kaiser Plz
 Oakland CA
 510 271-6611

(P-16166)
KAISER FOUNDATION HOSPITALS
280 Hospital Pkwy (95119-1103)
PHONE.....................408 972-6010
Rajan Bhandari, *Brnch Mgr*
EMP: 202
SALES (corp-wide): 68.1B **Privately Held**
Web: www.kaisercenter.com
SIC: **8062** General medical and surgical hospitals
HQ: Kaiser Foundation Hospitals Inc
 1 Kaiser Plz
 Oakland CA
 510 271-6611

PRODUCTS & SERVICES SECTION **8062 - General Medical And Surgical Hospitals (P-16185)**

(P-16167)
KAISER FOUNDATION HOSPITALS
Also Called: Antelope Valley Hospital
1600 W Avenue J (93534-2814)
PHONE..................................661 949-5000
Harriet R Lee, *Admn*
EMP: 67
SALES (corp-wide): 68.1B **Privately Held**
Web: www.kaisercenter.com
SIC: 8062 General medical and surgical hospitals
HQ: Kaiser Foundation Hospitals Inc
   1 Kaiser Plz
   Oakland CA
   510 271-6611

(P-16168)
KAISER FOUNDATION HOSPITALS
Also Called: Kaiser Prmanente Internet Svcs
5820 Owens Dr Bldg E-2 (94588-3900)
PHONE..................................925 598-2799
EMP: 111
SALES (corp-wide): 68.1B **Privately Held**
Web: www.kaisercenter.com
SIC: 8062 General medical and surgical hospitals
HQ: Kaiser Foundation Hospitals Inc
   1 Kaiser Plz
   Oakland CA
   510 271-6611

(P-16169)
KAISER FOUNDATION HOSPITALS
Also Called: Kaiser Permanente
9455 Clairemont Mesa Blvd (92123-1297)
PHONE..................................858 573-1504
EMP: 134
SALES (corp-wide): 68.1B **Privately Held**
Web: www.kaisercenter.com
SIC: 8062 8011 General medical and surgical hospitals; Medical centers
HQ: Kaiser Foundation Hospitals Inc
   1 Kaiser Plz
   Oakland CA
   510 271-6611

(P-16170)
KAISER FOUNDATION HOSPITALS
Also Called: Kaiser Permanente
3900 Freedom Cir Ste 201 (95054-1222)
PHONE..................................408 235-4005
Christopher L Boyd, *Sr VP*
EMP: 70
SALES (corp-wide): 68.1B **Privately Held**
Web: www.kaisercenter.com
SIC: 8062 General medical and surgical hospitals
HQ: Kaiser Foundation Hospitals Inc
   1 Kaiser Plz
   Oakland CA
   510 271-6611

(P-16171)
KAISER FOUNDATION HOSPITALS
Also Called: Kaiser Permanente
1650 Response Rd (95815-4807)
PHONE..................................916 973-5000
Sandra Lee Panora, *Brnch Mgr*
EMP: 571
SALES (corp-wide): 68.1B **Privately Held**
Web: www.kpivf.com
SIC: 8062 General medical and surgical hospitals
HQ: Kaiser Foundation Hospitals Inc
   1 Kaiser Plz
   Oakland CA
   510 271-6611

(P-16172)
KAISER FOUNDATION HOSPITALS
10990 San Diego Mission Rd (92108-2417)
PHONE..................................619 641-4663
Caroline Bonner, *Dir*
EMP: 73
SALES (corp-wide): 68.1B **Privately Held**
Web: www.kaisercenter.com
SIC: 8062 General medical and surgical hospitals
HQ: Kaiser Foundation Hospitals Inc
   1 Kaiser Plz
   Oakland CA
   510 271-6611

(P-16173)
KAISER FOUNDATION HOSPITALS
Also Called: Wildomar Medical Offices
36450 Inland Valley Dr Ste 204 (92595-9583)
PHONE..................................951 353-2000
Geoffrey Gomez, *Prin*
EMP: 231
SALES (corp-wide): 68.1B **Privately Held**
Web: www.kaisercenter.com
SIC: 8062 General medical and surgical hospitals
HQ: Kaiser Foundation Hospitals Inc
   1 Kaiser Plz
   Oakland CA
   510 271-6611

(P-16174)
KAISER FOUNDATION HOSPITALS
Also Called: Bostonia Medical Offices
1630 E Main St (92021-5204)
PHONE..................................619 528-5000
EMP: 152
SALES (corp-wide): 68.1B **Privately Held**
Web: www.kaisercenter.com
SIC: 8062 General medical and surgical hospitals
HQ: Kaiser Foundation Hospitals Inc
   1 Kaiser Plz
   Oakland CA
   510 271-6611

(P-16175)
KAISER FOUNDATION HOSPITALS
Also Called: Cudahy Medical Offices
7825 Atlantic Ave (90201-5022)
PHONE..................................323 562-6400
Karen Warren, *Mgr*
EMP: 105
SALES (corp-wide): 68.1B **Privately Held**
Web: www.kaisercenter.com
SIC: 8062 General medical and surgical hospitals
HQ: Kaiser Foundation Hospitals Inc
   1 Kaiser Plz
   Oakland CA
   510 271-6611

(P-16176)
KAISER FOUNDATION HOSPITALS
Also Called: Gardena Medical Offices
15446 S Western Ave (90249-4319)
PHONE..................................310 517-2956
Mary Mauch, *Mgr*
EMP: 178
SQ FT: 114,575
SALES (corp-wide): 68.1B **Privately Held**
Web: www.kaisercenter.com
SIC: 8062 General medical and surgical hospitals
HQ: Kaiser Foundation Hospitals Inc
   1 Kaiser Plz
   Oakland CA
   510 271-6611

(P-16177)
KAISER FOUNDATION HOSPITALS
Also Called: Erwin Street Medical Offices
5601 De Soto Ave (91367-6701)
PHONE..................................818 592-3100
Karen Kim, *Ofcr*
EMP: 70
SALES (corp-wide): 68.1B **Privately Held**
Web: www.kaisercenter.com
SIC: 8062 General medical and surgical hospitals
HQ: Kaiser Foundation Hospitals Inc
   1 Kaiser Plz
   Oakland CA
   510 271-6611

(P-16178)
KAISER FOUNDATION HOSPITALS
Also Called: Rancho Cordova Medical Offices
10725 International Dr (95670-7967)
PHONE..................................916 631-3088
David Haddad, *Prin*
EMP: 447
SALES (corp-wide): 68.1B **Privately Held**
Web: www.kaisercenter.com
SIC: 8062 General medical and surgical hospitals
HQ: Kaiser Foundation Hospitals Inc
   1 Kaiser Plz
   Oakland CA
   510 271-6611

(P-16179)
KAISER FOUNDATION HOSPITALS
20000 Rinaldi St (91326-4900)
PHONE..................................833 574-2273
EMP: 91
SALES (corp-wide): 68.1B **Privately Held**
Web: www.kaisercenter.com
SIC: 8062 General medical and surgical hospitals
HQ: Kaiser Foundation Hospitals Inc
   1 Kaiser Plz
   Oakland CA
   510 271-6611

(P-16180)
KAISER FOUNDATION HOSPITALS
Also Called: Kaiser Permanente Medical Ctr
4131 Geary Blvd (94118-3101)
PHONE..................................415 833-4393
EMP: 82
SALES (corp-wide): 68.1B **Privately Held**
Web: www.kaisercenter.com
SIC: 8062 General medical and surgical hospitals
HQ: Kaiser Foundation Hospitals Inc
   1 Kaiser Plz
   Oakland CA
   510 271-6611

(P-16181)
KAISER FOUNDATION HOSPITALS
Also Called: Kaiser Permanente Med Group
3505 Broadway (94611-5798)
PHONE..................................510 752-1000
EMP: 67
SALES (corp-wide): 68.1B **Privately Held**
Web: www.kaisercenter.com
SIC: 8062 8011 General medical and surgical hospitals; Medical centers
HQ: Kaiser Foundation Hospitals Inc
   1 Kaiser Plz
   Oakland CA
   510 271-6611

(P-16182)
KAISER FOUNDATION HOSPITALS
Also Called: Kaiser Permanente
501 Lennon Ln (94598-2414)
PHONE..................................925 906-2000
Christina Robinson, *Prin*
EMP: 307
SALES (corp-wide): 68.1B **Privately Held**
Web: www.kaisercenter.com
SIC: 8062 General medical and surgical hospitals
HQ: Kaiser Foundation Hospitals Inc
   1 Kaiser Plz
   Oakland CA
   510 271-6611

(P-16183)
KAISER FOUNDATION HOSPITALS
Also Called: Kaiser Permanente
7601 Stoneridge Dr (94588-4501)
PHONE..................................925 847-5000
Linsey Dicks, *Dir*
EMP: 8568
SALES (corp-wide): 68.1B **Privately Held**
Web: www.kaisercenter.com
SIC: 8062 General medical and surgical hospitals
HQ: Kaiser Foundation Hospitals Inc
   1 Kaiser Plz
   Oakland CA
   510 271-6611

(P-16184)
KAISER FOUNDATION HOSPITALS
Also Called: Kaiser Prmnnte Vallejo Med Ctr
975 Sereno Dr (94589-2441)
PHONE..................................707 651-1000
Katie Rickleff, *Prin*
EMP: 2649
SALES (corp-wide): 68.1B **Privately Held**
Web: www.kp2020.org
SIC: 8062 General medical and surgical hospitals
HQ: Kaiser Foundation Hospitals Inc
   1 Kaiser Plz
   Oakland CA
   510 271-6611

(P-16185)
KAISER FOUNDATION HOSPITALS
Also Called: Kaiser Prmnte San Jose Med Ct
275 Hospital Pkwy Ste 765a (95119-1106)
PHONE..................................408 972-6700
Diana Ochoa, *Brnch Mgr*
EMP: 119
SALES (corp-wide): 68.1B **Privately Held**
Web: www.kaisercenter.com
SIC: 8062 8021 General medical and surgical hospitals; Offices and clinics of dentists
HQ: Kaiser Foundation Hospitals Inc
   1 Kaiser Plz
   Oakland CA
   510 271-6611

8062 - General Medical And Surgical Hospitals (P-16186)

(P-16186)
KAISER FOUNDATION HOSPITALS
Also Called: Kaiser Permanente
1055 E Colorado Blvd Ste 100 (91106)
PHONE............................626 440-5659
Jeanine Boudakian, *Brnch Mgr*
EMP: 500
SALES (corp-wide): 68.1B **Privately Held**
Web: www.kaisercenter.com
SIC: 8062 General medical and surgical hospitals
HQ: Kaiser Foundation Hospitals Inc
1 Kaiser Plz
Oakland CA
510 271-6611

(P-16187)
KAISER FOUNDATION HOSPITALS
5800 Coliseum Way (94621-4043)
PHONE............................510 434-5835
Todd Scott, *Brnch Mgr*
EMP: 73
SALES (corp-wide): 68.1B **Privately Held**
Web: www.kaisercenter.com
SIC: 8062 General medical and surgical hospitals
HQ: Kaiser Foundation Hospitals Inc
1 Kaiser Plz
Oakland CA
510 271-6611

(P-16188)
KAISER FOUNDATION HOSPITALS
Also Called: Kaiser Permanente
1600 Eureka Rd (95661-3027)
PHONE............................916 784-4000
Douglas Freeman, *Brnch Mgr*
EMP: 2300
SALES (corp-wide): 68.1B **Privately Held**
Web: www.kaisercenter.com
SIC: 8062 General medical and surgical hospitals
HQ: Kaiser Foundation Hospitals Inc
1 Kaiser Plz
Oakland CA
510 271-6611

(P-16189)
KAISER FOUNDATION HOSPITALS
Also Called: Kaiser Permanente
250 W San Jose Ave (91711-5295)
PHONE............................888 750-0036
Bell Pacific, *Mgr*
EMP: 76
SQ FT: 17,908
SALES (corp-wide): 68.1B **Privately Held**
Web: www.kaisercenter.com
SIC: 8062 General medical and surgical hospitals
HQ: Kaiser Foundation Hospitals Inc
1 Kaiser Plz
Oakland CA
510 271-6611

(P-16190)
KAISER FOUNDATION HOSPITALS
Also Called: Kaiser Prmnnte Advice Ctr - Al
7300 Wyndham Dr (95823-4913)
PHONE............................916 525-6300
Tony Le, *Mgr*
EMP: 175
SALES (corp-wide): 68.1B **Privately Held**
Web: www.kaisercenter.com
SIC: 8062 General medical and surgical hospitals
HQ: Kaiser Foundation Hospitals Inc
1 Kaiser Plz
Oakland CA
510 271-6611

(P-16191)
KAISER FOUNDATION HOSPITALS
Also Called: Kaiser Permanente
7373 West Ln (95210-3377)
PHONE............................209 476-3101
Gene Long, *Brnch Mgr*
EMP: 1838
SALES (corp-wide): 68.1B **Privately Held**
Web: www.kaisercenter.com
SIC: 8062 General medical and surgical hospitals
HQ: Kaiser Foundation Hospitals Inc
1 Kaiser Plz
Oakland CA
510 271-6611

(P-16192)
KAISER FOUNDATION HOSPITALS
Also Called: Kaiser Prmnnte Snta Clara Med
710 Lawrence Expy (95051-5173)
PHONE............................408 851-1000
EMP: 3499
SALES (corp-wide): 68.1B **Privately Held**
Web: www.kaisercenter.com
SIC: 8062 General medical and surgical hospitals
HQ: Kaiser Foundation Hospitals Inc
1 Kaiser Plz
Oakland CA
510 271-6611

(P-16193)
KAISER FOUNDATION HOSPITALS
Also Called: Kaiser Permanente
43112 15th St W (93534-6219)
PHONE............................661 726-2500
Barbara Fordice, *Genl Mgr*
EMP: 570
SALES (corp-wide): 68.1B **Privately Held**
Web: www.kaisercenter.com
SIC: 8062 Hospital, affiliated with AMA residency
HQ: Kaiser Foundation Hospitals Inc
1 Kaiser Plz
Oakland CA
510 271-6611

(P-16194)
KAISER FOUNDATION HOSPITALS
Also Called: Permanente Medical Group
555 Castro St Fl 3 (94041-2009)
PHONE............................650 903-3000
Patricia Carpenter, *Dir*
EMP: 79
SALES (corp-wide): 68.1B **Privately Held**
Web: www.kaisercenter.com
SIC: 8062 Hospital, affiliated with AMA residency
HQ: Kaiser Foundation Hospitals Inc
1 Kaiser Plz
Oakland CA
510 271-6611

(P-16195)
KAISER PERMANENT
100 Smith Ranch Rd (94903-1900)
PHONE............................415 492-6311
EMP: 63 EST: 2014
SALES (est): 2.27MM **Privately Held**
SIC: 8062 General medical and surgical hospitals

(P-16196)
KAISER PERMANENTE WATTS C
1465 E 103rd St (90002-3306)
PHONE............................323 564-7911
Vikki Franklin, *Dir*
EMP: 96 EST: 2013
SALES (est): 8.23MM **Privately Held**
Web: community.kp.org
SIC: 8062 General medical and surgical hospitals

(P-16197)
KAWEAH DELTA HEALTH CARE DST
Also Called: KAWEAH DELTA HEALTH CARE DISTRICT
1014 San Juan Ave (93221-1312)
PHONE............................559 592-7128
EMP: 98
SALES (corp-wide): 857.31MM **Privately Held**
Web: www.kaweahhealth.org
SIC: 8062 General medical and surgical hospitals
PA: Kaweah Delta Health Care District Guild
400 W Mineral King Ave
Visalia CA
559 624-2000

(P-16198)
KAWEAH DELTA HEALTH CARE DST
Also Called: KAWEAH DELTA HEALTH CARE DISTRICT
1110 S Ben Maddox Way (93292-3643)
PHONE............................559 624-4800
EMP: 112
SALES (corp-wide): 857.31MM **Privately Held**
Web: www.kaweahhealthmedicalgroup.org
SIC: 8062 General medical and surgical hospitals
PA: Kaweah Delta Health Care District Guild
400 W Mineral King Ave
Visalia CA
559 624-2000

(P-16199)
KAWEAH DELTA HEALTH CARE DST
Also Called: KAWEAH DELTA HEALTH CARE DISTRICT
355 Monte Vista Dr (93618-9228)
PHONE............................559 591-5513
Gary K Herbst, *CFO*
EMP: 146
SALES (corp-wide): 857.31MM **Privately Held**
Web: www.kaweahhealth.org
SIC: 8062 Hospital, AMA approved residency
PA: Kaweah Delta Health Care District Guild
400 W Mineral King Ave
Visalia CA
559 624-2000

(P-16200)
KAWEAH DLTA HLTH CARE DST GILD (PA)
Also Called: Kaweah Delta Medical Center
400 W Mineral King Ave (93291-6237)
PHONE............................559 624-2000
Donna Archer, *CEO*
Lindsay K Mann, *
Gary Herbst, *
EMP: 1800 EST: 1961
SQ FT: 250,255
SALES (est): 857.31MM
SALES (corp-wide): 857.31MM **Privately Held**
Web: www.kaweahhealth.org
SIC: 8062 Hospital, AMA approved residency

(P-16201)
KECK HOSPITAL OF USC
1500 San Pablo St (90033-5313)
PHONE............................800 872-2273
Thomas E Jackiewicz, *CEO*
James J Uli Junior, *CFO*
▲ EMP: 921 EST: 2009
SALES (est): 1.13B **Privately Held**
Web: www.keckmedicine.org
SIC: 8062 General medical and surgical hospitals

(P-16202)
KECK SCHOOL
Also Called: Hoffman Medical Research Ctr
2011 Zonal Ave (90089-0110)
PHONE............................323 442-1179
Michael E Selsted, *Ch*
Fernando Zambrano, *CFO*
EMP: 82 EST: 2014
SALES (est): 7.22MM **Privately Held**
Web: www.keckmedicine.org
SIC: 8062 Hospital, med school affiliated with nursing and residency

(P-16203)
KENNETH CORP
Also Called: Garden Grove Hospital
12601 Garden Grove Blvd (92843-1908)
PHONE............................714 537-5160
Edward Mirzabegian, *CEO*
Hassan Alkhouli, *
EMP: 615 EST: 1951
SQ FT: 133,083
SALES (est): 76.84MM **Privately Held**
Web: www.gardengrovehospital.com
SIC: 8062 General medical and surgical hospitals

(P-16204)
KERN COUNTY HOSPITAL AUTHORITY (PA)
1700 Mount Vernon Ave (93306-4018)
PHONE............................661 326-2102
Russell Judd, *CEO*
Tyler Whitezell, *Admn Execs*
Andrew Cantu, *CFO*
EMP: 508 EST: 1865
SQ FT: 29,800
SALES (est): 47.39MM
SALES (corp-wide): 47.39MM **Privately Held**
Web: www.kernmedical.com
SIC: 8062 General medical and surgical hospitals

(P-16205)
KINDRED HEALTHCARE OPER LLC
Also Called: Kindred Hospital
2800 Benedict Dr (94577-6840)
PHONE............................510 357-8300
Wendy Mamoon, *CEO*
EMP: 450
SALES (corp-wide): 13.68B **Privately Held**
Web: www.kindredhealthcare.com
SIC: 8062 General medical and surgical hospitals
HQ: Kindred Healthcare Operating, Llc

8062 - General Medical And Surgical Hospitals (P-16224)

680 S 4th St
Louisville KY
502 596-7300

(P-16206)
KND DEVELOPMENT 55 LLC
Also Called: Kindred Hospital - Rancho
10841 White Oak Ave (91730-3817)
PHONE.................................909 581-6400
Miller Debroah, *Dir*
EMP: 108 EST: 2007
SALES (est): 35.86MM **Privately Held**
SIC: **8062** General medical and surgical hospitals

(P-16207)
KPC GLOBAL MEDICAL CENTERS INC (DH)
Also Called: PHH
1117 E Devonshire Ave (92543-3083)
PHONE.................................714 953-3500
Kali Chaudhuri, *Ch*
Sreenivasa Nakka, *
Ashok Agarwal, *
Kali Priyo Chaudhuri, *
Rakesh Gupta, *
EMP: 125 EST: 2009
SALES (est): 169.46MM **Privately Held**
Web: www.hemetglobalmedcenter.com
SIC: **8062** General medical and surgical hospitals
HQ: Kpc Healthcare, Inc.
1301 N Tustin Ave
Santa Ana CA
714 953-3652

(P-16208)
LA METROPOLITAN MEDICAL CENTER
2231 Southwest Dr (90043-4523)
PHONE.................................323 730-7300
TOLL FREE: 800
EMP: 600
Web: www.lammc.com
SIC: **8062** General medical and surgical hospitals

(P-16209)
LA PALMA HOSPITAL MEDICAL CENTER
Also Called: La Palma Intercommunity Hosp
7901 Walker St (90623-1764)
PHONE.................................714 670-7400
TOLL FREE: 800
EMP: 400
Web: www.lapalmaintercommunityhospital.com
SIC: **8062** General medical and surgical hospitals

(P-16210)
LAC USC COUNTY HOSPITAL
2051 Marengo St (90033-1352)
PHONE.................................323 226-2622
EMP: 92
SALES (est): 522.17K **Privately Held**
SIC: **8062** General medical and surgical hospitals

(P-16211)
LAC USC MEDICAL CENTER
Also Called: Los Angeles County Hospital
1200 N State St Rm 5250 (90089-1001)
P.O. Box 63 (90078-0063)
EMP: 143 EST: 1992
SALES (est): 54.37MM **Privately Held**
Web: www.usc.edu

SIC: **8062** 6324 General medical and surgical hospitals; Hospital and medical service plans

(P-16212)
LAKEWOOD REGIONAL MED CTR INC
Also Called: Lakewood Regional Medical Ctr
3700 South St (90712-1419)
P.O. Box 6070 (90714-6070)
PHONE.................................562 531-2550
John Grah, *CEO*
Ronald Galonsky, *
Mark Korth, *
Lani Dickinson, *
Michael Paul Amos, *
EMP: 900 EST: 2001
SALES (est): 139.55MM
SALES (corp-wide): 19.58B **Publicly Held**
SIC: **8062** Hospital, affiliated with AMA residency
PA: Tenet Healthcare Corporation
14201 Dallas Pkwy
Dallas TX
469 893-2200

(P-16213)
LELAND STANFORD JUNIOR UNIV
Also Called: Stanford University Medical
300 Pasteur Dr (94305-2200)
PHONE.................................650 723-4000
Martha Marsh, *Admn*
EMP: 214
SQ FT: 33,503
SALES (corp-wide): 15.13B **Privately Held**
Web: www.stanford.edu
SIC: **8062** 8011 8221 General medical and surgical hospitals; Offices and clinics of medical doctors; University
PA: Leland Stanford Junior University
450 Jane Stanford Way
Stanford CA
650 723-2300

(P-16214)
LINDA LOMA UNIV HLTH CARE (HQ)
11370 Anderson St Ste 3900 (92354-3450)
P.O. Box 2000 (92354-0200)
PHONE.................................909 558-2806
Richard Hart, *Pr*
Rosita Fike, *
EMP: 125 EST: 1967
SALES (est): 171.21MM
SALES (corp-wide): 388.6MM **Privately Held**
Web: www.lomalindafertility.com
SIC: **8062** 8011 8051 5999 Hospital, medical school affiliated with residency; Medical centers; Extended care facility; Convalescent equipment and supplies
PA: Loma Linda University
11060 Anderson St Mga
Loma Linda CA
909 558-4540

(P-16215)
LITTLE COMPANY MARY HOSPITAL
Also Called: Leader Drug Store
4101 Torrance Blvd (90503-4664)
PHONE.................................310 540-7676
Joseph Zanetta, *CEO*
Elizabeth Zuanich, *
▲ EMP: 1200 EST: 1957
SQ FT: 300,000
SALES (est): 18.03MM
SALES (corp-wide): 32.76MM **Privately Held**

SIC: **8062** 8051 General medical and surgical hospitals; Skilled nursing care facilities
HQ: Providence Health System-Southern California
1801 Lind Ave Sw
Renton WA
425 525-3355

(P-16216)
LITTLE COMPANY OF MARY HEALTH SERVICES
Also Called: Little Company Mary Svc Area
4101 Torrance Blvd (90503-4607)
PHONE.................................310 540-7676
EMP: 2946
SIC: **8062** 8741 General medical and surgical hospitals; Hospital management

(P-16217)
LODI MEMORIAL HOSP ASSN INC
Also Called: Loda Mem Hosp Occpational Hlth
975 S Fairmont Ave Ste 8 (95240-5118)
PHONE.................................209 339-7441
EMP: 67
SALES (corp-wide): 789.42MM **Privately Held**
Web: www.lodihealth.org
SIC: **8062** General medical and surgical hospitals
HQ: Lodi Memorial Hospital Association, Inc.
975 S Fairmont Ave
Lodi CA
209 334-3411

(P-16218)
LODI MEMORIAL HOSP ASSN INC
Also Called: Conrad Lab, The
1200 W Vine St (95240-5136)
PHONE.................................209 339-7583
Dave Mack, *Dir*
EMP: 67
SALES (corp-wide): 789.42MM **Privately Held**
Web: www.lodihealth.org
SIC: **8062** General medical and surgical hospitals
HQ: Lodi Memorial Hospital Association, Inc.
975 S Fairmont Ave
Lodi CA
209 334-3411

(P-16219)
LODI MEMORIAL HOSP ASSN INC
Also Called: Ione Primemed Clinic
395 Preston Ave (95640-9158)
P.O. Box 1580 (95640-1580)
PHONE.................................209 274-2183
Pam Schneider, *Dir*
EMP: 67
SALES (corp-wide): 789.42MM **Privately Held**
Web: www.lodihealth.org
SIC: **8062** General medical and surgical hospitals
HQ: Lodi Memorial Hospital Association, Inc.
975 S Fairmont Ave
Lodi CA
209 334-3411

(P-16220)
LODI MEMORIAL HOSP ASSN INC (HQ)
Also Called: Adventist Health Lodi Memorial
975 S Fairmont Ave (95240-5118)
P.O. Box 3004 (95241-1908)
PHONE.................................209 334-3411
Daniel Wolcott, *CEO*
Brooke Mccollough, *Pr*
Debbe Moreno, *
Terrence Deak, *
EMP: 700 EST: 1945
SQ FT: 97,057
SALES (est): 255.9MM
SALES (corp-wide): 789.42MM **Privately Held**
Web: www.lodihealth.org
SIC: **8062** Hospital, affiliated with AMA residency
PA: Adventist Health System/West, Corporation
1 Adventist Health Way
Roseville CA
844 574-5686

(P-16221)
LODI REGIONAL HLTH SYSTEMS INC
10200 Trinity Pkwy Ste 102 (95219-7286)
PHONE.................................209 948-0808
EMP: 347
SALES (corp-wide): 4.65MM **Privately Held**
SIC: **8062** General medical and surgical hospitals
PA: Lodi Regional Health Systems, Inc.
975 S Fairmont Ave
Lodi CA
800 323-3360

(P-16222)
LOMA LINDA UNIVERSITY MED CTR
26780 Barton Rd (92373-4308)
PHONE.................................909 558-4000
EMP: 79
SALES (corp-wide): 388.6MM **Privately Held**
Web: www.lluh.org
SIC: **8062** General medical and surgical hospitals
HQ: Loma Linda University Medical Center
11234 Anderson St
Loma Linda CA
909 558-4000

(P-16223)
LOMA LINDA UNIVERSITY MED CTR
11370 Anderson St (92354-3450)
P.O. Box 728 (92354-0728)
PHONE.................................909 558-4385
EMP: 86
SALES (corp-wide): 388.6MM **Privately Held**
Web: www.lluh.org
SIC: **8062** General medical and surgical hospitals
HQ: Loma Linda University Medical Center
11234 Anderson St
Loma Linda CA
909 558-4000

(P-16224)
LOMA LINDA UNIVERSITY MED CTR
Also Called: Loma Linda Pharmacy
11223 Campus St (92354-3203)
PHONE.................................909 558-4216

8062 - General Medical And Surgical Hospitals (P-16225)

Bill Robinson, *Mgr*
EMP: 107
SALES (corp-wide): 388.6MM **Privately Held**
Web: www.lluh.org
SIC: 8062 General medical and surgical hospitals
HQ: Loma Linda University Medical Center
11234 Anderson St
Loma Linda CA
909 558-4000

(P-16225)
LOMA LINDA UNIVERSITY MED CTR
Also Called: Loma Linda Community Hospital
25333 Barton Rd (92350-0210)
PHONE...............................909 796-0167
EMP: 105
SQ FT: 79,580
SALES (corp-wide): 388.6MM **Privately Held**
Web: www.lluh.org
SIC: 8062 General medical and surgical hospitals
HQ: Loma Linda University Medical Center
11234 Anderson St
Loma Linda CA
909 558-4000

(P-16226)
LOMA LINDA UNIVERSITY MED CTR (DH)
Also Called: LLUMC
11234 Anderson St (92354-2871)
P.O. Box 2000 (92354-0200)
PHONE...............................909 558-4000
TOLL FREE: 800
Richard H Hart, *CEO*
James Jesse, *
Richard Catalano, *
Noni Patchett, *
EMP: 4600 **EST:** 1967
SQ FT: 630,000
SALES (est): 1.59B
SALES (corp-wide): 388.6MM **Privately Held**
Web: www.lluh.org
SIC: 8062 8011 8051 5999 Hospital, medical school affiliated with residency; Medical centers; Extended care facility; Medical apparatus and supplies
HQ: Loma Linda University Health Care
11370 Anderson St # 3900
Loma Linda CA
909 558-2806

(P-16227)
LOMA LINDA UNIVERSITY MED CTR
Also Called: Loma Linda Catering Center
11175 Campos St (92350-1700)
PHONE...............................909 558-8244
Najwa Medina, *Mgr*
EMP: 69
SALES (corp-wide): 388.6MM **Privately Held**
Web: www.lluh.org
SIC: 8062 Hospital, medical school affiliation
HQ: Loma Linda University Medical Center
11234 Anderson St
Loma Linda CA
909 558-4000

(P-16228)
LOMA LINDA UNIVERSITY MED CTR
Also Called: Behavioral Medicine Center
1710 Barton Rd (92373-5304)
PHONE...............................909 558-9275

Ruthita Fike, *Mgr*
EMP: 90
SQ FT: 62,476
SALES (corp-wide): 388.6MM **Privately Held**
Web: www.lluh.org
SIC: 8062 8221 Hospital, medical school affiliation; University
HQ: Loma Linda University Medical Center
11234 Anderson St
Loma Linda CA
909 558-4000

(P-16229)
LOMA LNDA - INLAND EMPIRE CNSR
Also Called: Loma Linda University Med Ctr
11234 Anderson St (92354-2804)
PHONE...............................909 558-4000
Daniel Giang, *Pr*
EMP: 141 **EST:** 2013
SALES (est): 6.03MM **Privately Held**
SIC: 8062 Hospital, medical school affiliated with residency

(P-16230)
LOMPOC VALLEY MEDICAL CENTER
Also Called: Mammography Center
1111 E Ocean Ave Ste 2 (93436-2500)
PHONE...............................805 735-9229
Jim Raggio, *Brnch Mgr*
EMP: 173
SALES (corp-wide): 137.58MM **Privately Held**
Web: www.lompocvmc.com
SIC: 8062 General medical and surgical hospitals
PA: Lompoc Valley Medical Center
1515 E Ocean Ave
Lompoc CA
805 737-3300

(P-16231)
LOMPOC VALLEY MEDICAL CENTER (PA)
Also Called: Lompoc Skilled Care Center
1515 E Ocean Ave (93436-7092)
P.O. Box 1058 (93438-1058)
PHONE...............................805 737-3300
Jim Raggio, *CEO*
Naishadh Buch, *
Jayne Scalise, *
EMP: 325 **EST:** 1947
SQ FT: 150,000
SALES (est): 137.58MM
SALES (corp-wide): 137.58MM **Privately Held**
Web: www.lompocvmc.com
SIC: 8062 8051 Hospital, affiliated with AMA residency; Skilled nursing care facilities

(P-16232)
LONG BEACH MEDICAL CENTER
Also Called: Infusion Care
450 E Spring St Ste 11 (90806-1608)
PHONE...............................562 933-7701
Gerald Nichrossan, *Brnch Mgr*
EMP: 113
Web: www.memorialcare.org
SIC: 8062 General medical and surgical hospitals
HQ: Long Beach Medical Center
2801 Atlantic Ave Fl 2
Long Beach CA
562 933-2000

(P-16233)
LONG BEACH MEDICAL CENTER (HQ)
Also Called: Miller Children's Hospital
2801 Atlantic Ave Fl 2 (90806-1701)
PHONE...............................562 933-2000
John Bishop, *CEO*
Barry Arbuckle Ph.d., *Pr*
Judy Fix, *
Scott Joslyn, *CIO*
Thomas Poole, *
EMP: 2000 **EST:** 1907
SQ FT: 1,100,000
SALES (est): 633.63MM **Privately Held**
Web: www.memorialcare.org
SIC: 8062 General medical and surgical hospitals
PA: Memorial Health Services
17360 Brookhurst St # 160
Fountain Valley CA

(P-16234)
LONG BEACH MEDICAL CENTER
1720 Termino Ave (90804-2104)
PHONE...............................562 933-0085
EMP: 123
Web: www.memorialcare.org
SIC: 8062 General medical and surgical hospitals
HQ: Long Beach Medical Center
2801 Atlantic Ave Fl 2
Long Beach CA
562 933-2000

(P-16235)
LONG BEACH MEMORIAL HOSPI
24451 Health Center Dr (92653-3689)
PHONE...............................562 933-2000
Sabrina Sadler, *Prin*
EMP: 64 **EST:** 2009
SALES (est): 1.87MM **Privately Held**
Web: www.memorialcare.org
SIC: 8062 General medical and surgical hospitals

(P-16236)
LONG BEACH MEMORIAL MED CTR
Also Called: LONG BEACH MEMORIAL MEDICAL CENTER
1057 Pine Ave (90813-3118)
PHONE...............................562 933-0432
Renee May, *Brnch Mgr*
EMP: 113
Web: www.thechildrensclinic.org
SIC: 8062 General medical and surgical hospitals
HQ: Long Beach Medical Center
2801 Atlantic Ave Fl 2
Long Beach CA
562 933-2000

(P-16237)
LONGWOOD MANAGEMENT CORP
Also Called: Shea Convalescent Hospital
7716 Pickering Ave (90602-2001)
PHONE...............................562 693-5240
Richard Esconrias, *Mgr*
EMP: 97
SALES (corp-wide): 79.33MM **Privately Held**
Web: www.longwoodmgmt.com
SIC: 8062 8051 8011 General medical and surgical hospitals; Skilled nursing care facilities; Offices and clinics of medical doctors
PA: Longwood Management Corp.
4032 Wilshire Blvd Fl 6
Los Angeles CA
213 389-6900

(P-16238)
LONGWOOD MANAGEMENT CORP
Also Called: Northridge Nursing Center
7836 Reseda Blvd (91335-1902)
PHONE...............................818 881-7414
Deffie Biczi, *Genl Mgr*
EMP: 65
SALES (corp-wide): 79.33MM **Privately Held**
Web: www.longwoodmgmt.com
SIC: 8062 General medical and surgical hospitals
PA: Longwood Management Corp.
4032 Wilshire Blvd Fl 6
Los Angeles CA
213 389-6900

(P-16239)
LOS ALAMITOS MEDICAL CTR INC (HQ)
3751 Katella Ave (90720-3113)
P.O. Box 533 (90720-0533)
PHONE...............................714 826-6400
TOLL FREE: 800
Kent Clayton, *CEO*
Margaret Watkins, *
Alice Livingood Co, *President Elect*
EMP: 1100 **EST:** 1970
SQ FT: 900
SALES (est): 171.28MM
SALES (corp-wide): 19.58B **Publicly Held**
Web: www.losalamitosmri.com
SIC: 8062 General medical and surgical hospitals
PA: Tenet Healthcare Corporation
14201 Dallas Pkwy
Dallas TX
469 893-2200

(P-16240)
LOS ROBLES REGIONAL MED CTR (DH)
Also Called: Los Robles Hospital & Med Ctr
215 W Janss Rd (91360-1847)
PHONE...............................805 497-2727
Natalie Mussi, *CEO*
◆ **EMP:** 917 **EST:** 1978
SQ FT: 475
SALES (est): 334.05K **Publicly Held**
Web: www.losrobleshospital.com
SIC: 8062 General medical and surgical hospitals
HQ: Hca Inc.
1 Park Plz
Nashville TN
615 344-9551

(P-16241)
MADERA CMNTY HOSP FOUNDATION
1250 E Almond Ave (93637-5606)
P.O. Box 1328 (93639-1328)
PHONE...............................559 673-5101
Ray Gomes, *Ex Dir*
EMP: 79 **EST:** 1978
SQ FT: 225
SALES (est): 1.23MM **Privately Held**
Web: www.maderahospital.org
SIC: 8062 General medical and surgical hospitals

(P-16242)
MADERA COMMUNITY HOSPITAL
Also Called: Family Health Services Clinic

PRODUCTS & SERVICES SECTION
8062 - General Medical And Surgical Hospitals (P-16261)

1210 E Almond Ave Ste A (93637-5606)
PHONE..................................559 675-5530
Robert Kelly, *Brnch Mgr*
EMP: 119
SALES (corp-wide): 104.39MM **Privately Held**
Web: www.maderahospital.org
SIC: 8062 General medical and surgical hospitals
PA: Madera Community Hospital
1250 E Almond Ave
Madera CA
559 675-5555

(P-16243)
MADERA COMMUNITY HOSPITAL (PA)
Also Called: MCH
1250 E Almond Ave (93637-5606)
P.O. Box 1328 (93639-1328)
PHONE..................................559 675-5555
Karen Paolinelli, *CEO*
Mike Brink, *
EMP: 681 **EST:** 1975
SQ FT: 66,300
SALES (est): 104.39MM
SALES (corp-wide): 104.39MM **Privately Held**
Web: www.maderahospital.org
SIC: 8062 General medical and surgical hospitals

(P-16244)
MARIAN COMMUNITY CLINIC
117 W Bunny Ave (93458-2805)
P.O. Box 2400 (85002-2400)
PHONE..................................805 739-3867
Eugen Alarco, *CEO*
Lupe Terrones, *Dir*
EMP: 83 **EST:** 1997
SALES (est): 120.17MM **Privately Held**
Web: www.dignityhealth.org
SIC: 8062 General medical and surgical hospitals
HQ: Dignity Health
185 Berry St Ste 200
San Francisco CA
415 438-5500

(P-16245)
MARIAN MEDICAL CENTER
Also Called: Marian Regional Medical Center
1400 E Church St (93454-5906)
PHONE..................................805 739-3000
EMP: 1000
Web: www.supportmarianmedical.org
SIC: 8062 General medical and surgical hospitals

(P-16246)
MARIN GENERAL HOSPITAL
250 Bon Air Rd (94904-1784)
PHONE..................................415 925-7000
Lee Domonico, *CEO*
David Bradley, *
Theresa Daughton, *
EMP: 1100 **EST:** 1947
SQ FT: 125,000
SALES (est): 429.12MM
SALES (corp-wide): 531.12K **Privately Held**
Web: www.mymarinhealth.org
SIC: 8062 8011 General medical and surgical hospitals; Offices and clinics of medical doctors
PA: Marin Healthcare District
100 Drakes Landing Rd B
Greenbrae CA
415 464-2090

(P-16247)
MARIN HEALTHCARE DISTRICT (PA)
100b Drakes Landing Rd Ste 250 (94904-2404)
PHONE..................................415 464-2090
Barry Woerman, *Dir*
EMP: 171 **EST:** 2000
SALES (est): 531.12K
SALES (corp-wide): 531.12K **Privately Held**
Web: www.marinhealthcare.org
SIC: 8062 General medical and surgical hospitals

(P-16248)
MARK TWAIN MEDICAL CENTER (DH)
Also Called: Mark Twain St Joseph's Hospital
768 Mountain Ranch Rd (95249-9707)
PHONE..................................209 754-3521
Craig J Marks, *CEO*
Jacob Lews, *CFO*
Greg Jordan, *Pr*
Anita Paque, *VP*
Ruth Huffman, *Sec*
EMP: 225 **EST:** 1984
SQ FT: 40,000
SALES (est): 71.38MM **Privately Held**
Web: www.dignityhealth.org
SIC: 8062 General medical and surgical hospitals
HQ: Dignity Health
185 Berry St Ste 200
San Francisco CA
415 438-5500

(P-16249)
MARSHALL MEDICAL CENTER (PA)
Also Called: MARSHALL HOSPITAL
1100 Marshall Way (95667-6533)
P.O. Box 872 (95667-0872)
PHONE..................................530 622-1441
James Whipple, *CEO*
Laurie Eldridge, *CFO*
Shannon Truesdell, *COO*
EMP: 1000 **EST:** 1959
SQ FT: 124,000
SALES (est): 305.43MM
SALES (corp-wide): 305.43MM **Privately Held**
Web: www.marshallmedical.org
SIC: 8062 8071 8082 General medical and surgical hospitals; Medical laboratories; Home health care services

(P-16250)
MATER MISERICORDIAE HOSPITAL (PA)
Also Called: Mercy Medical Center Merced
333 Mercy Ave (95340-8319)
PHONE..................................209 564-5000
David Dunham, *CEO*
EMP: 668 **EST:** 1948
SQ FT: 60,000
SALES (est): 64.88MM
SALES (corp-wide): 64.88MM **Privately Held**
SIC: 8062 General medical and surgical hospitals

(P-16251)
MATERNAL CNNCTONS EL CMINO HOS
Also Called: El Camino Hospital
2110 Forest Ave Ste B (95128-1469)
PHONE..................................650 988-8287
Richard Warren, *CEO*
Lee Domonico, *CEO*
EMP: 69 **EST:** 1961
SALES (est): 4.62MM **Privately Held**
Web: www.elcaminohealth.org
SIC: 8062 General medical and surgical hospitals

(P-16252)
MEMORIAL HEALTH SERVICES (PA)
Also Called: Memorial Care Medical Centers
17360 Brookhurst St Ste 160 (92708-3720)
P.O. Box 20894 (92728-0894)
PHONE..................................714 377-2900
Barry Arbuckle, *Pr*
Diane Laird, *
Rick Graniere, *CIO*
Karen Testman, *
Terri Cammarano, *
EMP: 460 **EST:** 1937
SALES (est): 2.69B **Privately Held**
Web: www.memorialcare.org
SIC: 8062 General medical and surgical hospitals

(P-16253)
MEMORIAL HLTH SVCS - UNIV CAL (PA)
2801 Atlantic Ave (90806-1701)
PHONE..................................562 933-2000
Edward Quilligan, *CEO*
Diana Hendel, *
Darrel Brownell, *
EMP: 1138 **EST:** 1907
SQ FT: 1,000,000
SALES (est): 411.78MM
SALES (corp-wide): 411.78MM **Privately Held**
Web: www.memorialcare.org
SIC: 8062 8741 General medical and surgical hospitals; Management services

(P-16254)
MEMORIAL HOSPITAL LOS BANOS
520 W I St (93635-3419)
PHONE..................................209 826-0591
EMP: 160 **EST:** 1962
SALES (est): 101.31MM
SALES (corp-wide): 14.77B **Privately Held**
Web: www.memoriallosbanos.org
SIC: 8062 General medical and surgical hospitals
PA: Sutter Health
2200 River Plaza Dr
Sacramento CA
916 733-8800

(P-16255)
MEMORIAL HOSPITAL OF GARDENA
4060 Woody Blvd (90023)
PHONE..................................323 268-5514
EMP: 400
SIC: 8062 Hospital, affiliated with AMA residency

(P-16256)
MEMORIALCARE MEDICAL GROUP
Also Called: Orange Coast Medical Center
18111 Brookhurst St (92708-6728)
PHONE..................................714 378-7000
EMP: 96
SALES (est): 14.67MM **Privately Held**
Web: www.memorialcare.org
SIC: 8062 General medical and surgical hospitals

(P-16257)
MEMORLCARE SRGCAL CTR AT ORNGE
Also Called: Orange Coast Ctr For Surgl Cr
18111 Brookhurst St Ste 3200 (92708-6728)
PHONE..................................714 369-1100
Dana Pratt, *CEO*
EMP: 68 **EST:** 2011
SALES (est): 61.72MM
SALES (corp-wide): 324.16B **Publicly Held**
Web: www.orangecoastcenter.com
SIC: 8062 General medical and surgical hospitals
PA: Unitedhealth Group Incorporated
9900 Bren Rd E Ste 300w
Minnetonka MN
952 936-1300

(P-16258)
MENDOCINO COAST DISTRICT HOSP (PA)
700 River Dr (95437-5403)
PHONE..................................707 961-1234
Jonathan Baker, *CEO*
Camille Ranker, *Treas*
Patricia Jauregui Darland, *Ch*
John Kermen, *Prin*
Sean Hogan, *Sec*
▲ **EMP:** 300 **EST:** 1971
SQ FT: 71,500
SALES (est): 58.74MM
SALES (corp-wide): 58.74MM **Privately Held**
Web: www.mcdh.org
SIC: 8062 General medical and surgical hospitals

(P-16259)
MERCY HEALTHCARE SACRAMENTO
Also Called: Mercy San Juan Hospital
3400 Data Dr (95670-7956)
PHONE..................................916 379-2871
EMP: 6131
SIC: 8062 General medical and surgical hospitals

(P-16260)
MERCY HM SVCS A CAL LTD PARTNR (DH)
Also Called: Mercy Medical Center - Redding
2175 Rosaline Ave Ste A (96001-2549)
P.O. Box 496009 (96049-6009)
PHONE..................................530 225-6000
George A Govier, *CEO*
EMP: 700 **EST:** 1987
SQ FT: 250,000
SALES (est): 385.6MM **Privately Held**
Web: www.dignityhealth.org
SIC: 8062 Hospital, affiliated with AMA residency
HQ: Dignity Health
185 Berry St Ste 200
San Francisco CA
415 438-5500

(P-16261)
MERCY MEDICAL GROUP
Also Called: Mercy Medical Group, A Service
9394 Big Horn Blvd (95758-7977)
PHONE..................................916 691-8500
EMP: 66
Web: www.dignityhealth.org
SIC: 8062 General medical and surgical hospitals
HQ: Mercy Medical Group
3000 Q St

8062 - General Medical And Surgical Hospitals (P-16262)

PRODUCTS & SERVICES SECTION

Sacramento CA

(P-16262)
MERCY MEDICAL GROUP
Also Called: Dignity Health Medical Clinic
1700 Prairie City Rd (95630-9594)
PHONE..................916 351-4834
Mike Mcclintock, *Ex Dir*
EMP: 66
Web: www.dignityhealth.org
SIC: 8062 General medical and surgical hospitals
HQ: Mercy Medical Group
3000 Q St
Sacramento CA

(P-16263)
MERCY MEDICAL GROUP
4987 Golden Foothill Pkwy (95762-9364)
PHONE..................916 933-4222
EMP: 66
Web: www.dignityhealth.org
SIC: 8062 General medical and surgical hospitals
HQ: Mercy Medical Group
3000 Q St
Sacramento CA

(P-16264)
MERCY MEDICAL GROUP
8120 Timberlake Way Ste 107 (95823-5413)
PHONE..................916 681-6000
Katherine M Gillogley, *Dir*
EMP: 66
Web: www.dignityhealth.org
SIC: 8062 General medical and surgical hospitals
HQ: Mercy Medical Group
3000 Q St
Sacramento CA

(P-16265)
MERCY MEDICAL GROUP
8001 Madison Ave (95610-7901)
PHONE..................916 536-2420
Bruce Jensen Md, *Brnch Mgr*
EMP: 66
Web: www.dignityhealth.org
SIC: 8062 General medical and surgical hospitals
HQ: Mercy Medical Group
3000 Q St
Sacramento CA

(P-16266)
MERCY MEDICAL GROUP
6555 Coyle Ave Ste 110 (95608-0365)
PHONE..................916 536-3600
Janet Ankley, *Brnch Mgr*
EMP: 66
Web: www.dignityhealth.org
SIC: 8062 General medical and surgical hospitals
HQ: Mercy Medical Group
3000 Q St
Sacramento CA

(P-16267)
MERCY MEDICAL GROUP
2110 Professional Dr Ste 120 (95661)
PHONE..................916 536-2500
Tara Huff, *Brnch Mgr*
EMP: 66
Web: www.dignityhealth.org
SIC: 8062 General medical and surgical hospitals
HQ: Mercy Medical Group
3000 Q St
Sacramento CA

(P-16268)
MERCY MEDICAL GROUP (DH)
3000 Q St (95816-7058)
PHONE..................916 733-3333
David Marie-claude, *Prin*
Magna Kont, *
EMP: 87 **EST:** 2000
SALES (est): 480.49MM **Privately Held**
Web: www.dignityhealth.org
SIC: 8062 General medical and surgical hospitals
HQ: Dignity Health
185 Berry St Ste 200
San Francisco CA
415 438-5500

(P-16269)
MERCY SURGERY CENTER LP
2175 Rosaline Ave Ste A (96001-2510)
PHONE..................530 225-7400
Catholic Healthcare, *Pt*
Kristi Manutai, *Admn*
EMP: 62 **EST:** 2003
SALES (est): 14.57MM **Privately Held**
Web: www.mercy-sc.com
SIC: 8062 General medical and surgical hospitals

(P-16270)
METHODIST HOSPITAL OF S CA
300 W Huntington Dr (91007-3402)
P.O. Box 60016 (91066-6016)
PHONE..................626 574-3755
Dennis Lee, *Prin*
EMP: 76 **EST:** 2009
SALES (est): 52.66MM **Privately Held**
Web: www.uscarcadiahospital.org
SIC: 8062 General medical and surgical hospitals

(P-16271)
MILLS-PENINSULA HEALTH SERVICES
Also Called: Mills-Peninsula Hospitals
1501 Trousdale Dr (94010-4506)
PHONE..................650 696-5400
EMP: 2200
SIC: 8062 General medical and surgical hospitals

(P-16272)
MISSION HOSP REGIONAL MED CTR (PA)
Also Called: Mission Hospital
27700 Medical Center Rd (92691-6426)
PHONE..................949 364-1400
Seth Peigen, *CEO*
EMP: 1349 **EST:** 1941
SQ FT: 750,000
SALES (est): 765.86MM
SALES (corp-wide): 765.86MM **Privately Held**
Web: www.mission4health.com
SIC: 8062 General medical and surgical hospitals

(P-16273)
MODOC MEDICAL CENTER HOSP AUX (PA)
Also Called: Modoc Medical Center
1111 N Nagle St (96101-3840)
P.O. Box 190 (96101-0190)
PHONE..................530 708-8800
Kevin Kramer, *CEO*
Patrick Fields, *
Adam Willoughby, *
EMP: 99 **EST:** 2012
SQ FT: 56,094
SALES (est): 46.11MM **Privately Held**
Web: www.modocmedicalcenter.org
SIC: 8062 General medical and surgical hospitals

(P-16274)
MONTEREY PARK HOSPITAL
Also Called: Monterey Park Hospital
900 S Atlantic Blvd (91754-4780)
PHONE..................626 570-9000
Philip A Cohen, *CEO*
Robert M Dubbs, *
Robert W Fleming Junior, *Sr VP*
EMP: 150 **EST:** 1972
SQ FT: 90,575
SALES (est): 34.31MM
SALES (corp-wide): 476.02MM **Privately Held**
Web: www.ahmchealth.com
SIC: 8062 General medical and surgical hospitals
PA: Ahmc Healthcare Inc.
506 W Valley Blvd Ste 300
San Gabriel CA
626 943-7526

(P-16275)
MOTION PICTURE AND TV FUND (PA)
Also Called: Bob Hope Health Center
23388 Mulholland Dr Ste 200 (91364-2733)
P.O. Box 51151 (90051-5451)
PHONE..................818 876-1777
Robert Beitcher, *CEO*
Bob Pisano, *
Joseph Fischer, *
Jay Roth, *
EMP: 688 **EST:** 1924
SQ FT: 50,000
SALES (est): 29.84MM
SALES (corp-wide): 29.84MM **Privately Held**
Web: www.mptf.com
SIC: 8062 8051 8011 8351 General medical and surgical hospitals; Convalescent home with continuous nursing care; Medical centers; Child day care services

(P-16276)
MOUNTAIN CMMNTIES HLTH CARE DS (PA)
Also Called: Trinity Hospital
60 Easter Ave (96093-8054)
P.O. Box 1229 (96093-1229)
PHONE..................530 623-5541
Aaron Rogers, *CEO*
EMP: 86 **EST:** 2006
SALES (est): 27.26MM **Privately Held**
Web: www.mcmedical.org
SIC: 8062 General medical and surgical hospitals

(P-16277)
MOUNTAIN VIEW CHILD CARE INC (PA)
Also Called: Totally Kids Rhbilitation Hosp
1720 Mountain View Ave (92354-1799)
PHONE..................909 796-6915
Doug Pagett, *CEO*
Cynthia Capetillo, *
Donald Nydam, *
Hal Karlin, *
Loma Linda, *
EMP: 275 **EST:** 1972
SALES (est): 48.34MM **Privately Held**
Web: www.totallykids.com
SIC: 8062 8052 8051 General medical and surgical hospitals; Intermediate care facilities; Skilled nursing care facilities

(P-16278)
MOUNTAINS COMMUNITY HOSP FNDTN
Also Called: Mountains Community Hospital
29101 Hospital Rd (92352-9706)
P.O. Box 70 (92352-0070)
PHONE..................909 336-3651
Don Willerth, *CEO*
EMP: 180 **EST:** 1957
SQ FT: 18,500
SALES (est): 24.11MM **Privately Held**
Web: www.mchcares.com
SIC: 8062 8051 General medical and surgical hospitals; Skilled nursing care facilities

(P-16279)
NATIVIDAD MEDICAL CENTER
Also Called: OCCUPATIONAL MEDICINE
1441 Constitution Blvd Ste 200 (93906-3195)
PHONE..................831 755-4111
Charles Harris, *Interim Chief Executive Officer*
EMP: 659 **EST:** 1950
SALES (est): 62.77K **Privately Held**
Web: www.natividad.com
SIC: 8062 8011 8093 General medical and surgical hospitals; Offices and clinics of medical doctors; Specialty outpatient clinics, nec

(P-16280)
NAVY UNITED STATES DEPARTMENT
Also Called: Naval Medical Center
34800 Bob Wilson Dr (92134-1098)
PHONE..................619 532-6400
Esther Lynn, *Brnch Mgr*
EMP: 4250
Web: www.navy.mil
SIC: 8062 9711 General medical and surgical hospitals; Navy
HQ: United States Department Of The Navy
1200 Navy Pentagon
Washington DC

(P-16281)
NIX HOSPITALS SYSTEM LLC (HQ)
Also Called: Nix Healthcare System
3415 S Sepulveda Blvd # 900 (90034-6981)
PHONE..................210 271-1800
John F Strieby, *Pr*
Rob Elders, *
EMP: 108 **EST:** 2011
SALES (est): 113.34MM
SALES (corp-wide): 3.91B **Privately Held**
SIC: 8062 General medical and surgical hospitals
PA: Prospect Medical Holdings, Inc.
3415 S Sepulveda Blvd # 9
Los Angeles CA
310 943-4500

(P-16282)
NORTH KERN S TULARE HOSP DST
Also Called: Delano Dst Sklled Nrsing Fclty
1509 Tokay St (93215-3603)
PHONE..................661 720-2126
Silva Soto, *Pr*
Dio Telmo, *Admn*
Elson De Guzman, *Contrlr*
Jaime Mendoza, *Prin*
Femme Adebayo, *Prin*
EMP: 230 **EST:** 1966
SALES (est): 14.4MM **Privately Held**

Web: www.nksthd.org
SIC: 8062 General medical and surgical hospitals

(P-16283)
NORTH SONOMA COUNTY HOSP DST
Also Called: Healdsburg District Hospital
1375 University St (95448-3382)
PHONE.................................707 431-6500
Evan J Rayner, CEO
Dan Hull, *
EMP: 171 EST: 2001
SALES (est): 46.94MM Privately Held
Web: www.healdsburgdistricthospital.org
SIC: 8062 General medical and surgical hospitals

(P-16284)
NORTHBAY HEALTHCARE CORP (PA)
Also Called: Northbay Healthcare System
1200 B Gale Wilson Blvd (94533-3552)
PHONE.................................707 646-5000
Gary J Passama, Pr
Sheniece Smith, *
EMP: 114 EST: 1987
SQ FT: 24,000
SALES (est): 685.54MM
SALES (corp-wide): 685.54MM Privately Held
Web: www.northbay.org
SIC: 8062 8011 General medical and surgical hospitals; Offices and clinics of medical doctors

(P-16285)
NORTHBAY HEALTHCARE GROUP (HQ)
Also Called: NORTHBAY HEALTHCARE SYSTEM
1200 B Gale Wilson Blvd (94533-3552)
PHONE.................................707 646-5000
TOLL FREE: 888
Deborah Sugiyama, CEO
EMP: 900 EST: 1954
SQ FT: 125,000
SALES (est): 685.54MM
SALES (corp-wide): 685.54MM Privately Held
Web: www.northbay.org
SIC: 8062 General medical and surgical hospitals
PA: Northbay Healthcare Corporation
1200 B Gale Wilson Blvd
Fairfield CA
707 646-5000

(P-16286)
NORTHBAY HEALTHCARE GROUP
Also Called: Vaca Valley Hospital
1000 Nut Tree Rd (95687-4100)
PHONE.................................707 446-4000
Debra Sugiyama, Pr
EMP: 300
SQ FT: 59,000
SALES (corp-wide): 685.54MM Privately Held
Web: www.northbay.org
SIC: 8062 General medical and surgical hospitals
HQ: Northbay Healthcare Group
1200 B Gale Wilson Blvd
Fairfield CA
707 646-5000

(P-16287)
NORTHERN CAL RHBLTTION HOSP LL
2801 Eureka Way (96001-0222)
PHONE.................................530 246-9000
EMP: 62 EST: 2005
SALES (est): 39.95MM
SALES (corp-wide): 690.44MM Privately Held
Web: www.norcalrehab.com
SIC: 8062 General medical and surgical hospitals
PA: Vibra Healthcare, Llc
4600 Lena Dr
Mechanicsburg PA
717 591-5700

(P-16288)
NORTHERN INYO HEALTHCARE DST
Also Called: Northern Inyo Hospital
150 Pioneer Ln (93514-2556)
PHONE.................................760 873-5811
Stephen Delrossi, Interim Chief Executive Officer
M C Hubbard, *
Denise Hayden, *
D Scott Clark Md, Sec
Peter Watercott, *
EMP: 402 EST: 1946
SQ FT: 55,000
SALES (est): 103.68MM Privately Held
Web: www.nih.org
SIC: 8062 General medical and surgical hospitals

(P-16289)
NORTHRIDGE HOSP FOUNDATION AUX
18300 Roscoe Blvd (91325-4105)
PHONE.................................818 885-5341
Brian Hammel, Pr
Doctor Frederick Gruneck, Prin
EMP: 68 EST: 1959
SQ FT: 1,500
SALES (est): 8.38MM Privately Held
Web: www.supportnorthridge.org
SIC: 8062 General medical and surgical hospitals

(P-16290)
OAK VALLEY HOSPITAL DISTRICT (PA)
350 S Oak Ave (95361-3519)
PHONE.................................209 847-3011
John Mccormick, CEO
Bob Wikoff, *
Gail Sward, *
EMP: 325 EST: 1971
SQ FT: 55,000
SALES (est): 77.82MM
SALES (corp-wide): 77.82MM Privately Held
Web: www.oakvalleyhospital.com
SIC: 8062 8051 General medical and surgical hospitals; Skilled nursing care facilities

(P-16291)
OCONNOR HOSPITAL
Also Called: O'Connor Hosp Pdtric Ctr For L
2039 Forest Ave (95128-4817)
P.O. Box 1387 (94070-7387)
PHONE.................................408 947-2929
James F Dover, Pr
EMP: 148
Web: www.indianhealthcenter.org
SIC: 8062 General medical and surgical hospitals
HQ: O'connor Hospital
2105 Forest Ave
San Jose CA
408 947-2500

(P-16292)
OCONNOR HOSPITAL (HQ)
Also Called: O'Connor Wound Care Clinic
2105 Forest Ave (95128-1425)
PHONE.................................408 947-2500
Richard Adcock, CEO
James F Dover, *
Craig Rucker, *
David W Carroll, *
EMP: 1000 EST: 1889
SQ FT: 750,000
SALES (est): 201.44MM Privately Held
Web: och.sccgov.org
SIC: 8062 General medical and surgical hospitals
PA: County Of Santa Clara
70 W Hedding St
San Jose CA
408 299-5200

(P-16293)
OLYMPIA HEALTH CARE LLC
Also Called: Olympia Medical Center
5900 W Olympic Blvd (90036-4671)
P.O. Box 351209 (90035-9609)
PHONE.................................323 938-3161
Karen Knueven, *
Babur Ozkan, *
EMP: 875 EST: 2004
SQ FT: 500,000
SALES (est): 185.86MM Privately Held
Web: www.olympiamc.com
SIC: 8062 Hospital, affiliated with AMA residency
PA: Alecto Healthcare Services Llc
101 N Brand Blvd Ste 1920
Glendale CA

(P-16294)
ORANGE CAST MEM CARE BRAST CTR
9900 Talbert Ave Ste 102 (92708-5153)
PHONE.................................714 378-7955
Emily Randall, Dir
Marcella Buchheim, Dir
EMP: 71 EST: 1997
SQ FT: 145,064
SALES (est): 5.58MM Privately Held
Web: www.memorialcare.org
SIC: 8062 General medical and surgical hospitals

(P-16295)
ORANGE CNTY GLOBL MED CTR AUX (DH)
Also Called: Western Medical Center Aux
1301 N Tustin Ave (92705-8619)
PHONE.................................714 835-3555
Dan Brothman, CEO
Patricia Stites, *
EMP: 200 EST: 1998
SALES (est): 105.84MM Privately Held
Web: www.orangecountyglobalmedicalcenter.com
SIC: 8062 General medical and surgical hospitals
HQ: Kpc Healthcare, Inc.
1301 N Tustin Ave
Santa Ana CA
714 953-3652

(P-16296)
ORANGE CNTY GLOBL MED CTR INC
Also Called: KPC HEALTH
1001 N Tustin Ave (92705-3502)
P.O. Box 11913 (92711-1913)
PHONE.................................714 953-3500
Ann Abe, CEO
Derek Drake, COO
EMP: 84 EST: 2004
SALES (est): 12.29K Privately Held
Web: www.orangecountyglobalmedicalcenter.com
SIC: 8062 General medical and surgical hospitals
HQ: Kpc Healthcare, Inc.
1301 N Tustin Ave
Santa Ana CA
714 953-3652

(P-16297)
ORANGE COAST MEMORIAL MED CTR (HQ)
9920 Talbert Ave (92708-5153)
PHONE.................................714 378-7000
TOLL FREE: 888
Marcia Manker, Pr
Steve Mcnamara, CFO
Aaron Coley, *
EMP: 522 EST: 1995
SQ FT: 40,361
SALES (est): 377.3MM Privately Held
Web: www.memorialcare.org
SIC: 8062 General medical and surgical hospitals
PA: Memorial Health Services
17360 Brookhurst St # 160
Fountain Valley CA

(P-16298)
ORANGTREE CNVALESCENT HOSP INC
Also Called: Plott Family Care Centers
4000 Harrison St (92503-3514)
PHONE.................................951 785-6060
Elizabeth Plott, Pr
EMP: 120 EST: 1983
SALES (est): 7.67MM Privately Held
SIC: 8062 8051 General medical and surgical hospitals; Skilled nursing care facilities

(P-16299)
ORCHARD HOSPITAL
240 Spruce St (95948-2216)
P.O. Box 97 (95948-0097)
PHONE.................................530 846-9000
Steve Stark, CEO
Kristina Sanke, *
EMP: 235 EST: 1946
SQ FT: 12,000
SALES (est): 27.01MM Privately Held
Web: www.orchardhospital.com
SIC: 8062 General medical and surgical hospitals

(P-16300)
OROVILLE HOSPITAL (PA)
2767 Olive Hwy (95966-6118)
PHONE.................................530 533-8500
Robert J Wentz, CEO
Scott Chapple, *
Ashok Khanchandani, *
EMP: 732 EST: 1966
SQ FT: 68,133
SALES (est): 383.94MM
SALES (corp-wide): 383.94MM Privately Held
Web: www.orovillehospital.com
SIC: 8062 General medical and surgical hospitals

8062 - General Medical And Surgical Hospitals (P-16301)

(P-16301)
OROVILLE HOSPITAL
Also Called: Attic
2170 Bird St (95965-4915)
PHONE..................................530 532-8697
Kim Nixon, Dir
EMP: 280
SALES (corp-wide): 383.94MM Privately Held
Web: www.orovillehospital.com
SIC: 8062 General medical and surgical hospitals
PA: Oroville Hospital
2767 Olive Hwy
Oroville CA
530 533-8500

(P-16302)
ORTHOPAEDIC HOSPITAL (PA)
Also Called: Orthopaedic Inst For Children
403 W Adams Blvd (90007-2664)
P.O. Box 60132 (90060-0132)
PHONE..................................213 742-1000
Anthony A Scaduto, Pr
Diane Moon, *
EMP: 168 EST: 1923
SQ FT: 105,000
SALES (est): 13.5MM
SALES (corp-wide): 13.5MM Privately Held
Web: www.luskinoic.org
SIC: 8062 8011 General medical and surgical hospitals; Primary care medical clinic

(P-16303)
PACIFIC HEALTH CORPORATION
Also Called: Tustin Hospital
14642 Newport Ave (92780-6057)
PHONE..................................714 838-9600
EMP: 1700
Web: www.pacifichealthcorp.com
SIC: 8062 General medical and surgical hospitals

(P-16304)
PACIFICA OF VALLEY CORPORATION
Also Called: PACIFICA HOSPITAL OF THE VALLE
9449 San Fernando Rd (91352-1421)
PHONE..................................818 767-3310
Paul Tuft, Ch Bd
Ayman Mousa, *
EMP: 607 EST: 1996
SQ FT: 148,020
SALES (est): 97.12MM Privately Held
Web: www.pacificahospital.com
SIC: 8062 Hospital, affiliated with AMA residency

(P-16305)
PALO VERDE HEALTH CARE DST
Also Called: Palo Verde Hospital
250 N 1st St (92225-1702)
PHONE..................................760 922-4115
Sandra J Anaya, CEO
Dennis Rutherford, *
EMP: 180 EST: 1938
SALES (est): 23.8MM Privately Held
Web: www.paloverdehospital.org
SIC: 8062 8069 General medical and surgical hospitals; Specialty hospitals, except psychiatric

(P-16306)
PALO VERDE HOSPITAL ASSN
250 N 1st St (92225-1702)
PHONE..................................760 922-4115
Sandra J Anaya, CEO
Larry Blitz, *
Jim Carney, *
David Conejo, *
Beatrice Pinon, *
EMP: 135 EST: 1948
SQ FT: 44,000
SALES (est): 26.72MM Privately Held
Web: www.paloverdehospital.org
SIC: 8062 General medical and surgical hospitals

(P-16307)
PALOMAR HEALTH
Also Called: Patient Business Services
152255 Innovation Dr (92128)
PHONE..................................858 675-5218
Laurie Rose, Mgr
EMP: 300
SALES (corp-wide): 679.43K Privately Held
Web: www.palomarhealth.org
SIC: 8062 General medical and surgical hospitals
PA: Palomar Health
2125 Citracado Pkwy # 300
Escondido CA
442 281-5000

(P-16308)
PALOMAR HEALTH (PA)
Also Called: Palomar Medical Center
2125 Citracado Pkwy Ste 300 (92029-4159)
PHONE..................................442 281-5000
Doug Moir, Pr
Tanya Howell, *
EMP: 180 EST: 1950
SALES (est): 679.43K
SALES (corp-wide): 679.43K Privately Held
Web: www.palomarhealth.org
SIC: 8062 8059 General medical and surgical hospitals; Convalescent home

(P-16309)
PALOMAR HEALTH
Also Called: Palomar Medical Center
15615 Pomerado Rd (92064-2405)
PHONE..................................760 739-3000
Michael Covert, CEO
EMP: 1200
SALES (corp-wide): 679.43K Privately Held
Web: www.palomarhealth.org
SIC: 8062 General medical and surgical hospitals
PA: Palomar Health
2125 Citracado Pkwy # 300
Escondido CA
442 281-5000

(P-16310)
PALOMAR HEALTH
Also Called: Pomerado Hospital
15615 Pomerado Rd (92064-2405)
PHONE..................................858 613-4000
TOLL FREE: 800
Jim Flinn, Admn
EMP: 182
SALES (corp-wide): 679.43K Privately Held
Web: www.palomarhealth.org
SIC: 8062 General medical and surgical hospitals
PA: Palomar Health
2125 Citracado Pkwy # 300
Escondido CA
442 281-5000

(P-16311)
PALOMAR HEALTH MEDICAL GROUP (HQ)
Also Called: Arch Health Partners
15611 Pomerado Rd Ste 575 (92064-2440)
PHONE..................................858 675-3100
Deanna Kyrimis, CEO
Hugh King, *
Matt Niedzwiecki, *
EMP: 168 EST: 2009
SALES (est): 163.61MM
SALES (corp-wide): 679.43K Privately Held
Web: www.palomarhealthmedicalgroup.org
SIC: 8062 General medical and surgical hospitals
PA: Palomar Health
2125 Citracado Pkwy # 300
Escondido CA
442 281-5000

(P-16312)
PALOMAR HEALTH TECHNOLOGY INC
2140 Enterprise St (92029-2000)
PHONE..................................442 281-5000
Diane Hansen, CEO
EMP: 145 EST: 2011
SALES (est): 59.99MM
SALES (corp-wide): 679.43K Privately Held
Web: www.palomarhealth.org
SIC: 8062 General medical and surgical hospitals
PA: Palomar Health
2125 Citracado Pkwy # 300
Escondido CA
442 281-5000

(P-16313)
PALOMAR MEDICAL CENTER
Also Called: Pomerado Hospital
15615 Pomerado Rd (92064-2405)
PHONE..................................858 613-4000
Dianne Hansen, CEO
EMP: 281 EST: 2013
SALES (est): 218.46K
SALES (corp-wide): 679.43K Privately Held
Web: www.palomarhealth.org
SIC: 8062 General medical and surgical hospitals
PA: Palomar Health
2125 Citracado Pkwy # 300
Escondido CA
442 281-5000

(P-16314)
PAMC LTD (PA)
Also Called: Pamc Health Foundation
531 W College St (90012-2315)
PHONE..................................213 624-8411
John Edwards, CEO
EMP: 530 EST: 1989
SQ FT: 75,600
SALES (est): 19.13MM Privately Held
Web: www.pamc.net
SIC: 8062 General medical and surgical hospitals

(P-16315)
PARACLSUS LOS ANGLES CMNTY HOS
Also Called: LOS ANGELES COMMUNITY HOSPITAL
4081 E Olympic Blvd (90023-3330)
PHONE..................................323 267-0477
EMP: 250 EST: 1983
SALES (est): 194.63MM Privately Held
Web: www.lach-la.com
SIC: 8062 General medical and surgical hospitals

(P-16316)
PARADISE VALLEY HOSPITAL (PA)
2400 E 4th St (91950-2098)
PHONE..................................619 470-4100
Alan Soderblom, CEO
Luin Leon, *
Robert Carmen, *
Prem Reddy, *
Neerav Jadeja, *
EMP: 925 EST: 1904
SQ FT: 230,000
SALES (est): 140.77MM
SALES (corp-wide): 140.77MM Privately Held
Web: www.paradisevalleyhospital.net
SIC: 8062 General medical and surgical hospitals

(P-16317)
PARADISE VALLEY HOSPITAL
Also Called: West Health Care
180 Otay Lakes Rd Ste 100 (91902-2464)
PHONE..................................619 472-7474
Connie Mayo, Dir
EMP: 251
SALES (corp-wide): 140.77MM Privately Held
Web: www.paradisevalleyhospital.net
SIC: 8062 General medical and surgical hospitals
PA: Paradise Valley Hospital
2400 E 4th St
National City CA
619 470-4100

(P-16318)
PARKVIEW CMNTY HOSP MED CTR
3865 Jackson St (92503-3919)
PHONE..................................951 354-7404
Norm Martin, Pr
Doug Drumwright, *
EMP: 1149 EST: 1966
SQ FT: 132,651
SALES (est): 162.74MM
SALES (corp-wide): 162.74MM Privately Held
Web: www.ahmchealth.com
SIC: 8062 8011 General medical and surgical hospitals; Offices and clinics of medical doctors
PA: Doctors Hospital Of Riverside Llc
3865 Jackson St
Riverside CA
951 354-7404

(P-16319)
PASADENA HOSPITAL ASSN LTD (PA)
Also Called: Huntington Memorial Hospital
100 W California Blvd (91105-3010)
P.O. Box 440746 (77244-0746)
PHONE..................................626 397-5000
Lori J Morgan, CEO
Lois Matthews, *
Stephen A Ralph, *
Jim Noble, *
Jane Haderlein, *
EMP: 2100 EST: 1892
SQ FT: 928,000
SALES (est): 688.61MM
SALES (corp-wide): 688.61MM Privately Held
Web: www.huntingtonhealth.org

8062 - General Medical And Surgical Hospitals (P-16338)

SIC: 8062 General medical and surgical hospitals

(P-16320) PATIENTS HOSPITAL
2900 Eureka Way (96001-0220)
PHONE................................530 225-8700
James Daryl Tate Md, *Pr*
Shari Lejsek, *Admn*
EMP: 66 EST: 1993
SALES (est): 3.96MM **Privately Held**
Web: www.patientshospital.com
SIC: 8062 General medical and surgical hospitals

(P-16321) PERMANENTE MEDICAL GROUP INC
1550 Gateway Blvd (94533-6901)
PHONE................................707 427-4000
Laura Coffman, *Brnch Mgr*
EMP: 418
SALES (corp-wide): 68.1B **Privately Held**
Web: www.permanente.org
SIC: 8062 General medical and surgical hospitals
HQ: The Permanente Medical Group Inc
1950 Franklin St Fl 7th
Oakland CA
866 858-2226

(P-16322) PERRIS VALLEY CMNTY HOSP LLC
Also Called: Vista Hospital Riverside
10841 White Oak Ave (91730-3817)
PHONE................................909 581-6400
EMP: 227
SIC: 8062 General medical and surgical hospitals
PA: Perris Valley Community Hospital, Llc
2224 Medical Center Dr
Perris CA

(P-16323) PIH HEALTH INC (PA)
Also Called: Integrted Healthcare Dlvry Sys
12401 Washington Blvd (90602-1006)
PHONE................................562 698-0811
Jane Dicus, *Ch*
Richard Atwood, *Vice Chairman**
Efrain Aceves, *
Kenton Woods, *
Ronald Yoshihara, *
EMP: 1100 EST: 1981
SQ FT: 500,000
SALES (est): 923.01K
SALES (corp-wide): 923.01K **Privately Held**
SIC: 8062 8011 General medical and surgical hospitals; Offices and clinics of medical doctors

(P-16324) PIH HEALTH DOWNEY HOSPITAL (HQ)
Also Called: General Acute Care Hospital
11500 Brookshire Ave (90241-4917)
PHONE................................562 698-0811
James R West, *Pr*
Bryan Smolskis, *
Efrain Aceves, *
Kenton Woods, *
Peggy Chulack, *CAO**
EMP: 254 EST: 1956
SQ FT: 225,000
SALES (est): 203.49MM
SALES (corp-wide): 923.01K **Privately Held**

SIC: 8062 General medical and surgical hospitals
PA: Pih Health, Inc.
12401 Washington Blvd
Whittier CA
562 698-0811

(P-16325) PIH HEALTH GOOD SAMARITAN HOSP (HQ)
Also Called: INTEGRATED HEALTHCARE DELIVERY
1225 Wilshire Blvd (90017-1901)
PHONE................................213 977-2121
James West, *CEO*
Charles Munger, *
Alan Ino, *
▲ EMP: 1610 EST: 1885
SQ FT: 10,000
SALES (est): 435.92MM
SALES (corp-wide): 923.01K **Privately Held**
SIC: 8062 Hospital, affiliated with AMA residency
PA: Pih Health, Inc.
12401 Washington Blvd
Whittier CA
562 698-0811

(P-16326) PIH HEALTH HOSPITAL - WHITTI
Also Called: Downey Regional Medical Center
11500 Brookshire Ave (90241-4917)
PHONE................................562 904-5482
James R West, *CEO*
EMP: 1150
SALES (corp-wide): 923.01K **Privately Held**
SIC: 8062 8071 General medical and surgical hospitals; Medical laboratories
HQ: Pih Health Whittier Hospital
12401 Washington Blvd
Whittier CA
562 698-0811

(P-16327) PIH HEALTH WHITTIER HOSPITAL (HQ)
Also Called: General Acute Care Hospital
12401 Washington Blvd (90602-1006)
PHONE................................562 698-0811
James R West, *CEO*
Anita Chou, *
Ramona Pratt, *
EMP: 1900 EST: 1954
SQ FT: 500,000
SALES (est): 861.97MM
SALES (corp-wide): 923.01K **Privately Held**
SIC: 8062 General medical and surgical hospitals
PA: Pih Health, Inc.
12401 Washington Blvd
Whittier CA
562 698-0811

(P-16328) PIONEERS MEM HEALTHCARE DST (PA)
Also Called: PIONEERS MEMORIAL HOSPITAL
207 W Legion Rd (92227-7780)
PHONE................................760 351-3333
Richard L Mendoza, *CEO*
Daniel Heckathorne, *
Justina Aguirre, *
EMP: 571 EST: 1947
SQ FT: 171,445
SALES (est): 127.75MM
SALES (corp-wide): 127.75MM **Privately Held**

Web: www.pmhd.org
SIC: 8062 Hospital, affiliated with AMA residency

(P-16329) PIPELINE HEALTH LLC (PA)
898 N Pacific Coast Hwy Ste 700 (90245)
PHONE................................310 379-2134
EMP: 108 EST: 2014
SALES (est): 218.29MM
SALES (corp-wide): 218.29MM **Privately Held**
Web: www.pipelinehealth.us
SIC: 8062 General medical and surgical hospitals

(P-16330) PLUMAS HOSPITAL DISTRICT (PA)
1065 Bucks Lake Rd (95971-9507)
PHONE................................530 283-2121
Jodee Read, *CEO*
Doug Lafferty, *
▲ EMP: 180 EST: 1959
SQ FT: 30,000
SALES (est): 47.39MM
SALES (corp-wide): 47.39MM **Privately Held**
Web: www.pdh.org
SIC: 8062 Hospital, affiliated with AMA residency

(P-16331) POMONA VALLEY HOSPITAL MED CTR (PA)
Also Called: Pvhmc
1798 N Garey Ave (91767-2918)
PHONE................................909 865-9500
Richard E Yochum, *CEO*
Alan Smith, *
Michael Nelson, *
Kurt Weinmeister, *
EMP: 2121 EST: 1903
SQ FT: 362,000
SALES (est): 701.76MM
SALES (corp-wide): 701.76MM **Privately Held**
Web: www.pvhmc.org
SIC: 8062 Hospital, medical school affiliated with residency

(P-16332) PRIME HALTHCARE FOUNDATION INC (PA)
3480 E Guasti Rd (91761-7684)
PHONE................................909 235-4400
Prem Reddy, *CEO*
EMP: 107 EST: 2006
SALES (est): 1.03B
SALES (corp-wide): 1.03B **Privately Held**
Web: www.primehealthcare.com
SIC: 8062 General medical and surgical hospitals

(P-16333) PRIME HEALTHCARE ANAHEIM LLC
Also Called: West Anaheim Medical Center
3033 W Orange Ave (92804-3156)
PHONE................................714 827-3000
Virg Narbutas, *CEO*
Kora Guoyavatin, *
EMP: 800 EST: 1963
SQ FT: 180,000
SALES (est): 139.44MM
SALES (corp-wide): 1.03B **Privately Held**
Web: www.westanaheimmedctr.com
SIC: 8062 Hospital, affiliated with AMA residency

HQ: Prime Healthcare Services Inc
3480 E Guasti Rd
Ontario CA

(P-16334) PRIME HEALTHCARE CENTINELA LLC
Also Called: Centinela Hospital Medical Center
555 E Hardy St (90301-4011)
PHONE................................310 673-4660
Linda Bradley, *CEO*
Barbara Kokolowski, *SVS*
EMP: 1000 EST: 1952
SALES (est): 262.74MM
SALES (corp-wide): 1.03B **Privately Held**
Web: www.centinelamed.com
SIC: 8062 General medical and surgical hospitals
HQ: Prime Healthcare Services Inc
3480 E Guasti Rd
Ontario CA

(P-16335) PRIME HEALTHCARE SERVICES-MONT
5000 San Bernardino St (91763-2326)
PHONE................................909 625-5411
EMP: 1398
SALES (est): 108.8MM
SALES (corp-wide): 1.03B **Privately Held**
Web: www.montclair-hospital.org
SIC: 8062 General medical and surgical hospitals
PA: Prime Healthcare Foundation, Inc.
3480 E Guasti Rd
Ontario CA
909 235-4400

(P-16336) PRIME HLTHCARE HNTNGTON BCH LL
Also Called: Huntington Beach Hospital
17772 Beach Blvd (92647-6819)
PHONE................................714 843-5000
EMP: 480 EST: 1957
SQ FT: 100,000
SALES (est): 61.25MM
SALES (corp-wide): 1.03B **Privately Held**
Web: www.hbhospital.org
SIC: 8062 General medical and surgical hospitals
HQ: Prime Healthcare Services Inc
3480 E Guasti Rd
Ontario CA

(P-16337) PRIME HLTHCARE SRVCS-MNTCLAIR
Also Called: Urgent Care Center
5000 San Bernardino St (91763-2326)
PHONE................................909 625-5411
David Chu, *Mgr*
EMP: 216
SALES (corp-wide): 1.03B **Privately Held**
Web: www.montclair-hospital.org
SIC: 8062 General medical and surgical hospitals
HQ: Prime Healthcare Services-Montclair, Llc
5000 San Bernardino St
Montclair CA
909 625-5411

(P-16338) PRIME HLTHCARE SRVCS-MNTCLAIR (DH)
Also Called: Montclair Hospital Medical Center

8062 - General Medical And Surgical Hospitals (P-16339)

5000 San Bernardino St (91763-2326)
PHONE.................909 625-5411
Jennifer Ramirez, *Ex Sec*
Prem Reddy, *
EMP: 234 **EST:** 1999
SALES (est): 62.26MM
SALES (corp-wide): 1.03B **Privately Held**
Web: www.montclair-hospital.org
SIC: 8062 General medical and surgical hospitals
HQ: Prime Healthcare Services Inc
3480 E Guasti Rd
Ontario CA

(P-16339)
PRIME HLTHCARE SVCS - ENCINO H
16237 Ventura Blvd (91436-2201)
PHONE.................818 995-5000
Bockhi Park, *CEO*
Bockhi Park, *Prin*
Prem Reddy, *
EMP: 400 **EST:** 2008
SALES (est): 100.85MM
SALES (corp-wide): 1.03B **Privately Held**
Web: www.encinomed.org
SIC: 8062 General medical and surgical hospitals
HQ: Prime Healthcare Services Inc
3480 E Guasti Rd
Ontario CA

(P-16340)
PRIME HLTHCARE SVCS - PMPA LLC (DH)
Also Called: Pampa Regional Medical Center
3300 E Guasti Rd Ste 300 (91761-8654)
PHONE.................909 235-4400
Brad Morse, *CEO*
Steven Smith, *
Harsha Upadhyay, *
EMP: 149 **EST:** 1960
SQ FT: 150,000
SALES (est): 41.36MM
SALES (corp-wide): 1.03B **Privately Held**
Web: www.primehealthcare.com
SIC: 8062 General medical and surgical hospitals
HQ: Prime Healthcare Services Inc
3480 E Guasti Rd
Ontario CA

(P-16341)
PRIME HLTHCARE SVCS - SAN DMAS
Also Called: San Dimas Community Hospital
1350 W Covina Blvd (91773-3245)
PHONE.................909 599-6811
TOLL FREE: 800
Gregory Brentano, *CEO*
Harold Way, *
EMP: 350 **EST:** 1982
SQ FT: 90,000
SALES (est): 58.27MM
SALES (corp-wide): 1.03B **Privately Held**
Web: www.sandimashospital.com
SIC: 8062 General medical and surgical hospitals
HQ: Prime Healthcare Services Inc
3480 E Guasti Rd
Ontario CA

(P-16342)
PRIME HLTHCARE SVCS - SHRMAN O
Also Called: Sherman Oaks Hospital
4929 Van Nuys Blvd (91403-1702)
PHONE.................818 981-7111
Prem Reddy, *CEO*
John Deady, *CFO*
EMP: 500 **EST:** 2004
SQ FT: 36,000
SALES (est): 97.87MM
SALES (corp-wide): 1.03B **Privately Held**
Web: www.shermanoakshospital.org
SIC: 8062 General medical and surgical hospitals
HQ: Prime Healthcare Services Inc
3480 E Guasti Rd
Ontario CA

(P-16343)
PRIME HLTHCARE SVCS - SHSTA LL
Also Called: Shasta Regional Medical Center (SRMC)
1100 Butte St (96001-0852)
P.O. Box 491810 (96049-1810)
PHONE.................530 244-5400
Cyndy Gordon, *CEO*
EMP: 850 **EST:** 2004
SALES (est): 166.15MM
SALES (corp-wide): 1.03B **Privately Held**
Web: www.shastaregional.com
SIC: 8062 8011 General medical and surgical hospitals; Offices and clinics of medical doctors
HQ: Prime Healthcare Services Inc
3480 E Guasti Rd
Ontario CA

(P-16344)
PRIME HLTHCARE SVCS - ST JOHN (DH)
3500 S 4th St (91761)
PHONE.................913 680-6000
TOLL FREE: 800
Randall G Nyp, *CEO*
EMP: 252 **EST:** 1864
SQ FT: 96,000
SALES (est): 44.62MM
SALES (corp-wide): 1.03B **Privately Held**
Web: www.primehealthcare.com
SIC: 8062 General medical and surgical hospitals
HQ: Prime Healthcare Services Inc
3480 E Guasti Rd
Ontario CA

(P-16345)
PROGRESSIVE SUB-ACUTE CARE
Also Called: Sub-Acute Saratoga Hospital
13425 Sousa Ln (95070-4637)
PHONE.................408 378-8875
Michael Zarcone, *Pr*
EMP: 80 **EST:** 1987
SQ FT: 10,000
SALES (est): 19.1MM **Privately Held**
Web: www.chonc.org
SIC: 8062 General medical and surgical hospitals

(P-16346)
PROVIDENCE HEALTH & SVCS - ORE
540 23rd St (94612-1724)
PHONE.................510 444-0839
Tim Zaricznyj, *Dir*
EMP: 264
SALES (corp-wide): 32.76MM **Privately Held**
Web: www.providence.org
SIC: 8062 General medical and surgical hospitals
HQ: Providence Health & Services - Oregon
1801 Lind Ave Sw
Renton WA
425 525-3355

(P-16347)
PROVIDENCE HEALTH & SVCS - ORE
Also Called: Providence Holy Cross Med Ctr
15031 Rinaldi St (91345-1207)
PHONE.................818 365-8051
David Mast, *Brnch Mgr*
EMP: 4612
SALES (corp-wide): 32.76MM **Privately Held**
Web: www.providence.org
SIC: 8062 General medical and surgical hospitals
HQ: Providence Health & Services - Oregon
1801 Lind Ave Sw
Renton WA
425 525-3355

(P-16348)
PROVIDENCE HEALTH SYSTEM
Providence St Joseph Med Ctr
501 S Buena Vista St (91505-4809)
PHONE.................818 843-5111
Georgianne Johnson, *COO*
EMP: 2000
SALES (corp-wide): 32.76MM **Privately Held**
Web: www.providence.org
SIC: 8062 General medical and surgical hospitals
HQ: Providence Health System-Southern California
1801 Lind Ave Sw
Renton WA
425 525-3355

(P-16349)
PROVIDENCE HOLY CROSS MEDICAL (PA)
Also Called: Providence
15031 Rinaldi St (91345-1207)
PHONE.................818 365-8051
Lee Kanon Alpert, *Ch*
June E Drake, *
Jodi Hein, *
▲ **EMP:** 439 **EST:** 1960
SALES (est): 557.56MM
SALES (corp-wide): 557.56MM **Privately Held**
SIC: 8062 General medical and surgical hospitals

(P-16350)
PROVIDENCE MEDICAL FOUNDATION (DH)
Also Called: PROVIDENCE HOME HEALTH ORANGE
200 W Center Street Promenade Ste 800 (92805-3960)
PHONE.................714 712-3308
EMP: 150 **EST:** 1961
SALES (est): 1.09B
SALES (corp-wide): 32.76MM **Privately Held**
Web: www.psjhmedgroups.org
SIC: 8062 General medical and surgical hospitals
HQ: St. Joseph Health System
3345 Michelson Dr Ste 100
Irvine CA
949 381-4000

(P-16351)
PROVIDENCE ST JOHNS HLTH CTR
Also Called: St. John's Health Center
2121 Santa Monica Blvd (90404-2303)
PHONE.................971 268-7643
Marcel Loh, *CEO*
Donald Larsen Junior, *Chief Medical Officer*
Brian Anderson, *Contracts Director**
Guadalupe Martinez, *Finance**
EMP: 350 **EST:** 1940
SQ FT: 60,000
SALES (est): 401MM **Privately Held**
SIC: 8062 General medical and surgical hospitals

(P-16352)
PROVIDENCE TARZANA MEDICAL CTR
18321 Clark St (91356-3501)
PHONE.................818 881-0800
Dale Surowitz, *CEO*
Nick Lymberopoulos, *
EMP: 1300 **EST:** 1973
SALES (est): 291.91MM **Privately Held**
Web: www.tarzanacme.com
SIC: 8062 General medical and surgical hospitals

(P-16353)
PROVIDNCE HLTH SVCS FNDTN/ SAN
Also Called: Providnce Holy Cross Fundation
501 S Buena Vista St (91505-4809)
PHONE.................818 843-5111
Patricia Modrzejewski, *CEO*
Lee Kanon Alpert, *
Thomas Mcdevitt, *Contrlr*
EMP: 2000 **EST:** 1980
SALES (est): 63.69MM **Privately Held**
SIC: 8062 General medical and surgical hospitals

(P-16354)
QUEEN OF VLY MED CTR FUNDATION (DH)
1000 Trancas St (94558-2906)
PHONE.................707 252-4411
Lawrence Michael Coomes, *Pr*
Dick Green, *
Robert Eisen, *
Don Miller, *
Bob Diehl, *
EMP: 653 **EST:** 1953
SQ FT: 278,500
SALES (est): 268.19MM
SALES (corp-wide): 32.76MM **Privately Held**
Web: www.thequeen.org
SIC: 8062 General medical and surgical hospitals
HQ: St. Joseph Health System
3345 Michelson Dr Ste 100
Irvine CA
949 381-4000

(P-16355)
QUEEN OF VLY MED CTR FUNDATION
Also Called: Care Network
3448 Villa Ln Ste 102 (94558-6471)
PHONE.................707 251-2000
Cris Galleger, *Mgr*
EMP: 293
SALES (corp-wide): 32.76MM **Privately Held**
Web: www.thequeen.org
SIC: 8062 General medical and surgical hospitals
HQ: Queen Of The Valley Medical Center Foundation
1000 Trancas St
Napa CA
707 252-4411

PRODUCTS & SERVICES SECTION
8062 - General Medical And Surgical Hospitals (P-16374)

(P-16356)
RADY CHILDRENS HOSP & HLTH CTR (PA)
Also Called: Children's Hospital
3020 Childrens Way (92123-4223)
PHONE..............................858 576-1700
TOLL FREE: 800
Donald B Kearns, *Pr*
Irvin A Kaufman, *CMO**
Margareta E Norton, *
Roger G Roux, *
Nicholas Holmes, *
EMP: 1700 **EST:** 1980
SALES (est): 2.01B **Privately Held**
Web: www.rchsd.org
SIC: **8062** General medical and surgical hospitals

(P-16357)
RADY CHLD HOSPITAL-SAN DIEGO (HQ)
Also Called: CHILDREN'S HOSPITAL
3020 Childrens Way (92123-4223)
PHONE..............................858 576-1700
Donald Kearns, *CEO*
Jill Strickland, *CAO**
EMP: 2000 **EST:** 1952
SQ FT: 276,000
SALES (est): 1.91B **Privately Held**
Web: www.rchsd.org
SIC: **8062** General medical and surgical hospitals
PA: Rady Children's Hospital And Health Center
3020 Childrens Way
San Diego CA

(P-16358)
RAMONA RHBLTTION POST ACUTE CA
Also Called: Ramona Rhblttion Post Acute Ca
485 W Johnston Ave (92543-7012)
PHONE..............................951 652-0011
Stan Leland, *Pr*
Heidi Vickers, *
EMP: 120 **EST:** 1995
SQ FT: 30,000
SALES (est): 9.68MM **Privately Held**
Web: www.ramona-rehab.com
SIC: **8062** 8051 General medical and surgical hospitals; Convalescent home with continuous nursing care

(P-16359)
REDLANDS COMMUNITY HOSPITAL (PA)
350 Terracina Blvd (92373-4897)
PHONE..............................909 335-5500
EMP: 97 **EST:** 1927
SALES (est): 213.73MM **Privately Held**
Web: www.redlandshospital.org
SIC: **8062** General medical and surgical hospitals

(P-16360)
REDWOOD MEMORIAL HOSP FORTUNA (PA)
3300 Renner Dr (95540-3120)
PHONE..............................707 725-7327
Darian Harris, *CEO*
Bob Branigan, *
Kevin Clouder, *
EMP: 150 **EST:** 1954
SQ FT: 65,000
SALES (est): 22.56MM
SALES (corp-wide): 22.56MM **Privately Held**
SIC: **8062** Hospital, affiliated with AMA residency

(P-16361)
REEDLEY COMMUNITY HOSPITAL
Also Called: ADVENTIST MEDICAL CENTER-REEDL
372 W Cypress Ave (93654-2113)
PHONE..............................559 638-8155
Wayne Ferch, *Pr*
EMP: 87 **EST:** 2011
SALES (est): 175.23MM **Privately Held**
Web: www.adventisthealth.org
SIC: **8062** General medical and surgical hospitals

(P-16362)
RIDEOUT MEMORIAL HOSPITAL (HQ)
726 4th St (95901-5656)
P.O. Box 2128 (95901-0075)
PHONE..............................530 749-4416
Ronald M Sweeney, *Ch*
Theresa Hamilton, *
John Wright Chprsn, *Prin*
Lisa Del Pero, *
John Cary, *
EMP: 700 **EST:** 1907
SQ FT: 100,000
SALES (est): 453.74MM
SALES (corp-wide): 498.18MM **Privately Held**
Web: www.adventisthealth.org
SIC: **8062** 8082 General medical and surgical hospitals; Home health care services
PA: Freemont Rideout Health Group
989 Plumas St
Yuba City CA
530 751-4010

(P-16363)
RIDGECREST REGIONAL HOSPITAL (PA)
Also Called: Southern Sierra Medical Clinic
1081 N China Lake Blvd (93555-3130)
PHONE..............................760 446-3551
James A Suver, *CEO*
Donna Kiser, *
EMP: 470 **EST:** 1962
SQ FT: 80,000
SALES (est): 156.64MM
SALES (corp-wide): 156.64MM **Privately Held**
Web: www.rrh.org
SIC: **8062** General medical and surgical hospitals

(P-16364)
RIVERSIDE CMNTY HLTH SYSTEMS (DH)
Also Called: Riverside Community Hospital
4445 Magnolia Ave 6th Fl (92501-4135)
PHONE..............................951 788-3000
Partrick Brilliant, *Pr*
Tracey Fernandez, *
Doug Long, *
EMP: 1195 **EST:** 1901
SQ FT: 386,100
SALES (est): 162.72MM **Publicly Held**
Web: www.riversidecommunityhospital.com
SIC: **8062** 8011 General medical and surgical hospitals; Offices and clinics of medical doctors
HQ: Hca Inc.
1 Park Plz
Nashville TN
615 344-9551

(P-16365)
RIVERSIDE UNIV HLTH SYS FNDTIO (PA)
Also Called: Riverside Cnty Rgional Med Ctr
4065 County Circle Dr (92503-3410)
PHONE..............................951 358-5000
Douglas D Bagley, *CEO*
David Runke, *
Ellie Bennett, *
EMP: 459 **EST:** 1989
SALES (est): 4.17MM **Privately Held**
Web: www.ruhealth.org
SIC: **8062** General medical and surgical hospitals

(P-16366)
RIVERSIDE UNIVERSITY HEALTH
Also Called: Ruhs-Emergency Department
26520 Cactus Ave (92555-3927)
PHONE..............................951 486-4000
EMP: 341
Web: www.ruhealth.org
SIC: **8062** General medical and surgical hospitals
PA: Riverside University Health System Foundation
4065 County Circle Dr
Riverside CA

(P-16367)
SADDLEBACK MEMORIAL MED CTR (HQ)
Also Called: Memorlcare Heart Vascular Inst
24451 Health Center Dr Fl 1 (92653-3689)
PHONE..............................949 837-4500
Steve Geidt, *CEO*
Barry Arbuckle, *
Karen Testman, *
Rick Graniere, *
Adolfo Chanez, *
EMP: 1020 **EST:** 1969
SQ FT: 195,000
SALES (est): 349.15MM **Privately Held**
Web: www.memorialcare.org
SIC: **8062** 8011 8093 8099 General medical and surgical hospitals; Medical centers; Rehabilitation center, outpatient treatment; Blood related health services
PA: Memorial Health Services
17360 Brookhurst St # 160
Fountain Valley CA

(P-16368)
SAINT AGNES MEDICAL CENTER (HQ)
1303 E Herndon Ave (93720-3309)
PHONE..............................559 450-3000
Nancy R Hollingsworth, *CEO*
Christopher Pahlas, *
Andrew Laughlin, *
EMP: 1688 **EST:** 1929
SQ FT: 200,000
SALES (est): 635.34MM
SALES (corp-wide): 2.49B **Privately Held**
Web: www.samc.com
SIC: **8062** General medical and surgical hospitals
PA: Trinity Health Corporation
20555 Victor Pkwy Ste 100
Livonia MI
734 343-1000

(P-16369)
SAINT FRANCIS MEMORIAL HOSP (DH)
900 Hyde St (94109-4806)
PHONE..............................415 353-6000
Thomas G Hennessy, *CEO*
John G Williams, *
Cheryl A Fama R.n., *COO*
Tiffany Caster, *
Kim Brown Sims, *
EMP: 800 **EST:** 1905
SQ FT: 300,000
SALES (est): 187.94MM **Privately Held**
Web: www.dignityhealth.org
SIC: **8062** General medical and surgical hospitals
HQ: Dignity Health
185 Berry St Ste 200
San Francisco CA
415 438-5500

(P-16370)
SAINT JOHNS HEALTH CENTER FOUNDATION (DH)
Also Called: Saint John's Health Center
2121 Santa Monica Blvd (90404-2303)
PHONE..............................310 829-5511
TOLL FREE: 888
EMP: 1100 **EST:** 1942
SALES (est): 69.62MM
SALES (corp-wide): 10.75B **Privately Held**
Web: www.saintjohnsfoundation.org
SIC: **8062** General medical and surgical hospitals
HQ: Sisters Of Charity Of Leavenworth Health System, Inc.
500 Eldorado Blvd # 6300
Broomfield CO
303 813-5000

(P-16371)
SAINT LISE RGNAL HOSP FNDATION
9400 N Name Uno (95020-3528)
PHONE..............................408 848-4931
EMP: 489 **EST:** 2011
SALES (est): 8.04MM **Privately Held**
SIC: **8062** General medical and surgical hospitals
PA: Saint Louise Regional Hospital
9460 N Name Uno
Gilroy CA

(P-16372)
SAINT LOUISE HOSPITAL
9400 N Name Uno (95020-3528)
PHONE..............................408 848-2000
Jim Dober, *CEO*
Joanne Allan, *
Terry Curley, *
EMP: 500 **EST:** 2005
SALES (est): 90.68MM **Privately Held**
SIC: **8062** General medical and surgical hospitals

(P-16373)
SALINAS VALLEY HEALTH (PA)
Also Called: Salinas Valley Memorial Hosp
450 E Romie Ln (93901-4029)
P.O. Box 4760 (93912-4760)
PHONE..............................831 757-4333
Julie Jezowski, *CFO*
Henry Ornelas, *COO*
Kelly Richlin, *Sec*
▲ **EMP:** 1595 **EST:** 1947
SQ FT: 187,942
SALES (est): 255.85K
SALES (corp-wide): 255.85K **Privately Held**
Web: www.salinasvalleyhealth.com
SIC: **8062** Hospital, affiliated with AMA residency

(P-16374)
SAN ANTONIO REGIONAL HOSPITAL (PA)

8062 - General Medical And Surgical Hospitals (P-16375)

999 San Bernardino Rd (91786-4920)
PHONE..................................909 985-2811
John Chapman, *CEO*
Jim Milhiser, *
Wah-chung Hsu, *CFO*
▲ **EMP:** 1900 **EST:** 1920
SQ FT: 349,000
SALES (est): 424.66MM
SALES (corp-wide): 424.66MM **Privately Held**
Web: www.sarh.org
SIC: 8062 5912 General medical and surgical hospitals; Drug stores and proprietary stores

(P-16375)
SAN BENITO HEALTH CARE DST (PA)
Also Called: Hazel Hawkins Memorial Hosp
911 Sunset Dr (95023-5606)
▲ **EMP:** 270 **EST:** 1907
SQ FT: 42,000
SALES (est): 146.59MM
SALES (corp-wide): 146.59MM **Privately Held**
Web: www.hazelhawkins.com
SIC: 8062 8051 8059 General medical and surgical hospitals; Skilled nursing care facilities; Convalescent home

(P-16376)
SAN BENITO HEALTH CARE DST
Also Called: Hazel Hawkins North Side
900 Sunset Dr (95023-5603)
PHONE..................................831 635-1106
Mark Robinson, *Brnch Mgr*
EMP: 102
SALES (corp-wide): 146.59MM **Privately Held**
Web: www.hazelhawkins.com
SIC: 8062 8059 General medical and surgical hospitals; Convalescent home
PA: San Benito Health Care District
911 Sunset Dr
Hollister CA

(P-16377)
SAN BRUNOIDENCE OPCO LLC
Also Called: San Bruno Skilled Nursing
890 El Camino Real (94066-3137)
PHONE..................................650 583-7768
Jason Murray, *Prin*
Mark Hancock, *
EMP: 70 **EST:** 2014
SALES (est): 5MM
SALES (corp-wide): 1.53B **Privately Held**
Web: www.sanbrunoskillednursing.com
SIC: 8062 General medical and surgical hospitals
HQ: Providence Group North, Llc
262 N University Ave
Farmington UT
801 447-9829

(P-16378)
SAN GABRIEL VALLEY MEDICAL CTR
438 W Las Tunas Dr (91776-1216)
PHONE..................................626 289-5454
Thomas Mone, *CEO*
Edward Shuey, *
Richard Polver, *
Harold Way, *
EMP: 850 **EST:** 1964
SQ FT: 42,000
SALES (est): 106.77MM **Privately Held**
Web: www.ahmchealth.com
SIC: 8062 General medical and surgical hospitals
HQ: Dignity Health

185 Berry St Ste 200
San Francisco CA
415 438-5500

(P-16379)
SAN GORGONIO MEMORIAL HOSPITAL
600 N Highland Springs Ave (92220-3046)
PHONE..................................951 845-1121
Steve Barron, *CEO*
EMP: 819 **EST:** 1990
SALES (est): 57.5MM **Privately Held**
Web: www.sgmh.org
SIC: 8062 General medical and surgical hospitals

(P-16380)
SAN GRGNIO MEM HOSP FOUNDATION (PA)
600 N Highland Springs Ave (92220-3046)
PHONE..................................951 845-1121
Steven Barron, *CEO*
Jerilynn Kaibel, *
Denae Reagins, *
Olivia Hershey, *
Dorothy Ellis, *
EMP: 244 **EST:** 1990
SQ FT: 76,000
SALES (est): 88.29MM
SALES (corp-wide): 88.29MM **Privately Held**
Web: www.sgmh.org
SIC: 8062 Hospital, affiliated with AMA residency

(P-16381)
SAN JOAQUIN COMMUNITY HOSPITAL (PA)
Also Called: Adventist Health Bakersfield
2615 Chester Ave (93301-2014)
PHONE..................................661 395-3000
Sharlet Briggs, *Pr*
EMP: 850 **EST:** 1910
SQ FT: 137,000
SALES (est): 477.16MM
SALES (corp-wide): 477.16MM **Privately Held**
Web: www.adventisthealth.org
SIC: 8062 8011 General medical and surgical hospitals; Offices and clinics of medical doctors

(P-16382)
SAN JOAQUIN GENERAL HOSPITAL
500 W Hospital Rd (95231-9693)
P.O. Box 1020 (95201-3120)
PHONE..................................209 468-6000
David Cullberson, *CEO*
EMP: 500 **EST:** 2000
SALES (est): 36.11K **Privately Held**
Web: www.sanjoaquingeneral.org
SIC: 8062 General medical and surgical hospitals

(P-16383)
SAN JOSE HEALTHCARE SYSTEM LP
Also Called: Regional Medical Ctr San Jose
225 N Jackson Ave (95116-1603)
PHONE..................................408 259-5000
Kenneth West, *Pr*
EMP: 1200 **EST:** 1984
SQ FT: 203,685
SALES (est): 375.78MM **Publicly Held**
Web: www.regionalmedicalsanjose.com
SIC: 8062 General medical and surgical hospitals
HQ: Hca Inc.

1 Park Plz
Nashville TN
615 344-9551

(P-16384)
SAN JQUIN GEN HOSP FNDTION A C
Also Called: Healthcare Services
500 W Hospital Rd (95231-9693)
PHONE..................................209 468-6000
David Colberson, *CEO*
Ronald Kruetner, *
EMP: 1300 **EST:** 2001
SALES (est): 54.33MM **Privately Held**
Web: www.sanjoaquingeneral.org
SIC: 8062 General medical and surgical hospitals

(P-16385)
SAN LEANDRO HOSPITAL LP
13855 E 14th St (94578-2611)
PHONE..................................510 357-6500
Ronnie Bayduza, *CEO*
Janay Defer, *
EMP: 475 **EST:** 1994
SALES (est): 73.68MM **Privately Held**
Web: www.alamedahealthsystem.org
SIC: 8062 8361 General medical and surgical hospitals; Residential care
PA: Alameda Health System
1411 E 31st St
Oakland CA

(P-16386)
SAN PEDRO PENINSULA HOSPITAL
Also Called: Little Co Mary- San Pedro Hosp
1300 W 7th St (90732-3593)
PHONE..................................310 832-3311
EMP: 880
SIC: 8062 8051 5912 General medical and surgical hospitals; Skilled nursing care facilities; Drug stores

(P-16387)
SAN RAMON REGIONAL MED CTR LLC
6001 Norris Canyon Rd (94583-5400)
PHONE..................................925 275-9200
Beenu Chadha, *Interim Chief Executive Officer*
Shawn Dewers, *
Lee Huskins, *
Amber Campbell, *CSO**
EMP: 600 **EST:** 1983
SALES (corp-wide): 93MM
SALES (corp-wide): 19.58B **Publicly Held**
Web: validate.perfdrive.com
SIC: 8062 8093 General medical and surgical hospitals; Rehabilitation center, outpatient treatment
PA: Tenet Healthcare Corporation
14201 Dallas Pkwy
Dallas TX
469 893-2200

(P-16388)
SANTA BARBARA COTTAGE HOSPITAL
Pathology Department
400 W Pueblo St (93105-4353)
P.O. Box 689 (93102-0689)
PHONE..................................805 569-7367
Ron Werdt, *Pr*
EMP: 290
SALES (corp-wide): 152.81MM **Privately Held**
SIC: 8062 General medical and surgical hospitals

HQ: Santa Barbara Cottage Hospital Foundation
400 W Pueblo St
Santa Barbara CA
805 682-7111

(P-16389)
SANTA BRBARA CTTAGE HOSP FNDTI
Respiratory Care
400 W Pueblo St (93105-4353)
PHONE..................................805 569-7224
Doctor Phillip Michael, *Dir*
EMP: 340
SALES (corp-wide): 152.81MM **Privately Held**
SIC: 8062 General medical and surgical hospitals
HQ: Santa Barbara Cottage Hospital Foundation
400 W Pueblo St
Santa Barbara CA
805 682-7111

(P-16390)
SANTA BRBARA CTTAGE HOSP FNDTI
Also Called: Santa Barbara Cnty Social Svcs
2125 Centerpointe Pkwy (93455-1337)
PHONE..................................805 346-7135
Charlene Chase, *Dir*
EMP: 271
SALES (corp-wide): 152.81MM **Privately Held**
SIC: 8062 General medical and surgical hospitals
HQ: Santa Barbara Cottage Hospital Foundation
400 W Pueblo St
Santa Barbara CA
805 682-7111

(P-16391)
SANTA BRBARA CTTAGE HOSP FNDTI (HQ)
Also Called: Cottage Childrens Medical Ctr
400 W Pueblo St (93105-4353)
P.O. Box 689 (93102-0689)
PHONE..................................805 682-7111
Ronald C Werft, *CEO*
Steven Fellows, *
Brett Tande, *
EMP: 149 **EST:** 1982
SQ FT: 485,874
SALES (est): 772.02MM
SALES (corp-wide): 152.81MM **Privately Held**
SIC: 8062 Hospital, AMA approved residency
PA: Cottage Health
400 W Pueblo St
Santa Barbara CA
805 682-7111

(P-16392)
SANTA CLARA COUNTY OF
Also Called: St. Louise Regional Hospital
9400 No Name Uno (95020-3528)
PHONE..................................408 848-2000
EMP: 197
Web: home.sccgov.org
SIC: 8062 General medical and surgical hospitals
PA: County Of Santa Clara
70 W Hedding St
San Jose CA
408 299-5200

8062 - General Medical And Surgical Hospitals (P-16412)

(P-16393)
SANTA CRUZ MEDICAL FOUNDATION
2915 Chanticleer Ave (95065-1815)
PHONE.................831 477-2375
Steven Roberts, Mgr
EMP: 1197
SALES (corp-wide): 14.77B Privately Held
Web: www.sutterhealth.org
SIC: 8062 General medical and surgical hospitals
HQ: Santa Cruz Medical Foundation
2025 Soquel Ave
Santa Cruz CA
831 458-5537

(P-16394)
SANTA ROSA SURGERY CENTER LP
Also Called: Sutter Health
1111 Sonoma Ave Ste 214 (95405-4833)
PHONE.................707 575-5831
Dan Peterson, Admn
Jiries Mogannam, *
EMP: 98 EST: 1983
SQ FT: 8,000
SALES (est): 14.95MM Privately Held
Web: www.santarosasurgerycenter.com
SIC: 8062 General medical and surgical hospitals

(P-16395)
SANTA TERESITA INC (PA)
Also Called: MANOR AT SANTA TERESITA HOSPIT
819 Buena Vista St (91010-1703)
PHONE.................626 359-3243
Sister Mary Clare Mancini, CEO
EMP: 276 EST: 1955
SQ FT: 232,165
SALES (est): 11.71MM
SALES (corp-wide): 11.71MM Privately Held
Web: www.santa-teresita.org
SIC: 8062 8051 General medical and surgical hospitals; Skilled nursing care facilities

(P-16396)
SANTA YNEZ VLY CTTAGE HOSP INC
2050 Viborg Rd (93463-2220)
P.O. Box 689 (93102-0689)
PHONE.................805 688-6431
Ron Werft, Pr
EMP: 75 EST: 1962
SQ FT: 30,000
SALES (est): 24.49MM
SALES (corp-wide): 152.81MM Privately Held
Web: www.santaynezvalley.com
SIC: 8062 General medical and surgical hospitals
PA: Cottage Health
400 W Pueblo St
Santa Barbara CA
805 682-7111

(P-16397)
SCRIPPS CLINIC
12395 El Camino Real Ste 112 (92130-3082)
P.O. Box 2469 (92038-2469)
PHONE.................858 794-1250
Chris Van Gorder, CEO
Doctor Hubert Greenway, CEO
James Collins, Pr
EMP: 162 EST: 1999
SALES (est): 111.83MM Privately Held

(P-16398)
SCRIPPS HEALTH
Also Called: Scripps Ambulatory Surgery Ctr
320 Santa Fe Dr Ste 310 (92024-5140)
PHONE.................760 753-8413
Donna Danley, Prin
EMP: 70
SALES (corp-wide): 4.06B Privately Held
Web: www.scripps.org
SIC: 8062 General medical and surgical hospitals
PA: Scripps Health
10140 Campus Point Dr # 415
San Diego CA
800 727-4777

(P-16399)
SCRIPPS HEALTH
Also Called: Scripps Mercy Hospital
4077 5th Ave (92103-2105)
PHONE.................619 294-8111
Jacqueline Saucier, Dir
EMP: 109
SALES (corp-wide): 4.06B Privately Held
Web: www.scripps.org
SIC: 8062 General medical and surgical hospitals
PA: Scripps Health
10140 Campus Point Dr # 415
San Diego CA
800 727-4777

(P-16400)
SCRIPPS HEALTH
Also Called: Scripps Rancho Bernardo
15004 Innovation Dr (92128-3491)
PHONE.................858 271-9770
Melody Stewart, Admn
EMP: 83
SALES (corp-wide): 4.06B Privately Held
Web: www.scripps.org
SIC: 8062 General medical and surgical hospitals
PA: Scripps Health
10140 Campus Point Dr # 415
San Diego CA
800 727-4777

(P-16401)
SCRIPPS HEALTH
Also Called: Scripps Mem Hosp - Encinatas
354 Santa Fe Dr (92024-5142)
P.O. Box 230817 (92023-0817)
PHONE.................760 753-6501
Rebecca Ropchan, Brnch Mgr
EMP: 250
SALES (corp-wide): 4.06B Privately Held
Web: www.scripps.org
SIC: 8062 5912 General medical and surgical hospitals; Drug stores
PA: Scripps Health
10140 Campus Point Dr # 415
San Diego CA
800 727-4777

(P-16402)
SCRIPPS HEALTH
Also Called: Scripps Mercy Hospitals
435 H St (91910-4307)
PHONE.................619 691-7000
Pott Hoff, COO
EMP: 146
SALES (corp-wide): 4.06B Privately Held
Web: www.scripps.org
SIC: 8062 General medical and surgical hospitals

PA: Scripps Health
10140 Campus Point Dr # 415
San Diego CA
800 727-4777

(P-16403)
SCRIPPS HEALTH (PA)
10140 Campus Point Dr (92121-1520)
PHONE.................800 727-4777
Chris D Van Gorder, Pr
Brett Tande, *
Richard Sheridan, *
A Brent Eastman Md, Chief Medical Officer
John B Engle, Chief Development Officer*
EMP: 2514 EST: 1924
SQ FT: 95,000
SALES (est): 4.06B
SALES (corp-wide): 4.06B Privately Held
Web: www.scripps.org
SIC: 8062 8049 8042 8043 General medical and surgical hospitals; Physical therapist; Offices and clinics of optometrists; Offices and clinics of podiatrists

(P-16404)
SCRIPPS HEALTH
Also Called: Scripps Green Hospital
10666 N Torrey Pines Rd (92037-1027)
PHONE.................858 455-9100
Robin Brown, Brnch Mgr
EMP: 326
SALES (corp-wide): 4.06B Privately Held
Web: www.scripps.org
SIC: 8062 General medical and surgical hospitals
PA: Scripps Health
10140 Campus Point Dr # 415
San Diego CA
800 727-4777

(P-16405)
SCRIPPS HEALTH
Also Called: Scripps Mercy Hospital
4077 5th Ave (92103-2105)
PHONE.................619 294-8111
EMP: 110
SQ FT: 3,062
SALES (corp-wide): 4.06B Privately Held
Web: www.scripps.org
SIC: 8062 General medical and surgical hospitals
PA: Scripps Health
10140 Campus Point Dr # 415
San Diego CA
800 727-4777

(P-16406)
SCRIPPS HEALTH
Also Called: Scripps Torrey Pines
10666 N Torrey Pines Rd (92037-1027)
PHONE.................800 727-4777
Larry Harrison, Mgr
EMP: 61
SALES (corp-wide): 4.06B Privately Held
Web: www.scripps.org
SIC: 8062 General medical and surgical hospitals
PA: Scripps Health
10140 Campus Point Dr # 415
San Diego CA
800 727-4777

(P-16407)
SCRIPPS HEALTH
Also Called: Scripps Mem Hospital-La Jolla
9888 Genesee Ave (92037-1205)
PHONE.................858 626-6150
James Bruffey, Brnch Mgr
EMP: 326
SALES (corp-wide): 4.06B Privately Held

Web: www.scripps.org
SIC: 8062 General medical and surgical hospitals
PA: Scripps Health
10140 Campus Point Dr # 415
San Diego CA
800 727-4777

(P-16408)
SCRIPPS MERCY HOSPITAL
4077 5th Ave # Mer35 (92103-2105)
PHONE.................619 294-8111
Andrew C Ping, Prin
EMP: 93 EST: 2004
SALES (est): 708.46MM Privately Held
Web: www.scripps.org
SIC: 8062 General medical and surgical hospitals

(P-16409)
SCRIPPS MMRAL-XIMED MED CTR LP
Also Called: Scripps Health
9850 Genesee Ave Ste 900 (92037-1220)
PHONE.................858 882-8350
Brian Huizar, Prin
EMP: 88 EST: 1991
SALES (est): 17.9MM Privately Held
SIC: 8062 8049 General medical and surgical hospitals; Physical therapist

(P-16410)
SENECA HEALTHCARE DISTRICT (PA)
Also Called: SHD
130 Brentwood Dr (96020)
P.O. Box 737 (96020-0737)
PHONE.................530 258-2151
Linda Wagner, CEO
Cheryl Darnell, *
William Howe, *
Bob Caton, *
Loretta Gomez, *
EMP: 105 EST: 1952
SQ FT: 12,417
SALES (est): 26.39MM
SALES (corp-wide): 26.39MM Privately Held
Web: www.senecahospital.org
SIC: 8062 General medical and surgical hospitals

(P-16411)
SEQUOIA HEALTH SERVICES (DH)
Also Called: Sequoia Hospital
170 Alameda De Las Pulgas (94062-2751)
PHONE.................650 369-5811
Glenna Vaskellas, Admn
EMP: 306 EST: 1947
SQ FT: 350,000
SALES (est): 273.82MM Privately Held
Web: www.dignityhealth.org
SIC: 8062 General medical and surgical hospitals
HQ: Dignity Health
185 Berry St Ste 200
San Francisco CA
415 438-5500

(P-16412)
SEQUOIA HEALTH SERVICES
Also Called: Wipple Laboratories
2900 Whipple Ave Ste 110 (94062-2858)
PHONE.................650 367-5544
EMP: 861
Web: www.dignityhealth.org
SIC: 8062 General medical and surgical hospitals

8062 - General Medical And Surgical Hospitals (P-16413)

HQ: Sequoia Health Services
170 Alameda De Las Pulgas
Redwood City CA
650 369-5811

(P-16413)
SETON MEDICAL CTR FOUNDATION
1900 Sullivan Ave (94015-2200)
PHONE..................650 991-6464
Teresa Toymiguel, *CEO*
Frank Nalifrando, *Dir*
Wayne Silveria, *INTERIM DIRECTOR OF ACCOUNTING*
EMP: 560 **EST:** 1982
SQ FT: 1,800
SALES (est): 12.69MM **Privately Held**
Web: www.ahmchealth.com
SIC: 8062 General medical and surgical hospitals

(P-16414)
SHARP CHULA VISTA MEDICAL CTR
Also Called: Sharp Chula Vista Medical Ctr
751 Medical Center Ct (91911-6617)
PHONE..................619 502-5800
Chris Boyd, *CEO*
Michael Murphy, *
Rick King, *
EMP: 1600 **EST:** 1944
SQ FT: 270,205
SALES (est): 503.43MM
SALES (corp-wide): 2.37B **Privately Held**
Web: www.sharp.com
SIC: 8062 General medical and surgical hospitals
PA: Sharp Healthcare
8695 Spectrum Center Blvd
San Diego CA
858 499-4000

(P-16415)
SHARP CHULA VISTA MEDICAL CTR
8695 Spectrum Center Blvd (92123-1489)
PHONE..................858 499-5150
Chris Boyd, *CEO*
EMP: 99 **EST:** 2007
SALES (est): 4.69MM **Privately Held**
Web: www.sharp.com
SIC: 8062 General medical and surgical hospitals

(P-16416)
SHARP CORONADO HOSPITAL & HEALTHCARE CENTER
Also Called: Coronado Hospital
250 Prospect Pl (92118-1943)
PHONE..................619 522-3600
EMP: 550 **EST:** 1938
SALES (est): 155.84MM
SALES (corp-wide): 2.37B **Privately Held**
SIC: 8062 General medical and surgical hospitals
PA: Sharp Healthcare
8695 Spectrum Center Blvd
San Diego CA
858 499-4000

(P-16417)
SHARP HEALTHCARE
Also Called: Sharp Rees-Stealy
8008 Frost St Ste 106 (92123-4229)
PHONE..................858 939-5434
EMP: 151
SALES (corp-wide): 2.37B **Privately Held**
Web: www.sharp.com
SIC: 8062 General medical and surgical hospitals
PA: Sharp Healthcare
8695 Spectrum Center Blvd
San Diego CA
858 499-4000

(P-16418)
SHARP HEALTHCARE
Also Called: Birch Ptrick Convalescent Cntr
751 Medical Center Ct (91911-6617)
PHONE..................858 499-2000
Lily Reyes, *Dir*
EMP: 119
SALES (corp-wide): 2.37B **Privately Held**
Web: www.sharp.com
SIC: 8062 General medical and surgical hospitals
PA: Sharp Healthcare
8695 Spectrum Center Blvd
San Diego CA
858 499-4000

(P-16419)
SHARP HEALTHCARE ACO LLC
Also Called: SHARP HEALTHCARE ACO, LLC
7910 Frost St Ste 280 (92123-2752)
PHONE..................619 398-2988
EMP: 95
SALES (corp-wide): 2.37B **Privately Held**
Web: www.sharp.com
SIC: 8062 General medical and surgical hospitals
PA: Sharp Healthcare
8695 Spectrum Center Blvd
San Diego CA
858 499-4000

(P-16420)
SHARP HEALTHCARE ACO LLC
Also Called: Sharp Rees-Stealy Div
300 Fir St (92101-2327)
PHONE..................619 446-1575
Donna Mills, *Admn*
EMP: 223
SQ FT: 61,608
SALES (corp-wide): 2.37B **Privately Held**
Web: www.sharp.com
SIC: 8062 General medical and surgical hospitals
PA: Sharp Healthcare
8695 Spectrum Center Blvd
San Diego CA
858 499-4000

(P-16421)
SHARP HEALTHCARE ACO LLC
Also Called: Sharp Health Care
3554 Ruffin Rd Ste Soca (92123-2596)
PHONE..................858 627-5152
Alison Fleury, *Brnch Mgr*
EMP: 672
SALES (corp-wide): 2.37B **Privately Held**
Web: www.sharp.com
SIC: 8062 General medical and surgical hospitals
PA: Sharp Healthcare
8695 Spectrum Center Blvd
San Diego CA
858 499-4000

(P-16422)
SHARP MARY BIRCH H
3003 Health Center Dr (92123-2700)
PHONE..................858 939-3400
Trisha Khaleghi, *CEO*
EMP: 73 **EST:** 2004
SALES (est): 23.83MM **Privately Held**
Web: www.sharp.com
SIC: 8062 General medical and surgical hospitals
PA: Sharp Healthcare
8695 Spectrum Center Blvd
San Diego CA
858 499-4000

(P-16423)
SHARP MEMORIAL HOSPITAL (HQ)
7901 Frost St (92123-2701)
PHONE..................858 939-3636
Tim Smith, *CEO*
▲ **EMP:** 3000 **EST:** 1957
SALES (est): 1.44B
SALES (corp-wide): 2.37B **Privately Held**
Web: www.sharp.com
SIC: 8062 General medical and surgical hospitals
PA: Sharp Healthcare
8695 Spectrum Center Blvd
San Diego CA
858 499-4000

(P-16424)
SHERMAN OAKS HEALTH SYSTEM
Also Called: SHERMAN OAKS
4929 Van Nuys Blvd (91403-1702)
PHONE..................818 981-7111
David Levinsohn, *CEO*
EMP: 65 **EST:** 1997
SALES (est): 4.24MM **Privately Held**
Web: www.expertmri.com
SIC: 8062 General medical and surgical hospitals

(P-16425)
SHRINERS HSPITALS FOR CHILDREN
2425 Stockton Blvd (95817-2215)
PHONE..................916 453-2050
Margaret Bryan, *Admn*
EMP: 500
Web: www.shrinerschildrens.org
SIC: 8062 General medical and surgical hospitals
PA: Shriners Hospitals For Children
2900 N Rocky Point Dr
Tampa FL

(P-16426)
SIERRA KINGS DISTRICT HOSPITAL
Also Called: Sierra-Kings Health Care Dst
372 W Cypress Ave (93654-2113)
PHONE..................559 638-8155
▼ **EMP:** 290
Web: www.skdh.org
SIC: 8062 General medical and surgical hospitals

(P-16427)
SIERRA VIEW LOCAL HOSPITAL DST
Also Called: Sierra View District Hospital
283 Pearson Dr (93257-3353)
PHONE..................559 781-7877
Dennis Coleman, *Brnch Mgr*
EMP: 183
SALES (corp-wide): 98.83MM **Privately Held**
Web: www.sierra-view.com
SIC: 8062 General medical and surgical hospitals
PA: Sierra View District Hospital League, Inc.
465 W Putnam Ave
Porterville CA
559 784-1110

(P-16428)
SIERRA VISTA HOSPITAL INC (HQ)
Also Called: Sierra Vista Regional Med Ctr
1010 Murray Ave (93405-8801)
P.O. Box 1367 (93406-1367)
PHONE..................805 546-7600
Joseph Deschryver, *CEO*
Candace Markwith, *
Richard Phillips, *
Rollie Pirkl, *
Michael Keleman, *
EMP: 575 **EST:** 1968
SQ FT: 138,690
SALES (est): 150.01MM
SALES (corp-wide): 19.58B **Publicly Held**
SIC: 8062 General medical and surgical hospitals
PA: Tenet Healthcare Corporation
14201 Dallas Pkwy
Dallas TX
469 893-2200

(P-16429)
SIMI VLY HOSP & HLTH CARE SVCS
Also Called: Aspen Surgery Center
2750 Sycamore Dr (93065-1502)
PHONE..................805 955-6000
EMP: 562
SALES (corp-wide): 789.42MM **Privately Held**
Web: www.adventisthealth.org
SIC: 8062 General medical and surgical hospitals
HQ: Simi Valley Hospital And Health Care Services
2975 Sycamore Dr
Simi Valley CA

(P-16430)
SIMI VLY HOSP & HLTH CARE SVCS (HQ)
Also Called: Simi Vly Hosp & Hlth Care Svcs
2975 Sycamore Dr (93065-1201)
PHONE..................805 955-6000
Margaret Peterson, *Pr*
Caroline Esparza, *
Clif Patten, *
EMP: 228 **EST:** 1960
SALES (est): 199.33MM
SALES (corp-wide): 789.42MM **Privately Held**
Web: www.adventisthealth.org
SIC: 8062 General medical and surgical hospitals
PA: Adventist Health System/West, Corporation
1 Adventist Health Way
Roseville CA
844 574-5686

(P-16431)
SISKIYOU HOSPITAL INC
Also Called: Fairchild Medical Center
444 Bruce St (96097-3450)
PHONE..................530 842-4121
Dwayne Jones, *CEO*
Jonathon C Andrus, *
EMP: 560 **EST:** 1969
SALES (est): 101.23MM **Privately Held**
Web: www.fairchildmed.org
SIC: 8062 General medical and surgical hospitals

(P-16432)
SISTERS OF ST JOSEPH ORANGE
205 East St (95448-4434)

PRODUCTS & SERVICES SECTION
8062 - General Medical And Surgical Hospitals (P-16451)

PHONE.....................707 431-1135
EMP: 3874
SALES (corp-wide): 32.76MM **Privately Held**
Web: www.csjorange.org
SIC: 8062 General medical and surgical hospitals
HQ: Sisters Of St. Joseph Of Orange
480 S Batavia St
Orange CA
714 633-8121

(P-16433)
SOLLIS HEALTH LA PC A MED CORP
1005 Van Ness Ave (94109-6913)
PHONE.....................415 233-9901
Brad Oslon, *CEO*
EMP: 83
SALES (corp-wide): 795.97K **Privately Held**
Web: www.sollishealth.com
SIC: 8062 General medical and surgical hospitals
PA: Sollis Health La, P.C., A Medical Corporation
155 N San Vicente Blvd
Beverly Hills CA
310 870-0400

(P-16434)
SONOMA VALLEY HEALTH CARE DST (PA)
Also Called: Sonoma Valley Hospital
347 Andrieux St (95476-6811)
PHONE.....................707 935-5000
Carl Gerlach, *CEO*
Benjamin Armfield, *
EMP: 445 EST: 1946
SQ FT: 115,000
SALES (est): 49.22MM
SALES (corp-wide): 49.22MM **Privately Held**
Web: www.sonomavalleyhospital.org
SIC: 8062 General medical and surgical hospitals

(P-16435)
SONOMA WEST MEDICAL CENTER
501 Petaluma Ave (95472-4215)
PHONE.....................707 823-8511
EMP: 250
Web: www.sonomawestmedicalcenter.com
SIC: 8062 8051 General medical and surgical hospitals; Skilled nursing care facilities

(P-16436)
SOUTH COAST MEDICAL CENTER (PA)
2100 Douglas Blvd (95661-3804)
PHONE.....................916 781-2000
Bruce Christian, *Pr*
EMP: 690 EST: 1954
SQ FT: 220,000
SALES (est): 24.32MM
SALES (corp-wide): 24.32MM **Privately Held**
SIC: 8062 General medical and surgical hospitals

(P-16437)
SOUTHERN CAL HALTHCARE SYS INC
Also Called: Southern Cal Hosp At Culver Cy
3828 Delmas Ter (90232-2713)
PHONE.....................310 836-7000
EMP: 478

SALES (corp-wide): 3.91B **Privately Held**
SIC: 8062 General medical and surgical hospitals
HQ: Southern California Healthcare System, Inc.
3415 S Sepulveda Blvd 9thfl
Los Angeles CA

(P-16438)
SOUTHERN CAL HALTHCARE SYS INC (HQ)
3415 S Sepulveda Blvd 9th Fl (90034-6060)
PHONE.....................310 943-4500
David R Topper, *CEO*
EMP: 189 EST: 1998
SALES (est): 102.52MM
SALES (corp-wide): 3.91B **Privately Held**
SIC: 8062 General medical and surgical hospitals
PA: Prospect Medical Holdings, Inc.
3415 S Sepulveda Blvd # 9
Los Angeles CA
310 943-4500

(P-16439)
SOUTHERN CAL PRMNNTE MED GROUP
26415 Carl Boyer Dr (91350-5824)
PHONE.....................661 290-3100
EMP: 252
SALES (corp-wide): 68.1B **Privately Held**
Web: www.permanente.org
SIC: 8062 General medical and surgical hospitals
HQ: Southern California Permanente Medical Group
393 Walnut Dr
Pasadena CA
626 405-5704

(P-16440)
SOUTHERN CAL PRMNNTE MED GROUP
Also Called: S C P M G
9961 Sierra Ave (92335-6720)
PHONE.....................909 427-5000
Gerald Mccall, *Brnch Mgr*
EMP: 454
SALES (corp-wide): 68.1B **Privately Held**
Web: www.permanente.org
SIC: 8062 General medical and surgical hospitals
HQ: Southern California Permanente Medical Group
393 Walnut Dr
Pasadena CA
626 405-5704

(P-16441)
SOUTHERN CAL PRMNNTE MED GROUP
Also Called: Kaiser Permanente
9353 Imperial Hwy Garden Medical Bldg Flr 3 (90242-2812)
PHONE.....................562 657-2200
EMP: 475
SALES (corp-wide): 68.1B **Privately Held**
Web: www.permente.org
SIC: 8062 General medical and surgical hospitals
HQ: Southern California Permanente Medical Group
393 Walnut Dr
Pasadena CA
626 405-5704

(P-16442)
SOUTHERN CAL SPCIALTY CARE INC
Also Called: Kindred Hospital Santa Ana
1901 College Ave (92706-2334)
PHONE.....................714 564-7800
Rich Mccarthy, *Prin*
EMP: 250
SALES (corp-wide): 13.68B **Privately Held**
Web: www.kindredhospitals.com
SIC: 8062 General medical and surgical hospitals
HQ: Southern California Specialty Care, Llc
14900 Imperial Hwy
La Mirada CA

(P-16443)
SOUTHERN CAL SPCIALTY CARE INC
Also Called: Kindred Hospital La Mirata
845 N Lark Ellen Ave (91791-1069)
PHONE.....................626 339-5451
Nenda Estudillo, *Dir*
EMP: 250
SQ FT: 34,082
SALES (corp-wide): 13.68B **Privately Held**
SIC: 8062 General medical and surgical hospitals
HQ: Southern California Specialty Care, Llc
14900 Imperial Hwy
La Mirada CA

(P-16444)
SOUTHERN CAL SPCIALTY CARE LLC (DH)
Also Called: Southern Cal Spcialty Care Inc
14900 Imperial Hwy (90638-2172)
PHONE.....................562 944-1900
Ty Richardson, *Pr*
Robin Rapp, *Admn*
Judie Sheldon, *CCO*
George Burkley, *COO*
EMP: 100 EST: 1994
SQ FT: 74,074
SALES (est): 60.81MM
SALES (corp-wide): 13.68B **Privately Held**
SIC: 8062 General medical and surgical hospitals
HQ: Specialty Healthcare Services, Inc
680 S 4th St
Louisville KY
502 596-7300

(P-16445)
SOUTHERN HMBLDT CMNTY DST HOSP
Also Called: Southern Humboldt Cmnty Clinic
733 Cedar St (95542-3201)
PHONE.....................707 923-3921
Deborah Scaife, *Pr*
EMP: 63 EST: 1980
SQ FT: 17,000
SALES (est): 11.72MM **Privately Held**
Web: www.sohumhealth.org
SIC: 8062 General medical and surgical hospitals

(P-16446)
SOUTHERN HMBLDT CMNTY HLTH CAR
733 Cedar St (95542-3201)
PHONE.....................707 923-3921
Matt Rees, *CEO*
Kent Sown, *
Paul Eves, *CFO*
EMP: 85 EST: 2001
SALES (est): 907.29K **Privately Held**
Web: www.sohumhealth.org

SIC: 8062 General medical and surgical hospitals

(P-16447)
SOUTHERN INYO HEALTHCARE DST
501 E Locust St (93545-8044)
PHONE.....................760 876-5501
Peter Spiers, *CEO*
EMP: 112 EST: 1949
SQ FT: 29,000
SALES (est): 23.67MM **Privately Held**
Web: www.sihd.org
SIC: 8062 General medical and surgical hospitals

(P-16448)
SOUTHERN MNTREY CNTY MEM HOSP (PA)
Also Called: GEORGE L MEE MEMORIAL HOSPITAL
300 Canal St (93930-3431)
PHONE.....................831 385-6000
Lex T Smith, *CEO*
Susan Childers, *
Barbara Blalock, *
EMP: 495 EST: 1962
SQ FT: 5,000
SALES (est): 77.06MM
SALES (corp-wide): 77.06MM **Privately Held**
Web: www.meememorial.com
SIC: 8062 Hospital, affiliated with AMA residency

(P-16449)
SOUTHERN MONO HEALTHCARE DST
Also Called: MAMMOTH HOSPITAL
85 Sierra Park Rd (93546-2073)
P.O. Box 660 (93546-0660)
PHONE.....................760 934-3311
EMP: 350 EST: 1978
SQ FT: 20,000
SALES (est): 96.45MM **Privately Held**
Web: www.mammothhospital.org
SIC: 8062 General medical and surgical hospitals

(P-16450)
SOUTHWEST HEALTHCARE SYS AUX
Also Called: Business Department
38977 Sky Canyon Dr Ste 200 (92563-2681)
PHONE.....................800 404-6627
Paula Dalbeck, *Contrlr*
EMP: 712
SALES (corp-wide): 13.4B **Publicly Held**
Web: www.southwesthealthcare.com
SIC: 8062 General medical and surgical hospitals
HQ: Southwest Healthcare System Auxiliary
25500 Medical Center Dr
Murrieta CA

(P-16451)
SOUTHWEST HEALTHCARE SYS AUX (HQ)
Also Called: Rancho Springs Medical Center
25500 Medical Center Dr (92562-5965)
PHONE.....................951 696-6000
Brad Neet, *CEO*
Diane Moon, *
Barry Thorfenson, *
▲ EMP: 450 EST: 1989
SALES (est): 72.54K
SALES (corp-wide): 13.4B **Publicly Held**
Web: www.swranchosprings.com

8062 - General Medical And Surgical Hospitals (P-16452)

PRODUCTS & SERVICES SECTION

SIC: **8062** 8051 8059 4119 General medical and surgical hospitals; Skilled nursing care facilities; Convalescent home; Ambulance service
PA: Universal Health Services, Inc.
367 S Gulph Rd
King Of Prussia PA
610 768-3300

(P-16452)
SRM ALLIANCE HOSPITAL SERVICES (PA)
Also Called: Petaluma Valley Hospital
400 N Mcdowell Blvd (94954-2339)
PHONE.................................707 778-1111
Deborah A Proctor, Pr
Jane Reed, *
EMP: 400 EST: 1996
SQ FT: 50,000
SALES (est): 43.8MM
SALES (corp-wide): 43.8MM **Privately Held**
SIC: **8062** General medical and surgical hospitals

(P-16453)
ST BERNARDINE MED CTR AUX INC
Also Called: Inland Empire Heart Institute
2101 N Waterman Ave (92404-4836)
PHONE.................................909 881-4320
TOLL FREE: 877
Ed Langden, Dir
EMP: 107
Web: www.dignityhealth.org
SIC: **8062** General medical and surgical hospitals
HQ: St. Bernardine Medical Center Auxiliary, Inc.
2101 N Waterman Ave
San Bernardino CA
909 883-8711

(P-16454)
ST BERNARDINE MEDICAL CENTER
2101 N Waterman Ave (92404-4836)
PHONE.................................909 883-8711
Darryl Vandenbosch, Pr
Paul Steinke, CFO
Charlie Abraham, CMO
EMP: 87 EST: 1931
SQ FT: 433,484
SALES (est): 19.9MM **Privately Held**
Web: www.dignityhealth.org
SIC: **8062** General medical and surgical hospitals
HQ: Dignity Health
185 Berry St Ste 200
San Francisco CA
415 438-5500

(P-16455)
ST ELIZABETH COMMUNITY HOSP (DH)
2550 Sister Mary Columba Dr (96080-4327)
PHONE.................................530 529-7760
Todd Smith, CEO
John Halfhide, *
EMP: 201 EST: 1901
SQ FT: 98,000
SALES (est): 95.69MM **Privately Held**
Web: www.dignityhealth.org
SIC: **8062** 6513 General medical and surgical hospitals; Retirement hotel operation
HQ: Dignity Health
185 Berry St Ste 200
San Francisco CA
415 438-5500

(P-16456)
ST FRANCIS MEDICAL CENTER (DH)
Also Called: SFMC
3630 E Imperial Hwy (90262-2609)
P.O. Box 1387 (94070-7387)
PHONE.................................310 900-8900
Clay Farell, CEO
EMP: 354 EST: 2001
SALES (est): 532.13MM
SALES (corp-wide): 1.03B **Privately Held**
Web: www.stfrancismedicalcenter.com
SIC: **8062** General medical and surgical hospitals
HQ: Prime Healthcare Services Inc
3480 E Guasti Rd
Ontario CA

(P-16457)
ST HELENA HOSPITAL (HQ)
Also Called: ADVENTIST HEALTH
10 Woodland Rd (94574-9554)
P.O. Box 619002 (94574)
PHONE.................................707 963-3611
Steven Herber, CEO
Timothy J Kares, *
EMP: 750 EST: 1878
SQ FT: 200,000
SALES (est): 225.3MM
SALES (corp-wide): 789.42MM **Privately Held**
Web: www.adventisthealth.org
SIC: **8062** 8063 General medical and surgical hospitals; Psychiatric hospitals
PA: Adventist Health System/West, Corporation
1 Adventist Health Way
Roseville CA
844 574-5686

(P-16458)
ST JOSEPH HLTH NTHRN CAL LLC
Also Called: St. Joseph Dental
751 Lombardi Ct (95407-6798)
PHONE.................................707 547-2221
Kathy Ficco, Mgr
EMP: 238
SALES (corp-wide): 115.22MM **Privately Held**
SIC: **8062** General medical and surgical hospitals
PA: St. Joseph Health Northern California, Llc
1165 Montgomery Dr
Santa Rosa CA
949 381-4000

(P-16459)
ST JOSEPH HLTH NTHRN CAL LLC
Also Called: Montgomery Center
1170 Montgomery Dr (95405-4802)
PHONE.................................707 542-4704
Anne Katte, Brnch Mgr
EMP: 257
SALES (corp-wide): 115.22MM **Privately Held**
SIC: **8062** General medical and surgical hospitals
PA: St. Joseph Health Northern California, Llc
1165 Montgomery Dr
Santa Rosa CA
949 381-4000

(P-16460)
ST JOSEPH HLTH NTHRN CAL LLC
2700 Dolbeer St (95501-4736)
PHONE.................................707 525-5300
Tory Starr, Brnch Mgr
EMP: 257
SALES (corp-wide): 115.22MM **Privately Held**
Web: www.redwoodmemorial.org
SIC: **8062** General medical and surgical hospitals
PA: St. Joseph Health Northern California, Llc
1165 Montgomery Dr
Santa Rosa CA
949 381-4000

(P-16461)
ST JOSEPH HLTH NTHRN CAL LLC
Also Called: Providence Santa Rosa Mem Hosp
151 Sotoyome St (95405-4803)
PHONE.................................707 921-4717
Richard Afable, Pr
EMP: 257
SALES (corp-wide): 115.22MM **Privately Held**
SIC: **8062** General medical and surgical hospitals
PA: St. Joseph Health Northern California, Llc
1165 Montgomery Dr
Santa Rosa CA
949 381-4000

(P-16462)
ST JOSEPH HLTH NTHRN CAL LLC (PA)
Also Called: Santa Rosa Memorial Hospital
1165 Montgomery Dr (95405-4801)
PHONE.................................949 381-4000
Kevin Klockenga, CEO
EMP: 102 EST: 2016
SALES (est): 115.22MM
SALES (corp-wide): 115.22MM **Privately Held**
Web: www.stjoesonoma.org
SIC: **8062** General medical and surgical hospitals

(P-16463)
ST JOSEPH HOSPITAL
1000 W La Veta Ave (92868-4304)
PHONE.................................714 744-8601
Jay K Harness, Prin
EMP: 191 EST: 2008
SALES (est): 48.67MM **Privately Held**
Web: www.sjo.org
SIC: **8062** General medical and surgical hospitals

(P-16464)
ST JOSEPH HOSPITAL (PA)
2700 Dolbeer St (95501-4799)
PHONE.................................707 445-8121
TOLL FREE: 888
Darian Harris, CEO
David O'brien, Pr
Andrew Rybolt, CFO
▲ EMP: 444 EST: 1920
SQ FT: 125,000
SALES (est): 66.08MM
SALES (corp-wide): 66.08MM **Privately Held**
Web: www.stjoehumboldt.org
SIC: **8062** General medical and surgical hospitals

(P-16465)
ST JOSEPH HOSPITAL
Humboldt Central Laboratory
2700 Dolbeer St (95501-4799)
PHONE.................................707 445-8121
Sandeep Talwar, Owner
EMP: 101
SQ FT: 6,000
SALES (corp-wide): 66.08MM **Privately Held**
Web: www.stjoehumboldt.org
SIC: **8062** 8071 General medical and surgical hospitals; Pathological laboratory
PA: St. Joseph Hospital
2700 Dolbeer St
Eureka CA
707 445-8121

(P-16466)
ST JOSEPH HOSPITAL
Radiation Oncology Department
2700 Dolbeer St (95501-4799)
PHONE.................................707 445-8121
Doctor John W Harris, Dir
EMP: 101
SALES (corp-wide): 66.08MM **Privately Held**
Web: www.stjoehumboldt.org
SIC: **8062** 8011 General medical and surgical hospitals; Oncologist
PA: St. Joseph Hospital
2700 Dolbeer St
Eureka CA
707 445-8121

(P-16467)
ST JOSEPH HOSPITAL
Also Called: Neurosurgery
2752 Harrison Ave Ste A (95501-4738)
PHONE.................................707 268-0190
Maureen Lawlor, Mgr
EMP: 101
SALES (corp-wide): 66.08MM **Privately Held**
Web: www.stjoehumboldt.org
SIC: **8062** General medical and surgical hospitals
PA: St. Joseph Hospital
2700 Dolbeer St
Eureka CA
707 445-8121

(P-16468)
ST JOSEPH HOSPITAL
Also Called: Center For Women's Health Care
3645 E St (95503-5330)
PHONE.................................707 445-8121
Maggie Selenski, Dir
EMP: 101
SALES (corp-wide): 66.08MM **Privately Held**
Web: www.stjoehumboldt.org
SIC: **8062** 8011 General medical and surgical hospitals; Surgeon
PA: St. Joseph Hospital
2700 Dolbeer St
Eureka CA
707 445-8121

(P-16469)
ST JOSEPH HOSPITAL OF EUREKA
2700 Dolbeer St (95501-4736)
P.O. Box 5600 (92863-5600)
PHONE.................................707 445-8121
EMP: 667 EST: 2011
SALES (est): 149.63MM
SALES (corp-wide): 32.76MM **Privately Held**
Web: www.stjoehumboldt.org

PRODUCTS & SERVICES SECTION
8062 - General Medical And Surgical Hospitals (P-16487)

SIC: **8062** General medical and surgical hospitals
HQ: St. Joseph Hospital Of Orange
1100 W Stewart Dr
Orange CA
714 633-9111

(P-16470)
ST JOSEPH HOSPITAL OF ORANGE
Also Called: St Josephs Physical Rehab Svcs
1310 W Stewart Dr Ste 203 (92868-3837)
PHONE.................714 771-8222
Paul Pursell, *Ex Dir*
EMP: 91
SALES (corp-wide): 32.76MM **Privately Held**
Web: www.sjo.org
SIC: **8062** 8322 General medical and surgical hospitals; Rehabilitation services
HQ: St. Joseph Hospital Of Orange
1100 W Stewart Dr
Orange CA
714 633-9111

(P-16471)
ST JOSEPH HOSPITAL OF ORANGE
Also Called: Information Systems
363 S Main St Ste 211 (92868-3825)
PHONE.................714 771-8006
Dennise Masiello, *Dir*
EMP: 98
SQ FT: 15,605
SALES (corp-wide): 32.76MM **Privately Held**
Web: www.sjo.org
SIC: **8062** General medical and surgical hospitals
HQ: St. Joseph Hospital Of Orange
1100 W Stewart Dr
Orange CA
714 633-9111

(P-16472)
ST JOSEPH HOSPITAL OF ORANGE (DH)
1100 W Stewart Dr (92868-3891)
P.O. Box 5600 (92863-5600)
PHONE.................714 633-9111
Larry K Ainsworth, *Pr*
Jim Cora, *
Warren D Johnson, *
Tina Nycroft, *
Martin J Feldman, *Chief of Staff*
EMP: 2100 EST: 1929
SQ FT: 448,000
SALES (est): 627.27MM
SALES (corp-wide): 32.76MM **Privately Held**
Web: www.sjo.org
SIC: **8062** General medical and surgical hospitals
HQ: St. Joseph Health System
3345 Michelson Dr Ste 100
Irvine CA
949 381-4000

(P-16473)
ST JOSEPH HOSPITAL OF ORANGE
Also Called: Business Office
3345 Michelson Dr Ste 100 (92612-0693)
PHONE.................714 568-5500
Marina Lopez, *Mgr*
EMP: 127
SALES (corp-wide): 32.76MM **Privately Held**
Web: www.sjo.org

SIC: **8062** General medical and surgical hospitals
HQ: St. Joseph Hospital Of Orange
1100 W Stewart Dr
Orange CA
714 633-9111

(P-16474)
ST JOSEPH HOSPITAL OF ORANGE
Also Called: Renal Center
1100 W Stewart Dr (92868-3891)
P.O. Box 5600 (92863-5600)
PHONE.................714 771-8037
Mary Mckenzie, *Dir*
EMP: 88
SALES (corp-wide): 32.76MM **Privately Held**
Web: www.sjo.org
SIC: **8062** General medical and surgical hospitals
HQ: St. Joseph Hospital Of Orange
1100 W Stewart Dr
Orange CA
714 633-9111

(P-16475)
ST JOSEPHS BEHAVIORAL HLTH CTR (DH)
2510 N California St (95204-5502)
PHONE.................209 462-2826
Paul Rains, *Pr*
EMP: 73 EST: 1984
SALES (est): 47.51MM **Privately Held**
Web: www.dignityhealth.org
SIC: **8062** General medical and surgical hospitals
HQ: Dignity Health
185 Berry St Ste 200
San Francisco CA
415 438-5500

(P-16476)
ST JOSEPHS MED CTR STOCKTON
1800 N California St (95204-6019)
P.O. Box 213008 (95213-9008)
PHONE.................209 943-2000
Donald J Wiley, *Pr*
EMP: 2366 EST: 1899
SALES (est): 230.14MM **Privately Held**
SIC: **8062** General medical and surgical hospitals
HQ: Dignity Health
185 Berry St Ste 200
San Francisco CA
415 438-5500

(P-16477)
ST JOSEPHS MEDICAL CENTER INC
Also Called: A Hospital
1800 N California St (95204-6019)
P.O. Box 213008 (95213-9008)
PHONE.................209 943-2000
Donald J Wiley, *Pr*
Kathy Tohrnan, *STRATEGY**
Abby Newton V Pres Foundation, *Prin*
Nancy Vargas, *
Doctor Susan Mcdonald, *Medical Affairs Vice President*
EMP: 150 EST: 1995
SQ FT: 18,000
SALES (est): 100.65MM **Privately Held**
Web: www.dignityhealth.org
SIC: **8062** General medical and surgical hospitals
HQ: Dignity Health
185 Berry St Ste 200
San Francisco CA
415 438-5500

(P-16478)
ST JUDE HOSPITAL (DH)
Also Called: St Jude Medical Center
101 E Valencia Mesa Dr (92835-3875)
PHONE.................714 871-3280
TOLL FREE: 800
Robert Fraschetti, *Pr*
Lee Penrose, *
Doreen Dann, *
▲ EMP: 2582 EST: 1942
SQ FT: 190,000
SALES (est): 791.38MM
SALES (corp-wide): 32.76MM **Privately Held**
Web: www.stjudemedicalcenter.org
SIC: **8062** General medical and surgical hospitals
HQ: St. Joseph Health System
3345 Michelson Dr Ste 100
Irvine CA
949 381-4000

(P-16479)
ST LUKES HEALTH CARE CENTER
Also Called: St Lukes Neighborhood Clinic
1580 Valencia St Ste 506 (94110-4418)
PHONE.................415 647-8600
Judy Li, *Admn*
EMP: 101 EST: 1977
SALES (est): 4.94MM **Privately Held**
Web: www.cpmc.org
SIC: **8062** General medical and surgical hospitals

(P-16480)
ST LUKES HOSPITAL
2351 Clay St (94115-1931)
PHONE.................415 600-3959
EMP: 810
Web: www.unitypoint.org
SIC: **8062** General medical and surgical hospitals

(P-16481)
ST MARY MEDICAL CENTER (DH)
Also Called: St Mary's School of Nursing
1050 Linden Ave (90813-3321)
P.O. Box 887 (90801-0887)
PHONE.................562 491-9000
Trammie Mcmann, *CEO*
Tammie Mcmann, *CEO*
Ed S Engessers, *
Alan Garrett, *
Tiffany Caster, *
EMP: 1929 EST: 1924
SQ FT: 700,000
SALES (est): 254.75MM **Privately Held**
Web: www.stmarymed.com
SIC: **8062** Hospital, med school affiliated with nursing and residency
HQ: Dignity Health
185 Berry St Ste 200
San Francisco CA
415 438-5500

(P-16482)
ST MARY MEDICAL CENTER LLC
Also Called: Materals MGT At St Mary Med Ct
16000 Kasota Rd (92307)
P.O. Box 7025 (92307-0731)
PHONE.................760 946-8767
Leland Glisson, *Mgr*
EMP: 808
SALES (corp-wide): 377.15MM **Privately Held**
Web: www.stmaryapplevalley.com

SIC: **8062** General medical and surgical hospitals
PA: St. Mary Medical Center, Llc
18300 Us Highway 18
Apple Valley CA
760 242-2311

(P-16483)
ST MARY MEDICAL CENTER LLC (PA)
18300 Us Highway 18 (92307-2206)
PHONE.................760 242-2311
David Klein, *Pr*
Marilyn Drone, *
Tracey Fernandez, *
Kelly Linden, *
Judy Wagner, *
EMP: 542 EST: 1956
SQ FT: 92,000
SALES (est): 377.15MM
SALES (corp-wide): 377.15MM **Privately Held**
Web: www.stmaryapplevalley.com
SIC: **8062** General medical and surgical hospitals

(P-16484)
ST MARYS MED CTR FOUNDATION
450 Stanyan St (94117-1019)
P.O. Box 2400 (85002-2400)
PHONE.................415 668-1000
Ken Steele, *Pr*
James Wentz, *
EMP: 209 EST: 1983
SALES (est): 3.9MM **Privately Held**
Web: www.supportstmaryssf.org
SIC: **8062** Hospital, professional nursing school
HQ: Dignity Health
185 Berry St Ste 200
San Francisco CA
415 438-5500

(P-16485)
ST MARYS MEDICAL CENTER INC
Also Called: Surgery Department
450 Stanyan St (94117-1019)
PHONE.................415 668-1000
Ken Steele, *Pr*
EMP: 5032
SALES (corp-wide): 19.58B **Publicly Held**
Web: www.paleyinstitute.org
SIC: **8062** Hospital, affiliated with AMA residency
HQ: St. Mary's Medical Center, Inc.
901 45th St
Mangonia Park FL
561 844-6300

(P-16486)
STANFORD HEALTH CARE
Also Called: Stanford Schl Mdcine Jay McHae
1000 Welch Rd Ste 300 (94304-1812)
PHONE.................650 723-5171
EMP: 748
SALES (corp-wide): 15.13B **Privately Held**
Web: www.stanfordhealthcare.org
SIC: **8062** General medical and surgical hospitals
HQ: Stanford Health Care
300 Pasteur Dr
Stanford CA
650 723-4000

(P-16487)
STANFORD HEALTH CARE
300 Pasteur Dr (94305-2200)

8062 - General Medical And Surgical Hospitals (P-16488)

PHONE......................650 736-6661
EMP: 1382
SALES (corp-wide): 15.13B **Privately Held**
Web: www.stanfordhealthcare.org
SIC: 8062 General medical and surgical hospitals
HQ: Stanford Health Care
300 Pasteur Dr
Stanford CA
650 723-4000

(P-16488)
STANFORD HEALTH CARE
725 Welch Rd (94304-1601)
PHONE......................650 497-8953
EMP: 1383
SALES (corp-wide): 15.13B **Privately Held**
Web: www.stanfordhealthcare.org
SIC: 8062 General medical and surgical hospitals
HQ: Stanford Health Care
300 Pasteur Dr
Stanford CA
650 723-4000

(P-16489)
STANFORD HEALTH CARE
Hospital and Professional Svcs
300 Pasteur Dr (94305-2200)
PHONE......................650 723-4000
Noel Juaire, *Dir*
EMP: 112
SALES (corp-wide): 15.13B **Privately Held**
Web: www.stanfordhealthcare.org
SIC: 8062 General medical and surgical hospitals
HQ: Stanford Health Care
300 Pasteur Dr
Stanford CA
650 723-4000

(P-16490)
STANFORD HEALTH CARE
Also Called: Stanford Hospital
500 Pasteur Dr (94304-1048)
PHONE......................650 723-8561
EMP: 430
SALES (corp-wide): 15.13B **Privately Held**
Web: www.stanfordhealthcare.org
SIC: 8062 General medical and surgical hospitals
HQ: Stanford Health Care
300 Pasteur Dr
Stanford CA
650 723-4000

(P-16491)
STANFORD HEALTH CARE
Also Called: Shc Reference Laboratory
3375 Hillview Ave (94304-1204)
PHONE......................650 736-7844
EMP: 446
SALES (corp-wide): 15.13B **Privately Held**
Web: www.stanfordhealthcare.org
SIC: 8062 General medical and surgical hospitals
HQ: Stanford Health Care
300 Pasteur Dr
Stanford CA
650 723-4000

(P-16492)
STANFORD HEALTH CARE
1510 Page Mill Rd Ste 2 (94304-1133)
PHONE......................650 213-8360
Martha Marsh, *Pr*
EMP: 263
SALES (corp-wide): 15.13B **Privately Held**
Web: www.stanfordhealthcare.org
SIC: 8062 Hospital, medical school affiliated with residency
HQ: Stanford Health Care
300 Pasteur Dr
Stanford CA
650 723-4000

(P-16493)
STANFORD HEALTH CARE
Also Called: Quality Management
300 Pasteur Dr (94305-2200)
PHONE......................650 723-4000
EMP: 2523
SALES (corp-wide): 15.13B **Privately Held**
Web: www.stanfordhealthcare.org
SIC: 8062 8099 Hospital, medical school affiliated with residency; Childbirth preparation clinic
HQ: Stanford Health Care
300 Pasteur Dr
Stanford CA
650 723-4000

(P-16494)
STANFORD HEALTH CARE
Also Called: Stanford Cancer Center S Bay
2589 Samaritan Dr (95124-4102)
PHONE......................408 426-4900
Patrick Swift Md, *Brnch Mgr*
EMP: 858
SALES (corp-wide): 15.13B **Privately Held**
Web: www.stanfordhealthcare.org
SIC: 8062 Hospital, medical school affiliated with residency
HQ: Stanford Health Care
300 Pasteur Dr
Stanford CA
650 723-4000

(P-16495)
STANFORD HEALTH CARE
Valleycare Medical Center
5555 W Las Positas Blvd (94588-4000)
PHONE......................925 847-3000
David Entwistle, *CEO*
EMP: 881
SALES (corp-wide): 15.13B **Privately Held**
Web: www.stanfordhealthcare.org
SIC: 8062 Hospital, medical school affiliated with residency
HQ: Stanford Health Care
300 Pasteur Dr
Stanford CA
650 723-4000

(P-16496)
STANFORD HEALTH CARE
1300 Crane St (94025-4260)
PHONE......................650 498-7489
Karli Cleary D.o.s., *Brnch Mgr*
EMP: 82
SALES (corp-wide): 15.13B **Privately Held**
Web: www.stanfordhealthcare.org
SIC: 8062 Hospital, medical school affiliated with residency
HQ: Stanford Health Care
300 Pasteur Dr
Stanford CA
650 723-4000

(P-16497)
STANFORD HEALTH CARE (HQ)
Also Called: Stanford Medical Center
300 Pasteur Dr (94305-2200)
PHONE......................650 723-4000
David Entwistle, *CEO*
Marc E Jones, *
Lynda Hoff, *
Erica Yabokla, *CDO**
Norman Rizk Md, *CMO*
▲ **EMP:** 1027 **EST:** 1957
SALES (est): 7.41B
SALES (corp-wide): 15.13B **Privately Held**
Web: www.stanfordhealthcare.org
SIC: 8062 Hospital, medical school affiliated with residency
PA: Leland Stanford Junior University
450 Jane Stanford Way
Stanford CA
650 723-2300

(P-16498)
STANFORD HEALTH CARE
Also Called: Stanford Hlth Care Ctr For Edc
1850 Embarcadero Rd Ste B (94303-3308)
PHONE......................650 723-4000
EMP: 101
SALES (corp-wide): 15.13B **Privately Held**
Web: www.stanfordhealthcare.org
SIC: 8062 Hospital, medical school affiliation
HQ: Stanford Health Care
300 Pasteur Dr
Stanford CA
650 723-4000

(P-16499)
STANFORD HLTH CARE TRI-VALLEY
Also Called: Stanford Hlth Care - Vlleycare
1119 E Stanley Blvd (94550-4115)
PHONE......................925 447-7000
Marcy Feit, *Brnch Mgr*
EMP: 137
SALES (corp-wide): 15.13B **Privately Held**
Web: www.stanfordhealthcare.org
SIC: 8062 General medical and surgical hospitals
HQ: Stanford Health Care Tri-Valley
5555 W Las Positas Blvd
Pleasanton CA
925 847-3000

(P-16500)
STANISLAUS SURGICAL HOSP LLC (PA)
Also Called: Stanislaus Surgical Center
1421 Oakdale Rd (95355-3398)
PHONE......................209 572-2700
Douglas V Johnson, *CEO*
Timothy J Noakes, *Managing Member*
EMP: 140 **EST:** 1985
SQ FT: 50,000
SALES (est): 27MM
SALES (corp-wide): 27MM **Privately Held**
Web: www.stanislaussurgical.com
SIC: 8062 General medical and surgical hospitals

(P-16501)
SUMMIT MEDICAL CENTER
Also Called: Skilled Nursing Facility
3100 Summit St (94609-3412)
PHONE......................510 869-6758
Kathy Delaney, *Pr*
EMP: 200
SQ FT: 600
SALES (corp-wide): 14.77B **Privately Held**
Web: www.sutterhealth.org
SIC: 8062 General medical and surgical hospitals
HQ: Summit Medical Center
350 Hawthorne Ave
Oakland CA
510 655-4000

(P-16502)
SUMMIT MEDICAL CENTER (DH)
Also Called: SURGERY CENTER OF ALTA BATES S
350 Hawthorne Ave (94609-3108)
PHONE......................510 655-4000
EMP: 2000 **EST:** 1891
SALES (est): 511.48MM
SALES (corp-wide): 14.77B **Privately Held**
Web: www.sutterhealth.org
SIC: 8062 8221 5947 Hospital, professional nursing school; Professional schools; Gift, novelty, and souvenir shop
HQ: The Surgery Center Of Alta Bates Summit Medical Center Llc
2450 Ashby Ave
Berkeley CA
510 204-4444

(P-16503)
SUMMIT MEDICAL GROUP
350 Hawthorne Ave (94609-3108)
PHONE......................510 655-4000
Anthony Ravnik, *Pr*
EMP: 83 **EST:** 1980
SQ FT: 10,581
SALES (est): 2.13MM **Privately Held**
Web: www.altabatessummit.org
SIC: 8062 General medical and surgical hospitals

(P-16504)
SURGERY CTR OF ALTA BTES SMMIT (HQ)
Also Called: Alta Bates Summit Medical Ctr
2450 Ashby Ave (94705-2067)
PHONE......................510 204-4444
Warren Kirk, *Pr*
Robert Petrina, *
EMP: 653 **EST:** 1936
SQ FT: 749,000
SALES (est): 517.5MM
SALES (corp-wide): 14.77B **Privately Held**
Web: www.altabatessummit.org
SIC: 8062 General medical and surgical hospitals
PA: Sutter Health
2200 River Plaza Dr
Sacramento CA
916 733-8800

(P-16505)
SURPRISE VALLEY HLTH CARE DST
741 Main St (96104-1038)
P.O. Box 246 (96104-0246)
PHONE......................530 279-6111
Wanda Grove, *CEO*
Jason Diven, *
Carl Quigley, *
Cindy Linker, *
Bunne Hartmann, *
EMP: 72 **EST:** 1984
SQ FT: 13,330
SALES (est): 9.14MM **Privately Held**
Web: www.svhospital.org
SIC: 8062 General medical and surgical hospitals

(P-16506)
SUTTER AMADOR WOMENS SERVICES
Also Called: SUTTER AMADOR WOMENS SERVICES
255 New York Ranch Rd Ste C (95642-2171)
PHONE......................209 223-2034
Pat Simonson, *Brnch Mgr*
EMP: 989
SALES (corp-wide): 14.77B **Privately Held**
Web: www.sutteramador.org
SIC: 8062 General medical and surgical hospitals
HQ: Sutter Amador Women's Service
100 Mission Blvd Ste 2800

PRODUCTS & SERVICES SECTION
8062 - General Medical And Surgical Hospitals (P-16525)

Jackson CA
209 257-0177

(P-16507)
SUTTER BAY HOSPITALS (HQ)
Also Called: SUTTER C H S
475 Brannan St Ste 130 (94107-1731)
P.O. Box 7999 (94120-7999)
PHONE..............................415 600-6000
Jeff Gerard, *CEO*
Martin Brotman, *
EMP: 2578 **EST:** 1885
SALES (est): 4.84B
SALES (corp-wide): 14.77B **Privately Held**
Web: www.cpmcri.org
SIC: 8062 General medical and surgical hospitals
PA: Sutter Health
2200 River Plaza Dr
Sacramento CA
916 733-8800

(P-16508)
SUTTER BAY HOSPITALS
Also Called: Alta Bates Summit Medical Ctr
2420 Ashby Ave (94705-2002)
PHONE..............................510 869-6199
Sarah Love, *Prin*
EMP: 85
SALES (corp-wide): 14.77B **Privately Held**
Web: www.sutterhealth.org
SIC: 8062 General medical and surgical hospitals
HQ: Sutter Bay Hospitals
475 Brannan St Ste 130
San Francisco CA
415 600-6000

(P-16509)
SUTTER BAY HOSPITALS
Califrnia PCF Stnley Hlth Cntr
3801 Sacramento St Ste 61 (94118-1625)
PHONE..............................415 600-2403
Joyce Hansen, *Dir*
EMP: 113
SALES (corp-wide): 14.77B **Privately Held**
Web: www.cpmcri.org
SIC: 8062 General medical and surgical hospitals
HQ: Sutter Bay Hospitals
475 Brannan St Ste 130
San Francisco CA
415 600-6000

(P-16510)
SUTTER BAY HOSPITALS
Also Called: Alta Bates Summit Medical Ctr
350 Hawthorne Ave (94609-3108)
PHONE..............................510 655-4000
David Clark, *Brnch Mgr*
EMP: 113
SALES (corp-wide): 14.77B **Privately Held**
Web: www.altabatessummit.org
SIC: 8062 General medical and surgical hospitals
HQ: Sutter Bay Hospitals
475 Brannan St Ste 130
San Francisco CA
415 600-6000

(P-16511)
SUTTER BAY HOSPITALS
Also Called: Sutter Maternity & Surgery
2025 Soquel Ave (95062-1323)
PHONE..............................831 423-4111
EMP: 84
SALES (corp-wide): 14.77B **Privately Held**
Web: www.cpmcri.org
SIC: 8062 General medical and surgical hospitals
HQ: Sutter Bay Hospitals
475 Brannan St Ste 130
San Francisco CA
415 600-6000

(P-16512)
SUTTER CENTRAL VLY HOSPITALS
Also Called: Memorial Medical Center
1200 Scenic Dr Ste 200 (95350-6167)
PHONE..............................209 572-5900
EMP: 995
SALES (corp-wide): 14.77B **Privately Held**
Web: www.sutterhealth.org
SIC: 8062 General medical and surgical hospitals
HQ: Sutter Central Valley Hospitals
1700 Coffee Rd
Modesto CA
209 526-4500

(P-16513)
SUTTER CENTRAL VLY HOSPITALS (HQ)
Also Called: Memorial Medical Center
1700 Coffee Rd (95355-2803)
P.O. Box 942 (95353-0942)
PHONE..............................209 526-4500
James Conforti, *CEO*
Eric Dalton, *
Steve Mitchell, *
David P Benn, *
Todd Smith, *
EMP: 112 **EST:** 1947
SQ FT: 180,000
SALES (est): 772MM
SALES (corp-wide): 14.77B **Privately Held**
Web: www.sutterhealth.org
SIC: 8062 General medical and surgical hospitals
PA: Sutter Health
2200 River Plaza Dr
Sacramento CA
916 733-8800

(P-16514)
SUTTER CENTRAL VLY HOSPITALS
Also Called: Medi-Flight Northern Cal
1700 Coffee Rd (95355-2803)
PHONE..............................209 526-4500
Terry Sweeney, *Dir*
EMP: 988
SALES (corp-wide): 14.77B **Privately Held**
Web: www.sutterhealth.org
SIC: 8062 General medical and surgical hospitals
HQ: Sutter Central Valley Hospitals
1700 Coffee Rd
Modesto CA
209 526-4500

(P-16515)
SUTTER CENTRAL VLY HOSPITALS
1316 Celeste Dr Ste 104 (95355-2437)
PHONE..............................209 572-8270
David Benn, *CEO*
EMP: 861
SALES (corp-wide): 14.77B **Privately Held**
Web: www.sutterhealth.org
SIC: 8062 General medical and surgical hospitals
HQ: Sutter Central Valley Hospitals
1700 Coffee Rd
Modesto CA
209 526-4500

(P-16516)
SUTTER CENTRAL VLY HOSPITALS
1800 Coffee Rd Ste 30 (95355-2700)
P.O. Box 942 (95353-0942)
PHONE..............................209 569-7544
David P Benn, *Brnch Mgr*
EMP: 1052
SQ FT: 65,294
SALES (corp-wide): 14.77B **Privately Held**
Web: www.sutterhealth.org
SIC: 8062 Hospital, AMA approved residency
HQ: Sutter Central Valley Hospitals
1700 Coffee Rd
Modesto CA
209 526-4500

(P-16517)
SUTTER COAST HOSPITAL (HQ)
800 E Washington Blvd (95531-8359)
PHONE..............................707 464-8511
Eugene Suksi, *Pr*
Jim Strong, *
▲ **EMP:** 250 **EST:** 1985
SQ FT: 70,000
SALES (est): 108MM
SALES (corp-wide): 14.77B **Privately Held**
Web: www.suttercoast.org
SIC: 8062 General medical and surgical hospitals
PA: Sutter Health
2200 River Plaza Dr
Sacramento CA
916 733-8800

(P-16518)
SUTTER DELTA MEDICAL CENTER
3901 Lone Tree Way (94509-6200)
P.O. Box 3225 (94531-3225)
PHONE..............................925 779-7200
Linda Lee Rovai, *Pr*
Janice Falzano, *Assistant Administrator Finance*
Phil Gardiner, *
Tim Boslog, *
Admiral Linda Horn, *Prin*
EMP: 233 **EST:** 1927
SQ FT: 150,000
SALES (est): 221.66MM **Privately Held**
Web: www.sutterdelta.org
SIC: 8062 8082 8093 8069 General medical and surgical hospitals; Home health care services; Specialty outpatient clinics, nec; Orthopedic hospital

(P-16519)
SUTTER HEALTH
Also Called: Mamone James M
2 Medical Plaza Dr (95661-3043)
PHONE..............................916 797-4725
EMP: 107
SALES (corp-wide): 14.77B **Privately Held**
Web: www.sutterroseville.org
SIC: 8062 General medical and surgical hospitals
PA: Sutter Health
2200 River Plaza Dr
Sacramento CA
916 733-8800

(P-16520)
SUTTER HEALTH
Also Called: Cpmc
2395 Sacramento St (94115-2328)
P.O. Box 7999 (94120-7999)
PHONE..............................415 600-7034
EMP: 80
SALES (corp-wide): 14.77B **Privately Held**
Web: www.sutterhealth.org

SIC: 8062 8051 8011 6513 General medical and surgical hospitals; Skilled nursing care facilities; Offices and clinics of medical doctors; Retirement hotel operation
PA: Sutter Health
2200 River Plaza Dr
Sacramento CA
916 733-8800

(P-16521)
SUTTER HEALTH
1020 29th St Ste 600 (95816-5109)
PHONE..............................916 733-9588
EMP: 89
SALES (corp-wide): 14.77B **Privately Held**
Web: www.sutterhealth.org
SIC: 8062 General medical and surgical hospitals
PA: Sutter Health
2200 River Plaza Dr
Sacramento CA
916 733-8800

(P-16522)
SUTTER HEALTH
3901 Lone Tree Way (94509-6200)
PHONE..............................925 779-7273
EMP: 160
SALES (corp-wide): 14.77B **Privately Held**
Web: www.sutterhealth.org
SIC: 8062 General medical and surgical hospitals
PA: Sutter Health
2200 River Plaza Dr
Sacramento CA
916 733-8800

(P-16523)
SUTTER HEALTH
1301 Mission St (95060-3530)
PHONE..............................831 458-6310
EMP: 80
SALES (corp-wide): 14.77B **Privately Held**
Web: www.sutterhealth.org
SIC: 8062 General medical and surgical hospitals
PA: Sutter Health
2200 River Plaza Dr
Sacramento CA
916 733-8800

(P-16524)
SUTTER HEALTH
2340 Clay St Rm 121 (94115-1932)
P.O. Box 7999 (94120-7999)
PHONE..............................415 600-1020
EMP: 142
SALES (corp-wide): 14.77B **Privately Held**
Web: www.cpmc.org
SIC: 8062 General medical and surgical hospitals
PA: Sutter Health
2200 River Plaza Dr
Sacramento CA
916 733-8800

(P-16525)
SUTTER HEALTH
2880 Gateway Oaks Dr Ste 220 (95833-4338)
PHONE..............................916 566-4819
Vicki Flemming, *Brnch Mgr*
EMP: 213
SALES (corp-wide): 14.77B **Privately Held**
Web: www.suttermedicalcenter.org
SIC: 8062 General medical and surgical hospitals
PA: Sutter Health
2200 River Plaza Dr
Sacramento CA
916 733-8800

8062 - General Medical And Surgical Hospitals (P-16526)

(P-16526)
SUTTER HEALTH
Also Called: Sutter Elk Grove Surgery Ctr
8200 Laguna Blvd (95758-7956)
PHONE..................................916 544-5423
EMP: 80
SALES (corp-wide): 14.77B **Privately Held**
Web: www.suttermedicalcenter.org
SIC: 8062 General medical and surgical hospitals
PA: Sutter Health
2200 River Plaza Dr
Sacramento CA
916 733-8800

(P-16527)
SUTTER HEALTH
2015 Steiner St Fl 1 (94115-2627)
PHONE..................................415 600-4280
Dorothy Coleman-riese Md, *Pr*
EMP: 98
SALES (corp-wide): 14.77B **Privately Held**
Web: www.sutterpacific.org
SIC: 8062 General medical and surgical hospitals
PA: Sutter Health
2200 River Plaza Dr
Sacramento CA
916 733-8800

(P-16528)
SUTTER HEALTH
Also Called: Eden Medical Center
20103 Lake Chabot Rd (94546-5305)
PHONE..................................510 537-1234
Patricia Ryan, *CEO*
EMP: 763
SALES (corp-wide): 14.77B **Privately Held**
Web: www.edenmedcenter.org
SIC: 8062 General medical and surgical hospitals
PA: Sutter Health
2200 River Plaza Dr
Sacramento CA
916 733-8800

(P-16529)
SUTTER HEALTH
100 Rowland Way Ste 210 (94945-5040)
PHONE..................................415 897-8495
Vicki Del, *Brnch Mgr*
EMP: 178
SALES (corp-wide): 14.77B **Privately Held**
Web: www.sutterhealth.org
SIC: 8062 General medical and surgical hospitals
PA: Sutter Health
2200 River Plaza Dr
Sacramento CA
916 733-8800

(P-16530)
SUTTER HEALTH
2700 Gateway Oaks Dr (95833-4337)
PHONE..................................707 864-4660
Marcia Reissig, *Brnch Mgr*
EMP: 71
SALES (corp-wide): 14.77B **Privately Held**
Web: www.suttermedicalcenter.org
SIC: 8062 General medical and surgical hospitals
PA: Sutter Health
2200 River Plaza Dr
Sacramento CA
916 733-8800

(P-16531)
SUTTER HEALTH
3875 Telegraph Ave (94609-2428)
PHONE..................................510 547-2244
Aaron Adams, *Brnch Mgr*
EMP: 685
SALES (corp-wide): 14.77B **Privately Held**
Web: www.altabatessummit.org
SIC: 8062 General medical and surgical hospitals
PA: Sutter Health
2200 River Plaza Dr
Sacramento CA
916 733-8800

(P-16532)
SUTTER HEALTH
3000 Telegraph Ave (94609-3218)
PHONE..................................510 869-8777
Stefan Arnold, *Brnch Mgr*
EMP: 62
SALES (corp-wide): 14.77B **Privately Held**
Web: www.sutterhealth.org
SIC: 8062 General medical and surgical hospitals
PA: Sutter Health
2200 River Plaza Dr
Sacramento CA
916 733-8800

(P-16533)
SUTTER HEALTH
Also Called: Cpmc Van Ness Campus
1101 Van Ness Ave (94109-6919)
PHONE..................................415 600-6000
EMP: 71
SALES (corp-wide): 14.77B **Privately Held**
Web: www.sutterhealth.org
SIC: 8062 General medical and surgical hospitals
PA: Sutter Health
2200 River Plaza Dr
Sacramento CA
916 733-8800

(P-16534)
SUTTER HEALTH (PA)
Also Called: Sutter Health Sacsierra Region
2200 River Plaza Dr (95833-4134)
PHONE..................................916 733-8800
Patrick Fry, *Pr*
Jim Gray, *
Gordon Hunt Md, *Chief Medical Officer*
Gary F Loveridge, *Sr VP*
Robert D Reed, *Sr VP*
EMP: 900 EST: 1981
SALES (est): 14.77B
SALES (corp-wide): 14.77B **Privately Held**
Web: www.sutterhealth.org
SIC: 8062 8051 8011 6513 General medical and surgical hospitals; Skilled nursing care facilities; Offices and clinics of medical doctors; Retirement hotel operation

(P-16535)
SUTTER HEALTH
50 S San Mateo Dr Ste 470 (94401-3833)
PHONE..................................650 262-4262
EMP: 71
SALES (corp-wide): 14.77B **Privately Held**
Web: www.sutterhealth.org
SIC: 8062 General medical and surgical hospitals
PA: Sutter Health
2200 River Plaza Dr
Sacramento CA
916 733-8800

(P-16536)
SUTTER HEALTH
Also Called: Cpmc Mission Bernal Campus
1580 Valencia St Ste 237 (94110-4430)
PHONE..................................415 600-6000
Warren Browner Md, *CEO*
EMP: 169
SALES (corp-wide): 14.77B **Privately Held**
Web: www.sutterhealth.org
SIC: 8062 General medical and surgical hospitals
PA: Sutter Health
2200 River Plaza Dr
Sacramento CA
916 733-8800

(P-16537)
SUTTER HEALTH
2333 Buchanan St (94115-1925)
PHONE..................................415 600-6000
Michael P Holdsworth, *Mgr*
EMP: 107
SALES (corp-wide): 14.77B **Privately Held**
Web: www.sutterhealth.org
SIC: 8062 General medical and surgical hospitals
PA: Sutter Health
2200 River Plaza Dr
Sacramento CA
916 733-8800

(P-16538)
SUTTER HEALTH
701 E El Camino Real (94040-2833)
PHONE..................................650 934-7000
Ronald Hess, *Brnch Mgr*
EMP: 62
SALES (corp-wide): 14.77B **Privately Held**
Web: www.sutterhealth.org
SIC: 8062 General medical and surgical hospitals
PA: Sutter Health
2200 River Plaza Dr
Sacramento CA
916 733-8800

(P-16539)
SUTTER HEALTH
Also Called: Sutter Occupational Hlth Svcs
3 Medical Plaza Dr Ste 100 (95661-3088)
PHONE..................................916 797-4700
Dave Gladden, *Brnch Mgr*
EMP: 107
SALES (corp-wide): 14.77B **Privately Held**
Web: www.sutterhealth.org
SIC: 8062 General medical and surgical hospitals
PA: Sutter Health
2200 River Plaza Dr
Sacramento CA
916 733-8800

(P-16540)
SUTTER HLTH RHABILITATION SVCS
Also Called: Sutter Medical Ctr Sacramento
2801 L St Fl 3 (95816-5615)
P.O. Box 160727 (95816-0727)
PHONE..................................916 733-3040
Lisa Drewslucero, *Mgr*
EMP: 70 EST: 1980
SALES (est): 10.45MM **Privately Held**
Web: www.sutterhealth.org
SIC: 8062 General medical and surgical hospitals

(P-16541)
SUTTER HLTH SCRMNTO SIERRA REG
Also Called: Sutter West Foundation
2030 Sutter Pl Ste 2000 (95616-6216)
PHONE..................................530 747-5010
EMP: 199
SALES (corp-wide): 14.77B **Privately Held**
Web: www.sutterhealth.org
SIC: 8062 General medical and surgical hospitals
HQ: Sutter Health Sacramento Sierra Region
2200 River Plaza Dr
Sacramento CA
916 733-8800

(P-16542)
SUTTER HLTH SCRMNTO SIERRA REG
Also Called: Sutter Amador Hospital Lab
100 Mission Blvd (95642-2536)
PHONE..................................209 223-7540
Margie Souza, *Brnch Mgr*
EMP: 283
SALES (corp-wide): 14.77B **Privately Held**
Web: www.sutterhealth.org
SIC: 8062 General medical and surgical hospitals
HQ: Sutter Health Sacramento Sierra Region
2200 River Plaza Dr
Sacramento CA
916 733-8800

(P-16543)
SUTTER HLTH SCRMNTO SIERRA REG
701 Howe Ave Ste F20 (95825-4681)
PHONE..................................916 733-7080
Mary Ashuckian, *Brnch Mgr*
EMP: 230
SALES (corp-wide): 14.77B **Privately Held**
Web: www.sutterhealth.org
SIC: 8062 General medical and surgical hospitals
HQ: Sutter Health Sacramento Sierra Region
2200 River Plaza Dr
Sacramento CA
916 733-8800

(P-16544)
SUTTER HLTH SCRMNTO SIERRA REG (HQ)
Also Called: Sutter Memorial Hospital
2200 River Plaza Dr (95833-4134)
P.O. Box 160727 (95816-0727)
PHONE..................................916 733-8800
Patrick E Fry, *CEO*
▲ EMP: 300 EST: 1935
SQ FT: 20,000
SALES (est): 25.53MM
SALES (corp-wide): 14.77B **Privately Held**
Web: www.sutterhealth.org
SIC: 8062 8063 8052 General medical and surgical hospitals; Psychiatric hospitals; Intermediate care facilities
PA: Sutter Health
2200 River Plaza Dr
Sacramento CA
916 733-8800

(P-16545)
SUTTER HLTH SCRMNTO SIERRA REG
Also Called: Sutter Material Management
1600 Cebrian St (95691-3802)
PHONE..................................916 373-3400
Dan Javor, *Prin*
EMP: 293
SALES (corp-wide): 14.77B **Privately Held**
Web: www.sutterhealth.org
SIC: 8062 General medical and surgical hospitals
HQ: Sutter Health Sacramento Sierra Region
2200 River Plaza Dr
Sacramento CA
916 733-8800

8062 - General Medical And Surgical Hospitals (P-16565)

(P-16546)
SUTTER HLTH SCRMNTO SIERRA REG
Also Called: Sutter Memorial Hospital
5151 F St (95819-3223)
P.O. Box 160727 (95816-0727)
PHONE...............................916 454-2222
EMP: 272
SALES (corp-wide): 14.77B Privately Held
Web: www.suttermedicalcenter.org
SIC: 8062 8011 General medical and surgical hospitals; Offices and clinics of medical doctors
HQ: Sutter Health Sacramento Sierra Region
2200 River Plaza Dr
Sacramento CA
916 733-8800

(P-16547)
SUTTER HLTH SCRMNTO SIERRA REG
Also Called: Sutter Senior Care
1234 U St (95818-1433)
PHONE...............................916 446-3100
Janet Tedesco, Brnch Mgr
EMP: 419
SALES (corp-wide): 14.77B Privately Held
Web: www.sutterhealth.org
SIC: 8062 General medical and surgical hospitals
HQ: Sutter Health Sacramento Sierra Region
2200 River Plaza Dr
Sacramento CA
916 733-8800

(P-16548)
SUTTER HLTH SCRMNTO SIERRA REG
Also Called: Recruitment Service
2700 Gateway Oaks Dr (95833-4337)
PHONE...............................916 924-7666
Debbie Mareno, Mgr
EMP: 314
SALES (corp-wide): 14.77B Privately Held
Web: www.sutterhealth.org
SIC: 8062 General medical and surgical hospitals
HQ: Sutter Health Sacramento Sierra Region
2200 River Plaza Dr
Sacramento CA
916 733-8800

(P-16549)
SUTTER HLTH SCRMNTO SIERRA REG
300 Hospital Dr (94589-2574)
PHONE...............................707 554-4444
EMP: 419
SALES (corp-wide): 14.77B Privately Held
Web: www.sutterhealth.org
SIC: 8062 General medical and surgical hospitals
HQ: Sutter Health Sacramento Sierra Region
2200 River Plaza Dr
Sacramento CA
916 733-8800

(P-16550)
SUTTER HLTH SCRMNTO SIERRA REG
Also Called: Sutter Medical Center
2800 L St (95816-5616)
P.O. Box 160727 (95816-0727)
PHONE...............................916 733-3095
Sarah Krevans, Brnch Mgr
EMP: 502
SALES (corp-wide): 14.77B Privately Held
Web: www.sutterhealth.org
SIC: 8062 General medical and surgical hospitals
HQ: Sutter Health Sacramento Sierra Region
2200 River Plaza Dr
Sacramento CA
916 733-8800

(P-16551)
SUTTER HLTH SCRMNTO SIERRA REG
Also Called: Sutter Medical Center
475 Pioneer Ave Ste 100 (95776-4905)
PHONE...............................530 406-5616
Leefeldt Randall, Brnch Mgr
EMP: 199
SALES (corp-wide): 14.77B Privately Held
Web: www.sutterhealth.org
SIC: 8062 General medical and surgical hospitals
HQ: Sutter Health Sacramento Sierra Region
2200 River Plaza Dr
Sacramento CA
916 733-8800

(P-16552)
SUTTER LAKESIDE HOSPITAL
5176 Hill Rd E (95453-6357)
PHONE...............................707 262-5000
EMP: 380
Web: www.sutterlakeside.org
SIC: 8062 General medical and surgical hospitals

(P-16553)
SUTTER MEDICAL CENTER
Also Called: Sutter Medical Gen Campus Phrm
2825 Capitol Ave (95816-6039)
PHONE...............................916 887-0000
Joan Mengelkoch, Owner
EMP: 60 EST: 2002
SALES (est): 19.67MM Privately Held
Web: www.suttermedicalcenter.org
SIC: 8062 General medical and surgical hospitals

(P-16554)
SUTTER MTRNTY/SRGRY CTR-SNT CR
2900 Chanticleer Ave (95065-1816)
PHONE...............................831 477-2200
Larry De Ghetaldi, CEO
Richard Nichols, *
EMP: 86 EST: 1992
SALES (est): 86.85MM Privately Held
Web: www.suttersantacruz.org
SIC: 8062 General medical and surgical hospitals

(P-16555)
SUTTER N MED GROUP A PROF CORP (PA)
969 Plumas St Ste 205 (95991-4011)
PHONE...............................530 749-3661
Robert H Wright Junior Md, Pr
EMP: 82 EST: 1992
SQ FT: 30,096
SALES (est): 5.73MM Privately Held
Web: www.sutterhealth.org
SIC: 8062 General medical and surgical hospitals

(P-16556)
SUTTER ROSEVILLE MEDICAL CTR
1 Medical Plaza Dr (95661-3037)
PHONE...............................916 781-1000
Tammy Powers, CEO
EMP: 1700 EST: 1950
SALES (est): 96.08MM Privately Held
Web: www.sutterroseville.org
SIC: 8062 General medical and surgical hospitals

(P-16557)
SUTTER RSVLLE MED CTR FNDATION
1 Medical Plaza Dr (95661-3037)
PHONE...............................916 781-1000
Patricia Marquez, Pr
EMP: 383 EST: 1950
SALES (est): 2.32MM Privately Held
Web: www.sutterroseville.org
SIC: 8062 General medical and surgical hospitals

(P-16558)
SUTTER SOLANO MED CTR GUILD (HQ)
Also Called: SUTTER C H S
300 Hospital Dr (94589-2574)
PHONE...............................707 554-4444
Kelley Jaeger-jackson, CEO
EMP: 91 EST: 1957
SALES (est): 48.08K
SALES (corp-wide): 14.77B Privately Held
Web: www.suttersolano.org
SIC: 8062 General medical and surgical hospitals
PA: Sutter Health
2200 River Plaza Dr
Sacramento CA
916 733-8800

(P-16559)
SUTTER SOLANO MEDICAL CENTER
Also Called: SUTTER C H S
300 Hospital Dr (94589-2574)
PHONE...............................707 554-4444
Mary Ann Hayes, Prin
Brett Moore, *
Angie Hammons, Chief Nurse*
EMP: 560 EST: 1920
SQ FT: 94,000
SALES (est): 142.99MM
SALES (corp-wide): 14.77B Privately Held
Web: www.suttersolano.org
SIC: 8062 General medical and surgical hospitals
PA: Sutter Health
2200 River Plaza Dr
Sacramento CA
916 733-8800

(P-16560)
SUTTER VALLEY HOSPITALS (HQ)
2200 River Plaza Dr (95833-4134)
PHONE...............................916 733-8800
Anne Platt, CEO
EMP: 385 EST: 1993
SALES (est): 4.22B
SALES (corp-wide): 14.77B Privately Held
Web: www.sutterhealth.org
SIC: 8062 General medical and surgical hospitals
PA: Sutter Health
2200 River Plaza Dr
Sacramento CA
916 733-8800

(P-16561)
SUTTER VALLEY HOSPITALS
Also Called: Sutter Amador Hospital
200 Mission Blvd (95642-2564)
PHONE...............................209 223-7514
EMP: 385
SALES (corp-wide): 14.77B Privately Held
SIC: 8062 General medical and surgical hospitals
HQ: Sutter Valley Hospitals
2200 River Plaza Dr
Sacramento CA

(P-16562)
SUTTER WEST BAY HOSPITALS
100 Rowland Way Ste 310 (94945-5040)
P.O. Box 8010 (94912-8010)
PHONE...............................415 492-4800
Rojanne Sutsos, Brnch Mgr
EMP: 101
SALES (corp-wide): 14.77B Privately Held
Web: www.novatocommunity.org
SIC: 8062 General medical and surgical hospitals
HQ: Sutter West Bay Hospitals
180 Rowland Way
Novato CA
415 209-1300

(P-16563)
SUTTER WEST BAY HOSPITALS (HQ)
Also Called: Novato Community Hospital
180 Rowland Way (94945-5009)
P.O. Box 1108 (94948-1108)
PHONE...............................415 209-1300
Brian Alexander, CEO
David Bradley, *
▲ EMP: 329 EST: 1952
SQ FT: 50,000
SALES (est): 81.84MM
SALES (corp-wide): 14.77B Privately Held
Web: www.novatocommunity.org
SIC: 8062 General medical and surgical hospitals
PA: Sutter Health
2200 River Plaza Dr
Sacramento CA
916 733-8800

(P-16564)
SUTTER WEST BAY HOSPITALS
Also Called: Sutter Lakeside Hospital
5176 Hill Rd E (95453-6300)
PHONE...............................707 262-5000
EMP: 340
SALES (corp-wide): 14.77B Privately Held
Web: www.sutterlakeside.org
SIC: 8062 General medical and surgical hospitals
HQ: Sutter West Bay Hospitals
180 Rowland Way
Novato CA
415 209-1300

(P-16565)
SUTTERCARE CORPORATION
Also Called: Menlo Park Surgical Hospital
1501 Trousdale Dr (94010-4506)
PHONE...............................650 853-8500
EMP: 1096
SALES (corp-wide): 14.77B Privately Held
SIC: 8062 General medical and surgical hospitals
HQ: Suttercare Corporation
2200 River Plaza Dr
Sacramento CA
916 733-8800

8062 - General Medical And Surgical Hospitals (P-16566)

(P-16566)
TAHOE FOREST HOSPITAL DISTRICT
Also Called: Tahoe Workx
10956 Donner Pass Rd Ste 230 (96161)
PHONE.................................530 582-3277
Ricardo Fergazo, Dir
EMP: 118
SALES (corp-wide): 277.82MM Privately Held
Web: www.tfhd.com
SIC: 8062 8071 General medical and surgical hospitals; X-ray laboratory, including dental
PA: Tahoe Forest Hospital District
   10121 Pine Ave
   Truckee CA
   530 587-6011

(P-16567)
TAHOE FOREST HOSPITAL DISTRICT (PA)
10121 Pine Ave (96161-4856)
PHONE.................................530 587-6011
Robert Schapper, CEO
Crystal Betts, *
EMP: 302 EST: 1952
SQ FT: 120,000
SALES (est): 277.82MM
SALES (corp-wide): 277.82MM Privately Held
Web: www.tfhd.com
SIC: 8062 General medical and surgical hospitals

(P-16568)
TEAM HEALTH HOLDINGS INC
Also Called: Sharp Grssmont Hosp Emrgncy Ca
5555 Grossmont Center Dr (91942-3019)
PHONE.................................619 740-4401
EMP: 387
SALES (corp-wide): 3.6B Privately Held
Web: www.sharp.com
SIC: 8062 General medical and surgical hospitals
HQ: Team Health Holdings, Inc.
   265 Brkview Cntre Way Ste
   Knoxville TN
   865 693-1000

(P-16569)
TEMPLE HOSPITAL CORPORATION
Also Called: Temple Community Hospital
242 N Hoover St (90004-3628)
PHONE.................................213 355-3200
EMP: 350
Web: www.templecommunityhospital.com
SIC: 8062 General medical and surgical hospitals

(P-16570)
TENET HEALTH SYSTEMS NORRIS
Also Called: KENNETH NORRIS CANCER HOSPITAL
1441 Eastlake Ave (90089-1019)
PHONE.................................323 865-3000
Scott Evans, CEO
Strawn Steele, *
EMP: 352 EST: 1982
SQ FT: 175,000
SALES (est): 280.59MM Privately Held
Web: www.keckmedicine.org
SIC: 8062 General medical and surgical hospitals

(P-16571)
TENET HEALTHSYSTEM MEDICAL INC
Also Called: Irvine Regional Hospital
1400 S Douglass Rd Ste 250 (92806)
PHONE.................................714 428-6800
Donald Lorack, CEO
EMP: 230
SALES (corp-wide): 19.58B Publicly Held
Web: validate.perfdrive.com
SIC: 8062 General medical and surgical hospitals
HQ: Tenet Healthsystem Medical, Inc.
   14201 Dallas Pkwy
   Dallas TX
   469 893-2000

(P-16572)
TENET HEALTHSYSTEM MEDICAL INC
Cnty HSP/Rhb Ctr/Ls GTS-Srtg
815 Pollard Rd (95032-1438)
PHONE.................................408 378-6131
TOLL FREE: 888
Gary Honts, CEO
EMP: 416
SALES (corp-wide): 19.58B Publicly Held
Web: www.elcaminohealth.org
SIC: 8062 8011 General medical and surgical hospitals; Offices and clinics of medical doctors
HQ: Tenet Healthsystem Medical, Inc.
   14201 Dallas Pkwy
   Dallas TX
   469 893-2000

(P-16573)
TENNESSEE HOSPITALISTS INC
4605 Lankershim Blvd Ste 617 (91602-1818)
PHONE.................................888 447-2362
EMP: 72 EST: 2011
SALES (est): 3.44MM
SALES (corp-wide): 3.6B Privately Held
SIC: 8062 General medical and surgical hospitals
HQ: Ipc Healthcare, Inc.
   4605 Lankershim Blvd # 617
   North Hollywood CA
   888 447-2362

(P-16574)
THOUSAND OAKS SURGICAL HOSP LP
401 Rolling Oaks Dr (91361-1050)
PHONE.................................805 777-7750
Micheal Bass, Pt
EMP: 100 EST: 1999
SQ FT: 50,000
SALES (est): 13.98MM Privately Held
Web: www.losrobleshospital.com
SIC: 8062 General medical and surgical hospitals

(P-16575)
TORRANCE HEALTH ASSN INC (PA)
Also Called: Physician Office Support Svcs
3330 Lomita Blvd (90505-2002)
P.O. Box 13717 (90503-0717)
PHONE.................................310 325-9110
John Mcnamara, Sr VP
Bill Larson, *
Sally Eberhard, *
Bernadette Reid, *
EMP: 3000 EST: 1985
SQ FT: 180,000
SALES (est): 913.85MM Privately Held
Web: www.torrancememorialpa.org

(P-16576)
TORRANCE MEMORIAL MEDICAL CTR
3333 Skypark Dr Ste 200 (90505-5035)
PHONE.................................310 784-6316
EMP: 408
Web: www.torrancememorial.org
SIC: 8062 General medical and surgical hospitals
HQ: Torrance Memorial Medical Center
   3330 Lomita Blvd
   Torrance CA
   310 325-9110

(P-16577)
TORRANCE MEMORIAL MEDICAL CTR
Also Called: Torrance Memorial Breast Diagn
855 Manhattan Beach Blvd Ste 208 (90266-4965)
PHONE.................................310 939-7847
EMP: 408
Web: www.torrancememorial.org
SIC: 8062 General medical and surgical hospitals
HQ: Torrance Memorial Medical Center
   3330 Lomita Blvd
   Torrance CA
   310 325-9110

(P-16578)
TORRANCE MEMORIAL MEDICAL CTR
22411 Hawthorne Blvd (90505-2507)
PHONE.................................310 784-3740
EMP: 340
Web: www.torrancememorial.org
SIC: 8062 Hospital, affiliated with AMA residency
HQ: Torrance Memorial Medical Center
   3330 Lomita Blvd
   Torrance CA
   310 325-9110

(P-16579)
TORRANCE MEMORIAL MEDICAL CTR (HQ)
3330 Lomita Blvd (90505-5002)
PHONE.................................310 325-9110
Keith Hobbs, Pr
EMP: 1500 EST: 1925
SALES (est): 838.38MM Privately Held
Web: www.torrancememorial.org
SIC: 8062 Hospital, affiliated with AMA residency
PA: Torrance Health Association, Inc.
   3330 Lomita Blvd
   Torrance CA

(P-16580)
TRACY SUTTER COMMUNITY HOSP
1420 N Tracy Blvd (95376-3451)
PHONE.................................209 835-1500
David Thompson, Pr
Eric Dalton, *
▲ EMP: 400 EST: 1945
SQ FT: 80,000
SALES (est): 162.9MM
SALES (corp-wide): 14.77B Privately Held
Web: www.sutterhealth.org
SIC: 8062 8051 8011 General medical and surgical hospitals; Skilled nursing care facilities; Offices and clinics of medical doctors
PA: Sutter Health
   2200 River Plaza Dr
   Sacramento CA
   916 733-8800

(P-16581)
TRI-CITY HOSPITAL DISTRICT (PA)
Also Called: Tri-City Medical Center
4002 Vista Way (92056-4506)
PHONE.................................760 724-8411
Steve Dietlin, CEO
Ray Rivas, CFO
EMP: 2100 EST: 1957
SQ FT: 50,000
SALES (est): 319.28MM
SALES (corp-wide): 319.28MM Privately Held
Web: www.tricitymed.org
SIC: 8062 General medical and surgical hospitals

(P-16582)
TULARE LOCAL HEALTH CARE DST
Also Called: TULARE DISTRICT HOSPITAL
869 N Cherry St (93274-2207)
PHONE.................................559 685-3462
Shawn Bolouki, CEO
Fred Capozello, *
Prem Camboj, *
Sherrie Bell, *
EMP: 700 EST: 1951
SQ FT: 140,000
SALES (est): 65.33MM Privately Held
Web: www.adventisthealth.org
SIC: 8062 General medical and surgical hospitals

(P-16583)
TUSTIN HOSPITAL AND MEDICAL CENTER
Also Called: Newport Specialty Hospital
3699 Wilshire Blvd # 540 (90010-2723)
PHONE.................................714 619-7700
EMP: 360
SIC: 8062 General medical and surgical hospitals

(P-16584)
UC IRVINE HEALTH MKTG DEPT
333 City Blvd W Ste 1250 (92868-2990)
PHONE.................................714 456-6726
Uc Irvine, Prin
EMP: 63 EST: 2013
SALES (est): 18.07MM Privately Held
SIC: 8062 General medical and surgical hospitals

(P-16585)
UCLA HEALTH
Also Called: Ronald Reagan Building
757 Westwood Plz (90095-8358)
PHONE.................................310 825-9111
Doctor David T Feinberg, CEO
EMP: 65 EST: 2012
SALES (est): 118.75MM Privately Held
Web: www.uclahealth.org
SIC: 8062 General medical and surgical hospitals

(P-16586)
UCLA HEALTHCARE
1821 Wilshire Blvd Fl 6 (90403-5618)
PHONE.................................310 319-4560
Tami Dennis, Ex Dir
EMP: 77 EST: 2007
SALES (est): 23.15MM
SALES (corp-wide): 534.4MM Privately Held

PRODUCTS & SERVICES SECTION
8062 - General Medical And Surgical Hospitals (P-16603)

SIC: **8062** 9411 General medical and surgical hospitals; Administration of educational programs
HQ: University Of California, Los Angeles
405 Hilgard Ave
Los Angeles CA

(P-16587)
UHS-CORONA INC (HQ)
Also Called: Corona Regional Med Ctr Hosp
800 S Main St (92882-3420)
PHONE..................................951 737-4343
Marvin Pember, *CEO*
Ken Rivers, *
Alan B Miller, *
Kevan Metcalf, *
▲ **EMP:** 900 **EST:** 1978
SALES (est): 220.6MM
SALES (corp-wide): 13.4B **Publicly Held**
Web: www.swhcoronaregional.com
SIC: **8062** General medical and surgical hospitals
PA: Universal Health Services, Inc.
367 S Gulph Rd
King Of Prussia PA
610 768-3300

(P-16588)
UKIAH ADVENTIST HOSPITAL (HQ)
Also Called: Ukiah Valley Medical Center
275 Hospital Dr (95482-4531)
PHONE..................................707 462-3111
Terry Burns, *Pr*
Rod Grainger, *CFO*
EMP: 500 **EST:** 1967
SQ FT: 50,000
SALES (est): 169.52MM
SALES (corp-wide): 789.42MM **Privately Held**
Web: www.adventisthealth.org
SIC: **8062** General medical and surgical hospitals
PA: Adventist Health System/West, Corporation
1 Adventist Health Way
Roseville CA
844 574-5686

(P-16589)
UNIVERSITY CAL LOS ANGELES
Also Called: Ronald Reagan Ucla Medical Ctr
757 Westwood Plz (90095-8258)
PHONE..................................310 825-9111
EMP: 2056
SALES (corp-wide): 534.4MM **Privately Held**
Web: www.ucla.edu
SIC: **8062** 8221 9411 General medical and surgical hospitals; University; Administration of educational programs
HQ: University Of California, Los Angeles
405 Hilgard Ave
Los Angeles CA

(P-16590)
UNIVERSITY CAL SAN DIEGO
Also Called: Medical Center
200 W Arbor Dr Frnt (92103-9000)
PHONE..................................619 543-6654
Richard Likeweg, *Mgr*
EMP: 4000
SALES (corp-wide): 534.4MM **Privately Held**
Web: www.ucsd.edu
SIC: **8062** 8221 9411 General medical and surgical hospitals; University; Administration of educational programs
HQ: University Of California, San Diego
9500 Gilman Dr
La Jolla CA
858 534-2230

(P-16591)
UNIVERSITY CAL SAN DIEGO
Also Called: Ucsd Thornton Hospital
9300 Campus Point Dr (92037-1300)
P.O. Box 409 (92075-0409)
PHONE..................................858 657-7000
Paul Hensler, *Dir*
EMP: 1412
SALES (corp-wide): 534.4MM **Privately Held**
Web: www.ucsd.edu
SIC: **8062** 8221 9411 General medical and surgical hospitals; University; Administration of educational programs
HQ: University Of California, San Diego
9500 Gilman Dr
La Jolla CA
858 534-2230

(P-16592)
UNIVERSITY CAL SAN DIEGO
Also Called: U C S D Medical Center
402 Dickinson St Ste 380 (92103-6902)
PHONE..................................619 543-6170
Doctor Kenneth Kaushkay, *Ch*
EMP: 144
SALES (corp-wide): 534.4MM **Privately Held**
Web: www.ucsd.edu
SIC: **8062** 8221 9411 General medical and surgical hospitals; University; Administration of educational programs
HQ: University Of California, San Diego
9500 Gilman Dr
La Jolla CA
858 534-2230

(P-16593)
UNIVERSITY CAL SAN DIEGO
200 W Arbor Dr (92103-9000)
PHONE..................................619 471-9393
Carol Eimers, *Asst Dir*
EMP: 78
SALES (corp-wide): 534.4MM **Privately Held**
Web: www.ucsd.edu
SIC: **8062** 8221 9411 General medical and surgical hospitals; University; Administration of educational programs
HQ: University Of California, San Diego
9500 Gilman Dr
La Jolla CA
858 534-2230

(P-16594)
UNIVERSITY CAL SAN FRANCISCO
Ucsf Lngley Prter Psychtric In
401 Parnassus Ave (94143-2211)
PHONE..................................415 476-7000
Craig Van Dyke, *Mgr*
EMP: 124
SALES (corp-wide): 534.4MM **Privately Held**
Web: psych.ucsf.edu
SIC: **8062** 8221 9411 General medical and surgical hospitals; University; Administration of educational programs
HQ: University Cal San Francisco
513 Parnassus Ave 115f
San Francisco CA

(P-16595)
UNIVERSITY CAL SAN FRANCISCO
Also Called: Department of Urology
400 Parnassus Ave Ste A633 (94143-2202)
P.O. Box 738 (94104-0738)
PHONE..................................415 476-1611
Christine Mcdevitt, *Mgr*
EMP: 83
SALES (corp-wide): 534.4MM **Privately Held**
Web: www.ucsf.edu
SIC: **8062** 8221 9411 General medical and surgical hospitals; University; Administration of educational programs
HQ: University Cal San Francisco
513 Parnassus Ave 115f
San Francisco CA

(P-16596)
UNIVERSITY CAL SAN FRANCISCO
Also Called: Ucsf Medical Center At Mt Zion
1600 Divisadero St (94143-3010)
PHONE..................................415 567-6600
Mark Laret, *Mgr*
EMP: 239
SALES (corp-wide): 534.4MM **Privately Held**
Web: www.ucsfhealth.org
SIC: **8062** 8221 9411 General medical and surgical hospitals; University; Administration of educational programs, State government
HQ: University Cal San Francisco
513 Parnassus Ave 115f
San Francisco CA

(P-16597)
UNIVERSITY CAL SAN FRANCISCO
Also Called: Occupational Health Clinic
2550 23rd St Bldg 9 (94110-3504)
PHONE..................................415 206-8812
Mary Spangler, *Brnch Mgr*
EMP: 83
SALES (corp-wide): 534.4MM **Privately Held**
Web: orthosurgery.ucsf.edu
SIC: **8062** 8221 9411 General medical and surgical hospitals; University; Administration of educational programs
HQ: University Cal San Francisco
513 Parnassus Ave 115f
San Francisco CA

(P-16598)
UNIVERSITY CALIFORNIA DAVIS
Also Called: Medical Centre
4400 V St (95817-1445)
PHONE..................................916 734-3141
Doctor William Ellis, *Prin*
EMP: 73
SALES (corp-wide): 534.4MM **Privately Held**
Web: health.ucdavis.edu
SIC: **8062** 8221 9411 General medical and surgical hospitals; University; Administration of educational programs
HQ: University Of California, Davis
1 Shields Ave
Davis CA

(P-16599)
UNIVERSITY CALIFORNIA DAVIS
Also Called: Uc Davis Medical Center
2315 Stockton Blvd (95817-2201)
PHONE..................................916 734-2011
Mauda Butte, *Prin*
EMP: 228
SALES (corp-wide): 534.4MM **Privately Held**
Web: www.ucdavis.edu

SIC: **8062** 8221 9411 General medical and surgical hospitals; University; Administration of educational programs
HQ: University Of California, Davis
1 Shields Ave
Davis CA

(P-16600)
UNIVERSITY CALIFORNIA DAVIS
Also Called: Department Ansthslogy Pain Mdc
4150 V St Ste 1200 (95817-1460)
PHONE..................................916 734-5113
EMP: 82
SALES (corp-wide): 534.4MM **Privately Held**
Web: health.ucdavis.edu
SIC: **8062** 8221 9411 General medical and surgical hospitals; University; Administration of educational programs
HQ: University Of California, Davis
1 Shields Ave
Davis CA

(P-16601)
UNIVERSITY CALIFORNIA IRVINE
Also Called: UCI Cancer Center
101 The City Dr S (92868-3201)
PHONE..................................714 456-8000
Michael Lekawa, *Pr*
EMP: 478
SALES (corp-wide): 534.4MM **Privately Held**
Web: www.ucihealth.org
SIC: **8062** General medical and surgical hospitals
HQ: University Of California, Irvine
510 Aldrich Hall
Irvine CA
949 824-5011

(P-16602)
UNIVERSITY CALIFORNIA IRVINE
Also Called: Uc Irvine Medical Center
101 The City Dr S (92868-3201)
PHONE..................................714 456-6011
Mary Piccione, *Ex Dir*
EMP: 3000
SALES (corp-wide): 534.4MM **Privately Held**
Web: www.ucihealth.org
SIC: **8062** 8221 9411 General medical and surgical hospitals; University; Administration of educational programs, State government
HQ: University Of California, Irvine
510 Aldrich Hall
Irvine CA
949 824-5011

(P-16603)
UNIVERSITY CALIFORNIA IRVINE
Also Called: Irvine Medical Center
200 S Manchester Ave Ste 400 (92868-3220)
PHONE..................................714 456-5558
Joy Grosse, *Dir*
EMP: 114
SALES (corp-wide): 534.4MM **Privately Held**
Web: www.ucihealth.org
SIC: **8062** 8221 9411 General medical and surgical hospitals; University; Administration of educational programs
HQ: University Of California, Irvine
510 Aldrich Hall
Irvine CA
949 824-5011

8062 - General Medical And Surgical Hospitals (P-16604)

(P-16604)
UNIVERSITY CALIFORNIA IRVINE
Also Called: UCI Westminster Medical Center
15355 Brookhurst St Ste 102 (92683-7077)
PHONE.....................714 775-3066
TOLL FREE: 888
EMP: 137
SALES (corp-wide): 534.4MM **Privately Held**
Web: www.uci.edu
SIC: **8062** 8221 9411 General medical and surgical hospitals; University; Administration of educational programs
HQ: University Of California, Irvine
510 Aldrich Hall
Irvine CA
949 824-5011

(P-16605)
UNIVERSITY SOUTHERN CALIFORNIA
Also Called: Usc University Hospital
1500 San Pablo St (90033-5313)
PHONE.....................323 442-8500
Paul Vivano, *Dir*
EMP: 875
SALES (corp-wide): 5.57B **Privately Held**
Web: www.usc.edu
SIC: **8062** 8011 General medical and surgical hospitals; Offices and clinics of medical doctors
PA: University Of Southern California
3720 S Flower St Fl 3
Los Angeles CA
213 740-7762

(P-16606)
USC ARCADIA HOSPITAL (PA)
Also Called: Methodist Hospital
300 W Huntington Dr (91007-3402)
PHONE.....................626 898-8000
TOLL FREE: 800
Ikenna Mmeje, *Pr*
Steven A Sisto, *
William E Grigg, *
Clifford R Daniels, *
EMP: 933 EST: 1903
SQ FT: 100,000
SALES (est): 267.48MM
SALES (corp-wide): 267.48MM **Privately Held**
Web: www.uscarcadiahospital.org
SIC: **8062** General medical and surgical hospitals

(P-16607)
USC VERDUGO HILLS HOSPITAL LLC
1812 Verdugo Blvd (91208-1407)
PHONE.....................818 790-7100
Armand Dorian, *CEO*
Debbie Walsh, *
Cynthia Trousdale, *
Thomas Jackiewicz, *
Hack Lash, *
EMP: 750 EST: 2013
SQ FT: 45,000
SALES (est): 223.31MM
SALES (corp-wide): 5.57B **Privately Held**
Web: www.uscvhh.org
SIC: **8062** Hospital, affiliated with AMA residency
PA: University Of Southern California
3720 S Flower St Fl 3
Los Angeles CA
213 740-7762

(P-16608)
USC VRDUGO HLLS HOSP FUNDATION (HQ)
Also Called: U S C
1812 Verdugo Blvd (91208-1407)
PHONE.....................800 872-2273
TOLL FREE: 800
Paul Craig, *CEO*
Debbie L Walsh, *Pr*
EMP: 446 EST: 1947
SQ FT: 225,000
SALES (est): 891.27K
SALES (corp-wide): 5.57B **Privately Held**
Web: www.uscvhh.org
SIC: **8062** General medical and surgical hospitals
PA: University Of Southern California
3720 S Flower St Fl 3
Los Angeles CA
213 740-7762

(P-16609)
VALLEY CHILDRENS HOSPITAL
Also Called: Charlie Mitchell Chld Clinic
9300 Valley Childrens Pl (93636-8762)
PHONE.....................559 353-6425
Annette Humphrys, *Mgr*
EMP: 119
SALES (corp-wide): 1.13B **Privately Held**
Web: www.valleychildrens.org
SIC: **8062** General medical and surgical hospitals
PA: Valley Children's Hospital
9300 Valley Childrens Pl
Madera CA
559 353-3000

(P-16610)
VALLEY CHILDRENS HOSPITAL (PA)
9300 Valley Childrens Pl (93636-8762)
PHONE.....................559 353-3000
Todd Sunterapak, *Pr*
Michele Waldrin, *
Jessie Hudgins, *
Stephanie Scott, *
Gordon Alexander, *
EMP: 1500 EST: 1949
SQ FT: 300,000
SALES (est): 1.13B
SALES (corp-wide): 1.13B **Privately Held**
Web: www.valleychildrens.org
SIC: **8062** General medical and surgical hospitals

(P-16611)
VALLEY CHILDRENS HOSPITAL
Also Called: Children's Home Care
5085 E Mckinley Ave (93727-1964)
PHONE.....................559 353-7442
Harry Tozlian, *Mgr*
EMP: 119
SALES (corp-wide): 1.13B **Privately Held**
Web: www.valleychildrens.org
SIC: **8062** General medical and surgical hospitals
PA: Valley Children's Hospital
9300 Valley Childrens Pl
Madera CA
559 353-3000

(P-16612)
VALLEY HOSPITAL MEDICAL CENTER FOUNDATION
Also Called: Calex
18300 Roscoe Blvd (91325-4105)
PHONE.....................818 885-8500
EMP: 1000
Web: www.pvhmc.org
SIC: **8062** General medical and surgical hospitals

(P-16613)
VALLEY MED GROUP LOMPOC INC
Also Called: Bailey, Rollin C MD
136 N 3rd St (93436-7002)
PHONE.....................805 736-1253
William H Gausman Junior, *Pr*
Eldon Elam Md, *VP*
B J Coughlin Md, *Sec*
Admiral William Diebner, *Prin*
Thomas E Fritch, *
EMP: 69 EST: 1965
SQ FT: 10,700
SALES (est): 4.25MM **Privately Held**
Web: www.vmgoflompoc.com
SIC: **8062** General medical and surgical hospitals

(P-16614)
VALLEY PRESBYTERIAN HOSPITAL
Also Called: V P H
15107 Vanowen St (91405-4597)
PHONE.....................818 782-6600
Gustavo Valdespino, *CEO*
Ray Moss, *CIO*
Michelle Quigley, *VP*
Jean Rico, *Sr VP*
Norma Resneder, *Sr VP*
EMP: 1600 EST: 1948
SQ FT: 400,000
SALES (est): 475.76MM **Privately Held**
Web: www.valleypres.org
SIC: **8062** General medical and surgical hospitals

(P-16615)
VERDUGO HILLS HOSPITAL INC
1812 Verdugo Blvd (91208-1409)
PHONE.....................818 790-7100
Leonard Labella, *Pr*
EMP: 216 EST: 1947
SALES (est): 72.32MM **Privately Held**
Web: www.uscvhh.org
SIC: **8062** Hospital, affiliated with AMA residency

(P-16616)
VERITAS HEALTH SERVICES INC
Also Called: Chino Valley Medical Center
5451 Walnut Ave (91710-2609)
PHONE.....................909 464-8600
Parrish Scarboro, *CEO*
Irv E Edwards, *
EMP: 600 EST: 2000
SALES (est): 106.21MM
SALES (corp-wide): 1.03B **Privately Held**
Web: www.cvmc.com
SIC: **8062** General medical and surgical hospitals
HQ: Prime Healthcare Services Inc
3480 E Guasti Rd
Ontario CA

(P-16617)
VERITY HEALTH SYSTEM CAL INC
Also Called: O'Connor Hospital
2105 Forest Ave (95128-1425)
PHONE.....................408 947-2500
Robert Curry, *CEO*
EMP: 5983
SALES (corp-wide): 34.47MM **Privately Held**
SIC: **8062** General medical and surgical hospitals
PA: Verity Health System Of California, Inc.
6300 Canoga Ave Ste 1500
Woodland Hills CA

(P-16618)
VIBRA HEALTHCARE LLC
Also Called: Vibra Hospital Northern Cal
2801 Eureka Way (96001-0222)
PHONE.....................530 246-9000
EMP: 221
SALES (corp-wide): 690.44MM **Privately Held**
Web: www.norcalrehab.com
SIC: **8062** General medical and surgical hospitals
PA: Vibra Healthcare, Llc
4600 Lena Dr
Mechanicsburg PA
717 591-5700

(P-16619)
VIBRA HEALTHCARE LLC
Also Called: Vibra Hospital of San Diego
555 Washington St (92103-2289)
PHONE.....................619 260-8300
TOLL FREE: 800
Meeta Jones, *CEO*
EMP: 215
SALES (corp-wide): 690.44MM **Privately Held**
Web: www.vibrahealthcare.com
SIC: **8062** 8069 8322 General medical and surgical hospitals; Specialty hospitals, except psychiatric; Rehabilitation services
PA: Vibra Healthcare, Llc
4600 Lena Dr
Mechanicsburg PA
717 591-5700

(P-16620)
VIBRA HOSPITAL SACRAMENTO LLC
330 Montrose Dr (95630-2720)
PHONE.....................916 351-9151
Janet Biedrone, *CEO*
Brad E Hollinger, *Managing Member*
EMP: 246 EST: 2013
SQ FT: 22,000
SALES (est): 44.06MM
SALES (corp-wide): 690.44MM **Privately Held**
Web: www.vhsacramento.com
SIC: **8062** General medical and surgical hospitals
PA: Vibra Healthcare, Llc
4600 Lena Dr
Mechanicsburg PA
717 591-5700

(P-16621)
VINCENT-HAYLEY ENTERPRISES INC
Also Called: St Vincent Health Care
1810 N Fair Oaks Ave (91103-1619)
PHONE.....................626 398-8182
Rob Barrett, *Pr*
Cipriano Baustista, *
EMP: 75 EST: 1990
SALES (est): 11.28MM **Privately Held**
SIC: **8062** General medical and surgical hospitals

(P-16622)
VISTA SPCLTY HOSP STHERN CAL L
Also Called: Vista Hospital San Gabriel Vly
14148 Francisquito Ave (91706-6120)

PRODUCTS & SERVICES SECTION

8063 - Psychiatric Hospitals (P-16641)

PHONE..................626 388-2700
Marc C Ferrell, Pt
EMP: 88 EST: 2003
SQ FT: 44,400
SALES (est): 9.44MM **Privately Held**
SIC: 8062 General medical and surgical hospitals

(P-16623)
WASHINGTON CENTER LLC
14766 Washington Ave (94578-4220)
PHONE..................510 352-2211
EMP: 100 EST: 2019
SALES (est): 6.24MM **Privately Held**
Web: www.washingtoncenter.com
SIC: 8062 General medical and surgical hospitals

(P-16624)
WASHINGTON HOSP HEALTHCARE SYS
2000 Mowry Ave (94538-1716)
PHONE..................510 797-3342
Nancy Farber, CEO
Cathy Messman, *
EMP: 1600 EST: 1948
SQ FT: 250,000
SALES (est): 589.26MM **Privately Held**
Web: www.whhs.com
SIC: 8062 General medical and surgical hospitals

(P-16625)
WASHINGTON ON WHEELS
Also Called: Washington Hospital
2000 Mowry Ave (94538-1716)
PHONE..................510 494-7053
Ruth Young, Prin
EMP: 173 EST: 2002
SALES (est): 158.01MM **Privately Held**
Web: www.whhs.com
SIC: 8062 General medical and surgical hospitals

(P-16626)
WAVE PLASTIC SURGERY CTR INC
Also Called: Wave Plstic Srgery Ctr Arcadia
400 N Santa Anita Ave (91006-2874)
PHONE..................626 898-9711
EMP: 71
SALES (corp-wide): 21.31MM **Privately Held**
Web: www.waveplasticsurgery.com
SIC: 8062 8011 General medical and surgical hospitals; Plastic surgeon
PA: Wave Plastic Surgery Center Inc.
3680 Wilshire Blvd Fl 2
Los Angeles CA
213 383-4800

(P-16627)
WHITE MEMORIAL MEDICAL CENTER (HQ)
Also Called: CECILLA GONZALEZ DE AL HOYA CA
1720 E Cesar E Chavez Ave (90033-2414)
PHONE..................323 268-5000
Beth D Zachary, CEO
Terri Day, *
John G Raffoul, *
Roland Fargo, *
Mary Anne Chern, *
EMP: 1200 EST: 1913
SQ FT: 454,000
SALES (est): 412.24MM
SALES (corp-wide): 789.42MM **Privately Held**
Web: www.adventisthealth.org

SIC: 8062 General medical and surgical hospitals
PA: Adventist Health System/West, Corporation
1 Adventist Health Way
Roseville CA
844 574-5686

(P-16628)
WHITTIER HOSPITAL MED CTR INC
9080 Colima Rd (90605-1600)
PHONE..................562 945-3561
Richard Castro, CEO
EMP: 180 EST: 1962
SQ FT: 144,000
SALES (est): 27.14MM
SALES (corp-wide): 476.02MM **Privately Held**
Web: www.ahmchealth.com
SIC: 8062 General medical and surgical hospitals
PA: Ahmc Healthcare Inc.
506 W Valley Blvd Ste 300
San Gabriel CA
626 943-7526

(P-16629)
WILLITS HOSPITAL INC
Also Called: Howard Frank R Memorial Hosp
1 Marcela Dr (95490-5769)
PHONE..................707 459-6801
Rich Bockmann, CEO
Carlton Jacobsen, *
Bruce Andich, *
Ace Barash, *
William Bowen, *
EMP: 283 EST: 1928
SQ FT: 27,000
SALES (est): 96.4MM
SALES (corp-wide): 789.42MM **Privately Held**
Web: www.adventisthealth.org
SIC: 8062 General medical and surgical hospitals
PA: Adventist Health System/West, Corporation
1 Adventist Health Way
Roseville CA
844 574-5686

(P-16630)
WILLOW SPRINGS LLC
Heritage Oaks Hospital
4250 Auburn Blvd (95841-4100)
PHONE..................916 489-3336
Shawn Silva, CEO
EMP: 2147
SALES (corp-wide): 13.4B **Publicly Held**
Web: www.uhs.com
SIC: 8062 General medical and surgical hospitals
HQ: Willow Springs, Llc
6640 Carothers Pkwy # 400
Franklin TN
615 312-5700

(P-16631)
WOODLAND HEALTHCARE (DH)
1325 Cottonwood St (95695-5131)
PHONE..................530 662-3961
EMP: 460 EST: 1960
SALES (est): 213.53MM **Privately Held**
Web: www.dignityhealth.org
SIC: 8062 General medical and surgical hospitals
HQ: Dignity Health
185 Berry St Ste 200
San Francisco CA
415 438-5500

(P-16632)
WOODLAND HEALTHCARE
Also Called: Woodland Healthcare Home Hlth
261 California St (95695-2910)
PHONE..................530 669-5680
Claudia Owens, Mgr
EMP: 167
Web: www.dignityhealth.org
SIC: 8062 8082 General medical and surgical hospitals; Home health care services
HQ: Woodland Healthcare
1325 Cottonwood St
Woodland CA
530 662-3961

(P-16633)
WOODLAND HEALTHCARE
2660 W Covell Blvd (95616-5645)
PHONE..................530 756-2364
Kevin Mould, Brnch Mgr
EMP: 167
Web: www.dignityhealth.org
SIC: 8062 8011 General medical and surgical hospitals; Offices and clinics of medical doctors
HQ: Woodland Healthcare
1325 Cottonwood St
Woodland CA
530 662-3961

(P-16634)
WOODLAND HEALTHCARE
1207 Fairchild Ct (95695-4321)
PHONE..................530 668-2600
Bill Hunt, Prin
EMP: 197
Web: www.dignityhealth.org
SIC: 8062 8011 General medical and surgical hospitals; Offices and clinics of medical doctors
HQ: Woodland Healthcare
1325 Cottonwood St
Woodland CA
530 662-3961

8063 Psychiatric Hospitals

(P-16635)
ALTA HLLYWOOD CMNTY HOSP VAN N
14433 Emelita St (91401-4213)
PHONE..................818 787-1511
Irving Loube, Pr
Claude Lowen, *
EMP: 113 EST: 1969
SQ FT: 34,192
SALES (est): 6.5MM
SALES (corp-wide): 3.91B **Privately Held**
Web: www.sch-vannuys.com
SIC: 8063 Psychiatric hospitals
HQ: Southern California Healthcare System, Inc.
3415 S Sepulveda Blvd 9thf
Los Angeles CA

(P-16636)
AURORA - SAN DIEGO LLC (DH)
Also Called: MAGELLAN
11878 Avenue Of Industry (92128-3423)
PHONE..................858 487-3200
Jim Plummer, CEO
Jane Jones, *
EMP: 72 EST: 1986
SQ FT: 50,000
SALES (est): 36.83MM **Publicly Held**
Web: www.aurorasandiego.com
SIC: 8063 8069 Psychiatric hospitals; Drug addiction rehabilitation hospital

HQ: Magellan Health, Inc.
14100 Magellan Plz
Maryland Heights MO
800 642-1716

(P-16637)
AURORA BEHAVIORAL HEALTH CARE
Also Called: AURORA BEHAVIORAL HEALTH CARE
2900 E Del Mar Blvd (91107-4375)
PHONE..................818 515-4735
EMP: 78
Web: www.lasencinashospital.com
SIC: 8063 Psychiatric hospitals
HQ: Aurora - San Diego, Llc
11878 Avenue Of Industry
San Diego CA
858 487-3200

(P-16638)
AURORA CHRTR OAK - LOS ANGLES
1161 E Covina Blvd (91724-1523)
PHONE..................626 966-1632
Todd Smith, Prin
EMP: 65 EST: 2017
SALES (est): 15.41MM **Privately Held**
Web: www.charteroakhospital.com
SIC: 8063 Psychiatric hospitals

(P-16639)
AURORA LAS ENCINAS LLC
Also Called: Aurora Las Encinas Hospital
2900 E Del Mar Blvd (91107-4375)
PHONE..................626 795-9901
EMP: 236 EST: 1903
SQ FT: 132,000
SALES (est): 31.46MM **Publicly Held**
Web: www.lasencinashospital.com
SIC: 8063 8069 Mental hospital, except for the mentally retarded; Alcoholism rehabilitation hospital
HQ: Hca Inc.
1 Park Plz
Nashville TN
615 344-9551

(P-16640)
BAKERSFELD BHVRAL HLTHCARE HOS
5201 White Ln (93309-6200)
PHONE..................661 398-1800
Jeff Chinn, CEO
EMP: 235 EST: 2015
SALES (est): 18.72MM **Privately Held**
Web: www.bakersfieldbehavioral.com
SIC: 8063 8011 Psychiatric hospitals; Medical centers

(P-16641)
CALIFRNIA DEPT STATE HOSPITALS
Also Called: Coalinga State Hospital
24511 W Jayne Ave (93210-9503)
P.O. Box 5000 (93210-5000)
PHONE..................559 935-4300
Tom Voss, Dir
EMP: 1026
SALES (corp-wide): 534.4MM **Privately Held**
Web: dsh.ca.gov
SIC: 8063 9431 Psychiatric hospitals; Mental health agency administration, government
HQ: California Department Of State Hospitals
1600 9th St Ste 350
Sacramento CA

8063 - Psychiatric Hospitals (P-16642)

(P-16642)
CALIFRNIA DEPT STATE HOSPITALS
Also Called: Fairview Developmental Center
2501 Harbor Blvd (92626-6143)
PHONE....................714 957-5000
Michael Hatton, Prin
EMP: 1672
SALES (corp-wide): 534.4MM Privately Held
Web: dsh.ca.gov
SIC: **8063** 9431 Mental hospital, except for the mentally retarded; Mental health agency administration, government
HQ: California Department Of State Hospitals
1600 9th St Ste 350
Sacramento CA

(P-16643)
CALIFRNIA DEPT STATE HOSPITALS
Also Called: NAPA State Hospital
2100 Napa Vallejo Hwy (94558-6234)
PHONE....................707 253-5000
Sidney Herndon, Brnch Mgr
EMP: 937
SALES (corp-wide): 534.4MM Privately Held
Web: dsh.ca.gov
SIC: **8063** 9431 8361 Mental hospital, except for the mentally retarded; Mental health agency administration, government; Residential care
HQ: California Department Of State Hospitals
1600 9th St Ste 350
Sacramento CA

(P-16644)
CALIFRNIA DEPT STATE HOSPITALS
Also Called: Patton State Hospital
3102 E Highland Ave (92369-7813)
PHONE....................909 425-7000
Bruce Parks, Dir
EMP: 937
SALES (corp-wide): 534.4MM Privately Held
Web: dsh.ca.gov
SIC: **8063** 9431 Mental hospital, except for the mentally retarded; Mental health agency administration, government
HQ: California Department Of State Hospitals
1600 9th St Ste 350
Sacramento CA

(P-16645)
CALIFRNIA DEPT STATE HOSPITALS
Also Called: Atascadero State Hospital
10333 El Camino Real (93422-5808)
P.O. Box 7001 (93423-7001)
PHONE....................805 468-2000
John De Morales, Brnch Mgr
EMP: 1156
SALES (corp-wide): 534.4MM Privately Held
Web: dsh.ca.gov
SIC: **8063** 9431 8062 Mental hospital, except for the mentally retarded; Mental health agency administration, government; General medical and surgical hospitals
HQ: California Department Of State Hospitals
1600 9th St Ste 350
Sacramento CA

(P-16646)
CANYON RIDGE HOSPITAL INC
Also Called: UHS
5353 G St (91710-5250)
PHONE....................909 590-3700
Peggy Minnick, CEO
EMP: 396 EST: 1990
SALES (est): 46.67MM
SALES (corp-wide): 13.4B Publicly Held
Web: www.canyonridgehospital.com
SIC: **8063** 8093 Mental hospital, except for the mentally retarded; Mental health clinic, outpatient
HQ: Willow Springs, Llc
6640 Carothers Pkwy # 400
Franklin TN
615 312-5700

(P-16647)
CHARTER BHVRAL HLTH SYS S C/CH
Also Called: Charter Oak Hospital
1161 E Covina Blvd (91724-1523)
PHONE....................626 966-1632
Todd Smith, CEO
EMP: 104 EST: 1997
SALES (est): 18.68MM Privately Held
Web: www.charteroakhospital.com
SIC: **8063** Psychiatric hospitals

(P-16648)
COLLEGE HOSPITAL INC (PA)
Also Called: College Hospital Cerritos
10802 College Pl (90703-1579)
PHONE....................562 924-9581
TOLL FREE: 800
Stephen A Witt, Pr
Bessie Weiss, *
EMP: 300 EST: 1973
SQ FT: 60,000
SALES (est): 72.33MM
SALES (corp-wide): 72.33MM Privately Held
Web: www.chc.la
SIC: **8063** Mental hospital, except for the mentally retarded

(P-16649)
COUNTY OF SAN DIEGO
Also Called: Health & Human Services
3853 Rosecrans St (92110-3115)
PHONE....................619 692-8200
Karen Hogan, CEO
EMP: 253
Web: www.sandiegocounty.gov
SIC: **8063** 9431 Psychiatric hospitals; Administration of public health programs
PA: County Of San Diego
1600 Pacific Hwy Ste 209
San Diego CA
619 531-5880

(P-16650)
GATEWAYS HOSP MENTAL HLTH CTR (PA)
1891 Effie St (90026-1711)
PHONE....................323 644-2000
Mara Pelsman, CEO
Jeff Emery, *
EMP: 150 EST: 1953
SQ FT: 40,000
SALES (est): 37.02MM
SALES (corp-wide): 37.02MM Privately Held
Web: www.gatewayshospital.org
SIC: **8063** 8093 Mental hospital, except for the mentally retarded; Mental health clinic, outpatient

(P-16651)
KAISER FOUNDATION HOSPITALS
Also Called: Kaiser Mental Health Center
765 W College St (90012-1181)
PHONE....................213 580-7200
Kurt Hastings, Mgr
EMP: 170
SQ FT: 66,697
SALES (corp-wide): 68.1B Privately Held
Web: www.kaisercenter.com
SIC: **8063** Psychiatric hospitals
HQ: Kaiser Foundation Hospitals Inc
1 Kaiser Plz
Oakland CA
510 271-6611

(P-16652)
KAWEAH DLTA HLTH CARE DST GILD
1100 S Akers St (93277-8311)
PHONE....................559 624-3300
Don Myers, Dir
EMP: 182
SALES (corp-wide): 857.31MM Privately Held
Web: www.kaweahhealth.org
SIC: **8063** Psychiatric hospitals
PA: Kaweah Delta Health Care District Guild
400 W Mineral King Ave
Visalia CA
559 624-2000

(P-16653)
KEDREN COMMUNITY HLTH CTR INC (PA)
Also Called: Kedren Acute Psychtric Hosp Cm
4211 Avalon Blvd (90011-5622)
PHONE....................323 233-0425
John Griffith, Pr
John Griffith Ph.d., Pr
Lupe Ross, *
Robert Lawson, *
EMP: 400 EST: 1965
SQ FT: 144,000
SALES (est): 42.85MM
SALES (corp-wide): 42.85MM Privately Held
Web: www.kedren.org
SIC: **8063** 8093 Mental hospital, except for the mentally retarded; Specialty outpatient clinics, nec

(P-16654)
LANDMARK MEDICAL SERVICES INC
Also Called: Landmark Medical Center
2030 N Garey Ave (91767-2722)
PHONE....................909 593-2585
Rose Horsman, Pr
EMP: 100 EST: 1971
SQ FT: 27,500
SALES (est): 9.82MM Privately Held
Web: www.landmarkmedicalcenter.net
SIC: **8063** Mental hospital, except for the mentally retarded

(P-16655)
NORTHERN VLY INDIAN HLTH INC
175 W Court St (95695-2913)
PHONE....................530 661-4400
EMP: 62
SALES (corp-wide): 71.48MM Privately Held
Web: www.nvih.org
SIC: **8063** Psychiatric hospitals
PA: Northern Valley Indian Health, Inc.
207 N Butte St
Willows CA
530 934-9293

(P-16656)
PINE GROVE HOSPITAL CORP
9449 San Fernando Rd (91352-1421)
PHONE....................818 348-0500
Paul R Tuft, Pr
EMP: 180 EST: 1998
SALES (est): 2.55MM Privately Held
SIC: **8063** Psychiatric hospitals

(P-16657)
SHARP MEMORIAL HOSPITAL
Also Called: Sharp Mesa Vista Hospital
7850 Vista Hill Ave (92123-2717)
PHONE....................858 278-4110
Carolyn Mason, Dir
EMP: 250
SALES (corp-wide): 2.37B Privately Held
Web: www.sharp.com
SIC: **8063** 8069 8093 Psychiatric hospitals; Substance abuse hospitals; Specialty outpatient clinics, nec
HQ: Sharp Memorial Hospital
7901 Frost St
San Diego CA
858 939-3636

(P-16658)
TELECARE CORPORATION
1005 S Central Ave (90021-2039)
PHONE....................213 533-1050
EMP: 60
SALES (corp-wide): 440.9MM Privately Held
Web: www.telecarecorp.com
SIC: **8063** Psychiatric hospitals
PA: Telecare Corporation
1080 Marina Village Pkwy # 100
Alameda CA
510 337-7950

(P-16659)
TELECARE CORPORATION (PA)
1080 Marina Village Pkwy Ste 100 (94501-1041)
PHONE....................510 337-7950
Anne L Bakar, Pr
Ross Peterson, VP
Marshall Langfeld, CFO
Stacey Calhoun, VP Opers
Carol Caputo, VP
EMP: 234 EST: 1965
SQ FT: 15,000
SALES (est): 440.9MM
SALES (corp-wide): 440.9MM Privately Held
Web: www.telecarecorp.com
SIC: **8063** 8011 Psychiatric hospitals; Health maintenance organization

(P-16660)
UNIVERSITY CAL SAN FRANCISCO
Also Called: San Francisco General Hospital
1001 Potrero Ave Ste 7m (94110-3518)
PHONE....................415 206-8430
Dan Karasic, Brnch Mgr
EMP: 93
SALES (corp-wide): 534.4MM Privately Held
Web: www.ucsf.edu
SIC: **8063** 8221 9411 Psychiatric hospitals; University; Administration of educational programs
HQ: University Cal San Francisco
513 Parnassus Ave 115f
San Francisco CA

8069 Specialty Hospitals, Except Psychiatric

(P-16661)
AKUA BEHAVIORAL HEALTH INC (PA)
Also Called: Akua Mind & Body
20271 Sw Birch St Ste 200 (92660-1752)
PHONE................................949 777-2283
Stephen Mercurio, *CEO*
EMP: 65 EST: 2014
SALES (est): 15.66MM
SALES (corp-wide): 15.66MM **Privately Held**
Web: www.akuamindbody.com
SIC: **8069** 8322 Drug addiction rehabilitation hospital; Rehabilitation services

(P-16662)
ASIAN AMERCN RECOVERY SVCS INC
Also Called: Place Asian Amrcn Rcovery Svcs
1340 Tully Rd Ste 304 (95122-3055)
PHONE................................408 271-3900
EMP: 125
Web: www.healthright360.org
SIC: **8069** Drug addiction rehabilitation hospital
PA: Asian American Recovery Services, Inc.
1115 Mission Rd 2
South San Francisco CA

(P-16663)
BARLOW GROUP (PA)
Also Called: Barlow Respitory Hospital
2000 Stadium Way (90026-2606)
PHONE................................213 250-4200
Margaret W Crane, *CEO*
EMP: 250 EST: 1994
SALES (est): 21.07MM
SALES (corp-wide): 21.07MM **Privately Held**
Web: www.barlowhospital.org
SIC: **8069** 7389 8733 Specialty hospitals, except psychiatric; Fund raising organizations; Medical research

(P-16664)
BARLOW RESPIRATORY HOSPITAL (PA)
2000 Stadium Way (90026-2606)
PHONE................................213 250-4200
Margaret W Crane, *CEO*
Edward Engesser, *
EMP: 250 EST: 1902
SQ FT: 80,000
SALES (est): 68.31MM
SALES (corp-wide): 68.31MM **Privately Held**
Web: www.barlowhospital.org
SIC: **8069** Specialty hospitals, except psychiatric

(P-16665)
BARLOW RESPIRATORY HOSPITAL
12401 Washington Blvd (90602-1006)
PHONE................................562 698-0811
Priscilla Jahangiri, *Brnch Mgr*
EMP: 1650
SALES (corp-wide): 68.31MM **Privately Held**
Web: www.barlowhospital.org
SIC: **8069** Respiratory hospital
PA: Barlow Respiratory Hospital
2000 Stadium Way
Los Angeles CA
213 250-4200

(P-16666)
BAY AREA CLINICAL ASSOC PC
1530 Meridian Ave (95125-5318)
PHONE................................408 996-7950
Stephen Setterberg, *Prin*
EMP: 68 EST: 2017
SALES (est): 22.56MM **Privately Held**
Web: www.baca.org
SIC: **8069** Specialty hospitals, except psychiatric

(P-16667)
BEVERLY HLLS ONCLOGY MED GROUP
8900 Wilshire Blvd (90211-1958)
PHONE................................310 432-8900
Afshin Gabayan, *CEO*
EMP: 74 EST: 2007
SALES (est): 9.42MM **Privately Held**
Web: www.bhcancercenter.com
SIC: **8069** Cancer hospital

(P-16668)
CALIFRNIA DEPT DVLPMENTAL SVCS
Also Called: Sonoma Development Center
15000 Arnold Dr (95431-8900)
P.O. Box 1493 (95431-1493)
PHONE................................707 938-6000
Douglas Rice, *Dir*
EMP: 1636
SALES (corp-wide): 534.4MM **Privately Held**
Web: dds.ca.gov
SIC: **8069** 9431 Specialty hospitals, except psychiatric; Categorical health program administration, government
HQ: California Department Of Developmental Services
1215 O St
Sacramento CA

(P-16669)
CHAPMAN HOUSE INC
Also Called: Chapman House
1412 E Chapman Ave (92866-2229)
PHONE................................714 288-6100
Timothy P Chapman, *Pr*
EMP: 78 EST: 1985
SALES (est): 9.31MM **Privately Held**
Web: www.chapmanrehab.com
SIC: **8069** Drug addiction rehabilitation hospital

(P-16670)
CHILDRENS HEALTHCARE CAL (PA)
Also Called: Choc Children's
1201 W La Veta Ave (92868-4203)
PHONE................................714 997-3000
Kimberly C Cripe, *Pr*
Maria Minon Md, *VP*
Kerri Ruppert, *
Thomas Brotherton, *
EMP: 1500 EST: 1986
SALES (est): 30.63MM **Privately Held**
Web: www.choc.org
SIC: **8069** Childrens' hospital

(P-16671)
CHILDRENS HOSPITAL LOS ANGELES (PA)
4650 W Sunset Blvd (90027-6062)
PHONE................................323 660-2450
Richard Cordova, *Pr*
Lannie Tonnu, *
Alexandra Carter, *CDO**
Conrad Band, *CIO**
▲ EMP: 2212 EST: 1901
SQ FT: 750,000
SALES (est): 1.38B
SALES (corp-wide): 1.38B **Privately Held**
Web: www.chla.org
SIC: **8069** 8062 Childrens' hospital; General medical and surgical hospitals

(P-16672)
CHILDRENS RECOVERY CTR 1 LLC
Also Called: Childrens Rcvery Ctr Nthrn Cal
3777 S Bascom Ave (95008-7320)
PHONE................................408 558-3640
Ken Mcguire, *CEO*
EMP: 100 EST: 1997
SQ FT: 17,000
SALES (est): 24.96MM **Privately Held**
SIC: **8069** Childrens' hospital

(P-16673)
CLARE MATRIX (PA)
2644 30th St Ste 100 (90405-3009)
PHONE................................310 314-6200
Dan George, *CEO*
Kevin Fahy, *
EMP: 65 EST: 1970
SALES (est): 16.23MM
SALES (corp-wide): 16.23MM **Privately Held**
Web: www.clarematrix.org
SIC: **8069** Drug addiction rehabilitation hospital

(P-16674)
COMMUNITY HOSP OF MNTREY PNNSU (HQ)
23625 Holman Hwy (93940-5902)
P.O. Box Hh (93940)
PHONE................................831 624-5311
Steven J Packer, *Pr*
Terrill Lowe, *
Cynthia Peck, *
Tim Nylen, *
Shelley Post, *Sec*
EMP: 1500 EST: 1928
SQ FT: 550,000
SALES (est): 813.37MM
SALES (corp-wide): 947.23MM **Privately Held**
SIC: **8069** 8011 Geriatric hospital; Hematologist
PA: Montage Health
23625 Holman Hwy
Monterey CA
831 625-4830

(P-16675)
COUNTY OF LOS ANGELES
Also Called: Department of Health Services
1240 N Mission Rd (90033-1019)
PHONE................................323 226-3468
Barbara Oliver, *Ex Dir*
EMP: 108
SALES (corp-wide): 31.7B **Privately Held**
Web: www.lacounty.gov
SIC: **8069** 9431 8062 Specialty hospitals, except psychiatric; Administration of public health programs; General medical and surgical hospitals
PA: County Of Los Angeles
500 W Temple St Ste 437
Los Angeles CA
213 974-1101

(P-16676)
COUNTY OF LOS ANGELES
Also Called: Health Services, Dept of
30500 Arrastre Canyon Rd (93510-2160)
P.O. Box 25 (93510-0025)
PHONE................................661 223-8700
Suzanna Kassinger, *Admn*
EMP: 109
SALES (corp-wide): 31.7B **Privately Held**
Web: www.lacounty.gov
SIC: **8069** 9431 8361 Alcoholism rehabilitation hospital; Administration of public health programs; Residential care
PA: County Of Los Angeles
500 W Temple St Ste 437
Los Angeles CA
213 974-1101

(P-16677)
COUNTY OF LOS ANGELES
Also Called: Health Services, Dept of
38200 Lake Hughes Rd (91384-4100)
PHONE................................661 223-8700
Lynne Dahl, *Admn*
EMP: 99
SALES (corp-wide): 31.7B **Privately Held**
Web: www.lacounty.gov
SIC: **8069** 9431 Drug addiction rehabilitation hospital; Administration of public health programs
PA: County Of Los Angeles
500 W Temple St Ste 437
Los Angeles CA
213 974-1101

(P-16678)
COUNTY OF LOS ANGELES
515 E 6th St (90021-1009)
PHONE................................213 974-7284
Maria Lopez, *Mgr*
EMP: 73
SALES (corp-wide): 31.7B **Privately Held**
Web: www.lacounty.gov
SIC: **8069** 9111 Tuberculosis hospital; Executive offices
PA: County Of Los Angeles
500 W Temple St Ste 437
Los Angeles CA
213 974-1101

(P-16679)
CRC HEALTH LLC (DH)
20400 Stevens Creek Blvd 6th Fl (95014-2217)
PHONE................................877 272-8668
R Andrew Eckert, *Ch Bd*
Jerome E Rhodes, *CEO*
Leanne M Stewart, *CFO*
Philip L Herschman, *Chief Clinical Officer*
David Duerst, *VP Sls*
EMP: 80 EST: 2002
SALES (est): 495.35MM **Publicly Held**
Web: www.legalrecruiterdirectory.org
SIC: **8069** 8099 8322 8093 Drug addiction rehabilitation hospital; Medical services organization; General counseling services; Substance abuse clinics (outpatient)
HQ: Crc Health Group, Inc.
6100 Tower Cir Ste 1000
Franklin TN

(P-16680)
EL CAMINO HOSPITAL
Also Called: Occupational Health Services
1737 N 1st St Ste 220 (95112-4522)
PHONE................................650 988-4825
EMP: 157
SALES (corp-wide): 1.43B **Privately Held**
Web: www.elcaminohealth.org
SIC: **8069** Alcoholism rehabilitation hospital
PA: El Camino Hospital
2500 Grant Rd
Mountain View CA
650 940-7000

8069 - Specialty Hospitals, Except Psychiatric (P-16681)

(P-16681)
ENLIGHTICARE INC
Also Called: Elevate Addiction Services
138 Victoria Ln (95003-3027)
P.O. Box 1690 (95001-1690)
PHONE..............................831 750-3546
Daniel Manson, Pr
EMP: 90 EST: 2017
SALES (est): 4.99MM Privately Held
SIC: 8069 Substance abuse hospitals

(P-16682)
FRESNO SKLLED NRSING WLLNESS C
Also Called: Healthcare Centre of Fresno
1665 M St (93721-1121)
PHONE..............................559 268-5361
Lucille Epperson, Admn
Charles J Enoch, *
Glenn E Rose, *
Barbara H Rose, *
Laverne E Masten, *
EMP: 99 EST: 1960
SQ FT: 87,000
SALES (est): 8.52MM Privately Held
Web: www.hcfresno.com
SIC: 8069 8051 Specialty hospitals, except psychiatric; Convalescent home with continuous nursing care

(P-16683)
GOODEN CENTER
191 N El Molino Ave (91101-1804)
PHONE..............................626 356-0078
Thomas Mcnulty, Prin
Budd Williams, *
EMP: 85 EST: 1962
SALES (est): 7.04MM Privately Held
Web: www.goodencenter.org
SIC: 8069 8361 8093 Alcoholism rehabilitation hospital; Rehabilitation center, residential: health care incidental; Mental health clinic, outpatient

(P-16684)
JANUS OF SANTA CRUZ
200 7th Ave Ste 150 (95062-4669)
PHONE..............................831 462-1060
Rod Libbey, Ex Dir
EMP: 100 EST: 1976
SALES (est): 12.7MM Privately Held
Web: www.janussc.org
SIC: 8069 Drug addiction rehabilitation hospital

(P-16685)
KOREAN COMMUNITY SERVICES INC
Also Called: Kc Services
451 W Lincoln Ave Ste 100 (92805-2912)
PHONE..............................714 527-6561
Ellen Ahn, CEO
Ellen Ahn, Ex Dir
Kay Ahn, *
EMP: 120 EST: 1977
SALES (est): 8.12MM Privately Held
Web: www.kcsinc.org
SIC: 8069 8322 8011 Drug addiction rehabilitation hospital; Social service center; Offices and clinics of medical doctors

(P-16686)
LUCILE SLTER PCKARD CHLD HOSP (HQ)
Also Called: Lucile Packard Childrens Hosp
725 Welch Rd (94304-1601)
PHONE..............................650 497-8000
Christopher Dawes, Pr
Timothy W Carmack, *

▲ EMP: 868 EST: 1919
SALES (est): 2.36B
SALES (corp-wide): 15.13B Privately Held
Web: www.stanfordchildrens.org
SIC: 8069 8082 5912 Childrens' hospital; Home health care services; Drug stores and proprietary stores
PA: Leland Stanford Junior University
450 Jane Stanford Way
Stanford CA
650 723-2300

(P-16687)
MARINE CORPS UNITED STATES
Also Called: Camp Pendleton Hospital
Camp Pendleton (92055)
P.O. Box 555191 (92055-5191)
PHONE..............................760 725-1304
Richard R Jeffries, Mgr
EMP: 1000
Web: www.marines.mil
SIC: 8069 9711 Specialty hospitals, except psychiatric; Marine Corps
HQ: United States Marine Corps
Branch Hlth Clnic Bldg 5
Beaufort SC

(P-16688)
NEW START RCVERY SOLUTIONS INC
2167 Montgomery St Ste A (95965-4945)
P.O. Box 2456 (95965-2456)
PHONE..............................530 854-4119
Joseph Henderson, CEO
EMP: 80 EST: 2013
SALES (est): 30MM Privately Held
Web: www.newstartrecoverysolutions.com
SIC: 8069 Drug addiction rehabilitation hospital

(P-16689)
PALOMAR HEALTH
800 W Valley Pkwy Ste 201 (92025-2557)
PHONE..............................760 740-6311
Bob Henker, CEO
EMP: 206
SALES (corp-wide): 679.43K Privately Held
Web: www.palomarhealth.org
SIC: 8069 Specialty hospitals, except psychiatric
PA: Palomar Health
2125 Citracado Pkwy # 300
Escondido CA
442 281-5000

(P-16690)
PATHOLOGY ASSOCIATES
305 Park Creek Dr (93611-4426)
PHONE..............................559 326-2800
Katherine A Huber, Prin
EMP: 74 EST: 2009
SALES (est): 46.26MM Privately Held
Web: www.pathology-associates.com
SIC: 8069 Specialty hospitals, except psychiatric

(P-16691)
PSYCHNP CONSULTANTS INC
7880 Alta Valley Dr # 107 (95823-4900)
PHONE..............................800 205-6107
Vicky Magobet, CEO
EMP: 60 EST: 2013
SALES (est): 2.18MM Privately Held
SIC: 8069 8093 7371 Substance abuse hospitals; Substance abuse clinics (outpatient); Computer software development and applications

(P-16692)
ROSS HOSPITAL
1111 Sir Francis Dr (94904-1418)
PHONE..............................415 258-6900
EMP: 175 EST: 1917
SQ FT: 30,000
SALES (est): 3.52MM Privately Held
SIC: 8069 8063 Alcoholism rehabilitation hospital; Psychiatric hospitals

(P-16693)
SHARP MCDONALD CENTER
7989 Linda Vista Rd (92111-5106)
PHONE..............................858 637-6920
Daniel L Gross, Ex VP
EMP: 800 EST: 2001
SALES (est): 22.24MM
SALES (corp-wide): 2.37B Privately Held
Web: www.sharp.com
SIC: 8069 Drug addiction rehabilitation hospital
PA: Sharp Healthcare
8695 Spectrum Center Blvd
San Diego CA
858 499-4000

(P-16694)
SHIELDS FOR FAMILIES (PA)
Also Called: SHIELDS
11601 S Western Ave (90047-5006)
P.O. Box 59129 (90059-0129)
PHONE..............................323 242-5000
Kathryn S Icenhower, CEO
Xylina Bean Md, Pr
Norma Mtume, *
Charlene K Smith, *
Gerald Phillips, *
EMP: 82 EST: 1991
SALES (est): 26.21MM
SALES (corp-wide): 26.21MM Privately Held
Web: www.shieldsforfamilies.org
SIC: 8069 Drug addiction rehabilitation hospital

(P-16695)
SHRINERS HSPITALS FOR CHILDREN
3160 Genieva St (91020)
PHONE..............................213 368-3302
Frank Labonte, Dir
EMP: 287
Web: www.shrinerschildrens.org
SIC: 8069 8062 Childrens' hospital; General medical and surgical hospitals
PA: Shriners Hospitals For Children
2900 N Rocky Point Dr
Tampa FL

(P-16696)
SHRINERS HSPITALS FOR CHILDREN
Also Called: Shriner's Hospital
909 S Fair Oaks Ave (91105-2625)
PHONE..............................626 389-9300
Wendy Hill, Brnch Mgr
EMP: 347
Web: www.shrinerschildrens.org
SIC: 8069 8062 Childrens' hospital; General medical and surgical hospitals
PA: Shriners Hospitals For Children
2900 N Rocky Point Dr
Tampa FL

(P-16697)
SOCIAL SCIENCE SERVICE CENTER
Also Called: CEDAR HOUSE REHABILITATION CEN

18612 Santa Ana Ave (92316-2636)
PHONE..............................909 421-7120
Daniel Gakgolla, CEO
Allen Eisenman, *
EMP: 89 EST: 1973
SQ FT: 29,000
SALES (est): 8.12MM Privately Held
Web: www.cedarhouse.org
SIC: 8069 8322 Alcoholism rehabilitation hospital; Individual and family services

(P-16698)
STANFORD HLTH CARE TRI-VALLEY
Also Called: Valleycare Recovery Center
5698 Stoneridge Dr (94588-8501)
PHONE..............................925 416-3562
EMP: 137
SALES (corp-wide): 15.13B Privately Held
Web: www.stanfordhealthcare.org
SIC: 8069 Drug addiction rehabilitation hospital
HQ: Stanford Health Care Tri-Valley
5555 W Las Positas Blvd
Pleasanton CA
925 847-3000

(P-16699)
TENET HEALTHSYSTEM MEDICAL INC
Also Called: Placentia Linda Hospital
1301 N Rose Dr (92870-3802)
PHONE..............................714 993-2000
Kent Clayton, CEO
EMP: 334
SALES (corp-wide): 19.58B Publicly Held
Web: validate.perfdrive.com
SIC: 8069 8011 8062 Specialty hospitals, except psychiatric; Offices and clinics of medical doctors; General medical and surgical hospitals
HQ: Tenet Healthsystem Medical, Inc.
14201 Dallas Pkwy
Dallas TX
469 893-2000

(P-16700)
UNIVERSITY CAL SAN FRANCISCO
Also Called: Precision Cancer Medicine Bldg
1825 4th St (94143-2350)
PHONE..............................415 502-8516
Kira Chan, Mgr
EMP: 83
SALES (corp-wide): 534.4MM Privately Held
Web: www.ucsf.edu
SIC: 8069 Cancer hospital
HQ: University Cal San Francisco
513 Parnassus Ave 115f
San Francisco CA

(P-16701)
WOMENS CANCER CENTER
815 Pollard Rd (95032-1438)
PHONE..............................408 358-6500
Nicola Spirtos, Brnch Mgr
EMP: 60
Web: www.elcaminohealth.org
SIC: 8069 Cancer hospital
PA: Women's Cancer Center
170 Knowles Dr Ste 203
Los Gatos CA

8071 Medical Laboratories

(P-16702)
ADVANCED MEDICAL ANALYSIS LLC
1941 Walker Ave (91016-4846)
PHONE.....................626 301-0126
EMP: 75
Web: www.amalab.net
SIC: 8071 Medical laboratories

(P-16703)
ALLIANCE HEALTHCARE SVCS INC (DH)
Also Called: Alliance
18201 Von Karman Ave Ste 600 (92612-1000)
P.O. Box 19532 (92623-9532)
PHONE.....................800 544-3215
Rhonda Longmore Grund, CEO
Percy C Tomlinson, *
Laurie R Miller, *
Richard W Johns, *
EMP: 250 EST: 1983
SALES (est): 550.72MM
SALES (corp-wide): 824.12MM Privately Held
Web: www.alliancehealthcareservices-us.com
SIC: 8071 Ultrasound laboratory
HQ: Akumin Operating Corp.
8300 W Sunrise Blvd
Plantation FL

(P-16704)
ASSOCIATED PATHOLOGY MED GROUP
459 Monterey Ave (95030-5302)
P.O. Box 665 (95031-0665)
PHONE.....................408 399-5010
Robert Rinehart Md, Pr
Carlene A Hawksley, *
Julia Chan Md, Sec
Jeffrey Young, *
Warner Stamm, *
EMP: 63 EST: 1962
SQ FT: 3,000
SALES (est): 4.79MM Privately Held
Web: www.apmglab.com
SIC: 8071 Pathological laboratory

(P-16705)
BASS MEDICAL GROUP
2637 Shadelands Dr (94598-2512)
PHONE.....................925 690-5056
EMP: 243 EST: 2006
SALES (est): 11.28MM Privately Held
Web: www.bassmedicalgroup.com
SIC: 8071 Medical laboratories

(P-16706)
BILLIONTOONE INC
1035 Obrien Dr (94025-1408)
PHONE.....................650 460-2551
Oguzhan Atay, CEO
David Tsao, *
Nipun Soni, *
Tom Lynch, CCO*
EMP: 95 EST: 2016
SALES (est): 10.16MM Privately Held
Web: www.billiontoone.com
SIC: 8071 8731 Medical laboratories; Commercial physical research

(P-16707)
BIORA THERAPEUTICS INC (PA)
4330 La Jolla Village Dr Ste 300 (92122-6201)
P.O. Box 674425 (48267-4425)
PHONE.....................855 293-2639
Adi Mohanty, CEO
Jeffrey D Alter, *
Eric D'esparbes, CFO
Ariella Kelman, Chief Medical Officer
EMP: 98 EST: 2010
SQ FT: 25,800
SALES (est): 305K
SALES (corp-wide): 305K Publicly Held
Web: www.bioratherapeutics.com
SIC: 8071 8731 Medical laboratories; Biotechnical research, commercial

(P-16708)
CAP DIAGNOSTICS LLC
Also Called: Pathnostics
15545 Sand Canyon Ave (92618-3114)
PHONE.....................714 966-1221
Matt Tate, *
EMP: 172 EST: 2014
SALES (est): 25.57MM Privately Held
Web: www.pathnostics.com
SIC: 8071 Medical laboratories

(P-16709)
CARDIODX INC
3945 Freedom Cir Ste 560 (95054-1269)
PHONE.....................650 475-2788
EMP: 146
Web: www.cardiodx.com
SIC: 8071 2834 Medical laboratories; Drugs acting on the cardiovascular system, except diagnostic

(P-16710)
CAREDX INC (PA)
8000 Marina Blvd Fl 4 (94005-1883)
PHONE.....................415 287-2300
Reginald Seeto, Pr
Peter Maag, Ex Ch Bd
Alex Johnson, Chief Business Officer
EMP: 346 EST: 1998
SQ FT: 28,968
SALES (est): 321.79MM
SALES (corp-wide): 321.79MM Publicly Held
Web: www.caredx.com
SIC: 8071 8733 Medical laboratories; Noncommercial research organizations

(P-16711)
CLARIENT INC
Also Called: Chromavision Medical Systems
33171 Paseo Cerveza (92675-4870)
PHONE.....................949 445-7300
FAX: 949 443-3366
EMP: 201
SALES (est): 808.69K
SALES (corp-wide): 244.08MM Publicly Held
SIC: 8071 Biological laboratory
HQ: Clarient Diagnostic Services Inc
31 Columbia
Aliso Viejo CA
949 445-7300

(P-16712)
CONSOLDTED MED BO-ANALYSIS INC (PA)
Also Called: Cmb Laboratory
10700 Walker St (90630-4703)
P.O. Box 2369 (90630-1869)
PHONE.....................714 657-7369
Chin Kuo Fan, Pr
Cam Chinh Fan, Sr VP
Michelle Fan, *
Gloria Fan, Stockholder*
EMP: 100 EST: 1979
SQ FT: 11,000
SALES (est): 9.55MM
SALES (corp-wide): 9.55MM Privately Held
Web: www.cmblabs.com
SIC: 8071 Testing laboratories

(P-16713)
CSA SILICON VALLEY LLC
Also Called: Cannasafe
7027 Hayvenhurst Ave (91406-3802)
PHONE.....................818 922-2416
EMP: 61 EST: 2019
SALES (est): 653.31K Privately Held
SIC: 8071 Medical laboratories

(P-16714)
CURATIVE-KORVA LLC
605 E Huntington Dr (91016-6352)
PHONE.....................424 645-7575
Jonathan Martin, Managing Member
EMP: 85 EST: 2020
SALES (est): 8.88MM Privately Held
SIC: 8071 Medical laboratories

(P-16715)
DECIPHER CORP
6925 Lusk Blvd Ste 200 (92121-2789)
PHONE.....................888 975-4540
Tina Nova, CEO
Doug Dolginow, Prin
Brent Vetter, CFO
Elai Davicioni, Pr
EMP: 100 EST: 2012
SQ FT: 15,000
SALES (est): 23.62MM
SALES (corp-wide): 5.41MM Privately Held
Web: www.decipherbio.com
SIC: 8071 Biological laboratory
PA: Genomedx Biosciences Inc
430-1152 Mainland St
Vancouver BC
888 975-4540

(P-16716)
DR SYSTEMS INC
Also Called: Dominator Radiology Systems
10140 Mesa Rim Rd (92121-2914)
PHONE.....................858 625-3344
EMP: 205
SIC: 8071 Testing laboratories

(P-16717)
EISENHOWER MEDICAL CENTER
Also Called: Clinical Research
39000 Bob Hope Dr Frnt (92270-3230)
PHONE.....................760 773-1364
Lile Matthews, Dir
EMP: 124
SALES (corp-wide): 3.81MM Privately Held
Web: www.eisenhowerhealth.org
SIC: 8071 Medical laboratories
PA: Eisenhower Medical Center
39000 Bob Hope Dr
Rancho Mirage CA
760 340-3911

(P-16718)
EPIC SCIENCES INC
9381 Judicial Dr Ste 200 (92121-3832)
PHONE.....................858 356-6610
Lloyd Sanders, Pr
Michael Rodriguez, *
Mike Coward, *
Michael Giske, CIO*
Chockalingam Palaniappan, CIO*
EMP: 80 EST: 2008
SALES (est): 27.57MM Privately Held
Web: www.epicsciences.com
SIC: 8071 Blood analysis laboratory

(P-16719)
EXAGEN DIAGNOSTICS INC
Also Called: Exagen Diagnostics, Inc.
1221 Liberty Way Ste A (92081-8307)
PHONE.....................505 272-7966
Robert Mignatti, Pr
EMP: 134
SALES (corp-wide): 45.56MM Publicly Held
Web: www.exagen.com
SIC: 8071 Medical laboratories
PA: Exagen Inc.
1221 Liberty Way Ste C
Vista CA
760 560-1501

(P-16720)
EXQUISITE DENTAL TECHNOLOGY
4816 Temple City Blvd (91780-4235)
PHONE.....................626 237-0107
Ron Tsai, Pr
EMP: 70 EST: 2001
SQ FT: 920
SALES (est): 1.2MM Privately Held
SIC: 8071 Medical laboratories

(P-16721)
FOCUS DIAGNOSTICS INC
Also Called: Focus Diagnostics
11331 Valley View St Ste 150 (90630-5300)
PHONE.....................714 220-1900
John Hurrell Ph.d., Pr
EMP: 400 EST: 1978
SQ FT: 36,000
SALES (est): 48.61MM
SALES (corp-wide): 9.88B Publicly Held
Web: molecular.diasorin.com
SIC: 8071 Testing laboratories
PA: Quest Diagnostics Incorporated
500 Plaza Dr Ste G
Secaucus NJ
973 520-2700

(P-16722)
FULGENT GENETICS INC (PA)
4399 Santa Anita Ave (91731-1648)
PHONE.....................626 350-0537
Ming Hsieh, Ch Bd
Jian Xie, Pr
Paul Kim, CFO
Han Lin Gao, CSO
EMP: 893 EST: 2012
SQ FT: 12,000
SALES (est): 618.97MM
SALES (corp-wide): 618.97MM Publicly Held
Web: www.fulgentgenetics.com
SIC: 8071 Testing laboratories

(P-16723)
GENOMIC HEALTH INC (HQ)
Also Called: Genomic Health
301 Penobscot Dr (94063-4700)
PHONE.....................650 556-9300
Kevin T Conroy, Pr
Jeffrey T Elliott, *
EMP: 746 EST: 2000
SQ FT: 180,700
SALES (est): 394.11MM
SALES (corp-wide): 2.08B Publicly Held
Web: www.exactsciences.com
SIC: 8071 8731 Medical laboratories; Biotechnical research, commercial
PA: Exact Sciences Corporation
5505 Endeavor Ln
Madison WI
608 535-8815

8071 - Medical Laboratories (P-16724)

(P-16724)
GUARDANT HEALTH INC (PA)
Also Called: Guardant
3100 Hanover St (94304-1119)
PHONE..................................855 698-8887
Helmy Eltoukhy, *Ch Bd*
Amirali Talasaz, *
Michael Bell, *CFO*
Craig Eagle, *CMO*
Christopher Freeman, *CCO*
EMP: 275 **EST:** 2011
SQ FT: 249,500
SALES (est): 449.54MM
SALES (corp-wide): 449.54MM **Publicly Held**
Web: www.guardanthealth.com
SIC: 8071 Medical laboratories

(P-16725)
HEALTHQUEST CLINICAL LAB INC
9805 Research Dr (92618-4304)
PHONE..................................909 445-9727
Thomas Giancursio, *Brnch Mgr*
EMP: 93
SALES (corp-wide): 4.32MM **Privately Held**
Web: www.hqesoterics.com
SIC: 8071 Testing laboratories
PA: Healthquest Clinical Laboratory, Inc.
1800 Carnegie Ave
Santa Ana CA
714 418-5867

(P-16726)
HUNTER LABORATORIES INC
2605 Winchester Blvd (95008-5379)
PHONE..................................408 341-8600
EMP: 173
SIC: 8071 Medical laboratories

(P-16727)
IMMUNALYSIS CORPORATION
829 Towne Center Dr (91767-5901)
PHONE..................................909 482-0840
Kahi Luu, *Prin*
EMP: 80 **EST:** 1975
SALES (est): 5.61MM **Privately Held**
Web: www.immunalysis.com
SIC: 8071 Testing laboratories

(P-16728)
INVITAE CORPORATION (PA)
Also Called: INVITAE
1400 16th St (94103-5110)
PHONE..................................415 374-7782
EMP: 1416 **EST:** 2010
SQ FT: 103,000
SALES (est): 516.3MM **Publicly Held**
Web: www.invitae.com
SIC: 8071 Testing laboratories

(P-16729)
KAISER FOUNDATION HOSPITALS
Also Called: Kaiser Permanente
7373 West Ln (95210-3377)
PHONE..................................209 476-3646
EMP: 401
SALES (corp-wide): 68.1B **Privately Held**
Web: www.kaisercenter.com
SIC: 8071 Medical laboratories
HQ: Kaiser Foundation Hospitals Inc
1 Kaiser Plz
Oakland CA
510 271-6611

(P-16730)
KAISER FOUNDATION HOSPITALS
Also Called: Kaiser Permanente
2155 Iron Point Rd (95630-8707)
PHONE..................................916 817-5651
EMP: 76
SALES (corp-wide): 68.1B **Privately Held**
Web: www.kaisercenter.com
SIC: 8071 8099 Medical laboratories; Medical services organization
HQ: Kaiser Foundation Hospitals Inc
1 Kaiser Plz
Oakland CA
510 271-6611

(P-16731)
KAN-DI-KI LLC (HQ)
Also Called: Diagnostic Labs & Rdlgy
2820 N Ontario St (91504-2015)
PHONE..................................818 549-1880
David F Smith Iii, *Managing Member*
EMP: 95 **EST:** 2008
SQ FT: 7,000
SALES (est): 108.56MM **Privately Held**
Web: www.tridentcare.com
SIC: 8071 Testing laboratories
PA: Trident Usa Health Services, Llc
930 Ridgebrook Rd Fl 3
Sparks MD

(P-16732)
LATARA ENTERPRISE INC (PA)
Also Called: Foundation Laboratory
1716 W Holt Ave (91768-3333)
PHONE..................................909 623-9301
Stepan Vartanian, *CEO*
Linda Vartanian, *Prin*
Taleen Vartanian, *Prin*
Lala Vartanian, *Prin*
Ara Vartanian, *Treas*
EMP: 120 **EST:** 1966
SQ FT: 19,000
SALES (est): 25.34MM
SALES (corp-wide): 25.34MM **Privately Held**
Web: www.foundationlaboratory.com
SIC: 8071 Pathological laboratory

(P-16733)
LAWRENCE BERKELEY NATIONAL LAB
717 Potter St (94710-2722)
PHONE..................................347 425-3735
EMP: 1653
Web: www.lbl.gov
SIC: 8071 Biological laboratory
HQ: Lawrence Berkeley National Lab
1 Cyclotron Rd 50-413
Berkeley CA
510 486-5111

(P-16734)
LOTUS CLINICAL RESEARCH LLC
100 W California Blvd (91105-3010)
PHONE..................................626 381-9830
Neil Singla, *CSO*
Sonia Kaur D.o.s., *Dir*
Anne Arriaga, *
EMP: 100 **EST:** 2008
SALES (est): 11.47MM **Privately Held**
Web: www.lotuscr.com
SIC: 8071 Medical laboratories

(P-16735)
MIRACOR DIAGNOSTICS INC (PA)
Also Called: Medical Device Technologies
9191 Towne Centre Dr Ste 400 (92122-1225)
PHONE..................................858 455-7127
Ross S Seibert, *CEO*
Ross S Seibert, *CFO*
Howard W Salmon, *Ch Bd*
Leslie G Weber, *CMO*
▲ **EMP:** 75 **EST:** 1980
SALES (est): 8.78MM
SALES (corp-wide): 8.78MM **Privately Held**
SIC: 8071 8093 Medical laboratories; Specialty outpatient clinics, nec

(P-16736)
MOSS LANDING MARINE LABS
8272 Moss Landing Rd (95039-9647)
PHONE..................................831 771-4400
James Harvey, *Dir*
Kenneth H Coale, *
EMP: 87 **EST:** 1966
SALES (est): 9.3MM **Privately Held**
Web: mlml.sjsu.edu
SIC: 8071 Biological laboratory

(P-16737)
MYRIAD WOMENS HEALTH INC
180 Kimball Way (94080-6218)
PHONE..................................888 268-6795
Ramji Srinivasan, *CEO*
James Goldberg, *Chief Medical Officer*
Joel Jung, *
Noah Nasser, *CCO*
Eric A Evans, *
EMP: 281 **EST:** 2007
SALES (est): 46.59MM **Publicly Held**
Web: www.myriad.com
SIC: 8071 Medical laboratories
PA: Myriad Genetics, Inc.
322 N 2200 W
Salt Lake City UT

(P-16738)
NICHOLS INST REFERENCE LABS (DH)
33608 Ortega Hwy (92675-2042)
PHONE..................................949 728-4000
Douglas Harrington, *Pr*
Charles Olson, *
Murugan R Pandian, *Senior Science Director*
Chuck Miller, *
Michael O'gorman, *Supply Vice President*
EMP: 525 **EST:** 1971
SQ FT: 240,000
SALES (est): 43.15MM
SALES (corp-wide): 9.88B **Publicly Held**
Web: www.questdiagnostics.com
SIC: 8071 Testing laboratories
HQ: Quest Diagnostics Nichols Institute
33608 Ortega Hwy
San Juan Capistrano CA
949 728-4000

(P-16739)
PACIFIC TOXICOLOGY LABS
Also Called: Forensic Toxicology Associates
9348 De Soto Ave (91311-4926)
PHONE..................................818 598-3110
Jeff Lanzolatta, *CEO*
Greg Carroll, *
Sue Barbosa, *
Neil Patel Carroll, *
Bert Cohen, *
EMP: 75 **EST:** 1984
SQ FT: 19,000
SALES (est): 13.79MM **Privately Held**
Web: www.pactox.com
SIC: 8071 Testing laboratories

(P-16740)
PERSONALIS INC (PA)
6600 Dumbarton Cir (94555-3615)
PHONE..................................650 752-1300
John West, *Pr*
Jonathan Macquitty, *
Aaron Tachibana, *CFO*
Richard Chen, *CSO*
Clinton Musil, *Chief Business Officer*
EMP: 135 **EST:** 2011
SQ FT: 31,280
SALES (est): 65.05MM
SALES (corp-wide): 65.05MM **Publicly Held**
Web: www.personalis.com
SIC: 8071 Biological laboratory

(P-16741)
PHYSICIANS AUTOMATED LAB INC (DH)
Also Called: Central Coast Pathology Lab
820 34th St Ste 102 (93301-1933)
P.O. Box 1536 (93302-1536)
PHONE..................................661 325-0744
Ken Botta, *CEO*
Bruce Smith, *
William R Schmalhorst Md, *Pr*
Joyce Hulen, *
Mimi Breslin, *
EMP: 69 **EST:** 1967
SQ FT: 63,000
SALES (est): 30.25MM **Privately Held**
Web: www.westpaclab.com
SIC: 8071 Medical laboratories
HQ: Sonic Healthcare Services Pty Limited
L 22 225 George St
Sydney NSW

(P-16742)
PRECISION TOXICOLOGY
4215 Sorrento Valley Blvd (92121-1408)
PHONE..................................800 635-6901
EMP: 60 **EST:** 2011
SALES (est): 15.58MM
SALES (corp-wide): 45.4MM **Privately Held**
Web: www.precisiondxlab.com
SIC: 8071 Testing laboratories
PA: Belhealth Investment Partners, Llc
17713 32nd Ln N
Loxahatchee FL
347 308-7011

(P-16743)
PRIMEX CLINICAL LABS INC (PA)
16742 Stagg St Ste 120 (91406-1641)
EMP: 80 **EST:** 1996
SQ FT: 3,000
SALES (est): 24.69MM **Privately Held**
Web: www.primexlab.com
SIC: 8071 Blood analysis laboratory

(P-16744)
PROFORM INC
Also Called: Proform Labs
1140 S Rockefeller Ave (91761-2201)
PHONE..................................707 752-9010
Sean Phillip Thomas, *CEO*
EMP: 100 **EST:** 2016
SALES (est): 3.11MM **Privately Held**
SIC: 8071 Biological laboratory

(P-16745)
PTS DIAGNOSTICS CALIFORNIA INC
510 Oakmead Pkwy (94085-4022)
PHONE..................................877 870-5610
Robert Huffstodt, *CEO*

PRODUCTS & SERVICES SECTION
8071 - Medical Laboratories (P-16766)

EMP: 200 **EST:** 2016
SALES (est): 6.13MM **Privately Held**
Web: www.ptsdiagnostics.com
SIC: 8071 Medical laboratories

(P-16746)
RADIOLOGICAL ASSOCIATES OF SACRAMENTO MEDICAL GROUP INC
Also Called: Radiological Assoc Sacramento
1500 Expo Pkwy (95815-4227)
P.O. Box 160008 (95816-0008)
PHONE.................................916 646-8300
EMP: 1000
SIC: 8071 8011 Medical laboratories; Offices and clinics of medical doctors

(P-16747)
RADNET INC (PA)
1510 Cotner Ave (90025-3303)
PHONE.................................310 478-7808
Howard G Berger, *Ch Bd*
Mark D Stolper, *Ex VP*
Mital Patel, *Ex VP*
David J Katz, *CLO*
Ranjan Jayanathan, *CIO*
EMP: 520 **EST:** 1985
SQ FT: 21,500
SALES (est): 1.43B **Publicly Held**
Web: www.radnet.com
SIC: 8071 Ultrasound laboratory

(P-16748)
REDWOOD RGNAL MED GROUP DRG LL (PA)
Also Called: Redwood Regional Oncology Ctr
990 Sonoma Ave Ste 15 (95404-4813)
PHONE.................................707 525-4080
Mike Smith, *CFO*
EMP: 70 **EST:** 1996
SQ FT: 20,000
SALES (est): 11.15MM
SALES (corp-wide): 11.15MM **Privately Held**
SIC: 8071 8011 X-ray laboratory, including dental; Radiologist

(P-16749)
REDWOOD TOXICOLOGY LAB INC
3650 Westwind Blvd (95403-1066)
P.O. Box 5680 (95402-5680)
PHONE.................................707 577-7958
Albert Berger, *CEO*
Alber Berger, *
Wayne Ross, *Stockholder**
Barry Chapman, *
▲ **EMP:** 120 **EST:** 1994
SQ FT: 23,000
SALES (est): 35.4MM
SALES (corp-wide): 43.65B **Publicly Held**
Web: www.redwoodtoxicology.com
SIC: 8071 8734 Testing laboratories; Testing laboratories
HQ: Alere Inc.
51 Sawyer Rd Ste 200
Waltham MA
781 647-3900

(P-16750)
RHEUMATOLOGY DIAGNOSTICS LAB
Also Called: Rdl Reference Laboratory
324 S Beverly Dr (90212-4822)
P.O. Box 34020 (90034-0020)
PHONE.................................310 253-5455
Robert I Morris Md, *Pr*
Allan Metzger Md, *VP*
Barbara Rao, *Dir*

Laura Lehrhoff, *
EMP: 60 **EST:** 1976
SALES (est): 10.53MM **Privately Held**
SIC: 8071 Pathological laboratory

(P-16751)
SAMARITAN IMAGING CENTER
1245 Wilshire Blvd Ste 205 (90017-1901)
PHONE.................................213 977-2140
Andrew B Leeka, *CEO*
EMP: 5019 **EST:** 2010
SALES (est): 661.09K
SALES (corp-wide): 923.01K **Privately Held**
Web: www.samaritanimagingcenter.com
SIC: 8071 Medical laboratories
HQ: Pih Health Good Samaritan Hospital
1225 Wilshire Blvd
Los Angeles CA
213 977-2121

(P-16752)
SEQUENOM CTR FOR MLCLAR MDCINE
Also Called: Sequenom Laboratories
3595 John Hopkins Ct (92121-1121)
PHONE.................................858 202-9051
Jeffrey D Linton, *Sec*
Carolyn D Beaver, *
Kelly L Perez, *
Daniel Grosu, *
◆ **EMP:** 338 **EST:** 2008
SALES (est): 8.63MM **Publicly Held**
Web: womenshealth.labcorp.com
SIC: 8071 Medical laboratories
HQ: Sequenom, Inc.
3595 John Hopkins Ct
San Diego CA

(P-16753)
SPECIALTY LABORATORIES INC (DH)
Also Called: Quest Dgnstics Nchols Inst Vln
27027 Tourney Rd (91355-5386)
PHONE.................................661 799-6543
R Keith Laughman, *Pr*
Vicki Difrancesco, *
▲ **EMP:** 633 **EST:** 1975
SALES (est): 71.32MM
SALES (corp-wide): 9.88B **Publicly Held**
Web: www.questdiagnostics.com
SIC: 8071 Testing laboratories
HQ: Ameripath, Inc.
7108 Fairway Dr Ste 335
Palm Beach Gardens FL
561 712-6200

(P-16754)
SPECTRA LABORATORIES INC (DH)
525 Sycamore Dr (95035-7429)
PHONE.................................800 433-3773
EMP: 250 **EST:** 1982
SALES (est): 94.26MM
SALES (corp-wide): 20.15B **Privately Held**
Web: www.spectra-labs.com
SIC: 8071 Testing laboratories
HQ: Fresenius Medical Care Holdings, Inc.
920 Winter St
Waltham MA

(P-16755)
SPRING BIOSCIENCE CORP
4300 Hacienda Dr (94588-2722)
PHONE.................................925 474-8463
Meghan Lehrkamp, *Mgr*
EMP: 875 **EST:** 2002
SALES (est): 3.8MM **Privately Held**

SIC: 8071 Testing laboratories
HQ: Ventana Medical Systems, Inc.
1910 E Innovation Park Dr
Oro Valley AZ
520 887-2155

(P-16756)
THAIHOT INVESTMENT CO US LTD
18201 Von Karman Ave Ste 600 (92612-1000)
PHONE.................................949 242-5300
EMP: 2450 **EST:** 2017
SALES (est): 24.35MM **Privately Held**
SIC: 8071 Medical laboratories
PA: Tahoe Investment Group Co., Ltd.
No.333, Wusi North Road
Fuzhou FJ

(P-16757)
UNCHAINED LABS (PA)
Also Called: Optim
4747 Willow Rd (94588-2763)
PHONE.................................925 587-9800
Tim Harness, *CEO*
Terry Salyer, *CCO**
Jason Novi, *
Will Lachnit, *
Scott Lockard, *
EMP: 140 **EST:** 2014
SALES (est): 122.7MM
SALES (corp-wide): 122.7MM **Privately Held**
Web: www.unchainedlabs.com
SIC: 8071 3826 Medical laboratories; Analytical instruments

(P-16758)
UNILAB CORPORATION
470 27th St (94612-2413)
PHONE.................................510 444-5213
EMP: 910
SALES (corp-wide): 9.88B **Publicly Held**
Web: www.questdiagnostics.com
SIC: 8071 Medical laboratories
HQ: Unilab Corporation
8401 Fallbrook Ave
West Hills CA
818 737-6000

(P-16759)
UNILAB CORPORATION
Also Called: Physicians Clinical Lab
3160 Folsom Blvd (95816-5202)
PHONE.................................916 733-3330
Taylor Mckeyman, *Brnch Mgr*
EMP: 910
SALES (corp-wide): 9.88B **Publicly Held**
Web: www.questdiagnostics.com
SIC: 8071 Medical laboratories
HQ: Unilab Corporation
8401 Fallbrook Ave
West Hills CA
818 737-6000

(P-16760)
UNILAB CORPORATION
5325 N Fresno St Ste 106 (93710-6849)
PHONE.................................559 225-5076
Ramona Franco, *Brnch Mgr*
EMP: 910
SALES (corp-wide): 9.88B **Publicly Held**
Web: www.questdiagnostics.com
SIC: 8071 Medical laboratories
HQ: Unilab Corporation
8401 Fallbrook Ave
West Hills CA
818 737-6000

(P-16761)
UNILAB CORPORATION
3714 Northgate Blvd (95834-1617)
PHONE.................................916 927-9900
Surya Mohapatra, *CEO*
EMP: 1214
SALES (corp-wide): 9.88B **Publicly Held**
Web: www.questdiagnostics.com
SIC: 8071 Testing laboratories
HQ: Unilab Corporation
8401 Fallbrook Ave
West Hills CA
818 737-6000

(P-16762)
UNILAB CORPORATION
Also Called: Quest Diagnostics
51 N Sunrise Ave Ste 515 (95661)
PHONE.................................916 781-3031
Susan Spivey, *Brnch Mgr*
EMP: 1214
SALES (corp-wide): 9.88B **Publicly Held**
Web: www.questdiagnostics.com
SIC: 8071 Testing laboratories
HQ: Unilab Corporation
8401 Fallbrook Ave
West Hills CA
818 737-6000

(P-16763)
UNILAB CORPORATION (HQ)
Also Called: Quest Diagnostics
8401 Fallbrook Ave (91304-3226)
PHONE.................................818 737-6000
Surya Mohapatra, *CEO*
Robert Moverley, *
EMP: 400 **EST:** 1992
SALES (est): 118.21MM
SALES (corp-wide): 9.88B **Publicly Held**
Web: www.questdiagnostics.com
SIC: 8071 Testing laboratories
PA: Quest Diagnostics Incorporated
500 Plaza Dr Ste G
Secaucus NJ
973 520-2700

(P-16764)
UNILAB CORPORATION
6475 Camden Ave Ste 104 (95120-2847)
PHONE.................................408 927-8331
Ian Brotchie, *Pr*
EMP: 910
SALES (corp-wide): 9.88B **Publicly Held**
Web: www.questdiagnostics.com
SIC: 8071 Testing laboratories
HQ: Unilab Corporation
8401 Fallbrook Ave
West Hills CA
818 737-6000

(P-16765)
UNILAB CORPORATION
Also Called: Pathlab
1328 Natividad Rd (93906-3101)
PHONE.................................831 424-3858
EMP: 910
SALES (corp-wide): 9.88B **Publicly Held**
Web: www.questdiagnostics.com
SIC: 8071 Testing laboratories
HQ: Unilab Corporation
8401 Fallbrook Ave
West Hills CA
818 737-6000

(P-16766)
UNITED LAB SERVICES INC
2479 S Vicentia Ave (92882-5934)
PHONE.................................951 444-0467
Anabelle Myers, *CEO*
EMP: 80 **EST:** 2015

8071 - Medical Laboratories

SALES (est): 3.02MM **Privately Held**
SIC: 8071 Medical laboratories

(P-16767)
UNIVERSITY CALIFORNIA DAVIS
Also Called: Veterinary Genetics Laboratory
1 Shields Ave (95616-8500)
PHONE..................530 752-2314
Linda P B Katehi, *Brnch Mgr*
EMP: 64
SALES (corp-wide): 534.4MM **Privately Held**
Web: www.ucdavis.edu
SIC: 8071 8221 9411 Testing laboratories; University; Administration of educational programs
HQ: University Of California, Davis
   1 Shields Ave
   Davis CA

(P-16768)
VERACYTE INC (PA)
Also Called: VERACYTE
6000 Shoreline Ct Ste 300 (94080-7606)
PHONE..................650 243-6300
Marc Stapley, *CEO*
Bonnie H Anderson, *
Giulia C Kennedy, *CSO CMO*
Rob Brainin, *Chief Business Officer*
EMP: 86 EST: 2006
SQ FT: 59,000
SALES (est): 296.54MM
SALES (corp-wide): 296.54MM **Publicly Held**
Web: www.veracyte.com
SIC: 8071 8733 2835 Medical laboratories; Medical research; Cytology and histology diagnostic agents

8072 Dental Laboratories

(P-16769)
BURBANK DENTAL LABORATORY INC
2101 Floyd St (91504-3411)
PHONE..................818 841-2256
Anatony Sedler, *CEO*
Tony Sedler, *
Robert Vartanian, *
David French, *
▲ EMP: 175 EST: 1980
SALES (est): 22.59MM **Privately Held**
Web: www.burbankdental.com
SIC: 8072 Dental laboratories

(P-16770)
DLH DAVINCI LLC
22135 Roscoe Blvd Ste 101 (91304-3857)
PHONE..................818 703-5100
Thomas Rochefort, *VP Fin*
EMP: 65 EST: 2012
SALES (est): 604.68K **Privately Held**
SIC: 8072 Dental laboratories

(P-16771)
DURA-METRICS INC (PA)
2628 El Camino Ave Ste B1 (95821-5980)
P.O. Box 873 (95402-0763)
PHONE..................707 546-5138
EMP: 68 EST: 1968
SALES (est): 5.35MM
SALES (corp-wide): 5.35MM **Privately Held**
Web: www.dura-metrics.com
SIC: 8072 Dental laboratories

(P-16772)
GKY DENTAL ARTS INC (PA)
4212 Artesia Blvd (90504-3106)
PHONE..................310 214-8007
Glen Yamamoto, *Pr*
Kiichi Yamamoto, *
▲ EMP: 79 EST: 1982
SQ FT: 4,500
SALES (est): 9.88MM
SALES (corp-wide): 9.88MM **Privately Held**
Web: www.gkydentalarts.com
SIC: 8072 Crown and bridge production

(P-16773)
JAMES R GLDWELL DNTL CRMICS IN (PA)
Also Called: Glidewell Laboratories
4141 Macarthur Blvd (92660-2015)
PHONE..................949 440-2600
James R Glidewell, *CEO*
Jim Shuck, *
Glenn Sasaki, *
Greg Minzenmayer, *
Gary M Pritchard, *
▲ EMP: 1100 EST: 1969
SQ FT: 72,000
SALES (est): 460.81MM
SALES (corp-wide): 460.81MM **Privately Held**
Web: www.glidewelldental.com
SIC: 8072 Crown and bridge production

(P-16774)
KEATING DENTAL ARTS INC
Also Called: Keating Dental Lab
16881 Hale Ave Ste A (92606-5068)
PHONE..................949 955-2100
Shaun Keating, *Pr*
EMP: 105 EST: 2002
SQ FT: 26,000
SALES (est): 9.83MM **Privately Held**
Web: www.keatingdentallab.com
SIC: 8072 Crown and bridge production

(P-16775)
NOBEL BIOCARE USA LLC
22715 Savi Ranch Pkwy (92887-4609)
PHONE..................714 282-4800
Thomas Olsen, *Pr*
Frederick Walther, *Treas*
▲ EMP: 500 EST: 2004
SQ FT: 150,000
SALES (est): 101.09MM
SALES (corp-wide): 31.47B **Publicly Held**
Web: www.nobelbiocare.com
SIC: 8072 Dental laboratories
PA: Danaher Corporation
   2200 Penn Ave Nw Ste 800w
   Washington DC
   202 828-0850

(P-16776)
PRISMATIK DENTALCRAFT INC
4141 Macarthur Blvd (92660-2015)
PHONE..................949 399-1930
James R Glidewell, *CEO*
▲ EMP: 93 EST: 2005
SALES (est): 16.77MM
SALES (corp-wide): 460.81MM **Privately Held**
Web: www.glidewelldental.com
SIC: 8072 Dental laboratories
PA: James R. Glidewell, Dental Ceramics, Inc.
   4141 Macarthur Blvd
   Newport Beach CA
   949 440-2600

(P-16777)
SPRIG ORAL HEALTH TECHNOLOGIES
Also Called: EZ Pedo
6140 Horseshoe Bar Rd Ste L (95650-9774)
PHONE..................888 539-7336
Brenda Lee Hansen, *CEO*
Jeffrey Fisher, *
▼ EMP: 68 EST: 2009
SALES (est): 4.44MM **Privately Held**
Web: www.sprigusa.com
SIC: 8072 Crown and bridge production

(P-16778)
TRIDENT LABS LLC
Also Called: Trident Dental Laboratories
12000 Aviation Blvd (90250-3438)
PHONE..................310 915-9121
Laurence K Fishman, *Pr*
Richard B Mc Donald, *
▲ EMP: 125 EST: 1988
SQ FT: 16,000
SALES (est): 21.52MM
SALES (corp-wide): 165.17MM **Privately Held**
Web: www.tridentlab.com
SIC: 8072 Crown and bridge production
PA: Gdc Holdings, Inc.
   1701 Military Trl
   Jupiter FL
   763 398-0654

(P-16779)
WEST COAST DENTAL LABS LLC
12002 Aviation Blvd (90250-3438)
PHONE..................855 220-5600
Chuck Stapleton, *Genl Mgr*
EMP: 311 EST: 2017
SALES (est): 761.18K
SALES (corp-wide): 339.71MM **Privately Held**
Web: www.wcdlabs.com
SIC: 8072 Crown and bridge production
PA: National Dentex Labs Llc
   1701 Military Trl
   Jupiter FL
   561 537-8300

8082 Home Health Care Services

(P-16780)
365 HOME CARE
10225 Austin Dr Ste 208 (91978-1522)
PHONE..................310 908-5179
Ebele Enunwa, *Ex Dir*
EMP: 80 EST: 2020
SALES (est): 2.45MM **Privately Held**
SIC: 8082 Home health care services

(P-16781)
A CIRCLE OF CARE LLC
Also Called: A Passion For Care
16486 Bernardo Center Dr Ste 300 (92128-2518)
PHONE..................858 798-5005
Patricia Anne Melzer, *Pr*
Roland Melzer, *VP*
EMP: 60 EST: 2011
SALES (est): 2.03MM **Privately Held**
Web: www.apassionforcare.com
SIC: 8082 Home health care services

(P-16782)
A PLUS HOME HEALTH SPECIALISTS
Also Called: A Plus Home Health Specialist
1000 Lakes Dr Ste 170 (91790-2937)
PHONE..................626 918-9905
Manette Banares, *Pr*
EMP: 60 EST: 1994
SQ FT: 3,000
SALES (est): 1.6MM **Privately Held**
SIC: 8082 Home health care services

(P-16783)
ABC HOME HEALTH CARE LLC
5090 Shoreham Pl Ste 209 (92122-5935)
PHONE..................858 455-5000
Joseph Monteforte, *Ex Dir*
Hamideh F Panabi, *Managing Member*
Hamid Alebrahim, *Managing Member*
EMP: 125 EST: 1993
SALES (est): 1.11MM **Privately Held**
Web: www.bridgehh.com
SIC: 8082 7371 Home health care services; Computer software development and applications

(P-16784)
ABCSP LLC
Also Called: Always Best Care Senior Svcs
1406 Blue Oaks Blvd Ste 100 (95747-4002)
PHONE..................855 470-2273
Michael Newman, *Ex Ch Bd*
Jake Brown, *
Sheila Davis, *
Jason Wiedder, *Branches Vice President*
David J Caesar Vp Franchise Tr aining, *Prin*
EMP: 121 EST: 1996
SQ FT: 3,000
SALES (est): 17.63MM **Privately Held**
Web: www.alwaysbestcare.com
SIC: 8082 Home health care services

(P-16785)
ABRAHAM REST HOME
Also Called: ABRAHAM REST HOME
2832 Filbert Dr (94598-3819)
PHONE..................925 287-8382
Sara Abraham, *Brnch Mgr*
EMP: 87
SALES (corp-wide): 313.17K **Privately Held**
SIC: 8082 Home health care services
PA: Abraham Rest Home, Inc.
   14 Lommel Ct
   Walnut Creek CA
   925 944-9594

(P-16786)
ACCENTCARE INC
5050 Murphy Canyon Rd Ste 200 (92123)
PHONE..................858 576-7410
EMP: 413
SALES (corp-wide): 2.44B **Privately Held**
Web: www.accentcare.com
SIC: 8082 7389 Home health care services; Business Activities at Non-Commercial Site
HQ: Accentcare, Inc.
   17855 Dallas Pkwy
   Dallas TX
   800 834-3059

(P-16787)
ACCENTCARE HM HLTH EL CNTRO IN
2344 S 2nd St Ste A (92243-5606)
PHONE..................760 352-4022
Melanie Ihler, *CEO*
EMP: 245 EST: 1994
SALES (est): 2.44MM
SALES (corp-wide): 2.44B **Privately Held**
SIC: 8082 Home health care services
HQ: Accentcare Home Health, Inc.
   135 Technology Dr Ste 150

PRODUCTS & SERVICES SECTION
8082 - Home Health Care Services (P-16809)

Irvine CA

(P-16788)
ACCENTCARE HM HLTH SCRMNTO INC
Also Called: Accentcare
2880 Sunrise Blvd Ste 218 (95742-6101)
PHONE..................916 852-5888
Karin Stark, Pr
Rochelle Ward, *
EMP: 773 EST: 1993
SQ FT: 10,000
SALES (est): 13.61MM
SALES (corp-wide): 2.44B **Privately Held**
Web: www.accentcare.com
SIC: 8082 Visiting nurse service
HQ: Accentcare Home Health, Inc.
 135 Technology Dr Ste 150
 Irvine CA

(P-16789)
ACCENTCARE HOME HLTH YUMA INC
1455 Auto Center Dr Ste 125 (91761-2254)
PHONE..................909 605-7000
Connie Morris, Pr
Melanie Ihler, *
Anna Trappett, *
EMP: 495 EST: 1992
SALES (est): 9.3MM
SALES (corp-wide): 2.44B **Privately Held**
Web: www.accentcare.com
SIC: 8082 Home health care services
HQ: Accentcare Home Health, Inc.
 135 Technology Dr Ste 150
 Irvine CA

(P-16790)
ACCREDITED FMS INC
5955 De Soto Ave Ste 136 (91367-5122)
PHONE..................818 435-4200
EMP: 598 EST: 2012
SALES (est): 1.37MM
SALES (corp-wide): 1.79B **Publicly Held**
SIC: 8082 Home health care services
PA: Aveanna Healthcare Holdings Inc.
 400 Intrstate N Pkwy Se S
 Atlanta GA
 770 441-1580

(P-16791)
ACCREDITED NURSING SERVICES
Also Called: Accredited Nursing Care
3570 Camino Del Rio N Ste 108 (92108)
PHONE..................818 986-1234
Carol Speakman, Mgr
EMP: 147
SALES (corp-wide): 32.94MM **Privately Held**
Web: www.aveanna.com
SIC: 8082 Home health care services
PA: Accredited Nursing Services
 17141 Ventura Blvd # 201
 Encino CA
 818 986-6017

(P-16792)
ACCREDITED NURSING SERVICES
Also Called: Accredited Nursing Care
950 S Coast Dr Ste 215 (92626-1751)
PHONE..................714 973-1234
Meryll Jones, Mgr
EMP: 227
SALES (corp-wide): 32.94MM **Privately Held**
SIC: 8082 Home health care services
PA: Accredited Nursing Services
 17141 Ventura Blvd # 201
 Encino CA
 818 986-6017

(P-16793)
ACTION HLTH CARE PRSNNEL SVCS
3020 Old Ranch Pkwy # 30 (90740-2765)
PHONE..................562 799-5523
Renee Steele, CEO
EMP: 150 EST: 1977
SALES (est): 2.07MM **Privately Held**
SIC: 8082 Home health care services

(P-16794)
ADDUS HEALTHCARE INC
817 Coffee Rd Ste B1 (95355-4241)
PHONE..................209 526-8451
Linda Stinson, Brnch Mgr
EMP: 132
Web: www.addus.com
SIC: 8082 Home health care services
HQ: Addus Healthcare, Inc.
 2300 Warrenville Rd
 Downers Grove IL
 630 296-3400

(P-16795)
ADDUS HEALTHCARE INC
196 Cohasset Rd Ste 200 (95926-2287)
PHONE..................530 566-0405
Mary Gorman, Mgr
EMP: 120
Web: www.addus.com
SIC: 8082 Home health care services
HQ: Addus Healthcare, Inc.
 2300 Warrenville Rd
 Downers Grove IL
 630 296-3400

(P-16796)
ADVANCED HOME HEALTH INC
4354 Auburn Blvd (95841-4107)
PHONE..................916 978-0744
Angela Sehr, Pr
Angie Macadangdang, *
EMP: 75 EST: 1982
SQ FT: 4,000
SALES (est): 15.78MM **Privately Held**
Web: www.excelin.com
SIC: 8082 8621 Visiting nurse service; Nursing association

(P-16797)
ADVISORY BOARD COMPANY
23 Geary St (94108-5750)
PHONE..................415 671-7750
R W Musslewhite, Ch
EMP: 118
SALES (corp-wide): 324.16B **Publicly Held**
Web: www.advisory.com
SIC: 8082 Home health care services
HQ: The Advisory Board Company
 655 New York Ave Nw
 Washington DC
 202 266-5600

(P-16798)
AEGIS SENIOR COMMUNITIES LLC
Also Called: Aegis Gardens
36281 Fremont Blvd (94536-3509)
PHONE..................510 739-0909
Emily Poon, Mgr
EMP: 79
SALES (corp-wide): 137.21MM **Privately Held**
Web: www.aegisliving.com
SIC: 8082 8051 Home health care services; Skilled nursing care facilities
PA: Senior Aegis Communities Llc
 415 118th Ave Se
 Bellevue WA
 866 688-5829

(P-16799)
AEGIS SENIOR COMMUNITIES LLC
Also Called: Aegis Assisted Living
125 Heather Ter (95003-3825)
PHONE..................831 684-2700
Janice Ibaio, Mgr
EMP: 146
SALES (corp-wide): 137.21MM **Privately Held**
Web: www.aegisliving.com
SIC: 8082 8051 Home health care services; Skilled nursing care facilities
PA: Senior Aegis Communities Llc
 415 118th Ave Se
 Bellevue WA
 866 688-5829

(P-16800)
AEGIS SENIOR COMMUNITIES LLC
Also Called: Aegis of Ventura
4964 Telegraph Rd (93003-8181)
PHONE..................805 650-1114
Hugh Carter, Mgr
EMP: 79
SALES (corp-wide): 137.21MM **Privately Held**
Web: www.aegisliving.com
SIC: 8082 8051 Home health care services; Skilled nursing care facilities
PA: Senior Aegis Communities Llc
 415 118th Ave Se
 Bellevue WA
 866 688-5829

(P-16801)
AEGIS SENIOR COMMUNITIES LLC
Also Called: Aegis of South San Francisco
2280 Gellert Blvd (94080-5411)
PHONE..................650 952-6100
Charles Stevenson, Ex Dir
EMP: 106
SALES (corp-wide): 137.21MM **Privately Held**
Web: www.aegisliving.com
SIC: 8082 8051 Home health care services; Skilled nursing care facilities
PA: Senior Aegis Communities Llc
 415 118th Ave Se
 Bellevue WA
 866 688-5829

(P-16802)
AEGIS SENIOR COMMUNITIES LLC
Also Called: Aegis of Granada Hills
10801 Lindley Ave (91344-4441)
PHONE..................818 363-3373
Bill Phelps, Brnch Mgr
EMP: 119
SALES (corp-wide): 137.21MM **Privately Held**
Web: www.aegisliving.com
SIC: 8082 8052 8051 8361 Home health care services; Intermediate care facilities; Skilled nursing care facilities; Residential care
PA: Senior Aegis Communities Llc
 415 118th Ave Se
 Bellevue WA
 866 688-5829

(P-16803)
ALL VALLEY HOME HLTH CARE INC
Also Called: All Valley Home Care
3665 Ruffin Rd Ste 103 (92123-1871)
PHONE..................619 276-8001
EMP: 100 EST: 2013
SQ FT: 2,500
SALES (est): 3.71MM **Privately Held**
SIC: 8082 Home health care services

(P-16804)
ALTUS HEALTH INC
Also Called: Brightstar Healthcare
151 N Sunrise Ave Ste 1011 (95661-2930)
PHONE..................916 781-6500
Ignacio Cespedes, CEO
EMP: 150 EST: 2008
SALES (est): 6.89MM **Privately Held**
Web: www.brightstarcare.com
SIC: 8082 Home health care services

(P-16805)
ALWAYS HOME NURSING SVCS INC
Also Called: Always Home
7777 Greenback Ln Ste 208 (95610-5800)
PHONE..................916 989-6420
TOLL FREE: 800
Nancy Giachino, Pr
EMP: 200 EST: 1994
SALES (est): 8.99MM **Privately Held**
Web: www.alwayshomenursing.com
SIC: 8082 Visiting nurse service

(P-16806)
AMERICAN PRIVATE DUTY INC
Also Called: American Untd HM Care Crp-Priv
13111 Ventura Blvd Ste 100 (91604-2218)
PHONE..................818 386-6358
Ann Koshy, Pr
EMP: 80 EST: 1999
SALES (est): 4.29MM **Privately Held**
SIC: 8082 Visiting nurse service

(P-16807)
AMERICARE HOME HEALTH INC
16501 Sherman Way Ste 225 (91406-3787)
PHONE..................818 881-0005
Karo Yepremian, CEO
EMP: 99 EST: 2012
SALES (est): 2.39MM **Privately Held**
Web: www.americarehhinc.com
SIC: 8082 Home health care services

(P-16808)
ANGELS IN MOTION LLC
Also Called: Visiting Angels
13768 Roswell Ave (91710-1407)
PHONE..................909 590-9102
Dominique Alvarez, Managing Member
EMP: 70 EST: 2010
SALES (est): 2.35MM **Privately Held**
Web: www.visitingangels.com
SIC: 8082 Home health care services

(P-16809)
ASIAN AMERICAN HOME CARE INC
3410 Geary Blvd (94118-3356)
PHONE..................415 434-0138
Cindy Cao, Brnch Mgr
EMP: 111
SALES (corp-wide): 92.87B **Publicly Held**
Web: www.healthmatter.co

8082 - Home Health Care Services (P-16810)

SIC: 8082 8059 8049 Home health care services; Personal care home, with health care; Nurses and other medical assistants
HQ: Asian American Home Care, Inc.
1301 Marina Village Pkwy # 103
Alameda CA

(P-16810)
ASIAN AMERICAN HOME CARE INC
1840 The Alameda (95126-1731)
PHONE..............................408 283-5100
Cindy Cao, Brnch Mgr
EMP: 111
SALES (corp-wide): 92.87B **Publicly Held**
Web: www.healthmatter.co
SIC: 8082 Home health care services
HQ: Asian American Home Care, Inc.
1301 Marina Village Pkwy # 103
Alameda CA

(P-16811)
ASSISTED HOME RECOVERY INC
Also Called: ASSISTED HOME RECOVERY INC
1900 W Garvey Ave S Ste 210 (91790-2656)
PHONE..............................626 915-5595
EMP: 62
SALES (corp-wide): 11.42MM **Privately Held**
SIC: 8082 Home health care services
PA: Assisted Home Recovery, Inc.
8550 Balboa Blvd Lbby
Northridge CA
818 894-8117

(P-16812)
AT HOME NURSING CARE INC
531 Encinitas Blvd Ste 120 (92024-3741)
PHONE..............................760 634-8000
Lauren Reynolds, Pr
EMP: 65 EST: 2012
SALES (est): 5.12MM **Privately Held**
Web: www.athomenursingcare.com
SIC: 8082 Home health care services

(P-16813)
AXELACARE HOLDINGS INC
12604 Hiddencreek Way Ste C (90703-2137)
PHONE..............................714 522-8802
EMP: 182
SIC: 8082 Home health care services
PA: Axelacare Holdings, Inc.
15529 College Blvd
Lenexa KS

(P-16814)
BARBEE ELC
1406 Blue Oaks Blvd Ste 175 (95747-5199)
PHONE..............................916 884-1983
Daniel Barbee, Pr
EMP: 99 EST: 2017
SALES (est): 2.36MM **Privately Held**
SIC: 8082 Home health care services

(P-16815)
BARRY & TAFFY INC
Also Called: Accredited Home Care
5955 De Soto Ave Ste 160 (91367-5101)
PHONE..............................818 986-1234
Millette Arrendondo, Pr
EMP: 1993 EST: 2010
SALES (est): 3.84MM
SALES (corp-wide): 1.79B **Publicly Held**
SIC: 8082 Home health care services
PA: Aveanna Healthcare Holdings Inc.
400 Intrstate N Pkwy Se S
Atlanta GA
770 441-1580

(P-16816)
BAYWOOD COURT (PA)
Also Called: BAYWOOD COURT RETIREMENT CENTE
21966 Dolores St (94546-6961)
PHONE..............................510 733-2102
Kelly Wiest, Ex Dir
EMP: 78 EST: 1984
SALES (est): 22.73MM **Privately Held**
Web: www.baywoodcourt.org
SIC: 8082 8051 6513 Home health care services; Skilled nursing care facilities; Retirement hotel operation

(P-16817)
BEAR FLAG MARKETING CORP
Also Called: At Home Caregivers
7599 Redwood Blvd Ste 200 (94945-7706)
PHONE..............................415 899-8466
Peter L Rubens, CEO
EMP: 117 EST: 2000
SQ FT: 1,200
SALES (est): 4.54MM **Privately Held**
Web: www.bearflagmarketing.com
SIC: 8082 Home health care services

(P-16818)
BERGER INC
Also Called: Accredited Home Care
5955 De Soto Ave Ste 160 (91367-5101)
PHONE..............................818 986-1234
EMP: 5137 EST: 1980
SALES (est): 12.3MM
SALES (corp-wide): 1.79B **Publicly Held**
Web: www.aveanna.com
SIC: 8082 Home health care services
PA: Aveanna Healthcare Holdings Inc.
400 Intrstate N Pkwy Se S
Atlanta GA
770 441-1580

(P-16819)
BERKELEY COMMUNITY HEALTH PRJ
Also Called: BERKELEY FREE CLINIC
2339 Durant Ave (94704-1606)
PHONE..............................510 548-2570
TOLL FREE: 800
John Day, Pr
EMP: 61 EST: 1970
SALES (est): 439.75K **Privately Held**
Web: www.berkeleyfreeclinic.org
SIC: 8082 8322 Home health care services; Individual and family services

(P-16820)
BESTLIVING CARE LLC
2401 Merced St Ste 300 (94577-4200)
PHONE..............................510 862-3508
EMP: 60 EST: 2018
SALES (est): 2.53MM **Privately Held**
Web: www.bestlivingcare.com
SIC: 8082 Home health care services

(P-16821)
BJZ LLC
Also Called: Always Best Care Desert Cities
45150 Club Dr (92210-8806)
PHONE..............................760 851-0740
Neil Zwack, Admn
Neil Zwack, Managing Member
Bonnie Zwack, Managing Member*
EMP: 140 EST: 2013
SALES (est): 3.16MM **Privately Held**
Web: www.alwaysbestcare.com

SIC: 8082 Home health care services

(P-16822)
BLIZE HEALTHCARE CAL INC
Also Called: Blize Healthcare
750 Alfred Nobel Dr Ste 202 (94547-1836)
PHONE..............................800 343-2549
Ukeje Elendu, Pr
Blessing Elendu, *
EMP: 100 EST: 2010
SQ FT: 3,700
SALES (est): 8.49MM **Privately Held**
Web: www.blizecare.com
SIC: 8082 Home health care services

(P-16823)
BLOSSOM RIDGE HM HLTH AGCY LLC
520 9th St Ste 240 (95814-1327)
PHONE..............................800 991-6147
John Saruwatari, Managing Member
Gerald Agustin, Managing Member*
EMP: 86 EST: 2011
SALES (est): 10.61MM **Privately Held**
Web: www.blossomridge.com
SIC: 8082 Home health care services

(P-16824)
BLUEBRIDGE PROF SVCS INC
Also Called: Comfort Keepers
420 W Baseline Rd Ste D (91711-1621)
PHONE..............................909 625-6151
Michael Craig Ii, CEO
EMP: 68 EST: 2005
SALES (est): 2.2MM **Privately Held**
Web: www.comfortkeepers.com
SIC: 8082 Home health care services

(P-16825)
BRANLYN PROMINENCE INC
Also Called: Home Instead Senior Care
13334 Amargosa Rd (92392-8504)
PHONE..............................760 843-5655
Chris Parmelee, Genl Mgr
EMP: 130
SQ FT: 1,800
Web: www.homeinstead.com
SIC: 8082 Home health care services
PA: Branlyn Prominence, Inc.
9213 Archibald Ave
Rancho Cucamonga CA

(P-16826)
BRANLYN PROMINENCE INC (PA)
Also Called: Home Instead Senior Care
9213 Archibald Ave (91730-5207)
PHONE..............................909 476-9030
Brandi Johnson, CEO
Lynda Patriquin, *
EMP: 100 EST: 2000
SALES (est): 8.72MM **Privately Held**
Web: www.homeinstead.com
SIC: 8082 Home health care services

(P-16827)
BRIDGE HOME HEALTH LLC
5090 Shoreham Pl Ste 109 (92122-5934)
PHONE..............................858 277-5200
EMP: 91 EST: 2017
SALES (est): 5.91MM **Privately Held**
Web: www.bridgehh.com
SIC: 8082 Home health care services

(P-16828)
BRIGHTSTAR CARE LAKE FOREST
26023 Acero Ste 100 (92691-7942)
PHONE..............................949 837-7000
Mark Woodsum, CEO
Mark Woodsum, Prin
EMP: 275 EST: 2014
SALES (est): 8.34MM **Privately Held**
SIC: 8082 Home health care services

(P-16829)
BUENA VISTA MGT SVCS LLC
Also Called: Windward Life Care
2045 1st Ave (92101-2011)
P.O. Box 87371 (92138-7371)
PHONE..............................619 450-4300
Norman Hannay, Owner
Norman J Hannay, Owner
EMP: 130 EST: 2004
SQ FT: 2,000
SALES (est): 9.85MM **Privately Held**
Web: www.windwardlifecare.com
SIC: 8082 Home health care services

(P-16830)
BUTTE HOME HEALTH INC
Also Called: Butte Home Health & Hospice
10 Constitution Dr (95973-4903)
P.O. Box 5171 (95927-5171)
PHONE..............................530 895-0462
Brooke Quilici, Pr
Mike Quilici, *
Robert Love, *
EMP: 80 EST: 1984
SQ FT: 7,100
SALES (est): 7.23MM **Privately Held**
Web: www.buttehomehealth.com
SIC: 8082 Visiting nurse service

(P-16831)
BY THE BAY HEALTH (PA)
Also Called: Hospice of Marin
17 E Sir Francis Drake Blvd (94939-1708)
PHONE..............................415 927-2273
Kitty Whitaker, CEO
Sandra Lew, *
Denis Viscek, *
Dennis A Gilardi, *
Michelle Martinez, *
EMP: 220 EST: 1975
SQ FT: 8,000
SALES (est): 71.79MM
SALES (corp-wide): 71.79MM **Privately Held**
Web: www.bythebayhealth.org
SIC: 8082 Home health care services

(P-16832)
CALIFRNIA PRSON HLTHCARE RCVRS
501 J St Ste 100 (95814-2325)
P.O. Box 588500 (95758-8500)
PHONE..............................916 691-6721
J Clark Kelso, Pr
EMP: 66 EST: 2006
SALES (est): 2.6MM **Privately Held**
Web: cphcs.ca.gov
SIC: 8082 Home health care services

(P-16833)
CARE OPTIONS MANAGEMENT PLANS
7000 Village Pkwy Ste A (94568-2413)
PHONE..............................925 551-3227
Joanne Mccarley, Brnch Mgr
EMP: 778
Web: www.optioncarehealth.com
SIC: 8082 Home health care services
PA: Care Options Management Plans And Supportive Services, Llc
1020 Market St
Redding CA

PRODUCTS & SERVICES SECTION   8082 - Home Health Care Services (P-16856)

(P-16834)
CARE UNLIMITED HEALTH SVCS INC
1025 W Arrow Hwy Ste 103 (91740-5407)
PHONE.................................626 332-3767
Carol Wedderburn, *CEO*
EMP: 90 **EST:** 1995
SALES (est): 5.99MM **Privately Held**
Web: www.careunltd.com
SIC: 8082 Home health care services

(P-16835)
CASTRO VALLEY HEALTH INC
Also Called: Cvh Home Health Services
39 Beta Ct (94583-1201)
PHONE.................................510 690-1930
Mark R Parinas, *CEO*
Isobel Parinas, *
EMP: 200 **EST:** 2005
SALES (est): 17.74MM **Privately Held**
Web: www.cvhcare.com
SIC: 8082 Visiting nurse service

(P-16836)
CENTERWELL HEALTH SERVICES INC
Gentiva Health Services
1260 N Dutton Ave Ste 150 (95401-4680)
PHONE.................................707 545-7114
Linda Ecker, *Mgr*
EMP: 75
SALES (corp-wide): 4.82MM **Privately Held**
Web: www.gentivahs.com
SIC: 8082 Home health care services
PA: Centerwell Health Services, Inc.
  3350 Rvrwood Pkwy Se # 140
  Atlanta GA
  770 951-6450

(P-16837)
CENTRAL COAST VNA HOSPICE INC
45 Plaza Cir (93901-2902)
PHONE.................................831 758-8243
Raul Perez, *Mgr*
EMP: 184
SALES (corp-wide): 32.43MM **Privately Held**
Web: www.ccvna.com
SIC: 8082 Visiting nurse service
PA: Central Coast Vna & Hospice, Inc.
  5 Lower Ragsdale Dr # 10
  Monterey CA
  831 372-6668

(P-16838)
CENTRAL HEALTH PLAN CAL INC
1540 Bridgegate Dr (91765-3912)
PHONE.................................626 938-7120
Sam Kam, *Pr*
EMP: 175 **EST:** 2001
SQ FT: 16,144
SALES (est): 50.02MM
SALES (corp-wide): 2.41B **Publicly Held**
Web: www.centralhealthplan.com
SIC: 8082 Home health care services
PA: Bright Health Group, Inc.
  8000 Norman Center Dr # 120
  Minneapolis MN
  612 238-1321

(P-16839)
CHAROLAIS CARE V INC
Also Called: San Frncsco Bay Cmpssnate Cmnt
1426 Fillmore St Ste 207 (94115-4164)
PHONE.................................415 921-5038
Jim Everton, *CEO*
EMP: 85 **EST:** 2008
SALES (est): 2.12MM
SALES (corp-wide): 33.43MM **Privately Held**
SIC: 8082 Home health care services
PA: B.R.P. Health Management Systems, Inc.
  275 S 5th Ave Lowr Level
  Pocatello ID
  208 233-4673

(P-16840)
CLINICS ON DEMAND INC
11000 Wilshire Blvd (90024-3601)
PHONE.................................310 709-7355
Shahrouz Ghodsian, *CEO*
EMP: 81 **EST:** 2015
SALES (est): 8.5MM **Privately Held**
SIC: 8082 Home health care services

(P-16841)
COASTAL CMNTY SENIOR CARE LLC
Also Called: Home Instead Senior Care
5500 E Atherton St Ste 216 (90815-4016)
PHONE.................................562 596-4884
Donald Pierce, *Managing Member*
EMP: 140 **EST:** 2015
SQ FT: 2,300
SALES (est): 4.24MM **Privately Held**
Web: www.homeinstead.com
SIC: 8082 Home health care services

(P-16842)
COASTAL HOME CARE SERVICES INC
Also Called: Choice Home Health Care
80 Garden Ct Ste 105 (93940-5367)
PHONE.................................831 424-1344
Robert Levin, *CEO*
EMP: 141 **EST:** 1994
SALES (est): 8.21MM
SALES (corp-wide): 63.38MM **Privately Held**
Web: www.caremonterey.com
SIC: 8082 Home health care services
HQ: Rehabfocus Home Health, Inc.
  27071 Aliso Creek Rd
  Aliso Viejo CA
  209 524-8700

(P-16843)
COLLABRIA CARE
414 S Jefferson St (94559-4515)
PHONE.................................707 258-9080
Linda Gibson, *Pr*
EMP: 90 **EST:** 1997
SALES (est): 15.48MM **Privately Held**
Web: www.communityhealthnapavalley.org
SIC: 8082 Home health care services

(P-16844)
COMPETENT CARE INC
Also Called: Competent Care HM Hlth Nursing
2900 Bristol St Ste D107 (92626-5940)
PHONE.................................714 545-4818
TOLL FREE: 800
Lynett Laroche, *Pr*
EMP: 70 **EST:** 1988
SALES (est): 4.95MM **Privately Held**
Web: www.competentcare.com
SIC: 8082 7299 Visiting nurse service; Information services, consumer

(P-16845)
CONFIDO LLC
Also Called: 123 Home Care
1055 E Colorado Blvd (91106-2341)
PHONE.................................310 361-8558
Graeme Freeman, *CEO*
Ryan Baxter, *
Mark Schellinger, *
EMP: 1900 **EST:** 2018
SALES (est): 59.97MM **Privately Held**
Web: www.thekey.com
SIC: 8082 Home health care services

(P-16846)
CORAM HALTHCARE CORP NTHRN CAL
Also Called: Coram Healthcare
3160 Corporate Pl (94545-3916)
PHONE.................................415 292-6811
Patricia Igarashi, *Mgr*
EMP: 686
SALES (corp-wide): 322.47B **Publicly Held**
Web: www.coramhc.com
SIC: 8082 Home health care services
HQ: Coram Healthcare Corporation Of Northern California
  2100 E Lake Cook Rd # 120
  Buffalo Grove IL

(P-16847)
CORAM HEALTHCARE CORP NEVADA
Also Called: Coram Healthcare
9332 Tech Center Dr Ste 100 (95826-2562)
PHONE.................................916 857-7000
EMP: 72
SALES (corp-wide): 322.47B **Publicly Held**
SIC: 8082 Home health care services
HQ: Coram Healthcare Corporation Of Nevada
  101 N Pecos Rd Ste 106
  Las Vegas NV
  702 453-4546

(P-16848)
CORE HOLDINGS INC
Also Called: Maxin
17291 Irvine Blvd Ste 404 (92780-2932)
PHONE.................................714 969-2342
Ryan Dammieir, *CEO*
EMP: 250 **EST:** 1992
SQ FT: 1,320
SALES (est): 2.95MM **Privately Held**
SIC: 8082 Home health care services

(P-16849)
COUNTY OF ALAMEDA
Also Called: Health Care Fund
1411 E 31st St (94602-1018)
PHONE.................................510 437-4190
Carl N Lester, *Prin*
EMP: 147 **EST:** 2009
SALES (est): 13.32MM **Privately Held**
Web: www.acgov.org
SIC: 8082 Home health care services
PA: County Of Alameda
  1221 Oak St Ste 555
  Oakland CA
  510 272-6691

(P-16850)
COX ENTERPRISES LLC
Also Called: Home Helpers of North County
325 W 3rd Ave Ste 101 (92025-4140)
PHONE.................................858 822-8587
Christopher Cox, *Managing Member*
EMP: 80 **EST:** 2018
SALES (est): 2.25MM **Privately Held**
Web: www.homehelpershomecare.com
SIC: 8082 Home health care services

(P-16851)
CRESCENT HEALTHCARE INC
25901 Industrial Blvd (94545-2995)
PHONE.................................510 264-5454
Eileen Callaghan, *Dir*
EMP: 256
SALES (corp-wide): 139.08B **Publicly Held**
Web: www.optioncarehealth.com
SIC: 8082 Home health care services
HQ: Crescent Healthcare, Inc.
  11980 Telg Rd Ste 100
  Santa Fe Springs CA

(P-16852)
CRESCENT HEALTHCARE INC (DH)
11980 Telegraph Rd Ste 100 (90670)
PHONE.................................714 520-6300
Paul Mastrapa, *CEO*
William P Forster, *
Pamela Bowen, *CIO*
EMP: 150 **EST:** 1992
SQ FT: 26,000
SALES (est): 58.88MM
SALES (corp-wide): 139.08B **Publicly Held**
Web: www.crescenthealthcare.com
SIC: 8082 Home health care services
HQ: Walgreen Co.
  200 Wilmot Rd
  Deerfield IL
  800 925-4733

(P-16853)
CTSH LLC
640 N Tustin Ave Ste 201 (92705-3783)
PHONE.................................949 916-6705
EMP: 90 **EST:** 2014
SALES (est): 1.47MM **Privately Held**
Web: www.caretostayhome.com
SIC: 8082 Home health care services

(P-16854)
CVH CARE
39 Beta Ct (94583-1201)
PHONE.................................650 393-5657
EMP: 116 **EST:** 2015
SALES (est): 6.86MM **Privately Held**
Web: www.cvhcare.com
SIC: 8082 Home health care services

(P-16855)
DUNN & BERGER INC
Also Called: Accredited Nursing Care
5955 De Soto Ave Ste 160 (91367-5101)
PHONE.................................818 986-1234
Barry Berger, *Pr*
EMP: 500 **EST:** 1980
SALES (est): 24.01MM
SALES (corp-wide): 1.79B **Publicly Held**
SIC: 8082 Home health care services
PA: Aveanna Healthcare Holdings Inc.
  400 Intrstate N Pkwy Se S
  Atlanta GA
  770 441-1580

(P-16856)
DYNAMIC HOME CARE SERVICE INC (PA)
Also Called: Dynamic Home Care
14260 Ventura Blvd Ste 301 (91423-2734)
PHONE.................................818 981-4446
Nissan Pardo, *CEO*
Carol Silver, *

8082 - Home Health Care Services (P-16857)

EMP: 100 EST: 1987
SALES (est): 12.56MM Privately Held
Web: www.dynamicnursing.com
SIC: 8082 Visiting nurse service

(P-16857)
EISENHOWER MEDICAL CENTER
Also Called: Eisenhower Health Services
39000 Bob Hope Dr Ste 102 (92270-3221)
PHONE.................................760 773-1888
EMP: 206
SALES (corp-wide): 3.81MM Privately Held
Web: www.eisenhowerhealth.org
SIC: 8082 8062 Home health care services; General medical and surgical hospitals
PA: Eisenhower Medical Center
39000 Bob Hope Dr
Rancho Mirage CA
760 340-3911

(P-16858)
EL CAMINO HOSPITAL AUXILIARY
2500 Grant Rd (94040-4378)
P.O. Box 7025 (94039-7025)
PHONE.................................650 940-7214
Linda Heider, Pr
EMP: 600 EST: 1958
SQ FT: 2,000
SALES (est): 52.31K
SALES (corp-wide): 1.43B Privately Held
Web: www.elcaminohealth.org
SIC: 8082 Home health care services
PA: El Camino Hospital
2500 Grant Rd
Mountain View CA
650 940-7000

(P-16859)
ELIZABETH HOSPICE INC (PA)
800 W Valley Pkwy (92025-2557)
PHONE.................................760 737-2050
Sarah Mcspadden, CEO
Laura Miller, *
Kiprian Skavinski, *
Jan Jones, *
Andrea Goodwin, *
EMP: 200 EST: 1978
SALES (est): 41.15MM
SALES (corp-wide): 41.15MM Privately Held
Web: www.elizabethhospice.org
SIC: 8082 Home health care services

(P-16860)
ENLOE MEDICAL CENTER
Also Called: Enloe Homecare Services
1390 E Lassen Ave (95973-7823)
PHONE.................................530 332-6050
Leslie Gunghl, Dir
EMP: 163
SALES (corp-wide): 814.04MM Privately Held
Web: www.enloe.org
SIC: 8082 Home health care services
PA: Enloe Medical Center
1531 Esplanade
Chico CA
530 332-7300

(P-16861)
ESKATON
9722 Fair Oaks Blvd Ste A (95628-7039)
PHONE.................................916 536-3750
Marilyn Swick, Brnch Mgr
EMP: 216
SALES (corp-wide): 156.38MM Privately Held
Web: www.eskaton.org
SIC: 8082 Home health care services
PA: Eskaton
5105 Manzanita Ave Ste D
Carmichael CA
916 334-0296

(P-16862)
FAITH JONES & ASSOCIATES INC (PA)
Also Called: Aall Care In Home Services
7801 Mission Center Ct Ste 106 (92108)
PHONE.................................619 297-9601
Faith Jones, Pr
Norman Jones, *
EMP: 90 EST: 1995
SQ FT: 1,200
SALES (est): 9.69MM
SALES (corp-wide): 9.69MM Privately Held
Web: www.aallcare.com
SIC: 8082 Home health care services

(P-16863)
FAMILY MTTERS IN-HOME CARE LLC
2155 S Bascom Ave (95008-3200)
PHONE.................................408 824-1021
Jacob Laffen, Prin
EMP: 63 EST: 2015
SALES (est): 7.19MM Privately Held
Web: www.familymattershc.com
SIC: 8082 Home health care services

(P-16864)
FIRSTAT NURSING SERVICES INC
411 Camino Del Rio S Ste 100 (92108)
PHONE.................................619 220-7600
Linnea Goodrich, Owner
Kathleen Tickle, *
EMP: 105 EST: 1997
SQ FT: 1,800
SALES (est): 5.87MM Privately Held
Web: www.firstatofsandiego.com
SIC: 8082 Visiting nurse service

(P-16865)
FORTUNE SENIOR ENTERPRISES
Also Called: Comfort Keepers
6060 Sunrise Vista Dr Ste 1180 (95610-7053)
PHONE.................................916 560-9100
Vince Maffeo, CEO
EMP: 214 EST: 2002
SQ FT: 2,500
SALES (est): 9.27MM Privately Held
Web: www.comfortkeepers.com
SIC: 8082 Home health care services

(P-16866)
GRANDCARE HEALTH SERVICES LLC (PA)
3452 E Foothill Blvd Ste 700 (91107)
PHONE.................................866 554-2447
David Bell, Managing Member
EMP: 150 EST: 2014
SALES (est): 19.05MM
SALES (corp-wide): 19.05MM Privately Held
Web: www.grandcarehealth.com
SIC: 8082 Home health care services

(P-16867)
HELP & CARE LLC
Also Called: HELP & CARE LLC
20 S Santa Cruz Ave Ste 300 (95030-6830)
PHONE.................................408 384-4412
Markus Breitbach, Prin
EMP: 75
Web: www.helpandcare.com
SIC: 8082 Home health care services
PA: Help & Care, Llc
14417 Big Basin Way Ste B
Saratoga CA

(P-16868)
HELP AT HOME SENIOR CARE
255 Elm Ave (95603-4236)
PHONE.................................877 404-6636
Stephen Bowden, Prin
EMP: 72 EST: 2013
SALES (est): 7.3MM Privately Held
Web: www.hahcare.com
SIC: 8082 Home health care services

(P-16869)
HELP UNLMTED PERSONNEL SVC INC
Also Called: Help Unlimited
3202 E Ojai Ave (93023-9320)
PHONE.................................805 962-4646
Leanna Mcnealy, Mgr
EMP: 675
Web: www.arosacare.com
SIC: 8082 7363 Visiting nurse service; Medical help service
PA: Help Unlimited Personnel Service, Inc.
1957 Eastman Ave
Ventura CA

(P-16870)
HOME HEALTH CARE MGT INC
1398 Ridgewood Dr (95973-7801)
PHONE.................................530 343-0727
Barbara Hanna, Pr
EMP: 100 EST: 1985
SQ FT: 27,007
SALES (est): 9.78MM Privately Held
Web: www.homeandhealthcaremanagement.com
SIC: 8082 8322 Visiting nurse service; General counseling services

(P-16871)
HOSPICE OF SANTA CRUZ COUNTY (PA)
Also Called: HOSPICE CARING PROJECT
940 Disc Dr (95066-4544)
PHONE.................................831 430-3000
Michael Milward, CEO
EMP: 110 EST: 1978
SQ FT: 2,300
SALES (est): 19.29MM Privately Held
Web: www.hospicesantacruz.org
SIC: 8082 Home health care services

(P-16872)
HOSPICE OF SANTA CRUZ COUNTY
Also Called: Hospice Caring Project
65 Neilson St Ste 121 (95076-2491)
PHONE.................................831 430-3000
Michael Milward, CEO
EMP: 60
Web: www.hospicesantacruz.org
SIC: 8082 Home health care services
PA: Hospice Of Santa Cruz County
940 Disc Dr
Scotts Valley CA

(P-16873)
HUNTINGTON CARE LLC
Also Called: Huntington Home Care
3452 E Foothill Blvd Ste 760 (91107)
PHONE.................................877 405-6990

EMP: 184 EST: 2007
SALES (est): 1.73MM
SALES (corp-wide): 19.05MM Privately Held
Web: www.24hrcares.com
SIC: 8082 Home health care services
PA: Grandcare Health Services Llc
3452 E Fthill Blvd Ste 70
Pasadena CA
866 554-2447

(P-16874)
INFINITE HOME HEALTH INC
22151 Ventura Blvd Ste 102 (91364-5738)
PHONE.................................818 888-7772
Taimoor Bidari, Pr
EMP: 60 EST: 2003
SQ FT: 4,000
SALES (est): 2.53MM Privately Held
Web: www.infinitehha.com
SIC: 8082 Home health care services

(P-16875)
INTEGRITY HLTHCARE SLTIONS INC
5625 Ruffin Rd (92123-1395)
PHONE.................................760 432-9811
Wendy Olayvar, Pr
EMP: 74
Web: www.interimhealthcare.com
SIC: 8082 Home health care services
PA: Integrity Healthcare Solutions, Inc.
1551 Sawgrs Corp Pkwy
Sunrise FL

(P-16876)
INTERHEALTH SERVICES INC (HQ)
Also Called: Presbyterian Inter Cmnty Hosp
12401 Washington Blvd (90602-1006)
PHONE.................................562 698-0811
Daniel F Adams, Pr
Gary Koger, *
Peggy Chulack, *
Jim West, *
EMP: 143 EST: 1983
SQ FT: 1,000
SALES (est): 42.38MM
SALES (corp-wide): 923.01K Privately Held
SIC: 8082 8062 Home health care services; General medical and surgical hospitals
PA: Pih Health, Inc.
12401 Washington Blvd
Whittier CA
562 698-0811

(P-16877)
INTERIM HEALTHCARE INC
Also Called: Interim Services
2255 Watt Ave Ste 30 (95825-0504)
PHONE.................................916 486-8181
Marianne Ward, Brnch Mgr
EMP: 199
Web: www.interimhealthcare.com
SIC: 8082 Home health care services
PA: Interim Healthcare Inc.
1551 Sawgrs Corp Pkwy # 230
Sunrise FL

(P-16878)
INTERIM HEALTHCARE INC
Also Called: Interim Services
7000 Indiana Ave Ste 107 (92506-4153)
PHONE.................................951 684-6111
Marianne Thompson, Mgr
EMP: 105
SQ FT: 2,000
Web: www.interimhealthcare.com

PRODUCTS & SERVICES SECTION   **8082 - Home Health Care Services (P-16902)**

SIC: **8082** Home health care services
PA: Interim Healthcare Inc.
   1551 Sawgrs Corp Pkwy # 230
   Sunrise FL

(P-16879)
INTERIM HLTHCARE SAN DIEGO LLC
5625 Ruffin Rd Ste 225 (92123-6396)
PHONE..................................858 576-9501
EMP: 305 EST: 2020
SALES (est): 1.08MM **Privately Held**
SIC: **8082** Home health care services
PA: Interim Healthcare Inc.
   1551 Sawgrs Corp Pkwy # 230
   Sunrise FL

(P-16880)
JAMES REBECCA PROUTY ENTPS INC
Also Called: Always Best Care Temecula Vly
43980 Margarita Rd Ste 102 (92592-2782)
PHONE..................................951 292-9777
Rebecca Prouty, *Pr*
Rebecca Prouty, *Prin*
James Prouty, *
EMP: 80 EST: 2013
SALES (est): 1.38MM **Privately Held**
Web: www.alwaysbestcare.com
SIC: **8082** Home health care services

(P-16881)
K&B PICHETTE ENTERPRISES INC
Also Called: Interim Healthcare of Jackson
11992 State Highway 88 Ste 2046 (95642-9404)
PHONE..................................209 452-5999
Brenden Pichette, *Pr*
Katherine Pichette, *
EMP: 70 EST: 2017
SALES (est): 894.46K **Privately Held**
SIC: **8082** Home health care services

(P-16882)
KAISER FOUNDATION HOSPITALS
Also Called: Kaiser Permanente
50 Great Oaks Blvd (95119-1381)
PHONE..................................408 361-2100
EMP: 152
SALES (corp-wide): 68.1B **Privately Held**
Web: www.kaisercenter.com
SIC: **8082** 8011 Home health care services; Health maintenance organization
HQ: Kaiser Foundation Hospitals Inc
   1 Kaiser Plz
   Oakland CA
   510 271-6611

(P-16883)
KIDS OVERCOMING LLC
40029 St Ste 204 (94609)
PHONE..................................415 748-8052
Anne Swinney, *Managing Member*
EMP: 75 EST: 2013
SALES (est): 6.13MM **Privately Held**
Web: www.kadiant.com
SIC: **8082** Home health care services

(P-16884)
KIND HOMECARE INC
3705 Haven Ave Ste 104 (94025-1011)
P.O. Box 1914 (94042-1214)
PHONE..................................888 885-5463
Aida Bruun, *CEO*
EMP: 99 EST: 2016
SALES (est): 779.07K **Privately Held**

SIC: **8082** 7389 Home health care services; Business services, nec

(P-16885)
KINSA INC
535 Mission St Fl 18 (94105-3256)
PHONE..................................347 405-4315
EMP: 72 EST: 2012
SALES (est): 9.74MM **Privately Held**
Web: www.kinsahealth.com
SIC: **8082** Home health care services

(P-16886)
LAGUNA HOME HEALTH SVCS LLC
25411 Cabot Rd Ste 205 (92653-5525)
PHONE..................................949 707-5023
Michael Lovell, *Pr*
EMP: 133 EST: 2008
SALES (est): 2.22MM **Privately Held**
SIC: **8082** Home health care services

(P-16887)
LANDMARK HEALTH LLC
7755 Center Ave Ste 630 (92647-9152)
PHONE..................................657 237-2450
Nick Loporcaro, *CEO*
Carol Devol, *COO*
Brandon Kerns, *CFO*
Michael Le, *CMO*
Eric Van Horn, *Chief Business Officer*
EMP: 300 EST: 2013
SALES (est): 48.74MM
SALES (corp-wide): 324.16B **Publicly Held**
Web: www.landmarkhealth.org
SIC: **8082** Home health care services
PA: Unitedhealth Group Incorporated
   9900 Bren Rd E Ste 300w
   Minnetonka MN
   952 936-1300

(P-16888)
LIBERTY HEALTHCARE CAL INC
2251 San Diego Ave Ste B110 (92110-3003)
PHONE..................................610 668-8800
Tom Mcparland, *Prin*
Francis Ysla, *
EMP: 62 EST: 2015
SALES (est): 1.6MM **Privately Held**
Web: www.libertyhealthcare.com
SIC: **8082** Home health care services

(P-16889)
LIBERTY RESIDENTIAL SVCS INC
12700 Stowe Dr Ste 110 (92064-8875)
PHONE..................................858 500-0852
Herbert T Caskey, *Pr*
EMP: 100 EST: 2007
SALES (est): 12.51MM
SALES (corp-wide): 28.73MM **Privately Held**
SIC: **8082** Home health care services
PA: Liberty Healthcare Corporation
   401 E City Ave Ste 820
   Bala Cynwyd PA
   610 668-8500

(P-16890)
LIVHOME INC (PA)
Also Called: Arosa
5670 Wilshire Blvd Ste 500 (90036-5679)
PHONE..................................800 807-5854
TOLL FREE: 877
Mike Nicholson, *Ch Bd*
Cody D Legler, *Chief Clinical Officer*
EMP: 1299 EST: 1999

SQ FT: 7,454
SALES (est): 95.64MM
SALES (corp-wide): 95.64MM **Privately Held**
Web: www.arosacare.com
SIC: **8082** Home health care services

(P-16891)
MAXIM HEALTHCARE SERVICES INC
631 River Oaks Pkwy (95134-1907)
PHONE..................................408 914-7478
EMP: 146
Web: www.maximhealthcare.com
SIC: **8082** Home health care services
PA: Maxim Healthcare Services, Inc.
   7227 Lee Deforest Dr
   Columbia MD

(P-16892)
MAXIM HEALTHCARE SERVICES INC
3580 Wilshire Blvd Ste 1000 (90010-2501)
PHONE..................................866 465-5678
EMP: 292
Web: www.maximhealthcare.com
SIC: **8082** Home health care services
PA: Maxim Healthcare Services, Inc.
   7227 Lee Deforest Dr
   Columbia MD

(P-16893)
MAXIM HEALTHCARE SERVICES INC
Also Called: Poway Homecare
3111 Camino Del Rio N Ste 1200 (92108)
PHONE..................................619 299-9350
Jeremy Vanleeuwen, *Mgr*
EMP: 293
Web: www.maximhealthcare.com
SIC: **8082** Home health care services
PA: Maxim Healthcare Services, Inc.
   7227 Lee Deforest Dr
   Columbia MD

(P-16894)
MAXIM HEALTHCARE SERVICES INC
Also Called: Fresno Respite Companion Svcs
6051 N Fresno St Ste 102 (93710-5280)
PHONE..................................559 227-2250
Melissa Cantu, *Mgr*
EMP: 135
Web: www.maximhealthcare.com
SIC: **8082** Home health care services
PA: Maxim Healthcare Services, Inc.
   7227 Lee Deforest Dr
   Columbia MD

(P-16895)
MAXIM HEALTHCARE SERVICES INC
Also Called: Victorville Homecare
560 E Hospitality Ln Ste 400 (92408-3545)
PHONE..................................760 243-3377
Angie R Wiechert, *Mgr*
EMP: 146
Web: www.maximhealthcare.com
SIC: **8082** Home health care services
PA: Maxim Healthcare Services, Inc.
   7227 Lee Deforest Dr
   Columbia MD

(P-16896)
MISSION HM HLTH SAN DIEGO LLC
Also Called: Mission Healthcare
2365 Northside Ste 200 (92108-2703)

PHONE..................................619 757-2700
Kerry E Pawl, *CEO*
Brad Parrish, *
Todd Fontenot, *
Mag Vanoosten, *COO*
EMP: 85 EST: 2009
SALES (est): 10.37MM **Privately Held**
Web: www.homewithmission.com
SIC: **8082** Home health care services

(P-16897)
MISSION HSPICE SVCS SAN DEGO L
2385 Northside Dr Ste 200 (92108-2702)
PHONE..................................619 81. 4020
Marcus L Kimsey, *Prin*
Paul Verhoeve, *
EMP: 65 EST: 2011
SALES (est): 34.58MM **Privately Held**
Web: www.homewithmission.com
SIC: **8082** Home health care services

(P-16898)
MITRE CORPORATION
3550 General Atomics Ct (92121-1122)
PHONE..................................858 459-9701
EMP: 76
SALES (corp-wide): 990.87MM **Privately Held**
Web: www.mitre.org
SIC: **8082** Home health care services
PA: The Mitre Corporation
   202 Burlington Rd
   Bedford MA
   781 271-2000

(P-16899)
NO ORDINARY MOMENTS INC
16742 Gothard St Ste 115 (92647-4564)
PHONE..................................714 848-3800
Luis Pena, *Pr*
EMP: 86 EST: 1996
SALES (est): 9.52MM **Privately Held**
Web: www.noordinarymoments.com
SIC: **8082** 8322 Home health care services; Emergency social services

(P-16900)
NORTH COAST HOME CARE INC
Also Called: Homewatch Caregivers
5927 Balfour Ct Ste 111 (92008-7376)
PHONE..................................760 260-8700
Tanya Finnerty, *Pr*
Michael Finnerty, *
EMP: 80 EST: 2011
SQ FT: 1,000
SALES (est): 4.31MM **Privately Held**
Web: www.homewatchcaregivers.com
SIC: **8082** Home health care services

(P-16901)
NUEVACARE LLC
2100 Geng Rd Ste 210 (94303-3307)
PHONE..................................650 396-3596
EMP: 88
SALES (corp-wide): 5.44MM **Privately Held**
Web: www.thekey.com
SIC: **8082** Home health care services
PA: Nuevacare Llc
   1900 S Norfolk St Ste 350
   San Mateo CA
   650 539-2000

(P-16902)
OAK HILL CAPITAL PARTNERS LP
3000 Sand Hill Rd Ste 2-160 (94025-7145)

8082 - Home Health Care Services (P-16903)

PHONE..................650 234-0500
Steven B Gruber, Pr
EMP: 1071
SALES (corp-wide): 1.14B Privately Held
Web: www.oakhill.com
SIC: 8082 Home health care services
PA: Oak Hill Capital Partners, L.P.
65 E 55th St Fl 32
New York NY
212 527-8400

(P-16903)
OAKLAND HOSPICE INC
Also Called: Interim Hlthcare Hspice - Scrm
2233 Watt Ave Ste 330 (95825-0571)
PHONE..................916 779-0811
David Klaeser, CEO
EMP: 117 EST: 2020
SALES (est): 2.42MM Privately Held
SIC: 8082 Home health care services
PA: Interim Healthcare Inc.
1551 Sawgrs Corp Pkwy # 230
Sunrise FL

(P-16904)
OMADA HEALTH INC
500 Sansome St Ste 200 (94111-3215)
PHONE..................888 987-8337
EMP: 260 EST: 2011
SALES (est): 40.97MM Privately Held
Web: www.omadahealth.com
SIC: 8082 Home health care services

(P-16905)
ONEBODY INC
Also Called: Consensus Health
2000 Powell St Ste 555 (94608-1838)
P.O. Box 6219 (94570-6219)
PHONE..................510 285-2000
Kendall Lockhart, Ch Bd
Susan M Rowe, *
EMP: 60 EST: 1996
SALES (est): 1.25MM Privately Held
SIC: 8082 Home health care services

(P-16906)
PACIFIC COAST SERVICES INC
Also Called: Pacific Homecare Services
3202 W March Ln Ste D (95219-2351)
PHONE..................209 956-2532
Leticia Robles, Pr
Jorge Robles, *
Damian Gutierrez, *
EMP: 100 EST: 2007
SQ FT: 2,000
SALES (est): 10.53MM Privately Held
Web: www.pacifichomecare.com
SIC: 8082 Visiting nurse service

(P-16907)
PACIFICARE HEALTH SYSTEMS LLC (HQ)
Also Called: Pacificare Health Systems
5995 Plaza Dr (90630-5028)
PHONE..................714 952-1121
EMP: 550 EST: 1996
SQ FT: 104,000
SALES (est): 1.98B
SALES (corp-wide): 324.16B Publicly Held
Web: www.unitedhealthgroup.com
SIC: 8082 6321 Home health care services; Accident and health insurance carriers
PA: Unitedhealth Group Incorporated
9900 Bren Rd E Ste 300w
Minnetonka MN
952 936-1300

(P-16908)
PARAMOUNT HOME CARE INC
12235 Beach Blvd Ste 102 (90680-3943)
PHONE..................714 994-1250
Nickolas Lacson, CEO
Lordus Velez, *
EMP: 60 EST: 1994
SALES (est): 2.49MM Privately Held
Web: www.paramounthomecareinc.com
SIC: 8082 Home health care services

(P-16909)
PATIENT HOME MONITORING INC
550 Kearny St Ste 300 (94108-2597)
PHONE..................415 693-9690
David Hayes, CEO
Michael Dalsin, Ch Bd
Andrew Folmer, Pr
Cole Cox, CFO
Jess Cuthbert, COO
EMP: 171 EST: 2010
SALES (corp-wide): 97.75MM Publicly Held
SIC: 8082 Visiting nurse service
HQ: P H M Corp.
1019 Town Dr
Highland Heights KY
859 340-3114

(P-16910)
PEGASUS HM HLTH CARE A CAL COR
Also Called: Pegasus Home Health Services
505 N Brand Blvd Ste 1000 (91203-3924)
PHONE..................818 551-1932
Pamela Spiszman, Pr
▼ EMP: 80 EST: 1994
SALES (est): 9.91MM Privately Held
Web: www.pegasushomecare.com
SIC: 8082 Visiting nurse service

(P-16911)
PEOPLES CARE INC
Also Called: PEOPLE'S CARE INC.
13901 Amargosa Rd Ste 101 (92392-2409)
PHONE..................760 962-1900
Stacey Minwalla, Owner
EMP: 183
SALES (corp-wide): 62.27MM Privately Held
Web: www.peoplescare.com
SIC: 8082 Home health care services
PA: Peoples Care Inc.
13920 City Center Dr # 290
Chino Hills CA
855 773-6753

(P-16912)
PREMIER HEALTHCARE SVCS LLC (DH)
Also Called: Phs Staffing
3030 Old Ranch Pkwy Ste 100 (90740-2766)
PHONE..................626 204-7930
Anthony H Strange, CEO
EMP: 200 EST: 2005
SALES (est): 52.45MM
SALES (corp-wide): 1.79B Publicly Held
Web: www.aveanna.com
SIC: 8082 Home health care services
HQ: Aveanna Healthcare Llc
400 Intrstate N Pkwy Se S
Atlanta GA
770 441-1580

(P-16913)
PREMIER INFSION HLTHCARE SVCS
Also Called: Premier Infusion Care
19500 Normandie Ave (90502-1108)
PHONE..................310 328-3897
Saman Refua, CEO
EMP: 99 EST: 2004
SALES (est): 14.91MM Privately Held
Web: www.premierinfusion.com
SIC: 8082 Home health care services

(P-16914)
PROHEALTH HOME CARE INC (PA)
2700 Zanker Rd Ste 180 (95134-2140)
PHONE..................408 451-9055
Mohammed Marleen, CEO
Mohammed Marleen, Pr
Malalai Mohideen, VP
EMP: 63 EST: 2007
SQ FT: 7,000
SALES (est): 24.31MM Privately Held
Web: www.prohealth.us
SIC: 8082 Home health care services

(P-16915)
PROMEDICA HEALTH SYSTEM INC
Also Called: Heartland Hospice
2511 Garden Rd Ste A250 (93940-5331)
PHONE..................831 373-8442
EMP: 240
SALES (corp-wide): 187.07MM Privately Held
Web: www.gentivahs.com
SIC: 8082 Home health care services
PA: Promedica Health System, Inc.
100 Madison Ave
Toledo OH
567 585-9600

(P-16916)
PROMEDICA HEALTH SYSTEM INC
Also Called: Heartland Hospice
824 Bay Ave Ste 40 (95010-2104)
PHONE..................831 476-2158
EMP: 103
SALES (corp-wide): 187.07MM Privately Held
Web: www.heartlandhospice.com
SIC: 8082 Home health care services
PA: Promedica Health System, Inc.
100 Madison Ave
Toledo OH
567 585-9600

(P-16917)
PROVIDENT CARE INC
1025 14th St (95354-1001)
P.O. Box 3558 (95352-3558)
PHONE..................209 578-1210
Robin Conley, Pr
▲ EMP: 167 EST: 2001
SQ FT: 4,571
SALES (est): 11.96MM Privately Held
Web: www.providentcare.com
SIC: 8082 Home health care services

(P-16918)
RAMONA COMMUNITY SERVICES CORP (HQ)
Also Called: Ramona Vna & Hospice
890 W Stetson Ave Ste A (92543-7311)
PHONE..................951 658-9288
Patricia Mcbe, Brnch Mgr
Carol Wood, *
Patrick Searl, *
Mark Fredrickson, *
John Brudin, *
EMP: 150 EST: 1987

SQ FT: 14,000
SALES (est): 22.83MM Privately Held
SIC: 8082 Visiting nurse service
PA: Kpc Group Inc.
9 Kpc Pkwy 301
Corona CA

(P-16919)
RES-CARE INC
Also Called: Nightingale Nursing
101 Callan Ave Ste 208 (94577-4558)
PHONE..................510 357-4222
John Chin, Brnch Mgr
EMP: 62
SALES (corp-wide): 5.27B Privately Held
Web: www.rescare.com
SIC: 8082 Home health care services
HQ: Res-Care, Inc.
805 N Whittington Pkwy
Louisville KY
502 394-2100

(P-16920)
RES-CARE INC
3187 Red Hill Ave Ste 115 (92626-3480)
PHONE..................714 662-3075
Tara Ackley, Brnch Mgr
EMP: 68
SALES (corp-wide): 5.27B Privately Held
Web: www.rescare.com
SIC: 8082 Home health care services
HQ: Res-Care, Inc.
805 N Whittington Pkwy
Louisville KY
502 394-2100

(P-16921)
ROCK CANYON HEALTHCARE INC
Also Called: Riverwalk PST-Cute Rhblitation
27101 Puerta Real Ste 450 (92691-8566)
PHONE..................719 404-1000
Dave Jorgensen, Pr
Beverly Wittekind, *
Soon Burnam, *
Ron Cook, *
EMP: 250 EST: 2014
SALES (est): 19.22MM
SALES (corp-wide): 3.03B Publicly Held
Web: www.rockcanyonrehab.com
SIC: 8082 Home health care services
PA: The Ensign Group Inc
29222 Rncho Vejo Rd Ste 1
San Juan Capistrano CA
949 487-9500

(P-16922)
SAILS WASHINGTON INC
13920 City Center Dr Ste 290 (91709-5432)
P.O. Box 1026 (98014-1026)
PHONE..................425 333-4114
Michael Kaiser, CEO
Anthony Keuter, *
Matthew Cottrell, *
EMP: 500 EST: 2004
SALES (est): 22.29MM Privately Held
Web: www.sailswashington.com
SIC: 8082 Home health care services

(P-16923)
SAN DIEGO HOSPICE & PALLIATIVE CARE CORPORATION
Also Called: San Diego Hospice & Palliative
4311 3rd Ave (92103-1407)
P.O. Box 3008 (91944-3008)
PHONE..................619 688-1600
TOLL FREE: 866
EMP: 600

PRODUCTS & SERVICES SECTION
8082 - Home Health Care Services (P-16944)

Web: www.sdhospice.org
SIC: 8082 Home health care services

(P-16924)
SELECT HOME CARE
2393 Townsgate Rd Ste 100 (91361-2513)
PHONE.................805 777-3855
EMP: 100 EST: 2007
SALES (est): 9.7MM **Privately Held**
Web: www.selecthomecare.com
SIC: 8082 Home health care services

(P-16925)
SEQUOIA SENIOR SOLUTIONS INC
205 W Clay St (95482-5452)
PHONE.................707 621-9235
Stanton C Lawson, *Brnch Mgr*
EMP: 79
SALES (corp-wide): 9.75MM **Privately Held**
Web: www.sequoiaseniorsolutions.com
SIC: 8082 Home health care services
PA: Sequoia Senior Solutions, Inc.
1372 N Mcdowell Blvd S
Petaluma CA
707 763-6600

(P-16926)
SHARP HEALTHCARE ACO LLC
Also Called: Sharp Home Care
8080 Dagget St Ste 200 (92111-2333)
PHONE.................858 541-4850
Dan Gross, *Mgr*
EMP: 60
SALES (corp-wide): 2.37B **Privately Held**
Web: www.sharp.com
SIC: 8082 Home health care services
PA: Sharp Healthcare
8695 Spectrum Center Blvd
San Diego CA
858 499-4000

(P-16927)
SIERRA NEVADA MEM HM CARE INC
Also Called: Sierra Nevada Home Care
1020 Mccourtney Rd Ste A (95949-7343)
P.O. Box 1029 (95945-1029)
PHONE.................530 274-6350
Sharon Turner, *Dir*
EMP: 98 EST: 1986
SQ FT: 6,200
SALES (est): 21.4MM **Privately Held**
SIC: 8082 7361 Home health care services; Nurses' registry
HQ: Dignity Health
185 Berry St Ste 200
San Francisco CA
415 438-5500

(P-16928)
SISTERS OF ST JOSEPH ORANGE
111 Sonoma Ave Ste 308 (95405)
PHONE.................747 206-9124
EMP: 4981
SALES (corp-wide): 32.76MM **Privately Held**
Web: www.thecsd.org
SIC: 8082 Home health care services
HQ: Sisters Of St. Joseph Of Orange
480 S Batavia St
Orange CA
714 633-8121

(P-16929)
SISTERS OF ST JOSEPH ORANGE
Also Called: SISTERS OF ST JOSEPH OF ORANGE
2127 Harrison Ave Ste 3 (95501-3241)
PHONE.................707 443-9332
EMP: 5020
SALES (corp-wide): 32.76MM **Privately Held**
Web: www.thecsd.org
SIC: 8082 Visiting nurse service
HQ: Sisters Of St. Joseph Of Orange
480 S Batavia St
Orange CA
714 633-8121

(P-16930)
SOUTH BAY SENIOR SERVICES INC
Also Called: Homewatch Caregivers
8929 S Sepulveda Blvd Ste 314 (90045-3616)
PHONE.................310 338-8558
Richard Williams, *Pr*
Patricia Greaney, *
EMP: 77 EST: 2006
SQ FT: 700
SALES (est): 1.73MM **Privately Held**
Web: www.homewatchcaregivers.com
SIC: 8082 Home health care services

(P-16931)
SOUTH COAST BEHAVIORAL HEALTH
2220 University Dr (92660-3319)
PHONE.................714 312-5058
Charles A Mcphail, *CEO*
EMP: 60 EST: 2012
SALES (est): 7.82MM **Privately Held**
Web: www.scbh.com
SIC: 8082 Home health care services

(P-16932)
ST JOSEPH HEALTH PER CARE SVCS
1315 Corona Pointe Ct Ste 201 (92879-1785)
PHONE.................800 365-1110
Greg Henderson, *Prin*
EMP: 99
SALES (corp-wide): 7.78MM **Privately Held**
Web: www.nursenextdoor.com
SIC: 8082 Home health care services
PA: St Joseph Health Personal Care Services
200 W Center St Promenade
Anaheim CA
714 712-7100

(P-16933)
ST JOSEPH HOME CARE NETWORK (DH)
441 College Ave (95401-5141)
PHONE.................714 712-9500
Linda Glomp, *Dir*
Vincent Castaldo, *
EMP: 93 EST: 1982
SQ FT: 25,000
SALES (est): 48.89MM
SALES (corp-wide): 32.76MM **Privately Held**
Web: www.stjosephhomehealth.org
SIC: 8082 Home health care services
HQ: St. Joseph Health System
3345 Michelson Dr Ste 100
Irvine CA
949 381-4000

(P-16934)
ST JSEPH HLTH SYS HM CARE SVC
200 W Center St Promenade (92805-3960)
PHONE.................714 712-9500
Jeffrey Hammond, *Managing Member*
Susan Harvey, *
EMP: 800 EST: 2015
SALES (est): 71.9MM
SALES (corp-wide): 32.76MM **Privately Held**
SIC: 8082 Home health care services
HQ: St. Joseph Health System
3345 Michelson Dr Ste 100
Irvine CA
949 381-4000

(P-16935)
STAFF ASSISTANCE INC (PA)
Also Called: Staff Assistance
72 Moody Ct Ste 100 (91360-7426)
PHONE.................818 894-7879
Bill Donley, *Ch Bd*
Elaine S Donley, *
EMP: 300 EST: 1992
SQ FT: 800
SALES (est): 24.72MM **Privately Held**
SIC: 8082 Home health care services

(P-16936)
STEP UP ON SECOND STREET INC (PA)
1328 2nd St Ofc (90401-1123)
PHONE.................310 394-6889
Todd Lipka, *CEO*
Kim Carson, *
Barbara Bloom, *
EMP: 60 EST: 1984
SQ FT: 7,500
SALES (est): 27.98MM
SALES (corp-wide): 27.98MM **Privately Held**
Web: www.stepup.org
SIC: 8082 8052 8059 Home health care services; Home for the mentally retarded, with health care; Personal care home, with health care

(P-16937)
SUCCESS HEALTHCARE 1 LLC (PA)
Also Called: Silver Lake Medical Center
1711 W Temple St (90026-7329)
PHONE.................213 989-6100
Peter R Baronoff, *Ofcr*
Brian Dunn, *
James Hopwood, *
Lawrence Leder, *
EMP: 67 EST: 2008
SALES (est): 87.5MM
SALES (corp-wide): 87.5MM **Privately Held**
Web: www.silverlakemc.com
SIC: 8082 Home health care services

(P-16938)
SUTTER CARE & HOME
700 S Claremont St Ste 220 (94402-1452)
PHONE.................650 685-2800
Pat Murphy, *Dir*
EMP: 70 EST: 2000
SALES (est): 15.93MM **Privately Held**
SIC: 8082 Visiting nurse service

(P-16939)
SUTTER COAST HOSPITAL
983 3rd St Ste D (95531-4331)
PHONE.................707 464-8741
Chris Vancamp, *Brnch Mgr*
EMP: 275
SALES (corp-wide): 14.77B **Privately Held**
Web: www.suttercoast.org
SIC: 8082 Home health care services
HQ: Sutter Coast Hospital
800 E Washington Blvd
Crescent City CA

(P-16940)
SUTTER VSTING NRSE ASSN HSPICE
1625 Van Ness Ave (94109-3370)
PHONE.................415 600-6200
Cindy Brown, *Mgr*
EMP: 134
SALES (corp-wide): 14.77B **Privately Held**
SIC: 8082 8049 7361 Visiting nurse service; Nurses and other medical assistants; Nurses' registry
HQ: Sutter Visiting Nurse Association & Hospice
1900 Powell St Ste 300
Emeryville CA
866 652-9178

(P-16941)
SUTTER VSTING NRSE ASSN HSPICE
Respiratory Care & HM Med Eqp
2953 Teagarden St (94577-5718)
PHONE.................510 895-4403
EMP: 120
SALES (corp-wide): 14.77B **Privately Held**
SIC: 8082 Visiting nurse service
HQ: Sutter Visiting Nurse Association & Hospice
1900 Powell St Ste 300
Emeryville CA
866 652-9178

(P-16942)
SUTTER VSTING NRSE ASSN HSPICE
Also Called: SUTTER VISITING NURSE ASSOCIATION & HOSPICE
1316 Celeste Dr Ste 140 (95355-2437)
PHONE.................209 342-4048
Shannon Agulay, *Brnch Mgr*
EMP: 131
SALES (corp-wide): 14.77B **Privately Held**
SIC: 8082 Visiting nurse service
HQ: Sutter Visiting Nurse Association & Hospice
1900 Powell St Ste 300
Emeryville CA
866 652-9178

(P-16943)
SUTTER VSTING NRSE ASSN HSPICE
Also Called: Alliance Home Health
19045 Portola Dr Ste B (93908-1204)
PHONE.................831 455-8901
Rosemary S Allred, *Admn*
EMP: 128
SALES (corp-wide): 14.77B **Privately Held**
SIC: 8082 Visiting nurse service
HQ: Sutter Visiting Nurse Association & Hospice
1900 Powell St Ste 300
Emeryville CA
866 652-9178

(P-16944)
SUTTER VSTING NRSE ASSN HSPICE
Also Called: Sutter Vsiting Nurse Assn Hosp
5099 Commercial Cir Ste 20594520 (94520)

8082 - Home Health Care Services (P-16945)

PHONE...................925 677-4250
Windi Heaton, Mgr
EMP: 124
SALES (corp-wide): 14.77B Privately Held
SIC: 8082 Visiting nurse service
HQ: Sutter Visiting Nurse Association & Hospice
1900 Powell St Ste 300
Emeryville CA
866 652-9178

(P-16945)
TEXAS HOME HEALTH AMERICA LP (PA)
Also Called: Texas Home Health of America
1455 Auto Center Dr Ste 200 (91761-2254)
PHONE...................972 201-3800
Steve Abshire, Pt
Judy Bishop, Pt
Duff Whitaker, Pt
Mark Lamp, Pt
EMP: 100 EST: 1969
SQ FT: 18,000
SALES (est): 1.15MM
SALES (corp-wide): 1.15MM Privately Held
Web: www.accentcare.com
SIC: 8082 Home health care services

(P-16946)
THEKEY LLC
1802 Soscol Ave (94559-1346)
PHONE...................707 492-8411
EMP: 70
SALES (corp-wide): 84.59MM Privately Held
Web: www.thekey.com
SIC: 8082 8059 Home health care services; Personal care home, with health care
PA: Thekey, Llc
7777 Fay Ave Ste 210
La Jolla CA
650 462-9501

(P-16947)
THEKEY LLC
15734 Los Gatos Blvd (95032-2504)
PHONE...................408 356-0127
Kathy Johnson, Prin
EMP: 70
SALES (corp-wide): 84.59MM Privately Held
Web: www.thekey.com
SIC: 8082 8059 Home health care services; Personal care home, with health care
PA: Thekey, Llc
7777 Fay Ave Ste 210
La Jolla CA
650 462-9501

(P-16948)
THEKEY LLC
1330 Orange Ave Ste 300 (92118-3924)
PHONE...................858 842-1346
Ron Kinder, Mgr
EMP: 70
SALES (corp-wide): 84.59MM Privately Held
Web: www.thekey.com
SIC: 8082 Home health care services
PA: Thekey, Llc
7777 Fay Ave Ste 210
La Jolla CA
650 462-9501

(P-16949)
THEKEY LLC
2222 Francisco Dr Ste 610 (95762-3766)
PHONE...................916 358-3801
Glenn Krakow, Owner

EMP: 70
SALES (corp-wide): 84.59MM Privately Held
Web: www.thekey.com
SIC: 8082 8059 Home health care services; Personal care home, with health care
PA: Thekey, Llc
7777 Fay Ave Ste 210
La Jolla CA
650 462-9501

(P-16950)
THEKEY LLC
480 California Ave Ste 100 (94306-1623)
PHONE...................650 462-6900
Jim Johnson, Pr
EMP: 70
SALES (corp-wide): 84.59MM Privately Held
Web: www.thekey.com
SIC: 8082 Home health care services
PA: Thekey, Llc
7777 Fay Ave Ste 210
La Jolla CA
650 462-9501

(P-16951)
THERAEX REHAB SERVICES INC
1511 Sycamore Ave Ste M258 (94547-1767)
PHONE...................510 239-9614
EMP: 140
SALES (corp-wide): 10.4MM Privately Held
Web: www.theraexstaffing.com
SIC: 8082 Home health care services
PA: Theraex Rehab Services, Inc.
1320 Willow Pass Rd # 600
Concord CA
510 239-9614

(P-16952)
THRIVING SENIORS LLC
Also Called: Always Best Care Senior Svcs
479 Mason St Ste 109 (95688-4541)
PHONE...................707 317-1740
Rebecca Smith, Pr
EMP: 67 EST: 2016
SALES (est): 1.98MM Privately Held
Web: www.alwaysbestcare.com
SIC: 8082 Home health care services

(P-16953)
TIFFANY HOMECARE INC (PA)
Also Called: Always Right Home Care
9700 Reseda Blvd Ste 105 (91324-5516)
PHONE...................818 886-1602
Larry S Spaeter, CEO
EMP: 497 EST: 2003
SQ FT: 1,200
SALES (est): 8.14MM
SALES (corp-wide): 8.14MM Privately Held
SIC: 8082 Home health care services

(P-16954)
UCLA HEALTH AUXILIARY
10920 Wilshire Blvd Ste 400 (90024-6502)
PHONE...................310 267-4327
David T Feinberg, Pr
Patricia Kapur, *
Patty Cuen, *
EMP: 514 EST: 1981
SALES (est): 103.63MM Privately Held
Web: www.uclahealth.org
SIC: 8082 Home health care services

(P-16955)
ULTRACARE SERVICES LLC
1117 W Manchester Blvd Ste B (90301-1500)
PHONE...................818 266-9668
EMP: 94 EST: 2014
SALES (est): 2.28MM Privately Held
SIC: 8082 Home health care services

(P-16956)
UNI CARE HOME HEALTH INC
1510 S Escondido Blvd (92025-6017)
PHONE...................760 510-0055
Albert Keshavarzi, Pr
EMP: 70 EST: 2007
SALES (est): 5.2MM Privately Held
Web: www.unicarehospice.org
SIC: 8082 Home health care services

(P-16957)
UNIVERSAL HOME CARE INC
151 N San Vicente Blvd Ste 200 (90211-2323)
PHONE...................323 653-9222
Marina Greenberg, CEO
Stephen Shapiro Md, Medical Vice President
EMP: 200 EST: 1995
SALES (est): 3.55MM Privately Held
Web: www.universalhomecare.org
SIC: 8082 Home health care services

(P-16958)
UNIVERSITY HEALTHCARE ALLIANCE
Also Called: Stanford Medicine Partners
7999 Gateway Blvd Ste 200 (94560-1197)
PHONE...................510 974-8281
Rick Shumway, CEO
EMP: 235 EST: 2010
SALES (est): 113.74MM
SALES (corp-wide): 15.13B Privately Held
Web: www.stanfordmedicinepartners.org
SIC: 8082 Home health care services
HQ: Stanford Health Care
300 Pasteur Dr
Stanford CA
650 723-4000

(P-16959)
US CARENET SERVICES LLC
901 Campisi Way Ste 205 (95008-2348)
PHONE...................408 871-9860
Kelly Tripps, Prin
EMP: 102
SALES (corp-wide): 106.24MM Privately Held
SIC: 8082 Home health care services
HQ: Us Carenet Services, Llc
699 Broad St Ste 1001
Augusta GA

(P-16960)
US CARENET SERVICES LLC
815 Pollard Rd (95032-1438)
PHONE...................408 378-6131
Carol Parker, Brnch Mgr
EMP: 102
SALES (corp-wide): 106.24MM Privately Held
SIC: 8082 Home health care services
HQ: Us Carenet Services, Llc
699 Broad St Ste 1001
Augusta GA

(P-16961)
US CARENET SERVICES LLC
42225 10th St W Ste 2b (93534-7080)
PHONE...................661 945-7350

Michelle Shah, Dir
EMP: 102
SALES (corp-wide): 106.24MM Privately Held
SIC: 8082 Visiting nurse service
HQ: Us Carenet Services, Llc
699 Broad St Ste 1001
Augusta GA

(P-16962)
VISITING ANGELS
73700 Dinah Shore Dr Ste 105 (92211-0815)
PHONE...................800 365-4189
EMP: 120 EST: 2018
SALES (est): 940.52K Privately Held
Web: www.visitingangelspalmdesert.com
SIC: 8082 Home health care services

(P-16963)
VISITING NRSE ASSN OF INLAND C (PA)
Also Called: Vnaic
600 W Santa Ana Blvd Ste 114 (92701-4558)
P.O. Box 1649 (92502-1649)
PHONE...................951 413-1200
Mike A Rusnak, Pr
EMP: 720 EST: 1960
SALES (est): 35.35MM
SALES (corp-wide): 35.35MM Privately Held
Web: www.vnacalifornia.org
SIC: 8082 Visiting nurse service

(P-16964)
VISITING NRSE ASSN OF SNTA CRU (DH)
Also Called: Palo Alto Med Fndtion For Hlth
2880 Soquel Ave Ste 10 (95062-1423)
PHONE...................831 477-2600
Bella Hughes, Ex Dir
EMP: 100 EST: 1946
SQ FT: 19,000
SALES (est): 13.37MM
SALES (corp-wide): 14.77B Privately Held
Web: www.santacruzvna.org
SIC: 8082 Visiting nurse service
HQ: Sutter Bay Medical Foundation
795 El Camino Real
Palo Alto CA
650 321-4121

(P-16965)
VISITING NURSE & HOSPICE
512 E Gutierrez St (93103-5220)
PHONE...................805 965-5555
Karen M Wallace, CFO
EMP: 150 EST: 2017
SALES (est): 12.91MM Privately Held
Web: www.vna.health
SIC: 8082 Home health care services

(P-16966)
VISITING NURSE & HOSPICE CARE (PA)
Also Called: VISITING NURSE & HOSPICE CARE
509 E Montecito St Ste 200 (93103-3216)
PHONE...................805 965-5555
Lynda Tanner, CEO
Michelle Martinich, *
Rick Keith, *
Neil Levinson, *
Mary Pritchard, *
EMP: 122 EST: 1910
SQ FT: 13,765
SALES (est): 32.91MM
SALES (corp-wide): 32.91MM Privately Held

PRODUCTS & SERVICES SECTION
8092 - Kidney Dialysis Centers (P-16989)

Web: www.vna.health
SIC: 8082 Home health care services

(P-16967)
VIVIAN HEALTH INC
150 Spear St Ste 725 (94105-5112)
PHONE.................................415 851-1168
EMP: 88
SALES (est): 10.85MM **Privately Held**
Web: www.vivian.com
SIC: 8082 Home health care services

(P-16968)
VNA OF GREATER LOS ANGELES INC
17682 Mitchell N Ste 100 (92614-6037)
PHONE.................................951 252-5314
Rajnit Walia, *CEO*
EMP: 99 **EST:** 2005
SALES (est): 1.2MM **Privately Held**
SIC: 8082 Home health care services

(P-16969)
VNACARE
Also Called: Community Hospice Victor Vly
16147 Kamana Rd (92307-1377)
P.O. Box 908 (91711-0908)
PHONE.................................760 946-4730
Marsha Fox, *Prin*
EMP: 69
SALES (corp-wide): 22.47MM **Privately Held**
Web: www.chvv.org
SIC: 8082 Visiting nurse service
PA: Vnacare
   412 E Vanderbilt Way # 10
   San Bernardino CA
   909 624-3574

(P-16970)
VNACARE
Also Called: V N A & Hospice Southern Calif
412 E Vanderbilt Way (92408-3552)
PHONE.................................909 384-0737
TOLL FREE: 888
Marsha Fox, *Pr*
EMP: 69
SQ FT: 3,230
SALES (corp-wide): 22.47MM **Privately Held**
Web: www.vnacare.com
SIC: 8082 Visiting nurse service
PA: Vnacare
   412 E Vanderbilt Way # 10
   San Bernardino CA
   909 624-3574

(P-16971)
VNACARE (PA)
Also Called: Vna Private Duty Care
412 E Vanderbilt Way Ste 100
(92408-3552)
P.O. Box 908 (91711-0908)
PHONE.................................909 624-3574
Marsha Fox, *Pr*
EMP: 93 **EST:** 1952
SALES (est): 22.47MM
SALES (corp-wide): 22.47MM **Privately Held**
Web: www.vnacare.com
SIC: 8082 Visiting nurse service

(P-16972)
VYNCA INC
548 Market St Ste 83340 (94104-5401)
PHONE.................................650 427-0573
Jack Chiou, *Ex Dir*
EMP: 66 **EST:** 2015
SALES (est): 6.02MM **Privately Held**
Web: www.vyncacare.com

SIC: 8082 Home health care services

(P-16973)
WELBE HEALTH LLC
Also Called: Welbehealth Sierra Pace
582 E Harding Way (95204-6110)
PHONE.................................209 800-0621
EMP: 245
SALES (corp-wide): 27.51MM **Privately Held**
Web: www.welbehealth.com
SIC: 8082 Home health care services
PA: Welbe Health, Llc
   405 Claremont Way Ste 248
   Menlo Park CA
   650 862-6371

(P-16974)
WELL BEING SENIOR SOLUTIONS
Also Called: Holistic Homecare
55 Shaw Ave Ste 220 (93612-3819)
PHONE.................................559 321-8295
Rachelle Dyson, *Pr*
Marc Dyson, *CFO*
Janette Becerra, *Opers Mgr*
EMP: 80 **EST:** 2011
SALES (est): 5.37MM **Privately Held**
Web: www.wellbeingseniorsolutions.com
SIC: 8082 Home health care services

(P-16975)
WEST CONTRA COSTA HEALTHCARE DISTRICT
Also Called: Wcchd
2000 Vale Rd (94806-3808)
PHONE.................................510 970-5102
EMP: 1202
Web: wcchd.ca.gov
SIC: 8082 Home health care services

(P-16976)
WILLOW PASS HLTH CARE CTR INC
3318 Willow Pass Rd (94519-2316)
PHONE.................................925 689-9222
Pratap Poddatoori, *CEO*
EMP: 100 **EST:** 2003
SALES (est): 8.18MM **Privately Held**
Web: www.willowpasshc.net
SIC: 8082 8051 Home health care services;
   Skilled nursing care facilities
PA: Hycare, Inc.
   524 Callan Ave
   San Leandro CA

8092 Kidney Dialysis Centers

(P-16977)
APHERESIS CARE GROUP INC
570 N 2nd St (92021-6448)
PHONE.................................619 440-4612
Mats Wahlstrom, *Prin*
EMP: 86
SALES (corp-wide): 20.15B **Privately Held**
Web: www.freseniuskidneycare.com
SIC: 8092 Kidney dialysis centers
HQ: Apheresis Care Group, Inc.
   920 Winter St
   Waltham MA
   781 699-5000

(P-16978)
BIO-MDCAL APPLCTONS CMRLLO INC
Also Called: Camarillo Dialysis Center
3801 Las Posas Rd Ste 103 (93010-1425)
PHONE.................................805 388-2449

Josh Howard, *Brnch Mgr*
EMP: 63
SALES (corp-wide): 20.15B **Privately Held**
SIC: 8092 Kidney dialysis centers
HQ: Bio-Medical Applications Of Camarillo, Inc.
   920 Winter St
   Waltham MA

(P-16979)
DAVITA INC
Also Called: Davita Hesperia Dialysis Ctr
14135 Main St Ste 501 (92345-8090)
PHONE.................................310 536-2406
Javier J Rodriguez, *CEO*
EMP: 104 **EST:** 1994
SALES (est): 16.54MM **Privately Held**
Web: www.davita.com
SIC: 8092 Kidney dialysis centers

(P-16980)
DAVITA INC
15271 Laguna Canyon Rd (92618-3146)
PHONE.................................949 930-4400
Viki Anderson, *Brnch Mgr*
EMP: 270
Web: www.davita.com
SIC: 8092 Kidney dialysis centers
PA: Davita Inc.
   2000 16th St
   Denver CO

(P-16981)
EL CAMINO HOSPITAL
Also Called: Camino Dialysis Svcs Oak 110
2505 Hospital Dr Ste 1 (94040-4127)
PHONE.................................650 940-7310
George Ting Md, *Dir*
EMP: 87
SALES (corp-wide): 1.43B **Privately Held**
Web: www.elcaminohealth.org
SIC: 8092 Kidney dialysis centers
PA: El Camino Hospital
   2500 Grant Rd
   Mountain View CA
   650 940-7000

(P-16982)
FRESENIUS MED CARE CLOVIS LLC
Also Called: Fresenius Kidney Care Clovis
2585 Alluvial Ave (93611-9505)
PHONE.................................559 324-8023
EMP: 2981 **EST:** 2013
SALES (est): 471.67K
SALES (corp-wide): 20.15B **Privately Held**
SIC: 8092 Kidney dialysis centers
HQ: Fresenius Medical Care North America Holdings Limited Partnership
   920 Winter St
   Waltham MA

(P-16983)
FRESENIUS MED CARE SLANO CNTY
Also Called: Fresenius Med Care Solano Cnty
125 N Lincoln St Ste B (95620-3259)
PHONE.................................707 678-6433
Susan Lajoie, *Brnch Mgr*
EMP: 94
SALES (corp-wide): 3.3MM **Privately Held**
SIC: 8092 Kidney dialysis centers
PA: Fresenius Medical Care Solano County, Llc
   920 Winter St
   Waltham MA
   800 662-1237

(P-16984)
FRESENIUS MED CARE WDLND CAL L
Also Called: Fresenius Medical Care Wdlnd
35 W Main St (95695-3015)
PHONE.................................530 668-4503
Susan Lajoie, *Brnch Mgr*
EMP: 94
SALES (corp-wide): 4.46MM **Privately Held**
SIC: 8092 Kidney dialysis centers
PA: Fresenius Medical Care Woodland (California), Llc
   920 Winter St Ste A
   Waltham MA
   800 622-1237

(P-16985)
HANFORD DIALYSIS LLC
Also Called: Hanford Home Dialysis Pd
900 N Douty St (93230-3918)
PHONE.................................559 587-9014
Jim Hilger, *Brnch Mgr*
EMP: 98
SIC: 8092 Kidney dialysis centers
HQ: Hanford Dialysis, Llc
   2000 16th St
   Denver CO
   253 733-4501

(P-16986)
HARBOR-UCLA MED FOUNDATION INC
Also Called: Ucla Hbr Dlysis Ctr Med Fndtio
21602 S Vermont Ave (90502-1940)
PHONE.................................310 533-0413
Patricia Hall, *Mgr*
EMP: 300
Web: www.harbor-ucla.org
SIC: 8092 Kidney dialysis centers
PA: Harbor-Ucla Medical Foundation, Inc.
   21840 Normandie Ave Ste 1
   Torrance CA

(P-16987)
HEMODIALYSIS INC
Also Called: Holy Cross Renal Center
14901 Rinaldi St Ste 100 (91345-1253)
PHONE.................................818 365-6961
John R Depalma, *Brnch Mgr*
EMP: 75
SALES (corp-wide): 8.93MM **Privately Held**
Web: www.hemodialysis-inc.com
SIC: 8092 Kidney dialysis centers
PA: Hemodialysis, Inc.
   710 W Wilson Ave
   Glendale CA
   818 500-8736

(P-16988)
HOME DLYSIS THRAPIES SAN DIEGO
2060 Otay Lakes Rd Ste 120 (91915)
PHONE.................................619 422-0003
Maribel Rodriguez, *Brnch Mgr*
EMP: 62
SALES (corp-wide): 4.91MM **Privately Held**
Web: www.homedialysistherapies.com
SIC: 8092 Kidney dialysis centers
PA: Home Dialysis Therapies Of San Diego
   10672 Wexford St
   San Diego CA
   858 549-3400

(P-16989)
JAMBOOR MEDICAL CORPORATION

8092 - Kidney Dialysis Centers (P-16990)

Also Called: Desert Cities Dialysis
12675 Hesperia Rd (92395-5878)
PHONE.....................760 241-8063
Jay Shankar, *Pr*
Saguna Jayashankar, *
EMP: 65 **EST:** 1988
SQ FT: 7,000
SALES (est): 11.61MM **Privately Held**
Web: www.desertcitiesdialysis.com
SIC: 8092 Kidney dialysis centers

(P-16990)
PORTERVILLE DIALYSIS CENTER
Also Called: Porterville Hemodialysis
385 Pearson Dr (93257-3305)
PHONE.....................559 781-5551
Sonia Duran-aguilar, *CEO*
EMP: 174 **EST:** 1987
SALES (est): 574.74K
SALES (corp-wide): 857.31MM **Privately Held**
SIC: 8092 8051 Kidney dialysis centers; Skilled nursing care facilities
PA: Kaweah Delta Health Care District Guild
400 W Mineral King Ave
Visalia CA
559 624-2000

(P-16991)
RAI CARE CENTERS COLTON LLC
Also Called: Rai West C Colton
1275 W C St (92324-1916)
PHONE.....................909 430-0930
Monique Hartell, *Brnch Mgr*
EMP: 189
SALES (corp-wide): 20.15B **Privately Held**
Web: www.freseniuskidneycare.com
SIC: 8092 Kidney dialysis centers
HQ: Rai Care Centers Of Colton, Llc
920 Winter St
Waltham MA
781 699-9000

(P-16992)
RAI CARE CENTERS LYNWOOD LLC
Also Called: Fresenius Kidney Care Lynwood
7700 Imperial Hwy Ste R (90242-3466)
PHONE.....................562 401-0155
EMP: 105
SALES (corp-wide): 20.15B **Privately Held**
Web: www.fmcna.com
SIC: 8092 Kidney dialysis centers
HQ: Rai Care Centers Of Lynwood, Llc
920 Winter St
Waltham MA
781 699-9000

(P-16993)
RAI CARE CTRS STHERN CAL II LL
Also Called: Rai-Fletcher Parkway-El Cajon
858 Fletcher Pkwy (92020-1818)
PHONE.....................619 442-4122
Aida Smith, *Managing Member*
EMP: 128
SALES (corp-wide): 20.15B **Privately Held**
SIC: 8092 Kidney dialysis centers
HQ: Rai Care Centers Of Southern California Ii, Llc
920 Winter St
Waltham MA
781 699-9000

(P-16994)
RAI CARE CTRS STHERN CAL II LL
Rai Mission Gorge San Diego
7007 Mission Gorge Rd (92120-2422)
PHONE.....................619 229-1070
Monique Hartell, *Brnch Mgr*
EMP: 128
SALES (corp-wide): 20.15B **Privately Held**
SIC: 8092 Kidney dialysis centers
HQ: Rai Care Centers Of Southern California Ii, Llc
920 Winter St
Waltham MA
781 699-9000

(P-16995)
RAI CARE CTRS STHERN CAL II LL
Also Called: Rai Centinela Inglewood
1416 Centinela Ave (90302-1142)
PHONE.....................310 673-6865
Monique Hartell, *Brnch Mgr*
EMP: 128
SALES (corp-wide): 20.15B **Privately Held**
SIC: 8092 Kidney dialysis centers
HQ: Rai Care Centers Of Southern California Ii, Llc
920 Winter St
Waltham MA
781 699-9000

(P-16996)
RAI CARE CTRS STHERN CAL II LL
Also Called: Rai Corporate Way Palm Desert
41501 Corporate Way (92260-1974)
PHONE.....................760 346-7588
Monique Hartell, *Brnch Mgr*
EMP: 171
SALES (corp-wide): 20.15B **Privately Held**
SIC: 8092 Kidney dialysis centers
HQ: Rai Care Centers Of Southern California Ii, Llc
920 Winter St
Waltham MA
781 699-9000

(P-16997)
SANTA BRBARA ARTFL KDNEY CTR L
1704 State St (93101-2522)
PHONE.....................805 682-9942
Thomas Allen Md, *Pt*
Michael Fisher Md, *Pt*
EMP: 89 **EST:** 1987
SALES (est): 8.79MM **Privately Held**
SIC: 8092 Kidney dialysis centers

(P-16998)
SATELLITE HEALTHCARE INC (PA)
Also Called: SATELLITE DIALYSIS CENTERS
300 Santana Row Ste 300 (95128-2018)
PHONE.....................650 404-3600
Jeffrey Goffman, *CEO*
Norman S Coplon, *
Brigitte Schiller, *Chief Medical Officer**
Susan Del Bene, *
Robert A Lunbeck Junior, *VP*
EMP: 75 **EST:** 1973
SQ FT: 12,000
SALES (est): 281.09MM
SALES (corp-wide): 281.09MM **Privately Held**
Web: www.satellitehealthcare.com
SIC: 8092 Kidney dialysis centers

8093 Specialty Outpatient Clinics, Nec

(P-16999)
21ST CENTURY HEALTH CLUB (PA)
680a E Cotati Ave (94931-4092)
PHONE.....................707 795-0400
John Ford, *Pr*
Frank Ford, *
Elizabeth Gardner, *
Doctor Robert Gardner, *Treas*
▲ **EMP:** 70 **EST:** 1988
SQ FT: 20,000
SALES (est): 5.55MM **Privately Held**
Web: www.21stcenturyhealthclub.com
SIC: 8093 7991 Rehabilitation center, outpatient treatment; Health club

(P-17000)
ACCEL THERAPIES INC
1845 W Orangewood Ave Ste 101 (92868-2085)
PHONE.....................855 443-3822
Patrick Moynihan, *Admn*
EMP: 61 **EST:** 2005
SALES (est): 14.26MM **Privately Held**
Web: www.acceltherapies.com
SIC: 8093 Rehabilitation center, outpatient treatment

(P-17001)
ALCOTT CTR FOR MNTAL HLTH SVCS
10549 Jefferson Blvd (90232-3513)
PHONE.....................310 785-2121
Nicholas Maiorino, *CEO*
EMP: 75 **EST:** 1979
SALES (est): 5.77MM **Privately Held**
Web: www.alcottcenter.org
SIC: 8093 Mental health clinic, outpatient

(P-17002)
ALPINE CONVALESCENT CENTER INC
Also Called: Alpine Special Treatment Ctr
2120 Alpine Blvd (91901-2113)
PHONE.....................619 659-3120
Michael E Doyle, *CEO*
EMP: 100 **EST:** 1972
SQ FT: 15,000
SALES (est): 22.67MM **Privately Held**
Web: www.astci.com
SIC: 8093 Rehabilitation center, outpatient treatment

(P-17003)
AMANECER CMNTY CNSLING SVC A N
1200 Wilshire Blvd Ste 200 (90017-1908)
PHONE.....................213 481-7464
Tim Ryder, *Ex Dir*
Frank Chargualaf, * .
EMP: 100 **EST:** 1975
SALES (est): 11.26MM **Privately Held**
Web: www.amanecerla.org
SIC: 8093 Mental health clinic, outpatient

(P-17004)
ANKA BEHAVIORAL HEALTH INCORPORATED
3840 Buskirk Ave., Suite 300 (94523)
PHONE.....................925 825-4700
EMP: 900
Web: www.ankabhi.org
SIC: 8093 Mental health clinic, outpatient

(P-17005)
ASCEND HEALTHCARE LLC
4346 Empress Ave (91436-3507)
PHONE.....................747 247-2176
Joseph Essas, *Managing Member*
EMP: 64 **EST:** 2016
SALES (est): 16.07MM **Privately Held**
Web: www.ascendhc.com
SIC: 8093 7389 Mental health clinic, outpatient; Business Activities at Non-Commercial Site

(P-17006)
ASIAN COMMUNITY MENTAL HLTH BD
Also Called: Asian Cmnty Mental Hlth Svcs
310 8th St Ste 303 (94607-4253)
P.O. Box 10750 (94610-0750)
PHONE.....................510 869-6003
Lawrence Fong, *Pr*
Betty Hong, *
Sharon Sue, *
John Fong, *
EMP: 95 **EST:** 1974
SALES (est): 6.53MM **Privately Held**
Web: www.acmhs.org
SIC: 8093 Mental health clinic, outpatient

(P-17007)
AURORA BHVRAL HLTHCARE - STA R
1287 Fulton Rd (95401-4923)
PHONE.....................707 800-7700
Susan Rose, *CEO*
EMP: 75 **EST:** 2000
SQ FT: 50,000
SALES (est): 30.99MM **Publicly Held**
Web: www.norcalbehavioral.com
SIC: 8093 Mental health clinic, outpatient
HQ: Aurora Behavioral Healthcare Llc
4238 Green River Rd
Corona CA
951 549-8032

(P-17008)
AUTISM TREATMENT SOLUTIONS LLC
672 W 11th St Ste 339 (95376-3821)
PHONE.....................209 910-5038
EMP: 774 **EST:** 2012
SALES (est): 482.17K
SALES (corp-wide): 50.5MM **Privately Held**
Web: www.asdtreatments.com
SIC: 8093 Rehabilitation center, outpatient treatment
PA: Butterfly Effects, Llc
350 Fairway Dr Ste 101
Deerfield Beach FL
954 603-7885

(P-17009)
AXIS COMMUNITY HEALTH INC
4361 Railroad Ave (94566-6611)
PHONE.....................925 462-1755
Sue Compton, *CEO*
Kanwar Singh, *
Christina Mcfadden, *COO*
EMP: 99 **EST:** 1972
SALES (est): 30.67MM **Privately Held**
Web: www.axishealth.org
SIC: 8093 Mental health clinic, outpatient

(P-17010)
BAKER PLACES INC
101 Gough St (94102-5903)
PHONE.....................415 503-3137
EMP: 67
SALES (corp-wide): 20.54MM **Privately Held**

PRODUCTS & SERVICES SECTION
8093 - Specialty Outpatient Clinics, Nec (P-17032)

Web: www.prcsf.org
SIC: 8093 Substance abuse clinics (outpatient)
PA: Baker Places, Inc.
170 9th St
San Francisco CA
415 864-4655

(P-17011)
BEHAVIOR FRONTIERS LLC
2033 Gateway Pl Ste 500 (95110-3712)
PHONE.................310 856-0800
Helen Mader, *Prin*
EMP: 240
Web: www.behaviorfrontiers.com
SIC: 8093 Rehabilitation center, outpatient treatment
PA: Behavior Frontiers, Llc
100 N Pcf Cast Hwy Ste 14
El Segundo CA

(P-17012)
BEHAVIORAL HEALTH WORKS INC
1301 E Orangewood Ave (92805-6807)
PHONE.................800 249-1266
Robert Douk, *CEO*
EMP: 99 EST: 2011
SALES (est): 17.11MM **Privately Held**
Web: www.bhwcares.com
SIC: 8093 Mental health clinic, outpatient

(P-17013)
BEHAVIORAL LEARNING NETWRK LLC
10700 Santa Monica Blvd Ste 100 (90025-4768)
PHONE.................310 871-6800
Gregory Elsky, *Prin*
EMP: 92 EST: 2013
SALES (est): 2.34MM **Privately Held**
Web: www.blnautism.com
SIC: 8093 Mental health clinic, outpatient

(P-17014)
BETTY FORD CENTER (HQ)
39000 Bob Hope Dr (92270-3297)
P.O. Box 1560 (92270-1056)
PHONE.................760 773-4100
TOLL FREE: 800
Mark Mishek, *Pr*
James Blaha, *
Jim Steinhagen, *
EMP: 250 EST: 1983
SALES (est): 38.29MM
SALES (corp-wide): 236.83MM **Privately Held**
Web: www.hazeldenbettyford.org
SIC: 8093 Substance abuse clinics (outpatient)
PA: Hazelden Betty Ford Foundation
15251 Pleasant Valley Rd
Center City MN
651 213-4000

(P-17015)
BH-SD OPCO LLC (PA)
Also Called: ALVARADO PARKWAY INSTITUTE
7050 Parkway Dr (91942-1535)
PHONE.................619 465-4411
Patrick Ziemer, *CEO*
Chad Engbrecht, *
James Adamson, *
EMP: 94 EST: 2014
SALES (est): 30.95MM
SALES (corp-wide): 30.95MM **Privately Held**
Web: www.apibhs.com

SIC: 8093 Mental health clinic, outpatient

(P-17016)
BRAND THERAPY LLC
7376 W 88th St (90045-3466)
PHONE.................415 336-6411
Lisa Welch, *Prin*
EMP: 90 EST: 2018
SALES (est): 270.42K **Privately Held**
SIC: 8093 Rehabilitation center, outpatient treatment

(P-17017)
BRIGHTQEST TRTMNT CTRS - SAN D
5520 Wellesley St Ste 100 (91942-4401)
PHONE.................619 466-0547
EMP: 74 EST: 2019
SALES (est): 327.36K **Privately Held**
Web: www.brightquest.com
SIC: 8093 Mental health clinic, outpatient

(P-17018)
BUCKELEW PROGRAMS (PA)
201 Alameda Del Prado Ste 103 (94949-6698)
PHONE.................415 457-6964
Chris Kughn, *CEO*
EMP: 78 EST: 1970
SALES (est): 15.55MM
SALES (corp-wide): 15.55MM **Privately Held**
Web: www.buckelew.org
SIC: 8093 Substance abuse clinics (outpatient)

(P-17019)
CASA PALMERA LLC
14750 El Camino Real (92014-4204)
PHONE.................888 481-4481
Lee Johnson Mbr, *Mgr*
EMP: 70 EST: 2001
SALES (est): 6.14MM **Privately Held**
Web: www.casapalmera.com
SIC: 8093 Substance abuse clinics (outpatient)

(P-17020)
CENTER FOR ATISM RES EVLTION S
Also Called: Cares
8787 Complex Dr Ste 300 (92123-1453)
PHONE.................858 444-8823
Olanderia Brown, *Mgr*
EMP: 102 EST: 2007
SALES (est): 2.34MM
SALES (corp-wide): 33.56MM **Privately Held**
SIC: 8093 Mental health clinic, outpatient
PA: Fred Finch Youth Center
3800 Coolidge Ave
Oakland CA
510 773-6669

(P-17021)
CENTER FOR DSCOVERY ADOLESCENT
4136 Ann Arbor Rd (90712-3817)
PHONE.................562 425-6404
Craig Brown, *Dir*
EMP: 64 EST: 1997
SALES (est): 1.02MM **Privately Held**
Web: www.centerfordiscovery.com
SIC: 8093 Mental health clinic, outpatient

(P-17022)
CENTRAL VLY REGIONAL CTR INC
5441 W Cypress Ave (93277-8341)
PHONE.................559 738-2200
Lorraine Bortes, *Genl Mgr*
EMP: 120
SALES (corp-wide): 422.05MM **Privately Held**
Web: www.cvrc.org
SIC: 8093 8399 Mental health clinic, outpatient; Social service information exchange
PA: Central Valley Regional Center, Inc.
4615 N Marty Ave
Fresno CA
559 276-4300

(P-17023)
CENTRE FOR NEURO SKILLS (PA)
5215 Ashe Rd (93313-2069)
PHONE.................661 872-3408
Mark J Ashley, *CEO*
Ken Chief Strategy Diashyn, *Development Officer*
EMP: 450 EST: 1980
SQ FT: 14,000
SALES (est): 80.36MM
SALES (corp-wide): 80.36MM **Privately Held**
Web: www.neuroskills.com
SIC: 8093 Rehabilitation center, outpatient treatment

(P-17024)
CENTRO DE SALUD DE LA COMUNI (PA)
Also Called: San Ysidro Health
1601 Precision Park Ln (92173-1345)
PHONE.................619 428-4463
Kevin Mattson, *CEO*
Ed Martinez, *
M Gutierrez, *
EMP: 80 EST: 1969
SQ FT: 2,000
SALES (est): 69.69MM
SALES (corp-wide): 69.69MM **Privately Held**
Web: www.syhc.org
SIC: 8093 8011 Specialty outpatient clinics, nec; Offices and clinics of medical doctors

(P-17025)
CHILD AND FAMILY GUIDANCE CTR (PA)
Also Called: NORTHPOINT DAY TREATMENT SCH
9650 Zelzah Ave (91325-2003)
PHONE.................818 739-5140
Roy Marshall, *Ex Dir*
Russell Jones, *
Robert Garcia, *
Stephen J Howard Ph.d., *VP*
Bonnie Weissman, *
EMP: 200 EST: 1961
SQ FT: 35,000
SALES (est): 29.83MM
SALES (corp-wide): 29.83MM **Privately Held**
Web: www.childguidance.org
SIC: 8093 Mental health clinic, outpatient

(P-17026)
CHILD GUIDANCE CENTER INC
525 Cabrillo Park Dr Ste 300 (92701-5017)
PHONE.................714 953-4455
Lori Pack, *Ex Dir*
Christine Kiehl, *
EMP: 106 EST: 2008
SALES (est): 9.75MM **Privately Held**
Web: www.childguidancecenteroc.org

SIC: 8093 Mental health clinic, outpatient

(P-17027)
CHOICE IN AGING (PA)
Also Called: Mt Diblo Ctr Adult Day Hlth Ca
490 Golf Club Rd (94523-1553)
PHONE.................925 682-6330
Debbie Toth, *CEO*
EMP: 72 EST: 1949
SQ FT: 24,335
SALES (est): 6.53MM
SALES (corp-wide): 6.53MM **Privately Held**
Web: www.choiceinaging.org
SIC: 8093 8331 Rehabilitation center, outpatient treatment; Vocational rehabilitation agency

(P-17028)
CHOICES
Also Called: San Diego Psychiatric Hospital
3853 Rosecrans St (92110-3115)
PHONE.................619 692-8200
Isabella Karmach, *Dir*
EMP: 63 EST: 2001
SALES (est): 4.9MM **Privately Held**
Web: www.morechoicesd.org
SIC: 8093 Mental health clinic, outpatient

(P-17029)
CLEAR RECOVERY CENTER
18119 Prairie Ave Ste 102 (90504-3740)
PHONE.................310 318-2122
EMP: 63 EST: 2015
SALES (est): 9.26MM **Privately Held**
Web: www.clearrecoverycenter.com
SIC: 8093 Substance abuse clinics (outpatient)

(P-17030)
COMMUNITY ACTION MARIN
Also Called: Community Action Marine
1108 Tamalpais Ave (94901-3247)
PHONE.................415 459-6330
Michael Payne, *Pr*
EMP: 92
SALES (corp-wide): 19.8MM **Privately Held**
Web: www.camarin.org
SIC: 8093 Mental health clinic, outpatient
PA: Community Action Marin
555 Northgate Dr Ste 201
San Rafael CA
415 485-1489

(P-17031)
COMMUNITY ACTION PRTNR SAN LUI
Also Called: E O C Health Services
705 Grand Ave (93401-2639)
PHONE.................805 544-2478
Janice Wolf, *Mgr*
EMP: 127
SALES (corp-wide): 99.11MM **Privately Held**
Web: www.capslo.org
SIC: 8093 Family planning clinic
PA: Community Action Partnership Of San Luis Obispo County, Inc.
1030 Southwood Dr
San Luis Obispo CA
805 544-4355

(P-17032)
COMMUNITY MEDICAL CENTERS INC (PA)
7210 Murray Dr (95210-3339)
PHONE.................209 373-2800
Kathleen Marshall, *CEO*

8093 - Specialty Outpatient Clinics, Nec (P-17033)

EMP: 90 EST: 1978
SQ FT: 14,000
SALES (est): 107.61MM
SALES (corp-wide): 107.61MM Privately Held
Web: www.communitymedicalcenters.org
SIC: 8093 8011 Specialty outpatient clinics, nec; Offices and clinics of medical doctors

(P-17033)
COMPREHENSIVE CANCER CENTERS INC
8201 Beverly Blvd (90048-4505)
PHONE...............................323 966-3400
EMP: 120
SIC: 8093 Specialty outpatient clinics, nec

(P-17034)
CONSOLDTED TRIBAL HLTH PRJ INC
6991 N State St (95470-9629)
P.O. Box 387 (95418-0387)
PHONE...............................707 485-5115
Michael Knight, Ch
Donna Schuler, *
George Provencher, *
Debra Ramirez, *
EMP: 65 EST: 1984
SALES (est): 10.72MM Privately Held
Web: www.cthp.org
SIC: 8093 Mental health clinic, outpatient

(P-17035)
COUNTY OF IMPERIAL
Also Called: Imperial County Mental Health
202 N 8th St (92243-2302)
PHONE...............................760 482-4120
Rudy Lopez, Dir
EMP: 74
SALES (corp-wide): 404.81MM Privately Held
Web: www.imperialcountyced.com
SIC: 8093 9111 Mental health clinic, outpatient; County supervisors' and executives' office
PA: County Of Imperial
940 W Main St Ste 208
El Centro CA
760 482-4556

(P-17036)
COUNTY OF LOS ANGELES
Also Called: Health Dept
5850 S Main St (90003-1215)
PHONE...............................323 897-6187
Floretta Taylor, Dir
EMP: 475
SALES (corp-wide): 31.7B Privately Held
Web: www.lacounty.gov
SIC: 8093 9431 8011 Specialty outpatient clinics, nec; Administration of public health programs; Offices and clinics of medical doctors
PA: County Of Los Angeles
500 W Temple St Ste 437
Los Angeles CA
213 974-1101

(P-17037)
COUNTY OF LOS ANGELES
Also Called: Mental Health Dept of
17707 Studebaker Rd (90703-2640)
PHONE...............................562 402-0688
Latisha Guvman, Mgr
EMP: 63
SALES (corp-wide): 31.7B Privately Held
Web: www.lacounty.gov
SIC: 8093 9431 Specialty outpatient clinics, nec; Administration of public health programs
PA: County Of Los Angeles
500 W Temple St Ste 437
Los Angeles CA
213 974-1101

(P-17038)
COUNTY OF LOS ANGELES
Also Called: Health Services, Dept of
5205 Melrose Ave (90038-3144)
PHONE...............................323 769-7800
Rosa Pinon, Brnch Mgr
EMP: 63
SALES (corp-wide): 31.7B Privately Held
Web: www.lacounty.gov
SIC: 8093 9431 Family planning and birth control clinics; Administration of public health programs
PA: County Of Los Angeles
500 W Temple St Ste 437
Los Angeles CA
213 974-1101

(P-17039)
COUNTY OF LOS ANGELES
Also Called: Antelope Valley Health Center
335 E Avenue K6 Ste B (93535-4645)
PHONE...............................661 524-2005
Mary Nolan, Mgr
EMP: 63
SALES (corp-wide): 31.7B Privately Held
Web: www.lacounty.gov
SIC: 8093 Family planning clinic
PA: County Of Los Angeles
500 W Temple St Ste 437
Los Angeles CA
213 974-1101

(P-17040)
COUNTY OF LOS ANGELES
Also Called: Health Services, Dept of
7601 Imperial Hwy (90242-3456)
PHONE...............................562 401-7088
Valeria Orange, Dir
EMP: 592
SALES (corp-wide): 31.7B Privately Held
Web: www.lacounty.gov
SIC: 8093 9431 Rehabilitation center, outpatient treatment; Administration of public health programs, County government
PA: County Of Los Angeles
500 W Temple St Ste 437
Los Angeles CA
213 974-1101

(P-17041)
COUNTY OF SAN JOAQUIN
Also Called: Mental Health Services
1212 N California St (95202-1552)
PHONE...............................209 468-8750
Bruce Hopperstead, Prin
EMP: 216
SALES (corp-wide): 1.54B Privately Held
Web: www.sjgov.org
SIC: 8093 9111 8361 Mental health clinic, outpatient; County supervisors' and executives' office; Residential care
PA: County Of San Joaquin
44 N San Joaquin St # 374
Stockton CA
209 468-3203

(P-17042)
COUNTY OF SAN JOAQUIN
Also Called: Rehablttion Ctr At San Jquin G
500 W Hospital Rd (95231-9693)
PHONE...............................209 468-6280
Rachel Torres, Brnch Mgr
EMP: 65
SALES (corp-wide): 1.54B Privately Held
Web: www.sjgov.org
SIC: 8093 9431 Rehabilitation center, outpatient treatment; Communicable disease program administration, government
PA: County Of San Joaquin
44 N San Joaquin St # 374
Stockton CA
209 468-3203

(P-17043)
COUNTY OF STANISLAUS
Also Called: Department of Mental Health
2101 Geer Rd Ste 120 (95382-2456)
PHONE...............................209 664-8044
EMP: 67
Web: www.stancounty.com
SIC: 8093 9431 Mental health clinic, outpatient; Administration of public health programs
PA: County Of Stanislaus
1010 10th St Ste 5100
Modesto CA
209 525-6398

(P-17044)
COUNTY OF SUTTER
Also Called: Sutter Yuba Mental Health Svcs
1965 Live Oak Blvd (95991-8850)
P.O. Box 1520 (95992-1520)
PHONE...............................530 822-7250
Joann Hoss, Dir
EMP: 77
Web: www.suttercares.org
SIC: 8093 9431 Mental health clinic, outpatient; Mental health agency administration, government
PA: Sutter, County Of
1160 Civic Center Blvd A
Yuba City CA
530 822-7100

(P-17045)
CRC HEALTH CORPORATE (DH)
Also Called: Willamette Valley Trtmnt Ctr
20400 Stevens Creek Blvd Ste 600 (95014-2217)
PHONE...............................408 367-0044
R Andrew Eckert, CEO
James Hudak, CAO
Kevin Hogge, VP
Pamela B Burke, VP
Gary Fisher, CMO
EMP: 60 EST: 2002
SALES (est): 100.03MM Publicly Held
SIC: 8093 Substance abuse clinics (outpatient)
HQ: Crc Health Llc
20400 Stevns Crk Blvd 6
Cupertino CA
877 272-8668

(P-17046)
CRC HEALTH CORPORATE
Also Called: Recovery Solutions Santa Ana
2101 E 1st St (92705-4007)
PHONE...............................714 542-3581
Tfu Bach Tran, Mgr
EMP: 1318
Web: www.acadiahealthcare.com
SIC: 8093 Drug clinic, outpatient
HQ: Crc Health Corporate
20400 Stevns Crk Blvd
Cupertino CA
408 367-0044

(P-17047)
CRC HEALTH GROUP INC
256 E Hamilton Ave Ste I (95008-0237)
PHONE...............................408 866-8167
EMP: 68
SIC: 8093 Substance abuse clinics (outpatient)
HQ: Crc Health Group, Inc.
6100 Tower Cir Ste 1000
Franklin TN

(P-17048)
CRC HEALTH GROUP INC
Also Called: Sdhael Cajon Treatment Center
234 N Magnolia Ave (92020-3906)
PHONE...............................214 634-2722
EMP: 68
Web: www.ctcprograms.com
SIC: 8093 Substance abuse clinics (outpatient)
HQ: Crc Health Group, Inc.
6100 Tower Cir Ste 1000
Franklin TN

(P-17049)
CRC HEALTH GROUP INC
1021 W La Cadena Dr (92501-1413)
PHONE...............................951 784-8010
Tammy Elkins, Brnch Mgr
EMP: 140
SIC: 8093 Mental health clinic, outpatient
HQ: Crc Health Group, Inc.
6100 Tower Cir Ste 1000
Franklin TN

(P-17050)
DAVID HOWARD
Also Called: Veterans Affairs Palo Alto Hea
520 Abbie St (94566-7457)
PHONE...............................925 426-0979
Evan S Kletter, Prin
David Howard, Owner
EMP: 96 EST: 2011
SALES (est): 349.42K Privately Held
SIC: 8093 Substance abuse clinics (outpatient)

(P-17051)
DEL AMO HOSPITAL INC
Also Called: Del AMO Hospital
23700 Camino Del Sol (90505-5000)
PHONE...............................310 530-1151
TOLL FREE: 800
Lisa Moncen, CEO
Alan B Miller, *
Kirk E Gorman, *
Sidney Miller, *
EMP: 300 EST: 1991
SQ FT: 88,000
SALES (est): 45.01MM
SALES (corp-wide): 13.4B Publicly Held
Web: www.delamobehavioralhealth.com
SIC: 8093 Mental health clinic, outpatient
PA: Universal Health Services, Inc.
367 S Gulph Rd
King Of Prussia PA
610 768-3300

(P-17052)
DESTINATIONS FOR TEENS
20951 Burbank Blvd Ste D (91367-6696)
PHONE...............................818 737-2221
EMP: 84 EST: 2019
SALES (est): 1.01MM Privately Held
Web: www.destinationsforteens.com
SIC: 8093 Substance abuse clinics (outpatient)

PRODUCTS & SERVICES SECTION

8093 - Specialty Outpatient Clinics, Nec (P-17073)

(P-17053)
DEVEREUX FOUNDATION
Also Called: Devereux California Center
7055 Seaway Dr (93117-4358)
P.O. Box 6784 (93160-6784)
PHONE..................805 968-2525
Amy Evans, Prin
EMP: 274
SALES (corp-wide): 516.85MM Privately Held
Web: www.devereux.org
SIC: 8093 Mental health clinic, outpatient
PA: Devereux Foundation
444 Devereux Dr
Villanova PA
610 542-3057

(P-17054)
DISCOVERY PRACTICE MGT INC
Also Called: Center For Discovery
18401 Von Karman Ave Ste 500 (92612-1542)
PHONE..................714 828-1800
Craig Brown, CEO
Mark Hobbins, Pr
Robert Weitzman, CFO
Jennifer Gorman, Dir Opers
EMP: 434 EST: 2007
SALES (est): 40.52MM Privately Held
Web: www.centerfordiscovery.com
SIC: 8093 Mental health clinic, outpatient

(P-17055)
DRUG ABUSE ALTERNATIVES CENTER
Also Called: Redwood Empire Addctons Prgram
2403 Professional Dr Ste 103 (95403)
PHONE..................707 571-2233
Sushana Taylor, Pr
EMP: 101
SALES (corp-wide): 5.14MM Privately Held
Web: www.daacinfo.org
SIC: 8093 Drug clinic, outpatient
PA: Drug Abuse Alternatives Center
2403 Prof Dr Ste 102
Santa Rosa CA
707 544-3295

(P-17056)
DUAL DIAGNOSIS TRTMNT CTR INC (PA)
Also Called: Sovereign Health of California
1211 Puerta Del Sol # 200 (92673-6306)
PHONE..................949 276-5553
Tonmoy Sharma, CEO
Rishi Barkataki, *
EMP: 178 EST: 1983
SALES (est): 49.58MM
SALES (corp-wide): 49.58MM Privately Held
Web: www.alphabet-soup.net
SIC: 8093 Mental health clinic, outpatient

(P-17057)
DUNAMIS CENTER INC
Also Called: Dunamis Ctr Cunseling Wellness
1465 Victor Ave Ste B (96003-4856)
PHONE..................530 338-0087
Jill Clark, CEO
Jill Clarke, *
EMP: 90 EST: 2017
SQ FT: 4,000
SALES (est): 8.09MM Privately Held
Web: www.dunamiscenter.com
SIC: 8093 8322 8041 8049 Mental health clinic, outpatient; Rehabilitation services; Offices and clinics of chiropractors; Clinical psychologist

(P-17058)
EAST VALLEY CMNTY HLTH CTR INC (PA)
420 S Glendora Ave (91790-3001)
PHONE..................626 919-3402
Alicia Mardini, CEO
Alicia Thomas, *
Sophia Shavira, *
EMP: 65 EST: 1970
SQ FT: 24,000
SALES (est): 39.35MM
SALES (corp-wide): 39.35MM Privately Held
Web: www.evchc.org
SIC: 8093 Family planning clinic

(P-17059)
ED SUPPORTS LLC
Also Called: Juvo Atism Bhavioral Hlth Svcs
1045 Willow St (95125-2346)
PHONE..................201 478-8711
Adam Schreiber, Brnch Mgr
EMP: 60
SALES (corp-wide): 27.81MM Privately Held
SIC: 8093 Mental health clinic, outpatient
HQ: Ed Supports Llc
1200 Concord Ave Ste 100
Concord CA
510 832-4383

(P-17060)
ED SUPPORTS LLC
Also Called: Juvo Atism Bhavioral Hlth Svcs
6001 Telegraph Ave (94609-1310)
PHONE..................201 478-8711
Adam Schreiber, Brnch Mgr
EMP: 80
SALES (corp-wide): 27.81MM Privately Held
SIC: 8093 Mental health clinic, outpatient
HQ: Ed Supports Llc
1200 Concord Ave Ste 100
Concord CA
510 832-4383

(P-17061)
ENKI HEALTH AND RES SYSTEMS
3208 Rosemead Blvd Ste 100 (91731-2830)
PHONE..................626 227-7001
Daniel Guzman, Brnch Mgr
EMP: 64
SALES (corp-wide): 22.76MM Privately Held
Web: www.enkihealth.org
SIC: 8093 Mental health clinic, outpatient
PA: Enki Health And Research Systems
150 E Olive Ave Ste 203
Burbank CA
818 973-4899

(P-17062)
EVOLVE TREATMENT CENTERS
600 N Sepulveda Blvd (90049-2108)
PHONE..................310 622-1420
Michelle Gross, CEO
EMP: 90 EST: 2014
SALES (est): 814.05K Privately Held
Web: www.evolvetreatment.com
SIC: 8093 Mental health clinic, outpatient

(P-17063)
FAMILY HLTH CTRS SAN DIEGO INC (PA)
Also Called: Diamond Nghbrhood Fmly Hlth Ct
823 Gateway Center Way (92102-4541)
PHONE..................619 515-2303
Fran Butler-cohen, Pr
EMP: 65 EST: 1972
SQ FT: 32,000
SALES (est): 147.12MM
SALES (corp-wide): 147.12MM Privately Held
Web: www.fhcsd.org
SIC: 8093 Mental health clinic, outpatient

(P-17064)
FELD CARE THERAPY INC
31248 Oak Crest Dr Ste 120 (91361-4692)
PHONE..................818 926-9057
Randi Peled, CEO
EMP: 66 EST: 2016
SALES (est): 7.23MM Privately Held
Web: www.feldcareconnects.com
SIC: 8093 7371 Rehabilitation center, outpatient treatment; Computer software development and applications

(P-17065)
GOODWAGE THERAPY ASSOC LLC
1189 E Brandywine Ln Ste 110 (93720-1347)
PHONE..................559 434-1969
Kathryn Wage, Brnch Mgr
EMP: 72
SALES (corp-wide): 436.19K Privately Held
SIC: 8093 Rehabilitation center, outpatient treatment
PA: Goodwage Therapy Associates, Llc
2505 W Shaw Ave
Fresno CA
559 228-9100

(P-17066)
GRANITE WELLNESS CENTERS
Also Called: CORR
180 Sierra College Dr (95945-5768)
PHONE..................530 878-5166
Warren Daniels, Ex Dir
EMP: 92 EST: 1974
SALES (est): 11.34MM Privately Held
Web: www.granitewellness.org
SIC: 8093 Substance abuse clinics (outpatient)

(P-17067)
GREATER SACRAMENTO SUR
Also Called: Greater Sacramento Surgery Ctr
2288 Auburn Blvd Ste 201 (95821-1620)
PHONE..................916 929-7229
Marvin Kamras, Pt
EMP: 60 EST: 1983
SQ FT: 15,000
SALES (est): 10.62MM Privately Held
Web: www.gssc-asc.com
SIC: 8093 8011 Specialty outpatient clinics, nec; Ambulatory surgical center

(P-17068)
GREATER VALLEY MED GROUP INC (PA)
11600 Indian Hills Rd 300 (91345-1225)
PHONE..................818 838-4500
Don Rebhun Md, Pr
Howard Sawyer Md, Sec
Mohyi Soleiman Md, VP
EMP: 75 EST: 1977
SALES (est): 9.39MM
SALES (corp-wide): 9.39MM Privately Held
SIC: 8093 Specialty outpatient clinics, nec

(P-17069)
GREATER VALLEY MEDICAL GROUP
Also Called: Healthcare Partners
14600 Sherman Way Ste 300 (91405-2272)
PHONE..................818 781-7097
Cris Kalal, Mgr
EMP: 147
SALES (corp-wide): 9.39MM Privately Held
SIC: 8093 8011 Specialty outpatient clinics, nec; Offices and clinics of medical doctors
PA: Greater Valley Medical Group Incorporated
11600 Indian Hills Rd # 300
Mission Hills CA
818 838-4500

(P-17070)
HEALTHSOUTH CORPORATION
Also Called: HealthSouth
75 Scripps Dr (95825-6320)
PHONE..................916 929-9431
FAX: 916 929-0132
EMP: 60
SALES (corp-wide): 3.71B Publicly Held
SIC: 8093 Rehabilitation center, outpatient treatment
PA: Healthsouth Corporation
3660 Grandview Pkwy # 200
Birmingham AL
205 967-7116

(P-17071)
HELIX HEALTHCARE INC
Also Called: Alvarado Parkway Institute
7050 Parkway Dr (91942-1535)
PHONE..................619 465-4411
Roy Rodriguez, CEO
Mohammed Bari, *
Saleem Ishaque, *
Robert Sanders, Stockholder*
EMP: 310 EST: 2003
SQ FT: 37,354
SALES (est): 26.76MM Privately Held
Web: www.apibhs.com
SIC: 8093 Mental health clinic, outpatient

(P-17072)
HELP GROUP WEST (PA)
13130 Burbank Blvd (91401-6037)
PHONE..................818 781-0360
Barbara Firestone, Pr
Susan Berman Ph, Ex VP
Michael Love, *
EMP: 200 EST: 1999
SQ FT: 100,000
SALES (est): 17.88MM
SALES (corp-wide): 17.88MM Privately Held
Web: www.thehelpgroup.org
SIC: 8093 Speech defect clinic

(P-17073)
HILLVIEW MENTAL HEALTH CTR INC
12450 Van Nuys Blvd Ste 200 (91331-1352)
PHONE..................818 896-1161
Eva S Mccraven, Pr
Beth K Meltzer, *
Julie E Jones, *
Jack L Avila, *
Konstantinos N Tripodis, *
EMP: 80 EST: 1984
SQ FT: 17,600
SALES (est): 10.27MM Privately Held
Web: www.hillviewmhc.org
SIC: 8093 Mental health clinic, outpatient

8093 - Specialty Outpatient Clinics, Nec (P-17074)

(P-17074)
INIZIO INTERVENTIONS INC
17037 Chatsworth St Ste 206 (91344-5874)
PHONE......................................818 937-0882
Sally Torrens, *Admn*
EMP: 65 EST: 2014
SALES (est): 905.83K **Privately Held**
Web: www.iniziointerventions.com
SIC: **8093** Mental health clinic, outpatient

(P-17075)
INLAND VLY DRG ALCHOL RCVERY S (PA)
Also Called: ADMINISTRATIVE OFFICES
1260 E Arrow Hwy (91786-4910)
PHONE......................................909 932-1069
Tina Hughes, *CEO*
Ellen Davis, *
EMP: 75 EST: 1962
SALES (est): 8.92MM
SALES (corp-wide): 8.92MM **Privately Held**
Web: www.inlandvalleyrecovery.org
SIC: **8093** Substance abuse clinics (outpatient)

(P-17076)
INSTITUTE FOR BHVORAL HLTH INC
1905 Business Center Dr Ste 100 (92408)
PHONE......................................909 289-1041
Azadeh K Jebelli, *Pr*
EMP: 265 EST: 2013
SALES (est): 13.01MM **Privately Held**
Web: www.ibhcare.com
SIC: **8093** Mental health clinic, outpatient

(P-17077)
INTERSTATE RHBLTATION SVCS LLC
333 E Glenoaks Blvd Ste 204 (91207-2074)
PHONE......................................818 244-5656
Sandy Pietsch, *
EMP: 120 EST: 1986
SALES (est): 21.74MM **Privately Held**
Web: www.interstaterehab.com
SIC: **8093** Rehabilitation center, outpatient treatment

(P-17078)
JCYC
2012 Pine St (94115-2828)
PHONE......................................415 921-5537
EMP: 78 EST: 2019
SALES (est): 7.02MM **Privately Held**
Web: www.jcyc.org
SIC: **8093** Specialty outpatient clinics, nec

(P-17079)
KAISER FOUNDATION HOSPITALS
Also Called: Kaiser Permanente
3400 Delta Fair Blvd (94509-4004)
PHONE......................................925 779-5000
Dan Sonnier, *Mgr*
EMP: 360
SQ FT: 47,307
SALES (corp-wide): 68.1B **Privately Held**
Web: www.kaisercenter.com
SIC: **8093** 8011 8062 Specialty outpatient clinics, nec; General and family practice, physician/surgeon; General medical and surgical hospitals
HQ: Kaiser Foundation Hospitals Inc
1 Kaiser Plz
Oakland CA
510 271-6611

(P-17080)
KAISER FOUNDATION HOSPITALS
Also Called: Kaiser Permanente
23621 Main St (90745-5743)
PHONE......................................310 513-6707
Lora Griffin, *Brnch Mgr*
EMP: 117
SALES (corp-wide): 68.1B **Privately Held**
Web: www.kaisercenter.com
SIC: **8093** 8062 Specialty outpatient clinics, nec; General medical and surgical hospitals
HQ: Kaiser Foundation Hospitals Inc
1 Kaiser Plz
Oakland CA
510 271-6611

(P-17081)
KAISER FOUNDATION HOSPITALS
Chemical Dpndncy Rcvery Prgram
2829 Watt Ave Ste 150 (95821-6245)
PHONE......................................916 482-1132
Terry Obrien, *Brnch Mgr*
EMP: 251
SALES (corp-wide): 68.1B **Privately Held**
Web: www.kaisercenter.com
SIC: **8093** Detoxification center, outpatient
HQ: Kaiser Foundation Hospitals Inc
1 Kaiser Plz
Oakland CA
510 271-6611

(P-17082)
KERN COUNTY HOSPITAL AUTHORITY
1902 B St (93301-3526)
P.O. Box 3519 (93385-3519)
PHONE......................................661 843-7980
EMP: 492
SALES (corp-wide): 47.39MM **Privately Held**
Web: www.kernmedical.com
SIC: **8093** Mental health clinic, outpatient
PA: Kern County Hospital Authority
1700 Mount Vernon Ave
Bakersfield CA
661 326-2102

(P-17083)
KIMA W MEDICAL CENTER
535 Airport Rd (95546-9615)
P.O. Box 1288 (95546-1288)
PHONE......................................530 625-4114
Emmit Chase, *CEO*
Dennis Jones, *COO*
EMP: 80 EST: 1998
SQ FT: 11,000
SALES (est): 9.92MM **Privately Held**
Web: www.kimaw.org
SIC: **8093** 8399 Specialty outpatient clinics, nec; Health systems agency

(P-17084)
KINGSVIEW CORP
Also Called: Tuolomne Cnty Bhvral Hlth Rcve
2 S Green St (95370-4618)
PHONE......................................209 533-6245
Jack Tanebaum, *Ex Dir*
EMP: 154 EST: 2002
SALES (est): 1.83MM **Privately Held**
Web: www.kingsview.com
SIC: **8093** Mental health clinic, outpatient

(P-17085)
LA VENTANA TREATMENT PROGRAMS
1408 E Thousand Oaks Blvd (91362-2889)
PHONE......................................805 644-5745
Steve Zamarripa, *Owner*
EMP: 82 EST: 2019
SALES (est): 2.43MM **Privately Held**
Web: www.laventanatreatment.com
SIC: **8093** Mental health clinic, outpatient

(P-17086)
LINCOLN (PA)
Also Called: Lincoln
1266 14th St (94607-2247)
PHONE......................................510 273-4700
Nancy L Oakley, *
Allison Becwar, *
Enrico Hernandez, *
EMP: 99 EST: 1883
SQ FT: 40,000
SALES (est): 24.68MM
SALES (corp-wide): 24.68MM **Privately Held**
Web: www.lincolnfamilies.org
SIC: **8093** 8361 8049 Mental health clinic, outpatient; Orphanage; Psychiatric social worker

(P-17087)
MEDMARK TRTMNT CTRS - SCRMNTO
7240 E Southgate Dr Ste G (95823-2627)
PHONE......................................916 391-4293
David K White, *CEO*
Daniel Gutschenritter, *CFO*
Frank Baumann, *COO*
EMP: 90 EST: 2006
SALES (est): 2.12MM
SALES (corp-wide): 106.29MM **Privately Held**
Web: www.medmark.com
SIC: **8093** Substance abuse clinics (outpatient)
HQ: Medmark Services, Inc.
1720 Lakepointe Dr # 117
Lewisville TX
214 379-3300

(P-17088)
MENDOCINO COAST CLINICS INC
Also Called: MENDOCINO COAST CLINICS
205 South St (95437-5540)
PHONE......................................707 964-1251
Paula Cohen, *Ex Dir*
Jeff Warner, *
Richard Moon, *
Claudia Boudreau, *
▲ EMP: 93 EST: 1992
SQ FT: 5,000
SALES (est): 14.75MM **Privately Held**
Web: www.mendocinocoastclinics.org
SIC: **8093** Family planning and birth control clinics

(P-17089)
MENTAL HEALTH SYSTEMS INC (PA)
Also Called: MHS
9465 Farnham St (92123-1308)
PHONE......................................858 573-2600
James Callaghan Junior, *CEO*
EMP: 70 EST: 1978
SQ FT: 18,000
SALES (est): 95.19MM
SALES (corp-wide): 95.19MM **Privately Held**
Web: www.turnbhs.org
SIC: **8093** Mental health clinic, outpatient

(P-17090)
MENTAL HEALTH SYSTEMS INC
Also Called: Kinesis North
474 W Vermont Ave Ste 101 (92025-6584)
PHONE......................................760 737-7125
Nahvash Alami, *Mgr*
EMP: 62
SQ FT: 3,060
SALES (corp-wide): 95.19MM **Privately Held**
Web: www.turnbhs.org
SIC: **8093** Mental health clinic, outpatient
PA: Mental Health Systems, Inc.
9465 Farnham St
San Diego CA
858 573-2600

(P-17091)
MENTAL HLTH ASSN SAN FRANCISCO
870 Market St Ste 928 (94102-2923)
PHONE......................................415 421-2926
Quintin Mecke, *Pr*
Mason Turner, *Pr*
Eduardo Vega, *Ex Dir*
Jennifer Simon, *VP*
EMP: 76 EST: 1946
SQ FT: 2,600
SALES (est): 3.29MM **Privately Held**
Web: www.mentalhealthsf.org
SIC: **8093** Mental health clinic, outpatient

(P-17092)
MERU HEALTH HOLDING INC
720 S B St (94401-4245)
PHONE......................................760 841-8040
Kristian Ranta, *CEO*
EMP: 64 EST: 2015
SALES (est): 18.84MM **Privately Held**
Web: www.meruhealth.com
SIC: **8093** Mental health clinic, outpatient

(P-17093)
MHM SERVICES INC
155 Glen Cove Marina Rd E # 200 (94591-7342)
PHONE......................................707 652-2688
EMP: 160
Web: www.centurionmanagedcare.com
SIC: **8093** Mental health clinic, outpatient
HQ: Mhm Services, Inc.
1593 Spring Hill Rd # 600
Vienna VA
703 749-4600

(P-17094)
MHM SERVICES INC
230 Station Way (93420-3358)
PHONE......................................805 904-6678
EMP: 160
Web: www.centurionmanagedcare.com
SIC: **8093** Mental health clinic, outpatient
HQ: Mhm Services, Inc.
1593 Spring Hill Rd # 600
Vienna VA
703 749-4600

(P-17095)
MHM SERVICES INC
6041 N 1st St (93710-5444)
PHONE......................................559 412-8121
EMP: 160
Web: www.centurionmanagedcare.com
SIC: **8093** Mental health clinic, outpatient
HQ: Mhm Services, Inc.
1593 Spring Hill Rd # 600
Vienna VA
703 749-4600

(P-17096)
MHM SERVICES INC
2380 Professional Dr (95403-3016)
PHONE......................................707 623-9080

PRODUCTS & SERVICES SECTION

8093 - Specialty Outpatient Clinics, Nec (P-17119)

EMP: 240
Web: www.centurionmanagedcare.com
SIC: 8093 Mental health clinic, outpatient
HQ: Mhm Services, Inc.
    1593 Spring Hill Rd # 600
    Vienna VA
    703 749-4600

(P-17097)
MHM SERVICES INC
180 Redwood St (94102-3283)
PHONE.................415 416-6992
EMP: 160
Web: www.centurionmanagedcare.com
SIC: 8093 Mental health clinic, outpatient
HQ: Mhm Services, Inc.
    1593 Spring Hill Rd # 600
    Vienna VA
    703 749-4600

(P-17098)
MODERN LIFE INC (PA)
Also Called: Modern Health
650 California St Fl 7 (94108-2737)
PHONE.................617 980-9633
Alyson Watson, CEO
EMP: 74 EST: 2017
SALES (est): 12.37MM
SALES (corp-wide): 12.37MM Privately Held
Web: www.modernhealth.com
SIC: 8093 Mental health clinic, outpatient

(P-17099)
NATIONAL MED ASSN CMPRHNSIVE H
Also Called: Comprehensive Health Center
3177 Ocean View Blvd (92113-1432)
PHONE.................619 231-9300
EMP: 73
SALES (corp-wide): 9.47MM Privately Held
Web: www.syhc.org
SIC: 8093 Specialty outpatient clinics, nec
PA: National Medical Association Comprehensive Health Center
    1601 Precision Park Ln
    San Ysidro CA
    619 231-3200

(P-17100)
NATIONAL THERAPEUTIC SVCS INC (PA)
Also Called: Northbound Treatment Services
3822 Campus Dr Ste 100 (92660-2607)
PHONE.................866 311-0003
Michael Neatherton, Pr
Paul Alexander, *
Ray Pacini, *
David Allen Gates, *
Devon Wayt, *
EMP: 98 EST: 1995
SALES (est): 22.39MM
SALES (corp-wide): 22.39MM Privately Held
Web: www.northboundtreatment.com
SIC: 8093 Alcohol clinic, outpatient

(P-17101)
NEW BRIDGE FOUNDATION INC
2323 Hearst Ave (94709-1319)
PHONE.................510 548-7270
Kosta Markakis, CEO
Jenny Knowles, *
EMP: 65 EST: 1971
SALES (est): 7.2MM Privately Held
Web: www.newbridgefoundation.org
SIC: 8093 Substance abuse clinics (outpatient)

(P-17102)
OCTAVE HEALTH GROUP INC
625 Market St Fl 15 (94105-3316)
PHONE.................415 360-3833
Sandeep Acharya, CEO
EMP: 60 EST: 2017
SALES (est): 9.31MM Privately Held
Web: www.findoctave.com
SIC: 8093 Mental health clinic, outpatient

(P-17103)
OPEN DOOR COMMUNITY HLTH CTRS (PA)
1275 8th St (95521-5770)
PHONE.................707 826-8642
Sydney Fisher Larsen, CEO
EMP: 70 EST: 1971
SALES (est): 96.36MM Privately Held
Web: www.opendoorhealth.com
SIC: 8093 Smoking clinic

(P-17104)
OPTIONS RECOVERY SERVICES
1835 Allston Way (94703-1764)
PHONE.................510 666-9552
Davida Coady, Prin
EMP: 78 EST: 2019
SALES (est): 8.23MM Privately Held
Web: www.optionsrecoveryservices.com
SIC: 8093 Mental health clinic, outpatient

(P-17105)
PACIFIC CLNICS PSDENA CALWORKS
2550 E Foothill Blvd (91107-3406)
PHONE.................626 419-3228
Miriam Shenfeld, Prin
EMP: 146 EST: 2003
SALES (est): 1.96MM Privately Held
Web: www.pacificclinics.org
SIC: 8093 Mental health clinic, outpatient

(P-17106)
PASSAGES MALIBU
Also Called: Passages Mlibu DRG Rhab Alchol
6428 Meadows Ct (90265-4492)
P.O. Box 6302 (90264-6302)
PHONE.................888 777-8525
▲ EMP: 81 EST: 2010
SALES (est): 4.45MM Privately Held
Web: www.passagesmalibu.com
SIC: 8093 Substance abuse clinics (outpatient)

(P-17107)
PEDIATRIC THERAPY NETWORK
1815 W 213th St Ste 100 (90501-7803)
PHONE.................310 328-0276
Zoe Mailloux, Ex Dir
EMP: 119 EST: 1996
SQ FT: 20,000
SALES (est): 10.21MM Privately Held
Web: www.pediatrictherapynetwork.org
SIC: 8093 Rehabilitation center, outpatient treatment

(P-17108)
PLANNED PARENTHOOD LOS ANGELES (PA)
400 W 30th St (90007-3320)
PHONE.................213 284-3200
Sue Dunlap, Pr
Mark Kimura, *
Adrianne Black, *
Linda Pahl, *
EMP: 80 EST: 1965
SQ FT: 30,000
SALES (est): 99.98MM
SALES (corp-wide): 99.98MM Privately Held
Web: www.plannedparenthood.org
SIC: 8093 Family planning clinic

(P-17109)
PLANNED PRNTHOOD MAR MONTE INC
1746 The Alameda (95126-1727)
PHONE.................408 287-7532
Linda T Williams, Pr
EMP: 146
SALES (corp-wide): 120.33MM Privately Held
Web: www.plannedparenthood.org
SIC: 8093 Family planning clinic
PA: Planned Parenthood Mar Monte, Inc.
    1691 The Alameda
    San Jose CA
    408 287-7532

(P-17110)
PLANNED PRNTHOOD OF PCF STHWES (PA)
1075 Camino Del Rio S Ste 100 (92108-3516)
PHONE.................619 881-4500
Darrah Johnson, CEO
Len Dodson, CFO
EMP: 100 EST: 1964
SQ FT: 24,000
SALES (est): 146.19MM
SALES (corp-wide): 146.19MM Privately Held
Web: www.plannedparenthood.org
SIC: 8093 Family planning clinic

(P-17111)
PLANNED PRNTHOOD OF PCF STHWES
1964 Via Ctr (92081-6056)
PHONE.................619 881-4500
Darrah D Johnson, Mgr
EMP: 100
SALES (corp-wide): 146.19MM Privately Held
Web: www.pppswcareers.org
SIC: 8093 Family planning clinic
PA: Planned Parenthood Of The Pacific Southwest
    1075 Camino Del Rio S
    San Diego CA
    619 881-4500

(P-17112)
PLANNED PRNTHOOD OF PCF STHWES
4501 Mission Bay Dr Ste 1c (92109)
PHONE.................619 881-4652
Darrah D Johnson, Mgr
EMP: 100
SALES (corp-wide): 146.19MM Privately Held
Web: www.pppswcareers.org
SIC: 8093 Family planning clinic
PA: Planned Parenthood Of The Pacific Southwest
    1075 Camino Del Rio S
    San Diego CA
    619 881-4500

(P-17113)
POSITIVE BEHAVIOR STEPS CORP
Also Called: Positive Behavior Steps
675 Cliffside Dr (91773-2957)
PHONE.................626 940-5180
David Sandoval, CEO
David Alberto Sandoval, *
EMP: 73 EST: 2017
SALES (est): 6.78MM Privately Held
Web: www.pbxsteps.org
SIC: 8093 Mental health clinic, outpatient

(P-17114)
PRIME MSO LLC
550 N Brand Blvd Ste 900 (91203-4721)
PHONE.................818 937-9969
Shadi Yassine, Acctnt
Steven Dien Purchaser, Prin
EMP: 67 EST: 1998
SALES (est): 24.33MM Privately Held
Web: www.primemso.com
SIC: 8093 Specialty outpatient clinics, nec

(P-17115)
PURE AUTISM COUNSELING CTR INC
Also Called: Pacc
17702 Sierra Hwy (91351-1635)
PHONE.................661 360-7730
Arevik Karamyan, CEO
EMP: 65 EST: 2018
SALES (est): 2.2MM Privately Held
Web: www.paccenter.net
SIC: 8093 Mental health clinic, outpatient

(P-17116)
REHAB ALLIANCE
22995 Mill Creek Dr Ste A (92653-1271)
PHONE.................949 707-5555
Betsy Gazda, Prin
EMP: 97 EST: 2003
SALES (est): 6.47MM Privately Held
Web: www.rehaballiance.com
SIC: 8093 Rehabilitation center, outpatient treatment

(P-17117)
REIMAGINE NETWORK (PA)
Also Called: REHABILITATION INSTITUTE OF OR
1601 E Saint Andrew Pl (92705-4932)
PHONE.................714 633-7400
Praim S Singh, Dir
EMP: 130 EST: 1950
SALES (est): 12.18MM
SALES (corp-wide): 12.18MM Privately Held
Web: www.riorehab.org
SIC: 8093 Rehabilitation center, outpatient treatment

(P-17118)
RICHMOND AREA MLT-SERVICES INC
1282 Market St (94102-4801)
PHONE.................415 579-3021
Kenneth Choi, Brnch Mgr
EMP: 61
SALES (corp-wide): 27.9MM Privately Held
Web: www.ramsinc.org
SIC: 8093 Mental health clinic, outpatient
PA: Richmond Area Multi-Services, Inc.
    4355 Geary Blvd
    San Francisco CA
    415 800-0699

(P-17119)
RICHMOND AREA MLT-SERVICES INC (PA)
4355 Geary Blvd (94118-3003)
PHONE.................415 800-0699
Kavoos Bassiri, CEO
Lenore Williams, *
EMP: 76 EST: 1974

8093 - Specialty Outpatient Clinics, Nec (P-17120)

SQ FT: 8,400
SALES (est): 27.9MM
SALES (corp-wide): 27.9MM Privately Held
Web: ramsinc.blogspot.com
SIC: 8093 Mental health clinic, outpatient

(P-17120)
RIO
Also Called: Rehabltttion Inst Sthern Cal Ri
1601 E Saint Andrew Pl (92705-4940)
PHONE.................................714 633-7400
Glenn Motola, Ex Dir
Parim Singh, *
John Berry, *
EMP: 233 EST: 1964
SALES (est): 9.58MM Privately Held
Web: www.reimagineoc.org
SIC: 8093 8351 Rehabilitation center, outpatient treatment; Child day care services

(P-17121)
RIVER OAK CENTER FOR CHILDREN (PA)
5445 Laurel Hills Dr (95841-3105)
PHONE.................................916 609-5100
Laurie Clothier, CEO
EMP: 140 EST: 1966
SQ FT: 26,000
SALES (est): 14.82MM
SALES (corp-wide): 14.82MM Privately Held
Web: www.riveroak.org
SIC: 8093 8699 Mental health clinic, outpatient; Charitable organization

(P-17122)
RIVERSIDE-SAN BERNARDINO
11555 1/2 Potrero Rd (92220-6946)
PHONE.................................951 849-4761
EMP: 102
SALES (corp-wide): 92.69MM Privately Held
Web: www.rsbcihi.org
SIC: 8093 8011 Specialty outpatient clinics, nec; Offices and clinics of medical doctors
PA: Riverside-San Bernardino County Indian Health, Inc.
11980 Mount Vernon Ave
Grand Terrace CA
909 864-1097

(P-17123)
SAFE REFUGE
Also Called: SOBRIETY HOUSE
1041 Redondo Ave (90804-3928)
PHONE.................................562 987-5722
Kathryn Romo, Ex Dir
EMP: 80 EST: 1988
SQ FT: 2,300
SALES (est): 8.7MM Privately Held
Web: www.saferefuge.info
SIC: 8093 Substance abuse clinics (outpatient)

(P-17124)
SAN FERNANDO CITY OF INC
10605 Balboa Blvd Ste 100 (91344-6367)
PHONE.................................818 832-2400
Wendi Tovey, Brnch Mgr
EMP: 97
SALES (corp-wide): 40.97MM Privately Held
Web: ci.san-fernando.ca.us
SIC: 8093 9111 Mental health clinic, outpatient; County supervisors' and executives' office
PA: San Fernando, City Of Inc
117 N Macneil St
San Fernando CA
818 898-1201

(P-17125)
SAN JQUIN VLY RHBLTTION HOSP A (HQ)
7173 N Sharon Ave (93720-3329)
PHONE.................................559 436-3600
Edward C Palacios, Pt
EMP: 275 EST: 2000
SALES (est): 38.42MM
SALES (corp-wide): 690.44MM Privately Held
Web: www.sjvrehab.com
SIC: 8093 Rehabilitation center, outpatient treatment
PA: Vibra Healthcare, Llc
4600 Lena Dr
Mechanicsburg PA
717 591-5700

(P-17126)
SIERRA HLTH WELLNESS GROUP LLC
Also Called: New Start Recovery Solutions
9985 Folsom Blvd (95827-1405)
PHONE.................................530 854-4119
Joe Henderson, Managing Member
John Dolores, Managing Member*
Shawn Vang, *
EMP: 150 EST: 2019
SALES (est): 200K Privately Held
SIC: 8093 Mental health clinic, outpatient

(P-17127)
SOUTH BAYLO UNIVERSITY
Also Called: South Baylo Acupuncture Clinic
2727 W 6th St (90057-3111)
PHONE.................................213 999-0297
David J Park, Pr
EMP: 136
SALES (corp-wide): 4.43MM Privately Held
Web: www.southbaylo.edu
SIC: 8093 8221 8049 Specialty outpatient clinics, nec; University; Acupuncturist
PA: South Baylo University
1126 N Brookhurst St
Anaheim CA
714 533-1495

(P-17128)
SOUTH CNTL HLTH RHBLTTION PRGR
Also Called: Barbour & Floyd Medical Assoc
2620 Industry Way (90262-4024)
PHONE.................................310 667-4070
Jack M Barbour, Prin
EMP: 98
Web: www.barbourandfloydla.org
SIC: 8093 Rehabilitation center, outpatient treatment
PA: South Central Health & Rehabilitation Program
2610 Industry Way Ste A
Lynwood CA

(P-17129)
SOUTH COAST CHILDRENS SOC INC
24950 Redlands Blvd (92354-4032)
PHONE.................................909 478-3377
EMP: 186
SALES (corp-wide): 36.84MM Privately Held
Web: www.sccs4kids.org
SIC: 8093 Mental health clinic, outpatient
PA: South Coast Children's Society, Inc.
25910 Acero Ste 160
Mission Viejo CA
714 966-8650

(P-17130)
SOUTHERN CAL ALCHOL DRG PRGRAM (PA)
11500 Paramount Blvd (90241-4530)
PHONE.................................562 923-4545
Lynne Appel, Ex Dir
Gary Munger, *
Matt Matthews Ph.d., Sec
Leon Emerson, *
Judith Edwards, *
EMP: 60 EST: 1972
SALES (est): 12.49MM
SALES (corp-wide): 12.49MM Privately Held
Web: www.scadpinc.org
SIC: 8093 Substance abuse clinics (outpatient)

(P-17131)
SOUTHERN INDIAN HEALTH COUNCIL (PA)
4058 Willows Rd (91901-1668)
P.O. Box 2128 (91903-2128)
PHONE.................................619 445-1188
Laura Caswell, CEO
Carolina Monsano, *
Donna James, *
EMP: 100 EST: 1980
SQ FT: 11,000
SALES (est): 26.82MM
SALES (corp-wide): 26.82MM Privately Held
Web: www.sihc.org
SIC: 8093 Specialty outpatient clinics, nec

(P-17132)
ST JOSEPH HLTH NTHRN CAL LLC
Also Called: Centerism Memorial Hospital
1450 Medical Center Dr (94928-2924)
PHONE.................................707 584-0672
Mauree Rogers, Dir
EMP: 297
SQ FT: 14,560
SALES (corp-wide): 115.22MM Privately Held
SIC: 8093 8011 Specialty outpatient clinics, nec; Offices and clinics of medical doctors
PA: St. Joseph Health Northern California, Llc
1165 Montgomery Dr
Santa Rosa CA
949 381-4000

(P-17133)
SUBACUTE TRTMNT FOR ADLSCENT R (PA)
Also Called: Stars
545 Estudillo Ave (94577-4611)
PHONE.................................510 352-9200
EMP: 76 EST: 1996
SQ FT: 7,442
SALES (est): 11.41MM Privately Held
Web: www.starsinc.com
SIC: 8093 8051 Mental health clinic, outpatient; Mental retardation hospital

(P-17134)
SUCCESSFUL ALTRNTVES FOR ADDCT
795 Fletcher Ln (94544-1008)
PHONE.................................510 247-8300
David K White, CEO
Daniel Gutschenritter, CFO
Frank Baumann, COO
EMP: 71 EST: 1994

SQ FT: 1,700
SALES (est): 2.31MM
SALES (corp-wide): 106.29MM Privately Held
Web: www.medmark.com
SIC: 8093 Substance abuse clinics (outpatient)
HQ: Medmark Services, Inc.
1720 Lakepointe Dr # 117
Lewisville TX
214 379-3300

(P-17135)
SUTTER HEALTH
Sutter Health At Work
1201 Alhambra Blvd Ste 210 (95816-5238)
PHONE.................................916 220-1927
Colleen Cooke, Mgr
EMP: 142
SALES (corp-wide): 14.77B Privately Held
Web: www.sutterhealth.org
SIC: 8093 8011 Specialty outpatient clinics, nec; Offices and clinics of medical doctors
PA: Sutter Health
2200 River Plaza Dr
Sacramento CA
916 733-8800

(P-17136)
SUTTERCARE CORPORATION
1601 Trousdale Dr (94010-4520)
PHONE.................................650 696-5363
Janet Wagner, Mgr
EMP: 1096
SALES (corp-wide): 14.77B Privately Held
SIC: 8093 Substance abuse clinics (outpatient)
HQ: Suttercare Corporation
2200 River Plaza Dr
Sacramento CA
916 733-8800

(P-17137)
TARZANA TREATMENT CENTERS INC
320 E Palmdale Blvd (93550-4598)
PHONE.................................818 654-3815
Albert Senella, Pr
EMP: 79
SALES (corp-wide): 110.26MM Privately Held
Web: www.tarzanatc.org
SIC: 8093 Substance abuse clinics (outpatient)
PA: Tarzana Treatment Centers, Inc.
18646 Oxnard St
Tarzana CA
818 996-1051

(P-17138)
TARZANA TREATMENT CENTERS INC
Also Called: Tarzana Trtmnt Ctrs LNG Bch O
5190 Atlantic Ave (90805-6510)
PHONE.................................562 428-4111
EMP: 80
SALES (corp-wide): 110.26MM Privately Held
Web: www.tarzanatc.org
SIC: 8093 8299 Substance abuse clinics (outpatient); Airline training
PA: Tarzana Treatment Centers, Inc.
18646 Oxnard St
Tarzana CA
818 996-1051

(P-17139)
TARZANA TREATMENT CENTERS INC

PRODUCTS & SERVICES SECTION
8093 - Specialty Outpatient Clinics, Nec (P-17157)

2101 Magnolia Ave (90806-4521)
PHONE..................562 218-1868
Angela Knox, Brnch Mgr
EMP: 107
SQ FT: 11,482
SALES (corp-wide): 110.26MM Privately Held
Web: www.tarzanatc.org
SIC: 8093 Substance abuse clinics (outpatient)
PA: Tarzana Treatment Centers, Inc.
    18646 Oxnard St
    Tarzana CA
    818 996-1051

(P-17140)
TARZANA TREATMENT CENTERS INC
Also Called: Tarzana Treatment Ctr
44447 10th St W (93534-3324)
PHONE..................661 726-2630
Theresa Scott, Dir
EMP: 107
SALES (corp-wide): 110.26MM Privately Held
Web: www.tarzanatc.org
SIC: 8093 8069 8011 Drug clinic, outpatient; Drug addiction rehabilitation hospital; Clinic, operated by physicians
PA: Tarzana Treatment Centers, Inc.
    18646 Oxnard St
    Tarzana CA
    818 996-1051

(P-17141)
TARZANA TREATMENT CENTERS INC (PA)
18646 Oxnard St (91356-1411)
PHONE..................818 996-1051
TOLL FREE: 800
Albert Senella, Pr
Sylvia Cadena, *
Bobbi Sloan, *
EMP: 160 EST: 1972
SQ FT: 14,000
SALES (est): 110.26MM
SALES (corp-wide): 110.26MM Privately Held
Web: www.tarzanatc.org
SIC: 8093 8322 8063 Mental health clinic, outpatient; Individual and family services; Psychiatric hospitals

(P-17142)
TELECARE ACT 7
Also Called: Telecare
12440 Firestone Blvd Ste 3025 (90650-4328)
PHONE..................562 929-6688
Bryan Sawlsville, Dir
EMP: 74 EST: 1996
SALES (est): 4.32MM
SALES (corp-wide): 440.9MM Privately Held
Web: www.telecarecorp.com
SIC: 8093 Mental health clinic, outpatient
PA: Telecare Corporation
    1080 Marina Village Pkwy # 100
    Alameda CA
    510 337-7950

(P-17143)
TELECARE CORPORATION
Also Called: La Casa Mhrc
6060 N Paramount Blvd (90805-3711)
PHONE..................562 630-8672
Anne Bakar, CEO
EMP: 199 EST: 1965
SALES (est): 28.28MM
SALES (corp-wide): 440.9MM Privately Held
Web: www.telecarecorp.com
SIC: 8093 Mental health clinic, outpatient
PA: Telecare Corporation
    1080 Marina Village Pkwy # 100
    Alameda CA
    510 337-7950

(P-17144)
TRANSITIONS - MENTAL HLTH ASSN (PA)
Also Called: SLO TRANSITIONS
784 High St (93401-5243)
P.O. Box 15408 (93406-5408)
PHONE..................805 540-6500
Jill B White, Ex Dir
EMP: 60 EST: 1980
SQ FT: 8,000
SALES (est): 15.94MM Privately Held
Web: www.t-mha.org
SIC: 8093 Mental health clinic, outpatient

(P-17145)
TRI-CITY MENTAL HEALTH AUTH (PA)
Also Called: Tri City Mental Health Center
2008 N Garey Ave (91767-2722)
PHONE..................909 623-6131
TOLL FREE: 866
Antonette Navarro, Ex Dir
Diana Acosta, *
EMP: 85 EST: 1960
SQ FT: 12,000
SALES (est): 10.29MM
SALES (corp-wide): 10.29MM Privately Held
Web: www.tricitymhs.org
SIC: 8093 8322 Mental health clinic, outpatient; Individual and family services

(P-17146)
TRUVIDA RECOVERY
45 Timberland (92656-2108)
PHONE..................949 283-4679
Vince Bindi, Pt
EMP: 64 EST: 2016
SALES (est): 4.7MM Privately Held
SIC: 8093 Substance abuse clinics (outpatient)

(P-17147)
TULE RIVER INDIAN HLTH CTR INC
380 N Reservation Rd (93257-9673)
P.O. Box 768 (93258-0768)
PHONE..................559 784-2316
Zahid Sheikh, CEO
Casey Carrillo, *
EMP: 65 EST: 1973
SQ FT: 15,000
SALES (est): 17.24MM Privately Held
Web: www.trihci.org
SIC: 8093 Specialty outpatient clinics, nec

(P-17148)
TURNING POINT CMNTY PROGRAMS (PA)
10850 Gold Center Dr Ste 325 (95670-6034)
PHONE..................916 364-8395
Al Rowlett, CEO
Diana White, *
John Buck, *
Bruce Jefferson, *
Carol A Frezza, *
EMP: 65 EST: 1976
SQ FT: 6,000
SALES (est): 60.82MM
SALES (corp-wide): 60.82MM Privately Held

Web: www.telecarecorp.com
SIC: 8093 Mental health clinic, outpatient
PA: Telecare Corporation
    1080 Marina Village Pkwy # 100
    Alameda CA
    510 337-7950

(P-17149)
UHS-CORONA INC
Also Called: Corona Rgnal Med Ctr Rhbltion
730 Magnolia Ave (92879-3117)
PHONE..................951 736-7200
Pat Sanders, Dir
EMP: 200
SALES (corp-wide): 13.4B Publicly Held
Web: www.swhcoronaregional.com
SIC: 8093 8062 8069 8051 Rehabilitation center, outpatient treatment; General medical and surgical hospitals; Specialty hospitals, except psychiatric; Skilled nursing care facilities
HQ: Uhs-Corona, Inc.
    800 S Main St
    Corona CA
    951 737-4343

(P-17150)
UNITED AMRCN INDIAN INVLVMENT (PA)
1125 W 6th St Ste 103 (90017-1896)
PHONE..................213 202-3970
Joseph Quintana, Dir
Carrie Johnson Ph.d., Dir
David L Rambeau, *
EMP: 122 EST: 1974
SQ FT: 26,000
SALES (est): 10.38MM
SALES (corp-wide): 10.38MM Privately Held
Web: www.uaii.org
SIC: 8093 Rehabilitation center, outpatient treatment

(P-17151)
UNIVERSAL CARE INC (HQ)
Also Called: Smile Wide Dental
19762 Macarthur Blvd Ste 100 (92612-2424)
PHONE..................562 424-6200
Howard E Davis, CEO
Jay Davis, *
Jeffrey Davis, *
Mark Gunter, *
EMP: 350 EST: 1983
SQ FT: 73,000
SALES (est): 54.72MM
SALES (corp-wide): 2.41B Publicly Held
Web: www.bndhmo.com
SIC: 8093 Specialty outpatient clinics, nec
PA: Bright Health Group, Inc.
    8000 Norman Center Dr # 120
    Minneapolis MN
    612 238-1321

(P-17152)
UNIVERSITY CAL SAN FRANCISCO
982 Mission St (94103-2911)
PHONE..................415 597-8047
David Fariello, Prin
EMP: 73
SALES (corp-wide): 534.4MM Privately Held
Web: www.ucsf.edu
SIC: 8093 8221 9411 Specialty outpatient clinics, nec; University; Administration of educational programs
HQ: University Cal San Francisco
    513 Parnassus Ave 115f
    San Francisco CA

(P-17153)
VICTOR CMNTY SUPPORT SVCS INC
15095 Amargosa Rd Ste 201 (92394-1875)
PHONE..................760 987-8225
Angie R Wiechert, Mgr
EMP: 197
SALES (corp-wide): 69.1MM Privately Held
Web: www.victor.org
SIC: 8093 Mental health clinic, outpatient
PA: Victor Community Support Services, Inc.
    1360 E Lassen Ave
    Chico CA
    530 893-0758

(P-17154)
VICTOR CMNTY SUPPORT SVCS INC
900 E Main St Ste 201 (95945-5853)
PHONE..................530 273-2244
Rachel Pena, Ex Dir
EMP: 112
SALES (corp-wide): 69.1MM Privately Held
Web: www.victor.org
SIC: 8093 Mental health clinic, outpatient
PA: Victor Community Support Services, Inc.
    1360 E Lassen Ave
    Chico CA
    530 893-0758

(P-17155)
VICTOR CMNTY SUPPORT SVCS INC
1105 E Florida Ave (92543-4512)
PHONE..................951 212-1770
EMP: 158
SALES (corp-wide): 69.1MM Privately Held
Web: www.victor.org
SIC: 8093 Mental health clinic, outpatient
PA: Victor Community Support Services, Inc.
    1360 E Lassen Ave
    Chico CA
    530 893-0758

(P-17156)
VICTOR CMNTY SUPPORT SVCS INC
Also Called: Desert Mountain Fics
14360 St Andrews Dr Ste 11 (92395-4341)
PHONE..................760 245-4695
Alan Mann, Brnch Mgr
EMP: 107
SALES (corp-wide): 69.1MM Privately Held
Web: www.victor.org
SIC: 8093 Mental health clinic, outpatient
PA: Victor Community Support Services, Inc.
    1360 E Lassen Ave
    Chico CA
    530 893-0758

(P-17157)
VICTOR CMNTY SUPPORT SVCS INC
Also Called: San Bernardino Fics
1908 Business Center Dr Ste 109 (92408)
PHONE..................909 890-5930
Paula Quijano, Brnch Mgr
EMP: 107
SALES (corp-wide): 69.1MM Privately Held
Web: www.victor.org

8093 - Specialty Outpatient Clinics, Nec (P-17158)

SIC: 8093 Mental health clinic, outpatient
PA: Victor Community Support Services, Inc.
1360 E Lassen Ave
Chico CA
530 893-0758

(P-17158)
VICTOR CMNTY SUPPORT SVCS INC
Also Called: Stockton Fics
2495 W March Ln Ste 125 (95207-8224)
PHONE.....................209 465-1080
Debi Scott, Brnch Mgr
EMP: 113
SALES (corp-wide): 69.1MM Privately Held
Web: www.victor.org
SIC: 8093 Mental health clinic, outpatient
PA: Victor Community Support Services, Inc.
1360 E Lassen Ave
Chico CA
530 893-0758

(P-17159)
VICTOR CMNTY SUPPORT SVCS INC
Also Called: Butte Fics
1360 E Lassen Ave (95973-7823)
PHONE.....................530 267-1710
Trudi Engelhardt, Brnch Mgr
EMP: 94
SALES (corp-wide): 69.1MM Privately Held
Web: www.victor.org
SIC: 8093 Mental health clinic, outpatient
PA: Victor Community Support Services, Inc.
1360 E Lassen Ave
Chico CA
530 893-0758

(P-17160)
VISIONS UNLIMITED
8766 Williamson Dr (95624-1829)
PHONE.....................916 394-0800
Roleda Bates, Dir
EMP: 104 EST: 1978
SALES (est): 4.58MM Privately Held
Web: www.vuinc.org
SIC: 8093 Mental health clinic, outpatient

(P-17161)
WESTCOAST CHILDRENS CLINIC
3301 E 12th St Ste 259 (94601-2940)
P.O. Box 7026 (94601-0026)
PHONE.....................510 269-9030
Stacy Anne Katz, Ex Dir
EMP: 140 EST: 1979
SALES (est): 19.96MM Privately Held
Web: www.westcoastcc.org
SIC: 8093 Mental health clinic, outpatient

(P-17162)
WORKING WITH AUTISM INC
14724 Ventura Blvd Ste 1110 (91403-3511)
PHONE.....................818 501-4240
Jennifer Sabin, Dir
EMP: 100 EST: 1997
SALES (est): 5.2MM Privately Held
Web: www.workingwithautism.com
SIC: 8093 Mental health clinic, outpatient

8099 Health And Allied Services, Nec

(P-17163)
365 HLTHCARE STAFFING SVCS INC
25550 Hawthorne Blvd Ste 211 (90505-6825)
PHONE.....................310 436-3650
Aaron Mark Kasdorf, CEO
EMP: 76 EST: 2014
SALES (est): 10.88MM Privately Held
Web: www.365healthstaffing.com
SIC: 8099 Health and allied services, nec

(P-17164)
ABLE HEALTH GROUP LLC
41990 Cook St Ste 2004 (92211-6105)
PHONE.....................760 610-2093
Gilbert Mwansa, Admn
EMP: 80 EST: 2017
SALES (est): 1.68MM Privately Held
SIC: 8099 Health and allied services, nec

(P-17165)
ACCOUNTBLE HLTH CRE IPA A PROF
2525 Cherry Ave Ste 225 (90755-2057)
PHONE.....................562 435-3333
Thomas Lam, CEO
EMP: 113 EST: 1993
SALES (est): 985.73K Publicly Held
SIC: 8099 Physical examination and testing services
HQ: Apc-Lsma Designated Shareholder Medical Corporation
1668 S Garfield Ave Fl 2
Alhambra CA
626 282-0288

(P-17166)
AHMC HEALTHCARE INC
506 W Valley Blvd Ste 300 (91776-5716)
PHONE.....................626 248-3452
EMP: 200
SALES (corp-wide): 476.02MM Privately Held
Web: www.ahmchealth.com
SIC: 8099 8062 Blood bank; General medical and surgical hospitals
PA: Ahmc Healthcare Inc.
506 W Valley Blvd Ste 300
San Gabriel CA
626 943-7526

(P-17167)
AHMC HEALTHCARE INC
900 S Atlantic Blvd (91754-4716)
PHONE.....................626 570-9000
EMP: 100
SALES (corp-wide): 476.02MM Privately Held
Web: www.ahmchealth.com
SIC: 8099 Childbirth preparation clinic
PA: Ahmc Healthcare Inc.
506 W Valley Blvd Ste 300
San Gabriel CA
626 943-7526

(P-17168)
ALPHA HEALTH INC
400 Oyster Point Blvd Ste 222 (94080-1904)
PHONE.....................970 209-1462
EMP: 212 EST: 2018
SALES (est): 3.1MM Privately Held
Web: www.akasa.com
SIC: 8099 Health and allied services, nec

(P-17169)
ALTAMED HEALTH SERVICES CORP
1515 S Broadway Ste A (92707-2253)
PHONE.....................714 919-0280
Alberto Gedissman, Brnch Mgr
EMP: 65
SALES (corp-wide): 1.05B Privately Held
SIC: 8099 Blood related health services
PA: Altamed Health Services Corporation
2040 Camfield Ave
Commerce CA
323 725-8751

(P-17170)
ALTAMED HEALTH SERVICES CORP
Also Called: Altamed Med & Dntl Group Bell
8627 Atlantic Ave (90280-3501)
PHONE.....................323 562-6700
Erika Sockaci, Brnch Mgr
EMP: 144
SALES (corp-wide): 1.05B Privately Held
Web: www.altamed.org
SIC: 8099 8011 Medical services organization; Gynecologist
PA: Altamed Health Services Corporation
2040 Camfield Ave
Commerce CA
323 725-8751

(P-17171)
ALTAMED HEALTH SERVICES CORP
Also Called: Altamed Med Dntl Grp Whttier W
3945 Whittier Blvd (90023-2440)
PHONE.....................323 307-0400
Angela Arredondo, Brnch Mgr
EMP: 160
SALES (corp-wide): 1.05B Privately Held
Web: www.altamedfoundation.org
SIC: 8099 8011 Medical services organization; Gynecologist
PA: Altamed Health Services Corporation
2040 Camfield Ave
Commerce CA
323 725-8751

(P-17172)
ALTAMED HEALTH SERVICES CORP
Also Called: Altamed Ltc Trnsp Dept
5255 Pomona Blvd Ste 11 (90022-1770)
PHONE.....................323 890-8767
Gloria Marquez, Brnch Mgr
EMP: 72
SALES (corp-wide): 1.05B Privately Held
Web: www.altamedfoundation.org
SIC: 8099 8011 Medical services organization; Gynecologist
PA: Altamed Health Services Corporation
2040 Camfield Ave
Commerce CA
323 725-8751

(P-17173)
ALTAMED HEALTH SERVICES CORP
Also Called: Slauson Plaza Med Group
9436 Slauson Ave (90660-4748)
PHONE.....................562 949-8717
Alfredo Nunez, Brnch Mgr
EMP: 128
SALES (corp-wide): 1.05B Privately Held
Web: www.altamed.org

SIC: 8099 Health and allied services, nec
SIC: 8099 8011 Medical services organization; Clinic, operated by physicians
PA: Altamed Health Services Corporation
2040 Camfield Ave
Commerce CA
323 725-8751

(P-17174)
ALTAMED HEALTH SERVICES CORP
Also Called: Youth Services
711 E Wardlow Rd Ste 203 (90807-4650)
PHONE.....................562 595-8040
Galiah Richmond, Brnch Mgr
EMP: 64
SALES (corp-wide): 1.05B Privately Held
Web: www.altamed.org
SIC: 8099 8011 Medical services organization; Pediatrician
PA: Altamed Health Services Corporation
2040 Camfield Ave
Commerce CA
323 725-8751

(P-17175)
ALTAMED HEALTH SERVICES CORP
Also Called: Alta Med Health Services
10418 Valley Blvd Ste B (91731-3600)
PHONE.....................626 453-8466
EMP: 136
SALES (corp-wide): 1.05B Privately Held
Web: www.altamed.org
SIC: 8099 8011 Medical services organization; Gynecologist
PA: Altamed Health Services Corporation
2040 Camfield Ave
Commerce CA
323 725-8751

(P-17176)
AMBITIONS BEHAVIORAL HLTH LLC
2372 Morse Ave (92614-6234)
PHONE.....................408 373-6752
Billal Asghar, CEO
EMP: 64 EST: 2017
SALES (est): 6.06MM Privately Held
Web: www.ambitionsbh.com
SIC: 8099 Health and allied services, nec

(P-17177)
AMERICAN HLTHCARE ADM SVCS INC
Also Called: American Health Care
3850 Atherton Rd (95765-3700)
PHONE.....................916 773-7227
Lance Aizen, CEO
Christine Lee, CCO*
EMP: 490 EST: 1987
SQ FT: 8,000
SALES (est): 42.97MM Privately Held
Web: www.americanhealthcare.com
SIC: 8099 Medical services organization

(P-17178)
APREVA CORPORATION
Also Called: Apreva Hospice
1565 Hotel Cir S Ste 320 (92108-3425)
PHONE.....................619 450-4414
Noel Sullivan, CEO
EMP: 65 EST: 2008
SALES (est): 17.43MM Privately Held
Web: www.aprevahospice.com
SIC: 8099 Childbirth preparation clinic

8099 - Health And Allied Services, Nec (P-17201)

(P-17179)
ARBORMED INC (PA)
725 W Town And Country Rd (92868-4703)
PHONE..................................714 689-1500
EMP: 123 EST: 1995
SQ FT: 11,000
SALES (est): 14.55MM Privately Held
SIC: 8099 8742 Medical services organization; Management consulting services

(P-17180)
ASTIVA HEALTH INC
765 The City Dr S (92868-4955)
PHONE..................................858 707-5111
Viet Tran, Ex Dir
Viet Tran, Sec
EMP: 75 EST: 2019
SALES (est): 5.38MM Privately Held
Web: www.astivahealth.com
SIC: 8099 Health and allied services, nec

(P-17181)
ATLAS LIFT TECH INC
210 Porter Dr Ste 300 (94583-1534)
PHONE..................................415 283-1804
Eric Race, Pr
Wendy Mccollom, CFO
EMP: 150 EST: 2012
SALES (est): 25.4MM Privately Held
Web: www.atlaslifttech.com
SIC: 8099 Health screening service

(P-17182)
AYA LOCUMS SERVICES INC
5930 Cornerstone Ct W Ste 300 (92121-3772)
PHONE..................................866 687-7390
Alan Braynin, Pr
EMP: 585 EST: 2018
SALES (est): 288.11K Privately Held
SIC: 8099 Medical services organization
PA: Aya Healthcare, Inc.
5930 Cornerstone Ct W # 3
San Diego CA

(P-17183)
BAKERSFIELD FAMILY MED GROUP
5601 Auburn St Unit A. (93306-2977)
PHONE..................................661 846-3605
EMP: 65
SALES (corp-wide): 26.9MM Privately Held
Web: www.bfmc.com
SIC: 8099 Childbirth preparation clinic
PA: Bakersfield Family Medical Group, Inc
4580 California Ave
Bakersfield CA
661 327-4411

(P-17184)
BASS MEDICAL GROUP
3250 Beard Rd (94558-3406)
PHONE..................................707 346-5100
EMP: 98 EST: 2017
SALES (est): 630.25K Privately Held
Web: www.bassmedicalgroup.com
SIC: 8099 Health and allied services, nec

(P-17185)
BAY AREA COMMUNITY HEALTH
770 A St Ste 310 (94541-3956)
PHONE..................................510 770-8040
Sherol Gray, Mgr
EMP: 481
SALES (corp-wide): 110.22MM Privately Held
Web: www.bach.health

SIC: 8099 Blood related health services
PA: Bay Area Community Health
40910 Fremont Blvd
Fremont CA
510 770-8040

(P-17186)
BERKELEY EMRGNCY MED GROUP INC
2000 Crow Canyon Pl Ste 220 (94583-4633)
PHONE..................................925 962-1067
Teven Mark Sornsin, CEO
EMP: 80 EST: 1995
SQ FT: 3,000
SALES (est): 12MM Privately Held
Web: www.bemg.org
SIC: 8099 Blood related health services

(P-17187)
BHC ALHAMBRA HOSPITAL INC
Also Called: Bhc Alhambra Hospital
4619 Rosemead Blvd (91770-1478)
PHONE..................................626 286-1191
EMP: 350
SALES (est): 21.89MM Privately Held
Web: www.bhcalhambra.com
SIC: 8099 Blood related health services

(P-17188)
BIO-MEDICS INC
371 W Highland Ave (92405-4011)
PHONE..................................909 883-9501
Gary Crandall, Mgr
EMP: 121
SIC: 8099 Blood bank
PA: Bio-Medics, Inc.
2187 Monitor Dr
Park City UT

(P-17189)
BLOOD BANK OF REDWOODS (PA)
Also Called: Blood Center of The Pacific
3505 Industrial Dr (95403-2064)
PHONE..................................707 545-1222
Cathy Bryan, Admn
EMP: 109 EST: 1948
SQ FT: 13,540
SALES (est): 4.83MM
SALES (corp-wide): 4.83MM Privately Held
SIC: 8099 Blood bank

(P-17190)
BLOOD BNK SAN BRNRDINO RVRSIDE (HQ)
Also Called: Lifestream
384 W Orange Show Rd (92408-2028)
P.O. Box 1429 (92402-1429)
PHONE..................................909 885-6503
Frederick B Axelrod, CEO
Joseph Dunn, *
Susan Marquez, *
EMP: 240 EST: 1951
SQ FT: 50,000
SALES (est): 63.6MM
SALES (corp-wide): 526.62MM Privately Held
Web: www.lstream.org
SIC: 8099 2836 Blood bank; Blood derivatives
PA: Vitalant
9305 E Via De Ventura
Scottsdale AZ
800 288-2199

(P-17191)
BLOODSOURCE INC (PA)
10536 Peter A Mccuen Blvd (95655-4128)
PHONE..................................916 456-1500
Michael J Fuller, CEO
Dirk Johnson, *
Jim Eldridge, *
EMP: 325 EST: 1948
SQ FT: 105,000
SALES (est): 33.62MM
SALES (corp-wide): 33.62MM Privately Held
Web: www.vitalant.org
SIC: 8099 Blood bank

(P-17192)
BLOODSOURCE INC
Also Called: Bloodsource North Valley
555 Rio Lindo Ave (95926-1816)
PHONE..................................530 893-5433
Bettina Baur, Mgr
EMP: 60
SALES (corp-wide): 33.62MM Privately Held
Web: www.vitalant.org
SIC: 8099 Blood bank
PA: Bloodsource, Inc.
10536 Peter A Mccuen Blvd
Mather CA
916 456-1500

(P-17193)
BMS HEALTHCARE INC
8925 Mines Ave (90660-3006)
PHONE..................................562 942-7019
Mordechai Stock, Prin
EMP: 130 EST: 2010
SALES (est): 4.33MM Privately Held
SIC: 8099 Health and allied services, nec

(P-17194)
BUILDING CNNCTONS BHVORAL HLTH
811 San Ramon Valley Blvd Ste 100 (94526-4025)
PHONE..................................925 743-1678
Jeffrey Wilkinson, Prin
EMP: 62 EST: 2014
SALES (est): 1.31MM Privately Held
Web: www.bcbhinc.com
SIC: 8099 Health and allied services, nec

(P-17195)
CALIFORNIA CRYOBANK INC
Also Called: Califrnia Cryobank Lf Sciences
611 Gateway Blvd Ste 820 (94080-7029)
PHONE..................................650 635-1420
EMP: 300
SALES (corp-wide): 3.31B Publicly Held
Web: www.cryobank.com
SIC: 8099 Blood bank
HQ: California Cryobank Llc
11915 La Grange Ave
Los Angeles CA
310 496-5691

(P-17196)
CALIFORNIA CRYOBANK LLC (DH)
Also Called: Generate Life Sciences Co
11915 La Grange Ave (90025-5213)
PHONE..................................310 496-5691
TOLL FREE: 800
Richards Jennings, CEO
Pamela Richardson, *
Brian Rizkallah, *
EMP: 75 EST: 1977
SQ FT: 21,300
SALES (est): 92.08MM

SALES (corp-wide): 3.31B Publicly Held
Web: www.cryobank.com
SIC: 8099 Sperm bank
HQ: Coopersurgical, Inc.
75 Corporate Dr
Trumbull CT

(P-17197)
CALIFRNIA DEPT DVLPMENTAL SVCS
Also Called: CA Department Development Svc
696 Ramon (92234)
PHONE..................................760 770-6248
Kathleen Waegner, Dir
EMP: 446
SALES (corp-wide): 534.4MM Privately Held
SIC: 8099 Physical examination and testing services
HQ: California Department Of Developmental Services
1215 O St
Sacramento CA

(P-17198)
CALIFRNIA FRNSIC MED GROUP INC
2801 Meadow Lark Dr (92123-2709)
PHONE..................................858 694-4690
Penny Looper, Genl Mgr
EMP: 70
SALES (corp-wide): 10.38MM Privately Held
SIC: 8099 9223 Medical services organization; Jail, government
PA: California Forensic Medical Group, Incorporated
1283 Murfreesboro Pike # 500
Nashville TN
831 649-8994

(P-17199)
CALIFRNIA FRNSIC MED GROUP INC
800 S Victoria Ave (93009-0001)
PHONE..................................805 654-3343
Elaine Hustedt, VP
EMP: 186
SALES (corp-wide): 10.38MM Privately Held
SIC: 8099 Medical services organization
PA: California Forensic Medical Group, Incorporated
1283 Murfreesboro Pike # 500
Nashville TN
831 649-8994

(P-17200)
CAMDEN CENTER INC
10780 Santa Monica Blvd Ste 105 (90025-4749)
PHONE..................................310 526-3807
Jason Schiffman, Prin
EMP: 90 EST: 2011
SALES (est): 5.21MM Privately Held
Web: www.camdencenter.com
SIC: 8099 Health and allied services, nec

(P-17201)
CENPATICO BEHAVIORAL HLTH LLC
Also Called: Centene Advnced Bhavioral Hlth
1740 Creekside Oaks Dr Ste 200 (95833-3639)
PHONE..................................877 858-3855
Jason Harrold, Mgr
EMP: 82 EST: 2018
SALES (est): 2.03MM Publicly Held

8099 - Health And Allied Services, Nec (P-17202)

SIC: **8099** Health and allied services, nec
PA: Centene Corporation
7700 Forsyth Blvd Ste 800
Saint Louis MO

(P-17202)
CENTER TO PRMOTE HLTHCARE ACCE
Also Called: Social Interest Solutions
1 Capitol Mall Ste 300 (95814-3296)
PHONE..................................916 563-4004
John Caterham, *Pr*
EMP: 74
Web: www.socialinterest.org
SIC: **8099** Medical services organization
PA: The Center To Promote Healthcare Access Inc
1951 Webster St Fl 2
Oakland CA

(P-17203)
CENTRAL CALIFORNIA BLOOD CTR (PA)
4343 W Herndon Ave (93722-3794)
PHONE..................................559 389-5433
Christopher Staub, *Pr*
EMP: 180 EST: 1954
SQ FT: 53,000
SALES (est): 23.98MM
SALES (corp-wide): 23.98MM **Privately Held**
Web: www.donateblood.org
SIC: **8099** Blood bank

(P-17204)
CHARLES RVER LABS CELL SLTONS (HQ)
Also Called: Hemacare Corporation
8500 Balboa Blvd Ste 130 (91325-3503)
PHONE..................................877 310-0717
James C Foster, *Pr*
EMP: 93 EST: 1978
SQ FT: 19,600
SALES (est): 43.43MM
SALES (corp-wide): 3.98B **Publicly Held**
Web: www.hemacaredonorcenter.com
SIC: **8099** 5122 Blood related health services ; Blood plasma
PA: Charles River Laboratories International, Inc.
251 Ballardvale St
Wilmington MA
781 222-6000

(P-17205)
CHE BEHAVIORAL HEALTH SERVICES
5838 Edison Pl Ste 100 (92008-5520)
PHONE..................................760 300-3664
Lucy Janoyan, *COO*
EMP: 175 EST: 2018
SALES (est): 11.72MM **Privately Held**
Web: www.cheservices.com
SIC: **8099** Health and allied services, nec

(P-17206)
CITRUS VLY HLTH PARTNERS INC
Also Called: CITRUS VALLEY HEALTH PARTNERS, INC.
1325 N Grand Ave Ste 300 (91724-4046)
PHONE..................................626 732-3100
Carol Eaton, *Prin*
EMP: 407
Web: www.emanatehealth.com
SIC: **8099** Blood related health services
PA: Emanate Health Medical Group
210 W San Bernardino Rd
Covina CA

(P-17207)
COAST CARE PARTNERS
8033 Linda Vista Rd Ste 200 (92111-5119)
PHONE..................................619 354-2544
David Chong, *Prin*
Jodell Puckett, *Dir*
EMP: 71 EST: 2013
SALES (est): 912.68K **Privately Held**
Web: www.coastcarepartners.com
SIC: **8099** Childbirth preparation clinic

(P-17208)
COMPRHNSIVE INDUS DSBLITY MGT
Also Called: Cid Management
2555 Townsgate Rd Ste 125 (91361-2605)
P.O. Box 4379 (91359-1379)
PHONE..................................866 301-6568
Steven Cardinale, *CEO*
Andy Smith, *
EMP: 138 EST: 2002
SQ FT: 5,500
SALES (est): 8.35MM
SALES (corp-wide): 3.1B **Privately Held**
Web: www.genexservices.com
SIC: **8099** 8741 Medical services organization; Nursing and personal care facility management
HQ: Genex Services, Llc
440 E Swedesford Rd Ste 1
Wayne PA
610 964-5100

(P-17209)
CONTRA LOMA HEALTHCARE LLC
Also Called: Lone Tree Post Acute
4001 Lone Tree Way (94509-6232)
PHONE..................................925 754-0470
Jason Murray, *Prin*
Mark Hancock, *
EMP: 95 EST: 2020
SALES (est): 2.24MM
SALES (corp-wide): 1.53B **Privately Held**
Web: www.lonetreepa.com
SIC: **8099** Health and allied services, nec
PA: Providence Group, Inc.
262 N University Ave
Farmington UT
801 447-9829

(P-17210)
COPE HEALTH SOLUTIONS
1150 S Olive St Fl 12 (90015-4279)
PHONE..................................213 542-2250
Allen Miller, *CEO*
Andrew Snyder, *Chief Medical Officer*
EMP: 76 EST: 2013
SALES (est): 14.45MM **Privately Held**
Web: www.copehealthsolutions.com
SIC: **8099** Medical services organization

(P-17211)
CORTICA HEALTHCARE INC
7090 Miratech Dr (92121-3109)
PHONE..................................858 304-6440
EMP: 310 EST: 2017
SALES (est): 11.78MM **Privately Held**
Web: www.corticacare.com
SIC: **8099** Health and allied services, nec

(P-17212)
COUNTY OF LOS ANGELES
Also Called: Countywide Childrens Case MGT
600 S Commonwealth Ave Ste 700 (90005)
PHONE..................................213 739-2360
Bryan Mershon, *Brnch Mgr*
EMP: 63
SALES (corp-wide): 31.7B **Privately Held**
Web: www.lacounty.gov
SIC: **8099** Blood related health services
PA: County Of Los Angeles
500 W Temple St Ste 437
Los Angeles CA
213 974-1101

(P-17213)
COUNTY OF LOS ANGELES
Also Called: Specilzed Foster Care Pasadena
532 E Colorado Blvd Fl 8 (91101-2044)
PHONE..................................626 229-3825
Jonathan E Sherin, *Dir*
EMP: 63
SALES (corp-wide): 31.7B **Privately Held**
Web: www.lacounty.gov
SIC: **8099** Blood related health services
PA: County Of Los Angeles
500 W Temple St Ste 437
Los Angeles CA
213 974-1101

(P-17214)
COUNTY OF LOS ANGELES
Also Called: Los Angeles County Pub Works
5525 Imperial Hwy (90280-7417)
PHONE..................................562 861-0316
Phil Doudar, *Mgr*
EMP: 81
SALES (corp-wide): 31.7B **Privately Held**
Web: www.lacounty.gov
SIC: **8099** 9111 Blood related health services ; Executive offices
PA: County Of Los Angeles
500 W Temple St Ste 437
Los Angeles CA
213 974-1101

(P-17215)
COUNTY OF LOS ANGELES
Also Called: Specilzed Fster Care Chtsworth
20151 Nordhoff St (91311-6215)
PHONE..................................818 717-4644
Philip L Browning, *Dir*
EMP: 63
SALES (corp-wide): 31.7B **Privately Held**
Web: www.lacounty.gov
SIC: **8099** Childbirth preparation clinic
PA: County Of Los Angeles
500 W Temple St Ste 437
Los Angeles CA
213 974-1101

(P-17216)
COUNTY OF RIVERSIDE
Also Called: Public Nurse Office
47923 Oasis St (92201-6950)
PHONE..................................760 863-8450
Koen Brown, *Ex Dir*
EMP: 63
SALES (corp-wide): 4.58B **Privately Held**
Web: www.countyofriverside.us
SIC: **8099** Blood related health services
PA: County Of Riverside
4080 Lemon St Fl 11
Riverside CA
951 955-1110

(P-17217)
CUROLOGY INC (PA)
Also Called: Curology Medical Group
353 Sacramento St Ste 2000 (94111-3675)
PHONE..................................858 859-1188
Admiral David Nicholas Lortsch er, *Prin*
EMP: 68 EST: 2017
SALES (est): 49.59MM
SALES (corp-wide): 49.59MM **Privately Held**
Web: www.curology.com

SIC: **8099** Plasmapherous center

(P-17218)
DAVID-KLEIS II LLC
Also Called: PALM GROVE HEALTHCARE
1665 E Eighth St (92223-2512)
PHONE..................................951 845-3125
EMP: 86 EST: 2013
SALES (est): 6.72MM **Privately Held**
Web: www.pghsnf.com
SIC: **8099** Health and allied services, nec

(P-17219)
DCI DONOR SERVICES INC
Also Called: Sierra Eye Tissue Donor
3940 Industrial Blvd Ste 100 (95691-6505)
PHONE..................................877 401-2546
Keith Johnson, *Pr*
EMP: 95
Web: www.dcids.org
SIC: **8099** Organ bank
PA: Dci Donor Services, Inc.
566 Mainstream Dr Ste 300
Nashville TN

(P-17220)
DCI DONOR SERVICES INC
Also Called: Golden State Donor Services
3940 Industrial Blvd Ste 100 (95691-6505)
PHONE..................................916 567-1600
Helen Nels, *Mgr*
EMP: 85
Web: www.dcids.org
SIC: **8099** Organ bank
PA: Dci Donor Services, Inc.
566 Mainstream Dr Ste 300
Nashville TN

(P-17221)
DELTA BLOOD BANK LLC (HQ)
Also Called: American Nat Red Cross - Blood
65 N Commerce St (95202-2318)
P.O. Box 800 (95201-0800)
PHONE..................................800 244-6794
Benjamin Spindler, *CEO*
Robert Lawrence, *
Alfonso Figueroa, *
◆ EMP: 85 EST: 1954
SQ FT: 30,000
SALES (est): 17.02MM
SALES (corp-wide): 3.18B **Privately Held**
Web: www.deltabloodbank.org
SIC: **8099** Blood bank
PA: The American National Red Cross
431 18th St Nw
Washington DC
202 737-8300

(P-17222)
DIRECT FLOW MEDICAL INC
3945 Freedom Cir Ste 560 (95054-1269)
PHONE..................................707 576-0420
EMP: 170
Web: www.directflowmedical.com
SIC: **8099** Medical services organization

(P-17223)
DISCOVERY HEALTH SERVICES
Also Called: DISCOVERY MEDICAL STAFFING
5726 La Jolla Blvd Ste 104 (92037-7344)
PHONE..................................858 459-0785
Jeffrey Sternberg, *CEO*
Preston A Moreno, *
Lisa Hargrove, *
EMP: 286 EST: 2012
SALES (est): 17.18MM **Privately Held**
Web: www.discoveryhealthus.com
SIC: **8099** Blood related health services

PRODUCTS & SERVICES SECTION
8099 - Health And Allied Services, Nec (P-17246)

(P-17224)
DOCTOR ON DEMAND INC
9454 Wilshire Blvd Ste 803 (90212-2931)
PHONE..................310 988-2882
Kevin Rosenbloom, *Brnch Mgr*
EMP: 78
SALES (corp-wide): 105.52MM **Privately Held**
Web: www.doctorondemand.com
SIC: 8099 Physical examination and testing services
HQ: Doctor On Demand, Inc.
3033 Campus Dr Ste 225
Minneapolis MN
415 935-4447

(P-17225)
DONOR NETWORK WEST (PA)
12667 Alcosta Blvd Ste 500 (94583-4427)
PHONE..................925 480-3100
Cynthia D Siljestrom, *CEO*
Mark Borer, *
Jt Mason, *
Sean Van Slyck V Press, *Prin*
Jeremy Gimbel, *
EMP: 121 EST: 1987
SQ FT: 41,039
SALES (est): 121.44MM
SALES (corp-wide): 121.44MM **Privately Held**
Web: www.donornetworkwest.org
SIC: 8099 Medical services organization

(P-17226)
DOULAS BY BAY LLC
Also Called: Doulas By The Bay
1201 Liberty St (94530-2359)
PHONE..................415 510-9736
Shakila Marando, *Managing Member*
EMP: 85 EST: 2014
SALES (est): 1.94MM **Privately Held**
Web: www.doulasbythebay.com
SIC: 8099 Childbirth preparation clinic

(P-17227)
DRIP HYDRATION
11948 Gorham Ave Apt 3 (90049-5394)
PHONE..................323 333-9634
Abe Malkin, *Prin*
EMP: 89 EST: 2018
SALES (est): 4.99MM **Privately Held**
Web: www.driphydration.com
SIC: 8099 Health and allied services, nec

(P-17228)
DSSV INC
Also Called: Brightwheel
548 Market St Pmb 95237 (94104-5401)
PHONE..................415 216-8495
David Vasen, *CEO*
EMP: 350 EST: 2014
SALES (est): 24.68MM **Privately Held**
Web: www.mybrightwheel.com
SIC: 8099 Health and allied services, nec

(P-17229)
DUAL DIAGNOSIS TRTMNT CTR INC
Also Called: Sovereign Health
69640 Highway 111 (92270-2868)
PHONE..................949 324-4531
Tonmoy Sharma, *Brnch Mgr*
EMP: 194
SALES (corp-wide): 54.63MM **Privately Held**
Web: www.omacl.co.uk
SIC: 8099 Childbirth preparation clinic
PA: Dual Diagnosis Treatment Center, Inc.
1211 Puerta Del Sol # 200
San Clemente CA
949 276-5553

(P-17230)
EASTER SEAL SOC SUPERIOR CAL (PA)
Also Called: Easter Seals Main Office
9812 Old Winery Pl Ste 21 (95827-1732)
P.O. Box 254867 (95865-4867)
PHONE..................916 485-6711
Gary T Kasai, *Pr*
EMP: 100 EST: 1934
SQ FT: 28,500
SALES (est): 13.02MM
SALES (corp-wide): 13.02MM **Privately Held**
Web: www.easterseals.com
SIC: 8099 8093 Medical services organization; Rehabilitation center, outpatient treatment

(P-17231)
EASTERN PLMAS HLTH CARE FNDTIO (PA)
Also Called: Eastern Plumas Hospital
500 1st Ave (96122-9406)
PHONE..................530 832-4277
Tom Hayes, *CEO*
Virginia Luhring, *
Larry Fites, *
Gail Mcgrath, *Dir*
Jeri Nelson, *
EMP: 161 EST: 1992
SQ FT: 18,500
SALES (est): 97.3K
SALES (corp-wide): 97.3K **Privately Held**
Web: www.ephc.org
SIC: 8099 8011 8322 Medical services organization; Primary care medical clinic; Rehabilitation services

(P-17232)
EASY CARE MSO LLC
3780 Kilroy Airport Way Ste 530 (90806-2459)
PHONE..................562 676-9600
Michelle Bui, *Pr*
EMP: 103 EST: 2014
SALES (est): 3.9MM
SALES (corp-wide): 31.97B **Publicly Held**
Web: www.easycaremso.com
SIC: 8099 Medical services organization
PA: Molina Healthcare, Inc.
200 Oceangate Ste 100
Long Beach CA
562 435-3666

(P-17233)
EHEALTHWIRECOM INC
2450 Venture Oaks Way Ste 100 (95833-3292)
PHONE..................916 924-8092
Yousry Mekhamer, *Ch*
EMP: 250 EST: 1999
SQ FT: 17,000
SALES (est): 4.3MM **Privately Held**
SIC: 8099 Health screening service

(P-17234)
ELECTRONIC HEALTH PLANS INC
Also Called: Ehp Administrators
9131 Oakdale Ave Ste 150 (91311-6502)
P.O. Box 4449 (91313-4449)
PHONE..................818 734-4700
Alina Green, *VP*
EMP: 78
SALES (corp-wide): 4.97MM **Privately Held**
Web: www.electronichealthplans.com
SIC: 8099 Medical services organization
PA: Electronic Health Plans, Inc.

1111 Route 1110 Ste 378
Farmingdale NY
631 845-5680

(P-17235)
ELIZABETH GLASER PEDIA
16130 Ventura Blvd Ste 250 (91436-2503)
PHONE..................310 231-0400
Charles Lyons, *Brnch Mgr*
EMP: 457
SALES (corp-wide): 187.69MM **Privately Held**
Web: www.pedaids.org
SIC: 8099 Medical services organization
PA: Elizabeth Glaser Pediatric Aids Foundation
1140 Conn Ave Nw Ste 200
Washington DC
920 770-0103

(P-17236)
EVOLENT HEALTH INC
1 Kearny St Ste 300 (94108-5549)
PHONE..................571 389-6000
EMP: 400
SALES (corp-wide): 1.35B **Publicly Held**
Web: www.evolenthealth.com
SIC: 8099 Medical services organization
PA: Evolent Health, Inc.
800 N Glebe Rd Ste 500
Arlington VA
571 389-6000

(P-17237)
EXAMONE WORLD WIDE INC
Also Called: Examone
7480 Mission Valley Rd Ste 101 (92108-4433)
PHONE..................619 299-3926
EMP: 100
SALES (corp-wide): 9.88B **Publicly Held**
Web: www.myexamone.com
SIC: 8099 Physical examination service, insurance
HQ: Examone World Wide, Inc.
10101 Renner Blvd
Lenexa KS
913 888-1770

(P-17238)
FALCON CRTCAL CARE TRNSPT A NR
3508 San Pablo Dam Rd (94803-2728)
PHONE..................510 223-1171
Carin Johnson, *Pr*
Brian Johnson, *
Tammy Collins, *
Curtis Tuggle, *
EMP: 250 EST: 1998
SALES (est): 18.6MM **Privately Held**
Web: www.falconambulance.com
SIC: 8099 8082 Childbirth preparation clinic; Home health care services

(P-17239)
FAMILY HLTH CTRS SAN DIEGO INC
7592 Broadway (91945-1604)
PHONE..................619 515-2550
Elizabeth A Samuels, *Pr*
EMP: 348
SALES (corp-wide): 147.12MM **Privately Held**
Web: www.fhcsd.org
SIC: 8099 Blood related health services
PA: Family Health Centers Of San Diego, Inc.
823 Gateway Center Way
San Diego CA
619 515-2303

(P-17240)
FRAZIER MANAGEMENT LLC
70 Willow Rd Ste 200 (94025-3652)
PHONE..................650 325-5156
EMP: 167
Web: www.frazierhealthcare.com
SIC: 8099 Childbirth preparation clinic
PA: Frazier Management, L.L.C.
601 Union St Ste 3200
Seattle WA

(P-17241)
GOOD HEALTH INC
Also Called: Premier Pharmacy Service
410 Cloverleaf Dr (91706-6511)
PHONE..................714 961-7930
Stephen Edward Samuel, *CEO*
EMP: 187 EST: 1971
SALES (est): 32.49MM **Privately Held**
Web: www.premierpharmacyservices.com
SIC: 8099 Blood related health services

(P-17242)
GRIFOLS BIO SUPPLIES INC
980 Park Center Dr Ste F (92081-8351)
PHONE..................760 651-4042
Mark Viray, *Mgr*
EMP: 195
SALES (corp-wide): 92.52MM **Privately Held**
Web: www.interstatebloodbank.com
SIC: 8099 Blood bank
PA: Grifols Bio Supplies Inc.
5125 Elmore Rd Ste 6
Memphis TN
901 384-6200

(P-17243)
GRIFOLS WRLDWIDE OPRTONS USA I
13111 Temple Ave (91746-1500)
PHONE..................626 435-2600
Red Fredericksen, *Genl Mgr*
EMP: 70
SIC: 8099 Blood bank
HQ: Grifols Worldwide Operations Usa, Inc.
5555 Valley Blvd
Los Angeles CA
323 225-2221

(P-17244)
HARBOR HEALTH SYSTEMS LLC
3501 Jamboree Rd Ste 540 (92660-2950)
P.O. Box 1145 (60009-1145)
PHONE..................949 273-7020
EMP: 214 EST: 2001
SALES (est): 2.47MM **Privately Held**
Web: www.harborhealthsytems.com
SIC: 8099 7372 Blood related health services; Business oriented computer software
PA: One Call Medical, Inc.
841 Prudential Dr Ste 204
Jacksonville FL

(P-17245)
HEALTH IQ
2513 Charleston Rd # 102 (94043-1608)
PHONE..................917 770-2190
EMP: 93 EST: 2016
SALES (est): 14.23MM **Privately Held**
Web: www.healthiq.com
SIC: 8099 Health and allied services, nec

(P-17246)
HEALTH LF ORGNIZATION INC HALO
Also Called: Sacramento Community Clinic

8099 - Health And Allied Services, Nec (P-17247)

3030 Explorer Dr (95827-2728)
PHONE.....................916 428-3788
Jerry Bilatout, CEO
EMP: 80 EST: 2015
SALES (est): 1.75MM Privately Held
Web: www.halocares.org
SIC: 8099 Medical services organization

(P-17247)
HEALTH LINK
868 Brannan St Ste 307 (94103-5680)
PHONE.....................415 664-5500
Boris Reykhel, CEO
EMP: 90 EST: 2009
SALES (est): 5.08MM Privately Held
Web: www.healthlinkhha.com
SIC: 8099 Health and allied services, nec

(P-17248)
HEALTH SERVICES ADVISORY GROUP
700 N Brand Blvd Fl 1 (91203-3236)
PHONE.....................818 409-9220
Lawrence Shapiro, Prin
EMP: 184 EST: 2011
SALES (est): 2.27MM
SALES (corp-wide): 53.02MM Privately Held
Web: www.belderadvanced.com
SIC: 8099 Blood related health services
PA: Health Services Holdings, Inc.
3133 E Camelback Rd # 140
Phoenix AZ
602 264-6382

(P-17249)
HEALTHCARE TALENT
26090 Towne Centre Dr (92610-3441)
PHONE.....................714 341-1197
Keith J Hollis, Admn
EMP: 80 EST: 2017
SALES (est): 1.76MM Privately Held
Web: www.healthcaretalent.net
SIC: 8099 Health and allied services, nec

(P-17250)
HEALTHY MEDICAL SOLUTIONS INC
5943 Rhodes Ave (91607-1131)
PHONE.....................818 974-1980
Mori Bennissan, CEO
EMP: 77 EST: 2005
SALES (est): 2.37MM Privately Held
SIC: 8099 Childbirth preparation clinic

(P-17251)
HERITAGE MEDICAL GROUP
Also Called: HERITAGE MEDICAL GROUP
12370 Hesperia Rd Ste 6 (92395-4787)
PHONE.....................760 956-1286
Stanley Wohl, Brnch Mgr
EMP: 261
Web: www.bfmc.com
SIC: 8099 Blood related health services
PA: Heritage Medical Group, Inc.
4580 California Ave
Bakersfield CA

(P-17252)
HINGE HEALTH INC (PA)
455 Market St Ste 700 (94105-3350)
PHONE.....................855 902-7777
Daniel Perez, CEO
Gabriel Mecklenburg, *
Hassan Asghar Ciso, Prin
Ron Will, *
Mario Queiroz, CIO*
EMP: 760 EST: 2016
SALES (est): 98.6MM
SALES (corp-wide): 98.6MM Privately Held
Web: www.hingehealth.com
SIC: 8099 Physical examination and testing services

(P-17253)
INCLUDED HEALTH INC (PA)
1 California St Ste 2300 (94111-5424)
PHONE.....................800 929-0926
Owen Tripp, CEO
Robin Glass, *
Gabe Cortes, *
Ami Parekh, CHO
Wade Chambers, *
EMP: 110 EST: 2011
SALES (est): 105.52MM
SALES (corp-wide): 105.52MM Privately Held
Web: www.grandrounds.com
SIC: 8099 Physical examination and testing services

(P-17254)
INDUSTRIAL MEDICAL SUPPORT INC
3320 E Airport Way (90806-2410)
PHONE.....................877 878-9185
Michael Donoghue, CEO
Ryan La Bounty, *
EMP: 800 EST: 2014
SALES (est): 22.16MM Privately Held
SIC: 8099 Medical services organization

(P-17255)
INLAND BHAVIORAL HLTH SVCS INC (PA)
1963 N E St (92405-3919)
PHONE.....................909 881-6146
Temetry Ann Lindsey, Pr
Vernon Bragg Junior, Ch Bd
Peter Demel, *
John Wilson, *
EMP: 68 EST: 1978
SQ FT: 13,500
SALES (est): 11.19MM
SALES (corp-wide): 11.19MM Privately Held
Web: www.ibhealth.org
SIC: 8099 8093 Medical services organization; Drug clinic, outpatient

(P-17256)
INTEGRTED MLCLAR DGNSTICS PTHL
Also Called: IMD Path
3017 Telegraph Ave Ste 102 (94705)
PHONE.....................866 944-8050
Israel Villasenor, Managing Member
Israel Villasenor, CEO
EMP: 95 EST: 2016
SALES (est): 8.86MM Privately Held
Web: www.imdpath.com
SIC: 8099 8011 Medical services organization; Pathologist

(P-17257)
JOHN MUIR
3100 San Pablo Ave (94702-2498)
PHONE.....................510 922-9659
John Muir, Prin
EMP: 86 EST: 2018
SALES (est): 1.39MM Privately Held
Web: www.johnmuirhealth.com
SIC: 8099 Health and allied services, nec

(P-17258)
JWCH INSTITUTE INC
14371 Clark Ave (90706-2901)
PHONE.....................562 867-7999
Alvaro Ballesteros, Brnch Mgr
EMP: 177
SALES (corp-wide): 107.92MM Privately Held
Web: www.jwchinstitute.org
SIC: 8099 Blood related health services
PA: Jwch Institute, Inc.
5650 Jillson St
Commerce CA
323 477-1171

(P-17259)
JWCH INSTITUTE INC
8530 Firestone Blvd (90241-4926)
PHONE.....................562 862-1000
EMP: 178
SALES (corp-wide): 107.92MM Privately Held
Web: www.jwchinstitute.org
SIC: 8099 Childbirth preparation clinic
PA: Jwch Institute, Inc.
5650 Jillson St
Commerce CA
323 477-1171

(P-17260)
KAISER
4480 Hacienda Dr Bldg B-4 (94588-2761)
PHONE.....................925 924-6930
Elena Placido, Prin
EMP: 65 EST: 2010
SALES (est): 2.8MM Privately Held
Web: www.kaiserassociates.com
SIC: 8099 Health and allied services, nec

(P-17261)
KAISER FOUNDATION HOSPITALS
Also Called: Kaiser Foundation Health Plan
2055 Kellogg Ave (92879-3111)
PHONE.....................866 984-7483
Ruth Jasse, Admn
EMP: 79
SALES (corp-wide): 68.1B Privately Held
Web: www.kaisercenter.com
SIC: 8099 Childbirth preparation clinic
HQ: Kaiser Foundation Hospitals Inc
1 Kaiser Plz
Oakland CA
510 271-6611

(P-17262)
KAISER PERMANENTE
3772 Howe St (94611-5300)
PHONE.....................510 752-6198
EMP: 114 EST: 1997
SALES (est): 1.04MM Privately Held
SIC: 8099 Health and allied services, nec

(P-17263)
KAWEAH DLTA HLTH CARE DST GILD
4945 W Cypress Ave (93277-1592)
PHONE.....................559 624-3100
Robert Havard, Pr
EMP: 103
SALES (corp-wide): 857.31MM Privately Held
Web: www.kaweahhealth.org
SIC: 8099 Childbirth preparation clinic
PA: Kaweah Delta Health Care District Guild
400 W Mineral King Ave
Visalia CA
559 624-2000

(P-17264)
KELLY THOMAS MD UCSD HLTH CARE
Also Called: Ucsd
200 W Arbor Dr (92103-9000)
PHONE.....................619 543-2885
Lydia Ikeda, Prin
Ed Babakaian Md, Prin
EMP: 230 EST: 2001
SALES (est): 31.81MM Privately Held
Web: www.ucsd.edu
SIC: 8099 Childbirth preparation clinic

(P-17265)
KIMCO STAFFING SERVICES INC
1801 Oakland Blvd Ste 220 (94596-7033)
PHONE.....................925 945-1444
EMP: 779
SALES (corp-wide): 96.64MM Privately Held
Web: www.kimco.com
SIC: 8099 Medical services organization
PA: Kimco Staffing Services, Inc.
17872 Cowan
Irvine CA
949 331-1199

(P-17266)
LA CLINICA DE LA RAZA INC
Also Called: Billing & Registration
3451 E 12th St (94601-3463)
PHONE.....................510 535-3500
Jean Garcia, CEO
EMP: 299
SQ FT: 38,780
SALES (corp-wide): 144.12MM Privately Held
Web: www.laclinica.org
SIC: 8099 8011 Medical services organization; Medical centers
PA: La Clinica De La Raza, Inc.
1450 Fruitvale Ave Fl 3
Oakland CA
510 535-4000

(P-17267)
LA CLINICA DE LA RAZA INC
Also Called: Health Education
1537 Fruitvale Ave (94601-2322)
PHONE.....................510 535-4130
Berta Hernandez, Mgr
EMP: 200
SALES (corp-wide): 144.12MM Privately Held
Web: www.laclinica.org
SIC: 8099 8011 Medical services organization; Medical centers
PA: La Clinica De La Raza, Inc.
1450 Fruitvale Ave Fl 3
Oakland CA
510 535-4000

(P-17268)
LEGACY HEALTHCARE CENTER LLC
1570 N Fair Oaks Ave (91103-1822)
PHONE.....................626 798-0558
Raphael Oscherowitz, Prin
Dov Jacobs, *
EMP: 90 EST: 2016
SALES (est): 2.24MM Privately Held
SIC: 8099 Health and allied services, nec

(P-17269)
LIFE TIME FITNESS INC
Also Called: LIFE TIME FITNESS, INC.
28221 Crown Valley Pkwy (92677-1427)
PHONE.....................949 238-2700

PRODUCTS & SERVICES SECTION
8099 - Health And Allied Services, Nec (P-17293)

EMP: 169
SALES (corp-wide): 1.82B **Publicly Held**
Web: www.lifetime.life
SIC: **8099** 7991 7299 Nutrition services; Physical fitness clubs with training equipment; Personal appearance services
HQ: Life Time, Inc.
2902 Corporate Pl
Chanhassen MN

(P-17270)
LOS ANGLES CNTY DEPT MNTAL HLT
3205 N Lakewood Blvd (90808-1733)
PHONE..............................213 738-4431
Jonathan E Sherin, *Prin*
EMP: 89 EST: 2019
SALES (est): 1.29MM **Privately Held**
Web: dmh.lacounty.gov
SIC: **8099** Health and allied services, nec

(P-17271)
LOS ANGLES CNTY DVLPMNTAL SVCS
Also Called: FRANK D LANTERMAN REGIONAL CEN
3303 Wilshire Blvd Ste 700 (90010-1704)
PHONE..............................213 383-1300
Dianne Anand, *Ex Dir*
EMP: 180 EST: 1979
SQ FT: 80,000
SALES (est): 299.93MM **Privately Held**
Web: www.lanterman.org
SIC: **8099** 8322 8093 Medical services organization; Individual and family services; Mental health clinic, outpatient

(P-17272)
MARTIN LTHER KING JR-LOS ANGLE
Also Called: Martin Lther King Jr Cmnty Hos
1680 E 120th St (90059-3026)
PHONE..............................424 338-8000
EMP: 271 EST: 2010
SALES (est): 366.59MM **Privately Held**
Web: www.mlkch.org
SIC: **8099** Childbirth preparation clinic

(P-17273)
MDUSD
1936 Carlotta Dr (94519-1358)
PHONE..............................925 682-8000
Richard Nicoll, *Prin*
EMP: 65 EST: 2010
SALES (est): 2.78MM **Privately Held**
Web: www.mdusd.org
SIC: **8099** Nutrition services

(P-17274)
MEDASEND BIOMEDICAL INC (PA)
1402 Daisy Ave (90813-1521)
PHONE..............................800 200-3581
Steve Grand, *CEO*
Stephanie Harrison, *VP*
EMP: 150 EST: 1999
SQ FT: 10,000
SALES (est): 6.67MM
SALES (corp-wide): 6.67MM **Privately Held**
Web: www.medasend.com
SIC: **8099** 4953 Health screening service; Hazardous waste collection and disposal

(P-17275)
MEMORA HEALTH INC
38 Bluxome St (94107-1631)
PHONE..............................415 874-9390
EMP: 100 EST: 2019

SALES (est): 3.12MM **Privately Held**
Web: www.memorahealth.com
SIC: **8099** Health and allied services, nec

(P-17276)
MOLINA HEALTHCARE INC
9275 Sky Park Ct Ste 190 (92123-4386)
PHONE..............................858 614-1580
Lisa Ferrari, *Mgr*
EMP: 75
SALES (corp-wide): 31.97B **Publicly Held**
Web: www.molinahealthcare.com
SIC: **8099** Blood related health services
PA: Molina Healthcare, Inc.
200 Oceangate Ste 100
Long Beach CA
562 435-3666

(P-17277)
MOLINA HEALTHCARE INC
1 Golden Shore (90802-4202)
PHONE..............................562 435-3666
Sriram Bharadwaj, *Brnch Mgr*
EMP: 158
SALES (corp-wide): 31.97B **Publicly Held**
Web: www.molinahealthcare.com
SIC: **8099** Blood related health services
PA: Molina Healthcare, Inc.
200 Oceangate Ste 100
Long Beach CA
562 435-3666

(P-17278)
MONARCH HLTHCARE A MED GROUP I
2562 State St (92008-1663)
PHONE..............................760 730-9448
EMP: 119
SALES (corp-wide): 324.16B **Publicly Held**
Web: www.monarchhealthcare.com
SIC: **8099** Blood related health services
HQ: Monarch Healthcare, A Medical Group, Inc.
11 Technology Dr
Irvine CA

(P-17279)
MUIR WOOD LLC
Also Called: Muir WD Adolescent & Fmly Svcs
55 Shaver St Ste 200 (94901-2784)
PHONE..............................310 903-1155
Scott Sowle, *Ex Dir*
EMP: 60 EST: 2013
SALES (est): 25.98MM **Privately Held**
Web: www.muirwoodteen.com
SIC: **8099** Childbirth preparation clinic

(P-17280)
NALU MEDICAL INC
2320 Faraday Ave Ste 100 (92008-7241)
PHONE..............................760 603-8466
Earl R Fender, *Pr*
Keegan Harper, *Ch Bd*
EMP: 133 EST: 2015
SALES (est): 10.68MM **Privately Held**
Web: www.nalumed.com
SIC: **8099** Childbirth preparation clinic

(P-17281)
NAVY UNITED STATES DEPARTMENT
Also Called: Naval Hosp Twntynine Plms Gfeb
1145 Sturgis Rd (92278)
PHONE..............................760 830-2124
Eugene Dearstine, *CFO*
EMP: 99
Web: www.navy.mil

SIC: **8099** Blood related health services
HQ: United States Department Of The Navy
1200 Navy Pentagon
Washington DC

(P-17282)
NEIGHBORHOOD HEALTHCARE
401 E Valley Pkwy (92025-3317)
PHONE..............................760 737-6903
EMP: 100
SALES (corp-wide): 101.79MM **Privately Held**
Web: www.nhcare.org
SIC: **8099** Childbirth preparation clinic
PA: Neighborhood Healthcare
425 N Date St Ste 203
Escondido CA
760 520-8372

(P-17283)
NORTHERN ORNGE CNTY ENT MDCL
520 S Virgil Ave Ste 206 (90020-1425)
PHONE..............................213 252-0036
Jennifer Lee, *Brnch Mgr*
EMP: 60
SALES (corp-wide): 972.11K **Privately Held**
SIC: **8099** Blood related health services
PA: Northern Orange County Ent Medical Corp.
1955 Sunny Crest Dr # 108
Fullerton CA
714 441-0133

(P-17284)
NOVA SKILLED HOME HEALTH INC
3300 N San Fernando Blvd (91504-2530)
PHONE..............................323 658-6232
Nelson Aguilar, *CEO*
Julita Fraley, *
Carol Vega, *
EMP: 136 EST: 2018
SALES (est): 4.13MM **Privately Held**
SIC: **8099** Health and allied services, nec

(P-17285)
ON ASSIGNMENT HEALTHCARE
26745 Malibu Hills Rd (91301-5355)
PHONE..............................818 878-0683
Kevin Morse, *Prin*
EMP: 65 EST: 2011
SALES (est): 7.38MM **Privately Held**
Web: www.oxfordcorp.com
SIC: **8099** Health and allied services, nec

(P-17286)
ONELEGACY (PA)
1303 W Optical Dr (91702-3251)
EMP: 60 EST: 1977
SALES (est): 97.81MM
SALES (corp-wide): 97.81MM **Privately Held**
Web: www.onelegacy.org
SIC: **8099** Organ bank

(P-17287)
ONSITE HEALTH INC
6610 Goodyear Rd (94510-1250)
PHONE..............................888 411-2290
EMP: 78
SIC: **8099** Medical services organization
PA: Onsite Health, Inc.
85 Argonaut Ste 220
Aliso Viejo CA

(P-17288)
OPTUMCARE MANAGEMENT LLC
3501 S Harbor Blvd (92704-6919)
PHONE..............................714 964-6229
EMP: 73
SIC: **8099** Blood related health services
HQ: Optumcare Management, Llc
2175 Park Pl
El Segundo CA

(P-17289)
OPTUMCARE MANAGEMENT LLC
19066 Magnolia St (92646-2232)
PHONE..............................714 968-0068
Robert Hunn, *Prin*
EMP: 73
SIC: **8099** Medical services organization
HQ: Optumcare Management, Llc
2175 Park Pl
El Segundo CA

(P-17290)
OPTUMCARE MANAGEMENT LLC
Also Called: Talbert Medical Center
901 W Civic Center Dr Ste 120 (92703-2352)
PHONE..............................714 835-8501
Linda Journet, *Mgr*
EMP: 73
SIC: **8099** 8011 Medical services organization; General and family practice, physician/surgeon
HQ: Optumcare Management, Llc
2175 Park Pl
El Segundo CA

(P-17291)
OPTUMCARE MEDICAL GROUP
800 Corporate Dr Ste 100 (92694-1153)
PHONE..............................949 364-9112
EMP: 83 EST: 2019
SALES (est): 1.52MM **Privately Held**
Web: www.optum.com
SIC: **8099** Health and allied services, nec

(P-17292)
PANCRTIC CNCER ACTION NTWRK IN (PA)
Also Called: Pancan
1500 Rosecrans Ave Ste 200 (90266-3763)
PHONE..............................310 725-0025
Julie Fleshman, *Pr*
Jeanne Weaver Ruesch, *Ch Bd*
Michael Korengold, *
Megan Gordon Don, *VP*
Jenny Isaacson, *VP*
EMP: 79 EST: 1999
SALES (est): 52.93MM
SALES (corp-wide): 52.93MM **Privately Held**
Web: www.pancan.org
SIC: **8099** 8399 Medical services organization; Social service information exchange

(P-17293)
PATHWAYS HOME HEALTH
395 Oyster Point Blvd Ste 128 (94080-1928)
PHONE..............................650 634-0133
Mary Dias, *Mgr*
EMP: 86 EST: 1998
SALES (est): 903.22K **Privately Held**
Web: www.pathwayshealth.org
SIC: **8099** Health and allied services, nec

8099 - Health And Allied Services, Nec (P-17294)

(P-17294)
PEDIATRIC CARDIOLOGY MED GRP
5030 Business Center Dr Ste 230 (94534)
PHONE..................707 863-8190
Cindy Bennett, *Off Mgr*
EMP: 72
SALES (corp-wide): 191.35K **Privately Held**
SIC: 8099 Blood related health services
PA: Pediatric Cardiology Medical Group East Bay
    106 La Casa Via
    Walnut Creek CA
    925 295-1700

(P-17295)
PERFORMANCE HEALTH MED GROUP
13252 Garden Grove Blvd # 112 (92843-2270)
PHONE..................714 740-1778
Lanett Bell, *Mgr*
EMP: 146
SALES (corp-wide): 951.3K **Privately Held**
SIC: 8099 Blood related health services
PA: Performance Health Medical Group
    21707 Hawthorne Blvd # 20
    Torrance CA
    310 540-9699

(P-17296)
PERMANENTE MEDICAL GROUP INC (DH)
Also Called: Kaiser Permanente
1950 Franklin St 7th Fl (94612-5107)
PHONE..................866 858-2226
Richard S Isaacs, *CEO*
Pat Conolly, *
Sharon Levine, *
Gerard C Bajada, *
Nari Gopala, *Chief Digital Officer*
EMP: 500 EST: 1945
SQ FT: 10,000
SALES (est): 748.76MM
SALES (corp-wide): 68.1B **Privately Held**
Web: www.mmrpermanente.org
SIC: 8099 Medical services organization
HQ: Kaiser Foundation Hospitals Inc
    1 Kaiser Plz
    Oakland CA
    510 271-6611

(P-17297)
PERMANENTE MEDICAL GROUP INC
Also Called: Kaiser Permanente
4537 Valmonte Dr (95864-3168)
PHONE..................916 973-5175
EMP: 418
SALES (corp-wide): 68.1B **Privately Held**
Web: www.permanente.org
SIC: 8099 Medical services organization
HQ: The Permanente Medical Group Inc
    1950 Franklin St Fl 7th
    Oakland CA
    866 858-2226

(P-17298)
PPONEXT WEST INC
1501 Hughes Way Ste 400 (90810-1865)
PHONE..................888 446-6098
Barbara E Rodin Ph.d., *Pr*
EMP: 385 EST: 1999
SALES (est): 745.21K
SALES (corp-wide): 1.08B **Publicly Held**
SIC: 8099 Medical services organization
HQ: Beech Street Corporation
    25500 Cmmrcntre Dr Ste 20
    Lake Forest CA
    949 672-1000

(P-17299)
PROVIDENCE ST JOSEPHS HOME CR
3413 W Pacific Ave (91505-1585)
PHONE..................818 953-4494
EMP: 77 EST: 2019
SALES (est): 476.12K **Privately Held**
SIC: 8099 Health and allied services, nec

(P-17300)
PROVIDNCE FACEY MED FOUNDATION
11211 Sepulveda Blvd (91345-1115)
PHONE..................818 837-5677
Cathy Hawes, *Brnch Mgr*
EMP: 152
SALES (corp-wide): 91.37MM **Privately Held**
Web: www.facey.com
SIC: 8099 8042 8011 Medical services organization; Offices and clinics of optometrists; Offices and clinics of medical doctors
PA: Providence Facey Medical Foundation
    15451 San Frnndo Mssion B
    Mission Hills CA
    818 365-9531

(P-17301)
PROVIDNCE FACEY MED FOUNDATION
Also Called: Facey Medical Group
17909 Soledad Canyon Rd (91387-3210)
PHONE..................661 250-5225
Leslie Holland, *Brnch Mgr*
EMP: 122
SALES (corp-wide): 91.37MM **Privately Held**
Web: www.facey.com
SIC: 8099 8011 Medical services organization; Offices and clinics of medical doctors
PA: Providence Facey Medical Foundation
    15451 San Frnndo Mssion B
    Mission Hills CA
    818 365-9531

(P-17302)
PROVIDNCE FACEY MED FOUNDATION
Also Called: Marshall, Spector MD
1237 E Main St (91776)
PHONE..................626 576-0800
Ana Ventura, *Mgr*
EMP: 61
SALES (corp-wide): 91.37MM **Privately Held**
Web: www.facey.com
SIC: 8099 8011 Medical services organization; Pediatrician
PA: Providence Facey Medical Foundation
    15451 San Frnndo Mssion B
    Mission Hills CA
    818 365-9531

(P-17303)
PUBLIC HLTH FNDATION ENTPS INC
3648 E Olympic Blvd (90023-3129)
PHONE..................323 261-6388
EMP: 140
SALES (corp-wide): 92.05MM **Privately Held**
Web: www.helunahealth.org
SIC: 8099 Blood related health services
PA: Public Health Foundation Enterprises, Inc.
    13300 Crssrds Pkwy N
    City Of Industry CA
    800 201-7320

(P-17304)
PUBLIC HLTH FNDATION ENTPS INC
8666 Whittier Blvd (90660-2655)
PHONE..................562 801-2323
Nicolle Fevere, *Prin*
EMP: 140
SALES (corp-wide): 92.05MM **Privately Held**
Web: www.helunahealth.org
SIC: 8099 Blood related health services
PA: Public Health Foundation Enterprises, Inc.
    13300 Crssrds Pkwy N
    City Of Industry CA
    800 201-7320

(P-17305)
PUBLIC HLTH FNDATION ENTPS INC
1649 W Washington Blvd (90007-1116)
PHONE..................323 733-9381
Eloise Jenks, *Pr*
EMP: 140
SALES (corp-wide): 92.05MM **Privately Held**
Web: www.helunahealth.org
SIC: 8099 Blood related health services
PA: Public Health Foundation Enterprises, Inc.
    13300 Crssrds Pkwy N
    City Of Industry CA
    800 201-7320

(P-17306)
PUBLIC HLTH FNDATION ENTPS INC
125 E Anaheim St (90744-4590)
PHONE..................310 518-2835
EMP: 140
SALES (corp-wide): 92.05MM **Privately Held**
Web: www.phfewic.org
SIC: 8099 Blood related health services
PA: Public Health Foundation Enterprises, Inc.
    13300 Crssrds Pkwy N
    City Of Industry CA
    800 201-7320

(P-17307)
PUBLIC HLTH FNDATION ENTPS INC
Also Called: Wic
12781 Shama Rd (91732)
PHONE..................626 856-6618
Juan Chong, *Brnch Mgr*
EMP: 140
SALES (corp-wide): 92.05MM **Privately Held**
Web: www.phfewic.org
SIC: 8099 Blood related health services
PA: Public Health Foundation Enterprises, Inc.
    13300 Crssrds Pkwy N
    City Of Industry CA
    800 201-7320

(P-17308)
QTC MANAGEMENT INC (DH)
924 Overland Ct (91773-1742)
PHONE..................800 682-9701
Elizabeth Porter, *CEO*
▼ EMP: 99 EST: 1981
SQ FT: 20,000
SALES (est): 61.61MM **Publicly Held**
Web: www.qtcm.com
SIC: 8099 Medical services organization
HQ: Qtc Holdings Inc.
    9737 Washingtonian Blvd
    Gaithersburg MD
    909 859-2100

(P-17309)
QTC MDCAL GROUP INC A MED CORP
Also Called: Qtc Medical Group
924 Overland Ct (91773-1742)
PHONE..................800 260-1515
Brant Kim, *CEO*
EMP: 1000 EST: 1984
SALES (est): 51.09MM **Privately Held**
Web: www.qtcm.com
SIC: 8099 Medical services organization

(P-17310)
RALLY HEALTH INC
665 3rd St Ste 200 (94107-1985)
PHONE..................408 821-5414
EMP: 123
SALES (corp-wide): 324.16B **Publicly Held**
Web: www.rallyhealth.com
SIC: 8099 Physical examination and testing services
HQ: Rally Health, Inc.
    3000 K St Nw Ste 350
    Washington DC
    202 469-7728

(P-17311)
REE MEDICAL INC
3472 Calle Margarita (92024-6670)
PHONE..................760 641-4359
Adam Weissman, *CEO*
EMP: 66 EST: 2017
SALES (est): 3.87MM **Privately Held**
Web: www.reemedical.com
SIC: 8099 Health and allied services, nec

(P-17312)
REGENTS OF THE UNIVERSITY CAL
Also Called: Santa Monica Ucla Medical Ctr
1250 16th St (90404-1249)
PHONE..................310 267-9308
Johnese Spisso, *Prin*
Felicia Rue, *
Paul Staton, *
EMP: 99 EST: 1996
SALES (est): 10.89MM **Privately Held**
SIC: 8099 Health and allied services, nec

(P-17313)
RESCUE MISSION ALLIANCE
125 S Harrison Ave (93030-6038)
PHONE..................805 201-4341
Carol Roberg, *Prin*
EMP: 62 EST: 2009
SALES (est): 433.59K **Privately Held**
Web: www.vcrescuemission.org
SIC: 8099 Health and allied services, nec
PA: Rescue Mission Alliance
    315 N A St
    Oxnard CA

(P-17314)
RESTPADD HEALTH CORP
925 Walnut St (96080-3707)
PHONE..................530 727-9390
EMP: 75 EST: 2017
SALES (est): 4.33MM
SALES (corp-wide): 12.72MM **Privately Held**

PRODUCTS & SERVICES SECTION
8099 - Health And Allied Services, Nec (P-17337)

Web: www.restpaddhealth.com
SIC: 8099 Health and allied services, nec
PA: Restpadd Inc.
2750 Eureka Way
Redding CA
916 405-6016

(P-17315)
RIVERSIDE MEDICAL CLINIC INC
21634 Retreat Pkwy (92883-6100)
PHONE..................................951 277-0000
EMP: 65
SALES (corp-wide): 102.29MM Privately Held
Web: www.riversidemedicalclinic.com
SIC: 8099 Childbirth preparation clinic
PA: Riverside Medical Clinic, Inc.
3660 Arlington Ave
Riverside CA
951 683-6370

(P-17316)
ROBIN HEALTHCARE LLC
1845 Berkeley Way (94703-1576)
PHONE..................................310 601-6899
Noah Auerhahn, Prin
EMP: 131 EST: 2017
SALES (est): 11.9MM Privately Held
Web: www.robinhealthcare.com
SIC: 8099 Medical services organization

(P-17317)
ROLLING HILLS CLINIC
2540 Sister Mary Columba Dr (96080-4327)
PHONE..................................530 690-2334
Penny Costa, Brnch Mgr
EMP: 62
Web: www.rhclinic.org
SIC: 8099 Blood related health services
PA: Rolling Hills Clinic
740 Solano St
Corning CA

(P-17318)
SAN BRNRDINO CY UNFIED SCHL DS
Also Called: Nutrition Services
1257 Northpark Blvd (92407-2946)
PHONE..................................909 881-8000
EMP: 83
SALES (corp-wide): 952.38MM Privately Held
Web: www.sbcusd.com
SIC: 8099 8211 Nutrition services; Elementary school, nec
PA: San Bernardino City Unified School District
777 N F St
San Bernardino CA
909 381-1100

(P-17319)
SAN DIEGO BLOOD BANK (PA)
Also Called: San Diego Blood Bnk Foundation
3636 Gateway Center Ave Ste 100 (92102-4508)
PHONE..................................619 400-8132
TOLL FREE: 800
Ramona Walker, CEO
▲ EMP: 155 EST: 1950
SQ FT: 132,000
SALES (est): 41.12MM
SALES (corp-wide): 41.12MM Privately Held
Web: www.sandiegobloodbank.org
SIC: 8099 8071 Blood bank; Medical laboratories

(P-17320)
SAN MATEO HEALTH COMMISSION
Also Called: Health Plan of San Mateo
801 Gateway Blvd Ste 100 (94080-7408)
PHONE..................................650 616-0050
Maya Altman, CEO
Ron Robinson, *
EMP: 211 EST: 1986
SQ FT: 58,758
SALES (est): 42.97MM Privately Held
Web: www.hpsm.org
SIC: 8099 Physical examination service, insurance

(P-17321)
SANTA CLARA COUNTY OF
Also Called: Santa Clara Family Health
6201 San Ignacio Ave (95119-1325)
PHONE..................................408 362-9817
EMP: 204
Web: www.scfhp.com
SIC: 8099 Medical services organization
PA: County Of Santa Clara
70 W Hedding St
San Jose CA
408 299-5200

(P-17322)
SANTA CLARA VALLEY MEDICAL CTR
2220 Moorpark Ave (95128-2613)
PHONE..................................408 885-5730
EMP: 982
SIC: 8099 Childbirth preparation clinic
PA: Santa Clara Valley Medical Center
751 S Bascom Ave
San Jose CA

(P-17323)
SCRIBEAMERICA LLC
840 Apollo St Ste 231 (90245-4762)
PHONE..................................877 819-5900
Michael Murphy, Brnch Mgr
EMP: 306
Web: www.scribeamerica.com
SIC: 8099 Blood related health services
HQ: Scribeamerica, Llc
1200 E Las Olas Blvd # 201
Fort Lauderdale FL

(P-17324)
SENSEI WELLNESS HOLDINGS INC
1119 Colorado Ave Ste 18 (90401-3009)
PHONE..................................602 499-9862
Kevin Kelly, CEO
EMP: 92 EST: 2020
SALES (est): 11.33MM Privately Held
Web: www.sensei.com
SIC: 8099 Health screening service

(P-17325)
SIERRA HLTH WELLNESS CTRS LLC
2167 Montgomery St Ste A (95965-4945)
P.O. Box 2456 (95965-2456)
PHONE..................................530 854-4119
Joseph Henderson, Managing Member
Shawn Vang, Managing Member
EMP: 80 EST: 2019
SALES (est): 10.16MM Privately Held
Web: www.sierrahealthwellnesscenters.com
SIC: 8099 8322 Blood related health services; Rehabilitation services

(P-17326)
SILICON VALLEY MEDICAL DEV LLC
Also Called: El Camino Health
2500 Grant Rd (94040-4302)
PHONE..................................408 866-4000
Ramesh K Gopi, Prin
EMP: 65
SALES (est): 50.88MM Privately Held
Web: www.elcaminohealth.org
SIC: 8099 Health and allied services, nec

(P-17327)
SONIA CORINA INC
Also Called: Bay Respite Care
1100 Rose Dr Ste 140 (94510-3623)
PHONE..................................707 644-4491
Jodi Johnson, CEO
EMP: 69 EST: 2002
SALES (est): 3.25MM Privately Held
Web: www.soniacorina.org
SIC: 8099 Childbirth preparation clinic

(P-17328)
SOUTHERN CAL PRMNNTE MED GROUP
Also Called: SOUTHERN CALIFORNIA PERMANENTE MEDICAL GROUP
23781 Maquina (92691-2716)
PHONE..................................949 376-8619
EMP: 187
SALES (corp-wide): 68.1B Privately Held
Web: www.permanente.org
SIC: 8099 Blood related health services
HQ: Southern California Permanente Medical Group
393 Walnut Dr
Pasadena CA
626 405-5704

(P-17329)
STANFORD HEALTH CARE
450 Broadway St (94063-3132)
PHONE..................................650 723-5256
EMP: 1029
SALES (corp-wide): 15.13B Privately Held
Web: www.stanfordhealthcare.org
SIC: 8099 Childbirth preparation clinic
HQ: Stanford Health Care
300 Pasteur Dr
Stanford CA
650 723-4000

(P-17330)
STANFORD HEALTH CARE
866 Campus Dr (94305-8508)
PHONE..................................650 723-4841
EMP: 87
SALES (corp-wide): 15.13B Privately Held
Web: www.stanfordhealthcare.org
SIC: 8099 Childbirth preparation clinic
HQ: Stanford Health Care
300 Pasteur Dr
Stanford CA
650 723-4000

(P-17331)
STAR OF CA LLC
501 Marin St (91360-4266)
PHONE..................................805 379-1401
Doug Moes, Brnch Mgr
EMP: 94
SALES (corp-wide): 165.05MM Privately Held
Web: www.starofca.com
SIC: 8099 Medical services organization
HQ: Star Of Ca, Llc
4880 Market St
Ventura CA

(P-17332)
STAR OF CA LLC
15260 Ventura Blvd (91403-5307)
PHONE..................................818 986-7827
Alison Stanley, Brnch Mgr
EMP: 95
SALES (corp-wide): 165.05MM Privately Held
Web: www.starofca.com
SIC: 8099 Medical services organization
HQ: Star Of Ca, Llc
4880 Market St
Ventura CA

(P-17333)
STAR OF CA LLC (HQ)
4880 Market St (93003-7783)
PHONE..................................805 644-7827
Doug Moes, Pr
Quy Neel, CCO
Jennifer Johnson, Dir Opers
Tom Forde, Contrlr
EMP: 110 EST: 2006
SQ FT: 6,640
SALES (est): 53.82MM
SALES (corp-wide): 165.05MM Privately Held
Web: www.starofca.com
SIC: 8099 8049 8322 Medical services organization; Clinical psychologist; Individual and family services
PA: Pediatric Therapy Services, Llc
184 High St Ste 701
Boston MA
800 337-5965

(P-17334)
STAR OF CALIFORNIA
Also Called: STAR OF CALIFORNIA, A PROFESSIONAL PSYCHOLOGICAL CORPORATION
8834 Morro Rd (93422-3953)
PHONE..................................805 466-1638
EMP: 95
SALES (corp-wide): 165.05MM Privately Held
Web: www.starofca.com
SIC: 8099 Medical services organization
HQ: Star Of Ca, Llc
4880 Market St
Ventura CA

(P-17335)
SUTTER HEALTH
2950 Collier Canyon Rd (94551-9224)
PHONE..................................925 371-3800
Ronald D Workman, Brnch Mgr
EMP: 80
SALES (corp-wide): 14.77B Privately Held
Web: www.sutterhealth.org
SIC: 8099 Blood related health services
PA: Sutter Health
2200 River Plaza Dr
Sacramento CA
916 733-8800

(P-17336)
SWEATHEORY WELLNESS LLC
6427 W Sunset Blvd # 106 (90028-7314)
PHONE..................................310 844-3662
Julian Ledesma, Managing Member
EMP: 64 EST: 2018
SALES (est): 1.23MM Privately Held
Web: www.sweatheory.com
SIC: 8099 5812 Health and allied services, nec; Snack bar

(P-17337)
SWEETGRACE HOME HLTH SVCS LLC

8099 - Health And Allied Services, Nec (P-17338)

6101 Cherry Ave (92336-5362)
PHONE..................................909 463-7400
EMP: 65 EST: 2012
SALES (est): 1.69MM Privately Held
Web: www.sweetgracehomehealth.com
SIC: 8099 Health and allied services, nec

(P-17338)
SYNERGY HEALTH COMPANIES INC
1521 N Carpenter Rd Ste D1 (95351)
PHONE..................................209 577-4625
Ronald Murphy, CEO
Ronald Edward Murphy, *
Anita Murphy, *
EMP: 95 EST: 2013
SALES (est): 5.44MM Privately Held
SIC: 8099 Health and allied services, nec

(P-17339)
SYNERGY ORTHPD SPECIALISTS INC
4445 Eastgate Mall Ste 103 (92121)
PHONE..................................858 450-7118
Brent Noon, CEO
EMP: 83 EST: 2012
SALES (est): 5.36MM Privately Held
Web: www.synergysmg.com
SIC: 8099 Blood related health services

(P-17340)
TENDERLOIN HOUSING CLINIC INC
488 Ellis St (94102-1928)
PHONE..................................415 771-2427
Randall Shaw, Brnch Mgr
EMP: 175
Web: www.thclinic.org
SIC: 8099 Blood related health services
PA: Tenderloin Housing Clinic, Inc.
126 Hyde St
San Francisco CA

(P-17341)
TMS HEALTH SOLUTIONS
360 Post St Ste 500 (94108-4908)
PHONE..................................844 867-8444
Brad Hummel, CEO
EMP: 88 EST: 2016
SALES (est): 9.07MM Privately Held
Web: www.mindfulhealthsolutions.com
SIC: 8099 Health and allied services, nec

(P-17342)
UC IRVINE HEALTH
200 S Manchester Ave Ste 400 (92868-3220)
PHONE..................................714 456-6191
EMP: 100 EST: 2018
SALES (est): 2.71MM Privately Held
Web: www.ucihealth.org
SIC: 8099 Health and allied services, nec

(P-17343)
UNIVERSITY CALIFORNIA IRVINE
31865 Circle Dr (92651-6860)
PHONE..................................949 939-7106
EMP: 80
SALES (corp-wide): 534.4MM Privately Held
Web: www.uci.edu
SIC: 8099 Blood related health services
HQ: University Of California, Irvine
510 Aldrich Hall
Irvine CA
949 824-5011

(P-17344)
UNIVERSITY CALIFORNIA IRVINE
Also Called: UCI Health Blood Donor Center
106 B Student Ctr (92697-0001)
PHONE..................................949 824-2662
EMP: 80
SALES (corp-wide): 534.4MM Privately Held
Web: www.uci.edu
SIC: 8099 Blood donor station
HQ: University Of California, Irvine
510 Aldrich Hall
Irvine CA
949 824-5011

(P-17345)
VENTURA CNTY MD-CAL MNGED CARE
Also Called: Gold Coast Health Plan
711 E Daily Dr Ste 106 (93010-6082)
PHONE..................................888 301-1228
Michael P Engelhard, CEO
EMP: 87 EST: 2010
SALES (est): 51.41MM Privately Held
Web: www.goldcoasthealthplan.org
SIC: 8099 Medical services organization

(P-17346)
VITAL HEALTH SCIENCES INC
P.O. Box 910492 (92191-0492)
PHONE..................................619 675-5521
EMP: 61 EST: 2010
SALES (est): 157.49K Privately Held
Web: www.vitalhealthsciences.com
SIC: 8099 Health and allied services, nec

(P-17347)
VITALANT
Also Called: United Blood Svcs Cntl Coast
2223 Eastman Ave Ste A (93003-8050)
PHONE..................................805 654-1603
EMP: 60
SALES (corp-wide): 526.62MM Privately Held
Web: www.vitalant.org
SIC: 8099 Blood bank
PA: Vitalant
9305 E Via De Ventura
Scottsdale AZ
800 288-2199

(P-17348)
VITALANT RESEARCH INSTITUTE (PA)
Also Called: Shasta Blood Center
360 Spear St Ste 200 (94105-1756)
PHONE..................................415 923-5771
Nora Hirschler, Pr
Lage Anderson, *
EMP: 120 EST: 1941
SQ FT: 67,000
SALES (est): 47.97MM
SALES (corp-wide): 47.97MM Privately Held
Web: research.vitalant.org
SIC: 8099 Blood bank

(P-17349)
VITALANT RESEARCH INSTITUTE
Also Called: NAPA Solano Cmnty Blood Ctr
1325 Gateway Blvd Ste C1 (94533-6919)
PHONE..................................707 428-6001
Lana Dyson, Mgr
EMP: 66
SALES (corp-wide): 47.97MM Privately Held
Web: www.vitalant.org
SIC: 8099 Blood bank
PA: Vitalant Research Institute
360 Spear St Ste 200
San Francisco CA
415 923-5771

(P-17350)
VITALANT RESEARCH INSTITUTE
2680 Larkspur Ln (96002-1016)
PHONE..................................530 221-0600
Ellie Delgado, Brnch Mgr
EMP: 75
SALES (corp-wide): 47.97MM Privately Held
Web: research.vitalant.org
SIC: 8099 Blood bank
PA: Vitalant Research Institute
360 Spear St Ste 200
San Francisco CA
415 923-5771

(P-17351)
VU HOLDINGS LLC
55 Fair Dr (92626-6520)
PHONE..................................661 808-4004
EMP: 97 EST: 2014
SALES (est): 789.76K Privately Held
Web: www.vanguard.edu
SIC: 8099 Health and allied services, nec

(P-17352)
WEST HEALTH INCUBATOR INC
10350 N Torrey Pines Rd (92037-1018)
PHONE..................................858 535-7000
Shelley Lyford, CEO
EMP: 68 EST: 2012
SALES (est): 1.76MM Privately Held
Web: www.westhealth.org
SIC: 8099 Blood related health services

(P-17353)
WESTLAKE OAKS HEALTHCARE LLC
Also Called: Sherwood Oaks Post Acute
250 Fairview Rd (91361-2456)
PHONE..................................805 494-1233
EMP: 98 EST: 2020
SALES (est): 4.47MM
SALES (corp-wide): 1.53B Privately Held
SIC: 8099 Health and allied services, nec
PA: Providence Group, Inc.
262 N University Ave
Farmington UT
801 447-9829

8111 Legal Services

(P-17354)
A BUCHALTER PROFESSIONAL CORP (PA)
1000 Wilshire Blvd Ste 1500 (90017-2457)
PHONE..................................213 891-0700
Adam Bass, CEO
EMP: 209 EST: 1970
SQ FT: 84,000
SALES (est): 52.94MM
SALES (corp-wide): 52.94MM Privately Held
Web: www.buchalter.com
SIC: 8111 General practice law office

(P-17355)
AARON DOWLING INCORPORATED
8080 N Palm Ave Ste 300 (93711-5797)
P.O. Box 28902 (93729-8902)
PHONE..................................559 432-4500
Larry B Lindenau, CEO
Michael D Dowling, *
Richard M Aaron, *
William J Keeler Junior, Treas
EMP: 80 EST: 1977
SQ FT: 16,000
SALES (est): 12.32MM Privately Held
Web: www.fennemorelaw.com
SIC: 8111 General practice attorney, lawyer

(P-17356)
ABRAMSON LABOR GROUP
3580 Wilshire Blvd Ste 1260 (90010-2501)
PHONE..................................213 493-6300
Zev Abramson, Pt
EMP: 70 EST: 2021
SALES (est): 3.71MM Privately Held
Web: www.abramsonlaborgroup.com
SIC: 8111 General practice law office

(P-17357)
AKERMAN LLP
601 W 5th St Ste 300 (90071-3506)
PHONE..................................213 688-9500
Justin Balser, Office Managing Partner
EMP: 68
SALES (corp-wide): 178.89MM Privately Held
Web: www.akerman.com
SIC: 8111 General practice attorney, lawyer
PA: Akerman Llp
98 Se 7th St Ste 1100
Miami FL
305 374-5600

(P-17358)
AKIN GUMP STRUSS HUER FELD LLP
1999 Avenue Of The Stars Ste 600 (90067-6022)
PHONE..................................310 229-1000
EMP: 83 EST: 2017
SALES (est): 3MM Privately Held
Web: www.akingump.com
SIC: 8111 General practice law office

(P-17359)
ALBERT & MACKENZIE LLP (PA)
Also Called: Albert & Mackenzie
28216 Dorothy Dr Ste 200 (91301-4973)
PHONE..................................818 575-9876
Bruce Albert, Mng Pt
Bruce Albert, Pt
Peter Mackenzie, Pt
EMP: 75 EST: 2000
SALES (est): 23.43MM
SALES (corp-wide): 23.43MM Privately Held
Web: www.albmac.com
SIC: 8111 Real estate law

(P-17360)
ALDRIDGE PITE LLP
4375 Jutland Dr Ste 200 (92117-3600)
P.O. Box 17935 (92177-7923)
PHONE..................................858 750-7700
EMP: 431
SALES (corp-wide): 99.58MM Privately Held
Web: www.aldridgepite.com
SIC: 8111 Real estate law
PA: Aldridge Pite Llp
3575 Piedmont Rd Ne 15-500
Atlanta GA
404 994-7400

(P-17361)
ALEXANDRA LZANO IMMGRTION LAW

5800 S Eastern Ave Ste 270 (90040)
PHONE...................323 524-9944
Alexandra Lozano, *Governor*
EMP: 72
SALES (corp-wide): 14.48MM **Privately Held**
Web: www.abogadaalexandra.com
SIC: 8111 Immigration and naturalization law
PA: Alexandra Lozano Immigration Law, Pllc
6720 Fort Dent Way Ste 23
Tukwila WA
206 406-3068

(P-17362)
ALLEN MTKINS LECK GMBLE MLLORY (PA)
Also Called: Allen Matkins
865 S Figueroa St Ste 2800 (90017-2543)
PHONE...................213 622-5555
David L Osias, *Mng Pt*
Frederick L Allen, *Pt*
Michael L Matkins, *Pt*
John C Gamble, *Pt*
Richard C Mallory, *Pt*
EMP: 130 EST: 1986
SQ FT: 40,000
SALES (est): 51.83MM
SALES (corp-wide): 51.83MM **Privately Held**
Web: www.allenmatkins.com
SIC: 8111 General practice law office

(P-17363)
ALSTON & BIRD LLP
333 S Hope St Ste 1600 (90071-1410)
PHONE...................213 576-1000
Wayne Mitchell, *Brnch Mgr*
EMP: 77
SALES (corp-wide): 216.9MM **Privately Held**
Web: www.alston.com
SIC: 8111 General practice attorney, lawyer
PA: Alston & Bird Llp
1201 W Peachtree St Nw # 4000
Atlanta GA
404 881-7000

(P-17364)
ANDATHA INTERNATIONAL INC
Also Called: Evolve Discovery
611 Mission St Fl 4 (94105-3535)
EMP: 250
SIC: 8111 Legal services

(P-17365)
ANGELO KILDAY & KILDUFF
601 University Ave Ste 150 (95825-6706)
PHONE...................916 564-6100
EMP: 143 EST: 1997
SALES (est): 9.11MM **Privately Held**
Web: www.akk-law.com
SIC: 8111 General practice law office

(P-17366)
ARCHER NORRIS A PROFESSIONAL LAW CORPORATION
Also Called: Archer Norris
2033 N Main St Ste 800 (94596-3759)
P.O. Box 8035 (94596-8035)
PHONE...................925 930-6000
EMP: 205
Web: www.archernorris.com
SIC: 8111 General practice law office

(P-17367)
ARNOLD & PORTER PC
3 Embarcadero Ctr Fl 7 (94111-4003)
PHONE...................415 434-1600
Lawrence Rabkin, *Ch Bd*
Michelle Johnson, *
▲ EMP: 350 EST: 1957
SQ FT: 70,000
SALES (est): 24.69MM **Privately Held**
SIC: 8111 Corporate, partnership and business law

(P-17368)
ARNOLD PORTER KAYE SCHOLER LLP
Also Called: Arnold & Porter
777 S Figueroa St Ste 4400 (90017-5800)
PHONE...................213 243-4000
Peter Blinkley, *Brnch Mgr*
EMP: 96
SALES (corp-wide): 814.71K **Privately Held**
Web: www.arnoldporter.com
SIC: 8111 General practice attorney, lawyer
PA: Arnold & Porter Kaye Scholer Llp
601 Massachusetts Ave Nw
Washington DC
202 942-5000

(P-17369)
ATKINSON ANDLSON LOYA RUUD ROM (PA)
Also Called: Atkinson Andelson Loya
12800 Center Court Dr S Ste 300 (90703-9363)
PHONE...................562 653-3200
James C Romo, *CEO*
Steven Atkinson, *
Steven Andelson, *
Paul Loya, *
EMP: 150 EST: 1979
SALES (est): 38.23MM
SALES (corp-wide): 38.23MM **Privately Held**
Web: www.aalrr.com
SIC: 8111 General practice attorney, lawyer

(P-17370)
AUSTIN SIDLEY CA LLP
555 W 5th St Ste 4000 (90013-3000)
PHONE...................213 896-6000
Dan Clivner, *Pt*
EMP: 165 EST: 2001
SALES (est): 10.56MM
SALES (corp-wide): 511.15MM **Privately Held**
SIC: 8111 General practice attorney, lawyer
PA: Sidley Austin Llp
1 S Dearborn St Ste 900
Chicago IL
312 853-7000

(P-17371)
BAKER & HOSTETLER LLP
11601 Wilshire Blvd Fl 14 (90025-1744)
PHONE...................310 820-8800
John F Cermak Junior, *Mng Pt*
EMP: 85
SALES (corp-wide): 309.55K **Privately Held**
Web: www.bakerlaw.com
SIC: 8111 General practice attorney, lawyer
PA: Baker & Hostetler Llp
127 Public Sq Ste 2000
Cleveland OH
216 621-0200

(P-17372)
BAKER & HOSTETLER LLP
600 Anton Blvd Ste 900 (92626-7193)
PHONE...................714 754-6600
George T Mooradian, *Pt*
EMP: 85
SQ FT: 6,000
SALES (corp-wide): 309.55K **Privately Held**
Web: www.bakerlaw.com
SIC: 8111 General practice attorney, lawyer
PA: Baker & Hostetler Llp
127 Public Sq Ste 2000
Cleveland OH
216 621-0200

(P-17373)
BAKER & MCKENZIE LLP
2 Embarcadero Ctr Ste 1100 (94111-3911)
PHONE...................415 576-3000
Peter Engstrom, *Mgr*
EMP: 120
SALES (corp-wide): 782.22MM **Privately Held**
Web: www.bakermckenzie.com
SIC: 8111 Administrative and government law
PA: Baker & Mckenzie Llp
300 E Randolph St # 5000
Chicago IL
312 861-8000

(P-17374)
BAKER & MCKENZIE LLP
10250 Constellation Blvd Ste 1850 (90067-6278)
PHONE...................310 201-4728
EMP: 125
SALES (corp-wide): 782.22MM **Privately Held**
Web: www.bakermckenzie.com
SIC: 8111 General practice law office
PA: Baker & Mckenzie Llp
300 E Randolph St # 5000
Chicago IL
312 861-8000

(P-17375)
BAKER & MCKENZIE LLP
660 Hansen Way Ste 1 (94304-1045)
PHONE...................650 856-2400
Peter Engstrom, *Brnch Mgr*
EMP: 60
SALES (corp-wide): 782.22MM **Privately Held**
Web: www.bakermckenzie.com
SIC: 8111 8011 General practice law office; Medical centers
PA: Baker & Mckenzie Llp
300 E Randolph St # 5000
Chicago IL
312 861-8000

(P-17376)
BAKER MANOCK & JENSEN PC
Also Called: Baker Mnock Jnsen Attys At Law
5260 N Palm Ave Ste 201 (93704-2222)
PHONE...................559 432-5400
Bob Smittcamp, *CEO*
Kendall Manock, *
Douglas B Jensen, *
Donald P Fishbach, *
Craig A Houghton, *
EMP: 89 EST: 1904
SALES (est): 4.92MM **Privately Held**
Web: www.bakermanock.com
SIC: 8111 General practice law office

(P-17377)
BALLARD SPAHR LLP
2029 Century Park E Ste 1400 (90002-3076)
PHONE...................424 204-4400
Alan Petlak, *Brnch Mgr*
EMP: 76
SALES (corp-wide): 224.22MM **Privately Held**
Web: www.ballardspahr.com
SIC: 8111 General practice attorney, lawyer
PA: Ballard Spahr Llp
1735 Market St Fl 51
Philadelphia PA
215 665-8500

(P-17378)
BARNES & THORNBURG LLP
2029 Century Park E Ste 300 (90002-3076)
PHONE...................310 284-3880
EMP: 113
SALES (corp-wide): 85.65MM **Privately Held**
Web: www.btlaw.com
SIC: 8111 General practice attorney, lawyer
PA: Barnes & Thornburg Llp
11 S Meridian St Ste 1313
Indianapolis IN
317 236-1313

(P-17379)
BARNES FIRM LC
633 W 5th St Ste 1750 (90071-3547)
PHONE...................800 800-0000
Stephen E Barnes, *CEO*
EMP: 95 EST: 2017
SALES (est): 2.18MM **Privately Held**
Web: www.thebarnesfirm.com
SIC: 8111 General practice attorney, lawyer

(P-17380)
BARRY BISHOP
6001 Shellmound St Ste 875 (94608-1957)
PHONE...................510 596-0888
Nelson C Barry Senior, *Pr*
Rebecca B Ahern, *
Jeffrey N Haney, *
Nelson C Barry Iii, *VP*
Fredric W Trester, *
EMP: 60 EST: 1917
SQ FT: 14,000
SALES (est): 2.17MM **Privately Held**
Web: www.bishop-barry.com
SIC: 8111 General practice law office

(P-17381)
BARTKO ZNKEL BNZEL MLLER A PRO
1 Embarcadero Ctr Ste 800 (94111-3629)
PHONE...................415 956-1900
Richard T Tarrant, *Pr*
Martin I Zankel, *
John Bartko, *
Charles Miller, *
EMP: 80 EST: 1975
SQ FT: 18,000
SALES (est): 11.61MM **Privately Held**
Web: www.bzbm.com
SIC: 8111 Corporate, partnership and business law

(P-17382)
BD&J PC
9701 Wilshire Blvd Ste 630 (90212-2158)
PHONE...................855 906-3699
Kourosh Danesh Moghadam, *CEO*
EMP: 84 EST: 2007
SALES (est): 8.28MM **Privately Held**
Web: www.bdjinjurylawyers.com
SIC: 8111 General practice law office

(P-17383)
BERDING & WEIL LLP (PA)
2175 N California Blvd Ste 500 (94596-7336)
PHONE...................925 838-2090
Tyler Berding, *Pt*
EMP: 75 EST: 1988
SQ FT: 20,000

8111 - Legal Services (P-17384)

SALES (est): 16MM
SALES (corp-wide): 16MM Privately Held
Web: www.berding-weil.com
SIC: 8111 General practice attorney, lawyer

(P-17384)
BERGER KAHN A LAW CORPORATION (PA)
Also Called: Simon and Gladstone A Prof
1 Park Plz Ste 340 (92614-2511)
PHONE..................949 474-1880
Craig Simon, CEO
Leon J Gladstone, *
▲ EMP: 70 EST: 1928
SQ FT: 22,250
SALES (est): 15.65MM
SALES (corp-wide): 15.65MM Privately Held
Web: www.bergerkahn.com
SIC: 8111 General practice attorney, lawyer

(P-17385)
BERRY APPLEMAN & LEIDEN LLP (PA)
50 California St Fl 2 (94111-4632)
PHONE..................628 215-2800
EMP: 120 EST: 1980
SALES (est): 25.74MM
SALES (corp-wide): 25.74MM Privately Held
Web: www.bal.com
SIC: 8111 General practice attorney, lawyer

(P-17386)
BIRD MRLLA BXER WLPERT NSSIM
Also Called: Bird Marella
1875 Century Park E 23rd Fl (90067-2253)
PHONE..................310 201-2100
Vincent Marella, Pt
Terry Bird, *
Joel Boxer, *
Dorothy Wolpert, *
EMP: 60 EST: 1981
SALES (est): 10.15MM Privately Held
Web: www.birdmarella.com
SIC: 8111 General practice law office

(P-17387)
BLAKELY SOKOLOFF TAYLOR & ZAFMAN LLP
Also Called: Bstz
12400 Wilshire Blvd Ste 700 (90025-1019)
PHONE..................310 207-3800
EMP: 240
Web: www.womblebonddickinson.com
SIC: 8111 Specialized law offices, attorneys

(P-17388)
BLOMBERG BNSON GRRETT INC A LA
10300 4th St (91730-5808)
PHONE..................909 945-5000
David K Garrett, CEO
EMP: 70 EST: 1989
SALES (est): 1.87MM Privately Held
Web: www.lawbbg.com
SIC: 8111 General practice law office

(P-17389)
BMC GROUP INC
Also Called: Bankruptcy Management Cons
300 Continental Blvd Ste 570 (90245)
PHONE..................310 321-5555
Shawn Allen, Pr
EMP: 100
Web: www.bmcgroup.com

SIC: 8111 Bankruptcy referee
PA: The Bmc Group Inc
3732 W 120th St
Hawthorne CA

(P-17390)
BONNE BRDGES MLLER OKEFE NCHOL (PA)
355 S Grand Ave Ste 1750 (90071-1562)
PHONE..................213 480-1900
David J O'keefe, Pr
James D Nichols, *
George Peterson, *
EMP: 100 EST: 1961
SALES (est): 17.48MM
SALES (corp-wide): 17.48MM Privately Held
Web: www.bonnebridges.com
SIC: 8111 General practice attorney, lawyer

(P-17391)
BOOTH MITCHEL & STRANGE LLP
979 Osos St Ste C1 (93401-3253)
PHONE..................805 400-0703
Christpher Levwi, Brnch Mgr
EMP: 76
SALES (corp-wide): 7.29MM Privately Held
Web: www.boothmitchel.com
SIC: 8111 General practice law office
PA: Booth Mitchel & Strange, L.L.P.
707 Wilshire Blvd # 3000
Los Angeles CA
213 738-0100

(P-17392)
BRAYTON PURCELL APC (PA)
222 Rush Landing Rd (94945-2469)
P.O. Box 6169 (94948-6169)
PHONE..................415 898-1555
Alan Richard Brayton, CEO
EMP: 184 EST: 1982
SQ FT: 40,000
SALES (est): 22.68MM
SALES (corp-wide): 22.68MM Privately Held
Web: www.braytonlaw.com
SIC: 8111 General practice attorney, lawyer

(P-17393)
BRYAN CAVE LIGHTON PAISNER LLP
120 Broadway Ste 300 (90401-2386)
PHONE..................310 576-2100
Louise Caplan, Mgr
EMP: 77
SALES (corp-wide): 173.87K Privately Held
Web: www.bclplaw.com
SIC: 8111 General practice attorney, lawyer
PA: Bryan Cave Leighton Paisner Llp
1 Metropolitan Sq 211n
Saint Louis MO
314 259-2000

(P-17394)
BURKE WILLIAMS & SORENSEN LLP (PA)
Also Called: Burke
444 S Flower St Ste 2400 (90071-2953)
PHONE..................213 236-0600
John J Welsh, Mng Pt
James T Bradshaw Junior, Pt
Carl K Newton, Pt
Leland C Dolley, Pt
Neil F Yeager, Pt
EMP: 90 EST: 1927
SQ FT: 51,000

SALES (est): 25.16MM
SALES (corp-wide): 25.16MM Privately Held
Web: www.bwslaw.com
SIC: 8111 General practice attorney, lawyer

(P-17395)
BURNHAM BROWN A PROF CORP
Also Called: Burnham & Brown
1901 Harrison St Ste 1100 (94612-3648)
P.O. Box 119 (94604-0119)
PHONE..................510 444-6800
Gregory D Brown, Pr
Clark J Burnham, *
Robert J Lyman, *
Monica Del'osso, *
Schott C Finch, *
EMP: 120 EST: 1899
SQ FT: 50,000
SALES (est): 19.34MM Privately Held
Web: www.burnhambrown.com
SIC: 8111 General practice law office

(P-17396)
BURT L HOWE & ASSOCIATES
Also Called: Howe Construction Co
5415 E La Palma Ave (92807-2022)
PHONE..................714 701-9180
Bert L Howe, Pt
Susan A Howe, Pt
EMP: 61 EST: 1984
SALES (est): 3.14MM Privately Held
Web: www.berthowe.com
SIC: 8111 8711 Product liability law; Building construction consultant

(P-17397)
CALIFORNIA CITY SAN BERNARDINO (PA)
290 N D St (92401-1702)
PHONE..................909 384-7272
R Carey Davis, Mayor
Mark Scoth, *
Gigi Hannah, City Clerk*
David Kennedy, City Treasurer*
Gary Saiz, City Attorney*
EMP: 352 EST: 1854
SALES (est): 264.9MM
SALES (corp-wide): 264.9MM Privately Held
Web: www.sbcity.org
SIC: 8111 Administrative and government law

(P-17398)
CANAL ALLIANCE
91 Larkspur St (94901-4820)
PHONE..................415 485-3074
EMP: 105 EST: 2010
SALES (est): 13.07MM Privately Held
Web: www.canalalliance.org
SIC: 8111 Administrative and government law

(P-17399)
CARR MCCLELLAN PC (PA)
Also Called: Carr, McClellan
216 Park Rd (94010-4200)
P.O. Box 513 (94011-0513)
PHONE..................650 342-9600
Mark A Cassanego, Pr
Edward J Willig, Sec
EMP: 64 EST: 1946
SQ FT: 19,000
SALES (est): 9.03MM
SALES (corp-wide): 9.03MM Privately Held
Web: www.carr-mcclellan.com
SIC: 8111 General practice attorney, lawyer

(P-17400)
CARROLL BURDICK MC DONOUGH LLP (PA)
275 Battery St Ste 2600 (94111-3358)
PHONE..................415 989-5900
Angela Bradstreet, Pt
EMP: 142 EST: 1948
SQ FT: 50,000
SALES (est): 26.99MM
SALES (corp-wide): 26.99MM Privately Held
Web: www.squirepattonboggs.com
SIC: 8111 General practice attorney, lawyer

(P-17401)
CARSON KURTZMAN CONSULTANTS (DH)
Also Called: K C C
2335 Alaska Ave (90245-4808)
PHONE..................310 823-9000
Johnathan Carson, *
EMP: 180 EST: 2001
SQ FT: 46,000
SALES (est): 53.77MM Privately Held
Web: www.kccllc.com
SIC: 8111 Specialized legal services
HQ: Computershare Inc.
150 Royall St Ste 205
Canton MA

(P-17402)
CHILDRENS LAW CENTER CAL (PA)
101 Centre Plaza Dr (91754-2155)
PHONE..................323 980-8700
Leslie Starr Heimov, CEO
EMP: 88 EST: 1989
SALES (est): 73.27MM Privately Held
Web: www.clccal.org
SIC: 8111 Legal aid service

(P-17403)
CHRISTIE PARKER & HALE LLP (PA)
655 N Central Ave Ste 2300 (91203-1422)
P.O. Box 29001 (91209-9001)
PHONE..................626 795-9900
EMP: 130 EST: 1946
SALES (est): 18.85MM
SALES (corp-wide): 18.85MM Privately Held
Web: www.lewisroca.com
SIC: 8111 General practice attorney, lawyer

(P-17404)
CLARA SHORTRIDGE FOLTZ
9928 Flower St (90706-5453)
PHONE..................562 925-3039
EMP: 62
SALES (corp-wide): 5MM Privately Held
SIC: 8111 Specialized law offices, attorneys
PA: Clara Shortridge Foltz
210 W Temple St
Los Angeles CA
213 974-6141

(P-17405)
CLARKSON LAW FIRM PC
22525 Pacific Coast Hwy Ste 102 (90265)
PHONE..................213 788-4050
Ryan J Clarkson Esq, Prin
EMP: 69 EST: 2015
SALES (est): 2.18MM Privately Held
Web: www.clarksonlawfirm.com
SIC: 8111 General practice law office

PRODUCTS & SERVICES SECTION

8111 - Legal Services (P-17425)

(P-17406)
COBLENTZ PATCH DUFFY BASS LLP (PA)
1 Montgomery St Ste 3000 (94104-5500)
PHONE.................510 655-4598
Michael Meyers, *Pt*
Richard Patch, *Pt*
Paul Escobosa, *Pt*
Jim Mitchell, *Pt*
Jeffrey B Knowles, *Pt*
EMP: 100 **EST:** 1997
SQ FT: 30,000
SALES (est): 25.68MM
SALES (corp-wide): 25.68MM **Privately Held**
Web: www.coblentzlaw.com
SIC: 8111 General practice attorney, lawyer

(P-17407)
COLEMAN CHAVEZ & ASSOC LLP
1731 E Roseville Pkwy Ste 200 (95661)
PHONE.................916 787-2310
Chad Coleman, *Pt*
EMP: 75 **EST:** 2018
SALES (est): 5.43MM **Privately Held**
Web: www.cca-law.com
SIC: 8111 General practice law office

(P-17408)
COLLINSON LAW A PROF CORP
21515 Hawthorne Blvd Ste 800 (90503-6517)
PHONE.................424 212-7777
Lisa Collinson, *Brnch Mgr*
EMP: 185
SALES (corp-wide): 3.6MM **Privately Held**
Web: www.cdiglaw.com
SIC: 8111 General practice law office
PA: Collinson Law, A Professional Corporation
1600 Rosecrans Ave Fl 4
Manhattan Beach CA
310 321-7670

(P-17409)
COMMUNITY ACTION PARTNERSHIP
1152 E Grand Ave (93420-2583)
PHONE.................805 489-4026
Raye Flemming, *Brnch Mgr*
EMP: 64
SALES (corp-wide): 99.11MM **Privately Held**
Web: www.capslo.org
SIC: 8111 General practice law office
PA: Community Action Partnership Of San Luis Obispo County, Inc.
1030 Southwood Dr
San Luis Obispo CA
805 544-4355

(P-17410)
COMPEX LEGAL SERVICES INC (PA)
325 Maple Ave (90503-2602)
PHONE.................310 782-1801
Paul Boroditsch, *CEO*
Nitin Mehta, *Ch*
Anthony Bazurto, *Sr VP*
Humildad Pasimio, *VP*
Rajesh Rangaswamy, *VP*
▲ **EMP:** 120 **EST:** 1974
SQ FT: 47,740
SALES (est): 55.91MM
SALES (corp-wide): 55.91MM **Privately Held**
Web: www.compexlegal.com

SIC: 8111 7338 7334 Specialized legal services; Secretarial and court reporting; Photocopying and duplicating services

(P-17411)
COOKSEY TLEN GAGE DFFY WOOG A (PA)
535 Anton Blvd Fl 10 (92626-1912)
PHONE.................714 431-1100
David Cooksey, *Pr*
Robert L Toolen, *VP*
EMP: 91 **EST:** 1970
SALES (est): 9.85MM
SALES (corp-wide): 9.85MM **Privately Held**
Web: www.cookseylaw.com
SIC: 8111 General practice attorney, lawyer

(P-17412)
COOLEY LLP
Also Called: Cooley Godward Kronish
3 Embarcadero Ctr Fl 20 (94111-4004)
PHONE.................415 693-2000
Lee Benton, *Pt*
EMP: 100
SALES (corp-wide): 169.05MM **Privately Held**
Web: www.cooley.com
SIC: 8111 Specialized law offices, attorneys
PA: Cooley Llp
3175 Hanover St
Palo Alto CA
650 843-5000

(P-17413)
COOLEY LLP (PA)
3175 Hanover St (94304-1130)
PHONE.................650 843-5000
Joe Conroy, *Mng Pt*
Stephen Neal, *Pt*
Mark Pitchford, *Pt*
Janet L Callum, *Pt*
Fredrick Muto, *Pt*
EMP: 300 **EST:** 1935
SALES (est): 169.05MM
SALES (corp-wide): 169.05MM **Privately Held**
Web: www.cooley.com
SIC: 8111 General practice attorney, lawyer

(P-17414)
COOPER WHITE & COOPER LLP (PA)
50 California St Ste 2750 (94111-4616)
PHONE.................415 433-1900
Mark P Schreiber, *Pt*
Peter Sibley, *Pt*
Walter Hansell, *Pt*
Mark Tuft, *Pt*
Jed Solomon, *Pt*
EMP: 120 **EST:** 1895
SALES (est): 13.82MM
SALES (corp-wide): 13.82MM **Privately Held**
Web: www.womblebonddickinson.com
SIC: 8111 General practice attorney, lawyer

(P-17415)
COUNTY OF FRESNO
Also Called: Public Defender's Office
205 W Pontiac Way # 7 (93612-5609)
PHONE.................559 600-3546
Kenneth Taniguchi, *Brnch Mgr*
EMP: 71
SALES (corp-wide): 2.02B **Privately Held**
Web: www.fresnocountyca.gov
SIC: 8111 9222 Specialized law offices, attorneys; Public defenders' office
PA: County Of Fresno
2281 Tulare St Ste 304

Fresno CA
559 600-1710

(P-17416)
COUNTY OF LOS ANGELES
Also Called: Public Defender Administration
210 W Temple St Fl 19 (90012-3231)
PHONE.................213 974-2811
Ronald Brown, *Brnch Mgr*
EMP: 73
SALES (corp-wide): 31.7B **Privately Held**
Web: www.lacounty.gov
SIC: 8111 9222 Legal services; Public defenders' office
PA: County Of Los Angeles
500 W Temple St Ste 437
Los Angeles CA
213 974-1101

(P-17417)
COUNTY OF LOS ANGELES
Also Called: District Attorney
6230 Sylmar Ave Ste 201 (91401-2731)
PHONE.................818 374-2406
Nancy Lidamore, *Dir*
EMP: 63
SALES (corp-wide): 31.7B **Privately Held**
Web: www.lacounty.gov
SIC: 8111 9222 General practice attorney, lawyer; District attorneys' office
PA: County Of Los Angeles
500 W Temple St Ste 437
Los Angeles CA
213 974-1101

(P-17418)
COUNTY OF LOS ANGELES
Also Called: District Attorney
210 W Temple St Fl 18 (90012-3229)
PHONE.................213 974-3512
Jackie Lazey, *Mgr*
EMP: 117
SALES (corp-wide): 31.7B **Privately Held**
Web: www.lacounty.gov
SIC: 8111 9222 General practice attorney, lawyer; District attorneys' office
PA: County Of Los Angeles
500 W Temple St Ste 437
Los Angeles CA
213 974-1101

(P-17419)
COUNTY OF RIVERSIDE
Also Called: Public Defender- Main Office
4075 Main St (92501-3701)
PHONE.................951 955-6000
Gary Windom, *Admn*
EMP: 200
SALES (corp-wide): 4.58B **Privately Held**
Web: www.countyofriverside.us
SIC: 8111 9222 Legal services; Public defenders' office
PA: County Of Riverside
4080 Lemon St Fl 11
Riverside CA
951 955-1110

(P-17420)
COUNTY OF SAN DIEGO
Also Called: Public Defender, Alternate
450 B St Ste 900 (92101-8003)
PHONE.................619 446-2900
Timothy Chandler, *Dir*
EMP: 77
SALES (corp-wide): **Privately Held**
Web: www.sandiegocounty.gov
SIC: 8111 9222 Legal services; Public defenders' office
PA: County Of San Diego
1600 Pacific Hwy Ste 209
San Diego CA
619 531-5880

(P-17421)
COUNTY OF SAN DIEGO
District Attorney
330 W Broadway Ste 1020 (92101-3827)
PHONE.................619 531-4040
Steven Silva, *Sec*
EMP: 100
Web: www.sdcda.org
SIC: 8111 9222 Specialized legal services; District attorneys' office
PA: County Of San Diego
1600 Pacific Hwy Ste 209
San Diego CA
619 531-5880

(P-17422)
COVINGTON & BURLING LLP
3000 El Camino Real Ste 5-1000 (94306)
PHONE.................650 632-4700
Kurt G Calia, *Mgr*
EMP: 70
SALES (corp-wide): 422.72MM **Privately Held**
Web: www.cov.com
SIC: 8111 General practice law office
PA: Covington & Burling Llp
1 City Ctr 850 10th St Nw
Washington DC
202 662-6000

(P-17423)
COVINGTON & BURLING LLP
415 Mission St Ste 700 (94105-2597)
PHONE.................415 591-6000
Jim Snipes, *Pt*
EMP: 153
SALES (corp-wide): 422.72MM **Privately Held**
Web: www.cov.com
SIC: 8111 General practice law office
PA: Covington & Burling Llp
1 City Ctr 850 10th St Nw
Washington DC
202 662-6000

(P-17424)
COVINGTON & BURLING LLP
1999 Avenue Of The Stars # 3500 (90067-4643)
PHONE.................424 332-4800
Michelle Liffman, *Brnch Mgr*
EMP: 102
SALES (corp-wide): 422.72MM **Privately Held**
Web: www.cov.com
SIC: 8111 General practice law office
PA: Covington & Burling Llp
1 City Ctr 850 10th St Nw
Washington DC
202 662-6000

(P-17425)
COX CASTLE & NICHOLSON LLP (PA)
Also Called: Cox Castle
2029 Century Park E Ste 2100 (90002-3076)
PHONE.................310 284-2200
Gary A Glick, *Pt*
Edward F Quigley, *Pt*
David W Wensley, *Pt*
Mathew A Wyman, *Pt*
Marlene Goodfried, *Pt*
EMP: 165 **EST:** 1968
SQ FT: 60,000
SALES (est): 41.42MM
SALES (corp-wide): 41.42MM **Privately Held**
Web: www.coxcastle.com

8111 - Legal Services (P-17426)

SIC: 8111 General practice attorney, lawyer

(P-17426)
COX WTTON GRFFIN HNSEN PLOS LL
900 Front St (94111-1427)
PHONE..................415 438-4600
▲ EMP: 61 EST: 1996
SALES (est): 5.98MM Privately Held
Web: www.cwlfirm.com
SIC: 8111 Corporate, partnership and business law

(P-17427)
CROWELL & MORING LLP
515 S Flower St Ste 4000 (90071-2258)
PHONE..................213 622-4750
Mark Neighbor, Brnch Mgr
EMP: 113
SALES (corp-wide): 400MM Privately Held
Web: www.crowell.com
SIC: 8111 Specialized law offices, attorneys
PA: Crowell & Moring Llp
1001 Pennsylvania Ave Nw # 10
Washington DC
202 624-2500

(P-17428)
CROWELL & MORING LLP
3 Park Plz Ste 2000 (92614-2591)
PHONE..................949 263-8400
Daniel Sasse, Mgr
EMP: 120
SALES (corp-wide): 400MM Privately Held
Web: www.crowell.com
SIC: 8111 Specialized law offices, attorneys
PA: Crowell & Moring Llp
1001 Pennsylvania Ave Nw # 10
Washington DC
202 624-2500

(P-17429)
DANNING GILL DAMND KOLLITZ LLP
1901 Avenue Of The Stars Ste 450 (90067-6001)
PHONE..................310 277-0077
David A Gill, Pt
Richard K Diamond, *
Howard Kollitz, *
Eric P Israel Pc, Pt
David M Poitras, *
EMP: 70 EST: 1952
SALES (est): 11.02MM Privately Held
Web: www.danninggill.com
SIC: 8111 General practice law office

(P-17430)
DANNIS WLVER KLLEY A PROF CORP (PA)
275 Battery St Ste 1150 (94111-3333)
PHONE..................415 543-4111
Gregory Dannis, Pr
David Miller, *
EMP: 70 EST: 1976
SQ FT: 14,000
SALES (est): 10.94MM
SALES (corp-wide): 10.94MM Privately Held
Web: www.dwkesq.com
SIC: 8111 General practice attorney, lawyer

(P-17431)
DAVIS POLK & WARDWELL LLP
1600 El Camino Real Ste 100 (94025-4121)
PHONE..................650 752-2000
EMP: 92
SALES (corp-wide): 375.36MM Privately Held
Web: www.davispolk.com
SIC: 8111 General practice attorney, lawyer
PA: Davis Polk & Wardwell Llp
450 Lexington Ave Fl 10
New York NY
212 450-4000

(P-17432)
DAVIS WRIGHT TREMAINE LLP
50 California St Ste 2300 (94111-4795)
PHONE..................415 276-6500
Jeff Gray, Pt
EMP: 117
SALES (corp-wide): 238.76MM Privately Held
Web: www.dwt.com
SIC: 8111 General practice attorney, lawyer
PA: Davis Wright Tremaine Llp
920 5th Ave Ste 3300
Seattle WA
206 622-3150

(P-17433)
DAVIS WRIGHT TREMAINE LLP
865 S Figueroa St Ste 2400 (90017-2566)
PHONE..................213 633-6800
Mary Haas, Pt
EMP: 114
SALES (corp-wide): 238.76MM Privately Held
Web: www.dwt.com
SIC: 8111 General practice attorney, lawyer
PA: Davis Wright Tremaine Llp
920 5th Ave Ste 3300
Seattle WA
206 622-3150

(P-17434)
DE CASTRO W CHDROW MNDLER GLCK
10960 Wilshire Blvd Ste 1400 (90024-3702)
PHONE..................310 478-2541
Hugo Decastro, Pr
EMP: 65 EST: 1963
SQ FT: 19,400
SALES (est): 9.26MM Privately Held
Web: www.dwclaw.com
SIC: 8111 General practice law office

(P-17435)
DECHERT LLP
633 W 5th St Ste 4900 (90071-2032)
PHONE..................949 442-6000
Robert Roberton, Managing Member
EMP: 60
SALES (corp-wide): 230.88MM Privately Held
Web: www.dechert.com
SIC: 8111 General practice law office
PA: Dechert Llp
Cira Centre 2929 Arch St
Philadelphia PA
215 994-4000

(P-17436)
DECHERT LLP
1 Bush St Ste 1600 (94104-4422)
PHONE..................415 262-4500
John Randal, Off Mgr
EMP: 74
SALES (corp-wide): 230.88MM Privately Held
Web: www.dechert.com
SIC: 8111 8748 General practice law office; Business consulting, nec
PA: Dechert Llp
Cira Centre 2929 Arch St
Philadelphia PA
215 994-4000

(P-17437)
DENTONS US LLP
Also Called: A Dentons Innovation Wirthlin
601 S Figueroa St Ste 2500 (90017-5704)
PHONE..................213 623-9300
Edwin Reeser, Genl Mgr
EMP: 150
SALES (corp-wide): 473.25MM Privately Held
Web: www.dentons.com
SIC: 8111 Specialized law offices, attorneys
PA: Dentons Us Llp
233 S Wacker Dr Ste 5900
Chicago IL
312 876-8000

(P-17438)
DLA PIPER LLP (US)
2000 Avenue Of The Stars Ste 400n (90067-4735)
PHONE..................310 595-3000
Ronnie Decesare, Brnch Mgr
EMP: 102
Web: www.dlapiper.com
SIC: 8111 Corporate, partnership and business law
HQ: Dla Piper Llp (Us)
650 S Exeter St
Baltimore MD
410 580-3000

(P-17439)
DOMINGUEZ LAW GROUP PC
Also Called: Law Offices Juan J. Dominguez
3250 Wilshire Blvd Ste 1750 (90010-1613)
PHONE..................213 388-7788
Juan J Dominguez, Pr
EMP: 100 EST: 1988
SQ FT: 5,000
SALES (est): 12.3MM Privately Held
Web: www.dominguezfirm.com
SIC: 8111 General practice attorney, lawyer

(P-17440)
DONAHUE GALLAGER WOODS LLP (PA)
1999 Harrison St Ste 2500 (94612-4705)
PHONE..................415 381-4161
Lawrence K Rockwell, Pt
Wilfrid F Roberge Junior, Pt
Harrison S Robinson, Pt
Andrew W Lafrenz, Pt
George J Barron, Pt
EMP: 75 EST: 1918
SQ FT: 20,827
SALES (est): 4.4MM
SALES (corp-wide): 4.4MM Privately Held
Web: www.donahue.com
SIC: 8111 General practice attorney, lawyer

(P-17441)
DOWNEY BRAND LLP (PA)
621 Capitol Mall Fl 18 (95814-4719)
PHONE..................916 444-1000
Dale A Stern, Mng Pt
Stan Van Vleck, Pt
John Mccarron, Pt
EMP: 207 EST: 1926
SALES (est): 30.04MM
SALES (corp-wide): 30.04MM Privately Held
Web: www.downeybrand.com
SIC: 8111 General practice attorney, lawyer

(P-17442)
DREYER BABICH BUCCOLA WOOD CAM
195 Cherry Ave (95603-4811)
PHONE..................530 889-1800
Joseph Babich, Prin
EMP: 81
SALES (corp-wide): 8.26MM Privately Held
Web: www.dbbwc.com
SIC: 8111 General practice attorney, lawyer
PA: Dreyer Babich Buccola Wood Campora, Llp
20 Bicentennial Cir
Sacramento CA
916 379-3500

(P-17443)
DUANE MORRIS LLP
1 Market Plz Ste 2200 (94105-1127)
PHONE..................415 957-3000
EMP: 63
SALES (corp-wide): 206.81MM Privately Held
Web: www.duanemorris.com
SIC: 8111 General practice attorney, lawyer
PA: Duane Morris Llp
30 S 17th St Fl 5
Philadelphia PA
215 979-1000

(P-17444)
DUCKOR MTZGER WYNNE A PROF LAW
101 W Broadway Ste 1700 (92101-8289)
PHONE..................619 209-3000
Michael J Duckor, Pr
Gary J Spradling, *
Scott Metzger, *
EMP: 70 EST: 1977
SQ FT: 25,000
SALES (est): 9.77MM Privately Held
Web: www.dmwplc.com
SIC: 8111 General practice attorney, lawyer

(P-17445)
ELKINS KALT WNTRAUB RBEN GRTSI
10345 W Olympic Blvd (90064-2524)
PHONE..................310 746-4431
EMP: 81 EST: 2019
SALES (est): 4.42MM Privately Held
Web: www.elkinskalt.com
SIC: 8111 General practice attorney, lawyer

(P-17446)
ELLIS GRGE CPLLONE OBRIEN ANNG
2121 Avenue Of The Stars Fl 30 (90067-5010)
PHONE..................310 274-7100
Eric George, Mng Pt
Allen Browne, *
Peter Ross, Pt
EMP: 100 EST: 1985
SALES (est): 10.95MM Privately Held
Web: www.egcfirm.com
SIC: 8111 General practice law office

(P-17447)
ENGSTROM LIPSCOMB AND LACK A (PA)
10100 Santa Monica Blvd (90067-4113)
PHONE..................310 552-3800
Paul Engstrom, Pr
Lee G Lipscomb, *
Walter J Lack, *
EMP: 70 EST: 1974

SQ FT: 22,000
SALES (est): 10.84MM
SALES (corp-wide): 10.84MM **Privately Held**
Web: www.elllaw.com
SIC: 8111 General practice law office

(P-17448)
EPSTEIN BECKER & GREEN PC
655 Montgomery St Ste 1150 (94111-2646)
PHONE..............................415 398-3500
Bill Helvestine, *Mng Pt*
EMP: 67
SALES (corp-wide): 99.62MM **Privately Held**
Web: www.ebglaw.com
SIC: 8111 General practice attorney, lawyer
PA: Epstein Becker & Green, P.C.
    875 3rd Ave Fl 19
    New York NY
    212 351-4500

(P-17449)
EPSTEIN BECKER & GREEN PC
1875 Century Park E Ste 500 (90067-2253)
PHONE..............................310 556-8861
Sandy Siciliano, *Mgr*
EMP: 202
SALES (corp-wide): 99.62MM **Privately Held**
Web: www.ebglaw.com
SIC: 8111 General practice attorney, lawyer
PA: Epstein Becker & Green, P.C.
    875 3rd Ave Fl 19
    New York NY
    212 351-4500

(P-17450)
ESSEY LLC
140 Geary St (94108-5630)
PHONE..............................212 490-7400
EMP: 259
Web: www.tempositions.com
SIC: 8111 General practice law office
PA: Essey, Llc
    622 3rd Ave Fl 39
    New York NY

(P-17451)
EVERLAW INC (PA)
2101 Webster St Ste 1500 (94612-3011)
PHONE..............................844 383-7529
Aj Shankar, *CEO*
EMP: 387 EST: 2010
SALES (est): 2.63MM
SALES (corp-wide): 2.63MM **Privately Held**
Web: www.everlaw.com
SIC: 8111 Legal services

(P-17452)
FEDERAL DFENDERS SAN DIEGO INC (PA)
225 Broadway Ste 900 (92101-5030)
PHONE..............................619 234-8467
Jami Ferrara, *CEO*
Shereen J Charlick, *
EMP: 75 EST: 1971
SALES (est): 32.56MM
SALES (corp-wide): 32.56MM **Privately Held**
Web: www.fdsdi.com
SIC: 8111 General practice law office

(P-17453)
FENNEMORE CRAIG PC
Also Called: Fennemore Wendel
1500 J St (95354-1123)
PHONE..............................209 576-8888
EMP: 140

SALES (corp-wide): 29.44MM **Privately Held**
Web: www.wendel.com
SIC: 8111 General practice attorney, lawyer
PA: Fennemore Craig, P.C.
    2394 E Camelback Rd # 600
    Phoenix AZ
    602 916-5000

(P-17454)
FENNEMORE CRAIG PC
Also Called: Fennemore Wendel
1111 Broadway 24th Fl (94607-4139)
PHONE..............................510 834-6600
James Goodnow, *Brnch Mgr*
EMP: 110
SALES (corp-wide): 29.44MM **Privately Held**
Web: www.fennemorelaw.com
SIC: 8111 General practice attorney, lawyer
PA: Fennemore Craig, P.C.
    2394 E Camelback Rd # 600
    Phoenix AZ
    602 916-5000

(P-17455)
FENWICK & WEST LLP (PA)
801 California St (94041-1990)
PHONE..............................650 988-8500
Gordon K Davidson, *Genl Pt*
Laird H Simons, *
Ralph M Pais, *
Scott Pine, *
EMP: 375 EST: 1971
SALES (est): 139.39MM
SALES (corp-wide): 139.39MM **Privately Held**
Web: www.fenwick.com
SIC: 8111 General practice attorney, lawyer

(P-17456)
FENWICK & WEST LLP
555 California St Fl 12 (94104-1503)
PHONE..............................415 875-2300
EMP: 120
SALES (corp-wide): 139.39MM **Privately Held**
Web: www.fenwick.com
SIC: 8111 General practice attorney, lawyer
PA: Fenwick & West Llp
    801 California St
    Mountain View CA
    650 988-8500

(P-17457)
FIRM MCNAMARA LAW
3480 Buskirk Ave Ste 200 (94523-4342)
PHONE..............................925 939-5330
EMP: 73 EST: 2017
SALES (est): 2.34MM **Privately Held**
Web: www.mcnamaralaw.com
SIC: 8111 General practice law office

(P-17458)
FISH & RICHARDSON PC
500 Arguello St Ste 500 (94063-1568)
PHONE..............................650 839-5070
EMP: 147
SALES (corp-wide): 132.63MM **Privately Held**
Web: www.fr.com
SIC: 8111 General practice law office
PA: Fish & Richardson P.C.
    1 Marina Park Dr Ste 1700
    Boston MA
    617 542-5070

(P-17459)
FISH & RICHARDSON PC
12390 El Camino Real (92130-3162)

PHONE..............................858 678-5070
EMP: 153
SALES (corp-wide): 132.63MM **Privately Held**
Web: www.fr.com
SIC: 8111 General practice law office
PA: Fish & Richardson P.C.
    1 Marina Park Dr Ste 1700
    Boston MA
    617 542-5070

(P-17460)
FISHER & PHILLIPS LLP
2050 Main St Ste 1000 (92614-8240)
PHONE..............................949 851-2424
James Mcdonald, *Pt*
EMP: 88
SALES (corp-wide): 171.23MM **Privately Held**
Web: www.fisherphillips.com
SIC: 8111 General practice attorney, lawyer
PA: Fisher & Phillips Llp
    1230 Peachtree St Ne # 3300
    Atlanta GA
    404 231-1400

(P-17461)
FORD WLKER HAGGERTY BEHAR LLP (PA)
1 World Trade Ctr Ste 2700 (90831-2700)
PHONE..............................562 983-2500
William C Haggerty, *Prin*
Jeffrey S Behar, *Prin*
G Richard Ford Retired, *Prin*
Timothy Walker, *
EMP: 68 EST: 1991
SQ FT: 23,000
SALES (est): 14.03MM **Privately Held**
Web: www.fwhb.com
SIC: 8111 General practice attorney, lawyer

(P-17462)
FOX ROTHSCHILD LLP
1 Sansome St Ste 2850 (94104-4426)
PHONE..............................415 539-3336
Raquel L Sefton, *Brnch Mgr*
EMP: 70
SALES (corp-wide): 113.37MM **Privately Held**
Web: www.foxrothschild.com
SIC: 8111 Divorce and family law
PA: Fox Rothschild Llp
    2000 Market St Fl 20
    Philadelphia PA
    215 299-2000

(P-17463)
FREEMAN D AIUTO PROF LAW CORP
Also Called: Freeman Brown Sperry & D Aiuto
1818 Grand Canal Blvd Ste 4 (95207-8151)
PHONE..............................209 474-1818
Maxwell Freeman, *Pr*
EMP: 66 EST: 1965
SQ FT: 2,000
SALES (est): 6.63MM **Privately Held**
Web: www.freemanfirm.com
SIC: 8111 General practice attorney, lawyer

(P-17464)
FULWIDER AND PATTON LLP
111 W Ocean Blvd Ste 1510 (90802-4622)
PHONE..............................310 824-5555
Richard A Bardin, *Mng Pt*
Katherine Mcdaniel, *Pt*
David Pitman, *
Scott Hansen, *
EMP: 100 EST: 1938
SALES (est): 13.61MM **Privately Held**
Web: www.fulpat.com

SIC: 8111 General practice law office

(P-17465)
GIBBS GIDEN LOCHER
1880 Century Park E Ste 1200 (90067-1621)
PHONE..............................310 552-3400
Richard J Wittbrodt, *Prin*
Kenneth C Gibbs, *Prin*
Joseph M Giden, *Prin*
William D Locher, *Prin*
EMP: 70 EST: 1978
SQ FT: 27,000
SALES (est): 11.47MM **Privately Held**
Web: www.gibbsgiden.com
SIC: 8111 General practice attorney, lawyer

(P-17466)
GIBSON DUNN & CRUTCHER INC
333 S Grand Ave (90071-3197)
PHONE..............................213 229-7000
Kenneth M Doran, *Pr*
EMP: 153 EST: 1969
SALES (est): 157.07K
SALES (corp-wide): 2.06MM **Privately Held**
Web: www.gibsondunn.com
SIC: 8111 General practice law office
PA: Gibson, Dunn & Crutcher Llp
    333 S Grand Ave Ste 4600
    Los Angeles CA
    213 229-7000

(P-17467)
GIBSON DUNN & CRUTCHER LLP
1881 Page Mill Rd (94304-1146)
PHONE..............................650 849-5300
Russel Hansel, *Mng Pt*
EMP: 84
SALES (corp-wide): 2.06MM **Privately Held**
Web: www.gibsondunn.com
SIC: 8111 General practice law office
PA: Gibson, Dunn & Crutcher Llp
    333 S Grand Ave Ste 4600
    Los Angeles CA
    213 229-7000

(P-17468)
GIBSON DUNN & CRUTCHER LLP
3161 Michelson Dr Ste 1200 (92612-4400)
PHONE..............................949 451-3800
Karen Kubani, *Brnch Mgr*
EMP: 98
SALES (corp-wide): 2.06MM **Privately Held**
Web: www.gibsondunn.com
SIC: 8111 General practice law office
PA: Gibson, Dunn & Crutcher Llp
    333 S Grand Ave Ste 4600
    Los Angeles CA
    213 229-7000

(P-17469)
GIBSON DUNN & CRUTCHER LLP (PA)
333 S Grand Ave Ste 4600 (90071-1512)
PHONE..............................213 229-7000
Kenneth M Doran, *Prin*
Dan Mummery, *Prin*
M Sean Royall, *Prin*
Frederick Brown, *Prin*
Theodore B Olson, *Prin*
EMP: 500 EST: 1880
SQ FT: 250,000
SALES (est): 2.06MM

8111 - Legal Services (P-17470)

(P-17470)
GIBSON DUNN & CRUTCHER LLP
2029 Century Park E Ste 4000 (90002-3076)
PHONE..................310 552-8500
Julie Denton, *Genl Mgr*
EMP: 98
SALES (corp-wide): 2.06MM **Privately Held**
Web: www.gibsondunn.com
SIC: 8111 General practice law office
PA: Gibson, Dunn & Crutcher Llp
333 S Grand Ave Ste 4600
Los Angeles CA
213 229-7000

(P-17471)
GIBSON DUNN & CRUTCHER LLP
555 Mission St Ste 3000 (94105-0921)
PHONE..................415 393-8200
Mike Saad, *Mgr*
EMP: 83
SALES (corp-wide): 2.06MM **Privately Held**
Web: www.gibsondunn.com
SIC: 8111 General practice law office
PA: Gibson, Dunn & Crutcher Llp
333 S Grand Ave Ste 4600
Los Angeles CA
213 229-7000

(P-17472)
GILBERT KLLY CRWLEY JNNETT LLP (PA)
550 S Hope St Ste 2200 (90071-3200)
PHONE..................213 615-7000
Jon H Tisdale, *Mng Pt*
Paul Bigley, *
Arthur J Mc Keon Iii, *Pt*
Timothy Kenna, *
EMP: 75 EST: 1936
SQ FT: 30,000
SALES (est): 11.11MM
SALES (corp-wide): 11.11MM **Privately Held**
SIC: 8111 General practice law office

(P-17473)
GIPSON HFFMAN PNCONE A PROF CO
1901 Avenue Of The Stars Ste 1100 (90067-6001)
PHONE..................310 556-4660
Lawrence R Barnett, *Pr*
Robert E Gipson, *
Kenneth I Sidle, *
Robert H Steinberg, *
EMP: 70 EST: 1982
SQ FT: 27,000
SALES (est): 9.2MM **Privately Held**
Web: www.ghplaw.com
SIC: 8111 General practice attorney, lawyer

(P-17474)
GIRARDI KEESE (PA)
1126 Wilshire Blvd (90017-1904)
PHONE..................213 977-0211
Thomas V Girardi, *Pt*
Robert M Keese, *Pt*
EMP: 95 EST: 1976
SQ FT: 5,000
SALES (est): 9.67MM
SALES (corp-wide): 9.67MM **Privately Held**
Web: www.girardikeese.com
SIC: 8111 General practice law office

(P-17475)
GLASER WEIL FINK JACOBS (PA)
10250 Constellation Blvd Fl 19 (90067-6229)
PHONE..................310 553-3000
Terry Christensen, *Mng Pt*
Barry E Fink, *
Patricia L Glaser, *
Peter Weil, *
Allen Gilbert, *
EMP: 160 EST: 1988
SQ FT: 76,000
SALES (est): 34.42MM
SALES (corp-wide): 34.42MM **Privately Held**
Web: www.glaserweil.com
SIC: 8111 General practice law office

(P-17476)
GORDON REES SCULLY MANSUKHANI
Also Called: Gordon & Rees
1111 Broadway Ste 1700 (94607-4023)
PHONE..................510 463-8600
Dion N Cominos, *Prin*
EMP: 115
SALES (corp-wide): 271.79MM **Privately Held**
Web: www.grsm.com
SIC: 8111 Specialized law offices, attorneys
PA: Gordon Rees Scully Mansukhani, Llp.
275 Battery St Ste 2000
San Francisco CA
415 986-5900

(P-17477)
GORDON REES SCULLY MANSUKHANI
633 W 5th St 52nd Fl (90071-2005)
PHONE..................213 576-5000
Scott Sirlin, *Brnch Mgr*
EMP: 103
SALES (corp-wide): 271.79MM **Privately Held**
Web: www.grsm.com
SIC: 8111 Specialized law offices, attorneys
PA: Gordon Rees Scully Mansukhani, Llp.
275 Battery St Ste 2000
San Francisco CA
415 986-5900

(P-17478)
GORDON REES SCULLY MANSUKHANI
101 W Broadway Ste 1600 (92101-8217)
PHONE..................619 696-6700
Gary Zacher, *Mng Pt*
EMP: 138
SQ FT: 7,000
SALES (corp-wide): 271.79MM **Privately Held**
Web: www.grsm.com
SIC: 8111 Specialized law offices, attorneys
PA: Gordon Rees Scully Mansukhani, Llp.
275 Battery St Ste 2000
San Francisco CA
415 986-5900

(P-17479)
GORDON REES SCULLY MANSUKHANI (PA)
275 Battery St Ste 2000 (94111-3327)
PHONE..................415 986-5900
Dion N Cominos, *Mng Pt*
David C Capell, *Mng Pt*
Linda M Moroney, *Mng Pt*
EMP: 325 EST: 1974
SQ FT: 57,500
SALES (est): 271.79MM
SALES (corp-wide): 271.79MM **Privately Held**
Web: www.grsm.com
SIC: 8111 Corporate, partnership and business law

(P-17480)
GRAHAM & JAMES LLP
Also Called: Squires, Sanders and Dempsey
1 Maritime Plz Fl 3 (94111-3406)
PHONE..................415 954-0200
Tom Wobster, *Mgr*
EMP: 700 EST: 1925
SQ FT: 60,000
SALES (est): 26.86MM **Privately Held**
SIC: 8111 General practice law office

(P-17481)
GREENBERG GLSKER FLDS CLMAN MC
2049 Century Park E Ste 2600 (90067-3101)
PHONE..................310 553-3610
Jonathan R Fitzgarrald, *Prin*
Arthur N Greenberg, *Pt*
Stephen Claman, *Pt*
Bert Fields, *Pt*
Ricardo P Cestero, *Pt*
EMP: 200 EST: 1959
SQ FT: 80,000
SALES (est): 26.18MM **Privately Held**
Web: www.greenbergglusker.com
SIC: 8111 General practice attorney, lawyer

(P-17482)
GREENBERG TRAURIG LLP
101 2nd St Ste 2200 (94105-3668)
PHONE..................415 655-1300
Evan S Nadel, *Brnch Mgr*
EMP: 65
SALES (corp-wide): 495.87MM **Privately Held**
Web: www.gtlaw.com
SIC: 8111 General practice attorney, lawyer
HQ: Greenberg Traurig, Llp
1 Intl Pl Ste 2000
Boston MA

(P-17483)
GREENBERG TRAURIG LLP
1840 Century Park E Ste 1900 (90067-2101)
PHONE..................310 586-7708
Richard Rowan, *Brnch Mgr*
EMP: 76
SALES (corp-wide): 495.87MM **Privately Held**
Web: www.gtlaw.com
SIC: 8111 General practice attorney, lawyer
HQ: Greenberg Traurig, Llp
1 Intl Pl Ste 2000
Boston MA

(P-17484)
GREENBERG TRAURIG LLP
Also Called: Greenberg Traurig
1900 University Ave Fl 5 (94303-2283)
PHONE..................650 328-8500
Lance Joseph, *Brnch Mgr*
EMP: 73
SALES (corp-wide): 495.87MM **Privately Held**
Web: www.gtlaw.com
SIC: 8111 General practice attorney, lawyer
HQ: Greenberg Traurig, Llp
1 Intl Pl Ste 2000
Boston MA

(P-17485)
GREENBERG TRAURIG LLP
400 Capitol Mall (95814-4428)
PHONE..................916 442-1111
Kathy Kossak, *Mgr*
EMP: 148
SALES (corp-wide): 495.87MM **Privately Held**
Web: www.gtlaw.com
SIC: 8111 General practice attorney, lawyer
HQ: Greenberg Traurig, Llp
1 Intl Pl Ste 2000
Boston MA

(P-17486)
GREENBERG TRAURIG LLP
Also Called: Greenberg Traurig
18565 Jamboree Rd Ste 500 (92612-2562)
PHONE..................949 732-6500
Ray Lee, *Mng Pt*
EMP: 96
SALES (corp-wide): 495.87MM **Privately Held**
Web: www.gtlaw.com
SIC: 8111 General practice attorney, lawyer
HQ: Greenberg Traurig, Llp
1 Intl Pl Ste 2000
Boston MA

(P-17487)
GREENE RDVSKY MALONEY SHARE LP
4 Embarcadero Ctr Ste 4000 (94111-4106)
PHONE..................415 981-1400
Mark Hennigh, *Mng Pt*
Richard Green, *Sr Pt*
Joseph Rodovsky, *Pt*
Graham Maloney, *Pt*
Donald Share, *Pt*
EMP: 69 EST: 1984
SQ FT: 18,800
SALES (est): 9.89MM **Privately Held**
SIC: 8111 Specialized law offices, attorneys

(P-17488)
GUNDERSON DTTMER STUGH VLLNUVE (PA)
Also Called: Gunderson Dettmer
550 Allerton St (94063-1524)
PHONE..................650 321-2400
Robert Gunderson, *Pt*
Scott Dettmer, *Pt*
Brooks Stough, *Pt*
Thomas Villeneuve, *Pt*
Steve Franklin, *Pt*
▲ EMP: 200 EST: 1995
SALES (est): 78.02MM **Privately Held**
Web: www.gunder.com
SIC: 8111 General practice law office

(P-17489)
HAIGHT BROWN & BONESTEEL LLP (PA)
Also Called: Haight
555 S Flower St Ste 4500 (90071)
PHONE..................213 542-8000
S Christian Stouder, *Mng Pt*
Carolyn Harper, *CFO*
EMP: 80 EST: 1980
SQ FT: 36,265
SALES (est): 22.77MM
SALES (corp-wide): 22.77MM **Privately Held**
Web: www.hbblaw.com

SIC: 8111 General practice law office

(P-17490)
HANSON BRIDGETT LLP (PA)
Also Called: Hanson Bridgett
425 Market St Fl 26 (94105-2403)
PHONE..................................415 543-2055
EMP: 263 EST: 1958
SQ FT: 79,120
SALES (est): 49.34MM
SALES (corp-wide): 49.34MM **Privately Held**
Web: www.hansonbridgett.com
SIC: 8111 General practice attorney, lawyer

(P-17491)
HART KNLE PNTECOST A PROF CORP
4 Hutton Centre Dr Ste 900 (92707)
PHONE..................................714 432-8700
Robert S Coldren, Pr
William R Hart, *
Gary R King, *
EMP: 60 EST: 1982
SQ FT: 20,000
SALES (est): 7.96MM **Privately Held**
Web: www.hkplawfirm.com
SIC: 8111 General practice attorney, lawyer

(P-17492)
HASSARD BONNINGTON LLP (PA)
Also Called: HB
111 Pine St (94111-3912)
PHONE..................................415 288-9800
James M Goodman, Genl Pt
Phillip F Ward, Pt
EMP: 77 EST: 1945
SALES (est): 10.8MM
SALES (corp-wide): 10.8MM **Privately Held**
Web: www.hassard.com
SIC: 8111 General practice attorney, lawyer

(P-17493)
HIGGS FLETCHER & MACK LLP
Also Called: Goproto
401 W A St Ste 2600 (92101-3524)
PHONE..................................619 236-1551
John Morrell, Genl Pt
Anna F Roppo, Pt
Phillip C Samouis, Pt
EMP: 150 EST: 1939
SQ FT: 45,000
SALES (est): 25.77MM **Privately Held**
Web: www.higgslaw.com
SIC: 8111 General practice attorney, lawyer

(P-17494)
HILL FARRER & BURRILL
Also Called: One California Plaza
300 S Grand Ave Fl 37 (90071-3147)
PHONE..................................213 620-0460
Scott Gilmore, Pt
Jack R White, Pt
Kyle D Brown, Pt
William M Bitting, Pt
Stanley E Tobin, Pt
EMP: 100 EST: 1923
SQ FT: 32,000
SALES (est): 13.7MM **Privately Held**
Web: www.hillfarrer.com
SIC: 8111 General practice law office

(P-17495)
HOLLAND & KNIGHT LLP
400 S Hope St Ste 800 (90071-2809)
PHONE..................................213 896-2400
Maita Prout, Mgr

EMP: 99
SALES (corp-wide): 430.83MM **Privately Held**
Web: foundation.hklaw.com
SIC: 8111 General practice attorney, lawyer
PA: Holland & Knight Llp
524 Grand Regency Blvd
Brandon FL
813 901-4200

(P-17496)
HOPKINS & CARLEY A LAW CORP (PA)
70 S 1st St (95113-2406)
P.O. Box 1469 (95109-1469)
PHONE..................................408 286-9800
William S Klein, Prin
John F Hopkins, *
EMP: 80 EST: 1968
SQ FT: 33,000
SALES (est): 28.19MM
SALES (corp-wide): 28.19MM **Privately Held**
Web: www.hopkinscarley.com
SIC: 8111 Corporate, partnership and business law

(P-17497)
HUESTON HENNIGAN LLP
523 W 6th St Ste 400 (90014-1208)
PHONE..................................213 788-4340
Marshall A Camp, Pt
Douglas J Dixon, Pt
Alexander C D Giza, Pt
Brian J Hennigan, Pt
John C Hueston, Pt
EMP: 80 EST: 2015
SQ FT: 25,000
SALES (est): 10.7MM **Privately Held**
Web: www.hueston.com
SIC: 8111 General practice attorney, lawyer

(P-17498)
HUNTON ANDREWS KURTH LLP
50 California St Ste 1700 (94111-4604)
PHONE..................................415 975-3700
Fraser Mcalpine, Pt
EMP: 62
SALES (corp-wide): 402.45MM **Privately Held**
Web: www.huntonak.com
SIC: 8111 General practice attorney, lawyer
PA: Hunton Andrews Kurth Llp
951 E Byrd St Ste 200
Richmond VA
804 788-8200

(P-17499)
IMHOFF & ASSOCIATES PC
Also Called: Miller and Associates
12424 Wilshire Blvd Ste 770 (90025-1065)
PHONE..................................310 691-2200
Jim Stefanucci, Mgr
EMP: 100 EST: 2001
SALES (est): 10.95MM **Privately Held**
Web: www.criminalattorney.com
SIC: 8111 General practice law office

(P-17500)
IMMIGRANT DEFENDERS LAW CENTER
Also Called: IMMDEF
634 S Spring St Fl 10 (90014-1901)
PHONE..................................213 634-0999
Lindsay Toczylowski, Ex Dir
Susan Alva, *
EMP: 85 EST: 2015
SALES (est): 10.76MM **Privately Held**
Web: www.immdef.org
SIC: 8111 Legal services

(P-17501)
IRELL & MANELLA LLP
840 Newport Center Dr Ste 400 (92660)
PHONE..................................949 760-0991
Nancy Adams, Mgr
EMP: 365
SALES (corp-wide): 49.86MM **Privately Held**
Web: www.irell.com
SIC: 8111 General practice attorney, lawyer
PA: Irell & Manella Llp
1800 Avenue Of The Stars # 900
Los Angeles CA
310 277-1010

(P-17502)
IRELL & MANELLA LLP (PA)
1800 Avenue Of The Stars Ste 900 (90067-4276)
PHONE..................................310 277-1010
Keith Orso, Pt
Ben Hattenbach, Pt
Lisa Glasser, Pt
Matt Ashley, Ofcr
Thomas Edwards, Ex Dir
EMP: 185 EST: 1941
SQ FT: 154,000
SALES (est): 49.86MM
SALES (corp-wide): 49.86MM **Privately Held**
Web: www.irell.com
SIC: 8111 General practice law office

(P-17503)
JACKOWAY TYRMAN WRTHMER ASTEN
1925 Century Park E 2nd Fl (90067-2701)
PHONE..................................310 553-0305
Barry Hirsch, Pr
EMP: 100 EST: 1976
SQ FT: 3,000
SALES (est): 9.25MM **Privately Held**
Web: www.jtwamm.com
SIC: 8111 General practice law office

(P-17504)
JACOBY & MEYERS ATTYS LLP
10900 Wilshire Blvd Ste 930 (90024-6501)
PHONE..................................310 312-3300
Mirtha Lopez, Prin
EMP: 84 EST: 2019
SALES (est): 2.08MM **Privately Held**
Web: www.jacobymeyers.com
SIC: 8111 General practice attorney, lawyer

(P-17505)
JEFFER MNGELS BTLR MTCHELL LLP (PA)
Also Called: Jmbm
1900 Avenue Of The Stars Fl 7 (90067-4301)
PHONE..................................310 203-3080
Bruce P Jeffer, Managing Member
Bruce P Jeffer, Mng Pt
Robert E Mangels, Pt
James R Butler Junior, Pt
Mark Marmaro, Pt
▲ EMP: 190 EST: 1981
SALES (est): 46.29MM
SALES (corp-wide): 46.29MM **Privately Held**
Web: www.jmbm.com
SIC: 8111 General practice attorney, lawyer

(P-17506)
JONES DAY LIMITED PARTNERSHIP
Also Called: Jones Day
555 S Flower St Fl 50 (90071-2452)

PHONE..................................213 489-3939
Brian A Sun, Pt
EMP: 106
SALES (corp-wide): 541.17MM **Privately Held**
Web: www.jonesday.com
SIC: 8111 7389 General practice attorney, lawyer; Personal service agents, brokers, and bureaus
PA: Jones Day Limited Partnership
N Point 901 Lakeside Ave
Cleveland OH
216 586-3939

(P-17507)
JONES DAY LIMITED PARTNERSHIP
4655 Executive Dr Ste 1500 (92121-3106)
PHONE..................................858 314-1200
Karen P Hewitt, Pt
EMP: 60
SALES (corp-wide): 541.17MM **Privately Held**
Web: www.jonesday.com
SIC: 8111 General practice attorney, lawyer
PA: Jones Day Limited Partnership
N Point 901 Lakeside Ave
Cleveland OH
216 586-3939

(P-17508)
JP MORGAN & CO
1999 Avenue Of The Stars Ste 2600 (90067)
PHONE..................................213 485-1234
James Alexander, CFO
EMP: 63 EST: 2019
SALES (est): 509.24K **Privately Held**
Web: www.jpmorgan.com
SIC: 8111 Legal services

(P-17509)
JUSTICE DVRSITY CTR OF THE BAR
1360 Mission St (94103-2626)
PHONE..................................415 575-3130
Teresa Friend, Brnch Mgr
EMP: 71
Web: www.sfbar.org
SIC: 8111 Legal aid service
HQ: The Justice And Diversity Center Of The Bar Association Of San Francisco
201 Mission St Ste 400
San Francisco CA
415 982-1600

(P-17510)
K&L GATES LLP
4 Embarcadero Ctr Lbby 10 (94111-4124)
PHONE..................................415 882-8200
Michael Mccabe, Pr
EMP: 69
SALES (corp-wide): 1.18B **Privately Held**
Web: www.klgates.com
SIC: 8111 General practice attorney, lawyer
PA: K&L Gates Llp
210 6th Ave Ste 1100
Pittsburgh PA
412 355-6500

(P-17511)
K&L GATES LLP
10100 Santa Monica Blvd Ste 700 (90067-4104)
PHONE..................................310 552-5000
Karen Doyle, Mgr
EMP: 81
SALES (corp-wide): 1.18B **Privately Held**
Web: www.klgates.com

8111 - Legal Services (P-17512)

SIC: 8111 General practice law office
PA: K&L Gates Llp
  210 6th Ave Ste 1100
  Pittsburgh PA
  412 355-6500

(P-17512)
KAHANA & FELD LLP
2603 Main St Ste 900 (92614-4270)
PHONE..................................949 812-4781
EMP: 60 EST: 2019
SALES (est): 3.64MM Privately Held
Web: www.kahanafeld.com
SIC: 8111 Specialized law offices, attorneys

(P-17513)
KATTEN MUCHIN ROSENMAN LLP
2029 Century Park E Ste 2600 (90067-3012)
PHONE..................................310 788-4400
Tanya Russell, Brnch Mgr
EMP: 72
SALES (corp-wide): 12.72MM Privately Held
Web: www.katten.com
SIC: 8111 General practice law office
PA: Katten Muchin Rosenman Llp
  525 W Monroe St Ste 1900
  Chicago IL
  312 902-5200

(P-17514)
KAZAN MCCLAIN STTRLEY GRNWOOD
55 Harrison St Ste 400 (94607-3858)
PHONE..................................877 995-6372
Steven Kazan, Pt
David Mcclain, Pt
Joseph Satterley, *
Gordon Greenwood, *
Denise Abrams, *
EMP: 108 EST: 1975
SALES (est): 1.51MM Privately Held
Web: www.kazanlaw.com
SIC: 8111 General practice law office

(P-17515)
KEESAL YOUNG LOGAN A PROF CORP (PA)
400 Oceangate (90802-4325)
PHONE..................................562 436-2000
Samuel A Keesal Junior, CEO
J Stephen Young, *
EMP: 90 EST: 1970
SQ FT: 65,000
SALES (est): 10.57K
SALES (corp-wide): 10.57K Privately Held
Web: www.kyl.com
SIC: 8111 General practice law office

(P-17516)
KEKER VAN NEST & PETERS LLP
633 Battery St Bsmt 91 (94111-1801)
PHONE..................................415 391-5400
Robert A Van Nest, *
Jeffery R Chanin, *
Jan N Little, *
Susan J Harriman, *
EMP: 100 EST: 1978
SQ FT: 70,000
SALES (est): 170.25K Privately Held
Web: www.keker.com
SIC: 8111 Criminal law

(P-17517)
KILPATRICK TWNSEND STCKTON LLP
2 Embarcadero Ctr Ste 1900 (94111-3823)
PHONE..................................415 576-0200
EMP: 72
SALES (corp-wide): 235.05MM Privately Held
Web: www.kilpatricktownsend.com
SIC: 8111 General practice attorney, lawyer
PA: Kilpatrick Townsend & Stockton Llp
  1100 Peachtree St Ne # 28
  Atlanta GA
  404 815-6500

(P-17518)
KIMBALL TIREY & ST JOHN LLP (PA)
7676 Hazard Center Dr Ste 900 (92108-4515)
PHONE..................................619 234-1690
Theodore C Kimball, Pt
Leslie Mason, Prin
EMP: 70 EST: 1977
SQ FT: 6,000
SALES (est): 24.14MM
SALES (corp-wide): 24.14MM Privately Held
Web: www.kts-law.com
SIC: 8111 General practice attorney, lawyer

(P-17519)
KING & SPALDING LLP
601 California Ave (94304-1101)
PHONE..................................650 422-6700
Courtland Reichman, Brnch Mgr
EMP: 60
SALES (corp-wide): 248.84MM Privately Held
Web: www.kslaw.com
SIC: 8111 General practice law office
PA: King & Spalding Llp
  1180 Peachtree St
  Atlanta GA
  404 572-4600

(P-17520)
KING & SPALDING LLP
50 California St Ste 3300 (94111-4778)
PHONE..................................415 318-1200
Donald Zimmer, Pt
EMP: 63
SALES (corp-wide): 248.84MM Privately Held
Web: www.kslaw.com
SIC: 8111 General practice law office
PA: King & Spalding Llp
  1180 Peachtree St
  Atlanta GA
  404 572-4600

(P-17521)
KIRKLAND & ELLIS LLP
3330 Hillview Ave (94304-1059)
PHONE..................................650 859-7000
Alex Kaufman, Brnch Mgr
EMP: 378
SALES (corp-wide): 504.86MM Privately Held
Web: www.kirkland.com
SIC: 8111 General practice attorney, lawyer
PA: Kirkland & Ellis Llp
  300 N La Salle Dr # 2400
  Chicago IL
  312 862-2000

(P-17522)
KIRKLAND & ELLIS LLP
2049 Century Park E Ste 3700 (90067-3101)
PHONE..................................310 552-4200
EMP: 100
SALES (corp-wide): 504.86MM Privately Held
Web: www.kirkland.com
SIC: 8111 General practice attorney, lawyer
PA: Kirkland & Ellis Llp
  300 N La Salle Dr # 2400
  Chicago IL
  312 862-2000

(P-17523)
KIRKLAND & ELLIS LLP
555 S Flower St Ste 3700 (90071-2432)
PHONE..................................213 680-8400
EMP: 175
SALES (corp-wide): 504.86MM Privately Held
Web: www.kirkland.com
SIC: 8111 General practice attorney, lawyer
PA: Kirkland & Ellis Llp
  300 N La Salle Dr # 2400
  Chicago IL
  312 862-2000

(P-17524)
KIRKLAND & ELLIS LLP
555 California St Ste 2700 (94104-1503)
PHONE..................................415 439-1400
Caroline Recht, Mgr
EMP: 200
SALES (corp-wide): 504.86MM Privately Held
Web: www.kirkland.com
SIC: 8111 General practice attorney, lawyer
PA: Kirkland & Ellis Llp
  300 N La Salle Dr # 2400
  Chicago IL
  312 862-2000

(P-17525)
KIRKLAND & ELLIS LLP
333 S Hope St Ste 3000 (90071-3039)
PHONE..................................213 680-8400
Cynthia Barnes, Off Mgr
EMP: 500
SALES (corp-wide): 504.86MM Privately Held
Web: www.kirkland.com
SIC: 8111 General practice law office
PA: Kirkland & Ellis Llp
  300 N La Salle Dr # 2400
  Chicago IL
  312 862-2000

(P-17526)
KLEIN DENATALE GOLDNER (PA)
Also Called: Klein Dntale Gldner Cper Rsnli
10000 Stockdale Hwy Ste 200 (93311-3603)
P.O. Box 11172 (93389-1172)
PHONE..................................661 485-2100
Anthony J Klein, Pt
Barry L Goldner, Pt
Thomas V Denatale Junior, Pt
Jay L Rosenlieb, Pt
David J Cooper, Pt
EMP: 60 EST: 2007
SALES (est): 13.57MM
SALES (corp-wide): 13.57MM Privately Held
Web: www.kleinlaw.com
SIC: 8111 General practice attorney, lawyer

(P-17527)
KNIGHT LAW GROUP LLP
10250 Constellation Blvd Ste 2500 (90067-6225)
P.O. Box 512906 (90051-0906)
PHONE..................................424 355-1155
EMP: 87 EST: 2018
SALES (est): 9.46MM Privately Held
Web: www.lemonlawhelp.com
SIC: 8111 General practice law office

(P-17528)
KNOBBE MARTENS OLSON BEAR LLP
12790 El Camino Real Ste 100 (92130)
PHONE..................................858 707-4000
Wesly Pettus, Brnch Mgr
EMP: 64
SALES (corp-wide): 66.71MM Privately Held
Web: www.knobbe.com
SIC: 8111 Patent, trademark and copyright law
PA: Knobbe Martens Olson & Bear, Llp
  2040 Main St Fl 14
  Irvine CA
  949 760-0404

(P-17529)
KNOBBE MARTENS OLSON BEAR LLP (PA)
2040 Main St Fl 14 (92614-8214)
PHONE..................................949 760-0404
Steven J Nataupsky, Mng Pt
Steven Nataupsky, *
James B Bear, *
William B Bunker, *
William H Nieman, *
EMP: 350 EST: 1962
SQ FT: 120,000
SALES (est): 66.71MM
SALES (corp-wide): 66.71MM Privately Held
Web: www.knobbe.com
SIC: 8111 General practice law office

(P-17530)
KRAMER LVIN NFTLIS FRANKEL LLP
990 Marsh Rd (94025-1949)
PHONE..................................650 752-1700
Paul Andre, Mng Pt
EMP: 89
SALES (corp-wide): 100.08MM Privately Held
Web: www.kramerlevin.com
SIC: 8111 General practice attorney, lawyer
PA: Kramer Levin Naftalis & Frankel Llp
  1177 Ave Of The Americas
  New York NY
  212 715-9100

(P-17531)
KRONICK MSKVITZ TDMANN GRARD A (PA)
1331 Garden Hwy Ste 350 (95833-9774)
PHONE..................................916 321-4500
Robert Murphy, Ch
Michael A Grob, *
Thomas C Hughes Iii, VP
Thomas W Birmingham, *
Robin L Stewart, *
EMP: 98 EST: 1959
SALES (est): 20.87MM
SALES (corp-wide): 20.87MM Privately Held
Web: www.kmtg.com
SIC: 8111 General practice law office

(P-17532)
LA FOLETTE JOHNSON DEHASS SESL
865 S Figueroa St # 3200 (90017-2507)
PHONE..................................213 426-3600

PRODUCTS & SERVICES SECTION
8111 - Legal Services (P-17552)

Eva Cohen, *Dir Fin*
EMP: 88 EST: 2010
SALES (est): 2.82MM Privately Held
SIC: 8111 General practice attorney, lawyer

(P-17533)
LA FOLLTTE JHNSON DE HAAS FSLE (PA)
701 N Brand Blvd Ste 600 (91203-1213)
PHONE.................213 426-3600
Daren T Johnson, *Pr*
Louis De Haas Junior, *VP*
Don Fesler, *
Brian Birnie, *
Alfred Gerisch Junior, *Treas*
EMP: 105 EST: 1953
SALES (est): 17.99MM
SALES (corp-wide): 17.99MM Privately Held
Web: www.ljdfa.com
SIC: 8111 General practice law office

(P-17534)
LANAHAN & REILLEY LLP (PA)
600 Bicentennial Way # 300 (95403-7427)
P.O. Box 5227 (95402-5227)
PHONE.................415 856-4700
EMP: 119
SQ FT: 18,030
SALES (est): 9.28MM
SALES (corp-wide): 9.28MM Privately Held
Web: www.lanahan.com
SIC: 8111 General practice attorney, lawyer

(P-17535)
LATHAM & WATKINS LLP
12670 High Bluff Dr Ste 100 (92130-3086)
PHONE.................858 523-5400
Bruce Shepard, *Pt*
EMP: 335
SALES (corp-wide): 486.91MM Privately Held
Web: rg-www-prod-cd.azurewebsites.net
SIC: 8111 General practice attorney, lawyer
PA: Latham & Watkins Llp
 555 W 5th St Ste 300
 Los Angeles CA
 213 485-1234

(P-17536)
LATHAM & WATKINS LLP (PA)
555 W 5th St Ste 300 (90013-1020)
PHONE.................213 485-1234
David Gordon, *Pt*
John Clair, *Pt*
Allen Wang, *Pt*
Philip Rossetti, *Pt*
Jean Paul Poitras, *Pt*
EMP: 570 EST: 1934
SALES (est): 486.91MM
SALES (corp-wide): 486.91MM Privately Held
Web: rg-www-prod-cd.azurewebsites.net
SIC: 8111 General practice attorney, lawyer

(P-17537)
LATHAM & WATKINS LLP
555 W 5th St Ste 300 (90013-1020)
PHONE.................213 891-7108
EMP: 266
SALES (corp-wide): 486.91MM Privately Held
Web: rg-www-prod-cd.azurewebsites.net
SIC: 8111 General practice attorney, lawyer
PA: Latham & Watkins Llp
 555 W 5th St Ste 300
 Los Angeles CA
 213 485-1234

(P-17538)
LATHAM & WATKINS LLP
650 Town Center Dr Ste 2000 (92626-7135)
PHONE.................714 540-1235
Shayne Kennedy, *Mng Pt*
EMP: 317
SALES (corp-wide): 486.91MM Privately Held
Web: rg-www-prod-cd.azurewebsites.net
SIC: 8111 General practice attorney, lawyer
PA: Latham & Watkins Llp
 555 W 5th St Ste 300
 Los Angeles CA
 213 485-1234

(P-17539)
LATHAM & WATKINS LLP
505 Montgomery St Ste 2000 (94111-2562)
PHONE.................415 391-0600
Scott Haber, *Mng Pt*
EMP: 241
SALES (corp-wide): 486.91MM Privately Held
Web: rg-www-prod-cd.azurewebsites.net
SIC: 8111 General practice attorney, lawyer
PA: Latham & Watkins Llp
 555 W 5th St Ste 300
 Los Angeles CA
 213 485-1234

(P-17540)
LAUGHLIN FALBO LEVY MORESI LLP (PA)
1001 Galaxy Way Ste 200 (94520-5735)
PHONE.................510 628-0496
John Geyer, *Pt*
John Geyer, *Mng Pt*
John Bennett Junior, *Pt*
Phillip J Klein, *Pt*
James Wesolowski, *Pt*
EMP: 76 EST: 1985
SALES (est): 38.59MM
SALES (corp-wide): 38.59MM Privately Held
Web: www.lflm.com
SIC: 8111 General practice law office

(P-17541)
LAW OFFCES LES ZEVE A PROF COR
30 Corporate Park Ste 450 (92606-3401)
PHONE.................714 848-7920
Les Zieve, *Prin*
Mark Kayton, *
EMP: 105 EST: 1991
SQ FT: 1,000
SALES (est): 10.52MM Privately Held
SIC: 8111 General practice attorney, lawyer

(P-17542)
LAW OFFICES MICHAEL BURGIS PC
5900 Sepulveda Blvd Ste 215 (91411-2509)
PHONE.................818 994-9870
Michael Burgis, *Managing Member*
EMP: 60 EST: 2011
SALES (est): 5.77MM Privately Held
Web: www.burgislaw.com
SIC: 8111 General practice attorney, lawyer

(P-17543)
LEGAL SOLUTIONS HOLDINGS INC
Also Called: Getmedlegal
955 Overland Ct Ste 200 (91773-1747)
PHONE.................800 244-3495
Greg Webber, *CEO*
Kenneth Gleockler, *

Keahi Kakugawa, *
Harren Investors li Lp, *Prin*
Harren Investors li-b Lp, *Prin*
EMP: 237 EST: 1986
SALES (est): 9.35MM Privately Held
SIC: 8111 Legal services

(P-17544)
LEWIS BRSBOIS BSGARD SMITH LLP (PA)
633 W 5th St Ste 4000 (90071-2074)
PHONE.................213 250-1800
Robert F Lewis, *Mng Pt*
Roy M Brisbois, *Pt*
Christopher P Bisgaard, *Pt*
EMP: 650 EST: 1979
SQ FT: 80,000
SALES (est): 284.92MM
SALES (corp-wide): 284.92MM Privately Held
Web: www.lewisbrsbois.com
SIC: 8111 General practice law office

(P-17545)
LEWIS BRSBOIS BSGARD SMITH LLP
701 B St Ste 1900 (92101-8198)
PHONE.................619 233-1006
Susan O' Brien, *Mgr*
EMP: 168
SALES (corp-wide): 284.92MM Privately Held
Web: www.lewisbrsbois.com
SIC: 8111 General practice law office
PA: Lewis Brisbois Bisgaard & Smith Llp
 633 W 5th St Ste 4000
 Los Angeles CA
 213 250-1800

(P-17546)
LEWIS BRSBOIS BSGARD SMITH LLP
650 Town Center Dr Ste 1400 (92626-1989)
PHONE.................714 545-9200
Shawn Derfer, *Mgr*
EMP: 109
SALES (corp-wide): 284.92MM Privately Held
Web: www.lewisbrsbois.com
SIC: 8111 General practice law office
PA: Lewis Brisbois Bisgaard & Smith Llp
 633 W 5th St Ste 4000
 Los Angeles CA
 213 250-1800

(P-17547)
LEWIS BRSBOIS BSGARD SMITH LLP
333 Bush St (94104-2806)
PHONE.................415 362-2580
Cindy Aiello, *Mgr*
EMP: 115
SALES (corp-wide): 284.92MM Privately Held
Web: www.lewisbrsbois.com
SIC: 8111 General practice law office
PA: Lewis Brisbois Bisgaard & Smith Llp
 633 W 5th St Ste 4000
 Los Angeles CA
 213 250-1800

(P-17548)
LEWIS BRSBOIS BSGARD SMITH LLP
650 E Hospitality Ln Ste 600 (92408-3535)
PHONE.................909 387-1130
John Lowenthal, *Mgr*
EMP: 71

SQ FT: 6,203
SALES (corp-wide): 284.92MM Privately Held
Web: www.lewisbrsbois.com
SIC: 8111 General practice law office
PA: Lewis Brisbois Bisgaard & Smith Llp
 633 W 5th St Ste 4000
 Los Angeles CA
 213 250-1800

(P-17549)
LIEFF CBRSER HMANN BRNSTEIN LL (PA)
275 Battery St 29th Fl (94111-3305)
PHONE.................415 788-0245
Robert L Lieff, *Pt*
Richard M Heimann, *Pt*
Elizabeth J Cabraser, *Pt*
William Bernstein, *Pt*
James M Finberg, *Pt*
◆ EMP: 120 EST: 1972
SQ FT: 42,592
SALES (est): 24.41MM
SALES (corp-wide): 24.41MM Privately Held
Web: www.lieffcabraser.com
SIC: 8111 Antitrust and trade regulation law

(P-17550)
LINER LLP
Also Called: Liner Law
1100 Glendon Ave 14th (90024-3503)
PHONE.................310 500-3500
Stuart A Liner, *Mng Pt*
EMP: 104 EST: 1996
SQ FT: 21,000
SALES (est): 23.43MM Privately Held
Web: www.linerlawgroup.com
SIC: 8111 General practice law office
HQ: Dla Piper Llp (Us)
 650 S Exeter St
 Baltimore MD
 410 580-3000

(P-17551)
LITTLER MENDELSON PC (PA)
Also Called: Littler
333 Bush St Fl 34 (94104-2874)
P.O. Box 45547 (94145-0547)
PHONE.................415 433-1940
Erin Webber, *Pr*
Michael Wilder, *
Marko Mrkonich, *
Peter Susser, *
Steven R Mc Cown, *
EMP: 500 EST: 1942
SQ FT: 85,000
SALES (est): 481.15MM
SALES (corp-wide): 481.15MM Privately Held
Web: www.littler.com
SIC: 8111 General practice law office

(P-17552)
LLC BATES WHITE
322 8th St (92014-2807)
PHONE.................858 523-2150
Dorris Ballentine, *Brnch Mgr*
EMP: 130
SALES (corp-wide): 44.11MM Privately Held
Web: www.bateswhite.com
SIC: 8111 General practice attorney, lawyer
PA: Bates White, Llc
 2001 K St Nw Bldg Ste 5
 Washington DC
 202 747-1436

8111 - Legal Services (P-17553)

(P-17553)
LLP MAYER BROWN
2 Palo Alto Sq Ste 300 (94306-2122)
PHONE..................650 331-2000
Martin Collins, *Brnch Mgr*
EMP: 63
SALES (corp-wide): 456.54MM **Privately Held**
Web: www.mayerbrown.com
SIC: 8111 General practice attorney, lawyer
PA: Mayer Brown Llp
71 S Wacker Dr Ste 3300
Chicago IL
312 782-0600

(P-17554)
LLP MAYER BROWN
Also Called: Mayer Brown & Platt
350 S Grand Ave Ste 2500 (90071-3486)
PHONE..................213 229-9500
Jim Tancula, *Mgr*
EMP: 430
SALES (corp-wide): 456.54MM **Privately Held**
SIC: 8111 General practice attorney, lawyer
PA: Mayer Brown Llp
71 S Wacker Dr Ste 3300
Chicago IL
312 782-0600

(P-17555)
LLP RAINES FELDMAN
1900 Avenue Of The Stars (90067-4410)
PHONE..................310 440-4100
EMP: 77 **EST:** 2011
SALES (est): 5.33MM **Privately Held**
Web: www.raineslaw.com
SIC: 8111 General practice law office

(P-17556)
LOEB & LOEB LLP (PA)
Also Called: Loeb & Loeb
10100 Santa Monica Blvd Ste 2200 (90067-4120)
PHONE..................310 282-2000
Barry I Slotnick, *Ch*
Jerry Post, *Chief*
Kenneth B Anderson, *Pt*
Stan Johnson, *Ch*
Robert A Meyer, *Ch*
EMP: 134 **EST:** 1909
SALES (est): 66.83MM
SALES (corp-wide): 66.83MM **Privately Held**
Web: www.loeb.com
SIC: 8111 General practice attorney, lawyer

(P-17557)
LORBER GREENFIELD & POLITO LLP (PA)
12975 Brookprinter Pl Ste 200 (92064-8895)
PHONE..................858 486-6757
Bruce Lorber, *Mng Pt*
Joyia Greenfield, *
Steven Polito, *
EMP: 62 **EST:** 1980
SALES (est): 19.62MM
SALES (corp-wide): 19.62MM **Privately Held**
Web: www.lorberlaw.com
SIC: 8111 General practice law office

(P-17558)
LOZANO SMITH LLP
7404 N Spalding Ave (93720-3370)
PHONE..................559 431-5600
EMP: 167 **EST:** 1988
SALES (est): 30K **Privately Held**
Web: www.lozanosmith.com

SIC: 8111 Specialized law offices, attorneys

(P-17559)
LUBIN OLSON & NIEWIADOMSKI LLP
600 Montgomery St Fl 14 (94111-2701)
PHONE..................415 981-0550
EMP: 66 **EST:** 2015
SALES (est): 11.08MM **Privately Held**
Web: www.lubinolson.com
SIC: 8111 General practice attorney, lawyer

(P-17560)
MALCOLM & CISNEROS A LAW CORP
Also Called: Malcolm Cisneros
2112 Business Center Dr Ste 100 (92612-7137)
PHONE..................949 252-9400
William Malcolm, *CEO*
Arturo Cisneros, *
EMP: 110 **EST:** 1992
SALES (est): 12.31MM **Privately Held**
Web: www.malcolmcisneros.com
SIC: 8111 General practice law office

(P-17561)
MANATT PHELPS & PHILLIPS LLP (PA)
2049 Century Park E Ste 1700 (90067-3101)
PHONE..................310 312-4000
EMP: 420 **EST:** 1965
SALES (est): 137.56MM
SALES (corp-wide): 137.56MM **Privately Held**
Web: www.manatt.com
SIC: 8111 General practice law office

(P-17562)
MANNING KASS ELLROD RMREZ TRST (PA)
801 S Figueroa St 15th Fl (90017-5504)
PHONE..................213 624-6900
Steven D Manning, *Mng Pt*
EMP: 150 **EST:** 1994
SALES (est): 33.97MM **Privately Held**
Web: www.manningkass.com
SIC: 8111 General practice attorney, lawyer

(P-17563)
MATHENY SARS LINKERT JAIME LLP
3638 American River Dr (95864-5901)
PHONE..................916 978-3434
Richard S Linkert, *Pt*
Douglas A Sears, *
Matthew C Jamie, *
EMP: 66 **EST:** 1974
SQ FT: 12,000
SALES (est): 6.4MM **Privately Held**
Web: www.mathenysears.com
SIC: 8111 General practice law office

(P-17564)
MC NAMARA DDGE NEY BATT SLTTER (PA)
3480 Buskirk Ave Ste 250 (94523-7310)
PHONE..................925 939-5330
Richard Dodge, *Genl Pt*
Michael J Ney, *Pt*
Thomas G Beatty, *Pt*
Robert M Slattery, *Pt*
Thomas E Pfalzer, *Pt*
EMP: 70 **EST:** 1965
SQ FT: 9,500
SALES (est): 12.25MM
SALES (corp-wide): 12.25MM **Privately Held**

SIC: 8111 Specialized law offices, attorneys

(P-17565)
MCCORMICK BRSTOW SHPPARD WYTE (PA)
Also Called: McCormick Barstow
7647 N Fresno St (93720-2578)
P.O. Box 28912 (93729-8912)
PHONE..................559 433-1300
Jeffrey M Reid, *Mng Pt*
Matthew Hawkins, *Pt*
Todd Daxter, *Pt*
Gregory Mason, *Pt*
David Mcnamara, *Pt*
EMP: 194 **EST:** 1951
SQ FT: 67,000
SALES (est): 31.51MM
SALES (corp-wide): 31.51MM **Privately Held**
Web: www.mccormickbarstow.com
SIC: 8111 Antitrust and trade regulation law

(P-17566)
MED-LEGAL LLC
955 Overland Ct Ste 200 (91773-1747)
PHONE..................626 653-5160
Moonesh Arora, *CEO*
Michael Salzano, *
Kenneth E Gleockler, *
EMP: 150 **EST:** 2010
SALES (est): 9.6MM **Privately Held**
SIC: 8111 Legal aid service

(P-17567)
MEYERS NAVE A PROF CORP (PA)
1999 Harrison St Ste 900 (94612-3578)
PHONE..................510 351-4300
David W Skinner, *CEO*
Steven R Meyers, *
Adam U Lindgren, *
Michael S Riback, *
Clifford F Campbell, *
EMP: 100 **EST:** 1986
SALES (est): 25.5MM **Privately Held**
Web: www.meyersnave.com
SIC: 8111 Specialized law offices, attorneys

(P-17568)
MICHAEL SULLIVAN & ASSOC LLP
2401 E El Segundo Blvd (90245-4655)
P.O. Box 85059 (92186-5059)
PHONE..................310 337-4480
Michael W Sullivan, *Pt*
EMP: 147 **EST:** 2012
SALES (est): 11.05MM **Privately Held**
Web: www.sullivanattorneys.com
SIC: 8111 General practice attorney, lawyer

(P-17569)
MILBANK TWEED HDLEY MCCLOY LLP
Also Called: Milbank Global Securities
2029 Century Park E (90002-3076)
PHONE..................424 386-4000
David C Frauman, *Dir*
EMP: 120
SQ FT: 40,000
SALES (corp-wide): 133.63MM **Privately Held**
Web: www.milbank.com
SIC: 8111 Corporate, partnership and business law
PA: Milbank Llp
55 Hudson Yards
New York NY
212 530-5000

PRODUCTS & SERVICES SECTION

(P-17570)
MILLER STARR RGLIA A PROF LAW (PA)
1331 N California Blvd Fl 5 (94596-4502)
P.O. Box 8177 (94596-8177)
PHONE..................925 935-9400
Anthony M Leones, *CEO*
Richard Carlson, *
EMP: 90 **EST:** 1964
SQ FT: 30,000
SALES (est): 11.91MM
SALES (corp-wide): 11.91MM **Privately Held**
Web: www.msrlegal.com
SIC: 8111 General practice law office

(P-17571)
MINTZ LEVIN COHN FERRIS GL
Also Called: MINTZ, LEVIN, COHN, FERRIS, GLOVSKY AND POPEO, P.C.
3580 Carmel Mountain Rd Ste 300 (92130-6768)
PHONE..................858 314-1500
EMP: 100
SALES (corp-wide): 199.9MM **Privately Held**
Web: www.mintz.com
SIC: 8111 General practice law office
PA: Mintz, Levin, Cohn, Ferris, Glovsky And Popeo, P.C.
1 Financial Ctr
Boston MA
617 348-4951

(P-17572)
MITCHELL SILBERBERG KNUPP LLP (PA)
Also Called: Mitchell Slbrberg Knupp Fndtio
2049 Century Park E Fl 18 (90067-3120)
PHONE..................310 312-2000
Jeffrey K Eisen, *Prin*
Thomas P Lambert, *Mng Pt*
Kevin E Gaut, *COO*
Jerry Kaufman, *Ex Dir*
EMP: 198 **EST:** 1908
SALES (est): 38.88MM
SALES (corp-wide): 38.88MM **Privately Held**
Web: www.msk.com
SIC: 8111 General practice law office

(P-17573)
MOORE LAW GROUP A PROF CORP
3710 S Susan St Ste 210 (92704-6956)
P.O. Box 25145 (92799-5145)
PHONE..................714 431-2000
Harvey Moore, *Pr*
EMP: 65 **EST:** 2008
SALES (est): 10.02MM **Privately Held**
Web: www.collectmoore.com
SIC: 8111 General practice law office

(P-17574)
MORGAN LEWIS & BOCKIUS LLP
One Market Spear St Tower (94105)
PHONE..................415 442-1000
Brian C Rocca, *Mng Pt*
David Heilbron, *Pt*
EMP: 696 **EST:** 1880
SALES (est): 98.99K
SALES (corp-wide): 440.91K **Privately Held**
SIC: 8111 General practice law office
PA: Morgan, Lewis & Bockius Llp
2222 Market St
Philadelphia PA
215 963-5000

8111 - Legal Services (P-17595)

(P-17575)
MORRIS POLICH & PURDY LLP (PA)
1055 W 7th St Ste 2400 (90017-2550)
PHONE..................213 891-9100
Theodore D Levin, *Pt*
Douglas C Purdy, *Pt*
Walter Lipsman, *Pt*
Jeff Barron, *Pt*
James Chantland, *Pt*
EMP: 100 **EST:** 1969
SQ FT: 40,000
SALES (est): 18.97MM
SALES (corp-wide): 18.97MM **Privately Held**
Web: www.mpplaw.com
SIC: 8111 General practice attorney, lawyer

(P-17576)
MORRISON & FOERSTER LLP
Also Called: Morrison & Foerster
707 Wilshire Blvd Ste 6000 (90017-3501)
PHONE..................213 892-5200
Gregory Koltun, *Mng Pt*
EMP: 250
SALES (corp-wide): 392.26MM **Privately Held**
Web: www.mofo.com
SIC: 8111 General practice attorney, lawyer
PA: Morrison & Foerster Llp
   425 Market St Fl 32
   San Francisco CA
   415 268-7000

(P-17577)
MORRISON & FOERSTER LLP (PA)
Also Called: Mofo
425 Market St Fl 32 (94105-2467)
PHONE..................415 268-7000
Larren Nashelsky, *Mng Pt*
Patrick Cavaney, *Mng Pt*
Paul Friedman, *Mng Pt*
Craig Martin, *Mng Pt*
Eric Piesner, *Mng Pt*
EMP: 400 **EST:** 2000
SALES (est): 392.26MM
SALES (corp-wide): 392.26MM **Privately Held**
Web: www.mofo.com
SIC: 8111 General practice attorney, lawyer

(P-17578)
MORRISON & FOERSTER LLP
12531 High Bluff Dr Ste 100 (92130-3014)
PHONE..................858 720-5100
Mark Zebrowski, *Mng Pt*
EMP: 421
SALES (corp-wide): 392.26MM **Privately Held**
Web: www.mofo.com
SIC: 8111 General practice attorney, lawyer
PA: Morrison & Foerster Llp
   425 Market St Fl 32
   San Francisco CA
   415 268-7000

(P-17579)
MORRISON & FOERSTER LLP
Also Called: Morrison & Foerster - Library
755 Page Mill Rd (94304-1061)
PHONE..................650 813-5600
Alan Cope Johnston, *Mng Pt*
EMP: 429
SALES (corp-wide): 392.26MM **Privately Held**
Web: www.mofo.com
SIC: 8111 General practice law office
PA: Morrison & Foerster Llp
   425 Market St Fl 32
   San Francisco CA
   415 268-7000

(P-17580)
MUNGER TOLLES & OLSON LLP
350 S Grand Ave Fl 50 (90071-3426)
PHONE..................213 683-9100
Sandra Seville-jones Mng Ptrn, *Prin*
EMP: 482 **EST:** 2001
SALES (est): 28.97MM **Privately Held**
Web: www.mto.com
SIC: 8111 Corporate, partnership and business law

(P-17581)
MUNGER TOLLES OLSON FOUNDATION (PA)
350 S Grand Ave Fl 50 (90071-3426)
PHONE..................213 683-9100
O'malley M Miller, *CEO*
Robert Johnson, *
Bart Williams, *
Mark Helm, *
Steven B Weisburd, *
EMP: 420 **EST:** 1962
SQ FT: 100,000
SALES (est): 2.18MM
SALES (corp-wide): 2.18MM **Privately Held**
Web: www.mto.com
SIC: 8111 General practice attorney, lawyer

(P-17582)
MURCHISON & CUMMING LLP (PA)
Also Called: M & C
801 S Grand Ave Ste 900 (90017-4624)
PHONE..................213 623-7400
Friedrich W Seitz, *Pt*
Michael D Mc Evoy, *Sr Pt*
Michael Lawler, *Sr Pt*
Steven L Smilay, *Sr Pt*
Kenneth Moreno, *Sr Pt*
EMP: 100 **EST:** 1952
SQ FT: 30,000
SALES (est): 26.77MM
SALES (corp-wide): 26.77MM **Privately Held**
Web: www.murchisonlaw.com
SIC: 8111 General practice law office

(P-17583)
MURPHY & BEANE INC
5901 Green Valley Cir Ste 145 (90230-6991)
PHONE..................310 649-4470
Edward J Murphy Senior, *Mgr*
EMP: 63
SALES (corp-wide): 9.13MM **Privately Held**
Web: www.murphy-beane.com
SIC: 8111 6411 General practice attorney, lawyer; Insurance adjusters
PA: Murphy & Beane Inc
   15 Broad St Ste 305
   Boston MA
   617 723-0871

(P-17584)
MURTAUGH MYER NLSON TRGLIA LLP
2603 Main St Ste 900 (92614-4270)
P.O. Box 19627 (92623-9627)
PHONE..................949 794-4000
Michael J Nelson, *Mng Pt*
Mark S Himmelstein, *
Robert T Lemen, *Pt*
James A Murphy Iv, *Pt*
Harry A Halkowich, *Pt*
EMP: 60 **EST:** 1979
SALES (est): 9.16MM **Privately Held**
Web: www.murtaughlaw.com
SIC: 8111 General practice law office

(P-17585)
MUSICK PEELER & GARRETT LLP (PA)
624 S Grand Ave Ste 2000 (90023-1629)
PHONE..................213 629-7600
R Joseph De Briyn, *Mng Pt*
Wayne Littlefied, *Pt*
Gary Overstreet, *Pt*
Edward Landrey, *Pt*
Peter J Diedrich, *Pt*
EMP: 168 **EST:** 1937
SQ FT: 100,000
SALES (est): 24.72MM
SALES (corp-wide): 24.72MM **Privately Held**
Web: www.musickpeeler.com
SIC: 8111 General practice law office

(P-17586)
NATIONAL ATTNY COLLECTION SVCS
700 N Brand Blvd Fl 2 (91203-1247)
PHONE..................818 547-9760
A Donovan, *CEO*
John Weinstein, *
EMP: 251 **EST:** 2005
SALES (est): 9.29MM **Privately Held**
SIC: 8111 Debt collection law

(P-17587)
NATIONWIDE LEGAL LLC
Also Called: Sacramento
716 10th St Ste 102 (95814-1807)
PHONE..................916 443-4400
Alex Cain, *Brnch Mgr*
EMP: 74
Web: www.nationwidelegal.com
SIC: 8111 General practice attorney, lawyer
PA: Nationwide Legal, Llc
   1609 James M Wood Blvd
   Los Angeles CA

(P-17588)
NEWMEYER & DILLION LLP (PA)
895 Dove St Ste 500 (92660-2999)
PHONE..................949 854-7000
Gregory L Dillion, *Pt*
Thomas F Newmeyer, *Pt*
John A O Hara, *Pt*
Michael S Cucchissi, *Pt*
Joseph A Ferrentino, *Pt*
EMP: 115 **EST:** 1984
SQ FT: 52,000
SALES (est): 26.3MM **Privately Held**
Web: www.newmeyeranddillion.com
SIC: 8111 General practice attorney, lawyer

(P-17589)
NOSSAMAN LLP (PA)
777 S Figueroa St Ste 3400 (90017-5834)
PHONE..................213 612-7800
E George Joseph, *Mng Pt*
EMP: 74 **EST:** 1944
SQ FT: 20,000
SALES (est): 43.49MM
SALES (corp-wide): 43.49MM **Privately Held**
Web: www.nossaman.com
SIC: 8111 General practice attorney, lawyer

(P-17590)
NOSSAMAN LLP
Also Called: Bagley, William T
50 California St Ste 3400 (94111-4799)
PHONE..................415 398-3600
Susan Eres, *Mgr*
EMP: 68
SALES (corp-wide): 43.49MM **Privately Held**
Web: www.nossaman.com
SIC: 8111 General practice attorney, lawyer
PA: Nossaman Llp
   777 S Figueroa St # 3400
   Los Angeles CA
   213 612-7800

(P-17591)
NOSSAMAN LLP
18101 Von Karman Ave Ste 1800 (92612-0177)
PHONE..................949 833-7800
George Joseph, *Pt*
EMP: 68
SALES (corp-wide): 43.49MM **Privately Held**
Web: www.nossaman.com
SIC: 8111 General practice attorney, lawyer
PA: Nossaman Llp
   777 S Figueroa St # 3400
   Los Angeles CA
   213 612-7800

(P-17592)
OMELVENY & MYERS LLP
1999 Avenue Of The Stars Fl 8 (90067-6022)
PHONE..................310 553-6700
Jodi Yamada, *Mgr*
EMP: 66
SALES (corp-wide): 208.14MM **Privately Held**
Web: www.omm.com
SIC: 8111 General practice attorney, lawyer
PA: O'melveny & Myers Llp
   400 S Hope St Fl 18th
   Los Angeles CA
   213 430-6000

(P-17593)
OMELVENY & MYERS LLP (PA)
400 S Hope St 18th Fl (90071-1904)
PHONE..................213 430-6000
Arthur Culvahouse Junior, *Mng Pt*
Arthur Culvahouse Junior, *Managing Member*
Bradley Butwin, *Managing Member*
Stephen Brody, *
Chuck Diamond, *
EMP: 850 **EST:** 1885
SQ FT: 250,000
SALES (est): 208.14MM
SALES (corp-wide): 208.14MM **Privately Held**
Web: www.omm.com
SIC: 8111 General practice law office

(P-17594)
ONE LLP
9301 Wilshire Blvd Ph 2 (90210-6174)
PHONE..................310 866-5157
Peter R Afrasiabi, *Brnch Mgr*
EMP: 78
SALES (corp-wide): 6.03MM **Privately Held**
Web: www.onellp.com
SIC: 8111 Specialized law offices, attorneys
PA: One Llp
   23 Corporate Plaza Dr # 15
   Newport Beach CA
   949 502-2870

(P-17595)
ORRICK HRRINGTN SUT FOUNDTN

8111 - Legal Services (P-17596)

400 Capitol Mall Ste 3000 (95814-4497)
PHONE..................................916 329-7928
EMP: 67 EST: 1999
SALES (est): 1.3MM Privately Held
Web: www.orrick.com
SIC: 8111 General practice attorney, lawyer

(P-17596)
ORRICK HRRINGTON SUTCLIFFE LLP (PA)
Also Called: Orrick, Herrington & Sutcliffe
405 Howard St (94105-2625)
PHONE..................................415 773-5700
Ralph H Baxter Junior, Ch
Linda Havard, *
EMP: 1579 EST: 1863
SQ FT: 146,000
SALES (est): 490.64MM
SALES (corp-wide): 490.64MM Privately Held
Web: www.orrick.com
SIC: 8111 General practice attorney, lawyer

(P-17597)
ORRICK HRRINGTON SUTCLIFFE LLP
1000 Marsh Rd (94025-1015)
PHONE..................................650 614-7400
Don Keller, Brnch Mgr
EMP: 160
SALES (corp-wide): 490.64MM Privately Held
Web: www.orrick.com
SIC: 8111 General practice attorney, lawyer
PA: Orrick, Herrington & Sutcliffe, Llp
    405 Howard St
    San Francisco CA
    415 773-5700

(P-17598)
PACHULSKI STANG ZEHL JONES LLP (PA)
Also Called: Pszyjw
10100 Santa Monica Blvd Ste 1100 (90067-4114)
PHONE..................................310 277-6910
Richard M Pachulski, Pr
Dean A Ziehl, *
James I Stang, *
EMP: 90 EST: 1983
SQ FT: 21,000
SALES (est): 27.19MM Privately Held
Web: www.pszjlaw.com
SIC: 8111 General practice law office

(P-17599)
PALMIERI TYLER WNER WLHELM WLD
1900 Main St Ste 700 (92614-7328)
P.O. Box 19712 (92623-9712)
PHONE..................................949 851-9400
James E Wilhelm, Pt
Dennis Tyler, *
Alan Wiener, *
Mike Greene, *
Robert Ihrke, *
EMP: 100 EST: 1986
SQ FT: 34,000
SALES (est): 15.38MM Privately Held
Web: www.ptwww.com
SIC: 8111 General practice attorney, lawyer

(P-17600)
PARAGON LEGAL GROUP LLC
Also Called: Paragon Legal
601 Montgomery St Ste 2030 (94111-2668)
PHONE..................................415 738-7870
Trista Engel, CEO
Jessica Markowitz, *
EMP: 109 EST: 2018
SALES (est): 27.22MM Privately Held
Web: www.paragonlegal.com
SIC: 8111 7361 Legal services; Executive placement

(P-17601)
PARKER MLLKEN CLARK OHARA SMLI
555 S Flower St 30th Fl (90071-2300)
PHONE..................................818 784-8087
Larry Ivanjack, *
William M Reid, *
Richard D Robbins, *
Larry Ivanjack, *
EMP: 70 EST: 1914
SQ FT: 25,000
SALES (est): 10.21MM Privately Held
Web: www.parkermilliken.com
SIC: 8111 General practice law office

(P-17602)
PARKER STANBURY LLP (PA)
444 S Flower St Ste 1900 (90071-2909)
PHONE..................................619 528-1259
Robert Lo Presti, Pt
Thomas L Waddell, Pt
Douglas H Mori, Pt
Douglas M Degrade, Pt
Timothy D Lucas, Pt
EMP: 60 EST: 1922
SQ FT: 17,152
SALES (est): 9.19MM
SALES (corp-wide): 9.19MM Privately Held
Web: www.parkstan.com
SIC: 8111 General practice law office

(P-17603)
PAUL HASTINGS LLP (PA)
515 S Flower St Fl 25 (90071-2228)
PHONE..................................213 683-6000
Greg Nitzkowski, Pt
Seth M Zachary, *
Elena R Baca, *
EMP: 1884 EST: 2011
SQ FT: 209,000
SALES (est): 413.45MM
SALES (corp-wide): 413.45MM Privately Held
Web: www.paulhastings.com
SIC: 8111 General practice law office

(P-17604)
PAUL HASTINGS LLP
4747 Executive Dr Ste 1200 (92121-3114)
PHONE..................................858 458-3000
Craig Price, Admn
EMP: 98
SALES (corp-wide): 413.45MM Privately Held
Web: www.paulhastings.com
SIC: 8111 General practice law office
PA: Paul Hastings Llp
    515 S Flower St Fl 25
    Los Angeles CA
    213 683-6000

(P-17605)
PAUL HASTINGS LLP
101 California St (94111-5802)
PHONE..................................415 856-7000
Dennis Dehrens, Admn
EMP: 97
SALES (corp-wide): 413.45MM Privately Held
Web: www.paulhastings.com
SIC: 8111 General practice law office
PA: Paul Hastings Llp
    515 S Flower St Fl 25
    Los Angeles CA
    213 683-6000

(P-17606)
PEARLMAN BROWN & WAX LLP (PA)
15910 Ventura Blvd Fl 18 (91436-2819)
PHONE..................................818 501-4343
Barry S Pearlman, Pt
Elliot F Borska, Pt
Steven H Wax, Pt
Dean Brown, Pt
EMP: 60 EST: 1984
SQ FT: 4,000
SALES (est): 16.73MM
SALES (corp-wide): 16.73MM Privately Held
Web: www.pbw-law.com
SIC: 8111 General practice law office

(P-17607)
PETTI KOHN INGRASSIA & L PR CO
Also Called: Pettit Kohn Ingrassia & Lutz
11622 El Camino Real Ste 300 (92130-2049)
PHONE..................................310 649-5772
Andrew N Kohn, Pr
Douglas Pettit, *
Thomas S Ingrassia, *
Jeniffer Lutz, *
EMP: 66 EST: 2006
SALES (est): 20.06MM Privately Held
Web: www.pettitkohn.com
SIC: 8111 General practice law office

(P-17608)
PILLSBURY WINTHROP SHAW
4 Embarcadero Ctr Fl 22 (94111-5998)
PHONE..................................415 983-1000
Jeffrey M Vesely, Genl Pt
EMP: 194
SALES (corp-wide): 192.22MM Privately Held
Web: www.pillsburylaw.com
SIC: 8111 General practice law office
PA: Pillsbury Winthrop Shaw Pittman Llp
    31 W 52nd St Fl 29
    New York NY
    212 858-1000

(P-17609)
PILLSBURY WINTHROP SHAW
50 Fremont St Fl 5 (94105-2232)
P.O. Box 7880 (94120-7880)
PHONE..................................415 983-1075
Jeffrey M Vesely, Pt
EMP: 300
SALES (corp-wide): 192.22MM Privately Held
Web: www.pillsburylaw.com
SIC: 8111 General practice law office
PA: Pillsbury Winthrop Shaw Pittman Llp
    31 W 52nd St Fl 29
    New York NY
    212 858-1000

(P-17610)
PILLSBURY WNTHROP SHAW PTTMAN
500 Capitol Mall Ste 1800 (95814-4741)
PHONE..................................916 329-4700
Linda Magyar, Mgr
EMP: 76
SALES (corp-wide): 192.22MM Privately Held
Web: www.pillsburylaw.com
SIC: 8111 General practice law office
PA: Pillsbury Winthrop Shaw Pittman Llp
    31 W 52nd St Fl 29
    New York NY
    212 858-1000

(P-17611)
PILLSBURY WNTHROP SHAW PTTMAN
Also Called: Pillsbury
725 S Figueroa St Ste 2800 (90017-5524)
PHONE..................................213 488-7100
Melissa Burton, Admn
EMP: 128
SALES (corp-wide): 192.22MM Privately Held
Web: www.pillsburylaw.com
SIC: 8111 General practice law office
PA: Pillsbury Winthrop Shaw Pittman Llp
    31 W 52nd St Fl 29
    New York NY
    212 858-1000

(P-17612)
PILLSBURY WNTHROP SHAW PTTMAN
2550 Hanover St (94304-1115)
PHONE..................................650 233-4500
EMP: 82
SALES (corp-wide): 192.22MM Privately Held
Web: www.pillsburylaw.com
SIC: 8111 General practice law office
PA: Pillsbury Winthrop Shaw Pittman Llp
    31 W 52nd St Fl 29
    New York NY
    212 858-1000

(P-17613)
PIRCHER NICHOLS & MEEKS (PA)
1925 Century Park E Ste 1700 (90067-2740)
PHONE..................................310 201-0132
Gary Laughlin, Sr Pt
Leo Pircher, Sr Pt
Eugene Leone, Sr Pt
Stevens Carey, Sr Pt
EMP: 95 EST: 1983
SQ FT: 35,000
SALES (est): 17.16MM
SALES (corp-wide): 17.16MM Privately Held
Web: www.hklaw.com
SIC: 8111 General practice attorney, lawyer

(P-17614)
POLSINELLI PC
Also Called: Polsinelli LLP
2049 Century Park E Ste 2300 (90067-3101)
PHONE..................................310 556-1801
Norma Ayala, Admn
EMP: 70
SALES (corp-wide): 227.61MM Privately Held
Web: www.polsinelli.com
SIC: 8111 General practice attorney, lawyer
PA: Polsinelli Pc
    900 W 48th Pl Ste 900 # 900
    Kansas City MO
    816 753-1000

(P-17615)
PRICE LAW GROUP A PROF CORP (PA)
Also Called: Plg Law Group
15760 Ventura Blvd Ste 800 (91436-3044)
PHONE..................................818 995-4540
Stuart M Price, Pr
EMP: 115 EST: 1991

PRODUCTS & SERVICES SECTION

8111 - Legal Services (P-17637)

SQ FT: 15,000
SALES (est): 11.54MM **Privately Held**
Web: www.resolvelawgroup.com
SIC: 8111 General practice law office

(P-17616)
PRICE POSTEL AND PARMA LLP
200 E Carrillo St Ste 400 (93101-2105)
P.O. Box 99 (93102-0099)
PHONE.................................805 962-0011
Terry J Schwartz, *Pt*
Gerald S Thede, *Pt*
John Kerr Wilson, *Pt*
James H Hurley Junior, *Pt*
Lonni Meanley Collins, *Pt*
EMP: 60 EST: 1952
SQ FT: 5,000
SALES (est): 9.27MM **Privately Held**
Web: www.ppplaw.com
SIC: 8111 General practice attorney, lawyer

(P-17617)
PRINDLE DECKER & AMARO LLP (PA)
310 Golden Shore Fl 4 (90802-4232)
P.O. Box 22711 (90801-5711)
PHONE.................................562 436-3946
R J Decker, *Pt*
Michael Amaro, *Pt*
Kenneth Prindle, *Pt*
R Joseph Decker, *Pt*
EMP: 85 EST: 1990
SALES (est): 8.45MM **Privately Held**
Web: www.pdalaw.com
SIC: 8111 Specialized law offices, attorneys

(P-17618)
PROBER & RAPHAEL A LAW CORP
Also Called: Prober & Raphael, ALC
20750 Ventura Blvd Ste 100 (91364-2338)
P.O. Box 4365 (91365-4365)
PHONE.................................818 227-0100
Dean R Prober, *Pr*
Lee S Raphael, *
EMP: 70 EST: 1984
SALES (est): 5.07MM **Privately Held**
Web: www.pralc.com
SIC: 8111 General practice attorney, lawyer

(P-17619)
PROCOPIO CORY HARGREAVES & SAVITCH LLP (PA)
530 B St Ste 2200 (92101-4435)
PHONE.................................619 238-1900
EMP: 215 EST: 1946
SALES (est): 22.06MM
SALES (corp-wide): 22.06MM **Privately Held**
Web: www.procopio.com
SIC: 8111 General practice law office

(P-17620)
PUBLIC COUNSEL
610 S Ardmore Ave (90005-2322)
PHONE.................................213 385-2977
Margaret Morrow, *Pr*
Madaline Kleiner, *
EMP: 94 EST: 1970
SQ FT: 12,000
SALES (est): 17.52MM **Privately Held**
Web: www.publiccounsel.org
SIC: 8111 Specialized law offices, attorneys

(P-17621)
QUINN EMNUEL URQHART SLLVAN LL (PA)
Also Called: Quinn Emmanuel Trial Lawyers
865 S Figueroa St Fl 10 (90017-5003)
PHONE.................................213 443-3000
John B Quinn, *Pt*
Christopher Tayback, *Pt*
William Burck, *Co-Managing Partner*
Michael Carlinsky, *Co-Managing Partner*
EMP: 366 EST: 1986
SALES (est): 131MM
SALES (corp-wide): 131MM **Privately Held**
Web: www.quinnemanuel.com
SIC: 8111 Specialized law offices, attorneys

(P-17622)
REED SMITH LLP
355 S Grand Ave Ste 2900 (90071-1514)
PHONE.................................213 457-8000
Peter Kennedy, *Office Managing Partner*
EMP: 158
SALES (corp-wide): 488.93MM **Privately Held**
Web: www.reedsmith.com
SIC: 8111 General practice attorney, lawyer
PA: Reed Smith Llp
    225 5th Ave Ste 1200
    Pittsburgh PA
    412 288-3131

(P-17623)
REED SMITH LLP
101 2nd St Ste 1800 (94105-3659)
PHONE.................................415 543-8700
Bettie B Epstein, *Pt*
EMP: 158
SALES (corp-wide): 488.93MM **Privately Held**
Web: www.reedsmith.com
SIC: 8111 General practice attorney, lawyer
PA: Reed Smith Llp
    225 5th Ave Ste 1200
    Pittsburgh PA
    412 288-3131

(P-17624)
RICHARDS WTSON GRSHON A PROF C (PA)
Also Called: RW&g
355 S Grand Ave 40th Fl (90071-1560)
PHONE.................................213 626-8484
Laurence S Wiener, *CEO*
Kayser O Sume Cmb, *Prin*
James L Markman, *
Craig A Steele, *
William L Strausz, *
▲ EMP: 120 EST: 1954
SQ FT: 45,000
SALES (est): 17.44MM
SALES (corp-wide): 17.44MM **Privately Held**
Web: www.rwglaw.com
SIC: 8111 General practice law office

(P-17625)
ROBBINS GELLER RUDMAN DOWD LLP (PA)
655 W Broadway Ste 1900 (92101-8498)
PHONE.................................619 231-1058
Michael J Dowd, *
Darren J Robbins, *
Paul J Geller, *
Samuel H Rudman, *
EMP: 300 EST: 2004
SQ FT: 135,000
SALES (est): 45.41MM
SALES (corp-wide): 45.41MM **Privately Held**
Web: www.rgrdlaw.com
SIC: 8111 Corporate, partnership and business law

(P-17626)
ROBINSON CALCAGNIE INC
620 Newport Ctr Dr Ste 700 (92101)
PHONE.................................619 338-4060
Mark P Robinson, *Prin*
EMP: 60
SALES (corp-wide): 9.86MM **Privately Held**
Web: www.robinsonfirm.com
SIC: 8111 General practice attorney, lawyer
PA: Robinson Calcagnie, Inc.
    19 Corporate Plaza Dr
    Newport Beach CA
    949 720-1288

(P-17627)
ROPERS MAJESKI A PROF CORP (PA)
535 Middlefield Rd Ste 245 (94025-3468)
PHONE.................................650 364-8200
Jesshill E Love, *CEO*
Richard Wilson, *
Michael Ioannou, *
EMP: 81 EST: 1950
SALES (est): 5.2MM
SALES (corp-wide): 5.2MM **Privately Held**
Web: www.ropers.com
SIC: 8111 General practice law office

(P-17628)
ROPERS MAJESKI A PROF CORP
445 S Figueroa St Ste 3000 (90071-1602)
PHONE.................................213 312-2000
Allan Anderson, *Mgr*
EMP: 217
SALES (corp-wide): 5.2MM **Privately Held**
Web: www.ropers.com
SIC: 8111 General practice law office
PA: Ropers Majeski, A Professional Corporation
    535 Middlefield Rd # 245
    Menlo Park CA
    650 364-8200

(P-17629)
ROPES & GRAY LLP
1900 University Ave (94303-2299)
PHONE.................................650 617-4000
Kitty Dowgert, *Brnch Mgr*
EMP: 75
SALES (corp-wide): 310.78MM **Privately Held**
Web: www.ropesgray.com
SIC: 8111 General practice law office
PA: Ropes & Gray Llp
    Prudential Twr 800 Bylsto Prudential Tower
    Boston MA
    617 951-7000

(P-17630)
RUSS AUGUST & KABAT LLP
12424 Wilshire Blvd Ste 1200 (90025-1031)
PHONE.................................310 826-7474
Larry C Russ, *Prin*
Jules L Kabat, *
Laura K Stanton, *
Richard L August, *
Even Kent, *
EMP: 97 EST: 1981
SALES (est): 12.8MM **Privately Held**
Web: www.raklaw.com
SIC: 8111 General practice attorney, lawyer

(P-17631)
RUTAN & TUCKER LLP (PA)
18575 Jamboree Rd Ste 900 (92612-2526)
P.O. Box 1950 (92628-1950)
PHONE.................................714 641-5100
Richard Boden, *Managing Member*
Paul F Marx, *Managing Member*
Jodi Brooks, *Managing Member**
Tony Malkani, *Managing Member**
EMP: 265 EST: 1935
SALES (est): 48.58MM
SALES (corp-wide): 48.58MM **Privately Held**
Web: www.rutan.com
SIC: 8111 General practice attorney, lawyer

(P-17632)
SAUL EWING ARNSTEIN & LEHR LLP
Also Called: Saul Ewing Arnstein & Lehr LLP
1888 Century Park E Fl 19 (90067-1702)
PHONE.................................310 398-6100
EMP: 94
SALES (corp-wide): 120.22MM **Privately Held**
SIC: 8111 General practice law office
PA: Saul Ewing Llp
    1500 Market St Fl 38
    Philadelphia PA
    215 972-7777

(P-17633)
SCALE LLP
315 Montgomery St Fl 10 (94104-1823)
PHONE.................................415 735-5933
Adam Forest, *Pt*
David Reidy, *Pt*
Heather Phillips, *Pt*
EMP: 60 EST: 2021
SALES (est): 2.51MM **Privately Held**
Web: www.scalefirm.com
SIC: 8111 Legal services

(P-17634)
SCOTT A PORTER PROF CORP
350 University Ave Ste 200 (95825-6581)
PHONE.................................916 929-1481
Sherrie Cork, *Off Mgr*
A Irving Scott, *
Edwin T Weiberg, *
John W Delehant, *
Anthony Warburg, *
EMP: 85 EST: 1976
SALES (est): 11.4MM **Privately Held**
Web: www.porterscott.com
SIC: 8111 General practice attorney, lawyer

(P-17635)
SDCDA
2125 Park Blvd (92101-4753)
PHONE.................................619 459-9632
EMP: 187 EST: 2013
SALES (est): 625.95K **Privately Held**
Web: www.sdcda.org
SIC: 8111 Legal services

(P-17636)
SEDGWICK LLP
Also Called: Sedgwick
333 Bush St Fl 30 (94104-2834)
PHONE.................................415 781-7900
EMP: 834
Web: www.sedgwick.com
SIC: 8111 Real estate law

(P-17637)
SELMAN LCHNGER EDSON HSU NWMAN
11766 Wilshire Blvd (90025-6538)
PHONE.................................310 445-0800
Sheryl Leichenger, *Pt*
EMP: 70
SALES (est): 2.92MM **Privately Held**

8111 - Legal Services (P-17638)

SIC: 8111 Legal services

(P-17638)
SELTZER CPLAN MCMHON VTEK A LA (PA)
750 B St Ste 2100 (92101-8177)
PHONE.................................619 685-3003
Robert Caplan, *Pr*
Gerald L Mc Mahon, *
John H Alspaugh, *
Neal P Panish, *
EMP: 165 EST: 1970
SQ FT: 78,000
SALES (est): 15.68MM
SALES (corp-wide): 15.68MM **Privately Held**
Web: www.scmv.com
SIC: 8111 General practice attorney, lawyer

(P-17639)
SEVERSON & WERSON A PROF CORP (PA)
595 Market St Ste 2600 (94105-3413)
PHONE.................................415 398-3344
Mary Kate Sullivan, *CEO*
James B Werson, *
Robert L Lofts, *
Donald J Querio, *
Jan T Chilton, *
EMP: 132 EST: 1945
SQ FT: 40,000
SALES (est): 24.15MM
SALES (corp-wide): 24.15MM **Privately Held**
Web: www.severson.com
SIC: 8111 Labor and employment law

(P-17640)
SEYFARTH SHAW LLP
400 Capitol Mall Ste 2350 (95814-4428)
PHONE.................................916 448-0159
Rachel Miller, *Brnch Mgr*
EMP: 135
SALES (corp-wide): 474.05MM **Privately Held**
Web: www.seyfarth.com
SIC: 8111 General practice attorney, lawyer
PA: Seyfarth Shaw Llp
   233 S Wacker Dr Ste 8000
   Chicago IL
   312 460-5000

(P-17641)
SEYFARTH SHAW LLP
601 S Figueroa St Ste 3300 (90017-5704)
P.O. Box 17961 (90017-0961)
PHONE.................................213 270-9600
Arthur Wood Iv, *Brnch Mgr*
EMP: 69
SALES (corp-wide): 474.05MM **Privately Held**
Web: www.seyfarth.com
SIC: 8111 General practice law office
PA: Seyfarth Shaw Llp
   233 S Wacker Dr Ste 8000
   Chicago IL
   312 460-5000

(P-17642)
SEYFARTH SHAW LLP
2029 Century Park E Ste 3300 (90002-3076)
PHONE.................................310 277-7200
Sandy Abrahamian, *Brnch Mgr*
EMP: 200
SALES (corp-wide): 474.05MM **Privately Held**
Web: www.seyfarth.com
SIC: 8111 General practice law office
PA: Seyfarth Shaw Llp
   233 S Wacker Dr Ste 8000
   Chicago IL
   312 460-5000

(P-17643)
SEYFARTH SHAW LLP
560 Mission St Fl 31 (94105-2930)
PHONE.................................415 397-2823
William Dritsas, *Prin*
EMP: 100
SALES (corp-wide): 474.05MM **Privately Held**
Web: www.seyfarth.com
SIC: 8111 General practice law office
PA: Seyfarth Shaw Llp
   233 S Wacker Dr Ste 8000
   Chicago IL
   312 460-5000

(P-17644)
SHARTSIS FRIESE LLP
1 Maritime Plz Fl 18 (94111-3508)
PHONE.................................415 421-6500
Arthur J Shartsis, *Prin*
Robert Charles Friese, *
Mary Jo Shartsis, *
Douglas Hammer, *
Broadhurst John, *
EMP: 120 EST: 1975
SQ FT: 47,709
SALES (est): 24.17MM **Privately Held**
Web: www.sflaw.com
SIC: 8111 Patent, trademark and copyright law

(P-17645)
SHEPPARD MLLIN RCHTER HMPTON L
501 W Broadway Fl 19 (92101-8541)
PHONE.................................619 338-6500
Robert Sbardellati, *Brnch Mgr*
EMP: 89
SALES (corp-wide): 181.58MM **Privately Held**
Web: www.sheppardmullin.com
SIC: 8111 General practice law office
PA: Sheppard, Mullin, Richter & Hampton, Llp
   333 S Hope St Fl 43
   Los Angeles CA
   213 620-1780

(P-17646)
SHEPPARD MLLIN RCHTER HMPTON L (PA)
Also Called: Sheppard Mullin
333 S Hope St Fl 43 (90071-1422)
PHONE.................................213 620-1780
Guy N Halgren, *Ch Bd*
Robert Beall, *Administrative Partner*
Robert Zuber, *Ex Dir*
Lawrence Braun, *Pt*
Charles Barker, *Pt*
EMP: 370 EST: 1927
SQ FT: 52,820
SALES (est): 181.58MM
SALES (corp-wide): 181.58MM **Privately Held**
Web: www.sheppardmullin.com
SIC: 8111 General practice law office

(P-17647)
SHEPPARD MLLIN RCHTER HMPTON L
12275 El Camino Real Ste 100 (92130)
PHONE.................................858 720-8900
Shannon Petersen, *Brnch Mgr*
EMP: 84
SALES (corp-wide): 181.58MM **Privately Held**
Web: www.sheppardmullin.com
SIC: 8111 General practice law office
PA: Sheppard, Mullin, Richter & Hampton, Llp
   333 S Hope St Fl 43
   Los Angeles CA
   213 620-1780

(P-17648)
SHEPPARD MLLIN RCHTER HMPTON L
4 Embarcadero Ctr Ste 1700 (94111-4106)
PHONE.................................415 434-9100
Aline Pearl, *Admn*
EMP: 62
SALES (corp-wide): 181.58MM **Privately Held**
Web: www.sheppardmullin.com
SIC: 8111 General practice law office
PA: Sheppard, Mullin, Richter & Hampton, Llp
   333 S Hope St Fl 43
   Los Angeles CA
   213 620-1780

(P-17649)
SHEPPARD MLLIN RCHTER HMPTON L
1901 Avenue Of The Stars Ste 1600 (90067-6001)
PHONE.................................310 228-3700
Sherry Wilson, *Admn*
EMP: 78
SALES (corp-wide): 181.58MM **Privately Held**
Web: www.sheppardmullin.com
SIC: 8111 General practice law office
PA: Sheppard, Mullin, Richter & Hampton, Llp
   333 S Hope St Fl 43
   Los Angeles CA
   213 620-1780

(P-17650)
SHEPPARD MLLIN RCHTER HMPTON L
650 Town Center Dr Fl 10 (92626-1993)
PHONE.................................714 513-5100
EMP: 80
SALES (corp-wide): 181.58MM **Privately Held**
Web: www.sheppardmullin.com
SIC: 8111 General practice law office
PA: Sheppard, Mullin, Richter & Hampton, Llp
   333 S Hope St Fl 43
   Los Angeles CA
   213 620-1780

(P-17651)
SHOOK HARDY & BACON LLP
1 Montgomery St Ste 2700 (94104-5527)
PHONE.................................415 544-1900
Shannon Spangler, *Mng Pt*
EMP: 239
SALES (corp-wide): 147.91MM **Privately Held**
Web: www.shb.com
SIC: 8111 General practice law office
PA: Shook, Hardy & Bacon L.L.P.
   2555 Grand Blvd
   Kansas City MO
   816 474-6550

(P-17652)
SHOOK HARDY & BACON LLP
5 Park Plz Ste 1600 (92614-2546)
PHONE.................................949 475-1500
Michelle Fujimoto, *Mgr*
EMP: 239
SALES (corp-wide): 147.91MM **Privately Held**
Web: www.shb.com
SIC: 8111 General practice law office
PA: Shook, Hardy & Bacon L.L.P.
   2555 Grand Blvd
   Kansas City MO
   816 474-6550

(P-17653)
SIDEMAN & BANCROFT LLP
1 Embarcadero Ctr Fl 22 (94111-3711)
PHONE.................................415 392-1960
Jeffrey Hallam, *Genl Pt*
Kelly P Mccarthy, *Pt*
Hilary Pierce, *Pt*
EMP: 95 EST: 2004
SALES (est): 16.27MM **Privately Held**
Web: www.sideman.com
SIC: 8111 General practice law office

(P-17654)
SIDLEY AUSTIN LLP
1001 Page Mill Rd Bldg 1 (94304-1006)
PHONE.................................650 565-7000
Dorce Zimmermann, *Brnch Mgr*
EMP: 105
SALES (corp-wide): 511.15MM **Privately Held**
Web: www.sidley.com
SIC: 8111 General practice attorney, lawyer
PA: Sidley Austin Llp
   1 S Dearborn St Ste 900
   Chicago IL
   312 853-7000

(P-17655)
SKADDEN ARPS SLATE MEAGHER & F
300 S Grand Ave Ste 3400 (90071-3137)
PHONE.................................213 687-5000
Rand S April, *Pt*
EMP: 250
Web: www.skadden.com
SIC: 8111 General practice attorney, lawyer
HQ: Skadden, Arps, Slate, Meagher & Flom Llp
   One Mnhttan W 395 9th Ave
   New York NY
   212 735-3000

(P-17656)
SKADDEN ARPS SLATE MGHER FLOM
525 University Ave Ste A100 (94301-1925)
PHONE.................................650 470-4500
Kenton J King, *Pt*
EMP: 249
Web: www.skadden.com
SIC: 8111 General practice attorney, lawyer
HQ: Skadden, Arps, Slate, Meagher & Flom Llp
   One Mnhttan W 395 9th Ave
   New York NY
   212 735-3000

(P-17657)
SMS TRANSPORTATION INC
18516 S Broadway (90248-4615)
PHONE.................................310 527-9200
John W Harris, *Prin*
EMP: 100 EST: 2005
SALES (est): 4.94MM **Privately Held**
Web: www.smstransportation.net
SIC: 8111 Legal services

PRODUCTS & SERVICES SECTION

8111 - Legal Services (P-17678)

(P-17658)
SNELL & WILMER LLP
Also Called: Snell & Wilmer
600 Anton Blvd Ste 1400 (92626-7689)
PHONE.................................714 427-7000
Andrea Bryant, *Prin*
EMP: 75
SQ FT: 3,000
SALES (corp-wide): 80.35MM **Privately Held**
Web: www.swlaw.com
SIC: **8111** General practice attorney, lawyer
PA: Snell & Wilmer L.L.P.
1 E Washington St
Phoenix AZ
602 382-6000

(P-17659)
SOLOMON WARD SDNWURM SMITH LLP
401 B St Ste 1200 (92101-4295)
PHONE.................................619 231-0303
Herbert Solomon, *Pt*
Richard E Seidenwurm, *
Jeffrey H Silberman, *
Norman L Smith, *
Richard E Mccarthy, *Pt*
EMP: 60 EST: 1977
SQ FT: 17,000
SALES (est): 18.23MM **Privately Held**
Web: www.swsslaw.com
SIC: **8111** General practice attorney, lawyer

(P-17660)
SONOMA COUNTY OFFICE EDUCATION
Also Called: School & College Legal Svcs
5350 Skylane Blvd (95403-1082)
PHONE.................................707 524-2690
Alan Hersh, *Prin*
EMP: 71
SALES (corp-wide): 124.75MM **Privately Held**
Web: www.sclscal.org
SIC: **8111** 8211 Legal services; Elementary and secondary schools
PA: Sonoma County Office Of Education
5340 Skylane Blvd
Santa Rosa CA
707 524-2600

(P-17661)
STEELE CIS LLC
Also Called: Steele
1 Sansome St Ste 3500 (94104-4436)
PHONE.................................415 692-5000
Ken Kurtz, *Pr*
EMP: 350 EST: 2011
SALES (est): 11.77MM **Privately Held**
SIC: **8111** Legal services

(P-17662)
STRADLING YCCA CRLSON RUTH A P (PA)
660 Newport Center Dr Ste 1600 (92660)
PHONE.................................949 725-4000
John F Cannon, *Prin*
Nick E Yocca, *
William Rauth, *
Keith C Schaaf, *
Rick C Goodman, *
EMP: 200 EST: 1975
SQ FT: 64,000
SALES (est): 40.69MM
SALES (corp-wide): 40.69MM **Privately Held**
Web: www.stradlinglaw.com
SIC: **8111** General practice law office

(P-17663)
STRETTO INC (PA)
410 Exchange Ste 100 (92602-1331)
PHONE.................................949 222-1212
Steve Moore, *CEO*
Brian Soper, *Development*
Avid S Watkins, *Vice Chairman*
Rod Ennico, *CFO*
Ajay A Parikh, *
EMP: 73 EST: 2003
SALES (est): 44.53MM
SALES (corp-wide): 44.53MM **Privately Held**
Web: www.stretto.com
SIC: **8111** Bankruptcy referee

(P-17664)
STROOCK & STROOCK & LAVAN LLP
Also Called: Stroock & Stroock & Lavan
2029 Century Park E Ste 1800 (90002-3076)
PHONE.................................310 556-5800
Diane Cohen, *Brnch Mgr*
EMP: 150
SALES (corp-wide): 26.46K **Privately Held**
Web: www.stroock.com
SIC: **8111** General practice attorney, lawyer
PA: Stroock & Stroock & Lavan Llp
180 Maiden Ln Fl 26
New York NY
212 806-5400

(P-17665)
STUTMAN TRSTER GLATT PROF CORP
Also Called: Stutman Treister Glatt Prof Co
1901 Avenue Of The Stars Ste 200 (90067)
PHONE.................................310 228-5600
Scott H Yun, *CEO*
Robert A Greenfield, *
Charles D Axelrod, *
Theodore B Stolman, *
Isaac M Pachulski, *
EMP: 75 EST: 1969
SQ FT: 40,000
SALES (est): 9.78MM **Privately Held**
SIC: **8111** General practice law office

(P-17666)
THARPE & HOWELL (PA)
15250 Ventura Blvd Fl 9 (91403-3221)
PHONE.................................818 205-9955
John Maile, *Mng Pt*
Edgar Allen Tharpe Iii, *Pt*
Todd R Howell, *Pt*
Christopher P Ruiz, *Pt*
Christopher S Maile, *Pt*
EMP: 78 EST: 1977
SQ FT: 13,500
SALES (est): 8.47MM
SALES (corp-wide): 8.47MM **Privately Held**
Web: www.tharpe-howell.com
SIC: **8111** General practice law office

(P-17667)
THORSNES BARTOLOTTA & MCGUIRE
2550 5th Ave Ste 1100 (92103-6694)
PHONE.................................619 236-9363
Mickey Mcguire, *Pt*
Vincent Bartolotta, *Pt*
Mitchell Golub, *Pt*
Kevin Quinn, *Pt*
Darel Mazzerlla, *Pt*
EMP: 67 EST: 1978
SQ FT: 20,000
SALES (est): 9.05MM **Privately Held**
Web: www.tbmlawyers.com
SIC: **8111** Specialized law offices, attorneys

(P-17668)
TOBIN LUCKS A PROF CORP (PA)
Also Called: Tobin Lucks
8511 Fallbrook Ave Ste 400 (91304)
P.O. Box 4502 (91365-4502)
PHONE.................................818 226-3400
Irvin Lucks, *Mng Pt*
Donald Tobin, *
Irvin Lucks, *Pt*
Edwin Lucks, *
EMP: 97 EST: 1982
SALES (est): 24.04MM
SALES (corp-wide): 24.04MM **Privately Held**
Web: www.tobinlucks.com
SIC: **8111** General practice law office

(P-17669)
TROUTMAN PPPER HMLTON SNDERS L
Also Called: Troutman Sanders
5 Park Plz Ste 1400 (92614-2545)
PHONE.................................949 622-2700
David B Allen, *Pt*
EMP: 86
SALES (corp-wide): 161.17MM **Privately Held**
Web: www.troutman.com
SIC: **8111** General practice attorney, lawyer
PA: Troutman Pepper Hamilton Sanders Llp
600 Peachtree St Ne # 300
Atlanta GA
404 885-3000

(P-17670)
TROYGOULD PC
1801 Century Park E Ste 1600 (90067-2301)
PHONE.................................310 553-4441
Sanford J Hillsberg, *Prin*
Diane Gordon, *
EMP: 80 EST: 1970
SQ FT: 24,000
SALES (est): 12.43MM **Privately Held**
Web: www.troygould.com
SIC: **8111** General practice attorney, lawyer

(P-17671)
TYSON & MENDES
Also Called: Tyson
12520 High Bluff Dr Ste 360 (92130-2041)
PHONE.................................858 459-1476
Anastasia Ramirez, *Prin*
EMP: 66 EST: 2004
SALES (est): 430.03K **Privately Held**
Web: www.tysonmendes.com
SIC: **8111** Specialized law offices, attorneys

(P-17672)
VINSON & ELKINS LLP
1841 Page Mill Rd Fl 2 (94304-1255)
PHONE.................................650 617-8400
EMP: 138
SALES (corp-wide): 340.81MM **Privately Held**
Web: www.velaw.com
SIC: **8111** General practice attorney, lawyer
PA: Vinson & Elkins L.L.P.
845 Texas St Ste 4700
Houston TX
713 758-2222

(P-17673)
VISION LEGAL INC
4712 E 2nd St Ste 840 (90803-5950)
PHONE.................................310 469-4966
EMP: 67
SALES (corp-wide): 1.26MM **Privately Held**
Web: www.visionlegalinc.com
SIC: **8111** Legal services
PA: Vision Legal, Inc.
4470 W Sunset Blvd # 409
Los Angeles CA
323 663-9664

(P-17674)
WASSERMAN COMDEN & CASSELMAN (PA)
5567 Reseda Blvd Ste 330 (91356-2699)
P.O. Box 7033 (91357-7033)
PHONE.................................323 872-0995
Steve Wasserman, *Pt*
David B Casselman, *
Clifford H Pearson, *
Leonard J Comden, *
EMP: 88 EST: 1976
SQ FT: 15,000
SALES (est): 8.42MM
SALES (corp-wide): 8.42MM **Privately Held**
Web: www.wassermanlawgroup.com
SIC: **8111** General practice law office

(P-17675)
WEIL GOTSHAL & MANGES LLP
201 Redwood Shores Pkwy Ste 400 (94065)
PHONE.................................650 802-3000
Craig Adas, *Mng Pt*
EMP: 180
SALES (corp-wide): 290.51MM **Privately Held**
Web: www.weil.com
SIC: **8111** General practice law office
PA: Weil, Gotshal & Manges Llp
767 5th Ave Fl Conc1
New York NY
212 310-8000

(P-17676)
WEINBERG RGER RSNFELD A PROF C (PA)
1001 Marina Village Pkwy Ste 200 (94501-1091)
PHONE.................................510 337-1001
Stewart Weinberg, *Pr*
Andrea Laiacona, *
David Rosenfeld, *Stockholder**
EMP: 69 EST: 1964
SQ FT: 12,000
SALES (est): 9.98MM
SALES (corp-wide): 9.98MM **Privately Held**
Web: www.unioncounsel.net
SIC: **8111** General practice law office

(P-17677)
WHITE & CASE LLP
555 S Flower St Ste 2700 (90071-2433)
PHONE.................................213 620-7724
EMP: 103
SALES (corp-wide): 497.27MM **Privately Held**
Web: www.whitecase.com
SIC: **8111** General practice law office
PA: White & Case Llp
1221 Ave Of The Amrcas St
New York NY
212 819-8200

(P-17678)
WHITE & CASE LLP
3000 El Camino Real Ste 2-900 # & (94306-2113)

8111 - Legal Services (P-17679)

PHONE..............................650 213-0300
Krista Mancerelly, *Genl Mgr*
EMP: 60
SALES (corp-wide): 497.27MM **Privately Held**
Web: www.whitecase.com
SIC: 8111 General practice law office
PA: White & Case Llp
  1221 Ave Of The Amrcas St
  New York NY
  212 819-8200

(P-17679)
WILKE FLEURY HOFFELT GOULD & BIRNEY
Also Called: Powell, Matthew W
400 Capitol Mall Ste 2200 (95814-4403)
PHONE..............................916 441-2430
EMP: 61 EST: 1916
SALES (est): 1.09MM **Privately Held**
Web: www.wilkefleury.com
SIC: 8111 General practice law office

(P-17680)
WILSON ELSER MSKWITZ EDLMAN DC
555 S Flower St Ste 2900 (90071-2407)
PHONE..............................213 443-5100
Patrick M Kelly, *Mgr*
EMP: 68
SALES (corp-wide): 307.03MM **Privately Held**
Web: www.wilsonelser.com
SIC: 8111 General practice law office
PA: Wilson, Elser, Moskowitz, Edelman & Dicker Llp
  150 E 42nd St Fl 23
  New York NY
  212 490-3000

(P-17681)
WILSON SNSINI GDRICH RSATI PRO (PA)
650 Page Mill Rd (94304-1001)
PHONE..............................650 493-9300
Steven E Bochner, *CEO*
Larry W Sonsini, *
Jeff Saper, *
Donald E Bradley, *
Chris Groobey, *
EMP: 1100 EST: 1961
SQ FT: 184,000
SALES (est): 1.74MM
SALES (corp-wide): 1.74MM **Privately Held**
Web: www.wsgr.com
SIC: 8111 Corporate, partnership and business law

(P-17682)
WINGERT GRBING BRBKER JSTKIE L
1230 Columbia St Ste 400 (92101-8502)
PHONE..............................619 232-8151
Stephen Grebing, *Pr*
Charles Grebing, *Pt*
Michael Anello, *Pt*
Alan Brubaker, *Pt*
James Goodwin, *Pt*
EMP: 100 EST: 1974
SALES (est): 8.62MM **Privately Held**
Web: www.wingertlaw.com
SIC: 8111 General practice attorney, lawyer

(P-17683)
WINSTON & STRAWN LLP
101 California St Ste 3900 (94111-5894)
PHONE..............................415 591-1000
James Schwarz, *Dir*
EMP: 60
SALES (corp-wide): 445.94K **Privately Held**
Web: www.winston.com
SIC: 8111 General practice law office
PA: Winston & Strawn Llp
  35 W Wacker Dr Ste 4200
  Chicago IL
  312 558-5600

(P-17684)
WITHERS BERGMAN LLP
Also Called: Withers Bergman
12830 El Camino Real Ste 350 (92130-2977)
PHONE..............................203 974-0412
EMP: 348
Web: www.withersworldwide.com
SIC: 8111 General practice attorney, lawyer
HQ: Withers Bergman Llp
  157 Church St Fl 19
  New Haven CT
  203 789-1320

(P-17685)
WOLF RFKIN SHPIRO SCHLMAN RBK (PA)
Also Called: Grant, Richard S
11400 W Olympic Blvd Ste 900 (90064-1550)
PHONE..............................310 445-8817
Michael Wolf, *Sr Pt*
Leslie Marks, *Pt*
Roy Rifkin, *Pt*
Daniel Shapiro, *Pt*
Michael T Schulman, *Pt*
EMP: 67 EST: 1978
SALES (est): 14.21MM
SALES (corp-wide): 14.21MM **Privately Held**
Web: www.wrslawyers.com
SIC: 8111 General practice attorney, lawyer

(P-17686)
WOLF FIRM A LAW CORPORATION
Also Called: Wolf Firm
1651 E 4th St Ste 121 (92701-5117)
PHONE..............................949 720-9200
Alan S Wolf, *Pr*
EMP: 60 EST: 1993
SALES (est): 9.72MM **Privately Held**
Web: www.wolffirm.com
SIC: 8111 General practice law office

(P-17687)
WOMBLE BOND DICKINSON (US) LLP
12400 Wilshire Blvd Ste 600 (90025-1060)
PHONE..............................310 207-3800
EMP: 240
SALES (corp-wide): 218.48MM **Privately Held**
Web: www.womblebonddickinson.com
SIC: 8111 Specialized law offices, attorneys
PA: Womble Bond Dickinson (Us) Llp
  1 W 4th St
  Winston Salem NC
  336 721-3600

(P-17688)
WOODRUFF SPRADLIN & SMART
555 Anton Blvd Ste 1200 (92626-1912)
PHONE..............................714 558-7000
Ken Smart, *Pr*
Daniel K Spradlin, *
Thomas L Woodruff, *
Lois E Jeffrey, *

EMP: 62 EST: 1975
SALES (est): 8.4MM **Privately Held**
Web: www.wss-law.com
SIC: 8111 General practice attorney, lawyer

(P-17689)
WRIGHT FINLAY & ZAK LLP
4665 Macarthur Ct Ste 200 (92660-1811)
PHONE..............................949 477-5050
Robin P Wright, *Mng Pt*
Robert Finley, *Pt*
Jonathan Zak, *Pt*
EMP: 60 EST: 2002
SALES (est): 18.17MM **Privately Held**
Web: www.wrightlegal.net
SIC: 8111 General practice attorney, lawyer

(P-17690)
ZBS LAW LLP
30 Corporate Park Ste 450 (92606-3401)
PHONE..............................714 848-7920
Les Zieve, *Pt*
Paul Kim, *Prin*
EMP: 85 EST: 2020
SALES (est): 4.28MM **Privately Held**
Web: www.zbslaw.com
SIC: 8111 Real estate law

(P-17691)
ZIFFREN B B F G-L S&C FND
1801 Century Park W Fl 7 (90067-6401)
PHONE..............................310 552-3388
Kenneth Ziffren, *Owner*
Kenneth Ziffren, *Prin*
Harry M Brittenham, *
John G Branca, *
Dennis Luderer, *
EMP: 103 EST: 1979
SQ FT: 33,000
SALES (est): 17.17MM **Privately Held**
Web: www.ziffrenlaw.com
SIC: 8111 General practice law office

(P-17692)
ZWICKER & ASSOCIATES PC
1220 Concord Ave (94520-4906)
PHONE..............................925 689-7070
EMP: 68
Web: www.zwickerpc.com
SIC: 8111 General practice attorney, lawyer
PA: Zwicker & Associates, P.C.
  80 Minuteman Rd
  Andover MA

8211 Elementary And Secondary Schools

(P-17693)
ADAT ARI EL
Also Called: Adat ARI El Day School
12020 Burbank Blvd (91607-2198)
PHONE..............................818 766-4992
Joanne Klein, *Ex Dir*
EMP: 150 EST: 1938
SQ FT: 97,410
SALES (est): 9.16MM **Privately Held**
Web: www.aaedayschool.org
SIC: 8211 8661 8351 8299 Private elementary school; Temples; Montessori child development center; Religious school

(P-17694)
BEAUMONT UNFIED SCHL DST PUB F
Also Called: Community Day School
126 W Fifth St (92223-2142)
PHONE..............................951 845-6580
Douglas Walter, *Prin*

EMP: 341
SALES (corp-wide): 205.74MM **Privately Held**
Web: www.beaumontusd.us
SIC: 8211 8351 Public elementary and secondary schools; Group day care center
PA: Beaumont Unified School District
  Public Facilities Corporation
  350 W Brookside
  Cherry Valley CA
  951 845-1631

(P-17695)
BERKELEY HALL SCHL FOUNDATION
Also Called: Berkeley Hall School
16000 Mulholland Dr (90049-1123)
PHONE..............................310 476-6421
Sarah Colmaire, *Admn*
Caroline R Kuhn, *
EMP: 65 EST: 1911
SALES (est): 8.46MM **Privately Held**
Web: www.berkeleyhall.org
SIC: 8211 8351 Private elementary school; Nursery school

(P-17696)
BRAWLEY UNION HIGH SCHOOL DIST (PA)
480 N Imperial Ave (92227-1625)
PHONE..............................760 312-6068
Hasnik Danielian, *Superintnt*
Jenifer Layaye, *
EMP: 88 EST: 1908
SALES (est): 39.63MM
SALES (corp-wide): 39.63MM **Privately Held**
Web: www.brawleyhigh.org
SIC: 8211 8351 High school, junior or senior, nec; Preschool center

(P-17697)
CALIFORNIA SCHOOL OF MECH ARTS
Also Called: Lick Wilmerding High School
755 Ocean Ave (94112-1856)
PHONE..............................415 333-4021
Albert Adams Iii, *Headmaster*
EMP: 80 EST: 1895
SQ FT: 62,167
SALES (est): 32.89MM **Privately Held**
Web: www.lwhs.org
SIC: 8211 6512 Preparatory school; Commercial and industrial building operation

(P-17698)
CAMPBELL CHRISTIAN SCHOOL
1075 W Campbell Ave (95008-1753)
PHONE..............................408 370-4900
Shawn Stuart, *Admn*
Shawn Stewart, *
EMP: 64 EST: 1967
SALES (est): 7.4MM **Privately Held**
Web: www.campbellchristian.org
SIC: 8211 7032 Private elementary school; Summer camp, except day and sports instructional

(P-17699)
CAPE INC
Also Called: COMMUNITY ASSOC PRE-SCHOOL EDU
2406 Armstrong St (94551-7617)
PHONE..............................925 443-3434
Rosemary Almand, *Ex Dir*
EMP: 87 EST: 1962
SALES (est): 6.35MM **Privately Held**
Web: www.capeheadstart.org

PRODUCTS & SERVICES SECTION
8211 - Elementary And Secondary Schools (P-17719)

SIC: 8211 8351 8699 Elementary school, nec
; Preschool center; Charitable organization

(P-17700)
CEDARS OF MARIN (PA)
115 Upper Rd (94957-9686)
P.O. Box 947 (94957-0947)
PHONE..............................415 454-5310
Brenda Mcivor, *Ex Dir*
EMP: 94 EST: 1919
SQ FT: 35,000
SALES (est): 15.1MM
SALES (corp-wide): 15.1MM **Privately Held**
Web: www.cedarslife.org
SIC: 8211 8052 School for retarded, nec;
  Intermediate care facilities

(P-17701)
CHRISTIAN ARCADIA SCHOOL
Also Called: Christian Schl Soc of Arcadia
1900 S Santa Anita Ave (91006-4607)
PHONE..............................626 574-8229
Edward Limon, *Prin*
Steve Blankenship, *
Ryan Tungate, *
Greg Saltzer, *
EMP: 70 EST: 1945
SALES (est): 5.63MM **Privately Held**
Web: www.arcadiachristianschool.org
SIC: 8211 8351 Private elementary school;
  Preschool center

(P-17702)
CHRISTIAN MILPITAS SCHOOL (PA)
3435 Birchwood Ln (95132-1308)
PHONE..............................408 945-6530
Lu Gilbert, *CFO*
Clark Gilbert, *
Connie Segreto, *
Ken Van Meter, *
EMP: 126 EST: 1975
SQ FT: 2,000
SALES (est): 6.99MM
SALES (corp-wide): 6.99MM **Privately Held**
Web: www.milpitaschristian.org
SIC: 8211 8351 Private elementary and
  secondary schools; Child day care services

(P-17703)
CHRISTIAN TURLOCK SCHOOLS (PA)
1619 E Monte Vista Ave (95382-9184)
P.O. Box 1540 (95381-1540)
PHONE..............................209 632-2337
Karen Winters, *Superintnt*
Dave Schnurstein, *
EMP: 80 EST: 1979
SALES (est): 7.34MM
SALES (corp-wide): 7.34MM **Privately Held**
Web: www.turlockchristian.com
SIC: 8211 8351 Private elementary and
  secondary schools; Preschool center

(P-17704)
CLAIRBOURN SCHOOL
8400 Huntington Dr (91775-1154)
PHONE..............................626 286-3108
Robert Nafie, *Pr*
EMP: 60 EST: 1926
SQ FT: 24,403
SALES (est): 5.94MM **Privately Held**
Web: www.clairbourn.org
SIC: 8211 8351 Private elementary and
  secondary schools; Child day care services

(P-17705)
COMPTON UNIFIED SCHOOL DST
Also Called: Edward G Chester Adult Center
1104 E 148th St (90220-1339)
PHONE..............................310 898-6470
Saundra T Bishop, *Dir*
EMP: 61
SALES (corp-wide): 391.82MM **Privately Held**
Web: www.compton.k12.ca.us
SIC: 8211 8322 Public elementary and
  secondary schools; Adult day care center
PA: Compton Unified School District
  501 S Santa Fe Ave
  Compton CA
  310 639-4321

(P-17706)
COMPTON UNIFIED SCHOOL DST
2600 N Central Ave (90222-1640)
PHONE..............................310 639-4321
EMP: 64
SALES (corp-wide): 391.82MM **Privately Held**
Web: www.compton.k12.ca.us
SIC: 8211 7389 Public elementary and
  secondary schools; Personal service
  agents, brokers, and bureaus
PA: Compton Unified School District
  501 S Santa Fe Ave
  Compton CA
  310 639-4321

(P-17707)
CONTRA COSTA CNTY OFF EDUCATN (PA)
77 Santa Barbara Rd (94523-4215)
PHONE..............................925 942-3388
EMP: 130 EST: 1950
SALES (est): 123.44MM **Privately Held**
Web: www.cccoe.k12.ca.us
SIC: 8211 8741 8331 Public elementary and
  secondary schools; Management services;
  Job training and related services

(P-17708)
DIOCESE STOCKTON EDUCTL OFF
Also Called: Sacred Heart Pre-School
1250 Cooper Ave Ste 3 (95380-4174)
PHONE..............................209 634-8578
Debra Canella, *Dir*
EMP: 144
SALES (corp-wide): 121.08MM **Privately Held**
Web: www.dioceseofstockton.com
SIC: 8211 8351 Catholic elementary and
  secondary schools; Preschool center
PA: Diocese Of Stockton Educational Office
  212 N San Joaquin St
  Stockton CA
  209 466-0636

(P-17709)
DUBNOFF CTR FOR CHILD DEV EDCT (PA)
10526 Dubnoff Way (91606-3921)
PHONE..............................818 755-4950
Sandra Babcock, *Pr*
Sandra Sternig-babcock, *Pr*
EMP: 94 EST: 1948
SQ FT: 13,968
SALES (est): 5.59MM
SALES (corp-wide): 5.59MM **Privately Held**

SIC: 8211 8093 8361 Specialty education;
  Specialty outpatient clinics, nec; Residential
  care

(P-17710)
EGREMONT SCHOOLS INC
19850 Devonshire St (91311-3598)
PHONE..............................818 363-7803
Tina Struve, *Ex Dir*
EMP: 63 EST: 1936
SQ FT: 22,298
SALES (est): 2.44MM **Privately Held**
Web: www.egremont.org
SIC: 8211 8351 Private elementary school;
  Preschool center

(P-17711)
FIRST ASSMBLY OF GOD BKRSFIELD
Also Called: Stockdale Christian School
4901 California Ave (93309-1111)
PHONE..............................661 327-2227
Reverend Steven Hunt, *Ch Bd*
Kevin Harrel, *
Rick Roper, *
EMP: 90 EST: 1924
SQ FT: 60,000
SALES (est): 20.78MM **Privately Held**
Web: www.stockdalechristian.com
SIC: 8211 8351 Elementary and secondary
  schools; Preschool center

(P-17712)
GILLISPIE SCHOOL
7380 Girard Ave (92037-5139)
PHONE..............................858 459-3773
Alison Fleming, *Prin*
EMP: 60 EST: 1936
SALES (est): 10.02MM **Privately Held**
Web: www.gillispie.org
SIC: 8211 8351 Private elementary school;
  Preschool center

(P-17713)
GRACE YOKLEY MIDDLE SCHOOL
Also Called: Mountain View Schl Dist Grace
2947 S Turner Ave (91761-8146)
PHONE..............................909 947-6774
EMP: 63 EST: 2010
SALES (est): 451.29K **Privately Held**
Web: gys-mvsd-ca.schoolloop.com
SIC: 8211 8641 High school, junior or senior,
  nec; Parent-teachers' association

(P-17714)
GUADALUPE UNION SCHOOL DST (PA)
4465 9th St (93434-1436)
P.O. Box 788 (93434-0788)
PHONE..............................805 343-2114
Ed Cora, *Superintnt*
Celia Ramos, *
Jeffrey Alvarez, *
EMP: 114 EST: 1890
SALES (est): 36.96MM
SALES (corp-wide): 36.96MM **Privately Held**
Web: www.guadusd.org
SIC: 8211 8741 Public elementary school;
  Management services

(P-17715)
HAYWARD UNIFIED SCHOOL DST
Hayward High School
1633 East Ave (94541-5314)
PHONE..............................510 723-3170
David Seymour, *Prin*

EMP: 81
SALES (corp-wide): 418.63MM **Privately Held**
Web: hhs.husd.us
SIC: 8211 8351 Public junior high school;
  Preschool center
PA: Hayward Unified School District
  24411 Amador St
  Hayward CA
  510 784-2600

(P-17716)
HEMET UNIFIED SCHOOL DISTRICT
Also Called: Nutrition Services
2075 W Acacia Ave (92545-3746)
PHONE..............................951 765-5100
Kathy Anderson, *Brnch Mgr*
EMP: 80
SALES (corp-wide): 452.75MM **Privately Held**
Web: www.hemetusd.org
SIC: 8211 8734 Public elementary and
  secondary schools; Testing laboratories
PA: Hemet Unified School District
  1791 W Acacia Ave
  Hemet CA
  951 765-5100

(P-17717)
HEMET UNIFIED SCHOOL DISTRICT
Also Called: Santa Fe Middle School
985 N Cawston Ave (92545-1551)
P.O. Box 881 (92546-0881)
PHONE..............................951 765-6287
Todd Biggert, *Prin*
EMP: 80
SALES (corp-wide): 452.75MM **Privately Held**
Web: ranchoviejo.hemetusd.org
SIC: 8211 8699 Public elementary and
  secondary schools; Personal interest
  organization
PA: Hemet Unified School District
  1791 W Acacia Ave
  Hemet CA
  951 765-5100

(P-17718)
INCLUSIVE EDCATN CMNTY PRTNR I
Also Called: Iecp
2323 Roosevelt Blvd Apt 3 (93035-4480)
PHONE..............................805 985-4808
Rick B Clemens, *Pr*
Rick Clemens, *
EMP: 300 EST: 2002
SALES (est): 11.05MM **Privately Held**
Web: www.iecp.us
SIC: 8211 8351 Specialty education;
  Preschool center

(P-17719)
JEWISH CMNTY CTR SAN FRANCISCO (PA)
3200 California St (94118-1994)
PHONE..............................415 292-1200
Barry Finesone, *Pr*
Diane Walters, *
EMP: 243 EST: 1878
SQ FT: 35,000
SALES (est): 27.3MM
SALES (corp-wide): 27.3MM **Privately Held**
Web: www.jccsf.org
SIC: 8211 7032 8322 Preparatory school;
  Youth camps; Individual and family services

8211 - Elementary And Secondary Schools (P-17720)

(P-17720)
LAGUNA BLANCA SCHOOL (PA)
4125 Paloma Dr (93110-2146)
PHONE.....................................805 687-2461
Sue Smith, *Mgr*
EMP: 94 **EST:** 1933
SQ FT: 24,857
SALES (est): 19.66MM
SALES (corp-wide): 19.66MM **Privately Held**
Web: www.lagunablanca.org
SIC: 8211 8748 Private elementary and secondary schools; Business consulting, nec

(P-17721)
LINDEN UNIFIED SCHOOL DISTRICT
100 N Jack Tone Rd (95215-9575)
PHONE.....................................209 946-0707
Doctor Ronald Estes, *Admn*
EMP: 87
SALES (corp-wide): 57.96MM **Privately Held**
SIC: 8211 8744 Public elementary and secondary schools; Base maintenance (providing personnel on continuing basis)
PA: Linden Unified School District
18527 E Highway 26
Linden CA
209 887-3894

(P-17722)
LONG BEACH UNIFIED SCHOOL DST
Also Called: Muir Elementary School
3038 Delta Ave (90810-2843)
PHONE.....................................562 426-5571
Sophia Griffieth, *Prin*
EMP: 95
SALES (corp-wide): 788.46MM **Privately Held**
Web: www.lbschools.net
SIC: 8211 6531 Public junior high school; Rental agent, real estate
PA: Long Beach Unified School District
1515 Hughes Way
Long Beach CA
562 997-8000

(P-17723)
LOS ANGELES UNIFIED SCHOOL DST
Also Called: Granada Hills Sr High School
10535 Zelzah Ave (91344-5902)
PHONE.....................................818 360-2361
Brian Bauer, *Prin*
EMP: 61
SALES (corp-wide): 9.38B **Privately Held**
Web: www.laallcityband.com
SIC: 8211 8748 Elementary and secondary schools; Business consulting, nec
PA: Los Angeles Unified School District
333 S Beaudry Ave Ste 209
Los Angeles CA
213 241-1000

(P-17724)
LOS ANGELES UNIFIED SCHOOL DST
Also Called: West Valley Occupational Ctr
6200 Winnetka Ave (91367-3826)
PHONE.....................................818 346-3540
Candace Lee, *Prin*
EMP: 148
SALES (corp-wide): 9.38B **Privately Held**
Web: www.wvoc.net
SIC: 8211 8299 8331 Public elementary and secondary schools; Educational service, nondegree granting: continuing educ.; Job training and related services
PA: Los Angeles Unified School District
333 S Beaudry Ave Ste 209
Los Angeles CA
213 241-1000

(P-17725)
LYNWOOD UNIFIED SCHOOL DST
Also Called: Lindbergh Child Care Center
12120 Lindbergh Ave (90262-4701)
PHONE.....................................310 631-7308
Maria Noriega, *Dir*
EMP: 88
SQ FT: 3,790
SALES (corp-wide): 236.59MM **Privately Held**
Web: www.mylusd.org
SIC: 8211 8351 Public elementary and secondary schools; Child day care services
PA: Lynwood Unified School District
11321 Bullis Rd
Lynwood CA
310 886-1600

(P-17726)
MARIN COUNTY OFFICE EDUCATION (PA)
1111 Las Gallinas Ave (94903-1843)
P.O. Box 4925 (94913-4925)
PHONE.....................................415 472-4110
Mary Jane Burke, *Supervisor*
Tracee Edmunds, *
Terena Mares, *
EMP: 360 **EST:** 1854
SQ FT: 36,000
SALES (est): 55.22MM
SALES (corp-wide): 55.22MM **Privately Held**
Web: www.marinschools.org
SIC: 8211 8331 Public elementary and secondary schools; Job training and related services

(P-17727)
MERCED CITY SCHOOL DISTRICT
Also Called: Franklin Elementary School
2736 Franklin Rd (95348-9434)
PHONE.....................................209 385-6364
Lori Slaven, *Prin*
EMP: 65
SALES (corp-wide): 188.89MM **Privately Held**
Web: www.mcsd.k12.ca.us
SIC: 8211 8351 Public elementary school; Preschool center
PA: Merced City School District
444 W 23rd St
Merced CA
209 385-6600

(P-17728)
METROPOLITAN EDUCATION DST (PA)
760 Hillsdale Ave Bldg 6 (95136-1106)
PHONE.....................................408 723-6464
Alyssa Lynch, *Superintnt*
EMP: 86 **EST:** 1982
SQ FT: 240,000
SALES (est): 122.76K
SALES (corp-wide): 122.76K **Privately Held**
Web: www.metroed.net
SIC: 8211 8331 Public elementary and secondary schools; Job training and related services

(P-17729)
MILLER CREEK SCHOOL DISTRICT
Also Called: Dixie SC Dst Maint Dept
121 Marinwood Ave (94903-1521)
PHONE.....................................415 492-3776
Tim Walsh, *Dir*
EMP: 142
SALES (corp-wide): 32.11MM **Privately Held**
Web: www.millercreeksd.org
SIC: 8211 7349 Public elementary school; School custodian, contract basis
PA: Miller Creek School District Inc
380 Nova Albion Way
San Rafael CA
415 492-3700

(P-17730)
MILPITAS UNIFIED SCHOOL DST
Also Called: Rose Child Development Center
250a Roswell Dr (95035-5945)
PHONE.....................................408 635-2686
Kathy Lincoln, *Prin*
EMP: 63
SALES (corp-wide): 197.57MM **Privately Held**
Web: www.musd.org
SIC: 8211 8351 Public adult education school ; Child day care services
PA: Milpitas Unified School District
1331 E Calaveras Blvd
Milpitas CA
408 635-2600

(P-17731)
MOTHER OF DIVINE GRACE INC
407 Bryant Cir Ste B (93023-4228)
PHONE.....................................805 646-5818
Laura Berquist, *Pr*
EMP: 65 **EST:** 2007
SALES (est): 5.81MM **Privately Held**
Web: www.modg.org
SIC: 8211 8742 Catholic combined elementary and secondary school; School, college, university consultant

(P-17732)
MOUNTAIN VIEW ELMNTARY SCHL DS
Also Called: Mountain View Children'c Ctr
2109 Burkett Rd (91733-4113)
PHONE.....................................626 652-4250
Alma Gonzales, *Dir*
EMP: 63
SALES (corp-wide): 128.83MM **Privately Held**
Web: www.mtviewschools.com
SIC: 8211 8351 Public elementary school; Head Start center, except in conjunction with school
PA: Mountain View Elementary School District
3320 Gilman Rd
El Monte CA
626 652-4000

(P-17733)
MT DIABLO UNIFIED SCHOOL DST
Also Called: Mt Diablo Adult Education
1266 San Carlos Ave (94518-1102)
PHONE.....................................925 685-7340
Vittore Abbate, *Prin*
EMP: 67
SALES (corp-wide): 504.84MM **Privately Held**
Web: www.mdusd.org
SIC: 8211 8322 Public elementary and secondary schools; Adult day care center
PA: Mt. Diablo Unified School District School Facilities Corporation
1936 Carlotta Dr
Concord CA
925 682-8000

(P-17734)
NATIONAL SCHOOL DISTRICT
Also Called: Maintenance Operations Svc Ctr
1400 N Ave (91950-4825)
PHONE.....................................619 336-7770
Jerry O'hara, *Prin*
EMP: 202
SALES (corp-wide): 95.04MM **Privately Held**
Web: www.nsd.us
SIC: 8211 7349 Public elementary and secondary schools; School custodian, contract basis
PA: National School District
1500 N Ave
National City CA
619 336-7500

(P-17735)
NEWPORT MESA UNIFIED SCHL DST
Also Called: Nutrition Services Department
2985 Barrish St Bldg E (92626)
PHONE.....................................714 424-5090
Dale Ellis, *Dir*
EMP: 69
SALES (corp-wide): 443.34MM **Privately Held**
Web: www.nmusd.us
SIC: 8211 8099 Public combined elementary and secondary school; Nutrition services
PA: Newport Mesa Unified School District
2985 Bear St Ste A
Costa Mesa CA
714 424-5000

(P-17736)
NEWPORT MESA UNIFIED SCHL DST
Also Called: Harbor View Pre-School
900 Goldenrod Ave (92625-1503)
PHONE.....................................949 515-6940
Todd Schmidt, *Prin*
EMP: 69
SALES (corp-wide): 443.34MM **Privately Held**
Web: www.nmusd.us
SIC: 8211 8351 Public elementary school; Preschool center
PA: Newport Mesa Unified School District
2985 Bear St Ste A
Costa Mesa CA
714 424-5000

(P-17737)
OJAI VALLEY SCHOOL (PA)
Also Called: OVS
723 El Paseo Rd (93023-2498)
PHONE.....................................805 646-1423
EMP: 83 **EST:** 1911
SALES (est): 16.08MM
SALES (corp-wide): 16.08MM **Privately Held**
Web: www.ovs.org
SIC: 8211 8351 Private combined elementary and secondary school; Child day care services

(P-17738)
PAGE PRIVATE SCHOOL
419 S Robertson Blvd (90211-3603)
PHONE.....................................323 272-3429

PRODUCTS & SERVICES SECTION
8211 - Elementary And Secondary Schools (P-17757)

Janice Kim, *Prin*
EMP: 81
SQ FT: 7,074
SALES (corp-wide): 3.2MM **Privately Held**
Web: www.pageacademyca.com
SIC: 8211 8351 Private elementary school; Group day care center
PA: Page Private School
657 Victoria St
Costa Mesa CA
949 515-1700

(P-17739)
PALM VALLEY SCHOOL
35525 Da Vall Dr (92270-1822)
PHONE..................760 328-0861
Robert Graves, *Prin*
Grahm Hookey, *
EMP: 65 **EST:** 1958
SALES (est): 6.17MM **Privately Held**
Web: www.palmvalley-school.org
SIC: 8211 8748 Private elementary and secondary schools; Business consulting, nec

(P-17740)
POLYTECHNIC SCHOOL
1030 E California Blvd (91106-4042)
PHONE..................626 792-2147
John W Bracker, *Head of School*
Wendy Munger, *
EMP: 331 **EST:** 1907
SALES (est): 47.3MM **Privately Held**
Web: www.polytechnic.org
SIC: 8211 8351 Kindergarten; Preschool center

(P-17741)
PRESIDIO HILL SCHOOL
3839 Washington St (94118-1612)
PHONE..................415 213-8600
Kerry Davis, *Dir*
EMP: 95 **EST:** 1918
SQ FT: 6,596
SALES (est): 10.29MM **Privately Held**
Web: www.presidiohill.org
SIC: 8211 8351 Private combined elementary and secondary school; Child day care services

(P-17742)
PRINCE PEACE LUTHERAN CHURCH
Also Called: Prince Peace Lutheran School
38451 Fremont Blvd (94536-6030)
PHONE..................510 797-8186
Dan Dueck, *Prin*
Marcia Houseworth, *
EMP: 82 **EST:** 1980
SQ FT: 50,000
SALES (est): 10.66MM **Privately Held**
Web: www.popchristianschool.com
SIC: 8211 8661 8351 Private elementary and secondary schools; Lutheran Church; Preschool center

(P-17743)
ROMAN CTHLIC ARCHBSHOP OF SAN
Also Called: St Patricks School
120 King St (94939-1943)
PHONE..................415 924-0501
Linda Kinkade, *Prin*
EMP: 98
SALES (corp-wide): 91.44MM **Privately Held**
Web: www.stpatricksmarin.org
SIC: 8211 7371 Private elementary and secondary schools; Computer software development

PA: The Roman Catholic Archbishop Of San Francisco
1 Peter Yorke Way 1 # 1
San Francisco CA
415 614-5500

(P-17744)
ROMAN CTHLIC DIOCESE OF ORANGE
Also Called: Saint Cecilia School
1311 Sycamore Ave (92780-6276)
PHONE..................714 544-1533
Mary Alvarado, *Prin*
EMP: 132
SALES (corp-wide): 92.62MM **Privately Held**
Web: www.morethanschool.org
SIC: 8211 8351 Catholic combined elementary and secondary school; Preschool center
PA: The Roman Catholic Diocese Of Orange
13280 Chapman Ave
Garden Grove CA
714 282-3000

(P-17745)
ROMAN CTHLIC DIOCESE OF ORANGE
Also Called: St Josephs School
801 N Bradford Ave (92870-4515)
PHONE..................714 528-1794
Joann Telles, *Prin*
EMP: 229
SALES (corp-wide): 92.62MM **Privately Held**
Web: www.rcbo.org
SIC: 8211 8661 7389 Catholic junior high school; Catholic Church; Fund raising organizations
PA: The Roman Catholic Diocese Of Orange
13280 Chapman Ave
Garden Grove CA
714 282-3000

(P-17746)
SAN DIEGO CMNTY COLLEGE DST
Also Called: Cesar Chavez Center
1960 National Ave (92113-2116)
PHONE..................619 388-4850
Rudy Kastelic, *Brnch Mgr*
EMP: 106
SQ FT: 4,521
SALES (corp-wide): 146.65MM **Privately Held**
Web: www.sdccd.edu
SIC: 8211 8742 Public adult education school ; Management consulting services
PA: San Diego Community College District
3375 Camino Del Rio S
San Diego CA
619 388-6500

(P-17747)
SAN FRANCISCO UNIFIED SCHL DST (PA)
Also Called: Adminstrtion Offces For Schl D
555 Franklin St (94102-4414)
PHONE..................415 241-6000
Arlene Ackerman, *Superintnt*
▲ **EMP:** 250 **EST:** 1856
SQ FT: 14,000
SALES (est): 918.78MM
SALES (corp-wide): 918.78MM **Privately Held**
Web: www.sfusd.edu

SIC: 8211 8741 Public elementary and secondary schools; Administrative management

(P-17748)
SAN RAMON VLY UNIFIED SCHL DST
Also Called: Montivista
3131 Stone Valley Rd (94526-1129)
PHONE..................925 552-2880
Kevin Ahern, *Prin*
EMP: 78
SALES (corp-wide): 470.85MM **Privately Held**
Web: www.srvusd.net
SIC: 8211 8641 Public elementary school; Parent-teachers' association
PA: San Ramon Valley Unified School District
699 Old Orchard Dr
Danville CA
925 552-5500

(P-17749)
SIERRA CANYON INC
Also Called: Sierra Canyon Day Camp
11052 Independence Ave (91311-1562)
PHONE..................818 882-8121
Jim Skruneis, *Pr*
Howard Wang, *
Stephen Horwitz, *
EMP: 78 **EST:** 1971
SQ FT: 35,000
SALES (est): 5.66MM **Privately Held**
Web: www.sierracanyondaycamp.com
SIC: 8211 7999 Private elementary and secondary schools; Day camp

(P-17750)
SONOMA COUNTRY DAY SCHOOL
Also Called: Scds
4400 Day School Pl (95403-8221)
PHONE..................707 284-3200
Katie Murphy, *Ch*
EMP: 69 **EST:** 1983
SALES (est): 10.76MM **Privately Held**
Web: www.scds.org
SIC: 8211 8351 Private elementary and secondary schools; Group day care center

(P-17751)
SOUTH PNINSULA HEBREW DAY SCHL
Also Called: SPHDS
1030 Astoria Dr (94087-3008)
PHONE..................408 738-3060
Ann Goewert, *Prin*
Allen Selis, *
EMP: 65 **EST:** 1972
SALES (est): 7.19MM **Privately Held**
Web: www.sphds.org
SIC: 8211 8351 Private elementary and secondary schools; Preschool center

(P-17752)
ST MATTHEWS EPISCOPAL DAY SCHL
16 Baldwin Ave (94401-3807)
PHONE..................650 342-5436
Mark Hale, *Pt*
EMP: 115 **EST:** 1952
SALES (est): 28.46MM **Privately Held**
Web: www.episcopaldaysanmateo.org
SIC: 8211 8351 Private elementary school; Preschool center

(P-17753)
TEMECULA VLY UNIFIED SCHL DST
Also Called: Pauba Valley Elem. School
33125 Regina Dr (92592-1473)
PHONE..................951 302-5140
EMP: 70
SALES (corp-wide): 408.68MM **Privately Held**
Web: www.tvusd.k12.ca.us
SIC: 8211 8641 Public elementary school; Parent-teachers' association
PA: Temecula Valley Unified School District School Facilities Corporation
31350 Rancho Vista Rd
Temecula CA
951 676-2661

(P-17754)
TUSTIN UNIFIED SCHOOL DISTRICT
Also Called: Lestonnac Preschool
16791 E Main St (92780-4034)
PHONE..................714 542-4271
Sharon Lamtrecht, *Prin*
EMP: 66
SALES (corp-wide): 366.56MM **Privately Held**
Web: www.sjdlschool.com
SIC: 8211 8351 Public elementary and secondary schools; Preschool center
PA: Tustin Unified School District
300 S C St
Tustin CA
714 730-7515

(P-17755)
VALLEY MONTESSORI SCHOOL
Also Called: TRY VALLEY MONTESSORI SCHOOL
1273 N Livermore Ave (94551-1707)
PHONE..................925 455-8021
Ann Clark, *Dir*
Mary Ellen Kordas, *
EMP: 80 **EST:** 1976
SALES (est): 7.25MM **Privately Held**
Web: www.vmschool.org
SIC: 8211 8351 Private elementary and secondary schools; Montessori child development center

(P-17756)
VICTOR TREATMENT CENTERS INC
Also Called: Victor Treatment Centers
12755 N Highway 88 (95240-9323)
P.O. Box 330 (95253-0330)
PHONE..................209 465-1080
Terry Crumpacker, *Prin*
EMP: 74
SALES (corp-wide): 23.04MM **Privately Held**
Web: www.victor.org
SIC: 8211 8361 Specialty education; Emotionally disturbed home
PA: Victor Treatment Centers, Inc.
1360 E Lassen Ave
Chico CA
530 893-0758

(P-17757)
VISTA DEL MAR CHILD FMLY SVCS (PA)
3200 Motor Ave (90034-3710)
PHONE..................310 836-1223
Roosevelena Wilson, *CEO*
EMP: 262 **EST:** 1908
SQ FT: 100,000
SALES (est): 40.28MM

8211 - Elementary And Secondary Schools (P-17758)

SALES (corp-wide): 40.28MM **Privately Held**
Web: www.vistadelmar.org
SIC: **8211** 8361 Elementary and secondary schools; Mentally handicapped home

(P-17758)
WEST ANGELES CH GOD IN CHRST
Also Called: West Angeles Christian Academy
3010 Crenshaw Blvd (90016-4263)
PHONE..............................323 731-2567
Deloris A Dumbar, *Prin*
EMP: 152
SALES (corp-wide): 21.89MM **Privately Held**
Web: www.westa.org
SIC: **8211** 6512 Private elementary school; Theater building, ownership and operation
PA: West Angeles Church Of God In Christ
3045 Crenshaw Blvd
Los Angeles CA
323 733-8300

(P-17759)
WHITTIER UNION HIGH SCHL DIST
Also Called: Capc Adult Services
7200 Greenleaf Ave Ste 170 (90602-1367)
PHONE..............................562 693-8826
Dan Hulbert, *Dir*
EMP: 106
SALES (corp-wide): 206.51MM **Privately Held**
Web: www.wuhsd.org
SIC: **8211** 8322 Public elementary and secondary schools; Social services for the handicapped
PA: Whittier Union High School Dist
9401 Painter Ave
Whittier CA
562 698-8121

8221 Colleges And Universities

(P-17760)
AMERICAN CLLEGE OF TRDTNAL CHN (PA)
Also Called: Actcm
1453 Mission St (94103-2557)
PHONE..............................415 282-0316
Lixin Huang, *Pr*
EMP: 90 EST: 1980
SALES (est): 8.27MM
SALES (corp-wide): 8.27MM **Privately Held**
Web: www.actcm.edu
SIC: **8221** 8093 University; Mental health clinic, outpatient

(P-17761)
ASSOCIATED STUDENTS UCLA
Also Called: Ucla Dept of Design Media
11000 Kinross Ave Ave Ste 245 (90095-2000)
P.O. Box 951615 (90095-1615)
PHONE..............................310 206-8282
Diane Mills, *Prin*
EMP: 236
SALES (corp-wide): 47.49MM **Privately Held**
Web: asucla.ucla.edu
SIC: **8221** 7336 University; Graphic arts and related design
PA: Associated Students U.C.L.A.
308 Westwood Plz
Los Angeles CA
310 794-8836

(P-17762)
LELAND STANFORD JUNIOR UNIV (PA)
Also Called: Stanford University
450 Jane Stanford Way (94305-2004)
P.O. Box 20410 (94309-0410)
PHONE..............................650 723-2300
Richard Saller, *Pr*
Debra Zumwalt, *
Randall S Livingston, *
▲ EMP: 200 EST: 1891
SALES (est): 15.13B
SALES (corp-wide): 15.13B **Privately Held**
Web: www.stanford.edu
SIC: **8221** 8069 8062 University; Childrens' hospital; General medical and surgical hospitals

(P-17763)
LELAND STANFORD JUNIOR UNIV
Also Called: Stanford University - Et
505 Broadway St 4th Fl (94063-3122)
PHONE..............................650 935-5365
Marc Tessier-lavigne, *Pr*
EMP: 1000
SALES (corp-wide): 15.13B **Privately Held**
Web: www.stanford.edu
SIC: **8221** 8069 8062 University; Childrens' hospital; General medical and surgical hospitals
PA: Leland Stanford Junior University
450 Jane Stanford Way
Stanford CA
650 723-2300

(P-17764)
LELAND STANFORD JUNIOR UNIV
Also Called: Stanford School of Medicine
1291 Welch Rd (94305-5102)
PHONE..............................650 721-2726
EMP: 107
SALES (corp-wide): 15.13B **Privately Held**
Web: www.stanford.edu
SIC: **8221** 8062 University; General medical and surgical hospitals
PA: Leland Stanford Junior University
450 Jane Stanford Way
Stanford CA
650 723-2300

(P-17765)
LOS ANGELES UNIFIED SCHOOL DST
Also Called: Central Shop
1240 Naomi Ave (90021-2393)
PHONE..............................213 763-2900
Herman Perez, *Dir*
EMP: 84
SALES (corp-wide): 9.38B **Privately Held**
Web: www.laallcityband.com
SIC: **8221** 7349 Colleges and universities; Building maintenance services, nec
PA: Los Angeles Unified School District
333 S Beaudry Ave Ste 209
Los Angeles CA
213 241-1000

(P-17766)
MARSHALL B KETCHUM UNIVERSITY (PA)
Also Called: Eye Care Center, The
2575 Yorba Linda Blvd (92831-1699)
PHONE..............................714 463-7567
EMP: 160 EST: 1911
SALES (est): 42.57MM
SALES (corp-wide): 42.57MM **Privately Held**
Web: www.ketchum.edu
SIC: **8221** 8042 Professional schools; Offices and clinics of optometrists

(P-17767)
SAN DIEGO STATE UNIVERSITY
Also Called: K P B S
5200 Campanile Dr (92182-1901)
PHONE..............................619 594-1515
Tom Karlo, *Mgr*
EMP: 100
SALES (corp-wide): 534.4MM **Privately Held**
Web: www.kpbs.org
SIC: **8221** 9411 4832 University; Administration of educational programs, State government; Educational
HQ: San Diego State University
5500 Campanile Dr
San Diego CA

(P-17768)
SAN FRANCISCO ART INSTITUTE INC
Also Called: Sfai
800 Chestnut St (94133-2206)
PHONE..............................415 771-7020
▲ EMP: 184 EST: 1871
SALES (est): 7.74MM **Privately Held**
Web: www.sfai.edu
SIC: **8221** 8412 College, except junior; Museums and art galleries

(P-17769)
UNIVERSITY CAL LOS ANGELES
Tanms Engineering Research Ctr
420 Westwood Plz Rm 7702 (90095-0001)
PHONE..............................310 825-7852
EMP: 200
SALES (corp-wide): 534.4MM **Privately Held**
Web: www.ucla.edu
SIC: **8221** 8733 9411 University; Noncommercial research organizations; Administration of educational programs
HQ: University Of California, Los Angeles
405 Hilgard Ave
Los Angeles CA

(P-17770)
UNIVERSITY CAL SAN FRANCISCO
Also Called: Center For Rprductive Sciences
513 Parnassus Ave # 0556 (94143-2205)
PHONE..............................415 476-2695
Lan Pham, *Admn*
EMP: 83
SALES (corp-wide): 534.4MM **Privately Held**
Web: www.ucsf.edu
SIC: **8221** 9411 8011 Colleges and universities; Administration of educational programs; Offices and clinics of medical doctors
HQ: University Cal San Francisco
513 Parnassus Ave 115f
San Francisco CA

(P-17771)
UNIVERSITY CAL SAN FRANCISCO
Also Called: Ucsf Otlrynglogy - Head Neck S
2380 Sutter St Fl 3 (94115-3006)
PHONE..............................415 353-2757
EMP: 83
SALES (corp-wide): 534.4MM **Privately Held**
Web: ohns.ucsf.edu
SIC: **8221** 9411 8011 University; Administration of educational programs; Medical centers
HQ: University Cal San Francisco
513 Parnassus Ave 115f
San Francisco CA

(P-17772)
UNIVERSITY CAL SAN FRANCISCO
Also Called: Ucsf Design Construction
1100 Van Ness Ave (94109-6978)
PHONE..............................415 885-7257
Tim Mahaney, *Dir*
EMP: 83
SALES (corp-wide): 534.4MM **Privately Held**
Web: www.ucsf.edu
SIC: **8221** 9411 8011 University; Administration of educational programs; Medical centers
HQ: University Cal San Francisco
513 Parnassus Ave 115f
San Francisco CA

(P-17773)
UNIVERSITY CAL SAN FRANCISCO
Also Called: Clinical Pharmacy
521 Parnassus Ave Rm C152 (94143-2206)
P.O. Box 622 (94104-0622)
PHONE..............................415 476-3016
Debra Petrie, *Mgr*
EMP: 104
SALES (corp-wide): 534.4MM **Privately Held**
Web: nursing.ucsf.edu
SIC: **8221** 9411 8062 University; Administration of educational programs; General medical and surgical hospitals
HQ: University Cal San Francisco
513 Parnassus Ave 115f
San Francisco CA

(P-17774)
UNIVERSITY CAL SAN FRANCISCO
Also Called: Osher Ctr For Intgrtive Mdcine
1545 Divisadero St Fl 4 (94143-3400)
P.O. Box 1726 (94143)
PHONE..............................415 353-7700
Margareth Chesney, *Dir*
EMP: 114
SALES (corp-wide): 534.4MM **Privately Held**
Web: www.ucsf.edu
SIC: **8221** 9411 8011 University; Administration of educational programs; Medical centers
HQ: University Cal San Francisco
513 Parnassus Ave 115f
San Francisco CA

(P-17775)
UNIVERSITY CAL SAN FRANCISCO
Also Called: General Internal Medicine
1701 Divisadero St (94115-3011)
PHONE..............................415 353-7300
Margareth Chesney, *Dir*
EMP: 93
SALES (corp-wide): 534.4MM **Privately Held**
Web: www.ucsf.edu
SIC: **8221** 9411 8011 University; Administration of educational programs; Medical centers
HQ: University Cal San Francisco
513 Parnassus Ave 115f

PRODUCTS & SERVICES SECTION

8243 - Data Processing Schools (P-17792)

San Francisco CA

(P-17776)
UNIVERSITY CAL SAN FRANCISCO
Also Called: Ucsf Mmory Clnic Alzhimers Ctr
1500 Owens St Ste 320 (94158-2335)
PHONE.................................415 885-3668
Bruce Miller, *Dir*
EMP: 83
SALES (corp-wide): 534.4MM **Privately Held**
Web: www.ucsf.edu
SIC: 8221 9411 8011 University; Administration of educational programs; Medical centers
HQ: University Cal San Francisco
513 Parnassus Ave 115f
San Francisco CA

(P-17777)
UNIVERSITY CAL SAN FRANCISCO
Also Called: Ucsf/Mz Neurosurgery Abic
2233 Post St Ste 303 (94115-3471)
PHONE.................................415 885-7495
Charles Intyre, *Brnch Mgr*
EMP: 83
SALES (corp-wide): 534.4MM **Privately Held**
Web: www.ucsf.edu
SIC: 8221 9411 8011 University; Administration of educational programs; Medical centers
HQ: University Cal San Francisco
513 Parnassus Ave 115f
San Francisco CA

(P-17778)
UNIVERSITY CAL SAN FRANCISCO
Also Called: Ucsf/Obgyn Oncology
2356 Sutter St Fl 3 (94115-3006)
PHONE.................................415 885-3610
Wendy Miner, *Brnch Mgr*
EMP: 83
SALES (corp-wide): 534.4MM **Privately Held**
Web: www.ucsf.edu
SIC: 8221 9411 8011 University; Administration of educational programs; Medical centers
HQ: University Cal San Francisco
513 Parnassus Ave 115f
San Francisco CA

(P-17779)
UNIVERSITY CAL SAN FRANCISCO
Also Called: Ucsf Plstic Rcnstrctive Srgery
350 Parnassus Ave Ste 509 (94117-3608)
PHONE.................................415 476-3061
EMP: 73
SALES (corp-wide): 534.4MM **Privately Held**
Web: www.ucsf.edu
SIC: 8221 9411 8011 University; Administration of educational programs; Medical centers
HQ: University Cal San Francisco
513 Parnassus Ave 115f
San Francisco CA

(P-17780)
UNIVERSITY CAL SAN FRANCISCO
Also Called: Pulmonary Prctice At Parnassus
400 Parnassus Ave Fl 5 (94143-2202)
PHONE.................................415 353-2961

EMP: 83
SALES (corp-wide): 534.4MM **Privately Held**
Web: www.ucsf.edu
SIC: 8221 9411 8011 University; Administration of educational programs; Medical centers
HQ: University Cal San Francisco
513 Parnassus Ave 115f
San Francisco CA

(P-17781)
UNIVERSITY CAL SAN FRANCISCO
Also Called: Ucsf Mount Zion Cancer Center
2356 Sutter St (94115-3006)
PHONE.................................415 885-7478
EMP: 83
SALES (corp-wide): 534.4MM **Privately Held**
Web: www.ucsf.edu
SIC: 8221 9411 8011 University; Administration of educational programs; Medical centers
HQ: University Cal San Francisco
513 Parnassus Ave 115f
San Francisco CA

(P-17782)
UNIVERSITY CALIFORNIA DAVIS
Also Called: School of Veterinary Medicine
4112a Tupper Hall (95616)
PHONE.................................530 752-1653
R H Bondurant, *Ch*
EMP: 73
SALES (corp-wide): 534.4MM **Privately Held**
Web: www.ucdavis.edu
SIC: 8221 9411 8062 University; Administration of educational programs; General medical and surgical hospitals
HQ: University Of California, Davis
1 Shields Ave
Davis CA

(P-17783)
UNIVERSITY CALIFORNIA IRVINE
Also Called: Social Sciences
3151 Social Science Plz (92697-5100)
PHONE.................................949 824-7725
EMP: 159
SALES (corp-wide): 534.4MM **Privately Held**
Web: www.uci.edu
SIC: 8221 9411 8062 University; Administration of educational programs; General medical and surgical hospitals
HQ: University Of California, Irvine
510 Aldrich Hall
Irvine CA
949 824-5011

(P-17784)
VANGUARD UNIV SOUTHERN CAL
55 Fair Dr (92626-6520)
PHONE.................................714 668-6163
Michael Beals, *CEO*
EMP: 200 **EST:** 1921
SQ FT: 420,000
SALES (est): 100.21MM **Privately Held**
Web: www.vanguard.edu
SIC: 8221 8699 College, except junior; Charitable organization

8222 Junior Colleges

(P-17785)
CABRILLO CMNTY CLLEGE DST FING (PA)
Also Called: Cabrillo College
6500 Soquel Dr (95003-3119)
PHONE.................................831 479-6100
Dlaurel Jones, *Pr*
Laurel Jones, *Pr*
Brian King, *VP*
EMP: 980 **EST:** 1959
SQ FT: 8,000
SALES (est): 71.98MM
SALES (corp-wide): 71.98MM **Privately Held**
Web: www.cabrillo.edu
SIC: 8222 7922 8221 Community college; Theatrical producers and services; Colleges and universities

(P-17786)
SAN DIEGO CMNTY COLLEGE DST
Also Called: San Diego City College
1313 Twelfth Ave (92101-4712)
PHONE.................................619 388-3453
Terrence J Burgess, *Prin*
EMP: 82
SALES (corp-wide): 146.65MM **Privately Held**
Web: www.sdccd.edu
SIC: 8222 8641 Community college; Civic and social associations
PA: San Diego Community College District
3375 Camino Del Rio S
San Diego CA
619 388-6500

(P-17787)
SAN DIEGO CMNTY COLLEGE DST
Also Called: San Diego Mesa College
7250 Mesa College Dr (92111-4902)
PHONE.................................619 388-2600
Pamela Luster, *Pr*
EMP: 1500
SALES (corp-wide): 146.65MM **Privately Held**
Web: www.sdccd.edu
SIC: 8222 8412 Community college; Museums and art galleries
PA: San Diego Community College District
3375 Camino Del Rio S
San Diego CA
619 388-6500

(P-17788)
SANTA BRBARA CMNTY COLLEGE DST
Also Called: Academy of Cosmetology
525 Anacapa St (93101-1603)
PHONE.................................805 683-4191
Ben Partee, *Mgr*
EMP: 497
SALES (corp-wide): 82.58MM **Privately Held**
Web: www.sbcc.edu
SIC: 8222 7231 Community college; Cosmetology school
PA: Santa Barbara Community College District
721 Cliff Dr
Santa Barbara CA
805 965-0581

(P-17789)
STATE CENTER CMNTY COLLEGE DST
Also Called: Fresno City College Bus Off
1101 E University Ave (93704-6219)
PHONE.................................559 442-4600
Carole Goldsmith, *Pr*
EMP: 118
SALES (corp-wide): 117.41MM **Privately Held**
Web: www.scccd.edu
SIC: 8222 8721 Community college; Accounting, auditing, and bookkeeping
PA: State Center Community College District
1171 Fulton St
Fresno CA
559 226-0720

(P-17790)
WEST VLLY-MSSION CMNTY CLLEGE
Also Called: Mission College
3000 Mission College Blvd (95054-1804)
PHONE.................................408 988-2200
Linda Wilczewski, *Ex Dir*
EMP: 400
SALES (corp-wide): 8.54MM **Privately Held**
Web: mc.bncollege.com
SIC: 8222 8748 8221 Community college; Business consulting, nec; Colleges and universities
PA: West Valley-Mission Community College District
14000 Fruitvale Ave
Saratoga CA
408 867-2200

8231 Libraries

(P-17791)
HUNTINGTON LIB ART CLLCTONS BT
1151 Oxford Rd (91108-1218)
PHONE.................................626 405-2100
Robert F Erburu, *Ch Bd*
Robert Skotheim, *
Steve Koblik, *
Laurie Sowd, *
▲ **EMP:** 380 **EST:** 1919
SALES (est): 128.86MM **Privately Held**
Web: www.huntington.org
SIC: 8231 8412 8422 Public library; Art gallery, noncommercial; Botanical garden

8243 Data Processing Schools

(P-17792)
IT DIVISION INC
Also Called: Apeiro Technologies
9170 Irvine Center Dr Ste 200 (92618-4614)
PHONE.................................678 648-2709
Lavanya Nilagiri, *CEO*
Neeta Prasad, *
Shruti Nilagiri, *
Vivek Jaiswal, *
EMP: 103 **EST:** 2006
SALES (est): 2.61MM **Privately Held**
Web: www.apeiro.us
SIC: 8243 7371 7373 Software training, computer; Computer software systems analysis and design, custom; Systems software development services

8249 Vocational Schools, Nec

(P-17793)
ARDEN WOOD INC
445 Wawona St (94116-3058)
PHONE..................................415 681-5500
Ed Sage, *Ex Dir*
EMP: 80 **EST:** 1930
SQ FT: 50,000
SALES (est): 3.45MM **Privately Held**
Web: www.ardenwood.org
SIC: 8249 8361 Medical training services; Residential care

(P-17794)
CONCORDE CAREER COLLEGES INC
Concorde Career College
12412 Victory Blvd (91606-3134)
PHONE..................................818 766-8151
Carmen Bowen, *Dir*
EMP: 93
SQ FT: 5,500
SALES (corp-wide): 75.67MM **Privately Held**
Web: www.concorde.edu
SIC: 8249 8621 Medical and dental assistant school; Professional organizations
PA: Concorde Career Colleges, Inc
6701 W 64th St Ste 200
Mission KS
913 831-9977

(P-17795)
GEMOLOGICAL INSTITUTE AMER INC (PA)
Also Called: Gemological Institute America
5345 Armada Dr (92008-4602)
PHONE..................................760 603-4000
Susan M Jacques, *Pr*
Tom Moses, *LABORATORY Research*
David Tearle, *
EMP: 1000 **EST:** 1931
SQ FT: 300,000
SALES (est): 358.37MM
SALES (corp-wide): 358.37MM **Privately Held**
Web: www.gia.edu
SIC: 8249 8733 Trade school; Noncommercial research organizations

(P-17796)
SAN DIEGO ELEC TRAINING TR
Also Called: SAN DIEGO ELECTRICAL JATC
4675 Viewridge Ave (92123-1639)
PHONE..................................858 569-6633
Kevin Johnson, *CEO*
Rebecca Bennion, *
EMP: 65 **EST:** 1972
SQ FT: 32,000
SALES (est): 5.34MM **Privately Held**
Web: www.sdett.org
SIC: 8249 1731 Vocational schools, nec; Electrical work

(P-17797)
THE CODING SOURCE LLC
Also Called: Altegra Health
3415 S Sepulveda Blvd Ste 900 (90034-6981)
PHONE..................................866 235-7553
EMP: 250
Web: www.thecodingsource.com
SIC: 8249 7374 8331 7361 Medical training services; Data entry service; Job training and related services; Employment agencies

(P-17798)
UNIVERSAL TECHNICAL INST INC
Also Called: Uti
9494 Haven Ave (91730-5843)
PHONE..................................909 484-1929
EMP: 130
SALES (corp-wide): 418.76MM **Publicly Held**
Web: www.uti.edu
SIC: 8249 7389 Trade school; Personal service agents, brokers, and bureaus
PA: Universal Technical Institute, Inc.
4225 E Windrose Dr # 200
Phoenix AZ
623 445-9500

8299 Schools And Educational Services

(P-17799)
AMERICAN ASSN CRTCAL CARE NRSE
Also Called: A A C N
27071 Aliso Creek Rd (92656-3399)
PHONE..................................949 362-2000
Dana Woods, *CEO*
Vicki Good, *
Teri Lynn Kiss, *President Elect*
Michael Willett, *
Mary Zellinger, *
EMP: 128 **EST:** 1969
SALES (est): 38.31MM **Privately Held**
Web: www.aacn.org
SIC: 8299 8331 8621 Educational services; Job training and related services; Professional organizations

(P-17800)
AMERICAN JUSTICE SOLUTIONS INC
Also Called: Correctivesolutions
25910 Acero Ste 100 (92691-2777)
P.O. Box 3026 (92690-1026)
PHONE..................................949 369-6210
Mats Jonsson, *CEO*
Karl Jonsson, *
Karen Boyd, *
Kristy Silguero, *
EMP: 70 **EST:** 2014
SQ FT: 20,000
SALES (est): 4.49MM **Privately Held**
Web: www.correctivesolutions.org
SIC: 8299 8748 Educational service, nondegree granting: continuing educ.; Educational consultant

(P-17801)
ASSOCTED STDNTS OF THE UNIV CA (PA)
Also Called: A S U C, Berkeley
400 Eshleman Hall (94704)
PHONE..................................510 642-5420
Thomas Cordi, *Ex Dir*
Dedasan Permalul Md, *Owner*
EMP: 250 **EST:** 1887
SQ FT: 20,000
SALES (est): 10.93MM
SALES (corp-wide): 10.93MM **Privately Held**
Web: www.asuc.org
SIC: 8299 7999 Educational services; Billiard parlor

(P-17802)
AYUSA INTERNATIONAL
600 California St Fl 10 (94108-2730)
PHONE..................................888 552-9872
John Wilhelm, *CEO*
Takeshi Yokota, *
Lola Jung, *
EMP: 122 **EST:** 1982
SQ FT: 18,000
SALES (est): 4.53MM **Privately Held**
Web: www.ayusa.org
SIC: 8299 8699 Student exchange program; Charitable organization

(P-17803)
BOYS GRLS CLUBS GRDN GROVE INC (PA)
10540 Chapman Ave (92840-3101)
PHONE..................................714 530-0430
Mark Surmanian, *CEO*
EMP: 225 **EST:** 1952
SQ FT: 12,000
SALES (est): 11.91MM
SALES (corp-wide): 11.91MM **Privately Held**
Web: www.bgcgg.org
SIC: 8299 8699 Educational services; Charitable organization

(P-17804)
CALIFORNIA PARENTING INSTITUTE
Also Called: CHILD PARENT INSTITUTE
3650 Standish Ave (95407-8113)
PHONE..................................707 585-6108
Robin Bowen, *Dir*
EMP: 65 **EST:** 1978
SQ FT: 11,760
SALES (est): 3.94MM **Privately Held**
Web: www.calparents.org
SIC: 8299 8351 8322 Educational services; Child day care services; Family counseling services

(P-17805)
CALIFORNIA STATE UNIV LONG BCH
Also Called: Theatre Department
5201 N Maple Ave (93740-0001)
PHONE..................................559 278-2216
Melissa Gibson, *Admn*
EMP: 157
SALES (corp-wide): 534.4MM **Privately Held**
Web: www.csulb.edu
SIC: 8299 7922 8221 9411 Dramatic school; Theatrical producers and services; University; Administration of educational programs
HQ: California State University, Long Beach
1250 N Bellflower Blvd
Long Beach CA
562 985-4111

(P-17806)
CHRISTAN COMMUNITY THEATRE
Also Called: CHRISTIAN YOUTH THEATER
1545 Pioneer Way (92020-1637)
PHONE..................................619 588-0206
Sheryl Russell, *Pr*
Paul Russell, *
EMP: 75 **EST:** 1980
SQ FT: 11,000
SALES (est): 296.61K **Privately Held**
SIC: 8299 7922 Dramatic school; Legitimate live theater producers

(P-17807)
COMMUNITY COLLEGE FOUNDATION (PA)
1425 River Park Dr Ste 250 (95815-4515)
PHONE..................................916 418-5100
Richard Fowler, *Pr*
Kirk Turner, *
EMP: 98 **EST:** 1983
SALES (est): 5.56MM
SALES (corp-wide): 5.56MM **Privately Held**
Web: www.communitycollege.org
SIC: 8299 8748 Educational services; Business consulting, nec

(P-17808)
CROSSRADS CHRSTN SCHOLS CORONA
2380 Fullerton Ave (92881-3111)
PHONE..................................951 278-3199
Dough Husen, *Superintnt*
EMP: 145 **EST:** 2001
SQ FT: 1,088
SALES (est): 10.47MM **Privately Held**
Web: www.crossroadsschool.org
SIC: 8299 8211 8351 8699 Religious school; High school, junior or senior, nec; Preschool center; Charitable organization

(P-17809)
EMERSON COLLECTIVE LLC (PA)
555 Bryant St Ste 259 (94301-1704)
P.O. Box 10196 (94303-0996)
PHONE..................................650 422-2152
EMP: 85 **EST:** 2011
SALES (est): 10.59MM
SALES (corp-wide): 10.59MM **Privately Held**
Web: www.emersoncollective.com
SIC: 8299 7371 Educational services; Computer software development and applications

(P-17810)
GREENWOOD HALL INC
6230 Wilshire Blvd Ste 136 (90048-5126)
PHONE..................................310 905-8300
John Hall, *Ch Bd*
Bill Bradfield, *
EMP: 111 **EST:** 1997
SALES (est): 14.12MM **Privately Held**
Web: www.answernet.com
SIC: 8299 8741 8742 7374 Educational services; Management services; Management consulting services; Data processing service

(P-17811)
LOS GATOS SARATOGA DEPT OF COM
Also Called: LGS RECREATION
208 E Main St (95030-6107)
PHONE..................................408 354-8700
Nancy Rollett, *Ex Dir*
EMP: 225 **EST:** 1996
SQ FT: 15,000
SALES (est): 9.44MM **Privately Held**
Web: www.lgsrecreation.org
SIC: 8299 8351 Educational services; Child day care services

(P-17812)
MUSIC ACADEMY OF WEST
1070 Fairway Rd (93108-2899)
PHONE..................................805 969-4726
Nancybell Coe, *Pr*
Benjamin J Cohen, *
John Burgee, *
Barbara Robertson, *
James Davidson, *
EMP: 77 **EST:** 1947
SQ FT: 8,000
SALES (est): 15.44MM **Privately Held**

PRODUCTS & SERVICES SECTION

8322 - Individual And Family Services (P-17832)

Web: www.musicacademy.org
SIC: 8299 7929 Music school; Entertainers and entertainment groups

(P-17813)
NAPCA FOUNDATION
2600 W Olive Ave Ste 500 (91505-4525)
PHONE.................................800 799-4640
Aaron Smith, *Ex Dir*
EMP: 563 EST: 2012
SALES (est): 10.94MM **Privately Held**
Web: www.napcafoundation.org
SIC: 8299 8732 7999 8742 Educational services; Educational research; Instruction schools, camps, and services; School, college, university consultant

(P-17814)
PACIFIC AUTISM CTR FOR EDUCATN
Also Called: PACE
1880 Pruneridge Ave (95050-6514)
PHONE.................................408 245-3400
Kurt Ohlff, *Ex Dir*
EMP: 165 EST: 1982
SQ FT: 12,250
SALES (est): 13.85MM **Privately Held**
Web: www.pacificautism.org
SIC: 8299 8361 Arts and crafts schools; Residential care for children

(P-17815)
SAN FRNCSCO CNSERVATORY OF MUS (PA)
Also Called: Sfcm
50 Oak St (94102-6011)
PHONE.................................415 864-7326
David H Stull, *Pr*
Colin Murdoch, *
John Mccarthy, *Dir*
Jean Deleage, *
Kathryn Wittenmyer, *
EMP: 197 EST: 1917
SQ FT: 80,000
SALES (est): 59.35MM
SALES (corp-wide): 59.35MM **Privately Held**
Web: www.sfcm.edu
SIC: 8299 7929 Music school; Entertainers and entertainment groups

(P-17816)
SOUTHERN CAL PRMNNTE MED GROUP
1465 E 103rd St (90002-3306)
PHONE.................................323 564-7911
Joanne Robinson, *Dir*
EMP: 138
SALES (corp-wide): 68.1B **Privately Held**
Web: www.permanente.org
SIC: 8299 6324 8351 Educational services; Group hospitalization plans; Preschool center
HQ: Southern California Permanente Medical Group
393 Walnut Dr
Pasadena CA
626 405-5704

(P-17817)
THE ROMAN CATHOLIC ARCHBISHOP OF SAN FRANCISCO (PA)
Also Called: Archdiocese of San Francisco
1 Peter Yorke Way 1 (94109-6602)
PHONE.................................415 614-5500
▼ EMP: 120 EST: 1853
SALES (est): 91.44MM
SALES (corp-wide): 91.44MM **Privately Held**

Web: www.sfarchdiocese.org
SIC: 8299 7371 Religious school; Computer software development

(P-17818)
UNIVERSITY ENTERPRISES INC
Also Called: Sacramento State Sponsored RES
6000 J St (95819-2605)
PHONE.................................916 278-7001
James Reinhart, *Ex Dir*
Alexander Gonzalez, *
Ming Tung Mike Lee, *
Donald Taylor, *
Jim Reinhart, *
EMP: 1856 EST: 1951
SQ FT: 22,931
SALES (est): 98MM **Privately Held**
Web: enterprises.csus.edu
SIC: 8299 8741 Educational services; Management services

(P-17819)
VISTA HILL FOUNDATION
Also Called: Stein Sam & Rose Education Ctr
6145 Decena Dr (92120-3511)
PHONE.................................619 281-5511
Joan Richard, *Prin*
EMP: 90
SALES (corp-wide): 34.66MM **Privately Held**
Web: www.vistahill.org
SIC: 8299 8351 8093 Educational services; Child day care services; Mental health clinic, outpatient
PA: Vista Hill Foundation
8910 Clairemont Mesa Blvd
San Diego CA
585 514-5100

8322 Individual And Family Services

(P-17820)
ABILITYPATH
Also Called: Impact Business Service
350 Twin Dolphin Dr Ste 123 (94065-1458)
PHONE.................................650 259-8500
Sheryl Young, *CEO*
EMP: 120 EST: 1920
SQ FT: 25,000
SALES (est): 22.59MM **Privately Held**
Web: www.abilitypath.org
SIC: 8322 Social services for the handicapped

(P-17821)
ABILITYPATH HOUSING (PA)
Also Called: Abilities United
350 Twin Dolphin Dr Ste 123 (94065-1457)
PHONE.................................650 494-0550
Charlie Weidanz, *CEO*
Jane Machin, *
EMP: 85 EST: 1954
SALES (est): 5.27MM
SALES (corp-wide): 5.27MM **Privately Held**
Web: www.abilitypath.org
SIC: 8322 8361 Multi-service center; Residential care

(P-17822)
ABRAZAR INC
Also Called: ABRAZAR ELDERLY ASSISTANCE
7101 Wyoming St (92683-3811)
PHONE.................................714 893-3581
Gloria Reyes, *CEO*
Mario Ortega, *

EMP: 80 EST: 1975
SALES (est): 9.31MM **Privately Held**
Web: www.abrazarinc.com
SIC: 8322 Social service center

(P-17823)
ADVANCMENT THRUGH OPRTNTY KNWL
Also Called: CHILDREN, YOUTH & FAMILY COLLA
1200 W 37th Pl (90007-4220)
PHONE.................................323 730-9400
Lydia Templeton, *CEO*
EMP: 62 EST: 1993
SALES (est): 2.01MM **Privately Held**
Web: www.cyfcla.org
SIC: 8322 Social service center

(P-17824)
AIDS PROJECT LOS ANGELES (PA)
Also Called: Aids Project La
611 S Kingsley Dr (90005-2319)
PHONE.................................213 201-1600
Craig E Thompson, *CEO*
Robyn Goldman, *
EMP: 90 EST: 1983
SALES (est): 55.51MM
SALES (corp-wide): 55.51MM **Privately Held**
Web: www.aplahealth.org
SIC: 8322 Social service center

(P-17825)
ALAMEDA CNTY CMMNTY FD BNK INC
7900 Edgewater Dr (94621-2004)
P.O. Box 2599 (94614-0599)
PHONE.................................510 635-3663
Suzan Bateson, *Pr*
EMP: 70 EST: 1985
SQ FT: 118,000
SALES (est): 124.29MM **Privately Held**
Web: www.accfb.org
SIC: 8322 Social service center

(P-17826)
ALPHA PROJECT FOR HOMELESS
Also Called: Casa Raphael
993 Postal Way (92083-6945)
PHONE.................................760 630-9922
Margaret Larson, *Mgr*
EMP: 153
Web: www.alphaproject.org
SIC: 8322 8361 Community center; Halfway group home, persons with social or personal problems
PA: Alpha Project For The Homeless
3737 5th Ave Ste 203
San Diego CA

(P-17827)
ALTA CAL REGIONAL CTR INC
950 Tharp Rd (95993-8344)
PHONE.................................530 674-3070
Terry Rhoades, *Mgr*
EMP: 176
SALES (corp-wide): 602.69MM **Privately Held**
Web: www.altaregional.org
SIC: 8322 8699 General counseling services ; Charitable organization
PA: Alta California Regional Center, Inc.
2241 Harvard St Ste 100
Sacramento CA
916 978-6400

(P-17828)
ALTA CAL REGIONAL CTR INC
283 W Court St (95695-3096)
PHONE.................................530 666-3391
Mechelle Johnson, *Brnch Mgr*
EMP: 132
SALES (corp-wide): 602.69MM **Privately Held**
Web: www.altaregional.org
SIC: 8322 8082 Social service center; Home health care services
PA: Alta California Regional Center, Inc.
2241 Harvard St Ste 100
Sacramento CA
916 978-6400

(P-17829)
ALTA CAL REGIONAL CTR INC
Also Called: Alta California Regional Ctr
807 Douglas Blvd (95678-2762)
PHONE.................................916 786-8110
Jean Onesi, *Mgr*
EMP: 132
SALES (corp-wide): 602.69MM **Privately Held**
Web: www.altaregional.org
SIC: 8322 7389 Social service center; Fund raising organizations
PA: Alta California Regional Center, Inc.
2241 Harvard St Ste 100
Sacramento CA
916 978-6400

(P-17830)
AMERICAN NATIONAL RED CROSS
Also Called: American Nat Red Cross - Blood
6230 Claremont Ave (94618-1324)
PHONE.................................510 594-5100
Jay Winkenbach, *CEO*
EMP: 76
SQ FT: 42,714
SALES (corp-wide): 3.18B **Privately Held**
Web: www.redcross.org
SIC: 8322 Social service center
PA: The American National Red Cross
431 18th St Nw
Washington DC
202 737-8300

(P-17831)
AMERICAN NATIONAL RED CROSS
Also Called: American Nat Red Crss-Blood Sv
100 Red Cross Cir (91768-2580)
PHONE.................................909 859-7006
Joan Manning, *Genl Mgr*
EMP: 110
SALES (corp-wide): 3.18B **Privately Held**
Web: www.redcross.org
SIC: 8322 Social service center
PA: The American National Red Cross
431 18th St Nw
Washington DC
202 737-8300

(P-17832)
AMERICAN NATIONAL RED CROSS
Also Called: Red Cross
1450 S Central Ave (90021-2627)
PHONE.................................310 445-9900
EMP: 135
SALES (corp-wide): 3.18B **Privately Held**
Web: www.redcross.org
SIC: 8322 Social service center
PA: The American National Red Cross
431 18th St Nw
Washington DC
202 737-8300

8322 - Individual And Family Services (P-17833)

(P-17833)
AMERICAN RED CROSS LOS ANGLES (PA)
Also Called: American Red Cross
1320 Newton St (90021-2724)
PHONE..................310 445-9900
TOLL FREE: 800
Roger Dixon, *CEO*
Kirk Richard Hyde, *
William Niese, *
Thomas E Stephenson, *
Michelle Mccarthy, *Chief Financial*
EMP: 150 EST: 1916
SALES (est): 6.76MM
SALES (corp-wide): 6.76MM **Privately Held**
Web: www.redcross.org
SIC: 8322 Social service center

(P-17834)
AMERICAN RED CROSS SAN DG-MPRI (PA)
Also Called: American Red Cross
3950 Calle Fortunada (92123-1827)
PHONE..................858 309-1200
Joe Craver, *CEO*
EMP: 90 EST: 1898
SALES (est): 8.76MM
SALES (corp-wide): 8.76MM **Privately Held**
Web: www.redcross.org
SIC: 8322 Social service center

(P-17835)
AMIGO BABY INC
Also Called: Healthcare
1901 N Rice Ave Ste 325 (93030-7912)
P.O. Box 6757 (91359-6757)
PHONE..................805 901-1237
Pablo Velez, *CEO*
EMP: 80 EST: 2004
SALES (est): 5.82MM **Privately Held**
Web: www.amigobaby.com
SIC: 8322 8099 Social service center; Health and allied services, nec

(P-17836)
ARC - IMPERIAL VALLEY (PA)
298 E Ross Ave (92243-9303)
P.O. Box 1828 (92244-1828)
PHONE..................760 352-0180
Arturo Santos, *CEO*
Poli Flores, *
EMP: 60 EST: 1973
SQ FT: 22,000
SALES (est): 14.1MM
SALES (corp-wide): 14.1MM **Privately Held**
Web: www.arciv.org
SIC: 8322 4729 8361 Adult day care center; Carpool/vanpool arrangement; Mentally handicapped home

(P-17837)
ARC OF BUTTE COUNTY (PA)
Also Called: ARC of Butte County
2030 Park Ave (95928-6701)
P.O. Box 3697 (95927-3697)
PHONE..................530 891-5865
Courtney Casey, *CEO*
Michael Mcginnis, *Ex Dir*
Betty Lutz, *
Jean Campbell, *
EMP: 200 EST: 1962
SQ FT: 12,268
SALES (est): 11MM
SALES (corp-wide): 11MM **Privately Held**
Web: www.arcbutte.org
SIC: 8322 Individual and family services

(P-17838)
ARC OF SAN DIEGO
1280 Nolan Ave (91911-3738)
PHONE..................619 427-7524
Laura Orcutt, *Dir*
EMP: 60
SALES (corp-wide): 33.64MM **Privately Held**
Web: www.arc-sd.com
SIC: 8322 Social service center
PA: The Arc Of San Diego
3030 Market St
San Diego CA
619 685-1175

(P-17839)
ARTS AND SVCS FOR DISABLED INC
3626 E Pacific Coast Hwy (90804-2015)
PHONE..................562 377-0302
Kay Hagen, *Dir*
EMP: 60 EST: 1984
SALES (est): 3.45MM **Privately Held**
Web: www.artsandservices.org
SIC: 8322 Association for the handicapped

(P-17840)
ASSOCIATED STUDENTS INC (PA)
Also Called: ASSICIATED STUDENTS
University Union Bldg 65 (93407)
PHONE..................805 756-1281
Richard Johnson, *Ex Dir*
Dwayne Brummett, *
EMP: 70 EST: 1964
SQ FT: 110,000
SALES (est): 23.86MM
SALES (corp-wide): 23.86MM **Privately Held**
Web: www.calpoly.edu
SIC: 8322 8221 Multi-service center; Colleges and universities

(P-17841)
AUTISM OTRACH SOUTHERN CAL LLC
3110 Camino Del Rio S Ste 307 (92108)
PHONE..................619 795-9925
Abigail R Bun, *Mgr*
EMP: 75 EST: 2013
SALES (est): 4.55MM **Privately Held**
Web: www.mebefamily.com
SIC: 8322 Individual and family services

(P-17842)
AUTISM SPCTRUM INTRVNTIONS INC
713 W Commonwealth Ave Ste A (92832)
PHONE..................562 972-4846
Timothy M Prior, *Prin*
EMP: 116 EST: 2008
SALES (est): 4.56MM **Privately Held**
Web: www.asiautism.com
SIC: 8322 Individual and family services

(P-17843)
AVIVA FAMILY & CHILDRENS SVCS (PA)
1701 Camino Palmero St (90046-2902)
PHONE..................323 876-0550
Ira J Kruskol, *Dir*
EMP: 99 EST: 1976
SALES (est): 8.99MM
SALES (corp-wide): 8.99MM **Privately Held**
Web: www.aviva.org
SIC: 8322 Social service center

(P-17844)
AYA LIVING INC
1450 Frazee Rd (92108-4337)
PHONE..................619 446-6469
Matthew Williams, *Ex Dir*
EMP: 120 EST: 2010
SALES (est): 4MM **Privately Held**
Web: www.ayaliving.com
SIC: 8322 Individual and family services

(P-17845)
BAKER PLACES INC
Also Called: Grove Street
2157 Grove St (94117-1008)
PHONE..................415 387-2275
Silvia Dunning, *Dir*
EMP: 80
SALES (corp-wide): 20.54MM **Privately Held**
Web: www.prcsf.org
SIC: 8322 Social service center
PA: Baker Places, Inc.
170 9th St
San Francisco CA
415 864-4655

(P-17846)
BAY AREA COMMUNITY SVCS INC
Also Called: Bacs Adult Day Care
5714 Martin Luther King Jr Way (94609-1673)
PHONE..................510 601-1074
Rita Stuckey, *Brnch Mgr*
EMP: 74
SALES (corp-wide): 14.28MM **Privately Held**
Web: www.bayareacs.org
SIC: 8322 8399 Adult day care center; Advocacy group
PA: Bay Area Community Services, Inc.
390 40th St
Oakland CA
510 613-0330

(P-17847)
BAY AREA COMMUNITY SVCS INC
40963 Grimmer Blvd (94538-2846)
PHONE..................510 656-7742
Priscilla Mathews, *Brnch Mgr*
EMP: 99
SALES (corp-wide): 14.28MM **Privately Held**
Web: www.bayareacs.org
SIC: 8322 Social service center
PA: Bay Area Community Services, Inc.
390 40th St
Oakland CA
510 613-0330

(P-17848)
BAY AREA SENIOR SERVICES INC
Also Called: Peninsula Regent, The
1 Baldwin Ave Ofc (94401-3837)
PHONE..................650 579-5500
M Mannstab, *Ex Dir*
EMP: 151
SALES (corp-wide): 54.14MM **Privately Held**
Web: www.retirement.org
SIC: 8322 Senior citizens' center or association
HQ: Bay Area Senior Services, Inc.
1 Hawthorne St Ste 400
San Francisco CA
415 989-1111

(P-17849)
BEHAVRAL HLTHCARE SLUTIONS INC
9465 Farnham St (92123-1308)
PHONE..................858 573-2600
Kimberly Bond, *Pr*
EMP: 133 EST: 2010
SALES (est): 707.72K
SALES (corp-wide): 95.19MM **Privately Held**
SIC: 8322 Rehabilitation services
PA: Mental Health Systems, Inc.
9465 Farnham St
San Diego CA
858 573-2600

(P-17850)
BERKSHIRE HATHAWAY HOME SERVIC
231 S Glendora Ave (91741-3419)
PHONE..................626 335-6001
EMP: 82
SALES (corp-wide): 2.56MM **Privately Held**
Web: www.brucemulhearn.com
SIC: 8322 Homemakers' service
PA: Berkshire Hathaway Home Services Ca Roperties
18000 Studebaker Rd # 600
Cerritos CA
562 860-2625

(P-17851)
BERNARD OSHER MRIN JWISH CMNTY
Also Called: J C C
200 N San Pedro Rd (94903-4213)
PHONE..................415 444-8000
Marty Friedman, *Pr*
Deborah Stadtner, *
Karen Young, *
Michael Baumstein, *
Mark Goodman, *
EMP: 200 EST: 1995
SQ FT: 90,000
SALES (est): 13.16MM **Privately Held**
Web: www.marinjcc.org
SIC: 8322 Community center

(P-17852)
BLC RESIDENTIAL CARE INC
1455 W 112th St (90047-4926)
PHONE..................310 722-7541
Brenda Chandler, *Pr*
EMP: 80 EST: 2004
SALES (est): 701.41K **Privately Held**
SIC: 8322 Adult day care center

(P-17853)
BONITA HOUSE INC
6333 Telegraph Ave Ste 102 (94609)
PHONE..................510 923-0180
Rick Crispino, *Ex Dir*
EMP: 76 EST: 1971
SQ FT: 4,000
SALES (est): 7.04MM **Privately Held**
Web: www.bonitahouse.org
SIC: 8322 Association for the handicapped

(P-17854)
BRAILLE INSTITUTE AMERICA INC (PA)
Also Called: Braille Institute
741 N Vermont Ave (90029-3594)
PHONE..................323 663-1111
Lester M Sussman, *Ch Bd*
Les Stocker,
Peter Mindnich, *
Rezaur Rahman, *

PRODUCTS & SERVICES SECTION
8322 - Individual And Family Services (P-17874)

EMP: 208 EST: 1919
SQ FT: 167,079
SALES (est): 37.68MM
SALES (corp-wide): 37.68MM **Privately Held**
Web: www.brailleinstitute.org
SIC: **8322** 8231 2731 2759 Individual and family services; Specialized libraries; Textbooks: publishing and printing; Commercial printing, nec

(P-17855)
BREAKTHROUGH BEHAVIORAL INC
702 Marshall St Ste 340 (94063-1825)
PHONE..................888 282-2522
Julian Cohen, *Pr*
EMP: 134 EST: 2011
SALES (est): 946.26K
SALES (corp-wide): 180.52B **Publicly Held**
SIC: **8322** General counseling services
HQ: Mdlive, Inc.
3350 Sw 148th Ave Ste 300
Miramar FL

(P-17856)
BRIGHTLINE INC
400 Concar Dr (94402-2681)
PHONE..................650 769-5810
Naomi Allen, *CEO*
EMP: 197 EST: 2019
SALES (est): 13.69MM **Privately Held**
Web: www.hellobrightline.com
SIC: **8322** Individual and family services

(P-17857)
CALIFORNIA AUTISM CENTER
1630 E Shaw Ave Ste 190 (93710-8114)
PHONE..................559 475-7860
Amanda Nicholson Adams, *CEO*
William Forath, *Admn*
EMP: 92 EST: 2013
SALES (est): 10.26MM **Privately Held**
Web: www.calautismcenter.org
SIC: **8322** 6321 Individual and family services; Health insurance carriers

(P-17858)
CALIFRNIA DEPT CHILD SPPORT SV (DH)
11150 International Dr (95670-6072)
P.O. Box 419064 (95741-9064)
PHONE..................916 464-5000
Jan Sturla, *Dir*
EMP: 79 EST: 1999
SALES (est): 80.01MM
SALES (corp-wide): 534.4MM **Privately Held**
Web: childsupport.ca.gov
SIC: **8322** 9441 Family counseling services; Administration of social and manpower programs
HQ: California Health & Human Services Agency
1215 O St
Sacramento CA

(P-17859)
CAREWORKS HEALTH SERVICES
5151 Oceanus Dr Ste 102 (92649-1057)
PHONE..................949 859-4700
Anh Tu Dang, *Pr*
EMP: 65 EST: 2015
SALES (est): 4.81MM **Privately Held**
Web: www.careworkshealthservices.com
SIC: **8322** Senior citizens' center or association

(P-17860)
CAROLYN E WYLIE CTR FOR CHLDRE
4164 Brockton Ave (92501-3400)
PHONE..................951 683-5193
Mickey Rubinson, *CEO*
Melody Amaral, *
EMP: 100 EST: 1976
SQ FT: 3,000
SALES (est): 3.86MM **Privately Held**
Web: www.wyliecenter.org
SIC: **8322** 8093 8049 Individual and family services; Mental health clinic, outpatient; Psychotherapist, except M.D.

(P-17861)
CASA ALLEGRA COMMUNITY SVCS
35 Mitchell Blvd Ste 8 (94903-2012)
PHONE..................415 499-1116
EMP: 70 EST: 2011
SALES (est): 6.18MM **Privately Held**
Web: www.casaallegra.org
SIC: **8322** Social service center

(P-17862)
CASA CLINA HOSP CTRS FOR HLTHC
Also Called: Rancho Pino Verdi
11981 Midway Ave (92356-7517)
P.O. Box 1760 (92356-1760)
PHONE..................760 248-6245
Michael Stayer, *Mgr*
EMP: 149
SQ FT: 2,934
SALES (corp-wide): 136.57MM **Privately Held**
Web: www.casacolina.org
SIC: **8322** Rehabilitation services
HQ: Casa Colina Hospital And Centers For Healthcare
255 E Bonita Ave
Pomona CA
909 596-7733

(P-17863)
CASA COLINA INC (PA)
Also Called: Casa Clina Hosp Ctrs For Hlthc
255 E Bonita Ave (91767-1923)
PHONE..................909 596-7733
EMP: 800 EST: 1981
SALES (est): 136.57MM
SALES (corp-wide): 136.57MM **Privately Held**
Web: www.casacolina.org
SIC: **8322** 8011 Rehabilitation services; Ambulatory surgical center

(P-17864)
CASA PCFICA CTRS FOR CHLDREN F (PA)
Also Called: CASA PACIFICA
1722 S Lewis Rd (93012-8520)
PHONE..................805 482-3260
Shawna Morris, *CEO*
Felice Ginsberg, *
Michael Redard, *
EMP: 175 EST: 1988
SQ FT: 63,000
SALES (est): 27.97MM **Privately Held**
Web: www.casapacifica.org
SIC: **8322** 8361 8211 Child related social services; Residential care for children; Specialty education

(P-17865)
CATHOLIC CHRTIES OF THE DCESE
Also Called: Ombudsman Patients Advocate
2351 Tenaya Dr # D (95354-3925)
PHONE..................209 529-3784
Monica Raymos, *Mgr*
EMP: 73
SALES (corp-wide): 6.65MM **Privately Held**
Web: www.ccstockton.org
SIC: **8322** Social service center
PA: Catholic Charities Of The Diocese Of Stockton
1106 N El Dorado St
Stockton CA
209 444-5900

(P-17866)
CATHOLIC CHRTIES OF THE DCESE (PA)
Also Called: CATHOLIC CHARITIES OF EAST BAY
433 Jefferson St (94607-3539)
P.O. Box 23245 (94623-0245)
PHONE..................510 768-3100
Chuck Fernandez, *Ex Dir*
Solomon Belette, *
EMP: 83 EST: 1935
SQ FT: 10,376
SALES (est): 13.38MM **Privately Held**
Web: www.cceb.org
SIC: **8322** 8661 Social service center; Religious organizations

(P-17867)
CATHOLIC CHRTIES SNTA CLARA CN
Also Called: John Xxiii Snior Ntrtn Site Ct
195 E San Fernando St (95112-3503)
PHONE..................408 282-8600
Tatiana Colon, *Dir*
EMP: 110
SALES (corp-wide): 54.57MM **Privately Held**
Web: www.catholiccharitiessc.org
SIC: **8322** Social service center
PA: Catholic Charities Of Santa Clara County
2625 Zanker Rd Ste 200
San Jose CA
408 468-0100

(P-17868)
CATHOLIC CHRTIES SNTA CLARA CN (PA)
Also Called: CATHOLIC CHARITIES
2625 Zanker Rd Ste 200 (95134-2130)
PHONE..................408 468-0100
Gregory Kepferle, *CEO*
Margaret Williams, *CFO*
EMP: 200 EST: 1981
SQ FT: 50,000
SALES (est): 54.57MM
SALES (corp-wide): 54.57MM **Privately Held**
Web: www.catholiccharitiessc.org
SIC: **8322** Social service center

(P-17869)
CATHOLIC CHRTIES SNTA CLARA CN
Also Called: Catholic Charities
303 N Ventura Ave Ste A (93001-1961)
PHONE..................805 643-4694
Robert Batdazian, *Dir*
EMP: 88
SALES (corp-wide): 54.57MM **Privately Held**
Web: www.catholiccharitiessc.org
SIC: **8322** Social service center
PA: Catholic Charities Of Santa Clara County
2625 Zanker Rd Ste 200
San Jose CA
408 468-0100

(P-17870)
CENTER FOR HUMAN SERVICES (PA)
2000 W Briggsmore Ave Ste I (95350-3763)
PHONE..................209 526-1476
Linda Kovacs, *Ex Dir*
EMP: 72 EST: 1970
SQ FT: 8,000
SALES (est): 18.32MM
SALES (corp-wide): 18.32MM **Privately Held**
Web: www.centerforhumanservices.org
SIC: **8322** 8331 Child guidance agency; Job training services

(P-17871)
CENTER FOR LRNG ATISM SPPORT S
Also Called: Class
424 Peninsula Ave (94401-1653)
PHONE..................800 538-8365
Denise Pollard, *CEO*
Ross Berman, *
EMP: 400 EST: 2016
SALES (est): 23.34MM **Privately Held**
Web: www.classaba.com
SIC: **8322** Family counseling services

(P-17872)
CENTER FOR SOCIAL DYNAMICS LLC
Also Called: Csd Autism Services
150 Glen Cove Marina Rd E (94591-7292)
PHONE..................707 553-1784
EMP: 77
SALES (corp-wide): 46.84MM **Privately Held**
Web: www.csdautismservices.com
SIC: **8322** Family counseling services
PA: Center For Social Dynamics, Llc
1200 Concord Ave Ste 100
Concord CA
510 268-8120

(P-17873)
CENTRAL VLY TRAINING CTR INC
7603 Murray Dr (95210-5314)
PHONE..................209 951-1504
Crista Nylen, *Mgr*
EMP: 64
SALES (corp-wide): 19.01MM **Privately Held**
Web: www.cvtcinc.com
SIC: **8322** Social services for the handicapped
PA: Central Valley Training Center, Inc.
10100 Trinity Pkwy # 110
Stockton CA
209 951-1671

(P-17874)
CHILD & FAMILY CENTER
21545 Centre Pointe Pkwy (91350-2947)
PHONE..................661 259-9439
Joan Aschoff, *CEO*
Victor Chavira, *
Bert Paras, *
Evelyn Vega-aguilar, *Dir*
EMP: 120 EST: 1976
SQ FT: 26,581
SALES (est): 13.76MM **Privately Held**
Web: www.childfamilycenter.org

8322 - Individual And Family Services (P-17875) — PRODUCTS & SERVICES SECTION

SIC: **8322** 8099 8093 8049 Family counseling services; Childbirth preparation clinic; Mental health clinic, outpatient; Clinical psychologist

(P-17875)
CHILD ABUSE PRVNTION CNCIL SCR
4700 Roseville Rd Ste 102 (95660-5100)
PHONE....................................916 244-1900
Sheila Anderson, *Pr*
EMP: 83 **EST:** 1982
SALES (est): 9.71MM **Privately Held**
Web: www.thecapcenter.org
SIC: **8322** Child related social services

(P-17876)
CHILD CARE RESOURCE CENTER INC (PA)
20001 Prairie St (91311-6508)
PHONE....................................818 717-1000
Michael Olenick, *CEO*
Michael Olenick, *Pr*
Lorraine Schrag, *
Casey Quinn, *
Ellen Cervantes, *
EMP: 130 **EST:** 1976
SALES (est): 404.36MM
SALES (corp-wide): 404.36MM **Privately Held**
Web: www.ccrcca.org
SIC: **8322** Child related social services

(P-17877)
CHILD CARE RESOURCE CENTER INC
250 Grand Cypress Ave Ste 601 (93551-3675)
PHONE....................................661 723-3246
EMP: 204
SALES (corp-wide): 404.36MM **Privately Held**
Web: www.ccrcca.org
SIC: **8322** Child related social services
PA: Child Care Resource Center, Inc.
  20001 Prairie St
  Chatsworth CA
  818 717-1000

(P-17878)
CHILD DEV RSRCES OF VNTURA CNT (PA)
Also Called: C D R
221 Ventura Blvd (93036-0277)
PHONE....................................805 485-7878
Jack Hinojosa, *CEO*
EMP: 200 **EST:** 1974
SQ FT: 67,007
SALES (est): 62.02MM
SALES (corp-wide): 62.02MM **Privately Held**
Web: www.cdrv.org
SIC: **8322** 8699 Child guidance agency; Charitable organization

(P-17879)
CHILD DEVELOPMENT INSTITUTE
Also Called: CDI
18050 Vanowen St (91335-5638)
PHONE....................................818 888-4559
Joan Samaltese, *Ex Dir*
Dana Kalek, *
Steve Lenhert, *
Tessa Graham, *
EMP: 93 **EST:** 1995
SALES (est): 4.45MM **Privately Held**
Web: www.cdikids.org

SIC: **8322** Child related social services

(P-17880)
CHILDNET YOUTH & FMLY SVCS INC (PA)
Also Called: Childnet
3545 Long Beach Blvd Ste 200 (90807-3904)
P.O. Box 4550 (90804-0550)
PHONE....................................562 498-5500
Kathy L Hughes, *CEO*
EMP: 177 **EST:** 1970
SALES (est): 33.63MM
SALES (corp-wide): 33.63MM **Privately Held**
Web: www.childnet.net
SIC: **8322** Child related social services

(P-17881)
CHILDRENS BUREAU SOUTHERN CAL (PA)
1910 Magnolia Ave (90007-1220)
PHONE....................................213 342-0100
Alex Morales, *Pr*
Sona Chandwani, *
EMP: 107 **EST:** 1904
SQ FT: 43,000
SALES (est): 47.48MM
SALES (corp-wide): 47.48MM **Privately Held**
Web: www.all4kids.org
SIC: **8322** Child related social services

(P-17882)
CHILDRENS CUNCIL SAN FRANCISCO (PA)
445 Church St (94114-1720)
PHONE....................................415 343-3378
Sandee Blechman, *Ex Dir*
EMP: 86 **EST:** 1973
SALES (est): 112.16MM **Privately Held**
Web: www.childrenscouncil.org
SIC: **8322** 8351 Youth center; Child day care services

(P-17883)
CHILDRENS INST LOS ANGELES
679 S New Hampshire Ave (90005-1355)
PHONE....................................213 383-2765
Mary Emmons, *Brnch Mgr*
EMP: 850
SALES (corp-wide): 392.05K **Privately Held**
Web: www.childrensinstitute.org
SIC: **8322** Social service center
PA: Children's Institute Of Los Angeles
  2121 W Temple St
  Los Angeles CA
  213 385-5100

(P-17884)
CHILDRENS INSTITUTE INC (PA)
2121 W Temple St (90026-4915)
PHONE....................................213 385-5100
Martine Singer, *CEO*
Eugene Straub, *CFOO*
Todd Sosna, *CPO*
James Colon, *
EMP: 190 **EST:** 1906
SQ FT: 18,000
SALES (est): 75.05MM
SALES (corp-wide): 75.05MM **Privately Held**
Web: www.childrensinstitute.org
SIC: **8322** 8699 Child related social services; Charitable organization

(P-17885)
CHILDRENS RECVG HM SACRAMENTO
3555 Auburn Blvd (95821-2005)
PHONE....................................916 482-2370
David Ballard, *CEO*
Rich Bryan, *
EMP: 160 **EST:** 1944
SQ FT: 26,000
SALES (est): 5.21MM **Privately Held**
Web: www.crhkids.org
SIC: **8322** Social service center

(P-17886)
CITY OF BAKERSFIELD
Rabobank Arena Thter Cnvntion
1001 Truxtun Ave (93301-4714)
PHONE....................................661 852-7300
John Dorman, *Genl Mgr*
EMP: 118
SALES (corp-wide): 519.74MM **Privately Held**
Web: www.mechanicsbankarena.com
SIC: **8322** 9111 6512 Community center; Mayors' office; Nonresidential building operators
PA: City Of Bakersfield
  1600 Truxtun Ave Fl 5th
  Bakersfield CA
  661 326-3000

(P-17887)
CITY OF IRVINE
Also Called: Lakeview Senior Center
20 Lake Rd (92604-4567)
PHONE....................................949 724-6900
EMP: 72
Web: www.cityofirvine.org
SIC: **8322** Senior citizens' center or association
PA: City Of Irvine
  1 Civic Center Plz
  Irvine CA
  949 724-6000

(P-17888)
CITY OF OAKLAND
Also Called: Health & Human Services Dept
150 Frank H Ogawa Plz Ste 3354 (94612-2021)
PHONE....................................510 238-6796
Andrea Youngdahl, *Dir*
EMP: 63
SALES (corp-wide): 1.47B **Privately Held**
Web: www.oaklandcityid.com
SIC: **8322** 9441 Individual and family services; Administration of social and manpower programs
PA: City Of Oakland
  1 Frank H Ogawa Plz 2nd
  Oakland CA
  510 238-3280

(P-17889)
COMMUNITY ACTION PARTNERSHIP
3970 Short St (93401-7567)
PHONE....................................805 541-4122
EMP: 97
SALES (corp-wide): 99.11MM **Privately Held**
Web: www.capslo.org
SIC: **8322** Individual and family services
PA: Community Action Partnership Of San Luis Obispo County, Inc.
  1030 Southwood Dr
  San Luis Obispo CA
  805 544-4355

(P-17890)
COMMUNITY ACTION PRTNR ORNGE C
Also Called: OC FOOD BANK
11870 Monarch St (92841-2113)
PHONE....................................714 897-6670
Gregory C Scott, *CEO*
Caroline Coleman, *
EMP: 105 **EST:** 1965
SQ FT: 86,300
SALES (est): 38.93MM **Privately Held**
Web: www.capoc.org
SIC: **8322** Social service center

(P-17891)
COMMUNITY BRIDGES
Also Called: Golden Age Nutrition Program
114 E 5th St (95076-4309)
PHONE....................................831 724-2024
Valerie Rivera, *Prin*
EMP: 66
SALES (corp-wide): 16.62MM **Privately Held**
Web: www.communitybridges.org
SIC: **8322** Senior citizens' center or association
PA: Community Bridges
  519 Main St
  Watsonville CA
  831 688-8840

(P-17892)
COMMUNITY FOOD CONNECTION
14047 Twin Peaks Rd (92064-3039)
PHONE....................................858 751-4613
William Rearick, *Prin*
Kim Rearick, *
EMP: 80 **EST:** 2014
SALES (est): 529.5K **Privately Held**
Web: www.thecommunityfoodconnection.com
SIC: **8322** Social service center

(P-17893)
COMMUNITY INTERFACE SERVICES
981 Vale Terrace Dr (92084-5213)
PHONE....................................760 729-3866
Rose Mueller Hanson, *Pr*
EMP: 100 **EST:** 1983
SALES (est): 13.68MM **Privately Held**
Web: www.communityinterfaceservices.org
SIC: **8322** Social service center

(P-17894)
COMMUNITY SLTONS FOR CHLDREN F (PA)
9015 Murray Ave Ste 100 (95020-3617)
P.O. Box 546 (95038-0546)
PHONE....................................408 842-7138
Erin O'brien, *CEO*
Lynn Magruder, *
EMP: 120 **EST:** 1973
SALES (est): 39.52MM
SALES (corp-wide): 39.52MM **Privately Held**
Web: www.communitysolutions.org
SIC: **8322** Social service center

(P-17895)
COMMUNITY SUPPORT OPTIONS INC
1401 Poso Dr (93280-2584)
P.O. Box 8018 (93280-8108)
PHONE....................................661 758-5331
John Stockton, *CEO*
Anna Poggi, *

PRODUCTS & SERVICES SECTION
8322 - Individual And Family Services (P-17915)

Jose Hernandez, *
Ben Goosen, *
Violet Ratzlass, *
EMP: 102 **EST:** 1974
SQ FT: 9,000
SALES (est): 2.19MM **Privately Held**
Web: www.cso-svd.org
SIC: 8322 Association for the handicapped

(P-17896)
COMPASS FAMILY SERVICES
Also Called: Compass Family Shelter
626 Polk St (94102-3328)
PHONE.............................415 644-0504
Erica Kisch, Ex Dir
EMP: 80
SALES (corp-wide): 22.71MM **Privately Held**
Web: www.compass-sf.org
SIC: 8322 Family (marriage) counseling
PA: Compass Family Services
37 Grove St
San Francisco CA
415 644-0504

(P-17897)
COMPASS FAMILY SERVICES
Also Called: Compass Clara House
111 Page St (94102-5892)
PHONE.............................415 644-0504
EMP: 80
SALES (corp-wide): 22.71MM **Privately Held**
Web: www.compass-sf.org
SIC: 8322 General counseling services
PA: Compass Family Services
37 Grove St
San Francisco CA
415 644-0504

(P-17898)
CORE CMNTY ORGNZED RLIEF EFFOR
Also Called: Core
910 N Hill St (90012-1715)
PHONE.............................323 934-4400
Sean Penn, Ch Bd
Ann Young Lee, *
EMP: 400 **EST:** 2010
SALES (est): 62.01MM **Privately Held**
Web: www.coreresponse.org
SIC: 8322 Temporary relief service

(P-17899)
COUNCIL ON AGING - STHERN CAL
2 Executive Cir Ste 175 (92614-6773)
PHONE.............................714 479-0107
Lisa Wright Jenkins, CEO
EMP: 83 **EST:** 1973
SALES (est): 6.84MM **Privately Held**
Web: www.coasc.org
SIC: 8322 Senior citizens' center or association

(P-17900)
COUNTRY VILLA SERVICE CORP
3000 N Gate Rd (90740-2535)
PHONE.............................562 598-2477
Jennifer Rose, Brnch Mgr
EMP: 103
SALES (corp-wide): 88.5MM **Privately Held**
Web: www.evictionlawyer.com
SIC: 8322 8011 Rehabilitation services; Medical centers
PA: Country Villa Service Corp.
2400 E Katella Ave # 800
Anaheim CA
310 574-3733

(P-17901)
COUNTRY VILLA SERVICE CORP
Also Called: Cntry Vlla Merced Hlthcre Cntr
510 W 26th St (95340-2804)
PHONE.............................209 723-2911
Joel Saltzburg, CEO
EMP: 103
SALES (corp-wide): 88.5MM **Privately Held**
Web: www.evictionlawyer.com
SIC: 8322 8051 Rehabilitation services; Skilled nursing care facilities
PA: Country Villa Service Corp.
2400 E Katella Ave # 800
Anaheim CA
310 574-3733

(P-17902)
COUNTRY VLLA RNCHO MRAGE HLTHC
39950 Vista Del Sol (92270-3206)
PHONE.............................760 340-0053
Scott Gillis, Admn
EMP: 200 **EST:** 2007
SALES (est): 3.89MM **Privately Held**
Web: www.ranchomiragehcc.com
SIC: 8322 Rehabilitation services

(P-17903)
COUNTY OF FRESNO
Also Called: Probation Department
333 W Pontiac Way (93612-5613)
P.O. Box 453 (93709-0453)
PHONE.............................559 600-5127
Rick Chavez, Mgr
EMP: 82
SALES (corp-wide): 2.02B **Privately Held**
Web: www.fresnocountyca.gov
SIC: 8322 9441 Probation office; Administration of social and manpower programs, County government
PA: County Of Fresno
2281 Tulare St Ste 304
Fresno CA
559 600-1710

(P-17904)
COUNTY OF FRESNO
Also Called: Probation Department
2220 Tulare St Ste 1111 (93721-2124)
PHONE.............................559 600-2822
Rick Chavez, Mgr
EMP: 235
SALES (corp-wide): 2.02B **Privately Held**
Web: www.fresnocountyca.gov
SIC: 8322 9441 Probation office; Administration of social and manpower programs
PA: County Of Fresno
2281 Tulare St Ste 304
Fresno CA
559 600-1710

(P-17905)
COUNTY OF LOS ANGELES
Also Called: Public Social Services
12727 Norwalk Blvd (90650-3145)
PHONE.............................562 807-7860
Tony Iniguez, Dir
EMP: 63
SALES (corp-wide): 31.7B **Privately Held**
Web: www.lacounty.gov
SIC: 8322 9441 Individual and family services; Administration of social and manpower programs
PA: County Of Los Angeles
500 W Temple St Ste 437
Los Angeles CA
213 974-1101

(P-17906)
COUNTY OF LOS ANGELES
Also Called: Community & Senior Svcs
777 W Jackman St (93534-2419)
PHONE.............................661 948-2320
Nusun Muhamad, Mgr
EMP: 63
SALES (corp-wide): 31.7B **Privately Held**
Web: www.lacounty.gov
SIC: 8322 9441 Senior citizens' center or association; Administration of social and manpower programs
PA: County Of Los Angeles
500 W Temple St Ste 437
Los Angeles CA
213 974-1101

(P-17907)
COUNTY OF LOS ANGELES
Also Called: Department Children Fmly Svcs
501 Shatto Pl Ste 301 (90020-1749)
PHONE.............................213 351-7257
Bill Browning, Dir
EMP: 82
SALES (corp-wide): 31.7B **Privately Held**
Web: www.lacounty.gov
SIC: 8322 9111 Senior citizens' center or association; Executive offices
PA: County Of Los Angeles
500 W Temple St Ste 437
Los Angeles CA
213 974-1101

(P-17908)
COUNTY OF LOS ANGELES
Also Called: Child Support Services
5770 S Eastern Ave 4th Fl (90040-2948)
PHONE.............................323 889-3405
Steven Golightly, Mgr
EMP: 272
SALES (corp-wide): 31.7B **Privately Held**
Web: www.lacounty.gov
SIC: 8322 9441 Child related social services; Administration of social and manpower programs
PA: County Of Los Angeles
500 W Temple St Ste 437
Los Angeles CA
213 974-1101

(P-17909)
COUNTY OF LOS ANGELES
Also Called: Children & Family Svcs Dept
10355 Slusher Dr (90670-7353)
PHONE.............................562 903-5000
Barbara Betlem, Dir
EMP: 63
SALES (corp-wide): 31.7B **Privately Held**
Web: www.lacounty.gov
SIC: 8322 9441 Child related social services; Administration of social and manpower programs, level of governme
PA: County Of Los Angeles
500 W Temple St Ste 437
Los Angeles CA
213 974-1101

(P-17910)
COUNTY OF LOS ANGELES
Also Called: Children & Family Svcs Dept
510 S Vermont Ave Fl 1 (90020-1912)
PHONE.............................213 351-5600
Jackie Contreras, Dir
EMP: 63
SALES (corp-wide): 31.7B **Privately Held**
Web: www.lacounty.gov
SIC: 8322 9441 Child related social services; Administration of social and manpower programs
PA: County Of Los Angeles
500 W Temple St Ste 437
Los Angeles CA
213 974-1101

(P-17911)
COUNTY OF LOS ANGELES
Also Called: Los Angles Cnty Dept Mntal Hlt
19231 Victory Blvd Ste 100 (91335-6308)
PHONE.............................818 708-4500
Melaney Leland, Ex Dir
EMP: 63
SALES (corp-wide): 31.7B **Privately Held**
Web: www.lacounty.gov
SIC: 8322 Child guidance agency
PA: County Of Los Angeles
500 W Temple St Ste 437
Los Angeles CA
213 974-1101

(P-17912)
COUNTY OF LOS ANGELES
Also Called: Dept Children and Family Svcs
4060 Watson Plaza Dr (90712-4033)
PHONE.............................562 497-3500
Joy Russell, Admn
EMP: 99
SALES (corp-wide): 31.7B **Privately Held**
Web: dcfs.lacounty.gov
SIC: 8322 9111 Childrens' aid society; Executive offices
PA: County Of Los Angeles
500 W Temple St Ste 437
Los Angeles CA
213 974-1101

(P-17913)
COUNTY OF LOS ANGELES
Also Called: Probation Department
300 E Walnut St Dept 200 (91101-1584)
PHONE.............................626 356-5281
Diana Cunningham, Prin
EMP: 85
SALES (corp-wide): 31.7B **Privately Held**
Web: www.lacounty.gov
SIC: 8322 9199 Probation office; General government administration, County government
PA: County Of Los Angeles
500 W Temple St Ste 437
Los Angeles CA
213 974-1101

(P-17914)
COUNTY OF LOS ANGELES
Also Called: Probation Department
5300 W Avenue I (93536-8312)
PHONE.............................661 940-4181
Willie Doyle, Dir
EMP: 90
SALES (corp-wide): 31.7B **Privately Held**
Web: www.lacounty.gov
SIC: 8322 9223 Probation office; Correctional institutions
PA: County Of Los Angeles
500 W Temple St Ste 437
Los Angeles CA
213 974-1101

(P-17915)
COUNTY OF LOS ANGELES
Also Called: Probation Information Ctr Pic
9150 Imperial Hwy (90242-2835)
PHONE.............................562 940-2470
EMP: 82
SALES (corp-wide): 31.7B **Privately Held**
Web: www.lacounty.gov
SIC: 8322 Probation office
PA: County Of Los Angeles
500 W Temple St Ste 437
Los Angeles CA
213 974-1101

8322 - Individual And Family Services (P-17916)

PRODUCTS & SERVICES SECTION

(P-17916)
COUNTY OF LOS ANGELES
Also Called: Probation Dept
320 W Temple St Ste 1101 (90012-3289)
PHONE..........................213 974-9331
Mike Verilla, *Dir*
EMP: 73
SALES (corp-wide): 31.7B **Privately Held**
Web: www.lacounty.gov
SIC: 8322 9223 8093 Probation office; Correctional institutions; Mental health clinic, outpatient
PA: County Of Los Angeles
500 W Temple St Ste 437
Los Angeles CA
213 974-1101

(P-17917)
COUNTY OF LOS ANGELES
Also Called: La County Probation
8240 Broadway Ave (90606-3120)
PHONE..........................562 908-3119
Donna Rose, *Mgr*
EMP: 91
SALES (corp-wide): 31.7B **Privately Held**
Web: www.lacounty.gov
SIC: 8322 9111 Probation office; County supervisors' and executives' office
PA: County Of Los Angeles
500 W Temple St Ste 437
Los Angeles CA
213 974-1101

(P-17918)
COUNTY OF LOS ANGELES
236 E 58th St (90011-5316)
PHONE..........................323 235-7047
EMP: 63
SALES (corp-wide): 31.7B **Privately Held**
Web: www.lacounty.gov
SIC: 8322 Probation office
PA: County Of Los Angeles
500 W Temple St Ste 437
Los Angeles CA
213 974-1101

(P-17919)
COUNTY OF LOS ANGELES
Also Called: Probation Department
1601 Eastlake Ave (90033-1009)
PHONE..........................323 226-8511
Taula Heath, *Dir*
EMP: 91
SALES (corp-wide): 31.7B **Privately Held**
Web: www.lacounty.gov
SIC: 8322 Probation office
PA: County Of Los Angeles
500 W Temple St Ste 437
Los Angeles CA
213 974-1101

(P-17920)
COUNTY OF LOS ANGELES
Also Called: Probation Department
7285 Quill Dr (90242-2001)
PHONE..........................562 940-6856
Sheryl Cooke, *Superintnt*
EMP: 91
SALES (corp-wide): 31.7B **Privately Held**
Web: www.lacounty.gov
SIC: 8322 9223 Probation office; Correctional institutions
PA: County Of Los Angeles
500 W Temple St Ste 437
Los Angeles CA
213 974-1101

(P-17921)
COUNTY OF LOS ANGELES
Also Called: County Los Angles Prbtion Dept
1660 W Mission Blvd (91766-1200)
PHONE..........................909 469-4500
Lorraine Hubbard-johns, *Mgr*
EMP: 73
SALES (corp-wide): 31.7B **Privately Held**
Web: www.lacounty.gov
SIC: 8322 9223 Probation office; Correctional institutions
PA: County Of Los Angeles
500 W Temple St Ste 437
Los Angeles CA
213 974-1101

(P-17922)
COUNTY OF LOS ANGELES
Also Called: Probation Dept
1725 Main St Rm 125 (90401-3267)
PHONE..........................310 266-3711
Ernest P Gonzalez, *Brnch Mgr*
EMP: 82
SALES (corp-wide): 31.7B **Privately Held**
Web: www.lacounty.gov
SIC: 8322 9223 Probation office; Correctional institutions
PA: County Of Los Angeles
500 W Temple St Ste 437
Los Angeles CA
213 974-1101

(P-17923)
COUNTY OF LOS ANGELES
Also Called: Probation Dept
14414 Delano St (91401-2703)
PHONE..........................818 374-2000
Ed Johnson, *Dir*
EMP: 91
SALES (corp-wide): 31.7B **Privately Held**
Web: www.lacounty.gov
SIC: 8322 9223 Probation office; Correctional institutions
PA: County Of Los Angeles
500 W Temple St Ste 437
Los Angeles CA
213 974-1101

(P-17924)
COUNTY OF LOS ANGELES
Also Called: Probation Dept
4849 Civic Center Way (90022-1679)
PHONE..........................323 780-2185
Debbie Nelson, *Dir*
EMP: 145
SALES (corp-wide): 31.7B **Privately Held**
Web: www.lacounty.gov
SIC: 8322 9223 Probation office; Correctional institutions
PA: County Of Los Angeles
500 W Temple St Ste 437
Los Angeles CA
213 974-1101

(P-17925)
COUNTY OF LOS ANGELES
Also Called: Probation Dept
8526 Grape St (90001-4134)
PHONE..........................323 586-6469
Mark Garcia, *Dir*
EMP: 82
SALES (corp-wide): 31.7B **Privately Held**
Web: www.lacounty.gov
SIC: 8322 9223 Probation office; Correctional institutions
PA: County Of Los Angeles
500 W Temple St Ste 437
Los Angeles CA
213 974-1101

(P-17926)
COUNTY OF LOS ANGELES
Also Called: Probation Dept
200 W Compton Blvd Ste 300 (90220-6676)
PHONE..........................310 603-7311
Peggy May, *Dir*
EMP: 73
SALES (corp-wide): 31.7B **Privately Held**
Web: www.lacounty.gov
SIC: 8322 9223 Probation office; Correctional institutions
PA: County Of Los Angeles
500 W Temple St Ste 437
Los Angeles CA
213 974-1101

(P-17927)
COUNTY OF LOS ANGELES
Also Called: Probation Dept
199 N Euclid Ave (91101-1757)
PHONE..........................626 356-5281
Steve Yoder, *Dir*
EMP: 82
SALES (corp-wide): 31.7B **Privately Held**
Web: www.lacounty.gov
SIC: 8322 9223 Probation office; Correctional institutions
PA: County Of Los Angeles
500 W Temple St Ste 437
Los Angeles CA
213 974-1101

(P-17928)
COUNTY OF LOS ANGELES
200 W Woodward Ave (91801-3459)
PHONE..........................626 308-5542
Roger Fernandez, *Brnch Mgr*
EMP: 82
SALES (corp-wide): 31.7B **Privately Held**
Web: www.lacounty.gov
SIC: 8322 9111 Probation office; County supervisors' and executives' office
PA: County Of Los Angeles
500 W Temple St Ste 437
Los Angeles CA
213 974-1101

(P-17929)
COUNTY OF LOS ANGELES
Also Called: Camp Glenn Rocky
1900 Sycamore Canyon Rd (91773-1220)
PHONE..........................909 599-2391
EMP: 81
SALES (corp-wide): 31.7B **Privately Held**
Web: www.lacounty.gov
SIC: 8322 9111 Probation office; Executive offices
PA: County Of Los Angeles
500 W Temple St Ste 437
Los Angeles CA
213 974-1101

(P-17930)
COUNTY OF LOS ANGELES
Also Called: Health Services, Dept of
17171 Gale Ave (91745-1822)
PHONE..........................626 854-4987
Althea Shirley, *Dir*
EMP: 63
SALES (corp-wide): 31.7B **Privately Held**
Web: www.lacounty.gov
SIC: 8322 9431 Public welfare center; Administration of public health programs
PA: County Of Los Angeles
500 W Temple St Ste 437
Los Angeles CA
213 974-1101

(P-17931)
COUNTY OF LOS ANGELES
Also Called: Department Public Social Svcs
613 S Humphreys Ave (90022-2443)
PHONE..........................323 551-7224
Michael Sylvester, *Brnch Mgr*
EMP: 63
SALES (corp-wide): 31.7B **Privately Held**
Web: www.lacounty.gov
SIC: 8322 9441 Social service center; Administration of social and manpower programs, County government
PA: County Of Los Angeles
500 W Temple St Ste 437
Los Angeles CA
213 974-1101

(P-17932)
COUNTY OF LOS ANGELES
Also Called: Department of Social Services
530 12th St 1st Fl (93446-2201)
PHONE..........................805 237-3110
Michelle Chambers, *Mgr*
EMP: 63
SALES (corp-wide): 31.7B **Privately Held**
Web: www.lacounty.gov
SIC: 8322 Social service center
PA: County Of Los Angeles
500 W Temple St Ste 437
Los Angeles CA
213 974-1101

(P-17933)
COUNTY OF LOS ANGELES
Also Called: Latino Fmly Alchol DRG Abuse C
5801 E Beverly Blvd (90022-2876)
PHONE..........................323 722-4529
Germeen Duplesses, *Dir*
EMP: 63
SALES (corp-wide): 31.7B **Privately Held**
Web: www.lacounty.gov
SIC: 8322 9431 8093 Drug abuse counselor, nontreatment; Administration of public health programs; Rehabilitation center, outpatient treatment
PA: County Of Los Angeles
500 W Temple St Ste 437
Los Angeles CA
213 974-1101

(P-17934)
COUNTY OF ORANGE
Also Called: District Attorney
8141 13th St (92683-4576)
PHONE..........................714 896-7188
Gary Tackett, *Brnch Mgr*
EMP: 75
SALES (corp-wide): 5.2B **Privately Held**
Web: www.ocgov.com
SIC: 8322 9211 Substance abuse counseling ; Courts
PA: County Of Orange
400 W Civic Center Dr G36
Santa Ana CA
714 834-6200

(P-17935)
COUNTY OF RIVERSIDE
Also Called: Community Action Prtnr Rvrside
2038 Iowa Ave Ste 102 (92507-2471)
PHONE..........................951 955-4900
Maria Y Juarez, *Mgr*
EMP: 82
SALES (corp-wide): 4.58B **Privately Held**
Web: www.capriverside.org
SIC: 8322 9441 Individual and family services; Administration of social and manpower programs
PA: County Of Riverside
4080 Lemon St Fl 11
Riverside CA
951 955-1110

PRODUCTS & SERVICES SECTION
8322 - Individual And Family Services (P-17956)

(P-17936)
COUNTY OF RIVERSIDE
Also Called: Office On Aging Adrc Rvrside C
3610 Central Ave Ste 102 (92506-5904)
P.O. Box 12013 (92502-2213)
PHONE.................................800 510-2020
Edward Walsh, *Dir*
EMP: 63
SALES (corp-wide): 4.58B Privately Held
Web: www.countyofriverside.us
SIC: 8322 9441 Geriatric social service; Administration of social and manpower programs
PA: County Of Riverside
4080 Lemon St Fl 11
Riverside CA
951 955-1110

(P-17937)
COUNTY OF SAN DIEGO
Also Called: Probation Dept
330 W Broadway Ste 1100 (92101-3827)
P.O. Box 23596 (92193-3596)
PHONE.................................619 515-8202
Don Blevins, *Dir*
EMP: 892
Web: www.sdcda.org
SIC: 8322 9431 Probation office; Administration of public health programs
PA: County Of San Diego
1600 Pacific Hwy Ste 209
San Diego CA
619 531-5880

(P-17938)
COUNTY OF SAN JOAQUIN
Also Called: Dept of Child Support
409 E Market St (95202-3007)
PHONE.................................209 468-2601
Judy Grimes, *Brnch Mgr*
EMP: 76
SALES (corp-wide): 1.54B Privately Held
Web: www.sjgov.org
SIC: 8322 9441 Child related social services; Public welfare administration: nonoperating, government
PA: County Of San Joaquin
44 N San Joaquin St # 374
Stockton CA
209 468-3203

(P-17939)
COUNTY OF SAN JOAQUIN
Also Called: Mary Grahams Childrens Shelter
500 W Hospital Rd (95231-9693)
P.O. Box 201056 (95201-3006)
PHONE.................................209 468-6966
Brian Woods, *Dir*
EMP: 76
SALES (corp-wide): 1.54B Privately Held
Web: www.marygrahamfoundation.org
SIC: 8322 9512 Child related social services; Land conservation agencies
PA: County Of San Joaquin
44 N San Joaquin St # 374
Stockton CA
209 468-3203

(P-17940)
COUNTY OF SANTA CLARA
Also Called: Social Service Agency
333 W Julian St (95110-2314)
PHONE.................................408 299-5437
Norma Sparks, *Dir*
EMP: 320
Web: home.sccgov.org
SIC: 8322 Child related social services
PA: County Of Santa Clara
70 W Hedding St
San Jose CA
408 299-5200

(P-17941)
COUNTY OF SHASTA
Also Called: Shasta Family YMCA
1155 N Court St (96001-0437)
PHONE.................................530 246-9622
Kristen Lyns, *Ex Dir*
EMP: 71
SALES (corp-wide): 410.48MM Privately Held
Web: www.sfymca.org
SIC: 8322 8641 Individual and family services; Youth organizations
PA: County Of Shasta
1450 Court St Ste 308a
Redding CA
530 225-5561

(P-17942)
COUNTY OF VENTURA
Also Called: County Ventura Human Resources
800 S Victoria Ave (93009-0003)
PHONE.................................805 654-2561
Jodi Lee Prior, *Brnch Mgr*
EMP: 104
SALES (corp-wide): 165.04MM Privately Held
Web: www.ventura.org
SIC: 8322 9441 Individual and family services; Administration of social and human resources
PA: County Of Ventura
800 S Victoria Ave
Ventura CA
805 654-2644

(P-17943)
COUNTY OF YUBA
Also Called: Yuba Cnty Prbtion Chldren Fmli
209 6th St (95901-5570)
PHONE.................................530 741-6275
Jason Roper, *Prgrm Mgr*
EMP: 94
SALES (corp-wide): 233.12MM Privately Held
Web: www.yuba.org
SIC: 8322 9199 Probation office; General government administration, County government
PA: County Of Yuba
915 8th St Ste 109
Marysville CA
530 749-7575

(P-17944)
COUNTY OF YUBA
Also Called: Yuba County Probation Dept
215 5th St Ste 154 (95901-5737)
PHONE.................................530 749-7550
Jim Arnold, *Dir*
EMP: 124
SALES (corp-wide): 233.12MM Privately Held
Web: www.yuba.org
SIC: 8322 9199 Probation office; General government administration, County government
PA: County Of Yuba
915 8th St Ste 109
Marysville CA
530 749-7575

(P-17945)
COVIA AFFORDABLE COMMUNITIES
2185 N California Blvd Ste 215 (94596-3566)
PHONE.................................925 956-7400
Kevin Gerber, *CEO*
Jonathan Casey, *
EMP: 180 EST: 1980
SALES (est): 8.4MM Privately Held
SIC: 8322 6513 Individual and family services; Apartment building operators

(P-17946)
CRUCIBLE
1260 7th St (94607-2150)
PHONE.................................510 444-0919
Susan Mernit, *Ex Dir*
Michael Sturtz, *
Steven Young, *
EMP: 215 EST: 1997
SQ FT: 46,980
SALES (est): 3.44MM Privately Held
Web: www.thecrucible.org
SIC: 8322 8331 Outreach program; Skill training center

(P-17947)
CRYSTAL STAIRS INC (PA)
5110 W Goldleaf Cir Ste 150 (90056-1287)
PHONE.................................323 299-8998
Jackie B Majors, *CEO*
Dianna Torres, *
Doctor Karen Hill-scott, *Pr*
Carolyn Moultrie, *
Javier La Fianza, *
EMP: 330 EST: 1980
SQ FT: 83,000
SALES (est): 252.73MM
SALES (corp-wide): 252.73MM Privately Held
Web: www.crystalstairs.org
SIC: 8322 Social service center

(P-17948)
CV STARR COMMUNITY CENTER
300 S Lincoln St (95437-4416)
PHONE.................................707 964-9446
Dan Keyes, *Admn*
EMP: 99 EST: 2012
SALES (est): 2.21MM Privately Held
Web: www.mendocoastrec.org
SIC: 8322 Community center

(P-17949)
DAVIS STREET COMMUNITY CENTER (PA)
Also Called: DAVIS STREET FAMILY RESOURCE C
3081 Teagarden St (94577-5720)
PHONE.................................510 347-4620
EMP: 69 EST: 1971
SQ FT: 22,450
SALES (est): 19.46MM Privately Held
Web: www.davisstreet.org
SIC: 8322 8021 8011 8093 Community center; Dental clinic; Primary care medical clinic; Mental health clinic, outpatient

(P-17950)
DEAF CMNTY SVCS SAN DIEGO INC
Also Called: Sign Lnguage Interpreting Svcs
1545 Hotel Cir S Ste 300 (92108-3414)
PHONE.................................619 398-2441
Leslie K Elion, *Ch*
Matthew Baker, *
Tom Humphries, *
Patricia Sieglen-perry, *Sec*
EMP: 79 EST: 1984
SQ FT: 12,100
SALES (est): 3.98MM Privately Held
Web: www.deafcommunityservices.org
SIC: 8322 Social service center

(P-17951)
DESERT AIDS PROJECT (PA)
Also Called: REVIVALS THRIFT STORES
1695 N Sunrise Way Ste 101 (92262-3701)
P.O. Box 2890 (92263)
PHONE.................................760 323-2118
David Brinkman, *CEO*
Mary Park, *
EMP: 65 EST: 1984
SQ FT: 46,050
SALES (est): 72.25MM Privately Held
Web: www.daphealth.org
SIC: 8322 5932 8011 General counseling services; Used merchandise stores; Clinic, operated by physicians

(P-17952)
DESERT ARC
Also Called: DESERT VALLEY INDUSTRIES
73255 Country Club Dr (92260-2309)
PHONE.................................760 346-1611
Kurt Parish, *Admn*
Ruth Goodsell, *
Robin Keagen, *
Robert Anzalone, *
Rosemary Fausel, *
EMP: 256 EST: 1959
SQ FT: 12,000
SALES (est): 17.11MM Privately Held
Web: www.desertarc.org
SIC: 8322 Association for the handicapped

(P-17953)
DEVELOP DISABILITIES SVC ORG
Also Called: Community Integration Program
2331 Saint Marks Way G1 (95864-0626)
PHONE.................................916 973-1951
EMP: 75
SALES (est): 897.03K Privately Held
SIC: 8322 Association for the handicapped

(P-17954)
DIDI HIRSCH PSYCHIATRIC SVC (PA)
Also Called: Didi Hrsch Cmnty Mntal Hlth Ct
4760 Sepulveda Blvd (90230-4820)
PHONE.................................310 390-6612
Michael Wierwille, *Ch*
Kita S Curry, *
Andrew Rubin, *
John Mcgann, *VP Fin*
Martin Frank, *
EMP: 150 EST: 1944
SQ FT: 35,000
SALES (est): 56.18MM
SALES (corp-wide): 56.18MM Privately Held
Web: www.didihirsch.org
SIC: 8322 8093 Family counseling services; Mental health clinic, outpatient

(P-17955)
DISTRICT COUNCIL DC (PA)
Also Called: St Vincent De Paul
2272 San Pablo Ave (94612-1321)
PHONE.................................510 638-7600
Blase Bova, *Ex Dir*
EMP: 100 EST: 1938
SALES (est): 3.88MM
SALES (corp-wide): 3.88MM Privately Held
Web: www.svdp-alameda.org
SIC: 8322 Individual and family services

(P-17956)
DIVERSE JOURNEYS INC (PA)
525 S Douglas St Ste 210 (90245-4827)
PHONE.................................310 643-7403

8322 - Individual And Family Services (P-17957)

Amanda Gerhart, *Pr*
Laura Broderrick, *
EMP: 78 EST: 2005
SQ FT: 2,000
SALES (est): 5.6MM
SALES (corp-wide): 5.6MM **Privately Held**
Web: www.diversejourneys.org
SIC: 8322 Social services for the handicapped

(P-17957)
DONATIONS WITH CARE
6220 Winding Way (95608-1135)
PHONE.................916 544-3080
Serge Borodulin, *Prin*
Elle Rubinger, *
James Mitchell, *
Kay Ralston, *
EMP: 73 EST: 2020
SALES (est): 551.95K **Privately Held**
SIC: 8322 Individual and family services

(P-17958)
DOWNTOWN STREETS INC
Also Called: DOWNTOWN STREETS TEAM
1671 The Alameda (95126-2222)
PHONE.................650 462-1795
Eileen Richardson, *Ex Dir*
Chris Richardson, *
Andrew Hening, *
Jessica Orozco, *
EMP: 91 EST: 2005
SALES (est): 11.6MM **Privately Held**
Web: www.streetsteam.org
SIC: 8322 8399 Social service center; Community development groups

(P-17959)
DREW CHILD DEV CORP INC (PA)
1770 E 118th St (90059-2518)
PHONE.................323 249-2950
Michael Jackson, *Pr*
James Hays, *
EMP: 67 EST: 1987
SALES (est): 43.71MM **Privately Held**
Web: www.drewcdc.org
SIC: 8322 Child guidance agency

(P-17960)
EAST BAY ASIAN YOUTH CENTER
2025 E 12th St (94606-4925)
PHONE.................510 533-1092
Gianna Tran, *Pr*
EMP: 90
SALES (corp-wide): 7.12MM **Privately Held**
Web: www.ebayc.org
SIC: 8322 Youth center
PA: East Bay Asian Youth Center
2025 E 12th St
Oakland CA
510 533-1092

(P-17961)
EAST LOS ANGLES RMRKBLE CTZENS
Also Called: EL ARCA
3839 Selig Pl (90031-3143)
PHONE.................323 223-3079
Carlos Madrid, *Ex Dir*
John Menchaca, *
EMP: 100 EST: 1969
SQ FT: 23,360
SALES (est): 5.1MM **Privately Held**
Web: www.elarcainc.org
SIC: 8322 Social services for the handicapped

(P-17962)
EASTERN LOS ANGELES RE (PA)
1000 S Fremont Ave Unit 23 (91803-8800)
P.O. Box 7916 (91802-7916)
PHONE.................626 299-4700
Gloria Wong, *Ex Dir*
EMP: 242 EST: 1969
SQ FT: 31,704
SALES (est): 15.65MM
SALES (corp-wide): 15.65MM **Privately Held**
Web: www.elarc.org
SIC: 8322 Association for the handicapped

(P-17963)
ED SUPPORTS LLC
Also Called: Juvo Atism Bhavioral Hlth Svcs
1710 Prairie City Rd Ste 100 (95630)
PHONE.................201 478-8711
Adam Schreiber, *Brnch Mgr*
EMP: 60
SALES (corp-wide): 27.81MM **Privately Held**
SIC: 8322 Individual and family services
HQ: Ed Supports Llc
1200 Concord Ave Ste 100
Concord CA -
510 832-4383

(P-17964)
EGGLESTON YOUTH CENTERS INC (PA)
256 W Badillo St (91723-1906)
P.O. Box 638 (91706-0638)
PHONE.................626 480-8107
Clarence Brown, *Ex Dir*
Don Gutierrez, *
April Mitchell, *Brand President*
EMP: 90 EST: 1975
SQ FT: 7,616
SALES (est): 11.26MM
SALES (corp-wide): 11.26MM **Privately Held**
Web: www.egglestonyouthcenter.org
SIC: 8322 Social service center

(P-17965)
EL CAMINO HOSPITAL
1503 Grant Rd Ste 120 (94040-3293)
PHONE.................650 988-7444
Vicki Chryssos, *Ex Dir*
EMP: 70
SALES (corp-wide): 1.43B **Privately Held**
Web: www.elcaminohealth.org
SIC: 8322 Social worker
PA: El Camino Hospital
2500 Grant Rd
Mountain View CA
650 940-7000

(P-17966)
EL CONCILIO CALIFORNIA (PA)
Also Called: EL CONC!LIO
445 N San Joaquin St Ste A (95202-2026)
PHONE.................209 644-2600
Jose Rodriguez, *CEO*
Mark Apostolon, *Ofcr*
EMP: 136 EST: 1968
SQ FT: 8,000
SALES (est): 21.44MM
SALES (corp-wide): 21.44MM **Privately Held**
Web: www.elconcilio.org
SIC: 8322 Social service center

(P-17967)
EL NIDO FAMILY CENTERS (PA)
10200 Sepulveda Blvd Ste 350 (91345-3318)
PHONE.................818 830-3646
Liz Herrera, *Dir*
EMP: 130 EST: 1957
SQ FT: 3,650
SALES (est): 14.16MM
SALES (corp-wide): 14.16MM **Privately Held**
Web: www.elnidofamilycenters.org
SIC: 8322 Social service center

(P-17968)
ENCOMPASS COMMUNITY SERVICES
Also Called: Headstart
225 Westridge Dr (95076-4168)
P.O. Box 927 (95077-0927)
PHONE.................831 724-3885
Gloria Martinez, *Brnch Mgr*
EMP: 71
SALES (corp-wide): 30.21MM **Privately Held**
Web: www.encompasscs.org
SIC: 8322 8351 Social service center; Head Start center, except in conjunction with school
PA: Encompass Community Services
380 Encinal St Ste 2000
Santa Cruz CA
831 427-9670

(P-17969)
EPISCOPAL COMMUNITY SERVICES
Also Called: Ecs-National City Head Start
2432 E 18th St (91950-5143)
PHONE.................619 470-0720
Leanna Cobarrubias, *Dir*
EMP: 96
SALES (corp-wide): 32.67MM **Privately Held**
Web: www.ecscalifornia.org
SIC: 8322 Social service center
PA: Episcopal Community Services
401 Mile Of Cars Way
National City CA
619 228-2800

(P-17970)
ESKATON PROPERTIES INC
Also Called: Carmichael Adult Day Hlth Ctr
5105 Manzanita Ave Ste D (95608-0523)
PHONE.................916 334-0296
EMP: 122
SIC: 8322 Adult day care center
PA: Eskaton Properties Incorporated
5105 Manzanita Ave Ste A
Carmichael CA

(P-17971)
EXCEPTNL PRENTS UNLIMITED INC
Also Called: E P U
4440 N 1st St (93726-2304)
PHONE.................559 229-2000
Lowell Ens, *CEO*
EMP: 125 EST: 1976
SQ FT: 24,000
SALES (est): 9.06MM **Privately Held**
Web: www.epuchildren.org
SIC: 8322 Family counseling services

(P-17972)
FAMILIES CHICE HM CARE SVCS IN
545 N Mountain Ave Ste 209 (91786-5073)
PHONE.................909 303-9377
Kendal Ingram, *CEO*
EMP: 65 EST: 2014
SALES (est): 1.57MM **Privately Held**
Web: www.familieschoicehomecare.com
SIC: 8322 Individual and family services

(P-17973)
FAMILY & CHILDREN SERVICES
375 Cambridge Ave (94306-1613)
PHONE.................650 326-6576
Jim Welsh, *Pr*
EMP: 91 EST: 1948
SQ FT: 6,000
SALES (est): 2.83MM **Privately Held**
Web: www.fcservices.org
SIC: 8322 Child related social services

(P-17974)
FAMILY ASSISTANCE PROGRAM
Also Called: OUR HOUSE
15075 Seventh St (92395-3810)
PHONE.................760 843-0701
Darryl Evey, *CEO*
Darryl Evey, *Ex Dir*
Elsa Scott, *
EMP: 92 EST: 1985
SQ FT: 4,960
SALES (est): 8.51MM **Privately Held**
Web: www.familyassist.org
SIC: 8322 Social service center

(P-17975)
FAMILY ASSSSMENT CNSLING EDCAT
1651 E 4th St Ste 128 (92701-5117)
PHONE.................714 447-9024
Mary O Harris, *Brnch Mgr*
EMP: 69
Web: www.facescal.org
SIC: 8322 Family counseling services
PA: Family Assessment Counseling Education Services
2030 E 4th St
Santa Ana CA

(P-17976)
FAMILY BRIDGES INC
168 11th St (94607-4841)
PHONE.................510 839-2270
Corinne Jan, *Ex Dir*
Susanna Ng-lee, *VP*
Mary Marshall, *
EMP: 126 EST: 1968
SQ FT: 5,000
SALES (est): 7MM **Privately Held**
Web: www.familybridges.org
SIC: 8322 8641 Social service center; Civic and social associations

(P-17977)
FAMILY OPTIONS LLC
3245 W Figarden Dr (93711-3906)
PHONE.................559 275-2323
Yolanda Speed, *Managing Member*
EMP: 66 EST: 2008
SALES (est): 10.69MM **Privately Held**
Web: www.foptionsca.com
SIC: 8322 Social services for the handicapped

(P-17978)
FAMILY SVC AGCY OF MARIN CNTY (PA)
Also Called: Family Service Agency
555 Northgate Dr (94903-3680)
PHONE.................415 491-5700
Margret Hallett, *Dir*
EMP: 82 EST: 1952
SALES (est): 3.81MM
SALES (corp-wide): 3.81MM **Privately Held**
Web: www.fsamarin.org

8322 - Individual And Family Services (P-17999)

SIC: 8322 Family (marriage) counseling

(P-17979)
FAMILY SVC AGCY SNTA BRBARA CN
123 W Gutierrez St (93101-3274)
PHONE.................................805 965-1001
Denise Cicourel, Admn
EMP: 100 EST: 1901
SALES (est): 15.16MM Privately Held
Web: www.fsacares.org
SIC: 8322 Social service center

(P-17980)
FAR NRTHERN CRDNTING CNCIL ON
Also Called: Regional Center
1377 E Lassen Ave (95973-7824)
PHONE.................................530 895-8633
Laura Larson, Dir
EMP: 77
SALES (corp-wide): 212.13MM Privately Held
Web: www.farnothernrc.org
SIC: 8322 8399 Social services for the handicapped; Health and welfare council
PA: Far Northern Coordinating Council On Developmental Disabilities
1900 Churn Creek Rd # 114
Redding CA
530 222-4791

(P-17981)
FAR NRTHERN CRDNTING CNCIL ON (PA)
Also Called: FAR NORTHERN REGIONAL CENTER
1900 Churn Creek Rd Ste 114 (96002-0245)
P.O. Box 492418 (96049-2418)
PHONE.................................530 222-4791
Laura L Larson, Ex Dir
EMP: 100 EST: 1967
SALES (est): 212.13MM
SALES (corp-wide): 212.13MM Privately Held
Web: www.farnothernrc.org
SIC: 8322 Association for the handicapped

(P-17982)
FIRST 5 LA
750 N Alameda St Ste 300 (90012-3870)
PHONE.................................213 482-5920
Kim Belsh, Prin
EMP: 147 EST: 2008
SALES (est): 29.41MM Privately Held
Web: www.first5la.org
SIC: 8322 Child guidance agency

(P-17983)
FOOTHILL FAMILY SERVICE
3629 Santa Anita Ave Ste 201 (91731-2449)
PHONE.................................626 246-1240
EMP: 113
SALES (corp-wide): 29.83MM Privately Held
Web: www.foothillfamily.org
SIC: 8322 Family counseling services
PA: Foothill Family Service
2500 E Fthill Blvd Ste 30
Pasadena CA
626 993-3000

(P-17984)
FOOTHILL FAMILY SERVICE
2500 E Foothill Blvd Ste 300 (91107)
PHONE.................................626 795-6907
Helen Morran-wolf, Mgr
EMP: 113
SALES (corp-wide): 29.83MM Privately Held
Web: www.foothillfamily.org
SIC: 8322 Family counseling services
PA: Foothill Family Service
2500 E Fthill Blvd Ste 30
Pasadena CA
626 993-3000

(P-17985)
FRESH LIFELINES FOR YOUTH INC
568 Valley Way (95035-4106)
PHONE.................................408 263-2630
Christa Gannon, CEO
EMP: 89 EST: 2000
SALES (est): 7.85MM Privately Held
Web: www.flyprogram.org
SIC: 8322 Child guidance agency

(P-17986)
FRESNO CNTY ECNMIC OPPRTNTIES
3120 W Nielsen Ave (93706-1139)
PHONE.................................559 486-6587
George Egawa, Brnch Mgr
EMP: 61
SALES (corp-wide): 115.98MM Privately Held
Web: www.fresnoeoc.org
SIC: 8322 Social service center
PA: Fresno County Economic Opportunities Commission
1920 Mariposa Mall # 300
Fresno CA
559 263-1010

(P-17987)
FRESNO CNTY ECNMIC OPPRTNTIES
Also Called: Fresno Eoc
1900 Mariposa Mall Ste 300 (93721-2514)
PHONE.................................559 263-1000
Bryan Angus, CEO
EMP: 61
SALES (corp-wide): 115.98MM Privately Held
Web: www.fresnoeoc.org
SIC: 8322 Social service center
PA: Fresno County Economic Opportunities Commission
1920 Mariposa Mall # 300
Fresno CA
559 263-1010

(P-17988)
FRESNO CNTY ECNMIC OPPRTNTIES (PA)
Also Called: Fresno Eoc
1920 Mariposa Mall Ste 300 (93721-2504)
PHONE.................................559 263-1010
Brian Angus, CEO
Vongsavanh Mouanoutoua, *
Marina Magdaleno, *
Salam Nalia, *
EMP: 600 EST: 1965
SQ FT: 115,312
SALES (est): 115.98MM
SALES (corp-wide): 115.98MM Privately Held
Web: www.fresnoeoc.org
SIC: 8322 8399 Social service center; Community development groups

(P-17989)
FRESNO CNTY ECNMIC OPPRTNTIES
Also Called: Eoc Resource Development
1920 Mariposa Mall (93721-2504)
PHONE.................................559 263-1013
Roger Palomino, Mgr
EMP: 71
SALES (corp-wide): 115.98MM Privately Held
Web: www.fresnoeoc.org
SIC: 8322 Social service center
PA: Fresno County Economic Opportunities Commission
1920 Mariposa Mall # 300
Fresno CA
559 263-1010

(P-17990)
FRIENDS OUTSIDE
1148 W Fremont St (95203-2622)
P.O. Box 4085 (95204-0085)
PHONE.................................209 955-0701
Gretchen Newby, Ex Dir
EMP: 60 EST: 1963
SALES (est): 3.42MM Privately Held
Web: www.friendsoutside.org
SIC: 8322 Social service center

(P-17991)
FUTURES EXPLORED
2150 John Glenn Dr Ste 300 (94520-5633)
P.O. Box 418 (94522-0418)
PHONE.................................925 332-7183
Karen Smith, Ex Dir
Lindsey Dyba, *
EMP: 125 EST: 1964
SQ FT: 1,740
SALES (est): 11.27MM Privately Held
Web: www.futures-explored.org
SIC: 8322 Association for the handicapped

(P-17992)
G&L PENASQUITOS INC
Also Called: Arbors, The
10584 Rancho Carmel Dr (92128-3629)
PHONE.................................858 538-0802
Gary Penovich, Ex Dir
EMP: 934 EST: 1998
SQ FT: 48,685
SALES (est): 718.1K
SALES (corp-wide): 49.16MM Privately Held
SIC: 8322 Individual and family services
PA: G&L Realty Corp, Llc
439 N Bedford Dr
Beverly Hills CA
310 273-9930

(P-17993)
GOLDEN GATE REGIONAL CTR INC (PA)
1355 Market St Ste 220 (94103-1307)
PHONE.................................415 546-9222
Ron Fell, CEO
EMP: 120 EST: 1966
SQ FT: 16,901
SALES (est): 419.26MM
SALES (corp-wide): 419.26MM Privately Held
Web: www.ggrc.org
SIC: 8322 Referral service for personal and social problems

(P-17994)
GRASSHOPPER HOUSE PARTNERS LLC
Also Called: Passages
6428 Meadows Ct (90265-4492)
PHONE.................................310 589-2880
Pax Prentiss, *
EMP: 105 EST: 2000
SQ FT: 16,000
SALES (est): 11.28MM Privately Held
Web: www.passagesmalibu.com
SIC: 8322 Rehabilitation services

(P-17995)
HALLMARK REHABILITATION GP LLC
2 Park Plz Ste 225 (92614-2541)
PHONE.................................949 282-5900
Mark Whartley, *
Jimmy Sims, *
Laurie Thomas, Managing Member*
EMP: 62 EST: 2003
SALES (est): 4.07MM Privately Held
SIC: 8322 Rehabilitation services

(P-17996)
HAMILTON FAMILIES
1631 Hayes St (94117-1326)
PHONE.................................415 409-2100
Rosa Caspaneda, Fund Director
Rosa Castaneda, *
Jack Fagan, *
EMP: 65 EST: 1987
SALES (est): 18.99MM Privately Held
Web: www.hamiltonfamilies.org
SIC: 8322 Social service center

(P-17997)
HATHAWY-SYCMRES CHILD FMLY SVC
Also Called: Hathaway Children and Family
12502 Van Nuys Blvd Ste 120 (91331-1321)
PHONE.................................626 395-7100
Muriel Gaudin, Mgr
EMP: 211
SALES (corp-wide): 64.09MM Privately Held
Web: www.sycamores.org
SIC: 8322 Child related social services
PA: Hathaway-Sycamores Child And Family Services
100 W Walnut St Ste 375
Pasadena CA
626 395-7100

(P-17998)
HATHAWY-SYCMRES CHILD FMLY SVC
3741 Stocker St Ste 101 (90008-5150)
PHONE.................................323 733-0322
Debbie Manners, Brnch Mgr
EMP: 250
SALES (corp-wide): 64.09MM Privately Held
Web: www.sycamores.org
SIC: 8322 Child related social services
PA: Hathaway-Sycamores Child And Family Services
100 W Walnut St Ste 375
Pasadena CA
626 395-7100

(P-17999)
HEALTH TRUST
Also Called: Meals On Wheels
3180 Newberry Dr Ste 200 (95118-1566)
PHONE.................................408 513-8700
Michele Lew, CEO
EMP: 100
SALES (corp-wide): 27.94MM Privately Held
Web: www.healthtrust.org
SIC: 8322 Meal delivery program
PA: The Health Trust
3180 Newberry Dr Ste 200
San Jose CA
408 513-8700

8322 - Individual And Family Services (P-18000)

(P-18000)
HEARTLAND CHILD & FAMILY SVCS
Also Called: NORTH AREA COMMUNITY MENTAL HE
811 Grand Ave Ste D (95838-3466)
PHONE....................916 922-9868
Sarah Bailey, *CFO*
William Moss, *
William Benda, *
EMP: 70 **EST:** 1980
SALES (est): 8.9MM **Privately Held**
Web: www.doingwhateverittakes.org
SIC: 8322   General counseling services

(P-18001)
HELP CHILDREN WORLD FOUNDATION
Also Called: INTERNATIONAL CHILDREN'S CHARI
26500 Agoura Rd Ste 657 (91302-1952)
PHONE....................818 706-9848
Lev M Leznik, *Pr*
Andrew Grey, *
Veronica Duval, *
Michael Teilmann, *
EMP: 300 **EST:** 1991
SQ FT: 2,200
SALES (est): 10.68MM **Privately Held**
SIC: 8322   Childrens' aid society

(P-18002)
HILLSIDES
940 Avenue 64 (91105-2711)
PHONE....................323 254-2274
Joseph M Costa, *CEO*
Ryan Herren, *
Amy Ley-sanchez, *Ex VP*
EMP: 460 **EST:** 1913
SQ FT: 18,217
SALES (est): 51.1MM **Privately Held**
Web: www.recruiting.com
SIC: 8322   Individual and family services

(P-18003)
HOMEBOY INDUSTRIES (PA)
Also Called: Homeboy Bakery
130 Bruno St (90012-1815)
PHONE....................323 526-1254
Greg Boyle, *Ex Dir*
Thomas Vozzo, *Prin*
Jack Faherty, *
John Brady, *
EMP: 270 **EST:** 2000
SQ FT: 3,690
SALES (est): 33.03MM **Privately Held**
Web: www.homeboyindustries.org
SIC: 8322   Rehabilitation services

(P-18004)
HOMEBRIDGE INC
Also Called: IHSS Consortium, The
1035 Market St Ste L1 (94103-1666)
PHONE....................415 255-2079
Gay Kaplan, *CEO*
Gay Kaplan, *Prin*
Margaret Baran, *Prin*
Mark Burns, *Prin*
EMP: 500 **EST:** 1994
SALES (est): 30.74MM **Privately Held**
Web: www.homebridgeca.org
SIC: 8322   Homemakers' service

(P-18005)
HOMEFRST SVCS SANTA CLARA CNTY
Also Called: EHC LIFEBUILDERS
507 Valley Way (95035-4105)
PHONE....................408 539-2100
Jennifer Niklaus, *CEO*
EMP: 115 **EST:** 1980
SALES (est): 44.44MM **Privately Held**
Web: www.homefirstscc.org
SIC: 8322   Social service center

(P-18006)
HORRIGAN ENTERPRISES INC
Also Called: Crossroads Adult Day Hlth Care
7945 Cartilla Ave (91730-3076)
PHONE....................909 481-9663
EMP: 153
SALES (corp-wide): 4.74MM **Privately Held**
Web: www.industry386.com
SIC: 8322   Adult day care center
PA: Horrigan Enterprises, Inc.
    1636 Country Club Dr
    Redlands CA
    909 484-5561

(P-18007)
HOUSING MATTERS
115b Coral St (95060-2143)
PHONE....................831 458-6020
Monica Martinez, *Ex Dir*
EMP: 72 **EST:** 1986
SALES (est): 6.12MM **Privately Held**
Web: www.housingmattersc.org
SIC: 8322   Social service center

(P-18008)
HUMAN SERVICES ASSOCIATION (PA)
Also Called: HSA BELL GARDENS LAUP
6800 Florence Ave (90201-4957)
PHONE....................562 806-5400
Susanne Sundberg, *Prin*
EMP: 75 **EST:** 1940
SQ FT: 10,000
SALES (est): 28.13MM
SALES (corp-wide): 28.13MM **Privately Held**
Web: www.hsala.org
SIC: 8322   Social service center

(P-18009)
HUMBOLDT CMNTY ACCESS RSRCE CT
Also Called: Baybridge Employment Services
1707 E St Ste 2 (95501-7621)
PHONE....................707 443-7077
Ross Jantz, *Prin*
EMP: 93
SALES (corp-wide): 2.5MM **Privately Held**
Web: www.hcar.us
SIC: 8322   Referral service for personal and social problems
PA: Humboldt Community Access And Resource Center
    1707 East Ave Ste 2
    Eureka CA
    707 443-7077

(P-18010)
HUMBOLDT CMNTY ACCESS RSRCE CT
Also Called: Bay Center
1001 Searles St (95501-1236)
PHONE....................707 441-8625
Joanne Diaz, *Mgr*
EMP: 93
SALES (corp-wide): 2.5MM **Privately Held**
Web: www.hcar.us
SIC: 8322 8052   Social service center; Home for the mentally retarded, with health care
PA: Humboldt Community Access And Resource Center
    1707 East Ave Ste 2
    Eureka CA
    707 443-7077

(P-18011)
HUMBOLDT SNIOR RSOURCE CTR INC (PA)
1910 California St (95501-2870)
PHONE....................707 443-9747
Joyce Hayes, *Ex Dir*
EMP: 60 **EST:** 1974
SQ FT: 14,000
SALES (est): 31.41MM
SALES (corp-wide): 31.41MM **Privately Held**
Web: www.humsenior.org
SIC: 8322 8741   Senior citizens' center or association; Management services

(P-18012)
IN-ROADS CREATIVE PROGRAMS
9057 Arrow Rte Ste 120 (91730-4452)
PHONE....................909 989-9944
Sharon Barton, *Brnch Mgr*
EMP: 367
Web: www.in-roads.net
SIC: 8322   Adult day care center
PA: In-Roads Creative Programs, Inc
    7955 Webster St Ste 7
    Highland CA

(P-18013)
IN-ROADS CREATIVE PROGRAMS
1951 E Saint Andrews Dr (91761-6447)
PHONE....................909 947-9142
Sharon Barton, *Brnch Mgr*
EMP: 367
Web: www.in-roads.net
SIC: 8322   Childrens' aid society
PA: In-Roads Creative Programs, Inc
    7955 Webster St Ste 7
    Highland CA

(P-18014)
INCLUSION SERVICES LLC
Also Called: Inclusion Services
7255 Greenleaf Ave Ste 20 (90602-1340)
PHONE....................562 945-2000
Cesar Torres, *Managing Member*
Israel Ibenez, *Managing Member*
EMP: 103 **EST:** 2009
SALES (est): 9.49MM **Privately Held**
Web: www.inclusionsvs.org
SIC: 8322 8331   Social services for the handicapped; Skill training center

(P-18015)
INLAND CNTIES REGIONAL CTR INC (PA)
Also Called: Inland Regional Center
1365 S Waterman Ave (92408-2804)
P.O. Box 19037 (92423-9037)
PHONE....................909 890-3000
Carol A Fitzgibbons, *CEO*
Carol Fitzgibbons, *
EMP: 173 **EST:** 1971
SQ FT: 82,000
SALES (est): 744.4MM
SALES (corp-wide): 744.4MM **Privately Held**
Web: www.inlandrc.org
SIC: 8322   Social service center

(P-18016)
INSTITUTE ON AGING
Also Called: Irene Swndlls Adult Day Care P
3698 California St (94118-1702)
PHONE....................415 600-2690
Eureka CA
707 443-7077

Cindy Kauffman, *Admn*
EMP: 125
Web: www.ioaging.org
SIC: 8322   Senior citizens' center or association
PA: Institute On Aging
    3575 Geary Blvd
    San Francisco CA

(P-18017)
INSTITUTE ON AGING (PA)
Also Called: Mssp
3575 Geary Blvd (94118-3212)
PHONE....................415 750-4101
J Thomas Briody, *Pr*
Roxana Tsougarakis, *
Cindy Kauffman, *
EMP: 100 **EST:** 1985
SQ FT: 10,000
SALES (est): 68.01MM **Privately Held**
Web: www.ioaging.org
SIC: 8322   Senior citizens' center or association

(P-18018)
INTEGRATED COMMUNITY SERVICES
Also Called: I C S
523 4th St Ste 100 (94901-3347)
PHONE....................415 455-8481
EMP: 62 **EST:** 1994
SALES (est): 4.34MM **Privately Held**
Web: www.connectics.org
SIC: 8322 8699   Social services for the handicapped; Charitable organization

(P-18019)
INTERFACE COMMUNITY (PA)
Also Called: INTERFACE CHILDREN FAMILY SERV
4001 Mission Oaks Blvd Ste I (93012-5121)
PHONE....................805 485-6114
Charles T Watson, *Pr*
Dale Stoeber, *
Terryl Miller, *CPO*
EMP: 88 **EST:** 1975
SQ FT: 3,000
SALES (est): 13.2MM
SALES (corp-wide): 13.2MM **Privately Held**
Web: www.icfs.org
SIC: 8322   Social service center

(P-18020)
INTERFAITH COMMUNITY SVCS INC
Also Called: Interfaith Community Services
250 N Ash St (92027-3026)
PHONE....................760 489-6380
Greg Anglea, *Ex Dir*
Leonard Jacobson, *
Suzanne Pohlman, *
EMP: 100 **EST:** 1982
SALES (est): 30.32MM **Privately Held**
Web: www.interfaithservices.org
SIC: 8322   Social service center

(P-18021)
INTERNATIONAL MEDICAL CORPS (PA)
Also Called: IMC
12400 Wilshire Blvd Ste 1500 (90025-1019)
PHONE....................310 826-7800
Nancy Aossey, *Pr*
Ingrid Renaud, *
Ky Luu, *Ofcr*
EMP: 4500 **EST:** 1984
SALES (est): 220.72MM
SALES (corp-wide): 220.72MM **Privately Held**

PRODUCTS & SERVICES SECTION
8322 - Individual And Family Services (P-18042)

Web: www.internationalmedicalcorps.org
SIC: 8322 Disaster service

(P-18022)
INTERVAL HOUSE
6615 E Pacific Coast Hwy Ste 170 (90803)
P.O. Box 3356 (90740-2356)
PHONE..................................562 594-4555
Robert Armstrong, *Pr*
Carol Williams, *
Elizabeth Lambert, *
Christine Delabre, *
Sharon Wie, *
EMP: 91 EST: 1979
SALES (est): 10.35MM **Privately Held**
Web: www.intervalhouse.org
SIC: 8322 Emergency shelters

(P-18023)
JAY NOLAN COMMUNITY SVCS INC
1190 S Bascom Ave Ste 240 (95128)
PHONE..................................408 293-5002
EMP: 204
SALES (corp-wide): 23.76MM **Privately Held**
Web: www.jaynolan.org
SIC: 8322 8331 8361 Social services for the handicapped; Job training and related services; Residential care
PA: Jay Nolan Community Services, Inc.
15501 San Fernando Missio
Mission Hills CA
818 361-6400

(P-18024)
JEWISH COMMUNITY CTR LONG BCH
Also Called: ALPERT JEWISH COMMUNITY CENTRE
3801 E Willow St (90815-1734)
PHONE..................................562 426-7601
Gordon Lentzner, *Pr*
EMP: 150 EST: 1948
SQ FT: 90,000
SALES (est): 5.29MM **Privately Held**
Web: www.alpertjcc.org
SIC: 8322 Community center

(P-18025)
JEWISH FAMILY AND CHLD SVCS (PA)
Also Called: CLEANERIFIC
2150 Post St (94115-3508)
P.O. Box 159004 (94115-9004)
PHONE..................................415 449-1200
Anita Friedman, *Ex Dir*
Marga Dusedau, *
Michael R Zent, *
Javier Favela, *
Frank Jacobson, *
EMP: 80 EST: 1850
SALES (est): 51.7MM
SALES (corp-wide): 51.7MM **Privately Held**
Web: www.jfcs.org
SIC: 8322 Social service center

(P-18026)
JEWISH FAMILY AND CHLD SVCS
Also Called: Parentals Place Parent Educatn
600 5th Ave (94901-3348)
PHONE..................................415 449-3862
Gayle Zahler, *Dir*
EMP: 342
SALES (corp-wide): 51.7MM **Privately Held**
Web: www.jfcs.org

SIC: 8322 Social service center
PA: Jewish Family And Children's Services
2150 Post St
San Francisco CA
415 449-1200

(P-18027)
JEWISH FAMILY SVC LOS ANGELES
Also Called: Senior Nutrition Program
330 N Fairfax Ave (90036-2109)
PHONE..................................323 937-5900
Eileen Mccouliffe, *Dir*
EMP: 137
SALES (corp-wide): 55.36MM **Privately Held**
Web: www.jfla.org
SIC: 8322 Social service center
PA: Jewish Family Service Of Los Angeles
330 N Fairfax Ave
Los Angeles CA
323 761-8800

(P-18028)
JON K TAKATA CORPORATION (PA)
Also Called: Restoration Management Company
3090 Independence Dr (94551-9419)
PHONE..................................510 315-5400
Jon Takata, *Pr*
Dave Glover, *CFO*
EMP: 70 EST: 1985
SALES (est): 54.48MM **Privately Held**
Web: www.rmc.com
SIC: 8322 1799 4959 Disaster service; Asbestos removal and encapsulation; Environmental cleanup services

(P-18029)
JONI AND FRIENDS FOUNDATION (PA)
30009 Ladyface Ct (91301-2583)
PHONE..................................818 707-5664
Joni E Tada, *CEO*
Douglas Mazza, *
Billy Burnett, *
◆ EMP: 84 EST: 1979
SQ FT: 30,000
SALES (est): 38.02MM
SALES (corp-wide): 38.02MM **Privately Held**
Web: www.joniandfriends.org
SIC: 8322 Association for the handicapped

(P-18030)
JVS SOCAL
6505 Wilshire Blvd (90048-4906)
PHONE..................................323 761-8879
Alan Levey, *Prin*
EMP: 268 EST: 1931
SALES (est): 28.76MM **Privately Held**
Web: www.jvs-socal.org
SIC: 8322 Individual and family services

(P-18031)
JWCH INSTITUTE INC
Also Called: Jwch Medical Center
3591 E Imperial Hwy (90262-2654)
PHONE..................................310 223-1035
Al Basceros, *Mgr*
EMP: 178
SALES (corp-wide): 107.92MM **Privately Held**
Web: www.jwchinstitute.org
SIC: 8322 8093 Individual and family services; Family planning clinic
PA: Jwch Institute, Inc.
5650 Jillson St

Commerce CA
323 477-1171

(P-18032)
KAINOS HM TRNING CTR FOR DVLPM
Also Called: Kainos Work Activity Ctr
2761 Fair Oaks Ave Ste A (94063-3540)
PHONE..................................650 361-1355
Christen Rodgers, *Mgr*
EMP: 68
SALES (corp-wide): 9MM **Privately Held**
Web: www.kainosusa.org
SIC: 8322 Social services for the handicapped
PA: Kainos Home & Training Center For Developmentally Disabled Adults
3631 Jefferson Ave
Redwood City CA
650 363-2423

(P-18033)
KEDREN COMMUNITY HLTH CTR INC
3800 S Figueroa St (90037-1206)
PHONE..................................323 524-0634
John Griffith, *Pr*
EMP: 133
SALES (corp-wide): 42.85MM **Privately Held**
Web: www.kedren.org
SIC: 8322 Community center
PA: Kedren Community Health Center, Inc.
4211 Avalon Blvd
Los Angeles CA
323 233-0425

(P-18034)
KINGS CMNTY ACTION ORGNZTION I (PA)
Also Called: KCAO
1130 N 11th Ave Ca (93230-3608)
PHONE..................................559 582-4386
David Droker, *Ex Dir*
EMP: 93 EST: 1965
SQ FT: 15,000
SALES (est): 35.42MM
SALES (corp-wide): 35.42MM **Privately Held**
Web: www.kcao.org
SIC: 8322 8399 Individual and family services; Antipoverty board

(P-18035)
LA ASCCION NCNAL PRO PRSNAS MY
Also Called: National Assn For Hispanic
1452 W Temple St Ste 100 (90026-5649)
PHONE..................................213 202-5900
Zecia Soto, *Prin*
EMP: 703
SALES (corp-wide): 13.34MM **Privately Held**
SIC: 8322 7361 8611 Social service center; Employment agencies; Business associations
PA: La Asociacion Nacional Pro Personas Mayores
234 E Colo Blvd Ste 300
Pasadena CA
626 564-1988

(P-18036)
LA COUNTY
Also Called: Childrens Medical Center
9320 Telstar Ave Ste 226 (91731-2816)
PHONE..................................626 569-6459
Wesley Ford, *Dir*
Jeanie Johnson, *Dir Opers*

EMP: 66 EST: 2008
SALES (est): 1.15MM **Privately Held**
Web: www.lacounty.gov
SIC: 8322 Childrens' aid society

(P-18037)
LA FAMILIA COUNSELING CTR INC
5523 34th St (95820-4725)
PHONE..................................916 452-3601
Rachell R Rios, *Ex Dir*
EMP: 61 EST: 1975
SALES (est): 7.04MM **Privately Held**
Web: www.lafcc.org
SIC: 8322 Social service center

(P-18038)
LACBA COUNSEL FOR JUSTICE
200 S Spring St (90012-3710)
PHONE..................................951 489-2919
Stanley Bissey, *CEO*
EMP: 66 EST: 2015
SALES (est): 1.29MM **Privately Held**
Web: www.lacba.org
SIC: 8322 General counseling services

(P-18039)
LARKIN STREET YOUTH SERVICES
Also Called: Diamond Youth Shelter
6324 Geary Blvd (94121-1824)
PHONE..................................415 567-1020
Stanley Joseph, *Mgr*
EMP: 62
SQ FT: 2,650
SALES (corp-wide): 31.17MM **Privately Held**
Web: www.larkinstreetyouth.org
SIC: 8322 Youth center
PA: Larkin Street Youth Services
134 Golden Gate Ave
San Francisco CA
415 673-0911

(P-18040)
LAURAS HOUSE
33 Journey Ste 150 (92656-5364)
PHONE..................................949 361-3775
Margaret Bayston, *Ex Dir*
EMP: 92 EST: 1994
SALES (est): 4.04MM **Privately Held**
Web: www.laurashouse.org
SIC: 8322 Social service center

(P-18041)
LIFE STEPS FOUNDATION INC
Also Called: Santa Maria Wisdom Center
2255 S Depot St (93455-1216)
PHONE..................................805 349-9810
Susan Chang, *Brnch Mgr*
EMP: 71
Web: www.lifestepsfoundation.org
SIC: 8322 Social service center
PA: Life Steps Foundation, Inc.
5757 W Century Blvd # 575
Los Angeles CA

(P-18042)
LIFE STEPS FOUNDATION INC
500 E 4th St (90802-2501)
PHONE..................................562 436-0751
Kristine Engels, *Dir*
EMP: 93
Web: www.lifestepsfoundation.org
SIC: 8322 8399 Social service center; Community development groups
PA: Life Steps Foundation, Inc.
5757 W Century Blvd # 575
Los Angeles CA

8322 - Individual And Family Services (P-18043)

(P-18043)
LIFE STEPS FOUNDATION INC
1107 Johnson Ave (93401-3303)
PHONE..................805 549-0150
Virginia Franco, *Brnch Mgr*
EMP: 75
Web: www.lifestepsfoundation.org
SIC: 8322 Social service center
PA: Life Steps Foundation, Inc.
5757 W Century Blvd # 575
Los Angeles CA

(P-18044)
LIFEHOUSE INC (PA)
18 Professional Center Pkwy Fl 2 (94903-2753)
PHONE..................415 472-2373
Nancy Dow Moody, *CEO*
EMP: 83 EST: 1957
SALES (est): 32.25MM
SALES (corp-wide): 32.25MM **Privately Held**
Web: www.lifehouseagency.org
SIC: 8322 8361 Social services for the handicapped; Residential care for the handicapped

(P-18045)
LOS ANGELES HOMELESS SVCS AUTH
Also Called: L A H S A
707 Wilshire Blvd Ste 1000 (90017-3729)
PHONE..................213 683-3333
Heidi Marston, *Ex Dir*
EMP: 558 EST: 1993
SALES (est): 93.78MM **Privately Held**
Web: www.lahsa.org
SIC: 8322 Social service center

(P-18046)
LOS ANGELES REGIONAL FOOD BANK
1734 E 41st St (90058-1502)
PHONE..................323 234-3030
Michael Flood, *Pr*
Michael Flood, *Pr*
Czarina Luna, *
EMP: 185 EST: 1977
SALES (est): 251.17MM **Privately Held**
Web: www.lafoodbank.org
SIC: 8322 8699 Meal delivery program; Charitable organization

(P-18047)
LOS ANGLES FIREMAN RELIEF ASSN
Also Called: Widows Orphans Dsbled Frmens F
2900 W Temple St (90026-4516)
P.O. Box 41903 (90041-0903)
PHONE..................800 244-3439
Barry G Hedberg, *Pr*
John Kitchens, *
Leopoldo C Lacza, *
William Dillon, *
EMP: 66 EST: 1906
SQ FT: 10,000
SALES (est): 3.56MM **Privately Held**
Web: www.lafra.org
SIC: 8322 Emergency social services

(P-18048)
LUMINA ALLIANCE
Also Called: STAND STRONG
51 Zaca Ln Ste 150 (93401-7319)
P.O. Box 125 (93406-0125)
PHONE..................805 781-6400
Jennifer Adams, *CEO*
Marianne Kennedy, *
EMP: 75 EST: 2001
SALES (est): 3.5MM **Privately Held**
Web: www.luminaalliance.org
SIC: 8322 Social service center

(P-18049)
MARK 1 RESTORATION SERVICE LLC
3360 E La Palma Ave (92806-2814)
PHONE..................714 283-9990
EMP: 78 EST: 2020
SALES (est): 1.07MM **Privately Held**
SIC: 8322 Disaster service

(P-18050)
MARTHAS VILLAGE AND KITCHEN
83791 Date Ave (92201-4737)
PHONE..................760 347-4741
Joe Carol, *Pr*
Matthew Packard, *
Claudia Castorena, *
Gloria Gomez, *
EMP: 65 EST: 1999
SALES (est): 5.92MM **Privately Held**
Web: www.marthasvillage.org
SIC: 8322 Social service center

(P-18051)
MARTIS CAMP CLUB
7951 Fleur Du Lac Ct (96161-4261)
PHONE..................530 550-6000
Mark Johnson, *Pr*
Carla Yeager, *Treas*
EMP: 300 EST: 2011
SQ FT: 80,000
SALES (est): 28.61MM **Privately Held**
Web: www.martiscamp.com
SIC: 8322 Community center

(P-18052)
MEN TKING OVER RFRMING SOC INC
6630 Crenshaw Blvd (90043-4102)
PHONE..................323 338-6633
Toni Wells, *CEO*
Toni Wells, *Ex VP*
David Thomas, *
Ronald Burnette, *
Tylo James, *Development*
EMP: 61 EST: 2016
SALES (est): 1.91MM **Privately Held**
Web: www.operationbrightlights.org
SIC: 8322 Emergency shelters

(P-18053)
MEXICAN AMRCN OPRTNTY FNDATION (PA)
Also Called: MAOF
401 N Garfield Ave (90640-2901)
P.O. Box 4602 (90640-9311)
PHONE..................323 890-9600
Martin Vasquez Castro, *Pr*
Carlos J Viramontes, *
EMP: 100 EST: 1963
SQ FT: 25,000
SALES (est): 116.75MM
SALES (corp-wide): 116.75MM **Privately Held**
Web: www.maof.org
SIC: 8322 Social service center

(P-18054)
MEXICAN AMRCN OPRTNTY FNDATION
Also Called: Maof Commerce
5657 E Washington Blvd (90040-1405)
PHONE..................323 890-1555
Martin Castro, *Pr*
EMP: 86
SALES (corp-wide): 116.75MM **Privately Held**
Web: www.maof.org
SIC: 8322 Social service center
PA: Mexican American Opportunity Foundation
401 N Garfield Ave
Montebello CA
323 890-9600

(P-18055)
MHN GOVERNMENT SERVICES LLC
2370 Kerner Blvd (94901-5613)
P.O. Box 989730 (95798-9730)
PHONE..................916 294-4941
Billy Maynard, *Pr*
EMP: 482 EST: 2005
SQ FT: 67,000
SALES (est): 3.24MM **Publicly Held**
Web: www.mhn.com
SIC: 8322 Individual and family services
HQ: Health Net, Llc
21650 Oxnard St Fl 25
Woodland Hills CA
818 676-6000

(P-18056)
MIXTEC/NDGENA CMNTY ORGNZING P
Also Called: MICOP
135 Magnolia Ave (93030-5331)
P.O. Box 20543 (93034-0543)
PHONE..................805 483-1166
Arcenio Lopez, *Ex Dir*
Donna Foster, *
EMP: 75 EST: 2008
SALES (est): 7.16MM **Privately Held**
Web: www.mixteco.org
SIC: 8322 Social service center

(P-18057)
MOMENTUM WORK INC (PA)
Also Called: W O R K
5320 Carpinteria Ave Ste G (93013-2153)
PHONE..................805 566-9000
Kathy Webb, *Ex Dir*
EMP: 60 EST: 1968
SQ FT: 2,000
SALES (est): 12.55MM
SALES (corp-wide): 12.55MM **Privately Held**
Web: www.momentum4work.org
SIC: 8322 Social service center

(P-18058)
MYHHBS INC
237 N Central Ave Ste A (91203-3526)
PHONE..................888 969-4427
Khrist Kakosimidi, *Prin*
EMP: 85 EST: 2016
SALES (est): 1.19MM **Privately Held**
Web: www.myhhbs.com
SIC: 8322 Individual and family services

(P-18059)
NEIGHBORHOOD HOUSE ASSOCIATION (PA)
Also Called: N H A
5660 Copley Dr (92111-7902)
PHONE..................858 715-2642
Rudolph A Johnson Iii, *CEO*
EMP: 500 EST: 1914
SQ FT: 60,000
SALES (est): 106.3MM
SALES (corp-wide): 106.3MM **Privately Held**
Web: www.neighborhoodhouse.org
SIC: 8322 Neighborhood center

(P-18060)
NEIGHBORHOOD HOUSE ASSOCIATION
Also Called: Neighbrhood Hse Assn Fmly Svc
841 S 41st St (92113-1899)
PHONE..................619 263-7761
Ellen Brown, *Mgr*
EMP: 63
SALES (corp-wide): 106.3MM **Privately Held**
Web: www.neighborhoodhouse.org
SIC: 8322 8399 Neighborhood center; Community development groups
PA: The Neighborhood House Association
5660 Copley Dr
San Diego CA
858 715-2642

(P-18061)
NEW ALTERNATIVES INCORPORATED
8755 Aero Dr Ste 230 (92123-1750)
PHONE..................619 863-5855
EMP: 581
SALES (corp-wide): 65.42MM **Privately Held**
Web: www.newalternativesfund.com
SIC: 8322 Social service center
PA: New Alternatives, Incorporated
3589 4th Ave
San Diego CA
619 543-0293

(P-18062)
NEW DIRECTIONS INC (PA)
Also Called: New Directions For Veterans
11303 Wilshire Blvd Bldg 116 (90025-5069)
P.O. Box 25536 (90025-0536)
PHONE..................310 914-4045
EMP: 80 EST: 1989
SQ FT: 60,000
SALES (est): 15.31MM **Privately Held**
Web: www.ndvets.org
SIC: 8322 Substance abuse counseling

(P-18063)
NORTHEAST VALLEY HEALTH CORP (PA)
1172 N Maclay Ave (91340-1328)
PHONE..................818 898-1388
Kimberly Wyard, *CEO*
Nelson Wong, *
Irna Morales, *
Antonio Lugo, *
Patricia Moraga, *
EMP: 75 EST: 1971
SALES (est): 119.71MM
SALES (corp-wide): 119.71MM **Privately Held**
Web: www.eisnerhealth.org
SIC: 8322 Community center

(P-18064)
NORTHERN CALIFORNIA INALLIANCE
411 4th St (95692-9467)
PHONE..................530 633-9695
EMP: 75
SALES (corp-wide): 17.93MM **Privately Held**
Web: www.inallianceinc.com
SIC: 8322 Social service center
PA: Northern California Inalliance
6950 21st Ave
Sacramento CA
916 381-1300

8322 - Individual And Family Services (P-18086)

(P-18065)
NORTHERN CALIFORNIA INALLIANCE (PA)
Also Called: INALLIANCE
6950 21st Ave (95820-5948)
PHONE.................916 381-1300
Richard Royse, Ex Dir
EMP: 190 EST: 1968
SQ FT: 20,000
SALES (est): 17.93MM
SALES (corp-wide): 17.93MM Privately Held
Web: www.inallianceinc.com
SIC: 8322 Social service center

(P-18066)
NORTHERN CALIFORNIA INALLIANCE
Also Called: Inalliance
660 Main St (95667-5704)
PHONE.................530 344-1244
Van Traker, Mgr
EMP: 75
SQ FT: 28,324
SALES (corp-wide): 17.93MM Privately Held
Web: www.inallianceinc.com
SIC: 8322 Social service center
PA: Northern California Inalliance
6950 21st Ave
Sacramento CA
916 381-1300

(P-18067)
NORTHERN VLY CTHLIC SCIAL SVC
2400 Washington Ave (96001-2802)
PHONE.................530 241-0552
Jan Maurer Watkins, CEO
Don C Chapman, *
EMP: 151 EST: 2004
SALES (est): 13.79MM Privately Held
Web: www.nvcss.org
SIC: 8322 Social service center

(P-18068)
NOURISH INC
2170 Martin Ave (95050-2702)
PHONE.................917 572-6691
EMP: 80 EST: 2018
SALES (est): 10.15MM Privately Held
Web: www.nourishinc.com
SIC: 8322 Individual and family services

(P-18069)
OAK GROVE INST FOUNDATION INC
1251 N A St (92570-1911)
PHONE.................951 238-6022
EMP: 240
Web: www.oakgrovecenter.org
SIC: 8322 Child related social services
PA: Oak Grove Institute Foundation, Inc.
24275 Jefferson Ave
Murrieta CA

(P-18070)
ON MY OWN IND LIVING SVCS
Also Called: On My Own Ils Omo Omo Ils On M
6939 Sunrise Blvd Ste 215 (95610-3154)
PHONE.................916 726-0792
Michelle Ramirez, Prin
Linda Pierce, Prin
Danielle Reynolds, Prin
Darcy Hannibal, Prin
Debra Bishop, Prin
EMP: 62 EST: 2002
SALES (est): 1.12MM Privately Held
Web: www.onmyown-web.com
SIC: 8322 Social service center

(P-18071)
OPTIMA FAMILY SERVICES INC
253 N San Gabriel Blvd (91107-3429)
PHONE.................323 300-6066
Oscar A Carvajal, Prin
EMP: 178 EST: 2008
SALES (est): 6.83MM Privately Held
Web: www.optimafamilyservices.com
SIC: 8322 General counseling services

(P-18072)
ORANGE CNTY ADULT ACHVMENT CTR
Also Called: MY DAY COUNTS
225 W Carl Karcher Way (92801-2499)
PHONE.................714 744-5301
Michael Galliano, CEO
Patrick Faraday, *
Richard Farmer, *
Laurie Vinkavich, *
Jack Salseda, *
▲ EMP: 135 EST: 1955
SQ FT: 57,000
SALES (est): 9.73MM Privately Held
Web: www.mydaycounts.org
SIC: 8322 Social service center

(P-18073)
ORANGEWOOD FOUNDATION
1575 E 17th St (92705-8506)
PHONE.................714 619-0200
Chris Simonsen, CEO
John Luker, *
EMP: 85 EST: 1980
SQ FT: 22,340
SALES (est): 24.46MM Privately Held
Web: www.orangewoodfoundation.org
SIC: 8322 Child related social services

(P-18074)
OSHMAN FAMILY JEWISH CMNTY CTR
3921 Fabian Way (94303-4640)
PHONE.................650 223-8700
Alan Sataloff, Ex Dir
Paul Raczynski, *
Haim Hovav, *
EMP: 200 EST: 1988
SALES (est): 26.02MM Privately Held
Web: www.paloaltojcc.org
SIC: 8322 Community center

(P-18075)
OUTREACH & ESCORT INC (PA)
Also Called: OUTREACH
2221 Oakland Rd Ste 200 (95131-1415)
P.O. Box 640910 (95164-0910)
PHONE.................408 678-8585
Katheryn H Heatley, Pr
William Chawarz, *
EMP: 77 EST: 1979
SQ FT: 20,000
SALES (est): 1.54MM
SALES (corp-wide): 1.54MM Privately Held
Web: www.outreach1.org
SIC: 8322 Individual and family services

(P-18076)
PALOMAR HLTH RHBLTTION INST LL
2181 Citracado Pkwy (92029-4159)
PHONE.................442 277-6100
EMP: 150 EST: 2013
SALES (est): 6.11MM
SALES (corp-wide): 679.43K Privately Held
Web: www.palomarhealthrehabinstitute.com
SIC: 8322 Rehabilitation services
PA: Palomar Health
2125 Citracado Pkwy # 300
Escondido CA
442 281-5000

(P-18077)
PATH
340 N Madison Ave (90004-3504)
PHONE.................323 644-2216
Joel John Roberts, Pr
Jennifer Hark Dietz, *
Sandy Oluwek, *
Sarah Kolish, *
La Keishia Childers, *
EMP: 828 EST: 1984
SALES (est): 131.55MM Privately Held
Web: www.epath.org
SIC: 8322 Social service center

(P-18078)
PENINSULA FAMILY SERVICE
Also Called: Leo J Ryan Child Care Ctr
1200 Miller Ave (94080-1221)
PHONE.................650 952-6848
Liliya Sergiyemko, Brnch Mgr
EMP: 83
SALES (corp-wide): 17.3MM Privately Held
Web: www.peninsulafamilyservice.org
SIC: 8322 8351 Family (marriage) counseling ; Child day care services
PA: Peninsula Family Service
24 2nd Ave
San Mateo CA
650 403-4300

(P-18079)
PENINSULA JEWISH COMMUNITY CTR
800 Foster City Blvd (94404-2228)
PHONE.................650 212-7522
Paul Gedulig, CEO
Fred Weiner, *
EMP: 72 EST: 1995
SALES (est): 9.99MM Privately Held
Web: www.pjcc.org
SIC: 8322 Community center

(P-18080)
PEOPLE CONCERN
Safe Haven
1751 Cloverfield Blvd (90404-4007)
PHONE.................310 883-1222
Andrew Schwich, Dir
EMP: 174
SALES (corp-wide): 73.2MM Privately Held
Web: www.thepeopleconcern.org
SIC: 8322 Emergency shelters
PA: The People Concern
2116 Arlington Ave # 100
Los Angeles CA
323 334-9000

(P-18081)
PEOPLE CONCERN
Daybreak
1751 Cloverfield Blvd (90404-4007)
PHONE.................310 450-0650
Anya Booker, Dir
EMP: 174
SALES (corp-wide): 73.2MM Privately Held
Web: www.thepeopleconcern.org
SIC: 8322 Community center
PA: The People Concern
2116 Arlington Ave # 100
Los Angeles CA
323 334-9000

(P-18082)
PEOPLE CREATING SUCCESS INC
1607 E Palmdale Blvd Ste H (93550-7801)
PHONE.................661 225-9700
Robert Donery, Brnch Mgr
EMP: 99
SALES (corp-wide): 14.09MM Privately Held
Web: www.pcs-services.org
SIC: 8322 Individual and family services
PA: People Creating Success, Inc.
2585 Teller Rd
Newbury Park CA
805 375-9222

(P-18083)
PEOPLE CREATING SUCCESS INC
5350 Hollister Ave Ste I (93111-2326)
PHONE.................805 692-5290
Brian Fay, Mgr
EMP: 99
SALES (corp-wide): 14.09MM Privately Held
Web: www.pcs-services.org
SIC: 8322 Social service center
PA: People Creating Success, Inc.
2585 Teller Rd
Newbury Park CA
805 375-9222

(P-18084)
POMEROY RCRTION RHBLTATION CTR (PA)
Also Called: R C H
207 Skyline Blvd (94132-1025)
PHONE.................415 665-4100
John Mccue, Ex Dir
Henry Woo, *
EMP: 178 EST: 1954
SQ FT: 22,000
SALES (est): 13.48MM
SALES (corp-wide): 13.48MM Privately Held
Web: www.prrcsf.org
SIC: 8322 Social services for the handicapped

(P-18085)
PORTO INC
Also Called: A Quality In Home Care
12 S San Gorgonio Ave Ste 204 (92220-6015)
PHONE.................760 709-3737
Darrell R Marble, Ex Dir
EMP: 60 EST: 2015
SQ FT: 1,800
SALES (est): 949.5K Privately Held
SIC: 8322 Adult day care center

(P-18086)
PRIORITY CTR ENDING THE GNRTNA
Also Called: WELCOME BABY
1940 E Deere Ave Ste 100 (92705-5718)
PHONE.................714 543-4333
Scott Trotter, Ex Dir
Stephanie Enano, *
EMP: 99 EST: 1983
SALES (est): 8.84MM Privately Held
Web: www.theprioritycenter.org
SIC: 8322 Child related social services

8322 - Individual And Family Services (P-18087)

(P-18087)
PROJECT CONCERN INTERNATIONAL (PA)
Also Called: PCI
5151 Murphy Canyon Rd Ste 320 (92123-4330)
PHONE..................858 279-9690
Carrie Hessler-radelet, Pr
George Guimaraes, *
Kote Lomidze, *
Janine Schooley, *
Mark O Donnell, *
EMP: 124 EST: 1961
SQ FT: 12,000
SALES (est): 12.21MM
SALES (corp-wide): 12.21MM Privately Held
Web: www.pciglobal.org
SIC: 8322 Social service center

(P-18088)
PROJECT OPEN HAND (PA)
730 Polk St Fl 3 (94109-7813)
PHONE..................415 292-3400
Paul Hepfer, CEO
Teresa Ballete, *
EMP: 96 EST: 1986
SQ FT: 50,000
SALES (est): 16.61MM
SALES (corp-wide): 16.61MM Privately Held
Web: www.openhand.org
SIC: 8322 Social service center

(P-18089)
PROTOTYPES CENTERS FOR INNOV
Also Called: Prototypes
1000 N Alameda St Ste 390 (90012-1804)
PHONE..................213 542-3838
Cassandra Loch, Pr
Maryann Fraser, *
EMP: 250 EST: 1986
SQ FT: 8,400
SALES (est): 20.14MM Privately Held
Web: www.healthright360.org
SIC: 8322 General counseling services

(P-18090)
PUBLIC HLTH FNDATION ENTPS INC
13181 Crossroads Pkwy N (91746-3419)
PHONE..................626 856-6600
Eliose Jenks, Brnch Mgr
EMP: 140
SALES (corp-wide): 92.05MM Privately Held
Web: www.phfewic.org
SIC: 8322 Social service center
PA: Public Health Foundation Enterprises, Inc.
13300 Crssrds Pkwy N
City Of Industry CA
800 201-7320

(P-18091)
RADIANT HEALTH CENTERS
Also Called: AIDS WALK ORANGE COUNTY
17982 Sky Park Cir Ste J (92614-6482)
PHONE..................949 809-5700
Alan Witchey, Ex Dir
EMP: 66 EST: 1985
SQ FT: 16,051
SALES (est): 10.8MM Privately Held
Web: www.radianthealthcenters.org
SIC: 8322 8011 Social service center; Clinic, operated by physicians

(P-18092)
RAPHAEL HSE SAN FRANCISCO INC
Also Called: RAPHAEL HOUSE
1065 Sutter St (94109-5891)
PHONE..................415 345-7200
Kate Smith, Pr
Father David Lowell, *
Judy Davies, *
Karol K Denniston, *
EMP: 87 EST: 1977
SQ FT: 10,000
SALES (est): 2.81MM Privately Held
Web: www.raphaelhouse.org
SIC: 8322 8661 Emergency shelters; Nonchurch religious organizations

(P-18093)
RAPID RESPONSE FORCE LLC
Also Called: Rrf Tree Service
15105 Concord Cir Ste 210 (95037-5490)
PHONE..................408 612-8984
EMP: 64 EST: 2017
SALES (est): 2.13MM Privately Held
Web: www.rapidresponseforce.com
SIC: 8322 Disaster service

(P-18094)
READING PARTNERS
600 Valley Way (95035-4138)
PHONE..................408 945-5720
Michael Lombardo, Ex Dir
EMP: 69
SALES (corp-wide): 25.17MM Privately Held
Web: www.readingpartners.org
SIC: 8322 Individual and family services
PA: Reading Partners
638 3rd St
Oakland CA
510 444-9800

(P-18095)
REDWOOD COMMUNITY SERVICES INC
Also Called: Childrens Therapeutic Services
350 E Gobbi St (95482-5511)
PHONE..................707 472-2922
Dan Anderson, Off Mgr
EMP: 75
Web: www.redwoodcommunityservices.org
SIC: 8322 8059 Family service agency; Personal care home, with health care
PA: Redwood Community Services, Inc.
631 S Orchard Ave
Ukiah CA

(P-18096)
REGIONAL CENTER OF E BAY INC (PA)
Also Called: RCEB
500 Davis St Ste 100 (94577-2758)
PHONE..................510 618-6100
Kathy Hebert, CEO
EMP: 150 EST: 1975
SQ FT: 26,000
SALES (est): 613.77MM
SALES (corp-wide): 613.77MM Privately Held
Web: www.rceb.org
SIC: 8322 Social service center

(P-18097)
REGIONAL CENTER OF E BAY INC
Also Called: Rceb
1320 Willow Pass Rd Ste 300 (94520-5232)
PHONE..................925 691-2300
EMP: 100
SALES (corp-wide): 613.77MM Privately Held
Web: www.rceb.org
SIC: 8322 Social services for the handicapped
PA: Regional Center Of The East Bay, Inc.
500 Davis St Ste 100
San Leandro CA
510 618-6100

(P-18098)
RESOURCE CONNECTION OF AMADOR
Also Called: W I C
430 Sutter Hill Rd (95685-4149)
PHONE..................209 223-7685
Damian Wolin, Pr
EMP: 71
SALES (corp-wide): 11.77MM Privately Held
Web: www.trcac.org
SIC: 8322 Social service center
PA: The Resource Connection Of Amador And Calaveras Counties Incorporated
444 E Saint Charles St
San Andreas CA
209 754-3114

(P-18099)
REUTLINGER COMMUNITY
Also Called: REUTLINGER COMMUNITY FOR JEWIS
4000 Camino Tassajara (94506-4745)
PHONE..................925 964-2062
Jay Zimmer, CEO
EMP: 160 EST: 1972
SALES (est): 15.84MM Privately Held
Web: www.rcjl.org
SIC: 8322 Individual and family services

(P-18100)
ROWI USA INC
3155 Old Conejo Rd (91320-2151)
PHONE..................805 356-3372
Candice Feinberg, CEO
EMP: 70 EST: 2019
SALES (est): 1MM Privately Held
SIC: 8322 General counseling services

(P-18101)
RURAL CMNTY ASSISTANCE CORP (PA)
Also Called: Rcac
3120 Freeboard Dr Ste 201 (95691-5039)
PHONE..................916 447-2854
Stan Keasling, CEO
Kevin Mccumber, CFO
EMP: 60 EST: 1978
SALES (est): 25.43MM
SALES (corp-wide): 25.43MM Privately Held
Web: www.rcac.org
SIC: 8322 6111 Individual and family services; Federal and federally sponsored credit agencies

(P-18102)
SACRAMENTO AREA EMERG HOUSING
Also Called: Emergency Housing Chld Program
4516 Parker Ave (95820-4029)
PHONE..................916 455-2160
Bonnie Hager, Dir
EMP: 66
Web: www.nextmovesacramento.org
SIC: 8322 6513 Social service center; Apartment building operators
PA: Next Move Homeless Services
8001 Folsom Blvd
Sacramento CA

(P-18103)
SACRAMNTO CHNESE CMNTY SVC CTR
420 I St Ste 5 (95814-2309)
PHONE..................916 442-4228
Henry Kloczkowski, Dir
EMP: 200 EST: 1978
SQ FT: 2,000
SALES (est): 9.64MM Privately Held
Web: www.sccsc.org
SIC: 8322 8699 8611 Social service center; Charitable organization; Community affairs and services

(P-18104)
SAGE PROJECT INC
Also Called: Sage
68 12th St (94103-1297)
PHONE..................415 905-5050
Ellyn Green, Ex Dir
Francine Braae, Dir
Allen Wilson, Dir
EMP: 92 EST: 1995
SQ FT: 5,830
SALES (est): 1.53MM Privately Held
Web: www.sagesf.org
SIC: 8322 8069 Alcoholism counseling, nontreatment; Drug addiction rehabilitation hospital

(P-18105)
SALESFORCECOM/ FOUNDATION
The Landmark @ One Market Ste 300 (94105)
PHONE..................800 667-6389
Marc Benioff, CEO
Keith Block, *
Suzanne Dibianca, *
Jim Cavalieri, *
Monika Fahlbusch, *
EMP: 150 EST: 1999
SALES (est): 23.29MM Privately Held
SIC: 8322 Disaster service

(P-18106)
SALVATION ARMY (HQ)
Also Called: Salvation Army Western Ttry
30840 Hawthorne Blvd (90275-5301)
PHONE..................562 264-3600
James M Knaggs, CEO
Commissioner Carolyn R Knaggs Territorial, MINISTRIES*
Colonel David E Hudson, Chief Secretary*
Susan Lawrence, *
Kenneth Hodder, *
▼ EMP: 140 EST: 1865
SALES (est): 516.57K
SALES (corp-wide): 2.41B Privately Held
Web: www.salvationarmy.org
SIC: 8322 Social service center
PA: The Salvation Army National Corporation
615 Slaters Ln
Alexandria VA
703 684-5500

(P-18107)
SALVATION ARMY
Also Called: Salvation Army
10200 Pioneer St (92782-1418)
PHONE..................714 832-7100
EMP: 64
SALES (corp-wide): 2.41B Privately Held
Web: centralusa.salvationarmy.org

PRODUCTS & SERVICES SECTION
8322 - Individual And Family Services (P-18128)

SIC: 8322 8661 8699 Social service center; Religious organizations; Charitable organization
HQ: The Salvation Army
5550 Prairie Stone Pkwy # 130
Hoffman Estates IL
847 294-2000

(P-18108)
SAMARITAN VILLAGE INC
7700 Fox Rd (95326-9100)
P.O. Box 444 (95992-0444)
PHONE..................209 883-3212
Daniel Aguilar, *CEO*
Victor Savage, *CEO*
EMP: 115 EST: 2002
SALES (est): 9.79MM **Privately Held**
Web: www.svliving.org
SIC: 8322 Adult day care center

(P-18109)
SAN ANDREAS REGIONAL CENTER (PA)
6203 San Ignacio Ave Ste 200 (95119-1371)
P.O. Box 50002 (95150-0002)
PHONE..................408 374-9960
Mary Lu Gonzalez, *CEO*
Yoshiharu Kuroiwa, *
Lisa Lopez, *
Troy Hernandez, *
EMP: 174 EST: 1969
SQ FT: 29,000
SALES (est): 550.05MM
SALES (corp-wide): 550.05MM **Privately Held**
Web: www.sanandreasregional.org
SIC: 8322 Association for the handicapped

(P-18110)
SAN BRNRDINO CNTY PRBTION OFFC
4370 Hallmark Pkwy Ste 105 (92407-7710)
PHONE..................909 887-2544
Laura Pleasant, *VP*
EMP: 407 EST: 2007
SALES (est): 493.84K **Privately Held**
Web: www.sanbernardinocountyprobation.org
SIC: 8322 Probation office

(P-18111)
SAN DG-MPRIAL CNTIES DVLPMNTAL (PA)
4355 Ruffin Rd Ste 220 (92123-4308)
PHONE..................858 576-2996
Carlos Flores, *Ex Dir*
Judy Wallace Patton, *
Edward Kenney, *
EMP: 286 EST: 1982
SQ FT: 62,000
SALES (est): 522.22MM
SALES (corp-wide): 522.22MM **Privately Held**
Web: www.sdrc.org
SIC: 8322 Social services for the handicapped

(P-18112)
SAN FRANCISCO AIDS FOUNDATION (PA)
1035 Market St Ste 400 (94103-1665)
PHONE..................415 487-3000
Joe Hollendoner, *CEO*
Elizabeth Pesch, *
Robert Grant, *CMO*
EMP: 100 EST: 1982
SQ FT: 45,000
SALES (est): 48.97MM
SALES (corp-wide): 48.97MM **Privately Held**
Web: www.sfaf.org
SIC: 8322 Social service center

(P-18113)
SAN FRANCISCO FOOD BANK
Also Called: SF-MARIN FOOD BANK
900 Pennsylvania Ave (94107-3446)
PHONE..................415 282-1900
Paul Ash, *Ex Dir*
Leslie Bacho, *
Michael Braude, *
EMP: 80 EST: 1987
SQ FT: 55,000
SALES (est): 156.92MM **Privately Held**
Web: www.sfmfoodbank.org
SIC: 8322 Social service center

(P-18114)
SAN FRNCSCO PRTCLAR CNCIL OF T
525 5th St (94107-1012)
PHONE..................415 255-3525
EMP: 62
SALES (corp-wide): 11.66MM **Privately Held**
Web: www.svdp-sf.org
SIC: 8322 Social service center
PA: The San Francisco Particular Council Of The Society Of St Vincent De Paul
1175 Howard St
San Francisco CA
415 552-2943

(P-18115)
SAN GBRL/PMONA VLLEYS DVLPMNTA
Also Called: SAN GABRIEL/POMONA REGIONAL CE
75 Rancho Camino Dr (91766-4728)
PHONE..................909 620-7722
R Keith Penman, *Ex Dir*
R Keith Penman, *Ex Dir*
Carol Tomblin, *
John Hunt, *
EMP: 323 EST: 1986
SQ FT: 100,000
SALES (est): 320.15MM **Privately Held**
Web: www.sgprc.org
SIC: 8322 Social service center

(P-18116)
SAN JOAQUIN CNTY AGING & COMMU
102 S San Joaquin St (95202-3213)
P.O. Box 201056 (95201-3006)
PHONE..................209 468-9455
Michael Miller, *Human Service Director*
EMP: 120 EST: 2010
SALES (est): 10MM **Privately Held**
Web: www.sjchsa.org
SIC: 8322 Senior citizens' center or association

(P-18117)
SANTA CLRITA VLY CMMTTEE ON AG
Also Called: SANTA CLARITA VALLEY SENIOR CE
22900 Market St (91321-3608)
PHONE..................661 259-9444
Brad Berens, *Dir*
Jeff Pollard, *
Greg Kory, *
Don Kimball, *
EMP: 65 EST: 1976
SQ FT: 10,000
SALES (est): 10.5MM **Privately Held**
Web: www.myscvcoa.org
SIC: 8322 Senior citizens' center or association

(P-18118)
SANTEE SENIOR RETIREMENT COM
Also Called: Pointe At Lantern Crest, The
400 Lantern Crest Way (92071-4633)
PHONE..................619 955-0901
Kaan Ciftci, *Ex Dir*
EMP: 104
Web: www.lanterncrestseniorlivingsantee.com
SIC: 8322 Senior citizens' center or association
PA: Santee Senior Retirement Communities, Llc
8510 Railroad Ave
Santee CA

(P-18119)
SBCS CORPORATION
430 F St (91910-3711)
PHONE..................619 420-3620
Kathryn Lembo, *Ex Dir*
EMP: 200 EST: 1971
SQ FT: 2,900
SALES (est): 34.79MM **Privately Held**
Web: www.case-5-19-cv-07071.info
SIC: 8322 Social service center

(P-18120)
SECOND HRVEST FD BNK ORNGE CNT
8014 Marine Way (92618-2235)
PHONE..................949 653-2900
Claudia Bonilla Keller, *CEO*
Jerry Creekpaum, *COO*
Joyce Foley, *
EMP: 80 EST: 2008
SALES (est): 91.57MM **Privately Held**
Web: www.feedoc.org
SIC: 8322 Social service center

(P-18121)
SELF-HELP FOR ELDERLY
777 Stockton St Ste 110 (94108-2372)
PHONE..................415 391-3843
EMP: 70
SALES (corp-wide): 30.97MM **Privately Held**
Web: www.selfhelpelderly.org
SIC: 8322 Senior citizens' center or association
PA: Self-Help For The Elderly
731 Sansome St Ste 100
San Francisco CA
415 677-7600

(P-18122)
SELF-HELP FOR ELDERLY (PA)
Also Called: SAN FRANCISCO RESIDENTIAL CARE
731 Sansome St Ste 100 (94111-1703)
PHONE..................415 677-7600
Anni Chung, *Pr*
William Schulte, *
Janie Kaung, *Vice Chairman*
Linda Wang, *
Gerald Lee, *
EMP: 145 EST: 1980
SALES (est): 30.97MM
SALES (corp-wide): 30.97MM **Privately Held**
Web: www.selfhelpelderly.org
SIC: 8322 8361 8082 Senior citizens' center or association; Residential care; Home health care services

(P-18123)
SELF-HELP FOR ELDERLY
408 22nd Ave (94121-3014)
PHONE..................415 677-7556
EMP: 94
SALES (corp-wide): 30.97MM **Privately Held**
Web: www.selfhelpelderly.org
SIC: 8322 8011 Senior citizens' center or association; Clinic, operated by physicians
PA: Self-Help For The Elderly
731 Sansome St Ste 100
San Francisco CA
415 677-7600

(P-18124)
SENECA FAMILY OF AGENCIES
2130 N Ventura Rd (93036-2246)
PHONE..................805 278-0355
EMP: 215
SALES (corp-wide): 150.1MM **Privately Held**
Web: www.senecafoa.org
SIC: 8322 Social service center
PA: Seneca Family Of Agencies
8945 Golf Links Rd
Oakland CA
510 317-1444

(P-18125)
SENECA FAMILY OF AGENCIES
Also Called: Seneca Center
8945 Golf Links Rd (94605-4124)
PHONE..................510 317-1444
Ken Berrick, *CEO*
EMP: 215
SALES (corp-wide): 150.1MM **Privately Held**
Web: www.senecafoa.org
SIC: 8322 8361 Social service center; Residential care for children
PA: Seneca Family Of Agencies
8945 Golf Links Rd
Oakland CA
510 317-1444

(P-18126)
SENECA FAMILY OF AGENCIES
1234 Empire St (94533-5711)
PHONE..................707 429-4440
Ken Berrick, *Brnch Mgr*
EMP: 215
SALES (corp-wide): 150.1MM **Privately Held**
Web: www.senecafoa.org
SIC: 8322 Social service center
PA: Seneca Family Of Agencies
8945 Golf Links Rd
Oakland CA
510 317-1444

(P-18127)
SENECA FAMILY OF AGENCIES
Also Called: Building Blocks
3695 High St (94619-2105)
PHONE..................510 434-7990
EMP: 108
SALES (corp-wide): 150.1MM **Privately Held**
Web: www.senecafoa.org
SIC: 8322 8351 Social service center; Child day care services
PA: Seneca Family Of Agencies
8945 Golf Links Rd
Oakland CA
510 317-1444

(P-18128)
SER-JOBS FOR PRGRESS INC - SAN (PA)

8322 - Individual And Family Services (P-18129)

255 N Fulton St Ste 106 (93701-1600)
PHONE.................................559 452-0881
Rebecca Mendibles, *Ex Dir*
Michael Jimenez, *
Ofelia Gamez, *
EMP: 66 **EST:** 1973
SQ FT: 1,500
SALES (est): 7.4MM
SALES (corp-wide): 7.4MM **Privately Held**
Web: www.sercalifornia.org
SIC: 8322 Social service center

(P-18129)
SEXUAL RECOVERY INSTITUTE INC
1964 Westwood Blvd Ste 400 (90025-4695)
PHONE.................................310 360-0130
David A Sack, *CEO*
Robert Weiss, *
EMP: 305 **EST:** 1955
SALES (est): 8.01MM
SALES (corp-wide): 85.16MM **Privately Held**
Web: www.sexualrecovery.com
SIC: 8322 General counseling services
PA: Elements Behavioral Health, Inc.
5000 Arprt Plz Dr Ste 100
Long Beach CA
562 741-6470

(P-18130)
SHASCADE COMMUNITY SVCS INC
Also Called: Lorin Robinson Center
900 Twin View Blvd (96003-2006)
PHONE.................................530 247-8324
Ramone Valarde, *Ex Dir*
EMP: 99
SALES (corp-wide): 5.44MM **Privately Held**
Web: www.shascade.org
SIC: 8322 Social service center
PA: Shascade Community Services, Inc.
900 Twin View Blvd
Redding CA
530 243-1651

(P-18131)
SHASCADE COMMUNITY SVCS INC
1319 Sacramento St (96001-1916)
PHONE.................................530 243-1653
Ramon Velade, *Mgr*
EMP: 82
SALES (corp-wide): 5.44MM **Privately Held**
Web: www.shascade.org
SIC: 8322 Social services for the handicapped
PA: Shascade Community Services, Inc.
900 Twin View Blvd
Redding CA
530 243-1651

(P-18132)
SHELTER SOLANO INC
1333 Willow Pass Rd Ste 206 (94520-7930)
PHONE.................................925 957-7576
John Eckstrom, *CEO*
EMP: 99 **EST:** 2018
SALES (est): 735.72K **Privately Held**
Web: www.shelterinc.org
SIC: 8322 Social service center

(P-18133)
SIERRA FOREVER FAMILIES
Also Called: Sff
8912 Volunteer Ln (95826-3221)
PHONE.................................916 368-5114
Bob Herne, *Ex Dir*
EMP: 60 **EST:** 1982
SALES (est): 4.99MM **Privately Held**
Web: www.ssyaf.org
SIC: 8322 Adoption services

(P-18134)
SIERRA MOUNTAIN CNSTR INC
Also Called: Sierra Mountain
13919 Mono Way (95370-2807)
PHONE.................................209 928-1900
Douglas J Benton, *Pr*
EMP: 75 **EST:** 2003
SALES (est): 62.3MM **Privately Held**
Web: www.sierramtn.net
SIC: 8322 1389 Disaster service; Construction, repair, and dismantling services

(P-18135)
SOCIAL ADVCTES FOR YUTH SAN DE
4275 El Cajon Blvd Ste 101 (92105-1293)
PHONE.................................619 283-9624
Nancy G Hornberger, *CEO*
EMP: 177
SALES (corp-wide): 18.31MM **Privately Held**
Web: www.saysandiego.org
SIC: 8322 Social service center
PA: Social Advocates For Youth, San Diego, Inc.
4775 Viewridge Ave
San Diego CA
858 565-4148

(P-18136)
SOURCEWISE
3100 De La Cruz Blvd Ste 310 (95054-2452)
PHONE.................................408 350-3200
Stephen M Schmoll, *Dir*
Kimberly Marlar, *
Altamirano Manuel, *
EMP: 100 **EST:** 1974
SALES (est): 17.87MM **Privately Held**
Web: www.mysourcewise.com
SIC: 8322 Senior citizens' center or association

(P-18137)
SOUTH BAY CTR FOR COUNSELING
Also Called: SOUTH BAY CENTER FOR COMMUNITY
540 N Marine Ave (90744-5528)
PHONE.................................310 414-2090
Colleen Mooney, *Ex Dir*
Maria Lomibao, *
EMP: 90 **EST:** 1974
SALES (est): 7.76MM **Privately Held**
Web: www.sbccthrivela.org
SIC: 8322 General counseling services

(P-18138)
ST BRNBAS SNIOR CTR LOS ANGLE
Also Called: SAINT BARNABAS SENIOR SERVICES
675 S Carondelet St (90057-3309)
PHONE.................................213 388-4444
Rigo Sabareo, *Pr*
Nick Dumicreseu, *
EMP: 61 **EST:** 1908
SQ FT: 27,000
SALES (est): 5.25MM **Privately Held**
Web: www.sbssla.org

SIC: 8322 Senior citizens' center or association

(P-18139)
ST JOSEPH CENTER
Also Called: SAINT JOSEPH CENTER VOLUNTEER
204 Hampton Dr (90291-8633)
PHONE.................................310 396-6468
Felecia Adams, *VP*
Va Lecia Adams Kellum, *Ex Dir*
Paul Rubenstein, *
Tifara Monroe, *
John Mcgann, *CFO*
EMP: 85 **EST:** 1976
SQ FT: 32,000
SALES (est): 51.82MM **Privately Held**
Web: www.stjosephctr.org
SIC: 8322 8331 8351 Social service center; Job training services; Child day care services

(P-18140)
ST JOSEPH HOSPICE
Also Called: Saint Joseph Hlth Sys Hospice
200 W Center Street Promenade (92805-3960)
PHONE.................................714 712-7100
Linda Glomp, *Dir*
Ron Nagano, *
Maire Blaistell, *
EMP: 252 **EST:** 1994
SQ FT: 3,000
SALES (est): 3.8MM
SALES (corp-wide): 32.76MM **Privately Held**
Web: www.hospice.io
SIC: 8322 8063 Geriatric social service; Psychiatric hospitals
HQ: St. Joseph Home Care Network
441 College Ave
Santa Rosa CA
714 712-9500

(P-18141)
STAND FOR FMLIES FREE VOLENCE
3220 Blume Dr (94806-1767)
PHONE.................................510 964-7109
EMP: 61
Web: www.standffov.org
SIC: 8322 Crisis intervention center
PA: Stand For Families Free Of Violence
1410 Danzig Plz Fl 2
Concord CA

(P-18142)
STANFORD UNIV MED CTR AUX
300 Pasteur Dr (94305-2200)
PHONE.................................650 723-6636
Mary Dahlquist, *CEO*
Sarah Clark, *
EMP: 174 **EST:** 1959
SALES (est): 22.64MM
SALES (corp-wide): 15.13B **Privately Held**
Web: www.stanfordhealthcare.org
SIC: 8322 Adult day care center
PA: Leland Stanford Junior University
450 Jane Stanford Way
Stanford CA
650 723-2300

(P-18143)
STANFORD YOUTH SOLUTIONS (PA)
Also Called: Stanford Lthrop Mem HM For Frn
8912 Volunteer Ln (95826-3221)
PHONE.................................916 344-0199
Jovina Neves, *CFO*
Jovina Neves, *CFO*

SIC: 8322 Senior citizens' center or association

Laura Heintz, *
EMP: 84 **EST:** 1900
SQ FT: 30,000
SALES (est): 23.57MM
SALES (corp-wide): 23.57MM **Privately Held**
Web: www.ssyaf.org
SIC: 8322 Social service center

(P-18144)
STARVISTA
610 Elm St Ste 212 (94070-3070)
PHONE.................................650 591-9623
Michael Grb, *CEO*
EMP: 118 **EST:** 1989
SQ FT: 7,200
SALES (est): 17.11MM **Privately Held**
Web: www.star-vista.org
SIC: 8322 Substance abuse counseling

(P-18145)
STRAIGHT TALK INC
Also Called: Straight Talk Counseling Ctr
13710 La Mirada Blvd (90638-3028)
PHONE.................................562 943-0195
Meg Kalugan, *Mgr*
EMP: 90
SALES (corp-wide): 1.57MM **Privately Held**
Web: www.straighttalkcounseling.org
SIC: 8322 General counseling services
PA: Straight Talk Clinic, Incorporated
5712 Camp St
Cypress CA
714 828-2000

(P-18146)
STRENGTH UNITED
14651 Oxnard St (91411-3120)
PHONE.................................818 787-9700
EMP: 67 **EST:** 2015
SALES (est): 1.05MM **Privately Held**
Web: www.csun.edu
SIC: 8322 General counseling services

(P-18147)
SUMMITVIEW CHILD & FAMILY SVCS
670 Placerville Dr Ste 2 (95667-4200)
PHONE.................................530 644-2412
Carla Well, *Prin*
EMP: 80 **EST:** 2006
SALES (est): 13.3MM **Privately Held**
Web: www.summitviewcf.org
SIC: 8322 8093 Family counseling services; Mental health clinic, outpatient

(P-18148)
TEAM LOGIC IF LA W HOLLYWOOD
751 N Formosa Ave (90046-7609)
PHONE.................................310 292-0063
EMP: 71 **EST:** 2010
SALES (est): 294.12K **Privately Held**
Web: www.teamlogicit.com
SIC: 8322 General counseling services

(P-18149)
TERRA NOVA COUNSELING (PA)
5750 Sunrise Blvd Ste 100 (95610-7639)
PHONE.................................916 344-0249
Mary Stroube, *Ex Dir*
EMP: 80 **EST:** 1985
SQ FT: 4,789
SALES (est): 2.13MM **Privately Held**
Web: www.terranovacounseling.org
SIC: 8322 General counseling services

PRODUCTS & SERVICES SECTION
8322 - Individual And Family Services (P-18171)

(P-18150)
TESSIE CLVLAND CMNTY SVCS CORP
18220 S Broadway (90248-3534)
PHONE.................310 965-9759
EMP: 67
SALES (corp-wide): 20.76MM **Privately Held**
Web: www.tccsc.org
SIC: 8322 Individual and family services
PA: Tessie Cleveland Community Services Corporation
8019 Compton Ave Ste 219
Los Angeles CA
323 586-7333

(P-18151)
TLCS INC
Also Called: Hope Cooperative
650 Howe Ave Ste 400-A (95825-4732)
PHONE.................916 441-0123
Erin Johansen, *CEO*
Michael Lazar, *
EMP: 250 EST: 1981
SQ FT: 1,868
SALES (est): 22.01MM **Privately Held**
Web: www.hopecoop.org
SIC: 8322 Social service center

(P-18152)
TOOLWORKS INC
3075 Adeline St Ste 230 (94703-2578)
PHONE.................510 649-1322
Steve Crabiel, *Brnch Mgr*
EMP: 379
SALES (corp-wide): 19.44MM **Privately Held**
Web: www.toolworks.org
SIC: 8322 Social service center
PA: Toolworks Inc
25 Kearny St Ste 400
San Francisco CA
415 733-0990

(P-18153)
TOWARD MAXIMUM INDEPENDENCE (PA)
Also Called: T M I
4740 Murphy Canyon Rd Ste 300 (92123-4385)
PHONE.................858 467-0600
Kerby Wohlander, *Dir*
EMP: 125 EST: 1981
SQ FT: 5,700
SALES (est): 20.12MM **Privately Held**
Web: www.tmi-inc.org
SIC: 8322 Social services for the handicapped

(P-18154)
TRI-CNTIES ASSN FOR DVLPMNTLLY (PA)
Also Called: TRI-COUNTIES REGIONAL CENTER
520 E Montecito St (93103-3245)
PHONE.................805 962-7881
Bob Cobbs, *Pr*
Omar Noorzad, *
EMP: 60 EST: 1968
SQ FT: 16,000
SALES (est): 388.4MM
SALES (corp-wide): 388.4MM **Privately Held**
Web: www.tri-counties.org
SIC: 8322 Association for the handicapped

(P-18155)
TRI-CNTIES ASSN FOR DVLPMNTLLY
Also Called: Tri-Counties Regional Center
1146 Farmhouse Ln (93401-8362)
PHONE.................805 543-2833
Frank Bush, *Dir*
EMP: 108
SALES (corp-wide): 388.4MM **Privately Held**
Web: www.tri-counties.org
SIC: 8322 Association for the handicapped
PA: Tri-Counties Association For The Developmentally Disabled, Inc.
520 E Montecito St
Santa Barbara CA
805 962-7881

(P-18156)
TUPAZ DAY CARE SERVICES INC
Also Called: Great Endvors Adult Day Hlth C
3015 Union Ave (95124-2006)
PHONE.................408 377-1622
Rosario Tupaz, *Pr*
Beebe Tupaz, *
EMP: 75 EST: 2000
SALES (est): 2.41MM **Privately Held**
SIC: 8322 Adult day care center

(P-18157)
TURNING POINT CENTRAL CAL INC
Also Called: Visalia Youth Services
711 N Court St (93291-3638)
PHONE.................559 627-1490
Jose Ochoa, *Brnch Mgr*
EMP: 62
SALES (corp-wide): 66.45MM **Privately Held**
Web: www.tpocc.org
SIC: 8322 8093 Individual and family services; Mental health clinic, outpatient
PA: Turning Point Of Central California, Inc.
615 S Atwood St
Visalia CA
559 732-8086

(P-18158)
TURNING POINT FOR GOD
P.O. Box 3838 (92163-1838)
PHONE.................619 258-3600
David Jeremiah, *Prin*
EMP: 93 EST: 2010
SALES (est): 479.88K **Privately Held**
Web: www.davidjeremiah.ca
SIC: 8322 Individual and family services

(P-18159)
TURNING POINT MINISTRIES
Also Called: TURNING POINT COUNSELING
1370 Brea Blvd Ste 245 (92835-4173)
PHONE.................800 998-6329
TOLL FREE: 800
EMP: 93 EST: 1983
SQ FT: 2,500
SALES (est): 1.15MM **Privately Held**
Web: www.turningpointcounseling.org
SIC: 8322 Family counseling services

(P-18160)
UNITED CRBRAL PLSY ASSN ORNGE
Also Called: Ucp of Orange County
1251 E Dyer Rd Ste 150 (92705-5662)
PHONE.................949 333-6400
Ramin Baschshi, *CEO*
EMP: 400 EST: 1953
SQ FT: 5,000
SALES (est): 6.38MM **Privately Held**
SIC: 8322 Social service center

(P-18161)
UNITED CRBRAL PLSY ASSN SAN LU
Also Called: Ride On Transportation
3620 Sacramento Dr Ste 201 (93401-7215)
PHONE.................805 543-2039
Mark Shaffer, *Ex Dir*
EMP: 100 EST: 1991
SQ FT: 1,600
SALES (est): 6.02MM **Privately Held**
Web: www.ride-on.org
SIC: 8322 Social service center

(P-18162)
UNITY CARE GROUP
1400 Parkmoor Ave Ste 115 (95126-3797)
P.O. Box 730276 (95173-0276)
PHONE.................408 971-9822
Andre Chapman, *CEO*
Gary Rummelhoff, *
Linda Phillips, *
EMP: 70 EST: 1992
SALES (est): 8.05MM **Privately Held**
Web: www.unitycare.org
SIC: 8322 Child related social services

(P-18163)
UPLIFT FAMILY SERVICES
800 S Santa Anita Ave (91006-3536)
PHONE.................626 254-5000
Kathryn Mccarthy, *Pr*
EMP: 581
SALES (corp-wide): 147.1MM **Privately Held**
Web: www.pacificclinics.org
SIC: 8322 Individual and family services
PA: Uplift Family Services
251 Llewellyn Ave
Campbell CA
408 379-3790

(P-18164)
UPLIFT FAMILY SERVICES (PA)
Also Called: EMQ FAMILIESFIRST
251 Llewellyn Ave (95008-1940)
PHONE.................408 379-3790
Darrell Evora, *CEO*
Craig Wolfe, *CCO*
Kathy Mccarthy, *CLO CAO*
Jason D Gurahoo, *CFO*
EMP: 60 EST: 1973
SQ FT: 65,000
SALES (est): 147.1MM
SALES (corp-wide): 147.1MM **Privately Held**
Web: www.pacificclinics.org
SIC: 8322 Individual and family services

(P-18165)
URBAN ALCHEMY
1035 Market St Ste 150 (94103-1666)
PHONE.................415 757-0896
Lena Miller, *CEO*
EMP: 98 EST: 2019
SALES (est): 51.18MM **Privately Held**
Web: www.urban-alchemy.us
SIC: 8322 Social service center

(P-18166)
VALLEY VILLAGE (PA)
20830 Sherman Way (91306-2707)
PHONE.................818 587-9450
Debra Donovan, *Ex Dir*
EMP: 75 EST: 1973
SQ FT: 14,000
SALES (est): 21.42MM
SALES (corp-wide): 21.42MM **Privately Held**
Web: www.valleyvillage.org
SIC: 8322 Individual and family services

(P-18167)
VALLEY-MNTAIN REGIONAL CTR INC (PA)
702 N Aurora St (95202-2200)
P.O. Box 692290 (95269-2290)
PHONE.................209 473-0951
Paul Billodeau, *CEO*
Debra Roth, *
EMP: 160 EST: 1974
SQ FT: 63,000
SALES (est): 283.32MM
SALES (corp-wide): 283.32MM **Privately Held**
Web: www.vmrc.net
SIC: 8322 Multi-service center

(P-18168)
VALLEY-MNTAIN REGIONAL CTR INC
Cummins Drive (95350)
P.O. Box 692290 (95269-2290)
PHONE.................209 955-3207
Debra Roth, *Brnch Mgr*
EMP: 80
SALES (corp-wide): 283.32MM **Privately Held**
Web: www.vmrc.net
SIC: 8322 Multi-service center
PA: Valley-Mountain Regional Center, Inc.
702 N Aurora St
Stockton CA
209 473-0951

(P-18169)
VINTAGE SENIOR MANAGEMENT INC
Also Called: VINTAGE SENIOR MANAGEMENT, INC.
2721 W Willow St (91505-4544)
PHONE.................818 954-9500
Brian Flornes, *Brnch Mgr*
EMP: 832
SIC: 8322 Geriatric social service
PA: Senior Vintage Management Inc
23 Corporate Plaza Dr # 190
Newport Beach CA

(P-18170)
VISTA CARE GROUP LLC (PA)
Also Called: Vista Gardens
1863 Devon Pl (92084-7624)
PHONE.................760 295-3900
Avelen Delgado, *Admn*
Harry Crowell, *
Joe Balbas, *
EMP: 80 EST: 2010
SALES (est): 4.16MM
SALES (corp-wide): 4.16MM **Privately Held**
Web: www.vistagardensmemorycare.com
SIC: 8322 Senior citizens' center or association

(P-18171)
VISTA HILL FOUNDATION
4125 Alpha St (92113-4553)
PHONE.................619 266-0166
EMP: 90
SALES (corp-wide): 34.66MM **Privately Held**
Web: www.vistahill.org
SIC: 8322 8051 Geriatric social service; Skilled nursing care facilities
PA: Vista Hill Foundation
8910 Clairemont Mesa Blvd
San Diego CA
585 514-5100

8322 - Individual And Family Services (P-18172)

(P-18172)
VIVALON
Also Called: Whistlestop
930 Tamalpais Ave (94901-3325)
PHONE......................415 454-0964
Joe O'hehir, *CEO*
Linda Compton, *
Edward Fox, *
Nancy Geisse, *
Ashley Baker, *
EMP: 94 **EST:** 1954
SQ FT: 12,000
SALES (est): 11.53MM **Privately Held**
Web: www.vivalon.org
SIC: 8322 Senior citizens' center or association

(P-18173)
VOLUNTEERS OF AMER LOS ANGELES
Also Called: Volunteers of America
1032 W 18th St (90015-3324)
PHONE......................213 749-0362
Ernest Green, *Dir*
EMP: 104
SALES (corp-wide): 98.98MM **Privately Held**
Web: www.voala.org
SIC: 8322 Social service center
PA: Volunteers Of America Of Los Angeles
3600 Wilshire Blvd # 1500
Los Angeles CA
213 389-1500

(P-18174)
VOLUNTEERS OF AMER LOS ANGELES
Also Called: Volunteers of America
10896 Lehigh Ave (91331-2584)
PHONE......................818 834-9097
Paloma Cisneros, *Mgr*
EMP: 79
SALES (corp-wide): 98.98MM **Privately Held**
Web: www.voala.org
SIC: 8322 Social service center
PA: Volunteers Of America Of Los Angeles
3600 Wilshire Blvd # 1500
Los Angeles CA
213 389-1500

(P-18175)
VOLUNTEERS OF AMER LOS ANGELES
Also Called: Volunteers of America
522 N Dangler Ave (90022-1218)
PHONE......................323 780-3770
EMP: 103
SALES (corp-wide): 98.98MM **Privately Held**
Web: www.voala.org
SIC: 8322 Social service center
PA: Volunteers Of America Of Los Angeles
3600 Wilshire Blvd # 1500
Los Angeles CA
213 389-1500

(P-18176)
VOLUNTEERS OF AMER LOS ANGELES
Also Called: Volunteers of America
1760 W Cameron Ave Ste 104 (91790-2739)
PHONE......................626 337-9878
EMP: 103
SALES (corp-wide): 98.98MM **Privately Held**
Web: www.voala.org

SIC: 8322 Social service center
PA: Volunteers Of America Of Los Angeles
3600 Wilshire Blvd # 1500
Los Angeles CA
213 389-1500

(P-18177)
VOLUNTEERS OF AMER LOS ANGELES
Also Called: Volunteers of America
25141 Avenida Rondel (91355-3205)
PHONE......................661 290-2829
EMP: 77
SALES (corp-wide): 98.98MM **Privately Held**
Web: www.voala.org
SIC: 8322 Social service center
PA: Volunteers Of America Of Los Angeles
3600 Wilshire Blvd # 1500
Los Angeles CA
213 389-1500

(P-18178)
VOLUNTEERS OF AMER LOS ANGELES
Also Called: Voa Plainview Head Start
10819 Plainview Ave (91042-1633)
PHONE......................818 352-5974
EMP: 104
SALES (corp-wide): 98.98MM **Privately Held**
Web: www.voala.org
SIC: 8322 Social service center
PA: Volunteers Of America Of Los Angeles
3600 Wilshire Blvd # 1500
Los Angeles CA
213 389-1500

(P-18179)
VOLUNTEERS OF AMER LOS ANGELES
Also Called: Volunteers of America
2100 N Broadway Ste 300 (92706-2624)
PHONE......................714 426-9834
EMP: 78
SALES (corp-wide): 98.98MM **Privately Held**
Web: www.voala.org
SIC: 8322 Social service center
PA: Volunteers Of America Of Los Angeles
3600 Wilshire Blvd # 1500
Los Angeles CA
213 389-1500

(P-18180)
VOLUNTEERS OF AMER LOS ANGELES
Also Called: Volunteers of America
6724 Tujunga Ave (91606-1910)
PHONE......................818 769-3617
EMP: 104
SALES (corp-wide): 98.98MM **Privately Held**
Web: www.voala.org
SIC: 8322 Social service center
PA: Volunteers Of America Of Los Angeles
3600 Wilshire Blvd # 1500
Los Angeles CA
213 389-1500

(P-18181)
VOLUNTEERS OF AMER LOS ANGELES
Also Called: Maud Booth Family Center
11243 Kittridge St (91606-2605)
PHONE......................818 506-0597
Felix Cruz, *Mgr*
EMP: 130
SALES (corp-wide): 98.98MM **Privately Held**

Web: www.voala.org
SIC: 8322 Social service center
PA: Volunteers Of America Of Los Angeles
3600 Wilshire Blvd # 1500
Los Angeles CA
213 389-1500

(P-18182)
VOLUNTEERS OF AMER LOS ANGELES
Also Called: Voa
515 E 6th St Fl 9 (90021-1009)
PHONE......................213 627-8002
Jim Howat, *Dir*
EMP: 104
SQ FT: 15,346
SALES (corp-wide): 98.98MM **Privately Held**
Web: www.voala.org
SIC: 8322 Social service center
PA: Volunteers Of America Of Los Angeles
3600 Wilshire Blvd # 1500
Los Angeles CA
213 389-1500

(P-18183)
VOLUNTEERS OF AMER LOS ANGELES
Also Called: Volunteers of America
12550 Van Nuys Blvd (91331-1454)
PHONE......................818 834-8957
Letecia Aguirre, *Prin*
EMP: 80
SALES (corp-wide): 98.98MM **Privately Held**
Web: www.voala.org
SIC: 8322 Social service center
PA: Volunteers Of America Of Los Angeles
3600 Wilshire Blvd # 1500
Los Angeles CA
213 389-1500

(P-18184)
VOLUNTEERS OF AMER LOS ANGELES
Also Called: Volunteers of America
334 Figueroa St (90744-4804)
PHONE......................310 830-3404
EMP: 104
SALES (corp-wide): 98.98MM **Privately Held**
Web: www.voala.org
SIC: 8322 Social service center
PA: Volunteers Of America Of Los Angeles
3600 Wilshire Blvd # 1500
Los Angeles CA
213 389-1500

(P-18185)
VOLUNTERS AMER NTHRN CAL NTHRN
Also Called: Volunteers of America
624 14th St (94612-1219)
PHONE......................510 419-0360
Bobbie Johnson, *Mgr*
EMP: 71
SALES (corp-wide): 34.91MM **Privately Held**
Web: www.voa-ncnn.org
SIC: 8322 Social service center
PA: Volunteers Of America Northern California And Northern Nevada, Inc.
3434 Marconi Ave
Sacramento CA
916 265-3400

(P-18186)
VOLUNTERS AMER NTHRN CAL NTHRN

Also Called: Greenbriar
2844 Wright St (95821-4848)
PHONE......................916 488-0171
Vanessa Tran, *Brnch Mgr*
EMP: 62
SALES (corp-wide): 34.91MM **Privately Held**
Web: www.voa-ncnn.org
SIC: 8322 Social service center
PA: Volunteers Of America Northern California And Northern Nevada, Inc.
3434 Marconi Ave
Sacramento CA
916 265-3400

(P-18187)
WATTS LABOR COMMUNITY ACTION
Also Called: Wlcac
4142 Palmwood Dr Apt 11 (90008-2355)
PHONE......................323 563-5639
Timothy Watkins, *CEO*
EMP: 169
SALES (corp-wide): 24.79MM **Privately Held**
Web: www.wlcac.org
SIC: 8322 7299 Social service center; Handyman service
PA: Watts Labor Community Action Committee
10950 S Central Ave
Los Angeles CA
323 563-5639

(P-18188)
WAYMAKERS (PA)
440 Exchange (92602-1376)
PHONE......................714 492-1010
Margot R Carlson, *Ex Dir*
EMP: 60 **EST:** 1974
SALES (est): 26.24MM
SALES (corp-wide): 26.24MM **Privately Held**
Web: www.waymakersoc.org
SIC: 8322 Social service center

(P-18189)
WEINGART CENTER ASSOCIATION
Also Called: Weingart Center For Homeless
566 S San Pedro St (90013-2102)
PHONE......................213 622-6359
Kevin Murray, *Pr*
Warren Loui, *
Sonny Santa Ines, *
EMP: 150 **EST:** 1984
SQ FT: 175,000
SALES (est): 18.85MM **Privately Held**
Web: www.weingart.org
SIC: 8322 Emergency social services

(P-18190)
WELBE HEALTH LLC
Also Called: Welbe Health LLC
1649 Van Ness Ave (93721-1128)
PHONE......................559 777-6722
EMP: 245
SALES (corp-wide): 27.51MM **Privately Held**
Web: www.welbehealth.com
SIC: 8322 Senior citizens' center or association
PA: Welbe Health, Llc
405 Claremont Way Ste 248
Menlo Park CA
650 862-6371

PRODUCTS & SERVICES SECTION
8331 - Job Training And Related Services (P-18212)

(P-18191)
WELLNESS TOGETHER
1382 Blue Oaks Blvd Ste 213 (95678-7052)
PHONE..................877 412-8031
Marlon Morgan, *Ex Dir*
Brenda Duran, *
EMP: 150 **EST:** 2016
SALES (est): 5.86MM **Privately Held**
Web: www.wellnesstogether.org
SIC: 8322 General counseling services

(P-18192)
WELLNEST EMTONAL HLTH WELLNESS (PA)
3031 S Vermont Ave (90007-3033)
PHONE..................323 373-2400
Charlene Dimas-peinado, *CEO*
EMP: 110 **EST:** 1924
SALES (est): 30.2MM
SALES (corp-wide): 30.2MM **Privately Held**
Web: www.wellnestla.org
SIC: 8322 Child guidance agency

(P-18193)
WISE & HEALTHY AGING
23388 Mulholland Dr Stop 60 (91364-2733)
PHONE..................818 876-1402
Grace Cheng Braun, *Prin*
Charles Hardie, *
Molly Davies, *
Phyllis Amaral, *
EMP: 70 **EST:** 1972
SALES (est): 626.03K **Privately Held**
Web: www.wiseandhealthyaging.org
SIC: 8322 Senior citizens' center or association

(P-18194)
WOMANHAVEN
Also Called: CENTER FOR FAMILY SOLUTIONS
510 W Main St Ste 106 (92243-2900)
P.O. Box 2219 (92244-2219)
PHONE..................760 353-6922
Gina Vargas, *Ex Dir*
Yereida Soto, *
EMP: 90 **EST:** 1977
SALES (est): 3.29MM **Privately Held**
Web: www.womanhaven.org
SIC: 8322 Social service center

(P-18195)
WOMENS CTR - YOUTH & FMLY SVCS (PA)
620 N San Joaquin St (95202-2030)
PHONE..................209 941-2611
Joelle Gomez, *CEO*
EMP: 87 **EST:** 1978
SALES (est): 4.67MM
SALES (corp-wide): 4.67MM **Privately Held**
Web: www.weshallprevail.org
SIC: 8322 Child related social services

(P-18196)
WORK INC
3070 Skyway Dr Ste 104 (93455-1830)
PHONE..................805 739-0451
Ed Hartman, *Pr*
Kathy Webb, *Ex Dir*
EMP: 75 **EST:** 1968
SALES (est): 459.57K **Privately Held**
Web: www.momentum4work.org
SIC: 8322 Adult day care center
HQ: The Chimes Inc
    4815 Seton Dr
    Baltimore MD
    410 358-6400

(P-18197)
YOUTH FOR CHANGE (PA)
Also Called: Paradise Ridge Fmly Resources
260 Cohasset Rd Ste 120 (95926-2282)
P.O. Box 1476 (95967-1476)
PHONE..................530 877-8187
Dennis Cargile, *Prin*
George Siler, *
Michele Peterson, *
Alan White, *
Andy Martinez, *
EMP: 115 **EST:** 1990
SQ FT: 5,000
SALES (est): 16.63MM **Privately Held**
Web: www.youth4change.org
SIC: 8322 Youth center

(P-18198)
YUBA COMMUNITY COLLEGE DST
Also Called: Beale Air Force Base Outreach
2088 N Beale Rd (95901-7605)
PHONE..................530 788-0973
EMP: 64
SALES (corp-wide): 32.01MM **Privately Held**
Web: www.yccd.edu
SIC: 8322 Outreach program
PA: Yuba Community College District
    3301 E Onstott Rd
    Yuba City CA
    530 741-8949

(P-18199)
YUE FENG INC
145 S Fairfax Ave (90036-2166)
PHONE..................310 253-9795
Cheng Chen, *Pr*
EMP: 72 **EST:** 2013
SQ FT: 8,500
SALES (est): 981.06K **Privately Held**
SIC: 8322 Individual and family services

(P-18200)
YWCA CONTRA COSTA/ SACRAMENTO (PA)
Also Called: YWCA
1320 Arnold Dr Ste 170 (94553-4188)
PHONE..................925 372-4213
Nancy Atkinson, *CEO*
EMP: 60 **EST:** 1945
SQ FT: 8,000
SALES (est): 3.87MM
SALES (corp-wide): 3.87MM **Privately Held**
Web: www.ywcaccc.org
SIC: 8322 8641 8351 Individual and family services; Community membership club; Child day care services

(P-18201)
ZHOUG HONG
1 Harbor Dr (94965-1470)
PHONE..................415 647-7742
EMP: 60
SQ FT: 8,000
SALES (est): 5.3MM **Privately Held**
SIC: 8322 Travelers' aid

8331 Job Training And Related Services

(P-18202)
ABILITY COUNTS INC (PA)
775 Trademark Cir Ste 101 (92879-2084)
PHONE..................951 734-6595
Joyce Hearn, *CEO*
EMP: 99 **EST:** 1980
SQ FT: 28,000
SALES (est): 7.51MM
SALES (corp-wide): 7.51MM **Privately Held**
Web: www.abilitycounts.org
SIC: 8331 Sheltered workshop

(P-18203)
ADVOCACY FOR RSPECT CHICE - LO (PA)
Also Called: HILLSIDE ENTERPRISES - AR & C
4519 E Stearns St (90815-2540)
PHONE..................562 597-7716
Marion Lieberman, *CEO*
EMP: 81 **EST:** 1952
SQ FT: 35,000
SALES (est): 5.9MM
SALES (corp-wide): 5.9MM **Privately Held**
Web: www.hillsideenterprises.org
SIC: 8331 Sheltered workshop

(P-18204)
APPRENTICE JRNYMEN TRNING TR F
Also Called: COMPTON TRAINING CENTER
7850 Haskell Ave (91406-1907)
PHONE..................310 604-0892
Raymond Levangie Iii, *Ex Dir*
EMP: 222 **EST:** 1956
SALES (est): 30.36MM **Privately Held**
Web: www.ajtraining.org
SIC: 8331 Job training services

(P-18205)
ARC FRESNO/MADERA COUNTIES (PA)
4490 E Ashlan Ave (93726-2647)
PHONE..................559 226-6268
Lori Rmirez, *CEO*
Carolyn Wallace, *
Peter Mersino, *
Mike Takechi, *
Alan Lagunoff, *
EMP: 71 **EST:** 1953
SALES (est): 10.99MM
SALES (corp-wide): 10.99MM **Privately Held**
Web: www.arcfresno.org
SIC: 8331 Job training services

(P-18206)
ARC LOS ANGLES ORANGE COUNTIES (PA)
Also Called: SOUTHEAST INDUSTRIES
12049 Woodruff Ave (90241-5669)
PHONE..................562 803-1556
Kevin Mac Donald, *Ex Dir*
EMP: 75 **EST:** 1962
SQ FT: 9,800
SALES (est): 2.08MM
SALES (corp-wide): 2.08MM **Privately Held**
Web: www.thearclaoc.org
SIC: 8331 5932 Skill training center; Used merchandise stores

(P-18207)
ARC SAN FRANCISCO (PA)
1500 Howard St (94103-2525)
PHONE..................415 255-7200
Timothy Hornbecker, *Ex Dir*
Mark Kirk, *
Allan S Fox, *
Brian Wagman, *
Kirsten Mellor, *
EMP: 89 **EST:** 1951
SQ FT: 30,000
SALES (est): 14.08MM
SALES (corp-wide): 14.08MM **Privately Held**
Web: www.thearcsf.org
SIC: 8331 8361 7361 Job training services; Mentally handicapped home; Employment agencies

(P-18208)
ASIAN REHABILITATION SVC INC (PA)
750 E Green St Ste 301 (91101-2134)
PHONE..................562 632-1141
Joshua Yoon, *Ex Dir*
Si Ho, *
EMP: 62 **EST:** 1972
SALES (est): 2.14MM
SALES (corp-wide): 2.14MM **Privately Held**
Web: www.asianrehab.org
SIC: 8331 7349 Job counseling; Janitorial service, contract basis

(P-18209)
ASIAN REHABILITATION SVC INC
Also Called: ARS
312 N Spring St Ste B30 (90012-3152)
PHONE..................213 680-3790
EMP: 120
SALES (corp-wide): 2.14MM **Privately Held**
Web: www.asianrehab.org
SIC: 8331 Vocational rehabilitation agency
PA: Asian Rehabilitation Service, Inc.
    750 E Green St Ste 301
    Pasadena CA
    562 632-1141

(P-18210)
BAKERSFELD ASSN FOR RTRDED CTZ
2240 S Union Ave (93307-4158)
PHONE..................661 834-2272
Jim Baldwin, *Pr*
EMP: 98 **EST:** 1951
SQ FT: 30,000
SALES (est): 10.75MM **Privately Held**
SIC: 8331 Sheltered workshop

(P-18211)
BENEFITVISION INC
5550 Topanga Canyon Blvd (91367-6478)
PHONE..................818 348-3100
Terry Fuzue, *Brnch Mgr*
EMP: 73
SALES (corp-wide): 14.17MM **Privately Held**
Web: www.benefitvision.com
SIC: 8331 Job training and related services
PA: Benefitvision, Inc.
    4522 Rfd
    Long Grove IL
    877 737-5526

(P-18212)
BEST OPPORTUNITIES INC
Also Called: BEST OPPORTUNITIES
22450 Headquarters Ave (92307-4304)
PHONE..................760 628-0111
Karin Etheridge, *CEO*
Richard O'brien, *Pr*
EMP: 140 **EST:** 1981
SQ FT: 5,000
SALES (est): 6.12MM **Privately Held**
Web: www.bestopportunities.org
SIC: 8331 Vocational rehabilitation agency

8331 - Job Training And Related Services (P-18213)

(P-18213)
BUFFINI & COMPANY (PA)
6349 Palomar Oaks Ct (92011-1428)
PHONE..................................760 827-2100
Brian Buffini, *Ch Bd*
Beverly Buffini, *
EMP: 182 **EST:** 1995
SALES (est): 42.9MM **Privately Held**
Web: www.buffiniandcompany.com
SIC: 8331 Job training services

(P-18214)
CALIFORNIA HUMAN DEV CORP (PA)
Also Called: ANTHONY SOTO EMPLOYMENT TRAINI
3315 Airway Dr (95403-2005)
PHONE..................................707 523-1155
Miguel Mejia, *Ch*
Christopher Paige, *CEO*
Emila Aguilar, *Vice Chairman*
Hector Brambila, *Sec*
Doris Unsod, *Treas*
EMP: 140 **EST:** 1967
SQ FT: 15,000
SALES (est): 16.17MM
SALES (corp-wide): 16.17MM **Privately Held**
Web: www.californiahumandevelopment.org
SIC: 8331 7361 8399 7374 Job training services; Placement agencies; Community development groups; Calculating service (computer)

(P-18215)
CALIFRNIA DEPT DVLPMENTAL SVCS
Also Called: Fairview Developmental Center
2501 Harbor Blvd (92626-6143)
PHONE..................................714 957-5151
Bill Wilson, *Ex Dir*
EMP: 744
SALES (corp-wide): 534.4MM **Privately Held**
SIC: 8331 9431 8361 Job training and related services; Administration of public health programs; Residential care
HQ: California Department Of Developmental Services
1215 O St
Sacramento CA

(P-18216)
CALIFRNIA FIRE RSCUE TRNING AU
3121 Gold Canal Dr (95670-6111)
PHONE..................................916 475-1660
Joe Gear, *Ex Dir*
Sherri Martucci, *
EMP: 105 **EST:** 2011
SQ FT: 3,000
SALES (est): 5.15MM **Privately Held**
Web: fireandrescuetraining.ca.gov
SIC: 8331 Job training and related services

(P-18217)
CENTER FOR EMPLOYMENT TRAINING (PA)
Also Called: C E T
701 Vine St (95110-2940)
PHONE..................................408 287-7924
Hermelinda Sapien, *CEO*
Mohammad Aryanpour, *
EMP: 70 **EST:** 1967
SQ FT: 120,000
SALES (est): 32.92MM
SALES (corp-wide): 32.92MM **Privately Held**
Web: www.cetweb.edu
SIC: 8331 9721 Vocational training agency; Immigration services, government

(P-18218)
CENTRAL VALLEY OPRTNTY CTR INC (PA)
Also Called: CVOC
6838 Bridget Ct (95388)
P.O. Box 1389 (95388-1389)
PHONE..................................209 357-0062
Ernie Flores, *Ex Dir*
EMP: 63 **EST:** 1979
SQ FT: 27,000
SALES (est): 11.92MM
SALES (corp-wide): 11.92MM **Privately Held**
Web: www.cvoc.org
SIC: 8331 Vocational training agency

(P-18219)
CHINATOWN SERVICE CENTER
320 S Garfield Ave Ste 118 (91801)
PHONE..................................213 808-1700
Roy Jasso, *Brnch Mgr*
EMP: 69
SALES (corp-wide): 14.7MM **Privately Held**
Web: www.cscla.org
SIC: 8331 Job counseling
PA: Chinatown Service Center
767 N Hill St Ste 400
Los Angeles CA
213 808-1701

(P-18220)
CHINATOWN SERVICE CENTER (PA)
767 N Hill St Ste 400 (90012-2381)
PHONE..................................213 808-1701
Peter Ng, *CEO*
Peter Ng, *Pr*
Lawrence Lue, *
Henry Kwong, *
Gloria Tang, *
EMP: 80 **EST:** 1975
SQ FT: 20,000
SALES (est): 14.7MM
SALES (corp-wide): 14.7MM **Privately Held**
Web: www.cscla.org
SIC: 8331 8322 8011 Job counseling; Family (marriage) counseling; Clinic, operated by physicians

(P-18221)
CITY OF SANTA ANA
Also Called: Santa Ana Job Training Program
1000 E Santa Ana Blvd Ste 107 (92701-3900)
PHONE..................................714 647-6545
Judy Shenlee, *Mgr*
EMP: 87
SALES (corp-wide): 555.62MM **Privately Held**
Web: www.santa-ana.org
SIC: 8331 9111 Job training services; Mayors' office
PA: City Of Santa Ana
20 Civic Center Plz Fl 8
Santa Ana CA
714 647-5400

(P-18222)
CITY OF YUBA CITY
Also Called: Community Facilities District
1201 Civic Center Blvd (95993-3005)
PHONE..................................530 822-4601
EMP: 191 **EST:** 2010
SALES (est): 25.91MM
SALES (corp-wide): 61.57MM **Privately Held**
Web: www.yubacity.net
SIC: 8331 Community service employment training program
PA: City Of Yuba City
1201 Civic Center Blvd
Yuba City CA
530 822-4622

(P-18223)
COMMUNITY SERVICES AND EMPLOYMENT TRAINING INCORPORATED (PA)
Also Called: C-SET
312 Nw 3rd Ave (93291-3626)
P.O. Box 1350 (93279-1350)
PHONE..................................559 757-3539
EMP: 100 **EST:** 1976
SALES (est): 24.16MM
SALES (corp-wide): 24.16MM **Privately Held**
Web: www.cset.org
SIC: 8331 Job training services

(P-18224)
CONSERVATION CORPS LONG BEACH
340 Nieto Ave (90814-1845)
PHONE..................................562 986-1249
Samara Ashley, *Prin*
Mike Bassett, *
Mario R Beas, *
EMP: 165 **EST:** 1987
SQ FT: 10,000
SALES (est): 6.78MM **Privately Held**
Web: www.cclb-corps.org
SIC: 8331 8322 Community service employment training program; Individual and family services

(P-18225)
COUNTY OF RIVERSIDE
Also Called: County Rvrside Wrkfrce Dev Div
1325 Spruce St Ste 400 (92507-0506)
P.O. Box 553 (92502-0553)
PHONE..................................951 955-3434
Selicia Slournoy, *Dir*
EMP: 63
SALES (corp-wide): 4.58B **Privately Held**
Web: www.countyofriverside.us
SIC: 8331 9441 Skill training center; Administration of social and manpower programs
PA: County Of Riverside
4080 Lemon St Fl 11
Riverside CA
951 955-1110

(P-18226)
COUNTY OF STANISLAUS
Also Called: Department Workforce Dev
251 E Hackett Rd Ste 2 (95358-9800)
P.O. Box 3389 (95353-3389)
PHONE..................................209 558-2100
Doris Foster, *Dir*
EMP: 67
Web: www.stancounty.com
SIC: 8331 Job training and related services
PA: County Of Stanislaus
1010 10th St Ste 5100
Modesto CA
209 525-6398

(P-18227)
DREAMCTCHERS EMPWERMENT NETWRK
Also Called: Dreamcatchers Empowerment
1125 Missouri St (94533-6088)
PHONE..................................707 558-1775
Regina Keiser, *Ex Dir*
EMP: 580
SALES (corp-wide): 2.93MM **Privately Held**
Web: www.dreamcatchersnetwork.org
SIC: 8331 Vocational training agency
PA: Dreamcatchers Empowerment Network
7590 Shoreline Dr Ste B
Stockton CA
209 478-5291

(P-18228)
EDEN AREA RGNAL OCCPTNAL PRGRA
Also Called: Eden Area Rop School
26316 Hesperian Blvd (94545-2458)
PHONE..................................510 293-2900
Cyril Bonanno, *Ex Dir*
EMP: 83 **EST:** 1979
SQ FT: 74,000
SALES (est): 13.57MM **Privately Held**
Web: www.edenrop.org
SIC: 8331 8249 Vocational training agency; Vocational schools, nec

(P-18229)
EXCEPTIONAL CHLD FOUNDATION
Also Called: Par Services
1430 Venice Blvd (90006-4818)
PHONE..................................213 748-3556
Nanette Cruz, *Prin*
EMP: 219
SALES (corp-wide): 28.26MM **Privately Held**
Web: www.ecf.net
SIC: 8331 Job training and related services
PA: Exceptional Children's Foundation
5350 Machado Ln
Culver City CA
310 204-3300

(P-18230)
EXCEPTIONAL CHLD FOUNDATION (PA)
Also Called: PAR SERVICES
5350 Machado Ln (90230-8800)
PHONE..................................310 204-3300
Veronica Arteaga, *Pr*
EMP: 120 **EST:** 1946
SQ FT: 45,000
SALES (est): 28.26MM
SALES (corp-wide): 28.26MM **Privately Held**
Web: www.ecf.net
SIC: 8331 Vocational training agency

(P-18231)
GOODWILL INDS ORANGE CNTY CAL
Also Called: Goodwill Industries
5880 Edinger Ave (92649-1705)
PHONE..................................714 881-3986
EMP: 110
SALES (corp-wide): 49.48MM **Privately Held**
Web: www.ocgoodwill.org
SIC: 8331 Job training and related services
PA: Goodwill Industries Of Orange County, California
410 N Fairview St
Santa Ana CA
714 547-6308

(P-18232)
JEWISH VCTNAL CREER CNSLING SV
5106 Camden St (94619-3460)

PRODUCTS & SERVICES SECTION
8331 - Job Training And Related Services (P-18252)

PHONE.....................415 391-3600
Lisa Countryman-quiroz, *CEO*
Kathryn Beeley, *
EMP: 70 **EST:** 1974
SQ FT: 8,000
SALES (est): 14.3MM **Privately Held**
Web: www.jvs.org
SIC: 8331 Job counseling

(P-18233)
LINCOLN TRNING CTR RHBLTTION W
Also Called: LINCOLN TRAINING CENTER
2643 Loma Ave (91733-1419)
PHONE.....................626 442-0621
Judith Angelo, *CEO*
Eric Brown, *
David Nelson, *Vice Chairman* *
Judy Angelo, *
EMP: 85 **EST:** 1964
SQ FT: 30,000
SALES (est): 25.51MM **Privately Held**
Web: www.lincolntc.org
SIC: 8331 Vocational rehabilitation agency

(P-18234)
METROPLTAN AREA ADVSORY CMMTTE (PA)
Also Called: M A A C Project
1355 Third Ave (91911-4302)
PHONE.....................619 426-3595
Arnulfo Manriquez, *CEO*
Antonio Pizano, *
Austin Foye, *
EMP: 100 **EST:** 1965
SQ FT: 820,000
SALES (est): 62.25MM
SALES (corp-wide): 62.25MM **Privately Held**
Web: www.maacproject.org
SIC: 8331 8351 8748 Job training services; Head Start center, except in conjunction with school; Energy conservation consultant

(P-18235)
MID-CITIES ASSOCIATION INC (PA)
Also Called: Hub-Limited Workshop
14208 Towne Ave (90061-2653)
PHONE.....................310 537-4510
John Wagoner, *Ex Dir*
EMP: 60 **EST:** 1954
SALES (est): 4.19MM
SALES (corp-wide): 4.19MM **Privately Held**
Web: www.arcmidcities.org
SIC: 8331 Sheltered workshop

(P-18236)
MISSION ECONOMIC DEV AGCY
2301 Mission St Ste 301 (94110-1813)
PHONE.....................415 282-3334
Luis Granados, *CEO*
Luis Granados, *Dir*
EMP: 80 **EST:** 1973
SALES (est): 25.22MM **Privately Held**
Web: www.medasf.org
SIC: 8331 8322 8399 7299 Job training and related services; Social service center; Community development groups; Personal financial services

(P-18237)
NAPA VALLEY PSI INC
651 Trabajo Ln (94559-4258)
P.O. Box 600 (94559-0600)
PHONE.....................707 255-0177
Jeanne Fauquet, *Pr*
EMP: 80 **EST:** 1972

SQ FT: 43,800
SALES (est): 812.08K **Privately Held**
Web: www.napavalleypsi.com
SIC: 8331 2521 2511 Vocational rehabilitation agency; Filing cabinets (boxes), office: wood; Wood household furniture

(P-18238)
NORTH BAY DVLPMNTAL DSBLTIES S (PA)
Also Called: NORTH BAY REGIONAL CENTER
10 Exec Ct Ste A (94558-6331)
P.O. Box 3360 (94558-0295)
PHONE.....................707 256-1224
TOLL FREE: 888
Nancy Gardner, *Ex Dir*
EMP: 100 **EST:** 1972
SALES (est): 369.97MM
SALES (corp-wide): 369.97MM **Privately Held**
Web: www.nbrc.net
SIC: 8331 8322 Job training services; Individual and family services

(P-18239)
OPTIONS FOR ALL INC
5050 Murphy Canyon Rd Ste 220 (92123-4399)
PHONE.....................858 565-9870
Richard Gutierrez, *CFO*
EMP: 426
SALES (corp-wide): 23.36MM **Privately Held**
Web: www.optionsforall.org
SIC: 8331 Job training and related services
PA: Options For All, Inc.
5050 Murphy Canyon Rd # 220
San Diego CA
858 565-9870

(P-18240)
OWL EDUCATION AND TRAINING INC
2465 Campus Dr (92612-1502)
PHONE.....................949 797-2000
Gregory J Burden, *Pr*
Stephen Seastrom, *
EMP: 280 **EST:** 2005
SQ FT: 22,800
SALES (est): 2.46MM
SALES (corp-wide): 126.07MM **Privately Held**
Web: www.owlcompanies.com
SIC: 8331 Job training and related services
PA: Owl Companies
2465 Campus Dr
Irvine CA
949 797-2000

(P-18241)
PACE SOLANO
1955 W Texas St (94533-4462)
PHONE.....................707 426-6932
Kimberly Yarbor, *Brnch Mgr*
EMP: 83
SALES (corp-wide): 11.3MM **Privately Held**
Web: www.pacesolano.org
SIC: 8331 8361 Job training services; Mentally handicapped home
PA: Pace Solano
419 Mason St Ste 118
Vacaville CA
707 448-2283

(P-18242)
PACIFIC ASIAN CNSRTIUM IN EMPL (PA)
Also Called: P A C E
1055 Wilshire Blvd Ste 1475 (90017-2431)
PHONE.....................213 353-3982
Kerry N Doi, *Ex Dir*
EMP: 130 **EST:** 1976
SQ FT: 20,000
SALES (est): 30.46MM
SALES (corp-wide): 30.46MM **Privately Held**
Web: www.pacela.org
SIC: 8331 8322 7361 1521 Community service employment training program; Individual and family services; Labor contractors (employment agency); New construction, single-family houses

(P-18243)
PRIDE INDUSTRIES
Also Called: Auburn Pride
13080 Earhart Ave (95602-9536)
PHONE.....................530 888-0331
Vic Wursten, *Brnch Mgr*
EMP: 136
SQ FT: 5,000
SALES (corp-wide): 278.16MM **Privately Held**
Web: www.prideindustries.com
SIC: 8331 Sheltered workshop
PA: Pride Industries
10030 Foothills Blvd
Roseville CA
916 788-2100

(P-18244)
SACRAMENTO JOB CORP
3100 Meadowview Rd (95832-1498)
PHONE.....................916 391-1016
Tom Zender, *Ex Dir*
EMP: 78 **EST:** 2013
SALES (est): 9.2MM **Privately Held**
Web: www.jobcorps.gov
SIC: 8331 Job training and related services

(P-18245)
SACRAMNTO EMPLYMENT TRNING AGC
Also Called: Set A Head Start Westside
925 Del Paso Blvd Ste 100 (95815-3568)
PHONE.....................916 263-3800
Kathy Kossick, *Ex Dir*
EMP: 175
Web: www.seta.net
SIC: 8331 8351 Job training services; Head Start center, except in conjunction with school
PA: Sacramento Employment & Training Agency
925 Del Paso Blvd Ste 100
Sacramento CA

(P-18246)
SACRAMNTO EMPLYMENT TRNING AGC (PA)
Also Called: Seta
925 Del Paso Blvd Ste 100 (95815-3568)
PHONE.....................916 263-3800
EMP: 250 **EST:** 1978
SQ FT: 30,000
SALES (est): 21.77MM **Privately Held**
Web: www.seta.net
SIC: 8331 7361 8351 Job training services; Employment agencies; Child day care services

(P-18247)
SAN JOSE CONSERVATION CORPS
2650 Senter Rd (95111-1121)
PHONE.....................408 283-7171
Bob Hennessy, *CEO*
Erin Krueger, *
EMP: 81 **EST:** 1987
SQ FT: 1,800
SALES (est): 20.5MM **Privately Held**
Web: www.sjcccs.org
SIC: 8331 Community service employment training program

(P-18248)
SISKIYOU OPPORTUNITY CENTER (PA)
1516 S Mount Shasta Blvd (96067-2700)
P.O. Box 304 (96067-0304)
PHONE.....................530 926-4698
Daniel Chianello, *Dir*
EMP: 60 **EST:** 1970
SQ FT: 4,820
SALES (est): 2.55MM
SALES (corp-wide): 2.55MM **Privately Held**
Web: www.siskiyouoc.org
SIC: 8331 Job counseling

(P-18249)
SKILLSETS ONLINE CORPORATION
2010 Crow Canyon Pl Ste 200 (94583-4634)
PHONE.....................925 964-0531
EMP: 200 **EST:** 2007
SALES (est): 9.9MM **Privately Held**
Web: www.skillsetsonline.com
SIC: 8331 Job training and related services

(P-18250)
SPECIAL SERVICE FOR GROUPS INC (PA)
Also Called: Special Service For Groups Ssg
905 E 8th St (90021-1805)
PHONE.....................213 368-1888
Herbert K Hatanaka, *CEO*
Donna Wong, *
Donald A Kincey, *
EMP: 100 **EST:** 1952
SALES (est): 133.16MM
SALES (corp-wide): 133.16MM **Privately Held**
Web: www.ssg.org
SIC: 8331 8093 8399 Vocational rehabilitation agency; Mental health clinic, outpatient; Advocacy group

(P-18251)
ST MADELEINE SOPHIES CENTER
2119 E Madison Ave (92019-1111)
PHONE.....................619 442-5129
Debra Turner, *Ex Dir*
EMP: 70 **EST:** 1957
SQ FT: 13,092
SALES (est): 9.94MM **Privately Held**
Web: www.stmsc.org
SIC: 8331 Vocational training agency

(P-18252)
SUCCESS STRATEGIES INST INC
Also Called: Tom Ferry Your Coach
6 Hutton Centre Dr Ste 700 (92707)
PHONE.....................949 721-6808
Thomas Ferry, *Pr*
EMP: 70 **EST:** 2005
SALES (est): 24.37MM **Privately Held**

8331 - Job Training And Related Services (P-18253)

Web: www.tomferry.com
SIC: 8331 Job training and related services

(P-18253)
TOOLWORKS INC (PA)
25 Kearny St Ste 400 (94108-5518)
PHONE.................................415 733-0990
Steve Crabiel, *Ex Dir*
EMP: 91 EST: 1975
SQ FT: 3,500
SALES (est): 19.44MM
SALES (corp-wide): 19.44MM **Privately Held**
Web: www.toolworks.org
SIC: 8331 Vocational rehabilitation agency

(P-18254)
VALLEY LGHT CTR FOR SCIAL ADVN
Also Called: VALLEY LIGHT INDUSTRIES
109 W 6th St (91702-2875)
PHONE.................................626 337-6200
Sheryl Newman, *CEO*
EMP: 80 EST: 1970
SALES (est): 3.17MM **Privately Held**
Web: www.valleylight.org
SIC: 8331 Job training and related services

(P-18255)
VOCATION PLUS INC
3985 N Fresno St Ste 106 (93726-4000)
PHONE.................................559 221-8019
Judy Rogers, *Pr*
EMP: 125 EST: 1991
SQ FT: 5,000
SALES (est): 2.34MM **Privately Held**
Web: www.vocationplusconnections.com
SIC: 8331 Vocational rehabilitation agency

(P-18256)
VOCATIONAL IMPRV PROGRAM INC (PA)
9210 Rochester Ave (91730-5521)
PHONE.................................909 483-5924
Wendy A Rogina, *CEO*
Rick Rogina, *
M Stephen Cho, *
Christopher J Mcardle, *Treas*
EMP: 90 EST: 1986
SQ FT: 23,000
SALES (est): 19.46MM **Privately Held**
Web: www.vipsolutions.com
SIC: 8331 Vocational rehabilitation agency

(P-18257)
VOCATIONAL VISIONS
26041 Pala (92691-2705)
PHONE.................................949 837-7280
Joan Mckinney, *CEO*
Kathryn Hebel, *
EMP: 170 EST: 1975
SQ FT: 17,000
SALES (est): 8.32MM **Privately Held**
Web: www.vocationalvisions.org
SIC: 8331 Sheltered workshop

(P-18258)
VTC ENTERPRISES (PA)
2445 A St (93455-1401)
P.O. Box 1187 (93456-1187)
PHONE.................................805 928-5000
Jason Telander, *CEO*
Doctor Mark Malangko, *Pr*
Henry M Grennan, *
Lisa Walker, *
Cole Kinney, *
EMP: 96 EST: 1962
SQ FT: 21,093
SALES (est): 11.44MM

SALES (corp-wide): 11.44MM **Privately Held**
Web: www.vtc-sm.org
SIC: 8331 Vocational rehabilitation agency

(P-18259)
WESTVIEW SERVICES INC
1515 W Cameron Ave Ste 310 (91790-2726)
PHONE.................................626 962-0956
Patricia Stock, *Mgr*
EMP: 80
SALES (corp-wide): 14.51MM **Privately Held**
Web: www.westviewservices.org
SIC: 8331 5999 Job training and related services; Technical aids for the handicapped
PA: Westview Services, Inc
10522 Katella Ave
Anaheim CA
714 517-6606

(P-18260)
WESTVIEW SERVICES INC
Also Called: Starlight Educational Center
9421 Edinger Ave (92683-7426)
PHONE.................................714 418-2090
EMP: 79
SQ FT: 3,775
SALES (corp-wide): 14.51MM **Privately Held**
Web: www.westviewservices.org
SIC: 8331 8244 Community service employment training program; Business and secretarial schools
PA: Westview Services, Inc
10522 Katella Ave
Anaheim CA
714 517-6606

(P-18261)
WESTVIEW SERVICES INC
Also Called: Westview Vocational Services
27576 Commerce Center Dr Ste 103 (92590-2571)
PHONE.................................951 699-0047
Mary Radecki, *Dir*
EMP: 79
SALES (corp-wide): 14.51MM **Privately Held**
Web: www.westviewservices.org
SIC: 8331 8322 Vocational rehabilitation agency; Social services for the handicapped
PA: Westview Services, Inc
10522 Katella Ave
Anaheim CA
714 517-6606

(P-18262)
WESTVIEW SERVICES INC
Also Called: Westveiw Vo Ser
9776 Katella Ave (92804-6417)
PHONE.................................714 530-2703
Carol Cooper, *Mgr*
EMP: 68
SALES (corp-wide): 14.51MM **Privately Held**
Web: www.westviewservices.org
SIC: 8331 8249 Vocational rehabilitation agency; Vocational schools, nec
PA: Westview Services, Inc
10522 Katella Ave
Anaheim CA
714 517-6606

(P-18263)
WESTVIEW SERVICES INC
Also Called: Westview Vocational Services
1655 S Euclid St Ste A (92802-2400)
PHONE.................................714 635-2444

Greg Gann, *CEO*
EMP: 91
SQ FT: 5,952
SALES (corp-wide): 14.51MM **Privately Held**
Web: www.westviewservices.org
SIC: 8331 Vocational rehabilitation agency
PA: Westview Services, Inc
10522 Katella Ave
Anaheim CA
714 517-6606

(P-18264)
WORK2FUTURE FOUNDATION
Also Called: North San Jose Job Center
1901 Zanker Rd (95112-4217)
PHONE.................................408 216-6202
EMP: 167
SALES (corp-wide): 140.25K **Privately Held**
Web: www.work2futurefoundation.org
SIC: 8331 Job training services
PA: Work2future Foundation
38 N Almaden Blvd # 306
San Jose CA
408 794-1100

(P-18265)
WORK2FUTURE FOUNDATION
Also Called: Work2fture - Yuth Training Ctr
2072 Lucretia Ave (95122-3305)
PHONE.................................408 794-1234
EMP: 167
SALES (corp-wide): 140.25K **Privately Held**
Web: www.work2futurefoundation.org
SIC: 8331 Skill training center
PA: Work2future Foundation
38 N Almaden Blvd # 306
San Jose CA
408 794-1100

(P-18266)
WORK2FUTURE FOUNDATION
Also Called: Work2future - Gilroy Job Ctr
379 Tomkins Ct (95020-3631)
PHONE.................................408 758-3477
EMP: 167
SALES (corp-wide): 140.25K **Privately Held**
Web: www.work2futurefoundation.org
SIC: 8331 Skill training center
PA: Work2future Foundation
38 N Almaden Blvd # 306
San Jose CA
408 794-1100

8351 Child Day Care Services

(P-18267)
ALAMEDA FAMILY SERVICES
2325 Clement Ave (94501-7063)
PHONE.................................510 629-6300
Irene Kudarauskas, *Ex Dir*
EMP: 91 EST: 1970
SALES (est): 8.16MM **Privately Held**
Web: www.alamedafs.org
SIC: 8351 8322 Head Start center, except in conjunction with school; Youth self-help agency

(P-18268)
ALLIES FOR EVERY CHILD INC
5721 W Slauson Ave Ste 200 (90230-6554)
PHONE.................................310 846-4100
Heather Carrigan, *CEO*
Richard Klein, *
EMP: 88 EST: 1987
SQ FT: 18,000

SALES (est): 10.82MM **Privately Held**
Web: www.alliesforeverychild.org
SIC: 8351 8322 Child day care services; Child related social services

(P-18269)
BAY AREA HSPANO INST FOR ADVNC
Also Called: CENTRO VIDA
1000 Camelia St (94710-1514)
PHONE.................................510 525-1463
Beatriz Leyva Cutler, *Dir*
EMP: 66 EST: 1975
SQ FT: 1,200
SALES (est): 1.53MM **Privately Held**
Web: www.bahiainc.com
SIC: 8351 8299 Group day care center; Educational services

(P-18270)
BELMONT OAKS ACADEMY
2200 Carlmont Dr (94002-3310)
PHONE.................................650 593-6175
Pamela Clarke, *Pr*
Joanna Reames, *
EMP: 63 EST: 1946
SALES (est): 2.14MM **Privately Held**
Web: www.mmboa.org
SIC: 8351 8211 Preschool center; Private elementary school

(P-18271)
BOOKHEADED LEARNING LLC
610 Daniel Young Dr (95476-7278)
PHONE.................................707 996-3427
Robert Romano, *Prin*
EMP: 94 EST: 2010
SALES (est): 5.2MM **Privately Held**
Web: www.studysync.com
SIC: 8351 Group day care center

(P-18272)
BROOKSIDE CHRISTIAN SCHOOL INC (PA)
Also Called: Brookside Christn Jr /Sr High
3588 Brookside Rd (95219-2319)
PHONE.................................209 954-7650
Dennis Gibson, *Pr*
Gregory W Gibson, *
Monty Zorb, *
Bob Wise, *
Carol Hakeem, *
EMP: 65 EST: 1985
SALES (est): 1.09MM
SALES (corp-wide): 1.09MM **Privately Held**
Web: www.brooksidelittlelearners.com
SIC: 8351 Preschool center

(P-18273)
CALIFORNIA CHILDRENS ACADEMY
Also Called: Early Learning Center
233 N Breed St (90033-2902)
PHONE.................................323 263-3846
Monica Barahona, *Dir*
EMP: 144
Web: www.californiachildrensacademy.org
SIC: 8351 Preschool center
PA: California Children's Academy
2701 N Main St
Los Angeles CA

(P-18274)
CALVARY CHURCH SANTA ANA INC
1010 N Tustin Ave (92705-3598)
PHONE.................................714 973-4800
Pastor Michael Welles, *Prin*

PRODUCTS & SERVICES SECTION
8351 - Child Day Care Services (P-18294)

Michael Welles, *Executive Pastor*
EMP: 160 EST: 1932
SQ FT: 133,000
SALES (est): 11.48MM **Privately Held**
Web: www.calvarylife.org
SIC: **8351** 8661 Nursery school; Miscellaneous denomination church

(P-18275)
CAROUSEL CHILD CARE CORP
8333 Airport Blvd (90045-4244)
PHONE..................310 216-6641
Sandy Montano, *Brnch Mgr*
EMP: 107
SALES (corp-wide): 21.36MM **Privately Held**
Web: www.carouselschool.com
SIC: **8351** Preschool center
PA: Carousel Child Care Corporation
7899 La Tijera Blvd
Los Angeles CA
310 645-9222

(P-18276)
CATALYST FAMILY INC (PA)
Also Called: CDI CENTERS
350 Woodview Ave Ste 100 (95037-8105)
PHONE..................408 556-7300
Susan Dumars, *Pr*
Susan Blake, *
Eva Schulte, *
EMP: 75 EST: 1975
SQ FT: 10,000
SALES (est): 83.61MM
SALES (corp-wide): 83.61MM **Privately Held**
Web: www.catalystkids.org
SIC: **8351** 8399 Child day care services; Social service information exchange

(P-18277)
CATALYST FAMILY INC
Also Called: King City Child Dev Ctr
440 Jayne St Ofc (93930-2717)
PHONE..................831 385-4005
Patricia Reyes, *Brnch Mgr*
EMP: 463
SALES (corp-wide): 83.61MM **Privately Held**
Web: www.catalystkids.org
SIC: **8351** Preschool center
PA: Catalyst Family Inc.
350 Woodview Ave Ste 100
Morgan Hill CA
408 556-7300

(P-18278)
CHALLENGER SCHOOLS
4949 Harwood Rd (95124-5209)
PHONE..................408 723-0111
Josh Mckay, *Prin*
EMP: 103
SALES (corp-wide): 158.6MM **Privately Held**
Web: www.challengerschool.com
SIC: **8351** 8211 Preschool center; Private elementary school
PA: Challenger Schools
9424 S 300 W
Sandy UT
801 569-2700

(P-18279)
CHALLENGER SCHOOLS
3880 Middlefield Rd (94303-4716)
PHONE..................650 213-8245
Kamilah Abdul-haqq, *Prin*
EMP: 81
SALES (corp-wide): 158.6MM **Privately Held**

Web: www.challengerschool.com
SIC: **8351** 8211 Preschool center; Elementary and secondary schools
PA: Challenger Schools
9424 S 300 W
Sandy UT
801 569-2700

(P-18280)
CHALLENGER SCHOOLS
Also Called: Challenger School
39600 Cedar Blvd (94560-5487)
PHONE..................510 770-1771
Barbara Baker, *Bd of Dir*
EMP: 92
SALES (corp-wide): 158.6MM **Privately Held**
Web: www.challengerschool.com
SIC: **8351** Preschool center
PA: Challenger Schools
9424 S 300 W
Sandy UT
801 569-2700

(P-18281)
CHILD ACTION INC (PA)
10540 White Rock Rd Ste 180 (95670-6012)
PHONE..................916 369-0191
Tracey Strack, *Ex Dir*
Jaci White, *
EMP: 163 EST: 1976
SALES (est): 95.8MM
SALES (corp-wide): 95.8MM **Privately Held**
Web: wp.childaction.org
SIC: **8351** Child day care services

(P-18282)
CHILD CARE RESOURCE CENTER INC
Also Called: Volunteers America Head Start
454 S Kalisher St (91340-3535)
PHONE..................818 837-0097
EMP: 204
SALES (corp-wide): 404.36MM **Privately Held**
Web: www.ccrcca.org
SIC: **8351** Child day care services
PA: Child Care Resource Center, Inc.
20001 Prairie St
Chatsworth CA
818 717-1000

(P-18283)
CHILD DEVELOPMENT ASSOC INC
Also Called: Childrens Co
380 Telegraph Canyon Rd (91910-6334)
PHONE..................619 422-7115
Lili Torres, *Dir*
EMP: 77
SALES (corp-wide): 123.16MM **Privately Held**
Web: www.cdasd.org
SIC: **8351** Preschool center
PA: Child Development Associates, Incorporated
180 Otay Lakes Rd Ste 310
Bonita CA
619 427-4411

(P-18284)
CHILD DEVELOPMENT INCORPORATED
312 Gibson Rd (95695-4765)
PHONE..................530 666-4822
Diana Sorelle, *Brnch Mgr*
EMP: 362

SALES (corp-wide): 49.76MM **Privately Held**
Web: www.catalystkids.org
SIC: **8351** Preschool center
PA: Child Development Incorporated
350 Woodview Ave
Morgan Hill CA
408 556-7300

(P-18285)
CHILD DEVELOPMENT INCORPORATED
Also Called: Turtle Rock Cdc
5151 Amalfi Dr (92603-3443)
PHONE..................949 854-5060
Mindy Ho, *Dir*
EMP: 363
SALES (corp-wide): 49.76MM **Privately Held**
Web: www.catalystkids.org
SIC: **8351** Preschool center
PA: Child Development Incorporated
350 Woodview Ave
Morgan Hill CA
408 556-7300

(P-18286)
CHILD FAMILY & CMNTY SVCS INC
32980 Alvarado Niles Rd Ste 856 (94587-3106)
PHONE..................510 796-9512
Karen Deshayes, *Ex Dir*
EMP: 140 EST: 1973
SQ FT: 20,000
SALES (est): 17.07MM **Privately Held**
Web: www.cfcsinc.org
SIC: **8351** Preschool center

(P-18287)
CHILDREN OF RAINBOW INC (PA)
4890 Logan Ave (92113-3004)
PHONE..................619 615-0652
Gale R Walker, *Pr*
EMP: 64 EST: 1997
SQ FT: 8,500
SALES (est): 4.81MM **Privately Held**
Web: www.childrenoftherainbow.org
SIC: **8351** Group day care center

(P-18288)
CHILDRENS CRATIVE LRNG CTR INC
521 W Capitol Expy (95136-3914)
PHONE..................408 978-1500
Brandie Gonzales, *Mgr*
EMP: 387
Web: www.childrenscreativelearningcenter.com
SIC: **8351** Group day care center
PA: Children's Creative Learning Center, Inc.
794 E Duane Ave
Sunnyvale CA

(P-18289)
CHILDRENS CRATIVE LRNG CTR INC
1625 San Luis Ave (94043-3147)
PHONE..................650 968-2600
Kadie Albrecht, *Brnch Mgr*
EMP: 388
Web: www.childrenscreativelearningcenter.com
SIC: **8351** Group day care center
PA: Children's Creative Learning Center, Inc.
794 E Duane Ave

Sunnyvale CA

(P-18290)
CHILDRENS CRATIVE LRNG CTR INC
1608 Private Bolio Rd (93940-6915)
PHONE..................831 647-1880
Kari Galer, *Dir*
EMP: 485
Web: www.childrenscreativelearningcenter.com
SIC: **8351** Preschool center
PA: Children's Creative Learning Center, Inc.
794 E Duane Ave
Sunnyvale CA

(P-18291)
CHILDRENS CRATIVE LRNG CTR INC
Also Called: Downtown Palo Alto Kindercare
848 Ramona St (94301-2734)
PHONE..................650 473-1100
Nicole Ross, *Dir*
EMP: 388
Web: www.childrenscreativelearningcenter.com
SIC: **8351** Preschool center
PA: Children's Creative Learning Center, Inc.
794 E Duane Ave
Sunnyvale CA

(P-18292)
CHILDRENS HOSPITAL ORANGE CNTY
500 Superior Ave (92663-3657)
PHONE..................949 631-2062
EMP: 110
SALES (corp-wide): 1.11B **Privately Held**
Web: www.choc.org
SIC: **8351** Child day care services
PA: Children's Hospital Of Orange County
1201 W La Veta Ave
Orange CA
714 509-8300

(P-18293)
CHRISTIAN BROOKSIDE SCHOOLS
Also Called: United Chrisitan Schools
3588 Brookside Rd (95219-2319)
PHONE..................209 954-7656
Dennis Gibson, *Pr*
EMP: 60
SALES (corp-wide): 1.09MM **Privately Held**
Web: www.brooksidelittlelearners.com
SIC: **8351** Preschool center
PA: Brookside Christian School, Inc.
3588 Brookside Rd
Stockton CA
209 954-7650

(P-18294)
CLEMMIE GILL SCHL OF SCNCE CNS
Also Called: Granite Hills Child Dev Ctr
1701 E Putnam Ave (93257-8000)
PHONE..................559 782-0883
Connie Smith, *Dir*
EMP: 110
SALES (corp-wide): 291MM **Privately Held**
Web: www.tcoe.org
SIC: **8351** Child day care services
HQ: The Clemmie Gill School Of Science And Conservation
41569 Bear Creek Rd

8351 - Child Day Care Services (P-18295)

Springville CA

(P-18295)
COMMUNITY ACTION PRTNR MDERA C (PA)
1225 Gill Ave (93637-5234)
PHONE..................559 673-9173
Mattie Mendez, *Ex Dir*
Donna Tooley, *
Linda L Wright, *
EMP: 200 EST: 1965
SQ FT: 18,000
SALES (est): 31.43MM
SALES (corp-wide): 31.43MM Privately Held
Web: www.maderacap.org
SIC: 8351 Head Start center, except in conjunction with school

(P-18296)
COMMUNITY ACTION PRTNR SAN LUI
Also Called: San Jerardo Migrant
24495 Calle El Rosario (93908-9747)
PHONE..................831 751-9379
William Castiano, *Mgr*
EMP: 127
SALES (corp-wide): 99.11MM Privately Held
Web: www.capslo.org
SIC: 8351 Head Start center, except in conjunction with school
PA: Community Action Partnership Of San Luis Obispo County, Inc.
1030 Southwood Dr
San Luis Obispo CA
805 544-4355

(P-18297)
COMMUNITY ACTION PRTNR SAN LUI (PA)
1030 Southwood Dr (93401-5813)
PHONE..................805 544-4355
Anita Robinson, *Ch Bd*
Fran Coughon, *Vice Chairman*
Frances I Coughlin, *
Elizabeth Biz Steinberg, *
Santos Arrona, *
EMP: 72 EST: 1965
SQ FT: 20,000
SALES (est): 99.11MM
SALES (corp-wide): 99.11MM Privately Held
Web: www.capslo.org
SIC: 8351 Head Start center, except in conjunction with school

(P-18298)
COMMUNITY ACTION PRTNR SAN LUI
Also Called: Day Care Center
805 Fiero Ln Ste A (93401-8700)
PHONE..................805 541-2272
Sheri Wilson, *Dir*
EMP: 127
SALES (corp-wide): 99.11MM Privately Held
Web: www.capslo.org
SIC: 8351 Head Start center, except in conjunction with school
PA: Community Action Partnership Of San Luis Obispo County, Inc.
1030 Southwood Dr
San Luis Obispo CA
805 544-4355

(P-18299)
COMMUNITY ACTION PRTNR SAN LUI

Also Called: Soledad Migrant Headstart
160 Main St (93960-3024)
PHONE..................831 678-1584
EMP: 127
SALES (corp-wide): 99.11MM Privately Held
Web: www.capslo.org
SIC: 8351 Head Start center, except in conjunction with school
PA: Community Action Partnership Of San Luis Obispo County, Inc.
1030 Southwood Dr
San Luis Obispo CA
805 544-4355

(P-18300)
COMMUNITY CHILD CARE CNCIL SNO (PA)
Also Called: 4 CS
131a Stony Cir Ste 300 (95401-9513)
PHONE..................707 544-3077
Melanie Dodson, *Ex Dir*
Mary Ann Doan, *
EMP: 60 EST: 1972
SALES (est): 26.29MM
SALES (corp-wide): 26.29MM Privately Held
Web: www.sonoma4cs.org
SIC: 8351 Group day care center

(P-18301)
COMMUNITY DEV INST HEAD START
12988 Bowron Rd (92064-5790)
PHONE..................858 668-2985
EMP: 276
SALES (corp-wide): 73.75MM Privately Held
Web: www.cditeam.org
SIC: 8351 Head Start center, except in conjunction with school
PA: Community Development Institute Head Start
10065 E Harvard Ave # 700
Denver CO
720 747-5100

(P-18302)
COMPASS FAMILY SERVICES
Also Called: Compass Children's Center
144 Leavenworth St (94102-3806)
PHONE..................415 644-0504
Mary Mcnamara, *Dir*
EMP: 80
SQ FT: 12,143
SALES (corp-wide): 22.71MM Privately Held
Web: www.compass-sf.org
SIC: 8351 Child day care services
PA: Compass Family Services
37 Grove St
San Francisco CA
415 644-0504

(P-18303)
CREATIVE CHILD CARE INC
17 E Poplar St (95202-1607)
PHONE..................209 462-2282
Carolyn Ali, *Dir*
EMP: 295
Web: www.cccisj.com
SIC: 8351 Preschool center
PA: Creative Child Care, Inc.
4719 Quail Lakes Dr G-237
Stockton CA

(P-18304)
CREATIVE LRNG CTR PRESCHOOL

2100 Woods Ln (94024-7154)
P.O. Box 991 (94023-0991)
PHONE..................650 823-1496
Louise Emerson, *Prin*
EMP: 178 EST: 2009
SALES (est): 2.12MM Privately Held
SIC: 8351 Preschool center

(P-18305)
DER KINDER GARDEN PRESCHOOL
Also Called: Der Kinder Garden Pre-Schools
2700 Redondo Beach Blvd (90504-1530)
PHONE..................213 318-3838
Judith Hassoldt, *Pr*
William Hassoldt, *
EMP: 60 EST: 1973
SALES (est): 826.71K Privately Held
SIC: 8351 Child day care services

(P-18306)
DESERT SNDS UNFIED SCHL DST SC
Also Called: Early Childhood Education
47950 Dune Palms Rd (92253-4000)
PHONE..................760 777-4200
Debra Loukatos, *Prin*
EMP: 72
SALES (corp-wide): 527.09MM Privately Held
Web: www.dsusd.us
SIC: 8351 Preschool center
PA: Desert Sands Unified School District School Building Corporation
47950 Dune Palms Rd
La Quinta CA
760 777-4200

(P-18307)
DIANNE ADAIR DAY CARE CENTERS (PA)
Also Called: Dianne Adair
1862 Bailey Rd (94521-1349)
PHONE..................925 580-9704
Todd Porter, *CEO*
Brian Carbine, *
EMP: 100 EST: 1982
SALES (est): 5.02MM
SALES (corp-wide): 5.02MM Privately Held
Web: www.dianneadair.org
SIC: 8351 Group day care center

(P-18308)
DIOCESE FRESNO EDUCATION CORP
Also Called: Our Lady of Mercy Pre-School
1400 E 27th St (95340-3221)
PHONE..................209 722-7496
Judy Blackburn, *Prin*
EMP: 61
SALES (corp-wide): 83.07MM Privately Held
Web: www.olmlancers.com
SIC: 8351 8211 Preschool center; Catholic elementary school
PA: Diocese Of Fresno Education Corporation
1550 N Fresno St
Fresno CA
559 488-7400

(P-18309)
DREW CHILD DEV CORP INC
3737 Martin Luther King Jr Blvd Ste 201 (90262)
PHONE..................310 638-8108
Dianne Fauntleroy, *Brnch Mgr*
EMP: 74

Web: www.drewcdc.org
SIC: 8351 Head Start center, except in conjunction with school
PA: Drew Child Development Corporation, Inc.
1770 E 118th St
Los Angeles CA

(P-18310)
E CENTER
1506 Starr Dr (95993-2602)
PHONE..................530 634-1200
Kulraj Samra, *CEO*
Amanda Rhyne, *
EMP: 150 EST: 1973
SQ FT: 4,000
SALES (est): 29.47MM Privately Held
Web: www.ecenter.org
SIC: 8351 Head Start center, except in conjunction with school

(P-18311)
EAST BAY AGENCY FOR CHILDREN
Also Called: Ebac Therapeutic Nursery Schl
6117 Martin Luther King J (94609-1240)
PHONE..................510 655-4896
Timothy Desmond, *Mgr*
EMP: 63
SALES (corp-wide): 16.98MM Privately Held
Web: www.ebac.org
SIC: 8351 Child day care services
PA: East Bay Agency For Children
2828 Ford St
Oakland CA
510 268-3770

(P-18312)
EBEN-EZER CHLD DAY CARE CTR
Also Called: EBEN-EZER CHILDREN'S DAY CARE CENTER
3970 Maine Ave Bldg B (91706-4220)
PHONE..................626 960-7100
EMP: 91
SALES (corp-wide): 2.1MM Privately Held
Web: www.kids1st.org
SIC: 8351 Preschool center
PA: Eben-Ezer Children's Day Care Center
13232 Kagel Canyon St
Pacoima CA
818 897-5427

(P-18313)
ENVIRONMENTS FOR LEARNING INC (PA)
Also Called: Montessori On The Lake
24291 Muirlands Blvd (92630-3001)
PHONE..................949 855-5630
Sara Smith, *Pr*
EMP: 65 EST: 1988
SALES (est): 2.39MM Privately Held
Web: www.montessorionthelake.com
SIC: 8351 8211 Montessori child development center; Preparatory school

(P-18314)
FAMILY CARE NETWORK INC (PA)
1255 Kendall Rd (93401-8750)
PHONE..................805 503-6240
James Robert, *CEO*
Bobbie Boyer, *
Jonathan Nibbio, *
EMP: 71 EST: 1989
SQ FT: 2,600
SALES (est): 15.96MM
SALES (corp-wide): 15.96MM Privately Held

PRODUCTS & SERVICES SECTION

8351 - Child Day Care Services (P-18336)

Web: www.fcni.org
SIC: 8351 Child day care services

(P-18315)
FIRST BPTST CH OF LOS ALTOS TH
Also Called: Altos Oaks Day Care Center
625 Magdalena Ave (94024-5225)
PHONE.................................650 948-3738
Pastor Randy Wilson, Prin
John Benza, *
EMP: 60 EST: 1941
SQ FT: 63,000
SALES (est): 6.07MM Privately Held
Web: www.lacs.com
SIC: 8351 8661 8211 Child day care services ; Baptist Church; Private elementary school

(P-18316)
FOOTHILL CHILD DEV SVCS INC
16946 Sherman Way # 100 (91406-3613)
PHONE.................................818 353-3772
Mike Daldalyan, CEO
Emilia Broberg, *
Minas Daldalyan, *
Martiros Tngryan, *
EMP: 65 EST: 2005
SALES (est): 2.39MM Privately Held
Web: www.foothillchild.com
SIC: 8351 Preschool center

(P-18317)
FSA ARLANZA CHILD DEV CTR
8172 Magnolia Ave (92504-3441)
PHONE.................................951 353-0129
Vianca Hernandez, Brnch Mgr
EMP: 96
Web: www.fsaca.org
SIC: 8351 8322 Child day care services; Family counseling services
PA: Fsa Arlanza Child Dev Ctr
7801 Gramercy Pl
Riverside CA

(P-18318)
GARDEN GROVE UNIFIED SCHL DST
Also Called: Bryant Elementary School
8371 Orangewood Ave (92841-1517)
PHONE.................................714 663-6437
Sharon Hazelleaf, Prin
EMP: 86
SALES (corp-wide): 755.47MM Privately Held
Web: www.ggusd.us
SIC: 8351 Preschool center
PA: Garden Grove Unified School District
10331 Stanford Ave
Garden Grove CA
714 663-6000

(P-18319)
HARMONIUM INC (PA)
Also Called: EPICENTRE
5440 Morehouse Dr Ste 1000 (92121-6701)
PHONE.................................858 684-3080
Rosa Ana Lozada, CEO
Melinda Mallie, *
EMP: 150 EST: 1975
SALES (est): 10.15MM
SALES (corp-wide): 10.15MM Privately Held
Web: www.harmoniumsd.org
SIC: 8351 Preschool center

(P-18320)
HEAD START CHILD DEVELOPMENT COUNCIL INC
5361 N Pershing Ave Ste A (95207-5450)
P.O. Box 8280 (95208-0280)
EMP: 800
Web: www.hscdc.org
SIC: 8351 Preschool center

(P-18321)
IMMANUEL BPTST CH SAN BRNRDINO
Also Called: Immanuel Baptist Day School
28355 Baseline St (92346-5008)
PHONE.................................909 862-6641
Pastor Rob Zinn, Prin
EMP: 65 EST: 1953
SALES (est): 7.86MM Privately Held
Web: www.ibchighland.org
SIC: 8351 8661 Preschool center; Baptist Church

(P-18322)
KARE KLUB
9995 Carmel Mountain Rd Ste B8 (92129-2889)
PHONE.................................858 538-5437
Trudy Khodabande, Brnch Mgr
EMP: 105
SALES (corp-wide): 2.62MM Privately Held
Web: www.kidscareclub.com
SIC: 8351 Preschool center
PA: Kare Klub
10414 Craftsman Way
San Diego CA
858 675-7000

(P-18323)
KIDANGO INC
1824 Daytona Dr (95122-1719)
PHONE.................................408 258-9129
Paul Miller, Pr
EMP: 71
SALES (corp-wide): 68.44MM Privately Held
Web: www.kidango.org
SIC: 8351 Preschool center
PA: Kidango, Inc.
44000 Old Warm Sprng Blvd
Fremont CA
510 897-6900

(P-18324)
KIDANGO INC (PA)
44000 Old Warm Springs Blvd (94538-6145)
PHONE.................................510 897-6900
Scott Moore, CEO
Kate Breitzman, Operations Officer*
Nereyra Houle, *
Jennifer Pare, EARLY*
Andrea Garcia, *
EMP: 80 EST: 1979
SQ FT: 5,000
SALES (est): 68.44MM
SALES (corp-wide): 68.44MM Privately Held
Web: www.kidango.org
SIC: 8351 Preschool center

(P-18325)
KIDANGO INC
3720 E Hills Dr Rm M1 (95127-2418)
PHONE.................................408 353-0473
Kari Howley, Brnch Mgr
EMP: 72
SALES (corp-wide): 68.44MM Privately Held
Web: www.kidango.org
SIC: 8351 Preschool center
PA: Kidango, Inc.
44000 Old Warm Sprng Blvd
Fremont CA
510 897-6900

(P-18326)
KIDANGO INC
4700 Calaveras Ave (94538-1124)
PHONE.................................510 494-9601
Mai Ton, Brnch Mgr
EMP: 72
SALES (corp-wide): 68.44MM Privately Held
Web: www.kidango.org
SIC: 8351 Preschool center
PA: Kidango, Inc.
44000 Old Warm Sprng Blvd
Fremont CA
510 897-6900

(P-18327)
KIDS HAVEN
6056 Montgomery Bnd (95135-1429)
PHONE.................................408 274-8766
EMP: 134
SIC: 8351 Child day care services
PA: Kid's Haven
2059 Camden Ave
San Jose CA

(P-18328)
LEPORT EDUCATIONAL INST INC
Also Called: Leport Schools
1 Technology Dr Bldg A (92618-2350)
PHONE.................................914 374-8860
Ramandeep S Girn, CEO
EMP: 255 EST: 2000
SALES (est): 24.4MM Privately Held
Web: www.leportschools.com
SIC: 8351 Montessori child development center

(P-18329)
LEPORT SCHOOLS
1 Technology Dr Ste H100 (92618-5300)
PHONE.................................714 377-6035
Vanessa Stewart, Prin
EMP: 88 EST: 2015
SALES (est): 1.11MM Privately Held
Web: www.leportschools.com
SIC: 8351 Montessori child development center

(P-18330)
MARINE CORPS COMMUNITY SVCS
Also Called: Browne Child Development Ctr
202860 San Jacinto Rd (92054)
PHONE.................................760 725-2817
Maria Langlie, Dir
EMP: 140
Web: www.usmc-mccs.org
SIC: 8351 9711 Child day care services; Marine Corps
HQ: Marine Corps Community Services
3044 Catlin Ave
Quantico VA
703 432-0109

(P-18331)
MARINE CORPS COMMUNITY SVCS
Also Called: San Onofre Child Care Center
Basilone Rd Bldg 51080 (92055)
P.O. Box 555020 (92055-5020)
PHONE.................................760 725-7311
Kanoe Serguson, Dir
EMP: 160
Web: www.usmc-mccs.org
SIC: 8351 9711 Child day care services; Marine Corps
HQ: Marine Corps Community Services
3044 Catlin Ave
Quantico VA
703 432-0109

(P-18332)
MARYVALE DAY CARE CENTER
Also Called: Maryvale Edcatn Fmly Rsrce Ctr
2502 Huntington Dr (91010-2221)
PHONE.................................626 357-1514
Steve Gunther, Dir
EMP: 122
SALES (corp-wide): 14.48MM Privately Held
Web: www.maryvale.org
SIC: 8351 Preschool center
PA: Maryvale Day Care Center
1050 Maryvale Dr
Cheektowaga NY
626 280-6511

(P-18333)
MCKINLEY CHILD DEVELOPMENT CTR
Also Called: MCKINLEY CHILD DEVELOPMENT CENTER
6822 N Paramount Blvd (90805-1937)
PHONE.................................562 531-6182
EMP: 107
SALES (corp-wide): 75.08K Privately Held
SIC: 8351 Child day care services
PA: Mckinley Child Development Ctr
3401 Monroe St Ne
Albuquerque NM
505 888-8134

(P-18334)
MODESTOS NEIGHBORHOOD CHURCH
Also Called: Modesto Christian School
5921 Stoddard Rd (95356-9199)
PHONE.................................209 529-5510
Ralph Sudfeld, Pr
Scott Brown, *
Donna Shervington, *
EMP: 78 EST: 1957
SQ FT: 200
SALES (est): 9.84MM Privately Held
SIC: 8351 8211 8661 Group day care center; Private elementary and secondary schools; Assembly of God Church

(P-18335)
MONTE VISTA CHILD CARE CTR INC
7976 Beechwood Dr (91701-1830)
PHONE.................................909 476-6780
EMP: 104
SALES (corp-wide): 1.02MM Privately Held
SIC: 8351 Group day care center
PA: Monte Vista Child Care Center, Inc.
13342 Victoria St
Rancho Cucamonga CA
909 544-0040

(P-18336)
MOUNTAIN VIEW CHILD CARE INC
Also Called: Totally Kids Spcalty Hlth Care
10716 La Tuna Canyon Rd (91352-2130)
PHONE.................................818 252-5863
Michelle Nydam, Brnch Mgr
EMP: 150
Web: www.totallykids.com
SIC: 8351 Child day care services
PA: Mountain View Child Care, Inc.
1720 Mountain View Ave
Loma Linda CA

8351 - Child Day Care Services (P-18337)

(P-18337)
NAVY EXCHANGE SERVICE COMMAND
Also Called: Naval Station Child Dev Ctr
2375 Recreation Way (92136-5518)
PHONE..................................619 556-7466
Phylis Williams, *Dir*
EMP: 97
Web: www.mynavyexchange.com
SIC: 8351 9711 Child day care services; Navy
HQ: Navy Exchange Service Command
3280 Virginia Beach Blvd
Virginia Beach VA
757 463-6200

(P-18338)
NURTURING TOTS INC
535 Avenue B # A (90277-4827)
PHONE..................................818 996-1602
Eugene Cobuzzi, *Owner*
Eugene Cobuzzi, *Sec*
Linda Cobuzzi, *
Debra Dinielli, *
EMP: 60 EST: 2013
SALES (est): 567.62K **Privately Held**
Web: www.nurturingtots.com
SIC: 8351 Group day care center

(P-18339)
ONEGENERATION (PA)
Also Called: Onegenrtion Adult Dycare Chldc
17400 Victory Blvd (91406-5349)
PHONE..................................818 708-6625
Lawrence Gordon, *Ex Dir*
EMP: 73 EST: 1978
SALES (est): 10.02MM
SALES (corp-wide): 10.02MM **Privately Held**
Web: www.onegeneration.org
SIC: 8351 8322 Child day care services; Senior citizens' center or association

(P-18340)
ORANGE COUNTY HEAD START INC (PA)
2501 Pullman St (92705-5515)
P.O. Box 9269 (92728-9269)
PHONE..................................714 241-8920
Colleen Versteeg, *Ex Dir*
Loyal Sharp, *
EMP: 75 EST: 1965
SQ FT: 20,000
SALES (est): 40.1MM
SALES (corp-wide): 40.1MM **Privately Held**
Web: www.ochsinc.org
SIC: 8351 Head Start center, except in conjunction with school

(P-18341)
PACIFIC CLINICS HEAD START
171 N Altadena Dr (91107-7318)
PHONE..................................626 254-5000
Wassy Tesfa, *Ex Dir*
EMP: 130 EST: 2021
SALES (est): 1.64MM **Privately Held**
Web: www.headstartprogram.us
SIC: 8351 Head Start center, except in conjunction with school

(P-18342)
PALO ALTO COMMUNITY CHILD CARE
890 Escondido Rd (94305-7101)
PHONE..................................650 855-9828
Gary Prehn, *Prin*
EMP: 65
SALES (corp-wide): 11.08MM **Privately Held**
Web: www.paccc.org
SIC: 8351 Preschool center
PA: Palo Alto Community Child Care Inc
3990 Ventura Ct
Palo Alto CA
650 493-5990

(P-18343)
PENINSULA FAMILY SERVICE (PA)
24 2nd Ave (94401-3828)
PHONE..................................650 403-4300
Judy Swanson, *CEO*
Arne Croce, *
Laurie Wishard, *
Kimberly Hines, *
EMP: 100 EST: 1950
SALES (est): 17.3MM
SALES (corp-wide): 17.3MM **Privately Held**
Web: www.peninsulafamilyservice.org
SIC: 8351 8322 Group day care center; Family (marriage) counseling

(P-18344)
PEOPLES CARE INC
Also Called: PEOPLE'S CARE INC.
12215 Telegraph Rd Ste 208 (90670)
PHONE..................................562 320-0174
Torres Cesaer, *Prin*
EMP: 138
SALES (corp-wide): 62.27MM **Privately Held**
Web: www.peoplescare.com
SIC: 8351 Child day care services
PA: Peoples Care Inc.
13920 City Center Dr # 290
Chino Hills CA
855 773-6753

(P-18345)
PLAZA DE LA RAZA CHILD DEV SVC (PA)
13300 Crossroads Pkwy N Ste 440 (91746)
PHONE..................................562 776-1301
Anthony Rendon, *Ex Dir*
Rosalina Fine, *
EMP: 72 EST: 1965
SALES (est): 20.07MM
SALES (corp-wide): 20.07MM **Privately Held**
Web: www.plazadelaraza.info
SIC: 8351 Head Start center, except in conjunction with school

(P-18346)
PLAZA DE LA RAZA CHILD DEVELOP
225 N Avenue 25 (90031-1794)
PHONE..................................323 224-1788
EMP: 72
SALES (corp-wide): 20.07MM **Privately Held**
Web: www.plazadelaraza.info
SIC: 8351 Head Start center, except in conjunction with school
PA: Plaza De La Raza Child Development Services, Inc.
13300 Crssrads Pkwy N Ste
La Puente CA
562 776-1301

(P-18347)
PLAZA DE LA RAZA CHILD DEVELOP
6411 Norwalk Blvd (90606-1502)
PHONE..................................562 695-1070
Adriana Gonzalez, *Pr*
EMP: 71
SALES (corp-wide): 20.07MM **Privately Held**
Web: www.plazadelaraza.info
SIC: 8351 Head Start center, except in conjunction with school
PA: Plaza De La Raza Child Development Services, Inc.
13300 Crssrads Pkwy N Ste
La Puente CA
562 776-1301

(P-18348)
PRECIOUS ENTERPRISES INC
Also Called: Clement Preschool
14130 Douglass Ln (95070-5536)
PHONE..................................408 265-2226
Faz Ulla, *Owner*
Nilu Ulla, *
Shahana Shah, *
Husna Ulla, *
EMP: 62 EST: 1975
SQ FT: 7,500
SALES (est): 968.14K **Privately Held**
SIC: 8351 Preschool center

(P-18349)
PREGEL AMERICA INC
116 S Brent Cir (91789-3050)
PHONE..................................909 598-8980
EMP: 115
SALES (corp-wide): 161.91MM **Privately Held**
Web: www.pregelamerica.com
SIC: 8351 5149 Child day care services; Groceries and related products, nec
HQ: Pregel America, Inc.
4450 Fortune Ave Nw
Concord NC
704 707-0300

(P-18350)
PRIME HEALTH CARE
Also Called: San Dimas Community Hospital
1350 W Covina Blvd (91773-3245)
PHONE..................................909 394-2727
Prim Reddy, *Owner*
EMP: 140 EST: 2010
SALES (est): 6.15MM **Privately Held**
Web: www.primehealthcare.com
SIC: 8351 8062 Child day care services; General medical and surgical hospitals

(P-18351)
RGBX INC
Also Called: Heritage Oak Prvate Elmntary S
16971 Imperial Hwy (92886-1663)
PHONE..................................714 524-1350
Phyllis Cygan, *Pr*
Gregory Cygan, *
Latrese Jackson, *
Jennifer Tafolla, *
Kimberly Ford, *
EMP: 91 EST: 1992
SQ FT: 22,000
SALES (est): 6.54MM **Privately Held**
Web: www.heritageoak.org
SIC: 8351 8211 Preschool center; Elementary school, nec

(P-18352)
SIERRA CSCADE FMLY OPPRTNITIES (PA)
Also Called: HEAD START
424 N Mill Creek Rd (95971-9531)
PHONE..................................530 283-1242
Brenda Poteete, *Dir*
EMP: 65 EST: 1989
SQ FT: 2,600
SALES (est): 5.49MM **Privately Held**
Web: www.headstart4u.org

(P-18353)
SJB CHILD DEVELOPMENT CENTERS (PA)
Also Called: SICK CHILD CARE CENTER, THE
1400 Parkmoor Ave Ste 220 (95126-3429)
PHONE..................................408 538-0200
Victor Hassan, *CEO*
Kent Williams, *
EMP: 81 EST: 1971
SQ FT: 12,840
SALES (est): 16.72MM
SALES (corp-wide): 16.72MM **Privately Held**
Web: www.sjbcdc.org
SIC: 8351 Preschool center

(P-18354)
SOLANO FMLY & CHLD COUNCIL INC
Also Called: SOLANO FAMILY & CHILDREN'S SER
421 Executive Ct N (94534-4019)
PHONE..................................707 863-3950
Kathryn Lago, *Ex Dir*
EMP: 74 EST: 1978
SALES (est): 30.47MM **Privately Held**
Web: www.solanofamily.org
SIC: 8351 Child day care services

(P-18355)
STRATFORD SCHOOL INC
1999 S Bascom Ave Ste 400 (95008-2219)
PHONE..................................408 973-7320
Matthew Wulfstat, *CEO*
EMP: 357 EST: 2012
SALES (est): 26.21MM **Privately Held**
Web: www.stratfordschools.com
SIC: 8351 Preschool center

(P-18356)
SUNDALE FNDTION FOR STDNTS CMN
Also Called: Sundale School
13990 Avenue 240 (93274-9563)
PHONE..................................559 688-3419
Terri Rufert, *Pr*
Terry Rufert, *Superintnt*
Shirley Wasnick, *Sec*
EMP: 91 EST: 1950
SALES (est): 699.95K **Privately Held**
Web: www.sundaleschool.com
SIC: 8351 Head Start center, except in conjunction with school

(P-18357)
TEMPLE JDEA OF W SAN FRNNDO VL
Also Called: Temple Judea Nursery School
5429 Lindley Ave (91356-3703)
PHONE..................................818 758-3800
Margie Ipp, *Dir*
EMP: 77
SALES (corp-wide): 4.76MM **Privately Held**
Web: www.templejudea.com
SIC: 8351 8661 Child day care services; Synagogue
PA: Temple Judea Of The West San Fernando Valley
5429 Lindley Ave
Tarzana CA
818 758-3800

8361 - Residential Care (P-18379)

(P-18358)
TENET HEALTHSYSTEM MEDICAL INC
555 E Hardy St (90301-4011)
P.O. Box 720 (90312-6720)
PHONE.................310 673-4660
Steve Barker, *Brnch Mgr*
EMP: 67
SALES (corp-wide): 19.58B **Publicly Held**
Web: validate.perfdrive.com
SIC: 8351 Child day care services
HQ: Tenet Healthsystem Medical, Inc.
   14201 Dallas Pkwy
   Dallas TX
   469 893-2000

(P-18359)
THINK TOGETHER
202 E Airport Dr Ste 200 (92408-3429)
PHONE.................909 723-1400
EMP: 344
SALES (corp-wide): 75.71MM **Privately Held**
Web: www.thinktogether.org
SIC: 8351 Child day care services
PA: Think Together
   2101 E 4th St Ste 200b
   Santa Ana CA
   714 543-3807

(P-18360)
THINK TOGETHER
800 S Barranca Ave Ste 120 (91723-3625)
PHONE.................626 373-2311
Tom Lopez, *Brnch Mgr*
EMP: 345
SALES (corp-wide): 75.71MM **Privately Held**
Web: www.thinktogether.org
SIC: 8351 Child day care services
PA: Think Together
   2101 E 4th St Ste 200b
   Santa Ana CA
   714 543-3807

(P-18361)
THINK TOGETHER
22620 Goldencrest Dr Ste 104 (92553-9032)
PHONE.................951 571-9944
EMP: 345
SALES (corp-wide): 75.71MM **Privately Held**
Web: www.thinktogether.org
SIC: 8351 Child day care services
PA: Think Together
   2101 E 4th St Ste 200b
   Santa Ana CA
   714 543-3807

(P-18362)
TIGER WOODS LEARNING CENTER
1 Tiger Woods Way (92801-5039)
PHONE.................714 765-8040
Evan Tello, *Mgr*
EMP: 95 EST: 2006
SALES (est): 13.22MM **Privately Held**
SIC: 8351 Child day care services

(P-18363)
TUTOR TIME LEARNING CTRS LLC
5855 De Soto Ave (91367-5202)
PHONE.................818 710-1677
EMP: 189
Web: www.tutortime.com
SIC: 8351 Preschool center
HQ: Tutor Time Learning Centers, Llc
   21333 Haggerty Rd Ste 300
   Novi MI
   248 697-9000

(P-18364)
TUTOR TIME LEARNING CTRS LLC
5805 Corporate Ave (90630-4730)
PHONE.................714 484-1000
Jennifer Gardea, *Dir*
EMP: 177
Web: www.tutortime.com
SIC: 8351 Preschool center
HQ: Tutor Time Learning Centers, Llc
   21333 Haggerty Rd Ste 300
   Novi MI
   248 697-9000

(P-18365)
UNIPER CARE INC
3415 S Sepulveda Blvd (90034-6060)
PHONE.................888 471-7623
Rami Kirshblum, *CEO*
Avi Price, *COO*
EMP: 60 EST: 2020
SALES (est): 2.27MM **Privately Held**
Web: www.unipercare.com
SIC: 8351 Child day care services

(P-18366)
WE CARE SERVICES FOR CHILDREN
1450 Civic Ct Ste 200 (94520-7955)
PHONE.................925 685-0207
John Jones, *CEO*
EMP: 80
SALES (corp-wide): 3.88MM **Privately Held**
Web: www.wecarechildren.org
SIC: 8351 Preschool center
PA: We Care Services For Children
   2191 Kirker Pass Rd
   Concord CA
   925 671-0777

8361 Residential Care

(P-18367)
ADVENT GROUP MINISTRIES INC
90 Great Oaks Blvd Ste 108 (95119-1314)
PHONE.................408 281-0708
Jeff Davis, *Ch*
Mark Miller, *
Daniel Mahan, *Chief Administrator**
EMP: 63 EST: 1985
SQ FT: 4,400
SALES (est): 2.39MM **Privately Held**
Web: www.adventgm.org
SIC: 8361 Children's home

(P-18368)
AEGIS ASSSTED LIVING PRPTS LLC
Also Called: Aegis of Fremont
3850 Walnut Ave # 228 (94538-2263)
PHONE.................510 739-1515
Dave Peper, *Genl Mgr*
EMP: 117
SALES (corp-wide): 137.21MM **Privately Held**
Web: www.aegisliving.com
SIC: 8361 Aged home
HQ: Aegis Assisted Living Properties, Llc
   220 Concourse Blvd
   Santa Rosa CA
   707 535-3200

(P-18369)
AEGIS ASSSTED LIVING PRPTS LLC
Also Called: Aegis At Shadowridge
1440 S Melrose Dr (92056-5394)
PHONE.................760 806-3600
Gregory Case, *Mgr*
EMP: 117
SALES (corp-wide): 137.21MM **Privately Held**
Web: www.aegisliving.com
SIC: 8361 Aged home
HQ: Aegis Assisted Living Properties, Llc
   220 Concourse Blvd
   Santa Rosa CA
   707 535-3200

(P-18370)
AEGIS SENIOR COMMUNITIES LLC
Also Called: Aegis of Laguna Niguel
32170 Niguel Rd (92677-4264)
PHONE.................949 496-8080
Pamela Kerr, *Ex Dir*
EMP: 159
SALES (corp-wide): 137.21MM **Privately Held**
Web: www.aegisliving.com
SIC: 8361 Residential care
PA: Senior Aegis Communities Llc
   415 118th Ave Se
   Bellevue WA
   866 688-5829

(P-18371)
AEGIS SENIOR COMMUNITIES LLC
Also Called: Aegis of Moraga
950 Country Club Dr (94556-1922)
PHONE.................925 377-7900
Candice Moses, *Genl Mgr*
EMP: 147
SALES (corp-wide): 137.21MM **Privately Held**
Web: www.aegisliving.com
SIC: 8361 Aged home
PA: Senior Aegis Communities Llc
   415 118th Ave Se
   Bellevue WA
   866 688-5829

(P-18372)
ALLIANCE CHILDRENS SERVICES
Also Called: Mentor California
1001 Tower Way Ste 110 (93309-1586)
PHONE.................661 863-0350
Andretta Stokes, *Mgr*
EMP: 114
SALES (corp-wide): 4.3MM **Privately Held**
SIC: 8361 Mentally handicapped home
PA: Alliance Children's Services Inc
   313 Congress St Fl 5
   Boston MA
   617 790-4800

(P-18373)
APPLERIDGE ASSISTED LIVING INC
2030 23rd St (95818-1718)
PHONE.................916 451-1212
EMP: 151
SALES (corp-wide): 9.93MM **Privately Held**
Web: www.appleridgehome.com
SIC: 8361 Aged home
PA: Appleridge Assisted Living, Incorporated
   3950 Annadale Ln
   Sacramento CA
   916 489-6900

(P-18374)
ATRIA ASSISTED LIVING GROUP
Also Called: Atria Delsol
23792 Marguerite Pkwy (92692-1583)
PHONE.................949 427-8191
Michael D Ball, *Ex Dir*
Jeannine Sackett, *
Denise Platt, *
Iris Sanchez, *
EMP: 245 EST: 1983
SALES (est): 7.25MM
SALES (corp-wide): 4.13B **Publicly Held**
Web: www.atriaseniorliving.com
SIC: 8361 Aged home
HQ: Atria Management Company, Llc
   300 E Market St Ste 100
   Louisville KY

(P-18375)
ATRIA MANAGEMENT COMPANY LLC
5308 Monroe Ave (92115-3427)
PHONE.................619 326-0190
EMP: 124
SALES (corp-wide): 4.13B **Publicly Held**
Web: www.atriaseniorliving.com
SIC: 8361 Aged home
HQ: Atria Management Company, Llc
   300 E Market St Ste 100
   Louisville KY

(P-18376)
ATRIA MANAGEMENT COMPANY LLC
1342 N Escondido Blvd (92026-2508)
PHONE.................760 480-8155
EMP: 305
SALES (corp-wide): 4.13B **Publicly Held**
SIC: 8361 Aged home
HQ: Atria Management Company, Llc
   300 E Market St Ste 100
   Louisville KY

(P-18377)
ATRIA MANAGEMENT COMPANY LLC
Also Called: Atria Valley View
1228 Rossmoor Pkwy (94595-2532)
PHONE.................925 787-6149
EMP: 129
SALES (corp-wide): 4.13B **Publicly Held**
Web: www.atriaseniorliving.com
SIC: 8361 Aged home
HQ: Atria Management Company, Llc
   300 E Market St Ste 100
   Louisville KY

(P-18378)
ATRIA SENIOR LIVING INC
Also Called: Atria Park Pacific Palisades
15441 W Sunset Blvd (90272-3525)
PHONE.................310 573-9545
Elisa Brown, *Dir*
EMP: 60
SQ FT: 27,513
SALES (corp-wide): 4.13B **Publicly Held**
Web: www.atriaseniorliving.com
SIC: 8361 Aged home
HQ: Atria Senior Living Inc.
   300 E Market St Ste 100
   Louisville KY

(P-18379)
AVANTGARDE SENIOR LIVING
5645 Lindley Ave (91356-2557)
PHONE.................818 881-0055

8361 - Residential Care (P-18380)

Jason Adelman, *Prin*
EMP: 102 **EST:** 2010
SALES (est): 6.2MM **Privately Held**
Web: www.avantgardeseniorliving.com
SIC: 8361 Aged home

(P-18380)
BOYS REPUBLIC (PA)
Also Called: GIRLS REPUBLIC
1907 Boys Republic Dr (91709-5447)
PHONE.................909 902-6690
Dennis Slattery, *CEO*
Timothy J Kay, *
Robert Key, *
Jeff Seymour, *
Nadine Bosen, *
EMP: 150 **EST:** 1907
SQ FT: 173,000
SALES (est): 24.04MM
SALES (corp-wide): 24.04MM **Privately Held**
Web: www.boysrepublic.org
SIC: 8361 Group foster home

(P-18381)
BRETHREN HILLCREST HOMES
Also Called: HILLCREST
2705 Mountain View Dr Ofc (91750-4313)
PHONE.................909 593-4917
Matthew Neeley, *Pr*
Barbara Feliciano, *
EMP: 230 **EST:** 1947
SQ FT: 34,000
SALES (est): 28.63MM **Privately Held**
Web: www.livingathillcrest.org
SIC: 8361 8059 8051 Rest home, with health care incidental; Nursing home, except skilled and intermediate care facility; Extended care facility

(P-18382)
BRITTANY HOUSE LLC
5401 E Centralia St (90808-1452)
PHONE.................562 421-4717
Colleen Rosatti, *Ex Dir*
EMP: 107 **EST:** 1989
SQ FT: 43,018
SALES (est): 18.52MM
SALES (corp-wide): 40.58MM **Privately Held**
Web: www.activcareliving.com
SIC: 8361 Aged home
PA: Activcare Living, Inc.
10603 Rancho Bernardo Rd
San Diego CA
858 565-4424

(P-18383)
CALIFORNIA FRIENDS HOMES
Also Called: QUAKER GARDENS
12151 Dale Ave (90680-3889)
PHONE.................714 530-9100
Randy Brown, *CEO*
Gina Kolb, *
Glenda Hementiza, *
EMP: 315 **EST:** 1962
SQ FT: 10,000
SALES (est): 18.84MM **Privately Held**
Web: www.rowntreegardens.org
SIC: 8361 8051 Aged home; Convalescent home with continuous nursing care

(P-18384)
CARLTON SENIOR LIVING INC
380 Branham Ln Ofc Ofc (95136-4302)
PHONE.................408 972-1400
Mandi Farrell, *Dir*
EMP: 149
SALES (corp-wide): 45.36MM **Privately Held**
Web: www.carltonseniorliving.com
SIC: 8361 Residential care
PA: Senior Carlton Living Inc
4071 Port Chicago Hwy # 130
Concord CA
925 338-2434

(P-18385)
CARLTON SENIOR LIVING INC
Also Called: Senior Asssted Lving Cmnty Cht
175 Cleaveland Rd (94523-3875)
PHONE.................925 935-1001
Jeffrey Dillon, *Mgr*
EMP: 109
SALES (corp-wide): 45.36MM **Privately Held**
Web: www.carltonseniorliving.com
SIC: 8361 Residential care
PA: Senior Carlton Living Inc
4071 Port Chicago Hwy # 130
Concord CA
925 338-2434

(P-18386)
CARLTON SENIOR LIVING INC
1075 Fulton Ave Apt 208 (95825-4275)
PHONE.................916 971-4800
Timothy Macdonald, *Brnch Mgr*
EMP: 83
SALES (corp-wide): 45.36MM **Privately Held**
Web: www.carltonseniorliving.com
SIC: 8361 8052 8051 Residential care; Intermediate care facilities; Skilled nursing care facilities
PA: Senior Carlton Living Inc
4071 Port Chicago Hwy # 130
Concord CA
925 338-2434

(P-18387)
CASA DE AMPARO (PA)
325 Buena Creek Rd (92069-9679)
PHONE.................760 754-5500
Sharon Delphenich, *Ex Dir*
Tamara Fleck-myers, *Ex Dir*
Debbie Slattery, *
EMP: 74 **EST:** 1979
SQ FT: 25,000
SALES (est): 10.72MM
SALES (corp-wide): 10.72MM **Privately Held**
Web: www.casadeamparo.org
SIC: 8361 8351 Residential care; Child day care services

(P-18388)
CASA DE LAS CAMPANAS INC (PA)
18655 W Bernardo Dr (92127-3099)
PHONE.................858 451-9152
Jill Sorenson, *Ex Dir*
Robert L Reeves, *
David Johnson, *
EMP: 97 **EST:** 1988
SQ FT: 709,627
SALES (est): 49.52MM
SALES (corp-wide): 49.52MM **Privately Held**
Web: www.casadelascampanas.com
SIC: 8361 8052 8051 6513 Aged home; Intermediate care facilities; Skilled nursing care facilities; Apartment building operators

(P-18389)
CASA-PACIFICA INC
Also Called: Freedom Properties
2200 W Acacia Ave Ofc (92545-3737)
PHONE.................951 658-3369
Mary Ann Casino, *Dir*
EMP: 251
SALES (corp-wide): 26.84MM **Privately Held**
Web: www.casapacifica.org
SIC: 8361 8059 Geriatric residential care; Rest home, with health care
PA: Casa-Pacifica, Inc
23442 El Toro Rd
San Juan Capistrano CA
949 489-0430

(P-18390)
CASA-PACIFICA INC
Also Called: Freedom Properties Village
2400 W Acacia Ave (92545-3743)
PHONE.................951 766-5116
Valeria Machain, *Genl Mgr*
EMP: 251
SALES (corp-wide): 26.84MM **Privately Held**
Web: www.thevillageriversidecounty.com
SIC: 8361 8052 8051 6513 Aged home; Intermediate care facilities; Skilled nursing care facilities; Apartment building operators
PA: Casa-Pacifica, Inc
23442 El Toro Rd
San Juan Capistrano CA
949 489-0430

(P-18391)
CHAMBERLAINS CHILDREN CTR INC
1850 Cienega Rd (95023-5516)
P.O. Box 1269 (95024-1269)
PHONE.................831 636-2121
Robert Freiri, *Ex Dir*
EMP: 60 **EST:** 1965
SALES (est): 3.85MM **Privately Held**
Web: www.chamberlainsyouth.org
SIC: 8361 Residential care for children

(P-18392)
CHILDHELP INC
Also Called: Child Help Head Start Center
14700 Manzanita Rd (92223-3026)
P.O. Box 247 (92223-0247)
PHONE.................951 845-6737
Klara Pakozdi, *Mgr*
EMP: 126
SALES (corp-wide): 48.34MM **Privately Held**
Web: www.childhelp.org
SIC: 8361 Children's home
PA: Childhelp, Inc.
6730 N Scottsdale Rd # 150
Scottsdale AZ
480 922-8212

(P-18393)
CHILDRENS HOME OF STOCKTON
430 N Pilgrim St (95205-4428)
PHONE.................209 466-0853
Joelle Gomez, *CEO*
EMP: 140 **EST:** 1882
SQ FT: 10,000
SALES (est): 10.02MM **Privately Held**
Web: www.chstockton.org
SIC: 8361 Residential care

(P-18394)
CHRISTIAN CHURCH HOMES
Also Called: El-Bethel Terrace
1099 Fillmore St Apt6h (94115-4796)
PHONE.................415 814-2670
Babeth Avant, *Mgr*
EMP: 128
SALES (corp-wide): 25.11MM **Privately Held**
Web: www.cchnc.org
SIC: 8361 Aged home
PA: Christian Church Homes
1855 Olympic Blvd Ste 300
Walnut Creek CA
510 632-6712

(P-18395)
CLIFF VIEW TERRACE INC
Also Called: Mission Terrace
623 W Junipero St (93105-4213)
PHONE.................805 682-7443
Eve Murphy, *Mgr*
EMP: 83
SALES (corp-wide): 10.24MM **Privately Held**
Web: www.missionterracesb.com
SIC: 8361 8051 Aged home; Convalescent home with continuous nursing care
PA: Cliff View Terrace, Inc.
1020 Cliff Dr
Santa Barbara CA
805 963-7556

(P-18396)
CLIFF VIEW TERRACE INC
Also Called: Marin Terrace
297 Miller Ave (94941-2832)
PHONE.................415 388-9526
Araceli Pareja, *Dir*
EMP: 84
SQ FT: 2,534
SALES (corp-wide): 10.24MM **Privately Held**
Web: www.cliffviewterracesb.com
SIC: 8361 Aged home
PA: Cliff View Terrace, Inc.
1020 Cliff Dr
Santa Barbara CA
805 963-7556

(P-18397)
COLLWOOD TER STELLAR CARE INC
4518 54th St (92115-3527)
PHONE.................619 287-2920
Chris Cho, *Pr*
EMP: 90 **EST:** 2008
SALES (est): 4.38MM **Privately Held**
Web: www.stellarcaresd.com
SIC: 8361 Aged home

(P-18398)
COMMUNITY ACTION PARTNR KERN
1611 1st St (93304-2901)
PHONE.................661 336-5300
Aniko Matis, *Dir*
EMP: 69
SALES (corp-wide): 117.9MM **Privately Held**
Web: www.capk.org
SIC: 8361 Rehabilitation center, residential: health care incidental
PA: Community Action Partnership Of Kern
5005 Business Park N
Bakersfield CA
661 336-5236

(P-18399)
COMPASS HEALTH INC
Also Called: Wyndham Residence
222 S Elm St (93420-6012)
PHONE.................805 474-7260
Mark Woolpert, *Pr*
EMP: 155
Web: www.wyndhamresidence.com
SIC: 8361 Aged home
PA: Compass Health, Inc.
200 S 13th St Ste 208
Grover Beach CA

PRODUCTS & SERVICES SECTION

8361 - Residential Care (P-18420)

(P-18400)
CORECARE III
Also Called: Morningside of Fullerton
800 Morningside Dr (92835-3597)
PHONE.................714 256-8000
Carl Wilkins, *Admn*
EMP: 130 EST: 1989
SQ FT: 24,000
SALES (est): 13.7MM **Privately Held**
Web: www.morningsideoffullerton.com
SIC: **8361** 8052 Aged home; Intermediate care facilities

(P-18401)
COUNSELING AND RESEARCH ASSOC (PA)
Also Called: MASADA HOMES
108 W Victoria St (90248-3523)
P.O. Box 47001 (90247-6801)
PHONE.................310 715-2020
George Igi, *Ex Dir*
Bernard Smith, *
EMP: 125 EST: 1966
SQ FT: 2,500
SALES (est): 16.77MM
SALES (corp-wide): 16.77MM **Privately Held**
Web: www.masadahomes.org
SIC: **8361** Children's home

(P-18402)
COUNTY OF LOS ANGELES
1605 Eastlake Ave (90033-1009)
PHONE.................323 226-8611
Richard Shumsky, *Mgr*
EMP: 99
SALES (corp-wide): 31.7B **Privately Held**
Web: www.lacounty.gov
SIC: **8361** 9111 Juvenile correctional facilities ; Executive offices
PA: County Of Los Angeles
500 W Temple St Ste 437
Los Angeles CA
213 974-1101

(P-18403)
COUNTY OF LOS ANGELES
Also Called: San Fernando Juvenile Hall
16350 Filbert St (91342-1002)
PHONE.................818 364-2011
Dan Torres, *Superintnt*
EMP: 63
SALES (corp-wide): 31.7B **Privately Held**
Web: www.lacounty.gov
SIC: **8361** 9223 8093 Juvenile correctional home; Correctional institutions; Mental health clinic, outpatient
PA: County Of Los Angeles
500 W Temple St Ste 437
Los Angeles CA
213 974-1101

(P-18404)
COUNTY OF SAN DIEGO
Also Called: Health & Human Svcs
1255 Imperial Ave Ste 433 (92101-7404)
PHONE.................619 338-2558
Shirley Downs, *Brnch Mgr*
EMP: 69
Web: www.sandiegocounty.gov
SIC: **8361** 9441 Aged home; Administration of social and manpower programs
PA: County Of San Diego
1600 Pacific Hwy Ste 209
San Diego CA
619 531-5880

(P-18405)
COUNTY OF YUBA
Also Called: Yuba County Juvenile Hall
1023 14th St (95901-4115)
PHONE.................530 741-6371
Theresa Dove Weber, *Mgr*
EMP: 93
SQ FT: 2,293
SALES (corp-wide): 233.12MM **Privately Held**
Web: www.yuba.org
SIC: **8361** 9111 Juvenile correctional facilities ; County supervisors' and executives' office
PA: County Of Yuba
915 8th St Ste 109
Marysville CA
530 749-7575

(P-18406)
COVENANT HOUSE CALIFORNIA
Also Called: CHC
1325 N Western Ave (90027-5615)
PHONE.................323 461-3131
Luz Juan, *CEO*
George Lozano, *
Patrick S Mccabe, *Ex Dir*
EMP: 150 EST: 1986
SQ FT: 16,000
SALES (est): 20.29MM **Privately Held**
Web: www.covenanthousecalifornia.org
SIC: **8361** Children's home

(P-18407)
COVENANT LIVING WEST
Also Called: Covenant Living At Mt Miguel
325 Kempton St (91977-5810)
PHONE.................619 931-1114
Thad Rothrock, *Mgr*
EMP: 80
Web: www.covlivingmountmiguel.org
SIC: **8361** Aged home
HQ: Covenant Living West
5700 Old Orchard Rd # 10
Skokie IL

(P-18408)
COVENANT LIVING WEST
Also Called: Covenant Living At Samarkand
2550 Treasure Dr (93105-4148)
PHONE.................805 687-0701
Kenneth D Noreen, *Admn*
EMP: 80
Web: www.covliving.org
SIC: **8361** 8059 Aged home; Rest home, with health care
HQ: Covenant Living West
5700 Old Orchard Rd # 10
Skokie IL

(P-18409)
COVENANT LIVING WEST
Also Called: Covenant Living of Turlock
2125 N Olive Ave (95382-1947)
PHONE.................209 632-9976
Admiral Dwayne Gabrielson, *Brnch Mgr*
EMP: 80
Web: www.covlivingturlock.org
SIC: **8361** 8052 8051 Rest home, with health care incidental; Intermediate care facilities; Skilled nursing care facilities
HQ: Covenant Living West
5700 Old Orchard Rd # 10
Skokie IL

(P-18410)
CREATIVE ALTERNATIVES
2855 Geer Rd Ste A (95382-1102)
PHONE.................209 668-9361
Stephanie Biddle, *CEO*
EMP: 220 EST: 1976
SQ FT: 40,000
SALES (est): 14.93MM **Privately Held**
Web: www.creative-alternatives.org
SIC: **8361** 8211 8322 Children's home; Private special education school; Child related social services

(P-18411)
CREATIVE LIVING OPTIONS INC
2945 Ramco St Ste 120 (95691-5800)
PHONE.................916 372-2102
Joan Schmidt, *CEO*
Mary Anne Delaney, *
EMP: 115 EST: 2001
SALES (est): 4.81MM **Privately Held**
Web: www.creativelivingoptions.com
SIC: **8361** Physically handicapped home

(P-18412)
CRESTWOOD BEHAVIORAL HLTH INC
Also Called: 1170 Lompoc Mhrc
303 S C St (93436-7305)
PHONE.................805 308-8720
Charlotte Acosta, *Admn*
EMP: 85
SALES (corp-wide): 278.96MM **Privately Held**
Web: www.crestwoodbehavioralhealth.com
SIC: **8361** Residential care
PA: Crestwood Behavioral Health, Inc.
520 Capitol Mall Ste 800
Sacramento CA
209 955-2326

(P-18413)
CRI-HELP INC (PA)
Also Called: CRI HELP DRUG REHABILITATION
11027 Burbank Blvd (91601-2431)
P.O. Box 899 (91603-0899)
PHONE.................818 985-8323
Jack Bernstein, *Pr*
Markus Sola, *
Anthony Edmonson, *
EMP: 71 EST: 1971
SQ FT: 40,000
SALES (est): 10.37MM
SALES (corp-wide): 10.37MM **Privately Held**
Web: www.cri-help.org
SIC: **8361** 8069 Rehabilitation center, residential: health care incidental; Drug addiction rehabilitation hospital

(P-18414)
DAVID AND MARGARET HOME INC
Also Called: David Margaret Youth Fmly Svcs
1350 3rd St (91750-5299)
PHONE.................909 596-5921
Arun Tolia, *Pr*
Cindy Walkenbach, *
Charles C Rich, *
Timothy Evans, *
Sabina Sullivan, *
EMP: 240 EST: 1910
SQ FT: 40,000
SALES (est): 16.71MM **Privately Held**
Web: www.davidandmargaret.org
SIC: **8361** 8322 Emotionally disturbed home; Individual and family services

(P-18415)
DELANCEY STREET FOUNDATION (PA)
Also Called: DELANCEY STREET COACH SERVICE
600 The Embarcadero (94107-2116)
PHONE.................415 957-9800
Mimi Silbert, *Pr*
Jerry Raymond, *
EMP: 400 EST: 1971
SQ FT: 325,000
SALES (est): 7.45MM
SALES (corp-wide): 7.45MM **Privately Held**
Web: www.delanceystreetfoundation.org
SIC: **8361** 5199 8322 4212 Rehabilitation center, residential: health care incidental; Advertising specialties; Individual and family services; Moving services

(P-18416)
DEVELPMNTAL SVCS CONTINUUM INC
7944 Golden Ave (91945-1810)
PHONE.................619 460-7333
Elaine Lewis, *Pr*
EMP: 75 EST: 1982
SALES (est): 4.33MM **Privately Held**
SIC: **8361** Group foster home

(P-18417)
DOMINICAN HOSPITAL FOUNDATION
Also Called: Dominican Rehab Services
610 Frederick St (95062-2203)
PHONE.................831 457-7057
Debbie Hite, *Brnch Mgr*
EMP: 244
Web: www.dignityhealth.org
SIC: **8361** 8093 Rehabilitation center, residential: health care incidental; Rehabilitation center, outpatient treatment
HQ: Dominican Hospital Foundation
1555 Soquel Dr
Santa Cruz CA
831 462-7700

(P-18418)
DREAM HOME CARE INC
20695 S Western Ave Ste 132 (90501)
PHONE.................562 595-9021
Cora Manalang, *CEO*
Hazel Manalang, *
Reynaldo David, *
EMP: 60 EST: 1994
SALES (est): 3.14MM **Privately Held**
SIC: **8361** Group foster home

(P-18419)
E R I T INC (PA)
Also Called: TERI COMMON GROUNDS CAFE & COF
251 Airport Rd (92058-1201)
PHONE.................760 433-6024
Cheryl Kilmer, *Ex Dir*
William E Mara, *
EMP: 85 EST: 1980
SQ FT: 15,000
SALES (est): 24.07MM
SALES (corp-wide): 24.07MM **Privately Held**
Web: www.teriinc.org
SIC: **8361** Retarded home

(P-18420)
EDGEWOOD CTR FOR CHLDREN FMLIE (PA)
1801 Vicente St (94116-2923)
PHONE.................415 681-3211
Lynn Dolce, *CEO*
EMP: 224 EST: 1850
SQ FT: 100,000
SALES (est): 31.01MM
SALES (corp-wide): 31.01MM **Privately Held**

8361 - Residential Care (P-18421)

Web: www.edgewood.org
SIC: **8361** 8211 8322 8093 Emotionally disturbed home; Specialty education; Child related social services; Specialty outpatient clinics, nec

(P-18421)
ENSIGN GROUP INC
1405 E Main St (93454-4801)
PHONE.................................805 925-8713
Shawn Taylor, *Brnch Mgr*
EMP: 130
SALES (corp-wide): 3.03B **Publicly Held**
Web: www.ensigngroup.net
SIC: **8361** 6513 Geriatric residential care; Retirement hotel operation
PA: The Ensign Group Inc
  29222 Rncho Vejo Rd Ste 1
  San Juan Capistrano CA
  949 487-9500

(P-18422)
ESKATON
3421 Palmer Dr (95682-8200)
PHONE.................................530 672-8900
Orvile Bell, *Brnch Mgr*
EMP: 217
SQ FT: 23,400
SALES (corp-wide): 156.38MM **Privately Held**
Web: www.eskaton.org
SIC: **8361** Aged home
PA: Eskaton
  5105 Manzanita Ave Ste D
  Carmichael CA
  916 334-0296

(P-18423)
ESKATON
11390 Coloma Rd Ofc (95670-6324)
PHONE.................................916 852-7900
Tonae Hasik, *Mgr*
EMP: 216
SALES (corp-wide): 156.38MM **Privately Held**
Web: www.eskaton.org
SIC: **8361** Aged home
PA: Eskaton
  5105 Manzanita Ave Ste D
  Carmichael CA
  916 334-0296

(P-18424)
ESKATON PROPERTIES INC
Also Called: President James Monroe Manor
3225 Freeport Blvd Ofc (95818-4200)
PHONE.................................916 441-1015
Joe Dunham, *Pr*
EMP: 121
Web: www.eskaton.org
SIC: **8361** Aged home
PA: Eskaton Properties Incorporated
  5105 Manzanita Ave Ste A
  Carmichael CA

(P-18425)
ESKATON PROPERTIES INC
3421 Palmer Dr (95682-8200)
PHONE.................................530 677-5066
EMP: 122
Web: www.eskaton.org
SIC: **8361** Aged home
PA: Eskaton Properties Incorporated
  5105 Manzanita Ave Ste A
  Carmichael CA

(P-18426)
ESKATON PROPERTIES INC
Also Called: Eskaton Village Roseville
1650 Eskaton Loop (95747-5180)
PHONE.................................916 334-0810
Vicki Cross, *Mgr*
EMP: 122
Web: www.eskaton.org
SIC: **8361** Aged home
PA: Eskaton Properties Incorporated
  5105 Manzanita Ave Ste A
  Carmichael CA

(P-18427)
ESKATON PROPERTIES INC
Also Called: Homestead of Fair Oaks
11300 Fair Oaks Blvd (95628-5141)
PHONE.................................916 965-4663
Tom Coffey, *Mgr*
EMP: 122
SIC: **8361** Aged home
PA: Eskaton Properties Incorporated
  5105 Manzanita Ave Ste A
  Carmichael CA

(P-18428)
ESKATON PROPERTIES INC
Also Called: Eskaton Center of Greenhaven
455 Florin Rd (95831-2024)
PHONE.................................916 393-2550
Heather Craig, *Mgr*
EMP: 122
Web: www.eskaton.org
SIC: **8361** Aged home
PA: Eskaton Properties Incorporated
  5105 Manzanita Ave Ste A
  Carmichael CA

(P-18429)
ESKATON PROPERTIES INC (PA)
Also Called: 0EPI
5105 Manzanita Ave Ste A (95608-0523)
PHONE.................................916 334-0810
Todd Murch, *Pr*
Bill Pace, *
Betsy Donovan, *
Sheri Peifer, *
Charles Garcia, *
▲ **EMP:** 60 **EST:** 1983
SQ FT: 27,000
SALES (est): 101.97MM **Privately Held**
SIC: **8361** Aged home

(P-18430)
ESKATON PROPERTIES INC
Also Called: Eskaton Village Charmichael
3939 Walnut Ave Unit 399 (95608-7333)
PHONE.................................916 974-2000
EMP: 122
Web: www.eskaton.org
SIC: **8361** Aged home
PA: Eskaton Properties Incorporated
  5105 Manzanita Ave Ste A
  Carmichael CA

(P-18431)
EVOLVE GROWTH INITIATIVES LLC
Also Called: Evolve Treatment Centers
820 Moraga Dr (90049-1632)
PHONE.................................424 281-5000
Menachem Baron, *CEO*
EMP: 120 **EST:** 2014
SQ FT: 1,700
SALES (est): 3.54MM **Privately Held**
Web: www.evolvetreatment.com
SIC: **8361** 8093 Rehabilitation center, residential: health care incidental; Mental health clinic, outpatient

(P-18432)
FELLOWSHIP HOMES INC
Also Called: CASA DE MODESTO
1745 Eldena Way (95350-3568)
PHONE.................................209 529-4950
Carolyn Amaral, *Admn*
Curt Willems, *
EMP: 150 **EST:** 1965
SALES (est): 10.03MM **Privately Held**
Web: www.casademodesto.org
SIC: **8361** Aged home

(P-18433)
FIVE ACRES - THE BYS GRLS AID
Also Called: FIVE ACRES
760 Mountain View St (91001-4925)
PHONE.................................626 798-6793
Chanel W Boutakidis, *CEO*
Daniel Braun, *
Cathy Clement, *OF PHILANTHROPHY**
Robert A Ketch, *Executive Director Emeritus**
Kim Hutchigs, *
EMP: 419 **EST:** 1888
SQ FT: 70,000
SALES (est): 44.13MM **Privately Held**
SIC: **8361** 8322 8211 Children's home; Public welfare center; Public combined elementary and secondary school

(P-18434)
FLORENCE CRTTNTON SVCS ORNGE C
Also Called: CRITTENTON SERVICES FOR CHILDR
801 E Chapman Ave Ste 203 (92831-3846)
P.O. Box 9 (92836-0009)
PHONE.................................714 680-9000
Joyce Capelle, *CEO*
EMP: 320 **EST:** 1966
SALES (est): 36.22MM **Privately Held**
Web: www.crittentonsocal.org
SIC: **8361** Residential care for children

(P-18435)
FRONT PORCH COMMUNITIES & SVCS
100 Bay Pl Ofc (94610-4422)
PHONE.................................510 835-4700
Christopher Iechien, *Mgr*
EMP: 143
Web: www.covia.org
SIC: **8361** 8052 8051 Aged home; Intermediate care facilities; Skilled nursing care facilities
PA: Front Porch Communities And Services
  800 N Brand Blvd Fl 19
  Glendale CA

(P-18436)
FRONT PORCH COMMUNITIES & SVCS
651 Sinex Ave (93950-4253)
PHONE.................................831 373-3111
TOLL FREE: 800
Norma Brenbella, *Mgr*
EMP: 78
Web: www.covia.org
SIC: **8361** Aged home
PA: Front Porch Communities And Services
  800 N Brand Blvd Fl 19
  Glendale CA

(P-18437)
FRONT PORCH COMMUNITIES & SVCS
5555 Montgomery Dr (95409-8846)
P.O. Box 1105 (95416-1105)
PHONE.................................707 538-8400
Sharon York, *Mgr*
EMP: 198
Web: www.covia.org
SIC: **8361** 6531 8052 8051 Aged home; Real estate managers; Intermediate care facilities; Skilled nursing care facilities
PA: Front Porch Communities And Services
  800 N Brand Blvd Fl 19
  Glendale CA

(P-18438)
FRONT PORCH COMMUNITIES & SVCS
1661 Pine St Apt 911 (94109-0410)
PHONE.................................415 776-0500
Donna Teandler, *Brnch Mgr*
EMP: 182
Web: www.covia.org
SIC: **8361** 8052 8051 Aged home; Intermediate care facilities; Skilled nursing care facilities
PA: Front Porch Communities And Services
  800 N Brand Blvd Fl 19
  Glendale CA

(P-18439)
GENERATION CLOVIS LLC
Also Called: Carmel Village At Clovis
1650 Shaw Ave (93611-4201)
PHONE.................................559 297-4900
Erik Schuck, *Admn*
EMP: 150 **EST:** 2019
SALES (est): 9.14MM **Privately Held**
Web: www.generationsllc.com
SIC: **8361** Aged home

(P-18440)
GOOD SHEPHERD LUTHERAN HM OF W
1335 Mowry Ave (94538-1701)
PHONE.................................510 505-1244
Nina Bosley, *Mgr*
EMP: 93
SQ FT: 16,000
SALES (corp-wide): 14.31MM **Privately Held**
Web: www.grauranch.com
SIC: **8361** 8399 Residential care for the handicapped; Fund raising organization, non-fee basis
PA: Good Shepherd Lutheran Home Of The West
  24800 Chrisanta Dr # 250
  Mission Viejo CA
  559 791-2000

(P-18441)
GOOD SHEPHERD LUTHERAN HM OF W
2949 Alamo St (93063-2185)
PHONE.................................805 526-2482
Brian Dietrich, *Prin*
EMP: 163
SALES (corp-wide): 14.31MM **Privately Held**
Web: www.gsls-simi.com
SIC: **8361** 8059 Residential care for the handicapped; Personal care home, with health care
PA: Good Shepherd Lutheran Home Of The West
  24800 Chrisanta Dr # 250
  Mission Viejo CA
  559 791-2000

(P-18442)
GOOD SHEPHERD LUTHERAN HM OF W
1696 S Helm Ave (93727-5111)
PHONE.................................559 454-8514
EMP: 70
SALES (corp-wide): 14.31MM **Privately Held**

PRODUCTS & SERVICES SECTION

8361 - Residential Care (P-18463)

Web: www.grauranch.com
SIC: **8361** 8059 Residential care for the handicapped; Home for the mentally retarded, ex. skilled or intermediate
PA: Good Shepherd Lutheran Home Of The West
24800 Chrisanta Dr # 250
Mission Viejo CA
559 791-2000

(P-18443)
GREENRIDGE SENIOR CARE
2150 Pyramid Dr (94803-3220)
PHONE.................................510 758-9600
Linda Joseph, *Dir*
Linda Joseph, *Owner*
EMP: 110 EST: 2004
SALES (est): 7.71MM **Privately Held**
Web: www.greenridgeseniorcare.com
SIC: **8361** Aged home

(P-18444)
HAMBURGER HOME (PA)
Also Called: AVIVA CENTER
7120 Franklin Ave (90046-3002)
PHONE.................................323 876-0550
Regina Bette, *Pr*
EMP: 90 EST: 1915
SQ FT: 25,000
SALES (est): 17.58MM
SALES (corp-wide): 17.58MM **Privately Held**
Web: www.aviva.org
SIC: **8361** Children's home

(P-18445)
HARBOR HEALTH CARE INC
9461 Flower St (90706-5705)
PHONE.................................562 866-7054
Cheryl Hutchins, *Pr*
EMP: 200 EST: 1999
SALES (est): 10.04MM **Privately Held**
Web: www.harborhealthcare.org
SIC: **8361** Mentally handicapped home

(P-18446)
HATHAWY-SYCMRES CHILD FMLY SVC
840 N Avenue 66 (90042-1508)
PHONE.................................323 257-9600
Jim Cheney, *Pr*
EMP: 92
SALES (corp-wide): 64.09MM **Privately Held**
Web: www.sycamores.org
SIC: **8361** 8093 Emotionally disturbed home; Mental health clinic, outpatient
PA: Hathaway-Sycamores Child And Family Services
100 W Walnut St Ste 375
Pasadena CA
626 395-7100

(P-18447)
HATHAWY-SYCMRES CHILD FMLY SVC (PA)
Also Called: SYCAMORES
100 W Walnut St Ste 375 (91103-3744)
PHONE.................................626 395-7100
Michael Galper, *Ch Bd*
William Martone, *
EMP: 65 EST: 1920
SQ FT: 75,175
SALES (est): 64.09MM
SALES (corp-wide): 64.09MM **Privately Held**
Web: www.sycamores.org
SIC: **8361** 8093 Emotionally disturbed home; Mental health clinic, outpatient

(P-18448)
HAYNES FAMILY PROGRAMS INC
Also Called: LEROY HAYNES CENTER
233 Baseline Rd (91750-2353)
P.O. Box 400 (91750-0400)
PHONE.................................909 593-2581
Daniel Maydeck, *Pr*
Tony Williams, *
Frank Linebaugh, *
EMP: 125 EST: 1946
SQ FT: 72,466
SALES (est): 22.85MM **Privately Held**
Web: www.leroyhaynes.org
SIC: **8361** 8211 8099 Boys' towns; Specialty education; Medical services organization

(P-18449)
HEALTHVIEW INC (PA)
Also Called: Harbor View House
921 S Beacon St (90731-3740)
PHONE.................................310 638-4113
Susan Jane Major, *CEO*
EMP: 135 EST: 1965
SQ FT: 110,000
SALES (est): 4.67MM
SALES (corp-wide): 4.67MM **Privately Held**
Web: www.hvi.com
SIC: **8361** 8052 Mentally handicapped home; Home for the mentally retarded, with health care

(P-18450)
HOLLENBECK PALMS
Also Called: HOLLENBECK HOME FOR THE AGED
24431 Lyons Ave Apt 336 (91321-2342)
PHONE.................................323 263-6195
William G Heideman Junior, *Pr*
Johnny Young, *Contrlr*
Morris Shockley, *VP*
EMP: 170 EST: 1890
SALES (est): 21.48MM **Privately Held**
Web: www.hollenbeckpalms.com
SIC: **8361** Aged home

(P-18451)
HOME GUIDING HANDS CORPORATION (PA)
1908 Friendship Dr (92020-1129)
PHONE.................................619 938-2850
Mark Klaus, *CEO*
Carol A Fitzgibbons, *
Jan Adams, *
EMP: 266 EST: 1961
SALES (est): 29.77MM
SALES (corp-wide): 29.77MM **Privately Held**
Web: www.guidinghands.org
SIC: **8361** 8052 Residential care for the handicapped; Intermediate care facilities

(P-18452)
HOPE HSE FOR MLTPLE HNDCPPED I (PA)
Also Called: Schmitt House
4215 Peck Rd (91732-2113)
PHONE.................................626 443-1313
D Bernstein, *Ex Dir*
David Bernstein, *
EMP: 100 EST: 1963
SQ FT: 15,000
SALES (est): 9.55MM
SALES (corp-wide): 9.55MM **Privately Held**
Web: www.hopehouse.org
SIC: **8361** Residential care for the handicapped

(P-18453)
HUMANGOOD NORCAL
Also Called: San Joaquin Gardens
5555 N Fresno St (93710-6006)
PHONE.................................559 439-4770
Keli Swales, *Brnch Mgr*
EMP: 215
SALES (corp-wide): 27.02MM **Privately Held**
Web: www.humangood.org
SIC: **8361** 8051 Aged home; Skilled nursing care facilities
HQ: Humangood Norcal
1900 Huntington Dr
Duarte CA
925 924-7100

(P-18454)
HUMANGOOD NORCAL
Also Called: Grand Lake Gardens
401 Santa Clara Ave Apt 522 (94610-1967)
PHONE.................................510 893-8897
Adnan Hasan, *Mgr*
EMP: 222
SALES (corp-wide): 27.02MM **Privately Held**
Web: www.humangood.org
SIC: **8361** Aged home
HQ: Humangood Norcal
1900 Huntington Dr
Duarte CA
925 924-7100

(P-18455)
HUMANGOOD SOCAL
Also Called: White Sands Of La Jolla Clinic
7450 Olivetas Ave Ofc (92037-4900)
PHONE.................................858 454-4201
Wendy Matalon, *Brnch Mgr*
EMP: 233
SALES (corp-wide): 27.02MM **Privately Held**
Web: www.humangood.org
SIC: **8361** 8051 Aged home; Skilled nursing care facilities
HQ: Humangood Socal
1900 Huntington Dr
Duarte CA
925 924-7138

(P-18456)
HUMANGOOD SOCAL
Also Called: Buena Vista Manor
802 Buena Vista St (91010-1702)
PHONE.................................626 359-8141
Judy Phornkein, *Mgr*
EMP: 125
SALES (corp-wide): 27.02MM **Privately Held**
Web: www.humangood.org
SIC: **8361** Aged home
HQ: Humangood Socal
1900 Huntington Dr
Duarte CA
925 924-7138

(P-18457)
HUMANGOOD SOCAL
Also Called: Redwood Senior Homes & Svcs
710 W 13th Ave (92025-5511)
PHONE.................................760 747-4306
EMP: 215
SQ FT: 8,552
SALES (corp-wide): 27.02MM **Privately Held**
Web: www.humangood.org
SIC: **8361** Aged home
HQ: Humangood Socal
1900 Huntington Dr
Duarte CA
925 924-7138

(P-18458)
INDEPENDENT OPTIONS INC
2625 Sherwood Ave (92831-1418)
PHONE.................................714 738-4991
P Dennis Mattson, *Pr*
EMP: 100
SALES (corp-wide): 15.69MM **Privately Held**
Web: www.independentoptions.org
SIC: **8361** 8059 Mentally handicapped home; Personal care home, with health care
PA: Independent Options, Inc.
391 Corporate Terrace Cir # 102
Corona CA
951 279-2585

(P-18459)
INDEPENDENT OPTIONS INC
5095 Murphy Canyon Rd (92123-4348)
PHONE.................................858 598-5260
EMP: 99
SALES (corp-wide): 15.69MM **Privately Held**
Web: www.independentoptions.org
SIC: **8361** Mentally handicapped home
PA: Independent Options, Inc.
391 Corporate Terrace Cir # 102
Corona CA
951 279-2585

(P-18460)
INNOVATIVE INTEGRATED HLTH INC (PA)
Also Called: Fresno Pace
2042 Kern St (93721-2008)
PHONE.................................559 400-6420
Ibrahim Marouf, *Prin*
EMP: 150 EST: 2016
SALES (est): 11.17MM
SALES (corp-wide): 11.17MM **Privately Held**
Web: www.innovativeih.com
SIC: **8361** Residential care

(P-18461)
ISL EMPLOYEES INC
Also Called: Integral Senior Living
2333 State St Ste 300 (92008-1691)
PHONE.................................760 547-2863
Sue Farrow, *CEO*
Tracee Degrande, *
Collette Valentine, *
EMP: 71 EST: 2011
SALES (est): 8.57MM **Privately Held**
Web: www.islllc.com
SIC: **8361** Residential care

(P-18462)
J & L DAYCARE
Also Called: V.O.I.C.E.
24723 Redlands Blvd Ste A-C (92354)
PHONE.................................909 796-2656
Les Spoelstra, *Owner*
EMP: 65
SIC: **8361** Retarded home
PA: J & L Daycare
415 Tennessee St Ste U
Redlands CA

(P-18463)
KENSINGTON SIERRA MADRE LP
Also Called: Kensington At Sierra Madre
245 W Sierra Madre Blvd (91024-2355)
PHONE.................................626 355-5700
Dave Faeder, *Pt*
EMP: 71 EST: 2014
SALES (est): 12.27MM **Privately Held**

8361 - Residential Care (P-18464)

Web:
www.thekensingtonsierramadre.com
SIC: 8361 Aged home

(P-18464)
LAMP INC
Also Called: Lamp Community
2116 Arlington Ave Lbby (90018-1365)
PHONE................................213 488-9559
Donna Gallup, CEO
Kim Carson, *
EMP: 110 EST: 1985
SQ FT: 4,500
SALES (est): 14.53MM Privately Held
Web: www.lampcommunity.org
SIC: 8361 Residential care for the handicapped

(P-18465)
LAS VILLAS DEL NORTE
1325 Las Villas Way (92026-1946)
PHONE................................760 741-1047
Jolene M Farish, Ex Dir
EMP: 180 EST: 1989
SALES (est): 6.65MM Privately Held
Web:
www.lasvillasdelnorteseniorliving.com
SIC: 8361 8051 Geriatric residential care; Skilled nursing care facilities

(P-18466)
LBN LEISURE CARE LLC
Also Called: Woodlake, The
1445 Expo Pkwy (95815-5118)
PHONE................................916 604-3780
EMP: 81 EST: 2019
SALES (est): 5.4MM
SALES (corp-wide): 106.71MM Privately Held
Web: www.leisurecare.com
SIC: 8361 Aged home
HQ: Leisure Care, Llc
    999 3rd Ave Ste 4550
    Seattle WA
    206 436-7827

(P-18467)
LEISURE CARE LLC
Also Called: Heritage Estates-Livermore
800 E Stanley Blvd (94550-2800)
PHONE................................925 371-2300
EMP: 66
SALES (corp-wide): 106.71MM Privately Held
Web: www.leisurecare.com
SIC: 8361 Aged home
HQ: Leisure Care, Llc
    999 3rd Ave Ste 4550
    Seattle WA
    206 436-7827

(P-18468)
LEISURE CARE LLC
Also Called: Springfield Place
101 Ely Blvd S (94954-3861)
PHONE................................707 769-3300
Jeralyn May, Genl Mgr
EMP: 167
SALES (corp-wide): 106.71MM Privately Held
Web: www.leisurecare.com
SIC: 8361 Aged home
HQ: Leisure Care, Llc
    999 3rd Ave Ste 4550
    Seattle WA
    206 436-7827

(P-18469)
LEISURE CARE LLC
Also Called: Nohl Ranch Inn

380 S Anaheim Hills Rd Ofc (92807-4026)
PHONE................................714 974-1616
Wanda Reynolds, Brnch Mgr
EMP: 124
SQ FT: 82,222
SALES (corp-wide): 106.71MM Privately Held
Web: www.leisurecare.com
SIC: 8361 8051 Aged home; Skilled nursing care facilities
HQ: Leisure Care, Llc
    999 3rd Ave Ste 4550
    Seattle WA
    206 436-7827

(P-18470)
LEISURE CARE LLC
Also Called: Fairwinds Woodward Park
9525 N Fort Washington Rd (93730-0662)
PHONE................................559 434-1237
Coint Folwer, Brnch Mgr
EMP: 150
SALES (corp-wide): 106.71MM Privately Held
Web: www.leisurecare.com
SIC: 8361 Aged home
HQ: Leisure Care, Llc
    999 3rd Ave Ste 4550
    Seattle WA
    206 436-7827

(P-18471)
LEISURE CARE LLC
Also Called: Wellington Crt Asssted Lving C
601 Sunset Blvd (91007-6319)
PHONE................................626 447-0106
Tamara Pribble, Mgr
EMP: 118
SALES (corp-wide): 106.71MM Privately Held
Web: www.leisurecare.com
SIC: 8361 Aged home
HQ: Leisure Care, Llc
    999 3rd Ave Ste 4550
    Seattle WA
    206 436-7827

(P-18472)
LINCOLN CHILD CENTER INC
Also Called: Hope Contra Costa
51 Marina Blvd (94565-2068)
PHONE................................925 521-1270
Allison Staulcup, Prin
EMP: 80
SALES (corp-wide): 24.68MM Privately Held
Web: www.lincolnfamilies.org
SIC: 8361 Mentally handicapped home
PA: Lincoln
    1266 14th St
    Oakland CA
    510 273-4700

(P-18473)
LINCOLN GLEN MANOR LLC
Also Called: Lincoln Glen Skilled Nursing
2671 Plummer Ave Ste A (95125-4863)
PHONE................................408 267-1492
Loren Kroeker, Ex Dir
Barbara Filler, *
EMP: 86 EST: 1965
SQ FT: 68,000
SALES (est): 7.98MM Privately Held
Web: www.lgmanor.org
SIC: 8361 Aged home

(P-18474)
LITTLE SSTERS OF THE POOR OKLA
Also Called: ST ANNE'S HOME

300 Lake St (94118-1357)
PHONE................................415 751-6510
Patricia Metzgar, Pr
EMP: 90 EST: 1902
SQ FT: 110,000
SALES (est): 10.48MM Privately Held
Web:
www.littlesistersofthepoorsanfrancisco.org
SIC: 8361 8661 Aged home; Religious organizations

(P-18475)
LONGWOOD MANAGEMENT CORP
Also Called: Rosecrans Villa
14110 Cordary Ave (90250-8005)
PHONE................................310 675-9163
Boris Blumkin, Mgr
EMP: 85
SALES (corp-wide): 79.33MM Privately Held
Web: www.longwoodmgmt.com
SIC: 8361 Aged home
PA: Longwood Management Corp.
    4032 Wilshire Blvd Fl 6
    Los Angeles CA
    213 389-6900

(P-18476)
LOS ANGELES MISSION INC (PA)
303 E 5th St (90013-1505)
P.O. Box 55900 (90055-0630)
PHONE................................213 629-1227
Troy Vaughn, CEO
Herb Smith, *
Steve Kennedy, *
EMP: 77 EST: 1977
SALES (est): 21.41MM
SALES (corp-wide): 21.41MM Privately Held
Web: www.losangelesmission.org
SIC: 8361 Destitute home

(P-18477)
LOS ANGELES RESIDENTIAL COMM F
29890 Bouquet Canyon Rd (91390-5111)
PHONE................................661 296-8636
Kathy Sturky, Ex Dir
EMP: 85 EST: 1959
SQ FT: 5,000
SALES (est): 4.7MM Privately Held
Web: www.larcfoundation.org
SIC: 8361 8322 8051 Mentally handicapped home; Individual and family services; Skilled nursing care facilities

(P-18478)
MAGNOLIA OF MILLBRAE INC
201 Chadbourne Ave (94030-2570)
PHONE................................650 697-7700
Vincent Muzzi, Pr
EMP: 93 EST: 1986
SALES (est): 5.62MM Privately Held
Web: www.themagnolia.com
SIC: 8361 Aged home

(P-18479)
MARYVALE
7600 Graves Ave (91770-3414)
P.O. Box 1039 (91770-1000)
PHONE................................626 280-6510
Steve Gunter, CEO
EMP: 152 EST: 2011
SALES (est): 16.3MM Privately Held
Web: www.maryvale.org
SIC: 8361 8322 Residential care for children; Public welfare center

(P-18480)
MASONIC HOMES OF CALIFORNIA (PA)
1111 California St (94108-2252)
PHONE................................415 776-7000
Terry Quigley, Pr
Andrew Uehling, *
Allan L Casalou, *
Timothy A Wood, *
Dixie Reeve, *
EMP: 375 EST: 1898
SQ FT: 8,000
SALES (est): 41.94MM
SALES (corp-wide): 41.94MM Privately Held
Web: www.masonichome.org
SIC: 8361 Children's home

(P-18481)
MASONIC HOMES OF CALIFORNIA
Also Called: Masonic Home For Adults
34400 Mission Blvd (94587-3604)
PHONE................................510 441-3700
Gilbert Smart, Brnch Mgr
EMP: 350
SALES (corp-wide): 41.94MM Privately Held
Web: www.masonichome.org
SIC: 8361 8051 Rest home, with health care incidental; Skilled nursing care facilities
PA: Masonic Homes Of California Inc
    1111 California St
    San Francisco CA
    415 776-7000

(P-18482)
MCKINLEY CHILDRENS CENTER INC (PA)
180 Via Verde Ste 200 (91773-3901)
PHONE................................909 599-1227
Anil Vadatary, CEO
Michael Frazer, *
EMP: 190 EST: 1890
SALES (est): 31.38MM
SALES (corp-wide): 31.38MM Privately Held
Web: www.mckinleycc.org
SIC: 8361 8211 Boys' towns; Private elementary and secondary schools

(P-18483)
MEADOWBROOK VLG CHRSTN RTRMENT
100 Holland Gln (92026-1354)
PHONE................................760 746-2500
Jacob Bronwer, Pr
Sarah Rogh, *
EMP: 109 EST: 2004
SALES (est): 10.74MM Privately Held
Web: www.meadowbrookvillage.org
SIC: 8361 Aged home

(P-18484)
MERCEDES DIAZ HOMES INC
7239 Washington Ave Ste 100 (90602-1418)
PHONE................................562 945-4576
Mercedes Diaz, Pr
Ramon Diaz, *
EMP: 60 EST: 1980
SALES (est): 9.34MM Privately Held
Web: www.mdhnetwork.com
SIC: 8361 Residential care

(P-18485)
MERCY RETIREMENT AND CARE CTR

PRODUCTS & SERVICES SECTION

8361 - Residential Care (P-18506)

3431 Foothill Blvd (94601-3199)
PHONE.....................510 534-8540
Jesse Jantzen, CEO
EMP: 92 EST: 1872
SQ FT: 125,000
SALES (est): 21.84MM Privately Held
Web: www.eldercarealliance.org
SIC: 8361 8051 Aged home; Skilled nursing care facilities

(P-18486)
MGH CORPORATION
Also Called: Mitchells Group Home
1202 W 101st St (90044-1802)
PHONE.....................323 754-1408
EMP: 64 EST: 1985
SALES (est): 9.5MM Privately Held
Web: www.massgeneralbrigham.org
SIC: 8361 Geriatric residential care

(P-18487)
MILESTONE RTRMENT CMMNTIES LLC
20420 Rafferty Ct (95372-9783)
PHONE.....................209 533-4822
EMP: 90
SALES (corp-wide): 284.23MM Privately Held
Web: www.milestoneretirement.com
SIC: 8361 Aged home
PA: Milestone Retirement Communities, Llc
  12500 Se 2nd Cir Ste 205
  Vancouver WA
  360 882-4500

(P-18488)
MISSION HILLS SENIOR LIVING
34560 Bob Hope Dr (92270-1727)
PHONE.....................760 770-7737
Roland Gandy, Ex Dir
EMP: 62 EST: 2015
SALES (est): 865.03K Privately Held
Web: www.missionhillsseniorliving.com
SIC: 8361 Aged home

(P-18489)
MONTE VISTA GROVE HOMES
2889 San Pasqual St (91107-5364)
PHONE.....................626 796-6135
M Helen Baatz, Ex Dir
EMP: 85 EST: 1924
SQ FT: 12,000
SALES (est): 5.68MM Privately Held
Web: www.mvgh.org
SIC: 8361 Aged home

(P-18490)
MORNINGSTAR SENIOR MGT LLC
Also Called: Morningstar of Mission Viejo
28570 Marguerite Pkwy (92692-3713)
PHONE.....................949 298-3675
Dyan Summerell, Ex Dir
EMP: 119
SALES (corp-wide): 95.1MM Privately Held
Web: www.morningstarseniorliving.com
SIC: 8361 Residential care
PA: Morningstar Senior Management, Llc
  7555 E Hampden Ave # 501
  Denver CO
  303 750-5522

(P-18491)
MOTHER LODE RHBLTTION ENTPS IN
Also Called: MORE WORKSHOP
399 Placerville Dr (95667-3912)
PHONE.....................530 622-4848
Susie Davies, Ex Dir
EMP: 150 EST: 1969
SALES (est): 2.65MM Privately Held
Web: www.morerehab.org
SIC: 8361 8322 Rehabilitation center, residential: health care incidental; Individual and family services

(P-18492)
NATIONAL MENTOR HOLDINGS INC
Also Called: Horrigan Cole Enterprises
30033 Technology Dr (92563-3520)
PHONE.....................951 677-1453
EMP: 318
SALES (corp-wide): 1.7B Privately Held
Web: www.sevitahealth.com
SIC: 8361 Residential care
HQ: National Mentor Holdings, Inc.
  313 Congress St Fl 5
  Boston MA
  617 790-4800

(P-18493)
NINOS LATINO UNIDOS FSA
10016 Pioneer Blvd # 123 (90670-3245)
PHONE.....................562 801-5454
EMP: 60
SALES (est): 6.83MM Privately Held
Web: www.nlu.org
SIC: 8361 8322 Group foster home; Individual and family services

(P-18494)
NOIA RESIDENTIAL SERVICES INC
606 E Belmont Ave Ste 101 (93701-1527)
PHONE.....................559 485-5555
Lucia Noia, CEO
Bonda Aranas, *
EMP: 96 EST: 1986
SQ FT: 9,767
SALES (est): 2.15MM Privately Held
Web: noia-residential-services-inc.hub.biz
SIC: 8361 Destitute home

(P-18495)
NORTHERN CA RETIREDD OFCRS
Also Called: PARADISE VALLEY ESTATES
2600 Estates Dr (94533-9711)
PHONE.....................707 432-1200
James G Mertz, CEO
Debra Murphy, *
EMP: 225 EST: 1992
SALES (est): 24.91MM Privately Held
Web: www.pvestates.com
SIC: 8361 Aged home

(P-18496)
NORTHERN CALIFORNIA PRESBYTERI
Also Called: Sequoias, The
501 Portola Rd Ste 500 (94028-7654)
PHONE.....................650 851-1501
Jay Sumner, Dir
EMP: 155
SALES (corp-wide): 114.59MM Privately Held
Web: www.sequoialiving.org
SIC: 8361 Geriatric residential care
PA: Sequoia Living, Inc.
  1525 Post St
  San Francisco CA
  415 202-7808

(P-18497)
NURSECORE MANAGEMENT SVCS LLC
1010 S Broadway Ste A (93454-6600)
PHONE.....................805 938-7660
Veronica Aburto, Brnch Mgr
EMP: 571
Web: www.nursecore.com
SIC: 8361 8082 8049 7361 Residential care; Home health care services; Nurses and other medical assistants; Nurses' registry
PA: Nursecore Management Services, Llc
  2201 Brookhollow Plaza Dr # 450
  Arlington TX

(P-18498)
ODD FELLOW-REBEKAH CHLD HM CAL (PA)
Also Called: Rebekah Children's Services
290 I O O F Ave (95020-5204)
PHONE.....................408 846-2100
Nancy Johnson, CEO
Christophe Rebboah, *
EMP: 164 EST: 1897
SQ FT: 46,000
SALES (est): 25.07MM
SALES (corp-wide): 25.07MM Privately Held
Web: www.rcskids.org
SIC: 8361 8093 Emotionally disturbed home; Mental health clinic, outpatient

(P-18499)
ODD FELLOWS HOME CALIFORNIA
Also Called: SARATOGA RETIREMENT COMMUNITY
14500 Fruitvale Ave Bldg 1000 (95070-6129)
PHONE.....................408 741-7100
Admiral Cathy Schumacher, Prin
Cathy Schumacher, Executive Administrator
EMP: 275 EST: 1853
SALES (est): 77.36MM Privately Held
Web: www.saratogaretirement.org
SIC: 8361 8051 Aged home; Skilled nursing care facilities

(P-18500)
OLIVE CREST (PA)
Also Called: Olive Crest
2130 E 4th St Ste 200 (92705-3818)
PHONE.....................714 543-5437
Donald A Verleur, CEO
Lois Verleur, *
EMP: 300 EST: 1973
SQ FT: 40,000
SALES (est): 69.49MM
SALES (corp-wide): 69.49MM Privately Held
Web: www.olivecrest.org
SIC: 8361 8322 Emotionally disturbed home; Individual and family services

(P-18501)
OMNITRANS
Also Called: Omnitrans Access
234 S I St (92410-2408)
PHONE.....................909 383-1680
Brian Niemann, Prin
EMP: 219
SALES (corp-wide): 8.48MM Privately Held
Web: www.omnitrans.org
SIC: 8361 Physically handicapped home
PA: Omnitrans
  1700 W 5th St
  San Bernardino CA
  909 379-7100

(P-18502)
PACIFIC LODGE YOUTH SVCS INC
Also Called: Pacific Lodge Boy's Home
4900 Serrania Ave (91364-3301)
P.O. Box 308 (91365-0308)
PHONE.....................818 347-1577
Leslie King, Ch
Lisa Alegria, *
EMP: 110 EST: 1923
SQ FT: 22,634
SALES (est): 5.01K Privately Held
Web: www.oyhfs.org
SIC: 8361 Residential care

(P-18503)
PACIFIC RETIREMENT SVCS INC
Also Called: University Retirement Cmnty
1515 Shasta Dr Ofc (95616-6695)
PHONE.....................530 753-1450
Mark Blazer, Ex Dir
EMP: 758
Web: www.retirement.org
SIC: 8361 Aged home
PA: Pacific Retirement Services, Inc.
  1 W Main St Ste 303
  Medford OR

(P-18504)
PEPPERMINT RIDGE (PA)
Also Called: Ridge
825 Magnolia Ave (92879-3129)
PHONE.....................951 273-7320
Danette Mccarnes, Ex Dir
EMP: 83 EST: 1965
SQ FT: 25,000
SALES (est): 8.2MM
SALES (corp-wide): 8.2MM Privately Held
Web: www.peppermintridge.org
SIC: 8361 8322 Mentally handicapped home; Individual and family services

(P-18505)
PHOENIX HOUSES LOS ANGELES INC
Also Called: PHOENIX HOUSE
11600 Eldridge Ave (91342-6506)
PHONE.....................818 686-3000
Winifred Wechsler, Pr
EMP: 99 EST: 2000
SALES (est): 8.68MM
SALES (corp-wide): 16.69MM Privately Held
SIC: 8361 Rehabilitation center, residential: health care incidental
PA: Phoenix Houses Of California, Inc.
  11600 Eldridge Ave
  Sylmar CA
  818 896-1121

(P-18506)
PROFESSIONAL HEALTH CARE INC
Also Called: Monterey Bay Residental Care
555 Francis Ave (93955-5708)
PHONE.....................831 899-2644
Nerissa Ramos, Owner
EMP: 90
SALES (corp-wide): 4.47MM Privately Held
Web: www.anjelicasvilla.com
SIC: 8361 Aged home
PA: Professional Health Care, Inc.
  735 Pacific St
  Monterey CA
  831 373-1323

8361 - Residential Care (P-18507)

(P-18507)
RANCHO SAN ANTNIO RTRMENT HSIN
Also Called: Forum At Rancho San Antonio
23500 Cristo Rey Dr (95014-6503)
PHONE..................650 265-2637
Ken Fullmore, *Ex Dir*
EMP: 302 EST: 1990
SALES (est): 24.31MM **Privately Held**
Web: www.theforum-seniorliving.com
SIC: **8361** 8051 Rest home, with health care incidental; Skilled nursing care facilities

(P-18508)
RANCHO SAN ANTONIO BOYS HM INC (PA)
21000 Plummer St (91311-4903)
PHONE..................818 882-6400
Aubree Sweeney, *Ex Dir*
Brother John Crowe, *
Nicholas Rizzo, *Finance**
EMP: 100 EST: 1933
SALES (est): 15.32MM
SALES (corp-wide): 15.32MM **Privately Held**
Web: www.ranchosanantonio.org
SIC: **8361** Boys' towns

(P-18509)
REDWOOD ELDERLINK SCPH
Also Called: Redwood Elderlink & Homelink
710 W 13th Ave (92025-5511)
PHONE..................760 480-1030
Kurt Norden, *Dir*
Tom Vedvick, *Ch*
Dan Johnson, *Pr*
Fran Hillebrecht, *Treas*
Doug Best, *Sec*
EMP: 430 EST: 1989
SQ FT: 200,000
SALES (est): 4.6MM
SALES (corp-wide): 27.02MM **Privately Held**
Web: www.humangood.org
SIC: **8361** 8742 Aged home; Compensation and benefits planning consultant
HQ: Humangood Socal
1900 Huntington Dr
Duarte CA
925 924-7138

(P-18510)
REGENT ASSISTED LIVING INC
Also Called: Regent Senior Living W Covina
150 S Grand Ave Ofc (91791-2355)
PHONE..................626 332-3344
Lorena Arechiga, *Mgr*
EMP: 67
SIC: **8361** Aged home
PA: Regent Assisted Living, Inc.
121 Sw Morrison St # 950
Portland OR

(P-18511)
REGENT ASSISTED LIVING INC
Also Called: Sunshine Villa Assisted Living
80 Front St (95060-5098)
PHONE..................831 459-8400
EMP: 143
SIC: **8361** 8052 Aged home; Intermediate care facilities
PA: Regent Assisted Living, Inc.
121 Sw Morrison St # 950
Portland OR

(P-18512)
REMI VISTA INC
370 9th St (95531-3432)
PHONE..................707 464-4349
Doug Tippman, *Brnch Mgr*
EMP: 78
SALES (corp-wide): 12.63MM **Privately Held**
Web: www.remivistainc.org
SIC: **8361** 8063 Residential care for the handicapped; Psychiatric hospitals
PA: Vista Remi Inc
2701 Park Marina Dr
Redding CA
530 245-5805

(P-18513)
RES-CARE INC
611 S Central Ave (91204-2008)
PHONE..................818 637-7727
Michael Sowerby, *Mgr*
EMP: 68
SALES (corp-wide): 5.27B **Privately Held**
Web: www.rescare.com
SIC: **8361** Residential care
HQ: Res-Care, Inc.
805 N Whittington Pkwy
Louisville KY
502 394-2100

(P-18514)
ROSEMARY CHILDRENS SERVICES (PA)
36 S Kinneloa Ave # 200 (91107-3853)
PHONE..................626 844-3033
Greg Wessels, *Ex Dir*
Sungo Wang, *
Lynn Lu, *
Veronica Fuentes, *
Lesley Evangelista, *
EMP: 101 EST: 1920
SQ FT: 9,000
SALES (est): 4.42MM
SALES (corp-wide): 4.42MM **Privately Held**
Web: www.rosemarychildren.org
SIC: **8361** Emotionally disturbed home

(P-18515)
ROSS VALLEY HOMES INC
Also Called: TAMALPAIS
501 Via Casitas (94904-1901)
PHONE..................415 461-2300
David Berg, *CEO*
Don Meninga, *
Belinda Ong, *
EMP: 100 EST: 2002
SALES (est): 25.53MM **Privately Held**
Web: www.sequoialiving.org
SIC: **8361** Aged home

(P-18516)
RVM DAVIS HOUSING CORPORATION
Also Called: Shasta Point Retirement Cmnty
1501 Shasta Dr (95616-6696)
PHONE..................530 747-7095
EMP: 133 EST: 2007
SALES (est): 1.55MM **Privately Held**
SIC: **8361** Geriatric residential care
PA: Pacific Retirement Services, Inc.
1 W Main St Ste 303
Medford OR

(P-18517)
S L START AND ASSOCIATES LLC
Also Called: Pacific Place Retirement
3500 Lake Blvd (92056-4600)
PHONE..................760 414-9411
Ree Marina, *Dir*
EMP: 75
SALES (corp-wide): 25.08MM **Privately Held**

Web: www.slstart.com
SIC: **8361** Residential care for the handicapped
PA: S. L. Start And Associates Llc
5709 W Sunset Hwy Ste 100
Spokane WA
509 328-2740

(P-18518)
SACRAMENTO CHILDRENS HOME (PA)
2750 Sutterville Rd (95820-1024)
PHONE..................916 452-3981
Roy Alexander, *CEO*
Julia Chubb, *
EMP: 125 EST: 1867
SQ FT: 15,500
SALES (est): 26.91MM
SALES (corp-wide): 26.91MM **Privately Held**
Web: www.kidshome.org
SIC: **8361** Children's home

(P-18519)
SAN FRNCSCO LDIES PRTCTION RLI
Also Called: HERITAGE, THE
3400 Laguna St (94123-2271)
PHONE..................415 931-3136
Marla Hastings, *Admn*
EMP: 146 EST: 1853
SQ FT: 15,000
SALES (est): 14.95MM **Privately Held**
Web: www.heritageonthemarina.org
SIC: **8361** Aged home

(P-18520)
SENIOR KEIRO HEALTH CARE
Also Called: Japanese Retirement Home
325 S Boyle Ave (90033-3812)
PHONE..................323 263-9651
Shawn Miyake, *CEO*
George Aratani, *
Reverend David Shigekawa, *Treas*
EMP: 60 EST: 1974
SQ FT: 50,000
SALES (est): 6.82MM **Privately Held**
Web: www.keiro.org
SIC: **8361** Aged home

(P-18521)
SILVERADO SNIOR LVING HLDNGS
6400 Oak Cyn Ste 200 (92618-5201)
PHONE..................949 240-7200
Loren B Shook, *CEO*
Kristina Hulsey, *Chief Compliance Officer**
EMP: 4000 EST: 2010
SALES (est): 153.97MM **Privately Held**
Web: www.silverado.com
SIC: **8361** Aged home

(P-18522)
SISTERS OF NZARETH LOS ANGELES
3333 Manning Ave (90064-4804)
PHONE..................310 839-2361
Margarette Brody, *Admn*
EMP: 100 EST: 1935
SQ FT: 62,558
SALES (est): 6.65MM **Privately Held**
Web: www.sistersofnazareth.com
SIC: **8361** Aged home

(P-18523)
SOLHEIM LUTHERAN HOME
2236 Merton Ave (90041-1915)
PHONE..................323 257-7518
James Graunke, *Prin*

Norma Heaton, *
Antonio Davila, *
Sherry Wait, *
EMP: 185 EST: 1923
SQ FT: 82,591
SALES (est): 15.16MM **Privately Held**
Web: www.solheimlutheran.org
SIC: **8361** Aged home

(P-18524)
ST ANNES FAMILY SERVICES
155 N Occidental Blvd (90026-4641)
PHONE..................213 381-2931
Lorna Little, *Pr*
Mike Cazares, *CFO*
Janice Kanellis Cpoo, *Prin*
EMP: 158 EST: 1941
SQ FT: 100,000
SALES (est): 37.32MM **Privately Held**
Web: www.stannes.org
SIC: **8361** Rehabilitation center, residential: health care incidental

(P-18525)
ST PAULS EPISCOPAL HOME INC
2635 2nd Ave Ofc (92103-6597)
PHONE..................619 239-2097
EMP: 72
SALES (corp-wide): 34.55MM **Privately Held**
Web: www.stpaulseniors.org
SIC: **8361** Aged home
PA: St. Paul's Episcopal Home, Inc.
328 Maple St
San Diego CA
619 239-6900

(P-18526)
ST PAULS EPISCOPAL HOME INC
Also Called: St Paul's Villa
2700 E 4th St (91950-3006)
PHONE..................619 232-2996
Cheryl Wilson, *Dir*
EMP: 72
SALES (corp-wide): 34.55MM **Privately Held**
Web: www.stpaulseniors.org
SIC: **8361** Aged home
PA: St. Paul's Episcopal Home, Inc.
328 Maple St
San Diego CA
619 239-6900

(P-18527)
ST PAULS EPISCOPAL HOME INC
Saint Pauls Health Care Center
235 Nutmeg St (92103-6201)
PHONE..................619 239-8687
Ben Geske, *Mgr*
EMP: 72
SQ FT: 1,100
SALES (corp-wide): 34.55MM **Privately Held**
Web: www.stpaulseniors.org
SIC: **8361** 8051 Rest home, with health care incidental; Skilled nursing care facilities
PA: St. Paul's Episcopal Home, Inc.
328 Maple St
San Diego CA
619 239-6900

(P-18528)
SUNRISE SENIOR LIVING MGT INC
Also Called: Claremont Pl Assisted Living
120 W San Jose Ave (91711-5294)

8361 - Residential Care (P-18547)

PHONE..............................909 447-5259
Nancy Halleck, *Ex Dir*
EMP: 218
SQ FT: 4,900
SALES (corp-wide): 2.92B **Privately Held**
Web: www.sunriseseniorliving.com
SIC: 8361 8051 8082 Geriatric residential care; Skilled nursing care facilities; Home health care services
HQ: Sunrise Senior Living Management, Inc.
  7902 Westpark Dr
  Mc Lean VA
  703 273-7500

(P-18529)
SUPER HOME INC
Also Called: Maintnnce Repr For Rsdntial Hm
120 2nd St Ste 400 (94105-3602)
PHONE..............................844 997-8737
Jorey Ramer, *CEO*
Jorey Ramer, *Pr*
Cari Nick, *
Bianca Reyes, *
EMP: 100 **EST:** 2014
SALES (est): 5.49MM **Privately Held**
Web: www.hellosuper.com
SIC: 8361 Residential care

(P-18530)
SUSAN J HARRIS INC
Also Called: Therapy Specialist
344 F St Ste 100 (91910-2645)
PHONE..............................619 498-8450
EMP: 211
SALES (corp-wide): 21.68MM **Privately Held**
Web: www.therapyspecialists.net
SIC: 8361 8049 Rehabilitation center, residential: health care incidental; Occupational therapist
PA: New Life Physical Therapy Services San Diego, Inc.
  344 F St Ste 202
  Chula Vista CA
  858 514-0375

(P-18531)
THE REDWOODS A CMNTY SENIORS
Also Called: Redwoods, The
40 Camino Alto Ofc (94941-2997)
PHONE..............................415 383-2741
Barbara Solomon, *CEO*
Susan Badger, *
Alan Kern, *
Ron Bruno, *
EMP: 140 **EST:** 1970
SQ FT: 140,000
SALES (est): 25.75MM **Privately Held**
Web: www.theredwoods.org
SIC: 8361 Aged home

(P-18532)
TIERRA DEL SOL FOUNDATION (PA)
9919 Sunland Blvd (91040-1529)
PHONE..............................818 352-1419
Steve Miller, *Ex Dir*
EMP: 95 **EST:** 1971
SQ FT: 20,000
SALES (est): 21.23MM
SALES (corp-wide): 21.23MM **Privately Held**
Web: www.tierradelsol.org
SIC: 8361 8211 8322 Mentally handicapped home; Public special education school; Individual and family services

(P-18533)
TRINITY YOUTH SERVICES (PA)
201 N Indian Hill Blvd Ste 201 (91711-4610)
P.O. Box 1210 (91711-1210)
PHONE..............................909 825-5588
Cher Ofstedahl, *CEO*
John Neiuber, *
Nathan Mitakides, *
Aris Alexandre, *
John Alexandres, *
EMP: 60 **EST:** 1965
SQ FT: 7,600
SALES (est): 17.1MM
SALES (corp-wide): 17.1MM **Privately Held**
Web: www.trinityys.org
SIC: 8361 Halfway home for delinquents and offenders

(P-18534)
TULE RIVER ALCOHOLISM PROGRAM
Also Called: Tule River Tibal Council
1010 N Reservation Rd (93257-9680)
PHONE..............................559 781-8797
Joseph Garfield, *Dir*
EMP: 60 **EST:** 1979
SALES (est): 423.88K **Privately Held**
Web: www.tulerivertribe-nsn.gov
SIC: 8361 Rehabilitation center, residential: health care incidental

(P-18535)
UNIVERSITY CAL SAN FRNCSCO FND
Also Called: Ucsf Center On Deafness
3333 California St Ste 10 (94118-6200)
PHONE..............................415 775-2111
Nancy Moser, *Dir*
EMP: 72
SALES (corp-wide): 722.54MM **Privately Held**
Web: www.ucsf.edu
SIC: 8361 Deaf or blind home
PA: University Of California, San Francisco Foundation
  220 Montgomery St Ste 500
  San Francisco CA
  415 476-6922

(P-18536)
VALLEY TEEN RANCH
2610 W Shaw Ln Ste 105 (93711-2775)
PHONE..............................559 437-1144
Connie Clendenan, *Ex Dir*
EMP: 76 **EST:** 1983
SQ FT: 9,996
SALES (est): 3.88MM **Privately Held**
Web: www.valleyteenranch.org
SIC: 8361 8322 Group foster home; Individual and family services

(P-18537)
VALLEY-MNTAIN REGIONAL CTR INC
1620 Cummins Dr (95358-6400)
PHONE..............................209 529-2626
Richard Jacobs, *Brnch Mgr*
EMP: 90
SALES (corp-wide): 283.32MM **Privately Held**
Web: www.vmrc.net
SIC: 8361 Residential care for the handicapped
PA: Valley-Mountain Regional Center, Inc.
  702 N Aurora St
  Stockton CA
  209 473-0951

(P-18538)
VICTOR TREATMENT CENTERS INC
Also Called: Victor Treatment Centers
1053 N D St (92410-3521)
PHONE..............................951 436-5200
Jana Trew, *Brnch Mgr*
EMP: 74
SALES (corp-wide): 23.04MM **Privately Held**
Web: www.victor.org
SIC: 8361 Emotionally disturbed home
PA: Victor Treatment Centers, Inc.
  1360 E Lassen Ave
  Chico CA
  530 893-0758

(P-18539)
VICTOR TREATMENT CENTERS INC
Also Called: Willow Creek Treatment Center
341 Irwin Ln (95401-5603)
PHONE..............................707 360-1509
Gala Goodwin, *Brnch Mgr*
EMP: 110
SQ FT: 3,060
SALES (corp-wide): 23.04MM **Privately Held**
Web: www.victor.org
SIC: 8361 Emotionally disturbed home
PA: Victor Treatment Centers, Inc.
  1360 E Lassen Ave
  Chico CA
  530 893-0758

(P-18540)
VILLA SIENA
1855 Miramonte Ave # 117 (94040-4029)
PHONE..............................650 961-6484
Corrine Bernard, *CEO*
EMP: 68 **EST:** 1985
SQ FT: 40,000
SALES (est): 8.55MM **Privately Held**
Web: www.villa-siena.org
SIC: 8361 Aged home

(P-18541)
VILLAGE AT NORTHRIDGE
9222 Corbin Ave (91324-2409)
PHONE..............................818 514-4497
EMP: 111 **EST:** 2008
SALES (est): 20.69MM
SALES (corp-wide): 189.7MM **Privately Held**
Web: www.srgseniorliving.com
SIC: 8361 Aged home
PA: Senior Resource Group, Llc
  500 Stevens Ave Ste 100
  Solana Beach CA
  858 792-9300

(P-18542)
VILLAS DE CRLSBAD LTD A CAL LT
Also Called: Las Villas De Carlsbad
3500 Lake Blvd (92056-4600)
PHONE..............................760 434-7116
Jack Rowe, *Owner*
EMP: 97
SIC: 8361 Aged home
PA: Villas De Carlsbad, Ltd., A California Limited Partnership
  9619 Chesapeake Dr # 103
  San Diego CA

(P-18543)
VISTA DEL MAR CHILD FMLY SVCS
1533 Euclid St (90404-3306)
PHONE..............................310 836-1223
Louis Josephson, *Brnch Mgr*
EMP: 238
SALES (corp-wide): 40.28MM **Privately Held**
Web: www.vistadelmar.org
SIC: 8361 Mentally handicapped home
PA: Vista Del Mar Child And Family Services
  3200 Motor Ave
  Los Angeles CA
  310 836-1223

(P-18544)
WALDEN HOUSE INC
Also Called: Multi- Services
1735 Mission St (94103-2417)
PHONE..............................415 554-1131
Fermin Loza, *Brnch Mgr*
EMP: 170
SALES (corp-wide): 26.49MM **Privately Held**
Web: www.waldenhouse.org
SIC: 8361 8093 Group foster home; Specialty outpatient clinics, nec
PA: Walden House, Inc.
  520 Townsend St
  San Francisco CA
  415 554-1100

(P-18545)
WALDEN HOUSE INC
845 E Arrow Hwy (91767-2535)
PHONE..............................626 258-0300
Grace Gerarto, *Mgr*
EMP: 128
SALES (corp-wide): 26.49MM **Privately Held**
Web: www.waldenhouse.org
SIC: 8361 Group foster home
PA: Walden House, Inc.
  520 Townsend St
  San Francisco CA
  415 554-1100

(P-18546)
WALDEN HOUSE INC
Also Called: Walden House Adolescent
214 Haight St (94102-6127)
PHONE..............................415 554-1480
Bunny Cushman, *Dir*
EMP: 162
SQ FT: 24,000
SALES (corp-wide): 26.49MM **Privately Held**
Web: www.waldenhouse.org
SIC: 8361 Rehabilitation center, health care incidental
PA: Walden House, Inc.
  520 Townsend St
  San Francisco CA
  415 554-1100

(P-18547)
WESTMONT LIVING INC
Also Called: Terraces of Roseville, The
707 Sunrise Ave (95661-4524)
PHONE..............................916 786-3277
Andrew Plant, *Pr*
EMP: 239
SALES (corp-wide): 46.22MM **Privately Held**
Web: www.theterracesseniorliving.com
SIC: 8361 Aged home
PA: Westmont Living, Inc.
  7660 Fay Ave Ste N
  La Jolla CA
  858 456-1233

8361 - Residential Care (P-18548)

(P-18548)
WESTMONT LIVING INC (PA)
7660 Fay Ave Ste N (92037-4841)
PHONE..................................858 456-1233
Michael O Rourke, *CEO*
Andrew Plant, *
Leo Mckinley, *CFO*
EMP: 66 EST: 2008
SALES (est): 46.22MM
SALES (corp-wide): 46.22MM Privately Held
Web: www.westmontliving.com
SIC: 8361 Aged home

(P-18549)
WHITE RABBIT PARTNERS INC
9000 W Sunset Blvd Ste 1500 (90069-5815)
PHONE..................................310 975-1450
Andrew W Spanswick, *CEO*
Andrew William Spanswick, *CEO*
EMP: 150 EST: 2009
SALES (est): 3.82MM Privately Held
SIC: 8361 Residential care

(P-18550)
WIDER CIRCLE INC
50 Woodside Plz Ste 743 (94061-2500)
PHONE..................................650 924-2491
Moshe Pinto, *CEO*
EMP: 92 EST: 2016
SALES (est): 10.19MM Privately Held
Web: www.widercircle.com
SIC: 8361 Rehabilitation center, residential: health care incidental

(P-18551)
WORKING ALTERNATIVES INC
3465 Camino Del Rio S Ste 240 (92108)
PHONE..................................714 898-6400
Barry Rubin, *Pr*
EMP: 65 EST: 1988
SQ FT: 600
SALES (est): 4.24MM Privately Held
Web: workingalternativesinc.easyapply.co
SIC: 8361 Halfway group home, persons with social or personal problems

8399 Social Services, Nec

(P-18552)
ALAMEDA HEALTH SYSTEM (PA)
Also Called: Highland Hosp Hghland Wellness
1411 E 31st St (94602-1018)
PHONE..................................510 437-4800
James Jackson, *Interim Chief Executive Officer*
Jody Copeland, *
William T Peruzzi, *Chief Medical Officer*
David Cox, *
Carladenise A Edwards, *Chief Strategy Officer*
EMP: 99 EST: 2002
SALES (est): 317.8MM Privately Held
Web: www.alamedahealthsystem.org
SIC: 8399 Health systems agency

(P-18553)
ALEGRIA COMMUNITY LIVING
1201 Martin Luther King Jr Way (94612-1297)
PHONE..................................510 287-8488
Karen Toto, *Dir*
EMP: 105 EST: 2005
SALES (est): 9.46MM Privately Held
Web: www.alegriacl.org
SIC: 8399 Council for social agency

(P-18554)
AMADOR TLMNE CMNTY ACTION AGCY (PA)
Also Called: Atcaa
10590 State Highway 88 Ste 6 (95642-9470)
PHONE..................................209 296-2785
Shelly Hance, *Ex Dir*
Patty Cunningham, *Department Director*
EMP: 61 EST: 1981
SALES (est): 16.75MM
SALES (corp-wide): 16.75MM Privately Held
Web: www.atcaa.org
SIC: 8399 Community action agency

(P-18555)
AMADOR TLMNE CMNTY ACTION AGCY
Also Called: Aatcaa Headstart
427 Highway 49 Ste 305 (95370-5666)
PHONE..................................209 533-1397
Shelly Hance, *Ex Dir*
EMP: 79
SALES (corp-wide): 16.75MM Privately Held
Web: www.atcaa.org
SIC: 8399 Community action agency
PA: Amador Tuolumne Community Action Agency
10590 State Highway 88
Jackson CA
209 296-2785

(P-18556)
ANTI-RECIDIVISM COALITION
1320 E 7th St (90021-1114)
PHONE..................................213 955-5885
Scott Budnick, *Admn*
EMP: 67 EST: 2013
SALES (est): 8.46MM Privately Held
Web: www.antirecidivism.org
SIC: 8399 Advocacy group

(P-18557)
ARC OF SAN DIEGO (PA)
Also Called: ARC Enterprises
3030 Market St (92102-3230)
PHONE..................................619 685-1175
David W Schneider, *CEO*
Anthony J Desalis, *
Rich Coppa, *
Chad Lyle, *
Jennifer Bates Navarra, *
▲ EMP: 200 EST: 1953
SQ FT: 55,093
SALES (est): 33.64MM
SALES (corp-wide): 33.64MM Privately Held
Web: www.arc-sd.com
SIC: 8399 8351 8361 8322 Advocacy group; Child day care services; Retarded home; Individual and family services

(P-18558)
ARC OF SAN DIEGO
Also Called: ARC - SD E Cnty Training Ctrs
1855 John Towers Ave (92020-1116)
PHONE..................................619 448-2415
Millie Oveross, *Mgr*
EMP: 348
SALES (corp-wide): 33.64MM Privately Held
Web: www.arc-sd.com
SIC: 8399 8361 Advocacy group; Physically handicapped home
PA: The Arc Of San Diego
3030 Market St
San Diego CA
619 685-1175

(P-18559)
ARC OF SAN DIEGO
1336 Rancheros Dr Ste 100 (92069-3089)
PHONE..................................760 740-6800
Laura Orcutt, *Dir*
EMP: 464
SALES (corp-wide): 33.64MM Privately Held
Web: www.arc-sd.com
SIC: 8399 8322 Advocacy group; Association for the handicapped
PA: The Arc Of San Diego
3030 Market St
San Diego CA
619 685-1175

(P-18560)
ASIAN AMRCANS FOR CMNTY INVLVM (PA)
2400 Moorpark Ave Ste 300 (95128-2680)
PHONE..................................408 975-2730
Michele Lew, *Pr*
Brent Copen, *
Pancho Chang, *
Sone Silavong, *Account Clerk*
▲ EMP: 151 EST: 1973
SQ FT: 101,753
SALES (est): 28.26MM
SALES (corp-wide): 28.26MM Privately Held
Web: www.aaci.org
SIC: 8399 Health and welfare council

(P-18561)
ASSOCIATED STUDENTS UCLA (PA)
Also Called: Asucla
308 Westwood Plz (90095-8355)
PHONE..................................310 794-8836
Pouria Abbassi, *Ex Dir*
Donna Baker, *Finance*
EMP: 500 EST: 1919
SQ FT: 200,000
SALES (est): 47.49MM
SALES (corp-wide): 47.49MM Privately Held
Web: asucla.ucla.edu
SIC: 8399 5942 Council for social agency; Book stores

(P-18562)
ASSOCIATED STUDENTS UCLA
924 Westwood Blvd (90024-2910)
PHONE..................................310 794-0242
Roseanna P Malone, *Brnch Mgr*
EMP: 214
SALES (corp-wide): 47.49MM Privately Held
Web: www.ucla.edu
SIC: 8399 Council for social agency
PA: Associated Students U.C.L.A.
308 Westwood Plz
Los Angeles CA
310 794-8836

(P-18563)
AUTISM INTERVENTION PROFESSION
340 S Lemon Ave (91789-2706)
PHONE..................................909 245-9979
Rahima Shariff, *Owner*
EMP: 63 EST: 2016
SALES (est): 925.46K Privately Held
SIC: 8399 Advocacy group

(P-18564)
AUTOMTED RGNAL JSTICE INFO SYS
Also Called: Arjis
401 B St Ste 800 (92101-4231)
PHONE..................................619 533-4201
Pamela Scanlon, *Dir*
EMP: 65 EST: 2011
SALES (est): 1.16MM
SALES (corp-wide): 1.43MM Privately Held
Web: www.arjis.org
SIC: 8399 Regional planning organization
PA: Sourcepoint
401 B St Ste 800
San Diego CA
619 699-6900

(P-18565)
BAIL PROJECT
3107 Washington Blvd (90292-5550)
P.O. Box 750 (90294-0750)
PHONE..................................323 366-0799
David Gaspar, *CEO*
EMP: 66 EST: 2017
SALES (est): 18.51MM Privately Held
Web: www.bailproject.org
SIC: 8399 Advocacy group

(P-18566)
BEACH CITIES HEALTH DISTRICT
1200 Del Amo St (90277-3050)
PHONE..................................310 374-3426
Tom Bakaly, *Mgr*
Tom Bakaly, *CEO*
Monica Suua, *
EMP: 147 EST: 1955
SALES (est): 15.47MM Privately Held
Web: www.bchd.org
SIC: 8399 Health systems agency

(P-18567)
CALIFORNIA ENDOWMENT (PA)
1000 N Alameda St (90012-1804)
PHONE..................................213 928-8800
EMP: 80 EST: 1995
SQ FT: 110,000
SALES (est): 461.75MM Privately Held
Web: www.calendow.org
SIC: 8399 Fund raising organization, non-fee basis

(P-18568)
CALIFRNIA ATISM FOUNDATION INC
Also Called: Better Chance, A
982 Marlesta Rd (94564-2402)
PHONE..................................510 724-1751
John Clay, *Dir*
EMP: 106
SALES (corp-wide): 6.33MM Privately Held
Web: www.calautism.org
SIC: 8399 8322 Community development groups; Individual and family services
PA: The California Autism Foundation Inc
4138 Lakeside Dr
San Pablo CA
510 758-0433

(P-18569)
CALIFRNIA RUR INDIAN HLTH BD I
1020 Sundown Way (95661-4473)
PHONE..................................916 437-0104
James Crouch, *Ex Dir*
Jason C Lopez, *
Glenda Nelson, *
Laura Rambeau-lawson, *Treas*
EMP: 80 EST: 1969
SQ FT: 18,627
SALES (est): 72.12MM Privately Held

8399 - Social Services, Nec (P-18590)

(P-18570)
CAPC INC
Also Called: COMMUNITY ADVOCATE FOR PEOPLE'
7702 Washington Ave Ste A (90602)
PHONE.................................562 693-8826
Shauna Epting, *Ex Dir*
Carolyn Reggio, *
Paul Velasco, *
Cheryl Turner, *
Maria Segovia, *
EMP: 60 EST: 1995
SALES (est): 3.02MM **Privately Held**
Web: www.capcinc.org
SIC: 8399 Advocacy group

(P-18571)
CITY OF HOPE
City Hope Development Center
1500 Duarte Rd (91010-3012)
PHONE.................................213 202-5735
Kathleen Cane, *Brnch Mgr*
EMP: 392
SALES (corp-wide): 334.97MM **Privately Held**
Web: www.cityofhope.org
SIC: 8399 9532 Fund raising organization, non-fee basis; Urban and community development
PA: City Of Hope
1500 Duarte Rd
Duarte CA
626 256-4673

(P-18572)
COCOKIDS INC
1035 Detroit Ave Ste 200 (94518-2478)
PHONE.................................925 676-5442
John Jones, *Ex Dir*
Jay Perry, *
EMP: 105 EST: 1976
SALES (est): 53.02MM **Privately Held**
Web: www.cocokids.org
SIC: 8399 Community action agency

(P-18573)
COLUSA INDIAN CMNTY COUNCIL
Also Called: Colusa Casino
3740 State Highway 45 (95932-4030)
PHONE.................................530 458-6572
Laurie Costa, *Dir*
EMP: 393
Web: www.syix.com
SIC: 8399 7991 Community development groups; Health club
PA: Colusa Indian Community Council
3730 State Highway 45 B
Colusa CA

(P-18574)
COMMUNICATION SVC FOR DEAF INC
Also Called: Community Services For Deaf
81 W March Ln (95207-5723)
PHONE.................................209 475-5000
Rhasan Waser, *Mgr*
EMP: 81
SALES (corp-wide): 37.01MM **Privately Held**
Web: www.csd.org
SIC: 8399 Social service information exchange
PA: Communication Service For The Deaf, Inc.
901 S Mo Pac Expy 450
Austin TX
844 222-0002

(P-18575)
COMMUNITY ACTION PARTNR KERN
315 Stine Rd (93309-3268)
PHONE.................................661 835-5405
Luz Adams, *Brnch Mgr*
EMP: 82
SALES (corp-wide): 117.9MM **Privately Held**
Web: www.capk.org
SIC: 8399 Community action agency
PA: Community Action Partnership Of Kern
5005 Business Park N
Bakersfield CA
661 336-5236

(P-18576)
COMMUNITY ACTION PARTNR KERN
814 N Norma St (93555-3509)
PHONE.................................760 371-1469
Maria Harley, *Brnch Mgr*
EMP: 85
SALES (corp-wide): 117.9MM **Privately Held**
Web: www.capk.org
SIC: 8399 8351 Community action agency; Child day care services
PA: Community Action Partnership Of Kern
5005 Business Park N
Bakersfield CA
661 336-5236

(P-18577)
COMMUNITY ACTION PRTNR MDERA C
Also Called: Victims Services Center
1225 Gill Ave (93637-5234)
PHONE.................................559 661-1000
Tina Figueroa, *Off Mgr*
EMP: 125
SALES (corp-wide): 31.43MM **Privately Held**
Web: www.maderacap.org
SIC: 8399 Community action agency
PA: Community Action Partnership Of Madera County, Inc.
1225 Gill Ave
Madera CA
559 673-9173

(P-18578)
COMMUNITY ACTION PRTNR SAN BRN
Also Called: CAPSBC
696 S Tippecanoe Ave (92408-2607)
PHONE.................................909 723-1500
Patricia L Nickols, *CEO*
Richard Schmidt, *
Joanne Gilbert, *
Socorro Enriquez, *Vice Chairman*
Ammie Hines, *
EMP: 88 EST: 1965
SALES (est): 31.88MM **Privately Held**
Web: www.capsbc.org
SIC: 8399 8699 Community action agency; Charitable organization

(P-18579)
COMMUNITY ACTION PRTNR SNOMA C
141 Stony Cir Ste 210 (95401-4142)
PHONE.................................707 544-0120
Oscar Chavez, *Pr*
Karen Erickson, *
EMP: 84 EST: 1967
SQ FT: 18,000
SALES (est): 15.58MM **Privately Held**
Web: www.capsonoma.org
SIC: 8399 Antipoverty board

(P-18580)
COMMUNITY PARTNERS (PA)
1000 N Alameda St Ste 240 (90012-1804)
PHONE.................................213 346-3200
Paul Vandeventer, *Pr*
Gary Erickson, *
Janet Elliott, *
EMP: 198 EST: 1990
SALES (est): 87.39MM **Privately Held**
Web: www.communitypartners.org
SIC: 8399 Social service information exchange

(P-18581)
COUNTY OF DEL NORTE
Also Called: Health and Human Service
880 Northcrest Dr (95531-2313)
PHONE.................................707 464-3191
Gary Blatnick, *Dir*
EMP: 75
Web: www.visitdelnortecounty.com
SIC: 8399 Health systems agency
PA: County Of Del Norte
981 H St Ste 200
Crescent City CA
707 464-7204

(P-18582)
COUNTY OF LOS ANGELES
9668 Valley Blvd Ste 104 (91770-1598)
PHONE.................................626 291-2200
EMP: 63
SALES (corp-wide): 31.7B **Privately Held**
Web: www.lacounty.gov
SIC: 8399 Community development groups
PA: County Of Los Angeles
500 W Temple St Ste 437
Los Angeles CA
213 974-1101

(P-18583)
COUNTY OF STANISLAUS
Also Called: Behavioral Hlth Recovery Svcs
800 Scenic Dr (95350-6131)
PHONE.................................209 525-6225
Denise C Hunt, *Dir*
EMP: 67
Web: www.stancounty.com
SIC: 8399 Health and welfare council
PA: County Of Stanislaus
1010 10th St Ste 5100
Modesto CA
209 525-6398

(P-18584)
DEPARTMENT HMLSSNESS SPPRTIVE
440 Turk St (94102-3330)
P.O. Box 427400 (94142-7400)
PHONE.................................628 652-7700
Abigail Stewart-kahn, *Prin*
Derek Chan, *Prin*
EMP: 125 EST: 2016
SALES (est): 1.46MM **Privately Held**
Web: hsh.sfgov.org
SIC: 8399 Advocacy group

(P-18585)
DVEAL CORPORATION
Also Called: D'Veal Family and Youth Svcs
2750 E Washington Blvd Ste 230 (91107-1448)
P.O. Box 40255 (91114-7255)
PHONE.................................626 296-8900
John Mccall, *Ex Dir*
EMP: 107 EST: 1996
SQ FT: 7,500
SALES (est): 8.62MM **Privately Held**
Web: www.dveal.com
SIC: 8399 Community action agency

(P-18586)
ESSENTIAL ACCESS HEALTH (PA)
Also Called: Cfhc
3600 Wilshire Blvd Ste 600 (90010-2610)
PHONE.................................213 386-5614
Julie Rabinovitz, *Pr*
Nomsa Khalfani, *
Brenda Flores, *
Ron Frezieres, *
Amy Moy, *
EMP: 81 EST: 1968
SQ FT: 18,000
SALES (est): 28.71MM
SALES (corp-wide): 28.71MM **Privately Held**
Web: www.essentialaccess.org
SIC: 8399 8011 8099 Fund raising organization, non-fee basis; Primary care medical clinic; Medical services organization

(P-18587)
EXPENSIFYORG
88 Kearny St Ste 1600 (94108-5543)
PHONE.................................971 365-3939
David Barrett, *Prin*
EMP: 156 EST: 2019
SALES (est): 272.47K **Privately Held**
Web: www.expensify.org
SIC: 8399 Social services, nec

(P-18588)
FREMONT UN HIGH SCHOLS FNDTION
589 W Fremont Ave (94087-2556)
P.O. Box F (94087-0108)
PHONE.................................408 522-2200
Ann-marie Meacham, *Ex Dir*
Jeanne Bradford, *
Polly Bove, *
EMP: 800 EST: 1921
SQ FT: 15,078
SALES (est): 448.36K **Privately Held**
Web: www.fuhsfoundation.org
SIC: 8399 Fund raising organization, non-fee basis

(P-18589)
GREATER LOS ANGELES ZOO ASSN
Also Called: GLAZA
5333 Zoo Dr (90027-1451)
PHONE.................................323 644-4200
Connie M Morgan, *Pr*
Jeb Bonner, *
Genie Vasels, *
Eugenia Vasels, *
Phyllis Kupferstein, *
EMP: 100 EST: 1963
SQ FT: 8,200
SALES (est): 20.39MM **Privately Held**
Web: www.lazoo.org
SIC: 8399 7999 Fund raising organization, non-fee basis; Concession operator

(P-18590)
HABITAT FOR HMNITY E BY/ SLCON (PA)
Also Called: HABITAT FOR HUMANITY EAST BAY
2619 Broadway (94612-3107)
PHONE.................................866 450-4432
Janice Jenson, *Pr*
Lucinda Osullivan, *Dir*
EMP: 78 EST: 1987
SQ FT: 2,000

8399 - Social Services, Nec (P-18591)

SALES (est): 21.91MM **Privately Held**
Web: www.habitatebsv.org
SIC: **8399** Community development groups

(P-18591)
HABITAT FOR HMNITY GRTER SAN F
Also Called: HABITAT FOR HUMANITY
1 Embarcadero Ctr Ste Sl12 (94111-3628)
PHONE..............................415 625-1000
Maureen Sedonaen, *Ex Dir*
Jen Wilds, *
Darrell Byers, *CAO*
EMP: 98 EST: 1989
SALES (est): 8.97MM **Privately Held**
Web: www.habitatgsf.org
SIC: **8399** Community development groups

(P-18592)
HARBOR AREA GANG ALTRNTVES PRG
Also Called: GANG ALTERNATIVES PROGRAM
309 W Opp St (90744-3412)
P.O. Box 408 (90733-0408)
PHONE..............................310 519-7233
Sueann Ballat, *Ex Dir*
Douglas Semark, *
Thomas E Boles Ea, *Treas*
John Greenwood, *
Larry Kurtz, *
EMP: 66 EST: 1985
SALES (est): 4.41MM **Privately Held**
Web: www.gangfree.org
SIC: **8399** Community action agency

(P-18593)
HARBOR DVLPMNTL DSBLTIES FNDT
Also Called: HARBOR REGIONAL CENTER
21231 Hawthorne Blvd (90503-5501)
P.O. Box 2930 (90509-2930)
PHONE..............................310 540-1711
Judy Wada, *CFO*
EMP: 225 EST: 1977
SQ FT: 60,000
SALES (est): 301.25MM **Privately Held**
Web: www.harborrc.org
SIC: **8399** Council for social agency

(P-18594)
HEALTH ADVOCATES LLC
Also Called: Health Advocates
21540 Plummer St Ste B (91311-0888)
PHONE..............................818 995-9500
Al Leibovic, *Managing Member*
Aaron Leibovic, *Managing Member*
EMP: 371 EST: 1997
SQ FT: 40,900
SALES (est): 47.69MM **Privately Held**
Web: www.healthadvocates.com
SIC: **8399** Advocacy group

(P-18595)
I DID SMTHING GOOD TDAY FNDTIO
Also Called: Idsgt Foundation
527 W 7th St Ste 926 (90014-2561)
PHONE..............................888 491-0054
Kimberly Lewis, *CEO*
EMP: 150 EST: 2018
SALES (est): 2.48MM **Privately Held**
Web: www.ididsomethinggoodtoday.org
SIC: **8399** Social services, nec

(P-18596)
INTERNTNAL CHILD RSRCE EXCH IN (PA)
Also Called: INTERNATIONAL CHILD RESOURCE I
125 University Ave Ste 201 (94710-1601)
PHONE..............................510 644-1000
Ken Jaffe, *Dir*
EMP: 144 EST: 1981
SALES (est): 12.14MM
SALES (corp-wide): 12.14MM **Privately Held**
Web: www.icrichild.org
SIC: **8399** Social service information exchange

(P-18597)
INTERNTNAL FNDTION FOR KREA UN
3435 Wilshire Blvd Ste 480 (90010-1901)
PHONE..............................213 550-2182
Willie Wang-pyo Seung, *CEO*
EMP: 300 EST: 2016
SALES (est): 202.98K **Privately Held**
Web: www.ifku.org
SIC: **8399** Advocacy group

(P-18598)
INTOUCH TECHNOLOGIES INC (HQ)
Also Called: Intouch Health
7402 Hollister Ave (93117-2583)
PHONE..............................805 562-8686
Yulun Wang, *Ch*
Paul Evans, *
Michael Chan, *
Charles S Jordan, *
David Adornetto, *
EMP: 102 EST: 2002
SQ FT: 1,600
SALES (est): 60.31MM **Publicly Held**
Web: www.teladochealth.com
SIC: **8399** 7379 Health systems agency; Computer related consulting services
PA: Teladoc Health, Inc.
  2 Manhattanville Rd # 203
  Purchase NY

(P-18599)
JAPANESE CMNTY YOUTH COUNCIL (PA)
Also Called: CHIBI CHAN PRESCHOOL
2012 Pine St (94115-2828)
PHONE..............................415 202-7905
John Osaki, *Ex Dir*
EMP: 60 EST: 1969
SQ FT: 4,000
SALES (est): 19.04MM
SALES (corp-wide): 19.04MM **Privately Held**
Web: www.jcyc.org
SIC: **8399** Community action agency

(P-18600)
JEWISH CMNTY FDRTION OF SAN FR (PA)
121 Steuart St (94105-1206)
PHONE..............................415 777-0411
Jennifer Gorvitz, *CEO*
Bill Powers, *
EMP: 70 EST: 1921
SQ FT: 50,000
SALES (est): 255MM
SALES (corp-wide): 255MM **Privately Held**
Web: www.jewishfed.org
SIC: **8399** Fund raising organization, non-fee basis

(P-18601)
KERN REGIONAL CENTER (PA)
3200 N Sillect Ave (93308-6333)
P.O. Box 2536 (93303-2536)
PHONE..............................661 327-8531
TOLL FREE: 800
Michal Clark, *Ex Dir*
Jerry Bowman, *
Duane Law, *
EMP: 147 EST: 1971
SQ FT: 33,000
SALES (est): 231.95MM
SALES (corp-wide): 231.95MM **Privately Held**
Web: www.kernrc.org
SIC: **8399** Social service information exchange

(P-18602)
KEYSTONE NPS LLC (DH)
Also Called: Keystone Schools-Ramona
11980 Mount Vernon Ave (92313-5172)
PHONE..............................909 633-6354
Alfredo Alvarado, *Prin*
Martha Petrey, *
Don Whitfield, *
EMP: 100 EST: 1978
SALES (est): 22.49MM
SALES (corp-wide): 13.4B **Publicly Held**
SIC: **8399** Advocacy group
HQ: Children's Comprehensive Services, Inc.
  3401 West End Ave Ste 400
  Nashville TN
  615 250-0000

(P-18603)
KEYSTONE NPS LLC
Also Called: Keystone Educatn & Youth Svcs
9994 County Farm Rd (92503-3518)
PHONE..............................951 785-0504
EMP: 199
SALES (corp-wide): 13.4B **Publicly Held**
SIC: **8399** 8211 Advocacy group; Private elementary and secondary schools
HQ: Keystone Nps Llc
  11980 Mount Vernon Ave
  Grand Terrace CA
  909 633-6354

(P-18604)
KIPP FOUNDATION
135 Main St Ste 1875 (94105-1955)
PHONE..............................415 399-1556
Richard Barth, *CEO*
Tina Sachs, *
Tarun Bhatia, *
Jack Chorowsky, *
EMP: 110 EST: 2000
SALES (est): 130.7MM **Privately Held**
Web: www.kipp.org
SIC: **8399** Fund raising organization, non-fee basis

(P-18605)
LASH GROUP LLC
Also Called: Lash Group Healthcare Cons
999 Bayhill Dr Fl 3 (94066-3070)
PHONE..............................800 788-9637
Mike Busby, *Mgr*
EMP: 160
SALES (corp-wide): 238.59B **Publicly Held**
Web: www.lashgroup.com
SIC: **8399** 8742 Health systems agency; Hospital and health services consultant
HQ: The Lash Group Llc
  1800 Innovation Pt
  Fort Mill SC
  800 357-5274

(P-18606)
LAWRENCE FMLY JWISH CMNTY CTRS (PA)
4126 Executive Dr (92037-1348)
PHONE..............................858 362-1144
Craig Schluss, *Pr*
David Wax, *
Nancy Johnson, *
EMP: 150 EST: 1945
SALES (est): 12.11MM
SALES (corp-wide): 12.11MM **Privately Held**
Web: www.lfjcc.org
SIC: **8399** 8351 Community development groups; Child day care services

(P-18607)
LOS ANGELES EDUCATION PARTNR
1541 Wilshire Blvd Ste 200 (90017-2294)
PHONE..............................213 622-5237
Ellen Pais, *CEO*
EMP: 73 EST: 1984
SQ FT: 11,000
SALES (est): 7.4MM **Privately Held**
Web: www.laep.org
SIC: **8399** Fund raising organization, non-fee basis

(P-18608)
LOS ANGELES LGBT CENTER (PA)
Also Called: L.A. GAY & LESBIAN CENTER
1625 Schrader Blvd (90028-6213)
P.O. Box 2988 (90078-2988)
PHONE..............................323 993-7618
Lorri L Jean, *CEO*
Michael Holtzman, *
EMP: 148 EST: 1972
SQ FT: 45,000
SALES (est): 149.11MM
SALES (corp-wide): 149.11MM **Privately Held**
Web: www.lalgbtcenter.org
SIC: **8399** Advocacy group

(P-18609)
MARCH FOR OUR LVES ACTION FUND
16130 Ventura Blvd Ste 320 (91436-2503)
PHONE..............................801 815-1989
Deena Katz, *Pr*
EMP: 74 EST: 2018
SALES (est): 3.37MM **Privately Held**
Web: www.marchforourlives.com
SIC: **8399** Advocacy group

(P-18610)
MONTAGE HEALTH (PA)
23625 Holman Hwy (93940-5902)
P.O. Box Hh (93942-6032)
PHONE..............................831 625-4830
Steven Packer Md, *Pr*
Steven X Cabrales Md, *CMO*
EMP: 1650 EST: 1955
SQ FT: 350,000
SALES (est): 947.23MM
SALES (corp-wide): 947.23MM **Privately Held**
Web: www.montagehealth.org
SIC: **8399** Health and welfare council

(P-18611)
NEW ADVNCES FOR PPLE WITH DSBL
Also Called: Napd
4032 Jewett Ave (93301-1114)
PHONE..............................661 322-9735

PRODUCTS & SERVICES SECTION
8399 - Social Services, Nec (P-18631)

EMP: 106
SALES (corp-wide): 6.36MM Privately Held
Web: www.napd-bak.org
SIC: 8399 Community development groups
PA: New Advances For People With Disabilities
3400 N Sillect Ave
Bakersfield CA
661 395-1361

(P-18612)
NEW ADVNCES FOR PPLE WITH DSBL
Also Called: Center For Achievement Center
1120 21st St (93301-4613)
PHONE....................661 327-0188
EMP: 76
SALES (corp-wide): 6.36MM Privately Held
Web: www.napd-bak.org
SIC: 8399 Community development groups
PA: New Advances For People With Disabilities
3400 N Sillect Ave
Bakersfield CA
661 395-1361

(P-18613)
NORTHERN CAL INST FOR RES EDCA
Also Called: NCIRE
4150 Clement St (94121-1563)
PHONE....................415 750-6954
Robert Obana, Ex Dir
EMP: 300 EST: 1988
SQ FT: 1,650
SALES (est): 54.12MM Privately Held
Web: www.ncire.org
SIC: 8399 8741 Fund raising organization, non-fee basis; Management services

(P-18614)
ON THE RISE INC
305 E Buena Vista St (92311-2803)
P.O. Box 1169 (92312-1169)
PHONE....................760 964-7473
Kimberly Hammack, Ex Dir
Jessica Sims, *
Mike Parker, *
Ashley Dunkin, *
EMP: 63 EST: 2014
SALES (est): 3.39MM Privately Held
Web: www.ontheriseinc.com
SIC: 8399 Health and welfare council

(P-18615)
ORTHALLIANCE INC
Also Called: Orthalliances
21535 Hawthorne Blvd Ste 200 (90503-6604)
PHONE....................310 792-1300
Sam Westover, Pr
Paul H Hayase, *
James C Wilson, *
EMP: 1700 EST: 1996
SQ FT: 4,200
SALES (est): 23.92MM Privately Held
Web: www.orthalliance.com
SIC: 8399 8742 8741 Advocacy group; Management consulting services; Business management
PA: Orthosynetics, Inc.
3850 N Causeway Blvd # 800
Metairie LA

(P-18616)
PENNY LANE CENTERS (PA)
15305 Rayen St (91343-5117)
P.O. Box 2548 (91393-2548)
PHONE....................818 892-3423
Arthur Barr, Pr
Ivelise Markovits, *
Peter Padin, Assistant Executive Director*
EMP: 275 EST: 1967
SQ FT: 7,000
SALES (est): 57.33MM
SALES (corp-wide): 57.33MM Privately Held
Web: www.pennylane.org
SIC: 8399 Social service information exchange

(P-18617)
PJCC
800 Foster City Blvd (94404-2228)
PHONE....................650 212-7522
Mervyn Danker, CEO
EMP: 62 EST: 2011
SALES (est): 4.68MM Privately Held
Web: www.pjcc.org
SIC: 8399 Community development groups

(P-18618)
POLL EVERYWHERE INC
548 Market St Ste 17358 (94104-5401)
PHONE....................800 388-2039
Jeff Vyduna, CEO
Alejandro Alec Nunez, Dir Opers
EMP: 60 EST: 2012
SALES (est): 9.86MM Privately Held
Web: www.polleverywhere.com
SIC: 8399 Social service information exchange

(P-18619)
PREMIER DISABILITY SVCS LLC
909 N Pacific Coast Hwy Fl 11 (90245-2724)
PHONE....................310 280-4000
Robert N Brisco, Mgr
EMP: 99 EST: 2020
SALES (est): 1.01MM Privately Held
Web: www.premierdisability.com
SIC: 8399 Advocacy group

(P-18620)
REACH OUT WEST END
1126 W Foothill Blvd Ste 250 (91786-3778)
PHONE....................909 982-8641
Diana Fox, Dir
EMP: 60 EST: 1969
SQ FT: 12,232
SALES (est): 7.25MM Privately Held
Web: www.we-reachout.org
SIC: 8399 Social change association

(P-18621)
SAN DIEGO RESCUE MISSION INC (PA)
Also Called: CITY RESCUE MISSION
299 17th St (92101-7665)
P.O. Box 80427 (92138-0427)
PHONE....................619 819-1880
Herb Johnson, CEO
John Suderman, *
Shari Finney Houser, *
C Greg Helton, *
Cathy Christianson, *
EMP: 99 EST: 1955
SALES (est): 26.9MM
SALES (corp-wide): 26.9MM Privately Held
Web: www.sdrescue.org
SIC: 8399 5932 8322 Social change association; Used merchandise stores; Emergency shelters

(P-18622)
SHARP HEALTHCARE FOUNDATION
8695 Spectrum Center Blvd (92123-1489)
PHONE....................858 499-4800
William Littlejohn, CEO
Marsha Lubick, *
EMP: 168 EST: 1979
SALES (est): 23.93MM
SALES (corp-wide): 2.37B Privately Held
Web: www.sharp.com
SIC: 8399 Fund raising organization, non-fee basis
PA: Sharp Healthcare
8695 Spectrum Center Blvd
San Diego CA
858 499-4000

(P-18623)
SOUTH CNTL LOS ANGLES RGNAL CT (PA)
Also Called: SCLARC
2500 S Western Ave (90018-2609)
PHONE....................213 744-7000
Dexter Henderson, CEO
Roy Doronila, *
EMP: 104 EST: 1983
SQ FT: 110,470
SALES (est): 455.32MM
SALES (corp-wide): 455.32MM Privately Held
Web: www.sclarc.org
SIC: 8399 Health and welfare council

(P-18624)
SOUTH CNTL LOS ANGLES RGNAL CT
650 W Adams Blvd (90007-2580)
PHONE....................231 744-8484
EMP: 131
SALES (corp-wide): 455.32MM Privately Held
Web: www.sclarc.org
SIC: 8399 Health and welfare council
PA: South Central Los Angeles Regional Center For Developmentally Disabled Persons, Inc.
2500 S Western Ave
Los Angeles CA
213 744-7000

(P-18625)
SOUTHLAND INTEGRATED SVCS INC (PA)
Also Called: VIETNAMESE COMMUNITY OF ORANGE
9862 Chapman Ave (92841-2711)
PHONE....................714 558-6009
Tricia Nguyen, CEO
EMP: 68 EST: 1979
SALES (est): 13.66MM
SALES (corp-wide): 13.66MM Privately Held
Web: www.southlandintegrated.org
SIC: 8399 8322 8351 8011 Community development groups; Senior citizens' center or association; Preschool center; Primary care medical clinic

(P-18626)
SPANISH SPKING UNITY CNCIL ALM
Also Called: Thurgood Mrshall Erly Head Sta
1117 10th St (94607-2707)
PHONE....................510 836-0543
Elizabeth Crocker, Dir
EMP: 125
SALES (corp-wide): 34.32MM Privately Held
Web: www.unitycouncil.org
SIC: 8399 8351 Social change association; Child day care services
PA: Spanish Speaking Unity Council Of Alameda County, Inc.
1900 Fruitvale Ave Ste 2a
Oakland CA
510 535-6900

(P-18627)
SPECIAL SERVICE FOR GROUPS INC
520 S La Fayette Park Pl # 30 (90057-1607)
PHONE....................213 553-1800
Herbert Hatanaka, Brnch Mgr
EMP: 131
SALES (corp-wide): 133.16MM Privately Held
Web: www.ssg.org
SIC: 8399 Community development groups
PA: Special Service For Groups, Inc.
905 E 8th St
Los Angeles CA
213 368-1888

(P-18628)
SPECIAL SERVICE FOR GROUPS INC
Also Called: Occupational Therapy Training
19401 S Vermont Ave Ste A200 (90502-4418)
PHONE....................310 323-6887
Sarah Bream, Brnch Mgr
EMP: 132
SALES (corp-wide): 133.16MM Privately Held
Web: www.ssg.org
SIC: 8399 8322 Community action agency; Individual and family services
PA: Special Service For Groups, Inc.
905 E 8th St
Los Angeles CA
213 368-1888

(P-18629)
SUPPORTLOGIC INC (PA)
356 Santana Row Ste 1000 (95128-2034)
PHONE....................408 471-4710
Krishnaraj Raja, CEO
EMP: 81 EST: 2016
SALES (est): 9.94MM
SALES (corp-wide): 9.94MM Privately Held
Web: www.supportlogic.com
SIC: 8399 7371 Advocacy group; Computer software development and applications

(P-18630)
TIDES INC (PA)
Also Called: TIDES SHARED SPACES
1012 Torney Ave (94129-1704)
P.O. Box 29198 (94129-0198)
PHONE....................415 561-6400
Melissa Bradley, CEO
Nick Hodges, *
China Brotsky, *
EMP: 90 EST: 2002
SQ FT: 180,000
SALES (est): 3.61MM
SALES (corp-wide): 3.61MM Privately Held
Web: www.tides.org
SIC: 8399 Community development groups

(P-18631)
UNITED CRBRAL PLSY ASSN SAN JQ
134 S Pacific Rd (95337-5114)

8399 - Social Services, Nec (P-18632)

PHONE..................209 239-3066
Corinne Fielder, *Mgr*
EMP: 65
SALES (corp-wide): 1.74MM **Privately Held**
Web: www.ucpsj.org
SIC: 8399 Fund raising organization, non-fee basis
PA: United Cerebral Palsy Association Of San Joaquin County
333 W Benjamin Holt Dr # 1
Stockton CA
209 956-0290

(P-18632)
UNITED WAY INC (PA)
Also Called: United Way Greater Los Angeles
1150 S Olive St Ste T-500 (90015-2481)
PHONE..................213 808-6220
Caroline W Nahas, *Ch Bd*
Elise Buik, *
Les Brockhurst, *
Alicia Lara, *
Mae Tuck, *
▲ **EMP:** 95 **EST:** 1962
SQ FT: 40,000
SALES (est): 49.6MM
SALES (corp-wide): 49.6MM **Privately Held**
Web: 100.unitedwayla.org
SIC: 8399 Fund raising organization, non-fee basis

(P-18633)
WESTSIDE JEWISH CMNTY CTR INC (PA)
5870 W Olympic Blvd (90036-4657)
PHONE..................323 938-2531
Brian Greene, *Ex Dir*
EMP: 200 **EST:** 1932
SQ FT: 150,000
SALES (est): 2.31MM
SALES (corp-wide): 2.31MM **Privately Held**
Web: www.westsidejcc.org
SIC: 8399 8641 8322 Community development groups; Civic and social associations; Individual and family services

(P-18634)
YUBA CY UNFIED SCHL DST FING C
Also Called: YCUSD
425 Plumas Blvd (95991-5085)
PHONE..................530 822-7601
Steven Scriven, *Pr*
Nancy Aaberg, *
Lonetta Riley, *
EMP: 2000 **EST:** 1966
SALES (est): 214.09MM **Privately Held**
Web: www.ycusd.org
SIC: 8399 Fund raising organization, non-fee basis

8412 Museums And Art Galleries

(P-18635)
ACADEMY MUSEUM MOTION PICTURES
6067 Wilshire Blvd (90036-3604)
PHONE..................310 247-3000
Bill Kramer, *Pr*
EMP: 212 **EST:** 2021
SALES (est): 6.1MM **Privately Held**
Web: www.academymuseum.org
SIC: 8412 Museum

(P-18636)
AIRCRAFT CRIER HRNET FUNDATION
Pier 3 Alameda Point (94501)
P.O. Box 460 (94501-9560)
PHONE..................510 521-8448
Jon Stanley, *Pr*
EMP: 68 **EST:** 1995
SALES (est): 4.11MM **Privately Held**
Web: www.uss-hornet.org
SIC: 8412 Museum

(P-18637)
ARMAND HMMER MSEUM OF ART CLTR
Also Called: HAMMER MUSEUM
10899 Wilshire Blvd (90024-4343)
PHONE..................310 443-7000
Michael Rubel, *Dir*
Steven A Olsen, *
▲ **EMP:** 101 **EST:** 1989
SQ FT: 20,000
SALES (est): 34.99MM **Privately Held**
Web: hammer.ucla.edu
SIC: 8412 Museum

(P-18638)
ASIAN ART MSEUM FNDTION SAN FR
Also Called: Asian Art Meusuem of SF
200 Larkin St (94102-4734)
PHONE..................415 581-3500
▲ **EMP:** 140 **EST:** 1969
SALES (est): 35.44MM **Privately Held**
Web: www.asianart.org
SIC: 8412 Museum

(P-18639)
AUTRY MUSEUM OF AMERICAN WEST
Also Called: AUTRY MUSEUM
4700 Western Heritage Way (90027-1462)
PHONE..................323 667-2000
Richard West, *Prin*
Richard West, *Pr*
Robert Caragher, *
Maren Dougherty, *
Susan Harlow, *
EMP: 140 **EST:** 1984
SQ FT: 144,000
SALES (est): 12.35MM **Privately Held**
Web: www.theautry.org
SIC: 8412 5947 5812 6512 Museum; Gift shop; Cafeteria; Theater building, ownership and operation

(P-18640)
CALIFRNIA CTR FOR ARTS ESCNDID
340 N Escondido Blvd (92025-2600)
PHONE..................760 839-4138
Vicky Basehore, *Pr*
Lee Cavell Board, *Prin*
EMP: 185 **EST:** 1989
SALES (est): 5.23MM **Privately Held**
Web: www.artcenter.org
SIC: 8412 5999 Arts or science center; Art dealers

(P-18641)
CALIFRNIA SCNCE CTR FOUNDATION
700 Exposition Park Dr (90037-1210)
PHONE..................213 744-2545
Jeffrey N Rudolph, *Pr*
Cynthia Pygin, *
EMP: 260 **EST:** 1949
SALES (est): 28.6MM
SALES (corp-wide): 534.4MM **Privately Held**
SIC: 8412 7832 5947 Museum; Motion picture theaters, except drive-in; Gifts and novelties
HQ: California Natural Resources Agency
1416 9th St Ste 1311
Sacramento CA

(P-18642)
CHARLES W BOWERS MUSEUM CORP
Also Called: BOWERS MUSEUM
2002 N Main St (92706-2731)
PHONE..................714 567-3600
Peter C Keller, *Pr*
▲ **EMP:** 72 **EST:** 1936
SALES (est): 8.28MM **Privately Held**
Web: www.bowers.org
SIC: 8412 Museum

(P-18643)
CHILDRENS CREATIVITY MUSEUM
221 4th St (94103-3116)
PHONE..................415 820-3320
Adrienne Pon, *CEO*
Michael Nobleza, *
Laney Whitcanack, *
John Gonzalez, *
Bill Rusitzky, *
EMP: 65 **EST:** 1992
SALES (est): 1.9MM **Privately Held**
Web: www.creativity.org
SIC: 8412 5947 Museum; Gift shop

(P-18644)
CITY & COUNTY SAN FRANCISCO
Also Called: Asian Art Museum
200 Larkin St (94102-4734)
PHONE..................415 581-3500
Emily Sano, *Dir*
EMP: 60
SALES (corp-wide): 7.18B **Privately Held**
Web: www.asianart.org
SIC: 8412 9199 Museum; General government administration
PA: City & County Of San Francisco
1 Dr Carlton B Goodlett P
San Francisco CA
415 554-7500

(P-18645)
CORPORTION OF FINE ARTS MSEUMS
Also Called: Fine Arts Mseums San Francisco
75 Tea Garden Dr (94118-4501)
PHONE..................415 750-3600
Harry S Parker Iii, *Prin*
EMP: 61
Web: www.famsf.org
SIC: 8412 Museum
PA: Corporation Of The Fine Arts Museums
50 Hagiwara Tea Garden Dr
San Francisco CA

(P-18646)
CORPORTION OF FINE ARTS MSEUMS
Also Called: Fine Arts Museum San Francisco
100 Pine St 11th Fl (94111-5102)
PHONE..................415 750-3600
EMP: 123
Web: www.famsf.org
SIC: 8412 Museum
PA: Corporation Of The Fine Arts Museums
50 Hagiwara Tea Garden Dr
San Francisco CA

(P-18647)
CORPORTION OF FINE ARTS MSEUMS
Also Called: Palace of The Legion Honor
50 Hagiwara Tea Garden Dr (94118-4502)
PHONE..................415 750-3600
John Duchanan, *Mgr*
EMP: 92
Web: www.famsf.org
SIC: 8412 Museum
PA: Corporation Of The Fine Arts Museums
50 Hagiwara Tea Garden Dr
San Francisco CA

(P-18648)
CORPORTION OF FINE ARTS MSEUMS
Also Called: M H Deyoung Memorial
50 Golden Gate Ave (94118)
PHONE..................415 750-3600
Debbie Albuquerque, *Brnch Mgr*
EMP: 123
Web: www.famsf.org
SIC: 8412 Museum
PA: Corporation Of The Fine Arts Museums
50 Hagiwara Tea Garden Dr
San Francisco CA

(P-18649)
CORPORTION OF FINE ARTS MSEUMS (PA)
Also Called: Deyoung Museum
50 Hagiwara Tea Garden Dr (94118-4502)
PHONE..................415 750-3600
Michelle Gutierrez, *CFO*
Colin Bailey, *
▲ **EMP:** 145 **EST:** 1987
SQ FT: 300,000
SALES (est): 39.48MM **Privately Held**
Web: www.famsf.org
SIC: 8412 Museum

(P-18650)
DISCOVERY SCNCE CTR ORNGE CNTY
2500 N Main St (92705-6600)
PHONE..................866 552-2823
Daniel Bolar, *Ch Bd*
Joseph Adams, *Pr*
▲ **EMP:** 135 **EST:** 1998
SALES (est): 12.79MM **Privately Held**
Web: www.discoverycube.org
SIC: 8412 Museum

(P-18651)
EASTERN CALIFORNIA MUSEUM (PA)
155 N Grant St (93526)
PHONE..................760 878-0292
Margaret Mairs, *Ch Bd*
Del Hubbs, *
Leah Kirk, *
William Michaels, *
EMP: 348 **EST:** 1928
SQ FT: 3,200
SALES (est): 2.18MM
SALES (corp-wide): 2.18MM **Privately Held**
Web: www.inyocounty.us
SIC: 8412 Museum

(P-18652)
EXPLORATORIUM
17 Pier Ste 100 (94111-1455)
PHONE..................415 528-4462
Chris Flink, *Ex Dir*
Laura Zander, *
Roberta Katz, *

8412 - Museums And Art Galleries (P-18674)

◆ EMP: 298 EST: 1968
SQ FT: 200,000
SALES (est): 79.57MM Privately Held
Web: www.exploratorium.edu
SIC: 8412 Museum

(P-18653)
KIDSPCE A PRTICIPATORY MUSEUM
Also Called: KIDSPACE
480 N Arroyo Blvd (91103-3269)
PHONE...................626 449-9144
EMP: 83 EST: 1979
SALES (est): 4.39MM Privately Held
Web: www.kidspacemuseum.org
SIC: 8412 Museum

(P-18654)
LONG BCH MUSEUM ART FOUNDATION
2300 E Ocean Blvd (90803-2442)
PHONE...................562 439-2119
Ronald B Nelson, Dir
Ronald C Nelson, *
▲ EMP: 62 EST: 1950
SQ FT: 24,000
SALES (est): 1.95MM Privately Held
Web: www.lbma.org
SIC: 8412 Museum

(P-18655)
LOS ANGELES CNTY MSEUM OF ART
Also Called: Lacma
5905 Wilshire Blvd (90036-4504)
PHONE...................323 857-6000
Michael Govan, CEO
Ann Rowland, *
John Bowsher, *
Jane Burrell, *
Fred Goldstein, *
▲ EMP: 430 EST: 2011
SALES (est): 11.58MM Privately Held
Web: www.lacma.org
SIC: 8412 Museum

(P-18656)
LUCAS MUSEUM OF NARRATIVE ART
700 S Flower St Ste 2400 (90017-4211)
PHONE...................831 566-9332
EMP: 61 EST: 2019
SALES (est): 200.32MM Privately Held
Web: www.lucasmuseumconstruction.org
SIC: 8412 Museum

(P-18657)
MEXICAN HERITG CTR GALLERY INC
111 S Sutter St (95202-3220)
P.O. Box 77985 (95267-1285)
PHONE...................209 969-9306
Gracie Madrid, Pr
EMP: 75 EST: 1997
SQ FT: 6,799
SALES (est): 392.54K Privately Held
Web: www.mexicanheritagecenter.org
SIC: 8412 Museum

(P-18658)
MUSEUM ASSOCIATES
Also Called: La County Museum of Art
5905 Wilshire Blvd (90036-4504)
PHONE...................323 857-6172
Michael Gavin, Dir
EMP: 400 EST: 1938
SALES (est): 230.97MM Privately Held
Web: www.lacma.org

SIC: 8412 Museum

(P-18659)
MUSEUM CNTMPRARY ART SAN DIEGO (PA)
Also Called: MCASD
1100 Kettner Blvd (92101-3306)
PHONE...................858 454-3541
Hugh M Davies, CEO
▼ EMP: 69 EST: 1941
SQ FT: 45,200
SALES (est): 13.72MM
SALES (corp-wide): 13.72MM Privately Held
Web: www.mcasd.org
SIC: 8412 Museum

(P-18660)
MUSEUM OF CONTEMPORARY ART (PA)
250 S Grand Ave (90012-3021)
PHONE...................213 626-6222
Charles Young, CEO
Michael Harrison, *
Jeffrey Deitch, *
▲ EMP: 150 EST: 1979
SQ FT: 100,000
SALES (est): 28.96MM
SALES (corp-wide): 28.96MM Privately Held
Web: www.moca.org
SIC: 8412 Museum

(P-18661)
NEW CHILDRENS MUSEUM
200 W Island Ave (92101-6850)
PHONE...................619 233-8792
Judy Forrester, Ex Dir
Kay Wagner, *
Robert Sain, *
Rachel Teagle, *
Julianne Markow, *
EMP: 90 EST: 1981
SQ FT: 50,000
SALES (est): 4.09MM Privately Held
Web: www.thinkplaycreate.org
SIC: 8412 Museum

(P-18662)
NORTON SMON MSEUM ART AT PSDEN
411 W Colorado Blvd (91105-1825)
PHONE...................626 449-6840
Ronald H Dykhuizen, Prin
Jennifer J Simon, *
Walter W Timoshuk, *
Robert Walker, *
▲ EMP: 100 EST: 1924
SQ FT: 70,000
SALES (est): 8.6MM Privately Held
Web: www.nortonsimon.org
SIC: 8412 Museum

(P-18663)
OAKLAND MUSEUM OF CALIFORNIA
1000 Oak St (94607-4892)
PHONE...................510 318-8400
Lori Fogarty, CEO
Ariel Weintraub, *
Lori G Fogarty, *
EMP: 100 EST: 1969
SQ FT: 150,000
SALES (est): 18.57MM Privately Held
Web: www.museumca.org
SIC: 8412 Museum

(P-18664)
PACIFIC METRO LLC (PA)
Also Called: Thomas Kinkade Company, The
18715 Madrone Pkwy (95037-2876)
PHONE...................408 201-5000
Eric H Halvorson, Pr
Anthony D Thomopoulos, Ch
Herbert D Montgomery Es, VP
Rose Capistran, Pers/VP
Steve Paszkiewicz, Manufacturing Business Unit President
▲ EMP: 350 EST: 1993
SALES (est): 14.7MM Privately Held
SIC: 8412 Art gallery

(P-18665)
PALM SPRINGS ART MUSEUM INC
101 N Museum Dr (92262-5659)
P.O. Box 2310 (92263-2310)
PHONE...................760 322-4800
Donna Macmillan, Ch Bd
Rochelle Steinerm, Chief Curator*
Adam Lerner, *
▲ EMP: 96 EST: 1938
SQ FT: 75,000
SALES (est): 8.92MM Privately Held
Web: www.psmuseum.org
SIC: 8412 Museum

(P-18666)
REUBEN H FLEET SCIENCE CENTER
1875 El Prado (92101-1625)
P.O. Box 33303 (92163-3303)
PHONE...................619 238-1233
Gary Thomas Phillips, CEO
Jeffrey Kirsch, *
Craig A Blower, *
EMP: 105 EST: 1957
SQ FT: 93,500
SALES (est): 7.32MM Privately Held
Web: www.fleetscience.org
SIC: 8412 Museum

(P-18667)
RONALD RGAN PRSDNTIAL FNDTION
Also Called: Ronald Rgan Prsdntial Lib Fndt
40 Presidential Dr Ste 200 (93065-0600)
PHONE...................805 522-2977
TOLL FREE: 800
Glenn Baker, CFO
John Heubusch, *
Cary L Garman, *
Joanne Drake, Chief of Staff*
EMP: 70 EST: 1985
SQ FT: 225,000
SALES (est): 31.83MM Privately Held
Web: www.reaganfoundation.org
SIC: 8412 8231 5947 8399 Museum; Public library; Gifts and novelties; Community development groups

(P-18668)
SAN DEGO SOC OF NTURAL HISTORY
Also Called: SAN DIEGO NATURAL HISTORY MUSE
1788 El Prado (92101-1624)
P.O. Box 121390 (92112-1390)
PHONE...................619 232-3821
Michael W Hager, CEO
George Gonyer, *
Susan Loveall, *
▲ EMP: 70 EST: 1874
SQ FT: 60,000
SALES (est): 15.38MM Privately Held
Web: www.sdnhm.org

SIC: 8412 5047 Museum; Dental equipment and supplies

(P-18669)
SAN DIEGO AIR & SPACE MUSEUM
2001 Pan American Plz (92101-1636)
PHONE...................619 234-8291
James Kidrick, Pr
▼ EMP: 75 EST: 1961
SQ FT: 105,000
SALES (est): 7.58MM Privately Held
Web: www.sandiegoairandspace.org
SIC: 8412 5947 Museum; Souvenirs

(P-18670)
SAN DIEGO MUSEUM OF ART
1450 El Prado (92101-1618)
P.O. Box 122107 (92112-2107)
PHONE...................619 696-1909
Philip Tom Gildred, CEO
Roxanna Velasquez, *
Reed Viekerman, Asst Dir
▲ EMP: 82 EST: 1925
SQ FT: 96,278
SALES (est): 14MM Privately Held
Web: www.sdmart.org
SIC: 8412 Museum

(P-18671)
SAN FRANCISCO MUSEUM MODRN ART (PA)
Also Called: SFMOMA MUSEUM STORE
151 3rd St (94103-3107)
PHONE...................415 357-4035
Robert J Fisher, Pr
Charles R Schwab, *
Neal Benezra, *
Dennis J Wong, *
▲ EMP: 355 EST: 1921
SQ FT: 225,000
SALES (est): 89.77MM
SALES (corp-wide): 89.77MM Privately Held
Web: www.sfmoma.org
SIC: 8412 5942 Museum; Book stores

(P-18672)
SAN JOSE CHLD DISCOVERY MUSEUM
Also Called: Children's Discovery Museum
180 Woz Way (95110-2722)
PHONE...................408 298-5437
William Sullivan, CEO
EMP: 85 EST: 1983
SQ FT: 52,000
SALES (est): 6.15MM Privately Held
Web: www.cdm.org
SIC: 8412 Museum

(P-18673)
SAN JOSE MUSEUM OF ART ASSN
110 S Market St (95113-2307)
PHONE...................408 271-6840
Daniel Keegan, Dir
▲ EMP: 70 EST: 1969
SQ FT: 80,000
SALES (est): 5.29MM Privately Held
Web: www.sjmusart.org
SIC: 8412 5942 5947 Museum; Book stores; Gift shop

(P-18674)
SANTA BARBARA MUSEUM OF ART (PA)
Also Called: FINE ARTS MUSEUM
1130 State St (93101-2746)

8412 - Museums And Art Galleries (P-18675)

PHONE.................805 963-4364
Larry J Feinberg, *CEO*
Larry Feinberg, *
Kenneth Anderson, *
Robert Frankel, *
James Owen, *
▲ **EMP:** 60 **EST:** 1939
SQ FT: 50,000
SALES (est): 18.95MM
SALES (corp-wide): 18.95MM **Privately Held**
Web: www.sbma.net
SIC: 8412 Museum

(P-18675)
SANTA BRBARA MSEUM NTRAL HSTOR
2559 Puesta Del Sol (93105-2936)
PHONE.................805 682-4711
Luke Swetland, *CEO*
Karl Hutterer, *
Diane Wondowloski, *
Palmer Jackson Junior, *Pr*
Carolyn Chandler, *
EMP: 95 **EST:** 1916
SALES (est): 7.85MM **Privately Held**
Web: www.sbnature.org
SIC: 8412 Museum

(P-18676)
SKIRBALL CULTURAL CENTER
Also Called: SKIRBALL CULTURAL CENTER
2701 N Sepulveda Blvd (90049-6833)
PHONE.................310 440-4500
Uri D Herscher, *Pr*
Leslie K Johnson, *
▲ **EMP:** 150 **EST:** 1995
SQ FT: 65,000
SALES (est): 16.43MM **Privately Held**
Web: www.skirball.org
SIC: 8412 Museum

(P-18677)
TECH INTERACTIVE (PA)
Also Called: TECH
201 S Market St (95113-2008)
PHONE.................408 795-6116
Peter Friess, *CEO*
Donald Gralnek, *Sec*
Christopher Digiorgio, *Ch Bd*
Tim Ritchie, *Pr*
Naresh Kapahi, *CFO*
◆ **EMP:** 102 **EST:** 1983
SQ FT: 130,000
SALES (est): 16.98MM
SALES (corp-wide): 16.98MM **Privately Held**
Web: www.thetech.org
SIC: 8412 Arts or science center

(P-18678)
TECH INTERACTIVE
145 W San Carlos St (95113-2006)
PHONE.................408 795-6168
Bill Bailor, *Dir*
EMP: 62
SALES (corp-wide): 16.98MM **Privately Held**
Web: www.thetech.org
SIC: 8412 Arts or science center
PA: The Tech Interactive
   201 S Market St
   San Jose CA
   408 795-6116

(P-18679)
THE J PAUL GETTY TRUST (PA)
Also Called: Getty Publications
1200 Getty Center Dr Ste 500 (90049-1657)
PHONE.................310 440-7300
▲ **EMP:** 1431 **EST:** 1953
SALES (est): 149.74MM
SALES (corp-wide): 149.74MM **Privately Held**
Web: www.getty.edu
SIC: 8412 Museums and art galleries

(P-18680)
THE ORIGIN PROJECT INC
2121 Vallejo St (94123-4814)
PHONE.................415 601-2409
Nancy Fisher, *Ex Dir*
Adriana Trigiani, *
EMP: 75 **EST:** 2016
SALES (est): 144.59K **Privately Held**
SIC: 8412 Museums and art galleries

(P-18681)
USS HORNET MUSEUM
94 Chatham Pt (94502-6504)
PHONE.................510 521-8448
Jon Stanley, *Ch*
EMP: 60 **EST:** 2008
SALES (est): 470.04K **Privately Held**
Web: www.uss-hornet.org
SIC: 8412 Museum

(P-18682)
WALT DISNEY FAMILY MUSEUM
104 Montgomery St (94129-1718)
PHONE.................415 345-6800
Ronald W Miller, *Pr*
Kirsten Komoroske, *
Joanna Miller, *
Jennifer Miller-goff, *Sec*
EMP: 60 **EST:** 2007
SALES (est): 13MM **Privately Held**
Web: www.waltdisney.org
SIC: 8412 Museum

8422 Botanical And Zoological Gardens

(P-18683)
AQUARIUM OF PACIFIC (PA)
100 Aquarium Way (90802-8126)
PHONE.................562 590-3100
▲ **EMP:** 220 **EST:** 1997
SQ FT: 10,000
SALES (est): 55.28MM **Privately Held**
Web: www.aquariumofpacific.org
SIC: 8422 Aquarium

(P-18684)
BAYORG
Also Called: Aquarium of The Bay, The
Embarcadero At Beach St Pier 39 (94133)
PHONE.................415 623-5300
EMP: 99 **EST:** 2010
SALES (est): 11.59MM **Privately Held**
Web: www.aquariumofthebay.org
SIC: 8422 Aquarium

(P-18685)
CALIFORNIA ACADEMY SCIENCES (PA)
55 Music Concourse Dr (94118-4503)
PHONE.................415 379-8000
John Hafernik, *Pr*
Alison Brown, *
EMP: 635 **EST:** 1853
SQ FT: 410,000
SALES (est): 62.97MM
SALES (corp-wide): 62.97MM **Privately Held**
Web: www.calacademy.org

SIC: 8422 2721 8412 Aquarium; Periodicals, publishing only; Museums and art galleries

(P-18686)
CITY OF SAN JOSE
Also Called: Visitor Services & Facilities
1300 Senter Rd (95112-2520)
PHONE.................408 794-6400
Randy Adams Park, *Supervisor*
EMP: 60
SALES (corp-wide): 2.14B **Privately Held**
Web: www.happyhollow.org
SIC: 8422 9512 Zoological garden, noncommercial; Recreational program administration, government
PA: City Of San Jose
   200 E Santa Clara St 13th
   San Jose CA
   408 535-3500

(P-18687)
CONSERVATION SOCIETY CAL
Also Called: OAKLAND ZOO IN KNOWLAND PARK
9777 Golf Links Rd (94605-4925)
P.O. Box 5238 (94605-0238)
PHONE.................510 632-9525
Joel J Parrott, *CEO*
Steven E Kane, *
William L Marchant, *
Jonathan M Harris, *Treas*
EMP: 215 **EST:** 1936
SQ FT: 1,000
SALES (est): 35.36MM **Privately Held**
Web: www.oaklandzoo.org
SIC: 8422 Botanical and zoological gardens

(P-18688)
FRESNOS CHAFFEE ZOO CORP
Also Called: FRESNO'S CHAFFEE ZOO
894 W Belmont Ave (93728-2807)
PHONE.................559 498-5910
Scott Barton, *CEO*
Brian Goldman, *
◆ **EMP:** 121 **EST:** 2005
SALES (est): 20.42MM **Privately Held**
Web: www.fresnochaffeezoo.org
SIC: 8422 Animal and reptile exhibit

(P-18689)
LIVING DESERT
47900 Portola Ave (92260-6156)
PHONE.................760 346-5694
Allen Monroe, *CEO*
Terrie Correll, *
Dwight Middendorf, *
Sarah Clapp, *
Peter Siminski, *
EMP: 124 **EST:** 1970
SQ FT: 1,700
SALES (est): 34.59MM **Privately Held**
Web: www.livingdesert.org
SIC: 8422 5947 Aquariums and zoological gardens; Gift shop

(P-18690)
LOS ANGLES ARBRTUM FNDTION INC
301 N Baldwin Ave (91007-2697)
PHONE.................626 821-3222
Richard Schulhof, *CEO*
Jennifer Williams, *
EMP: 65 **EST:** 1948
SALES (est): 6.98MM **Privately Held**
Web: www.arboretum.org
SIC: 8422 Arboretum

(P-18691)
MONTALVO ASSOCIATION
Also Called: VILLA MONTALVO
15400 Montalvo Rd (95070-6327)
P.O. Box 158 (95071-0158)
PHONE.................408 961-5800
Angela Mcconnell, *CEO*
EMP: 65 **EST:** 1952
SQ FT: 13,000
SALES (est): 7.48MM **Privately Held**
Web: www.montalvoarts.org
SIC: 8422 8412 Arboretum; Art gallery, noncommercial

(P-18692)
MONTEREY BAY AQAR FOUNDATION (PA)
Also Called: MONTEREY BAY AQUARIUM
886 Cannery Row (93940-1023)
PHONE.................831 648-4800
Peter Bing, *Ch Bd*
Julie E Packard, *
Edward Prohaska, *
Barbara P Wright, *
EMP: 372 **EST:** 1978
SQ FT: 326,000
SALES (est): 114.46MM
SALES (corp-wide): 114.46MM **Privately Held**
Web: www.montereybayaquarium.org
SIC: 8422 Aquarium

(P-18693)
RANCHO SANTA ANA BOTANIC GRDN
Also Called: CALIFORNIA BOTANIC GARDEN
1500 N College Ave (91711-3157)
PHONE.................909 625-8767
Lucinda Mcdade, *Ex Dir*
Clement Hamilton, *
Richard Grant, *
Sonja Evensen, *
EMP: 75 **EST:** 1927
SQ FT: 30,000
SALES (est): 6.57MM **Privately Held**
Web: www.calbg.org
SIC: 8422 Botanical garden

(P-18694)
SANTA BRBARA ZLGCAL FOUNDATION
Also Called: SANTA BARBARA ZOO
500 Ninos Dr (93103-3759)
PHONE.................805 962-1673
Yul Vanek, *CEO*
Nancy Mctoldridge, *COO*
Carol Bedford, *
Fred Clough, *
Diane Pearson, *
▲ **EMP:** 130 **EST:** 1961
SQ FT: 1,200
SALES (est): 18.28MM **Privately Held**
Web: www.sbzoo.org
SIC: 8422 Zoological garden, noncommercial

(P-18695)
ZOOLOGICAL SOCIETY SAN DIEGO
Also Called: San Diego Zoo
2920 Zoo Dr (92101-1646)
P.O. Box 120551 (92112-0551)
PHONE.................619 744-3325
Richard Farrar, *Dir*
EMP: 152
SALES (corp-wide): 422.09MM **Privately Held**
Web: www.sandiegozoowildlifealliance.org

PRODUCTS & SERVICES SECTION
8611 - Business Associations (P-18715)

SIC: **8422** Botanical and zoological gardens
PA: Zoological Society Of San Diego
2920 Zoo Dr
San Diego CA
619 231-1515

(P-18696)
ZOOLOGICAL SOCIETY SAN DIEGO
Also Called: San Diego Wild Animal Park
15500 San Pasqual Valley Rd (92027-7017)
PHONE..................760 747-8702
Robert Mcclure, *Mgr*
EMP: 228
SALES (corp-wide): 422.09MM **Privately Held**
Web: www.sandiegozoowildlifealliance.org
SIC: **8422** 7999 Animal and reptile exhibit; Tourist attraction, commercial
PA: Zoological Society Of San Diego
2920 Zoo Dr
San Diego CA
619 231-1515

(P-18697)
ZOOLOGICAL SOCIETY SAN DIEGO
Also Called: San Diego Zoo
10946 Willow Ct Ste 200 (92127-2417)
PHONE..................619 231-1515
Janet Matsuura, *Dir*
EMP: 152
SALES (corp-wide): 422.09MM **Privately Held**
Web: www.sandiegozoowildlifealliance.org
SIC: **8422** Animal and reptile exhibit
PA: Zoological Society Of San Diego
2920 Zoo Dr
San Diego CA
619 231-1515

(P-18698)
ZOOLOGICAL SOCIETY SAN DIEGO (PA)
Also Called: San Diego Zoo Wildlife Aliance
2920 Zoo Dr (92101-1646)
P.O. Box 120551 (92112-0551)
PHONE..................619 231-1515
Paul Baribault, *CEO*
Shawn Dixon, *COO*
David Franco, *CFO*
◆ EMP: 1500 EST: 1916
SALES (est): 422.09MM
SALES (corp-wide): 422.09MM **Privately Held**
Web: www.sandiegozoowildlifealliance.org
SIC: **8422** Aquarium

8611 Business Associations

(P-18699)
ALL STATE ASSOCIATION INC
11487 San Fernando Rd (91340-3406)
PHONE..................877 425-2558
Steve Avetyan, *CEO*
Alfred Megrabyan, *
Armen Karibyan, *
EMP: 250 EST: 2003
SALES (est): 9.56MM **Privately Held**
SIC: **8611** Trade associations

(P-18700)
CALIFORNIA ASSN REALTORS INC (PA)
525 S Virgil Ave (90020-1403)
PHONE..................213 739-8200
Joel S Singer, *
Joel S Singer, *
Lefrancis Arnold, *
Don Flyn, *
Don Faught, *
EMP: 110 EST: 1907
SQ FT: 52,000
SALES (est): 49.8MM
SALES (corp-wide): 49.8MM **Privately Held**
Web: zfp.car.org
SIC: **8611** 8742 Real estate board; Real estate consultant

(P-18701)
CALIFORNIA CHAMBER COMMERCE (PA)
Also Called: CAL CHAMBER
1215 K St Ste 1400 (95814-3953)
P.O. Box 1736 (95812-1736)
PHONE..................916 444-6670
Allan Zaremberg, *Pr*
Lawrence M Dicke, *Ex VP*
Dave Kilby, *Executive Corporate Affairs Vice President*
Jeanne Cain, *POLICY*
EMP: 65 EST: 1890
SQ FT: 26,000
SALES (est): 25.46MM
SALES (corp-wide): 25.46MM **Privately Held**
Web: www.calchamber.com
SIC: **8611** Chamber of Commerce

(P-18702)
CALIFORNIA RE ASSN INC
Also Called: California Real Estate
525 S Virgil Ave (90020-1403)
PHONE..................213 739-8200
EMP: 85 EST: 1996
SQ FT: 52,000
SALES (est): 1.9MM
SALES (corp-wide): 49.8MM **Privately Held**
SIC: **8611** Real estate board
PA: California Association Of Realtors, Inc.
525 S Virgil Ave
Los Angeles CA
213 739-8200

(P-18703)
CALIFRNIA RDVLPMENT ASSN FNDTI
801 12th St (95814-2947)
PHONE..................916 449-6229
EMP: 67 EST: 1979
SALES (est): 2.77MM **Privately Held**
Web: www.calredevelop.org
SIC: **8611** Trade associations

(P-18704)
CITY ORANGE POLICE ASSN INC
1107 N Batavia St (92867-4615)
P.O. Box 906 (92856-6906)
PHONE..................714 457-5340
EMP: 216 EST: 1980
SALES (est): 390.11K **Privately Held**
Web: www.copa33.org
SIC: **8611** Business associations

(P-18705)
CONTENTFUL INC
101 Montgomery St Ste 2050 (94104-4151)
PHONE..................415 248-7801
Sascha Konietzke, *CEO*
Bridget Perry, *CMO*
EMP: 82 EST: 2016
SALES (est): 9.91MM **Privately Held**
Web: www.contentful.com
SIC: **8611** Growers' marketing advisory service

(P-18706)
CWS UTILITY SERVICES CORP
1720 N 1st St (95112-4508)
PHONE..................408 367-8200
Robert W Foye, *Prin*
EMP: 79 EST: 2005
SALES (est): 832.27K
SALES (corp-wide): 846.43MM **Publicly Held**
SIC: **8611** Public utility association
PA: California Water Service Group
1720 N 1st St
San Jose CA
408 367-8200

(P-18707)
ELECTRA OWNERS ASSOC
700 W E St (92101-5984)
PHONE..................619 236-3310
J E Martin, *Prin*
EMP: 197 EST: 2008
SALES (est): 999.58K
SALES (corp-wide): 90.39MM **Privately Held**
Web: electraownersassociation.buildinglink.com
SIC: **8611** Business associations
PA: Action Property Management, Inc.
2603 Main St Ste 500
Irvine CA
949 450-0202

(P-18708)
ELECTRIC & GAS INDUSTRIES ASSOCIATION (PA)
Also Called: E G I A
3800 Watt Ave Ste 105 (95821-2613)
PHONE..................916 609-5300
EMP: 90 EST: 1966
SALES (est): 15.18MM
SALES (corp-wide): 15.18MM **Privately Held**
Web: www.egia.org
SIC: **8611** Trade associations

(P-18709)
EPSILON SYSTEMS SOLUTIONS INC
2101 Haffley Ave # A (91950-6416)
PHONE..................619 474-3252
Robert Duran, *Brnch Mgr*
EMP: 142
SALES (corp-wide): 110MM **Privately Held**
Web: www.epsilonsystems.com
SIC: **8611** Shipping and steamship company association
PA: Epsilon Systems Solutions, Inc.
9444 Balboa Ave Ste 100
San Diego CA
619 702-1700

(P-18710)
HUMBOLDT BAY FIRE JINT PWERS A
533 C St (95501-0340)
PHONE..................707 441-4000
Kenneth Woods, *Chief*
Kathi Hendricks, *Ex Sec*
EMP: 60 EST: 2012
SQ FT: 18,700
SALES (est): 399.58K **Privately Held**
Web: www.hbfire.org
SIC: **8611** 8099 Business associations; Medical services organization

(P-18711)
INSTITUTE OF ELEC ELEC ENGNERS
Also Called: Ieee Computer Society
10662 Los Vaqueros Cir (90720-2513)
P.O. Box 3014 (90720-1314)
PHONE..................714 821-8380
Linda Ashworth, *Admn*
EMP: 85
SALES (corp-wide): 524.8MM **Privately Held**
Web: ieeeshutpages.s3-website-us-west-2.amazonaws.com
SIC: **8611** Trade associations
PA: The Institute Of Electrical And Electronics Engineers Incorporated
445 Hoes Ln
Piscataway NJ
212 419-7900

(P-18712)
LOS ANGLES AREA CHMBER CMMERCE
350 S Bixel St (90017-1418)
PHONE..................213 580-7500
Maria S Salinas, *Pr*
Gary Toebben, *CEO*
David Eads, *COO*
Benjamin Stilp, *CFO*
Mark Louchheim, *Ch Bd*
EMP: 85 EST: 2009
SALES (est): 6.08MM **Privately Held**
Web: www.lachamber.com
SIC: **8611** Chamber of Commerce

(P-18713)
MENS APPAREL GUILD IN CAL INC
Also Called: Magic International
2901 28th St Ste 100 (90405-2975)
PHONE..................310 857-7500
Joe Loggia, *Pr*
EMP: 117 EST: 1932
SALES (est): 2.4MM
SALES (corp-wide): 2.72B **Privately Held**
SIC: **8611** Manufacturers' institute
HQ: Advanstar Communications Inc.
2501 Colorado Ave Ste 280
Santa Monica CA
310 857-7500

(P-18714)
MERCHANT VALLEY CORPORATION
Also Called: Best Western Apricot Inn
1808 Avondale Dr (95747-8390)
PHONE..................916 786-7227
Mahmood Merchant, *Prin*
EMP: 125 EST: 1997
SALES (est): 9.91MM **Privately Held**
SIC: **8611** Merchants' association

(P-18715)
MERCY HOUSE LIVING CENTERS
Also Called: Mercy Hse Trnstnal Living Ctrs
807 N Garfield St (92701-3821)
P.O. Box 1905 (92702-1905)
PHONE..................714 836-7188
Larry Haynes, *Ex Dir*
Jerome Karcher, *
Carrie Delaurie, *
EMP: 170 EST: 1988
SQ FT: 19,000
SALES (est): 19.91MM **Privately Held**
Web: www.mercyhouse.net
SIC: **8611** Community affairs and services

8611 Business Associations

(P-18716)
MIDI MANUFACTURERS ASSN INC
Also Called: Midi Association, The
85 Matisse Cir (92656-3864)
PHONE..................714 227-0068
Athan Billias, Pr
Lee Whitmore, Treas
Jean-baptiste Thiebaut, Sec
EMP: 98 EST: 1985
SALES (est): 629.62K Privately Held
SIC: 8611 Trade associations

(P-18717)
MOUNTAIN HOUSE CMNTY SVCS DST
251 E Main St (95391-3050)
PHONE..................209 831-2300
Eric Payne, Pr
EMP: 96 EST: 2009
SALES (est): 30.05MM Privately Held
Web: www.mountainhousecsd.org
SIC: 8611 Community affairs and services

(P-18718)
NATIONAL ASSN MUS MRCHANTS INC
Also Called: NAMM
5790 Armada Dr (92008-4608)
PHONE..................760 438-8001
Joe Lamond, Pr
Larry Manley, *
Kevin Cranley, Vice Chairman*
Larry Morton, *
EMP: 62 EST: 1901
SQ FT: 38,000
SALES (est): 7.16MM Privately Held
Web: www.namm.org
SIC: 8611 Trade associations

(P-18719)
RH COMMUNITY BUILDERS LP
2550 W Clinton Ave B-142 (93705-4206)
PHONE..................559 492-1373
Wayne Rutledge, CEO
Brad Hardie, Pr
EMP: 100 EST: 2019
SALES (est): 2.08MM Privately Held
Web: www.rhcommunitybuilders.com
SIC: 8611 8082 Community affairs and services; Home health care services

(P-18720)
SAN DIEGO ASSN GOVERNMENTS (PA)
Also Called: Regional Transportation Comm
401 B St Ste 800 (92101-4231)
PHONE..................619 699-1900
Jack Dale, Ch
Jim Janney, *
Don Higginson, *
Gary L Gallegos, *
EMP: 250 EST: 1972
SQ FT: 20,000
SALES (est): 222.55MM
SALES (corp-wide): 222.55MM Privately Held
Web: www.sandag.org
SIC: 8611 Business associations

(P-18721)
SATICOY LEMON ASSOCIATION
600 E 3rd St (93030-6001)
P.O. Box 46 (93061-0046)
PHONE..................805 654-6543
EMP: 99
SALES (corp-wide): 26.61MM Privately Held
Web: www.saticoylemon.com
SIC: 8611 Growers' associations
PA: Saticoy Lemon Association
103 N Peck Rd
Santa Paula CA
805 654-6500

(P-18722)
SEMI (PA)
673 S Milpitas Blvd (95035-5473)
PHONE..................408 943-6900
Ajit Manocha, Pr
Richard Salsman, *
Bertrand Loy, *
Kevin Crofton, *
Mary G Puma, *
EMP: 133 EST: 1970
SALES (est): 57.59MM
SALES (corp-wide): 57.59MM Privately Held
Web: www.semi.org
SIC: 8611 Trade associations

(P-18723)
SOUTHLAND RGNAL ASSN RLTORS IN (PA)
7232 Balboa Blvd (91406-2701)
PHONE..................818 786-2110
James Link, Ex VP
Brian Paul, *
Rob Schwab, *
Chuck Nickerson, *
Steve White, *
EMP: 72 EST: 1957
SQ FT: 25,000
SALES (est): 9.1MM
SALES (corp-wide): 9.1MM Privately Held
Web: www.srar.com
SIC: 8611 Real estate board

(P-18724)
SPECIALTY EQUIPMENT MKT ASSN (PA)
Also Called: Sema
1575 Valley Vista Dr (91765-3914)
PHONE..................909 396-0289
Bill Miller, Interim CAO
Mike Spagnola, Interim CAO*
Linda Czarkowski, *
George Afremow, *
EMP: 70 EST: 1963
SQ FT: 23,000
SALES (est): 20.61MM
SALES (corp-wide): 20.61MM Privately Held
Web: www.sema.org
SIC: 8611 Trade associations

(P-18725)
SURPLUS LINE ASSOCIATION CAL
12667 Alcosta Blvd Ste 450 (94583-4427)
PHONE..................415 434-4900
Ted Pierce, Ex Dir
Joy Laughery, *
EMP: 111 EST: 1937
SQ FT: 8,400
SALES (est): 15.51MM Privately Held
Web: www.slacal.com
SIC: 8611 Trade associations

(P-18726)
WESTERN GROWERS ASSOCIATION (PA)
Also Called: W G A
6501 Irvine Center Dr (92618-2134)
P.O. Box 57089 (92619-7089)
PHONE..................949 863-1000
Tom A Nassif, CEO
Steve Patricio, *
Matt Mcinerney, Ex VP
Ward Kennedy, *
Dave Puglia, *
EMP: 150 EST: 1926
SALES (est): 42.45MM
SALES (corp-wide): 42.45MM Privately Held
Web: www.wga.com
SIC: 8611 8111 Growers' associations; Legal services

(P-18727)
WONDERFUL CITRUS COOPERATIVE
5001 California Ave Ste 230 (93309-1671)
PHONE..................661 720-2400
EMP: 520
Web: www.wonderfulcitrus.com
SIC: 8611 Growers' marketing advisory service
PA: Wonderful Citrus Cooperative
1901 S Lexington St
Delano CA

8621 Professional Organizations

(P-18728)
ACADEMY MPIC ARTS & SCIENCES (PA)
8949 Wilshire Blvd (90211-1907)
PHONE..................310 247-3000
Dawn Hudson, CEO
Janet Yang, *
Bruce Davis, *
Andy Horn, *
Meredith Shea Chief Membership Impact Industry, Ofcr
EMP: 100 EST: 1927
SQ FT: 35,000
SALES (est): 287.95MM
SALES (corp-wide): 287.95MM Privately Held
Web: www.oscars.org
SIC: 8621 7819 8611 Professional organizations; Services allied to motion pictures; Business associations

(P-18729)
AMERICAN ACDEMY OPHTHLMLOGY IN (PA)
655 Beach St Fl 1 (94109-1342)
P.O. Box 7424 (94120-7424)
PHONE..................415 561-8500
David W Parke Ii, CEO
Keith Carter, *
Jill Boyett, *
EMP: 160 EST: 1896
SQ FT: 66,000
SALES (est): 63.35MM
SALES (corp-wide): 63.35MM Privately Held
Web: www.aao.org
SIC: 8621 Medical field-related associations

(P-18730)
ANOVA EDCATN BEHAVIORAL CNSLTN
Also Called: ANOVA EDUCATION & BEHAVIORAL CONSULTATION INC
3033 Cleveland Ave Ste 240 (95403-2126)
PHONE..................707 527-0183
Mary Ludwig, Prin
EMP: 61
SALES (corp-wide): 10.56MM Privately Held
Web: www.anovaeducation.org
SIC: 8621 Professional organizations
PA: Anova Education And Behavior Consultation, Inc.
475 Aviation Blvd
Santa Rosa CA
707 527-7032

(P-18731)
ASSOCTION MXCAN AMRCN EDCATORS
Also Called: Norwalk Unified School Dst
12820 Pioneer Blvd (90650-2875)
PHONE..................562 868-0431
Hasmik Danielian, Superintnt
EMP: 93
Web: www.nlmusd.org
SIC: 8621 Education and teacher association
PA: Association Of Mexican American Educators
2511 W 3rd St
Los Angeles CA

(P-18732)
ATTAINMENT HOLDCO LLC
Also Called: Instride
700 S Flower St Ste 1800 (90017-4205)
PHONE..................310 954-1578
Stephen Chu, Managing Member
Jonathan Lau, COO
Dan Bock, CCO
Jeff Stark, CFO
EMP: 151 EST: 2019
SALES (est): 11.83MM Privately Held
Web: www.instride.com
SIC: 8621 Education and teacher association

(P-18733)
BAR ASSCATION OF SAN FRANCISCO (PA)
201 Mission St Ste 400 (94105-1832)
PHONE..................415 982-1600
James Donato, Pr
Dan Burkhardt, *
Jonathan Bond, *
EMP: 85 EST: 1949
SALES (est): 7.82MM Privately Held
Web: www.sfbar.org
SIC: 8621 Bar association

(P-18734)
BVOH LLC
Also Called: Bvoh Fin & Accounting Search
5 3rd St Ste 1225 (94103-3228)
PHONE..................415 738-0901
EMP: 62 EST: 2004
SALES (est): 10.62MM
SALES (corp-wide): 539.88MM Privately Held
Web: www.bvoh.com
SIC: 8621 Professional organizations
PA: Vaco Llc
5501 Virginia Way Ste 120
Brentwood TN
615 301-4099

(P-18735)
CALIFORNIA CANCER SPECIALISTS MEDICAL GROUP INC
1333 S Mayflower Ave # 200 (91016-4032)
PHONE..................626 775-3200
EMP: 320
SIC: 8621 7389 Medical field-related associations; Financial services

(P-18736)
CALIFORNIA DENTAL ASSOCIATION (PA)

PRODUCTS & SERVICES SECTION
8621 - Professional Organizations (P-18756)

1201 K St Fl 14 (95814-3906)
PHONE..............................916 443-0505
Peter A Dubois, *CEO*
Carol Summerhayes, *
Cynthia Schneider, *
EMP: 120 **EST:** 1873
SQ FT: 28,932
SALES (est): 15.89MM
SALES (corp-wide): 15.89MM Privately Held
Web: www.cda.org
SIC: 8621 Dental association

(P-18737)
CALIFORNIA HEALTH BENEFIT EXCH
Also Called: California Health Insur Exch
1601 Exposition Blvd (95815-5103)
PHONE..............................916 228-8210
EMP: 99 **EST:** 2012
SALES (est): 12.8MM Privately Held
Web: www.coveredca.com
SIC: 8621 Health association

(P-18738)
CALIFORNIA MEDICAL ASSOCIATION (PA)
Also Called: C M A
1201 K Ste 800 (95814-3906)
PHONE..............................916 444-5532
Dustin Corcoren, *CEO*
Lance Lewis, *
Nick Birtcil, *
EMP: 73 **EST:** 1856
SALES (est): 29.62MM
SALES (corp-wide): 29.62MM Privately Held
Web: www.cmadocs.org
SIC: 8621 Medical field-related associations

(P-18739)
CALIFORNIA NURSES ASSOCIATION (PA)
Also Called: National Nurses United
155 Grand Ave (94612-3724)
PHONE..............................510 273-2200
Rose Anne Demoro, *CEO*
Deborah Burger, *
Nikki Dones, *
Mike Griffing, *
EMP: 100 **EST:** 1907
SQ FT: 36,000
SALES (est): 139.57MM
SALES (corp-wide): 139.57MM Privately Held
Web: www.nationalnursesunited.org
SIC: 8621 Nursing association

(P-18740)
CALIFORNIA SCHOOL BOARDS ASSN
Also Called: CSBA
3251 Beacon Blvd (95691-3475)
PHONE..............................800 266-3382
Vernon M Billy, *CEO*
Scott Plotkin, *
Cindy Marks, *
Jesus Holguin, *
Stephen Pogemiller, *
EMP: 100 **EST:** 1931
SQ FT: 15,000
SALES (est): 114.69K Privately Held
Web: www.csba.org
SIC: 8621 Education and teacher association

(P-18741)
CALIFORNIA TEACHERS ASSN (PA)
1705 Murchison Dr (94010-4504)

P.O. Box 921 (94011-0921)
PHONE..............................650 697-1400
Carolyn Doggett, *Ex Dir*
EMP: 210 **EST:** 1907
SALES (est): 39.4K
SALES (corp-wide): 39.4K Privately Held
Web: www.cta.org
SIC: 8621 8631 Education and teacher association; Labor organizations

(P-18742)
CALIFRNIA ASSN HSPTALS HLTH SY (PA)
Also Called: California Hospital Assn Cha
1215 K St Ste 700 (95814-3946)
PHONE..............................916 443-7401
Carmela Coyle, *Pr*
Lois M Suder, *
Dietmar Grellmann, *
Anne Mcleod, *Sr VP*
EMP: 74 **EST:** 1934
SALES (est): 31.12MM
SALES (corp-wide): 31.12MM Privately Held
Web: www.calhospital.org
SIC: 8621 8011 Health association; Group health association

(P-18743)
CAPITAL INVSTMNTS VNTURES CORP (PA)
Also Called: Civco
30151 Tomas (92688-2125)
PHONE..............................949 858-0647
Drew Richardson, *Pr*
Gary Prenovost, *
Marjorie Kelso Int'l, *Prs Dir*
Brian Cronin, *
◆ **EMP:** 195 **EST:** 1975
SQ FT: 95,000
SALES (est): 64.57MM
SALES (corp-wide): 64.57MM Privately Held
Web: www.padi.com
SIC: 8621 4724 Professional organizations; Travel agencies

(P-18744)
CEP AMERICA-CALIFORNIA (PA)
2100 Powell St Ste 900 (94608-1872)
PHONE..............................510 350-2700
EMP: 80 **EST:** 1975
SALES (est): 500MM
SALES (corp-wide): 500MM Privately Held
Web: www.vituity.com
SIC: 8621 Professional organizations

(P-18745)
CONSOLIDATED NETWORKS CORP
1031 Aldridge Rd Ste E (95688-8721)
PHONE..............................707 422-0791
John Kowalsky, *Brnch Mgr*
EMP: 96
SALES (corp-wide): 25.91MM Privately Held
Web: www.cnc-usa.com
SIC: 8621 Professional organizations
PA: Consolidated Networks Corporation
       722 N Broadway Ave # 203
       Oklahoma City OK
       405 879-2322

(P-18746)
COOPERTIVE AMRCN PHYSCIANS INC (PA)
Also Called: Cap-Mpt
333 S Hope St Fl 8 (90071-3001)

PHONE..............................213 473-8600
James Weidner, *CEO*
Thomas Andrem, *VP*
Cindy Belcher, *COO*
Nancy Brusegaard Johnson, *Sr VP*
John Donaldson, *CFO*
EMP: 100 **EST:** 1975
SALES (est): 29.98MM
SALES (corp-wide): 29.98MM Privately Held
Web: www.capphysicians.com
SIC: 8621 Medical field-related associations

(P-18747)
COUNTY OF LOS ANGELES
313 N Figueroa St 9th Fl (90012-2602)
PHONE..............................213 240-8412
Thomas L Garthwaite, *Brnch Mgr*
EMP: 117
SALES (corp-wide): 31.7B Privately Held
Web: www.lacounty.gov
SIC: 8621 9431 Professional organizations; Prenatal (maternity) health program administration, govt.
PA: County Of Los Angeles
       500 W Temple St Ste 437
       Los Angeles CA
       213 974-1101

(P-18748)
DEMAND GEN INC ✪
1147 Groen Ct (95366-3335)
PHONE..............................415 373-2450
Derek Rey, *CEO*
EMP: 80 **EST:** 2022
SALES (est): 1.31MM Privately Held
SIC: 8621 7389 Professional organizations; Business services, nec

(P-18749)
HOSPITALITY BENNETT GROUP LLC
Also Called: Bennett's Kitchen Bar Market
1595 Eureka Rd (95661-3040)
PHONE..............................916 750-5150
Brian Bennett, *Managing Member*
EMP: 177
SALES (corp-wide): 4.93MM Privately Held
Web: www.bennettskitchen.com
SIC: 8621 Bar association
PA: Bennett Hospitality Group, Llc
       4521 Longview Dr
       Rocklin CA
       916 750-5150

(P-18750)
LEIGHTON GROUP INC
75450 Gerald Ford Dr Ste 301 (92211-6022)
PHONE..............................760 776-4192
EMP: 165
SALES (corp-wide): 163.28MM Privately Held
Web: www.leightongroup.com
SIC: 8621 Professional organizations
HQ: Leighton Group, Inc.
       2600 Michelson Dr Ste 400
       Irvine CA
       949 250-1421

(P-18751)
LOS ANGELES COUNTY BAR ASSN (PA)
Also Called: LOS ANGELES LAWYER MAGAZINE
444 S Flower St (90071-2926)
P.O. Box 55020 (90055-2020)
PHONE..............................213 627-2727
Paul R Kiesel, *Pr*

Sally Suchil, *
▲ **EMP:** 85 **EST:** 1878
SALES (est): 8.13MM
SALES (corp-wide): 8.13MM Privately Held
Web: www.lacba.org
SIC: 8621 Bar association

(P-18752)
MEDIMPACT HLTHCARE SYSTEMS INC (HQ)
10181 Scripps Gateway Ct (92131-5152)
PHONE..............................858 566-2727
Frederick Howe, *Ch Bd*
James Gollaher, *CFO*
EMP: 160 **EST:** 1989
SQ FT: 100,000
SALES (est): 134.05MM Privately Held
Web: www.medimpact.com
SIC: 8621 Medical field-related associations
PA: Medimpact Holdings, Inc.
       10181 Scripps Gateway Ct
       San Diego CA

(P-18753)
NATIONAL NOTARY ASSOCIATION
Also Called: Nna Insurance Services
9350 De Soto Ave (91311-4926)
PHONE..............................800 876-6827
EMP: 204 **EST:** 1984
SALES (est): 26.08MM Privately Held
Web: www.nationalnotary.org
SIC: 8621 Professional organizations

(P-18754)
ORANGE CNTY HLTH AUTH A PUB AG
Also Called: Orange County Health Authority
505 City Pkwy W (92868-2924)
PHONE..............................714 246-8500
Richard Chambers, *CEO*
Michael Schrader, *
Richard Helmer, *Chief Medical Officer*
Ladan Khamseh, *
EMP: 432 **EST:** 1994
SQ FT: 200,000
SALES (est): 103.83MM Privately Held
Web: www.caloptima.org
SIC: 8621 Professional organizations

(P-18755)
ORANGE COUNTY HEALTH CARE AGCY
405 W 5th St Ste 700 (92701-4534)
PHONE..............................714 568-5683
Jenny Qian, *Prin*
EMP: 99 **EST:** 2014
SALES (est): 10.34MM Privately Held
Web: www.ochealthinfo.com
SIC: 8621 Health association

(P-18756)
PADI AMERICAS INC
Also Called: Padi
30151 Tomas (92688-2125)
P.O. Box 7005 (92688-7005)
PHONE..............................949 858-7234
Drew Richardson, *Prin*
◆ **EMP:** 200 **EST:** 1967
SQ FT: 96,000
SALES (est): 51.74MM
SALES (corp-wide): 64.57MM Privately Held
Web: www.padi.com
SIC: 8621 Education and teacher association
HQ: Padi Worldwide Corp.
       30151 Tomas
       Rcho Sta Marg CA
       949 858-7234

(PA)=Parent Co (HQ)=Headquarters
✪ = New Business established in last 2 years

8621 - Professional Organizations (P-18757)

(P-18757)
POMONA COMMUNITY HEALTH CENTER
Also Called: PARKTREE COMMUNITY HEALTH CENT
1450 E Holt Ave (91767-5822)
PHONE..................909 630-7927
EMP: 60 **EST:** 2010
SALES (est): 14.16MM Privately Held
Web: www.parktreechc.org
SIC: 8621 Health association

(P-18758)
REGAL MEDICAL GROUP INC (PA)
Also Called: Heritage California Aco
8510 Balboa Blvd Ste 275 (91325-5809)
PHONE..................818 654-3400
EMP: 111 **EST:** 1986
SALES (est): 66.89MM Privately Held
Web: www.regalmed.com
SIC: 8621 Medical field-related associations

(P-18759)
ROCKBLUE
601 Foothill Rd (93023-1765)
PHONE..................703 314-0208
Peter Macy, *Pr*
Satish Menon, *
Richard Noth, *
Chris Fahlin, *
Shannon Roxborough, *
EMP: 75 **EST:** 2021
SALES (est): 801.27K Privately Held
SIC: 8621 Professional organizations

(P-18760)
SAN FRANCISCO HEALTH AUTHORITY (PA)
Also Called: Hsf Programme
50 Beale St Fl 12 (94105-1823)
P.O. Box 194247 (94119-4247)
PHONE..................415 615-4407
EMP: 99 **EST:** 1996
SQ FT: 26,000
SALES (est): 26.65MM Privately Held
Web: www.sfhp.org
SIC: 8621 Health association

(P-18761)
SHARP COMMUNITY MEDICAL GROUP
Also Called: SCMG
8695 Spectrum Center Blvd (92123-1489)
PHONE..................858 499-4525
Kenneth Roth, *Pr*
EMP: 200 **EST:** 1989
SALES (est): 552.32MM
SALES (corp-wide): 2.37B Privately Held
Web: www.scmg.org
SIC: 8621 Professional organizations
PA: Sharp Healthcare
  8695 Spectrum Center Blvd
  San Diego CA
  858 499-4000

(P-18762)
STANFORD HEALTH CARE
Also Called: Stanford Cancer Center
875 Blake Wilbur Dr (94304-2205)
PHONE..................650 498-5032
Quynh-thu Le, *Prin*
EMP: 225
SALES (corp-wide): 15.13B Privately Held
Web: www.stanfordhealthcare.org
SIC: 8621 Professional standards review board
HQ: Stanford Health Care
  300 Pasteur Dr
  Stanford CA
  650 723-4000

(P-18763)
STATE BAR OF CALIFORNIA
845 S Figueroa St (90017-2515)
PHONE..................213 765-1520
EMP: 93
SALES (corp-wide): 91.35MM Privately Held
Web: calbar.ca.gov
SIC: 8621 Bar association
PA: State Bar Of California
  180 Howard St Fl Grnd
  San Francisco CA
  415 538-2000

(P-18764)
STATE BAR OF CALIFORNIA (PA)
180 Howard St (94105-6155)
PHONE..................415 538-2000
Bill Hebert, *Pr*
Peggy Van Horn, *
Ellin Davtyan, *
EMP: 296 **EST:** 1927
SQ FT: 72,000
SALES (est): 91.35MM
SALES (corp-wide): 91.35MM Privately Held
Web: calbar.ca.gov
SIC: 8621 Bar association

(P-18765)
STATE BAR OF CALIFORNIA
755 Santa Rosa St Ste 310 (93401-4805)
PHONE..................805 544-7551
EMP: 92
SALES (corp-wide): 91.35MM Privately Held
Web: calbar.ca.gov
SIC: 8621 Bar association
PA: State Bar Of California
  180 Howard St Fl Grnd
  San Francisco CA
  415 538-2000

(P-18766)
TRUCK UNDERWRITERS ASSOCIATION (DH)
4680 Wilshire Blvd (90010-3807)
PHONE..................323 932-3200
Leonard H Gelfand, *Pr*
Gerald Faulwell, *
Martin Feinstein, *
John Lynch, *
Jason Katz, *
EMP: 1767 **EST:** 1935
SALES (est): 51MM Privately Held
SIC: 8621 Professional organizations
HQ: Farmers Group, Inc.
  6301 Owensmouth Ave # 300
  Woodland Hills CA
  323 932-3200

(P-18767)
TSIA
17065 Camino San Bernardo Ste 200 (92127)
PHONE..................858 674-5491
EMP: 81 **EST:** 2019
SALES (est): 2.55MM Privately Held
Web: www.tsia.com
SIC: 8621 Professional organizations

(P-18768)
UNITED CEREBRAL PALSY ASSOC (PA)
Also Called: Cerebral Palsy Assn San Joaqui
333 W Benjamin Holt Dr Ste 1 (95207-3906)
PHONE..................209 956-0290
Ray All, *Ex Dir*
EMP: 110 **EST:** 1954
SQ FT: 15,000
SALES (est): 1.74MM
SALES (corp-wide): 1.74MM Privately Held
Web: www.ucpsj.org
SIC: 8621 Professional organizations

(P-18769)
WOMENS RCVERY ASSN SAN MTEO CN
Also Called: Womens Recovery Association
2015 Pioneer Ct (94403-1781)
PHONE..................650 348-6603
EMP: 147 **EST:** 1970
SQ FT: 12,000
SALES (est): 2.42MM
SALES (corp-wide): 145.84MM Privately Held
Web: www.healthright360.org
SIC: 8621 Professional organizations
PA: Healthright 360 Foundation
  1563 Mission St Fl 4
  San Francisco CA
  415 762-3700

8631 Labor Organizations

(P-18770)
ALLIANCE HEALTH CARE UNIONS (PA)
Also Called: Unac/Uhcp
955 Overland Ct Ste 150 (91773-1718)
PHONE..................909 599-8622
Ken Deitz, *Pr*
Denise Duncan, *
Charmaine Morales, *
Jettie Deden-castillo, *Treas*
EMP: 63 **EST:** 1972
SALES (est): 8.25MM
SALES (corp-wide): 8.25MM Privately Held
Web: www.ahcunions.org
SIC: 8631 Employees' association

(P-18771)
AMERICAN FDRTION MSCANS LCAL 4
Also Called: AMERICAN FEDERATION OF MUSICIA
3220 Winona Ave (91504-2544)
PHONE..................323 462-2161
John Acosta, *Pr*
Rick Baptist, *
Gary Lasley, *
EMP: 95 **EST:** 1897
SALES (est): 3.47MM
SALES (corp-wide): 13.67MM Privately Held
Web: www.afm47.org
SIC: 8631 Labor union
PA: American Federation Of Musicians Of The United States & Canada (Inc)
  1501 Broadway Fl 9
  New York NY
  212 869-1330

(P-18772)
ART DRCTORS GILD ITSE LCAL 876
11969 Ventura Blvd Ste 200 (91604-2630)
PHONE..................818 762-9995
Mimi Gramatky, *Pr*
Scott Roth, *Dir*
Jim Wallis, *VP*
Cate Bangs, *Treas*
Judy Cosgrove, *Sec*
EMP: 127 **EST:** 1937
SQ FT: 19,040
SALES (est): 11.3MM Privately Held
Web: www.adg.org
SIC: 8631 Labor organizations

(P-18773)
CALIF SCHL EMPLYEES ASSOC RTRE
2045 Lundy Ave (95131-1825)
PHONE..................408 473-1000
EMP: 67 **EST:** 2011
SALES (est): 326.44K Privately Held
Web: www.csea.com
SIC: 8631 Labor union

(P-18774)
CALIFORNIA SCHL EMPLOYEES ASSN (PA)
Also Called: CSEA
2045 Lundy Ave (95131-1825)
PHONE..................408 473-1000
TOLL FREE: 800
Keith Pace, *CEO*
Steve Brashear, *CFO*
EMP: 180 **EST:** 1927
SQ FT: 65,000
SALES (est): 8.64MM
SALES (corp-wide): 8.64MM Privately Held
Web: www.csea.com
SIC: 8631 Labor union

(P-18775)
CALIFRNIA CRRCTNAL PACE OFFCER (PA)
Also Called: Ccpoa
755 Riverpoint Dr (95605-1626)
PHONE..................916 372-6060
Chuck Alexander, *Pr*
James Martin, *
Perry Speth, *
EMP: 60 **EST:** 1957
SQ FT: 32,000
SALES (est): 13.82MM
SALES (corp-wide): 13.82MM Privately Held
Web: www.ccpoa.org
SIC: 8631 8111 Labor union; Legal services

(P-18776)
CALIFRNIA DEPT INDUS RELATIONS
301 Howard St Ste 700 (94105-6604)
P.O. Box 420603 (94142-0603)
PHONE..................415 703-5133
EMP: 67
SALES (corp-wide): 534.4MM Privately Held
SIC: 8631 Labor organizations
HQ: California Department Of Industrial Relations
  455 Golden Gate Ave Fl 10
  San Francisco CA

(P-18777)
CALIFRNIA DEPT INDUS RELATIONS
25347 S Schulte Rd (95377-9710)
PHONE..................209 830-7200
Michael Height, *Brnch Mgr*
EMP: 94
SALES (corp-wide): 534.4MM Privately Held
SIC: 8631 8249 Labor union; Vocational apprentice training
HQ: California Department Of Industrial Relations
  455 Golden Gate Ave Fl 10

PRODUCTS & SERVICES SECTION
8631 - Labor Organizations (P-18800)

San Francisco CA

(P-18778)
CALIFRNIA STATE EMPLOYEES ASSN (PA)
Also Called: Csea
3000 Advantage Way (95834-9707)
PHONE..................................916 444-8134
Dave Hart, Pr
Debbie Cotton, *
Dave Okunura, *
EMP: 80 EST: 1932
SQ FT: 30,000
SALES (est): 3.02K
SALES (corp-wide): 3.02K Privately Held
Web: www.calcsea.org
SIC: 8631 Labor union

(P-18779)
FREQUENCE INC
155 E Dana St (94041-1507)
PHONE..................................650 520-6114
Tom Cheli, CEO
Oliver Jacob, Pr
EMP: 169 EST: 2011
SALES (est): 6.38MM Privately Held
Web: www.frequence.com
SIC: 8631 Labor organizations

(P-18780)
IATSE AFFL PRPRTY CRFTSPRSON L
12021 Riverside Dr (91607-3726)
PHONE..................................818 769-2500
Erik Nelson, Pr
EMP: 138 EST: 1939
SQ FT: 17,947
SALES (est): 11.16MM Privately Held
Web: www.local44.org
SIC: 8631 Labor union

(P-18781)
INTERNTIONAL UN OPER ENGINEERS (PA)
1121 L St Ste 401 (95814-3969)
PHONE..................................916 444-6880
Tim Neep, Dir
EMP: 67 EST: 2014
SALES (est): 70.57MM
SALES (corp-wide): 70.57MM Privately Held
SIC: 8631 Labor union

(P-18782)
INTERNTIONAL UN OPER ENGINEERS
Also Called: Local 12
3935 Normal St (92103-3585)
PHONE..................................619 295-3186
Dan Hawn, Mgr
EMP: 594
SQ FT: 4,500
SALES (corp-wide): 70.57MM Privately Held
SIC: 8631 Labor union
PA: International Union Of Operating Engineers
1121 L St Ste 401
Sacramento CA
916 444-6880

(P-18783)
INTERNTIONAL UN OPER ENGINEERS
Also Called: Local 12
1647 W Lugonia Ave (92374-2048)
PHONE..................................909 307-8700
Ron Sikroski, Mgr

EMP: 595
SALES (corp-wide): 70.57MM Privately Held
Web: www.oefi.org
SIC: 8631 Labor union
PA: International Union Of Operating Engineers
1121 L St Ste 401
Sacramento CA
916 444-6880

(P-18784)
INTERNTNAL BRTHD ELC WKR LCAL (PA)
Also Called: AFL-CIO #1245
30 Orange Tree Cir (95687-3105)
PHONE..................................707 452-2700
Ed Mallory, Pr
James Mcculley, VP
Michael J Davis, Northern Area Member*
Kathy Tindall, Northern Area Member*
EMP: 64 EST: 1948
SALES (est): 49.11MM
SALES (corp-wide): 49.11MM Privately Held
Web: www.ibew1245.com
SIC: 8631 Labor union

(P-18785)
INTERNTNAL UN OPER ENGNERS LCA
Also Called: Operating Engners Lcal Un No 3
1620 S Loop Rd (94502-7085)
PHONE..................................510 748-7400
EMP: 300 EST: 1896
SALES (est): 60.31MM Privately Held
Web: www.oe3.org
SIC: 8631 Labor union

(P-18786)
LABORERS FNDS ADMNSTRTIVE OFFI (PA)
Also Called: Laborers Trust Funds Nthrn Cal
5672 Stoneridge Dr Ste 100 (94588-8501)
PHONE..................................707 864-2800
Edward Smith, Sec
EMP: 100 EST: 1963
SQ FT: 43,000
SALES (est): 404.61MM
SALES (corp-wide): 404.61MM Privately Held
Web: www.norcalaborers.org
SIC: 8631 Labor union

(P-18787)
LOS ANGLES CNTY EMPLOYEES ASSN
Also Called: Service Employee Intl Un
1545 Wilshire Blvd (90017-4501)
PHONE..................................213 368-8660
Annelle Grajeda, Pr
Bob Schoonover, *
Annette Jeffrief, *
Kathleen Austria, *
EMP: 71 EST: 1950
SQ FT: 40,000
SALES (est): 9.19MM Privately Held
Web: www.seiu721.org
SIC: 8631 Labor union

(P-18788)
NORTHERN CAL CRPNTERS RGNAL CN
Also Called: NCCRC
265 Hegenberger Rd Ste 200 (94621-1409)
PHONE..................................510 568-4788
Bob Alvarado, Asstg
EMP: 70 EST: 2008
SALES (est): 85.72MM Privately Held

Web: www.norcalcarpenters.org
SIC: 8631 Labor union

(P-18789)
SEIU LOCAL 2015 (PA)
2910 Beverly Blvd (90057-1012)
PHONE..................................213 985-0384
Laphonza Butler, Pr
EMP: 61 EST: 2015
SALES (est): 22.6MM
SALES (corp-wide): 22.6MM Privately Held
Web: www.seiu2015.org
SIC: 8631 Labor union

(P-18790)
SEIU LOCAL 2015
681 W Capitol Ave (95605-2835)
PHONE..................................213 985-0419
EMP: 149
SALES (corp-wide): 22.6MM Privately Held
Web: www.seiu2015.org
SIC: 8631 Labor union
PA: Seiu Local 2015
2910 Beverly Blvd
Los Angeles CA
213 985-0384

(P-18791)
SEIU LOCAL 521
2302 Zanker Rd (95131-1115)
PHONE..................................650 801-3500
Gwen Harshaw, Pr
EMP: 84 EST: 2008
SALES (est): 33.06MM Privately Held
Web: www.seiu521.org
SIC: 8631 Labor union

(P-18792)
SEIU LOCAL 721
1545 Wilshire Blvd Ste 100 (90017-4510)
PHONE..................................213 368-8660
Annelle Grajeda, Owner
EMP: 175 EST: 2007
SALES (est): 142.29K Privately Held
Web: www.seiu721.org
SIC: 8631 Labor union

(P-18793)
SEIU UNITED HEALTHCARE WORKERS (PA)
560 Thomas L Berkley Way (94612-1602)
PHONE..................................510 251-1250
Dave Regan, Pr
Debbie M Schneider, Deputy Trustee*
Eliseo Medina, *
Edgard Tajina, *
Stanley Lyles, *
EMP: 140 EST: 1923
SQ FT: 33,000
SALES (est): 48.12MM
SALES (corp-wide): 48.12MM Privately Held
Web: www.seiu-uhw.org
SIC: 8631 Labor union

(P-18794)
SEIU UNTD HLTHCARE WRKRS-WEST
Also Called: Seiu Uhw-West
5480 Ferguson Dr (90022-5119)
PHONE..................................323 734-8399
Liza Leyva, Dir
EMP: 79
SALES (corp-wide): 48.12MM Privately Held
Web: www.seiu-uhw.org
SIC: 8631 Labor union

PA: Seiu United Healthcare Workers-West Local 2005
560 Thomas L Berkley Way
Oakland CA
510 251-1250

(P-18795)
SOUTHERN CAL IBW-NECA HLTH TR
100 Corson St Ste 200 (91103-3841)
PHONE..................................323 221-5861
EMP: 89 EST: 2010
SALES (est): 139.15MM
SALES (corp-wide): 139.15MM Privately Held
Web: www.scibew-neca.org
SIC: 8631 Labor union
PA: Southern California Ibew-Neca Administrative Corporation
100 Corson St Ste 200
Pasadena CA
323 221-5861

(P-18796)
SOUTHWEST CRPNTERS TRNING FUND
533 S Fremont Ave Ste 700 (90071-1712)
PHONE..................................213 386-8590
EMP: 81 EST: 2012
SALES (est): 36.64MM Privately Held
Web: www.swmsctf.org
SIC: 8631 Labor union

(P-18797)
SOUTHWEST RGNAL CNCIL CRPNTERS
7111 Firestone Blvd (90621-2958)
PHONE..................................714 571-0449
EMP: 92
SALES (corp-wide): 26.99MM Privately Held
Web: www.swcarpenters.org
SIC: 8631 Labor union
PA: Southwest Regional Council Of Carpenters
533 S Fremont Ave Fl 10
Los Angeles CA
213 385-1457

(P-18798)
TEMPORARY STAFFING UNION
19800 Macarthur Blvd Ste 300 (92612-2421)
PHONE..................................714 728-5186
Veronica Lake, CEO
Fe Santos, *
EMP: 4000 EST: 2018
SQ FT: 1,500
SALES (est): 7.05MM Privately Held
SIC: 8631 Labor union

(P-18799)
UA LOCAL 342 JATC
2450 Whitman Rd (94518-2543)
PHONE..................................925 686-0730
EMP: 138 EST: 2019
SALES (est): 9.1MM Privately Held
Web: www.ua342.org
SIC: 8631 Labor union

(P-18800)
UA LOCAL 38 PENSION TR FUND
1625 Market St (94103-1217)
PHONE..................................415 626-2000
EMP: 69 EST: 2014
SALES (est): 360.54K Privately Held
Web: www.ualocal38.org
SIC: 8631 Labor union

8631 - Labor Organizations (P-18801)

PRODUCTS & SERVICES SECTION

(P-18801)
UNITE HAIR
2870 Whiptail Loop Ste 100 (92010-6709)
PHONE.................................760 585-1800
EMP: 94 EST: 2017
SALES (est): 527.04K Privately Held
Web: www.unitehair.com
SIC: 8631 Labor organizations

(P-18802)
UNITED FARM WORKERS AMERICA (PA)
29700 Woodford Tehachapi Rd (93531)
P.O. Box 62 (93531-0062)
PHONE.................................661 822-5571
Arturo Rodriguez, *Pr*
Irv Hershenbaum, *
Tanis Ybarra, *
Liz Villarino, *
EMP: 110 EST: 1966
SQ FT: 5,000
SALES (est): 9.96MM
SALES (corp-wide): 9.96MM Privately Held
Web: www.ufw.org
SIC: 8631 Labor union

(P-18803)
UNITED FOOD & COMMERCL WORKERS (PA)
8530 Stanton Ave (90620-3930)
P.O. Box 5004 (90622-5004)
PHONE.................................714 995-4601
Greg Conger, *Pr*
EMP: 61 EST: 1936
SQ FT: 45,000
SALES (est): 2.07MM
SALES (corp-wide): 2.07MM Privately Held
Web: www.ufcw324.org
SIC: 8631 Labor union

(P-18804)
UNITED FOOD AND COMMERCIAL (PA)
Also Called: Ufcw Local 770
630 Shatto Pl Ste 300 (90005-1301)
P.O. Box 770 (90078-0770)
PHONE.................................213 487-7070
Ricardo F Icaza, *Pr*
Rodney Diamond, *
EMP: 60 EST: 1937
SALES (est): 9.31MM
SALES (corp-wide): 9.31MM Privately Held
Web: www.ufcw770.org
SIC: 8631 Labor union

(P-18805)
UNITED FRFGHTERS LOS ANGLES CY
1571 Beverly Blvd (90026-5704)
PHONE.................................213 489-1300
Pat Macoscar, *Pr*
Kenneth Buzzell, *Pr*
Michael Mc Oster, *VP*
Dan Mccarthy, *VP*
Don Forest, *Sec*
EMP: 63 EST: 1972
SQ FT: 8,500
SALES (est): 1.75MM Privately Held
Web: www.uflac.org
SIC: 8631 Labor union

(P-18806)
UNITED TEACHERS-LOS ANGELES
Also Called: U T L A
3303 Wilshire Blvd Fl 10 (90010-1794)
PHONE.................................213 487-5560
Aj Duffy, *Pr*
Ana Valencia, *
Joshua Pechthalt, *
David Goldburg, *
Betty Forrester, *
EMP: 72 EST: 1970
SQ FT: 144,000
SALES (est): 53.01MM Privately Held
Web: www.utla.net
SIC: 8631 Labor union

(P-18807)
WRITERS GUILD AMERICA WEST INC
7000 W 3rd St (90048-4321)
PHONE.................................323 951-4000
David Young, *CEO*
David Weiss, *Prin*
Elias Davis, *Sec*
David Young, *Ex Dir*
Chris Keyser, *Prin*
EMP: 160 EST: 1954
SQ FT: 67,000
SALES (est): 38.7MM Privately Held
Web: www.wga.org
SIC: 8631 Labor union

8641 Civic And Social Associations

(P-18808)
21515 HAWTHORNE OWNER LLC
21535 Hawthorne Blvd Ste 100 (90503-6604)
PHONE.................................310 406-3730
Margaret Powell, *
Jenny Blanchart, *
EMP: 100 EST: 2014
SALES (est): 1.06MM Privately Held
SIC: 8641 Dwelling-related associations

(P-18809)
ACLU FNDATION SOUTHERN CAL LLC
Also Called: American Cvil Lbrties Un Sther
765 The City Dr S Ste 360 (92868-6913)
PHONE.................................213 977-9500
James Gilliam, *Managing Member*
Mark Rosenbaum, *Managing Member**
EMP: 83 EST: 2007
SALES (est): 18.83MM Privately Held
Web: www.aclusocal.org
SIC: 8641 Civic and social associations

(P-18810)
AFRICAN WOMEN RISING
801 Cold Springs Rd (93108-1016)
PHONE.................................415 278-1784
EMP: 200 EST: 2007
SALES (est): 1.5MM Privately Held
Web: www.africanwomenrising.org
SIC: 8641 Civic and social associations

(P-18811)
AMERICAN HIGH SCHL BOOSTER CLB
36300 Fremont Blvd (94536-3511)
PHONE.................................510 796-1776
EMP: 110 EST: 1972
SALES (est): 14.91K Privately Held
Web: www.achineseschool.org
SIC: 8641 Booster club

(P-18812)
AMERICAN LGION POST NO 108 AMB
Also Called: AMERICAN LEGION HALL
11350 American Legion Dr (95642-9764)
P.O. Box 100 (95685-0100)
PHONE.................................209 223-2963
Alan Mcnany, *Pr*
Al Lennox, *
EMP: 84 EST: 1929
SQ FT: 800
SALES (est): 13.91MM Privately Held
Web: www.legion.org
SIC: 8641 Veterans' organization

(P-18813)
ARMED SERVICES YMCA OF USA
3293 Santo Rd (92124-3340)
PHONE.................................858 751-5755
Kim Ney, *Ex Dir*
EMP: 121
SALES (corp-wide): 7.42MM Privately Held
Web: www.asymca.org
SIC: 8641 Youth organizations
PA: Armed Services Ymca Of The U.S.A.
   14040 Central Loop B
   Woodbridge VA
   703 445-3986

(P-18814)
ASSOCIATED STUDENTS STANFORD (PA)
Also Called: A S S U
201 Tresidder Un (94305)
PHONE.................................650 723-4331
Linda Whitcomb, *Dir*
Alice Willoughby, *
EMP: 63 EST: 1914
SALES (est): 1.52MM
SALES (corp-wide): 1.52MM Privately Held
Web: www.stanford.edu
SIC: 8641 University club

(P-18815)
ASSOCTED STDNTS CAL STATE UNIV
Also Called: A S I
1212 N Bellflower Blvd Ste 220 (90815-4148)
PHONE.................................562 985-4994
Richard Haller, *Ex Dir*
EMP: 222 EST: 1956
SQ FT: 184,000
SALES (est): 16.84MM Privately Held
Web: www.asicsulb.org
SIC: 8641 University club

(P-18816)
BEAR VALLEY SPRINGS ASSN
29541 Rollingoak Dr (93561-7133)
PHONE.................................661 821-5537
Todd Lander, *Pr*
Terry Quinn, *
Larry Thompson, *
Tim Hawkins, *
EMP: 200 EST: 1970
SQ FT: 2,000
SALES (est): 7.45MM Privately Held
Web: www.bvsa.org
SIC: 8641 Homeowners' association

(P-18817)
BODEGA HARBOUR HOMEOWNERS ASSN
Also Called: Bodega Harbour Golf Links
21301 Heron Dr (94923)
P.O. Box 368 (94923-0368)
PHONE.................................707 875-3519
Judith A Steeves, *Admn Mgr*
EMP: 65 EST: 1971
SQ FT: 10,000
SALES (est): 4.5MM Privately Held
Web: www.bodegaharbourgolf.com
SIC: 8641 5812 5813 7997 Homeowners' association; American restaurant; Bars and lounges; Yacht club, membership

(P-18818)
BOHEMIAN CLUB (PA)
Also Called: BOHEMIAN GROVE
624 Taylor St (94102-1075)
PHONE.................................415 885-2440
Robert L Spence, *CEO*
Matt Ogerio, *
EMP: 100 EST: 1872
SQ FT: 20,000
SALES (est): 11.06MM
SALES (corp-wide): 11.06MM Privately Held
Web: www.bc-owl.org
SIC: 8641 Social club, membership

(P-18819)
BOYS & GIRLS CLUBS OF N VLY
601 Wall St (95928-5626)
PHONE.................................530 899-0335
Rashell Brobst, *CEO*
EMP: 80 EST: 1995
SQ FT: 14,000
SALES (est): 3.81MM Privately Held
Web: www.bgcnv.org
SIC: 8641 Youth organizations

(P-18820)
BOYS & GIRLS CLUBS SOUTH CNTY
847 Encina Ave (91932-2135)
P.O. Box 520 (91933-0520)
PHONE.................................619 424-2266
Ken Blinsman, *Pr*
EMP: 100 EST: 1982
SALES (est): 4.85MM Privately Held
Web: www.bgcscounty.org
SIC: 8641 5812 Youth organizations; Eating places

(P-18821)
BOYS CLUB OF FALLBROOK
Also Called: BOYS & GIRLS CLUBS OF NORTH CO
445 E Ivy St (92028-2122)
P.O. Box 2665 (92088-2665)
PHONE.................................760 728-5871
Allison Barclay, *CEO*
Linda J Gerber, *
EMP: 65 EST: 1963
SALES (est): 2.02MM Privately Held
Web: www.bgcnorthcounty.org
SIC: 8641 Youth organizations

(P-18822)
BOYS GIRLS CLUBS OF KERN CNTY
Also Called: Boy's & Girls Club Bakersfield
801 Niles St (93305-4419)
PHONE.................................661 325-3730
Zane Smith, *Dir*
Ed Kuhn, *
Bill Campbell, *
Craig Stickler, *
Tricia Ceccarill, *
EMP: 500 EST: 1971
SALES (est): 9.29MM Privately Held
Web: www.bgclubsofkerncounty.org

PRODUCTS & SERVICES SECTION
8641 - Civic And Social Associations (P-18843)

SIC: 8641 8322 Boy Scout organization; Individual and family services

(P-18823)
BOYS GRLS CLB BRBANK GRTER E V
300 E Angeleno Ave (91502-1311)
PHONE.................................818 842-9333
Shanna Warren, CEO
Shannon Warren, *
EMP: 99 EST: 1994
SQ FT: 6,000
SALES (est): 3.15MM Privately Held
Web: www.bgcburbank.org
SIC: 8641 Youth organizations

(P-18824)
BOYS GRLS CLB SNTA MONICA INC
Also Called: BOYS & GIRLS CLUBS OF SANTA MO
1220 Lincoln Blvd (90401-1704)
PHONE.................................310 361-8500
Aaron Young, Dir
EMP: 83 EST: 1943
SQ FT: 6,000
SALES (est): 3.03MM Privately Held
Web: www.smbgc.org
SIC: 8641 7997 Youth organizations; Membership sports and recreation clubs

(P-18825)
BOYS GRLS CLUBS CNTL ORNGE CAS
17701 Cowan Ste 110 (92614-6061)
PHONE.................................714 543-5540
Robert Santana, CEO
John Brewster, *
EMP: 60 EST: 1957
SQ FT: 15,150
SALES (est): 53.75K Privately Held
Web: www.boysandgirlsclub.com
SIC: 8641 Youth organizations

(P-18826)
BOYS GRLS CLUBS HUNTINGTON VLY (PA)
Also Called: BOYS & GIRLS CLUBS OF HUNTINGT
16582 Brookhurst St (92708-2353)
PHONE.................................714 531-2582
Tanya Hoxsie, Pr
EMP: 89 EST: 1967
SALES (est): 8.67MM Privately Held
Web: www.bgchv.com
SIC: 8641 Youth organizations

(P-18827)
CALI CALMECAC LANGUAGE ACADEMY
9491 Starr Rd (95492-9460)
PHONE.................................707 837-7747
EMP: 60 EST: 2010
SALES (est): 102.47K Privately Held
Web: ccla.wusd.org
SIC: 8641 8211 Parent-teachers' association; Elementary and secondary schools

(P-18828)
CALIFORNIA CLUB
538 S Flower St (90071-2501)
PHONE.................................213 622-1391
Robert C Baker, CEO
EMP: 185 EST: 1888
SALES (est): 16.26MM Privately Held
Web: www.californiaclub.org
SIC: 8641 7041 Business persons club; Residence club, organization

(P-18829)
CASSY
544 Valley Way (95035-4106)
PHONE.................................408 493-5289
Elizabeth Moore Schoeben, Admn
EMP: 68 EST: 2013
SALES (est): 4.02MM Privately Held
Web: www.cassybayarea.org
SIC: 8641 Civic and social associations

(P-18830)
CATHOLIC EDUCATION FOUNDA
3424 Wilshire Blvd Ste 24 (90010-2263)
PHONE.................................213 637-7475
Kathleen Ash, Prin
EMP: 82 EST: 2014
SALES (est): 1.12MM Privately Held
Web: www.cefdn.org
SIC: 8641 Civic and social associations

(P-18831)
CCOF FOUNDATION
2155 Delaware Ave Ste 150 (95060-5732)
PHONE.................................831 423-2263
Cathy Calfo, Ex Dir
EMP: 67 EST: 2008
SALES (est): 764.46K Privately Held
Web: www.ccof.org
SIC: 8641 Civic and social associations

(P-18832)
CENTRAL COAST YMCA
Also Called: YMCA San Benito County
351 Tres Pinos Rd Ste 201a (95023)
PHONE.................................831 637-8600
Mayra Yerena, Prin
EMP: 96
SALES (corp-wide): 8.22MM Privately Held
Web: www.centralcoastymca.org
SIC: 8641 Youth organizations
PA: Central Coast Ymca
600 Camino El Estero
Monterey CA
831 757-4633

(P-18833)
CENTRAL COAST YMCA
Also Called: YMCA
27 Sudden St (95076-4322)
PHONE.................................831 728-9622
Jeanette Mattos, Dir
EMP: 109
SALES (corp-wide): 8.22MM Privately Held
Web: www.centralcoastymca.org
SIC: 8641 7991 8351 7032 Youth organizations; Physical fitness facilities; Child day care services; Youth camps
PA: Central Coast Ymca
600 Camino El Estero
Monterey CA
831 757-4633

(P-18834)
CHANNEL ISLNDS YUNG MNS CHRSTN
301 W Figueroa St (93101-3632)
PHONE.................................805 963-8775
Teri Bradford Rouse, Brnch Mgr
EMP: 87
SALES (corp-wide): 19.77MM Privately Held
Web: www.ciymca.org
SIC: 8641 Youth organizations
PA: Channel Islands Young Men's Christian Association
1180 Eugenia Pl
Carpinteria CA
805 569-1103

(P-18835)
CHANNEL ISLNDS YUNG MNS CHRSTN
Also Called: Lompoc Family YMCA
201 W College Ave (93436-4415)
PHONE.................................805 736-3483
Dan Powell, Brnch Mgr
EMP: 87
SALES (corp-wide): 19.77MM Privately Held
Web: www.ciymca.org
SIC: 8641 7991 8351 7032 Youth organizations; Physical fitness facilities; Child day care services; Youth camps
PA: Channel Islands Young Men's Christian Association
1180 Eugenia Pl
Carpinteria CA
805 569-1103

(P-18836)
CHANNEL ISLNDS YUNG MNS CHRSTN
Also Called: Camarillo Family YMCA
3111 Village Park Dr (93012)
PHONE.................................805 484-0423
Marge Castellano, Dir
EMP: 88
SALES (corp-wide): 19.77MM Privately Held
Web: www.ciymca.org
SIC: 8641 7991 8351 7032 Youth organizations; Physical fitness facilities; Child day care services; Youth camps
PA: Channel Islands Young Men's Christian Association
1180 Eugenia Pl
Carpinteria CA
805 569-1103

(P-18837)
CHANNEL ISLNDS YUNG MNS CHRSTN
Also Called: Santa Barbara Family YMCA
36 Hitchcock Way (93105-3102)
PHONE.................................805 687-7727
Tim Hardy, Brnch Mgr
EMP: 88
SALES (corp-wide): 19.77MM Privately Held
Web: www.ciymca.org
SIC: 8641 7991 8351 7032 Youth organizations; Physical fitness facilities; Child day care services; Youth camps
PA: Channel Islands Young Men's Christian Association
1180 Eugenia Pl
Carpinteria CA
805 569-1103

(P-18838)
CHANNEL ISLNDS YUNG MNS CHRSTN
Also Called: Montecito Family YMCA
591 Santa Rosa Ln (93108-2145)
PHONE.................................805 969-3288
Yvonne Rubio, Dir
EMP: 88
SALES (corp-wide): 19.77MM Privately Held
Web: www.ciymca.org
SIC: 8641 7991 8351 7032 Youth organizations; Physical fitness facilities; Child day care services; Youth camps
PA: Channel Islands Young Men's Christian Association
1180 Eugenia Pl
Carpinteria CA
805 569-1103

(P-18839)
CHANNEL ISLNDS YUNG MNS CHRSTN
Also Called: Ventura Family YMCA
3760 Telegraph Rd (93003-3421)
PHONE.................................805 484-0423
Sarah Abrams, Dir
EMP: 88
SALES (corp-wide): 19.77MM Privately Held
Web: www.ciymca.org
SIC: 8641 7991 8351 7032 Youth organizations; Physical fitness facilities; Child day care services; Youth camps
PA: Channel Islands Young Men's Christian Association
1180 Eugenia Pl
Carpinteria CA
805 569-1103

(P-18840)
CHANNEL ISLNDS YUNG MNS CHRSTN
Also Called: Stuart C. Gildred Family YMCA
900 N Refugio Rd (93460-9314)
PHONE.................................805 686-2037
Paula Parisotto, Brnch Mgr
EMP: 88
SALES (corp-wide): 19.77MM Privately Held
Web: www.ciymca.org
SIC: 8641 7991 8351 7032 Youth organizations; Physical fitness facilities; Child day care services; Youth camps
PA: Channel Islands Young Men's Christian Association
1180 Eugenia Pl
Carpinteria CA
805 569-1103

(P-18841)
CHICO STATE ENTERPRISES
25 Main St Unit 203 (95928-5388)
PHONE.................................530 898-6811
Jessica Bourne, Ex Dir
EMP: 2000 EST: 1996
SQ FT: 15,000
SALES (est): 46.86MM Privately Held
Web: www.csuchico.edu
SIC: 8641 Civic and social associations

(P-18842)
CITY OF STOCKTON
Also Called: Public Works Association
1465 S Lincoln St (95206-1941)
PHONE.................................209 937-8453
Gordon Mackay, Mgr
EMP: 108
SALES (corp-wide): 509.91MM Privately Held
Web: www.stocktonca.gov
SIC: 8641 Civic and social associations
PA: City Of Stockton
425 N El Dorado St
Stockton CA
209 937-8212

(P-18843)
CLOUD NATIVE CMPT FOUNDATION
1 Letterman Dr Ste D4700 (94129-1494)
PHONE.................................415 723-9709
Priyanka Sharma, Genl Mgr
EMP: 148 EST: 2015
SALES (est): 526.7K Privately Held
Web: www.cncf.io
SIC: 8641 Civic and social associations
PA: The Linux Foundation
548 Market St Pmb 57274

8641 - Civic And Social Associations (P-18844)

San Francisco CA

(P-18844)
CODING SCHOOL
12438 Landale St (91604-1220)
PHONE..................................424 339-3977
Kiera Peltz, *CEO*
EMP: 70 **EST:** 2014
SALES (est): 1.35MM Privately Held
Web: www.codeconnects.org
SIC: 8641 Civic and social associations

(P-18845)
COUNTY OF RIVERSIDE
Also Called: Riverside Crona Rsrce Cnsrvtio
4500 Glenwood Dr Ste A (92501-3066)
PHONE..................................951 683-7691
Shelli Lamb, *Dist Mgr*
EMP: 119
SALES (corp-wide): 4.58B Privately Held
Web: www.rcrcd.org
SIC: 8641 9512 Environmental protection organization; Land, mineral, and wildlife conservation, County government
PA: County Of Riverside
4080 Lemon St Fl 11
Riverside CA
951 955-1110

(P-18846)
COUNTY OF SACRAMENTO
Also Called: Parks and Recreation Dept
7801 Auburn Blvd (95610-2115)
PHONE..................................916 725-1585
Terry Jewell, *Brnch Mgr*
EMP: 362
SALES (corp-wide): 3.56B Privately Held
Web: www.sunriseparks.com
SIC: 8641 9512 7999 7299 Recreation association; Recreational program administration, government; Recreation center; Banquet hall facilities
PA: County Of Sacramento
700 H St Ste 7650
Sacramento CA
916 874-8515

(P-18847)
COWELL HOMEOWNERS ASSN INC (PA)
Also Called: Walnut Country
4498 Lawson Ct (94521-4410)
PHONE..................................925 825-0250
Rhinan Harris, *Genl Mgr*
Michael Demeo, *
EMP: 60 **EST:** 1972
SQ FT: 2,300
SALES (est): 2.39MM
SALES (corp-wide): 2.39MM Privately Held
Web: www.walnutcountry.com
SIC: 8641 8351 Homeowners' association; Child day care services

(P-18848)
CRESCENTA-CANADA YMCA (PA)
Also Called: YMCA Crescenta-Canada
1930 Foothill Blvd (91011-1933)
PHONE..................................818 790-0123
Larry Hall, *CEO*
Ken Gorvetzian, *
EMP: 150 **EST:** 1953
SALES (est): 115.62K
SALES (corp-wide): 115.62K Privately Held
Web: www.ymcafoothills.org
SIC: 8641 7991 8351 7032 Youth organizations; Physical fitness facilities; Child day care services; Youth camps

(P-18849)
CRESCENTA-CANADA YMCA
Also Called: Learning Tree Pre-School
6840 Foothill Blvd (91042-2711)
PHONE..................................818 352-3255
Kathi Brink, *Brnch Mgr*
EMP: 130
SALES (corp-wide): 115.62K Privately Held
Web: www.ymcafoothills.org
SIC: 8641 7991 8351 7032 Youth organizations; Physical fitness facilities; Child day care services; Youth camps
PA: Crescenta-Canada Ymca
1930 Foothill Blvd
La Canada CA
818 790-0123

(P-18850)
D A V INDUSTRIES
1049 Elkelton Blvd (91977-4720)
PHONE..................................619 337-9244
William D Mudd, *Pr*
Bernard Bandish, *
Clifford Caldwell, *
Donald Pouliot, *
EMP: 100 **EST:** 1967
SQ FT: 8,000
SALES (est): 11.28MM Privately Held
Web: www.davveteransthriftstores.com
SIC: 8641 5932 Veterans' organization; Clothing, secondhand

(P-18851)
DEEPMIND FOUNDATION
19503 Stevens Creek Blvd Ste 107 (95014)
PHONE..................................408 887-1605
Hsiao-pin Su, *CEO*
EMP: 78 **EST:** 2017
SALES (est): 230.76K Privately Held
Web: www.deepmind.com
SIC: 8641 Civic and social associations

(P-18852)
DS LAKESHORE LP
200 Baker St Ste 100 (92626-4551)
PHONE..................................916 286-5231
Patrick S Donahue, *Pt*
Trina Perales, *Pt*
EMP: 99 **EST:** 2019
SALES (est): 268.71K Privately Held
SIC: 8641 Civic and social associations

(P-18853)
EACH ONE TEACH ONE FOUNDATION
1800 59th Ave (95822-4216)
PHONE..................................916 428-5627
Jewel Watson, *Prin*
EMP: 71 **EST:** 2007
SALES (est): 63.57K Privately Held
Web: www.eachoneteachone.is
SIC: 8641 Civic and social associations

(P-18854)
EARTHJUSTICE (PA)
Also Called: Earthjustice Legal Def Fund
50 California St Ste 500 (94111-4608)
PHONE..................................415 217-2000
EMP: 78 **EST:** 1970
SALES (est): 135.32MM
SALES (corp-wide): 135.32MM Privately Held
Web: www.earthjustice.org
SIC: 8641 8111 Civic and social associations, Specialized legal services

(P-18855)
EHDD
1 Pier Ste 2 (94111-2028)
PHONE..................................415 285-9193
EMP: 78 **EST:** 2020
SALES (est): 2.83MM Privately Held
Web: www.ehdd.com
SIC: 8641 Veterans' organization

(P-18856)
ELIZABETH GLSER PDTRIC AIDS FN
2950 31st St Ste 125 (90405-3098)
PHONE..................................310 593-0047
Jeff Gaffney, *Brnch Mgr*
EMP: 457
SALES (corp-wide): 187.69MM Privately Held
Web: www.pedaids.org
SIC: 8641 Civic and social associations
PA: Elizabeth Glaser Pediatric Aids Foundation
1140 Conn Ave Nw Ste 200
Washington DC
920 770-0103

(P-18857)
ENVIRNMENT NTRAL RESOURCES DIV
301 Howard St Ste 1050 (94105-6607)
PHONE..................................415 744-6491
David B Glazer, *Mgr*
EMP: 1336
SIC: 8641 Environmental protection organization
HQ: Environment & Natural Resources Division
601 D St Nw Rm 2729
Washington DC

(P-18858)
EXCEPTIONAL CHLD FOUNDATION
11124 Fairbanks Way (90230-4945)
PHONE..................................310 915-6606
EMP: 110
SALES (corp-wide): 28.26MM Privately Held
Web: www.ecf.net
SIC: 8641 Civic and social associations
PA: Exceptional Children's Foundation
5350 Machado Ln
Culver City CA
310 204-3300

(P-18859)
FOUNDTION FOR STDNTS RSING ABO
2 Embarcadero Ctr Fl 8 (94111-3833)
P.O. Box 192492 (94119-2492)
PHONE..................................415 333-4222
EMP: 63 **EST:** 2003
SALES (est): 5.03MM Privately Held
Web: www.studentsrisingabove.org
SIC: 8641 8699 Youth organizations; Charitable organization

(P-18860)
FRIENDS SANTA CRUZ STATE PARKS
1543 Pacific Ave Ste 206 (95060-3962)
PHONE..................................831 429-1840
EMP: 80 **EST:** 1975
SALES (est): 8.03MM Privately Held
Web: www.thatsmypark.org
SIC: 8641 Environmental protection organization

(P-18861)
GIRL SCOUTS HEART CENTRAL CAL
Also Called: GIRL SCOUTS
6601 Elvas Ave (95819-4339)
PHONE..................................916 452-9181
Linda Farley, *CEO*
Kerry Koyasako, *
EMP: 127 **EST:** 1965
SALES (est): 8.88MM Privately Held
Web: www.girlscoutshcc.org
SIC: 8641 Girl Scout organization

(P-18862)
GIRL SCOUTS NORTHERN CAL (PA)
Also Called: GIRL SCOUTS
1650 Harbor Bay Pkwy Ste 100 (94502-3013)
PHONE..................................510 562-8470
Marina Park, *CEO*
Robin Macgillivray, *
Dianne Lamendola, *
Diana Bell, *
Ellen Richey, *
EMP: 70 **EST:** 1963
SQ FT: 17,000
SALES (est): 29.58MM
SALES (corp-wide): 29.58MM Privately Held
Web: www.gsnorcal.org
SIC: 8641 Girl Scout organization

(P-18863)
GIRL SCUTS GREATER LOS ANGELES (PA)
423 N La Brea Ave (90302-3408)
PHONE..................................626 677-2265
Lise Luttgens, *CEO*
Sylvia Rosenberger, *
Christa Weddle, *
Emily Ausbrook Chief Mission D elivery, *Ofcr*
EMP: 114 **EST:** 1924
SALES (est): 25.32MM
SALES (corp-wide): 25.32MM Privately Held
Web: www.girlscoutsla.org
SIC: 8641 Girl Scout organization

(P-18864)
GIRL SCUTS SAN DG-MPRIAL CNCIL (PA)
Also Called: GIRL SCOUTS SAN DIEGO
1231 Upas St (92103-5127)
PHONE..................................619 610-0751
Jo Dee C Jacob, *CEO*
▼ **EMP:** 94 **EST:** 1917
SQ FT: 7,926
SALES (est): 9.99MM
SALES (corp-wide): 9.99MM Privately Held
Web: www.sdgirlscouts.org
SIC: 8641 Girl Scout organization

(P-18865)
GOLDEN GATE NAT PRKS CNSRVANCY
680 Point Lobos Ave (94121-1477)
PHONE..................................415 933-6760
EMP: 118
Web: www.parksconservancy.org
SIC: 8641 Environmental protection organization
PA: Golden Gate National Parks Conservancy
201 Fort Mason
San Francisco CA

8641 - Civic And Social Associations (P-18887)

(P-18866)
GOLDEN RAIN FOUNDATION
800 Rockview Dr (94595-3002)
PHONE..................925 988-7800
Warren Thurlow Salmons, *Brnch Mgr*
EMP: 260
SQ FT: 24,100
SALES (corp-wide): 24.44MM **Privately Held**
Web: www.rossmoor.org
SIC: 8641 Homeowners' association
PA: Golden Rain Foundation Of Walnut Creek
    1001 Golden Rain Rd
    Walnut Creek CA
    925 988-7700

(P-18867)
GORDON BETTY MOORE FOUNDATION
1661 Page Mill Rd (94304-1209)
P.O. Box 29910 (94129-0910)
PHONE..................650 213-3000
Steve Mccormick, *Pr*
Steve Mccormick, *Pr*
EMP: 89 **EST:** 2010
SALES (est): 10.34MM **Privately Held**
Web: www.moore.org
SIC: 8641 Civic and social associations

(P-18868)
GREATER LOS ANGLES AREA CNCIL (PA)
Also Called: BOY SCOUTS OF AMERICA
2333 Scout Way (90026-4912)
PHONE..................213 413-4400
Cash Sutton, *Pr*
EMP: 93 **EST:** 1935
SALES (est): 7.98MM
SALES (corp-wide): 7.98MM **Privately Held**
Web: www.glaacbsa.org
SIC: 8641 Boy Scout organization

(P-18869)
HENTREL GREATHOUSE FOUNDATION
1861 E Main St (92311-3234)
PHONE..................302 513-4056
David Taylor, *CEO*
Allen Jefferson, *
EMP: 62 **EST:** 2015
SQ FT: 15,000
SALES (est): 1.95MM **Privately Held**
SIC: 8641 Civic and social associations

(P-18870)
IDEOORG
320 Florida St (94110-1411)
PHONE..................415 426-7080
EMP: 70 **EST:** 2011
SALES (est): 13.8MM **Privately Held**
Web: www.ideo.org
SIC: 8641 Social associations

(P-18871)
JAMESTOWN COMMUNITY CENTER INC
2929 19th St (94110-2019)
PHONE..................415 647-4709
Nelly Sapinski, *Ex Dir*
Evelyn Davison, *
EMP: 60 **EST:** 1994
SALES (est): 5.35MM **Privately Held**
Web: www.jamestownsf.org
SIC: 8641 Youth organizations

(P-18872)
JEWISH CMNTY FNDTION LOS ANGLE (PA)
6505 Wilshire Blvd Ste 1150 (90048-4906)
PHONE..................323 761-8700
Richard V Sandler, *Ch Bd*
Leslie E Bider, *
J Sanderson, *
Arlene Freedman, *
Jack Klein, *
EMP: 150 **EST:** 1937
SQ FT: 100,000
SALES (est): 43.79MM
SALES (corp-wide): 43.79MM **Privately Held**
Web: www.jewishla.org
SIC: 8641 8661 Community membership club ; Religious organizations

(P-18873)
JONATHAN CLUB (PA)
545 S Figueroa St (90071-1704)
PHONE..................213 624-0881
Gregory J Dumas, *Pr*
James Abbott, *
Norm Rich, *
Randolph P Sinnott, *
◆ **EMP:** 200 **EST:** 1895
SQ FT: 230,276
SALES (est): 30.26MM
SALES (corp-wide): 30.26MM **Privately Held**
Web: www.jc.org
SIC: 8641 Social club, membership

(P-18874)
LA COUNTY SHERIFF PDC NO
211 W Temple St (90012-4086)
PHONE..................661 294-6312
EMP: 224 **EST:** 2018
SALES (est): 1.03MM **Privately Held**
Web: www.lasd.org
SIC: 8641 Civic and social associations

(P-18875)
LAKE FREST NO II MSTR HMWNERS
Also Called: SUN & SAIL CLUB
24752 Toledo Ln (92630-2318)
PHONE..................949 586-0860
Sonny Morper, *Pr*
Ted Brackez, *
Terri Graham, *
Ken Hedge, *
EMP: 80 **EST:** 1971
SQ FT: 9,000
SALES (est): 4.71MM **Privately Held**
Web: www.liveinlakeforest.com
SIC: 8641 Homeowners' association

(P-18876)
LAKE MISSION VIEJO ASSOCIATION
22555 Olympiad Rd (92692-1118)
PHONE..................949 770-1313
Fred Mellenbruch, *Pr*
Jane Chadburn, *
Senator Jeff Miklaus, *VP*
Wayne Dunn, *
Sid Wittenberg, *
EMP: 90 **EST:** 1978
SQ FT: 7,400
SALES (est): 9.02MM **Privately Held**
Web: www.lakemissionviejo.org
SIC: 8641 Homeowners' association

(P-18877)
LAKE WILDWOOD ASSOCIATION
Also Called: LAKE WILDWOOD GOLF COURSE.
11255 Cottontail Way (95946-9409)
PHONE..................530 432-1152
Tom Cross, *CEO*
William Haushalter, *
EMP: 120 **EST:** 1971
SQ FT: 10,000
SALES (est): 8.95MM **Privately Held**
Web: www.lwwa.org
SIC: 8641 7997 Homeowners' association; Golf club, membership

(P-18878)
LEGION TECHNOLOGIES INC
3101 Park Blvd (94306-2233)
PHONE..................408 605-2603
Sanish Mondkar, *Prin*
EMP: 103 **EST:** 2016
SALES (est): 6.02MM **Privately Held**
Web: www.legion.co
SIC: 8641 Veterans' organization

(P-18879)
LELAND STANFORD JUNIOR UNIV
Also Called: Stanford Alumni Association
326 Galvez St (94305-6105)
PHONE..................650 723-2021
Howard Wolf, *Brnch Mgr*
EMP: 250
SALES (corp-wide): 15.13B **Privately Held**
Web: www.stanford.edu
SIC: 8641 8221 Alumni association; University
PA: Leland Stanford Junior University
    450 Jane Stanford Way
    Stanford CA
    650 723-2300

(P-18880)
MARAVILLA FOUNDATION (PA)
5729 Union Pacific Ave (90022-5134)
PHONE..................323 721-4162
Alex M Sotomayor, *CEO*
Paul Lopez, *
Robert Lagunas, *
George Ross, *
EMP: 151 **EST:** 1967
SQ FT: 30,000
SALES (est): 13.93MM
SALES (corp-wide): 13.93MM **Privately Held**
Web: www.maravilla.org
SIC: 8641 Civic and social associations

(P-18881)
MIDNIGHT MISSION (PA)
601 S San Pedro St (90014-2415)
PHONE..................213 624-9258
Michael Arnold, *CEO*
R Stephen Doan, *
Larry Adamson, *
Clancy Imislund, *
Arpit Jain, *
EMP: 69 **EST:** 1926
SQ FT: 11,550
SALES (est): 6.52MM
SALES (corp-wide): 6.52MM **Privately Held**
Web: www.midnightmission.org
SIC: 8641 8322 Veterans' organization; Senior citizens' center or association

(P-18882)
MILKEN FAMILY FOUNDATION
1250 4th St Fl 1 (90401-1418)
PHONE..................310 570-4800
Lowell J Milken, *Pr*
Susan Fox, *
EMP: 200 **EST:** 1986
SALES (est): 8.45MM **Privately Held**
Web: www.mff.org
SIC: 8641 Civic and social associations

(P-18883)
MISSION BAY YOUTH WTR SPT CAMP
Also Called: Mission Bay Aquatic Center
1001 Santa Clara Pl (92109-7228)
PHONE..................858 539-2003
EMP: 75 **EST:** 1978
SALES (est): 1.15MM **Privately Held**
Web: www.mbaquaticcenter.com
SIC: 8641 Youth organizations

(P-18884)
MORNINGSIDE COMMUNITY ASSN
82 Mayfair Dr (92270-2562)
PHONE..................760 328-3323
M Abdelnour, *Genl Mgr*
Michelle Abdelnour, *
EMP: 73 **EST:** 1983
SQ FT: 3,500
SALES (est): 5.27MM **Privately Held**
Web: www.morningsideca.com
SIC: 8641 Homeowners' association

(P-18885)
NATURE CONSERVANCY
Also Called: California Field Office
201 Mission St Ste 400 (94105-1832)
PHONE..................415 777-0487
Mark Burget, *Ex Dir*
EMP: 80
SQ FT: 2,500
SALES (corp-wide): 992.11MM **Privately Held**
Web: www.nature.org
SIC: 8641 Environmental protection organization
PA: The Nature Conservancy
    4245 Fairfax Dr Ste 100
    Arlington VA
    703 841-5300

(P-18886)
OAKLEY UNION SCHOOL DISTRICT
Also Called: Pta Clfrnia Cngress Prnts Tche
1100 Ohara Ave (94561-3502)
PHONE..................925 625-5060
Colleen Crestwell, *Pr*
EMP: 67
SALES (corp-wide): 84.3MM **Privately Held**
Web: www.ouesd.k12.ca.us
SIC: 8641 Parent-teachers' association
PA: Oakley Union School District
    91 Mercedes Ln
    Oakley CA
    925 625-5057

(P-18887)
OLYMPIC CLUB (PA)
524 Post St (94102-1295)
PHONE..................415 345-5100
John M Jack, *CEO*
Jay Bedsworth, *
EMP: 200 **EST:** 1879
SQ FT: 160,000
SALES (est): 49.42MM
SALES (corp-wide): 49.42MM **Privately Held**
Web: www.olyclub.com
SIC: 8641 7997 5812 Civic and social associations; Golf club, membership; Health food restaurant

8641 - Civic And Social Associations (P-18888)

(P-18888)
OLYMPIC CLUB
Also Called: Lakeside Clubhouse
599 Skyline Dr (94015-4611)
PHONE..................415 404-4300
EMP: 83
SALES (corp-wide): 49.42MM Privately Held
Web: www.olyclub.com
SIC: 8641 5812 Civic and social associations; Health food restaurant
PA: The Olympic Club
  524 Post St
  San Francisco CA
  415 345-5100

(P-18889)
ORANGE CNTY CNCIL BOY SCUTS AM (PA)
Also Called: BOY SCOUTS OF AMERICA
2 Irvine Park Rd (92869-1000)
PHONE..................714 546-4990
Les Baron, *Pr*
Jan Borja, *
Jeffrie A Herrmann, *
Robert Neal, *
Larry Behm, *
EMP: 65 **EST:** 1910
SALES (est): 13.09MM
SALES (corp-wide): 13.09MM Privately Held
Web: www.ocbsa.org
SIC: 8641 Boy Scout organization

(P-18890)
OXNARD POLICE DEPARTMENT
251 S C St (93030-5789)
PHONE..................805 385-8300
EMP: 350 **EST:** 1960
SALES (est): 10.08MM Privately Held
Web: www.oxnardpd.org
SIC: 8641 Veterans' organization

(P-18891)
PACIFIC NEUROSCIENCE INST LLC
2125 Arizona Ave (90404-1337)
PHONE..................310 829-8271
Daniel F Kelly, *Mgr*
EMP: 79 **EST:** 2014
SALES (est): 3.21MM Privately Held
Web: www.pacificneuroscienceinstitute.org
SIC: 8641 Civic and social associations

(P-18892)
PALM DESERT GREENS ASSOCIATION
73750 Country Club Dr (92260-8663)
PHONE..................760 346-8005
Roberta Hollingsworth, *Genl Mgr*
Mal Sinclair, *
Ken Dobson, *
EMP: 75 **EST:** 1971
SQ FT: 12,400
SALES (est): 9.12MM Privately Held
Web: www.pdgcc.com
SIC: 8641 Homeowners' association

(P-18893)
PAZLO EDUCATION FOUNDATION
Also Called: APEX ACADEMY
1309 N Wilton Pl Fl 3 (90028-8526)
PHONE..................323 817-6550
Cesar Arturo Lopez, *Admn*
Margret Woelke-guevara, *Dir*
EMP: 60 **EST:** 2015
SALES (est): 8.46MM Privately Held
Web: www.apexacademyla.org
SIC: 8641 Civic and social associations

(P-18894)
PINE MOUNTAIN LAKE ASSOCIATION (PA)
Also Called: Pine Mountain Lake
19228 Pine Mountain Dr (95321-9497)
PHONE..................209 962-4080
Brian Sweeney, *Pr*
Joe Powell, *
Ian Morcott, *
Jerry Dickson, *
Dana Chavarria, *
EMP: 129 **EST:** 1969
SQ FT: 20,000
SALES (est): 13.13MM
SALES (corp-wide): 13.13MM Privately Held
Web: www.pinemountainlake.com
SIC: 8641 Homeowners' association

(P-18895)
PRIMARY SCHOOL
2086 Clarke Ave (94303-1916)
PHONE..................510 606-4563
Alison Kjeldgaard, *Prin*
EMP: 88 **EST:** 2018
SALES (est): 4MM Privately Held
Web: www.theprimaryschool.org
SIC: 8641 Civic and social associations

(P-18896)
PRO-YOUTH
Also Called: Pro-Youth Heart
505 N Court St (93291-4912)
P.O. Box 387 (93279-0387)
PHONE..................559 374-2030
Daryn Davis, *
Don Goodyear, *VP*
David Lari, *Treas*
Renee Whitson, *Corporate Secretary*
Charlie Saponara, *At Large*
EMP: 260 **EST:** 1993
SQ FT: 1,400
SALES (est): 29.51MM Privately Held
Web: www.proyouthexpandedlearning.org
SIC: 8641 Youth organizations

(P-18897)
PUBLIC HLTH FNDATION ENTPS INC
277 S Atlantic Blvd (90022-1734)
PHONE..................323 263-0262
Laurie Hill, *Prin*
EMP: 140
SALES (corp-wide): 92.05MM Privately Held
Web: www.phfewic.org
SIC: 8641 Civic and social associations
PA: Public Health Foundation Enterprises, Inc.
  13300 Crssrds Pkwy N
  City Of Industry CA
  800 201-7320

(P-18898)
PUBLIC HLTH FNDATION ENTPS INC
Also Called: Wic
1640 W Carson St Ste G (90501-3877)
PHONE..................310 320-5215
EMP: 140
SALES (corp-wide): 92.05MM Privately Held
Web: www.helunahealth.org
SIC: 8641 Civic and social associations
PA: Public Health Foundation Enterprises, Inc.
  13300 Crssrds Pkwy N
  City Of Industry CA
  800 201-7320

(P-18899)
PUBLIC HLTH FNDATION ENTPS INC (PA)
Also Called: Heluna Health
13300 Crossroads Pkwy N Ste 450 (91746)
PHONE..................800 201-7320
Blain Cutler, *Pr*
Eric Ramanathan, *
Devecchio Finley, *Vice Chairman*
Robert Jenks, *
Tamara Joseph, *
EMP: 177 **EST:** 1968
SQ FT: 25,000
SALES (est): 92.05MM
SALES (corp-wide): 92.05MM Privately Held
Web: www.helunahealth.org
SIC: 8641 Civic and social associations

(P-18900)
READING AND BEYOND
4670 E Butler Ave (93702-4608)
PHONE..................559 840-1068
Luis Santana, *Pr*
EMP: 76 **EST:** 1999
SALES (est): 7.51MM Privately Held
Web: www.readingandbeyond.org
SIC: 8641 Youth organizations

(P-18901)
RECREATIONAL ASSN CORCORAN
Also Called: RAC
900 Dairy Ave (93212-2114)
P.O. Box 176 (93212-0176)
PHONE..................559 992-5171
S S Brown, *Ex Dir*
Jim Razor, *Pr*
EMP: 63 **EST:** 2015
SALES (est): 1.88MM Privately Held
Web: www.cityofcorcoran.com
SIC: 8641 8699 Recreation association; Charitable organization

(P-18902)
REDWOOD FOREST FOUNDATION INC
2979 Santos Ln (94597-7545)
PHONE..................510 459-1131
Mark R Welther, *Brnch Mgr*
EMP: 76
SALES (corp-wide): 2.7MM Privately Held
Web: www.rffi.org
SIC: 8641 Environmental protection organization
PA: Redwood Forest Foundation, Inc.
  90 W Redwood Ave
  Fort Bragg CA
  707 409-5144

(P-18903)
ROSE FMLY CRTIVE EMPWRMENT CTR
7000 Franklin Blvd Ste 1000 (95823-1820)
PHONE..................916 376-7916
Jacqueline Rose, *CEO*
EMP: 99 **EST:** 2014
SALES (est): 1.71MM Privately Held
SIC: 8641 Civic and social associations

(P-18904)
SAN DIEGO COUNTRY ESTATES ASSN
Also Called: SAN VICENTE INN & GOLF CLUB
24157 San Vicente Rd (92065-4166)
PHONE..................760 789-3788
Jim Piva, *Pr*
EMP: 147 **EST:** 1972
SQ FT: 14,000
SALES (est): 12.16MM Privately Held
Web: www.sdcea.net
SIC: 8641 7997 7992 7011 Homeowners' association; Membership sports and recreation clubs; Public golf courses; Vacation lodges

(P-18905)
SAN LUIS OBISPO COUNTY YMCA
5785 Los Ranchos Rd (93401-8247)
PHONE..................805 544-7225
EMP: 72
SALES (corp-wide): 3.17MM Privately Held
Web: www.sloymca.org
SIC: 8641 7991 8351 7032 Youth organizations; Physical fitness facilities; Child day care services; Youth camps
PA: San Luis Obispo County Ymca Inc
  1020 Southwood Dr
  San Luis Obispo CA
  805 543-8235

(P-18906)
SAVICE INC
30052 Tomas (92688-2127)
PHONE..................949 888-2444
Phu Hoang, *Prin*
EMP: 98 **EST:** 2008
SALES (est): 71K Privately Held
SIC: 8641 Civic and social associations

(P-18907)
SHRINERS INTERNATIONAL
Also Called: Shriners Hspitals For Children
909 S Fair Oaks Ave (91105-2625)
PHONE..................626 389-9300
EMP: 139
Web: www.shrinerschildrens.org
SIC: 8641 Fraternal associations
PA: Shriners Hospitals For Children
  2900 N Rocky Point Dr
  Tampa FL

(P-18908)
SIERRA CLUB (PA)
Also Called: SIERRA CLUB BOOKS
2101 Webster St Ste 1300 (94612-3011)
PHONE..................415 977-5500
Robin Mann, *Pr*
David Scott, *
Michael Brune, *
Donna Buell, *
Allison Chin, *
EMP: 175 **EST:** 1892
SQ FT: 43,500
SALES (est): 119.89MM
SALES (corp-wide): 119.89MM Privately Held
Web: www.sierraclub.org
SIC: 8641 8399 Environmental protection organization; Advocacy group

(P-18909)
SILICON VLY CMNTY FOUNDATION (PA)
Also Called: Svcf
444 Castro St (94041-2073)
PHONE..................650 450-5400
Nicole Taylor, *Pr*
EMP: 127 **EST:** 2006
SALES (est): 5.61B
SALES (corp-wide): 5.61B Privately Held
Web: www.siliconvalleycf.org

PRODUCTS & SERVICES SECTION
8641 - Civic And Social Associations (P-18930)

SIC: 8641 Civic and social associations

(P-18910)
SILICON VLY CMNTY FOUNDATION
1300 S El Camino Real (94402-2963)
PHONE..................................650 458-2660
Johanna Wise, Prin
EMP: 105
SALES (corp-wide): 5.61B Privately Held
Web: www.siliconvalleycf.org
SIC: 8641 Civic and social associations
PA: Silicon Valley Community Foundation
444 Castro St Ste 140
Mountain View CA
650 450-5400

(P-18911)
SILVER LAKES ASSOCIATION
Also Called: Homeowners Association
15273 Orchard Hill Ln (92342-7824)
P.O. Box 179 (92342-0179)
PHONE..................................760 245-1606
Michael Bennett, Genl Mgr
EMP: 90 EST: 1976
SQ FT: 3,000
SALES (est): 5.02MM Privately Held
Web: www.silverlakesassociation.com
SIC: 8641 Homeowners' association

(P-18912)
SUN CITY PALM DSERT CMNTY ASSN (PA)
Also Called: Palm Desert Community Assn
38180 Del Webb Blvd (92211-1256)
PHONE..................................760 200-2100
Helen Mcenerney, Pr
EMP: 80 EST: 1992
SQ FT: 4,000
SALES (est): 16.7MM Privately Held
Web: www.scpdca.com
SIC: 8641 7992 7997 Dwelling-related associations; Public golf courses; Country club, membership

(P-18913)
SUTTER CLUB
1220 9th St (95814-4897)
PHONE..................................916 442-0456
Tom Narozonick, Genl Mgr
EMP: 75 EST: 1889
SQ FT: 45,000
SALES (est): 7.59MM Privately Held
Web: www.sutterclub.org
SIC: 8641 Social club, membership

(P-18914)
SUTTER REGIONAL MED FOUNDATION
127 Hospital Dr Ste 102 (94589-2500)
PHONE..................................707 551-3616
Bobbi Underhill, Prin
EMP: 187
SALES (corp-wide): 45.62MM Privately Held
SIC: 8641 Civic and social associations
PA: Sutter Regional Medical Foundation Inc
2702 Low Ct
Fairfield CA
707 427-4900

(P-18915)
TECHSOUP GLOBAL (PA)
Also Called: DISCOUNT TECH
435 Brannan St Ste 100 (94107-1780)
PHONE..................................800 659-3579
Rebecca Masisak, CEO
Daniel Ben-horin, Prin
Marnie Webb, *
EMP: 172 EST: 1988
SALES (est): 54.44MM Privately Held
Web: www.techsoup.org
SIC: 8641 Social associations

(P-18916)
THE LINUX FOUNDATION (PA)
548 Market St Pmb 57274 (94104-5401)
PHONE..................................415 723-9709
Jim Zemlin, CEO
Alan Clark, Sec
Lisbeth Mcnabb, CFO
EMP: 82 EST: 2007
SALES (est): 139.97MM Privately Held
Web: www.linuxfoundation.org
SIC: 8641 Civic and social associations

(P-18917)
THEATER ARTS FNDTION SAN DEGO
Also Called: LA JOLLA PLAYHOUSE
2910 La Jolla Village Dr (92093-5100)
P.O. Box 12039 (92039-2039)
PHONE..................................858 623-3366
Jeffrey Ressler Ch Person, Prin
Steven Libman, *
Lynelle Lynch Ch Person, Prin
Tim Scott Ch Person, Prin
Michael Bartell, *
EMP: 250 EST: 1954
SQ FT: 1,440
SALES (est): 6.05MM Privately Held
Web: www.lajollaplayhouse.org
SIC: 8641 7922 Civic associations; Theatrical producers and services

(P-18918)
UNITED BYS GRLS CLUBS SNTA BRB
Also Called: Boys & Girls Club
5701 Hollister Ave (93117-3420)
P.O. Box 1485 (93102-1485)
PHONE..................................805 967-1612
EMP: 71
SALES (corp-wide): 3.73MM Privately Held
Web: www.unitedbg.com
SIC: 8641 8351 Bars and restaurants, members only; Child day care services
PA: United Boys And Girls Clubs Of Santa Barbara County
1124 Castillo St
Santa Barbara CA
805 681-1315

(P-18919)
UPLAND HIGHLANDERS HIGH PTSA
565 W 11th St (91786-4660)
PHONE..................................909 949-7880
EMP: 88 EST: 2010
SALES (est): 50.15K Privately Held
Web: uhs.upland.k12.ca.us
SIC: 8641 Parent-teachers' association

(P-18920)
URBAN CORPS SAN DIEGO COUNTY
3127 Jefferson St (92110-4422)
P.O. Box 80156 (92138-0156)
PHONE..................................619 235-6884
Sam Duran, CEO
Michael Sterns, *
EMP: 132 EST: 1989
SQ FT: 25,000
SALES (est): 14.3MM Privately Held
Web: www.urbancorpssd.org
SIC: 8641 Youth organizations

(P-18921)
VALLEY HUNT CLUB
520 S Orange Grove Blvd (91105-1709)
PHONE..................................626 793-7134
David Mole, CEO
Donald F Crumrine, *
EMP: 85 EST: 1888
SQ FT: 40,000
SALES (est): 6.71MM Privately Held
Web: www.valleyhuntclub.com
SIC: 8641 Social club, membership

(P-18922)
VETERANS MED RES FNDTION SAN D
3350 La Jolla Village Dr Ste 151a (92161-0002)
PHONE..................................858 642-3080
Kerstin B Lynam, CEO
Barabara Dovenbarger, *
EMP: 250 EST: 1986
SALES (est): 16.37MM Privately Held
Web: www.vmrf.org
SIC: 8641 Civic and social associations

(P-18923)
VETERANS OF FOREIGN WARS OF US
1525 W Oakland Ave (92543-2682)
PHONE..................................951 202-3792
EMP: 65
SALES (corp-wide): 105.25MM Privately Held
SIC: 8641 Veterans' organization
PA: Veterans Of Foreign Wars Of The United States
406 W 34th St Fl 11
Kansas City MO
816 756-3390

(P-18924)
VETERANS OF FOREIGN WARS OF US
12235 California St (92399-4349)
PHONE..................................909 797-1898
EMP: 62
SALES (corp-wide): 105.25MM Privately Held
SIC: 8641 Veterans' organization
PA: Veterans Of Foreign Wars Of The United States
406 W 34th St Fl 11
Kansas City MO
816 756-3390

(P-18925)
VETERANS OF FOREIGN WARS OF US
9136 Elk Grove Blvd # 100 (95624-2075)
PHONE..................................916 786-7757
EMP: 65
SALES (corp-wide): 105.25MM Privately Held
SIC: 8641 Veterans' organization
PA: Veterans Of Foreign Wars Of The United States
406 W 34th St Fl 11
Kansas City MO
816 756-3390

(P-18926)
VETERANS OF FOREIGN WARS OF US
1251 Oregon St (96001-0414)
PHONE..................................530 241-9168
EMP: 62
SALES (corp-wide): 105.25MM Privately Held
SIC: 8641 Veterans' organization
PA: Veterans Of Foreign Wars Of The United States
406 W 34th St Fl 11
Kansas City MO
816 756-3390

(P-18927)
VIETNAM VETERANS OF SAN DIEGO (PA)
Also Called: VETERANS VILLAGE OF SAN DIEGO
4141 Pacific Hwy (92110-2030)
PHONE..................................619 497-0142
Phil Landis, Pr
Harry Guess, *
Andre Simpson, *
EMP: 65 EST: 1981
SQ FT: 35,719
SALES (est): 19.29MM
SALES (corp-wide): 19.29MM Privately Held
Web: www.vvsd.net
SIC: 8641 Veterans' organization

(P-18928)
VILLA MARIN HOMEOWNERS ASSN
Also Called: Villa Mrin Rtrement Residences
100 Thorndale Dr (94903-4599)
PHONE..................................415 499-8711
Danel Walker, CEO
Dan Walker, CEO
EMP: 170 EST: 1982
SQ FT: 500,000
SALES (est): 17.38MM Privately Held
Web: www.villa-marin.com
SIC: 8641 8051 8059 Homeowners' association; Skilled nursing care facilities; Personal care home, with health care

(P-18929)
WEST END YUNG MNS CHRISTN ASSN
Also Called: Ontario/Montclair YMCA
1257 E D St (91764-4329)
P.O. Box 3220 (91761-0922)
PHONE..................................909 477-2780
Dianna Lee-mitchell, Dir
EMP: 115
SALES (corp-wide): 4.73MM Privately Held
Web: www.weymca.org
SIC: 8641 7991 8351 7032 Youth organizations; Physical fitness facilities; Child day care services; Youth camps
PA: West End Young Men's Christian Association Inc
1150 E Foothill Blvd
Upland CA
909 481-0722

(P-18930)
WEST END YUNG MNS CHRISTN ASSN
Also Called: Chino Valley YMCA
5665 Edison Ave (91710-9051)
PHONE..................................909 597-7445
EMP: 115
SALES (corp-wide): 4.73MM Privately Held
Web: www.weymca.org
SIC: 8641 7991 8351 7032 Youth organizations; Physical fitness facilities; Child day care services; Youth camps
PA: West End Young Men's Christian Association Inc
1150 E Foothill Blvd
Upland CA
909 481-0722

8641 - Civic And Social Associations (P-18931)

(P-18931)
WOODBRIDGE VILLAGE ASSOCIATION
31 Creek Rd (92604-4793)
PHONE..................................949 786-1800
Kevin Chudy, *Ex Dir*
EMP: 65 **EST:** 1976
SQ FT: 15,000
SALES (est): 10.59MM **Privately Held**
SIC: 8641 Homeowners' association

(P-18932)
WORLD MVIE AWRDS ORGNZTION WMA
9171 Wilshire Blvd # 500a (90210-5530)
PHONE..................................833 375-5857
Lily Alphonsis, *CEO*
Royal Vincent, *
EMP: 99 **EST:** 2018
SALES (est): 198.74K **Privately Held**
SIC: 8641 Civic and social associations

(P-18933)
YMCA OF EAST VALLEY (PA)
500 E Citrus Ave (92373-5285)
PHONE..................................909 798-9622
Darwin Barnett, *CEO*
Ken Stein, *
Perry Mecate, *
Doug Thorne, *
Carmen Barney, *
EMP: 125 **EST:** 1887
SQ FT: 100,000
SALES (est): 15.69MM
SALES (corp-wide): 15.69MM **Privately Held**
Web: www.ymcaeastvalley.org
SIC: 8641 Youth organizations

(P-18934)
YMCA OF EAST VALLEY
Also Called: YMCA Camp Edwards
42842 Jenks Lake Rd E (92305-9769)
P.O. Box 277 (92305-0277)
PHONE..................................909 794-1702
Loren Werner, *Dir*
EMP: 117
SALES (corp-wide): 15.69MM **Privately Held**
Web: www.ymcaeastvalley.org
SIC: 8641 7991 8351 7032 Youth organizations; Physical fitness facilities; Child day care services; Youth camps
PA: Ymca Of The East Valley
500 E Citrus Ave
Redlands CA
909 798-9622

(P-18935)
YMCA OF EAST VALLEY
Also Called: San Bernardino Family YMCA
808 E 21st St (92404-4874)
PHONE..................................909 881-9622
Bill Blank, *Dir*
EMP: 127
SALES (corp-wide): 15.69MM **Privately Held**
Web: www.ymcaeastvalley.org
SIC: 8641 7991 8351 7032 Youth organizations; Physical fitness facilities; Child day care services; Youth camps
PA: Ymca Of The East Valley
500 E Citrus Ave
Redlands CA
909 798-9622

(P-18936)
YMCA OF EAST VALLEY
Also Called: Young Mens Christn Assocation
7793 Central Ave (92346-4106)
PHONE..................................909 425-9622
Ursula Walsh, *Brnch Mgr*
EMP: 61
SALES (corp-wide): 15.69MM **Privately Held**
Web: www.ymcaeastvalley.org
SIC: 8641 7991 8351 7032 Youth organizations; Physical fitness facilities; Child day care services; Youth camps
PA: Ymca Of The East Valley
500 E Citrus Ave
Redlands CA
909 798-9622

(P-18937)
YMCA OF SAN DIEGO COUNTY
Also Called: Toby Wells YMCA
5105 Overland Ave (92123-1238)
PHONE..................................858 496-9622
EMP: 67
SALES (corp-wide): 391K **Privately Held**
Web: www.ymcasd.org
SIC: 8641 Youth organizations
PA: Ymca Of San Diego County
3708 Ruffin Rd
San Diego CA
858 292-9622

(P-18938)
YMCA OF SAN DIEGO COUNTY
Also Called: La Jolla YMCA
8355 Cliffridge Ave (92037-2107)
PHONE..................................858 453-3483
Sam Wurtzbacher, *Dir*
EMP: 314
SALES (corp-wide): 391K **Privately Held**
Web: www.ymca.org
SIC: 8641 8351 7997 Youth organizations; Child day care services; Membership sports and recreation clubs
PA: Ymca Of San Diego County
3708 Ruffin Rd
San Diego CA
858 292-9622

(P-18939)
YMCA OF SAN DIEGO COUNTY (PA)
Also Called: Y, The
3708 Ruffin Rd (92123-1812)
PHONE..................................858 292-9622
Todd Tibbits, *Pr*
John Merritt, *
Charmaine Carter, *
EMP: 292 **EST:** 1882
SQ FT: 19,600
SALES (est): 391K
SALES (corp-wide): 391K **Privately Held**
Web: www.ymcasd.org
SIC: 8641 Youth organizations

(P-18940)
YMCA OF SAN DIEGO COUNTY
Also Called: Borderview Y M C A
3085 Beyer Blvd Ste 105 (92154-3479)
PHONE..................................619 428-1168
Mauricio Gonzalez, *Ex Dir*
EMP: 138
SALES (corp-wide): 391K **Privately Held**
Web: www.ymcasd.org
SIC: 8641 7991 8351 7032 Youth organizations; Physical fitness facilities; Child day care services; Youth camps
PA: Ymca Of San Diego County
3708 Ruffin Rd
San Diego CA
858 292-9622

(P-18941)
YMCA OF SAN DIEGO COUNTY
Also Called: Pelomar Family YMCA
200 Saxony Rd (92024-2720)
PHONE..................................760 745-7490
Alfredo Velasco, *Mgr*
EMP: 220
SALES (corp-wide): 391K **Privately Held**
Web: www.ymcasd.org
SIC: 8641 7991 8351 7032 Youth organizations; Physical fitness facilities; Child day care services; Youth camps
PA: Ymca Of San Diego County
3708 Ruffin Rd
San Diego CA
858 292-9622

(P-18942)
YMCA OF SAN DIEGO COUNTY
Also Called: Young Mens Christn Assocation
8881 Dallas St (91942-3297)
PHONE..................................619 464-1323
Steve Rowe, *Ex Dir*
EMP: 231
SALES (corp-wide): 391K **Privately Held**
Web: www.ymcasd.org
SIC: 8641 7991 8351 7032 Youth organizations; Physical fitness facilities; Child day care services; Youth camps
PA: Ymca Of San Diego County
3708 Ruffin Rd
San Diego CA
858 292-9622

(P-18943)
YMCA OF SAN DIEGO COUNTY
Also Called: Copley Family YMCA
5505 Friars Rd (92110-2682)
PHONE..................................619 280-9622
Kischa Hill, *Dir*
EMP: 287
SALES (corp-wide): 391K **Privately Held**
Web: www.ymcasd.org
SIC: 8641 7991 8351 7032 Youth organizations; Physical fitness facilities; Child day care services; Youth camps
PA: Ymca Of San Diego County
3708 Ruffin Rd
San Diego CA
858 292-9622

(P-18944)
YMCA OF SAN DIEGO COUNTY
Also Called: Magdalena Ecke Family YMCA
200 Saxony Rd (92024-2720)
PHONE..................................858 292-4034
Susan J Cocke, *Brnch Mgr*
EMP: 372
SALES (corp-wide): 391K **Privately Held**
Web: www.ymca.org
SIC: 8641 8351 8322 7997 Youth organizations; Child day care services; Youth center; Membership sports and recreation clubs
PA: Ymca Of San Diego County
3708 Ruffin Rd
San Diego CA
858 292-9622

(P-18945)
YMCA OF SAN DIEGO COUNTY
Also Called: YMCA Youth & Family Services
2927 Meade Ave (92116-4251)
PHONE..................................619 281-8313
Cesar Marcano, *Ex Dir*
EMP: 135
SALES (corp-wide): 391K **Privately Held**
Web: www.ymcasd.org
SIC: 8641 7991 8351 7032 Youth organizations; Physical fitness facilities; Child day care services; Youth camps
PA: Ymca Of San Diego County
3708 Ruffin Rd
San Diego CA
858 292-9622

(P-18946)
YMCA OF SAN DIEGO COUNTY
Also Called: Peninsula Family YMCA Sunshine
2150 Beryl St Ste 18 (92109-3617)
PHONE..................................619 226-8888
Andrea Sanchez, *Dir*
EMP: 326
SQ FT: 3,500
SALES (corp-wide): 391K **Privately Held**
Web: www.ymcasd.org
SIC: 8641 8322 Youth organizations; Individual and family services
PA: Ymca Of San Diego County
3708 Ruffin Rd
San Diego CA
858 292-9622

(P-18947)
YMCA OF SAN DIEGO COUNTY
Also Called: Jackie Robinson Family YMCA
5505 Friars Rd (92110-2682)
PHONE..................................619 264-0144
Mike Brunker, *Ex Dir*
EMP: 202
SALES (corp-wide): 391K **Privately Held**
Web: www.ymcasd.org
SIC: 8641 7991 8351 7032 Youth organizations; Physical fitness facilities; Child day care services; Youth camps
PA: Ymca Of San Diego County
3708 Ruffin Rd
San Diego CA
858 292-9622

(P-18948)
YMCA OF SAN DIEGO COUNTY
Also Called: YMCA Child Care Resource Svcs
3333 Camino Del Rio S Ste 400 (92108-3837)
PHONE..................................619 521-3055
Debbie Macdonald, *Dir*
EMP: 180
SALES (corp-wide): 391K **Privately Held**
Web: www.ymcasd.org
SIC: 8641 7991 8351 7032 Youth organizations; Physical fitness facilities; Child day care services; Youth camps
PA: Ymca Of San Diego County
3708 Ruffin Rd
San Diego CA
858 292-9622

(P-18949)
YMCA OF SAN DIEGO COUNTY
Also Called: YMCA Overnight Camp
4761 Pine Hills Rd (92036)
P.O. Box 2440 (92036-2440)
PHONE..................................760 765-0642
Thomas Madeyski, *Ex Dir*
EMP: 174
SALES (corp-wide): 391K **Privately Held**
Web: www.ymcasd.org
SIC: 8641 7991 8351 7032 Youth organizations; Physical fitness facilities; Child day care services; Youth camps
PA: Ymca Of San Diego County
3708 Ruffin Rd
San Diego CA
858 292-9622

PRODUCTS & SERVICES SECTION
8641 - Civic And Social Associations (P-18968)

(P-18950)
YMCA OF SAN DIEGO COUNTY
Also Called: Mission Valley YMCA
5505 Friars Rd (92110-2682)
PHONE.................................619 298-3576
Dick Webster, Mgr
EMP: 315
SALES (corp-wide): 391K **Privately Held**
Web: www.ymcasd.org
SIC: **8641** 7997 Youth organizations; Membership sports and recreation clubs
PA: Ymca Of San Diego County
3708 Ruffin Rd
San Diego CA
858 292-9622

(P-18951)
YMCA OF SAN DIEGO COUNTY
Also Called: Joe & Mary Mottino YMCA
200 Saxony Rd (92024-2720)
PHONE.................................760 758-0808
Jeff Guzzardo, Brnch Mgr
EMP: 157
SALES (corp-wide): 391K **Privately Held**
Web: www.ymcasd.org
SIC: **8641** 8322 Youth organizations; Individual and family services
PA: Ymca Of San Diego County
3708 Ruffin Rd
San Diego CA
858 292-9622

(P-18952)
YMCA OF SAN DIEGO COUNTY
Also Called: Oz North Coast Y M C A
215 Barnes St (92054-3472)
PHONE.................................760 721-8930
Kim Morgan, Mgr
EMP: 141
SQ FT: 3,567
SALES (corp-wide): 391K **Privately Held**
Web: www.ymcasd.org
SIC: **8641** 7991 8351 7032 Youth organizations; Physical fitness facilities; Child day care services; Youth camps
PA: Ymca Of San Diego County
3708 Ruffin Rd
San Diego CA
858 292-9622

(P-18953)
YOSEMITE LAKES OWNERS ASSN
30250 Yosemite Springs Pkwy Unit A (93614-9369)
PHONE.................................559 658-7466
Steve Payne, Genl Mgr
EMP: 70 EST: 1970
SQ FT: 10,000
SALES (est): 5.94MM **Privately Held**
Web: www.yosemitelakespark.org
SIC: **8641** Homeowners' association

(P-18954)
YOUNG MENS CHRISTIAN ASSOCIATION OF THE EAST BAY
2350 Broadway (94612-2415)
PHONE.................................510 451-8039
◆ EMP: 852
SIC: **8641** 7991 8351 7032 Youth organizations; Physical fitness facilities; Child day care services; Youth camps

(P-18955)
YOUNG MNS CHRSTN ASSN BRBANK C (PA)
321 E Magnolia Blvd (91502-1132)
PHONE.................................818 845-8551
Mary Cutone, CEO
Bryan Snodgrasss, *
EMP: 100 EST: 1924
SQ FT: 47,000
SALES (est): 5.91MM
SALES (corp-wide): 5.91MM **Privately Held**
Web: www.burbankymca.org
SIC: **8641** 7991 8351 7032 Youth organizations; Physical fitness facilities; Child day care services; Youth camps

(P-18956)
YOUNG MNS CHRSTN ASSN GLNDALE
Also Called: GLENDALE YMCA SWIM SCHOOL
140 N Louise St (91206-4226)
PHONE.................................818 484-8256
Tom Tyler, CEO
EMP: 86 EST: 1924
SQ FT: 15,000
SALES (est): 3.86MM **Privately Held**
Web: www.glendaleymca.org
SIC: **8641** Youth organizations

(P-18957)
YOUNG MNS CHRSTN ASSN MTRO LOS
Also Called: YMCA
2900 Sepulveda Blvd (90505-2804)
PHONE.................................310 325-5885
Steve Macaller, Ex Dir
EMP: 71
SALES (corp-wide): 73.8MM **Privately Held**
Web: www.ymcala.org
SIC: **8641** 7997 Youth organizations; Membership sports and recreation clubs
PA: Young Men's Christian Association Of Metropolitan Los Angeles
625 S New Hampshire Ave
Los Angeles CA
213 380-6448

(P-18958)
YOUNG MNS CHRSTN ASSN MTRO LOS
Also Called: Mid-Valley Y M C A
6901 Lennox Ave (91405-4002)
PHONE.................................818 989-3800
Wendy Sunders, Ex Dir
EMP: 64
SQ FT: 37,223
SALES (corp-wide): 73.8MM **Privately Held**
Web: www.ymcala.org
SIC: **8641** 7991 8351 7032 Youth organizations; Physical fitness facilities; Child day care services; Youth camps
PA: Young Men's Christian Association Of Metropolitan Los Angeles
625 S New Hampshire Ave
Los Angeles CA
213 380-6448

(P-18959)
YOUNG MNS CHRSTN ASSN MTRO LOS
Also Called: South East Rio Vista YMCA
4801 E 58th St (90270-3014)
PHONE.................................323 588-2256
Renee Breswilla, Dir
EMP: 75
SALES (corp-wide): 73.8MM **Privately Held**
Web: www.ymcala.org
SIC: **8641** 8322 Youth organizations; Youth center
PA: Young Men's Christian Association Of Metropolitan Los Angeles
625 S New Hampshire Ave
Los Angeles CA
213 380-6448

(P-18960)
YOUNG MNS CHRSTN ASSN MTRO LOS (PA)
Also Called: YMCA
625 S New Hampshire Ave (90005-1342)
PHONE.................................213 380-6448
Alan Hostrup, Pr
Stephen Meier, *
W J Ellison, *
Dan Cooper, *
EMP: 70 EST: 1887
SQ FT: 16,000
SALES (est): 73.8MM
SALES (corp-wide): 73.8MM **Privately Held**
Web: www.ymcala.org
SIC: **8641** Youth organizations

(P-18961)
YOUNG MNS CHRSTN ASSN MTRO LOS
Also Called: YMCA of Westchester
8015 S Sepulveda Blvd (90045-2940)
PHONE.................................310 216-9036
Patricia De Frelice, Ex Dir
EMP: 76
SALES (corp-wide): 73.8MM **Privately Held**
Web: www.ymcala.org
SIC: **8641** 8322 Youth organizations; Individual and family services
PA: Young Men's Christian Association Of Metropolitan Los Angeles
625 S New Hampshire Ave
Los Angeles CA
213 380-6448

(P-18962)
YOUNG MNS CHRSTN ASSN MTRO LOS
Also Called: National Fitness Testing
1553 Schrader Blvd (90028)
PHONE.................................323 467-4161
Rosa Najera, Brnch Mgr
EMP: 133
SALES (corp-wide): 73.8MM **Privately Held**
Web: www.ymcala.org
SIC: **8641** Youth organizations
PA: Young Men's Christian Association Of Metropolitan Los Angeles
625 S New Hampshire Ave
Los Angeles CA
213 380-6448

(P-18963)
YOUNG MNS CHRSTN ASSN OF E BAY
Also Called: Urban Services YMCA
3265 Market St (94608-4332)
PHONE.................................510 654-9622
Chris Chatmon, Ex Dir
EMP: 297
SALES (corp-wide): 64.62MM **Privately Held**
Web: www.ymcaeastbay.org
SIC: **8641** 7991 8351 7032 Youth organizations; Physical fitness facilities; Child day care services; Youth camps
PA: Young Men's Christian Association Of The East Bay
2330 Broadway
Oakland CA
510 549-4515

(P-18964)
YOUNG MNS CHRSTN ASSN OF E BAY
200 Lake Ave (94572-1063)
PHONE.................................510 412-5644
Pamela Williams, Brnch Mgr
EMP: 196
SALES (corp-wide): 64.62MM **Privately Held**
Web: www.ymcaeastbay.org
SIC: **8641** Youth organizations
PA: Young Men's Christian Association Of The East Bay
2330 Broadway
Oakland CA
510 549-4515

(P-18965)
YOUNG MNS CHRSTN ASSN OF E BAY
1250 23rd St (94804-1011)
PHONE.................................510 412-5640
Kathy Hardy, Brnch Mgr
EMP: 295
SALES (corp-wide): 64.62MM **Privately Held**
Web: www.ymcaeastbay.org
SIC: **8641** Youth organizations
PA: Young Men's Christian Association Of The East Bay
2330 Broadway
Oakland CA
510 549-4515

(P-18966)
YOUNG MNS CHRSTN ASSN OF E BAY
Also Called: Berkeley Albany YMCA
1705 Thornwood Dr (94521-1915)
PHONE.................................925 609-7971
EMP: 196
SALES (corp-wide): 64.62MM **Privately Held**
Web: www.ymcaeastbay.org
SIC: **8641** Youth organizations
PA: Young Men's Christian Association Of The East Bay
2330 Broadway
Oakland CA
510 549-4515

(P-18967)
YOUNG MNS CHRSTN ASSN OF E BAY
Also Called: YMCA of East Bay
2350 Broadway (94612-2415)
PHONE.................................510 451-8039
Fran Gallati, Pr
EMP: 852
SALES (corp-wide): 64.62MM **Privately Held**
Web: www.ymcaeastbay.org
SIC: **8641** 7991 8351 7032 Youth organizations; Physical fitness facilities; Child day care services; Youth camps
PA: Young Men's Christian Association Of The East Bay
2330 Broadway
Oakland CA
510 549-4515

(P-18968)
YOUNG MNS CHRSTN ASSN OF E BAY
Also Called: Emery Marina
4727 San Pablo Ave (94608-3035)
PHONE.................................510 601-8674
Henry Der, Brnch Mgr
EMP: 296

8641 - Civic And Social Associations (P-18969)

SALES (corp-wide): 64.62MM **Privately Held**
Web: www.ymcaeastbay.org
SIC: **8641** 7991 8351 7032 Youth organizations; Physical fitness facilities; Child day care services; Youth camps
PA: Young Men's Christian Association Of The East Bay
2330 Broadway
Oakland CA
510 549-4515

(P-18969)
YOUNG MNS CHRSTN ASSN OF E BAY
Also Called: Y M C A Metro Clinic
2111 Martin Luther King Jr Way (94704-1108)
PHONE...................510 486-8400
Larry Bush, *Mgr*
EMP: 296
SALES (corp-wide): 64.62MM **Privately Held**
Web: www.ymcaeastbay.org
SIC: **8641** 7991 8351 7032 Youth organizations; Physical fitness facilities; Child day care services; Youth camps
PA: Young Men's Christian Association Of The East Bay
2330 Broadway
Oakland CA
510 549-4515

(P-18970)
YOUNG MNS CHRSTN ASSN OF E BAY
Also Called: YMCA Head Start
2009 10th St (94710-2119)
PHONE...................510 848-9092
Pamela Shaw, *Dir*
EMP: 394
SALES (corp-wide): 64.62MM **Privately Held**
Web: www.ymcaeastbay.org
SIC: **8641** 7991 8351 7032 Youth organizations; Physical fitness facilities; Child day care services; Youth camps
PA: Young Men's Christian Association Of The East Bay
2330 Broadway
Oakland CA
510 549-4515

(P-18971)
YOUNG MNS CHRSTN ASSN OF E BAY
Also Called: Downtown Berkeley YMCA
2001 Allston Way (94704-1417)
PHONE...................510 848-9622
Fran Gallati, *Ex Dir*
EMP: 1380
SQ FT: 70,135
SALES (corp-wide): 64.62MM **Privately Held**
Web: www.ymcaeastbay.org
SIC: **8641** 7991 8351 7032 Youth organizations; Physical fitness facilities; Child day care services; Youth camps
PA: Young Men's Christian Association Of The East Bay
2330 Broadway
Oakland CA
510 549-4515

(P-18972)
YOUNG MNS CHRSTN ASSN OF E BAY
Also Called: YMCA Pre School Hillview
3800 Clark Rd (94803-3145)
PHONE...................510 223-7070
EMP: 197
SALES (corp-wide): 64.62MM **Privately Held**
Web: www.ymcaeastbay.org
SIC: **8641** Youth organizations
PA: Young Men's Christian Association Of The East Bay
2330 Broadway
Oakland CA
510 549-4515

(P-18973)
YOUNG MNS CHRSTN ASSN OF E BAY
Also Called: Kids' Club YMCA Oxford School
1130 Oxford St (94707-2624)
PHONE...................510 526-2146
Stephanie Hochman, *Brnch Mgr*
EMP: 296
SALES (corp-wide): 64.62MM **Privately Held**
Web: www.ymcaeastbay.org
SIC: **8641** 7991 8351 7032 Youth organizations; Physical fitness facilities; Child day care services; Youth camps
PA: Young Men's Christian Association Of The East Bay
2330 Broadway
Oakland CA
510 549-4515

(P-18974)
YOUNG MNS CHRSTN ASSN OF E BAY
Also Called: YMCA Elementary School
505 Escuela Ave (94040-2006)
PHONE...................650 526-3500
Lucia Medina, *Brnch Mgr*
EMP: 296
SALES (corp-wide): 64.62MM **Privately Held**
Web: www.ymcaeastbay.org
SIC: **8641** 7991 8351 7032 Youth organizations; Physical fitness facilities; Child day care services; Youth camps
PA: Young Men's Christian Association Of The East Bay
2330 Broadway
Oakland CA
510 549-4515

(P-18975)
YOUNG MNS CHRSTN ASSN OF E BAY
Also Called: Y M C A
2241 Russell St (94705-1029)
PHONE...................510 644-6290
Fran Gallati, *Pr*
EMP: 197
SALES (corp-wide): 64.62MM **Privately Held**
Web: www.ymcaeastbay.org
SIC: **8641** Youth organizations
PA: Young Men's Christian Association Of The East Bay
2330 Broadway
Oakland CA
510 549-4515

(P-18976)
YOUNG MNS CHRSTN ASSN OF E BAY
Also Called: YMCA Child Care Chadbourne
801 Plymouth Ave (94539-4637)
PHONE...................510 656-7243
Santofh Mahavni, *Mgr*
EMP: 296
SALES (corp-wide): 64.62MM **Privately Held**
Web: www.ymcaeastbay.org

(P-18977)
YOUNG MNS CHRSTN ASSN OF E BAY
Also Called: West Contra Costa YMCA
4300 Lakeside Dr Ste 150 (94806-5717)
PHONE...................510 222-9622
Bria Cartwright, *Ex Dir*
EMP: 2858
SQ FT: 45,343
SALES (corp-wide): 64.62MM **Privately Held**
Web: www.ymcaeastbay.org
SIC: **8641** 7991 8351 7032 Youth organizations; Physical fitness facilities; Child day care services; Youth camps
PA: Young Men's Christian Association Of The East Bay
2330 Broadway
Oakland CA
510 549-4515

(P-18978)
YOUNG MNS CHRSTN ASSN OF E BAY
Also Called: Coronado YMCA
263 S 20th St (94804-2709)
PHONE...................510 412-5647
Don Lau, *Brnch Mgr*
EMP: 788
SQ FT: 16,338
SALES (corp-wide): 64.62MM **Privately Held**
Web: www.ymcaeastbay.org
SIC: **8641** Youth organizations
PA: Young Men's Christian Association Of The East Bay
2330 Broadway
Oakland CA
510 549-4515

(P-18979)
YOUNG MNS CHRSTN ASSN OF E BAY
Also Called: Hilltop Family YMCA
4300 Lakeside Dr (94806-5717)
PHONE...................510 222-9622
Linda Cook, *Brnch Mgr*
EMP: 394
SALES (corp-wide): 64.62MM **Privately Held**
Web: www.ymcaeastbay.org
SIC: **8641** Youth organizations
PA: Young Men's Christian Association Of The East Bay
2330 Broadway
Oakland CA
510 549-4515

(P-18980)
YOUNG MNS CHRSTN ASSN OF E BAY
Also Called: Tri-Valley YMCA
5000 Pleasanton Ave Ste 200 (94566-7052)
PHONE...................925 475-6100
Kelley O'lague, *Brnch Mgr*
EMP: 296
SALES (corp-wide): 64.62MM **Privately Held**
Web: www.ymcaeastbay.org

SIC: **8641** Youth organizations
PA: Young Men's Christian Association Of The East Bay
2330 Broadway
Oakland CA
510 549-4515

(P-18981)
YOUNG MNS CHRSTN ASSN OF E BAY
Also Called: Urban Services Eastlake YMCA
1612 45th Ave (94601-4520)
PHONE...................510 534-7441
Chris Chatmon, *Mgr*
EMP: 394
SALES (corp-wide): 64.62MM **Privately Held**
Web: www.ymcaeastbay.org
SIC: **8641** Youth organizations
PA: Young Men's Christian Association Of The East Bay
2330 Broadway
Oakland CA
510 549-4515

(P-18982)
YOUNG MNS CHRSTN ASSN OF E BAY
41811 Blacow Rd (94538-3352)
PHONE...................510 683-9165
Deepa Meata, *Mgr*
EMP: 296
SALES (corp-wide): 64.62MM **Privately Held**
Web: www.ymcaeastbay.org
SIC: **8641** 7991 8351 7032 Youth organizations; Physical fitness facilities; Child day care services; Youth camps
PA: Young Men's Christian Association Of The East Bay
2330 Broadway
Oakland CA
510 549-4515

(P-18983)
YOUNG MNS CHRSTN ASSN OF E BAY
Also Called: YMCA Sch Age Pgrm Durham
40292 Leslie St 402 (94538-3520)
PHONE...................510 683-9107
Melda Shaffer, *Dir*
EMP: 197
SALES (corp-wide): 64.62MM **Privately Held**
Web: www.ymcaeastbay.org
SIC: **8641** 7991 8351 7032 Youth organizations; Physical fitness facilities; Child day care services; Youth camps
PA: Young Men's Christian Association Of The East Bay
2330 Broadway
Oakland CA
510 549-4515

(P-18984)
YOUNG MNS CHRSTN ASSN OF E BAY
Also Called: Metro YMCA Leitch
47100 Fernald St 471 (94539-7005)
PHONE...................510 683-9147
Ericka Mckinnon, *Dir*
EMP: 197
SALES (corp-wide): 64.62MM **Privately Held**
Web: www.ymcaeastbay.org
SIC: **8641** 7991 8351 7032 Youth organizations; Physical fitness facilities; Child day care services; Youth camps
PA: Young Men's Christian Association Of The East Bay

2330 Broadway
Oakland CA
510 549-4515

(P-18985)
YOUNG MNS CHRSTN ASSN OF E BAY
Also Called: YMCA
2001 Allston Way (94704-1417)
PHONE..................510 848-6800
Peter Gerharz, *Brnch Mgr*
EMP: 197
SALES (corp-wide): 64.62MM **Privately Held**
Web: www.ymcaeastbay.org
SIC: 8641 7991 8351 7032 Youth organizations; Physical fitness facilities; Child day care services; Youth camps
PA: Young Men's Christian Association Of The East Bay
2330 Broadway
Oakland CA
510 549-4515

(P-18986)
YOUNG MNS CHRSTN ASSN OF E BAY
Also Called: YMCA After School-Olinda
5855 Olinda Rd (94803-3543)
PHONE..................510 262-6588
EMP: 197
SALES (corp-wide): 64.62MM **Privately Held**
Web: www.ymcaeastbay.org
SIC: 8641 7991 8351 7032 Youth organizations; Physical fitness facilities; Child day care services; Youth camps
PA: Young Men's Christian Association Of The East Bay
2330 Broadway
Oakland CA
510 549-4515

(P-18987)
YOUNG MNS CHRSTN ASSN OF E BAY
Also Called: YMCA
1422 San Pablo Ave (94702-1024)
PHONE..................510 559-2090
EMP: 296
SALES (corp-wide): 64.62MM **Privately Held**
Web: www.ymcaeastbay.org
SIC: 8641 8322 8351 Youth organizations; Individual and family services; Head Start center, except in conjunction with school
PA: Young Men's Christian Association Of The East Bay
2330 Broadway
Oakland CA
510 549-4515

(P-18988)
YOUNG MNS CHRSTN ASSN OF FTHLL
Also Called: YMCA OF THE FOOTHILLS
1930 Foothill Blvd (91011-1933)
PHONE..................818 790-0123
Tyler Wright, *CEO*
Mark Skeehan, *Finance*
Linden Katherine, *Prin*
EMP: 68 **EST:** 1957
SALES (est): 7.85MM **Privately Held**
Web: www.ymcafoothills.org
SIC: 8641 Youth organizations

(P-18989)
YOUNG MNS CHRSTN ASSN ORNGE CN
Also Called: YMCA
2300 University Dr (92660-3313)
PHONE..................949 642-9990
Joy Hyde, *Genl Mgr*
EMP: 93
SQ FT: 17,976
SALES (corp-wide): 33.29MM **Privately Held**
Web: www.ymcaoc.org
SIC: 8641 7991 Youth organizations; Physical fitness facilities
PA: Young Men's Christian Association Of Orange County
13821 Newport Ave Ste 200
Tustin CA
714 549-9622

(P-18990)
YOUNG MNS CHRSTN ASSN ORNGE CN
Also Called: Saddle Back Valley YMCA
27341 Trabuco Cir (92692-1939)
PHONE..................949 859-9622
Mary J Goodrick, *Ex Dir*
EMP: 92
SALES (corp-wide): 33.29MM **Privately Held**
Web: www.ymcaoc.org
SIC: 8641 7991 8351 7032 Youth organizations; Physical fitness facilities; Child day care services; Youth camps
PA: Young Men's Christian Association Of Orange County
13821 Newport Ave Ste 200
Tustin CA
714 549-9622

(P-18991)
YOUNG MNS CHRSTN ASSN SAN FRNC
Also Called: Ymcasf
1500 Los Gamos Dr (94903-1841)
PHONE..................415 492-9622
EMP: 74
SALES (corp-wide): 91.37MM **Privately Held**
Web: www.ymcasf.org
SIC: 8641 8351 7991 Community membership club; Child day care services; Physical fitness facilities
PA: Young Men's Christian Association Of San Francisco
50 California St Ste 650
San Francisco CA
415 777-9622

(P-18992)
YOUNG MNS CHRSTN ASSN SAN FRNC
Also Called: Presido YMCA
63 Funston Ave (94129-1110)
PHONE..................415 447-9622
Robert Sindelar, *Ex Dir*
EMP: 78
SALES (corp-wide): 91.37MM **Privately Held**
Web: www.ymcasf.org
SIC: 8641 7999 Youth organizations; Tennis services and professionals
PA: Young Men's Christian Association Of San Francisco
50 California St Ste 650
San Francisco CA
415 777-9622

(P-18993)
YOUNG MNS CHRSTN ASSN SAN FRNC
Also Called: Peninsula YMCA
1877 S Grant St (94402-2647)
PHONE..................650 286-9622
Rachel Del Monte, *Mgr*
EMP: 114
SALES (corp-wide): 91.37MM **Privately Held**
Web: www.ymcasf.org
SIC: 8641 7991 8351 Youth organizations; Physical fitness facilities; Child day care services
PA: Young Men's Christian Association Of San Francisco
50 California St Ste 650
San Francisco CA
415 777-9622

(P-18994)
YOUNG MNS CHRSTN ASSN SAN FRNC
Also Called: Camp Jones Gulch YMCA
11000 Pescadero Rd (94020-9711)
PHONE..................650 747-1200
Peter Jones, *Ex Dir*
EMP: 114
SALES (corp-wide): 91.37MM **Privately Held**
Web: www.ymcasf.org
SIC: 8641 8322 Youth organizations; Individual and family services
PA: Young Men's Christian Association Of San Francisco
50 California St Ste 650
San Francisco CA
415 777-9622

(P-18995)
YOUNG MNS CHRSTN ASSN SAN FRNC
Also Called: YMCA
169 Steuart St (94105-1206)
PHONE..................415 957-9622
Larry Bush, *Brnch Mgr*
EMP: 193
SQ FT: 54,186
SALES (corp-wide): 91.37MM **Privately Held**
Web: www.ymcasf.org
SIC: 8641 7991 8351 7032 Youth organizations; Physical fitness facilities; Child day care services; Youth camps
PA: Young Men's Christian Association Of San Francisco
50 California St Ste 650
San Francisco CA
415 777-9622

(P-18996)
YOUNG MNS CHRSTN ASSN SAN FRNC
Also Called: Shih Yu-Lang Central YMCA
246 Eddy St (94102-2716)
PHONE..................415 885-0460
Carmela Gold, *Ex Dir*
EMP: 91
SALES (corp-wide): 91.37MM **Privately Held**
Web: www.ymcasf.org
SIC: 8641 7997 8322 7999 Youth organizations; Membership sports and recreation clubs; Senior citizens' center or association; Swimming instruction
PA: Young Men's Christian Association Of San Francisco
50 California St Ste 650
San Francisco CA
415 777-9622

(P-18997)
YOUNG MNS CHRSTN ASSN SAN FRNC
Also Called: YMCA Pt Bnita Otdoor Cnfrnce C
981 Fort Barry (94965)
PHONE..................415 331-9622
Mary Perkins, *Ex Dir*
EMP: 62
SALES (corp-wide): 91.37MM **Privately Held**
Web: www.ymcasf.org
SIC: 8641 7991 8351 7032 Youth organizations; Physical fitness facilities; Child day care services; Youth camps
PA: Young Men's Christian Association Of San Francisco
50 California St Ste 650
San Francisco CA
415 777-9622

(P-18998)
YOUNG MNS CHRSTN ASSN SAN FRNC
Also Called: Mission YMCA
4080 Mission St (94112-1017)
PHONE..................415 586-6900
EMP: 148
SQ FT: 6,833
SALES (corp-wide): 91.37MM **Privately Held**
Web: www.ymcasf.org
SIC: 8641 7991 8351 7032 Youth organizations; Physical fitness facilities; Child day care services; Youth camps
PA: Young Men's Christian Association Of San Francisco
50 California St Ste 650
San Francisco CA
415 777-9622

(P-18999)
YOUNG MNS CHRSTN ASSN SLCON VL (PA)
80 Saratoga Ave (95051-7303)
PHONE..................408 351-6400
Kathy Riggins, *Pr*
Ed Barrantes, *
EMP: 60 **EST:** 1867
SQ FT: 5,000
SALES (est): 28.49MM
SALES (corp-wide): 28.49MM **Privately Held**
Web: www.ymcasv.org
SIC: 8641 7991 8351 7032 Youth organizations; Physical fitness facilities; Child day care services; Youth camps

(P-19000)
YOUNG MNS CHRSTN ASSN SLCON VL
Also Called: Young Mens Christn Assocation
1922 The Alameda Ste 300 (95126-1430)
PHONE..................650 493-9622
EMP: 80
SALES (corp-wide): 28.49MM **Privately Held**
Web: www.ymcasv.org
SIC: 8641 7991 8351 7032 Youth organizations; Physical fitness facilities; Child day care services; Youth camps
PA: Young Men's Christian Association Of Silicon Valley
80 Saratoga Ave
Santa Clara CA
408 351-6400

(P-19001)
YOUNG MNS CHRSTN ASSN SLCON VL
Also Called: Central Branch YMCA
1717 The Alameda (95126-1726)
PHONE..................408 298-1717
Barbara Cardinez, *Mgr*
EMP: 245

8641 - Civic And Social Associations (P-19002)

SQ FT: 52,715
SALES (corp-wide): 28.49MM **Privately Held**
Web: www.ymcasv.org
SIC: **8641** 8351 8322 7997 Youth organizations; Child day care services; Individual and family services; Membership sports and recreation clubs
PA: Young Men's Christian Association Of Silicon Valley
80 Saratoga Ave
Santa Clara CA
408 351-6400

(P-19002)
YOUNG MNS CHRSTN ASSN SLCON VL
Also Called: El Camino YMCA
2400 Grant Rd (94040-4301)
PHONE.................................650 969-9622
Elaine Glissmeyer, *Dir*
EMP: 191
SALES (corp-wide): 28.49MM **Privately Held**
Web: www.ymcasv.org
SIC: **8641** 7991 8351 7032 Youth organizations; Physical fitness facilities; Child day care services; Youth camps
PA: Young Men's Christian Association Of Silicon Valley
80 Saratoga Ave
Santa Clara CA
408 351-6400

(P-19003)
YOUNG MNS CHRSTN ASSN SLCON VL
Also Called: YMCA of Santa Clara Valley
5632 Santa Teresa Blvd (95123-2633)
PHONE.................................408 226-9622
Rick Valdez, *Ex Dir*
EMP: 188
SALES (corp-wide): 28.49MM **Privately Held**
Web: www.ymcasv.org
SIC: **8641** 7991 8351 7032 Youth organizations; Physical fitness facilities; Child day care services; Youth camps
PA: Young Men's Christian Association Of Silicon Valley
80 Saratoga Ave
Santa Clara CA
408 351-6400

(P-19004)
YOUNG MNS CHRSTN ASSN SLCON VL
Also Called: YMCA of Santa Clara Valley
1855 Majestic Way (95132-1940)
PHONE.................................408 729-4223
Rick Valdez, *Brnch Mgr*
EMP: 81
SALES (corp-wide): 28.49MM **Privately Held**
Web: www.ymcasv.org
SIC: **8641** 7991 8351 7032 Youth organizations; Physical fitness facilities; Child day care services; Youth camps
PA: Young Men's Christian Association Of Silicon Valley
80 Saratoga Ave
Santa Clara CA
408 351-6400

(P-19005)
YOUNG MNS CHRSTN ASSN SLCON VL
Also Called: YMCA of Redwoods
16275 Highway 9 (95006-9652)
PHONE.................................831 338-2128

Mike Wentz, *Dir*
EMP: 299
SALES (corp-wide): 28.49MM **Privately Held**
Web: www.ymcasv.org
SIC: **8641** 7991 8351 7032 Youth organizations; Physical fitness facilities; Child day care services; Youth camps
PA: Young Men's Christian Association Of Silicon Valley
80 Saratoga Ave
Santa Clara CA
408 351-6400

(P-19006)
YOUNG MNS CHRSTN ASSN STHAST V
Also Called: Young Men's Christian Assoc
4031 N Moorpark Rd (91360-2660)
PHONE.................................805 523-7613
Kelly Dulek, *Dir*
EMP: 62
SALES (corp-wide): 8.13MM **Privately Held**
Web: www.sevymca.org
SIC: **8641** 7997 8351 Youth organizations; Membership sports and recreation clubs; Child day care services
PA: Young Men's Christian Association Of Southeast Ventura County
31105 E Thusand Oaks Blvd
Thousand Oaks CA
805 497-3081

(P-19007)
YOUNG WNS CHRSTN ASSN GRTER LO
Also Called: YWCA
2501 W Vernon Ave (90008-3927)
PHONE.................................323 295-4280
EMP: 116
SALES (corp-wide): 12.45MM **Privately Held**
Web: www.ywcagla.org
SIC: **8641** Youth organizations
PA: Young Women's Christian Association Of Greater Los Angeles, California
1020 S Olive St Fl 7
Los Angeles CA
213 365-2991

(P-19008)
YOUNG WNS CHRSTN ASSN GRTER LO
Also Called: Angeles Mesa YWCA Chldren Lrng
2519 W Vernon Ave (90008-3927)
PHONE.................................323 295-4288
Hertistine Taylor, *Dir*
EMP: 132
SALES (corp-wide): 12.45MM **Privately Held**
SIC: **8641** 8351 Youth organizations; Child day care services
PA: Young Women's Christian Association Of Greater Los Angeles, California
1020 S Olive St Fl 7
Los Angeles CA
213 365-2991

(P-19009)
YWCA GOLDEN GATE SILICON VLY
Also Called: YWCA
375 S 3rd St (95112-3649)
PHONE.................................408 295-4011
Keri Procunier Mclain, *Pr*
Tanis Crosby, *
Christine Jeffers, *Development**
Sue Barnes, *

Adriana Caldera, *
EMP: 83 EST: 1905
SALES (est): 15.12MM **Privately Held**
Web: www.yourywca.org
SIC: **8641** 8322 Community membership club; Individual and family services

8651 Political Organizations

(P-19010)
KENNEDY TEAM INC ✪
Also Called: Recruit Bobby
600 W Broadway Ste 1400 (92101-3377)
PHONE.................................619 921-5582
Matthew Sanders, *CEO*
EMP: 60 EST: 2023
SALES (est): 260.98K **Privately Held**
SIC: **8651** Political organizations

8661 Religious Organizations

(P-19011)
BIG VLLEY GRACE CMNTY CH INC M (PA)
Also Called: Big Valley Christian School
4040 Tully Rd Ste D (95356-8835)
PHONE.................................209 577-1604
Pastor Rick Countryman, *Prin*
Bob Yovino, *
EMP: 69 EST: 1966
SALES (est): 15.6MM
SALES (corp-wide): 15.6MM **Privately Held**
Web: www.bigvalleygrace.org
SIC: **8661** 8211 8351 Non-denominational church; Private elementary school; Preschool center

(P-19012)
CALIFRNIA STHERN BPTST CNVNTIO
Also Called: Southern Bptst Jnness Pk Encmp
29005 State Highway 108 (95335-9737)
PHONE.................................209 965-3735
EMP: 83
SQ FT: 23,904
SALES (corp-wide): 9.86MM **Privately Held**
Web: www.csbc.com
SIC: **8661** 7032 Religious organizations; Sporting and recreational camps
PA: California Southern Baptist Convention
678 E Shaw Ave
Fresno CA
559 229-9533

(P-19013)
CENTURY ASSEMBLY INC (PA)
Also Called: Century Christian School
550 W Century Blvd (95240-6602)
PHONE.................................209 334-3230
Pastor Richard Dale Edwards, *Prin*
Nadeen Zerbe, *
Phillip Orosco, *
EMP: 76 EST: 1930
SQ FT: 10,000
SALES (est): 2.37MM
SALES (corp-wide): 2.37MM **Privately Held**
Web: www.centuryassembly.com
SIC: **8661** 8351 Assembly of God Church; Preschool center

(P-19014)
CERRITOS CHURCH OF NAZARENE
Also Called: Sunshine Preschool
12229 Del Amo Blvd (90703-7633)

PHONE.................................562 809-4143
Pastor James Payton, *Prin*
EMP: 67 EST: 1936
SQ FT: 30,552
SALES (est): 3.8MM **Privately Held**
Web: www.cerritosnazarene.com
SIC: **8661** 8351 Miscellaneous denomination church; Preschool center

(P-19015)
COMMUNITY PRESBT CH DANVILLE (PA)
222 W El Pintado (94526-2513)
PHONE.................................925 837-5525
Pastor Scott Farmer, *Prin*
EMP: 120 EST: 1928
SQ FT: 140,000
SALES (est): 9.17MM
SALES (corp-wide): 9.17MM **Privately Held**
Web: www.cpcdanville.org
SIC: **8661** 8351 Presbyterian Church; Child day care services

(P-19016)
CONGRGTION BETH ISRAEL SAN DEG
Also Called: Sid Rubin Preschool
9001 Towne Centre Dr (92122-1222)
PHONE.................................858 535-1111
Benjamin Kamin, *Pr*
EMP: 78 EST: 1876
SQ FT: 20,000
SALES (est): 8.77MM **Privately Held**
Web: www.cbisd.org
SIC: **8661** 8351 Synagogue; Child day care services

(P-19017)
CRENSHAW CHRSTN CTR CH LOS ANG (PA)
Also Called: Ever Increasing Faith Ministry
7901 S Vermont Ave (90044-3531)
P.O. Box 90000 (90009-9201)
PHONE.................................323 758-3777
Frederick K C Price, *CEO*
Angela Evans, *
Craig Hays, *
Cheryl Price, *
Jeanette Fant, *
▲ EMP: 294 EST: 1973
SALES (est): 14.19MM
SALES (corp-wide): 14.19MM **Privately Held**
Web: www.crenshawchristiancenter.net
SIC: **8661** 7812 Community Church; Motion picture and video production

(P-19018)
CRYSTAL CATHEDRAL MINISTRIES (PA)
12901 Lewis St (92840-6207)
P.O. Box 100 (92842-0100)
PHONE.................................714 622-2900
Robert V Schuller, *CEO*
Fred Southard, *
▲ EMP: 250 EST: 1955
SQ FT: 135,000
SALES (est): 9.95MM
SALES (corp-wide): 9.95MM **Privately Held**
Web: www.hourofpower.org
SIC: **8661** 7812 Apostolic Church; Television film production

(P-19019)
GOOD SHEPHERD LUTHERAN CH CORP
Also Called: Good Shpherd Lthran Ch Prschoo

PRODUCTS & SERVICES SECTION
8699 - Membership Organizations, Nec (P-19037)

4800 Irvine Center Dr (92604-3300)
PHONE..................................949 552-1967
Pastor James Hale, *Prin*
EMP: 90 **EST:** 1977
SQ FT: 2,700
SALES (est): 8.36MM **Privately Held**
Web: www.goodshepherdirvine.com
SIC: 8661 8351 Lutheran Church; Preschool center

(P-19020)
HOSPITLLER ORDER OF ST JOHN GO
2468 S St Andrews Pl (90018-2042)
PHONE..................................323 731-0641
Arlene De Guzman Hospitaller, *Prin*
EMP: 362 **EST:** 2009
SALES (est): 1.08MM **Privately Held**
SIC: 8661 8399 Religious organizations; Health and welfare council

(P-19021)
HOUSE MODESTO (PA)
Also Called: Calvary Temple Academy
1601 Coffee Rd (95355-2801)
PHONE..................................209 529-7346
Glen Berteau, *Pr*
EMP: 73 **EST:** 1935
SQ FT: 15,000
SALES (est): 9.84MM
SALES (corp-wide): 9.84MM **Privately Held**
Web: www.thehousemodesto.com
SIC: 8661 8211 8351 Assembly of God Church; Private elementary school; Group day care center

(P-19022)
INTERNTNAL CH OF FRSQARE GOSPL (PA)
Also Called: Foursquare International
1910 W Sunset Blvd (90026-3275)
P.O. Box 26902 (90026-0176)
PHONE..................................714 701-1818
Glenn C Burris Junior, *Pr*
Jared Roth, *
James C Scott Junior, *VP*
Sterling Brackett, *
Tammy Dunahoo, *
▲ **EMP:** 100 **EST:** 1921
SQ FT: 110,000
SALES (est): 175.95MM
SALES (corp-wide): 175.95MM **Privately Held**
Web: www.foursquare.org
SIC: 8661 6512 7032 8211 Miscellaneous denomination church; Nonresidential building operators; Sporting and recreational camps; Elementary and secondary schools

(P-19023)
LOS ANGELES INTL CH CHRST
Also Called: Los Angeles Church of Christ
2716 Ocean Park Blvd Ste 2006 (90405-5207)
PHONE..................................213 351-2300
Brian Gold, *COO*
Chris Yen, *
Michael Wooten, *Co-Secretary*
EMP: 160 **EST:** 1989
SALES (est): 13MM **Privately Held**
Web: www.laicc.net
SIC: 8661 7371 Miscellaneous denomination church; Computer software development and applications

(P-19024)
NEIGHBORHOOD CHURCH CASTRO VLY
Also Called: Cathedral At The Crossroads
20600 John Dr (94546-5196)
PHONE..................................510 537-4690
Reverend Larry Vold, *Pastor*
David Von Rotz, *
EMP: 65 **EST:** 1935
SALES (est): 8.57MM **Privately Held**
Web: www.3crosses.org
SIC: 8661 5942 5943 7371 Miscellaneous denomination church; Books, religious; Stationery stores; Computer software development and applications

(P-19025)
ROMAN CATHLIC BISHP SACRAMENTO
Also Called: Catholic Social Service
125 Corporate Pl (94590-6285)
PHONE..................................707 556-9317
Kurt Chifmark, *Dir*
EMP: 190
SALES (corp-wide): 33.66MM **Privately Held**
Web: www.scd.org
SIC: 8661 8322 8111 Catholic Church; Senior citizens' center or association; Immigration and naturalization law
PA: Roman Catholic Bishop Of Sacramento
2110 Broadway
Sacramento CA
916 733-0100

(P-19026)
SAN DEGO CHRSTN FOUNDATION INC
Also Called: CANYON VILLAS
4282 Balboa Ave Ofc (92117-5510)
PHONE..................................858 273-1306
Edsel Hughes, *Pr*
Bert Wahlen, *
S J Harris, *
Kevin Withem, *
EMP: 68 **EST:** 1977
SQ FT: 600
SALES (est): 5.37MM **Privately Held**
Web: www.cvretirement.org
SIC: 8661 8059 Religious organizations; Rest home, with health care

(P-19027)
SINAI TEMPLE (PA)
Also Called: Mt Sinai Mem Pk & Mortuary
10400 Wilshire Blvd (90024-4600)
PHONE..................................310 474-1518
Howard Lesner, *Admn*
Howard Lesner, *Ex Dir*
Joel Weinstein, *
EMP: 300 **EST:** 1908
SQ FT: 100,000
SALES (est): 53.77MM
SALES (corp-wide): 53.77MM **Privately Held**
Web: www.registrar-transfers.com
SIC: 8661 7261 5947 Synagogue; Funeral service and crematories; Gift shop

(P-19028)
SISTERS OF ST JOSEPH ORANGE
240 Ocean Ave (90740-6029)
PHONE..................................562 430-4638
Catherine Gray, *Prin*
EMP: 2767
SALES (corp-wide): 32.76MM **Privately Held**
Web: www.csjorange.org
SIC: 8661 8062 Convent; General medical and surgical hospitals
HQ: Sisters Of St. Joseph Of Orange
480 S Batavia St
Orange CA
714 633-8121

(P-19029)
ST JHNS LTHRAN CH BAKERSFIELD
Also Called: St Johns Lthran Schl Chldren C
4500 Buena Vista Rd (93311-9702)
PHONE..................................661 665-7815
Pastor Dennis Hilken, *Prin*
Eric Van Scharrel, *
Evan Anwyl, *
Mike Kinsey, *
EMP: 105 **EST:** 1904
SQ FT: 40,000
SALES (est): 7MM **Privately Held**
Web: www.sjlchurch.org
SIC: 8661 8211 7371 Lutheran Church; Private elementary school; Computer software development and applications

(P-19030)
WILSHIRE BOULEVARD TEMPLE
4334 Whittier Blvd (90023-2019)
PHONE..................................323 261-6135
Carol J Bova, *Mgr*
EMP: 75
SALES (corp-wide): 36.21MM **Privately Held**
Web: www.wbtla.org
SIC: 8661 6553 7261 Temples; Cemetery subdividers and developers; Funeral service and crematories
PA: Wilshire Boulevard Temple
3663 Wilshire Blvd
Los Angeles CA
213 388-2401

(P-19031)
YOUNG MEN CHRSTN ASSOC W SAN G (PA)
Also Called: YMCA
401 Corto St (91801-4553)
PHONE..................................626 576-0226
Valarie Gomez, *CEO*
EMP: 70 **EST:** 1912
SQ FT: 17,000
SALES (est): 1.18MM
SALES (corp-wide): 1.18MM **Privately Held**
Web: www.wsgvymca.org
SIC: 8661 8322 Religious organizations; Youth center

8699 Membership Organizations, Nec

(P-19032)
AFFINITY DEVELOPMENT GROUP INC
Also Called: A D G
10590 W Ocean Air Dr Ste 300 (92130)
PHONE..................................858 643-9324
Jeff Skeen, *Pr*
Gary Drean, *
Greg Siebenthal, *
Eric Campbell, *CSO*
EMP: 120 **EST:** 1997
SALES (est): 22.94MM **Privately Held**
Web: www.affinitydev.com
SIC: 8699 Automobile owners' association

(P-19033)
AGUA CLNTE BAND CHILLA INDIANS (PA)
5401 Dinah Shore Dr (92264-5970)
PHONE..................................760 699-6800
Jeff L Grubbe, *Ch*
Larry N Olinger, *Vice Chairman*
Vincent Gonzales Iii, *Sec*
EMP: 696 **EST:** 1988
SALES (est): 83.82MM
SALES (corp-wide): 83.82MM **Privately Held**
Web: www.dwa.org
SIC: 8699 6552 7999 Reading rooms and other cultural organizations; Subdividers and developers, nec; Tour and guide services

(P-19034)
ANITA BORG INST FOR WOMEN TECH
1650 S Amphlett Blvd Ste 110 (94402-2517)
PHONE..................................650 236-4756
Brenda D Wilkerson, *Pr*
Doctor Anita Borg, *Pr*
Cindy Georal, *
Ahmed Reza Khan, *
EMP: 67 **EST:** 1998
SALES (est): 26.48MM **Privately Held**
Web: www.anitab.org
SIC: 8699 Charitable organization

(P-19035)
ASSOCTED STDNTS SAN DEGO STATE (PA)
Also Called: Mission Bay Aquatic Center
5500 Campanile Dr (92182-0001)
PHONE..................................619 594-0234
Christina Brown, *Ex Dir*
EMP: 900 **EST:** 1897
SALES (est): 36.31MM
SALES (corp-wide): 36.31MM **Privately Held**
Web: www.mbaquaticcenter.com
SIC: 8699 Automobile owners' association

(P-19036)
ASSOCTED STDNTS SAN DEGO STATE
Also Called: Associated Students & Faculty
San Diego State University (92182-0001)
PHONE..................................619 594-5200
Lana Heck, *Prin*
EMP: 190
SALES (corp-wide): 36.31MM **Privately Held**
Web: www.mbaquaticcenter.com
SIC: 8699 Automobile owners' association
PA: Associated Students, San Diego State University
5500 Campanile Dr
San Diego CA
619 594-0234

(P-19037)
ASYLUM ACCESS
344 Thomas L Berkley Way Ste 111 (94612-3544)
P.O. Box 14205 (94114-0205)
PHONE..................................510 891-8700
Emily Arnold-fernandez, *CEO*
Emily E Arnold-fernandez, *Pr*
EMP: 69 **EST:** 2005
SALES (est): 5.32MM **Privately Held**
Web: www.asylumaccess.org
SIC: 8699 Charitable organization

8699 - Membership Organizations, Nec (P-19038)

(P-19038)
AUTOMOBILE CLUB SOUTHERN CAL
3712 State St (93105-3135)
PHONE..................................805 682-5811
Nancy Alexander, *Brnch Mgr*
EMP: 115
SALES (corp-wide): 1.08B **Privately Held**
Web: ace.aaa.com
SIC: 8699 Automobile owners' association
PA: Automobile Club Of Southern California
   2601 S Figueroa St
   Los Angeles CA
   213 741-3686

(P-19039)
AUTOMOBILE CLUB SOUTHERN CAL
Also Called: AAA
4973 Clairemont Dr Ste C (92117-2793)
P.O. Box 17527 (92177-7527)
PHONE..................................858 483-4960
Thomas Mckernan, *Brnch Mgr*
EMP: 155
SALES (corp-wide): 1.08B **Privately Held**
Web: ace.aaa.com
SIC: 8699 Automobile owners' association
PA: Automobile Club Of Southern California
   2601 S Figueroa St
   Los Angeles CA
   213 741-3686

(P-19040)
AUTOMOBILE CLUB SOUTHERN CAL
Also Called: AAA
1445 Calle Joaquin (93405-7203)
PHONE..................................805 543-6454
Darlene Lair, *Brnch Mgr*
EMP: 78
SALES (corp-wide): 1.08B **Privately Held**
Web: ace.aaa.com
SIC: 8699 Automobile owners' association
PA: Automobile Club Of Southern California
   2601 S Figueroa St
   Los Angeles CA
   213 741-3686

(P-19041)
AUTOMOBILE CLUB SOUTHERN CAL
Also Called: AAA
100 E Wilbur Rd (91360-5564)
P.O. Box 1046 (91358-0046)
PHONE..................................805 497-0911
Chris Davis, *Brnch Mgr*
EMP: 78
SALES (corp-wide): 1.08B **Privately Held**
Web: ace.aaa.com
SIC: 8699 Automobile owners' association
PA: Automobile Club Of Southern California
   2601 S Figueroa St
   Los Angeles CA
   213 741-3686

(P-19042)
AUTOMOBILE CLUB SOUTHERN CAL
Also Called: AAA
23001 Hawthorne Blvd (90505-3702)
P.O. Box 4298 (90510-4298)
PHONE..................................310 325-3111
Bud Hudson, *Brnch Mgr*
EMP: 136
SQ FT: 34,720
SALES (corp-wide): 1.08B **Privately Held**
Web: ace.aaa.com
SIC: 8699 Automobile owners' association
PA: Automobile Club Of Southern California
   2601 S Figueroa St
   Los Angeles CA
   213 741-3686

(P-19043)
AUTOMOBILE CLUB SOUTHERN CAL
Also Called: AAA
420 N Euclid St (92801-5505)
PHONE..................................714 774-2392
Conny Kuhm, *Mgr*
EMP: 97
SALES (corp-wide): 1.08B **Privately Held**
Web: ace.aaa.com
SIC: 8699 Automobile owners' association
PA: Automobile Club Of Southern California
   2601 S Figueroa St
   Los Angeles CA
   213 741-3686

(P-19044)
AUTOMOBILE CLUB SOUTHERN CAL
Also Called: AAA
2440 Hotel Cir N Ste 100 (92108-2823)
PHONE..................................619 233-1000
Jill Clark, *Mgr*
EMP: 97
SALES (corp-wide): 1.08B **Privately Held**
Web: ace.aaa.com
SIC: 8699 Automobile owners' association
PA: Automobile Club Of Southern California
   2601 S Figueroa St
   Los Angeles CA
   213 741-3686

(P-19045)
AUTOMOBILE CLUB SOUTHERN CAL
Also Called: AAA
1301s S Grand Ave (91740-5040)
PHONE..................................626 963-8531
Connie Stelzer, *Mgr*
EMP: 78
SQ FT: 8,261
SALES (corp-wide): 1.08B **Privately Held**
Web: ace.aaa.com
SIC: 8699 Automobile owners' association
PA: Automobile Club Of Southern California
   2601 S Figueroa St
   Los Angeles CA
   213 741-3686

(P-19046)
AUTOMOBILE CLUB SOUTHERN CAL
Also Called: AAA
1500 Commercial Way (93309-0625)
PHONE..................................661 327-4661
Jeff Goldsmith, *Brnch Mgr*
EMP: 78
SALES (corp-wide): 1.08B **Privately Held**
Web: ace.aaa.com
SIC: 8699 Automobile owners' association
PA: Automobile Club Of Southern California
   2601 S Figueroa St
   Los Angeles CA
   213 741-3686

(P-19047)
AUTOMOBILE CLUB SOUTHERN CAL
Also Called: AAA
9440 Reseda Blvd (91324-6014)
PHONE..................................818 993-1616
EMP: 78
SQ FT: 15,624
SALES (corp-wide): 1.08B **Privately Held**
Web: ace.aaa.com

(P-19048)
AUTOMOBILE CLUB SOUTHERN CAL
Also Called: AAA
8223 Firestone Blvd (90241-4809)
PHONE..................................562 904-5970
Mirtha Rodriguez, *Brnch Mgr*
EMP: 116
SALES (corp-wide): 1.08B **Privately Held**
Web: ace.aaa.com
SIC: 8699 Automobile owners' association
PA: Automobile Club Of Southern California
   2601 S Figueroa St
   Los Angeles CA
   213 741-3686

(P-19049)
AUTOMOBILE CLUB SOUTHERN CAL
Also Called: A A A Automobile Club So Cal
3330 Vista Way (92056-3752)
P.O. Box 1128 (92051-1128)
PHONE..................................760 433-6261
Carolyn Tsuida, *Mgr*
EMP: 78
SQ FT: 10,240
SALES (corp-wide): 1.08B **Privately Held**
Web: ace.aaa.com
SIC: 8699 Automobile owners' association
PA: Automobile Club Of Southern California
   2601 S Figueroa St
   Los Angeles CA
   213 741-3686

(P-19050)
AUTOMOBILE CLUB SOUTHERN CAL
Also Called: AAA
700 S Aviation Blvd (90266-7106)
PHONE..................................310 376-0521
John Dm, *Mgr*
EMP: 116
SQ FT: 7,815
SALES (corp-wide): 1.08B **Privately Held**
Web: ace.aaa.com
SIC: 8699 Automobile owners' association
PA: Automobile Club Of Southern California
   2601 S Figueroa St
   Los Angeles CA
   213 741-3686

(P-19051)
AUTOMOBILE CLUB SOUTHERN CAL
Also Called: A A A Automobile Club So Cal
801 E Union St (91101-1885)
PHONE..................................626 795-0601
Teresa Martinez, *Mgr*
EMP: 78
SQ FT: 12,326
SALES (corp-wide): 1.08B **Privately Held**
Web: ace.aaa.com
SIC: 8699 Automobile owners' association
PA: Automobile Club Of Southern California
   2601 S Figueroa St
   Los Angeles CA
   213 741-3686

(P-19052)
AUTOMOBILE CLUB SOUTHERN CAL
3880 Birch St (92660-2669)
PHONE..................................949 476-8880
Cindy Kitchens, *Mgr*
EMP: 78
SQ FT: 14,794
SALES (corp-wide): 1.08B **Privately Held**
Web: ace.aaa.com
SIC: 8699 Automobile owners' association
PA: Automobile Club Of Southern California
   2601 S Figueroa St
   Los Angeles CA
   213 741-3686

(P-19053)
AUTOMOBILE CLUB SOUTHERN CAL
Also Called: AAA
22708 Victory Blvd (91367-1697)
PHONE..................................818 883-2660
Glenn Lumley, *Brnch Mgr*
EMP: 78
SQ FT: 15,624
SALES (corp-wide): 1.08B **Privately Held**
Web: ace.aaa.com
SIC: 8699 4724 6331 Automobile owners' association; Travel agencies; Fire, marine, and casualty insurance
PA: Automobile Club Of Southern California
   2601 S Figueroa St
   Los Angeles CA
   213 741-3686

(P-19054)
AUTOMOBILE CLUB SOUTHERN CAL
Also Called: A A A Automobile Club So Cal
1234 Centinela Ave (90302-1138)
PHONE..................................310 673-5170
Lola Nix, *Brnch Mgr*
EMP: 78
SQ FT: 11,228
SALES (corp-wide): 1.08B **Privately Held**
Web: ace.aaa.com
SIC: 8699 Automobile owners' association
PA: Automobile Club Of Southern California
   2601 S Figueroa St
   Los Angeles CA
   213 741-3686

(P-19055)
AUTOMOBILE CLUB SOUTHERN CAL
Also Called: AAA
16041 Whittier Blvd (90603-2526)
P.O. Box 4766 (90607-4766)
PHONE..................................562 698-3721
Velia Garcia, *Mgr*
EMP: 78
SALES (corp-wide): 1.08B **Privately Held**
Web: ace.aaa.com
SIC: 8699 4724 6331 Automobile owners' association; Travel agencies; Fire, marine, and casualty insurance
PA: Automobile Club Of Southern California
   2601 S Figueroa St
   Los Angeles CA
   213 741-3686

(P-19056)
AUTOMOBILE CLUB SOUTHERN CAL
3700 Central Ave (92506-2421)
P.O. Box 2217 (92516-2217)
PHONE..................................951 684-4250
Richard Meyer, *Brnch Mgr*
EMP: 97
SALES (corp-wide): 1.08B **Privately Held**
Web: ace.aaa.com
SIC: 8699 Automobile owners' association
PA: Automobile Club Of Southern California
   2601 S Figueroa St
   Los Angeles CA
   213 741-3686

PRODUCTS & SERVICES SECTION
8699 - Membership Organizations, Nec (P-19077)

(P-19057)
AUTOMOBILE CLUB SOUTHERN CAL
Also Called: AAA
5402 Philadelphia St Ste A (91710-2488)
P.O. Box 1846 (91708-1846)
PHONE..................................909 591-9451
Tim Irwin, Mgr
EMP: 116
SALES (corp-wide): 1.08B Privately Held
Web: ace.aaa.com
SIC: 8699 Automobile owners' association
PA: Automobile Club Of Southern California
2601 S Figueroa St
Los Angeles CA
213 741-3686

(P-19058)
AUTOMOBILE CLUB SOUTHERN CAL
Also Called: AAA
800 La Terraza Blvd (92025-3817)
PHONE..................................760 745-2124
Theresa Tentschert, Mgr
EMP: 116
SQ FT: 49,100
SALES (corp-wide): 1.08B Privately Held
Web: ace.aaa.com
SIC: 8699 Automobile owners' association
PA: Automobile Club Of Southern California
2601 S Figueroa St
Los Angeles CA
213 741-3686

(P-19059)
AUTOMOBILE CLUB SOUTHERN CAL
Also Called: AAA
638 Camino De Los Mares Ste E100 (92673)
PHONE..................................949 489-5572
Cindy Colter, Brnch Mgr
EMP: 78
SALES (corp-wide): 1.08B Privately Held
Web: ace.aaa.com
SIC: 8699 Automobile owners' association
PA: Automobile Club Of Southern California
2601 S Figueroa St
Los Angeles CA
213 741-3686

(P-19060)
AUTOMOBILE CLUB SOUTHERN CAL
Also Called: A A A Automobile Club So Cal
25181 Paseo De Alicia (92653-4614)
PHONE..................................949 951-1400
Cindy Raymond, Mgr
EMP: 78
SQ FT: 13,948
SALES (corp-wide): 1.08B Privately Held
Web: ace.aaa.com
SIC: 8699 Automobile owners' association
PA: Automobile Club Of Southern California
2601 S Figueroa St
Los Angeles CA
213 741-3686

(P-19061)
AUTOMOBILE CLUB SOUTHERN CAL
Also Called: AAA
12630 Sabre Springs Pkwy Ste 301 (92128-4129)
PHONE..................................858 486-0786
Jill Clark Gregory, Mgr
EMP: 78
SQ FT: 7,000
SALES (corp-wide): 1.08B Privately Held
Web: ace.aaa.com
SIC: 8699 Automobile owners' association
PA: Automobile Club Of Southern California
2601 S Figueroa St
Los Angeles CA
213 741-3686

(P-19062)
AUTOMOBILE CLUB SOUTHERN CAL
Also Called: A A A Automobile Club So Cal
450 W Stetson Ave (92543-7328)
PHONE..................................951 652-6202
EMP: 78
SALES (corp-wide): 1.08B Privately Held
Web: ace.aaa.com
SIC: 8699 Automobile owners' association
PA: Automobile Club Of Southern California
2601 S Figueroa St
Los Angeles CA
213 741-3686

(P-19063)
AUTOMOBILE CLUB SOUTHERN CAL
2730 Santa Monica Blvd (90404-2408)
PHONE..................................310 453-1909
Vasile Dejeu, Mgr
EMP: 136
SQ FT: 10,000
SALES (corp-wide): 1.08B Privately Held
Web: ace.aaa.com
SIC: 8699 Automobile owners' association
PA: Automobile Club Of Southern California
2601 S Figueroa St
Los Angeles CA
213 741-3686

(P-19064)
AUTOMOBILE CLUB SOUTHERN CAL
1170 El Camino Ave (92879-1761)
PHONE..................................951 808-9624
EMP: 78
SALES (corp-wide): 1.08B Privately Held
Web: ace.aaa.com
SIC: 8699 Automobile owners' association
PA: Automobile Club Of Southern California
2601 S Figueroa St
Los Angeles CA
213 741-3686

(P-19065)
AUTOMOBILE CLUB SOUTHERN CAL
525 W Central Ave (93436-2836)
PHONE..................................805 735-2731
EMP: 78
SALES (corp-wide): 1.08B Privately Held
Web: ace.aaa.com
SIC: 8699 Automobile owners' association
PA: Automobile Club Of Southern California
2601 S Figueroa St
Los Angeles CA
213 741-3686

(P-19066)
AUTOMOBILE CLUB SOUTHERN CAL
Also Called: A A A Automobile Club So Cal
4800 Airport Plaza Dr Ste 100 (90815-1274)
PHONE..................................562 425-8350
Susan Dabinett, Mgr
EMP: 78
SQ FT: 7,200
SALES (corp-wide): 1.08B Privately Held
Web: ace.aaa.com
SIC: 8699 Automobile owners' association
PA: Automobile Club Of Southern California
2601 S Figueroa St
Los Angeles CA
213 741-3686

(P-19067)
AUTOMOBILE CLUB SOUTHERN CAL
Also Called: AAA
18642 Gridley Rd (90701-5441)
PHONE..................................562 924-6636
Diane Ruiz, Brnch Mgr
EMP: 78
SQ FT: 12,960
SALES (corp-wide): 1.08B Privately Held
Web: ace.aaa.com
SIC: 8699 Automobile owners' association
PA: Automobile Club Of Southern California
2601 S Figueroa St
Los Angeles CA
213 741-3686

(P-19068)
AUTOMOBILE CLUB SOUTHERN CAL
Also Called: AAA
8761 Santa Monica Blvd (90069-4538)
PHONE..................................323 525-0018
Randy Miller, Mgr
EMP: 97
SALES (corp-wide): 1.08B Privately Held
Web: ace.aaa.com
SIC: 8699 Automobile owners' association
PA: Automobile Club Of Southern California
2601 S Figueroa St
Los Angeles CA
213 741-3686

(P-19069)
BACR
171 Carlos Dr (94903-2005)
PHONE..................................415 444-5580
Tiffany Chin, Prin
EMP: 61 EST: 2010
SALES (est): 1.16MM Privately Held
Web: www.bacr.org
SIC: 8699 Charitable organization

(P-19070)
BEST FRIENDS ANIMAL SOCIETY
1845 Pontius Ave (90025-4305)
PHONE..................................818 643-3989
Marc Peralta, Mgr
EMP: 246
Web: www.bestfriends.org
SIC: 8699 Animal humane society
PA: Best Friends Animal Society
5001 Angel Canyon Rd
Kanab UT

(P-19071)
BRIARPATCH COOP NEV CNTY INC
Also Called: Briarpatch Coop-Community Mkt
290 Sierra College Drive (95945-5762)
PHONE..................................530 272-5333
Christopher Maher, CEO
EMP: 180 EST: 1976
SALES (est): 11.81MM Privately Held
Web: www.briarpatch.coop
SIC: 8699 Food co-operative

(P-19072)
CALIF STAT UNIV FRES FOUN
Also Called: California State University
5370 N Chestnut Ave (93725)
PHONE..................................559 278-0850
Linda Alatorre, Brnch Mgr
EMP: 168
SALES (corp-wide): 96.36MM Privately Held
Web: auxiliary.fresnostate.edu
SIC: 8699 Amateur sports promotion
PA: California State University, Fresno Foundation
4910 N Chestnut Ave
Fresno CA
559 278-0850

(P-19073)
CALIFORNIA STATE AUTOMOBILE ASSOCIATION INTER-INSURANCE BUREAU (HQ)
Also Called: American Atmble Assn Nrthrn CA
1276 S California Blvd (94596-5123)
P.O. Box 22221 (94623-2221)
PHONE..................................925 287-7600
EMP: 1600 EST: 1902
SALES (est): 79.09MM
SALES (corp-wide): 420.02MM Privately Held
Web: csaa-insurance.aaa.com
SIC: 8699 Automobile owners' association
PA: American Automobile Association of Northern California, Nevada & Utah
1277 Treat Blvd Ste 1000
Walnut Creek CA
800 922-8228

(P-19074)
CALIFRNIA YUTH SOCCER ASSN INC
Also Called: CAL NORTH
2081 Arena Blvd (95834-2309)
PHONE..................................925 426-5437
Kenyatta Scott, Ch
EMP: 87 EST: 1972
SALES (est): 1.75MM Privately Held
Web: www.calnorth.org
SIC: 8699 Personal interest organization

(P-19075)
CARE 2
203 Redwood Shores Pkwy Ste 230 (94065)
PHONE..................................650 622-0860
Randy Paynter, Prin
EMP: 97 EST: 2011
SALES (est): 2.2MM Privately Held
Web: www.care2.com
SIC: 8699 Charitable organization

(P-19076)
CARLSBAD FIREFIGHTERS ASSN
2560 Orion Way (92010-7240)
P.O. Box 945 (92018-0945)
PHONE..................................760 729-3730
Josh Clark, Pr
EMP: 80 EST: 1970
SALES (est): 205.96K Privately Held
Web: www.carlsbadfdf.org
SIC: 8699 Charitable organization

(P-19077)
CHG FOUNDATION
740 Bay Blvd (91910-5254)
PHONE..................................619 422-0422
Sheila Martz, Dir
EMP: 372 EST: 1999
SALES (est): 1.2B Privately Held
SIC: 8699 Charitable organization

8699 - Membership Organizations, Nec (P-19078)

(P-19078)
COUNTY OF MONTEREY
Also Called: Monterey County Sheriffs Dept
1414 Natividad Rd (93906-3102)
PHONE..................831 755-3856
EMP: 103
SALES (corp-wide): 1.04B **Privately Held**
Web: www.montereysheriff.org
SIC: **8699** Personal interest organization
PA: County Of Monterey
    168 W Alisal St Fl 3
    Salinas CA
    831 755-5040

(P-19079)
CROCKER ART MUSEUM ASSOCIATION
Also Called: CROCKER ART MUSEUM
216 O St (95814-5324)
PHONE..................916 808-7000
Lial Jones, CEO
EMP: 66 EST: 1875
SQ FT: 150,000
SALES (est): 9.22MM **Privately Held**
Web: www.crockerart.org
SIC: **8699** 5942 8412 Art council; Book stores; Museum

(P-19080)
DAVID LCILE PACKARD FOUNDATION
343 2nd St (94022-3639)
PHONE..................650 948-7658
Julie Packard, Dir
EMP: 162 EST: 2015
SALES (est): 12.74MM **Privately Held**
Web: www.packard.org
SIC: **8699** Charitable organization

(P-19081)
DREAM CORPS
436 14th St Ste 920 (94612-2711)
PHONE..................510 663-6500
Nisha Anand, CEO
EMP: 61 EST: 2015
SALES (est): 4.69MM **Privately Held**
Web: www.dream.org
SIC: **8699** Charitable organization

(P-19082)
EARTH ISLAND INSTITUTE INC
2150 Allston Way Ste 460 (94704-1375)
PHONE..................510 859-9100
Michael Mitrani, CEO
John A Knox, *
David Phillips, *
EMP: 76 EST: 1982
SQ FT: 4,400
SALES (est): 23.68MM **Privately Held**
Web: www.earthisland.org
SIC: **8699** 8748 8641 Charitable organization; Business consulting, nec; Environmental protection organization

(P-19083)
FRIENDS LONG BCH ANMAL SHELTER
3815 Atlantic Ave Ste 4 (90807-3505)
P.O. Box 92736 (90809-2736)
PHONE..................562 988-7647
Shirley Vaughan, Prin
EMP: 75 EST: 2008
SALES (est): 190.35K **Privately Held**
Web: www.folba.org
SIC: **8699** Animal humane society

(P-19084)
FUSE CORPS
235 Montgomery St Ste 1110 (94104-3304)
P.O. Box 26070 (94126-6070)
PHONE..................855 687-9905
EMP: 67 EST: 2014
SALES (est): 11.75MM **Privately Held**
Web: www.fuse.org
SIC: **8699** Charitable organization

(P-19085)
GOODWILL INDS SAN DIEGO CNTY
Also Called: Goodwill Industries
3841 Plaza Dr Ste 902 (92056-4649)
PHONE..................760 806-7670
Tim Hurley, Mgr
EMP: 85
SALES (corp-wide): 70.31MM **Privately Held**
Web: www.sdgoodwill.org
SIC: **8699** 8331 5932 Charitable organization; Vocational rehabilitation agency; Used merchandise stores
PA: Goodwill Industries Of San Diego County
    3663 Rosecrans St
    San Diego CA
    619 225-2200

(P-19086)
HAAS JR EVELYN & WALTER FUND
114 Sansome St Fl 6 (94104-3814)
P.O. Box 1459 (94530-4459)
PHONE..................415 856-1400
Ira S Hershfeild, Pr
EMP: 63 EST: 1953
SQ FT: 22,000
SALES (est): 62.23MM **Privately Held**
Web: www.haasjr.org
SIC: **8699** Charitable organization

(P-19087)
HENRY J KAISER FMLY FOUNDATION (PA)
Also Called: Kaiser Family Foundation
185 Berry St Ste 2000 (94107-1704)
PHONE..................650 854-9400
Drew Altman, Pr
Timothy Ortez, *
Koonal Gandhi, *
EMP: 124 EST: 1948
SQ FT: 185,000
SALES (est): 60MM
SALES (corp-wide): 60MM **Privately Held**
Web: www.kff.org
SIC: **8699** Charitable organization

(P-19088)
HEWLETT WLLIAM FLORA FNDATION
Also Called: Hewlett Foundation
2121 Sand Hill Rd (94025-6909)
PHONE..................650 234-4500
Paul Brest, Pr
EMP: 60 EST: 1966
SALES (est): 20.11MM **Privately Held**
Web: www.hewlett.org
SIC: **8699** Charitable organization

(P-19089)
HOPLAND BAND POMO INDIANS INC (PA)
3000 Shanel Rd (95449-9809)
PHONE..................707 472-2100
Romen Carrillo, Pr
Rachel Whetstone, *
EMP: 79 EST: 1976
SQ FT: 3,800
SALES (est): 17.41MM
SALES (corp-wide): 17.41MM **Privately Held**
Web: www.hoplandtribe.com
SIC: **8699** Personal interest organization

(P-19090)
HUMANE SOCIETY SILICON VALLEY
Also Called: Pet Pourri
901 Ames Ave (95035-6326)
PHONE..................408 262-2133
Carol Novello, CEO
Christine B Arnold, *
Peter N Detkin, *
EMP: 85 EST: 1929
SQ FT: 3,000
SALES (est): 19.19MM **Privately Held**
Web: www.hssv.org
SIC: **8699** Animal humane society

(P-19091)
INLAND EMPIRE CHPTR-SSCTION CR
2210 E Route 66 (91740-4661)
PHONE..................512 478-9000
EMP: 82 EST: 2009
SALES (est): 4.13K **Privately Held**
SIC: **8699** Membership organizations, nec

(P-19092)
LOS ANGELES MEM COLISEUM COMM
Also Called: La Sports Arena
3911 S Figueroa St (90037-1207)
PHONE..................213 747-7111
Kevin Daly, Admn
Don Knabe, *
Gregory Hellmold, *
John Sandbrook, *
EMP: 500 EST: 1923
SQ FT: 2,000
SALES (est): 21.59MM **Privately Held**
Web: www.lacoliseum.com
SIC: **8699** Athletic organizations

(P-19093)
MARIN HUMANE SOCIETY
171 Bel Marin Keys Blvd (94949-6105)
PHONE..................415 883-4621
Suzanne Golt, Ex Dir
Marilyn Castellblanch, *
EMP: 91 EST: 1907
SQ FT: 42,500
SALES (est): 9.85MM **Privately Held**
Web: www.marinhumane.org
SIC: **8699** Animal humane society

(P-19094)
MEMORIAL MEDICAL CENTER FOUNDATION
Also Called: MILLER CHILDREN'S HOSPITAL
2801 Atlantic Ave (90806-1701)
P.O. Box 1428 (90801-1428)
PHONE..................562 933-2273
EMP: 906 EST: 1964
SALES (est): 14.33MM **Privately Held**
Web: www.memorialcare.org
SIC: **8699** Charitable organization
HQ: Long Beach Medical Center
    2801 Atlantic Ave Fl 2
    Long Beach CA
    562 933-2000

(P-19095)
OPEN PHILANTHROPY PROJECT
182 Howard St Ste 225 (94105-1611)
PHONE..................415 429-0423
EMP: 72 EST: 2017
SALES (est): 1.01MM **Privately Held**
Web: www.openphilanthropy.org
SIC: **8699** Charitable organization

(P-19096)
PASADENA HUMANE SOCIETY
361 S Raymond Ave (91105-2687)
PHONE..................626 792-7151
Steven R Mc Nall, Pr
EMP: 70 EST: 1903
SQ FT: 26,000
SALES (est): 17.26MM **Privately Held**
Web: www.pasadenahumane.org
SIC: **8699** 0752 Animal humane society; Animal specialty services

(P-19097)
PENINSULA HUMANE SOC & SPCA
1450 Rollins Rd (94010-2307)
PHONE..................650 340-7022
EMP: 74
SALES (corp-wide): 19.23MM **Privately Held**
Web: www.phs-spca.org
SIC: **8699** Animal humane society
PA: Peninsula Humane Society And Spca
    12 Airport Blvd
    San Mateo CA
    650 340-7022

(P-19098)
PLAY VERSUS INC
Also Called: Playvs
2236 S Barrington Ave Ste A (90064-1231)
PHONE..................949 636-4193
Jon Chapman, CEO
EMP: 95 EST: 2018
SALES (est): 7.56MM **Privately Held**
Web: www.playvs.com
SIC: **8699** Amateur sports promotion

(P-19099)
RESCUE MISSION ALLIANCE (PA)
Also Called: Mission Bargain Center
315 N A St (93030-4901)
P.O. Box 5545 (93031-5545)
PHONE..................805 487-1234
Gary Gray, Pr
Jim Ownes, *
Brian Elster, Vice Chairman*
Andy Stay, *
David Chittenden, *
EMP: 77 EST: 1972
SQ FT: 30,000
SALES (est): 28.24MM **Privately Held**
Web: www.erescuemission.org
SIC: **8699** Charitable organization

(P-19100)
SACRAMNTO SOC FOR THE PRVNTION
Also Called: SSPCA
6201 Florin Perkins Rd (95828-1012)
PHONE..................916 383-7387
Maryann Subbotin, Interim Director
EMP: 76 EST: 1894
SQ FT: 40,000
SALES (est): 9.98MM **Privately Held**
Web: www.sspca.org
SIC: **8699** Animal humane society

PRODUCTS & SERVICES SECTION

8711 - Engineering Services (P-19125)

(P-19101)
SAN DIEGO HUMANE SOC & SPCA
5500 Gaines St (92110-2572)
PHONE..................619 299-7012
Gary L Weitzman, *Pr*
Renee Harris, *
Kelly Riseley, *
Kim Shannon, *
EMP: 65 **EST:** 1880
SQ FT: 44,500
SALES (est): 59.37MM **Privately Held**
Web: www.sdhumane.org
SIC: 8699 Animal humane society

(P-19102)
SAN FRANCISCO SPCA
2500 26th Ave (94116-2905)
PHONE..................415 554-3000
Daniel Crain, *Pr*
EMP: 72 **EST:** 2007
SALES (est): 5.95MM **Privately Held**
Web: www.sfspca.org
SIC: 8699 Animal humane society

(P-19103)
SAN FRNCSCO SOC FOR THE PRVNTI (PA)
Also Called: SAN FRANCISCO SPCA
201 Alabama St (94103-4217)
PHONE..................415 554-3000
Katherine Brown, *Ch Bd*
Eric Roberts, *
Jane Mchugh-smith, *Pr*
David Tateosian, *
EMP: 199 **EST:** 1868
SQ FT: 57,000
SALES (est): 51.61MM
SALES (corp-wide): 51.61MM **Privately Held**
Web: www.sfspca.org
SIC: 8699 Animal humane society

(P-19104)
SERVE PEOPLE INC
Also Called: SERVE THE PEOPLE COMMUNITY HEA
1206 E 17th St Ste 101 (92701-2641)
PHONE..................714 352-2911
Dimitri Sirakoff, *Prin*
EMP: 61 **EST:** 2009
SALES (est): 10.53MM **Privately Held**
Web: www.serve-the-people.com
SIC: 8699 Charitable organization

(P-19105)
SOCIETY OF ST VNCENT DE PAUL A (PA)
2272 San Pablo Ave (94612-1321)
PHONE..................510 638-7600
Blase Bova, *Ex Dir*
Ron Dean, *
EMP: 80 **EST:** 1938
SALES (est): 6.34MM **Privately Held**
Web: www.svdp-alameda.org
SIC: 8699 Charitable organization

(P-19106)
SOCIETY OF ST VNCENT DE PAUL C (PA)
Also Called: St Vincent De Paul Soc Los Ang
210 N Avenue 21 (90031-1713)
PHONE..................323 226-9645
David Garcia, *Ex Dir*
Susana Santana, *Deputy Executive Director*
EMP: 77 **EST:** 1908
SQ FT: 108,000
SALES (est): 16.4MM
SALES (corp-wide): 16.4MM **Privately Held**
Web: www.svdpla.org
SIC: 8699 Charitable organization

(P-19107)
STANFORD HLTH CARE TRI-VALLEY
Also Called: Stanford Hlth Care - Vlleycare
2586 Regent Rd (94550-6539)
PHONE..................925 447-1919
Kathryn M Eggers, *Brnch Mgr*
EMP: 137
SALES (corp-wide): 15.13B **Privately Held**
Web: www.stanfordhealthcare.org
SIC: 8699 Charitable organization
HQ: Stanford Health Care Tri-Valley
5555 W Las Positas Blvd
Pleasanton CA
925 847-3000

(P-19108)
STARTX
2627 Hanover St (94304-1118)
PHONE..................408 230-3300
Cameron Teitelman, *Dir*
EMP: 60 **EST:** 2012
SALES (est): 2.6MM **Privately Held**
Web: www.startx.com
SIC: 8699 Charitable organization

(P-19109)
SYNOPSYS FOUNDATION
675 Almanor Ave (94085-2925)
PHONE..................650 584-5000
EMP: 94 **EST:** 2011
SALES (est): 16.73MM **Privately Held**
Web: www.synopsys.com
SIC: 8699 Charitable organization

(P-19110)
TEAM RUBICON USA
300 Continental Blvd Ste 100 (90245-5043)
PHONE..................310 906-1636
EMP: 71 **EST:** 2016
SALES (est): 5.5MM **Privately Held**
Web: www.teamrubiconusa.org
SIC: 8699 Charitable organization

(P-19111)
THE DAVID LCILE PCKARD FNDTION
300 2nd St (94022-3621)
PHONE..................650 917-7167
Carol S Larson, *Pr*
Julie Packard, *Ex Dir*
Katy Lnp, *Prin*
▲ **EMP:** 85 **EST:** 1964
SALES (est): 13.38MM **Privately Held**
Web: www.packard.org
SIC: 8699 Personal interest organization

(P-19112)
THINK TOGETHER
17270 Bear Valley Rd Ste 103 (92395-5881)
PHONE..................760 269-1230
EMP: 344
SALES (corp-wide): 75.71MM **Privately Held**
Web: www.thinktogether.org
SIC: 8699 8351 Charitable organization; Child day care services
PA: Think Together
2101 E 4th St Ste 200b
Santa Ana CA
714 543-3807

(P-19113)
U C SAN DIEGO FOUNDATION
Also Called: UC SAN DIEGO
9500 Gilman Dr (92093-5004)
PHONE..................858 534-1032
EMP: 218 **EST:** 1972
SALES (est): 216.43MM **Privately Held**
Web: www.ucsd.edu
SIC: 8699 Charitable organization

(P-19114)
UC HASTINGS FOUNDATION
200 Mcallister St (94102-4707)
PHONE..................415 565-4704
EMP: 193 **EST:** 2010
SALES (est): 9.23MM **Privately Held**
Web: www.uclawsf.edu
SIC: 8699 Charitable organization

(P-19115)
UNITED STATES ENRGY FOUNDATION
55 2nd St (94105-3492)
PHONE..................415 561-6700
Jason Mark, *Dir*
EMP: 80 **EST:** 2021
SALES (est): 181.89MM **Privately Held**
SIC: 8699 Charitable organization

(P-19116)
UNITOGETHER INC
1253 Gray Hawk Ln (94585-3789)
PHONE..................707 208-7602
Riair Levelle Hamilton, *Pr*
EMP: 60 **EST:** 2020
SALES (est): 244.6K **Privately Held**
SIC: 8699 Membership organizations, nec

(P-19117)
USA TRAVEL SERVICES LLC
714 Washington Blvd (90292-5543)
PHONE..................207 899-8803
EMP: 800 **EST:** 2016
SALES (est): 6.27MM **Privately Held**
SIC: 8699 Travel club

(P-19118)
VICTORIA PLACE COMMUNITY ASSN
195 N Euclid Ave (91786-6036)
PHONE..................909 981-4131
John Melcher, *Pr*
EMP: 75 **EST:** 2008
SALES (est): 2.53MM **Privately Held**
SIC: 8699 Membership organizations, nec

(P-19119)
VITAMIN ANGEL ALLIANCE INC
Also Called: VITAMIN ANGEL
6500 Hollister Ave Ste 130 (93117-3019)
P.O. Box 4490 (93140-4490)
PHONE..................805 564-8400
Peter Van Stolk, *CEO*
Howard Schiffer, *
Bonnie Forssel, *
Caterinia Cellis, *
EMP: 66 **EST:** 2010
SALES (est): 131.1MM **Privately Held**
Web: www.vitaminangels.org
SIC: 8699 5122 Charitable organization; Vitamins and minerals

(P-19120)
WIKIMEDIA FOUNDATION INC
1 Montgomery St Ste 1600 (94104-5516)
PHONE..................415 839-6885
Katherine Maher, *Ex Dir*
Jaime Villagomez, *
Eileen Hershenov, *
EMP: 284 **EST:** 2003
SALES (est): 167.91MM **Privately Held**
Web: www.wikimediafoundation.org
SIC: 8699 6732 Charitable organization; Trusts: educational, religious, etc.

(P-19121)
WORLD VISION INTERNATIONAL (PA)
800 W Chestnut Ave (91016-3198)
P.O. Box 9716 (98063-9716)
PHONE..................626 303-8811
Andrew Morley, *CEO*
Kevin Jenkins, *
Valdir Steuernagel, *
Denis St Amour, *
▼ **EMP:** 196 **EST:** 1977
SQ FT: 94,000
SALES (est): 62.03MM
SALES (corp-wide): 62.03MM **Privately Held**
Web: www.wvi.org
SIC: 8699 Charitable organization

(P-19122)
YOUNG MNS CHRSTN ASSN SLCON VL
Also Called: Southwest YMCA
13500 Quito Rd (95070-4749)
PHONE..................408 370-1877
Maria Drake, *Ex Dir*
EMP: 245
SALES (corp-wide): 28.49MM **Privately Held**
Web: www.ymcasv.org
SIC: 8699 8641 Personal interest organization; Youth organizations
PA: Young Men's Christian Association Of Silicon Valley
80 Saratoga Ave
Santa Clara CA
408 351-6400

8711 Engineering Services

(P-19123)
A-C ELECTRIC COMPANY
Also Called: Automated Ctrl Technical Svcs
315 30th St (93301-2511)
P.O. Box 81376 (93380-1376)
PHONE..................661 633-5368
Dave Morton, *Mgr*
EMP: 76
SALES (corp-wide): 96.92MM **Privately Held**
Web: www.a-celectric.com
SIC: 8711 Engineering services
PA: A-C Electric Company
2921 Hanger Way
Bakersfield CA
661 410-0000

(P-19124)
ABM FACILITY SERVICES LLC
Also Called: A B M
152 Technology Dr (92618-2401)
PHONE..................949 330-1555
EMP: 1391
SIC: 8711 Engineering services

(P-19125)
ABS CONSULTING INC
Also Called: ABS Group
420 Exchange Ste 200 (92602-1319)
PHONE..................714 734-4242
Doug Frazier, *CEO*
Peter Yanev, *Pr*
Jim Johnson, *COO*

8711 - Engineering Services (P-19126)

George Reitter, *CFO*
EMP: 100 **EST:** 1970
SALES (est): 9.25MM
SALES (corp-wide): 455.19MM **Privately Held**
Web: www.abs-group.com
SIC: 8711 8742 Consulting engineer; Management consulting services
HQ: Abs Group Of Companies, Inc.
1701 City Plaza Dr
Spring TX

(P-19126)
ACER CLOUD TECHNOLOGY INC
333 W San Carlos St Ste 1500 (95110-2738)
PHONE.................408 830-9809
J T Wang, *CEO*
EMP: 5043 **EST:** 2011
SALES (est): 2.69MM **Privately Held**
Web: www.acer.com
SIC: 8711 Engineering services
HQ: Acer American Holdings Corp.
1730 N 1st St Ste 400
San Jose CA

(P-19127)
ACRONICS SYSTEMS INC
2102 Commerce Dr (95131-1804)
PHONE.................408 432-0888
Kim Tran, *CEO*
EMP: 110 **EST:** 1994
SQ FT: 16,000
SALES (est): 16.44MM **Privately Held**
Web: www.acronics.com
SIC: 8711 7373 Electrical or electronic engineering; Systems engineering, computer related

(P-19128)
ADVANTEDGE TECHNOLOGY INC
271 Market St Ste 15 (93041-3219)
PHONE.................805 488-0405
Tim Edward Huggins, *CEO*
Vickie Dewolfe, *
Tim Huggins, *
Bruce Underwood, *
EMP: 60 **EST:** 2004
SQ FT: 2,000
SALES (est): 14.36MM **Privately Held**
Web: www.advantedgetechnology.com
SIC: 8711 Engineering services

(P-19129)
AECOM GLOBAL II LLC (HQ)
300 S Grand Ave Ste 900 (90071-3135)
PHONE.................213 593-8100
Michael Burke, *Managing Member*
◆ **EMP:** 65 **EST:** 1976
SALES (est): 3.11B
SALES (corp-wide): 13.15B **Publicly Held**
Web: www.aecom.com
SIC: 8711 8712 8741 Engineering services; Architectural engineering; Construction management
PA: Aecom
13355 Noel Rd Ste 400
Dallas TX
972 788-1000

(P-19130)
AECOM-TSE JOINT VENTURE
300 Lakeside Dr Ste 400 (94612-3573)
PHONE.................510 285-6639
Simon Kim, *VP*
Etty Mercurio, *
Paul Van Der Wel, *
EMP: 99 **EST:** 2017
SQ FT: 150,000
SALES (est): 1.78MM **Privately Held**
SIC: 8711 Engineering services

(P-19131)
AEROSPACE ENGINEERING CORP LLC
2141 S Standard Ave (92707-3034)
PHONE.................714 641-5884
EMP: 70 **EST:** 2018
SALES (est): 9.65MM **Privately Held**
Web: www.karman-sd.com
SIC: 8711 Engineering services

(P-19132)
AHNTECH INC (PA)
745 Distel Dr Ste 104 (94022-1523)
PHONE.................650 861-3987
Eugene Ahn, *CEO*
Sam Ahn, *
Soo Myung Ahn, *Prin*
EMP: 70 **EST:** 1984
SALES (est): 38.94MM
SALES (corp-wide): 38.94MM **Privately Held**
Web: www.ahntech.com
SIC: 8711 3674 3679 3699 Engineering services; Semiconductors and related devices; Electronic circuits; Electronic training devices

(P-19133)
AIR LIQUIDE ELECTRONICS US LP
Also Called: Air Lquide Globl E C Solutions
1831 Carnegie Ave (92705-5528)
PHONE.................713 624-8000
EMP: 4366
SALES (corp-wide): 109.44MM **Privately Held**
Web: engineering.airliquide.com
SIC: 8711 Engineering services
HQ: Air Liquide Electronics U.S. Lp
9101 Lyndon B Johnson Fwy # 800
Dallas TX
972 301-5200

(P-19134)
ALBERT A WEBB ASSOCIATES (PA)
Also Called: Webb
3788 Mccray St (92506-2927)
PHONE.................951 686-1070
A Hubert Webb, *Ch*
Matt Webb, *
Scott Webb, *
Roger D Prend Pe, *
Todd R Smith, *
EMP: 127 **EST:** 1949
SQ FT: 20,000
SALES (est): 32.56MM
SALES (corp-wide): 32.56MM **Privately Held**
Web: www.webbassociates.com
SIC: 8711 Civil engineering

(P-19135)
ALFA TECH CNSLTING ENGNERS INC (PA)
Also Called: Alfa Tech Consulting Entps
1321 Ridder Park Dr No 50 (95131-2306)
PHONE.................408 487-1200
Jeff Fini, *Ch Bd*
Reza Zare, *
EMP: 67 **EST:** 1987
SQ FT: 22,000
SALES (est): 48.02MM **Privately Held**
Web: www.atce.com

SIC: 8711 Consulting engineer

(P-19136)
ALLEN ENGINEERING CONTRACTOR INC
1655 Riverview Dr (92408-3016)
PHONE.................909 478-5500
EMP: 165
Web: www.allenec.com
SIC: 8711 Construction and civil engineering

(P-19137)
AME UNMANNED AIR SYSTEMS INC
Also Called: Lockheed Martin Unmndd
125 Venture Dr Ste 110 (93401-9103)
PHONE.................805 541-4448
EMP: 80
Web: www.ameuas.com
SIC: 8711 Aviation and/or aeronautical engineering

(P-19138)
AMEC GEOMATRIX INC
2101 Webster St Ste 1200 (94612-3066)
PHONE.................510 663-4100
EMP: 450
Web: www.amecgeomatrixinc.com
SIC: 8711 8999 8744 Engineering services; Earth science services; Facilities support services

(P-19139)
AMERESCO SOLAR LLC
42175 Zevo Dr (92590-2503)
PHONE.................888 967-6527
EMP: 479
Web: www.ameresco.com
SIC: 8711 Energy conservation engineering
HQ: Ameresco Solar Llc
111 Speen St Ste 410
Framingham MA
508 661-2200

(P-19140)
AMERICAN TECHNICAL SVCS INC
20384 Via Mantua (91326-4441)
PHONE.................951 372-9664
Alen Petrossian, *Pr*
EMP: 70 **EST:** 2004
SQ FT: 2,040
SALES (est): 6.73MM **Privately Held**
Web: www.atspage.com
SIC: 8711 Consulting engineer

(P-19141)
APPLIED INNOVATION GROUP INC
1919 Monterey Hwy Ste 70 (95112-6147)
PHONE.................408 452-5716
EMP: 103
Web: www.aig-tech.com
SIC: 8711 Engineering services
PA: Applied Innovation Group Inc.
2365 Paragon Dr Ste C
San Jose CA

(P-19142)
APTIM CORP
4005 Port Chicago Hwy (94520-1180)
PHONE.................925 288-9898
EMP: 181
SALES (corp-wide): 2.2B **Privately Held**
SIC: 8711 8734 8748 Engineering services; Testing laboratories; Business consulting, nec
HQ: Aptim Corp.

10001 Woodloch Forest Dr # 450
The Woodlands TX
832 823-2700

(P-19143)
ARIA GROUP INCORPORATED
17395 Daimler St (92614-5510)
PHONE.................949 475-2915
Clive Hawkins, *Pr*
EMP: 70 **EST:** 1995
SQ FT: 45,489
SALES (est): 11.6MM **Privately Held**
Web: www.aria-group.com
SIC: 8711 Consulting engineer

(P-19144)
ARUP NORTH AMERICA LIMITED
12777 W Jefferson Blvd Ste 300 (90066-7034)
PHONE.................310 578-4182
Tony Panossian, *Brnch Mgr*
EMP: 291
Web: www.arup.com
SIC: 8711 Consulting engineer
HQ: Arup North America Limited
560 Mission St Fl 7
San Francisco CA

(P-19145)
ARUP NORTH AMERICA LIMITED (DH)
Also Called: Arup
560 Mission St Fl 7 (94105-0915)
PHONE.................415 957-9445
Mahadev Ramen, *Pr*
Andrew Howard, *
James Quiter, *
EMP: 200 **EST:** 1987
SALES (est): 322.98MM **Privately Held**
Web: www.arup.com
SIC: 8711 Consulting engineer
HQ: Arup Americas Inc.
77 Water St
New York NY

(P-19146)
ASHLEY & VANCE ENGINEERING INC
1229 Carmel St (93401-3814)
PHONE.................805 545-0010
Truitt Vance, *Prin*
EMP: 75 **EST:** 2008
SALES (est): 6.49MM **Privately Held**
Web: www.ashleyvance.com
SIC: 8711 Civil engineering

(P-19147)
ATA ENGINEERING INC (PA)
13290 Evening Creek Dr S Ste 250 (92128-4695)
PHONE.................858 480-2000
Joshua Davis, *Pr*
Mary Baker, *
Ralph Brillhart, *
Thomas Deiters, *
Paul A Blelloch, *
EMP: 60 **EST:** 2000
SQ FT: 50,215
SALES (est): 49.94MM
SALES (corp-wide): 49.94MM **Privately Held**
Web: www.ata-e.com
SIC: 8711 Consulting engineer

(P-19148)
ATKINS NORTH AMERICA INC
9275 Sky Park Ct Ste 200 (92123-4905)
PHONE.................858 874-1810
Marc Cavallero, *Brnch Mgr*

PRODUCTS & SERVICES SECTION
8711 - Engineering Services (P-19170)

EMP: 65
SALES (corp-wide): 5.62B **Privately Held**
Web: www.atkinsglobal.com
SIC: 8711 Consulting engineer
HQ: Atkins North America, Inc.
4030 W Boy Scout Blvd
Tampa FL
813 282-7275

(P-19149)
AUSGAR TECHNOLOGIES INC
10721 Treena St Ste 100 (92131-1185)
PHONE.....................855 428-7427
Jonathan Dien, *Pr*
Karen Dien, *
Eric Lofgren, *
Saul Dien, *
EMP: 115 **EST:** 2003
SQ FT: 16,000
SALES (est): 21.88MM **Privately Held**
Web: www.ausgar.com
SIC: 8711 7371 7373 7379 Consulting engineer; Custom computer programming services; Computer integrated systems design; Computer related consulting services

(P-19150)
B&C TRANSIT INC (HQ)
Also Called: B & C
1924 Franklin St Ste 200 (94612-2913)
PHONE.....................510 483-3560
Alberto Fernandez, *Pr*
Steven Falk, *
Tanya Powell, *
Jerome S Furman, *
Rita Roquez, *
EMP: 60 **EST:** 1999
SQ FT: 25,000
SALES (est): 37.92MM **Privately Held**
Web: www.bnctransit.com
SIC: 8711 Electrical or electronic engineering
PA: Alstom
Rue Albert Dhalenne
St Ouen Sur Seine

(P-19151)
BAE SYSTEMS MARITIME ENGINEERING & SERVICES INC
7330 Engineer Rd Ste A (92111-1434)
P.O. Box 13308 (92170-3308)
PHONE.....................619 238-1000
EMP: 370
SIC: 8711 Engineering services

(P-19152)
BIGGS CARDOSA ASSOCIATES INC (PA)
865 The Alameda (95126-3133)
PHONE.....................408 296-5515
Steven A Biggs, *Pr*
Mark Cardosa, *
EMP: 70 **EST:** 1986
SQ FT: 7,237
SALES (est): 12.44MM
SALES (corp-wide): 12.44MM **Privately Held**
Web: www.biggscardosa.com
SIC: 8711 Civil engineering

(P-19153)
BINOPTICS LLC
977 S Meridian Ave (91803-1250)
PHONE.....................607 257-3200
Norman Kwong, *Brnch Mgr*
EMP: 134
SIC: 8711 Engineering services
HQ: Binoptics, Llc
9 Brown Rd
Ithaca NY
607 257-3200

(P-19154)
BIT MEDTECH LLC
15870 Bernardo Center Dr (92127-2320)
PHONE.....................858 613-1200
EMP: 60 **EST:** 1999
SALES (est): 4.65MM **Privately Held**
SIC: 8711 3841 Engineering services; Surgical and medical instruments

(P-19155)
BKF ENGINEERS (PA)
255 Shoreline Dr Ste 200 (94065-1428)
PHONE.....................650 482-6300
Greg Hurd, *CEO*
Dave Evans, *
Janine O'flaherty, *VP*
Max Keech, *
Maureen Nevin, *
EMP: 90 **EST:** 1915
SQ FT: 18,155
SALES (est): 100.83MM
SALES (corp-wide): 100.83MM **Privately Held**
Web: www.bkf.com
SIC: 8711 8713 Civil engineering; Surveying services

(P-19156)
BKF ENGINEERS/AGS
Also Called: BKF ENGINEERS/AGS
4675 Macarthur Ct Ste 400 (92660-8834)
PHONE.....................949 526-8400
Isaac Kontorovsky, *Brnch Mgr*
EMP: 99
SALES (corp-wide): 100.83MM **Privately Held**
Web: www.bkf.com
SIC: 8711 Civil engineering
PA: Bkf Engineers
255 Shoreline Dr Ste 200
Redwood City CA
650 482-6300

(P-19157)
BKF/FLI
150 California St Ste 600 (94111-4564)
PHONE.....................415 930-7900
EMP: 61 **EST:** 2019
SALES (est): 347.79K **Privately Held**
SIC: 8711 Civil engineering

(P-19158)
BOYLE ENGINEERING CORPORATION
999 W Town And Country Rd (92868-4713)
PHONE.....................949 476-3300
EMP: 400
SIC: 8711 8712 Engineering services; Architectural engineering

(P-19159)
BRIDGE DESIGN LLC
375 Alabama St Ste 410 (94110-1391)
PHONE.....................415 487-7100
William Evans, *Pr*
Stacy Evans, *Sec*
EMP: 67 **EST:** 1992
SQ FT: 1,300
SALES (est): 1.47MM **Privately Held**
Web: www.redswan.com
SIC: 8711 7389 7373 Designing: ship, boat, machine, and product; Design, commercial and industrial; Computer-aided design (CAD) systems service
PA: Ximedica, Llc
55 Dupont Dr
Providence RI

(P-19160)
BRINDERSON LLC (DH)
18841 S Broadwick St (90220-6429)
PHONE.....................714 466-7100
William Gary, *CEO*
EMP: 150 **EST:** 1993
SALES (est): 292.81MM **Privately Held**
Web: www.aegion.com
SIC: 8711 1629 Engineering services; Dams, waterways, docks, and other marine construction
HQ: Brock Holdings Iii, Llc
10343 Sam Houston Park Dr
Houston TX
281 807-8200

(P-19161)
BROSAMER & WALL INC
1777 Oakland Blvd Ste 300 (94596-4063)
PHONE.....................925 932-7900
Robert Brosamer, *Ch Bd*
Charles Wall, *
Jeffrey Turner, *
EMP: 140 **EST:** 2012
SQ FT: 13,000
SALES (est): 22.86MM **Privately Held**
Web: www.brosamerwall.com
SIC: 8711 Engineering services

(P-19162)
BROWN AND CALDWELL (PA)
201 N Civic Dr Ste 115 (94596-3865)
Rural Route 1527 Cole Blvd S (80401)
PHONE.....................925 937-9010
Richard D'amato, *CEO*
James Miller, *V Ch Bd*
Richard D' Amanto, *Pr*
Sachin Gajwani, *VP*
Marc Damikolas, *COO*
▲ **EMP:** 131 **EST:** 1944
SQ FT: 24,000
SALES (est): 374.67MM
SALES (corp-wide): 374.67MM **Privately Held**
Web: www.brownandcaldwell.com
SIC: 8711 Civil engineering

(P-19163)
BSK ASSOCIATES
Also Called: B S K Analytical Laboratories
687 N Laverne Ave (93727-6820)
PHONE.....................559 497-2888
Jeff Koelewyn, *Dir*
EMP: 63
SALES (corp-wide): 49.3MM **Privately Held**
Web: www.bskassociates.com
SIC: 8711 8734 Professional engineer; Testing laboratories
PA: Bsk Associates
691 N Laverne Ave
Fresno CA
559 497-2880

(P-19164)
BURNS & MCDONNELL INC
140 S State College Blvd Ste 100 (92821-5850)
PHONE.....................714 256-1595
Ken Gerling, *Brnch Mgr*
EMP: 80
SALES (corp-wide): 1.26B **Privately Held**
Web: www.burnsmcd.com
SIC: 8711 Consulting engineer
PA: Burns & Mcdonnell, Inc.
9400 Ward Pkwy
Kansas City MO
816 333-9400

(P-19165)
BURO HAPPOLD CONSULTING ENGINE
140 Geary St Fl 8 (94108-5619)
PHONE.....................310 945-4808
Joyce Engebretsen, *Prin*
EMP: 127
SALES (corp-wide): 360.99MM **Privately Held**
Web: www.burohappold.com
SIC: 8711 Consulting engineer
HQ: Buro Happold Consulting Engineers, Inc.
800 Wilshire Blvd Fl 16
Los Angeles CA

(P-19166)
C D LYON CONSTRUCTION INC (PA)
380 W Stanley Ave (93001-1350)
P.O. Box 1456 (93002-1456)
PHONE.....................805 653-0173
Christopher D Lyon, *CEO*
Debra C Lyon, *
EMP: 80 **EST:** 1986
SALES (est): 21.22MM
SALES (corp-wide): 21.22MM **Privately Held**
Web: www.cdlyon.com
SIC: 8711 Petroleum engineering

(P-19167)
CALIFORNIA ENVMTL SYSTEMS INC
12265 Locksley Ln (95602-2055)
PHONE.....................530 820-3693
Carter Pierce, *Prin*
EMP: 70 **EST:** 2011
SQ FT: 10,000
SALES (est): 12.22MM **Privately Held**
Web: www.calenvirosys.com
SIC: 8711 Engineering services

(P-19168)
CALIFORNIA MFG TECH CONSULTING
Also Called: Cmtc
3760 Kilroy Airport Way Ste 450 (90806-2443)
PHONE.....................310 263-3060
EMP: 74 **EST:** 1994
SQ FT: 10,000
SALES (est): 31.61MM **Privately Held**
Web: www.cmtc.com
SIC: 8711 8742 Consulting engineer; Marketing consulting services

(P-19169)
CALIFORNIA PROF ENGRG INC
19062 San Jose Ave (91748-1412)
PHONE.....................626 810-1338
Van Nguyen, *Pr*
EMP: 65 **EST:** 2000
SALES (est): 9.62MM **Privately Held**
Web: www.cpengineeringinc.com
SIC: 8711 1611 1731 Engineering services; Highway and street construction; Voice, data, and video wiring contractor

(P-19170)
CALIFORNIA SEMICONDUCTOR TECH
Also Called: Calsemi
429 Santa Monica Blvd (90401-3401)
PHONE.....................310 579-2939
Antonio Garcia, *CEO*
Jose Luis Lopez, *
EMP: 120 **EST:** 2013

8711 - Engineering Services (P-19171)

PRODUCTS & SERVICES SECTION

SALES (est): 3.4MM **Privately Held**
Web: www.calsemi-tech.com
SIC: **8711** Engineering services

(P-19171)
CAPITAL ENGINEERING CONS INC (PA)
Also Called: Capital Engineering Cons
11020 Sun Center Dr Ste 100 (95670-6114)
PHONE..................................916 851-3500
Lowell E Shields, *Pr*
John Lionakis, *
Thomas Duval, *
EMP: 72 EST: 1947
SQ FT: 6,800
SALES (est): 10.93MM
SALES (corp-wide): 10.93MM **Privately Held**
Web: www.capital-engineering.com
SIC: **8711** Consulting engineer

(P-19172)
CAPITAL ENGINEERING LLC
Also Called: Capital Engineering
2830 Temple Ave (90806-2213)
PHONE..................................562 612-1302
EMP: 76
SALES (corp-wide): 5.62B **Privately Held**
Web: www.capital-engineering.com
SIC: **8711** Consulting engineer
HQ: Capital Engineering Llc
436 Creamery Way Ste H100
Exton PA
219 791-1984

(P-19173)
CARBON LIGHTHOUSE INC
343 Sansome St Ste 700 (94104-5614)
PHONE..................................415 787-3550
Brenden Millstein, *Prin*
Raphael Rosen, *Prin*
EMP: 139 EST: 2010
SALES (est): 18.66MM **Privately Held**
Web: www.carbonlighthouse.com
SIC: **8711** Energy conservation engineering

(P-19174)
CARLSON BARBEE & GIBSON INC
2633 Camino Ramon (94583-9139)
PHONE..................................925 866-0322
David Carlson, *Pr*
Michael Barbee, *
Grant Gibson, *
EMP: 100 EST: 1989
SQ FT: 6,800
SALES (est): 11.92MM **Privately Held**
Web: www.cbandg.com
SIC: **8711** Civil engineering

(P-19175)
CAROLLO ENGINEERS INC (PA)
Also Called: Carollo Engineers
2795 Mitchell Dr (94598-1601)
PHONE..................................925 932-1710
Balakrishnan Narayanan, *Pr*
Kristi Powers, *
Michael W Barnes, *
EMP: 100 EST: 2010
SQ FT: 20,000
SALES (est): 198.71MM
SALES (corp-wide): 198.71MM **Privately Held**
Web: www.carollo.com
SIC: **8711** Consulting engineer

(P-19176)
CARTER & BURGESS INC
2033 Gateway Pl 6th Fl (95110-3709)

PHONE..................................408 428-2010
Dan Potter, *Brnch Mgr*
EMP: 63
SALES (corp-wide): 14.92B **Publicly Held**
Web: www.c-b.com
SIC: **8711** Civil engineering
HQ: Carter & Burgess, Inc.
777 Main St Ste 2500
Fort Worth TX
817 735-6000

(P-19177)
CDM CONSTRUCTORS INC
9220 Cleveland Ave Ste 100 (91730-8560)
PHONE..................................909 579-3500
Joyce Jackson, *Brnch Mgr*
EMP: 90
SALES (corp-wide): 1.42B **Privately Held**
Web: www.cdmsmith.com
SIC: **8711** Consulting engineer
HQ: Cdm Constructors Inc.
75 State St Ste 701
Boston MA

(P-19178)
CITY OF GLENDALE
Also Called: Engineering Public Works
633 E Broadway Ste 205 (91206-4310)
PHONE..................................818 548-3945
Lou Le Blanc, *Dir*
EMP: 112
SALES (corp-wide): 390.24MM **Privately Held**
Web: www.glendaleca.gov
SIC: **8711** 9511 Engineering services; Air, water, and solid waste management
PA: City Of Glendale
141 N Glendale Ave Fl 2
Glendale CA
818 548-2085

(P-19179)
CONCEPT TECHNOLOGY INC (PA)
895 Dove St 3rd Fl (92660-2941)
PHONE..................................949 854-7047
Mahesh P Badani, *Pr*
▲ EMP: 60 EST: 1981
SALES (est): 4.82MM
SALES (corp-wide): 4.82MM **Privately Held**
Web: www.concepttechnologyinc.com
SIC: **8711** 3599 8742 3825 Consulting engineer; Machine shop, jobbing and repair; Management information systems consultant; Radio frequency measuring equipment

(P-19180)
CONCEPT TECHNOLOGY INC
2941 W Macarthur Blvd Ste 136 (92704-6952)
PHONE..................................949 851-6550
EMP: 430
SALES (corp-wide): 4.82MM **Privately Held**
Web: www.concepttechnology.com
SIC: **8711** Consulting engineer
PA: Concept Technology, Inc.
895 Dove St Fl 3
Newport Beach CA
949 854-7047

(P-19181)
CONSOR NORTH AMERICA INC
11017 Cobblerock Dr Ste 100 (95670-6049)
PHONE..................................916 368-9181
EMP: 62
SALES (corp-wide): 728.53MM **Privately Held**

Web: www.consoreng.com
SIC: **8711** 4785 Civil engineering; Transportation inspection services
HQ: Consor North America, Inc.
155 N Wacker Dr Ste 1500
Chicago IL
888 451-6822

(P-19182)
CONSOR PMCM INC
1663 Mission St Ste 425 (94103-2486)
PHONE..................................415 596-5399
EMP: 100
SALES (corp-wide): 728.53MM **Privately Held**
SIC: **8711** 4785 Civil engineering; Transportation inspection services
HQ: Consor Pmcm, Inc.
155 N Wacker Dr Ste 41
Chicago IL
888 451-6822

(P-19183)
CONSTRUCTION TSTG & ENGRG INC
Also Called: CONSTRUCTION TESTING & ENGINEERING, INC.
14538 Meridian Pkwy Ste A (92518-3018)
PHONE..................................951 571-4081
Vincent Patula, *Brnch Mgr*
EMP: 359
SALES (corp-wide): 462.96MM **Privately Held**
Web: www.teamues.com
SIC: **8711** Civil engineering
HQ: Construction Testing & Engineering, Inc.
1441 Montiel Rd Ste 115
Escondido CA

(P-19184)
COOPER VALI & ASSOCIATES INC (HQ)
1850 Gateway Blvd Ste 100 (94520-8447)
PHONE..................................510 446-8301
Gary Bedey, *CEO*
Agnes Weber, *Chief Strategy Officer*
Hank Doll, *
John Collins, *
Connie Fremier, *
EMP: 80 EST: 1987
SQ FT: 3,000
SALES (est): 19.83MM
SALES (corp-wide): 482.42MM **Privately Held**
SIC: **8711** Construction and civil engineering
PA: Trc Companies, Inc.
21 Griffin Rd N
Windsor CT
860 298-9692

(P-19185)
COUNTY OF FRESNO
Also Called: Public Works and Planning
2220 Tulare St Fl 6 (93721-2127)
PHONE..................................559 600-4078
EMP: 129
SALES (corp-wide): 2.02B **Privately Held**
Web: www.fresnocountyca.gov
SIC: **8711** 9199 Engineering services; General government administration, County government
PA: County Of Fresno
2281 Tulare St Ste 304
Fresno CA
559 600-1710

(P-19186)
COUNTY OF LOS ANGELES
Also Called: Engineering Division
44933 Fern Ave (93534-2461)
PHONE..................................661 723-6088
Bert Perry, *Brnch Mgr*
EMP: 135
SALES (corp-wide): 31.7B **Privately Held**
Web: www.lacounty.gov
SIC: **8711** 9111 Engineering services; Executive offices
PA: County Of Los Angeles
500 W Temple St Ste 437
Los Angeles CA
213 974-1101

(P-19187)
COUNTY OF LOS ANGELES
Public Works, Dept of
14747 Ramona Blvd (91706-3435)
PHONE..................................626 337-1277
William Wolfer, *Brnch Mgr*
EMP: 82
SALES (corp-wide): 31.7B **Privately Held**
Web: www.lacounty.gov
SIC: **8711** 9199 Engineering services; General government administration
PA: County Of Los Angeles
500 W Temple St Ste 437
Los Angeles CA
213 974-1101

(P-19188)
COUNTY OF PLACER
Also Called: Public Works Dept
3091 County Center Dr Ste 220 (95603-2610)
PHONE..................................530 889-7500
Ken Grehm, *Dir*
EMP: 60
SALES (corp-wide): 803.78MM **Privately Held**
Web: placer.ca.gov
SIC: **8711** 9511 Structural engineering; Air, water, and solid waste management, County government
PA: County Of Placer
2986 Richardson Dr
Auburn CA
530 889-4200

(P-19189)
CROWN ENERGY SERVICES INC
Also Called: Able Engineering Services
2003 Diamond Blvd Rm 31209 (94520-5701)
PHONE..................................925 827-6299
EMP: 182
SALES (corp-wide): 7.81B **Publicly Held**
SIC: **8711** Engineering services
HQ: Crown Energy Services, Inc.
600 Harrison St Ste 600 # 600
San Francisco CA

(P-19190)
CROWN ENERGY SERVICES INC
Also Called: Able Services
611 Gateway Blvd (94080-7017)
PHONE..................................415 546-6534
EMP: 170
SALES (corp-wide): 7.81B **Publicly Held**
SIC: **8711** Engineering services
HQ: Crown Energy Services, Inc.
600 Harrison St Ste 600 # 600
San Francisco CA

(P-19191)
CURTISS-WRGHT CNTRLS ELCTRNIC
28965 Avenue Penn (91355-4185)

PRODUCTS & SERVICES SECTION
8711 - Engineering Services (P-19212)

PHONE..............................661 257-4430
Val Zarov, *Brnch Mgr*
EMP: 194
SALES (corp-wide): 2.56B **Publicly Held**
Web: www.curtisswright.com
SIC: 8711 Engineering services
HQ: Curtiss-Wright Controls Electronic Systems, Inc.
  28965 Avenue Penn
  Santa Clarita CA
  661 702-1494

(P-19192)
CURTISS-WRGHT CNTRLS INTGRTED (DH)
Also Called: Avionics & Electronics
28965 Avenue Penn (91355-4185)
PHONE..............................661 257-4430
Thomas Quinly, *CEO*
John Kuperhand, *
Tony Sozutek, *
Anabele Cloud, *
EMP: 69 **EST:** 1978
SQ FT: 27,000
SALES (est): 24.09MM
SALES (corp-wide): 2.56B **Publicly Held**
Web: www.cw-sensors.com
SIC: 8711 Engineering services
HQ: Curtiss-Wright Controls, Inc.
  201 Old Boiling Sprng Rd
  Shelby NC
  704 869-4600

(P-19193)
CYGNA GROUP INC
2101 Webster St (94612-3011)
PHONE..............................510 419-5000
James Edwards, *CEO*
Marc Tipermas, *
Pete Offringa, *
EMP: 250 **EST:** 1974
SALES (est): 10.48MM
SALES (corp-wide): 107.87MM **Publicly Held**
SIC: 8711 8741 8748 Consulting engineer; Construction management; Business consulting, nec
PA: Kaiser Group Holdings, Inc.
  1943 50th St N
  Birmingham AL
  404 593-1025

(P-19194)
DCS CORPORATION
137 W Drummond Ave Ste C (93555-3583)
PHONE..............................760 384-5600
Charles Faris, *Brnch Mgr*
EMP: 71
SALES (corp-wide): 196.63MM **Privately Held**
Web: www.dcscorp.com
SIC: 8711 Consulting engineer
PA: Dcs Corporation
  6909 Metro Park Dr # 500
  Alexandria VA
  571 227-6000

(P-19195)
DEGENKOLB ENGINEERS (PA)
375 Beale St Ste 500 (94105-2177)
PHONE..............................415 392-6952
Stacy Bartoletti, *CEO*
Robert Beggs, *
James O Malley, *
Andrew Scott, *
Chris Poland, *
EMP: 66 **EST:** 1940
SQ FT: 22,800
SALES (est): 48.19MM
SALES (corp-wide): 48.19MM **Privately Held**

Web: www.degenkolb.com
SIC: 8711 Structural engineering

(P-19196)
DELTA PROJECT MANAGEMENT INC
400 Concar Dr (94402-2681)
PHONE..............................415 590-3202
Feras Al-zubaidy, *Ofcr*
Scott Kobayashi, *
EMP: 60 **EST:** 2006
SALES (est): 5.56MM **Privately Held**
Web: www.verista.com
SIC: 8711 Consulting engineer

(P-19197)
DEVELOPMENT RESOURCE CONS INC (PA)
160 S Old Springs Rd Ste 210 (92808-1260)
PHONE..............................714 685-6860
Lawrence Gates, *Pr*
EMP: 90 **EST:** 1997
SQ FT: 12,000
SALES (est): 12.4MM
SALES (corp-wide): 12.4MM **Privately Held**
SIC: 8711 Civil engineering

(P-19198)
DEWBERRY ENGINEERS INC
Also Called: Drake Haglan & Associates
11060 White Rock Rd Ste 200 (95670-6046)
PHONE..............................916 363-4210
Craig C Drake, *Brnch Mgr*
EMP: 62
Web: www.dewberry.com
SIC: 8711 Civil engineering
HQ: Dewberry Engineers Inc.
  8401 Arlington Blvd Ste 1
  Fairfax VA
  973 338-9100

(P-19199)
DEX CORPORATION
Also Called: Data Exchange
3600 Via Pescador (93012-5051)
PHONE..............................805 388-1711
Sheldon Malchiconfqs, *CEO*
EMP: 150 **EST:** 2015
SQ FT: 100,000
SALES (est): 12.06MM **Privately Held**
Web: www.dex.com
SIC: 8711 5065 Engineering services; Electronic parts

(P-19200)
DIVERGENT TECHNOLOGIES INC
Also Called: Divergent 3d
19601 Hamilton Ave (90502-1309)
PHONE..............................424 542-2158
Kevin Czinger, *Pr*
Ursula Ster, *
EMP: 150 **EST:** 2021
SALES (est): 32.04MM **Privately Held**
Web: www.divergent3d.com
SIC: 8711 Mechanical engineering

(P-19201)
DIVERSIFIED PRJ SVCS INTL INC (PA)
5351 Olive Dr Ste 100 (93308-2926)
PHONE..............................661 371-2800
Robert Chambers, *Pr*
EMP: 80 **EST:** 2007
SALES (est): 15.65MM
SALES (corp-wide): 15.65MM **Privately Held**

Web: www.dpsiinc.com
SIC: 8711 Consulting engineer

(P-19202)
DMS FACILITY SERVICES LLC
2861 E Coronado St (92806-2504)
PHONE..............................949 975-1366
Richard E Dotts, *Brnch Mgr*
EMP: 684
Web: www.dmsfacilityservices.com
SIC: 8711 Engineering services
PA: Dms Facility Services, Llc
  1040 Arroyo Dr
  South Pasadena CA

(P-19203)
DMS FACILITY SERVICES LLC
5735 Kearny Villa Rd Ste 108 (92123)
PHONE..............................858 560-4191
John Harris, *Brnch Mgr*
EMP: 661
Web: www.dmsfacilityservices.com
SIC: 8711 7349 0781 Engineering services; Janitorial service, contract basis; Landscape services
PA: Dms Facility Services, Llc
  1040 Arroyo Dr
  South Pasadena CA

(P-19204)
DOKKEN ENGINEERING (PA)
110 Blue Ravine Rd Ste 200 (95630-4713)
PHONE..............................916 858-0642
Richard Dokken, *CEO*
Richard Liptak, *
Cathy Chan, *
Bradley Dokken, *
EMP: 70 **EST:** 1986
SQ FT: 12,931
SALES (est): 28.08MM
SALES (corp-wide): 28.08MM **Privately Held**
Web: www.dokkenengineering.com
SIC: 8711 8741 Civil engineering; Construction management

(P-19205)
DSP CONCEPTS INC (PA)
3235 Kifer Rd Ste 100 (95051-0821)
PHONE..............................408 747-5200
Chin Beckmann, *CEO*
Paul Beckmann, *
Chris Reed, *
Yuchun Lee, *
David Daggett, *
EMP: 104 **EST:** 2015
SQ FT: 2,400
SALES (est): 15MM
SALES (corp-wide): 15MM **Privately Held**
Web: www.dspconcepts.com
SIC: 8711 Consulting engineer

(P-19206)
DUDEK INC (PA)
605 3rd St (92024-3513)
PHONE..............................760 942-5147
Joseph Monaco, *CEO*
Eric Wilson, *
Christine Moore, *
Emily Hart, *
Helder Guimaraes, *
EMP: 100 **EST:** 1980
SQ FT: 50,000
SALES (est): 132.78MM
SALES (corp-wide): 132.78MM **Privately Held**
Web: www.dudek.com
SIC: 8711 8748 Civil engineering; Environmental consultant

(P-19207)
E2 CONSULTING ENGINEERS INC
2100 Powell St Ste 850 (94608-1894)
PHONE..............................510 652-1164
EMP: 97
SALES (corp-wide): 68.06MM **Privately Held**
Web: www.e2.com
SIC: 8711 Consulting engineer
PA: E2 Consulting Engineers, Inc.
  450 E 17th Ave Unit 200
  Denver CO
  510 652-1164

(P-19208)
EDSI
700 Ammunition Rd Bldg 103 (92028-3187)
PHONE..............................760 731-3501
Rick Lengerke, *Brnch Mgr*
EMP: 94
SALES (corp-wide): 22.28MM **Privately Held**
Web: www.edsi.com
SIC: 8711 Engineering services
PA: Edsi
  22835 Savi Ranch Pkwy F
  Yorba Linda CA
  951 272-8689

(P-19209)
EICHLEAY INC
500 N State College Blvd # 1205 (92868-1637)
PHONE..............................562 256-8600
Lori M Lofstrom, *Brnch Mgr*
EMP: 149
Web: www.eichleay.com
SIC: 8711 Consulting engineer
PA: Eichleay, Inc.
  1390 Willow Pass Rd # 60
  Concord CA

(P-19210)
EICHLEAY INC (PA)
1390 Willow Pass Rd Ste 600 (94520-5200)
PHONE..............................925 689-7000
George F Eichleay Junior, *CEO*
George F Eichleay Junior, *Pr*
EMP: 150 **EST:** 2007
SQ FT: 17,000
SALES (est): 67.85MM **Privately Held**
Web: www.eichleay.com
SIC: 8711 Consulting engineer

(P-19211)
EICHLEAY ENGINEERS INC
1390 Willow Pass Rd Ste 600 (94520-7936)
P.O. Box 238 (15071-0238)
PHONE..............................925 689-7000
John Borman, *VP*
John Eichleay Junior, *Sec*
Theodore Nelson Junior, *Treas*
EMP: 77 **EST:** 1945
SALES (est): 2.93MM **Privately Held**
Web: www.eichleay.com
SIC: 8711 Consulting engineer

(P-19212)
EMBEE PROCESSING LLC
Also Called: Embee Plating
2158 S Hathaway St (92705-5249)
PHONE..............................714 546-9842
Michael Coburn, *CEO*
Scott Chrisman, *
Derek Watson, *
▲ **EMP:** 385 **EST:** 1947
SQ FT: 100,000

8711 - Engineering Services (P-19213)

SALES (est): 23.51MM **Privately Held**
Web: www.embee.com
SIC: **8711** 3398 3479 8734 Aviation and/or aeronautical engineering; Shot peening (treating steel to reduce fatigue); Coating of metals and formed products; Metallurgical testing laboratory

(P-19213)
ENCORE SEMI INC
7310 Miramar Rd Ste 410 (92126-4226)
PHONE.................................858 225-4993
EMP: 67 EST: 2011
SALES (est): 8.07MM **Privately Held**
Web: www.encoresemi.com
SIC: **8711** 3674 Engineering services; Integrated circuits, semiconductor networks, etc.

(P-19214)
ENGEO INCORPORATED
6399 San Ignacio Ave Ste 150 (95119-1244)
PHONE.................................408 574-4900
Uri Eliahu, *Pr*
EMP: 120
SALES (corp-wide): 45.8MM **Privately Held**
Web: www.engeo.com
SIC: **8711** Consulting engineer
PA: Engeo Incorporated
    2010 Crow Canyon Pl # 250
    San Ramon CA
    925 866-9000

(P-19215)
ENGINEERING PARTNERS INC
Also Called: E P I
10150 Meanley Dr Ste 200 (92131-3008)
PHONE.................................858 824-1761
Romeo Flores, *Pr*
EMP: 95 EST: 1985
SQ FT: 2,500
SALES (est): 9.45MM **Privately Held**
Web: www.engineeringpartners.com
SIC: **8711** Consulting engineer

(P-19216)
ENGINRING SFTWR SYS SLTONS INC (PA)
Also Called: E S 3
600 B St (92101-4501)
PHONE.................................619 338-0380
Teri Sgammato, *Pr*
Chuck Dahms, *
Doug Wiser, *
Craig Edwards, *
EMP: 80 EST: 2001
SALES (est): 22.78MM
SALES (corp-wide): 22.78MM **Privately Held**
Web: www.es3inc.com
SIC: **8711** Engineering services

(P-19217)
ENVIRONMENTAL CHEMICAL CORP (PA)
Also Called: Ecc
1240 Bayshore Hwy (94010-1805)
PHONE.................................650 347-1555
Manjiv S Vohra, *Pr*
August Ochabauer, *
Tom Delmastro, *
▼ EMP: 75 EST: 1985
SQ FT: 21,000
SALES (est): 689.17MM **Privately Held**
Web: www.ecc.net
SIC: **8711** 1542 8744 Engineering services; Commercial and office building contractors ; Environmental remediation

(P-19218)
EPSILON SYSTEMS SLTONS MSSION
9242 Lightwave Ave Ste 100 (92123-6402)
PHONE.................................619 702-1700
Alan Stewart, *CFO*
Robin Nordberg, *
EMP: 99 EST: 2011
SALES (est): 3.33MM **Privately Held**
Web: www.epsilonsystems.com
SIC: **8711** Electrical or electronic engineering

(P-19219)
EPSILON SYSTEMS SOLUTIONS INC (PA)
9444 Balboa Ave Ste 100 (92123-4351)
PHONE.................................619 702-1700
Bryan Min, *CEO*
Joe Quinn, *
EMP: 100 EST: 1990
SQ FT: 50,000
SALES (est): 110MM
SALES (corp-wide): 110MM **Privately Held**
Web: www.epsilonsystems.com
SIC: **8711** Engineering services

(P-19220)
ERM-WEST INC (DH)
Also Called: Environmental Resources MGT
1277 Treat Blvd Ste 500 (94597-7989)
PHONE.................................925 946-0455
Jennifer Lee, *Pr*
Jonathan Beevers, *VP*
Marlene Dawes, *VP*
Alexandra Fraser, *VP*
Andra Kidd, *VP*
EMP: 305 EST: 1984
SQ FT: 19,455
SALES (est): 179.87MM
SALES (corp-wide): 673.68MM **Privately Held**
SIC: **8711** 8742 Consulting engineer; Management consulting services
HQ: Erm-Delaware, Inc.
    1105 N Market St Ste 1300
    Wilmington DE
    302 651-8300

(P-19221)
ES ENGINEERING SERVICES LLC
4 Park Plz Ste 790 (92614-5262)
PHONE.................................949 988-3500
Vijay Menthripragada, *CEO*
EMP: 85 EST: 2015
SALES (est): 4.71MM
SALES (corp-wide): 544.42MM **Publicly Held**
SIC: **8711** 8748 Engineering services; Systems analysis and engineering consulting services
PA: Montrose Environmental Group, Inc.
    5120 Northshore Dr
    North Little Rock AR
    501 900-6400

(P-19222)
EXPONENT INC (PA)
149 Commonwealth Dr (94025-1133)
PHONE.................................650 326-9400
TOLL FREE: 888
Catherine Ford Corrigan, *Pr*
Catherine Ford Corrigan, *Pr*
Paul R Johnston, *
Richard L Schlenker Junior, *Corporate Secretary*
Sally B Shepard, *Chief Human Resources Officer*
EMP: 231 EST: 1967
SQ FT: 153,738
SALES (est): 513.29MM **Publicly Held**
Web: www.exponent.com
SIC: **8711** 8742 8999 Consulting engineer; Management consulting services; Scientific consulting

(P-19223)
FALCON TECHNOLOGIES INC
3233 Luyung Dr (95742-6862)
PHONE.................................916 638-1221
William J Delgado, *Pr*
Patrick Quarry, *Business Development**
Jeff Jordeson, *
Dave Stolecki, *
EMP: 63 EST: 1991
SALES (est): 1.84MM **Privately Held**
Web: www.falcontechusa.com
SIC: **8711** Engineering services

(P-19224)
FEHR & PEERS (PA)
Also Called: Fehr & Peers
100 Pringle Ave Ste 600 (94596-3582)
PHONE.................................925 977-3200
Matthew Henry, *CEO*
Alan Telford, *
Steven Brown, *
Marion Donnelly, *
EMP: 60 EST: 1985
SQ FT: 16,000
SALES (est): 45.89MM
SALES (corp-wide): 45.89MM **Privately Held**
Web: www.fehrandpeers.com
SIC: **8711** Consulting engineer

(P-19225)
FLINT ENERGY SERVICES INC
1999 Avenue Of The Stars Ste 2600 (90067-6022)
PHONE.................................213 593-8000
EMP: 107
SALES (corp-wide): 13.15B **Publicly Held**
Web: www.aecom.com
SIC: **8711** Engineering services
HQ: Flint Energy Services Inc.
    7595 E Technology Way # 200
    Denver CO
    918 294-3030

(P-19226)
FLUOR CORPORATION
Also Called: Trs Staffing Solutions
3 Polaris Way (92656-5338)
PHONE.................................949 349-2000
Tim Kirk, *Prin*
EMP: 99
SALES (corp-wide): 13.74B **Publicly Held**
Web: www.fluor.com
SIC: **8711** 7363 Engineering services; Help supply services
PA: Fluor Corporation
    6700 Las Colinas Blvd
    Irving TX
    469 398-7000

(P-19227)
FLUOR ENTERPRISES INC
3 Polaris Way (92656-5338)
PHONE.................................949 349-2000
Ronald Albright, *Brnch Mgr*
EMP: 61
SALES (corp-wide): 13.74B **Publicly Held**
Web: www.fluor.com
SIC: **8711** Engineering services
HQ: Fluor Enterprises, Inc.
    6700 Las Colinas Blvd
    Irving TX
    469 398-7000

(P-19228)
FLUOR ENTERPRISES INC
611 Gateway Blvd Ste 950 (94080-7040)
PHONE.................................925 307-1200
Annette Baird, *Mgr*
EMP: 70
SALES (corp-wide): 13.74B **Publicly Held**
Web: www.fluor.com
SIC: **8711** Engineering services
HQ: Fluor Enterprises, Inc.
    6700 Las Colinas Blvd
    Irving TX
    469 398-7000

(P-19229)
FLUOR PLANT SERVICES INTL INC
Also Called: Fluor Daniel
1 Enterprise (92656-2606)
PHONE.................................949 349-2000
D Michael Steuert, *CFO*
EMP: 100 EST: 1900
SALES (est): 26.72MM
SALES (corp-wide): 13.74B **Publicly Held**
Web: www.microsemi.com
SIC: **8711** Engineering services
PA: Fluor Corporation
    6700 Las Colinas Blvd
    Irving TX
    469 398-7000

(P-19230)
FORWARD SLOPE INCORPORATED
Also Called: Forward Slope.
2020 Camino Del Rio N Ste 400 (92108)
PHONE.................................619 299-4400
Carlos Persichetti, *Pr*
Kevin Noonan, *VP*
EMP: 80 EST: 1997
SALES (est): 26.22MM **Privately Held**
Web: www.forwardslope.com
SIC: **8711** 7371 7389 Consulting engineer; Software programming applications; Financial services

(P-19231)
FRICTION MATERIALS LLC
2525 W 190th St (90504-6002)
PHONE.................................248 362-3600
Andre Bezuszka, *Managing Member*
EMP: 132 EST: 2002
SALES (est): 10.02MM
SALES (corp-wide): 3.63B **Privately Held**
SIC: **8711** Engineering services
PA: Garrett Motion Inc.
    47548 Halyard Dr
    Plymouth MI
    734 359-5901

(P-19232)
FTI CONSULTING INC
350 S Grand Ave Ste 3000 (90071-3424)
PHONE.................................213 689-1200
Stewart Kahn, *Pr*
EMP: 80
SALES (corp-wide): 3.03B **Publicly Held**
Web: www.fticonsulting.com
SIC: **8711** 8748 8742 Consulting engineer; Business consulting, nec; Management consulting services
PA: Fti Consulting, Inc.
    555 12th St Nw Ste 700
    Washington DC
    202 312-9100

(P-19233)
FUGRO WILLIAM LETTIS ASSOC INC (DH)

PRODUCTS & SERVICES SECTION

8711 - Engineering Services (P-19254)

Also Called: Fugro USA Land
1777 Botelho Dr Ste 262 (94596-5132)
PHONE..................925 256-6070
William Lettis, Pr
Keith Kelson, VP
Jeffrey R Unruh, VP
Jeff Bachhuber, VP
EMP: 81 EST: 1990
SQ FT: 5,000
SALES (est): 7.83MM
SALES (corp-wide): 1.02B Privately Held
SIC: 8711 Consulting engineer
HQ: Fugro (Usa) Holdings Inc.
   6100 Hillcroft St Ste 700
   Houston TX
   713 369-5600

(P-19234)
FUSCOE ENGINEERING INC (PA)
15535 Sand Canyon Ave (92618-3114)
PHONE..................949 474-1960
Patrick Fuscoe, Pr
EMP: 85 EST: 1992
SALES (est): 20.61MM Privately Held
Web: www.fuscoe.com
SIC: 8711 Civil engineering

(P-19235)
FUTURE ENERGY CORPORATION
9701 Elk Grove Florin Rd (95624-2277)
PHONE..................916 685-4200
EMP: 70
SALES (corp-wide): 24.18MM Privately Held
Web: www.futureenergysavers.com
SIC: 8711 Building construction consultant
PA: Future Energy Corporation
   8980 Grant Line Rd
   Elk Grove CA
   800 985-0733

(P-19236)
GARRETT J GENTRY GEN ENGRG INC
1297 W 9th St (91786-5706)
PHONE..................909 693-3391
Garrett J Gentry, Pr
Bryan Copping, *
EMP: 100 EST: 2013
SALES (est): 15.82MM Privately Held
Web: www.gjgentry.com
SIC: 8711 Acoustical engineering

(P-19237)
GAS TRANSMISSION SYSTEMS INC (HQ)
Also Called: GTS
130 Amber Grove Dr Ste 134 (95973-5880)
PHONE..................530 893-6711
Ben Campbell, Pr
Mark Cabral, VP
EMP: 86 EST: 2001
SQ FT: 4,500
SALES (est): 16.35MM
SALES (corp-wide): 458.93MM Privately Held
Web: www.gtsinc.us
SIC: 8711 Professional engineer
PA: The Kleinfelder Group Inc
   770 1st Ave Ste 400
   San Diego CA
   619 831-4600

(P-19238)
GENER8 LLC (PA)
2560 Junction Ave (95134-1902)
PHONE..................650 940-9898
Jerry Jurkiewicz, CEO
▲ EMP: 85 EST: 2002
SALES (est): 103.43MM
SALES (corp-wide): 103.43MM Privately Held
Web: www.gener8.net
SIC: 8711 3429 Engineering services; Locks or lock sets

(P-19239)
GEOCON INCORPORATED
6960 Flanders Dr (92121-3992)
PHONE..................858 558-6900
Joesph Vettel, CEO
Michael Chapin, *
William Lydon, *
EMP: 100 EST: 1971
SALES (est): 18.42MM Privately Held
Web: www.geoconinc.com
SIC: 8711 Consulting engineer

(P-19240)
GEOLOGIC ASSOCIATES INC
143 Spring Hill Dr Ste E (95945-5969)
PHONE..................530 272-2448
Scott Purdy, Brnch Mgr
EMP: 73
Web: www.geo-logic.com
SIC: 8711 Consulting engineer
PA: Geologic Associates, Inc.
   2777 E Guasti Rd Ste 1
   Ontario CA

(P-19241)
GEORGE G SHARP INC
1065 Bay Blvd Ste D (91911-1626)
PHONE..................619 425-4211
EMP: 75
SALES (corp-wide): 32.11MM Privately Held
SIC: 8711 Consulting engineer
PA: George G. Sharp, Inc.
   160 Broadway Rm 800
   New York NY
   212 732-2800

(P-19242)
GILBANE FEDERAL (DH)
Also Called: Gilbane Federal Company
1220 Concord Ave (94520-4906)
PHONE..................925 946-3100
Sarabjit Singh, CEO
Jon Verlinde, *
▲ EMP: 110 EST: 1994
SALES (est): 79.43MM
SALES (corp-wide): 5.6B Privately Held
SIC: 8711 8748 Building construction consultant; Environmental consultant
HQ: Gilbane Building Company
   7 Jackson Walkway Ste 2
   Providence RI
   401 456-5800

(P-19243)
GLENN A RICK ENGRG & DEV CO (PA)
Also Called: Rick Engineering Company
5620 Friars Rd (92110-2513)
PHONE..................619 291-0708
Roger Ball, Prin
Paul J Iezzi, *
Robert A Stockton, *
Dennis C Bowling, *
Deborah B Ragione, *
EMP: 212 EST: 1955
SQ FT: 50,000
SALES (est): 48.11MM
SALES (corp-wide): 48.11MM Privately Held
Web: www.rickengineering.com
SIC: 8711 Civil engineering

(P-19244)
GLOBAL SOLUTIONS INTEGRATION
Also Called: Gsico
26632 Towne Centre Dr Ste 300 (92610-2813)
PHONE..................949 307-1849
Cel Esmundi, Pr
EMP: 75 EST: 2016
SQ FT: 3,000
SALES (est): 5.9MM Privately Held
SIC: 8711 Engineering services

(P-19245)
GRADIENT ENGINEERS INC
Also Called: Leighton & Associates
17781 Cowan Ste 140 (92614-6009)
PHONE..................949 477-0555
EMP: 156 EST: 1996
SALES (est): 325.55K
SALES (corp-wide): 154.82MM Privately Held
SIC: 8711 8744 Consulting engineer; Environmental remediation
HQ: Leighton Group, Inc.
   2600 Michelson Dr Ste 400
   Irvine CA
   949 250-1421

(P-19246)
GRYPHON MARINE LLC
Also Called: Gryphon
694 Moss St (91911-1616)
PHONE..................619 407-4010
Ms. Karlovic, CEO
EMP: 90
SALES (corp-wide): 2.52B Privately Held
Web: www.mantech.com
SIC: 8711 Engineering services
HQ: Gryphon Marine, Llc
   4600 Village Ave Ste 100
   Norfolk VA
   757 763-6666

(P-19247)
HARRIS & ASSOCIATES INC (PA)
Also Called: Harris & Associates Cnstr MGT
1401 Willow Pass Rd Ste 500 (94520)
PHONE..................925 827-4900
Lisa Larrabee, CEO
Carl Harris, *
Guy Erickson, *
Byron Tobey Junior, Sr VP
Vernon Phillips, *
▲ EMP: 104 EST: 1974
SQ FT: 23,000
SALES (est): 55.53MM
SALES (corp-wide): 55.53MM Privately Held
Web: www.weareharris.com
SIC: 8711 8712 Construction and civil engineering; Architectural engineering

(P-19248)
HENKEL US OPERATIONS CORP
Also Called: Aerospace Material Division
2850 Willow Pass Rd (94565-3237)
P.O. Box 312 (94565-0031)
PHONE..................925 458-8086
EMP: 170
SQ FT: 6,325
SALES (corp-wide): 23.26B Privately Held
Web: www.henkel.com
SIC: 8711 Engineering services
HQ: Henkel Us Operations Corporation
   1 Henkel Way
   Rocky Hill CT
   860 571-5100

(P-19249)
HETHERINGTON ENGINEERING (PA)
4333 Apache St (92056-2913)
PHONE..................760 931-1917
Mark Hetherington, Pr
EMP: 227 EST: 1986
SALES (est): 2.56MM
SALES (corp-wide): 2.56MM Privately Held
Web: www.hetheringtonengineering.com
SIC: 8711 Consulting engineer

(P-19250)
HIGHBURY DEFENSE GROUP
2725 Congress St Ste 1m (92110-2766)
PHONE..................619 316-7979
Andrew Nugent, CEO
EMP: 76 EST: 2012
SALES (est): 4.7MM Privately Held
Web: www.highbury-defense.com
SIC: 8711 7382 Engineering services; Security systems services

(P-19251)
HII FLEET SUPPORT GROUP LLC
131 W 33rd St Ste 100a (91950-7266)
PHONE..................619 474-8820
Suliman Haidar, Mgr
EMP: 180
SIC: 8711 Engineering services
HQ: Hii Fleet Support Group Llc
   5701 Cleveland St
   Virginia Beach VA
   757 463-6666

(P-19252)
HMS CONSTRUCTION INC (PA)
Also Called: HMS
2885 Scott St (92081-8547)
PHONE..................760 727-9808
Michael High, Pr
Ian High, *
Sharon High, *
Carla Sims, *
EMP: 75 EST: 1996
SQ FT: 5,200
SALES (est): 40.22MM
SALES (corp-wide): 40.22MM Privately Held
Web: www.hmsconco.com
SIC: 8711 1781 1731 Engineering services; Geothermal drilling; Electrical work

(P-19253)
HNTB CORPORATION
401 B St Ste 510 (92101-4285)
PHONE..................619 684-6586
Joanne Manthey, Brnch Mgr
EMP: 86
SALES (corp-wide): 1.53B Privately Held
Web: www.hntb.com
SIC: 8711 Consulting engineer
HQ: Hntb Corporation
   715 Kirk Dr
   Kansas City MO
   816 472-1201

(P-19254)
HNTB CORPORATION
3633 Inland Empire Blvd (91764-4922)
PHONE..................909 727-5600
Craig Denson, Brnch Mgr
EMP: 83
SALES (corp-wide): 1.53B Privately Held
Web: www.hntb.com
SIC: 8711 Consulting engineer
HQ: Hntb Corporation
   715 Kirk Dr
   Kansas City MO
   816 472-1201

8711 - Engineering Services (P-19255)

(P-19255)
HNTB CORPORATION
1732 N 1st St Ste 400 (95112-4538)
PHONE.................................408 451-7300
Steve Whitaker, *Brnch Mgr*
EMP: 103
SALES (corp-wide): 1.53B **Privately Held**
Web: www.hntb.com
SIC: 8711 Consulting engineer
HQ: Hntb Corporation
 715 Kirk Dr
 Kansas City MO
 816 472-1201

(P-19256)
HNTB CORPORATION
6 Hutton Centre Dr Ste 500 (92707)
PHONE.................................714 460-1600
Andres Ocon, *Brnch Mgr*
EMP: 116
SALES (corp-wide): 1.53B **Privately Held**
Web: www.hntb.com
SIC: 8711 Consulting engineer
HQ: Hntb Corporation
 715 Kirk Dr
 Kansas City MO
 816 472-1201

(P-19257)
HNTB CORPORATION
2101 Webster St (94612-3267)
PHONE.................................510 208-4599
Steve Whitaker, *Mgr*
EMP: 139
SALES (corp-wide): 1.53B **Privately Held**
Web: www.hntb.com
SIC: 8711 Consulting engineer
HQ: Hntb Corporation
 715 Kirk Dr
 Kansas City MO
 816 472-1201

(P-19258)
HNTB GERWICK WATER SOLUTIONS
200 Sandpointe Ave (92707-5751)
PHONE.................................714 460-1600
EMP: 150
SALES (est): 3.78MM **Privately Held**
SIC: 8711 8712 Consulting engineer; Architectural services

(P-19259)
HOLMES & NARVER INC (HQ)
999 W Town And Country Rd (92868-4713)
P.O. Box 6240 (92863-6240)
PHONE.................................714 567-2400
Danny Seal, *CEO*
Raymond Landy, *
Dennis Deslatte, *
Tina Clugston, *
EMP: 250 **EST:** 1933
SQ FT: 100,000
SALES (est): 24.57MM
SALES (corp-wide): 13.15B **Publicly Held**
SIC: 8711 8742 8741 1542 Engineering services; Training and development consultant; Construction management; Nonresidential construction, nec
PA: Aecom
 13355 Noel Rd Ste 400
 Dallas TX
 972 788-1000

(P-19260)
HSA & ASSOCIATES INC
1906 W Garvey Ave S Ste 200
(91790-2652)
PHONE.................................626 521-9931
EMP: 66 **EST:** 2019
SALES (est): 5.64MM **Privately Held**
Web: www.hsaassociates.com
SIC: 8711 Consulting engineer

(P-19261)
HUNSAKER & ASSOC IRVINE INC
2900 Adams St Ste A15 (92504-4337)
PHONE.................................951 352-7200
Brad Hay, *Brnch Mgr*
EMP: 300
SALES (corp-wide): 54.08MM **Privately Held**
Web: www.hnagi.com
SIC: 8711 Civil engineering
PA: Hunsaker & Associates Irvine, Inc.
 3 Hughes
 Irvine CA
 949 583-1010

(P-19262)
HUNSAKER & ASSOC IRVINE INC (PA)
Also Called: Hunsaker & Associates
3 Hughes (92618-2021)
PHONE.................................949 583-1010
Richard Hunsaker, *CEO*
Douglas Snyder, *
Kamal Karam, *
Doug Staley, *
EMP: 100 **EST:** 1976
SQ FT: 27,000
SALES (est): 54.08MM
SALES (corp-wide): 54.08MM **Privately Held**
Web: www.hnagi.com
SIC: 8711 8713 Civil engineering; Surveying services

(P-19263)
HYUNDAI AMER TECHNICAL CTR INC
Also Called: Kia Design Center America
101 Peters Canyon Rd (92606-1790)
PHONE.................................734 337-2500
EMP: 113
Web: www.hatci.com
SIC: 8711 8734 Designing; ship, boat, machine, and product; Automobile proving and testing ground
HQ: Hyundai America Technical Center Incorporated
 6800 Geddes Rd
 Ypsilanti MI
 734 337-2500

(P-19264)
IMEG CONSULTANTS CORP
222 S Harbor Blvd Ste 800 (92805-3715)
PHONE.................................714 490-5555
Albert Chiu, *Brnch Mgr*
EMP: 63
SALES (corp-wide): 141.33MM **Privately Held**
Web: www.imegcorp.com
SIC: 8711 Consulting engineer
PA: Imeg Consultants Corp.
 623 26th Ave
 Rock Island IL
 309 788-0673

(P-19265)
INDUS TECHNOLOGY INC
2243 San Diego Ave Ste 200 (92110-2069)
PHONE.................................619 299-2555
James B Lasswell, *Pr*
Will Nevilles, *
Eric Macgregor, *
Jan Perez, *
Rebecca Spane, *
EMP: 230 **EST:** 1991
SQ FT: 12,000
SALES (est): 49.51MM **Privately Held**
Web: www.industechnology.com
SIC: 8711 Engineering services

(P-19266)
INDUSTRIAL AUTOMTN GROUP LLC
Also Called: Automation Group
4400 Sisk Rd (95356-8729)
PHONE.................................209 579-7527
Brad Stegmann, *CEO*
Brad Stegmann, *Pr*
EMP: 75 **EST:** 2012
SALES (est): 15.39MM **Privately Held**
Web: www.automationgroup.com
SIC: 8711 Mechanical engineering

(P-19267)
INFRASTRUCTURE ENGRG CORP
301 Mission Ave Ste 202 (92054-2591)
PHONE.................................760 529-0795
Preston Lewis, *Brnch Mgr*
EMP: 61
SALES (corp-wide): 109.75MM **Privately Held**
Web: www.ardurra.com
SIC: 8711 Consulting engineer
HQ: Infrastructure Engineering Corporation
 14271 Danielson St
 Poway CA
 858 413-2400

(P-19268)
INGENIUM TECHNOLOGIES CORP
5665 Oberlin Dr Ste 202 (92121-1739)
PHONE.................................858 227-4422
Duane Wingate, *Prin*
EMP: 79
SALES (corp-wide): 18.73MM **Privately Held**
Web: www.ingeniumtech.com
SIC: 8711 Consulting engineer
PA: Ingenium Technologies Corp.
 4216 Maray Dr
 Rockford IL
 815 399-8803

(P-19269)
INNOVATIVE ENGRG SYSTEMS INC (PA)
Also Called: Ies Engineering
8800 Crippen St (93311-9686)
P.O. Box 20610 (93390-0610)
PHONE.................................661 381-7800
David Wolfer, *Pr*
EMP: 100 **EST:** 2002
SQ FT: 20,000
SALES (est): 26.33MM **Privately Held**
Web: www.agilitechgroup.com
SIC: 8711 1731 Consulting engineer; Electrical work

(P-19270)
INSPIRIA INC (PA)
Also Called: Audiovisions
140 Technology Dr Ste 100 (92618-2427)
PHONE.................................949 206-0606
Mark Hoffenberg, *Pr*
Bob Walpert, *
Ted Taylor, *General Vice President*
EMP: 64 **EST:** 1989
SALES (est): 24.57MM **Privately Held**
SIC: 8711 Electrical or electronic engineering

(P-19271)
INTERNATIONAL ENERGY SERVICES USA INC
Also Called: International Energy Svcs Co
3445 Kashiwa St (90505-4024)
PHONE.................................310 257-8222
EMP: 200
SIC: 8711 Engineering services

(P-19272)
IQA SOLUTIONS INC
4089 E Conant St (90808-1777)
PHONE.................................562 420-1000
Mohsem H Hashemi, *CEO*
Andrew Stasio, *
EMP: 62 **EST:** 2003
SQ FT: 8,500
SALES (est): 14.14MM **Privately Held**
Web: www.iqasolutions.com
SIC: 8711 Consulting engineer

(P-19273)
J D PASQUETTI ENGINEERING
Also Called: JD Pasquetti Engineering
3032 Thunder Valley Ct Ste 200
(95648-9395)
PHONE.................................916 543-9401
Jason Pasquetti, *CEO*
EMP: 70 **EST:** 2006
SALES (est): 11.33MM **Privately Held**
Web: www.jdpasquetti.com
SIC: 8711 Engineering services

(P-19274)
JACOBS ATCS FEMA A JOINT VENTR
155 N Lake Ave Fl 5 (91101-1849)
PHONE.................................571 218-1115
Ed Pogreba, *Prin*
EMP: 99 **EST:** 2017
SALES (est): 1.53MM **Privately Held**
SIC: 8711 8712 8748 8741 Consulting engineer; Architectural services; Business consulting, nec; Management services

(P-19275)
JACOBS CIVIL INC
1500 Hughes Way Ste B400 (90810-1882)
PHONE.................................310 847-2500
EMP: 229
SALES (corp-wide): 14.92B **Publicly Held**
SIC: 8711 Consulting engineer
HQ: Jacobs Civil Inc.
 501 N Broadway
 Saint Louis MO

(P-19276)
JACOBS ENGINEERING COMPANY
1111 S Arroyo Pkwy (91105-3254)
P.O. Box 7084 (91109-7084)
PHONE.................................626 449-2171
EMP: 4000 **EST:** 1979
SALES (est): 42.54MM
SALES (corp-wide): 14.09B **Publicly Held**
SIC: 8711 1629 Engineering services; Chemical plant and refinery construction
HQ: Jacobs Engineering Group Inc.
 1999 Bryan St Ste 1200
 Dallas TX
 214 583-8500

(P-19277)
JACOBS ENGINEERING GROUP INC
2600 Michelson Dr Ste 500 (92612-6506)
PHONE.................................949 224-7500
Dan Grubb, *Brnch Mgr*

PRODUCTS & SERVICES SECTION
8711 - Engineering Services (P-19297)

EMP: 88
SALES (corp-wide): 14.92B **Publicly Held**
Web: www.jacobs.com
SIC: 8711 Consulting engineer
HQ: Jacobs Engineering Group Inc.
1999 Bryan St Ste 3500
Dallas TX
214 583-8500

(P-19278)
JACOBS ENGINEERING GROUP INC
1737 N 1st St Ste 300 (95112-4585)
PHONE.................408 436-4936
EMP: 88
SALES (corp-wide): 12.74B **Publicly Held**
SIC: 8711 Consulting engineer
PA: Jacobs Engineering Group Inc.
1999 Bryan St Ste 1200
Dallas TX
214 583-8500

(P-19279)
JACOBS ENGINEERING GROUP INC
1111 S Arroyo Pkwy (91105-3254)
P.O. Box 7084 (91109-7084)
PHONE.................626 578-3300
EMP: 89
SALES (corp-wide): 14.92B **Publicly Held**
Web: www.jacobs.com
SIC: 8711 Consulting engineer
HQ: Jacobs Engineering Group Inc.
1999 Bryan St Ste 3500
Dallas TX
214 583-8500

(P-19280)
JACOBS ENGINEERING INC (DH)
155 N Lake Ave (91101-1849)
P.O. Box 7084 (91109-7084)
PHONE.................626 578-3300
Craig L Martin, *CEO*
Noel G Watson, *
EMP: 161 **EST:** 1971
SALES (est): 110.24MM
SALES (corp-wide): 14.92B **Publicly Held**
Web: www.jacobs.com
SIC: 8711 Consulting engineer
HQ: Jacobs Engineering Group Inc.
1999 Bryan St Ste 3500
Dallas TX
214 583-8500

(P-19281)
JACOBS GOVERNMENT SERVICES CO
2600 Michelson Dr Ste 500 (92612-6506)
PHONE.................949 224-7500
Issam Khalaf, *VP*
EMP: 230
SALES (corp-wide): 14.92B **Publicly Held**
Web: www.jacobs.com
SIC: 8711 Engineering services
HQ: Jacobs Government Services Company
155 N Lake Ave Ste 150
Pasadena CA

(P-19282)
JACOBS INTERNATIONAL LTD INC
155 N Lake Ave Ste 800 (91101-1857)
P.O. Box 7084 (91109-7084)
PHONE.................626 578-3300
Craig Martin, *Pr*
Jeff Sanders, *
John W Prosser Junior, *Treas*
EMP: 300 **EST:** 2002

SQ FT: 120,000
SALES (est): 71.22MM
SALES (corp-wide): 14.92B **Publicly Held**
SIC: 8711 Consulting engineer
HQ: Jacobs Engineering Group Inc.
1999 Bryan St Ste 3500
Dallas TX
214 583-8500

(P-19283)
JACOBS PROJECT MANAGEMENT CO
4 Embarcadero Ctr Ste 3800 (94111-4106)
PHONE.................949 224-7908
David Roberts, *Prod Manager*
EMP: 61
SALES (corp-wide): 14.92B **Publicly Held**
Web: www.jacobs.com
SIC: 8711 8712 8748 8742 Consulting engineer; Architectural services; Business consulting, nec; Construction project management consultant
HQ: Jacobs Project Management Co.
501 N Broadway Ste 185
Saint Louis MO

(P-19284)
JACOBS PROJECT MANAGEMENT CO
2600 Michelson Dr Ste 500 (92612-6506)
PHONE.................949 224-7695
Les Steinberger, *Mgr*
Frank Joyce, *
EMP: 99 **EST:** 2008
SALES (est): 4.45MM
SALES (corp-wide): 14.92B **Publicly Held**
SIC: 8711 Consulting engineer
HQ: Jacobs Engineering Group Inc.
1999 Bryan St Ste 3500
Dallas TX
214 583-8500

(P-19285)
JACOBS TECHNOLOGY INC
Building 227 Room 117a (94035)
P.O. Box 336 (94035-0336)
PHONE.................650 604-3784
Michael D Weiss, *Mgr*
EMP: 121
SALES (corp-wide): 14.92B **Publicly Held**
Web: www.jacobstechnology.com
SIC: 8711 Aviation and/or aeronautical engineering
HQ: Jacobs Technology Inc.
600 William Northern Blvd
Tullahoma TN
931 455-6400

(P-19286)
JBA CONSULTING ENGINEERS INC
163 Technology Dr Ste 100 (92618-2486)
PHONE.................949 419-3030
Ed Butera, *Mgr*
EMP: 60
SALES (corp-wide): 786.78MM **Publicly Held**
Web: www.nv5.com
SIC: 8711 Mechanical engineering
HQ: J.B.A. Consulting Engineers, Inc.
5155 W Patrick Ln
Las Vegas NV
702 362-9200

(P-19287)
JOHN A MARTIN & ASSOCIATES INC
950 S Grand Ave Ste 400 (90015-1422)
PHONE.................213 483-6490

Kurt Clandening, *Pr*
EMP: 68 **EST:** 1985
SALES (est): 12.48MM **Privately Held**
Web: www.johnmartin.com
SIC: 8711 Consulting engineer

(P-19288)
JSL TECHNOLOGIES INC
1451 N Rice Ave Ste A (93030-7991)
PHONE.................805 985-7700
Joseph T Black Iii, *Pr*
Ben Fujikawa, *
Jed Williams, *
EMP: 305 **EST:** 2008
SQ FT: 22,155
SALES (est): 28MM **Privately Held**
Web: www.jsltechinc.com
SIC: 8711 Consulting engineer

(P-19289)
JT3 LLC
190 S Wolfe Ave Bldg 1260 (93524-6501)
PHONE.................661 277-4900
James Tedeschi, *Mgr*
EMP: 1340
SALES (corp-wide): 150MM **Privately Held**
SIC: 8711 Engineering services
PA: Jt3, L.L.C.
821 Grier Dr
Las Vegas NV
704 492-2181

(P-19290)
K&B ELECTRIC LLC
Also Called: K&B Engineering
290 Corporate Terrace Cir Ste 200 (92879-6033)
PHONE.................951 808-9501
Sandee Gibbs, *Managing Member*
Trey Gibbs, *
EMP: 158 **EST:** 2011
SALES (est): 3.77MM **Privately Held**
Web: www.kbeng.net
SIC: 8711 Engineering services

(P-19291)
K&B ENGINEERING
290 Corporate Terrace Cir Ste 200 (92879-6033)
PHONE.................951 808-9501
Trey Gibbs, *Owner*
EMP: 200 **EST:** 2007
SALES (est): 24.61MM **Privately Held**
Web: www.kbeng.net
SIC: 8711 Consulting engineer

(P-19292)
KAGA FEI AMERICA INC (DH)
Also Called: F E A
2349 Bering Dr (95131-1125)
▲ **EMP:** 84 **EST:** 2001
SQ FT: 49,000
SALES (est): 25.75MM **Privately Held**
SIC: 8711 5065 Engineering services; Electronic parts and equipment, nec
HQ: Kaga Fei Co. Ltd.
2-100-45, Shinyokohama, Kohoku-Ku
Yokohama KNG

(P-19293)
KENNEDY/JENKS CONSULTANTS INC (PA)
Also Called: Kennedy Jenks
303 2nd St Ste 300s (94107-3632)
PHONE.................415 243-2150
Gary Carlton, *Ch*
Keith A London, *
Patrick J Courtney, *
Lynn Takaichi, *

Anthony Brown, *
EMP: 100 **EST:** 1919
SQ FT: 45,000
SALES (est): 82.42MM
SALES (corp-wide): 82.42MM **Privately Held**
Web: www.kennedyjenks.com
SIC: 8711 Consulting engineer

(P-19294)
KLEINFELDER INC (HQ)
Also Called: Kleinfelder
770 1st Ave Ste 400 (92101-6171)
P.O. Box 51958 (90051-6258)
PHONE.................619 831-4600
John Murphy, *CFO*
Deborah Butera, *
Carl Lowman, *
Daniel Brockman, *
Lisa Millet, *Central Division*
EMP: 160 **EST:** 1962
SQ FT: 5,000
SALES (est): 249.41MM
SALES (corp-wide): 458.93MM **Privately Held**
Web: www.kleinfelder.com
SIC: 8711 8712 Consulting engineer; Architectural engineering
PA: The Kleinfelder Group Inc
770 1st Ave Ste 400
San Diego CA
619 831-4600

(P-19295)
KLEINFELDER INC
Also Called: Ganda
63 Hermit Ln (94904-2514)
PHONE.................415 458-5803
Louis Armstrong, *Brnch Mgr*
EMP: 175
SALES (corp-wide): 458.93MM **Privately Held**
Web: www.kleinfelder.com
SIC: 8711 Consulting engineer
HQ: Kleinfelder, Inc.
770 1st Ave Ste 400
San Diego CA
619 831-4600

(P-19296)
KLEINFELDER ASSOCIATES
550 W C St Ste 1200 (92101-3532)
PHONE.................619 831-4600
George J Pierson, *Pr*
Russ Carey, *
John Pilkington, *
Bart Patton, *
Larry Peterson, *
EMP: 99 **EST:** 1985
SALES (est): 15.66MM
SALES (corp-wide): 458.93MM **Privately Held**
Web: www.kleinfelder.com
SIC: 8711 Consulting engineer
PA: The Kleinfelder Group Inc
770 1st Ave Ste 400
San Diego CA
619 831-4600

(P-19297)
KLEINFELDER GROUP INC (PA)
770 1st Ave Ste 400 (92101-6171)
PHONE.................619 831-4600
Louis Armstrong, *Pr*
Lisa Millet, *Ex VP*
Jeff Hill, *Dist Vice President*
Ann Masey, *Prin*
Erik Soderquist, *Ex VP*
EMP: 175 **EST:** 1985
SALES (est): 458.93MM
SALES (corp-wide): 458.93MM **Privately Held**

8711 - Engineering Services (P-19298)

Web: www.kleinfelder.com
SIC: 8711 Consulting engineer

(P-19298)
KODIAK ROBOTICS INC
1049 Terra Bella Ave (94043-1829)
PHONE.................................781 626-2729
Paz Eshel, *Pr*
EMP: 80 EST: 2018
SALES (est): 11.09MM **Privately Held**
Web: www.kodiak.ai
SIC: 8711 Engineering services

(P-19299)
KPFF INC
K P F F Consulting Engineers
18500 Von Karman Ave Ste 1000 (92612-0527)
PHONE.................................949 252-1022
Roger Young, *Prin*
EMP: 87
SALES (corp-wide): 108.51MM **Privately Held**
Web: www.kpff.com
SIC: 8711 Consulting engineer
PA: Kpff, Inc.
    1601 5th Ave Ste 1300
    Seattle WA
    206 225-2980

(P-19300)
KPFF INC
Also Called: Kpff Consulting Engineers
45 Fremont St Fl 28 (94105-2209)
PHONE.................................415 989-1004
Marc Press, *Mgr*
EMP: 96
SALES (corp-wide): 108.51MM **Privately Held**
Web: www.kpff.com
SIC: 8711 Consulting engineer
PA: Kpff, Inc.
    1601 5th Ave Ste 1300
    Seattle WA
    206 225-2980

(P-19301)
KRATOS TECH TRNING SLTIONS INC (HQ)
10680 Treena St Ste 600 (92131-2433)
PHONE.................................858 812-7300
Eric M Demarco, *Pr*
Deanna H Lund, *Ex VP*
Laura L Siegal, *Corporate Controller**
Deborah S Butera, *Sec*
Phil Carrai, *VP Opers*
EMP: 94 EST: 1966
SQ FT: 25,000
SALES (est): 121.41MM **Publicly Held**
Web: www.kratosdefense.com
SIC: 8711 Engineering services
PA: Kratos Defense & Security Solutions, Inc.
    10680 Treena St Ste 600
    San Diego CA

(P-19302)
KRATOS UNMNNED ARIAL SYSTEMS I (HQ)
5381 Raley Blvd (95838-1701)
PHONE.................................916 431-7977
Eric M Demarco, *CEO*
Amy Fournier, **
Michel M Fournier, **
▲ EMP: 227 EST: 1963
SQ FT: 60,000
SALES (est): 96.36MM **Publicly Held**
Web: www.kratosdefense.com
SIC: 8711 3761 Engineering services; Guided missiles and space vehicles

PA: Kratos Defense & Security Solutions, Inc.
    10680 Treena St Ste 600
    San Diego CA

(P-19303)
L3 MARIPRO INC
1522 Cook Pl (93117-3124)
PHONE.................................805 683-3881
EMP: 90
SIC: 8711 Marine engineering

(P-19304)
LASH CONSTRUCTION INC
721 Carpinteria St (93103-3623)
P.O. Box 4640 (93140-4640)
PHONE.................................805 963-3553
EMP: 99 EST: 1978
SALES (est): 4.44MM **Privately Held**
Web: www.lashconstruction.com
SIC: 8711 1623 Engineering services; Underground utilities contractor

(P-19305)
LEA & BRAZE ENGINEERING INC (PA)
2495 Industrial Pkwy W (94545-5007)
PHONE.................................510 887-4086
Gregory F Braze, *Pr*
Jeffrey C Lea, **
EMP: 83 EST: 1984
SALES (est): 15.85MM
SALES (corp-wide): 15.85MM **Privately Held**
Web: www.leabraze.com
SIC: 8711 8713 Civil engineering; Surveying services

(P-19306)
LINQUEST CORPORATION (PA)
5140 W Goldleaf Cir Ste 400 (90056-1299)
PHONE.................................323 924-1600
Timothy Dills, *Pr*
Matthew Klein, **
Greg Young, **
Douglas Manya, **
Richard Martin, *CIO**
EMP: 200 EST: 2003
SQ FT: 20,000
SALES (est): 116.91MM
SALES (corp-wide): 116.91MM **Privately Held**
Web: www.linquest.com
SIC: 8711 Aviation and/or aeronautical engineering

(P-19307)
LOCKHEED MARTIN SERVICES LLC
Also Called: Lockheed Martin
645 Marsat Ct Ste D (91911-7141)
PHONE.................................619 271-9831
EMP: 440
SIC: 8711 Engineering services
HQ: Lockheed Martin Services, Llc
    700 N Frederick Ave
    Gaithersburg MD

(P-19308)
LOPEZGARCIA GROUP INC (DH)
300 California St (94104-1407)
PHONE.................................415 796-8100
Rudy M Garcia, *Pr*
Wendy A Lopez, **
Devarati Rastogi, **
Douglas C Mikeworth, *Stockholder**
Jerry D Smiley, *Stockholder**
▲ EMP: 148 EST: 1988
SQ FT: 40,345
SALES (est): 20.56MM
SALES (corp-wide): 13.15B **Publicly Held**
SIC: 8711 8713 8741 8748 Consulting engineer; Surveying services; Management services; Environmental consultant
HQ: Aecom Global Ii, Llc
    300 S Grand Ave Ste 900
    Los Angeles CA
    213 593-8100

(P-19309)
LOS ANGELES ENGINEERING INC
633 N Barranca Ave (91723-1229)
PHONE.................................626 869-1400
Henry Angus O'brien, *Pr*
Henry Angus O'brien, *Pr*
Aaron O'brien, *VP*
Beth Ballard, **
Melody Turner, **
EMP: 110 EST: 1987
SQ FT: 33,000
SALES (est): 47.57MM **Privately Held**
Web: www.laeng.net
SIC: 8711 1622 Construction and civil engineering; Bridge, tunnel, and elevated highway construction

(P-19310)
LUND CONSTRUCTION CO
5302 Roseville Rd (95660-5000)
PHONE.................................916 344-5800
Jerry A Lund, *Ch Bd*
Jerry A Lund, *Pr*
Kevin Lund, **
Jeff Lund, **
Alta M Lund, **
EMP: 155 EST: 1959
SQ FT: 7,500
SALES (est): 70.69MM **Privately Held**
Web: www.lundconst.com
SIC: 8711 1794 1623 4212 Construction and civil engineering; Excavation and grading, building construction; Underground utilities contractor; Hazardous waste transport

(P-19311)
MACAULAY BROWN INC
Also Called: Macb
2933 Bunker Hill Ln Ste 220 (95054-1124)
PHONE.................................937 426-3421
EMP: 1500 EST: 2011
SALES (est): 35.73MM **Privately Held**
SIC: 8711 Consulting engineer

(P-19312)
MACKAY SMPS CVIL ENGINEERS INC (PA)
5142 Franklin Dr Ste C (94588-3355)
PHONE.................................925 416-1790
James C Ray, *Pr*
Bob Chan, **
John F Kuzia, **
EMP: 62 EST: 1953
SALES (est): 10.9MM
SALES (corp-wide): 10.9MM **Privately Held**
Web: www.msce.com
SIC: 8711 Civil engineering

(P-19313)
MALEMA
2329 Zanker Rd (95131-1109)
PHONE.................................408 970-3419
EMP: 67 EST: 2015
SALES (est): 827.12K
SALES (corp-wide): 8.51B **Publicly Held**
Web: www.malema.com
SIC: 8711 Engineering services
HQ: Malema Engineering Corporation
    1060 S Rogers Cir
    Boca Raton FL
    561 995-0595

(P-19314)
MANGAN INC (PA)
3901 Via Oro Ave (90810-1800)
PHONE.................................310 835-8080
Richard D Mangan, *Ch Bd*
Richard D Mangan, *Prin*
Russell Seward, **
Amin Solehjou, **
Christopher Lopez, **
EMP: 90 EST: 1991
SQ FT: 15,000
SALES (est): 50.72MM **Privately Held**
Web: www.manganinc.com
SIC: 8711 Consulting engineer

(P-19315)
MARQUES GEN ENGRG INC A CAL CO
7225 26th St (95673-1814)
PHONE.................................916 923-3434
Jeremy Jaeger, *CEO*
EMP: 350 EST: 1999
SQ FT: 2,000
SALES (est): 200MM **Privately Held**
Web: www.marquespipeline.com
SIC: 8711 Engineering services

(P-19316)
MARTIN ASSOCIATES GROUP INC (PA)
Also Called: Martin, John A & Associates
950 S Grand Ave Fl 4 (90015-1422)
PHONE.................................213 483-6490
John A Martin Junior, *CEO*
Barry Schindler, **
EMP: 63 EST: 1961
SQ FT: 70,000
SALES (est): 84.18MM
SALES (corp-wide): 84.18MM **Privately Held**
Web: www.johnmartin.com
SIC: 8711 Consulting engineer

(P-19317)
MARVIN ENGINEERING CO INC (PA)
Also Called: Marvin Group, The
261 W Beach Ave (90302-2904)
PHONE.................................310 674-5030
Howard Gussman, *CEO*
Ariel Lechter, **
Craig Snaguski, **
▲ EMP: 580 EST: 1963
SQ FT: 300,000
SALES (est): 149.54MM
SALES (corp-wide): 149.54MM **Privately Held**
Web: www.marvingroup.com
SIC: 8711 Consulting engineer

(P-19318)
MAXAR SPACE ROBOTICS LLC
1250 Lincoln Ave Ste 100 (91103-2466)
PHONE.................................626 296-1373
EMP: 65
SALES (corp-wide): 1.6B **Privately Held**
Web: www.maxar.com
SIC: 8711 8731 Aviation and/or aeronautical engineering; Commercial physical research
HQ: Maxar Space Robotics Llc
    1250 Lincoln Ave Ste 100
    Pasadena CA
    626 296-1373

PRODUCTS & SERVICES SECTION

8711 - Engineering Services (P-19340)

(P-19319)
MDS CONSULTING (PA)
17320 Red Hill Ave Ste 350 (92614-5644)
PHONE..............................949 251-8821
Stanley C Morse, *Ch*
Stanley C Morse, *Owner*
Jerry R Schultz, *
EMP: 71 **EST:** 1976
SQ FT: 8,837
SALES (est): 4.58MM
SALES (corp-wide): 4.58MM **Privately Held**
Web: www.mdsconsulting.net
SIC: 8711 Civil engineering

(P-19320)
MESA ASSOCIATES INC
3670 W Temple Ave Ste 152 (91768-2588)
PHONE..............................909 979-6609
Brad Hoy, *Brnch Mgr*
EMP: 67
Web: www.mesainc.com
SIC: 8711 8712 Consulting engineer; Architectural services
PA: Mesa Associates, Inc.
480 Production Ave
Madison AL

(P-19321)
MICHAEL BAKER INTERNATIONAL INC (DH)
5 Hutton Centre Dr Ste 500 (92707)
Rural Route 57057 (92619)
PHONE..............................949 472-3505
EMP: 350 **EST:** 1944
SALES (est): 48.71MM
SALES (corp-wide): 1.03B **Privately Held**
Web: www.mbakerintl.com
SIC: 8711 8713 Civil engineering; Surveying services
HQ: Michael Baker International Holdco Corporation
100 Airside Dr
Moon Township PA
412 269-6300

(P-19322)
MILLERICK ENGINEERING INC
735 E Main St (95380-4521)
P.O. Box 3338 (95381-3338)
PHONE..............................209 664-9111
Chris Millerick, *Pr*
Ciara Millerick, *Stockholder*
Jogre B Suasin, *
EMP: 70 **EST:** 1997
SALES (est): 7.17MM **Privately Held**
Web: www.millerickeng.com
SIC: 8711 Industrial engineers

(P-19323)
MKA INTERNATIONAL INC
Also Called: Construction Consulting Svcs
100 Pringle Ave Ste 340 (94596-3512)
PHONE..............................925 934-3235
Michael Bischof, *Prin*
EMP: 185 **EST:** 1987
SALES (est): 2.02MM **Privately Held**
Web: www.mkainc.com
SIC: 8711 Engineering services

(P-19324)
MNS ENGINEERS INC (PA)
201 N Calle Cesar Chavez Ste 300 (93103-3256)
PHONE..............................805 692-6921
James A Salvito, *CEO*
Mark E Reinhardt, *
Gregory A Chelini, *
Jeffrey L Edwards, *
Shawn M Kowalewski, *
EMP: 94 **EST:** 1962
SQ FT: 7,000
SALES (est): 26.35MM
SALES (corp-wide): 26.35MM **Privately Held**
Web: www.mnsengineers.com
SIC: 8711 8713 Civil engineering; Surveying services

(P-19325)
MOBILENET SERVICES INC (PA)
18 Morgan Ste 200 (92618-2074)
PHONE..............................949 951-4444
Richard Grant, *Pr*
Eugene Powell, *
Edward Krol, *
Lorenzo Mills, *
Rodelio Santos, *
EMP: 180 **EST:** 2002
SQ FT: 17,500
SALES (est): 38.03MM
SALES (corp-wide): 38.03MM **Privately Held**
Web: www.mobilenet.net
SIC: 8711 4813 Engineering services; Telephone communication, except radio

(P-19326)
MOFFATT & NICHOL
Also Called: Moffatt & Nichol
555 Anton Blvd Ste 400 (92626-7667)
PHONE..............................657 261-2699
Eric Nichol, *CEO*
EMP: 70
SALES (corp-wide): 126.34MM **Privately Held**
Web: www.moffattnichol.com
SIC: 8711 Structural engineering
PA: Eric Nichol
4225 E Conant St Ste 101
Long Beach CA
562 590-6500

(P-19327)
MORTON & PITALO INC (PA)
600 Coolidge Dr Ste 140 (95630-4211)
PHONE..............................916 984-7621
Eddie Kho, *Pr*
Gregory J Bardini, *
Christopher J Gorges, *
EMP: 64 **EST:** 1977
SALES (est): 9.27MM
SALES (corp-wide): 9.27MM **Privately Held**
Web: www.mpengr.com
SIC: 8711 Civil engineering

(P-19328)
MOTIV POWER SYSTEMS INC
Also Called: Motiv
330 Hatch Dr (94404-1106)
PHONE..............................650 458-4804
Tim Krauskopf, *CEO*
Prasad Ramakrishnan, *COO*
Kristen Magnuson, *CFO*
EMP: 158 **EST:** 2009
SALES (corp-wide): 11.1MM **Privately Held**
Web: www.motivps.com
SIC: 8711 Engineering services

(P-19329)
MOTIVO ENGINEERING LLC (PA)
17700 S Figueroa St (90248-4207)
PHONE..............................844 668-4861
Dean Banks, *
EMP: 69 **EST:** 2010
SALES (est): 10.49MM
SALES (corp-wide): 10.49MM **Privately Held**
Web: www.motivo.com

SIC: 8711 Electrical or electronic engineering

(P-19330)
NATIONAL SECURITY TECH LLC
5520 Ekwill St Ste B (93111-2335)
PHONE..............................805 681-2432
EMP: 493
SALES (corp-wide): 497.8MM **Privately Held**
Web: www.nstec.com
SIC: 8711 1629 Civil engineering; Industrial plant construction
PA: National Security Technologies, Llc
2621 Losee Rd
North Las Vegas NV
702 295-1000

(P-19331)
NATIONAL SECURITY TECH LLC
Also Called: Bechtel
161 S Vasco Rd Ste A (94551-5131)
PHONE..............................925 960-2500
Gary Still, *Brnch Mgr*
EMP: 704
SALES (corp-wide): 497.8MM **Privately Held**
Web: www.nstec.com
SIC: 8711 1629 Civil engineering; Industrial plant construction
PA: National Security Technologies, Llc
2621 Losee Rd
North Las Vegas NV
702 295-1000

(P-19332)
NATIONAL TELECONSULTANTS INC
550 N Brand Blvd Fl 17 (91203-1904)
PHONE..............................818 265-4400
Eliot P Graham, *Managing Member*
Charles C Phelan, *
Peter Adamiak, *
EMP: 108 **EST:** 1981
SQ FT: 35,400
SALES (est): 21.46MM **Privately Held**
Web: www.ntc.com
SIC: 8711 Electrical or electronic engineering

(P-19333)
NAVAL FACILITIES ENGINEER COMM
1220 Pacific Hwy (92132-5101)
PHONE..............................619 532-1158
Shahraam Plaseied, *Prin*
Nancy Wright, *Acctnt*
Captain Darius Banaji, *COO*
EMP: 99 **EST:** 2014
SQ FT: 4,000
SALES (est): 2.46MM **Privately Held**
SIC: 8711 1623 8744 Pollution control engineering; Underground utilities contractor ; Base maintenance (providing personnel on continuing basis)

(P-19334)
NEST PARENT INC
2125 E Katella Ave Ste 250 (92806-6072)
PHONE..............................310 551-0101
Gerald L Parsky, *Pr*
John T Mapes, *
EMP: 1207 **EST:** 2012
SALES (est): 23.1MM **Privately Held**
SIC: 8711 Consulting engineer

(P-19335)
NOVARIANT INC
Also Called: Autofarm
46610 Landing Pkwy (94538-6420)
PHONE..............................510 933-4800

Dave Vaughn, *Pr*
Mike Manning, *Interim Vice President*
EMP: 95 **EST:** 1994
SQ FT: 20,000
SALES (est): 21.78MM **Privately Held**
Web: www.novariant.com
SIC: 8711 Engineering services

(P-19336)
NV5 INC (DH)
Also Called: Nolte Associates
2525 Natomas Park Dr Ste 300 (95833-2927)
PHONE..............................916 641-9100
Dickerson Wright, *CEO*
EMP: 80 **EST:** 1949
SQ FT: 27,000
SALES (est): 40.73MM
SALES (corp-wide): 786.78MM **Publicly Held**
Web: www.nv5.com
SIC: 8711 Civil engineering
HQ: Nv5, Inc
200 S Park Rd Ste 350
Hollywood FL

(P-19337)
NV5 INC
Also Called: Nolte, George S & Associates
15092 Avenue Of Science # 200 (92128-3404)
PHONE..............................858 385-0500
Carmen Kasmer, *Dir*
EMP: 200
SALES (corp-wide): 786.78MM **Publicly Held**
Web: www.nv5.com
SIC: 8711 8713 Civil engineering; Surveying services
HQ: Nv5, Inc.
2525 Natomas Park Dr # 300
Sacramento CA
916 641-9100

(P-19338)
OASIS MATERIALS COMPANY LLC
Also Called: Oasis Precision
4130 Citrus Ave Ste 17 (95677-4006)
PHONE..............................858 842-1338
EMP: 108
SALES (corp-wide): 147.68MM **Privately Held**
Web: www.fralock.com
SIC: 8711 Engineering services
HQ: Oasis Materials Company Llc
12131 Community Rd
Poway CA
858 486-8846

(P-19339)
OASIS SYSTEMS LLC
4125 Market St Ste 12 (93003-5642)
PHONE..............................805 644-2191
EMP: 107
SALES (corp-wide): 98.12MM **Privately Held**
Web: www.oasissystems.com
SIC: 8711 Marine engineering
PA: Oasis Systems, Llc
200 Summit Dr Ste 510
Burlington MA
781 676-7333

(P-19340)
ONCORE MANUFACTURING LLC (HQ)
Also Called: Neo Tech
9340 Owensmouth Ave (91311-6915)
PHONE..............................818 734-6500

8711 - Engineering Services (P-19341)

Sudesh Arora, *Pr*
Laura Siegal, *CFO*
Kunal Sharma, *COO*
David Brakenwagen Csmo, *Prin*
▲ **EMP:** 700 **EST:** 2001
SALES (est): 146.23MM
SALES (corp-wide): 1.43B **Privately Held**
Web: www.neotech.com
SIC: 8711 3672 Electrical or electronic engineering; Printed circuit boards
PA: Natel Engineering Company, Llc
9340 Owensmouth Ave
Chatsworth CA
818 495-8617

(P-19341)
ONE SUN POWER INC
3451 Via Montebello Ste 511 (92009-8492)
PHONE..............................844 360-9600
James Joseph Holmes, *CEO*
EMP: 3231 **EST:** 2017
SALES (est): 37.94MM **Privately Held**
SIC: 8711 Energy conservation engineering

(P-19342)
OPERATING ENGINEERS LOCA
325 Digital Dr (95037-2878)
PHONE..............................408 782-9803
Lisa Kunkel, *Brnch Mgr*
EMP: 127
SALES (corp-wide): 411.32K **Privately Held**
Web: www.oe3.org
SIC: 8711 Engineering services
PA: Operating Engineers Local Union No. 3 Scholarship Foundation
1620 S Loop Rd
Alameda CA
510 748-7400

(P-19343)
OSI ENGINEERING INC
901 Campisi Way Ste 160 (95008-2365)
PHONE..............................408 550-2800
EMP: 120 **EST:** 2010
SALES (est): 10.03MM **Privately Held**
Web: www.osiengineering.com
SIC: 8711 Consulting engineer

(P-19344)
P2S INC
4660 La Jolla Village Dr (92122-4605)
PHONE..............................562 497-2999
EMP: 195
Web: www.p2sinc.com
SIC: 8711 Consulting engineer
PA: P2s Inc.
5000 E Spring St Ste 800
Long Beach CA

(P-19345)
PACE ENGINEERING INC
5155 Venture Pkwy (96002-9034)
PHONE..............................530 244-0202
Paul J Reuter, *Pr*
Fred Lucero, *
EMP: 67 **EST:** 1976
SALES (est): 15.37MM **Privately Held**
Web: www.paceengineering.us
SIC: 8711 8713 Consulting engineer; Surveying services

(P-19346)
PACIFIC ADVNCED CVIL ENGRG INC (PA)
17520 Newhope St Ste 200 (92708-8206)
PHONE..............................714 481-7300
Mark E Krebs, *Pr*
Andy Komor, *
James Matthews, *
Michael Krebs, *
Cory Severson, *
EMP: 73 **EST:** 1987
SQ FT: 18,254
SALES (est): 10.85MM
SALES (corp-wide): 10.85MM **Privately Held**
Web: www.pacewater.com
SIC: 8711 Civil engineering

(P-19347)
PACIFIC HYDROTECH CORPORATION
314 E 3rd St (92570-2225)
PHONE..............................951 943-8803
J Kirk Harns, *Pr*
Sean Finnegan, *
Bobby Owens, *
Joselito Guintu, *
Dale Mckay, *VP*
EMP: 135 **EST:** 1987
SQ FT: 1,500
SALES (est): 65.73MM **Privately Held**
Web: www.pachydro.com
SIC: 8711 Construction and civil engineering

(P-19348)
PACIFICA SERVICES INC
106 S Mentor Ave Ste 200 (91106-2931)
PHONE..............................626 405-0131
Ernest M Camacho, *Pr*
Stephen Caropino, *
EMP: 84 **EST:** 1979
SQ FT: 15,000
SALES (est): 8.55MM **Privately Held**
Web: www.pacificaservices.com
SIC: 8711 7629 8741 Civil engineering; Electronic equipment repair; Construction management

(P-19349)
PAE CONSULTING ENGINEERS INC
444 Spear St (94105-1684)
PHONE..............................503 226-2921
Christian Agulles, *Brnch Mgr*
EMP: 74
SALES (corp-wide): 70.02MM **Privately Held**
Web: www.pae-engineers.com
SIC: 8711 Engineering services
PA: Pae Consulting Engineers, Inc.
151 Sw 1st Ave Ste 300
Portland OR
503 226-2921

(P-19350)
PANASONIC AVIONICS CORPORATION (DH)
3347 Michelson Dr Ste 100 (92612-0661)
PHONE..............................949 672-2000
Kenneth W Sain, *CEO*
Seigo Tada, *
Jessica L Hodkinson, *
▲ **EMP:** 400 **EST:** 1990
SQ FT: 20,000
SALES (est): 925.13MM **Privately Held**
Web: www.panasonic.aero
SIC: 8711 3728 Aviation and/or aeronautical engineering; Aircraft parts and equipment, nec
HQ: Panasonic Corporation Of North America
2 Riverfront Plz Ste 200
Newark NJ
201 348-7000

(P-19351)
PARSONS ENGRG SCIENCE INC (DH)
100 W Walnut St (91103-3696)
P.O. Box 88954 (60695-1954)
PHONE..............................626 440-2000
Charles Harrington, *CEO*
Mary Ann Hopkins, *
Curtis A Bower, *
Nicholas L Presecan, *
Gary L Stone, *
EMP: 500 **EST:** 1946
SALES (est): 494.32MM
SALES (corp-wide): 4.2B **Publicly Held**
Web: www.parsons.com
SIC: 8711 Consulting engineer
HQ: Parsons Government Services Inc.
5875 Trinity Pkwy Ste 230
Centreville VA
703 988-8500

(P-19352)
PARSONS GOVERNMENT SVCS INC
525 B St Ste 1600 (92101-4401)
PHONE..............................619 685-0085
Christopher Bush, *VP*
EMP: 301
SALES (corp-wide): 4.2B **Publicly Held**
Web: www.parsons.com
SIC: 8711 Engineering services
HQ: Parsons Government Services Inc.
5875 Trinity Pkwy Ste 230
Centreville VA
703 988-8500

(P-19353)
PARSONS INTL CAYMAN ISLANDS
100 W Walnut St (91124-0001)
PHONE..............................626 440-6000
William E Hall, *Pr*
EMP: 2000 **EST:** 1994
SALES (est): 29.54MM
SALES (corp-wide): 4.2B **Publicly Held**
Web: www.parsons.com
SIC: 8711 8741 Engineering services; Management services
HQ: Parsons Government Services Inc.
5875 Trinity Pkwy Ste 230
Centreville VA
703 988-8500

(P-19354)
PARSONS SERVICE CORPORATION
100 W Walnut St (91124-0001)
PHONE..............................626 440-2000
Geoge L Ball, *Prin*
EMP: 797 **EST:** 1977
SALES (est): 9.01MM **Privately Held**
Web: www.parsons.com
SIC: 8711 Construction and civil engineering

(P-19355)
PARSONS WTR INFRASTRUCTURE INC
100 W Walnut St (91124-0001)
PHONE..............................626 440-7000
Virginia Grebbien, *CEO*
Anthony F Leketa, *
EMP: 82 **EST:** 2003
SQ FT: 1,220,000
SALES (est): 2.45MM
SALES (corp-wide): 4.2B **Publicly Held**
Web: www.parsons.com
SIC: 8711 Consulting engineer
PA: The Parsons Corporation
5875 Trinity Pkwy Ste 300
Centreville VA
703 988-8500

(P-19356)
PEARL AUTOMATION INC
100 Enterprise Way A101 (95066-3248)
PHONE..............................831 316-5207
EMP: 80 **EST:** 2014
SALES (est): 3.6MM **Privately Held**
SIC: 8711 Electrical or electronic engineering

(P-19357)
PENFIELD & SMITH ENGINEERS INC
Also Called: Penfield & Smith
111 E Victoria St (93101-2072)
P.O. Box 98 (93102-0098)
PHONE..............................805 963-9532
EMP: 80
SIC: 8711 8713 Civil engineering; Surveying services

(P-19358)
PHG ENGINEERING SERVICES LLC
27481 Ganso (92691-3646)
PHONE..............................714 283-8288
EMP: 100 **EST:** 2017
SALES (est): 3.34MM **Privately Held**
SIC: 8711 Engineering services

(P-19359)
PHOENIX ENGINEERING TECH LLC
17117 Leal Ave (90703-1337)
PHONE..............................714 918-0630
Kadambari Ayithi, *
EMP: 65 **EST:** 2017
SALES (est): 1.54MM **Privately Held**
Web: www.phoenixetech.com
SIC: 8711 Engineering services

(P-19360)
PHOTON RESEARCH ASSOCIATES INC
9985 Pacific Heights Blvd Ste 200 (92121)
PHONE..............................858 455-9741
EMP: 187
SIC: 8711 5045 8733 Aviation and/or aeronautical engineering; Computer software; Scientific research agency

(P-19361)
POWER CONSTRUCTORS INC
Also Called: PCI
2934 Gold Pan Ct Ste 4 (95670-6136)
PHONE..............................916 858-8601
Chris Kayne, *Mgr*
EMP: 65
SALES (corp-wide): 2.35MM **Privately Held**
SIC: 8711 1623 1731 Consulting engineer; Water, sewer, and utility lines; Communications specialization
PA: Power Constructors, Inc.
3940 Glenbrook Dr
Hailey ID
208 788-3456

(P-19362)
PRINCIPAL SVC SOLUTIONS INC
4285 Spyres Way Ste B (95356-9270)
PHONE..............................209 408-1982
Timothy Wylie, *Pr*
Gina Wylie, *
Jeff Hamilton, *
Neal Landsburgh, *
EMP: 200 **EST:** 2010

PRODUCTS & SERVICES SECTION

8711 - Engineering Services (P-19385)

SALES (est): 14.3MM **Privately Held**
Web: www.psstechnical.com
SIC: 8711 Engineering services

(P-19363)
PROCESSES UNLIMITED INTERNATIONAL INC
Also Called: Processes Unlimited
5500 Ming Ave Ste 400 (93309-9119)
PHONE.....................661 396-3770
EMP: 330
SIC: 8711 Engineering services

(P-19364)
PROVOST & PRITCHARD ENGINEERING GROUP INC (PA)
Also Called: Provost and Pritchard
286 W Cromwell Ave (93711-6162)
PHONE.....................559 449-2700
EMP: 120 EST: 1968
SALES (est): 25.74MM
SALES (corp-wide): 25.74MM **Privately Held**
Web: www.provostandpritchard.com
SIC: 8711 8713 Civil engineering; Surveying services

(P-19365)
PTEC SOLUTIONS INC (PA)
48633 Warm Springs Blvd (94539-7782)
PHONE.....................510 358-3578
▲ EMP: 167 EST: 2010
SQ FT: 25,000
SALES (est): 23.69MM **Privately Held**
Web: www.ptecsolutions.com
SIC: 8711 3357 3599 3679 Engineering services; Fiber optic cable (insulated); Machine shop, jobbing and repair; Harness assemblies, for electronic use: wire or cable

(P-19366)
PTSI MANAGED SERVICES INC
100 W Walnut St (91124-0001)
PHONE.....................626 440-3118
Mary Ann Hopkins, Pr
EMP: 99 EST: 1983
SALES (est): 4.71MM
SALES (corp-wide): 4.2B **Publicly Held**
Web: www.parsons.com
SIC: 8711 Engineering services
PA: The Parsons Corporation
5875 Trinity Pkwy Ste 300
Centreville VA
703 988-8500

(P-19367)
QLM INC
Also Called: Constuction
94 Umbarger Rd (95111-2021)
P.O. Box 33162 (95031-3162)
PHONE.....................408 265-0904
Darrell Qualls, CEO
Darrell Quails, *
EMP: 150 EST: 1982
SALES (est): 23.4MM **Privately Held**
Web: www.qlm-inc.com
SIC: 8711 1542 0782 1771 Engineering services; Commercial and office building contractors; Landscape contractors; Concrete work

(P-19368)
QUARTUS ENGINEERING INC (PA)
9689 Towne Centre Dr (92121-1964)
PHONE.....................858 875-6000
John Williams, CEO
Mark Stabb, *
Chris Flanigan, *
Doug Botos, *
Jeff Frantz, *
EMP: 159 EST: 1997
SQ FT: 3,100
SALES (est): 36.79MM
SALES (corp-wide): 36.79MM **Privately Held**
Web: www.quartus.com
SIC: 8711 Consulting engineer

(P-19369)
R AND L LOPEZ ASSOCIATES INC (PA)
Also Called: Lopez & Associates Engineers
3649 Tyler Ave (91731-2505)
PHONE.....................626 330-5296
Lourdes P Lopez, Pr
Remberto Lopez, *
EMP: 80 EST: 1979
SQ FT: 2,700
SALES (est): 2.37MM **Privately Held**
SIC: 8711 Consulting engineer

(P-19370)
R JOY INC
Also Called: Richard Joy Engineering
1584 Wolf Meadows Ln (96122-7080)
PHONE.....................530 832-5760
Richard Joy, Owner
EMP: 100 EST: 2009
SALES (est): 3.42MM **Privately Held**
SIC: 8711 Engineering services

(P-19371)
RADIUS PRODUCT DEVELOPMENT INC
6375 San Ignacio Ave (95119-1200)
PHONE.....................408 361-6000
John Van Akkeren, Pr
EMP: 441 EST: 2015
SALES (est): 953.23K
SALES (corp-wide): 34.7B **Publicly Held**
Web: www.radiusinnovation.com
SIC: 8711 7389 8742 Designing: ship, boat, machine, and product; Design services; Marketing consulting services
HQ: Nypro Inc.
101 Union St
Clinton MA
978 365-9721

(P-19372)
RAXIUM INC
1250 Reliance Way (94539-6100)
PHONE.....................510 296-9935
Rick Dodd, CEO
EMP: 70 EST: 2018
SALES (est): 10.11MM
SALES (corp-wide): 282.84B **Publicly Held**
Web: www.raxium.com
SIC: 8711 Engineering services
HQ: Google Llc
1600 Amphitheatre Pkwy
Mountain View CA
650 253-0000

(P-19373)
RAYTHEON SECURE INFORMATION SYSTEMS LLC
Also Called: Raytheon
2000 E El Segundo Blvd (90245-4501)
PHONE.....................310 647-9438
EMP: 226
SIC: 8711 Electrical or electronic engineering

(P-19374)
REY ENGINEERS INC
905 Sutter St Ste 200 (95630-2479)
PHONE.....................916 366-3040
Robert Huun, Pr
EMP: 70 EST: 1998
SALES (est): 11.38MM **Privately Held**
Web: www.reyengineers.com
SIC: 8711 7389 Civil engineering; Photogrammatic mapping

(P-19375)
RIALTO BIOENERGY FACILITY LLC
5780 Fleet St Ste 310 (92008-4700)
PHONE.....................760 436-8870
Arun Sharma, Managing Member
EMP: 250 EST: 2013
SQ FT: 12,937
SALES (est): 22.37MM
SALES (corp-wide): 121.24MM **Privately Held**
Web: www.anaergia.com
SIC: 8711 Energy conservation engineering
PA: Anaergia Inc
4210 South Service Rd
Burlington ON
905 766-3333

(P-19376)
RICHARD BRADY & ASSOCIATES INC
18837 Brookhurst St # 103 (92708-7301)
PHONE.....................657 204-9124
EMP: 65
SALES (corp-wide): 67.13MM **Privately Held**
SIC: 8711 Consulting engineer
PA: Richard Brady & Associates, Inc.
3710 Ruffin Rd
San Diego CA
858 496-0500

(P-19377)
RIPCORD INC
30955 Huntwood Ave (94544-7005)
PHONE.....................408 838-7446
Sam Fahmy, CEO
Ronald Sorisho, *
Ahson Ahmad, Chief Product Officer*
Wasim Khan, CDO*
EMP: 147 EST: 2015
SALES (est): 41.7MM **Privately Held**
Web: www.ripcord.com
SIC: 8711 7374 Engineering services; Data processing and preparation

(P-19378)
ROVE ENGINEERING INC
398 E Aurora Dr (92243-9603)
PHONE.....................760 425-0001
Steven Eugenio, Pr
EMP: 95 EST: 2018
SALES (est): 20.32MM **Privately Held**
SIC: 8711 1611 Engineering services; General contractor, highway and street construction

(P-19379)
SAALEX CORP (PA)
Also Called: Saalex Solutions
811 Camarillo Springs Rd Ste A (93012-9465)
PHONE.....................805 482-1070
Travis Mack, Pr
Elaine Reese, *
Lisa Cortes, *
EMP: 245 EST: 1999
SQ FT: 7,000
SALES (est): 96.07MM
SALES (corp-wide): 96.07MM **Privately Held**
Web: www.saalex.com

SIC: 8711 7379 Consulting engineer; Computer related consulting services

(P-19380)
SABRE SYSTEMS INC
3111 Camino Del Rio N Ste 400 (92108)
PHONE.....................619 528-2226
EMP: 87
Web: www.sabresystems.com
SIC: 8711 Engineering services
PA: Sabre Systems, Inc.
125 County Line Rd # 180
Warminster PA

(P-19381)
SAN DIEGO COMPOSITES INC
9220 Activity Rd Ste 100 (92126-4420)
PHONE.....................858 751-0450
Marc Duvall, CEO
Jeff Murphy, *
EMP: 70 EST: 2003
SQ FT: 70,000
SALES (est): 18.96MM
SALES (corp-wide): 189.21MM **Privately Held**
Web: www.appliedcomposites.com
SIC: 8711 8734 3761 3764 Consulting engineer; Testing laboratories; Guided missiles and space vehicles; Space propulsion units and parts
PA: Applied Composites Holdings, Llc
25692 Atlantic Ocean Dr
Lake Forest CA
949 716-3511

(P-19382)
SAN DIEGO SERVICES LLC
Also Called: Paragon Services Engineering
5415 Oberlin Dr (92121-1716)
PHONE.....................858 654-0102
Rosemary Dymek, Prin
Wesley S Dymek, Prin
EMP: 150 EST: 1999
SQ FT: 2,477
SALES (est): 17.32MM **Privately Held**
Web: paragonservices.us.com
SIC: 8711 Engineering services

(P-19383)
SC WRIGHT CONSTRUCTION INC
3838 Camino Del Rio N Ste 370 (92108)
P.O. Box 3250 (91944-3250)
PHONE.....................619 698-6909
Steven C Wright, Pr
EMP: 400 EST: 1997
SALES (est): 27.86MM **Privately Held**
Web: www.scwright.com
SIC: 8711 Building construction consultant

(P-19384)
SEMICONDUCTOR TOOLING SERVICES LLC
Also Called: Watlow
6781 Via Del Oro (95119-1360)
PHONE.....................408 776-6646
EMP: 85
SIC: 8711 Engineering services

(P-19385)
SERCO INC
9350 Waxie Way Ste 400 (92123-1056)
PHONE.....................858 569-8979
Kent Brown, Brnch Mgr
EMP: 132
SALES (corp-wide): 5.46B **Privately Held**
Web: www.serco.com
SIC: 8711 Engineering services
HQ: Serco Inc.

8711 - Engineering Services (P-19386)

12930 Worldgate Dr # 600
Herndon VA

(P-19386)
SHN CNSLTING ENGNERS GLGSTS IN (PA)
812 W Wabash Ave (95501-2138)
PHONE.................................707 441-8855
Michael Foget, *CEO*
EMP: 60 **EST:** 1979
SQ FT: 14,000
SALES (est): 15.77MM
SALES (corp-wide): 15.77MM **Privately Held**
Web: www.shn-engr.com
SIC: 8711 8999 Consulting engineer; Geological consultant

(P-19387)
SHUMS CODA ASSOCIATES INC
5776 Stoneridge Mall Rd Ste 150 (94588)
PHONE.................................925 463-0651
David Basinger, *CEO*
EMP: 75 **EST:** 2006
SALES (est): 10.44MM **Privately Held**
Web: www.shumscoda.com
SIC: 8711 Consulting engineer

(P-19388)
SIA ENGINEERING (USA) INC
7001 W Imperial Hwy (90045-6313)
PHONE.................................310 957-2928
Chandra Nair, *CEO*
Cheng Hian Tan, *
Chiuyen Tseng, *
EMP: 151 **EST:** 2008
SALES (est): 10.39MM **Privately Held**
SIC: 8711 Consulting engineer

(P-19389)
SITESOL
Also Called: Site Sltions Cnstr Integration
7372 Sycamore Canyon Blvd (92508-2335)
P.O. Box 91747 (90809-1747)
PHONE.................................562 746-5884
Kristine Glaeser, *CEO*
Peter Glaeser, *
EMP: 85 **EST:** 2010
SALES (est): 2.46MM **Privately Held**
Web: www.sitesol.us
SIC: 8711 Construction and civil engineering

(P-19390)
SIX3 ADVANCED SYSTEMS INC
2933 Bunker Hill Ln (95054-1124)
PHONE.................................408 878-4920
Robert A Coleman, *Brnch Mgr*
EMP: 105
SALES (corp-wide): 6.7B **Publicly Held**
SIC: 8711 Engineering services
HQ: Six3 Advanced Systems, Inc.
   45200 Business Ct Ste 100
   Dulles VA
   703 742-7660

(P-19391)
SONIC INDUSTRIES INC
Also Called: Airframer R
20030 Normandie Ave (90502-1210)
PHONE.................................310 532-8382
Jamie King, *CEO*
▲ **EMP:** 150 **EST:** 1966
SQ FT: 65,000
SALES (est): 23.56MM
SALES (corp-wide): 1.47B **Publicly Held**
SIC: 8711 7699 Machine tool design; Aviation propeller and blade repair
HQ: Roller Bearing Company Of America, Inc.
   102 Willenbrock Rd
   Oxford CT
   203 267-7001

(P-19392)
SPEC SERVICES INC
10540 Talbert Ave Ste 100e (92708-6051)
PHONE.................................714 963-8077
Kim R Henry, *Pr*
Dan Letcher, *
Chuck Lake, *
EMP: 290 **EST:** 1981
SQ FT: 16,000
SALES (est): 49.39MM **Privately Held**
Web: www.specservices.com
SIC: 8711 Consulting engineer

(P-19393)
SSC CONSTRUCTION INC
4195 Chino Hills Pkwy (91709-2618)
PHONE.................................951 278-1177
Gregory E Larkin, *CEO*
Neil Nehmens, *
EMP: 80 **EST:** 1999
SALES (est): 4.44MM **Privately Held**
Web: www.sscconstruction.net
SIC: 8711 Engineering services

(P-19394)
STANTEC ARCHITECTURE INC
300 Montgomery St Ste 1200 (94104-1902)
PHONE.................................415 882-9500
Michael Gambucci, *CEO*
EMP: 915
SALES (corp-wide): 4.23B **Privately Held**
Web: www.stantec.com
SIC: 8711 8712 Engineering services; Architectural services
HQ: Stantec Architecture Inc.
   224 S Michigan Ave # 1400
   Chicago IL
   336 714-7413

(P-19395)
STANTEC CONSULTING SVCS INC
3301 C St Ste 1900 (95816-3394)
PHONE.................................916 924-8844
EMP: 67
SALES (corp-wide): 3.18B **Privately Held**
SIC: 8711 Engineering services
HQ: Stantec Consulting Services Inc.
   475 5th Ave Fl 12
   New York NY
   212 352-5160

(P-19396)
STANTEC CONSULTING SVCS INC
300 N Lake Ave Ste 400 (91101-4169)
PHONE.................................626 796-9141
Paul Boulos, *Brnch Mgr*
EMP: 79
SALES (corp-wide): 4.23B **Privately Held**
Web: www.stantec.com
SIC: 8711 Engineering services
HQ: Stantec Consulting Services Inc.
   410 17th St Ste 1400
   Denver CO
   303 410-4000

(P-19397)
STANTEC CONSULTING SVCS INC
1340 Treat Blvd Ste 525 (94597-7984)
PHONE.................................925 627-4500
Stacey Robinson, *Off Mgr*
EMP: 170
SALES (corp-wide): 4.23B **Privately Held**
Web: www.stantec.com
SIC: 8711 Consulting engineer
HQ: Stantec Consulting Services Inc.
   410 17th St Ste 1400
   Denver CO
   303 410-4000

(P-19398)
STATCOMM INC
939 San Rafael Ave Ste C (94043-1941)
PHONE.................................650 988-9508
Richard Schwanck, *Pr*
Rich Schwank, *
Mark Andrade, *
William Wood, *
EMP: 96 **EST:** 1991
SQ FT: 5,000
SALES (est): 17.9MM
SALES (corp-wide): 17.9MM **Privately Held**
Web: www.statcomm.com
SIC: 8711 Engineering services
PA: Performance Systems Integration, Llc
   7324 Sw Durham Rd
   Portland OR
   503 641-2222

(P-19399)
STEARNS CONRAD AND SCHMIDT CONSULTING ENGINEERS INC (PA)
Also Called: Scs Engineers
3900 Kilroy Airport Way Ste 100 (90806-2453)
PHONE.................................562 426-9544
EMP: 100 **EST:** 1970
SALES (est): 438.81MM
SALES (corp-wide): 438.81MM **Privately Held**
Web: www.scsengineers.com
SIC: 8711 1541 8748 Consulting engineer; Industrial buildings, new construction, nec; Environmental consultant

(P-19400)
STRATEGIC COMMAND US
9406 Stargaze Ave (92129-3801)
PHONE.................................858 603-8901
EMP: 72
SIC: 8711 7389 Consulting engineer; Business services, nec
HQ: Strategic Command, United States
   901 Sac Blvd Ste 1a1
   Omaha NE
   402 294-4130

(P-19401)
SUMARIA SYSTEMS LLC
105 13th St (93437-5209)
PHONE.................................805 606-4973
EMP: 78
SALES (corp-wide): 100.85MM **Privately Held**
Web: www.sumaria.com
SIC: 8711 Consulting engineer
PA: Sumaria Systems, Llc
   8 Essex Center Dr Ste 210
   Peabody MA
   978 739-4200

(P-19402)
SYSTEMS & TECHNOLOGY RES LLC
Also Called: Str
1808 Aston Ave Ste 180 (92008-7369)
PHONE.................................844 204-0963
EMP: 74
Web: www.str.us
SIC: 8711 Engineering services
PA: Systems & Technology Research Llc
   600 W Cummings Park # 1075
   Woburn MA

(P-19403)
SYSTEMS APPLICATION & TECH INC
Also Called: Sa-Tech
1000 Town Center Dr Ste 110 (93036-1100)
P.O. Box 25 (93044-0025)
PHONE.................................805 487-7373
Geoff Dezavala, *Sr VP*
EMP: 80
Web: www.sa-techinc.com
SIC: 8711 Consulting engineer
PA: Systems Application & Technologies, Inc.
   1101 Merc Ln Ste 200
   Largo MD

(P-19404)
T Y LIN INTERNATIONAL (HQ)
345 California St Fl 23 (94104-2646)
PHONE.................................415 291-3700
Man Chung Tang, *Ch*
Allison Bagby, *
Robert A Peterson, *
John M Young, *
Veronica Fennie, *Chief Accounting Officer**
EMP: 84 **EST:** 1964
SQ FT: 30,159
SALES (est): 102.33MM
SALES (corp-wide): 175.24MM **Privately Held**
Web: www.tylin.com
SIC: 8711 Consulting engineer
PA: T.Y.Lin International Group, Ltd.
   345 California St Fl 23
   San Francisco CA
   415 291-3700

(P-19405)
TECHNIP USA INC
Also Called: TP USA
555 W Arrow Hwy (91711-4805)
PHONE.................................909 447-3600
Gary Keyser, *Brnch Mgr*
EMP: 400
Web: www.technipfmc.com
SIC: 8711 Petroleum engineering
PA: Technip Energies Usa, Inc.
   11720 Katy Fwy
   Houston TX

(P-19406)
TEECOM
Also Called: Teecom, Inc.
50 California St Ste 1500 (94111-4612)
PHONE.................................510 337-2800
EMP: 153 **EST:** 1997
SQ FT: 12,600
SALES (est): 14.98MM **Privately Held**
Web: www.teecom.com
SIC: 8711 Consulting engineer

(P-19407)
TEN STONE WBSTER PRCESS TECH
555 W Arrow Hwy (91711-4805)
PHONE.................................909 447-3600
Gary Keyser, *Brnch Mgr*
EMP: 281
Web: www.ten.com
SIC: 8711 Chemical engineering
HQ: T.En Stone & Webster Process Technology, Inc.
   11740 Katy Fwy Ste 100
   Houston TX
   281 870-1111

PRODUCTS & SERVICES SECTION

8711 - Engineering Services (P-19427)

(P-19408)
TERAWAVE COMMUNICATION INC
30680 Huntwood Ave (94544-7022)
PHONE..................................510 429-5300
Raymond C Lin, *Ch Bd*
Donald Stalter, *
Boris Auerbuch, *
▲ **EMP:** 100 **EST:** 1999
SQ FT: 61,800
SALES (est): 5.85MM **Privately Held**
Web: www.terawave.com
SIC: 8711 Engineering services

(P-19409)
TETRA TECH INC (PA)
Also Called: Tetra Tech
3475 E Foothill Blvd (91107-6024)
PHONE..................................626 351-4664
Dan L Batrack, *Ch Bd*
Jill Hudkins, *Pr*
Steven M Burdick, *Ex VP*
Leslie L Shoemaker, *SUSTAIN LEADERSHIP Development*
Preston Hopson, *CCO*
EMP: 200 **EST:** 1966
SALES (est): 3.5B
SALES (corp-wide): 3.5B **Publicly Held**
Web: www.tetratech.com
SIC: 8711 Engineering services

(P-19410)
TETRA TECH INC
17885 Von Karman Ave Ste 500 (92614-5227)
PHONE..................................949 263-0846
Jack Chicca, *Brnch Mgr*
EMP: 85
SALES (corp-wide): 3.5B **Publicly Held**
Web: www.tetratech.com
SIC: 8711 Consulting engineer
PA: Tetra Tech, Inc.
3475 E Foothill Blvd
Pasadena CA
626 351-4664

(P-19411)
TETRA TECH BAS INC (HQ)
Also Called: B A S
21700 Copley Dr Ste 200 (91765-2219)
PHONE..................................909 860-7777
Bryan A Stirrat, *Pr*
Ira Snyder, *
Jeanne Stirrat, *
EMP: 65 **EST:** 1985
SALES (est): 35.2MM
SALES (corp-wide): 3.5B **Publicly Held**
SIC: 8711 Civil engineering
PA: Tetra Tech, Inc.
3475 E Foothill Blvd
Pasadena CA
626 351-4664

(P-19412)
TETRA TECH EM INC
135 Main St Ste 1800 (94105-1850)
PHONE..................................415 265-3715
EMP: 194 **EST:** 2005
SALES (est): 540.94K **Privately Held**
Web: www.tetratech.com
SIC: 8711 Consulting engineer

(P-19413)
TETRA TECH NUS INC
3475 E Foothill Blvd (91107-6024)
PHONE..................................412 921-7090
Dan L Batrack, *CEO*
Janet Mandel, *
John Trepanowski, *
Steven M Burdick, *

Ronald Chu, *
▲ **EMP:** 149 **EST:** 1960
SALES (est): 2.44MM
SALES (corp-wide): 3.5B **Publicly Held**
Web: www.tetratech.com
SIC: 8711 Consulting engineer
PA: Tetra Tech, Inc.
3475 E Foothill Blvd
Pasadena CA
626 351-4664

(P-19414)
TGCON INC (DH)
50 Contractors St (94551-4863)
PHONE..................................925 449-5764
William L Gates, *Pr*
Scott Blaine, *Sr VP*
Brian L Gates, *Ex VP*
Brian Gates, *Ex VP*
Frank Williams, *VP*
EMP: 82 **EST:** 1989
SQ FT: 25,000
SALES (est): 51.94MM
SALES (corp-wide): 600MM **Privately Held**
Web: www.goodfellowbros.com
SIC: 8711 Construction and civil engineering
HQ: Goodfellow Bros. Llc
135 N Wenatchee Ave
Wenatchee WA
509 662-7111

(P-19415)
THERMAL ENGRG INTL USA INC (HQ)
Also Called: Thermal Engineering
18000 Studebaker Rd Ste 400 (90703-2691)
PHONE..................................323 726-0641
Kenneth Murakoshi, *CEO*
Thomas Richardson, *
Micael D Leclair, *
William J Ferguson Junior, *Law Vice President*
Kenneth Murakoshi, *Sr VP*
◆ **EMP:** 70 **EST:** 1969
SQ FT: 18,000
SALES (est): 47.06MM
SALES (corp-wide): 509.03MM **Privately Held**
Web: www.babcockpower.com
SIC: 8711 3443 Professional engineer; Air coolers, metal plate
PA: Babcock Power Inc.
222 Rosewood Dr
Danvers MA
978 646-3300

(P-19416)
TK1SC
15231 Laguna Canyon Rd Ste 100 (92618-3146)
PHONE..................................949 751-5800
Roger A Carter, *CEO*
Larry Sun, *Prin*
EMP: 213 **EST:** 2002
SALES (est): 23.46MM
SALES (corp-wide): 8.88B **Privately Held**
Web: www.tk1sc.com
SIC: 8711 8712 Engineering services; Architectural services
PA: Groupe Wsp Global Inc
1600 Boul Rene-Levesque O 11e etage
Montreal QC
514 340-0046

(P-19417)
TOYON RESEARCH CORPORATION (PA)
6800 Cortona Dr (93117-3139)

PHONE..................................805 968-6787
Kevin Sullivan, *
Dave Wright, *
Paul Castleberg, *
Chuck Nardo, *
EMP: 200 **EST:** 1980
SQ FT: 16,000
SALES (est): 49.8MM
SALES (corp-wide): 49.8MM **Privately Held**
Web: www.toyon.com
SIC: 8711 7371 Electrical or electronic engineering; Custom computer programming services

(P-19418)
TRANSTECH ENGINEERS INC (PA)
13367 Benson Ave (91710-5246)
PHONE..................................909 595-8599
Allen Cayir, *Pr*
Sybil Cayir, *
EMP: 85 **EST:** 1989
SQ FT: 10,000
SALES (est): 10.25MM **Privately Held**
Web: www.transtech.org
SIC: 8711 Civil engineering

(P-19419)
TRI STAR ENGINEERING INC
6774 Calle De Linea Ste 106 (92154-8020)
PHONE..................................619 710-8038
Alfred Lybred, *Mgr*
EMP: 86
Web: www.star3.com
SIC: 8711 Engineering services
PA: Tri Star Engineering, Inc.
1801 S Liberty Dr Ste 200
Bloomington IN

(P-19420)
TRUST AUTOMATION INC
125 Venture Dr Ste 110 (93401-9103)
PHONE..................................805 544-0761
Ty Safreno, *CEO*
Trudie Safreno, *
Brett Keegan, *
Chuck Kass, *
Dave Rennie, *
▲ **EMP:** 65 **EST:** 1990
SQ FT: 100,000
SALES (est): 21.38MM **Privately Held**
Web: www.trustautomation.com
SIC: 8711 3812 3731 3621 Machine tool design; Antennas, radar or communications; Submersible marine robots, manned or unmanned; Generators for gas-electric or oil-electric vehicles

(P-19421)
TTG ENGINEERS
Also Called: Mbe
300 N Lake Ave Fl 14 (91101-4164)
PHONE..................................626 463-2800
▲ **EMP:** 350
SIC: 8711 Consulting engineer

(P-19422)
TYLIN INTL GROUP LTD (PA)
345 California St Fl 23 (94104-2646)
PHONE..................................415 291-3700
Matthew G Cummings, *Pr*
Sheila Jordan, *CMO*
EMP: 109 **EST:** 1961
SQ FT: 34,000
SALES (est): 175.24MM
SALES (corp-wide): 175.24MM **Privately Held**
Web: www.tylin.com

SIC: 8711 Consulting engineer

(P-19423)
UCI CONSTRUCTION INC
3900 Fruitvale Ave (93308-5114)
PHONE..................................661 587-0192
David Krugh, *Brnch Mgr*
EMP: 98
SALES (corp-wide): 46.43MM **Privately Held**
Web: www.uciconstruction.com
SIC: 8711 Professional engineer
PA: U.C.I. Construction, Inc.
167 Grobric Ct
Fairfield CA
925 370-9808

(P-19424)
URS GROUP INC
Also Called: URS
3995 Via Oro Ave (90810-1869)
PHONE..................................562 420-2933
Wilfrido Simbol, *Brnch Mgr*
EMP: 89
SALES (corp-wide): 13.15B **Publicly Held**
Web: www.aecom.com
SIC: 8711 8712 Structural engineering; Architectural engineering
HQ: Urs Group, Inc.
300 S Grand Ave Ste 900
Los Angeles CA
213 593-8000

(P-19425)
URS GROUP INC
Also Called: URS
300 Lakeside Dr Ste 400 (94612-3573)
PHONE..................................510 893-3600
Louise Armstrong, *Mgr*
EMP: 502
SALES (corp-wide): 13.15B **Publicly Held**
Web: www.aecom.com
SIC: 8711 4953 Consulting engineer; Refuse systems
HQ: Urs Group, Inc.
300 S Grand Ave Ste 900
Los Angeles CA
213 593-8000

(P-19426)
URS GROUP INC
Also Called: URS
300 Lakeside Dr Ste 400 (94612-3573)
PHONE..................................925 446-3800
Sam Capps, *Brnch Mgr*
EMP: 67
SALES (corp-wide): 13.15B **Publicly Held**
Web: www.aecom.com
SIC: 8711 8712 8741 Consulting engineer; Architectural engineering; Construction management
HQ: Urs Group, Inc.
300 S Grand Ave Ste 900
Los Angeles CA
213 593-8000

(P-19427)
URS GROUP INC
Also Called: URS
4 N 2nd St (95113-1308)
PHONE..................................408 297-9585
William Hadaya, *Brnch Mgr*
EMP: 78
SALES (corp-wide): 13.15B **Publicly Held**
Web: www.aecom.com
SIC: 8711 Consulting engineer
HQ: Urs Group, Inc.
300 S Grand Ave Ste 900
Los Angeles CA
213 593-8000

8711 - Engineering Services (P-19428)

(P-19428)
URS GROUP INC
Also Called: URS
1360 E Spruce Ave Ste 101 (93720-3378)
PHONE...................................559 255-2541
Ralph Boyakin, *Mgr*
EMP: 89
SALES (corp-wide): 13.15B **Publicly Held**
Web: www.aecom.com
SIC: 8711 Consulting engineer
HQ: Urs Group, Inc.
    300 S Grand Ave Ste 900
    Los Angeles CA
    213 593-8000

(P-19429)
URS HOLDINGS INC (DH)
600 Montgomery St Fl 25 (94111-2701)
PHONE...................................415 774-2700
Thomas Walter Bishop, *CEO*
Martin M Koffel, *
EMP: 470 EST: 1991
SALES (est): 1.5B
SALES (corp-wide): 13.15B **Publicly Held**
SIC: 8711 7389 6531 8249 Consulting engineer; Financial services; Real estate agents and managers; Aviation school
HQ: Aecom Global Ii, Llc
    300 S Grand Ave Ste 900
    Los Angeles CA
    213 593-8100

(P-19430)
UTILITY TRAFFIC SERVICES LLC
2845 E Spring St (90806-2417)
PHONE...................................562 264-2355
Ed Barrera, *Managing Member*
EMP: 287 EST: 2020
SALES (est): 928.77K **Privately Held**
SIC: 8711 Consulting engineer
PA: Traffic Management, Inc.
    4900 Arprt Plz Dr Ste 300
    Long Beach CA

(P-19431)
VANGUARD SPACE TECH INC
Also Called: Alliance Spacesystems
4398 Corporate Center Dr (90720-2537)
PHONE...................................858 587-4210
Frank Belknap, *CEO*
Ronald Miller, *
John Richer, *
EMP: 101 EST: 1994
SQ FT: 50,000
SALES (est): 13.8MM
SALES (corp-wide): 211MM **Publicly Held**
Web: www.appliedcomposites.com
SIC: 8711 Aviation and/or aeronautical engineering
HQ: Solaero Technologies Corp.
    10420 Res Rd Se Bldg 1
    Albuquerque NM
    505 332-5000

(P-19432)
VSA AND ASSOCIATES INC
Also Called: Health Care Resource Group
6571 Altura Blvd Ste 100 (90620-1020)
PHONE...................................562 698-2468
Mahabir S Atwal, *Pr*
Vicky Sumnogum, *
Kaunenaka Jain, *
EMP: 61 EST: 1987
SQ FT: 12,000
SALES (est): 4.36MM **Privately Held**
SIC: 8711 8742 Acoustical engineering; Business planning and organizing services

(P-19433)
VT MILCOM INC
1660 Logan Ave Ste 2 (92113-1044)
PHONE...................................619 424-9024
Brian Upthegrove, *Brnch Mgr*
EMP: 100
SALES (corp-wide): 1.59B **Privately Held**
Web: www.mlupino.com
SIC: 8711 Engineering services
HQ: Vt Milcom Inc.
    448 Viking Dr Ste 350
    Virginia Beach VA
    757 463-2800

(P-19434)
W M LYLES CO
2810 Unicorn Rd (93308-6853)
PHONE...................................661 387-1600
Mike Burson, *Pr*
EMP: 113
SALES (corp-wide): 17.85MM **Privately Held**
Web: www.wmlylesco.com
SIC: 8711 1623 Engineering services; Pipeline construction, nsk
HQ: W. M. Lyles Co.
    525 W Alluvial Ave
    Fresno CA
    559 441-1900

(P-19435)
WALLACE-KUHL INVESTMENTS LLC (PA)
3050 Industrial Blvd (95691-3470)
P.O. Box 1137 (95691-1137)
PHONE...................................916 372-1434
Thomas S Wallace, *
EMP: 65 EST: 1984
SQ FT: 11,300
SALES (est): 11.07MM **Privately Held**
Web: www.teamues.com
SIC: 8711 8748 Civil engineering; Business consulting, nec

(P-19436)
WATLOW ELECTRIC MFG CO
6781 Via Del Oro (95119-1360)
PHONE...................................408 776-6646
EMP: 85
SALES (corp-wide): 607.48MM **Privately Held**
Web: www.watlow.com
SIC: 8711 Engineering services
PA: Watlow Electric Manufacturing Company
    12001 Lackland Rd
    Saint Louis MO
    314 878-4600

(P-19437)
WEST YOST & ASSOCIATES INC (PA)
2020 Research Park Dr Ste 100 (95618)
PHONE...................................530 756-5905
Charles Duncan, *Pr*
Bruce West, *
Jim Yost, *
Steven R Dalrymple, *
EMP: 76 EST: 1990
SQ FT: 25,000
SALES (est): 19.5MM **Privately Held**
Web: www.westyost.com
SIC: 8711 Civil engineering

(P-19438)
WESTERN ALLIED MECHANICAL INC
33210 Central Ave (94587-2010)
PHONE...................................650 326-0750
Zachary Russi, *CEO*
EMP: 175 EST: 2003
SALES (est): 77.26MM **Privately Held**
Web: www.westernallied.com
SIC: 8711 Mechanical engineering

(P-19439)
WESTWIND ENGINEERING INC
625 Esplanade Unit 70 (90277-4150)
PHONE...................................310 831-3454
Mary Anne Graves, *CEO*
Carl Graves, *
EMP: 150 EST: 1992
SQ FT: 2,400
SALES (est): 13MM **Privately Held**
Web: www.westwind111.com
SIC: 8711 7363 Engineering services; Temporary help service

(P-19440)
WILLDAN ENGINEERING
9281 Office Park Cir Ste 100 (95758-8068)
PHONE...................................916 661-3520
EMP: 62
SALES (corp-wide): 429.14MM **Publicly Held**
Web: www.willdan.com
SIC: 8711 Civil engineering
HQ: Willdan Engineering
    2401 E Katella Ave # 300
    Anaheim CA
    714 978-8200

(P-19441)
WILLDAN ENGINEERING
2240 Douglas Blvd Ste 270 (95661-3874)
PHONE...................................916 924-7000
Robert Keefe, *Brnch Mgr*
EMP: 62
SALES (corp-wide): 429.14MM **Publicly Held**
Web: www.willdan.com
SIC: 8711 8742 Civil engineering; Business planning and organizing services
HQ: Willdan Engineering
    2401 E Katella Ave # 300
    Anaheim CA
    714 978-8200

(P-19442)
WILLDAN ENGINEERING
374 Poli St Ste 101 (93001-2605)
PHONE...................................805 653-6597
Roxanne Hughes, *Brnch Mgr*
EMP: 62
SALES (corp-wide): 429.14MM **Publicly Held**
Web: www.willdan.com
SIC: 8711 8742 Civil engineering; Business planning and organizing services
HQ: Willdan Engineering
    2401 E Katella Ave # 300
    Anaheim CA
    714 978-8200

(P-19443)
WILLDAN GROUP INC (PA)
2401 E Katella Ave Ste 300 (92806-5909)
PHONE...................................800 424-9144
Thomas D Brisbin, *Ch Bd*
Michael A Bieber, *
Daniel Chow, *
Creighton Early, *
Micah Chen, *
EMP: 116 EST: 1964
SQ FT: 18,000
SALES (est): 429.14MM
SALES (corp-wide): 429.14MM **Publicly Held**
Web: www.willdan.com
SIC: 8711 8748 Civil engineering; Urban planning and consulting services

(P-19444)
WOOD RODGERS INC (PA)
3301 C St Ste 100b (95816-3342)
PHONE...................................916 341-7760
Mark Rodgers, *Pr*
Steve Balbierz, *
Mark Rayback, *
Gerardo Calvillo, *
EMP: 120 EST: 1996
SQ FT: 5,500
SALES (est): 50.36MM
SALES (corp-wide): 50.36MM **Privately Held**
Web: www.woodrodgers.com
SIC: 8711 Civil engineering

(P-19445)
WSP USA INC
Also Called: Odeh Engineers
15231 Laguna Canyon Rd (92618-7714)
PHONE...................................714 973-4880
Charline Talmer, *Genl Mgr*
EMP: 100
SALES (corp-wide): 8.88B **Privately Held**
Web: www.wsp.com
SIC: 8711 Consulting engineer
HQ: Wsp Usa Inc.
    250 W 34th St Fl 4
    New York NY
    212 465-5000

(P-19446)
YOUNGDAHL CONSULTING GROUP INC
1234 Glenhaven Ct (95762-5709)
PHONE...................................916 933-0633
John Youngdahl, *Pr*
Scott Youngdahl, *
Martha Mcdonald Stkhldrs, *Prin*
EMP: 70 EST: 1984
SQ FT: 9,500
SALES (est): 10.02MM **Privately Held**
Web: www.youngdahl.net
SIC: 8711 8748 Consulting engineer; Environmental consultant

(P-19447)
ZOHO CORPORATION
Also Called: Manageengine
4900 Hopyard Rd Ste 310 (94588-3337)
PHONE...................................925 924-9500
Sridhar Vembu, *CEO*
EMP: 395
Web: www.site24x7.com
SIC: 8711 Engineering services
HQ: Zoho Corporation
    4141 Hacienda Dr
    Pleasanton CA

8712 Architectural Services

(P-19448)
5 DESIGN INC
Also Called: 5design
6161 Santa Monica Blvd Ste 208 (90038-4404)
PHONE...................................323 308-3558
Stanley Russell Hathaway, *Pr*
Arthur Benedetti Junior, *VP*
Michael Ellis, *Treas*
Tim Magill, *Sec*
EMP: 76 EST: 2005
SALES (est): 15.1MM **Privately Held**
Web: www.5plusdesign.com
SIC: 8712 Architectural engineering

8712 - Architectural Services (P-19470)

(P-19449)
AECOM SERVICES INC (HQ)
300 S Grand Ave Ste 900 (90071-3135)
PHONE.................213 593-8000
Michael S Burke, *CEO*
Raymond Landy, *Pr*
Kelly Olson, *VP*
Paul Steinke, *Ex VP*
Deborah Klem, *Sr VP*
EMP: 250 **EST:** 1946
SALES (est): 2.12B
SALES (corp-wide): 13.15B **Publicly Held**
Web: www.aecom.com
SIC: 8712 8741 8711 Architectural services; Management services; Engineering services
PA: Aecom
  13355 Noel Rd Ste 400
  Dallas TX
  972 788-1000

(P-19450)
ALTOON PARTNERS LLP (PA)
Also Called: Altoon Porter
617 W 7th St Ste 400 (90017-3889)
PHONE.................213 225-1900
Ronald A Altoon, *Pt*
Gary Dempster, *Pt*
James Auld, *Pt*
William Sebring, *Pt*
EMP: 67 **EST:** 1984
SQ FT: 20,000
SALES (est): 8.01MM
SALES (corp-wide): 8.01MM **Privately Held**
Web: www.altoon.com
SIC: 8712 Architectural engineering

(P-19451)
ARCHITECTS ORANGE INC
Also Called: Ao
144 N Orange St (92866-1400)
PHONE.................714 639-9860
Jack Selman, *Sr Pt*
Darrel Hebenstreit, *
Hugh Rose, *
Jim Dietze, *
Rc Alley Iii, *Pt*
EMP: 200 **EST:** 1973
SQ FT: 10,000
SALES (est): 37.4MM **Privately Held**
Web: www.aoarchitects.com
SIC: 8712 Architectural engineering

(P-19452)
ARCHITECTURAL MTLS USA INC
4025 Camino Del Rio S Ste 300 (92108)
PHONE.................888 219-2126
Greg Romine, *CEO*
Serhan Emre, *
EMP: 70 **EST:** 1997
SALES (est): 2.39MM **Privately Held**
Web: www.architecturalmaterials.com
SIC: 8712 3999 3211 5039 Architectural engineering; Barber and beauty shop equipment; Construction glass; Prefabricated structures

(P-19453)
AUSTIN VEUM RBBINS PRTNERS INC (PA)
501 W Broadway Ste A (92101-3562)
PHONE.................619 231-1960
Douglas H Austin Faia, *CEO*
Randy Robbins, *
Chris Vium, *
Jeffrey Parshalle, *
Doreen Deen Austin, *CFO*
EMP: 83 **EST:** 1995
SQ FT: 12,500
SALES (est): 5.97MM **Privately Held**
SIC: 8712 Architectural engineering

(P-19454)
BAR ARCHITECTS
77 Geary St Ste 200 (94108-5724)
PHONE.................415 293-5700
Robert Hunter, *Pr*
Earl Wilson, *
EMP: 80 **EST:** 1966
SALES (est): 8.53MM **Privately Held**
Web: www.bararch.com
SIC: 8712 Architectural engineering

(P-19455)
BASSENIAN/LAGONI ARCHITECTS
2031 Orchard Dr Ste 100 (92660-0753)
PHONE.................949 553-9100
Aram Bassenian, *CEO*
Carl Lagoni, *
Lee R Rogaliner, *
Robert Chavez, *
EMP: 65 **EST:** 1979
SQ FT: 22,800
SALES (est): 9.48MM **Privately Held**
Web: www.bassenianlagoni.com
SIC: 8712 Architectural engineering

(P-19456)
BJARKE INGELS GROUP NYC LLC
310 Wilshire Blvd (90401-1312)
PHONE.................347 549-4141
EMP: 196
SALES (corp-wide): 101.84MM **Privately Held**
SIC: 8712 Architectural services
HQ: Bjarke Ingels Group Nyc Llc
  45 Main St Fl 900
  Brooklyn NY
  917 287-4326

(P-19457)
BLACKSTONE DEVELOPMENT INC
801 Ygnacio Valley Rd Ste 100 (94596-3856)
PHONE.................925 718-3126
David J Tognela, *CEO*
Nancy Tognela, *Sec*
EMP: 100 **EST:** 2002
SALES (est): 12MM **Privately Held**
SIC: 8712 8711 1522 1541 Architectural engineering; Engineering services; Residential construction, nec; Industrial buildings and warehouses

(P-19458)
CARRIER JOHNSON (PA)
Also Called: Culture
185 W F St Ste 600 (92101-4012)
PHONE.................619 236-9462
Gordon Carrier, *Pr*
Michael Johnson, *
EMP: 68 **EST:** 1977
SALES (est): 8.56MM
SALES (corp-wide): 8.56MM **Privately Held**
Web: www.carrierjohnson.com
SIC: 8712 7389 Architectural engineering; Interior design services

(P-19459)
CARTER & BURGESS INC
300 Frank H Ogawa Plz Ste 10 (94612-2037)
PHONE.................510 457-0027
Robert Turley, *Brnch Mgr*
EMP: 84
SALES (corp-wide): 14.92B **Publicly Held**
Web: www.c-b.com
SIC: 8712 8713 8711 Architectural engineering; Surveying services; Civil engineering
HQ: Carter & Burgess, Inc.
  777 Main St Ste 2500
  Fort Worth TX
  817 735-6000

(P-19460)
CGL COMPANIES LLC
2260 Del Paso Rd Ste 100 (95834-9713)
PHONE.................916 678-7890
Robert Glass, *Ex VP*
Joe E Lee, *
EMP: 70 **EST:** 2017
SALES (est): 2.36MM **Privately Held**
Web: www.cglcompanies.com
SIC: 8712 Architectural services

(P-19461)
CO ARCHITECTS (PA)
5750 Wilshire Blvd Ste 550 (90036-3677)
PHONE.................323 525-0500
EMP: 74 **EST:** 1996
SALES (est): 10.55MM
SALES (corp-wide): 10.55MM **Privately Held**
Web: www.coarchitects.com
SIC: 8712 Architectural services

(P-19462)
DAHLIN GROUP INC (PA)
5865 Owens Dr (94588-3939)
PHONE.................925 251-7200
Nancy K Keenan, *Pr*
Nancy K Keenan, *CEO*
Charles Meyer, *
John Thatch, *
Karl Danielson, *
EMP: 60 **EST:** 1972
SQ FT: 300,000
SALES (est): 17.12MM
SALES (corp-wide): 17.12MM **Privately Held**
Web: www.dahlingroup.com
SIC: 8712 Architectural engineering

(P-19463)
DARDEN ARCHITECTS INC
6790 N West Ave Ste 104 (93711-4306)
PHONE.................559 448-8051
Martin Dietz, *Pr*
EMP: 75 **EST:** 1959
SQ FT: 5,000
SALES (est): 6.89MM **Privately Held**
Web: www.dardenarchitects.com
SIC: 8712 7389 Architectural engineering; Interior designer

(P-19464)
DELAWIE
1515 Morena Blvd (92110-3731)
PHONE.................619 299-6690
Frank Ternasky, *CEO*
Michael L Asaro, *
Paul E Schroeder, *
EMP: 61 **EST:** 1961
SQ FT: 19,000
SALES (est): 8.98MM **Privately Held**
Web: www.delawie.com
SIC: 8712 7389 Architectural engineering; Interior design services

(P-19465)
DES ARCHITECTS ENGINEERS INC
Also Called: Lightfiction
399 Bradford St Ste 300 (94063-1529)
P.O. Box 3599 (94064-3599)
PHONE.................650 364-6453
Thomas Gilman, *Pr*
Stephen D Mincey, *
Craig Ivancovich, *
EMP: 115 **EST:** 1973
SQ FT: 35,000
SALES (est): 17.99MM **Privately Held**
Web: www.des-ae.com
SIC: 8712 8711 Architectural engineering; Engineering services

(P-19466)
DLR GROUP INC (HQ)
700 S Flower St Ste 2200 (90017)
PHONE.................213 800-9400
Adrian O Cohen, *Pr*
Daniel A Munn, *
Jon P Anderson, *
Darrell L Stelling, *
Pamela Touschner, *
EMP: 140 **EST:** 1997
SALES (est): 24.79MM
SALES (corp-wide): 183.73MM **Privately Held**
Web: www.dlrgroup.com
SIC: 8712 8711 Architectural engineering; Engineering services
PA: Dlr Holding Company
  6457 Frances St Ste 200
  Omaha NE
  402 393-4100

(P-19467)
FORGE ARCHITECTURE
Also Called: Fee Munson Ebert Architects
500 Montgomery St (94111-6523)
PHONE.................415 434-0320
Jack Munson, *Pt*
Andrew Wilson, *
EMP: 63 **EST:** 1980
SQ FT: 6,800
SALES (est): 3.53MM **Privately Held**
Web: www.forge-arch.com
SIC: 8712 7389 Architectural services; Interior design services

(P-19468)
GEHRY PARTNERS LLP
12541 Beatrice St (90066-7001)
PHONE.................310 482-3000
Frank Gehry, *Pt*
Berta Gehry, *
Brian Aamoth, *
John Bowers, *
Anand Devarajan, *
EMP: 130 **EST:** 2001
SQ FT: 12,100
SALES (est): 21.66MM **Privately Held**
Web: www.foga.com
SIC: 8712 Architectural services

(P-19469)
GENSLER ASSCTS/ NTRNATIONAL LTD (HQ)
220 Montgomery St (94104-3402)
PHONE.................415 433-3700
EMP: 75 **EST:** 1988
SALES (est): 57.22MM
SALES (corp-wide): 1.84B **Privately Held**
Web: www.gensler.com
SIC: 8712 Architectural engineering
PA: M. Arthur Gensler Jr. & Associates, Inc.
  220 Montgomery St Ste 200
  San Francisco CA
  415 433-3700

(P-19470)
GKK CORPORATION
1775 Hancock St (92110-2034)

8712 - Architectural Services (P-19471)

PHONE.................................619 398-0215
EMP: 62
SIC: 8712 Architectural engineering
PA: Gkk Corporation
2355 Main St Ste 220
Irvine CA

(P-19471)
GKK CORPORATION (PA)
Also Called: Gkkworks
2355 Main St Ste 220 (92614-4251)
PHONE.................................949 250-1500
Praful Kulkarni, *Pr*
David Hunt, *
Mike Helton, *Prin*
Sam Porter, *Prin*
EMP: 85 **EST**: 1991
SQ FT: 11,000
SALES (est): 32.74MM **Privately Held**
SIC: 8712 8711 Architectural engineering; Building construction consultant

(P-19472)
GOULD EVANS P C
156 S Park St (94107-1809)
PHONE.................................415 503-1411
Robert M Baum, *Admn*
EMP: 75
SALES (corp-wide): 17.4MM **Privately Held**
Web: www.multi.studio
SIC: 8712 Architectural engineering
PA: Gould Evans, P C
4200 Pennsylvania Ave # 150
Kansas City MO
816 931-6655

(P-19473)
GRUEN ASSOCIATES INC
Also Called: Gruen Assoc Archtects Planners
6330 San Vicente Blvd Ste 200 (90048-5441)
PHONE.................................323 937-4270
Ki Suh Park, *Pt*
Michael Enomoto, *
EMP: 75 **EST**: 1947
SQ FT: 14,000
SALES (est): 10.6MM **Privately Held**
Web: www.gruenassociates.com
SIC: 8712 Architectural engineering

(P-19474)
HAWKINS BROWN USA INC
8500 Steller Dr Ste 1 (90232-2453)
PHONE.................................310 600-2695
Matthew Ollier, *Prin*
EMP: 276 **EST**: 2017
SALES (est): 4.77MM **Privately Held**
Web: www.hawkinsbrown.com
SIC: 8712 Architectural engineering

(P-19475)
HELLMUTH OBATA & KASSABAUM INC (DH)
Also Called: H O K
1 Bush St Ste 200 (94104-4404)
PHONE.................................415 243-0555
Patrick Macleamy, *CEO*
William Hellmuth, *
Lisa Green, *
Peter Mosanyi, *
Thomas Robson, *
EMP: 193 **EST**: 1966
SALES (est): 98.4MM
SALES (corp-wide): 457.53MM **Privately Held**
Web: www.hok.com

SIC: 8712 8711 8742 7389 Architectural engineering; Engineering services; Management consulting services; Interior design services
HQ: Hok, Inc.
10 S Broadway Ste 200
Saint Louis MO

(P-19476)
HELLMUTH OBATA & KASSABAUM INC
757 S Alameda St (90021-1679)
PHONE.................................310 838-9555
EMP: 97
SALES (corp-wide): 457.53MM **Privately Held**
Web: www.hok.com
SIC: 8712 8711 Architectural engineering; Engineering services
HQ: Hellmuth, Obata & Kassabaum, Inc.
1 Bush St Ste 200
San Francisco CA

(P-19477)
HMC GROUP (HQ)
Also Called: HMC Architects
3546 Concours (91764-5584)
PHONE.................................909 989-9979
Brian Staton, *CEO*
▲ **EMP**: 165 **EST**: 1941
SQ FT: 58,000
SALES (est): 53.1MM
SALES (corp-wide): 93.14MM **Privately Held**
Web: www.hmcarchitects.com
SIC: 8712 Architectural engineering
PA: Hmc Holdings, Inc.
3546 Concours
Ontario CA
909 989-9979

(P-19478)
HOK GROUP INC
Also Called: Hok
757 S Alameda St (90021-1670)
PHONE.................................310 838-9555
John L Conley, *Brnch Mgr*
EMP: 60
SALES (corp-wide): 457.53MM **Privately Held**
Web: www.hok.com
SIC: 8712 Architectural engineering
PA: Hok Group, Inc
10 S Broadway Ste 200
Saint Louis MO
314 421-2000

(P-19479)
HUNTSMAN ARCHITECTURAL GROUP (PA)
50 California St 7th Fl (94111-4624)
PHONE.................................415 394-1212
Sascha Wagner, *Pr*
Susan Williams, *
Linda H Parker, *
EMP: 83 **EST**: 1981
SQ FT: 19,000
SALES (est): 21MM
SALES (corp-wide): 21MM **Privately Held**
Web: www.huntsmanag.com
SIC: 8712 Architectural engineering

(P-19480)
INTERIOR ARCHITECTS INC (PA)
Also Called: IA
500 Sansome St Fl 8 (94111-3241)
PHONE.................................415 434-3305
EMP: 64 **EST**: 1984
SALES (est): 148.99MM
SALES (corp-wide): 148.99MM **Privately Held**

Web: www.interiorarchitects.com
SIC: 8712 Architectural services

(P-19481)
JEFFREY ROME & ASSOCIATES
1715 Port Charles Pl (92660-5319)
PHONE.................................949 760-3929
Jeffery Rome, *Pr*
EMP: 60 **EST**: 1991
SALES (est): 5.33MM **Privately Held**
Web: www.jeffreyromeassociates.com
SIC: 8712 Architectural engineering

(P-19482)
JOHNSON FAIN INC
1201 N Broadway (90012-1407)
PHONE.................................323 224-6000
R Scott Johnson, *
Sherry Miller, *
EMP: 80 **EST**: 1950
SQ FT: 26,000
SALES (est): 8.66MM **Privately Held**
Web: www.johnsonfain.com
SIC: 8712 7389 Architectural engineering; Interior design services

(P-19483)
KTGY GROUP INC (PA)
Also Called: Ktgy Architecture Planning
17911 Von Karman Ave Ste 200 (92614-6209)
PHONE.................................949 851-2133
Tricia Esser, *CEO*
Stan Braden, *Pr*
Brittany Choisnet, *Sec*
EMP: 70 **EST**: 1991
SQ FT: 21,000
SALES (est): 29.2MM **Privately Held**
Web: www.ktgy.com
SIC: 8712 Architectural engineering

(P-19484)
LAMAR JHNSON COLLABORATIVE INC
8590 National Blvd (90232-2443)
PHONE.................................424 361-3960
EMP: 209
SALES (corp-wide): 878.7MM **Privately Held**
SIC: 8712 Architectural engineering
HQ: The Lamar Johnson Collaborative Inc
35 E Wacker Dr Ste 1300
Chicago IL
312 429-0400

(P-19485)
LEE BURKHART LIU INC
5510 Lincoln Blvd # 250 (90094-3008)
PHONE.................................310 829-2249
Kenneth Lee, *Pr*
Erich Burkart, *
Ken Liu, *
EMP: 75 **EST**: 1986
SQ FT: 11,000
SALES (est): 4.8MM **Privately Held**
SIC: 8712 Architectural engineering

(P-19486)
LIONAKIS (PA)
Also Called: Architecture
2025 19th St (95818-1618)
PHONE.................................916 558-1901
Andrew Deeble, *Ex Dir*
Tim Fry, *
Dave Younger, *
EMP: 150 **EST**: 1909
SALES (est): 29.96MM
SALES (corp-wide): 29.96MM **Privately Held**
Web: www.lionakis.com

SIC: 8712 7389 8711 Architectural services; Interior design services; Structural engineering

(P-19487)
LPA INC (PA)
5301 California Ave Ste 100 (92617-3224)
PHONE.................................949 261-1001
Wendy Rogers, *CEO*
Dan Heinfeld, *
James Kelly, *
Charles Pruitt, *
◆ **EMP**: 180 **EST**: 1971
SQ FT: 33,700
SALES (est): 36.63MM
SALES (corp-wide): 36.63MM **Privately Held**
Web: www.lpadesignstudios.com
SIC: 8712 8711 0781 Architectural engineering; Engineering services; Landscape counseling and planning

(P-19488)
LPAS INC
723 S St (95811-7021)
PHONE.................................916 443-0335
Theressa Page, *Owner*
David Brady Smith, *
Ronald Metzker, *
Curtis Owyang, *
EMP: 61 **EST**: 1975
SALES (est): 9.21MM **Privately Held**
Web: www.lpas.com
SIC: 8712 Architectural engineering

(P-19489)
M ARTHUR GENSLER JR ASSOC INC (PA)
Also Called: Gensler
220 Montgomery St Ste 200 (94104-3504)
PHONE.................................415 433-3700
Diane Hoskins, *
Greg M Richart, *
Joseph Brancato, *
EMP: 360 **EST**: 1965
SQ FT: 57,000
SALES (est): 1.84B
SALES (corp-wide): 1.84B **Privately Held**
Web: www.gensler.com
SIC: 8712 Architectural services

(P-19490)
M ARTHUR GENSLER JR ASSOC INC
Also Called: Gensler and Associates
500 S Figueroa St (90071-1705)
PHONE.................................213 927-3600
Rob Jernigan, *Brnch Mgr*
EMP: 249
SALES (corp-wide): 1.84B **Privately Held**
Web: www.gensler.com
SIC: 8712 7389 Architectural engineering; Design, commercial and industrial
PA: M. Arthur Gensler Jr. & Associates, Inc.
220 Montgomery St Ste 200
San Francisco CA
415 433-3700

(P-19491)
M ARTHUR GENSLER JR ASSOC INC
Also Called: Gensler
4675 Macarthur Ct Ste 100 (92660-8811)
PHONE.................................949 863-9434
Kim Graham, *Brnch Mgr*
EMP: 108
SALES (corp-wide): 1.84B **Privately Held**
Web: www.gensler.com

PRODUCTS & SERVICES SECTION **8712 - Architectural Services (P-19513)**

SIC: 8712 Architectural engineering
PA: M. Arthur Gensler Jr. & Associates, Inc.
220 Montgomery St Ste 200
San Francisco CA
415 433-3700

(P-19492)
MARMOL RDZNER AN ARCHTCTRAL CO
12210 Nebraska Ave (90025-3620)
PHONE..............................310 826-6222
Ron Radziner, *CEO*
Leo Marmol, *
EMP: 70 EST: 1989
SQ FT: 6,500
SALES (est): 12MM Privately Held
Web: www.marmol-radziner.com
SIC: 8712 1521 1542 Architectural engineering; General remodeling, single-family houses; Commercial and office building, new construction

(P-19493)
MARTIN AC PARTNERS INC
444 S Flower St Ste 1200 (90071-1802)
PHONE..............................213 683-1900
Robert Newsom, *Pr*
Christopher C Martin, *
David C Martin, *
EMP: 116 EST: 1906
SALES (est): 12.69MM Privately Held
Web: www.acmartin.com
SIC: 8712 Architectural services

(P-19494)
MARTIN ATI-AC INC (PA)
Also Called: ATI Architects & Engineers
4305 Hacienda Dr Ste 500 (94588-8586)
PHONE..............................925 648-8800
Paul Didonato, *Pr*
Olliver Santos, *
EMP: 74 EST: 1989
SALES (est): 10.34MM Privately Held
Web: www.acmartin.com
SIC: 8712 8711 Architectural engineering; Structural engineering

(P-19495)
MBH ARCHITECTS INC
Also Called: Mbh Arch
960 Atlantic Ave Ste 100 (94501-1066)
PHONE..............................510 865-8663
Dennis Heath, *Pr*
Joseph Smart, *
Clay Fry, *
John Mcnulty, *Prin*
EMP: 210 EST: 1989
SQ FT: 55,000
SALES (est): 36.86MM Privately Held
Web: www.mbharch.com
SIC: 8712 Architectural engineering

(P-19496)
MORPHOSIS ARCHITECTS
Also Called: Morphosis
3440 Wesley St (90232-2328)
PHONE..............................310 453-2247
Thom Mayne, *Pr*
Blythe Allison Mayne, *
EMP: 62 EST: 1975
SQ FT: 10,000
SALES (est): 9.35MM Privately Held
Web: www.morphosis.net
SIC: 8712 Architectural engineering

(P-19497)
MYLES STEVENS ARCHITECTURE
Also Called: Stevens and Associates

855 Sansome St Ste 200 (94111-1532)
PHONE..............................415 397-6500
Myles Stevens, *Owner*
EMP: 62 EST: 1980
SQ FT: 4,000
SALES (est): 215.9K Privately Held
Web: www.stevens-arch.com
SIC: 8712 0781 Architectural engineering; Landscape architects

(P-19498)
NEWMAN GARRISON + PARTNERS INC
3100 Bristol St Ste 400 (92626-7333)
PHONE..............................949 756-0818
Kevin Newman, *Ch*
Donald J Meeks, *
EMP: 70 EST: 1974
SQ FT: 7,000
SALES (est): 4.47MM Privately Held
Web: www.nggpartners.com
SIC: 8712 Architectural engineering

(P-19499)
NTD ARCHITECTS
Also Called: NTD Architecture
9665 Chesapeake Dr # 365 (92123-1367)
PHONE..............................858 565-4440
EMP: 98
SIC: 8712 Architectural services

(P-19500)
PERKINS + WILL INC
Also Called: Perkins & Will
2 Bryant St Ste 300 (94105-1641)
PHONE..............................415 856-3000
Russ Drinker, *Brnch Mgr*
EMP: 60
SALES (corp-wide): 606MM Privately Held
Web: www.perkinswill.com
SIC: 8712 Architectural services
HQ: Will Perkins Inc
1222 22nd St Nw Ste 200
Washington DC

(P-19501)
RDC-S111 INC (PA)
Also Called: Perkowitz & Ruth Architects
245 E 3rd St (90802-3141)
PHONE..............................562 628-8000
Bradley Williams, *CEO*
Ian Denny, *
Brian Wolfe, *
EMP: 74 EST: 1979
SALES (est): 28.62MM
SALES (corp-wide): 28.62MM Privately Held
Web: www.rdcollaborative.com
SIC: 8712 Architectural engineering

(P-19502)
RO ROCKET DESIGN INC
1306 Bridgeway Fl 2 (94965-1959)
PHONE..............................415 289-0830
Jason Ro, *Brnch Mgr*
EMP: 124
SALES (corp-wide): 2.04MM Privately Held
Web: www.rorockettdesign.com
SIC: 8712 Architectural services
PA: Ro Rocket Design Inc.
1031 W Mnchstr Blvd
Inglewood CA
213 784-0014

(P-19503)
RRM DESIGN GROUP (PA)
3765 S Higuera St Ste 102 (93401-7437)
PHONE..............................805 439-0442

Victor Montgomery, *Ch Bd*
John Wilbanks, *
Keith Gurnee, *
EMP: 99 EST: 1973
SQ FT: 23,000
SALES (est): 17.86MM
SALES (corp-wide): 17.86MM Privately Held
Web: www.rrmdesign.com
SIC: 8712 Architectural engineering

(P-19504)
SKIDMORE OWINGS & MERRILL LLP
1 Maritime Plz Fl 5 (94111-3408)
PHONE..............................415 981-1555
Gene Schnair, *Pt*
EMP: 240
SALES (corp-wide): 224.51K Privately Held
Web: www.som.com
SIC: 8712 Architectural engineering
PA: Skidmore, Owings & Merrill Llp
224 S Michigan Ave # 1000
Chicago IL
312 554-9090

(P-19505)
SMITHGROUP INC
Also Called: Smithgroupjjr
301 Battery St Fl 7 (94111-3237)
PHONE..............................313 442-8351
Michael Medici, *Pr*
EMP: 146
SALES (corp-wide): 210.44MM Privately Held
Web: www.smithgroup.com
SIC: 8712 Architectural engineering
HQ: Smithgroup, Inc.
1700 New York Ave Nw # 100
Washington DC
202 842-2100

(P-19506)
STANTEC ARCHITECTURE INC
38 Technology Dr Ste 200 (92618-5310)
PHONE..............................949 923-6000
Eric Nielsen, *VP*
EMP: 279
SALES (corp-wide): 4.23B Privately Held
Web: www.stantec.com
SIC: 8712 8711 4111 Architectural services; Engineering services; Local and suburban transit
HQ: Stantec Architecture Inc.
224 S Michigan Ave # 1400
Chicago IL
336 714-7413

(P-19507)
STANTEC ARCHITECTURE INC
300 N Lake Ave Ste 400 (91101-4169)
PHONE..............................626 796-9141
Simon Bluestone, *Brnch Mgr*
EMP: 88
SALES (corp-wide): 4.23B Privately Held
Web: www.stantec.com
SIC: 8712 Architectural services
HQ: Stantec Architecture Inc.
224 S Michigan Ave # 1400
Chicago IL
336 714-7413

(P-19508)
STANTEC ARCHITECTURE INC
555 Capitol Mall Ste 650 (95814-4583)
PHONE..............................916 442-3230
Jason Marshall, *Brnch Mgr*
EMP: 651
SALES (corp-wide): 4.23B Privately Held

Web: www.stantec.com
SIC: 8712 8711 Architectural services; Engineering services
HQ: Stantec Architecture Inc.
224 S Michigan Ave # 1400
Chicago IL
336 714-7413

(P-19509)
STANTEC ARCHITECTURE INC
1383 N Mcdowell Blvd Ste 250 (94954-1187)
PHONE..............................707 765-1660
EMP: 186
SALES (corp-wide): 4.23B Privately Held
Web: www.stantec.com
SIC: 8712 8711 Architectural services; Engineering services
HQ: Stantec Architecture Inc.
224 S Michigan Ave # 1400
Chicago IL
336 714-7413

(P-19510)
STANTEC CONSULTING SVCS INC
38 Technology Dr Ste 100 (92618-5312)
PHONE..............................949 923-6000
Bob Gomes, *Brnch Mgr*
EMP: 117
SALES (corp-wide): 4.23B Privately Held
Web: www.stantec.com
SIC: 8712 8711 Architectural services; Engineering services
HQ: Stantec Consulting Services Inc.
410 17th St Ste 1400
Denver CO
303 410-4000

(P-19511)
STEINBERG HART (PA)
Also Called: Steinberg Architects
818 W 7th St Ste 1100 (90017-3404)
PHONE..............................408 295-5446
David Hart, *Pr*
Robert Steinberg, *
Ernest Yamana, *
EMP: 74 EST: 1953
SQ FT: 14,000
SALES (est): 14.69MM
SALES (corp-wide): 14.69MM Privately Held
Web: www.steinberghart.com
SIC: 8712 Architectural engineering

(P-19512)
STV ARCHITECTS INC
1055 W 7th St Ste 3150 (90017-2556)
PHONE..............................213 482-9444
Wagih Andraos, *Mgr*
EMP: 156
SALES (corp-wide): 261.09MM Privately Held
Web: www.stvinc.com
SIC: 8712 8742 8711 Architectural engineering; Transportation consultant; Consulting engineer
HQ: Stv Architects Inc
205 W Welsh Dr
Douglassville PA
610 385-8200

(P-19513)
STV INCORPORATED
505 14th St Ste 1060 (94612-1406)
PHONE..............................510 763-1313
EMP: 406
SALES (corp-wide): 261.09MM Privately Held
Web: www.stvinc.com

8712 - Architectural Services (P-19514)

PRODUCTS & SERVICES SECTION

SIC: 8712 Architectural engineering
HQ: Stv Incorporated
 225 Park Ave S Fl 5
 New York NY
 212 529-2722

(P-19514)
THE JERDE PARTNERSHIP INC
Also Called: Jerde Partnership Intl
601 W 5th St Ste 500 (90071-2045)
PHONE..................310 399-1987
EMP: 70 **EST:** 1977
SALES (est): 5.21MM **Privately Held**
Web: www.jerde.com
SIC: 8712 Architectural services

(P-19515)
UNIVERSITY CAL SAN DIEGO
Also Called: Ucsd Fac & Design
10280 N Torrey Pines Rd Ste 470 (92037-1033)
PHONE..................858 534-2177
M Boone Hellmann, Brnch Mgr
EMP: 97
SALES (corp-wide): 534.4MM **Privately Held**
Web: www.ucsd.edu
SIC: 8712 8221 9411 Architectural services; University; Administration of educational programs
HQ: University Of California, San Diego
 9500 Gilman Dr
 La Jolla CA
 858 534-2230

(P-19516)
URS GLOBAL HOLDINGS INC
600 Montgomery St Fl 28 (94111-2803)
PHONE..................415 774-2700
EMP: 60 **EST:** 2009
SALES (est): 3.23MM
SALES (corp-wide): 13.15B **Publicly Held**
SIC: 8712 8741 8711 Architectural engineering; Construction management; Consulting engineer
HQ: Aecom Global Ii, Llc
 300 S Grand Ave Ste 900
 Los Angeles CA
 213 593-8100

(P-19517)
WARE MALCOMB (PA)
10 Edelman (92618-4312)
PHONE..................949 660-9128
Kenneth Wink, CEO
Lawrence R Armstrong, *
Jay Todisco, *
Matthew Brady, *
Tobin Sloane, *
▲ **EMP:** 137 **EST:** 1972
SQ FT: 22,000
SALES (est): 52.53MM
SALES (corp-wide): 52.53MM **Privately Held**
Web: www.waremalcomb.com
SIC: 8712 7336 8711 7389 Architectural engineering; Commercial art and graphic design; Civil engineering; Interior design services

(P-19518)
WILL PERKINS INC
617 W 7th St Fl 12 (90017-3807)
PHONE..................213 270-8400
Gabriella Bullock, Prin
EMP: 63
SALES (corp-wide): 606MM **Privately Held**
Web: www.perkinswill.com

SIC: 8712 Architectural services
HQ: Will Perkins Inc
 1222 22nd St Nw Ste 200
 Washington DC

(P-19519)
WILLIAM HZMLHLCH ARCHTECTS INC
Also Called: Wha
680 Newport Center Dr Ste 300 (92660)
PHONE..................949 250-0607
William Hezmalhalch, CEO
EMP: 75 **EST:** 1986
SALES (est): 12.69MM **Privately Held**
Web: www.whainc.com
SIC: 8712 Architectural engineering

(P-19520)
WIMBERLY ALLSON TONG GOO NA IN
Also Called: Watg
300 Spectrum Center Dr Ste 500 (92618-4989)
PHONE..................949 574-8500
Mike Seyle, CEO
Monica Cuervo, *
EMP: 98 **EST:** 2006
SALES (est): 6.81MM **Privately Held**
Web: www.watg.com
SIC: 8712 Architectural services

(P-19521)
WOODS BAGOT ARCHITECTS PC
128 Spear St Lbby (94105-5160)
PHONE..................415 277-3000
EMP: 159
SALES (corp-wide): 16.4MM **Privately Held**
Web: www.woodsbagot.com
SIC: 8712 Architectural engineering
PA: Woods Bagot Architects, P.C.
 30 Broad St Fl 7
 New York NY
 646 756-3300

(P-19522)
ZIMMER GNSUL FRSCA ARCHTCTS LL
Also Called: Zimmer Gnsul Frsca Partnr Amer
515 S Flower St Ste 3700 (90071-2221)
PHONE..................213 617-1901
Rachel Morris, Mgr
EMP: 118
SALES (corp-wide): 48.63MM **Privately Held**
SIC: 8712 7389 Architectural engineering; Interior designer
PA: Zimmer Gunsul Frasca Architects Llp
 1223 Sw Washington St # 200
 Portland OR
 503 224-3860

8713 Surveying Services

(P-19523)
CANNON CORPORATION (PA)
Also Called: Cannon
1050 Southwood Dr (93401-5813)
PHONE..................805 544-7407
Michael F Cannon, CEO
Daniel Hutchinson, *
EMP: 60 **EST:** 1975
SQ FT: 4,200
SALES (est): 18.94MM
SALES (corp-wide): 18.94MM **Privately Held**
Web: www.cannoncorp.us

SIC: 8713 8711 1611 Surveying services; Civil engineering; Highway and street construction

(P-19524)
F3 AND ASSOCIATES INC (PA)
701 E H St (94510-3567)
P.O. Box 5099 (94955-5099)
PHONE..................707 748-4300
Fred Feickert, Pr
Sean Finn, *
Gene Feickert, *
EMP: 70 **EST:** 2004
SALES (est): 16.29MM
SALES (corp-wide): 16.29MM **Privately Held**
Web: www.f3-inc.com
SIC: 8713 Surveying services

(P-19525)
PSOMAS
Also Called: Bonterra Psomas
5 Hutton Centre Dr Ste 300 (92707)
PHONE..................714 751-7373
Ryan Mclean, Mgr
EMP: 121
SALES (corp-wide): 67.87MM **Privately Held**
Web: www.psomas.com
SIC: 8713 8711 Surveying services; Consulting engineer
PA: Psomas
 865 S Figueroa St # 3200
 Los Angeles CA
 213 223-1400

(P-19526)
PSOMAS (PA)
865 S Figueroa St (90017-2507)
PHONE..................213 223-1400
Ryan Mclean, Pr
EMP: 125 **EST:** 1946
SALES (est): 67.87MM
SALES (corp-wide): 67.87MM **Privately Held**
Web: www.psomas.com
SIC: 8713 8711 Surveying services; Engineering services

(P-19527)
SANDIS CVIL ENGNERS SRVYORS PL (PA)
Also Called: Sandis
1700 Winchester Blvd Ste 200 (95008-1163)
PHONE..................408 636-0900
Ken Olcott, Pr
Jeff Setera, *
Tony Brubaker, *
EMP: 61 **EST:** 1965
SQ FT: 12,000
SALES (est): 24.77MM
SALES (corp-wide): 24.77MM **Privately Held**
Web: www.sandis.net
SIC: 8713 8711 Surveying services; Civil engineering

(P-19528)
YOUGOV AMERICA INC
Also Called: Yougov & Polimetrix Co
999 Main St Ste 101 (94063-1903)
PHONE..................650 462-8000
Stephen Shakespeare, CEO
Sundip Chahal, COO
Ray Martin, Chief Executive Officer Americas
EMP: 300 **EST:** 2007
SALES (est): 34.64MM
SALES (corp-wide): 269.63MM **Privately Held**

Web: today.yougov.com
SIC: 8713 7311 Surveying services; Advertising agencies
PA: Yougov Plc
 50 Featherstone Street
 London
 207 012-6000

8721 Accounting, Auditing, And Bookkeeping

(P-19529)
ABBOTT STRNGHAM LYNCH A PROF A
1530 Meridian Ave # 2 (95125-5350)
PHONE..................408 377-8700
Morgan Lynch, Pr
Robert G Simmons, *
Raymond E Schaeffer, *
Doug Taylor, In Charge*
Ray Scheaffer, *
EMP: 125 **EST:** 1977
SALES (est): 15.22MM **Privately Held**
Web: www.aslcpa.com
SIC: 8721 Accounting services, except auditing

(P-19530)
ARMANDO C IBRRA CPA A PROF COR
310 Third Ave Ste Aa (91910-3976)
PHONE..................619 422-1348
Armando C Ibarra Senior, Pr
Armando C Ibarra Junior, VP
Oscar Ibarra, *
EMP: 60 **EST:** 1984
SALES (est): 1.69MM **Privately Held**
Web: www.icscpas.com
SIC: 8721 7291 Accounting services, except auditing; Tax return preparation services

(P-19531)
ARMANINO LLP
11766 Wilshire Blvd Fl 9 (90025-6538)
PHONE..................310 478-4148
EMP: 321
SALES (corp-wide): 311.23MM **Privately Held**
Web: www.armanino.com
SIC: 8721 Certified public accountant
PA: Armanino Llp
 2700 Camino Ramon Ste 350
 San Ramon CA
 925 790-2600

(P-19532)
ARMANINO LLP
50 W San Fernando St Ste 500 (95113-2438)
PHONE..................408 200-6400
EMP: 271
SALES (corp-wide): 311.23MM **Privately Held**
Web: www.armanino.com
SIC: 8721 8742 Certified public accountant; Management consulting services
PA: Armanino Llp
 2700 Camino Ramon Ste 350
 San Ramon CA
 925 790-2600

(P-19533)
ARMANINO LLP (PA)
Also Called: AMF Media Group
2700 Camino Ramon Ste 350 (94583-5004)
PHONE..................925 790-2600
Matt Armanino, CEO

8721 - Accounting, Auditing, And Bookkeeping (P-19554)

Chris Carlberg, *COO*
Carol Ann Nash, *CPO*
EMP: 160 **EST:** 2017
SQ FT: 5,500
SALES (est): 311.23MM
SALES (corp-wide): 311.23MM **Privately Held**
Web: www.armanino.com
SIC: 8721 8742 Certified public accountant; Management consulting services

(P-19534)
BAKER TILLY US LLP
15760 Ventura Blvd Ste 1100 (91436-3000)
PHONE..................................818 981-2600
William Wolf, *Brnch Mgr*
EMP: 292
Web: www.bakertilly.com
SIC: 8721 Certified public accountant
HQ: Baker Tilly Us, Llp
 205 N Michigan Ave # 2800
 Chicago IL
 312 729-8000

(P-19535)
BAKER TILLY US LLP
11150 Santa Monica Blvd Ste 600 (90025-0479)
PHONE..................................310 826-4474
Lew Thomashaw, *Brnch Mgr*
EMP: 760
Web: www.bakertilly.com
SIC: 8721 Certified public accountant
HQ: Baker Tilly Us, Llp
 205 N Michigan Ave # 2800
 Chicago IL
 312 729-8000

(P-19536)
BAKER TILLY US LLP
3655 Nobel Dr Ste 300 (92122-1050)
PHONE..................................858 597-4100
Vanessa Liguzinski, *Brnch Mgr*
EMP: 292
Web: www.bakertilly.com
SIC: 8721 Certified public accountant
HQ: Baker Tilly Us, Llp
 205 N Michigan Ave # 2800
 Chicago IL
 312 729-8000

(P-19537)
BAKER TILLY US LLP
Also Called: Baker Tilly California
18500 Von Karman Ave Fl 10 (92612-0527)
PHONE..................................949 222-2999
Thomas Bennett, *Mng Pt*
EMP: 351
Web: www.bakertilly.com
SIC: 8721 Certified public accountant
HQ: Baker Tilly Us, Llp
 205 N Michigan Ave # 2800
 Chicago IL
 312 729-8000

(P-19538)
BMS PARENT INC (PA)
1220 Dewey Way Ste F (91786-1101)
PHONE..................................909 981-2341
John Wallace, *CEO*
Barbara Gillet, *
EMP: 68 **EST:** 1997
SQ FT: 9,000
SALES (est): 3.27MM
SALES (corp-wide): 3.27MM **Privately Held**
SIC: 8721 5045 Billing and bookkeeping service; Computer software

(P-19539)
BOOS & ASSOCIATES A PROF CORP
Also Called: Boostest
5250 N Palm Ave Ste 120 (93704-2200)
PHONE..................................559 449-7688
Wayne Boos, *Pr*
EMP: 60 **EST:** 2009
SALES (est): 5.42MM **Privately Held**
Web: www.booscpa.com
SIC: 8721 Certified public accountant

(P-19540)
BPM LLP
10 Almaden Blvd Ste 1000 (95113-2238)
PHONE..................................408 961-6300
James Wallace, *Pt*
EMP: 100 **EST:** 2017
SALES (est): 4.05MM **Privately Held**
Web: www.bpm.com
SIC: 8721 Accounting, auditing, and bookkeeping

(P-19541)
BRAULT
Also Called: Emergency Groups' Office
180 Via Verde Ste 100 (91773-3993)
PHONE..................................626 447-0296
EMP: 200 **EST:** 2015
SALES (est): 10.21MM **Privately Held**
Web: www.brault.us
SIC: 8721 Billing and bookkeeping service

(P-19542)
BROWN ARMSTRONG ACCNTANCY CORP
Also Called: Brown Armstrong Cpas
4200 Truxtun Ave Ste 300 (93309-0668)
PHONE..................................661 324-4971
Andrew J Paulden, *Pr*
Peter C Brown, *
Burton H Armstrong, *
Benjamin P Reyes, *
Jerry E Randall, *
EMP: 65 **EST:** 1974
SQ FT: 30,000
SALES (est): 10.1MM **Privately Held**
Web: www.ba.cpa
SIC: 8721 Certified public accountant

(P-19543)
BURR PILGER MAYER INC (PA)
600 California St Fl 600 (94108-2752)
PHONE..................................415 421-5757
James Wallace, *CEO*
EMP: 110 **EST:** 1986
SQ FT: 20,824
SALES (est): 50.33MM
SALES (corp-wide): 50.33MM **Privately Held**
Web: www.bpmllp.com
SIC: 8721 Certified public accountant

(P-19544)
BURR PILGER MAYER INC
4200 Bohannon Dr Ste 250 (94025-1021)
PHONE..................................650 855-6800
Mark Loveless, *Brnch Mgr*
EMP: 76
SALES (corp-wide): 50.33MM **Privately Held**
Web: www.bpm.com
SIC: 8721 Certified public accountant
PA: Burr Pilger Mayer, Inc.
 600 California St Fl 600 # 600
 San Francisco CA
 415 421-5757

(P-19545)
CACHET FINANCIAL SERVICES
175 S Lake Ave Unit 200 (91101-2629)
PHONE..................................626 578-9400
Aberash Asfaw, *Pr*
Alden Blowers, *Pr*
EMP: 95 **EST:** 2001
SALES (est): 4.51MM
SALES (corp-wide): 7.62MM **Privately Held**
Web: www.cachetservices.com
SIC: 8721 Payroll accounting service
PA: Financial Business Group Holdings
 1932 E Deere Ave Ste 200
 Santa Ana CA
 949 225-3000

(P-19546)
CALIFORNIA BUSINESS BUREAU INC (PA)
Also Called: Medical Billing Services
1711 S Mountain Ave (91016-4256)
P.O. Box 5010 (91017-7110)
PHONE..................................626 303-1515
Michael J Sigal, *Pr*
EMP: 132 **EST:** 1973
SQ FT: 24,000
SALES (est): 12.43MM
SALES (corp-wide): 12.43MM **Privately Held**
Web: www.cbbinc.com
SIC: 8721 Billing and bookkeeping service

(P-19547)
CALIFORNIA STATE UNIV LONG BCH
Also Called: Bursar's Office
1250 N Bellflower Blvd Bh155 (90840-0004)
PHONE..................................562 985-1764
Randy Nielson, *Supervisor*
EMP: 202
SALES (corp-wide): 534.4MM **Privately Held**
Web: www.csulb.edu
SIC: 8721 8221 9411 Accounting, auditing, and bookkeeping; University; Administration of educational programs
HQ: California State University, Long Beach
 1250 N Bellflower Blvd
 Long Beach CA
 562 985-4111

(P-19548)
CAPINCROUSE LLP
Also Called: CAPINCROUSE LLP
5990 Stoneridge Dr (94588-4517)
PHONE..................................925 201-1187
EMP: 88
SALES (corp-wide): 9.74MM **Privately Held**
Web: www.capincrouse.com
SIC: 8721 Certified public accountant
PA: Capin Crouse Llp
 9511 Angola Ct Ste 221
 Indianapolis IN
 317 885-2620

(P-19549)
CAST & CREW LLC (PA)
Also Called: Cast and Crew Entrmt Svcs
2300 W Empire Ave Ste 500 (91504-5399)
PHONE..................................818 570-6180
Eric Belcher, *Pr*
Sally Knutson, *
Shardell Cavaliere, *LIFE SERVCS**
Andrew Patterson, *
EMP: 195 **EST:** 1976
SQ FT: 12,000
SALES (est): 58.77MM
SALES (corp-wide): 58.77MM **Privately Held**
Web: www.castandcrew.com
SIC: 8721 Payroll accounting service

(P-19550)
CFGI LLC
600 California St Fl 14 (94108-2709)
PHONE..................................415 670-9041
Greg Lynch, *Mgr*
EMP: 75
SALES (corp-wide): 24.9MM **Privately Held**
Web: www.cfgi.com
SIC: 8721 7291 Accounting, auditing, and bookkeeping; Tax return preparation services
PA: Cfgi, Llc
 1 Lincoln St Ste 1301
 Boston MA
 617 531-8270

(P-19551)
CLIFTONLARSONALLEN LLP
925 Highland Pointe Dr Ste 450 (95678-5427)
PHONE..................................916 784-7800
EMP: 300
SALES (corp-wide): 966.83MM **Privately Held**
Web: www.claconnect.com
SIC: 8721 Certified public accountant
PA: Cliftonlarsonallen Llp
 220 S 6th St Ste 300
 Minneapolis MN
 612 376-4500

(P-19552)
CLIFTONLARSONALLEN LLP
Also Called: Nsbn
1925 Century Park E 16th Fl (90067-2701)
PHONE..................................310 273-2501
Randy Wells, *Brnch Mgr*
EMP: 91
SALES (corp-wide): 966.83MM **Privately Held**
Web: www.claconnect.com
SIC: 8721 Accounting services, except auditing
PA: Cliftonlarsonallen Llp
 220 S 6th St Ste 300
 Minneapolis MN
 612 376-4500

(P-19553)
COLLABRUS INC
Also Called: M Squared Consulting
180 Montgomery St Ste 2380 (94104-4228)
P.O. Box 210100 (94121-0100)
PHONE..................................415 288-1826
Alex Todd, *CEO*
Russel Orelowitz, *
EMP: 240 **EST:** 1995
SALES (est): 22.78MM
SALES (corp-wide): 77.7MM **Privately Held**
Web: www.collabrus.com
SIC: 8721 Billing and bookkeeping service
HQ: M Squared Consulting, Inc.
 180 Montgomery St # 2380
 San Francisco CA
 415 391-1038

(P-19554)
COMPUTERIZED MGT SVCS INC
Also Called: CMS
4100 Guardian St Ste 205 (93063-6721)
P.O. Box 190 (93062-0190)
PHONE..................................805 522-5940
J Daryl Favale, *Pr*

8721 - Accounting, Auditing, And Bookkeeping (P-19555)

PRODUCTS & SERVICES SECTION

EMP: 100 EST: 1985
SQ FT: 7,500
SALES (est): 6.67MM
SALES (corp-wide): 49.46MM Privately Held
Web: www.xifin.com
SIC: 8721 Billing and bookkeeping service
PA: Xifin, Inc.
  12225 El Camino Real
  San Diego CA
  858 793-5700

(P-19555)
CONSIDINE CNSDINE AN ACCNTNCY
8989 Rio San Diego Dr Ste 250 (92108-1629)
PHONE.............................619 231-1977
Perry S Wright, CEO
Timothy Considine, *
Don Bonk, *
Jerry Hotz, *
Charles E Considine, *
EMP: 109 EST: 1946
SQ FT: 20,000
SALES (est): 198.03K Privately Held
Web: www.cccpa.com
SIC: 8721 Certified public accountant

(P-19556)
COUNTY OF LOS ANGELES
Also Called: Internal Services Department
1100 N Eastern Ave (90063-3200)
PHONE.............................323 267-2136
Scott Minnix, Dir
EMP: 1800
SALES (corp-wide): 31.7B Privately Held
Web: www.lacounty.gov
SIC: 8721 Accounting, auditing, and bookkeeping
PA: County Of Los Angeles
  500 W Temple St Ste 437
  Los Angeles CA
  213 974-1101

(P-19557)
COUNTY OF SANTA CLARA
Also Called: Valley Med Ctr Billing Dept
2325 Enborg Ln Fl 4 (95128-2628)
PHONE.............................408 885-7200
Mary Wells, Dir
EMP: 211
Web: home.sccgov.org
SIC: 8721 9311 Billing and bookkeeping service; Finance, taxation, and monetary policy
PA: County Of Santa Clara
  70 W Hedding St
  San Jose CA
  408 299-5200

(P-19558)
COUNTY OF SANTA CLARA
Also Called: Santa Clara Vly Hlth Hosp Syst
751 S Bascom Ave 4th Fl (95128-2604)
PHONE.............................408 885-7354
EMP: 95
Web: home.sccgov.org
SIC: 8721 9431 Billing and bookkeeping service; Administration of public health programs
PA: County Of Santa Clara
  70 W Hedding St
  San Jose CA
  408 299-5200

(P-19559)
COUNTY OF VENTURA
Auditor /controller
800 S Victoria Ave Ste 1540 (93009-0001)
PHONE.............................805 654-3152
Christine Cohens, Mgr
EMP: 74
SALES (corp-wide): 165.04MM Privately Held
Web: www.ventura.org
SIC: 8721 9311 Auditing services; Controllers' office, government
PA: County Of Ventura
  800 S Victoria Ave
  Ventura CA
  805 654-2644

(P-19560)
DELOITTE & TOUCHE LLP
12830 El Camino Real Ste 600 (92130)
PHONE.............................619 232-6500
Cathy Jennings, Mgr
EMP: 1321
SALES (corp-wide): 677.45K Privately Held
Web: www.deloitte.com
SIC: 8721 7291 Certified public accountant; Tax return preparation services
HQ: Deloitte & Touche Llp
  30 Rockefeller Plz # 4350
  New York NY
  212 492-4000

(P-19561)
DELOITTE & TOUCHE LLP
225 W Santa Clara St Ste 600 (95113-1728)
PHONE.............................408 704-4000
Jonathan Tharmapalan, Mgr
EMP: 450
SALES (corp-wide): 677.45K Privately Held
Web: www.deloitte.com
SIC: 8721 8742 6282 Certified public accountant; Management consulting services; Investment advice
HQ: Deloitte & Touche Llp
  30 Rockefeller Plz # 4350
  New York NY
  212 492-4000

(P-19562)
DELOITTE & TOUCHE LLP
555 W 5th St Ste 2700 (90013-1024)
PHONE.............................213 688-0800
Byron David, Brnch Mgr
EMP: 1000
SALES (corp-wide): 677.45K Privately Held
Web: www.deloitte.com
SIC: 8721 Accounting services, except auditing
HQ: Deloitte & Touche Llp
  30 Rockefeller Plz # 4350
  New York NY
  212 492-4000

(P-19563)
DELOITTE & TOUCHE LLP
695 Town Center Dr Ste 1200 (92626-7188)
PHONE.............................714 436-7419
Bob Grant, Mgr
EMP: 221
SALES (corp-wide): 677.45K Privately Held
Web: www.deloitte.com
SIC: 8721 7291 Accounting services, except auditing; Tax return preparation services
HQ: Deloitte & Touche Llp
  30 Rockefeller Plz # 4350
  New York NY
  212 492-4000

(P-19564)
DELOITTE & TOUCHE LLP
555 Mission St Ste 1400 (94105-0942)
PHONE.............................415 783-4000
Mark Edmonds, Brnch Mgr
EMP: 429
SALES (corp-wide): 677.45K Privately Held
Web: www.deloitte.com
SIC: 8721 Accounting services, except auditing
HQ: Deloitte & Touche Llp
  30 Rockefeller Plz # 4350
  New York NY
  212 492-4000

(P-19565)
DELOITTE TAX LLP
555 W 5th St Ste 2700 (90013-1024)
PHONE.............................404 885-6754
EMP: 104
SALES (corp-wide): 677.45K Privately Held
Web: www.deloitte.com
SIC: 8721 Auditing services
HQ: Deloitte Tax Llp
  30 Rockefeller Plz
  New York NY
  212 492-4000

(P-19566)
DELOITTE TAX LLP
Also Called: Deloitte
555 Mission St Ste 1400 (94105-0942)
PHONE.............................415 783-4000
EMP: 294
SALES (corp-wide): 677.45K Privately Held
Web: www.deloitte.com
SIC: 8721 Auditing services
HQ: Deloitte Tax Llp
  30 Rockefeller Plz
  New York NY
  212 492-4000

(P-19567)
DELOITTE TAX LLP
225 W Santa Clara St Ste 600 (95113-1728)
PHONE.............................408 704-4000
EMP: 294
SALES (corp-wide): 677.45K Privately Held
Web: www.deloitte.com
SIC: 8721 Certified public accountant
HQ: Deloitte Tax Llp
  30 Rockefeller Plz
  New York NY
  212 492-4000

(P-19568)
EGO INC
Also Called: Emergency Groups Office
180 Via Verde Ste 100 (91773-3993)
PHONE.............................626 447-0296
Andrea Brault, Pr
Del Brault, *
Jane Brault, *
James Blakeman, *
EMP: 150 EST: 1990
SQ FT: 8,500
SALES (est): 24.04MM Privately Held
Web: www.brault.us
SIC: 8721 Billing and bookkeeping service

(P-19569)
EIDE BAILLY LLP
10681 Foothill Blvd Ste 300 (91730)
PHONE.............................909 466-4410
Dave Stende, Mng Pt
EMP: 300
SALES (corp-wide): 537.56MM Privately Held
Web: www.eidebailly.com
SIC: 8721 Certified public accountant
PA: Eide Bailly Llp
  4310 17th Ave S
  Fargo ND
  701 239-8500

(P-19570)
EISNERAMPER LLP
1 Market Ste 620 (94105-5105)
PHONE.............................415 974-6000
John Williamson, Mng Pt
EMP: 237
SALES (corp-wide): 350.25MM Privately Held
Web: www.eisnramper.com
SIC: 8721 Certified public accountant
PA: Eisneramper Llp
  733 3rd Ave Fl 9
  New York NY
  212 949-8700

(P-19571)
EISNERAMPER LLP
3001 Douglas Blvd Ste 350 (95661-4230)
PHONE.............................916 563-7790
Charles Weinstein, Brnch Mgr
EMP: 190
SALES (corp-wide): 350.25MM Privately Held
Web: www.eisnramper.com
SIC: 8721 Certified public accountant
PA: Eisneramper Llp
  733 3rd Ave Fl 9
  New York NY
  212 949-8700

(P-19572)
ELECTRONIC MEDICAL MANAGEMENT (PA)
Also Called: Emmi
3116 W March Ln Ste 200 (95219-2370)
PHONE.............................209 473-6555
Cyril Seligman, Pr
Brian Seligman, *
EMP: 65 EST: 1989
SQ FT: 14,000
SALES (est): 4.76MM Privately Held
Web: www.emmicorp.com
SIC: 8721 5734 Billing and bookkeeping service; Software, business and non-game

(P-19573)
ENTERTAINMENT PARTNERS INC (PA)
2950 N Hollywood Way (91505-1072)
PHONE.............................818 955-6000
Mark Goldstein, CEO
George Vaughan, *
EMP: 295 EST: 1992
SQ FT: 38,000
SALES (est): 55.81MM Privately Held
Web: www.ep.com
SIC: 8721 Payroll accounting service

(P-19574)
ERNST & YOUNG LLP
Also Called: Ey
725 S Figueroa St Ste 200 (90017-5403)
PHONE.............................213 977-3200
Jeff Kaufman, Mgr
EMP: 1000
SALES (corp-wide): 27.95MM Privately Held
Web: www.ey.com

PRODUCTS & SERVICES SECTION
8721 - Accounting, Auditing, And Bookkeeping (P-19596)

SIC: 8721 8742 7291 Certified public accountant; Business management consultant; Tax return preparation services
PA: Ernst & Young Llp
1 Manhattan W Fl 6
New York NY
703 747-0049

(P-19575)
ERNST & YOUNG LLP
Also Called: Ey
303 Almaden Blvd Ste 1000 (95110-2721)
PHONE..................408 947-5500
Teri Shaffer, Brnch Mgr
EMP: 155
SALES (corp-wide): 27.95MM **Privately Held**
Web: www.ey.com
SIC: 8721 8742 Certified public accountant; Business management consultant
PA: Ernst & Young Llp
1 Manhattan W Fl 6
New York NY
703 747-0049

(P-19576)
ERNST & YOUNG LLP
Also Called: Ey
18101 Von Karman Ave Ste 1700 (92612-0164)
PHONE..................949 794-2300
Linda Minx, Off Mgr
EMP: 450
SALES (corp-wide): 27.95MM **Privately Held**
Web: www.ey.com
SIC: 8721 8742 Certified public accountant; Business management consultant
PA: Ernst & Young Llp
1 Manhattan W Fl 6
New York NY
703 747-0049

(P-19577)
FILM PAYROLL SERVICES INC (PA)
Also Called: Quantos Payroll
500 S Sepulveda Blvd Fl 4 (90049-3550)
PHONE..................310 440-9600
Gregory Pickert, CEO
EMP: 100 EST: 1978
SQ FT: 5,000
SALES (est): 16.28MM **Privately Held**
Web: www.mediaservices.com
SIC: 8721 Payroll accounting service

(P-19578)
GATTO POPE WALWICK LLP
3131 Camino Del Rio N Ste 1200 (92108)
PHONE..................619 282-7366
Charlie Pope, Mng Pt
Daniel Gatto, Pt
Kirk Walwick, Pt
Thomas Mcfadden, Pt
EMP: 70 EST: 1983
SALES (est): 4.41MM **Privately Held**
Web: www.gpwcpas.com
SIC: 8721 8111 Certified public accountant; General practice attorney, lawyer

(P-19579)
GENENTECH INC
Also Called: Genentech Procurement Dept
1 Dna Way Stop 35 (94080-4990)
P.O. Box 4354 (97208-4354)
PHONE..................650 225-1000
EMP: 713
Web: www.gene.com
SIC: 8721 Accounting services, except auditing
HQ: Genentech, Inc.
1 Dna Way
South San Francisco CA
650 225-1000

(P-19580)
GILBERT ASSOCIATES INC
2880 Gateway Oaks Dr Ste 100 (95833-4329)
PHONE..................916 646-6464
David L June, Pr
David Ljung, Pr
Linda Geery, VP
Sarah Ellis, CFO
Kevin Wong, Sec
EMP: 95 EST: 2010
SALES (est): 4.46MM **Privately Held**
Web: www.gilbertcpa.com
SIC: 8721 Certified public accountant

(P-19581)
GREEN HASSON & JANKS LLP
700 S Flower St Ste 3300 (90017-3701)
PHONE..................310 873-1600
Leon Janks, Pt
William Cline, *
EMP: 120 EST: 1953
SALES (est): 25.68MM **Privately Held**
Web: www.ghjadvisors.com
SIC: 8721 Certified public accountant

(P-19582)
GRIMBLEBY CLMAN CRTIF PUB ACCN
200 W Roseburg Ave (95350-5255)
PHONE..................209 527-4220
Clive T Grimbleby, Pr
EMP: 94 EST: 1981
SQ FT: 1,000
SALES (est): 9.47MM **Privately Held**
Web: www.grimbleby-coleman.com
SIC: 8721 Certified public accountant

(P-19583)
GURSEY SCHNEIDER & CO LLC (PA)
1888 Century Park E Ste 900 (90067-1702)
PHONE..................310 552-0960
Donald Gursey, *
David Blumenthal, *
Robert Watts, *
Rosanna Purzycki, *
EMP: 117 EST: 1964
SQ FT: 12,000
SALES (est): 179.49K
SALES (corp-wide): 179.49K **Privately Held**
Web: www.gursey.com
SIC: 8721 Certified public accountant

(P-19584)
HAGEN STREIFF NEWTON & OSHIRO ACCOUNTANTS PC
4667 Macarthur Blvd Ste 400 (92660-1817)
PHONE..................949 390-7647
EMP: 99
SIC: 8721 Calculating and statistical service

(P-19585)
HOLTHOUSE CARLIN VAN TRIGT LLP (PA)
Also Called: H C V T
11444 W Olympic Blvd Fl 11 (90064-1500)
PHONE..................310 566-1900
Philip Holthouse, Mng Pt
James Carlin, *
John Van Trigt, *
Zach Shuman, *
Blake Christian, *
EMP: 110 EST: 1991
SALES (est): 36.22MM **Privately Held**
Web: www.hcvt.com
SIC: 8721 Certified public accountant

(P-19586)
HOOD & STRONG LLP (PA)
275 Battery St Ste 900 (94111-3332)
PHONE..................415 781-0793
Robert Raffo, Mng Pt
Raul Hernandez, Pt
Steve Piuma, Pt
EMP: 75 EST: 1917
SQ FT: 13,000
SALES (est): 13.97MM
SALES (corp-wide): 13.97MM **Privately Held**
Web: www.hoodstrong.com
SIC: 8721 Certified public accountant

(P-19587)
HOTTA LIESENBERG SAITO LLP
970 W 190th St Ste 900 (90502-1053)
PHONE..................424 246-2000
George Liesenberg, Prin
EMP: 68 EST: 2010
SALES (est): 5.19MM **Privately Held**
Web: www.hls-global.com
SIC: 8721 Certified public accountant

(P-19588)
INFINEON TECH AMERICAS CORP
Interntnal Rctfr/Ccunting Dept
222 Kansas St (90245-4315)
PHONE..................310 726-8000
Michael Mcgee, Mgr
EMP: 699
SALES (corp-wide): 14.17B **Privately Held**
Web: www.infineon.com
SIC: 8721 3674 Accounting, auditing, and bookkeeping; Semiconductors and related devices
HQ: Infineon Technologies Americas Corp.
101 N Pacific Coast Hwy
El Segundo CA
310 726-8200

(P-19589)
INFOSEND INC (PA)
4240 E La Palma Ave (92807-1816)
PHONE..................714 993-2690
Mahmood Rezai, Pr
Rusteen Rezai, COO
EMP: 68 EST: 1997
SALES (est): 18.28MM
SALES (corp-wide): 18.28MM **Privately Held**
Web: www.infosend.com
SIC: 8721 7338 2732 2741 Billing and bookkeeping service; Stenographic services; Pamphlets: printing only, not published on site; Business service newsletters: publishing and printing

(P-19590)
INNOVTIVE EMPLYEE SLUTIONS INC (PA)
2307 Fenton Pkwy 107-615 (92108-4746)
PHONE..................858 715-5100
Karla Hertzog, CEO
Darlene Bruder, *
Tania Fiero, *
Peter Limone, *
Trevor Foster, *
EMP: 69 EST: 1987
SQ FT: 6,641
SALES (est): 43.78MM
SALES (corp-wide): 43.78MM **Privately Held**
Web: www.innovativeemployeesolutions.com
SIC: 8721 Payroll accounting service

(P-19591)
JS HELD LLC
4667 Macarthur Blvd Ste 400 (92660-1817)
PHONE..................949 390-7647
EMP: 99
SALES (corp-wide): 200MM **Privately Held**
Web: www.jsheld.com
SIC: 8721 Calculating and statistical service
PA: J.S. Held Llc
50 Jericho Quadrangle # 117
Jericho NY
516 621-2900

(P-19592)
KBKG INC
225 S Lake Ave Ste 400 (91101-3010)
PHONE..................626 449-4225
EMP: 160 EST: 2001
SALES (est): 12.07MM **Privately Held**
Web: www.kbkg.com
SIC: 8721 Certified public accountant

(P-19593)
KELLOGG ANDLSON ACCNTANCY CORP (PA)
Also Called: Kellog
21700 Oxnard St Ste 800 (91367-7500)
PHONE..................818 971-5100
Christian Payne, CEO
James F Walters, *
William Wall, *
EMP: 60 EST: 1939
SALES (est): 10.96MM
SALES (corp-wide): 10.96MM **Privately Held**
SIC: 8721 Certified public accountant

(P-19594)
KPMG LLP
4464 Jasmine Ave (90232-3429)
PHONE..................703 286-8175
Daniel Smith, Mgr
EMP: 99
SALES (corp-wide): 1.34B **Privately Held**
Web: www.home.kpmg
SIC: 8721 Certified public accountant
PA: Kpmg Llp
345 Park Ave
New York NY
212 758-9700

(P-19595)
KPMG LLP
20 Pacifica Ste 700 (92618-3391)
PHONE..................949 885-5400
EMP: 120
SALES (corp-wide): 1.34B **Privately Held**
Web: www.home.kpmg
SIC: 8721 Certified public accountant
PA: Kpmg Llp
345 Park Ave
New York NY
212 758-9700

(P-19596)
KROST (PA)
Also Called: Krost Bumgarten Kniss Guerrero
225 S Lake Ave Ste 400 (91101-3010)
PHONE..................626 449-4225
Richard B Krost, CEO
Gregory Kniss, *
EMP: 170 EST: 1936
SALES (est): 13.73MM
SALES (corp-wide): 13.73MM **Privately Held**

8721 - Accounting, Auditing, And Bookkeeping (P-19597)

Web: www.krostcpas.com
SIC: 8721 Accounting services, except auditing

(P-19597)
LANCE SOLL & LUNGHARD LLP
203 N Brea Blvd Ste 203 (92821-4056)
PHONE..................714 672-0022
Ronald Stumpf, Pr
Gregory N Lewis, *
Edward J Leiber, *
Sherry Radmore, *
Yen Nguyen, *
EMP: 100 EST: 1968
SQ FT: 7,000
SALES (est): 5.54MM Privately Held
Web: www.lslcpas.com
SIC: 8721 Certified public accountant

(P-19598)
LAWRENCE BERKELEY NATIONAL LAB
1 Cyclotron Rd # 90j0106 (94720-8099)
PHONE..................510 486-6954
EMP: 1653
Web: www.lbl.gov
SIC: 8721 Accounting, auditing, and bookkeeping
HQ: Lawrence Berkeley National Lab
1 Cyclotron Rd 50-413
Berkeley CA
510 486-5111

(P-19599)
LLP MOSS ADAMS
2882 Prospect Park Dr Ste 300 (95670-6059)
PHONE..................916 503-8100
Robert Ahern, Brnch Mgr
EMP: 75
SALES (corp-wide): 317.2MM Privately Held
Web: www.mossadams.com
SIC: 8721 Certified public accountant
PA: Moss Adams Llp
999 3rd Ave Ste 2800
Seattle WA
206 302-6800

(P-19600)
LLP MOSS ADAMS
3121 W March Ln Ste 100 (95219-2367)
PHONE..................209 955-6100
David Gellerman, Prin
EMP: 72
SALES (corp-wide): 317.2MM Privately Held
Web: www.mossadams.com
SIC: 8721 Certified public accountant
PA: Moss Adams Llp
999 3rd Ave Ste 2800
Seattle WA
206 302-6800

(P-19601)
LLP MOSS ADAMS
101 2nd St Ste 900 (94105-3650)
PHONE..................415 956-1500
Joy Robinson, Brnch Mgr
EMP: 69
SALES (corp-wide): 317.2MM Privately Held
Web: www.mossadams.com
SIC: 8721 Certified public accountant
PA: Moss Adams Llp
999 3rd Ave Ste 2800
Seattle WA
206 302-6800

(P-19602)
LLP MOSS ADAMS
635 Campbell Technology Pkwy Ste 100 (95008-5071)
PHONE..................408 369-2400
Vid Lock, Pt
EMP: 74
SALES (corp-wide): 317.2MM Privately Held
Web: www.mossadams.com
SIC: 8721 Certified public accountant
PA: Moss Adams Llp
999 3rd Ave Ste 2800
Seattle WA
206 302-6800

(P-19603)
LLP MOSS ADAMS
21700 Oxnard St Ste 300 (91367-7561)
PHONE..................310 477-0450
Rod Green, Pt
EMP: 150
SALES (corp-wide): 317.2MM Privately Held
Web: www.mossadams.com
SIC: 8721 Certified public accountant
PA: Moss Adams Llp
999 3rd Ave Ste 2800
Seattle WA
206 302-6800

(P-19604)
LLP MOSS ADAMS
2040 Main St Ste 900 (92614-8213)
PHONE..................949 221-4000
Roger Weninger, Brnch Mgr
EMP: 115
SALES (corp-wide): 317.2MM Privately Held
Web: www.mossadams.com
SIC: 8721 Certified public accountant
PA: Moss Adams Llp
999 3rd Ave Ste 2800
Seattle WA
206 302-6800

(P-19605)
LLP MOSS ADAMS
4747 Executive Dr Ste 1300 (92121-3114)
PHONE..................858 627-1400
Laura Roos, Pt
EMP: 91
SALES (corp-wide): 317.2MM Privately Held
Web: www.mossadams.com
SIC: 8721 Certified public accountant
PA: Moss Adams Llp
999 3rd Ave Ste 2800
Seattle WA
206 302-6800

(P-19606)
MACIAS GINI & OCONNELL LLP
700 S Flower St Ste 800 (90017-4105)
PHONE..................213 408-8700
EMP: 105
Web: www.mgocpa.com
SIC: 8721 Certified public accountant
PA: Macias Gini & O'connell Llp
500 Capitol Mall Ste 2200
Sacramento CA

(P-19607)
MACIAS GINI & OCONNELL LLP
Also Called: Beverly Office of Mgo
2121 Avenue Of The Stars Ste 2200 (90067-5046)
PHONE..................323 653-8300
EMP: 104
Web: www.mgocpa.com
SIC: 8721 Certified public accountant
PA: Macias Gini & O'connell Llp
500 Capitol Mall Ste 2200
Sacramento CA

(P-19608)
MACIAS GINI & OCONNELL LLP (PA)
Also Called: Mgo
500 Capitol Mall Ste 2200 (95814-4759)
PHONE..................310 277-3373
Kevin O'connell, Pt
Kenneth A Macias, Pt
Ernest Gini, Pt
Kevin O Connell, Pt
Jan Rosati, Pt
EMP: 75 EST: 1989
SQ FT: 12,000
SALES (est): 78.53MM Privately Held
Web: www.mgocpa.com
SIC: 8721 Certified public accountant

(P-19609)
MACIAS GINI & OCONNELL LLP
Also Called: Mgo
2121 Avenue Of The Stars Ste 2200 (90067-5046)
PHONE..................916 928-4600
EMP: 104
Web: www.mgocpa.com
SIC: 8721 Certified public accountant
PA: Macias Gini & O'connell Llp
500 Capitol Mall Ste 2200
Sacramento CA

(P-19610)
MAZE & ASSOC ACCOUNTING CORP
3478 Buskirk Ave (94523-4344)
PHONE..................925 930-0902
Timothy Kirsch, CEO
Timothy J Krisch, *
Chris Hunt, *
Katherine Yuen, *
EMP: 60 EST: 1979
SALES (est): 9.89MM Privately Held
Web: www.mazeassociates.com
SIC: 8721 7299 Accounting services, except auditing; Information services, consumer

(P-19611)
MED-DATA INCORPORATED
3741 Douglas Blvd (95661-4241)
PHONE..................916 771-1362
Bruce Stewart, Brnch Mgr
EMP: 100
SALES (corp-wide): 11.32MM Privately Held
Web: www.elevatepfs.com
SIC: 8721 Accounting services, except auditing
PA: Med-Data, Incorporated
3326 160th Ave Se Ste 440
Bellevue WA
800 261-0048

(P-19612)
MILLER KAPLAN ARASE LLP (PA)
Also Called: Cahn, Jsph/Miller Kaplan Arase
4123 Lankershim Blvd (91602-2828)
PHONE..................818 769-2010
EMP: 129 EST: 1940
SALES (est): 17.38MM
SALES (corp-wide): 17.38MM Privately Held
Web: www.millerkaplan.com
SIC: 8721 Certified public accountant

(P-19613)
MURPHY MURPHY & MURPHY INC
6261 Katella Ave (90630-5200)
PHONE..................562 594-6678
Patrick G Murphy, CEO
EMP: 92 EST: 2009
SALES (est): 8.52MM Privately Held
Web: www.murphy3.com
SIC: 8721 Certified public accountant

(P-19614)
NASIF HICKS HARRIS & CO LLP
Also Called: Harris, Jeffery P
104 W Anapamu St Ste B (93101-3126)
PHONE..................805 966-1521
William Nasif, Pt
Jeffrey Hicks, Pt
Steven Hicks, Pt
EMP: 64 EST: 1988
SQ FT: 2,400
SALES (est): 6.3MM Privately Held
Web: www.nhhco.com
SIC: 8721 Certified public accountant

(P-19615)
NEW TALCO ENTERPRISES LLC
Also Called: Caps Payroll
2300 W Empire Ave (91504-3341)
PHONE..................310 280-0755
Doug Sylvester, CEO
Frank Devito, *
David Lee, CIO*
Fran Lucci-pannozzo, CMO
Anne Plechner, *
EMP: 97 EST: 2010
SALES (est): 2.31MM
SALES (corp-wide): 58.77MM Privately Held
SIC: 8721 Payroll accounting service
PA: Cast & Crew Llc
2300 W Empire Ave Ste 500
Burbank CA
818 570-6180

(P-19616)
NIGRO KRLIN SGAL FLDSTEIN BLNO
1 Embarcadero Ctr Ste 3840 (94111-3628)
PHONE..................415 463-1300
EMP: 257
SALES (corp-wide): 213.24K Privately Held
Web: www.nksfb.com
SIC: 8721 Certified public accountant
PA: Nigro Karlin Segal Feldstein & Bolno, Llc.
10960 Wilshire Blvd Fl 5
Los Angeles CA
310 277-4657

(P-19617)
NOVOGRADAC & COMPANY LLP (PA)
1160 Battery St Ste 225 (94111)
P.O. Box 7833 (94120-7833)
PHONE..................415 356-8000
EMP: 120 EST: 1989
SALES (est): 47.09MM Privately Held
Web: www.novoco.com
SIC: 8721 Certified public accountant

(P-19618)
OMEGA ACCOUNTING SOLUTIONS INC
15101 Alton Pkwy Ste 450 (92618-2372)
PHONE..................949 348-2433
Jay Woods, Prin
EMP: 78 EST: 2008

8721 - Accounting, Auditing, And Bookkeeping (P-19641)

SALES (est): 3.34MM **Privately Held**
Web: www.omega-accounting.com
SIC: **8721** Accounting, auditing, and bookkeeping

(P-19619)
OPTIMA OFFICE INC
5120 Shoreham Pl Ste 285 (92122-5992)
PHONE..................................858 361-0481
EMP: 76 EST: 2018
SALES (est): 2.75MM **Privately Held**
Web: www.optimaoffice.com
SIC: **8721** Accounting, auditing, and bookkeeping

(P-19620)
PAYCHEX INC
50 Iron Point Cir Ste 200 (95630-8594)
PHONE..................................916 983-0303
Anita Mc Afee, *Brnch Mgr*
EMP: 70
SALES (corp-wide): 5.01B **Publicly Held**
Web: www.paychex.com
SIC: **8721** Payroll accounting service
PA: Paychex, Inc.
    911 Panorama Trl S
    Rochester NY
    585 385-6666

(P-19621)
PHYSICIAN SUPPORT SYSTEMS INC (DH)
1131 W 6th St Ste 300 (91762-1118)
PHONE..................................717 653-5340
Douglas Estock, *Pr*
EMP: 400 EST: 1991
SALES (est): 16.49MM
SALES (corp-wide): 276.71B **Publicly Held**
Web: www.pssbilling.com
SIC: **8721** Billing and bookkeeping service
HQ: Ndchealth Corporation
    1564 Northeast Expy Ne
    Brookhaven GA
    404 728-2000

(P-19622)
PHYSICIANS CHOICE LLC
21860 Burbank Blvd Ste 120 (91367-6477)
P.O. Box 4419 (91365-4419)
PHONE..................................818 340-9988
EMP: 80 EST: 1999
SQ FT: 10,000
SALES (est): 4.82MM **Privately Held**
Web: www.physchoice.com
SIC: **8721** Billing and bookkeeping service

(P-19623)
PRICEWATERHOUSECOOPERS LLP
488 Almaden Blvd Ste 1800 (95110-2768)
PHONE..................................408 817-3700
Don Mcgovern, *Brnch Mgr*
EMP: 700
SALES (corp-wide): 6.79B **Privately Held**
Web: www.pwc.com
SIC: **8721** Certified public accountant
PA: Pricewaterhousecoopers Llp
    300 Madison Ave
    New York NY
    646 471-4000

(P-19624)
PRO BACK OFFICE LLC
Also Called: Pbo Advisory Group
3655 Nobel Dr Ste 520 (92122-1051)
PHONE..................................858 622-1681
Michael R Ford, *Prin*
EMP: 63 EST: 2012

SALES (est): 6.97MM **Privately Held**
Web: www.pboadvisory.com
SIC: **8721** Certified public accountant

(P-19625)
QUALITY REIMBURSEMENT SERVICES
150 N Santa Anita Ave Ste 570a (91006-3113)
PHONE..................................626 445-5092
James C Ravindran, *CEO*
EMP: 75 EST: 1988
SALES (est): 7.48MM **Privately Held**
Web: www.qualityreimbursement.com
SIC: **8721** Auditing services

(P-19626)
RBZ LLP
11766 Wilshire Blvd Fl 9 (90025-6548)
PHONE..................................310 478-4148
EMP: 150
Web: www.armanino.com
SIC: **8721** Certified public accountant

(P-19627)
RECURLY INC (PA)
201 Spear St (94105-6164)
PHONE..................................844 732-8759
EMP: 61 EST: 2009
SALES (est): 36.45MM **Privately Held**
Web: www.recurly.com
SIC: **8721** Billing and bookkeeping service

(P-19628)
RSM US LLP
100 W San Fernando St (95113-2219)
PHONE..................................408 572-4440
EMP: 84
SALES (corp-wide): 2.44B **Privately Held**
SIC: **8721** Certified public accountant
PA: Rsm Us Llp
    1 S Wacker Dr Ste 800
    Chicago IL
    312 384-6000

(P-19629)
SEILER LLP (PA)
3 Lagoon Dr Ste 400 (94065-1561)
P.O. Box 8043 (94063-0943)
PHONE..................................650 365-4646
George Marinos, *Pt*
George Marinos, *CEO*
Kevin Paul, *COO*
James G B Demartini Iii, *Pt*
Brian J Dinsmore, *Pt*
EMP: 102 EST: 1957
SQ FT: 31,142
SALES (est): 2.55MM
SALES (corp-wide): 2.55MM **Privately Held**
Web: www.seiler.com
SIC: **8721** Certified public accountant

(P-19630)
SEMA LLC (PA)
Also Called: Cell Business Equipment
4 Mason Ste A (92618-2554)
PHONE..................................949 830-1400
TOLL FREE: 800
Tarek Abdulhafiz, *Pr*
▲ EMP: 74 EST: 1993
SQ FT: 18,000
SALES (est): 31.78MM **Privately Held**
Web: www.cbesolutions.com
SIC: **8721** 5044 Accounting, auditing, and bookkeeping; Photocopy machines

(P-19631)
SIGNATURE ANALYTICS LLC
10120 Pacific Heights Blvd Ste 110 (92121)
PHONE..................................888 284-3842
EMP: 84 EST: 2016
SALES (est): 1.1MM **Privately Held**
Web: www.signatureanalytics.com
SIC: **8721** Accounting, auditing, and bookkeeping

(P-19632)
SINGERLEWAK LLP (PA)
Also Called: Singerlewak
10960 Wilshire Blvd Fl 7 (90024-3710)
PHONE..................................310 477-3924
Jim Pitrat, *Mng Pt*
Jim Pitrat Mng Pttnr, *Prin*
Norman Greenbaum, *Pt*
William D Simon, *Pt*
David Free, *Pt*
◆ EMP: 120 EST: 1959
SALES (est): 48.95MM
SALES (corp-wide): 48.95MM **Privately Held**
Web: www.singerlewak.com
SIC: **8721** 8742 Certified public accountant; Business management consultant

(P-19633)
TEAM COMPANIES LLC (PA)
Also Called: Team Services
2300 W Empire Ave Ste 500 (91504-3350)
PHONE..................................818 558-3261
Greg Smith, *Pr*
An De Vooght, *
Geoffrey Matus, *
EMP: 90 EST: 1992
SALES (est): 22.8MM
SALES (corp-wide): 22.8MM **Privately Held**
Web: www.theteamcompanies.com
SIC: **8721** Payroll accounting service

(P-19634)
TGG ACCOUNTING
10188 Telesis Ct Ste 130 (92121-4779)
PHONE..................................760 697-1033
Andrew Ruff, *Pr*
Andrew Ruff, *Pr*
Matt Garrett, *CEO*
EMP: 83 EST: 2013
SALES (est): 4.36MM **Privately Held**
Web: www.tgg-accounting.com
SIC: **8721** 8748 Payroll accounting service; Business consulting, nec

(P-19635)
THOMAS WIRIG DOLL & CO CPAS
Also Called: Thomas Doll & Company
165 Lennon Ln Ste 200 (94598-2447)
P.O. Box 30307 (94598-9307)
PHONE..................................925 939-2500
Brent P Thomas, *Pr*
Sherman Doll, *
EMP: 66 EST: 1988
SQ FT: 9,000
SALES (est): 8.59MM **Privately Held**
Web: www.thomasdoll.com
SIC: **8721** Certified public accountant

(P-19636)
UNIVERSITY CALIFORNIA IRVINE
Also Called: Accounting and Fiscal Services
120 Theory Ste 200 (92617-3210)
PHONE..................................949 824-6828
Griselda Duran Optns, *Mgr*
EMP: 80

SALES (corp-wide): 534.4MM **Privately Held**
Web: www.uci.edu
SIC: **8721** Accounting, auditing, and bookkeeping
HQ: University Of California, Irvine
    510 Aldrich Hall
    Irvine CA
    949 824-5011

(P-19637)
UNIVERSITY CALIFORNIA IRVINE
Also Called: UCI Division Plastic Surgery
200 S Manchester Ave Ste 650 (92868-3220)
PHONE..................................714 456-6655
EMP: 80
SALES (corp-wide): 534.4MM **Privately Held**
Web: www.uciplasticsurgery.com
SIC: **8721** 8221 9411 Accounting, auditing, and bookkeeping; University; Administration of educational programs
HQ: University Of California, Irvine
    510 Aldrich Hall
    Irvine CA
    949 824-5011

(P-19638)
VASQUEZ & COMPANY LLP (PA)
655 N Central Ave Ste 1550 (91203-1451)
PHONE..................................213 873-1700
Gilbert Vasquez, *Mng Pt*
Linda Narciso Audit, *Pt*
EMP: 61 EST: 1980
SALES (est): 13.7MM
SALES (corp-wide): 13.7MM **Privately Held**
Web: www.vasquez.cpa
SIC: **8721** Certified public accountant

(P-19639)
WINDES INC (PA)
3780 Kilroy Airport Way Ste 600 (90806-2451)
P.O. Box 87 (90801-0087)
PHONE..................................562 435-1191
John L Dicarlo, *CEO*
Scott J Dionne, *
EMP: 100 EST: 1926
SQ FT: 26,560
SALES (est): 21.23MM
SALES (corp-wide): 21.23MM **Privately Held**
Web: www.windes.com
SIC: **8721** Certified public accountant

(P-19640)
WITHUMSMITH+BROWN PC
601 California St Ste 1800 (94108-2834)
PHONE..................................415 434-3744
EMP: 68
SALES (corp-wide): 132.85K **Privately Held**
Web: www.withum.com
SIC: **8721** Certified public accountant
PA: Withumsmith+Brown, Pc
    506 Carnegie Ctr Ste 400
    Princeton NJ
    609 520-1188

(P-19641)
WRIGHT FORD YOUNG & CO
16140 Sand Canyon Ave (92618-3715)
PHONE..................................949 910-2727
EMP: 85 EST: 2019
SALES (est): 3.13MM **Privately Held**
Web: www.cpa-wfy.com

SIC: 8721 Certified public accountant

8731 Commercial Physical Research

(P-19642)
10X GENOMICS INC (PA)
Also Called: 10X GENOMICS
6230 Stoneridge Mall Rd (94588-3260)
PHONE..................................925 401-7300
Serge Saxonov, *CEO*
John R Stuelpnagel, *
Benjamin J Hindson, *CSO*
Justin J Mcanear, *CFO*
Bradford J Crutchfield, *CCO*
EMP: 216 EST: 2012
SQ FT: 200,000
SALES (est): 516.41MM
SALES (corp-wide): 516.41MM **Publicly Held**
Web: www.10xgenomics.com
SIC: 8731 Commercial physical research

(P-19643)
4D MOLECULAR THERAPEUTICS INC
5858 Horton St Ste 455 (94608-2072)
PHONE..................................510 505-2680
David Kirn, *CEO*
John F Milligan, *
Fred Kamal, *Pr*
Theresa Janke, *Chief Strategy Officer*
EMP: 78 EST: 2013
SALES (est): 3.13MM **Privately Held**
Web: www.4dmoleculartherapeutics.com
SIC: 8731 Biological research

(P-19644)
ACEA BIOSCIENCES INC
6779 Mesa Ridge Rd Ste 100 (92121-2996)
PHONE..................................858 724-0928
Xiao Xu, *Pr*
Xiaobo Wang, *
▲ EMP: 85 EST: 2001
SALES (est): 19.76MM
SALES (corp-wide): 6.85B **Publicly Held**
SIC: 8731 Biotechnical research, commercial
PA: Agilent Technologies, Inc.
    5301 Stevens Creek Blvd
    Santa Clara CA
    800 227-9770

(P-19645)
ADVANCED CELL DIAGNOSTICS INC
Also Called: Acd
7707 Gateway Blvd Ste 200 (94560-1268)
PHONE..................................510 576-8800
Yuling Luo, *Pr*
Steve Chen, *COO*
Jessie Qian Wang, *CFO*
Tom Olenic, *CCO*
Rob Monroe, *CMO*
EMP: 90 EST: 2006
SQ FT: 2,500
SALES (est): 10.35MM
SALES (corp-wide): 1.14B **Publicly Held**
SIC: 8731 2835 Biotechnical research, commercial; Microbiology and virology diagnostic products
PA: Bio-Techne Corporation
    614 Mckinley Pl Ne
    Minneapolis MN
    612 379-8854

(P-19646)
AEROSPACE CORPORATION
P.O. Box 91337 (90009-1337)
PHONE..................................310 336-7270
EMP: 88
SALES (corp-wide): 1.2B **Privately Held**
Web: www.aerospace.org
SIC: 8731 Commercial physical research
PA: The Aerospace Corporation
    2310 E El Segundo Blvd
    El Segundo CA
    310 336-5000

(P-19647)
AGENDIA INC
22 Morgan (92618-2022)
PHONE..................................949 540-6300
Mark R Straley, *CEO*
Brian Dow, *CFO*
Kurt Schmidt, *CFO*
Glen Fredenberg, *CFO*
Neil M Barth, *Chief Medical Officer*
EMP: 107 EST: 2008
SALES (est): 58.42MM
SALES (corp-wide): 57.46MM **Privately Held**
Web: www.agendia.com
SIC: 8731 Biotechnical research, commercial
PA: Agendia N.V.
    Radarweg 60
    Amsterdam NH
    204621500

(P-19648)
AGOURON PHARMACEUTICALS INC
3550 General Atomics Ct Bldg 9 (92121-1122)
PHONE..................................858 455-3200
Peter Johnson, *Pr*
EMP: 130
SALES (corp-wide): 100.33B **Publicly Held**
Web: www.agi.org
SIC: 8731 5122 Biotechnical research, commercial; Pharmaceuticals
HQ: Agouron Pharmaceuticals, Inc.
    10777 Science Center Dr
    San Diego CA
    858 622-3000

(P-19649)
AGOURON PHARMACEUTICALS INC
3301 N Torrey Pines Ct (92037-1022)
PHONE..................................858 622-3000
Evaristo Cruz, *Mgr*
EMP: 409
SALES (corp-wide): 100.33B **Publicly Held**
Web: www.agi.org
SIC: 8731 Biotechnical research, commercial
HQ: Agouron Pharmaceuticals, Inc.
    10777 Science Center Dr
    San Diego CA
    858 622-3000

(P-19650)
ALIMENTIV US INC
10581 Roselle St Ste 110 (92121-1521)
PHONE..................................858 356-5665
Denise Stark, *Prin*
EMP: 86 EST: 2013
SALES (est): 914.15K
SALES (corp-wide): 52.45MM **Privately Held**
Web: www.alimentiv.com
SIC: 8731 8011 Biotechnical research, commercial; General and family practice, physician/surgeon
PA: Alimentiv Inc.
    100 Dundas St Suite 200
    London ON
    226 270-7868

(P-19651)
ALKAHEST INC
125 Shoreway Rd Ste D (94070-2789)
PHONE..................................650 801-0474
Karoly Nikolich, *CEO*
Tamara Kent, *
Sam Jackson, *
Helen Jenkins, *
Michael Byrnes, *
EMP: 95 EST: 2014
SALES (est): 10.15MM **Privately Held**
Web: www.alkahest.com
SIC: 8731 Biotechnical research, commercial

(P-19652)
ALLELE BIO & PHARMACEUTICALS
6868 Nancy Ridge Dr (92121-2217)
PHONE..................................858 410-0299
Jiwu Wang, *CEO*
EMP: 237
SALES (corp-wide): 8.97MM **Privately Held**
Web: www.allelebiotech.com
SIC: 8731 Biotechnical research, commercial
PA: Allele Biotechnology And Pharmaceuticals, Inc.
    6404 Nancy Ridge Dr
    San Diego CA
    858 587-6645

(P-19653)
ALLOGENE THERAPEUTICS INC
7400 Gateway Blvd (94560-8003)
PHONE..................................650 457-2700
EMP: 85
SALES (corp-wide): 243K **Publicly Held**
Web: ir.allogene.com
SIC: 8731 Biological research
PA: Allogene Therapeutics, Inc.
    210 E Grand Ave
    South San Francisco CA
    650 457-2700

(P-19654)
ALTOR BSCNCE LLC AN INDRECT WH
9920 Jefferson Blvd (90232-3506)
PHONE..................................310 733-7107
Richard Adcock, *CEO*
Hing Wong, *
Rick Greene, *
Peter Rhode, *
EMP: 65 EST: 2002
SQ FT: 25,000
SALES (est): 9.67MM **Privately Held**
Web: www.immunitybio.com
SIC: 8731 Biotechnical research, commercial

(P-19655)
AMBYS MEDICINES INC
131 Oyster Point Blvd Ste 200 (94080-1910)
PHONE..................................408 373-4030
Ronald Park, *CEO*
Jeffrey K Tong, *Ch Bd*
Ran Xiao, *CFO*
Amanda Valentino, *CPO*
Nancy Shulman, *VP*
EMP: 79 EST: 2016
SALES (est): 10.36MM **Privately Held**
Web: www.cytotheryx.com
SIC: 8731 Biological research

(P-19656)
APPLIED RESEARCH ASSOC INC
10833 Valley View St Ste 250 (90630-5045)
PHONE..................................505 881-8074
Robert H Sues, *Brnch Mgr*
EMP: 99
SALES (corp-wide): 418.64MM **Privately Held**
Web: www.ara.com
SIC: 8731 Commercial physical research
HQ: Applied Research Associates, Inc.
    4300 San Mateo Blvd Ne
    Albuquerque NM
    505 883-3636

(P-19657)
ARCHIMDES TECH GROUP HLDNGS LL
5660 Eastgate Dr (92121-2816)
PHONE..................................858 642-9170
David Gerson, *
Scott Tierney, *
EMP: 71 EST: 1998
SQ FT: 20,000
SALES (est): 2.82MM **Privately Held**
SIC: 8731 Environmental research

(P-19658)
ARCTURUS THERAPEUTICS INC
10628 Science Center Dr Ste 250 (92121-1150)
PHONE..................................858 900-2660
Joseph Payne, *Pr*
Andrew Sassine, *
Steve Hughes, *CDO*
Lance Kurata, *CLO*
EMP: 150 EST: 2013
SALES (est): 29.73MM **Privately Held**
Web: www.arcturusrx.com
SIC: 8731 Biotechnical research, commercial

(P-19659)
ARCUS BIOSCIENCES INC (PA)
Also Called: ARCUS BIOSCIENCES
3928 Point Eden Way (94545-3719)
PHONE..................................510 694-6200
Terry Rosen, *Ch Bd*
Juan Carlos Jaen, *Pr*
Rekha Hemrajani, *CAO*
Eric Hoefer, *CCO*
Dimitry S A Nuyten, *Chief Medical Officer*
EMP: 87 EST: 2015
SQ FT: 70,100
SALES (est): 112MM
SALES (corp-wide): 112MM **Publicly Held**
Web: www.arcusbio.com
SIC: 8731 Biotechnical research, commercial

(P-19660)
ARIOSA DIAGNOSTICS INC
5945 Optical Ct (95138-1400)
PHONE..................................408 229-7500
Kenneth Song Md, *CEO*
Thomas Musci Md, *CMO*
Dave Mullarkey, *
Arnold Oliphant, *CSO*
EMP: 140 EST: 2008
SALES (est): 22.15MM **Publicly Held**
SIC: 8731 Biotechnical research, commercial
HQ: Bio-Reference Laboratories, Inc.
    481 Edward H Ross Dr
    Elmwood Park NJ
    800 229-5227

(P-19661)
AVERY CORP
207 N Goode Ave Fl 6 (91203-1364)
PHONE..................................626 304-2000
Dean Scarborough, *Pr*
EMP: 200 EST: 1968
SALES (est): 16.14MM
SALES (corp-wide): 9.04B **Publicly Held**
Web: www.avery.com

PRODUCTS & SERVICES SECTION
8731 - Commercial Physical Research (P-19683)

SIC: 8731 Biological research
PA: Avery Dennison Corporation
8080 Norton Pkwy
Mentor OH
440 534-6000

(P-19662)
BIODURO LLC
72 Fairbanks (92618-1668)
PHONE......................858 529-6600
Kent M Payne, *Brnch Mgr*
EMP: 264
Web: www.bioduro-sundia.com
SIC: 8731 Biotechnical research, commercial
PA: Bioduro Llc
11011 Torreyana Rd
San Diego CA

(P-19663)
BIOLEGEND INC (HQ)
8999 Biolegend Way (92121-2284)
PHONE......................858 455-9588
Gene Lay, *Pr*
Kent Johnson, *
◆ EMP: 101 EST: 2002
SQ FT: 75,000
SALES (est): 93.5MM
SALES (corp-wide): 3.31B **Publicly Held**
Web: www.biolegend.com
SIC: 8731 Biotechnical research, commercial
PA: Revvity, Inc.
940 Winter St
Waltham MA
781 663-6900

(P-19664)
BIOSPACE INC
Also Called: Inbody
13850 Cerritos Corporate Dr Ste C (90703-2467)
PHONE......................323 932-6503
Ki Chul Cha, *Pr*
Hak Hee Yun, *
▲ EMP: 86 EST: 2000
SQ FT: 35,319
SALES (est): 18.64MM **Privately Held**
Web: www.inbody.com
SIC: 8731 3821 Energy research; Calibration tapes, for physical testing machines
PA: Shenzhen Longgang District Baolong Kangxing Fruit Firm
No.419-420, Chishi Gang Xiaoqu Tongfu Road, Longxin Community, B
Shenzhen GD

(P-19665)
BIS RESEARCH INC
39111 Paseo Padre Pkwy Ste 313 (94538-1672)
PHONE......................510 404-8135
Mohammad Faisal Ahmad, *CEO*
Rupen Suri, *VP*
EMP: 130 EST: 2018
SALES (est): 10.43MM **Privately Held**
Web: www.bisresearch.com
SIC: 8731 Commercial physical research

(P-19666)
BRIDGEBIO SERVICES INC
421 Kipling St (94301-1530)
PHONE......................650 438-1302
Neil Kumar, *CEO*
Brian Stephenson, *
Frank Mccormick Cmn, *Prin*
Richard Scheller Cmn, *Prin*
Uma Sinha, *
EMP: 96 EST: 2015
SALES (est): 9.66MM
SALES (corp-wide): 77.65MM **Publicly Held**

Web: www.bridgebio.com
SIC: 8731 Biotechnical research, commercial
PA: Bridgebio Pharma, Inc.
3160 Porter Dr Ste 250
Palo Alto CA
650 391-9740

(P-19667)
CALICO LIFE SCIENCES LLC
Also Called: California Life Company
1170 Veterans Blvd (94080-1985)
PHONE......................650 754-6200
Arthur Levinson, *CEO*
EMP: 258 EST: 2013
SALES (est): 23.38MM
SALES (corp-wide): 282.84B **Publicly Held**
Web: www.calicolabs.com
SIC: 8731 Biotechnical research, commercial
HQ: Google Llc
1600 Amphitheatre Pkwy
Mountain View CA
650 253-0000

(P-19668)
CATALYST BIO INC
290 Utah St (94103-4842)
PHONE......................650 871-0761
Charles Craik, *Brnch Mgr*
EMP: 443
SIC: 8731 Biotechnical research, commercial
HQ: Catalyst Bio, Inc.
611 Gateway Blvd Ste 120
South San Francisco CA
650 266-8679

(P-19669)
CELLANOME INC
Also Called: Cellanome
1810 Embarcadero Rd Ste 200 (94303-3398)
PHONE......................510 736-0922
Ali Agah, *CEO*
EMP: 75 EST: 2020
SALES (est): 2.92MM **Privately Held**
Web: www.cellanome.com
SIC: 8731 Biotechnical research, commercial

(P-19670)
CGI TECHNOLOGIES SOLUTIONS INC
860 Stillwater Rd Ste 210 (95605-1684)
PHONE......................916 281-3200
EMP: 64
SALES (corp-wide): 9.87B **Privately Held**
SIC: 8731 Commercial physical research
HQ: Cgi Technologies And Solutions Inc.
11325 Rndom Hills Rd Fl 8 Flr 8
Fairfax VA
703 267-5111

(P-19671)
CHARLES RIVER LABORATORIES INC
Also Called: Charles Rver Acclrator Dev Lab
1300 Rancho Conejo Blvd (91320-1405)
PHONE......................877 274-8371
EMP: 70
SALES (corp-wide): 3.98B **Publicly Held**
Web: criver.dejobs.org
SIC: 8731 Biotechnical research, commercial
HQ: Charles River Laboratories, Inc.
10792 Roselle St
San Diego CA
978 658-6000

(P-19672)
CIBUS GLOBAL LTD
6455 Nancy Ridge Dr (92121-2249)

PHONE......................858 450-0008
Peter Beetham, *Pr*
Rory Riggs, *
Gerhard Prante, *
Greg Gocal, *CSO*
Jim Hinrichs, *CFO*
EMP: 134 EST: 2001
SQ FT: 53,000
SALES (est): 7.41MM **Privately Held**
Web: www.cibus.com
SIC: 8731 Biotechnical research, commercial

(P-19673)
CRL TECHNOLOGIES INC
543 W Graaf Ave B (93555-2529)
PHONE......................760 495-3000
Carlos M Velez, *Brnch Mgr*
EMP: 71
Web: www.crltechnologies.com
SIC: 8731 Commercial physical research
PA: Crl Technologies, Inc
9426 Ferry Landing Ct
Alexandria VA

(P-19674)
CUBERG INC
2020 Williams St Unit E (94577-2335)
PHONE......................510 725-4200
Richard Wang, *CEO*
EMP: 150 EST: 2015
SALES (est): 31.26MM
SALES (corp-wide): 103.26MM **Privately Held**
Web: www.cuberg.net
SIC: 8731 Commercial physical research
PA: Northvolt Ab
Alstromergatan 20
Stockholm
730592916

(P-19675)
CULTURE BIOSCIENCES INC
269 E Grand Ave (94080-4804)
PHONE......................919 622-5123
Will Patrick, *CEO*
EMP: 79 EST: 2016
SALES (est): 9.38MM **Privately Held**
Web: www.culturebiosciences.com
SIC: 8731 Commercial physical research

(P-19676)
CURTIS & TOMPKINS LTD
2323 5th St (94710-2407)
PHONE......................510 486-0900
EMP: 66
SIC: 8731 Commercial research laboratory

(P-19677)
DEEPCELL INC
4025 Bohannon Dr (94025-1004)
PHONE......................617 447-1067
Mahdokht Masaeli, *CEO*
Mahyar Salha, *
EMP: 63 EST: 2015
SALES (est): 10.77MM **Privately Held**
Web: www.deepcell.com
SIC: 8731 Biotechnical research, commercial

(P-19678)
DEPOSITION SCIENCES INC
Also Called: D S I
3300 Coffey Ln (95403-1917)
PHONE......................707 573-6700
Lee Bartolomei, *Pr*
Thomas Chambers, *
EMP: 96 EST: 1997
SQ FT: 8,400
SALES (est): 15.54MM **Publicly Held**
Web: www.depsci.com

SIC: 8731 3827 Industrial laboratory, except testing; Lens coating equipment
PA: Lockheed Martin Corporation
6801 Rockledge Dr
Bethesda MD

(P-19679)
DERMTECH OPERATIONS INC
12340 El Camino Real Ste 200 (92130)
PHONE......................866 450-4223
EMP: 260 EST: 1995
SQ FT: 9,000
SALES (est): 1.72MM
SALES (corp-wide): 14.52MM **Publicly Held**
Web: www.dermtech.com
SIC: 8731 Biotechnical research, commercial
PA: Dermtech, Inc.
12340 El Camino Real
San Diego CA
866 450-4223

(P-19680)
DICE THERAPEUTICS INC
400 E Jamie Ct Ste 300 (94080-6230)
PHONE......................650 566-1402
J Kevin Judice, *CEO*
Richard Scheller, *
Scott Robertson, *Chief Business Officer*
John Jacobsen, *CSO*
Timothy Lu, *CMO*
EMP: 71 EST: 2013
SQ FT: 33,331
SALES (est): 1.13MM
SALES (corp-wide): 28.54B **Publicly Held**
Web: www.dicetherapeutics.com
SIC: 8731 Biotechnical research, commercial
PA: Eli Lilly And Company
Lilly Corporate Ctr
Indianapolis IN
317 276-2000

(P-19681)
DISNEY RESEARCH PITTSBURGH
532 Paula Ave (91201-2328)
PHONE......................412 623-1800
EMP: 207 EST: 2011
SALES (est): 892.38K
SALES (corp-wide): 82.72B **Publicly Held**
SIC: 8731 Commercial research laboratory
HQ: Walt Disney Imagineering Research & Development, Inc.
1401 Flower St
Glendale CA
818 544-6500

(P-19682)
DNA TWOPOINTO INC
Also Called: Dna2.0
37950 Central Ct (94560-3463)
PHONE......................650 853-8347
Jeremy Minshull, *CEO*
Claes Gustafsson, *
Sridhar Govindarajan, *
Jon Ness, *
▼ EMP: 68 EST: 2003
SQ FT: 40,000
SALES (est): 14.6MM **Privately Held**
Web: www.atum.bio
SIC: 8731 Biotechnical research, commercial

(P-19683)
DSM BIOMEDICAL INC
Also Called: Polymer Technology Group, The
2810 7th St (94710-2703)
PHONE......................510 841-8800
EMP: 120
Web: www.dsm.com

8731 - Commercial Physical Research (P-19684)

SIC: 8731 2836 Commercial physical research; Biological products, except diagnostic

(P-19684)
DUPONT DISPLAYS INC
600 Ward Dr Ste C (93111-2300)
PHONE...........................805 562-5400
Steve Quindlen, *Brnch Mgr*
EMP: 135
SALES (corp-wide): 17.45B **Publicly Held**
Web: www.dupont.com
SIC: 8731 Commercial physical research
HQ: Dupont Displays, Inc.
  974 Centre Rd
  Wilmington DE

(P-19685)
EBIOSCIENCE INC
Also Called: Affymetrix
10255 Science Center Dr (92121-1117)
PHONE...........................858 642-2058
EMP: 200
Web: www.thermofisher.com
SIC: 8731 Biotechnical research, commercial

(P-19686)
EMERALD CLOUD LAB INC
844 Dubuque Ave (94080-1804)
PHONE...........................650 257-7554
Daniel Kleinbaum, *Pr*
Daniel Jerome Kleinbaum, *
Brian Frezza, *
EMP: 90 EST: 2009
SALES (est): 10.92MM **Privately Held**
Web: www.emeraldcloudlab.com
SIC: 8731 Biotechnical research, commercial

(P-19687)
ENVIRONMENTAL SCIENCE ASSOC (PA)
Also Called: ESA
575 Market St Ste 3700 (94105-5827)
PHONE...........................415 896-5900
Leslie Moulton, *Pr*
Gary Oates, *
EMP: 65 EST: 1969
SALES (est): 62.52MM
SALES (corp-wide): 62.52MM **Privately Held**
Web: www.esassoc.com
SIC: 8731 8748 Environmental research; Environmental consultant

(P-19688)
ENVIRONMENTAL SCIENCE ASSOC
Also Called: ESA
626 Wilshire Blvd Ste 1100 (90017-2934)
PHONE...........................213 599-4300
Melissa Gross, *Mgr*
EMP: 135
SALES (corp-wide): 62.52MM **Privately Held**
Web: www.esassoc.com
SIC: 8731 8748 Environmental research; Environmental consultant
PA: Environmental Science Associates
  575 Market St Ste 3700
  San Francisco CA
  415 896-5900

(P-19689)
EPRI INTERNATIONAL INC (HQ)
Also Called: Epri
3420 Hillview Ave (94304-1338)
P.O. Box 10412 (94303-0813)
PHONE...........................650 855-2000
Mary Nakama, *Pr*
EMP: 73 EST: 2001
SALES (est): 17.87MM
SALES (corp-wide): 441.37MM **Privately Held**
Web: www.eprijournal.com
SIC: 8731 Energy research
PA: Electric Power Research Institute, Inc.
  3420 Hillview Ave
  Palo Alto CA
  650 855-2000

(P-19690)
ESTUDYSITE
752 Medical Center Ct Ste 304 (91911-6658)
PHONE...........................619 955-5246
Tom Wardle, *CEO*
EMP: 86
SQ FT: 4,000
SALES (corp-wide): 34.11MM **Privately Held**
Web: www.velocityclinical.com
SIC: 8731 Biotechnical research, commercial
HQ: Estudysite
  5565 Grossmont Center Dr
  La Mesa CA
  619 704-2750

(P-19691)
EUROFINS DISCOVERX PDTS LLC
42501 Albrae St (94538-3394)
PHONE...........................510 979-1415
EMP: 60 EST: 2019
SALES (est): 4.57MM
SALES (corp-wide): 220.81K **Privately Held**
Web: www.discoverx.com
SIC: 8731 Biotechnical research, commercial
PA: Eurofins Scientific Se
  Val Fleuri 23
  Luxembourg
  2618531

(P-19692)
F6S NETWORK LIMITED
16935 Encino Hills Dr (91436-4007)
PHONE...........................619 818-4363
Sean Kane, *CEO*
EMP: 80 EST: 2020
SALES (est): 1.28MM **Privately Held**
SIC: 8731 Commercial physical research

(P-19693)
FERRING RESEARCH INSTITUTE INC
4245 Sorrento Valley Blvd (92121-1408)
PHONE...........................858 657-1400
Pierre Riviere, *Pr*
EMP: 65 EST: 1995
SQ FT: 30,000
SALES (est): 10.13MM
SALES (corp-wide): 2.67MM **Privately Held**
Web: www.ferringusa.com
SIC: 8731 Biotechnical research, commercial
HQ: Ferring Pharmaceuticals Sa
  Chemin De La Vergognausaz 50
  Saint-Prex VD

(P-19694)
FORM ENERGY INC
2810 7th St (94710-2703)
PHONE...........................844 367-6462
EMP: 60
SALES (corp-wide): 10.98MM **Privately Held**
Web: www.formenergy.com
SIC: 8731 8711 Energy research; Energy conservation engineering
PA: Form Energy, Inc.
  30 Dane St
  Somerville MA
  844 367-6462

(P-19695)
FUJIFILM DIMATIX INC
2230 Martin Ave (95050-2704)
PHONE...........................408 565-0670
EMP: 95
Web: www.dimatix.com
SIC: 8731 Commercial physical research
HQ: Fujifilm Dimatix, Inc.
  2250 Martin Ave
  Santa Clara CA
  408 565-9150

(P-19696)
FUJITSU RESEARCH AMERICA INC (PA)
350 Cobalt Way (94085-5426)
PHONE...........................800 385-4878
Yoichi Koyanagi, *CEO*
Hiromu Hayashi, *
Nobuaki Kawato, *
EMP: 80 EST: 1994
SALES (est): 56.49MM **Privately Held**
Web: www.fujitsu.com
SIC: 8731 Commercial physical research

(P-19697)
GARRETT MOTION INC
Garrett Advancing Motion
2525 W 190th St (90504-6002)
PHONE...........................310 512-5424
Craig Balis, *Brnch Mgr*
EMP: 132
SALES (corp-wide): 3.63B **Privately Held**
Web: www.garrettmotion.com
SIC: 8731 Commercial research laboratory
PA: Garrett Motion Inc.
  47548 Halyard Dr
  Plymouth MI
  734 359-5901

(P-19698)
GENENTECH INC
611 Gateway Blvd (94080-7017)
PHONE...........................650 225-1000
EMP: 1284
Web: www.gene.com
SIC: 8731 Commercial physical research
HQ: Genentech, Inc.
  1 Dna Way
  South San Francisco CA
  650 225-1000

(P-19699)
GENERAL ATOMICS
Also Called: Shipping and Receiving
3483 Dunhill St (92121-1200)
P.O. Box 85608 (92186-5608)
PHONE...........................858 455-4141
Jene Spence, *Mgr*
EMP: 88
Web: www.ga.com
SIC: 8731 Commercial physical research
HQ: General Atomics
  3550 General Atomics Ct
  San Diego CA
  858 455-2810

(P-19700)
GENERAL ATOMICS
16969 Mesamint St (92127-2407)
PHONE...........................858 676-7100
Anthony Navarra, *Co-Vice President*
EMP: 99
Web: www.ga.com
SIC: 8731 Commercial physical research
HQ: General Atomics
  3550 General Atomics Ct
  San Diego CA
  858 455-2810

(P-19701)
GENERAL ATOMICS
Also Called: General Atomics Energy Pdts
4949 Greencraig Ln (92123-1675)
PHONE...........................858 455-4000
Joel Ennis, *Genl Mgr*
EMP: 170
Web: www.ga.com
SIC: 8731 7371 3823 Commercial physical research; Custom computer programming services; Process control instruments
HQ: General Atomics
  3550 General Atomics Ct
  San Diego CA
  858 455-2810

(P-19702)
GENOMICS INST OF NVRTIS RES FN
10675 John J Hopkins Dr (92121-1127)
PHONE...........................858 812-1805
Genevieve Welch, *Prin*
EMP: 73 EST: 2013
SALES (est): 9.54MM **Privately Held**
Web: www.gnf.org
SIC: 8731 Biotechnical research, commercial

(P-19703)
GENTEX CORPORATION
Also Called: Western Operations
9859 7th St (91730-5244)
PHONE...........................909 481-7667
Robert Mccay, *Brnch Mgr*
EMP: 90
SALES (corp-wide): 97.07MM **Privately Held**
Web: www.gentexcorp.com
SIC: 8731 3845 3841 Commercial research laboratory; Electromedical equipment; Surgical and medical instruments
PA: Gentex Corporation
  324 Main St
  Simpson PA
  570 282-3550

(P-19704)
HALOZYME INC
Also Called: Halozyme Therapeutics
12390 El Camino Real (92130-3190)
PHONE...........................858 794-8889
Helen I Torley, *CEO*
Harry J Leonhardt, *Sec*
Laureen Stelzer, *CFO*
EMP: 216 EST: 1998
SALES (est): 24.93MM
SALES (corp-wide): 660.12MM **Publicly Held**
Web: www.halozyme.com
SIC: 8731 Biotechnical research, commercial
PA: Halozyme Therapeutics, Inc.
  12390 El Camino Real # 150
  San Diego CA
  858 794-8889

(P-19705)
HELIX HOLDINGS I LLC
1 Circle Star Way Fl 2 (94070-6234)
PHONE...........................415 805-3360
Robin Thurston, *CEO*
EMP: 100 EST: 2015
SALES (est): 3.3MM **Privately Held**
SIC: 8731 Biological research

PRODUCTS & SERVICES SECTION
8731 - Commercial Physical Research (P-19728)

(P-19706)
HELIX OPCO LLC
101 S Ellsworth Ave Ste 350 (94401-3911)
PHONE..............................415 805-3360
Marc Stapley, *CEO*
Robin Thurston, *
EMP: 106 **EST:** 2015
SALES (est): 18.96MM **Privately Held**
Web: www.helix.com
SIC: 8731 Biotechnical research, commercial

(P-19707)
HII FLEET SUPPORT GROUP LLC
9444 Balboa Ave Ste 400 (92123-4378)
PHONE..............................858 522-6319
Michelle Wurl, *Dir*
EMP: 258
SIC: 8731 8711 Commercial physical research; Engineering services
HQ: Hii Fleet Support Group Llc
5701 Cleveland St
Virginia Beach VA
757 463-6666

(P-19708)
HOWARD HUGHES MEDICAL INST
1550 4th St Rm 190 (94143-2324)
PHONE..............................415 476-9668
John Flickinger, *Brnch Mgr*
EMP: 83
SALES (corp-wide): 6.69B **Privately Held**
Web: www.hhmi.org
SIC: 8731 Biological research
PA: Howard Hughes Medical Institute Inc
4000 Jones Bridge Rd
Chevy Chase MD
301 215-8500

(P-19709)
IMS - INSURANCE MED SVCS INC
Also Called: IMS
37600 Central Ct Ste 201 (94560-3456)
PHONE..............................510 490-6211
Saeed Uddin, *CEO*
Bilal Saeed, *
Cherry Ansari, *
Rina Albelda, *
EMP: 124 **EST:** 1993
SALES (est): 10.22MM **Privately Held**
Web: www.imsparamed.com
SIC: 8731 Commercial physical research

(P-19710)
INOVA DIAGNOSTICS INC (HQ)
Also Called: Werfen
9900 Old Grove Rd (92131-1638)
PHONE..............................858 586-9900
Carlos Pascual, *CEO*
Javier Gomez, *
▲ **EMP:** 285 **EST:** 1987
SQ FT: 81,000
SALES (est): 93.05MM **Privately Held**
Web: www.werfen.com
SIC: 8731 2835 Medical research, commercial; In vitro diagnostics
PA: Werfen S.A.
Plaza Europa, 21 - 23
L'hospitalet De Llobregat B

(P-19711)
INSITRO INC
279 E Grand Ave Ste 200 (94080-4304)
PHONE..............................650 730-7074
Daphne Koller, *CEO*
Mary M Rozenman, *Chief Business Officer*
Allison Lai, *VP Fin*
Stephen Meadows, *Business Operations Manager*
EMP: 202 **EST:** 2018
SALES (est): 20.48MM **Privately Held**
Web: www.insitro.com
SIC: 8731 Commercial physical research

(P-19712)
INTERNATIONAL BUS MCHS CORP
Also Called: IBM
650 Harry Rd (95120-6001)
PHONE..............................408 927-1080
Mark Dean, *VP*
EMP: 500
SALES (corp-wide): 60.53B **Publicly Held**
Web: www.ibm.com
SIC: 8731 Commercial research laboratory
PA: International Business Machines Corporation
1 New Orchard Rd Ste 1 # 1
Armonk NY
914 499-1900

(P-19713)
INVASIX INC
Also Called: Inmode Aesthetic Solutions
17 Hughes (92618-1902)
PHONE..............................855 418-5306
Moshe Mizrahy, *CEO*
Shakil Lakhani, *
Yair Malca, *
EMP: 99 **EST:** 2008
SALES (est): 9.4MM **Privately Held**
Web: www.inmodemd.com
SIC: 8731 5047 Medical research, commercial; Electro-medical equipment

(P-19714)
IOTA BIOSCIENCES INC
1020 Atlantic Ave (94501-1147)
PHONE..............................831 229-3524
EMP: 97 **EST:** 2017
SALES (est): 5.46MM **Privately Held**
Web: www.iota.bio
SIC: 8731 Commercial physical research

(P-19715)
ISE CORPORATION
Also Called: I S E
12302 Kerran St (92064-6884)
PHONE..............................858 413-1720
▲ **EMP:** 140
SIC: 8731 3621 Commercial physical research; Electric motor and generator parts

(P-19716)
ISOTIS ORTHOBIOLOGICS INC
2 Goodyear Ste A (92618-2052)
PHONE..............................949 595-8710
Keith Valentine, *CEO*
Peter J Arduini, *
Christian S Schade, *
▲ **EMP:** 150 **EST:** 1990
SALES (est): 22.65MM **Privately Held**
Web: www.seaspine.com
SIC: 8731 5047 Biotechnical research, commercial; Surgical equipment and supplies
HQ: Isotis International Sarl
C/O Fidulem Sa
Lausanne VD

(P-19717)
JANSSEN ALZHEIMER IMMUNOTHERA
700 Gateway Blvd (94080-7020)
PHONE..............................650 794-2500
Doctor Stefaan Heylen, *Pr*
EMP: 100 **EST:** 2009
SALES (est): 14.49MM
SALES (corp-wide): 94.94B **Publicly Held**
SIC: 8731 Commercial physical research
HQ: Janssen Research & Development, Llc
920 Us Highway 202
Raritan NJ
908 704-4000

(P-19718)
KARIUS INC
975 Island Dr Ste 100 (94065-5147)
PHONE..............................866 452-7487
Michael Kertesz, *Pr*
EMP: 154 **EST:** 2015
SALES (est): 7.71MM **Privately Held**
Web: www.kariusdx.com
SIC: 8731 Biotechnical research, commercial

(P-19719)
KARTOS THERAPEUTICS INC
275 Shoreline Dr Ste 100 (94065-1412)
PHONE..............................650 542-0130
Jesse Mcgreivy, *CEO*
Srdan Verstovsek, *Chief Medical Officer*
EMP: 78 **EST:** 2017
SALES (est): 5.52MM **Privately Held**
Web: www.kartosthera.com
SIC: 8731 Commercial physical research

(P-19720)
KITE PHARMA INC (HQ)
Also Called: Kite, A Gilead Company
2400 Broadway Ste 100 (90404-3058)
PHONE..............................310 824-9999
EMP: 99 **EST:** 2009
SQ FT: 20,000
SALES (est): 66.52MM
SALES (corp-wide): 27.28B **Publicly Held**
Web: www.kitepharma.com
SIC: 8731 2836 Biotechnical research, commercial; Biological products, except diagnostic
PA: Gilead Sciences, Inc.
333 Lakeside Dr
Foster City CA
650 574-3000

(P-19721)
KONICA MINOLTA LABORATORY USA INC
2855 Campus Dr Ste 100 (94403-2512)
PHONE..............................650 522-9619
▲ **EMP:** 85
Web: research.konicaminolta.us
SIC: 8731 Commercial physical research

(P-19722)
L3 APPLIED TECHNOLOGIES INC
2700 Merced St (94577-5602)
PHONE..............................510 577-7100
Janet Luna, *Dir*
EMP: 109
SALES (corp-wide): 17.06B **Publicly Held**
SIC: 8731 Commercial physical research
HQ: L3 Applied Technologies, Inc.
10180 Barnes Canyon Rd # 10
San Diego CA
858 404-7824

(P-19723)
LAB-GISTICS LLC
885 Pacific Ave (95126-4821)
PHONE..............................650 309-2627
EMP: 200 **EST:** 2012
SQ FT: 60,000
SALES (est): 5.24MM **Privately Held**
SIC: 8731 Computer (hardware) development

(P-19724)
LABCYTE INC
Also Called: Echo
170 Rose Orchard Way Ste 200 (95134-1374)
PHONE..............................408 747-2000
Mark F Colbrie, *Pr*
Richard Ellson, *
EMP: 74 **EST:** 2000
SQ FT: 19,200
SALES (est): 25.45K
SALES (corp-wide): 31.47B **Publicly Held**
Web: www.beckman.com
SIC: 8731 Biotechnical research, commercial
HQ: Beckman Coulter, Inc.
250 S Kraemer Blvd
Brea CA
714 993-5321

(P-19725)
LEIDOS INC
Also Called: Saic
10260 Campus Point Dr Bldg C (92121-1522)
PHONE..............................703 676-4300
Jere Drummond, *Dir*
EMP: 107
Web: www.leidos.com
SIC: 8731 7373 Commercial physical research; Systems software development services
HQ: Leidos, Inc.
1750 Presidents St
Reston VA
571 526-6000

(P-19726)
LEIDOS INC
Also Called: Reveal Imaging
2985 Scott St (92081-8339)
PHONE..............................858 826-9090
EMP: 130
Web: www.leidos.com
SIC: 8731 3829 3826 Commercial physical research; Measuring and controlling devices, nec; Analytical instruments
HQ: Leidos, Inc.
1750 Presidents St
Reston VA
571 526-6000

(P-19727)
LEIDOS INC
Also Called: Saic
Naval Air Station (92135)
PHONE..............................858 826-6000
EMP: 66
Web: www.leidos.com
SIC: 8731 7373 8742 3679 Commercial physical research; Systems engineering, computer related; Training and development consultant; Recording and playback apparatus, including phonograph
HQ: Leidos, Inc.
1750 Presidents St
Reston VA
571 526-6000

(P-19728)
LEIDOS INC
4161 Campus Point Ct Stop Em3 (92121-1513)
PHONE..............................858 826-9416
Paul Chang, *Mgr*
EMP: 109
Web: www.leidos.com
SIC: 8731 Commercial physical research
HQ: Leidos, Inc.
1750 Presidents St
Reston VA
571 526-6000

8731 - Commercial Physical Research (P-19729)

(P-19729)
LEIDOS ENGRG & SCIENCES LLC
1330 30th St Ste A (92154-3471)
PHONE..................619 542-3130
Karen Parizeau, *Mgr*
EMP: 129
SIC: 8731 Natural resource research
HQ: Leidos Engineering & Sciences, Llc
   9737 Washingtonian Blvd
   Gaithersburg MD
   301 240-7000

(P-19730)
LS9 INC
600 Gateway Blvd (94080-7014)
PHONE..................650 243-5400
EMP: 62 EST: 2005
SALES (est): 5.84MM **Privately Held**
Web: www.ls9.com
SIC: 8731 Commercial research laboratory

(P-19731)
LYELL IMMUNOPHARMA INC
401 E Jamie Ct (94080-6204)
PHONE..................650 383-5381
Richard Klausner, *Brnch Mgr*
EMP: 72
SALES (corp-wide): 84.68MM **Publicly Held**
Web: www.lyell.com
SIC: 8731 Biotechnical research, commercial
PA: Lyell Immunopharma, Inc.
   201 Haskins Way
   South San Francisco CA
   650 695-0677

(P-19732)
MAMMOTH BIOSCIENCES INC
1000 Marina Blvd. Ste 600 (94005-1803)
PHONE..................770 655-1937
Trevor Martin, *CEO*
Ashley Tehranchi, *
Lucas Harrington, *
Janice Chen, *
Jennifer Doudna, *
EMP: 67 EST: 2017
SALES (est): 10.13MM **Privately Held**
Web: www.mammoth.bio
SIC: 8731 Biotechnical research, commercial

(P-19733)
MARAVAI LF SCNCES HOLDINGS LLC (HQ)
10770 Wateridge Cir Ste 100 (92121)
PHONE..................650 697-3600
Eric Tardif, *Pr*
EMP: 148 EST: 2014
SALES (est): 32.29MM
SALES (corp-wide): 883MM **Publicly Held**
Web: www.maravai.com
SIC: 8731 Commercial physical research
PA: Maravai Lifesciences Holdings, Inc.
   10770 Wtridge Cir Ste 200
   San Diego CA
   858 546-0004

(P-19734)
MEMBRANE TECHNOLOGY & RES INC (PA)
Also Called: M T R
39630 Eureka Dr (94560-4805)
PHONE..................650 328-2228
Colin Bailey, *Ch*
Hans Wijmans, *
Meryl Rains, *
Richard W Baker, *
◆ EMP: 69 EST: 1982
SQ FT: 60,000
SALES (est): 17.92MM
SALES (corp-wide): 17.92MM **Privately Held**
Web: www.mtrinc.com
SIC: 8731 3823 Commercial research laboratory; On-stream gas/liquid analysis instruments, industrial

(P-19735)
MEMORIAL HEALHTEC LABRATORIES
9920 Talbert Ave (92708-5153)
PHONE..................714 962-4677
Marcia Manker, *Mgr*
EMP: 2502
Web: www.memorialcare.org
SIC: 8731 Commercial physical research
HQ: Memorial Healthtec Laboratories Inc
   2865 Atlantic Ave Ste 203
   Long Beach CA

(P-19736)
MENDEL BIOTECHNOLOGY INC
3935 Point Eden Way (94545-3720)
PHONE..................510 264-0280
EMP: 75
SIC: 8731 Commercial physical research

(P-19737)
MESA BIOTECH INC
6190 Cornerstone Ct E Ste 220 (92121-4701)
PHONE..................858 800-4929
Ingo Chakravarty, *Pr*
Hong Cai, *
William R Brody, *
Tom Willardson, *
John Monroe, *
EMP: 60 EST: 2015
SALES (est): 23.9MM
SALES (corp-wide): 44.91B **Publicly Held**
Web: www.thermofisher.com
SIC: 8731 7389 Biotechnical research, commercial; Air pollution measuring service
PA: Thermo Fisher Scientific Inc.
   168 3rd Ave
   Waltham MA
   781 622-1000

(P-19738)
METABIOTA INC
425 California St Ste 1200 (94104-2114)
PHONE..................415 398-4712
Nathan Wolfe Md, *CEO*
Robert Mann, *
EMP: 82 EST: 2008
SQ FT: 8,000
SALES (est): 9.31MM **Privately Held**
Web: www.metabiota.com
SIC: 8731 Biotechnical research, commercial

(P-19739)
MOTECH AMERICAS LLC
Also Called: GE Energy
1300 Valley Vista Dr Ste 207 (91765-3940)
PHONE..................302 451-7500
▲ EMP: 320
Web: www.motech-americas.com
SIC: 8731 3674 Energy research; Solar cells

(P-19740)
MYST THERAPEUTICS INC
570 Westwood Plz Bldg 114 (90095-8352)
PHONE..................415 516-8450
Sammy Farah, *CEO*
EMP: 93 EST: 2019
SALES (est): 485.83K
SALES (corp-wide): 5.25MM **Publicly Held**
SIC: 8731 Medical research, commercial
PA: Turnstone Biologics Corp.
   9310 Athena Cir Ste 300
   La Jolla CA
   347 897-5988

(P-19741)
NANTCELL INC
9920 Jefferson Blvd (90232-3506)
PHONE..................562 397-3639
Richard Adcock, *CEO*
EMP: 371 EST: 2014
SALES (est): 151.69K **Publicly Held**
Web: www.immunitybio.com
SIC: 8731 Biological research
PA: Immunitybio, Inc.
   3530 John Hopkins Ct
   San Diego CA

(P-19742)
NAUTILUS BIOTECHNOLOGY INC
Also Called: Nautilus Biotechnology
835 Industrial Rd Ste 200 (94070-3333)
PHONE..................206 333-2001
Sujal Patel, *CEO*
Matt Murphy, *
EMP: 106 EST: 2016
SALES (est): 16.98MM **Publicly Held**
Web: www.nautilus.bio
SIC: 8731 Biotechnical research, commercial
PA: Nautilus Biotechnology, Inc.
   425 Pontius Ave N Ste 202
   Seattle WA
   206 333-2001

(P-19743)
NAVIGATE BIOPHARMA SVCS INC
1890 Rutherford Rd (92008-7326)
PHONE..................866 992-4939
Kevin Zou, *CEO*
EMP: 180 EST: 2016
SALES (est): 26.61MM **Privately Held**
Web: www.navigatebp.com
SIC: 8731 Biotechnical research, commercial
HQ: Novartis Finance Corporation
   1 Health Plz
   East Hanover NJ

(P-19744)
NAVY UNITED STATES DEPARTMENT
Also Called: Naval Health Researc
Naval Training Ctr Bldg 287 (92133)
PHONE..................619 524-6727
EMP: 63
Web: www.navy.mil
SIC: 8731 9711 Medical research, commercial; Navy
HQ: United States Department Of The Navy
   1200 Navy Pentagon
   Washington DC

(P-19745)
NEBULA INC
Also Called: Nebula Systems
1100 La Avenida St (94043-1452)
PHONE..................650 539-9900
EMP: 67
Web: www.nebula.com
SIC: 8731 7373 Computer (hardware) development; Computer integrated systems design

(P-19746)
NORTHROP GRMMN SPCE & MSSN SYS
Space Technology Sector
862 E Hospitality Ln (92408-3530)
PHONE..................909 382-6800
FAX: 909 382-6249
EMP: 200
SIC: 8731 7373 Commercial physical research; Computer integrated systems design
HQ: Northrop Grumman Space & Mission Systems Corp.
   6379 San Ignacio Ave
   San Jose CA
   703 280-2900

(P-19747)
NOVARTIS INST FOR FNCTNAL GNMI
Also Called: Nibr
10675 John J Hopkins Dr (92121-1127)
PHONE..................858 812-1500
Hans Seidel, *Pr*
Timothy Smith, *VP*
Karl Olsen, *CFO*
Robert Downs, *Ex Dir*
Daniel Vasella Md, *Prin*
EMP: 735 EST: 1998
SALES (est): 49.86MM **Privately Held**
Web: www.gnf.org
SIC: 8731 Biotechnical research, commercial
HQ: Novartis Institutes For Biomedical Research, Inc.
   700 Main St
   Cambridge MA
   617 777-8276

(P-19748)
NOYMED CORP
1101 N Pacific Ave Ste 303 (91202)
PHONE..................800 224-2090
Armen Margaryan, *CEO*
Tatevik Simonyan, *
EMP: 130 EST: 2020
SALES (est): 8MM **Privately Held**
Web: www.noymed.com
SIC: 8731 Commercial physical research

(P-19749)
NURIX THERAPEUTICS INC (PA)
Also Called: Nurix
1700 Owens St Ste 205 (94158-0006)
PHONE..................415 660-5320
Arthur T Sands, *Pr*
David Lacey, *
Hans Van Houte, *CFO*
Pierre Beaurang, *Chief Business Officer*
Gwenn Hansen, *CSO*
EMP: 84 EST: 2009
SQ FT: 49,991
SALES (est): 38.63MM
SALES (corp-wide): 38.63MM **Publicly Held**
Web: www.nurixtx.com
SIC: 8731 Biotechnical research, commercial

(P-19750)
OMNIAB INC (PA)
5980 Horton St Ste 600 (94608-2061)
PHONE..................510 250-7800
Matthew W Foehr, *CEO*
John L Higgins, *
Kurt A Gustafson, *VP Fin*
Charles S Berkman, *CLO*
Donna Ventura, *Corporate Controller*
EMP: 74 EST: 2012
SALES (est): 59.08MM
SALES (corp-wide): 59.08MM **Publicly Held**
SIC: 8731 Biological research

PRODUCTS & SERVICES SECTION
8731 - Commercial Physical Research (P-19771)

(P-19751)
OMNIOME INC
Also Called: Omniome North
1600 Adams Dr Ste 230 (94025-1449)
PHONE.................................510 935-3021
Robert Wicke, *CEO*
EMP: 80
SALES (corp-wide): 128.3MM **Publicly Held**
Web: www.pacb.com
SIC: 8731 Biotechnical research, commercial
HQ: Omniome, Inc.
    6965 Lusk Blvd Ste 100
    San Diego CA
    858 459-2428

(P-19752)
ONE LAMBDA INC (HQ)
22801 Roscoe Blvd (91304-3200)
PHONE.................................747 494-1000
Seth H Hoogasian, *CEO*
George M Ayoub, *
Don Arii, *
James Keegan, *
Emiko Terasaki, *Corporate Secretary**
EMP: 82 **EST:** 1984
SQ FT: 53,000
SALES (est): 51.05MM
SALES (corp-wide): 44.91B **Publicly Held**
Web: www.thermofisher.com
SIC: 8731 Biotechnical research, commercial
PA: Thermo Fisher Scientific Inc.
    168 3rd Ave
    Waltham MA
    781 622-1000

(P-19753)
ORCA BIOSYSTEMS INC
3400 Business Dr Ste 140 (95820-2180)
PHONE.................................916 822-4235
Ivan K Dimov, *CEO*
EMP: 69
SALES (corp-wide): 12.27MM **Privately Held**
Web: www.orcabio.com
SIC: 8731 Biotechnical research, commercial
PA: Orca Biosystems, Inc.
    3475 Edison Way Ste C
    Menlo Park CA
    650 246-9601

(P-19754)
PALL FORTEBIO LLC
47661 Fremont Blvd (94538-6577)
PHONE.................................650 322-1360
▼ **EMP:** 94
Web: www.fortebio.com
SIC: 8731 Biotechnical research, commercial

(P-19755)
PALO ALTO RESEARCH CENTER INC
Also Called: Parc
3333 Coyote Hill Rd (94304-1314)
PHONE.................................650 812-4000
Naresh Shanker, *CEO*
Mark Bernstein, *Pr*
John Pauksta, *CFO*
Jonathan R Wolter, *CFO*
Damon C Matteo, *VP*
EMP: 220 **EST:** 1998
SQ FT: 200,000
SALES (est): 49.65MM
SALES (corp-wide): 7.11B **Publicly Held**
Web: www.parc.com
SIC: 8731 Medical research, commercial
HQ: Xerox Corporation
    201 Merritt 7 Ste 20
    Norwalk CT
    203 849-5216

(P-19756)
PAREXEL INTERNATIONAL CORP
Also Called: PAREXEL INTERNATIONAL CORPORATION
1560 E Chevy Chase Dr Ste 140
(91206-4105)
PHONE.................................818 254-7076
Mollie Barrett, *Dir*
EMP: 108
SALES (corp-wide): 2.44B **Privately Held**
Web: www.parexel.com
SIC: 8731 Biotechnical research, commercial
HQ: Parexel International (Ma) Corporation
    275 Grove St Ste 3101
    Auburndale MA
    617 454-9300

(P-19757)
PETER H MATTSON & CO INC
Also Called: Mattson
343 Hatch Dr (94404-1162)
PHONE.................................650 356-2500
Steve Gundrum, *Pr*
Peter H Mattson, *
Samson Hsia, *
Patricia Mattson, *
Justin Shimek, *
EMP: 70 **EST:** 1977
SQ FT: 20,000
SALES (est): 15.6MM **Privately Held**
Web: www.mattsonco.com
SIC: 8731 Food research

(P-19758)
PHARMARON INC
6 Venture Ste 250 (92618-7354)
PHONE.................................949 788-0586
Boliang Lou, *Owner*
EMP: 18585
Web: www.pharmaron.com
SIC: 8731 Biotechnical research, commercial
HQ: Pharmaron, Inc.
    201 E Jefferson St # 304
    Louisville KY
    502 569-1047

(P-19759)
PHARMRON SAN DEGO LAB SVCS LLC
7901 Vickers St (92111-1916)
PHONE.................................858 560-9000
Patrick Dentinger, *Ex Dir*
Patrick Dentinger, *Pr*
Ismael Hidalgo, *
Patrick F Carr, *
Sid Bhoopathy, *
EMP: 66 **EST:** 1999
SQ FT: 25,000
SALES (est): 10.17MM
SALES (corp-wide): 20.46MM **Privately Held**
Web: www.absorption.com
SIC: 8731 Biotechnical research, commercial
PA: Pharmaron (Exton) Lab Services Llc
    436 Creamery Way Ste 600
    Exton PA
    610 280-7300

(P-19760)
PORTOLA PHARMACEUTICALS INC (DH)
270 E Grand Ave (94080-4811)
PHONE.................................650 246-7300
Scott Garland, *CEO*
Hollings Renton, *
Mardi Dier, *Chief Business Officer**
Sheldon Koenig, *CCO**
Glenn Brame, *Chief Technician**
EMP: 113 **EST:** 2003
SQ FT: 74,000
SALES (est): 116.64MM
SALES (corp-wide): 44.35B **Privately Held**
Web: www.portola.com
SIC: 8731 Biotechnical research, commercial
HQ: Alexion Pharmaceuticals, Inc.
    121 Seaport Blvd
    Boston MA

(P-19761)
PROMAB BIOTECHNOLOGIES INC
2600 Hilltop Dr (94806-1971)
PHONE.................................510 860-4615
Lijun Wu, *Pr*
EMP: 80 **EST:** 2001
SALES (est): 7.29MM **Privately Held**
Web: www.promab.com
SIC: 8731 Biotechnical research, commercial

(P-19762)
PROSCIENTO INC (PA)
855 Third Ave Ste 3340 (91911-1350)
PHONE.................................619 427-1300
Marcus Hompesch, *CEO*
Linda Morrow, *COO*
Markus Hofmann, *CFO*
Christian Weyer, *Chief Development Officer*
EMP: 170 **EST:** 2002
SQ FT: 20,000
SALES (est): 30.74MM
SALES (corp-wide): 30.74MM **Privately Held**
Web: www.prosciento.com
SIC: 8731 Biotechnical research, commercial

(P-19763)
RIPPLE FOODS PBC
901 Gilman St Ste A (94710-1423)
PHONE.................................510 269-2563
Laura Flanagan, *CEO*
EMP: 82 **EST:** 2015
SQ FT: 10,000
SALES (est): 17.37MM **Privately Held**
Web: www.ripplefoods.com
SIC: 8731 Food research

(P-19764)
ROCHE MOLECULAR SYSTEMS INC (DH)
Also Called: Roche Molecular Solutions
4300 Hacienda Dr (94588-2722)
P.O. Box 9002 (94566-9002)
PHONE.................................925 730-8000
Brad Moore, *Pr*
◆ **EMP:** 400 **EST:** 1991
SALES (est): 458.1MM **Privately Held**
Web: diagnostics.roche.com
SIC: 8731 Biotechnical research, commercial
HQ: Roche Holdings, Inc.
    1 Dna Way
    South San Francisco CA
    650 225-1000

(P-19765)
ROCHE NIMBLEGEN INC
4300 Hacienda Dr (94588-2722)
PHONE.................................608 316-3890
Frank Pitzer, *Pr*
Robert J Palay, *
Rebecca Selzer, *
Steve Oldham, *
Mark Schaller, *
EMP: 121 **EST:** 2000
SALES (est): 22.58MM **Privately Held**
SIC: 8731 Biotechnical research, commercial
HQ: Roche Holding Ag
    Grenzacherstrasse 124
    Basel BS

(P-19766)
SAMSUNG RESEARCH AMERICA INC (DH)
Also Called: Sisa
665 Clyde Ave (94043-2235)
PHONE.................................650 210-1001
Joonhyun Lee, *Pr*
Sungyu Hahm, *
Seungbeom Choi, *
◆ **EMP:** 140 **EST:** 1977
SQ FT: 130,000
SALES (est): 90.78MM **Privately Held**
Web: sra.samsung.com
SIC: 8731 7371 Computer (hardware) development; Computer software development and applications
HQ: Samsung Electronics America, Inc.
    85 Challenger Rd
    Ridgefield Park NJ
    201 229-4000

(P-19767)
SEMINIS INC (DH)
2700 Camino Del Sol (93030-7967)
PHONE.................................805 485-7317
◆ **EMP:** 300 **EST:** 1995
SALES (est): 90.74MM
SALES (corp-wide): 52.7B **Privately Held**
Web: vegetables.bayer.com
SIC: 8731 8742 2099 Agricultural research; Productivity improvement consultant; Food preparations, nec
HQ: Bayer Northern Production Co., Llc
    800 N Lindbergh Blvd
    Saint Louis MO
    314 694-1000

(P-19768)
SEMPRIUS INC
Also Called: Semprius
1100 La Avenida St Ste A (94043-1453)
PHONE.................................919 433-9980
EMP: 64
SIC: 8731 3674 Electronic research; Solar cells

(P-19769)
SEQUENOM INC (HQ)
3595 John Hopkins Ct (92121-1121)
PHONE.................................858 202-9000
EMP: 80 **EST:** 1994
SALES (est): 43.43MM **Publicly Held**
Web: womenshealth.labcorp.com
SIC: 8731 Biological research
PA: Laboratory Corporation Of America Holdings
    358 S Main St
    Burlington NC

(P-19770)
SHORELINE BIOSCIENCES INC
11555 Sorrento Valley Rd Ste 101
(92121-1331)
PHONE.................................619 890-0383
Carlos Espinoza, *Brnch Mgr*
EMP: 75
SALES (corp-wide): 8.11MM **Privately Held**
Web: www.shorelinebio.com
SIC: 8731 Commercial physical research
PA: Shoreline Biosciences, Inc.
    10220 Sorrento Valley Rd
    San Diego CA
    619 890-0383

(P-19771)
SIMBOL INC
Also Called: Simbol Materials
6920 Koll Center Pkwy Ste 216
(94566-3156)

8731 - Commercial Physical Research (P-19772)

PHONE.....................925 226-7400
Luka Erceg, Pr
EMP: 100 EST: 2007
SALES (est): 10.16MM Privately Held
Web: www.simbolmaterials.com
SIC: 8731 Natural resource research

(P-19772)
SOLOPOWER INC
5981 Optical Ct (95138-1400)
P.O. Box 731229 (95173-1229)
PHONE.....................503 388-3710
EMP: 135
SIC: 8731 Energy research

(P-19773)
SPREADTRUM CMMNCATIONS USA INC
Also Called: Spreadtrum
10180 Telesis Ct Ste 500 (92121-2787)
PHONE.....................858 546-0895
EMP: 70 EST: 2003
SALES (est): 12.14MM Privately Held
SIC: 8731 Electronic research
HQ: Spreadtrum Communications (Shanghai) Co., Ltd.
Building 1, Spreadtrum Center, Lane 2288, Zuchongzhi Road, China
Shanghai SH

(P-19774)
STELLARTECH RESEARCH CORP (PA)
560 Cottonwood Dr (95035-7403)
PHONE.....................408 331-3000
Roger Stern, Pr
Vincent Sullivan, *
Jerome Jackson, *
Jerry Smith, *
EMP: 109 EST: 1988
SQ FT: 68,000
SALES (est): 35MM Privately Held
Web: www.stellartechresearch.com
SIC: 8731 3841 8732 8733 Commercial physical research; Surgical and medical instruments; Sociological research; Physical research, noncommercial

(P-19775)
SUNSYSTEM TECHNOLOGY LLC
2025 N Gateway Blvd Ste 112 (93727-1619)
PHONE.....................559 412-7870
Kurtis Bank, Brnch Mgr
EMP: 160
SALES (corp-wide): 49.25MM Privately Held
Web: www.sstsolar.com
SIC: 8731 7374 Commercial physical research; Data processing and preparation
PA: Sunsystem Technology, Llc
2731 Citrus Rd Ste D
Rancho Cordova CA
916 671-3351

(P-19776)
SYMYX TECHNOLOGIES INC
2804 Mission College Blvd (95054-1842)
PHONE.....................408 764-2000
EMP: 460
SIC: 8731 7372 Commercial physical research; Business oriented computer software

(P-19777)
TAE LIFE SCIENCES US LLC (PA)
19571 Pauling (92610-2619)

P.O. Box 7010 (92688-7010)
PHONE.....................949 344-6112
Bruce Bauer, Managing Member
EMP: 90 EST: 2017
SALES (est): 3.49MM
SALES (corp-wide): 3.49MM Privately Held
Web: www.taelifesciences.com
SIC: 8731 Biotechnical research, commercial

(P-19778)
TAE TECHNOLOGIES INC (PA)
Also Called: Tae Technologies
19631 Pauling (92610-2607)
P.O. Box 7010 (92688-7010)
PHONE.....................949 830-2117
Michl Binderbauer, CEO
Mark J Lewis, Pr
EMP: 155 EST: 2002
SALES (est): 60.78MM
SALES (corp-wide): 60.78MM Privately Held
Web: www.tae.com
SIC: 8731 Energy research

(P-19779)
TALON THERAPEUTICS INC
18200 Von Karman Ave Ste 700 (92612-1023)
PHONE.....................949 788-6700
Joseph W Turgeon, CEO
EMP: 89 EST: 2002
SQ FT: 50,000
SALES (est): 5.11MM Privately Held
SIC: 8731 2834 Commercial physical research; Pharmaceutical preparations
PA: Spectrum Pharmaceuticals, Inc.
2 Atlantic Ave Fl 6
Boston MA

(P-19780)
TANVEX BIOPHARMA USA INC (PA)
Also Called: L J B
10394 Pacific Center Ct (92121-4340)
PHONE.....................858 210-4100
Allen Chao, CEO
Chi-chuan Chen, Pr
EMP: 134 EST: 1984
SALES (est): 49.54MM
SALES (corp-wide): 49.54MM Privately Held
Web: www.tanvex.com
SIC: 8731 Biotechnical research, commercial

(P-19781)
TEGILE SYSTEMS INC
7999 Gateway Blvd Ste 120 (94560-1005)
PHONE.....................510 791-7900
Rohit Kshetrapal, CEO
Ian Edmundson, *
Rajesh Nair, *
Narayan Venkat, CMO*
Michael Morgan, *
EMP: 130 EST: 2010
SQ FT: 6,500
SALES (est): 22.22MM Privately Held
Web: www.ddn.com
SIC: 8731 3572 Computer (hardware) development; Computer storage devices

(P-19782)
TELEDYNE SCENTIFIC IMAGING LLC
Also Called: Teledyne Judson Technologies
5212 Verdugo Way (93012-8662)
PHONE.....................805 373-4979
James Beletic, Pr
EMP: 90
SQ FT: 54,295

SALES (corp-wide): 5.46B Publicly Held
Web: www.teledyne-si.com
SIC: 8731 Commercial physical research
HQ: Teledyne Scientific & Imaging, Llc
1049 Camino Dos Rios
Thousand Oaks CA

(P-19783)
TELEDYNE SCENTIFIC IMAGING LLC (HQ)
Also Called: Teledyne Scientific Company
1049 Camino Dos Rios (91360-2362)
PHONE.....................805 373-4545
EMP: 125 EST: 1962
SQ FT: 161,000
SALES (est): 97.3MM
SALES (corp-wide): 5.46B Publicly Held
Web: www.teledyne-si.com
SIC: 8731 8732 8733 Commercial physical research; Commercial nonphysical research; Noncommercial research organizations
PA: Teledyne Technologies Inc
1049 Camino Dos Rios
Thousand Oaks CA
805 373-4545

(P-19784)
THE SALK INSTITUTE FOR BIOLOGICAL STUDIES SAN DIEGO CALIFORNIA
Also Called: SALK INSTITUTE, THE
10010 N Torrey Pines Rd (92037-1002)
P.O. Box 85800 (92186-5800)
PHONE.....................858 453-4100
EMP: 1100 EST: 1960
SALES (est): 162.33MM Privately Held
Web: www.salk.edu
SIC: 8731 Commercial physical research

(P-19785)
TISSUE-GROWN CORPORATION
15245 W Telegraph Rd (93060-3039)
PHONE.....................805 525-1975
Carolyn Sluis, Pr
◆ EMP: 85 EST: 1986
SQ FT: 10,500
SALES (est): 2MM Privately Held
Web: www.tissuegrown.com
SIC: 8731 Biotechnical research, commercial

(P-19786)
TNK THERAPEUTICS INC (HQ)
9380 Judicial Dr (92121-3830)
PHONE.....................858 210-3700
Henry Ji, CEO
EMP: 191 EST: 2015
SALES (est): 9.07MM
SALES (corp-wide): 62.84MM Publicly Held
Web: www.sorrentotherapeutics.com
SIC: 8731 Medical research, commercial
PA: Sorrento Therapeutics, Inc.
4955 Directors Pl Ste 100
San Diego CA
858 203-4100

(P-19787)
TRILINK BIOTECHNOLOGIES LLC
10770 Wateridge Cir Ste 200 (92121)
PHONE.....................800 863-6801
EMP: 159 EST: 1996
SQ FT: 40,000
SALES (est): 44.23MM
SALES (corp-wide): 883MM Publicly Held
Web: www.trilinkbiotech.com
SIC: 8731 8748 Biotechnical research, commercial; Test development and evaluation service

PA: Maravai Lifesciences Holdings, Inc.
10770 Wtridge Cir Ste 200
San Diego CA
858 546-0004

(P-19788)
TRUVIAN SCIENCES INC
10300 Campus Point Dr Ste 190 (92121-1511)
PHONE.....................858 251-3646
Jeff Hawkins, CEO
Conner Hargrave, *
Dena Marrinucci, *
Katherine Atkinson, CCO*
Ria Francisco, *
EMP: 74 EST: 2015
SQ FT: 1,500
SALES (est): 10.17MM Privately Held
Web: www.truvianhealth.com
SIC: 8731 Biotechnical research, commercial

(P-19789)
TURNING POINT THERAPEUTICS INC
10300 Campus Point Dr (92121-1504)
PHONE.....................858 926-5251
Athena Countouriotis, Pr
Andrew Partridge, CCO
Annette North, Ex VP
Brian Baker, VP Fin
EMP: 87 EST: 2013
SALES (est): 30.83MM
SALES (corp-wide): 46.16B Publicly Held
Web: www.bms.com
SIC: 8731 Biotechnical research, commercial
PA: Bristol-Myers Squibb Company
430 E 29th St Fl 14
New York NY
212 546-4000

(P-19790)
TWIST BIOSCIENCE CORPORATION (PA)
681 Gateway Blvd (94080-7015)
PHONE.....................800 719-0671
Emily M Leproust, Ch Bd
Patrick Finn, Pr
James M Thorburn, CFO
William Banyai, OF ADVANCED Development*
Dennis Cho, Sr VP
EMP: 293 EST: 2013
SQ FT: 91,791
SALES (est): 203.56MM
SALES (corp-wide): 203.56MM Publicly Held
Web: www.twistbioscience.com
SIC: 8731 Biotechnical research, commercial

(P-19791)
UNITED STTES DEPT ENRGY LVRMOR
Also Called: Lawrence Livermore Nat Lab
741 S H St (94550-4635)
P.O. Box 5012 (94551-5012)
PHONE.....................925 423-1521
EMP: 598
Web: www.llnl.gov
SIC: 8731 Commercial research laboratory
HQ: United States Department Of Energy Livermore Office
7000 East Ave
Livermore CA
925 422-1100

(P-19792)
UNIVERSITY CALIFORNIA DAVIS
Division of Agriculture
2801 2nd St (95618-7717)

PRODUCTS & SERVICES SECTION
8732 - Commercial Nonphysical Research (P-19813)

PHONE.................530 750-1313
Barbara Allen-diaz, *VP*
EMP: 155
SALES (corp-wide): 534.4MM **Privately Held**
Web: www.ucanr.edu
SIC: 8731 8221 9411 Agricultural research; University; Administration of educational programs
HQ: University Of California, Davis
   1 Shields Ave
   Davis CA

(P-19793)
UNIVERSITY CALIFORNIA IRVINE
Also Called: Henry Samueli School Engrg
2220 Engineering Gtwy (92697-0001)
PHONE.................949 824-2819
Doctor G P Li, *Dir*
EMP: 603
SALES (corp-wide): 534.4MM **Privately Held**
Web: www.uci.edu
SIC: 8731 8221 9411 Electronic research; University; Administration of educational programs
HQ: University Of California, Irvine
   510 Aldrich Hall
   Irvine CA
   949 824-5011

(P-19794)
VACUUM PROCESS ENGINEERING INC
150 Commerce Cir (95815-4208)
PHONE.................916 925-6100
Carl P Schalansky, *Brnch Mgr*
EMP: 74
SALES (corp-wide): 15.74MM **Privately Held**
Web: www.vpei.com
SIC: 8731 Commercial physical research
PA: Vacuum Process Engineering, Inc.
   110 Commerce Cir
   Sacramento CA
   916 925-6100

(P-19795)
VELODYNE LIDAR INC
Also Called: Velodyne Labs
1210 Marina Village Pkwy (94501-6477)
PHONE.................510 522-2351
EMP: 127
SALES (corp-wide): 95.92MM **Privately Held**
Web: www.velodynelidar.com
SIC: 8731 Electronic research
HQ: Velodyne Lidar Usa, Inc.
   5521 Hellyer Ave
   San Jose CA
   669 275-2251

(P-19796)
VIR BIOTECHNOLOGY INC (PA)
1800 Owens St Fl 11 (94158-2388)
PHONE.................415 906-4324
George Scangos, *Pr*
Vicki Sato, *
Howard Horn, *CFO*
Phil Pang, *CMO*
EMP: 135 **EST:** 2016
SALES (est): 1.62B
SALES (corp-wide): 1.62B **Publicly Held**
Web: www.vir.bio
SIC: 8731 Biotechnical research, commercial

(P-19797)
VIRIDENT SYSTEMS INC
1745 Tech Dr Ste 700 (95110)
PHONE.................408 573-5000
Mike Gustafson, *Sr VP*
Kumar Ganapathy, *Global Vice President*
Vijay Karamcheti, *
Bruce Horn, *
Ken Grohe, *
EMP: 110 **EST:** 2006
SALES (est): 24.57MM
SALES (corp-wide): 12.32B **Publicly Held**
SIC: 8731 Computer (hardware) development
HQ: Hgst, Inc.
   5601 Great Oaks Pkwy
   San Jose CA
   408 717-6000

(P-19798)
VIRIDOS INC
250 W Schrimpf Rd (92233-9745)
PHONE.................858 754-2900
EMP: 99
Web: www.viridos.com
SIC: 8731 Biotechnical research, commercial
HQ: Viridos, Inc.
   11149 N Torrey Pines Rd
   La Jolla CA

(P-19799)
WCCT GLOBAL INC
5630 Cerritos Ave (90630-4721)
PHONE.................714 252-0700
EMP: 67
Web: participantsla.altasciences.com
SIC: 8731 Biotechnical research, commercial
PA: Wcct Global, Inc.
   5630 Cerritos Ave
   Cypress CA

8732 Commercial Nonphysical Research

(P-19800)
BERKELEY NUTRITIONAL MFG CORP (PA)
Also Called: Protein Research
1852 Rutan Dr (94551-7635)
PHONE.................925 243-6300
Robert Matheson, *Pr*
Gary Troxel, *
Ashley Matheson, *
▲ **EMP:** 60 **EST:** 1972
SQ FT: 53,900
SALES (est): 11.18MM
SALES (corp-wide): 11.18MM **Privately Held**
Web: www.proteinresearch.com
SIC: 8732 Market analysis or research

(P-19801)
BLOOMBERG LP
Pier Three 101 (94111)
PHONE.................415 283-4872
Jeff Taylor, *Prin*
EMP: 137 **EST:** 2012
SALES (est): 582.32K
SALES (corp-wide): 1.39B **Privately Held**
Web: www.bloomberg.com
SIC: 8732 Commercial nonphysical research
PA: Bloomberg L.P.
   731 Lexington Ave
   New York NY
   212 318-2000

(P-19802)
C3 NANO INC
3988 Trust Way (94545-3716)
PHONE.................510 259-9650
Cliff Morris, *CEO*
Paul Larose, *
Ajay Virkar, *
EMP: 85 **EST:** 2010
SALES (est): 6.89MM **Privately Held**
Web: www.c3nano.com
SIC: 8732 Research services, except laboratory

(P-19803)
CENTRAK INC
68 Willow Rd (94025-3653)
PHONE.................215 860-2928
Ari Naim, *Pr*
EMP: 192
SALES (corp-wide): 2.23B **Privately Held**
Web: www.centrak.com
SIC: 8732 Commercial nonphysical research
HQ: Centrak, Inc.
   826 Newtown Yardley Rd # 101
   Newtown PA
   215 860-2928

(P-19804)
CHASE GROUP LLC
Also Called: Simi Vly Care & Rehabilitation
5270 E Los Angeles Ave (93063-4137)
PHONE.................805 522-9155
Phil Chase, *Mgr*
EMP: 295
Web: www.chasegroup.us
SIC: 8732 8742 Research services, except laboratory; Management consulting services
PA: The Chase Group Llc
   5374 Long Shadow Ct
   Westlake Village CA

(P-19805)
CIC RESEARCH INC
Also Called: CIC Research
8361 Vickers St Ste 308 (92111-2112)
PHONE.................858 637-4000
Gordon H Kubota Ph.d., *Pr*
Joyce G Revlett, *
Warren L Hull, *
EMP: 65 **EST:** 1965
SQ FT: 15,000
SALES (est): 4.67MM **Privately Held**
Web: www.cicresearch.com
SIC: 8732 Economic research

(P-19806)
CORNERSTONE RESEARCH INC
555 W 5th St Ste 3800 (90013-3016)
PHONE.................213 553-2500
Richard Dalbeck, *VP*
EMP: 77
SALES (corp-wide): 94.84MM **Privately Held**
Web: www.cornerstone.com
SIC: 8732 Market analysis, business, and economic research
PA: Cornerstone Research, Inc.
   1000 Coleman Ave Ste 25
   Menlo Park CA
   650 853-1660

(P-19807)
DAVIS RESEARCH LLC
26610 Agoura Rd Ste 240 (91302-1954)
PHONE.................818 591-2408
William A Davis Iii, *Managing Member*
EMP: 150 **EST:** 1970
SALES (est): 14.07MM **Privately Held**
Web: www.davisresearch.com

(P-19808)
DISQO INC
Also Called: Survey Junkie
400 N Brand Blvd Ste 600 (91203-2359)
PHONE.................818 237-2186
Armen Adjemian, *CEO*
Drew Kutcharian, *
Jean-philippe Durrios, *CFO*
EMP: 60 **EST:** 2018
SALES (est): 6.45MM **Privately Held**
Web: www.disqo.com
SIC: 8732 7375 Market analysis or research; On-line data base information retrieval

(P-19809)
GATOR BIO INC
2455 Faber Pl (94303-3316)
PHONE.................650 800-7651
Hong Tan, *CEO*
EMP: 100 **EST:** 2017
SALES (est): 3MM **Privately Held**
Web: www.gatorbio.com
SIC: 8732 Business research service

(P-19810)
GENERAL ATOMICS (HQ)
3550 General Atomics Ct (92121-1194)
P.O. Box 85608 (92186-5608)
PHONE.................858 455-2810
J Neal Blue, *Pr*
Linden Blue, *
Liam Kelly, *
Robert S Forney, *
Jeffrey Quintenz, *
▲ **EMP:** 2015 **EST:** 1955
SQ FT: 1,000,000
SALES (est): 1.2B **Privately Held**
Web: www.ga.com
SIC: 8732 Commercial sociological and educational research
PA: General Atomic Technologies Corporation
   3550 General Atomics Ct
   San Diego CA

(P-19811)
GFK ETILIZE INC
34145 Pacific Coast Hwy 636 (92629-2808)
PHONE.................888 608-1212
Azhar Hameed, *Brnch Mgr*
EMP: 87
Web: www.etilize.com
SIC: 8732 Market analysis or research
HQ: Gfk Etilize, Inc.
   18662 Macarthur Blvd # 20
   Irvine CA

(P-19812)
GLASS LEWIS & CO LLC (HQ)
255 California St Ste 1100 (94111-4924)
PHONE.................415 678-4110
Carrie Busch, *Pr*
Stephen Gray, *
John Wieck, *
Dan Concannon, *CCO*
Eric Shostal, *
EMP: 60 **EST:** 2003
SALES (est): 20.79MM **Privately Held**
Web: www.glasslewis.com
SIC: 8732 Business analysis
PA: Peloton Capital Management Inc
   200-250 University Ave
   Toronto ON

(P-19813)
GLOBAL INDUSTRY ANALYSTS INC
6150 Hellyer Ave Ste 100 (95138-1072)

8732 - Commercial Nonphysical Research (P-19814)

PHONE.................408 528-9966
Kalakoti S Reddy, *CEO*
▲ **EMP:** 60 **EST:** 1992
SALES (est): 4.38MM **Privately Held**
Web: www.strategyr.com
SIC: 8732 Market analysis or research

(P-19814)
GUIDELINE INC
Also Called: Gdln
1412 Chapin Ave (94010-4003)
PHONE.................888 228-3491
EMP: 172 **EST:** 2015
SALES (est): 9.7MM **Privately Held**
Web: www.guideline.com
SIC: 8732 Commercial nonphysical research

(P-19815)
HENKEL US OPERATIONS CORP
14000 Jamboree Rd (92606-1730)
PHONE.................714 368-8000
Jim Heaton, *Brnch Mgr*
EMP: 104
SALES (corp-wide): 23.26B **Privately Held**
Web: www.henkel.com
SIC: 8732 Business research service
HQ: Henkel Us Operations Corporation
  1 Henkel Way
  Rocky Hill CT
  860 571-5100

(P-19816)
HI LLC (PA)
Also Called: Kernel
10361 Jefferson Blvd (90232-3511)
PHONE.................757 655-4113
Bryan Johnson, *Managing Member*
EMP: 90 **EST:** 2016
SQ FT: 3,500
SALES (est): 4.23MM
SALES (corp-wide): 4.23MM **Privately Held**
SIC: 8732 Business research service

(P-19817)
HIGH DSERT PRTNR IN ACDMIC EXC
Also Called: Lewis Center For Eductl RES
17500 Mana Rd (92307-2181)
PHONE.................760 946-5414
Lisa Lamb, *CEO*
Teresa Dowd, *
EMP: 350 **EST:** 1992
SQ FT: 35,000
SALES (est): 35.41MM **Privately Held**
Web: www.lewiscenter.org
SIC: 8732 Commercial nonphysical research

(P-19818)
HONDA R&D AMERICAS LLC
Also Called: Honda
1900 Harpers Way (90501-1521)
PHONE.................310 781-5500
▲ **EMP:** 1537
Web: www.hondaresearch.com
SIC: 8732 Market analysis or research

(P-19819)
HRL LABORATORIES LLC
Also Called: Hughes Research Laboratories
3011 Malibu Canyon Rd (90265-4797)
PHONE.................310 317-5000
Penrose Albright, *Pr*
Roger Gronwald, *CFO*
◆ **EMP:** 647 **EST:** 1997
SQ FT: 250,000
SALES (est): 106.52MM **Privately Held**
Web: www.hrl.com

SIC: 8732 Commercial sociological and educational research

(P-19820)
INCLIN INC (PA)
155 Bovet Rd Ste 660 (94402-3152)
PHONE.................650 961-3422
Brian Horger, *CEO*
Arnold Wong, *
Taylor Kilfoil, *CIO*
George Faurot, *
Ryan Clift, *
EMP: 88 **EST:** 1998
SALES (est): 8.64MM
SALES (corp-wide): 8.64MM **Privately Held**
Web: www.inclin.com
SIC: 8732 8731 Research services, except laboratory; Biotechnical research, commercial

(P-19821)
INFORMA RESEARCH SERVICES INC (HQ)
26565 Agoura Rd Ste 300 (91302-1958)
PHONE.................818 880-8877
Michael E Adler, *Pr*
Charles A Miwa, *
Lori Jomsky, *
EMP: 193 **EST:** 1993
SQ FT: 16,000
SALES (est): 50.64MM
SALES (corp-wide): 2.72B **Privately Held**
Web: financialintelligence.informa.com
SIC: 8732 Market analysis or research
PA: Informa Plc
  5 Howick Place
  London
  208 052-0400

(P-19822)
INNER CIRCLE LABS LLC
333 1st St Ste A (94105-2661)
P.O. Box 77851 (94107-0851)
PHONE.................415 684-9400
Julie A Neri, *Managing Member*
EMP: 74 **EST:** 2014
SALES (est): 3.92MM **Privately Held**
Web: www.highwirepr.com
SIC: 8732 Research services, except laboratory

(P-19823)
INSTANTLY INC
Also Called: Usamp
16501 Ventura Blvd # 300 (91436-2067)
PHONE.................866 872-4006
EMP: 200
SIC: 8732 Market analysis or research

(P-19824)
INTERVIEWING SERVICE AMER LLC (PA)
Also Called: ISA
15400 Sherman Way Ste 400 (91406-4211)
PHONE.................818 989-1044
Michael Halberstam, *Ch*
Tony Kretzmer, *
John Fitzpatrick, *
Vicky Agalsoff, *
EMP: 250 **EST:** 1982
SQ FT: 20,000
SALES (est): 21.54MM
SALES (corp-wide): 21.54MM **Privately Held**
Web: www.isacorp.com
SIC: 8732 Market analysis or research

(P-19825)
IPSOS OTX CORPORATION (HQ)
300 Corporate Pointe Ste 500 (90230)
PHONE.................310 736-3400
Shelley Zalis, *CEO*
Jeff Dean, *
EMP: 210 **EST:** 2003
SALES (est): 31.23MM
SALES (corp-wide): 426.25K **Privately Held**
Web: www.ipsosotx.com
SIC: 8732 Market analysis or research
PA: Ipsos
  35 Rue Du Val De Marne
  Paris
  141989000

(P-19826)
IQVIA INC
135 Main St Fl 22 (94105-1856)
PHONE.................415 692-9898
Telia Mangrai, *Off Mgr*
EMP: 100
Web: www.iqvia.com
SIC: 8732 Market analysis or research
HQ: Iqvia Inc.
  100 Ims Dr
  Parsippany NJ
  203 448-4600

(P-19827)
IQVIA INC (DH)
Also Called: SK&a
2601 Main St Ste 650 (92614-4228)
PHONE.................866 267-4479
David Escalante Junior, *Pr*
Al M Cosentino, *
Jaqueline Aguilera, *
Albert Chang, *
EMP: 87 **EST:** 1998
SQ FT: 12,000
SALES (est): 11.88MM
SALES (corp-wide): 8.5MM **Privately Held**
Web: www.onekeydata.com
SIC: 8732 Market analysis or research
HQ: Cegedim Inc.
  1425 Us Highway 206
  Bedminster NJ

(P-19828)
JD POWER AND ASSOCIATES INC
2625 Townsgate Rd Ste 100 (91361-5737)
PHONE.................805 418-8000
Dan Sullivan, *Prin*
EMP: 118 **EST:** 2018
SALES (est): 5.2MM **Privately Held**
Web: www.jdpower.com
SIC: 8732 Commercial nonphysical research

(P-19829)
KNOWLEDGE NETWORKS INC
2100 Geng Rd Ste 210 (94303-3307)
PHONE.................650 289-2000
EMP: 647
SIC: 8732 Market analysis or research

(P-19830)
LUTH RESEARCH INC (PA)
Also Called: Surveysavvy
404 Camino Del Rio S Ste 505 (92108)
P.O. Box 12557 (92112-3557)
PHONE.................619 234-5884
Roseanne Luth, *Pr*
Charles Rosen, *
EMP: 305 **EST:** 1977
SALES (est): 46.58MM
SALES (corp-wide): 46.58MM **Privately Held**
Web: www.luthresearch.com

SIC: 8732 Market analysis or research

(P-19831)
MATERIAL HOLDINGS LLC (PA)
Also Called: Lrw Group
1900 Avenue Of The Stars Ste 1600 (90067-4606)
PHONE.................310 553-0550
David Sackman, *Ch*
Arnold Fishman, *
Cathy Lindquist, *
EMP: 140 **EST:** 1973
SQ FT: 24,560
SALES (est): 65.39MM
SALES (corp-wide): 65.39MM **Privately Held**
Web: www.lrwonline.com
SIC: 8732 Market analysis or research

(P-19832)
MATHEMATICA INC
505 14th St Ste 800 (94612-1475)
PHONE.................510 830-3700
Paul Decker, *Mgr*
EMP: 134
SALES (corp-wide): 290MM **Privately Held**
Web: www.mathematica.org
SIC: 8732 Market analysis or research
HQ: Mathematica Inc.
  600 Alexander Park # 100
  Princeton NJ
  609 799-3535

(P-19833)
NATIONAL OPINION RESEARCH CTR
50 California St Ste 1500 (94111-4612)
PHONE.................415 315-2000
EMP: 108
SALES (corp-wide): 293.76MM **Privately Held**
Web: www.norc.org
SIC: 8732 Research services, except laboratory
PA: National Opinion Research Center
  55 E Monroe St Fl 30
  Chicago IL
  312 759-4266

(P-19834)
NATIONAL OPINION RESEARCH CTR
1250 Borregas Ave (94089-1309)
PHONE.................415 315-3800
EMP: 108
SALES (corp-wide): 293.76MM **Privately Held**
Web: www.norc.org
SIC: 8732 Research services, except laboratory
PA: National Opinion Research Center
  55 E Monroe St Fl 30
  Chicago IL
  312 759-4266

(P-19835)
NATIONAL RESEARCH GROUP INC
Also Called: National Research Group
12101 Bluff Creek Dr (90094-2627)
PHONE.................323 406-6200
Jon Penn, *CEO*
Jeff Hall, *
James Mcnamara, *Ex VP*
Jenny Swisher, *
Ray Ydoyaga, *
EMP: 278 **EST:** 1977
SALES (est): 22.69MM

PRODUCTS & SERVICES SECTION
8732 - Commercial Nonphysical Research (P-19857)

SALES (corp-wide): 2.69B **Publicly Held**
SIC: 8732 Market analysis or research
HQ: A + N Real Estate & Business
Management Corporation
1 World Trade Ctr
New York NY

(P-19836)
NIELSEN MOBILE LLC (DH)
Also Called: Nielsen Mobile
1010 Battery St (94111-1224)
PHONE..................917 435-9301
Sid Gorham, *Pr*
Tom Stahl, *COO*
EMP: 180 **EST:** 2000
SQ FT: 38,000
SALES (est): 26.8MM
SALES (corp-wide): 2.06B **Privately Held**
Web: global.nielsen.com
SIC: 8732 Market analysis or research
HQ: The Nielsen Company Us Llc
675 6th Ave
New York NY

(P-19837)
NITTO DENKO TECHNICAL CORP
Also Called: Nitto
501 Via Del Monte (92058-1251)
PHONE..................760 435-7011
Kenji Matsumoto, *Pr*
EMP: 99 **EST:** 1985
SALES (est): 16.11MM **Privately Held**
Web: www.ndtcorp.com
SIC: 8732 3089 3462 Research services, except laboratory; Automotive parts, plastic; Automotive and internal combustion engine forgings
PA: Nitto Denko Corporation
4-20, Ofukacho, Kita-Ku
Osaka OSK

(P-19838)
NOVOZYMES INC (DH)
Also Called: Novo Nordisk Biotech
1445 Drew Ave (95618-4880)
PHONE..................530 757-8100
Peder Holk Nielsen, *CEO*
Ejner B Jensen, *
EMP: 109 **EST:** 1992
SQ FT: 64,000
SALES (est): 31.36MM
SALES (corp-wide): 2.45B **Privately Held**
Web: www.novozymes.com
SIC: 8732 Commercial nonphysical research
HQ: Novozymes North America, Inc.
77 Perry Chapel Church Rd
Franklinton NC
919 494-2014

(P-19839)
ORANGE SILICON VALLEY LLC
Also Called: Orange Labs
60 Spear St Ste 1100 (94105-1599)
PHONE..................415 284-9765
Valerie Bar, *
EMP: 65 **EST:** 1999
SALES (est): 26.12MM
SALES (corp-wide): 23.35B **Privately Held**
Web: siliconvalley.orange.com
SIC: 8732 Market analysis or research
PA: Orange
111 Quai Du President Roosevelt
Issy Les Moulineaux

(P-19840)
OTR GLOBAL HOLDINGS II INC
155 Montgomery St Ste 501 (94104-4110)
PHONE..................415 675-7660
EMP: 142

Web: www.otrglobal.com
SIC: 8732 Market analysis or research
PA: Otr Global Holdings Ii, Inc.
4 Manhattanville Rd
Purchase NY

(P-19841)
PALLADIUM VALLEY GLOBAL INC ✪
3857 Birch St Ste 9017 (92660-2616)
PHONE..................949 723-9613
Jason Wilhite, *Ex Dir*
EMP: 75 **EST:** 2023
SALES (est): 1.28MM **Privately Held**
SIC: 8732 Merger, acquisition, and reorganization research

(P-19842)
PARAGON BIOMEDICAL INC
9685 Research Dr (92618-4657)
PHONE..................949 224-2800
EMP: 65
Web: www.parabio.com
SIC: 8732 8742 Business research service; Management consulting services

(P-19843)
PIVOT BIO INC
Also Called: Gatc
2910 7th St Ste 100 (94710-2700)
PHONE..................515 436-4462
EMP: 268 **EST:** 2010
SALES (est): 38.38MM **Privately Held**
Web: www.pivotbio.com
SIC: 8732 Commercial nonphysical research

(P-19844)
PROSEARCH STRATEGIES LLC
3250 Wilshire Blvd Ste 301 (90010-1577)
PHONE..................877 447-7291
Julia Kim Hasenzahl, *CEO*
EMP: 139 **EST:** 2005
SALES (est): 17.82MM **Privately Held**
Web: www.prosearchstrategies.com
SIC: 8732 Research services, except laboratory

(P-19845)
QUINTILES PACIFIC INCORPORATED
10201 Wateridge Cir Ste 300 (92121)
PHONE..................858 552-3400
EMP: 371
SIC: 8732 Market analysis or research
HQ: Quintiles Pacific Incorporated
448 E Middlefield Rd
Mountain View CA
650 567-2000

(P-19846)
QY RESEARCH INC
17890 Castleton St (91748-1756)
PHONE..................626 295-2442
Song Chunming, *Pr*
Diao Hongwei, *
Zhang Dong, *
EMP: 61 **EST:** 2016
SALES (est): 2.32MM **Privately Held**
Web: www.qyresearchglobal.com
SIC: 8732 Market analysis or research

(P-19847)
SMARTREVENUECOM INC
Also Called: Smartrevenue
101 Cooper St Ste 205 (95060-4526)
PHONE..................203 733-9156
EMP: 492
SALES (corp-wide): 50.29MM **Privately Held**

SIC: 8732 Market analysis or research
PA: Smartrevenue.Com, Inc.
60 Twin Ridge Rd
Ridgefield CT
203 733-9156

(P-19848)
SOLEIL COMMUNICATIONS LLC
Also Called: Prodata Research
2655 Camino Del Rio N Ste 110 (92108)
PHONE..................619 624-2888
Michael Gehrig, *Managing Member*
EMP: 137 **EST:** 2002
SALES (est): 778K
SALES (corp-wide): 47.43MM **Privately Held**
SIC: 8732 Market analysis or research
PA: The Welk Group Inc
11400 W Olympic Blvd # 1450
Los Angeles CA
760 749-3000

(P-19849)
SPHERE INSTITUTE
500 Airport Blvd Ste 340 (94010-1934)
PHONE..................650 558-3980
Thomas Ma Curdy, *Pr*
Greg Boro, *Treas*
EMP: 290 **EST:** 1996
SQ FT: 2,000
SALES (est): 29.25MM **Privately Held**
Web: www.sphereinstitute.org
SIC: 8732 Market analysis or research

(P-19850)
STREAMELEMENTS INC
11400 W Olympic Blvd (90064-1550)
PHONE..................323 928-7848
Udi Hoffmann, *Managing Member*
Udi Hoffmann, *CFO*
EMP: 99 **EST:** 2017
SALES (est): 4.02MM **Privately Held**
SIC: 8732 Commercial nonphysical research

(P-19851)
SUNING CMMERCE R D CTR USA INC
Also Called: Suning USA
845 Page Mill Rd (94304-1011)
PHONE..................650 834-9800
Enlong Hou, *CEO*
Jin Ming, *
EMP: 60 **EST:** 2013
SQ FT: 9,800
SALES (est): 3.84MM **Privately Held**
Web: www.ussuning.com
SIC: 8732 Commercial nonphysical research
PA: Suning.Com Co.,Ltd.
No.1,Suning Avenue,Xuewu Dist.
Nanjing JS

(P-19852)
TOASTER LLC
Also Called: Crosswalk
7083 Hollywood Blvd Fl 5 (90028-8908)
PHONE..................917 655-6440
EMP: 64
SALES (corp-wide): 2.09MM **Privately Held**
Web: www.crosswalknyc.com
SIC: 8732 Market analysis, business, and economic research
PA: Toaster, Llc
115 Brdway Ste 3 127 Fl 3
New York NY
662 316-5673

(P-19853)
TRENDSOURCE INC
Also Called: Examine Your Practice
4891 Pacific Hwy Ste 200 (92110-4026)
PHONE..................619 718-7467
Rodney Moll, *Ch Bd*
Rodney Moll, *Ch*
Neil A Wykes, *
Bob Post, *
EMP: 60 **EST:** 1989
SQ FT: 7,500
SALES (est): 7.13MM **Privately Held**
Web: www.trendsource.com
SIC: 8732 Market analysis or research

(P-19854)
UNIVERSITY CAL RIVERSIDE
Also Called: Uc Riverside RES Economic Dev
1160 University Ave (92507-4545)
PHONE..................951 827-4801
Stan Fletcher, *Dir*
EMP: 231
SALES (corp-wide): 534.4MM **Privately Held**
Web: www.ucr.edu
SIC: 8732 8221 9411 Economic research; University; Administration of educational programs
HQ: University Of California, Riverside, Alumni Association
900 University Ave
Riverside CA
951 827-1012

(P-19855)
VERANCE CORPORATION
6046 Cornerstone Ct W Ste 216 (92121-4734)
PHONE..................858 202-2800
Nilesh Shah, *CEO*
Clifford Friedman, *
Doctor Joe Winograd, *Ex VP*
F Mario Petrocco, *
EMP: 65 **EST:** 1995
SALES (est): 7.11MM **Privately Held**
Web: www.verance.com
SIC: 8732 Research services, except laboratory

(P-19856)
VERVE GROUP INC
350 Marine Pkwy Ste 220 (94065-5223)
PHONE..................760 536-8350
Remco Westermann, *CEO*
EMP: 103
SALES (corp-wide): 2.73MM **Privately Held**
Web: www.verve.com
SIC: 8732 Business analysis
PA: Verve Group, Inc.
5740 Fleet St Ste 100
Carlsbad CA
760 536-8350

(P-19857)
XDBS CORPORATION
Also Called: Xdbsb2b
3501 Jack Northrop Ave (90250-4433)
PHONE..................844 932-7356
Julie Strong, *CEO*
Kartik Anand, *
EMP: 157 **EST:** 2012
SQ FT: 4,000
SALES (est): 952.45K **Privately Held**
Web: www.xdbsworldwide.com
SIC: 8732 7389 5963 8742 Survey service: marketing, location, etc.; Telemarketing services; Direct sales, telemarketing; Sales (including sales management) consultant

8732 - Commercial Nonphysical Research (P-19858)

(P-19858)
ZEFR INC
Also Called: Movieclips.com
4101 Redwood Ave (90066-5603)
PHONE....................310 392-3555
Rich Raddon, *CEO*
Toby Byrne, *
EMP: 437 EST: 2010
SALES (est): 27.52MM Privately Held
Web: www.zefr.com
SIC: 8732 7371 Market analysis, business, and economic research; Software programming applications

8733 Noncommercial Research Organizations

(P-19859)
ABBVIE STEMCENTRX LLC
Also Called: Abbvie
1000 Gateway Blvd (94080-7028)
PHONE....................415 298-9242
Brian Slingerland, *CEO*
Scott J Dylla, *
James N Strabridge, *
Julia Hong, *Prin*
EMP: 138 EST: 2008
SALES (est): 18.93MM
SALES (corp-wide): 58.05B Publicly Held
Web: www.abbvie.com
SIC: 8733 2834 Medical research; Proprietary drug products
PA: Abbvie Inc.
1 N Waukegan Rd
North Chicago IL
847 932-7900

(P-19860)
AEROSPACE CORPORATION
200 S Los Robles Ave Ste 150 (91101-4614)
PHONE....................626 873-7700
Matthew Hart, *Brnch Mgr*
EMP: 72
SALES (corp-wide): 1.2B Privately Held
Web: www.aerospace.org
SIC: 8733 8711 8731 Scientific research agency; Engineering services; Commercial physical research
PA: The Aerospace Corporation
2310 E El Segundo Blvd
El Segundo CA
310 336-5000

(P-19861)
ALCON RESEARCH LLC
20511 Lake Forest Dr (92630-7741)
PHONE....................800 862-5266
EMP: 61
Web: www.alcon.com
SIC: 8733 Noncommercial research organizations
HQ: Alcon Research, Llc
6201 South Fwy
Fort Worth TX
817 551-4555

(P-19862)
ALPHA TEKNOVA INC
Also Called: Teknova
205 Apollo Way (95023-2507)
PHONE....................831 637-1100
EMP: 162
Web: www.teknova.com
SIC: 8733 Biotechnical research, noncommercial
PA: Alpha Teknova, Inc.
2451 Bert Dr
Hollister CA

(P-19863)
ASIA FOUNDATION (PA)
465 California St Fl 9 (94104-1892)
P.O. Box 193223 (94119-3223)
PHONE....................415 982-4640
David D Arnold, *Pr*
Richard H Fuller, *
Gordon Hein, *
Ken Krug, *
Suzanne Siskel, *
◆ EMP: 90 EST: 1951
SQ FT: 17,207
SALES (est): 101.64MM
SALES (corp-wide): 101.64MM Privately Held
Web: www.asiafoundation.org
SIC: 8733 Noncommercial research organizations

(P-19864)
BAY AREA ENVMTL RES INST
Also Called: BAER INSTITUTE
Nasa Research Park, Bldg 18, Room 101, 385 Bushnell St (94035)
P.O. Box 25 (94035-0025)
PHONE....................707 938-9387
Robert W Bergstrom, *Pr*
Mark Sittloh, *
▲ EMP: 83 EST: 1993
SQ FT: 750
SALES (est): 21.98MM Privately Held
Web: www.baeri.org
SIC: 8733 Medical research

(P-19865)
BEHAVIOR CHANGE INSTITUTE LLC
4096 Piedmont Ave Ste 161 (94611-5221)
PHONE....................866 273-2451
Joy S Pollard, *Pr*
EMP: 76 EST: 2014
SALES (est): 1.11MM Privately Held
Web: www.behaviorchangeinstitute.com
SIC: 8733 Noncommercial research organizations

(P-19866)
BIOSPLICE THERAPEUTICS INC
9360 Towne Centre Dr (92121-3057)
PHONE....................858 926-2900
Osman Kibar, *CEO*
EMP: 82 EST: 2007
SALES (est): 11.2MM Privately Held
Web: www.biosplice.com
SIC: 8733 Medical research

(P-19867)
BRENTWOOD BMDICAL RES INST INC
11301 Wilshire Blvd Bldg 114 (90073-1003)
P.O. Box 25027 (90025-0027)
PHONE....................310 312-1554
Kenneth Hickman, *CEO*
Thoyd Ellis, *
EMP: 130 EST: 1988
SQ FT: 1,500
SALES (est): 4.85MM Privately Held
Web: www.brentwoodresearch.org
SIC: 8733 Medical research

(P-19868)
BUCK INST FOR RES ON AGING (PA)
8001 Redwood Blvd (94945-1400)
PHONE....................415 209-2000
Eric M Verdin, *Pr*
Dale Bredesen Md, *Pr*
Nancy Derr, *
Remy Gross Iii, *VP*
Ralph O Rear, *
EMP: 172 EST: 1986
SQ FT: 185,000
SALES (est): 43.95MM Privately Held
Web: www.buckinstitute.org
SIC: 8733 Medical research

(P-19869)
CALIFORNIA CMPLTE CNT CNSUS
400 R St Ste 350 (95811-6233)
PHONE....................916 852-2020
Ditas Katague, *Prin*
EMP: 60 EST: 2018
SALES (est): 1.41MM Privately Held
Web: census.ca.gov
SIC: 8733 Noncommercial research organizations

(P-19870)
CALIFORNIA DEPT WTR RESOURCES
Division of Flood Management
3310 El Camino Ave Ste 200 (95821)
PHONE....................916 574-1423
Jon Ericson, *Div Mgr*
EMP: 100
SALES (corp-wide): 534.4MM Privately Held
Web: water.ca.gov
SIC: 8733 Research institute
HQ: California Department Of Water Resources
715 P St
Sacramento CA
916 653-9394

(P-19871)
CALIFORNIA INSTITUTE FOR BIOMEDICAL RESEARCH
Also Called: California Institute For
11119 N Torrey Pines Rd (92037-1046)
PHONE....................858 242-1000
EMP: 110
Web: www.calibr.org
SIC: 8733 Medical research

(P-19872)
CALIFORNIA INSTITUTE TECH
Also Called: Jet Propulsion Laboratory
4800 Oak Grove Dr (91109-8001)
PHONE....................818 354-9154
Michael Watkins, *Dir*
EMP: 6000
SALES (corp-wide): 3.31B Privately Held
Web: www.caltech.edu
SIC: 8733 Research institute
PA: California Institute Of Technology
1200 E California Blvd
Pasadena CA
626 395-6811

(P-19873)
CANCER PREVENTION INST CAL (PA)
Also Called: Greater Bay Area Cncer Rgistry
1 Blackfield Dr (94920-2053)
PHONE....................510 608-5000
Matt O'grady, *Interim Chief Executive Officer*
EMP: 115 EST: 1974
SALES (est): 13.22K
SALES (corp-wide): 13.22K Privately Held
Web: www.cpic.org
SIC: 8733 Medical research

(P-19874)
CARNEGIE INSTITUTION WASH
Also Called: Observatories of The Carnegie
813 Santa Barbara St (91101-1232)
PHONE....................626 577-1122
Wendy L Freedman, *Dir*
EMP: 100
SQ FT: 24,075
SALES (corp-wide): 164.74MM Privately Held
Web: obs.carnegiescience.edu
SIC: 8733 7999 Scientific research agency; Observation tower operation
PA: Carnegie Institution Of Washington
1530 P St Nw
Washington DC
202 387-6400

(P-19875)
CENTER FOR CIVIC EDUCATION (PA)
5115 Douglas Fir Rd Ste J (91302-2590)
PHONE....................818 591-9321
Christopher R Riano, *Ex Dir*
EMP: 60 EST: 1980
SQ FT: 16,000
SALES (est): 2.92MM
SALES (corp-wide): 2.92MM Privately Held
Web: www.civiced.org
SIC: 8733 8748 Educational research agency; Educational consultant

(P-19876)
CHAN ZUCKERBERG BIOHUB INC
499 Illinois St (94158-2518)
PHONE....................628 200-3246
Stephen Quake, *Pr*
Melinda Griffith, *CLO*
EMP: 166 EST: 2017
SALES (est): 10.31MM Privately Held
Web: www.czbiohub.org
SIC: 8733 Medical research

(P-19877)
CHILDRENS INST LOS ANGELES (PA)
2121 W Temple St (90026-4915)
PHONE....................213 385-5100
Bradley Myslinski, *Pr*
Martine Singer, *
Eugene Straub, *
EMP: 150 EST: 2011
SALES (est): 392.05K
SALES (corp-wide): 392.05K Privately Held
Web: www.childrensinstitute.org
SIC: 8733 Noncommercial research organizations

(P-19878)
COMPLETE GENOMICS INC (HQ)
2904 Orchard Pkwy (95134-2009)
PHONE....................408 648-2560
Clifford A Reid Ph.d., *Ch Bd*
Bruce Martin, *
Keith Raffel, *CCO**
Arthur W Homan, *
Ethan Knowlden, *
EMP: 214 EST: 2005
SQ FT: 66,000
SALES (est): 67.63MM Privately Held
Web: completegenomics.mgiamericas.com
SIC: 8733 Biotechnical research, noncommercial
PA: Beijing Genomics Institute At Shenzhen Comprehensive Building, Beishan Industrial Zone, Yantian Street, Shenzhen GD

8733 - Noncommercial Research Organizations (P-19900)

(P-19879)
DOHENY EYE INSTITUTE (PA)
150 N Orange Grove Blvd (91103-3534)
PHONE.....................323 342-7120
EMP: 100 EST: 1947
SALES (est): 20.91MM
SALES (corp-wide): 20.91MM Privately Held
Web: www.doheny.org
SIC: 8733 Medical research

(P-19880)
ELECTRIC POWER RES INST INC (PA)
3420 Hillview Ave (94304-1338)
P.O. Box 10412 (94303-0813)
PHONE.....................650 855-2000
Arshad Mansoor, CEO
Stanley W Connally Junior, Vice Chairman
Michael Howard, CEO
Terry Boston, Pr
Jim Kerr, Dir
EMP: 600 EST: 1973
SQ FT: 300,000
SALES (est): 441.37MM
SALES (corp-wide): 441.37MM Privately Held
Web: www.epri.com
SIC: 8733 Research institute

(P-19881)
ELEMENT SCIENCE INC
200 Kansas St Ste 210 (94103-5146)
PHONE.....................415 872-6500
Uday N Kumar, Pr
Michael Mcsweeney, Regulatory Affairs
EMP: 70 EST: 2011
SALES (est): 5.19MM Privately Held
Web: www.elementscience.com
SIC: 8733 8011 Medical research; Surgeon

(P-19882)
GENENTECH INC (DH)
1 Dna Way (94080-4990)
P.O. Box 4354 (97208-4354)
PHONE.....................650 225-1000
Ian Clark, CEO
◆ EMP: 2000 EST: 1986
SALES (est): 1.2B Privately Held
Web: www.gene.com
SIC: 8733 Medical research
HQ: Roche Holdings, Inc.
    1 Dna Way
    South San Francisco CA
    650 225-1000

(P-19883)
HEALTHPOINT CAPITAL LLC (PA)
9920 Pacific Heights Blvd Ste 150 (92121)
PHONE.....................212 935-7780
John H Foster, CEO
Mike Mogul, *
EMP: 160 EST: 2002
SALES (est): 8.27MM
SALES (corp-wide): 8.27MM Privately Held
Web: www.healthpointcapital.com
SIC: 8733 Medical research

(P-19884)
HISAMITSU PHARMACEUTICAL CO INC
2730 Loker Ave W (92010-6603)
PHONE.....................760 931-1756
EMP: 626
SIC: 8733 Medical research

(P-19885)
HOUSE RESEARCH INSTITUTE
2100 W 3rd St Ste 500 (90057-1922)
PHONE.....................213 353-7012
EMP: 160
SIC: 8733 Medical research

(P-19886)
IMPAQ INTERNATIONAL LLC
1333 Broadway Ste 300 (94612-1922)
PHONE.....................510 597-2400
Sharon R Benus, Brnch Mgr
EMP: 140
SALES (corp-wide): 305.83MM Privately Held
Web: www.air.org
SIC: 8733 7371 7373 7379 Noncommercial research organizations; Custom computer programming services; Computer integrated systems design; Computer related maintenance services
HQ: Impaq International, Llc
    10420 Lttle Ptxent Pkwy S
    Columbia MD
    443 259-5500

(P-19887)
INSTITUTE FOR DEFENSE ANALYSES
Center For Communications RES
4320 Westerra Ct (92121-1969)
PHONE.....................858 622-5439
Joe Buhler, Mgr
EMP: 170
SALES (corp-wide): 311.3MM Privately Held
Web: www.ida.org
SIC: 8733 Research institute
PA: Institute For Defense Analyses Inc
    730 E Glebe Rd
    Alexandria VA
    703 845-2000

(P-19888)
IONPATH INC
1455 Adams Dr 1036 (94025-1438)
PHONE.....................650 336-3058
EMP: 87
SALES (corp-wide): 7.6MM Privately Held
Web: www.ionpath.com
SIC: 8733 Noncommercial research organizations
PA: Ionpath, Inc.
    960 Obrien Dr
    Menlo Park CA
    650 521-1763

(P-19889)
J CRAIG VENTER INSTITUTE INC (PA)
4120 Capricorn Ln (92037-3498)
PHONE.....................301 795-7000
J Craig Venter, CEO
Karen Nelson, *
Reid Adler, *
Kathleen L Mattis, *
Robert Friedman, *
EMP: 275 EST: 1993
SQ FT: 125,000
SALES (est): 25.45MM
SALES (corp-wide): 25.45MM Privately Held
Web: www.jcvi.org
SIC: 8733 8731 Research institute; Biological research

(P-19890)
JACKSON LABORATORY
1650 Santa Ana Ave (95838-1752)
PHONE.....................800 422-6423
Elise Bonker, Mgr
EMP: 90
SALES (corp-wide): 572.87MM Privately Held
Web: www.jax.org
SIC: 8733 Medical research
PA: The Jackson Laboratory
    600 Main St
    Bar Harbor ME
    207 288-6000

(P-19891)
JWCH INSTITUTE INC
6912 Ajax Ave (90201-4057)
PHONE.....................323 562-5813
Annabel Munoz, Mgr
EMP: 178
SALES (corp-wide): 107.92MM Privately Held
Web: www.jwchinstitute.org
SIC: 8733 Noncommercial research organizations
PA: Jwch Institute, Inc.
    5650 Jillson St
    Commerce CA
    323 477-1171

(P-19892)
JWCH INSTITUTE INC
12360 Firestone Blvd (90650-4324)
PHONE.....................562 281-0306
Oyamendan Itohan, COO
EMP: 178
SALES (corp-wide): 107.92MM Privately Held
Web: www.jwchinstitute.org
SIC: 8733 Noncommercial research organizations
PA: Jwch Institute, Inc.
    5650 Jillson St
    Commerce CA
    323 477-1171

(P-19893)
LA JOLLA INST FOR IMMUNOLOGY
Also Called: La Jolla Inst For Allrgy Immnl
9420 Athena Cir (92037-1387)
PHONE.....................858 752-6500
Erica Ollmann Saphire, Pr
Stephen Wilson Ph.d., Ex VP
Michael Dollar, CFO
Eric Zwisler, Ch Bd
Skip Carpowich, CFO
EMP: 400 EST: 1988
SQ FT: 87,000
SALES (est): 102.02MM Privately Held
Web: www.lji.org
SIC: 8733 8731 Medical research; Biotechnical research, commercial

(P-19894)
LUNDQUIST INSTITUTE FOR BIOMEDICAL INNOVATION AT HARBOR-UCLA MEDICAL CENTER
Also Called: LA BIOMED
1124 W Carson St (90502-2006)
PHONE.....................877 452-2674
EMP: 800 EST: 1952
SALES (est): 85.15MM Privately Held
Web: www.lundquist.org
SIC: 8733 Medical research

(P-19895)
MIND RESEARCH INSTITUTE
Also Called: Music Intllgnce Neuro Dev Inst
5281 California Ave Ste 300 (92617-3219)
PHONE.....................949 345-8700
Brett Woudenberg, CEO
Matthew Peterson Crdo, Prin
Josephine Garrett, CFO
EMP: 160 EST: 2000
SALES (est): 24.87MM Privately Held
Web: www.mindresearch.org
SIC: 8733 Medical research

(P-19896)
MITRE CORPORATION
2401 E El Segundo Blvd Ste 400 (90245-4670)
PHONE.....................310 297-8350
Jason Providakes, Prin
EMP: 60
SALES (corp-wide): 990.87MM Privately Held
Web: www.mitre.org
SIC: 8733 Noncommercial research organizations
PA: The Mitre Corporation
    202 Burlington Rd
    Bedford MA
    781 271-2000

(P-19897)
MITRE CORPORATION
Also Called: Washington C3 Center
2756 Locust St (92106-1447)
PHONE.....................619 758-7818
David Coomber, Mgr
EMP: 99
SALES (corp-wide): 990.87MM Privately Held
Web: www.mitre.org
SIC: 8733 Research institute
PA: The Mitre Corporation
    202 Burlington Rd
    Bedford MA
    781 271-2000

(P-19898)
MONTEREY BAY AQUARIUM RES INST
Also Called: Mbari
7700 Sandholdt Rd (95039-9644)
PHONE.....................831 775-1700
Christopher A Scholin, Pr
Marcia Mcnutt, Pr
Julie Packard, *
Marsha Mcnutt, Sec
▲ EMP: 220 EST: 1987
SQ FT: 17,000
SALES (est): 66.11MM Privately Held
Web: www.mbari.org
SIC: 8733 Research institute

(P-19899)
NANOCOMPOSIX LLC
4878 Ronson Ct Ste J (92111-1806)
PHONE.....................858 565-4227
Steven Oldenburg, Pr
EMP: 90 EST: 2004
SQ FT: 16,000
SALES (est): 14MM
SALES (corp-wide): 14MM Privately Held
Web: www.nanocomposix.com
SIC: 8733 Scientific research agency
PA: Fortis Life Sciences, Llc
    222 Berkeley St Fl 18
    Boston MA

(P-19900)
NANTCELL INC
2040 E Mariposa Ave (90245-5027)
PHONE.....................310 883-1300
Patrick Soon-shiong, CEO
EMP: 224 EST: 2014
SALES (est): 10.17MM

8733 - Noncommercial Research Organizations (P-19901)

SALES (corp-wide): 158.26K **Publicly Held**
SIC: 8733 Bacteriological research
PA: Nantworks, Llc
9920 Jefferson Blvd
Culver City CA
310 883-1300

(P-19901)
NATIONAL FOOD LABORATORY LLC
365 N Canyons Pkwy Ste 201 (94551-7703)
PHONE...................925 828-1440
Austin Sharp, *Pr*
Kevin Waters, *
Mindy Hungerman, *
Carolyn Graham, *
Jena Roberts, *
EMP: 85 **EST:** 1991
SQ FT: 21,000
SALES (est): 5.17MM **Privately Held**
SIC: 8733 Scientific research agency

(P-19902)
PALO ALTO VTERANS INST FOR RES
Also Called: PAVIR
3801 Miranda Ave Bldg 101 (94304-1207)
PHONE...................650 858-3970
Kerstin Lynam, *CEO*
Mary Thornton, *
EMP: 218 **EST:** 1988
SQ FT: 5,500
SALES (est): 29.92MM **Privately Held**
Web: www.pavir.org
SIC: 8733 Medical research

(P-19903)
PARKINSONS INSTITUTE
2500 Hospital Dr Bldg 10 (94040-4106)
P.O. Box 70727 (94086-0727)
PHONE...................650 770-0201
TOLL FREE: 800
EMP: 85
Web: www.thepi.org
SIC: 8733 8011 Medical research; Clinic, operated by physicians

(P-19904)
POINT REYES BIRD OBSERVATORY
Also Called: PRBO
3820 Cypress Dr Ste 11 (94954-6964)
PHONE...................707 781-2555
Ellie M Cohen, *Pr*
Steven Thal, *
Laurie Tahcott, *
Edward Sarti, *
EMP: 85 **EST:** 1965
SQ FT: 2,000
SALES (est): 15.54MM **Privately Held**
Web: www.pointblue.org
SIC: 8733 8748 Noncommercial biological research organization; Business consulting, nec

(P-19905)
PUBLIC HEALTH INSTITUTE (PA)
555 12th St Ste 600 (94607-4067)
PHONE...................510 285-5500
Mary Pittman, *Pr*
Bob Wolfson, *
Anthony B Iton, *
Melange Matthews, *
Carmen Nevarez, *
EMP: 100 **EST:** 1964
SQ FT: 50,000
SALES (est): 112.18MM

SALES (corp-wide): 112.18MM **Privately Held**
Web: www.phi.org
SIC: 8733 Scientific research agency

(P-19906)
RANCHO RESEARCH INSTITUTE
Also Called: RRI
7601 Imperial Hwy (90242-3456)
P.O. Box 3500 (90242-3500)
PHONE...................562 401-8111
Julia Laplount, *CEO*
Yaga Szlachcic, *
EMP: 175 **EST:** 1956
SQ FT: 15,000
SALES (est): 9.21MM **Privately Held**
Web: www.ranchoresearch.org
SIC: 8733 Educational research agency

(P-19907)
REGULUS THERAPEUTICS INC
4224 Campus Point Ct Ste 210 (92121-1555)
PHONE...................858 202-6300
Stelios Papadopoulos, *Ch Bd*
Joseph P Hagan, *
Daniel Chevallard, *CAO*
Denis Drygin, *CSO*
EMP: 63 **EST:** 2008
SQ FT: 59,000
Web: www.regulusrx.com
SIC: 8733 Biotechnical research, noncommercial

(P-19908)
SANFORD BRNHAM PRBYS MED DSCVE (PA)
Also Called: SBP
10901 N Torrey Pines Rd (92037-1005)
PHONE...................858 795-5000
C Randal Mills, *CEO*
Kristiina Vuori, *
Robin Ryan, *
Gary Chessum, *
EMP: 966 **EST:** 1976
SQ FT: 397,000
SALES (est): 98.58MM
SALES (corp-wide): 98.58MM **Privately Held**
Web: www.sbpdiscovery.org
SIC: 8733 Research institute

(P-19909)
SCRIPPS RESEARCH INSTITUTE
Also Called: Calibr A Division Scripps RES
11119 N Torrey Pines Rd Ste 100 (92037-1046)
PHONE...................858 242-1000
EMP: 99
Web: www.scripps.edu
SIC: 8733 Medical research
PA: The Scripps Research Institute
10550 N Torrey Pines Rd
La Jolla CA

(P-19910)
SCRIPPS RESEARCH INSTITUTE (PA)
10550 N Torrey Pines Rd (92037-1000)
PHONE...................858 784-1000
Peter G Schultz, *CEO*
John D Diekman, *
Steve A Kay, *
Cary E Thomas, *
Donna J Weston, *
EMP: 90 **EST:** 1990
SALES (est): 652.04MM **Privately Held**
Web: www.scripps.edu
SIC: 8733 Research institute

(P-19911)
SETI INSTITUTE
Also Called: Seti Institute, The
339 Bernardo Ave Ste 200 (94043-5232)
PHONE...................650 961-6633
Matthew Doan, *Pr*
Edna Devor, *
Doctor Greg Papadopolous, *Ch*
Doctor John Billingham, *Vice Chairman*
Shannon Atkinson, *
EMP: 115 **EST:** 1984
SQ FT: 19,737
SALES (est): 25.93MM **Privately Held**
Web: www.seti.org
SIC: 8733 Research institute

(P-19912)
SINGULEX INC
Also Called: Singulex
1701 Harbor Bay Pkwy Ste 200 (94502-3087)
PHONE...................510 995-9000
EMP: 260 **EST:** 1998
SALES (est): 25.3MM **Privately Held**
Web: www.singulex.com
SIC: 8733 8071 3841 Scientific research agency; Blood analysis laboratory; Diagnostic apparatus, medical

(P-19913)
SMARTMATIC USA CORP
2450 Colorado Ave (90404-3575)
PHONE...................424 581-6604
EMP: 68
SALES (corp-wide): 3.22MM **Privately Held**
SIC: 8733 Noncommercial research organizations
PA: Smartmatic Usa Corp
1001 Broken Sound Pkwy Nw
Boca Raton FL
561 862-0747

(P-19914)
SOUTHERN CAL INST FOR RES EDCA
Also Called: S C I R E
5901 E 7th St 151 (90822-5201)
P.O. Box 15298 (90815-0298)
PHONE...................562 826-8139
Timothy R Morgan, *Pr*
Moti Kashyap Md, *Treas*
EMP: 80 **EST:** 1989
SALES (est): 3.4MM **Privately Held**
Web: www.scire-lb.org
SIC: 8733 Medical research

(P-19915)
SRI INTERNATIONAL (PA)
333 Ravenswood Ave (94025-3493)
P.O. Box 2203 (94026-2203)
PHONE...................650 859-2000
William Jeffrey, *CEO*
Denise Glyn Borders, *Pr*
Stephen Ciesinski, *Pr*
Manish Kothari, *Pr*
Erin Andre, *CPO*
▲ **EMP:** 1430 **EST:** 1946
SQ FT: 1,300,000
SALES (est): 249.22MM
SALES (corp-wide): 249.22MM **Privately Held**
Web: www.sri.com
SIC: 8733 8748 Scientific research agency; Business consulting, nec

(P-19916)
STANFORD UNIV FRMAN SPGLI INST
616 Jane Stanford Way (94305-6008)
PHONE...................650 723-8681
Michael Mcfaul, *Dir*
EMP: 250 **EST:** 2017
SALES (est): 6.35MM **Privately Held**
Web: fsi.stanford.edu
SIC: 8733 Research institute

(P-19917)
TAKEDA DEV CTR AMERICAS INC (HQ)
Also Called: Tcal
9625 Towne Centre Dr (92121-1964)
PHONE...................858 622-8528
Keith Wilson, *Pr*
Tetsuyuki Maruyama, *Dir*
James Morley, *Dir*
David J Weitz J.d., *Genl Mgr*
EMP: 151 **EST:** 2001
SALES (est): 41.41MM **Privately Held**
Web: www.pint.com
SIC: 8733 2834 Biotechnical research, noncommercial; Pharmaceutical preparations
PA: Takeda Pharmaceutical Company Limited
2-1-1, Nihombashihoncho
Chuo-Ku TKY

(P-19918)
THE AEROSPACE CORPORATION (PA)
2310 E El Segundo Blvd (90245-4609)
P.O. Box 92957 (90009-2957)
PHONE...................310 336-5000
EMP: 2313 **EST:** 1960
SALES (est): 1.2B
SALES (corp-wide): 1.2B **Privately Held**
Web: www.aerospace.org
SIC: 8733 8711 8731 Scientific research agency; Engineering services; Commercial physical research

(P-19919)
THE J DAVID GLADSTONE INSTITUTES
1650 Owens St (94158-2261)
PHONE...................415 734-2000
▲ **EMP:** 370 **EST:** 1971
SALES (est): 101.11MM **Privately Held**
Web: www.gladstone.org
SIC: 8733 Medical research

(P-19920)
THE RAND CORPORATION (PA)
Also Called: Rand
1776 Main St (90401-3297)
P.O. Box 2138 (90407-2138)
PHONE...................310 393-0411
EMP: 900 **EST:** 1948
SALES (est): 399.09MM
SALES (corp-wide): 399.09MM **Privately Held**
Web: www.rand.org
SIC: 8733 8732 8742 Noncommercial research organizations; Commercial nonphysical research; Management consulting services

(P-19921)
TMT INTRNTONAL OBSERVATORY LLC
100 W Walnut St Ste 300 (91124-0001)
PHONE...................626 395-1651
Henry Yang, *Managing Member*
Edward Stone, *Managing Member**
Dean Currie, *
Fiona Harrison, *
B Thomas Soifer, *

PRODUCTS & SERVICES SECTION   8733 - Noncommercial Research Organizations (P-19941)

EMP: 80 EST: 2014
SALES (est): 25.56MM **Privately Held**
Web: www.tmt.org
SIC: 8733 Scientific research agency

(P-19922)
TRANSFAIR USA
Also Called: FAIR TRADE USA
360 Grand Ave Unit 311 (94610-4840)
PHONE......................510 663-5260
Paul Rice, CEO
Paul Rice, Pr
Dave Rochlin, *
Joan Catherine Braun, *
Katarzyna Syta, *
EMP: 144 EST: 1996
SALES (est): 24.01MM **Privately Held**
Web: www.fairtradecertified.org
SIC: 8733 Noncommercial social research organization

(P-19923)
UNITED STTES DEPT ENRGY BRKLEY
Also Called: Lawrence Berkeley National Lab
555 W Imperial Hwy (92821-4802)
PHONE......................510 486-7089
EMP: 153
Web: www.es.net
SIC: 8733 9611 Noncommercial research organizations; Energy development and conservation agency, government
HQ: United States Department Of Energy
  Berkeley Office
  1 Cyclotron Rd
  Berkeley CA
  510 486-5784

(P-19924)
UNITED STTES DEPT ENRGY BRKLEY
Also Called: Lawrence Berkeley National Lab
1226 Cornell Ave (94706-2308)
PHONE......................510 701-1089
EMP: 153
Web: www.es.net
SIC: 8733 9611 Noncommercial research organizations; Energy development and conservation agency, government
HQ: United States Department Of Energy
  Berkeley Office
  1 Cyclotron Rd
  Berkeley CA
  510 486-5784

(P-19925)
UNITED STTES DEPT ENRGY BRKLEY
Also Called: Lawrence Berkeley National Lab
419 Latimer Hall (94720-1461)
PHONE......................510 486-4033
EMP: 153
Web: www.es.net
SIC: 8733 9611 Noncommercial research organizations; Energy development and conservation agency, government
HQ: United States Department Of Energy
  Berkeley Office
  1 Cyclotron Rd
  Berkeley CA
  510 486-5784

(P-19926)
UNITED STTES DEPT ENRGY LVRMOR
Also Called: Lawrence Livermore Nat Lab
539 Peralta Ave (94110-5338)
PHONE......................415 648-3878
EMP: 598

Web: www.llnl.gov
SIC: 8733 9611 Noncommercial research organizations; Energy development and conservation agency, government
HQ: United States Department Of Energy
  Livermore Office
  7000 East Ave
  Livermore CA
  925 422-1100

(P-19927)
UNITED STTES DEPT ENRGY LVRMOR
Also Called: Lawrence Livermore Nat Lab
1413 Willowtree Ct (95118-1155)
PHONE......................408 267-1413
David Zalk, Brnch Mgr
EMP: 598
Web: www.llnl.gov
SIC: 8733 9611 Noncommercial research organizations; Energy development and conservation agency, government
HQ: United States Department Of Energy
  Livermore Office
  7000 East Ave
  Livermore CA
  925 422-1100

(P-19928)
UNIVERSITY CAL RVRSIDE ALMNI A
Also Called: Kearney Agricultural Center
9240 S Riverbend Ave (93648-9757)
PHONE......................559 646-6500
Jeff Ehlberg, Dir
EMP: 73
SALES (corp-wide): 534.4MM **Privately Held**
Web: www.ucr.edu
SIC: 8733 8221 9411 Research institute; University; Administration of educational programs
HQ: University Of California, Riverside, Alumni Association
  900 University Ave
  Riverside CA
  951 827-1012

(P-19929)
UNIVERSITY CAL SAN DIEGO
Also Called: Health Services Research Ctr
5440 Morehouse Dr Ste 2600 (92121-1798)
PHONE......................858 622-1771
Theodore Ganiats, Ex Dir
EMP: 89
SALES (corp-wide): 534.4MM **Privately Held**
Web: www.ucsd.edu
SIC: 8733 8221 9411 Noncommercial research organizations; University; Administration of educational programs
HQ: University Of California, San Diego
  9500 Gilman Dr
  La Jolla CA
  858 534-2230

(P-19930)
UNIVERSITY CAL SAN FRANCISCO
Also Called: Ucsf Ward 86
995 Potrero Ave (94110-2859)
PHONE......................628 206-2400
EMP: 73
SALES (corp-wide): 534.4MM **Privately Held**
Web: www.ucsf.edu
SIC: 8733 Noncommercial research organizations
HQ: University Cal San Francisco
  513 Parnassus Ave 115f

  San Francisco CA

(P-19931)
UNIVERSITY CAL SAN FRANCISCO
Also Called: Ucsf Neuro Epidemiology Lab
1450 3rd St (94143-2197)
PHONE......................415 476-9323
EMP: 83
SALES (corp-wide): 534.4MM **Privately Held**
Web: www.ucsf.edu
SIC: 8733 8221 9411 Medical research; University; Administration of educational programs
HQ: University Cal San Francisco
  513 Parnassus Ave 115f
  San Francisco CA

(P-19932)
URS GROUP INC
Also Called: URS
1550 Humboldt Rd Ste 2 (95928-9115)
PHONE......................530 893-9675
Elena Nilsson, Brnch Mgr
EMP: 78
SALES (corp-wide): 13.15B **Publicly Held**
Web: www.aecom.com
SIC: 8733 Archeological expeditions
HQ: Urs Group, Inc.
  300 S Grand Ave Ste 900
  Los Angeles CA
  213 593-8000

(P-19933)
USC INFORMATION SCIENCES INST
4676 Admiralty Way Ste 1001 (90292-6622)
PHONE......................310 448-9438
Jerry R Hobbs, Prin
EMP: 243 EST: 2015
SALES (est): 3.65MM **Privately Held**
Web: www.isi.edu
SIC: 8733 Research institute

(P-19934)
WCCT GLOBAL INC (PA)
5630 Cerritos Ave (90630-4738)
PHONE......................714 668-1500
Gregory Hanson, CEO
Bill Taaffe, *
Kenneth T Kim, Managing Member*
EMP: 66 EST: 2005
SALES (est): 24.69MM **Privately Held**
Web: participantsla.altasciences.com
SIC: 8733 8731 8721 Research institute; Biological research; Calculating and statistical service

(P-19935)
WESTED
300 Lakeside Dr 25th Fl (94612-3534)
PHONE......................510 302-4200
Teresa Johnson, Brnch Mgr
EMP: 60
SALES (corp-wide): 115.65MM **Privately Held**
Web: www.wested.org
SIC: 8733 8732 Educational research agency ; Commercial nonphysical research
PA: Wested
  730 Harrison St Ste 500
  San Francisco CA
  415 565-3000

(P-19936)
WESTED
180 Harbor Dr Ste 112 (94965-2845)

PHONE......................415 289-2300
Peter Mangione, Brnch Mgr
EMP: 60
SALES (corp-wide): 115.65MM **Privately Held**
Web: www.wested.org
SIC: 8733 8732 Educational research agency ; Commercial nonphysical research
PA: Wested
  730 Harrison St Ste 500
  San Francisco CA
  415 565-3000

(P-19937)
WESTED (PA)
730 Harrison St (94107-1242)
PHONE......................415 565-3000
Glen H Harvey, CEO
EMP: 115 EST: 1995
SQ FT: 85,000
SALES (est): 115.65MM
SALES (corp-wide): 115.65MM **Privately Held**
Web: www.wested.org
SIC: 8733 Educational research agency

(P-19938)
WESTERN STATES INFO NETWRK INC
1825 Bell St Ste 205 (95825-1020)
PHONE......................916 263-1188
Karen Aumond, Ex Dir
EMP: 78 EST: 2009
SALES (est): 5.43MM **Privately Held**
SIC: 8733 Noncommercial research organizations

(P-19939)
WHITTIER INST FOR DIABETES
10140 Campus Point Dr (92121-1520)
PHONE......................877 944-8843
Athena Tsimikas, Ex Dir
EMP: 65 EST: 1980
SALES (est): 819.75K
SALES (corp-wide): 4.06B **Privately Held**
Web: www.scripps.org
SIC: 8733 Medical research
PA: Scripps Health
  10140 Campus Point Dr # 415
  San Diego CA
  800 727-4777

(P-19940)
XQ INSTITUTE
248 3rd St Ste 319 (94607-4375)
PHONE......................844 825-5297
EMP: 79 EST: 2015
SALES (est): 493.15K **Privately Held**
Web: www.xqsuperschool.org
SIC: 8733 Noncommercial research organizations

(P-19941)
ZONARE MEDICAL SYSTEMS INC
Also Called: Zonare
420 Bernardo Ave (94043-5209)
P.O. Box 760 (95002-0760)
PHONE......................650 230-2800
Donald Southard, CEO
Timothy A Marcotte, *
Glen W Mclaughlin, VP
Priscilla J Ryland, *
Steve Edwards, *
EMP: 65 EST: 1999
SALES (est): 13.19MM **Privately Held**
Web: www.mindraynorthamerica.com
SIC: 8733 5047 Research institute; Hospital equipment and supplies, nec
PA: Mindray Medical International Limited

8734 - Testing Laboratories (P-19942)

C/O: Conyers Trust Company
(Cayman) Limited
George Town GR CAYMAN

8734 Testing Laboratories

(P-19942)
911 HEALTH INC
701 Santa Monica Blvd # 300 (90401-2624)
PHONE..................................310 560-8509
Steve Farzam, *COO*
EMP: 99
SALES (est): 3.27MM **Privately Held**
SIC: 8734 Testing laboratories

(P-19943)
ACCION LABS US INC
4633 Old Ironsides Dr Ste 304
(95054-1807)
PHONE..................................408 970-9809
William Flavin, *Genl Mgr*
EMP: 1452
SALES (corp-wide): 45.16MM **Privately Held**
Web: www.accionlabs.com
SIC: 8734 Testing laboratories
PA: Accion Labs Us, Inc.
1225 Wash Pike Ste 401
Bridgeville PA
724 260-5139

(P-19944)
AIRCRAFT XRAY LABORATORIES INC
5216 Pacific Blvd (90255-2595)
PHONE..................................323 587-4141
Gary G Newton, *CEO*
James Newton, *
Sandi Spelic, *
Justin Guzman, *
EMP: 80 **EST:** 1938
SQ FT: 60,000
SALES (est): 8.29MM **Privately Held**
Web: www.aircraftxray.com
SIC: 8734 7384 3471 Testing laboratories;
Photograph developing and retouching;
Plating and polishing

(P-19945)
ALCON VISION LLC
20521 Lake Forest Dr (92630-7741)
PHONE..................................949 505-6890
EMP: 489
Web: www.alcon.com
SIC: 8734 Testing laboratories
HQ: Alcon Vision, Llc
6201 South Fwy
Fort Worth TX
817 293-0450

(P-19946)
ALS GROUP USA CORP
Also Called: Bioscreen Testing Services
3904 Del Amo Blvd (90503-2160)
PHONE..................................310 214-0043
Ranil Femando, *Genl Mgr*
EMP: 70
SIC: 8734 8731 Testing laboratories;
Commercial physical research
HQ: Als Group Usa, Corp.
10450 Stncliff Rd Ste 210
Houston TX
281 530-5656

(P-19947)
ANALYSTS INC
Also Called: Analysts Maintenance and Labs
3401 Jack Northrop Ave (90250-4428)
P.O. Box 2955 (90509-2955)
PHONE..................................800 424-0099
EMP: 148
Web: www.oil-testing.com
SIC: 8734 Product testing laboratory, safety or performance

(P-19948)
ANALYTICAL PACE SERVICES LLC
4100 Atlas Ct (93308-4510)
PHONE..................................800 878-4911
Stuart Buttram, *Brnch Mgr*
EMP: 104
Web: www.pacelabs.com
SIC: 8734 Water testing laboratory
HQ: Pace Analytical Services, Llc
2665 Long Lake Rd Ste 300
Saint Paul MN

(P-19949)
APTIM CORP
18100 Von Karman Ave # 450
(92612-0169)
PHONE..................................949 261-6441
EMP: 502
SALES (corp-wide): 2.2B **Privately Held**
SIC: 8734 Pollution testing
HQ: Aptim Corp.
10001 Woodloch Forest Dr # 450
The Woodlands TX
832 823-2700

(P-19950)
ARCEO LABS INC (PA)
55 2nd St Ste 1950 (94105-3451)
PHONE..................................332 203-4971
Vishaal Hariprasad, *CEO*
Raj Shah, *
Matthew Hall, *
EMP: 132 **EST:** 2016
SALES (est): 22.49MM
SALES (corp-wide): 22.49MM **Privately Held**
Web: www.cyberresilience.com
SIC: 8734 Testing laboratories

(P-19951)
ATLAS ENGINEERING WEST INC (DH)
6280 Riverdale St (92120-3308)
PHONE..................................619 280-4321
John Kirschbaum, *Pr*
EMP: 66 **EST:** 1959
SQ FT: 15,482
SALES (est): 35.06MM
SALES (corp-wide): 1.47B **Privately Held**
Web: www.oneatlas.com
SIC: 8734 8711 Testing laboratories;
Engineering services
HQ: Atlas Technical Consultants, Inc.
13215 Bee Cave Pkwy B230
Austin TX
512 851-1501

(P-19952)
BABCOCK LABORATORIES INC
Also Called: E. S. Babcock & Sons
6100 Quail Valley Ct (92507-0704)
P.O. Box 432 (92502-0432)
PHONE..................................951 653-3351
Allison Mackenzie, *CEO*
Marianna Etcheverria, *
Lawrence Chrystal, *
EMP: 70 **EST:** 1978
SQ FT: 20,000
SALES (est): 13.84MM **Privately Held**
Web: www.babcocklabs.com
SIC: 8734 Water testing laboratory

(P-19953)
CALIFORNIA LAB SCIENCES LLC
Also Called: West Pacific Medical Lab
10200 Pioneer Blvd Ste 500 (90670-6000)
PHONE..................................562 758-6900
EMP: 300 **EST:** 2009
SALES (est): 23.13MM **Privately Held**
SIC: 8734 Testing laboratories

(P-19954)
CATALENT SAN DIEGO INC
7330 Carroll Rd Ste 200 (92121-2364)
PHONE..................................858 805-6383
Timothy Scott, *Pr*
Bryan Knox, *OF PHARMACEUTICS**
Jason Everett, *
EMP: 120 **EST:** 1999
SQ FT: 6,600
SALES (est): 22.99MM **Publicly Held**
Web: www.catalent.com
SIC: 8734 8731 Testing laboratories;
Commercial research laboratory
HQ: Catalent Pharma Solutions, Inc.
14 Schoolhouse Rd
Somerset NJ

(P-19955)
CENTRAL COUNTIES
241 Business Park Way (95301-9487)
PHONE..................................209 356-0355
Christine Hackler, *Prin*
EMP: 70 **EST:** 2005
SALES (est): 2.33MM **Privately Held**
Web: www.valleytechlogic.com
SIC: 8734 Testing laboratories

(P-19956)
CERTIFIED LABORATORIES LLC
3125 N Damon Way (91505-1016)
PHONE..................................818 845-0070
Doug Shepard, *Mgr*
EMP: 1503
SALES (corp-wide): 43.93MM **Privately Held**
Web: www.certified-laboratories.com
SIC: 8734 Food testing service
PA: Certified Laboratories, Llc
65 Marcus Dr
Melville NY
516 576-1400

(P-19957)
CLARIENT DIAGNOSTIC SVCS INC
31 Columbia (92656-1460)
PHONE..................................888 443-3310
Cindy Collins, *CEO*
Michael Brown, *
Mark Machulcz, *
Renika Seghal, *
EMP: 182 **EST:** 2004
SALES (est): 1.98MM
SALES (corp-wide): 509.73MM **Publicly Held**
Web: www.neogenomics.com
SIC: 8734 Testing laboratories
HQ: Clarient, Inc.
31 Columbia
Aliso Viejo CA
949 445-7300

(P-19958)
COLOR DESIGN LABORATORY INC (PA)
Also Called: Color Design Labs
21329 Nordhoff St (91311-5819)
PHONE..................................818 341-5100
Gilberto Amparo, *CEO*
Maria Amparo, *
Maria Gonzalez, *
▲ **EMP:** 100 **EST:** 2010
SQ FT: 9,000
SALES (est): 11MM **Privately Held**
Web: www.colordesignlaboratory.com
SIC: 8734 Testing laboratories

(P-19959)
CONSTRUCTION TSTG & ENGRG INC
Also Called: C T E
3628 Madison Ave Ste 22 (95660-5071)
PHONE..................................916 331-6030
Terry Haagensen, *Mgr*
EMP: 279
SALES (corp-wide): 462.96MM **Privately Held**
Web: www.teamues.com
SIC: 8734 Testing laboratories
HQ: Construction Testing & Engineering, Inc.
1441 Montiel Rd Ste 115
Escondido CA

(P-19960)
CONSUMER SAFETY ANALYTICS LLC
Also Called: Cannasafe
7027 Hayvenhurst Ave (91406-3802)
PHONE..................................818 922-2416
Aaron Riley, *Prin*
Antonio Frazier, *Prin*
Bosco Ramirez, *Prin*
EMP: 99 **EST:** 2017
SALES (est): 4.73MM **Privately Held**
SIC: 8734 Testing laboratories

(P-19961)
COUNTY OF LOS ANGELES
Also Called: Hertzbrg-Dvis Frnsic Scnce Ctr
1800 Paseo Rancho Castilla (90032-4210)
PHONE..................................323 267-6167
Joseph Hourigan, *Brnch Mgr*
EMP: 154
SALES (corp-wide): 31.7B **Privately Held**
Web: www.lacounty.gov
SIC: 8734 8731 Forensic laboratory;
Commercial physical research
PA: County Of Los Angeles
500 W Temple St Ste 437
Los Angeles CA
213 974-1101

(P-19962)
CRITERION LABS INC
10907 Magnolia Blvd (91601-3904)
P.O. Box 140 (95367-0140)
PHONE..................................818 506-8332
Glenn H Hanson, *Pr*
Phil Castor, *
Arnold Collins, *
Llinda Mannor, *
Benjamin Tennor, *
▲ **EMP:** 62 **EST:** 1985
SQ FT: 7,200
SALES (est): 2.49MM **Privately Held**
Web: www.freebitco.in
SIC: 8734 Product testing laboratory, safety or performance

(P-19963)
CSA AMERICA STANDARDS INC
Also Called: Csa America
2805 Barranca Pkwy (92606-5114)
PHONE..................................949 733-4300
Mark Christopherson, *Mgr*
EMP: 74
SALES (corp-wide): 367.35MM **Privately Held**

PRODUCTS & SERVICES SECTION
8734 - Testing Laboratories (P-19982)

Web: www.csagroup.org
SIC: 8734 Testing laboratories
HQ: Csa America Standards, Inc.
8501 E Pleasant Valley Rd
Independence OH
216 524-4990

(P-19964)
CSA AMERICA STANDARDS INC
International Approval Svcs
2805 Barranca Pkwy (92606-5114)
PHONE..............................949 733-4300
EMP: 74
SALES (corp-wide): 367.35MM **Privately Held**
Web: www.csagroup.org
SIC: 8734 Testing laboratories
HQ: Csa America Standards, Inc.
8501 E Pleasant Valley Rd
Independence OH
216 524-4990

(P-19965)
DICKSON TESTING CO INC (DH)
11126 Palmer Ave (90280-7410)
PHONE..............................562 862-8378
Robert Lyddon, Pr
Jim Scanell, *
EMP: 80 EST: 1970
SQ FT: 40,000
SALES (est): 19.46MM
SALES (corp-wide): 302.09B **Publicly Held**
Web: www.dicksontesting.com
SIC: 8734 Metallurgical testing laboratory
HQ: Precision Castparts Corp.
5885 Meadows Rd Ste 620
Lake Oswego OR
503 946-4800

(P-19966)
EAG HOLDINGS LLC
2710 Walsh Ave (95051-0963)
PHONE..............................408 530-3500
Siddhartha Kadia, CEO
EMP: 700 EST: 2006
SQ FT: 70,000
SALES (est): 41.74MM **Privately Held**
Web: www.eag.com
SIC: 8734 Testing laboratories

(P-19967)
ELEMENT MATERIALS (DH)
15062 Bolsa Chica St (92649-1023)
PHONE..............................714 892-1961
Charles Noall, Pr
Pete Regan, *
Jo Wetz, *
Jeff Joyce, *
Eelco Niermeijer, *
▲ EMP: 80 EST: 1997
SQ FT: 4,500
SALES (est): 23.05MM **Privately Held**
Web: www.element.com
SIC: 8734 Metallurgical testing laboratory
HQ: Element Materials Technology Group Us Holdings, Inc.
15062 Bolsa Chica St
Huntington Beach CA
714 892-1961

(P-19968)
ELEMENT MTRLS TECH HB INC
Also Called: Element Rancho Dominguez
18100 S Wilmington Ave (90220-5909)
PHONE..............................310 632-8500
Chuck Gee, Genl Mgr
EMP: 86
Web: www.element.com
SIC: 8734 Metallurgical testing laboratory
HQ: Element Materials Technology Huntington Beach Llc
15062 Bolsa Chica St
Huntington Beach CA
714 892-1961

(P-19969)
ELLISON INSTITUTE LLC (PA)
Also Called: Ellisson Institute Technology
12414 Exposition Blvd (90064-1016)
PHONE..............................310 228-6400
Paul Marinelli, CEO
Jason Bowman, *
EMP: 118 EST: 2019
SQ FT: 80,000
SALES (est): 10.43MM
SALES (corp-wide): 10.43MM **Privately Held**
Web: www.eitm.org
SIC: 8734 Testing laboratories

(P-19970)
ETL TESTING LABORATORIES
Also Called: Intertechsynco
1365 Adams Ct (94025-1443)
PHONE..............................650 463-2900
Richard Nelson, CEO
Richard Adams, Genl Mgr
EMP: 232 EST: 2000
SALES (est): 514.86K **Privately Held**
Web: www.intertek.com
SIC: 8734 Testing laboratories

(P-19971)
EUROFINS EAG ENGRG SCIENCE LLC (DH)
2710 Walsh Ave (95051-0963)
PHONE..............................408 588-0050
Stefan Karnavas, Pr
EMP: 100 EST: 2018
SALES (est): 23.67MM
SALES (corp-wide): 220.81K **Privately Held**
Web: www.eag.com
SIC: 8734 Testing laboratories
HQ: Eurofins Eag Materials Science Us Holding, Inc.
4747 Executive Dr Ste 700
San Diego CA
949 521-6200

(P-19972)
EUROFINS EAG MTLS SCIENCE LLC (DH)
Also Called: Eurofins Eag Laboratories
810 Kifer Rd (94086-5203)
PHONE..............................408 454-4600
Stefan Karnavas, Pr
EMP: 110 EST: 2008
SQ FT: 70,000
SALES (est): 114.79MM
SALES (corp-wide): 220.81K **Privately Held**
Web: www.eag.com
SIC: 8734 Product testing laboratories
HQ: Eurofins Eag Materials Science Us Holding, Inc.
4747 Executive Dr Ste 700
San Diego CA
949 521-6200

(P-19973)
EUROFINS EATON ANALYTICAL LLC (DH)
750 Royal Oaks Dr Ste 100 (91016-3629)
PHONE..............................626 386-1100
Wilson Hershey, Ch
Bosco Ramirez, *
Andrew Eaton, *
Yongtao Bruce Li, Dir
EMP: 93 EST: 2012
SALES (est): 24.27MM
SALES (corp-wide): 220.81K **Privately Held**
Web: www.eurofinsus.com
SIC: 8734 Testing laboratories
HQ: Eurofins Lancaster Laboratories, Inc.
2425 New Holland Pike
Lancaster PA
717 656-2300

(P-19974)
EUROFINS EPK BILT ENVMT TSTG L (DH)
Also Called: Eurofins Emlab P&K Fairfax Co
2841 Dow Ave Ste 300 (92780-7211)
P.O. Box 2912 (44720-0912)
PHONE..............................330 497-9396
David Spurlock, Pr
Heather Collins Villemaire, *
Frank Conicella, *
Justin Dudas, Finance*
Brian Williams, *
EMP: 69 EST: 2010
SALES (est): 19.94MM
SALES (corp-wide): 220.81K **Privately Held**
Web: www.eurofinsus.com
SIC: 8734 Testing laboratories
HQ: Testamerica Holdings, Inc.
4101 Shuffel St Nw # 100
North Canton OH
330 497-9396

(P-19975)
EUROFINS FD CHMSTRY TSTG MDSON
Covance Food Solutions
2441 Constitution Dr (94551-7573)
PHONE..............................609 452-4440
EMP: 4167
SALES (corp-wide): 189.2MM **Privately Held**
Web: www.eurofinsus.com
SIC: 8734 Testing laboratories
PA: Eurofins Food Chemistry Testing Madison, Inc.
6304 Ronald Reagan Ave
Madison WI
800 675-8375

(P-19976)
EVANS ANALYTICAL GROUP LLC
Also Called: Wildlife International
2710 Walsh Ave (95051-0963)
PHONE..............................408 454-4600
Siddhartha C Kadia, Prin
Steve Hall, *
Prasad Raje, Prin
Tomoya Aoyama, Prin
Patricia M Lindley Ph.d., Prin
EMP: 81 EST: 2012
SALES (est): 31.79MM
SALES (corp-wide): 220.81K **Privately Held**
Web: www.eag.com
SIC: 8734 Assaying service
HQ: Eurofins Eag Materials Science, Llc
810 Kifer Rd
Sunnyvale CA
408 454-4600

(P-19977)
FORENSIC ANALYTICAL SPC INC
Also Called: Forensic Analytical
20535 Belshaw Ave (90746-3505)
PHONE..............................310 763-2374
Bruce White, Prin
EMP: 94
SALES (corp-wide): 11.18MM **Privately Held**
Web: www.forensicanalytical.com
SIC: 8734 8748 8731 8071 Forensic laboratory; Environmental consultant; Commercial physical research; Medical laboratories
PA: Forensic Analytical Specialties Incorporated
3777 Depot Rd Ste 409
Hayward CA
510 887-8828

(P-19978)
FOUND HEALTH INC
1 Letterman Dr Ste C3500 (94129-1494)
PHONE..............................415 854-3296
Sarah Jones Simmer, CEO
Emily Yudofsky, *
Chester Ng, *
Andrew Dudum, *
Teresa Starin, *
EMP: 70 EST: 2019
SALES (est): 2.3MM **Privately Held**
Web: www.foundhealth.com
SIC: 8734 Testing laboratories

(P-19979)
FUZZY PET HEALTH INC
1355 Market St Ste 488 (94103-1337)
PHONE..............................415 692-1875
EMP: 65 EST: 2019
SALES (est): 9.27MM **Privately Held**
Web: www.fuzzy.com
SIC: 8734 Testing laboratories

(P-19980)
GARWOOD LABORATORIES INC
Also Called: Garwood Labs
143 Calle Iglesia (92672-7501)
PHONE..............................562 949-2727
EMP: 65
Web: www.garwoodlabs.com
SIC: 8734 Testing laboratories

(P-19981)
HOUND LABS INC
47000 Warm Springs Blvd Ste 290 (94539-7467)
P.O. Box 526 (94604-0526)
PHONE..............................408 893-2654
Mike Lynn, CEO
Bob Capwell, VP
John Lindgren, CFO
EMP: 81 EST: 2015
SALES (est): 5.03MM **Privately Held**
Web: www.houndlabs.com
SIC: 8734 Testing laboratories

(P-19982)
HYUNDAI AMER TECHNICAL CTR INC
Also Called: Hyundai America/Tech Center
12610 E End Ave (91710-3006)
PHONE..............................909 627-3525
Scott Kin, Mgr
EMP: 113
SQ FT: 19,620
Web: www.hatci.com
SIC: 8734 8711 Product testing laboratories; Mechanical engineering
HQ: Hyundai America Technical Center Incorporated
6800 Geddes Rd
Ypsilanti MI
734 337-2500

8734 - Testing Laboratories (P-19983)

(P-19983)
INTERTEK TESTING SVCS NA INC
Also Called: Inchcape Testing Services
1365 Adams Ct (94025-1443)
PHONE..................650 463-2900
Jeff Turcotte, Brnch Mgr
EMP: 76
SALES (corp-wide): 3.84B Privately Held
Web: www.intertek.com
SIC: 8734 Testing laboratories
HQ: Intertek Testing Services Na, Inc.
3933 Us Route 11
Cortland NY
607 753-6711

(P-19984)
INTERTEK USA INC
Also Called: Intertek Pharmaceutical Svcs
10420 Wateridge Cir (92121-5773)
PHONE..................858 558-2599
Arron Xu, Mgr
EMP: 100
SALES (corp-wide): 3.84B Privately Held
Web: www.intertek.com
SIC: 8734 Testing laboratories
HQ: Intertek Usa Inc.
200 Westlake Park Blvd # 1010
Houston TX
713 543-3600

(P-19985)
ISE LABS INC (DH)
46800 Bayside Pkwy (94538-6592)
PHONE..................510 687-2500
Tien Wu, CEO
Jeff Thompson, VP
EMP: 200 EST: 1999
SQ FT: 69,000
SALES (est): 53.58MM Privately Held
Web: www.iselabs.com
SIC: 8734 3672 Calibration and certification;
Printed circuit boards
HQ: Ase Test Limited
C/O: Allen & Gledhill Llp
Singapore

(P-19986)
MCCAMPBELL ANALYTICAL INC
1534 Willow Pass Rd (94565-1701)
PHONE..................925 252-9262
Edward Hamilton, CEO
EMP: 63 EST: 1991
SQ FT: 12,896
SALES (est): 10.29MM Privately Held
Web: www.mccampbell.com
SIC: 8734 Testing laboratories

(P-19987)
MICHELSON LABORATORIES INC (PA)
6280 Chalet Dr (90040-3704)
PHONE..................562 928-0553
Grant Michelson, Pr
Jack E Michelson, *
EMP: 70 EST: 1970
SQ FT: 20,000
SALES (est): 11.44MM
SALES (corp-wide): 11.44MM Privately Held
Web: www.michelsonlab.com
SIC: 8734 Food testing service

(P-19988)
MICRO PRCISION CALIBRATION INC
Also Called: Micro Precision
2165 N Glassell St (92865-3307)
PHONE..................714 901-5659
EMP: 153
SALES (corp-wide): 66.84MM Privately Held
Web: www.microprecision.com
SIC: 8734 Calibration and certification
PA: Micro Precision Calibration, Inc.
22835 Industrial Pl
Grass Valley CA
530 268-1860

(P-19989)
MILLENNIUM HEALTH LLC
16981 Via Tazon Ste F (92127-1645)
PHONE..................877 451-3534
Jennifer Strickland, CEO
Howard Appel, *
David Cohen, *
Martin Price, *
Janna Sipes, Regional COMP*
EMP: 258 EST: 2007
SALES (est): 79.25MM Privately Held
Web: www.millenniumhealth.com
SIC: 8734 Testing laboratories

(P-19990)
MOORE TWINING ASSOCIATES INC (PA)
2527 Fresno St (93721-1804)
PHONE..................559 268-7021
Harry D Moore, Pr
Ruth E Moore, *
EMP: 85 EST: 1898
SQ FT: 22,500
SALES (est): 9.16MM
SALES (corp-wide): 9.16MM Privately Held
Web: www.mooretwining.com
SIC: 8734 8711 Testing laboratories;
Engineering services

(P-19991)
NATIONAL GENETICS INSTITUTE
2440 S Sepulveda Blvd Ste 235 (90064-1748)
PHONE..................310 996-6610
Mike Aicher, CEO
Geri Cox, *
EMP: 200 EST: 1991
SQ FT: 35,000
SALES (est): 10.71MM Publicly Held
Web: plasma.labcorp.com
SIC: 8734 Testing laboratories
PA: Laboratory Corporation Of America Holdings
358 S Main St
Burlington NC

(P-19992)
NORTH AMERCN SCIENCE ASSOC INC
N A M S A
9 Morgan (92618-2005)
PHONE..................949 951-3110
Dennis Nivens, VP
EMP: 60
SQ FT: 40,000
SALES (corp-wide): 90.42MM Privately Held
Web: www.namsa.com
SIC: 8734 8071 8999 Testing laboratories;
Medical laboratories; Chemical consultant
PA: North American Science Associates, Llc
6750 Wales Rd
Northwood OH
419 666-9455

(P-19993)
PACIFIC BIOLABS INC
551 Linus Pauling Dr (94547-1817)
PHONE..................510 964-9000
EMP: 89 EST: 1982
SALES (est): 12.26MM Privately Held
Web: www.pacificbiolabs.com
SIC: 8734 Testing laboratories

(P-19994)
PHAMATECH INCORPORATED
15175 Innovation Dr (92128-3401)
PHONE..................888 635-5840
▲ EMP: 200 EST: 1991
SQ FT: 50,000
SALES (est): 22.68MM Privately Held
Web: www.phamatech.com
SIC: 8734 5047 Forensic laboratory; Medical laboratory equipment

(P-19995)
PIXEL LABS LLC
Also Called: Helium 10
500 Technology Dr Ste 450 (92618-1384)
PHONE..................512 560-5961
EMP: 93 EST: 2016
SALES (est): 3.64MM Privately Held
Web: www.helium10.com
SIC: 8734 Testing laboratories

(P-19996)
PSYCHEMEDICS CORPORATION
5750 Hannum Ave Ste 100 (90230-6666)
PHONE..................310 216-7776
Michael Schaffer, Mgr
EMP: 63
SALES (corp-wide): 25.24MM Publicly Held
Web: www.psychemedics.com
SIC: 8734 Testing laboratories
PA: Psychemedics Corporation
289 Great Rd Ste 200
Acton MA
978 206-8220

(P-19997)
SCANTIBODIES LABORATORY INC (PA)
9336 Abraham Way (92071-2861)
PHONE..................619 258-9300
Thomas L Cantor, CEO
John Van Duzer, *
▲ EMP: 240 EST: 1976
SQ FT: 60,500
SALES (est): 53.95MM
SALES (corp-wide): 53.95MM Privately Held
Web: www.scantibodies.com
SIC: 8734 Testing laboratories

(P-19998)
SE LABORATORIES INC
Also Called: S E Labs
1065 Comstock St (95054-3439)
PHONE..................408 727-3286
Anil R Singh, Pr
Marilyn Singh, *
Richard Terrell, *
Agnes Lewis, *
EMP: 60 EST: 1978
SQ FT: 11,450
SALES (est): 5.94MM Privately Held
Web: www.trescal.us
SIC: 8734 7629 Calibration and certification; Electronic equipment repair

(P-19999)
SEMICONDUCTOR TECHNOLOGIES INC
3901 N 1st St (95134-1506)
PHONE..................408 240-7000
EMP: 360
SIC: 8734 3674 Testing laboratories; Semiconductors and related devices

(P-20000)
SHOGUN LABS INC (PA)
340 S Lemon Ave # 1085 (91789-2706)
PHONE..................317 676-2719
Finbarr Taylor, CEO
EMP: 146 EST: 2015
SALES (est): 12.55MM
SALES (corp-wide): 12.55MM Privately Held
Web: www.getshogun.com
SIC: 8734 Testing laboratories

(P-20001)
SILLIKER INC
Also Called: Dsl Laboratories
5262 Pirrone Ct (95368-9072)
PHONE..................209 549-7508
Heather Hawke, Brnch Mgr
EMP: 60
SQ FT: 14,652
SALES (corp-wide): 7.5MM Privately Held
Web: www.merieuxnutrisciences.com
SIC: 8734 Food testing service
HQ: Silliker, Inc.
401 N Michigan Ave # 1400
Chicago IL

(P-20002)
TWINING INC (PA)
Also Called: Twining Laboratories
2883 E Spring St Ste 300 (90806-2417)
PHONE..................562 426-3355
Edward Butch M Twining Junior, CEO
Brian Kramer, *
Robert M Ryan, *
Boris Stein D Sc, VP
Linas Vitkus, *
EMP: 82 EST: 1959
SQ FT: 13,600
SALES (est): 24.71MM
SALES (corp-wide): 24.71MM Privately Held
Web: www.twininginc.com
SIC: 8734 Testing laboratories

(P-20003)
UNITED MFG ASSEMBLY INC
44169 Fremont Blvd (94538-6044)
PHONE..................510 490-4680
Yonwen Chou, Pr
May Mah, *
Arlene Chou, *
EMP: 95 EST: 1987
SALES (est): 9.17MM Privately Held
Web: www.umai.com
SIC: 8734 3672 Testing laboratories; Printed circuit boards

(P-20004)
WECK ANLYTICAL ENVMTL SVCS INC
Also Called: Weck Laboratories
14859 Clark Ave (91745-1379)
PHONE..................626 336-2139
Alfredo Pierri, Pr
Alfredo E Pierri, *
Cecilia G Pierri, *
EMP: 74 EST: 1964
SQ FT: 27,000
SALES (est): 10.82MM Privately Held
Web: weck-analytical-environmental.sbcontract.com
SIC: 8734 Testing laboratories

PRODUCTS & SERVICES SECTION

8741 - Management Services (P-20027)

(P-20005)
WESTPAC LABS INC
10200 Pioneer Blvd # 500 (90670-6000)
PHONE..................................562 906-5227
EMP: 452
SALES (est): 53MM Privately Held
Web: www.westpaclab.com
SIC: 8734 8071 Testing laboratories; Pathological laboratory

(P-20006)
XCOM LABS INC
9450 Carroll Park Dr (92121-5201)
PHONE..................................858 987-9266
Paul E Jacobs, Prin
Derek Aberle, *
Matt Grob, *
EMP: 70 EST: 2019
SALES (est): 6.49MM Privately Held
Web: www.xcom-labs.com
SIC: 8734 Testing laboratories

8741 Management Services

(P-20007)
360 HEALTH PLAN INC
Also Called: 360 Clinic
13800 Arizona St Ste 104 (92683-3951)
PHONE..................................800 446-8888
Vince Pien, CEO
David Ngo, CFO
Mike Lee, COO
EMP: 200 EST: 2020
SALES (est): 5.85MM Privately Held
Web: www.360clinic.md
SIC: 8741 Hospital management

(P-20008)
360 SUPPORT SERVICES
306 S Myrtle Ave (91016-2849)
P.O. Box 801238 (91380-1238)
PHONE..................................866 360-6348
Kelly Martinez, CEO
Ola Ostlund, *
Renee Fields, *
EMP: 72 EST: 2016
SALES (est): 2.4MM Privately Held
SIC: 8741 7349 Nursing and personal care facility management; Building cleaning service

(P-20009)
ACTIVCARE LIVING INC (PA)
10603 Rancho Bernardo Rd (92127-5722)
PHONE..................................858 565-4424
William Major Chance, CEO
D Kevin Moriarty, VP
Frank A Virgadamo, *
B Renee Barnard, *
Todd A Shetter, *
EMP: 180 EST: 1979
SQ FT: 9,000
SALES (est): 40.58MM
SALES (corp-wide): 40.58MM Privately Held
Web: www.activcareliving.com
SIC: 8741 Nursing and personal care facility management

(P-20010)
ACTIVE WELLNESS LLC
600 California St Fl 11 (94108-2727)
P.O. Box 2358 (94126-2358)
PHONE..................................415 741-3300
Jill Stevens Kinney, Ch
William Joseph Mcbride Iii, Pr
Carey White, *
EMP: 1100 EST: 2015
SQ FT: 1,000
SALES (est): 45.73MM Privately Held
Web: www.activewellness.com
SIC: 8741 7991 Hospital management; Health club

(P-20011)
ADVANCED BIOSERVICES LLC (PA)
19255 Vanowen St (91335-5070)
PHONE..................................818 342-0100
EMP: 65 EST: 2004
SALES (est): 11.55MM Privately Held
SIC: 8741 Administrative management

(P-20012)
ADVANCED MEDICAL MGT INC
5000 Airport Plaza Dr Ste 150 (90815)
PHONE..................................562 766-2000
Stephen Hegstrom, Ch
Kathy Hegstrom, *
Paul Pew, *
EMP: 60 EST: 1982
SALES (est): 13.62MM Privately Held
Web: www.amm.cc
SIC: 8741 8721 Hospital management; Accounting, auditing, and bookkeeping

(P-20013)
AEG MANAGEMENT LACC LLC
Also Called: Los Angeles Convention Center
1201 S Figueroa St (90015-1308)
PHONE..................................213 741-1151
Brad Gessner, Sr VP
Greg Rosicky, *
Carisa Malanum, *
Ellen Schwartz, *
Keith Hilsgen, *
EMP: 220 EST: 2013
SALES (est): 44.87MM
SALES (corp-wide): 16.52K Privately Held
Web: www.lacclink.com
SIC: 8741 Business management
PA: Aeg Facilities, Llc
800 W Olympic Blvd # 305
Los Angeles CA
213 763-7700

(P-20014)
AJIT HEALTHCARE INC
316 S Westlake Ave (90057-2906)
PHONE..................................213 484-0510
Jasvant N Modi, Pr
Sagar Parikh, Prin
EMP: 80 EST: 2004
SALES (est): 3.99MM Privately Held
Web: www.wlchospital.com
SIC: 8741 Nursing and personal care facility management

(P-20015)
ALLEGIS RESIDENTIAL SVCS INC
Also Called: Aspm-Sandiego
9340 Hazard Way Ste B2 (92123-1218)
PHONE..................................858 430-5700
Karen Martinez, CEO
Jorge Martinez, *
Steve Howe, *
EMP: 80 EST: 1971
SQ FT: 4,000
SALES (est): 13.14MM Privately Held
Web: www.aspm-sandiego.com
SIC: 8741 Business management
PA: S.H.E. Manages Properties, Inc.
9340 Hazard Way Ste B2
San Diego CA

(P-20016)
ALLIANT INSURANCE SERVICES INC
Also Called: Nationwide
100 Pine St Ste 1100 (94111-5113)
PHONE..................................415 403-1400
Mimi Long, Prin
EMP: 70 EST: 2013
SALES (est): 2.51MM Privately Held
Web: www.csurma.org
SIC: 8741 6411 Management services; Insurance agents, brokers, and service

(P-20017)
ALLZONE MANAGEMENT SVCS INC
Also Called: Allzone Management Solutions
3795 La Crescenta Ave Ste 200 (91208-1057)
PHONE..................................213 291-8879
Jonathan Rodrigues, Pr
EMP: 500 EST: 2011
SALES (est): 11.76MM Privately Held
Web: www.allzonems.com
SIC: 8741 Management services

(P-20018)
ALTER MANAGEMENT LLC
Also Called: Alter Health Group
34232 Pacific Coast Hwy Ste D (92629-3854)
PHONE..................................949 629-0214
Michael Castanon, Prin
EMP: 100 EST: 2018
SALES (est): 2.29MM Privately Held
SIC: 8741 Management services

(P-20019)
ALTURA MANAGEMENT SERVICES LLC
1401 N Montebello Blvd (90640-2584)
PHONE..................................323 768-2898
Jose Esparza, CFO
EMP: 375 EST: 2015
SALES (est): 9.77MM Privately Held
SIC: 8741 Management services

(P-20020)
AMERICAN INTGRTED RSOURCES INC
Also Called: Air Demolition and Envmtl
2341 N Pacific St (92865-2601)
PHONE..................................714 921-4100
Thomas C Stevens, CEO
EMP: 80 EST: 2013
SALES (est): 9.95MM Privately Held
Web: www.american-integrated.com
SIC: 8741 Construction management

(P-20021)
AMERICAN MANAGEMENT SVCS W LLC
1240 Bethel Ln (93458-8386)
PHONE..................................805 352-1921
EMP: 130
SALES (corp-wide): 146.69MM Privately Held
SIC: 8741 Management services
PA: American Management Services West Llc
11235 Se 6th St
Bellevue WA
206 215-9700

(P-20022)
AMERICAN MZHOU DNGPO GROUP INC
4520 Maine Ave (91706-2671)
PHONE..................................626 820-9239
Gang Wang, CEO
EMP: 100 EST: 2012
SALES (est): 2.21MM Privately Held
SIC: 8741 Restaurant management

(P-20023)
ANGLEPOINT GROUP INC (PA)
2261 Market St Pmb 4723 (94114-1612)
PHONE..................................855 512-6453
Ron Brill, Ch Bd
Ron Brill, CEO
Ravi Kohli, *
Brian Papay, *
EMP: 163 EST: 2009
SQ FT: 4,000
SALES (est): 25.62MM
SALES (corp-wide): 25.62MM Privately Held
Web: www.anglepoint.com
SIC: 8741 Business management

(P-20024)
APPLECARE MEDICAL MGT LLC
18 Centerpointe Dr Ste 100 (90623-1028)
P.O. Box 6014 (90702-6014)
PHONE..................................714 443-4507
EMP: 108 EST: 2010
SALES (est): 15.02MM
SALES (corp-wide): 324.16B Publicly Held
Web: www.applecaremedical.com
SIC: 8741 Nursing and personal care facility management
PA: Unitedhealth Group Incorporated
9900 Bren Rd E Ste 300w
Minnetonka MN
952 936-1300

(P-20025)
ARCHIVES MANAGEMENT CORP (PA)
Also Called: Bay Management
2301 S El Camino Real (94403-2213)
PHONE..................................650 544-2200
Harlan Shapers, Pr
EMP: 180 EST: 1981
SQ FT: 12,000
SALES (est): 3.63MM
SALES (corp-wide): 3.63MM Privately Held
SIC: 8741 8742 Business management; Management consulting services

(P-20026)
ASPEN
28528 Constellation Rd (91355-5082)
PHONE..................................661 476-5138
EMP: 77 EST: 2017
SALES (est): 101.54K Privately Held
Web: www.aspentech.com
SIC: 8741 Management services

(P-20027)
ASSET MANAGEMENT TR SVCS LLC
Also Called: A Mediation & Resolution Ctr
1455 Frazee Rd Ste 500 (92108-4350)
PHONE..................................858 457-2202
Steven K Dony, Managing Member
Rochelle O'donnell Juarez, Managing Member
EMP: 72 EST: 1983
SALES (est): 4.3MM Privately Held
Web: amediationresoluti.wixsite.com
SIC: 8741 Financial management for business

8741 - Management Services (P-20028)

(P-20028)
AVIATION CONSULTANTS INC (PA)
Also Called: Epic Jet Centre
4751 Aviadores Way (93401-8221)
PHONE..................805 782-9722
William Borgsmiller, CEO
EMP: 72 EST: 1998
SALES (est): 43.44MM
SALES (corp-wide): 43.44MM Privately Held
Web: www.acijet.com
SIC: 8741 7363 Management services; Pilot service, aviation

(P-20029)
AVSC INTLLCTUAL PRPRTY MGT INC
111 W Ocean Blvd Ste 1110 (90802-4688)
PHONE..................562 366-1924
J Michael Mcilwain, CEO
EMP: 303 EST: 1998
SALES (est): 1.99MM
SALES (corp-wide): 460.08MM Privately Held
SIC: 8741 Business management
HQ: Audio Visual Services Co.
    5100 River Rd Ste 300
    Schiller Park IL
    847 222-9800

(P-20030)
AWI MANAGEMENT CORPORATION
1800 E Lakeshore Dr (92530-4469)
PHONE..................951 674-8200
Angelica Chaidez, Brnch Mgr
EMP: 241
SALES (corp-wide): 29.21MM Privately Held
Web: www.awimc.com
SIC: 8741 Business management
PA: Awi Management Corporation
    120 Center St
    Auburn CA
    530 745-6170

(P-20031)
AZUL HOSPITALITY GROUP INC
800 W Ivy St Ste D (92101-1771)
PHONE..................619 223-4200
Alvaro Fraile, CEO
Douglas Leiber, *
Mark Crisci, *
EMP: 166 EST: 2007
SALES (est): 12.66MM Privately Held
Web: www.azulhospitalitygroup.com
SIC: 8741 Business management

(P-20032)
BAYPOINTE MANAGEMENT INC
Also Called: Baypointe Management, Inc.
220 Newport Center Dr # 11 (92660-7506)
PHONE..................813 503-5551
EMP: 68
SALES (corp-wide): 214.16K Privately Held
SIC: 8741 Business management
PA: Baypointe Asset Management, Inc.
    100 Newport Center Dr
    Newport Beach CA
    949 720-0030

(P-20033)
BECHTEL CAPITAL MGT CORP
50 Beale St (94105-1813)
PHONE..................415 768-1234
Riley Bechtel, Ch
Bill Dudley, CEO
Brendan Bechtel, Pr
Peter Dawson, CFO
Anshul Maheshwari, Treas
EMP: 67 EST: 1987
SQ FT: 600,000
SALES (est): 8.28MM
SALES (corp-wide): 5.07B Privately Held
Web: www.bechtel.com
SIC: 8741 Financial management for business
PA: Bechtel Group, Inc.
    12011 Sunset Hills Rd # 1
    Reston VA
    734 205-9093

(P-20034)
BEECH STREET CORPORATION (HQ)
25550 Commercentre Dr Ste 200 (92630)
PHONE..................949 672-1000
William Fickling Junior, Ch
William Hale, *
Norm Werthwein, *
Rick Markus, *
Jon Bird, *
EMP: 350 EST: 1951
SQ FT: 60,000
SALES (est): 45.39MM
SALES (corp-wide): 1.08B Publicly Held
SIC: 8741 Administrative management
PA: Multiplan Corporation
    640 5th Ave Fl 12
    New York NY
    212 380-7500

(P-20035)
BEETS HOSPITALITY GROUP
316 Stealth Ct (94551-9303)
PHONE..................925 294-8667
Pam Yarolimek, Prin
EMP: 62 EST: 2010
SALES (est): 1.43MM Privately Held
Web: www.beetshospitality.com
SIC: 8741 Hotel or motel management

(P-20036)
BELLWETHER ASSET MGT INC (PA)
200 N Pacific Coast Hwy Ste 1400 (90245)
PHONE..................310 525-3022
Dennis Grzeskowiak, CEO
EMP: 74 EST: 2013
SALES (est): 5.51MM
SALES (corp-wide): 5.51MM Privately Held
Web: www.bellwetheram.com
SIC: 8741 Financial management for business

(P-20037)
BERNARDS INC
555 1st St (91340-3051)
PHONE..................818 898-1521
Jeff Bernards, CEO
Doug Bernards, *
Greg Simons, *
EMP: 60 EST: 2009
SALES (est): 1.75MM Privately Held
SIC: 8741 1542 Construction management; Commercial and office building contractors

(P-20038)
BJS RESTAURANT OPERATIONS CO
Also Called: BJ's Restaurant & Brewhouse
7755 Center Ave Ste 300 (92647-3084)
PHONE..................714 500-2400
EMP: 401 EST: 2017
SALES (est): 2.45MM
SALES (corp-wide): 1.28B Publicly Held
SIC: 8741 Restaurant management
PA: Bj's Restaurants, Inc.
    7755 Center Ave Ste 300
    Huntington Beach CA
    714 500-2400

(P-20039)
BON APPETIT MANAGEMENT CO
4125 Hopyard Rd (94588-8534)
PHONE..................925 730-3653
EMP: 188
SALES (corp-wide): 29.97B Privately Held
Web: www.bamco.com
SIC: 8741 Management services
HQ: Bon Appetit Management Co.
    201 Rdwood Shres Pkwy Ste
    Redwood City CA
    650 798-8000

(P-20040)
BON APPETIT MANAGEMENT CO
500 El Camino Real 500 (95050-4345)
PHONE..................408 554-2728
Cathy Staub, Mgr
EMP: 210
SALES (corp-wide): 29.97B Privately Held
Web: www.bamco.com
SIC: 8741 Management services
HQ: Bon Appetit Management Co.
    201 Rdwood Shres Pkwy Ste
    Redwood City CA
    650 798-8000

(P-20041)
BON APPETIT MANAGEMENT CO
Also Called: Bon Appetit
1200 Getty Center Dr (90049-1657)
PHONE..................310 440-6052
EMP: 198
SALES (corp-wide): 29.97B Privately Held
Web: www.bamco.com
SIC: 8741 Management services
HQ: Bon Appetit Management Co.
    201 Rdwood Shres Pkwy Ste
    Redwood City CA
    650 798-8000

(P-20042)
BON APPETIT MANAGEMENT CO
1050 N Mills Ave (91711-3908)
PHONE..................909 607-2788
EMP: 209
SALES (corp-wide): 29.97B Privately Held
Web: www.bamco.com
SIC: 8741 Management services
HQ: Bon Appetit Management Co.
    201 Rdwood Shres Pkwy Ste
    Redwood City CA
    650 798-8000

(P-20043)
BON APPETIT MANAGEMENT CO
301 Market St (95053-0001)
PHONE..................408 554-5771
EMP: 187
SALES (corp-wide): 29.97B Privately Held
Web: www.bamco.com
SIC: 8741 Management services
HQ: Bon Appetit Management Co.
    201 Rdwood Shres Pkwy Ste
    Redwood City CA
    650 798-8000

(P-20044)
BON APPETIT MANAGEMENT CO
383 E Grand Ave (94080-6234)
PHONE..................650 467-3767
EMP: 210
SALES (corp-wide): 29.97B Privately Held
Web: www.bamco.com
SIC: 8741 Restaurant management
HQ: Bon Appetit Management Co.
    201 Rdwood Shres Pkwy Ste
    Redwood City CA
    650 798-8000

(P-20045)
BON APPETIT MANAGEMENT CO
Also Called: Getty Center
1200 Getty Center Dr Ste 100 (90049-1657)
PHONE..................310 440-6209
Javier Ramirez, Mgr
EMP: 176
SALES (corp-wide): 29.97B Privately Held
Web: www.bamco.com
SIC: 8741 Restaurant management
HQ: Bon Appetit Management Co.
    201 Rdwood Shres Pkwy Ste
    Redwood City CA
    650 798-8000

(P-20046)
BRIGHTSOURCE CONSTRUCTION MANAGEMENT INC
1999 Harrison St Ste 2150 (94612-3500)
PHONE..................510 550-8161
EMP: 316 EST: 2007
SALES (est): 1.28MM Privately Held
SIC: 8741 Management services
PA: Brightsource Energy, Inc.
    1999 Harrison St Ste 2150
    Oakland CA

(P-20047)
BUCKLAND VINEYARD MGT INC
4560 Slodusty Rd (95633-9244)
PHONE..................530 333-1534
Alfred Buckland, Pr
EMP: 65 EST: 1984
SALES (est): 2.49MM Privately Held
Web: www.bucklandvineyards.com
SIC: 8741 Management services

(P-20048)
BUFFALO SPOT MGT GROUP LLC
7245 Garden Grove Blvd (92841-4216)
PHONE..................949 354-0884
Ivan Flores, Managing Member
EMP: 110 EST: 2016
SALES (est): 9.01MM Privately Held
SIC: 8741 Restaurant management

(P-20049)
BUYERZONECOM LLC
Also Called: Business.com
12130 Millennium (90094-2945)
PHONE..................888 393-5000
Doug Llewellyn, CEO
Jason Teebagy, *
EMP: 60 EST: 1992
SALES (est): 8.66MM
SALES (corp-wide): 60.59MM Privately Held
Web: www.buyerzone.com
SIC: 8741 Business management
PA: Centerfield Media Holdings, Llc

PRODUCTS & SERVICES SECTION

8741 - Management Services (P-20071)

12130 Millennium Ste 600
Los Angeles CA
310 341-4420

(P-20050)
CAL STATE LA UNIV AUX SVCS INC
Also Called: UAS
5151 State University Dr (90032-4226)
PHONE.................323 343-2531
Tariq Marji, *Ex Dir*
▲ **EMP:** 600 **EST:** 1954
SQ FT: 108,000
SALES (est): 22.54MM **Privately Held**
Web: www.calstatela.edu
SIC: 8741 5942 5651 5812 Business management; College book stores; Unisex clothing stores; Cafeteria

(P-20051)
CAMARILLO HEALTHCARE CENTER
205 Granada St (93010-7715)
PHONE.................805 482-9805
Erica Olsen, *Admn*
Angie Chavz, *Admn*
EMP: 97 **EST:** 2007
SALES (est): 8.31MM
SALES (corp-wide): 3.03B **Publicly Held**
Web: www.camarillohealthcare.com
SIC: 8741 Nursing and personal care facility management
PA: The Ensign Group Inc
29222 Rncho Vejo Rd Ste 1
San Juan Capistrano CA
949 487-9500

(P-20052)
CAMERON ENERGY SERVICES CORP
4040 Capitol Ave (90601-1735)
PHONE.................562 321-9183
Steve Gassen, *Pr*
Hinda Gharbi, *Dir*
Scott Osterling, *Dir*
EMP: 68 **EST:** 2019
SALES (est): 2.37MM **Privately Held**
SIC: 8741 Management services

(P-20053)
CAREMORE MEDICAL MANAGEMENT COMPANY A CALIFORNIA LIMITED PARTNERSHIP
Also Called: Caremore AP
12900 Park Plaza Dr # 150 (90703-9329)
PHONE.................562 741-4300
EMP: 900
SIC: 8741 5047 Business management; Medical equipment and supplies

(P-20054)
CGP MAINTENANCE CNSTR SVCS INC
8614 Siesta Rd (92071-4537)
PHONE.................858 454-7326
Jim Robinson, *Pr*
EMP: 70 **EST:** 1982
SQ FT: 3,000
SALES (est): 9.64MM **Privately Held**
Web: www.cgpconstruction.com
SIC: 8741 Construction management

(P-20055)
CHAN FAMILY PARTNERSHIP LP
801 S Grand Ave Apt 1811 (90017-4673)
PHONE.................626 322-7132
Ann Chan, *Pt*
EMP: 100 **EST:** 2017
SALES (est): 2.4MM **Privately Held**
SIC: 8741 Restaurant management

(P-20056)
CIRCLE WOOD SERVICES INC
3670 W Temple Ave (91768-2588)
PHONE.................909 784-0733
Don Watson, *Pr*
EMP: 63 **EST:** 2007
SQ FT: 1,400
SALES (est): 5.86MM **Privately Held**
Web: www.circlewood.net
SIC: 8741 Business management

(P-20057)
CITY OF HOPE (PA)
1500 Duarte Rd (91010-3012)
PHONE.................626 256-4673
TOLL FREE: 800
EMP: 260 **EST:** 1929
SALES (est): 334.97MM
SALES (corp-wide): 334.97MM **Privately Held**
Web: www.cityofhope.org
SIC: 8741 8399 Hospital management; Fund raising organization, non-fee basis

(P-20058)
CITY OF MENIFEE
29844 Haun Rd (92586-6539)
PHONE.................951 672-6777
Kathy Benett, *City Clerk*
EMP: 90 **EST:** 2008
SALES (est): 123.4MM **Privately Held**
Web: www.cityofmenifee.us
SIC: 8741 Personnel management

(P-20059)
CLOROX SERVICES COMPANY
Also Called: Clorox
4900 Johnson Dr (94588-3308)
PHONE.................925 368-6000
R A Llenado, *Ch Bd*
EMP: 167
SALES (corp-wide): 7.39B **Publicly Held**
Web: www.thecloroxcompany.com
SIC: 8741 Management services
HQ: Clorox Services Company
1221 Broadway
Oakland CA

(P-20060)
COLLECTIVE MGT GROUP LLC
Also Called: Collective Management Group
8383 Wilshire Blvd Ste 1050 (90211-2425)
PHONE.................323 655-8585
Reza Izad, *
Gary Binkow, *
Jordan Berliant, *
Jordan Toplitzky, *
EMP: 206 **EST:** 1999
SQ FT: 15,000
SALES (est): 7.41MM **Privately Held**
SIC: 8741 Management services

(P-20061)
COLUSA REGIONAL MEDICAL CENTER INC
Also Called: Women's Health Center
199 E Webster St Ste 1 (95932-2954)
PHONE.................530 458-5821
EMP: 180
SIC: 8741 8062 Hospital management; General medical and surgical hospitals

(P-20062)
CORNERSTONE HOTEL MANAGEMENT (DH)
222 Kearny St Ste 200 (94108-4537)
PHONE.................415 397-5572
Tom La Tour, *Pr*
J Kirke Wrench, *
Nir Margalit, *
EMP: 75 **EST:** 1985
SALES (est): 44.86MM **Privately Held**
SIC: 8741 Management services
HQ: Alexis Hotel Management Inc
222 Kearny St Ste 200
San Francisco CA

(P-20063)
CORVEL CORPORATION
Also Called: Corvel
1100 W Town And Country Rd Ste 400 (92868-4645)
PHONE.................714 385-8500
Laurie Wright, *Brnch Mgr*
EMP: 72
Web: www.corvel.com
SIC: 8741 Management services
PA: Corvel Corporation
5128 Apache Plume Rd # 4
Fort Worth TX

(P-20064)
COUNTRY VILLA SERVICE CORP
615 W Duarte Rd (91016-4436)
PHONE.................626 358-4547
Sam Chia, *Brnch Mgr*
EMP: 102
SALES (corp-wide): 88.5MM **Privately Held**
Web: www.evictionlawyer.com
SIC: 8741 Management services
PA: Country Villa Service Corp.
2400 E Katella Ave # 800
Anaheim CA
310 574-3733

(P-20065)
COUNTRY VILLA SERVICE CORP
3002 Rowena Ave (90039-2005)
PHONE.................323 666-1544
Stephen Rissman, *Pr*
EMP: 103
SALES (corp-wide): 88.5MM **Privately Held**
Web: www.evictionlawyer.com
SIC: 8741 8051 Nursing and personal care facility management; Skilled nursing care facilities
PA: Country Villa Service Corp.
2400 E Katella Ave # 800
Anaheim CA
310 574-3733

(P-20066)
COUNTRY VILLA SERVICE CORP (PA)
Also Called: Country Villa Health Services
2400 E Katella Ave Ste 800 (92806-5945)
PHONE.................310 574-3733
Stephen Reissman, *CEO*
Diane Reissman, *
Cheryl Petterson, *
EMP: 80 **EST:** 1972
SQ FT: 24,000
SALES (est): 88.5MM
SALES (corp-wide): 88.5MM **Privately Held**
Web: www.evictionlawyer.com
SIC: 8741 Nursing and personal care facility management

(P-20067)
COUNTRY VILLA SERVICE CORP
1730 Grand Ave (90804-2011)
PHONE.................562 597-8817

EMP: 102
SALES (corp-wide): 88.5MM **Privately Held**
Web: www.evictionlawyer.com
SIC: 8741 Nursing and personal care facility management
PA: Country Villa Service Corp.
2400 E Katella Ave # 800
Anaheim CA
310 574-3733

(P-20068)
COUNTRY VILLA SERVICE CORP
Also Called: Country Villa E Convalescent
2415 S Western Ave (90018-2608)
PHONE.................323 734-1101
Phadra Johnson, *Mgr*
EMP: 102
SALES (corp-wide): 88.5MM **Privately Held**
Web: www.evictionlawyer.com
SIC: 8741 8051 8011 8059 Nursing and personal care facility management; Skilled nursing care facilities; Clinic, operated by physicians; Convalescent home
PA: Country Villa Service Corp.
2400 E Katella Ave # 800
Anaheim CA
310 574-3733

(P-20069)
COUNTRY VILLA SERVICE CORP
3233 W Pico Blvd (90019-3640)
PHONE.................323 734-9122
Mike Demchuck, *Mgr*
EMP: 102
SALES (corp-wide): 88.5MM **Privately Held**
Web: www.evictionlawyer.com
SIC: 8741 8051 Nursing and personal care facility management; Skilled nursing care facilities
PA: Country Villa Service Corp.
2400 E Katella Ave # 800
Anaheim CA
310 574-3733

(P-20070)
COUNTY OF LOS ANGELES
Also Called: Social Service Dept- Admin
12900 Crossroads Pkwy S Ste 200 (91746)
PHONE.................562 908-8400
Phillip Browning, *Dir*
EMP: 63
SALES (corp-wide): 31.7B **Privately Held**
Web: www.lacounty.gov
SIC: 8741 9441 Management services; Administration of social and manpower programs, County government
PA: County Of Los Angeles
500 W Temple St Ste 437
Los Angeles CA
213 974-1101

(P-20071)
COUNTY OF LOS ANGELES
Also Called: Internal Services Department
9150 Imperial Hwy (90242-2835)
PHONE.................562 940-2907
Dave Chittenten, *Dir*
EMP: 108
SALES (corp-wide): 31.7B **Privately Held**
Web: www.lacounty.gov
SIC: 8741 9199 Administrative management; General government administration
PA: County Of Los Angeles
500 W Temple St Ste 437
Los Angeles CA
213 974-1101

8741 - Management Services (P-20072)

(P-20072)
CURATIVE INC
605 E Huntington Dr (91016-6353)
PHONE.................................650 713-8928
EMP: 802 EST: 2020
SALES (est): 24.62MM Privately Held
Web: www.curative.com
SIC: 8741 Management services

(P-20073)
D7 LLC
Also Called: Dawson D7, LLC
200 Spectrum Center Dr Ste 1210
(92618-5003)
PHONE.................................808 630-9169
EMP: 61 EST: 2021
SALES (est): 1.52MM Privately Held
Web: www.d7consulting.com
SIC: 8741 Construction management

(P-20074)
DAICEL AMERICA HOLDINGS INC
21515 Hawthorne Blvd Ste 600
(90503-6501)
PHONE.................................480 798-6737
Kenichi Tanaka, Brnch Mgr
EMP: 338
Web: www.daicelamerica.com
SIC: 8741 Administrative management
HQ: Daicel America Holdings, Inc.
    1 Parker Plz
    Fort Lee NJ
    201 461-4466

(P-20075)
DCL MARITIME LLC
Also Called: Disney Cruise Line
500 S Buena Vista St (91521-0001)
PHONE.................................818 560-1000
EMP: 178 EST: 2016
SALES (est): 4.94MM
SALES (corp-wide): 82.72B Publicly Held
SIC: 8741 Management services
PA: The Walt Disney Company
    500 S Buena Vista St
    Burbank CA
    818 560-1000

(P-20076)
DELTA ELECTRONICS AMERICAS LTD (DH)
46101 Fremont Blvd (94538-6468)
PHONE.................................510 668-5111
Kelvin Huang, CEO
Chia-shien Chen, CFO
Chung-hsiu Yao, Sec
James Tang, Dir
Wilson Huang, Dir
◆ EMP: 100 EST: 1985
SALES (est): 462.92MM Privately Held
Web: www.delta-americas.com
SIC: 8741 5065 5045 5063 Management services; Electronic parts and equipment, nec; Computer peripheral equipment; Electrical apparatus and equipment
HQ: Delta America Ltd
    46101 Fremont Blvd
    Fremont CA

(P-20077)
DEMANDBLUE INC
5 Corporate Park Ste 140 (92606-3163)
PHONE.................................909 402-3453
EMP: 61 EST: 2021
SALES (est): 702.92K Privately Held
Web: www.demandblue.com
SIC: 8741 Financial management for business

(P-20078)
DEWOLF REALTY CO INC
4330 California St (94118-1316)
P.O. Box 591540 (94159-1540)
PHONE.................................415 221-2032
William A Talmage, Pr
Marie Wayne, *
Aaron Sinel, *
EMP: 60 EST: 1879
SALES (est): 5.34MM Privately Held
Web: www.dewolfsf.com
SIC: 8741 6531 Management services; Appraiser, real estate

(P-20079)
DFA OF CALIFORNIA
Also Called: American Cncil For Fd Sfety Ql
2037 Morgan Dr (93631-2753)
PHONE.................................559 233-7249
Michael Hurley, Dir
EMP: 71
SALES (corp-wide): 6.76MM Privately Held
Web: www.safefoodalliance.com
SIC: 8741 8734 Administrative management; Food testing service
PA: Dfa Of California
    710 Striker Ave
    Sacramento CA
    916 561-5900

(P-20080)
DHS CONSULTING LLC
1820 E 1st St Ste 410 (92705-8311)
PHONE.................................714 276-1135
EMP: 140 EST: 2012
SQ FT: 6,000
SALES (est): 27.82MM Privately Held
Web: www.anseradvisory.com
SIC: 8741 Construction management
HQ: Anser Advisory, Llc
    2677 N Main St Ste 400
    Santa Ana CA
    310 351-8907

(P-20081)
DIGITAL MEDIA MANAGEMENT INC
6555 Barton Ave Ste 200 (90038-2587)
PHONE.................................323 378-6505
EMP: 65 EST: 2011
SALES (est): 10.49MM Privately Held
Web: www.digitalmediamanagement.com
SIC: 8741 Management services

(P-20082)
ENTEGRIS INC
4175 Santa Fe Rd (93401-8159)
PHONE.................................805 541-9299
EMP: 63
SALES (corp-wide): 3.28B Publicly Held
Web: www.entegris.com
SIC: 8741 3674 Management services; Semiconductors and related devices
PA: Entegris, Inc.
    129 Concord Rd
    Billerica MA
    978 436-6500

(P-20083)
EPIC MANAGEMENT LP (PA)
1615 Orange Tree Ln (92374-2804)
P.O. Box 19020 (92423-9020)
PHONE.................................909 799-1818
EMP: 86 EST: 1995
SALES (est): 45.17MM Privately Held
Web: www.epicmanagementlp.com
SIC: 8741 Nursing and personal care facility management

(P-20084)
EVOLUTION HOSPITALITY LLC (HQ)
1211 Puerta Del Sol Ste 170 (92673-6353)
PHONE.................................949 325-1350
John Murphy, Pr
William Loughran, *
Matt Raine, *
EMP: 77 EST: 2010
SALES (est): 50.04MM
SALES (corp-wide): 819.71MM Privately Held
Web: www.evolutionhospitality.com
SIC: 8741 7011 Hotel or motel management; Hotels and motels
PA: Aimbridge Hospitality, Llc
    5301 Headquarters Dr
    Plano TX
    972 952-0200

(P-20085)
FAR EAST NATIONAL BANK
977 N Broadway Ste 306 (90012-1786)
P.O. Box Po Box 54198 (90099-0001)
PHONE.................................213 687-1300
EMP: 354
SIC: 8741 6021 Management services; National commercial banks

(P-20086)
FINANCIAL GROUP INC
1991 Country Pl (93023-4190)
PHONE.................................805 646-7974
EMP: 130
SALES (corp-wide): 1.47B Publicly Held
SIC: 8741 Management services
HQ: The Financial Group Inc
    2555 Severn Ave Ste 100
    Metairie LA
    504 456-0101

(P-20087)
FIRSTSRVICE RSIDENTIAL CAL LLC
3415 S Sepulveda Blvd Ste 720 (90034-6060)
PHONE.................................213 213-0886
Gregg Evangelho, Brnch Mgr
EMP: 110
SALES (corp-wide): 3.75B Privately Held
Web: www.fsresidential.com
SIC: 8741 6531 Business management; Real estate managers
HQ: Firstservice Residential California, Llc
    15241 Laguna Canyon Rd
    Irvine CA
    949 448-6000

(P-20088)
FIRSTSRVICE RSIDENTIAL CAL LLC
43100 Cook St Ste 103 (92211-3124)
PHONE.................................760 834-2480
Daniel Farrar, Brnch Mgr
EMP: 66
SALES (corp-wide): 3.75B Privately Held
Web: www.fsresidential.com
SIC: 8741 6531 Business management; Real estate managers
HQ: Firstservice Residential California, Llc
    15241 Laguna Canyon Rd
    Irvine CA
    949 448-6000

(P-20089)
FIRSTSRVICE RSIDENTIAL CAL LLC
12009 Foundation Pl (95670-4533)
PHONE.................................916 293-4740
Leon Castiaux, Brnch Mgr
EMP: 66
SALES (corp-wide): 3.75B Privately Held
Web: www.fsresidential.com
SIC: 8741 6531 Business management; Real estate managers
HQ: Firstservice Residential California, Llc
    15241 Laguna Canyon Rd
    Irvine CA
    949 448-6000

(P-20090)
FLATIRON CONSTRUCTION CORP
1200 Concord Ave (94520-4915)
PHONE.................................707 742-6270
John Diedurcio, CEO
Bob French, *
Paul Driscoll, *
Blair Brandon, *
Lars Leitner, *
EMP: 138 EST: 1990
SALES (est): 23.36MM Privately Held
Web: www.flatironcorp.com
SIC: 8741 Construction management

(P-20091)
FORT JAMES CORPORATION
Also Called: Fort James Communications Pprs
2000 Powell St (94608-1804)
PHONE.................................510 594-4900
Miles Marsh, Brnch Mgr
EMP: 664
SALES (corp-wide): 36.93B Privately Held
SIC: 8741 Administrative management
HQ: Fort James Corporation
    133 Peachtree St Ne
    Atlanta GA
    404 652-4000

(P-20092)
FORTE ENTERPRISES INC (PA)
Also Called: ST FRANCIS PAVILLION
99 Escuela Dr (94015-4003)
PHONE.................................650 994-3200
Thomas J Nico, Pr
EMP: 240 EST: 1982
SQ FT: 14,000
SALES (est): 23.12MM
SALES (corp-wide): 23.12MM Privately Held
SIC: 8741 8721 Nursing and personal care facility management; Accounting, auditing, and bookkeeping

(P-20093)
FOUR SISTERS INNS
Also Called: Blue Lantern Inn
34343 Blue Lantern St (92629-2703)
PHONE.................................949 661-1304
Lin Mcmahon, Mgr
EMP: 63
SALES (corp-wide): 24.21MM Privately Held
Web: www.foursisters.com
SIC: 8741 7011 Hotel or motel management; Hotels and motels
PA: Four Sisters Inns
    460 Alma St Ste 100
    Monterey CA
    831 649-0908

(P-20094)
FRONT LINE MGT GROUP INC
1100 Glendon Ave Ste 2000 (90024-3524)
PHONE.................................310 209-3100
Irving Azoff, Pr
EMP: 67 EST: 2004
SALES (est): 3.39MM Publicly Held

PRODUCTS & SERVICES SECTION

8741 - Management Services (P-20116)

SIC: **8741** Management services
HQ: Flmg Holdings Corp.
9348 Civic Center Dr
Beverly Hills CA
310 867-7000

(P-20095)
FUJITEC AMERICA INC
12170 Mora Dr Ste 1 (90670-7339)
PHONE..................................310 464-8270
Timothy Mooney, *Mgr*
EMP: 122
Web: www.fujitecamerica.com
SIC: **8741** 1796 Business management; Elevator installation and conversion
HQ: Fujitec America Inc
7258 Innovation Way
Mason OH
513 755-6100

(P-20096)
GAFCON INC (PA)
10301 Meanley Dr # 225 (92131-3011)
PHONE..................................858 875-0010
Yehudi Gaffen, *CEO*
Pam Gaffen, *
Paul Najar, *
Robin Duveen, *
Bryan Benso, *CDO**
EMP: 60 EST: 1987
SALES (est): 24.92MM **Privately Held**
Web: www.gafcon.com
SIC: **8741** 8111 Construction management; Legal services

(P-20097)
GAR BENNETT LLC (PA)
8246 Crawford Ave (93654-9550)
PHONE..................................559 638-6311
EMP: 218 EST: 1929
SALES (est): 154.25MM
SALES (corp-wide): 154.25MM **Privately Held**
Web: www.garbennett.com
SIC: **8741** 5191 1629 1711 Management services; Fertilizer and fertilizer materials; Irrigation system construction; Irrigation sprinkler system installation

(P-20098)
GHP MANAGEMENT CORPORATION
270 N Canon Dr (90210-5323)
PHONE..................................310 432-1441
Geoffrey H Palmer, *Brnch Mgr*
EMP: 202
SALES (corp-wide): 23.93MM **Privately Held**
Web: www.ghpmgmt.com
SIC: **8741** Business management
PA: Ghp Management Corporation
1082 W 7th St
Los Angeles CA
213 213-0190

(P-20099)
GILARDI & CO LLC
1 Mcinnis Pkwy (94903-2797)
PHONE..................................415 798-5900
Eric Barberio, *Pr*
Bryan Butvick, *
Daniel Burke, *
Lara Mcdermott, *Ex VP*
Kim Wagner, *
EMP: 80 EST: 1997
SQ FT: 16,000
SALES (est): 530.88K **Privately Held**
Web: www.gilardi.com
SIC: **8741** 8111 Management services; Legal services

HQ: Kurtzman Carson Consultants, Inc
2335 Alaska Ave
El Segundo CA
310 823-9000

(P-20100)
GLOBAL-DINING INC CALIFORNIA
1212 3rd Street Promenade (90401-1308)
PHONE..................................310 576-9922
Kozo Hasegawa, *CEO*
EMP: 85 EST: 1990
SALES (est): 8.64MM **Privately Held**
Web: www.globaldiningca.com
SIC: **8741** Restaurant management
PA: Global-Dining, Inc.
7-1-5, Minamiaoyama
Minato-Ku TKY

(P-20101)
GONZALEZ MANAGEMENT CO INC
10147 San Fernando Rd (91331-2617)
PHONE..................................818 485-0596
Luis Gonzalez, *Pr*
EMP: 65 EST: 2004
SQ FT: 20,000
SALES (est): 2.07MM **Privately Held**
SIC: **8741** Management services

(P-20102)
GRANITE POWER INC
580 W Beach St (95076-5107)
P.O. Box 50085 (95077-5085)
PHONE..................................831 724-1011
EMP: 300 EST: 2019
SALES (est): 12.43MM **Publicly Held**
Web: www.graniteconstruction.com
SIC: **8741** Construction management
PA: Granite Construction Incorporated
585 W Beach St
Watsonville CA

(P-20103)
GREYSTAR LP
821 W El Camino Real (94040-2511)
PHONE..................................650 386-6438
EMP: 5843
SALES (corp-wide): 117.7K **Privately Held**
Web: www.greystar.com
SIC: **8741** Management services
PA: Greystar, Lp
465 Meeting St Ste 500
Charleston SC
843 579-9400

(P-20104)
GRIFFIN GROUP LLC
4 Rebelo Ln Ste D (94947-3629)
PHONE..................................415 892-4569
Tony Foglio, *
Crystal Marty, *
Lynn Lackey, *
Chad Farmer, *
EMP: 110 EST: 2007
SALES (est): 2.49MM **Privately Held**
Web: tgg.us.com
SIC: **8741** Business management

(P-20105)
GRIMMWAY ENTERPRISES INC
Grimmway Fresh Processing
14141 Di Giorgio Rd (93203-9518)
P.O. Box 81498 (93380-1498)
PHONE..................................661 854-6200
Jeff Meger, *Pr*
EMP: 89
SALES (corp-wide): 1.86B **Privately Held**
Web: www.grimmway.com

SIC: **8741** 2099 2037 Management services; Food preparations, nec; Frozen fruits and vegetables
PA: Grimmway Enterprises, Inc.
14141 Di Giorgio Rd
Arvin CA
800 301-3101

(P-20106)
HABER CORP CRTIF PUB ACCNTANTS
16830 Ventura Blvd # 501 (91436-1731)
PHONE..................................818 783-9200
Gary Haber, *CEO*
EMP: 64 EST: 1980
SQ FT: 7,000
SALES (est): 3.97MM **Privately Held**
SIC: **8741** 8721 Business management; Certified public accountant

(P-20107)
HALL MANAGEMENT CORP
Also Called: Land & Personnel Management
759 S Madera Ave (93630-1744)
PHONE..................................559 846-7382
Stacy Hampton, *Pr*
James Randles, *
EMP: 2000 EST: 2001
SQ FT: 5,000
SALES (est): 21.94MM **Privately Held**
SIC: **8741** Personnel management

(P-20108)
HANDS WORKING VIRTUALLY INC
74710 Highway 111 Ste 102 (92260-3806)
PHONE..................................760 459-8138
Jamie E Lacy, *CEO*
EMP: 69 EST: 2013
SALES (est): 2.68MM **Privately Held**
Web: www.handsworkingvirtually.com
SIC: **8741** Business management

(P-20109)
HARBOR-UCLA MED FOUNDATION INC (PA)
Also Called: Harbor Ucla Med Foundation
21840 Normandie Ave Ste 100 (90502-2047)
PHONE..................................310 222-5015
Chester Choi, *CEO*
EMP: 100 EST: 1967
SQ FT: 45,000
SALES (est): 4.17MM **Privately Held**
Web: www.harbor-ucla.org
SIC: **8741** Hospital management

(P-20110)
HOTCHKIS WILEY CAPITL MGT LLC (PA)
725 S Figueroa St Ste 3900 (90017-5439)
PHONE..................................213 430-1000
EMP: 139 EST: 1980
SQ FT: 12,000
SALES (est): 24.1MM
SALES (corp-wide): 24.1MM **Privately Held**
Web: www.hwcm.com
SIC: **8741** 6211 Financial management for business; Security brokers and dealers

(P-20111)
HOTEL MANAGERS GROUP LLC
Also Called: Hotel Managers Group
11590 W Bernardo Ct Ste 211 (92127-1622)
PHONE..................................858 673-1534
Joel Biggs, *Managing Member*
Charles W Giacomini, *Managing Member**

Michelle Demayo, *
EMP: 400 EST: 1996
SALES (est): 23.42MM **Privately Held**
Web: www.hotelmanagersgroup.com
SIC: **8741** 7011 7041 Hotel or motel management; Hotels and motels; Membership-basis organization hotels

(P-20112)
IKEA PURCHASING SVCS US INC
600 N San Fernando Blvd (91502-1021)
PHONE..................................818 841-3500
Chris Maynard, *Mgr*
EMP: 104
Web: www.ikea.com
SIC: **8741** 8721 5712 Administrative management; Accounting, auditing, and bookkeeping; Furniture stores
HQ: Ikea Purchasing Services (Us) Inc.
7810 Katy Fwy
Houston TX

(P-20113)
INLAND CNTIES REGIONAL CTR INC
Also Called: Inland Regional Center
1500 Iowa Ave Ste 100 (92507-2165)
PHONE..................................951 826-2600
Lavina Johnson, *Brnch Mgr*
EMP: 224
SALES (corp-wide): 744.4MM **Privately Held**
Web: www.inlandrc.org
SIC: **8741** Management services
PA: Inland Counties Regional Center, Inc.
1365 S Waterman Ave
San Bernardino CA
909 890-3000

(P-20114)
INTEGRATED PAIN MAN
4053 Lone Tree Way (94531-6210)
PHONE..................................925 238-0020
EMP: 95
SALES (corp-wide): 55MM **Privately Held**
Web: www.boomeranghc.com
SIC: **8741** Management services
PA: Integrated Pain Management Medical Group, Inc.
450 N Wiget Ln
Walnut Creek CA
925 691-9806

(P-20115)
INTEGRATED PAIN MAN
4530 Balfour Rd (94513-1581)
PHONE..................................925 666-8972
Jacob Rosenberg, *Brnch Mgr*
EMP: 95
SALES (corp-wide): 55MM **Privately Held**
Web: www.boomeranghc.com
SIC: **8741** Management services
PA: Integrated Pain Management Medical Group, Inc.
450 N Wiget Ln
Walnut Creek CA
925 691-9806

(P-20116)
INTEGRATED PAIN MANAGEMEN
165 Lennon Ln Ste 100 (94598-2478)
PHONE..................................925 691-9806
EMP: 108 EST: 2020
SALES (est): 3.8MM **Privately Held**
SIC: **8741** Management services

8741 - Management Services (P-20117)

(P-20117)
INTEGRTED PAIN MGT MED GROUP I
333 University Ave # 140 (95825-6531)
PHONE................916 333-5800
EMP: 96
SALES (corp-wide): 55MM **Privately Held**
Web: www.boomeranghc.com
SIC: 8741 Management services
PA: Integrated Pain Management Medical Group, Inc.
450 N Wiget Ln
Walnut Creek CA
925 691-9806

(P-20118)
INTELLECTUAL VENTURES LLC
Also Called: Intellectual Ventures
200 California Ave Ste 200 (94306-1635)
PHONE................650 941-1330
EMP: 269
SALES (corp-wide): 47.05MM **Privately Held**
Web: www.intellectualventures.com
SIC: 8741 Management services
PA: Intellectual Ventures, Llc
3150 139th Ave Se Ste 500
Bellevue WA
425 467-2300

(P-20119)
JC RESORTS LLC
Also Called: Surf Sand Hotel
1555 S Coast Hwy (92651-3226)
PHONE................949 376-2779
Blaise Bartell, *Brnch Mgr*
EMP: 646
Web: www.surfandsandresort.com
SIC: 8741 5813 5812 7011 Hotel or motel management; Drinking places; Eating places; Hotels
PA: Jc Resorts Llc
533 Coast Blvd S
La Jolla CA

(P-20120)
JC RESORTS LLC
Also Called: Encinitas Ranch Golf Course
4154 Maryland St (92103-2330)
PHONE................760 944-1936
Rod Landville, *Mgr*
EMP: 325
Web: www.jcgolf.com
SIC: 8741 7992 Hotel or motel management; Public golf courses
PA: Jc Resorts Llc
533 Coast Blvd S
La Jolla CA

(P-20121)
JC RESORTS LLC
Also Called: Rancho Bernardo Inn
17550 Bernardo Oaks Dr (92128-2112)
PHONE................858 675-8500
Jhon Gates, *Brnch Mgr*
EMP: 219
Web: www.ranchobernardoinn.com
SIC: 8741 7991 5813 5812 Hotel or motel management; Physical fitness facilities; Drinking places; Eating places
PA: Jc Resorts Llc
533 Coast Blvd S
La Jolla CA

(P-20122)
JEWISH SENIOR LIVING GROUP
302 Silver Ave (94112-1510)
PHONE................415 334-2500
EMP: 60 EST: 2008
SALES (est): 7.92MM **Privately Held**
Web: www.sfcjl.org
SIC: 8741 Nursing and personal care facility management

(P-20123)
JIPC MANAGEMENT INC
Also Called: John's Incredible Pizza Co
22342 Avenida Empresa Ste 220 (92688)
PHONE................949 916-2000
John M Parlet, *Pr*
EMP: 1000 EST: 1998
SALES (est): 36MM **Privately Held**
Web: www.johnspizza.com
SIC: 8741 Restaurant management

(P-20124)
JOIE DE VIVRE HOSPITALITY LLC
Also Called: Hotel Drisco
2901 Pacific Ave (94115-1011)
PHONE................415 346-2880
Jerard Lespinette, *Prin*
EMP: 178
SALES (corp-wide): 83.61MM **Privately Held**
Web: www.hoteldrisco.com
SIC: 8741 7011 Hotel or motel management; Hotels
PA: Joie De Vivre Hospitality, Llc
1750 Geary Blvd
San Francisco CA
415 922-6000

(P-20125)
JOIE DE VIVRE HOSPITALITY LLC
Also Called: Maxwell Hotel, The
386 Geary St (94102-1802)
PHONE................415 986-2000
Steven Conley, *Mgr*
EMP: 62
SALES (corp-wide): 83.61MM **Privately Held**
Web: www.jdvhotels.com
SIC: 8741 7011 Hotel or motel management; Motels
PA: Joie De Vivre Hospitality, Llc
1750 Geary Blvd
San Francisco CA
415 922-6000

(P-20126)
JOIE DE VIVRE HOSPITALITY LLC
Also Called: Costanoa
2001 Rossi Rd (94060-9732)
PHONE................650 879-1100
Daniel Medellin, *Brnch Mgr*
EMP: 79
SALES (corp-wide): 83.61MM **Privately Held**
Web: www.jdvhotels.com
SIC: 8741 Hotel or motel management
PA: Joie De Vivre Hospitality, Llc
1750 Geary Blvd
San Francisco CA
415 922-6000

(P-20127)
JOIE DE VIVRE HOSPITALITY LLC
Also Called: Wild Palms Hotel, The
910 E Fremont Ave (94087-3702)
PHONE................408 738-0500
Karen Acero, *Genl Mgr*
EMP: 88
SALES (corp-wide): 83.61MM **Privately Held**
Web: www.jdvhotels.com
SIC: 8741 7011 Hotel or motel management; Hotels and motels
PA: Joie De Vivre Hospitality, Llc
1750 Geary Blvd
San Francisco CA
415 922-6000

(P-20128)
JPL MANAGEMENT LLC
Also Called: Jpl Management
6427 W Sunset Blvd # 101 (90028-7314)
PHONE................310 844-3662
Julian Ledesma, *CEO*
EMP: 72 EST: 2018
SALES (est): 2.3MM **Privately Held**
SIC: 8741 8748 Management services; Business consulting, nec

(P-20129)
JT2 INTEGRATED RESOURCES (PA)
333 Hegenberger Rd # 650 (94621-1420)
P.O. Box 8021 (94588-8604)
PHONE................925 556-7012
Jeff Sandford, *Ch Bd*
John Casas, *
Tabatha Bettencourt, *
Theresa Fernandez, *
EMP: 62 EST: 1989
SQ FT: 4,200
SALES (est): 6.71MM **Privately Held**
Web: www.jt2.com
SIC: 8741 Administrative management

(P-20130)
JUVENILE JUSTICE DIVISION CAL
Also Called: Ventura Yuth Crrctional Fcilty
3100 Wright Rd (93010-8307)
PHONE................805 485-7951
Vivian Craford, *Superintnt*
EMP: 804
SALES (corp-wide): 534.4MM **Privately Held**
SIC: 8741 9223 Office management; House of correction, government
HQ: Juvenile Justice Division, California
1515 S St Ste 502s
Sacramento CA

(P-20131)
KA MANAGEMENT II INC
5820 Oberlin Dr Ste 201 (92121-3743)
PHONE................858 404-6080
Kayvon Agahnia, *CEO*
Kambiz Agahnia, *Ch*
Ken Assi, *CIO*
EMP: 90 EST: 2015
SALES (est): 8.48MM **Privately Held**
SIC: 8741 Financial management for business

(P-20132)
KEIRO SERVICES
Also Called: KEIRO SENIOR HEALTH CARE
420 E 3rd St Ste 1000 (90013-1648)
PHONE................213 873-5700
Shawn Miyake, *CEO*
EMP: 500 EST: 1984
SQ FT: 26,000
SALES (est): 1.59MM **Privately Held**
Web: www.keiro.org
SIC: 8741 Nursing and personal care facility management

(P-20133)
KELLEYAMERIT HOLDINGS INC (PA)
Also Called: Kelleyamerit Fleet Services
1331 N California Blvd Ste 150 (94596-4535)
PHONE................877 512-6374
Dan Williams, *CEO*
Robert Brauer, *
Kent Bates, *
Amein Punjani, *
EMP: 71 EST: 2010
SQ FT: 10,000
SALES (est): 180MM **Privately Held**
Web: www.ameritfleetsolutions.com
SIC: 8741 Management services

(P-20134)
LA 1000 SANTA FE LLC
1000 S Santa Fe Ave (90021-1741)
PHONE................213 205-1000
EMP: 210 EST: 2019
SALES (est): 8.68MM **Privately Held**
SIC: 8741 Hotel or motel management

(P-20135)
LAKE MRRITT HEALTHCARE CTR LLC
309 Macarthur Blvd (94610-3233)
PHONE................510 227-1806
Admiral Edna Cortez, *Prin*
EMP: 80 EST: 2016
SALES (est): 2.26MM **Privately Held**
SIC: 8741 Hospital management

(P-20136)
LAKESIDE SYSTEMS INC
Also Called: Lakeside Medical Systems
8510 Balboa Blvd Ste 150 (91325-5810)
PHONE................866 654-3471
Richard Merkin, *CEO*
EMP: 700 EST: 1991
SQ FT: 20,000
SALES (est): 24.69MM
SALES (corp-wide): 58.33MM **Privately Held**
SIC: 8741 8742 6411 Management services; Management consulting services; Insurance agents, brokers, and service
PA: Heritage Provider Network Inc
8510 Balboa Blvd Ste 285
Northridge CA
818 654-3461

(P-20137)
LEGACY PRTNERS RESIDENTIAL INC
5141 California Ave Ste 100 (92617-3060)
PHONE................949 930-6600
Deborah Dodd, *Brnch Mgr*
EMP: 205
SALES (corp-wide): 49.67MM **Privately Held**
Web: www.legacypartners.com
SIC: 8741 Management services
PA: Legacy Partners Residential, Inc.
950 Tower Ln Ste 900
Foster City CA
650 571-2250

(P-20138)
LEGACY PRTNERS RESIDENTIAL INC (PA)
950 Tower Ln Ste 900 (94404-2125)
PHONE................650 571-2250
C Preston Butcher, *CEO*
Gary J Rossi, *
EMP: 180 EST: 1995
SALES (est): 49.67MM
SALES (corp-wide): 49.67MM **Privately Held**
Web: www.legacypartners.com

8741 - Management Services (P-20161)

SIC: **8741** Management services

(P-20139)
LEWIS MANAGEMENT CORP
1154 N Mountain Ave (91786-3633)
PHONE.................................909 985-0971
John M Goodman, *CEO*
EMP: 131 **EST:** 2017
SALES (est): 7.43MM **Privately Held**
Web: www.lewisgroupofcompanies.com
SIC: **8741** Management services

(P-20140)
LEXXIOM INC
99 N San Antonio Ave Ste 330 (91786-4575)
PHONE.................................909 581-7313
Robert Lemelin, *Pr*
Brian Lemelin, *
Leo Lemelin, *
EMP: 360 **EST:** 2000
SALES (est): 13.56MM **Privately Held**
Web: www.lexxiom.com
SIC: **8741** Administrative management

(P-20141)
LFC CORPORATE SERVICES INC
17 Corporate Plaza Dr Ste 200 (92660-7902)
PHONE.................................949 640-4950
Alisha A Lange, *Pr*
EMP: 93 **EST:** 1994
SALES (est): 3.98MM **Privately Held**
Web: www.lfc.com
SIC: **8741** Management services

(P-20142)
LION-VALLEN LTD PARTNERSHIP
22 Area Aven A Bldg #2234 (92055)
P.O. Box 555045 (92055-5045)
PHONE.................................760 385-4885
EMP: 95
SALES (corp-wide): 13.99MM **Privately Held**
SIC: **8741** Management services
HQ: Lion-Vallen Limited Partnership
7200 Poe Ave Ste 400
Dayton OH

(P-20143)
LIVINGSTON MEM VNA HLTH CORP
Also Called: Livingston Mem Vsting Nrse Ass
1996 Eastman Ave Ste 101 (93003-5768)
PHONE.................................805 642-0319
Lanyard K Dial Md, *Pr*
Judy Hecox, *
Charles Hair Md, *Ch Bd*
Jeffrey Paul, *
EMP: 292 **EST:** 1947
SQ FT: 12,600
SALES (est): 16.68MM **Privately Held**
Web: www.lmvna.org
SIC: **8741** 8082 Hospital management; Home health care services

(P-20144)
LOS ANGELES RAMS LLC
Also Called: La Rams Football Club
10271 W Pico Blvd (90064-2606)
P.O. Box 69216 (90069-0216)
PHONE.................................310 277-4700
John Shaw, *Prin*
EMP: 104
SALES (corp-wide): 1.23MM **Privately Held**
Web: www.therams.com
SIC: **8741** 7941 Administrative management; Football club
PA: The Los Angeles Rams Llc
29899 Agoura Rd
Agoura Hills CA
314 982-7267

(P-20145)
MARINER HEALTH CARE INC
Also Called: Palm Springs Health Care Ctr
277 S Sunrise Way (92262-6738)
PHONE.................................760 327-8541
Darrin Tharp, *Admn*
EMP: 105
SALES (corp-wide): 1.02B **Privately Held**
Web: www.marinerhealthcare.com
SIC: **8741** 8322 Nursing and personal care facility management; Rehabilitation services
PA: Mariner Health Care, Inc.
3060 Mercer University Dr # 200
Atlanta GA
678 443-7000

(P-20146)
MASSACHUSETTS ELECTRIC COMPANY
1925 Wright Ave Ste C (91750-5847)
PHONE.................................909 962-6001
EMP: 83
SALES (corp-wide): 26.03B **Privately Held**
SIC: **8741** Construction management
HQ: Massachusetts Electric Company
40 Sylvan Rd
Waltham MA
781 907-1000

(P-20147)
MATRIX ABSENCE MANAGEMENT INC
3979 Freedom Cir (95054-1203)
PHONE.................................408 330-0754
EMP: 83
Web: www.reliancematrix.com
SIC: **8741** Management services
HQ: Matrix Absence Management, Inc.
2421 W Peoria Ave Ste 200
Phoenix AZ

(P-20148)
MATRIX ABSENCE MANAGEMENT INC
1420 Rocky Ridge Dr Ste 270 (95661-2877)
PHONE.................................916 773-5737
EMP: 83
Web: www.reliancematrix.com
SIC: **8741** Management services
HQ: Matrix Absence Management, Inc.
2421 W Peoria Ave Ste 200
Phoenix AZ

(P-20149)
MEDICAL NETWORK INC
Also Called: MBC Systems
1809 E Dyer Rd Ste 311 (92705-5740)
PHONE.................................949 863-0022
David Conrad, *Pr*
Michael Weinstein, *Ch*
EMP: 80 **EST:** 1993
SQ FT: 3,500
SALES (est): 9.98MM **Privately Held**
Web: www.mbcsystems.com
SIC: **8741** Hospital management

(P-20150)
MENTOR MDIA USA SUP CHAIN MGT
865 S Washington Ave (92408-2237)
PHONE.................................909 930-0800
Kok Khoon Lim, *CEO*
▲ **EMP:** 80 **EST:** 2008
SALES (est): 21.15MM
SALES (corp-wide): 7.13B **Privately Held**
SIC: **8741** 8742 Business management; Business planning and organizing services
HQ: Mentor Media Ltd
47 Jalan Buroh
Singapore

(P-20151)
MERITAGE GROUP LP
1 Ferry Building (94111-4289)
PHONE.................................415 399-5330
EMP: 1500 **EST:** 2007
SALES (est): 26.96MM **Privately Held**
Web: www.meritagegroup.com
SIC: **8741** Management services

(P-20152)
MIG MANAGEMENT SERVICES LLC
660 Newport Center Dr Ste 1300 (92660-6401)
PHONE.................................949 474-5800
EMP: 80 **EST:** 2010
SALES (est): 6.65MM
SALES (corp-wide): 25.45MM **Privately Held**
Web: www.migcap.com
SIC: **8741** Management services
PA: Mig Capital, Llc
660 Nwport Ctr Dr Ste 13
Newport Beach CA
949 474-5800

(P-20153)
MIKE ROVNER CONSTRUCTION INC
22600 Lambert St (92630-6201)
PHONE.................................949 458-1562
Mike Rovner, *Brnch Mgr*
EMP: 141
Web: www.rovnerconstruction.com
SIC: **8741** 1522 1521 Construction management; Residential construction, nec; Single-family housing construction
PA: Mike Rovner Construction, Inc.
5400 Tech Cir
Moorpark CA

(P-20154)
MONTAGE HOTELS & RESORTS LLC
Also Called: Montage Laguna Beach
30801 Coast Hwy (92651-4221)
PHONE.................................949 715-6000
Alan Fuerstman, *CEO*
EMP: 600
SALES (corp-wide): 110.64MM **Privately Held**
Web: www.montagehotels.com
SIC: **8741** 7011 5813 5812 Hotel or motel management; Hotels; Drinking places; Eating places
PA: Montage Hotels & Resorts, Llc
3 Ada Ste 100
Irvine CA
949 715-5002

(P-20155)
MORGNER TECHNOLOGY MANAGEMENT
Also Called: Morgner Construction MGT
1880 Century Park E Ste 1402 (90067-1630)
PHONE.................................323 900-0030
Monique Morgner, *CEO*
Andrea D'alfonso, *COO*
EMP: 68 **EST:** 1992
SALES (est): 8.9MM **Privately Held**
Web: www.morgnerco.com
SIC: **8741** Construction management

(P-20156)
MTC FINANCIAL INC
Also Called: Trustee Corps
17100 Gillette Ave (92614-5603)
PHONE.................................949 252-8300
Rande Johnsen, *CEO*
EMP: 90 **EST:** 1992
SALES (est): 9.4MM **Privately Held**
Web: www.trusteecorps.com
SIC: **8741** Management services

(P-20157)
NAVIGATORS MANAGEMENT CO INC
19100 Von Karman Ave (92612-1539)
PHONE.................................949 255-4860
EMP: 166
SIC: **8741** Management services
HQ: Navigators Management Company, Inc.
6 International Dr # 100
Port Chester NY
412 995-2255

(P-20158)
NCN MANAGEMENT LLC
5838 Edison Pl Ste 100 (92008-5520)
PHONE.................................800 275-3243
Michael Lawler, *CEO*
Vu Nguyen, *CIO*
EMP: 175 **EST:** 2015
SALES (est): 4.67MM **Privately Held**
SIC: **8741** Management services

(P-20159)
NELSON BROS PROPERTY MGT INC
Also Called: Nelson Brothers Property MGT
16b Journey Ste 200 (92656-3317)
PHONE.................................949 916-7300
Patrick Nelson, *Pr*
EMP: 134 **EST:** 2007
SALES (est): 8.94MM **Privately Held**
Web: www.nelson-brotherscm.com
SIC: **8741** Management services

(P-20160)
NETWORK MANAGEMENT GROUP INC (PA)
1100 S Flower St Ste 3110 (90015-2287)
PHONE.................................323 263-2632
John Park, *Pr*
EMP: 160 **EST:** 1997
SQ FT: 2,039
SALES (est): 3.17MM
SALES (corp-wide): 3.17MM **Privately Held**
SIC: **8741** 8742 Business management; Management consulting services

(P-20161)
NETWORK MEDICAL MANAGEMENT INC
1668 S Garfield Ave Ste 100 (91801)
PHONE.................................626 282-0288
Gary Augusta, *Pr*
Hing Ang, *COO*
Mihir Shah, *CFO*
EMP: 130 **EST:** 1994
SQ FT: 14,000
SALES (est): 15.03MM **Publicly Held**
Web: www.networkmedicalmanagement.com
SIC: **8741** Hospital management
PA: Apollo Medical Holdings, Inc.

8741 - Management Services (P-20162)

1668 S Garfield Ave Fl 2
Alhambra CA

(P-20162)
NORTH AMERICAN CLIENT SVCS INC (PA)
25910 Acero Ste 350 (92691-7908)
PHONE.....................949 240-2423
Darian Dahl, *Pr*
Jonathan Sloey, *
Jeffrey Daly, *
John L Sorensen, *
Timothy J Paulsen, *
▲ EMP: 175 EST: 1989
SALES (est): 48.37MM **Privately Held**
Web: www.nahci.com
SIC: 8741 Nursing and personal care facility management

(P-20163)
NORTH AMERICAN MED MGT CAL INC (DH)
Also Called: Optum
3990 Concours Ste 500 (91764-7983)
PHONE.....................909 605-8000
EMP: 75 EST: 1995
SALES (est): 35.74MM
SALES (corp-wide): 324.16B **Publicly Held**
Web: www.nammcal.com
SIC: 8741 Nursing and personal care facility management
HQ: Namm Holdings, Inc.
3281 E Guasti Rd Ste 700
Ontario CA

(P-20164)
NORTHSTAR SENIOR LIVING INC
Also Called: Woodmont Senior Living
2334 Washington Ave Ste A (96001-2159)
PHONE.....................530 242-8300
Rick Jensen, *CEO*
Brian Uhlir, *
EMP: 586 EST: 2008
SALES (est): 25.05MM **Privately Held**
Web: www.northstarseniorliving.com
SIC: 8741 Nursing and personal care facility management

(P-20165)
ONNI PROPERTIES LLC
Also Called: Level Furnished Living
888 S Olive St (90014-3006)
PHONE.....................213 568-0278
Javier Sepeda, *Genl Mgr*
EMP: 206
SALES (corp-wide): 26.35MM **Privately Held**
Web: www.onni.com
SIC: 8741 Business management
PA: Onni Properties Llc
5055 N 32nd St
Phoenix AZ
602 595-4810

(P-20166)
ONTRAPORT INC
2040 Alameda Padre Serra Ste 220 (93103-1704)
PHONE.....................805 568-1424
Landon Ray, *CEO*
Lena Requist, *
EMP: 142 EST: 2012
SQ FT: 35,000
SALES (est): 18.85MM **Privately Held**
Web: www.ontraport.com
SIC: 8741 Business management

(P-20167)
OREQ CORPORATION
Also Called: Orchem Division
42306 Remington Ave (92590-2512)
PHONE.....................951 296-5076
Jess L Hetzner, *CEO*
Ron Hetzner, *
▲ EMP: 82 EST: 1999
SALES (est): 12.76MM **Privately Held**
Web: www.oreqcorp.com
SIC: 8741 5941 5091 Business management; Water sport equipment; Spa equipment and supplies

(P-20168)
PACIFIC GARDENS MED CTR LLC
21530 Pioneer Blvd (90716-2608)
PHONE.....................562 860-0401
EMP: 250 EST: 2017
SALES (est): 21.65MM **Privately Held**
SIC: 8741 Hospital management

(P-20169)
PACIFIC LIFE FUND ADVISORS LLC
Pacific Asset Management
700 Newport Center Dr (92660-6307)
PHONE.....................949 260-9000
Rex Olson, *Prin*
EMP: 239
SALES (corp-wide): 12.84B **Privately Held**
Web: www.pacificlife.com
SIC: 8741 Financial management for business
HQ: Pacific Life Fund Advisors Llc
700 Newport Center Dr
Newport Beach CA

(P-20170)
PACIFIC PARK MANAGEMENT
Also Called: PACIFIC PARK MANAGEMENT
1300 Fillmore St (94115-4113)
PHONE.....................415 440-4840
EMP: 84
Web: www.pacificparkonline.com
SIC: 8741 7521 Business management; Indoor parking services
PA: Pacific Park Management Inc
311 California St Ste 310
San Francisco CA

(P-20171)
PACIFIC PARTNERS MGT SVCS INC
Also Called: Pacific Partners MSI
1051 E Hillsdale Blvd Ste 750 (94404-1640)
P.O. Box 5860 (94402-5860)
PHONE.....................650 358-5804
Lori Vatcher, *CEO*
M Lawrence Bonham Md, *Pr*
EMP: 100 EST: 1997
SALES (est): 12.74MM **Publicly Held**
SIC: 8741 8748 Business management; Business consulting, nec
PA: Hca Healthcare, Inc.
1 Park Plz
Nashville TN

(P-20172)
PACIFIC VENTURES LTD
Also Called: Jacmar Companies, The
2200 W Valley Blvd (91803-1928)
PHONE.....................626 576-0737
William H Tilley, *CEO*
Jim Dalpozzo, *
Randy Hill, *
EMP: 250 EST: 1976
SQ FT: 20,000
SALES (est): 8.24MM **Privately Held**
SIC: 8741 6722 Restaurant management; Management investment, open-end

(P-20173)
PARSONS CONSTRUCTORS INC
Also Called: PARSONS
100 W Walnut St (91103-3697)
PHONE.....................626 440-2000
Chuck Harrington, *CEO*
Robert Camp, *
EMP: 1786 EST: 1978
SALES (est): 6.33MM
SALES (corp-wide): 4.2B **Publicly Held**
Web: www.parsons.com
SIC: 8741 8711 Management services; Engineering services
PA: The Parsons Corporation
5875 Trinity Pkwy Ste 300
Centreville VA
703 988-8500

(P-20174)
PEN-CAL ADMINISTRATORS INC
Also Called: P C A
7633 Southfront Rd Ste 120 (94551)
PHONE.....................925 251-3400
Kirk Penland, *CEO*
Stephen Schwaderer, *Prin*
EMP: 75 EST: 1980
SQ FT: 15,000
SALES (est): 10.22MM
SALES (corp-wide): 5.92B **Publicly Held**
SIC: 8741 Financial management for business
PA: Voya Financial, Inc.
230 Park Ave Fl 14
New York NY
212 309-8200

(P-20175)
PERSONA IDENTITIES INC (PA)
201 Post St (94108-5092)
PHONE.....................415 355-4050
Richard Song, *CEO*
Vincent Tsao, *Pr*
Charles Yeh, *Sec*
EMP: 205 EST: 2018
SALES (est): 9.79MM
SALES (corp-wide): 9.79MM **Privately Held**
Web: www.withpersona.com
SIC: 8741 Personnel management

(P-20176)
PFC MANAGEMENT LLC
10880 Wilshire Blvd (90024-4128)
PHONE.....................310 401-1926
Miles Collins, *Pr*
Brittany Collins, *
Gregory Wiles, *
EMP: 63 EST: 2018
SALES (est): 3.25MM **Privately Held**
SIC: 8741 8011 Hospital management; Fertility specialist, physician

(P-20177)
PIPELINE GROUP LLC
2850 Redhill Ave Ste 110 (92705-5537)
PHONE.....................949 296-8375
David Sundling, *CEO*
Raju Patel, *Sec*
EMP: 151 EST: 2011
SALES (est): 2.94MM
SALES (corp-wide): 37.72MM **Privately Held**
Web: www.gopipeline.com
SIC: 8741 Management services
HQ: Pegasus Sub-Intermediate Corp

1 Letterman Dr Bldg C
San Francisco CA
919 378-2215

(P-20178)
PREMIER HLTHCARE SOLUTIONS INC
Also Called: Premier IMS Insurance Services
12225 El Camino Real (92130-2084)
PHONE.....................858 569-8629
Susan Devore, *Brnch Mgr*
EMP: 81
SALES (corp-wide): 1.34B **Publicly Held**
Web: www.premierinc.com
SIC: 8741 Management services
HQ: Premier Healthcare Solutions, Inc.
13034 Balntyn Corp Pl
Charlotte NC
704 357-0022

(P-20179)
PRIMARY CARE ASSOD MED GROUP I
3998 Vista Way Ste B (92056-4514)
PHONE.....................760 724-1033
Jeannette Brody, *Mgr*
EMP: 112
SALES (corp-wide): 4.52MM **Privately Held**
SIC: 8741 Administrative management
PA: Primary Care Associated Medical Group, Inc.
1635 Lake San Marcos Dr
San Marcos CA
760 471-7505

(P-20180)
PRIMARY CARE ASSOD MED GROUP I (PA)
1635 Lake San Marcos Dr Ste 201 (92078-4661)
PHONE.....................760 471-7505
Robert Mongeon, *Pr*
EMP: 70 EST: 1992
SALES (est): 4.52MM
SALES (corp-wide): 4.52MM **Privately Held**
SIC: 8741 Administrative management

(P-20181)
PRIMARY PROVIDER MGT CO INC (HQ)
Also Called: Ppmc
2115 Compton Ave Ste 301 (92881-7272)
PHONE.....................951 280-7700
Robert Dukes Md, *CEO*
Robert Dukes, *CEO*
Maureen B Tyson, *
EMP: 90 EST: 1983
SQ FT: 23,500
SALES (est): 28.35MM
SALES (corp-wide): 2.71B **Publicly Held**
SIC: 8741 Business management
PA: Agilon Health, Inc.
6210 E Hwy 290 Ste 450
Austin TX
562 256-3800

(P-20182)
PRIMED MGT CONSULTING SVCS INC
Also Called: Primed
2409 Camino Ramon (94583-4285)
P.O. Box 5080 (94583-0980)
PHONE.....................925 327-6710
David Joyner, *CEO*
Steve Mcdermott, *Pr*
Robert Ramsey, *
Wendy Chow, *

PRODUCTS & SERVICES SECTION

8741 - Management Services (P-20204)

Tim Richards, *
EMP: 488 EST: 1984
SQ FT: 30,000
SALES (est): 60.91MM **Privately Held**
Web: www.hillphysicians.com
SIC: 8741 8742 Management services;
 Management consulting services
PA: Hill Physicians Medical Group, Inc.
 2409 Camino Ramon
 San Ramon CA

(P-20183)
PROACTIVE BUS SOLUTIONS INC
1290 B St Ste 208 (94541-2996)
PHONE.....................510 302-0120
Deidrie Towery, *CEO*
EMP: 250 EST: 1998
SQ FT: 3,000
SALES (est): 12.49MM **Privately Held**
Web: www.proactiveok.com
SIC: 8741 8742 Business management;
 Business management consultant

(P-20184)
PROACTIVE RISK MANAGEMENT INC
22617 Hawthorne Blvd (90505-2510)
PHONE.....................213 840-8856
Benoit Grenier, *CEO*
EMP: 100 EST: 2014
SALES (est): 4.93MM **Privately Held**
Web: www.parminc.com
SIC: 8741 Business management

(P-20185)
PROFESSIONAL COMMUNITY MGT CAL
Also Called: Pcm
23081 Via Campo Verde (92656)
PHONE.....................949 380-0725
Richard Lee, *Brnch Mgr*
EMP: 110
SALES (corp-wide): 49.19MM **Privately Held**
Web: www.pcminternet.com
SIC: 8741 6519 Business management;
 Real property lessors, nec
PA: Professional Community Management
 Of California, Inc.
 27051 Twne Cntre Dr Ste 2
 Foothill Ranch CA
 800 369-7260

(P-20186)
PROSPECT MEDICAL GROUP INC (HQ)
1920 E 17th St Ste 200 (92705-8626)
PHONE.....................714 796-5900
Jacob Y Terner Md, *Pr*
Mitchell Lew Md, *CEO*
Mike Heather, *
Stewart Kahn, *
EMP: 350 EST: 1986
SQ FT: 2,420
SALES (est): 32.89MM
SALES (corp-wide): 3.91B **Privately Held**
Web: www.prospectmedical.com
SIC: 8741 Hospital management
PA: Prospect Medical Holdings, Inc.
 3415 S Sepulveda Blvd # 9
 Los Angeles CA
 310 943-4500

(P-20187)
PROSPECT MEDICAL SYSTEMS INC (HQ)
Also Called: Genesis Health Care
600 City Pkwy W Ste 800 (92868-2915)
PHONE.....................714 667-8156
Mitchell Lew Md, *CEO*
Brice Keyser Senior, *Dir Fin*
EMP: 127 EST: 1996
SALES (est): 43.01MM
SALES (corp-wide): 3.91B **Privately Held**
Web: www.prospectmedical.com
SIC: 8741 Hospital management
PA: Prospect Medical Holdings, Inc.
 3415 S Sepulveda Blvd # 9
 Los Angeles CA
 310 943-4500

(P-20188)
PROVIDENT FINANCIAL MANAGEMENT
3130 Wilshire Blvd Ste 600 (90403-2349)
P.O. Box 4084 (90411-4084)
PHONE.....................310 282-0477
Ivan Axelrod, *Mng Pt*
Barry Siegel, *
EMP: 95 EST: 1981
SQ FT: 34,000
SALES (est): 2.61MM **Privately Held**
Web: www.providentfm.com
SIC: 8741 Financial management for
 business

(P-20189)
PS24 INC
Also Called: Grove - Design District, The
690 Mission St (94105-4014)
PHONE.....................415 834-5105
Kenneth Zankel, *CEO*
Anna Zankel, *
EMP: 100 EST: 2017
SALES (est): 3.56MM **Privately Held**
SIC: 8741 Restaurant management

(P-20190)
RAINMAKER SYSTEMS INC
Also Called: Rmkr
1821 S Bascom Ave Ste 385 (95008-2309)
PHONE.....................408 659-1800
EMP: 150
Web: www.rainmakersystems.com
SIC: 8741 8742 Management services;
 Marketing consulting services

(P-20191)
RAYMOND GROUP (PA)
Also Called: Orange Cnty George M
Raymond N
520 W Walnut Ave (92868-2233)
PHONE.....................714 771-7670
Travis Winsor, *CEO*
James Watson, *
Mary Raymond, *
Tom Obrien, *
Michael Potter, *
EMP: 95 EST: 1955
SQ FT: 20,000
SALES (est): 36.98MM
SALES (corp-wide): 36.98MM **Privately Held**
Web: www.raymondgroup.com
SIC: 8741 Construction management

(P-20192)
RELATED MANAGEMENT CORPORATION
303 Checkers Dr (95133-2290)
PHONE.....................408 272-0356
EMP: 72
SALES (corp-wide): 2.05B **Privately Held**
Web: www.related.com
SIC: 8741 Management services
HQ: Related Management Corporation
 423 W 55th St Fl 10
 New York NY
 212 319-1200

(P-20193)
RELOCITY INC
10250 Constellation Blvd Ste 100
(90067-6200)
PHONE.....................323 207-9160
Klaus Siegmann, *CEO*
EMP: 120 EST: 2016
SQ FT: 800
SALES (est): 17.43MM **Privately Held**
Web: www.relocity.com
SIC: 8741 Management services

(P-20194)
RENOVO SOLUTIONS LLC (PA)
4 Executive Cir Ste 185 (92614-6791)
PHONE.....................714 599-7969
Joseph Happ, *CIO**
Donald K Carson, *OF WEST COAST**
Haresh Saitiani, *
Fernando Castorena, *
EMP: 300 EST: 2009
SQ FT: 5,400
SALES (est): 73.08MM
SALES (corp-wide): 73.08MM **Privately Held**
Web: www.renovo1.com
SIC: 8741 Hospital management

(P-20195)
RHS CORP
Also Called: REDLANDS COMMUNITY HOSPITAL
350 Terracina Blvd (92373-4850)
PHONE.....................909 335-5500
James R Holmes, *Pr*
EMP: 1450 EST: 1985
SQ FT: 265,000
SALES (est): 550.43K **Privately Held**
Web: www.redlandshospital.org
SIC: 8741 Hospital management

(P-20196)
RIM CORPORATION
Also Called: Rim Hospitality
915 17th St (95354-1207)
PHONE.....................209 523-8331
EMP: 3000
SIC: 8741 Hotel or motel management

(P-20197)
ROCKPORT ADM SVCS LLC (PA)
Also Called: Rockport Healthcare Services
5900 Wilshire Blvd Ste 1600 (90036-5016)
PHONE.....................323 330-6500
EMP: 75 EST: 2010
SALES (est): 66.76MM **Privately Held**
SIC: 8741 Administrative management

(P-20198)
SAGA KAPITAL GROUP INC
108 Saybrook (92620-7307)
PHONE.....................714 294-4132
Ashish Kapoor, *CEO*
EMP: 75 EST: 2019
SALES (est): 2.36MM **Privately Held**
Web: www.sagakgi.com
SIC: 8741 Business management

(P-20199)
SAN FRNCSCO CMNTY CLNIC CNSRTI
Also Called: Sfccc
170c Capp St (94110-1210)
PHONE.....................415 355-2222
John Gressman, *Resident Chief Executive Officer*
Maria Powers, *
Pat Dunn, *
EMP: 68 EST: 1983
SALES (est): 13.64MM **Privately Held**
Web: www.sfccc.org
SIC: 8741 Management services

(P-20200)
SAN JOSE ARENA MANAGEMENT LLC
44388 Old Warm Springs Blvd
(94538-6148)
PHONE.....................408 28, 7070
Greg Jamison, *Brnch Mgr*
EMP: 81
SALES (corp-wide): 21.61MM **Privately Held**
Web: www.sapcenter.com
SIC: 8741 Management services
PA: San Jose Arena Management, Llc
 525 W Santa Clara St
 San Jose CA
 408 287-7070

(P-20201)
SAN JOSE EARTHQUAKES MGT LLC
Also Called: SAN JOSE EARTHQUAKES
451 El Camino Real Ste 220 (95050)
PHONE.....................408 556-7700
Lew Wolff, *Owner*
John Fisher Majority, *Stockholder*
Dave Kaval, *Pr*
Robert Bardin, *Prin*
EMP: 106 EST: 2011
SALES (est): 348.32K **Privately Held**
Web: www.sjearthquakes.com
SIC: 8741 Management services

(P-20202)
SANTA CLRITA HLTH CARE ASSN IN (PA)
23845 Mcbean Pkwy (91355-2001)
PHONE.....................661 253-8000
Roger Seaver, *Pr*
C R Hudson, *
Paul Salomon, *
John Barstis, *
James D Hicken, *
EMP: 65 EST: 1975
SQ FT: 130,000
SALES (est): 21.77MM
SALES (corp-wide): 21.77MM **Privately Held**
SIC: 8741 Hospital management

(P-20203)
SCRIPPS CLINIC MED GROUP INC
12395 El Camino Real Ste 112 (92130)
PHONE.....................858 554-9000
Doctor Hugh Greenway, *CEO*
EMP: 160 EST: 1999
SALES (est): 17.86MM
SALES (corp-wide): 4.06B **Privately Held**
Web: www.scripps.org
SIC: 8741 Management services
PA: Scripps Health
 10140 Campus Point Dr # 415
 San Diego CA
 800 727-4777

(P-20204)
SEABREEZE MANAGEMENT CO INC (PA)
26840 Aliso Viejo Pkwy Ste 100
(92656-2624)
PHONE.....................949 855-1800
Isaiah S Henry, *CEO*
Karen Inman, *
Jake Parvino, *VP*
EMP: 69 EST: 1987

8741 - Management Services (P-20205) — PRODUCTS & SERVICES SECTION

SQ FT: 22,000
SALES (est): 32.88MM
SALES (corp-wide): 32.88MM **Privately Held**
Web: www.seabreezemgmt.com
SIC: 8741 Management services

(P-20205)
SETHI MANAGEMENT INC
6156 Innovation Way (92009-1728)
P.O. Box 235927 (92023-5927)
PHONE.....................760 692-5288
Jeetander Sethi, *CEO*
EMP: 154 EST: 2009
SALES (est): 40MM **Privately Held**
Web: www.sethimanagement.com
SIC: 8741 Business management

(P-20206)
SMILE BRANDS GROUP INC (PA)
Also Called: Bright Now Dental
100 Spectrum Center Dr Ste 1500 (92618-4963)
PHONE.....................714 668-1300
Steven C Bilt, *CEO*
Stan Andrakowicz, *
Robert C Crim, *CDO*
George Suda, *CIO*
Cheryl Dore, *Chief Human Resource Officer*
EMP: 90 EST: 1978
SQ FT: 15,000
SALES (est): 295.09MM
SALES (corp-wide): 295.09MM **Privately Held**
Web: www.smilebrands.com
SIC: 8741 8021 Management services; Dental clinics and offices

(P-20207)
SMITH BROADCASTING GROUP INC (PA)
2315 Red Rose Way (93109-1259)
PHONE.....................805 965-0400
Debrah Egar, *Ex Sec*
David A Fitz, *
EMP: 165 EST: 1985
SALES (est): 6.69MM
SALES (corp-wide): 6.69MM **Privately Held**
SIC: 8741 8742 Business management; Management consulting services

(P-20208)
SNF MANAGEMENT
1901 Avenue Of The Stars (90067-4608)
PHONE.....................310 385-1090
Lee Samson, *Pr*
EMP: 94 EST: 2010
SALES (est): 9.87MM **Privately Held**
Web: www.windsorcares.com
SIC: 8741 Management services

(P-20209)
SODEXO MANAGEMENT INC
Also Called: Cific Energy Center
851 Howard St (94103-3009)
PHONE.....................925 325-9657
Jim Wasley, *Brnch Mgr*
EMP: 1342
SALES (corp-wide): 206.19MM **Privately Held**
Web: www.sodexo.com
SIC: 8741 Management services
HQ: Sodexo Management Inc.
9801 Washingtonian Blvd
Gaithersburg MD

(P-20210)
SODEXO MANAGEMENT INC
1 University Cir (95382-3200)
PHONE.....................209 667-3634
EMP: 1618
SALES (corp-wide): 206.19MM **Privately Held**
Web: www.sodexo.com
SIC: 8741 Management services
HQ: Sodexo Management Inc.
9801 Washingtonian Blvd
Gaithersburg MD

(P-20211)
SOLPAC CONSTRUCTION INC
Also Called: Soltek Pacific Construction Co
2424 Congress St (92110-2819)
PHONE.....................619 296-6247
Stephen Thompson, *CEO*
Brandon Richie, *
John Myers, *
Kevin Cammall, *
Robert Thompson, *
EMP: 130 EST: 2005
SQ FT: 12,291
SALES (est): 177.75MM **Privately Held**
Web: www.soltekpacific.com
SIC: 8741 1542 1611 Construction management; Commercial and office building contractors; General contractor, highway and street construction

(P-20212)
SOUTH COAST PLAZA SECURITY
695 Town Center Dr Ste 50 (92626-1924)
PHONE.....................714 435-2180
Craig Farrow, *Mgr*
EMP: 120 EST: 1989
SALES (est): 4.84MM **Privately Held**
SIC: 8741 Management services

(P-20213)
SOUTHERN CALIFORNIA PHYSICIA
6760 Top Gun St Ste 100 (92121-4114)
PHONE.....................858 824-7000
Joyce Cook, *CEO*
Marcia Aeschaleman, *
EMP: 65 EST: 1996
SQ FT: 17,000
SALES (est): 6.62MM **Privately Held**
Web: www.scpmcs.org
SIC: 8741 Administrative management

(P-20214)
SOUTHERN IMPLANTS INC
5 Holland Ste 209 (92618-2576)
PHONE.....................949 273-8505
Michael Kehoe, *Pr*
Michael Nealon, *
EMP: 125 EST: 2007
SALES (est): 4.78MM **Privately Held**
Web: www.southernimplants.us
SIC: 8741 Management services

(P-20215)
SPEARMINT RHINO CMPNIES WRLDWI
1875 Tandem (92860-3606)
PHONE.....................951 371-3788
Dyanna Gray, *CEO*
Kathy Vercher, *Pr*
Kathy Mcdonald, *VP*
Dena Hernandez, *CFO*
EMP: 88 EST: 1996
SQ FT: 5,000
SALES (est): 6.62MM **Privately Held**
Web: www.spearmintrhino.com

SIC: 8741 Business management

(P-20216)
STANDISH MANAGEMENT LLC
Also Called: Standish Management
750 Battery St Ste 600 (94111-1567)
PHONE.....................925 300-3277
EMP: 203
SALES (corp-wide): 22.89MM **Privately Held**
Web: www.standishmanagement.com
SIC: 8741 Management services
PA: Standish Management, Llc
750 Battery St
San Francisco CA
415 273-6810

(P-20217)
STANFORD HLTH CARE TRI-VALLEY (DH)
Also Called: The Hsptal Cmmttee For Lvrmr-P
5555 W Las Positas Blvd (94588-4000)
PHONE.....................925 847-3000
Scott Gregerson, *CEO*
Gina Teeples, *
Kyle Wichelmann, *
EMP: 500 EST: 1958
SALES (est): 419.87MM
SALES (corp-wide): 15.13B **Privately Held**
Web: www.stanfordhealthcare.org
SIC: 8741 8062 Hospital management; General medical and surgical hospitals
HQ: Stanford Health Care
300 Pasteur Dr
Stanford CA
650 723-4000

(P-20218)
STREAMLAND MEDIA LLC
1117 W Isabel St (91506-1405)
PHONE.....................416 909-2103
EMP: 103
SALES (corp-wide): 5.51MM **Privately Held**
Web: www.streamlandmedia.com
SIC: 8741 Management services
PA: Streamland Media Llc
1132 Vine St
Los Angeles CA

(P-20219)
SUNA SOLUTIONS INC
530 B St Ste 300 (92101-4431)
PHONE.....................888 223-4788
Michael Larkins, *CEO*
EMP: 63 EST: 2009
SALES (est): 6.52MM **Privately Held**
Web: www.suna.com
SIC: 8741 Management services

(P-20220)
SUNAMERICA INVESTMENTS INC (DH)
Also Called: SunAmerica
1 Sun America Ctr Fl 37 (90067-6100)
PHONE.....................310 772-6000
Eli Broad, *Pr*
EMP: 80 EST: 1978
SQ FT: 76,000
SALES (est): 22.67MM
SALES (corp-wide): 56.44B **Publicly Held**
SIC: 8741 6211 6282 7311 Administrative management; Security brokers and dealers; Investment advisory service; Advertising agencies
HQ: Sunamerica Inc.
1 Sun America Ctr Fl 38
Los Angeles CA
310 772-6000

(P-20221)
SUNROAD ASSET MANAGEMENT INC
4445 Eastgate Mall Ste 400 (92121)
PHONE.....................858 362-8500
Dan Feldman, *Pr*
EMP: 119 EST: 1986
SALES (est): 2.23MM **Privately Held**
Web: www.sunroadenterprises.com
SIC: 8741 Business management
PA: Sunroad Holding Corporation
8620 Spectrum Center Blvd
San Diego CA

(P-20222)
SUTTER VALLEY MED FOUNDATION
Also Called: Padilla, David A MD
568 N Sunrise Ave Ste 250 (95661-3097)
PHONE.....................916 865-1140
Susan Paez, *Mgr*
EMP: 165
Web: www.sutterhealth.org
SIC: 8741 8011 Hospital management; Internal medicine, physician/surgeon
PA: Sutter Valley Medical Foundation
2700 Gateway Oaks Dr
Sacramento CA

(P-20223)
SYLMARK INC (PA)
Also Called: Sylmark Group
7821 Orion Ave Ste 200 (91406-2032)
PHONE.....................818 217-2000
Peter Spiegel, *Pr*
Steven Ober, *
Mark Funk, *
EMP: 90 EST: 1998
SALES (est): 20.39MM
SALES (corp-wide): 20.39MM **Privately Held**
Web: www.sylmark.com
SIC: 8741 Management services

(P-20224)
T3W BUSINESS SOLUTIONS INC
3921 Ampudia St (92110-2813)
PHONE.....................619 298-0888
Lisa Carman, *Pr*
Holly Andrews, *
EMP: 65 EST: 2004
SQ FT: 2,523
SALES (est): 9.79MM **Privately Held**
Web: www.t3w.com
SIC: 8741 8713 8711 7371 Business management; Surveying services; Engineering services; Custom computer programming services

(P-20225)
TATUM MANAGEMENT COMPANY LLC
1781 E Fir Ave Ste 102 (93720-3865)
PHONE.....................559 577-4474
Matthew Tatum, *Mgr*
EMP: 90 EST: 2019
SALES (est): 1.71MM **Privately Held**
SIC: 8741 Management services

(P-20226)
TCT MOBILE INC
189 Technology Dr (92618-2402)
PHONE.....................949 892-2990
Xin Zhang, *Pr*
Juanjuan Feng, *
Qian Wen, *
EMP: 100 EST: 2008
SALES (est): 16.74MM
SALES (corp-wide): 4.15MM **Privately Held**

PRODUCTS & SERVICES SECTION
8741 - Management Services (P-20249)

Web: us.alcatelmobile.com
SIC: **8741** 8711 7389 8721 Management services; Engineering services; Financial services; Accounting, auditing, and bookkeeping
HQ: Tcl Communication Technology Holdings Limited
C/O: Conyers Trust Company (Cayman) Limited
George Town GR CAYMAN

(P-20227)
TEAM GROUP LLC
4076 Flat Rock Dr (92505-5858)
PHONE..................951 688-8593
EMP: 78 EST: 2018
SALES (est): 1.89MM
SALES (corp-wide): 4.28MM **Privately Held**
Web: www.teamcorpint.com
SIC: **8741** Management services
PA: Total Educational Activity Model Corp
4076 Flat Rock Dr
Riverside CA
951 977-9690

(P-20228)
TEICHERT ENRGY UTLTIES GROUP I
3780 Kilroy Airport Way (90806-2457)
PHONE..................916 484-3011
Thomas J Griffith, *CEO*
EMP: 97 EST: 2019
SALES (est): 2.62MM **Privately Held**
Web: www.teichert.com
SIC: **8741** Construction management

(P-20229)
TILTON PACIFIC CNSTR INC
2216 The Alameda (95050-6034)
PHONE..................408 551-0492
James Tilton, *Brnch Mgr*
EMP: 60
Web: www.tiltonpacific.com
SIC: **8741** 1521 Construction management; Single-family housing construction
PA: Tilton Pacific Construction, Inc.
595 Menlo Dr
Rocklin CA

(P-20230)
TRADESMEN INTERNATIONAL LLC
Also Called: Tradesmen International
11145 Knott Ave Ste G (90630-5140)
PHONE..................949 588-3280
Jason Hammer, *Brnch Mgr*
EMP: 60
Web: www.tradesmeninternational.com
SIC: **8741** 7361 Construction management; Employment agencies
PA: Tradesmen International, Llc
9760 Shepard Rd
Macedonia OH

(P-20231)
TRANSCOSMOS OMNICONNECT LLC
879 W 190th St Ste 1050 (90248-4224)
PHONE..................310 630-0072
EMP: 100 EST: 2019
SALES (est): 6.52MM
SALES (corp-wide): 23.83MM **Privately Held**
SIC: **8741** Management services
PA: Trans Cosmos America, Inc.
879 W 190th St Ste 410
Gardena CA
310 630-0072

(P-20232)
TRICOM MANAGEMENT INC
Also Called: United Owners Services
4025 E La Palma Ave Ste 101 (92807-1734)
PHONE..................714 630-2029
Woody Cary, *Pr*
EMP: 200 EST: 1979
SQ FT: 9,000
SALES (est): 7.95MM **Privately Held**
Web: www.tricommanagement.com
SIC: **8741** 7389 Management services; Time-share condominium exchange

(P-20233)
TRILAR MANAGEMENT GROUP
1025 S Gilbert St (92543-7090)
PHONE..................951 925-2021
Susan A York, *Brnch Mgr*
EMP: 127
SALES (corp-wide): 11.89MM **Privately Held**
Web: www.ctmmanagement.com
SIC: **8741** Business management
PA: Trilar Management Group
2225 Faraday Ave Ste A
Carlsbad CA
760 603-3205

(P-20234)
TRIPALINK CORP
600 Wilshire Blvd Ste 1540 (90005-3983)
PHONE..................323 717-9139
Donghal Li, *Prin*
EMP: 133 EST: 2016
SALES (est): 5.03MM **Privately Held**
Web: www.tripalink.com
SIC: **8741** Management services

(P-20235)
TROON GOLF LLC
Also Called: Indian Wells Golf Resort
44500 Indian Wells Ln (92210-8746)
PHONE..................760 346-4653
Rich Carter, *Genl Mgr*
EMP: 130
Web: www.indianwellsgolfresort.com
SIC: **8741** 7997 Management services; Country club, membership
PA: Troon Golf, L.L.C.
15044 N Scottsdale Rd # 300
Scottsdale AZ

(P-20236)
TWENTY4SEVEN HOTELS CORP
520 Newport Center Dr Ste 520 (92660)
PHONE..................949 734-6400
David Wani, *CEO*
Drew Hardy, *
EMP: 500 EST: 2002
SQ FT: 15,000
SALES (est): 25.73MM **Privately Held**
Web: www.247hotels.com
SIC: **8741** Hotel or motel management

(P-20237)
UNITED BEHAVIORAL HEALTH (HQ)
595 Market St (94105-2835)
PHONE..................415 547-1403
Saul Feldman, *Ch Bd*
Keith Dickson, *
William Goldman Senior, *Ex VP*
Ann Mc Clanathan, *
Michael Swanson, *CIO**
EMP: 250 EST: 1979
SALES (est): 28.74MM
SALES (corp-wide): 324.16B **Publicly Held**

SIC: **8741** 8742 Management services; Management consulting services
PA: Unitedhealth Group Incorporated
9900 Bren Rd E Ste 300w
Minnetonka MN
952 936-1300

(P-20238)
UNITED PARADYNE CORPORATION
Bldg 7525, Utah & 10th St (93437)
P.O. Box 5398 (93437-0398)
PHONE..................805 734-4734
George Kennedy, *Genl Mgr*
EMP: 69
Web: www.unitedparadyne.com
SIC: **8741** Industrial management
PA: United Paradyne Corporation
340 James Way Ste 230
Pismo Beach CA

(P-20239)
UNIVERSITY OF CALIFORNIA
1 Shields Ave (95616-8500)
PHONE..................530 752-0503
EMP: 157 EST: 2019
SALES (est): 28.85MM **Privately Held**
Web: www.ucdavis.edu
SIC: **8741** Management services

(P-20240)
UTILITY LINE MGT SVCS INC
2315 W Foothill Blvd Ste 4 (91786-3572)
PHONE..................909 920-0812
Tom F Shiflett, *Pr*
Jim Deason, *Mgr*
EMP: 65 EST: 1999
SQ FT: 500
SALES (est): 1.03MM
SALES (corp-wide): 17.07B **Publicly Held**
Web: www.ulmservices.com
SIC: **8741** Construction management
PA: Quanta Services, Inc.
2727 North Loop W Ste 100
Houston TX
713 629-7600

(P-20241)
VANIR CONSTRUCTION MGT INC (PA)
4540 Duckhorn Dr Ste 300 (95834-2597)
PHONE..................916 444-3700
Dorene C Dominguez, *Ch Bd*
John Kuprenas, *
Mansour Aliabadi, *
Alex Leon, *
Ray Nez, *
EMP: 70 EST: 1980
SQ FT: 16,000
SALES (est): 47.89MM
SALES (corp-wide): 47.89MM **Privately Held**
Web: www.vanir.com
SIC: **8741** Construction management

(P-20242)
VENDO LLC
11601 Wilshire Blvd Ste 1818 (90025-0509)
PHONE..................310 300-2810
EMP: 78 EST: 2017
SALES (est): 3.63MM **Privately Held**
Web: www.vendocommerce.com
SIC: **8741** Business management

(P-20243)
VENTURA MEDICAL MANAGEMENT LLC
2601 E Main St (93003-2801)
PHONE..................805 477-6220

EMP: 325 EST: 2002
SALES (est): 23.13MM **Privately Held**
Web: www.ventura.org
SIC: **8741** Hospital management

(P-20244)
VETERANS HEALTH ADMINISTRATION
Also Called: VA Palo Alto Healthcare System
3801 Miranda Ave (94304-1207)
PHONE..................650 493-5000
Vanessa Amasol, *Brnch Mgr*
EMP: 109
Web: benefits.va.gov
SIC: **8741** 9451 Hospital management; Administration of veterans' affairs, Federal government
HQ: Veterans Health Administration
810 Vermont Ave Nw
Washington DC

(P-20245)
VILLAGE MANAGEMENT SVCS INC
24351 El Toro Rd (92637-4901)
PHONE..................949 597-4360
EMP: 94 EST: 2016
SALES (est): 2.37MM **Privately Held**
Web: www.lagunawoodsvillage.com
SIC: **8741** Management services

(P-20246)
VIVA SOMA LESSEE INC
Also Called: Park Central Ht San Francisco
50 3rd St (94103-3106)
PHONE..................415 974-6400
John Anderson, *Brnch Mgr*
EMP: 511
SIC: **8741** Hotel or motel management
HQ: Viva Soma Lessee, Inc.
7550 Wisconsin Ave Fl 10
Bethesda MD

(P-20247)
VPM MANAGEMENT INC
2400 Main St Ste 201 (92614-6271)
PHONE..................949 863-1500
Philip H Mcnamee, *CEO*
Scott J Barker, *Managing Member**
Steve Tomlin, *
Mark Ellis, *
EMP: 150 EST: 1997
SALES (est): 9.34MM **Privately Held**
Web: www.vpmmanagement.com
SIC: **8741** Management services

(P-20248)
WARMINGTON MR 14 ASSOC LLC
Also Called: Warmington
3090 Pullman St (92626-5901)
PHONE..................714 557-5511
EMP: 87 EST: 2013
SALES (est): 5.07MM **Privately Held**
Web: www.homesbywarmington.com
SIC: **8741** Business management

(P-20249)
WARNER BROS DISTRIBUTING INC
Warner Bros. Pictures Domestic
4000 Warner Blvd Bldg 154 (91522-0002)
PHONE..................818 954-6000
Dan Fellman, *Brnch Mgr*
EMP: 418
SIC: **8741** 7822 Management services; Distribution, exclusive of production: motion picture
HQ: Warner Bros. Distributing Inc.

8741 - Management Services (P-20250)

4000 Warner Blvd
Burbank CA

(P-20250)
WESTERN NATIONAL CONTRACTORS
8 Executive Cir (92614-6746)
PHONE.............................949 862-6200
Michael Hayde, *CEO*
Jeffrey R Scott, *
John Townsend, *
Randy Avery, *
Larry Johnson, *
EMP: 88 EST: 2004
SALES (est): 14.11MM **Privately Held**
Web: www.wng.com
SIC: 8741 Construction management

(P-20251)
WESTLAKE DEVELOPMENT GROUP LLC
520 El Camino Real Fl 9 (94002-2121)
PHONE.............................650 579-1010
T M Chang, *Brnch Mgr*
EMP: 102
SQ FT: 600
SALES (corp-wide): 17.8MM **Privately Held**
Web: www.westlake-realty.com
SIC: 8741 Administrative management
PA: Westlake Development Group, Llc
520 S El Camino Real # 900
San Mateo CA
650 579-1010

(P-20252)
WESTREC PROPERTIES INC
16633 Ventura Blvd Fl 6 (91436-1826)
PHONE.............................818 907-0400
Michael M Sachs, *Pr*
EMP: 477 EST: 1990
SALES (est): 1.02MM **Privately Held**
SIC: 8741 Administrative management
PA: Westrec Financial, Inc.
16633 Ventura Blvd Fl 6
Encino CA

(P-20253)
WHISKEY GIRL
702 5th Ave (92101-6918)
PHONE.............................619 236-1616
Jerry Lopez, *Genl Mgr*
EMP: 152 EST: 2011
SALES (est): 1.55MM
SALES (corp-wide): 9.95MM **Privately Held**
Web: www.whiskeygirl.com
SIC: 8741 5813 Restaurant management; Night clubs
PA: Buffalo Joe's, L. P.
1620 5th Ave Ste 770
San Diego CA
619 235-6796

(P-20254)
WOLF & RAVEN LLC
206 W 4th St Ste 439 (92701-4679)
PHONE.............................800 431-6471
Josue B Vazquez, *CEO*
EMP: 99 EST: 2021
SALES (est): 2.2MM **Privately Held**
SIC: 8741 8742 Business management; Business management consultant

(P-20255)
WURL INC
591 Lytton Ave (94301-1538)
PHONE.............................662 649-8825
Sean P Doherty, *CEO*

Yuval Fisher, *
EMP: 71 EST: 2011
SALES (est): 879.57K **Privately Held**
Web: www.wurl.com
SIC: 8741 Management services

(P-20256)
ZA MANAGEMENT
101 N Robertson Blvd (90211-2191)
PHONE.............................310 271-2200
Alexander Zaks, *CEO*
EMP: 90 EST: 2001
SALES (est): 2.42MM **Privately Held**
SIC: 8741 Management services

(P-20257)
ZERO GRAVITY MANAGEMENT
11110 Ohio Ave Ste 100 (90025-3329)
PHONE.............................310 656-9440
EMP: 84 EST: 2016
SALES (est): 1.05MM **Privately Held**
Web: www.zerogravitymanagement.com
SIC: 8741 Management services

8742 Management Consulting Services

(P-20258)
AA BLOCKS LLC
9823 Pacific Heights Blvd Ste F (92121)
PHONE.............................858 523-8231
Branden G Lee, *Mgr*
EMP: 92 EST: 2017
SALES (est): 2.44MM **Privately Held**
Web: www.aablocks.com
SIC: 8742 Business management consultant

(P-20259)
ACCENTURE FEDERAL SERVICES LLC
Also Called: Accenture National SEC Svcs
1615 Murray Canyon Rd Ste 400 (92108-4314)
PHONE.............................619 574-2400
Jim Wangler, *Brnch Mgr*
EMP: 1461
Web: www.accenture.com
SIC: 8742 7361 8711 7373 Business management consultant; Employment agencies; Engineering services; Computer integrated systems design
HQ: Accenture Federal Services Llc
800 N Glebe Rd Ste 300
Arlington VA
703 947-2000

(P-20260)
ACCENTURE LLP
415 Mission St Ste 3300 (94105-5422)
PHONE.............................415 537-5000
Christopher S Digiorgio, *Prin*
EMP: 104
Web: www.accenture.com
SIC: 8742 Business management consultant
HQ: Accenture Llp
500 W Madison St
Chicago IL
312 693-0161

(P-20261)
ADIVO ASSOCIATES LLC
44 Montgomery St Ste 4050 (94104-4824)
PHONE.............................415 992-1449
Maik Klasen, *Brnch Mgr*
EMP: 90
SALES (corp-wide): 3.17MM **Privately Held**
Web: www.adivoassociates.com

SIC: 8742 Business management consultant
PA: Adivo Associates Llc
1429 Plymouth Ave
San Francisco CA
650 743-6226

(P-20262)
ADVANTAGE SALES & MKTG INC (DH)
Also Called: Advantage Solutions
15310 Barranca Pkwy Ste 100 (92618-2236)
PHONE.............................949 797-2900
David Peacock, *CEO*
Robert Murray, *
Chris Growe, *
Bryce Robinson, *
Humberto Domingues, *
▲ EMP: 250 EST: 1997
SQ FT: 48,000
SALES (est): 1.56B
SALES (corp-wide): 4.71B **Publicly Held**
Web: www.advantagesolutions.net
SIC: 8742 Business management consultant
HQ: Advantage Solutions Inc.
15310 Barranca Pkwy # 100
Irvine CA
949 797-2900

(P-20263)
ADVANTAGE SALES & MKTG LLC (DH)
Also Called: Advantage Solutions
15310 Barranca Pkwy Ste 100 (92618-2236)
PHONE.............................949 797-2900
Dave Peacock, *CEO*
Chris Growe, *
Bryce Robinson, *
Kelli Hammersmith, *Chief Communication Officer*
Pamela Morris-thompson, *Chief Human Resources Officer*
EMP: 250 EST: 1987
SALES (est): 1.38B
SALES (corp-wide): 4.71B **Publicly Held**
Web: www.advantagesolutions.net
SIC: 8742 8743 8732 7311 Marketing consulting services; Sales promotion; Market analysis or research; Advertising agencies
HQ: Advantage Solutions Inc.
15310 Barranca Pkwy # 100
Irvine CA
949 797-2900

(P-20264)
AGAMA SOLUTIONS INC
39159 Paseo Padre Pkwy Ste 215 (94538-1608)
PHONE.............................510 796-9300
Pankaj Kalra, *CEO*
Shivani G Sanan, *
Tanu Kalra, *
Ashish Sanan, *
Pankaj Kalra, *VP*
EMP: 126 EST: 2006
SQ FT: 9,000
SALES (est): 4.13MM **Privately Held**
Web: www.agamasolutions.com
SIC: 8742 7371 Business management consultant; Computer software development

(P-20265)
AKI TECHNOLOGIES
375 Alabama St (94110-1360)
PHONE.............................415 624-3253
EMP: 62 EST: 2019
SALES (est): 2.49MM **Privately Held**
Web: www.a.ki

SIC: 8742 Marketing consulting services

(P-20266)
AKQA INC (HQ)
360 3rd St Ste 500 (94107-2165)
PHONE.............................415 645-9400
Tom Bedecarre, *CEO*
EMP: 400 EST: 1990
SQ FT: 28,000
SALES (est): 349.95MM
SALES (corp-wide): 17.37B **Privately Held**
Web: www.akqa.com
SIC: 8742 Marketing consulting services
PA: Wpp Plc
22 Grenville Street
Jersey
370 707-1411

(P-20267)
ALAN B WHITSON COMPANY INC
1507 W Alton Ave (92704-7219)
P.O. Box 9229 (92728-9229)
PHONE.............................949 955-1200
Alan B Whitson, *Pr*
EMP: 750 EST: 1990
SQ FT: 18,000
SALES (est): 9.92MM **Privately Held**
SIC: 8742 1389 5411 Corporation organizing consultant; Servicing oil and gas wells; Convenience stores, chain

(P-20268)
ALTAIS CLINICAL SERVICES (HQ)
601 12th St Fl 16 (94607-3885)
PHONE.............................510 607-4000
Jeffrey Bailet, *CEO*
Nishant Anand, *
Kara Ricci, *
Claire Tamo, *
Robert Van Tuyl, *
EMP: 78 EST: 2020
SALES (est): 112.64MM
SALES (corp-wide): 8.08B **Privately Held**
Web: www.altais.com
SIC: 8742 Management consulting services
PA: California Physicians' Service
601 12th St
Oakland CA
510 607-2000

(P-20269)
ALTRUIST CORP
3030 La Cienega Blvd (90232-7315)
PHONE.............................949 370-5096
EMP: 104 EST: 2008
SALES (est): 7.17MM **Privately Held**
Web: www.altruist.com
SIC: 8742 Financial consultant

(P-20270)
ALVAREZ MRSAL BUS CNSLTING LLC
Also Called: ALVAREZ & MARSAL BUSINESS CONSULTING LLC
2029 Century Park E (90002-3076)
PHONE.............................310 975-2600
Dora Alverez, *Prin*
EMP: 191
SALES (corp-wide): 1.22B **Privately Held**
Web: www.alvarezandmarsal.com
SIC: 8742 Management consulting services
PA: Alvarez & Marsal Corporate Performance Improvement, Llc
600 Madison Ave Fl 8
New York NY
212 759-4433

8742 - Management Consulting Services (P-20293)

(P-20271)
AMCO FOODS INC
601 E Glenoaks Blvd Ste 108 (91207-1760)
PHONE..................818 247-4716
Bobken Amirian, *Pr*
Nick Amirian, *
Brian Polthow, *
Nareg Amirian, *
EMP: 475 **EST:** 1999
SALES (est): 9.89MM **Privately Held**
SIC: 8742 Business management consultant

(P-20272)
AMPM SYSTEMS INC
16520 Harbor Blvd (92708-1360)
PHONE..................949 629-7800
Hirbod Davari, *Prin*
EMP: 75
SALES (est): 1.09MM **Privately Held**
SIC: 8742 Management information systems consultant

(P-20273)
AMPUSH MEDIA INC
450 9th St Fl 2 (94103-4411)
PHONE..................415 638-9663
EMP: 83 **EST:** 2010
SQ FT: 3,000
SALES (est): 12.08MM
SALES (corp-wide): 62.25MM **Privately Held**
SIC: 8742 Marketing consulting services
PA: Tinuiti, Inc.
111 W 33rd St Ste 1510
New York NY
833 846-8484

(P-20274)
AMS VENTURES INC
Also Called: Nichols Research
39055 Hastings St Ste 205 (94538-1599)
PHONE..................301 980-5087
Stephen Zuppas, *CFO*
EMP: 70 **EST:** 2018
SALES (est): 4.74MM **Privately Held**
Web: www.nicholsresearch.com
SIC: 8742 Marketing consulting services

(P-20275)
AMTEX SUPPLY HOLDINGS INC
736 Inland Center Dr (92408-1806)
PHONE..................909 985-8918
EMP: 120
SALES (corp-wide): 17.12MM **Privately Held**
SIC: 8742 Management consulting services
PA: Amtex Supply Holdings, Inc.
544 Lakeview Pkwy Ste 300
Vernon Hills IL
800 766-6676

(P-20276)
ANDRESSEN HRWITZ LSV FUND II L
2865 Sand Hill Rd (94025-7022)
PHONE..................650 798-5800
Alex Immerman, *Pt*
EMP: 580 **EST:** 2020
SALES (est): 19.3MM **Privately Held**
SIC: 8742 Business management consultant

(P-20277)
APEX SITE SOLUTIONS INC
9749 Kent St (95624-2416)
PHONE..................916 685-8619
Kenny Blakeslee, *Pr*
Brooke Blakeslee, *
EMP: 67 **EST:** 2010
SQ FT: 12,100
SALES (est): 11.57MM **Privately Held**
Web: www.apexsitesolutions.com
SIC: 8742 Management consulting services

(P-20278)
APN BUSINESS RESOURCES INC
21418 Osborne St (91304-1520)
PHONE..................818 717-9980
Michael Noori, *CEO*
Khosrow Noori, *
EMP: 85 **EST:** 2011
SALES (est): 15MM **Privately Held**
SIC: 8742 8748 Business planning and organizing services; Business consulting, nec

(P-20279)
ARCHETYPE CONSULTING INC
530 Divisadero St Ste 310 (94117-2213)
PHONE..................888 644-8445
EMP: 84
SALES (corp-wide): 10.14MM **Privately Held**
Web: www.archetypeconsulting.com
SIC: 8742 Financial consultant
PA: Archetype Consulting, Inc.
180 Canal St Ste 600
Boston MA
857 350-4369

(P-20280)
ARTEMIS CONSULTING LLC
Also Called: Artemis Consulting
1012 W Washington St (92103-1808)
PHONE..................619 573-6328
Adam Svoboda, *Managing Member*
▲ **EMP:** 81 **EST:** 2005
SALES (est): 11.71MM **Privately Held**
Web: www.consultartemis.com
SIC: 8742 8741 8748 Management engineering; Administrative management; Systems analysis and engineering consulting services

(P-20281)
ARTIZEN INC
460 City Center Dr (94928-2186)
PHONE..................707 595-5998
Rosanna Hayden, *CEO*
Parker Painter, *
EMP: 250 **EST:** 1991
SALES (est): 9.96MM **Privately Held**
Web: www.artizen.com
SIC: 8742 7371 7363 Management consulting services; Computer software development and applications; Temporary help service

(P-20282)
ASPIREIQ INC
550 Montgomery St Ste 800 (94111-6548)
PHONE..................415 445-3567
Anand Kishore, *CEO*
EMP: 100 **EST:** 2013
SALES (est): 7.06MM **Privately Held**
Web: www.aspire.io
SIC: 8742 Marketing consulting services

(P-20283)
ASSET MKTG SYSTEMS INSUR SVCS
Also Called: AMS
15050 Avenue Of Science Ste 100 (92128-3417)
PHONE..................888 303-8755
Mike Botkin, *CEO*
Dee Costa, *Pr*
Jeff Stemler, *Ex VP*
Louise Kinard Erdman, *CFO*
EMP: 70 **EST:** 2003
SQ FT: 19,000
SALES (est): 16.84MM **Privately Held**
Web: www.assetmarketingsystems.com
SIC: 8742 Marketing consulting services

(P-20284)
AVASANT LLC (PA)
1960 E Grand Ave Ste 1050 (90245-5096)
PHONE..................310 643-3030
Kevin Parikh, *Managing Member*
Robert Randolph, *
EMP: 80 **EST:** 2006
SQ FT: 6,000
SALES (est): 16.77MM
SALES (corp-wide): 16.77MM **Privately Held**
Web: www.avasant.com
SIC: 8742 Marketing consulting services

(P-20285)
AVETA HEALTH SOLUTION INC
3990 Concours Ste 500 (91764-7983)
PHONE..................909 605-8000
Tim O'rourke, *Pr*
Rod St Clair, *Chief Medical Officer*
Marcia Anderson, *
Carol Hairston, *Health Service Vice President*
EMP: 366 **EST:** 2010
SALES (est): 384.16K
SALES (corp-wide): 1.8MM **Privately Held**
SIC: 8742 Hospital and health services consultant
HQ: Innovacare Services Company Llc
6900 Tavistock Lakes Blvd
Orlando FL

(P-20286)
AVISO INC
805 Veterans Blvd Ste 300 (94063-1737)
PHONE..................650 567-5470
K V Rao, *CEO*
Rahul Pathak, *VP*
Mandar Parikh, *VP*
EMP: 60 **EST:** 2011
SALES (est): 8.45MM **Privately Held**
Web: www.aviso.com
SIC: 8742 8748 8732 Marketing consulting services; Business consulting, nec; Business research service

(P-20287)
BAIN & COMPANY INC
1901 Avenue Of The Stars Ste 2000 (90067-6021)
PHONE..................310 229-3000
Kevin Badkoubehi, *Brnch Mgr*
EMP: 85
SALES (corp-wide): 995.84MM **Privately Held**
Web: www.bain.com
SIC: 8742 Business management consultant
PA: Bain & Company, Inc.
131 Dartmouth St Ste 901
Boston MA
617 572-2000

(P-20288)
BAIN & COMPANY INC
415 Mission St Ste 4700 (94105-2604)
PHONE..................415 627-1000
Vernon Altman, *Mgr*
EMP: 164
SALES (corp-wide): 995.84MM **Privately Held**
Web: www.bain.com
SIC: 8742 Business management consultant
PA: Bain & Company, Inc.
131 Dartmouth St Ste 901
Boston MA
617 572-2000

(P-20289)
BARONHR LLC
1005 S Hacienda Blvd (91745-1502)
PHONE..................626 209-8888
EMP: 62
SALES (corp-wide): 50.76MM **Privately Held**
Web: www.baronhr.com
SIC: 8742 Management consulting services
PA: Baronhr, Llc
8101 E Kaiser Blvd
Anaheim CA
714 860-7800

(P-20290)
BARONHR LLC
35 E Romie Ln (93901-3123)
PHONE..................831 272-7980
EMP: 62
SALES (corp-wide): 50.76MM **Privately Held**
Web: www.baronhr.com
SIC: 8742 Human resource consulting services
PA: Baronhr, Llc
8101 E Kaiser Blvd
Anaheim CA
714 860-7800

(P-20291)
BASKETBALL MARKETING CO INC
Also Called: and 1
101 Enterprise Ste 100 (92656-2604)
PHONE..................610 249-2255
Kevin Wulff, *Pr*
▲ **EMP:** 137 **EST:** 2006
SALES (est): 2.26MM
SALES (corp-wide): 2.97B **Publicly Held**
SIC: 8742 Management consulting services
HQ: American Sporting Goods Corp
101 Enterprise Ste 200
Aliso Viejo CA
949 267-2800

(P-20292)
BEACON RESOURCES LLC
17300 Red Hill Ave (92614-5643)
PHONE..................949 955-1773
Mike Kelly, *
EMP: 244 **EST:** 2010
SALES (est): 16.64MM
SALES (corp-wide): 166.95MM **Privately Held**
Web: www.addisongroup.com
SIC: 8742 Business planning and organizing services
HQ: David M. Lewis Company, Llc
20750 Ventura Blvd # 300
Woodland Hills CA

(P-20293)
BENEFITCOMPASS LLC
1 Venture Ste 220 (92618-7413)
PHONE..................949 289-9300
Alison Mccallum, *Prin*
EMP: 62 **EST:** 2014
SALES (est): 586.72K **Privately Held**
SIC: 8742 Planning consultant
PA: Edgewood Partners Insurance Center
1 California St Ste 400
San Francisco CA

8742 - Management Consulting Services (P-20294)

(P-20294)
BERGERSON GROUP
Also Called: Channel Impact
1030 Country Club Dr B (94556-1950)
PHONE.................................925 948-8110
EMP: 70 EST: 2005
SALES (est): 5.87MM Privately Held
Web: www.channel-impact.com
SIC: 8742 Marketing consulting services

(P-20295)
BETTERUP INC (PA)
1200 Folsom St (94103-3817)
PHONE.................................415 862-0708
Alexi Robichaux, CEO
Eduardo Medina, *
Gabriella Rosen Kellerman, *
Ryan Sonnek, Prin
Vinh Le, *
EMP: 223 EST: 2013
SALES (est): 70.01MM
SALES (corp-wide): 70.01MM Privately Held
Web: www.betterup.com
SIC: 8742 Training and development consultant

(P-20296)
BITE COMMUNICATIONS LLC (HQ)
100 Montgomery St Ste 1100 (94104-4388)
PHONE.................................415 365-0222
Tim Dyson, Managing Member
David Dewhurst, Managing Member*
Will Willis, *
Alisa Macdonnell, *
EMP: 75 EST: 1992
SQ FT: 10,000
SALES (est): 26.6MM
SALES (corp-wide): 866.9MM Privately Held
Web: www.biteglobal.com
SIC: 8742 8743 Marketing consulting services; Public relations services
PA: Next 15 Group Plc
60 Great Portland Street
London
203 128-8000

(P-20297)
BLACKSTONE CONSULTING INC (PA)
Also Called: BCI Alabama
11726 San Vicente Blvd Ste 550 (90049-5089)
PHONE.................................310 826-4389
Ronald Joseph Blackstone, Pr
EMP: 71 EST: 1991
SQ FT: 1,500
SALES (est): 49.69MM Privately Held
Web: www.blackstone-consulting.com
SIC: 8742 Management consulting services

(P-20298)
BLANCHARD TRAINING AND DEV INC (PA)
Also Called: Ken Blanchard Companies, The
125 State Pl (92029-1323)
PHONE.................................760 489-5005
Thomas J Mckee, CEO
Howard Farfel, *
Deborah K Blanchard, *
Scott Blanchard, *
▼ EMP: 200 EST: 1978
SALES (est): 61.26MM
SALES (corp-wide): 61.26MM Privately Held
Web: www.blanchard.com

SIC: 8742 Training and development consultant

(P-20299)
BON APPETIT MANAGEMENT CO
1259 E Colton Ave (92374-3755)
PHONE.................................909 748-8970
Bret Martin, Genl Mgr
EMP: 243
SALES (corp-wide): 29.97B Privately Held
Web: www.bamco.com
SIC: 8742 Administrative services consultant
HQ: Bon Appetit Management Co.
201 Rdwood Shres Pkwy Ste
Redwood City CA
650 798-8000

(P-20300)
BRANDED GROUP INC
Also Called: Facilities MGT & Coml RPS Svcs
222 S Harbor Blvd Ste 500 (92805-3702)
PHONE.................................323 940-1444
Mike Kurland, CEO
Kiira Esposito, *
Jerry Jonathan Thomas Iii, Pr
EMP: 218 EST: 2014
SQ FT: 13,372
SALES (est): 11.89MM Privately Held
Web: www.branded-group.com
SIC: 8742 8741 Maintenance management consultant; Construction management

(P-20301)
BRANDWATCH LLC
445 Bush St Fl 8 (94108-3729)
PHONE.................................415 429-5800
EMP: 205
SALES (corp-wide): 934.8MM Privately Held
Web: www.brandwatch.com
SIC: 8742 Marketing consulting services
HQ: Brandwatch Llc
200 Vesey St Fl 19
New York NY
212 229-2240

(P-20302)
BRIDGWTER CONSULTING GROUP INC
18881 Von Karman Ave Ste 1450 (92612-8517)
PHONE.................................949 535-1755
Mark Montgomery, CEO
EMP: 90 EST: 2015
SQ FT: 1,600
SALES (est): 9.41MM Privately Held
Web: www.bridgewcg.com
SIC: 8742 7379 Management consulting services; Online services technology consultants

(P-20303)
BRIOTIX
515 Marin St Ste 318 (91360-4116)
PHONE.................................805 864-2711
EMP: 85 EST: 2016
SALES (est): 510.03K Privately Held
Web: www.briotix.com
SIC: 8742 Management consulting services

(P-20304)
BROWN AND STREZA LLP
40 Pacifica Ste 1500 (92618-7496)
PHONE.................................949 453-2900
Richard Streza, Pr
David Brown, *
EMP: 60 EST: 1979
SQ FT: 1,000

SALES (est): 9.16MM Privately Held
Web: www.brownandstreza.com
SIC: 8742 8111 Business planning and organizing services; General practice attorney, lawyer

(P-20305)
CAERUS MARKETING GROUP LLC
17875 Von Karman Ave Ste 200 (92614-6273)
PHONE.................................877 627-2509
Matt Miller, Pr
Jodee Essensa, *
EMP: 70 EST: 2013
SALES (est): 25MM
SALES (corp-wide): 5.39B Privately Held
SIC: 8742 Marketing consulting services
PA: Syneos Health, Inc.
1030 Sync St
Morrisville NC
919 876-9300

(P-20306)
CAL GOLDEN HEALTHCARE LLC
Also Called: Central Gardens Post Acute
1355 Ellis St (94115-4215)
PHONE.................................415 567-2967
Mark Hancock, Prin
EMP: 69 EST: 2018
SALES (est): 710.65K
SALES (corp-wide): 1.53B Privately Held
SIC: 8742 Business management consultant
PA: Providence Group, Inc.
262 N University Ave
Farmington UT
801 447-9829

(P-20307)
CAPITOL SERVICES INC
3609 Bradshaw Rd Ste H # 343 (95827-3275)
PHONE.................................916 443-0657
Shauna Krause, CEO
EMP: 158 EST: 1982
SALES (est): 3.46MM Privately Held
Web: www.capitolservices.com
SIC: 8742 Industry specialist consultants

(P-20308)
CAPTAIN MARKETING INC
3577 N Figueroa St (90065-2445)
PHONE.................................310 402-9709
EMP: 73
SALES (corp-wide): 9.93MM Privately Held
Web: www.captainmarketing.com
SIC: 8742 Marketing consulting services
PA: Captain Marketing, Inc.
337 Ne Emerson Ave
Bend OR
888 297-9977

(P-20309)
CASHMERE AGENCY INC
5242 W Adams Blvd (90016-2628)
PHONE.................................323 928-5080
Ryan Ford, Pr
Eric Enjem, CFO
EMP: 154 EST: 2021
SALES (est): 3.55MM Privately Held
Web: www.cashmereagency.com
SIC: 8742 Marketing consulting services

(P-20310)
CATALYST GROUP LLC
2285 W Hearn Ave (95407-7377)
PHONE.................................707 527-8551
EMP: 63

SIC: 8742 Management consulting services
PA: Catalyst Group Llc
2945 Griffith St
San Francisco CA

(P-20311)
CATALYST SPEECH LLC
Also Called: Catalyst Spech Lngage Pthology
205 S Broadway Ste 217 (90012-3607)
PHONE.................................213 346-9945
Ji Soo Kim, CEO
EMP: 397 EST: 2015
SALES (est): 635.61K
SALES (corp-wide): 165.05MM Privately Held
SIC: 8742 Hospital and health services consultant
PA: Pediatric Therapy Services, Llc
184 High St Ste 701
Boston MA
800 337-5965

(P-20312)
CELERITY CONSULTING GROUP LLC (PA)
2 Gough St Ste 300 (94103-1215)
PHONE.................................415 986-8850
Rachelle Yowell, CEO
Christopher Yowell, *
Norman Yee, *
Steffani Aranas, *
Christopher Purdy, *
EMP: 61 EST: 2001
SQ FT: 28,000
SALES (est): 14.69MM
SALES (corp-wide): 14.69MM Privately Held
Web: www.consultcelerity.com
SIC: 8742 7371 7379 7375 Management consulting services; Computer software development and applications; Data processing consultant; On-line data base information retrieval

(P-20313)
CERTIFIEDSAFETY INC
Also Called: CERTIFIEDSAFETY, INC.
3070 Bay Vista Courtste B (94510)
PHONE.................................707 747-9400
EMP: 78
SALES (corp-wide): 14.05MM Privately Held
Web: www.carefreeindustries.com
SIC: 8742 Business management consultant
PA: Certifiedsafety, Llc
906 W 13th St
Deer Park TX
281 680-1200

(P-20314)
CHASE GROUP LLC
Also Called: Center At Parkwest, The
6740 Wilbur Ave (91335-5179)
PHONE.................................818 708-3533
Phil Chase, Brnch Mgr
EMP: 295
Web: www.chasegroup.us
SIC: 8742 8049 Management consulting services; Nurses and other medical assistants
PA: The Chase Group Llc
5374 Long Shadow Ct
Westlake Village CA

(P-20315)
CIENCE TECHNOLOGIES INC
548 Market St # 99737 (94104-5401)
PHONE.................................949 424-2906
John Girard, CEO
EMP: 60 EST: 2018

PRODUCTS & SERVICES SECTION **8742 - Management Consulting Services (P-20338)**

SALES (est): 668.91K **Privately Held**
Web: www.cience.com
SIC: 8742 Marketing consulting services

(P-20316)
CITY OF IRVINE
Also Called: Dept of Public Works
6427 Oak Cyn (92618-5202)
P.O. Box 19575 (92623-9575)
PHONE...............................949 724-7600
Allison Hart, Mgr
EMP: 163
Web: www.cityofirvine.org
SIC: 8742 9111 8748 7349 Public utilities consultant; Mayors' office; Business consulting, nec; Building maintenance services, nec
PA: City Of Irvine
1 Civic Center Plz
Irvine CA
949 724-6000

(P-20317)
CITY OF OXNARD (PA)
Also Called: Oxnard City Hall
300 W 3rd St (93030-5729)
PHONE...............................805 385-7803
Doctor Thomas E Holden, Mayor
▲ EMP: 150 EST: 1903
SQ FT: 11,000
SALES (est): 301.04MM
SALES (corp-wide): 301.04MM **Privately Held**
Web: www.oxnard.org
SIC: 8742 Industrial and labor consulting services

(P-20318)
CITY OF RIVERSIDE
5901 Payton Ave (92504-1003)
PHONE...............................951 826-5485
David Wright, Dir
EMP: 65
SALES (corp-wide): 402.47MM **Privately Held**
Web: www.riversideca.gov
SIC: 8742 Business planning and organizing services
PA: City Of Riverside
3900 Main St Fl 7
Riverside CA
951 826-5311

(P-20319)
CLOUD9 ESPORTS INC
Also Called: London Spitfire
2720 Neilson Way Unt 5697 (90405-4060)
PHONE...............................424 256-8391
Jack Etienne, CEO
Tricia Sugita, CMO
EMP: 99 EST: 2016
SALES (est): 2.56MM **Privately Held**
Web: www.cloud9.gg
SIC: 8742 Business management consultant

(P-20320)
CO-PRODUCTION INTL INC
8716 Sherwood Ter (92154-7718)
PHONE...............................619 429-4344
EMP: 2300 EST: 1997
SALES (est): 23MM **Privately Held**
Web: www.co-production.net
SIC: 8742 Marketing consulting services
PA: Co-Production De Tijuana, S.A. De C.V.
Blvd. Carretera Libre Antiguo Camino
Tijuana
Tijuana BCN

(P-20321)
COCKRAM CONSTRUCTION INC
605 8th St (91340-1400)
PHONE...............................818 650-0999
David Judd, Pr
Malcolm W Batten, *
Robert Sirgiovanni, *
Louis E Sciuto, *
Rene Alicea, *
EMP: 315 EST: 2000
SALES (est): 16.79MM **Privately Held**
Web: www.cockram.com
SIC: 8742 8741 1541 Construction project management consultant; Construction management; Food products manufacturing or packing plant construction
HQ: Kajima Cockram International Pty Ltd
Level 2 6 Palmer Parade
Cremorne VIC

(P-20322)
CODA PROJECT INC
888 Villa St Fl 4 (94041-1260)
PHONE...............................561 267-1403
Shishir Samir Mehrotra, CEO
EMP: 74 EST: 2014
SALES (est): 8.48MM **Privately Held**
Web: www.coda.io
SIC: 8742 Management consulting services

(P-20323)
CODE FOR AMERICA LABS INC
Also Called: Code For America
972 Mission St Fl 5 (94103-2994)
PHONE...............................415 816-1286
EMP: 80 EST: 2009
SALES (est): 15.16MM **Privately Held**
Web: www.codeforamerica.org
SIC: 8742 Marketing consulting services

(P-20324)
COLLEGE TRACK
483 9th St (94607-4051)
PHONE...............................510 834-3295
EMP: 191 EST: 1997
SALES (est): 27.54MM **Privately Held**
Web: www.collegetrack.org
SIC: 8742 School, college, university consultant

(P-20325)
CONSUMER RESOURCE NETWORK LLC
Also Called: Launchpad Communications
4420 E Miraloma Ave Ste J (92807-1839)
PHONE...............................800 291-4794
EMP: 340 EST: 1995
SALES (est): 19.49MM **Privately Held**
SIC: 8742 Marketing consulting services

(P-20326)
CONTEMPORARY SERVICES CORP
1821 Marina Blvd (94577-4225)
PHONE...............................650 524-8889
EMP: 1339
SALES (corp-wide): 297.45MM **Privately Held**
SIC: 8742 Industry specialist consultants
HQ: Contemporary Services Corp
100 Alfred Lerner Way
Cleveland OH
718 736-4242

(P-20327)
CONTINUUMGLOBAL INC
1200 Gough St Unit 3a (94109-6613)
PHONE...............................415 685-3301
EMP: 787
SALES (corp-wide): 30.22MM **Privately Held**
Web: www.continuumglobal.com
SIC: 8742 Marketing consulting services
PA: Continuumglobal, Inc.
3723 Haven Ave
Menlo Park CA
415 685-3302

(P-20328)
COOPERATIVE PERSONNEL SERVICES (PA)
Also Called: CPS Hr Consulting
2450 Del Paso Rd Ste 220 (95834-9711)
PHONE...............................916 263-3600
Jerry Greenwell, CEO
Tim Howald, *
EMP: 139 EST: 1985
SQ FT: 34,000
SALES (est): 24.89MM
SALES (corp-wide): 24.89MM **Privately Held**
Web: www.cpshr.us
SIC: 8742 Personnel management consultant

(P-20329)
CORE-MARK INTERNATIONAL INC
Also Called: Core-Mark International
3030 Mulvany Pl (95691-5745)
PHONE...............................916 374-8677
EMP: 65
SALES (corp-wide): 57.25B **Publicly Held**
Web: www.core-mark.com
SIC: 8742 Marketing consulting services
HQ: Core-Mark International, Inc.
1500 Solana Blvd Ste 3400
Westlake TX
650 589-9445

(P-20330)
CORPORATE VISIONS INC
2705 Avenida De Anita Apt 29 (92010-8355)
PHONE...............................760 458-0914
Mark Valle, Prin
EMP: 155
SALES (corp-wide): 28.8MM **Privately Held**
Web: www.corporatevisions.com
SIC: 8742 Marketing consulting services
PA: Corporate Visions Inc
5455 Kietzke Ln
Reno NV
415 464-4400

(P-20331)
COUNTY OF SAN JOAQUIN
7585 Longe St (95206-4940)
P.O. Box 1020 (95201-3120)
PHONE...............................209 472-7127
John Meek, Prin
EMP: 108
SALES (corp-wide): 1.54B **Privately Held**
Web: www.sjgov.org
SIC: 8742 Business planning and organizing services
PA: County Of San Joaquin
44 N San Joaquin St # 374
Stockton CA
209 468-3203

(P-20332)
COVARIO INC
9255 Towne Centre Dr # 600 (92121-3039)
PHONE...............................858 397-1500
EMP: 96
SIC: 8742 Marketing consulting services

(P-20333)
CPE HR INC
9000 W Sunset Blvd Ste 900 (90069-5801)
PHONE...............................310 270-9800
Harold Walt, CEO
Faith Branvold, *
Grace Drulias, *
EMP: 90 EST: 1982
SALES (est): 10.98MM **Privately Held**
Web: www.modernhr.com
SIC: 8742 Human resource consulting services

(P-20334)
CRETELLIGENT INC
11344 Coloma Rd Ste 870 (95670-6308)
PHONE...............................916 288-8177
Anthony Romano, CEO
EMP: 65 EST: 2014
SALES (est): 5.06MM **Privately Held**
Web: www.cretelligent.com
SIC: 8742 Real estate consultant

(P-20335)
CROMETRICS
1112 Sir Francis Drake Blvd (94904-1419)
PHONE...............................415 482-8899
Chris Neumann, Prin
EMP: 75 EST: 2017
SALES (est): 5.6MM **Privately Held**
Web: www.crometrics.com
SIC: 8742 Marketing consulting services

(P-20336)
CROWN GOLF PROPERTIES LP
Also Called: Tustin Ranch Golf Club
12442 Tustin Ranch Rd (92782-1000)
PHONE...............................714 730-1611
Steve Plummer, Mgr
EMP: 241
SALES (corp-wide): 92.11MM **Privately Held**
Web: www.tustinranchgolf.com
SIC: 8742 7997 7992 Business management consultant; Membership sports and recreation clubs; Public golf courses
PA: Crown Golf Properties, Lp
222 N La Salle St # 2000
Chicago IL
312 395-7701

(P-20337)
CYDCOR LLC (PA)
29899 Agoura Rd Ste 100 (91301-2493)
PHONE...............................805 277-5500
Gary Polson, Pr
Ron Nathanson, *
Vera Quinn, *
Jim Majeski, *
Stephen Semprevivo Csgo, Prin
EMP: 69 EST: 1994
SALES (est): 22.73MM
SALES (corp-wide): 22.73MM **Privately Held**
Web: www.cydcor.com
SIC: 8742 Marketing consulting services

(P-20338)
DATAKNOX SOLUTIONS INC
38505 Cherry St Ste A (94560-4700)
PHONE...............................510 673-7070
Ankush Dham, CEO
EMP: 70 EST: 2019
SALES (est): 2.53MM **Privately Held**
Web: www.dataknox.io
SIC: 8742 Business management consultant

8742 - Management Consulting Services (P-20339)

(P-20339)
DCW SERVICES LLC
20500 Denker Ave (90501-1645)
PHONE..................................310 324-3147
EMP: 75 EST: 2021
SALES (est): 2.02MM Privately Held
SIC: 8742 Distribution channels consultant

(P-20340)
DELOITTE CONSULTING LLP
Also Called: Bersin By Deloitte
555 Mission St (94105-0920)
PHONE..................................510 251-4400
Joshua Bersin, Prin
EMP: 141
SALES (corp-wide): 677.45K Privately Held
Web: www.deloittedigital.com
SIC: 8742 Financial consultant
HQ: Deloitte Consulting Llp
30 Rockefeller Plz
New York NY
212 492-4000

(P-20341)
DELOITTE CONSULTING LLP
225 W Santa Clara St (95113-1723)
PHONE..................................212 492-4000
EMP: 125
SALES (corp-wide): 677.45K Privately Held
SIC: 8742 Financial consultant
HQ: Deloitte Consulting Llp
30 Rockefeller Plz
New York NY
212 492-4000

(P-20342)
DEMA CONSULTING & MGT LLC
1000 Apollo Way Ste 165 (95407-5462)
PHONE..................................707 757-5010
EMP: 92 EST: 2021
SALES (est): 2.42MM Privately Held
SIC: 8742 Management consulting services

(P-20343)
DENKEN SOLUTIONS INC
9170 Irvine Center Dr Ste 200
(92618-4614)
PHONE..................................949 630-5263
Rajendra Maddula, CEO
Eddie Gallardo, *
Rajendra Maddula, Dir
EMP: 250 EST: 2010
SQ FT: 4,000
SALES (est): 16.8MM Privately Held
Web: www.denkensolutions.com
SIC: 8742 8748 7371 7361 Management consulting services; Systems analysis and engineering consulting services; Computer software systems analysis and design, custom; Employment agencies

(P-20344)
DEVCOOL INC
7901 Stoneridge Dr Ste 220 (94588-3671)
PHONE..................................408 372-4313
Sandeep Deokule, Pr
EMP: 100 EST: 2006
SALES (est): 9.05MM
SALES (corp-wide): 45.89MM Publicly Held
Web: www.devcool.com
SIC: 8742 Management consulting services
PA: Healthcare Triangle, Inc.
7901 Stoneridge Dr # 220
Pleasanton CA
925 592-1100

(P-20345)
DIAGNOSTIC HEALTH CORPORATION
Also Called: Diagnostic Health Los Angeles
6801 Park Ter (90045-1543)
PHONE..................................310 665-7180
Janet Bateman, Prin
EMP: 192
SALES (corp-wide): 1.81B Privately Held
SIC: 8742 Hospital and health services consultant
HQ: Diagnostic Health Corporation
22 Inverness Pkwy Ste 425
Birmingham AL

(P-20346)
DIGITALTHINK INC (DH)
601 Brannan St (94107-1511)
PHONE..................................415 625-4000
EMP: 250 EST: 1996
SQ FT: 51,000
SALES (est): 40.64MM
SALES (corp-wide): 6.32B Publicly Held
Web: www.andrecoelho.com
SIC: 8742 Marketing consulting services
HQ: Convergys Customer Management Group Inc.
201 E 4th St Bsmt
Cincinnati OH
513 723-6104

(P-20347)
DOUBLE FORTE
351 California St Ste 450 (94104-2426)
PHONE..................................415 863-4900
Lee Mcenany Caraher, Pr
EMP: 63 EST: 2002
SALES (est): 4.54MM Privately Held
Web: www.double-forte.com
SIC: 8742 Marketing consulting services

(P-20348)
DOWLING ADVISORY GROUP
3579 E Foothill Blvd Ste 651 (91107-3119)
PHONE..................................626 319-1369
James Dowling, Owner
EMP: 100 EST: 2010
SALES (est): 2.78MM Privately Held
Web: www.dowlingadvisorygroup.com
SIC: 8742 Business management consultant

(P-20349)
DRAWBRIDGE INC
479 N Pastoria Ave (94085-4112)
PHONE..................................650 513-2323
Kamakshi Sivaramakrishnan, CEO
EMP: 85 EST: 2010
SALES (est): 10.93MM
SALES (corp-wide): 211.91B Publicly Held
SIC: 8742 Marketing consulting services
HQ: Linkedin Corporation
1000 W Maude Ave
Sunnyvale CA
650 687-3600

(P-20350)
EASTERN GOLDFIELDS INC
1660 Hotel Cir N Ste 207 (92108-2803)
PHONE..................................619 497-2555
Michael Mcchesney, CEO
EMP: 218 EST: 1998
SALES (est): 4.83MM Privately Held
Web: www.easterngoldfields.com
SIC: 8742 Management consulting services

(P-20351)
ECG MANAGEMENT CONSULTANT
11512 El Camino Real Ste 200 (92130)
PHONE..................................206 689-2200
EMP: 121 EST: 2019
SALES (est): 5.99MM Privately Held
Web: www.ecgmc.com
SIC: 8742 Business management consultant

(P-20352)
EDELMAN FINANCIAL ENGINES LLC (HQ)
Also Called: Financial Engines
1050 Enterprise Way Ste 300 (94089-1415)
PHONE..................................408 498-6000
Lawrence M Raffone, Pr
John B Bunch, *
Lewis E Antone Junior, Ex VP
Christopher Jones, *
Hamesh Chawla, *
EMP: 170 EST: 1996
SQ FT: 80,995
SALES (est): 260.28MM
SALES (corp-wide): 480.51MM Privately Held
Web: www.edelmanfinancialengines.com
SIC: 8742 6282 6411 Financial consultant; Investment advice; Pension and retirement plan consultants
PA: Financial Engines Edelman, L.P.
6500 Sheridan Dr Ste 110
Buffalo NY
800 706-3916

(P-20353)
EGON ZEHNDER INTERNATIONAL
350 S Grand Ave Ste 3580 (90071-3456)
P.O. Box 27264 (90027-0264)
PHONE..................................213 337-1500
A Daniel Meiland, CEO
EMP: 342 EST: 1987
SQ FT: 4,300
SALES (est): 3.05MM Privately Held
Web: www.egonzehnder.com
SIC: 8742 7361 Personnel management consultant; Executive placement
HQ: Egon Zehnder International Inc.
520 Madison Ave Fl 23
New York NY
212 519-6000

(P-20354)
EK HEALTH SERVICES INC (PA)
992 S De Anza Blvd Ste 101 (95129-2777)
PHONE..................................408 973-0888
Eunhee Kim, Pr
Douglas Benner, CMO
Kerri Wilson, Pr
EMP: 130 EST: 1998
SQ FT: 6,500
SALES (est): 11.95MM
SALES (corp-wide): 11.95MM Privately Held
Web: www.ekhealth.com
SIC: 8742 Hospital and health services consultant

(P-20355)
ENBIO CORP
150 E Olive Ave Ste 114 (91502-1849)
PHONE..................................818 953-9976
Arthur Zenian, CEO
◆ EMP: 142 EST: 2008
SQ FT: 1,500
SALES (est): 11.77MM Privately Held
Web: www.enbiocorp.com
SIC: 8742 Hospital and health services consultant

(P-20356)
END TO END ANALYTICS LLC
2595 E Bayshore Rd Ste 150 (94303)
PHONE..................................650 331-9659
Colin Kessinger, *
Allan Gray, *
Heiko Piper, *
Gianpaolo Callioni, *
EMP: 60 EST: 2005
SQ FT: 3,200
SALES (est): 10.21MM Privately Held
Web: www.accenture.com
SIC: 8742 Business management consultant
HQ: Accenture Inc.
161 N Clark St Ste 1100
Chicago IL
312 693-0161

(P-20357)
ENDORS TOI PBC
Also Called: Western Flower Company
600 F St Ste 3 (95521-6301)
PHONE..................................434 987-0919
Arthur Lichtenberger, CEO
EMP: 60 EST: 2019
SALES (est): 1.56MM Privately Held
SIC: 8742 Business management consultant

(P-20358)
ENERGY EXPERTS INTERNATIONAL
12657 Alcosta Blvd # 470 (94583-4438)
PHONE..................................925 242-0446
Kelley White, Brnch Mgr
EMP: 74
SALES (corp-wide): 43.89MM Privately Held
Web: www.eeintl.com
SIC: 8742 Business management consultant
PA: Energy Experts International
555 Twin Dolphin Dr # 150
Redwood City CA
650 593-4261

(P-20359)
ENGAGE3 INC
501 2nd St (95616-4618)
PHONE..................................530 231-5485
EMP: 90 EST: 2012
SALES (est): 2.82MM Privately Held
Web: www.engage3.com
SIC: 8742 Marketing consulting services

(P-20360)
ENGLEWOOD MARKETING GROUP INC
127 W Jurupa Ave (92316-3510)
PHONE..................................909 875-3649
Jack Tuttle, Pr
EMP: 80
SALES (corp-wide): 160.32MM Privately Held
Web: www.emg-usa.com
SIC: 8742 Marketing consulting services
HQ: Englewood Marketing Group Inc
1471 Partnership Rd
Green Bay WI

(P-20361)
ENTERPRISE EVENTS GROUP INC
950 Northgate Dr Ste 100 (94903-3430)
PHONE..................................415 499-4444
EMP: 150 EST: 1995
SQ FT: 18,000
SALES (est): 29.04MM Privately Held
Web: www.eeginc.com
SIC: 8742 8743 Incentive or award program consultant; Promotion service

PRODUCTS & SERVICES SECTION
8742 - Management Consulting Services (P-20383)

(P-20362)
EOS IT MGT SOLUTIONS INC
30826 Santana St (94544-7060)
PHONE..................................510 600-4188
Adrian Strain, *CEO*
EMP: 570 EST: 2014
SALES (est): 100.8MM
SALES (corp-wide): 31.47MM **Privately Held**
Web: www.eosits.com
SIC: **8742** 7379 7376 Business management consultant; Online services technology consultants; Computer facilities management
PA: Eos It Holdings Limited
105 Culcavy Road
Hillsborough
284 065-1006

(P-20363)
ESSEX NATIONAL SECURITIES LLC
550 Gateway Dr Ste 210 (94558-7578)
PHONE..................................707 258-5000
Stephen Amarante, *Pr*
EMP: 97
Web: www.infinexgroup.com
SIC: **8742** Financial consultant
HQ: Essex National Securities, Llc
538 Preston Ave
Meriden CT

(P-20364)
ETHOS EVENT COLLECTIVE LLC
2269 Chestnut St Ste 260 (94123-2600)
PHONE..................................415 762-9773
EMP: 68
SALES (corp-wide): 753.93K **Privately Held**
SIC: **8742** Management consulting services
PA: Ethos Event Collective, Llc
265 S Federal Hwy Ste 183
Deerfield Beach FL
888 390-4436

(P-20365)
EVA AUTOMATION INC
3945 Freedom Cir Ste 560 (95054-1269)
PHONE..................................650 513-6875
David Liu, *Prin*
EMP: 400 EST: 2014
SALES (est): 11.45MM **Privately Held**
SIC: **8742** Automation and robotics consultant

(P-20366)
EXCEL MANAGED CARE DISA
3840 Watt Ave Bldg C (95821-2640)
PHONE..................................916 944-7185
Brenda Smith, *Pr*
Steve Smetana, *Director Customer Relations*
EMP: 125 EST: 1992
SQ FT: 3,600
SALES (est): 12.92MM
SALES (corp-wide): 3.1B **Privately Held**
Web: www.excelmanagedcare.com
SIC: **8742** Hospital and health services consultant
HQ: Genex Services, Llc
440 E Swedesford Rd Ste 1
Wayne PA
610 964-5100

(P-20367)
EXERTUS FNCL PRTNERS INSUR AGC
830 Hillview Ct Ste 140 (95035-4552)
PHONE..................................408 458-8418
Allan Lorenzo, *Prin*
EMP: 80 EST: 2016
SALES (est): 2.69MM **Privately Held**
Web: www.exertusacademy.com
SIC: **8742** 6411 Financial consultant; Insurance agents, brokers, and service

(P-20368)
EXPITRANS INC
Also Called: Aloha Data Systems
22412 Gilberto Ste B (92688-2179)
PHONE..................................949 650-4600
Scott Vickers, *Pr*
EMP: 62 EST: 2006
SALES (est): 5.03MM **Privately Held**
Web: www.expitrans.com
SIC: **8742** 7389 Management consulting services

(P-20369)
EXPRESSWORKS INTERNATIONAL LLC (PA)
2410 Camino Ramon Ste 167 (94583-4328)
PHONE..................................925 244-0900
Stephen Zaruba, *Managing Member*
EMP: 100 EST: 1984
SQ FT: 12,000
SALES (est): 13.2MM **Privately Held**
Web: www.expressworks.com
SIC: **8742** Marketing consulting services

(P-20370)
EXULT INC
121 Innovation Dr Ste 200 (92617-3094)
P.O. Box 6300 (92658-6300)
PHONE..................................949 856-8800
James C Madden V, *Ch Bd*
Kevin Campbell, *
John Adams, *
Stephen M Unterberger, *Executive Business Model Operations Vice President*
Robert E Ball, *CPO*
EMP: 2424 EST: 1998
SQ FT: 22,000
SALES (est): 86.89MM
SALES (corp-wide): 3.13B **Publicly Held**
Web: www.exult.net
SIC: **8742** Human resource consulting services
HQ: Alight (Us), Llc
200 E Randolph St Ll3
Chicago IL
312 381-1000

(P-20371)
EY-PARTHENON
555 California St Lbby (94104-1503)
PHONE..................................415 486-3600
Mala Bingham, *Mgr*
EMP: 182
SALES (corp-wide): 27.95MM **Privately Held**
Web: www.parthenon.com
SIC: **8742** Business management consultant
HQ: Ey-Parthenon
50 Rowes Wharf
Boston MA

(P-20372)
F2 CONSULTING (PA)
Also Called: F2 Strategy
849 Almar Ave Ste C (95060-5875)
PHONE..................................415 844-0641
Doug Fritz, *CEO*
EMP: 60 EST: 2016
SALES (est): 8.23MM
SALES (corp-wide): 8.23MM **Privately Held**

SIC: **8742** Management consulting services

(P-20373)
FAIRWAY TECHNOLOGIES LLC (PA)
4370 La Jolla Village Dr Ste 500 (92122-1249)
PHONE..................................858 454-4471
Brett Humphrey, *CEO*
EMP: 90 EST: 2002
SALES (est): 9.24MM
SALES (corp-wide): 9.24MM **Privately Held**
Web: www.accenture.com
SIC: **8742** Business management consultant

(P-20374)
FDSI LOGISTICS LLC
Also Called: Fdsi Logistics
27680 Avenue Mentry # 2 (91355-1200)
PHONE..................................818 971-3300
David Kolchins, *VP*
Dee Weller, *
John Hudson, *
EMP: 75 EST: 2000
SALES (est): 24.63MM
SALES (corp-wide): 205.01B **Publicly Held**
SIC: **8742** 4731 Transportation consultant; Freight transportation arrangement
PA: Cardinal Health, Inc.
7000 Cardinal Pl
Dublin OH
614 757-5000

(P-20375)
FERRY INTERNATIONAL LLC
Also Called: Tom Ferry Coaching
6 Hutton Centre Dr Ste 700 (92707)
PHONE..................................888 866-3377
EMP: 82 EST: 2018
SALES (est): 5.72MM **Privately Held**
Web: www.tomferry.com
SIC: **8742** Management consulting services

(P-20376)
FINANCIAL TECH SLTONS INTL INC
Also Called: Ftsi
406 E Huntington Dr Ste 100 (91016-3638)
PHONE..................................818 241-9571
Susan Baird Napier, *CEO*
Susan Baird Napier, *Pr*
John De La Pena, *
EMP: 140 EST: 2000
SALES (est): 38.98MM **Privately Held**
Web: www.ftsius.com
SIC: **8742** Banking and finance consultant

(P-20377)
FIREWOOD MARKETING INC
311 California St Ste 200 (94104-2604)
PHONE..................................415 872-5132
Lanya Zambrano, *Prin*
Juan Zambrano, *Prin*
EMP: 157 EST: 2011
SALES (est): 10.04MM **Privately Held**
Web: www.firewoodmarketing.com
SIC: **8742** Marketing consulting services

(P-20378)
FIRST ALLIED HOLDINGS INC
655 W Broadway Fl 11 (92101-8487)
PHONE..................................800 499-5489
Adam Antoniades, *CEO*
Gregg S Glaser, *CFO*
Tiy Oneal, *COO*
EMP: 76 EST: 2011
SALES (est): 512.03K
SALES (corp-wide): 512.03K **Privately Held**
Web: www.cetera.com
SIC: **8742** Financial consultant
PA: Rcap Holdings, Llc
405 Park Ave Fl 3
New York NY
212 415-6500

(P-20379)
FIRST CAPITOL CONSULTING INC
Also Called: Trusaic
520 S Grand Ave (90071-2655)
PHONE..................................213 382-1115
Robert Sheen, *Pr*
EMP: 73 EST: 1999
SALES (est): 8.87MM **Privately Held**
Web: www.trusaic.com
SIC: **8742** Management consulting services

(P-20380)
FIRSTCALL
1350 Treat Blvd Ste 250 (94597-8802)
PHONE..................................415 781-4300
Todd Lane, *CFO*
EMP: 220
Web: www.firstcallcss.com
SIC: **8742** 7381 Management consulting services; Detective and armored car services
PA: Firstcall
1 Sansome St Ste 3500
San Francisco CA

(P-20381)
FISHERIES RESOURCE VLNTR CORPS
109 Stanford Ln (90740-2533)
PHONE..................................562 596-9261
Thomas J Walsh, *Pr*
EMP: 113 EST: 2011
SALES (est): 2.3MM **Privately Held**
Web: www.frvc.org
SIC: **8742** Business planning and organizing services

(P-20382)
FIVE STARS LOYALTY INC
60 Francisco St (94133-2104)
PHONE..................................860 578-2770
Victor Ho, *CEO*
EMP: 181 EST: 2010
SALES (est): 19.68MM
SALES (corp-wide): 2.67MM **Privately Held**
Web: www.fivestars.com
SIC: **8742** Marketing consulting services
HQ: Sumup Payments Limited
32-34 Great Marlborough Street
London
203 510-0160

(P-20383)
FNI INTERNATIONAL INC
1300 Ethan Way (95825-2211)
PHONE..................................916 643-1400
Bob Taylor, *Mgr*
EMP: 98
SALES (corp-wide): 23.75MM **Privately Held**
SIC: **8742** Financial consultant
PA: Fni International, Inc.
200 N Pacific Coast Hwy
El Segundo CA
310 326-3100

8742 - Management Consulting Services (P-20384)

(P-20384)
FORTUNA BUS MGT CONSULTING INC
Also Called: Fortuna BMC
4926 43rd St Ste 120 (95652-2619)
P.O. Box 2110 (95677-8110)
PHONE..................916 458-0991
Jack R Smith Ii, *Pr*
Steve Hill, *
EMP: 750 **EST:** 2009
SALES (est): 26.56MM **Privately Held**
Web: www.fortunabmc.com
SIC: 8742 7379 8748 Management consulting services; Computer related consulting services; Systems analysis and engineering consulting services

(P-20385)
FOUNDATION LEAD GROUP LLC
Also Called: Doctor Genius
16800 Aston Ste 270 (92606-4839)
PHONE..................877 477-2311
Christopher M Lopez, *Managing Member*
Joseph Alcaraz, *
EMP: 66 **EST:** 2009
SALES (est): 6MM **Privately Held**
Web: www.doctorgenius.com
SIC: 8742 Marketing consulting services

(P-20386)
FPG SERVICES LLC
Also Called: Ovation Fertility
15821 Ventura Blvd Ste 625 (91436-4780)
PHONE..................818 858-1080
EMP: 140 **EST:** 2015
SALES (est): 1.85MM **Privately Held**
SIC: 8742 Management consulting services

(P-20387)
FREDERICK LABS LLC
535 Mission St (94105-2997)
PHONE..................646 738-8303
Josh Mccarter, *CEO*
EMP: 169 **EST:** 2014
SALES (est): 365.63K **Privately Held**
SIC: 8742 Marketing consulting services
HQ: Booker Software, Inc.
  1 Liberty Plz Ste 702
  New York NY
  866 966-9798

(P-20388)
FREEDOM EQUITY GROUP
1500 E Hamilton Ave Ste 215 (95008-0835)
PHONE..................408 340-5672
Ronald Petrinovich, *Prin*
EMP: 60 **EST:** 2013
SALES (est): 2.11MM **Privately Held**
Web: www.freedomequitygroup.com
SIC: 8742 Marketing consulting services

(P-20389)
FRONTRANGE SOLUTIONS INC
490 N Mccarthy Blvd Ste 100 (95035-5118)
PHONE..................408 601-2800
EMP: 383
SIC: 8742 Management consulting services

(P-20390)
GANZ USA LLC
16525 Sherman Way Ste C5 (91406-3753)
PHONE..................818 901-0077
Marilyn Smith, *Brnch Mgr*
EMP: 107
SIC: 8742 5199 Management consulting services; Gifts and novelties
HQ: Ganz U.S.A., Llc
  3855 Shallowford Rd # 220
  Marietta GA

(P-20391)
GAVIN DE BECKER & ASSOC GP LLC
Also Called: Gavin De Becker & Associates
350 N Glendale Ave Ste 517 (91206-3794)
PHONE..................818 505-0177
Gavin De Becker, *Managing Member*
Michael La Fever, *
EMP: 180 **EST:** 1979
SQ FT: 1,600
SALES (est): 39.15MM **Privately Held**
Web: www.gdba.com
SIC: 8742 Business management consultant

(P-20392)
GCORP CONSULTING
2831 Camino Del Rio S Ste 311 (92108)
PHONE..................619 587-3160
Alba Graham, *CEO*
James Graham, *
EMP: 147 **EST:** 2011
SALES (est): 12.32MM **Privately Held**
Web: www.gcorpconsulting.com
SIC: 8742 8711 7379 8243 Management consulting services; Engineering services; Online services technology consultants; Software training, computer

(P-20393)
GEOGRAPHIC SOLUTIONS INC
234 Capitol St Ste A (93901-2600)
PHONE..................831 757-4400
Deane Toler, *Mgr*
EMP: 311
Web: www.geographicsolutions.com
SIC: 8742 Business management consultant
PA: Geographic Solutions, Inc.
  2570 Coral Landings Blvd
  Palm Harbor FL

(P-20394)
GLOBAL RISK MGT SOLUTIONS LLC
5271 California Ave Ste 290 (92617-3222)
PHONE..................949 759-8500
Gerard Smith, *Managing Member*
EMP: 100 **EST:** 2013
SALES (est): 6.94MM **Privately Held**
Web: www.globalrms.com
SIC: 8742 General management consultant

(P-20395)
GOETZMAN GROUP INC
21333 Oxnard St Ste 200 (91367-5194)
PHONE..................818 595-1112
Greg Goetzman, *Pr*
EMP: 90 **EST:** 1998
SALES (est): 7.82MM **Privately Held**
Web: www.goetzmangroup.com
SIC: 8742 8721 Management consulting services; Accounting, auditing, and bookkeeping

(P-20396)
GREENHOUSE AGENCY INC
4100 Birch St Ste 500 (92660-2273)
PHONE..................949 752-7542
Sean Roche, *Prin*
EMP: 224 **EST:** 2012
SALES (est): 6.04MM **Privately Held**
Web: www.greenhouseagency.com
SIC: 8742 Marketing consulting services

(P-20397)
GSL HOLDINGS INC
Also Called: A Development Stage Company
333 S Alameda St Ste 234 (90013-1740)
PHONE..................213 625-2588
Mai Wang, *Ch*
Luis Chang, *
EMP: 64 **EST:** 2002
SALES (est): 2.41MM **Privately Held**
SIC: 8742 Industry specialist consultants

(P-20398)
H&H CATERING LP
111 Pine St (94111-5602)
PHONE..................408 354-1964
Patti Wilson, *Brnch Mgr*
EMP: 88
SALES (corp-wide): 126.46MM **Privately Held**
Web: www.wolfgangpuck.com
SIC: 8742 Human resource consulting services
PA: H&H Catering, L.P.
  6801 Hollywood Blvd
  Los Angeles CA
  323 491-1250

(P-20399)
HAPAG-LLOYD (AMERICA) LLC
180 Grand Ave Ste 1535 (94612-3702)
PHONE..................510 286-1940
Manfred Braun, *Mgr*
EMP: 103
SALES (corp-wide): 35.88B **Privately Held**
Web: www.hapag-lloyd.com
SIC: 8742 4499 Transportation consultant; Marine salvaging and surveying services
HQ: Hapag-Lloyd (America) Llc
  3 Ravinia Dr Ste 1600
  Atlanta GA
  732 562-1800

(P-20400)
HARBOR INDUSTRIES INC
74 W Neal St Ste 102 (94566-6661)
PHONE..................925 461-1366
EMP: 120
SALES (corp-wide): 55.6MM **Privately Held**
Web: www.harbor-ind.com
SIC: 8742 Marketing consulting services
PA: Harbor Industries, Inc.
  14130 172nd Ave
  Grand Haven MI
  616 842-5330

(P-20401)
HARRIS MYCFO INC
2200 Geng Rd Ste 100 (94303-3358)
PHONE..................480 348-7725
Michael Montgomery, *Pr*
EMP: 90 **EST:** 2003
SALES (est): 7.45MM **Privately Held**
SIC: 8742 Financial consultant

(P-20402)
HAWKE MEDIA VENTURES LLC (PA)
2231 S Barrington Ave (90064-1205)
PHONE..................310 451-7295
Erik Huberman, *CEO*
EMP: 202 **EST:** 2013
SALES (est): 9.61MM
SALES (corp-wide): 9.61MM **Privately Held**
Web: www.hawkemedia.com
SIC: 8742 Marketing consulting services

(P-20403)
HEALTHCARE FINANCE DIRECT LLC
1707 Eye St Ste 300 (93301-5208)
PHONE..................661 616-4400
Tyler Johnson, *CEO*
Mark Weighall, *CFO*
EMP: 84 **EST:** 2009
SALES (est): 7.15MM **Privately Held**
Web: www.gohfd.com
SIC: 8742 Financial consultant

(P-20404)
HEIDELBERG INVESTMENT GROUP IN ✪
4957 Onaknoll Ave (90043-1020)
PHONE..................213 884-7747
Laron Heidelberg, *CEO*
Whitney Cornell, *
Paul Heidelberg, *
EMP: 122 **EST:** 2022
SALES (est): 8.7MM **Privately Held**
SIC: 8742 7389 Real estate consultant; Business Activities at Non-Commercial Site

(P-20405)
HP CAPITAL LLC
3111 Camino Del Rio N Ste 400 (92108-5720)
PHONE..................858 753-8486
EMP: 65 **EST:** 2016
SQ FT: 600
SALES (est): 3.98MM **Privately Held**
SIC: 8742 Management consulting services

(P-20406)
HR&A ADVISORS INC
700 S Flower St Ste 2995 (90017-4217)
PHONE..................310 581-0900
George Bogakos, *Brnch Mgr*
EMP: 75
Web: www.hraadvisors.com
SIC: 8742 Business management consultant
PA: Hr&A Advisors, Inc.
  99 Hudson St Rm 3l
  New York NY

(P-20407)
HUMAN RESOURCE CAPITL CONS INC
Also Called: Hrc Consultants
6236 Paseo Colina (92009-2103)
PHONE..................760 518-8816
Anisa D Towns, *Pr*
Pierre A Towns, *
EMP: 142 **EST:** 2003
SALES (est): 424.49K **Privately Held**
Web: www.hrcconsultants.com
SIC: 8742 Training and development consultant
PA: Onyx Global Hr Llc
  110 Pine Ave Ste 920
  Long Beach CA

(P-20408)
HYKSO INC
Also Called: Fightcamp
936 W 17th St (92627-4403)
PHONE..................213 785-3372
Khalil Zahar, *CEO*
EMP: 60 **EST:** 2021
SALES (est): 15.51MM **Privately Held**
Web: www.joinfightcamp.com
SIC: 8742 Business management consultant

(P-20409)
ICF JONES & STOKES INC
1 Ada Ste 100 (92618-5339)
PHONE..................949 333-6600
David Freytag, *Mgr*
EMP: 74
SALES (corp-wide): 1.78B **Publicly Held**
Web: www.icf.com

PRODUCTS & SERVICES SECTION
8742 - Management Consulting Services (P-20432)

SIC: 8742 8748 Business management consultant; Business consulting, nec
HQ: Icf Jones & Stokes, Inc
1902 Reston Metro Plz
Reston VA
703 934-3000

(P-20410)
INDEPENDENT FINCL GROUP LLC
12671 High Bluff Dr Ste 200 (92130-3018)
PHONE.................................858 436-3180
EMP: 106 EST: 2003
SALES (est): 5.71MM **Privately Held**
Web: www.ifgsd.com
SIC: 8742 Financial consultant

(P-20411)
INDUCTIVE AUTOMATION LLC
90 Blue Ravine Rd (95630-4715)
PHONE.................................800 266-7798
Steve Hechtman, Pr
Wendi-lynn Hechtman, VP
Don Pearson, CSO
Katharina Jeschke, CAO
Carl Gould, Dir
EMP: 100 EST: 2011
SALES (est): 30.06MM **Privately Held**
Web: www.inductiveautomation.com
SIC: 8742 5734 Automation and robotics consultant; Computer software and accessories

(P-20412)
INFOSPAN
31878 Del Obispo St Ste 118 (92675-3223)
PHONE.................................949 260-9990
Farooq Bajwa, Pr
P Kyle Moody, *
Rizwan Uraizee, *
Dan Johnson, *
Gregory J White, *
EMP: 750 EST: 2003
SQ FT: 8,000
SALES (est): 12.92MM **Privately Held**
Web: www.ispaninc.org
SIC: 8742 Management consulting services

(P-20413)
INKLING SYSTEMS INC
535 Mission St Fl 14 (94105-3253)
PHONE.................................415 975-4420
Jeff Carr, CEO
Matt Macinnis, *
Charles Macinnis, *
EMP: 66 EST: 2009
SALES (est): 10.19MM **Privately Held**
Web: www.inkling.com
SIC: 8742 Management consulting services
PA: Marlin Equity Partners, Llc
1301 Manhattan Ave
Hermosa Beach CA

(P-20414)
INQUIRING SYSTEMS INC
Also Called: ISI
887 Sonoma Ave Apt 23 (95404-6509)
P.O. Box 2037 (95476-2037)
PHONE.................................707 939-3900
Pamela Campbell, CEO
Pamela Campbell, Pr
Connie Grauds, *
Kurk Marckwald, *
Gil Friend, *
EMP: 72 EST: 1978
SQ FT: 750
SALES (est): 8.36MM **Privately Held**
Web: www.inquiringsystems.org
SIC: 8742 8748 Business management consultant; Environmental consultant

(P-20415)
INTELITY INC
16501 Ventura Blvd (91436-2067)
PHONE.................................310 596-8160
EMP: 61 EST: 2014
SALES (est): 3.87MM **Privately Held**
Web: www.intelity.com
SIC: 8742 General management consultant

(P-20416)
INTRAVAS INC
Also Called: Review Boost
6300 Yarrow Dr (92011-1542)
PHONE.................................760 650-4040
Guillermo Rivas, CEO
EMP: 65 EST: 2007
SALES (est): 5.42MM **Privately Held**
Web: www.reputationboost.com
SIC: 8742 Marketing consulting services

(P-20417)
INVISION COMMUNICATIONS INC (PA)
Also Called: Invision
1280 Civic Dr 3rd Fl (94596-7244)
PHONE.................................925 944-1211
EMP: 90 EST: 1991
SALES (est): 28.8MM **Privately Held**
Web: www.iv.com
SIC: 8742 Management consulting services

(P-20418)
ISLAND GLOBAL HOLDINGS INC
6100 Bandini Blvd (90040-3112)
PHONE.................................301 742-0775
Raymond Landgraf, CEO
EMP: 63 EST: 2016
SALES (est): 2.04MM
SALES (corp-wide): 118.58MM **Privately Held**
SIC: 8742 Retail trade consultant
PA: 4front Ventures Inc
5060 N 40th St Ste 120
Phoenix AZ
312 593-3311

(P-20419)
ISYS SOLUTIONS INC
2601 Saturn St Ste 302 (92821-6702)
P.O. Box 189 (92822-0189)
PHONE.................................714 521-7656
Chris Loumakis, CEO
EMP: 69 EST: 1997
SALES (est): 10MM **Privately Held**
Web: www.isyscm.com
SIC: 8742 Hospital and health services consultant

(P-20420)
JACK NADEL INC (PA)
Also Called: Jack Nadel International
5820 Uplander Way (90230-6608)
P.O. Box 8342 (91109-8342)
PHONE.................................310 815-2600
Jack Nadel, Ch
Craig Nadel, *
Debbie Abergel, *
Craig Reese, *
Steve Widdicombe, *
◆ EMP: 70 EST: 1953
SQ FT: 30,000
SALES (est): 45.5MM
SALES (corp-wide): 45.5MM **Privately Held**
Web: www.nadel.com
SIC: 8742 5199 Marketing consulting services; Advertising specialties

(P-20421)
JETTY MARKETING LLC
1137 57th Ave (94621-4427)
PHONE.................................310 867-9911
EMP: 61 EST: 2018
SALES (est): 2.8MM **Privately Held**
Web: www.jettyextracts.com
SIC: 8742 Management consulting services

(P-20422)
JNR INC
19900 Macarthur Blvd Ste 700 (92612-8416)
PHONE.................................949 476-2788
James Jalet Iii, CEO
Greg Moody, CFO
Luann Jalet, COO
EMP: 60 EST: 1980
SQ FT: 15,000
SALES (est): 12.2MM **Privately Held**
Web: www.jnrcorp.com
SIC: 8742 7389 4724 Incentive or award program consultant; Convention and show services; Tourist agency arranging transport, lodging and car rental

(P-20423)
JUMPSTART DIGITAL MKTG INC (DH)
Also Called: Jumpstart Automotive Media
550 Kearny St Ste 500 (94108-2595)
PHONE.................................415 844-6336
Nick Matarazzo, CEO
EMP: 80 EST: 1996
SQ FT: 3,600
SALES (est): 24.3MM
SALES (corp-wide): 4.29B **Privately Held**
SIC: 8742 7311 Marketing consulting services; Advertising agencies
HQ: Hearst Communications, Inc.
300 W 57th St
New York NY
212 649-2000

(P-20424)
KINGS GARDEN LLC
Also Called: Kings Garden Royal Deliveries
3540 N Anza Rd (92262-1606)
PHONE.................................760 275-4969
Lauri Kibby, Managing Member
Michael King, Managing Member
EMP: 180 EST: 2018
SALES (est): 7.88MM **Privately Held**
Web: www.kingsgarden.com
SIC: 8742 Marketing consulting services

(P-20425)
KINSALE HOLDINGS INC (PA)
Also Called: Validant
388 Market St Ste 860 (94111-5314)
P.O. Box 75 (94104-0075)
PHONE.................................415 400-2600
Patrick Ronan, CEO
John Mcshane, Mng Pt
Kimberly Snyder, *
Sanny Kataoka, *
EMP: 213 EST: 2005
SALES (est): 24.22MM
SALES (corp-wide): 24.22MM **Privately Held**
Web: www.validant.com
SIC: 8742 Management consulting services

(P-20426)
KORN FERRY (US) (HQ)
Also Called: Hay Group
1900 Avenue Of The Stars Ste 2600 (90067-4507)
PHONE.................................310 552-1834
EMP: 250 EST: 1963
SALES (est): 101.24MM
SALES (corp-wide): 2.86B **Publicly Held**
SIC: 8742 Human resource consulting services
PA: Korn Ferry
1900 Avenue Of The Stars # 2600
Los Angeles CA
310 552-1834

(P-20427)
KPC GROUP INC (PA)
9 Kpc Pkwy # 301 (92879-7102)
PHONE.................................951 782-8812
Michael O'brien, Pr
EMP: 167 EST: 2006
SALES (est): 573.02MM **Privately Held**
Web: www.thekpcgroup.com
SIC: 8742 Financial consultant

(P-20428)
KVC GROUP LLC
1551 N Tustin Ave Ste 550 (92705-8637)
PHONE.................................855 438-0377
Kim Vo, Managing Member
EMP: 75 EST: 2018
SALES (est): 2.83MM **Privately Held**
Web: www.corporatefinanceliability.com
SIC: 8742 Marketing consulting services

(P-20429)
KYO AUTISM THERAPY LLC
1155 Broadway St Ste 218 (94063-3127)
PHONE.................................877 264-6747
Melissa Willa, Brnch Mgr
EMP: 239
Web: www.kyocare.com
SIC: 8742 Hospital and health services consultant
PA: Kyo Autism Therapy, Llc
295 89th St Ste 306
Daly City CA

(P-20430)
KYO AUTISM THERAPY LLC
121 Paul Dr (94903-2047)
PHONE.................................877 264-6747
Melissa Willa, Brnch Mgr
EMP: 239
Web: www.kyocare.com
SIC: 8742 Hospital and health services consultant
PA: Kyo Autism Therapy, Llc
295 89th St Ste 306
Daly City CA

(P-20431)
LATENTVIEW ANALYTICS CORP
2540 N 1st St Ste 108 (95131-1016)
PHONE.................................408 493-6653
Venkat Viswanathan, Pr
EMP: 70
Web: www.latentview.com
SIC: 8742 Marketing consulting services
HQ: Latentview Analytics Corporation
5 Independence Way # 418
Princeton NJ

(P-20432)
LBA INC
Also Called: Lba Realty
3333 Michelson Dr Ste 230 (92612-8803)
PHONE.................................949 833-0400
EMP: 73
Web: www.lbarealty.com
SIC: 8742 Real estate consultant
PA: Lba Inc.
3347 Michelson Dr Ste 200
Irvine CA

8742 - Management Consulting Services (P-20433)

(P-20433)
LEADCRUNCH INC
3830 Valley Centre Dr # 705-823 (92130)
PHONE..............................888 708-6649
Olin Hyde, CEO
EMP: 69
SALES (corp-wide): 7.5MM Privately Held
Web: www.getrev.ai
SIC: 8742 Marketing consulting services
PA: Leadcrunch Inc.
750 B St Ste 1630
San Diego CA
888 708-6649

(P-20434)
LEEKILPATRICK MANAGEMENT INC
Also Called: Management Success
324 S Myrtle Ave (91016-2849)
PHONE..............................818 500-9631
Bill Kilpatrick, Pr
EMP: 60 EST: 1993
SQ FT: 18,200
SALES (est): 9.53MM Privately Held
Web: www.driveshops.com
SIC: 8742 7538 Business management consultant; General automotive repair shops

(P-20435)
LEGACY MARKETING GROUP (PA)
5341 Old Redwood Hwy Ste 400 (94954-7127)
PHONE..............................707 778-8638
Lynda R Pitts, CEO
Preston Pitts, *
Chris Eaken, *
Dayna Wells, *
EMP: 215 EST: 1993
SALES (est): 10.73MM Privately Held
Web: www.legacynet.com
SIC: 8742 Marketing consulting services

(P-20436)
LIGHTSPEED MANAGEMENT CO LLC
2200 Sand Hill Rd Ste 100 (94025-6955)
PHONE..............................650 234-8300
EMP: 69 EST: 2005
SALES (est): 1.05MM Privately Held
SIC: 8742 Management consulting services

(P-20437)
LINEA SOLUTIONS INC
4551 Glencoe Ave Ste 140 (90292-7921)
PHONE..............................310 443-4191
Akio Tagawa, Pr
Brian Colker, CFO
EMP: 79 EST: 1999
SALES (est): 10.57MM Privately Held
Web: www.lineasolutions.com
SIC: 8742 Business management consultant

(P-20438)
LINQIA INC
965 Mission St (94103-2921)
PHONE..............................415 913-7179
Nader Alizadeh, CEO
EMP: 100 EST: 2012
SALES (est): 9.87MM Privately Held
Web: www.linqia.com
SIC: 8742 Marketing consulting services

(P-20439)
LIVERAMP INC (HQ)
225 Bush St Fl 17 (94104-4248)
PHONE..............................866 352-3267
Scott Howe, CEO
James Arra, Chief Commercial Officer
Dave Yaffe, Chief Growth Officer
EMP: 717 EST: 2005
SALES (est): 31.76MM
SALES (corp-wide): 596.58MM Publicly Held
Web: www.liveramp.com
SIC: 8742 7374 Marketing consulting services; Data processing service
PA: Liveramp Holdings, Inc.
225 Bush St Ste 1700
San Francisco CA
888 987-6764

(P-20440)
LOLLICUP FRANCHISING LLC
6185 Kimball Ave (91708-9126)
PHONE..............................626 965-8882
Alan Yu, Prin
EMP: 159 EST: 2009
SALES (est): 1.35MM
SALES (corp-wide): 364.24MM Publicly Held
Web: www.lollicupfresh.com
SIC: 8742 5149 Food and beverage consultant; Coffee and tea
PA: Karat Packaging Inc.
6185 Kimball Ave
Chino CA
626 965-8882

(P-20441)
LOTUS WORKFORCE LLC
Also Called: Human Capital Select, LLC
5930 Cornerstone Ct W Ste 300 (92121-3741)
PHONE..............................480 264-0773
Martha White, Pr
EMP: 745 EST: 2012
SALES (est): 1.07MM Privately Held
Web: www.hcselect.com
SIC: 8742 Human resource consulting services
PA: Aya Healthcare, Inc.
5930 Cornerstone Ct W # 3
San Diego CA

(P-20442)
LPL HOLDINGS INC (HQ)
Also Called: Lpl Holdings
4707 Executive Dr (92121-3091)
PHONE..............................858 450-9606
Mark Casady, Ch
EMP: 90 EST: 1989
SALES (est): 619.96MM Publicly Held
Web: www.lpl.com
SIC: 8742 Financial consultant
PA: Lpl Financial Holdings Inc.
4707 Executive Dr
San Diego CA

(P-20443)
LTA RESEARCH & EXPLORATION LLC (PA)
642 N Pastoria Ave (94085-3521)
P.O. Box 2048 (94042-2048)
PHONE..............................408 396-0577
Alan Weston, CEO
EMP: 77 EST: 2014
SALES (est): 45.41MM
SALES (corp-wide): 45.41MM Privately Held
Web: www.ltaresearch.com
SIC: 8742 3721 New products and services consultants; Research and development on aircraft by the manufacturer

(P-20444)
M F SALTA CO INC (PA)
Also Called: Atlas Advertising
20 Executive Park Ste 150 (92614-4732)
PHONE..............................562 421-2512
Mike Salta, Pr
James Smith, *
EMP: 70 EST: 1959
SALES (est): 2.38MM
SALES (corp-wide): 2.38MM Privately Held
SIC: 8742 Management consulting services

(P-20445)
MAGICLINKS INC
361 Vernon Ave Ste 6 (90291-8648)
PHONE..............................626 808-2215
Brian Nickerson, Prin
EMP: 72 EST: 2019
SALES (est): 10.49MM Privately Held
Web: www.magiclinks.com
SIC: 8742 Marketing consulting services

(P-20446)
MANAGEMENT TRUST ASSN INC
12607 Hiddencreek Way Ste R (90703-2146)
PHONE..............................562 926-3372
Christie Alviso, Admn
EMP: 145
Web: www.managementtrust.com
SIC: 8742 8741 Management consulting services; Business management
PA: The Management Trust Association Inc
15661 Red Hill Ave # 201
Tustin CA

(P-20447)
MANIFOLD LLC
Also Called: Manifold
531 Howard St Fl 3 (94105-3036)
PHONE..............................415 978-9500
Brian Mullin, Pt
EMP: 92 EST: 2010
SQ FT: 2,000
SALES (est): 1.4MM Privately Held
Web: www.wearemanifold.com
SIC: 8742 7311 Marketing consulting services; Advertising consultant

(P-20448)
MAPP DIGITAL US LLC
4660 La Jolla Village Dr Ste 100 (92122-4625)
PHONE..............................619 342-4340
Steve Warren, CEO
Jonah Sulak, *
Cody Kase, *
Eric Hinkle, *
Juhan Lee, *
EMP: 308 EST: 2000
SALES (est): 50MM Privately Held
Web: www.mapp.com
SIC: 8742 Marketing consulting services
PA: Marlin Equity Partners, Llc
1301 Manhattan Ave
Hermosa Beach CA

(P-20449)
MARCUS EVANS INC
13520 Evening Creek Dr N Ste 370 (92128-8105)
PHONE..............................858 679-1275
David Mc Carthy, Mgr
EMP: 68
SALES (corp-wide): 2.12MM Privately Held
Web: www.marcusevans.com
SIC: 8742 Business management consultant
HQ: Marcus Evans Inc.
455 N Cityfront Plaza Dr # 900
Chicago IL

(P-20450)
MARKETBRIDGE CORP
Also Called: MARKETBRIDGE CORP.
601 Montgomery St Ste 650 (94111-2608)
PHONE..............................240 752-1800
Ashok Nayyar, Brnch Mgr
EMP: 96
Web: www.market-bridge.com
SIC: 8742 Marketing consulting services
PA: Marketbridge Llc
3 Bethesda Metro Ctr # 95
Bethesda MD

(P-20451)
MARKETERHIRE LLC
660 4th St (94107-1618)
PHONE..............................312 870-0008
EMP: 110 EST: 2018
SALES (est): 738.26K Privately Held
Web: www.marketerhire.com
SIC: 8742 Marketing consulting services

(P-20452)
MARKETING PRACTICE INC
Also Called: The Marketing Practice Inc
101 Broadway (94607-3745)
PHONE..............................415 793-8370
EMP: 98
SALES (corp-wide): 12.6MM Privately Held
Web: www.themarketingpractice.com
SIC: 8742 Marketing consulting services
PA: The Marketing Practice Inc
2231 1st Ave
Seattle WA
206 792-5544

(P-20453)
MARKSYS LLC
3725 Cincinnati Ave Ste 200 (95765-1220)
PHONE..............................916 745-4883
EMP: 60 EST: 2012
SQ FT: 45,000
SALES (est): 34MM Privately Held
Web: www.themarksys.com
SIC: 8742 Marketing consulting services

(P-20454)
MARKSYS HOLDINGS LLC
3725 Cincinnati Ave Ste 200 (95765-1220)
PHONE..............................916 745-4883
Tabrez Rajani, Managing Member
EMP: 60 EST: 2018
SALES (est): 2.36MM Privately Held
SIC: 8742 Marketing consulting services

(P-20455)
MARS & CO CONSULTING LLC
600 Montgomery St Ste 1500 (94111-2801)
PHONE..............................415 288-6970
EMP: 181
Web: www.marsandco.com
SIC: 8742 Management consulting services
PA: Mars & Co. Consulting Llc
124 Mason St Ste 1
Greenwich CT

(P-20456)
MATT CONSTRUCTION CORPORATION (PA)
9814 Norwalk Blvd Ste 100 (90670-2997)
PHONE..............................562 903-2277
Paul J Matt, CEO
Steve F Matt, *
Alan B Matt, *
EMP: 108 EST: 1991
SQ FT: 21,000
SALES (est): 38.53MM Privately Held
Web: www.mattconstruction.com

PRODUCTS & SERVICES SECTION
8742 - Management Consulting Services (P-20479)

SIC: 8742 Construction project management consultant

(P-20457)
MCCLELLAN BUSINESS PARK LLC
Also Called: Mp Holdings
3140 Peacekeeper Way (95652-2508)
PHONE...................916 965-7100
Frank Myers, *
Jay Hecklivenly, *
Alan Hersh, *
Debra Compton, *
EMP: 99 EST: 1999
SQ FT: 22,000
SALES (est): 16.97MM **Privately Held**
Web: www.mcclellanpark.com
SIC: 8742 Real estate consultant

(P-20458)
MCINTYRE
14680 Wicks Blvd (94577-6716)
PHONE...................510 614-5890
Jo Farsight, Owner
EMP: 96 EST: 2019
SALES (est): 6.56MM **Privately Held**
SIC: 8742 Manufacturing management consultant

(P-20459)
MCKINSEY & COMPANY INC
555 California St Ste 4700 (94104-1779)
PHONE...................415 981-0250
Gary Pinkus, Mgr
EMP: 300
SALES (corp-wide): 2.98B **Privately Held**
Web: www.mckinsey.com
SIC: 8742 Business management consultant
PA: Mckinsey & Company, Inc.
3 World Trade Ctr
New York NY
212 446-7000

(P-20460)
MDH NETWORK INC
7239 Washington Ave (90602-1420)
PHONE...................562 945-4576
EMP: 101 EST: 2020
SALES (est): 6.44MM **Privately Held**
Web: www.mdhnetwork.com
SIC: 8742 Management consulting services

(P-20461)
MEDAMERICA INC (HQ)
2100 Powell St Ste 900 (94608-1844)
PHONE...................510 350-2600
EMP: 100 EST: 1975
SALES (est): 21.25MM
SALES (corp-wide): 500MM **Privately Held**
Web: www.medamerica.com
SIC: 8742 Hospital and health services consultant
PA: Cep America-California
2100 Powell St Ste 400
Emeryville CA
510 350-2700

(P-20462)
MEDICAL MANAGEMENT CONS INC
Also Called: MMC
6046 Cornerstone Ct W (92121-4758)
PHONE...................858 587-0609
Mister Rahmani, Mgr
EMP: 4950
SALES (corp-wide): 39.85MM **Privately Held**
Web: www.mmchr.com

SIC: 8742 Hospital and health services consultant
PA: Medical Management Consultants, Inc.
8150 Beverly Blvd
Los Angeles CA
310 659-3835

(P-20463)
MEDICAL SPC MANAGERS INC
Also Called: Medical Specialty Billing
1 City Blvd W Ste 1100 (92868-3647)
PHONE...................714 571-5000
Matt Haberman, CEO
Barry Haberman, *
Uri Klugman, *
Monica Bahr, *
Randy Brooks, *
EMP: 115 EST: 1990
SQ FT: 29,000
SALES (est): 17.71MM **Privately Held**
Web: www.msmhealth.com
SIC: 8742 8721 Hospital and health services consultant; Billing and bookkeeping service

(P-20464)
MERCER (US) INC
17901 Von Karman Ave Ste 1100 (92614-6297)
PHONE...................949 222-1300
Kathy Spear, Mgr
EMP: 75
SALES (corp-wide): 20.72B **Publicly Held**
Web: www.mercer.com
SIC: 8742 Compensation and benefits planning consultant
HQ: Mercer (Us) Inc.
1166 Ave Of The Amrcas Fl
New York NY
212 345-7000

(P-20465)
MERIDIAN KNWLDGE SOLUTIONS LLC (DH)
Also Called: Meridian
80 Iron Point Cir Ste 100 (95630-8592)
PHONE...................916 985-9625
Jonna Ward, CEO
EMP: 74 EST: 2006
SQ FT: 9,000
SALES (est): 13.99MM **Privately Held**
Web: www.meridianks.com
SIC: 8742 Training and development consultant
HQ: Visionary Integration Professionals, Llc
80 Iron Point Cir Ste 100
Folsom CA
916 985-9625

(P-20466)
MESMERIZE LLC
Also Called: Brite Media
350 Frank H Ogawa Plz Ste 310 (94612-2084)
PHONE...................415 374-8298
EMP: 106
Web: www.mesmerize.com
SIC: 8742 Sales (including sales management) consultant
PA: Mesmerize, Llc
505 8th Ave
New York NY

(P-20467)
METRIC THEORY LLC
311 California St Ste 200 (94104-2604)
PHONE...................415 659-8600
EMP: 62 EST: 2013
SALES (est): 4.54MM **Privately Held**
Web: www.metrictheory.com

SIC: 8742 Marketing consulting services

(P-20468)
METROSTUDY INC
Also Called: Zonda Intelligence
4000 Macarthur Blvd Ste 40 (92660-2543)
PHONE...................714 619-7800
Jeff Meyers, CEO
Diana Stewart, *
EMP: 184 EST: 2013
SALES (est): 19.88MM **Privately Held**
Web: www.zondahome.com
SIC: 8742 7379 Real estate consultant; Computer related consulting services

(P-20469)
MF SERVICES COMPANY LLC (HQ)
4350 Von Karman Ave Ste 400 (92660-2007)
PHONE...................949 474-5800
Paul Merage, Managing Member
EMP: 60 EST: 2005
SALES (est): 7.89MM
SALES (corp-wide): 25.45MM **Privately Held**
SIC: 8742 Financial consultant
PA: Mig Capital, Llc
660 Nwport Ctr Dr Ste 13
Newport Beach CA
949 474-5800

(P-20470)
MGID INC
1149 3rd St Ste 210 (90403-7201)
PHONE...................424 322-8059
Ben Artikov, Acctnt
EMP: 91 EST: 2011
SALES (est): 1.87MM **Privately Held**
Web: www.mgid.com
SIC: 8742 Marketing consulting services

(P-20471)
MICHAELSON CONNOR & BOUL (PA)
5312 Bolsa Ave (92649-1062)
PHONE...................714 230-3600
EMP: 100 EST: 1994
SQ FT: 12,500
SALES (est): 12.95MM **Privately Held**
Web: www.mcbreo.com
SIC: 8742 Real estate consultant

(P-20472)
MINDLANCE INC
Also Called: MINDLANCE INC.
10679 Westview Pkwy Fl 2 (92126-2961)
PHONE...................858 433-9298
EMP: 1735
SALES (corp-wide): 198.49MM **Privately Held**
Web: www.mindlance.com
SIC: 8742 Human resource consulting services
PA: Mindlance, Inc.
1095 Morris Ave Ste 101
Union NJ
201 386-5400

(P-20473)
MODERN HR INC
7590 N Glenoaks Blvd (91504-1011)
PHONE...................877 842-4988
Dana Holmes, Prin
EMP: 95 EST: 2019
SALES (est): 4.42MM **Privately Held**
Web: www.modernhr.com
SIC: 8742 Business planning and organizing services

(P-20474)
MODSQUAD INC (PA)
Also Called: Metaverse Mod Squad
1300 S St Ste B (95811-7142)
PHONE...................916 913-4465
Amelia Pritchard, CEO
Michael Pinkerton, COO
Amy Kennedy, CMO
EMP: 245 EST: 2009
SALES (est): 21.85MM **Privately Held**
Web: www.modsquad.com
SIC: 8742 7389 Management consulting services; Telephone answering service

(P-20475)
MORRIS & WILLNER PARTNERS
Also Called: Mw Partners
2151 Michelson Dr Ste 185 (92612-1371)
PHONE...................949 705-0682
Divya Pyreddy, CEO
EMP: 100 EST: 2010
SALES (est): 7.18MM **Privately Held**
Web: www.mwpartners.net
SIC: 8742 Management consulting services

(P-20476)
MOTOROLA GOOD TECHNOLOGY GROUP
101 Redwood Shores Pkwy Ste 400 (94065-1176)
PHONE...................408 327-6000
Christy Wyatt, CEO
EMP: 60 EST: 2011
SALES (est): 545.65K **Privately Held**
SIC: 8742 Marketing consulting services

(P-20477)
MUNISERVICES LLC (DH)
Also Called: Avenu Muniservices
7625 N Palm Ave Ste 108 (93711-5785)
PHONE...................800 800-8181
Steve Roberts, Pr
Doug Jensen, *
EMP: 113 EST: 1978
SQ FT: 16,000
SALES (est): 22.25MM
SALES (corp-wide): 95.06MM **Privately Held**
Web: www.avenuinsights.com
SIC: 8742 Industry specialist consultants
HQ: Avenu Insights & Analytics, Llc
555 Madison Ave Fl 16
New York NY
757 519-9300

(P-20478)
MUTH MACHINE WORKS
4510 Rutile St (92509-2649)
PHONE...................951 685-1521
Dwayne Gleason, Mgr
EMP: 80
SALES (corp-wide): 54.49MM **Privately Held**
SIC: 8742 Manufacturing management consultant
HQ: Muth Machine Works
8042 Katella Ave
Stanton CA

(P-20479)
MV MEDICAL MANAGEMENT
1860 Colorado Blvd Ste 200 (90041)
PHONE...................323 257-7637
Eva Vargas, Pr
Evy Vargas, *
Alma Moreno, *
EMP: 60 EST: 1996
SQ FT: 7,400
SALES (est): 5.66MM **Privately Held**
Web: www.mvmedical.com

8742 - Management Consulting Services (P-20480)

SIC: **8742** Marketing consulting services

(P-20480)
MYERS-BRIGGS COMPANY (PA)
185 N Wolfe Rd (94086-5212)
PHONE.................650 969-8901
Jeffrey Hayes, *CEO*
Carl Thoresen, *
Jeffrey Hayes, *Pr*
Andrew Bell, *
Calvin W Finch, *
EMP: 100 **EST:** 1956
SQ FT: 16,000
SALES (est): 25.14MM
SALES (corp-wide): 25.14MM **Privately Held**
Web: status.themyersbriggs.com
SIC: **8742** 5999 Management consulting services; Educational aids and electronic training materials

(P-20481)
MYTHIC INC
333 Twin Dolphin Dr Ste 300 (94065-1449)
PHONE.................734 707-7339
Paul Lopez, *Dir Fin*
EMP: 91
SALES (corp-wide): 17.32MM **Privately Held**
Web: www.mythic.ai
SIC: **8742** Management consulting services
PA: Mythic Inc.
   1905 Kramer Ln Ste A200
   Austin TX
   650 388-0824

(P-20482)
NATIONAL CLEARING CORPORATION (PA)
Also Called: J B Oxford & Co
9665 Wilshire Blvd (90212-2340)
PHONE.................310 385-2165
Christopher Garrett, *Pr*
EMP: 70 **EST:** 2003
SQ FT: 20,400
SALES (est): 4.14MM
SALES (corp-wide): 4.14MM **Privately Held**
SIC: **8742** Financial consultant

(P-20483)
NATIONSBENEFITS LLC
1540 Scenic Ave (92626-1408)
PHONE.................877 439-2665
EMP: 95
SALES (corp-wide): 125.57MM **Privately Held**
Web: www.nationsbenefits.com
SIC: **8742** 6371 6411 Management consulting services; Pension, health, and welfare funds; Insurance agents, brokers, and service
PA: Nationsbenefits, Llc
   1700 N University Dr
   Plantation FL
   877 439-2665

(P-20484)
NBC CONSULTING INC
Also Called: Pacific Health and Welness
2110 Artesia Blvd Ste 323 (90278-3073)
PHONE.................310 798-5000
Neal M Bychek, *Pr*
Robin Bychek, *
EMP: 100 **EST:** 2004
SALES (est): 1MM **Privately Held**
Web: www.nbc-consulting.com
SIC: **8742** Hospital and health services consultant

(P-20485)
NCOMPASS INTERNATIONAL LLC
Also Called: Ncompass International
12101 Crenshaw Blvd Ste 800 (90250-3458)
PHONE.................323 785-1700
Donna Direnzo Graves, *Pr*
Kae Erickson, *
EMP: 138 **EST:** 2003
SALES (est): 24.53MM **Privately Held**
Web: www.ncompassonline.com
SIC: **8742** Marketing consulting services

(P-20486)
NEARDATA INC
Also Called: Neardata Systems
3730 Park Pl (91020-1623)
PHONE.................818 249-2469
Samuel S Chilingurian, *Pr*
EMP: 76 **EST:** 2005
SALES (est): 4.03MM **Privately Held**
Web: www.neardata.net
SIC: **8742** 7371 Management consulting services; Computer software development

(P-20487)
NEW AMERICA FUNDING LLC
Also Called: New American Funding
3558 Round Barn Blvd Ste 200 (95403-1780)
PHONE.................707 392-4254
EMP: 71
Web: www.newamericanfunding.com
SIC: **8742** 6162 Financial consultant; Bond and mortgage companies
PA: New American Funding, Llc
   14511 Myford Rd Ste 100
   Tustin CA

(P-20488)
NORTHBOUND LLC
961 E Arques Ave (94085-4521)
PHONE.................408 333-9780
Hetel Mehta, *Managing Member*
Leena Menon, *Managing Member*
EMP: 128 **EST:** 2003
SQ FT: 20,000
SALES (est): 12.29MM **Privately Held**
Web: www.northboundllc.com
SIC: **8742** Management information systems consultant

(P-20489)
NORTHGATE GONZALEZ INC
425 S Soto St (90033-4315)
PHONE.................323 262-0595
Estela Gonz Lez De Ortiz, *Prin*
EMP: 394
SALES (corp-wide): 512.69MM **Privately Held**
Web: www.northgatemarket.com
SIC: **8742** 5411 Marketing consulting services; Grocery stores
PA: Northgate Gonzalez, Inc.
   1201 N Magnolia Ave
   Anaheim CA
   714 778-3784

(P-20490)
NVE INC
912 N La Cienega Blvd 2nd Fl (90069-4848)
PHONE.................323 512-8400
Brett Nathan Hyman, *CEO*
EMP: 100 **EST:** 2005
SALES (est): 10.71MM **Privately Held**
Web: www.experiencenve.com

SIC: **8742** Marketing consulting services

(P-20491)
OCTAGON INC
1840 Century Park E Ste 200 (90067-2101)
PHONE.................310 967-2473
EMP: 191
SALES (corp-wide): 10.93B **Publicly Held**
Web: www.octagon.com
SIC: **8742** Marketing consulting services
HQ: Octagon, Inc.
   290 Harbor Dr Fl 3
   Stamford CT
   203 354-7400

(P-20492)
ODME SOLUTIONS LLC
1963 Christy Ln (92014-2239)
PHONE.................619 227-0059
EMP: 90 **EST:** 2012
SALES (est): 7.01MM **Privately Held**
Web: www.odmesolutions.com
SIC: **8742** 8748 7389 Management consulting services; Business consulting, nec; Business Activities at Non-Commercial Site

(P-20493)
OMEGA WASTE MANAGEMENT INC
Also Called: Omega Management Services
957 Colusa St (96021-2224)
P.O. Box 495 (96021-0495)
PHONE.................530 824-1890
Robert O'conner, *Pr*
Karen O'conner, *VP*
Dan O'connor, *VP*
EMP: 68 **EST:** 1989
SQ FT: 6,000
SALES (est): 9.35MM **Privately Held**
Web: www.omegawaste.com
SIC: **8742** Management consulting services

(P-20494)
ONE HEART WORLDWIDE
Also Called: One H.E.A.R.T.
8141 El Extenso Ct (92119-1134)
PHONE.................415 379-4762
David Murphy, *CEO*
Arlene Samen, *
Toshiko Dignam, *
Julie Dargis, *
Sibylle Kristensen, *
EMP: 85 **EST:** 2006
SALES (est): 2.28MM **Privately Held**
Web: www.oneheartworldwide.org
SIC: **8742** Training and development consultant

(P-20495)
ONLINE MARKETING GROUP LLC
Also Called: Zoek
530 Technology Dr Ste 100 (92618-1350)
PHONE.................888 737-9635
Samuel Riemer, *CEO*
Doug Powell, *
EMP: 106 **EST:** 2015
SALES (est): 7.7MM **Privately Held**
Web: www.gozoek.com
SIC: **8742** Marketing consulting services

(P-20496)
OPEN UP RESOURCES
Also Called: K12 Oer Collaborative, The
1600 El Camino Real Ste 155 (94025)
PHONE.................650 450-3445
Larry Singer, *CEO*
EMP: 72 **EST:** 2017

SALES (est): 15.04MM **Privately Held**
Web: www.openupresources.org
SIC: **8742** Business planning and organizing services

(P-20497)
OPERAM INC
1041 N Formosa Ave 500 (90046-6703)
PHONE.................855 673-7261
Johnny Wong, *Prin*
EMP: 84 **EST:** 2015
SQ FT: 23,000
SALES (est): 9.44MM **Privately Held**
Web: www.operam.com
SIC: **8742** Marketing consulting services

(P-20498)
P K B INVESTMENTS INC
Also Called: Home Instead Senior Care
745 E Locust Ave Ste 105 (93720-3000)
PHONE.................559 243-1224
David Phillips, *Pr*
Patrick Cavanaugh, *
April Cavanaugh, *
EMP: 140 **EST:** 1995
SALES (est): 8.22MM **Privately Held**
Web: www.homeinstead.com
SIC: **8742** 8322 Management consulting services; Individual and family services

(P-20499)
PACIFIC SECURED EQUITIES INC
Also Called: Intercare Holdings Insur Svcs
6020 West Oaks Blvd Ste 100 (95765-5472)
P.O. Box 579 (95661-0579)
PHONE.................916 677-2500
EMP: 300 **EST:** 1994
SQ FT: 21,000
SALES (est): 25.71MM **Privately Held**
SIC: **8742** Administrative services consultant

(P-20500)
PANDORA MARKETING LLC
Also Called: Timeshare Compliance
26970 Aliso Viejo Pkwy Ste 150 (92656-2621)
PHONE.................800 705-6856
EMP: 75 **EST:** 2016
SALES (est): 8.53MM **Privately Held**
Web: www.timesharecompliance.com
SIC: **8742** Marketing consulting services

(P-20501)
PARA SEMPRE INC
11322 Idaho Ave Ste 202 (90025-3170)
P.O. Box 45 (90406-0045)
PHONE.................310 444-0555
Tahj Zeekvrotzkii, *CEO*
EMP: 74 **EST:** 2021
SALES (est): 1.65MM **Privately Held**
SIC: **8742** Management consulting services

(P-20502)
PATHOLOGY INC
19951 Mariner Ave Ste 150 (90503-1738)
PHONE.................310 769-0561
EMP: 356
Web: www.pathologyinc.com
SIC: **8742** 8071 Hospital and health services consultant; Medical laboratories

(P-20503)
PENSINMARK RTIREMENT GROUP LLC
24 E Cota St Ste 200 (93101-1665)
PHONE.................805 456-6260
Troy G Hammond, *Managing Member*

PRODUCTS & SERVICES SECTION
8742 - Management Consulting Services (P-20527)

EMP: 132 EST: 2008
SALES (est): 1.81MM **Privately Held**
Web: www.pensionmark.com
SIC: 8742 Financial consultant

(P-20504)
PERMANENTE FEDERATION LLC
1 Kaiser Plz 27th Fl (94612-3610)
PHONE..................510 625-6920
Cal James, *CEO*
Claire Tamo, *CFO*
Nancy Gin, *Executive Vice President COS*
Edward Lee, *CIO*
EMP: 80 EST: 1997
SQ FT: 18,663
SALES (est): 7.26MM **Privately Held**
Web: www.permanente.org
SIC: 8742 Management consulting services

(P-20505)
PHENOMENON MKTG & ENTRMT LLC (PA)
5900 Wilshire Blvd Fl 28 (90036-5013)
PHONE..................323 648-4000
EMP: 60 EST: 2006
SQ FT: 15,289
SALES (est): 16.2MM **Privately Held**
Web: www.phenomenon.com
SIC: 8742 Marketing consulting services

(P-20506)
PHOENIX AMERICAN INCORPORATED (PA)
125 E Sir Francis Drake Blvd Ste 301 (94939-1860)
PHONE..................415 485-4500
Gus Constantin, *Ch Bd*
Lisa A Olsen, *
Andrew N Gregson, *
EMP: 100 EST: 1972
SQ FT: 60,000
SALES (est): 46.59MM
SALES (corp-wide): 46.59MM **Privately Held**
Web: www.phxa.com
SIC: 8742 Financial consultant

(P-20507)
PHYSICIANS DATATRUST INC
17215 Studebaker Rd Ste 220 (90703-2548)
PHONE..................562 860-8771
Marla Lease, *Mgr*
EMP: 125
SALES (corp-wide): 9.24MM **Privately Held**
Web: www.pdtrust.com
SIC: 8742 Hospital and health services consultant
PA: Physicians Datatrust, Inc.
161 Thunder Dr Ste 212
Vista CA
760 941-7309

(P-20508)
PLUG CONNECTION LLC
3742 Blue Bird Canyon Rd (92084-7432)
PHONE..................760 631-0992
Ken Altman, *Managing Member*
EMP: 106 EST: 2016
SALES (est): 2.6MM **Privately Held**
Web: www.plugconnection.com
SIC: 8742 Business management consultant

(P-20509)
PMCS GROUP INC
2600 E Pacific Coast Hwy Ste 160 (90804)
PHONE..................562 498-0808
Walid Azar, *Pr*
Violene Azar, *
Walid Azar, *VP*
EMP: 100 EST: 2005
SALES (est): 7.97MM **Privately Held**
Web: www.pmcsgroup.net
SIC: 8742 Construction project management consultant

(P-20510)
POSTALIO INC
75 Higuera St Ste 240 (93401-5425)
PHONE..................408 616-9284
Erik Kostelnik, *CEO*
EMP: 72 EST: 2019
SALES (est): 3.56MM **Privately Held**
Web: www.postal.com
SIC: 8742 5734 7372 Marketing consulting services; Software, business and non-game ; Business oriented computer software

(P-20511)
POWER DIGITAL MARKETING INC (PA)
2251 San Diego Ave Ste A250 (92110-2927)
PHONE..................619 501-1211
Grayson Lafrenz, *CEO*
Sasha Dagayev, *Ex VP*
Corey Eulas, *CSO*
EMP: 340 EST: 2012
SALES (est): 89.21MM
SALES (corp-wide): 89.21MM **Privately Held**
Web: www.powerdigitalmarketing.com
SIC: 8742 Marketing consulting services

(P-20512)
POWERSOURCE TALENT LLC
12655 W Jefferson Blvd Ste 400 (90066-7008)
PHONE..................424 835-0878
Lisa Tran Mckee, *CEO*
Mike Bassignani, *
EMP: 101 EST: 2017
SALES (est): 3.4MM **Privately Held**
Web: www.powersourcetalent.com
SIC: 8742 Management consulting services

(P-20513)
PRO SAFETY & RESCUE INC
3700 Pegasus Dr Ste 200 (93308-6805)
PHONE..................888 269-5095
Sarah Pierce, *Pr*
Jessie Pierce, *TRESR**
EMP: 70 EST: 2014
SALES (est): 4.64MM **Privately Held**
Web: www.prosafetyandrescue.com
SIC: 8742 8999 Training and development consultant; Search and rescue service

(P-20514)
PROMOTE MEDIA LP
9200 W Sunset Blvd Ste 950 (90069-3506)
PHONE..................323 433-7950
EMP: 60 EST: 2017
SALES (est): 2.61MM **Privately Held**
Web: www.promoteroi.com
SIC: 8742 Marketing consulting services

(P-20515)
PROTIVITI INC (HQ)
2884 Sand Hill Rd Ste 200 (94025-7072)
PHONE..................650 234-6000
Joseph Tarantino, *Pr*
Brian Christensen, *
Andrew Clinton, *
James Pajakowski, *
Jose Saenz, *Business**
EMP: 100 EST: 2002
SALES (est): 630.97MM
SALES (corp-wide): 7.24B **Publicly Held**
Web: www.protiviti.com
SIC: 8742 8721 Industry specialist consultants; Auditing services
PA: Robert Half Inc.
2884 Sand Hill Rd Ste 200
Menlo Park CA
650 234-6000

(P-20516)
PULSEPOINT INC
115 Sansome St Ste 1002 (94104-3602)
PHONE..................415 937-8208
Sloan Gaon, *CEO*
EMP: 216
SALES (corp-wide): 23.11MM **Privately Held**
Web: www.pulsepoint.com
SIC: 8742 7313 Marketing consulting services; Electronic media advertising representatives
PA: Pulsepoint, Inc.
283-299 Market St Fl 4
Newark NJ
212 706-4800

(P-20517)
PWC STRATEGY& (US) LLC
3 Embarcadero Ctr Ste 1150 (94111-4003)
PHONE..................415 498-5000
Ralph W Shrader, *Brnch Mgr*
EMP: 122
SALES (corp-wide): 6.79B **Privately Held**
Web: www.pwc.com
SIC: 8742 Management consulting services
HQ: Pwc Strategy& (Us) Llc
101 Park Ave Fl 18
New York NY

(P-20518)
PWC STRATEGY& (US) LLC
601 S Figueroa St Ste 900 (90017-5743)
PHONE..................213 356-6000
EMP: 113
SALES (corp-wide): 6.79B **Privately Held**
Web: www.pwc.com
SIC: 8742 Management consulting services
HQ: Pwc Strategy& (Us) Llc
101 Park Ave Fl 18
New York NY

(P-20519)
Q ANALYSTS LLC (PA)
4320 Stevens Creek Blvd Ste 130 (95129-1280)
PHONE..................408 907-8500
Thuy To, *
Stephen Graziani, *
EMP: 70 EST: 2003
SALES (est): 14.25MM
SALES (corp-wide): 14.25MM **Privately Held**
Web: www.qanalysts.com
SIC: 8742 7379 Quality assurance consultant ; Computer related consulting services

(P-20520)
QB3 LLC
29 Hunter Crk (94930-1355)
PHONE..................415 515-3595
Andrew Kimball, *Brnch Mgr*
EMP: 90
SALES (corp-wide): 220.77K **Privately Held**
SIC: 8742 Management consulting services
PA: Qb3, Llc
824 E St
San Rafael CA
415 459-7459

(P-20521)
R3 STRATEGIC SUPPORT GROUP INC
1050 B Ave Ste A (92118-3430)
PHONE..................800 418-2040
Randall Packard, *Pr*
Randall Packard, *Pr*
Mark Sanders, *
Clark Nichols, *
EMP: 67 EST: 2007
SALES (est): 9.75MM **Privately Held**
Web: www.r3ssg.com
SIC: 8742 Business management consultant

(P-20522)
RAINDROP AGENCY INC
8276 Ronson Rd (92111-2015)
PHONE..................661 724-6237
EMP: 67 EST: 2018
SALES (est): 2.29MM **Privately Held**
Web: www.raindrop.agency
SIC: 8742 Marketing consulting services

(P-20523)
RALIS SERVICES CORP
Also Called: Ralis
1 City Blvd W Ste 600 (92868-3639)
PHONE..................844 347-2547
Delbert O Meeks, *CEO*
Mike Chiang, *
EMP: 150 EST: 2014
SALES (est): 6MM **Privately Held**
Web: www.ralisservices.com
SIC: 8742 7371 8721 Human resource consulting services; Custom computer programming services; Accounting services, except auditing

(P-20524)
RALPH BRENNAN REST GROUP LLC
Also Called: Red Fish Grill
1590 S Disneyland Dr (92802-2319)
PHONE..................714 776-5200
Kiki Lungquist, *Brnch Mgr*
EMP: 125
Web: www.neworleans-food.com
SIC: 8742 Restaurant and food services consultants
PA: The Ralph Brennan Restaurant Group Llc
550 Bienville St
New Orleans LA

(P-20525)
RED PEAK GROUP LLC
23975 Park Sorrento # 410 (91302-4031)
PHONE..................818 222-7762
EMP: 90 EST: 2009
SALES (est): 5.32MM **Privately Held**
SIC: 8742 Marketing consulting services

(P-20526)
REDSTONE PRINT & MAIL INC
910 Riverside Pkwy Ste 40 (95605-1510)
PHONE..................916 318-6450
Ledi Cody, *Pr*
EMP: 60 EST: 2015
SALES (est): 4.74MM **Privately Held**
Web: www.redstoneprintmail.com
SIC: 8742 Marketing consulting services

(P-20527)
RESOURCES CONNECTION INC (PA)
Also Called: Resources Global Professionals
17101 Armstrong Ave Ste 100 (92614-5742)

8742 - Management Consulting Services (P-20528)

PRODUCTS & SERVICES SECTION

PHONE..................714 430-6400
Kate W Duchene, *Pr*
Donald B Murray, *
Jennifer Ryu, *Ex VP*
John D Bower, *CAO*
EMP: 198 **EST:** 1996
SQ FT: 56,200
SALES (est): 775.64MM **Publicly Held**
Web: www.rgp.com
SIC: 8742 7389 8721 Business management consultant; Financial services; Accounting, auditing, and bookkeeping

(P-20528)
RIVIERA DATA CORP
Also Called: Social Intelligence
735 State St Ste 600 (93101-7065)
PHONE..................805 456-7082
Max Drucker, *CEO*
Jeff Andrews, *
EMP: 64 **EST:** 2010
SQ FT: 2,500
SALES (est): 12MM **Privately Held**
Web: www.carpe.io
SIC: 8742 Human resource consulting services

(P-20529)
RK LOGISTICS GROUP INC (PA)
Also Called: Rk Logistics
41707 Christy St (94538-4195)
P.O. Box 610670 (95161-0670)
PHONE..................408 942-8107
Rodney F Kalune, *Pr*
EMP: 64 **EST:** 2004
SQ FT: 180,000
SALES (est): 27.24MM
SALES (corp-wide): 27.24MM **Privately Held**
Web: www.rklogisticsgroup.com
SIC: 8742 4214 4225 Transportation consultant; Local trucking with storage; General warehousing and storage

(P-20530)
RMD GROUP INC
2311 E South St (90805-4424)
PHONE..................562 866-9288
Ralph Holguin, *Pr*
EMP: 300 **EST:** 2008
SALES (est): 20.24MM **Privately Held**
Web: www.rmdgroupinc.com
SIC: 8742 Marketing consulting services

(P-20531)
ROCHE MOLECULAR SYSTEMS INC
2801 Scott Blvd (95050-2549)
PHONE..................408 217-5400
EMP: 113 **EST:** 1991
SALES (est): 4.37MM **Privately Held**
SIC: 8742 Business management consultant

(P-20532)
ROCKY POINT INVESTMENTS LLC (HQ)
Also Called: Creative Channel Services LLC
6601 Center Dr W Ste 400 (90045-1577)
PHONE..................310 482-6500
Andy Restivo, *CEO*
George Plumb, *
Hanoz Gandhi, *
Michael Butler, *
EMP: 105 **EST:** 1995
SALES (est): 99.11MM
SALES (corp-wide): 14.29B **Publicly Held**
SIC: 8742 Marketing consulting services
PA: Omnicom Group Inc.
280 Park Ave Fl 31w
New York NY
212 415-3600

(P-20533)
ROOFSTOCK INC (PA)
2001 Broadway 4th Fl (94612-2301)
PHONE..................510 269-9400
Gary Beasley, *CEO*
EMP: 208 **EST:** 2015
SALES (est): 9.94MM
SALES (corp-wide): 9.94MM **Privately Held**
Web: www.roofstock.com
SIC: 8742 6798 Business management consultant; Real estate investment trusts

(P-20534)
ROSERYAN INC
1999 S Bascom Ave Ste 700 (95008-2205)
PHONE..................510 456-3056
David Roberson, *CEO*
Kathleen Ryan, *
EMP: 97 **EST:** 1994
SALES (est): 9.49MM
SALES (corp-wide): 48.97MM **Privately Held**
Web: www.roseryan.com
SIC: 8742 Financial consultant
PA: Zrg Partners, Llc
365 W Passaic St Ste 465
Rochelle Park NJ
201 560-9900

(P-20535)
S E O P INC
1621 Alton Pkwy Ste 150 (92606-4875)
PHONE..................949 682-7906
Gary Hagins, *CEO*
Rhonda Spears, *
EMP: 150 **EST:** 2001
SALES (est): 13.88MM **Privately Held**
Web: www.seop.com
SIC: 8742 Marketing consulting services

(P-20536)
S P S INC
245 Medio Ave (94019-5335)
PHONE..................650 685-5913
Steve Semprevivo, *Pr*
EMP: 70 **EST:** 1997
SALES (est): 1.39MM **Privately Held**
SIC: 8742 Marketing consulting services

(P-20537)
SABAN BRANDS LLC (HQ)
10100 Santa Monica Blvd Ste 500 (90067-4003)
PHONE..................310 557-5230
Elie Dekel, *Managing Member*
William Kehoe, *Managing Member*
Nina Leong, *Managing Member*
Kirk Bloomgarden, *Managing Member*
Rami Yanni, *Managing Member*
EMP: 88 **EST:** 2010
SQ FT: 605,000
SALES (est): 16.5MM
SALES (corp-wide): 54.98MM **Privately Held**
Web: www.saban.com
SIC: 8742 General management consultant
PA: Global Reach 18, Inc.
10100 Santa Monica Blvd
Los Angeles CA
310 203-5850

(P-20538)
SAVIYNT INC (PA)
1301 E El Segundo Blvd Ste D (90245-4303)
PHONE..................310 641-1664
Sachin Nayyar, *CEO*
Paul Zolfaghari, *Pr*
Amit Saha, *CGO*
Shankar Ganapathy, *COO*
Jim Jackson, *CFO*
EMP: 122 **EST:** 2011
SQ FT: 10,000
SALES (est): 73.1MM
SALES (corp-wide): 73.1MM **Privately Held**
Web: www.saviynt.com
SIC: 8742 Business management consultant

(P-20539)
SCORPION DESIGN LLC (PA)
27750 Entertainment Dr (91355-1091)
PHONE..................661 702-0100
Rustin Kretz, *CEO*
Daniel Street, *Pr*
Raj Ramanan, *COO*
EMP: 585 **EST:** 2003
SQ FT: 100,000
SALES (est): 117.78MM
SALES (corp-wide): 117.78MM **Privately Held**
Web: www.scorpion.co
SIC: 8742 Marketing consulting services

(P-20540)
SEEK CAPITAL LLC
6420 Wilshire Blvd (90048-5562)
PHONE..................855 978-6106
Roy Ferman, *CEO*
EMP: 75 **EST:** 2014
SALES (est): 5.73MM **Privately Held**
Web: www.seekcapital.com
SIC: 8742 Management consulting services

(P-20541)
SENDLANE INC
10620 Treena St Ste 250 (92131-1141)
PHONE..................301 520-3812
EMP: 75 **EST:** 2018
SALES (est): 5.16MM **Privately Held**
Web: www.sendlane.com
SIC: 8742 Marketing consulting services

(P-20542)
SHANNON RANCHES INC
12601 E Highway 20 (95423-8312)
P.O. Box 2037 (95423-2037)
PHONE..................707 998-9656
Clay Shannon, *Pr*
Craig Shannon, *
Margarita Shannon, *
EMP: 250 **EST:** 1993
SQ FT: 2,100
SALES (est): 22.53MM **Privately Held**
SIC: 8742 Administrative services consultant

(P-20543)
SHEIN TECHNOLOGY LLC (PA)
777 S Alameda St Fl 2 (90021-1657)
PHONE..................213 628-4008
EMP: 500 **EST:** 2021
SALES (est): 56.93MM
SALES (corp-wide): 56.93MM **Privately Held**
SIC: 8742 Management consulting services

(P-20544)
SHELL OIL COMPANY
Also Called: Shell
511 N Brookhurst St (92801-5231)
P.O. Box 4848 (92803-4848)
PHONE..................714 991-9200
Roger Underwood, *Brnch Mgr*
EMP: 125
SALES (corp-wide): 381.31B **Privately Held**
Web: www.shell.com
SIC: 8742 Industry specialist consultants
HQ: Shell Usa, Inc.
150 N Dairy Ashford Rd
Houston TX
832 337-2000

(P-20545)
SIGMAWAYS INC
39737 Paseo Padre Pkwy (94538-2957)
PHONE..................510 573-4208
Prakash Sadasivam, *CEO*
Sudha Kadirvelu, *
EMP: 60 **EST:** 2006
SQ FT: 5,000
SALES (est): 5.95MM **Privately Held**
Web: www.sigmaways.com
SIC: 8742 7379 7373 Management consulting services; Computer related consulting services; Systems software development services

(P-20546)
SIMPLELEGAL INC
488 Ellis St (94043-2204)
PHONE..................949 887-2900
EMP: 69 **EST:** 2013
SALES (est): 852K **Privately Held**
Web: www.simplelegal.com
SIC: 8742 Business management consultant

(P-20547)
SIMPSON SMPSON MGT CNSLTING IN
718 S Date Ave Ste A1 (91803-1412)
PHONE..................626 282-4000
Hamid Taheri, *Admn*
Carl P Simpson, *
EMP: 74 **EST:** 2001
SQ FT: 2,000
SALES (est): 4.49MM **Privately Held**
Web: www.ssmci.net
SIC: 8742 Business management consultant

(P-20548)
SITE HELPERS LLC
25232 Steinbeck Ave (91381-1240)
PHONE..................877 217-5395
Danika Weber, *Managing Member*
EMP: 100 **EST:** 2021
SALES (est): 1.32MM **Privately Held**
SIC: 8742 7389 Marketing consulting services; Business services, nec

(P-20549)
SITRICK BRINCKO GROUP LLC
1840 Century Park E # 800 (90067-2101)
PHONE..................310 788-2850
EMP: 60
SALES (est): 3.66MM **Publicly Held**
SIC: 8742 8743 Management consulting services; Public relations services
PA: Resources Connection, Inc.
17101 Armstrong Ave # 100
Irvine CA

(P-20550)
SKIN LAUNDRY HOLDINGS INC
130 Lomita St (90245-4113)
PHONE..................424 220-8826
Gregg Throgmartin, *CEO*
Christopher Carey, *COO*
Paul Pugh, *CFO*
EMP: 330 **EST:** 2015
SALES (est): 13.92MM **Privately Held**
Web: www.skinlaundry.com
SIC: 8742 7371 Business management consultant; Computer software development and applications

PRODUCTS & SERVICES SECTION
8742 - Management Consulting Services (P-20573)

(P-20551)
SL BLUE GARDEN CORP
3790 Keri Way (92028-8139)
PHONE.................626 633-2672
Susan Luo, *CEO*
EMP: 126 **EST:** 2014
SALES (est): 4.11MM **Privately Held**
SIC: 8742 Management consulting services

(P-20552)
SLALOM LLC
Also Called: SLALOM, LLC
100 Pine St Ste 2500 (94111-5211)
PHONE.................415 593-3450
Pat Meade, *Genl Mgr*
EMP: 416
Web: www.slalom.com
SIC: 8742 Business management consultant
PA: Slalom, Inc.
   821 2nd Ave Ste 1900
   Seattle WA

(P-20553)
SMART CIRCLE INTERNATIONAL LLC (PA)
Also Called: Smart Circle, The
4490 Von Karman Ave (92660-2008)
PHONE.................949 587-9207
Michael Meryash, *CEO*
George Graffy, *
Jigna Patel, *
Paul Sunny, *
EMP: 90 **EST:** 2007
SQ FT: 10,700
SALES (est): 327.12MM **Privately Held**
Web: www.smartcircle.com
SIC: 8742 Marketing consulting services

(P-20554)
SMARTZIP ANALYTICS INC
6200 Stoneridge Mall Rd Ste 300 (94588)
PHONE.................855 661-1064
Tom Glassanos, *Pr*
Frank Richards, *
Scott Baumgartner, *
EMP: 77 **EST:** 2008
SALES (est): 10.77MM **Privately Held**
Web: www.smartzip.com
SIC: 8742 Marketing consulting services

(P-20555)
SMG HOLDINGS LLC
Also Called: Palm Springs Convention Center
277 N Avenida Caballeros (92262-6440)
PHONE.................760 325-6611
Jim Dunn, *Brnch Mgr*
EMP: 84
SALES (corp-wide): 422MM **Privately Held**
Web: www.visitpalmsprings.com
SIC: 8742 7389 Business management consultant; Convention and show services
HQ: Smg Holdings, Llc
   300 Cnshohckn State Rd # 450
   Conshohocken PA

(P-20556)
SMITH-EMERY INTERNATIONAL INC (PA)
791 E Washington Blvd Fl 3 (90021-3043)
PHONE.................213 741-8500
James E Patridge, *Pr*
Helen Choe, *
EMP: 222 **EST:** 1976
SQ FT: 32,380
SALES (est): 41.71MM **Privately Held**
Web: www.smithemeryinternational.com
SIC: 8742 Management consulting services

(P-20557)
SOCIALCOM INC
Also Called: Audiencex
13468 Beach Ave (90292-5624)
PHONE.................310 289-4477
Reeve Benaron, *CEO*
EMP: 73 **EST:** 2013
SALES (est): 10.16MM **Privately Held**
Web: www.audiencex.com
SIC: 8742 Marketing consulting services

(P-20558)
SODEXO MANAGEMENT INC
450 World Way (90045-5812)
PHONE.................310 646-3738
EMP: 1633
SALES (corp-wide): 206.19MM **Privately Held**
Web: www.sodexo.com
SIC: 8742 Food and beverage consultant
HQ: Sodexo Management Inc.
   9801 Washingtonian Blvd
   Gaithersburg MD

(P-20559)
SOLUTIONS INC
Also Called: Kind Lending
4 Hutton Centre Dr (92707-8706)
PHONE.................949 899-0448
EMP: 119 **EST:** 2020
SALES (est): 10.74MM **Privately Held**
Web: www.kindlending.com
SIC: 8742 Business management consultant

(P-20560)
SOLUTIONZ INC ✪
1029 Swarthmore Ave (90272-2506)
PHONE.................888 815-0322
EMP: 227 **EST:** 2022
SALES (est): 6.04MM **Privately Held**
Web: www.solutionzinc.com
SIC: 8742 Business management consultant

(P-20561)
SPOTIFY USA INC
555 Mateo St (90013-2647)
PHONE.................213 505-3040
EMP: 558
SALES (corp-wide): 2.67MM **Privately Held**
SIC: 8742 Management consulting services
HQ: Spotify Usa Inc.
   150 Greenwich St Fl 62
   New York NY

(P-20562)
SQA SERVICES INC
Also Called: Sqa Services
425 Via Corta Ste 203 (90274-1358)
P.O. Box 5220 (90274-9672)
PHONE.................800 333-6180
EMP: 267 **EST:** 1995
SQ FT: 8,000
SALES (est): 26.71MM **Privately Held**
Web: www.sqaservices.com
SIC: 8742 Quality assurance consultant

(P-20563)
ST MARYS MEDICAL CENTER
Also Called: ST MARY'S MEDICAL CENTER
1050 Linden Ave (90813-3321)
PHONE.................562 491-9230
EMP: 3694
SALES (corp-wide): 19.58B **Publicly Held**
Web: validate.perfdrive.com
SIC: 8742 Hospital and health services consultant
HQ: St. Mary's Medical Center, Inc.
   901 45th St
   Mangonia Park FL
   561 844-6300

(P-20564)
STAGE 4 SOLUTIONS INCORPORATED
19200 Portos Dr (95070-5123)
PHONE.................408 868-9739
Niti Agrawal, *CEO*
EMP: 100 **EST:** 2001
SALES (est): 5.28MM **Privately Held**
Web: www.stage4solutions.com
SIC: 8742 New products and services consultants

(P-20565)
STARDUST STUDIOS INC
1823 Colorado Ave (90404-3411)
PHONE.................310 399-6047
Matthew Marquis, *Pt*
Jake Banks, *Pt*
EMP: 86 **EST:** 2003
SALES (est): 2.91MM **Privately Held**
Web: www.stardust.tv
SIC: 8742 7374 Marketing consulting services; Computer graphics service

(P-20566)
STAT REVENUE PROFESSIONAL CORP
2200 Powell St (94608-1809)
PHONE.................510 597-1800
Kevin Scott Lee, *Prin*
EMP: 64 **EST:** 2016
SALES (est): 2.81MM **Privately Held**
Web: www.pararevenue.com
SIC: 8742 Hospital and health services consultant

(P-20567)
STERLING CONSULTING GROUP LLC
Also Called: Sterling Brand
600 California St Fl 8 (94108-2726)
PHONE.................415 248-7900
Austin Mcghie, *Mgr*
EMP: 84
Web: www.sterlingbrands.com
SIC: 8742 Marketing consulting services
PA: Sterling Consulting Group Llc
   75 Varick St Fl 8
   New York NY

(P-20568)
STERLING HEALTHCARE SVCS LLC
19925 Stevens Creek Blvd Ste 100 (95014-2384)
P.O. Box 472 (40059-0472)
PHONE.................502 262-2914
Ramesh Datla, *CEO*
Vanitha Datla, *
Richard Beatty, *
Snayhil Rana, *
EMP: 1000 **EST:** 2008
SALES (est): 10MM
SALES (corp-wide): 322.47B **Publicly Held**
Web: www.sterlinghcs.com
SIC: 8742 Hospital and health services consultant
PA: Cvs Health Corporation
   1 Cvs Dr
   Woonsocket RI
   401 765-1500

(P-20569)
STRATEGIC BUS INSIGHTS INC (PA)
333 Ravenswood Ave (94025-3453)
PHONE.................650 859-4600
William Guns, *CEO*
William Ralston, *
EMP: 63 **EST:** 2000
SQ FT: 10,000
SALES (est): 11.78MM
SALES (corp-wide): 11.78MM **Privately Held**
Web: www.strategicbusinessinsights.com
SIC: 8742 Business management consultant

(P-20570)
STRATEOS INC (PA)
930 Guinda St (94301-3318)
PHONE.................650 763-8432
Mark Colbrie, *CEO*
Max Hodak, *
Alexander K Arrow, *
EMP: 77 **EST:** 2012
SALES (est): 9.46MM
SALES (corp-wide): 9.46MM **Privately Held**
Web: www.strateos.com
SIC: 8742 7371 8731 Automation and robotics consultant; Computer software development and applications; Biological research

(P-20571)
SULLIVNCRTSMNROE INSUR SVCS LL (PA)
Also Called: Nationwide
1920 Main St Ste 600 (92614-7200)
P.O. Box 19763 (92623-9763)
PHONE.................800 427-3253
John Monroe, *CEO*
David Kummer, *
Shawn Kraatz, *
Jeannine Coronado, *
William Curtis, *
EMP: 103 **EST:** 1987
SQ FT: 22,000
SALES (est): 38.34MM
SALES (corp-wide): 38.34MM **Privately Held**
Web: www.sullivancurtismonroe.com
SIC: 8742 6411 Management consulting services; Insurance brokers, nec

(P-20572)
SUN PACIFIC MARKETING COOP INC
33502 Lerdo Hwy (93308-9438)
PHONE.................213 612-9957
Berne H Evans Iii, *Brnch Mgr*
EMP: 395
SALES (corp-wide): 92.65MM **Privately Held**
Web: www.sunpacific.com
SIC: 8742 Marketing consulting services
PA: Sun Pacific Marketing Cooperative, Inc.
   1095 E Green St
   Pasadena CA
   213 612-9957

(P-20573)
SUTTER PHYSICIAN SERVICES (HQ)
10470 Old Placerville Rd Ste 100 (95827-2539)
P.O. Box 211584 (55121-2884)
PHONE.................916 854-6600
Jeremy Eaves, *CEO*
EMP: 800 **EST:** 1989

8742 - Management Consulting Services (P-20574)

SQ FT: 87,000
SALES (est): 11.49MM
SALES (corp-wide): 14.77B **Privately Held**
Web: www.sutterphysicianservices.org
SIC: 8742 8741 8721 Hospital and health services consultant; Management services; Accounting, auditing, and bookkeeping
PA: Sutter Health
2200 River Plaza Dr
Sacramento CA
916 733-8800

(P-20574)
SWINERTON RENEWABLE ENERGY
16680 W Bernardo Dr (92127-1900)
PHONE.................................858 622-4040
EMP: 108 **EST:** 2021
SALES (est): 3.34MM **Privately Held**
Web: www.swinerton.com
SIC: 8742 Business management consultant

(P-20575)
SYMPHONY COMM SVCS LLC (PA)
640 W California Ave Ste 200 (94086-3624)
PHONE.................................650 733-6660
Brad Levy, *CEO*
Ben Chrnelich, *Pr*
Eran Barack, *COO*
EMP: 178 **EST:** 2014
SALES (est): 49.68MM
SALES (corp-wide): 49.68MM **Privately Held**
Web: www.symphony.com
SIC: 8742 7389 7373 Financial consultant; Financial services; Systems integration services

(P-20576)
T G T ENTERPRISES INC
Also Called: Anderson
12650 Danielson Ct (92064-6822)
PHONE.................................858 413-0300
Randy Dale, *CEO*
Scott Hopkins, *Ex VP*
Todd Stoker, *COO*
EMP: 145 **EST:** 1976
SQ FT: 77,000
SALES (est): 33.92MM **Privately Held**
Web: www.andersondd.com
SIC: 8742 2759 7311 Marketing consulting services; Commercial printing, nec; Advertising agencies

(P-20577)
TAPETECH TOOL COMPANY
Also Called: Tapetech Tool Company
2190 Meridian Park Blvd (94520-5789)
PHONE.................................925 676-7002
EMP: 633
SALES (corp-wide): 5.33B **Publicly Held**
Web: www.amestools.com
SIC: 8742 5082 Marketing consulting services; Contractor's materials
HQ: Ames Tools Corporation
1327 Northbrook Pkwy # 400
Suwanee GA

(P-20578)
TECHNOLOGY ASSOCIATES EC INC
3129 Tiger Run Ct Ste 206 (92010-6512)
PHONE.................................760 765-5275
EMP: 74 **EST:** 2010
SALES (est): 6.76MM **Privately Held**
Web: www.taec.net
SIC: 8742 General management consultant

(P-20579)
TECOLOTE RESEARCH INC
2120 E Grand Ave Ste 200 (90245-2565)
PHONE.................................310 640-4700
James Takayesu, *Pr*
EMP: 99
SALES (corp-wide): 47.38MM **Privately Held**
Web: www.tecolote.com
SIC: 8742 8731 Management consulting services; Commercial physical research
PA: Tecolote Research, Inc.
420 S Fairview Ave # 201
Goleta CA
805 571-6366

(P-20580)
TECOLOTE RESEARCH INC
Also Called: Santa Barbara Group
5266 Hollister Ave Ste 301 (93111-2089)
PHONE.................................805 964-6963
James Suttle, *Brnch Mgr*
EMP: 142
SALES (corp-wide): 47.38MM **Privately Held**
Web: www.tecolote.com
SIC: 8742 Marketing consulting services
PA: Tecolote Research, Inc.
420 S Fairview Ave # 201
Goleta CA
805 571-6366

(P-20581)
TELESECTOR RESOURCES GROUP INC
Also Called: Verizon
5010 Azusa Canyon Rd (91706-1830)
PHONE.................................626 813-4538
Nancy Cano, *Mgr*
EMP: 393
SALES (corp-wide): 136.84B **Publicly Held**
SIC: 8742 Management consulting services
HQ: Telesector Resources Group, Inc.
140 West St
New York NY
212 395-1000

(P-20582)
TELUS HEALTH (US) LTD INC
27715 Jefferson Ave Ste 103 (92590-2636)
PHONE.................................888 577-3784
EMP: 65
SALES (corp-wide): 13.71B **Privately Held**
Web: www.telus.com
SIC: 8742 Human resource consulting services
HQ: Telus Health (Us) Ltd. Inc.
250 Royall St Ste 210w
Canton MA

(P-20583)
THOMAS ST JOHN INC
10877 Wilshire Blvd Ste 1550 (90024-4351)
PHONE.................................424 273-1172
Laura Skinner, *Prin*
EMP: 81 **EST:** 2009
SALES (est): 8.84MM **Privately Held**
Web: www.thomasstjohn.com
SIC: 8742 Quality assurance consultant

(P-20584)
TITANUM HEALTH CARE
1414 S Grand Ave (90015-3067)
PHONE.................................213 765-8123
Gray William Miller, *CEO*
EMP: 81 **EST:** 2016
SALES (est): 528.84K **Privately Held**
Web: www.tihealthcare.com
SIC: 8742 Hospital and health services consultant

(P-20585)
TOPIA MOBILITY INC (PA)
Also Called: Polaris Global Mobility
1900 S Norfolk St Ste 350 (94403-1171)
PHONE.................................415 666-2130
Shawn Farshchi, *CEO*
Marcus Womersley, *
Kristof Stolarek, *
EMP: 68 **EST:** 2001
SALES (est): 6.71MM
SALES (corp-wide): 6.71MM **Privately Held**
Web: www.topia.com
SIC: 8742 8721 Financial consultant; Payroll accounting service

(P-20586)
TORRID MERCHANDISING INC
18501 San Jose Ave (91748-1330)
PHONE.................................626 667-1002
Lisa Harper, *CEO*
Tim Martin, *
Chinwe Abaelu, *
Elizabeth Munoz, *Chief Creative Officer**
▲ **EMP:** 429 **EST:** 2015
SALES (est): 4.73MM **Publicly Held**
SIC: 8742 5621 Merchandising consultant; Ready-to-wear apparel, women's
HQ: Torrid Holdings Inc.
18501 San Jose Ave
City Of Industry CA
626 667-1002

(P-20587)
TOTAL RECON SOLUTIONS INC
27 Oakbrook (92679-4741)
PHONE.................................949 584-8417
EMP: 90 **EST:** 2011
SALES (est): 2.06MM **Privately Held**
SIC: 8742 Management consulting services

(P-20588)
TRACE3 INC
Also Called: TRACE3, INC.
2120 E Grand Ave Ste 145 (90245-2565)
PHONE.................................310 220-0164
Teresa Chavez, *Off Mgr*
EMP: 78
SALES (corp-wide): 583.64MM **Privately Held**
Web: www.trace3.com
SIC: 8742 Sales (including sales management) consultant
HQ: Trace3, Llc
7505 Irvine Center Dr # 100
Irvine CA
949 333-2300

(P-20589)
TRACE3 LLC
Also Called: Trace3
12636 High Bluff Dr Ste 300 (92130-2022)
PHONE.................................858 345-2650
EMP: 65
SALES (corp-wide): 583.64MM **Privately Held**
Web: www.trace3.com
SIC: 8742 Management consulting services
HQ: Trace3, Llc
7505 Irvine Center Dr # 100
Irvine CA
949 333-2300

(P-20590)
TRANSIRIS CORPORATION
Also Called: Retina Communications
530 Sycamore St (94070-2047)
PHONE.................................650 303-3495
Silvian Centiu, *CEO*
Ted Kohnen, *
Silvian Centiu, *Prin*
Simona Nan, *
EMP: 60 **EST:** 2012
SALES (est): 4.94MM **Privately Held**
Web: www.retinab2.com
SIC: 8742 Marketing consulting services

(P-20591)
TRI-AD ACTUARIES INC
Also Called: Tri-Ad
221 W Crest St Ste 300 (92025-1728)
PHONE.................................760 743-7555
Thad Hamilton, *CEO*
Curtis Hamilton, *
Judy Simons, *
Thad Hamilton, *VP*
Robert Krier, *
EMP: 117 **EST:** 1973
SQ FT: 17,500
SALES (est): 9.25MM **Privately Held**
Web: www.tri-ad.com
SIC: 8742 6411 Human resource consulting services; Pension and retirement plan consultants

(P-20592)
TRINAMIX INC (PA)
35 Amoret Dr (92602-0770)
PHONE.................................408 507-3583
Amit Sharma, *CEO*
Molly Chakraborty, *Pr*
Sandeep Goyal, *CFO*
EMP: 289 **EST:** 2008
SALES (est): 15.25MM
SALES (corp-wide): 15.25MM **Privately Held**
Web: www.trinamix.com
SIC: 8742 7379 7361 Management consulting services; Computer related consulting services; Labor contractors (employment agency)

(P-20593)
TRINET GROUP INC (PA)
Also Called: Trinet
1 Park Pl Ste 600 (94568-7983)
PHONE.................................510 352-5000
Burton M Goldfield, *Pr*
David C Hodgson, *
Kelly Tuminelli, *Ex VP*
Jay Venkat, *DIGITAL Innovation*
Samantha Wellington, *CLO*
EMP: 2700 **EST:** 1988
SALES (est): 4.88B **Publicly Held**
Web: www.trinet.com
SIC: 8742 8748 Human resource consulting services; Communications consulting

(P-20594)
TROVE RECOMMERCE INC
240 Valley Dr (94005-9811)
PHONE.................................925 726-3316
Andrew Ruben, *CEO*
EMP: 200 **EST:** 2019
SALES (est): 14.26MM **Privately Held**
Web: www.trove.co
SIC: 8742 Business management consultant

(P-20595)
TRUOG-RYDING COMPANY INC
2659 Townsgate Rd Ste 101 (91361-2797)
PHONE.................................805 371-9222
David Ryding, *Pr*
Irene Ryding, *VP*
EMP: 62 **EST:** 1975
SQ FT: 3,200
SALES (est): 7.6MM **Privately Held**

Web: www.trco.com
SIC: **8742** 6411 Administrative services consultant; Pension and retirement plan consultants

(P-20596)
TSMC NORTH AMERICA (HQ)
2851 Junction Ave (95134-1910)
PHONE.................................408 382-8000
Richard B Cassidy Ii, *CEO*
Rick Cassidy, *
Edward Ross, *
EMP: 395 **EST:** 1987
SALES (est): 183.1MM **Privately Held**
SIC: **8742** 8711 5065 3674 Marketing consulting services; Consulting engineer; Electronic parts and equipment, nec; Semiconductor circuit networks
PA: Taiwan Semiconductor Manufacturing Company Limited
No. 8, Li-Hsin Rd. 6, Hsinchu Science Park,
Hsinchu City

(P-20597)
TUBULAR LABS INC (HQ)
153 Castro St Ste 300 (94041-1201)
P.O. Box 391304 (94039-1304)
PHONE.................................650 260-8823
Robert Gabel, *CEO*
Michael Kamprath, *
Matt Hunter, *CPO*
EMP: 103 **EST:** 2012
SALES (est): 10.26MM **Privately Held**
Web: www.tubularlabs.com
SIC: **8742** Marketing consulting services
PA: Chartbeat, Inc.
826 Broadway Fl 6
New York NY

(P-20598)
UNITED INNOVATION SERVICES INC
950 Tower Ln (94404-2121)
PHONE.................................831 334-0673
Tingting Du, *CEO*
EMP: 84 **EST:** 2017
SALES (est): 2.3MM **Privately Held**
Web: www.uisus.com
SIC: **8742** Management consulting services

(P-20599)
UNIVERSITY OF CALIFORNIA
Also Called: MEMORY AND AGING CENTER
1500 Owens St Ste 320 (94158-2335)
PHONE.................................415 353-2057
Michael V Drake, *Pr*
EMP: 152 **EST:** 2019
SALES (est): 38.9B **Privately Held**
Web: www.ucsf.edu
SIC: **8742** Business management consultant

(P-20600)
UPSTREM INC
1253 University Ave Ste 1003 (92103-3389)
PHONE.................................858 229-2979
Jacob Risman, *CEO*
Steven Maman, *
EMP: 70 **EST:** 2018
SQ FT: 1,500
SALES (est): 18MM **Privately Held**
Web: www.upstrem.com
SIC: **8742** Sales (including sales management) consultant

(P-20601)
VARIS LLC
9245 Sierra College Blvd # 100
(95661-5919)
PHONE.................................916 294-0860
Dean B Wilkie, *Mgr*
EMP: 70
SALES (corp-wide): 10.17MM **Privately Held**
Web: www.varis1.com
SIC: **8742** Hospital and health services consultant
PA: Varis Llc
9245 Sierra College Blvd
Roseville CA
916 294-0860

(P-20602)
VENTURA COUNTY MEDICAL CENTER
825 N 10th St (93060-1309)
PHONE.................................805 677-5184
EMP: 98
SALES (corp-wide): 77.09MM **Privately Held**
Web: www.vchca.org
SIC: **8742** Business planning and organizing services
PA: Ventura County Medical Center
3291 Loma Vista Rd
Ventura CA
805 652-6000

(P-20603)
VERIFI INC
8391 Beverly Blvd Ste 310 (90048-2633)
P.O. Box 310 (90078-0310)
PHONE.................................323 655-5789
Matthew G Katz, *CEO*
Sara Craven, *
Tony Wootton, *CRO*
Hitesh Anand, *CPO*
Ronald B Cushey, *
EMP: 65 **EST:** 2005
SALES (est): 24.15MM **Publicly Held**
Web: www.verifi.com
SIC: **8742** Quality assurance consultant
PA: Visa Inc.
900 Metro Center Blvd
Foster City CA

(P-20604)
VISIONAIRE GROUP INC
Also Called: Tvgla
400 Corporate Pointe Ste 700 (90230)
PHONE.................................310 823-1800
Dimitry Ioffe, *CEO*
Bryan Pettigrew, *
EMP: 60 **EST:** 2007
SALES (est): 5.97MM **Privately Held**
Web: www.tvgla.com
SIC: **8742** Marketing consulting services

(P-20605)
VISTAGE INTERNATIONAL INC (PA)
Also Called: Executive Committee, The
4840 Eastgate Mall (92121-1977)
PHONE.................................858 523-6800
Rafael Pastor, *CEO*
Rafael Pastor, *Ch Bd*
Leon Shapiro, *
Richard Carr, *
Ruby Randall, *
EMP: 88 **EST:** 1998
SALES (est): 42.39MM
SALES (corp-wide): 42.39MM **Privately Held**
Web: www.vistage.com
SIC: **8742** Business planning and organizing services

(P-20606)
VISTANCIA MARKETING LLC
Also Called: Shea Homes Ltd Prtnershp
655 Brea Canyon Rd (91789-3078)
PHONE.................................909 594-9500
John Francisshea, *Prin*
EMP: 166 **EST:** 2003
SALES (est): 1.6MM
SALES (corp-wide): 2.1B **Privately Held**
Web: www.jfshea.com
SIC: **8742** Marketing consulting services
HQ: Shea Homes Limited Partnership, A California Limited Partnership
655 Brea Canyon Rd
Walnut CA

(P-20607)
VULCAN CYBER INC
2345 Yale St Fl 1 (94306-1449)
PHONE.................................415 429-4311
Yaniv Bar-dayan, *CEO*
EMP: 83 **EST:** 2018
SALES (est): 2MM **Privately Held**
Web: www.vulcan.io
SIC: **8742** Business management consultant

(P-20608)
WASSERMAN MEDIA GROUP LLC (PA)
Also Called: Wasserman
10900 Wilshire Blvd Ste 1200 (90024-6548)
PHONE.................................310 407-0200
Casey Wasserman, *Managing Member*
Tim Chadwick, *
Dean Christopher, *
EMP: 115 **EST:** 2003
SQ FT: 40,000
SALES (est): 116.26MM
SALES (corp-wide): 116.26MM **Privately Held**
Web: www.teamwass.com
SIC: **8742** Marketing consulting services

(P-20609)
WATTS HEALTH SYSTEMS INC (PA)
3405 W Imperial Hwy (90303-2219)
PHONE.................................310 424-2220
Clyde W Oden, *Pr*
EMP: 700 **EST:** 1983
SALES (est): 70.19MM
SALES (corp-wide): 70.19MM **Privately Held**
Web: www.wattshealthsystems.com
SIC: **8742** Hospital and health services consultant

(P-20610)
WELLMADE INC
Also Called: Polagram
800 E 12th St (90021-2198)
PHONE.................................213 221-1123
Jin Kim, *Pr*
EMP: 100 **EST:** 2018
SALES (est): 3.46MM **Privately Held**
Web: www.wellmadeusa.com
SIC: **8742** Business management consultant

(P-20611)
WENTE BROS (PA)
Also Called: Wente Vineyards
5565 Tesla Rd (94550-9149)
PHONE.................................925 456-2300
Carolyn Wente, *Ch Bd*
Jean Wente, *
Eric P Wente, *
Carolyn Wente, *Pr*
Philip Wente, *
◆ **EMP:** 100 **EST:** 1900
SQ FT: 168,000
SALES (est): 88.64MM
SALES (corp-wide): 88.64MM **Privately Held**
Web: www.wentevineyards.com
SIC: **8742** 2084 Restaurant and food services consultants; Wines

(P-20612)
WESTERN HEALTH RESOURCES
100 San Hedrin Cir (95490-8753)
PHONE.................................707 459-1818
William G Wiedemann, *Brnch Mgr*
EMP: 101
SALES (corp-wide): 66.06MM **Privately Held**
SIC: **8742** 8741 Business planning and organizing services; Administrative management
PA: Western Health Resources
2100 Douglas Blvd
Roseville CA
916 781-4685

(P-20613)
WILLIS NORTH AMERICA INC
Also Called: Willis Insurance Services Cal
18101 Von Karman Ave Ste 600 (92612-1012)
PHONE.................................909 476-3300
Bryan Fitzpatrick, *Prin*
EMP: 104
Web: www.wtwco.com
SIC: **8742** Management consulting services
HQ: Willis North America Inc.
200 Liberty St Fl 7
New York NY
212 915-8888

(P-20614)
WILSHIRE ADVISORS LLC (PA)
1299 Ocean Ave Ste 700 (90401-1061)
PHONE.................................310 451-3051
Dennis A Tito, *CEO*
John C Hindman, *
Michael Wauters, *
Renna Lalji, *
EMP: 210 **EST:** 1972
SQ FT: 57,530
SALES (est): 51.6MM
SALES (corp-wide): 51.6MM **Privately Held**
Web: www.wilshire.com
SIC: **8742** Financial consultant

(P-20615)
WILSON EMERY CORPORATION
Also Called: Sterling Management Systems
350 Arden Ave Ste 200 (91203-1110)
PHONE.................................818 245-6387
Kevin Wilson, *Ch Bd*
EMP: 67 **EST:** 1983
SQ FT: 8,500
SALES (est): 3.69MM **Privately Held**
Web: www.sterling.us
SIC: **8742** Business management consultant

(P-20616)
WORK HEALTH
Also Called: Queen of The Valley Hospital
3421 Villa Ln Ste 2a (94558-3060)
P.O. Box 2340 (94558-0688)
PHONE.................................707 257-4084
Deborah Morrissey, *Owner*
EMP: 61 **EST:** 1999
SALES (est): 7.28MM **Privately Held**
Web: www.thequeen.org

8742 - Management Consulting Services (P-20617)

SIC: 8742 8049 8011 Compensation and benefits planning consultant; Occupational therapist; Occupational and industrial specialist, physician/surgeon

(P-20617)
WPROMOTE LLC (PA)
101 Continental Blvd (90245-4516)
PHONE..................310 421-4844
Michael Mothner, *Pr*
Paul Rappoport, *
Michael Block, *
Paul Dumais, *
Michael Stone, *CRO*
EMP: 98 EST: 2004
SALES (est): 55.47MM
SALES (corp-wide): 55.47MM Privately Held
Web: www.wpromote.com
SIC: 8742 Marketing consulting services

(P-20618)
XDBS CORPORATION
2400 Broadway St Ste 130 (94063-1588)
PHONE..................415 513-0068
Julie Strong, *Prin*
EMP: 68 EST: 2018
SALES (est): 536.93K Privately Held
Web: www.xdbsworldwide.com
SIC: 8742 Marketing consulting services

(P-20619)
YMARKETING LLC
4000 Macarthur Blvd Ste 350 (92660-2517)
PHONE..................714 545-2550
Ryan Lash, *CEO*
Brian Yun, *COO*
Jennifer Jee, *Chief Relations Officer*
EMP: 70 EST: 2007
SALES (est): 8.93MM
SALES (corp-wide): 51.34MM Privately Held
SIC: 8742 Marketing consulting services
HQ: The Sandbox Group Llc
200 E Randolph St # 3450
Chicago IL
312 803-1900

(P-20620)
YOUNG & RUBICAM LLC
1735 Irvine Center Dr (92618)
PHONE..................949 224-6300
David Murphy, *Pr*
EMP: 300
SALES (corp-wide): 17.37B Privately Held
Web: www.vmlyr.com
SIC: 8742 Marketing consulting services
HQ: Young & Rubicam Llc
3 Columbus Cir Fl 3 # 3
New York NY
212 210-3017

(P-20621)
YOUR PRACTICE ONLINE LLC (PA)
4590 Macarthur Blvd Ste 500 (92660-2030)
PHONE..................877 388-8569
Doctor Prem Lobo, *Managing Member*
EMP: 109 EST: 2004
SALES (est): 8.31MM Privately Held
Web: www.yourpracticeonline.net
SIC: 8742 Marketing consulting services

(P-20622)
ZENLEADS INC
Also Called: Apollo.io
440 N Barranca Ave # 4750 (91723-1722)
PHONE..................415 640-9303
Tianyuan Zheng, *CEO*
Malvin Hoxhallari, *
EMP: 500 EST: 2016
SALES (est): 22.58MM Privately Held
Web: www.apollo.io
SIC: 8742 Marketing consulting services

(P-20623)
ZILLOW INC
535 Mission St (94105-3333)
PHONE..................877 215-8423
Spencer Rascoff, *CEO*
EMP: 62
SALES (corp-wide): 1.96B Publicly Held
Web: www.zillow.com
SIC: 8742 Real estate consultant
HQ: Zillow, Inc.
1301 2nd Ave Fl 31
Seattle WA
206 470-7000

(P-20624)
ZIMENO INC
Also Called: Monarch Tractor
203 Lawrence Dr Ste A (94551-5152)
PHONE..................833 247-4797
Praveen Penmetsa, *CEO*
EMP: 196 EST: 2017
SALES (est): 28.32MM Privately Held
SIC: 8742 Management consulting services

(P-20625)
ZIPLINE INTERNATIONAL INC
Also Called: Zipline
333 Corey Way (94080-6706)
PHONE..................408 475-8625
Keller Rinaudo, *CEO*
Keenan Wyrobek, *
EMP: 150 EST: 2011
SALES (est): 25.71MM Privately Held
Web: www.flyzipline.com
SIC: 8742 Automation and robotics consultant

(P-20626)
ZIPRECRUITER INC
Also Called: ZIPRECRUITER
604 Arizona Ave (90401-1610)
PHONE..................877 252-1062
EMP: 1150 EST: 2010
SQ FT: 60,000
SALES (est): 904.65MM Privately Held
Web: www.ziprecruiter.com
SIC: 8742 7371 Human resource consulting services; Custom computer programming services

(P-20627)
ZOHO CORPORATION
Manage Engine
4141 Hacienda Dr (94588-8549)
PHONE..................925 924-9500
Sridhar Vembu, *CEO*
EMP: 395
Web: www.site24x7.com
SIC: 8742 Management information systems consultant
HQ: Zoho Corporation
4141 Hacienda Dr
Pleasanton CA

8743 Public Relations Services

(P-20628)
ACCESS PUBLIC RELATIONS LLC
Also Called: Access Brand Communications
720 California St Fl 5 (94108-2453)
PHONE..................415 904-7070
Matt Afflixio, *
EMP: 64 EST: 1982
SQ FT: 17,000
SALES (est): 20.09MM
SALES (corp-wide): 14.29B Publicly Held
Web: www.accesspr.com
SIC: 8743 Public relations and publicity
HQ: Ketchum, Inc.
1285 Avenue Of The Americ
New York NY
646 935-3900

(P-20629)
ATOMIC PUBLIC RELATIONS (HQ)
Also Called: Atomic P R
735 Market St Fl 4 (94103-2034)
PHONE..................415 402-0230
Andy Getsey, *CEO*
James Hannon, *CIO*
EMP: 67 EST: 1999
SALES (est): 1.43MM
SALES (corp-wide): 5.57MM Privately Held
Web: www.atomicpr.com
SIC: 8743 Public relations and publicity
PA: Huntsworth Limited
Holborn Gate
London

(P-20630)
BNI ENTERPRISES INC
Also Called: B N I
545 College Commerce Way (91786-4377)
PHONE..................909 305-1818
Ivan Misner, *Ch*
EMP: 600 EST: 1985
SQ FT: 33,000
SALES (est): 47.78MM Privately Held
SIC: 8743 Promotion service

(P-20631)
BRAND AMP LLC
1945 Placentia Ave Ste C (92627-6274)
PHONE..................949 438-1060
Todd Brooks, *Managing Member*
Karen Schaefer, *
EMP: 74 EST: 2012
SQ FT: 16,069
SALES (est): 7.75MM Privately Held
Web: www.thebrandamp.com
SIC: 8743 8742 Public relations and publicity; Marketing consulting services

(P-20632)
CALIBRE INTERNATIONAL LLC (PA)
Also Called: High Caliber Line
6250 N Irwindale Ave (91702-3208)
PHONE..................626 969-4660
Catherine Oas, *
◆ EMP: 120 EST: 1998
SQ FT: 100,000
SALES (est): 23.2MM
SALES (corp-wide): 23.2MM Privately Held
Web: www.highcaliberline.com
SIC: 8743 2759 Promotion service; Promotional printing

(P-20633)
CHICEXECS
820 Los Vallecitos Blvd Ste A-C (92069-1408)
PHONE..................760 484-2116
EMP: 78 EST: 2017
SALES (est): 1.04MM Privately Held
Web: www.chicexecs.com
SIC: 8743 Public relations and publicity

(P-20634)
HAVAS FORMULA LLC
1215 Cushman Ave (92110-3904)
PHONE..................619 234-0345
EMP: 100 EST: 2014
SQ FT: 2,700
SALES (est): 23.62MM Privately Held
Web: www.havasformula.com
SIC: 8743 Public relations and publicity
HQ: Havas
29 30
Puteaux
158478000

(P-20635)
IGEL TECHNOLOGY CORPORATION
594 Howard St Ste 200 (94105-3026)
PHONE..................845 589-5900
Jedediah Dierke Ayres, *CEO*
Christiane Ohlgart, *
EMP: 108 EST: 2014
SALES (est): 22.45MM
SALES (corp-wide): 355.83K Privately Held
Web: www.igel.com
SIC: 8743 Sales promotion
HQ: Igel Technology Gmbh
Hermann-Ritter-Str. 110
Bremen HB
421520940

(P-20636)
KETCHUM INCORPORATED
Also Called: KETCHUM INCORPORATED
600 California St Fl 1 (94108-2734)
PHONE..................415 984-6100
Melissa Kinch, *Dir*
EMP: 75
SALES (corp-wide): 14.29B Publicly Held
Web: www.ketchum.com
SIC: 8743 Public relations and publicity
HQ: Ketchum, Inc.
1285 Avenue Of The Americ
New York NY
646 935-3900

(P-20637)
LEAGUE OF CALIFORNIA CITIES (PA)
Also Called: Western City Magazine
1400 K St Fl 4 (95814-3916)
PHONE..................916 658-8200
Carolyn Coleman, *Ex Dir*
Norman Coppinger, *
EMP: 65 EST: 1932
SQ FT: 32,000
SALES (est): 12.85MM
SALES (corp-wide): 12.85MM Privately Held
Web: www.calcities.org
SIC: 8743 2721 Lobbyist; Magazines: publishing only, not printed on site

(P-20638)
MAGIC WORKFORCE SOLUTIONS LLC
9100 Wilshire Blvd Ste 700e (90212)
PHONE..................310 246-6153
Earvin Johnson, *CEO*
Eric Holoman, *
Kawanna Brown, *
EMP: 611 EST: 2007
SALES (est): 327.89K
SALES (corp-wide): 72.76MM Privately Held
SIC: 8743 Promotion service
PA: Magic Johnson Enterprises, Inc.
9100 Wilshire Blvd 700e

PRODUCTS & SERVICES SECTION
8744 - Facilities Support Services (P-20661)

Beverly Hills CA
310 247-2033

(P-20639)
OGILVY PUB RLATIONS WORLD WIDE
800 El Camino Real (94025-4887)
PHONE.................................650 324-7015
Kate Osullivan, *VP*
EMP: 119
SALES (corp-wide): 17.37B **Privately Held**
SIC: 8743 Public relations and publicity
HQ: Ogilvy Public Relations World Wide
  3340 Peachtree Rd Ne # 300
  Atlanta GA

(P-20640)
OUTCAST AGENCY LLC
100 Montgomery St Ste 1200 (94104-4331)
PHONE.................................415 392-8282
Darlyn Phillips, *
EMP: 120 **EST:** 2012
SALES (est): 10.39MM **Privately Held**
Web: www.thisisoutcast.com
SIC: 8743 Public relations services

(P-20641)
PEDERSEN MEDIA GROUP INC
Also Called: Intrepid
1115 3rd St (94901-3017)
PHONE.................................415 512-9800
Mark Pedersen, *Pr*
Maureen Kumar, *Treas*
EMP: 113 **EST:** 1982
SALES (est): 4.9MM **Privately Held**
Web: www.pedersen.com
SIC: 8743 7812 Public relations services;
  Video tape production

(P-20642)
R/GA MEDIA GROUP INC
35 Park St (94110-5833)
PHONE.................................415 913-7531
Barry Wacksman, *Brnch Mgr*
EMP: 70
SALES (corp-wide): 10.93B **Publicly Held**
SIC: 8743 Public relations and publicity
HQ: R/Ga Media Group, Inc.
  450 W 33rd St Fl 12
  New York NY
  212 946-4000

(P-20643)
RADIUMONE INC
601 Montgomery St Fl 16 (94111-2620)
PHONE.................................415 418-2840
EMP: 167
SIC: 8743 Promotion service

(P-20644)
YOUNG & RUBICAM LLC
Also Called: Burson Marsteller
100 Pine St Ste 2300 (94111-5209)
PHONE.................................650 287-4000
Dave Chapman, *Genl Mgr*
EMP: 150
SALES (corp-wide): 17.37B **Privately Held**
Web: www.vmlyr.com
SIC: 8743 Public relations services
HQ: Young & Rubicam Llc
  3 Columbus Cir Fl 3 # 3
  New York NY
  212 210-3017

8744 Facilities Support Services

(P-20645)
ACEPEX MANAGEMENT CORPORATION
2707 Saturn St (92821-6705)
PHONE.................................909 625-6900
Henry C Rhee, *CEO*
EMP: 150 **EST:** 1989
SALES (est): 22.88MM **Privately Held**
Web: www.acepex.com
SIC: 8744 Base maintenance (providing personnel on continuing basis)

(P-20646)
ADVANCED CLEANUP TECH INC
Also Called: Acti
230 E C St (90744-6612)
PHONE.................................310 763-1423
Ruben Garcia, *CEO*
EMP: 260 **EST:** 1992
SALES (est): 15.68MM **Privately Held**
Web: www.actihazmat.com
SIC: 8744 Environmental remediation

(P-20647)
AMERIKO INC (PA)
Also Called: Ameriko Industries
980 S Arroyo Pkwy Ste 240 (91105-3928)
PHONE.................................626 795-7988
Chase C Rhee, *Pr*
Socorro Rhee, *Sec*
EMP: 60 **EST:** 1972
SQ FT: 5,000
SALES (est): 4.25MM
SALES (corp-wide): 4.25MM **Privately Held**
Web: www.ameriko.com
SIC: 8744 7349 Facilities support services; Building maintenance services, nec

(P-20648)
AMERIT FLEET SOLUTIONS INC
1331 N Calif Blvd Ste 150 (94596-4535)
PHONE.................................877 512-6374
EMP: 200
SALES (est): 7.09MM **Privately Held**
Web: www.ameritfleetsolutions.com
SIC: 8744 Base maintenance (providing personnel on continuing basis)

(P-20649)
AMERITAC INC (PA)
24 Toscana Way W (92270-1978)
P.O. Box 2550 (92270-1088)
PHONE.................................925 989-2942
Isiah Harris, *Pr*
Lawrence Stevens, *
EMP: 80 **EST:** 1994
SQ FT: 2,024
SALES (est): 5.33MM **Privately Held**
Web: www.ameritac.net
SIC: 8744 Base maintenance (providing personnel on continuing basis)

(P-20650)
ARGUS MANAGEMENT COMPANY LLC
Also Called: Argus Medical Management
5150 E Pacific Coast Hwy Ste 500 (90804)
PHONE.................................562 299-5200
EMP: 300 **EST:** 1995
SQ FT: 2,500
SALES (est): 23.01MM **Privately Held**
Web: www.argusmso.com
SIC: 8744 Facilities support services

(P-20651)
CAMSTON WRATHER LLC
2856 Whiptail Loop (92010-6708)
PHONE.................................858 525-9999
Dirk Wray, *CEO*
Mark Evans, *
Aaron Kamenash, *
EMP: 250 **EST:** 2014
SQ FT: 1,000
SALES (est): 6.64MM **Privately Held**
Web: www.camstonwrather.com
SIC: 8744 8711 1629 1041   Environmental remediation; Mining engineer; Land reclamation; Placer gold mining

(P-20652)
CHUGACH GOVERNMENT SVCS INC
9466 Black Mountain Rd Ste 240 (92126-4550)
PHONE.................................858 578-0276
Kevin Terry, *Mgr*
EMP: 487
SALES (corp-wide): 1.41B **Privately Held**
Web: www.chugach.com
SIC: 8744 Facilities support services
HQ: Chugach Government Services, Inc.
  3800 Cntrpint Dr Ste 1200
  Anchorage AK

(P-20653)
ENGINRNG/RMDTION RSRCES GROUP
Also Called: Errg-Er J V
456 Montgomery St Ste 900 (94104-1242)
PHONE.................................415 395-9974
EMP: 151
SALES (corp-wide): 58.92MM **Privately Held**
Web: www.errg.com
SIC: 8744 Environmental remediation
PA: Engineering/Remediation Resources Group, Inc.
  4585 Pacheco Blvd Ste 200
  Martinez CA
  925 839-2200

(P-20654)
HENRY CALL INC
Bldg 861 Clark And Arguello (93437)
PHONE.................................805 734-2762
Robert Clark, *Mgr*
EMP: 153
Web: www.callhenry.com
SIC: 8744 7371 8742 Base maintenance (providing personnel on continuing basis); Computer software development; Management consulting services
PA: Call Henry Inc
  1425 Chaffee Dr Ste 3
  Titusville FL

(P-20655)
INDYNE INC
1036 California Blvd Bldg 11013 (93437-6202)
PHONE.................................805 606-7225
Kenneth A Cinal, *Brnch Mgr*
EMP: 326
SALES (corp-wide): 97.78MM **Privately Held**
Web: www.indyneinc.com
SIC: 8744 Base maintenance (providing personnel on continuing basis)
PA: Indyne, Inc.
  46561 Expedition Dr 100
  Lexington Park MD
  703 903-6900

(P-20656)
INNOVATIVE CNSTR SOLUTIONS
575 Anton Blvd Ste 850 (92626-1912)
PHONE.................................714 893-6366
Hirad Emadi, *Pr*
John R White, *
EMP: 105 **EST:** 1999
SQ FT: 2,000
SALES (est): 25.05MM **Privately Held**
Web: www.icsinc.tv
SIC: 8744 1795   Environmental remediation; Demolition, buildings and other structures

(P-20657)
JLS ENVIRONMENTAL SERVICES INC
3460 Swetzer Rd (95650-7624)
PHONE.................................916 660-1525
John Sheehan, *Pr*
Larry Walker, *
John G Sheehan, *
David Locke, *
EMP: 86 **EST:** 2002
SALES (est): 10.69MM **Privately Held**
Web: www.jlsinc.com
SIC: 8744 8999   Environmental remediation; Earth science services

(P-20658)
M & E TECHNICAL SERVICES L L C
Also Called: Mets//
3601 Bayview Dr (90266-3225)
PHONE.................................256 964-6486
EMP: 100
Web: www.metechservices.com
SIC: 8744 4225 4731 7539 Facilities support services; General warehousing and storage ; Freight transportation arrangement; Automotive repair shops, nec

(P-20659)
MILITARY CALIFORNIA DEPARTMENT
Also Called: CA Arng 115th Rsg
11300 Lexington Dr Bldg 1000 (90720-5002)
PHONE.................................562 795-2065
Chi Huynh, *Brnch Mgr*
EMP: 500
SALES (corp-wide): 534.4MM **Privately Held**
SIC: 8744 Facilities support services
HQ: Department Of Military California
  9800 Goethe Rd 10
  Sacramento CA

(P-20660)
OLYMPUS BUILDING SERVICES INC
Also Called: OLYMPUS BUILDING SERVICES INC
441 La Moree Rd (92078-5017)
PHONE.................................760 750-4629
Anthony Hipple, *Brnch Mgr*
EMP: 920
SALES (corp-wide): 620.83MM **Privately Held**
Web: www.olympusinc.com
SIC: 8744 Facilities support services
HQ: Olympus Building Services, Llc
  1430 E Missouri Ave B205
  Phoenix AZ
  480 284-8018

(P-20661)
PRISTINE ENVIRONMENTS INC (PA)

8744 - Facilities Support Services (P-20662)

3605 Ocean Ranch Blvd Ste 200 (92056-2696)
PHONE.................................703 245-4751
Shaun R Gordon, *Prin*
Brian M Snow, *Prin*
Eric C Miller, *Prin*
Vincent Troisi, *Prin*
Naser Gjeloshi, *Prin*
EMP: 66 **EST:** 2011
SALES (est): 51.04MM
SALES (corp-wide): 51.04MM **Privately Held**
Web: www.kbs-services.com
SIC: 8744 Facilities support services

(P-20662)
PRO ENERGY SERVICES GROUP LLC
2060 Aldergrove Ave (92029-1301)
PHONE.................................760 789-7149
EMP: 290 **EST:** 2012
SALES (est): 21.48MM **Privately Held**
Web: www.proeservices.com
SIC: 8744 Facilities support services

(P-20663)
SMG
Also Called: Smg Stockton
3445 S El Dorado St (95206)
PHONE.................................209 937-7433
Kandra Clark, *Genl Mgr*
EMP: 400 **EST:** 2010
SQ FT: 25,000
SALES (est): 24.61MM
SALES (corp-wide): 422MM **Privately Held**
Web: www.stocktonmaintenance.com
SIC: 8744 Facilities support services
HQ: Smg Holdings, Llc
  300 Cnshohckn State Rd # 450
  Conshohocken PA

(P-20664)
SWISS PORT CORP
Also Called: Swissport
11001 Aviation Blvd (90045-6123)
PHONE.................................310 417-0258
Armin Unternaehrer, *VP*
▲ **EMP:** 290 **EST:** 1958
SALES (est): 9.71MM **Privately Held**
Web: www.swissport.com
SIC: 8744 4581 Facilities support services; Airports, flying fields, and services

(P-20665)
TECHFLOW INC (PA)
Also Called: Techflow Scntfic A Div Tchflow
9889 Willow Creek Rd Ste 100 (92131-1119)
PHONE.................................858 412-8000
Robert Baum, *CEO*
Mark Carter, *
Lorie Atoe, *
EMP: 104 **EST:** 1995
SQ FT: 19,000
SALES (est): 48.08MM
SALES (corp-wide): 48.08MM **Privately Held**
Web: www.techflow.com
SIC: 8744 8711 8748 Facilities support services; Engineering services; Systems analysis and engineering consulting services

(P-20666)
ULTURA INC
Also Called: Ultura
3605 Long Beach Blvd Ste 201 (90807-4024)
PHONE.................................562 661-4999
EMP: 128
SIC: 8744 3399 Environmental remediation; Iron ore recovery from open hearth slag

(P-20667)
WORKCARE INC
300 S Harbor Blvd Ste 600 (92805-3718)
PHONE.................................714 978-7488
Doctor Peter P Greaney, *CEO*
William E Nixon, *
Paula Sandrock, *
Mason D Harrell Iii, *Chief Medical Officer*
EMP: 181 **EST:** 1997
SQ FT: 11,000
SALES (est): 25.83MM **Privately Held**
Web: www.workcare.com
SIC: 8744 8011 Facilities support services; Offices and clinics of medical doctors

(P-20668)
ZERO WASTE SOLUTIONS INC
Also Called: Zero Waste Solutions
1850 Gateway Blvd Ste 1030 (94520-3279)
P.O. Box 5097 (94524-0097)
PHONE.................................925 270-3339
Shavila Singh, *Pr*
EMP: 200 **EST:** 2002
SQ FT: 3,000
SALES (est): 19.49MM **Privately Held**
Web: www.zerowastesolutions.com
SIC: 8744 Facilities support services

8748 Business Consulting, Nec

(P-20669)
2DREAM INC
5729 Sonoma Dr Ste Z (94566-8312)
P.O. Box 6065 (94538-0665)
PHONE.................................650 943-2366
Hongfei Yin, *Prin*
EMP: 70 **EST:** 2017
SALES (est): 2.02MM **Privately Held**
Web: www.2dreaminc.com
SIC: 8748 Business consulting, nec

(P-20670)
3E COMPANY ENV EC N ENG (PA)
Also Called: 3e
3207 Grey Hawk Ct (92010-6662)
PHONE.................................760 602-8700
Gregory Gartland, *CEO*
Justin Byron, *
Audrey Jean, *
EMP: 102 **EST:** 1985
SQ FT: 38,139
SALES (est): 118.07MM **Privately Held**
Web: www.3eco.com
SIC: 8748 8731 8711 Environmental consultant; Environmental research; Consulting engineer

(P-20671)
8020 CONSULTING LLC
6303 Owensmouth Ave Fl 10 (91367-2262)
PHONE.................................818 523-3201
David Lewis, *CEO*
Kelly Swartzel, *
EMP: 89 **EST:** 2013
SALES (est): 3.58MM **Privately Held**
Web: www.8020consulting.com
SIC: 8748 Business consulting, nec

(P-20672)
ACC-GWG LLC
Also Called: American Commodity Co.
6133 Abel Rd (95987-5816)
P.O. Box 236 (95987-0236)
PHONE.................................530 473-2827
Chris Crutchfield, *Pr*
Nicole Montna Van Vleck, *Sec*
EMP: 60 **EST:** 2005
SALES (est): 9.8MM **Privately Held**
Web: www.accrice.com
SIC: 8748 Agricultural consultant

(P-20673)
ACCENT COMPUTER SOLUTIONS LLC
8438 Red Oak St (91730-3815)
PHONE.................................909 825-2772
Marlin J Kaufman, *CEO*
Debbie Kaufman, *Sec*
EMP: 70 **EST:** 1987
SQ FT: 4,000
SALES (est): 11.66MM **Privately Held**
Web: www.vc3.com
SIC: 8748 1623 Systems engineering consultant, ex. computer or professional; Cable laying construction
PA: Vc3, Inc.
  1301 Gervais St Ste 1800
  Columbia SC

(P-20674)
ACRT PACIFIC LLC
3443 Deer Park Dr Ste B (95219-2306)
PHONE.................................330 945-7500
Alan Rothenbuecher, *
EMP: 450 **EST:** 2017
SALES (est): 50MM **Privately Held**
Web: pacific.acrt.com
SIC: 8748 Business consulting, nec

(P-20675)
ADVISORYCLOUD INC
7 Hamilton Landing Ste 100 (94949-8209)
PHONE.................................415 289-7115
EMP: 156 **EST:** 2018
SALES (est): 12.63MM **Privately Held**
Web: www.advisorycloud.com
SIC: 8748 Business consulting, nec

(P-20676)
AE & ASSOCIATES LLC
506 Queensland Cir (92879-1381)
PHONE.................................951 278-3477
EMP: 63 **EST:** 1999
SQ FT: 3,755
SALES (est): 8.74MM **Privately Held**
Web: www.aeandassociatesllc.com
SIC: 8748 Business consulting, nec

(P-20677)
AECOM TECHNICAL SERVICES INC (HQ)
300 S Grand Ave Fl 9 (90071-3135)
PHONE.................................213 593-8100
Timothy H Keener, *CEO*
▲ **EMP:** 100 **EST:** 1970
SQ FT: 43,000
SALES (est): 1.18B
SALES (corp-wide): 13.15B **Publicly Held**
Web: www.aecom.com
SIC: 8748 4953 8742 8711 Environmental consultant; Refuse systems; Industry specialist consultants; Engineering services
PA: Aecom
  13355 Noel Rd Ste 400
  Dallas TX
  972 788-1000

(P-20678)
AECOM USA INC
515 S Figueroa St Ste 400 (90071-3323)
PHONE.................................213 330-7200
EMP: 98
SALES (corp-wide): 13.15B **Publicly Held**
Web: www.aecom.com
SIC: 8748 Business consulting, nec
HQ: Aecom Usa, Inc.
  605 3rd Ave
  New York NY
  212 973-2900

(P-20679)
AECOM USA INC
401 W A St Ste 1200 (92101-7905)
PHONE.................................858 947-7144
Frederick William Werner, *Brnch Mgr*
EMP: 142
SALES (corp-wide): 13.15B **Publicly Held**
SIC: 8748 8741 Business consulting, nec; Construction management
HQ: Aecom Usa, Inc.
  605 3rd Ave
  New York NY
  212 973-2900

(P-20680)
AECOM USA INC
300 S Grand Ave Ste 900 (90071-3135)
PHONE.................................213 593-8000
Frederick Werner, *Brnch Mgr*
EMP: 98
SALES (corp-wide): 13.15B **Publicly Held**
Web: www.aecom.com
SIC: 8748 Business consulting, nec
HQ: Aecom Usa, Inc.
  605 3rd Ave
  New York NY
  212 973-2900

(P-20681)
AECOM USA INC
999 W Town And Country Rd (92868-4713)
PHONE.................................714 567-2501
Bruce Toro, *Mgr*
EMP: 98
SALES (corp-wide): 13.15B **Publicly Held**
SIC: 8748 Business consulting, nec
HQ: Aecom Usa, Inc.
  605 3rd Ave
  New York NY
  212 973-2900

(P-20682)
AKVARR INC
672 W 11th St Ste 325 (95376-3821)
PHONE.................................240 370-4182
EMP: 164
Web: www.akvarr.com
SIC: 8748 Systems analysis and engineering consulting services
PA: Akvarr, Inc.
  101 Lkforest Blvd Ste 400
  Gaithersburg MD

(P-20683)
ALIANTEL INC
1940 W Corporate Way (92801-5373)
PHONE.................................714 829-1650
EMP: 90 **EST:** 1996
SALES (est): 12.95MM **Privately Held**
SIC: 8748 7389 Telecommunications consultant; Telephone services

(P-20684)
ALLIANT INSURANCE SERVICES INC (PA)
Also Called: Nationwide
18100 Von Karman Ave Ste 1000 (92612-7196)
P.O. Box 6450 (92658-6450)
PHONE.................................949 756-0271
Thomas Corbett, *Ch Bd*

PRODUCTS & SERVICES SECTION
8748 - Business Consulting, Nec (P-20708)

Greg Zimmer, *
Ilene Anders, *
Peter Carpenter, *
Diana Kiehl, *
EMP: 175 **EST:** 1925
SALES (est): 1.15B
SALES (corp-wide): 1.15B **Privately Held**
Web: www.alliant.com
SIC: 8748 6411 Business consulting, nec; Insurance agents, nec

(P-20685)
ALLIANT INSURANCE SERVICES INC
Also Called: Nationwide
701 B St Fl 6 (92101-8156)
PHONE..................619 238-1828
Robert Campbell, Mgr
EMP: 75
SALES (corp-wide): 1.15B **Privately Held**
Web: www.alliant.com
SIC: 8748 6411 Business consulting, nec; Insurance agents and brokers
PA: Alliant Insurance Services, Inc.
  18100 Von Karman Ave # 1000
  Irvine CA
  949 756-0271

(P-20686)
ALLIED INDUSTRIES INC (PA)
Also Called: Allied Environmental Services
21650 Oxnard St Ste 500 (91367-4911)
PHONE..................800 605-5323
Ernesto Gutierrez, Pr
Fernando Gutierrez, COO
EMP: 150 **EST:** 1998
SQ FT: 11,000
SALES (est): 24.7MM
SALES (corp-wide): 24.7MM **Privately Held**
Web: www.alliedlead.com
SIC: 8748 Environmental consultant

(P-20687)
AMATEL INC (PA)
915 N Todd Ave (91702-2226)
PHONE..................323 801-0199
Joe Nwankwo, CEO
EMP: 63 **EST:** 1998
SALES (est): 11.59MM
SALES (corp-wide): 11.59MM **Privately Held**
Web: www.amatel.com
SIC: 8748 8711 Telecommunications consultant; Engineering services

(P-20688)
AMPLUS GROUP
400 Crenshaw Blvd Ste 200 (90503-1736)
PHONE..................424 316-5913
EMP: 60 **EST:** 2020
SALES (est): 1.52MM **Privately Held**
Web: www.amplusgrp.com
SIC: 8748 Business consulting, nec

(P-20689)
ANCHOR CNSLING EDCATN SLTONS L
19200 Von Karman Ave Ste 600 (92612-8553)
PHONE..................213 505-6322
Guillermo Valdez Ii, CEO
EMP: 70 **EST:** 2015
SALES (est): 2.52MM **Privately Held**
Web: www.anchorcounseling.solutions
SIC: 8748 7389 Educational consultant; Business Activities at Non-Commercial Site

(P-20690)
ANKURA CONSULTING GROUP LLC
633 W 5th St Fl 28 (90071-3502)
PHONE..................213 223-2109
Shannon Nolan, Prin
EMP: 136
SALES (corp-wide): 110MM **Privately Held**
Web: www.ankura.com
SIC: 8748 Business consulting, nec
HQ: Ankura Consulting Group, Llc
  485 Lexington Ave Fl 10
  New York NY
  212 818-1555

(P-20691)
APTIM CORP
18100 Von Karman Ave # 450 (92612-0169)
PHONE..................949 261-6441
EMP: 63
SALES (corp-wide): 2.2B **Privately Held**
SIC: 8748 Business consulting, nec
HQ: Aptim Corp.
  10001 Woodloch Forest Dr # 450
  The Woodlands TX
  832 823-2700

(P-20692)
APTIM CORP
4005 Port Chicago Hwy (94520-1180)
PHONE..................925 288-9898
EMP: 220
SALES (corp-wide): 2.2B **Privately Held**
SIC: 8748 Business consulting, nec
HQ: Aptim Corp.
  10001 Woodloch Forest Dr # 450
  The Woodlands TX
  832 823-2700

(P-20693)
APTIM CORP
1230 Columbia St Ste 1200 (92101-8517)
PHONE..................619 239-1690
EMP: 260
SALES (corp-wide): 2.2B **Privately Held**
SIC: 8748 Environmental consultant
HQ: Aptim Corp.
  10001 Woodloch Forest Dr # 450
  The Woodlands TX
  832 823-2700

(P-20694)
ASTRYA GLOBAL INC
4655 Cass St Ste 112 (92109-2810)
PHONE..................888 808-3138
Joseph Ventura, Pr
EMP: 60 **EST:** 2014
SALES (est): 15MM **Privately Held**
Web: www.astryaglobal.com
SIC: 8748 Business consulting, nec

(P-20695)
ATLAS TECHNICAL CONS LLC
Also Called: Consolidated Engineering Labs
2001 Crow Canyon Rd Ste 110 (94583-5368)
PHONE..................925 314-7100
EMP: 350
SALES (corp-wide): 1.47B **Privately Held**
Web: www.oneatlas.com
SIC: 8748 Testing services
HQ: Atlas Technical Consultants Llc
  13215 Bee Cave Pkwy B230
  Austin TX
  866 858-4499

(P-20696)
AVA THE RABBIT HAVEN INC
Also Called: RABBIT HAVEN THE
1261 S Mary St (95067)
P.O. Box 66594 (95067-6594)
PHONE..................831 600-7479
EMP: 80 **EST:** 2010
SALES (est): 90.34K **Privately Held**
Web: www.therabbithaven.org
SIC: 8748 Testing service, educational or personnel

(P-20697)
AXIOM GLOBAL TECHNOLOGIES INC
220 N Wiget Ln (94598-2404)
PHONE..................925 393-5800
Mohit Sishu Arora, CEO
Priya Arora, *
EMP: 125 **EST:** 2001
SALES (est): 10.22MM **Privately Held**
Web: www.axiomglobal.com
SIC: 8748 Business consulting, nec

(P-20698)
B & L CONSULTING LLC
164 N 2nd Ave # 9 (91786-6001)
PHONE..................682 238-6994
EMP: 63 **EST:** 1995
SQ FT: 5,000
SALES (est): 1.98MM **Privately Held**
SIC: 8748 Business consulting, nec

(P-20699)
BAY AREA AIR QUALITY (PA)
375 Beale St Ste 600 (94105-2001)
P.O. Box 420434 (94142-0434)
PHONE..................415 749-4900
Jack Broadbent, CEO
Ricardo Cardenas, *
EMP: 250 **EST:** 1955
SQ FT: 101,000
SALES (est): 60.13MM
SALES (corp-wide): 60.13MM **Privately Held**
Web: www.baaqmd.gov
SIC: 8748 Environmental consultant

(P-20700)
BAY AREA AIR QUALITY MGT DST
375 Beale St Ste 600 (94105-2097)
PHONE..................415 749-4900
Jack Broadbent, Prin
EMP: 400 **EST:** 2014
SALES (est): 11.15MM **Privately Held**
Web: www.baaqmd.gov
SIC: 8748 8741 5722 Environmental consultant; Business management; Electric household appliances

(P-20701)
BE SMITH INC
12400 High Bluff Dr Ste 100 (92130-3077)
PHONE..................913 341-9116
John Doug Smith, CEO
Lisa Carr, *
Colleen Chapp, *
Brian Christianson, *
Mark Madden, *
EMP: 271 **EST:** 1980
SALES (est): 22.81MM
SALES (corp-wide): 5.24B **Publicly Held**
Web: www.besmith.com
SIC: 8748 Business consulting, nec
PA: Amn Healthcare Services, Inc.
  2999 Olympus Blvd Ste 500
  Coppell TX
  866 871-8519

(P-20702)
BEHAVIORAL SCIENCE TECHNOLOGY INC (PA)
Also Called: Dekra Insight
1000 Town Center Dr Ste 600 (93036-1100)
PHONE..................805 646-0166
EMP: 82 **EST:** 1981
SALES (est): 22.24MM
SALES (corp-wide): 22.24MM **Privately Held**
SIC: 8748 Safety training service

(P-20703)
BERKELEY RESEARCH GROUP LLC (PA)
2200 Powell St Ste 1200 (94608-1833)
PHONE..................510 285-3300
EMP: 157 **EST:** 2010
SALES (est): 306.51MM **Privately Held**
Web: www.thinkbrg.com
SIC: 8748 Business consulting, nec

(P-20704)
BEYONDSOFT CONSULTING INC
2953 Bunker Hill Ln Ste 400 (95054-1104)
PHONE..................408 806-0715
EMP: 120
Web: www.beyondsoft.com
SIC: 8748 Business consulting, nec
HQ: Beyondsoft Consulting, Inc.
  10700 Northup Way Ste 120
  Bellevue WA
  425 332-4520

(P-20705)
BEYONDSOFT CONSULTING INC
19009 S Laurel Park Rd Spc 6 (90220-6054)
PHONE..................310 532-2822
EMP: 120
Web: www.beyondsoft.com
SIC: 8748 Business consulting, nec
HQ: Beyondsoft Consulting, Inc.
  10700 Northup Way Ste 120
  Bellevue WA
  425 332-4520

(P-20706)
BIOLA FRESH INC
5887 N Sycamore Ave (93723-8111)
PHONE..................559 970-8881
Sandra Olds, CEO
EMP: 60 **EST:** 2018
SALES (est): 2.5MM **Privately Held**
SIC: 8748 Agricultural consultant

(P-20707)
BISHOP FOX INC
85 2nd St Ste 750 (94105-3465)
PHONE..................480 621-8967
EMP: 167
SALES (corp-wide): 10.28MM **Privately Held**
Web: www.bishopfox.com
SIC: 8748 Business consulting, nec
HQ: Bishop Fox Inc.
  8240 S Kyrene Rd Ste 113
  Tempe AZ
  480 621-8967

(P-20708)
BMV DIRECT II LP
17190 Bernardo Center Dr (92128-7030)
PHONE..................858 485-9840
EMP: 83 **EST:** 2014
SALES (est): 2.04MM

8748 - Business Consulting, Nec (P-20709)

SALES (corp-wide): 264.45MM **Privately Held**
SIC: 8748 Business consulting, nec
HQ: Biomed Realty, L.P.
4570 Executive Dr Ste 400
San Diego CA
858 485-9840

(P-20709)
BOOSTED ECOMMERCE INC
9903 Santa Monica Blvd Ste 605 (90212-1606)
PHONE....................310 721-6316
Keith H Richman, *CEO*
Martin Dunstheimer, *CFO*
EMP: 69 **EST:** 2019
SALES (est): 11.37MM **Privately Held**
Web: www.boostedcommerce.com
SIC: 8748 Business consulting, nec

(P-20710)
BROADBAND TELECOM INC
515 S Flower St Fl 36 (90071-2221)
PHONE....................818 450-5714
EMP: 203
SALES (corp-wide): 34.06MM **Privately Held**
Web: www.broadbandtele.net
SIC: 8748 Telecommunications consultant
HQ: Broadband Telecom, Inc.
100 Quentin Roosevelt Blv
Garden City NY
718 713-8417

(P-20711)
BURKLAND CONSULTING INC
340 W Baltimore Ave (94939-2128)
PHONE....................415 944-8215
Richard Burkland, *Prin*
EMP: 209 **EST:** 2011
SALES (est): 1.29MM **Privately Held**
Web: www.burklandassociates.com
SIC: 8748 Business consulting, nec

(P-20712)
BUXTON CONSULTING
2010 Crow Canyon Pl Ste 100 (94583-1344)
PHONE....................925 467-0700
James T Buxton, *Pr*
Chandra Reddy, *
EMP: 90 **EST:** 1981
SALES (est): 10.88MM **Privately Held**
Web: www.buxtonconsulting.com
SIC: 8748 Systems engineering consultant, ex. computer or professional

(P-20713)
BY REFERRAL ONLY INC
2035 Corte Del Nogal Ste 200 (92011-1445)
PHONE....................760 707-1300
Joseph F Stumpf, *Pr*
EMP: 100 **EST:** 1991
SALES (est): 9.65MM **Privately Held**
Web: www.byreferralonly.com
SIC: 8748 Educational consultant

(P-20714)
C M E CORP
1051 S East St (92805-5749)
PHONE....................714 632-6939
EMP: 195
SALES (corp-wide): 22.17MM **Privately Held**
Web: www.cmecorp.com
SIC: 8748 Business consulting, nec
PA: C. M. E. Corp.
1206 Jefferson Blvd
Warwick RI
800 338-2372

(P-20715)
CAL SOUTHERN ASSN GOVERNMENTS (PA)
Also Called: S C A G
900 Wilshire Blvd Ste 1700 (90017-4701)
PHONE....................213 236-1800
Hasan Ikhrata, *Ex Dir*
Basil Panas, *
EMP: 116 **EST:** 1965
SQ FT: 50,000
SALES (est): 15.54MM
SALES (corp-wide): 15.54MM **Privately Held**
Web: scag.ca.gov
SIC: 8748 Urban planning and consulting services

(P-20716)
CALIFORNIA DEPARTMENT TRNSP
Also Called: Caltrans District 1
1656 Union St (95501-2229)
P.O. Box 3700 (95502-3700)
PHONE....................707 445-6600
Charlie Fielder, *Dir*
EMP: 140
SALES (corp-wide): 534.4MM **Privately Held**
Web: dot.ca.gov
SIC: 8748 4789 9621 Business consulting, nec; Railroad maintenance and repair services; Regulation, administration of transportation, State government
HQ: California, Department Of Transportation
1120 N St
Sacramento CA

(P-20717)
CAPITAL OVERSIGHT INC (PA)
Also Called: Capital Oversight
2118 Wilshire Blvd Ste 1000 (90403-5704)
PHONE....................310 453-8000
Dayne Williams, *CEO*
Kenneth Mays, *
Patricia Sewell, *
Douglas Rand, *
Matthew Denti, *
EMP: 65 **EST:** 2002
SQ FT: 11,000
SALES (est): 3.96MM
SALES (corp-wide): 3.96MM **Privately Held**
Web: www.capitaloversight.com
SIC: 8748 7323 7389 7299 Business consulting, nec; Credit clearinghouse; Personal financial services

(P-20718)
CAPSTONE PARTNERS
4695 Macarthur Ct Ste 1000 (92660-1865)
PHONE....................949 660-1717
EMP: 79 **EST:** 2013
SALES (est): 1.1MM **Privately Held**
Web: www.capstonepartnersfinancial.com
SIC: 8748 Business consulting, nec

(P-20719)
CASK NX LLC
Also Called: Cask
8910 University Center Ln Ste 400 (92122-1029)
P.O. Box 927170 (92192-7170)
PHONE....................858 232-8900
Mark Larsen, *Pr*
Jayson Rosenfeld, *
Craig Amundsen, *
Kent Moddelmog, *
Jason Young, *
EMP: 200 **EST:** 2018
SALES (est): 22.4MM **Privately Held**
Web: www.casknx.com
SIC: 8748 Business consulting, nec

(P-20720)
CAVISSON SYSTEMS INC
5201 Great America Pkwy Ste 320 (95054-1122)
PHONE....................800 701-6125
Anil Kumar, *Pr*
EMP: 500 **EST:** 2002
SQ FT: 10,000
SALES (est): 39.87MM **Privately Held**
Web: www.cavisson.com
SIC: 8748 Systems analysis and engineering consulting services

(P-20721)
CBA SITE SERVICES INC
11387 Pyrites Way (95670-4595)
PHONE....................925 754-7633
Michael Mcwhirter, *Pr*
EMP: 62 **EST:** 1980
SQ FT: 70,000
SALES (est): 8.91MM **Privately Held**
Web: www.legacy-wireless.com
SIC: 8748 Telecommunications consultant

(P-20722)
CBR GROUP
59 Skipping Rock Way (94558-7006)
PHONE....................415 806-2323
Christy Beltran Roberts, *Prin*
EMP: 66 **EST:** 2010
SALES (est): 5.86MM **Privately Held**
Web: www.thecbrgroup.com
SIC: 8748 Telecommunications consultant

(P-20723)
CDSNET LLC
Also Called: Fmsinfoserv
6053 W Century Blvd (90045-6430)
PHONE....................310 981-9500
Michael Griffus, *Pr*
Francis G Homan, *CFO*
EMP: 411 **EST:** 2006
SALES (est): 940.63K
SALES (corp-wide): 4.23MM **Privately Held**
SIC: 8748 Business consulting, nec
HQ: Keolis Transit America, Inc.
53 State St Fl 11
Boston MA

(P-20724)
CENTER FOR SUSTAINABLE ENERGY
3980 Sherman St Ste 170 (92110-4314)
PHONE....................858 244-1177
Michael Akavan, *Bd*
Mary Mcgroarty, *Ch Bd*
Lawrence E Goldenhersh, *
Michael Akavan Former, *BD*
Nick Leibham, *Vice Chairman*
EMP: 87 **EST:** 2001
SALES (est): 246.28MM **Privately Held**
Web: www.energycenter.org
SIC: 8748 Energy conservation consultant

(P-20725)
CETECOM INC
411 Dixon Landing Rd (95035-2579)
PHONE....................408 586-6200
Maan Ghanma, *CEO*
Willfried Klassmann, *
Heiko Strehlow, *
Clorinda Sammis, *
EMP: 110 **EST:** 1998
SQ FT: 48,000
SALES (est): 24.94MM
SALES (corp-wide): 300.28MM **Privately Held**
Web: www.cetecomadvanced.com
SIC: 8748 8734 Telecommunications consultant; Testing laboratories
HQ: Cetecom Advanced Gmbh
Unterturkheimer Str. 6-10
Saarbruecken SL
205495190

(P-20726)
CHAMBERS GROUP INC (PA)
5 Hutton Centre Dr Ste 750 (92707)
PHONE....................949 261-5414
EMP: 80 **EST:** 1978
SALES (est): 10.2MM **Privately Held**
Web: www.chambersgroupinc.com
SIC: 8748 Environmental consultant

(P-20727)
CHANNELWAVE SOFTWARE INC
27081 Aliso Creek Rd (92656-5365)
PHONE....................949 448-4500
Rob Hagen, *Mgr*
EMP: 83
Web: www.channelwave.com
SIC: 8748 8742 Business consulting, nec; Management consulting services
HQ: Channelwave Software, Inc.
1 Kendall Sq Bldg 200
Cambridge MA

(P-20728)
CITY OF NORCO
Also Called: Successor Agcy To Nrco Cmnty R
2870 Clark Ave (92860-1903)
PHONE....................951 270-5617
EMP: 100
SALES (corp-wide): 49.71MM **Privately Held**
Web: www.norco.ca.us
SIC: 8748 Urban planning and consulting services
PA: City Of Norco
2870 Clark Ave
Norco CA
951 270-5617

(P-20729)
CLEAN HARBORS ENVMTL SVCS INC
4101 Industrial Way (94510-1211)
PHONE....................707 747-6699
Kevin Carnahan, *Pr*
EMP: 100
SALES (corp-wide): 5.17B **Publicly Held**
Web: www.cleanharbors.com
SIC: 8748 Environmental consultant
HQ: Clean Harbors Environmental Services, Inc.
42 Longwater Dr
Norwell MA
781 792-5000

(P-20730)
CLEARESULT OPERATING LLC
807 N Park View Dr # 150 (90245-4932)
PHONE....................508 836-9500
Kimberly Simpson, *Brnch Mgr*
EMP: 79
SALES (corp-wide): 499.94MM **Privately Held**
SIC: 8748 Energy conservation consultant
HQ: Clearesult Operating, Llc
6504 Bridge Point Pkwy # 42
Austin TX
512 327-9200

PRODUCTS & SERVICES SECTION
8748 - Business Consulting, Nec (P-20754)

(P-20731)
COHEN VENTURES INC (PA)
Also Called: Energy Solutions
449 15th St # 400 (94612-2801)
PHONE.....................................510 482-4420
Samuel D Cohen, *Pr*
EMP: 74 **EST:** 1995
SQ FT: 11,000
SALES (est): 13.57MM
SALES (corp-wide): 13.57MM **Privately Held**
Web: www.energy-solution.com
SIC: 8748 Energy conservation consultant

(P-20732)
CONNOR CONSULTING CORP (PA)
300 Brannan St Ste 511 (94107-1874)
PHONE.....................................415 678-5002
Viresh Chana, *CEO*
Rich Reyes, *Ex VP*
Vannessa James, *Opers Mgr*
EMP: 143 **EST:** 2009
SALES (est): 14.16MM
SALES (corp-wide): 14.16MM **Privately Held**
Web: www.connor-consulting.com
SIC: 8748 Business consulting, nec

(P-20733)
CONTROLLER CONSULTING SVCS INC
1577 Aldacourrou St (95304-5872)
PHONE.....................................408 221-2492
Eric Fan, *Pr*
EMP: 150 **EST:** 2007
SALES (est): 3.97MM **Privately Held**
Web: www.controllerconsulting.com
SIC: 8748 Business consulting, nec

(P-20734)
CORNERSTONE RESEARCH INC (PA)
1000 El Camino Real Ste 250 (94025-2339)
PHONE.....................................650 853-1660
Cynthia Zollinger, *Ch*
Michael E Burton, *
Michael Keeley, *
Catherine Galley, *
Allan Kleidon, *
EMP: 100 **EST:** 1989
SQ FT: 40,000
SALES (est): 94.84MM
SALES (corp-wide): 94.84MM **Privately Held**
Web: www.cornerstone.com
SIC: 8748 7389 Economic consultant; Financial services

(P-20735)
CRA INTERNATIONAL INC
12424 Wilshire Blvd Ste 600 (90025-1052)
PHONE.....................................310 393-5530
EMP: 60
SALES (corp-wide): 590.9MM **Publicly Held**
Web: www.crai.com
SIC: 8748 8111 Economic consultant; Legal services
PA: Cra International, Inc.
200 Clarendon St
Boston MA
617 425-3000

(P-20736)
DATATRACE TITLE
200 Commerce (92602-5000)
PHONE.....................................800 221-2056
EMP: 97 **EST:** 2019
SALES (est): 829.81K **Privately Held**
SIC: 8748 Business consulting, nec

(P-20737)
DELOITTE CONSULTING LLP
350 S Grand Ave Ste 200 (90071-3469)
PHONE.....................................212 489-1600
Laura Conlin, *Brnch Mgr*
EMP: 230
SALES (corp-wide): 677.45K **Privately Held**
SIC: 8748 Business consulting, nec
HQ: Deloitte Consulting Llp
30 Rockefeller Plz
New York NY
212 492-4000

(P-20738)
DETECON INC
351 California St (94104-2418)
PHONE.....................................415 549-6999
Daniel Kellmereit, *CEO*
Lars Bodenheimer, *
EMP: 271 **EST:** 2008
SALES (est): 5.13MM
SALES (corp-wide): 118.6B **Privately Held**
Web: www.detecon.com
SIC: 8748 Telecommunications consultant
HQ: Detecon International Gmbh
Bayenwerft 12-14
Koln NW
22191610

(P-20739)
DISRUPTIVE VISIONS LLC
23456 Madero Ste 210 (92691-2783)
PHONE.....................................949 502-3800
Marc Anthony, *Managing Member*
EMP: 60 **EST:** 2016
SALES (est): 1.12MM **Privately Held**
SIC: 8748 Telecommunications consultant

(P-20740)
ECO BAY SERVICES INC
1501 Minnesota St (94107-3521)
PHONE.....................................415 643-7777
Trent Scott Michels, *CEO*
EMP: 150 **EST:** 2007
SQ FT: 80,000
SALES (est): 44.56MM **Privately Held**
Web: www.ecobayservices.com
SIC: 8748 Environmental consultant

(P-20741)
EDGE MORTGAGE ADVISORY CO LLC
2125 E Katella Ave Ste 350 (92806-6072)
PHONE.....................................714 564-5800
Doug Speaker, *
EMP: 88 **EST:** 2009
SALES (est): 9.89MM **Privately Held**
Web: www.edgemac.com
SIC: 8748 Business consulting, nec

(P-20742)
ENERGY EXPERTS INTERNATIONAL
7111 N Fresno St Ste 260 (93720-2959)
PHONE.....................................559 449-1124
EMP: 74
SALES (corp-wide): 43.89MM **Privately Held**
Web: www.eeintl.com
SIC: 8748 8742 Energy conservation consultant; Management consulting services
PA: Energy Experts International
555 Twin Dolphin Dr # 150
Redwood City CA
650 593-4261

(P-20743)
ENTERPRISE SOLUTIONS INC
2855 Kifer Rd (95051-0814)
PHONE.....................................408 727-3627
Lucy Phang, *CFO*
EMP: 344
Web: www.enterprisesolutioninc.com
SIC: 8748 Systems engineering consultant, ex. computer or professional
PA: Enterprise Solutions, Inc.
700 E Diehl Rd
Naperville IL

(P-20744)
ENVENT CORPORATION (PA)
3220 E 29th St (90806-2321)
PHONE.....................................562 997-9465
Steve Sellinger, *Pr*
Tom L Kerscher, *Sr VP*
Joe Stonecipher, *Prin*
Brian Miller, *Prin*
Keith Lyons, *Prin*
EMP: 93 **EST:** 1992
SQ FT: 6,400
SALES (est): 38.89MM **Privately Held**
Web: www.enventcorporation.com
SIC: 8748 Environmental consultant

(P-20745)
ENVIRONMENTAL RESOLUTIONS INC
Also Called: Cardno Eri
25371 Commercentre Dr Ste 250 (92630)
PHONE.....................................949 457-8950
Steve M Zigan, *CEO*
Robert L Kroeger, *VP*
EMP: 300 **EST:** 1989
SQ FT: 14,100
SALES (est): 22.46MM **Privately Held**
Web: www.eri-us.com
SIC: 8748 8744 Environmental consultant; Environmental remediation
HQ: Cardno Usa, Inc.
8310 S Valley Hwy Ste 300
Englewood CO

(P-20746)
ENVIRONMENTAL SCIENCE ASSOC
9191 Towne Centre Dr Ste 340 (92122)
PHONE.....................................858 638-0900
Ralene Cavataio, *Brnch Mgr*
EMP: 105
SALES (corp-wide): 62.52MM **Privately Held**
Web: www.esassoc.com
SIC: 8748 Environmental consultant
PA: Environmental Science Associates
575 Market St Ste 3700
San Francisco CA
415 896-5900

(P-20747)
ETONIEN LLC (PA)
Also Called: Etonien
1230 Rosecrans Ave Ste 530 (90266-2486)
PHONE.....................................310 321-5800
Joseph E Davis, *CEO*
EMP: 68 **EST:** 2008
SALES (est): 5.37MM
SALES (corp-wide): 5.37MM **Privately Held**
Web: www.etonien.com
SIC: 8748 Business consulting, nec

(P-20748)
FAME ASSISTANCE CORPORATION
2270 S Harvard Blvd (90018-2142)
PHONE.....................................323 373-7720
Denise Hunter, *Pr*
EMP: 75 **EST:** 1988
SQ FT: 33,748
SALES (est): 1.89MM **Privately Held**
Web: www.famecorporations.org
SIC: 8748 Business consulting, nec

(P-20749)
FIRST STEP HOUSING
Also Called: First Step Communities
139 Blakeslee Way (95630-4629)
PHONE.....................................916 769-8877
Stephen Watters, *CEO*
EMP: 77 **EST:** 2015
SALES (est): 331.3K **Privately Held**
SIC: 8748 Urban planning and consulting services

(P-20750)
FRANCSCO PRTNERS III CAYMAN LP
1 Letterman Dr Bldg C (94129-1492)
PHONE.....................................415 418-2900
Dipanjan Dj Deb, *CEO*
Tom Ludwig, *COO*
EMP: 64 **EST:** 2016
SALES (est): 3.12MM **Privately Held**
Web: www.franciscopartners.com
SIC: 8748 Business consulting, nec

(P-20751)
FREMOUW ENVIRONMENTAL SVCS INC
6940 Tremont Rd (95620-9603)
PHONE.....................................707 448-3700
Ted Fremouw, *CEO*
Phillip A Fremouw, *
Marty Mosley, *
Stu E Jordan, *
Nancy Fremouw, *
EMP: 60 **EST:** 1996
SQ FT: 4,000
SALES (est): 12.94MM **Privately Held**
Web: www.fremouwenvironmental.com
SIC: 8748 4212 Environmental consultant; Hazardous waste transport

(P-20752)
FRYMAN MANAGEMENT INC
18 Goodyear Ste 105 (92618-3749)
PHONE.....................................949 481-5211
Ross Fryman, *Pr*
EMP: 88 **EST:** 2014
SALES (est): 5.24MM **Privately Held**
Web: www.frymanmanagement.com
SIC: 8748 Traffic consultant

(P-20753)
FTI CONSULTING INC
50 California St Ste 1900 (94111-4620)
PHONE.....................................415 283-4200
Jerry Keeler, *Mgr*
EMP: 80
SALES (corp-wide): 3.03B **Publicly Held**
Web: www.fticonsulting.com
SIC: 8748 Business consulting, nec
PA: Fti Consulting, Inc.
555 12th St Nw Ste 700
Washington DC
202 312-9100

(P-20754)
FUNGIBLE INC
3201 Scott Blvd (95054-3008)
PHONE.....................................669 292-5522
Pradeep Sindhu, *CEO*
Jai Menon, *Chief Scientist**
EMP: 219 **EST:** 2015

8748 - Business Consulting, Nec (P-20755)

SALES (est): 24.09MM
SALES (corp-wide): 211.91B **Publicly Held**
Web: blogs.microsoft.com
SIC: 8748 Business consulting, nec
PA: Microsoft Corporation
1 Microsoft Way
Redmond WA
425 882-8080

(P-20755)
FUSE PROJECT LLC
1401 16th St (94103-5109)
PHONE.................................415 908-1492
Yves Behar, *Pr*
Mitch Pergola, *
Helen Fu Thomas, *
▲ **EMP:** 60 **EST:** 1998
SQ FT: 22,000
SALES (est): 12.88MM **Privately Held**
Web: www.fuseproject.com
SIC: 8748 Business consulting, nec

(P-20756)
FUTUREWEI TECHNOLOGIES INC (HQ)
2220 Central Expy (95050-2516)
PHONE.................................469 277-5700
Jason Chao, *Pr*
Xing Yang, *
▲ **EMP:** 140 **EST:** 2000
SALES (est): 81.31MM
SALES (corp-wide): 31.02B **Privately Held**
Web: www.futurewei.com
SIC: 8748 8731 Telecommunications consultant; Electronic research
PA: Huawei Technologies Cooperatief U.A.
Herikerbergweg 36
Amsterdam NH
204300808

(P-20757)
GARCIA AND ASSOCIATES
Also Called: Ganda
1 Saunders Ave (94960-1719)
PHONE.................................415 458-5803
EMP: 175
Web: www.kleinfelder.com
SIC: 8748 Environmental consultant

(P-20758)
GARRAD HASSAN AMERICA INC (DH)
Also Called: GL
9665 Chesapeake Dr Ste 435 (92123-1378)
PHONE.................................858 836-3370
Carole Barbeau, *CEO*
EMP: 70 **EST:** 2002
SQ FT: 1,380
SALES (est): 8.86MM **Privately Held**
Web: www.dnv.com
SIC: 8748 Energy conservation consultant
HQ: Garrad Hassan Group Limited
One Linear Park, Avon Street
Bristol

(P-20759)
GATEB CONSULTING INC
815 Hampton Dr Unit 1b (90291-5702)
PHONE.................................310 526-8323
Sarah Iskander, *CEO*
EMP: 90 **EST:** 2013
SALES (est): 3.82MM **Privately Held**
Web: www.gateb.com
SIC: 8748 Business consulting, nec

(P-20760)
GEOCON CONSULTANTS INC (PA)
Also Called: Geocon
6960 Flanders Dr (92121-3992)
PHONE.................................858 558-6900
Michael Chapin, *CEO*
Joe Vettel, *
John Hoobs, *
John Juhrend, *
Neal Berliner, *
EMP: 85 **EST:** 1987
SQ FT: 10,000
SALES (est): 27.86MM **Privately Held**
Web: www.geoconinc.com
SIC: 8748 8711 Environmental consultant; Engineering services

(P-20761)
GEOLOGICS CORPORATION
25375 Orchard Village Rd Ste 102 (91355-3000)
PHONE.................................661 259-5767
Fernando Arroyo, *Mgr*
EMP: 182
Web: www.geologics.com
SIC: 8748 8711 7379 Systems analysis and engineering consulting services; Consulting engineer; Computer related consulting services
PA: Geologics Corporation
5500 Cherokee Ave Ste 400
Alexandria VA

(P-20762)
GI PARTNERS LLC (PA)
Also Called: Global Innovation Advisors
4 Embarcadero Ctr Ste 3200 (94111-4188)
PHONE.................................415 688-4800
EMP: 3450 **EST:** 1998
SALES (est): 1.47B
SALES (corp-wide): 1.47B **Privately Held**
Web: www.gipartners.com
SIC: 8748 Business consulting, nec

(P-20763)
GIBSON OVERSEAS INC
7776 Tippecanoe Ave (92410-4537)
PHONE.................................323 832-8900
EMP: 169
SALES (corp-wide): 221.89MM **Privately Held**
Web: www.gibsonhomewares.com
SIC: 8748 Business consulting, nec
PA: Gibson Overseas, Inc.
2410 Yates Ave
Commerce CA
323 832-8900

(P-20764)
GLOBAL INFOTECH CORPORATION
2890 Zanker Rd Ste 202 (95134-2118)
PHONE.................................408 567-0600
Atul Sharma, *Pr*
Nitin Prasad, *
EMP: 300 **EST:** 1995
SQ FT: 3,000
SALES (est): 21.71MM
SALES (corp-wide): 53.13MM **Privately Held**
Web: www.global-infotech.com
SIC: 8748 Systems analysis and engineering consulting services
PA: Intelliswift Software, Inc.
39600 Balentine Dr # 200
Newark CA
510 370-2600

(P-20765)
GOALBOOK
234 7th Ave Unit 200 (94401-4217)
PHONE.................................650 207-9388
Justin Su, *Prin*
EMP: 87 **EST:** 2017
SALES (est): 2.11MM **Privately Held**
Web: www.goalbookapp.com
SIC: 8748 Educational consultant

(P-20766)
GOLDMAN DATA LLC
2156 N Shaffer St (92865-3407)
PHONE.................................714 283-5889
EMP: 87
SALES (corp-wide): 5.81MM **Privately Held**
Web: www.goldmandata.com
SIC: 8748 Business consulting, nec
PA: Goldman Data, Llc
1407 N Batavia St Ste 106
Orange CA

(P-20767)
GORDON E BTTY I MORE FUNDATION
Also Called: Moore Foundation
1661 Page Mill Rd (94304-1209)
PHONE.................................650 213-3000
Lewis W Coleman, *Pr*
Chris Mccrum, *CAO*
Denise Strack, *
EMP: 75 **EST:** 2001
SALES (est): 804.91MM **Privately Held**
Web: www.moore.org
SIC: 8748 Economic consultant

(P-20768)
GREATER LOS ANGLES CNTY VCTOR
12545 Florence Ave (90670-3919)
PHONE.................................562 944-7976
Trucmai Nguyen-dever, *Mgr*
EMP: 132 **EST:** 2019
SALES (est): 12.84MM **Privately Held**
Web: www.glamosquito.org
SIC: 8748 Environmental consultant

(P-20769)
HALEY & ALDRICH INC
5333 Mission Center Rd Ste 300 (92108)
PHONE.................................619 280-9210
Anita Broughton, *Brnch Mgr*
EMP: 60
SALES (corp-wide): 78.95MM **Privately Held**
Web: www.haleyaldrich.com
SIC: 8748 8711 Environmental consultant; Engineering services
PA: Haley & Aldrich, Inc.
70 Blanchard Rd Ste 204
Burlington MA
781 685-2115

(P-20770)
HIGHER GROUND EDUCATION INC (PA)
10 Orchard Ste 200 (92630-8309)
PHONE.................................949 836-9401
Ramandeep Grin, *CEO*
Ramandeep Girn, *
Rebecca Girn, *
Guy Barnett, *
EMP: 307 **EST:** 2016
SALES (est): 53.85MM
SALES (corp-wide): 53.85MM **Privately Held**
Web: www.tohigherground.com

SIC: 8748 8299 Business consulting, nec; Educational services

(P-20771)
HQE SYSTEMS INC
27419 Via Industria (92590-3752)
PHONE.................................800 967-3036
Qais Alkurdi, *CEO*
Henry Hernandez, *
EMP: 65 **EST:** 2013
SALES (est): 5.02MM **Privately Held**
Web: www.hqesystems.com
SIC: 8748 7629 3669 3571 Systems analysis and engineering consulting services; Telecommunication equipment repair (except telephones); Emergency alarms; Electronic computers

(P-20772)
HUMANO LLC
4231 Balboa Ave (92117-5504)
PHONE.................................844 448-6266
EMP: 87 **EST:** 2018
SALES (est): 4.22MM **Privately Held**
Web: www.humano.net
SIC: 8748 Business consulting, nec

(P-20773)
HUMBOLDT STATE UNIV SPNSRED PR
Also Called: Hsu Foundation
1 Harpst St Rm 427 (95521)
P.O. Box 1185 (95518-1185)
PHONE.................................707 826-4189
Steven Karp, *Ex Dir*
EMP: 100 **EST:** 1952
SALES (est): 36.74MM **Privately Held**
Web: www.humboldt.edu
SIC: 8748 Educational consultant

(P-20774)
ICF JONES & STOKES INC
525 B St Ste 1700 (92101-4478)
PHONE.................................858 578-8964
Tevon Muto, *Brnch Mgr*
EMP: 111
SALES (corp-wide): 1.78B **Publicly Held**
Web: www.icf.com
SIC: 8748 Environmental consultant
HQ: Icf Jones & Stokes, Inc
1902 Reston Metro Plz
Reston VA
703 934-3000

(P-20775)
IES COMMERCIAL INC
Also Called: Ies
9211 Irvine Blvd (92618-1645)
PHONE.................................949 222-0320
EMP: 86
Web: www.ielectric.com
SIC: 8748 Business consulting, nec
HQ: Ies Commercial, Inc.
2801 S Fair Ln Ste 101
Tempe AZ
480 379-6200

(P-20776)
IN MONTROSE WTR SSTNBLITY SVCS
Also Called: Mwss
4 Park Plz Ste 790 (92614-5262)
PHONE.................................949 988-3500
Vijay Manthripragada, *Pr*
Jose Revuelta, *
Nasym Afsari, *
Allan Dicks, *
EMP: 90 **EST:** 2019
SALES (est): 16.22MM

PRODUCTS & SERVICES SECTION
8748 - Business Consulting, Nec (P-20799)

SALES (corp-wide): 544.42MM **Publicly Held**
Web: www.montrose-env.com
SIC: **8748** 8744 Environmental consultant; Environmental remediation
PA: Montrose Environmental Group, Inc.
5120 Northshore Dr
North Little Rock AR
501 900-6400

(P-20777)
INDIE LLC
32 Journey Ste 100 (92656-5329)
PHONE.............................949 608-0854
EMP: 170 EST: 2017
SALES (est): 972.08K
SALES (corp-wide): 110.8MM **Publicly Held**
Web: www.indiesemi.com
SIC: **8748** Business consulting, nec
PA: Indie Semiconductor, Inc.
32 Journey Ste 100
Aliso Viejo CA
949 608-0854

(P-20778)
INFLECTIONCOM INC
303 Twin Dolphin Dr Ste 600 (94065-1497)
PHONE.............................650 618-9910
Max Wesman, *VP*
Jared Waterman, *
EMP: 168 EST: 2014
SQ FT: 7,000
SALES (est): 24.91MM
SALES (corp-wide): 473.9MM **Privately Held**
Web: www.inflection.com
SIC: **8748** Business consulting, nec
PA: Checkr, Inc.
1 Montgomery St Ste 2400
San Francisco CA
844 824-3257

(P-20779)
INFOSOFT INC
7891 Westwood Dr Ste 113 (95020-4786)
PHONE.............................408 659-4326
Ashish Chopra, *Pr*
Raj Rajneesh Chopra, *VP*
EMP: 80 EST: 2005
SALES (est): 5.55MM **Privately Held**
Web: www.infosoft-inc.com
SIC: **8748** 7361 Systems engineering consultant, ex. computer or professional; Placement agencies

(P-20780)
INNOVATIVE VHCL SOLUTIONS LLC
5831 Research Dr (92649-1349)
PHONE.............................714 896-8267
Lisa Kuhn, *Mgr*
EMP: 116
SALES (corp-wide): 11.91MM **Privately Held**
Web: www.innovativevehicle.com
SIC: **8748** Business consulting, nec
PA: Innovative Vehicle Solutions Llc
3241 Benchmark Dr
Ladson SC
843 376-3822

(P-20781)
INSIGNIA ENVIRONMENTAL
545 Middlefield Rd Ste 210 (94025-3400)
PHONE.............................650 321-6783
Anne Marie Mcgraw, *Pr*
Alex Mcgraw, *VP*
EMP: 65 EST: 2004
SALES (est): 16.2MM **Privately Held**
Web: www.insigniaenvironmental.com
SIC: **8748** Environmental consultant

(P-20782)
IRVINE TECHNOLOGY CORPORATION
2850 Redhill Ave Ste 230 (92705-5550)
PHONE.............................714 445-2624
Nicole Mcmackin, *Pr*
Janet Thornby, *
Michael Rose, *
Kevin Orlando, *
EMP: 160 EST: 2000
SALES (est): 19.05MM **Privately Held**
Web: www.irvinetechcorp.com
SIC: **8748** 7363 7371 7379 Business consulting, nec; Temporary help service; Software programming applications; Computer related consulting services

(P-20783)
ITC SRVICE GROUP ACQSITION LLC
108 N East St (95776-5911)
PHONE.............................530 717-0485
EMP: 141
Web: www.callitc.com
SIC: **8748** Telecommunications consultant
HQ: Itc Service Group Acquisition Llc
7777 Greenback Ln Ste 201
Citrus Heights CA
877 370-4482

(P-20784)
IVY ENTERPRISES INC
5564 E 61st St (90040-3406)
PHONE.............................323 887-8661
Jane Kim, *Mgr*
EMP: 440
Web: www.myivyusa.com
SIC: **8748** Business consulting, nec
HQ: Ivy Enterprises, Inc.
25 Harbor Park Dr
Port Washington NY

(P-20785)
JAG PROFESSIONAL SERVICES INC
2008 Walnut Ave (90266-2841)
P.O. Box 3007 (90245-8107)
PHONE.............................310 945-5648
Judith Hinkley, *CEO*
EMP: 126 EST: 2001
SQ FT: 1,000
SALES (est): 2.77MM **Privately Held**
Web: www.jagprof.com
SIC: **8748** Business consulting, nec

(P-20786)
JOHNSON JOHNSON INNOVATION LLC
Also Called: Jlabs
3210 Merryfield Row (92121-1126)
PHONE.............................858 242-1504
Tom Heyman, *Pr*
EMP: 96 EST: 2016
SALES (est): 43.66MM
SALES (corp-wide): 94.94B **Publicly Held**
SIC: **8748** Test development and evaluation service
PA: Johnson & Johnson
1 Johnson And Johnson Plz
New Brunswick NJ
732 524-0400

(P-20787)
JONES IT CONSULTING LLC
Also Called: Jones It
3435 Cesar Chavez Ste Ph (94110-4554)
PHONE.............................415 578-7111
EMP: 208 EST: 2011
SQ FT: 2,300
SALES (est): 10.49MM **Privately Held**
Web: www.itjones.com
SIC: **8748** 5734 Business consulting, nec; Computer and software stores

(P-20788)
KADIANT LLC
155 Grand Ave Ste 500 (94612-3747)
P.O. Box 399318 (94139-9318)
PHONE.............................209 521-4791
EMP: 243 EST: 2019
SALES (est): 6.4MM **Privately Held**
Web: www.kadiant.com
SIC: **8748** Business consulting, nec

(P-20789)
KARMAN TOPCO LP (PA)
18100 Von Karman Ave Ste 1000 (92612-0169)
PHONE.............................949 797-2900
EMP: 64 EST: 2014
SALES (est): 4.71B
SALES (corp-wide): 4.71B **Publicly Held**
SIC: **8748** Business consulting, nec

(P-20790)
KCCTECH LLC
1630 N Main St Ste 305 (94596-4609)
PHONE.............................628 400-2420
Ahmet Cark, *Managing Member*
Hakan Kavlak, *
EMP: 150 EST: 2016
SQ FT: 2,500
SALES (est): 8.12MM **Privately Held**
Web: www.kcctech.com
SIC: **8748** 8742 8711 1799 Telecommunications consultant; Management consulting services; Engineering services; Construction site cleanup

(P-20791)
KEYSTONE STRATEGY LLC
Also Called: KEYSTONE STRATEGY, LLC
150 Spear St Ste 1750 (94105-1541)
PHONE.............................877 419-2623
Henry Liu, *Prin*
EMP: 80
Web: www.keystone.ai
SIC: **8748** Business consulting, nec
PA: Keystone Strategy Llc
150 Cambridgepark Dr # 704
Cambridge MA

(P-20792)
KINKISHARYO INTERNATIONAL
2825 E Avenue P (93550-2177)
PHONE.............................661 265-1647
EMP: 116 EST: 2014
SALES (est): 6.51MM **Privately Held**
Web: www.kinkisharyo.com
SIC: **8748** Business consulting, nec
HQ: Kinkisharyo International, L.L.C.
1960 E Grand Ave Ste 1210
El Segundo CA
424 276-1803

(P-20793)
KRAZAN & ASSOCIATES (PA)
215 W Dakota Ave (93612-5608)
PHONE.............................559 348-2200
Dean L Alexander, *Pr*
August Hioco, *
Thomas P Krazan, *
Emilo Vargas, *
EMP: 68 EST: 1982
SQ FT: 21,000
SALES (est): 35.05MM
SALES (corp-wide): 35.05MM **Privately Held**
Web: www.krazan.com
SIC: **8748** 8734 8742 Environmental consultant; Product testing laboratory, safety or performance; Management engineering

(P-20794)
KROS-WISE
435 E Carmel St (92078-4362)
PHONE.............................619 607-2899
Lily Aragon, *Pr*
EMP: 150 EST: 2004
SALES (est): 18.7MM **Privately Held**
Web: www.kros-wise.com
SIC: **8748** Business consulting, nec

(P-20795)
KRUZE CONSULTING INC
3561 Jackson St (94118-1807)
PHONE.............................415 601-6967
Vanessa Kruze, *Pr*
EMP: 66 EST: 2015
SALES (est): 2.52MM **Privately Held**
Web: www.kruzeconsulting.com
SIC: **8748** Business consulting, nec

(P-20796)
LAGUNA SAPPHIRE LLC
1200 S Coast Hwy Ste 105b (92651-3183)
PHONE.............................949 715-3300
EMP: 90 EST: 2007
SALES (est): 211.99K
SALES (corp-wide): 4.28MM **Privately Held**
Web: www.sapphirelaguna.com
SIC: **8748** Business consulting, nec
PA: Ag Consulting Llc.
1200 S Coast Hwy Ste 105b
Laguna Beach CA
949 715-9888

(P-20797)
LAND DESIGN CONSULTANTS INC
2700 E Foothill Blvd Ste 200 (91107)
PHONE.............................626 578-7000
Robert Sims, *Pr*
Steve Hunter, *
Larry Mar, *
EMP: 70 EST: 1992
SALES (est): 1.75MM **Privately Held**
Web: www.ldcla.com
SIC: **8748** 8711 8713 Urban planning and consulting services; Civil engineering; Surveying services

(P-20798)
LEAF COMMUNICATIONS LLC
1000 Calle Cordillera (92673-6235)
PHONE.............................949 388-0192
Frederick Dan Leaf, *Pr*
EMP: 64 EST: 2016
SALES (est): 9.43MM **Privately Held**
Web: www.leafcomm.com
SIC: **8748** 1623 Communications consulting; Transmitting tower (telecommunication) construction

(P-20799)
LESLEY FOUNDATION
701 Arnold Way Bldg A (94019-2199)
PHONE.............................650 726-4888
Catherine Evans, *Ex Dir*
EMP: 73 EST: 2004
SALES (est): 8.33MM **Privately Held**
Web: www.lesleyseniorcommunities.org

8748 - Business Consulting, Nec (P-20800)

SIC: 8748 Urban planning and consulting services

(P-20800)
LSA ASSOCIATES INC (PA)
Also Called: L S A
3210 El Camino Real Ste 100 (92602-1366)
PHONE..................................949 553-0666
Les Card, CEO
Rob Mccann, Pr
James Baum, *
EMP: 110 EST: 1974
SALES (est): 39.11MM
SALES (corp-wide): 39.11MM Privately Held
Web: www.lsa.net
SIC: 8748 Environmental consultant

(P-20801)
LYLE COMPANY
3140 Gold Camp Dr Ste 30 (95670-6192)
P.O. Box 2255 (95741-2255)
PHONE..................................916 266-7000
Lanny G Lyle, Ch Bd
EMP: 60 EST: 1989
SALES (est): 9.36MM Privately Held
Web: www.lyleco.com
SIC: 8748 Business consulting, nec

(P-20802)
MACKIN CONSULTANCY LLC
Also Called: Mackin Talent
2880 Zanker Rd Ste 203 (95134-2122)
PHONE..................................828 755-4073
Andy Mackin, CEO
Fiona Donnelly, *
Leniece Lane, *
EMP: 150 EST: 2014
SALES (est): 4.71MM Privately Held
Web: www.mackinconsultancy.com
SIC: 8748 Business consulting, nec

(P-20803)
MARSH CONSULTING GROUP
2626 Summer Ranch Rd (93446-8473)
PHONE..................................239 433-5500
Brad Heinrichs, Pr
EMP: 70 EST: 2005
SALES (est): 4.26MM
SALES (corp-wide): 6.98MM Privately Held
Web: www.mcgteam.com
SIC: 8748 Business consulting, nec
PA: Foster & Foster Consulting Actuaries, Inc.
    13420 Parker Commons Blvd
    Fort Myers FL
    239 433-5500

(P-20804)
MIDNIGHT SUN ENTERPRISES INC
Also Called: Spearmint Rhino Gentlemens CLB
19900 Normandie Ave (90502-1113)
PHONE..................................310 532-2427
Kathy Vercher, Prin
EMP: 86 EST: 2008
SALES (est): 2.33MM Privately Held
SIC: 8748 Business consulting, nec

(P-20805)
MONTROSE ENVIRONMENTAL CORP
2825 Verne Roberts Cir (94509-7902)
PHONE..................................925 680-4300
Wei Marcus Tan, Prin
EMP: 333
Web: www.montrose-env.com
SIC: 8748 Environmental consultant
PA: Montrose Environmental Corporation
    4 Park Plz Ste 790
    Irvine CA

(P-20806)
MOORE IACOFANO GOLTSMAN INC (PA)
Also Called: M I G
800 Hearst Ave (94710-2018)
PHONE..................................510 845-7549
Susan M Goltsman, Pr
Daniel Iacofano, *
Carolyn Verheyen, *
EMP: 63 EST: 1981
SQ FT: 6,000
SALES (est): 22.22MM
SALES (corp-wide): 22.22MM Privately Held
Web: www.migcom.com
SIC: 8748 Environmental consultant

(P-20807)
MSLA MANAGEMENT LLC
1294 E Colorado Blvd (91106-1901)
PHONE..................................626 824-6020
Michael Lambert, CEO
Sahniah Siciarz-lambert, Pr
Robert Worth Oberrender, *
EMP: 612 EST: 2016
SALES (est): 766.87K
SALES (corp-wide): 324.16B Publicly Held
SIC: 8748 Business consulting, nec
HQ: Optumserve Health Services, Inc.
    328 Front St S
    La Crosse WI
    866 284-8788

(P-20808)
MULTIFAMILY UTILITY CO INC
4891 Pacific Hwy Ste 102 (92110-4003)
P.O. Box 86531 (92138-6531)
PHONE..................................858 442-7783
Brian Anthony Stone, Pr
EMP: 65 EST: 2007
SQ FT: 6,000
SALES (est): 5.08MM Privately Held
Web: www.multifamilyutility.com
SIC: 8748 Energy conservation consultant

(P-20809)
MULTIPLIER
981 Mission St (94103-2912)
PHONE..................................415 421-3774
Laura Deaton, Ex Dir
Mellissa Clack, *
EMP: 70 EST: 2001
SALES (est): 10.49MM Privately Held
Web: www.multiplier.org
SIC: 8748 8699 Environmental consultant; Animal humane society

(P-20810)
MURJ INC
3912 Portola Dr Ste 9 (95062-5231)
PHONE..................................831 588-4462
Todd Butka, Admn
EMP: 74 EST: 2014
SALES (est): 2.09MM Privately Held
Web: www.murj.com
SIC: 8748 Business consulting, nec

(P-20811)
NAVIS CORPORATION (PA)
32980 Alvarado Niles Rd (94587-3186)
PHONE..................................510 267-5000
Rob Dillon, Interim Chief Executive Officer
Rob Dillon, Interim Chief Executive Officer
Bruce Jacquemard, CRO
Sunaina Lobo, CHO
EMP: 66 EST: 1988
SALES (est): 28.62MM
SALES (corp-wide): 28.62MM Privately Held
Web: www.kaleris.com
SIC: 8748 7371 Systems analysis and engineering consulting services; Custom computer programming services

(P-20812)
NETFORTRIS ACQUISITION CO INC
11954 S La Cienega Blvd (90250-3465)
PHONE..................................877 366-2548
Grant Evans, CEO
EMP: 80
SALES (corp-wide): 32.6MM Privately Held
Web: www.sangoma.com
SIC: 8748 Telecommunications consultant
PA: Netfortris Acquisition Co., Inc.
    5340 Legacy Dr
    Plano TX
    877 366-2548

(P-20813)
NETFORTRIS ACQUISITION CO INC
200 Corporate Pointe Ste 300 (90230)
PHONE..................................310 861-4300
Chris Vuillaume, Brnch Mgr
EMP: 80
SALES (corp-wide): 32.6MM Privately Held
Web: www.sangoma.com
SIC: 8748 Telecommunications consultant
PA: Netfortris Acquisition Co., Inc.
    5340 Legacy Dr
    Plano TX
    877 366-2548

(P-20814)
NEWFIELD WIRELESS INC (DH)
2855 Telegraph Ave Ste 200 (94705)
PHONE..................................510 848-8248
Marc Bensadoun, CEO
Matthew Ehrenman, *
Petrit Nahi, *
Chris Haidet, *
Kethees Ketheesan, *
EMP: 75 EST: 1995
SALES (est): 3.96MM
SALES (corp-wide): 914.53MM Publicly Held
Web: www.netscout.com
SIC: 8748 7361 Telecommunications consultant; Employment agencies
HQ: Netscout Systems Texas, Llc
    2200 Penn Ave Nw Ste 800w
    Washington DC
    202 828-0850

(P-20815)
NINJIO LLC
880 Hampshire Rd Ste B (91361-2836)
PHONE..................................805 864-1992
Tim Acker, CRO
EMP: 65 EST: 2017
SALES (est): 1.57MM Privately Held
Web: www.ninjio.com
SIC: 8748 Business consulting, nec

(P-20816)
NINYO MORE GTCHNCAL ENVMTL SCN (PA)
5710 Ruffin Rd (92123-1013)
PHONE..................................858 576-1000
Avram Ninyo, CEO
EMP: 80 EST: 1986
SQ FT: 24,000
SALES (est): 51.87MM
SALES (corp-wide): 51.87MM Privately Held
Web: www.ninyoandmoore.com
SIC: 8748 Environmental consultant

(P-20817)
NORTH LA COUNTY REGIONAL CTR (PA)
9200 Oakdale Ave Ste 100 (91311-6505)
PHONE..................................818 778-1900
George Stevens, Dir
Ellen Stein, *
EMP: 280 EST: 1974
SQ FT: 57,000
SALES (est): 645.13MM Privately Held
Web: www.nlacrc.org
SIC: 8748 Test development and evaluation service

(P-20818)
O C JONES & SONS INC
155 Filbert St Ste 209 (94607-2524)
PHONE..................................510 663-6911
Carla Radosta, Brnch Mgr
EMP: 100
SALES (corp-wide): 99.77MM Privately Held
Web: www.ocjones.com
SIC: 8748 Business consulting, nec
PA: O. C. Jones & Sons, Inc.
    1520 4th St
    Berkeley CA
    510 526-3424

(P-20819)
OCEAN PARK COMMUNITY CENTER
Turning Point
1447 16th St (90404-2715)
PHONE..................................310 828-6717
Patricia Bauman, Dir
EMP: 175
SALES (corp-wide): 73.2MM Privately Held
Web: www.thepeopleconcern.org
SIC: 8748 Urban planning and consulting services
PA: The People Concern
    2116 Arlington Ave # 100
    Los Angeles CA
    323 334-9000

(P-20820)
OMRON STI MACHINE SERVICES INC
6550 Dumbarton Cir (94555-3605)
PHONE..................................714 693-1041
EMP: 68
Web: www.stimachineservices.com
SIC: 8748 7699 Safety training service; Industrial machinery and equipment repair

(P-20821)
ONE DIVERSIFIED LLC
3275 Edward Ave (95054-2340)
PHONE..................................408 969-1972
EMP: 91
SALES (corp-wide): 1.21B Privately Held
Web: www.onediversified.com
SIC: 8748 7373 Systems analysis and engineering consulting services; Systems integration services
PA: One Diversified, Llc
    2975 Northwoods Pkwy
    Peachtree Corners GA
    770 447-1001

PRODUCTS & SERVICES SECTION
8748 - Business Consulting, Nec (P-20844)

(P-20822)
OPENPOPCOM INC (PA)
12539 Carson St (90716-1607)
PHONE.................................714 249-7044
Sun Jong Baek, *Pr*
EMP: 75 EST: 1999
SALES (est): 2.07MM
SALES (corp-wide): 2.07MM **Privately Held**
Web: www.openpop.com
SIC: 8748 Telecommunications consultant

(P-20823)
PACIFIC METRICS LLC
1 Lower Ragsdale Dr Ste 150 (93940-5749)
PHONE.................................831 646-6400
EMP: 109
Web: www.pacificmetrics.com
SIC: 8748 Educational consultant

(P-20824)
PARAGON PARTNERS CONS INC (PA)
5660 Katella Ave Ste 100 (90630-5058)
PHONE.................................714 379-3376
Neilia La Valle, *Pr*
Neilia A La Valle, *
Joel Sewell, *
EMP: 65 EST: 1993
SQ FT: 10,000
SALES (est): 18.49MM **Privately Held**
Web: www.paragon-partners.com
SIC: 8748 Business consulting, nec

(P-20825)
PATRIOT WASTEWATER LLC
314 W Freedom Ave (92865-2647)
PHONE.................................714 921-4545
Richard Yukihiro, *Mgr*
EMP: 153 EST: 2015
SALES (est): 328.53K **Privately Held**
Web: www.patriotenvironmental.com
SIC: 8748 Environmental consultant
HQ: Patriot Environmental Services, Inc.
508 East E St Ste A
Wilmington CA
562 436-2614

(P-20826)
PCS LINK INC
Also Called: Greenwood & Hall
12424 Wilshire Blvd Ste 1030 (90025-1031)
PHONE.................................949 655-5000
EMP: 310 EST: 1997
SALES (est): 9.55MM **Privately Held**
SIC: 8748 Communications consulting

(P-20827)
PEOPLES SELF-HELP HOUSING CORP
Also Called: Los Adobes De Maria
1026 W Boone St (93458-5499)
PHONE.................................805 349-9341
John Fowler, *Dir*
EMP: 65
SALES (corp-wide): 17.63MM **Privately Held**
Web: www.pshhc.org
SIC: 8748 Urban planning and consulting services
PA: Peoples' Self-Help Housing Corporation
1060 Kendall Rd
San Luis Obispo CA
805 781-3088

(P-20828)
PEOPLESHORES PBC
2033 Gateway Pl Ste 500 (95110-3712)
PHONE.................................408 431-4686
Murali Vullaganti, *Pr*
EMP: 84 EST: 2017
SALES (est): 4.53MM **Privately Held**
Web: www.peopleshores.com
SIC: 8748 Business consulting, nec

(P-20829)
PLUTO7 CONSULTING INC
Also Called: Planning In A Box
174 Hobbs Ct (95035-7725)
PHONE.................................408 824-9213
Manjunath Devadas, *CEO*
EMP: 65 EST: 2005
SALES (est): 3.1MM **Privately Held**
Web: www.pluto7.com
SIC: 8748 7379 7374 8742 Business consulting, nec; Data processing consultant ; Data processing service; Management consulting services

(P-20830)
POPULARMEDIA INC
1550 Bryant St Ste 220 (94103-4853)
PHONE.................................415 928-5880
Jim Calhoun, *CEO*
Sage Bray, *
Bob Tekiela, *
EMP: 80 EST: 2006
SALES (est): 806.98K
SALES (corp-wide): 609.02MM **Privately Held**
Web: www.popularmedia.com
SIC: 8748 Business consulting, nec
HQ: Selligent Inc.
11 Lea Ave
Nashville TN
615 292-5888

(P-20831)
PROFIT RECOVERY PARTNERS LLC
Also Called: P R P
3501 W Sunflower Ave Ste 100 (92704-6918)
PHONE.................................949 851-2777
Bill Carpou, *
Teresa Madden, *
Edward Lyon, *
Marty Bozarth, *
EMP: 75 EST: 1997
SALES (est): 11.79MM **Privately Held**
Web: www.prpllc.com
SIC: 8748 Business consulting, nec

(P-20832)
PROJECT DESIGN CONSULTANTS LLC
Also Called: PDC A Bowman Company
701 B St Ste 800 (92101-8162)
PHONE.................................619 235-6471
Gregory M Shields, *CEO*
William R Dick, *
Debby Reece, *
EMP: 92 EST: 1976
SQ FT: 22,000
SALES (est): 10.8MM **Publicly Held**
Web: www.projectdesign.com
SIC: 8748 8711 8713 Urban planning and consulting services; Civil engineering; Surveying services
PA: Bowman Consulting Group Ltd.
12355 Sunrise Valley Dr # 5
Reston VA

(P-20833)
PSI SERVICES LLC (PA)
Also Called: PSI
611 N Brand Blvd Ste 10 (91203-3290)
PHONE.................................818 847-6180
EMP: 80 EST: 2001
SALES (est): 160.35MM
SALES (corp-wide): 160.35MM **Privately Held**
Web: www.psiexams.com
SIC: 8748 Testing services

(P-20834)
QMETRY INC
3200 Patrick Henry Dr Ste 250 (95054-1875)
PHONE.................................408 727-1101
Agnelo Rodrigues, *Managing Member*
EMP: 110 EST: 2018
SALES (est): 3MM **Privately Held**
Web: www.qmetry.com
SIC: 8748 Testing services

(P-20835)
QUALIA LABS INC
Also Called: Qualia Software
50 Fremont St Fl 36 (94105-2239)
PHONE.................................440 477-5625
Nathan Baker, *Pr*
EMP: 216 EST: 2015
SALES (est): 24.5MM **Privately Held**
Web: www.qualia.com
SIC: 8748 Business consulting, nec

(P-20836)
QUORUM ONE LLC
Also Called: Professional Services
5758 Geary Blvd Ste 141 (94121-2112)
PHONE.................................760 786-7861
Hank Holiday, *Managing Member*
EMP: 60 EST: 2021
SALES (est): 1.5MM **Privately Held**
Web: www.quorum.one
SIC: 8748 Business consulting, nec

(P-20837)
QUOVA INC
401 Castro St Fl 3 (94041-2089)
PHONE.................................650 965-2898
Marie Alexander, *Pr*
Gary P Jackson, *
Jean-louis Casabonne, *CFO*
EMP: 60 EST: 2000
SQ FT: 10,000
SALES (est): 6.07MM
SALES (corp-wide): 3.71B **Publicly Held**
Web: www.home.neustar
SIC: 8748 Business consulting, nec
HQ: Neustar, Inc.
1906 Reston Metro Plz # 5
Reston VA
571 434-5400

(P-20838)
REACH ADULT DEVELOPMENT INC
3280 Ramos Cir (95827-2513)
PHONE.................................916 203-6246
Sean Suh, *CEO*
EMP: 64
SALES (corp-wide): 6.55MM **Privately Held**
Web: www.reachdayprogram.com
SIC: 8748 Business consulting, nec
PA: Reach Adult Development, Inc.
2204 Kausen Dr Ste 120
Elk Grove CA
916 683-6565

(P-20839)
RECON ENVIRONMENTAL INC (PA)
Also Called: Recon
3111 Camino Del Rio N Ste 600 (92108)
PHONE.................................619 308-9333
Robert Hobbs, *Pr*
Michael Page, *
Lee Sherwood, *
Jennifer Campos, *
Charles Bull, *
EMP: 82 EST: 1977
SALES (est): 20.4MM
SALES (corp-wide): 20.4MM **Privately Held**
Web: www.recon-us.com
SIC: 8748 Environmental consultant

(P-20840)
RESOURCE INNOVATIONS INC (DH)
719 Main St Ste A (94019-1924)
PHONE.................................415 369-1000
Lauren Casentini, *CEO*
EMP: 80 EST: 1999
SALES (est): 57.42MM
SALES (corp-wide): 124.51MM **Privately Held**
Web: www.resource-innovations.com
SIC: 8748 Energy conservation consultant
HQ: Bv Ri Acquisitionco, Llc
125 High St Fl 17
Boston MA
617 224-0057

(P-20841)
RICHARD HEATH & ASSOCIATES INC (PA)
Also Called: R H A
590 W Locust Ave Ste 103 (93650-1079)
PHONE.................................559 447-7000
EMP: 97 EST: 1979
SALES (est): 46.03MM
SALES (corp-wide): 46.03MM **Privately Held**
Web: www.rhainc.com
SIC: 8748 Energy conservation consultant

(P-20842)
RINCON CONSULTANTS INC
1530 Monterey St Ste D (93401-2969)
PHONE.................................805 547-0900
John Rickenvach, *Mgr*
EMP: 238
Web: www.rinconconsultants.com
SIC: 8748 Environmental consultant
PA: Rincon Consultants, Inc.
180 N Ashwood Ave
Ventura CA

(P-20843)
SACRAMENTO HOUSING DEV CORP (PA)
Also Called: HOUSING AUTHORITY OF SACRAMENT
801 12th St (95814-2929)
P.O. Box 1834 (95812-1834)
PHONE.................................916 440-1333
David Ossont, *Pr*
EMP: 97 EST: 1951
SQ FT: 33,000
SALES (est): 4.21MM
SALES (corp-wide): 4.21MM **Privately Held**
Web: www.shra.org
SIC: 8748 Urban planning and consulting services

(P-20844)
SACRAMNTO MTRO A QULTY MGT DST
777 12th St Ste 300 (95814-1928)
PHONE.................................916 874-4800
Larry Greene, *Ex Dir*

8748 - Business Consulting, Nec (P-20845)

EMP: 86 EST: 2012
SALES (est): 26.71MM Privately Held
Web: www.airquality.org
SIC: 8748 Environmental consultant

(P-20845)
SAN JOSE REDEVELOPMENT AGENCY
200 E Santa Clara St 14th Fl (95113-1903)
PHONE...............................408 535-8500
Harry Mavrogenes, Ex Dir
Julie Amato, Development Officer*
John Wise, *
EMP: 140 EST: 1987
SQ FT: 10,045
SALES (est): 243.27MM
SALES (corp-wide): 2.14B Privately Held
Web: www.sjredevelopment.org
SIC: 8748 Urban planning and consulting services
PA: City Of San Jose
   200 E Santa Clara St 13th
   San Jose CA
   408 535-3500

(P-20846)
SAN JQUIN VLY UNFIED A PLLTION (PA)
Also Called: Valley Air District
1990 E Gettysburg Ave (93726-0244)
PHONE...............................559 230-6000
Seyed Sadredin, Ex Dir
Cindi Hamm, *
EMP: 200 EST: 1992
SQ FT: 60,000
SALES (est): 26.8MM Privately Held
Web: www.valleyair.org
SIC: 8748 Environmental consultant

(P-20847)
SANYO NORTH AMERICA CORP
Also Called: Sanyo Fisher Company
2055 Sanyo Ave (92154-6234)
PHONE...............................619 661-1134
◆ EMP: 400
SIC: 8748 3632 Business consulting, nec; Household refrigerators and freezers

(P-20848)
SLALOM LLC
Also Called: SLALOM, LLC
300 Spectrum Center Dr Ste 1500 (92618-3095)
PHONE...............................949 450-1100
EMP: 208
Web: www.slalom.com
SIC: 8748 Business consulting, nec
PA: Slalom, Inc.
   821 2nd Ave Ste 1900
   Seattle WA

(P-20849)
SLR INTERNATIONAL CORPORATION
20 Corporate Park Ste 200 (92606-3111)
PHONE...............................949 553-8417
Rebecca Hjelm, Brnch Mgr
EMP: 615
SALES (corp-wide): 2.14MM Privately Held
Web: www.slrconsulting.com
SIC: 8748 Environmental consultant
HQ: Slr International Corporation
   22118 20th Ave Se Ste G20
   Bothell WA
   425 402-8800

(P-20850)
SMART SFTWR TSTG SOLUTIONS INC
11750 Dublin Blvd Ste 200 (94568-2820)
PHONE...............................833 778-7872
Pankaj Goel, CEO
EMP: 60 EST: 2016
SALES (est): 3.03MM Privately Held
SIC: 8748 7371 Testing services; Computer software development and applications

(P-20851)
SONOMA TECHNOLOGY INC
1450 N Mcdowell Blvd Ste 200 (94954-6515)
PHONE...............................707 665-9900
Lyle R Chinkin, Pr
Fred Lurmann, *
Barbara A Austin, *
Paul T Roberts, *
Timothy S Dye, *
EMP: 65 EST: 1982
SQ FT: 29,011
SALES (est): 14.83MM Privately Held
Web: www.sonomatech.com
SIC: 8748 Environmental consultant

(P-20852)
SOURCE 44 LLC
Also Called: Source Intelligence
4660 La Jolla Village Dr Ste 100 (92122-4604)
PHONE...............................877 916-6337
Glenn Trout, CEO
Matt Thorn, *
Lina Ramos, *
Jennifer Kraus, *
Dan Dague, Chief Development Officer*
EMP: 130 EST: 2009
SALES (est): 12.18MM
SALES (corp-wide): 12.18MM Privately Held
Web: www.sourceintelligence.com
SIC: 8748 7371 Environmental consultant; Computer software development
PA: Pg Source Acquisition, Inc.
   4660 La Jolla Village Dr # 1
   San Diego CA
   877 916-6337

(P-20853)
SOUTH CAST A QLTY MGT DST BLDG (PA)
Also Called: A Q M D
21865 Copley Dr (91765-4178)
P.O. Box 4940 (91765-0940)
PHONE...............................909 396-2000
Raymond E Robinson, CEO
Barry R Wallerstein, *
EMP: 720 EST: 1955
SQ FT: 350
SALES (est): 449.02MM
SALES (corp-wide): 449.02MM Privately Held
Web: www.aqmd.gov
SIC: 8748 Environmental consultant

(P-20854)
SOUTHEAST FRESNO RAD LP
4430 E Hamilton Ave (93702-4535)
PHONE...............................559 443-8400
Preston Prince, CEO
EMP: 225 EST: 2014
SALES (est): 9.83MM Privately Held
SIC: 8748 Urban planning and consulting services

(P-20855)
SPECTRUM SERVICES GROUP INC
3841 N Freeway Blvd Ste 120 (95834-1949)
PHONE...............................916 760-7913
Tasawwar Ali, CEO
Shane Ali, *
EMP: 85 EST: 1999
SQ FT: 2,000
SALES (est): 10.5MM Privately Held
Web: www.spectrum-inc.net
SIC: 8748 8744 8741 Business consulting, nec; Facilities support services; Construction management

(P-20856)
STOK LLC
26 Ofarrell St Fl 2 (94108-5813)
PHONE...............................415 265-2366
Jacob Arlein, Managing Member
EMP: 84 EST: 2016
SALES (est): 5.65MM Privately Held
Web: www.stok.com
SIC: 8748 Business consulting, nec

(P-20857)
SUREFOX NORTH AMERICA INC
655 3rd St (94107-1901)
PHONE...............................650 665-1852
Brian Sweigart, CEO
EMP: 207 EST: 2020
SALES (est): 2.12MM Privately Held
Web: www.surefox.com
SIC: 8748 Business consulting, nec

(P-20858)
SYMPHONY TECHNOLOGY GROUP LLC (DH)
428 University Ave (94301-1812)
P.O. Box 51770 (94303-0720)
PHONE...............................650 935-9500
Jim Obsitnik, CEO
Bill Diaz, *
Romesh Wadhwani, *
Stephen Henkenmeier, *
William Chisholm, *
EMP: 5775 EST: 2000
SQ FT: 15,000
SALES (est): 4.25B
SALES (corp-wide): 694.97MM Privately Held
Web: www.stg.com
SIC: 8748 6719 Business consulting, nec; Investment holding companies, except banks
HQ: Surveymonkey Global Inc.
   1 Curiosity Way
   San Mateo CA
   650 543-8400

(P-20859)
SYNERGY COMPANIES
2626 West Ln # 100 (95205-2887)
PHONE...............................800 439-9610
EMP: 132 EST: 2013
SALES (est): 1.68MM Privately Held
Web: www.synergycompanies.com
SIC: 8748 Energy conservation consultant

(P-20860)
SYSTEMS EXPERIENCE INC
6033 W Century Blvd Ste 820 (90045-6424)
PHONE...............................310 215-9000
Richard L Jivery, Pr
EMP: 65 EST: 1979
SQ FT: 3,600
SALES (est): 4.41MM Privately Held
Web: www.systemsexperience.com
SIC: 8748 Business consulting, nec

(P-20861)
T-FORCE INC (PA)
Also Called: T-Force
4695 Macarthur Ct (92660-1882)
PHONE...............................949 208-1527
Raid Al-khawaldeh, Pr
EMP: 98 EST: 2004
SALES (est): 9.73MM
SALES (corp-wide): 9.73MM Privately Held
Web: www.tforcelogistics.com
SIC: 8748 7379 Telecommunications consultant; Online services technology consultants

(P-20862)
TANGOE-PL INC
9920 Pacific Heights Blvd Ste 200 (92121)
P.O. Box 509088 (92150-9088)
EMP: 235
SIC: 8748 Telecommunications consultant

(P-20863)
TEAM RISK MGT STRATEGIES LLC
Also Called: Trust Employee ADM & MGT
3131 Camino Del Rio N Ste 650 (92108)
PHONE...............................877 767-8728
Terence J Keating, Pr
Arthur D Candland, *
Cheryl Doss, *
EMP: 2500 EST: 2003
SALES (est): 83.61MM Privately Held
Web: www.teamemployer.com
SIC: 8748 Employee programs administration

(P-20864)
TEMPEST TELECOM SOLUTIONS LLC (HQ)
Also Called: Tempest
136 W Canon Perdido St Ste 100 (93101-3242)
PHONE...............................805 879-4800
Jessica Firestone, CEO
Richard Smith, *
Julie Lubin, *
Dan Firestone, *
EMP: 60 EST: 2005
SQ FT: 9,000
SALES (est): 28.87MM Privately Held
Web: www.tempestns.com
SIC: 8748 Systems analysis and engineering consulting services
PA: Pfingsten Partners, L.L.C.
   151 N Franklin St # 2150
   Chicago IL

(P-20865)
THE SOURCE GROUP INC
Also Called: Sgi Environmental
3478 Buskirk Ave Ste 100 (94523-7311)
PHONE...............................925 944-2856
EMP: 75
SIC: 8748 Environmental consultant

(P-20866)
TRC SOLUTIONS
10680 White Rock Rd Ste 100 (95670-6175)
PHONE...............................916 962-7001
Lisa Heschong, Prin
Douglas Mahone, *
EMP: 144 EST: 1993
SALES (est): 14.28MM
SALES (corp-wide): 482.42MM Privately Held

PRODUCTS & SERVICES SECTION

8999 - Services, Nec (P-20886)

Web: www.imbsen.com
SIC: **8748** Energy conservation consultant
PA: Trc Companies, Inc.
21 Griffin Rd N
Windsor CT
860 298-9692

(P-20867)
TRC SOLUTIONS INC (HQ)
Also Called: Alton Geoscience
9685 Research Dr Ste 100 (92618-4657)
PHONE..............................949 753-0101
Christopher P Vincze, *CEO*
Thomas W Bennet Junior, *CFO*
John Cowdery, *
Martin H Dodd, *
Ed Wiegele, *
EMP: 125 **EST:** 1981
SQ FT: 47,000
SALES (est): 21.32MM
SALES (corp-wide): 482.42MM **Privately Held**
SIC: **8748** 8711 Environmental consultant; Engineering services
PA: Trc Companies, Inc.
21 Griffin Rd N
Windsor CT
860 298-9692

(P-20868)
TULE RIVER ECONOMIC DEV
Also Called: TREDC
31071 Highway 190 (93257-9168)
PHONE..............................559 781-4271
Dennis Ickes, *CEO*
Dennis Ickes, *Prin*
Isacc Manuel, *
William Hayter, *
Kellie Carrillo, *
EMP: 80 **EST:** 2001
SALES (est): 770.21K **Privately Held**
Web: www.tuleriveredc.com
SIC: **8748** 8711 Economic consultant; Consulting engineer

(P-20869)
VALLEJO FLOOD & WASTEWATER DST
450 Ryder St (94590-7217)
PHONE..............................707 644-8949
Melissa Morton, *Mgr*
Jeff Tucker, *
Mj Brown, *
Mark Tomko, *
Alexandria Bell, *
EMP: 96 **EST:** 2018
SALES (est): 39.49MM **Privately Held**
Web: www.vallejowastewater.org
SIC: **8748** Environmental consultant

(P-20870)
VALLEJO FLOOD WSTWTER DST FING
450 Ryder St (94590-7217)
PHONE..............................707 644-8949
Melissa Morton, *CEO*
Holly M Charlety, *
Mary A Morris, *
EMP: 86 **EST:** 1952
SQ FT: 10,000
SALES (est): 32.78MM **Privately Held**
Web: www.vallejowastewater.org
SIC: **8748** Environmental consultant

(P-20871)
VENTEGRA INC A CAL BENEFT CORP
450 N Brand Blvd Ste 600 (91203-2349)
PHONE..............................858 551-8111
Robert Taketomo, *Pr*
Mariana Ritchie, *
Don Schoenly, *
Mike Gannon, *
Michele Yoon, *
EMP: 85 **EST:** 2004
SALES (est): 6.07MM **Privately Held**
Web: www.ventegra.com
SIC: **8748** Business consulting, nec

(P-20872)
VERIDIAM ALLIED SWISS
4645 North Ave (92056-3593)
PHONE..............................760 941-1702
Thomas Cresante, *Owner*
EMP: 67 **EST:** 2007
SALES (est): 4.1MM
SALES (corp-wide): 206.12MM **Privately Held**
Web: www.veridiam.com
SIC: **8748** Business consulting, nec
HQ: Veridiam, Inc.
1717 N Cuyamaca St
El Cajon CA
619 448-1000

(P-20873)
VETERANS EZ INFO INC
Also Called: Veterans EZ Info
1901 1st Ave Ste 192 (92101-2322)
PHONE..............................866 839-1329
James Miner, *Ch Bd*
Phonprapha Miner, *
EMP: 138 **EST:** 2012
SQ FT: 1,200
SALES (est): 24MM **Privately Held**
Web: www.vetsez.com
SIC: **8748** 7371 7373 Business consulting, nec; Computer software development; Computer systems analysis and design

(P-20874)
VIMO INC (PA)
Also Called: Getinsured.com
1305 Terra Bella Ave (94043-1851)
PHONE..............................650 618-4600
Srinivasan Krishnan, *CEO*
Whitney Chang, *
Shankar Srinivasan, *
EMP: 69 **EST:** 2005
SQ FT: 20,000
SALES (est): 102.92K **Privately Held**
Web: company.getinsured.com
SIC: **8748** 6411 7371 7373 Business consulting, nec; Insurance brokers, nec; Computer software development and applications; Systems software development services

(P-20875)
VINCULUMS SERVICES LLC
Also Called: Vinculums
10 Pasteur Ste 100 (92618-3823)
PHONE..............................949 783-3552
Paul Foster, *CEO*
Lisa Di Giovanna, *
Brian Woodward, *
Norm Alexander, *
EMP: 220 **EST:** 2005
SQ FT: 8,000
SALES (est): 32.7MM
SALES (corp-wide): 753.86MM **Privately Held**
Web: www.qualtekservices.com
SIC: **8748** Telecommunications consultant
HQ: Qualtek Llc
475 Sentry Pkwy E # 1000
Blue Bell PA
484 804-4500

(P-20876)
VOLT TELECOM GROUP INC
Also Called: Volt Telecom Group
218 Helicopter Cir (92878-5031)
PHONE..............................951 493-8900
EMP: 260
SALES (corp-wide): 885.39MM **Privately Held**
Web: www.volt-telecom.com
SIC: **8748** Telecommunications consultant
HQ: Volt Telecommunications Group, Inc.
2400 Meadowbrook Pkwy
Duluth GA
212 704-2400

(P-20877)
VSC SPORTS INC
Also Called: Yorba Bena Ice Skting Bowl Ctr
750 Folsom St (94107-1276)
PHONE..............................415 820-3525
Michael Paikin, *Owner*
EMP: 60
SALES (corp-wide): 2.47MM **Privately Held**
SIC: **8748** Business consulting, nec
PA: Vsc Sports Inc
11401 Topanga Canyon Blvd # 125
Chatsworth CA
818 994-3229

(P-20878)
WARNER BROS CONSUMER PDTS INC (DH)
4001 W Olive Ave (91505-4272)
PHONE..............................818 954-7980
Brad Globe, *Pr*
Dan Romanelli, *Pr*
Randy Blotky, *Sr VP*
John Schulman, *Sec*
▲ **EMP:** 112 **EST:** 2003
SALES (est): 26.86MM **Publicly Held**
SIC: **8748** 5961 Business consulting, nec; Novelty merchandise, mail order
HQ: Warner Bros. Entertainment Inc.
4000 Warner Blvd
Burbank CA
818 954-6000

(P-20879)
WESTERVELT COMPANY
Westervelt Ecological Services
3636 American River Dr (95864-5952)
PHONE..............................916 646-3644
Greg Sutter, *Mgr*
EMP: 123
SALES (corp-wide): 130.03MM **Privately Held**
Web: www.westerveltproperties.com
SIC: **8748** Environmental consultant
PA: Westervelt Company
1400 Jack Warner Pkwy Ne
Tuscaloosa AL
205 562-5295

(P-20880)
YGRENE ENERGY FUND INC
2600 Capitol Ave Ste 100 (95816-5928)
PHONE..............................916 444-9700
EMP: 254
SALES (corp-wide): 26.84MM **Privately Held**
Web: www.ygrene.com
SIC: **8748** Energy conservation consultant
PA: Ygrene Energy Fund Inc.
2100 S Mcdowell Blvd
Petaluma CA
866 634-1358

(P-20881)
YUCAIPA COMPANIES LLC (PA)
9130 W Sunset Blvd (90069-3110)
PHONE..............................310 789-7200
Ronald W Burkle, *Managing Member*
Scott Stedman, *
EMP: 150 **EST:** 1986
SALES (est): 247.94MM
SALES (corp-wide): 247.94MM **Privately Held**
Web: www.yucaipaco.com
SIC: **8748** 6719 6726 Business consulting, nec; Investment holding companies, except banks; Investment offices, nec

(P-20882)
ZERO GRAVITY CONSULTING LLC
458 N Doheny Dr (90069-7563)
PHONE..............................310 989-7989
Jonathan Cohen, *Pr*
EMP: 713 **EST:** 2015
SALES (est): 25MM **Privately Held**
SIC: **8748** Business consulting, nec

8999 Services, Nec

(P-20883)
AGORA LAB INC
Also Called: Agora.io
2804 Mission College Blvd Ste 110 (95054-1803)
PHONE..............................408 879-5885
Tony Zhao, *CEO*
Reggie Yativ, *COO*
EMP: 88 **EST:** 2014
SALES (est): 9MM **Privately Held**
Web: www.agora.io
SIC: **8999** Communication services

(P-20884)
DATA TRACE INFO SVCS LLC (HQ)
4 First American Way (92707-5913)
PHONE..............................714 250-6700
EMP: 100 **EST:** 2000
SALES (est): 9.34MM **Publicly Held**
Web: www.datatracetitle.com
SIC: **8999** Information bureau
PA: First American Financial Corporation
1 First American Way
Santa Ana CA

(P-20885)
ENGEO INCORPORATED
27742 Hancock Pkwy (91355-6020)
PHONE..............................661 257-4004
Uri Eliahu, *Pr*
EMP: 69
SALES (corp-wide): 45.8MM **Privately Held**
Web: www.engeo.com
SIC: **8999** 8711 Earth science services; Engineering services
PA: Engeo Incorporated
2010 Crow Canyon Pl # 250
San Ramon CA
925 866-9000

(P-20886)
ENVIRONMENTAL REMEDIES INC
22390 Thunderbird Pl (94545-1314)
P.O. Box 10416 (94588-0416)
PHONE..............................925 461-3285
Scott Tamayo, *Ex Dir*
EMP: 65 **EST:** 2004
SALES (est): 2.29MM **Privately Held**

8999 - Services, Nec (P-20887)

Web: www.environmentalremediesinc.com
SIC: 8999 Earth science services

(P-20887)
ESSENSE
Also Called: Maxus USA
6300 Wilshire Blvd Ste 720 (90048-5204)
PHONE..................................323 202-4650
EMP: 711 EST: 2015
SALES (est): 242.78K
SALES (corp-wide): 17.37B Privately Held
SIC: 8999 Communication services
HQ: Maxus Communications Llc
    498 Fashion Ave
    New York NY
    212 297-8300

(P-20888)
GLOBAL BUILDING SERVICES INC
17618 Murphy Pkwy (95330-8629)
PHONE..................................209 858-9501
EMP: 1039
SALES (corp-wide): 29.17MM Privately Held
Web: www.globalbuildingservices.com
SIC: 8999 Actuarial consultant
PA: Global Building Services, Inc.
    27433 Tourney Rd Ste 280
    Valencia CA
    800 675-6643

(P-20889)
GMU GEOTECHNICAL INC
Also Called: Gmu Construction Management
30336 Esperanza (92688-2118)
PHONE..................................949 888-6513
Greg Silver, Pr
EMP: 60 EST: 1978
SALES (est): 5.06MM Privately Held
Web: www.gmugeo.com
SIC: 8999 8711 Geological consultant;
    Consulting engineer

(P-20890)
GOLDEN GATE NAT PRKS CNSRVANCY
1600 Los Gamos Dr (94903-1806)
PHONE..................................415 785-4787
EMP: 79
Web: www.parksconservancy.org
SIC: 8999 Natural resource preservation service
PA: Golden Gate National Parks
    Conservancy
    201 Fort Mason
    San Francisco CA

(P-20891)
GOLDEN GATE NAT PRKS CNSRVANCY (PA)
201 Fort Mason (94123-1307)
PHONE..................................415 561-3000
Greg Moore, CEO
Nicolas Elsishans, *
Cathie Barner, *
J Mark Jenkins, *
▲ EMP: 70 EST: 1981
SQ FT: 5,000
SALES (est): 56.66MM Privately Held
Web: www.parksconservancy.org
SIC: 8999 Natural resource preservation service

(P-20892)
HEALTHCARE SERVICES GROUP INC
5199 E Pacific Coast Hwy Ste 402
(90804-3309)
PHONE..................................562 494-7939
Mike Hammond, Prin
EMP: 1080
SALES (corp-wide): 1.76B Publicly Held
Web: www.hcsgcorp.com
SIC: 8999 Artists and artists' studios
PA: Healthcare Services Group Inc
    3220 Tillman Dr Ste 300
    Bensalem PA
    215 639-4274

(P-20893)
INTERIM INC
Also Called: Interim Services
339 Pajaro St (93901-3400)
PHONE..................................831 754-3838
Fred Harris, Brnch Mgr
EMP: 75
SALES (corp-wide): 24.17MM Privately Held
Web: www.interiminc.org
SIC: 8999 Personal services
PA: Interim, Inc.
    604 Pearl St Frnt
    Monterey CA
    831 649-4399

(P-20894)
KLINGSTUBBINS INC
160 Spear St Ste 330 (94105-1543)
PHONE..................................415 356-2040
Peter Dugo, Mgr
EMP: 62
SALES (corp-wide): 14.92B Publicly Held
SIC: 8999 Artists and artists' studios
HQ: Klingstubbins, Inc.
    2301 Chestnut St
    Philadelphia PA
    215 569-2900

(P-20895)
MGM AND UA SERVICES COMPANY
245 N Beverly Dr (90210-5319)
PHONE..................................310 449-3000
Gary Barber, Pr
EMP: 560 EST: 1994
SALES (est): 3.51MM Publicly Held
SIC: 8999 Artists and artists' studios
HQ: Metro-Goldwyn-Mayer, Inc.
    245 N Beverly Dr
    Beverly Hills CA

(P-20896)
MIDPENNSULA RGNAL OPEN SPACE D
5050 El Camino Real (94022-1525)
PHONE..................................650 691-1200
Craig Britton, Pr
EMP: 65 EST: 1972
SQ FT: 12,000
SALES (est): 69.73MM Privately Held
Web: www.openspace.org
SIC: 8999 Natural resource preservation service

(P-20897)
ORANGEPEOPLE LLC
300 Spectrum Center Dr Ste 400
(92618-4925)
PHONE..................................949 535-1308
Raghav Putrevu, Pr
EMP: 76 EST: 2004
SQ FT: 8,000
SALES (est): 9.66MM Privately Held
Web: www.orangepeople.com
SIC: 8999 7374 7371 8742 Cloud seeding;
    Data processing service; Computer
    software development; Construction project
    management consultant

(P-20898)
OVERSEAS SERVICE CORPORATION
Also Called: Ocean Service
8221 Arjons Dr Ste B2 (92126-6319)
PHONE..................................858 408-0751
Paul Hogan, Pr
EMP: 232
SALES (corp-wide): 36.64MM Privately Held
Web: www.oscweb.com
SIC: 8999 Actuarial consultant
PA: Overseas Service Corporation
    1100 Nrthpint Pkwy Ste 20
    West Palm Beach FL
    561 683-4090

(P-20899)
PRESIDIO TRUST
1750 Lincoln Blvd (94129-1801)
P.O. Box 29052 (94129-0052)
PHONE..................................415 561-5300
Craig Middleton, CEO
Craig Mdleton, CEO
William Ellison Grayson, Ch Bd
David H Grubb, VP
EMP: 241 EST: 1996
SALES (est): 27.31MM Privately Held
Web: www.presidio.gov
SIC: 8999 Natural resource preservation service

(P-20900)
RIVERSIDE CNTY FLOOD CTRL WTR
1995 Market St (92501-1719)
PHONE..................................951 955-1200
Jason Uhley, Prin
EMP: 210 EST: 1945
SALES (est): 87.05MM Privately Held
Web: www.rcflood.org
SIC: 8999 Natural resource preservation service

(P-20901)
RUBIO ARTS CORPORATION
1313 S Harbor Blvd (92802-2309)
PHONE..................................407 849-1643
EMP: 111
SALES (corp-wide): 2.27MM Privately Held
SIC: 8999 Artist
PA: Rubio Arts Corporation
    8100 Chancellor Dr # 100
    Orlando FL
    407 849-1643

(P-20902)
STORMGEO (DH)
Also Called: Awt Worlwide
140 Kifer Ct (94086-5120)
P.O. Box 61779 (94088-1779)
PHONE..................................408 731-8600
EMP: 166 EST: 1996
SQ FT: 19,000
SALES (est): 21.33MM Privately Held
Web: www.stormgeo.com
SIC: 8999 Weather forecasting
HQ: Stormgeo As
    Nordre Nostekaien 1
    Bergen

(P-20903)
TRIDENT CONSULTING
6101 Bollinger Canyon Rd Ste 330
(94583-5110)
PHONE..................................925 352-3885
Shabanna Siraj, Admn
EMP: 61 EST: 2005

SALES (est): 923.6K Privately Held
Web: www.tridentconsultinginc.com
SIC: 8999 7319 7311 Scientific consulting;
    Display advertising service; Advertising agencies

(P-20904)
UNION EDITORIAL LLC
12200 W Olympic Blvd Ste 140
(90064-1000)
PHONE..................................310 481-2200
EMP: 78 EST: 2003
SALES (est): 6.41MM Privately Held
Web: www.unioneditorial.com
SIC: 8999 Editorial service

(P-20905)
VERIZON MEDIA INC
701 First Ave (94089-1019)
PHONE..................................310 907-3016
EMP: 1715
SALES (corp-wide): 10.97B Publicly Held
Web: www.yahooinc.com
SIC: 8999 Communication services
HQ: Verizon Media Inc.
    11995 Bluff Creek Dr
    Los Angeles CA
    310 907-3016

(P-20906)
WEAPON X SECURITY INC
297 Country Club Dr (93065-6632)
P.O. Box 940835 (93094-0835)
PHONE..................................818 818-9950
Mish Marie, CEO
Sayed Sadat, *
EMP: 80 EST: 2018
SALES (est): 962.55K Privately Held
Web: www.weaponxsecurity.com
SIC: 8999 1731 7381 Personal services;
    Safety and security specialization; Security guard service

(P-20907)
WESTAMERICA COMMUNICATIONS INC
26012 Atlantic Ocean Dr (92630-8843)
PHONE..................................949 340-8942
Douglas Grant, CEO
EMP: 79 EST: 1975
SALES (est): 11.86MM Privately Held
Web: www.mywestamerica.com
SIC: 8999 Communication services

(P-20908)
WESTVIEW SERVICES INC
1650 Spruce St (92507-7403)
PHONE..................................951 343-2356
Greg Drann, Brnch Mgr
EMP: 68
SALES (corp-wide): 14.51MM Privately Held
Web: www.westviewservices.org
SIC: 8999 Artists and artists' studios
PA: Westview Services, Inc
    10522 Katella Ave
    Anaheim CA
    714 517-6606

(P-20909)
ZENO GROUP INC
275 Shoreline Dr Ste 530 (94065-1413)
PHONE..................................650 801-7950
Todd Irwin, Brnch Mgr
EMP: 95
SALES (corp-wide): 1.53B Privately Held
Web: www.zenogroup.com
SIC: 8999 Personal services
HQ: Zeno Group, Inc.
    130 E Randolph St # 3000

PRODUCTS & SERVICES SECTION

9221 - Police Protection (P-20928)

Chicago IL
312 396-9700

(P-20910)
ZOE HOLDING COMPANY INC
44 Montgomery St (94104-4602)
PHONE......................415 421-4900
John Unick, *Brnch Mgr*
EMP: 126
SALES (corp-wide): 48.96MM **Privately Held**
Web: www.zoeholding.com
SIC: 8999 Artists and artists' studios
PA: Zoe Holding Company, Inc.
7025 N Scottsdale Rd # 250
Scottsdale AZ
602 508-1883

9111 Executive Offices

(P-20911)
CITY OF BRAWLEY (PA)
400 Main St (92227-2434)
PHONE......................760 344-8941
Rayan Kelley, *Mayor*
EMP: 69 **EST:** 1908
SQ FT: 6,000
Web: www.brawley-ca.gov
SIC: 9111 8611 Mayors' office; Business associations

(P-20912)
CITY OF CERRITOS
Also Called: Cerritos Ctr For Prfrmg Arts
18125 Bloomfield Ave (90703-8577)
PHONE......................562 916-8500
TOLL FREE: 800
EMP: 150
SALES (corp-wide): 100.13MM **Privately Held**
Web: www.cerritoscenter.com
SIC: 9111 7922 Executive offices, Local government; Legitimate live theater producers
PA: City Of Cerritos
18125 Bloomfield Ave
Cerritos CA
562 860-0311

(P-20913)
CITY OF CULVER CITY
Also Called: Transportation Department
4343 Duquesne Ave (90232-2944)
PHONE......................310 253-6525
Steven Cunningham, *Mgr*
EMP: 100
SALES (corp-wide): 147.32MM **Privately Held**
Web: www.culvercity.org
SIC: 9111 8611 Executive offices, state and local; Business associations
PA: City Of Culver City
9770 Culver Blvd
Culver City CA
310 253-5640

(P-20914)
CITY OF REDDING (PA)
777 Cypress Ave (96001-2718)
P.O. Box 496071 (96049-6071)
PHONE......................530 225-4079
Kristen Schreder, *Mayor*
Francie Sullivan, *
▲ **EMP:** 802 **EST:** 1887
SQ FT: 105,000
SALES (est): 127.55MM
SALES (corp-wide): 127.55MM **Privately Held**
Web: www.cityofredding.org

SIC: 9111 8999 8399 City and town managers' office; Search and rescue service; Community action agency

(P-20915)
CITY OF TORRANCE
Also Called: Torrance Cultural Art Center
3350 Civic Center Dr N Ste 201 (90503-5016)
PHONE......................310 781-7150
Sheryl Ballieu, *Brnch Mgr*
EMP: 63
SALES (corp-wide): 303.18MM **Privately Held**
Web: arts.torranceca.gov
SIC: 9111 6512 City and town managers' office; Auditorium and hall operation
PA: City Of Torrance
3031 Torrance Blvd
Torrance CA
310 328-5310

(P-20916)
COUNTY OF SAN JOAQUIN
Also Called: Sewer Maintenance
1702 E Scotts Ave (95205-6240)
PHONE......................209 468-3090
Ron Rall, *Brnch Mgr*
EMP: 76
SALES (corp-wide): 1.54B **Privately Held**
Web: www.sjgov.org
SIC: 9111 1623 County supervisors' and executives' office; Water, sewer, and utility lines
PA: County Of San Joaquin
44 N San Joaquin St # 374
Stockton CA
209 468-3203

(P-20917)
COUNTY OF VENTURA
Also Called: Family Care Center
3291 Loma Vista Rd (93003-3099)
PHONE......................805 652-6100
Judy Mullins, *Mgr*
EMP: 80
SALES (corp-wide): 165.04MM **Privately Held**
Web: www.ventura.org
SIC: 9111 8322 Executive offices, County government; Adult day care center
PA: County Of Ventura
800 S Victoria Ave
Ventura CA
805 654-2644

(P-20918)
LOS ANGLES CNTY MSEUM NTRAL HS (PA)
900 Exposition Blvd (90007-4057)
PHONE......................213 763-3466
Lori Bettison-varga, *Pr*
Egbert Gutierrez, *
EMP: 210 **EST:** 1913
SQ FT: 450,000
SALES (est): 64.34MM
SALES (corp-wide): 64.34MM **Privately Held**
Web: www.nhm.org
SIC: 9111 8399 8412 County supervisors' and executives' office; Fund raising organization, non-fee basis; Museums and art galleries

9131 Executive And Legislative Combined

(P-20919)
SAN PSQUAL BAND MSSION INDIANS (PA)
16400 Kumeyaay Way (92082-6796)
P.O. Box 365 (92082-0365)
PHONE......................760 749-3200
Allen Lawson, *Ch*
EMP: 99 **EST:** 1971
Web: www.sanpasqualbandofmissionindians.org
SIC: 9131 6733 Indian Reservation; Trusts, nec

9199 General Government, Nec

(P-20920)
CALIFORNIA DEPT OF PUB HLTH
681 S Parker St Ste 200 (92868-4719)
PHONE......................714 567-2906
Jacqueline Lincer, *Brnch Mgr*
EMP: 206
SALES (corp-wide): 534.4MM **Privately Held**
Web: cdph.ca.gov
SIC: 9199 8051 General government administration, State government; Extended care facility
HQ: The California Department Of Public Health
1615 Capitol Ave
Sacramento CA
916 558-1784

(P-20921)
CALIFRNIA DEPT INDUS RELATIONS
28 Civic Center Plz Ste 239 (92701-4024)
PHONE......................714 558-4121
George Gomez, *Mgr*
EMP: 67
SALES (corp-wide): 534.4MM **Privately Held**
SIC: 9199 8322 General government administration, State government; Rehabilitation services
HQ: California Department Of Industrial Relations
455 Golden Gate Ave Fl 10
San Francisco CA

(P-20922)
CITY OF LANCASTER
Also Called: Aerospace Walk of Honor
44933 Fern Ave (93534-2483)
PHONE......................661 723-6008
Mark Bovigan, *Mgr*
EMP: 66
Web: www.cityoflancasterca.org
SIC: 9199 8699 General government administration, Local government; Charitable organization
PA: City Of Lancaster
44933 Fern Ave
Lancaster CA

(P-20923)
COUNTY OF FRESNO
Also Called: Cemetery District- Clovis
305 N Villa Ave (93612-0278)
PHONE......................559 299-6057
Anna Herrera, *Mgr*
EMP: 224

SALES (corp-wide): 2.02B **Privately Held**
Web: fresno.courts.ca.gov
SIC: 9199 6553 General government administration; Cemetery association
PA: County Of Fresno
2281 Tulare St Ste 304
Fresno CA
559 600-1710

(P-20924)
COUNTY OF SAN DIEGO
5560 Overland Ave Ste 410 (92123-1204)
PHONE......................858 505-6100
Danielle Enriquez, *CFO*
EMP: 87
SQ FT: 10,000
Web: www.sdcda.org
SIC: 9199 6531 General government administration; Real estate brokers and agents
PA: County Of San Diego
1600 Pacific Hwy Ste 209
San Diego CA
619 531-5880

(P-20925)
COUNTY OF VENTURA
Also Called: Juvenile Facilities
4333 E Vineyard Ave (93036-1013)
PHONE......................805 981-5521
Patty Moruawiddows, *Brnch Mgr*
EMP: 62
SALES (corp-wide): 165.04MM **Privately Held**
Web: www.ventura.org
SIC: 9199 8322 General government administration; Child guidance agency
PA: County Of Ventura
800 S Victoria Ave
Ventura CA
805 654-2644

(P-20926)
COUNTY OF VENTURA
Also Called: Department Animal Regulation
600 Aviation Dr (93010-8550)
PHONE......................805 388-4341
Kathy Jenks, *Dir*
EMP: 68
SALES (corp-wide): 165.04MM **Privately Held**
Web: www.ventura.org
SIC: 9199 8699 General government administration, County government; Animal humane society
PA: County Of Ventura
800 S Victoria Ave
Ventura CA
805 654-2644

(P-20927)
PASKENTA BAND NOMLAKI INDIANS
22580 Olivewood Rd (96021-9726)
P.O. Box 709 (96021-0709)
PHONE......................530 670-1750
Andrew Alejandre, *Ch*
EMP: 493 **EST:** 1994
Web: www.paskenta-nsn.gov
SIC: 9199 7011 General government administration; Casino hotel

9221 Police Protection

(P-20928)
CITY OF LIVERMORE
Also Called: Livermoore Police Facility
1110 S Livermore Ave (94550-9315)
PHONE......................925 371-4848

9221 - Police Protection (P-20929)

EMP: 63
SALES (corp-wide): 147.69MM **Privately Held**
Web: www.livermoreca.gov
SIC: **9221** 0752 Police protection, Local government; Animal specialty services
PA: City Of Livermore
1052 S Livermore Ave
Livermore CA
925 960-4020

(P-20929)
COUNTY OF CONTRA COSTA
Also Called: Office of The Sheriff
1850 Muir Rd (94553-4719)
PHONE.................................925 655-0000
EMP: 76
SQ FT: 3,200
SALES (corp-wide): 2.51B **Privately Held**
Web: www.cc-courts.org
SIC: **9221** 8111 Sheriffs' office; Legal services
PA: County Of Contra Costa
625 Court St Ste 100
Martinez CA
925 957-5280

(P-20930)
SAN DIEGO UNIFIED PORT DST
Also Called: San Diego Unified Hbr Police
3380 N Harbor Dr (92101-1023)
PHONE.................................619 686-6585
Betty Kelepecz, *Brnch Mgr*
EMP: 107
SALES (corp-wide): 167.04MM **Privately Held**
Web: www.portofsandiego.org
SIC: **9221** 4491 Police protection; Marine cargo handling
PA: San Diego Unified Port District
3165 Pacific Hwy
San Diego CA
619 686-6200

9222 Legal Counsel And Prosecution

(P-20931)
COUNTY OF LOS ANGELES
Also Called: District Attorney
42011 4th St W Ste 3530 (93534-7196)
PHONE.................................661 974-7700
Steve Cooley, *Admn*
EMP: 82
SALES (corp-wide): 31.7B **Privately Held**
Web: www.lacounty.gov
SIC: **9222** 8111 District attorneys' office; General practice attorney, lawyer
PA: County Of Los Angeles
500 W Temple St Ste 437
Los Angeles CA
213 974-1101

(P-20932)
COUNTY OF RIVERSIDE
Also Called: District Attorney's Office
2001 Iowa Ave Ste 218 (92507-2480)
P.O. Box 1260 (92502-1260)
PHONE.................................951 955-5659
John Replogle, *Brnch Mgr*
EMP: 63
SALES (corp-wide): 4.58B **Privately Held**
Web: www.countyofriverside.us
SIC: **9222** 8322 District attorneys' office; Child related social services
PA: County Of Riverside
4080 Lemon St Fl 11
Riverside CA
951 955-1110

9224 Fire Protection

(P-20933)
CITY OF PLEASANTON
Also Called: Livermore Pleasanton Fire Dept
3560 Nevada St (94566-6267)
PHONE.................................925 454-2341
Bill Cody, *Superintnt*
EMP: 64
SALES (corp-wide): 142.65MM **Privately Held**
Web: www.cityofpleasantonca.gov
SIC: **9224** 8748 Fire protection, Local government; Business consulting, nec
PA: City Of Pleasanton
123 Main St
Pleasanton CA
925 931-5002

(P-20934)
COUNTY OF PLACER
Also Called: South Plcer Fire Prtection Dst
6900 Eureka Rd (95746-6531)
PHONE.................................916 791-7059
Eric Walter, *Chief*
EMP: 158
SQ FT: 2,908
SALES (corp-wide): 803.78MM **Privately Held**
Web: www.southplacerfire.org
SIC: **9224** 8322 Fire department, not including volunteer; First aid service
PA: County Of Placer
2986 Richardson Dr
Auburn CA
530 889-4200

(P-20935)
KAISER FOUNDATION HOSPITALS
3200 Arden Way (95825-2015)
PHONE.................................916 974-6211
EMP: 523
SALES (corp-wide): 68.1B **Privately Held**
Web: www.kaisercenter.com
SIC: **9224** 9221 8742 8699 Fire protection; Police protection; Hospital and health services consultant; Charitable organization
HQ: Kaiser Foundation Hospitals Inc
1 Kaiser Plz
Oakland CA
510 271-6611

(P-20936)
NORTH BAY FIRE
4500 Hessel Rd (95472-6267)
PHONE.................................707 823-1084
Mike Mickelson, *Pr*
Mike Mickelson, *Prin*
Bill Newman, *
Terri Bolduc, *
Tiffanie Palmer, *
EMP: 85 EST: 1982
Web: www.goldridgefire.org
SIC: **9224** 0851 Fire protection; Fire prevention services, forest

9431 Administration Of Public Health Programs

(P-20937)
CITY OF LONG BEACH
Also Called: Long Bch Dept Hlth & Humn Svcs
2525 Grand Ave (90815-1765)
PHONE.................................562 570-4000
Ronald Arias, *Dir*
EMP: 62
SQ FT: 56,733
Web: www.longbeach.gov
SIC: **9431** 8322 Administration of public health programs, Local government; Individual and family services
PA: City Of Long Beach
1800 E Wardlow Rd
Long Beach CA
562 570-6450

(P-20938)
COUNTY OF LOS ANGELES
Also Called: Department of Mental Health
510 S Vermont Ave Fl 1 (90020-1912)
PHONE.................................213 738-4601
Richard Kushi, *Brnch Mgr*
EMP: 108
SALES (corp-wide): 31.7B **Privately Held**
Web: www.lacounty.gov
SIC: **9431** 8093 Mental health agency administration, government; Mental health clinic, outpatient
PA: County Of Los Angeles
500 W Temple St Ste 437
Los Angeles CA
213 974-1101

(P-20939)
COUNTY OF RIVERSIDE
Also Called: Children & Families Commission
585 Technology Ct (92507-2192)
PHONE.................................951 248-0014
Harry Freedman, *Mgr*
EMP: 69
SALES (corp-wide): 4.58B **Privately Held**
Web: www.countyofriverside.us
SIC: **9431** 8322 Child health program administration, government; Parole office
PA: County Of Riverside
4080 Lemon St Fl 11
Riverside CA
951 955-1110

(P-20940)
REGIONAL CTR ORANGE CNTY INC (PA)
Also Called: DEVELOPMENT DISABILITIES CENTE
1525 N Tustin Ave (92705-8621)
P.O. Box 22010 (92702-2010)
PHONE.................................714 796-5100
William J Bowman, *Ex Dir*
EMP: 309 EST: 1977
SQ FT: 41,128
SALES (est): 522.74MM
SALES (corp-wide): 522.74MM **Privately Held**
Web: www.rcocdd.com
SIC: **9431** 8322 Mental health agency administration, government; Individual and family services

9441 Administration Of Social And Manpower Programs

(P-20941)
CALIFORNIA DEPT SOCIAL SVCS
Also Called: Community Care Licensing
3737 Main St Ste 700 (92501-3349)
PHONE.................................951 782-4200
Robert Gonzales, *Brnch Mgr*
EMP: 71
SALES (corp-wide): 534.4MM **Privately Held**
Web: cdss.ca.gov
SIC: **9441** 8322 Administration of social and manpower programs; Offender self-help agency
HQ: California Dept Of Social Services
744 P St
Sacramento CA

(P-20942)
COUNTY OF KERN
Also Called: Employers Training Resource
1600 E Belle Ter Ste 5 (93307-3872)
PHONE.................................661 336-6871
Verna Lewis, *Ex Dir*
EMP: 118
Web: www.kerncounty.com
SIC: **9441** 8331 Administration of social and manpower programs; Job training and related services
PA: County Of Kern
1115 Truxtun Ave Rm 505
Bakersfield CA
661 868-3690

(P-20943)
COUNTY OF RIVERSIDE
Also Called: Community Health Agency
4065 County Circle Dr (92503-3410)
P.O. Box 7849 (92513-7849)
PHONE.................................951 358-5000
Gary Feldman, *Asst Dir*
EMP: 119
SALES (corp-wide): 4.58B **Privately Held**
Web: www.countyofriverside.us
SIC: **9441** 8621 Public welfare administration: nonoperating, government; Health association
PA: County Of Riverside
4080 Lemon St Fl 11
Riverside CA
951 955-1110

(P-20944)
FIRST 5 ALAMEDA COUNTY
1115 Atlantic Ave (94501-1145)
PHONE.................................510 227-6900
Janis Burger, *CEO*
EMP: 60 EST: 2014
Web: www.first5alameda.org
SIC: **9441** 8322 Administration of social and manpower programs; Family service agency

9512 Land, Mineral, And Wildlife Conservation

(P-20945)
COUNTY OF SAN JOAQUIN
Also Called: Micke Grove Park & Zoo
11793 N Micke Grove Rd (95240-8104)
PHONE.................................209 331-7270
Marcia Cunningham, *Dir*
EMP: 87
SALES (corp-wide): 1.54B **Privately Held**
Web: www.mgzoo.com
SIC: **9512** 8412 Wildlife conservation agencies; Museums and art galleries
PA: County Of San Joaquin
44 N San Joaquin St # 374
Stockton CA
209 468-3203

(P-20946)
COUNTY OF SANTA CLARA
Also Called: SCC Open Space Authority
6980 Santa Teresa Blvd Ste 100 (95119-1393)
PHONE.................................408 224-7476
Adrea Manie, *Genl Mgr*
EMP: 87
Web: www.openspaceauthority.org

PRODUCTS & SERVICES SECTION 9641 - Regulation Of Agricultural Marketing (P-20949)

SIC: 9512 8641 Land conservation agencies; Civic and social associations
PA: County Of Santa Clara
70 W Hedding St
San Jose CA
408 299-5200

9532 Urban And Community Development

(P-20947)
FORMOSA TOGETHER ✪
8430 Pine River Way (95823-7233)
PHONE.................................916 661-8835
Daniel Wright, *CEO*
EMP: 300 **EST:** 2022
SIC: 9532 7389 Community and rural development; Business services, nec

9621 Regulation, Administration Of Transportation

(P-20948)
CITY OF LOS ANGELES
Harbor Dept- Port Los Angeles
425 S Palos Verdes St (90731-3309)
P.O. Box 151 (90733-0151)
PHONE.................................310 732-3734
EMP: 650
Web: www.lacity.org
SIC: 9621 8721 Water vessels and port regulating agencies; Accounting services, except auditing
PA: City Of Los Angeles
200 N Spring St Ste 303
Los Angeles CA
213 978-0600

9641 Regulation Of Agricultural Marketing

(P-20949)
CALIFORNIA DEPT FD AGRICULTURE
Also Called: Del Mar Fair Grounds
2260 Jimmy Durante Blvd (92014-2216)
PHONE.................................858 755-1161
Carlene Moore, *CEO*
EMP: 758
SALES (corp-wide): 534.4MM **Privately Held**
Web: www.sdfair5k.com
SIC: 9641 7948 Food inspection agency, government; Racing, including track operation
HQ: California Department Of Food And Agriculture
1220 N St Fl 4
Sacramento CA

(PA)=Parent Co (HQ)=Headquarters
✪ = New Business established in last 2 years

ALPHABETIC SECTION

> **R & R Sealants (HQ)** .... C 818 247-6319
> 651 Tally Blvd, Burbank 91505 *(P-1710)*
> **Rake, J R Co** .... D 310 542-3000
> 21 45th, Malibu 90265 *(P-1715)*
> **Ready Box Co (HQ)** .... A 310 999-4444
> 704 Lawrence Rd, Venice 90294 *(P-17231)*

- Address, city & ZIP
- Designates this location as a headquarters
- Business phone
- Indicates approximate employment figure:
  A = over 500 employees
  B = 251-500, C = 101-250
  D = 51-100, E = 20-50
  F = 10-19, G = 1-9
- Product & Services Section entry number where full company information appears

See footnotes for symbols and codes identification.
- Companies listed alphabetically.
- Complete physical or mailing address.

(415 Location), San Francisco *Also Called: Leemah Electronics Inc (P-4583)*

(AN EXPLORATION STAGE COMPANY), San Francisco *Also Called: Colombia Energy Resources Inc (P-576)*

0EPI, Carmichael *Also Called: Eskaton Properties Inc (P-18429)*

1-800 Radiator & A/C LLC (DH) .... D 707 747-7400
4401 Park Rd Benicia (94510) *(P-5020)*

1-800-Radiator, Benicia *Also Called: 1-800 Radiator & A/C LLC (P-5020)*

1-Carasight Surveillance, San Diego *Also Called: Inseego North America LLC (P-12469)*

1000 Executive Parkway LLC .... C 530 533-7335
1000 Executive Pkwy Oroville (95966) *(P-15313)*

101communications LLC (HQ) .... D 818 734-1520
9201 Oakdale Ave Ste 101 Chatsworth (91311) *(P-10698)*

10632 Bolsa Avenue LP .... D 949 673-1221
500 Nwport Ctr Dr Ste 200 Newport Beach (92660) *(P-8786)*

10up Inc (PA) .... D 888 571-7130
2765 Carradale Dr Roseville (95661) *(P-12412)*

10up.com, Roseville *Also Called: 10up Inc (P-12412)*

10X GENOMICS, Pleasanton *Also Called: 10x Genomics Inc (P-19642)*

10x Genomics Inc (PA) .... C 925 401-7300
6230 Stoneridge Mall Rd Pleasanton (94588) *(P-19642)*

10x Hvac of Ca LLC .... D 760 343-7488
31170 Reserve Dr Thousand Palms (92276) *(P-1326)*

11 Main Inc .... C 530 892-9191
527 Flume St Chico (95928) *(P-4246)*

1101 Stockton Accounting Off, Stockton *Also Called: Crestwood Behavioral Hlth Inc (P-15417)*

1105 Government Group, Chatsworth *Also Called: 101communications LLC (P-10698)*

1106 Sacramento Mhrc, Sacramento *Also Called: Crestwood Behavioral Hlth Inc (P-15838)*

1107 San Jose Mhrc, San Jose *Also Called: Crestwood Behavioral Hlth Inc (P-15837)*

1111 6th Ave LLC .... D 312 283-3683
1111 6th Ave Ste 102 San Diego (92101) *(P-13164)*

1112 Modesto Snf/STP, Modesto *Also Called: Crestwood Behavioral Hlth Inc (P-15413)*

1115 Bakersfield Mhrc, Bakersfield *Also Called: Crestwood Behavioral Hlth Inc (P-15842)*

1116 Angwin Mhrc, Angwin *Also Called: Crestwood Behavioral Hlth Inc (P-15841)*

1120 Fremont Snf, Fremont *Also Called: Crestwood Behavioral Hlth Inc (P-15416)*

1122 Redding IMD, Redding *Also Called: Crestwood Behavioral Hlth Inc (P-15414)*

1125 Sir Frncis Drake Blvd Ope .... C 415 456-9680
1125 Sir Francis Drake Blvd Kentfield (94904) *(P-15914)*

1134 Alameda Snf/STP, Fremont *Also Called: Crestwood Behavioral Hlth Inc (P-15415)*

1135 N Leisure Ct Inc .... D 714 772-1353
1135 N Leisure Ct Anaheim (92801) *(P-15314)*

1140 Kingsburg Mhrc, Kingsburg *Also Called: Crestwood Behavioral Hlth Inc (P-15836)*

1154 San Diego Mhrc, San Diego *Also Called: Crestwood Behavioral Hlth Inc (P-15839)*

1167 Fallbrook Mhrc, Fallbrook *Also Called: Crestwood Behavioral Hlth Inc (P-15840)*

1170 Lompoc Mhrc, Lompoc *Also Called: Crestwood Behavioral Hlth Inc (P-18412)*

1221 Ocean Ave Apartments, Santa Monica *Also Called: Irvine APT Communities LP (P-8830)*

123 Home Care, Pasadena *Also Called: Confido LLC (P-16845)*

1260 Bb Property LLC .... B 805 969-2261
1260 Channel Dr Santa Barbara (93108) *(P-9585)*

1334 Partners LP .... D 310 546-5656
1330 Park View Ave Manhattan Beach (90266) *(P-14318)*

14766 Wash Ave Operations LLC .... D 510 352-2211
14766 Washington Ave San Leandro (94578) *(P-15807)*

1651 Tiburon Hotel LLC .... D 401 946-4600
1651 Tiburon Blvd Belvedere Tiburon (94920) *(P-9586)*

17400 Inc .... D 626 913-1800
17400 Chestnut St City Of Industry (91748) *(P-3577)*

180Ia LLC .... C 310 382-1400
12555 W Jefferson Blvd Ste 200 Los Angeles (90066) *(P-10584)*

1835 Columbia Street LP .... D 619 564-3993
1835 Columbia St San Diego (92101) *(P-9587)*

1855 S Hbr Blvd Drv Hldngs LLC .... C 714 750-1811
1855 S Harbor Blvd Anaheim (92802) *(P-9588)*

1928 Jewelry Company, Burbank *Also Called: Mel Bernie and Company Inc (P-6023)*

1life Healthcare Inc (HQ) .... D 415 814-0927
1 Embarcadero Ctr Ste 1900 San Francisco (94111) *(P-14591)*

1st Century Bancshares Inc .... D 310 270-9500
1875 Century Park E Ste 1400 Los Angeles (90067) *(P-7650)*

1st Class Laundry .... C 510 487-8297
33485 Western Ave Union City (94587) *(P-10475)*

1st Class Laundry Services, Union City *Also Called: 1st Class Laundry (P-10475)*

1st Team Real Estate, Tustin *Also Called: First Team RE - Orange Cnty (P-9015)*

1st United Credit Union (PA) .... D 800 649-0193
5901 Gibraltar Dr Pleasanton (94588) *(P-7750)*

20/20 Mobile Corp .... D 909 587-2973
3380 La Sierra Ave Riverside (92503) *(P-4180)*

20/20 Plumbing & Heating Inc (PA) .... D 951 396-2020
7343 Orangewood Dr Ste B Riverside (92504) *(P-1327)*

20/20 Plumbing & Heating Inc .... C 760 535-3101
674 Rancheros Dr San Marcos (92069) *(P-1328)*

20th Century Fox Studio, Los Angeles *Also Called: Fox Net Inc (P-13851)*

2100 Freedom Inc (HQ) .... D 714 796-7000
625 N Grand Ave Santa Ana (92701) *(P-2535)*

2100 Trust LLC (PA) .... C 877 469-7344
625 N Grand Ave Santa Ana (92701) *(P-9419)*

211 La County, San Gabriel *Also Called: Informtion Rfrral Fdrtion of L (P-10552)*

21515 Hawthorne Owner LLC .... D 310 406-3730
21535 Hawthorne Blvd Ste 100 Torrance (90503) *(P-18808)*

21st Century Health Club (PA) .... D 707 795-0400
680a E Cotati Ave Cotati (94931) *(P-16999)*

21st Century Insurance, Woodland Hills *Also Called: 21st Century Life Insurance Co (P-8475)*

21st Century Lf & Hlth Co Inc (PA) .... C 818 887-4436
21600 Oxnard St Ste 1500 Woodland Hills (91367) *(P-8254)*

21st Century Life Insurance Co (DH) .... A 877 310-5687
6301 Owensmouth Ave Ste 700 Woodland Hills (91367) *(P-8475)*

22nd Century Technologies Inc .... B 866 537-9191
6203 San Ignacio Ave Ste 110 San Jose (95119) *(P-11365)*

ALPHABETIC SECTION

2310 Catalina LLC .... D...... 818 696-2040
1507 Western Ave Glendale (91201) *(P-13165)*

23627 Calabasas Road LLC .... D...... 818 222-5300
23627 Calabasas Rd Calabasas (91302) *(P-9589)*

23andme Inc (HQ) .... A...... 650 961-7152
349 Oyster Point Blvd South San Francisco (94080) *(P-12648)*

24 7ai Inc (PA) .... C...... 650 385-2247
2105 S Bascom Ave Ste 195 Campbell (95008) *(P-12715)*

24 Hour Fitness, Carlsbad *Also Called: 24 Hour Fitness Usa LLC (P-14168)*

24 Hour Fitness Usa LLC (HQ) .... C...... 925 543-3100
1265 Laurel Tree Ln Ste 200 Carlsbad (92011) *(P-14168)*

24 Hour Fitness Worldwide Inc .... A...... 925 543-3100
1265 Laurel Tree Ln Ste 200 Carlsbad (92011) *(P-14169)*

24 Hour In Motion Fitness, Chico *Also Called: IBAM INC (P-14207)*

24-Hour Med Staffing Svcs LLC .... C...... 909 895-8960
1370 Valley Vista Dr Ste 280 Diamond Bar (91765) *(P-11066)*

24/7 Medstaff, Sacramento *Also Called: Epn Enterprises Inc (P-11285)*

2733 Idylwood Care Center, Sunnyvale *Also Called: Helios Healthcare LLC (P-15512)*

29 Palms Enterprises Corp .... A...... 760 775-5566
46200 Harrison Pl Coachella (92236) *(P-14486)*

2dream Inc .... D...... 650 943-2366
5729 Sonoma Dr Ste Z Pleasanton (94566) *(P-20669)*

2h Construction Inc .... D...... 562 424-4567
2653 Walnut Ave Signal Hill (90755) *(P-858)*

2k Games Inc C
10 Hamilton Landing Novato (94949) *(P-5984)*

2wire Inc (DH) .... C...... 408 235-5500
2450 Walsh Ave Santa Clara (95051) *(P-4247)*

3-Downtown Bars Inc .... D...... 530 898-9898
191 E 2nd St Chico (95928) *(P-10527)*

3-Way Air Charter, Santa Clara *Also Called: Three Way Inc (P-3598)*

313 Acquisition LLC .... A...... 801 234-6374
1111 Citrus St Ste 1 Riverside (92507) *(P-13081)*

314e Corporation (PA) .... C...... 510 371-6736
6701 Koll Center Pkwy Ste 340 Pleasanton (94566) *(P-11366)*

360 Clinic, Westminster *Also Called: 360 Health Plan Inc (P-20007)*

360 Health Plan Inc .... C...... 800 446-8888
13800 Arizona St Ste 104 Westminster (92683) *(P-20007)*

360 Support Services .... D...... 866 360-6468
306 S Myrtle Ave Monrovia (91016) *(P-20008)*

360s2g, San Francisco *Also Called: Etech-360 Inc (P-12183)*

360zebra, City Of Industry *Also Called: Gels Logistics Inc (P-4023)*

365 Delivery Inc .... D...... 818 815-5005
440 E Huntington Dr Ste 300 Arcadia (91006) *(P-3359)*

365 Hlthcare Staffing Svcs Inc .... D...... 310 436-3650
25550 Hawthorne Blvd Ste 211 Torrance (90505) *(P-17163)*

365 Home Care .... D...... 310 908-5179
10225 Austin Dr Ste 208 Spring Valley (91978) *(P-16780)*

3dconnexion Inc .... D...... 510 713-6000
6505 Kaiser Dr Fremont (94555) *(P-2821)*

3dna Corp (PA) .... C...... 213 992-4809
750 W 7th St Ste 201 Los Angeles (90017) *(P-11367)*

3e, Carlsbad *Also Called: 3E Company Env Ec n Eng (P-20670)*

3E Company Env Ec n Eng (PA) .... C...... 760 602-8700
3207 Grey Hawk Ct Carlsbad (92010) *(P-20670)*

3k Technologies LLC .... C...... 408 716-5900
1114 Cadillac Ct Milpitas (95035) *(P-11368)*

3M Company .... B...... 949 863-1360
2111 Mcgaw Ave Irvine (92614) *(P-3066)*

3vr Security Inc .... D...... 415 513-4577
1 Kaiser Plz Ste 1030 Oakland (94612) *(P-13082)*

4 CS, Santa Rosa *Also Called: Community Child Care Cncil Sno (P-18300)*

4 Earth Farms LLC (PA) .... B...... 323 201-5800
5555 E Olympic Blvd Commerce (90022) *(P-6511)*

4 Wheel Parts Performance Ctrs, Compton *Also Called: Tap Worldwide LLC (P-5064)*

4 Wheel Parts Wholesalers LLC .... B...... 310 900-7725
400 W Artesia Blvd Compton (90220) *(P-5021)*

40 Hours Staffing, San Jose *Also Called: 40 Hrs Inc (P-11067)*

40 Hrs Inc .... A...... 408 414-0158
1669 Flanigan Dr San Jose (95121) *(P-11067)*

417 Stockton St LLC .... D...... 323 327-9656
1180 S Beverly Dr Ste 508 Los Angeles (90035) *(P-9590)*

4290 El Camino Properties LP .... C...... 650 857-0787
4290 El Camino Real Palo Alto (94306) *(P-9591)*

48123 CA Investors LLC .... C...... 831 667-2331
48123 Highway 1 Big Sur (93920) *(P-9592)*

4d Inc .... C...... 408 557-4600
95 S Market St Ste 240 San Jose (95113) *(P-11369)*

4d Molecular Therapeutics Inc .... D...... 510 505-2680
5858 Horton St Ste 455 Emeryville (94608) *(P-19643)*

4g Wireless Inc (PA) .... D...... 949 748-6100
775 Laguna Canyon Rd Laguna Beach (92651) *(P-4181)*

4inkjets, Long Beach *Also Called: Ld Products Inc (P-2510)*

4liberty Inc .... D...... 619 400-1000
7675 Dagget St Ste 200 San Diego (92111) *(P-1648)*

4th & Folsom Associates LP .... B...... 415 417-3086
201 Eddy St San Francisco (94102) *(P-8787)*

5 Arches LLC .... D...... 949 387-8092
19800 Macarthur Blvd Irvine (92612) *(P-8029)*

5 Day Business Forms Mfg Inc .... D...... 714 632-8674
2921 E La Cresta Ave Anaheim (92806) *(P-6061)*

5 Design Inc .... C...... 323 308-3558
6161 Santa Monica Blvd Ste 208 Los Angeles (90038) *(P-19448)*

5 Palms LLC .... C...... 650 457-0539
800 S B St Fl 1 San Mateo (94401) *(P-13166)*

5 Star Job Source .... D...... 562 788-7391
12025 Garfield Ave South Gate (90280) *(P-11068)*

500 Startups Management Co LLC .... C...... 650 743-4738
3478 Buskirk Ave Ste 1000 Pleasant Hill (94523) *(P-9481)*

51 Minds Entertainment LLC .... D...... 818 643-8200
5200 Lankershim Blvd Ste 200 North Hollywood (91601) *(P-14075)*

51st St & 8th Ave Corp .... C...... 619 424-4000
4000 Coronado Bay Rd Coronado (92118) *(P-9593)*

550 Flower St Operations LLC .... C...... 213 892-8080
550 S Flower St Los Angeles (90071) *(P-9594)*

5525 E Pacific Coast Hwy Inc .... C...... 323 669-9090
2016 Riverside Dr Los Angeles (90039) *(P-9461)*

5design, Los Angeles *Also Called: 5 Design Inc (P-19448)*

6 Sense Insights Inc (PA) .... D...... 415 212-9225
450 Mission St Ste 201 San Francisco (94105) *(P-12546)*

6417 Selma Hotel LLC .... C...... 323 844-6417
6417 Selma Ave Los Angeles (90028) *(P-9595)*

6500 Hllister Ave Partners LLC .... D...... 805 722-1362
6500 Hollister Ave Goleta (93117) *(P-8697)*

6sense, San Francisco *Also Called: 6 Sense Insights Inc (P-12546)*

6wind Usa Inc .... D...... 408 816-1366
2445 Augustine Dr Ste 150 Santa Clara (95054) *(P-11370)*

7 Diamonds Clothing, Tustin *Also Called: M & S Trading Inc (P-6180)*

7 Up / R C Bottling Co, Vernon *Also Called: American Bottling Company (P-2402)*

716 Management Inc .... D...... 818 471-4956
3900 W Alameda Ave # 120 Burbank (91505) *(P-744)*

76, San Diego *Also Called: Cosco Fire Protection Inc (P-1409)*

7th & C Investments LLC .... C...... 619 233-7327
404 14th St San Diego (92101) *(P-9482)*

7th Standard Ranch Company .... B...... 661 399-0416
33374 Lerdo Hwy Bakersfield (93308) *(P-67)*

80 Twenty LLC .... D...... 415 592-7773
369 Pine St Ste 208 San Francisco (94104) *(P-11069)*

8020 Consulting LLC .... D...... 818 523-3201
6303 Owensmouth Ave Fl 10 Woodland Hills (91367) *(P-20671)*

8110 Aero Holding LLC .... C...... 858 277-8888
8110 Aero Dr San Diego (92123) *(P-9596)*

8minutenergy US Solar LLC .... D...... 916 608-9060
4370 Town Center Blvd Ste 110 El Dorado Hills (95762) *(P-1329)*

8X8, Campbell *Also Called: 8x8 Inc (P-4248)*

8x8 Inc (PA) .... A...... 408 727-1885
675 Creekside Way Campbell (95008) *(P-4248)*

901 West Olympic Blvd Ltd Prtn .... C...... 347 992-5707
901 W Olympic Blvd Los Angeles (90015) *(P-9597)*

911 Health Inc .... D...... 310 560-8509
701 Santa Monica Blvd # 300 Santa Monica (90401) *(P-19942)*

ALPHABETIC SECTION

911 Restoration Entps Inc .... B....... 832 887-2582
  6932 Gross Ave West Hills (91307) *(P-10845)*
99 Cents Only Stores, Commerce *Also Called: 99 Cents Only Stores LLC (P-6885)*
99 Cents Only Stores LLC (HQ) .... B....... 323 980-8145
  4000 Union Pacific Ave Commerce (90023) *(P-6885)*
99designs Inc (PA) .... C....... 415 539-1088
  2201 Broadway Ste 815 Oakland (94612) *(P-10797)*
A & B Construction, Oakland *Also Called: Andrew M Jordan Inc (P-2212)*
A & B Equipment, Corona *Also Called: Boudreau Pipeline Corporation (P-1198)*
A & D Fire Protection Inc .... D....... 619 258-7697
  7130 Convoy Ct San Diego (92111) *(P-1330)*
A & E Arborists Tree Care Inc .... B....... 530 790-5312
  225 Butte Ave Yuba City (95993) *(P-550)*
A & H Communications Inc .... C....... 949 250-4555
  15 Chrysler Irvine (92618) *(P-1191)*
A & I Color Laboratory, Burbank *Also Called: Jake Hey Incorporated (P-13160)*
A & P Towing-Metropro Rd Svcs, Costa Mesa *Also Called: Metropro Road Services Inc (P-13717)*
A & R Wholesale Distrs Inc .... D....... 714 777-7742
  1765 W Penhall Way Anaheim (92801) *(P-6452)*
A & S Metal Recycling Inc (PA) .... D....... 213 623-9443
  2261 E 15th St Los Angeles (90021) *(P-3360)*
A & S Technologies, Northridge *Also Called: Ikano Communications Inc (P-12581)*
A A A Automobile Club So Cal, Irvine *Also Called: Automobile Club Southern Cal (P-8502)*
A A A Automobile Club So Cal, Los Angeles *Also Called: Automobile Club Southern Cal (P-8505)*
A A A Automobile Club So Cal, Oceanside *Also Called: Automobile Club Southern Cal (P-19049)*
A A A Automobile Club So Cal, Pasadena *Also Called: Automobile Club Southern Cal (P-19051)*
A A A Automobile Club So Cal, Inglewood *Also Called: Automobile Club Southern Cal (P-19054)*
A A A Automobile Club So Cal, Laguna Hills *Also Called: Automobile Club Southern Cal (P-19060)*
A A A Automobile Club So Cal, Hemet *Also Called: Automobile Club Southern Cal (P-19062)*
A A A Automobile Club So Cal, Long Beach *Also Called: Automobile Club Southern Cal (P-19066)*
A A C N, Aliso Viejo *Also Called: American Assn Crtcal Care Nrse (P-17799)*
A A Gonzalez Inc .... D....... 818 367-2242
  13264 Ralston Ave Rancho Cascades (91342) *(P-1898)*
A B C D Associates .... C....... 916 363-4843
  10410 Coloma Rd Rancho Cordova (95670) *(P-15315)*
A B C Design Rugs, Los Angeles *Also Called: ABC Carpet Co Inc (P-7427)*
A B C Pediatrics .... C....... 650 579-6500
  50 S San Mateo Dr Ste 260 San Mateo (94401) *(P-14592)*
A B M, Irvine *Also Called: ABM Facility Services LLC (P-19124)*
A B S, City Of Industry *Also Called: Magnell Associate Inc (P-5327)*
A Buchalter Professional Corp (PA) .... C....... 213 891-0700
  1000 Wilshire Blvd Ste 1500 Los Angeles (90017) *(P-17354)*
A C G, Laguna Hills *Also Called: American Capital Group Inc (P-7914)*
A C I Communications, Calabasas *Also Called: Able Cable Inc (P-13731)*
A C M, Santa Ana *Also Called: Advanced Clnroom McRclean Corp (P-10849)*
A C T, Hawthorne *Also Called: All Cartage Transportation Inc (P-3578)*
A C T, San Francisco *Also Called: American Conservatory Theater (P-7571)*
A Circle of Care LLC .... D....... 858 798-5005
  16486 Bernardo Center Dr Ste 300 San Diego (92128) *(P-16781)*
A Clark/Mccarthy Joint Venture .... A....... 714 429-9779
  18201 Von Karman Ave # 800 Irvine (92612) *(P-649)*
A Community of Friends .... D....... 213 480-0809
  3701 Wilshire Blvd Ste 700 Los Angeles (90010) *(P-8788)*
A D A C Laboratories (inc) .... A....... 408 321-9100
  3860 N 1st St San Jose (95134) *(P-3039)*
A D G, San Diego *Also Called: Affinity Development Group Inc (P-19032)*
A D S, Los Angeles *Also Called: Advanced Digital Services Inc (P-13815)*
A Deluxe Entrmt Svcs Group Co, Burbank *Also Called: Deluxe Encore Inc (P-4364)*
A Dentons Innovation Wirthlin, Los Angeles *Also Called: Dentons US LLP (P-17437)*
A Development Stage Company, San Francisco *Also Called: Brience Inc (P-11474)*
A Development Stage Company, Los Angeles *Also Called: Gsl Holdings Inc (P-20397)*
A F Evans Company Inc .... D....... 925 937-1700
  1700 Tice Valley Blvd Ofc Walnut Creek (94595) *(P-13167)*

A F Evans Development Inc .... B....... 510 267-4612
  2033 N Main St Ste 340 Walnut Creek (94596) *(P-9242)*
A Filml Inc .... D....... 213 977-8600
  737 N Western Ave # 101 Los Angeles (90029) *(P-13924)*
A G A, Fremont *Also Called: Homelegance Inc (P-5090)*
A G Hacienda Incorporated .... B....... 661 792-2418
  32794 Sherwood Ave Mc Farland (93250) *(P-3361)*
A Hospital, Stockton *Also Called: St Josephs Medical Center Inc (P-16477)*
A Is For Apple Inc .... C....... 877 991-0009
  1420 Koll Cir San Jose (95112) *(P-15267)*
A J Excavation Inc .... C....... 559 408-5908
  514 N Brawley Ave Fresno (93706) *(P-2211)*
A J Parent Company Inc (PA) .... D....... 714 521-1100
  6910 Aragon Cir Ste 6 Buena Park (90620) *(P-13168)*
A L Gilbert Company (PA) .... D....... 209 847-1721
  304 N Yosemite Ave Oakdale (95361) *(P-6817)*
A Lighting By Design, La Habra *Also Called: Albd Electric and Cable (P-1658)*
A M I Encn-Trzana Rgnal Med Ce, Tarzana *Also Called: AMI-Hti Trzana Encino Jint Vnt (P-15943)*
A M Ortega Construction Inc .... D....... 951 360-1352
  58 Kellogg St Ventura (93001) *(P-650)*
A M Ortega Construction Inc (PA) .... C....... 619 390-1988
  10125 Channel Rd Lakeside (92040) *(P-1649)*
A M R, Riverside *Also Called: American Med Rspnse Ambince Sv (P-3228)*
A M S Partnership (PA) .... D....... 310 312-6698
  1517 S Sepulveda Blvd Los Angeles (90025) *(P-9243)*
A Mediation & Resolution Ctr, San Diego *Also Called: Asset Management Tr Svcs LLC (P-20027)*
A O Reed & Co LLC .... B....... 858 565-4131
  4777 Ruffner St San Diego (92111) *(P-1331)*
A Oseguera Company Inc .... B....... 831 443-4155
  1099 Rogge Rd Salinas (93906) *(P-11070)*
A P R Consulting Inc .... A....... 714 544-3696
  17852 17th St Ste 206 Tustin (92780) *(P-12716)*
A P R Inc .... C....... 805 379-3400
  100 E Thousand Oaks Blvd Ste 240 Thousand Oaks (91360) *(P-11265)*
A Passion For Care, San Diego *Also Called: A Circle of Care LLC (P-16781)*
A Plus Home Health Specialist, West Covina *Also Called: A Plus Home Health Specialists (P-16782)*
A Plus Home Health Specialists .... D....... 626 918-9905
  1000 Lakes Dr Ste 170 West Covina (91790) *(P-16782)*
A Plus International Inc (PA) .... D....... 909 591-5168
  5138 Eucalyptus Ave Chino (91710) *(P-5394)*
A Plus Tree LLC .... C....... 707 644-1672
  985 Walnut Ave Vallejo (94592) *(P-551)*
A Preman Roofing, San Diego *Also Called: A Preman Roofing Inc (P-2041)*
A Preman Roofing Inc .... D....... 619 276-1700
  875 34th St San Diego (92102) *(P-2041)*
A Q M D, Diamond Bar *Also Called: South Cast A Qlty MGT Dst Bldg (P-20853)*
A Quality In Home Care, Banning *Also Called: Porto Inc (P-18085)*
A R C O, La Palma *Also Called: Atlantic Richfield Company (P-7383)*
A Rudin Inc (PA) .... D....... 323 589-5547
  6062 Alcoa Ave Vernon (90058) *(P-2488)*
A Rudin Designs, Vernon *Also Called: A Rudin Inc (P-2488)*
A S I, Long Beach *Also Called: Assocted Stdnts Cal State Univ (P-18815)*
A S S U, Stanford *Also Called: Associated Students Stanford (P-18814)*
A S U C, Berkeley, Berkeley *Also Called: Assocted Stdnts of The Univ CA (P-17801)*
A Speedcast Co, San Diego *Also Called: Ultisat Inc (P-12540)*
A SUNRISE HORIZON, Covina *Also Called: West Covina Foster Family Agcy (P-8685)*
A T A, Paso Robles *Also Called: Applied Technologies Assoc Inc (P-3042)*
A Transportation, Tarzana *Also Called: Airey Enterprises LLC (P-5954)*
A V Nursing Care Center, Lancaster *Also Called: Antelope Vly Retirement HM Inc (P-15810)*
A-1 Advantage Asphalt Inc .... D....... 916 388-2020
  10308 Placer Ln Ste 100 Sacramento (95827) *(P-1069)*
A-1 Delivery Co .... D....... 909 444-1220
  1777 S Vintage Ave Ontario (91761) *(P-3362)*
A-1 Door & Building Solutions, North Highlands *Also Called: Sacramento A-1 Door (P-5186)*
A-1 Hospice Care Inc .... D....... 818 237-2700
  217 E Alameda Ave Ste 306 Burbank (91502) *(P-15744)*

A-1 Pomona Linen — ALPHABETIC SECTION

A-1 Pomona Linen, Paramount Also Called: Braun Linen Service (P-10432)

A-Able Inc (PA) .... D....... 323 658-5779
17801 Ventura Blvd Encino (91316) *(P-10826)*

A-C Electric Company .... D....... 559 233-2208
2560 S East Ave Fresno (93706) *(P-1650)*

A-C Electric Company .... D....... 661 633-5368
315 30th St Bakersfield (93301) *(P-19123)*

A-Check America LLC (HQ) .... C....... 951 750-1501
1501 Research Park Dr Riverside (92507) *(P-10755)*

A-Check America, Member Act 1, Riverside Also Called: A-Check America LLC (P-10755)

A-G Sod Farms Inc .... D....... 951 687-7581
2900 Adams St Ste C120 Riverside (92504) *(P-119)*

A-LINE MESSENGER SERVICE, Chatsworth Also Called: M & N Consulting Inc (P-3619)

A-Mark, El Segundo Also Called: A-Mark Precious Metals Inc (P-6018)

A-Mark Precious Metals Inc (PA) .... D....... 310 587-1477
2121 Rosecrans Ave Ste 6300 El Segundo (90245) *(P-6018)*

A-Para Transit Corp .... C....... 510 562-5500
1400 Doolittle Dr San Leandro (94577) *(P-3119)*

A-Team Delivers LLC .... D....... 858 254-8401
12127 Mall Blvd Ste A322 Victorville (92392) *(P-3363)*

A-Z Bus Sales Inc (PA) .... D....... 951 781-7188
1900 S Riverside Ave Colton (92324) *(P-4998)*

A.B.C. Carpet & Home, Los Angeles Also Called: ABC Home Furnishings Inc (P-7418)

A.G. Ferrari Foods, San Leandro Also Called: Rof Ferrari Lending 1 LLC (P-7148)

A&W Restaurant, Campbell Also Called: Harman Management Corporation (P-7485)

A1 Protective Services Inc .... D....... 415 467-7200
5 Thomas Mellon Cir San Francisco (94134) *(P-12914)*

A10, San Jose Also Called: A10 Networks Inc (P-12717)

A10 Networks Inc (PA) .... A....... 408 325-8668
2300 Orchard Pkwy San Jose (95131) *(P-12717)*

A3 Smart Home LP .... C....... 800 669-7779
1277 Treat Blvd Ste 1000 Walnut Creek (94597) *(P-12915)*

Aa, San Leandro Also Called: Aa/Acme Locksmiths Inc (P-1651)

AA Blocks LLC .... D....... 858 523-8231
9823 Pacific Heights Blvd Ste F San Diego (92121) *(P-20258)*

Aa Equipment, Montclair Also Called: Cascade Turf LLC (P-5807)

Aa Leasing, Los Angeles Also Called: Vahe Enterprises Inc (P-2969)

Aa/Acme Locksmiths Inc .... D....... 510 483-6584
1660 Factor Ave San Leandro (94577) *(P-1651)*

AAA, Santa Maria Also Called: Automobile Club Southern Cal (P-8503)

AAA, San Diego Also Called: Automobile Club Southern Cal (P-19039)

AAA, San Luis Obispo Also Called: Automobile Club Southern Cal (P-19040)

AAA, Thousand Oaks Also Called: Automobile Club Southern Cal (P-19041)

AAA, Torrance Also Called: Automobile Club Southern Cal (P-19042)

AAA, Anaheim Also Called: Automobile Club Southern Cal (P-19043)

AAA, San Diego Also Called: Automobile Club Southern Cal (P-19044)

AAA, Glendora Also Called: Automobile Club Southern Cal (P-19045)

AAA, Bakersfield Also Called: Automobile Club Southern Cal (P-19046)

AAA, Northridge Also Called: Automobile Club Southern Cal (P-19047)

AAA, Downey Also Called: Automobile Club Southern Cal (P-19048)

AAA, Manhattan Beach Also Called: Automobile Club Southern Cal (P-19050)

AAA, Woodland Hills Also Called: Automobile Club Southern Cal (P-19053)

AAA, Whittier Also Called: Automobile Club Southern Cal (P-19055)

AAA, Chino Also Called: Automobile Club Southern Cal (P-19057)

AAA, Escondido Also Called: Automobile Club Southern Cal (P-19058)

AAA, San Clemente Also Called: Automobile Club Southern Cal (P-19059)

AAA, San Diego Also Called: Automobile Club Southern Cal (P-19061)

AAA, Artesia Also Called: Automobile Club Southern Cal (P-19067)

AAA, West Hollywood Also Called: Automobile Club Southern Cal (P-19068)

AAA Auto Club, Costa Mesa Also Called: Automobile Club Southern Cal (P-8504)

AAA Elctrcal Cmmunications Inc (PA) .... C....... 800 892-4784
25007 Anza Dr Valencia (91355) *(P-1652)*

AAA Facility Services, Valencia Also Called: AAA Elctrcal Cmmunications Inc (P-1652)

AAA Fire Protection Service, Union City Also Called: AAA Restaurant Fire Ctrl Inc (P-13169)

AAA Network Solutions Inc .... D....... 714 484-2711
8401 Page St Buena Park (90621) *(P-1653)*

AAA Plating & Inspection Inc .... D....... 323 979-8930
424 E Dixon St Compton (90222) *(P-2756)*

AAA Quality Services Inc (PA) .... C....... 559 594-1128
321 Noble Ave Farmersville (93223) *(P-11011)*

AAA Restaurant Fire Ctrl Inc .... D....... 510 786-9555
30113 Union City Blvd Union City (94587) *(P-13169)*

AAA Services, Farmersville Also Called: AAA Quality Services Inc (P-11011)

AAA Smart Home, Walnut Creek Also Called: A3 Smart Home LP (P-12915)

Aadlen Bros Auto Wrecking Inc (PA) .... D....... 323 875-1400
11590 Tuxford St Sun Valley (91352) *(P-6002)*

Aall Care In Home Services, San Diego Also Called: Faith Jones & Associates Inc (P-16862)

AAM, Anaheim Also Called: Anaheim Arena Management LLC (P-14123)

Aarki Inc (PA) .... C....... 408 382-1180
530 Lakeside Dr Ste 260 Sunnyvale (94085) *(P-12413)*

Aaron Dowling Incorporated .... D....... 559 432-4500
8080 N Palm Ave Ste 300 Fresno (93711) *(P-17355)*

Aaron Thomas, Garden Grove Also Called: Aaron Thomas Company Inc (P-13170)

Aaron Thomas Company Inc (PA) .... C....... 714 894-4468
7421 Chapman Ave Garden Grove (92841) *(P-13170)*

Aatcaa Headstart, Sonora Also Called: Amador Tlmne Cmnty Action Agcy (P-18555)

AB Cellular Holding LLC .... A....... 562 468-6846
1452 Edinger Ave Tustin (92780) *(P-4249)*

Abacus Data Systems Inc (PA) .... C....... 858 452-4280
9171 Towne Centre Dr Ste 200 San Diego (92122) *(P-11371)*

Abacus Data Systems Inc .... D....... 858 529-0020
3262 Holiday Ct Ste 101 La Jolla (92037) *(P-11372)*

Abacus Service Corporation .... B....... 916 288-8948
1725 23rd St Sacramento (95816) *(P-11373)*

Abacusnext, San Diego Also Called: Abacus Data Systems Inc (P-11371)

Abacusnext, La Jolla Also Called: Abacus Data Systems Inc (P-11372)

Abb Inc .... D....... 808 497-7240
6650 Goodyear Rd Benicia (94510) *(P-5532)*

ABB - Los Gatos Research, San Jose Also Called: ABB Enterprise Software Inc (P-5463)

ABB Enterprise Software Inc .... B....... 408 770-8968
3055 Orchard Dr San Jose (95134) *(P-5463)*

ABB Optical Group, Alameda Also Called: Abb/Con-Cise Optical Group LLC (P-5462)

ABB, INC., Benicia Also Called: Abb Inc (P-5532)

Abb/Con-Cise Optical Group LLC .... B....... 510 483-9400
1750 N Loop Rd Ste 150 Alameda (94502) *(P-5462)*

Abbey-Properties LLC (PA) .... D....... 562 435-2100
12447 Lewis St Ste 203 Garden Grove (92840) *(P-8698)*

Abbott Laboratories .... A....... 408 845-3000
3200 Lakeside Dr Santa Clara (95054) *(P-3045)*

Abbott Manco Inc .... D....... 831 250-7397
100 Clock Tower Pl Ste 210 Carmel (93923) *(P-8892)*

Abbott Strngham Lynch A Prof A .... C....... 408 377-8700
1530 Meridian Ave # 2 San Jose (95125) *(P-19529)*

Abbott Vascular, Santa Clara Also Called: Abbott Laboratories (P-3045)

Abbvie, South San Francisco Also Called: Abbvie Stemcentrx LLC (P-19859)

Abbvie Stemcentrx LLC .... C....... 415 298-9242
1000 Gateway Blvd South San Francisco (94080) *(P-19859)*

Abbyson Living Corp .... C....... 805 465-5500
26500 Agoura Rd Ste 102 Calabasas (91302) *(P-5077)*

Abbyy USA, Milpitas Also Called: Abbyy USA Software House Inc (P-11374)

Abbyy USA Software House Inc (HQ) .... C....... 408 457-9777
860 Hillview Ct Ste 330 Milpitas (95035) *(P-11374)*

ABC, Burbank Also Called: ABC Cable Networks Group (P-4369)

ABC, San Francisco Also Called: ABC Cable Networks Group (P-4409)

ABC 30, Fresno Also Called: Kfsn Television LLC (P-4443)

ABC Bus Inc .... C....... 714 444-5888
1485 Dale Way Costa Mesa (92626) *(P-4999)*

ABC Bus Inc .... D....... 650 368-3364
3508 Haven Ave Redwood City (94063) *(P-5000)*

ABC Cable Networks Group (HQ) .... C....... 818 460-7477
500 S Buena Vista St Burbank (91521) *(P-4369)*

ABC Cable Networks Group .... C....... 415 954-7911
900 Front St San Francisco (94111) *(P-4409)*

ABC Carpet Co Inc (PA) .... D....... 212 473-3000
11111 Santa Monica Blvd Los Angeles (90025) *(P-7427)*

ABC Family, Burbank Also Called: ABC Family Worldwide Inc (P-13814)

ABC Family Worldwide Inc (HQ) .... B....... 818 560-1000
500 S Buena Vista St Burbank (91521) *(P-13814)*

ALPHABETIC SECTION

A

ABC Home Furnishings Inc (PA) .... A 212 473-3000
 11111 Santa Monica Blvd Los Angeles (90025) *(P-7418)*
ABC Home Health Care Llc .... C 858 455-5000
 5090 Shoreham Pl Ste 209 San Diego (92122) *(P-16783)*
ABC Sacramento Striker, Sacramento *Also Called: Amerisourcebergen Drug Corp* *(P-6095)*
ABC School Equipment Inc .... D 951 817-2200
 1451 E 6th St Corona (92879) *(P-5464)*
ABC Security Service Inc .... C 510 436-0666
 1840 Embarcadero Oakland (94606) *(P-12916)*
ABC Signature Studios Inc .... D 818 560-1000
 500 S Buena Vista St Burbank (91521) *(P-4410)*
ABC Valencia, Corona *Also Called: Amerisourcebergen Drug Corp* *(P-6094)*
Abco Insulation, Azusa *Also Called: Oj Insulation LP* *(P-1950)*
Abcsp LLC .... C 855 470-2273
 1406 Blue Oaks Blvd Ste 100 Roseville (95747) *(P-16784)*
Abd Insurance & Fincl Svcs Inc (PA) .... D 650 488-8565
 777 Mariners Island Blvd Ste 250 San Mateo (94404) *(P-8476)*
Abhe & Svoboda Inc .... D 619 659-1320
 880 Tavern Rd Alpine (91901) *(P-859)*
ABI Attorneys Service Inc (PA) .... D 909 793-0613
 2015 W Park Ave Redlands (92373) *(P-10781)*
ABI Document Support Service, Rancho Cordova *Also Called: ABI Document Support Svcs LLC* *(P-13171)*
ABI Document Support Services, Loma Linda *Also Called: ABI Document Support Svcs LLC* *(P-13172)*
ABI Document Support Svcs LLC .... D 909 793-0613
 11010 White Rock Rd Ste 1 Rancho Cordova (95670) *(P-13171)*
ABI Document Support Svcs LLC .... D 909 793-0613
 10459 Mountain View Ave Ste E Loma Linda (92354) *(P-13172)*
ABI VIP Attorney Service, Redlands *Also Called: ABI Attorneys Service Inc* *(P-10781)*
Abilities United, Redwood City *Also Called: Abilitypath Housing* *(P-17821)*
Ability Counts Inc (PA) .... D 951 734-6595
 775 Trademark Cir Ste 101 Corona (92879) *(P-18202)*
Abilitypath .... C 650 259-8500
 350 Twin Dolphin Dr Ste 123 Redwood City (94065) *(P-17820)*
Abilitypath Housing (PA) .... D 650 494-0550
 350 Twin Dolphin Dr Ste 123 Redwood City (94065) *(P-17821)*
Abjayon Inc .... C 510 824-3260
 42808 Christy St Ste 228 Fremont (94538) *(P-11375)*
Able Building Maintenance, Tustin *Also Called: Crown Building Maintenance Co* *(P-10882)*
Able Building Maintenance, Sacramento *Also Called: Crown Building Maintenance Co* *(P-10885)*
Able Cable Inc (PA) .... C 818 223-3600
 5115 Douglas Fir Rd Ste A Calabasas (91302) *(P-13731)*
Able Engineering Services, Los Angeles *Also Called: Crown Energy Services Inc* *(P-10886)*
Able Engineering Services, Concord *Also Called: Crown Energy Services Inc* *(P-19189)*
Able Freight Services LLC (PA) .... D 310 568-8883
 5340 W 104th St Los Angeles (90045) *(P-3974)*
Able Health Group LLC .... D 760 610-2093
 41990 Cook St Ste 2004 Palm Desert (92211) *(P-17164)*
Able Patrol & Guard, San Diego *Also Called: Locator Services Inc* *(P-12998)*
Able Services, South San Francisco *Also Called: Crown Energy Services Inc* *(P-19190)*
ABM Aviation Inc .... D 650 872-5400
 601 Gateway Blvd Ste 1145 South San Francisco (94080) *(P-3870)*
ABM Elctrcal Ltg Solutions Inc .... D 408 399-3030
 6940 Koll Center Pkwy Ste 100 Pleasanton (94566) *(P-10846)*
ABM Facility Services LLC .... A 949 330-1555
 152 Technology Dr Irvine (92618) *(P-19124)*
ABM Janitorial Services Inc .... D 559 651-1612
 1335 N Plaza Dr Ste C Visalia (93291) *(P-10847)*
ABM Onsite Services Inc .... A 949 863-9100
 3337 Michelson Dr Ste Cn7 Irvine (92612) *(P-12917)*
ABM Parking Services Inc .... A 213 284-7600
 1150 S Olive St Fl 19 Los Angeles (90015) *(P-13600)*
ABM Security Services Inc .... D 916 614-9571
 830 Riverside Pkwy Ste 30 West Sacramento (95605) *(P-13083)*
Abnormal Security Corporation (PA) .... B 415 690-7347
 185 Clara St Ste 100 San Francisco (94107) *(P-5264)*
Abode Communities LLC .... C 213 629-2702
 1149 S Hill St Fl 7 Los Angeles (90015) *(P-8893)*

Abraham Rest Home .... D 925 287-8382
 2832 Filbert Dr Walnut Creek (94598) *(P-16785)*
ABRAHAM REST HOME, Walnut Creek *Also Called: Abraham Rest Home* *(P-16785)*
Abramson Labor Group .... D 213 493-6300
 3580 Wilshire Blvd Ste 1260 Los Angeles (90010) *(P-17356)*
Abrazar Inc .... D 714 893-3581
 7101 Wyoming St Westminster (92683) *(P-17822)*
ABRAZAR ELDERLY ASSISTANCE, Westminster *Also Called: Abrazar Inc* *(P-17822)*
ABS .... D 805 453-9359
 79 E Daily Dr Camarillo (93010) *(P-1654)*
ABS Capital Partners III LP .... B 415 617-2800
 101 California St Fl 24 San Francisco (94111) *(P-9483)*
ABS Consulting Inc .... D 714 734-4242
 420 Exchange Ste 200 Irvine (92602) *(P-19125)*
ABS Group, Irvine *Also Called: ABS Consulting Inc* *(P-19125)*
ABS-Cbn International (DH) .... C 800 527-2820
 432 N Canal St Ste 21 South San Francisco (94080) *(P-4472)*
Abso .... C 800 943-2589
 101 Creekside Ridge Ct Fl 2 Roseville (95678) *(P-11071)*
Absolutdata Technologies Inc .... D 510 748-9922
 1320 Harbor Bay Pkwy Ste 170 Alameda (94502) *(P-13173)*
Absolute Return Portfolio .... A 800 800-7646
 700 Newport Center Dr Newport Beach (92660) *(P-9350)*
Absolutely Zero Corporation .... B 949 269-3300
 1 City Blvd W Ste 1000 Orange (92868) *(P-8894)*
Abx Engineering Inc .... D 650 552-2300
 875 Stanton Rd Burlingame (94010) *(P-5617)*
AC By Marriott Palo Alto, Palo Alto *Also Called: M10 Dev LLC* *(P-9994)*
AC Enterprises, Hayward *Also Called: Andrew Chekene Enterprises Inc* *(P-654)*
AC Hotel San Jose Downtown, San Jose *Also Called: Avr San Jose Downtown Ht LLC* *(P-9623)*
AC Hotel San Jose Snnyvale Cpr, Sunnyvale *Also Called: K3 Dev LLC* *(P-9931)*
AC Hotel Sunnyvale, Sunnyvale *Also Called: K3 Dev LLC* *(P-9932)*
AC Irrigation Holdco LLC .... C 661 368-3550
 10000 Stockdale Hwy # 100 Bakersfield (93311) *(P-240)*
AC Pro Inc (PA) .... **C 951 360-7849**
 11700 Industry Ave Fontana (92337) *(P-5765)*
AC Square Inc .... B 650 293-2730
 371 Foster City Blvd Foster City (94404) *(P-1655)*
AC Transit, Oakland *Also Called: Alameda-Contra Costa Trnst Dst* *(P-3122)*
Acacia Pharma Inc .... D 317 941-9576
 440 Stevens Ave Ste 200 Solana Beach (92075) *(P-13174)*
ACACIA PHARMA, INC., Solana Beach *Also Called: Acacia Pharma Inc* *(P-13174)*
Academy Mpic Arts & Sciences (PA) .... D 310 247-3000
 8949 Wilshire Blvd Beverly Hills (90211) *(P-18728)*
Academy Museum Motion Pictures .... C 310 247-3000
 6067 Wilshire Blvd Los Angeles (90036) *(P-18635)*
Academy of Cosmetology, Santa Barbara *Also Called: Santa Brbara Cmnty College Dst* *(P-17788)*
Acapulco Mxican Rest Escondido, Escondido *Also Called: Acapulco Restaurants Inc* *(P-7453)*
Acapulco Mxican Rest Y Cantina, Moreno Valley *Also Called: Acapulco Restaurants Inc* *(P-7452)*
Acapulco Restaurants Inc .... D 951 653-8809
 12625 Frederick St Ste T Moreno Valley (92553) *(P-7452)*
Acapulco Restaurants Inc .... D 562 346-1200
 1541 E Valley Pkwy Escondido (92027) *(P-7453)*
ACC West Coast, Benicia *Also Called: American Cvil Cnstrs W Cast LL* *(P-1075)*
ACC-Gwg LLC .... D 530 473-2827
 6133 Abel Rd Williams (95987) *(P-20672)*
Accel Therapies Inc .... D 855 443-3822
 1845 W Orangewood Ave Ste 101 Orange (92868) *(P-17000)*
Accel-KKR, Menlo Park *Also Called: Accel-KKR Company LLC* *(P-9484)*
Accel-KKR Company LLC (PA) .... **C 650 289-2460**
 2180 Sand Hill Rd Ste 300 Menlo Park (94025) *(P-9484)*
Accela Inc (PA) .... **C 925 659-3200**
 2633 Camino Ramon Ste 500 San Ramon (94583) *(P-12071)*
Accellion, San Mateo *Also Called: Accellion Inc* *(P-12718)*
Accellion Inc .... C 650 485-4300
 1510 Fashion Island Blvd San Mateo (94404) *(P-12718)*

Accent Computer Solutions LLC — ALPHABETIC SECTION

Accent Computer Solutions LLC .... D 909 825-2772
8438 Red Oak St Rancho Cucamonga (91730) *(P-20673)*

Accent Hospitality Group LLC .... C 415 286-2867
2830 I St Ste 104 Sacramento (95816) *(P-3957)*

Accentcare, Rancho Cordova *Also Called: Accentcare HM Hlth Scrmnto Inc (P-16788)*

Accentcare Inc .... B 858 576-7410
5050 Murphy Canyon Rd Ste 200 San Diego (92123) *(P-16786)*

Accentcare HM Hlth El Cntro In .... C 760 352-4022
2344 S 2nd St Ste A El Centro (92243) *(P-16787)*

Accentcare HM Hlth Scrmnto Inc .... A 916 852-5888
2880 Sunrise Blvd Ste 218 Rancho Cordova (95742) *(P-16788)*

Accentcare Home Hlth Yuma Inc .... B 909 605-7000
1455 Auto Center Dr Ste 125 Ontario (91761) *(P-16789)*

Accenture Federal Services LLC .... A 619 574-2400
1615 Murray Canyon Rd Ste 400 San Diego (92108) *(P-20259)*

Accenture LLP .... C 415 537-5000
415 Mission St Ste 3300 San Francisco (94105) *(P-20260)*

Accenture National SEC Svcs, San Diego *Also Called: Accenture Federal Services LLC (P-20259)*

Access Brand Communications, San Francisco *Also Called: Access Public Relations LLC (P-20628)*

Access Business Group LLC .... B 808 422-9482
12825 Leffingwell Ave Santa Fe Springs (90670) *(P-6700)*

Access Business Group LLC .... B 714 562-6200
5600 Beach Blvd Buena Park (90621) *(P-6701)*

Access Business Group LLC .... B 714 562-7914
5609 River Way Buena Park (90621) *(P-6702)*

Access Control Security Inc .... D 714 826-3800
2622 W Lincoln Ave Ste 108 Anaheim (92801) *(P-12918)*

Access Dental Centers, Orange *Also Called: Access Dental Plan (P-15214)*

Access Dental Plan (PA) .... D 916 922-5000
530 S Main St Orange (92868) *(P-15214)*

Access Info Holdings LLC .... A 909 459-1417
12135 Davis St Moreno Valley (92557) *(P-3788)*

Access Logistics, Santa Fe Springs *Also Called: Access Business Group LLC (P-6700)*

Access Nurses Inc .... D 858 458-4400
5935 Cornerstone Ct W Ste 300 San Diego (92121) *(P-11072)*

ACCESS PARATRANSIT, El Monte *Also Called: Access Services (P-3120)*

Access Public Relations LLC .... D 415 904-7070
720 California St Fl 5 San Francisco (94108) *(P-20628)*

Access Self Storage SE, Santa Monica *Also Called: William Warren Properties Inc (P-8873)*

Access Services .... D 213 270-6000
3449 Santa Anita Ave El Monte (91731) *(P-3120)*

Access Spclty Animal Hospitals .... D 310 558-6100
9599 Jefferson Blvd Culver City (90232) *(P-321)*

Access Systems Americas Inc .... D 408 400-3000
3965 Freedom Cir Ste 200 Santa Clara (95054) *(P-11376)*

Accessory Power, Westlake Village *Also Called: AP Global Inc (P-5625)*

Accion Labs Us Inc .... A 408 970-9809
4633 Old Ironsides Dr Ste 304 Santa Clara (95054) *(P-19943)*

Acclamation Insurance Mgt Svcs .... D 559 227-9891
4450 N Brawley Ave Fresno (93722) *(P-8477)*

Acco, Pasadena *Also Called: Acco Engineered Systems Inc (P-1334)*

Acco Engineered Systems Inc .... C 831 423-9522
250 Harvey West Blvd Santa Cruz (95060) *(P-1332)*

Acco Engineered Systems Inc .... C 510 346-4300
1133 Aladdin Ave San Leandro (94577) *(P-1333)*

Acco Engineered Systems Inc (PA) .... A 818 244-6571
888 E Walnut St Pasadena (91101) *(P-1334)*

Acco Management Company .... C 408 241-3000
100 Buckingham Dr Ofc Santa Clara (95051) *(P-8895)*

Accor Corp .... C 310 278-5444
8555 Beverly Blvd Los Angeles (90048) *(P-7454)*

Accor Services US LLC (HQ) .... A 415 772-5000
950 Mason St San Francisco (94108) *(P-9598)*

Accord Logistics Llc .... D 281 687-1181
3165 Indian Fig Dr San Diego (92115) *(P-4141)*

Accountants International, San Jose *Also Called: Randstad Professionals Us LLC (P-11215)*

Accountble Hlth Cre IPA A Prof .... C 562 435-3333
2525 Cherry Ave Ste 225 Signal Hill (90755) *(P-17165)*

Accountble Hlthcare Stffing In .... C 916 286-7667
7777 Greenback Ln Ste 205 Citrus Heights (95610) *(P-11073)*

Accountble Hlthcare Stffing In .... B 408 377-9960
1999 S Bascom Ave Ste 590 Campbell (95008) *(P-11074)*

Accounting and Fiscal Services, Irvine *Also Called: University California Irvine (P-19636)*

Accounts Payable Department, Ontario *Also Called: Vantiva Sup Chain Slutions Inc (P-13957)*

Accredited Debt Relief, San Diego *Also Called: Beyond Finance LLC (P-10530)*

Accredited Fms Inc .... A 818 435-4200
5955 De Soto Ave Ste 136 Woodland Hills (91367) *(P-16790)*

Accredited Home Care, Woodland Hills *Also Called: Barry & Taffy Inc (P-16815)*

Accredited Home Care, Woodland Hills *Also Called: Berger Inc (P-16818)*

Accredited Nursing Care, Pasadena *Also Called: Accredited Nursing Services (P-15316)*

Accredited Nursing Care, San Diego *Also Called: Accredited Nursing Services (P-15317)*

Accredited Nursing Care, San Diego *Also Called: Accredited Nursing Services (P-16791)*

Accredited Nursing Care, Costa Mesa *Also Called: Accredited Nursing Services (P-16792)*

Accredited Nursing Care, Woodland Hills *Also Called: Dunn & Berger Inc (P-16855)*

Accredited Nursing Services .... C 626 573-1234
80 S Lake Ave Ste 630 Pasadena (91101) *(P-15316)*

Accredited Nursing Services .... D 619 265-1234
591 Camino De La Reina Ste 421 San Diego (92108) *(P-15317)*

Accredited Nursing Services .... C 818 986-1234
3570 Camino Del Rio N Ste 108 San Diego (92108) *(P-16791)*

Accredited Nursing Services .... C 714 973-1234
950 S Coast Dr Ste 215 Costa Mesa (92626) *(P-16792)*

Accrete Solutions LLC .... B 877 849-5838
1027 Calaveras Ridge Dr Milpitas (95035) *(P-12719)*

Accriva Dgnostics Holdings Inc (DH) .... B 858 404-8203
6260 Sequence Dr San Diego (92121) *(P-3046)*

Acct Holdings LLC .... A 916 971-1981
5949 Fair Oaks Blvd Carmichael (95608) *(P-13175)*

Accu, Glendora *Also Called: Americas Christian Credit Un (P-7754)*

Accurate Background LLC (PA) .... B 800 784-3911
200 Spectrum Center Dr Ste 1100 Irvine (92618) *(P-12649)*

Accurate Firestop Inc .... C 925 701-8600
1057 Serpentine Ln Ste A Pleasanton (94566) *(P-13176)*

Accurate Firestop & Insulation, Pleasanton *Also Called: Accurate Firestop Inc (P-13176)*

Accuret Equipment, Pomona *Also Called: Ol Old Company (P-5849)*

Acd, Newark *Also Called: Advanced Cell Diagnostics Inc (P-19645)*

Ace Cash Express, Riverside *Also Called: Populus Financial Group Inc (P-7859)*

Ace Clearwater Enterprises Inc (PA) .... D 310 323-2140
19815 Magellan Dr Torrance (90502) *(P-2986)*

Ace Fence Company, La Puente *Also Called: AZ Construction Inc (P-658)*

Ace Hardware, Fresno *Also Called: Fresno Plumbing & Heating Inc (P-1446)*

Ace Hardware, San Jose *Also Called: County Building Materials Inc (P-5152)*

Ace Hardware, Baldwin Park *Also Called: Nichols Lumber & Hardware Co (P-5174)*

Ace Hardware, Morgan Hill *Also Called: D & J Lumber Co Inc (P-7117)*

Ace Hardware, Fontana *Also Called: Foothill Home Improvement Center Inc (P-7118)*

Ace Industrial Supply Inc (PA) .... D 818 252-1981
7535 N San Fernando Rd Burbank (91505) *(P-651)*

Ace Relocation Systems, San Diego *Also Called: Ace Relocation Systems Inc (P-3364)*

Ace Relocation Systems Inc (PA) .... D 858 677-5500
5608 Eastgate Dr San Diego (92121) *(P-3364)*

Ace Sushi, Torrance *Also Called: Asiana Cuisine Enterprises Inc (P-2430)*

Ace Wireless & Trading Inc .... B 949 748-5700
3031 Orange Ave Ste B Santa Ana (92707) *(P-5618)*

Acea Biosciences Inc .... D 858 724-0928
6779 Mesa Ridge Rd Ste 100 San Diego (92121) *(P-19644)*

Acepex Management Corporation .... C 909 625-6900
2707 Saturn St Brea (92821) *(P-20645)*

Acer America Corporation (DH) .... D 408 533-7700
1730 N 1st St Ste 400 San Jose (95112) *(P-12720)*

Acer Cloud Technology Inc .... A 408 830-9809
333 W San Carlos St Ste 1500 San Jose (95110) *(P-19126)*

Acera, Oakland *Also Called: Alameda Cnty Emplyees Rtrment (P-8482)*

Ach Mechanical Contractors Inc .... D 909 307-2850
411 Business Center Ct Redlands (92373) *(P-1335)*

Achates Power Inc .... D 858 535-9920
4060 Sorrento Valley Blvd Ste A San Diego (92121) *(P-2970)*

Achates Security, Salinas *Also Called: J Waters Inc (P-12991)*

Aci International (PA) .... D 310 889-3400
844 Moraga Dr Los Angeles (90049) *(P-6226)*

ALPHABETIC SECTION — Adelfi Credit Union

Aci Jet, Santa Ana *Also Called: Aviation Consultants Inc (P-3879)*
Aclu Fndation Southern Cal LLC .... D....... 213 977-9500
   765 The City Dr S Ste 360 Orange (92868) *(P-18809)*
Acme, San Jose *Also Called: United Site Services Cal Inc (P-11059)*
Acme Building Maint Co Inc (DH)... D....... 408 263-5911
   941 Catherine St Alviso (95002) *(P-10848)*
Acme Metals, Gardena *Also Called: Jayem Enterprises Inc (P-5498)*
Acme Staffing, El Centro *Also Called: I N C Builders Inc (P-11291)*
Acorn Paper Products Co., Los Angeles *Also Called: Oak Paper Products Co Inc (P-6081)*
Acorns, Irvine *Also Called: Acorns Grow Incorporated (P-9396)*
Acorns Grow Incorporated (PA)... B....... 949 251-0095
   5300 California Ave Irvine (92617) *(P-9396)*
Acosta Inc .... C....... 714 988-1500
   480 Apollo St Ste C Brea (92821) *(P-6235)*
Acosta Inc .... D....... 925 600-3500
   5735 W Las Positas Blvd Ste 300 Pleasanton (94588) *(P-6236)*
Acosta and Sons Inc .... D....... 209 322-3181
   736 Wakefield Ct Oakdale (95361) *(P-1989)*
Acosta Sales & Marketing, Brea *Also Called: Acosta Inc (P-6235)*
Acqua Hotel, Mill Valley *Also Called: Joie De Vivre Hospitality LLC (P-9924)*
Acrobat Staffing, Rocklin *Also Called: SE Scher Corporation (P-11226)*
Acrobat Staffing, San Diego *Also Called: SE Scher Corporation (P-11227)*
Acronics Systems Inc .... C....... 408 432-0888
   2102 Commerce Dr San Jose (95131) *(P-19127)*
Acrt Pacific LLC .... B....... 330 945-7500
   3443 Deer Park Dr Ste B Stockton (95219) *(P-20674)*
ACS, Antioch *Also Called: Allied Container Systems Inc (P-2746)*
ACS, Los Angeles *Also Called: Authorized Cellular Service (P-13732)*
ACS Communications Inc .... D....... 310 767-2145
   680 Knox St Ste 150 Torrance (90502) *(P-1656)*
Act 1 Group Inc (PA).. D....... 310 750-3400
   1999 W 190th St Torrance (90504) *(P-11075)*
Act Computer Services, Fresno *Also Called: Ekc Enterprises Inc (P-7443)*
Act Fulfillment Inc (PA)... C....... 909 930-9083
   3155 Universe Dr Jurupa Valley (91752) *(P-3669)*
Actcm, San Francisco *Also Called: American Cllege of Trdtnal Chn (P-17760)*
Acti, Wilmington *Also Called: Advanced Cleanup Tech Inc (P-20646)*
Actiance, Redwood City *Also Called: Smarsh Inc (P-12353)*
Actiance Inc .... C....... 650 631-6300
   900 Veterans Blvd Ste 500 Redwood City (94063) *(P-12072)*
Action Crash Parts, Santa Fe Springs *Also Called: Global Trade Alliance Inc (P-7349)*
Action Hlth Care Prsnnel Svcs .... C....... 562 799-5523
   3020 Old Ranch Pkwy # 30 Seal Beach (90740) *(P-16793)*
Action Messenger Service, Los Angeles *Also Called: Peach Inc (P-3626)*
Action Property Management, Irvine *Also Called: Action Property Management Inc (P-8875)*
Action Property Management Inc (PA).................................... D....... 949 450-0202
   2603 Main St Ste 500 Irvine (92614) *(P-8875)*
Action Roofing, Santa Barbara *Also Called: JM Roofing Company Inc (P-2070)*
Activcare Living Inc (PA)... C....... 858 565-4424
   10603 Rancho Bernardo Rd San Diego (92127) *(P-20009)*
Active Video, San Jose *Also Called: Ictv (P-12467)*
Active Wellness LLC .... A....... 415 741-3300
   600 California St Fl 11 San Francisco (94108) *(P-20010)*
Activevideo Networks LLC (DH).. D....... 408 931-9200
   333 W San Carlos St Ste 900 San Jose (95110) *(P-12414)*
Actividentity Corporation .... C....... 510 574-0100
   6623 Dumbarton Cir Fremont (94555) *(P-12547)*
Actividentity Inc .... B....... 510 574-0100
   6623 Dumbarton Cir Fremont (94555) *(P-11377)*
Activision Blizzard, Santa Monica *Also Called: Activision Blizzard Inc (P-12073)*
Activision Blizzard Inc (HQ)... B....... 310 255-2000
   2701 Olympic Blvd Bldg B Santa Monica (90404) *(P-12073)*
Activision Blizzard Inc .... D....... 949 955-1380
   3 Blizzard Irvine (92618) *(P-12074)*
Activision Blizzard Media LLC .... D....... 206 890-4996
   405 Howard St Ste 400 San Francisco (94105) *(P-4528)*
Actuate Corporation (HQ).. D....... 650 645-3000
   951 Mariners Island Blvd Ste 600 San Mateo (94404) *(P-11378)*
Acumen LLC .... C....... 650 558-8882
   500 Airport Blvd Ste 100 Burlingame (94010) *(P-12415)*

Acura Pleasanton, Pleasanton *Also Called: Hendrick Automotive Group (P-7232)*
Acute Psychiatric Hospital, Rosemead *Also Called: Success Healthcare 1 LLC (P-15103)*
ACWD, Fremont *Also Called: Alameda County Water District (P-4763)*
Acx Intermodal Inc .... C....... 310 241-6229
   920 E Pacific Coast Hwy Wilmington (90744) *(P-6818)*
Ad Art Inc (PA).. D....... 415 869-6460
   150 Executive Park Blvd Ste 2100 San Francisco (94134) *(P-13177)*
Ad Art Sign Company, San Francisco *Also Called: Ad Art Inc (P-13177)*
Ad Populum LLC (PA)... D....... 619 818-7644
   1234 6th St Apt 410 Santa Monica (90401) *(P-10585)*
AD Receivables Corp (PA).. D....... 323 296-8787
   5457 Crenshaw Blvd Los Angeles (90043) *(P-1336)*
Adac Medical Systems, San Jose *Also Called: A D A C Laboratories (inc) (P-3039)*
Adactive Media Ca Inc .... D....... 818 465-7500
   14724 Ventura Blvd Ste 1110 Sherman Oaks (91403) *(P-10699)*
Adams Comm & Engrg Tech Inc .... C....... 301 861-5000
   1875 Century Park E Ste 1130 Los Angeles (90067) *(P-12721)*
Adams International Mtls Corp .... D....... 714 630-8901
   3200 E Frontera St Anaheim (92806) *(P-6003)*
Adams Pool Specialties, Sacramento *Also Called: Dave Gross Enterprises Inc (P-2272)*
Adams Steel, Anaheim *Also Called: Self Serve Auto Dismantlers (P-6015)*
Adaptamed LLC .... C....... 877 478-7773
   6699 Alvarado Rd Ste 2301 San Diego (92120) *(P-11379)*
Adaptive Insights LLC (HQ)... C....... 650 528-7500
   2300 Geng Rd Ste 100 Palo Alto (94303) *(P-12075)*
Adara Inc (PA)... D....... 408 876-6360
   2625 Middlefield Rd Ste 827 Palo Alto (94306) *(P-12076)*
Adarsh Kaur DDS Inc .... D....... 530 892-1218
   3423 Ashbourne Cir San Ramon (94583) *(P-15215)*
Adas Investment Holdings Inc .... D....... 805 483-2341
   1114 Industrial Ave Oxnard (93030) *(P-6882)*
Adat ARI El .... C....... 818 766-4992
   12020 Burbank Blvd Valley Village (91607) *(P-17693)*
Adat ARI El Day School, Valley Village *Also Called: Adat ARI El (P-17693)*
ADB Industries .... B....... 310 679-9193
   1400 Manhattan Ave Fullerton (92831) *(P-2727)*
Adchemy Inc .... C....... 650 581-4600
   1001 E Hillsdale Blvd Fl 7 Foster City (94404) *(P-4250)*
Adcolony Inc .... D....... 650 625-1262
   11400 W Olympic Blvd # 1200 Los Angeles (90064) *(P-11380)*
Adcom Express Inc .... D....... 626 606-5160
   33830 Channel St Temecula (92592) *(P-3975)*
Adcom Express Inc .... D....... 714 870-7447
   1404 E Walnut Ave # A Fullerton (92831) *(P-3976)*
Adcom Interactive Media Inc .... D....... 800 296-7104
   21200 Oxnard St # 429 Woodland Hills (91367) *(P-12722)*
Adconion Media Inc (PA).. C....... 310 382-5521
   3301 Exposition Blvd Fl 1 Santa Monica (90404) *(P-10586)*
Adconion Media Group, Santa Monica *Also Called: Adconion Media Inc (P-10586)*
Add-On Cmpt Peripherals Inc .... C....... 949 546-8200
   15775 Gateway Cir Tustin (92780) *(P-2822)*
Add-On Cmpt Peripherals LLC .... C....... 949 546-8200
   15775 Gateway Cir Tustin (92780) *(P-2815)*
Addink Turf, Riverside *Also Called: A-G Sod Farms Inc (P-119)*
Addisn-Pnzak Jwish Cmnty Ctr S .... C....... 408 358-3636
   14855 Oka Rd Ste 201 Los Gatos (95032) *(P-14170)*
Addon Networks, Tustin *Also Called: Add-On Cmpt Peripherals LLC (P-2815)*
Addus Healthcare Inc .... C....... 209 526-8451
   817 Coffee Rd Ste B1 Modesto (95355) *(P-16794)*
Addus Healthcare Inc .... C....... 530 566-0405
   196 Cohasset Rd Ste 200 Chico (95926) *(P-16795)*
Adecco Employment Services .... C....... 949 586-2342
   25301 Cabot Rd Ste 214 Aliso Viejo (92653) *(P-11076)*
Adecco Employment Services .... D....... 209 474-0443
   1231 W Robinhood Dr Stockton (95207) *(P-11266)*
Adecco Staffing, Chula Vista *Also Called: Ado Staffing Inc (P-11267)*
Adelante Media Group LLC .... D....... 801 908-8777
   500 Media Pl Sacramento (95815) *(P-4370)*
Adelfi Credit Union .... C....... 714 671-5700
   955 W Imperial Hwy Ste 100 Brea (92821) *(P-7819)*

Adesa Auction — ALPHABETIC SECTION

Adesa Auction, Sacramento *Also Called: Adesa Corporation LLC (P-5001)*
  Adesa Corporation LLC .... D 916 388-8899
    8649 Kiefer Blvd Sacramento (95826) *(P-5001)*
  Adesa Corporation LLC .... D 619 661-5565
    2175 Cactus Rd San Diego (92154) *(P-5002)*
  Adesso Inc .... C 909 839-2929
    20659 Valley Blvd Walnut (91789) *(P-5265)*
ADI, Compton *Also Called: American Dawn Inc (P-2448)*
ADI, San Bernardino *Also Called: Aviation & Defense Inc (P-3877)*
Adiana Inc .... B 650 421-2900
  1240 Elko Dr Sunnyvale (94089) *(P-2578)*
Adicio Inc .... D 760 602-9502
  5857 Owens Ave Ste 300 Carlsbad (92008) *(P-4251)*
Adivo Associates LLC 415 992-1449
  44 Montgomery St Ste 4050 San Francisco (94104) *(P-20261)*
Adj Products LLC (PA) .... C 323 582-2650
  6122 S Eastern Ave Commerce (90040) *(P-5533)*
Adler Dev LLC .... D 707 229-3162
  2554 Front St Apt 3 San Diego (92103) *(P-11381)*
Admar Corporation .... C 714 953-9600
  1551 N Tustin Ave Ste 300 Santa Ana (92705) *(P-8274)*
Admedia, Woodland Hills *Also Called: Adcom Interactive Media Inc (P-12722)*
ADMINISTRATIVE OFFICES, Upland *Also Called: Inland Vly DRG Alchol Rcvery S (P-17075)*
Administrative Svcs Coop Inc .... C 310 715-1968
  1515 W 190th St Ste 200 Gardena (90248) *(P-3307)*
Administrative Systems Inc .... D 916 563-1121
  1651 Response Rd Ste 350 Sacramento (95815) *(P-13178)*
Adminstrtion Offces For Schl D, San Francisco *Also Called: San Francisco Unified Schl Dst (P-17747)*
  Adminsure Inc .... C 909 718-1200
    3380 Shelby St Ontario (91764) *(P-8478)*
Admiral Refrigeration Inc .... D 661 505-7913
  20867 Alaminos Dr Saugus (91350) *(P-1337)*
Admiral Security Services Inc .... B 888 471-1128
  2151 Salvio St Ste 260 Concord (94520) *(P-13084)*
Ado Staffing Inc .... C 619 691-3659
  850 Lagoon Dr Bldg 99a Chula Vista (91910) *(P-11267)*
Adobe Animal Hospital .... D 650 948-9661
  4470 El Camino Real Los Altos (94022) *(P-322)*
Adobe Animal Hospital .... D 408 357-8000
  15965 Los Gatos Blvd Ste 100 Los Gatos (95032) *(P-323)*
Adobe Inc (PA) .... A 408 536-6000
  345 Park Ave San Jose (95110) *(P-12077)*
Adopt-A-Beach, Costa Mesa *Also Called: Adopt-A-Highway Maintenance (P-1070)*
Adopt-A-Highway Maintenance .... C 800 200-0003
  3158 Red Hill Ave Ste 200 Costa Mesa (92626) *(P-1070)*
ADP, Irvine *Also Called: Automatic Data Processing Inc (P-12551)*
ADP, San Dimas *Also Called: Automatic Data Processing Inc (P-12552)*
Adroll, San Francisco *Also Called: Nextroll Inc (P-12290)*
ADS Techonlogy, Walnut *Also Called: Adesso Inc (P-5265)*
ADT LLC .... C 714 450-6461
  731 E Ball Rd Anaheim (92805) *(P-13085)*
ADT LLC .... C 818 464-5001
  9201 Oakdale Ave Ste 100 Chatsworth (91311) *(P-13086)*
ADT LLC .... C 626 593-1020
  475 N Muller St Anaheim (92801) *(P-13087)*
ADT LLC .... D 818 574-3809
  9555 Owensmouth Ave Chatsworth (91311) *(P-13088)*
ADT LLC .... C 951 824-7205
  1808 Commercenter W Ste E San Bernardino (92408) *(P-13089)*
ADT LLC .... D 925 602-0500
  4071 Port Chicago Hwy Ste 150 Concord (94520) *(P-13090)*
ADT LLC .... C 818 373-6200
  26074 Avenue Hall Ste 1 Valencia (91355) *(P-13091)*
ADT LLC .... C 951 782-6900
  1120 Palmyrita Ave Ste 280 Riverside (92507) *(P-13092)*
ADT Security Services, Chatsworth *Also Called: ADT LLC (P-13088)*
ADT Security Services, San Bernardino *Also Called: ADT LLC (P-13089)*
Advance Beverage Co Inc .... D 661 833-3783
  5200 District Blvd Bakersfield (93313) *(P-6748)*

Advance Construction Tech Inc .... D 510 876-8403
  48995 Milmont Dr Fremont (94538) *(P-745)*
Advance Disposal Company, Hesperia *Also Called: Best Way Disposal Co Inc (P-4864)*
Advance Services Inc .... A 408 767-2797
  8021 Kern Ave Gilroy (95020) *(P-13750)*
Advance Staffing Inc .... B 408 205-6154
  2060 Walsh Ave Ste 101 Santa Clara (95050) *(P-11077)*
Advanced Air, Hawthorne *Also Called: Advanced Air LLC (P-3862)*
Advanced Air LLC .... C 310 644-3344
  12101 Crenshaw Blvd Ste 100 Hawthorne (90250) *(P-3862)*
Advanced Bioservices LLC (PA) .... D 818 342-0100
  19255 Vanowen St Reseda (91335) *(P-20011)*
Advanced Cell Diagnostics Inc .... D 510 576-8800
  7707 Gateway Blvd Ste 200 Newark (94560) *(P-19645)*
Advanced Chemical Trnspt Inc .... C 951 790-7989
  600 Iowa St Redlands (92373) *(P-3365)*
Advanced Cleanup Tech Inc .... B 310 763-1423
  230 E C St Wilmington (90744) *(P-20646)*
Advanced Clnroom McRclean Corp .... C 714 751-1152
  3250 S Susan St Ste A Santa Ana (92704) *(P-10849)*
Advanced Crtcal Care Emrgncy S .... C 310 558-6111
  9599 Jefferson Blvd Culver City (90232) *(P-324)*
Advanced Digital Services Inc (PA) .... D 323 962-8585
  948 N Cahuenga Blvd Los Angeles (90038) *(P-13815)*
Advanced Electronic Solutions, Irvine *Also Called: Patric Communications Inc (P-1801)*
Advanced Fabrication Tech, Hayward *Also Called: R2g Enterprises Inc (P-2079)*
Advanced Gases and Eqp Inc .... D 530 344-0771
  4639 Missouri Flat Rd Placerville (95667) *(P-7569)*
Advanced HM Hlth & Hospice Inc .... C 916 978-0744
  4354 Auburn Blvd Sacramento (95841) *(P-15745)*
Advanced Home Health Inc .... D 916 978-0744
  4354 Auburn Blvd Sacramento (95841) *(P-16796)*
ADVANCED HOME HOUSE, Sacramento *Also Called: Advanced HM Hlth & Hospice Inc (P-15745)*
Advanced Image Direct, Fullerton *Also Called: Real Estate Image Inc (P-10774)*
Advanced Industrial Services, Bakersfield *Also Called: CL Knox Inc (P-611)*
Advanced Industrial Svcs Cal, Paramount *Also Called: Advanced Industrial Svcs Inc (P-1602)*
Advanced Industrial Svcs Inc .... D 562 940-8305
  7831 Alondra Blvd Paramount (90723) *(P-1602)*
Advanced Innovative Tech Corp .... D 417 831-9444
  1675 W Park Ave Redlands (92373) *(P-13654)*
Advanced Integrated Pest Management .... C 916 786-2404
  205 Kenroy Ln Roseville (95678) *(P-10827)*
Advanced Integrated Pest MGT, Roseville *Also Called: Advanced Integrated Pest Management (P-10827)*
Advanced Lubrication Spc, Richmond *Also Called: Advanced Lubrication Spc Inc (P-6721)*
Advanced Lubrication Spc Inc .... D 215 244-2114
  810 Wright Ave Richmond (94804) *(P-6721)*
Advanced Med Prsonnel Svcs Inc .... D 386 756-4395
  12400 High Bluff Dr Ste 100 San Diego (92130) *(P-11078)*
Advanced Medical Analysis LLC .... C 626 301-0126
  1941 Walker Ave Monrovia (91016) *(P-16702)*
Advanced Medical MGT Inc .... D 562 766-2000
  5000 Airport Plaza Dr Ste 150 Long Beach (90815) *(P-20012)*
Advanced Medical Reviews, Culver City *Also Called: Advanced Medical Reviews LLC (P-11268)*
Advanced Medical Reviews LLC .... D 310 575-0900
  600 Corporate Pointe Ste 300 Culver City (90230) *(P-11268)*
Advanced Micro Devices Inc (PA) .... A 408 749-4000
  2485 Augustine Dr Santa Clara (95054) *(P-5266)*
Advanced Mnlythic Ceramics Inc .... D 818 364-9800
  15191 Bledsoe St Sylmar (91342) *(P-5619)*
Advanced Mp Technology LLC (DH) .... C 800 492-3113
  27271 Las Ramblas Ste 300 Mission Viejo (92691) *(P-5620)*
Advanced Multimodal Dist Inc .... C 800 838-3058
  14822 Central Ave Chino (91710) *(P-4142)*
Advanced Office, Irvine *Also Called: Integrus LLC (P-5247)*
Advanced Prof Imging Med Group .... C 818 244-4646
  1109 S Central Ave Glendale (91204) *(P-14593)*
Advanced Protection Inds LLC .... C 800 662-1711
  25341 Commercentre Dr Lake Forest (92630) *(P-13093)*

ALPHABETIC SECTION — Aecom Usa Inc

Advanced Restoration Inc .... C....... 916 888-9816
  8880 Cal Center Dr Sacramento (95826) *(P-860)*
Advanced Strlztion Pdts Lgstic, Fontana Also Called: Advanced Strlztion Pdts Svcs I *(P-3670)*
Advanced Strlztion Pdts Svcs I .... B....... 909 350-6987
  13135 Napa St Fontana (92335) *(P-3670)*
Advanced Test Eqp Rentals, San Diego Also Called: Advanced Test Equipment Corp *(P-11012)*
Advanced Test Equipment Corp .... D....... 858 558-6500
  10401 Roselle St San Diego (92121) *(P-11012)*
Advancment Through Oprtnty Knwl .... D....... 323 730-9400
  1200 W 37th Pl Los Angeles (90007) *(P-17823)*
Advanstar Communications Inc .... D....... 714 513-8400
  2525 Main St Ste 300 Irvine (92614) *(P-2543)*
Advanstar Communications Inc (DH) .... C....... 310 857-7500
  2501 Colorado Ave Ste 280 Santa Monica (90404) *(P-13179)*
Advanstar Global, Santa Monica Also Called: Advanstar Communications Inc *(P-13179)*
Advantage Asphalt, Sacramento Also Called: A-1 Advantage Asphalt Inc *(P-1069)*
Advantage Ford, Duarte Also Called: Advantage Ford Lincoln Mercury *(P-7164)*
Advantage Ford Lincoln Mercury .... D....... 626 305-9188
  1031 Central Ave Duarte (91010) *(P-7164)*
Advantage Logistics Inc .... C....... 408 943-6300
  2071 Ringwood Ave Ste D San Jose (95131) *(P-3977)*
Advantage Mailing LLC (PA) .... C....... 714 538-3881
  1600 N Kraemer Blvd Anaheim (92806) *(P-10766)*
Advantage Mailing Service, Anaheim Also Called: Advantage Mailing LLC *(P-10766)*
Advantage Media Services Inc .... C....... 661 705-7588
  28220 Industry Dr Valencia (91355) *(P-3671)*
Advantage Media Services Inc (PA) .... D....... 661 775-0611
  29010 Commerce Center Dr Valencia (91355) *(P-4124)*
Advantage Pntg Solutions Inc .... D....... 951 739-9204
  14734 Yorba Ct Chino (91710) *(P-1603)*
Advantage Sales & Mktg Inc (DH) .... C....... 949 797-2900
  15310 Barranca Pkwy Ste 100 Irvine (92618) *(P-20262)*
Advantage Sales & Mktg LLC (DH) .... C....... 949 797-2900
  15310 Barranca Pkwy Ste 100 Irvine (92618) *(P-20263)*
Advantage Solutions, Irvine Also Called: Advantage Sales & Mktg Inc *(P-20262)*
Advantage Solutions, Irvine Also Called: Advantage Sales & Mktg LLC *(P-20263)*
Advantage Workforce Svcs LLC .... C....... 415 212-6464
  55 Hawthorne St San Francisco (94105) *(P-11269)*
Advantage-Crown Sls & Mktg LLC (DH) .... A....... 714 780-3000
  1400 S Douglass Rd Ste 200 Anaheim (92806) *(P-6237)*
Advantech, Milpitas Also Called: Advantech Corporation *(P-11382)*
Advantech Corporation (HQ) .... B....... 408 519-3800
  380 Fairview Way Milpitas (95035) *(P-11382)*
Advantedge Technology Inc .... D....... 805 488-0405
  271 Market St Ste 15 Port Hueneme (93041) *(P-19128)*
Advantel Incorporated .... C....... 800 377-4911
  48377 Fremont Blvd # 117 Fremont (94538) *(P-7570)*
Advantel Networks, Fremont Also Called: Advantel Incorporated *(P-7570)*
Advantest America Corporation (holding Co) .... B....... 408 456-3600
  3061 Zanker Rd San Jose (95134) *(P-5621)*
Advantest America Inc .... B....... 408 988-7700
  3201 Scott Blvd Santa Clara (95054) *(P-5622)*
Advantis, Mill Valley Also Called: Advantis Global Inc *(P-12723)*
Advantis Global Inc (PA) .... C....... 415 612-3338
  20 Sunnyside Ave Ste E Mill Valley (94941) *(P-12723)*
Advent Group Ministries Inc .... D....... 408 281-0708
  90 Great Oaks Blvd Ste 108 San Jose (95119) *(P-18367)*
Advent Resources Inc .... D....... 310 241-1500
  235 W 7th St San Pedro (90731) *(P-11383)*
Advent Software Inc (HQ) .... C....... 415 543-7696
  600 Townsend St Fl 4 San Francisco (94103) *(P-11384)*
ADVENTIST HEALTH, Tulare Also Called: Adventist Health Tulare *(P-15919)*
Adventist Health, Roseville Also Called: Adventist Hlth Systm/West Corp *(P-15922)*
ADVENTIST HEALTH, Hanford Also Called: Adventist Med Center-Hanford *(P-15925)*
ADVENTIST HEALTH, Saint Helena Also Called: St Helena Hospital *(P-16457)*
Adventist Health Bakersfield, Bakersfield Also Called: San Joaquin Community Hospital *(P-16381)*
Adventist Health Clearlake, Clearlake Also Called: Adventist Hlth Clrlake Hosp In *(P-15921)*
Adventist Health Cmnty. Care, Dinuba Also Called: Adventist Health System *(P-14594)*

Adventist Health Delano .... D....... 661 758-4184
  2300 7th St Wasco (93280) *(P-9420)*
Adventist Health Delano (HQ) .... A....... 661 725-4800
  1401 Garces Hwy Delano (93215) *(P-15915)*
Adventist Health Delano .... C....... 661 721-5337
  1205 Garces Hwy Ste 208 Delano (93215) *(P-15916)*
Adventist Health Lodi Memorial, Lodi Also Called: Lodi Memorial Hosp Assn Inc *(P-16220)*
Adventist Health Med Tehachapi (PA) .... C....... 661 750-4848
  305 S Robinson St Tehachapi (93561) *(P-15917)*
Adventist Health Selma, Selma Also Called: Hanford Community Hospital *(P-16118)*
Adventist Health Sonora (HQ) .... A....... 209 532-5000
  1000 Greenley Rd Sonora (95370) *(P-15918)*
Adventist Health System .... B....... 559 595-9890
  250 W El Monte Way Dinuba (93618) *(P-14594)*
Adventist Health System/West .... D....... 619 475-5040
  2700 E 4th St National City (91950) *(P-8789)*
ADVENTIST HEALTH SYSTEM/WEST, National City Also Called: Adventist Health System/West *(P-8789)*
Adventist Health Tulare .... B....... 559 688-0821
  869 N Cherry St Tulare (93274) *(P-15919)*
Adventist Hlth Clrlake Hosp In .... C....... 707 994-6486
  15140 Lakeshore Dr Clearlake (95422) *(P-15920)*
Adventist Hlth Clrlake Hosp In (HQ) .... B....... 707 994-6486
  15630 18th Ave Clearlake (95422) *(P-15921)*
Adventist Hlth Systm/West Corp (PA) .... B....... 844 574-5686
  1 Adventist Health Way Roseville (95661) *(P-15922)*
Adventist Hlth Systm/West Corp .... B....... 661 316-6000
  3001 Sillect Ave Bakersfield (93308) *(P-15923)*
Adventist Hlth Systm/West Corp .... D....... 707 994-6486
  18th Ave Hwy 53 Clearlake (95422) *(P-15924)*
Adventist Med Center-Hanford (HQ) .... C....... 559 582-9000
  115 Mall Dr Hanford (93230) *(P-15925)*
Adventist Med Center-Hanford .... C....... 559 537-1377
  125 Mall Dr Hanford (93230) *(P-15926)*
Adventist Media Center Inc (PA) .... C....... 805 955-7777
  11291 Pierce St Riverside (92505) *(P-14025)*
ADVENTIST MEDICAL CENTER-REEDL, Reedley Also Called: Reedley Community Hospital *(P-16361)*
Adventure City Inc .... D....... 714 821-3311
  1238 S Beach Blvd Anaheim (92804) *(P-14487)*
Advertise Purple .... D....... 424 272-7400
  1431 7th St Ste 302 Santa Monica (90401) *(P-10587)*
Adverum, Redwood City Also Called: Adverum Biotechnologies Inc *(P-2616)*
Adverum Biotechnologies Inc (PA) .... C....... 650 656-9323
  100 Cardinal Way Redwood City (94063) *(P-2616)*
Adviceperiod .... D....... 424 281-3600
  2121 Avenue Of The Stars Ste 2400 Los Angeles (90067) *(P-8182)*
Advintist Hlth Clearlake Hosp .... C....... 707 994-6486
  18th Ave & Hwy 53 Clearlake (95422) *(P-15927)*
Advise Health Holdings LLC .... D....... 415 723-1723
  476 Jackson St Fl 2 San Francisco (94111) *(P-8255)*
Advisorsquare, Culver City Also Called: Liveoffice LLC *(P-12256)*
Advisory Board Company .... C....... 415 671-7750
  23 Geary St San Francisco (94108) *(P-16797)*
Advisorycloud Inc .... C....... 415 289-7115
  7 Hamilton Landing Ste 100 Novato (94949) *(P-20675)*
Advocacy For Rspect Chice - Lo (PA) .... D....... 562 597-7716
  4519 E Stearns St Long Beach (90815) *(P-18203)*
Ae & Associates LLC .... D....... 951 278-3477
  506 Queensland Cir Corona (92879) *(P-20676)*
Aechelon Technology Inc (PA) .... C....... 415 255-0120
  611 Gateway Blvd Ste 300 South San Francisco (94080) *(P-11385)*
Aecom Global II LLC (HQ) .... D....... 213 593-8100
  300 S Grand Ave Ste 900 Los Angeles (90071) *(P-19129)*
Aecom Services Inc (HQ) .... C....... 213 593-8000
  300 S Grand Ave Ste 900 Los Angeles (90071) *(P-19449)*
Aecom Technical Services Inc (HQ) .... D....... 213 593-8100
  300 S Grand Ave Fl 9 Los Angeles (90071) *(P-20677)*
Aecom Usa Inc .... D....... 213 330-7200
  515 S Figueroa St Ste 400 Los Angeles (90071) *(P-20678)*
Aecom Usa Inc .... C....... 858 947-7144
  401 W A St Ste 1200 San Diego (92101) *(P-20679)*

ALPHABETIC SECTION

Aecom Usa Inc .... D....... 213 593-8000
300 S Grand Ave Ste 900 Los Angeles (90071) *(P-20680)*

Aecom Usa Inc .... D....... 714 567-2501
999 W Town And Country Rd Orange (92868) *(P-20681)*

Aecom-TSE Joint Venture 510 285-6639
300 Lakeside Dr Ste 400 Oakland (94612) *(P-19130)*

AEG Management Lacc LLC .... C....... 213 741-1151
1201 S Figueroa St Los Angeles (90015) *(P-20013)*

AEG Presents, Los Angeles Also Called: AEG Presents LLC *(P-14026)*

AEG Presents LLC (DH) .... C....... 323 930-5700
425 W 11th St Los Angeles (90015) *(P-14026)*

AEG Worldwide, Los Angeles Also Called: Anschutz Entrmt Group Inc *(P-14076)*

Aegis Assisted Living, Aptos Also Called: Aegis Senior Communities LLC *(P-16799)*

Aegis Asssted Living Prpts LLC .... C....... 510 739-1515
3850 Walnut Ave # 228 Fremont (94538) *(P-18368)*

Aegis Asssted Living Prpts LLC .... C....... 760 806-3600
1440 S Melrose Dr Oceanside (92056) *(P-18369)*

Aegis At Shadowridge, Oceanside Also Called: Aegis Asssted Living Prpts LLC *(P-18369)*

Aegis Fire Systems, Pleasanton Also Called: Aegis Fire Systems LLC *(P-1338)*

Aegis Fire Systems LLC .... D....... 925 417-5550
500 Boulder Ct Ste A Pleasanton (94566) *(P-1338)*

Aegis Gardens, Fremont Also Called: Aegis Senior Communities LLC *(P-16798)*

Aegis of Fremont, Fremont Also Called: Aegis Asssted Living Prpts LLC *(P-18368)*

Aegis of Granada Hills, Granada Hills Also Called: Aegis Senior Communities LLC *(P-16802)*

Aegis of Laguna Niguel, Laguna Niguel Also Called: Aegis Senior Communities LLC *(P-18370)*

Aegis of Moraga, Moraga Also Called: Aegis Senior Communities LLC *(P-18371)*

Aegis of South San Francisco, South San Francisco Also Called: Aegis Senior Communities LLC *(P-16801)*

Aegis of Ventura, Ventura Also Called: Aegis Senior Communities LLC *(P-16800)*

Aegis SEC & Investigations Inc .... C....... 310 838-2787
10866 Washington Blvd Ste 308 Culver City (90232) *(P-12919)*

Aegis Senior Communities LLC .... D....... 510 739-0909
36281 Fremont Blvd Fremont (94536) *(P-16798)*

Aegis Senior Communities LLC .... C....... 831 684-2700
125 Heather Ter Aptos (95003) *(P-16799)*

Aegis Senior Communities LLC .... D....... 805 650-1114
4964 Telegraph Rd Ventura (93003) *(P-16800)*

Aegis Senior Communities LLC .... C....... 650 952-6100
2280 Gellert Blvd South San Francisco (94080) *(P-16801)*

Aegis Senior Communities LLC .... C....... 818 363-3373
10801 Lindley Ave Granada Hills (91344) *(P-16802)*

Aegis Senior Communities LLC .... C....... 949 496-8080
32170 Niguel Rd Laguna Niguel (92677) *(P-18370)*

Aegis Senior Communities LLC .... C....... 925 377-7900
950 Country Club Dr Moraga (94556) *(P-18371)*

Aem Corporation, Camarillo Also Called: Applied Engineering MGT Corp *(P-11415)*

Aemi Holdings LLC .... D....... 858 481-0210
6610 Cobra Way San Diego (92121) *(P-2860)*

AEP Span Inc .... D....... 916 372-0933
2110 Enterprise Blvd West Sacramento (95691) *(P-2042)*

Aer Logistics, Brea Also Called: Aer Technologies Inc *(P-13760)*

Aer Technologies Inc .... B....... 714 871-7357
650 Columbia St Brea (92821) *(P-13760)*

Aera Energy LLC .... A....... 661 665-5000
10000 Ming Ave Bakersfield (93311) *(P-579)*

Aera Energy LLC .... D....... 661 334-3100
19590 7th Standard Rd Mc Kittrick (93251) *(P-580)*

Aera Energy Services Company (HQ) .... A....... 661 665-5000
10000 Ming Ave Bakersfield (93311) *(P-589)*

Aera Energy Services Company .... C....... 661 665-4400
59231 Main Camp Rd Mc Kittrick (93251) *(P-590)*

Aera Energy Services Company .... C....... 661 665-3200
29235 Highway 33 Maricopa (93252) *(P-591)*

Aera Energy Services Company .... C....... 559 935-7418
29010 Shell Rd Coalinga (93210) *(P-2774)*

Aera Energy South Midway, Maricopa Also Called: Aera Energy Services Company *(P-591)*

Aera Technology Inc (PA) .... D....... 408 524-2222
707 California St Mountain View (94041) *(P-11386)*

Aercap Global Aviation Trust (HQ) .... C....... 310 788-1999
10250 Constellation Blvd Ste 3400 Los Angeles (90067) *(P-11013)*

Aerial Topco LP .... A....... 415 983-2700
1 Embarcadero Ctr Ste 3900 San Francisco (94111) *(P-12650)*

Aeris Communications Inc (PA) .... C....... 408 557-1900
1731 Technology Dr Ste 800 San Jose (95110) *(P-4252)*

Aero Bending Company .... D....... 661 948-2363
560 Auto Center Dr Ste A Palmdale (93551) *(P-2743)*

Aero Port Services Inc (PA) .... A....... 310 623-8230
216 W Florence Ave Inglewood (90301) *(P-13094)*

Aeroground Inc (DH) .... A....... 650 266-6965
270 Lawrence Ave South San Francisco (94080) *(P-3871)*

Aerojet Rcketdyne Holdings Inc (HQ) .... D....... 310 252-8100
222 N Pacific Coast Hwy Ste 500 El Segundo (90245) *(P-3000)*

Aerospace Corporation .... D....... 310 336-7270
Los Angeles (90009) *(P-19646)*

Aerospace Corporation .... D....... 626 873-7700
200 S Los Robles Ave Ste 150 Pasadena (91101) *(P-19860)*

Aerospace Engineering Corp LLC .... D....... 714 641-5884
2141 S Standard Ave Santa Ana (92707) *(P-19131)*

Aerospace Material Division, Bay Point Also Called: Henkel US Operations Corp *(P-19248)*

Aerospace Systems, Redondo Beach Also Called: Northrop Grumman Systems Corp *(P-2982)*

Aerospace Walk of Honor, Lancaster Also Called: City of Lancaster *(P-20922)*

Aerotransporte De Carge Union .... B....... 310 649-0069
5625 W Imperial Hwy Los Angeles (90045) *(P-3827)*

Aerounion, Los Angeles Also Called: Aerotransporte De Carge Union *(P-3827)*

AES, Chico Also Called: Alternative Energy Systems Inc *(P-1352)*

AES, Long Beach Also Called: AES Alamitos LLC *(P-4560)*

AES Alamitos LLC .... D....... 562 493-7891
690 N Studebaker Rd Long Beach (90803) *(P-4560)*

AES Generator Depot, South San Francisco Also Called: AES Heavy Equipment Rental Inc *(P-5373)*

AES Generator Depot, San Francisco Also Called: AES Heavy Equipment Rental Inc *(P-5374)*

AES Heavy Equipment Rental Inc .... D....... 817 615-1044
611 Gateway Blvd South San Francisco (94080) *(P-5373)*

AES Heavy Equipment Rental Inc .... D....... 817 615-1044
1390 Market St San Francisco (94102) *(P-5374)*

AES Networks, San Jose Also Called: Thales Esecurity Inc *(P-12895)*

Aetna, San Francisco Also Called: Aetna International Inc *(P-2253)*

Aetna, Concord Also Called: Aetna Health California Inc *(P-8275)*

Aetna Health California Inc (DH) .... C....... 925 543-9223
1401 Willow Pass Rd Ste 600 Concord (94520) *(P-8275)*

Aetna International Inc (DH) .... D....... 415 575-0912
1616 16th St Ste 200 San Francisco (94103) *(P-2253)*

AEVA, Mountain View Also Called: Aeva Technologies Inc *(P-2971)*

Aeva Technologies Inc (PA) .... C....... 650 481-7070
555 Ellis St Mountain View (94043) *(P-2971)*

Afc Distribution Corp .... C....... 310 604-3630
19205 S Laurel Park Rd Rancho Dominguez (90220) *(P-6238)*

Afc First Consumer Discount Co, Oakland Also Called: Renew Financial Corp II *(P-8015)*

Afc-Bpi Inc .... B....... 541 441-2847
729 Green Valley Rd Watsonville (95076) *(P-6819)*

Affiliate Traction .... C....... 831 464-1441
2125 Delaware Ave Ste E Santa Cruz (95060) *(P-10725)*

Affinity Auto Programs Inc .... B....... 858 643-9324
10251 Vista Sorrento Pkwy Ste 300 San Diego (92121) *(P-13180)*

Affinity Development Group Inc .... C....... 858 643-9324
10590 W Ocean Air Dr Ste 300 San Diego (92130) *(P-19032)*

Affirm, San Francisco Also Called: Affirm Holdings Inc *(P-7889)*

Affirm Inc (HQ) .... C....... 415 984-0490
650 California St Fl 12 San Francisco (94108) *(P-7888)*

Affirm Holdings Inc (PA) .... A....... 415 984-0490
650 California St Fl 12 San Francisco (94108) *(P-7889)*

Affirm Identity, San Francisco Also Called: Affirm Inc *(P-7888)*

Affymetrix, San Diego Also Called: Ebioscience Inc *(P-19685)*

AFL-CIO #1245, Vacaville Also Called: Interntnal Brthd Elc Wkr Lcal *(P-18784)*

AFLAC .... C....... 800 992-3522
4325 Main St Kelseyville (95451) *(P-8479)*

Afm & Sg-Ftra Intllctual Prprt .... D....... 818 255-7980
4705 Laurel Canyon Blvd Ste 400 Valley Village (91607) *(P-13181)*

Afr Apparel International Inc .... D....... 818 773-5000
25365 Prado De La Felicidad Calabasas (91302) *(P-2462)*

ALPHABETIC SECTION — Air Demolition and Envmtl

Afresh Technologies Inc .... D....... 415 651-5068
33 New Montgomery St Ste 1100 San Francisco (94105) *(P-12078)*

African Women Rising .... C....... 415 278-1784
801 Cold Springs Rd Santa Barbara (93108) *(P-18810)*

Aftco Mfg Co Inc .... D....... 949 660-8757
2400 S Garnsey St Santa Ana (92707) *(P-5972)*

After-Party2 Inc .... D....... 408 457-1187
22674 Broadway # A Sonoma (95476) *(P-11014)*

After-Party2 Inc (DH) .... C....... 310 202-0011
901 W Hillcrest Blvd Inglewood (90301) *(P-11015)*

After-Party6 Inc .... C....... 310 966-4900
901 W Hillcrest Blvd Inglewood (90301) *(P-11016)*

Aftershock La Studios Inc .... D....... 650 450-9660
3633 Lenawee Ave Ste 100 Los Angeles (90016) *(P-11387)*

AG Rx (PA) .... D....... 805 487-0696
751 S Rose Ave Oxnard (93030) *(P-6820)*

Ag-Wise Enterprises Inc (PA) .... C....... 661 325-1567
5100 California Ave Ste 209 Bakersfield (93309) *(P-371)*

Agama Solutions Inc .... C....... 510 796-9300
39159 Paseo Padre Pkwy Ste 215 Fremont (94538) *(P-20264)*

Agc Inc .... D....... 408 369-6305
745 Camden Ave Ste B Campbell (95008) *(P-1339)*

Agency For Performing Arts Inc (PA) .... D....... 310 557-9049
405 S Beverly Dr Ste 500 Beverly Hills (90212) *(P-14027)*

Agencycom LLC .... B....... 415 817-3800
5353 Grosvenor Blvd Los Angeles (90066) *(P-12079)*

Agendia Inc .... C....... 949 540-6300
22 Morgan Irvine (92618) *(P-19647)*

Agent Franchise LLC .... C....... 949 930-5025
9518 9th St Ste C2 Rancho Cucamonga (91730) *(P-8256)*

Agent Image Inc .... B....... 310 577-9222
1700 E Walnut Ave El Segundo (90245) *(P-11388)*

Agia Affinity, Carpinteria *Also Called: AGIA Inc (P-8480)*

AGIA Inc (PA) .... C....... 805 566-9191
1155 Eugenia Pl Carpinteria (93013) *(P-8480)*

Agile, Corona *Also Called: Agile Sourcing Partners Inc (P-4757)*

Agile Occupational Medicine PC .... D....... 949 464-4036
710 N Euclid St Ste 107 Anaheim (92801) *(P-14595)*

Agile Sourcing Partners Inc .... C....... 951 279-4154
2385 Railroad St Corona (92878) *(P-4757)*

Agilent, Santa Clara *Also Called: Agilent Technologies Inc (P-3028)*

Agilent Technologies Inc (PA) .... A....... 800 227-9770
5301 Stevens Creek Blvd Santa Clara (95051) *(P-3028)*

Agileone, Torrance *Also Called: Act 1 Group Inc (P-11075)*

Agilepoint Inc (PA) .... D....... 650 968-6789
1916 Old Middlefield Way Ste B Mountain View (94043) *(P-12080)*

Agiliti Inc .... C....... 952 465-9993
960 Riverside Pkwy West Sacramento (95605) *(P-5395)*

Agility Holdings Inc (DH) .... D....... 714 617-6300
310 Commerce Ste 250 Irvine (92602) *(P-3978)*

Agility Logistics, Irvine *Also Called: Agility Holdings Inc (P-3978)*

Agility Logistics Corp (DH) .... D....... 714 617-6300
310 Commerce Ste 250 Irvine (92602) *(P-3979)*

Agiloft Inc (PA) .... B....... 650 459-5637
303 Twin Dolphin Dr Fl 6 Redwood City (94065) *(P-12081)*

AGM California Inc .... C....... 661 328-0118
1400 Easton Dr Ste 144 Bakersfield (93309) *(P-4371)*

Agora Lab Inc .... D....... 408 879-5885
2804 Mission College Blvd Ste 110 Santa Clara (95054) *(P-20883)*

Agora.io, Santa Clara *Also Called: Agora Lab Inc (P-20883)*

Agoura Hills Renaissance Hotel, Agoura Hills *Also Called: Davidson Hotel Partners Lp (P-9739)*

Agouron Pharmaceuticals Inc .... C....... 858 455-3200
3550 General Atomics Ct Bldg 9 San Diego (92121) *(P-19648)*

Agouron Pharmaceuticals Inc .... B....... 858 622-3000
3301 N Torrey Pines Ct La Jolla (92037) *(P-19649)*

Agri-Empire .... C....... 951 654-7311
630 W 7th St San Jacinto (92583) *(P-6512)*

Agricultural Supply, Escondido *Also Called: B J T C Inc (P-5806)*

Agua Caliente Casino & Resort, Rancho Mirage *Also Called: Agua Clnte Band Chilla Indians (P-9599)*

Agua Clnte Band Chilla Indians .... A....... 760 321-2000
32250 Bob Hope Dr Rancho Mirage (92270) *(P-9599)*

Agua Clnte Band Chilla Indians .... B....... 800 854-1279
401 E Amado Rd Palm Springs (92262) *(P-9600)*

Agua Clnte Band Chilla Indians (PA) .... A....... 760 699-6800
5401 Dinah Shore Dr Palm Springs (92264) *(P-19033)*

Agurto Corporation .... C....... 408 564-6196
888 N 1st St San Jose (95112) *(P-10828)*

Ah Capital Management LLC .... A....... 650 798-5800
2865 Sand Hill Rd Ste 101 Menlo Park (94025) *(P-8064)*

Ah Parallel Fund V LP .... B....... 650 798-3900
2865 Sand Hill Rd Ste 101 Menlo Park (94025) *(P-9485)*

Aha Labs Inc .... D....... 650 575-1425
20 Gloria Cir Menlo Park (94025) *(P-12082)*

Ahern Agribusiness Inc .... D....... 619 661-9450
9465 Customhouse Plz Ste G San Diego (92154) *(P-6821)*

Ahern International, San Diego *Also Called: Ahern Agribusiness Inc (P-6821)*

AHFCU, Long Beach *Also Called: Allied Healthcare Federal Cr Un (P-7751)*

Ahg Inc .... B....... 703 596-0111
340 S Lemon Ave 6633 Walnut (91789) *(P-10518)*

Ahm Gemch Inc .... C....... 626 579-7777
1701 Santa Anita Ave El Monte (91733) *(P-15928)*

Ahmc, Anaheim *Also Called: Anaheim Regional Medical Ctr (P-15947)*

Ahmc Anaheim Rgional Med Ctr LP .... A....... 714 774-1450
1111 W La Palma Ave Anaheim (92801) *(P-15929)*

Ahmc Anaheim Rgional Med Ctr LP (PA) .... A....... 714 774-1450
1111 W La Palma Ave Anaheim (92801) *(P-15930)*

Ahmc Garfield Medical Ctr LP .... C....... 626 573-2222
525 N Garfield Ave Monterey Park (91754) *(P-15318)*

Ahmc Healthcare Inc (PA) .... C....... 626 943-7526
506 W Valley Blvd Ste 300 San Gabriel (91776) *(P-15931)*

Ahmc Healthcare Inc .... C....... 626 579-7777
1701 Santa Anita Ave South El Monte (91733) *(P-15932)*

Ahmc Healthcare Inc .... C....... 626 248-3452
506 W Valley Blvd Ste 300 San Gabriel (91776) *(P-17166)*

Ahmc Healthcare Inc .... D....... 626 570-9000
900 S Atlantic Blvd Monterey Park (91754) *(P-17167)*

Ahmc Inc .... D....... 626 570-1606
100 S Raymond Ave Alhambra (91801) *(P-14596)*

Ahmc Seton Medical Center LLC .... B....... 650 563-7100
600 Marine Blvd Moss Beach (94038) *(P-15933)*

Ahmc Whittier Hosp Med Ctr LP .... A....... 562 945-3561
9080 Colima Rd Whittier (90605) *(P-15934)*

Ahntech Inc (PA) .... D....... 650 861-3987
745 Distel Dr Ste 104 Los Altos (94022) *(P-19132)*

Ahtna Facility Services Inc .... C....... 916 375-0199
3100 Beacon Blvd West Sacramento (95691) *(P-10850)*

Aicent Inc .... C....... 408 324-1316
900 E Hamilton Ave # 600 Campbell (95008) *(P-12724)*

Aidash Inc (PA) .... C....... 408 703-1099
3031 Tisch Way Ste 110pw San Jose (95128) *(P-11389)*

Aidells Sausage, San Lorenzo *Also Called: Aidells Sausage Company Inc (P-2341)*

Aidells Sausage Company Inc .... A....... 510 614-5450
2411 Baumann Ave San Lorenzo (94580) *(P-2341)*

Aids Project La, Los Angeles *Also Called: Aids Project Los Angeles (P-17824)*

Aids Project Los Angeles (PA) .... D....... 213 201-1600
611 S Kingsley Dr Los Angeles (90005) *(P-17824)*

AIDS WALK ORANGE COUNTY, Irvine *Also Called: Radiant Health Centers (P-18091)*

AIG, Walnut Creek *Also Called: Western National Life Insur Co (P-8253)*

AIG Capital Services Inc .... D....... 800 445-7862
21650 Oxnard St Ste 750 Woodland Hills (91367) *(P-9397)*

AIG Direct Insurance Svcs Inc .... B....... 858 309-3000
9640 Granite Ridge Dr Ste 200 San Diego (92123) *(P-8481)*

Aim Mail Centers, Rancho Cordova *Also Called: Automotive Importing Manufacturing Inc (P-5026)*

Aimloan.com, A Direct Lender, San Diego *Also Called: American Internet Mortgage Inc (P-7928)*

Aio Acquisition Inc (HQ) .... D....... 800 333-3795
3200 E Guasti Rd Ste 300 Ontario (91761) *(P-2552)*

Air Cargo Handling Service, South San Francisco *Also Called: Aeroground Inc (P-3871)*

Air Demolition and Envmtl, Orange *Also Called: American Intgrted Rsources Inc (P-20020)*

ALPHABETIC SECTION

Air Electro Inc (PA)..D....... 818 407-5400
   9452 De Soto Ave Chatsworth (91311) *(P-5623)*
Air Express Intl USA Inc ....D....... 310 297-4401
   19900 S Vermont Ave Ste A Torrance (90502) *(P-3980)*
Air Force Village West Inc ....B....... 951 697-2000
   17050 Arnold Dr Riverside (92518) *(P-15319)*
Air Group Leasing Inc ....A....... 310 684-4095
   1111 E Watson Center Rd Ste C Carson (90745) *(P-3981)*
Air Lease Corporation (PA)..D....... 310 553-0555
   2000 Avenue Of The Stars Ste 1000n Los Angeles (90067) *(P-11017)*
Air Liquide Electronics US LP ....A....... 310 549-7079
   1502 W Anaheim St Wilmington (90744) *(P-2571)*
Air Liquide Electronics US LP ....A....... 713 624-8000
   1831 Carnegie Ave Santa Ana (92705) *(P-19133)*
Air Lquide Globl E C Solutions, Santa Ana *Also Called: Air Liquide Electronics US LP*
(P-19133)
Air Methods ....D....... 909 382-0045
   2885 U St San Bernardino (92408) *(P-3226)*
Air New Zealand Limited ....D....... 310 648-7000
   222 N Pacific Coast Hwy Ste 900 El Segundo (90245) *(P-3828)*
Air Products, Santa Clara *Also Called: Air Products and Chemicals Inc (P-6703)*
Air Products and Chemicals Inc ....D....... 408 988-6263
   1515 Norman Ave Frnt Santa Clara (95054) *(P-6703)*
Air Systems Inc ....B....... 408 280-1666
   940 Remillard Ct Frnt San Jose (95122) *(P-1340)*
Air Systems Svc & Cnstr LLC ....C....... 916 368-0336
   10381 Old Placerville Rd Ste 100 Sacramento (95827) *(P-1341)*
Air Treatment, Brea *Also Called: Air Treatment Corporation (P-5766)*
Air Treatment Corporation (PA)...D....... 909 869-7975
   640 N Puente St Brea (92821) *(P-5766)*
Air-Sea Forwarders Inc (PA)...D....... 310 216-1616
   9009 S La Cienega Blvd Inglewood (90301) *(P-3982)*
Air-TEC, Carson *Also Called: Clay Dunn Enterprises Inc (P-1400)*
Air-Tro Air Conditioning & Htg, Monrovia *Also Called: Air-Tro Incorporated (P-1342)*
Air-Tro Incorporated ....D....... 626 357-3535
   1630 S Myrtle Ave Monrovia (91016) *(P-1342)*
Aira Tech, Carlsbad *Also Called: Aira Tech Corp (P-12083)*
Aira Tech Corp ....D....... 800 835-1934
   3451 Via Montebello Ste 192 Pmb 214 Carlsbad (92009) *(P-12083)*
Airbase Inc ....B....... 415 625-6222
   548 Market St Ste 93249 San Francisco (94104) *(P-12084)*
Airbnb, San Francisco *Also Called: Airbnb Inc (P-13182)*
Airbnb Inc (PA)...A....... 415 510-4027
   888 Brannan St Fl 4 San Francisco (94103) *(P-13182)*
Airbnb Payments Inc ....D....... 415 861-2325
   888 Brannan St San Francisco (94103) *(P-7839)*
Airborne Security Patrol Inc ....D....... 916 599-8120
   9462 Rush Creek Ct Elk Grove (95624) *(P-12920)*
Airborne Technologies, Camarillo *Also Called: Airborne Technologies Inc (P-2987)*
Airborne Technologies Inc ....C....... 805 389-3700
   999 Avenida Acaso Camarillo (93012) *(P-2987)*
Airbyte Inc ....D....... 415 307-4864
   2261 Market St Pmb 4381 San Francisco (94114) *(P-11390)*
Airco Mechanical Inc (PA)...C....... 916 381-4523
   8210 Demetre Ave Sacramento (95828) *(P-1343)*
Aircraft Crier Hrnet Fundation ....D....... 510 521-8448
   Pier 3 Alameda Point Alameda (94501) *(P-18636)*
Aircraft Spruce Speciality Co, Corona *Also Called: Irwin International Inc (P-7400)*
Aircraft Xray Laboratories Inc ....D....... 323 587-4141
   5216 Pacific Blvd Huntington Park (90255) *(P-19944)*
Aire-Rite AC & Rfrgn LLC ....D....... 714 895-2338
   15122 Bolsa Chica St Huntington Beach (92649) *(P-1344)*
Airey Enterprises LLC ....C....... 818 530-3362
   5530 Corbin Ave Ste 325 Tarzana (91356) *(P-5954)*
Airfield Supply Co, San Jose *Also Called: Captain Kirk Services Inc (P-6033)*
Airframer R, Torrance *Also Called: Sonic Industries Inc (P-19391)*
Airgas, Riverside *Also Called: Airgas Specialty Products Inc (P-6704)*
Airgas Specialty Products Inc ....D....... 951 353-2390
   6270 Wilderness Ave Riverside (92504) *(P-6704)*
Airgas Usa LLC ....A....... 562 497-1991
   3737 Worsham Ave Long Beach (90808) *(P-5817)*

Airline Coach Service, Burlingame *Also Called: Jeremiah Phillips LLC (P-3142)*
Airport, San Jose *Also Called: City of San Jose (P-3884)*
Airport Blvd Hotels LLC ....C....... 650 342-9200
   1177 Airport Blvd Burlingame (94010) *(P-9601)*
Airport Cinemas 12, Santa Rosa *Also Called: North American Cinemas Inc (P-14004)*
Airport Connection Inc ....C....... 805 389-8196
   95 Dawson Dr Camarillo (93012) *(P-3121)*
Airport Express, Santa Rosa *Also Called: Sonoma County Airport Ex Inc (P-3215)*
Airport Honda, Los Angeles *Also Called: Noarus Investments Inc (P-7269)*
Airport Marina Ford, Los Angeles *Also Called: Fox Hills Auto Inc (P-7212)*
Airport Terminal MGT Inc ....B....... 310 988-1492
   6851 W Imperial Hwy Los Angeles (90045) *(P-3872)*
Airports Dept, Sacramento *Also Called: County of Sacramento (P-3889)*
Airtable, San Francisco *Also Called: Formagrid Inc (P-4273)*
Airtech Advanced Mtls Group, Huntington Beach *Also Called: Airtech International Inc (P-2988)*
Airtech International Inc (PA)..C....... 714 899-8100
   5700 Skylab Rd Huntington Beach (92647) *(P-2988)*
Ais Construction Company ....D....... 805 928-9467
   7015 Vista Del Rincon Dr Ventura (93001) *(P-861)*
Aisera Inc ....C....... 650 667-4308
   1121 San Antonio Rd Ste C202 Palo Alto (94303) *(P-11391)*
Aisha Academy ....D....... 310 908-1962
   706 S Pershing Ave Stockton (95203) *(P-10390)*
Aizon LLC ....C....... 312 285-4605
   44 Montgomery St Ste 3 San Francisco (94104) *(P-12416)*
AJ Kirkwood & Associates Inc ....B....... 714 505-1977
   4300 N Harbor Blvd Fullerton (92835) *(P-1657)*
Ajilon LLC ....C....... 949 955-0100
   4590 Macarthur Blvd Newport Beach (92660) *(P-12725)*
Ajinomoto Foods North Amer Inc ....C....... 909 477-4700
   4200 Concours Ste 100 Ontario (91764) *(P-2356)*
Ajit Healthcare Inc ....D....... 213 484-0510
   316 S Westlake Ave Los Angeles (90057) *(P-20014)*
AJM Packaging Corporation ....D....... 619 448-4007
   1160 Vernon Way El Cajon (92020) *(P-6886)*
Ajr Trucking Inc ....D....... 310 707-1120
   435 E Weber Ave Compton (90222) *(P-3366)*
AK Constructors Inc ....D....... 951 280-0269
   1751 Jenks Dr Corona (92878) *(P-862)*
AK Electrical Services, Corona *Also Called: AK Constructors Inc (P-862)*
AK Landscaping Maint Inc ....D....... 760 347-9747
   42929 Madio St Indio (92201) *(P-472)*
Akcea Therapeutics, Carlsbad *Also Called: Akcea Therapeutics Inc (P-2579)*
Akcea Therapeutics Inc (HQ)..D....... 617 207-0202
   2850 Gazelle Ct Carlsbad (92010) *(P-2579)*
Akerman LLP ....D....... 213 688-9500
   601 W 5th St Ste 300 Los Angeles (90071) *(P-17357)*
Akh Company Inc ....D....... 909 748-5016
   1647 W Redlands Blvd Ste C Redlands (92373) *(P-7339)*
Akh Company Inc ....C....... 951 924-5356
   23316 Sunnymead Blvd Moreno Valley (92553) *(P-7340)*
Akh Company Inc ....B....... 818 691-1978
   7120 Laurel Canyon Blvd North Hollywood (91605) *(P-13680)*
Aki Technologies ....D....... 415 624-3253
   375 Alabama St San Francisco (94110) *(P-20265)*
Akin Gump Struss Huer Feld LLP ....D....... 310 229-1000
   1999 Avenue Of The Stars Ste 600 Los Angeles (90067) *(P-17358)*
Akkodis Inc ....C....... 415 896-5566
   135 Main St Ste 1040 San Francisco (94105) *(P-11392)*
Akkodis Inc ....B....... 408 441-7144
   2055 Gateway Pl Ste 300 San Jose (95110) *(P-11393)*
Akkodis Inc ....C....... 818 546-2848
   801 N Brand Blvd Ste 250 Glendale (91203) *(P-11394)*
Akland Healthcare Wellness Ctr, Oakland *Also Called: Oakland Healthcare & Wellness (P-15602)*
Akqa Inc (HQ)...B....... 415 645-9400
   360 3rd St Ste 500 San Francisco (94107) *(P-20266)*
Akshaya Inc (PA)..C....... 925 914-7395
   415 Boulder Ct Ste 100 Pleasanton (94566) *(P-12726)*

ALPHABETIC SECTION

Aktana Inc (PA) .... B....... 888 707-3125
207 Powell St Ste 800 San Francisco (94102) *(P-12085)*

Akua Behavioral Health Inc (PA) .... D....... 949 777-2283
20271 Sw Birch St Ste 200 Newport Beach (92660) *(P-16661)*

Akua Mind & Body, Newport Beach *Also Called: Akua Behavioral Health Inc (P-16661)*

Akvarr Inc .... C....... 240 370-4182
672 W 11th St Ste 325 Tracy (95376) *(P-20682)*

Al Hewitt Inc .... C....... 661 945-7050
4009 Mission Oaks Blvd Camarillo (93012) *(P-8183)*

Alabbasi, Perris *Also Called: Mamco Inc (P-1132)*

Aladdin Bail Bonds, Carlsbad *Also Called: Two Jinn Inc (P-13522)*

Alakor Healthcare LLC .... C....... 626 408-9800
323 S Heliotrope Ave Monrovia (91016) *(P-15935)*

Alameda Alliance For Health .... C....... 510 747-4555
1240 S Loop Rd Alameda (94502) *(P-8276)*

Alameda Bureau Elec Imprv Corp (HQ) .... D....... 510 748-3902
2000 Grand St Alameda (94501) *(P-4561)*

Alameda Chapel of The Chimes, Hayward *Also Called: Chapel of Chimes (P-9282)*

Alameda Cnty Cmnty Fd Bnk Inc .... D....... 510 635-3663
7900 Edgewater Dr Oakland (94621) *(P-17825)*

Alameda Cnty Emplyees Rtrment .... D....... 510 628-3000
475 14th St Ste 1000 Oakland (94612) *(P-8482)*

Alameda County AG Fair Assn .... D....... 925 426-7600
4501 Pleasanton Ave Pleasanton (94566) *(P-14488)*

Alameda County Fair, Pleasanton *Also Called: Alameda County AG Fair Assn (P-14488)*

Alameda County Industries LLC .... D....... 510 357-7282
610 Aladdin Ave San Leandro (94577) *(P-4855)*

Alameda County Water District (PA) .... C....... 510 668-4200
43885 S Grimmer Blvd Fremont (94538) *(P-4763)*

Alameda Family Services .... D....... 510 629-6300
2325 Clement Ave Alameda (94501) *(P-18267)*

Alameda Halthcare Wellness Ctr, Alameda *Also Called: Alameda Hlthcare & Wellnss Ctr (P-15320)*

Alameda Health System (PA) .... D....... 510 437-4800
1411 E 31st St Oakland (94602) *(P-18552)*

Alameda Hlthcare & Wellnss Ctr .... D....... 510 523-8857
430 Willow St Alameda (94501) *(P-15320)*

Alameda Hospital, Alameda *Also Called: City Alameda Health Care Corp (P-16003)*

Alameda Municipal Power, Alameda *Also Called: Alameda Bureau Elec Imprv Corp (P-4561)*

Alameda-Contra Costa Trnst Dst (PA) .... C....... 510 891-4777
1600 Franklin St Oakland (94612) *(P-3122)*

Alameda-Contra Costa Trnst Dst .... A....... 510 577-8816
10626 International Blvd Oakland (94603) *(P-3354)*

Alamitos Blmont Rhblttion Hosp, Long Beach *Also Called: Alamitos-Belmont Rehab Inc (P-15321)*

Alamitos W Convalescent Hosp, Los Alamitos *Also Called: Katella Properties (P-15528)*

Alamitos-Belmont Rehab Inc .... C....... 562 434-8421
3901 E 4th St Long Beach (90814) *(P-15321)*

Alamo Rent A Car, Anaheim *Also Called: Alamo Rental (us) Inc (P-13572)*

Alamo Rent A Car, Inglewood *Also Called: Alamo Rental (us) Inc (P-13573)*

Alamo Rent A Car, Burbank *Also Called: Alamo Rental (us) Inc (P-13574)*

Alamo Rent A Car, Ontario *Also Called: Alamo Rental (us) Inc (P-13575)*

Alamo Rent A Car, Solana Beach *Also Called: Alamo Rental (us) Inc (P-13576)*

Alamo Rent A Car, San Francisco *Also Called: Alamo Rental (us) Inc (P-13577)*

Alamo Rent A Car, Palm Springs *Also Called: Alamo Rental (us) Inc (P-13578)*

Alamo Rental (us) Inc .... D....... 714 748-7368
711 W Katella Ave Anaheim (92802) *(P-13572)*

Alamo Rental (us) Inc .... C....... 310 649-2242
9020 Aviation Blvd Inglewood (90301) *(P-13573)*

Alamo Rental (us) Inc .... D....... 818 953-5438
2627 N Hollywood Way Unit 9 Burbank (91505) *(P-13574)*

Alamo Rental (us) Inc .... D....... 888 826-6893
3450 E Airport Dr Ste 300 Ontario (91761) *(P-13575)*

Alamo Rental (us) Inc .... D....... 858 792-2522
617 S Highway 101 Solana Beach (92075) *(P-13576)*

Alamo Rental (us) Inc .... D....... 415 693-0191
750 Bush St San Francisco (94108) *(P-13577)*

Alamo Rental (us) Inc .... D....... 760 778-6271
3400 E Tahquitz Canyon Way Ste 5 Palm Springs (92262) *(P-13578)*

Alan B Whitson Company Inc .... A....... 949 955-1200
1507 W Alton Ave Santa Ana (92704) *(P-20267)*

Alan Smith Pool Plastering Inc .... D....... 714 628-9494
227 W Carleton Ave Orange (92867) *(P-1899)*

Alarcon Bohm Corp .... D....... 510 893-4405
5301 Adeline St Oakland (94608) *(P-2228)*

Alation Inc (PA) .... B....... 650 779-4440
3 Lagoon Dr Ste 300 Redwood City (94065) *(P-12086)*

Alba Wheels Up Intl LLC .... D....... 650 952-0815
839 Mitten Rd San Bruno (94066) *(P-3983)*

Albany Ford Inc (PA) .... D....... 510 528-1244
718 San Pablo Ave Albany (94706) *(P-7165)*

Albany Subaru, Albany *Also Called: Albany Ford Inc (P-7165)*

Albd Electric and Cable .... D....... 949 440-1216
1031 S Leslie St La Habra (90631) *(P-1658)*

Albert & Mackenzie, Agoura Hills *Also Called: Albert & Mackenzie LLP (P-17359)*

Albert & Mackenzie LLP (PA) .... D....... 818 575-9876
28216 Dorothy Dr Ste 200 Agoura Hills (91301) *(P-17359)*

Albert A Webb Associates (PA) .... C....... 951 686-1070
3788 Mccray St Riverside (92506) *(P-19134)*

Albert D Seeno Cnstr Co Inc .... D....... 925 671-7711
3240 Stone Valley Rd W Ste 2 Alamo (94507) *(P-652)*

Albert Y LI MD Appintment Line, Riverside *Also Called: Riverside Medical Clinic Inc (P-15021)*

Albertson's Distribution Ctr, Irvine *Also Called: Albertsons LLC (P-3672)*

Albertsons LLC .... D....... 949 855-2465
9300 Toledo Way Irvine (92618) *(P-3672)*

Albireo Energy, Poway *Also Called: Electronic Control Systems LLC (P-1727)*

Alcal Specialty Contg Inc .... D....... 916 929-3100
946 N Market Blvd Sacramento (95834) *(P-1900)*

Alcal Specialty Contg Inc .... D....... 510 477-9380
42950 Osgood Rd Fremont (94539) *(P-1901)*

Alcatraz Cruises LLC .... D....... 415 981-7625
Pier 33 Hornblower Alcatraz Landing San Francisco (94111) *(P-3958)*

Alchemy, Los Angeles *Also Called: Our Alchemy LLC (P-13976)*

Alco Designs, Gardena *Also Called: Vege-Mist Inc (P-2846)*

Alco Iron & Metal Co (PA) .... D....... 510 562-1107
2140 Davis St San Leandro (94577) *(P-6004)*

Alco Service, Los Angeles *Also Called: Automatic Leasing Inc (P-5600)*

Alcon Research LLC .... D....... 800 862-5266
20511 Lake Forest Dr Lake Forest (92630) *(P-19861)*

Alcon Surgical, Irvine *Also Called: Alcon Vision LLC (P-3047)*

Alcon Vision LLC .... A....... 949 753-6488
15800 Alton Pkwy Irvine (92618) *(P-3047)*

Alcon Vision LLC .... B....... 949 505-6890
20521 Lake Forest Dr Lake Forest (92630) *(P-19945)*

Alcone Marketing Group Inc (HQ) .... D....... 949 595-5322
4 Studebaker Irvine (92618) *(P-10588)*

Alcorn Fence Company (PA) .... D....... 818 983-0650
1088 Hamilton Rd Duarte (91010) *(P-2254)*

Alcott Ctr For Mntal Hlth Svcs .... D....... 310 785-2121
10549 Jefferson Blvd Culver City (90232) *(P-17001)*

Alderson Convalescent Hospital, Woodland *Also Called: United Health Systems Inc (P-15711)*

Aldoc Inc .... D....... 714 836-8477
910 E Orangefair Ln Anaheim (92801) *(P-1345)*

Aldon Inc .... D
1333 E 223rd St Carson (90745) *(P-9296)*

Aldon Ter Convalsent Hosptial, Los Angeles *Also Called: Longwood Management Corp (P-15870)*

Aldridge Pite LLP .... B....... 858 750-7700
4375 Jutland Dr Ste 200 San Diego (92117) *(P-17360)*

Alegre Trucking, Stockton *Also Called: California Bulk Inc (P-3451)*

Alegria Community Living .... C....... 510 287-8488
1201 Martin Luther King Jr Way Oakland (94612) *(P-18553)*

Alert Insulation Company Inc .... D....... 626 961-9113
15913 Old Valley Blvd Ste A La Puente (91744) *(P-1902)*

Alertenterprise Inc (PA) .... C....... 510 440-0840
4350 Starboard Dr Fremont (94538) *(P-12087)*

Alesia Viticulture Svcs LLC .... D....... 650 333-5490
7620 Alpine Rd La Honda (94020) *(P-363)*

Alessandro Electric Inc .... D....... 916 283-6966
11335 Sunrise Gold Cir Rancho Cordova (95742) *(P-1659)*

Alexander Dennis Incorporated   **ALPHABETIC SECTION**

Alexander Dennis Incorporated .... A....... 951 244-9429
   31566 Railroad Canyon Rd Ste 3 Canyon Lake (92587) *(P-5003)*

Alexander's Moving & Storage, Tustin *Also Called: Stanley G Alexander Inc (P-3545)*

Alexandra Lzano Immgrtion Law .... D....... 323 524-9944
   5800 S Eastern Ave Ste 270 Commerce (90040) *(P-17361)*

Alfa Tech Cnslting Engners Inc (PA) .... D....... 408 487-1200
   1321 Ridder Park Dr No 50 San Jose (95131) *(P-19135)*

Alfa Tech Consulting Entps, San Jose *Also Called: Alfa Tech Cnslting Engners Inc (P-19135)*

Alfresco Software Americas Inc .... C....... 888 317-3395
   428 University Ave Palo Alto (94301) *(P-11395)*

Alhambra Hospital Med Ctr LP .... C....... 626 570-1606
   100 S Raymond Ave Alhambra (91801) *(P-15936)*

Alhambra Hospital Medical Ctr, Alhambra *Also Called: Alhambra Hospital Med Ctr LP (P-15936)*

Alhambra Motors Inc .... C....... 626 576-1114
   1400 W Main St Alhambra (91801) *(P-7166)*

Aliantel Inc .... D....... 714 829-1650
   1940 W Corporate Way Anaheim (92801) *(P-20683)*

Aligned Company .... D....... 917 558-4565
   360 E 2nd St Ste 809 Los Angeles (90012) *(P-12548)*

Alignment Health, Orange *Also Called: Alignment Healthcare Inc (P-8278)*

Alignment Health Plan .... D....... 323 728-7232
   1100 W Town And Country Rd Ste 1600 Orange (92868) *(P-8277)*

Alignment Healthcare Inc (PA) .... D....... 844 310-2247
   1100 W Town And Country Rd Ste 1600 Orange (92868) *(P-8278)*

Aligntech .... D....... 714 605-7114
   2820 Orchard Pkwy San Jose (95134) *(P-13655)*

Alimentiv US Inc .... D....... 858 356-5665
   10581 Roselle St Ste 110 San Diego (92121) *(P-19650)*

Alinor Holdings Inc .... D....... 650 393-4865
   4 W 4th Ave Fl 6 San Mateo (94402) *(P-11396)*

Aliph, San Francisco *Also Called: Aliphcom (P-5624)*

Aliphcom .... B....... 415 230-7600
   99 Rhode Island St Fl 3 San Francisco (94103) *(P-5624)*

Alisal Guest Ranch, Solvang *Also Called: Alisal Properties (P-10397)*

Alisal Properties (PA) .... C....... 805 688-6411
   1054 Alisal Rd Solvang (93463) *(P-10397)*

Aliso Viejo Medical Offices, Aliso Viejo *Also Called: Kaiser Foundation Hospitals (P-14796)*

Aliso Viejo Stadium Cinemas 10, Aliso Viejo *Also Called: Edwards Theatres Circuit Inc (P-13990)*

Alkahest Inc .... D....... 650 801-0474
   125 Shoreway Rd Ste D San Carlos (94070) *(P-19651)*

All About Parking .... D....... 650 508-8886
   100 S Ellsworth Ave Ste 203 San Mateo (94401) *(P-13601)*

All About Produce Company .... D....... 805 543-9000
   712 Fiero Ln Ste 30 San Luis Obispo (93401) *(P-6513)*

All Access Rental, Santa Ana *Also Called: County of Orange (P-10996)*

All American Agrigate, Corona *Also Called: All American Asphalt (P-1071)*

All American Asphalt (PA) .... D....... 951 736-7600
   400 E 6th St Corona (92879) *(P-1071)*

All American Asphalt .... C....... 951 736-7617
   1776 All American Way Corona (92879) *(P-1072)*

All American Asphalt .... D....... 951 736-7617
   1776 All American Way Corona (92879) *(P-1073)*

All California Title Escrow Co .... D....... 800 626-0106
   1001 Wilshire Blvd Los Angeles (90017) *(P-8896)*

All Care Medical Group Inc .... D....... 408 278-3550
   31 Crescent St Huntington Park (90255) *(P-14597)*

All Cartage Transportation Inc (PA) .... D....... 310 970-0600
   12621 Chadron Ave Hawthorne (90250) *(P-3578)*

All Counties Courier Inc .... C....... 714 599-9300
   1900 S State College Blvd Ste 450 Anaheim (92806) *(P-3605)*

All Covered Inc .... B....... 650 486-5000
   1051 E Hillsdale Blvd Ste 510 Foster City (94404) *(P-12727)*

All Fab Prcsion Sheetmetal Inc .... D....... 408 279-1099
   1980 Senter Rd San Jose (95112) *(P-2043)*

All Guard Alarm Systems Inc (PA) .... D....... 800 255-4273
   1306 Stealth St Livermore (94551) *(P-1660)*

All Health Services Corp (PA) .... D....... 559 583-9101
   11104 Bonneyview Ln Hanford (93230) *(P-11079)*

All Metals Processing of San Diego Inc .... C....... 714 828-8238
   8401 Standustrial St Stanton (90680) *(P-2757)*

All Mtals Proc Orange Cnty LLC .... C....... 714 828-8238
   8401 Standustrial St Stanton (90680) *(P-2758)*

All Phase Security Inc .... D....... 916 919-3859
   2959 Promenade St Ste 200 West Sacramento (95691) *(P-12921)*

ALI Roofg Mtls Long Bch Inc .... D....... 805 656-6319
   1435 Walter St Ventura (93003) *(P-5217)*

ALI Roofg Mtls Long Bch Inc .... D....... 562 595-7377
   3100 Orange Ave Long Beach (90755) *(P-5218)*

All Saints Maubert, San Leandro *Also Called: Maubertidence Opco LLC (P-15773)*

All Saintsidence Opco LLC .... B....... 510 481-3200
   1652 Mono Ave San Leandro (94578) *(P-15322)*

All Snts Sbcute Trnstonal Care, San Leandro *Also Called: All Saintsidence Opco LLC (P-15322)*

All Star Parking .... C....... 310 337-1944
   9700 Bellanca Ave Los Angeles (90045) *(P-13602)*

All Starz Stffing Cnslting Inc .... D....... 909 870-9559
   9375 Archibald Ave Ste 202 Rancho Cucamonga (91730) *(P-11270)*

All State Association Inc .... C....... 877 425-2558
   11487 San Fernando Rd San Fernando (91340) *(P-18699)*

All Tmperatures Controlled Inc .... D....... 818 882-1478
   9720 Topanga Canyon Pl Chatsworth (91311) *(P-1346)*

All Valley Home Care, San Diego *Also Called: All Valley Home Hlth Care Inc (P-16803)*

All Valley Home Hlth Care Inc .... D....... 619 276-8001
   3665 Ruffin Rd Ste 103 San Diego (92123) *(P-16803)*

All Valley Washer Service Inc .... D....... 818 787-1100
   15008 Delano St Van Nuys (91411) *(P-10460)*

All Wall Inc .... D....... 760 600-5108
   46150 Commerce St Ste 102 Indio (92201) *(P-1903)*

All Weather Inc .... D....... 916 928-1000
   1065 National Dr Ste 1 Sacramento (95834) *(P-3040)*

All-Battery.com, Fremont *Also Called: Tenergy Corporation (P-2950)*

All-Coast Forest Products Inc (PA) .... D....... 707 894-4281
   250 Asti Rd Cloverdale (95425) *(P-5145)*

All-In Prdctons Csino Rntals L .... D....... 866 875-8628
   7222 Garden Grove Blvd Westminster (92683) *(P-11018)*

All-Points Petroleum LLC .... D....... 707 745-1116
   640 Noyes Ct Benicia (94510) *(P-6722)*

All-Pro Bail Bonds Inc .... D....... 760 512-1969
   530 Hacienda Dr Ste 104d Vista (92081) *(P-13183)*

All-Rite Leasing Company Inc .... B....... 714 957-1822
   950 S Coast Dr Ste 110 Costa Mesa (92626) *(P-10851)*

Allan Company, Baldwin Park *Also Called: Cedarwood-Young Company (P-4876)*

Allaquaria LLC .... D....... 310 645-1107
   5420 W 104th St Los Angeles (90045) *(P-6887)*

Allcloud USA LLC .... D....... 510 717-3785
   155 Montgomery St Ste 810 San Francisco (94104) *(P-12728)*

Alldata LLC .... B....... 916 684-5200
   9650 W Taron Dr Ste 100 Elk Grove (95757) *(P-12088)*

Allegis Residential Svcs Inc .... D....... 858 430-5700
   9340 Hazard Way Ste B2 San Diego (92123) *(P-20015)*

Allegretto Vineyard Resort, Paso Robles *Also Called: Ayres - Paso Robles LP (P-9624)*

Allele Bio & Pharmaceuticals .... C....... 858 410-0299
   6868 Nancy Ridge Dr San Diego (92121) *(P-19652)*

Allen Associates, Santa Barbara *Also Called: Dennis Allen Associates (P-672)*

Allen Development Partners LLC (PA) .... D....... 559 732-5425
   125 Sbridge 100 Visalia (93291) *(P-9244)*

Allen Distribution (PA) .... C....... 717 258-3040
   4580 Logistics Dr Stockton (95215) *(P-3673)*

Allen Drywall & Associates .... D....... 650 579-0664
   380 Lang Rd Burlingame (94010) *(P-1904)*

Allen Engineering Contractor Inc .... C....... 909 478-5500
   1655 Riverview Dr San Bernardino (92408) *(P-19136)*

Allen Gwynn Chevrolet, Glendale *Also Called: Allen Gwynn Chevrolet Inc (P-7167)*

Allen Gwynn Chevrolet Inc .... D....... 818 240-0000
   1400 S Brand Blvd Glendale (91204) *(P-7167)*

Allen Lund Company LLC (HQ) .... D....... 818 777-6142
   4529 Angeles Crest Hwy Ste 300 La Canada Flintridge (91011) *(P-3984)*

Allen Matkins, Los Angeles *Also Called: Allen Mtkins Leck Gmble Mllory (P-17362)*

Allen Mtkins Leck Gmble Mllory (PA) .... C....... 213 622-5555
   865 S Figueroa St Ste 2800 Los Angeles (90017) *(P-17362)*

Allen Transportation Co, Sacramento *Also Called: Amador Stage Lines Inc (P-3315)*

ALPHABETIC SECTION — Aloha Data Systems

Allen/Clark Cadillac .... D....... 626 966-7441
2700 E Garvey Ave S West Covina (91791) *(P-7168)*

Alliance, Irvine *Also Called: Alliance Healthcare Svcs Inc (P-16703)*

Alliance Childrens Services .... C....... 661 863-0350
1001 Tower Way Ste 110 Bakersfield (93309) *(P-18372)*

Alliance Ground Intl LLC .... A....... 310 646-2446
6181 W Imperial Hwy Los Angeles (90045) *(P-3873)*

Alliance Ground Intl LLC .... B....... 650 821-0855
648 West Field Rd San Francisco (94128) *(P-3874)*

Alliance Health Care Unions (PA) .... D....... 909 599-8622
955 Overland Ct Ste 150 San Dimas (91773) *(P-18770)*

Alliance Healthcare Svcs Inc (DH) .... C....... 800 544-3215
18201 Von Karman Ave Ste 600 Irvine (92612) *(P-16703)*

Alliance Home Health, Salinas *Also Called: Sutter Vsting Nrse Assn Hspice (P-16943)*

Alliance Medical Center Inc .... D....... 707 431-8234
1381 University St Healdsburg (95448) *(P-14598)*

Alliance Nrsing Rhbltation Ctr, El Monte *Also Called: Georgia Atkison Snf LLC (P-15494)*

Alliance Rdwods Cnfrnce Grunds .... C....... 707 874-3507
6250 Bohemian Hwy Occidental (95465) *(P-10398)*

Alliance Residential LLC .... D....... 818 841-2441
1200 W Riverside Dr Ofc Burbank (91506) *(P-8699)*

Alliance Spacesystems, Los Alamitos *Also Called: Vanguard Space Tech Inc (P-19431)*

Alliance Title, Glendale *Also Called: Wfg National Title Insur Co (P-9241)*

Alliancebernstein LP .... C....... 310 286-6000
1999 Avenue Of The Stars Ste 2150 Los Angeles (90067) *(P-9351)*

Alliant Asset MGT Co LLC (HQ) .... D....... 818 668-2805
26050 Mureau Rd Calabasas (91302) *(P-8897)*

Alliant Insurance Services Inc .... D....... 415 403-1400
100 Pine St Ste 1100 San Francisco (94111) *(P-20016)*

Alliant Insurance Services Inc (PA) .... C....... 949 756-0271
18100 Von Karman Ave Ste 1000 Irvine (92612) *(P-20684)*

Alliant Insurance Services Inc .... D....... 619 238-1828
701 B St Fl 6 San Diego (92101) *(P-20685)*

Allianz Global Investors of America LP .... A....... 949 219-2200
680 Nwport Ctr Dr Ste 250 Newport Beach (92660) *(P-8184)*

Allianz Globl Risks US Insur .... B....... 415 899-3758
1465 N Mcdowell Blvd Petaluma (94954) *(P-8374)*

Allianz Globl Risks US Insur (DH) C
2350 W Empire Ave Ste 200 Burbank (91504) *(P-8375)*

Allianz Insurance Company, Petaluma *Also Called: Allianz Globl Risks US Insur (P-8374)*

Allianz Insurance Company, Burbank *Also Called: Allianz Globl Risks US Insur (P-8375)*

Allianz Reinsurance Amer Inc .... B....... 415 899-2000
1465 N Mcdowell Blvd Petaluma (94954) *(P-8257)*

Allied Artists International, City Of Industry *Also Called: Allied Entertainment Group Inc (P-13816)*

Allied Avocados & Citrus Inc .... D....... 805 625-7155
1203 S Sespe St Fillmore (93015) *(P-253)*

Allied Company Holdings Inc (PA) .... D....... 818 493-6400
13235 Golden State Rd Sylmar (91342) *(P-6749)*

Allied Company Holdings Inc .... C....... 661 510-6533
28311 Constellation Rd Santa Clarita (91355) *(P-6750)*

Allied Construction Services, Livermore *Also Called: Csrw Inc (P-2270)*

Allied Container Systems Inc .... C....... 925 944-7600
511 Wilbur Ave Ste B4 Antioch (94509) *(P-2746)*

Allied Digital Services LLC .... C....... 310 431-2361
1075 Mt Vernon Ave Riverside (92507) *(P-12692)*

Allied Entertainment Group Inc (PA) .... B....... 626 330-0600
273 W Allen Ave City Of Industry (91746) *(P-13816)*

Allied Environmental Services, Woodland Hills *Also Called: Allied Industries Inc (P-20686)*

Allied Farming Company, Exeter *Also Called: Sun Pacific Farming Coop Inc (P-381)*

Allied Fire Protection .... C....... 510 533-5516
555 High St Oakland (94601) *(P-1347)*

Allied Framers Inc .... C....... 707 452-7050
4990 Allison Pkwy Vacaville (95688) *(P-1990)*

Allied Gardens Towing Inc (PA) .... D....... 619 563-4060
9150 Chesapeake Dr Ste 240 San Diego (92123) *(P-13706)*

Allied Hlthcare Federal Cr Un .... D....... 562 933-0370
2801 Atlantic Ave Long Beach (90806) *(P-7751)*

Allied Heating & Air Conditioning Co Inc .... C....... 415 459-5232
12 De Luca Pl San Rafael (94901) *(P-1348)*

Allied High Tech Products Inc .... D....... 310 635-2466
16207 Carmenita Rd Cerritos (90703) *(P-5888)*

Allied Industries Inc (PA) .... C....... 800 605-5323
21650 Oxnard St Ste 500 Woodland Hills (91367) *(P-20686)*

Allied Insurance .... B....... 916 924-4000
1601 Exposition Blvd Sacramento (95815) *(P-8376)*

Allied Intl San Franisco, Hayward *Also Called: Nor-Cal Moving Services (P-3591)*

Allied Landscape Services, Morgan Hill *Also Called: New Path Landscape Svcs Inc (P-450)*

Allied Lube Inc .... D....... 949 651-8814
3087 Edinger Ave Tustin (92780) *(P-13656)*

Allied Lube Inc .... D....... 408 779-8969
17010 Walnut Grove Dr Morgan Hill (95037) *(P-13707)*

Allied Mechanical, San Rafael *Also Called: Allied Heating & Air Conditioning Co Inc (P-1348)*

Allied Protection Services Inc .... C....... 310 330-8314
24303 Berendo Ave Harbor City (90710) *(P-12922)*

Allied Steel Co Inc .... C....... 951 241-7000
1027 Palmyrita Ave Riverside (92507) *(P-2176)*

Allied Trench Shoring Service, Newport Beach *Also Called: Traffic Control Service Inc (P-11058)*

Allied Universal .... C....... 619 444-0219
9320 Hazard Way Ste A1 San Diego (92123) *(P-1661)*

Allied Universal .... D....... 650 223-3221
533 Airport Blvd Ste 303 Burlingame (94010) *(P-12923)*

Allied Universal, Irvine *Also Called: Universal Services America LP (P-13066)*

Allied Universal Event Svcs, Westminster *Also Called: Staff Pro Inc (P-13148)*

Allied Universal Security Svcs, San Francisco *Also Called: Universal Protection Svc LP (P-13063)*

Allied Universal Topco LLC .... A....... 209 472-0455
5308 Pacific Ave Stockton (95207) *(P-12924)*

Allies For Every Child Inc .... D....... 310 846-4100
5721 W Slauson Ave Ste 200 Culver City (90230) *(P-18268)*

Allmark Inc (PA) .... D....... 909 989-7556
10070 Arrow Rte Rancho Cucamonga (91730) *(P-8898)*

Allmodular Systems Inc .... D....... 510 887-9000
21005 Cabot Blvd Hayward (94545) *(P-5241)*

ALLOGENE THERAPEUTICS, South San Francisco *Also Called: Allogene Therapeutics Inc (P-2617)*

Allogene Therapeutics Inc (PA) .... C....... 650 457-2700
210 E Grand Ave South San Francisco (94080) *(P-2617)*

Allogene Therapeutics Inc .... C....... 650 457-2700
7400 Gateway Blvd Newark (94560) *(P-19653)*

Alloy Technologies Inc (PA) .... D....... 415 990-5140
548 Market St San Francisco (94104) *(P-5267)*

Allspring Funds Distr LLC .... D....... 415 396-8000
525 Market St Fl 10 San Francisco (94105) *(P-8185)*

Allstate, Los Angeles *Also Called: Allstate Financial Svcs LLC (P-8483)*

Allstate Financial Svcs LLC .... D....... 323 981-8520
5161 Pomona Blvd Ste 212 Los Angeles (90022) *(P-8483)*

Allstate Floral Inc .... C....... 562 926-2989
15928 Commerce Way Cerritos (90703) *(P-8484)*

Allstate Imaging Inc (PA) .... D....... 818 678-4550
21621 Nordhoff St Chatsworth (91311) *(P-5242)*

Allzone Management Solutions, Glendale *Also Called: Allzone Management Svcs Inc (P-20017)*

Allzone Management Svcs Inc .... B....... 213 291-8879
3795 La Crescenta Ave Ste 200 Glendale (91208) *(P-20017)*

Almaden Golf & Country Club .... D....... 408 323-4812
6663 Hampton Dr San Jose (95120) *(P-14319)*

Almaden Health & Rehab Ctr, San Jose *Also Called: Mariner Health Care Inc (P-15576)*

Almaden Valley Athletic Club .... D....... 408 445-4900
5400 Camden Ave San Jose (95124) *(P-14171)*

ALMAVIA OF CAMARILLO, Camarillo *Also Called: Elder Care Alliance Camarillo (P-15431)*

Aloft, Millbrae *Also Called: Aloft Ht San Francisco Arprt (P-9602)*

Aloft Ht San Francisco Arprt .... D....... 650 443-5500
401 E Millbrae Ave Millbrae (94030) *(P-9602)*

Alogent, Carlsbad *Also Called: Alogent Holdings Inc (P-11397)*

Alogent Holdings Inc .... D....... 760 410-9000
5868 Owens Ave Ste 200 Carlsbad (92008) *(P-11397)*

Aloha Beach Resort, San Francisco *Also Called: Equinox Hotel Management Inc (P-9785)*

Aloha Data Systems, Rcho Sta Marg *Also Called: Expitrans Inc (P-20368)*

Alois LLC .... C....... 215 297-4492
548 Market St Ste 47970 San Francisco (94104) *(P-11080)*

Alois Staffing, San Francisco *Also Called: Alois LLC (P-11080)*

Alom Technologies, Fremont *Also Called: Alom Technologies Corporation (P-4125)*

Alom Technologies Corporation (PA) .... C....... 510 360-3600
48105 Warm Springs Blvd Fremont (94539) *(P-4125)*

Alorica Customer Care Inc .... D....... 619 298-7103
8885 Rio San Diego Dr Ste 107 San Diego (92108) *(P-13184)*

Alorica Customer Care Inc .... C....... 941 906-9000
5161 California Ave Ste 100 Irvine (92617) *(P-13185)*

Alorica Inc (PA) .... D....... 866 256-7422
5161 California Ave Ste 100 Irvine (92617) *(P-13186)*

Alpase, Chino *Also Called: Tst Inc (P-2722)*

Alpert & Alpert Iron & Metal Inc (PA) .... D....... 323 265-4040
1815 S Soto St Los Angeles (90023) *(P-5472)*

ALPERT JEWISH COMMUNITY CENTRE, Long Beach *Also Called: Jewish Community Ctr Long Bch (P-18024)*

Alpha Health Inc .... C....... 970 209-1462
400 Oyster Point Blvd Ste 222 South San Francisco (94080) *(P-17168)*

Alpha Innotech Corp .... C....... 408 510-5500
3040 Oakmead Village Dr Santa Clara (95051) *(P-5396)*

Alpha Mechanical Inc .... C....... 858 278-3500
4990 Greencraig Ln Ste A San Diego (92123) *(P-1349)*

Alpha Mechanical Inc (PA) .... D....... 858 278-3500
1866 Friendship Dr El Cajon (92020) *(P-1350)*

Alpha Mechanical Heating & Air Conditioning Inc .... C....... 858 279-1300
4885 Greencraig Ln San Diego (92123) *(P-1351)*

Alpha Net Consulting Llc (PA) .... C....... 408 550-5686
3211 Scott Blvd Ste 203 Santa Clara (95054) *(P-11398)*

Alpha Professional Resources, Thousand Oaks *Also Called: A P R Inc (P-11265)*

Alpha Project For Homeless .... C....... 760 630-9922
993 Postal Way Vista (92083) *(P-17826)*

Alpha Teknova Inc .... C....... 831 637-1100
205 Apollo Way Hollister (95023) *(P-19862)*

Alphabet, Mountain View *Also Called: Alphabet Inc (P-11399)*

Alphabet Inc (PA) .... B....... 650 253-0000
1600 Amphitheatre Pkwy Mountain View (94043) *(P-11399)*

Alphabold .... D....... 949 637-7148
2011 Palomar Airport Rd Ste 305 Carlsbad (92011) *(P-12729)*

Alphatec Spine Inc (HQ) .... C....... 760 431-9286
1950 Camino Vida Roble Carlsbad (92008) *(P-3062)*

Alphatech General Inc .... D....... 626 337-4640
4750 Littlejohn St Baldwin Park (91706) *(P-13761)*

Alpine Allrgy Asthma Assoc Inc .... D....... 530 888-1016
3254 Professional Dr Auburn (95602) *(P-14599)*

Alpine Animal Hospital, Mountain View *Also Called: Animus Inc (P-327)*

Alpine Convalescent Center Inc .... D....... 619 659-3120
2120 Alpine Blvd Alpine (91901) *(P-17002)*

Alpine Inn Restaurant, Torrance *Also Called: Alpine Village (P-8700)*

Alpine Invstors Cnfrnce Call H .... D....... 415 392-9100
3 Embarcadero Ctr Ste 2330 San Francisco (94111) *(P-9486)*

Alpine Special Treatment Ctr, Alpine *Also Called: Alpine Convalescent Center Inc (P-17002)*

Alpine Village .... C....... 310 327-4384
23670 Hawthorne Blvd Torrance (90505) *(P-8700)*

Alquest Technologies Inc .... D....... 909 592-8708
1760 Yeager Ave La Verne (91750) *(P-12701)*

Als Group Usa Corp .... C....... 310 214-0043
3904 Del Amo Blvd Torrance (90503) *(P-19946)*

Alsco - Geyer Irrigation Inc .... D....... 530 476-2253
700 5th St Arbuckle (95912) *(P-5805)*

Alston & Bird LLP .... D....... 213 576-1000
333 S Hope St Ste 1600 Los Angeles (90071) *(P-17363)*

Alston Construction Co Inc (PA) .... D....... 916 340-2400
400 Capitol Mall Sacramento (95814) *(P-863)*

Alstyle AP & Activewear MGT Co (HQ) .... A....... 714 765-0400
1501 E Cerritos Ave Anaheim (92805) *(P-6194)*

Alta Bates Medical Center, Berkeley *Also Called: Ocadian Care Centers LLC (P-15603)*

Alta Bates Summit Medical Ctr, Berkeley *Also Called: Surgery Ctr of Alta Btes Smmit (P-16504)*

Alta Bates Summit Medical Ctr, Berkeley *Also Called: Sutter Bay Hospitals (P-16508)*

Alta Bates Summit Medical Ctr, Oakland *Also Called: Sutter Bay Hospitals (P-16510)*

Alta Cal Regional Ctr Inc .... C....... 530 674-3070
950 Tharp Rd Yuba City (95993) *(P-17827)*

Alta Cal Regional Ctr Inc .... C....... 530 666-3391
283 W Court St Woodland (95695) *(P-17828)*

Alta Cal Regional Ctr Inc .... C....... 916 786-8110
807 Douglas Blvd Roseville (95678) *(P-17829)*

Alta California Regional Ctr, Roseville *Also Called: Alta Cal Regional Ctr Inc (P-17829)*

Alta Healthcare System LLC (HQ) .... C....... 323 267-0477
4081 E Olympic Blvd Los Angeles (90023) *(P-15937)*

Alta Hllywood Cmnty Hosp Van N .... C....... 818 787-1511
14433 Emelita St Van Nuys (91401) *(P-16635)*

Alta Hospitals System LLC .... A....... 714 619-7700
14662 Newport Ave Tustin (92780) *(P-15938)*

Alta Med Health Services, El Monte *Also Called: Altamed Health Services Corp (P-17175)*

Alta Mira Hotel & Restaurant, Sausalito *Also Called: Alta Mira Recovery Ctrs LLC (P-7455)*

Alta Mira Recovery Ctrs LLC .... D....... 415 332-1350
125 Bulkley Ave Sausalito (94965) *(P-7455)*

Alta One Fcu, Ridgecrest *Also Called: Altaone Federal Credit Union (P-7752)*

Alta Vista Country Club LLC .... D....... 714 524-1591
777 Alta Vista St Placentia (92870) *(P-14320)*

Alta-Dena Certified Dairy LLC (DH) .... B....... 626 964-6401
17637 E Valley Blvd City Of Industry (91744) *(P-213)*

Altadena Town and Country Club .... D....... 626 345-9088
2290 Country Club Dr Altadena (91001) *(P-14321)*

Altair Lighting, Compton *Also Called: Jimway Inc (P-2876)*

Altais Clinical Services (HQ) .... D....... 510 607-4000
601 12th St Fl 16 Oakland (94607) *(P-20268)*

Altamed Adhc Golden Age, Lynwood *Also Called: Altamed Health Services Corp (P-14602)*

Altamed Health Services Corp .... C....... 323 980-4466
5427 Whittier Blvd Los Angeles (90022) *(P-14600)*

Altamed Health Services Corp .... C....... 562 923-9414
1500 Hughes Way Ste A150 Long Beach (90810) *(P-14601)*

Altamed Health Services Corp .... C....... 310 632-0415
3820 Martin Luther King Jr Blvd Lynwood (90262) *(P-14602)*

Altamed Health Services Corp .... D....... 714 635-0593
1325 N Anaheim Blvd # 101 Anaheim (92801) *(P-14603)*

Altamed Health Services Corp .... C....... 323 277-7678
6330 Rugby Ave Ste 200 Huntington Park (90255) *(P-14604)*

Altamed Health Services Corp .... D....... 714 426-5400
2720 S Bristol St Santa Ana (92704) *(P-14605)*

Altamed Health Services Corp (PA) .... C....... 323 725-8751
2040 Camfield Ave Commerce (90040) *(P-14606)*

Altamed Health Services Corp .... C....... 323 728-0411
5425 Pomona Blvd Los Angeles (90022) *(P-14607)*

Altamed Health Services Corp .... C....... 323 269-0421
2219 E 1st St Los Angeles (90033) *(P-14608)*

Altamed Health Services Corp .... D....... 714 919-0280
1515 S Broadway Ste A Santa Ana (92707) *(P-17169)*

Altamed Health Services Corp .... C....... 323 562-6700
8627 Atlantic Ave South Gate (90280) *(P-17170)*

Altamed Health Services Corp .... C....... 323 307-0400
3945 Whittier Blvd Los Angeles (90023) *(P-17171)*

Altamed Health Services Corp .... D....... 323 890-8767
5255 Pomona Blvd Ste 11 Los Angeles (90022) *(P-17172)*

Altamed Health Services Corp .... C....... 562 949-8717
9436 Slauson Ave Pico Rivera (90660) *(P-17173)*

Altamed Health Services Corp .... D....... 562 595-8040
711 E Wardlow Rd Ste 203 Long Beach (90807) *(P-17174)*

Altamed Health Services Corp .... C....... 626 453-8466
10418 Valley Blvd Ste B El Monte (91731) *(P-17175)*

Altamed Ltc Trnsp Dept, Los Angeles *Also Called: Altamed Health Services Corp (P-17172)*

Altamed Med & Dntl Group Bell, South Gate *Also Called: Altamed Health Services Corp (P-17170)*

Altamed Med Dntl Grp Whttier W, Los Angeles *Also Called: Altamed Health Services Corp (P-17171)*

Altametrics, Costa Mesa *Also Called: Altametrics Hosting LLC (P-5268)*

Altametrics Hosting LLC .... C....... 800 676-1281
3191 Red Hill Ave Ste 100 Costa Mesa (92626) *(P-5268)*

Altaone Federal Credit Union (PA) .... C....... 760 371-7000
701 S China Lake Blvd Ridgecrest (93555) *(P-7752)*

ALPHABETIC SECTION

Altec Products Inc (PA) .... D....... 949 727-1248
23422 Mill Creek Dr Ste 225 Laguna Hills (92653) *(P-13187)*

Altech Services Inc .... B....... 888 725-8324
400 Continental Blvd Fl 6 El Segundo (90245) *(P-11271)*

Altegra Health, Los Angeles *Also Called: The Coding Source LLC (P-17797)*

Alten Construction Inc .... D....... 510 234-4200
1141 Marina Way S Richmond (94804) *(P-653)*

Alter Health Group, Dana Point *Also Called: Alter Management LLC (P-20018)*

Alter Management LLC .... D....... 949 629-0214
34232 Pacific Coast Hwy Ste D Dana Point (92629) *(P-20018)*

Altera, San Jose *Also Called: Altera Corporation (P-2912)*

Altera Corporation (HQ) .... B....... 408 544-7000
101 Innovation Dr San Jose (95134) *(P-2912)*

Altergy Systems .... D....... 916 458-8590
140 Blue Ravine Rd Folsom (95630) *(P-9297)*

Alternative Energy Systems Inc .... D....... 530 345-6980
13620 State Highway 99 N Chico (95973) *(P-1352)*

Alternative Ira Services LLC .... C....... 877 936-7175
15303 Ventura Blvd Ste 1060 Sherman Oaks (91403) *(P-13188)*

Alterntive Protective Svcs Inc .... D....... 818 456-0989
7301 Topanga Canyon Blvd Ste 350 Canoga Park (91303) *(P-5534)*

Alterra Spcalty Insur Svcs Ltd .... C....... 415 490-4615
201 California St San Francisco (94111) *(P-8231)*

Altexsoft Inc .... C....... 877 777-9097
6590 Lockheed Dr Redding (96002) *(P-12730)*

Altigen Communications Inc .... C....... 408 597-9000
670 N Mccarthy Blvd Ste 200 Milpitas (95035) *(P-2884)*

Altium Inc (HQ) .... D....... 858 864-1500
4225 Executive Sq Ste 800 La Jolla (92037) *(P-11400)*

Altman Flowers, Fallbrook *Also Called: Altman Specialty Plants LLC (P-6849)*

Altman Plants, Vista *Also Called: Altman Specialty Plants LLC (P-6848)*

Altman Specialty Plants LLC .... A....... 831 758-4850
20460 Spence Rd Salinas (93908) *(P-6847)*

Altman Specialty Plants LLC (PA) .... A....... 800 348-4881
3742 Blue Bird Canyon Rd Vista (92084) *(P-6848)*

Altman Specialty Plants LLC .... B....... 800 348-4881
2575 Olive Hill Rd Fallbrook (92028) *(P-6849)*

Alto Lucero Transitional Care, Santa Barbara *Also Called: Compass Health Inc (P-15386)*

Alton Geoscience, Irvine *Also Called: TRC Solutions Inc (P-20867)*

Altoon Partners LLP (PA) .... D....... 213 225-1900
617 W 7th St Ste 400 Los Angeles (90017) *(P-19450)*

Altoon Porter, Los Angeles *Also Called: Altoon Partners LLP (P-19450)*

Altor Bscnce LLC An Indrect Wh .... D....... 310 733-7107
9920 Jefferson Blvd Culver City (90232) *(P-19654)*

Altos Oaks Day Care Center, Los Altos Hills *Also Called: First Bptst Ch of Los Altos Th (P-18315)*

Altour International Inc (PA) .... D....... 310 571-6000
12100 W Olympic Blvd Ste 300 Los Angeles (90064) *(P-3924)*

Altour International Inc .... B....... 310 571-6000
10635 Santa Monica Blvd Ste 200 Los Angeles (90025) *(P-3925)*

Altour Travel Master, Los Angeles *Also Called: Altour International Inc (P-3925)*

Altro Usa Inc .... D....... 562 944-8292
12648 Clark St Santa Fe Springs (90670) *(P-3104)*

Altruist Corp .... C....... 949 370-5096
3030 La Cienega Blvd Culver City (90232) *(P-20269)*

Altura Centers For Health .... D....... 559 686-9097
1201 N Cherry St Tulare (93274) *(P-14609)*

Altura Management Services LLC .... B....... 323 768-2898
1401 N Montebello Blvd Montebello (90640) *(P-20019)*

Altus Health Inc .... C....... 916 781-6500
151 N Sunrise Ave Ste 1011 Roseville (95661) *(P-16804)*

Aluminum Precision Pdts Inc .... C....... 805 488-4401
1001 Mcwane Blvd Oxnard (93033) *(P-5473)*

Alvah Contractors Inc .... B....... 650 741-6785
263 S Maple Ave South San Francisco (94080) *(P-1662)*

Alvarado Hospital LLC (DH) .... C....... 619 287-3270
6655 Alvarado Rd San Diego (92120) *(P-15939)*

Alvarado Hospital Med Ctr Inc .... A....... 619 287-3270
6655 Alvarado Rd San Diego (92120) *(P-15940)*

ALVARADO PARKWAY INSTITUTE, La Mesa *Also Called: Bh-SD Opco LLC (P-17015)*

Alvarado Parkway Institute, La Mesa *Also Called: Helix Healthcare Inc (P-17071)*

ALVAREZ & MARSAL BUSINESS CONSULTING LLC, Los Angeles *Also Called: Alvarez Mrsal Bus Cnslting LLC (P-20270)*

Alvarez Mrsal Bus Cnslting LLC .... C....... 310 975-2600
2029 Century Park E Los Angeles (90002) *(P-20270)*

Alviso Health Center, Alviso *Also Called: Gardner Family Hlth Netwrk Inc (P-14758)*

Always Best Care Desert Cities, Indian Wells *Also Called: Bjz LLC (P-16821)*

Always Best Care Senior Svcs, Roseville *Also Called: Abcsp LLC (P-16784)*

Always Best Care Senior Svcs, Vacaville *Also Called: Thriving Seniors LLC (P-16952)*

Always Best Care Temecula Vly, Temecula *Also Called: James Rebecca Prouty Entps Inc (P-16880)*

Always Home, Citrus Heights *Also Called: Always Home Nursing Svcs Inc (P-16805)*

Always Home Nursing Svcs Inc .... C....... 916 989-6420
7777 Greenback Ln Ste 208 Citrus Heights (95610) *(P-16805)*

Always Right Home Care, Northridge *Also Called: Tiffany Homecare Inc (P-16953)*

Am-Pac Tire Dist Inc (DH) .... D
51 Moreland Rd Simi Valley (93065) *(P-7341)*

Am-PM Sewer & Drain Cleaning, San Diego *Also Called: Bill Howe Plumbing Inc (P-1378)*

Am/PM Mini Market, La Palma *Also Called: Prestige Stations Inc (P-7147)*

Amada America Inc (HQ) .... D....... 714 739-2111
7025 Firestone Blvd Buena Park (90621) *(P-5818)*

Amada Capital Corporation .... D....... 714 739-2111
7025 Firestone Blvd Buena Park (90621) *(P-11019)*

Amada Enterprises Inc .... C....... 323 757-1881
12619 Avalon Blvd Los Angeles (90061) *(P-15323)*

Amador Stage Lines Inc .... D....... 916 444-7880
1331 C St Sacramento (95814) *(P-3315)*

Amador Tlmne Cmnty Action Agcy (PA) .... D....... 209 296-2785
10590 State Highway 88 Ste 6 Jackson (95642) *(P-18554)*

Amador Tlmne Cmnty Action Agcy .... D....... 209 533-1397
427 Highway 49 Ste 305 Sonora (95370) *(P-18555)*

Amanecer Cmnty Cnsling Svc A N .... D....... 213 481-7464
1200 Wilshire Blvd Ste 200 Los Angeles (90017) *(P-17003)*

Amaral Ranches, Chualar *Also Called: C & G Farms Inc (P-25)*

Amatel Inc (PA) .... D....... 323 801-0199
915 N Todd Ave Azusa (91702) *(P-20687)*

Amatix, Sun Valley *Also Called: Marfred Industries (P-2520)*

Amawaterways LLC (PA) .... C....... 800 626-0126
4500 Park Granada # 200 Calabasas (91302) *(P-3926)*

Amax Computer, Fremont *Also Called: Amax Engineering Corporation (P-5269)*

Amax Engineering Corporation (PA) .... C....... 510 651-8886
1565 Reliance Way Fremont (94539) *(P-5269)*

Amaya Curiel Corporation .... A....... 619 661-1230
9775 Marconi Dr Ste G San Diego (92154) *(P-803)*

Amaya Curiel Y CIA S.A., San Diego *Also Called: Amaya Curiel Corporation (P-803)*

Amazing Coachella Inc .... D....... 760 398-0151
85810 Peter Rabbit Ln Coachella (92236) *(P-19)*

Amazing Facts Inc .... D....... 916 434-3880
1203 W Sunset Blvd Rocklin (95765) *(P-2548)*

Amazing Facts International .... D....... 916 434-3880
6615 Sierra College Blvd Roseville (95746) *(P-4372)*

Amazing Facts Ministries, Rocklin *Also Called: Amazing Facts Inc (P-2548)*

AMAZING FACTS MINISTRIES, Roseville *Also Called: Amazing Facts International (P-4372)*

Amazon Processing LLC .... C....... 858 565-1135
4619 Viewridge Ave Ste C San Diego (92123) *(P-12549)*

Amazon Studios LLC .... C....... 818 804-0884
9336 Washington Blvd Culver City (90232) *(P-11401)*

Amazon.Com, San Bernardino *Also Called: Amazoncom Inc (P-3674)*

Amazoncom Inc .... D....... 626 260-6954
1910 E Central Ave San Bernardino (92408) *(P-3674)*

Amber Holding Inc .... D....... 603 324-3000
1601 Cloverfield Blvd Santa Monica (90404) *(P-12089)*

Amber Holdings Inc .... A....... 415 765-6500
150 California St San Francisco (94111) *(P-11402)*

Amberwood Convalescent Hosp .... D....... 323 254-3407
6071 York Blvd Los Angeles (90042) *(P-15808)*

Ambiance Apparel, Los Angeles *Also Called: Ambiance USA Inc (P-2458)*

Ambiance Transportation LLC .... D....... 818 955-5757
6901 San Fernando Rd Glendale (91201) *(P-4143)*

Ambiance USA Inc (PA) .... D...... 323 587-0007
2415 E 15th St Los Angeles (90021) *(P-2458)*

Ambitions Behavioral Hlth LLC .... D...... 408 373-6752
2372 Morse Ave Irvine (92614) *(P-17176)*

Ambius, San Marcos *Also Called: Rentokil North America Inc (P-532)*

Amblin Partners .... D...... 818 733-9665
100 Universal City Plz Universal City (91608) *(P-13817)*

Ambulnz Health LLC .... B...... 877 311-5555
12531 Vanowen St North Hollywood (91605) *(P-3227)*

Ambys Medicines Inc .... D...... 408 373-4030
131 Oyster Point Blvd Ste 200 South San Francisco (94080) *(P-19655)*

AMC, Stanton *Also Called: All Metals Processing of San Diego Inc (P-2757)*

AMC, Sylmar *Also Called: Advanced Mnlythic Ceramics Inc (P-5619)*

Amco Foods Inc .... B...... 818 247-4716
601 E Glenoaks Blvd Ste 108 Glendale (91207) *(P-20271)*

Amcom Food Service, City Of Industry *Also Called: Klm Management Company (P-6439)*

AMD, Santa Clara *Also Called: Advanced Micro Devices Inc (P-5266)*

AME Unmanned Air Systems Inc .... D...... 805 541-4448
125 Venture Dr Ste 110 San Luis Obispo (93401) *(P-19137)*

AME-Gyu Co Ltd .... A...... 310 214-9572
20000 Mariner Ave Ste 500 Torrance (90503) *(P-9298)*

Amec Geomatrix Inc .... B...... 510 663-4100
2101 Webster St Ste 1200 Oakland (94612) *(P-19138)*

Amen Clinics Inc A Med Corp (PA) .... D...... 888 564-2700
3150 Bristol St Ste 400 Costa Mesa (92626) *(P-14610)*

Amenities Development Co .... C...... 626 350-9588
1089 Santa Anita Ave El Monte (91733) *(P-9603)*

Ameresco Solar LLC .... B...... 888 967-6527
42175 Zevo Dr Temecula (92590) *(P-19139)*

Ameri-Kleen .... C...... 831 722-8888
313 W Beach St Watsonville (95076) *(P-10852)*

Ameri-Kleen .... C...... 805 546-0706
1023 E Grand Ave Arroyo Grande (93420) *(P-10853)*

Ameri-Kleen Building Services, Watsonville *Also Called: Ameri-Kleen (P-10852)*

Ameri-Kleen Building Services, Arroyo Grande *Also Called: Ameri-Kleen (P-10853)*

American Academic Hlth Sys LLC .... A...... 310 414-7200
222 N Pacific Coast Hwy Ste 900 El Segundo (90245) *(P-9299)*

American Acdemy Ophthlmlogy In (PA) .... C...... 415 561-8500
655 Beach St Fl 1 San Francisco (94109) *(P-18729)*

American Agcredit Flca (PA) .... D...... 707 545-1200
400 Aviation Blvd Ste 100 Santa Rosa (95403) *(P-7913)*

American Air, Visalia *Also Called: American Incorporated (P-864)*

American Air Liquide Inc (DH) .... D...... 510 624-4000
46409 Landing Pkwy Fremont (94538) *(P-2572)*

American Airlines Inc .... D...... 650 877-6000
International Airport San Francisco (94128) *(P-3829)*

American Airlines Inc .... B...... 310 646-4553
400 World Way Ste F Los Angeles (90045) *(P-3830)*

American Airlines/Eagle, Long Beach *Also Called: Piedmont Airlines Inc (P-3840)*

American Airlines/Eagle, Fresno *Also Called: Piedmont Airlines Inc (P-3841)*

American Ambulance, Fresno *Also Called: KWPH Enterprises (P-3269)*

American Asp Repr Rsrfcing Inc (PA) .... D...... 510 723-0280
24200 Clawiter Rd Hayward (94545) *(P-1074)*

American Asphalt, Hayward *Also Called: American Asp Repr Rsrfcing Inc (P-1074)*

American Assn Crtcal Care Nrse .... C...... 949 362-2000
27071 Aliso Creek Rd Aliso Viejo (92656) *(P-17799)*

American Atmble Assn Nrthrn CA, Walnut Creek *Also Called: California State Automobile Association Inter-Insurance Bureau (P-19073)*

American Beef Packers Inc .... C...... 909 628-4888
13677 Yorba Ave Chino (91710) *(P-355)*

American Bldg Maint Co of Ill .... B...... 510 573-1618
44870 Osgood Rd Fremont (94539) *(P-10854)*

American Bldg Maint Co-West (HQ) .... C...... 415 733-4000
75 Broadway Ste 111 San Francisco (94111) *(P-10855)*

American Bottling Company .... D...... 951 341-7500
1188 Mt Vernon Ave Riverside (92507) *(P-2398)*

American Bottling Company .... D...... 661 323-7921
230 E 18th St Bakersfield (93305) *(P-2399)*

American Bottling Company .... D...... 818 898-1471
1166 Arroyo St San Fernando (91340) *(P-2400)*

American Bottling Company .... C...... 714 974-8560
1166 Arroyo St Orange (92865) *(P-2401)*

American Bottling Company .... C...... 323 268-7779
3220 E 26th St Vernon (90058) *(P-2402)*

American Bottling Company .... D...... 510 346-3777
2009 Farallon Dr San Leandro (94577) *(P-6599)*

American Bridge/Fluor Enterprises Inc .... D...... 510 808-4623
1390 Willow Pass Rd # 33 Concord (94520) *(P-1178)*

American Building Maintenance, San Francisco *Also Called: American Bldg Maint Co-West (P-10855)*

American Building Service Inc .... D...... 510 483-5120
4578 Crow Canyon Pl Castro Valley (94552) *(P-10856)*

American Building Supply, Rialto *Also Called: Jeld-Wen Inc (P-5171)*

American Business Bank .... D...... 909 919-2040
3633 Inland Empire Blvd Ste 720 Ontario (91764) *(P-7651)*

American Business Bank .... D...... 310 808-1200
970 W 190th St Ste 850 Torrance (90502) *(P-7652)*

American Capital Group Inc .... D...... 949 271-5800
23382 Mill Creek Dr # 115 Laguna Hills (92653) *(P-7914)*

American Civil Constrs LLC .... D...... 707 746-8028
3701 Mallard Dr Benicia (94510) *(P-1284)*

American Cllege of Trdtnal Chn (PA) .... D...... 415 282-0316
1453 Mission St San Francisco (94103) *(P-17760)*

American Cmmrcal Clims Admnstr .... C...... 415 782-3933
1200 Fulsome St San Francisco (94104) *(P-8485)*

American Cmpus Communities Inc .... D...... 949 854-0900
62600 Arroyo Dr Irvine (92617) *(P-10391)*

American Cncil For Fd Sfety Ql, Kingsburg *Also Called: Dfa of California (P-20079)*

American Commodity Co., Williams *Also Called: ACC-Gwg LLC (P-20672)*

American Concrete Washouts Inc .... D...... 916 496-2798
8620 Antelope North Rd Antelope (95843) *(P-2094)*

American Conservatory Theater (PA) .... D...... 415 749-2228
30 Grant Ave Fl 7 San Francisco (94108) *(P-7571)*

American Contractors Inc .... D...... 714 282-5700
404 W Blueridge Ave Orange (92865) *(P-1353)*

American Contrs Indemnity Co (DH) .... C...... 213 330-1309
801 S Figueroa St Ste 700 Los Angeles (90017) *(P-8427)*

American Copak Corporation .... C...... 818 576-1000
9175 Eton Ave Chatsworth (91311) *(P-13189)*

American Crane Rental Inc .... D...... 209 838-8815
17800 Comconex Rd Manteca (95336) *(P-10992)*

American Cvil Cnstrs W Cast LL .... D...... 707 746-8028
2990 Bay Vista Ct Ste D Benicia (94510) *(P-1075)*

American Cvil Lbrties Un Sther, Orange *Also Called: Aclu Fndation Southern Cal LLC (P-18809)*

American Dawn Inc (PA) .... D...... 800 821-2221
401 W Artesia Blvd Compton (90220) *(P-2448)*

American De Rosa Lamparts LLC .... D...... 800 777-4440
10650 4th St Rancho Cucamonga (91730) *(P-804)*

American Development Corp (PA) .... D...... 562 989-3730
3605 Long Beach Blvd Ste 410 Long Beach (90807) *(P-8899)*

American Dj Group of Companies, Commerce *Also Called: D J American Supply Inc (P-6039)*

American Eagle Protective Svcs, Inglewood *Also Called: American Egle Prtctive Svcs In (P-12925)*

American Egle Prtctive Svcs In .... D...... 310 412-0019
425 W Kelso St Inglewood (90301) *(P-12925)*

American Electric Supply Inc (PA) .... D...... 951 734-7910
361 S Maple St Corona (92878) *(P-5535)*

American Electronics, Carson *Also Called: Ducommun Labarge Tech Inc (P-2990)*

American Engrg Contrs Inc .... C...... 209 229-1591
25445 S Schulte Rd Tracy (95377) *(P-1663)*

American Etc Inc .... B...... 650 873-5353
1140 San Mateo Ave South San Francisco (94080) *(P-10422)*

American Farms LLC .... D...... 831 424-1815
1107 Harkins Rd Salinas (93901) *(P-10)*

American Fdrtion Mscans Lcal 4 .... D...... 323 462-2161
3220 Winona Ave Burbank (91504) *(P-18771)*

AMERICAN FEDERATION OF MUSICIA, Burbank *Also Called: American Fdrtion Mscans Lcal 4 (P-18771)*

American Fencing, Fresno *Also Called: A J Excavation Inc (P-2211)*

American Financial Network Inc (PA) .... C...... 714 831-4000
10 Pointe Dr Ste 330 Brea (92821) *(P-7927)*

ALPHABETIC SECTION — American Recovery Service

American First Credit Union (PA) .... D....... 562 691-1112
  6 Pointe Dr Ste 400 Brea (92821) *(P-7753)*

American Fish and Seafood, Los Angeles *Also Called: Prospect Enterprises Inc (P-6477)*

American Freightways LP .... D....... 866 326-5902
  10845 Rancho Bernardo Rd Ste 100 San Diego (92127) *(P-3441)*

American Fruits & Flavors LLC .... B....... 818 899-9574
  510 Park Ave San Fernando (91340) *(P-10528)*

American Funds Distrs Inc (DH) .... C....... 213 486-9200
  333 S Hope St Ste Levb Los Angeles (90071) *(P-9352)*

American Funds Service Company (DH) .... B....... 949 975-5000
  6455 Irvine Center Dr Irvine (92618) *(P-8229)*

American Furniture Alliance, Corona *Also Called: Widly Inc (P-2494)*

American Future Tech Corp .... C....... 888 462-3899
  529 Baldwin Park Blvd City Of Industry (91746) *(P-5270)*

American Golf Construction, Canoga Park *Also Called: American Landscape Inc (P-386)*

American Golf Corporation .... D....... 925 672-9737
  1001 Peacock Creek Dr Clayton (94517) *(P-14322)*

American Golf Corporation (HQ) .... C....... 310 664-4000
  909 N Pacific Coast Hwy Ste 650 El Segundo (90245) *(P-14323)*

American Guard Services Inc (PA) .... B....... 310 645-6200
  1125 W 190th St Gardena (90248) *(P-12926)*

American Health Care, Rocklin *Also Called: American Hlthcare ADM Svcs Inc (P-17177)*

American Health Connection .... A....... 424 226-0420
  8484 Wilshire Blvd Ste 501 Beverly Hills (90211) *(P-13190)*

American Heritage, Irvine *Also Called: American Heritage Lf Insur Co (P-8486)*

American Heritage Lf Insur Co .... D....... 800 753-9227
  400 Exchange Ste 210 Irvine (92602) *(P-8486)*

American High Schl Booster CLB .... C....... 510 796-1776
  36300 Fremont Blvd Fremont (94536) *(P-18811)*

American Hlthcare ADM Svcs Inc .... B....... 916 773-7227
  3850 Atherton Rd Rocklin (95765) *(P-17177)*

American Hlthcare Systems Corp (PA) .... B....... 818 646-9933
  505 N Brand Blvd Ste 1110 Glendale (91203) *(P-15941)*

American Honda, Torrance *Also Called: American Honda Motor Co Inc (P-5004)*

AMERICAN HONDA, Torrance *Also Called: American Honda Finance Corp (P-7869)*

American Honda Finance Corp (DH) .... C....... 310 972-2239
  1919 Torrance Blvd Torrance (90501) *(P-7869)*

American Honda Motor Co Inc (HQ) .... A....... 310 783-2000
  1919 Torrance Blvd Torrance (90501) *(P-5004)*

American Hospital Mgt Corp (PA) .... B....... 707 822-3621
  3800 Janes Rd Arcata (95521) *(P-15942)*

American Incorporated (PA) .... C....... 559 651-1776
  1345 N American St Visalia (93291) *(P-864)*

American Industrial Partners LP .... A....... 415 788-7354
  1 Maritime Plz Ste 1925 San Francisco (94111) *(P-2788)*

American Industrial Source Inc .... D....... 800 661-0622
  15759 Strathern St Ste 1 Van Nuys (91406) *(P-5889)*

American International Inds, Commerce *Also Called: Glamour Industries Co (P-6109)*

American Internet Mortgage Inc .... C....... 888 411-4246
  4121 Camino Del Rio S Ste 200 San Diego (92108) *(P-7928)*

American Intgrted Rsources Inc .... D....... 714 921-4100
  2341 N Pacific St Orange (92865) *(P-20020)*

American Justice Solutions Inc .... D....... 949 369-6210
  25910 Acero Ste 100 Mission Viejo (92691) *(P-17800)*

American Kal Enterprises Inc (PA) .... D....... 626 338-7308
  4265 Puente Ave Baldwin Park (91706) *(P-5720)*

American Koyu Corporation .... C....... 626 793-0669
  1733 S Anaheim Blvd Anaheim (92805) *(P-9604)*

American Landscape Inc .... C....... 818 999-2041
  7013 Owensmouth Ave Canoga Park (91303) *(P-386)*

American Landscape MGT Inc (PA) .... C....... 818 999-2041
  7013 Owensmouth Ave Canoga Park (91303) *(P-387)*

American Landscape MGT Inc .... D....... 805 647-5077
  1607 Los Angeles Ave Ste I Ventura (93004) *(P-473)*

American Legal Copy - Oc LLC .... D....... 415 777-4449
  655 W Broadway Ste 200 San Diego (92101) *(P-10782)*

AMERICAN LEGION HALL, Jackson *Also Called: American Lgion Post No 108 Amb (P-18812)*

American Lgion Post No 108 Amb .... D....... 209 223-2963
  11350 American Legion Dr Jackson (95642) *(P-18812)*

American Management Svcs W LLC .... C....... 805 352-1921
  1240 Bethel Ln Santa Maria (93458) *(P-20021)*

American Marketing Systems Inc .... D....... 800 747-7784
  2800 Van Ness Ave San Francisco (94109) *(P-8900)*

American Med Rspnse Amblnce Sv (DH) .... D....... 303 495-1217
  879 Marlborough Ave Riverside (92507) *(P-3228)*

American Med Rspnse Inland Emp .... A....... 530 241-2686
  4451 Caterpillar Rd Ste 1 Redding (96003) *(P-3229)*

American Med Rspnse Inland Emp .... A....... 831 423-7030
  116 Hubbard St Santa Cruz (95060) *(P-3230)*

American Med Rspnse Inland Emp (HQ) .... D....... 951 782-5200
  879 Marlborough Ave Riverside (92507) *(P-3231)*

American Medical Response, Palm Springs *Also Called: American Medical Response Inc (P-3232)*

American Medical Response Inc .... C....... 760 883-5000
  1111 Montalvo Way Palm Springs (92262) *(P-3232)*

American Medical Response Inc .... C....... 415 794-9204
  13992 Catalina St San Leandro (94577) *(P-3233)*

American Medical Tech Inc .... D....... 949 553-0359
  17595 Cartwright Rd Irvine (92614) *(P-5397)*

American Mobile Healthcare, San Diego *Also Called: Amn Healthcare Inc (P-11081)*

American Modular Systems Inc .... D....... 209 825-1921
  787 Spreckels Ave Manteca (95336) *(P-2485)*

American Mortgage Network, Chula Vista *Also Called: Amnet Esop Corporation (P-7931)*

American Multimedia TV USA .... D....... 626 466-1038
  530 S Lake Ave Unit 368 Pasadena (91101) *(P-4411)*

American Mutual Fund .... C....... 213 486-9200
  333 S Hope St Fl 51 Los Angeles (90071) *(P-9353)*

American Mzhou Dngpo Group Inc .... D....... 626 820-9239
  4520 Maine Ave Baldwin Park (91706) *(P-20022)*

American Nat Red Cross - Blood, Stockton *Also Called: Delta Blood Bank LLC (P-17221)*

American Nat Red Cross - Blood, Oakland *Also Called: American National Red Cross (P-17830)*

American Nat Red Crss-Blood Sv, Pomona *Also Called: American National Red Cross (P-17831)*

American National Red Cross .... D....... 510 594-5100
  6230 Claremont Ave Oakland (94618) *(P-17830)*

American National Red Cross .... C....... 909 859-7006
  100 Red Cross Cir Pomona (91768) *(P-17831)*

American National Red Cross .... A....... 310 445-9900
  1450 S Central Ave Los Angeles (90021) *(P-17832)*

American Nuts LLC .... C....... 818 364-8855
  12950 San Fernando Rd Sylmar (91342) *(P-6453)*

American Pacific Mortgage Corp (PA) .... C....... 916 960-1325
  3000 Lava Ridge Ct Ste 200 Roseville (95661) *(P-7929)*

American Paper & Plastics LLC .... C....... 626 444-0000
  550 S 7th Ave City Of Industry (91746) *(P-6888)*

American Paper & Provisions, City Of Industry *Also Called: American Paper & Plastics LLC (P-6888)*

American Peptide Company Inc .... D....... 408 733-7604
  1271 Avenida Chelsea Vista (92081) *(P-2618)*

American Plumbing Contractors, Orange *Also Called: American Contractors Inc (P-1353)*

American Portwell Tech Inc (PA) .... D....... 510 403-3399
  44200 Christy St Fremont (94538) *(P-5271)*

American Power SEC Svc Inc .... D....... 866 974-9994
  1451 Rimpau Ave Ste 207 Corona (92879) *(P-12927)*

American Private Duty Inc .... D....... 818 386-6358
  13111 Ventura Blvd Ste 100 Studio City (91604) *(P-16806)*

American Prof Ambulance Corp .... D....... 818 996-2200
  16945 Sherman Way Van Nuys (91406) *(P-3234)*

American Property Management .... C....... 925 463-8000
  7050 Johnson Dr Pleasanton (94588) *(P-9605)*

American Protection Group Inc (PA) .... C....... 818 279-2433
  8741 Van Nuys Blvd Ste 202 Panorama City (91402) *(P-12928)*

American Prprty-Mnagement Corp .... A....... 619 232-3121
  326 Broadway San Diego (92101) *(P-9606)*

American Prtctive Svcs Invstgt .... C....... 626 705-8600
  12471 Balsam Rd Victorville (92395) *(P-12929)*

American Rag Compagnie .... D....... 323 935-3154
  150 S La Brea Ave Los Angeles (90036) *(P-7403)*

American Ready Mix, Escondido *Also Called: Superior Ready Mix Concrete LP (P-2713)*

American Recovery Service, El Dorado Hills *Also Called: Patrick K Willis and Co Inc (P-13421)*

American Recovery Service Inc   **ALPHABETIC SECTION**

American Recovery Service Inc (DH)... C....... 805 379-8500
   555 Saint Charles Dr Ste 100 Thousand Oaks (91360) *(P-10734)*

American Red Cross, Los Angeles *Also Called: American Red Cross Los Angles (P-17833)*

American Red Cross, San Diego *Also Called: American Red Cross San Dg-Mpri (P-17834)*

American Red Cross Los Angles (PA).. C....... 310 445-9900
   1320 Newton St Los Angeles (90021) *(P-17833)*

American Red Cross San Dg-Mpri (PA)... D....... 858 309-1200
   3950 Calle Fortunada San Diego (92123) *(P-17834)*

American Restoration Services, Hayward *Also Called: ATI Restoration LLC (P-2258)*

American Retirement Corp .... C....... 310 399-3227
   2107 Ocean Ave Santa Monica (90405) *(P-15324)*

American River Packaging, Madera *Also Called: Pk1 Inc (P-2522)*

American Rsdntial Svcs Ind Inc .... B....... 650 409-1986
   24800 Industrial Blvd Hayward (94545) *(P-1354)*

American Rver Care Rhblttion C, Carmichael *Also Called: Sunbrdge Brttany Rhblttion Ctr (P-15686)*

American Sanitary Supply Inc .... D....... 714 632-3010
   3800 E Miraloma Ave Anaheim (92806) *(P-5935)*

American Scaffold Inc (PA)... D....... 619 231-4898
   3210 Commercial St San Diego (92113) *(P-2245)*

American Security Bank .... D....... 949 440-5200
   1401 Dove St Ste 100 Newport Beach (92660) *(P-7653)*

American Security Products Co .... C....... 951 685-9680
   11925 Pacific Ave Fontana (92337) *(P-2765)*

American Solar Direct Inc .... C....... 424 214-6700
   11766 Wilshire Blvd Ste 500 Los Angeles (90025) *(P-1664)*

American Spclty Hlth Group Inc .... B....... 858 754-2000
   10221 Wateridge Cir Ste 201 San Diego (92121) *(P-8279)*

American Spclty Hlth Plans Cal .... B....... 619 297-8100
   10221 Wateridge Cir San Diego (92121) *(P-8487)*

American States Water Company (PA)... A....... 909 394-3600
   630 E Foothill Blvd San Dimas (91773) *(P-4764)*

American Suzuki Motor Corporation .... C....... 714 996-7040
   3251 E Imperial Hwy Brea (92821) *(P-7169)*

American Technical Svcs Inc .... D....... 951 372-9664
   20384 Via Mantua Porter Ranch (91326) *(P-19140)*

American Textile Maint Co .... D....... 562 438-7656
   3001 E Anaheim St Long Beach (90804) *(P-10426)*

American Textile Maint Co .... D....... 562 438-1126
   3001 E Anaheim St Long Beach (90804) *(P-10427)*

American Textile Maint Co .... C....... 323 735-1661
   1664 W Washington Blvd Los Angeles (90007) *(P-10428)*

American Textile Maint Co .... D....... 213 749-4433
   1705 Hooper Ave Los Angeles (90021) *(P-10429)*

American Textile Maint Co .... D....... 562 424-1607
   2201 E Carson St Long Beach (90807) *(P-10476)*

American Tire Depot, Vernon *Also Called: Atv Canter LLC (P-7342)*

American Tooth Industries .... D....... 805 487-9868
   1200 Stellar Dr Oxnard (93033) *(P-5398)*

American Trading Intl Inc .... D....... 310 445-2000
   10780 Santa Monica Blvd Ste 370 Los Angeles (90025) *(P-6454)*

American Transportation Co LLC .... D....... 818 660-2343
   635 W Colorado St Ste 108a Glendale (91204) *(P-4144)*

American Travel Solutions LLC (PA).. D....... 818 359-6514
   27509 Agoura Rd Ste 100 Agoura Hills (91301) *(P-3927)*

American Two-Way, North Hollywood *Also Called: Emergency Technologies Inc (P-13112)*

American Untd HM Care Crp-Priv, Studio City *Also Called: American Private Duty Inc (P-16806)*

American Vision Baths, Simi Valley *Also Called: American Vision Windows Inc (P-13762)*

American Vision Windows Inc .... C....... 805 582-1833
   2125 N Madera Rd Ste A Simi Valley (93065) *(P-13762)*

American West Worldwide Ex Inc (PA).. D....... 800 788-4534
   51 Zaca Ln Ste 120 San Luis Obispo (93401) *(P-3579)*

American Wholesale Ltg Inc .... D....... 510 252-1088
   1725 Rutan Dr Livermore (94551) *(P-5536)*

American Wrecking Inc .... D....... 626 350-8303
   2459 Lee Ave South El Monte (91733) *(P-2229)*

American-Way Services Corp .... C....... 408 223-8912
   110 N Bascom Ave San Jose (95128) *(P-15325)*

Americantours Intl LLC (HQ)... C....... 310 641-9953
   6053 W Century Blvd Ste 700 Los Angeles (90045) *(P-3928)*

Americare Ambulance .... C....... 760 739-9723
   10730 Thornmint Rd San Diego (92127) *(P-3235)*

AMERICARE AMBULANCE, San Diego *Also Called: Americare Ambulance (P-3235)*

Americare Ambulance Service, Huntington Beach *Also Called: Americare Medservices Inc (P-3236)*

Americare Hlth Retirement Inc .... C....... 760 744-4484
   1550 Security Pl Ofc San Marcos (92078) *(P-8701)*

Americare Home Health Inc .... D....... 818 881-0005
   16501 Sherman Way Ste 225 Van Nuys (91406) *(P-16807)*

Americare Medservices Inc .... D....... 310 632-1141
   6524 Fremont Cir Huntington Beach (92648) *(P-3236)*

Americas Christian Credit Un (PA)... D....... 626 208-5400
   2100 E Route 66 Ste 100 Glendora (91740) *(P-7754)*

Americas Finest Carpet Company, Chula Vista *Also Called: Home Carpet Investment Inc (P-2034)*

Americas Printer.com, Buena Park *Also Called: A J Parent Company Inc (P-13168)*

Americold Logistics LLC .... C....... 909 937-2200
   5401 Santa Ana St Ontario (91761) *(P-3651)*

Americold Logistics LLC .... D....... 909 390-4950
   700 Malaga St Ontario (91761) *(P-3652)*

Americold Realty, Ontario *Also Called: Americold Logistics LLC (P-3652)*

Americor Funding Inc .... C....... 866 333-8686
   18200 Von Karman Ave Ste 600 Irvine (92612) *(P-10529)*

Americore, Hilmar *Also Called: Americore Inc (P-3048)*

Americore Inc .... D....... 209 632-5679
   19705 August Ave Hilmar (95324) *(P-3048)*

Ameriflight LLC .... C....... 818 847-0000
   4700 W Empire Ave Burbank (91505) *(P-3831)*

Amerihome Inc .... A....... 888 469-0810
   1 Baxter Way Ste 300 Westlake Village (91362) *(P-7930)*

Amerihome Mortgage, Westlake Village *Also Called: Amerihome Mortgage Company LLC (P-8065)*

Amerihome Mortgage Company LLC .... A....... 888 469-0810
   1 Baxter Way Ste 300 Westlake Village (91362) *(P-8065)*

Ameriko Inc (PA)... D....... 626 795-7988
   980 S Arroyo Pkwy Ste 240 Pasadena (91105) *(P-20647)*

Ameriko Industries, Pasadena *Also Called: Ameriko Inc (P-20647)*

Ameripark LLC .... B....... 949 279-7525
   17165 Von Karman Ave Ste 110 Irvine (92614) *(P-13603)*

Ameripride Services Inc .... C....... 323 587-3941
   5950 Alcoa Ave Vernon (90058) *(P-10430)*

Ameripride Services Inc .... C....... 916 689-1111
   7620 Wilbur Way Sacramento (95828) *(P-10431)*

Ameripride Services Inc .... C....... 559 266-0627
   1050 W Whites Bridge Ave Fresno (93706) *(P-10477)*

AMERIPRIDE SERVICES, INC., Vernon *Also Called: Ameripride Services Inc (P-10430)*

AMERIPRIDE SERVICES, INC., Sacramento *Also Called: Ameripride Services Inc (P-10431)*

Ameripride Uniform Services, Fresno *Also Called: Ameripride Services Inc (P-10477)*

Amerisourcebergen Drug Corp .... C....... 951 371-2000
   1851 California Ave Corona (92881) *(P-6094)*

Amerisourcebergen Drug Corp .... C....... 916 830-4500
   1325 W Striker Ave Sacramento (95834) *(P-6095)*

Amerit Fleet Solutions Inc .... A....... 909 357-0100
   15325 Manila St Fontana (92337) *(P-13708)*

Amerit Fleet Solutions Inc (HQ)... D....... 877 512-6374
   1333 N California Blvd Walnut Creek (94596) *(P-13709)*

Amerit Fleet Solutions Inc .... C....... 877 512-6374
   1331 N Calif Blvd Ste 150 Walnut Creek (94596) *(P-20648)*

Ameritac Inc (PA).. D....... 925 989-2942
   24 Toscana Way W Rancho Mirage (92270) *(P-20649)*

Ames Construction Inc .... B....... 951 356-1275
   391 N Main St Ste 302 Corona (92878) *(P-7419)*

Ametek Intellipower, Orange *Also Called: Intellipower Inc (P-5664)*

Ametek-Ameron, Baldwin Park *Also Called: Alphatech General Inc (P-13761)*

AMF Media Group, San Ramon *Also Called: Armanino LLP (P-19533)*

AMG Construction Group .... D....... 800 310-2609
   1103 W Gardena Blvd Unit 201 Gardena (90248) *(P-1076)*

AMG Data Services .... D....... 707 822-4888
   5440 Ericson Way Ste B Arcata (95521) *(P-12550)*

AMI Manufacturing, Sacramento *Also Called: Airco Mechanical Inc (P-1343)*

ALPHABETIC SECTION

AMI-Hti Trzana Encino Jint Vnt .... D....... 818 881-0800
   18321 Clark St Tarzana (91356) *(P-15943)*

Amigo Baby Inc .... D....... 805 901-1237
   1901 N Rice Ave Ste 325 Oxnard (93030) *(P-17835)*

Aminco International USA Inc .... D....... 949 457-3261
   20571 Crescent Bay Dr Lake Forest (92630) *(P-3086)*

Amisub, Tarzana *Also Called: Amisub of California Inc (P-15944)*

Amisub of California Inc (DH) .... A....... 818 881-0800
   18321 Clark St Tarzana (91356) *(P-15944)*

Amity Foundation, Los Angeles *Also Called: Epidaurus (P-9425)*

Amk Foodservices Inc .... C....... 805 544-7600
   830 Capitolio Way San Luis Obispo (93401) *(P-6239)*

Amko Service Company .... D....... 760 246-3600
   17909 Adelanto Rd Adelanto (92301) *(P-13763)*

Amkotron Inc (PA) .... D....... 562 921-3330
   16220 Bloomfield Ave Cerritos (90703) *(P-12702)*

Amn Healthcare Inc (HQ) .... B....... 858 792-0711
   12400 High Bluff Dr Ste 100 San Diego (92130) *(P-14611)*

Amn Healthcare Inc .... D....... 800 282-0300
   12235 El Camino Real Ste 200 San Diego (92130) *(P-11081)*

Amnet Esop Corporation .... C....... 877 354-1110
   347 Third Ave Fl 2 Chula Vista (91910) *(P-7931)*

Amnet Mortgage LLC .... A....... 858 909-1200
   10421 Wateridge Cir Ste 250 San Diego (92121) *(P-7932)*

AMP Technologies LLC .... C....... 877 442-2824
   445 Melrose Ct San Ramon (94582) *(P-11403)*

Ampam Parks Mechanical Inc .... A....... 310 835-1532
   17036 Avalon Blvd Carson (90746) *(P-1355)*

Ampco Airport Parking, Los Angeles *Also Called: ABM Parking Services Inc (P-13600)*

Ampco Contracting Inc .... C....... 949 955-2255
   17991 Cowan Irvine (92614) *(P-4974)*

Ampla Health (PA) .... C....... 530 674-4261
   935 Market St Yuba City (95991) *(P-15216)*

Ample Inc (PA) .... D....... 617 504-3557
   100 Hooper St Ste 25 San Francisco (94107) *(P-13191)*

Amplitude Inc (PA) .... D....... 650 988-5131
   201 3rd St Ste 200 San Francisco (94103) *(P-11404)*

Amplitude Analytics, San Francisco *Also Called: Amplitude Inc (P-11404)*

Amplus Group .... D....... 424 316-5913
   400 Crenshaw Blvd Ste 200 Torrance (90503) *(P-20688)*

Ampm Systems Inc .... D....... 949 629-7800
   16520 Harbor Blvd Fountain Valley (92708) *(P-20272)*

Ampronix LLC .... D....... 949 273-8000
   15 Whatney Irvine (92618) *(P-3071)*

Ampush Media Inc .... D....... 415 638-9663
   450 9th St Fl 2 San Francisco (94103) *(P-20273)*

AMR, Fullerton *Also Called: Dorean Enterprises Inc (P-10610)*

Amro Fabricating Corporation (PA) .... C....... 626 579-2200
   1430 Amro Way South El Monte (91733) *(P-2989)*

Amron, Vista *Also Called: Amron International Inc (P-3091)*

Amron International Inc (PA) .... D....... 760 208-6500
   1380 Aspen Way Vista (92081) *(P-3091)*

AMS, Manteca *Also Called: American Modular Systems Inc (P-2485)*

AMS, Anaheim *Also Called: Walnut Investment Corp (P-5193)*

AMS, San Diego *Also Called: Asset Mktg Systems Insur Svcs (P-20283)*

AMS American Mech Svcs MD Inc .... C....... 714 888-6820
   2116 E Walnut Ave Fullerton (92831) *(P-1356)*

AMS Electric Inc .... D....... 925 961-1600
   6905 Sierra Ct Ste A Dublin (94568) *(P-1665)*

AMS Fulfillment, Valencia *Also Called: Advantage Media Services Inc (P-4124)*

AMS Fulfillment, Valencia *Also Called: Advantage Media Services Inc (P-3671)*

AMS Ventures Inc .... D....... 301 980-5087
   39055 Hastings St Ste 205 Fremont (94538) *(P-20274)*

Amsec, Fontana *Also Called: American Security Products Co (P-2765)*

Amsi Real Estate Services, San Francisco *Also Called: American Marketing Systems Inc (P-8900)*

Amsurg, Glendale *Also Called: Glendale Eye Medical Group (P-14762)*

Amsurg, Colton *Also Called: Premier Otptent Srgery Ctr Inc (P-14998)*

Amtech Elevator Services, Los Angeles *Also Called: Pacific Coast Elevator Corp (P-13790)*

Amtex Supply Holdings Inc .... C....... 909 985-8918
   736 Inland Center Dr San Bernardino (92408) *(P-20275)*

Amtrav, Agoura Hills *Also Called: American Travel Solutions LLC (P-3927)*

Amtrend Corporation .... D....... 714 630-2070
   1458 Manhattan Ave Fullerton (92831) *(P-2499)*

Amtv USA, Pasadena *Also Called: American Multimedia TV USA (P-4411)*

Amwest Funding Corp .... C....... 714 831-3333
   6 Pointe Dr Ste 300 Brea (92821) *(P-7890)*

Amwins Brkg Wash Henrico Co, Woodland Hills *Also Called: Amwins Insurance Brkg Cal LLC (P-8489)*

Amwins Connect Insur Svcs LLC .... D....... 714 460-5153
   2677 N Main St Ste 800 Santa Ana (92705) *(P-8471)*

Amwins Connect Insur Svcs LLC (PA) .... D....... 650 348-4131
   1600 W Hillsdale Blvd Ste 201 San Mateo (94402) *(P-8488)*

Amwins Insurance Brkg Cal LLC (HQ) .... D....... 818 772-1774
   21550 Oxnard St Ste 1100 Woodland Hills (91367) *(P-8489)*

An Open Check, Costa Mesa *Also Called: North American Acceptance Corp (P-7882)*

Ana Nacapa Surgical Associates, Ventura *Also Called: Ventura County Medical Center (P-15183)*

Anabella Hotel The, Anaheim *Also Called: Fjs Inc (P-9798)*

Anabelle Hotel Inc .... D....... 818 845-7800
   2011 W Olive Ave Burbank (91506) *(P-9607)*

Anaheim - 1855 S Hbr Blvd Owne .... D....... 714 750-1811
   1855 S Harbor Blvd Anaheim (92802) *(P-9608)*

Anaheim Arena, Anaheim *Also Called: City of Anaheim (P-8709)*

Anaheim Arena Management LLC .... A....... 714 704-2400
   2695 E Katella Ave Anaheim (92806) *(P-14123)*

Anaheim Ca LLC .... D....... 714 634-4500
   100 The City Dr S Orange (92868) *(P-9609)*

Anaheim Ducks, Corona Del Mar *Also Called: Anaheim Ducks Hockey Club LLC (P-14124)*

Anaheim Ducks Hockey Club LLC .... D....... 714 940-2900
   2101 E Coast Hwy Fl 3 Corona Del Mar (92625) *(P-14124)*

Anaheim Ducks Hockey Club LLC (PA) .... D....... 714 940-2900
   2695 E Katella Ave Anaheim (92806) *(P-14125)*

Anaheim Global Medical Center .... A....... 714 533-6220
   1025 S Anaheim Blvd Anaheim (92805) *(P-15945)*

Anaheim Healthcare Center, Anaheim *Also Called: Anaheim Healthcare Center LLC (P-15326)*

Anaheim Healthcare Center LLC .... D....... 714 816-0540
   501 S Beach Blvd Anaheim (92804) *(P-15326)*

Anaheim Hills Auto Body Inc .... D....... 714 632-8266
   3500 E La Palma Ave Anaheim (92806) *(P-13631)*

Anaheim Hotel, The, Anaheim *Also Called: Anaheim Plaza Hotel Inc (P-9611)*

Anaheim Ice .... D....... 714 535-7465
   300 W Lincoln Ave Anaheim (92805) *(P-14489)*

Anaheim Inn, Anaheim *Also Called: Best Western Stovalls Inn (P-9645)*

Anaheim Majestic Garden Hotel, Anaheim *Also Called: Ken Real Estate Lease Ltd (P-9937)*

Anaheim Park Hotel .... C....... 714 992-1700
   222 W Houston Ave Fullerton (92832) *(P-9610)*

Anaheim Plaza Hotel Inc .... D....... 714 772-5900
   1700 S Harbor Blvd Anaheim (92802) *(P-9611)*

Anaheim Regional Medical Ctr .... C....... 714 774-1450
   1111 W La Palma Ave Anaheim (92801) *(P-15946)*

Anaheim Regional Medical Ctr .... D....... 714 999-3847
   1211 W La Palma Ave Anaheim (92801) *(P-15947)*

Anaheim Regional Medical Ctr, Anaheim *Also Called: Ahmc Anheim Rgional Med Ctr LP (P-15930)*

Anaheim Urgent Care Inc .... D....... 714 533-2273
   831 S State College Blvd Anaheim (92806) *(P-14612)*

Analysts Inc .... C....... 800 424-0099
   3401 Jack Northrop Ave Hawthorne (90250) *(P-19947)*

Analysts Maintenance and Labs, Hawthorne *Also Called: Analysts Inc (P-19947)*

Analytical Pace Services LLC .... C....... 800 878-4911
   4100 Atlas Ct Bakersfield (93308) *(P-19948)*

Anaplan, San Francisco *Also Called: Anaplan Inc (P-12731)*

Anaplan Inc (PA) .... B....... 415 742-8199
   50 Hawthorne St San Francisco (94105) *(P-12731)*

ANBERRY REHABILITATION HOSPITA, Atwater *Also Called: Tjd LLC (P-15903)*

Anberry Transitional Care LLC .... C....... 209 357-3420
   1000 W Yosemite Ave Merced (95348) *(P-15327)*

Anc Technology Inc .... D....... 805 530-3958
   10195 Stockton Rd Moorpark (93021) *(P-2905)*

Ancca Corporation   ALPHABETIC SECTION

Ancca Corporation .... D...... 949 553-0084
   7 Goddard Irvine (92618) *(P-1905)*

Ancestry.com, San Francisco *Also Called: Ancestrycom LLC (P-12651)*

Ancestrycom LLC .... B...... 415 795-6000
   153 Townsend St Ste 800 San Francisco (94107) *(P-12651)*

Anchor Blue, Corona *Also Called: Hub Distributing Inc (P-7402)*

Anchor Cnsling Edcatn Sltons L .... D...... 213 505-6322
   19200 Von Karman Ave Ste 600 Irvine (92612) *(P-20689)*

Anchor General Insur Agcy Inc .... C...... 858 527-3600
   10256 Meanley Dr San Diego (92131) *(P-8490)*

Anchor Loans LP .... C...... 310 395-0010
   1 Baxter Way # 220 Westlake Village (91362) *(P-7933)*

Anchor Nationwide Loans, Westlake Village *Also Called: Anchor Loans LP (P-7933)*

Ancon Marine LLC .... C...... 562 326-5900
   2735 Rose Ave Signal Hill (90755) *(P-3367)*

Ancon Services, Signal Hill *Also Called: Ancon Marine LLC (P-3367)* and 1, Aliso Viejo *Also Called: Basketball Marketing Co Inc (P-20291)*

Andari, El Monte *Also Called: Andari Fashion Inc (P-2453)*

Andari Fashion Inc .... C...... 626 575-2759
   9626 Telstar Ave El Monte (91731) *(P-2453)*

Andatha International Inc C
   611 Mission St Fl 4 San Francisco (94105) *(P-17364)*

Andaz Sandiego, San Diego *Also Called: Hyatt Corporation (P-9898)*

Andaz West Hollywood .... D...... 323 656-1234
   8401 W Sunset Blvd Los Angeles (90069) *(P-9612)*

Andersen, Vina *Also Called: Andersen & Sons Shelling Inc (P-254)*

Andersen & Sons Shelling Inc .... D...... 530 839-2236
   4530 Rowles Rd Vina (96092) *(P-254)*

Andersen Commercial Plbg Inc .... C...... 909 599-5950
   1608 Yeager Ave La Verne (91750) *(P-1357)*

Andersen Tax LLC .... C...... 213 593-2300
   400 S Hope St Ste 2000 Los Angeles (90071) *(P-10519)*

Anderson, Poway *Also Called: T G T Enterprises Inc (P-20576)*

Anderson Rowe & Buckley Inc .... C...... 415 282-1625
   2833 3rd St San Francisco (94107) *(P-1358)*

Anderson & Howard Electric Inc .... C...... 949 250-4555
   15 Chrysler Irvine (92618) *(P-1666)*

Anderson Air Conditioning LP .... D...... 714 998-6850
   2100 E Walnut Ave Fullerton (92831) *(P-1359)*

Anderson Assoc Staffing Corp (PA) .... C...... 323 930-3170
   8200 Wilshire Blvd Ste 200 Beverly Hills (90211) *(P-11272)*

Anderson Burton Cnstr Inc (PA) .... D...... 805 481-5096
   121 Nevada St Arroyo Grande (93420) *(P-865)*

Anderson Howard, Irvine *Also Called: Anderson & Howard Electric Inc (P-1666)*

Anderson Kayne Capital .... B...... 800 231-7414
   1800 Avenue Of The Stars Ste 200 # 3rd Los Angeles (90067) *(P-8186)*

Anderson Logging Inc .... D...... 707 964-2770
   1296 N Main St Fort Bragg (95437) *(P-2473)*

Anderson PCF Engrg Cnstr Inc .... D...... 408 970-9900
   1370 Norman Ave Santa Clara (95054) *(P-1285)*

Anderson Physical Therapy Inc .... D...... 530 265-8100
   202 Providence Mine Rd Ste 206 Nevada City (95959) *(P-15268)*

Anderson Plbg Htg A Condition, El Cajon *Also Called: Walter Anderson Plumbing Inc (P-1594)*

Anderson Systems Inc .... D...... 805 683-6133
   5958 Corta St Goleta (93117) *(P-1360)*

Andpak Inc .... D...... 408 776-1072
   400 Jarvis Dr Ste A Morgan Hill (95037) *(P-13192)*

Andreessen Horowitz, Menlo Park *Also Called: Ah Capital Management LLC (P-8064)*

Andressen Hrwtz Lsv Fund II L .... A...... 650 798-5800
   2865 Sand Hill Rd Menlo Park (94025) *(P-20276)*

Andrew Chekene Enterprises Inc .... C...... 650 588-1001
   21965 Meekland Ave Hayward (94541) *(P-654)*

Andrew L Youngquist Cnstr Inc .... D...... 949 862-5611
   3187 Red Hill Ave Ste 200 Costa Mesa (92626) *(P-866)*

Andrew Lauren Company Inc .... C...... 949 861-4222
   15225 Alton Pkwy Unit 300 Irvine (92618) *(P-13193)*

Andrew M Jordan Inc .... D...... 510 999-6000
   225 3rd St Oakland (94607) *(P-2212)*

Andrews International Inc .... B...... 310 575-4844
   11601 Wilshire Blvd Ste 500 Los Angeles (90025) *(P-12930)*

Andrews International Inc (DH) .... A...... 818 487-4060
   455 N Moss St Burbank (91502) *(P-12931)*

Andwin Corporation (PA) .... D...... 818 999-2828
   167 W Cochran St Simi Valley (93065) *(P-6073)*

Andwin Scientific, Simi Valley *Also Called: Andwin Corporation (P-6073)*

Andy Anand Chocolates, Chino *Also Called: Hira Paris Inc (P-2375)*

Anemostat Products, Carson *Also Called: Mestek Inc (P-2843)*

Anesthsia Med Group Snta Brbar .... D...... 805 682-7751
   514 W Pueblo St Fl 2 Santa Barbara (93105) *(P-14613)*

Anesthsia Med Group Snta Brbar, Santa Barbara *Also Called: Anesthsia Med Group Snta Brbar (P-14613)*

Anfinson Lumber Sales Inc (PA) .... D...... 951 681-4707
   13041 Union Ave Fontana (92337) *(P-5146)*

Angaza Design Inc (PA) .... D...... 415 993-5595
   315 Montgomery St Fl 10 San Francisco (94104) *(P-11405)*

Angel Island Co, Red Bluff *Also Called: Concessionaires Urban Park (P-14507)*

Angeles Mesa YWCA Chldren Lrng, Los Angeles *Also Called: Young Wns Chrstn Assn Grter Lo (P-19008)*

Angelo Kilday & Kilduff .... C...... 916 564-6100
   601 University Ave Ste 150 Sacramento (95825) *(P-17365)*

Angels Baseball LP (PA) .... A...... 714 940-2000
   2000 E Gene Autry Way Anaheim (92806) *(P-14126)*

Angels In Motion LLC .... D...... 909 590-9102
   13768 Roswell Ave Chino (91710) *(P-16808)*

Anglepoint Group Inc (PA) .... C...... 855 512-6453
   2261 Market St Pmb 4723 San Francisco (94114) *(P-20023)*

Anheuser-Busch, Rocklin *Also Called: Bi Warehousing Inc (P-7344)*

Anheuser-Busch, Van Nuys *Also Called: Anheuser-Busch LLC (P-13194)*

Anheuser-Busch LLC .... B...... 805 381-4700
   15800 Roscoe Blvd Van Nuys (91406) *(P-13194)*

Anil Garde M.D., Riverside *Also Called: Riverside Medical Clinic Inc (P-15025)*

Animal Care & Control, Gardena *Also Called: County of Los Angeles (P-331)*

Animal Care & Control, Baldwin Park *Also Called: County of Los Angeles (P-332)*

Animal Care & Control, Castaic *Also Called: County of Los Angeles (P-361)*

Animal Care Services, Marysville *Also Called: County of Yuba (P-333)*

Animal Rescue Squad Intl II .... A...... 530 761-6008
   5122 Hamel St Davis (95618) *(P-325)*

Animal Specialty Group .... D...... 818 244-7977
   4641 Colorado Blvd Los Angeles (90039) *(P-326)*

Animal Specialty Group, San Diego *Also Called: VCA Animal Hospitals Inc (P-347)*

Animoto LLC .... D...... 415 987-3139
   333 Kearny St Fl 6 San Francisco (94108) *(P-11406)*

Animus Inc .... C...... 650 969-8555
   2460 W El Camino Real Mountain View (94040) *(P-327)*

Anita Borg Inst For Women Tech .... D...... 650 236-4756
   1650 S Amphlett Blvd Ste 110 San Mateo (94402) *(P-19034)*

Anitsa Inc .... C...... 213 237-0533
   6032 Shull St Bell Gardens (90201) *(P-10423)*

Anixter Inc .... D...... 800 854-2088
   7140 Opportunity Rd San Diego (92111) *(P-5537)*

Anjana Software Solutions Inc .... D...... 805 583-0121
   1445 E Los Angeles Ave Ste 305 Simi Valley (93065) *(P-11407)*

Anka Behavioral Health Incorporated .... A...... 925 825-4700
   3840 Buskirk Ave., Suite 300 Pleasant Hill (94523) *(P-17004)*

Ankura Consulting Group LLC .... C...... 213 223-2109
   633 W 5th St Fl 28 Los Angeles (90071) *(P-20690)*

Annabelles Bar & Bistro, San Francisco *Also Called: Mosser Vctrian Ht Arts Mus Inc (P-7497)*

Annandale Golf Club .... C...... 626 796-6125
   1 N San Rafael Ave Pasadena (91105) *(P-14324)*

Annapurna Pictures LLC .... D...... 310 385-7701
   817 Hilldale Ave West Hollywood (90069) *(P-13925)*

Annas Linens, Costa Mesa *Also Called: Annas Linens Inc (P-7434)*

Annas Linens Inc .... A...... 714 850-0504
   3550 Hyland Ave Costa Mesa (92626) *(P-7434)*

Annie Golf Club, Goleta *Also Called: Glen Annie Golf Club (P-14263)*

Annies Homegrown Inc .... D...... 510 558-7500
   1610 5th St Berkeley (94710) *(P-6600)*

Anning-Johnson Company .... C...... 510 670-0100
   22955 Kidder St Hayward (94545) *(P-1906)*

Anomali Incorporated .... C...... 844 484-7328
   808 Winslow St Redwood City (94063) *(P-13095)*

ALPHABETIC SECTION — Apigee Corporation

Anonymous Content LLC (PA)...D....... 310 558-6000
 8501 Washington Blvd Culver City (90232) *(P-13818)*
Anova Edcatn Behavioral Cnsltn ....D....... 707 527-0183
 3033 Cleveland Ave Ste 240 Santa Rosa (95403) *(P-18730)*
ANOVA EDUCATION & BEHAVIORAL CONSULTATION INC, Santa Rosa Also Called: Anova Edcatn Behavioral Cnsltn *(P-18730)*
Anre Tech, Altadena Also Called: Anre Technologies Inc *(P-11408)*
Anre Technologies Inc ....C....... 818 627-5433
 741 W Woodbury Rd Altadena (91001) *(P-11408)*
Anritsu Americas Sales Company ....A....... 408 778-2000
 490 Jarvis Dr Morgan Hill (95037) *(P-5819)*
Anritsu Company, Morgan Hill Also Called: Anritsu US Holding Inc *(P-3023)*
Anritsu US Holding Inc (HQ)..B....... 408 778-2000
 490 Jarvis Dr Morgan Hill (95037) *(P-3023)*
Ansar Gallery Inc ....C....... 949 220-0000
 2505 El Camino Rd Tustin (92782) *(P-6240)*
Anschutz Entrmt Group Inc (HQ)...C....... 213 763-7700
 800 W Olympic Blvd Ste 305 Los Angeles (90015) *(P-14076)*
Anschutz Sthern Cal Spt Cmplex ....C....... 310 630-2000
 18400 Avalon Blvd Ste 100 Carson (90746) *(P-14490)*
Answer Financial Inc (HQ)..C....... 818 644-4000
 15910 Ventura Blvd Fl 6 Encino (91436) *(P-13195)*
Antelope Valley Health Care Di (PA).....................................A....... 661 949-5000
 1600 W Avenue J Lancaster (93534) *(P-15948)*
Antelope Valley Health Center, Lancaster Also Called: County of Los Angeles *(P-17039)*
Antelope Valley Hlth Care Dst, Lancaster Also Called: Antelope Valley Hospital Inc *(P-15950)*
Antelope Valley Home Care, Lancaster Also Called: Antelope Valley Hospital Inc *(P-15949)*
Antelope Valley Hospital, Lancaster Also Called: Kaiser Foundation Hospitals *(P-16167)*
Antelope Valley Hospital Inc ....B....... 661 726-6180
 1600 W Avenue J Lancaster (93534) *(P-14614)*
Antelope Valley Hospital Inc ....C....... 661 949-5936
 44335 Lowtree Ave Lancaster (93534) *(P-15949)*
Antelope Valley Hospital Inc ....C....... 661 949-5000
 44335 Lowtree Ave Lancaster (93534) *(P-15950)*
Antelope Valley Hospital Inc ....C....... 661 726-6050
 44105 15th St W Ste 100 Lancaster (93534) *(P-15951)*
Antelope Valley Lincoln, Lancaster Also Called: Johnson Ford *(P-7243)*
Antelope Vly Cntry CLB Imprv ....C....... 661 947-3142
 39800 Country Club Dr Palmdale (93551) *(P-14325)*
Antelope Vly Convalecent Hosp, Lancaster Also Called: Antelope Vly Retirement HM Inc *(P-15809)*
Antelope Vly Retirement HM Inc ....C....... 661 949-5584
 44523 15th St W Lancaster (93534) *(P-15328)*
Antelope Vly Retirement HM Inc ....C....... 661 948-7501
 44445 15th St W Lancaster (93534) *(P-15809)*
Antelope Vly Retirement HM Inc ....C....... 661 949-5524
 44567 15th St W Lancaster (93534) *(P-15810)*
Antelope Vly Retirement Manor, Lancaster Also Called: Antelope Vly Retirement HM Inc *(P-15328)*
Antelope Vly Schl Trnsp Agcy ....C....... 661 952-3106
 670 W Avenue L8 Lancaster (93534) *(P-3322)*
Antenna Audio Inc (PA)..A....... 203 523-0320
 555 W 5th St Ste 3725 Los Angeles (90013) *(P-3959)*
Antenna International, Los Angeles Also Called: Antenna Audio Inc *(P-3959)*
Anthem, Fresno Also Called: Anthem Insurance Companies Inc *(P-8280)*
Anthem, San Francisco Also Called: Anthem Insurance Companies Inc *(P-8281)*
Anthem Insurance Companies Inc ....D....... 559 230-6200
 5260 N Palm Ave Ste 215 Fresno (93704) *(P-8280)*
Anthem Insurance Companies Inc ....D....... 415 617-1700
 2 Embarcadero Ctr Ste 1310 San Francisco (94111) *(P-8281)*
Anthony Inc ....C....... 818 365-9451
 12812 Arroyo St Sylmar (91342) *(P-2691)*
Anthony Electric, Santa Fe Springs Also Called: RGA Electric Inc *(P-1821)*
Anthony International, Sylmar Also Called: Anthony Inc *(P-2691)*
ANTHONY SOTO EMPLOYMENT TRAINI, Santa Rosa Also Called: California Human Dev Corp *(P-18214)*
Anthony Vineyards Inc ....D....... 760 391-5488
 52301 Enterprise Way Coachella (92236) *(P-68)*
Anti-Recidivism Coalition ....D....... 213 955-5885
 1320 E 7th St Los Angeles (90021) *(P-18556)*

Antioch Convalescent Hospital, Antioch Also Called: Norcal Care Centers Inc *(P-15882)*
Antioch Dunes Healthcare LLC ....D....... 925 757-8787
 1210 A St Antioch (94509) *(P-15329)*
Antis Roofg Waterproofing LLC ....D....... 949 461-9222
 2649 Campus Dr Irvine (92612) *(P-2255)*
Antis Roofing, Irvine Also Called: Antis Roofg Waterproofing LLC *(P-2255)*
Antonelli & Sons Fish & Poultry ....D....... 650 952-7413
 119 S Linden Ave South San Francisco (94080) *(P-6465)*
Anvil Builders Inc ....C....... 415 285-5000
 1550 Park Ave Emeryville (94608) *(P-1077)*
Anvil Iron, Gardena Also Called: Anvil Steel Corporation *(P-2177)*
Anvil Steel Corporation ....D....... 310 329-5811
 134 W 168th St Gardena (90248) *(P-2177)*
Anvilogic Inc ....D....... 650 665-7707
 644 Emerson St Ste 100 Palo Alto (94301) *(P-11409)*
Anyscale Inc ....D....... 650 248-8086
 55 Hawthorne St Fl 9 San Francisco (94105) *(P-11410)*
Anza A Calabasas Hotel, The, Calabasas Also Called: 23627 Calabasas Road LLC *(P-9589)*
Ao, Orange Also Called: Architects Orange Inc *(P-19451)*
AOA Technology Partners ....D....... 888 828-6426
 342 Linda Way Mill Valley (94941) *(P-11411)*
Aoc LLC ....D....... 951 657-5161
 19991 Seaton Ave Perris (92570) *(P-2447)*
AOC California Plant, Perris Also Called: Aoc LLC *(P-2447)*
AOC Technologies Inc ....B....... 925 875-0808
 6900 Koll Center Pkwy Ste 401 Pleasanton (94566) *(P-5474)*
AON, San Francisco Also Called: AON Consulting & Insur Svcs *(P-8491)*
AON, Los Angeles Also Called: AON/Albert G Ruben Insur Svcs *(P-8492)*
AON Consulting & Insur Svcs ....C....... 415 486-7500
 199 Fremont St Fl 14 San Francisco (94105) *(P-8491)*
AON/Albert G Ruben Insur Svcs (DH)..................................D....... 310 234-6800
 10880 Wilshire Blvd Ste 700 Los Angeles (90024) *(P-8492)*
AP Global Inc ....D....... 818 707-3167
 2326 Townsgate Rd Westlake Village (91361) *(P-5625)*
AP Tech, Fremont Also Called: American Portwell Tech Inc *(P-5271)*
Apartment Seo LLC ....D....... 877 309-7363
 111 W Ocean Blvd Ste 1040 Long Beach (90802) *(P-10700)*
Apco Paving Company ....D....... 925 827-9850
 1790 Farm Bureau Rd Concord (94519) *(P-1078)*
Apeel Sciences, Goleta Also Called: Apeel Technology Inc *(P-255)*
Apeel Technology Inc (PA)..B....... 805 203-0146
 71 S Los Carneros Rd Goleta (93117) *(P-255)*
Apeiro Technologies, Irvine Also Called: It Division Inc *(P-17792)*
Aperto Property Management Inc ....B....... 626 965-1961
 17351 Main St La Puente (91744) *(P-8790)*
APEX ACADEMY, Los Angeles Also Called: Pazlo Education Foundation *(P-18893)*
Apex Bulk Commodities, Adelanto Also Called: Apex Bulk Commodities Inc *(P-3368)*
Apex Bulk Commodities Inc (PA)..C....... 760 246-6077
 12531 Violet Rd Ste A Adelanto (92301) *(P-3368)*
Apex Computer Systems Inc ....D....... 562 926-6820
 13875 Cerritos Corporate Dr Ste A Cerritos (90703) *(P-12703)*
Apex Janitorial Solutions, San Francisco Also Called: Billing Svcs Plus DBA Apex Jnt *(P-10862)*
Apex Logistics Intl Inc (PA)...C....... 310 665-0288
 18554 S Susana Rd Compton (90221) *(P-3985)*
Apex Mechanical Systems Inc ....D....... 858 536-8700
 7440 Trade St Ste A San Diego (92121) *(P-1361)*
Apex Site Solutions Inc ....D....... 916 685-8619
 9749 Kent St Elk Grove (95624) *(P-20277)*
Apex USA, Compton Also Called: Apex Logistics Intl Inc *(P-3985)*
Apffels Coffee, Santa Fe Springs Also Called: Apffels Coffee Inc *(P-2425)*
Apffels Coffee Inc ....D....... 562 309-0400
 12115 Pacific St Santa Fe Springs (90670) *(P-2425)*
Apg, Panorama City Also Called: American Protection Group Inc *(P-12928)*
Apheresis Care Group Inc ....D....... 619 440-4612
 570 N 2nd St El Cajon (92021) *(P-16977)*
Apical Industries Inc ....D....... 760 724-5300
 3030 Enterprise Ct Ste A Vista (92081) *(P-5955)*
Apigee Corporation ....B....... 408 343-7300
 1600 Amphitheatre Pkwy Mountain View (94043) *(P-11412)*

APL Logistics Americas Ltd   **ALPHABETIC SECTION**

APL Logistics Americas Ltd .... D...... 209 836-0302
   1550 N Chrisman Rd Tracy (95304) *(P-3675)*

APM Terminals Pacific LLC .... B...... 310 221-4000
   2500 Navy Way Pier 400 San Pedro (90731) *(P-3986)*

APn Business Resources Inc .... D...... 818 717-9980
   21418 Osborne St Canoga Park (91304) *(P-20278)*

Apollo Couriers Inc (PA) .... D...... 310 337-0377
   1039 W Hillcrest Blvd Inglewood (90301) *(P-3606)*

Apollo Electric .... D...... 714 256-8414
   330 N Basse Ln Brea (92821) *(P-1667)*

Apollo.io, Covina *Also Called: Zenleads Inc (P-20622)*

App Orchid Inc .... C...... 833 277-6724
   6111 Bollinger Canyon Rd Ste 570 San Ramon (94583) *(P-5272)*

App Wholesale LLC .... B...... 323 980-8315
   3686 E Olympic Blvd Los Angeles (90023) *(P-6601)*

Appdynamics, San Francisco *Also Called: Appdynamics LLC (P-11413)*

Appdynamics LLC (HQ) .... B...... 408 526-4000
   500 Terry A Francois Blvd Fl 3 San Francisco (94158) *(P-11413)*

Appetize Technologies Inc .... C...... 877 559-4225
   100 California St San Francisco (94111) *(P-12090)*

APPFOLIO, Santa Barbara *Also Called: Appfolio Inc (P-12092)*

Appfolio Inc .... D...... 866 648-1536
   9201 Spectrum Center Blvd Ste 100 San Diego (92123) *(P-12091)*

Appfolio Inc (PA) .... B...... 805 364-6093
   70 Castilian Dr Santa Barbara (93117) *(P-12092)*

Apple, Cupertino *Also Called: Apple Inc (P-2891)*

Apple Farm Collections-Slo Inc (PA) .... B...... 805 544-2040
   2015 Monterey St San Luis Obispo (93401) *(P-7456)*

Apple Freight Inc .... D...... 510 423-4000
   223 W 5th St Ripon (95366) *(P-3442)*

Apple Inc (PA) .... A...... 408 996-1010
   1 Apple Park Way Cupertino (95014) *(P-2891)*

Apple Store Glendale Galleria, Glendale *Also Called: Glendale Associates Ltd (P-8722)*

Applecare Medical MGT LLC .... C...... 714 443-4507
   18 Centerpointe Dr Ste 100 La Palma (90623) *(P-20024)*

Appleone Employment Services, Glendale *Also Called: AppleOne Inc (P-11082)*

Appleone Employment Services, Glendale *Also Called: AppleOne Inc (P-11083)*

AppleOne Inc (HQ) .... C...... 818 240-8688
   327 W Broadway Glendale (91204) *(P-11082)*

AppleOne Inc .... C...... 818 240-8688
   325 W Broadway Glendale (91204) *(P-11083)*

Appleridge Assisted Living Inc .... C...... 916 451-1212
   2030 23rd St Sacramento (95818) *(P-18373)*

Applied Biosystems, Carlsbad *Also Called: Applied Biosystems LLC (P-12093)*

Applied Biosystems LLC (DH) C
   5791 Van Allen Way Carlsbad (92008) *(P-12093)*

Applied Computer Solutions (DH) .... D...... 714 861-2200
   110 Progress Irvine (92618) *(P-11414)*

Applied Engineering MGT Corp .... C...... 805 484-1909
   760 Paseo Camarillo Ste 101 Camarillo (93010) *(P-11415)*

Applied Fusion LLC .... D...... 510 351-8314
   1915 Republic Ave San Leandro (94577) *(P-13764)*

Applied Innovation Group Inc .... C...... 408 452-5716
   1919 Monterey Hwy Ste 70 San Jose (95112) *(P-19141)*

Applied Intuition Inc (PA) .... D...... 630 935-8986
   145 E Dana St Mountain View (94041) *(P-11416)*

Applied Materials, Roseville *Also Called: Cokeva Inc (P-12705)*

Applied Membranes Inc .... C...... 760 727-3711
   2450 Business Park Dr Vista (92081) *(P-2847)*

Applied Physics Systems Inc (PA) .... C...... 650 965-0500
   425 Clyde Ave Mountain View (94043) *(P-3041)*

Applied Process Cooling, Modesto *Also Called: Process Cooling Intl Inc (P-1537)*

Applied Research Assoc Inc .... D...... 505 881-8074
   10833 Valley View St Ste 250 Cypress (90630) *(P-19656)*

Applied Silicone, Carpinteria *Also Called: Applied Silicone Company LLC (P-6705)*

Applied Silicone Company LLC .... D...... 805 525-5657
   1050 Cindy Ln Carpinteria (93013) *(P-6705)*

Applied Statistics & MGT Inc .... C...... 951 699-4600
   32848 Wolf Store Rd Ste A Temecula (92592) *(P-12094)*

Applied Technologies Assoc Inc (HQ) .... C...... 805 239-9100
   3025 Buena Vista Dr Paso Robles (93446) *(P-3042)*

Applimotion Inc .... D...... 916 652-3118
   5915 Jetton Ln Loomis (95650) *(P-5538)*

Applovin Corporation (PA) .... C...... 800 839-9646
   1100 Page Mill Rd Palo Alto (94304) *(P-12095)*

Apprentice Jrnymen Trning Tr F .... C...... 310 604-0892
   7850 Haskell Ave Van Nuys (91406) *(P-18204)*

Appsflyer Inc .... C...... 408 367-9938
   100 1st St Ste 2500 San Francisco (94105) *(P-11417)*

Appsflyer Ltd .... D...... 415 636-9430
   111 New Montgomery St Ste 400 San Francisco (94105) *(P-10701)*

Appstar Financial, San Diego *Also Called: Amazon Processing LLC (P-12549)*

Apreva Corporation .... D...... 619 450-4414
   1565 Hotel Cir S Ste 320 San Diego (92108) *(P-17178)*

Apreva Hospice, San Diego *Also Called: Apreva Corporation (P-17178)*

Apria Healthcare LLC .... D...... 530 677-2713
   1450 Expo Pkwy Ste D Sacramento (95815) *(P-10989)*

Apstra Inc (HQ) .... D...... 650 307-3245
   1137 Innovation Way Sunnyvale (94089) *(P-12732)*

Apteligent Inc .... D...... 415 371-1402
   1100 La Avenida St Ste A Mountain View (94043) *(P-11418)*

Aptim Corp .... C...... 925 288-9898
   4005 Port Chicago Hwy Concord (94520) *(P-19142)*

Aptim Corp .... A...... 949 261-6441
   18100 Von Karman Ave # 450 Irvine (92612) *(P-19949)*

Aptim Corp .... D...... 949 261-6441
   18100 Von Karman Ave # 450 Irvine (92612) *(P-20691)*

Aptim Corp .... C...... 925 288-9898
   4005 Port Chicago Hwy Concord (94520) *(P-20692)*

Aptim Corp .... B...... 619 239-1690
   1230 Columbia St Ste 1200 San Diego (92101) *(P-20693)*

Aptim Federal Services LLC .... A...... 925 288-9898
   4005 Port Chicago Hwy Concord (94520) *(P-655)*

Aptim Federal Services LLC .... A...... 619 239-1690
   1230 Columbia St Ste 1200 San Diego (92101) *(P-656)*

Aptina LLC .... A...... 408 660-2699
   2660 Zanker Rd San Jose (95134) *(P-2913)*

Aptina Imaging, San Jose *Also Called: Aptina LLC (P-2913)*

Aptiv Digital LLC .... D...... 818 295-6789
   2160 Gold St San Jose (95002) *(P-12096)*

Apttus Corporation (PA) .... A...... 650 445-7700
   3001 Bishop Dr San Ramon (94583) *(P-12417)*

Apu Inc (PA) .... D...... 661 948-2880
   14939 Oxnard St Van Nuys (91411) *(P-5022)*

Apw Knox-Seeman Warehouse Inc (HQ) .... D...... 310 604-4373
   1073 E Artesia Blvd Carson (90746) *(P-5023)*

Aquaclean Janitorial .... D...... 858 537-9090
   9403 Compass Point Dr S San Diego (92126) *(P-10857)*

Aqualine Piping Inc .... D...... 408 745-7100
   2108 Bering Dr Ste C San Jose (95131) *(P-1362)*

Aquarium of Pacific (PA) .... C...... 562 590-3100
   100 Aquarium Way Long Beach (90802) *(P-18683)*

Aquarium of The Bay, The, San Francisco *Also Called: Bayorg (P-18684)*

Aquatic Co .... C...... 714 993-1220
   8101 E Kaiser Blvd Ste 200 Anaheim (92808) *(P-2666)*

Aquinas Corporation .... C...... 408 248-7100
   3580 Payne Ave San Jose (95117) *(P-15330)*

Aquire, Norwalk *Also Called: Aquirecorps Norwalk Auto Auctn (P-5005)*

Aquirecorps Norwalk Auto Auctn .... C...... 562 864-7464
   12405 Rosecrans Ave Norwalk (90650) *(P-5005)*

Arabella Philanthropic .... C...... 415 677-9700
   340 Pine St Ste 401 San Francisco (94104) *(P-9487)*

ARABELLA PHILANTHROPIC INVESTMENT ADVISORS, LLC, San Francisco *Also Called: Arabella Philanthropic (P-9487)*

Araco Enterprises LLC .... B...... 818 767-0675
   9189 De Garmo Ave Sun Valley (91352) *(P-4856)*

Aragon Commercial Ldscpg Inc .... C...... 408 998-0600
   2305 S Vasco Rd Livermore (94550) *(P-474)*

Arakelian Enterprises Inc .... C...... 818 768-2644
   11121 Pendleton St Sun Valley (91352) *(P-3369)*

Arakelian Enterprises Inc .... B...... 626 336-3636
   15045 Salt Lake Ave City Of Industry (91746) *(P-4857)*

ALPHABETIC SECTION

Arden Wood Inc

Arakelian Enterprises Inc .... C....... 951 342-3300
   687 Iowa Ave Riverside (92507) *(P-4858)*

Arakelian Enterprises Inc (PA) .... B....... 626 336-3636
   14048 Valley Blvd City Of Industry (91746) *(P-4859)*

Aramark, Fresno *Also Called: Vestis Corporation (P-10458)*

Aramark, Burbank *Also Called: Aramark Unf & Career AP LLC (P-10478)*

Aramark, Los Angeles *Also Called: Aramark Facility Services LLC (P-10858)*

Aramark, San Jose *Also Called: Aramark Spt & Entrmt Group LLC (P-14077)*

Aramark Facility Services LLC .... D....... 213 740-8968
   941 W 35th St Los Angeles (90007) *(P-10858)*

Aramark Spt & Entrmt Group LLC .... D....... 408 999-5735
   525 W Santa Clara St San Jose (95113) *(P-14077)*

Aramark Unf & Career AP LLC .... A....... 818 973-3700
   115 N First St Ste 203 Burbank (91502) *(P-10478)*

Ararat Convalescent Hospital, Los Angeles *Also Called: Ararat Home Los Angeles Inc (P-15811)*

Ararat Home Los Angeles Inc .... C....... 323 256-8012
   2373 Colorado Blvd Los Angeles (90041) *(P-15811)*

Ararat Home Los Angeles Inc .... C....... 818 837-1800
   15099 Mission Hills Rd Mission Hills (91345) *(P-15812)*

Ararat Nursing Facility, Mission Hills *Also Called: Ararat Home Los Angeles Inc (P-15812)*

Arb Inc (HQ) .... C....... 949 598-9242
   26000 Commercentre Dr Lake Forest (92630) *(P-1192)*

Arbitech LLC .... D....... 949 376-6650
   64 Fairbanks Irvine (92618) *(P-5273)*

Arbor Glen Care Center, Glendora *Also Called: Harbor Glen Care Center (P-15506)*

Arbor Glen Care Center, Glendora *Also Called: Ensign San Dimas LLC (P-15843)*

Arbor Hills Nursing Center, La Mesa *Also Called: Life Gnerations Healthcare LLC (P-15544)*

Arbor Post Acute, Chico *Also Called: Arbor Post Acute LLC (P-15331)*

Arbor Post Acute LLC .... D....... 530 342-4885
   1200 Springfield Dr Chico (95928) *(P-15331)*

Arbormed Inc (PA) .... C....... 714 689-1500
   725 W Town And Country Rd Orange (92868) *(P-17179)*

Arbors, The, San Diego *Also Called: G&L Penasquitos Inc (P-17992)*

Arborwell Inc (PA) .... C....... 510 881-4260
   2337 American Ave Hayward (94545) *(P-552)*

ARC, Torrance *Also Called: Good Sports Plus Ltd (P-11628)*

ARC - Imperial Valley (PA) .... D....... 760 352-0180
   298 E Ross Ave El Centro (92243) *(P-17836)*

ARC - SD E Cnty Training Ctrs, El Cajon *Also Called: ARC of San Diego (P-18558)*

ARC Document Solutions LLC .... A....... 951 445-4480
   41521 Date St Apt 101 Murrieta (92562) *(P-10783)*

ARC Enterprises, San Diego *Also Called: ARC of San Diego (P-18557)*

ARC Fresno/Madera Counties (PA) .... D....... 559 226-6268
   4490 E Ashlan Ave Fresno (93726) *(P-18205)*

ARC Los Angeles Orange Counties (PA) .... D....... 562 803-1556
   12049 Woodruff Ave Downey (90241) *(P-18206)*

ARC of Butte County (PA) .... C....... 530 891-5865
   2030 Park Ave Chico (95928) *(P-17837)*

ARC of Butte County, Chico *Also Called: ARC of Butte County (P-17837)*

ARC of San Diego .... D....... 619 427-7524
   1280 Nolan Ave Chula Vista (91911) *(P-17838)*

ARC of San Diego (PA) .... C....... 619 685-1175
   3030 Market St San Diego (92102) *(P-18557)*

ARC of San Diego .... B....... 619 448-2415
   1855 John Towers Ave El Cajon (92020) *(P-18558)*

ARC of San Diego .... B....... 760 740-6800
   1336 Rancheros Dr Ste 100 San Marcos (92069) *(P-18559)*

ARC San Francisco (PA) .... D....... 415 255-7200
   1500 Howard St San Francisco (94103) *(P-18207)*

Arcadia Convalescent Hosp Inc .... D....... 818 352-4438
   10158 Sunland Blvd Sunland (91040) *(P-15332)*

Arcadia Convalescent Hosp Inc (PA) .... C....... 626 445-2170
   1601 S Baldwin Ave Arcadia (91007) *(P-15813)*

Arcadia Eye Center, Arcadia *Also Called: Arcadia Eye Ctr (P-14615)*

Arcadia Eye Ctr .... D....... 626 445-4873
   622 W Duarte Rd Ste 103 Arcadia (91007) *(P-14615)*

Arcadia Gardens MGT Corp .... D....... 626 574-8571
   720 W Camino Real Ave Arcadia (91007) *(P-15746)*

Arcadia Health Care Center, Arcadia *Also Called: Arcadia Convalescent Hosp Inc (P-15813)*

Arcaris Inc (PA) .... C....... 415 854-3801
   530 Lawrence Expy Sunnyvale (94085) *(P-12097)*

Arceo Labs Inc (PA) .... C....... 332 203-4971
   55 2nd St Ste 1950 San Francisco (94105) *(P-19950)*

Arch Health Partners, Poway *Also Called: Palomar Health Medical Group (P-16311)*

Archdiocese of San Francisco, San Francisco *Also Called: The Roman Catholic Archbishop of San Francisco (P-17817)*

Archer Norris, Walnut Creek *Also Called: Archer Norris A Professional Law Corporation (P-17366)*

Archer Norris A Professional Law Corporation .... C....... 925 930-6000
   2033 N Main St Ste 800 Walnut Creek (94596) *(P-17366)*

Archetype Consulting Inc .... D....... 888 644-8445
   530 Divisadero St Ste 310 San Francisco (94117) *(P-20279)*

Archimdes Tech Group Hldngs LL .... D....... 858 642-9170
   5660 Eastgate Dr San Diego (92121) *(P-19657)*

Archipelago Development Inc .... D....... 858 699-6272
   Rancho Santa Fe (92067) *(P-9245)*

Archipelago Lighting Inc .... D....... 909 627-5333
   4615 State St Montclair (91763) *(P-5539)*

Architects Orange Inc .... C....... 714 639-9860
   144 N Orange St Orange (92866) *(P-19451)*

Architectural GL & Alum Co Inc (PA) .... C....... 925 583-2460
   6400 Brisa St Livermore (94550) *(P-5475)*

Architectural Glass & Aluminum, Livermore *Also Called: Architectural GL & Alum Co Inc (P-5475)*

Architectural Mtls USA Inc .... D....... 888 219-2126
   4025 Camino Del Rio S Ste 300 San Diego (92108) *(P-19452)*

Architectural Window Shades .... D....... 626 578-1936
   9900 Gidley St El Monte (91731) *(P-7435)*

Architectural Woodworking Co .... D....... 626 570-4125
   582 Monterey Pass Rd Monterey Park (91754) *(P-2500)*

Architecture, Sacramento *Also Called: Lionakis (P-19486)*

Archives Management Corp (PA) .... C....... 650 544-2200
   2301 S El Camino Real San Mateo (94403) *(P-20025)*

Archkey Technologies, San Jose *Also Called: Sprig Electric Co (P-1848)*

Archlynk LLC (PA) .... D....... 408 214-3140
   550 S Winchester Blvd Ste 605 San Jose (95128) *(P-5274)*

Arciero Brothers Inc .... C....... 714 238-6600
   5614 E La Palma Ave Anaheim (92807) *(P-2095)*

Arcline Elvtion Svcs Hldngs LL .... A....... 860 805-2025
   4 Embarcadero Ctr Ste 3460 San Francisco (94111) *(P-13765)*

Arconix USA, Camarillo *Also Called: Arconix/Usa Inc (P-5890)*

Arconix/Usa Inc .... C....... 805 388-2525
   880 Avenida Acaso Ste 100 Camarillo (93012) *(P-5890)*

Arcoro Holdings Corp .... C....... 818 222-1836
   9452 Telephone Rd Pmb 227 Ventura (93004) *(P-12098)*

Arcs Commercial Mortgage, Calabasas *Also Called: Arcs Commercial Mortgage Co LP (P-7934)*

Arcs Commercial Mortgage Co LP (DH) .... C....... 818 676-3274
   26901 Agoura Rd Ste 200 Calabasas (91301) *(P-7934)*

Arctic Wolf Networks Inc .... C....... 888 272-8429
   111 W Evelyn Ave Ste 115 Sunnyvale (94086) *(P-12099)*

Arcticom Group Rfrgn LLC .... B....... 916 484-3190
   3675 De Forest Cir Jurupa Valley (91752) *(P-13723)*

Arctouch LLC .... C....... 415 944-2000
   1001 Front St San Francisco (94111) *(P-11419)*

Arcturus Therapeutics Inc .... C....... 858 900-2660
   10628 Science Center Dr Ste 250 San Diego (92121) *(P-19658)*

Arcules Inc .... D....... 949 439-0053
   17875 Von Karman Ave Ste 450 Irvine (92614) *(P-11420)*

ARCUS BIOSCIENCES, Hayward *Also Called: Arcus Biosciences Inc (P-19659)*

Arcus Biosciences Inc (PA) .... D....... 510 694-6200
   3928 Point Eden Way Hayward (94545) *(P-19659)*

Arden Health & Rehab Ctr, Sacramento *Also Called: Mariner Health Care Inc (P-15562)*

Arden Hills, Sacramento *Also Called: Arden Hills Country Club Inc (P-7457)*

Arden Hills Country Club Inc .... D....... 916 482-6111
   1220 Arden Hills Ln Sacramento (95864) *(P-7457)*

Arden Realty Inc .... B....... 310 966-2600
   11601 Wilshire Blvd Fl 5 Los Angeles (90025) *(P-8702)*

Arden Wood Inc .... D....... 415 681-5500
   445 Wawona St San Francisco (94116) *(P-17793)*

Ardenbrook Inc — 5016 Paseo Padre Pkwy Fremont (94555) *(P-8901)* .... D...... 510 794-1020

Ardent Companies Inc — 4842 Airport Dr Bakersfield (93308) *(P-1668)* .... D...... 661 633-1465

Ardenwood Rental Condominiums, Fremont Also Called: Ardenbrook Inc *(P-8901)*

Ardwin Freight, Burbank Also Called: Ardwin Inc *(P-3443)*

Ardwin Inc — 2940 N Hollywood Way Burbank (91505) *(P-3443)* .... C...... 818 767-7777

Are/Cal-Sd Region No 62 LLC — 26 N Euclid Ave Pasadena (91101) *(P-9488)* .... D...... 626 578-0777

Area 1 Security Inc — 101 Townsend St San Francisco (94107) *(P-12100)* .... D...... 650 924-1637

Arecont Vision Costar LLC — 1801 Highland Ave Duarte (91010) *(P-13096)* .... D...... 818 937-0700

Arena Event Services Inc — 454 S Abbott Ave Milpitas (95035) *(P-11020)* .... D...... 408 856-3232

Arena Painting Contractors Inc — 525 E Alondra Blvd Gardena (90248) *(P-1604)* .... D...... 310 316-2446

Arena Stuart Rentals Inc — 454 S Abbott Ave Milpitas (95035) *(P-7555)* .... C...... 408 856-3232

Ares, Los Angeles Also Called: Ares Management Corporation *(P-9354)*

Ares Management Corporation (PA) — 2000 Avenue Of The Stars Fl 12 Los Angeles (90067) *(P-9354)* .... C...... 310 201-4100

Ares Management LLC (HQ) — 2000 Avenue Of The Stars Fl 12 Los Angeles (90067) *(P-9355)* .... D...... 310 201-4100

Arey Jones Eductl Solutions, San Diego Also Called: Broadway Typewriter Co Inc *(P-5284)*

Argent Hotel, The, San Francisco Also Called: L-O Soma Hotel Inc *(P-9959)*

Argent Management LLC (PA) — 4131 S Main St Santa Ana (92707) *(P-8902)* .... D...... 949 777-4000

Argent Management LLC — 4131 S Main St Santa Ana (92707) *(P-8903)* .... D...... 949 777-4070

Argonaut Constructors Inc — 360 Sutton Pl Santa Rosa (95407) *(P-1193)* .... C...... 707 542-4862

Argonaut Mfg Svcs Inc — 2841 Loker Ave E Carlsbad (92010) *(P-5399)* .... D...... 888 834-8892

Argus Management Company LLC — 5150 E Pacific Coast Hwy Ste 500 Long Beach (90804) *(P-20650)* .... B...... 562 299-5200

Argus Medical Management, Long Beach Also Called: Argus Management Company LLC *(P-20650)*

Aria, San Francisco Also Called: Aria Systems Inc *(P-11421)*

Aria Group Incorporated — 17395 Daimler St Irvine (92614) *(P-19143)* .... D...... 949 475-2915

Aria Systems Inc (PA) — 575 Market St Fl 4 San Francisco (94105) *(P-11421)* .... C...... 415 852-7250

Ariat International Inc (PA) — 1500 Alvarado St Ste 100 San Leandro (94577) *(P-2687)* .... A...... 510 477-7000

Ariba Inc (DH) — 3420 Hillview Ave Palo Alto (94304) *(P-12101)* .... C...... 650 849-4000

Aricent Inc — 303 Twin Dolphin Dr # 600 Redwood City (94065) *(P-11422)* .... A...... 650 632-4310

Aricent US Inc — 303 Twin Dolphin Dr Ste 600 Redwood City (94065) *(P-11423)* .... C...... 650 632-4310

Aries Industries Inc — 5748 E Shields Ave Ste 101 Fresno (93727) *(P-4845)* .... C...... 559 291-0383

Ariosa Diagnostics Inc — 5945 Optical Ct San Jose (95138) *(P-19660)* .... C...... 408 229-7500

Arista, Santa Clara Also Called: Arista Networks Inc *(P-2823)*

Arista Networks Inc (PA) — 5453 Great America Pkwy Santa Clara (95054) *(P-2823)* .... B...... 408 547-5500

Aristotle Credit Partners LLC — 11100 Santa Monica Blvd Ste 1700 Los Angeles (90025) *(P-9356)* .... D...... 310 478-4005

Arizona Channel Isla — 300 W 9th St Oxnard (93030) *(P-14491)* .... D...... 480 788-0755

Arizona Pipeline Company (PA) — 17372 Lilac St Hesperia (92345) *(P-1194)* .... B...... 760 244-8212

Arizona Pipeline Company — 1745 Sampson Ave Corona (92879) *(P-1195)* .... C...... 951 270-3100

Arizona Portland Cement, Glendora Also Called: Calportland Company *(P-2696)*

Arjis, San Diego Also Called: Automted Rgnal Jstice Info Sys *(P-18564)*

Arjo Inc — 17502 Fabrica Way Cerritos (90703) *(P-5400)* .... B...... 714 412-1170

Arkebauer Properties, Irvine Also Called: Western National Prpts LLC *(P-785)*

Arkose Labs Holdings Inc (PA) — 400 Concar Dr San Mateo (94402) *(P-13097)* .... C...... 415 917-8701

ARLO, Carlsbad Also Called: Arlo Technologies Inc *(P-2877)*

Arlo Technologies Inc (PA) — 2200 Faraday Ave Ste 150 Carlsbad (92008) *(P-2877)* .... D...... 408 890-3900

Armand Hmmer Mseum of Art Cltr — 10899 Wilshire Blvd Los Angeles (90024) *(P-18637)* .... C...... 310 443-7000

Armando C Ibrra CPA A Prof Cor — 310 Third Ave Ste Aa Chula Vista (91910) *(P-19530)* .... D...... 619 422-1348

Armanino LLP — 11766 Wilshire Blvd Fl 9 Los Angeles (90025) *(P-19531)* .... B...... 310 478-4148

Armanino LLP — 50 W San Fernando St Ste 500 San Jose (95113) *(P-19532)* .... B...... 408 200-6400

Armanino LLP (PA) — 2700 Camino Ramon Ste 350 San Ramon (94583) *(P-19533)* .... C...... 925 790-2600

Armc, Colton Also Called: Arrowhead Regional Medical Ctr *(P-15952)*

Armed Guard Private SEC Inc — 50 Landing Cir Chico (95973) *(P-12932)* .... D...... 530 751-3218

Armed Services YMCA of USA — 3293 Santo Rd San Diego (92124) *(P-18813)* .... C...... 858 751-5755

Armed/Xctive Prtction Armed Un, Harbor City Also Called: Allied Protection Services Inc *(P-12922)*

Armis Federal LLC — 300 Hamilton Ave Fl 5 Palo Alto (94301) *(P-13098)* .... B...... 888 452-4011

Armorblox Inc — 100 S Murphy Ave Ste 200 Sunnyvale (94086) *(P-11424)* .... D...... 831 428-2124

Armorous — 3550 Round Barn Blvd Ste 313 Santa Rosa (95403) *(P-12933)* .... D...... 707 387-4400

Armstrong Construction Company, Emeryville Also Called: Armstrong Instlltion Svc A Cal *(P-1605)*

Armstrong Instlltion Svc A Cal — 4575 San Pablo Ave Emeryville (94608) *(P-1605)* .... C...... 408 777-1234

Arnaudo Bros Transport Inc (PA) — 16505 S Tracy Blvd Tracy (95304) *(P-166)* .... D...... 209 835-0406

Arnaudo Bros Trucking, Tracy Also Called: Arnaudo Bros Transport Inc *(P-166)*

Arnold & Porter, Los Angeles Also Called: Arnold Porter Kaye Scholer LLP *(P-17368)*

Arnold & Porter PC — 3 Embarcadero Ctr Fl 7 San Francisco (94111) *(P-17367)* .... B...... 415 434-1600

Arnold Porter Kaye Scholer LLP — 777 S Figueroa St Ste 4400 Los Angeles (90017) *(P-17368)* .... D...... 213 243-4000

Aroma Housewares, San Diego Also Called: Mirama Enterprises Inc *(P-5124)*

Aroma Spa & Sports LLC — 3680 Wilshire Blvd Ste 301 Los Angeles (90010) *(P-14492)* .... D...... 213 387-2111

Aroma Wilshire Center, Los Angeles Also Called: Aroma Spa & Sports LLC *(P-14492)*

Arosa, Los Angeles Also Called: Livhome Inc *(P-16890)*

Arose Recruiting Co Inc — 2429 W Coast Hwy Ste 208 Newport Beach (92663) *(P-11084)* .... D...... 949 642-2696

Around The Clock Care, Bakersfield Also Called: Vasinda Investments Inc *(P-11347)*

Arrcus Inc — 2077 Gateway Pl Ste 400 San Jose (95110) *(P-11425)* .... D...... 408 884-1965

Arriaga Usa Inc (PA) — 12000 Sherman Way North Hollywood (91605) *(P-1974)* .... D...... 818 982-9559

Arris Composites Inc — 745 Heinz Ave Berkeley (94710) *(P-11426)* .... C...... 510 730-0067

Arrival Communications Inc (DH) — 1800 19th St Bakersfield (93301) *(P-13196)* .... D...... 661 716-2100

Arrowhead Brass & Plumbing LLC — 5147 Alhambra Ave Los Angeles (90032) *(P-1363)* .... D...... 800 332-4267

Arrowhead Central Credit Union — 8686 Haven Ave Rancho Cucamonga (91730) *(P-7755)* .... B...... 866 212-4333

Arrowhead Gen Insur Agcy Inc (HQ) — 701 B St Ste 2100 San Diego (92101) *(P-8377)* .... C...... 619 881-8600

Arrowhead Regional Medical Ctr — 400 N Pepper Ave Colton (92324) *(P-15952)* .... A...... 909 580-1000

Arrowhead Water, Orange Also Called: Bluetriton Brands Inc *(P-6610)*

Arroyo Grande Care Center, Arroyo Grande Also Called: Compass Health Inc *(P-15383)*

Arroyo Grande Community Hospital — 345 S Halcyon Rd Arroyo Grande (93420) *(P-15953)* .... B...... 805 473-7626

Arroyo Seco Medical Group (PA) — 301 S Fair Oaks Ave Ste 300 Pasadena (91105) *(P-14616)* .... D...... 626 795-7556

ALPHABETIC SECTION — Asian Health Services

Arroyo Vista Family Health Ctr, Los Angeles *Also Called: Arroyo Vsta Fmly Hlth Fndation* *(P-14617)*
Arroyo Vsta Fmly Hlth Fndation .... D....... 323 224-2188
  2411 N Broadway Los Angeles (90031) *(P-14617)*
ARS, Los Angeles *Also Called: Asian Rehabilitation Svc Inc (P-18209)*
ARS National Services Inc (PA) .... C....... 800 456-5053
  201 W Grand Ave Escondido (92025) *(P-10735)*
Arsi of California, Thousand Oaks *Also Called: American Recovery Service Inc (P-10734)*
Art Drctors Gild Itse Lcal 876 .... C....... 818 762-9995
  11969 Ventura Blvd Ste 200 Studio City (91604) *(P-18772)*
Art Piccadilly Shaw LLC .... C....... 559 375-7760
  5115 E Mckinley Ave Fresno (93727) *(P-9613)*
Art Piccadilly Shaw LLC .... C....... 559 224-4200
  4961 N Cedar Ave Fresno (93726) *(P-9614)*
Artemis Consulting, San Diego *Also Called: Artemis Consulting LLC (P-20280)*
Artemis Consulting LLC .... D....... 619 573-6328
  1012 W Washington St San Diego (92103) *(P-20280)*
Artemis Inst For Clncal RES LL 858 278-3647
  770 Washington St Ste 300 San Diego (92103) *(P-15255)*
Artesia Christian Home Inc .... C....... 562 865-5218
  11614 183rd St Artesia (90701) *(P-15814)*
Arthur J Gallagher & Co .... D....... 818 539-2300
  500 N Brand Blvd Ste 100 Glendale (91203) *(P-8493)*
Arthur J Gallagher & Co 559 733-1181
  501 W Main St Visalia (93291) *(P-8494)*
Arthur J Gallagher Risk Mgmt .... D....... 818 539-2300
  500 N Brand Blvd Ste 100 Glendale (91203) *(P-8495)*
Arthur Loussararian MD, Mission Viejo *Also Called: Mission Internal Med Group Inc (P-14902)*
Arthur Schawlow Center, Chico *Also Called: California Vocations Inc (P-15826)*
Artic Sentinel Inc .... D....... 310 227-8230
  1700 E Walnut Ave Ste 200 El Segundo (90245) *(P-11427)*
Artichoke Joe's Casino, San Bruno *Also Called: Artichoke Joes (P-14493)*
Artichoke Joes .... B....... 650 589-8812
  659 Huntington Ave San Bruno (94066) *(P-14493)*
Artimex Iron Inc .... C....... 619 444-3155
  315 Cypress Ln El Cajon (92020) *(P-2178)*
Artisan Bakers .... D....... 707 939-1765
  940 Riverside Pkwy Ste 50 West Sacramento (95605) *(P-6602)*
Artisan Bistro Foods Inc .... D....... 949 797-0014
  1882 Mcgaw Ave Ste A Irvine (92614) *(P-6416)*
Artisan Entertainment Inc .... A....... 310 449-9200
  2700 Colorado Ave Ste 200 Santa Monica (90404) *(P-13819)*
Artisan Glass and Design Inc .... D....... 714 542-0507
  2665 W Woodland Dr Anaheim (92801) *(P-2256)*
Artisan Partners Ltd Partnr .... B....... 415 283-2444
  100 Pine St Ste 2950 San Francisco (94111) *(P-8179)*
Artistic Entrmt Svcs LLC .... D....... 626 334-9388
  120 N Aspan Ave Azusa (91702) *(P-14078)*
Artizen Inc .... C....... 707 595-5998
  460 City Center Dr Rohnert Park (94928) *(P-20281)*
Arts and Svcs For Disabled Inc .... D....... 562 377-0302
  3626 E Pacific Coast Hwy Long Beach (90804) *(P-17839)*
Aruba Networks Inc (HQ) .... B....... 408 941-4300
  6280 America Center Dr San Jose (95002) *(P-2824)*
Aruba Networks Inc .... A....... 408 227-4500
  390 W Caribbean Dr Sunnyvale (94089) *(P-2892)*
Aruba Networks Cafe, San Jose *Also Called: Aruba Networks Inc (P-2824)*
Arup, San Francisco *Also Called: Arup North America Limited (P-19145)*
Arup North America Limited .... B....... 310 578-4182
  12777 W Jefferson Blvd Ste 300 Los Angeles (90066) *(P-19144)*
Arup North America Limited (DH) .... C....... 415 957-9445
  560 Mission St Fl 7 San Francisco (94105) *(P-19145)*
Arvato Digital Services, Los Gatos *Also Called: Arvato USA LLC (P-10784)*
Arvato USA LLC .... D....... 408 402-3469
  750 University Ave Los Gatos (95032) *(P-10784)*
Arvato USA LLC .... C....... 502 356-8063
  2053 E Jay St Ontario (91764) *(P-13197)*
Arvee Bros Inc 650 583-3935
  1375 El Camino Real Millbrae (94030) *(P-9615)*
Arya Ice Cream Distrg Co Inc .... D....... 323 234-2994
  914 E 31st St Los Angeles (90011) *(P-6429)*

Aryaka Networks Inc (PA) .... B....... 888 692-7925
  1850 Gateway Dr Ste 500 San Mateo (94404) *(P-12418)*
Aryzta Sweet Life, Santa Ana *Also Called: The Sweet Life Enterprises Inc (P-2360)*
Asab Inc (DH) .... C....... 818 551-7300
  500 N Brand Blvd Fl 3 Glendale (91203) *(P-10824)*
Asana, San Francisco *Also Called: Asana Inc (P-12733)*
Asana Inc (PA) .... A....... 415 525-3888
  633 Folsom St Ste 100 San Francisco (94107) *(P-12733)*
Asbestos Instant Response Inc .... D....... 323 733-0508
  3517 W Washington Blvd Los Angeles (90018) *(P-2257)*
Asbury, La Mirada *Also Called: Orange Courier Inc (P-13410)*
Asbury Environmental Services (PA) .... D....... 310 886-3400
  1300 S Santa Fe Ave Compton (90221) *(P-3370)*
Asbury Park Nursing, Sacramento *Also Called: Asbury Pk Nrsing Rhblttion Ctr (P-15333)*
Asbury Pk Nrsing Rhblttion Ctr .... C....... 916 649-2000
  2257 Fair Oaks Blvd Sacramento (95825) *(P-15333)*
ASC Building Products, West Sacramento *Also Called: ASC Profiles LLC (P-5476)*
ASC Profiles LLC (DH) .... D....... 916 376-2800
  2110 Enterprise Blvd West Sacramento (95691) *(P-5476)*
Ascend Distribution, City Of Industry *Also Called: Eforcity Corporation (P-5647)*
Ascend Healthcare LLC .... D....... 747 247-2176
  4346 Empress Ave Encino (91436) *(P-17005)*
Ascender Software Inc .... C....... 877 561-7501
  8885 Rio San Diego Dr Ste 270 San Diego (92108) *(P-12102)*
Ascot Hotel LP .... C....... 310 476-6411
  170 N Church Ln Los Angeles (90049) *(P-9616)*
Ash Holdings LLC .... D....... 909 793-2609
  1620 W Fern Ave Redlands (92373) *(P-15334)*
Ashbury Market Inc .... D....... 650 952-8889
  179 Starlite St South San Francisco (94080) *(P-6603)*
Ashford Trs Fremont LLC .... C....... 510 413-3700
  46100 Landing Pkwy Fremont (94538) *(P-9617)*
Ashford Trs Seven LLC .... D....... 760 776-0050
  38305 Cook St Palm Desert (92211) *(P-9618)*
Ashley & Vance Engineering Inc .... D....... 805 545-0010
  1229 Carmel St San Luis Obispo (93401) *(P-19146)*
Ashley Furniture, Redlands *Also Called: Ashley Furniture Inds LLC (P-3676)*
Ashley Furniture Inds LLC .... B....... 909 825-4900
  2250 W Lugonia Ave Redlands (92374) *(P-3676)*
Ashton-Tate LLC .... C....... 415 639-5873
  403 Main St San Francisco (94105) *(P-12419)*
Ashunya Inc .... D....... 714 385-1900
  642 N Eckhoff St Orange (92868) *(P-11428)*
ASI Hastings Inc .... C....... 619 590-9300
  4870 Viewridge Ave Ste 200 San Diego (92123) *(P-1364)*
Asi Heating, Air and Solar, San Diego *Also Called: ASI Hastings Inc (P-1364)*
Asia Foundation (PA) .... D....... 415 982-4640
  465 California St Fl 9 San Francisco (94104) *(P-19863)*
Asiainfo-Linkage Inc .... A....... 408 970-9788
  5201 Great America Pkwy Ste 4209 Santa Clara (95054) *(P-4253)*
Asian Amercn Recovery Svcs Inc .... C....... 408 271-3900
  1340 Tully Rd Ste 304 San Jose (95122) *(P-16662)*
Asian American Home Care Inc .... C....... 415 434-0138
  3410 Geary Blvd San Francisco (94118) *(P-16809)*
Asian American Home Care Inc .... C....... 408 283-5100
  1840 The Alameda San Jose (95126) *(P-16810)*
Asian Amrcans For Cmnty Invlvm (PA) .... C....... 408 975-2730
  2400 Moorpark Ave Ste 300 San Jose (95128) *(P-18560)*
Asian Art Meuseum of SF, San Francisco *Also Called: Asian Art Mseum Fndtion San Fr (P-18638)*
Asian Art Mseum Fndtion San Fr .... C....... 415 581-3500
  200 Larkin St San Francisco (94102) *(P-18638)*
Asian Art Museum, San Francisco *Also Called: City & County San Francisco (P-18644)*
Asian Cmnty Mental Hlth Svcs, Oakland *Also Called: Asian Community Mental Hlth Bd (P-17006)*
Asian Community Mental Hlth Bd .... D....... 510 869-6003
  310 8th St Ste 303 Oakland (94607) *(P-17006)*
Asian European Products Inc .... C....... 949 553-3900
  18071 Fitch Fl 250 Irvine (92614) *(P-5024)*
Asian Health Services (PA) .... C....... 510 986-6800
  101 8th St Oakland (94607) *(P-14618)*

Asian Pacific Family Center, Rosemead *Also Called: Uplift Family Services (P-15169)*

Asian Rehabilitation Svc Inc (PA)..D...... 562 632-1141
750 E Green St Ste 301 Pasadena (91101) *(P-18208)*

Asian Rehabilitation Svc Inc ....C...... 213 680-3790
312 N Spring St Ste B30 Los Angeles (90012) *(P-18209)*

Asiana Cuisine Enterprises Inc ....A...... 310 327-2223
22771 S Western Ave Ste 100 Torrance (90501) *(P-2430)*

Asics America Corporation (HQ)...C...... 949 453-8888
7755 Irvine Center Dr Ste 400 Irvine (92618) *(P-6227)*

Asics Tiger, Irvine *Also Called: Asics America Corporation (P-6227)*

Asig, Ontario *Also Called: Menzies Aviation (texas) Inc (P-3900)*

Ask Media Group LLC ....D...... 212 524-8716
1955 Broadway Ste 350 Oakland (94612) *(P-4254)*

Ask.com, Oakland *Also Called: IAC Search & Media Inc (P-12666)*

Asmb LLC ....D...... 949 347-7100
2021 Arizona Ave Santa Monica (90404) *(P-15335)*

Asomeo Envmtl Rstrtion Indust ....D...... 530 434-6869
2151 River Plaza Dr Ste 105 Sacramento (95833) *(P-5782)*

Asp Henry Holdings Inc ....A...... 310 955-9200
999 N Pacific Coast Hwy Ste 800 El Segundo (90245) *(P-9300)*

Aspect Development Inc (DH)..B...... 650 428-2700
1395 Charleston Rd Mountain View (94043) *(P-11429)*

Aspect Ratio Inc (HQ)..D...... 323 467-2121
5161 Lankershim Blvd Ste 300 North Hollywood (91601) *(P-13926)*

Aspen ....D...... 661 476-5138
28528 Constellation Rd Valencia (91355) *(P-20026)*

Aspen Surgery Center, Simi Valley *Also Called: Simi Vly Hosp & Hlth Care Svcs (P-16429)*

Aspire Bakeries LLC ....B...... 661 832-0409
6501 District Blvd Bakersfield (93313) *(P-6604)*

Aspire Bakeries LLC ....C...... 909 472-3500
1220 S Baker Ave Ontario (91761) *(P-6605)*

Aspire Bakeries LLC ....B...... 510 494-1700
6500 Overlake Pl Newark (94560) *(P-6606)*

Aspire General Insurance Co ....D...... 877 789-4742
2721 Citrus Rd Ste B Rancho Cordova (95742) *(P-8496)*

Aspireiq Inc ....D...... 415 445-3567
550 Montgomery St Ste 800 San Francisco (94111) *(P-20282)*

Aspirez Inc ....D...... 714 485-8104
1440 N Harbor Blvd Ste 900 Fullerton (92835) *(P-11430)*

Aspm-Sandiego, San Diego *Also Called: Allegis Residential Svcs Inc (P-20015)*

Asrc Aerospace Corp ....B...... 650 604-5946
Nasa Ames Research Center Mountain View (94035) *(P-3001)*

ASRC AEROSPACE CORP, Mountain View *Also Called: Asrc Aerospace Corp (P-3001)*

Assa Abloy Rsdential Group Inc (HQ)...C...... 626 961-0413
12801 Schabarum Ave Irwindale (91706) *(P-5721)*

Assa Abloy Rsdential Group Inc ....A...... 626 369-4718
600 Baldwin Park Blvd City Of Industry (91746) *(P-5722)*

Asset Management Tr Svcs LLC ....D...... 858 457-2202
1455 Frazee Rd Ste 500 San Diego (92108) *(P-20027)*

Asset Mktg Systems Insur Svcs ....D...... 888 303-8755
15050 Avenue Of Science Ste 100 San Diego (92128) *(P-20283)*

ASset Private Security Inc ....D...... 831 809-9779
36 Quail Run Cir Unit 100 Salinas (93907) *(P-12934)*

Assi Security (PA)..D...... 949 955-0244
1370 Reynolds Ave Ste 201 Irvine (92614) *(P-1669)*

ASSICIATED STUDENTS, San Luis Obispo *Also Called: Associated Students Inc (P-17840)*

Assign Corporation ....C...... 818 247-7100
200 N Maryland Ave Ste 204 Glendale (91206) *(P-12734)*

Assisted Home Care, Northridge *Also Called: Assisted Home Recovery Inc (P-11085)*

Assisted Home Care, Thousand Oaks *Also Called: Staff Assistance Inc (P-11236)*

Assisted Home Recovery Inc (PA)..C...... 818 894-8117
8550 Balboa Blvd Lbby Northridge (91325) *(P-11085)*

Assisted Home Recovery Inc ....D...... 626 915-5595
1900 W Garvey Ave S Ste 210 West Covina (91790) *(P-16811)*

ASSISTED HOME RECOVERY INC, West Covina *Also Called: Assisted Home Recovery Inc (P-16811)*

Associate Mech Contrs Inc ....C...... 760 294-3517
622 S Vinewood St Escondido (92029) *(P-1365)*

Associated Desert Shoppers Inc (DH)...D...... 760 346-1729
73400 Highway 111 Palm Desert (92260) *(P-2553)*

Associated Fmly Physicians Inc ....D...... 916 689-4111
8110 Timberlake Way Sacramento (95823) *(P-14619)*

Associated Group, Los Angeles *Also Called: Assocted Ldscp Dsplay Group In (P-13198)*

Associated Intl Insur Co, Woodland Hills *Also Called: Markel Corp (P-8605)*

Associated Materials Inc ....A...... 415 788-5111
1 Maritime Plz 12th Fl San Francisco (94111) *(P-2670)*

Associated Pathology Med Group ....D...... 408 399-5010
459 Monterey Ave Los Gatos (95030) *(P-16704)*

Associated Students & Faculty, San Diego *Also Called: Assocted Stdnts San Dego State (P-19036)*

Associated Students Inc (PA)..D...... 805 756-1281
University Union Bldg 65 San Luis Obispo (93407) *(P-17840)*

Associated Students Stanford (PA)..D...... 650 723-4331
201 Tresidder Un Stanford (94305) *(P-18814)*

Associated Students UCLA ....D...... 310 825-9451
650 Charles Young Dr S Rm 23120 Los Angeles (90095) *(P-14620)*

Associated Students UCLA ....C...... 310 206-8282
11000 Kinross Ave Ave Ste 245 Los Angeles (90095) *(P-17761)*

Associated Students UCLA (PA)...B...... 310 794-8836
308 Westwood Plz Los Angeles (90095) *(P-18561)*

Associated Students UCLA ....C...... 310 794-0242
924 Westwood Blvd Los Angeles (90024) *(P-18562)*

Associated Third Party Administrators Inc ....B
222 N Pacific Coast Hwy # 2000 El Segundo (90245) *(P-8456)*

Associates First Capital Corp ....D...... 818 248-7055
3634 5th Ave Glendale (91214) *(P-7870)*

Assocted Fgn Exch Holdings Inc (HQ)..D...... 818 386-2702
21045 Califa St Woodland Hills (91367) *(P-7840)*

Assocted Ldscp Dsplay Group In ....D...... 714 558-6100
1005 Mateo St Los Angeles (90021) *(P-13198)*

Assocted Stdnts Cal State Univ (PA)...A...... 530 898-6815
101 Hazel St Rm 218 Chico (95928) *(P-7545)*

Assocted Stdnts Cal State Univ ....C...... 562 985-4994
1212 N Bellflower Blvd Ste 220 Long Beach (90815) *(P-18815)*

Assocted Stdnts of The Univ CA (PA)..C...... 510 642-5420
400 Eshleman Hall Berkeley (94704) *(P-17801)*

Assocted Stdnts San Dego State (PA)..A...... 619 594-0234
5500 Campanile Dr San Diego (92182) *(P-19035)*

Assocted Stdnts San Dego State 619 594-5200
San Diego State University San Diego (92182) *(P-19036)*

Assocted Vtrnary Practices Inc ....C...... 925 634-1177
4519 Ohara Ave Brentwood (94513) *(P-328)*

Assoction Mxcan Amrcn Edcators ....D...... 562 868-0431
12820 Pioneer Blvd Norwalk (90650) *(P-18731)*

Assured Insurance Tech Inc ....D...... 650 753-1070
650 Page Mill Rd Palo Alto (94304) *(P-8497)*

Assured Relocation Inc ....C...... 888 670-9700
50 Woodside Plz Ste 441 Redwood City (94061) *(P-13199)*

AST Sportswear Inc ....B...... 714 223-2030
Anaheim (92817) *(P-10767)*

Astiva Health Inc ....D...... 858 707-5111
765 The City Dr S Orange (92868) *(P-17180)*

Astra Oil Company Inc ....C...... 714 969-6569
301 Main St Ste 201 Huntington Beach (92648) *(P-6723)*

Astro Mechanical Contractors Inc ....D...... 619 442-9686
603 S Marshall Ave El Cajon (92020) *(P-1366)*

Astronic ....C...... 949 454-1180
2 Orion Aliso Viejo (92656) *(P-2906)*

Astrya Global Inc ....D...... 888 808-3138
4655 Cass St Ste 112 San Diego (92109) *(P-20694)*

Astute Business Solutions ....C...... 925 997-3267
11501 Dublin Blvd Ste 200 Dublin (94568) *(P-11431)*

Asucla, Los Angeles *Also Called: Associated Students UCLA (P-18561)*

Asus Computer International ....C...... 510 739-3777
48720 Kato Rd Fremont (94538) *(P-5275)*

Asylum Access ....D...... 510 891-8700
344 Thomas L Berkley Way Ste 111 Oakland (94612) *(P-19037)*

At & T Wireless Service, Tustin *Also Called: AB Cellular Holding LLC (P-4249)*

At Home Caregivers, Novato *Also Called: Bear Flag Marketing Corp (P-16817)*

At Home Nursing Care Inc ....D...... 760 634-8000
531 Encinitas Blvd Ste 120 Encinitas (92024) *(P-16812)*

ALPHABETIC SECTION — Atria Valley View

At Road Inc .... A 510 668-1638
  888 Tasman Dr Milpitas (95035) *(P-12420)*

At Work, Tustin *Also Called: B2 Services Llc (P-11087)*

At-Bay Specialty Insurance Co .... C 888 338-9522
  1 Post St Fl 14 San Francisco (94104) *(P-8498)*

AT&T, San Diego *Also Called: New Cingular Wireless Svcs Inc (P-4219)*

AT&T, Santa Rosa *Also Called: New Cingular Wireless Svcs Inc (P-4220)*

AT&T Corp .... B 925 823-6949
  330 R San Ramon (94583) *(P-4182)*

AT&T Corp .... B 714 284-2878
  Rm 620 Anaheim (92805) *(P-4183)*

AT&T Corp .... D 303 596-8431
  2260 E Imperial Hwy El Segundo (90245) *(P-4184)*

Ata Engineering Inc (PA) .... D 858 480-2000
  13290 Evening Creek Dr S Ste 250 San Diego (92128) *(P-19147)*

Ata Retail Services LLC .... C 925 621-4700
  7133 Koll Center Pkwy Ste 100 Pleasanton (94566) *(P-6889)*

Atac (PA) .... D 408 736-2822
  2770 De La Cruz Blvd Santa Clara (95050) *(P-12421)*

Atara Bio, Thousand Oaks *Also Called: Atara Biotherapeutics Inc (P-2619)*

Atara Biotherapeutics Inc (PA) .... A 650 278-8930
  2380 Conejo Spectrum St Ste 200 Thousand Oaks (91320) *(P-2619)*

Atascadero State Hospital, Atascadero *Also Called: Califrnia Dept State Hospitals (P-16645)*

Atcaa, Jackson *Also Called: Amador Tlmne Cmnty Action Agcy (P-18554)*

Atec Spine, Carlsbad *Also Called: Alphatec Spine Inc (P-3062)*

Atech Logistics Inc .... C 707 526-1910
  7 College Ave Santa Rosa (95401) *(P-3987)*

Atech Logistics & Distribution, Santa Rosa *Also Called: Atech Logistics Inc (P-3987)*

Atech Warehousing & Dist Inc (PA) .... D 707 526-1910
  7 College Ave Santa Rosa (95401) *(P-3444)*

Atel 14 LLC .... D 415 989-8800
  600 California St Fl 6 San Francisco (94108) *(P-7915)*

Atel Capital Group (PA) .... D 800 543-2835
  505 Montgomery St Fl 11 San Francisco (94111) *(P-7916)*

Atel Corporation .... D 415 989-8800
  600 Montgomery St Fl 9 San Francisco (94111) *(P-13200)*

Aten Technology Inc .... D 949 453-8782
  15365 Barranca Pkwy Irvine (92618) *(P-5276)*

Athas Capital Group Inc .... C 877 877-1477
  27001 Agoura Rd Ste 200 Agoura Hills (91301) *(P-7935)*

Athens Administrators, Concord *Also Called: Athens Insurance Service Inc (P-8499)*

Athens Disposal Company Inc (PA) .... B 626 336-3636
  14048 Valley Blvd La Puente (91746) *(P-4860)*

Athens Environmental Services, Sun Valley *Also Called: Araco Enterprises Inc (P-4856)*

Athens Insurance, Concord *Also Called: James C Jenkins Insur Svc Inc (P-8595)*

Athens Insurance Service Inc .... C 925 826-1000
  2552 Stanwell Dr Ste 100 Concord (94520) *(P-8499)*

Athens Services, Sun Valley *Also Called: Arakelian Enterprises Inc (P-3369)*

Athens Services, City Of Industry *Also Called: Arakelian Enterprises Inc (P-4857)*

Athens Services, City Of Industry *Also Called: Arakelian Enterprises Inc (P-4859)*

Atherton Baptist Homes .... C 626 863-1710
  214 S Atlantic Blvd Alhambra (91801) *(P-15336)*

Athletics Investment Group LLC (PA) .... C 510 638-4900
  7000 Coliseum Way Ste 3 Oakland (94621) *(P-14127)*

ATI, Anaheim *Also Called: ATI Restoration LLC (P-2259)*

ATI, Los Angeles *Also Called: American Trading Intl Inc (P-6454)*

ATI Architects & Engineers, Pleasanton *Also Called: Martin ATI-AC Inc (P-19494)*

ATI Restoration LLC .... D 510 429-5000
  25000 Industrial Blvd Hayward (94545) *(P-2258)*

ATI Restoration LLC (PA) .... C 714 283-9990
  3360 E La Palma Ave Anaheim (92806) *(P-2259)*

ATI Systems International Inc .... A 858 715-8484
  8807 Complex Dr San Diego (92123) *(P-12935)*

Atk Audiotek, Valencia *Also Called: Sound River Corporation (P-1842)*

Atk Space Systems LLC .... D 626 351-0205
  370 N Halstead St Pasadena (91107) *(P-3002)*

Atkins North America Inc .... D 858 874-1810
  9275 Sky Park Ct Ste 200 San Diego (92123) *(P-19148)*

Atkinson Andelson Loya, Cerritos *Also Called: Atkinson Andlson Loya Ruud Rom (P-17369)*

Atkinson Andlson Loya Ruud Rom (PA) .... C 562 653-3200
  12800 Center Court Dr S Ste 300 Cerritos (90703) *(P-17369)*

Atkinson Construction Inc .... B 303 410-2540
  18201 Von Karman Ave Ste 800 Irvine (92612) *(P-1079)*

Atlantic Aviation Fbo Inc .... C 408 297-7552
  1250 Aviation Ave San Jose (95110) *(P-3875)*

Atlantic Aviation Holding Corp .... D 310 396-6770
  2828 Donald Douglas Loop N Lbby Santa Monica (90405) *(P-3876)*

Atlantic Express of California, Long Beach *Also Called: Atlantic Express Trnsp (P-3237)*

Atlantic Express Trnsp .... C 562 997-6868
  2450 Long Beach Blvd Long Beach (90806) *(P-3237)*

Atlantic Mem Healthcare Ctr, Long Beach *Also Called: Atlantic Mem Hlthcare Assoc In (P-15337)*

Atlantic Mem Hlthcare Assoc In (HQ) .... D 562 424-8101
  2750 Atlantic Ave Long Beach (90806) *(P-15337)*

Atlantic Richfield Company (DH) .... A 800 333-3991
  4 Centerpointe Dr La Palma (90623) *(P-7383)*

Atlas Advertising, Irvine *Also Called: M F Salta Co Inc (P-20444)*

Atlas Capital Group LLC .... D 213 988-8890
  1318 E 7th St Ste 200 Los Angeles (90021) *(P-8187)*

Atlas Construction Supply Inc (PA) .... D 858 277-2100
  4640 Brinnell St San Diego (92111) *(P-5195)*

Atlas Copco, Santa Maria *Also Called: Atlas Copco Mafi-Trench Co LLC (P-2795)*

Atlas Copco Mafi-Trench Co LLC (DH) .... C 805 928-5757
  3037 Industrial Pkwy Santa Maria (93455) *(P-2795)*

Atlas Disposal Industries LLC .... D 916 455-2800
  3035 Prospect Park Dr Ste 40 Rancho Cordova (95670) *(P-4861)*

Atlas Engineering West Inc (DH) .... D 619 280-4321
  6280 Riverdale St San Diego (92120) *(P-19951)*

Atlas General Insur Svcs LLC .... C 858 529-6700
  6165 Greenwich Dr Ste 200 San Diego (92122) *(P-8500)*

Atlas Hospitality Group .... D 949 622-3400
  1901 Main St Ste 175 Irvine (92614) *(P-8904)*

Atlas Hotels Inc .... A 619 291-2232
  500 Hotel Cir N San Diego (92108) *(P-9619)*

Atlas Lift Tech Inc .... C 415 283-1804
  210 Porter Dr Ste 300 San Ramon (94583) *(P-17181)*

Atlas Mechanical Inc (PA) .... D 858 554-0700
  8260 Camino Santa Fe Ste B San Diego (92121) *(P-1367)*

Atlas Operations Group .... D 844 414-2857
  240 N Main St Ste 388 Alturas (96101) *(P-12936)*

Atlas Sales and Rentals Inc .... D 510 713-3313
  47233 Fremont Blvd Fremont (94538) *(P-5599)*

Atlas Technical Cons LLC .... B 925 314-7100
  2001 Crow Canyon Rd Ste 110 San Ramon (94583) *(P-20695)*

Atlas/Eastern Van Lines, Pomona *Also Called: W Why W Enterprises Inc (P-3604)*

Atm Consultants, Claremont *Also Called: Atmc Incorporated (P-1670)*

Atmc Incorporated .... D 909 390-0470
  725 W Baseline Rd Claremont (91711) *(P-1670)*

Atob Asset Vehicle I LLC .... D 703 663-0658
  4 Embarcadero Ctr Ste 140 San Francisco (94111) *(P-12103)*

Atomic P R, San Francisco *Also Called: Atomic Public Relations (P-20629)*

Atomic Public Relations (HQ) .... D 415 402-0230
  735 Market St Fl 4 San Francisco (94103) *(P-20629)*

Atpa, El Segundo *Also Called: Associated Third Party Administrators Inc (P-8456)*

Atrenta Inc (HQ) .... D 408 453-3333
  690 E Middlefield Rd Mountain View (94043) *(P-11432)*

Atria Assisted Living Group .... C 949 427-8191
  23792 Marguerite Pkwy Mission Viejo (92692) *(P-18374)*

Atria Delsol, Mission Viejo *Also Called: Atria Assisted Living Group (P-18374)*

Atria Management Company LLC .... C 619 326-0190
  5308 Monroe Ave San Diego (92115) *(P-18375)*

Atria Management Company LLC .... B 760 480-8155
  1342 N Escondido Blvd Escondido (92026) *(P-18376)*

Atria Management Company LLC .... C 925 787-6149
  1228 Rossmoor Pkwy Walnut Creek (94595) *(P-18377)*

Atria Park Pacific Palisades, Pacific Palisades *Also Called: Atria Senior Living Inc (P-18378)*

Atria Senior Living Inc .... D 310 573-9545
  15441 W Sunset Blvd Pacific Palisades (90272) *(P-18378)*

Atria Valley View, Walnut Creek *Also Called: Atria Management Company LLC (P-18377)*

Atrium Door & Win Co Ariz Inc .... C...... 714 693-0601
  5455 E La Palma Ave Ste A Anaheim (92807) *(P-5147)*
Atrium Finance I LP .... A...... 916 446-0100
  300 J St Sacramento (95814) *(P-9620)*
Atrium Hotel, Irvine *Also Called: Golden Hotels Ltd Partnership (P-9811)*
Atrium Plaza LLC .... D...... 650 653-6000
  1770 S Amphlett Blvd San Mateo (94402) *(P-9621)*
Ats, Cotati *Also Called: Ats Medical Services LLC (P-3238)*
Ats Medical Services LLC .... A...... 815 963-5001
  720 Portal St Cotati (94931) *(P-3238)*
Attainment Holdco LLC .... C...... 310 954-1578
  700 S Flower St Ste 1800 Los Angeles (90017) *(P-18732)*
Atterdag Village of Solvang, Solvang *Also Called: Solvang Lutheran Home Inc (P-15677)*
Attic, Oroville *Also Called: Oroville Hospital (P-16301)*
Attivo Networks Inc .... D...... 510 623-1000
  444 Castro St Mountain View (94041) *(P-5277)*
Attn Inc .... C...... 323 413-2878
  5700 Wilshire Blvd Ste 375 Los Angeles (90036) *(P-10702)*
Attorney Network Services, Los Angeles *Also Called: Attorney Network Services Inc (P-11086)*
Attorney Network Services Inc .... D...... 213 430-0440
  725 S Figueroa St Ste 3065 Los Angeles (90017) *(P-11086)*
Attorney Recovery Systems Inc (PA) .... D...... 818 774-1420
  18757 Burbank Blvd Ste 300 Tarzana (91356) *(P-10736)*
Atv Canter LLC (PA) .... D...... 562 977-8565
  4490 Ayers Ave Vernon (90058) *(P-7342)*
Auberge Du Soleil Resort, Rutherford *Also Called: Terre Du Soleil Ltd (P-10308)*
Auburn Area Recreation Pk Dst .... D...... 530 537-2185
  471 Maidu Dr Ste 200 Auburn (95603) *(P-14494)*
Auburn Constructors LLC .... D...... 916 924-0344
  730 W Stadium Ln Sacramento (95834) *(P-1286)*
Auburn Dermatology Center, Auburn *Also Called: Alpine Allrgy Asthma Assoc Inc (P-14599)*
Auburn Oaks Care Center .... D...... 650 949-7777
  3400 Bell Rd Auburn (95603) *(P-15338)*
Auburn Pride, Auburn *Also Called: Pride Industries (P-18243)*
Auction.com, Irvine *Also Called: Auctioncom Inc (P-8905)*
Auction.com, Irvine *Also Called: Auctioncom LLC (P-8906)*
Auctioncom Inc .... C...... 800 499-6199
  1 Mauchly Ste 27 Irvine (92618) *(P-8905)*
Auctioncom LLC (PA) .... C...... 949 859-2777
  1 Mauchly Irvine (92618) *(P-8906)*
Auctioncom LLC .... C...... 949 609-5376
  2121 S El Camino Real Ste 900 San Mateo (94403) *(P-8907)*
Audacy Inc .... C...... 916 766-5000
  3010 Lava Ridge Ct Ste 220 Roseville (95661) *(P-4373)*
Audiencex, Marina Del Rey *Also Called: Socialcom Inc (P-20557)*
Audiovisions, Irvine *Also Called: Inspiria Inc (P-19270)*
Auditboard Inc (PA) .... D...... 877 769-5444
  12900 Park Plaza Dr Ste 200 Cerritos (90703) *(P-11433)*
Audrey's Boutique, Carlsbad *Also Called: Omni La Costa Resort & Spa LLC (P-10066)*
Augmedix Inc (PA) .... A...... 888 669-4885
  111 Sutter St Fl 13 San Francisco (94104) *(P-12104)*
Augmedix Operating Corporation .... D...... 855 720-2929
  111 Sutter St Fl 13 San Francisco (94104) *(P-13201)*
Augora Hills 8 Cinema Center, Agoura Hills *Also Called: Weststar Cinemas Inc (P-14011)*
August Hall & Fifth Arrow, San Francisco *Also Called: Jasper Hall LLC (P-10556)*
Augustine Casino, Coachella *Also Called: Augustine Gaming MGT Corp (P-11434)*
Augustine Gaming MGT Corp .... D...... 760 391-9500
  84001 Avenue 54 Coachella (92236) *(P-11434)*
AUL Corp (DH) .... C...... 707 257-9700
  1250 Main St Ste 300 Napa (94559) *(P-13757)*
Auptix and Flock Freight, Encinitas *Also Called: Flock Freight Inc (P-4020)*
Aura Hardwood Lumber Inc .... D...... 800 411-2872
  620 Quinn Ave San Jose (95112) *(P-5148)*
Aurelio Felix Barreto III .... D...... 951 354-9528
  169 Radio Rd Corona (92879) *(P-7412)*
Aurora, Pico Rivera *Also Called: Aurora World Inc (P-5985)*
Aurora - San Diego LLC (DH) .... D...... 858 487-3200
  11878 Avenue Of Industry San Diego (92128) *(P-16636)*

Aurora Behavioral Health Care .... D...... 818 515-4735
  2900 E Del Mar Blvd Pasadena (91107) *(P-16637)*
AURORA BEHAVIORAL HEALTH CARE, Pasadena *Also Called: Aurora Behavioral Health Care (P-16637)*
Aurora Bhvral Hlthcare - STA R .... D...... 707 800-7700
  1287 Fulton Rd Santa Rosa (95401) *(P-17007)*
Aurora Casting & Engrg Inc .... D...... 805 933-2761
  1790 E Lemonwood Dr Santa Paula (93060) *(P-5477)*
Aurora Chrtr Oak - Los Angles .... D...... 626 966-1632
  1161 E Covina Blvd Covina (91724) *(P-16638)*
Aurora Innovation Inc .... B...... 646 725-4999
  77 Stillman St San Francisco (94107) *(P-12105)*
AURORA INNOVATION, INC., San Francisco *Also Called: Aurora Innovation Inc (P-12105)*
Aurora Las Encinas LLC .... C...... 626 795-9901
  2900 E Del Mar Blvd Pasadena (91107) *(P-16639)*
Aurora Las Encinas Hospital, Pasadena *Also Called: Aurora Las Encinas LLC (P-16639)*
Aurora Operations Inc .... D...... 888 583-9506
  280 Bernardo Ave Mountain View (94043) *(P-12422)*
Aurora World Inc .... C...... 562 205-1222
  8820 Mercury Ln Pico Rivera (90660) *(P-5985)*
Ausgar Technologies Inc .... C...... 855 428-7427
  10721 Treena St Ste 100 San Diego (92131) *(P-19149)*
Austin Commercial LP .... C...... 619 446-5637
  402 W Broadway Ste 400 San Diego (92101) *(P-867)*
Austin Commercial LP .... C...... 310 421-0269
  5901 W Century Blvd Ste 600 Los Angeles (90045) *(P-868)*
Austin Sidley CA LLP .... C...... 213 896-6000
  555 W 5th St Ste 4000 Los Angeles (90013) *(P-17370)*
Austin Veum Rbbins Prtners Inc (PA) .... D...... 619 231-1960
  501 W Broadway Ste A San Diego (92101) *(P-19453)*
Authorized Cellular Service .... D...... 310 466-4144
  8808 S Sepulveda Blvd Los Angeles (90045) *(P-13732)*
Autism Intervention Profession .... D...... 909 245-9979
  340 S Lemon Ave Walnut (91789) *(P-18563)*
Autism Otrach Southern Cal LLC .... D...... 619 795-9925
  3110 Camino Del Rio S Ste 307 San Diego (92108) *(P-17841)*
Autism Spctrum Intrvntions Inc .... C...... 562 972-4846
  713 W Commonwealth Ave Ste A Fullerton (92832) *(P-17842)*
Autism Treatment Solutions LLC .... A...... 209 910-5038
  672 W 11th St Ste 339 Tracy (95376) *(P-17008)*
Auto Club Enterprises (PA) .... A...... 714 850-5111
  3333 Fairview Rd Ms A451 Costa Mesa (92626) *(P-8258)*
Auto Club Enterprises .... B...... 310 914-8500
  8761 Santa Monica Blvd West Hollywood (90069) *(P-8259)*
Auto Edge Solutions, Pacoima *Also Called: Moc Products Company Inc (P-2645)*
Auto Insurance Specialists LLC (DH) .... C...... 562 345-6247
  17785 Center Court Dr N Ste 110 Cerritos (90703) *(P-8501)*
Auto Pride, Anaheim *Also Called: Cal-State Auto Parts Inc (P-5031)*
Auto Value, San Bernardino *Also Called: Metropolitan Automotive Warehouse (P-5049)*
Autobody Depot, San Diego *Also Called: Tcp Global Corporation (P-6884)*
Autocrib Inc .... C...... 714 274-0400
  2882 Dow Ave Tustin (92780) *(P-13202)*
Autodesk, San Francisco *Also Called: Autodesk Inc (P-12106)*
Autodesk Inc (PA) .... B...... 415 507-5000
  1 Market St Ste 400 San Francisco (94105) *(P-12106)*
Autodesk Inc .... D...... 415 356-0700
  1 Market St San Francisco (94105) *(P-12107)*
Autofarm, Fremont *Also Called: Novariant Inc (P-19335)*
Automated Ctrl Technical Svcs, Bakersfield *Also Called: A-C Electric Company (P-19123)*
Automatic Data Processing Inc .... C...... 949 751-0360
  3972 Barranca Pkwy Ste J610 Irvine (92606) *(P-12551)*
Automatic Data Processing Inc .... C...... 800 225-5237
  400 W Covina Blvd San Dimas (91773) *(P-12552)*
Automatic Leasing Inc (PA) .... D...... 213 746-4117
  445 S Figueroa St Los Angeles (90071) *(P-5600)*
Automatic Leasing Inc .... B...... 559 233-2444
  260 Fulton St Fresno (93721) *(P-10461)*
Automatic Screw Mch Pdts Co, Brea *Also Called: Nelson Stud Welding Inc (P-5915)*
Automation Anywhere Inc (PA) .... B...... 888 484-3535
  633 River Oaks Pkwy San Jose (95134) *(P-11435)*

ALPHABETIC SECTION
Avanquest North America LLC

Automation Group, Modesto *Also Called: Industrial Automtn Group LLC (P-19266)*

Automation Holdco Inc .... D....... 858 967-8650
10815 Rancho Bernardo Rd Ste 102 San Diego (92127) *(P-12423)*

Automobile Club Southern Cal .... C....... 714 973-1211
13331 Jamboree Rd Irvine (92602) *(P-8502)*

Automobile Club Southern Cal .... D....... 805 922-5731
2033b S Broadway Santa Maria (93454) *(P-8503)*

Automobile Club Southern Cal .... C....... 714 885-1343
3333 Fairview Rd Costa Mesa (92626) *(P-8504)*

Automobile Club Southern Cal (PA) .... C....... 213 741-3686
2601 S Figueroa St Los Angeles (90007) *(P-8505)*

Automobile Club Southern Cal .... C....... 805 682-5811
3712 State St Santa Barbara (93105) *(P-19038)*

Automobile Club Southern Cal .... C....... 858 483-4960
4973 Clairemont Dr Ste C San Diego (92117) *(P-19039)*

Automobile Club Southern Cal .... D....... 805 543-6454
1445 Calle Joaquin San Luis Obispo (93405) *(P-19040)*

Automobile Club Southern Cal .... D....... 805 497-0911
100 E Wilbur Rd Thousand Oaks (91360) *(P-19041)*

Automobile Club Southern Cal .... C....... 310 325-3111
23001 Hawthorne Blvd Torrance (90505) *(P-19042)*

Automobile Club Southern Cal .... D....... 714 774-2392
420 N Euclid St Anaheim (92801) *(P-19043)*

Automobile Club Southern Cal .... D....... 619 233-1000
2440 Hotel Cir N Ste 100 San Diego (92108) *(P-19044)*

Automobile Club Southern Cal .... D....... 626 963-8531
1301s S Grand Ave Glendora (91740) *(P-19045)*

Automobile Club Southern Cal .... D....... 661 327-4661
1500 Commercial Way Bakersfield (93309) *(P-19046)*

Automobile Club Southern Cal .... D....... 818 993-1616
9440 Reseda Blvd Northridge (91324) *(P-19047)*

Automobile Club Southern Cal .... C....... 562 904-5970
8223 Firestone Blvd Downey (90241) *(P-19048)*

Automobile Club Southern Cal .... D....... 760 433-6261
3330 Vista Way Oceanside (92056) *(P-19049)*

Automobile Club Southern Cal .... C....... 310 376-0521
700 S Aviation Blvd Manhattan Beach (90266) *(P-19050)*

Automobile Club Southern Cal .... D....... 626 795-0601
801 E Union St Pasadena (91101) *(P-19051)*

Automobile Club Southern Cal .... D....... 949 476-8880
3880 Birch St Newport Beach (92660) *(P-19052)*

Automobile Club Southern Cal .... D....... 818 883-2660
22708 Victory Blvd Woodland Hills (91367) *(P-19053)*

Automobile Club Southern Cal .... D....... 310 673-5170
1234 Centinela Ave Inglewood (90302) *(P-19054)*

Automobile Club Southern Cal .... D....... 562 698-3721
16041 Whittier Blvd Whittier (90603) *(P-19055)*

Automobile Club Southern Cal .... D....... 951 684-4250
3700 Central Ave Riverside (92506) *(P-19056)*

Automobile Club Southern Cal .... C....... 909 591-9451
5402 Philadelphia St Ste A Chino (91710) *(P-19057)*

Automobile Club Southern Cal .... C....... 760 745-2124
800 La Terraza Blvd Escondido (92025) *(P-19058)*

Automobile Club Southern Cal .... D....... 949 489-5572
638 Camino De Los Mares Ste E100 San Clemente (92673) *(P-19059)*

Automobile Club Southern Cal .... D....... 949 951-1400
25181 Paseo De Alicia Laguna Hills (92653) *(P-19060)*

Automobile Club Southern Cal .... D....... 858 486-0786
12630 Sabre Springs Pkwy Ste 301 San Diego (92128) *(P-19061)*

Automobile Club Southern Cal .... D....... 951 652-6202
450 W Stetson Ave Hemet (92543) *(P-19062)*

Automobile Club Southern Cal .... C....... 310 453-1909
2730 Santa Monica Blvd Santa Monica (90404) *(P-19063)*

Automobile Club Southern Cal .... D....... 951 808-9624
1170 El Camino Ave Corona (92879) *(P-19064)*

Automobile Club Southern Cal .... D....... 805 735-2731
525 W Central Ave Lompoc (93436) *(P-19065)*

Automobile Club Southern Cal .... D....... 562 425-8350
4800 Airport Plaza Dr Ste 100 Long Beach (90815) *(P-19066)*

Automobile Club Southern Cal .... D....... 562 924-6636
18642 Gridley Rd Artesia (90701) *(P-19067)*

Automobile Club Southern Cal .... D....... 323 525-0018
8761 Santa Monica Blvd West Hollywood (90069) *(P-19068)*

Automotive Aftermarket Inc .... D....... 310 793-0046
15912 Hawthorne Blvd Lawndale (90260) *(P-5025)*

Automotive Importing Manufacturing Inc (PA) .... B....... 916 985-8505
3920 Security Park Dr Rancho Cordova (95742) *(P-5026)*

Automotive Tstg & Dev Svcs Inc (PA) .... C....... 909 390-1100
400 Etiwanda Ave Ontario (91761) *(P-13710)*

Automotivemastermind Inc .... D....... 646 679-3441
201 Mission St Fl 10 San Francisco (94105) *(P-11436)*

Automotus Inc .... D....... 805 504-5750
3415 S Sepulveda Blvd Ste 1166 Los Angeles (90034) *(P-11437)*

Automted Rgnal Jstice Info Sys .... D....... 619 533-4201
401 B St Ste 800 San Diego (92101) *(P-18564)*

Autonation Finance, Irvine *Also Called: Cig Financial LLC (P-7872)*

Autonation Ford Valencia, Valencia *Also Called: Magic Acquisition Corp (P-7255)*

Autonomic LLC (PA) .... D....... 650 823-1806
3251 Hillview Ave # 200 Palo Alto (94304) *(P-11438)*

Autonomy Interwoven, Sunnyvale *Also Called: Entco LLC (P-12181)*

Autostore Integrator, Valencia *Also Called: Sdi Industries Inc (P-2776)*

Autovitals Inc .... D....... 866 949-2848
4141 Jutland Dr Ste 300 San Diego (92117) *(P-12735)*

Autozone, Gardena *Also Called: Autozone Inc (P-7343)*

Autozone Inc .... D....... 310 525-2333
1361 W 190th St Gardena (90248) *(P-7343)*

AUTRY MUSEUM, Los Angeles *Also Called: Autry Museum of American West (P-18639)*

Autry Museum of American West .... C....... 323 667-2000
4700 Western Heritage Way Los Angeles (90027) *(P-18639)*

Autumn Hills Convalescent Home, Glendale *Also Called: Mariner Health Care Inc (P-15571)*

Auxilary of Mssion Hosp Mssion .... A....... 949 364-1400
27700 Medical Center Rd Mission Viejo (92691) *(P-15954)*

Auxilio Inc .... D....... 949 614-0731
27271 Las Ramblas Ste 200 Mission Viejo (92691) *(P-12736)*

AV Fenix Llc .... D....... 805 279-3457
6464 Wood Rd Port Hueneme (93041) *(P-167)*

Ava The Rabbit Haven Inc .... D....... 831 600-7479
1261 S Mary St Scotts Valley (95067) *(P-20696)*

Avac, San Jose *Also Called: Almaden Valley Athletic Club (P-14171)*

Avadyne Health, San Diego *Also Called: H & R Accounts Inc (P-11636)*

Avago Technologies, San Jose *Also Called: Avago Technologies US Inc (P-5626)*

Avago Technologies US Inc (HQ) .... B....... 800 433-8778
1320 Ridder Park Dr San Jose (95131) *(P-5626)*

Avalon Building Maint Inc .... B....... 714 693-2407
1832 Commercenter Cir San Bernardino (92408) *(P-10859)*

Avalon Care Cen .... C....... 209 723-1056
3170 M St Merced (95348) *(P-15339)*

Avalon Care Center - Modesto .... C....... 209 526-1775
1900 Coffee Rd Modesto (95355) *(P-15340)*

Avalon Care Ctr - Chwchlla LLC .... C....... 559 665-4826
1010 Ventura Ave Chowchilla (93610) *(P-15341)*

Avalon Care Ctr - Mrced Frncsc .... D....... 209 722-6231
3169 M St Merced (95348) *(P-15342)*

Avalon Care Ctr - Newman LLC .... D....... 209 862-2862
709 N St Newman (95360) *(P-15343)*

Avalon Care Ctr - San Andreas .... D....... 209 754-3823
900 Mountain Ranch Rd San Andreas (95249) *(P-15344)*

Avalon Care Ctr - Sonora LLC .... C....... 209 533-2500
19929 Greenley Rd Sonora (95370) *(P-15345)*

Avalon Glass & Mirror, Carson *Also Called: Avalon Glass & Mirror Company (P-2692)*

Avalon Glass & Mirror Company .... D....... 323 321-8806
642 Alondra Blvd Carson (90746) *(P-2692)*

AVALON HEALTH CARE GROUP, San Andreas *Also Called: Avalon Care Ctr - San Andreas (P-15344)*

AVALON HEALTH CARE GROUP, Sonora *Also Called: Avalon Care Ctr - Sonora LLC (P-15345)*

Avalon Hotel, Beverly Hills *Also Called: Honeymoon Real Estate LP (P-9867)*

Avalon Transportation Co, Culver City *Also Called: Virgin Fish Inc (P-3303)*

Avamar Technologies Inc .... D....... 949 743-5100
135 Technology Dr Irvine (92618) *(P-11439)*

Avanquest North America LLC (HQ) .... D....... 818 591-9600
23801 Calabasas Rd Ste 2005 Calabasas (91302) *(P-11440)*

Avante Health Solutions   ALPHABETIC SECTION

Avante Health Solutions, San Clemente *Also Called: Pacific Medical Group Inc (P-5438)*

Avantgarde Senior Living .... C...... 818 881-0055
5645 Lindley Ave Tarzana (91356) *(P-18379)*

Avasant LLC (PA) .... D...... 310 643-3030
1960 E Grand Ave Ste 1050 El Segundo (90245) *(P-20284)*

Avast Software Inc (PA) .... D...... 844 340-9251
501 E Middlefield Rd Mountain View (94043) *(P-12108)*

Avco Financial, Glendale *Also Called: Associates First Capital Corp (P-7870)*

Avenu Muniservices, Fresno *Also Called: Muniservices LLC (P-20477)*

Avenue of Arts Wyndham Hotel, Costa Mesa *Also Called: Rosanna Inc (P-10172)*

Averitt Express Inc .... D...... 310 970-9520
3133 W 131st St Hawthorne (90250) *(P-3445)*

Avery Corp .... C...... 626 304-2000
207 N Goode Ave Fl 6 Glendale (91203) *(P-19661)*

Avery Group Inc .... B...... 310 217-1070
8941 Dalton Ave Los Angeles (90047) *(P-7564)*

Avery Transport Inc .... D...... 661 948-3627
43120 Venture St Lancaster (93535) *(P-3446)*

Aveta Health Solution Inc .... B...... 909 605-8000
3990 Concours Ste 500 Ontario (91764) *(P-20285)*

Aveva Software LLC .... C...... 760 268-7700
5850 El Camino Real Carlsbad (92008) *(P-11441)*

Aveva Software LLC (DH) .... B...... 949 727-3200
26561 Rancho Pkwy S Lake Forest (92630) *(P-12424)*

AVI-Spl LLC .... A...... 510 344-5618
44911 Industrial Dr Fremont (94538) *(P-12425)*

Aviara Fsrc Associates Limited .... A...... 760 603-6800
7100 Aviara Resort Dr Carlsbad (92011) *(P-9622)*

Aviation & Defense Inc .... C...... 909 382-3487
255 S Leland Norton Way San Bernardino (92408) *(P-3877)*

Aviation Consultants Inc .... D...... 805 596-0212
4900 Wing Way Paso Robles (93446) *(P-3878)*

Aviation Consultants Inc .... D...... 949 201-2550
19301 Campus Dr Santa Ana (92707) *(P-3879)*

Aviation Consultants Inc (PA) .... D...... 805 782-9722
4751 Aviadores Way San Luis Obispo (93401) *(P-20028)*

Aviation Maintenance Group Inc .... D...... 714 469-0515
8352 Kimball Ave Hngr 3 Chino (91708) *(P-3880)*

Avid Bioservices, Tustin *Also Called: Pphm Inc (P-6139)*

Avidbank Holdings Inc .... C...... 408 200-7390
1732 N 1st St Fl 6 San Jose (95112) *(P-7654)*

Avidex Industries LLC .... D...... 949 428-6333
20382 Hermana Cir Lake Forest (92630) *(P-12737)*

Avilas Garden Art (PA) .... D...... 909 350-4546
14608 Merrill Ave Fontana (92335) *(P-2701)*

Avionics & Electronics, Valencia *Also Called: Curtiss-Wrght Cntrls Intgrted (P-19192)*

Aviso Inc .... D...... 650 567-5470
805 Veterans Blvd Ste 300 Redwood City (94063) *(P-20286)*

Avita Medical, Valencia *Also Called: Avita Medical Americas LLC (P-5401)*

Avita Medical Americas LLC .... C...... 661 367-9170
28159 Avenue Stanford Ste 220 Valencia (91355) *(P-5401)*

Avitex Inc (PA) .... C...... 818 994-6487
20362 Plummer St Chatsworth (91311) *(P-2444)*

AVIVA CENTER, Los Angeles *Also Called: Hamburger Home (P-18444)*

Aviva Family & Childrens Svcs (PA) .... D...... 323 876-0550
1701 Camino Palmero St Los Angeles (90046) *(P-17843)*

Avjet Corporation (DH) .... D...... 818 841-6190
4301 W Empire Ave Burbank (91505) *(P-3863)*

Avmc, Lancaster *Also Called: Antelope Valley Health Care Di (P-15948)*

Avocado Packer & Shipper, Murrieta *Also Called: West Pak Avocado Inc (P-314)*

Avocado Post Acute, El Cajon *Also Called: Eldorado Care Center LP (P-15433)*

Avr Global Tech, Escondido *Also Called: Avr Global Technologies Inc (P-2939)*

Avr Global Technologies Inc (PA) .... C...... 949 391-1180
500 La Terraza Blvd Ste 150 Escondido (92025) *(P-2939)*

Avr San Jose Downtown Ht LLC .... D...... 408 924-0900
350 W Santa Clara St San Jose (95113) *(P-9623)*

Avsc Intllctual Prprty MGT Inc .... B...... 562 366-1924
111 W Ocean Blvd Ste 1110 Long Beach (90802) *(P-20029)*

Awe, San Diego *Also Called: Herring Networks Inc (P-4440)*

Awesome Office Inc .... D...... 310 845-7750
3415 S Sepulveda Blvd Ste 1100 Los Angeles (90034) *(P-6455)*

Awhap Acquisition Corp .... C...... 888 611-4328
28358 Constellation Rd Ste 698 Valencia (91355) *(P-1368)*

AWI, Sacramento *Also Called: All Weather Inc (P-3040)*

AWI Management Corporation .... C...... 951 674-8200
1800 E Lakeshore Dr Lake Elsinore (92530) *(P-20030)*

AWR, San Dimas *Also Called: American States Water Company (P-4764)*

AWR, San Dimas *Also Called: Golden State Water Company (P-4794)*

Awt Construction Group Inc .... D...... 707 746-7500
4740 E 2nd St Ste 22 Benicia (94510) *(P-657)*

Awt Worlwide, Sunnyvale *Also Called: Stormgeo (P-20902)*

Axa Rosenberg Inv MGT LLC .... C...... 925 253-3300
4 Orinda Way Bldg E Orinda (94563) *(P-9357)*

Axelacare Holdings Inc .... C...... 714 522-8802
12604 Hiddencreek Way Ste C Cerritos (90703) *(P-16813)*

Axim Geospatial LLC .... D...... 608 352-4180
2701 Loker Ave W Carlsbad (92010) *(P-13203)*

Axiom Global Technologies Inc .... C...... 925 393-5800
220 N Wiget Ln Walnut Creek (94598) *(P-20697)*

Axiom Memory Solutions Inc .... D...... 949 581-1450
16 Goodyear Ste 120 Irvine (92618) *(P-5278)*

Axis, Culver City *Also Called: Rick Solomon Enterprises Inc (P-6185)*

Axis Community Health Inc .... D...... 925 462-1755
4361 Railroad Ave Pleasanton (94566) *(P-17009)*

Axis Construction, Hayward *Also Called: Axis Services Inc (P-746)*

Axis Mechanical Inc .... D...... 408 573-7400
908 Bern Ct San Jose (95112) *(P-1369)*

Axis Services Inc .... C...... 510 732-6111
2544 Barrington Ct Hayward (94545) *(P-746)*

Axxcelera, Fremont *Also Called: Axxcelera Brdband Wireless Inc (P-4529)*

Axxcelera Brdband Wireless Inc .... C...... 510 573-4708
48389 Fremont Blvd Fremont (94538) *(P-4529)*

Aya Healthcare Inc (PA) .... B...... 858 458-4410
5930 Cornerstone Ct W Ste 300 San Diego (92121) *(P-11273)*

Aya Living Inc .... C...... 619 446-6469
1450 Frazee Rd San Diego (92108) *(P-17844)*

Aya Locums Services Inc .... A...... 866 687-7390
5930 Cornerstone Ct W Ste 300 San Diego (92121) *(P-17182)*

Aylesva Inc .... C...... 562 688-0592
14537 Garfield Ave Paramount (90723) *(P-6228)*

Ayoob & Peery Plumbing Co Inc .... D...... 415 550-0975
975 Indiana St San Francisco (94107) *(P-1370)*

Ayres - Paso Robles LP .... C...... 714 850-0409
2700 Buena Vista Dr Paso Robles (93446) *(P-9624)*

Ayres Group .... D...... 949 455-2545
28941 Los Alisos Blvd Mission Viejo (92692) *(P-9625)*

Ayres Group .... D...... 310 220-6447
14400 Hindry Ave Hawthorne (90250) *(P-9626)*

Ayres Hotel Laguna Woods, Laguna Woods *Also Called: Countryside Inn-Corona LP (P-9721)*

Ayres Hotel Manhattan Beach, Hawthorne *Also Called: Ayres Group (P-9626)*

Ayres Suites Mission Viejo, Mission Viejo *Also Called: Ayres Group (P-9625)*

Ayusa International .... C...... 888 552-9872
600 California St Fl 10 San Francisco (94108) *(P-17802)*

Ayzenberg Group Inc .... D...... 626 584-4070
49 E Walnut St Pasadena (91103) *(P-10589)*

AZ Construction Inc (PA) .... C...... 626 333-0727
727 Glendora Ave La Puente (91744) *(P-658)*

Azad Professional Dental Corp .... D...... 661 558-0022
4221 S H St Bakersfield (93304) *(P-15217)*

Azimc Investments Inc .... C...... 818 678-1200
8901 Canoga Ave Canoga Park (91304) *(P-5027)*

Aztec Landscaping Inc (PA) .... C...... 619 464-3303
7980 Lemon Grove Way Lemon Grove (91945) *(P-475)*

Azteca Landscape .... D...... 951 369-9210
4073 Mennes Ave Riverside (92509) *(P-388)*

Aztecs Telecom Inc .... D...... 714 373-1560
1353 Walker Ln Corona (92879) *(P-13204)*

Azuga, Fremont *Also Called: Azuga Inc (P-12426)*

Azuga Inc (DH) .... B...... 866 497-2512
42840 Christy St Ste 205 Fremont (94538) *(P-12426)*

ALPHABETIC SECTION

Azul Hospitality Group Inc .... C....... 619 223-4200
  800 W Ivy St Ste D San Diego (92101) *(P-20031)*

Azul Systems Inc (PA) .... D....... 650 230-6500
  385 Moffett Park Dr Ste 115 Sunnyvale (94089) *(P-12109)*

Azulworks Inc .... C....... 415 558-1507
  1400 Egbert Ave San Francisco (94124) *(P-4765)*

Azuma Foods Intl Inc USA (HQ) .... D....... 510 782-1112
  20201 Mack St Hayward (94545) *(P-2418)*

Azuma Foods Intl Inc USA, Hayward *Also Called: Azuma Foods Intl Inc USA (P-2418)*

Azumio Inc (PA) .... D....... 719 310-3774
  255 Shoreline Dr Ste 130 Redwood City (94065) *(P-11442)*

Azumo, Portola Valley *Also Called: Azumo LLC (P-11443)*

Azumo LLC .... C....... 415 610-7002
  3130 Alpine Rd Ste 288 # 485 Portola Valley (94028) *(P-11443)*

Azusa Lights & Water Dept, Azusa *Also Called: City of Azusa (P-4770)*

B & B Concrete, Santa Clara *Also Called: Robert A Bothman Inc (P-2153)*

B & B Nurseries Inc .... C....... 951 352-8383
  9505 Cleveland Ave Riverside (92503) *(P-6850)*

B & B Specialties Inc .... D....... 714 985-3075
  4321 E La Palma Ave Anaheim (92807) *(P-5723)*

B & B Specialty Metals, Bakersfield *Also Called: B & B Surplus Inc (P-5478)*

B & B Surplus Inc (PA) .... D....... 661 589-0381
  7020 Rosedale Hwy Bakersfield (93308) *(P-5478)*

B & C, Oakland *Also Called: B&C Transit Inc (P-19150)*

B & E Convalescent Center Inc (PA) .... D....... 562 923-9449
  11627 Telegraph Rd Ste 200 Santa Fe Springs (90670) *(P-15815)*

B & G Delivery System Inc .... C....... 916 921-4401
  2549 Harris Ave Sacramento (95838) *(P-3371)*

B & L Consulting LLC .... C....... 682 238-6994
  164 N 2nd Ave # 9 Upland (91786) *(P-20698)*

B & M Contractors Inc .... D....... 805 581-5480
  4473 Cochran St Simi Valley (93063) *(P-2096)*

B & W, Carlsbad *Also Called: Equity International Inc (P-5648)*

B A S, Diamond Bar *Also Called: Tetra Tech Bas Inc (P-19411)*

B B Blu, Los Angeles *Also Called: Treivush Industries Inc (P-2461)*

B B S I, San Diego *Also Called: Barrett Business Services Inc (P-11089)*

B C S, Canoga Park *Also Called: Buyers Consultation Svc Inc (P-5637)*

B Capital Group US LLC .... D....... 310 698-1270
  1240 Rosecrans Ave Ste 120 Manhattan Beach (90266) *(P-9489)*

B H R Operations LLC .... A....... 408 321-9500
  777 Bellew Dr Milpitas (95035) *(P-9627)*

B J T C Inc .... D....... 760 737-2442
  1435 Simpson Way Escondido (92029) *(P-5806)*

B L S Limousine Service, Los Angeles *Also Called: Bls Lmsine Svc Los Angeles Inc (P-3242)*

B M D, Galt *Also Called: Building Material Distrs Inc (P-5150)*

B M W of Riverside, Riverside *Also Called: David A Campbell Corporation (P-7191)*

B N I, Upland *Also Called: Bni Enterprises Inc (P-20630)*

B R Funsten & Co .... D....... 209 825-5375
  105 Industrial Park Dr Manteca (95337) *(P-5110)*

B Riley Securities Inc .... C....... 310 966-1444
  11100 Santa Monica Blvd Los Angeles (90025) *(P-13205)*

B S K Analytical Laboratories, Fresno *Also Called: BSK Associates (P-19163)*

B Spot, Los Angeles *Also Called: Game Play Network Inc (P-11612)*

B T Mancini Co Inc (PA) .... D....... 408 942-7900
  876 S Milpitas Blvd Milpitas (95035) *(P-2029)*

B T Mancini Co Inc .... C....... 916 381-3660
  8571 23rd Ave Sacramento (95826) *(P-5111)*

B Young Enterprises Inc .... D....... 858 748-0935
  12254 Iavelli Way Poway (92064) *(P-2479)*

B-K Lighting Inc .... C....... 559 438-5800
  40429 Brickyard Dr Madera (93636) *(P-2871)*

B-Spring Valley LLC .... D....... 619 797-3991
  9009 Campo Rd Spring Valley (91977) *(P-15346)*

B.T. Mancini Company, Milpitas *Also Called: B T Mancini Co Inc (P-2029)*

B&C Liquidating Corp (HQ) .... C....... 626 799-7000
  3475 E Foothill Blvd Ste 100 Pasadena (91107) *(P-8506)*

B&C Transit Inc (HQ) .... D....... 510 483-3560
  1924 Franklin St Ste 200 Oakland (94612) *(P-19150)*

B2 Services Llc .... D....... 714 363-3481
  17291 Irvine Blvd Ste 258 Tustin (92780) *(P-11087)*

B2b Industrial Products LLC .... D....... 510 887-4586
  23271 Eichler St Hayward (94545) *(P-6890)*

B2b Industrial Products LLC .... C....... 630 396-6300
  340 El Camino Real S Ste 35b Salinas (93901) *(P-6891)*

B2b Payroll Services, Cypress *Also Called: B2b Staffing Services Inc (P-11274)*

B2b Staffing Services Inc .... B....... 714 243-4104
  4501 Cerritos Ave Ste 201 Cypress (90630) *(P-11274)*

Ba Leasing & Capital Corp (DH) .... C....... 415 765-1804
  555 California St Fl 4 San Francisco (94104) *(P-11021)*

Ba Sports Nutrition LLC .... D....... 718 357-7402
  630 Clinton Pl Beverly Hills (90210) *(P-14172)*

Babcock Laboratories Inc .... D....... 951 653-3351
  6100 Quail Valley Ct Riverside (92507) *(P-19952)*

Baby Phat, Commerce *Also Called: BP Clothing LLC (P-6195)*

Babycenter LLC (DH) .... D....... 415 537-0900
  163 Freelon St San Francisco (94107) *(P-7572)*

Babyfirst Americas LLC .... D....... 310 442-9853
  10390 Santa Monica Blvd Ste 310 Los Angeles (90025) *(P-11444)*

Babylon Security Services Inc .... D....... 818 766-8122
  6032 One Half Vineland Ave North Hollywood (91606) *(P-12937)*

Bacara Resorts and Spa, Santa Barbara *Also Called: Bcra Resort Services Inc (P-9635)*

Back of House Inc .... D....... 415 550-8626
  2020 Union St San Francisco (94123) *(P-13206)*

Backblaze Inc .... C....... 650 352-3738
  201 Baldwin Ave San Mateo (94401) *(P-12652)*

Backbone Capital Advisors LLC .... C....... 818 769-8016
  4084 Camellia Ave Studio City (91604) *(P-9490)*

Backroads (PA) .... D....... 510 527-1555
  801 Cedar St Berkeley (94710) *(P-3960)*

Baco Realty Corporation .... D....... 916 974-9898
  6310 Stockton Blvd Sacramento (95824) *(P-3677)*

Baco Realty Corporation .... D....... 925 275-0100
  2071 Camino Ramon San Ramon (94583) *(P-3678)*

Bacon's Multivision, Oakland *Also Called: Multivision Inc (P-13386)*

Bacr .... D....... 415 444-5580
  171 Carlos Dr San Rafael (94903) *(P-19069)*

Bacs Adult Day Care, Oakland *Also Called: Bay Area Community Svcs Inc (P-17846)*

Bad Boys Bail Bonds Inc (PA) .... D....... 408 298-3333
  595 Park Ave Ste 200 San Jose (95110) *(P-13207)*

Bad Robot Productions Inc .... D....... 310 664-3456
  1221 Olympic Blvd Santa Monica (90404) *(P-13961)*

Bae Systems, San Diego *Also Called: Bae Systems Info Elctrnic Syst (P-3024)*

Bae Systems Info Elctrnic Syst .... A....... 858 592-5000
  10920 Technology Pl San Diego (92127) *(P-3024)*

Bae Systems Maritime Engineering & Services Inc .... B....... 619 238-1000
  7330 Engineer Rd Ste A San Diego (92111) *(P-19151)*

Bae Systems National Security Solutions Inc .... A....... 858 592-5000
  10920 Technology Pl San Diego (92127) *(P-3025)*

Bae Systems Srra Dtroit Desl A (HQ) .... D....... 510 635-8991
  1755 Adams Ave San Leandro (94577) *(P-13657)*

BAER INSTITUTE, Moffett Field *Also Called: Bay Area Envmtl Res Inst (P-19864)*

Baggage & Air Freight Service, Fresno *Also Called: Skywest Airlines Inc (P-3845)*

Baggage Service, Los Angeles *Also Called: China Airlines Ltd (P-3833)*

Baggu Corporation .... D....... 800 605-0759
  2415 3rd St Ste 239 San Francisco (94107) *(P-6892)*

Bagley, William T, San Francisco *Also Called: Nossaman LLP (P-17590)*

Bahare .... C....... 516 472-1457
  11769 W Sunset Blvd Los Angeles (90049) *(P-11445)*

Bahia Resort Hotels, San Diego *Also Called: Bh Partnership LP (P-9648)*

Baidu USA LLC .... C....... 669 224-6400
  1195 Bordeaux Dr Sunnyvale (94089) *(P-12738)*

Bail Project .... D....... 323 366-0799
  3107 Washington Blvd Marina Del Rey (90292) *(P-18565)*

Bailey, Rollin C MD, Lompoc *Also Called: Valley Med Group Lompoc Inc (P-16613)*

Bain & Company Inc .... D....... 310 229-3000
  1901 Avenue Of The Stars Ste 2000 Los Angeles (90067) *(P-20287)*

Bain & Company Inc .... C....... 415 627-1000
  415 Mission St Ste 4700 San Francisco (94105) *(P-20288)*

Bain Capitl Ventr Partners LLC .... C....... 415 213-2400
  590 Howard St San Francisco (94105) *(P-9491)*

Bairesdev LLC — ALPHABETIC SECTION

Bairesdev LLC .... A....... 847 796-1636
1999 S Bascom Ave Campbell (95008) *(P-11446)*

Baja Construction Co Inc (PA).................................... D....... 925 229-0732
223 Foster St Martinez (94553) *(P-2179)*

Baja Designs, San Marcos *Also Called: Bestop Baja LLC (P-7396)*

Baja Duty Free, Oakland *Also Called: Fairn & Swanson Inc (P-6107)*

Baja Fresh, Chino Hills *Also Called: Gateway Fresh LLC (P-9313)*

Baja Fresh Supermarket .... B....... 760 843-7730
14827 Seventh St Victorville (92395) *(P-232)*

Bakbone Software Inc (HQ)....................................... D....... 858 450-9009
9540 Towne Centre Dr Ste 100 San Diego (92121) *(P-11447)*

Bakell LLC .... D....... 800 292-2137
24723 Redlands Blvd Ste F Loma Linda (92354) *(P-805)*

Bakemark, Pico Rivera *Also Called: Bakemark USA LLC (P-6607)*

Bakemark USA LLC (PA)... C....... 562 949-1054
7351 Crider Ave Pico Rivera (90660) *(P-6607)*

Baker & Hostetler LLP .... D....... 310 820-8800
11601 Wilshire Blvd Fl 14 Los Angeles (90025) *(P-17371)*

Baker & Hostetler LLP .... D....... 714 754-6600
600 Anton Blvd Ste 900 Costa Mesa (92626) *(P-17372)*

Baker & McKenzie LLP .... C....... 415 576-3000
2 Embarcadero Ctr Ste 1100 San Francisco (94111) *(P-17373)*

Baker & McKenzie LLP .... C....... 310 201-4728
10250 Constellation Blvd Ste 1850 Los Angeles (90067) *(P-17374)*

Baker & McKenzie LLP .... D....... 650 856-2400
660 Hansen Way Ste 1 Palo Alto (94304) *(P-17375)*

Baker & Taylor LLC .... C....... 858 457-2500
10350 Barnes Canyon Rd Ste 100 San Diego (92121) *(P-6840)*

Baker & Taylor Holdings LLC .... A....... 858 457-2500
10350 Barnes Canyon Rd San Diego (92121) *(P-5279)*

Baker & Taylor Marketing Svc, San Diego *Also Called: Baker & Taylor Holdings LLC (P-5279)*

Baker Electric & Renewables LLC .... A....... 760 745-2001
1298 Pacific Oaks Pl Escondido (92029) *(P-1671)*

Baker Manock & Jensen Pc .... D....... 559 432-5400
5260 N Palm Ave Ste 201 Fresno (93704) *(P-17376)*

Baker Mnock Jnsen Attys At Law, Fresno *Also Called: Baker Manock & Jensen Pc (P-17376)*

Baker Places Inc .... D....... 415 503-3137
101 Gough St San Francisco (94102) *(P-17010)*

Baker Places Inc .... D....... 415 387-2275
2157 Grove St San Francisco (94117) *(P-17845)*

Baker Tilly California, Irvine *Also Called: Baker Tilly Us LLP (P-19537)*

Baker Tilly Us LLP .... B....... 818 981-2600
15760 Ventura Blvd Ste 1100 Encino (91436) *(P-19534)*

Baker Tilly Us LLP .... A....... 310 826-4474
11150 Santa Monica Blvd Ste 600 Los Angeles (90025) *(P-19535)*

Baker Tilly Us LLP .... B....... 858 597-4100
3655 Nobel Dr Ste 300 San Diego (92122) *(P-19536)*

Baker Tilly Us LLP .... B....... 949 222-2999
18500 Von Karman Ave Fl 10 Irvine (92612) *(P-19537)*

Bakersfeld Assn For Rtrded Ctz .... D....... 661 834-2272
2240 S Union Ave Bakersfield (93307) *(P-18210)*

Bakersfeld Bhvral Hlthcare Hos .... C....... 661 398-1800
5201 White Ln Bakersfield (93309) *(P-16640)*

Bakersfeld Hlthcare Wllness CN .... D....... 661 872-2121
2211 Mount Vernon Ave Bakersfield (93306) *(P-15347)*

Bakersfeld Mem Hosp Foundation .... D....... 661 327-4647
420 34th St Bakersfield (93301) *(P-15955)*

Bakersfield Country Club .... C....... 661 871-4000
4200 Country Club Dr Bakersfield (93306) *(P-14326)*

Bakersfield District Office, Bakersfield *Also Called: State Compensation Insur Fund (P-8410)*

Bakersfield Family Med Group .... D....... 661 846-3605
5601 Auburn St Unit A Bakersfield (93306) *(P-17183)*

Bakersfield Family Medical Ctr, Bakersfield *Also Called: Bakersfield Family Medical Group Inc (P-14621)*

Bakersfield Family Medical Group Inc (PA)................. D....... 661 327-4411
4580 California Ave Bakersfield (93309) *(P-14621)*

Bakersfield Heart Hospital, Bakersfield *Also Called: Adventist Hlth Systm/West Corp (P-15923)*

Bakersfield Hospitality LLC .... D....... 661 393-1277
6141 Knudsen Dr Bakersfield (93308) *(P-9628)*

Bakersfield Inn Inc .... D....... 661 323-1900
801 Truxtun Ave Bakersfield (93301) *(P-9629)*

Bakersfield Mazda, Bakersfield *Also Called: Cjm Automotive Group Inc (P-7185)*

Bakersfield Memorial Hospital .... A....... 661 327-1792
420 34th St Bakersfield (93301) *(P-15956)*

Bakersfield Respite Homecare, Bakersfield *Also Called: Maxim Healthcare Services Inc (P-11309)*

Bakersfield Shingles Wholesale Inc .... D....... 661 327-3727
4 P St Bakersfield (93304) *(P-5226)*

Bakersfield Well & Pump Co, Fresno *Also Called: Zim Industries Inc (P-1283)*

Bakersfield Westwind Corp .... C....... 661 327-2121
1810 Westwind Dr Bakersfield (93301) *(P-8908)*

Bakersfieldidence Opco LLC .... C....... 661 399-2472
5151 Knudsen Dr Bakersfield (93308) *(P-15348)*

Bakery Ex Southern Cal LLC .... D....... 714 446-9470
1910 W Malvern Ave Fullerton (92833) *(P-6608)*

Balance, Concord *Also Called: Consumer Cr Cnsling Svc San Fr (P-10539)*

Balance Staffing, San Jose *Also Called: Staffing Solutions Inc (P-11237)*

Balbix Inc .... D....... 866 936-3180
3031 Tisch Way Ste 800 San Jose (95128) *(P-11448)*

Balboa Bay Club Inc (HQ)...................................... B....... 949 645-5000
1221 W Coast Hwy Newport Beach (92663) *(P-14327)*

Balboa Bay Club and Resort, Newport Beach *Also Called: International Bay Clubs LLC (P-14384)*

Balboa Capital Corporation (DH)............................. C....... 949 756-0800
575 Anton Blvd Ste 1200 Costa Mesa (92626) *(P-7891)*

Balboa Enterprises Inc .... D....... 650 961-6161
2530 Solace Pl Mountain View (94040) *(P-15349)*

Balboa Intrmdiate Holdings LLC (PA)....................... A....... 650 846-1000
3307 Hillview Ave Palo Alto (94304) *(P-11449)*

Balboa Nphrology Med Group Inc .... C....... 858 810-8000
4225 Executive Sq Ste 450 La Jolla (92037) *(P-14622)*

Baldwin Hospitality LLC .... D....... 626 446-2988
14635 Baldwin Park Towne Ctr Baldwin Park (91706) *(P-9630)*

Balfour Beatty Cnstr LLC .... D....... 858 635-7400
13520 Evening Creek Dr N Ste 270 San Diego (92128) *(P-869)*

Bali Construction Inc .... D....... 626 442-8003
9852 Joe Vargas Way South El Monte (91733) *(P-1196)*

Ballard Rehabilitation Hosp, San Bernardino *Also Called: Robert Ballard Rehab Hospital (P-15305)*

Ballard Spahr LLP .... D....... 424 204-4400
2029 Century Park E Ste 1400 Los Angeles (90002) *(P-17377)*

Ballena Technologies .... B....... 510 521-0720
1150 Ballena Blvd Ste 250 Alameda (94501) *(P-4473)*

Balletto Ranch Inc (PA).. C....... 707 568-2455
5700 Occidental Rd Santa Rosa (95401) *(P-20)*

Balletto Ranch Inc .... C....... 707 568-2455
3800 Guerneville Rd Santa Rosa (95401) *(P-69)*

Balletto Ranch Shop, Santa Rosa *Also Called: Balletto Ranch Inc (P-69)*

Bally Total Fitness, Norwalk *Also Called: Bally Total Fitness Corporation (P-14173)*

Bally Total Fitness Corporation .... A....... 562 484-2000
12440 Imperial Hwy # 300 Norwalk (90650) *(P-14173)*

Baloian Farm, Fresno *Also Called: Baloian Packing Co Inc (P-21)*

Baloian Farms, Fresno *Also Called: Baloian Packing Co Inc (P-22)*

Baloian Packing Co Inc (PA)................................. D....... 559 485-9200
446 N Blythe Ave Fresno (93706) *(P-21)*

Baloian Packing Co Inc .... D....... 559 441-7043
3138 W Whites Bridge Ave A Fresno (93706) *(P-22)*

Balt Usa LLC .... D....... 949 788-1443
29 Parker Ste 100 Irvine (92618) *(P-5402)*

Bam Advisor Services LLC .... D....... 800 366-7266
10 Almaden Blvd Fl 15 San Jose (95113) *(P-8188)*

Bamko, Los Angeles *Also Called: Bamko Inc (P-10695)*

Bamko Inc .... C....... 310 470-5859
11620 Wilshire Blvd Ste 610 Los Angeles (90025) *(P-10695)*

Bana Home Loan Servicing .... A....... 213 345-7975
31303 Agoura Rd Westlake Village (91361) *(P-7603)*

Banamex USA Bancorp (DH)................................... C....... 310 203-3440
787 W 5th St Los Angeles (90071) *(P-9294)*

Banc America Lsg & Capitl LLC (DH)........................ C....... 415 765-7349
555 California St Fl 4 San Francisco (94104) *(P-7604)*

Banc California National Assn (HQ)......................... D....... 877 770-2262
3 Macarthur Pl Ste 100 Santa Ana (92707) *(P-7605)*

Banc of California Inc (PA) .... C....... 855 361-2262
  3 Macarthur Pl Ste 100 Santa Ana (92707) *(P-7606)*
Bancolmbia PR Intrnacional Inc .... C....... 323 582-2255
  2625 E Florence Ave Ste E Huntington Park (90255) *(P-13208)*
Bandai Namco Entrmt Amer Inc .... C....... 408 235-2000
  23 Odyssey Irvine (92618) *(P-5986)*
Bandy Ranch Floral Corp 805 757-9905
  2755 Dos Aarons Way Ste B Vista (92081) *(P-6851)*
Bang Zoom Entertainment Inc .... D....... 818 295-3939
  1100 N Hollywood Way Ste A Burbank (91505) *(P-14079)*
Bangkit (usa) Inc .... D....... 626 672-0888
  10511 Valley Blvd El Monte (91731) *(P-6062)*
Banister Electrical Inc .... D....... 925 778-7801
  2532 Verne Roberts Cir Antioch (94509) *(P-1672)*
Bank of America, San Francisco *Also Called: Bankamerica Financial Inc (P-7892)*
Bank of Cardiff, San Diego *Also Called: Commercial Fin Lsg Bnk Crdiff (P-7730)*
Bank of Hope (HQ) .... C....... 213 639-1700
  3200 Wilshire Blvd Ste 1400 Los Angeles (90010) *(P-7607)*
Bank of Manhattan .... C....... 310 606-8000
  2141 Rosecrans Ave Ste 1100 El Segundo (90245) *(P-7728)*
Bank of Marin Bancorp (PA) .... C....... 415 763-4520
  504 Redwood Blvd Ste 100 Novato (94947) *(P-7655)*
Bank of Orient Foundation (HQ) .... C....... 415 338-0668
  100 Pine St Ste 600 San Francisco (94111) *(P-7656)*
Bank of Sacramento .... D....... 916 648-2100
  1750 Howe Ave Ste 100 Sacramento (95825) *(P-7742)*
Bank of Sierra (HQ) .... C....... 559 782-4300
  90 N Main St Porterville (93257) *(P-7657)*
Bank of Stockton (HQ) .... C....... 209 929-1600
  301 E Miner Ave Stockton (95202) *(P-7658)*
BANK OF STOCKTON, Stockton *Also Called: Bank of Stockton (P-7658)*
Bankamerica Financial Inc .... D....... 415 622-3521
  315 Montgomery St San Francisco (94104) *(P-7892)*
Bankcard Services (PA) .... C....... 213 365-1122
  21281 S Western Ave Torrance (90501) *(P-13209)*
Bankcard Services, Torrance *Also Called: Credit Card Services Inc (P-13251)*
Bankcard USA Merchant Srvc .... D....... 818 597-7000
  5701 Lindero Canyon Rd Westlake Village (91362) *(P-13210)*
Bankruptcy Management Cons, El Segundo *Also Called: BMC Group Inc (P-17389)*
Banks Pest Control .... B....... 661 323-7858
  7440 District Blvd Ste A Bakersfield (93313) *(P-10829)*
Banner Lassen Medical Center, Susanville *Also Called: Banner Lssen Med Ctr Fndtion I (P-15957)*
Banner Lssen Med Ctr Fndtion I .... C....... 530 252-2000
  1800 Spring Ridge Dr Susanville (96130) *(P-15957)*
Banyan Solutions Inc .... D....... 650 766-9338
  2809 Blue Oak Ct Brentwood (94513) *(P-11275)*
Banyon Transcription, Brentwood *Also Called: Banyan Solutions Inc (P-11275)*
Bapko Metal Inc .... D....... 714 639-9380
  721 S Parker St Ste 300 Orange (92868) *(P-2180)*
Bar Architects 415 293-5700
  77 Geary St Ste 200 San Francisco (94108) *(P-19454)*
Bar Asscation of San Francisco (PA) .... D....... 415 982-1600
  201 Mission St Ste 400 San Francisco (94105) *(P-18733)*
Barbee Elc .... D....... 916 884-1983
  1406 Blue Oaks Blvd Ste 175 Roseville (95747) *(P-16814)*
Barber Beale, Marysville *Also Called: Gino Morena Enterprises LLC (P-10511)*
Barber Volkeswagen, Ventura *Also Called: R E Barber-Ford (P-7284)*
Barbier Security Group .... C....... 415 747-8473
  20 Galli Dr # 9-10 Novato (94949) *(P-12938)*
Barbour & Floyd Medical Assoc, Lynwood *Also Called: South Cntl Hlth Rhbltion Prgr (P-17128)*
Barcelon Associates MGT Corp .... C....... 925 627-7000
  590 Lennon Ln Ste 110 Walnut Creek (94598) *(P-8909)*
Bargain Rent-A-Car .... C....... 562 865-7447
  18800 Studebaker Rd Cerritos (90703) *(P-7170)*
Barker Management Incorporated .... D....... 619 236-8130
  438 3rd Ave Apt 312 San Diego (92101) *(P-8791)*
Barlow Group (PA) .... C....... 213 250-4200
  2000 Stadium Way Los Angeles (90026) *(P-16663)*
Barlow Respiratory Hospital (PA) .... C....... 213 250-4200
  2000 Stadium Way Los Angeles (90026) *(P-16664)*
Barlow Respiratory Hospital .... A....... 562 698-0811
  12401 Washington Blvd Whittier (90602) *(P-16665)*
Barlow Respitory Hospital, Los Angeles *Also Called: Barlow Group (P-16663)*
Barnard Bessac Joint Venture .... D....... 650 212-8957
  395 Shoreway Rd Redwood City (94065) *(P-1287)*
Barnes & Thornburg LLP .... C....... 310 284-3880
  2029 Century Park E Ste 300 Los Angeles (90002) *(P-17378)*
Barnes Firm LC .... D....... 800 800-0000
  633 W 5th St Ste 1750 Los Angeles (90071) *(P-17379)*
Barney & Barney Inc .... C....... 800 321-4696
  9171 Twne Cntre Dr 500 San Diego (92122) *(P-8507)*
Barnhart Inc .... B....... 858 635-7400
  10620 Treena St Ste 300 San Diego (92131) *(P-870)*
Barnstorm Vfx Inc .... D....... 818 792-1899
  2860 N Naomi St Burbank (91504) *(P-13820)*
Barnum & Celillo Electric Inc (PA) .... C....... 916 646-4661
  135 Main Ave Sacramento (95838) *(P-1673)*
Barona Resort & Casino .... A....... 619 443-2300
  1932 Wildcat Canyon Rd Lakeside (92040) *(P-9631)*
Baronhr LLC .... D....... 909 517-3800
  13085 Central Ave Ste 4 Chino (91710) *(P-11088)*
Baronhr LLC .... D....... 626 209-8888
  1005 S Hacienda Blvd Hacienda Heights (91745) *(P-20289)*
Baronhr LLC .... D....... 831 272-7980
  35 E Romie Ln Salinas (93901) *(P-20290)*
Barr Engineering Inc .... D....... 562 944-1722
  19 Castano Rcho Sta Marg (92688) *(P-1371)*
Barr, Ronald J MD /UCI Med Gro, Orange *Also Called: University California Irvine (P-15165)*
Barra LLC (HQ) .... B....... 510 548-5442
  2100 Milvia St Berkeley (94704) *(P-12110)*
Barracuda, Campbell *Also Called: Barracuda Networks Inc (P-12111)*
Barracuda Holdings LLC .... A....... 408 342-5400
  3175 Winchester Blvd Campbell (95008) *(P-9301)*
Barracuda Networks Inc (PA) .... C....... 408 342-5400
  3175 Winchester Blvd Campbell (95008) *(P-12111)*
Barranca Medical Offices, Irvine *Also Called: Kaiser Foundation Hospitals (P-16148)*
Barrett Business Services, San Mateo *Also Called: Barrett Business Services Inc (P-11091)*
Barrett Business Services Inc .... A....... 858 314-1100
  8880 Rio San Diego Dr Ste 800 San Diego (92108) *(P-11089)*
Barrett Business Services Inc .... A....... 909 890-3633
  862 E Hospitality Ln San Bernardino (92408) *(P-11090)*
Barrett Business Services Inc .... A....... 650 653-7588
  1840 Gateway Dr San Mateo (94404) *(P-11091)*
Barrett Business Services Inc .... A....... 805 987-0331
  815 Camarillo Springs Rd Ste C Camarillo (93012) *(P-11092)*
Barrington Associates, Los Angeles *Also Called: Wells Fargo Securities LLC (P-7647)*
Barry & Taffy Inc .... A....... 818 986-1234
  5955 De Soto Ave Ste 160 Woodland Hills (91367) *(P-16815)*
Barry Bishop .... D....... 510 596-0888
  6001 Shellmound St Ste 875 Emeryville (94608) *(P-17380)*
Barry Swenson Builders, Santa Cruz *Also Called: Green Valley Corporation (P-924)*
Barry's Boot Camp, Los Angeles *Also Called: Barrys Bootcamp LLC (P-14174)*
Barrys Bootcamp LLC (PA) .... D....... 323 452-0037
  7373 Beverly Blvd Los Angeles (90036) *(P-14174)*
Barrys Security Services Inc (PA) .... C....... 951 789-7575
  16739 Van Buren Blvd Riverside (92504) *(P-12939)*
Barstow Community Hospital, Barstow *Also Called: Hospital of Barstow Inc (P-16136)*
Bart .... D....... 510 421-3768
  150 California St Ste 275 San Francisco (94111) *(P-3123)*
BART, Oakland *Also Called: San Frncsco Bay Area Rpid Trns (P-3199)*
Bart Manufacturing Inc .... C....... 408 250-4975
  1300 E Victor Rd Lodi (95240) *(P-13211)*
Bartco Lighting Inc .... D....... 714 230-3200
  5761 Research Dr Huntington Beach (92649) *(P-5540)*
Bartell Hotels .... D....... 619 291-6700
  1960 Harbor Island Dr San Diego (92101) *(P-9632)*
Bartko Znkel Bnzel Mller A Pro .... C....... 415 956-1900
  1 Embarcadero Ctr Ste 800 San Francisco (94111) *(P-17381)*
Barton Home Health and Hospice, South Lake Tahoe *Also Called: Barton Memorial Hospital (P-15958)*

Barton Memorial Hospital .... A..... 530 543-5581
2092 Lake Tahoe Blvd Ste 500 South Lake Tahoe (96150) *(P-15958)*

Barton Ranch Inc .... D..... 209 838-8930
22398 Mcbride Rd Escalon (95320) *(P-233)*

Basepoint Analytics LLC .... B..... 760 602-4971
703 Palomar Airport Rd Ste 350 Carlsbad (92011) *(P-10756)*

Basic Agency, San Diego *Also Called: Thinkbasic Inc (P-10819)*

Basic Solutions Corp .... C..... 510 573-3658
46724 Fremont Blvd Fremont (94538) *(P-12739)*

Basket Basics, Carson *Also Called: Kole Imports (P-6922)*

Basketball Marketing Co Inc .... C..... 610 249-2255
101 Enterprise Ste 100 Aliso Viejo (92656) *(P-20291)*

Bass Medical Group .... C..... 925 690-5056
2637 Shadelands Dr Walnut Creek (94598) *(P-16705)*

Bass Medical Group .... D..... 707 346-5100
3250 Beard Rd Napa (94558) *(P-17184)*

Bass Tickets, Concord *Also Called: Bay Area Seating Service Inc (P-14495)*

Bassenian/Lagoni Architects .... D..... 949 553-9100
2031 Orchard Dr Ste 100 Newport Beach (92660) *(P-19455)*

Basso Distributing Co inc .... D..... 805 656-1946
2505 Pleasant Valley Rd Camarillo (93012) *(P-6751)*

Batchmaster Software, Irvine *Also Called: Eworkplace Manufacturing Inc (P-5304)*

Battery Systems Inc .... C..... 714 667-9320
12322 Monarch St Garden Grove (92841) *(P-5028)*

Battery Systems Inc .... D..... 818 474-1500
16725 Roscoe Blvd North Hills (91343) *(P-5541)*

Battery Systems Inc .... D..... 951 894-2960
26151 Jefferson Ave Ste A Murrieta (92562) *(P-5627)*

Batth Farms, Caruthers *Also Called: Batth Farms Inc (P-89)*

Batth Farms Inc .... D..... 559 864-9421
5434 W Kamm Ave Caruthers (93609) *(P-89)*

Battle-Tested Strategies LLC .... C..... 661 802-6509
650 Commerce Ave Ste E Palmdale (93551) *(P-3607)*

Bauers Intelligent Trnsp Inc (PA) .... C..... 415 263-4020
50 Pier San Francisco (94158) *(P-3239)*

Bavarian Lion Company Cal (PA) .... C..... 707 545-8530
2777 4th St Santa Rosa (95405) *(P-9633)*

Baxalta US Inc .... B..... 805 498-8664
1700 Rancho Conejo Blvd Thousand Oaks (91320) *(P-3049)*

Baxalta US Inc .... C..... 949 474-6301
17511 Armstrong Ave Irvine (92614) *(P-13212)*

Baxter Healthcare Corporation .... C..... 805 372-3000
1 Baxter Way Ste 100 Westlake Village (91362) *(P-6096)*

Bay 101, San Jose *Also Called: Sutters Place Inc (P-7511)*

Bay Alarm Company (PA) .... D..... 925 935-1100
5130 Commercial Cir Concord (94520) *(P-1674)*

Bay Area Air Quality (PA) .... C..... 415 749-4900
375 Beale St Ste 600 San Francisco (94105) *(P-20699)*

Bay Area Air Quality MGT Dst .... B..... 415 749-4900
375 Beale St Ste 600 San Francisco (94105) *(P-20700)*

Bay Area Beverage Company, Richmond *Also Called: T F Louderback Inc (P-6784)*

Bay Area Clinical Assoc PC .... D..... 408 996-7950
1530 Meridian Ave San Jose (95125) *(P-16666)*

Bay Area Community Health (PA) .... C..... 510 770-8040
40910 Fremont Blvd Fremont (94538) *(P-14623)*

Bay Area Community Health .... B..... 510 770-8040
770 A St Ste 310 Hayward (94541) *(P-17185)*

Bay Area Community Med Group, Los Angeles *Also Called: Santa Monica Bay Physicians He (P-15050)*

Bay Area Community Svcs Inc .... D..... 510 601-1074
5714 Martin Luther King Jr Way Oakland (94609) *(P-17846)*

Bay Area Community Svcs Inc .... D..... 510 656-7742
40963 Grimmer Blvd Fremont (94538) *(P-17847)*

Bay Area Concrete LLC .... D..... 510 294-0220
1580 Chabot Ct Hayward (94545) *(P-4862)*

Bay Area Envmtl Res Inst .... D..... 707 938-9387
Nasa Research Park, Bldg 18, Room 101, 385 Bushnell St Moffett Field (94035) *(P-19864)*

Bay Area Hspano Inst For Advnc .... D..... 510 525-1463
1000 Camelia St Berkeley (94710) *(P-18269)*

Bay Area Seating Service Inc .... B..... 925 671-4000
1855 Gateway Blvd Ste 630 Concord (94520) *(P-14495)*

Bay Area Senior Services Inc .... C..... 650 579-5500
1 Baldwin Ave Ofc San Mateo (94401) *(P-17848)*

Bay Area Srgcal Spclsts Inc A .... C..... 925 350-4044
2637 Shadelands Dr Walnut Creek (94598) *(P-14624)*

Bay Area Techworkers (PA) .... D..... 925 359-2200
2000 Crow Canyon Pl Ste 150 Ste Walnut Creek (94596) *(P-11093)*

Bay Bread LLC .... D..... 415 440-0356
2325 Pine St San Francisco (94115) *(P-6609)*

Bay Center, Eureka *Also Called: Humboldt Cmnty Access Rsrce CT (P-18010)*

Bay Cities Container Corp (PA) .... D..... 562 948-3751
5138 Industry Ave Pico Rivera (90660) *(P-2512)*

Bay Cities Logistics, Pico Rivera *Also Called: Bay Cities Container Corp (P-2512)*

Bay Cities Pav & Grading Inc .... C..... 925 687-6666
1450 Civic Ct Bldg B Concord (94520) *(P-2213)*

Bay Cities Produce Inc .... C..... 510 346-4943
2109 Williams St San Leandro (94577) *(P-6514)*

Bay City Equipment Inds Inc .... D..... 619 938-8200
13625 Danielson St Poway (92064) *(P-5542)*

Bay City Mechanical Inc (PA) .... C..... 510 233-7000
870 Harbour Way S Richmond (94804) *(P-1372)*

Bay City Television Inc (PA) .... D..... 858 279-6666
8253 Ronson Rd San Diego (92111) *(P-4412)*

Bay Club America Inc .... C..... 415 781-1874
1 Lombard St Ste 201 San Francisco (94111) *(P-14328)*

Bay Club Financial District, San Francisco *Also Called: Bay Clubs Company LLC (P-14335)*

Bay Club Marin, Corte Madera *Also Called: Bay Clubs Company LLC (P-14333)*

Bay Clubs Company LLC (HQ) .... D..... 415 781-1874
1 Lombard St San Francisco (94111) *(P-14175)*

Bay Clubs Company LLC .... B..... 408 738-2582
3250 Central Expy Santa Clara (95051) *(P-14176)*

Bay Clubs Company LLC .... B..... 805 778-0888
19867 Prairie St Ste 200 Chatsworth (91311) *(P-14177)*

Bay Clubs Company LLC .... B..... 310 216-3060
6833 Park Ter Los Angeles (90045) *(P-14178)*

Bay Clubs Company LLC .... B..... 650 593-1112
200 Redwood Shores Pkwy Redwood City (94065) *(P-14179)*

Bay Clubs Company LLC .... B..... 805 964-0556
6144 Calle Real Goleta (93117) *(P-14329)*

Bay Clubs Company LLC .... B..... 805 965-0999
21 W Carrillo St Santa Barbara (93101) *(P-14330)*

Bay Clubs Company LLC .... B..... 310 643-6878
2250 Park Pl Thousand Oaks (91362) *(P-14331)*

Bay Clubs Company LLC .... B..... 805 563-8700
3908 State St Santa Barbara (93105) *(P-14332)*

Bay Clubs Company LLC .... B..... 415 945-3000
220 Corte Madera Town Ctr Corte Madera (94925) *(P-14333)*

Bay Clubs Company LLC .... B..... 858 509-9933
12000 Carmel Country Rd San Diego (92130) *(P-14334)*

Bay Clubs Company LLC .... B..... 415 362-7800
555 California St San Francisco (94104) *(P-14335)*

Bay Clubs Company LLC .... B..... 310 541-2582
51 Peninsula Ctr Ste 51d Rancho Palos Verdes (90275) *(P-14336)*

Bay Clubs Company LLC .... B..... 310 829-4995
2425 Olympic Blvd Ste 100 Santa Monica (90404) *(P-14337)*

Bay Company, The, San Francisco *Also Called: Portco Inc (P-7504)*

Bay Counties Waste Svcs Inc .... D..... 408 565-9900
3355 Thomas Rd Santa Clara (95054) *(P-4863)*

Bay Federal Credit Union (PA) .... D..... 831 479-6000
3333 Clares St Capitola (95010) *(P-7756)*

Bay Imaging Cons Med Group Inc (PA) .... D..... 925 296-7150
2125 Oak Grove Rd Ste 200 Walnut Creek (94598) *(P-14625)*

Bay Management, San Mateo *Also Called: Archives Management Corp (P-20025)*

Bay Medic Transportation Inc .... C..... 800 689-9511
959 Detroit Ave Concord (94518) *(P-3240)*

Bay Medical Management LLC .... C..... 925 296-7150
2125 Oak Grove Rd Ste 200 Walnut Creek (94598) *(P-14626)*

Bay Photo Inc .... C..... 831 475-6090
2959 Park Ave Ste A Soquel (95073) *(P-10489)*

BAY PHOTO, INC, Soquel *Also Called: Bay Photo Inc (P-10489)*

Bay Respite Care, Benicia *Also Called: Sonia Corina Inc (P-17327)*

Bay Standard Inc .... D..... 925 634-1181
24485 Marsh Creek Rd Brentwood (94513) *(P-5891)*

ALPHABETIC SECTION — Bear Valley Ski Co

Bay Valley Medical Group Inc (PA) .... D...... 510 785-5000
319 Diablo Rd Ste 105 Danville (94526) *(P-14627)*

Bay Valley Mortgage, La Mirada *Also Called: Pacific Bay Lending Group (P-8049)*

Bay View Rhbilitation Hosp LLC .... D...... 510 521-5600
516 Willow St Alameda (94501) *(P-15350)*

Bay Vista Senior Housing .... B...... 925 924-7100
1900 Huntington Dr Duarte (91010) *(P-8792)*

Bayberry Inc .... D...... 707 995-1643
15120 Lakeshore Dr # C Clearlake (95422) *(P-7573)*

BAYBERRY INC, Clearlake *Also Called: Bayberry Inc (P-7573)*

Baybridge Employment Services, Eureka *Also Called: Humboldt Cmnty Access Rsrce CT (P-18009)*

Baymarr Constructors Inc .... C...... 661 395-1676
6950 Mcdivitt Dr Bakersfield (93313) *(P-2097)*

Bayone Solutions .... C...... 408 930-1600
4637 Chabot Dr Ste 250 Pleasanton (94588) *(P-11450)*

Bayonet/Blackhorse Golf Course, Seaside *Also Called: Bsl Golf Corp (P-14247)*

Bayorg .... D...... 415 623-5300
Embarcadero At Beach St Pier 39 San Francisco (94133) *(P-18684)*

Baypoint Trading, San Francisco *Also Called: Btig LLC (P-8068)*

Baypointe Management Inc .... D...... 813 503-5551
220 Newport Center Dr # 11 Newport Beach (92660) *(P-20032)*

Baypointe Management, Inc., Newport Beach *Also Called: Baypointe Management Inc (P-20032)*

Bayscape Management Inc .... D...... 408 288-2940
1350 Pacific Ave Alviso (95002) *(P-389)*

Bayshore Healthcare Inc .... C...... 805 544-5100
3033 Augusta St San Luis Obispo (93401) *(P-15351)*

Bayside Care Center, Morro Bay *Also Called: Compass Health Inc (P-15382)*

Bayside Healthcare Inc .... C...... 619 426-8611
553 F St Chula Vista (91910) *(P-15352)*

Bayside Insulation, Concord *Also Called: Bayside Insulation & Cnstr Inc (P-871)*

Bayside Insulation & Cnstr Inc .... D...... 925 288-8960
1635 Challenge Dr Concord (94520) *(P-871)*

Bayside Interiors Inc (PA) .... D...... 510 438-9171
3220 Darby Cmn Fremont (94539) *(P-1907)*

Baysport Inc .... C...... 650 593-2800
200 Redwood Shores Pkwy Redwood City (94065) *(P-14628)*

Baysport Physical Therapy, Redwood City *Also Called: Baysport Inc (P-14628)*

Bayview Engrg & Cnstr Co Inc .... D...... 916 939-8986
5040 Robert J Mathews Pkwy El Dorado Hills (95762) *(P-1373)*

Bayview Environmental Svcs Inc .... C...... 510 562-6181
6925 San Leandro St Oakland (94621) *(P-2260)*

Bayview Farms, Salinas *Also Called: Norcal Harvesting LLC (P-57)*

Bayview Hosp Mntal Hlth System .... C...... 619 426-6310
330 Moss St Chula Vista (91911) *(P-15959)*

Bayview Properties Inc (PA) .... D...... 831 394-3321
2600 Sand Dunes Dr Monterey (93940) *(P-9634)*

Baywood Court (PA) .... D...... 510 733-2102
21966 Dolores St Castro Valley (94546) *(P-16816)*

BAYWOOD COURT RETIREMENT CENTE, Castro Valley *Also Called: Baywood Court (P-16816)*

Bazic Product, El Monte *Also Called: Bangkit (usa) Inc (P-6062)*

Bbam Arcft Holdings 139 Labuan, San Francisco *Also Called: Bbam US LP (P-8066)*

Bbam US LP .... B...... 415 267-1600
50 California St Fl 14 San Francisco (94111) *(P-8066)*

Bbcn Bank .... A...... 213 251-2222
3731 Wilshire Blvd Los Angeles (90010) *(P-7608)*

BBDO, San Francisco *Also Called: BBDO Worldwide Inc (P-10590)*

BBDO Worldwide Inc .... C...... 415 808-6200
600 California St Fl 8 San Francisco (94108) *(P-10590)*

Bbk Performance Inc .... D...... 951 296-1771
27427 Bostik Ct Temecula (92590) *(P-5029)*

Bbm Fairway Inc (PA) C
3520 Challenger St Torrance (90503) *(P-2544)*

Bbsi Camarillo, Camarillo *Also Called: Barrett Business Services Inc (P-11092)*

Bc Labor Contractors .... C...... 831 751-6000
2272 Alisal Rd Salinas (93908) *(P-11094)*

Bcci Construction LLC .... C...... 650 543-8900
150 E Dana St Mountain View (94041) *(P-659)*

Bcd Tofu House, Los Angeles *Also Called: Wilshire Kingsley Inc (P-8784)*

Bcfs Health and Human Services .... B...... 707 422-8802
2301 Pennsylvania Ave Fairfield (94533) *(P-357)*

BCI Alabama, Los Angeles *Also Called: Blackstone Consulting Inc (P-20297)*

BCM Construction Company Inc .... D...... 530 342-1722
2990 State Highway 32 Ste 100 Chico (95973) *(P-806)*

BCM Customer Service .... D...... 858 679-5757
12155 Kirkham Rd Poway (92064) *(P-1374)*

Bcp Systems Inc .... D...... 714 202-3900
1560 S Sinclair St Anaheim (92806) *(P-12704)*

Bcra Resort Services Inc .... C...... 805 571-3176
8301 Hollister Ave Santa Barbara (93117) *(P-9635)*

Bd Carefusion, San Diego *Also Called: Carefusion Corporation (P-3074)*

BD&j PC .... D...... 855 906-3699
9701 Wilshire Blvd Ste 630 Beverly Hills (90212) *(P-17382)*

Bdi Inc .... C...... 626 442-8948
9917 Gidley St Unit A El Monte (91731) *(P-5892)*

BDR Industries Inc (PA) .... D...... 661 940-8554
820 E Avenue L12 Lancaster (93535) *(P-4474)*

Be School Inc .... C...... 650 576-5263
12 Grace St Fl 3 San Francisco (94103) *(P-12740)*

BE Smith Inc .... B...... 913 341-9116
12400 High Bluff Dr Ste 100 San Diego (92130) *(P-20701)*

Bea Systems Inc (HQ) .... A...... 650 506-7000
2315 N 1st St San Jose (95131) *(P-11451)*

Beach & Tennis Club, Pebble Beach *Also Called: Lone Cypress Company LLC (P-14396)*

Beach Area Family Health Ctr, San Diego *Also Called: Family Hlth Ctrs San Diego Inc (P-14749)*

Beach Cities Health District .... C...... 310 374-3426
1200 Del Amo St Redondo Beach (90277) *(P-18566)*

Beach Club .... D...... 310 395-3254
201 Palisades Beach Rd Santa Monica (90402) *(P-14338)*

Beach Creek Post-Acute, Anaheim *Also Called: Oceanside Harbor Holdings LLC (P-15609)*

Beach State, Moorpark *Also Called: Picnic Time Inc (P-3111)*

Beachbody, El Segundo *Also Called: Beachbody LLC (P-10704)*

Beachbody LLC .... D...... 310 883-9000
400 Continental Blvd Ste 400 El Segundo (90245) *(P-10703)*

Beachbody LLC (HQ) .... B...... 310 883-9000
400 Continental Blvd Ste 400 El Segundo (90245) *(P-10704)*

Beachbody Company Inc (PA) .... C...... 310 883-9000
3301 Exposition Blvd Santa Monica (90404) *(P-10705)*

Beacon Electric Supply .... D...... 858 279-9770
9630 Chesapeake Dr San Diego (92123) *(P-5543)*

Beacon Pacific Inc .... C...... 714 288-1974
675 N Batavia St Orange (92868) *(P-5219)*

Beacon Park School .... D...... 949 936-8400
200 Cultivate Irvine (92618) *(P-14496)*

Beacon Resources LLC .... C...... 949 955-1773
17300 Red Hill Ave Irvine (92614) *(P-20292)*

Beacon Roofing Supply Inc .... D...... 818 768-4661
8501 Telfair Ave Sun Valley (91352) *(P-5893)*

Beador Construction Co Inc .... D...... 951 674-7352
2900 Bristol St Costa Mesa (92626) *(P-1080)*

Beale Air Force Base Outreach, Marysville *Also Called: Yuba Community College Dst (P-18198)*

Bear Communications Inc .... D...... 619 263-2159
8290 Vickers St Ste D San Diego (92111) *(P-5628)*

Bear Communications Inc .... D...... 310 854-2327
8584 Venice Blvd Los Angeles (90034) *(P-5629)*

Bear Communications Inc .... C...... 415 656-2327
150 N Hill Dr Ste 19 Brisbane (94005) *(P-5630)*

Bear Flag Marketing Corp .... C...... 415 899-8466
7599 Redwood Blvd Ste 200 Novato (94945) *(P-16817)*

Bear Nash Productions .... D...... 310 428-5167
521 E Sycamore Ave El Segundo (90245) *(P-13927)*

Bear River Casino .... C...... 707 733-9644
11 Bear Paws Way Loleta (95551) *(P-9636)*

Bear River Casino Hotel, Loleta *Also Called: Bear River Casino (P-9636)*

Bear Valley Mountain Resort, Bear Valley *Also Called: Bear Valley Ski Co (P-14497)*

Bear Valley Ski Co .... B...... 209 753-2301
2280 State Rte 207 Bear Valley (95223) *(P-14497)*

Bear Valley Springs Assn — ALPHABETIC SECTION

Bear Valley Springs Assn .... C...... 661 821-5537
  29541 Rollingoak Dr Tehachapi (93561) *(P-18816)*
Bear Vly Cmnty Healthcare Dst (PA)....................................... C...... 909 866-6501
  41870 Garstin Dr Big Bear Lake (92315) *(P-15960)*
Bearcom Wireless Worldwide, San Diego *Also Called: Bear Communications Inc (P-5628)*
Bearcom Wireless Worldwide, Los Angeles *Also Called: Bear Communications Inc (P-5629)*
Bearcom Wireless Worldwide, Brisbane *Also Called: Bear Communications Inc (P-5630)*
Beatbox Beverages, Acampo *Also Called: Constlltion Brnds US Oprtons I (P-6792)*
Beating Wall Street Inc (PA)... C...... 818 332-9696
  20121 Ventura Blvd Ste 305 Woodland Hills (91364) *(P-8189)*
Beats Music LLC .... D...... 415 590-5104
  235 2nd St San Francisco (94105) *(P-12112)*
Beauchamp Distributing Company .... D...... 310 639-5320
  1911 S Santa Fe Ave Compton (90221) *(P-6752)*
Beaumont Unified Schl Dst Pub F .... B...... 951 845-6580
  126 W Fifth St Beaumont (92223) *(P-17694)*
Beauty 21 Cosmetics Inc .... C...... 909 945-2220
  2021 S Archibald Ave Ontario (91761) *(P-6097)*
Beauty Barrage LLC .... C...... 949 771-3399
  4340 Von Karman Ave Ste 240 Newport Beach (92660) *(P-10491)*
Beauty Bazar Inc .... D...... 650 326-8522
  36 Stanford Shopping Ctr Palo Alto (94304) *(P-10492)*
Beauty Boutique Inc .... C...... 619 442-3407
  1073 E Main St El Cajon (92021) *(P-10493)*
Beaver Dam Health Care Center .... D...... 949 642-0387
  340 Victoria St Costa Mesa (92627) *(P-15353)*
Beaver Dam Health Care Center .... D...... 707 546-0471
  1221 Rosemarie Ln Stockton (95207) *(P-15354)*
Beaver Dam Health Care Center .... C...... 209 368-0693
  950 S Fairmont Ave Lodi (95240) *(P-15355)*
Beaver Medical Clinic, Highland *Also Called: Beaver Medical Group LP (P-14630)*
Beaver Medical Clinic Inc (PA).. C...... 909 793-3311
  1615 Orange Tree Ln Redlands (92374) *(P-14629)*
Beaver Medical Group LP (HQ)... C...... 909 425-3321
  7000 Boulder Ave Highland (92346) *(P-14630)*
Beazer, Brea *Also Called: Beazer Mortgage Corporation (P-787)*
Beazer Mortgage Corporation .... D...... 714 480-1635
  1800 E Imperial Hwy Ste 200 Brea (92821) *(P-787)*
Becho Inc .... D...... 818 362-8391
  15901 Olden St Rancho Cascades (91342) *(P-1081)*
Bechtel, Livermore *Also Called: National Security Tech LLC (P-19331)*
Bechtel Capital MGT Corp .... D...... 415 768-1234
  50 Beale St San Francisco (94105) *(P-20033)*
Beckman RES Inst of The Cy Hop .... C...... 626 359-8111
  1500 Duarte Rd Duarte (91010) *(P-14631)*
Bedrock Company .... D...... 951 273-1931
  2970 Myers St Riverside (92503) *(P-2098)*
Bedrosian's Tiles & Stone, Anaheim *Also Called: Paragon Industries Inc (P-7112)*
Bee Sweet Citrus Inc .... C...... 559 834-5345
  416 E South Ave Fowler (93625) *(P-256)*
Beech Street Corporation (HQ)... B...... 949 672-1000
  25550 Commercentre Dr Ste 200 Lake Forest (92630) *(P-20034)*
Beets Hospitality Group .... D...... 925 294-8667
  316 Stealth Ct Livermore (94551) *(P-20035)*
Behavior Change Institute LLC .... D...... 866 273-2451
  4096 Piedmont Ave Ste 161 Oakland (94611) *(P-19865)*
Behavior Frontiers LLC .... C...... 310 856-0800
  2033 Gateway Pl Ste 500 San Jose (95110) *(P-17011)*
Behavioral Health Works Inc .... D...... 800 249-1266
  1301 E Orangewood Ave Anaheim (92805) *(P-17012)*
Behavioral Hlth Recovery Svcs, Modesto *Also Called: County of Stanislaus (P-18583)*
Behavioral Learning Netwrk LLC .... D...... 310 871-6800
  10700 Santa Monica Blvd Ste 100 Los Angeles (90025) *(P-17013)*
Behavioral Medicine Center, Redlands *Also Called: Loma Linda University Med Ctr (P-16228)*
Behavioral Science Technology Inc (PA)................................ D...... 805 646-0166
  1000 Town Center Dr Ste 600 Oxnard (93036) *(P-20702)*
Behaviosec Inc .... B...... 833 248-6732
  160 W Santa Clara St Ste 1100 San Jose (95113) *(P-11452)*
Behavral Hlthcare Slutions Inc .... C...... 858 573-2600
  9465 Farnham St San Diego (92123) *(P-17849)*

Behringer Harvard Wilshire Blv .... D...... 310 475-8711
  10740 Wilshire Blvd Los Angeles (90024) *(P-9637)*
BEI Industrial Encoders, Thousand Oaks *Also Called: Sensata Technologies Inc (P-12874)*
Beigene Usa Inc .... B...... 877 828-5568
  1840 Gateway Dr Fl 3 San Mateo (94404) *(P-2580)*
Bejac Corporation (PA).. D...... 714 528-6224
  569 S Van Buren St Placentia (92870) *(P-5820)*
Bel Air Inv Advisors LLC .... D...... 310 229-1500
  1999 Avenue Of The Stars Ste 2800 Los Angeles (90067) *(P-8190)*
Bel Air Market 525, Elk Grove *Also Called: Bel Air Mart (P-7142)*
Bel Air Mart .... D...... 916 714-6996
  9435 Elk Grove Blvd Elk Grove (95624) *(P-7142)*
Bel Tren Vlla Cnvalescent Hosp, Bellflower *Also Called: Life Care Centers America Inc (P-15541)*
Bel Vista Healthcare Center, Long Beach *Also Called: Villa De La Mar Inc (P-15910)*
Bel-Air Bay Club Ltd .... C...... 310 230-4700
  16801 Pacific Coast Hwy Pacific Palisades (90272) *(P-14339)*
Bel-Air Country Club .... C...... 310 472-9563
  10768 Bellagio Rd Los Angeles (90077) *(P-14340)*
Belectric Inc .... D...... 510 896-3940
  951 Mariners Island Blvd Ste 300 San Mateo (94404) *(P-1288)*
Belkin Components, El Segundo *Also Called: Belkin International Inc (P-2825)*
Belkin International Inc (DH)... B...... 310 751-5100
  555 S Aviation Blvd Ste 180 El Segundo (90245) *(P-2825)*
Bell Gardens Bicycle Club Inc .... A...... 562 806-4646
  888 Bicycle Casino Dr Bell Gardens (90201) *(P-14498)*
Bell Products Inc .... D...... 707 255-1811
  722 Soscol Ave Napa (94559) *(P-1375)*
Bell Villa Care Associates LLC .... D...... 562 925-4252
  9028 Rose St Bellflower (90706) *(P-15356)*
Bella Collina San Clemente .... D...... 949 498-6604
  200 Avenida La Pata San Clemente (92673) *(P-14341)*
Bella Terra Nursery Inc .... D...... 619 585-1118
  302 Hollister St San Diego (92154) *(P-6852)*
Bella Vsta Trnstional Care Ctr, San Luis Obispo *Also Called: Bayshore Healthcare Inc (P-15351)*
Bellami Hair, Chatsworth *Also Called: Bellami Hair LLC (P-10494)*
Bellami Hair LLC .... D...... 844 235-5264
  21123 Nordhoff St Chatsworth (91311) *(P-10494)*
Bellevue Club .... C...... 510 451-1000
  525 Bellevue Ave Oakland (94610) *(P-7458)*
Bellflower Dental Group, Bellflower *Also Called: Peter Wylan DDS (P-15247)*
Bellflower Medical Center, Los Angeles *Also Called: Jupiter Bellflower Doctors Hospital (P-16146)*
Bellota US Corp .... C...... 951 737-6515
  22440 Temescal Canyon Rd Corona (92883) *(P-9358)*
Bellus Academy, El Cajon *Also Called: Beauty Boutique Inc (P-10493)*
Bellwether Asset MGT Inc (PA)... D...... 310 525-3022
  200 N Pacific Coast Hwy Ste 1400 El Segundo (90245) *(P-20036)*
Belmond El Encanto, Santa Barbara *Also Called: El Encanto Inc (P-9777)*
Belmont Oaks Academy .... D...... 650 593-6175
  2200 Carlmont Dr Belmont (94002) *(P-18270)*
Belshire, Foothill Ranch *Also Called: Belshire Trnsp Svcs Inc (P-3372)*
Belshire Trnsp Svcs Inc .... C...... 949 460-5200
  25971 Towne Centre Dr Foothill Ranch (92610) *(P-3372)*
Belvedere Hotel Partnership .... B...... 310 551-2888
  9882 Santa Monica Blvd Beverly Hills (90212) *(P-9638)*
Belvedere Partnership .... B...... 310 551-2888
  9882 Santa Monica Blvd Beverly Hills (90212) *(P-9639)*
Belville Enterprises Inc .... D...... 858 652-6960
  6225 Nancy Ridge Dr San Diego (92121) *(P-14632)*
Bemus Landscape Inc .... B...... 714 557-7910
  951 Calle Negocio Ste D San Clemente (92673) *(P-1289)*
Ben Bennett Inc (PA)... C...... 949 209-9712
  3419 Via Lido # 646 Newport Beach (92663) *(P-15816)*
Ben F Smith Inc .... C...... 858 271-4320
  8655 Miramar Pl Ste B San Diego (92121) *(P-2099)*
Ben Group Inc .... B...... 310 342-1500
  14724 Ventura Blvd Ste 1200 Sherman Oaks (91403) *(P-11453)*
Benbow Gifts, Garberville *Also Called: Benbow Valley Investments LLC (P-9640)*

ALPHABETIC SECTION

Benbow Valley Investments LLC .... D....... 707 923-2124
445 Lake Benbow Dr Garberville (95542) *(P-9640)*

Bench Depot, Tecate *Also Called: Benchpro Inc (P-5078)*

Benchmark Contractors, Santa Monica *Also Called: Morley Builders Inc (P-835)*

Benchmark Landscape Svcs Inc .... C....... 858 513-7190
12575 Stowe Dr Poway (92064) *(P-390)*

Benchpro Inc .... C....... 619 478-9400
23949 Tecate Mission Rd Tecate (91980) *(P-5078)*

Benefit & Risk Management Svcs .... C....... 888 326-2555
80 Iron Point Cir Ste 200 Folsom (95630) *(P-8508)*

Benefit Cosmetics LLC (DH) .... D....... 415 781-8153
225 Bush St Fl 20 San Francisco (94104) *(P-6098)*

Benefit Programs ADM, City Of Industry *Also Called: Management Applied Prgrm Inc (P-12591)*

Benefitcompass LLC .... D....... 949 289-9300
1 Venture Ste 220 Irvine (92618) *(P-20293)*

Benefits Prgram Adminsitration .... D....... 562 463-5000
13191 Concords Pkwy N Ste 205 City Of Industry (91746) *(P-9421)*

Benefitstreet Inc .... D....... 925 831-0800
12677 Alcosta Blvd San Ramon (94583) *(P-8509)*

Benefitvision Inc .... D....... 818 348-3100
5550 Topanga Canyon Blvd Woodland Hills (91367) *(P-18211)*

Benetech Inc (PA) .... D....... 916 484-6811
3841 N Freeway Blvd Ste 185 Sacramento (95834) *(P-8510)*

Benetrac, San Diego *Also Called: Paychex Benefit Tech Inc (P-4328)*

Benihana 24, Encino *Also Called: Benihana Inc (P-7459)*

Benihana Inc .... D....... 818 788-7121
16226 Ventura Blvd Encino (91436) *(P-7459)*

Benjamin Moore Authorized Ret, Corona *Also Called: Ganahl Lumber Company (P-6961)*

Benjamin Moore Authorized Ret, Buena Park *Also Called: Ganahl Lumber Company (P-7119)*

Benjamin Moore Authorized Ret, Los Alamitos *Also Called: Ganahl Lumber Company (P-7120)*

Benjamin Moore Authorized Ret, Lake Forest *Also Called: Ganahl Lumber Company (P-7121)*

Bennett Entps A Cal Ldscp Cntg .... D....... 310 534-3543
25889 Belle Porte Ave Harbor City (90710) *(P-391)*

Bennett Landscape, Harbor City *Also Called: Bennett Entps A Cal Ldscp Cntg (P-391)*

Bennett's Kitchen Bar Market, Roseville *Also Called: Hospitality Bennett Group LLC (P-18749)*

Bennion Deville Fine Homes Inc .... B....... 760 674-3452
74850 Us Highway 111 Indian Wells (92210) *(P-8910)*

Benq, Costa Mesa *Also Called: Benq America Corp (P-5280)*

Benq America Corp (HQ) .... D....... 714 559-4900
3200 Park Center Dr Ste 150 Costa Mesa (92626) *(P-5280)*

Bens Asphalt & Maint Co Inc .... D....... 951 248-1103
2537 Rubidoux Blvd Riverside (92509) *(P-1082)*

Bento Box Entertainment LLC .... B....... 818 333-7700
5161 Lankershim Blvd Ste 120 North Hollywood (91601) *(P-13821)*

Benz - One Complete Operation, Tehachapi *Also Called: Pjbs Holdings Inc (P-4920)*

Berberian Bros Inc .... D....... 209 944-5514
3755 Nw Ln Stockton (95204) *(P-7171)*

Berding & Weil LLP (PA) .... D....... 925 838-2090
2175 N California Blvd Ste 500 Walnut Creek (94596) *(P-17383)*

Berg Lacquer Co (PA) .... D....... 323 261-8114
3150 E Pico Blvd Los Angeles (90023) *(P-6883)*

Bergelectric Corp (PA) .... D....... 760 638-2374
3182 Lionshead Ave Carlsbad (92010) *(P-1675)*

Bergelectric Corp .... A....... 760 746-1003
3182 Lionshead Ave Carlsbad (92010) *(P-1676)*

Bergelectric Corp .... D....... 760 746-1003
2210 Meyers Ave Escondido (92029) *(P-1677)*

Bergelectric Corp .... D....... 760 291-8100
955 Borra Pl Escondido (92029) *(P-1678)*

Bergelectric Corp .... D....... 559 860-2590
750 W Pinedale Ave Fresno (93711) *(P-1679)*

Bergelectric Corp .... D....... 510 314-8590
46740 Lakeview Blvd Fremont (94538) *(P-1680)*

Bergelectric Corp .... C....... 916 636-1880
11333 Sunrise Park Dr Rancho Cordova (95742) *(P-1681)*

Bergelectric Corp .... C....... 949 250-7005
15776 Gateway Cir Tustin (92780) *(P-1682)*

Bergensons Property Svcs Inc .... A....... 760 631-5111
3605 Ocean Ranch Blvd Ste 200 Oceanside (92056) *(P-10860)*

Berger Inc .... A....... 818 986-1234
5955 De Soto Ave Ste 160 Woodland Hills (91367) *(P-16818)*

Berger Bros Inc .... B....... 626 334-2699
154 N Aspan Ave Azusa (91702) *(P-1908)*

Berger Kahn A Law Corporation (PA) .... D....... 949 474-1880
1 Park Plz Ste 340 Irvine (92614) *(P-17384)*

Bergerson Group .... D....... 925 948-8110
1030 Country Club Dr B Moraga (94556) *(P-20294)*

Bergman Kprs LLC (PA) .... C....... 714 924-7000
2850 Saturn St Ste 100 Brea (92821) *(P-872)*

Berkel & Company Contrs Inc .... D....... 415 495-3627
81 Langton St Unit 15 San Francisco (94103) *(P-2100)*

Berkeley .... B....... 510 845-7300
2086 Allston Way Berkeley (94704) *(P-9641)*

Berkeley Albany YMCA, Concord *Also Called: Young MNS Chrstn Assn of E Bay (P-18966)*

Berkeley Cement Inc .... C....... 510 525-8175
1200 6th St Berkeley (94710) *(P-2101)*

Berkeley Community Health Prj .... D....... 510 548-2570
2339 Durant Ave Berkeley (94704) *(P-16819)*

Berkeley Country Club .... D....... 510 233-7550
7901 Cutting Blvd El Cerrito (94530) *(P-14342)*

Berkeley Downtown Ht Owner LLC .... D....... 510 982-2100
2121 Center St Berkeley (94704) *(P-9642)*

Berkeley E Convalescent Hosp .... C....... 310 829-5377
2021 Arizona Ave Santa Monica (90404) *(P-15817)*

Berkeley E Convalescent Hosp, Santa Monica *Also Called: Berkeley E Convalescent Hosp (P-15817)*

Berkeley Emrgncy Med Group Inc .... D....... 925 962-1067
2000 Crow Canyon Pl Ste 220 San Ramon (94583) *(P-17186)*

Berkeley Farms LLC .... B....... 510 265-8600
17637 E Valley Blvd City Of Industry (91744) *(P-2351)*

BERKELEY FREE CLINIC, Berkeley *Also Called: Berkeley Community Health Prj (P-16819)*

Berkeley Hall Schl Foundation .... D....... 310 476-6421
16000 Mulholland Dr Los Angeles (90049) *(P-17695)*

Berkeley Hall School, Los Angeles *Also Called: Berkeley Hall Schl Foundation (P-17695)*

Berkeley Nutritional Mfg Corp (PA) .... D....... 925 243-6300
1852 Rutan Dr Livermore (94551) *(P-19800)*

Berkeley Research Group LLC (PA) .... C....... 510 285-3300
2200 Powell St Ste 1200 Emeryville (94608) *(P-20703)*

Berkeley Student Coop Inc .... D....... 510 848-1936
2424 Ridge Rd Berkeley (94709) *(P-10418)*

Berkeley Unified School Dst .... D....... 510 644-6250
1707 Russell St Berkeley (94703) *(P-10861)*

Berkley East Healthcare Center, Santa Monica *Also Called: Asmb LLC (P-15335)*

Berkshire Hathaway Home Servic .... D....... 562 809-1331
11409 Carson St Lakewood (90715) *(P-8378)*

Berkshire Hathaway Home Servic .... D....... 626 335-6001
231 S Glendora Ave Glendora (91741) *(P-17850)*

Berkshire Hathaway Homestates (HQ) .... C....... 415 433-1650
1 California St Ste 600 San Francisco (94111) *(P-8511)*

Berkshire Hthway HM Svcs CA Rp .... D....... 562 307-5636
9836 Atlantic Ave South Gate (90280) *(P-8911)*

Berkshire Hthway HM Svcs Cal P .... C....... 619 302-8082
2365 Northside Dr Ste 200 San Diego (92108) *(P-7936)*

Berkshire Hthway Hmsrvces Trot, Lancaster *Also Called: V Troth Inc (P-9207)*

Bernard Hodes Group Inc .... B....... 212 999-9000
720 Market St San Francisco (94102) *(P-10591)*

Bernard Osher Mrin Jwish Cmnty .... C....... 415 444-8000
200 N San Pedro Rd San Rafael (94903) *(P-17851)*

Bernardo Hts Healthcare Inc .... C....... 858 673-0101
11895 Avenue Of Industry San Diego (92128) *(P-15818)*

Bernards Builders Inc .... B....... 818 898-1521
555 1st St San Fernando (91340) *(P-747)*

Bernards Inc .... D....... 818 898-1521
555 1st St San Fernando (91340) *(P-20037)*

Bernel Inc .... C....... 714 778-6070
501 W Southern Ave Orange (92865) *(P-1376)*

Bernstein, Los Angeles *Also Called: Alliancebernstein LP (P-9351)*

Berry Appleman & Leiden LLP (PA) .... C....... 628 215-2800
50 California St Fl 2 San Francisco (94111) *(P-17385)*

ALPHABETIC SECTION

Berry Man Inc .... D...... 805 543-9000
  712 Fiero Ln San Luis Obispo (93401) *(P-6515)*

Berry Seed & Feed, Oakdale *Also Called: A L Gilbert Company (P-6817)*

Bersin By Deloitte, San Francisco *Also Called: Deloitte Consulting LLP (P-20340)*

Bert E Jessup Transportation .... D...... 408 848-3390
  641 Old Gilroy St Gilroy (95020) *(P-3447)*

Best Choice LLC .... C...... 510 862-4989
  22568 Mission Blvd Ste 344 Hayward (94541) *(P-13213)*

Best Contracting Services Inc .... D...... 510 886-7240
  4301 Bettencourt Way Union City (94587) *(P-2044)*

Best Contracting Services Inc (PA) .... B...... 310 328-9176
  19027 S Hamilton Ave Gardena (90248) *(P-2045)*

Best Financial, The, Signal Hill *Also Called: First American Team Realty Inc (P-9006)*

Best Friends Animal Hospital .... D...... 818 766-2140
  4925 Longridge Ave Sherman Oaks (91423) *(P-329)*

Best Friends Animal Society .... C...... 818 643-3989
  1845 Pontius Ave Los Angeles (90025) *(P-19070)*

Best Interiors Inc .... D...... 858 715-3760
  4395 Murphy Canyon Rd San Diego (92123) *(P-1909)*

Best Interiors Inc (PA) .... C...... 714 490-7999
  2100 E Via Burton Anaheim (92806) *(P-1910)*

Best Life and Health Insur Co .... D...... 949 253-4080
  2435 E Coast Hwy Ste 4 Corona Del Mar (92625) *(P-8232)*

BEST OPPORTUNITIES, Apple Valley *Also Called: BEST Opportunities Inc (P-18212)*

BEST Opportunities Inc .... C...... 760 628-0111
  22450 Headquarters Ave Apple Valley (92307) *(P-18212)*

Best Overnight Express, Irwindale *Also Called: Best Overnite Express Inc (P-3448)*

Best Overnite Express Inc (PA) .... D...... 626 256-6340
  406 Live Oak Ave Irwindale (91706) *(P-3448)*

Best Rest Management Inc .... D...... 619 543-1130
  1955 San Diego Ave San Diego (92110) *(P-9643)*

Best Sac Homes Grp At Big Blck .... D...... 916 891-2641
  550 Howe Ave Ste 150 Sacramento (95825) *(P-8912)*

Best Way Disposal Co Inc .... C...... 760 244-9773
  17105 Mesa St Hesperia (92345) *(P-4864)*

Best Western, San Francisco *Also Called: Best Western Hotel Tomo (P-9644)*

Best Western, Santa Barbara *Also Called: Encina Pepper Tree Joint Ventr (P-9782)*

Best Western, Santa Barbara *Also Called: Encina Pepper Tree Joint Ventr (P-9783)*

Best Western, South San Francisco *Also Called: Grosvenor Properties Ltd (P-9828)*

Best Western, Costa Mesa *Also Called: Newport Mesa Inn LLC (P-10044)*

Best Western, Aptos *Also Called: Seacliff Inn Inc (P-10213)*

Best Western Amador Inn, Jackson *Also Called: Sita Ram LLC (P-10242)*

Best Western Apricot Inn, Roseville *Also Called: Merchant Valley Corporation (P-18714)*

Best Western Bayside Inn, San Diego *Also Called: Tic Hotels Inc (P-10312)*

Best Western Golden Sails Ht, Torrance *Also Called: Long Beach Golden Sails Inc (P-9984)*

Best Western Hotel Tomo .... C...... 415 921-4000
  1800 Sutter St San Francisco (94115) *(P-9644)*

Best Western Stovalls Inn (PA) .... D...... 714 956-4430
  1110 W Katella Ave Anaheim (92802) *(P-9645)*

Best Western, The Beach Resort, Monterey *Also Called: Bayview Properties Inc (P-9634)*

Best Wstn Carmel Mission Inn, Carmel *Also Called: Trevi Partners A Calif LP (P-10321)*

Best Wstn Fireside Inn By Sea, Cambria *Also Called: Moonstone Bch Innvstors A Cal (P-10028)*

Best-Way Distributing Co, Sylmar *Also Called: Allied Company Holdings Inc (P-6749)*

Bestit, Simi Valley *Also Called: Bestitcom Inc (P-12741)*

Bestitcom Inc (PA) .... D...... 602 667-5613
  1464 Madera Rd Simi Valley (93065) *(P-12741)*

Bestliving Care LLC .... D...... 510 862-3508
  2401 Merced St Ste 300 San Leandro (94577) *(P-16820)*

Bestop Baja LLC .... C...... 760 560-2252
  2950 Norman Strasse Rd San Marcos (92069) *(P-7396)*

Beta Soft Systems Inc .... C...... 408 766-0000
  2570 N 1st St 2nd Fl San Jose (95131) *(P-11454)*

Bethany Adult Day Care, Ripon *Also Called: Bethany HM Soc San Jquin Cnty (P-15357)*

Bethany HM Soc San Jquin Cnty .... C...... 209 599-7670
  368 S Wilma Ave Ripon (95366) *(P-15357)*

Bethar Corporation C
  17625 Railroad St City Of Industry (91748) *(P-9302)*

Bethel Lutheran Home Inc .... D...... 559 896-4900
  2280 Dockery Ave Selma (93662) *(P-15819)*

Bethlehem Construction Inc .... D...... 661 758-1001
  425 J St Wasco (93280) *(P-807)*

Better Chance, A, Pinole *Also Called: Califrnia Atism Foundation Inc (P-18568)*

Better Night LLC .... D...... 619 299-6299
  5471 Kearny Villa Rd Ste 200 San Diego (92123) *(P-5403)*

Better Place Forests .... D...... 888 958-7674
  3727 Buchanan St Fl 4 San Francisco (94123) *(P-9281)*

Betterdoctor Inc .... C...... 844 668-2543
  945 Bryant St Ste 350 San Francisco (94103) *(P-12653)*

Betterup Inc (PA) .... C...... 415 862-0708
  1200 Folsom St San Francisco (94103) *(P-20295)*

Betterworks, Menlo Park *Also Called: Betterworks Systems Inc (P-11455)*

Betterworks Systems Inc .... D...... 650 656-9013
  101 Jefferson Dr 1st Fl Menlo Park (94025) *(P-11455)*

Betty Ford Center (HQ) .... C...... 760 773-4100
  39000 Bob Hope Dr Rancho Mirage (92270) *(P-17014)*

Beverages & More Inc .... C...... 949 643-3020
  28011 Greenfield Dr Laguna Niguel (92677) *(P-2403)*

Beverages & More Inc .... C...... 714 891-1242
  6820 Katella Ave Cypress (90630) *(P-5776)*

Beverages & More Inc .... C...... 714 990-2060
  875 E Birch St Ste A Brea (92821) *(P-7530)*

Beverages & More Inc .... C...... 714 279-8131
  2000 N Tustin St Orange (92865) *(P-7531)*

Beverly and Company Inc .... D...... 323 422-3253
  15301 Ventura Blvd B305 Sherman Oaks (91403) *(P-8913)*

Beverly Center, Los Angeles *Also Called: La Cienega Associates (P-9067)*

Beverly Community Hosp Assn (PA) .... A...... 323 726-1222
  309 W Beverly Blvd Montebello (90640) *(P-15961)*

Beverly Healthcare, Costa Mesa *Also Called: Beaver Dam Health Care Center (P-15353)*

Beverly Healthcare, Lodi *Also Called: Beaver Dam Health Care Center (P-15355)*

Beverly Hills BMW, Los Angeles *Also Called: FAA Beverly Hills Inc (P-7204)*

Beverly Hills Collection .... D...... 310 276-1022
  604 N Arden Dr Beverly Hills (90210) *(P-9646)*

Beverly Hills Hotel, Beverly Hills *Also Called: Sajahtera Inc (P-10191)*

Beverly Hills Luxury Hotel LLC .... B...... 310 274-9999
  1801 Century Park E Ste 1200 Los Angeles (90067) *(P-9647)*

Beverly Hills Luxury Interiors, Los Angeles *Also Called: Kenneth Brdwick Intr Dsgns Inc (P-13335)*

Beverly Hills Plaza Hotel, Los Angeles *Also Called: Donald T Sterling Corporation (P-9762)*

Beverly Hls Oncology Med Group .... D...... 310 432-8900
  8900 Wilshire Blvd Beverly Hills (90211) *(P-16667)*

Beverly Hospital, Montebello *Also Called: Beverly Community Hosp Assn (P-15961)*

Beverly Office of Mgo, Los Angeles *Also Called: Macias Gini & OConnell LLP (P-19607)*

Beverly Pl Memory Care Cmnty, Los Angeles *Also Called: Silverado Senior Living Inc (P-15673)*

Beverly West Health Care Inc .... D...... 323 938-2451
  1020 S Fairfax Ave Los Angeles (90019) *(P-15358)*

Bevmo, Laguna Niguel *Also Called: Beverages & More Inc (P-2403)*

Bexel, Van Nuys *Also Called: Nep Bexel Inc (P-13943)*

Beyond Finance LLC .... A...... 800 282-7186
  9525 Towne Centre Dr Ste 100 San Diego (92121) *(P-10530)*

Beyond Franchise Group Inc .... C...... 949 398-7338
  220 Technology Dr Ste 120 Irvine (92618) *(P-7460)*

Beyondid Inc .... D...... 415 878-6210
  535 Mission St Fl 14 San Francisco (94105) *(P-12742)*

Beyondsoft Consulting Inc .... C...... 408 806-0715
  2953 Bunker Hill Ln Ste 400 Santa Clara (95054) *(P-20704)*

Beyondsoft Consulting Inc .... C...... 310 532-2822
  19009 S Laurel Park Rd Spc 6 Compton (90220) *(P-20705)*

BFI Waste Systems N Amer Inc .... D...... 408 432-1234
  1601 Dixon Landing Rd Bldg 1 Milpitas (95035) *(P-3373)*

BFI Waste Systems N Amer Inc .... D...... 510 657-1350
  42600 Boyce Rd Fremont (94538) *(P-4865)*

BFI Waste Systems N Amer Inc .... D...... 831 775-3850
  271 Rianda St Salinas (93901) *(P-4866)*

BFI Waste Systems N Amer Inc .... D...... 323 321-1722
  9200 Glenoaks Blvd Sun Valley (91352) *(P-4867)*

Bfp Fire Protection Inc .... D...... 831 461-1100
  17 Janis Way Scotts Valley (95066) *(P-1377)*

ALPHABETIC SECTION — Biomed Realty Trust Inc

Bgk Equities Inc (HQ) .... D 505 982-2184
  2000 Avenue Of The Stars Los Angeles (90067) *(P-8914)*

Bgm, San Jose *Also Called: Brilliant General Maint Inc (P-10865)*

Bh Partnership LP (PA) .... B 858 539-7635
  998 W Mission Bay Dr San Diego (92109) *(P-9648)*

Bh-SD Opco LLC (PA) .... D 619 465-4411
  7050 Parkway Dr La Mesa (91942) *(P-17015)*

Bhc Alhambra Hospital, Rosemead *Also Called: Bhc Alhambra Hospital Inc (P-17187)*

Bhc Alhambra Hospital Inc .... B 626 286-1191
  4619 Rosemead Blvd Rosemead (91770) *(P-17187)*

Bhr Operations LLC .... C 415 771-9000
  495 Bay St San Francisco (94133) *(P-9649)*

Bhr Operations LLC .... C 619 232-3861
  1355 N Harbor Dr San Diego (92101) *(P-9650)*

Bhr Trs Tahoe LLC .... C 530 562-3045
  13031 Ritz Carlton Highlands Ct Truckee (96161) *(P-9651)*

Bi Nutraceuticals Inc .... C 310 669-2100
  2384 E Pacifica Pl Rancho Dominguez (90220) *(P-2415)*

Bi Technologies Corporation (HQ) .... B 714 447-2300
  120 S State College Blvd Ste 175 Brea (92821) *(P-2940)*

Bi Warehousing Inc (PA) .... D 916 624-0654
  5404 Pacific St Rocklin (95677) *(P-7344)*

Bi Warehousing Inc .... C 916 624-0654
  5404 Pacific St Ste B Rocklin (95677) *(P-7345)*

Bi-Rite Foodservice Distrs, Brisbane *Also Called: Bi-Rite Restaurant Sup Co Inc (P-6241)*

Bi-Rite Restaurant Sup Co Inc .... B 415 656-0187
  123 S Hill Dr Brisbane (94005) *(P-6241)*

Bianchi Ag Services Inc .... D 530 923-7675
  3056 Colusa Hwy Yuba City (95993) *(P-372)*

BIANCHI AG. SERVICES, INC., Yuba City *Also Called: Bianchi Ag Services Inc (P-372)*

Biarca Inc (PA) .... D 408 564-4465
  333 W San Carlos St Ste 600 San Jose (95110) *(P-12743)*

Bicara Ltd .... B 310 316-6222
  318 Avenue I Ste 65 Redondo Beach (90277) *(P-6489)*

Bickmore and Associates Inc (DH) .... D 916 244-1100
  1750 Creekside Oaks Dr Ste 200 Sacramento (95833) *(P-8512)*

Bickmore Risk Svcs Consulting, Sacramento *Also Called: Bickmore and Associates Inc (P-8512)*

Bicycle Club Casino, Bell Gardens *Also Called: Bell Gardens Bicycle Club Inc (P-14498)*

Bien Air, Irvine *Also Called: Bien Air Usa Inc (P-3067)*

Bien Air Usa Inc .... D 949 477-6050
  8861 Research Dr Ste 100 Irvine (92618) *(P-3067)*

BIENVENIDOS COMMUNITY HEALTH C, Los Angeles *Also Called: Via Care Cmnty Hlth Ctr Inc (P-15193)*

Big Canyon Country Club .... C 949 644-5404
  1 Big Canyon Dr Newport Beach (92660) *(P-14343)*

Big Dog Sportswear, Los Angeles *Also Called: Walking Company Holdings Inc (P-7409)*

Big Eight, Lancaster *Also Called: City of Lancaster (P-14301)*

Big Four Restaurant, San Francisco *Also Called: Nob Hill Properties Inc (P-10047)*

Big Health Inc .... C 707 653-5570
  461 Bush St Ste 200 San Francisco (94108) *(P-15747)*

Big Joe California North Inc (PA) .... C 510 785-6900
  25932 Eden Landing Rd Hayward (94545) *(P-5821)*

Big Joe Handling Systems, Hayward *Also Called: Big Joe California North Inc (P-5821)*

Big Lgue Dreams Consulting LLC .... C 760 324-5600
  33700 Date Palm Dr Cathedral City (92234) *(P-10399)*

Big Lgue Dreams Consulting LLC .... C 619 846-8855
  2155 Trumble Rd Perris (92571) *(P-14128)*

Big Lgue Dreams Consulting LLC .... C 626 839-1100
  2100 S Azusa Ave West Covina (91792) *(P-14129)*

Big Lgue Dreams Consulting LLC .... C 530 223-1177
  20155 Viking Way Redding (96003) *(P-14344)*

Big Poppy Holdings Inc .... C 707 636-9020
  6580 Oakmont Dr Ste A Santa Rosa (95409) *(P-7659)*

Big Poppy Holdings Inc .... C 707 836-1588
  9230 Old Redwood Hwy Windsor (95492) *(P-7660)*

Big Sandy Rancheria, Auberry *Also Called: Mono Wind Casino (P-10023)*

Big Star, South Gate *Also Called: Koos Manufacturing Inc (P-13340)*

Big Switch Networks LLC .... C 650 322-6510
  5453 Great America Pkwy Santa Clara (95054) *(P-12113)*

Big Token Inc .... D 310 569-6553
  456 Seaton St Los Angeles (90013) *(P-10592)*

Big Tray, San Francisco *Also Called: Trimark Erf Inc (P-5390)*

Big Valley Christian School, Modesto *Also Called: Big Vlley Grace Cmnty Ch Inc M (P-19011)*

Big Valley Ford Inc .... C 209 870-4400
  3282 Auto Center Cir Stockton (95212) *(P-7172)*

Big Valley Mortgage, Roseville *Also Called: American Pacific Mortgage Corp (P-7929)*

Big Vlley Grace Cmnty Ch Inc M (PA) .... D 209 577-1604
  4040 Tully Rd Ste D Modesto (95356) *(P-19011)*

Big3 Basketball LLC .... D 213 417-2013
  13351 Riverside Dr Sherman Oaks (91423) *(P-14130)*

Bigfix Inc .... C 510 652-6700
  1480 64th St Ste 200 Emeryville (94608) *(P-12114)*

Bigge Crane and Rigging Co (PA) .... C 510 638-8100
  10700 Bigge St San Leandro (94577) *(P-2246)*

Bigge Group .... C 714 523-4092
  14511 Industry Cir La Mirada (90638) *(P-10993)*

Biggs Cardosa Associates Inc (PA) .... D 408 296-5515
  865 The Alameda San Jose (95126) *(P-19152)*

Bigham Taylor Roofing Corp .... D 510 886-0197
  22721 Alice St Hayward (94541) *(P-2046)*

Bighorn Golf Club Charities .... C 760 773-2468
  255 Palowet Dr Palm Desert (92260) *(P-14345)*

Bijan, Beverly Hills *Also Called: Fashion World Incorporated (P-6173)*

Bikes Online Inc .... D 650 272-3378
  2711 Loker Ave W Carlsbad (92010) *(P-5973)*

Bill & Daves Ldscp Maint Inc .... C 714 850-0213
  1401 E Edinger Ave Santa Ana (92705) *(P-392)*

Bill Brown Construction Co .... D 408 297-3738
  242 Phelan Ave San Jose (95112) *(P-660)*

Bill Holdings Inc (PA) .... B 650 621-7700
  6220 America Center Dr Ste 100 San Jose (95002) *(P-12115)*

Bill Howe Plumbing Inc .... D 800 245-5469
  9210 Sky Park Ct San Diego (92123) *(P-1378)*

Bill Sharp Electrical Contr .... D 530 338-1735
  5136 Caterpillar Rd Redding (96003) *(P-1683)*

Bill.com, San Jose *Also Called: Bill Holdings Inc (P-12115)*

Billabong, Huntington Beach *Also Called: Boardriders Inc (P-2454)*

Billcom LLC (HQ) .... C 650 353-3301
  6220 America Center Dr Ste 100 San Jose (95002) *(P-12116)*

Billing & Registration, Oakland *Also Called: La Clinica De La Raza Inc (P-17266)*

Billing Svcs Plus DBA Apex Jnt .... D 415 604-3515
  70 Dorman Ave San Francisco (94124) *(P-10862)*

Billiontoone Inc .... D 650 460-2551
  1035 Obrien Dr Menlo Park (94025) *(P-16706)*

Bilt-Well Roofing & Mtl Co, Los Angeles *Also Called: Sbb Roofing Inc (P-2084)*

Binding Site Inc (HQ) .... D 858 453-9177
  6730 Mesa Ridge Rd Ste B San Diego (92121) *(P-5404)*

BINEX, Torrance *Also Called: Binex Line Corp (P-3988)*

Binex Line Corp (PA) .... D 310 416-8600
  19515 S Vermont Ave Torrance (90502) *(P-3988)*

Binoptics LLC .... C 607 257-3200
  977 S Meridian Ave Alhambra (91803) *(P-19153)*

Bio-Mdcal Applctons Cmrllo Inc .... D 805 388-2449
  3801 Las Posas Rd Ste 103 Camarillo (93010) *(P-16978)*

Bio-Med Services Inc .... D 909 235-4400
  3300 E Guasti Rd Ontario (91761) *(P-15962)*

Bio-Medics Inc .... C 909 883-9501
  371 W Highland Ave San Bernardino (92405) *(P-17188)*

Biocare Medical LLC (PA) .... C 925 603-8000
  60 Berry Dr Pacheco (94553) *(P-2611)*

Bioclinica, San Mateo *Also Called: Synarc Inc (P-11960)*

Bioduro LLC .... B 858 529-6600
  72 Fairbanks Irvine (92618) *(P-19662)*

Biola Fresh Inc .... D 559 970-8881
  5887 N Sycamore Ave Fresno (93723) *(P-20706)*

Biolegend Inc (HQ) .... C 858 455-9588
  8999 Biolegend Way San Diego (92121) *(P-19663)*

Biomed Realty, San Diego *Also Called: Biomed Realty Trust Inc (P-9462)*

Biomed Realty Trust Inc (PA) .... B 858 207-2513
  4570 Executive Dr Ste 400 San Diego (92121) *(P-9462)*

ALPHABETIC SECTION

Bioness Inc .... C....... 661 362-4850
25103 Rye Canyon Loop Valencia (91355) *(P-3072)*

Bionic Stork Inc .... C....... 650 600-1494
2345 Yale St Palo Alto (94306) *(P-11456)*

Biora Therapeutics Inc (PA) .... D....... 855 293-2639
4330 La Jolla Village Dr Ste 300 San Diego (92122) *(P-16707)*

Bioscreen Testing Services, Torrance Also Called: Als Group Usa Corp *(P-19946)*

Biosite Inc .... C....... 510 683-9063
9975 Summers Ridge Rd San Diego (92121) *(P-5405)*

Biospace Inc .... D....... 323 932-6503
13850 Cerritos Corporate Dr Ste C Cerritos (90703) *(P-19664)*

Biosplice Therapeutics Inc .... D....... 858 926-2900
9360 Towne Centre Dr San Diego (92121) *(P-19866)*

Biovail Technologies Ltd .... D....... 703 995-2400
1 Enterprise Aliso Viejo (92656) *(P-2581)*

Birch Ptrick Convalescent Cntr, Chula Vista Also Called: Sharp Healthcare *(P-16418)*

Bird Mrlla Bxer Wlpert Nssim .... D....... 310 201-2100
1875 Century Park E 23rd Fl Los Angeles (90067) *(P-17386)*

Bird Marella, Los Angeles Also Called: Bird Mrlla Bxer Wlpert Nssim *(P-17386)*

Bird Rides Inc .... D....... 866 205-2442
2501 Colorado Ave Santa Monica (90404) *(P-11457)*

Birkenstock Usa Lp .... C....... 415 884-3200
100 Wood Hollow Dr Ste 100 Novato (94945) *(P-6229)*

Birnam Wood Golf Club (PA) .... D....... 805 969-2223
1941 E Valley Rd Santa Barbara (93108) *(P-14346)*

Birst Inc .... B....... 415 766-4800
45 Fremont St Ste 1800 San Francisco (94105) *(P-11458)*

Bis Research Inc .... C....... 510 404-8135
39111 Paseo Padre Pkwy Ste 313 Fremont (94538) *(P-19665)*

Bisco Inc .... C....... 714 693-2901
5065 E Hunter Ave Anaheim (92807) *(P-5631)*

Bisco Industries Inc (HQ) .... D....... 800 323-1232
5065 E Hunter Ave Anaheim (92807) *(P-5632)*

Biscuit Filmworks LLC .... D....... 323 856-9200
7026 Santa Monica Blvd West Hollywood (90038) *(P-14028)*

Bishop Fox Inc .... C....... 480 621-8967
85 2nd St Ste 750 San Francisco (94105) *(P-20707)*

Bishop Paiute Gaming Corp .... C....... 760 872-6005
2742 N Sierra Hwy Bishop (93514) *(P-9652)*

Bishop Ranch, San Ramon Also Called: Sunset Development Company *(P-8767)*

Bishop Ranch Veterinary Center .... D....... 925 743-9300
2000 Bishop Dr San Ramon (94583) *(P-330)*

Bissell Bros Bldg Maint Servic, Rancho Cordova Also Called: Bissell Brothers Janitorial *(P-10863)*

Bissell Brothers Janitorial .... D....... 916 635-1852
3207 Luyung Dr Rancho Cordova (95742) *(P-10863)*

Bista Solutions Inc (PA) .... C....... 858 401-2332
39180 Liberty St Ste 101 Fremont (94538) *(P-11459)*

Bit Medtech LLC .... D....... 858 613-1200
15870 Bernardo Center Dr San Diego (92127) *(P-19154)*

Bitalign Inc .... D....... 415 395-9525
95 Minna St Fl 4 San Francisco (94105) *(P-11460)*

Bitcentral, Newport Beach Also Called: Bitcentral Inc *(P-5633)*

Bitcentral Inc .... D....... 949 253-9000
4340 Von Karman Ave # 410 Newport Beach (92660) *(P-5633)*

Bitco Cnstr Insur Agcy Inc .... D....... 626 683-5200
225 S Lake Ave Ste 1050 Pasadena (91101) *(P-8513)*

Bitcoin Ira, Sherman Oaks Also Called: Alternative Ira Services LLC *(P-13188)*

Bite Communications LLC (HQ) .... D....... 415 365-0222
100 Montgomery St Ste 1100 San Francisco (94104) *(P-20296)*

Bitglass Inc .... C....... 408 337-0190
675 Campbell Technology Pkwy Ste 225 Campbell (95008) *(P-11461)*

Bitwarden Inc .... D....... 904 664-9194
1 N Calle Cesar Chavez Ste 102 Santa Barbara (93103) *(P-11462)*

Biu Inc .... D....... 909 556-1311
9268 1/2 Hall Rd Downey (90241) *(P-13214)*

Bizcom Electronics Inc (HQ) .... C....... 408 262-7877
1361 El Camino Real Santa Clara (95050) *(P-5281)*

BJ's Restaurant & Brewhouse, Huntington Beach Also Called: BJs Restaurant Operations Co *(P-20038)*

Bjarke Ingels Group Nyc LLC .... C....... 347 549-4141
310 Wilshire Blvd Santa Monica (90401) *(P-19456)*

Bjork Construction Company Inc (PA) .... C....... 510 656-4688
4420 Enterprise Pl Fremont (94538) *(P-873)*

BJs Restaurant Operations Co .... B....... 714 500-2440
7755 Center Ave Ste 300 Huntington Beach (92647) *(P-20038)*

Bjz LLC .... C....... 760 851-0740
45150 Club Dr Indian Wells (92210) *(P-16821)*

Bkf Engineers (PA) .... D....... 650 482-6300
255 Shoreline Dr Ste 200 Redwood City (94065) *(P-19155)*

Bkf Engineers/Ags .... D....... 949 526-8400
4675 Macarthur Ct Ste 400 Newport Beach (92660) *(P-19156)*

BKF ENGINEERS/AGS, Newport Beach Also Called: Bkf Engineers/Ags *(P-19156)*

Bkf/Fli .... D....... 415 930-7900
150 California St Ste 600 San Francisco (94111) *(P-19157)*

BKM Diablo 227 LLC .... D....... 602 688-6409
1701 Quail St Ste 100 Newport Beach (92660) *(P-8915)*

BKM Officeworks, San Diego Also Called: BKM Officeworks LLC *(P-5079)*

BKM Officeworks LLC (PA) .... D....... 858 569-4700
4780 Eastgate Mall Ste 100 San Diego (92121) *(P-5079)*

BKM Total Office of Texas, Santa Fe Springs Also Called: New Tangram LLC *(P-5095)*

Blach, San Jose Also Called: Blach Construction Company *(P-808)*

Blach Construction Company (PA) .... D....... 408 244-7100
2244 Blach Pl Ste 100 San Jose (95131) *(P-808)*

Black Box Inc .... D....... 760 804-3300
371 2nd St Ste 1 Encinitas (92024) *(P-6166)*

Black Box Network Services, Los Angeles Also Called: Scottel Voice & Data Inc *(P-13744)*

Black Diamond Electric Inc .... D....... 925 777-3440
1300 Verne Roberts Cir Antioch (94509) *(P-1684)*

Black Dot Wireless LLC .... D....... 949 502-3800
23456 Madero Ste 210 Mission Viejo (92691) *(P-4185)*

Black Jack Farms, Santa Maria Also Called: Blackjack Frms De La Csta Cntl *(P-168)*

Black Knight Infoserv LLC .... C....... 904 854-5100
2500 Redhill Ave Ste 100 Santa Ana (92705) *(P-12553)*

Black Knight Infoserv LLC .... C....... 415 989-9800
601 California St Ste 980 San Francisco (94108) *(P-13215)*

Black Oak Casino .... D....... 209 928-9300
19400 Tuolumne Rd N Tuolumne (95379) *(P-14499)*

Black Tie Transportation LLC .... C....... 925 847-0747
7080 Commerce Dr Pleasanton (94588) *(P-3241)*

Blackbeard's Family Fun Center, Fresno Also Called: GLad Entertainment Inc *(P-14528)*

Blackberry Corporation .... A....... 650 564-0016
331 Fairchild Dr Mountain View (94043) *(P-12117)*

Blackberry Corporation (HQ) .... D....... 972 650-6126
3001 Bishop Dr San Ramon (94583) *(P-12118)*

Blackhawk, Pleasanton Also Called: Blackhawk Network Holdings Inc *(P-7842)*

Blackhawk Country Club .... C....... 925 736-6500
599 Blackhawk Club Dr Danville (94506) *(P-14347)*

Blackhawk Network Inc (DH) .... A....... 925 226-9990
6220 Stoneridge Mall Rd Pleasanton (94588) *(P-7841)*

Blackhawk Network Holdings Inc (HQ) .... B....... 925 226-9990
6220 Stoneridge Mall Rd Pleasanton (94588) *(P-7842)*

Blackink., Irvine Also Called: Clear Mortgage Capital Inc *(P-8034)*

Blackjack Frms De La Csta Cntl 805 347-1333
2385 A St Santa Maria (93455) *(P-168)*

Blackline, Woodland Hills Also Called: Blackline Inc *(P-12119)*

Blackline Inc (PA) .... C....... 818 223-9008
21300 Victory Blvd Fl 12 Woodland Hills (91367) *(P-12119)*

Blackrock Funds III .... C....... 415 597-2000
400 Howard St San Francisco (94105) *(P-9359)*

Blackrock Global Investors .... A....... 415 670-2000
400 Howard St San Francisco (94105) *(P-9360)*

Blackrock Instnl Tr Nat Assn (HQ) .... A....... 415 597-2000
400 Howard St San Francisco (94105) *(P-9361)*

Blackrock Logistics, Fontana Also Called: Blackrock Logistics Inc *(P-3990)*

Blackrock Logistics Inc (PA) .... D....... 925 523-3878
7031 Koll Center Pkwy Ste 250 Pleasanton (94566) *(P-3989)*

Blackrock Logistics Inc .... C....... 909 259-5357
14601 Slover Ave Fontana (92337) *(P-3990)*

Blackstone Consulting Inc (PA) .... D....... 310 826-4389
11726 San Vicente Blvd Ste 550 Los Angeles (90049) *(P-20297)*

Blackstone Development Inc .... D....... 925 718-3126
801 Ygnacio Valley Rd Ste 100 Walnut Creek (94596) *(P-19457)*

ALPHABETIC SECTION

Blackstone Technology Group (PA)..D....... 415 837-1400
  1141 Capuchino Ave Burlingame (94010) *(P-8067)*
Blackwater Cellular Corp ....C....... 415 526-2200
  125 E Sir Francis Drake Blvd # 4 Larkspur (94939) *(P-4186)*
Bladium Inc (PA)...D....... 510 814-4999
  800 W Tower Ave Bldg 40 Alameda (94501) *(P-14180)*
Bladium Sports Clubs, Alameda *Also Called: Bladium Inc (P-14180)*
Blakely Sokoloff Taylor & Zafman LLP ....C....... 310 207-3800
  12400 Wilshire Blvd Ste 700 Los Angeles (90025) *(P-17387)*
Blanchard Training and Dev Inc (PA)...C....... 760 489-5005
  125 State Pl Escondido (92029) *(P-20298)*
Bland A/C & Heating Inc (PA)..D....... 661 836-3880
  4303 E Brundage Ln Bakersfield (93307) *(P-1379)*
Bland Solar & Air, Bakersfield *Also Called: Bland A/C & Heating Inc (P-1379)*
Blast Motion, San Marcos *Also Called: Blast Motion Inc (P-11463)*
Blast Motion Inc ....D....... 760 803-2724
  1780 La Costa Meadows Dr Ste 101 San Marcos (92078) *(P-11463)*
Blaze Solutions Inc ....D....... 415 964-5689
  155 N Riverview Dr Anaheim (92808) *(P-11464)*
BlazerWilkinsonGee LLC ....B....... 831 455-3700
  19040 Portola Dr Salinas (93908) *(P-6516)*
Blazona Concrete Cnstr Inc ....C....... 916 375-8337
  525 Harbor Blvd Ste 10 West Sacramento (95691) *(P-2102)*
Blc Residential Care Inc ....D....... 310 722-7541
  1455 W 112th St Los Angeles (90047) *(P-17852)*
Blend, San Francisco *Also Called: Blend Insurance Agency Inc (P-7937)*
Blend Insurance Agency Inc ....C....... 650 550-4810
  415 Kearny St San Francisco (94108) *(P-7937)*
Blh Construction Company ....C....... 818 905-3837
  20750 Ventura Blvd Ste 155 Woodland Hills (91364) *(P-748)*
Bligh Pacific, Santa Fe Springs *Also Called: Bligh Roof Co (P-2047)*
Bligh Roof Co ....D....... 562 944-9753
  11043 Forest Pl Santa Fe Springs (90670) *(P-2047)*
Blind Decker Productions Inc ....D....... 310 264-4247
  3000 Olympic Blvd Santa Monica (90404) *(P-13822)*
Bliss World LLC ....D....... 415 217-7047
  39 Pier San Francisco (94133) *(P-6019)*
Bliss World LLC ....D....... 323 500-0921
  6250 Hollywood Blvd Fl 4 Los Angeles (90028) *(P-14181)*
Blize Healthcare, Hercules *Also Called: Blize Healthcare Cal Inc (P-16822)*
Blize Healthcare Cal Inc ....D....... 800 343-2549
  750 Alfred Nobel Dr Ste 202 Hercules (94547) *(P-16822)*
Blizzard Entertainment Inc (DH)..D....... 949 955-1380
  1 Blizzard Irvine (92618) *(P-12120)*
Blocka Construction Inc ....D....... 510 657-3686
  445 Boulder Ct Pleasanton (94566) *(P-1380)*
Blockade Medical, Irvine *Also Called: Balt Usa LLC (P-5402)*
Blois Construction Inc ....C....... 805 485-0011
  3201 Sturgis Rd Oxnard (93030) *(P-1197)*
Blomberg Bnson Grrett Inc A La ....D....... 909 945-5000
  10300 4th St Rancho Cucamonga (91730) *(P-17388)*
Blood Bank of Redwoods (PA)..C....... 707 545-1222
  3505 Industrial Dr Santa Rosa (95403) *(P-17189)*
Blood Bnk San Brnrdino Rvrside (HQ)......................................C....... 909 885-6503
  384 W Orange Show Rd San Bernardino (92408) *(P-17190)*
Blood Center of The Pacific, Santa Rosa *Also Called: Blood Bank of Redwoods (P-17189)*
Bloodsource Inc (PA)...B....... 916 456-1500
  10536 Peter A Mccuen Blvd Mather (95655) *(P-17191)*
Bloodsource Inc ....D....... 530 893-5433
  555 Rio Lindo Ave Chico (95926) *(P-17192)*
Bloodsource North Valley, Chico *Also Called: Bloodsource Inc (P-17192)*
Bloomberg LP ....C....... 415 283-4872
  Pier Three 101 San Francisco (94111) *(P-19801)*
Blossom Ridge HM Hlth Agcy LLC ....D....... 800 991-6147
  520 9th St Ste 240 Sacramento (95814) *(P-16823)*
Blossom Valley Cnstr Inc ....D....... 408 993-0766
  1125 Mabury Rd San Jose (95133) *(P-476)*
Blowfish LLC ....D....... 310 566-5700
  6065 Bristol Pkwy # 100 Culver City (90230) *(P-6230)*
Blowfish Footwear, Culver City *Also Called: Blowfish LLC (P-6230)*

Bls Lmsine Svc Los Angeles Inc ....B....... 323 644-7166
  2860 Fletcher Dr Los Angeles (90039) *(P-3242)*
BLT, Los Angeles *Also Called: BLT & Associates Inc (P-10798)*
BLT & Associates Inc ....C....... 323 860-4000
  6430 W Sunset Blvd Ste 800 Los Angeles (90028) *(P-10798)*
BLT Cmmnctions LLC A Ltd Lblty ....C....... 323 860-4000
  6430 W Sunset Blvd Ste 800 Los Angeles (90028) *(P-10706)*
Blu Digital Group Inc (PA)..C....... 818 527-2763
  2233 N Ontario St # 130 Burbank (91504) *(P-11465)*
Blue and Gold Fleet ....D....... 415 705-8200
  Pier 41 Marine Terminal San Francisco (94133) *(P-3805)*
Blue Beacon of Wheeler Ridge, Arvin *Also Called: Blue Beacon USA LP (P-13684)*
Blue Beacon USA LP ....C....... 661 858-2090
  5831 Santa Elena Dr Arvin (93203) *(P-13684)*
Blue Beacon USA LP II ....D....... 213 477-1060
  1630 Mcgarry St Los Angeles (90021) *(P-13685)*
Blue Bus Tours LLC ....C....... 415 353-5310
  10 Industrial Way Brisbane (94005) *(P-3961)*
Blue Chip Stamps Inc ....A....... 626 585-6700
  301 E Colorado Blvd Ste 300 Pasadena (91101) *(P-5479)*
Blue Coat LLC ....A....... 408 220-2200
  350 Ellis St Mountain View (94043) *(P-12121)*
Blue Cross, Woodland Hills *Also Called: Blue Cross of California (P-8282)*
Blue Cross of California (HQ)...C....... 805 557-6050
  21215 Burbank Blvd Ste 630 Woodland Hills (91367) *(P-8282)*
Blue Diamond Growers ....D....... 559 251-4044
  10840 E Mckinley Ave Sanger (93657) *(P-257)*
Blue Diamond Growers ....C....... 209 545-6221
  4800 Sisk Rd Modesto (95356) *(P-258)*
Blue Diamond Materials, Brea *Also Called: Sully-Miller Contracting Co (P-1166)*
Blue Lake Casino ....D....... 707 668-5101
  777 Casino Way Blue Lake Blue Lake (95525) *(P-9653)*
Blue Lantern Inn, Dana Point *Also Called: Four Sisters Inns (P-20093)*
Blue Mountain Air, Vacaville *Also Called: Blue Mountain Cnstr Svcs Inc (P-1381)*
Blue Mountain Cnstr Svcs Inc ....C....... 800 889-2085
  707 Aldridge Rd Ste B Vacaville (95688) *(P-1381)*
Blue Oak Energy, Sacramento *Also Called: Blue Oak Energy LLC (P-1382)*
Blue Oak Energy LLC ....D....... 530 747-2026
  3947 Lennane Dr Ste 130 Sacramento (95834) *(P-1382)*
Blue Print Service, San Francisco *Also Called: Bps Reprographics Services (P-10785)*
Blue Shield Cal Lf Hlth Insur ....A....... 800 660-3007
  4005 Manzanita Ave Ste 6 Carmichael (95608) *(P-8283)*
Blue Shield Cal Lf Hlth Insur ....A....... 619 686-4200
  2275 Rio Bonito Way Ste 250 San Diego (92108) *(P-8284)*
Blue Shield of CA ....D....... 916 841-0584
  3300 Zinfandel Dr Rancho Cordova (95670) *(P-8285)*
Blue Shield of California, Oakland *Also Called: California Physicians Service (P-8286)*
Blue Shield of California, Long Beach *Also Called: California Physicians Service (P-8288)*
Blue Shield of California, Woodland Hills *Also Called: California Physicians Service (P-8289)*
Blue Shield of California, Fresno *Also Called: California Physicians Service (P-8290)*
Blue Sky The Clor Imgntion LLC ....D....... 714 389-7700
  410 Exchange Ste 250 Irvine (92602) *(P-6063)*
Blue White Robotics US Inc (PA)..C....... 559 731-2239
  3731 W Ashcroft Ave Fresno (93722) *(P-5822)*
Bluebeam Inc (PA)...C....... 626 788-4100
  443 S Raymond Ave Pasadena (91105) *(P-11466)*
Bluebird Office Supplies, Los Angeles *Also Called: Image Source Inc (P-6066)*
Bluebridge Prof Svcs Inc ....D....... 909 625-6151
  420 W Baseline Rd Ste D Claremont (91711) *(P-16824)*
Bluecrew LLC ....D....... 510 684-7362
  821 Folsom St Ste 102 San Francisco (94107) *(P-11095)*
Blueline Construction, Rancho Cordova *Also Called: Ron Nurss Inc (P-2154)*
Bluemark Inc ....C....... 323 230-0770
  27909 Hancock Pkwy Valencia (91355) *(P-6893)*
Blues Roofing Co ....D....... 408 240-0680
  182 Topaz St Milpitas (95035) *(P-2048)*
Blueshift Labs Inc ....C....... 844 258-3735
  433 California St Ste 600 San Francisco (94130) *(P-12122)*
Bluetriton Brands Inc ....C....... 714 532-6220
  619 N Main St Orange (92868) *(P-6610)*

Bluevine, Redwood City *Also Called: Bluevine Capital Inc* **(P-8030)**
Bluevine Capital Inc .... B...... 888 216-9619
   401 Warren St Ste 300 Redwood City (94063) *(P-8030)*
Bluewater Envmtl Svcs Inc .... D...... 510 346-8800
   2075 Williams St San Leandro (94577) *(P-2230)*
Bluewater Wear, Santa Ana *Also Called: Aftco Mfg Co Inc* **(P-5972)**
Bluewhite, Fresno *Also Called: Blue White Robotics US Inc* **(P-5822)**
Blufi Lending Corporation C
   9909 Mira Mesa Blvd # 160 San Diego (92131) *(P-7938)*
Blufocus, Burbank *Also Called: Blu Digital Group Inc* **(P-11465)**
Blumenthal Distributing Inc (PA) .... C...... 909 930-2000
   1901 S Archibald Ave Ontario (91761) *(P-5080)*
Blur Studio Inc .... D...... 424 258-3145
   3960 Ince Blvd Culver City (90232) *(P-11467)*
Blyth/Wndsor Cntry Pk Hlthcare .... D...... 310 385-1090
   3232 E Artesia Blvd Long Beach (90805) *(P-15748)*
Bmb 1 LLC .... D...... 951 741-0663
   495 E Rincon St Ste 211 Corona (92879) *(P-15820)*
BMC Group Inc .... D...... 310 321-5555
   300 Continental Blvd Ste 570 El Segundo (90245) *(P-17389)*
Bmi Inc .... D...... 530 749-0808
   4060 Alvis Ct Rocklin (95677) *(P-2735)*
Bmo Bank NA .... C...... 415 765-4886
   180 Montgomery St San Francisco (94104) *(P-7661)*
Bmp, Glendale *Also Called: Bunim-Murray Productions* **(P-13826)**
Bms Catastrophe Inc .... C...... 877 730-1948
   30964 San Benito St Hayward (94544) *(P-10864)*
BMS CATASTROPHE, INC., Hayward *Also Called: Bms Catastrophe Inc* **(P-10864)**
Bms Healthcare Inc .... C...... 562 942-7019
   8925 Mines Ave Pico Rivera (90660) *(P-17193)*
Bms Parent Inc (PA) .... D...... 909 981-2341
   1220 Dewey Way Ste F Upland (91786) *(P-19538)*
Bmv Direct II LP .... D...... 858 485-9840
   17190 Bernardo Center Dr San Diego (92128) *(P-20708)*
BMW Fresno, Fresno *Also Called: Weber Motors Fresno Inc* **(P-7332)**
BMW of San Francisco, San Francisco *Also Called: German Motors Corporation* **(P-7220)**
Bni Enterprises Inc .... A...... 909 305-1818
   545 College Commerce Way Upland (91786) *(P-20630)*
Bnn, Los Angeles *Also Called: Breitbart News Network LLC* **(P-10707)**
Bny Mellon National Assn .... A...... 310 551-7600
   10250 Constellation Blvd Ste 2100 Los Angeles (90067) *(P-7609)*
Bny Mellon National Assn .... A...... 877 420-6377
   1600 Newport Center Dr Ste 200 Newport Beach (92660) *(P-7662)*
Boardriders Inc (HQ) .... A...... 714 889-5404
   5600 Argosy Ave Ste 100 Huntington Beach (92649) *(P-2454)*
Boardriders Wholesale LLC (DH) .... D...... 714 889-2200
   5600 Argosy Ave Ste 100 Huntington Beach (92649) *(P-6167)*
Boardwalk Solutions, Gardena *Also Called: Ocean Direct LLC* **(P-2422)**
Bob Baker Chrysler-Plymouth, Carlsbad *Also Called: Bob Baker Volkswagen* **(P-7173)**
Bob Baker Volkswagen .... D...... 760 438-2200
   5500 Paseo Del Norte Carlsbad (92008) *(P-7173)*
Bob Hope Health Center, Woodland Hills *Also Called: Motion Picture and TV Fund* **(P-16275)**
Bob Stall Chevrolet .... C...... 619 460-1311
   7601 Alvarado Rd La Mesa (91942) *(P-7174)*
Bobbi Boss, Cerritos *Also Called: Midway International Inc* **(P-6928)**
Boboli International, Stockton *Also Called: Boboli International LLC* **(P-6611)**
Boboli International LLC .... D...... 209 473-3507
   5530 El Greco Dr Stockton (95212) *(P-6611)*
Bockmon & Woody Elc Co Inc .... C...... 209 464-4878
   1528 El Pinal Dr Stockton (95205) *(P-1685)*
Bodega Bay Lodge, Bodega Bay *Also Called: NAPA Valley Lodge LP* **(P-10037)**
Bodega Harbour Golf Links, Bodega Bay *Also Called: Bodega Harbour Homeowners Assn* **(P-18817)**
Bodega Harbour Homeowners Assn .... D...... 707 875-3519
   21301 Heron Dr Bodega Bay (94923) *(P-18817)*
Bodhtree Solutions Inc .... C...... 844 409-0510
   74 W Neal St Ste 100 Pleasanton (94566) *(P-12744)*
Body Beautiful Car Wash Inc .... D...... 858 748-4400
   13236 Poway Rd Poway (92064) *(P-13686)*
Body Fit Plus Inc .... C...... 925 226-7744
   440 N Wolfe Rd Sunnyvale (94085) *(P-11096)*

Boerner Truck Center, Huntington Park *Also Called: Fred M Boerner Motor Co* **(P-7348)**
Boething Treeland Farms Inc (PA) .... D...... 818 883-1222
   23475 Long Valley Rd Woodland Hills (91367) *(P-564)*
Boething Treeland Farms Inc .... D...... 209 727-3741
   20601 E Kettleman Ln Lodi (95240) *(P-565)*
Boething Treeland Nursery, Lodi *Also Called: Boething Treeland Farms Inc* **(P-565)**
Bohemian Club (PA) .... D...... 415 885-2440
   624 Taylor St San Francisco (94102) *(P-18818)*
BOHEMIAN GROVE, San Francisco *Also Called: Bohemian Club* **(P-18818)**
Boiling Crab Operations LLC .... B...... 714 636-4885
   5811 Mcfadden Ave Huntington Beach (92649) *(P-7461)*
Boiling Crab, The, Huntington Beach *Also Called: Boiling Crab Operations LLC* **(P-7461)**
Boiling Point Rest S CA Inc .... B...... 626 551-5181
   13668 Valley Blvd Unit C2 City Of Industry (91746) *(P-11097)*
Boise Cascade, Riverside *Also Called: Boise Cascade Company* **(P-6958)**
Boise Cascade Company .... D...... 951 343-3000
   7145 Arlington Ave Riverside (92503) *(P-6958)*
Boku Inc (PA) .... C...... 415 375-3160
   660 Market St Ste 400 San Francisco (94104) *(P-11468)*
Boldt Company .... D...... 415 762-8300
   375 Beale St Ste 500 San Francisco (94105) *(P-874)*
Boldyn Networks US Services LL .... B...... 877 999-7070
   121 Innovation Dr Ste 200 Irvine (92617) *(P-4255)*
Boldyn Ntwrks US Oprations LLC .... C...... 949 515-1500
   121 Innovation Dr Irvine (92617) *(P-4256)*
Bolide International, San Dimas *Also Called: Bolide Technology Group Inc* **(P-13099)**
Bolide Technology Group Inc .... D...... 909 305-8889
   468 S San Dimas Ave San Dimas (91773) *(P-13099)*
Bolt .... D...... 650 804-0633
   1235 Howard St Ste D San Francisco (94103) *(P-11469)*
Bolthouse Farms .... A...... 661 366-7205
   3200 E Brundage Ln Bakersfield (93304) *(P-23)*
Bolthouse Farms, Bakersfield *Also Called: Wm Bolthouse Farms Inc* **(P-49)**
Bomel Construction Co Inc .... D...... 760 431-6360
   701 Palomar Airport Rd Ste 270 Carlsbad (92011) *(P-875)*
Bomel Construction Co Inc .... D...... 909 923-3319
   939 E Francis St Ontario (91761) *(P-876)*
Bon Appetit, Los Angeles *Also Called: Bon Appetit Management Co* **(P-20041)**
Bon Appetit Management Co .... C...... 925 730-3653
   4125 Hopyard Rd Pleasanton (94588) *(P-20039)*
Bon Appetit Management Co .... C...... 408 554-2728
   500 El Camino Real 500 Santa Clara (95050) *(P-20040)*
Bon Appetit Management Co .... C...... 310 440-6052
   1200 Getty Center Dr Los Angeles (90049) *(P-20041)*
Bon Appetit Management Co .... C...... 909 607-2788
   1050 N Mills Ave Claremont (91711) *(P-20042)*
Bon Appetit Management Co .... C...... 408 554-5771
   301 Market St Santa Clara (95053) *(P-20043)*
Bon Appetit Management Co .... C...... 650 467-3767
   383 E Grand Ave South San Francisco (94080) *(P-20044)*
Bon Appetit Management Co .... C...... 310 440-6209
   1200 Getty Center Dr Ste 100 Los Angeles (90049) *(P-20045)*
Bon Appetit Management Co .... C...... 909 748-8970
   1259 E Colton Ave Redlands (92374) *(P-20299)*
Bonander Auto Truck & Trlr Inc (PA) .... D...... 209 632-8871
   231 S Center St Turlock (95380) *(P-7175)*
Bonander Pontiac-Buick-Gmc, Turlock *Also Called: Bonander Auto Truck & Trlr Inc* **(P-7175)**
Bond Manufacturing Co Inc (PA) .... D...... 866 771-2663
   2516 Verne Roberts Cir Ste H3 Antioch (94509) *(P-2702)*
Bonded Carpet, San Diego *Also Called: Bonded Inc* **(P-10469)**
Bonded Inc (PA) .... D...... 858 576-8400
   7590 Carroll Rd San Diego (92121) *(P-10469)*
Boneso Brothers Cnstr Inc .... D...... 805 227-4450
   2758 Concrete Ct Paso Robles (93446) *(P-1383)*
Bonita Golf Club, Bonita *Also Called: Crockett & Coinc* **(P-14255)**
Bonita House Inc .... D...... 510 923-0180
   6333 Telegraph Ave Ste 102 Oakland (94609) *(P-17853)*
Bonne Brdges Mller Okefe Nchol (PA) .... D...... 213 480-1900
   355 S Grand Ave Ste 1750 Los Angeles (90071) *(P-17390)*
Bonnie Brae Cnvlscent Hosp Inc (PA) .... D...... 213 483-8144
   420 S Bonnie Brae St Los Angeles (90057) *(P-15821)*

ALPHABETIC SECTION — Boys Republic

Bonterra Psomas, Santa Ana *Also Called: Psomas (P-19525)*

Bookheaded Learning LLC .... D....... 707 996-3427
610 Daniel Young Dr Sonoma (95476) *(P-18271)*

Booking Com .... C....... 323 801-4200
5700 Wilshire Blvd Ste 285 Los Angeles (90036) *(P-3929)*

Boomerang Commerce Inc (PA) .... C....... 602 459-2578
2100 Geng Rd Ste 210 Palo Alto (94303) *(P-12123)*

Boomerang Ex Dry Clg & Dlvry, South San Francisco *Also Called: Inter-City Cleaners LLC (P-10467)*

Boomr LLC .... A....... 877 687-6228
660 Menlo Oaks Dr Menlo Park (94025) *(P-11470)*

Boos & Associates A Prof Corp .... D....... 559 449-7688
5250 N Palm Ave Ste 120 Fresno (93704) *(P-19539)*

Boost Mobile, Fresno *Also Called: Dish Wireless LLC (P-4214)*

Boost Mobile LLC .... A....... 949 451-1563
6316 Irvine Blvd Irvine (92620) *(P-13216)*

Boosted Ecommerce Inc .... D....... 310 721-6316
9903 Santa Monica Blvd Ste 605 Beverly Hills (90212) *(P-20709)*

Boostest, Fresno *Also Called: Boos & Associates A Prof Corp (P-19539)*

Booth Mitchel & Strange LLP .... D....... 805 400-0703
979 Osos St Ste C1 San Luis Obispo (93401) *(P-17391)*

Booth Ranches LLC .... D....... 559 626-4472
440 Anchor Ave Orange Cove (93646) *(P-234)*

Boral Industries, Oceanside *Also Called: Royal Westlake Roofing LLC (P-2083)*

Borbon Incorporated .... C....... 714 994-0170
2560 W Woodland Dr Anaheim (92801) *(P-1606)*

Border Valley Trading, Brawley *Also Called: Border Valley Trading Ltd (P-6822)*

Border Valley Trading Ltd .... D....... 760 344-6700
604 Mead Rd Brawley (92227) *(P-6822)*

Borderview Y M C A, San Diego *Also Called: YMCA of San Diego County (P-18940)*

Boreal Ridge Corporation .... C....... 530 426-1012
19749 Boreal Ridge Rd Soda Springs (95728) *(P-9654)*

Boreal Ski Area, Soda Springs *Also Called: Boreal Ridge Corporation (P-9654)*

Borg Produce Sales, Los Angeles *Also Called: Pacific Trellis Fruit LLC (P-6568)*

Borg Produce Sales LLC .... C....... 213 624-2674
1601 E Olympic Blvd Ste 100 Los Angeles (90021) *(P-6517)*

Borrego Cmnty Hlth Foundation (PA) .... C....... 855 436-1234
587 Palm Canyon Dr Ste 208 Borrego Springs (92004) *(P-14633)*

Borrego Cmnty Hlth Foundation .... C....... 760 466-1080
1121 E Washington Ave Escondido (92025) *(P-14634)*

Borrego Cmnty Hlth Foundation .... C....... 951 487-8506
651 N State St Ste 5 San Jacinto (92583) *(P-14635)*

Borrego Cmnty Hlth Foundation .... C....... 760 251-0044
11750 Cholla Dr Ste B Desert Hot Springs (92240) *(P-14636)*

Borrego Health, San Jacinto *Also Called: Borrego Cmnty Hlth Foundation (P-14635)*

Borrego Medical Center, Borrego Springs *Also Called: Borrego Cmnty Hlth Foundation (P-14633)*

Boskovich Farms Inc .... C....... 805 987-1443
4224 Pleasant Valley Rd Camarillo (93012) *(P-24)*

Boskovich Farms Inc (PA) .... C....... 805 487-2299
711 Diaz Ave Oxnard (93030) *(P-259)*

Boskovich Fresh Cut LLC .... C....... 805 487-2299
711 Diaz Ave Oxnard (93030) *(P-6518)*

Bosman Dairy LLC .... C....... 559 752-7018
6802 Avenue 120 # A Tipton (93272) *(P-214)*

Bosque Joe L Del Jr .... B....... 209 364-6428
51481 W Shields Ave Firebaugh (93622) *(P-246)*

Bossa Nova Robotics Inc (HQ) .... D....... 415 234-5136
610 22nd St Ste 250 San Francisco (94107) *(P-6029)*

Bossa Nova Robotics Inc .... C....... 415 234-5136
709 N Shoreline Blvd Mountain View (94043) *(P-6030)*

Boston Properties Ltd Partnr .... D....... 415 772-0700
4 Embarcadero Ctr Lbby Level San Francisco (94111) *(P-9246)*

Boston Scntfc Nrmdlation Corp (HQ) .... B....... 661 949-4310
25155 Rye Canyon Loop Valencia (91355) *(P-3063)*

Bostonia Medical Offices, El Cajon *Also Called: Kaiser Foundation Hospitals (P-16174)*

Boswell Properties Inc .... B....... 626 583-3000
101 W Walnut St Pasadena (91103) *(P-247)*

Bottomley Distributing Co Inc .... D....... 408 945-0660
755 Yosemite Dr Milpitas (95035) *(P-6753)*

Boudreau Pipeline Corporation .... B....... 951 493-6780
463 N Smith Ave Corona (92878) *(P-1198)*

BOULDER CREEK POST ACUTE, Poway *Also Called: Pomerado Operations LLC (P-15632)*

Boulevard Automotive Group (PA) .... D....... 562 492-1000
2850 Cherry Ave Signal Hill (90755) *(P-7176)*

Boulevard Collision Center, Signal Hill *Also Called: Boulevard Automotive Group (P-7176)*

Bouqs Company .... D....... 888 320-2687
4094 Glencoe Ave Marina Del Rey (90292) *(P-6853)*

Boutique Air Inc (PA) .... D....... 415 449-0505
5 3rd St Ste 925 San Francisco (94103) *(P-3864)*

Bouton Construction Inc .... D....... 408 375-0829
420 E Mcglincy Ln Campbell (95008) *(P-5783)*

BOWERS MUSEUM, Santa Ana *Also Called: Charles W Bowers Museum Corp (P-18642)*

Bowie Enterprises (PA) .... D....... 559 227-6221
4411 N Blackstone Ave Fresno (93726) *(P-13687)*

Bowie Enterprises .... D....... 559 292-6565
801 W Shaw Ave Clovis (93612) *(P-13688)*

Box Inc (PA) .... A....... 877 729-4269
900 Jefferson Ave Redwood City (94063) *(P-12124)*

Boxunion, Santa Monica *Also Called: Boxunion Santa Monica LLC (P-14182)*

Boxunion Santa Monica LLC (PA) .... C....... 310 882-5508
1755 Ocean Ave Santa Monica (90401) *(P-14182)*

BOY SCOUTS OF AMERICA, Los Angeles *Also Called: Greater Los Angles Area Cncil (P-18868)*

BOY SCOUTS OF AMERICA, Orange *Also Called: Orange Cnty Cncil Boy Scuts AM (P-18889)*

Boy's & Girls Club Bakersfield, Bakersfield *Also Called: Boys Girls Clubs of Kern Cnty (P-18822)*

Boyd and Associates .... D....... 805 988-8298
445 E Esplanade Dr Ste 210 Oxnard (93036) *(P-12940)*

Boyd and Associates (PA) .... C....... 818 752-1888
2191 E Thompson Blvd Ventura (93001) *(P-12941)*

Boyd Dental Corporation .... D....... 909 890-0421
362 E Vanderbilt Way San Bernardino (92408) *(P-15218)*

Boyett, Hayward *Also Called: Boyett Construction Inc (P-1911)*

Boyett Construction Inc (PA) .... D....... 510 264-9100
2404 Tripaldi Way Hayward (94545) *(P-1911)*

Boykin Mgt Co Ltd Lblty Co .... D....... 619 299-6633
3888 Greenwood St San Diego (92110) *(P-9655)*

Boykin Mgt Co Ltd Lblty Co .... D....... 510 548-7920
200 Marina Blvd Berkeley (94710) *(P-9656)*

Boyle Engineering Corporation .... B....... 949 476-3300
999 W Town And Country Rd Orange (92868) *(P-19158)*

Boys & Girls Club, Goleta *Also Called: United Bys Grls Clubs Snta BRB (P-18918)*

BOYS & GIRLS CLUBS OF HUNTINGT, Fountain Valley *Also Called: Boys Grls Clubs Huntington Vly (P-18826)*

Boys & Girls Clubs of N Vly .... D....... 530 899-0335
601 Wall St Chico (95928) *(P-18819)*

BOYS & GIRLS CLUBS OF NORTH CO, Fallbrook *Also Called: Boys Club of Fallbrook (P-18821)*

BOYS & GIRLS CLUBS OF SANTA MO, Santa Monica *Also Called: Boys Grls CLB Snta Monica Inc (P-18824)*

Boys & Girls Clubs South Cnty .... D....... 619 424-2266
847 Encina Ave Imperial Beach (91932) *(P-18820)*

Boys Club of Fallbrook .... D....... 760 728-5871
445 E Ivy St Fallbrook (92028) *(P-18821)*

Boys Girls Clubs of Kern Cnty .... B....... 661 325-3730
801 Niles St Bakersfield (93305) *(P-18822)*

Boys Girls Clubs of Peninsula .... D....... 650 322-6255
401 Pierce Rd Menlo Park (94025) *(P-14348)*

Boys Grls CLB Brbank Grter E V .... D....... 818 842-9333
300 E Angeleno Ave Burbank (91502) *(P-18823)*

Boys Grls CLB Snta Monica Inc .... D....... 310 361-8500
1220 Lincoln Blvd Santa Monica (90401) *(P-18824)*

Boys Grls Clubs Cntl Ornge Cas .... D....... 714 543-5540
17701 Cowan Ste 110 Irvine (92614) *(P-18825)*

Boys Grls Clubs Grdn Grove Inc (PA) .... C....... 714 530-0430
10540 Chapman Ave Garden Grove (92840) *(P-17803)*

Boys Grls Clubs Huntington Vly (PA) .... D....... 714 531-2582
16582 Brookhurst St Fountain Valley (92708) *(P-18826)*

Boys Republic (PA) .... C....... 909 902-6690
1907 Boys Republic Dr Chino Hills (91709) *(P-18380)*

Employee Codes: A=Over 500 employees, B=251-500, C=101-250, D=51-100, E=20-50, F=10-19, G=1-9

BP Clothing LLC C
3424 Garfield Ave Commerce (90040) *(P-6195)*

Bpaz Holdings 18 LLC .... D...... 972 354-6250
1 Sansome St Fl 15 San Francisco (94104) *(P-9303)*

Bpaz Holdings 6 LLC .... D...... 415 295-8080
1 Sansome St Ste 1500 San Francisco (94104) *(P-9304)*

Bpm LLP .... D...... 408 961-6300
10 Almaden Blvd Ste 1000 San Jose (95113) *(P-19540)*

Bpo Management Services Inc (PA) .... D...... 714 972-2670
8175 E Kaiser Blvd # 100 Anaheim (92808) *(P-11471)*

Bpoms/Hro Inc (HQ) .... D...... 714 974-2670
8175 E Kaiser Blvd # 100 Anaheim (92808) *(P-12125)*

Bpr Properties Berkeley LLC .... D...... 650 424-1400
953 Industrial Ave Ste 100 Palo Alto (94303) *(P-8703)*

Bps Reprographics Services .... C...... 415 495-8700
945 Bryant St San Francisco (94103) *(P-10785)*

Bps Supply Group (PA) .... D...... 661 589-9141
3301 Zachary Ave Shafter (93263) *(P-5480)*

BQE Software Inc .... D...... 310 602-4020
3825 Del Amo Blvd Torrance (90503) *(P-12126)*

BR Building Resources Co .... C...... 626 963-4880
2247 Lindsay Way Glendora (91740) *(P-877)*

BR Funsten, Manteca *Also Called: B R Funsten & Co (P-5110)*

Braddock & Logan Services Inc .... C...... 925 736-4000
4155 Blackhawk Plaza Cir Ste 201 Danville (94506) *(P-878)*

Braddock Logan Ventr Group LP (PA) .... C...... 925 736-4000
4155 Blackhawk Plaza Cir Danville (94506) *(P-788)*

Braden Prtners LP A Cal Ltd PR (HQ) .... D...... 415 893-1518
1304 Southpoint Blvd Ste 130 Petaluma (94954) *(P-5406)*

Bradford Messenger Service .... D...... 559 252-0775
4955 E Andersen Ave # 118 Fresno (93727) *(P-13217)*

Bradley Court .... D...... 619 448-6633
675 E Bradley Ave El Cajon (92021) *(P-15822)*

Bradley Court, Chula Vista *Also Called: Healthcare Management Systems Inc (P-15510)*

Bradshaw Home, Rancho Cucamonga *Also Called: Bradshaw International Inc (P-5112)*

Bradshaw International Inc (PA) .... B...... 909 476-3884
9409 Buffalo Ave Rancho Cucamonga (91730) *(P-5112)*

Brady Company/San Diego Inc .... B...... 619 462-2600
8100 Center St La Mesa (91942) *(P-1912)*

Brady Socal Incorporated .... D...... 619 462-2600
8100 Center St La Mesa (91942) *(P-1913)*

Braemac (ca) LLC .... D...... 510 687-1000
43134 Osgood Rd Fremont (94539) *(P-5634)*

Braemar Country Club, Tarzana *Also Called: Braemar Country Club Inc (P-14349)*

Braemar Country Club Inc .... C...... 323 873-6880
4001 Reseda Blvd Tarzana (91356) *(P-14349)*

Braemar Partnership .... B...... 858 488-1081
3999 Mission Blvd San Diego (92109) *(P-9657)*

Brafton Incorporated .... D...... 617 206-3040
220 Montgomery St Ste 917 San Francisco (94104) *(P-4257)*

Braga Fresh Family Farms Inc (PA) .... D...... 831 675-2154
33750 Moranda Rd Soledad (93960) *(P-169)*

Braga Fresh Family Farms Inc .... C...... 760 353-1155
817 W Hackleman Rd El Centro (92243) *(P-170)*

Braga Fresh Family Farms Inc .... C...... 831 675-2361
500 S Alta St Gonzales (93926) *(P-6519)*

Braga Fresh Gonzales 2, Gonzales *Also Called: Braga Fresh Family Farms Inc (P-6519)*

Braga Fresh Imperial, El Centro *Also Called: Braga Fresh Family Farms Inc (P-170)*

Bragg Crane, Fontana *Also Called: Bragg Investment Company Inc (P-10994)*

Bragg Crane & Rigging, Long Beach *Also Called: Bragg Investment Company Inc (P-10995)*

Bragg Investment Company Inc .... D...... 805 485-2106
1930 Lockwood St Oxnard (93036) *(P-5030)*

Bragg Investment Company Inc .... C...... 909 350-3738
13188 Dahlia St Fontana (92337) *(P-10994)*

Bragg Investment Company Inc (PA) .... B...... 562 984-2400
6251 N Paramount Blvd Long Beach (90805) *(P-10995)*

Braille Institute, Los Angeles *Also Called: Braille Institute America Inc (P-17854)*

Braille Institute America Inc (PA) .... C...... 323 663-1111
741 N Vermont Ave Los Angeles (90029) *(P-17854)*

Brain Corporation .... C...... 858 689-7600
10182 Telesis Ct Ste 100 San Diego (92121) *(P-11472)*

Brain Technologies Inc .... B...... 650 918-2245
400 S El Camino Real Ste 250 San Mateo (94402) *(P-11473)*

Brainstorm Corporation .... C...... 888 370-8882
1620 Proforma Ave Ontario (91761) *(P-5282)*

Brake Depot Systems Inc .... B...... 714 623-9030
1205 E 1st St Santa Ana (92701) *(P-13658)*

Bramasol Inc .... D...... 408 831-0046
5201 Great America Pkwy Ste 220 Santa Clara (95054) *(P-5283)*

Branch Medical Center, San Diego *Also Called: NAVY UNITED STATES DEPARTMENT (P-14916)*

Branch Metrics Inc (PA) .... B...... 650 209-6461
195 Page Mill Rd Ste 101 Palo Alto (94306) *(P-12554)*

Brand Amp LLC .... D...... 949 438-1060
1945 Placentia Ave Ste C Costa Mesa (92627) *(P-20631)*

Brand Therapy LLC .... D...... 415 336-6411
7376 W 88th St Los Angeles (90045) *(P-17016)*

Branded Entrmt Netwrk Inc (PA) .... C...... 310 342-1500
14724 Ventura Blvd Ste 1200 Sherman Oaks (91403) *(P-10795)*

Branded Group Inc .... C...... 323 940-1444
222 S Harbor Blvd Ste 500 Anaheim (92805) *(P-20300)*

Brandel Manor, Turlock *Also Called: Covenant Living West (P-16034)*

Brandes Inv Partners Inc (PA) .... C...... 858 755-0239
11988 El Camino Real Ste 300 San Diego (92131) *(P-8191)*

Brandt Consolidated Inc .... D...... 559 499-2100
3654 S Willow Ave Fresno (93725) *(P-2638)*

Brandvia Alliance Inc (HQ) .... D...... 408 955-0500
2901 Tasman Dr Ste 110 Santa Clara (95054) *(P-10593)*

Brandvia Powered By Halo, Santa Clara *Also Called: Brandvia Alliance Inc (P-10593)*

Brandwatch LLC .... C...... 415 429-5800
445 Bush St Fl 8 San Francisco (94108) *(P-20301)*

Branlyn Prominence Inc .... C...... 760 843-5655
13334 Amargosa Rd Victorville (92392) *(P-16825)*

Branlyn Prominence Inc (PA) .... D...... 909 476-9030
9213 Archibald Ave Rancho Cucamonga (91730) *(P-16826)*

Bratton Masonry Inc (PA) .... D...... 559 291-9423
2763 N Argyle Ave Fresno (93727) *(P-1880)*

Brault .... C...... 626 447-0296
180 Via Verde Ste 100 San Dimas (91773) *(P-19541)*

Braun Linen Service (PA) .... C...... 909 623-2678
16514 Garfield Ave Paramount (90723) *(P-10432)*

Bravante Produce, Reedley *Also Called: Cal Packing and Storage LP (P-3653)*

Brawley Union High School Dist (PA) .... D...... 760 312-6068
480 N Imperial Ave Brawley (92227) *(P-17696)*

Brayer Electric Company (PA) .... D...... 800 581-2544
15095 Wicks Blvd San Leandro (94577) *(P-1686)*

Brayton Purcell APC (PA) .... C...... 415 898-1555
222 Rush Landing Rd Novato (94945) *(P-17392)*

Bre Properties Inc .... A...... 415 445-6530
525 Market St Fl 4 San Francisco (94105) *(P-9463)*

Bre/Japantown Owner LLC .... D...... 415 922-3200
1625 Post St San Francisco (94115) *(P-9658)*

Break Media, Beverly Hills *Also Called: Nextpoint Inc (P-4320)*

Breakthrough Behavioral Inc .... C...... 888 282-2522
702 Marshall St Ste 340 Redwood City (94063) *(P-17855)*

Breakthru Beverage Cal LLC (HQ) .... B...... 800 331-2829
6550 E Washington Blvd Commerce (90040) *(P-6787)*

Breakthru Beverage Cal LLC .... D...... 510 236-2233
912 Harbour Way S Richmond (94804) *(P-6788)*

Brecht BMW, Escondido *Also Called: Brecht Enterprises Inc (P-7177)*

Brecht Enterprises Inc .... D...... 760 745-3000
1555 Auto Park Way Escondido (92029) *(P-7177)*

Brehm Communities (PA) .... D...... 760 448-2420
1935 Camino Vida Roble Ste 200 Carlsbad (92008) *(P-661)*

Breitbart News Network LLC .... D...... 424 371-0585
149 S Barrington Ste 735 Los Angeles (90049) *(P-10707)*

Breitburn Energy Partners LP .... A...... 213 225-5900
707 Wilshire Blvd Ste 4600 Los Angeles (90017) *(P-581)*

Brenden Theatre Corporation (PA) .... C...... 925 677-0462
1985 Willow Pass Rd Ste C Concord (94520) *(P-13977)*

Brenden Theatre Corporation .... C...... 707 469-0180
531 Davis St Vacaville (95688) *(P-13978)*

ALPHABETIC SECTION

Brenden Theatre Corporation .... D....... 209 491-7770
   1021 10th St Frnt Modesto (95354) *(P-13979)*

Brennan International Trnspt, Long Beach *Also Called: Vanguard Lgistics Svcs USA Inc* *(P-4117)*

Brenntag Pacific Inc (DH) .... D....... 562 903-9626
   10747 Patterson Pl Santa Fe Springs (90670) *(P-6706)*

Brentwood Bmdical RES Inst Inc .... C....... 310 312-1554
   11301 Wilshire Blvd Bldg 114 Los Angeles (90073) *(P-19867)*

Brentwood Builders, Burbank *Also Called: 716 Management Inc (P-744)*

BRENTWOOD COUNTRY CLUB, Los Angeles *Also Called: Brentwood Country Club Los Angeles (P-14350)*

Brentwood Country Club Los Angeles .... D....... 310 451-8011
   590 S Burlingame Ave Los Angeles (90049) *(P-14350)*

BRENTWOOD HEALTH CARE CENTER, Santa Monica *Also Called: Coastal Health Care Inc (P-15376)*

Brentwood Home LLC (PA) .... C....... 562 949-3759
   701 Burning Tree Rd Ste A Fullerton (92833) *(P-2493)*

Brentwood Veterinary Hospital, Brentwood *Also Called: Assocted Vtrnary Practices Inc (P-328)*

Brer Affiliates LLC (DH) .... C....... 949 794-7900
   18500 Von Karman Ave Ste 400 Irvine (92612) *(P-9452)*

Brethren Hillcrest Homes .... C....... 909 593-4917
   2705 Mountain View Dr Ofc La Verne (91750) *(P-18381)*

Brett V Crtis MD A Prof Corp I .... D....... 415 924-4525
   101 Casa Buena Dr Corte Madera (94925) *(P-14637)*

Brewer Crane & Rigging, Lakeside *Also Called: LLC Brewer Crane (P-11002)*

Brex Inc (PA) .... A....... 844 725-9569
   115 Sansome St Ste 1200 San Francisco (94104) *(P-13218)*

Brex Technologies, San Francisco *Also Called: Brex Inc (P-13218)*

Briarpatch Coop Nev Cnty Inc .... C....... 530 272-5333
   290 Sierra College Drive Grass Valley (95945) *(P-19071)*

Briarpatch Coop-Community Mkt, Grass Valley *Also Called: Briarpatch Coop Nev Cnty Inc (P-19071)*

Bridge Bank, San Jose *Also Called: Western Alliance Bank (P-7725)*

Bridge Bank National Association .... D....... 408 423-8500
   55 Almaden Blvd Ste 200 San Jose (95113) *(P-7663)*

Bridge Bay Resort, Redding *Also Called: Bridge Bay Resort & Marina (P-9659)*

Bridge Bay Resort & Marina .... D....... 530 275-3021
   10300 Bridge Bay Rd Redding (96003) *(P-9659)*

Bridge Design LLC .... D....... 415 487-7100
   375 Alabama St Ste 410 San Francisco (94110) *(P-19159)*

Bridge Group Hh Inc .... C....... 858 455-5000
   3636 Nobel Dr Ste 450 San Diego (92122) *(P-9305)*

Bridge Home Health LLC .... D....... 858 277-5200
   5090 Shoreham Pl Ste 109 San Diego (92122) *(P-16827)*

Bridge Housing Corporation (PA) .... D....... 415 989-1111
   600 California St Fl 900 San Francisco (94108) *(P-8916)*

BRIDGEBIO, Palo Alto *Also Called: Bridgebio Pharma Inc (P-2582)*

Bridgebio Pharma Inc (PA) .... C....... 650 391-9740
   3160 Porter Dr Ste 250 Palo Alto (94304) *(P-2582)*

Bridgebio Services Inc .... D....... 650 438-1302
   421 Kipling St Palo Alto (94301) *(P-19666)*

Bridges At Gale Ranch LLC .... D....... 925 735-4253
   9000 S Gale Ridge Rd San Ramon (94582) *(P-14246)*

Bridges Golf Club, The, San Ramon *Also Called: Bridges At Gale Ranch LLC (P-14246)*

Bridgestone Living LLC .... D....... 949 487-9500
   27101 Puerta Real Ste 450 Mission Viejo (92691) *(P-15359)*

Bridgewest Group, The, San Diego *Also Called: Bridgewest Ventures LLC (P-9398)*

Bridgewest Ventures LLC (PA) .... A....... 858 529-6600
   7310 Miramar Rd Ste 500 San Diego (92126) *(P-9398)*

Bridgford Marketing Company (DH) .... D....... 714 526-5533
   1308 N Patt St Anaheim (92801) *(P-6490)*

Bridgwter Consulting Group Inc .... D....... 949 535-1755
   18881 Von Karman Ave Ste 1450 Irvine (92612) *(P-20302)*

Brience Inc (DH) .... D....... 415 974-5300
   128 Spear St Fl 3 San Francisco (94105) *(P-11474)*

Briggs Electric Inc (PA) .... D....... 714 544-2500
   14381 Franklin Ave Tustin (92780) *(P-1687)*

Bright Event Rentals LLC (PA) .... C....... 310 202-0011
   1640 W 190th St Ste A Torrance (90501) *(P-11022)*

Bright Health Physicians (PA) .... C....... 562 947-8478
   15725 Whittier Blvd Ste 500 Whittier (90603) *(P-14638)*

Bright Now Dental, Irvine *Also Called: Smile Brands Group Inc (P-20206)*

Brightcloud Inc .... B....... 858 652-4803
   4370 La Jolla Village Dr Ste 820 San Diego (92122) *(P-13100)*

Brighterion Inc .... D....... 415 986-5600
   123 Mission St Ste 1700 San Francisco (94105) *(P-11475)*

Brightline Inc .... C....... 650 769-5810
   400 Concar Dr San Mateo (94402) *(P-17856)*

Brighton, Modesto *Also Called: Del Rio Golf & Country Club (P-14369)*

Brighton Convalescent Center .... D....... 626 798-9124
   1836 N Fair Oaks Ave Pasadena (91103) *(P-15823)*

Brighton Place Spring Valley, Spring Valley *Also Called: B-Spring Valley LLC (P-15346)*

Brightqest Trtmnt Ctrs - San D .... D....... 619 466-0547
   5520 Wellesley St Ste 100 La Mesa (91942) *(P-17017)*

Brightroll Inc .... B....... 415 677-9222
   343 Sansome St Ste 600 San Francisco (94104) *(P-10594)*

Brightsource Construction Management Inc .... B....... 510 550-8161
   1999 Harrison St Ste 2150 Oakland (94612) *(P-20046)*

Brightstar Care Lake Forest .... B....... 949 837-7000
   26023 Acero Ste 100 Mission Viejo (92691) *(P-16828)*

Brightstar Care Oxnard Cmrllo, Oxnard *Also Called: Tripod Inc (P-11343)*

Brightstar Healthcare, Roseville *Also Called: Altus Health Inc (P-16804)*

Brightview Companies LLC .... C....... 714 437-1586
   11555 Coley River Cir Fountain Valley (92708) *(P-477)*

Brightview Companies LLC (DH) .... C....... 818 223-8500
   27001 Agoura Rd Ste 350 Calabasas (91301) *(P-1290)*

Brightview Golf Maint Inc .... C....... 805 968-6400
   405 Glen Annie Rd Santa Barbara (93117) *(P-393)*

Brightview Golf Maint Inc (DH) .... D....... 818 223-8500
   27001 Agoura Rd Ste 350 Agoura Hills (91301) *(P-394)*

Brightview Landscape Dev Inc .... B....... 858 458-9900
   8450 Miramar Pl San Diego (92121) *(P-395)*

Brightview Landscape Dev Inc .... C....... 925 463-0700
   7039 Commerce Cir Ste A Pleasanton (94588) *(P-396)*

Brightview Landscape Dev Inc .... C....... 916 386-4875
   20 Business Park Way Ste 200 Sacramento (95828) *(P-397)*

Brightview Landscape Dev Inc .... D....... 818 838-4700
   13691 Vaughn St San Fernando (91340) *(P-1384)*

Brightview Landscape Dev Inc .... C....... 714 546-7975
   8 Hughes Ste 125 Irvine (92618) *(P-1385)*

Brightview Landscape Svcs Inc .... D....... 510 487-4826
   20551b Corsair Blvd Hayward (94545) *(P-398)*

Brightview Landscape Svcs Inc .... D....... 951 684-2730
   715 W La Cadena Dr Riverside (92501) *(P-399)*

Brightview Landscape Svcs Inc .... D....... 714 215-7423
   1900 S Lewis St Anaheim (92805) *(P-400)*

Brightview Landscape Svcs Inc .... D....... 714 546-7843
   32202 Paseo Adelanto San Juan Capistrano (92675) *(P-401)*

Brightview Landscape Svcs Inc .... B....... 909 946-3196
   8726 Calabash Ave Fontana (92335) *(P-402)*

Brightview Landscape Svcs Inc .... D....... 916 415-1004
   4030 Alvis Ct Rocklin (95677) *(P-403)*

Brightview Landscape Svcs Inc .... C....... 858 458-1900
   8500 Miramar Pl San Diego (92121) *(P-404)*

Brightview Landscape Svcs Inc .... C....... 925 957-8831
   4677 Pacheco Blvd Martinez (94553) *(P-405)*

Brightview Landscape Svcs Inc .... D....... 619 474-4478
   415 W 30th St National City (91950) *(P-406)*

Brightview Landscape Svcs Inc .... B....... 714 546-7843
   1960 S Yale St Santa Ana (92704) *(P-407)*

Brightview Landscape Svcs Inc .... D....... 650 289-9324
   825 Mahler Rd Burlingame (94010) *(P-408)*

Brightview Landscape Svcs Inc .... D....... 714 939-6600
   17846 Van Buren Blvd Riverside (92508) *(P-409)*

Brightview Landscape Svcs Inc .... D....... 925 243-0288
   5779 Preston Ave Livermore (94551) *(P-410)*

Brightview Landscape Svcs Inc .... C....... 408 453-5904
   825 Mabury Rd San Jose (95133) *(P-411)*

Brightview Landscape Svcs Inc .... C....... 916 381-2800
   5745 Alder Ave Sacramento (95828) *(P-412)*

Brightview Landscape Svcs Inc .... C....... 805 642-9300
   2064 Eastman Ave Ste 104 Ventura (93003) *(P-413)*

Brightview Landscape Svcs Inc .... D...... 949 480-4187
1 University Dr Aliso Viejo (92656) *(P-414)*

Brightview Landscape Svcs Inc .... C...... 925 924-8900
7039 Commerce Cir Ste B Pleasanton (94588) *(P-415)*

Brightview Landscape Svcs Inc .... C...... 310 327-8700
17813 S Main St Ste 105 Gardena (90248) *(P-416)*

Brightview Landscape Svcs Inc .... D...... 310 829-4707
47 Plateau Aliso Viejo (92656) *(P-417)*

Brightview Tree Care Svcs Inc .... D...... 951 684-2730
715 W La Cadena Dr Riverside (92501) *(P-418)*

Brightview Tree Company .... D...... 760 955-2560
Apple Valley (92307) *(P-419)*

Brightview Tree Company .... D...... 209 886-5511
28915 E Funck Rd Farmington (95230) *(P-420)*

Brightview Tree Company .... D...... 818 951-5500
9500 Foothill Blvd Sunland (91040) *(P-566)*

Brightview Tree Company .... D...... 714 546-7975
3200 W Telegraph Rd Fillmore (93015) *(P-567)*

Brightview Tree Company .... D...... 925 862-2485
8501 Calaveras Rd Sunol (94586) *(P-568)*

Brightwheel, San Francisco *Also Called: Dssv Inc (P-17228)*

Brilliant General Maint Inc (PA) .... D...... 408 287-6708
954 Chestnut St San Jose (95110) *(P-10865)*

Brilliant Lighting Products, Livermore *Also Called: American Wholesale Ltg Inc (P-5536)*

Brillius Technologies Inc .... C...... 510 379-9027
4305 Hacienda Dr Pleasanton (94588) *(P-12427)*

Brillstein Entrmt Partners LLC (HQ) .... D...... 310 205-5100
9150 Wilshire Blvd Ste 350 Beverly Hills (90212) *(P-13823)*

Brillstein Grey Entertainment, Beverly Hills *Also Called: Brillstein Entrmt Partners LLC (P-13823)*

Brinderson LLC (DH) .... C...... 714 466-7100
18841 S Broadwick St Compton (90220) *(P-19160)*

Brink's, Garden Grove *Also Called: Brinks Incorporated (P-12942)*

Brinks Incorporated .... C...... 714 903-9272
7191 Patterson Dr Garden Grove (92841) *(P-12942)*

Briotix .... D...... 805 864-2711
515 Marin St Ste 318 Thousand Oaks (91360) *(P-20303)*

Brisam Lax (de) LLC .... D...... 310 649-5151
9901 S La Cienega Blvd Los Angeles (90045) *(P-9660)*

Brisan LLC .... D...... 559 233-6650
1055 Van Ness Ave Fresno (93721) *(P-9661)*

Brisbane Mechanical, Brisbane *Also Called: Fred Will and Bill Inc (P-1442)*

Brislan, Fresno *Also Called: Valley Iron Inc (P-5529)*

Bristlecone Incorporated .... A...... 650 386-4000
10 Almaden Blvd Ste 600 San Jose (95113) *(P-11476)*

Brita, Oakland *Also Called: Brita Products Company (P-5741)*

Brita Products Company .... D...... 510 271-7000
1221 Broadway Ste 290 Oakland (94612) *(P-5741)*

Brite Industries Inc .... C...... 510 250-9330
1746 13th St Oakland (94607) *(P-3105)*

Brite Labs, Oakland *Also Called: Brite Industries Inc (P-3105)*

Brite Media, Oakland *Also Called: Mesmerize LLC (P-20466)*

Britelab Inc .... D...... 650 961-0671
6341 San Ignacio Ave San Jose (95119) *(P-3020)*

Briteworks, Covina *Also Called: Briteworks Inc (P-10866)*

Briteworks Inc .... D...... 626 337-0099
620 N Commercial Ave Covina (91723) *(P-10866)*

Britex, San Jose *Also Called: Britelab Inc (P-3020)*

Britive Inc .... D...... 213 915-4142
450 N Brand Blvd Ste 600 Glendale (91203) *(P-11477)*

Brittany House LLC .... C...... 562 421-4717
5401 E Centralia St Long Beach (90808) *(P-18382)*

Brix Group Inc (PA) .... D...... 559 457-4700
838 N Laverne Ave Fresno (93727) *(P-5635)*

Brixton LLC .... D...... 866 264-4245
3821 Ocean Ranch Blvd Oceanside (92056) *(P-6168)*

Broadband Telecom Inc .... C...... 818 450-5714
515 S Flower St Fl 36 Los Angeles (90071) *(P-20710)*

Broadmoor Hotel (PA) .... D...... 415 776-7034
1499 Sutter St San Francisco (94109) *(P-9662)*

Broadmoor Hotel .... D...... 415 673-8445
1465 65th St Apt 274 Emeryville (94608) *(P-9663)*

Broadmoor Hotel .... D...... 415 673-2511
1000 Sutter St San Francisco (94109) *(P-9664)*

Broadrach Cpitl Prtners Fund I .... A...... 650 331-2500
248 Homer Ave Palo Alto (94301) *(P-9362)*

Broadreach Capitl Partners LLC .... A...... 310 691-5760
6430 W Sunset Blvd Ste 504 Los Angeles (90028) *(P-9492)*

Broadreach Capitl Partners LLC (PA) .... D...... 650 331-2500
885 Oak Grove Ave Ste 206 Menlo Park (94025) *(P-9493)*

Broadreach Capitl Partners LLC .... A...... 415 354-4640
235 Montgomery St Ste 1018 San Francisco (94104) *(P-9494)*

Broadstone Raquet Club, Folsom *Also Called: Spare-Time Inc (P-14459)*

Broadview Networks Inc .... D...... 818 939-0015
7731 Hayvenhurst Ave Van Nuys (91406) *(P-4258)*

Broadway By Bay .... C...... 650 579-5565
1972 2nd Ave Walnut Creek (94597) *(P-14029)*

Broadway Manor Care Center, Glendale *Also Called: Longwood Management Corp (P-15868)*

Broadway Mech - Contrs Inc .... C...... 510 746-4000
873 81st Ave Oakland (94621) *(P-1386)*

Broadway Sacramento .... C...... 916 446-5880
1419 H St Sacramento (95814) *(P-8704)*

Broadway Sacramento (PA) .... C...... 916 446-5880
1510 J St Ste 200 Sacramento (95814) *(P-14030)*

Broadway Typewriter Co Inc .... D...... 800 998-9199
1055 6th Ave Ste 101 San Diego (92101) *(P-5284)*

Broadway Villa Post Acute, Sonoma *Also Called: Ensign Sonoma LLC (P-15459)*

Brocade Cmmnctions Systems LLC (DH) .... A...... 408 333-8000
1320 Ridder Park Dr San Jose (95131) *(P-2826)*

Bromic Heating Pty Limited .... D...... 855 552-7432
7595 Irvine Center Dr Ste 100 Irvine (92618) *(P-1387)*

Bronco Wine Company (PA) .... C...... 209 538-3131
6342 Bystrum Rd Ceres (95307) *(P-6789)*

Brookdale Clairemont, San Diego *Also Called: Emeritus Corporation (P-15437)*

Brookfeld Bay Area Hldings LLC .... D...... 925 743-8000
12657 Alcosta Blvd San Ramon (94583) *(P-9247)*

Brookfeld Sthland Holdings LLC .... C...... 714 427-6868
3200 Park Center Dr Ste 1000 Costa Mesa (92626) *(P-662)*

Brookfield Homes, San Ramon *Also Called: Brookfeld Bay Area Hldings LLC (P-9247)*

Brookfield Residential, Costa Mesa *Also Called: Brookfeld Sthland Holdings LLC (P-662)*

Brookside Christian School Inc (PA) .... D...... 209 954-7650
3588 Brookside Rd Stockton (95219) *(P-18272)*

Brookside Christn Jr /Sr High, Stockton *Also Called: Brookside Christian School Inc (P-18272)*

Brookside Country Club .... D...... 209 956-6200
3603 Saint Andrews Dr Stockton (95219) *(P-14351)*

Brosamer & Wall Inc .... C...... 925 932-7900
1777 Oakland Blvd Ste 300 Walnut Creek (94596) *(P-19161)*

Brotman Medical Center Inc .... B...... 310 836-7000
3828 Delmas Ter Culver City (90232) *(P-15963)*

Broward Builders Inc .... D...... 530 666-5635
1200 E Kentucky Ave Woodland (95776) *(P-879)*

Brower Hale, Laguna Hills *Also Called: Valley Insurance Service Inc (P-8679)*

Brown & Toland Medical Group .... C...... 415 923-3015
2100 Webster St Ste 117 San Francisco (94115) *(P-14639)*

Brown & Toland Medical Group .... C...... 415 752-8038
3905 Sacramento St Ste 301 San Francisco (94118) *(P-14640)*

BROWN & TOLAND MEDICAL GROUP INC, San Francisco *Also Called: Brown & Toland Medical Group (P-14639)*

BROWN & TOLAND MEDICAL GROUP INC, San Francisco *Also Called: Brown & Toland Medical Group (P-14640)*

Brown and Caldwell (PA) .... C...... 925 937-9010
201 N Civic Dr Ste 115 Walnut Creek (94596) *(P-19162)*

Brown and Streza LLP .... D...... 949 453-2900
40 Pacifica St 1500 Irvine (92618) *(P-20304)*

Brown Armstrong Accntancy Corp .... D...... 661 324-4971
4200 Truxtun Ave Ste 300 Bakersfield (93309) *(P-19542)*

Brown Armstrong Cpas, Bakersfield *Also Called: Brown Armstrong Accntancy Corp (P-19542)*

Brown Construction Inc .... D...... 916 374-8616
1465 Enterprise Blvd Ste 100 West Sacramento (95691) *(P-880)*

Brown Construction Inc A Cal, West Sacramento *Also Called: Brown Construction Inc (P-880)*

ALPHABETIC SECTION

Brown Tland Physcn Svcs Orgnzt (DH) .... C....... 415 972-4162
   1221 Broadway Ste 700 Oakland (94612) *(P-14641)*

Brownco Construction, Anaheim *Also Called: Brownco Construction Co Inc (P-663)*

Brownco Construction Co Inc .... D....... 714 935-9600
   1000 E Katella Ave Anaheim (92805) *(P-663)*

Browne Child Development Ctr, Oceanside *Also Called: Marine Corps Community Svcs (P-18330)*

Browning-Ferris Inds Cal Inc .... D....... 925 313-8901
   951 Waterbird Way Martinez (94553) *(P-4868)*

Browning-Ferris Inds Cal Inc .... C....... 650 726-1819
   12310 San Mateo Rd Half Moon Bay (94019) *(P-4869)*

Brownstone Companies Inc .... A....... 310 297-3600
   2629 Manhattan Beach Blvd # 100 Redondo Beach (90278) *(P-5636)*

Brownstone Security, Redondo Beach *Also Called: Brownstone Companies Inc (P-5636)*

Bruck Lighting Systems, Irvine *Also Called: Ledra Brands Inc (P-5121)*

Bruckheimer, Jerry Films, Santa Monica *Also Called: Jerry Bruckheimer Inc (P-13858)*

Bruker Cellular Analysis Inc (HQ) .... C....... 510 858-2855
   5858 Horton St Ste 320 Emeryville (94608) *(P-3029)*

Brusco Tug & Barge Inc .... C....... 805 986-1600
   170 E Port Hueneme Rd Port Hueneme (93041) *(P-3821)*

Brutoco Engineering, Covina *Also Called: Brutoco Engineering & Construction Inc (P-1083)*

Brutoco Engineering & Construction Inc C
   1272 Center Court Dr Ste 101 Covina (91724) *(P-1083)*

Bryan Cave Lighton Paisner LLP .... D....... 310 576-2100
   120 Broadway Ste 300 Santa Monica (90401) *(P-17393)*

Bryant Elementary School, Garden Grove *Also Called: Garden Grove Unified Schl Dst (P-18318)*

Brymax Construction Svcs Inc .... D....... 949 200-9619
   7436 Lorge Cir Huntington Beach (92647) *(P-1388)*

Bsh Home Appliances Corp (DH) .... C....... 949 440-7100
   1901 Main St Ste 600 Irvine (92614) *(P-13733)*

BSK Associates .... D....... 559 497-2888
   687 N Laverne Ave Fresno (93727) *(P-19163)*

Bsl Golf Corp .... C....... 831 899-7271
   1 Mcclure Way Seaside (93955) *(P-14247)*

Bssp, Sausalito *Also Called: Butler Shine Stern Prtners LLC (P-10595)*

Bstz, Los Angeles *Also Called: Blakely Sokoloff Taylor & Zafman LLP (P-17387)*

Bsw Roofing Contractors, Bakersfield *Also Called: Bakersfield Shingles Wholesale Inc (P-5226)*

BT Infonet, El Segundo *Also Called: Infonet Services Corporation (P-4299)*

BT Ins Inc .... A....... 408 330-2700
   1600 Memorex Dr Ste 200 Santa Clara (95050) *(P-12745)*

BTG S CORP (PA) .... D....... 323 582-4444
   2801 E Vernon Ave Vernon (90058) *(P-6894)*

Btig LLC (PA) .... D....... 415 248-2200
   600 Montgomery St Fl 6 San Francisco (94111) *(P-8068)*

Buchanan Street Partners LP .... D....... 949 721-1414
   3501 Jamboree Rd Ste 4200 Newport Beach (92660) *(P-8917)*

Buck Inst For RES On Aging (PA) .... C....... 415 209-2000
   8001 Redwood Blvd Novato (94945) *(P-19868)*

Buckelew Programs (PA) .... D....... 415 457-6964
   201 Alameda Del Prado Ste 103 Novato (94949) *(P-17018)*

Buckeye Fire Equipment Company .... B....... 510 483-1815
   2416 Teagarden St San Leandro (94577) *(P-5823)*

Buckingham Property Management .... D....... 559 322-1105
   12609 Moffatt Ln Fresno (93730) *(P-10531)*

Buckland Vineyard MGT Inc .... D....... 530 333-1534
   4560 Slodusty Rd Garden Valley (95633) *(P-20047)*

Buddy Group Inc .... D....... 949 468-0042
   7 Studebaker Irvine (92618) *(P-11478)*

Buddy Stoopid Stoodios LLC .... C....... 818 333-8600
   220 S Flower St Burbank (91502) *(P-13824)*

Budget Blinds LLC (DH) .... D....... 949 404-1100
   19000 Macarthur Blvd Ste 100 Irvine (92612) *(P-7436)*

Budget Electric, Tracy *Also Called: American Engrg Contrs Inc (P-1663)*

Budget Motel, San Luis Obispo *Also Called: Travelodge Downtown (P-10318)*

Buds Ice Cream San Francisco, City Of Industry *Also Called: Berkeley Farms LLC (P-2351)*

Buena Ventura Care Center Inc .... D....... 818 247-4476
   1505 Colby Dr Glendale (91205) *(P-15824)*

Buena Vista Business Svcs LP (PA) .... D....... 908 452-9002
   1276 Lincoln Ave Ste 107 San Jose (95125) *(P-10495)*

Buena Vista Care Center, Santa Barbara *Also Called: Covenant Care California LLC (P-15404)*

Buena Vista Cnstr Group Inc .... D....... 916 354-9832
   14958 Venado Dr Rancho Murieta (95683) *(P-664)*

Buena Vista Food Products Inc (DH) .... C....... 626 815-8859
   823 W 8th St Azusa (91702) *(P-6612)*

Buena Vista Gaming Authority .... B....... 866 915-0777
   4640 Coal Mine Rd Ione (95640) *(P-9665)*

Buena Vista International Inc .... C....... 818 295-5200
   350 S Buena Vista St Burbank (91521) *(P-13825)*

Buena Vista Manor, Duarte *Also Called: Humangood Socal (P-18456)*

Buena Vista MGT Svcs LLC .... C....... 619 450-4300
   2045 1st Ave San Diego (92101) *(P-16829)*

Buena Vista Television (DH) .... C....... 818 560-1878
   500 S Buena Vista St Burbank (91521) *(P-13155)*

Buena Vista TV Advg Sls, Burbank *Also Called: Buena Vista Television (P-13155)*

Buenaventura 6, Ventura *Also Called: Weststar Cinemas Inc (P-14010)*

Bueno Beverage Company, Visalia *Also Called: Sequoia Beverage Company LP (P-6782)*

Buffalo, Chatsworth *Also Called: Piege Co (P-6216)*

Buffalo Market, Los Angeles *Also Called: Buffalo Market Inc (P-6242)*

Buffalo Market Inc .... C....... 650 337-0078
   1439 N Highland Ave Los Angeles (90028) *(P-6242)*

Buffalo Spot MGT Group LLC .... C....... 949 354-0884
   7245 Garden Grove Blvd Garden Grove (92841) *(P-20048)*

Buffalo Wild Wings, Beverly Hills *Also Called: BW Hotel LLC (P-7462)*

Buffini & Company (PA) .... C....... 760 827-2100
   6349 Palomar Oaks Ct Carlsbad (92011) *(P-18213)*

Build Group Inc (PA) .... D....... 415 367-9399
   160 S Van Ness Ave San Francisco (94103) *(P-881)*

Build Group Inc .... D....... 408 986-8711
   1210 Coleman Ave Santa Clara (95050) *(P-882)*

Build Group Inc .... D....... 415 367-9399
   2121 N California Blvd Ste 301 Walnut Creek (94596) *(P-883)*

Build Sjc, Santa Clara *Also Called: Build Group Inc (P-882)*

Buildcom Inc .... B....... 800 375-3403
   402 Otterson Dr Ste 100 Chico (95928) *(P-5742)*

Builders Firstsource Inc .... B....... 916 481-5030
   4300 Jetway Ct North Highlands (95660) *(P-5149)*

Builders Trdsmens Insur Svcs I .... D....... 916 772-9200
   6610 Sierra College Blvd Rocklin (95677) *(P-8514)*

Building Blocks, Oakland *Also Called: Seneca Family of Agencies (P-18127)*

Building Cnnctons Bhvoral Hlth .... D....... 925 7'3-1678
   811 San Ramon Valley Blvd Ste 100 Danville (94526) *(P-17194)*

Building Material Distrs Inc (PA) .... C....... 800 356-3001
   225 Elm Ave Galt (95632) *(P-5150)*

Bulk Transportation (PA) .... D....... 909 594-2855
   415 S Lemon Ave Walnut (91789) *(P-3449)*

Bulldoc Korean Fusion, Fresno *Also Called: Nabiekim Enterprises Inc (P-13388)*

Bunim-Murray Productions .... C....... 818 756-5100
   1015 Grandview Ave Glendale (91201) *(P-13826)*

Bunzl, Anaheim *Also Called: Bunzl Distribution Cal LLC (P-6074)*

Bunzl Distribution Cal LLC (DH) .... D....... 714 688-1900
   3310 E Miraloma Ave Anaheim (92806) *(P-6074)*

Burbank Airport Mariott Hotel, Burbank *Also Called: PHF II Burbank LLC (P-10116)*

Burbank Dental Laboratory Inc .... C....... 818 841-2256
   2101 Floyd St Burbank (91504) *(P-16769)*

Burbank Partners LLC .... C....... 818 263-8704
   15433 Ventura Blvd Sherman Oaks (91403) *(P-9666)*

Burbank Water & Power, Burbank *Also Called: City of Burbank (P-4749)*

Burdick Painting .... D....... 408 567-1330
   705 Nuttman St Santa Clara (95054) *(P-2261)*

Burger Physcl Therapy Svcs Inc (HQ) .... C....... 916 983-5900
   1301 E Bidwell St Ste 201 Folsom (95630) *(P-15269)*

Burger Physcl Thrapy Rhblttion, Folsom *Also Called: Burger Physcl Therapy Svcs Inc (P-15269)*

Burger Rhblitation Systems Inc (PA) .... C....... 800 900-8491
   1301 E Bidwell St Ste 201 Folsom (95630) *(P-15270)*

Burgett Incorporated (PA) .... D....... 916 567-9999
   4111a N Freeway Blvd Sacramento (95834) *(P-6031)*

Burke, Los Angeles *Also Called: Burke Williams & Sorensen LLP (P-17394)*

Burke Engineering Co — ALPHABETIC SECTION

Burke Engineering Co .... D....... 626 579-6763
9700 Factorial Way El Monte (91733) *(P-5743)*

Burke Williams & Sorensen LLP (PA)................................... D....... 213 236-0600
444 S Flower St Ste 2400 Los Angeles (90071) *(P-17394)*

Burkland Consulting Inc .... C....... 415 944-8215
340 W Baltimore Ave Larkspur (94939) *(P-20711)*

Burleigh Point LLC .... C....... 949 428-3200
5600 Argosy Ave Ste 100 Huntington Beach (92649) *(P-8918)*

Burleigh Point, Ltd., Huntington Beach *Also Called: Burleigh Point LLC (P-8918)*

Burlingame Country Club .... D....... 650 696-8100
80 New Place Rd Hillsborough (94010) *(P-14352)*

Burlingame Industries Inc .... C....... 209 464-9001
4555 Mckinley Ave Stockton (95206) *(P-5220)*

Burlingame Industries Inc (PA)....................................... D....... 909 355-7000
3546 N Riverside Ave Rialto (92377) *(P-10414)*

Burlingame Industries Inc .... C....... 909 887-7038
277 Lytle Creek Rd Lytle Creek (92358) *(P-10415)*

Burlington Coat Factory, Arcadia *Also Called: Burlington Coat Fctry Whse of (P-7406)*

Burlington Coat Fctry Whse of .... C....... 626 447-8784
1201 S Baldwin Ave Arcadia (91007) *(P-7406)*

Burlington Convalescent Hosp (PA).................................... D....... 213 381-5585
845 S Burlington Ave Los Angeles (90057) *(P-15360)*

Burlington Convalescent Hosp .... C....... 323 295-7737
3737 Don Felipe Dr Los Angeles (90008) *(P-15361)*

Burnham & Brown, Oakland *Also Called: Burnham Brown A Prof Corp (P-17395)*

Burnham Benefits Insur Svcs .... D....... 310 370-5000
15901 Hawthorne Blvd Ste 200 Lawndale (90260) *(P-8515)*

Burnham Bnefits Insur Svcs LLC (PA).................................. D....... 805 772-7965
2211 Michelson Dr Ste 1200 Irvine (92612) *(P-8516)*

Burnham Brown A Prof Corp .... C....... 510 444-6800
1901 Harrison St Ste 1100 Oakland (94612) *(P-17395)*

Burnham Risk Insurance, Lawndale *Also Called: Burnham Benefits Insur Svcs (P-8515)*

Burnham Wgb Insur Solutions, Tustin *Also Called: Wood Gutmann Bogart Insur Brks (P-8692)*

Burns & McDonnell Inc .... D....... 714 256-1595
140 S State College Blvd Ste 100 Brea (92821) *(P-19164)*

Burns and Sons Trucking Inc .... D....... 619 460-5394
9210 Olive Dr Spring Valley (91977) *(P-3374)*

Buro Happold Consulting Engine .... C....... 310 945-4808
140 Geary St Fl 8 San Francisco (94108) *(P-19165)*

Burr Pilger Mayer Inc (PA)... C....... 415 421-5757
600 California St Fl 600 San Francisco (94108) *(P-19543)*

Burr Pilger Mayer Inc .... D....... 650 855-6800
4200 Bohannon Dr Ste 250 Menlo Park (94025) *(P-19544)*

Burrtec, Fontana *Also Called: Burrtec Waste Industries Inc (P-4870)*

Burrtec Waste Industries Inc (HQ).................................... C....... 909 429-4200
9890 Cherry Ave Fontana (92335) *(P-4870)*

Burrtec Waste Industries Inc .... C....... 909 889-1969
5455 Industrial Pkwy San Bernardino (92407) *(P-4871)*

Bursar's Office, Long Beach *Also Called: California State Univ Long Bch (P-19547)*

Burson Marsteller, San Francisco *Also Called: Young & Rubicam LLC (P-20644)*

Burt L Howe & Associates .... D....... 714 701-9180
5415 E La Palma Ave Anaheim (92807) *(P-17396)*

Burtech Pipeline Incorporated .... D....... 760 634-2822
1325 Pipeline Dr Vista (92081) *(P-1199)*

Burtech Plumbing, Vista *Also Called: Burtech Pipeline Incorporated (P-1199)*

Burton Way Hotels LLC .... D....... 310 273-2222
300 S Doheny Dr Los Angeles (90048) *(P-9667)*

Burton Way Htels Ltd A Cal Ltd .... C....... 818 575-3000
2 Dole Dr Westlake Village (91362) *(P-9668)*

Burton-Way House Ltd A CA .... C....... 310 273-2222
300 S Doheny Dr Los Angeles (90048) *(P-9669)*

Busa Servicing Inc (PA).. C....... 310 203-3400
787 W 5th St Los Angeles (90071) *(P-7664)*

Bushnell Gardens .... D....... 916 791-4199
5255 Douglas Blvd Granite Bay (95746) *(P-6854)*

Bushnell's Landscape Creations, Granite Bay *Also Called: Bushnell Gardens (P-6854)*

Business Department, Murrieta *Also Called: Southwest Healthcare Sys Aux (P-16450)*

Business Objects Inc .... A....... 650 849-4000
3410 Hillview Ave Palo Alto (94304) *(P-5285)*

Business Office, Irvine *Also Called: St Joseph Hospital of Orange (P-16473)*

Business Services Network Corp .... D....... 415 282-8161
1275 Fairfax Ave Ste 103 San Francisco (94124) *(P-10768)*

Business Wire, San Francisco *Also Called: Business Wire Inc (P-13156)*

Business Wire Inc (HQ)... C....... 415 986-4422
101 California St Fl 20 San Francisco (94111) *(P-13156)*

Business.com, Playa Vista *Also Called: Buyerzonecom LLC (P-20049)*

Busy Bee LLC .... D....... 951 404-9900
36798 Pictor Ave Murrieta (92563) *(P-10830)*

Butcher's Brand, San Leandro *Also Called: Webers Quality Meats Inc (P-6508)*

Butler America Holdings Inc .... B....... 951 563-0020
12625 Frederick St Ste E2 Moreno Valley (92553) *(P-11098)*

Butler America Holdings Inc .... B....... 909 417-3660
8647 Haven Ave Ste 100 Rancho Cucamonga (91730) *(P-11099)*

Butler International Inc (PA).. C....... 805 882-2200
3820 State St Ste A Santa Barbara (93105) *(P-11100)*

Butler Service Group Inc (HQ).. D....... 201 891-5312
3820 State St Ste A Santa Barbara (93105) *(P-11276)*

Butler Shine Stern Prtners LLC .... C....... 415 331-6049
20 Liberty Ship Way Sausalito (94965) *(P-10595)*

Butler-Johnson Corporation .... C....... 800 776-2167
2200 Zanker Rd Ste 130 San Jose (95131) *(P-5113)*

Butte County Assn Governments .... D....... 530 809-4616
326 Huss Dr Ste 150 Chico (95928) *(P-3124)*

Butte County Facillities Svcs, Oroville *Also Called: County of Butte (P-10879)*

Butte Fics, Chico *Also Called: Victor Cmnty Support Svcs Inc (P-17159)*

Butte Home Health Inc .... D....... 530 895-0462
10 Constitution Dr Chico (95973) *(P-16830)*

Butte Home Health & Hospice, Chico *Also Called: Butte Home Health Inc (P-16830)*

Butterfield Electric Inc .... C....... 530 666-2116
2101 Freeway Dr Ste A Woodland (95776) *(P-1688)*

Button Transportation Inc .... C....... 707 678-7434
7000 Button Ln Dixon (95620) *(P-3450)*

Buxton Consulting .... D....... 925 467-0700
2010 Crow Canyon Pl Ste 100 San Ramon (94583) *(P-20712)*

Buy Fresh Produce Inc .... D....... 323 796-0127
6636 E 26th St Commerce (90040) *(P-6520)*

Buyefficient LLC .... C....... 949 382-3129
903 Calle Amanecer Ste 200 San Clemente (92673) *(P-5375)*

Buyerlink, Walnut Creek *Also Called: One Planet Ops Inc (P-10659)*

Buyers Consultation Svc Inc (PA)..................................... D....... 818 341-4820
8735 Remmet Ave Canoga Park (91304) *(P-5637)*

Buyerzonecom LLC .... D....... 888 393-5000
12130 Millennium Playa Vista (90094) *(P-20049)*

Buzztime Inc .... C....... 760 476-1976
2231 Rutherford Rd Ste 210 Carlsbad (92008) *(P-4413)*

BV General Inc .... D....... 818 244-2323
413 E Cypress St Glendale (91205) *(P-8793)*

Bvk Gaming Inc .... D....... 707 644-8853
3466 Broadway St American Canyon (94503) *(P-14500)*

Bvoh LLC .... D....... 415 738-0901
5 3rd St Ste 1225 San Francisco (94103) *(P-18734)*

Bvoh Fin & Accounting Search, San Francisco *Also Called: Bvoh LLC (P-18734)*

BW Hotel LLC .... A....... 310 275-5200
9500 Wilshire Blvd Beverly Hills (90212) *(P-7462)*

By Referral Only Inc .... D....... 760 707-1300
2035 Corte Del Nogal Ste 200 Carlsbad (92011) *(P-20713)*

By The Bay Health (PA)... C....... 415 927-2273
17 E Sir Francis Drake Blvd Larkspur (94939) *(P-16831)*

By The Blue Sea LLC .... B....... 310 458-0030
1 Pico Blvd Santa Monica (90405) *(P-9670)*

Bycor General Contractors, San Diego *Also Called: Bycor General Contractors Inc (P-884)*

Bycor General Contractors Inc .... D....... 858 587-1901
6490 Marindustry Dr San Diego (92121) *(P-884)*

Byers Enterprises Inc .... D....... 530 272-7777
11773 Slow Poke Ln Grass Valley (95945) *(P-2049)*

Byers Leafguard Gutter Systems, Grass Valley *Also Called: Byers Enterprises Inc (P-2049)*

Bynd LLC .... D....... 415 944-2293
100 Montgomery St Ste 1102 San Francisco (94104) *(P-11479)*

Bynder .... D....... 415 227-4886
734 El Camino Real San Carlos (94070) *(P-11480)*

ALPHABETIC SECTION

Byron Park, Walnut Creek *Also Called: A F Evans Company Inc (P-13167)*

Bzya Corporation .... B....... 949 656-3220
100 Spectrum Center Dr Ste 900 Irvine (92618) *(P-10867)*

C & B Delivery Service .... D....... 909 623-4708
1405 E Franklin Ave Pomona (91766) *(P-3679)*

C & D Wax Inc .... C....... 858 292-5954
9353 Waxie Way San Diego (92123) *(P-8705)*

C & G Farms Inc .... C....... 831 679-2978
25453 Iverson Rd Chualar (93925) *(P-25)*

C & H Enterprises, Fremont *Also Called: Colleen & Herb Enterprises Inc (P-2850)*

C & I, Spring Valley *Also Called: Commercial Indus Roofg Co Inc (P-2053)*

C & L Refrigeration Corp .... C....... 800 901-4822
4111 N Palm St Fullerton (92835) *(P-1389)*

C & S Draperies Inc .... C....... 209 466-5371
4210 Kiernan Ave Modesto (95356) *(P-10470)*

C A A, Los Angeles *Also Called: Creative Artsts Agcy Hldngs LL (P-14035)*

C B Coast Newport Properties .... A....... 949 644-1600
840 Newport Center Dr Ste 100 Newport Beach (92660) *(P-8919)*

C B S, San Marcos *Also Called: Winchster Intrcnnect CM CA Inc (P-2726)*

C B Tool & Supply Inc .... D....... 916 568-7514
1045 Memorex Dr Santa Clara (95050) *(P-7115)*

C C C S D, Martinez *Also Called: Central Contra Costa Sanitary District Facilities Financing Authority (P-4847)*

C C Myers Inc .... C....... 916 635-9370
3286 Fitzgerald Rd Rancho Cordova (95742) *(P-1179)*

C D C, Costa Mesa *Also Called: Creative Design Consultants (P-13249)*

C D I, Sacramento *Also Called: Creative Design Interiors Inc (P-2030)*

C D Listening Bar Inc .... A....... 949 225-1170
17822 Gillette Ave Ste A Irvine (92614) *(P-6032)*

C D Lyon Construction Inc (PA) .... D....... 805 653-0173
380 W Stanley Ave Ventura (93001) *(P-19166)*

C D R, Oxnard *Also Called: Child Dev Rsrces of Vntura CNT (P-17878)*

C D Video, Santa Ana *Also Called: CD Video Manufacturing Inc (P-2952)*

C E D, Orange *Also Called: County Whl Elc Co Los Angeles (P-5550)*

C E I, Oakland *Also Called: Center For Elders Independence (P-8291)*

C E T, Gardena *Also Called: Charles E Thomas Company Inc (P-892)*

C E T, San Jose *Also Called: Center For Employment Training (P-18217)*

C E Toland & Son .... C....... 707 747-1000
5300 Industrial Way Benicia (94510) *(P-2262)*

C Enterprises, San Diego *Also Called: C Enterprises Inc (P-2827)*

C Enterprises .... D....... 760 599-5111
16868 Via Del Campo Ct San Diego (92127) *(P-2827)*

C H I, Modesto *Also Called: Community Hospice Inc (P-15751)*

C H Reynolds Electric Inc (PA) .... B....... 408 436-9280
1281 Wayne Ave San Jose (95131) *(P-1689)*

C I Container Line, Monterey Park *Also Called: Carmichael International Svc (P-3994)*

C I Design, Lake Forest *Also Called: Commercial Indus Design Co Inc (P-5286)*

C I G A, Glendale *Also Called: Califrnia Insur Guarantee Assn (P-8519)*

C L A, Van Nuys *Also Called: Clay Lacy Aviation Inc (P-3885)*

C M A, Sacramento *Also Called: California Medical Association (P-18738)*

C M E Corp .... C....... 714 632-6939
1051 S East St Anaheim (92805) *(P-20714)*

C M P, San Leandro *Also Called: Peggy S Lane Inc (P-2669)*

C Mondavi & Family (PA) .... D....... 707 967-2200
2800 Main St Saint Helena (94574) *(P-2378)*

C N B Commercial Banking Ctr, Riverside *Also Called: City National Bank (P-7618)*

C N B Commercial Banking Ctr, Burlingame *Also Called: City National Bank (P-7619)*

C N B Real Estate Group, Los Angeles *Also Called: City National Bank (P-7621)*

C N L Hotel Del Partners LP .... D....... 619 522-8299
1500 Orange Ave San Diego (92118) *(P-9671)*

C N P Signs & Graphics, El Cajon *Also Called: California Neon Products (P-3099)*

C Overaa & Co (PA) .... C....... 510 234-0926
200 Parr Blvd Richmond (94801) *(P-885)*

C P S Express .... C....... 951 685-1041
4375 E Lowell St Ste G Ontario (91761) *(P-3375)*

C P Shades Inc .... B....... 510 647-9605
2633 Ashby Ave Berkeley (94705) *(P-13219)*

C R Laurence Co Inc (HQ) .... B....... 323 588-1281
2503 E Vernon Ave Vernon (90058) *(P-2972)*

C R S Drywall Inc .... D....... 408 998-4360
135 San Jose Ave San Jose (95125) *(P-1914)*

C S C, Northridge *Also Called: Contemporary Services Corp (P-12949)*

C S I, Santa Fe Springs *Also Called: Csi Electrical Contractors Inc (P-1715)*

C S Transport Inc .... D....... 760 666-5661
425 E Heber Rd Ste 200 Heber (92249) *(P-3376)*

C T and F Inc .... D....... 562 927-2339
7228 Scout Ave Bell Gardens (90201) *(P-1690)*

C T E, North Highlands *Also Called: Construction Tstg & Engrg Inc (P-19959)*

C T I, Rancho Cucamonga *Also Called: Collection Technology Inc (P-10739)*

C V S Optical Lab Div, Rancho Cordova *Also Called: Vision Service Plan (P-8372)*

C W Brower Inc (PA) .... D....... 209 523-1828
413 S Riverside Dr Ste A Modesto (95354) *(P-7384)*

C W Driver Incorporated .... C....... 619 696-5100
7588 Metropolitan Dr San Diego (92108) *(P-886)*

C W Driver LLC (PA) .... D....... 626 351-8800
468 N Rosemead Blvd Pasadena (91107) *(P-887)*

C W Hotels Ltd .... C....... 310 395-9700
1740 Ocean Ave Santa Monica (90401) *(P-9672)*

C W S, San Diego *Also Called: Communction Wirg Spcalists Inc (P-1703)*

C-28, Corona *Also Called: Aurelio Felix Barreto III (P-7412)*

C-Cure, Ontario *Also Called: Western States Wholesale Inc (P-2700)*

C-SET, Visalia *Also Called: Community Services and Employment Training Incorporated (P-18223)*

C. W. DRIVER, INCORPORATED, San Diego *Also Called: C W Driver Incorporated (P-886)*

C&C Jewelry Mfg Inc .... D....... 213 623-6800
323 W 8th St Fl 4 Los Angeles (90014) *(P-6020)*

C&J Well Services LLC .... A....... 661 589-5220
3752 Allen Rd Bakersfield (93314) *(P-608)*

C&S Wholesale Grocers Inc .... B....... 916 383-5275
8301 Fruitridge Rd Sacramento (95826) *(P-3680)*

C&S Wholesale Grocers Inc .... C....... 559 442-4700
2797 S Orange Ave Fresno (93725) *(P-6243)*

C&S WHOLESALE GROCERS, INC., Sacramento *Also Called: C&S Wholesale Grocers Inc (P-3680)*

C&S WHOLESALE GROCERS, INC., Fresno *Also Called: C&S Wholesale Grocers Inc (P-6243)*

C&W Facility Services Inc .... A....... 805 267-7123
3011 Townsgate Rd Ste 410 Westlake Village (91361) *(P-10868)*

C&W Facility Services Inc .... A....... 408 600-4169
10 Almaden Blvd Ste 400 San Jose (95113) *(P-10869)*

C2 Financial, Clovis *Also Called: C2 Financial Corporation (P-8193)*

C2 Financial Corporation .... C....... 925 938-1300
3000 Citrus Cir Ste 118 Walnut Creek (94598) *(P-8192)*

C2 Financial Corporation .... C....... 559 824-2300
978 Burlingame Ave Clovis (93612) *(P-8193)*

C2 Financial Corporation .... C....... 858 220-2112
703 Sunset Ct San Diego (92109) *(P-8194)*

C2 Imaging, Costa Mesa *Also Called: Crisp Enterprises Inc (P-10787)*

C3 Nano Inc .... D....... 510 259-9650
3988 Trust Way Hayward (94545) *(P-19802)*

C3AI INC (PA) .... A....... 650 503-2200
1400 Seaport Blvd Ste 100 Redwood City (94063) *(P-12127)*

CA, Santa Clara *Also Called: Ca Inc (P-12128)*

Ca Inc .... C....... 800 225-5224
3965 Freedom Cir Fl 6 Santa Clara (95054) *(P-12128)*

CA Arng 115th Rsg, Los Alamitos *Also Called: Military California Department (P-20659)*

CA Department Development Svc, Cathedral City *Also Called: Califrnia Dept Dvlpmental Svcs (P-17197)*

CA Landscape and Design, Upland *Also Called: California Ldscp & Design Inc (P-480)*

CA Station Management Inc .... C....... 909 245-6251
3200 E Guasti Rd Ste 100 Ontario (91761) *(P-1200)*

Ca'del Sole, Toluca Lake *Also Called: Tre Venezie Inc (P-7514)*

Cabana Hotel, Palo Alto *Also Called: 4290 El Camino Properties LP (P-9591)*

Cabazon Band Mission Indians .... A....... 760 342-5000
84245 Indio Springs Dr Indio (92203) *(P-9673)*

Cabe Brothers .... D....... 562 595-7411
2895 Long Beach Blvd Long Beach (90806) *(P-7178)*

Cabe Toyota, Long Beach *Also Called: Cabe Brothers (P-7178)*

Cabinets 2000 LLC .... C 562 868-0909
11100 Firestone Blvd Norwalk (90650) *(P-2480)*

Cable Com, Fresno *Also Called: Cablecom LLC (P-13734)*

Cablecom, Mcclellan *Also Called: Cablecom LLC (P-13736)*

Cablecom LLC .... D 559 412-8720
5745 E Fountain Way Fresno (93727) *(P-13734)*

Cablecom LLC .... D 714 666-2400
1251 N Jefferson St Anaheim (92807) *(P-13735)*

Cablecom LLC .... D 916 891-2400
5337 Luce Ave Mcclellan (95652) *(P-13736)*

Cableconn, San Diego *Also Called: Cableconn Industries Inc (P-5544)*

Cableconn Industries Inc .... D 858 571-7111
7198 Convoy Ct San Diego (92111) *(P-5544)*

Cabrillo Cmnty Cllege Dst Fing (PA) .... A **831 479-6100**
6500 Soquel Dr Aptos (95003) *(P-17785)*

Cabrillo College, Aptos *Also Called: Cabrillo Cmnty Cllege Dst Fing (P-17785)*

Cabrillo Crdolgy Med Group Inc .... D 805 983-0922
2241 Wankel Way Ste C Oxnard (93030) *(P-14642)*

Cabrillo Hoist, Fontana *Also Called: Engel Holdings Inc (P-913)*

Cache Creek Casino Resort .... A 530 796-3118
14455 State Highway 16 Brooks (95606) *(P-9674)*

Cachet Financial Services .... D 626 578-9400
175 S Lake Ave Unit 200 Pasadena (91101) *(P-19545)*

Caci Enterprise Solutions LLC .... B 619 881-6000
1455 Frazee Rd Ste 700 San Diego (92108) *(P-12428)*

Cacique, La Puente *Also Called: Cacique Distributors US (P-6430)*

Cacique, La Puente *Also Called: Cacique Foods LLC (P-6431)*

Cacique Distributors US .... C 626 961-3399
14923 Proctor Ave La Puente (91746) *(P-6430)*

Cacique Foods LLC .... C 626 961-3399
14923 Proctor Ave La Puente (91746) *(P-6431)*

Cadence, San Jose *Also Called: Cadence Design Systems Inc (P-12129)*

Cadence Design Systems Inc (PA) .... A **408 943-1234**
2655 Seely Ave Bldg 5 San Jose (95134) *(P-12129)*

Cadent Inc .... C 408 470-1000
2560 Orchard Pkwy San Jose (95131) *(P-12429)*

Caerus Marketing Group LLC .... D 877 627-2509
17875 Von Karman Ave Ste 200 Irvine (92614) *(P-20305)*

Caesars Entrtnment Oprting Inc .... A 760 751-3100
777 Harrahs Rincon Way Valley Center (92082) *(P-14501)*

Caffe DAmore Inc C
1916 S Tubeway Ave Commerce (90040) *(P-2426)*

Cafvina Coffee & Tea, Garden Grove *Also Called: Quoc Viet Foods Inc (P-2441)*

Cagwin & Dorward LLC .... D 415 892-7710
887 Howe Rd Ste A Martinez (94553) *(P-478)*

Cahill Contractors Inc (PA) .... D **415 986-0600**
425 California St Ste 2200 San Francisco (94104) *(P-888)*

Cahill Contractors LLC .... D 415 986-0600
425 California St Ste 2200 # 2200 San Francisco (94104) *(P-889)*

Cahn, Jsph/Miller Kaplan Arase, North Hollywood *Also Called: Miller Kaplan Arase LLP (P-19612)*

Cahuilla Creek Casino, Anza *Also Called: Cahuilla Creek Rest & Casino (P-14502)*

Cahuilla Creek Rest & Casino .... C 951 763-1200
52702 Us Highway 371 Anza (92539) *(P-14502)*

Caine & Weiner, Sherman Oaks *Also Called: Caine & Weiner Company Inc (P-10737)*

Caine & Weiner Company Inc (PA) .... D **818 226-6000**
5805 Sepulveda Blvd Fl 4 Sherman Oaks (91411) *(P-10737)*

Cake Mortgage Corp .... D 818 812-5150
9200 Oakdale Ave Ste 501 Chatsworth (91311) *(P-7939)*

CAL CHAMBER, Sacramento *Also Called: California Chamber Commerce (P-18701)*

Cal Coast Financial Inc .... D 510 683-9850
39355 California St Ste 101 Fremont (94538) *(P-7940)*

Cal Coffee Shop, Lakewood *Also Called: Nationwide Theatres Corp (P-14120)*

Cal Consolidated Communications .... B 916 786-6141
211 Lincoln St Roseville (95678) *(P-4259)*

Cal Custom Tile .... D 559 875-1460
1300 Commerce Way Sanger (93657) *(P-1975)*

Cal Golden Healthcare LLC .... D 415 567-2967
1355 Ellis St San Francisco (94115) *(P-20306)*

Cal Insurance and Assoc Inc .... D 415 661-6500
2311 Taraval St San Francisco (94116) *(P-8517)*

Cal Mutual Inc .... D 888 700-4650
34077 Temecula Creek Rd Temecula (92592) *(P-7941)*

CAL NORTH, Sacramento *Also Called: Califrnia Yuth Soccer Assn Inc (P-19074)*

Cal Packing and Storage LP .... D 559 638-2929
1356 S Buttonwillow Ave Reedley (93654) *(P-3653)*

Cal Rehab, Carlsbad *Also Called: Physical Rhbltation Netwrk LLC (P-15299)*

Cal Shakes, Orinda *Also Called: California Shakespeare Theater (P-14031)*

Cal Southern Assn Governments (PA) .... C **213 236-1800**
900 Wilshire Blvd Ste 1700 Los Angeles (90017) *(P-20715)*

Cal Southern Sound Image Inc (PA) .... D **760 737-3900**
2425 Auto Park Way Escondido (92029) *(P-5638)*

Cal Southern United Food .... C 714 220-2297
6425 Katella Ave Ste 100 Cypress (90630) *(P-8457)*

Cal State La Univ Aux Svcs Inc .... A 323 343-2531
5151 State University Dr Los Angeles (90032) *(P-20050)*

Cal Strs, West Sacramento *Also Called: Califrnia State Tchers Rtrment (P-8459)*

Cal Tech Emplyees Fderal Cr Un (PA) .... D **818 952-4444**
528 Foothill Blvd La Canada Flintridge (91011) *(P-7757)*

Cal Treehouse Almonds LLC .... C 661 725-6334
2115 Road 144 Delano (93215) *(P-260)*

Cal West Enterprises, San Diego *Also Called: Wamc Company Inc (P-8869)*

Cal West Underground Inc .... D 951 371-6775
951 6th St Norco (92860) *(P-1291)*

Cal Western Foreclosure Svcs, El Cajon *Also Called: EC Closing Corp (P-7957)*

Cal-A-Vie, Vista *Also Called: Spa Havens LP (P-14232)*

Cal-Med Ambulance, South El Monte *Also Called: California Med Response Inc (P-3243)*

Cal-Organic Farms, Lamont *Also Called: Grimmway Enterprises Inc (P-6558)*

Cal-State Auto Parts Inc (PA) .... C **714 630-5950**
1361 N Red Gum St Anaheim (92806) *(P-5031)*

Cal-State Steel Corporation .... C 310 632-2772
1397 Lynnmere Dr Thousand Oaks (91360) *(P-2181)*

Cal-Steam Supply .... D 510 512-7700
1595 Crocker Ave Hayward (94544) *(P-5744)*

Cal-West Concrete Cutting Inc .... C 209 823-2236
1153 Vanderbilt Cir Manteca (95337) *(P-2103)*

Cal-West Nurseries Inc .... C 951 270-0667
138 North Dr Norco (92860) *(P-479)*

Cal/Pac Pntngs Ctngs Acqstion .... D 714 628-1514
608 N Eckhoff St Orange (92868) *(P-1607)*

Cala Health Inc .... D 415 890-3961
1800 Gateway Dr Ste 300 San Mateo (94404) *(P-3073)*

Calabasas Memory Care Cmnty, Calabasas *Also Called: Silverado Senior Living Inc (P-15672)*

Calabasas Stadium 6, Calabasas *Also Called: Edwards Theatres Inc (P-13988)*

Calabria Group Inc (PA) .... C **916 773-3900**
920 Reserve Dr Ste 150 Roseville (95678) *(P-11101)*

CALAMP, Irvine *Also Called: Calamp Corp (P-12130)*

Calamp Corp (PA) .... D **949 600-5600**
15635 Alton Pkwy Ste 250 Irvine (92618) *(P-12130)*

Calance, Anaheim *Also Called: Partners Information Tech (P-12853)*

Calaveras County Water Dst .... D 209 754-3543
120 Toma Ct San Andreas (95249) *(P-4766)*

Calavo, Santa Paula *Also Called: Calavo Growers Inc (P-2431)*

Calavo Growers Inc (PA) .... D **805 525-1245**
1141 Cummings Rd Ste A Santa Paula (93060) *(P-2431)*

Calbee America Incorporated .... D 310 370-2500
3625 Del Amo Blvd Ste 235 Torrance (90503) *(P-6456)*

Calcom Energy, Fresno *Also Called: California Coml Solar Inc (P-1390)*

Calderon Drywall Contrs Inc .... D 714 696-2977
1931 E Meats Ave Trlr 127 Orange (92865) *(P-1915)*

Calenergy LLC .... B 402 231-1527
7030 Gentry Rd Calipatria (92233) *(P-1691)*

Calex, Northridge *Also Called: Valley Hospital Medical Center Foundation (P-16612)*

Calex Engineering Inc .... D 661 254-1866
23651 Pine St Newhall (91321) *(P-2214)*

Calex Engineering Co., Newhall *Also Called: Calex Engineering Inc (P-2214)*

Calftech Corporation .... D 559 752-2302
13939 Rd L52 Tipton (93272) *(P-210)*

Calhot Illinios LLC .... D 310 536-9800
5250 W El Segundo Blvd Hawthorne (90250) *(P-9675)*

ALPHABETIC SECTION — California Family Fitness

Cali Beach Bears LLC .... D....... 805 361-0260
335 E Betteravia Rd Santa Maria (93454) *(P-13220)*

Cali Calmecac Language Academy .... D....... 707 837-7747
9491 Starr Rd Windsor (95492) *(P-18827)*

CALIBER BODYWORKS OF TEXAS, INC., Hesperia *Also Called: Caliber Bodyworks Texas Inc (P-13632)*

Caliber Bodyworks Texas Inc .... D....... 760 949-6269
11182 I Ave Hesperia (92345) *(P-13632)*

Caliber Bodyworks Texas Inc .... D....... 714 665-3905
5 Auto Center Dr Tustin (92782) *(P-13633)*

Caliber Bodyworks Texas Inc .... D....... 408 972-0300
3517 Hillcap Ave San Jose (95136) *(P-13634)*

Caliber Cllsion - 1127 Mdesto, Modesto *Also Called: Wand Topco Inc (P-13652)*

Caliber Collision, Burlingame *Also Called: Wand Topco Inc (P-13651)*

Caliber Collision Centers, Tustin *Also Called: Caliber Bodyworks Texas Inc (P-13633)*

Caliber Collision Centers, San Jose *Also Called: Caliber Bodyworks Texas Inc (P-13634)*

Caliber Holdings Corporation .... D....... 323 913-4000
3020 Riverside Dr Los Angeles (90039) *(P-13635)*

Caliber Home Loans Inc .... D....... 707 432-1000
3700 Hilborn Rd Ste 700 Fairfield (94534) *(P-7942)*

Calibr A Division Scripps RES, La Jolla *Also Called: Scripps Research Institute (P-19909)*

Calibre International LLC (PA) .... C....... 626 969-4660
6250 N Irwindale Ave Irwindale (91702) *(P-20632)*

Calico, Irvine *Also Called: Calico Building Services Inc (P-10870)*

Calico Building Services Inc .... C....... 949 380-8707
15550 Rockfield Blvd Ste C Irvine (92618) *(P-10870)*

Calico Life Sciences LLC .... B....... 650 754-6200
1170 Veterans Blvd South San Francisco (94080) *(P-19667)*

Calidad Industries Inc .... B....... 510 698-7200
1700 Park St Ste 220 Alameda (94501) *(P-10871)*

Calidental, Bakersfield *Also Called: Azad Professional Dental Corp (P-15217)*

Caliente Creek Prtners A Cal L (PA) .... D....... 559 651-1000
8445 W Elowin Ct Visalia (93291) *(P-8920)*

Caliente Farms, Delano *Also Called: M Caratan Disc Inc (P-80)*

Calif Schl Emplyees Assoc Rtre .... D....... 408 473-1000
2045 Lundy Ave San Jose (95131) *(P-18773)*

Calif Stat Univ Fres Foun .... C....... 559 278-0850
5370 N Chestnut Ave Fresno (93725) *(P-19072)*

California Academy Sciences (PA) .... A....... 415 379-8000
55 Music Concourse Dr San Francisco (94118) *(P-18685)*

California Arb, Inc., Lake Forest *Also Called: Arb Inc (P-1192)*

California Armenian Home, Fresno *Also Called: California HM For The Aged Inc (P-15825)*

California Assn Realtors Inc (PA) .... C....... 213 739-8200
525 S Virgil Ave Los Angeles (90020) *(P-18700)*

California Autism Center .... D....... 559 475-7860
1630 E Shaw Ave Ste 190 Fresno (93710) *(P-17857)*

California Baking Company .... B....... 619 591-8289
681 Anita St Chula Vista (91911) *(P-6613)*

California Bancorp (PA) .... C....... 510 457-3737
1300 Clay St Ste 500 Oakland (94612) *(P-7665)*

California Bank & Trust .... A....... 801 844-7637
11622 El Camino Real San Diego (92130) *(P-7666)*

California Basic, Santa Fe Springs *Also Called: Mias Fashion Mfg Co Inc (P-6208)*

CALIFORNIA BOTANIC GARDEN, Claremont *Also Called: Rancho Santa Ana Botanic Grdn (P-18693)*

California Box II .... D....... 909 944-9202
8949 Toronto Ave Rancho Cucamonga (91730) *(P-6075)*

California Bread Co., Chula Vista *Also Called: California Baking Company (P-6613)*

California Broadcast Ctr LLC .... D....... 310 233-2425
3800 Via Oro Ave Long Beach (90810) *(P-4475)*

California Bulk Inc .... C....... 209 983-1069
3939 Producers Dr Stockton (95206) *(P-3451)*

California Business Bureau Inc (PA) .... C....... 626 303-1515
1711 S Mountain Ave Monrovia (91016) *(P-19546)*

California Cancer Specialists Medical Group Inc .... B....... 626 775-3200
1333 S Mayflower Ave # 200 Monrovia (91016) *(P-18735)*

California Capital Insur Co (HQ) .... C....... 831 233-5500
2300 Garden Rd Monterey (93940) *(P-8379)*

California Casualty, San Mateo *Also Called: California Casualty Mgt Co (P-8380)*

California Casualty Mgt Co (HQ) .... C....... 650 574-4000
1875 S Grant St Ste 800 San Mateo (94402) *(P-8380)*

California Center Bank, Los Angeles *Also Called: Bbcn Bank (P-7608)*

California Chamber Commerce (PA) .... D....... 916 444-6670
1215 K St Ste 1400 Sacramento (95814) *(P-18701)*

California Childrens Academy .... C....... 323 263-3846
233 N Breed St Los Angeles (90033) *(P-18273)*

California Choice, Orange *Also Called: Choic Admini Insur Servi (P-8526)*

California City San Bernardino (PA) .... B....... 909 384-7272
290 N D St San Bernardino (92401) *(P-17397)*

California Closet Co, Huntington Beach *Also Called: California Closet Company Inc (P-2263)*

California Closet Company Inc .... C....... 714 899-4905
5921 Skylab Rd Huntington Beach (92647) *(P-2263)*

California Club .... C....... 213 622-1391
538 S Flower St Los Angeles (90071) *(P-18828)*

California Cmplte CNT Cnsus .... D....... 916 852-2020
400 R St Ste 350 Sacramento (95811) *(P-19869)*

California Coast Credit Union (PA) .... D....... 858 495-1600
9201 Spectrum Center Blvd Ste 300 San Diego (92123) *(P-7820)*

California Coml Solar Inc .... C....... 559 667-9200
9479 N Fort Washington Rd Ste 105 Fresno (93730) *(P-1390)*

California Commerce Club Inc .... A....... 323 721-2100
6131 Telegraph Rd Commerce (90040) *(P-9676)*

California Convalescent Center, Los Angeles *Also Called: Bonnie Brae Cnvlscent Hosp Inc (P-15821)*

California Credit Union .... D....... 858 769-7369
503 Telegraph Canyon Rd Chula Vista (91910) *(P-7758)*

California Credit Union (PA) .... C....... 818 291-6700
701 N Brand Blvd Fl 7 Glendale (91203) *(P-7821)*

California Cryobank Inc .... B....... 650 635-1420
611 Gateway Blvd Ste 820 South San Francisco (94080) *(P-17195)*

California Cryobank LLC (DH) .... D....... 310 496-5691
11915 La Grange Ave Los Angeles (90025) *(P-17196)*

California Dairies Inc .... C....... 559 752-5200
11894 Avenue 120 Pixley (93256) *(P-6432)*

California Dental Association (PA) .... C....... 916 443-0505
1201 K St Fl 14 Sacramento (95814) *(P-18736)*

California Department Tech .... C....... 916 464-3747
3101 Gold Camp Dr Rancho Cordova (95670) *(P-12746)*

California Department Tech (DH) .... C....... 916 319-9223
1325 J St Ste 1600 Sacramento (95814) *(P-12747)*

California Department Trnsp .... C....... 707 428-2031
2019 W Texas St Fairfield (94533) *(P-1084)*

California Department Trnsp .... D....... 562 692-0823
1940 Workman Mill Rd Whittier (90601) *(P-1085)*

California Department Trnsp .... D....... 760 352-1129
1607 Adams Ave El Centro (92243) *(P-1086)*

California Department Trnsp .... C....... 707 445-6600
1656 Union St Eureka (95501) *(P-20716)*

California Dept Fd Agriculture .... A....... 858 755-1161
2260 Jimmy Durante Blvd Del Mar (92014) *(P-20949)*

California Dept of Pub Hlth .... B....... 510 231-7408
850 Marina Bay Pkwy F175 Richmond (94804) *(P-14643)*

California Dept of Pub Hlth .... C....... 714 567-2906
681 S Parker St Ste 200 Orange (92868) *(P-20920)*

California Dept Social Svcs .... D....... 951 782-4200
3737 Main St Ste 700 Riverside (92501) *(P-20941)*

California Dept Wtr Resources .... D....... 916 574-1423
3310 El Camino Ave Ste 200 Sacramento (95821) *(P-19870)*

California Drywall Co (PA) .... C....... 408 292-7500
2290 S 10th St San Jose (95112) *(P-1916)*

California Eastern Labs Inc (PA) .... D....... 408 919-2500
5201 Great America Pkwy Ste 320 Santa Clara (95054) *(P-5639)*

California Endive Farm, Rio Vista *Also Called: California Vegetable Spc Inc (P-6521)*

California Endowment (PA) .... D....... 213 928-8800
1000 N Alameda St Los Angeles (90012) *(P-18567)*

California Envmtl Systems Inc .... D....... 530 820-3693
12265 Locksley Ln Auburn (95602) *(P-19167)*

California Eye Institute .... C....... 559 449-5000
1360 E Herndon Ave Ste 230 Fresno (93720) *(P-14644)*

California Fair Plan Assn .... D....... 213 487-0111
725 S Figueroa St Ste 3900 Los Angeles (90017) *(P-8518)*

California Family Fitness, Orangevale *Also Called: California Family Health LLC (P-14183)*

California Family Foods LLC — ALPHABETIC SECTION

California Family Foods LLC .... D...... 530 476-3326
   6550 Struckmeyer Rd Arbuckle (95912) *(P-2362)*

California Family Health LLC (PA) .... C...... 916 987-2030
   8680 Greenback Ln Ste 108 Orangevale (95662) *(P-14183)*

California Field Office, San Francisco *Also Called: Nature Conservancy (P-18885)*

California Friends Homes .... B...... 714 530-9100
   12151 Dale Ave Stanton (90680) *(P-18383)*

California Glass, San Francisco *Also Called: United California Glass & Door (P-13807)*

California Health Benefit Exch .... D...... 916 228-8210
   1601 Exposition Blvd Sacramento (95815) *(P-18737)*

California Health Insur Exch, Sacramento *Also Called: California Health Benefit Exch (P-18737)*

California Hlth Collaborative (PA) .... D...... 559 221-6315
   1680 W Shaw Ave Fresno (93711) *(P-13221)*

California HM For The Aged Inc .... C...... 559 251-8414
   6720 E Kings Canyon Rd Fresno (93727) *(P-15825)*

California Hornblower, San Francisco *Also Called: Hornblower Yachts LLC (P-3934)*

California Hospital Assn Cha, Sacramento *Also Called: Califrnia Assn Hsptals Hlth Sy (P-18742)*

California Human Dev Corp (PA) .... C...... 707 523-1155
   3315 Airway Dr Santa Rosa (95403) *(P-18214)*

California Imaging Nework, Los Angeles *Also Called: Oaks Diagnostics Inc (P-14930)*

California Institute For, La Jolla *Also Called: California Institute For Biomedical Research (P-19871)*

California Institute For Biomedical Research .... C...... 858 242-1000
   11119 N Torrey Pines Rd La Jolla (92037) *(P-19871)*

California Institute Tech .... A...... 818 354-9154
   4800 Oak Grove Dr Pasadena (91109) *(P-19872)*

California Internet LP (PA) .... C...... 805 225-4638
   251 Camarillo Ranch Rd Camarillo (93012) *(P-4260)*

California ISO, Folsom *Also Called: Califrnia Ind Sys Oprator Corp (P-4562)*

California Kit Cab Door Corp .... D...... 408 776-1105
   105 Cochrane Cir Morgan Hill (95037) *(P-8706)*

California Lab Sciences LLC .... B...... 562 758-6900
   10200 Pioneer Blvd Ste 500 Santa Fe Springs (90670) *(P-19953)*

California Ldscp & Design Inc .... C...... 909 949-1601
   273 N Benson Ave Upland (91786) *(P-480)*

California Life Company, South San Francisco *Also Called: Calico Life Sciences LLC (P-19667)*

California Linen Service, Pasadena *Also Called: Dy-Dee Service Pasadena Inc (P-10485)*

California Marine Cleaning Inc (PA) .... C...... 619 231-8788
   2049 Main St San Diego (92113) *(P-4872)*

California Marketing, San Diego *Also Called: Mabie Marketing Group Inc (P-13360)*

California Med Response Inc .... D...... 562 968-1818
   1557 Santa Anita Ave South El Monte (91733) *(P-3243)*

California Medical Association (PA) .... D...... 916 444-5532
   1201 K St Ste 800 Sacramento (95814) *(P-18738)*

California Mfg Tech Consulting .... D...... 310 263-3060
   3760 Kilroy Airport Way Ste 450 Long Beach (90806) *(P-19168)*

California Natural Products .... B...... 209 858-2525
   1250 Lathrop Rd Lathrop (95330) *(P-2432)*

California Neon Products .... D...... 619 283-2191
   9944 Blossom Valley Rd El Cajon (92021) *(P-3099)*

California Northern RR Co .... D...... 530 406-8981
   600 M St Ste 3 Patterson (95363) *(P-3991)*

California Nurses Association (PA) .... D...... 510 273-2200
   155 Grand Ave Oakland (94612) *(P-18739)*

CALIFORNIA NURSING & REHABILIT, Palm Springs *Also Called: Califrnia Nrsing Rhbltton Ctr (P-15363)*

California Oregon Broadcasting (HQ) .... D...... 530 243-7777
   755 Auditorium Dr Redding (96001) *(P-4414)*

California Parenting Institute .... D...... 707 585-6108
   3650 Standish Ave Santa Rosa (95407) *(P-17804)*

California Physicians Service (PA) .... A...... 510 607-2000
   601 12th St Oakland (94607) *(P-8286)*

California Physicians Service .... D...... 530 351-6115
   4700 Bechelli Ln Redding (96002) *(P-8287)*

California Physicians Service .... D...... 310 744-2668
   3840 Kilroy Airport Way Long Beach (90806) *(P-8288)*

California Physicians Service .... C...... 818 598-8000
   6300 Canoga Ave Ste A Woodland Hills (91367) *(P-8289)*

California Physicians Service .... D...... 559 440-4000
   5250 N Palm Ave Ste 120 Fresno (93704) *(P-8290)*

California Pools, Coachella *Also Called: Teserra (P-2320)*

California Portland Cement, Mojave *Also Called: Calportland Company (P-2695)*

California Premium Incentives, Lake Forest *Also Called: Aminco International USA Inc (P-3086)*

California Prof Engrg Inc .... D...... 626 810-1338
   19062 San Jose Ave La Puente (91748) *(P-19169)*

California Rain, Los Angeles *Also Called: California Rain Company Inc (P-6196)*

California Rain Company Inc .... D...... 213 623-6061
   1213 E 14th St Los Angeles (90021) *(P-6196)*

California RE Assn Inc .... D...... 213 739-8200
   525 S Virgil Ave Los Angeles (90020) *(P-18702)*

California Real Estate, Los Angeles *Also Called: California RE Assn Inc (P-18702)*

California Republic Bank .... B...... 949 270-9700
   18400 Von Karman Ave # 630 Irvine (92612) *(P-7667)*

California Resources Corp (PA) .... D...... 888 848-4754
   1 World Trade Ctr Ste 1500 Long Beach (90831) *(P-582)*

California Resources Prod Corp (HQ) .... C...... 661 869-8000
   27200 Tourney Rd Ste 200 Santa Clarita (91355) *(P-583)*

California Schl Employees Assn (PA) .... C...... 408 473-1000
   2045 Lundy Ave San Jose (95131) *(P-18774)*

California School Boards Assn .... D...... 800 266-3382
   3251 Beacon Blvd West Sacramento (95691) *(P-18740)*

California School of Mech Arts .... D...... 415 333-4021
   755 Ocean Ave San Francisco (94112) *(P-17697)*

California Schools Veba .... D...... 888 276-0250
   1843 Hotel Cir S San Diego (92108) *(P-14645)*

California Semiconductor Tech .... C...... 310 579-2939
   429 Santa Monica Blvd Santa Monica (90401) *(P-19170)*

California Shakespeare Theater (PA) .... D...... 510 548-3422
   100 California Shakespear Theater Way Orinda (94563) *(P-14031)*

California Sheet Metal, El Cajon *Also Called: California Shtmtl Works Inc (P-809)*

California Shellfish Co Inc .... C...... 707 542-9490
   1280 Columbus Ave #300r San Francisco (94133) *(P-6466)*

California Shirt Printer Inc .... D...... 714 898-9946
   12221 Monarch St Garden Grove (92841) *(P-6169)*

California Shtmtl Works Inc .... D...... 619 562-7010
   1020 N Marshall Ave El Cajon (92020) *(P-809)*

California Skateparks .... C...... 909 949-1601
   285 N Benson Ave Upland (91786) *(P-421)*

California Skin Institute .... D...... 408 736-0441
   603 S Knickerbocker Dr Sunnyvale (94087) *(P-14646)*

California Skin Institute .... D...... 510 881-7822
   20400 Lake Chabot Rd Ste 202 Castro Valley (94546) *(P-14647)*

California Sportservice Inc .... B...... 619 795-5000
   100 Park Blvd San Diego (92101) *(P-14131)*

California State Automobile Association Inter-Insurance Bureau (HQ) ... A...... 925 287-7600
   1276 S California Blvd Walnut Creek (94596) *(P-19073)*

California State Univ Long Bch .... C...... 559 278-2216
   5201 N Maple Ave Fresno (93740) *(P-17805)*

California State Univ Long Bch .... C...... 562 985-1764
   1250 N Bellflower Blvd Bh155 Long Beach (90840) *(P-19547)*

California State University, Fresno *Also Called: Calif Stat Univ Fres Foun (P-19072)*

California Steel and Tube .... C...... 626 968-5511
   16049 Stephens St City Of Industry (91745) *(P-5481)*

California Strl Concepts Inc .... D...... 661 257-6903
   28358 Constellation Rd Ste 660 Valencia (91355) *(P-890)*

California Sun Inc .... D...... 916 789-1034
   8265 Sierra College Blvd Roseville (95661) *(P-10532)*

California Supply Inc .... D...... 310 532-2500
   491 E Compton Blvd Gardena (90248) *(P-6076)*

California Teachers Assn (PA) .... C...... 650 697-1400
   1705 Murchison Dr Burlingame (94010) *(P-18741)*

California Traffic Control .... D...... 562 595-7575
   3333 Cherry Ave Long Beach (90807) *(P-13222)*

California Traffic Ctrl Svcs, Long Beach *Also Called: California Traffic Control (P-13222)*

California Transit Inc .... D...... 323 234-8750
   1900 S Alameda St Vernon (90058) *(P-3125)*

California Transport Enterprises Inc .... D
   2610 Wisconsin Ave South Gate (90280) *(P-3377)*

ALPHABETIC SECTION

California United Mech Inc (PA) .... B 408 232-9000
2185 Oakland Rd San Jose (95131) *(P-1391)*

California Valley Land Co Inc (PA) .... D 559 945-9292
18036 Gale Huron (93234) *(P-241)*

California Vegetable Spc Inc .... D 707 374-2111
15 Poppy House Rd Rio Vista (94571) *(P-6521)*

California Vocations Inc .... C 530 877-0937
564 Rio Lindo Ave Ste 204 Chico (95926) *(P-15826)*

California Waste Services LLC .... C 310 538-5998
621 W 152nd St Gardena (90247) *(P-4873)*

California Waste Solutions Inc (PA) .... D 408 292-0830
1005 Timothy Dr San Jose (95133) *(P-4874)*

California Water Service Co (HQ) .... C 408 367-8200
1720 N 1st St San Jose (95112) *(P-4767)*

California Water Service Group (PA) .... C 408 367-8200
1720 N 1st St San Jose (95112) *(P-4768)*

California Watercress Inc (PA) .... D 805 524-4808
550 E Telegraph Rd Fillmore (93015) *(P-26)*

Califrnia Artchoke Vgtble Grwe .... D 831 633-2144
10855 Ocean Mist Pkwy Castroville (95012) *(P-171)*

Califrnia Assn Hsptals Hlth Sy (PA) .... D 916 443-7401
1215 K St Ste 700 Sacramento (95814) *(P-18742)*

Califrnia Atism Foundation Inc .... C 510 724-1751
982 Marlesta Rd Pinole (94564) *(P-18568)*

Califrnia Auto Dalers Exch LLC .... B 714 996-2400
1320 N Tustin Ave Anaheim (92807) *(P-5006)*

Califrnia Clnic Plstic Surgery .... C 760 346-0611
73180 El Paseo Palm Desert (92260) *(P-13223)*

Califrnia Cncer Care A Med Gro .... C 415 925-5000
1350 S Eliseo Dr Ste 200 Greenbrae (94904) *(P-14648)*

Califrnia Crrctnal Pace Offcer (PA) .... D 916 372-6060
755 Riverpoint Dr West Sacramento (95605) *(P-18775)*

Califrnia Crtive Solutions Inc (PA) .... D 458 208-4131
13475 Danielson St Ste 230 Poway (92064) *(P-12748)*

Califrnia Cryobank Lf Sciences, South San Francisco *Also Called: California Cryobank Inc* *(P-17195)*

Califrnia Cslty Indemnity Exch (PA) .... C 650 574-4000
1900 Alameda De Las Pulgas San Mateo (94403) *(P-8381)*

Califrnia Ctr For Arts Escndid .... C 760 839-4138
340 N Escondido Blvd Escondido (92025) *(P-18640)*

Califrnia Dept Child Spport Sv (DH) .... D 916 464-5000
11150 International Dr Rancho Cordova (95670) *(P-17858)*

Califrnia Dept Dvlpmental Svcs .... A 559 782-2222
26501 Avenue 140 Porterville (93257) *(P-15362)*

Califrnia Dept Dvlpmental Svcs .... A 707 938-6000
15000 Arnold Dr Eldridge (95431) *(P-16668)*

Califrnia Dept Dvlpmental Svcs .... B 760 770-6248
696 Ramon Cathedral City (92234) *(P-17197)*

Califrnia Dept Dvlpmental Svcs .... A 714 957-5151
2501 Harbor Blvd Costa Mesa (92626) *(P-18215)*

Califrnia Dept Indus Relations .... D 510 286-7000
1515 Clay St Ste 1201 Oakland (94612) *(P-4145)*

Califrnia Dept Indus Relations .... D 415 703-5133
301 Howard St Ste 700 San Francisco (94105) *(P-18776)*

Califrnia Dept Indus Relations .... D 209 830-7200
25347 S Schulte Rd Tracy (95377) *(P-18777)*

Califrnia Dept Indus Relations .... D 714 558-4121
28 Civic Center Plz Ste 239 Santa Ana (92701) *(P-20921)*

Califrnia Dept State Hospitals .... A 559 935-4300
24511 W Jayne Ave Coalinga (93210) *(P-16641)*

Califrnia Dept State Hospitals .... A 714 957-5000
2501 Harbor Blvd Costa Mesa (92626) *(P-16642)*

Califrnia Dept State Hospitals .... A 707 253-5000
2100 Napa Vallejo Hwy Napa (94558) *(P-16643)*

Califrnia Dept State Hospitals .... A 909 425-7000
3102 E Highland Ave Patton (92369) *(P-16644)*

Califrnia Dept State Hospitals .... A 805 468-2000
10333 El Camino Real Atascadero (93422) *(P-16645)*

Califrnia Erctors Bay Area Inc .... D 707 746-1990
4500 California Ct Benicia (94510) *(P-2182)*

Califrnia Fire Rscue Trning Au .... C 916 475-1660
3121 Gold Canal Dr Rancho Cordova (95670) *(P-18216)*

Califrnia Frnsic Med Group Inc .... D 858 694-4690
2801 Meadow Lark Dr San Diego (92123) *(P-17198)*

Califrnia Frnsic Med Group Inc .... C 805 654-3343
800 S Victoria Ave Ventura (93009) *(P-17199)*

Califrnia Golf CLB San Frncsco .... D 650 588-9021
844 W Orange Ave South San Francisco (94080) *(P-14353)*

Califrnia Grnhse Frm Il Ltd PR .... D 949 715-3987
17712 Adobe Rd Bakersfield (93307) *(P-13224)*

Califrnia Gvrnment Oprtons Agc, Sacramento *Also Called: Califrnia Pub Emplyees Rtrment* *(P-8458)*

Califrnia High Speed Rail Auth .... D 916 324-1541
770 L St Ste 620 Sacramento (95814) *(P-3115)*

Califrnia Hosp Med Ctr Fndtion .... A 213 742-5867
1401 S Grand Ave Los Angeles (90015) *(P-15964)*

Califrnia Ind Sys Oprator Corp (PA) .... B 916 351-4400
250 Outcropping Way Folsom (95630) *(P-4562)*

Califrnia Insur Guarantee Assn .... C 818 844-4300
330 N Brand Blvd Ste 500 Glendale (91203) *(P-8519)*

Califrnia Mrtime Acdemy Fndtio .... C 707 654-1000
200 Maritime Academy Dr Vallejo (94590) *(P-9411)*

Califrnia Nrsing Rhbltttion Ctr .... D 760 325-2937
2299 N Indian Ave Palm Springs (92262) *(P-15363)*

Califrnia Odd Fllows Hsing Nap (PA) .... D 707 257-7885
1800 Atrium Pkwy Napa (94559) *(P-8794)*

Califrnia Odd Fllows Hsing Nap .... D 707 257-7885
1800 Atrium Pkwy Napa (94559) *(P-8795)*

Califrnia Prson Hlthcare Rcvrs .... D 916 691-6721
501 J St Ste 100 Sacramento (95814) *(P-16832)*

Califrnia Pub Emplyees Rtrment (DH) .... A 916 795-3000
400 Q St Sacramento (95811) *(P-8458)*

Califrnia Rdvlpment Assn Fndti .... D 916 449-6229
801 12th St Sacramento (95814) *(P-18703)*

Califrnia Rhblitation Inst LLC .... D 424 363-1003
2070 Century Park E Los Angeles (90067) *(P-15965)*

Califrnia Rsrces Elk Hills LLC .... B 661 412-0000
27200 Tourney Rd Ste 200 Santa Clarita (91355) *(P-596)*

Califrnia Rsurces Long Bch Inc .... D 888 848-4754
27200 Tourney Rd Ste 200 Santa Clarita (91355) *(P-597)*

Califrnia Rur Indian Hlth Bd I .... D 916 437-0104
1020 Sundown Way Roseville (95661) *(P-18569)*

Califrnia Scnce Ctr Foundation .... B 213 744-2545
700 Exposition Park Dr Los Angeles (90037) *(P-18641)*

Califrnia Shock Truma A Rescue (PA) .... D 916 921-4000
4933 Bailey Loop Mcclellan (95652) *(P-3244)*

Califrnia State Employees Assn (PA) .... D 916 444-8134
3000 Advantage Way Sacramento (95834) *(P-18778)*

Califrnia State Tchers Rtrment (DH) .... B 858 258-5077
100 Waterfront Pl West Sacramento (95605) *(P-8459)*

Califrnia Sthern Bptst Cnvntio .... D 209 965-3735
29005 State Highway 108 Long Barn (95335) *(P-19012)*

Califrnia Suthland Private SEC .... C 714 367-4005
1818 S State College Blvd Anaheim (92806) *(P-12943)*

Califrnia Yuth Soccer Assn Inc .... D 925 426-5437
2081 Arena Blvd Sacramento (95834) *(P-19074)*

Califrnia-Nevada Methdst Homes .... C 831 657-5200
551 Gibson Ave Pacific Grove (93950) *(P-8796)*

Califrnia-Nevada Methdst Homes .... C 510 835-5511
1850 Alice St Ofc Oakland (94612) *(P-15827)*

Califrnias Gnite Pool Plst Inc .... D 925 960-9500
510 Greenville Rd Livermore (94550) *(P-2264)*

Calimesa Operations LLC .... C 909 795-2421
13542 2nd St Yucaipa (92399) *(P-15364)*

CALIMESA POST ACUTE, Yucaipa *Also Called: Calimesa Operations LLC (P-15364)*

Calistoga Spa Inc .... D 707 942-6269
1006 Washington St Calistoga (94515) *(P-14184)*

Calistoga Spa Hot Springs, Calistoga *Also Called: Calistoga Spa Inc (P-14184)*

Calix, San Jose *Also Called: Calix Inc (P-4530)*

Calix Inc (PA) .... A 408 514-3000
2777 Orchard Pkwy San Jose (95134) *(P-4530)*

Call To Action Partners Llc (PA) .... D 310 996-7200
11601 Wilshire Blvd Fl 23 Los Angeles (90025) *(P-9495)*

Call-The-Car ALPHABETIC SECTION

Call-The-Car .... D....... 855 282-6968
   3100 New York Dr Ste 100 Pasadena (91107) *(P-3245)*

Callan LLC (PA) .... C....... 415 974-5060
   1 Bush St San Francisco (94104) *(P-8195)*

Calleguas Mncpl Wtr Dst Pub Fc .... D....... 805 526-9323
   2100 E Olsen Rd Thousand Oaks (91360) *(P-4769)*

Callfire Inc .... D....... 213 221-2289
   548 Market St Ste 44523 San Francisco (94104) *(P-11481)*

Callisto Media Inc .... D....... 510 253-0500
   918 Parker St Berkeley (94710) *(P-4531)*

Calmat Co .... C....... 661 858-2673
   16101 Hwy 156 Maricopa (93252) *(P-634)*

Calmat Co (DH) .... D....... 818 553-8821
   500 N Brand Blvd Ste 500 Glendale (91203) *(P-2648)*

Calmet Inc (PA) .... C....... 323 721-8120
   7202 Petterson Ln Paramount (90723) *(P-4875)*

Calnet Inc .... D....... 530 672-1078
   4101 Wild Chaparral Dr Shingle Springs (95682) *(P-4261)*

Calpaco Papers Inc (PA) .... C....... 323 767-2800
   3155 Universe Dr Jurupa Valley (91752) *(P-2533)*

Calpers, Sacramento *Also Called: Public Employees Retirement (P-8466)*

Calpine Energy Solutions LLC (DH) .... C....... 877 273-6772
   401 W A St Ste 500 San Diego (92101) *(P-4748)*

Calportland Company .... C....... 661 824-2401
   9350 Oak Creek Rd Mojave (93501) *(P-2695)*

Calportland Company (DH) .... D....... 626 852-6200
   2025 E Financial Way Glendora (91741) *(P-2696)*

Calsemi, Santa Monica *Also Called: California Semiconductor Tech (P-19170)*

Calstar, Mcclellan *Also Called: Califrnia Shock Truma A Rescue (P-3244)*

CALTECH EFCU, La Canada Flintridge *Also Called: Cal Tech Emplyees Fderal Cr Un (P-7757)*

CALTRAIN, San Carlos *Also Called: Peninsula Crrdor Jint Pwers Bd (P-3189)*

Caltrans, Fairfield *Also Called: California Department Trnsp (P-1084)*

Caltrans District 1, Eureka *Also Called: California Department Trnsp (P-20716)*

Caltrans Eastern Reg Rd Maint, Whittier *Also Called: California Department Trnsp (P-1085)*

Caltronics Business Systems, Rancho Cordova *Also Called: JJR Enterprises Inc (P-13741)*

Calvary Church Santa Ana Inc .... C....... 714 973-4800
   1010 N Tustin Ave Santa Ana (92705) *(P-18274)*

Calvary Temple Academy, Modesto *Also Called: House Modesto (P-19021)*

Calvey Incorporated .... D....... 916 681-4800
   8670 Fruitridge Rd Ste 300 Sacramento (95826) *(P-6895)*

Calvin Dubois .... D....... 909 222-6662
   9057 Arrow Rte Rancho Cucamonga (91730) *(P-1392)*

Camanche Recreation-North, Ione *Also Called: Concessionaires Urban Park (P-14508)*

Camarena Health (PA) .... D....... 559 664-4000
   344 E 6th St Madera (93638) *(P-14649)*

Camarillo Dialysis Center, Camarillo *Also Called: Bio-Mdcal Applctons Cmrllo Inc (P-16978)*

Camarillo Family YMCA, Camarillo *Also Called: Channel Islnds Yung MNS Chrstn (P-18836)*

Camarillo Healthcare Center .... D....... 805 482-9805
   205 Granada St Camarillo (93010) *(P-20051)*

Cambium Business Group Inc (PA) .... C....... 714 670-1171
   6950 Noritsu Ave Buena Park (90620) *(P-5081)*

Cambium Networks Inc .... C....... 847 640-3809
   2010 N 1st St San Jose (95131) *(P-4532)*

Cambria Pines Lodge, Cambria *Also Called: Pacific Cambria Inc (P-10077)*

Cambridge Sierra Holdings LLC .... B....... 909 370-4411
   1350 Reche Canyon Rd Colton (92324) *(P-15365)*

Camden Center Inc .... D....... 310 526-3807
   10780 Santa Monica Blvd Ste 105 Los Angeles (90025) *(P-17200)*

Camden Development Inc .... C....... 949 427-4674
   27261 Las Ramblas Mission Viejo (92691) *(P-8921)*

Camellia Gardens Care Center, Pasadena *Also Called: Highland Hlthcare Cmllia Grdns (P-15515)*

Camelot Theatres, Palm Springs *Also Called: Metropolitan Theatres Corp (P-14003)*

Cameron Energy Services Corp .... D....... 562 321-9183
   4040 Capitol Ave City Of Industry (90601) *(P-20052)*

Cameron Health Inc .... D....... 949 940-4000
   905 Calle Amanecer # 300 San Clemente (92673) *(P-5407)*

Cameron Intrstate Pipeline LLC .... C....... 619 696-3110
   488 8th Ave San Diego (92101) *(P-1201)*

CAMERON PARK COUNTRY CLUB, Cameron Park *Also Called: Cameron Park Country Club Inc (P-14354)*

Cameron Park Country Club Inc .... D....... 530 672-9840
   3201 Royal Dr Cameron Park (95682) *(P-14354)*

Cameron Surface Systems, Bakersfield *Also Called: Cameron West Coast Inc (P-5784)*

Cameron West Coast Inc .... D
   4315 Yeager Way Bakersfield (93313) *(P-5784)*

Camflor Inc .... C....... 831 726-1330
   2364 Riverside Rd Watsonville (95076) *(P-6855)*

Camico Mutual Insurance Co (PA) .... D....... 800 652-1772
   1800 Gateway Dr Ste 200 San Mateo (94404) *(P-8428)*

Camino Dialysis Svcs Oak 110, Mountain View *Also Called: El Camino Hospital (P-16981)*

Camino Ruiz Suite 235, San Diego *Also Called: Operation Samahan Inc (P-14939)*

Camp Bow Wow, Los Angeles *Also Called: Camp Bow Wow Franchising Inc (P-358)*

Camp Bow Wow Franchising Inc .... C....... 310 571-6500
   12401 W Olympic Blvd Los Angeles (90064) *(P-358)*

Camp Glenn Rocky, San Dimas *Also Called: County of Los Angeles (P-17929)*

Camp Jones Gulch YMCA, La Honda *Also Called: Young MNS Chrstn Assn San Fmc (P-18994)*

Camp Pendleton Hospital, Oceanside *Also Called: Marine Corps United States (P-16687)*

Campaign Monitor, San Francisco *Also Called: Marigold (P-11732)*

Campbell Christian School .... D....... 408 370-4900
   1075 W Campbell Ave Campbell (95008) *(P-17698)*

Campbell Construction, Chino *Also Called: Campbell Painting Inc (P-1608)*

Campbell Painting Inc .... D....... 919 591-4300
   14175 Telephone Ave Ste M Chino (91710) *(P-1608)*

Campbell-Ewald Company .... C....... 310 358-4800
   1840 Century Park E Ste 1600 Los Angeles (90067) *(P-10596)*

Campbell-Ewald-West, Los Angeles *Also Called: Campbell-Ewald Company (P-10596)*

Campo Band Missions Indians .... B....... 619 938-6000
   1800 Golden Acorn Way Campo (91906) *(P-14297)*

Campos Bros Farms .... B....... 559 864-9488
   15516 S Walnut Ave Caruthers (93609) *(P-90)*

Campos Bros. Farms, Caruthers *Also Called: Campos Bros Farms (P-90)*

Campos Family Farms LLC .... D....... 559 275-3000
   4726 W Jacquelyn Ave Fresno (93722) *(P-172)*

Campton Place Hotel, San Francisco *Also Called: Southbourne Inc (P-10257)*

Campton Place, A Taj Hotel, San Francisco *Also Called: Ihms (sf) LLC (P-9907)*

Campus By The Sea, Avalon *Also Called: Intervrsity Chrstn Fllwshp/Usa (P-10405)*

Campus Commons Imaging, Sacramento *Also Called: Sutter Health (P-15112)*

Camstar International Inc .... D....... 909 931-2540
   939 W 9th St Upland (91786) *(P-5724)*

Camston Wrather LLC .... C....... 858 525-9999
   2856 Whiptail Loop Carlsbad (92010) *(P-20651)*

Can-AM Plumbing Inc .... C....... 925 846-1833
   151 Wyoming St Pleasanton (94566) *(P-1393)*

Canaccord Genuity LLC .... C....... 415 229-7171
   44 Montgomery St Ste 1600 San Francisco (94104) *(P-8069)*

Canada Pension Plan Inv Bd, San Francisco *Also Called: Cppib America Inc (P-9503)*

Canal Alliance .... C....... 415 485-3074
   91 Larkspur St San Rafael (94901) *(P-17398)*

Canandaigua Wine Company Inc .... D....... 559 673-7071
   12667 Road 24 Madera (93637) *(P-6790)*

Cancer Center of Santa Barbara .... D....... 805 898-2182
   2410 Fletcher Ave Ste 104 Santa Barbara (93105) *(P-14650)*

Cancer Prevention Inst Cal (PA) .... C....... 510 608-5000
   1 Blackfield Dr Belvedere Tiburon (94920) *(P-19873)*

Cancom USA, Fremont *Also Called: HPM Incorporated (P-5312)*

Candlewood Suites, Turlock *Also Called: Turlock Hospitality LLC (P-10329)*

Candy Cane Inn, Anaheim *Also Called: Cinderella Motel (P-9703)*

Canepas Car Wash .... D....... 209 951-9772
   642 N Hunter St Stockton (95202) *(P-13689)*

Canine Cmpnons For Indpendence (PA) .... D....... 707 577-1700
   2965 Dutton Ave Santa Rosa (95407) *(P-359)*

Cannasafe, Van Nuys *Also Called: Csa Silicon Valley LLC (P-16713)*

Cannasafe, Van Nuys *Also Called: Consumer Safety Analytics LLC (P-19960)*

Cannon, San Luis Obispo *Also Called: Cannon Corporation (P-19523)*

Cannon Corporation (PA) .... D....... 805 544-7407
   1050 Southwood Dr San Luis Obispo (93401) *(P-19523)*

Canon Business Solutions-West Inc .... B....... 310 217-3000
   110 W Walnut St Gardena (90248) *(P-5243)*

ALPHABETIC SECTION — Captiva Software Corporation

Canon Medical Systems USA Inc (DH) .... B 714 730-5000
  2441 Michelle Dr Tustin (92780) *(P-5408)*
Canon Recruiting Group LLC .... B 661 252-7400
  27651 Lincoln Pl Ste 250 Santa Clarita (91387) *(P-11277)*
Canon USA Inc .... B 949 753-4000
  15955 Alton Pkwy Irvine (92618) *(P-5235)*
Canopy By Hlton San Frncsco So, San Francisco *Also Called: Paradigm Hotels Group LLC (P-10097)*
Canopy Energy, Van Nuys *Also Called: Energy Enterprises USA Inc (P-1429)*
Canteen Refreshment Services, Hayward *Also Called: Compass Group Usa Inc (P-13240)*
Canteen Vending, Garden Grove *Also Called: Compass Group Usa Inc (P-11027)*
Canteen Vending - San Diego .... A 619 527-1900
  5515 Market St San Diego (92114) *(P-6457)*
Canterbury Hotel Corp .... D 415 345-3200
  750 Sutter St San Francisco (94109) *(P-9677)*
Canterbury, The, Pls Vrds Pnsl *Also Called: Episcopal Communities & Servic (P-15464)*
Canton Food Co Inc .... C 213 688-7707
  750 S Alameda St Los Angeles (90021) *(P-6244)*
Canvas Worldwide LLC .... C 424 303-4300
  12015 Bluff Creek Dr Playa Vista (90094) *(P-10708)*
Canyon, Los Angeles *Also Called: Canyon Partners Incorporated (P-8070)*
Canyon Crest Country Club Inc .... D 951 274-7900
  975 Country Club Dr Riverside (92506) *(P-14355)*
Canyon Partners Incorporated (HQ) .... D 310 272-1000
  2000 Ave Of The Strs 11 Fl Los Angeles (90067) *(P-8070)*
Canyon Ridge Hospital Inc .... B 909 590-3700
  5353 G St Chino (91710) *(P-16646)*
Canyon Springs Pkwy Qsr LLC .... D 951 413-6081
  6231 Valley Springs Pkwy Riverside (92507) *(P-13225)*
Canyon View Capital, Santa Cruz *Also Called: Canyon View Capital Inc (P-9464)*
Canyon View Capital Inc .... D 831 480-6335
  331 Soquel Ave Ste 100 Santa Cruz (95062) *(P-9464)*
CANYON VILLAS, San Diego *Also Called: San Dego Chrstn Foundation Inc (P-19026)*
Cap Diagnostics LLC .... C 714 966-1221
  15545 Sand Canyon Ave Irvine (92618) *(P-16708)*
Cap-Mpt (PA) .... C 213 473-8600
  333 S Hope St Fl 8 Los Angeles (90071) *(P-8429)*
Cap-Mpt, Los Angeles *Also Called: Coopertive Amrcn Physcians Inc (P-18746)*
Capable Transport Inc .... D 310 697-0198
  3528 Torrance Blvd Ste 220 Torrance (90503) *(P-3992)*
Capay Fruits and Vegetables, Capay *Also Called: Capay Incorporated (P-6522)*
Capay Incorporated (PA) .... D 530 796-0730
  23804 State Highway 16 Capay (95607) *(P-6522)*
Capay Organic, West Sacramento *Also Called: Farm Fresh To You LLC (P-178)*
Capc Inc .... D 562 693-8826
  7702 Washington Ave Ste A Whittier (90602) *(P-18570)*
Capc Adult Services, Whittier *Also Called: Whittier Union High Schl Dist (P-17759)*
Capcom Entertainment Inc .... D 650 350-6500
  185 Berry St San Francisco (94107) *(P-5987)*
Capcom U S A Inc (HQ) .... C 650 350-6500
  185 Berry St Ste 1200 San Francisco (94107) *(P-5988)*
Capcom U.S.a, San Francisco *Also Called: Capcom Entertainment Inc (P-5987)*
Cape Inc .... D 925 443-3434
  2406 Armstrong St Livermore (94551) *(P-17699)*
Capgemini America Inc .... D 415 796-6777
  427 Brannan St San Francisco (94107) *(P-12749)*
Capincrouse LLP .... D 925 201-1187
  5990 Stoneridge Dr Pleasanton (94588) *(P-19548)*
CAPINCROUSE LLP, Pleasanton *Also Called: Capincrouse LLP (P-19548)*
Capiot Software Inc .... C 408 216-7010
  2055 Laurelwood Rd Ste 210 Santa Clara (95054) *(P-12750)*
Capistrano Volkswagen, San Juan Capistrano *Also Called: Mission Volkswagen Inc (P-7260)*
Capital Beverage Company (PA) .... C 916 371-8164
  2500 Del Monte St West Sacramento (95691) *(P-6754)*
Capital City Drywall Inc .... D 916 331-9200
  6525 32nd St Ste B1 North Highlands (95660) *(P-1917)*
Capital Commercial Property, Culver City *Also Called: Property Management Assoc Inc (P-9147)*
Capital Drywall LP .... C 909 599-6818
  333 S Grand Ave Ste 4070 Los Angeles (90071) *(P-1918)*

Capital Engineering, Long Beach *Also Called: Capital Engineering LLC (P-19172)*
Capital Engineering Cons, Rancho Cordova *Also Called: Capital Engineering Cons Inc (P-19171)*
Capital Engineering Cons Inc (PA) .... D 916 851-3500
  11020 Sun Center Dr Ste 100 Rancho Cordova (95670) *(P-19171)*
Capital Engineering LLC .... D 562 612-1302
  2830 Temple Ave Long Beach (90806) *(P-19172)*
Capital Eye Medical Group .... C 916 241-9378
  6620 Coyle Ave Ste 408 Carmichael (95608) *(P-14651)*
Capital Group, Irvine *Also Called: American Funds Service Company (P-8229)*
Capital Group Companies Inc (PA) .... A 213 486-9200
  333 S Hope St Fl 55 Los Angeles (90071) *(P-8196)*
Capital Group, The, Los Angeles *Also Called: Capital Group Companies Inc (P-8196)*
Capital Guardian Trust Company (HQ) .... D 213 486-9200
  333 S Hope St Fl 52 Los Angeles (90071) *(P-9422)*
Capital Insurance Group, Monterey *Also Called: California Capital Insur Co (P-8379)*
Capital Intl Investors .... D 213 486-9200
  333 S Hope St Ste 2500 Los Angeles (90071) *(P-9496)*
Capital Invstmnts Vntures Corp (PA) .... C 949 858-0647
  30151 Tomas Rcho Sta Marg (92688) *(P-18743)*
Capital Mortgage Services, Ventura *Also Called: E&S Financial Group Inc (P-7956)*
Capital Network Funding Svcs, Los Angeles *Also Called: Capnet Financial Services Inc (P-7918)*
Capital Oversight, Santa Monica *Also Called: Capital Oversight Inc (P-20717)*
Capital Oversight Inc (PA) .... D 310 453-8000
  2118 Wilshire Blvd Ste 1000 Santa Monica (90403) *(P-20717)*
Capital Research and MGT Co (HQ) .... B 213 486-9200
  333 S Hope St Fl 55 Los Angeles (90071) *(P-8197)*
Capital Transitional Care, Sacramento *Also Called: Covenant Care California LLC (P-15398)*
Capitalsource Bank .... C 714 989-4600
  130 S State College Blvd Brea (92821) *(P-7668)*
Capitalsource Inc .... A 213 443-7700
  633 W 5th St 33rd Fl Los Angeles (90071) *(P-7917)*
Capitol Barricade Inc (PA) .... D 916 451-5176
  6001 Elvas Ave Sacramento (95819) *(P-5824)*
Capitol Builders Hardware Inc (HQ) .... D 916 451-2821
  4699 24th St Sacramento (95822) *(P-1991)*
Capitol Casino .... C 916 446-0700
  411 N 16th St Sacramento (95811) *(P-14503)*
Capitol Door Service, Sacramento *Also Called: Capitol Builders Hardware Inc (P-1991)*
Capitol Drive-In, San Jose *Also Called: Century Theatres Inc (P-13983)*
Capitol Records, Los Angeles *Also Called: Medholdings of Newnan LLC (P-13367)*
Capitol Regency LLC .... B 916 443-1234
  1209 L St Sacramento (95814) *(P-9678)*
Capitol Services Inc .... C 916 443-0657
  3609 Bradshaw Rd Ste H # 343 Sacramento (95827) *(P-20307)*
Capitola Imports Inc .... C 831 462-4200
  4200 Auto Plaza Dr Capitola (95010) *(P-7179)*
Capnet Financial Services Inc (PA) .... D 877 980-0558
  11901 Santa Monica Blvd Los Angeles (90025) *(P-7918)*
Cappstone Inc .... C 415 821-6757
  1699 Valencia St San Francisco (94110) *(P-10872)*
Caps Payroll, Burbank *Also Called: New Talco Enterprises LLC (P-19615)*
CAPSBC, San Bernardino *Also Called: Community Action Prtnr San Brn (P-18578)*
Capstone Logistics, Moreno Valley *Also Called: Capstone Logistics LLC (P-4146)*
Capstone Logistics LLC .... C 770 414-1929
  12661 Aldi Pl Moreno Valley (92555) *(P-4146)*
Capstone Logistics LLC .... C 209 858-1401
  16888 Mckinley Ave Lathrop (95330) *(P-4147)*
Capstone Partners .... D 949 660-1717
  4695 Macarthur Ct Ste 1000 Newport Beach (92660) *(P-20718)*
Capsule Manufacturing Inc .... D 949 245-4151
  1399 N Miller St Anaheim (92806) *(P-609)*
Capsule Mfg, Anaheim *Also Called: Capsule Manufacturing Inc (P-609)*
Captain Kirk Services Inc .... D 408 320-0230
  1190 Coleman Ave San Jose (95110) *(P-6033)*
Captain Marketing Inc .... D 310 402-9709
  3577 N Figueroa St Los Angeles (90065) *(P-20308)*
Captiva Software Corporation (DH) .... D 858 320-1000
  10145 Pacific Heights Blvd San Diego (92121) *(P-12430)*

Captivateiq Inc .... D 650 930-0619
480 2nd St Ste 100 San Francisco (94107) *(P-11482)*

Car Wash Partners Inc .... C 661 377-1020
2619 Mount Vernon Ave Bakersfield (93306) *(P-13690)*

Car Wash Partners Inc .... D 661 231-3689
5375 Olive Dr Bakersfield (93308) *(P-13691)*

CAR WASH PARTNERS INC., Bakersfield *Also Called: Car Wash Partners Inc (P-13691)*

CAR WASH PARTNERS, INC., Bakersfield *Also Called: Car Wash Partners Inc (P-13690)*

Cara Communications LLC .... D 310 442-5600
12233 W Olympic Blvd Ste 170 Los Angeles (90064) *(P-13928)*

Carat N Amer Dntsu Ageis Ntwrk .... D 310 255-1000
5800 Bristol Pkwy 5th Fl Culver City (90230) *(P-10726)*

Carbon Five, San Francisco *Also Called: Carbonfive Incorporated (P-11483)*

Carbon Health Technologies Inc .... C 805 226-4222
500 First St Paso Robles (93446) *(P-14652)*

Carbon Health Technologies Inc .... C 650 318-3384
500 E Remington Dr Ste 20 Sunnyvale (94087) *(P-14653)*

Carbon Health Technologies Inc .... C 714 710-3030
1421 W Macarthur Blvd Ste E Santa Ana (92704) *(P-14654)*

Carbon Health Technologies Inc .... C 760 603-3221
6971 El Camino Real Ste 101 Carlsbad (92009) *(P-15256)*

Carbon Health Technologies Inc .... C 510 844-4097
411 Grand Ave Oakland (94610) *(P-15966)*

Carbon Lighthouse Inc .... C 415 787-3550
343 Sansome St Ste 700 San Francisco (94104) *(P-19173)*

Carbonfive Incorporated .... D 415 546-0500
201 Mission St Ste 1800 San Francisco (94105) *(P-11483)*

Cardiac Noninvasive Laboratory, Los Angeles *Also Called: Cedars-Sinai Medical Center (P-14662)*

Cardiac Unit, Anaheim *Also Called: Anaheim Regional Medical Ctr (P-15946)*

Cardiff Transportation, Palm Desert *Also Called: Gary Cardiff Enterprises Inc (P-3265)*

Cardinal C G, Moreno Valley *Also Called: Cardinal Glass Industries Inc (P-2688)*

Cardinal Glass Industries Inc .... C 951 485-9007
24100 Cardinal Ave Moreno Valley (92551) *(P-2688)*

Cardinal Health Inc .... D 916 372-9880
3238 Dwight Rd Elk Grove (95758) *(P-6099)*

Cardinal Health Inc .... D 661 295-6100
27680 Avenue Mentry Valencia (91355) *(P-6100)*

Cardinal Transportation, Gardena *Also Called: First Student Inc (P-3344)*

Cardio Vascular Associates .... D 559 439-6808
1313 E Herndon Ave Ste 203 Fresno (93720) *(P-14655)*

Cardiodx Inc .... C 650 475-2788
3945 Freedom Cir Ste 560 Santa Clara (95054) *(P-16709)*

Cardiology, Long Beach *Also Called: Memorial Crdolgy Med Group Inc (P-14893)*

Cardionet Inc .... D 619 243-7500
750 B St Ste 1400 San Diego (92101) *(P-14656)*

CARDIONET, INC., San Diego *Also Called: Cardionet Inc (P-14656)*

Cardiovascular Consultants Hea .... D 559 432-4303
1207 E Herndon Ave Fresno (93720) *(P-14657)*

Cardno Eri, Lake Forest *Also Called: Environmental Resolutions Inc (P-20745)*

Cardservice International Inc (DH) .... B
5898 Condor Dr # 220 Moorpark (93021) *(P-13226)*

Care 1st Health Plan (PA) .... C 323 889-6638
601 Potrero Grande Dr Fl 2 Monterey Park (91755) *(P-8260)*

Care 2 .... D 650 622-0860
203 Redwood Shores Pkwy Ste 230 Redwood City (94065) *(P-19075)*

Care A Van Transport, Carlsbad *Also Called: CAV Inc (P-3248)*

Care Ambulance, San Diego *Also Called: Care Medical Trnsp Inc (P-3246)*

Care Ambulance, Orange *Also Called: Lifestar Response of Alabama (P-3273)*

Care Choice Health Systems Inc .... D 760 798-4508
2236 Lone Oak Ln Vista (92084) *(P-15828)*

Care Choice Home Care, Vista *Also Called: Care Choice Health Systems Inc (P-15828)*

Care Management Services, Sacramento *Also Called: Davis Uc Medical Center (P-16036)*

Care Medical Trnsp Inc .... C 858 653-4520
9770 Candida St San Diego (92126) *(P-3246)*

Care Network, Napa *Also Called: Queen of Vly Med Ctr Fundation (P-16355)*

Care Options Management Plans .... A 925 551-3227
7000 Village Pkwy Ste A Dublin (94568) *(P-16833)*

Care Stffing Professionals Inc .... D 909 906-2060
2151 E Convention Center Way Ste 204 Ontario (91764) *(P-11278)*

Care Unlimited Health Svcs Inc .... D 626 332-3767
1025 W Arrow Hwy Ste 103 Glendora (91740) *(P-16834)*

Carecredit LLC .... C 800 300-3046
555 Anton Blvd Ste 700 Costa Mesa (92626) *(P-13227)*

Caredx Inc (PA) .... B 415 287-2300
8000 Marina Blvd Fl 4 Brisbane (94005) *(P-16710)*

Career Group Inc (PA) .... A 310 277-8188
10100 Santa Monica Blvd Ste 900 Los Angeles (90067) *(P-11102)*

Career Group Inc .... C 415 781-8188
345 California St Ste 1650 San Francisco (94104) *(P-11103)*

Career Strategies Tmpry Inc .... C 909 230-4504
9267 Haven Ave Ste 225 Rancho Cucamonga (91730) *(P-11104)*

Career Strategies Tmpry Inc .... C 818 883-0440
21031 Ventura Blvd Ste 1005 Woodland Hills (91364) *(P-11105)*

Career Strategies Tmpry Inc .... C 925 296-9600
1990 N California Blvd # 8 Walnut Creek (94596) *(P-11106)*

Career Strategies Tmpry Inc .... C 760 564-5959
78060 Calle Estado La Quinta (92253) *(P-11107)*

Career Strategies Tmpry Inc .... C 925 296-9600
1755 Locust St Walnut Creek (94596) *(P-11108)*

Career Strategies Tmpry Inc .... C 714 824-6840
575 Anton Blvd Ste 630 Costa Mesa (92626) *(P-11109)*

Carefree Communities, Newbury Park *Also Called: Carefree Communities Inc (P-8879)*

Carefree Communities Inc .... C 805 498-2612
1251 Old Conejo Rd Newbury Park (91320) *(P-8879)*

Carefusion 207 Inc .... B 760 778-7200
1100 Bird Center Dr Palm Springs (92262) *(P-3050)*

Carefusion Corporation (HQ) .... B 858 617-2000
3750 Torrey View Ct San Diego (92130) *(P-3074)*

Careismatic Brands Inc (PA) .... C 818 671-2100
9800 De Soto Ave Chatsworth (91311) *(P-2684)*

Carelon Bhavioral Hlth Cal Inc .... A 800 228-1286
12898 Towne Center Dr Cerritos (90703) *(P-8520)*

Carelon Med Benefits MGT Inc .... A 847 310-0366
505 N Brand Blvd Glendale (91203) *(P-8261)*

Caremore AP, Cerritos *Also Called: Caremore Medical Management Company A California Limited Partnership (P-20053)*

Caremore Health Plan (HQ) .... C 562 622-2950
12900 Park Plaza Dr Ste 150 Cerritos (90703) *(P-8262)*

Caremore Insurance Services, Cerritos *Also Called: Caremore Health Plan (P-8262)*

Caremore Medical Management Company A California Limited Partnership 562 741-4300
12900 Park Plaza Dr # 150 Cerritos (90703) *(P-20053)*

Careonsite Inc .... B 562 437-0381
1805 Arnold Dr Martinez (94553) *(P-14658)*

Careray USA, Santa Clara *Also Called: Compass Innovations Inc (P-2660)*

Cares, San Diego *Also Called: Center For Atism RES Evltion S (P-17020)*

Cares Community Health .... C 916 443-3299
1500 21st St Sacramento (95811) *(P-14659)*

Careworks Health Services .... D 949 859-4700
5151 Oceanus Dr Ste 102 Huntington Beach (92649) *(P-17859)*

Cargo Service Center, Los Angeles *Also Called: Swissport Cargo Services LP (P-3914)*

Cargo Solution Brokerage Inc .... C 909 350-1644
14587 Valley Blvd Fontana (92335) *(P-3378)*

Cargo Solution Express Inc (PA) .... C 909 350-1644
14587 Valley Blvd # 89 Fontana (92335) *(P-3452)*

Cargomatic Inc (PA) .... C 866 513-2343
211 E Ocean Blvd Ste 350 Long Beach (90802) *(P-3993)*

Carinet, San Diego *Also Called: Fortitude Technology Inc (P-4274)*

Carl Ziss X-Ray Microscopy Inc .... D 925 701-3600
5300 Central Pkwy Dublin (94568) *(P-3070)*

Carl's Jr., Carpinteria *Also Called: Carls Jr Restaurants LLC (P-7463)*

Carls Jr Restaurants LLC .... D 805 684-6388
6307 Carpinteria Ave Ste A Carpinteria (93013) *(P-7463)*

Carlsbad By The Sea, Carlsbad *Also Called: Front Porch Communities & Svcs (P-8814)*

Carlsbad Firefighters Assn .... D 760 729-3730
2560 Orion Way Carlsbad (92010) *(P-19076)*

Carlsbad Premium Outlets, Carlsbad *Also Called: Premium Outlet Partners LP (P-8750)*

Carlsbad Properties Inc .... D 760 438-7880
850 Palomar Airport Rd Carlsbad (92011) *(P-9679)*

Carlson Barbee & Gibson Inc .... D 925 866-0322
2633 Camino Ramon San Ramon (94583) *(P-19174)*

ALPHABETIC SECTION

Carlton Senior Living Inc .... C....... 408 972-1400
380 Branham Ln Ofc Ofc San Jose (95136) *(P-18384)*

Carlton Senior Living Inc .... C....... 925 935-1001
175 Cleaveland Rd Pleasant Hill (94523) *(P-18385)*

Carlton Senior Living Inc .... D....... 916 971-4800
1075 Fulton Ave Apt 208 Sacramento (95825) *(P-18386)*

Carlyle Group Inc (PA) .... D....... 310 550-8656
9073 Nemo St Ste 100 West Hollywood (90069) *(P-8922)*

Carmax Inc .... C....... 951 387-3887
25560 Madison Ave Murrieta (92562) *(P-7337)*

Carmel Hills Care Center, Monterey *Also Called: Pater Dignitas Inc (P-15623)*

Carmel Mission Inn, Carmel *Also Called: Khp V Carmel Trs LLC (P-9938)*

Carmel Mtn Rhab Healthcare Ctr, San Diego *Also Called: Bernardo Hts Healthcare Inc (P-15818)*

Carmel Partners LLC .... C....... 916 479-5286
530 Wilshire Blvd Ste 203 Santa Monica (90401) *(P-9363)*

Carmel Rlty Carmel Vly Sls Off 831 622-1000
4 E Carmel Valley Rd Carmel Valley (93924) *(P-8923)*

CARMEL VALLEY MANOR, Carmel *Also Called: Northern Cal Cngrgtnal Rtrment (P-15883)*

Carmel Valley Ranch, Carmel *Also Called: Cvr Hsge LLC (P-9736)*

Carmel Village At Clovis, Clovis *Also Called: Generation Clovis LLC (P-18439)*

Carmichael Adult Day Hlth Ctr, Carmichael *Also Called: Eskaton Properties Inc (P-17970)*

Carmichael International Svc (DH) .... D....... 213 353-0800
1200 Corporate Center Dr Ste 200 Monterey Park (91754) *(P-3994)*

Carmichael Rcrtion Pk Dst Fndt .... D....... 916 485-5322
5750 Grant Ave Carmichael (95608) *(P-14504)*

Carmike Cinemas, Thousand Oaks *Also Called: Carmike Cinemas LLC (P-13980)*

Carmike Cinemas LLC .... D....... 805 494-4702
166 W Hillcrest Dr Thousand Oaks (91360) *(P-13980)*

Carnegie Agency Inc .... D....... 805 445-1470
2535 W Hillcrest Dr Newbury Park (91320) *(P-8521)*

Carnegie General Insur Agcy, Newbury Park *Also Called: Carnegie Agency Inc (P-8521)*

Carnegie Institution Wash .... D....... 626 577-1122
813 Santa Barbara St Pasadena (91101) *(P-19874)*

Carnegie Mortgage LLC .... B....... 949 379-7000
15480 Laguna Canyon Rd Ste 100 Irvine (92618) *(P-8031)*

Carneros Inn LLC .... B....... 707 299-4880
4048 Sonoma Hwy Napa (94559) *(P-9680)*

Carol Electric Company Inc .... D....... 562 431-1870
3822 Cerritos Ave Los Alamitos (90720) *(P-1692)*

Carolense Entrmt Group LLC .... D....... 405 493-1120
506 S Spring St Los Angeles (90013) *(P-3082)*

Carollo Engineers, Walnut Creek *Also Called: Carollo Engineers Inc (P-19175)*

Carollo Engineers Inc (PA) .... D....... 925 932-1710
2795 Mitchell Dr Walnut Creek (94598) *(P-19175)*

Carolyn E Wylie Ctr For Chldre 951 683-5193
4164 Brockton Ave Riverside (92501) *(P-17860)*

Carone & Company Inc .... D....... 925 602-8800
5009 Forni Dr Ste A Concord (94520) *(P-2215)*

Carousel Child Care Corp .... C....... 310 216-6641
8333 Airport Blvd Los Angeles (90045) *(P-18275)*

Carpenter Fnds Admnstrtive Off 510 633-0333
265 Hegenberger Rd Ste 100 Oakland (94621) *(P-9423)*

Carpenters Southwest ADM Corp .... C....... 805 688-5581
376 Avenue Of The Flags Buellton (93427) *(P-7464)*

Carpenters Southwest ADM Corp (PA) .... D....... 213 386-8590
533 S Fremont Ave Los Angeles (90071) *(P-9681)*

Carpet USA Ltd (PA) .... D....... 310 390-8570
9310 S La Cienega Blvd Inglewood (90301) *(P-7428)*

Carr McClellan PC (PA) 650 342-9600
216 Park Rd Burlingame (94010) *(P-17399)*

Carr, McClellan, Burlingame *Also Called: Carr McClellan PC (P-17399)*

Carrara Marble Co Amer Inc (PA) .... D....... 626 961-6010
15939 Phoenix Dr City Of Industry (91745) *(P-5196)*

Carrentalscom Inc .... D....... 866 468-9473
655 Montgomery St Ste 600 San Francisco (94111) *(P-3247)*

Carriage Inn, Daly City *Also Called: Reneson Hotels Inc (P-10153)*

Carrier Fire SEC Americas Corp .... C....... 949 737-7800
2955 Red Hill Ave Ste 100 Costa Mesa (92626) *(P-2900)*

Carrier Johnson (PA) .... D....... 619 236-9462
185 W F St Ste 600 San Diego (92101) *(P-19458)*

Carrington Mortgage Svcs LLC .... C....... 559 261-1724
7600 N Ingram Ave Ste 205 Fresno (93711) *(P-8071)*

Carrington Mortgage Svcs LLC .... C....... 909 226-7963
10370 Commerce Center Dr Ste 140 Rancho Cucamonga (91730) *(P-8072)*

Carrington Mrtg Holdings LLC .... C....... 888 267-0584
1600 S Douglass Rd Ste 110 Anaheim (92806) *(P-7943)*

Carroll Burdick Mc Donough LLP (PA) .... C....... 415 989-5900
275 Battery St Ste 2600 San Francisco (94111) *(P-17400)*

Carroll Fulmer Logistics Corp .... B....... 626 435-9940
13773 Algranti Ave Sylmar (91342) *(P-3995)*

Carroll Shelby Licensing Inc .... D....... 310 914-1843
19021 S Figueroa St Gardena (90248) *(P-3681)*

Carrot Behavioral Health, San Carlos *Also Called: Pivot Health Technologies Inc (P-11829)*

Carson Kurtzman Consultants (DH) .... C....... 310 823-9000
2335 Alaska Ave El Segundo (90245) *(P-17401)*

Carson Landscape Industries, Sacramento *Also Called: Frank Carson Ldscp & Maint Inc (P-431)*

Carson Medical Offices, Gardena *Also Called: Kaiser Foundation Hospitals (P-14812)*

Carson Operating Company LLC .... D....... 310 830-9200
2 Civic Plaza Dr Carson (90745) *(P-9682)*

Cartel Marketing Inc .... C....... 818 483-1130
5230 Las Virgenes Rd Ste 250 Calabasas (91302) *(P-8522)*

Cartel Transport LLC .... C....... 209 892-3880
154 Poppy Ave Patterson (95363) *(P-3379)*

Carter & Burgess Inc .... D....... 408 428-2010
2033 Gateway Pl 6th Fl San Jose (95110) *(P-19176)*

Carter & Burgess Inc .... D....... 510 457-0027
300 Frank H Ogawa Plz Ste 10 Oakland (94612) *(P-19459)*

Carter Aston Inc .... C....... 916 431-3922
1601 Response Rd Ste 100 Sacramento (95815) *(P-11110)*

Caruso MGT Ltd A Cal Ltd Prtnr (PA) .... D....... 323 900-8100
101 The Grove Dr Los Angeles (90036) *(P-8924)*

Caruthers Raisin Pkg Co Inc (PA) .... D....... 559 864-9448
12797 S Elm Ave Caruthers (93609) *(P-2354)*

Casa Acquisition Corp .... C....... 400 207-9499
99 Almaden Blvd Ste 400 San Jose (95113) *(P-665)*

Casa Allegra Community Svcs .... D....... 415 499-1116
35 Mitchell Blvd Ste 8 San Rafael (94903) *(P-17861)*

Casa Clina Ctrs For Rhbltation, Pomona *Also Called: Casa Clina Hosp Ctrs For Hlthc (P-15967)*

Casa Clina Hosp Ctrs For Hlthc .... C....... 626 334-8735
910 E Alosta Ave Azusa (91702) *(P-15271)*

Casa Clina Hosp Ctrs For Hlthc (HQ) .... B....... 909 596-7733
255 E Bonita Ave Pomona (91767) *(P-15967)*

Casa Clina Hosp Ctrs For Hlthc .... C....... 760 248-6245
11981 Midway Ave Lucerne Valley (92356) *(P-17862)*

Casa Clina Hosp Ctrs For Hlthc, Pomona *Also Called: Casa Colina Inc (P-17863)*

Casa Colina Inc (PA) .... A....... 909 596-7733
255 E Bonita Ave Pomona (91767) *(P-17863)*

Casa Coloma Health Care Center, Rancho Cordova *Also Called: A B C D Associates (P-15315)*

Casa De Amparo (PA) .... D....... 760 754-5500
325 Buena Creek Rd San Marcos (92069) *(P-18387)*

Casa De Las Campanas Inc (PA) .... D....... 858 451-9152
18655 W Bernardo Dr San Diego (92127) *(P-18388)*

Casa De Manana, La Jolla *Also Called: Front Porch Communities & Svcs (P-8813)*

CASA DE MODESTO, Modesto *Also Called: Fellowship Homes Inc (P-18432)*

Casa Dorinda, Santa Barbara *Also Called: Montecito Retirement Assn (P-15590)*

Casa Logistics LLC 949 636-3391
1403 Jinette San Clemente (92673) *(P-4148)*

Casa Madrona Hotel and Spa, Sausalito *Also Called: Casa Madrona Hotel and Spa LLC (P-9683)*

Casa Madrona Hotel and Spa LLC .... A....... 415 332-0502
801 Bridgeway Sausalito (94965) *(P-9683)*

CASA PACIFICA, Camarillo *Also Called: Casa Pcfica Ctrs For Chldren F (P-17864)*

Casa Palmera LLC .... D....... 888 481-4481
14750 El Camino Real Del Mar (92014) *(P-17019)*

Casa Pcfica Ctrs For Chldren F (PA) .... C....... 805 482-3260
1722 S Lewis Rd Camarillo (93012) *(P-17864)*

Casa Raphael, Vista *Also Called: Alpha Project For Homeless (P-17826)*

Casa Sandoval, Hayward *Also Called: Casa Sandoval LLC (P-8797)*

Casa Sandoval LLC   **ALPHABETIC SECTION**

Casa Sandoval LLC .... D...... 510 727-1700
   1200 Russell Way Hayward (94541) *(P-8797)*

Casa-Pacifica Inc .... B...... 951 658-3369
   2200 W Acacia Ave Ofc Hemet (92545) *(P-18389)*

Casa-Pacifica Inc .... B...... 951 766-5116
   2400 W Acacia Ave Hemet (92545) *(P-18390)*

Casabella Holdings LLC .... D...... 845 348-0012
   9409 Buffalo Ave Rancho Cucamonga (91730) *(P-5082)*

Casanova Publicidad LLC .... D...... 949 271-6344
   3337 Susan St Ste 200 Costa Mesa (92626) *(P-10597)*

Casanoval/Mccann, Costa Mesa *Also Called: Casanova Publicidad LLC (P-10597)*

Casas, San Diego *Also Called: Casas International Brkg Inc (P-3682)*

Casas International Brkg Inc (PA) .... D...... 619 661-6162
   9355 Airway Rd Ste 4 San Diego (92154) *(P-3682)*

Cascade Turf LLC .... C...... 909 626-8586
   4811 Brooks St Montclair (91763) *(P-5807)*

Case Dealer Holding Company, Sacramento *Also Called: Case Power and Equipment (P-5785)*

Case Medical Group, Sacramento *Also Called: Central Ansthsia Svc Exch Med (P-14665)*

Case Power and Equipment .... C...... 916 649-0096
   1751 Bell Ave Sacramento (95838) *(P-5785)*

Casecentral Inc (DH) .... D...... 415 989-2300
   1055 E Colorado Blvd Ste 400 Pasadena (91106) *(P-13228)*

Casecentral.com, Pasadena *Also Called: Casecentral Inc (P-13228)*

Casela Technologies USA .... D...... 650 892-8480
   1525 Mccarthy Blvd Ste 1000 Milpitas (95035) *(P-4533)*

Casestack LLC (HQ) .... D...... 310 473-8885
   3000 Ocean Park Blvd Ste 1000 Santa Monica (90405) *(P-3683)*

Casetext Inc .... C...... 317 407-0790
   330 Townsend St Ste 100 San Francisco (94107) *(P-11484)*

Casey Company (PA) .... C...... 562 436-9685
   180 E Ocean Blvd Ste 1010 Long Beach (90802) *(P-6724)*

Casey Securities Inc (PA) .... C...... 415 544-5030
   301 Pine St San Francisco (94104) *(P-8073)*

Casey-Fogli Con Contrs Inc (PA) .... D...... 510 887-0837
   1970 National Ave Hayward (94545) *(P-2104)*

Cash It Here, Santa Ana *Also Called: Continental Currency Svcs Inc (P-7843)*

Cashcall Inc .... A...... 949 752-4600
   1 City Blvd W Ste 102 Orange (92868) *(P-7871)*

Cashedge Inc .... D...... 408 541-3900
   525 Almanor Ave Ste 150 Sunnyvale (94085) *(P-13229)*

Cashmere Agency Inc .... C...... 323 928-5080
   5242 W Adams Blvd Los Angeles (90016) *(P-20309)*

Cashnet, Oakland *Also Called: Higher One Payments Inc (P-12222)*

Casino, Hopland *Also Called: Hopland Band Pomo Indians Inc (P-14534)*

Casino San Pablo, San Pablo *Also Called: Lytton Rancheria (P-9992)*

Casino Table Rentals, Westminster *Also Called: All-In Prdctons Csino Rntals L (P-11018)*

Cask, San Diego *Also Called: Cask Nx LLC (P-20719)*

Cask Nx LLC .... C...... 858 232-8900
   8910 University Center Ln Ste 400 San Diego (92122) *(P-20719)*

Casper Company .... C...... 619 589-6001
   3825 Bancroft Dr Spring Valley (91977) *(P-2105)*

Caspian Commercial Plbg Inc .... D...... 818 649-2500
   711 Ivy St Glendale (91204) *(P-1394)*

Cass, El Cajon *Also Called: Cass Construction Inc (P-1202)*

Cass Inc (PA) .... D...... 510 893-6476
   2730 Peralta St Oakland (94607) *(P-6005)*

Cass Construction Inc (PA) .... B...... 619 590-0929
   1100 Wagner Dr El Cajon (92020) *(P-1202)*

Cassy .... C...... 408 493-5289
   544 Valley Way Milpitas (95035) *(P-18829)*

Cast & Crew LLC (PA) .... C...... 818 570-6180
   2300 W Empire Ave Ste 500 Burbank (91504) *(P-19549)*

Cast and Crew Entrmt Svcs, Burbank *Also Called: Cast & Crew LLC (P-19549)*

Cast Iron Systems Inc .... D...... 914 499-1900
   4400 N 1st St San Jose (95134) *(P-12431)*

Castaway Restaurant, The, Burbank *Also Called: Specialty Restaurants Corp (P-7509)*

Castle & Cooke Investments Inc .... C...... 310 208-3636
   1 Dole Dr Westlake Village (91362) *(P-891)*

Castle Access Inc .... D...... 858 836-0200
   9606 Aero Dr Ste 1900 San Diego (92123) *(P-4262)*

Castle Creek Country Club Inc .... D...... 760 749-2877
   8797 Circle R Dr Escondido (92026) *(P-14356)*

Castle Global Inc .... C...... 401 523-9531
   575 Market St Fl 15 San Francisco (94105) *(P-11485)*

Castle Manor Inc .... D...... 619 791-7900
   541 S V Ave National City (91950) *(P-15366)*

CASTLE MANOR CONVALESCENT CENT, National City *Also Called: Castle Manor Inc (P-15366)*

Castle Metals Aerospace, Paramount *Also Called: Transtar Metals Corp (P-5528)*

Castle Rock Winery, Sonoma *Also Called: South Bay Wine Group LLC (P-6806)*

Castlehill Properties Inc .... D...... 209 472-9700
   3252 W March Ln Stockton (95219) *(P-9684)*

Castlewood Country Club .... C...... 925 846-2871
   707 Country Club Cir Pleasanton (94566) *(P-14357)*

Castlight Health Inc (HQ) .... D...... 415 829-1400
   150 Spear St Ste 400 San Francisco (94105) *(P-12555)*

Caston Inc .... D...... 909 381-1619
   354 S Allen St San Bernardino (92408) *(P-1919)*

Castro Valley Health Inc .... C...... 510 690-1930
   39 Beta Ct San Ramon (94583) *(P-16835)*

Catalent San Diego Inc .... C...... 858 805-6383
   7330 Carroll Rd Ste 200 San Diego (92121) *(P-19954)*

Catalina Canyon Resort, Avalon *Also Called: Pacific Catalina Hotel Inc (P-10078)*

Catalina Channel Express Inc (HQ) .... C...... 310 519-7971
   385 E Swinford St San Pedro (90731) *(P-3806)*

Catalina Express Cruises, San Pedro *Also Called: Catalina Channel Express Inc (P-3806)*

Catalina Offshore Products Inc .... D...... 619 297-9797
   5202 Lovelock St San Diego (92110) *(P-6467)*

Catalyst Bio Inc .... B...... 650 871-0761
   290 Utah St San Francisco (94103) *(P-19668)*

Catalyst Family Inc (PA) .... D...... 408 556-7300
   350 Woodview Ave Ste 100 Morgan Hill (95037) *(P-18276)*

Catalyst Family Inc .... B...... 831 385-4005
   440 Jayne St Ofc King City (93930) *(P-18277)*

Catalyst Group LLC .... D...... 707 527-8551
   2285 W Hearn Ave Santa Rosa (95407) *(P-20310)*

Catalyst Spech Lngage Pthology, Los Angeles *Also Called: Catalyst Speech LLC (P-20311)*

Catalyst Speech LLC .... B...... 213 346-9945
   205 S Broadway Ste 217 Los Angeles (90012) *(P-20311)*

Catamaran Resort Hotel, San Diego *Also Called: Braemar Partnership (P-9657)*

Catamorphic Co (PA) .... C...... 415 579-3275
   1999 Harrison St Ste 1100 Oakland (94612) *(P-11486)*

Catamunt Brdcstg Chc-Rdding In (PA) .... C...... 530 893-2424
   3460 Silverbell Rd Chico (95973) *(P-4415)*

Catania Worldwide .... B...... 559 664-8400
   21801 Ave Ste 16 Madera (93637) *(P-6523)*

Cataphora Inc (PA) .... D...... 650 622-9840
   3425 Edison Way Menlo Park (94025) *(P-11487)*

Catered Fit Corp 855 400-2348
   13631 Saticoy St Van Nuys (91402) *(P-3380)*

Caterpillar Authorized Dealer, West Sacramento *Also Called: Holt of California (P-5792)*

Caterpillar Authorized Dealer, Stockton *Also Called: Holt of California (P-5793)*

Caterpillar Authorized Dealer, Riverside *Also Called: Johnson Machinery Co (P-5794)*

Caterpillar Authorized Dealer, Corcoran *Also Called: Quinn Company (P-5798)*

Caterpillar Authorized Dealer, Bakersfield *Also Called: Quinn Company (P-5800)*

Caterpillar Authorized Dealer, Oxnard *Also Called: Quinn Company (P-5801)*

Caterpillar Authorized Dealer, Santa Maria *Also Called: Quinn Company (P-5802)*

Caterpillar Authorized Dealer, City Of Industry *Also Called: Quinn Shepherd Machinery (P-5803)*

Caterpillar Authorized Dealer, San Diego *Also Called: Hawthorne Rent-It Service (P-11000)*

Cathay Bank (HQ) .... C...... 626 279-3698
   777 N Broadway Los Angeles (90012) *(P-7669)*

Cathay Capital Trust II .... D...... 213 625-4700
   9650 Flair Dr El Monte (91731) *(P-7670)*

Cathay General Bancorp (PA) .... C...... 213 625-4700
   777 N Broadway Los Angeles (90012) *(P-7671)*

Cathedral At The Crossroads, Castro Valley *Also Called: Neighborhood Church Castro Vly (P-19024)*

Cathedral Pioneer Church Homes (PA) .... D...... 916 442-4906
   415 P St Ofc Sacramento (95814) *(P-15367)*

ALPHABETIC SECTION

CATHOLIC CHARITIES, San Jose *Also Called: Catholic Chrties Snta Clara CN (P-17868)*
Catholic Charities, Ventura *Also Called: Catholic Chrties Snta Clara CN (P-17869)*
CATHOLIC CHARITIES OF EAST BAY, Oakland *Also Called: Catholic Chrties of The Dcese (P-17866)*
Catholic Chrties of The Dcese .... D....... 209 529-3784
  2351 Tenaya Dr # D Modesto (95354) *(P-17865)*
Catholic Chrties # of The Dcese (PA) .... D....... 510 768-3100
  433 Jefferson St Oakland (94607) *(P-17866)*
Catholic Chrties Snta Clara CN .... C....... 408 282-8600
  195 E San Fernando St San Jose (95112) *(P-17867)*
Catholic Chrties Snta Clara CN (PA) .... C....... 408 468-0100
  2625 Zanker Rd Ste 200 San Jose (95134) *(P-17868)*
Catholic Chrties Snta Clara CN .... D....... 805 643-4694
  303 N Ventura Ave Ste A Ventura (93001) *(P-17869)*
Catholic Education Founda .... D....... 213 637-7475
  3424 Wilshire Blvd Ste 24 Los Angeles (90010) *(P-18830)*
Catholic Healthcare West .... A....... 415 668-1000
  450 Stanyan St San Francisco (94117) *(P-15968)*
Catholic Hlthcare W Sthern Cal (HQ) .... C....... 562 491-9000
  1050 Linden Ave Long Beach (90813) *(P-15969)*
Catholic Social Service, Vallejo *Also Called: Roman Cathlic Bishp Sacramento (P-19025)*
Cato Networks Inc .... D....... 646 975-9243
  3031 Tisch Way 110 Plz W San Jose (95128) *(P-12131)*
Cats U S A Pest Control, North Hollywood *Also Called: Cats USA Inc (P-10831)*
Cats USA Inc .... D....... 818 506-1000
  5683 Whitnall Hwy North Hollywood (91601) *(P-10831)*
Catta Verdera Country Club LLC .... D....... 916 645-7200
  1111 Catta Verdera Lincoln (95648) *(P-14358)*
Cattlemens .... D....... 925 447-1224
  2882 Kitty Hawk Rd Livermore (94551) *(P-10533)*
Cattlemens Restaurant, Livermore *Also Called: Cattlemens (P-10533)*
Cattrac, Fontana *Also Called: Cattrac Construction Inc (P-1292)*
Cattrac Construction Inc .... D....... 909 355-1146
  15030 Slover Ave Fontana (92337) *(P-1292)*
Causeway Capital MGT LLC .... C....... 310 231-6100
  11111 Santa Monica Blvd Fl 15 Los Angeles (90025) *(P-9364)*
CAV Inc .... D....... 760 729-5199
  5931 Sea Lion Pl Ste 110 Carlsbad (92010) *(P-3248)*
Cavalier Inn Inc .... D....... 805 927-4688
  9415 Hearst Dr San Simeon (93452) *(P-9685)*
Cavalier Oceanfront Resort, San Simeon *Also Called: Cavalier Inn Inc (P-9685)*
Cavisson Systems Inc .... B....... 800 701-6125
  5201 Great America Pkwy Ste 320 Santa Clara (95054) *(P-20720)*
Caylent Inc .... C....... 800 215-9124
  4521 Campus Dr Ste 344 Irvine (92612) *(P-12751)*
CB Controls, Jurupa Valley *Also Called: Christian Brothers Mechanical Services Inc (P-1396)*
CB Richard Ellis Strgc Prtners .... D....... 213 683-4200
  515 S Flower St Ste 3100 Los Angeles (90071) *(P-8707)*
CB Tang MD Incorporated .... D....... 562 437-0831
  1250 Pacific Ave Long Beach (90813) *(P-14660)*
Cb-1 Hotel .... D....... 415 633-3838
  757 Market St San Francisco (94103) *(P-9686)*
CBA Site Services Inc .... D....... 925 754-7633
  11387 Pyrites Way Rancho Cordova (95670) *(P-20721)*
Cbabr Inc (PA) .... D....... 951 640-7056
  31620 Railroad Canyon Rd Ste A Canyon Lake (92587) *(P-8925)*
Cbec, San Diego *Also Called: Clear Blue Energy Corp (P-2875)*
Cbem LLC Corporate Office .... D....... 415 454-3700
  1101 5th Ave San Rafael (94901) *(P-15272)*
Cbf Electric & Data, San Francisco *Also Called: CBF Inc (P-1693)*
CBF Inc .... C....... 415 495-3085
  735 Battery St Fl 2 San Francisco (94111) *(P-1693)*
Cbiz Life Insur Solutions Inc .... C....... 858 444-3100
  13500 Evening Creek Dr N Ste 450 San Diego (92128) *(P-8523)*
Cbol Corporation .... C....... 818 704-8200
  19850 Plummer St Chatsworth (91311) *(P-5640)*
Cbr Electric Inc .... C....... 949 455-0331
  22 Rancho Cir Lake Forest (92630) *(P-1694)*
Cbr Group .... C....... 415 806-2323
  59 Skipping Rock Way Napa (94558) *(P-20722)*

Cbre, Newport Beach *Also Called: Cbre Globl Value Investors LLC (P-8929)*
Cbre Inc .... D....... 916 446-6800
  500 Capitol Mall Ste 2400 Sacramento (95814) *(P-8926)*
Cbre Inc .... C....... 858 546-4600
  4301 La Jolla Village Dr # 3000 San Diego (92122) *(P-8927)*
Cbre Globl Value Investors LLC (DH) .... C....... 213 683-4200
  601 S Figueroa St Ste 49 Los Angeles (90017) *(P-8928)*
Cbre Globl Value Investors LLC .... C....... 949 725-8500
  3501 Jamboree Rd Ste 100 Newport Beach (92660) *(P-8929)*
CBS, Colton *Also Called: Entercom Media Corp (P-4379)*
CBS, Fresno *Also Called: Entercom Media Corp (P-4380)*
CBS, San Francisco *Also Called: Entercom Media Corp (P-4381)*
CBS, Los Angeles *Also Called: Entercom Media Corp (P-4382)*
CBS, Sacramento *Also Called: Entercom Media Corp (P-4383)*
CBS, San Francisco *Also Called: CBS Broadcasting Inc (P-4416)*
CBS, Studio City *Also Called: CBS Broadcasting Inc (P-4417)*
CBS Broadcasting Inc .... D....... 415 765-0928
  855 Battery St San Francisco (94111) *(P-4416)*
CBS Broadcasting Inc .... C....... 818 655-8500
  4024 Radford Ave Bldg 4 Studio City (91604) *(P-4417)*
CBS Films Inc .... D
  8560 W Sunset Blvd Fl 5 West Hollywood (90069) *(P-4418)*
CBS Interactive Inc (HQ) .... A....... 415 344-2000
  680 Folsom St San Francisco (94107) *(P-10727)*
CBS Maxpreps Inc .... D....... 530 676-6440
  4364 Town Center Blvd Ste 320 El Dorado Hills (95762) *(P-4263)*
CBS Network News, Los Angeles *Also Called: Merlot Film Productions Inc (P-13864)*
CBS Studio Center, Studio City *Also Called: Radford Studio Center LLC (P-14059)*
CBS Studios Inc .... B....... 661 964-6020
  27420 Avenue Scott Ste A Santa Clarita (91355) *(P-4419)*
CBS Studios Inc .... C....... 818 655-5160
  4024 Radford Ave Studio City (91604) *(P-13827)*
Cbsi, San Francisco *Also Called: CBS Interactive Inc (P-10727)*
CC Co Health Cntr Information .... C....... 925 431-2300
  2311 Loveridge Rd Pittsburg (94565) *(P-14661)*
CCC Property Holdings LLC .... C....... 310 609-1957
  7223 Alondra Blvd Paramount (90723) *(P-9306)*
Cccc Growth Fund LLC .... D....... 626 441-8770
  899 El Centro St South Pasadena (91030) *(P-9497)*
CCH Incorporated .... A....... 310 800-9800
  2050 W 190th St Torrance (90504) *(P-12556)*
Cchh Burlingame LLC .... D....... 650 696-2607
  1333 Bayshore Hwy Burlingame (94010) *(P-9687)*
CCM Enterprises (PA) .... D....... 619 562-2605
  10848 Wheatlands Ave Santee (92071) *(P-2501)*
Cco Holdings LLC .... C....... 209 585-1001
  1645 Countryside Dr Turlock (95380) *(P-4476)*
Cco Holdings LLC .... C....... 559 560-5323
  375 N Main St Porterville (93257) *(P-4477)*
Cco Holdings LLC .... C....... 626 500-1214
  3106 San Gabriel Blvd Rosemead (91770) *(P-4478)*
Cco Holdings LLC .... C....... 530 646-4026
  1636 Market St Redding (96001) *(P-4479)*
Cco Holdings LLC .... C....... 310 589-3008
  23841 Malibu Rd Malibu (90265) *(P-4480)*
Cco Holdings LLC .... C....... 562 239-2761
  12319 Norwalk Blvd Norwalk (90650) *(P-4481)*
Cco Holdings LLC .... C....... 559 202-1001
  825 W Henderson Ave Porterville (93257) *(P-4482)*
Cco Holdings LLC .... C....... 626 513-0204
  1151 N Azusa Ave Azusa (91702) *(P-4483)*
Cco Holdings LLC .... C....... 408 413-0317
  681 Leavesley Rd Ste 175 Gilroy (95020) *(P-4484)*
Cco Holdings LLC .... C....... 805 904-1047
  1128 W Branch St Arroyo Grande (93420) *(P-4485)*
Cco Holdings LLC .... C....... 805 400-1002
  1131 Creston Rd Paso Robles (93446) *(P-4486)*
Cco Holdings LLC .... C....... 760 810-4076
  21898 Us Highway 18 Apple Valley (92307) *(P-4487)*
Cco Holdings LLC .... C....... 864 679-1745
  5835 Eastside Rd Redding (96001) *(P-4488)*

Cco Holdings LLC

Cco Holdings LLC .... C....... 805 232-5887
51 W Main St Ste F Ventura (93001) *(P-4489)*

Cco Holdings LLC .... C....... 562 228-1262
2310 N Bellflower Blvd Long Beach (90815) *(P-4490)*

Cco Holdings LLC .... C....... 714 509-5861
2684 N Tustin St Orange (92865) *(P-4491)*

Cco Holdings LLC .... C....... 909 742-8273
26827 Baseline St Highland (92346) *(P-4492)*

Ccof Foundation .... D....... 831 423-2263
2155 Delaware Ave Ste 150 Santa Cruz (95060) *(P-18831)*

Ccpoa, West Sacramento Also Called: Califrnia Crrctnal Pace Offcer *(P-18775)*

Ccpu, San Diego Also Called: Continuous Computing Corp *(P-2803)*

CCS Global Tech, Poway Also Called: Califrnia Crtive Solutions Inc *(P-12748)*

Ccts, Santa Ana Also Called: Satellite Management Co *(P-9175)*

Ccv Engineering & Mfg, Fresno Also Called: Aries Industries Inc *(P-4845)*

CCWD, Concord Also Called: Contra Costa Water District *(P-4778)*

CD, Culver City Also Called: Charles David of California *(P-7410)*

CD Video Manufacturing Inc .... D....... 714 265-0770
12650 Westminster Ave Santa Ana (92706) *(P-2952)*

Cdc San Francisco LLC .... D....... 415 616-6512
888 Howard St San Francisco (94103) *(P-9688)*

Cdcf III PCF Lndmark Scrmnto L .... D....... 310 552-7211
515 S Flower St 44th Fl Los Angeles (90071) *(P-8708)*

CDF Parkway LLC (PA) .... C....... 408 842-7282
10021 Pacheco Pass Hwy Hollister (95023) *(P-7156)*

CDI, Reseda Also Called: Child Development Institute *(P-17879)*

CDI CENTERS, Morgan Hill Also Called: Catalyst Family Inc *(P-18276)*

CDM Constructors Inc .... D....... 909 579-3500
9220 Cleveland Ave Ste 100 Rancho Cucamonga (91730) *(P-19177)*

CDS Moving Equipment Inc (PA) .... D....... 310 631-1100
375 W Manville St Rancho Dominguez (90220) *(P-5825)*

Cds Packing Solutions, Rancho Dominguez Also Called: CDS Moving Equipment Inc *(P-5825)*

Cdsnet LLC .... B....... 310 981-9500
6053 W Century Blvd Los Angeles (90045) *(P-20723)*

Cecelia Packing Corporation .... C....... 559 626-5000
24780 E South Ave Orange Cove (93646) *(P-6524)*

CECILIA GONZALEZ DE AL HOYA CA, Los Angeles Also Called: White Memorial Medical Center *(P-16627)*

Cedar Creek Corporation .... C....... 530 364-2143
15875 Jellys Ferry Rd Red Bluff (96080) *(P-1203)*

Cedar Fair LP .... C....... 408 988-1776
4701 Great America Pkwy Santa Clara (95054) *(P-14300)*

Cedar Holdings LLC .... D....... 909 862-0611
7534 Palm Ave Highland (92346) *(P-15368)*

CEDAR HOUSE REHABILITATION CEN, Bloomington Also Called: Social Science Service Center *(P-16697)*

Cedar Mountain Post Acute, Yucaipa Also Called: Cedar Operations LLC *(P-15369)*

Cedar Operations LLC .... C....... 909 790-2273
11970 4th St Yucaipa (92399) *(P-15369)*

Cedar Sinai .... D....... 310 285-7268
9090 Wilshire Blvd Ste 200 Beverly Hills (90211) *(P-11279)*

Cedars of Marin (PA) .... D....... 415 454-5310
115 Upper Rd Ross (94957) *(P-17700)*

Cedars Surgical Research Ctr, West Hollywood Also Called: Cedars-Sinai Medical Center *(P-15971)*

Cedars-Sinai Home Care, Los Angeles Also Called: Cedars-Sinai Medical Center *(P-15980)*

Cedars-Sinai Medical Center .... B....... 310 423-3849
127 S San Vicente Blvd Rm 3417 Los Angeles (90048) *(P-14662)*

Cedars-Sinai Medical Center .... D....... 310 423-7900
8631 W 3rd St # 800-E Los Angeles (90048) *(P-14663)*

Cedars-Sinai Medical Center .... D....... 310 423-4208
8720 Beverly Blvd Lower Level Ste Ac1010 Los Angeles (90048) *(P-14664)*

Cedars-Sinai Medical Center .... A....... 310 824-3664
8635 W 3rd St Ste 1195 Los Angeles (90048) *(P-15970)*

Cedars-Sinai Medical Center .... B....... 310 855-7701
8700 Beverly Blvd # 4018 West Hollywood (90048) *(P-15971)*

Cedars-Sinai Medical Center .... C....... 310 423-5468
8797 Beverly Blvd Ste 220 West Hollywood (90048) *(P-15972)*

Cedars-Sinai Medical Center .... C....... 310 423-6451
8727 W 3rd St Los Angeles (90048) *(P-15973)*

Cedars-Sinai Medical Center .... C....... 310 423-2587
8730 Alden Dr West 220 Los Angeles (90048) *(P-15974)*

Cedars-Sinai Medical Center .... B....... 310 423-8965
8723 Alden Dr Los Angeles (90048) *(P-15975)*

Cedars-Sinai Medical Center .... C....... 310 423-5841
8700 Beverly Blvd Ste 8211 West Hollywood (90048) *(P-15976)*

Cedars-Sinai Medical Center .... D....... 310 423-5147
8700 Beverly Blvd Ste 2216 West Hollywood (90048) *(P-15977)*

Cedars-Sinai Medical Center .... C....... 310 423-9310
310 N San Vicente Blvd West Hollywood (90048) *(P-15978)*

Cedars-Sinai Medical Center .... C....... 310 967-1884
99 N La Cienega Blvd Ste Mezz Beverly Hills (90211) *(P-15979)*

Cedars-Sinai Medical Center .... B....... 310 423-3277
8635 W 3rd St Ste 1165w Los Angeles (90048) *(P-15980)*

Cedars-Sinai Medical Center .... B....... 310 423-9520
444 S San Vicente Blvd Ste 1001 Los Angeles (90048) *(P-15981)*

Cedars-Sinai Medical Center .... A....... 310 967-1900
4100 W 190th St Torrance (90504) *(P-15982)*

Cedars-Sinai Medical Center .... A....... 310 385-3400
250 N Robertson Blvd # 101 Beverly Hills (90211) *(P-15983)*

Cedars-Sinai Medical Center .... C....... 310 423-8780
8700 Beverly Blvd Ste 1103 West Hollywood (90048) *(P-15984)*

Cedars-Snai Imging Med Group A .... D....... 310 423-8000
8700 Beverly Blvd West Hollywood (90048) *(P-15985)*

Cedarwood-Young Company (PA) .... C....... 626 962-4047
14620 Joanbridge St Baldwin Park (91706) *(P-4876)*

Cederlind Farms LP .... D....... 209 606-8586
2514 Kenney Ave Winton (95388) *(P-70)*

Cei, San Jose Also Called: Cupertino Electric Inc *(P-1717)*

Celebrity Casinos Inc .... B....... 310 631-3838
123 E Artesia Blvd Compton (90220) *(P-9689)*

Celebrtions Pty Rentals Tents, Roseville Also Called: Wright Celebrations Inc *(P-11065)*

Celerity Consulting Group LLC (PA) .... D....... 415 986-8850
2 Gough St Ste 300 San Francisco (94103) *(P-20312)*

Celestial-Saturn Parent Inc (PA) .... C....... 949 214-1000
40 Pacifica Irvine (92618) *(P-12557)*

Celestix Networks Inc .... D....... 510 668-0700
4125 Hopyard Rd Ste 225 Pleasanton (94588) *(P-12432)*

Celex Solutions, Brea Also Called: Contract Services Group Inc *(P-10878)*

Cell Business Equipment, Irvine Also Called: Sema LLC *(P-19630)*

Cell-Crete, Monrovia Also Called: Cell-Crete Corporation *(P-2106)*

Cell-Crete Corporation (PA) .... D....... 626 357-3500
135 Railroad Ave Monrovia (91016) *(P-2106)*

Cellanome, Palo Alto Also Called: Cellanome Inc *(P-19669)*

Cellanome Inc .... D....... 510 736-0922
1810 Embarcadero Rd Ste 200 Palo Alto (94303) *(P-19669)*

Cellco Partnership .... D....... 925 245-0494
2428 Las Positas Rd Livermore (94551) *(P-4187)*

Cellco Partnership .... D....... 530 477-8042
682 Freeman Ln Grass Valley (95949) *(P-4188)*

Cellco Partnership .... D....... 916 838-9525
5815 Stockton Blvd Ste D Sacramento (95824) *(P-4189)*

Cellco Partnership .... D....... 714 564-0050
691 S Main St Ste 80 Orange (92868) *(P-4190)*

Cellco Partnership .... D....... 310 603-0101
237 E Compton Blvd Compton (90220) *(P-4191)*

Cellco Partnership .... D....... 559 321-8116
300 W Shaw Ave Clovis (93612) *(P-4192)*

Cellco Partnership .... D....... 831 475-3100
1440 41st Ave Ste B Capitola (95010) *(P-4193)*

Cellco Partnership .... D....... 714 256-6015
2500 E Imperial Hwy Ste 178 Brea (92821) *(P-4194)*

Cellco Partnership .... D....... 760 642-0430
258 N El Camino Real Ste A Encinitas (92024) *(P-4195)*

Cellco Partnership .... D....... 661 296-7585
26445 Bouquet Canyon Rd Santa Clarita (91350) *(P-4196)*

Cellco Partnership .... D....... 661 765-5397
407 Kern St Taft (93268) *(P-4197)*

Cellco Partnership .... D....... 951 205-4170
20 City Blvd W Orange (92868) *(P-4198)*

Cellco Partnership .... D....... 323 662-0009
2921 Los Feliz Blvd Los Angeles (90039) *(P-4199)*

ALPHABETIC SECTION **Central Coast Pathology Lab**

Cellco Partnership ....D....... 408 846-5170
   6965 Camino Arroyo Ste 60 Gilroy (95020) *(P-4200)*

Cellco Partnership ....D....... 760 568-5542
   71800 Highway 111 Ste A110 Rancho Mirage (92270) *(P-4201)*

Cellco Partnership ....D....... 949 472-0700
   23718 El Toro Rd Ste A Lake Forest (92630) *(P-4202)*

Cellco Partnership ....D....... 714 258-8870
   2687 Park Ave Tustin (92782) *(P-4203)*

Cellco Partnership ....D....... 209 474-9071
   10952 Trinity Pkwy Stockton (95219) *(P-4204)*

Cellco Partnership ....D....... 562 244-8814
   11902 Gem St Norwalk (90650) *(P-4205)*

Cellco Partnership ....D....... 760 662-5914
   12821 Main St Hesperia (92345) *(P-4206)*

Cellco Partnership ....D....... 909 591-9740
   3825 Grand Ave Chino (91710) *(P-4207)*

Cellmark Inc (DH) ....**D....... 415 927-1700**
   88 Rowland Way Ste 300 Novato (94945) *(P-6034)*

Cellmark Pulp & Paper Inc ....D....... 415 927-1700
   22 Pelican Way San Rafael (94901) *(P-6035)*

Cellular One, Larkspur *Also Called: Blackwater Cellular Corp (P-4186)*

Celmol Inc ....D....... 714 259-1000
   1611 E Saint Andrew Pl Santa Ana (92705) *(P-6896)*

Celtic Commercial Finance, Irvine *Also Called: Celtic Leasing Corp (P-11023)*

Celtic Leasing Corp ....D....... 949 263-3880
   4 Park Plz Ste 300 Irvine (92614) *(P-11023)*

Cement Cutting Inc ....D....... 619 296-9592
   3610 Hancock St Frnt San Diego (92110) *(P-2107)*

Cemetery District- Clovis, Clovis *Also Called: County of Fresno (P-20923)*

Cemex, Pleasanton *Also Called: RMC Pacific Materials LLC (P-2697)*

Cemex Cement Inc ....C....... 626 969-1747
   1201 W Gladstone St Azusa (91702) *(P-5197)*

Cemex Corp ....C....... 800 992-3639
   22101 W Sunset Ave Los Banos (93635) *(P-5198)*

Cemex Corp ....C....... 800 992-3639
   808 Gilman St Berkeley (94710) *(P-5199)*

Cen Cal Plastering Inc ....B....... 209 981-5265
   15300 East Wyman Rd Lathrop (95330) *(P-1920)*

Cencal Health, Santa Barbara *Also Called: Santa Brbara San Luis Obspo RG (P-8270)*

Cencora Inc ....C....... 610 727-7000
   1368 Metropolitan Dr Orange (92868) *(P-6101)*

Cenket Inc ....D
   449 Littlefield Ave South San Francisco (94080) *(P-5032)*

Cenpatico Behavioral Hlth LLC ....D....... 877 858-3855
   1740 Creekside Oaks Dr Ste 200 Sacramento (95833) *(P-17201)*

Centene Advnced Bhaviorial Hlth, Sacramento *Also Called: Cenpatico Behavioral Hlth LLC (P-17201)*

Center At Parkwest, The, Reseda *Also Called: Chase Group Llc (P-20314)*

Center Automotive Inc ....D....... 818 907-9995
   5201 Van Nuys Blvd Sherman Oaks (91401) *(P-7180)*

Center B M W, Sherman Oaks *Also Called: Center Automotive Inc (P-7180)*

Center For Achievement Center, Bakersfield *Also Called: New Advnces For Pple With Dsbl (P-18612)*

Center For Atism RES Evltion S ....C....... 858 444-8823
   8787 Complex Dr Ste 300 San Diego (92123) *(P-17020)*

Center For Civic Education (PA)...**D....... 818 591-9321**
   5115 Douglas Fir Rd Ste J Calabasas (91302) *(P-19875)*

Center For Discovery, Irvine *Also Called: Discovery Practice MGT Inc (P-17054)*

Center For Dscovery Adoloscent ....D....... 562 425-6404
   4136 Ann Arbor Rd Lakewood (90712) *(P-17021)*

Center For Elders Independence ....C....... 510 433-1150
   510 17th St Ste 400 Oakland (94612) *(P-8291)*

Center For Employment Training (PA)...D....... 408 287-7924
   701 Vine St San Jose (95110) *(P-18217)*

CENTER FOR FAMILY SOLUTIONS, El Centro *Also Called: Womanhaven (P-18194)*

Center For Human Services (PA)...D....... 209 526-1476
   2000 W Briggsmore Ave Ste I Modesto (95350) *(P-17870)*

Center For Lrng Atism Spport S ....B....... 800 538-8365
   424 Peninsula Ave San Mateo (94401) *(P-17871)*

Center For Rprductive Sciences, San Francisco *Also Called: University Cal San Francisco (P-17770)*

Center For Social Dynamics LLC ....D....... 916 382-4447
   10390 Coloma Rd Ste A Rancho Cordova (95670) *(P-15273)*

Center For Social Dynamics LLC ....D....... 408 843-9350
   9360 N Name Uno Gilroy (95020) *(P-15274)*

Center For Social Dynamics LLC ....D....... 408 320-2590
   3170 De La Cruz Blvd Ste 107 Santa Clara (95054) *(P-15275)*

Center For Social Dynamics LLC ....D....... 650 243-9849
   1001 Sneath Ln Ste 200 San Bruno (94066) *(P-15276)*

Center For Social Dynamics LLC ....D....... 707 553-1784
   150 Glen Cove Marina Rd E Vallejo (94591) *(P-17872)*

Center For Sustainable Energy ....D....... 858 244-1177
   3980 Sherman St Ste 170 San Diego (92110) *(P-20724)*

Center For Women's Health Care, Eureka *Also Called: St Joseph Hospital (P-16468)*

Center Thtre Group Los Angeles (PA)..**C....... 213 972-7344**
   601 W Temple St Los Angeles (90012) *(P-14032)*

Center To Prmote Hlthcare Acce ....D....... 916 563-4004
   1 Capitol Mall Ste 300 Sacramento (95814) *(P-17202)*

Centerbeam Inc C
   710 Lakeway Dr Ste 195 Sunnyvale (94085) *(P-12752)*

Centerfield Media, Los Angeles *Also Called: Qology Direct LLC (P-13440)*

Centerism Memorial Hospital, Rohnert Park *Also Called: St Joseph Hlth Nthrn Cal LLC (P-17132)*

Centerline Mortgage Capitl Inc ....B....... 949 221-6685
   18300 Von Karman Ave Ste 600 Irvine (92612) *(P-9498)*

Centerline Wood Products ....D....... 760 246-4530
   15447 Anacapa Rd Ste 102 Victorville (92392) *(P-6036)*

Centerplate, San Francisco *Also Called: Volume Services Inc (P-14582)*

Centerwell Health Services Inc ....D....... 707 545-7114
   1260 N Dutton Ave Ste 150 Santa Rosa (95401) *(P-16836)*

Centinela Frman Rgonal Med Ctr, Marina Del Rey *Also Called: Cfhs Holdings Inc (P-15988)*

Centinela Frman Rgonal Med Ctr, Marina Del Rey *Also Called: Cfhs Holdings Inc (P-15989)*

Centinela Frman Rgonal Med Ctr, Inglewood *Also Called: Cfhs Holdings Inc (P-15990)*

Centinela Hospital Medical Center, Inglewood *Also Called: Prime Healthcare Centinela LLC (P-16334)*

Centinela Skld Nrng Wlns Cntr, Inglewood *Also Called: West Cntinela Vly Care Ctr Inc (P-15730)*

Centinela Sklled Nrsing Wllnes ....D....... 310 674-3216
   950 S Flower St Inglewood (90301) *(P-15370)*

Centon, Aliso Viejo *Also Called: Centon Electronics Inc (P-2816)*

Centon Electronics Inc (PA)..**D....... 949 855-9111**
   27412 Aliso Viejo Pkwy Aliso Viejo (92656) *(P-2816)*

Centrak Inc ....C....... 215 860-2928
   68 Willow Rd Menlo Park (94025) *(P-19803)*

Central Ansthsia Svc Exch Med ....D....... 916 481-6800
   3315 Watt Ave Sacramento (95821) *(P-14665)*

Central Branch YMCA, San Jose *Also Called: Young MNS Chrstn Assn Slcon Vl (P-19001)*

Central Business Solutions Inc (PA)..D....... 510 573-5500
   37600 Central Ct Ste 214 Newark (94560) *(P-12753)*

Central Cal Ear Nose Throat ME ....D....... 559 432-3724
   1351 E Spruce Ave Fresno (93720) *(P-14666)*

Central Cal Fclty Med Group In ....D....... 559 435-6600
   2335 E Kashian Ln Ste 220 Fresno (93701) *(P-14667)*

Central Cal Fclty Med Group In ....D....... 559 435-4700
   6311 N Fresno St Fresno (93710) *(P-14668)*

Central Cal Fclty Med Group In (PA)..**D....... 559 453-5200**
   2625 E Divisadero St Fresno (93721) *(P-14669)*

Central Cal Fclty Med Group In ....D....... 559 320-1090
   2828 Fresno St Ste 203 Fresno (93721) *(P-14670)*

Central Cal Healthcare Sys, Fresno *Also Called: Veterans Health Administration (P-15187)*

Central California Blood Ctr (PA)...**C....... 559 389-5433**
   4343 W Herndon Ave Fresno (93722) *(P-17203)*

Central Cardiology Med Clinic ....C....... 661 395-0000
   2901 Sillect Ave Ste 100 Bakersfield (93308) *(P-14671)*

Central Cast Crdlgy A Med Corp ....C....... 831 758-2100
   230 San Jose St Salinas (93901) *(P-14672)*

Central Cntra Csta Sani Dst Em ....B....... 925 228-9500
   5019 Imhoff Pl Martinez (94553) *(P-4846)*

Central Coast Distributing LLC ....D....... 805 922-2108
   815 S Blosser Rd Santa Maria (93458) *(P-6755)*

Central Coast Pathology Lab, Bakersfield *Also Called: Physicians Automated Lab Inc (P-16741)*

Central Coast Seafoods — ALPHABETIC SECTION

Central Coast Seafoods .... C....... 805 462-3474
  5495 Traffic Way Atascadero (93422) *(P-6468)*

Central Coast Vna Hospice Inc .... C....... 831 758-8243
  45 Plaza Cir Salinas (93901) *(P-16837)*

CENTRAL COAST WINE COMPANY .... C....... 707 745-8500
  4301 Industrial Way Benicia (94510) *(P-6791)*

Central Coast YMCA .... D....... 831 637-8600
  351 Tres Pinos Rd Ste 201a Hollister (95023) *(P-18832)*

Central Coast YMCA .... C....... 831 728-9622
  27 Sudden St Watsonville (95076) *(P-18833)*

Central Contra Costa Sanitary District Facilities Financing Authority ... C....... 925 228-9500
  5019 Imhoff Pl Martinez (94553) *(P-4847)*

Central Counties .... C....... 209 356-0355
  241 Business Park Way Atwater (95301) *(P-19955)*

Central Gardens Post Acute, San Francisco *Also Called: Cal Golden Healthcare LLC* *(P-20306)*

Central Health Plan Cal Inc .... C....... 626 938-7120
  1540 Bridgegate Dr Diamond Bar (91765) *(P-16838)*

Central Prcss 4140, Los Angeles *Also Called: US Foods Inc (P-6687)*

Central Purchasing LLC (HQ) .... B....... 800 444-3353
  26677 Agoura Rd Calabasas (91302) *(P-5894)*

Central Roofing Company, Gardena *Also Called: Claud Townsley Inc (P-2051)*

Central Shop, Los Angeles *Also Called: Los Angeles Unified School Dst (P-17765)*

Central States Logistics Inc .... C....... 661 295-7222
  28338 Constellation Rd Ste 940 Valencia (91355) *(P-3381)*

Central Striping Service Inc .... D....... 916 635-5175
  3489 Luyung Dr Rancho Cordova (95742) *(P-1087)*

Central Valley AG Trnspt Inc, Oakdale *Also Called: Central Valley AG Trnspt LLC (P-261)*

Central Valley AG Trnspt LLC .... D....... 209 544-9246
  5509 Langworth Rd Oakdale (95361) *(P-261)*

Central Valley Cheese Inc .... D....... 209 664-1080
  115 S Kilroy Rd Turlock (95380) *(P-6433)*

Central Valley Cmnty Bancorp (PA) .... C....... 559 298-1775
  7100 N Financial Dr Ste 101 Fresno (93720) *(P-7672)*

Central Valley Community Bank (HQ) .... C....... 800 298-1775
  7100 N Financial Dr Ste 101 Fresno (93720) *(P-7673)*

Central Valley Concrete Inc (PA) .... C....... 209 723-8846
  3823 N State Highway 59 Merced (95348) *(P-3382)*

Central Valley Fund, The, Davis *Also Called: Cvf Capital Partners Inc (P-9505)*

Central Valley General Hosp (HQ) .... B....... 559 583-2100
  1025 N Douty St Hanford (93230) *(P-15986)*

Central Valley Indian Hlth Inc (PA) .... D....... 559 299-2578
  2740 Herndon Ave Clovis (93611) *(P-14673)*

Central Valley Oprtnty Ctr Inc (PA) .... D....... 209 357-0062
  6838 Bridget Ct Winton (95388) *(P-18218)*

Central Valley Presort Inc .... D....... 559 906-2003
  4215 S Dans St Visalia (93277) *(P-10769)*

Central Valley Trlr Repr Inc .... D....... 559 233-8444
  2974 S East Ave Fresno (93725) *(P-7181)*

Central Valley Trucking, Merced *Also Called: Central Valley Concrete Inc (P-3382)*

Central Vly Regional Ctr Inc .... C....... 559 738-2200
  5441 W Cypress Ave Visalia (93277) *(P-17022)*

Central Vly Specialty Hosp Inc .... C....... 209 248-7700
  730 17th St Modesto (95354) *(P-15987)*

Central Vly Training Ctr Inc .... D....... 209 951-1504
  7603 Murray Dr Stockton (95210) *(P-17873)*

Central Wholesale Electrical Distributors Inc .... C....... 925 245-9310
  6611 Preston Ave Ste E Livermore (94551) *(P-5545)*

Centre For Neuro Skills (PA) .... B....... 661 872-3408
  5215 Ashe Rd Bakersfield (93313) *(P-17023)*

Centrescapes Inc .... D....... 909 392-3303
  165 Gentry St Pomona (91767) *(P-481)*

Centro De Salud De La Comuni (PA) .... D....... 619 428-4463
  1601 Precision Park Ln San Diego (92173) *(P-17024)*

CENTRO VIDA, Berkeley *Also Called: Bay Area Hspano Inst For Advnc (P-18269)*

Centurion Group Inc (PA) .... C....... 760 471-8536
  365 S Rancho Santa Fe Rd San Marcos (92078) *(P-8074)*

Centurion Group, The, Los Angeles *Also Called: Mulholland SEC & Patrol Inc (P-13002)*

Century 14, Vallejo *Also Called: Century Theatres Inc (P-13981)*

Century 20, Milpitas *Also Called: Century Theatres Inc (P-14013)*

Century 21, South Gate *Also Called: Century 21 A Better Svc Rlty (P-8930)*

Century 21, Visalia *Also Called: Jordan - Link & Company (P-9063)*

Century 21, Redlands *Also Called: Lois Lauer Realty (P-9076)*

Century 21, Fremont *Also Called: Mission-Bishop Real Estate Inc (P-9100)*

Century 21 A Better Svc Rlty .... D....... 562 806-1000
  5831 Firestone Blvd Ste J South Gate (90280) *(P-8930)*

Century 21 Crest, Sunland *Also Called: EAM Enterprises Inc (P-8989)*

Century 21 Hill Top Realtors, Simi Valley *Also Called: First & La Realty Corp (P-9003)*

Century 21 Showcase, Boulder Creek *Also Called: Cortlandt Liquidating LLC (P-8953)*

Century 8, North Hollywood *Also Called: Century Theatres Inc (P-14018)*

Century Assembly Inc (PA) .... D....... 209 334-3230
  550 W Century Blvd Lodi (95240) *(P-19013)*

Century Blinds Inc .... D....... 951 734-3762
  300 S Promenade Ave Corona (92879) *(P-2508)*

Century Christian School, Lodi *Also Called: Century Assembly Inc (P-19013)*

Century Cinema, Mountain View *Also Called: Century Theatres Inc (P-14019)*

Century Downtown 10, Ventura *Also Called: Century Theatres Inc (P-14016)*

Century Gaming Management Inc .... A....... 310 330-2800
  3883 W Century Blvd Inglewood (90303) *(P-9690)*

Century Hlth Staffing Svcs Inc .... C....... 661 322-0606
  1701 Westwind Dr Ste 101 Bakersfield (93301) *(P-11111)*

Century Laguna 16, Elk Grove *Also Called: Century Theatres Inc (P-14012)*

Century National, Westlake Village *Also Called: Kramer-Wilson Company Inc (P-8389)*

Century National Properties (PA) .... D....... 818 760-0880
  12200 Sylvan St Ste 250 North Hollywood (91606) *(P-9691)*

Century Pacific Realty Corp .... C....... 310 729-9922
  9401 Wilshire Blvd Ste 1250 Beverly Hills (90212) *(P-9248)*

Century Pk Capitl Partners LLC (PA) .... C....... 310 867-2210
  2101 Rosecrans Ave Ste 4275 El Segundo (90245) *(P-9399)*

Century Pk Capitl Partners LLC .... D....... 650 324-1956
  1010 El Camino Real Ste 300 Menlo Park (94025) *(P-9499)*

Century Presidio, San Francisco *Also Called: Century Theatres Inc (P-14017)*

Century Snacks LLC .... B....... 323 278-9578
  5560 E Slauson Ave Commerce (90040) *(P-6458)*

Century Theatres Inc .... C....... 707 648-3456
  109 Plaza Dr Vallejo (94591) *(P-13981)*

Century Theatres Inc .... C....... 714 373-4573
  7777 Edinger Ave Ste 170 Huntington Beach (92647) *(P-13982)*

Century Theatres Inc .... C....... 408 226-2251
  3630 Hillcap Ave San Jose (95136) *(P-13983)*

Century Theatres Inc .... B....... 916 683-5290
  9349 Big Horn Blvd Elk Grove (95758) *(P-14012)*

Century Theatres Inc .... B....... 408 942-7441
  1010 Great Mall Dr Milpitas (95035) *(P-14013)*

Century Theatres Inc .... C....... 866 322-4547
  825 Middlefield Rd Redwood City (94063) *(P-14014)*

Century Theatres Inc .... B....... 510 758-9626
  3200 Klose Way Richmond (94806) *(P-14015)*

Century Theatres Inc .... B....... 805 641-6555
  555 E Main St Ventura (93001) *(P-14016)*

Century Theatres Inc .... C....... 415 776-2388
  2340 Chestnut St San Francisco (94123) *(P-14017)*

Century Theatres Inc .... B....... 818 508-1943
  12827 Victory Blvd North Hollywood (91606) *(P-14018)*

Century Theatres Inc .... B....... 650 961-3828
  1500 N Shoreline Blvd Mountain View (94043) *(P-14019)*

Century Theatres Inc .... B....... 916 332-2622
  6233 Garfield Ave Sacramento (95841) *(P-14020)*

Century Theatres Inc .... B....... 415 661-2539
  85 West Portal Ave San Francisco (94127) *(P-14021)*

Century Theatres Inc .... C....... 916 363-6572
  9616 Oates Dr Sacramento (95827) *(P-14022)*

Century Theatres Anchorage, San Rafael *Also Called: Century Theatres Inc (P-13984)*

Century Theatres Inc .... A....... 415 448-8400
  150 Pelican Way San Rafael (94901) *(P-13984)*

CENTURY THEATRES, INC, Huntington Beach *Also Called: Century Theatres Inc (P-13982)*

CENTURY THEATRES, INC, Redwood City *Also Called: Century Theatres Inc (P-14014)*

CENTURY THEATRES, INC, Richmond *Also Called: Century Theatres Inc (P-14015)*

Century West LLC .... D....... 818 432-5800
  4245 Lankershim Blvd North Hollywood (91602) *(P-7182)*

ALPHABETIC SECTION

Century West Concrete Inc .... B 951 712-4065
9782 Indiana Ave Riverside (92503) *(P-2108)*

Century West Plumbing, Westlake Village *Also Called: Sdg Enterprises (P-1556)*

Century Wire & Cable Inc .... D 800 999-5566
7400 E Slauson Ave Commerce (90040) *(P-2724)*

Century-National Insurance Co (DH) .... B 818 760-0880
16650 Sherman Way Ste 200 Van Nuys (91406) *(P-8524)*

Cenveo Worldwide Limited .... B 626 369-4921
705 Baldwin Park Blvd City Of Industry (91746) *(P-6064)*

Cep America - Illinois LLP .... D 510 350-2777
2100 Powell St Ste 400 Emeryville (94608) *(P-14674)*

Cep America LLC .... D 510 350-2691
2100 Powell St # 400 Emeryville (94608) *(P-14675)*

Cep America-California (PA) .... D 510 350-2700
2100 Powell St Ste 900 Emeryville (94608) *(P-18744)*

Cequent Towing Products, Fresno *Also Called: Horizon Global Americas Inc (P-13715)*

Ceramic Tile Art Inc .... D 818 767-9088
11601 Pendleton St Sun Valley (91352) *(P-1976)*

Cerebral Palsy Assn San Joaqui, Stockton *Also Called: United Cerebral Palsy Assoc (P-18768)*

Cerebras Systems Inc .... C 650 933-4980
1237 E Arques Ave Sunnyvale (94085) *(P-12433)*

Cerenzia Foods Inc .... D 909 989-4000
8585 White Oak Ave Rancho Cucamonga (91730) *(P-6245)*

Ceridian, Fountain Valley *Also Called: Ceridian Tax Service Inc (P-10520)*

Ceridian Tax Service Inc .... B 714 963-1311
17390 Brookhurst St Fountain Valley (92708) *(P-10520)*

Cerium Systems Inc, San Jose *Also Called: Tech Mahindra Cerium Systems (P-12893)*

Cerritos Church of Nazarene .... D 562 809-4143
12229 Del Amo Blvd Cerritos (90703) *(P-19014)*

Cerritos Ctr For Prfrmg Arts, Cerritos *Also Called: City of Cerritos (P-20912)*

Certified Aviation Svcs LLC .... D 650 588-8665
612 West Field Rd San Francisco (94128) *(P-3881)*

Certified Coatings Company .... D 707 639-4414
2320 Cordelia Rd Fairfield (94534) *(P-1609)*

Certified Distribution Svcs, Santa Fe Springs *Also Called: Contract Transportation Sys Co (P-3456)*

Certified Frt Logistics Inc (PA) .... C 800 592-5906
1344 White Ct Santa Maria (93458) *(P-3453)*

Certified Laboratories LLC .... A 818 845-0070
3125 N Damon Way Burbank (91505) *(P-19956)*

Certified Transportation, Santa Ana *Also Called: Certified Trnsp Svcs Inc (P-3316)*

Certified Trnsp Svcs Inc .... D 714 835-8676
1038 N Custer St Santa Ana (92701) *(P-3316)*

Certifiedsafety Inc .... D 707 747-9400
3070 Bay Vista Courtste B Benicia (94510) *(P-20313)*

CERTIFIEDSAFETY, INC., Benicia *Also Called: Certifiedsafety Inc (P-20313)*

Certinia, San Jose *Also Called: Financialforcecom Inc (P-11599)*

Cesar Chavez Center, San Diego *Also Called: San Diego Cmnty College Dst (P-17640)*

Cetecom Inc .... C 408 586-6200
411 Dixon Landing Rd Milpitas (95035) *(P-20725)*

Cetera Financial Group Inc (PA) .... C 866 489-3100
655 W Broadway Ste 1680 San Diego (92101) *(P-13230)*

Ceva Logistics LLC .... B 310 223-6500
19600 S Western Ave Torrance (90501) *(P-3996)*

CF Merced La Sierra LLC .... D 209 723-4224
2424 M St Merced (95340) *(P-15371)*

CF Susanville LLC .... D 530 257-5341
2005 River St Susanville (96130) *(P-15372)*

Cfgi LLC .... D 415 670-9041
600 California St Fl 14 San Francisco (94108) *(P-19550)*

Cfhc, Los Angeles *Also Called: Essential Access Health (P-18586)*

Cfhs Holdings Inc .... A 310 823-8911
4650 Lincoln Blvd Marina Del Rey (90292) *(P-15988)*

Cfhs Holdings Inc .... A 310 448-7800
4640 Admiralty Way Ste 650 Marina Del Rey (90292) *(P-15989)*

Cfhs Holdings Inc .... A 310 673-4660
555 E Hardy St Inglewood (90301) *(P-15990)*

Cfp Fire Protection Inc .... D 949 727-3277
153 Technology Dr Ste 200 Irvine (92618) *(P-1395)*

Cfr Rinkens LLC (PA) .... D 310 639-7725
444 W Ocean Blvd Ste 1200 Long Beach (90802) *(P-3997)*

Cfr Rinkens, Long Beach *Also Called: Cfr Rinkens LLC (P-3997)*

Cfwf Inc .... C 310 221-6280
842 Flint Ave Wilmington (90744) *(P-2419)*

CGB, Gardena *Also Called: Pulp Studio Incorporated (P-10817)*

Cgi Federal Inc .... D 619 260-0602
7480 Mission Valley Rd Ste 100 San Diego (92108) *(P-12754)*

Cgi Technologies Solutions Inc .... C 916 830-1100
621 Capitol Mall Ste 2025 Sacramento (95814) *(P-12755)*

Cgi Technologies Solutions Inc .... D 916 281-3200
860 Stillwater Rd Ste 210 West Sacramento (95605) *(P-19670)*

Cgl Companies LLC .... D 916 678-7890
2260 Del Paso Rd Ste 100 Sacramento (95834) *(P-19460)*

Cgp Holdings LLC .... D 760 764-1300
2 Gill Station Coastal Rd Little Lake (93542) *(P-4985)*

Cgp Maintenance Cnstr Svcs Inc .... D 858 454-7326
8614 Siesta Rd Santee (92071) *(P-20054)*

Ch Reynolds, San Jose *Also Called: C H Reynolds Electric Inc (P-1689)*

Cha Health Systems Inc (PA) .... A 213 487-3211
3731 Wilshire Blvd Ste 850 Los Angeles (90010) *(P-14676)*

Cha Hollywood Medical Ctr LP .... A 213 413-3000
4636 Fountain Ave Los Angeles (90029) *(P-15373)*

Cha La Mirada LLC .... C 714 739-8500
14299 Firestone Blvd La Mirada (90638) *(P-9692)*

Cha Renetative Medicine, Los Angeles *Also Called: Cha Health Systems Inc (P-14676)*

Cha-Dor Realty LLC .... C 530 544-2237
2763 Lake Tahoe Blvd South Lake Tahoe (96150) *(P-7116)*

Challenger School, Newark *Also Called: Challenger Schools (P-18280)*

Challenger Schools .... C 408 723-0111
4949 Harwood Rd San Jose (95124) *(P-18278)*

Challenger Schools .... D 650 213-8245
3880 Middlefield Rd Palo Alto (94303) *(P-18279)*

Challenger Schools .... D 510 770-1771
39600 Cedar Blvd Newark (94560) *(P-18280)*

Challenger Sheet Metal Inc .... D 619 596-8040
9353 Abraham Way Ste A Santee (92071) *(P-2050)*

Chalone Vineyard, Healdsburg *Also Called: Treasury Chateau & Estates (P-2396)*

Cham-Cal Engineering Co .... D 714 898-9721
12722 Western Ave Garden Grove (92841) *(P-2693)*

Chamberlains Children Ctr Inc .... D 831 636-2121
1850 Cienega Rd Hollister (95023) *(P-18391)*

Chambers Group Inc (PA) .... D 949 261-5414
5 Hutton Centre Dr Ste 750 Santa Ana (92707) *(P-20726)*

Chameleon Beverage Company Inc (PA) .... D 323 724-8223
6444 E 26th St Commerce (90040) *(P-2404)*

Chaminade Ltd .... C 831 475-5600
1 Chaminade Ln Santa Cruz (95065) *(P-9693)*

Chaminade At Santa Cruz, Santa Cruz *Also Called: Chaminade Ltd (P-9693)*

Champagne Landscape Nurs Inc .... D 559 277-8188
3233 N Cornelia Ave Fresno (93722) *(P-482)*

Champion Electric Inc .... D 951 276-9619
3950 Garner Rd Riverside (92501) *(P-1695)*

Champion Home Builders Inc .... D 951 256-4617
299 N Smith Ave Corona (92878) *(P-666)*

Champion Investment Corp .... D 917 712-7807
12809 Oakfield Way Poway (92064) *(P-9694)*

Champion Mortgage, San Diego *Also Called: Integrity Mortgage Group (P-7984)*

Champion Scaffold, Richmond *Also Called: Champion Scaffold Services Inc (P-2265)*

Champion Scaffold Services Inc .... D 510 708-4731
112 Railroad Ave Richmond (94801) *(P-2265)*

Chan Family Partnership LP .... D 626 322-7132
801 S Grand Ave Apt 1811 Los Angeles (90017) *(P-20055)*

Chan Zuckerberg Biohub Inc .... C 628 200-3246
499 Illinois St San Francisco (94158) *(P-19876)*

Chancellor Hlth Care of Cal IV .... B 209 367-8870
2220 W Kettleman Ln Ofc Lodi (95242) *(P-15374)*

Chancellor Place of Lodi, Lodi *Also Called: Chancellor Hlth Care of Cal IV (P-15374)*

Chandler Packaging A Transpak Company .... D 858 292-5674
7595 Raytheon Rd San Diego (92111) *(P-4126)*

Change Home Loans — ALPHABETIC SECTION

Change Home Loans, Anaheim *Also Called: Change Lending LLC (P-7947)*
Change Lending LLC .... D...... 831 460-0202
523 Capitola Ave Capitola (95010) *(P-7944)*
Change Lending LLC .... D...... 949 769-3526
32 Discovery Ste 160 Irvine (92618) *(P-7945)*
Change Lending LLC .... D...... 530 282-1166
970 Executive Way Redding (96002) *(P-7946)*
Change Lending LLC (PA) .... D...... **949 423-6814**
175 N Riverview Dr Anaheim (92808) *(P-7947)*
Change Lending LLC .... D...... 858 500-3060
6265 Greenwich Dr Ste 215 San Diego (92122) *(P-8032)*
Change Lending LLC .... D...... 707 596-5111
100 Stony Point Rd Ste 290 Santa Rosa (95401) *(P-8033)*
Changeorg Inc (PA) .... C...... 415 817-1840
383 Rhode Island St Ste 300 San Francisco (94103) *(P-12654)*
Channel 40 Inc .... C...... 916 454-4422
4655 Fruitridge Rd Sacramento (95820) *(P-4420)*
Channel Impact, Moraga *Also Called: Bergerson Group (P-20294)*
Channel Intelligence Inc .... C...... 321 939-5600
1600 Amphitheatre Pkwy Mountain View (94043) *(P-4264)*
Channel Islands Post Acute, Santa Barbara *Also Called: Powers Park Healthcare Inc (P-15633)*
Channel Islnds Vgtble Frms Inc (PA) .... D...... 805 984-1910
595 Victoria Ave Oxnard (93030) *(P-160)*
Channel Islnds Yung MNS Chrstn .... D...... 805 963-8775
301 W Figueroa St Santa Barbara (93101) *(P-18834)*
Channel Islnds Yung MNS Chrstn .... D...... 805 736-3483
201 W College Ave Lompoc (93436) *(P-18835)*
Channel Islnds Yung MNS Chrstn .... D...... 805 484-0423
3111 Village Park Dr Camarillo (93012) *(P-18836)*
Channel Islnds Yung MNS Chrstn .... D...... 805 687-7727
36 Hitchcock Way Santa Barbara (93105) *(P-18837)*
Channel Islnds Yung MNS Chrstn .... D...... 805 969-3288
591 Santa Rosa Ln Santa Barbara (93108) *(P-18838)*
Channel Islnds Yung MNS Chrstn .... D...... 805 484-0423
3760 Telegraph Rd Ventura (93003) *(P-18839)*
Channel Islnds Yung MNS Chrstn .... D...... 805 686-2037
900 N Refugio Rd Santa Ynez (93460) *(P-18840)*
Channelwave Software Inc .... D...... 949 448-4500
27081 Aliso Creek Rd Aliso Viejo (92656) *(P-20727)*
Channing House .... D...... 650 327-0950
850 Webster St Ofc Palo Alto (94301) *(P-15829)*
CHAP, Pasadena *Also Called: Community Hlth Alance Pasadena (P-16008)*
Chapa-De Indian Hlth Prgram In (PA) .... D...... 530 887-2800
11670 Atwood Rd Auburn (95603) *(P-14677)*
Chapa-De Indian Hlth Prgram In .... D...... 530 477-8545
1350 E Main St Grass Valley (95945) *(P-15219)*
Chaparral Foundation .... D...... 510 848-8774
1309 Allston Way Berkeley (94702) *(P-15375)*
Chaparral House, Berkeley *Also Called: Chaparral Foundation (P-15375)*
Chaparral Motorsports, San Bernardino *Also Called: Ocelot Engineering Inc (P-7398)*
Chapel of Chimes (DH) .... D...... 510 471-3363
32992 Mission Blvd Hayward (94544) *(P-9282)*
Chapel of Chimes .... D...... 650 349-4411
10600 Skyline Blvd Redwood City (94062) *(P-9283)*
Chapman Family Health, Orange *Also Called: Chapman Global Medical Ctr Inc (P-15991)*
Chapman Global Medical Ctr Inc .... B...... 714 633-0011
2601 E Chapman Ave Orange (92869) *(P-15991)*
Chapman Golf Development LLC .... D...... 760 564-8723
78505 Avenue 52 La Quinta (92253) *(P-14248)*
Chapman House, Orange *Also Called: Chapman House Inc (P-16669)*
Chapman House Inc .... D...... 714 288-6100
1412 E Chapman Ave Orange (92866) *(P-16669)*
Chapmn/Lnard Stdio Eqp Cnada I (PA) .... C...... 323 877-5309
12950 Raymer St North Hollywood (91605) *(P-13929)*
Chapter Seven Lending, Orange *Also Called: Cashcall Inc (P-7871)*
Chardnnay Golf CLB Vnyrds - NA, Napa *Also Called: NAPA Golf Associates LLC (P-14412)*
Charger Investment Partners LP .... D...... 310 372-5525
880 Apollo St Ste 347 El Segundo (90245) *(P-8075)*
Chargers Football Company LLC (PA) .... D...... **619 280-2121**
3333 Susan St Costa Mesa (92626) *(P-14132)*

Charles & Cynthia Eberly Inc .... D...... 323 937-6468
8383 Wilshire Blvd Ste 906 Beverly Hills (90211) *(P-8798)*
Charles David of California (PA) .... D...... **310 348-5050**
5731 Buckingham Pkwy Culver City (90230) *(P-7410)*
Charles Dunn RE Svcs Inc (PA) .... D...... **213 270-6200**
800 W 6th St Ste 600 Los Angeles (90017) *(P-8931)*
Charles E Thomas Company Inc (PA) .... D...... **310 323-6730**
13701 Alma Ave Gardena (90249) *(P-892)*
Charles Krug Winery, Saint Helena *Also Called: C Mondavi & Family (P-2378)*
Charles Matoian Entps Inc (PA) .... D...... **559 445-8600**
1888 Se Ave Fresno (93721) *(P-3684)*
Charles McMurray Co (PA) .... D...... **559 292-5751**
2520 N Argyle Ave Fresno (93727) *(P-5725)*
Charles Pnkow Bldrs Ltd A Cal .... B...... 510 893-5170
1111 Broadway Ste 200 Oakland (94607) *(P-893)*
Charles River Laboratories Inc .... D...... 877 274-8371
1300 Rancho Conejo Blvd Thousand Oaks (91320) *(P-19671)*
Charles Rver Acclrator Dev Lab, Thousand Oaks *Also Called: Charles River Laboratories Inc (P-19671)*
Charles Rver Labs Cell Sltons (HQ) .... D...... **877 310-0717**
8500 Balboa Blvd Ste 130 Northridge (91325) *(P-17204)*
Charles Schwab, Temecula *Also Called: Charles Schwab Corporation (P-8076)*
Charles Schwab, Los Angeles *Also Called: Charles Schwab Corporation (P-8077)*
Charles Schwab, Roseville *Also Called: Charles Schwab Corporation (P-8078)*
Charles Schwab, San Diego *Also Called: Charles Schwab Corporation (P-8079)*
Charles Schwab, San Diego *Also Called: Charles Schwab Corporation (P-9400)*
Charles Schwab Corporation .... C...... 800 435-4000
27580 Ynez Rd Ste A Temecula (92591) *(P-8076)*
Charles Schwab Corporation .... D...... 800 435-4000
1900 Avenue Of The Stars Ste 101 Los Angeles (90067) *(P-8077)*
Charles Schwab Corporation .... D...... 916 789-2120
3741 Douglas Blvd Ste 190 Roseville (95661) *(P-8078)*
Charles Schwab Corporation .... D...... 800 435-4000
7510 Hazard Center Dr Ste 407 San Diego (92108) *(P-8079)*
Charles Schwab Corporation .... D...... 800 435-4000
10920 Via Frontera Ste 100 San Diego (92127) *(P-9400)*
Charles Schwab Family of Funds .... B...... 415 627-7000
211 Main St San Francisco (94105) *(P-9365)*
Charles W Bowers Museum Corp .... D...... 714 567-3600
2002 N Main St Santa Ana (92706) *(P-18642)*
Charlie Mitchell Chld Clinic, Madera *Also Called: Valley Childrens Hospital (P-16609)*
Charlies Specialties Inc .... C...... 724 346-2350
501 Airpark Dr Fullerton (92833) *(P-2370)*
Charming Trim & Packaging .... A...... 415 302-7021
5889 Rickenbacker Rd Commerce (90040) *(P-6153)*
Charolais Care V Inc .... D...... 415 921-5038
1426 Fillmore St Ste 207 San Francisco (94115) *(P-16839)*
Charter Bhvral Hlth Sys S C/Ch .... C...... 626 966-1632
1161 E Covina Blvd Covina (91724) *(P-16647)*
Charter Communications, Ventura *Also Called: Cco Holdings LLC (P-4489)*
Charter Communications, Long Beach *Also Called: Cco Holdings LLC (P-4490)*
Charter Hospice Colton LLC .... C...... 909 825-2969
1007 E Cooley Dr Ste 100 Colton (92324) *(P-15749)*
Charter Oak Hospital, Covina *Also Called: Charter Bhvral Hlth Sys S C/Ch (P-16647)*
Chase, Fresno *Also Called: Chase Inc (P-7610)*
Chase Inc .... D...... 559 275-7331
3754 W Holland Ave Fresno (93722) *(P-7610)*
Chase Care Center, Los Angeles *Also Called: Chase Care Center Inc (P-15830)*
Chase Care Center Inc .... D...... 323 935-8490
1101 Crenshaw Blvd Los Angeles (90019) *(P-15830)*
Chase Chevrolet Co Inc .... D...... 209 475-6600
6441 Holman Rd Stockton (95212) *(P-7183)*
Chase Chvrlet Chevy Trck World, Stockton *Also Called: Chase Chevrolet Co Inc (P-7183)*
Chase Group Llc .... B...... 805 522-9155
5270 E Los Angeles Ave Simi Valley (93063) *(P-19804)*
Chase Group Llc .... B...... 818 708-3533
6740 Wilbur Ave Reseda (91335) *(P-20314)*
Chase Manhattan, Santa Rosa *Also Called: Chase Manhattan Mortgage Corp (P-7948)*
Chase Manhattan, San Francisco *Also Called: Chase Manhattan Mortgage Corp (P-7949)*
Chase Manhattan Mortgage Corp .... C...... 707 525-5060
2245 Mendocino Ave Ste 202 Santa Rosa (95403) *(P-7948)*

ALPHABETIC SECTION — Child Development Incorporated

Chase Manhattan Mortgage Corp .... C 858 605-3300
  560 Mission St Fl 2 San Francisco (94105) *(P-7949)*

Chase Suite Hotel .... D 858 314-7910
  12555 High Bluff Dr Ste 330 San Diego (92130) *(P-9695)*

Chases LLC .... D 909 596-6810
  2079 Bonita Ave La Verne (91750) *(P-7729)*

Chateau At River's Edge, Sacramento *Also Called: Hank Fisher Properties Inc (P-15853)*

Chateau La Salle, San Jose *Also Called: Mobilehome Communities America (P-8880)*

Chateau Lk San Mrcos Hmwners A .... D 760 471-0083
  1502 Circa Del Lago San Marcos (92078) *(P-8799)*

Chatmeter Inc .... D 619 300-1050
  225 Broadway Ste 2200 San Diego (92101) *(P-12132)*

CHATSWORTH PARK HEALTH CARE CE, Chatsworth *Also Called: Cpcc Inc (P-15835)*

Chattopadhyay Runi MD .... D 650 853-2946
  795 El Camino Real Palo Alto (94301) *(P-14678)*

CHC, Los Angeles *Also Called: Covenant House California (P-18406)*

Che Behavioral Health Services .... C 760 300-3664
  5838 Edison Pl Ste 100 Carlsbad (92008) *(P-17205)*

Che Snior Psychlogical Svcs PC .... C 888 307-0893
  4929 Wilshire Blvd Ste 510 Los Angeles (90010) *(P-15277)*

Check Point Software, San Carlos *Also Called: Check Point Software Tech Inc (P-12133)*

Check Point Software Tech Inc (HQ) .... C 650 628-2000
  959 Skyway Rd Ste 300 San Carlos (94070) *(P-12133)*

Checkout Holding Corp .... A 415 788-5111
  1 Maritime Plz Ste 1200 San Francisco (94111) *(P-10728)*

Checkr Inc (PA) .... C 844 824-3257
  1 Montgomery St Ste 2400 San Francisco (94104) *(P-13231)*

Cheema Logistics .... D 559 702-1444
  968 Sierra St Ste 130 Kingsburg (93631) *(P-3802)*

Chef Works Inc (PA) .... C 858 643-5600
  12325 Kerran St # A Poway (92064) *(P-6170)*

Chelbay Schuler & Chelbay (PA) .... D 408 288-4400
  6800 Santa Teresa Blvd Ste 100 San Jose (95119) *(P-8460)*

Chem Quip Inc .... D 800 821-1678
  2551 Land Ave Sacramento (95815) *(P-5974)*

Chem-Tronics, El Cajon *Also Called: GKN Aerospace Chem-Tronics Inc (P-2985)*

Chembridge Corporation (PA) .... B 858 451-7400
  11199 Sorrento Valley Rd Ste 206 San Diego (92121) *(P-6707)*

Chemical Waste Management Inc .... C 559 386-9711
  35251 Old Skyline Rd Kettleman City (93239) *(P-4877)*

Chemtool Incorporated .... C 661 823-7190
  1300 Goodrick Dr Tehachapi (93561) *(P-2652)*

Chen & Huang Partners LP .... D 714 557-8700
  1400 S Bristol St Santa Ana (92704) *(P-9696)*

Chen Dvid MD Dgnstc Med Group .... D 626 288-8029
  208 N Garfield Ave Monterey Park (91754) *(P-14679)*

Cher Ae Heights Casino, Trinidad *Also Called: Cher-Ae Heights Indian Cmnty (P-14505)*

Cher-Ae Heights Indian Cmnty .... C 707 677-3611
  27 Scenic Dr Trinidad (95570) *(P-14505)*

Cherokee Freight Lines, Stockton *Also Called: Scan-Vino LLC (P-3542)*

Cherokee Uniform, Chatsworth *Also Called: Careismatic Brands Inc (P-2684)*

Cherokee Uniforms, Chatsworth *Also Called: Strategic Distribution L P (P-2452)*

Cherry City Electric, City Of Industry *Also Called: Morrow-Meadows Corporation (P-1782)*

Chesapeake Lodging Trust .... C 415 296-2900
  333 Battery St Lbby San Francisco (94111) *(P-9697)*

Chester C Lehmann Co Inc (PA) .... D 408 293-5818
  1135 Auzerais Ave San Jose (95126) *(P-5546)*

Chestnut Ridge Energy Company C
  18101 Von Karman Ave Ste 920 Irvine (92612) *(P-4563)*

Chevron, San Ramon *Also Called: Chevron Corporation (P-2646)*

Chevron, El Segundo *Also Called: Chevron Corporation (P-7385)*

Chevron, San Ramon *Also Called: Chevron Shipping Company LLC (P-7386)*

Chevron, Tracy *Also Called: Chevron Stations Inc (P-7387)*

Chevron, San Ramon *Also Called: Chevron Stations Inc (P-7388)*

Chevron, Fresno *Also Called: Bowie Enterprises (P-13687)*

Chevron, Stockton *Also Called: Canepas Car Wash (P-13689)*

Chevron, San Jose *Also Called: Lark Avenue Car Wash (P-13697)*

Chevron, Campbell *Also Called: Lark Avenue Car Wash (P-13698)*

Chevron Corporation (PA) .... A 925 326-2189
  6001 Bollinger Canyon Rd San Ramon (94583) *(P-2646)*

Chevron Corporation .... A 310 615-5000
  324 W El Segundo Blvd El Segundo (90245) *(P-7385)*

Chevron Energy Solutions Co, San Francisco *Also Called: Chevron Energy Solutions LP (P-3013)*

Chevron Energy Solutions LP .... B 415 894-4188
  345 California St Fl 18 San Francisco (94104) *(P-3013)*

Chevron Global Energy Inc (HQ) .... D 925 842-1000
  6001 Bollinger Canyon Rd San Ramon (94583) *(P-2647)*

Chevron Global Lubricants, San Ramon *Also Called: Chevron Global Energy Inc (P-2647)*

Chevron Mining Inc .... C 760 856-7625
  67750 Bailey Rd Mountain Pass (92366) *(P-575)*

Chevron Shipping Company LLC .... D 925 842-1000
  6001 Bollinger Canyon Rd San Ramon (94583) *(P-7386)*

Chevron Stations Inc .... C 209 830-0370
  755 S Tracy Blvd Tracy (95376) *(P-7387)*

Chevron Stations Inc .... C 925 328-0292
  18060 San Ramon Valley Blvd San Ramon (94583) *(P-7388)*

CHG Foundation .... B 619 422-0422
  740 Bay Blvd Chula Vista (91910) *(P-19077)*

Chiala, George Packing, Morgan Hill *Also Called: George Chiala Farms Inc (P-33)*

CHIBI CHAN PRESCHOOL, San Francisco *Also Called: Japanese Cmnty Youth Council (P-18599)*

Chicago Title, San Jose *Also Called: Chicago Title Company (P-8436)*

Chicago Title, Campbell *Also Called: Chicago Title Insurance Co (P-8437)*

Chicago Title, Santa Barbara *Also Called: Chicago Title Insurance Co (P-8438)*

Chicago Title Company .... C 408 292-4212
  675 N 1st St Ste 400 San Jose (95112) *(P-8436)*

Chicago Title Insurance Co .... A 408 371-4100
  1500 E Hamilton Ave Ste 104 Campbell (95008) *(P-8437)*

Chicago Title Insurance Co (HQ) .... C 805 565-6900
  4050 Calle Real Santa Barbara (93110) *(P-8438)*

Chicexecs .... D 760 484-2116
  820 Los Vallecitos Blvd Ste A-C San Marcos (92069) *(P-20633)*

Chick-Fil-A, Rohnert Park *Also Called: Chick-Fil-A Inc (P-7465)*

Chick-Fil-A Inc .... D 707 585-7462
  5080 Redwood Dr Rohnert Park (94928) *(P-7465)*

Chicken of Sea International, El Segundo *Also Called: Tri-Union Seafoods LLC (P-6487)*

Chico Area Recreation & Pk Dst (PA) .... C 530 895-4711
  545 Vallombrosa Ave Chico (95926) *(P-14506)*

Chico Electric Inc .... D 530 891-1933
  36 W Eaton Rd Chico (95973) *(P-1696)*

Chico Nut Company .... D 530 894-5441
  2020 Esplanade Chico (95926) *(P-91)*

Chico Produce Inc (PA) .... C 530 893-0596
  70 Pepsi Way Durham (95938) *(P-6525)*

Chico State Enterprises .... A 530 898-6811
  25 Main St Unit 203 Chico (95928) *(P-18841)*

Child & Family Center .... C 661 259-9439
  21545 Centre Pointe Pkwy Santa Clarita (91350) *(P-17874)*

Child Abuse Prvntion Cncil SCR .... D 916 244-1900
  4700 Roseville Rd Ste 102 North Highlands (95660) *(P-17875)*

Child Action Inc (PA) .... C 916 369-0191
  10540 White Rock Rd Ste 180 Rancho Cordova (95670) *(P-18281)*

Child and Family Guidance Ctr (PA) .... C 818 739-5140
  9650 Zelzah Ave Northridge (91325) *(P-17025)*

Child Care Resource Center Inc (PA) .... C 818 717-1000
  20001 Prairie St Chatsworth (91311) *(P-17876)*

Child Care Resource Center Inc .... C 661 723-3246
  250 Grand Cypress Ave Ste 601 Palmdale (93551) *(P-17877)*

Child Care Resource Center Inc .... C 818 837-0097
  454 S Kalisher St San Fernando (91340) *(P-18282)*

Child Dev Rsrces of Vntura CNT (PA) .... C 805 485-7878
  221 Ventura Blvd Oxnard (93036) *(P-17878)*

Child Development Assoc Inc .... D 619 422-7115
  380 Telegraph Canyon Rd Chula Vista (91910) *(P-18283)*

Child Development Incorporated .... B 714 842-4064
  17341 Jacquelyn Ln Huntington Beach (92647) *(P-8932)*

Child Development Incorporated .... B 530 666-4822
  312 Gibson Rd Woodland (95695) *(P-18284)*

Child Development Incorporated .... B 949 854-5060
  5151 Amalfi Dr Irvine (92603) *(P-18285)*

Child Development Institute   **ALPHABETIC SECTION**

Child Development Institute .... D....... 818 888-4559
   18050 Vanowen St Reseda (91335) *(P-17879)*

Child Family & Cmnty Svcs Inc .... C....... 510 796-9512
   32980 Alvarado Niles Rd Ste 856 Union City (94587) *(P-18286)*

Child Guidance Center Inc .... C....... 714 953-4455
   525 Cabrillo Park Dr Ste 300 Santa Ana (92701) *(P-17026)*

Child Help Head Start Center, Beaumont *Also Called: Childhelp Inc (P-18392)*

CHILD PARENT INSTITUTE, Santa Rosa *Also Called: California Parenting Institute (P-17804)*

Child Support Services, Commerce *Also Called: County of Los Angeles (P-17908)*

Childcare Careers LLC .... A....... 650 372-0211
   2000 Sierra Point Pkwy Ste 702 Brisbane (94005) *(P-11280)*

Childhelp Inc .... C....... 951 845-6737
   14700 Manzanita Rd Beaumont (92223) *(P-18392)*

Childnet, Long Beach *Also Called: Childnet Youth & Fmly Svcs Inc (P-17880)*

Childnet Youth & Fmly Svcs Inc (PA) .... C....... 562 498-5500
   3545 Long Beach Blvd Ste 200 Long Beach (90807) *(P-17880)*

Children & Families Commission, Riverside *Also Called: County of Riverside (P-20939)*

Children & Family Svcs Dept, Santa Fe Springs *Also Called: County of Los Angeles (P-17909)*

Children & Family Svcs Dept, Los Angeles *Also Called: County of Los Angeles (P-17910)*

Children of Rainbow Inc (PA) .... D....... 619 615-0652
   4890 Logan Ave San Diego (92113) *(P-18287)*

CHILDREN, YOUTH & FAMILY COLLA, Los Angeles *Also Called: Advancment Thrugh Oprtnty Knwl (P-17823)*

Children's Discovery Museum, San Jose *Also Called: San Jose Chld Discovery Museum (P-18672)*

Children's Health Center, Chico *Also Called: Enloe Medical Center (P-16087)*

Children's Home Care, Fresno *Also Called: Valley Childrens Hospital (P-16611)*

Children's Hospital, San Diego *Also Called: Rady Childrens Hosp & Hlth Ctr (P-16356)*

CHILDREN'S HOSPITAL, San Diego *Also Called: Rady Chld Hospital-San Diego (P-16357)*

Childrens Associated Med Group, San Diego *Also Called: Childrens Spclsts of San Dego (P-14683)*

Childrens Bureau Southern Cal (PA) .... C....... 213 342-0100
   1910 Magnolia Ave Los Angeles (90007) *(P-17881)*

Childrens Clnic Srving Chldren .... B....... 562 264-4638
   701 E 28th St Ste 200 Long Beach (90806) *(P-14680)*

Childrens Co, Chula Vista *Also Called: Child Development Assoc Inc (P-18283)*

Childrens Crative Lrng Ctr Inc .... B....... 408 978-1500
   521 W Capitol Expy San Jose (95136) *(P-18288)*

Childrens Crative Lrng Ctr Inc .... B....... 650 968-2600
   1625 San Luis Ave Mountain View (94043) *(P-18289)*

Childrens Crative Lrng Ctr Inc .... B....... 831 647-1880
   1608 Private Bolio Rd Monterey (93940) *(P-18290)*

Childrens Crative Lrng Ctr Inc .... B....... 650 473-1100
   848 Ramona St Palo Alto (94301) *(P-18291)*

Childrens Creativity Museum .... D....... 415 820-3320
   221 4th St San Francisco (94103) *(P-18643)*

Childrens Cuncil San Francisco (PA) .... D....... 415 343-3378
   445 Church St San Francisco (94114) *(P-17882)*

Childrens Healthcare Cal .... B....... 714 997-3000
   455 S Main St Orange (92868) *(P-14681)*

Childrens Healthcare Cal (PA) .... A....... 714 997-3000
   1201 W La Veta Ave Orange (92868) *(P-16670)*

Childrens Home of Stockton .... C....... 209 466-0853
   430 N Pilgrim St Stockton (95205) *(P-18393)*

Childrens Hosp Los Angles Med (PA) .... D....... 323 361-2336
   6430 W Sunset Blvd Ste 600 Los Angeles (90028) *(P-15992)*

Childrens Hosp Okland Res Inst .... D....... 510 450-7600
   5700 Martin Luther King Jr Way Oakland (94609) *(P-15993)*

Childrens Hosp RES Ctr At Okla (PA) .... A....... 510 428-3000
   747 52nd St Oakland (94609) *(P-15994)*

Childrens Hosp RES Ctr At Okla, Oakland *Also Called: Childrens Hosp Okland Res Inst (P-15993)*

Childrens Hospital Los Angeles .... B....... 323 361-2751
   4661 W Sunset Blvd Los Angeles (90027) *(P-15995)*

Childrens Hospital Los Angeles (PA) .... A....... 323 660-2450
   4650 W Sunset Blvd Los Angeles (90027) *(P-16671)*

CHILDRENS HOSPITAL LOS ANGELES, Los Angeles *Also Called: Childrens Hosp Los Angles Med (P-15992)*

Childrens Hospital Orange Cnty .... B....... 714 638-5990
   10602 Chapman Ave Ste 200 Garden Grove (92840) *(P-15996)*

Childrens Hospital Orange Cnty (PA) .... A....... 714 509-8300
   1201 W La Veta Ave Orange (92868) *(P-15997)*

Childrens Hospital Orange Cnty .... B....... 949 365-2416
   455 S Main St Orange (92868) *(P-15998)*

Childrens Hospital Orange Cnty .... C....... 949 387-2586
   980 Roosevelt Irvine (92620) *(P-15999)*

Childrens Hospital Orange Cnty .... C....... 949 631-2062
   500 Superior Ave Newport Beach (92663) *(P-18292)*

Childrens Inst Los Angeles .... A....... 213 383-2765
   679 S New Hampshire Ave Los Angeles (90005) *(P-17883)*

Childrens Inst Los Angeles (PA) .... C....... 213 385-5100
   2121 W Temple St Los Angeles (90026) *(P-19877)*

Childrens Institute Inc (PA) .... C....... 213 385-5100
   2121 W Temple St Los Angeles (90026) *(P-17884)*

Childrens Law Center Cal (PA) .... D....... 323 980-8700
   101 Centre Plaza Dr Monterey Park (91754) *(P-17402)*

Childrens Medical Center, El Monte *Also Called: La County (P-18036)*

Childrens Oncology Group .... C....... 626 447-0064
   800 Royal Oaks Dr Ste 101 Monrovia (91016) *(P-14682)*

Childrens Rcvery Ctr Nthrn Cal, Campbell *Also Called: Childrens Recovery Ctr 1 LLC (P-16672)*

Childrens Recovery Ctr 1 LLC .... D....... 408 558-3640
   3777 S Bascom Ave Campbell (95008) *(P-16672)*

Childrens Recvg Hm Sacramento .... C....... 916 482-2370
   3555 Auburn Blvd Sacramento (95821) *(P-17885)*

Childrens Spclsts of San Dego (PA) .... B....... 858 576-1700
   3020 Childrens Way San Diego (92123) *(P-14683)*

Childrens Therapeutic Services, Ukiah *Also Called: Redwood Community Services Inc (P-18095)*

China Airlines Ltd .... C....... 310 484-1818
   5651 W 96th St Los Angeles (90045) *(P-3832)*

China Airlines Ltd .... C....... 310 646-4293
   380 World Way Ste S14 Los Angeles (90045) *(P-3833)*

Chinatown Service Center .... D....... 213 808-1700
   320 S Garfield Ave Ste 118 Alhambra (91801) *(P-18219)*

Chinatown Service Center (PA) .... D....... 213 808-1701
   767 N Hill St Ste 400 Los Angeles (90012) *(P-18220)*

Chinese Consumer Yellow Pages, Rosemead *Also Called: Chinese Overseas Mktg Svc Corp (P-2554)*

Chinese Hospital Association (PA) .... B....... 415 982-2400
   845 Jackson St San Francisco (94133) *(P-16000)*

Chinese Overseas Mktg Svc Corp (PA) .... D....... 626 280-8588
   3940 Rosemead Blvd Rosemead (91770) *(P-2554)*

Chino Medical Group Inc .... D....... 909 591-6446
   5475 Walnut Ave Chino (91710) *(P-14684)*

Chino Valley Medical Center, Chino *Also Called: Veritas Health Services Inc (P-16616)*

Chino Valley YMCA, Chino *Also Called: West End Yung MNS Christn Assn (P-18930)*

Chino-Pacific Warehouse Corp (PA) .... D....... 909 545-8100
   3601 Jurupa St Ontario (91761) *(P-3685)*

Chipper, San Francisco *Also Called: Chipper Cash Inc (P-11488)*

Chipper Cash Inc .... D....... 844 386-3753
   180 Montgomery St Ste 1860 San Francisco (94104) *(P-11488)*

Chipton-Ross Inc .... D....... 310 414-7800
   420 Culver Blvd Playa Del Rey (90293) *(P-2981)*

Chiro Inc (PA) .... C....... 909 879-1160
   2260 S Vista Ave Bloomington (92316) *(P-5936)*

Chirotech Inc .... C....... 619 528-0040
   9265 Sky Park Ct Ste 200 San Diego (92123) *(P-15261)*

Chirotouch, San Diego *Also Called: Chirotech Inc (P-15261)*

Chivaroli & Assoc Inc .... D....... 208 338-6640
   200 N Westlake Blvd Ste 101 Westlake Village (91362) *(P-8525)*

Chm Productions Inc .... D....... 818 972-8433
   8033 W Sunset Blvd Ste 875 Los Angeles (90046) *(P-13828)*

Chme Inc .... D....... 650 931-8713
   780 Montague Expy Ste 704 San Jose (95131) *(P-14685)*

Choc, Orange *Also Called: Childrens Hospital Orange Cnty (P-15997)*

Choc Childern's, Garden Grove *Also Called: Childrens Hospital Orange Cnty (P-15996)*

Choc Children's, Orange *Also Called: Childrens Healthcare Cal (P-16670)*

Choc Mission, Orange *Also Called: Childrens Hospital Orange Cnty (P-15998)*

Choic Admini Insur Servi .... B....... 714 542-4200
   721 S Parker St Ste 200 Orange (92868) *(P-8526)*

ALPHABETIC SECTION

Choice Home Health Care, Monterey *Also Called: Coastal Home Care Services Inc (P-16842)*
Choice In Aging (PA) .... D....... 925 682-6330
490 Golf Club Rd Pleasant Hill (94523) *(P-17027)*
Choicepoint, Irvine *Also Called: Lexisnexis Risk Assets Inc (P-8603)*
Choices .... D....... 619 692-8200
3853 Rosecrans St San Diego (92110) *(P-17028)*
Chop Stop Inc .... D....... 818 369-7350
601 N Glendale Ave Glendale (91206) *(P-7466)*
Chopra Global LLC .... D....... 760 494-1604
6451 El Camino Real Ste A Carlsbad (92009) *(P-14185)*
Choura Events .... D....... 310 320-6200
540 Hawaii Ave Torrance (90503) *(P-11024)*
Choura Venue Services .... D....... 562 426-0555
4101 E Willow St Long Beach (90815) *(P-10534)*
Choura Vnue Svcs At Carson Ctr, Long Beach *Also Called: Choura Venue Services (P-10534)*
Chowchilla Conv. Center, Chowchilla *Also Called: Avalon Care Ctr - Chwchlla LLC (P-15341)*
Chownow Inc .... D....... 888 707-2469
12181 Bluff Creek Dr Ste W200 Playa Vista (90094) *(P-12134)*
Chp .... D....... 909 213-3788
11338 Walnut St Redlands (92374) *(P-13962)*
Chrisp Company (PA) .... D....... 510 656-2840
43650 Osgood Rd Fremont (94539) *(P-1088)*
Christan Community Theatre .... D....... 619 588-0206
1545 Pioneer Way El Cajon (92020) *(P-17806)*
Christian Arcadia School .... D....... 626 574-8229
1900 S Santa Anita Ave Arcadia (91006) *(P-17701)*
Christian Brookside Schools .... D....... 209 954-7656
3588 Brookside Rd Stockton (95219) *(P-18293)*
Christian Bros Flrg Interiors, Lakeside *Also Called: Christian Bros Flrg Intrors In (P-7429)*
Christian Bros Flrg Intrors In .... D....... 619 443-9500
12086 Woodside Ave Lakeside (92040) *(P-7429)*
Christian Brothers Mechanical Services Inc .... C....... 951 361-2247
11140 Thurston Ln Jurupa Valley (91752) *(P-1396)*
Christian Church Homes .... D....... 510 420-8802
6400 San Pablo Ave Oakland (94608) *(P-8800)*
Christian Church Homes .... C....... 415 814-2670
1099 Fillmore St Apt6h San Francisco (94115) *(P-18394)*
Christian Community Credit Un (PA) .... D....... 626 915-7551
255 N Lone Hill Ave San Dimas (91773) *(P-7822)*
Christian Conference Grounds, Mount Hermon *Also Called: Mount Hermon Association Inc (P-10408)*
Christian Milpitas School (PA) .... C....... 408 945-6530
3435 Birchwood Ln San Jose (95132) *(P-17702)*
Christian Schl Soc of Arcadia, Arcadia *Also Called: Christian Arcadia School (P-17701)*
Christian Turlock Schools (PA) .... D....... 209 632-2337
1619 E Monte Vista Ave Turlock (95382) *(P-17703)*
CHRISTIAN YOUTH THEATER, El Cajon *Also Called: Christan Community Theatre (P-17806)*
Christie Dgtal Systems USA Inc (HQ) .... D....... 714 236-8610
10550 Camden Dr Cypress (90630) *(P-5236)*
Christie Digital Systems Inc (HQ) .... D....... 714 236-8610
10550 Camden Dr Cypress (90630) *(P-3083)*
Christie Parker & Hale LLP (PA) .... C....... 626 795-9900
655 N Central Ave Ste 2300 Glendale (91203) *(P-17403)*
Christopher Ranch LLC (PA) .... C....... 408 847-1100
305 Bloomfield Ave Gilroy (95020) *(P-11)*
Chromalloy San Diego Corp .... C....... 858 877-2800
7007 Consolidated Way San Diego (92121) *(P-13766)*
Chromavision Medical Systems, San Juan Capistrano *Also Called: Clarient Inc (P-16711)*
Chrome River Technologies Inc .... C....... 888 781-0088
5757 Wilshire Blvd Ste 270 Los Angeles (90036) *(P-12135)*
Chromium Dental II LLC .... C....... 949 733-3111
1524 Brookhollow Dr Santa Ana (92705) *(P-15220)*
Chronicle Broadcasting Co .... B....... 415 561-8000
900 Front St San Francisco (94111) *(P-4421)*
Chronicle LLC .... D....... 650 214-5199
250 Mayfield Ave Mountain View (94043) *(P-13101)*
Chrontel Inc (PA) .... D....... 408 383-9328
2210 Otoole Ave Ste 100 San Jose (95131) *(P-2914)*
Chsp Trs Fisherman Wharf LLC .... B....... 415 563-1234
555 N Point St San Francisco (94133) *(P-9698)*

Chubb, Los Angeles *Also Called: Pacific Indemnity Company (P-8634)*
Chugach Government Svcs Inc .... B....... 858 578-0276
9466 Black Mountain Rd Ste 240 San Diego (92126) *(P-20652)*
Chukchansi Gold Resort Casino .... A....... 866 794-6946
711 Lucky Ln Coarsegold (93614) *(P-9699)*
Chula Vista Electric Co .... D....... 619 420-4500
9344 Wheatlands Rd Ste A Santee (92071) *(P-1697)*
Church & Larsen Inc .... C....... 626 303-8741
16103 Avenida Padilla Irwindale (91702) *(P-1921)*
Church Brothers LLC (PA) .... D....... 831 796-1000
19065 Portola Dr Ste C Salinas (93908) *(P-6526)*
Chuwa American, Santa Clara *Also Called: Ryzlink Corp (P-11890)*
Chuze Fitness, Anaheim *Also Called: Rachas Inc (P-14224)*
Ci, Mather *Also Called: Construction Innovations LLC (P-2955)*
Cibus Inc .... C....... 858 450-0008
6455 Nancy Ridge Dr San Diego (92121) *(P-2640)*
Cibus Global Ltd .... C....... 858 450-0008
6455 Nancy Ridge Dr San Diego (92121) *(P-19672)*
CIC Research, San Diego *Also Called: CIC Research Inc (P-19805)*
CIC Research Inc .... D....... 858 637-4000
8361 Vickers St Ste 308 San Diego (92111) *(P-19805)*
Cicoil LLC .... C....... 661 295-1295
24960 Avenue Tibbitts Valencia (91355) *(P-5641)*
Cid Management, Westlake Village *Also Called: Comprhnsive Indus Dsblity MGT (P-17208)*
Cidara, San Diego *Also Called: Cidara Therapeutics Inc (P-2620)*
Cidara Therapeutics Inc (PA) .... D....... 858 752-6170
6310 Nancy Ridge Dr Ste 101 San Diego (92121) *(P-2620)*
Cience Technologies Inc .... D....... 949 424-2906
548 Market St # 99737 San Francisco (94104) *(P-20315)*
Cific Energy Center, San Francisco *Also Called: Sodexo Management Inc (P-20209)*
Cig Financial LLC .... C....... 877 244-4442
6 Executive Cir Ste 100 Irvine (92614) *(P-7872)*
Cigna, Glendale *Also Called: Cigna Behavioral Health of Cal (P-8292)*
Cigna, Glendale *Also Called: Cigna Healthcare Cal Inc (P-8293)*
Cigna Behavioral Health of Cal .... B....... 800 753-0540
450 N Brand Blvd Ste 500 Glendale (91203) *(P-8292)*
Cigna Healthcare Cal Inc (DH) .... B....... 818 500-6262
400 N Brand Blvd Ste 400 Glendale (91203) *(P-8293)*
Cignex Holding Corp .... C....... 408 327-9900
2350 Mission College Blvd Ste 490 Santa Clara (95054) *(P-11489)*
Cim Group LP (PA) .... C....... 323 860-4900
4700 Wilshire Blvd Ste 1 Los Angeles (90010) *(P-9700)*
Cim/H & H Hotel LP .... B....... 323 856-1200
1755 N Highland Ave Los Angeles (90028) *(P-9701)*
Cim/Oakland City Center LLC .... D....... 510 451-4000
1001 Broadway Oakland (94607) *(P-9702)*
Cimarron Group, The, Los Angeles *Also Called: Cimarron Partner Associates LLC (P-10598)*
Cimarron Partner Associates LLC .... C....... 323 337-0300
6855 Santa Monica Blvd Los Angeles (90038) *(P-10598)*
Cimatron Gibbs LLC .... D....... 805 523-0004
2545 W Hillcrest Dr Ste 210 Newbury Park (91320) *(P-11490)*
Cimc Intermodal Equipment, South Gate *Also Called: Cimc Intermodal Equipment LLC (P-2978)*
Cimc Intermodal Equipment LLC (HQ) .... D....... 562 904-8600
10530 Sessler St South Gate (90280) *(P-2978)*
Cinderella Motel .... D....... 559 432-0118
1747 S Harbor Blvd Anaheim (92802) *(P-9703)*
Cinedome 9, Sacramento *Also Called: Century Theatres Inc (P-14020)*
Cinema Secrets Inc .... D....... 818 846-0579
6639 Odessa Ave Van Nuys (91406) *(P-7574)*
Cinnabar .... C....... 818 842-8190
4571 Electronics Pl Los Angeles (90039) *(P-10799)*
Cinnabar, Los Angeles *Also Called: Cinnabar California Inc (P-10800)*
Cinnabar California Inc .... D....... 818 842-8190
4571 Electronics Pl Los Angeles (90039) *(P-10800)*
Cinnabar Hills Golf Club, San Jose *Also Called: Traditions Golf LLC (P-14294)*
Cintas, San Diego *Also Called: Cintas Corporation No 3 (P-7414)*
Cintas, Whittier *Also Called: Cintas Corporation No 3 (P-7415)*
Cintas, Stockton *Also Called: Cintas Corporation No 3 (P-7416)*

Cintas ALPHABETIC SECTION

Cintas, Santa Ana *Also Called: Cintas Sales Corporation* **(P-10433)**
  Cintas Corporation .... D...... 714 646-2550
  4320 E Miraloma Ave Anaheim (92807) **(P-7413)**
  Cintas Corporation No 3 .... C...... 619 239-1001
  675 32nd St San Diego (92102) **(P-7414)**
  Cintas Corporation No 3 .... D...... 562 692-8741
  2829 Workman Mill Rd Whittier (90601) **(P-7415)**
  Cintas Corporation No 3 .... D...... 209 922-0500
  1877 Industrial Dr Stockton (95206) **(P-7416)**

Cintas Fire, Anaheim *Also Called: Cintas Corporation* **(P-7413)**
  Cintas Sales Corporation .... D...... 714 957-2852
  2618 Oak St Santa Ana (92707) **(P-10433)**
  Ciphercloud Inc (HQ) .... D...... 408 687-4350
  2581 Junction Ave Ste 200 San Jose (95134) **(P-12136)**
  Ciphertrace Inc .... D...... 650 996-2142
  140 Victory Ln Los Gatos (95030) **(P-12756)**
  Circle K Ranch LP (PA) .... D...... 559 834-1571
  8640 E Manning Ave Selma (93662) **(P-104)**
  Circle Talent Agency LLC .... D...... 323 424-4970
  8383 Wilshire Blvd Beverly Hills (90211) **(P-14033)**
  Circle Wood Services Inc .... D...... 909 784-0733
  3670 W Temple Ave Pomona (91768) **(P-20056)**
  Circor Aerospace Inc (HQ) .... C...... 951 270-6200
  2301 Wardlow Cir Corona (92878) **(P-2764)**
  Circor Naval Solutions LLC (HQ) .... D...... 413 436-7711
  656 Marsat Ct Ste A Chula Vista (91911) **(P-2792)**
  Circulating Air Inc (PA) .... D...... 818 764-0530
  7337 Varna Ave North Hollywood (91605) **(P-1397)**
  Circulating Air Inc .... D...... 661 942-2048
  1109 W Columbia Way Lancaster (93534) **(P-1398)**
  Ciri - Stroup Inc .... C...... 949 488-3104
  25135 Park Lantern Dana Point (92629) **(P-10535)**
  Cirks Construction Inc .... D...... 916 362-5460
  3300 Industrial Blvd West Sacramento (95691) **(P-894)**

Cirpa Radiology Management, El Segundo *Also Called: Radiology Partners Inc* **(P-15007)**
  Cirrus Asset Management Inc (PA) .... D...... 818 222-4840
  20720 Ventura Blvd Ste 300 Woodland Hills (91364) **(P-8933)**
  Cirrus Health II LP .... C...... 949 855-0562
  24331 El Toro Rd Ste 150 Laguna Hills (92637) **(P-14686)**

CIS Security, Fresno *Also Called: Geil Enterprises Inc* **(P-12977)**
Cisco, San Jose *Also Called: Cisco Systems Capital Corp* **(P-13232)**
Cisco Meraki, San Francisco *Also Called: Meraki LLC* **(P-12836)**
Cisco Systems, San Jose *Also Called: Cisco Systems Inc* **(P-2828)**
Cisco Systems, San Jose *Also Called: Cisco Systems LLC* **(P-12137)**
  Cisco Systems Inc (PA) .... A...... 408 526-4000
  170 W Tasman Dr San Jose (95134) **(P-2828)**
  Cisco Systems Capital Corp (HQ) .... C...... 610 386-5870
  170 W Tasman Dr San Jose (95134) **(P-13232)**
  Cisco Systems LLC (HQ) .... B...... 650 989-6500
  170 W Tasman Dr San Jose (95134) **(P-12137)**
  Cisco Webex LLC (HQ) .... A...... 408 526-4000
  170 W Tasman Dr San Jose (95134) **(P-13233)**
  CIT Bank NA .... D...... 310 399-9262
  2827 Main St Santa Monica (90405) **(P-7611)**
  CIT Bank NA (HQ) .... D...... 626 859-5400
  75 N Fair Oaks Ave Ste C Pasadena (91103) **(P-7612)**
  Citadel Entp Americas LLC .... B...... 415 354-7200
  1 Market Spear Fl 38 San Francisco (94105) **(P-9500)**
  Citadel Panda Express Inc .... D...... 626 799-9898
  899 El Centro St Ste 201 South Pasadena (91030) **(P-7467)**

Citibank, San Francisco *Also Called: Citibank FSB* **(P-7613)**
Citibank, Long Beach *Also Called: Citibank FSB* **(P-7614)**
Citibank, San Francisco *Also Called: Citibank FSB* **(P-7615)**
  Citibank FSB (HQ) .... B...... 415 627-6000
  1 Sansome St San Francisco (94104) **(P-7613)**
  Citibank FSB .... C...... 562 999-3453
  1 World Trade Ctr Ste 100 Long Beach (90831) **(P-7614)**
  Citibank FSB .... C...... 415 649-6971
  2000 Irving St San Francisco (94122) **(P-7615)**

Citifinancial, Yuba City *Also Called: Citifinancial Credit Company* **(P-7873)**
Citifinancial, City Of Industry *Also Called: Citifinancial Credit Company* **(P-7874)**
  Citifinancial Credit Company .... D...... 530 671-7970
  1054 Harter Pkwy Ste 4 Yuba City (95993) **(P-7873)**
  Citifinancial Credit Company .... D...... 626 712-8780
  2655 Del Vista Dr City Of Industry (91745) **(P-7874)**
  Citigroup Global Markets Inc .... D...... 408 947-2200
  225 W Santa Clara St Ste 900 San Jose (95113) **(P-8080)**
  Citiguard Inc .... B...... 800 613-5903
  22736 Vanowen St Ste 300 West Hills (91307) **(P-12944)**

Citiscape, San Francisco *Also Called: Citiscape Prprty MGT Group LLC* **(P-8934)**
  Citiscape Prprty MGT Group LLC .... D...... 415 401-2000
  3450 3rd St Ste 1a San Francisco (94124) **(P-8934)**
  Citivest Inc .... D...... 949 705-0420
  4350 Von Karman Ave Ste 200 Newport Beach (92660) **(P-8935)**

Citizen Watch America, Torrance *Also Called: Citizen Watch Company of America Inc* **(P-6021)**
  Citizen Watch Company of America Inc (HQ) ..... C...... 800 321-1023
  1000 W 190th St Torrance (90502) **(P-6021)**
  Citizens Business Bank (HQ) .... C...... 909 980-4030
  701 N Haven Ave Ste 280 Ontario (91764) **(P-7674)**

Citizens Choice Health Plan, Orange *Also Called: Alignment Health Plan* **(P-8277)**
Citrix Online Group, Goleta *Also Called: Citrix Online LLC* **(P-11491)**
  Citrix Online LLC .... B...... 805 690-6400
  7414 Hollister Ave Goleta (93117) **(P-11491)**

Citrus Ford, Ontario *Also Called: Citrus Motors Ontario Inc* **(P-7184)**
  Citrus Motors Ontario Inc (PA) .... C...... 909 390-0930
  1375 S Woodruff Way Ontario (91761) **(P-7184)**
  Citrus North Venture LLC .... D...... 256 428-2000
  6591 Collins Dr Ste E11 Moorpark (93021) **(P-9704)**
  Citrus Restaurant LLC .... C...... 858 277-8888
  8110 Aero Dr San Diego (92123) **(P-7468)**

CITRUS VALLEY HEALTH PARTNERS, INC., Covina *Also Called: Citrus Vly Hlth Partners Inc* **(P-17206)**
Citrus Vly Hlth Care Partners, Glendora *Also Called: Emanate Health* **(P-16073)**
  Citrus Vly Hlth Partners Inc .... A...... 626 962-4011
  1115 S Sunset Ave West Covina (91790) **(P-16001)**
  Citrus Vly Hlth Partners Inc .... B...... 626 732-3100
  1325 N Grand Ave Ste 300 Covina (91724) **(P-17206)**
  City & County San Francisco .... A...... 415 206-8000
  1001 Potrero Ave San Francisco (94110) **(P-16002)**
  City & County San Francisco .... D...... 415 581-3500
  200 Larkin St San Francisco (94102) **(P-18644)**
  City Alameda Health Care Corp .... A...... 510 522-3700
  2070 Clinton Ave Alameda (94501) **(P-16003)**

City Center Grill, Oakland *Also Called: Cim/Oakland City Center LLC* **(P-9702)**
  City Chevrolet of San Diego .... C...... 619 276-6171
  2111 Morena Blvd San Diego (92110) **(P-13659)**

City Chevrolet of Volkswagen, San Diego *Also Called: City Chevrolet of San Diego* **(P-13659)**
City Corporation Yard, Delano *Also Called: City of Delano* **(P-14249)**
  City Electric Supply .... C...... 707 523-4600
  360 Tesconi Cir Santa Rosa (95401) **(P-5547)**
  City Fibers Inc (PA) .... D...... 323 583-1013
  2500 E 24th St Vernon (90058) **(P-6006)**
  City Hope National Medical Ctr (HQ) .... A...... 626 256-4673
  1500 Duarte Rd Duarte (91010) **(P-16004)**
  City Mechanical Inc .... D...... 510 724-9088
  724 Alfred Nobel Dr Hercules (94547) **(P-13724)**
  City Moving Inc (PA) .... C...... 888 794-8808
  2507 Medford St Los Angeles (90033) **(P-3580)**
  City National Bank (DH) .... B...... 310 888-6000
  555 S Flower St Ste 2500 Los Angeles (90071) **(P-7616)**
  City National Bank .... D...... 949 223-4000
  18111 Von Karman Ave Ste 100 Irvine (92612) **(P-7617)**
  City National Bank .... D...... 951 276-8800
  3484 Central Ave Riverside (92506) **(P-7618)**
  City National Bank .... D...... 650 696-6404
  1450 Chapin Ave Fl 100 Burlingame (94010) **(P-7619)**
  City National Bank .... D...... 310 888-6150
  400 N Roxbury Dr Beverly Hills (90210) **(P-7620)**
  City National Bank .... C...... 310 888-6500
  555 S Flower St Ste 2500 Los Angeles (90071) **(P-7621)**

ALPHABETIC SECTION   Civicactions Inc

City National Corporation .... A
  555 S Flower St Los Angeles (90071) *(P-7622)*

City National Securities Inc .... C....... 310 888-6393
  400 N Roxbury Dr Ste 400 Beverly Hills (90210) *(P-7623)*

City of Anaheim .... D....... 714 254-0125
  201 S Anaheim Blvd Anaheim (92805) *(P-4986)*

City of Anaheim .... D....... 714 704-2400
  2695 E Katella Ave Anaheim (92806) *(P-8709)*

City of Azusa .... D....... 626 969-4408
  729 N Azusa Ave Azusa (91702) *(P-4770)*

City of Bakersfield .... C....... 661 852-7300
  1001 Truxtun Ave Bakersfield (93301) *(P-17886)*

City of Brawley (PA) .... D....... 760 344-8941
  400 Main St Brawley (92227) *(P-20911)*

City of Burbank .... B....... 818 238-3550
  164 W Magnolia Blvd Burbank (91502) *(P-4749)*

City of Burbank .... D....... 818 238-3838
  124 S Lake St Burbank (91502) *(P-13660)*

City of Cerritos .... C....... 562 916-8500
  18125 Bloomfield Ave Cerritos (90703) *(P-20912)*

City of Coronado .... D....... 619 522-7380
  101 B Ave Coronado (92118) *(P-4750)*

City of Culver City .... D....... 310 253-6525
  4343 Duquesne Ave Culver City (90232) *(P-20913)*

City of Delano .... D....... 661 721-3350
  725 S Lexington St Delano (93215) *(P-14249)*

City of Downey .... D....... 562 529-5465
  7209 Rosecrans Ave Paramount (90723) *(P-3323)*

City of Downey .... C....... 562 861-8211
  8435 Firestone Blvd Downey (90241) *(P-14034)*

City of Fairfield .... C....... 707 428-7680
  5110 Peabody Rd Fairfield (94533) *(P-4771)*

City of Folsom .... C....... 916 355-8395
  1300 Leidesdorff St Folsom (95630) *(P-3126)*

City of Fresno .... B....... 559 621-7433
  2223 G St Fresno (93706) *(P-3127)*

City of Fresno .... C....... 559 621-5300
  1910 E University Ave Fresno (93703) *(P-4772)*

City of Glendale .... D....... 818 548-3980
  634 Bekins Way Glendale (91201) *(P-4564)*

City of Glendale .... D....... 818 548-2011
  800 Air Way Glendale (91201) *(P-4773)*

City of Glendale .... C....... 818 548-3945
  633 E Broadway Ste 205 Glendale (91206) *(P-19178)*

City of Hope .... C....... 626 396-2900
  209 Fair Oaks Ave South Pasadena (91030) *(P-14687)*

City of Hope .... B....... 213 202-5735
  1500 Duarte Rd Duarte (91010) *(P-18571)*

City of Hope (PA) .... B....... 626 256-4673
  1500 Duarte Rd Duarte (91010) *(P-20057)*

City of Hope Corona, Duarte *Also Called: City Hope National Medical Ctr* *(P-16004)*

City of Hope Medical Group, South Pasadena *Also Called: City of Hope* *(P-14687)*

City of Huntington Beach .... D....... 714 846-4450
  16782 Graham St Huntington Beach (92649) *(P-14250)*

City of Irvine .... D....... 949 724-6900
  20 Lake Rd Irvine (92604) *(P-17887)*

City of Irvine .... C....... 949 724-7600
  6427 Oak Cyn Irvine (92618) *(P-20316)*

City of Lancaster .... C....... 661 723-6071
  43011 N 10th St W Lancaster (93534) *(P-14301)*

City of Lancaster .... D....... 661 723-6008
  44933 Fern Ave Lancaster (93534) *(P-20922)*

City of Livermore .... D....... 925 371-4848
  1110 S Livermore Ave Livermore (94550) *(P-20928)*

City of Lodi (PA) .... D....... 209 333-6700
  221 W Pine St Lodi (95240) *(P-13234)*

City of Long Beach .... D....... 562 570-2600
  4100 E Donald Douglas Dr # 2 Long Beach (90808) *(P-3882)*

City of Long Beach .... D....... 562 570-4000
  2525 Grand Ave Long Beach (90815) *(P-20937)*

City of Los Angeles .... A....... 310 732-3734
  425 S Palos Verdes St San Pedro (90731) *(P-20948)*

City of Menifee .... D....... 951 672-6777
  29844 Haun Rd Menifee (92586) *(P-20058)*

City of Norco .... D....... 951 270-5617
  2870 Clark Ave Norco (92860) *(P-20728)*

City of Oakland .... D....... 510 351-5812
  11450 Golf Links Rd Oakland (94605) *(P-14251)*

City of Oakland .... D....... 510 238-6796
  150 Frank H Ogawa Plz Ste 3354 Oakland (94612) *(P-17888)*

City of Oxnard (PA) .... C....... 805 385-7803
  300 W 3rd St Oxnard (93030) *(P-20317)*

City of Paso Robles .... D....... 805 237-3999
  747 Spring St Ste B Paso Robles (93446) *(P-1089)*

City of Pleasanton .... D....... 925 454-2341
  3560 Nevada St Pleasanton (94566) *(P-20933)*

City of Redding (PA) .... A....... 530 225-4079
  777 Cypress Ave Redding (96001) *(P-20914)*

City of Riverside .... D....... 951 826-5312
  3901 Orange St Riverside (92501) *(P-4774)*

City of Riverside .... D....... 951 826-5485
  5901 Payton Ave Riverside (92504) *(P-20318)*

City of Sacramento .... C....... 916 808-4949
  2812 Meadowview Rd Sacramento (95832) *(P-4878)*

City of Sacramento .... B....... 916 808-4044
  5730 24th St Bldg 9 Sacramento (95822) *(P-10873)*

City of Sacramento .... C....... 916 808-5291
  1401 K St Sacramento (95814) *(P-13235)*

City of San Diego .... C....... 619 527-7482
  2781 Caminito Chollas San Diego (92105) *(P-1090)*

City of San Diego .... B....... 619 795-5000
  100 Park Blvd San Diego (92101) *(P-14133)*

City of San Jose .... D....... 408 392-3600
  1701 Airport Blvd Ste B1130 San Jose (95110) *(P-3883)*

City of San Jose .... C....... 650 965-4156
  801 N 1st St San Jose (95110) *(P-3884)*

City of San Jose .... D....... 408 441-4653
  1560 Oakland Rd San Jose (95131) *(P-14252)*

City of San Jose .... D....... 408 794-6400
  1300 Senter Rd San Jose (95112) *(P-18686)*

City of San Mateo .... D....... 650 522-7300
  1949 Pacific Blvd San Mateo (94403) *(P-10874)*

City of Santa Ana .... D....... 714 647-6545
  1000 E Santa Ana Blvd Ste 107 Santa Ana (92701) *(P-18221)*

City of Santa Clara .... D....... 408 615-2300
  1500 Warburton Ave Santa Clara (95050) *(P-4565)*

City of Santa Clara .... D....... 408 615-2046
  1705 Martin Ave Santa Clara (95050) *(P-4566)*

City of Stockton .... C....... 209 937-8453
  1465 S Lincoln St Stockton (95206) *(P-18842)*

City of Torrance .... D....... 310 781-7150
  3350 Civic Center Dr N Ste 201 Torrance (90503) *(P-20915)*

City of Ukiah .... C....... 707 467-2818
  300 Plant Rd Ukiah (95482) *(P-1204)*

City of Ukiah .... C....... 707 463-6233
  1320 Airport Rd Ukiah (95482) *(P-4775)*

City of Yuba City .... C....... 530 822-4601
  1201 Civic Center Blvd Yuba City (95993) *(P-18222)*

City Orange Police Assn Inc .... C....... 714 457-5340
  1107 N Batavia St Orange (92867) *(P-18704)*

City Park, San Francisco *Also Called: Imperial Parking (us) LLC* *(P-13606)*

CITY RESCUE MISSION, San Diego *Also Called: San Diego Rescue Mission Inc* *(P-18621)*

City Rise LLC .... D....... 209 334-2703
  18826 N Lower Sacramento Rd Woodbridge (95258) *(P-13236)*

City View At Metreon .... C....... 415 369-6142
  135 4th St Ste 4000 San Francisco (94103) *(P-14134)*

City Wire Cloth, Fontana *Also Called: Daniel Gerard Worldwide Inc* *(P-5487)*

City-Wide Electronic Systems Inc .... D....... 619 444-0219
  440 Highland Ave El Cajon (92020) *(P-1698)*

Civco, Rcho Sta Marg *Also Called: Capital Invstmnts Vntures Corp* *(P-18743)*

CIVIC THEATRE, San Diego *Also Called: San Diego Theatres Inc* *(P-8755)*

Civicactions Inc .... D....... 510 408-7510
  3527 Mt Diablo Blvd Ste 269 Lafayette (94549) *(P-12757)*

Civicorps — ALPHABETIC SECTION

Civicorps .... C 510 992-7800
   6315 San Leandro St Oakland (94621) *(P-4879)*

CJ Berry Well Services MGT LLC .... A 661 589-5220
   3752 Allen Rd Bakersfield (93314) *(P-610)*

CJ Logistics America LLC .... C 909 605-7233
   12350 Philadelphia Ave Eastvale (91752) *(P-3383)*

CJ Logistics America LLC .... D 909 363-4354
   1895 Marigold Ave Redlands (92374) *(P-3454)*

CJ Logistics America LLC .... C 209 362-2232
   1565 N Macarthur Dr Tracy (95376) *(P-3686)*

CJ Logistics America LLC .... D 847 390-6800
   3800 Fanucchi Way E. Shafter (93263) *(P-3687)*

CJ Logistics America LLC .... C 540 377-2302
   5690 Industrial Pkwy San Bernardino (92407) *(P-3998)*

Cjm Automotive Group Inc .... D 661 832-3000
   3101 Cattle Dr Bakersfield (93313) *(P-7185)*

Cjs Model Home Maint Inc .... D 925 485-3280
   240 Spring St Pleasanton (94566) *(P-10875)*

CK Imports Inc .... C 915 225-5747
   530 Alameda Del Prado Ste C10 Novato (94949) *(P-5083)*

CL Knox Inc .... D 661 837-0477
   34933 Imperial Ave Bakersfield (93308) *(P-611)*

Claims Management Inc .... C 916 631-1250
   1101 Creekside Ridge Dr Ste 100 Roseville (95678) *(P-8527)*

Clairbourn School .... D 626 286-3108
   8400 Huntington Dr San Gabriel (91775) *(P-17704)*

Clara Shortridge Foltz .... C 562 925-3039
   9928 Flower St Bellflower (90706) *(P-17404)*

Clare Matrix (PA) .... D 310 314-6200
   2644 30th St Ste 100 Santa Monica (90405) *(P-16673)*

Claremont Club, The, Claremont *Also Called: Claremont Tennis Club (P-14360)*

Claremont Country Club .... D 510 653-6789
   5295 Broadway Ter Oakland (94618) *(P-14359)*

Claremont Hotel Club & Spa, Berkeley *Also Called: Claremont Hotel Properties LLC (P-9705)*

Claremont Hotel Properties LLC .... A 510 843-3000
   41 Tunnel Rd Berkeley (94705) *(P-9705)*

Claremont Pl Assisted Living, Claremont *Also Called: Sunrise Senior Living MGT Inc (P-18528)*

Claremont Tennis Club .... C 909 625-9515
   1777 Monte Vista Ave Claremont (91711) *(P-14360)*

Claremont Toyota, Claremont *Also Called: R&C Motor Corporation (P-13673)*

Clarendon Specialty Fas Inc .... D 714 842-2603
   2180 Temple Ave Long Beach (90804) *(P-5726)*

Clari Inc (PA) .... A 650 265-2111
   1154 Sonora Ct Sunnyvale (94086) *(P-11492)*

Clarient Inc .... C 949 445-7300
   33171 Paseo Cerveza San Juan Capistrano (92675) *(P-16711)*

Clarient Diagnostic Svcs Inc .... C 888 443-3310
   31 Columbia Aliso Viejo (92656) *(P-19957)*

Clarion Hotel, Anaheim *Also Called: Comfort California Inc (P-9717)*

Claris International Inc (HQ) .... C 800 725-2747
   1 Apple Park Way Cupertino (95014) *(P-11493)*

Clarity Services Inc .... D 727 489-7266
   475 Anton Blvd Costa Mesa (92626) *(P-10757)*

Clark - Pacific Corporation (PA) .... B 916 371-0305
   710 Riverpoint Ct Ste 100 West Sacramento (95605) *(P-5200)*

Clark & Sullivan Builders Inc .... C 916 338-7707
   1340 Blue Oaks Blvd Ste 150 Roseville (95678) *(P-895)*

Clark & Sullivan Constrs Inc .... C 916 338-7707
   2024 Opportunity Dr Ste 150 Roseville (95678) *(P-896)*

Clark Bros Inc .... D 209 392-6144
   745 Broadway St Fresno (93721) *(P-1293)*

Clark Cnstr Group - Cal Inc .... B 714 754-0764
   18201 Von Karman Ave Ste 800 Irvine (92612) *(P-810)*

Clark Cnstr Group - Cal LP .... B 714 429-9779
   18201 Von Karman Ave # 800 Irvine (92612) *(P-897)*

Clark Pacific, West Sacramento *Also Called: Clark - Pacific Corporation (P-5200)*

Clark Pest Ctrl Stockton Inc (HQ) .... D 209 368-7152
   555 N Guild Ave Lodi (95240) *(P-10832)*

Clark Pest Ctrl Stockton Inc .... D 209 524-6384
   480 E Service Rd Modesto (95358) *(P-10833)*

Clarke & Rush Mechanical Inc .... D 916 306-5835
   4411 Auburn Blvd Sacramento (95841) *(P-1399)*

Clarklift-West Inc .... C 916 381-5674
   4750 Illinois Ave Fair Oaks (95628) *(P-5826)*

Clarkson Law Firm PC .... D 213 788-4050
   22525 Pacific Coast Hwy Ste 102 Malibu (90265) *(P-17405)*

Class, San Mateo *Also Called: Center For Lrng Atism Spport S (P-17871)*

Classic Bev Southern Cal LLC .... B 626 934-3700
   120 Puente Ave City Of Industry (91746) *(P-6756)*

Classic Camaro Inc .... C 714 847-6887
   18460 Gothard St Huntington Beach (92648) *(P-7346)*

Classic Catering, Monterey *Also Called: Cox & Young Ventures LLC (P-7470)*

Classic Collision Center 2, Los Angeles *Also Called: Caliber Holdings Corporation (P-13635)*

Classic Components, Torrance *Also Called: I C Class Components Corp (P-5661)*

Classic Containers Inc .... B 909 930-3610
   1700 S Hellman Ave Ontario (91761) *(P-2663)*

Classic Custom Vacations, San Jose *Also Called: Classic Vacations LLC (P-3962)*

Classic Firebird, Huntington Beach *Also Called: Classic Camaro Inc (P-7346)*

Classic Installs Inc .... D 951 678-9906
   41755 Elm St Murrieta (92562) *(P-2247)*

Classic Parking Inc .... A 408 278-1444
   34 S Autumn St San Jose (95110) *(P-13604)*

Classic Party Rentals, Inglewood *Also Called: After-Party2 Inc (P-11015)*

Classic Party Rentals, Inglewood *Also Called: After-Party6 Inc (P-11016)*

Classic Party Rentals, Inglewood *Also Called: Classic Party Rentals Inc (P-11025)*

Classic Party Rentals Inc .... A 310 966-4900
   901 W Hillcrest Blvd A Inglewood (90301) *(P-11025)*

Classic Rsdence Mgt Ltd Partnr .... D 831 373-0101
   200 Glenwood Cir Ofc Monterey (93940) *(P-9706)*

Classic Tents, Torrance *Also Called: Classic/Prime Inc (P-11026)*

Classic Vacations LLC .... C 408 287-4550
   5669 Snell Ave Ste 343 San Jose (95123) *(P-3962)*

Classic Wines of California, Ceres *Also Called: Bronco Wine Company (P-6789)*

Classic/Prime Inc .... D 310 328-5060
   540 Hawaii Ave Torrance (90503) *(P-11026)*

Classy, San Diego *Also Called: Classy Inc (P-12138)*

Classy Inc .... C 619 961-1892
   350 10th Ave Ste 1300 San Diego (92101) *(P-12138)*

Claud Townsley Inc .... D 310 527-6770
   555 W 182nd St Gardena (90248) *(P-2051)*

Clauss Construction .... D 619 390-4940
   9911 Maine Ave Lakeside (92040) *(P-2231)*

Clay Dunn Enterprises Inc .... C 310 549-1698
   1606 E Carson St Carson (90745) *(P-1400)*

Clay Lacy Aviation Inc (PA) .... B 818 989-2900
   7435 Valjean Ave Van Nuys (91406) *(P-3885)*

Clean Cut Technologies, Anaheim *Also Called: Oliver Healthcare Packaging Co (P-5850)*

Clean Energy .... A 949 437-1000
   4675 Macarthur Ct Ste 800 Newport Beach (92660) *(P-4722)*

Clean Energy Fuels Corp (PA) .... D 949 437-1000
   4675 Macarthur Ct Ste 800 Newport Beach (92660) *(P-4755)*

Clean Harbors Envmtl Svcs Inc .... D 707 747-6699
   4101 Industrial Way Benicia (94510) *(P-20729)*

Clean Power Finance Inc C
   50 Osgood Pl Ste 400 San Francisco (94133) *(P-13767)*

CLEANERIFIC, San Francisco *Also Called: Jewish Family and Chld Svcs (P-18025)*

Cleanrite Inc .... D 530 246-4886
   5601 Cedars Rd Ste I Redding (96001) *(P-10471)*

Cleanrite Inc .... D 916 381-1321
   814 Striker Ave Ste B Sacramento (95834) *(P-10834)*

Cleanscapessf, San Francisco *Also Called: Recology King County Inc (P-10953)*

Cleansmart Solutions Inc (DH) .... D 510 413-4700
   47422 Kato Rd Fremont (94538) *(P-6059)*

Cleanstreet LLC .... C 800 225-7316
   1918 W 169th St Gardena (90247) *(P-4975)*

Clear Blue Energy Corp .... D 858 451-1549
   17150 Via Del Campo Ste 203 San Diego (92127) *(P-2875)*

Clear Channel Entertainment, Beverly Hills *Also Called: Live Nation Worldwide Inc (P-14148)*

Clear Group Inc .... C 603 325-5600
   408 N Avalon Blvd Los Angeles (90074) *(P-9707)*

ALPHABETIC SECTION   Cloudstaff LLC

Clear Mortgage Capital Inc .... D....... 866 239-8068
   19800 Macarthur Blvd Irvine (92612) *(P-8034)*

Clear Recovery Center .... D....... 310 318-2122
   18119 Prairie Ave Ste 102 Torrance (90504) *(P-17029)*

Clear View Sanitarium, Gardena Also Called: Clear View Sanitarium Inc *(P-15831)*

Clear View Sanitarium Inc .... C....... 310 538-2323
   15823 S Western Ave Gardena (90247) *(P-15831)*

Clear View Windows & Doors Inc .... D....... 661 257-5050
   28106 Avenue Crocker Santa Clarita (91355) *(P-1992)*

Clearcaptions, Roseville Also Called: Clearcaptions LLC *(P-4265)*

Clearcaptions LLC .... B....... 866 868-8695
   3001 Lava Ridge Ct Ste 100 Roseville (95661) *(P-4265)*

Clearchoice MGT Svcs LLC .... D....... 916 742-6055
   9225 Sierra College Blvd Roseville (95661) *(P-15221)*

Clearchoice MGT Svcs LLC .... D....... 408 288-7710
   1655 The Alameda San Jose (95126) *(P-15222)*

Clearchoice MGT Svcs LLC .... D....... 424 337-1178
   21525 Hawthorne Blvd Torrance (90503) *(P-15223)*

Clearedge Lending .... D....... 562 708-7706
   65 Enterprise Aliso Viejo (92656) *(P-7950)*

Clearesult Operating LLC .... D....... 508 836-9500
   807 N Park View Dr # 150 El Segundo (90245) *(P-20730)*

Clearkin Inc .... C....... 925 838-2551
   4115 Blackhawk Plaza Cir Ste 100 Danville (94506) *(P-422)*

Clearlake Capital Group LP (PA) .... B....... 310 400-8800
   233 Wilshire Blvd Ste 800 Santa Monica (90401) *(P-9366)*

Clearlake Capital Partners .... A....... 310 400-8800
   233 Wilshire Blvd Ste 800 Santa Monica (90401) *(P-12139)*

Clearpath Lending .... C....... 949 502-3577
   15635 Alton Pkwy Ste 300 Irvine (92618) *(P-8035)*

Clearpath Lending, Irvine Also Called: Clearpath Lending *(P-8035)*

Clearpath Workforce MGT Inc .... C....... 209 239-8700
   1215 W Center St Ste 102 Manteca (95337) *(P-11281)*

Clearview Capital LLC .... A....... 310 806-9555
   12100 Wilshire Blvd Ste 800 Los Angeles (90025) *(P-9501)*

Clearwater Living, Newport Beach Also Called: Csl Berkshire Operating Co LLC *(P-8954)*

Clearxchange LLC .... D....... 415 813-4801
   275 Sacramento St # 400 San Francisco (94111) *(P-13237)*

Clement Preschool, Saratoga Also Called: Precious Enterprises Inc *(P-18348)*

Clemmie Gill Schl of Scnce Cns .... C....... 559 782-0883
   1701 E Putnam Ave Porterville (93257) *(P-18294)*

Cleo Labs Inc .... C....... 415 234-3437
   85 2nd St Ste 710 San Francisco (94105) *(P-11494)*

Cleveland Wrecking Company .... A....... 510 674-2600
   1580 Chabot Ct Hayward (94545) *(P-2232)*

Clfrn/Clrd/Flrd/rgon I Comcast .... C....... 925 424-0273
   3011 Comcast Pl Livermore (94551) *(P-4208)*

Cli, Indio Also Called: Commercial Lighting Inds Inc *(P-5548)*

Clickbrand, Newport Beach Also Called: Saritasa LLC *(P-12622)*

Clickup, San Diego Also Called: Mango Technologies Inc *(P-11729)*

Client Direct Mortgage, Walnut Creek Also Called: Mortgage Solutions Fcs Inc *(P-8003)*

Clif Bar & Company LLC (HQ) .... B....... 510 596-6300
   1451 66th St Emeryville (94608) *(P-2373)*

Cliff House Restaurant, Fort Bragg Also Called: Tradewinds Lodge *(P-10317)*

Cliff View Terrace Inc .... D....... 805 682-7443
   623 W Junipero St Santa Barbara (93105) *(P-18395)*

Cliff View Terrace Inc .... D....... 415 388-9526
   297 Miller Ave Mill Valley (94941) *(P-18396)*

Clift Hotel Four Season, San Francisco Also Called: Morgans Hotel Group MGT LLC *(P-10031)*

Clift Royal Sonesta Hotel, The, San Francisco Also Called: Sonesta Intl Hotels Corp *(P-10252)*

Cliftonlarsonallen LLP .... B....... 916 784-7800
   925 Highland Pointe Dr Ste 450 Roseville (95678) *(P-19551)*

Cliftonlarsonallen LLP .... D....... 310 273-2501
   1925 Century Park E 16th Fl Los Angeles (90067) *(P-19552)*

Clima-Tech Inc .... D....... 909 613-5550
   1820 Town And Country Dr Norco (92860) *(P-13725)*

Climate Corporation (DH) .... D....... 415 363-0500
   201 3rd St Ste 1010 San Francisco (94103) *(P-12140)*

Climate Fieldview, San Francisco Also Called: Climate Corporation *(P-12140)*

Climate Pros LLC .... C....... 510 784-8990
   3550 Arden Rd Hayward (94545) *(P-1401)*

Climatec LLC .... D....... 858 391-7000
   13715 Stowe Dr Poway (92064) *(P-1699)*

Climatec LLC .... D....... 818 855-8528
   16735 Saticoy St Ste 111 Van Nuys (91406) *(P-1700)*

Clinch-On Cornerbead Company, Orange Also Called: Continuous Coating Corp *(P-2759)*

Clinic Inc .... D....... 323 730-1920
   3834 S Western Ave Los Angeles (90062) *(P-14688)*

Clinica Sierra Vista (PA) .... D....... 661 635-3050
   1430 Truxtun Ave Ste 400 Bakersfield (93301) *(P-14689)*

Clinica Sierra Vista .... D....... 661 845-3717
   8787 Hall Rd Lamont (93241) *(P-14690)*

Clinica Srra Vsta Adult Mntal, Lamont Also Called: Clinica Sierra Vista *(P-14690)*

Clinical Pharmacy, San Francisco Also Called: University Cal San Francisco *(P-17773)*

Clinical Research, Rancho Mirage Also Called: Eisenhower Medical Center *(P-16717)*

Clinical Translational RES Ctr, Los Angeles Also Called: Cedars-Sinai Medical Center *(P-15975)*

Clinicas De Slud Del Peblo Inc (PA) .... D....... 760 344-9951
   852 E Danenberg Dr El Centro (92243) *(P-14691)*

Clinicomp International Inc (PA) .... D....... 858 546-8202
   9655 Towne Centre Dr San Diego (92121) *(P-12434)*

Clinics On Demand Inc .... D....... 310 709-7355
   11000 Wilshire Blvd Los Angeles (90024) *(P-16840)*

Clipboard Health, Covina Also Called: Twomagnets Inc *(P-11249)*

Cliq Inc .... D....... 714 361-1900
   2900 Bristol St Ste F Costa Mesa (92626) *(P-13238)*

Clock Shark LLC .... D....... 530 433-0981
   900 Fortress St Ste 100 Chico (95973) *(P-11495)*

Clockparts, Culver City Also Called: Innovation Specialties *(P-13324)*

Clorox, Oakland Also Called: Clorox Services Company *(P-2623)*

Clorox, Pleasanton Also Called: Clorox Services Company *(P-20059)*

Clorox Services Company (HQ) .... D....... 510 271-7000
   1221 Broadway Oakland (94612) *(P-2623)*

Clorox Services Company .... C....... 925 368-6000
   4900 Johnson Dr Pleasanton (94588) *(P-20059)*

Closet Factory Inc (PA) .... D....... 310 516-7000
   12800 S Bdwy Los Angeles (90061) *(P-2266)*

Closet World Inc .... D....... 626 855-0846
   14438 Don Julian Rd City Of Industry (91746) *(P-1993)*

Closet World Inc .... D....... 800 576-7717
   320 S 6th Ave City Of Industry (91746) *(P-2267)*

Closet World, The, City Of Industry Also Called: Home Organizers Inc *(P-2002)*

Closingcorp Inc .... D....... 858 551-1500
   9645 Granite Ridge Dr Ste 300 San Diego (92123) *(P-12758)*

Cloud Automation Division, Aliso Viejo Also Called: Quest Software Inc *(P-12331)*

Cloud Creations Inc .... D....... 800 951-7651
   301 N Lake Ave Ste 600 Pasadena (91101) *(P-12759)*

Cloud Native Cmpt Foundation .... C....... 415 723-9709
   1 Letterman Dr Ste D4700 San Francisco (94129) *(P-18843)*

Cloud9 Esports Inc .... D....... 424 256-8391
   2720 Neilson Way Unt 5697 Santa Monica (90405) *(P-20319)*

Cloudera Inc .... D....... 650 362-0488
   5470 Great America Pkwy Santa Clara (95054) *(P-11496)*

Cloudflare, San Francisco Also Called: Cloudflare Inc *(P-12141)*

Cloudflare Inc (PA) .... A....... 888 993-5273
   101 Townsend St San Francisco (94107) *(P-12141)*

Cloudinary Inc .... B....... 650 772-1833
   3400 Central Expy Ste 110 Santa Clara (95051) *(P-12760)*

Cloudradiant Corp (PA) .... C....... 408 256-1527
   12 Fuchsia Lake Forest (92630) *(P-6897)*

Cloudradiant Corp .... A....... 408 256-1527
   1111 Di Napoli Dr San Jose (95129) *(P-6898)*

Cloudshield Technologies LLC .... C....... 408 331-6640
   212 Gibraltar Dr Sunnyvale (94089) *(P-12142)*

Cloudsimple Inc .... D....... 412 568-3487
   1600 Amphitheatre Pkwy Mountain View (94043) *(P-12143)*

Cloudstaff LLC .... B....... 888 551-5339
   26895 Aliso Creek Rd # B-209 Aliso Viejo (92656) *(P-10536)*

ALPHABETIC SECTION

Cloudwick Technologies Inc (PA)..D...... 650 346-5788
39899 Balentine Dr Ste 345 Newark (94560) *(P-12761)*

Clover Envmtl Solutions LLC...A...... 815 431-8100
9414 Eton Ave Chatsworth (91311) *(P-5895)*

Clover Network Inc..D...... 650 210-7888
415 N Mathilda Ave Sunnyvale (94085) *(P-2841)*

Clover Sonoma, Petaluma *Also Called: Clover-Stornetta Farms LLC (P-6614)*

Clover-Stornetta Farms LLC (PA)..C...... 707 769-3282
1800 S Mcdowell Boulevard Ext Ste 100 Petaluma (94954) *(P-6614)*

Cloverdale Healthcare Center, Cloverdale *Also Called: Ensign Cloverdale LLC (P-15450)*

Clovis Community Medical Ctr, Clovis *Also Called: Fresno Cmnty Hosp & Med Ctr (P-14755)*

Cls Landscape Management, Montclair *Also Called: Cls Landscape Management Inc (P-553)*

Cls Landscape Management Inc..B...... 909 628-3005
4329 State St Ste B Montclair (91763) *(P-553)*

Cls Trnsprttion Los Angles LLC (HQ).....................................C...... 310 414-8189
600 S Allied Way El Segundo (90245) *(P-3249)*

Club Assist North America Inc (DH)......................................D...... 213 388-4333
888 W 6th St Ste 300 Los Angeles (90017) *(P-5033)*

Club At Los Gatos Inc...D...... 408 354-4808
285 E Main St Los Gatos (95030) *(P-14186)*

Club At Pasadera The, Monterey *Also Called: Pasadera Club Oc LLC (P-14422)*

Club Corp Incorporated..D...... 925 240-2990
120 Guthrie Ln Brentwood (94513) *(P-14187)*

Club One Casino, Fresno *Also Called: Club One Casino Inc (P-9708)*

Club One Casino Inc..B...... 559 497-3000
3950 N Cedar Ave Ste 101 Fresno (93726) *(P-9708)*

Club One Fitness, San Francisco *Also Called: Club One Inc (P-14188)*

Club One Inc..A...... 415 477-3000
555 Market St Fl 13 San Francisco (94105) *(P-14188)*

Club Quarters MGT Co LLC...D...... 415 392-7400
424 Clay St San Francisco (94111) *(P-10419)*

Clubsport of Pleasanton, Pleasanton *Also Called: Cs-Pleasanton LLC (P-14366)*

Clubsport San Ramon LLC...D...... 925 283-4000
4000 Mt Diablo Blvd Lafayette (94549) *(P-14189)*

Clubsport San Ramon LLC (PA)...C...... 925 735-1182
350 Bollinger Canyon Ln San Ramon (94582) *(P-14190)*

Clumio Inc...D...... 603 321-2495
4555 Great America Pkwy Ste 101 Santa Clara (95054) *(P-11497)*

Clune Construction Company LP..C...... 415 395-7245
1 Post St Ste 300 San Francisco (94104) *(P-898)*

Clutter Inc (PA)..C...... 800 805-4023
3526 Hayden Ave Culver City (90232) *(P-10537)*

CM Laundry LLC..D...... 310 436-6170
14919 S Figueroa St Gardena (90248) *(P-10484)*

Cmb Laboratory, Cypress *Also Called: Consoldted Med Bo-Analysis Inc (P-16712)*

CMC, Goleta *Also Called: CMC Rescue Inc (P-7575)*

CMC Rebar West..D...... 714 692-7082
10840 Norwalk Blvd Santa Fe Springs (90670) *(P-811)*

CMC Rebar West..C...... 707 863-3933
1060 Kaiser Rd Napa (94558) *(P-812)*

CMC Rebar West..C...... 858 737-7700
7326 Mission Gorge Rd San Diego (92120) *(P-813)*

CMC Rebar West..C...... 707 759-1400
5160 Fulton Dr Fairfield (94534) *(P-5482)*

CMC Rebar West..C...... 909 713-1130
5425 Industrial Pkwy San Bernardino (92407) *(P-5483)*

CMC Rescue Inc...D...... 805 562-9120
6740 Cortona Dr Goleta (93117) *(P-7575)*

Cmf Inc..D...... 714 637-2409
1317 W Grove Ave Orange (92865) *(P-2052)*

Cmg, San Ramon *Also Called: Cmg Mortgage Inc (P-8036)*

Cmg Financial Services...A...... 925 983-3073
3160 Crow Canyon Rd Ste 400 San Ramon (94583) *(P-7951)*

Cmg Mortgage Inc (PA)..B...... 619 554-1327
3160 Crow Canyon Rd Ste 400 San Ramon (94583) *(P-8036)*

CMI, San Jose *Also Called: Critchfield Mechanical Inc (P-1414)*

Cmre Financial Services Inc..B...... 714 528-3200
3075 E Imperial Hwy Ste 200 Brea (92821) *(P-10738)*

CMS, Simi Valley *Also Called: Computerized Mgt Svcs Inc (P-19554)*

Cmt, Camino *Also Called: Coastal Mountain Timber Inc (P-554)*

Cmtc, Long Beach *Also Called: California Mfg Tech Consulting (P-19168)*

Cncml A California Ltd Partnr..D...... 530 583-1578
1920 Squaw Valley Rd Olympic Valley (96146) *(P-9709)*

Cnet Express...C...... 949 357-5475
15134 Indiana Ave Apt 38 Paramount (90723) *(P-3384)*

Cnet Networks Inc..A...... 415 344-2000
235 2nd St San Francisco (94105) *(P-12435)*

Cnet Technology Corporation..C...... 408 392-9966
26291 Production Ave Ste 205 Hayward (94545) *(P-5642)*

Cni Thl Propco Fe LLC...D...... 661 325-9700
5101 California Ave Bakersfield (93309) *(P-9710)*

Cnn, Los Angeles *Also Called: Cnn America Inc (P-4422)*

Cnn America Inc..C...... 323 993-5000
6430 W Sunset Blvd Ste 300 Los Angeles (90028) *(P-4422)*

Cns Inc..D...... 661 872-3408
5215 Ashe Rd Bakersfield (93313) *(P-14692)*

Cntry Vlla Merced Hlthcre Cntr, Merced *Also Called: Country Villa Service Corp (P-17901)*

Co Architects (PA)..D...... 323 525-0500
5750 Wilshire Blvd Ste 550 Los Angeles (90036) *(P-19461)*

Co Ltd, All Nippon Airways, Torrance *Also Called: Nippon Express (P-4065)*

Co-Op Solutions, Rancho Cucamonga *Also Called: CU Cooperative Systems Inc (P-7824)*

Co-Production Intl Inc..A...... 619 429-4344
8716 Sherwood Ter San Diego (92154) *(P-20320)*

Coach Usa Inc..D...... 626 357-7912
5640 Peck Rd Arcadia (91006) *(P-3317)*

Coachella Valley Water Dst, Palm Desert *Also Called: Coachlla Vly Wtr Dst Pub Fclti (P-4776)*

Coachlla Vly Wtr Dst Pub Fclti (PA)......................................C...... 760 398-2651
75515 Hovley Ln E Palm Desert (92211) *(P-4776)*

Coachlla Vly Wtr Dst Pub Fclti..C...... 760 398-2651
75525 Hovley Ln E Palm Desert (92260) *(P-4777)*

Coaction, Glendale *Also Called: Coaction Spclty Insur Group In (P-8528)*

Coaction Spclty Insur Group In..D...... 818 230-8200
101 N Brand Blvd Ste 1900 Glendale (91203) *(P-8528)*

Coadna Holdings Inc..D...... 408 736-1100
1020 Stewart Dr Sunnyvale (94085) *(P-9307)*

Coalinga Feed Yard Inc..C...... 559 935-0836
35244 Oil City Rd Coalinga (93210) *(P-209)*

Coalinga Regional Med Ctr Aux..C...... 559 935-6400
1191 Phelps Ave Coalinga (93210) *(P-16005)*

Coalinga State Hospital, Coalinga *Also Called: Califrnia Dept State Hospitals (P-16641)*

Coast Aluminum, Santa Fe Springs *Also Called: Coast Aluminum Inc (P-5484)*

Coast Aluminum Inc (PA)..C...... 562 946-6061
10628 Fulton Wells Ave Santa Fe Springs (90670) *(P-5484)*

Coast Care Partners...D...... 619 354-2544
8033 Linda Vista Rd Ste 200 San Diego (92111) *(P-17207)*

Coast Central Credit Union (PA)...D...... 707 445-8801
2650 Harrison Ave Eureka (95501) *(P-7759)*

Coast Citrus Distributors (PA)..D...... 619 661-7950
7597 Bristow Ct San Diego (92154) *(P-6527)*

Coast Group Financial, San Marcos *Also Called: Centurion Group Inc (P-8074)*

Coast Landscape Management, Alviso *Also Called: Bayscape Management Inc (P-389)*

Coast Lm Inc..C...... 800 578-8810
7400 Folsom Blvd Sacramento (95826) *(P-423)*

Coast Oil Company LLC...D...... 408 252-7720
4250 Williams Rd San Jose (95129) *(P-6725)*

Coast Personnel Services Inc (PA).......................................A...... 408 653-2100
2295 De La Cruz Blvd Santa Clara (95050) *(P-11282)*

Coast Plz Dctors Hosp A Cal Lt (DH)...................................D...... 562 868-3751
13100 Studebaker Rd Norwalk (90650) *(P-16006)*

Coast Produce Company (PA)...C...... 213 955-4900
1791 Bay St Los Angeles (90021) *(P-6528)*

Coast To Coast Cmpt Pdts Inc..C...... 805 244-9500
4277 Valley Fair St Simi Valley (93063) *(P-7441)*

Coast Tropical, San Diego *Also Called: Coast Citrus Distributors (P-6527)*

Coastal Alliance Holdings Inc...C...... 562 370-1000
1650 Ximeno Ave Ste 120 Long Beach (90804) *(P-8936)*

Coastal Building Services Inc...B...... 714 775-2855
1433 W Central Park Ave N Anaheim (92802) *(P-10876)*

Coastal Cmnty Senior Care LLC...C...... 562 596-4884
5500 E Atherton St Ste 216 Long Beach (90815) *(P-16841)*

ALPHABETIC SECTION — Coldwell Bnkr Rsdntial Rfrral

Coastal Cocktails Inc (PA) .... D....... 949 250-8951
1920 E Deere Ave Ste 100 Santa Ana (92705) *(P-6615)*

Coastal Community Hospital, Santa Ana *Also Called: Health Resources Corp (P-16122)*

Coastal Health Care Inc .... D....... 310 828-5596
1321 Franklin St Santa Monica (90404) *(P-15376)*

Coastal Home Care Services Inc .... C....... 831 424-1344
80 Garden Ct Ste 105 Monterey (93940) *(P-16842)*

Coastal International, Tustin *Also Called: Coastal Intl Holdings LLC (P-13239)*

Coastal Intl Holdings LLC .... B....... 714 635-1200
2832 Walnut Ave Ste B Tustin (92780) *(P-13239)*

Coastal Mountain Timber Inc .... D....... 530 303-3378
3737 Carson Rd Unit A Camino (95709) *(P-554)*

Coastal Pacific Fd Distrs Inc .... D....... 909 947-2066
1520 E Mission Blvd Ste B Ontario (91761) *(P-3688)*

Coastal Pacific Fd Distrs Inc (PA) .... C....... 909 947-2066
1015 Performance Dr Stockton (95206) *(P-6246)*

Coastal Pacific Foods, Ontario *Also Called: Coastal Pacific Fd Distrs Inc (P-3688)*

Coastal Rdtion Onclogy Med Gro .... D....... 805 494-4483
1240 S Westlake Blvd Ste 103 Westlake Village (91361) *(P-14693)*

Coastal The, Sherman Oaks *Also Called: Coastal Tile Inc (P-1977)*

Coastal Tile Inc .... D....... 818 988-6134
13226 Moorpark St Apt 104 Sherman Oaks (91423) *(P-1977)*

Coastal View Halthcare Ctr LLC .... D....... 805 642-4101
4904 Telegraph Rd Ventura (93003) *(P-15377)*

Coastal View Healthcare Center, Ventura *Also Called: Coastal View Halthcare Ctr LLC (P-15377)*

Coasthills Credit Union (PA) .... D....... 805 733-7600
1075 E Betteravia Rd Santa Maria (93454) *(P-7823)*

Coastline Cnstr & Awng Co Inc .... D....... 714 891-9798
5742 Research Dr Huntington Beach (92649) *(P-667)*

Coastline Equipment, Oxnard *Also Called: Bragg Investment Company Inc (P-5030)*

Cobalt Construction Company .... D....... 805 577-6222
2259 Ward Ave Ste 200 Simi Valley (93065) *(P-749)*

Cobalt Southwest Company, Simi Valley *Also Called: Cobalt Construction Company (P-749)*

Cobblestone Fruit .... C....... 559 524-1005
730 N Oliver Ave Sanger (93657) *(P-2352)*

Cobe Chemical Co Inc .... D....... 877 691-3590
1016 S Vail Ave Montebello (90640) *(P-2626)*

Cobe Laboratories, Montebello *Also Called: Cobe Chemical Co Inc (P-2626)*

Coblentz Patch Duffy Bass LLP (PA) .... D....... 510 655-4598
1 Montgomery St Ste 3000 San Francisco (94104) *(P-17406)*

Cobrapro, Orange *Also Called: Word & Brown Insurance Administrators Inc (P-8694)*

Coca-Cola, Downey *Also Called: Reyes Coca-Cola Bottling LLC (P-2408)*

Coca-Cola, Rancho Cucamonga *Also Called: Reyes Coca-Cola Bottling LLC (P-2409)*

Coca-Cola, San Diego *Also Called: Reyes Coca-Cola Bottling LLC (P-2410)*

Cockram Construction Inc .... B....... 818 650-0999
605 8th St San Fernando (91340) *(P-20321)*

Cocokids Inc .... C....... 925 676-5442
1035 Detroit Ave Ste 200 Concord (94518) *(P-18572)*

Coda Project Inc .... D....... 561 267-1403
888 Villa St Fl 4 Mountain View (94041) *(P-20322)*

Codazen, Irvine *Also Called: Codazen Inc (P-11498)*

Codazen Inc .... D....... 949 916-6266
60 Bunsen Irvine (92618) *(P-11498)*

Coddingtontown, Santa Rosa *Also Called: Korvalabs Inc (P-13341)*

Code For America, San Francisco *Also Called: Code For America Labs Inc (P-20323)*

Code For America Labs Inc .... D....... 415 816-1286
972 Mission St Fl 5 San Francisco (94103) *(P-20323)*

Codesignal Inc .... C....... 669 200-9704
201 California St San Francisco (94111) *(P-11499)*

CODEXIS, Redwood City *Also Called: Codexis Inc (P-2573)*

Codexis Inc (PA) .... D....... 650 421-8100
200 Penobscot Dr Redwood City (94063) *(P-2573)*

Codility US Inc .... C....... 415 568-5055
575 Market St Fl 4 San Francisco (94105) *(P-11500)*

Coding School .... D....... 424 339-3977
12438 Landale St Studio City (91604) *(P-18844)*

Cofa Media Group LLC .... D....... 877 293-2007
5650 El Camino Real Ste 100a Carlsbad (92008) *(P-12558)*

Coffee Bean & Tea Leaf, The, Los Angeles *Also Called: International Coffee & Tea LLC (P-7488)*

Coffman Specialties Inc (PA) .... C....... 858 536-3100
9685 Via Excelencia Ste 200 San Diego (92126) *(P-2109)*

Cofiroute, Irvine *Also Called: Cofiroute Usa LLC (P-4137)*

Cofiroute Usa LLC .... C....... 949 754-0198
100 Progress Ste 110 Irvine (92618) *(P-4137)*

Cognitive Medical Systems Inc (PA) .... D....... 858 509-4949
9920 Pacific Heights Blvd Ste 150 # 5604 San Diego (92121) *(P-11501)*

Cognitiveclouds Software Inc .... D....... 415 234-3611
5433 Ontario Cmn Fremont (94555) *(P-11502)*

Cognizant Trizetto .... D....... 949 719-2200
567 San Nicolas Dr Ste 360 Newport Beach (92660) *(P-12762)*

Cognizant Trzttto Sftwr Group I .... C....... 714 481-0396
3631 S Harbor Blvd Ste 200 Santa Ana (92704) *(P-12436)*

Cohen Ventures Inc (PA) .... D....... 510 482-4420
449 15th St # 400 Oakland (94612) *(P-20731)*

Coherent Aerospace & Def Inc .... D....... 714 247-7100
14192 Chambers Rd Tustin (92780) *(P-3035)*

Cohesity Inc .... C....... 650 968-4470
1880 Fallen Leaf Ln Los Altos (94024) *(P-9424)*

Cohesity Inc (PA) .... B....... 855 926-4374
300 Park Ave Ste 1700 San Jose (95110) *(P-11503)*

Coinlist .... D....... 408 230-4375
900 Kearny St Ste 500 San Francisco (94133) *(P-8710)*

Coit, Burlingame *Also Called: Coit Services Inc (P-10466)*

Coit, Sacramento *Also Called: Coit Services Inc (P-10472)*

Coit Restoration Services, Modesto *Also Called: C & S Draperies Inc (P-10470)*

Coit Services Inc .... D....... 916 731-7006
1755 Helena Ave Ste C Sacramento (95815) *(P-10472)*

Coit Services Inc (PA) .... C....... 650 697-5471
897 Hinckley Rd Burlingame (94010) *(P-10466)*

Cokeva Inc .... C....... 916 462-6001
9000 Foothills Blvd Roseville (95747) *(P-12705)*

Cold Stone Creamery, Vallejo *Also Called: Park Management Corp (P-14309)*

Coldwater Care Center LLC .... C....... 818 766-6105
12750 Riverside Dr North Hollywood (91607) *(P-15378)*

Coldwell Banker, Bakersfield *Also Called: Bakersfield Westwind Corp (P-8908)*

Coldwell Banker, Canyon Lake *Also Called: Cbabr Inc (P-8925)*

Coldwell Banker, Victorville *Also Called: Coldwell Banker Home Source (P-8937)*

Coldwell Banker, Santa Barbara *Also Called: Coldwell Banker Premier Prpts (P-8938)*

Coldwell Banker, San Jose *Also Called: Coldwell Banker RE LLC (P-8939)*

Coldwell Banker, Mission Viejo *Also Called: Coldwell Banker Residential (P-8940)*

Coldwell Banker, Arcadia *Also Called: Coldwell Banker Residential RE (P-8941)*

Coldwell Banker, Concord *Also Called: Coldwell Bnkr Residential Brkg (P-8942)*

Coldwell Banker, Greenbrae *Also Called: Coldwell Bnkr Rsdntial RE Svcs (P-8943)*

Coldwell Banker, Mission Viejo *Also Called: Coldwell Bnkr Rsdntial Rfrral (P-8944)*

Coldwell Banker, Newport Beach *Also Called: Coldwell Bnkr Rsdntial Rfrral (P-8945)*

Coldwell Banker, Bakersfield *Also Called: Preferred Brokers Inc (P-9138)*

Coldwell Banker Coastl Aliance, Long Beach *Also Called: Coastal Alliance Holdings Inc (P-8936)*

Coldwell Banker Home Source .... D....... 760 684-8100
15500 W Sand St Ste 2 Victorville (92392) *(P-8937)*

Coldwell Banker Premier Prpts .... D....... 805 565-2200
1498 E Valley Rd Santa Barbara (93108) *(P-8938)*

Coldwell Banker RE LLC .... D....... 408 723-3300
1712 Meridian Ave Ste C San Jose (95125) *(P-8939)*

Coldwell Banker Residential (DH) .... D....... 949 837-5700
27742 Vista Del Lago Ste J1 Mission Viejo (92692) *(P-8940)*

Coldwell Banker Residential BR, San Diego *Also Called: Dorothy Sarkozy (P-8987)*

Coldwell Banker Residential RE .... C....... 626 445-5500
15 E Foothill Blvd Arcadia (91006) *(P-8941)*

Coldwell Banker Royal Realty, Chula Vista *Also Called: Palanging International Inc (P-9123)*

Coldwell Banker Solano Pacific, Benicia *Also Called: Solano Pacific Corporation (P-9181)*

Coldwell Bnkr Residential Brkg (DH) .... D....... 925 275-3000
1855 Gateway Blvd Ste 750 Concord (94520) *(P-8942)*

Coldwell Bnkr Rsdntial RE Svcs .... B....... 415 461-2020
500 Sir Francis Drake Blvd Greenbrae (94904) *(P-8943)*

Coldwell Bnkr Rsdntial Rfrral (DH) .... B....... 949 367-1800
27271 Las Ramblas Mission Viejo (92691) *(P-8944)*

Coldwell Bnkr Rsdntial Rfrral .... A....... 949 673-8700
201 Marine Ave Newport Beach (92662) *(P-8945)*

Coldwell Bnkr Rsdntial Rfrral, Newport Beach *Also Called: C B Coast Newport Properties* (P-8919)

Cole, Norman Anne, Anaheim *Also Called: House Seven Gables RE Inc* (P-9041)

Coleman Chavez & Assoc LLP .... D...... 916 787-2310
1731 E Roseville Pkwy Ste 200 Roseville (95661) (P-17407)

Collab Inc (PA) .... D...... 310 991-0062
155 W Washington Blvd Ste 417 Los Angeles (90015) (P-10599)

Collabria Care .... D...... 707 258-9080
414 S Jefferson St Napa (94559) (P-16843)

Collabrus Inc .... C...... 415 288-1826
180 Montgomery St Ste 2380 San Francisco (94104) (P-19553)

Collection Technology Inc .... D...... 800 743-4284
10801 6th St Ste 200 Rancho Cucamonga (91730) (P-10739)

Collective Digital Studio, LLC, Beverly Hills *Also Called: Studio 71 LP* (P-10720)

Collective Health, San Francisco *Also Called: Collectivehealth Inc* (P-8529)

Collective Management Group, Beverly Hills *Also Called: Collective MGT Group LLC* (P-20060)

Collective MGT Group LLC .... C...... 323 655-8585
8383 Wilshire Blvd Ste 1050 Beverly Hills (90211) (P-20060)

Collectivehealth Inc (PA) .... C...... 844 265-3288
45 Fremont St Ste 1200 San Francisco (94105) (P-8529)

Collectors Universe, Santa Ana *Also Called: Collectors Universe Inc* (P-13768)

Collectors Universe Inc (PA) .... C...... 949 567-1234
1610 E Saint Andrew Pl Santa Ana (92705) (P-13768)

Colleen & Herb Enterprises Inc .... C...... 510 226-6083
46939 Bayside Pkwy Fremont (94538) (P-2850)

College Hospital Inc (PA) .... B...... 562 924-9581
10802 College Pl Cerritos (90703) (P-16648)

COLLEGE HOSPITAL CERRITOS, Costa Mesa *Also Called: College Hospital Costa Mesa Mso Inc* (P-16007)

College Hospital Cerritos, Cerritos *Also Called: College Hospital Inc* (P-16648)

College Hospital Costa Mesa Mso Inc (HQ) .... D...... 949 642-2734
301 Victoria St Costa Mesa (92627) (P-16007)

College Park Realty Inc (PA) .... D...... 562 594-6753
10791 Los Alamitos Blvd Los Alamitos (90720) (P-8946)

College Track .... C...... 510 834-3295
483 9th St Oakland (94607) (P-20324)

College Works Painting, Irvine *Also Called: Cwpnc Inc* (P-1610)

Colliers International .... D...... 415 788-3100
101 2nd St Ste 1100 San Francisco (94105) (P-8947)

Collins & Collins .... D...... 626 243-1100
790 E Colorado Blvd Ste 600 Pasadena (91101) (P-8711)

Collins Electrical Company Inc (PA) .... C...... 209 466-3691
3412 Metro Dr Stockton (95215) (P-1701)

Collinson Law A Prof Corp .... C...... 424 212-7777
21515 Hawthorne Blvd Ste 800 Torrance (90503) (P-17408)

Collwood Ter Stellar Care Inc .... D...... 619 287-2920
4518 54th St San Diego (92115) (P-18397)

Colombia Energy Resources Inc C
1 Embarcadero Ctr Ste 500 San Francisco (94111) (P-576)

Colombo Construction Co Inc .... D...... 661 316-0100
3211 Rio Mirada Dr Bakersfield (93308) (P-899)

Colonial Care Center, Long Beach *Also Called: Longwood Management Corp* (P-15873)

Colonial Gardens Nursing Home, Pico Rivera *Also Called: Rivera Sanatarium Inc* (P-15640)

Colony Dstrssed Cr Spcial Stto, Los Angeles *Also Called: Cdcf III PCF Lndmark Scrmnto L* (P-8708)

Colony MB Partners LP .... D...... 310 282-8820
1999 Avenue Of The Stars Ste 1200 Los Angeles (90067) (P-8712)

Colony Palms Hotel LLC .... D...... 760 969-1800
572 N Indian Canyon Dr Palm Springs (92262) (P-9711)

Color Concepts, Canoga Park *Also Called: Rte Enterprises Inc* (P-1639)

Color Design Laboratory Inc (PA) .... D...... 818 341-5100
21329 Nordhoff St Chatsworth (91311) (P-19958)

Color Design Labs, Chatsworth *Also Called: Color Design Laboratory Inc* (P-19958)

Color Genomic Danny, Burlingame *Also Called: Color Health Inc* (P-5409)

Color Health Inc .... A...... 650 651-7116
831 Mitten Rd Ste 100 Burlingame (94010) (P-5409)

Color Laser R&D, Chatsworth *Also Called: Clover Envmtl Solutions LLC* (P-5895)

Color Spot Holdings Inc (PA) .... A...... 760 695-1430
3742 Blue Bird Canyon Rd Vista (92084) (P-120)

Color Spot Lodi, Lodi *Also Called: Csn Winddown Inc* (P-122)

Color Spot Nurseries, Vista *Also Called: Color Spot Holdings Inc* (P-120)

Colorado River Adventures Inc (PA) .... C...... 760 663-3737
2715 Parker Dam Rd Earp (92242) (P-10416)

COLORADO RIVER MEDICAL CENTER, Needles *Also Called: Community Hlthcare Partner Inc* (P-14702)

Colorama Wholesale Nursery, Azusa *Also Called: Richard Wilson Wellington* (P-151)

Coloredge .... C...... 818 842-1121
3520 W Valhalla Dr Burbank (91505) (P-13159)

Colorescience Inc .... C...... 866 426-5673
2141 Palomar Airport Rd Ste 200 Carlsbad (92011) (P-6102)

Colorgraphics, Los Angeles *Also Called: Madisn/Grham Clor Graphics Inc* (P-2562)

Coloserve, San Jose *Also Called: Gogrid LLC* (P-4289)

Colosseum Athletics, Compton *Also Called: Colosseum Athletics Corp* (P-6171)

Colosseum Athletics Corp .... D...... 310 667-8341
2400 S Wilmington Ave Compton (90220) (P-6171)

Colour Concepts Inc C
1225 Los Angeles St Glendale (91204) (P-2559)

Colrich Communities Inc .... C...... 858 350-7672
444 W Beech St Ste 300 San Diego (92101) (P-9249)

Colsa Corporation .... C...... 619 553-0031
2727 Cmino Del Rio S Ste San Diego (92108) (P-11504)

Colt Services Inc .... D...... 858 271-9910
9655 Via Excelencia San Diego (92126) (P-10473)

Columbia Hospitality Inc .... B...... 415 362-8878
665 Bush St San Francisco (94108) (P-9712)

Columbia Hospitality Inc .... A...... 831 646-8900
652 Cannery Row Monterey (93940) (P-9713)

Columbia Hospitality Inc .... A...... 831 373-5700
300 Pacific St Monterey (93940) (P-9714)

Columbia Hospitality Inc .... B...... 630 366-2309
242 Cannery Row Monterey (93940) (P-9715)

Columbia Pictures, Culver City *Also Called: Columbia Pictures Inds Inc* (P-13830)

Columbia Pictures Inds Inc .... D...... 818 655-5820
4024 Radford Ave Studio City (91604) (P-13829)

Columbia Pictures Inds Inc (DH) .... C...... 310 244-4000
10202 Washington Blvd Culver City (90232) (P-13830)

Columbia Showcase & Cab Co Inc .... C...... 818 765-9710
11034 Sherman Way Ste A Sun Valley (91352) (P-2502)

Columbia Spclty A Trstar Indus, Long Beach *Also Called: Trstar Industrial LLC* (P-5932)

Columbia Specialty Company Inc .... D...... 562 634-6425
5875 Obispo Ave Long Beach (90805) (P-5896)

Columbus Foods LLC .... B...... 510 921-3400
30977 San Antonio St Hayward (94544) (P-2338)

Colusa Casino, Colusa *Also Called: Colusa Indian Cmnty Council* (P-18573)

Colusa Casino Resort, Colusa *Also Called: New Colusa Indian Bingo* (P-10041)

Colusa Indian Cmnty Council .... D...... 530 458-5787
3720 State Highway 45 Colusa (95932) (P-14694)

Colusa Indian Cmnty Council .... C...... 530 458-5501
3710 State Highway 45 Ste A Colusa (95932) (P-14695)

Colusa Indian Cmnty Council .... B...... 530 458-6572
3740 State Highway 45 Colusa (95932) (P-18573)

Colusa Produce Corporation .... D...... 530 696-0121
1954 Progress Rd Meridian (95957) (P-6616)

Colusa Regional Medical Center Inc .... C...... 530 458-5821
199 E Webster St Ste 1 Colusa (95932) (P-20061)

Com Dev Usa LLC .... D...... 424 456-8000
2333 Utah Ave El Segundo (90245) (P-5956)

Com2us Usa Inc .... D...... 310 416-1100
999 N Pacific Coast Hwy Ste 450 El Segundo (90245) (P-11505)

Comav LLC .... C...... 760 523-5100
18260 Phantom W Victorville (92394) (P-3886)

Comav Aviation, Victorville *Also Called: Comav LLC* (P-3886)

Comav Technical Services LLC .... C...... 760 530-2400
18438 Readiness St Victorville (92394) (P-3887)

Comcast, Livermore *Also Called: Clfrn/Clrd/Flrd/rgon I Comcast* (P-4208)

Comcast, Ontario *Also Called: Comcast Corporation* (P-4493)

Comcast Corporation .... D...... 909 890-0886
1205 S Dupont Ave Ontario (91761) (P-4493)

Comcast Slcon Vly Innvtion Ctr, Sunnyvale *Also Called: Plaxo Inc* (P-4518)

ALPHABETIC SECTION — Community College Foundation

Comcast Sprtsnet Bay Area Hldn .... C....... 415 896-2557
360 3rd St 2nd Fl San Francisco (94107) *(P-4423)*

Come Land Maint Svc Co Inc .... A....... 818 567-2455
1419 N San Fernando Blvd Ste 250 Burbank (91504) *(P-10877)*

Comedy Club Oxnard LLC .... D....... 805 535-5400
591 Collection Blvd Oxnard (93036) *(P-14361)*

Comet Building Maintenance Inc .... D....... 415 382-1150
21 Commercial Blvd Ste 12 Novato (94949) *(P-424)*

Comet Electric Inc .... C....... 818 340-0965
21625 Prairie St Chatsworth (91311) *(P-1702)*

Comet Medical, Ventura *Also Called: Peter Brasseler Holdings LLC* *(P-5442)*

Comfort Air Inc .... D....... 209 466-4601
1607 French Camp Tpke Stockton (95206) *(P-1402)*

Comfort California Inc .... C....... 415 928-5000
2775 Van Ness Ave San Francisco (94109) *(P-9716)*

Comfort California Inc .... C....... 714 750-3131
616 W Convention Way Anaheim (92802) *(P-9717)*

Comfort Inn, San Diego *Also Called: Best Rest Management Inc* *(P-9643)*

Comfort Inn, San Francisco *Also Called: Comfort California Inc* *(P-9716)*

Comfort Inn, Palo Alto *Also Called: Comfort Inn Palo Alto* *(P-9718)*

Comfort Inn Palo Alto .... D....... 650 493-3142
3945 El Camino Real Palo Alto (94306) *(P-9718)*

Comfort Keepers, Claremont *Also Called: Bluebridge Prof Svcs Inc* *(P-16824)*

Comfort Keepers, Citrus Heights *Also Called: Fortune Senior Enterprises* *(P-16865)*

Comity Designs Inc .... D....... 415 967-1530
41 Marvin Ave Los Altos (94022) *(P-12763)*

Command Gard Srvces Wsa Srvces, Gardena *Also Called: United Facility Solutions Inc* *(P-13059)*

Command Packaging, Vernon *Also Called: Revoltion Cnsmr Sltions CA LLC* *(P-6943)*

Commerce Casino, Commerce *Also Called: California Commerce Club Inc* *(P-9676)*

Commercial Casting Co, Covina *Also Called: Hartman Industries* *(P-5497)*

Commercial Crrers Insur Agcy I .... D....... 562 404-4900
4 Centerpointe Dr Ste 300 La Palma (90623) *(P-8530)*

Commercial Door Company Inc .... D....... 714 529-2179
1374 E 9th St Pomona (91766) *(P-1994)*

Commercial Fin Lsg Bnk Crdiff .... D....... 888 234-0166
12626 High Bluff Dr Ste 370 San Diego (92130) *(P-7730)*

Commercial Fueling Network .... D....... 800 899-2236
1510 Fashion Island Blvd Ste 130 San Mateo (94404) *(P-6726)*

Commercial Indus Design Co Inc .... D....... 949 273-6199
20372 N Sea Cir Lake Forest (92630) *(P-5286)*

Commercial Indus Roofg Co Inc .... D....... 619 465-3737
9239 Olive Dr Spring Valley (91977) *(P-2053)*

Commercial Inv MGT Group, Los Angeles *Also Called: Cim Group LP* *(P-9700)*

Commercial Lbr & Pallet Co Inc (PA) .... C....... 626 968-0631
135 Long Ln City Of Industry (91746) *(P-2483)*

Commercial Lighting Inds Inc .... D....... 800 755-0155
81161 Indio Blvd Indio (92201) *(P-5548)*

Commercial Property MGT Inc (PA) .... D....... 213 739-2000
3251 W 6th St Ste 109 Los Angeles (90020) *(P-8948)*

Commercial Protective Services, Gardena *Also Called: Construction Protective Services Inc* *(P-12948)*

Commercial Protective Svcs Inc .... A....... 310 515-5290
17215 Studebaker Rd Ste 205 Cerritos (90703) *(P-12945)*

Commercial RE Exch Inc .... C....... 888 273-0423
5510 Lincoln Blvd Playa Vista (90094) *(P-11506)*

Commercial Rsdntial Rofg Contr, Oceanside *Also Called: Regan Roofing Inc* *(P-2081)*

Commercial Wood Products Company .... C....... 760 246-4530
10019 Yucca Rd Adelanto (92301) *(P-1995)*

Commodity Sales Co .... C....... 323 980-5463
517 S Clarence St Los Angeles (90033) *(P-2343)*

Commodore Dining Cruises Inc .... D....... 510 337-9000
Mainers Sq Alameda (94501) *(P-3807)*

COMMODORE DINING CRUISES INC, Alameda *Also Called: Commodore Dining Cruises Inc* *(P-3807)*

Common Grounds Holdings LLC .... D....... 760 206-7861
6790 Embarcadero Ln Ste 100 Carlsbad (92011) *(P-8949)*

Commons At Calabasas, The, Los Angeles *Also Called: Caruso MGT Ltd A Cal Ltd Prtnr* *(P-8924)*

Commonwealth Central Credit Un (PA) .... D....... 408 531-3100
5890 Silver Creek Valley Rd San Jose (95138) *(P-7760)*

Communction Wirg Spcalists Inc .... D....... 858 278-4545
8909 Complex Dr Ste F San Diego (92123) *(P-1703)*

Communicare Health Centers (PA) .... D....... **530 758-2060**
2051 John Jones Rd Davis (95616) *(P-14696)*

Communicare Health Centers .... C....... 530 753-3498
215 W Beamer St Woodland (95695) *(P-14697)*

Communicare Health Centers .... D....... 530 758-2060
2051 John Jones Rd Davis (95616) *(P-14698)*

Communicare Health Centers .... D....... 530 758-2060
2040 Sutter Pl Davis (95616) *(P-14699)*

Communication & Info Tech, Sacramento *Also Called: County of Sacramento* *(P-12694)*

Communication Svc For Deaf Inc .... D....... 209 475-5000
81 W March Ln Stockton (95207) *(P-18574)*

Communication Tech Svcs LLC .... B....... 508 382-2700
1590 S Milliken Ave Ste H Ontario (91761) *(P-1704)*

Communications & Pwr Inds LLC .... D....... 530 662-7553
1318 Commerce Ave Woodland (95776) *(P-13737)*

Communications Supply Corp .... D....... 714 670-7711
6251 Knott Ave Buena Park (90620) *(P-4534)*

Community & Senior Svcs, Lancaster *Also Called: County of Los Angeles* *(P-17906)*

Community Action Marin .... D....... 415 459-6330
1108 Tamalpais Ave San Rafael (94901) *(P-17030)*

Community Action Marine, San Rafael *Also Called: Community Action Marin* *(P-17030)*

Community Action Partnership .... D....... 805 489-4026
1152 E Grand Ave Arroyo Grande (93420) *(P-17409)*

Community Action Partnership .... D....... 805 541-4122
3970 Short St San Luis Obispo (93401) *(P-17889)*

Community Action Partnr Kern .... D....... 661 336-5300
1611 1st St Bakersfield (93304) *(P-18398)*

Community Action Partnr Kern .... D....... 661 835-5405
315 Stine Rd Bakersfield (93309) *(P-18575)*

Community Action Partnr Kern .... D....... 760 371-1469
814 N Norma St Ridgecrest (93555) *(P-18576)*

Community Action Prtnr Mdera C (PA) .... C....... **559 673-9173**
1225 Gill Ave Madera (93637) *(P-18295)*

Community Action Prtnr Mdera C .... C....... 559 661-1000
1225 Gill Ave Madera (93637) *(P-18577)*

Community Action Prtnr Ornge C .... C....... 714 897-6670
11870 Monarch St Garden Grove (92841) *(P-17890)*

Community Action Prtnr Rvrside, Riverside *Also Called: County of Riverside* *(P-17935)*

Community Action Prtnr San Brn .... D....... 909 723-1500
696 S Tippecanoe Ave San Bernardino (92408) *(P-18578)*

Community Action Prtnr San Lui .... C....... 805 544-2478
705 Grand Ave San Luis Obispo (93401) *(P-17031)*

Community Action Prtnr San Lui .... C....... 831 751-9379
24495 Calle El Rosario Salinas (93908) *(P-18296)*

Community Action Prtnr San Lui (PA) .... D....... **805 544-4355**
1030 Southwood Dr San Luis Obispo (93401) *(P-18297)*

Community Action Prtnr San Lui .... C....... 805 541-2272
805 Fiero Ln Ste A San Luis Obispo (93401) *(P-18298)*

Community Action Prtnr San Lui .... C....... 831 678-1584
160 Main St Soledad (93960) *(P-18299)*

Community Action Prtnr Snoma C .... D....... 707 544-0120
141 Stony Cir Ste 210 Santa Rosa (95401) *(P-18579)*

COMMUNITY ADVOCATE FOR PEOPLE', Whittier *Also Called: Capc Inc* *(P-18570)*

COMMUNITY ASSOC PRE-SCHOOL EDU, Livermore *Also Called: Cape Inc* *(P-17699)*

Community Bank .... B....... 626 577-1700
460 Sierra Madre Villa Ave Pasadena (91107) *(P-7675)*

Community Bridges .... D....... 831 724-2024
114 E 5th St Watsonville (95076) *(P-17891)*

COMMUNITY CARE AND REHABILITAT, Newport Beach *Also Called: Ben Bennett Inc* *(P-15816)*

Community Care Center .... D....... 619 465-0702
8665 La Mesa Blvd La Mesa (91942) *(P-15379)*

Community Care Licensing, Riverside *Also Called: California Dept Social Svcs* *(P-20941)*

Community Care On Palm Rvrside .... D....... 951 686-9001
4768 Palm Ave Riverside (92501) *(P-15380)*

Community Child Care Cncil Sno (PA) .... D....... **707 544-3077**
131a Stony Cir Ste 300 Santa Rosa (95401) *(P-18300)*

Community Cnvlscent Hosp Mntcl, Montclair *Also Called: US Skillserve Inc* *(P-15713)*

Community College Foundation (PA) .... D....... **916 418-5100**
1425 River Park Dr Ste 250 Sacramento (95815) *(P-17807)*

Community Day School — ALPHABETIC SECTION

Community Day School, Beaumont Also Called: Beaumont Unfied Schl Dst Pub F *(P-17694)*
Community Dev Inst Head Start .... B....... 858 668-2985
  12988 Bowron Rd Poway (92064) *(P-18301)*
Community Facilities District, Yuba City Also Called: City of Yuba City *(P-18222)*
Community Food Connection .... D....... 858 751-4613
  14047 Twin Peaks Rd Poway (92064) *(P-17892)*
Community Health Agency, Moreno Valley Also Called: County of Riverside *(P-14715)*
Community Health Agency, Riverside Also Called: County of Riverside *(P-20943)*
COMMUNITY HEALTH CENTER, Bakersfield Also Called: Omni Family Health *(P-14935)*
Community Health Group .... C....... 800 224-7766
  2420 Fenton St Ste 100 Chula Vista (91914) *(P-14700)*
Community Health System, Fresno Also Called: Community Hospitals Centl Cal *(P-16013)*
COMMUNITY HEALTH SYSTEM, Fresno Also Called: Fresno Cmnty Hosp & Med Ctr *(P-16096)*
Community Health Systems Inc .... C....... 951 571-2300
  21801 Alessandro Blvd Moreno Valley (92553) *(P-14701)*
Community Hlth Alance Pasadena (PA) .... D....... 626 398-6300
  1855 N Fair Oaks Ave Ste 200 Pasadena (91103) *(P-16008)*
Community Hlth Plan Off MGT Ca, Alhambra Also Called: County of Los Angeles *(P-8294)*
Community Hlthcare Partner Inc .... D....... 760 326-4531
  1401 Bailey Ave Needles (92363) *(P-14702)*
Community Home Partners LLC .... D....... 408 985-5252
  2384 Pacific Dr Santa Clara (95051) *(P-15750)*
Community Hosp Mntrey Pninsula .... C....... 831 625-4500
  23625 Holman Hwy Monterey (93940) *(P-16009)*
Community Hosp of Mntrey Pnnsu (HQ) .... A....... 831 624-5311
  23625 Holman Hwy Monterey (93940) *(P-16674)*
Community Hosp San Bernardino (DH) .... B....... 909 887-6333
  1805 Medical Center Dr San Bernardino (92411) *(P-16010)*
Community Hospice Inc (PA) .... C....... 209 578-6300
  4368 Spyres Way Modesto (95356) *(P-15751)*
Community Hospice Victor Vly, Apple Valley Also Called: Vnacare *(P-16969)*
Community Hospital, Long Beach Also Called: Community Hospital Long Beach *(P-16011)*
Community Hospital Long Beach .... A....... 562 494-0600
  1760 Termino Ave Ste 105 Long Beach (90804) *(P-16011)*
Community Hospital Monterey .... C....... 831 625-4600
  23625 Holman Hwy Monterey (93940) *(P-16012)*
COMMUNITY HOSPITAL OF MONTEREY PENINSULA, Monterey Also Called: Community Hosp Mntrey Pninsula *(P-16009)*
Community Hospitals Centl Cal (PA) .... A....... 559 459-6000
  2823 Fresno St Fresno (93721) *(P-16013)*
Community Hospitals Centl Cal .... A....... 559 459-6000
  2823 Fresno St Fresno (93721) *(P-16014)*
Community Integration Program, Sacramento Also Called: Develop Disabilities Svc Org *(P-17953)*
Community Interface Services .... D....... 760 729-3866
  981 Vale Terrace Dr Vista (92084) *(P-17893)*
Community Medical Centers Inc (PA) .... D....... 209 373-2800
  7210 Murray Dr Stockton (95210) *(P-17032)*
Community Mem Hosp San Bnvntur .... D....... 805 652-5072
  147 N Brent St Ventura (93003) *(P-16015)*
Community Memorial Health Sys (PA) .... A....... 805 652-5011
  147 N Brent St Ventura (93003) *(P-16016)*
Community Memorial Health Sys .... C....... 805 646-1401
  1306 Maricopa Hwy Ojai (93023) *(P-16017)*
Community Memorial Hospital, Ventura Also Called: Community Memorial Health Sys *(P-16016)*
Community Orthpd Med Group Prt .... D....... 949 348-4000
  26401 Crown Valley Pkwy Ste 101 Mission Viejo (92691) *(P-14703)*
Community Partners (PA) .... C....... 213 346-3200
  1000 N Alameda St Ste 240 Los Angeles (90012) *(P-18580)*
Community Partners Intl .... C....... 510 225-9676
  580 California St Fl 16 San Francisco (94104) *(P-9412)*
Community Patrol Inc .... D....... 657 247-4744
  1420 E Edinger Ave Ste 213 Santa Ana (92705) *(P-12946)*
Community Presbt Ch Danville (PA) .... C....... 925 837-5525
  222 W El Pintado Danville (94526) *(P-19015)*
Community Psychiatry MGT LLC (PA) .... D....... 855 501-1004
  3835 N Freeway Blvd Ste 100 Sacramento (95834) *(P-15278)*
Community Regional Medical Ctr .... D....... 559 459-2415
  1560 E Shaw Ave Fresno (93710) *(P-14704)*
Community Regional Medical Ctr, Fresno Also Called: Community Hospitals Centl Cal *(P-16014)*
Community Services and Employment Training Incorporated (PA) .... D....... 559 757-3539
  312 Nw 3rd Ave Visalia (93291) *(P-18223)*
Community Services For Deaf, Stockton Also Called: Communication Svc For Deaf Inc *(P-18574)*
Community Sltons For Chldren F (PA) .... C....... 408 842-7138
  9015 Murray Ave Ste 100 Gilroy (95020) *(P-17894)*
Community Support Options Inc .... C....... 661 758-5331
  1401 Poso Dr Wasco (93280) *(P-17895)*
Community Transit Services, El Monte Also Called: First Student Inc *(P-3128)*
Community Trnstional Resources .... D....... 209 529-2200
  1209 Woodrow Ave Ste B10 Modesto (95350) *(P-14705)*
Communty Hsptal of The Mntrey .... D....... 831 596-8986
  109 San Benancio Rd Salinas (93908) *(P-16018)*
Commure Inc (PA) .... D....... 888 994-2443
  2261 Market St # 4072 San Francisco (94114) *(P-11507)*
Compas Health, Templeton Also Called: Compass Health Inc *(P-15385)*
Compass .... D....... 818 629-9776
  9454 Wilshire Blvd Beverly Hills (90212) *(P-8950)*
Compass Children's Center, San Francisco Also Called: Compass Family Services *(P-18302)*
Compass Clara House, San Francisco Also Called: Compass Family Services *(P-17897)*
Compass Components Inc (PA) .... C....... 510 656-4700
  48133 Warm Springs Blvd Fremont (94539) *(P-2941)*
Compass Family Services .... D....... 415 644-0504
  626 Polk St San Francisco (94102) *(P-17896)*
Compass Family Services 415 644-0504
  111 Page St San Francisco (94102) *(P-17897)*
Compass Family Services .... D....... 415 644-0504
  144 Leavenworth St San Francisco (94102) *(P-18302)*
Compass Family Shelter, San Francisco Also Called: Compass Family Services *(P-17896)*
Compass Flooring, Santa Fe Springs Also Called: Altro Usa Inc *(P-3104)*
Compass Group Usa Inc .... C....... 714 899-2520
  12640 Knott St Garden Grove (92841) *(P-11027)*
Compass Group Usa Inc .... B....... 510 259-0416
  20929 Cabot Blvd Hayward (94545) *(P-13240)*
Compass Health Inc .... C....... 805 543-0210
  1425 Woodside Dr San Luis Obispo (93401) *(P-15381)*
Compass Health Inc .... C....... 805 772-7372
  1405 Teresa Dr Morro Bay (93442) *(P-15382)*
Compass Health Inc .... C....... 805 489-8137
  1212 Farroll Ave Arroyo Grande (93420) *(P-15383)*
Compass Health Inc .... C....... 805 466-9254
  10805 El Camino Real Atascadero (93422) *(P-15384)*
Compass Health Inc .... C....... 805 434-3035
  290 Heather Ct Templeton (93465) *(P-15385)*
Compass Health Inc .... C....... 805 687-6651
  3880 Via Lucero Santa Barbara (93110) *(P-15386)*
Compass Health Inc .... C....... 805 474-7260
  222 S Elm St Arroyo Grande (93420) *(P-18399)*
Compass Innovations Inc 408 418-3985
  2352 Walsh Ave Santa Clara (95051) *(P-2660)*
Compass Manufacturing Service, Fremont Also Called: Compass Components Inc *(P-2941)*
Compass Transportation Charter, San Jose Also Called: Sfo Airporter Inc *(P-3211)*
Competent Care Inc .... D....... 714 545-4818
  2900 Bristol St Ste D107 Costa Mesa (92626) *(P-16844)*
Competent Care HM Hlth Nursing, Costa Mesa Also Called: Competent Care Inc *(P-16844)*
Compex Legal Services Inc (PA) .... C....... 310 782-1801
  325 Maple Ave Torrance (90503) *(P-17410)*
Compex Legal Services LLC .... C....... 650 833-0460
  1225 Pear Ave # 110 Mountain View (94043) *(P-10786)*
Complete Coach Works .... C....... 800 300-3751
  42882 Ivy St Murrieta (92562) *(P-13711)*
Complete Genomics Inc (HQ) .... C....... 408 648-2560
  2904 Orchard Pkwy San Jose (95134) *(P-19878)*
Complete Linen Services, South San Francisco Also Called: Medical Linen Service Inc *(P-10437)*
Complete Logistics Company .... D....... 619 661-9610
  1207 Air Wing Rd San Diego (92154) *(P-3455)*
Complete Office, Cerritos Also Called: Complete Office California Inc *(P-5084)*

ALPHABETIC SECTION

Complete Office California Inc .... D....... 714 880-1222
  12724 Moore St Cerritos (90703) *(P-5084)*

Completely Fresh Foods Inc .... C....... 323 722-9136
  4401 S Downey Rd Vernon (90058) *(P-6617)*

Completes Plus, Lawndale Also Called: Automotive Aftermarket Inc *(P-5025)*

Complianceonline, San Jose Also Called: Metricstream Inc *(P-12271)*

Component Control Systems, San Diego Also Called: Component Controlcom Inc *(P-11508)*

Component Controlcom Inc .... D....... 619 696-5400
  1731 Kettner Blvd San Diego (92101) *(P-11508)*

Composite Software LLC (DH) .... D....... 800 553-6387
  755 Sycamore Dr Milpitas (95035) *(P-12144)*

Comprehensive Blood Cancer Ctr, Bakersfield Also Called: Ravi Patel MD Inc *(P-15011)*

Comprehensive Cancer Centers Inc .... C....... 323 966-3400
  8201 Beverly Blvd Los Angeles (90048) *(P-17033)*

Comprehensive Dist Svcs Inc .... C....... 310 523-1546
  18726 S Western Ave Ste 300 Gardena (90248) *(P-4149)*

Comprehensive Health Center, San Diego Also Called: National Med Assn Cmprhnsive H *(P-17099)*

Comprehensive SEC Svcs Inc (PA) .... D....... 916 683-3605
  10535 E Stockton Blvd Ste G Elk Grove (95624) *(P-12947)*

Comprhnsive Indus Dsblity MGT .... C....... 866 301-6568
  2555 Townsgate Rd Ste 125 Westlake Village (91361) *(P-17208)*

Compton Service Center, Compton Also Called: Southern California Edison Co *(P-4688)*

COMPTON TRAINING CENTER, Van Nuys Also Called: Apprentice Jrnymen Trning Tr F *(P-18204)*

Compton Unified School Dst .... D....... 310 898-6470
  1104 E 148th St Compton (90220) *(P-17705)*

Compton Unified School Dst .... D....... 310 639-4321
  2600 N Central Ave Compton (90222) *(P-17706)*

Compulink Business Systems Inc (PA) .... C....... 805 446-2050
  1100 Business Center Cir Newbury Park (91320) *(P-12145)*

Compulink Healthcare Solutions, Newbury Park Also Called: Compulink Business Systems Inc *(P-12145)*

Compulink Management Ctr Inc (PA) .... C....... 562 988-1688
  3443 Long Beach Blvd Long Beach (90807) *(P-11509)*

Compumail Information Svcs Inc .... D....... 925 689-7100
  4057 Port Chicago Hwy Ste 300 Concord (94520) *(P-13241)*

Compushare Inc .... C....... 714 427-1000
  3 Hutton Centre Dr Ste 700 Santa Ana (92707) *(P-12559)*

Computacenter US Inc (HQ) .... A....... 714 861-2200
  2 Bryant St Ste 150 San Francisco (94105) *(P-12764)*

Computer Proc Unlimited Inc .... C....... 858 530-0875
  9235 Activity Rd Ste 104 San Diego (92126) *(P-11510)*

Computer Sciences Corporation .... C....... 702 558-8092
  1520 Railroad Ave Walnut Creek (94595) *(P-12693)*

Computer Software Development, San Diego Also Called: Cognitive Medical Systems Inc *(P-11501)*

Computer Tech Resources Inc .... C....... 714 665-6507
  16 Technology Dr Ste 202 Irvine (92618) *(P-12437)*

Computerized Mgt Svcs Inc .... D....... 805 522-5940
  4100 Guardian St Ste 205 Simi Valley (93063) *(P-19554)*

Computershare Inc .... C....... 800 522-6645
  2335 Alaska Ave El Segundo (90245) *(P-8230)*

Computerworks Technologies, Burbank Also Called: Global Service Resources Inc *(P-11623)*

Computrition Inc (HQ) .... D....... 818 961-3999
  8521 Fallbrook Ave Ste 100 Canoga Park (91304) *(P-11511)*

Compwest Insurance Company .... C....... 415 593-5100
  100 Pringle Ave Ste 515 Walnut Creek (94596) *(P-8382)*

Comtel Systems Technology Inc .... D....... 408 543-5600
  1292 Hammerwood Ave Sunnyvale (94089) *(P-1705)*

Con J Franke Electric Inc .... D....... 209 462-0717
  317 N Grant St Stockton (95202) *(P-1706)*

Conam Management Corporation (PA) .... C....... 858 614-7200
  3990 Ruffin Rd Ste 100 San Diego (92123) *(P-8951)*

CONCENTRIX, Fremont Also Called: Concentrix Corporation *(P-13242)*

Concentrix Corporation (PA) .... A....... 800 747-0583
  44111 Nobel Dr Fremont (94538) *(P-13242)*

Concept Technology Inc (PA) .... D....... 949 854-7047
  895 Dove St 3rd Fl Newport Beach (92660) *(P-19179)*

Concept Technology Inc .... B....... 949 851-6550
  2941 W Macarthur Blvd Ste 136 Santa Ana (92704) *(P-19180)*

Concessionaires Urban Park (PA) .... B....... 530 529-1512
  2150 Main St Ste 5 Red Bluff (96080) *(P-14507)*

Concessionaires Urban Park .... C....... 209 763-5121
  2000 Camanche Rd Ofc Ofc Ione (95640) *(P-14508)*

Concessionaires Urban Park .... D....... 530 529-1513
  2150 Main St Red Bluff (96080) *(P-14509)*

Conco Cement Co, Fontana Also Called: Gonsalves & Santucci Inc *(P-2121)*

Conco Companies .... D....... 303 996-9841
  5141 Commercial Cir Concord (94520) *(P-2110)*

Concord Foods Inc (HQ) .... D....... 909 975-2000
  4601 E Guasti Rd Ontario (91761) *(P-6247)*

Concord Hotel LLC .... D....... 925 521-3751
  45 John Glenn Dr Concord (94520) *(P-9719)*

Concord Toyota, Concord Also Called: FAA Concord T Inc *(P-7205)*

Concord Veranda Cinema LLC .... C....... 707 762-0990
  2035 Diamond Blvd Ste 150 Concord (94520) *(P-13831)*

Concord Worldwide Inc .... D....... 415 689-5488
  177 Post St Ste 910 San Francisco (94108) *(P-11512)*

Concorde Career Colleges Inc .... D....... 818 766-8151
  12412 Victory Blvd North Hollywood (91606) *(P-17794)*

Concorse Ht At Los Angles Arpr, Los Angeles Also Called: Humnit Hotel At Lax LLC *(P-9879)*

Concrete Construction, San Diego Also Called: Ben F Smith Inc *(P-2099)*

Concrete Craft, San Rafael Also Called: Ghilotti Bros Inc *(P-2217)*

Concrete North Inc .... D....... 209 745-7400
  10274 Iron Rock Way Elk Grove (95624) *(P-2111)*

Concrete Tie, Compton Also Called: Concrete Tie Industries Inc *(P-5201)*

Concrete Tie Industries Inc (PA) .... D....... 310 628-2328
  130 E Oris St Compton (90222) *(P-5201)*

Concreteworks Studio Inc .... D....... 510 534-7141
  1998 Republic Ave San Leandro (94577) *(P-7420)*

Condon-Johnson & Assoc Inc .... D....... 858 530-9165
  3434 Grove St Lemon Grove (91945) *(P-750)*

Condor Productions LLC .... C....... 310 449-3000
  245 N Beverly Dr Beverly Hills (90210) *(P-13930)*

Condor Trading LP .... A....... 415 248-2200
  600 Montgomery St Fl 6 San Francisco (94111) *(P-9308)*

Conduent State Lcal Sltons Inc .... A....... 415 486-2409
  455 The Embarcadero Ste 103 San Francisco (94111) *(P-12438)*

Conduit Lngage Specialists Inc .... D....... 859 299-3178
  22720 Ventura Blvd Ste 100 Woodland Hills (91364) *(P-10538)*

Conexant Holdings Inc .... A....... 415 983-2706
  4000 Macarthur Blvd Newport Beach (92660) *(P-2915)*

Conexis Bnfits Admnstrators LP (HQ) .... C....... 714 835-5006
  721 S Parker St Ste 300 Orange (92868) *(P-8531)*

Confab, Van Nuys Also Called: Consolidated Fabricators Corp *(P-2742)*

Confido LLC .... A....... 310 361-8558
  1055 E Colorado Blvd Pasadena (91106) *(P-16845)*

Confie, Huntington Beach Also Called: Confie Holding II Co *(P-8532)*

Confie Holding II Co (PA) .... C....... 714 252-2500
  7711 Center Ave Ste 200 Huntington Beach (92647) *(P-8532)*

Confluent Inc (PA) .... A....... 800 439-3207
  899 W Evelyn Ave Mountain View (94041) *(P-12146)*

Congaree Health Holdings LLC .... D....... 949 487-9500
  29222 Rancho Viejo Rd Ste 127 San Juan Capistrano (92675) *(P-15387)*

Congregation Emanu-El .... C....... 650 755-4700
  1299 El Camino Real Colma (94014) *(P-9284)*

Congrgtion Beth Israel San Deg .... D....... 858 535-1111
  9001 Towne Centre Dr San Diego (92122) *(P-19016)*

Conifer Securities LLC .... D....... 415 677-1500
  1 Ferry Building Ste 255 San Francisco (94111) *(P-8081)*

Connect Computers, Anaheim Also Called: General Procurement Inc *(P-5309)*

Connecticut Ctr Plastic Surg .... D....... 760 779-9595
  73260 El Paseo Ste 2b Palm Desert (92260) *(P-7568)*

Conner Logistics, Fresno Also Called: Conner Logistics Inc *(P-3999)*

Conner Logistics Inc .... D....... 888 939-4637
  4069 W Shaw Ave Ste 103 Fresno (93722) *(P-3999)*

Connexity Inc (DH) .... C....... 310 571-1235
  2120 Colorado Ave Ste 400 Santa Monica (90404) *(P-4266)*

Connor Consulting Corp (PA) .... C....... 415 678-5002
  300 Brannan St Ste 511 San Francisco (94107) *(P-20732)*

Conquistador International LLC .... D...... 424 249-9304
  21200 Oxnard St Ste 492 Woodland Hills (91365) *(P-6103)*
Conrad Lab, The, Lodi *Also Called: Lodi Memorial Hosp Assn Inc (P-16218)*
Conrad Los Angeles, Los Angeles *Also Called: Core/Related Gala Retail LLC (P-9720)*
Consensus Cloud Solutions Inc (PA).. D...... 323 860-9200
  700 S Flower St Fl 15 Los Angeles (90017) *(P-12147)*
Consensus Health, Emeryville *Also Called: Onebody Inc (P-16905)*
Conservation Corps Long Beach .... C...... 562 986-1249
  340 Nieto Ave Long Beach (90814) *(P-18224)*
Conservation Society Cal .... C...... 510 632-9525
  9777 Golf Links Rd Oakland (94605) *(P-18687)*
Conservis, Clovis *Also Called: Conservis Corp (P-11513)*
Conservis Corp .... D...... 612 424-6300
  352 W Spruce Ave Clovis (93611) *(P-11513)*
Considine Cnsdine An Accntncy .... C...... 619 231-1977
  8989 Rio San Diego Dr Ste 250 San Diego (92108) *(P-19555)*
Consoldted Fire Protection LLC (HQ).. A...... 949 727-3277
  153 Technology Dr Ste 200 Irvine (92618) *(P-13243)*
Consoldted Med Bo-Analysis Inc (PA).. D...... 714 657-7369
  10700 Walker St Cypress (90630) *(P-16712)*
Consoldted Tribal Hlth Prj Inc .... D...... 707 485-5115
  6991 N State St Redwood Valley (95470) *(P-17034)*
Consolidated Communications, Roseville *Also Called: Cal Consolidated Communications (P-4259)*
Consolidated Contg Svcs Inc .... D...... 949 498-7500
  181 Avenida La Pata Ste 200 San Clemente (92673) *(P-900)*
Consolidated Engineering Labs, San Ramon *Also Called: Atlas Technical Cons LLC (P-20695)*
Consolidated Fabricators Corp (PA).. C...... 800 635-8335
  14620 Arminta St Van Nuys (91402) *(P-2742)*
Consolidated Networks Corp .... D...... 707 422-0791
  1031 Aldridge Rd Ste E Vacaville (95688) *(P-18745)*
Consolidated Svc Distrs Inc .... D...... 908 687-5800
  777 S Central Ave Los Angeles (90021) *(P-6459)*
Consor North America Inc .... D...... 916 368-9181
  11017 Cobblerock Dr Ste 100 Rancho Cordova (95670) *(P-19181)*
Consor Pmcm Inc .... D...... 415 596-5399
  1663 Mission St Ste 425 San Francisco (94103) *(P-19182)*
Consortium For Community Svcs, Fresno *Also Called: Quality Group Homes Inc (P-710)*
Constlltion Brnds US Oprtons I .... D...... 209 294-4110
  5950 E Woodbridge Rd Acampo (95220) *(P-6792)*
Constlltion Brnds US Oprtons I .... A...... 559 485-0141
  12667 Road 24 Madera (93637) *(P-6793)*
Constrction - Tile Instllation, Sacramento *Also Called: National Crmic Tile Stone Corp (P-1986)*
Construction, Fresno *Also Called: Quiring General LLC (P-997)*
Construction, Gardena *Also Called: Best Contracting Services Inc (P-2045)*
Construction, Poway *Also Called: D and D Concrete Cnstr Inc (P-2113)*
Construction Consulting Svcs, Walnut Creek *Also Called: Mka International Inc (P-19323)*
Construction Innovations LLC .... C...... 855 725-9555
  10630 Mather Blvd Ste 200 Mather (95655) *(P-2955)*
Construction Protective Services Inc (PA)....................................... A...... 800 257-5512
  436 W Walnut St Gardena (90248) *(P-12948)*
CONSTRUCTION TESTING & ENGINEERING, INC., Riverside *Also Called: Construction Tstg & Engrg Inc (P-19183)*
Construction Tstg & Engrg Inc .... B...... 951 571-4081
  14538 Meridian Pkwy Ste A Riverside (92518) *(P-19183)*
Construction Tstg & Engrg Inc .... B...... 916 331-6030
  3628 Madison Ave Ste 22 North Highlands (95660) *(P-19959)*
Constuction, San Jose *Also Called: Qlm Inc (P-19367)*
Consumer Cr Cnsling Svc San Fr (PA)... D...... 888 456-2227
  1655 Grant St Ste 1300 Concord (94520) *(P-10539)*
Consumer Loan Dept, Tustin *Also Called: Schoolsfirst Federal Credit Un (P-7803)*
Consumer Resource Network LLC .... B...... 800 291-4794
  4420 E Miraloma Ave Ste J Anaheim (92807) *(P-20325)*
Consumer Safety Analytics LLC .... D...... 818 922-2416
  7027 Hayvenhurst Ave Van Nuys (91406) *(P-19960)*
Contemporary Services Corp .... A...... 818 885-5150
  17101 Superior St Northridge (91325) *(P-12949)*
Contemporary Services Corp .... C...... 310 320-8418
  369 Van Ness Way Ste 702 Torrance (90501) *(P-13102)*
Contemporary Services Corp .... A...... 650 524-8889
  1821 Marina Blvd San Leandro (94577) *(P-20326)*
Content Guru Inc .... B...... 408 559-3988
  900 E Hamilton Ave Ste 510 Campbell (95008) *(P-12439)*
Contentful Inc .... D...... 415 248-7801
  101 Montgomery St Ste 2050 San Francisco (94104) *(P-18705)*
Contessa Liquidating Co Inc C
  222 W 6th St Fl 8 San Pedro (90731) *(P-6417)*
Contessa Premium Foods Inc .... C...... 310 832-8000
  5980 Alcoa Ave Vernon (90058) *(P-6418)*
Conti Materials Service LLC .... D...... 209 467-0626
  3932 Newton Rd Stockton (95205) *(P-5151)*
Contiki Holidays, Cypress *Also Called: Contiki US Holdings Inc (P-3963)*
Contiki US Holdings Inc .... D...... 714 935-0808
  5551 Katella Ave Cypress (90630) *(P-3963)*
Continental Airlines, Los Angeles *Also Called: United Airlines Inc (P-3847)*
Continental Currency Svcs Inc (PA)... D...... 714 667-6699
  1108 E 17th St Santa Ana (92701) *(P-7843)*
Continental Data Graphics, Long Beach *Also Called: Continental Graphics Corp (P-10801)*
Continental Exch Solutions Inc .... D...... 562 790-8532
  14601 Lakewood Blvd Paramount (90723) *(P-7844)*
Continental Exch Solutions Inc .... D...... 714 530-3582
  12891 Harbor Blvd Garden Grove (92840) *(P-7845)*
Continental Exch Solutions Inc (HQ)... D...... 714 522-7044
  6565 Knott Ave Buena Park (90620) *(P-7846)*
Continental Exch Solutions Inc .... D...... 415 824-4280
  2796 Mission St San Francisco (94110) *(P-7847)*
Continental Exch Solutions Inc .... D...... 559 655-7583
  662 Oller St Mendota (93640) *(P-7848)*
Continental Exch Solutions Inc .... D...... 909 622-0500
  1575 E Holt Ave Pomona (91767) *(P-7849)*
Continental Exch Solutions Inc .... D...... 562 345-2156
  860 E Alisal St Ste D Salinas (93905) *(P-7850)*
Continental Exch Solutions Inc .... D...... 626 969-4130
  960 W Arrow Hwy Covina (91722) *(P-7851)*
Continental Exch Solutions Inc .... D...... 562 345-2100
  7001 Village Dr Ste 200 Buena Park (90621) *(P-13244)*
Continental Exch Solutions Inc .... D...... 805 965-0663
  506 N Milpas St Santa Barbara (93103) *(P-13245)*
Continental Graphics Corp (PA).. C...... 714 503-4200
  4060 N Lakewood Blvd Bldg 801 Long Beach (90808) *(P-10801)*
Continental Pacific Bank .... D...... 707 448-1200
  555 Mason St Ste 280 Vacaville (95688) *(P-7676)*
Continental Sales Co., Los Angeles *Also Called: Val-Pro Inc (P-6589)*
Continental Vitamin Co Inc .... D...... 323 581-0176
  4510 S Boyle Ave Vernon (90058) *(P-2583)*
Continuing Lf Communities LLC (PA)... D...... 760 704-6400
  1940 Levante St Carlsbad (92009) *(P-11112)*
Continuous Coating Corp (PA).. D...... 714 637-4642
  500 W Grove Ave Orange (92865) *(P-2759)*
Continuous Computing Corp .... C...... 858 882-8800
  10431 Wateridge Cir Ste 110 San Diego (92121) *(P-2803)*
Continuumglobal Inc .... A...... 415 685-3301
  1200 Gough St Unit 3a San Francisco (94109) *(P-20327)*
Contra Costa Cnty Off Educatn (PA).. C...... 925 942-3388
  77 Santa Barbara Rd Pleasant Hill (94523) *(P-17707)*
Contra Costa Country Club .... D...... 925 798-7135
  801 Golf Club Rd Pleasant Hill (94523) *(P-14362)*
Contra Costa County .... B...... 925 313-1323
  30 Douglas Dr Martinez (94553) *(P-4209)*
Contra Costa Electric Inc (DH)... B...... 925 229-4250
  825 Howe Rd Martinez (94553) *(P-1707)*
Contra Costa Electric Inc .... C...... 661 322-4036
  3208 Landco Dr Bakersfield (93308) *(P-1708)*
Contra Costa Water District (PA).. C...... 925 688-8000
  1331 Concord Ave Concord (94520) *(P-4778)*
Contra Csta Rgonal Med Ctr Aux .... B...... 925 370-5000
  2500 Alhambra Ave Martinez (94553) *(P-14706)*
Contra Loma Healthcare LLC .... D...... 925 754-0470
  4001 Lone Tree Way Antioch (94509) *(P-17209)*
Contract Interiors, Fresno *Also Called: Contract Interiors San Diego (P-5085)*

ALPHABETIC SECTION — Corelogic Inc

Contract Interiors San Diego .... D....... 559 276-0561
4450 N Brawley Ave Ste 125 Fresno (93722) *(P-5085)*

Contract Services Group Inc .... C....... 714 582-1800
480 Capricorn St Brea (92821) *(P-10878)*

Contract Transportation Sys Co .... D....... 562 696-3262
12500 Slauson Ave Ste B2 Santa Fe Springs (90670) *(P-3456)*

Contractor, Petaluma *Also Called: Simply Solar (P-1562)*

Contractors Cargo Company (PA) .... D....... 310 609-1957
7223 Alondra Blvd Paramount (90723) *(P-3457)*

Contractors Cargo Company, Paramount *Also Called: CCC Property Holdings LLC (P-9306)*

Contractors Flrg Svc Cal Inc .... C....... 714 556-6100
300 E Dyer Rd Santa Ana (92707) *(P-5114)*

Contractors Rigging & Erectors, Paramount *Also Called: Contractors Cargo Company (P-3457)*

Control Air Conditioning Corporation .... B....... 714 777-8600
5200 E La Palma Ave Anaheim (92807) *(P-1403)*

Control Air Enterprises LLC .... B....... 510 441-1800
30655 San Clemente St Hayward (94544) *(P-1404)*

Control Air Enterprises LLC .... B....... 760 744-2727
1390 Armorlite Dr San Marcos (92069) *(P-13726)*

Control Air North Inc .... D....... 510 441-1800
30655 San Clemente St Hayward (94544) *(P-1405)*

Control Group Media Co LLC .... D....... 858 242-1350
375 Camino De La Reina Ste 400 San Diego (92101) *(P-10600)*

Controller Consulting Svcs Inc .... C....... 408 221-2492
1577 Aldacourrou St Tracy (95304) *(P-20733)*

Controltec Inc .... D....... 760 975-9750
101 State Pl Ste Q Escondido (92029) *(P-12765)*

Convaid Products LLC .... D....... 310 618-0111
2830 California St Torrance (90503) *(P-5410)*

Convention & Cultural Services, Sacramento *Also Called: City of Sacramento (P-13235)*

Convention Center, San Diego *Also Called: San Dego Cnvntion Ctr Corp Inc (P-13459)*

Conventus Lending LLC .... D....... 415 923-8069
111 Potrero Ave San Francisco (94103) *(P-8037)*

Converse Inc .... D....... 310 451-0314
1437 3rd Street Promenade 39 Santa Monica (90401) *(P-6231)*

Conversio Health, San Luis Obispo *Also Called: Integrated Health Concepts Inc (P-6113)*

Conversionpoint Holdings Inc .... D....... 888 706-6764
840 Newport Center Dr Ste 450 Newport Beach (92660) *(P-12148)*

Convex Labs Inc .... D....... 408 692-0852
703 Market St Ste 17 San Francisco (94103) *(P-11514)*

Convrgd Data Tech Inc .... C....... 650 461-4488
999 Commercial St Ste 202 Palo Alto (94303) *(P-5287)*

Cook King, La Mirada *Also Called: Stainless Stl Fabricators Inc (P-5870)*

Cooke & Associates Inc .... B....... 408 842-0602
4101 Dublin Blvd Ste F Pmb 337 Dublin (94568) *(P-12950)*

Cookingcom Inc .... C....... 310 664-1283
1960 E Grand Ave Ste 60 El Segundo (90245) *(P-7437)*

Cooksey Tlen Gage Dffy Woog A (PA) .... D....... 714 431-1100
535 Anton Blvd Fl 10 Costa Mesa (92626) *(P-17411)*

Cool Roofing Systems Inc .... D....... 209 825-0818
1286 Dupont Ct Manteca (95336) *(P-2054)*

Cooland Inc .... D....... 424 329-3550
16830 S Main St Gardena (90248) *(P-1406)*

Cooley Godward Kronish, San Francisco *Also Called: Cooley LLP (P-17412)*

Cooley LLP .... D....... 415 693-2000
3 Embarcadero Ctr Fl 20 San Francisco (94111) *(P-17412)*

Cooley LLP (PA) .... B....... 650 843-5000
3175 Hanover St Palo Alto (94304) *(P-17413)*

Coolish Holdings LLC .... D....... 818 575-7280
21160 Califa St Woodland Hills (91367) *(P-2366)*

Coolsys Coml Indus Sltions Inc (DH) .... C....... 714 510-9609
145 S State College Blvd Ste 200 Brea (92821) *(P-1407)*

Coolwater Generating Station, Daggett *Also Called: NRG California South LP (P-4593)*

Cooper Bussmann LLC .... C....... 925 924-8500
5735 W Las Positas Blvd Ste 100 Pleasanton (94588) *(P-2869)*

Cooper Bussmann-Automotive, Pleasanton *Also Called: Cooper Bussmann LLC (P-2869)*

Cooper Lighting LLC .... C....... 760 357-4760
285 Rood Rd Ste 101 Calexico (92231) *(P-1709)*

Cooper Vali & Associates Inc (HQ) .... D....... 510 446-8301
1850 Gateway Blvd Ste 100 Concord (94520) *(P-19184)*

Cooper White & Cooper LLP (PA) .... C....... 415 433-1900
50 California St Ste 2750 San Francisco (94111) *(P-17414)*

Cooperative Personnel Services (PA) .... C....... 916 263-3600
2450 Del Paso Rd Ste 220 Sacramento (95834) *(P-20328)*

Coopertive Amrcn Physcians Inc (PA) .... D....... 213 473-8600
333 S Hope St Fl 8 Los Angeles (90071) *(P-18746)*

Cope Health Solutions .... D....... 213 542-2250
1150 S Olive St Fl 12 Los Angeles (90015) *(P-17210)*

Copley Family YMCA, San Diego *Also Called: YMCA of San Diego County (P-18943)*

Copley Newspapers, La Jolla *Also Called: The Copley Press Inc (P-13158)*

Coppel, Calexico *Also Called: Coppel Corporation (P-5086)*

Coppel Corporation .... D....... 760 357-3707
503 Scaroni Ave Calexico (92231) *(P-5086)*

Coppersmith Global Logistics, El Segundo *Also Called: L E Coppersmith Inc (P-4048)*

Copypage, Los Angeles *Also Called: CP Document Technologies LLC (P-5643)*

Coram Hlthcare Corp Nthrn Cal .... A....... 415 292-6811
3160 Corporate Pl Hayward (94545) *(P-16846)*

Coram Healthcare, Hayward *Also Called: Coram Hlthcare Corp Nthrn Cal (P-16846)*

Coram Healthcare, Sacramento *Also Called: Coram Healthcare Corp Nevada (P-16847)*

Coram Healthcare Corp Nevada .... D....... 916 857-7000
9332 Tech Center Dr Ste 100 Sacramento (95826) *(P-16847)*

Corcoran District Hospital Foundation .... D....... 559 992-3300
1310 Hanna Ave Corcoran (93212) *(P-16019)*

Corcoran Global Living, Ladera Ranch *Also Called: Exclusive Lifestyles Inc (P-8998)*

Cordelia Lighting Inc .... C....... 310 886-3490
20101 S Santa Fe Ave Compton (90221) *(P-5549)*

Cordevalle Golf Club LLC .... A....... 408 695-4500
1 Cordevalle Club Dr San Martin (95046) *(P-14363)*

Cordial Experience Inc .... D....... 619 793-9787
402 W Broadway Ste 700 San Diego (92101) *(P-11515)*

Cordoba Corporation .... D....... 213 895-0224
1401 N Broadway Los Angeles (90012) *(P-12440)*

Core, Los Angeles *Also Called: Core Cmnty Orgnzed Rlief Effor (P-17898)*

Core -Mark International, West Sacramento *Also Called: Core-Mark International Inc (P-20329)*

Core & Main Inc .... C....... 650 366-3833
939 Broadway St Redwood City (94063) *(P-6037)*

Core & Main Inc .... B....... 530 662-7700
1425 E Beamer St Woodland (95776) *(P-6038)*

Core Bts Inc .... C....... 818 766-2400
5250 Lankershim Blvd Ste 620 North Hollywood (91601) *(P-12441)*

Core Cmnty Orgnzed Rlief Effor .... B....... 323 934-4400
910 N Hill St Los Angeles (90012) *(P-17898)*

Core Holdings Inc .... C....... 714 969-2342
17291 Irvine Blvd Ste 404 Tustin (92780) *(P-16848)*

Core Med Staff .... D....... 213 382-5550
3946 Wilshire Blvd Los Angeles (90010) *(P-14707)*

Core Realty Holdings MGT Inc .... D....... 949 863-1031
1600 Dove St Ste 450 Newport Beach (92660) *(P-8952)*

Core Systems, Poway *Also Called: Rugged Systems Inc (P-2812)*

Core-Mark International Inc .... C....... 661 366-2673
200 Coremark Ct Bakersfield (93307) *(P-6618)*

Core-Mark International Inc .... C....... 323 583-6531
2311 E 48th St Vernon (90058) *(P-6619)*

Core-Mark International Inc .... D....... 509 535-9768
3970 Pell Cir Sacramento (95838) *(P-6620)*

Core-Mark International Inc .... C....... 510 487-3000
31300 Medallion Dr Hayward (94544) *(P-6621)*

Core-Mark International Inc .... D....... 916 374-8677
3030 Mulvany Pl West Sacramento (95691) *(P-20329)*

Core/Related Gala Retail LLC .... D....... 213 349-8585
100 S Grand Ave Los Angeles (90012) *(P-9720)*

Corecare I I I .... C....... 714 256-8000
800 Morningside Dr Fullerton (92835) *(P-18400)*

Corecare V A Cal Ltd Partnr .... D....... 714 256-1000
2525 Brea Blvd Fullerton (92835) *(P-15388)*

Corelation Inc .... D....... 619 876-5074
2305 Historic Decatur Rd Ste 300 San Diego (92106) *(P-11516)*

Corelogic Inc .... D....... 916 431-2146
11010 White Rock Rd Ste 200 Rancho Cordova (95670) *(P-10758)*

Corelogic Credco — ALPHABETIC SECTION

Corelogic Credco, Irvine Also Called: Corelogic Credco LLC (P-10759)
Corelogic Credco LLC (DH) .... C....... 800 255-0792
  40 Pacifica Ste 900 Irvine (92618) *(P-10759)*
Corelogic Credco LLC .... B....... 619 938-7028
  9645 Granite Ridge Dr Ste 300 San Diego (92123) *(P-10760)*
Corelogic Dorado, Irvine Also Called: Dorado Network Systems Corp (P-12163)
Corelogic Info Solutions, Rancho Cordova Also Called: Corelogic Inc (P-10758)
Coresite LLC .... B....... 213 327-1231
  624 S Grand Ave Ste 1800 Los Angeles (90023) *(P-9465)*
Corinthian Intl Prkg Svcs Inc (PA) .... B....... 408 867-7275
  19925 Stevens Creek Blvd Ste 126 Cupertino (95014) *(P-13103)*
Corinthian Parking Services, Cupertino Also Called: Corinthian Intl Prkg Svcs Inc (P-13103)
Corinthian Title Company Inc .... D....... 619 299-4800
  5030 Camino De La Siesta Ste 100 San Diego (92108) *(P-9227)*
Corkys Pest Control Inc .... D....... 760 432-8801
  909 Rancheros Dr San Marcos (92069) *(P-10835)*
Cornerstone, Santa Monica Also Called: Cornerstone Ondemand Inc (P-12149)
Cornerstone Concrete Inc .... D....... 951 279-2221
  255 Benjamin Dr Corona (92879) *(P-2112)*
Cornerstone Hotel Management (DH) .... D....... 415 397-5572
  222 Kearny St Ste 200 San Francisco (94108) *(P-20062)*
Cornerstone Ondemand Inc (HQ) .... B....... 310 752-0200
  1601 Cloverfield Blvd Ste 620s Santa Monica (90404) *(P-12149)*
Cornerstone Protective Svcs .... C....... 888 848-4791
  400 Continental Blvd Ste 6056 El Segundo (90245) *(P-12951)*
Cornerstone Research Inc .... D....... 213 553-2500
  555 W 5th St Ste 3800 Los Angeles (90013) *(P-19806)*
Cornerstone Research Inc (PA) .... D....... 650 853-1660
  1000 El Camino Real Ste 250 Menlo Park (94025) *(P-20734)*
Corodata Records MGT Inc .... D....... 858 748-1100
  12375 Kerran St Poway (92064) *(P-3789)*
Corona - Cllege Hts Ornge Lmon .... B....... 951 359-6451
  8000 Lincoln Ave Riverside (92504) *(P-262)*
Corona Clipper Inc .... D....... 951 737-6515
  22440 Temescal Canyon Rd Ste 102 Corona (92883) *(P-5727)*
Corona Regional Med Ctr Hosp, Corona Also Called: Uhs-Corona Inc (P-16587)
Corona Regional Med Ctr LLC .... C....... 951 737-4343
  800 S Main St Corona (92882) *(P-14708)*
Corona Rgnal Med Ctr Rhbltion, Corona Also Called: Uhs-Corona Inc (P-17149)
Corona Tools, Corona Also Called: Corona Clipper Inc (P-5727)
Coronado Hospital, Coronado Also Called: Sharp Coronado Hospital & Healthcare Center (P-16416)
Coronado YMCA, Richmond Also Called: Young MNS Chrstn Assn of E Bay (P-18978)
Corovan Corporation (PA) .... C....... 858 762-8100
  12302 Kerran St Poway (92064) *(P-3581)*
Corovan Moving & Storage Co (HQ) .... D....... 858 748-1100
  12302 Kerran St Poway (92064) *(P-3582)*
Corp., R.g Barry, Fontana Also Called: DSV Solutions LLC (P-4010)
Corpinfo Services, Santa Monica Also Called: K-Micro Inc (P-5320)
Corporate Alnce Strategies Inc .... C....... 877 777-7487
  3410 La Sierra Ave Ste F244 Riverside (92503) *(P-13104)*
Corporate Real Estate Advisors, San Diego Also Called: Cushman & Wakefield Cal Inc (P-8958)
Corporate Security Service Inc .... C....... 415 626-9271
  901 Mission St Ste 80b San Francisco (94103) *(P-12952)*
Corporate Visions Inc .... C....... 760 458-0914
  2705 Avenida De Anita Apt 29 Carlsbad (92010) *(P-20330)*
Corporate Yard, San Mateo Also Called: City of San Mateo (P-10874)
Corportion of Fine Arts Mseums .... D....... 415 750-3600
  75 Tea Garden Dr San Francisco (94118) *(P-18645)*
Corportion of Fine Arts Mseums .... D....... 415 750-3600
  100 Pine St 11th Fl San Francisco (94111) *(P-18646)*
Corportion of Fine Arts Mseums .... D....... 415 750-3600
  50 Hagiwara Tea Garden Dr San Francisco (94118) *(P-18647)*
Corportion of Fine Arts Mseums .... C....... 415 750-3600
  50 Golden Gate Ave San Francisco (94118) *(P-18648)*
Corportion of Fine Arts Mseums (PA) .... C....... 415 750-3600
  50 Hagiwara Tea Garden Dr San Francisco (94118) *(P-18649)*
Corptax LLC .... C....... 818 316-2400
  21550 Oxnard St Ste 700 Woodland Hills (91367) *(P-11517)*

CORR, Grass Valley Also Called: Granite Wellness Centers (P-17066)
Corral De Tierra Country Club .... D....... 831 484-1325
  81 Corral De Tierra Rd Salinas (93908) *(P-14364)*
Correctivesolutions, Mission Viejo Also Called: American Justice Solutions Inc (P-17800)
Corridor Capital LLC (PA) .... C....... 310 442-7000
  12400 Wilshire Blvd Ste 645 Los Angeles (90025) *(P-9502)*
Corru Kraft Buena Pk Div 5058, Buena Park Also Called: Orora Packaging Solutions (P-6087)
Cortica Healthcare Inc .... B....... 858 304-6440
  7090 Miratech Dr San Diego (92121) *(P-17211)*
Cortlandt Liquidating LLC .... C....... 831 338-4500
  13117 Highway 9 Boulder Creek (95006) *(P-8953)*
Corvel, Orange Also Called: Corvel Corporation (P-20063)
Corvel Corporation .... D....... 714 385-8500
  1100 W Town And Country Rd Ste 400 Orange (92868) *(P-20063)*
Corventis Inc .... C....... 408 790-9300
  2033 Gateway Pl Ste 100 San Jose (95110) *(P-12655)*
Cosco Fire Protection Inc .... B....... 559 275-3795
  4223 W Sierra Madre Ave Ste 108 Fresno (93722) *(P-1408)*
Cosco Fire Protection Inc .... D....... 858 444-2000
  4990 Greencraig Ln San Diego (92123) *(P-1409)*
Cosco Fire Protection Inc .... D....... 925 455-2751
  7455 Longard Rd Livermore (94551) *(P-1710)*
Cosmetic Laboratories America, Chatsworth Also Called: Cosmetic Laboratories of America LLC (P-7576)
Cosmetic Laboratories of America LLC .... B....... 818 717-6140
  20245 Sunburst St Chatsworth (91311) *(P-7576)*
Coso Operating Company LLC .... D....... 760 764-1300
  2 Gill Station Coso Rd. Little Lake (93542) *(P-4567)*
Costa Del Sol Healthcare, Los Angeles Also Called: East Los Angles Healthcare LLC (P-15428)
Costa Mesa Country Club, Costa Mesa Also Called: Mesa Verde Partners (P-14275)
Costa Mesa Healthcare Inc .... D....... 949 631-4282
  2570 Newport Blvd Costa Mesa (92627) *(P-15389)*
Costanoa, Pescadero Also Called: King-Reynolds Ventures LLC (P-13337)
Costanoa, Pescadero Also Called: Joie De Vivre Hospitality LLC (P-20126)
Costco, Montebello Also Called: Costco Wholesale Corporation (P-7140)
Costco Auto Program, San Diego Also Called: Affinity Auto Programs Inc (P-13180)
Costco Wholesale Corporation .... A....... 951 361-3606
  11600 Riverside Dr Ste A Jurupa Valley (91752) *(P-3689)*
Costco Wholesale Corporation .... C....... 323 890-1904
  1345 N Montebello Blvd Montebello (90640) *(P-7140)*
Cosumnes Community Svcs Dst .... B....... 916 405-7150
  9355 E Stockton Blvd Ste 185 Elk Grove (95624) *(P-14510)*
Cottage Bakery Inc .... B....... 209 334-3616
  1831 S Stockton St Lodi (95240) *(P-2367)*
Cottage Childrens Medical Ctr, Santa Barbara Also Called: Santa Brbara Cttage Hosp Fndti (P-16391)
Cottage Health .... D....... 805 688-6432
  2050 Viborg Rd Solvang (93463) *(P-16020)*
Cottage Health System, Santa Barbara Also Called: Goleta Valley Cottage Hosp Aux (P-16109)
Cotton Heritage, Commerce Also Called: Roochi Traders Incorporated (P-6186)
Cottrell Paul Enterprises LLC (PA) .... C....... 661 212-2357
  16654 Soledad Canyon Rd Ste 233 Santa Clarita (91387) *(P-12953)*
COUCHBASE, Santa Clara Also Called: Couchbase Inc (P-11518)
Couchbase Inc (PA) .... C....... 650 417-7500
  3250 Olcott St Santa Clara (95054) *(P-11518)*
Council On Aging - Sthern Cal .... D....... 714 479-0107
  2 Executive Cir Ste 175 Irvine (92614) *(P-17899)*
Counseling and Research Assoc (PA) .... C....... 310 715-2020
  108 W Victoria St Gardena (90248) *(P-18401)*
Counter Hospitality Group LLC .... D....... 559 228-9735
  8398 N Fresno St Ste 101 Fresno (93720) *(P-7469)*
Country Archer Jerky, San Bernardino Also Called: S&E Gourmet Cuts Inc (P-6464)
Country Builders Inc .... C....... 925 373-1020
  5915 Graham Ct Livermore (94550) *(P-751)*
Country Builders Construction, Livermore Also Called: Country Builders Inc (P-751)
Country Club Lanes, Sacramento Also Called: Pinsetters Inc (P-14121)
Country Club Mortgage Inc .... D....... 559 636-3333
  525 N Hall St # B Visalia (93291) *(P-7952)*

ALPHABETIC SECTION — County of Los Angeles

COUNTRY CLUB OF RANCHO BERNARD, San Diego Also Called: Rancho Bernardo Golf Club *(P-14552)*

Country Floral Supply Inc (PA)..D....... 805 520-8026
3802 Weatherly Cir Westlake Village (91361) *(P-6856)*

Country Furnishings, Westlake Village Also Called: Country Floral Supply Inc *(P-6856)*

Country Hills Health Care Inc ....C....... 619 441-8745
1580 Broadway El Cajon (92021) *(P-15390)*

Country Hills Post Acute, El Cajon Also Called: Country Hills Health Care Inc *(P-15390)*

Country Oaks Care Center Inc ....D....... 805 922-6657
830 E Chapel St Santa Maria (93454) *(P-15391)*

Country Villa E Convalescent, Los Angeles Also Called: Country Villa Service Corp *(P-20068)*

Country Villa Health Services, Anaheim Also Called: Country Villa Service Corp *(P-20066)*

COUNTRY VILLA NURSING & REHABI, Los Angeles Also Called: Country Villa Nursing Ctr Inc *(P-15392)*

Country Villa Nursing Ctr Inc ....C....... 213 484-9730
340 S Alvarado St Los Angeles (90057) *(P-15392)*

Country Villa Service Corp ....C....... 760 340-0053
39950 Vista Del Sol Rancho Mirage (92270) *(P-13246)*

Country Villa Service Corp ....C....... 818 246-5516
1208 S Central Ave Glendale (91204) *(P-15393)*

Country Villa Service Corp ....C....... 626 445-2421
400 W Huntington Dr Arcadia (91007) *(P-15394)*

Country Villa Service Corp ....C....... 310 537-2500
3611 E Imperial Hwy Lynwood (90262) *(P-15395)*

Country Villa Service Corp ....C....... 626 285-2165
112 E Broadway San Gabriel (91776) *(P-15832)*

Country Villa Service Corp ....C....... 562 598-2477
3000 N Gate Rd Seal Beach (90740) *(P-17900)*

Country Villa Service Corp ....C....... 209 723-2911
510 W 26th St Merced (95340) *(P-17901)*

Country Villa Service Corp ....C....... 626 358-4547
615 W Duarte Rd Monrovia (91016) *(P-20064)*

Country Villa Service Corp ....C....... 323 666-1544
3002 Rowena Ave Los Angeles (90039) *(P-20065)*

Country Villa Service Corp (PA)..D....... 310 574-3733
2400 E Katella Ave Ste 800 Anaheim (92806) *(P-20066)*

Country Villa Service Corp ....C....... 562 597-8817
1730 Grand Ave Long Beach (90804) *(P-20067)*

Country Villa Service Corp ....C....... 323 734-1101
2415 S Western Ave Los Angeles (90018) *(P-20068)*

Country Villa Service Corp ....C....... 323 734-9122
3233 W Pico Blvd Los Angeles (90019) *(P-20069)*

Country Villa Terrace (PA)..D....... 323 653-3980
6050 W Pico Blvd Los Angeles (90035) *(P-15833)*

COUNTRY VILLA WESTWOOD NURSING, Los Angeles Also Called: Westwood Healthcare Center LP *(P-15734)*

Country VIla Convalescent Hosp, Los Angeles Also Called: Country Villa Terrace *(P-15833)*

Country VIla Mar Vsta Nrsing C, Los Angeles Also Called: Rrt Enterprises LP *(P-15646)*

Country VIla Rncho Mrage Hlthc ....C....... 760 340-0053
39950 Vista Del Sol Rancho Mirage (92270) *(P-17902)*

Country VIla Rvrview Rhab Hlth, Susanville Also Called: CF Susanville LLC *(P-15372)*

Countryside Inn-Corona LP ....D....... 949 588-0131
24341 El Toro Rd Laguna Woods (92637) *(P-9721)*

Countrywide, Thousand Oaks Also Called: Countrywide Home Loans Inc *(P-7953)*

Countrywide, Glendale Also Called: Countrywide Home Loans Inc *(P-7954)*

Countrywide Home Loans Inc (HQ)..A
225 W Hillcrest Dr Thousand Oaks (91360) *(P-7953)*

Countrywide Home Loans Inc ....A....... 818 550-8700
801 N Brand Blvd Ste 750 Glendale (91203) *(P-7954)*

County Building Materials Inc ....D....... 408 274-4920
2927 S King Rd San Jose (95122) *(P-5152)*

County Ford North Inc (PA)...C....... 760 945-9900
450 W Vista Way Vista (92083) *(P-7186)*

County General Hospital, San Luis Obispo Also Called: County of San Luis Obispo *(P-16029)*

County Landfill, Woodland Also Called: County of Yolo *(P-4880)*

County Los Angles Prbtion Dept, Pomona Also Called: County of Los Angeles *(P-17921)*

County of Alameda ....C....... 510 670-5455
399 Elmhurst St Hayward (94544) *(P-1091)*

County of Alameda ....D....... 510 670-6466
399 Elmhurst St Hayward (94544) *(P-4779)*

County of Alameda ....B....... 510 895-4200
15400 Foothill Blvd San Leandro (94578) *(P-16021)*

County of Alameda ....C....... 510 437-4190
1411 E 31st St Oakland (94602) *(P-16849)*

County of Butte ....D....... 530 538-7407
2081 2nd St Oroville (95965) *(P-10879)*

County of Contra Costa ....D....... 510 313-7077
2467 Waterbird Way Martinez (94553) *(P-13661)*

County of Contra Costa ....C....... 925 370-5000
2500 Alhambra Ave Martinez (94553) *(P-16022)*

County of Contra Costa ....D....... 925 655-0000
1850 Muir Rd Martinez (94553) *(P-20929)*

County of Del Norte ....D....... 707 464-3191
880 Northcrest Dr Crescent City (95531) *(P-18581)*

County of El Dorado, Placerville Also Called: El Dorado County Health Dept *(P-14736)*

County of Fresno ....D....... 559 600-3546
205 W Pontiac Way # 7 Clovis (93612) *(P-17415)*

County of Fresno ....D....... 559 600-5127
333 W Pontiac Way Clovis (93612) *(P-17903)*

County of Fresno ....C....... 559 600-2822
2220 Tulare St Ste 1111 Fresno (93721) *(P-17904)*

County of Fresno ....C....... 559 600-4078
2220 Tulare St Fl 6 Fresno (93721) *(P-19185)*

County of Fresno ....C....... 559 299-6057
305 N Villa Ave Clovis (93612) *(P-20923)*

County of Imperial ....D....... 760 482-4120
202 N 8th St El Centro (92243) *(P-17035)*

County of Kern ....A....... 661 326-2054
1700 Mount Vernon Ave Bakersfield (93306) *(P-16023)*

County of Kern ....C....... 661 336-6871
1600 E Belle Ter Ste 5 Bakersfield (93307) *(P-20942)*

County of Los Angeles ....D....... 310 523-9566
216 W Victoria St Gardena (90248) *(P-331)*

County of Los Angeles ....D....... 626 962-3577
4275 Elton St Baldwin Park (91706) *(P-332)*

County of Los Angeles ....D....... 562 658-2085
11258 Garfield Ave Downey (90242) *(P-360)*

County of Los Angeles ....D....... 661 257-3191
31044 Charlie Canyon Rd Castaic (91384) *(P-361)*

County of Los Angeles ....D....... 626 458-1700
1525 Alcazar St Bldg 1 Los Angeles (90033) *(P-1092)*

County of Los Angeles ....C....... 562 945-2581
9402 Greenleaf Ave Whittier (90605) *(P-3324)*

County of Los Angeles ....D....... 626 458-1707
1537 Alcazar St Los Angeles (90033) *(P-3690)*

County of Los Angeles ....D....... 213 367-3176
6801 E 2nd St Long Beach (90803) *(P-4780)*

County of Los Angeles ....B....... 626 458-4000
900 S Fremont Ave Alhambra (91803) *(P-4781)*

County of Los Angeles ....D....... 661 942-6042
45712 Division St Lancaster (93535) *(P-4848)*

County of Los Angeles ....D....... 626 299-5300
1000 S Fremont Ave Unit 4 Alhambra (91803) *(P-8294)*

County of Los Angeles ....D....... 562 985-4687
6300 E State University Dr Ste 104 Long Beach (90815) *(P-9413)*

County of Los Angeles ....D....... 818 340-2633
7326 Jordan Ave Canoga Park (91303) *(P-10400)*

County of Los Angeles ....C....... 213 922-6210
1 Gateway Plz Los Angeles (90012) *(P-10802)*

County of Los Angeles ....A....... 562 940-4324
1100 N Eastern Ave Los Angeles (90063) *(P-11519)*

County of Los Angeles ....C....... 562 462-2094
12400 Imperial Hwy Norwalk (90650) *(P-12560)*

County of Los Angeles ....C....... 213 974-0515
320 W Temple St Fl 9 Los Angeles (90012) *(P-12656)*

County of Los Angeles ....D....... 323 267-2771
1100 N Eastern Ave Los Angeles (90063) *(P-13247)*

County of Los Angeles ....C....... 909 231-0549
1875 Fairplex Dr Pomona (91768) *(P-14253)*

County of Los Angeles ....A....... 323 226-7131
1900 Zonal Ave Los Angeles (90033) *(P-14709)*

County of Los Angeles — ALPHABETIC SECTION

County of Los Angeles .... D...... 213 744-3919
2829 S Grand Ave Los Angeles (90007) *(P-14710)*

County of Los Angeles .... D...... 626 968-3711
15930 Central Ave Ste 100 La Puente (91744) *(P-14711)*

County of Los Angeles .... D...... 562 804-8111
10005 Flower St Bellflower (90706) *(P-14712)*

County of Los Angeles .... D...... 626 969-7885
150 N Azusa Ave Azusa (91702) *(P-14713)*

County of Los Angeles .... C...... 310 222-2401
1000 W Carson St 8th Fl Palos Verdes Peninsu (90274) *(P-16024)*

County of Los Angeles .... B...... 310 668-4545
12025 Wilmington Ave Los Angeles (90059) *(P-16025)*

County of Los Angeles .... C...... 323 226-6021
1100 N Mission Rd Rm 236 Los Angeles (90033) *(P-16026)*

County of Los Angeles .... C...... 213 473-6100
450 Bauchet St Los Angeles (90012) *(P-16027)*

County of Los Angeles .... C...... 323 226-3468
1240 N Mission Rd Los Angeles (90033) *(P-16675)*

County of Los Angeles .... C...... 661 223-8700
30500 Arrastre Canyon Rd Acton (93510) *(P-16676)*

County of Los Angeles .... D...... 661 223-8700
38200 Lake Hughes Rd Castaic (91384) *(P-16677)*

County of Los Angeles .... D...... 213 974-7284
515 E 6th St Los Angeles (90021) *(P-16678)*

County of Los Angeles .... B...... 323 897-6187
5850 S Main St Los Angeles (90003) *(P-17036)*

County of Los Angeles .... D...... 562 402-0688
17707 Studebaker Rd Artesia (90703) *(P-17037)*

County of Los Angeles .... D...... 323 769-7800
5205 Melrose Ave Los Angeles (90038) *(P-17038)*

County of Los Angeles .... D...... 661 524-2005
335 E Avenue K6 Ste B Lancaster (93535) *(P-17039)*

County of Los Angeles .... A...... 562 401-7088
7601 Imperial Hwy Downey (90242) *(P-17040)*

County of Los Angeles .... D...... 213 739-2360
600 S Commonwealth Ave Ste 700 Los Angeles (90005) *(P-17212)*

County of Los Angeles .... D...... 626 229-3825
532 E Colorado Blvd Fl 8 Pasadena (91101) *(P-17213)*

County of Los Angeles .... D...... 562 861-0316
5525 Imperial Hwy South Gate (90280) *(P-17214)*

County of Los Angeles .... D...... 818 717-4644
20151 Nordhoff St Chatsworth (91311) *(P-17215)*

County of Los Angeles .... D...... 213 974-2811
210 W Temple St Fl 19 Los Angeles (90012) *(P-17416)*

County of Los Angeles .... D...... 818 374-2406
6230 Sylmar Ave Ste 201 Van Nuys (91401) *(P-17417)*

County of Los Angeles .... C...... 213 974-3512
210 W Temple St Fl 18 Los Angeles (90012) *(P-17418)*

County of Los Angeles .... D...... 562 807-7860
12727 Norwalk Blvd Norwalk (90650) *(P-17905)*

County of Los Angeles .... D...... 661 948-2320
777 W Jackman St Lancaster (93534) *(P-17906)*

County of Los Angeles .... D...... 213 351-7257
501 Shatto Pl Ste 301 Los Angeles (90020) *(P-17907)*

County of Los Angeles .... B...... 323 889-3405
5770 S Eastern Ave 4th Fl Commerce (90040) *(P-17908)*

County of Los Angeles .... D...... 562 903-5000
10355 Slusher Dr Santa Fe Springs (90670) *(P-17909)*

County of Los Angeles .... D...... 213 351-5600
510 S Vermont Ave Fl 1 Los Angeles (90020) *(P-17910)*

County of Los Angeles .... D...... 818 708-4500
19231 Victory Blvd Ste 100 Reseda (91335) *(P-17911)*

County of Los Angeles .... D...... 562 497-3500
4060 Watson Plaza Dr Lakewood (90712) *(P-17912)*

County of Los Angeles .... D...... 626 356-5281
300 E Walnut St Dept 200 Pasadena (91101) *(P-17913)*

County of Los Angeles .... D...... 661 940-4181
5300 W Avenue I Lancaster (93536) *(P-17914)*

County of Los Angeles .... D...... 562 940-2470
9150 Imperial Hwy Downey (90242) *(P-17915)*

County of Los Angeles .... D...... 213 974-9331
320 W Temple St Ste 1101 Los Angeles (90012) *(P-17916)*

County of Los Angeles .... D...... 562 908-3119
8240 Broadway Ave Whittier (90606) *(P-17917)*

County of Los Angeles .... D...... 323 235-7047
236 E 58th St Los Angeles (90011) *(P-17918)*

County of Los Angeles .... D...... 323 226-8511
1601 Eastlake Ave Los Angeles (90033) *(P-17919)*

County of Los Angeles .... D...... 562 940-6856
7285 Quill Dr Downey (90242) *(P-17920)*

County of Los Angeles .... D...... 909 469-4500
1660 W Mission Blvd Pomona (91766) *(P-17921)*

County of Los Angeles .... D...... 310 266-3711
1725 Main St Rm 125 Santa Monica (90401) *(P-17922)*

County of Los Angeles .... D...... 818 374-2000
14414 Delano St Van Nuys (91401) *(P-17923)*

County of Los Angeles .... C...... 323 780-2185
4849 Civic Center Way Los Angeles (90022) *(P-17924)*

County of Los Angeles .... D...... 323 586-6469
8526 Grape St Los Angeles (90001) *(P-17925)*

County of Los Angeles .... D...... 310 603-7311
200 W Compton Blvd Ste 300 Compton (90220) *(P-17926)*

County of Los Angeles .... D...... 626 356-5281
199 N Euclid Ave Pasadena (91101) *(P-17927)*

County of Los Angeles .... D...... 626 308-5542
200 W Woodward Ave Alhambra (91801) *(P-17928)*

County of Los Angeles .... D...... 909 599-2391
1900 Sycamore Canyon Rd San Dimas (91773) *(P-17929)*

County of Los Angeles .... D...... 626 854-4987
17171 Gale Ave City Of Industry (91745) *(P-17930)*

County of Los Angeles .... D...... 323 551-7224
613 S Humphreys Ave Los Angeles (90022) *(P-17931)*

County of Los Angeles .... D...... 805 237-3110
530 12th St 1st Fl Paso Robles (93446) *(P-17932)*

County of Los Angeles .... D...... 323 722-4529
5801 E Beverly Blvd Los Angeles (90022) *(P-17933)*

County of Los Angeles .... D...... 323 226-8611
1605 Eastlake Ave Los Angeles (90033) *(P-18402)*

County of Los Angeles .... D...... 818 364-2011
16350 Filbert St Sylmar (91342) *(P-18403)*

County of Los Angeles .... D...... 626 291-2200
9668 Valley Blvd Ste 104 Rosemead (91770) *(P-18582)*

County of Los Angeles .... C...... 213 240-8412
313 N Figueroa St 9th Fl Los Angeles (90012) *(P-18747)*

County of Los Angeles .... C...... 661 723-6088
44933 Fern Ave Lancaster (93534) *(P-19186)*

County of Los Angeles .... D...... 626 337-1277
14747 Ramona Blvd Baldwin Park (91706) *(P-19187)*

County of Los Angeles .... A...... 323 267-2136
1100 N Eastern Ave Los Angeles (90063) *(P-19556)*

County of Los Angeles .... C...... 323 267-6167
1800 Paseo Rancho Castilla Los Angeles (90032) *(P-19961)*

County of Los Angeles .... D...... 562 908-8400
12900 Crossroads Pkwy S Ste 200 City Of Industry (91746) *(P-20070)*

County of Los Angeles .... C...... 562 940-2907
9150 Imperial Hwy Downey (90242) *(P-20071)*

County of Los Angeles .... D...... 661 974-7700
42011 4th St W Ste 3530 Lancaster (93534) *(P-20931)*

County of Los Angeles .... C...... 213 738-4601
510 S Vermont Ave Fl 1 Los Angeles (90020) *(P-20938)*

County of Monterey .... C...... 831 755-4201
1441 Constitution Blvd Ste 100 Salinas (93906) *(P-16028)*

County of Monterey .... C...... 831 755-3856
1414 Natividad Rd Salinas (93906) *(P-19078)*

County of Orange .... C...... 949 252-5006
3160 Airway Ave Costa Mesa (92626) *(P-3888)*

County of Orange .... D...... 714 647-1552
1631 E Wilshire Ave Santa Ana (92705) *(P-10996)*

County of Orange .... D...... 714 834-6021
405 W 5th St Ofc Santa Ana (92701) *(P-15752)*

County of Orange .... D...... 714 896-7188
8141 13th St Westminster (92683) *(P-17934)*

County of Placer .... D...... 530 889-7500
3091 County Center Dr Ste 220 Auburn (95603) *(P-19188)*

ALPHABETIC SECTION — Coursera Inc

County of Placer .... C...... 916 791-7059
6900 Eureka Rd Granite Bay (95746) *(P-20934)*

County of Riverside .... D...... 951 955-4800
3450 14th St Riverside (92501) *(P-668)*

County of Riverside .... A...... 951 486-4000
26520 Cactus Ave Moreno Valley (92555) *(P-14714)*

County of Riverside .... B...... 951 486-4000
26520 Cactus Ave Moreno Valley (92555) *(P-14715)*

County of Riverside .... C...... 951 955-0840
5256 Mission Blvd Riverside (92509) *(P-14716)*

County of Riverside .... D...... 760 863-8450
47923 Oasis St Indio (92201) *(P-17216)*

County of Riverside .... C...... 951 955-6000
4075 Main St Riverside (92501) *(P-17419)*

County of Riverside .... D...... 951 955-4900
2038 Iowa Ave Ste 102 Riverside (92507) *(P-17935)*

County of Riverside .... D...... 800 510-2020
3610 Central Ave Ste 102 Riverside (92506) *(P-17936)*

County of Riverside .... D...... 951 955-3434
1325 Spruce St Ste 400 Riverside (92507) *(P-18225)*

County of Riverside .... D...... 951 683-7691
4500 Glenwood Dr Ste A Riverside (92501) *(P-18845)*

County of Riverside .... D...... 951 955-5659
2001 Iowa Ave Ste 218 Riverside (92507) *(P-20932)*

County of Riverside .... D...... 951 248-0014
585 Technology Ct Riverside (92507) *(P-20939)*

County of Riverside .... C...... 951 358-5000
4065 County Circle Dr Riverside (92503) *(P-20943)*

County of Sacramento .... B...... 916 874-0912
6900 Airport Blvd Sacramento (95837) *(P-3889)*

County of Sacramento .... B...... 916 874-7752
799 G St Sacramento (95814) *(P-12694)*

County of Sacramento .... B...... 916 725-1585
7801 Auburn Blvd Citrus Heights (95610) *(P-18846)*

County of San Diego .... C...... 858 694-2960
5510 Overland Ave Ste 410 San Diego (92123) *(P-13248)*

County of San Diego .... D...... 619 956-2800
9065 Edgemoor Dr Santee (92071) *(P-15396)*

County of San Diego .... B...... 619 692-8200
3853 Rosecrans St San Diego (92110) *(P-16649)*

County of San Diego .... D...... 619 446-2900
450 B St Ste 900 San Diego (92101) *(P-17420)*

County of San Diego .... D...... 619 531-4040
330 W Broadway Ste 1020 San Diego (92101) *(P-17421)*

County of San Diego .... A...... 619 515-8202
330 W Broadway Ste 1100 San Diego (92101) *(P-17937)*

County of San Diego .... D...... 619 338-2558
1255 Imperial Ave Ste 433 San Diego (92101) *(P-18404)*

County of San Diego .... D...... 858 505-6100
5560 Overland Ave Ste 410 San Diego (92123) *(P-20924)*

County of San Joaquin .... C...... 209 468-8750
1212 N California St Stockton (95202) *(P-17041)*

County of San Joaquin .... D...... 209 468-6280
500 W Hospital Rd French Camp (95231) *(P-17042)*

County of San Joaquin .... D...... 209 468-2601
409 E Market St Stockton (95202) *(P-17938)*

County of San Joaquin .... D...... 209 468-6966
500 W Hospital Rd French Camp (95231) *(P-17939)*

County of San Joaquin .... C...... 209 472-7127
7585 Longe St Stockton (95206) *(P-20331)*

County of San Joaquin .... D...... 209 468-3090
1702 E Scotts Ave Stockton (95205) *(P-20916)*

County of San Joaquin .... D...... 209 331-7270
11793 N Micke Grove Rd Lodi (95240) *(P-20945)*

County of San Luis Obispo .... D...... 805 781-4753
2180 Johnson Ave San Luis Obispo (93401) *(P-16029)*

County of San Mateo .... A...... 650 208-3480
222 W 39th Ave San Mateo (94403) *(P-14717)*

County of San Mateo .... C...... 650 573-2662
222 W 39th Ave San Mateo (94403) *(P-14718)*

County of Santa Clara .... B...... 408 573-2400
101 Skyport Dr San Jose (95110) *(P-4976)*

County of Santa Clara .... C...... 408 355-2200
298 Garden Hill Dr Los Gatos (95032) *(P-14511)*

County of Santa Clara .... A...... 408 885-5000
751 S Bascom Ave San Jose (95128) *(P-14719)*

County of Santa Clara .... D...... 408 885-7470
2325 Enborg Ln 2h260 San Jose (95128) *(P-16030)*

County of Santa Clara .... B...... 408 299-5437
333 W Julian St San Jose (95110) *(P-17940)*

County of Santa Clara .... C...... 408 885-7200
2325 Enborg Ln Fl 4 San Jose (95128) *(P-19557)*

County of Santa Clara .... D...... 408 885-7354
751 S Bascom Ave 4th Fl San Jose (95128) *(P-19558)*

County of Santa Clara .... D...... 408 224-7476
6980 Santa Teresa Blvd Ste 100 San Jose (95119) *(P-20946)*

County of Shasta .... D...... 530 246-9622
1155 N Court St Redding (96001) *(P-17941)*

County of Solano .... C...... 707 451-6090
810 Vaca Valley Pkwy Ste 203 Vacaville (95688) *(P-4782)*

County of Solano .... D...... 707 421-6055
3255 N Texas St Fairfield (94533) *(P-5485)*

County of Sonoma .... C...... 707 823-8511
501 Petaluma Ave Sebastopol (95472) *(P-16031)*

County of Stanislaus .... D...... 209 522-4098
2000 Santa Fe Ave Modesto (95357) *(P-4977)*

County of Stanislaus .... C...... 209 525-7000
830 Scenic Dr Modesto (95350) *(P-16032)*

County of Stanislaus .... D...... 209 664-8044
2101 Geer Rd Ste 120 Turlock (95382) *(P-17043)*

County of Stanislaus .... D...... 209 558-2100
251 E Hackett Rd Ste 2 Modesto (95358) *(P-18226)*

County of Stanislaus .... D...... 209 525-6225
800 Scenic Dr Modesto (95350) *(P-18583)*

County of Sutter .... D...... 530 822-7250
1965 Live Oak Blvd Yuba City (95991) *(P-17044)*

County of Ventura .... C...... 805 654-2561
800 S Victoria Ave Ventura (93009) *(P-17942)*

County of Ventura .... D...... 805 654-3152
800 S Victoria Ave Ste 1540 Ventura (93009) *(P-19559)*

County of Ventura .... D...... 805 652-6100
3291 Loma Vista Rd Ventura (93003) *(P-20917)*

County of Ventura .... D...... 805 981-5521
4333 E Vineyard Ave Oxnard (93036) *(P-20925)*

County of Ventura .... D...... 805 388-4341
600 Aviation Dr Camarillo (93010) *(P-20926)*

County of Yolo .... C...... 530 661-0816
350 Industrial Way Woodland (95776) *(P-4000)*

County of Yolo .... D...... 530 666-8729
44090 County Road 28h Woodland (95776) *(P-4880)*

County of Yuba .... D...... 530 741-6478
5245 Feather River Blvd Marysville (95901) *(P-333)*

County of Yuba .... D...... 530 741-6275
209 6th St Marysville (95901) *(P-17943)*

County of Yuba .... C...... 530 749-7550
215 5th St Ste 154 Marysville (95901) *(P-17944)*

County of Yuba .... D...... 530 741-6371
1023 14th St Marysville (95901) *(P-18405)*

County Rvrside Wrkfrce Dev Div, Riverside *Also Called: County of Riverside (P-18225)*

County Ventura Human Resources, Ventura *Also Called: County of Ventura (P-17942)*

County Whl Elc Co Los Angeles .... D...... 714 633-3801
560 N Main St Orange (92868) *(P-5550)*

Countywide Childrens Case MGT, Los Angeles *Also Called: County of Los Angeles (P-17212)*

Countywide Mech Systems LLC .... C...... 619 449-9900
1400 N Johnson Ave Ste 104-115 El Cajon (92020) *(P-1410)*

Coupa, San Mateo *Also Called: Coupa Software Incorporated (P-12150)*

Coupa Software Incorporated (HQ) .... C...... 650 931-3200
1855 S Grant St San Mateo (94402) *(P-12150)*

Courseco Inc .... A...... 707 255-4333
2295 Streblow Dr Napa (94558) *(P-14254)*

COURSERA, Mountain View *Also Called: Coursera Inc (P-12151)*

Coursera Inc (PA) .... A...... 650 963-9884
381 E Evelyn Ave Mountain View (94041) *(P-12151)*

ALPHABETIC SECTION

Courtesy Chevrolet Center .... D....... 619 297-4321
750 Camino Del Rio N San Diego (92108) *(P-7187)*

Courtesy Motors Auto Ctr Inc .... D....... 530 345-9444
2520 Cohasset Rd Chico (95973) *(P-7188)*

Courtesy Moving and Storage, Fresno *Also Called: Rich Harvest Inc (P-113)*

Courtesy Security Inc .... D....... 888 572-5545
2252 Erie Ct Tracy (95304) *(P-12954)*

Courthuse Tours-Docent Council, Santa Barbara *Also Called: Santa Barbara City of (P-3967)*

Courtney Inc (PA) .... D....... 949 222-2050
16781 Millikan Ave Irvine (92606) *(P-2268)*

Courtside Club, Los Gatos *Also Called: Courtside Tennis Club (P-14365)*

Courtside Tennis Club .... D....... 408 395-7111
14675 Winchester Blvd Los Gatos (95032) *(P-14365)*

Courtyard By Marriott .... D....... 925 866-2900
18090 San Ramon Valley Blvd San Ramon (94583) *(P-9722)*

Courtyard By Marriott, Baldwin Park *Also Called: Baldwin Hospitality LLC (P-9630)*

Courtyard By Marriott, Sherman Oaks *Also Called: Burbank Partners LLC (P-9666)*

Courtyard By Marriott, Los Angeles *Also Called: Courtyard By Marriott/Lax (P-9723)*

Courtyard By Marriott, Richmond *Also Called: Pacific Hotel Management LLC (P-10083)*

Courtyard By Marriott, San Diego *Also Called: RPC Old Town Jffrson Owner LLC (P-10180)*

Courtyard By Marriott Irvine, Irvine *Also Called: Courtyard Management Corp (P-9725)*

Courtyard By Marriott Stockton, Stockton *Also Called: Castlehill Properties Inc (P-9684)*

Courtyard By Marriott/Lax .... D....... 310 981-2350
6161 W Century Blvd Los Angeles (90045) *(P-9723)*

Courtyard By Mrrott Los Angles, Monrovia *Also Called: Sage Hospitality Resources LLC (P-10188)*

Courtyard La LLC .... D....... 917 913-8333
3302 Griffith Park Blvd Los Angeles (90027) *(P-9724)*

Courtyard Little Chico Creek, Chico *Also Called: Hignell Incorporated (P-9255)*

Courtyard Management Corp .... D....... 949 453-1033
7955 Irvine Center Dr Irvine (92618) *(P-9725)*

Courtyard Marriott, Fairfield *Also Called: Embassy Investments LLC (P-9779)*

Courtyard Marriott Mission Vly, San Diego *Also Called: Mbp Land LLC (P-10011)*

Courtyard Oxnard .... D....... 805 988-3600
600 E Esplanade Dr Oxnard (93036) *(P-9726)*

Courtyard Sacramento-Midtown, Sacramento *Also Called: Cy Sac Operator LLC (P-9738)*

Courtyard San Dego Gslmp/Cnvnt, San Diego *Also Called: Cy Gaslamp LLC (P-9737)*

Courtyard San Dego Mssion Vlly, San Diego *Also Called: Mhf Mv Operating VI LLC (P-10018)*

Courtyard Santa Barbara Dwntwn, Santa Barbara *Also Called: Marriott Intl Hotels Inc (P-10007)*

Couts Heating & Cooling Inc .... C....... 951 278-5560
1693 Rimpau Ave Corona (92881) *(P-1411)*

Covan World-Wide Moving Inc .... D....... 858 558-0439
10015 Waples Ct Ste B San Diego (92121) *(P-3583)*

Covanta Long Bch Rnwble Enrgy .... C....... 562 436-0636
118 Pier S Ave Long Beach (90802) *(P-4881)*

Covario Inc .... D....... 858 397-1500
9255 Towne Centre Dr # 600 San Diego (92121) *(P-20332)*

Cove Electric Inc .... D....... 760 568-9924
77971 Wildcat Dr Ste F Palm Desert (92211) *(P-1711)*

Covenant Aviation Security LLC .... A....... 650 219-3473
1000 Marina Blvd Ste 100 Brisbane (94005) *(P-12955)*

Covenant Care LLC .... D....... 831 476-0770
1935 Wharf Rd Capitola (95010) *(P-15397)*

Covenant Care California LLC .... D....... 916 391-6011
6821 24th St Sacramento (95822) *(P-15398)*

Covenant Care California LLC .... C....... 209 477-5252
9289 Branstetter Pl Stockton (95209) *(P-15399)*

Covenant Care California LLC .... D....... 415 327-0511
911 Bryant St Palo Alto (94301) *(P-15400)*

Covenant Care California LLC .... D....... 408 248-3736
410 N Winchester Blvd Santa Clara (95050) *(P-15401)*

Covenant Care California LLC .... D....... 323 589-5941
6425 Miles Ave Huntington Park (90255) *(P-15402)*

Covenant Care California LLC .... D....... 559 251-8463
577 S Peach Ave Fresno (93727) *(P-15403)*

Covenant Care California LLC .... D....... 805 964-4871
160 S Patterson Ave Santa Barbara (93111) *(P-15404)*

Covenant Care California LLC .... D....... 209 632-3821
1111 E Tuolumne Rd Turlock (95382) *(P-15405)*

Covenant Care California LLC .... D....... 408 842-9311
8170 Murray Ave Gilroy (95020) *(P-15406)*

Covenant Care California LLC .... C....... 650 941-5255
809 Fremont Ave Los Altos (94024) *(P-15407)*

Covenant Care California LLC .... C....... 209 521-2094
3620 Dale Rd Ste B Modesto (95356) *(P-15834)*

Covenant Care California LLC .... C....... 650 964-0543
1949 Grant Rd Mountain View (94040) *(P-16033)*

Covenant Care La Jolla LLC .... C....... 858 453-5810
2552 Torrey Pines Rd Ste 1 La Jolla (92037) *(P-15408)*

Covenant Care LLC (PA) .... B....... 949 349-1200
120 Vantis Dr Ste 200 Aliso Viejo (92656) *(P-15409)*

Covenant House California .... C....... 323 461-3131
1325 N Western Ave Los Angeles (90027) *(P-18406)*

Covenant Living At Mt Miguel, Spring Valley *Also Called: Covenant Living West (P-18407)*

Covenant Living At Samarkand, Santa Barbara *Also Called: Covenant Living West (P-18408)*

Covenant Living of Turlock, Turlock *Also Called: Covenant Living West (P-18409)*

Covenant Living West .... D....... 209 667-5600
1801 N Olive Ave Turlock (95382) *(P-16034)*

Covenant Living West .... D....... 619 931-1114
325 Kempton St Spring Valley (91977) *(P-18407)*

Covenant Living West .... D....... 805 687-0701
2550 Treasure Dr Santa Barbara (93105) *(P-18408)*

Covenant Living West .... D....... 209 632-9976
2125 N Olive Ave Turlock (95382) *(P-18409)*

COVENANT RETIREMENT COMMUNITIES, Santa Barbara *Also Called: Covenant Rtirement Communities (P-15410)*

Covenant Rtirement Communities .... D....... 805 687-0701
2550 Treasure Dr Santa Barbara (93105) *(P-15410)*

Covenant Transport, Pomona *Also Called: Covenant Transport Inc (P-3458)*

Covenant Transport Inc .... A....... 909 469-0130
1300 E Franklin Ave Pomona (91766) *(P-3458)*

Coventry Court Health Center .... C....... 714 636-2800
2040 S Euclid St Anaheim (92802) *(P-15411)*

Coventry Cove Apartments, Fresno *Also Called: Buckingham Property Management (P-10531)*

Coveo Software Corp .... D....... 800 635-5476
44 Montgomery St San Francisco (94104) *(P-11520)*

Coverance Insur Solutions Inc .... C....... 310 856-9925
1343 6th St Manhattan Beach (90266) *(P-8533)*

Coveris, Hanford *Also Called: Hood Packaging Corporation (P-6915)*

Coverking, Anaheim *Also Called: Shrin LLC (P-5060)*

Covestic LLC .... D....... 425 803-9889
3101 Skyway Ct Fremont (94539) *(P-12766)*

Covey Auto Express Inc (PA) .... D....... 253 826-0461
1444 El Pinal Dr Stockton (95205) *(P-13712)*

Covey, The, Carmel *Also Called: Quail Lodge Inc (P-10132)*

Covia Affordable Communities .... C....... 925 956-7400
2185 N California Blvd Ste 215 Walnut Creek (94596) *(P-17945)*

Covid Clinic Inc .... B....... 877 219-8378
16541 Gothard St Huntington Beach (92647) *(P-14720)*

Covina Rehabilitation Center .... C....... 626 967-3874
261 W Badillo St Covina (91723) *(P-15412)*

Covina Service Center, San Dimas *Also Called: Southern California Edison Co (P-4696)*

Covington & Burling LLP .... D....... 650 632-4700
3000 El Camino Real Ste 5-1000 Palo Alto (94306) *(P-17422)*

Covington & Burling LLP .... C....... 415 591-6000
415 Mission St Ste 700 San Francisco (94105) *(P-17423)*

Covington & Burling LLP .... C....... 424 332-4800
1999 Avenue Of The Stars # 3500 Los Angeles (90067) *(P-17424)*

Cowell Homeowners Assn Inc (PA) .... D....... 925 825-0250
4498 Lawson Ct Concord (94521) *(P-18847)*

Cox Castle & Nicholson LLP (PA) .... C....... 310 284-2200
2029 Century Park E Ste 2100 Los Angeles (90002) *(P-17425)*

Cox & Young Ventures LLC .... D....... 831 647-0114
447 Figueroa St Monterey (93940) *(P-7470)*

Cox Castle, Los Angeles *Also Called: Cox Castle & Nicholson LLP (P-17425)*

Cox Communications Cal LLC .... B....... 619 262-1122
5159 Federal Blvd San Diego (92105) *(P-4494)*

Cox Enterprises LLC .... D....... 858 822-8587
325 W 3rd Ave Ste 101 Escondido (92025) *(P-16850)*

ALPHABETIC SECTION

Cox Petroleum Transport, Cudahy *Also Called: HF Cox Inc (P-3404)*

Cox Petroleum Transport, Bakersfield *Also Called: HF Cox Inc (P-3490)*

Cox Wtton Grffin Hnsen Plos LL .... D....... 415 438-4600
900 Front St San Francisco (94111) *(P-17426)*

Coyote Creek Consulting, Morgan Hill *Also Called: Coyote Creek Consulting LLC (P-12767)*

Coyote Creek Consulting LLC .... D....... 408 383-9200
1057 Cochrane Rd Ste 160 Pmb 1017 Morgan Hill (95037) *(P-12767)*

Cozad Trailer Sales LLC 209 931-3000
4907 E Waterloo Rd Stockton (95215) *(P-2979)*

CP Document Technologies LLC (PA) .... D....... 213 617-4040
800 W 6th St Ste 1400 Los Angeles (90017) *(P-5643)*

CP Employer Inc (PA) .... C....... 415 273-2900
1000 Sansome St Fl 1 San Francisco (94111) *(P-752)*

CP Multifamily Cnstr Cal Inc .... C....... 415 273-2900
1000 Sansome St Fl 1 San Francisco (94111) *(P-753)*

Cpacket Networks Inc 650 969-9500
2130 Gold St Ste 200 Alviso (95002) *(P-12768)*

Cpcc Inc .... D....... 818 882-3200
10610 Owensmouth Ave Chatsworth (91311) *(P-15835)*

Cpe Hr Inc .... D....... 310 270-9800
9000 W Sunset Blvd Ste 900 West Hollywood (90069) *(P-20333)*

Cph Monarch Hotel LLC .... A....... 949 234-3200
1 Monarch Beach Resort Dana Point (92629) *(P-9727)*

CPI Econco Division 530 662-7553
1318 Commerce Ave Woodland (95776) *(P-13738)*

CPI International .... D....... 707 521-6327
5580 Skylane Blvd Santa Rosa (95403) *(P-5465)*

Cpl Holdings LLC .... C....... 310 348-6800
12181 Bluff Creek Dr Ste 250 Playa Vista (90094) *(P-7136)*

Cpmc, San Francisco *Also Called: Sutter Health (P-16520)*

Cpmc Mission Bernal Campus, San Francisco *Also Called: Sutter Health (P-16536)*

Cpmc Van Ness Campus, San Francisco *Also Called: Sutter Health (P-16533)*

Cppib America Inc (DH) .... D....... 646 564-4900
100 1st St Ste 2600 San Francisco (94105) *(P-9503)*

CPS, San Mateo *Also Called: Kotobuki-Ya Inc (P-3145)*

CPS Hr Consulting, Sacramento *Also Called: Cooperative Personnel Services (P-20328)*

CPS Security, Cerritos *Also Called: Commercial Protective Svcs Inc (P-12945)*

CPS Security Solutions Inc .... B....... 510 806-7227
799 Fletcher Ln Ste 201 Hayward (94544) *(P-12956)*

Cpu Medical Management Systems, San Diego *Also Called: Computer Proc Unlimited Inc (P-11510)*

Cputer Inc .... D....... 844 394-1538
2110 Artesia Blvd Redondo Beach (90278) *(P-12769)*

Cr Drywall, San Jose *Also Called: C R S Drywall Inc (P-1914)*

CR&r Incorporated 951 634-8079
1706 Goetz Rd Perris (92570) *(P-4882)*

CRA International Inc .... D....... 310 393-5530
12424 Wilshire Blvd Ste 600 Los Angeles (90025) *(P-20735)*

Craft, San Francisco *Also Called: Craft Machine Inc (P-11521)*

Craft Machine Inc (PA) .... D....... 650 862-9580
564 Market St Ste 150 San Francisco (94104) *(P-11521)*

Craftsman Lath and Plaster Inc .... B....... 951 685-9922
8325 63rd St Riverside (92509) *(P-1996)*

Crafty Apes LLC (PA) .... A....... 310 837-3900
127 Lomita St El Segundo (90245) *(P-13832)*

Crain Walnut Shelling LP .... B....... 530 529-1585
10695 Decker Ave Los Molinos (96055) *(P-814)*

Crane Acquisition Inc .... A....... 415 922-1666
2700 Geary Blvd San Francisco (94118) *(P-10836)*

Crane Pest Control, San Francisco *Also Called: Crane Acquisition Inc (P-10836)*

CRC, Long Beach *Also Called: California Resources Corp (P-582)*

CRC Health Corporate (DH) .... D....... 408 367-0044
20400 Stevens Creek Blvd Ste 600 Cupertino (95014) *(P-17045)*

CRC Health Corporate .... A....... 714 542-3581
2101 E 1st St Santa Ana (92705) *(P-17046)*

CRC Health Group Inc .... D....... 408 866-8167
256 E Hamilton Ave Ste I Campbell (95008) *(P-17047)*

CRC Health Group Inc .... D....... 214 634-2722
234 N Magnolia Ave El Cajon (92020) *(P-17048)*

CRC Health Group Inc .... C....... 951 784-8010
1021 W La Cadena Dr Riverside (92501) *(P-17049)*

CRC Health LLC (DH) .... D....... 877 272-8668
20400 Stevens Creek Blvd 6th Fl Cupertino (95014) *(P-16679)*

CRC Insurance Services Inc .... D....... 415 986-5050
50 California St Ste 2000 San Francisco (94111) *(P-8534)*

Crdn of Southern La County, Long Beach *Also Called: Foasberg Laundry and Clrs Inc (P-10434)*

Createme, Newark *Also Called: Createme Technologies LLC (P-7417)*

Createme Technologies LLC .... C....... 646 880-8625
6701 Mowry Ave Newark (94560) *(P-7417)*

Creative Alternatives .... C....... 209 668-9361
2855 Geer Rd Ste A Turlock (95382) *(P-18410)*

Creative Artsts Agcy Hldngs LL (PA) .... A....... 424 288-2000
2000 Avenue Of The Stars Ste 100 Los Angeles (90067) *(P-14035)*

Creative Channel Services LLC, Los Angeles *Also Called: Rocky Point Investments LLC (P-20532)*

Creative Child Care Inc .... B....... 209 462-2282
17 E Poplar St Stockton (95202) *(P-18303)*

Creative Design Consultants (PA) .... D....... 714 641-4868
2915 Red Hill Ave Ste G201 Costa Mesa (92626) *(P-13249)*

Creative Design Industries .... C....... 619 710-2525
2587 Otay Center Dr San Diego (92154) *(P-2450)*

Creative Design Interiors Inc (PA) .... D....... 916 641-1121
737 Del Paso Rd Sacramento (95834) *(P-2030)*

Creative Energy Foods Inc .... D....... 510 638-8668
9957 Medford Ave Ste 4 Oakland (94603) *(P-6622)*

Creative Inflatables, South El Monte *Also Called: Promotnal Design Concepts Inc (P-2659)*

Creative Labs Inc (DH) .... C....... 408 428-6600
1900 Mccarthy Blvd Ste 103 Milpitas (95035) *(P-5288)*

Creative Living Options Inc .... C....... 916 372-2102
2945 Ramco St Ste 120 West Sacramento (95691) *(P-18411)*

Creative Lrng Ctr Preschool .... C....... 650 823-1496
2100 Woods Ln Los Altos (94024) *(P-18304)*

Creative Machine Technology, Corona *Also Called: Cremach Tech Inc (P-2780)*

Creative Maintenance Systems .... D....... 949 852-2871
1340 Reynolds Ave Ste 111 Irvine (92614) *(P-10880)*

Creative Park Productions LLC .... C....... 818 622-3702
100 Universal City Plz Universal City (91608) *(P-13833)*

Creative Recrtl Systems Inc .... D....... 916 638-5375
2377 Gold Meadow Way Ste 100 Gold River (95670) *(P-5975)*

Creative Security Company Inc .... B....... 408 295-2600
150 Barack Obama Blvd Ste B San Jose (95110) *(P-12957)*

Creative Solutions Svcs LLC .... C....... 646 495-1558
1745 N Vista St Los Angeles (90046) *(P-11113)*

Credibility Corp .... A....... 310 456-8271
22761 Pacific Coast Hwy Malibu (90265) *(P-13250)*

Credit Card Services Inc (PA) .... D....... 213 365-1122
21281 S Western Ave Torrance (90501) *(P-13251)*

Credit Karma LLC (HQ) .... C....... 415 510-5059
1100 Broadway Ste 1800 Oakland (94607) *(P-13252)*

Credit Karma Inc .... A....... 415 510-5059
760 Market St Fl 2 San Francisco (94102) *(P-13253)*

Credit Union Southern Cal (PA) .... D....... 562 698-8326
8101 E Kaiser Blvd Ste 300 Anaheim (92808) *(P-7761)*

Credo Mobile Inc .... D....... 415 369-2000
101 Market St Ste 700 San Francisco (94105) *(P-4210)*

Creekside Center, Stockton *Also Called: Genesis Healthcare LLC (P-15492)*

Cremach Tech Inc (PA) .... D....... 951 735-3194
369 Meyer Cir Corona (92879) *(P-2780)*

Crenshaw Chrstn Ctr Ch Los Ang (PA) .... B....... 323 758-3777
7901 S Vermont Ave Los Angeles (90044) *(P-19017)*

Crenshaw Nursing, Los Angeles *Also Called: Longwood Management Corp (P-15553)*

Crescent Cy Convalescent Hosp, Crescent City *Also Called: North Shore Investment Inc (P-15597)*

Crescent Healthcare Inc .... B....... 510 264-5454
25901 Industrial Blvd Hayward (94545) *(P-16851)*

Crescent Healthcare Inc (DH) .... C....... 714 520-6300
11980 Telegraph Rd Ste 100 Santa Fe Springs (90670) *(P-16852)*

Crescenta-Canada YMCA (PA) .... C....... 818 790-0123
1930 Foothill Blvd La Canada (91011) *(P-18848)*

Crescenta-Canada YMCA .... C....... 818 352-3255
6840 Foothill Blvd Tujunga (91042) *(P-18849)*

Crescentone Inc (HQ)..C....... 310 563-7000
200 Continental Blvd Fl 3 El Segundo (90245) *(P-11522)*

Crest Beverage LLC...B....... 858 452-2300
1348 47th St San Diego (92102) *(P-6757)*

Crest Beverage Company Inc..B....... 858 452-2300
3840 Via De La Valle Ste 300 Del Mar (92014) *(P-6758)*

Crest Chevrolet, San Bernardino Also Called: Harbill Inc *(P-7230)*

Crest Financial Corporation (DH)..D....... 562 733-6500
12641 166th St Cerritos (90703) *(P-8535)*

Crest R E O & Relocation, La Crescenta Also Called: EAM Enterprises Inc *(P-8990)*

Crest Steel, Riverside Also Called: Crest Steel Corporation *(P-5486)*

Crest Steel Corporation..D....... 951 727-2600
6580 General Rd Riverside (92509) *(P-5486)*

Crestline Hotels & Resorts Inc (HQ)..C....... 213 629-1200
120 S Los Angeles St 11 Los Angeles (90012) *(P-9728)*

Crestmont Capital LLC...C....... 949 537-3882
1422 Edinger Ave Ste 210 Tustin (92780) *(P-9504)*

Creston Village, Paso Robles Also Called: Emeritus Corporation *(P-8806)*

Crestview Cadillac, West Covina Also Called: Allen/Clark Cadillac *(P-7168)*

Crestview Landscape Inc..D....... 818 962-7771
13915 Saticoy St Panorama City (91402) *(P-425)*

Crestwood Behavioral Hlth Inc..B....... 209 526-8050
1400 Celeste Dr Modesto (95355) *(P-15413)*

Crestwood Behavioral Hlth Inc..C....... 530 221-0976
3062 Churn Creek Rd Redding (96002) *(P-15414)*

Crestwood Behavioral Hlth Inc..B....... 510 651-1244
4303 Stevenson Blvd Fremont (94538) *(P-15415)*

Crestwood Behavioral Hlth Inc..C....... 510 793-8383
2171 Mowry Ave Fremont (94538) *(P-15416)*

Crestwood Behavioral Hlth Inc..D....... 209 478-5291
7590 Shoreline Dr Stockton (95219) *(P-15417)*

Crestwood Behavioral Hlth Inc..D....... 559 238-6981
1200 Smith St Kingsburg (93631) *(P-15836)*

Crestwood Behavioral Hlth Inc..C....... 408 275-1067
1425 Fruitdale Ave San Jose (95128) *(P-15837)*

Crestwood Behavioral Hlth Inc..D....... 916 452-1431
2600 Stockton Blvd Sacramento (95817) *(P-15838)*

Crestwood Behavioral Hlth Inc..C....... 619 481-6790
5550 University Ave Ste A San Diego (92105) *(P-15839)*

Crestwood Behavioral Hlth Inc..C....... 760 451-4165
624 E Elder St Fallbrook (92028) *(P-15840)*

Crestwood Behavioral Hlth Inc..D....... 707 965-2461
295 Pine Breeze Dr Angwin (94508) *(P-15841)*

Crestwood Behavioral Hlth Inc..D....... 661 363-8127
6700 Eucalyptus Dr Ste A Bakersfield (93306) *(P-15842)*

Crestwood Behavioral Hlth Inc..D....... 805 308-8720
303 S C St Lompoc (93436) *(P-18412)*

Cretelligent Inc...D....... 916 288-8177
11344 Coloma Rd Ste 870 Gold River (95670) *(P-20334)*

Crevier Classics LLC...B....... 714 835-3171
1500 Auto Mall Dr Santa Ana (92705) *(P-7189)*

Crew Builders Inc...C....... 619 587-2033
8130 Commercial St La Mesa (91942) *(P-901)*

Crew Inc..D....... 310 608-6860
19618 S Susana Rd Compton (90221) *(P-2216)*

Crexi, Playa Vista Also Called: Commercial RE Exch Inc *(P-11506)*

Crh Management, Newport Beach Also Called: Core Realty Holdings MGT Inc *(P-8952)*

CRI HELP DRUG REHABILITATION, North Hollywood Also Called: Cri-Help Inc *(P-18413)*

Cri-Help Inc (PA)..D....... 818 985-8323
11027 Burbank Blvd North Hollywood (91601) *(P-18413)*

Cricket Communications LLC (DH)..D
7337 Trade St San Diego (92121) *(P-4211)*

Cricket Wireless, San Diego Also Called: Cricket Communications LLC *(P-4211)*

Cricket Wireless, Oakland Also Called: Tks Wireless Inc *(P-4237)*

Crime Prevention Patrol, Sacramento Also Called: Wade Casey *(P-13074)*

Crimetek, Turlock Also Called: Crimetek Security Inc *(P-12958)*

Crimetek Security Inc..C....... 209 668-6208
3448 N Golden State Blvd Ste G Turlock (95382) *(P-12958)*

Crisp Enterprises Inc (PA)...D....... 714 668-5955
3180 Pullman St Costa Mesa (92626) *(P-10787)*

Critchfeld Mech Inc Sthern Cal..D....... 949 390-2900
15391 Springdale St Huntington Beach (92649) *(P-1412)*

Critchfield Mechanical Inc..B....... 650 321-7801
4085 Campbell Ave Menlo Park (94025) *(P-1413)*

Critchfield Mechanical Inc (PA)...D....... 408 437-7000
1901 Junction Ave San Jose (95131) *(P-1414)*

Criterion Labs Inc..D....... 818 506-8332
10907 Magnolia Blvd North Hollywood (91601) *(P-19962)*

CRITTENTON SERVICES FOR CHILDR, Fullerton Also Called: Florence Crttnton Svcs Ornge C *(P-18434)*

Crl, Vernon Also Called: C R Laurence Co Inc *(P-2972)*

Crl Technologies Inc..D....... 760 495-3000
543 W Graaf Ave B Ridgecrest (93555) *(P-19673)*

Crmc, Coalinga Also Called: Coalinga Regional Med Ctr Aux *(P-16005)*

Crmls LLC..C....... 909 859-2040
15325 Fairfield Ranch Rd Ste 200 Chino Hills (91709) *(P-8713)*

CROCKER ART MUSEUM, Sacramento Also Called: Crocker Art Museum Association *(P-19079)*

Crocker Art Museum Association...D....... 916 808-7000
216 O St Sacramento (95814) *(P-19079)*

Crockett & Coinc..D....... 619 267-1103
5540 Sweetwater Rd Bonita (91902) *(P-14255)*

Crockett Garbage Service, Richmond Also Called: Richmond Sanitary Service Inc *(P-13795)*

Crocodile Restaurant, Santa Barbara Also Called: Paradise Hotel Inc *(P-10098)*

Crocus Holdings LLC...D....... 916 782-1238
1161 Cirby Way Roseville (95661) *(P-15418)*

Cromer Inc..B....... 510 534-6566
4701 Oakport St Oakland (94601) *(P-5827)*

Cromer Material Handling, Oakland Also Called: Cromer Inc *(P-5827)*

Crometrics..D....... 415 482-8899
1112 Sir Francis Drake Blvd Kentfield (94904) *(P-20335)*

Cronos USA Client Services LLC..C....... 323 843-2741
322 Culver Blvd Playa Del Rey (90293) *(P-9309)*

Cross Link Inc...D....... 415 495-3191
50 Pier Bldg C San Francisco (94158) *(P-3822)*

Cross Match Inc...C....... 650 474-4000
6607 Kaiser Dr Fremont (94555) *(P-11523)*

Crosscircles Inc..D....... 626 341-8469
627 E Calaveras Blvd Pmb 1005 Milpitas (95035) *(P-11114)*

Crossfit LLC..C....... 619 540-5017
1101 Pacific Ave Ste 230 Santa Cruz (95060) *(P-14191)*

Crossing Guard Company..A....... 310 202-8284
10440 Pioneer Blvd Ste 5 Santa Fe Springs (90670) *(P-12959)*

Crossrads Adult Day Hlth Care, Rancho Cucamonga Also Called: Horrigan Enterprises Inc *(P-18006)*

Crossrads Chrstn Schols Corona...C....... 951 278-3199
2380 Fullerton Ave Corona (92881) *(P-17808)*

Crossroad Services Inc..B....... 714 728-3915
2360 Alvarado St San Leandro (94577) *(P-6899)*

Crossroads Diversfd Svcs Inc..D....... 916 676-2540
7011 Sylvan Rd Ste A Citrus Heights (95610) *(P-11115)*

Crosstown Elec & Data Inc..D....... 626 813-6693
5454 Diaz St Baldwin Park (91706) *(P-1712)*

Crosswalk, Los Angeles Also Called: Toaster LLC *(P-19852)*

Crothall Services Group...A....... 909 991-4887
8190 Murray Ave Gilroy (95020) *(P-10462)*

Crothall Services Group...A....... 714 562-9275
14710 Northam St La Mirada (90638) *(P-13769)*

Crowdstaffing...D....... 844 467-2300
6030 Hellyer Ave Ste 100 San Jose (95138) *(P-11116)*

Crowdstrike Inc..C....... 888 512-8906
15440 Laguna Canyon Rd Ste 250 Irvine (92618) *(P-12770)*

Crowdstrike Inc..C....... 888 512-8906
15441 Laguna Canyon Rd, Ste 260 Irvine (92618) *(P-12771)*

Crowdstrike Inc..C....... 888 512-8906
400 Continental Blvd Ste 275 El Segundo (90245) *(P-12772)*

Crowell & Moring LLP..C....... 213 622-4750
515 S Flower St Ste 4000 Los Angeles (90071) *(P-17427)*

Crowell & Moring LLP..C....... 949 263-8400
3 Park Plz Ste 2000 Irvine (92614) *(P-17428)*

Crowley Marine Services Inc...B....... 310 732-6500
86 Berth 300 S Harbor Blvd San Pedro (90731) *(P-4001)*

ALPHABETIC SECTION — CU Direct Corporation

Crown Bolt, Aliso Viejo *Also Called: Hd Supply Distribution Services LLC (P-5729)*

Crown Building Maintenance Co .... B....... 916 920-9556
1832 Tribute Rd Ste H Sacramento (95815) *(P-10881)*

Crown Building Maintenance Co .... B....... 714 434-9494
14201 Franklin Ave Tustin (92780) *(P-10882)*

Crown Building Maintenance Co .... B....... 303 680-3713
600 Harrison St Ste 600 San Francisco (94107) *(P-10883)*

Crown Building Maintenance Co .... B....... 858 560-5785
5482 Complex St Ste 108 San Diego (92123) *(P-10884)*

Crown Building Maintenance Co .... B....... 415 546-6534
1143 N Market Blvd Ste 3 Sacramento (95834) *(P-10885)*

Crown Energy Services Inc .... A....... 213 765-7800
2601 S Figueroa St Bldg 1 Los Angeles (90007) *(P-10886)*

Crown Energy Services Inc .... C....... 925 827-6299
2003 Diamond Blvd Rm 31209 Concord (94520) *(P-19189)*

Crown Energy Services Inc .... C....... 415 546-6534
611 Gateway Blvd South San Francisco (94080) *(P-19190)*

Crown Fence Co .... D....... 562 864-5177
12070 Telegraph Rd Ste 340 Santa Fe Springs (90670) *(P-2269)*

Crown Golf Properties LP .... C....... 714 730-1611
12442 Tustin Ranch Rd Tustin (92782) *(P-20336)*

Crown Management Services Inc .... D....... 510 537-8470
22660 Main St Hayward (94541) *(P-9729)*

Crown Media Holdings Inc (HQ) .... D....... 888 390-7474
12700 Ventura Blvd Ste 200 Studio City (91604) *(P-4495)*

Crown Painting Inc .... D....... 209 322-3275
641 Galaxy Way Modesto (95356) *(P-2495)*

Crown Plaza, Milpitas *Also Called: B H R Operations LLC (P-9627)*

Crown Plaza La Harbor Hotel, San Pedro *Also Called: Spf Capital Real Estate LLC (P-10261)*

Crown Plaza Los Angeles, Los Angeles *Also Called: Ihg Management (maryland) LLC (P-9905)*

Crown Vly Precision Machining, Irwindale *Also Called: Sinecera Inc (P-13477)*

Crowne Plaza Concord, Concord *Also Called: Concord Hotel LLC (P-9719)*

Crowne Plaza Hotel, Foster City *Also Called: Founders Management II Corp (P-9801)*

Crowne Plaza San Francisco Int, Burlingame *Also Called: Airport Blvd Hotels LLC (P-9601)*

Crowne Plaza Ventura Beach, Ventura *Also Called: Ventura Hsptality Partners LLC (P-10343)*

Crowne Plz Los Angeles Hbr Ht, Long Beach *Also Called: Nhca Inc (P-10045)*

Crowne Transportation, Oakland *Also Called: GSC Logistics Inc (P-4028)*

Crp Centinela LP .... D....... 901 821-4117
6161 W Centinela Ave Culver City (90230) *(P-9730)*

CRST Expedited Inc .... B....... 209 249-4403
2577 W Yosemite Ave Manteca (95337) *(P-3459)*

CRST Expedited Inc .... B....... 909 563-5606
1219 E Elm St Ontario (91761) *(P-3460)*

CRST Expedited Inc .... C....... 909 563-5606
9032 Merrill Ave Chino (91708) *(P-3461)*

Crucible .... C....... 510 444-0919
1260 7th St Oakland (94607) *(P-17946)*

Cruise LLC (HQ) .... D....... 415 335-4097
1201 Bryant St San Francisco (94103) *(P-3250)*

Crump Insurance, San Francisco *Also Called: CRC Insurance Services Inc (P-8534)*

Crunch LLC .... C....... 415 543-1110
61 New Montgomery St San Francisco (94105) *(P-14192)*

Crunch LLC .... D....... 415 495-1939
345 Spear St Ste 104 San Francisco (94105) *(P-14193)*

Crunch Fitness .... D....... 805 522-5454
19867 Prairie St Ste 200 Chatsworth (91311) *(P-14194)*

Crunch Fitness, San Francisco *Also Called: Crunch LLC (P-14192)*

Crunchyroll, San Francisco *Also Called: Ellation LLC (P-11569)*

Crunchyroll LLC (DH) .... D....... 972 355-7300
10202 Washington Blvd Culver City (90232) *(P-13834)*

Cruz Modular Inc (PA) .... D....... 714 283-2890
249 W Baywood Ave Ste B Orange (92865) *(P-3584)*

Crydom Inc (DH) .... D....... 619 210-1590
2320 Paseo De Las Americas Ste 201 San Diego (92154) *(P-2864)*

Crystal Art Gallery, Vernon *Also Called: Rggd Inc (P-6049)*

Crystal Casino & Hotel, Compton *Also Called: Celebrity Casinos Inc (P-9689)*

Crystal Cathedral Ministries (PA) .... C....... 714 622-2900
12901 Lewis St Garden Grove (92840) *(P-19018)*

Crystal Creamery, Modesto *Also Called: Foster Dairy Farms (P-6437)*

Crystal Geyser Water Company .... D....... 661 323-6296
1233 E California Ave Bakersfield (93307) *(P-2405)*

Crystal Organic Farms LLC .... A....... 661 845-5200
10000 Stockdale Hwy Ste 200 Bakersfield (93311) *(P-173)*

Crystal Stairs Inc (PA) .... B....... 323 299-8998
5110 W Goldleaf Cir Ste 150 Los Angeles (90056) *(P-17947)*

Cs-Pleasanton LLC .... A....... 925 463-2822
7090 Johnson Dr Pleasanton (94588) *(P-14366)*

Csa America, Irvine *Also Called: Csa America Standards Inc (P-19963)*

Csa America Standards Inc .... D....... 949 733-4300
2805 Barranca Pkwy Irvine (92606) *(P-19963)*

Csa America Standards Inc .... D....... 949 733-4300
2805 Barranca Pkwy Irvine (92606) *(P-19964)*

Csa Silicon Valley LLC .... D....... 818 922-2416
7027 Hayvenhurst Ave Van Nuys (91406) *(P-16713)*

Csaa Insurance Exchange (PA) .... D....... 925 279-2300
3055 Oak Rd Walnut Creek (94597) *(P-8536)*

Csaa Insurance Group, Walnut Creek *Also Called: Csaa Insurance Services Inc (P-8537)*

Csaa Insurance Services Inc (HQ) .... D....... 925 279-3153
3055 Oak Rd Walnut Creek (94597) *(P-8537)*

Csac Excess Insurance Auth .... D....... 916 850-7300
75 Iron Point Cir Ste 200 Folsom (95630) *(P-8538)*

CSBA, West Sacramento *Also Called: California School Boards Assn (P-18740)*

CSC Serviceworks Inc .... D....... 626 389-0169
14426 Bonelli St City Of Industry (91746) *(P-10463)*

Cscu, Santa Maria *Also Called: Coasthills Credit Union (P-7823)*

Csd Autism Services, Rancho Cordova *Also Called: Center For Social Dynamics LLC (P-15273)*

Csd Autism Services, Gilroy *Also Called: Center For Social Dynamics LLC (P-15274)*

Csd Autism Services, Santa Clara *Also Called: Center For Social Dynamics LLC (P-15275)*

Csd Autism Services, San Bruno *Also Called: Center For Social Dynamics LLC (P-15276)*

Csd Autism Services, Vallejo *Also Called: Center For Social Dynamics LLC (P-17872)*

Cse Holdings Inc .... C....... 408 436-1907
650 Brennan St San Jose (95131) *(P-5937)*

CSEA, San Jose *Also Called: California Schl Employees Assn (P-18774)*

Csea, Sacramento *Also Called: Califrnia State Employees Assn (P-18778)*

Cshg Holdings, Temecula *Also Called: Hines Growers Inc (P-130)*

Csi Electrical Contractors Inc .... B....... 661 723-0869
41769 11th St W Ste B Palmdale (93551) *(P-1713)*

Csi Electrical Contractors Inc .... B....... 760 227-0577
310 Via Vera Cruz Ste 106 San Marcos (92078) *(P-1714)*

Csi Electrical Contractors Inc (HQ) .... C....... 562 946-0700
10623 Fulton Wells Ave Santa Fe Springs (90670) *(P-1715)*

Csi Vegas, Santa Clarita *Also Called: CBS Studios Inc (P-4419)*

Csl Berkshire Operating Co LLC 949 333-8580
5000 Birch St Ste 400 Newport Beach (92660) *(P-8954)*

Csn Winddown Inc .... D....... 831 444-0523
420 Espinosa Rd Salinas (93907) *(P-121)*

Csn Winddown Inc .... D....... 209 369-3018
5400 E Harney Ln Lodi (95240) *(P-122)*

CSRA LLC .... A....... 703 641-2000
524 Logue Ave Mountain View (94043) *(P-11524)*

Csrw Inc .... D....... 925 724-2324
7602 National Dr Livermore (94550) *(P-2270)*

CT Commodities Inc .... D....... 559 757-3996
217 W Terra Bella Ave Pixley (93256) *(P-8180)*

Ctac Research 60901, Irwindale *Also Called: Southern California Edison Co (P-4698)*

Ctc Group Inc (DH) .... C....... 310 540-0500
21333 Hawthorne Blvd Torrance (90503) *(P-9731)*

Ctour Holiday LLC .... B....... 323 261-8811
222 E Huntington Dr Ste 105 Monrovia (91016) *(P-14512)*

Ctpartners Exec Search Inc .... C....... 949 754-2821
8001 Irvine Center Dr Irvine (92618) *(P-11117)*

CTS Advantage Logistics, San Jose *Also Called: Advantage Logistics Inc (P-3977)*

Ctsh LLC .... D....... 949 916-6705
640 N Tustin Ave Ste 201 Santa Ana (92705) *(P-16853)*

CU Cooperative Systems Inc (PA) .... B....... 909 948-2500
9692 Haven Ave Rancho Cucamonga (91730) *(P-7824)*

CU Direct Corporation (PA) .... C....... 833 908-0121
2855 E Guasti Rd Ste 500 Ontario (91761) *(P-11525)*

Cuberg Inc — ALPHABETIC SECTION

Cuberg Inc .... C...... 510 725-4200
2020 Williams St Unit E San Leandro (94577) *(P-19674)*

Cubework, City Of Industry *Also Called: Cubeworkcom Inc (P-8955)*

Cubeworkcom Inc .... C...... 909 991-6669
900 Turnbull Canyon Rd City Of Industry (91745) *(P-8955)*

Cubic, San Diego *Also Called: Cubic Corporation (P-3003)*

Cubic, San Diego *Also Called: Cubic Trnsp Systems Inc (P-11526)*

Cubic Corporation (HQ) .... A...... 858 277-6780
9233 Balboa Ave San Diego (92123) *(P-3003)*

Cubic Corporation .... A...... 858 277-6780
9233 Balboa Ave San Diego (92123) *(P-12442)*

Cubic Defense Applications Inc .... C...... 858 505-2870
9233 Balboa Ave San Diego (92123) *(P-2956)*

Cubic Defense Systems, San Diego *Also Called: Cubic Corporation (P-12442)*

Cubic Secure Communications I .... B...... 858 505-2000
9233 Balboa Ave San Diego (92123) *(P-4212)*

Cubic Trnsp Systems Inc (DH) .... A...... 858 268-3100
9233 Balboa Ave San Diego (92123) *(P-11526)*

Cucamonga Valley Water Dst .... D...... 909 987-2591
10440 Ashford St Rancho Cucamonga (91730) *(P-4783)*

Cucina Holdings Inc (DH) .... B...... 916 565-5500
1300 Del Paso Rd Sacramento (95834) *(P-7471)*

Cudahy Medical Offices, Cudahy *Also Called: Kaiser Foundation Hospitals (P-16175)*

Cudc, Ontario *Also Called: CU Direct Corporation (P-11525)*

Culinary Hispanic Foods Inc .... A...... 619 955-6101
805 Bow St Chula Vista (91914) *(P-6623)*

Cultura Technologies Inc .... D...... 209 923-6278
1810 Mesquite Ct Tracy (95376) *(P-12773)*

Culture, San Diego *Also Called: Carrier Johnson (P-19458)*

Culture Biosciences Inc .... D...... 919 622-5123
269 E Grand Ave South San Francisco (94080) *(P-19675)*

Culver Personnel Agencies Inc .... C...... 888 600-5733
445 Marine View Ave Ste 101 Del Mar (92014) *(P-11118)*

Culver Personnel Services, Del Mar *Also Called: Culver Personnel Agencies Inc (P-11118)*

Culver West Health Center LLC .... D...... 310 390-9506
4035 Grand View Blvd Los Angeles (90066) *(P-15419)*

Cummings Transportation, Shafter *Also Called: Cummings Vacuum Service Inc (P-612)*

Cummings Vacuum Service Inc .... D...... 661 746-1786
19605 Broken Ct Shafter (93263) *(P-612)*

Cummins, Irvine *Also Called: Cummins Pacific LLC (P-2767)*

Cummins, San Leandro *Also Called: Cummins West Inc (P-5828)*

Cummins Pacific LLC (HQ) .... D...... 949 253-6000
1939 Deere Ave Irvine (92606) *(P-2767)*

Cummins West Inc .... B...... 510 351-6101
14775 Wicks Blvd San Leandro (94577) *(P-5828)*

Cumulus Networks, Mountain View *Also Called: Cumulus Networks Inc (P-12152)*

Cumulus Networks Inc (PA) .... C...... 650 383-6700
185 E Dana St Mountain View (94041) *(P-12152)*

Cunha Draying Inc .... D...... 209 858-1400
1500 Madruga Rd Lathrop (95330) *(P-3462)*

Cupertino Electric, Felton *Also Called: Cupertino Electric Inc (P-1716)*

Cupertino Electric Inc .... A...... 408 808-8260
350 Lenore Way Felton (95018) *(P-1716)*

Cupertino Electric Inc (PA) .... B...... 408 808-8000
1132 N 7th St San Jose (95112) *(P-1717)*

Cupertino Electric Inc .... A...... 415 970-3400
1740 Cesar Chavez Fl 2 San Francisco (94124) *(P-1718)*

Cupertino Hlthcare Wllness Ctr .... D...... 408 253-9034
22590 Voss Ave Fl 1 Cupertino (95014) *(P-15420)*

Cupertino Hlthcare Wllness Ctr, Cupertino *Also Called: Cupertino Hlthcare Wllness Ctr (P-15420)*

Cupertino Hspitality Assoc LLC .... C...... 408 777-8787
10741 N Wolfe Rd Cupertino (95014) *(P-9732)*

Cupertino Lessee LLC .... C...... 908 253-8900
10050 S De Anza Blvd Cupertino (95014) *(P-9733)*

Curation Foods Inc (HQ) .... D...... 800 454-1355
2811 Airpark Dr Santa Maria (93455) *(P-2433)*

Curative Inc .... A...... 650 713-8928
605 E Huntington Dr Monrovia (91016) *(P-20072)*

Curative-Korva LLC .... D...... 424 645-7575
605 E Huntington Dr Monrovia (91016) *(P-16714)*

Curiosity Ink Media LLC .... C...... 561 287-5776
478 Ellis St Pasadena (91105) *(P-5897)*

Curology Inc .... B...... 617 959-2480
5717 Pacific Center Blvd Ste 200 San Diego (92121) *(P-14721)*

Curology Inc (PA) .... D...... 858 859-1188
353 Sacramento St Ste 2000 San Francisco (94111) *(P-17217)*

Curology Medical Group, San Francisco *Also Called: Curology Inc (P-17217)*

Current Tv LLC .... C...... 415 995-8328
118 King St San Francisco (94107) *(P-13254)*

Curtin Maritime Corp .... B...... 562 983-7257
725 Pier T Ave Long Beach (90802) *(P-1294)*

Curtis, Walnut Creek *Also Called: LN Curtis and Sons (P-5944)*

Curtis & Tompkins Ltd .... D...... 510 486-0900
2323 5th St Berkeley (94710) *(P-19676)*

Curtis Winery, Los Olivos *Also Called: Firestone Vineyard LP (P-2386)*

Curtiss-Wrght Cntrls Elctrnic (DH) .... C...... 661 702-1494
28965 Avenue Penn Santa Clarita (91355) *(P-2865)*

Curtiss-Wrght Cntrls Elctrnic .... C...... 661 257-4430
28965 Avenue Penn Santa Clarita (91355) *(P-19191)*

Curtiss-Wrght Cntrls Elctrnic, Santa Clarita *Also Called: Curtiss-Wrght Cntrls Elctrnic (P-2865)*

Curtiss-Wrght Cntrls Intgrted (DH) .... D...... 661 257-4430
28965 Avenue Penn Valencia (91355) *(P-19192)*

Curvature LLC (DH) .... B...... 800 230-6638
7418 Hollister Ave Ste 110 Santa Barbara (93117) *(P-5289)*

Cushman & Wakefield, San Francisco *Also Called: Cushman & Wakefield Cal Inc (P-8957)*

Cushman & Wakefield, San Jose *Also Called: Cushman & Wakefield Cal Inc (P-8964)*

Cushman & Wakefield, Ontario *Also Called: Cushman & Wakefield Cal Inc (P-8965)*

Cushman & Wakefield Inc .... D...... 415 781-8100
425 Market St Ste 2300 San Francisco (94105) *(P-8956)*

Cushman & Wakefield Cal Inc (DH) .... C...... 408 275-6730
1 Maritime Plz Ste 900 San Francisco (94111) *(P-8957)*

Cushman & Wakefield Cal Inc .... A...... 858 452-6500
12830 El Camino Real Ste 100 San Diego (92130) *(P-8958)*

Cushman & Wakefield Cal Inc .... B...... 805 418-5811
3011 Townsgate Rd Westlake Village (91361) *(P-8959)*

Cushman & Wakefield Cal Inc .... B...... 714 591-0451
7281 Garden Grove Blvd Ste G Garden Grove (92841) *(P-8960)*

Cushman & Wakefield Cal Inc .... B...... 408 572-4134
1357 Hillcrest Dr San Jose (95120) *(P-8961)*

Cushman & Wakefield Cal Inc .... A...... 510 763-4900
555 12th St Ste 1400 Oakland (94607) *(P-8962)*

Cushman & Wakefield Cal Inc .... B...... 805 322-7244
770 Paseo Camarillo 315 Camarillo (93010) *(P-8963)*

Cushman & Wakefield Cal Inc .... B...... 408 436-5500
560 S Winchester Blvd Ste 200 San Jose (95128) *(P-8964)*

Cushman & Wakefield Cal Inc .... B...... 909 483-0077
3800 Concours Ste 300 Ontario (91764) *(P-8965)*

Cushman & Wakefield Cal Inc .... B...... 909 980-3781
901 Via Piemonte Ste 200 Ontario (91764) *(P-8966)*

Cushman & Wakefield Cal Inc .... B...... 925 935-0770
1333 N California Blvd Ste 550 Walnut Creek (94596) *(P-8967)*

Cushman & Wakefield Cal Inc .... B...... 310 556-1805
10250 Constellation Blvd Ste 2200 Los Angeles (90067) *(P-8968)*

Cushman & Wakefield Cal Inc .... B...... 562 276-1400
3760 Kilroy Airport Way Long Beach (90806) *(P-8969)*

Cushman & Wakefield Cal Inc .... A...... 949 474-4004
18111 Von Karman Ave Ste 1000 Irvine (92612) *(P-8970)*

Cushman & Wakefield Cal Inc .... B...... 415 397-1700
2125 Hamilton Ave San Jose (95125) *(P-8971)*

Cushman & Wakefield Cal Inc .... A...... 415 828-1923
455 Market St Ste 530 San Francisco (94105) *(P-8972)*

Cushman & Wakefield California, Garden Grove *Also Called: Cushman & Wakefield Cal Inc (P-8960)*

Cushman Realty Corporation .... C...... 213 627-4700
601 S Figueroa St Ste 4700 Los Angeles (90017) *(P-8973)*

Custom Building Products LLC .... C...... 323 582-0846
6511 Salt Lake Ave Bell (90201) *(P-2642)*

Custom Business Solutions Inc (PA) .... D...... 949 380-7674
1 Studebaker Irvine (92618) *(P-5244)*

Custom Chrome, Morgan Hill *Also Called: Custom Chrome Manufacturing (P-5034)*

Custom Chrome Manufacturing .... B....... 408 825-5000
15750 Vineyard Blvd Ste 100 Morgan Hill (95037) *(P-5034)*

Custom Comfort Mattress Co, Orange *Also Called: Custom Comfort Mattress Co Inc (P-5087)*

Custom Comfort Mattress Co Inc (PA) .... D....... 714 693-6161
581 N Batavia St Orange (92868) *(P-5087)*

Custom Cooler Inc (HQ) .... D....... 909 592-1111
420 E Arrow Hwy San Dimas (91773) *(P-5777)*

Custom Drywall Inc .... D....... 408 263-1616
1570 Gladding Ct Milpitas (95035) *(P-1922)*

Custom Goods LLC .... D....... 310 241-6700
907 E 236th St Carson (90745) *(P-3691)*

Custom Goods LLC .... D....... 310 241-6700
809 E 236th St Carson (90745) *(P-3692)*

Custom Hotel, Los Angeles *Also Called: Playa Proper Jv LLC (P-10123)*

Custom Hotel LLC .... B....... 310 645-0400
8639 Lincoln Blvd Los Angeles (90045) *(P-9734)*

Custom House Hotel LP .... C....... 831 649-4511
2 Portola Plz Monterey (93940) *(P-9735)*

Custom Lawn Services, Canoga Park *Also Called: American Landscape MGT Inc (P-387)*

Custom Lawn Services, Ventura *Also Called: American Landscape MGT Inc (P-473)*

Custom Metal Fabricators, Orange *Also Called: Cmf Inc (P-2052)*

Custom Power LLC .... D....... 714 962-7600
10910 Talbert Ave Fountain Valley (92708) *(P-5551)*

Custom Produce Sales (HQ) .... C....... 559 254-5800
13475 E Progress Dr Parlier (93648) *(P-6529)*

Customer Loan Depot, Foothill Ranch *Also Called: Loandepotcom LLC (P-7999)*

Customized Performance Inc .... C....... 408 437-1720
780 Montague Expy Ste 201 San Jose (95131) *(P-10887)*

Customripe Avocado Company, Escondido *Also Called: Henry Avocado Corporation (P-117)*

Customzed Svcs Admnstrtors Inc .... C....... 858 810-2004
9797 Aero Dr Ste 300 San Diego (92123) *(P-8539)*

Cut N Clean Greens, Oxnard *Also Called: San Miguel Produce Inc (P-39)*

Cutting Edge Creative LLC .... D....... 562 907-7007
9944 Flower St Bellflower (90706) *(P-2505)*

Cv Logistics Inc .... D
2741 Riverside Blvd Sacramento (95818) *(P-3693)*

Cv Starr Community Center .... D....... 707 964-9446
300 S Lincoln St Fort Bragg (95437) *(P-17948)*

Cvb Financial Corp (PA) .... C....... 909 980-4030
701 N Haven Ave Ste 350 Ontario (91764) *(P-7677)*

Cvc Construction Corp .... B....... 559 276-6050
1544 N Maple Ave Fresno (93703) *(P-669)*

Cvc Specialties, Vernon *Also Called: Continental Vitamin Co Inc (P-2583)*

Cvf Capital Partners Inc .... C....... 530 757-7004
1590 Drew Ave Ste 110 Davis (95618) *(P-9505)*

Cvh Care .... C....... 650 393-5657
39 Beta Ct San Ramon (94583) *(P-16854)*

Cvh Home Health Services, San Ramon *Also Called: Castro Valley Health Inc (P-16835)*

Cvl, Sacramento *Also Called: Cv Logistics Inc (P-3693)*

CVOC, Winton *Also Called: Central Valley Oprtnty Ctr Inc (P-18218)*

Cvp Southern Properties, Fowler *Also Called: Bee Sweet Citrus Inc (P-256)*

Cvpartners Inc (HQ) .... C....... 415 543-8600
655 Montgomery St Ste 1200 San Francisco (94111) *(P-11119)*

Cvr Hsge LLC .... C....... 831 625-9500
1 Old Ranch Rd Carmel (93923) *(P-9736)*

Cvtr, Fresno *Also Called: Central Valley Trlr Repr Inc (P-7181)*

Cw Network LLC (HQ) .... C....... 818 977-2500
3300 W Olive Ave Fl 3 Burbank (91505) *(P-4424)*

Cwp, Adelanto *Also Called: Commercial Wood Products Company (P-1995)*

Cwp Cabinets Inc .... C....... 760 246-4530
15447 Anacapa Rd Ste 102 Victorville (92392) *(P-1997)*

Cwpnc Inc .... D....... 714 564-7904
1682 Langley Ave Irvine (92614) *(P-1610)*

Cws Utility Services Corp .... D....... 408 367-8200
1720 N 1st St San Jose (95112) *(P-18706)*

Cwtv, Burbank *Also Called: Cw Network LLC (P-4424)*

Cxapp Inc .... C....... 650 575-4456
4 Palo Alto Sq Ste 200 Palo Alto (94306) *(P-12153)*

Cy Gaslamp LLC .... D....... 619 544-1004
453 6th Ave San Diego (92101) *(P-9737)*

Cy Sac Operator LLC .... D....... 916 455-6800
4422 Y St Sacramento (95817) *(P-9738)*

Cyan Inc .... C....... 707 735-2300
1383 N Mcdowell Blvd # 300 Petaluma (94954) *(P-5644)*

Cyara, Redwood City *Also Called: Cyara Solutions Corp (P-5290)*

Cyara, Redwood City *Also Called: Cyara Inc (P-12154)*

Cyara Inc (PA) .... C....... 650 549-8522
805 Veterans Blvd Ste 105 Redwood City (94063) *(P-12154)*

Cyara Solutions Corp .... C....... 650 549-8522
805 Veterans Blvd Ste 105 Redwood City (94063) *(P-5290)*

Cyber Infrastructure Inc .... D....... 408 364-6849
2880 Zanker Rd Ste 20 San Jose (95134) *(P-12561)*

Cyber-Pro Systems Inc .... C....... 562 256-3800
2121 S Towne Centre Pl Ste 200 Anaheim (92806) *(P-12562)*

Cybercoders Inc .... C....... 949 885-5151
6591 Irvine Center Dr Ste 200 Irvine (92618) *(P-11120)*

Cybercoders Staffing Svcs LLC .... C....... 949 885-5151
6591 Irvine Center Dr Ste 200 Irvine (92618) *(P-11121)*

Cybercsi Inc .... D....... 408 727-2900
3511 Thomas Rd Ste 5 Santa Clara (95054) *(P-5291)*

Cybernet Entertainment LLC .... C....... 415 865-0230
1800 Mission St San Francisco (94103) *(P-13835)*

Cyberpolicy Inc .... C....... 877 626-9991
19584 Pine Valley Ave Porter Ranch (91326) *(P-8540)*

Cyberscientific, Irvine *Also Called: Cybercoders Inc (P-11120)*

Cybersource Corporation (HQ) .... C....... 650 432-7350
900 Metro Center Blvd Foster City (94404) *(P-12563)*

Cydcor LLC (PA) .... D....... 805 277-5500
29899 Agoura Rd Ste 100 Agoura Hills (91301) *(P-20337)*

Cygna Group Inc .... C....... 510 419-5000
2101 Webster St Oakland (94612) *(P-19193)*

Cylance Inc (DH) .... D....... 949 375-3380
3001 Bishop Dr Ste 400 San Ramon (94583) *(P-12155)*

Cypress Communications Inc .... D....... 415 962-4500
1999 Harrison St Ste 101 Oakland (94612) *(P-4496)*

Cypress Creek Holdings LLC .... D....... 310 581-6299
3250 Ocean Park Blvd Ste 355 Santa Monica (90405) *(P-4568)*

Cypress Creek Renewables LLC .... C....... 415 306-5300
445 Bush St Fl 7 San Francisco (94108) *(P-4569)*

Cypress Lawn Cemetery Assn .... D....... 650 755-0580
1370 El Camino Real Colma (94014) *(P-9285)*

CYPRESS LAWN MEMORIAL PARK, Colma *Also Called: Cypress Lawn Cemetery Assn (P-9285)*

Cypress Pnt-Rrowhead Gen Insur .... D....... 619 681-0560
2365 Northside Dr Ste 450 San Diego (92108) *(P-8541)*

Cypress Private Security, San Jose *Also Called: Cypress Security LLC (P-12962)*

Cypress Private Security LP (DH) .... D....... 866 345-1277
478 Tehama St San Francisco (94103) *(P-12960)*

Cypress Private Security LP .... D....... 562 222-4197
9926 Pioneer Blvd Ste 106 Santa Fe Springs (90670) *(P-12961)*

Cypress Security LLC .... D....... 408 217-6063
1762 Tech Dr Ste 122 San Jose (95110) *(P-12962)*

Cys Knship Sneca Tstin Wrprund, Santa Ana *Also Called: Seneca Family of Agencies (P-8657)*

CYTOKINETICS, South San Francisco *Also Called: Cytokinetics Incorporated (P-2584)*

Cytokinetics Incorporated (PA) .... C....... 650 624-3000
350 Oyster Point Blvd South San Francisco (94080) *(P-2584)*

Cznd Inc .... D....... 323 378-6505
8444 Wilshire Blvd Fl 5 Beverly Hills (90211) *(P-14080)*

D - Link, Irvine *Also Called: D-Link Systems Incorporated (P-5292)*

D & D Cahill Inc .... D....... 559 708-7601
2626 Terrace Ave Sanger (93657) *(P-13255)*

D & D Saw Works Inc C
1445 Engineer St Ste 110 Vista (92081) *(P-5898)*

D & D Tool & Supply, Vista *Also Called: D & D Saw Works Inc (P-5898)*

D & J Lumber Co Inc (PA) .... D....... 408 778-1550
600 Tennant Ave Morgan Hill (95037) *(P-7117)*

D & J Tile Company Inc .... D....... 650 632-4000
1045 Terminal Way San Carlos (94070) *(P-1978)*

D & K Engineering (PA) .... C....... 858 451-8999
16990 Goldentop Rd San Diego (92127) *(P-3021)*

D A McCosker Construction Co .... C...... 925 686-1780
  3911 Laura Alice Way Concord (94520) *(P-1093)*

D A V Industries .... D...... 619 337-9244
  1049 Elkelton Blvd Spring Valley (91977) *(P-18850)*

D and D Concrete Cnstr Inc .... D...... 858 748-5011
  13795 Blaisdell Pl Ste 201 Poway (92064) *(P-2113)*

D B Specialty Farms, Santa Maria *Also Called: Darensberries LLC (P-50)*

D C S, Brea *Also Called: Diversfied Cmmnctions Svcs Inc (P-4269)*

D C Shower Doors Inc .... C...... 661 257-1177
  26121 Avenue Hall Valencia (91355) *(P-3463)*

D C Vient Inc (PA) .... D...... 209 578-1224
  1556 Cummins Dr Modesto (95358) *(P-1611)*

D D N, Chatsworth *Also Called: Datadirect Networks Inc (P-11528)*

D E M Enterprises Inc .... D...... 650 401-6200
  15 S Bayshore Blvd San Mateo (94401) *(P-12564)*

D E X, Camarillo *Also Called: Data Exchange Corporation (P-5293)*

D G A, Los Angeles *Also Called: Directors Guild America Inc (P-13932)*

D G X, E Rncho Dmngz *Also Called: Dependable Global Express Inc (P-4004)*

D J American Supply Inc .... C...... 323 582-2650
  6122 S Eastern Ave Commerce (90040) *(P-6039)*

D Line Constructors, Oakland *Also Called: D-Line Constructors Inc (P-815)*

D Longo Inc .... B...... 626 580-6000
  3534 Peck Rd El Monte (91731) *(P-7190)*

D M S, Fremont *Also Called: DMS Facility Services Inc (P-10891)*

D P S Inc .... D...... 888 278-8200
  1682 Langley Ave Irvine (92614) *(P-1612)*

D R I, Irvine *Also Called: Dri Commercial Corporation (P-2057)*

D S I, Brea *Also Called: Delivery Solutions Inc (P-3386)*

D S I, Santa Rosa *Also Called: Deposition Sciences Inc (P-19678)*

D S T Macdonald, Valencia *Also Called: Whi Solutions Inc (P-5370)*

D W Nicholson Corporation (PA) .... C...... 510 887-0900
  24747 Clawiter Rd Hayward (94545) *(P-1415)*

D-Line Constructors Inc .... D...... 510 251-6400
  498 Embarcadero W Ste 8 Oakland (94607) *(P-815)*

D-Link Systems Incorporated .... C...... 714 885-6000
  14420 Myford Rd Ste 100 Irvine (92606) *(P-5292)*

D-Wave Quantum Inc .... C...... 604 630-1428
  2650 E Bayshore Rd Palo Alto (94303) *(P-12156)*

D'Andrea Graphics, Cypress *Also Called: DAndrea Graphic Corportion (P-10803)*

D'Veal Family and Youth Svcs, Pasadena *Also Called: DVeal Corporation (P-18585)*

D&A Endeavors Inc .... D...... 310 390-7540
  8484 Wilshire Blvd Ste 605 Beverly Hills (90211) *(P-2271)*

D&D Wholesale Distributors LLC .... D...... 626 333-2111
  777 Baldwin Park Blvd City Of Industry (91746) *(P-6530)*

D&E Propogators, Encinitas *Also Called: Dramm and Echter Inc (P-124)*

D3 Equipment, El Cajon *Also Called: Denardi Machinery Inc (P-5786)*

D3 Go, Encino *Also Called: D3publisher of America Inc (P-12157)*

D3publisher of America Inc .... D...... 310 268-0820
  15910 Ventura Blvd Ste 800 Encino (91436) *(P-12157)*

D7 LLC .... D...... 808 630-9169
  200 Spectrum Center Dr Ste 1210 Irvine (92618) *(P-20073)*

D7 Roofing Services, Rancho Cordova *Also Called: D7 Roofing Services Inc (P-2055)*

D7 Roofing Services Inc .... D...... 916 447-2175
  2851 Gold Tailings Ct Rancho Cordova (95670) *(P-2055)*

Da Vinci Schools Fund .... C...... 310 725-5800
  201 N Douglas St El Segundo (90245) *(P-13256)*

Dacor .... D...... 626 961-2256
  14525 Clark Ave City Of Industry (91745) *(P-13739)*

Daggett Solar Power 3 LLC .... C...... 415 627-1600
  100 California St Ste 400 San Francisco (94111) *(P-1416)*

Dahl-Beck Electric Co .... D...... 510 237-2325
  2775 Goodrick Ave Richmond (94801) *(P-5552)*

Dahlin Group Inc (PA) .... D...... 925 251-7200
  5865 Owens Dr Pleasanton (94588) *(P-19462)*

Daicel America Holdings Inc .... B...... 480 798-6737
  21515 Hawthorne Blvd Ste 600 Torrance (90503) *(P-20074)*

Dailey & Associates .... D...... 323 490-3847
  8687 Melrose Ave Ste G300 West Hollywood (90069) *(P-10601)*

Daily Co .... D...... 855 660-1224
  548 Market St Unit 39113 San Francisco (94104) *(P-11527)*

DAILY CALIFORNIAN, Berkeley *Also Called: Indepndent Brkley Stdnt Pubg I (P-2538)*

Daily Journal Corporation (PA) .... D...... 213 229-5300
  915 E 1st St Los Angeles (90012) *(P-2536)*

Daily Manufacturing, La Verne *Also Called: Ten Days Manufacturing (P-5930)*

Daily Transcript, Laguna Niguel *Also Called: San Diego Daily Transcript (P-2511)*

Dairyland Produce LLC .... C...... 415 647-2991
  453 Valley Dr Brisbane (94005) *(P-6531)*

Daiso California LLC .... D...... 510 679-5121
  7000 El Cerrito Plz El Cerrito (94530) *(P-8974)*

Daiwa Corporation .... D...... 562 375-6800
  20155 Ellipse Foothill Ranch (92610) *(P-5976)*

Daiwa Golf Company Division, Foothill Ranch *Also Called: Daiwa Corporation (P-5976)*

Dako North America Inc .... B...... 805 566-6655
  6392 Via Real Carpinteria (93013) *(P-6104)*

Daleys Drywall and Taping Inc .... B...... 408 378-9500
  960 Camden Ave Campbell (95008) *(P-1923)*

Dalinghaus Construction Inc .... D...... 877 360-9227
  445 Birch St Lake Elsinore (92530) *(P-670)*

Dalton Trucking Inc (PA) .... C...... 909 823-0663
  13560 Whittram Ave Fontana (92335) *(P-3694)*

Dameron Hospital Association (HQ) .... A...... 209 944-5550
  525 W Acacia St Stockton (95203) *(P-16035)*

Dan Avila & Sons Farms Inc .... D...... 209 495-3899
  2718 Roberts Rd Ceres (95307) *(P-27)*

Dan Freitas Electric Inc .... D...... 559 686-9572
  983 E Levin Ave Tulare (93274) *(P-1719)*

Dan R Costa Incorporated .... C...... 209 234-2004
  17239 Louise Ave Escalon (95320) *(P-174)*

Dana Capital Group Inc (PA) .... D...... 949 789-0200
  300 Spectrum Center Dr Ste 1200 Irvine (92618) *(P-8038)*

Dana Innovations (PA) .... C...... 949 492-7777
  991 Calle Amanecer San Clemente (92673) *(P-2878)*

Danco Builders .... D...... 707 822-9000
  5251 Ericson Way Ste A Arcata (95521) *(P-754)*

DAndrea Graphic Corportion .... D...... 310 642-0260
  6100 Gateway Dr Cypress (90630) *(P-10803)*

Dane Karno Inc .... D...... 619 813-8585
  1798 Larkhaven Gln Escondido (92026) *(P-13257)*

Danell Bros Inc .... D...... 559 582-1251
  8265 Hanford Armona Rd Hanford (93230) *(P-248)*

Danell Custom Harvesting LLC .... C...... 559 582-1251
  8265 Hanford Armona Rd Hanford (93230) *(P-249)*

Daniel Gerard Worldwide Inc .... D...... 951 361-1111
  13055 Jurupa Ave Fontana (92337) *(P-5487)*

Danisco US Inc (HQ) .... C...... 650 846-7500
  925 Page Mill Rd Palo Alto (94304) *(P-2612)*

Danish Care Center, Atascadero *Also Called: Compass Health Inc (P-15384)*

Danmer Custom Shutters, Van Nuys *Also Called: Danmer Inc (P-2477)*

Danmer Inc .... C...... 516 670-5125
  8000 Woodley Ave Van Nuys (91406) *(P-2477)*

Danning Gill Damnd Kollitz LLP .... D...... 310 277-0077
  1901 Avenue Of The Stars Ste 450 Los Angeles (90067) *(P-17429)*

Dannis Wlver Klley A Prof Corp (PA) .... D...... 415 543-4111
  275 Battery St Ste 1150 San Francisco (94111) *(P-17430)*

Danny Letner Inc .... C...... 714 633-0030
  1490 N Glassell St Orange (92867) *(P-2056)*

Danny Ryan Precision Contg Inc .... D...... 949 642-6664
  16782 Millikan Ave Irvine (92606) *(P-2233)*

Darco Construction, Stanton *Also Called: Denver D Darling Inc (P-816)*

Darden Architects Inc .... D...... 559 448-8051
  6790 N West Ave Ste 104 Fresno (93711) *(P-19463)*

Darensberries LLC .... C...... 805 937-8000
  714 S Blosser Rd Santa Maria (93458) *(P-50)*

Dark Burn Creative LLC .... D...... 818 471-4948
  21122 Erwin St Woodland Hills (91367) *(P-13836)*

DArrigo Bros Co California .... B...... 831 455-2913
  20911 Harris Rd Salinas (93962) *(P-28)*

DART, Ridgecrest *Also Called: Desert Area Resources Training (P-7532)*

Dart Aerospace, Vista *Also Called: Apical Industries Inc (P-5955)*

Dart Entities, Commerce *Also Called: Dart International A Corp (P-3695)*

ALPHABETIC SECTION

Dart International A Corp (HQ) .... C 323 264-8746
  1430 S Eastman Ave Commerce (90023) *(P-3695)*
Dart Warehouse Corporation (HQ) .... B 323 264-1011
  1430 S Eastman Ave Commerce (90023) *(P-3696)*
Dash Radio, Los Angeles *Also Called: Dash Radio Inc (P-4374)*
Dash Radio Inc .... D 310 456-9993
  6230 Wilshire Blvd # 118 Los Angeles (90048) *(P-4374)*
Data 911, Poway *Also Called: Hubb Systems LLC (P-12465)*
Data Council LLC .... D 904 512-3200
  15310 Barranca Pkwy Ste 100 Irvine (92618) *(P-13258)*
Data Domain LLC .... A 408 980-4800
  2421 Mission College Blvd Santa Clara (95054) *(P-12443)*
Data Exchange, Camarillo *Also Called: Dex Corporation (P-19199)*
Data Exchange Corporation (PA) .... B 805 388-1711
  3600 Via Pescador Camarillo (93012) *(P-5293)*
Data Trace Info Svcs LLC (HQ) .... D 714 250-6700
  4 First American Way Santa Ana (92707) *(P-20884)*
Database Marketing Group Inc .... D 714 727-0800
  300 Commerce Ste 200 Irvine (92602) *(P-10770)*
Datadirect Networks Inc (PA) .... C 818 700-7600
  9351 Deering Ave Chatsworth (91311) *(P-11528)*
Datadivider, Carlsbad *Also Called: Exois Inc (P-12791)*
Datagrail .... D 650 781-3680
  164 Townsend St Unit 12 San Francisco (94107) *(P-12774)*
Dataknox Solutions Inc .... D 510 673-7070
  38505 Cherry St Ste A Newark (94560) *(P-20338)*
Datallegro Inc .... D 949 680-3000
  85 Enterprise Ste 200 Aliso Viejo (92656) *(P-5294)*
Datapipe, Mountain View *Also Called: Rackspace Hosting Inc (P-12612)*
Datapipe, San Jose *Also Called: Rackspace Hosting Inc (P-12613)*
Datastax Inc (PA) .... B 650 389-6000
  2755 Augustine Dr 8th Fl Santa Clara (95054) *(P-11529)*
Datatrace Title .... D 800 221-2056
  200 Commerce Irvine (92602) *(P-20736)*
Datavant Inc (PA) .... C 415 520-1171
  44 Montgomery St Ste 300 San Francisco (94104) *(P-11530)*
Datavisor Inc .... D 408 331-9886
  967 N Shoreline Blvd Mountain View (94043) *(P-12158)*
Daughters Charity Health Sys, Los Altos Hills *Also Called: Ministry Services of The Daugh (P-9438)*
Dav El Chuffeured Trnsp Networ, San Francisco *Also Called: Dav-El Reservations System Inc (P-3251)*
Dav-El Reservations System Inc .... D 415 206-7950
  2025 Mckinnon Ave San Francisco (94124) *(P-3251)*
Davalan Fresh, Los Angeles *Also Called: Davalan Sales Inc (P-6532)*
Davalan Sales Inc .... C 213 623-2500
  1601 E Olympic Blvd Ste 325 Los Angeles (90021) *(P-6532)*
Dave Calhoun and Assoc LLC .... C 925 688-1234
  2575 Stanwell Dr Ste 100 Concord (94520) *(P-10888)*
Dave Gross Enterprises Inc .... D 916 388-2000
  7 Wayne Ct Sacramento (95829) *(P-2272)*
Dave Inc (PA) .... C 844 857-3283
  1265 S Cochran Ave Los Angeles (90019) *(P-12159)*
Dave Williams Plbg & Elec Inc .... C 760 296-1397
  75140 Saint Charles Pl Ste C Palm Desert (92211) *(P-1417)*
Davey Tree Surgery Company (HQ) .... A 925 443-1723
  2617 S Vasco Rd Livermore (94550) *(P-555)*
David & Goliath LLC .... C 310 445-5200
  909 N Pacific Coast Hwy Ste 700 El Segundo (90245) *(P-10602)*
David A Campbell Corporation .... C 951 785-4444
  3060 Adams St Riverside (92504) *(P-7191)*
David and Margaret Home Inc .... C 909 596-5921
  1350 3rd St La Verne (91750) *(P-18414)*
David D Bohannon Organization (PA) .... D 650 345-8222
  60 31st Ave San Mateo (94403) *(P-8714)*
David Howard .... D 925 426-0979
  520 Abbie St Pleasanton (94566) *(P-17050)*
David L Gates & Associates Inc .... D 925 736-8176
  1655 N Main St Ste 365 Walnut Creek (94596) *(P-426)*
David Lcile Packard Foundation .... C 650 948-7658
  343 2nd St Los Altos (94022) *(P-19080)*

David Margaret Youth Fmly Svcs, La Verne *Also Called: David and Margaret Home Inc (P-18414)*
David Morse & Assoc., Glendale *Also Called: Dma Claims Management Inc (P-8546)*
David Shield Security Inc .... D 310 849-4950
  23945 Calabasas Rd Ste 102 Calabasas (91302) *(P-12963)*
David Toma DDS Inc .... D 858 583-6147
  645 Sweetwater Rd Spring Valley (91977) *(P-15224)*
David Wilson's Villa Ford, Orange *Also Called: Villa Ford Inc (P-7323)*
David Wood and Associates Inc .... C 415 296-8050
  1160 Battery St Ste 400 San Francisco (94111) *(P-10709)*
David-Kleis II LLC .... D 951 845-3125
  1665 E Eighth St Beaumont (92223) *(P-17218)*
Davidson Hotel Partners Lp .... A 818 707-1220
  30100 Agoura Rd Agoura Hills (91301) *(P-9739)*
Davies Public Affairs, Santa Barbara *Also Called: Perceptioneering Inc (P-10660)*
Davis Cmmnity Clnic Dntl Prgra, Davis *Also Called: Communicare Health Centers (P-14699)*
Davis Construction Plbg Inc .... D 661 269-4325
  32120 Mountain Shadow Rd Acton (93510) *(P-1418)*
Davis Medical Group, Sacramento *Also Called: University California Davis (P-15158)*
Davis Medical Offices, Davis *Also Called: Kaiser Foundation Hospitals (P-14831)*
Davis Polk & Wardwell LLP .... D 650 752-2000
  1600 El Camino Real Ste 100 Menlo Park (94025) *(P-17431)*
Davis Research LLC .... C 818 591-2408
  26610 Agoura Rd Ste 240 Calabasas (91302) *(P-19807)*
Davis Street Community Center (PA) .... D 510 347-4620
  3081 Teagarden St San Leandro (94577) *(P-17949)*
DAVIS STREET FAMILY RESOURCE C, San Leandro *Also Called: Davis Street Community Center (P-17949)*
Davis Uc Medical Center .... C 916 734-2011
  4800 2nd Ave # 3010 Sacramento (95817) *(P-16036)*
Davis Wholesale Electric Inc .... D 818 392-2400
  11581 Vanowen St North Hollywood (91605) *(P-5553)*
Davis Wright Tremaine LLP .... C 415 276-6500
  50 California St Ste 2300 San Francisco (94111) *(P-17432)*
Davis Wright Tremaine LLP .... C 213 633-6800
  865 S Figueroa St Ste 2400 Los Angeles (90017) *(P-17433)*
Daviselen Advertising Inc (PA) .... C 213 688-7000
  865 S Figueroa St Ste 1200 Los Angeles (90017) *(P-10603)*
Davita Hesperia Dialysis Ctr, Hesperia *Also Called: Davita Inc (P-16979)*
Davita Inc .... C 310 536-2406
  14135 Main St Ste 501 Hesperia (92345) *(P-16979)*
Davita Inc .... B 949 930-4400
  15271 Laguna Canyon Rd Irvine (92618) *(P-16980)*
Davita Magan Management Inc (DH) .... C 626 331-6411
  420 W Rowland St Covina (91723) *(P-14722)*
Dawson D7, LLC, Irvine *Also Called: D7 LLC (P-20073)*
Dawson Delivery LLC .... D 505 385-1074
  27240 Turnberry Ln Ste 200 Valencia (91355) *(P-3385)*
Day Care Center, San Luis Obispo *Also Called: Community Action Prtnr San Lui (P-18298)*
Day Designer, Irvine *Also Called: Blue Sky The Clor Imgntion LLC (P-6063)*
Daybreak, San Diego *Also Called: Daybreak Game Company LLC (P-11531)*
Daybreak Game Company LLC .... B 858 239-0500
  13500 Evening Creek Dr N Ste 300 San Diego (92128) *(P-11531)*
Daylight Foods Inc .... C 510 931-4207
  30200 Whipple Rd Union City (94587) *(P-6533)*
Daylight Solutions Inc (DH) .... C 858 432-7500
  16465 Via Esprillo Ste 100 San Diego (92127) *(P-2916)*
Daymark Properties Realty, San Diego *Also Called: Daymark Realty Advisors Inc (P-8975)*
Daymark Realty Advisors Inc .... B 714 975-2999
  750 B St Ste 2620 San Diego (92101) *(P-8975)*
Daymen US Inc .... D 707 827-4053
  1435 N Mcdowell Blvd Ste 200 Petaluma (94954) *(P-5237)*
Days Inn, Los Angeles *Also Called: Hollywood Partnership (P-9864)*
Days Inn, Glendale *Also Called: JP Allen Extended Stay (P-9930)*
Days Inn, Encinitas *Also Called: Trigild International Inc (P-10326)*
Dayton Dmh Inc .... C 858 350-4400
  121 Spinnaker Ct Del Mar (92014) *(P-8876)*
Daytona Surfise, North Hollywood *Also Called: Century National Properties (P-9691)*
Daz, Los Angeles *Also Called: Daz Systems LLC (P-11532)*

Daz Systems LLC — ALPHABETIC SECTION

Daz Systems LLC .... B...... 310 640-1300
  1003 E 4th Pl Ste 800 Los Angeles (90013) *(P-11532)*
Dazz Inc .... D...... 800 956-8019
  2345 Yale St Palo Alto (94306) *(P-5295)*
Dbi Beverage San Francisco .... C...... 415 643-9900
  245 S Spruce Ave Ste 100 South San Francisco (94080) *(P-6759)*
DC Power Systems, Rohnert Park *Also Called: Solarnet LLC (P-5760)*
DC Solar Solutions Inc .... D...... 925 203-1088
  4901 Park Rd Benicia (94510) *(P-1419)*
Dcc General Engrg Contrs Inc .... D...... 760 480-7400
  2180 Meyers Ave Escondido (92029) *(P-2703)*
DCH Acura of Temecula .... D...... 877 847-9532
  26705 Ynez Rd Temecula (92591) *(P-7192)*
DCH California Motors Inc .... D...... 805 988-7900
  1631 Auto Center Dr Oxnard (93036) *(P-7193)*
DCH Gardena Honda .... C...... 310 515-5700
  15541 S Western Ave Gardena (90249) *(P-7194)*
DCI Donor Services Inc .... D...... 877 401-2546
  3940 Industrial Blvd Ste 100 West Sacramento (95691) *(P-17219)*
DCI Donor Services Inc .... D...... 916 567-1600
  3940 Industrial Blvd Ste 100 West Sacramento (95691) *(P-17220)*
Dcl Maritime LLC .... C...... 818 560-1000
  500 S Buena Vista St Burbank (91521) *(P-20075)*
Dcli, Huntington Beach *Also Called: Direct Chassislink Inc (P-11029)*
Dcm Ventures LLC .... D...... 650 233-1400
  2420 Sand Hill Rd Menlo Park (94025) *(P-9506)*
Dcor, Oxnard *Also Called: Dcor LLC (P-598)*
Dcor LLC (PA) .... C...... **805 535-2000**
  1000 Town Center Dr Fl 6 Oxnard (93036) *(P-598)*
Dcpi, Glendale *Also Called: Disney Cnsmr Pdts Intrctive MD (P-11544)*
DCS, Lathrop *Also Called: Performant Recovery Inc (P-10747)*
DCS Corporation .... D...... 760 384-5600
  137 W Drummond Ave Ste C Ridgecrest (93555) *(P-19194)*
Dcw Dcw Inc .... D...... 310 324-3147
  20500 Denker Ave Torrance (90501) *(P-4002)*
Dcw Services LLC .... D...... 310 324-3147
  20500 Denker Ave Torrance (90501) *(P-20339)*
DDB Worldwide .... C...... 415 732-3600
  600 California St Fl 7 San Francisco (94108) *(P-10604)*
DDB WORLDWIDE COMMUNICATIONS GROUP, INC., San Francisco *Also Called: DDB Worldwide (P-10604)*
DDB Wrldwide Cmmnctns Group L .... D...... 310 907-1500
  340 Main St Venice (90291) *(P-10605)*
De Castro W Chdrow Mndler Glck .... D...... 310 478-2541
  10960 Wilshire Blvd Ste 1400 Los Angeles (90024) *(P-17434)*
De Mattei Construction Inc .... D...... 408 295-7516
  1794 The Alameda San Jose (95126) *(P-671)*
De Well Container Shipping Inc .... D...... 310 735-8600
  5553 Bandini Blvd Unit A Bell (90201) *(P-4003)*
Deadline Hollywood Media LLC .... D...... 310 321-5000
  11175 Santa Monica Blvd Los Angeles (90025) *(P-11533)*
Deaf Cmnty Svcs San Diego Inc .... D...... 619 398-2441
  1545 Hotel Cir S Ste 300 San Diego (92108) *(P-17950)*
Dealertrack Clltral MGT Svcs I .... C...... 916 368-5300
  9750 Goethe Rd Sacramento (95827) *(P-11534)*
Dealey Renton and Associates .... D...... 510 465-3090
  530 Water St 7th Fl Oakland (94607) *(P-8542)*
Dealpath Inc .... D...... 415 876-8441
  300 California St Ste 200 San Francisco (94104) *(P-12444)*
Deanco Healthcare LLC .... A...... 818 787-2222
  14850 Roscoe Blvd Panorama City (91402) *(P-16037)*
Deasy Penner Podley .... D...... 626 408-1280
  30 N Baldwin Ave Sierra Madre (91024) *(P-8976)*
Debisys Inc (PA) .... D...... **949 699-1401**
  27442 Portola Pkwy Ste 150 Foothill Ranch (92610) *(P-7852)*
Debtmerica LLC .... D...... 714 389-4200
  3100 S Harbor Blvd Ste 250 Santa Ana (92704) *(P-10540)*
Debtmerica Relief, Santa Ana *Also Called: Debtmerica LLC (P-10540)*
Decathlon Club, Santa Clara *Also Called: Bay Clubs Company LLC (P-14176)*
Decatur Electronics, San Diego *Also Called: D & K Engineering (P-3021)*
Decentral TV Corporation .... D...... 415 480-6800
  442 Post St Fl 10 San Francisco (94102) *(P-4267)*

Dechert LLP .... D...... 949 442-6000
  633 W 5th St Ste 4900 Los Angeles (90071) *(P-17435)*
Dechert LLP .... D...... 415 262-4500
  1 Bush St Ste 1600 San Francisco (94104) *(P-17436)*
Decimal Inc .... D...... 855 980-6612
  1160 Battery St Ste 350 San Francisco (94111) *(P-13259)*
Decipher Corp .... D...... 888 975-4540
  6925 Lusk Blvd Ste 200 San Diego (92121) *(P-16715)*
Decision Sciences, Poway *Also Called: Decision Sciences Intl Corp (P-5645)*
Decision Sciences Intl Corp .... D...... 858 571-1900
  12345 First American Way Ste 100 Poway (92064) *(P-5645)*
Decker Electric Co Inc Electrical Contractors (PA) ...... D...... **415 552-1622**
  1282 Folsom St San Francisco (94103) *(P-1720)*
Decker Landscaping Inc .... D...... 916 652-1780
  13265 Bill Francis Dr Auburn (95603) *(P-483)*
Declara Inc .... D...... 877 216-0604
  977 Commercial St Palo Alto (94303) *(P-12775)*
Decton Inc .... D...... 310 838-7246
  555 W Redondo Beach Blvd Ste 205 Gardena (90248) *(P-11122)*
Decurion Corporation (PA) .... D...... **310 659-9432**
  120 N Robertson Blvd Fl 3 Los Angeles (90048) *(P-13985)*
Dedicated Dental Systems Inc .... D...... 661 397-5513
  9800 S La Cienega Blvd Ste 800 Inglewood (90301) *(P-15225)*
Dedicted Dfned Benefit Svcs LLC .... C...... 415 931-1990
  550 N Brand Blvd Ste 1610 Glendale (91203) *(P-8543)*
Deem Inc (DH) .... D...... **415 590-8300**
  1330 Broadway Fl 7 Oakland (94612) *(P-12160)*
Deep Security, San Jose *Also Called: Trend Micro Incorporated (P-5363)*
Deepcell Inc .... D...... 617 447-1067
  4025 Bohannon Dr Menlo Park (94025) *(P-19677)*
Deepgram Inc .... D...... 415 302-7624
  548 Market St Ste 25104 San Francisco (94104) *(P-11535)*
Deepmind Foundation .... D...... 408 887-1605
  19503 Stevens Creek Blvd Ste 107 Cupertino (95014) *(P-18851)*
Defenseweb Technologies Inc .... D...... 858 272-8505
  10188 Telesis Ct Ste 300 San Diego (92121) *(P-12776)*
Degenkolb Engineers (PA) .... D...... **415 392-6952**
  375 Beale St Ste 500 San Francisco (94105) *(P-19195)*
Dekra Insight, Oxnard *Also Called: Behavioral Science Technology Inc (P-20702)*
Dekra-Lite Industries Inc .... D...... 714 436-0705
  3102 W Alton Ave Santa Ana (92704) *(P-13260)*
DEL AMO GARDENS CONVALESCENT H, Torrance *Also Called: Del AMO Grdns Cnvlscent Hosp S (P-15421)*
Del AMO Grdns Cnvlscent Hosp S .... D...... 310 378-4233
  22419 Kent Ave Torrance (90505) *(P-15421)*
Del AMO Hospital, Torrance *Also Called: Del AMO Hospital Inc (P-17051)*
Del AMO Hospital Inc .... B...... 310 530-1151
  23700 Camino Del Sol Torrance (90505) *(P-17051)*
Del Contes Landscaping Inc .... D...... 510 353-6030
  41900 Boscell Rd Fremont (94538) *(P-427)*
Del Mar Convalescent Hospital, Brea *Also Called: Gibraltar Cnvalescent Hosp Inc (P-15849)*
Del Mar Country Club Inc .... D...... 858 759-5500
  6001 Clubhouse Dr Rancho Santa Fe (92067) *(P-14367)*
Del Mar Fair Grounds, Del Mar *Also Called: California Dept Fd Agriculture (P-20949)*
Del Mar Fairgrounds .... D...... 858 792-4288
  2260 Jimmy Durante Blvd Del Mar (92014) *(P-10541)*
Del Mar Holding LLC .... A...... 313 659-7300
  1022 Bay Marina Dr 10 National City (91950) *(P-6491)*
Del Mar Seafoods Inc .... C...... 805 850-0421
  1449 Spinnaker Dr Ventura (93001) *(P-6469)*
Del Mar Thoroughbred Club .... B...... 858 755-1141
  2260 Jimmy Durante Blvd Del Mar (92014) *(P-14163)*
Del Monaco Foods LLC .... D...... 408 500-4100
  18675 Madrone Pkwy Ste 150 Morgan Hill (95037) *(P-6248)*
Del Monaco Foods, Inc., Morgan Hill *Also Called: Del Monaco Foods LLC (P-6248)*
Del Monte Foods, Walnut Creek *Also Called: Del Monte Foods Inc (P-6624)*
Del Monte Foods Inc (HQ) .... C...... **925 949-2772**
  205 N Wiget Ln Walnut Creek (94598) *(P-6624)*
Del Paso Country Club .... C...... 916 489-3681
  3333 Marconi Ave Sacramento (95821) *(P-14368)*
Del Rio Convalescent, Bell Gardens *Also Called: Del Rio Sanitarium Inc (P-15422)*

ALPHABETIC SECTION

Del Rio Golf & Country Club .... C....... 209 341-2414
  801 Stewart Rd Modesto (95356) *(P-14369)*

Del Rio Sanitarium Inc .... C....... 562 927-6586
  7002 Gage Ave Bell Gardens (90201) *(P-15422)*

Del Rosa Villa, San Bernardino *Also Called: Del Rosa Villaidence Opco LLC (P-15753)*

Del Rosa Villa Inc .... D....... 909 885-3261
  2018 Del Rosa Ave San Bernardino (92404) *(P-15423)*

Del Rosa Villaidence Opco LLC .... B....... 909 885-3261
  2018 Del Rosa Ave San Bernardino (92404) *(P-15753)*

Del Taco, Lake Forest *Also Called: Del Taco Restaurants Inc (P-7472)*

Del Taco Restaurants Inc (PA) .... C....... 949 462-9300
  25521 Commercentre Dr Ste 200 Lake Forest (92630) *(P-7472)*

Del Webb Corporation .... C....... 925 513-2640
  772 Centennial Pl Brentwood (94513) *(P-9250)*

Delafield Corporation (PA) .... C....... 626 303-0740
  1520 Flower Ave Duarte (91010) *(P-2851)*

Delafield Fluid Technology, Duarte *Also Called: Delafield Corporation (P-2851)*

DELANCEY STREET COACH SERVICE, San Francisco *Also Called: Delancey Street Foundation (P-18415)*

Delancey Street Foundation (PA) .... B....... 415 957-9800
  600 The Embarcadero San Francisco (94107) *(P-18415)*

Delano Dst Sklled Nrsing Fclty .... C....... 661 720-2100
  1509 Tokay St Delano (93215) *(P-15424)*

Delano Dst Sklled Nrsing Fclty, Delano *Also Called: North Kern S Tulare Hosp Dst (P-16282)*

Delano Regional Medical Center, Delano *Also Called: Adventist Health Delano (P-15915)*

Delano Regional Medical Center, Delano *Also Called: Adventist Health Delano (P-15916)*

Delart Technology Services LLC .... D....... 949 229-2786
  312 Arizona Ave Santa Monica (90401) *(P-12445)*

Delave Inc (PA) .... D....... 408 293-7200
  311 E Reed St Apt 13 San Jose (95112) *(P-7567)*

Delave Periodicals, San Jose *Also Called: Delave Inc (P-7567)*

Delawie .... D....... 619 299-6690
  1515 Morena Blvd San Diego (92110) *(P-19464)*

Delegata Corporation .... D....... 916 609-5400
  2450 Venture Oaks Way Ste 400 Sacramento (95833) *(P-12446)*

Deleon Realty Inc .... D....... 650 543-8500
  1717 Embarcadero Rd Ste 5000 Palo Alto (94303) *(P-8977)*

Delicate Productions Inc (PA) .... D....... 415 484-1174
  874 Verdulera St Camarillo (93010) *(P-14036)*

Delinea Inc (HQ) .... C....... 669 444-5200
  221 Main St Ste 1300 San Francisco (94105) *(P-11536)*

Deliver-It, Anaheim *Also Called: Di Overnite LLC (P-3609)*

Deliverimates LLC .... D....... 857 445-7736
  5311 Escover Ln San Jose (95118) *(P-4150)*

Deliverr Inc .... B....... 213 534-8686
  307 S Wilson Ave Apt 6 Pasadena (91106) *(P-6249)*

Delivery Solutions Inc .... D....... 800 335-6557
  595 Tamarack Ave Ste D Brea (92821) *(P-3386)*

Dell, San Jose *Also Called: Force10 Networks Global Inc (P-12456)*

Dell Wyse, Santa Clara *Also Called: Wyse Technology LLC (P-5372)*

Della Maggiore Tile Inc .... D....... 408 286-3991
  87 N 30th St San Jose (95116) *(P-1979)*

Deloitte, San Francisco *Also Called: Deloitte Tax LLP (P-19566)*

Deloitte & Touche LLP .... A....... 619 232-6500
  12830 El Camino Real Ste 600 San Diego (92130) *(P-19560)*

Deloitte & Touche LLP .... B....... 408 704-4000
  225 W Santa Clara St Ste 600 San Jose (95113) *(P-19561)*

Deloitte & Touche LLP .... A....... 213 688-0800
  555 W 5th St Ste 2700 Los Angeles (90013) *(P-19562)*

Deloitte & Touche LLP .... C....... 714 436-7419
  695 Town Center Dr Ste 1200 Costa Mesa (92626) *(P-19563)*

Deloitte & Touche LLP .... B....... 415 783-4000
  555 Mission St Ste 1400 San Francisco (94105) *(P-19564)*

Deloitte Consulting LLP .... C....... 510 251-4400
  555 Mission St San Francisco (94105) *(P-20340)*

Deloitte Consulting LLP .... C....... 212 492-4000
  225 W Santa Clara St San Jose (95113) *(P-20341)*

Deloitte Consulting LLP .... C....... 212 489-1600
  350 S Grand Ave Ste 200 Los Angeles (90071) *(P-20737)*

Deloitte Tax LLP .... C....... 404 885-6754
  555 W 5th St Ste 2700 Los Angeles (90013) *(P-19565)*

Deloitte Tax LLP .... B....... 415 783-4000
  555 Mission St Ste 1400 San Francisco (94105) *(P-19566)*

Deloitte Tax LLP .... B....... 408 704-4000
  225 W Santa Clara St Ste 600 San Jose (95113) *(P-19567)*

Delphi Downtown La, The, Los Angeles *Also Called: 550 Flower St Operations LLC (P-9594)*

Delphi Productions Inc .... C....... 510 748-7494
  950 W Tower Ave Alameda (94501) *(P-13261)*

Delphic Enterprises Inc .... D....... 661 254-2000
  23026 Soledad Canyon Rd Santa Clarita (91350) *(P-334)*

Delphix Corp (PA) .... A....... 650 494-1645
  1450 Veterans Blvd Ste 120 Redwood City (94063) *(P-11537)*

Delta America Ltd (HQ) .... C....... 510 668-5100
  46101 Fremont Blvd Fremont (94538) *(P-5646)*

Delta Blood Bank LLC (HQ) .... D....... 800 244-6794
  65 N Commerce St Stockton (95202) *(P-17221)*

Delta Computer Consulting .... C....... 310 541-9440
  25550 Hawthorne Blvd Ste 106 Torrance (90505) *(P-12777)*

Delta Corey Inc .... C....... 707 747-7500
  4931 Park Rd Benicia (94510) *(P-1420)*

Delta Creative Inc .... C....... 800 423-4135
  2690 Pellissier Pl City Of Industry (90601) *(P-5989)*

Delta Dental of California (PA) .... B....... 415 972-8300
  560 Mission St Ste 1300 San Francisco (94105) *(P-8295)*

Delta Dental of California .... D....... 916 853-7373
  11155 International Dr Sacramento (95826) *(P-8296)*

Delta Dental Plan, Sacramento *Also Called: Delta Dental of California (P-8296)*

Delta Diablo Sanitation District .... D....... 925 756-1900
  2500 Pittsburg Antioch Hwy Antioch (94509) *(P-4978)*

Delta Disposal Service Co, Tracy *Also Called: Tracy Dlta Solid Waste Mgt Inc (P-4946)*

Delta Electronics Americas Ltd (DH) .... D....... 510 668-5111
  46101 Fremont Blvd Fremont (94538) *(P-20076)*

Delta Floral Distributors Inc .... C....... 323 751-8116
  6810 West Blvd Los Angeles (90043) *(P-6857)*

Delta Galil USA Inc .... C....... 949 296-0380
  16912 Von Karman Ave Irvine (92606) *(P-6197)*

Delta Health Systems, Stockton *Also Called: Wm Michael Stemler Inc (P-8689)*

Delta Personnel Services Inc .... D....... 925 356-3034
  1820 Galindo St Ste 3 Concord (94520) *(P-12964)*

Delta Products, Fremont *Also Called: Delta America Ltd (P-5646)*

Delta Project Management Inc .... D....... 415 590-3202
  400 Concar Dr San Mateo (94402) *(P-19196)*

Delta Radiology Medical Group .... D....... 209 334-4416
  1031 S Fairmont Ave Lodi (95240) *(P-14723)*

Delta Rubber Co Inc .... D....... 209 948-0511
  2648 Teepee Dr Stockton (95205) *(P-5899)*

Delta Scientific Corporation (PA) .... C....... 661 575-1100
  40355 Delta Ln Palmdale (93551) *(P-13105)*

Delta Sierra Beverage LLC .... B....... 209 522-9011
  3700 Finch Rd Modesto (95357) *(P-6760)*

Delta Tau Data Systems Inc Cal (HQ) .... C....... 818 998-2095
  21314 Lassen St Chatsworth (91311) *(P-2799)*

Delta Truck Center, French Camp *Also Called: Fresno Truck Center (P-5010)*

Delta Valley Athletic Club, Brentwood *Also Called: Club Corp Incorporated (P-14187)*

Delta Valley Health Club .... D....... 925 240-2990
  120 Guthrie Ln Brentwood (94513) *(P-14195)*

Delta View Post Acute, Antioch *Also Called: Antioch Dunes Healthcare LLC (P-15329)*

Delta-T Group Inc .... C....... 619 543-0556
  4420 Hotel Circle Ct Ste 205 San Diego (92108) *(P-11123)*

Delu Vineyards Inc .... D....... 209 334-6660
  15175 N Devries Rd Lodi (95242) *(P-71)*

Deluxe Auto Carriers Inc .... D....... 909 746-0900
  4788 Brookhollow Cir Jurupa Valley (92509) *(P-3387)*

Deluxe Digital Studios, Burbank *Also Called: Deluxe Media Inc (P-13931)*

Deluxe Encore Inc .... C....... 323 466-7663
  2400 W Empire Ave Ste 400 Burbank (91504) *(P-4364)*

Deluxe Media Inc (PA) .... D....... 818 565-3697
  2130 N Hollywood Way Burbank (91505) *(P-13931)*

Deluxe Media Services LLC .... C....... 323 462-6171
  1377 N Serrano Ave Los Angeles (90027) *(P-13837)*

Deluxe Nms Inc .... C....... 310 760-8500
  4499 Glencoe Ave Marina Del Rey (90292) *(P-13963)*

Dema Consulting & MGT LLC   **ALPHABETIC SECTION**

Dema Consulting & MGT LLC .... D...... 707 757-5010
   1000 Apollo Way Ste 165 Santa Rosa (95407) *(P-20342)*

Demand Gen Inc .... D...... 415 373-2450
   1147 Groen Ct Ripon (95366) *(P-18748)*

Demandblue Inc .... D...... 909 402-3453
   5 Corporate Park Ste 140 Irvine (92606) *(P-20077)*

Demandtec LLC .... B...... 914 499-1900
   1 Franklin Pkwy Bldg 910 San Mateo (94403) *(P-11538)*

Demandwhiz LLC .... D...... 408 600-2720
   4079 Middle Park Dr San Jose (95135) *(P-12161)*

Demcon Concrete Contractor, Poway *Also Called: Demcon Concrete Contrs Inc (P-2114)*

Demcon Concrete Contrs Inc .... D...... 858 748-5090
   13795 Blaisdell Pl Ste 202 Poway (92064) *(P-2114)*

Demler Brothers LLC .... D...... 760 789-2457
   25818 Highway 78 Ramona (92065) *(P-224)*

Demptos Glass, Concord *Also Called: Saxco-Demptos Inc (P-6946)*

Denardi Machinery Inc .... C...... 619 749-0039
   1475 Pioneer Way El Cajon (92020) *(P-5786)*

Denevi Digital, San Jose *Also Called: Far Western Graphics Inc (P-10788)*

Denios Rsvlle Frmrs Mkt Actn I .... C...... 916 782-2704
   2013 Opportunity Dr Roseville (95678) *(P-13262)*

Denken Solutions Inc .... C...... 949 630-5263
   9170 Irvine Center Dr Ste 200 Irvine (92618) *(P-20343)*

Dennis & Leen, Los Angeles *Also Called: EC Group Inc (P-5088)*

Dennis Allen Associates (PA) .... D...... 805 884-8777
   201 N Milpas St Santa Barbara (93103) *(P-672)*

Dennis M McCoy & Sons Inc .... D...... 818 874-3872
   32107 Lindero Canyon Rd Ste 212 Westlake Village (91361) *(P-1094)*

Denova Home Sales Inc .... D...... 925 852-0545
   1500 Willow Pass Ct Concord (94520) *(P-8978)*

Denova Homes, Concord *Also Called: Denova Home Sales Inc (P-8978)*

Denso Pdts & Svcs Americas Inc (DH) .... B...... 310 834-6352
   3900 Via Oro Ave Long Beach (90810) *(P-5035)*

Dentalville, Bell *Also Called: Leonid M Glsman DDS A Dntl Cor (P-15234)*

Dentists Insurance Company (HQ) .... C...... 916 443-4567
   1201 K St Ste 1600 Sacramento (95814) *(P-8297)*

Dentons US LLP .... C...... 213 623-9300
   601 S Figueroa St Ste 2500 Los Angeles (90017) *(P-17437)*

Denver D Darling Inc .... D...... 714 761-8299
   8402 Katella Ave Stanton (90680) *(P-816)*

Department Animal Care & Ctrl, Downey *Also Called: County of Los Angeles (P-360)*

Department Animal Regulation, Camarillo *Also Called: County of Ventura (P-20926)*

Department Ansthslogy Pain Mdc, Sacramento *Also Called: University California Davis (P-16600)*

Department Children Fmly Svcs, Los Angeles *Also Called: County of Los Angeles (P-17907)*

Department Hmlssness Spprtive .... C...... 628 652-7700
   440 Turk St San Francisco (94102) *(P-18584)*

Department of Arprts of The Cy .... A...... 855 463-5252
   1 World Way Los Angeles (90045) *(P-3890)*

Department of Health Services, Martinez *Also Called: County of Contra Costa (P-16022)*

Department of Health Services, Los Angeles *Also Called: County of Los Angeles (P-16675)*

Department of Mental Health, Los Angeles *Also Called: County of Los Angeles (P-12656)*

Department of Mental Health, Turlock *Also Called: County of Stanislaus (P-17043)*

Department of Mental Health, Los Angeles *Also Called: County of Los Angeles (P-20938)*

Department of Public Health .... B...... 619 338-2493
   1500 Capitol Ave 5 Fl Ms 7610 San Diego (92101) *(P-14724)*

Department of Public Works, Alhambra *Also Called: County of Los Angeles (P-4781)*

Department of Public Works, Sacramento *Also Called: City of Sacramento (P-4878)*

Department of Public Works, Sacramento *Also Called: City of Sacramento (P-10873)*

Department of Social Services, Paso Robles *Also Called: County of Los Angeles (P-17932)*

Department of Urology, San Francisco *Also Called: University Cal San Francisco (P-16595)*

Department Public Social Svcs, Los Angeles *Also Called: County of Los Angeles (P-17931)*

Department Workforce Dev, Modesto *Also Called: County of Stanislaus (P-18226)*

Dependable Companies .... C...... 800 548-8608
   2555 E Olympic Blvd Los Angeles (90023) *(P-3464)*

Dependable Disposal and Recycl, Spring Valley *Also Called: Burns and Sons Trucking Inc (P-3374)*

Dependable Global Express Inc (PA) .... C...... 310 537-2000
   19201 S Susana Rd E Rncho Dmngz (90221) *(P-4004)*

Dependable Highway Express Inc (PA) .... B...... 323 526-2200
   2555 E Olympic Blvd Los Angeles (90023) *(P-3465)*

Dependable Logistics Services, Los Angeles *Also Called: Dependable Highway Express Inc (P-3465)*

Dependble Break Rm Sltions Inc .... D...... 909 982-5933
   1431 W 9th St Ste B Upland (91786) *(P-5376)*

Deplabs, Walnut Creek *Also Called: Deplabs Inc (P-12778)*

Deplabs Inc .... D...... 415 456-5600
   2872 Ygnacio Valley Rd Ste 241 Walnut Creek (94598) *(P-12778)*

Deposition Sciences Inc .... D...... 707 573-6700
   3300 Coffey Ln Santa Rosa (95403) *(P-19678)*

Dept Children and Family Svcs, Lakewood *Also Called: County of Los Angeles (P-17912)*

Dept of Cardiologist, Los Angeles *Also Called: Kaiser Fndtion Hosp Gift Shppe (P-8306)*

Dept of Child Support, Stockton *Also Called: County of San Joaquin (P-17938)*

Dept of Public Works, Irvine *Also Called: City of Irvine (P-20316)*

Der Kinder Garden Pre-Schools, Torrance *Also Called: Der Kinder Garden Preschool (P-18305)*

Der Kinder Garden Preschool .... D...... 213 318-3838
   2700 Redondo Beach Blvd Torrance (90504) *(P-18305)*

Der Manouel Insurance Group, Fresno *Also Called: Hub Intrntional Insur Svcs Inc (P-8587)*

Derek and Constance Lee Corp (PA) .... D...... 909 595-8831
   19355 San Jose Ave City Of Industry (91748) *(P-2342)*

Derivative Path Inc .... D...... 415 992-8200
   2001 N Main St Ste 250 Walnut Creek (94596) *(P-13263)*

Dermtech Operations Inc .... B...... 866 450-4223
   12340 El Camino Real Ste 200 San Diego (92130) *(P-19679)*

Derouen Enterprises LLC .... D...... 925 360-5743
   1547 Palos Verdes Mall Walnut Creek (94597) *(P-13264)*

Des Architects Engineers Inc .... C...... 650 364-6453
   399 Bradford St Ste 300 Redwood City (94063) *(P-19465)*

DES PERES HOSPITAL, INC., Indio *Also Called: John F Kennedy Mem Hosp Aux (P-16142)*

Descanso Gardens Guild Inc .... D...... 818 952-4408
   1418 Descanso Dr La Canada (91011) *(P-7125)*

Desert Aids Project (PA) .... D...... 760 323-2118
   1695 N Sunrise Way Ste 101 Palm Springs (92262) *(P-17951)*

Desert ARC .... B...... 760 346-1611
   73255 Country Club Dr Palm Desert (92260) *(P-17952)*

Desert Area Resources Training (PA) .... D...... 760 375-9787
   201 E Ridgecrest Blvd Ridgecrest (93555) *(P-7532)*

Desert Cardiology Cons Med G, Rancho Mirage *Also Called: Desert Crdlgy Cons Med Group I (P-14725)*

Desert Cities Dialysis, Victorville *Also Called: Jamboor Medical Corporation (P-16989)*

Desert Crdlgy Cons Med Group I .... C...... 760 346-0642
   39000 Bob Hope Dr Rancho Mirage (92270) *(P-14725)*

Desert Haven Enterprises .... A...... 661 948-8402
   43437 Copeland Cir Lancaster (93535) *(P-484)*

DESERT HORIZONS COUNTRY CLUB, Indian Wells *Also Called: Dhccnp (P-14370)*

Desert Hot Springs Spa Hotel, Desert Hot Springs *Also Called: Desert Hot Sprng Real Prpts In (P-8715)*

Desert Hot Springs Spa Hotel, Desert Hot Springs *Also Called: Whatever It Takes Inc (P-10366)*

Desert Hot Sprng Real Prpts In .... D...... 760 329-6000
   10805 Palm Dr Desert Hot Springs (92240) *(P-8715)*

Desert Inn & Suites, Anaheim *Also Called: SAI Management Co Inc (P-10190)*

Desert Knlls Convalescent Hosp, Victorville *Also Called: Knolls Convalescent Hosp Inc (P-15530)*

Desert Mechanical Inc .... A...... 702 873-7333
   15870 Olden St Rancho Cascades (91342) *(P-1421)*

Desert Medical Group Inc (PA) .... C...... 760 320-8814
   275 N El Cielo Rd Ste D-402 Palm Springs (92262) *(P-14726)*

Desert Mountain Fics, Victorville *Also Called: Victor Cmnty Support Svcs Inc (P-17156)*

Desert Oasis Healthcare, Palm Springs *Also Called: Desert Medical Group Inc (P-14726)*

Desert Orthpd Ctr A Med Group (PA) .... D...... 760 568-2684
   39000 Bob Hope Dr Ste W301 Rancho Mirage (92270) *(P-14727)*

Desert Regional Med Ctr Inc (HQ) .... A...... 760 323-6511
   1150 N Indian Canyon Dr Palm Springs (92262) *(P-16038)*

Desert Regional Med Ctr Inc .... D...... 760 416-4613
   1180 N Indian Canyon Dr Ste W110 Palm Springs (92262) *(P-16039)*

Desert Snds Unified Schl Dst SC .... D...... 760 777-4200
   47950 Dune Palms Rd La Quinta (92253) *(P-18306)*

Desert Sun Science Center, The, Idyllwild *Also Called: Guided Discoveries Inc* ***(P-10402)***

Desert Valley Date LLC .... D....... 760 398-0999
86740 Industrial Way Coachella (92236) ***(P-6625)***

Desert Valley Hospital Inc (DH) .... **C....... 760 241-8000**
16850 Bear Valley Rd Victorville (92395) ***(P-16040)***

DESERT VALLEY INDUSTRIES, Palm Desert *Also Called: Desert ARC* ***(P-17952)***

Desert Valley Med Group Inc (PA) .... **B....... 760 241-8000**
16850 Bear Valley Rd Victorville (92395) ***(P-14728)***

Desert Valley Medical Group, Victorville *Also Called: Desert Valley Med Group Inc* ***(P-14728)***

Desert Water Agency Fing Corp .... D....... 760 323-4971
1200 S Gene Autry Trl Palm Springs (92264) ***(P-4784)***

Desert Willow Golf Course, Palm Desert *Also Called: Desert Willow Golf Resort Inc* ***(P-14257)***

Desert Willow Golf Resort .... D....... 760 346-7060
38500 Portola Ave Palm Desert (92260) ***(P-14256)***

Desert Willow Golf Resort Inc .... C....... 760 346-0015
38995 Desert Willow Dr Palm Desert (92260) ***(P-14257)***

Deserve, Palo Alto *Also Called: Deserve Inc* ***(P-13265)***

Deserve Inc .... C....... 800 418-7353
195 Page Mill Rd Ste 109 Palo Alto (94306) ***(P-13265)***

Design Collection Inc .... D....... 323 277-9200
2209 S Santa Fe Ave Los Angeles (90058) ***(P-6154)***

Design Electric, Pleasanton *Also Called: Pmn Design Electric Inc* ***(P-1807)***

Design Made Easy, Los Angeles *Also Called: Emser Tile LLC* ***(P-5204)***

Design Masonry Inc .... D....... 661 252-2784
20703 Santa Clara St Canyon Country (91351) ***(P-1881)***

Design People Inc .... C....... 800 969-5799
1700 E Walnut Ave Ste 400 El Segundo (90245) ***(P-12565)***

Design Veronique, Richmond *Also Called: My True Image Mfg Inc* ***(P-5433)***

Design West Technologies Inc .... D....... 714 731-0201
2701 Dow Ave Tustin (92780) ***(P-2671)***

Designory, Long Beach *Also Called: Designory Inc* ***(P-10804)***

Designory Inc (HQ) .... **C....... 562 624-0200**
211 E Ocean Blvd Ste 100 Long Beach (90802) ***(P-10804)***

Desilva Gates Construction, Dublin *Also Called: Desilva Gates Construction LP* ***(P-1095)***

Desilva Gates Construction LP (PA) .... **D....... 925 361-1380**
11555 Dublin Blvd Dublin (94568) ***(P-1095)***

Dessert Cancer Care, Yucca Valley *Also Called: Eisenhower Medical Center* ***(P-14734)***

Destination Moon LP .... D....... 415 675-7777
615 Battery St Fl 6 San Francisco (94111) ***(P-10805)***

Destination Residences LLC .... B....... 760 346-4647
45750 San Luis Rey Ave Palm Desert (92260) ***(P-9740)***

Destination Residences LLC .... B....... 858 550-1000
9700 N Torrey Pines Rd La Jolla (92037) ***(P-10542)***

Destinations For Teens .... D....... 818 737-2221
20951 Burbank Blvd Ste D Woodland Hills (91367) ***(P-17052)***

Detecon Inc .... B....... 415 549-6999
351 California St San Francisco (94104) ***(P-20738)***

Deutsch La Inc .... D....... 310 862-3000
12901 W Jefferson Blvd Los Angeles (90066) ***(P-10606)***

Deutsche Bank National Tr Co .... D....... 714 247-6054
1761 E Saint Andrew Pl Santa Ana (92705) ***(P-7837)***

Deutsche Bank National Tr Co .... D....... 310 788-6200
1999 Avenue Of The Stars Ste 3750 Los Angeles (90067) ***(P-7863)***

Devcon Construction Inc (PA) .... **B....... 408 942-8200**
690 Gibraltar Dr Milpitas (95035) ***(P-902)***

Devcool Inc .... D....... 408 372-4313
7901 Stoneridge Dr Ste 220 Pleasanton (94588) ***(P-20344)***

Develop Disabilities Svc Org .... D....... 916 973-1951
2331 Saint Marks Way G1 Sacramento (95864) ***(P-17953)***

Developers Surety Indemnity Co (DH) .... **D....... 949 263-3300**
17771 Cowan Ste 100 Irvine (92614) ***(P-8430)***

Developers Surety Indemnity Co, Irvine *Also Called: Insco Insurance Services Inc* ***(P-8589)***

Developlus Inc .... C....... 951 738-8595
1575 Magnolia Ave Corona (92879) ***(P-3106)***

Development Design Mgmt, San Francisco *Also Called: Forma LLC* ***(P-13292)***

DEVELOPMENT DISABILITIES CENTE, Santa Ana *Also Called: Regional Ctr Orange Cnty Inc* ***(P-20940)***

Development Resource Cons Inc (PA) .... **D....... 714 685-6860**
160 S Old Springs Rd Ste 210 Anaheim (92808) ***(P-19197)***

Development Services, Lancaster *Also Called: Lancaster Cmnty Svcs Fndtion I* ***(P-13665)***

Develpmntal Svcs Continuum Inc .... D....... 619 460-7333
7944 Golden Ave Lemon Grove (91945) ***(P-18416)***

Devereux California Center, Goleta *Also Called: Devereux Foundation* ***(P-17053)***

Devereux Foundation .... B....... 805 968-2525
7055 Seaway Dr Goleta (93117) ***(P-17053)***

Deviation Games LLC .... D....... 310 873-5225
12100 Wilshire Blvd Ste 1150 Los Angeles (90025) ***(P-11539)***

Devil Mountain Whl Nurs LLC .... D....... 949 496-9356
29001 Ortega Hwy San Juan Capistrano (92675) ***(P-123)***

Devine & Son Trucking Co Inc (PA) .... **C....... 559 486-7440**
3870 Channel Dr West Sacramento (95691) ***(P-3803)***

Devine Intermodal, West Sacramento *Also Called: Devine & Son Trucking Co Inc* ***(P-3803)***

Devron H Char MD .... D....... 415 522-0700
45 Castro St Ste 309 San Francisco (94114) ***(P-14729)***

Dewberry Engineers Inc .... D....... 916 363-4210
11060 White Rock Rd Ste 200 Rancho Cordova (95670) ***(P-19198)***

Dewitt Stern Group Inc .... C....... 818 933-2700
5990 Sepulvda Blvd # 550 Van Nuys (91411) ***(P-8544)***

Dewolf Realty Co Inc .... D....... 415 221-2032
4330 California St San Francisco (94118) ***(P-20078)***

Dex Corporation .... C....... 805 388-1711
3600 Via Pescador Camarillo (93012) ***(P-19199)***

Dexyp, Glendale *Also Called: Yellowpagescom LLC* ***(P-13561)***

Deyoung Museum, San Francisco *Also Called: Corportion of Fine Arts Mseums* ***(P-18649)***

Df One Operator LLC .... D....... 310 961-9739
11 Via Santanella Rancho Mirage (92270) ***(P-13266)***

Dfa Dairy Brands Fluid LLC .... B....... 800 395-7004
17851 Railroad St City Of Industry (91748) ***(P-6434)***

Dfa of California .... D....... 559 233-7249
2037 Morgan Dr Kingsburg (93631) ***(P-20079)***

Dfds International Corporation .... D....... 310 414-1516
898 Sepulveda Blvd, 6th Floor El Segundo (90245) ***(P-4005)***

Dfds Transport US, El Segundo *Also Called: Dfds International Corporation* ***(P-4005)***

Dfm Dietary Food Management, Canoga Park *Also Called: Computrition Inc* ***(P-11511)***

Dfs Flooring Inc (PA) .... **D....... 818 374-5200**
15651 Saticoy St Van Nuys (91406) ***(P-2031)***

DG Performance Spc Inc .... D....... 714 961-8850
4100 E La Palma Ave Anaheim (92807) ***(P-2999)***

Dg Real Estate Inc .... D....... 818 591-8800
4766 Park Granada Ste 214 Calabasas (91302) ***(P-8979)***

Dgn Technologies Inc (PA) .... **D....... 510 252-0346**
46500 Fremont Blvd Ste 708 Fremont (94538) ***(P-11540)***

Dgwb Inc .... D....... 714 881-2300
217 N Main St Ste 200 Santa Ana (92701) ***(P-10607)***

Dgwb Advg & Communications, Santa Ana *Also Called: Dgwb Inc* ***(P-10607)***

DH Smith Company Inc .... D....... 408 532-7617
6000 Hellyer Ave Ste 150 San Jose (95138) ***(P-1924)***

Dharma Ventures Group Inc (PA) .... **B....... 661 294-4200**
24700 Avenue Rockefeller Valencia (91355) ***(P-7577)***

Dhb Delivery LLC .... D....... 626 588-7562
1134 N Chestnut Ln Azusa (91702) ***(P-3608)***

Dhccnp .... D....... 760 340-4646
44900 Desert Horizons Dr Indian Wells (92210) ***(P-14370)***

Dhl Express (usa) Inc .... D....... 415 826-7338
401 23rd St San Francisco (94107) ***(P-3852)***

Dhl Global Forwarding, Torrance *Also Called: Air Express Intl USA Inc* ***(P-3980)***

Dhs Consulting LLC .... C....... 714 276-1135
1820 E 1st St Ste 410 Santa Ana (92705) ***(P-20080)***

Dhx-Dependable Hawaiian Ex Inc .... D....... 510 686-2600
3623 Munster St Hayward (94545) ***(P-4006)***

Dhx-Dependable Hawaiian Ex Inc (PA) .... **C....... 310 537-2000**
19201 S Susana Rd Compton (90221) ***(P-4007)***

Di Overnite LLC .... D....... 877 997-7447
1900 S State College Blvd Ste 450 Anaheim (92806) ***(P-3609)***

Di-Sep Systems Intl Inc (HQ) .... **D....... 562 407-3432**
15519 Blackburn Ave Norwalk (90650) ***(P-5745)***

Diablo Lodge Partnership, Danville *Also Called: Braddock Logan Ventr Group LP* ***(P-788)***

Diablo Realty .... C....... 925 933-9300
1301 Ygnacio Valley Rd Ste 100 Walnut Creek (94598) ***(P-8980)***

Diablo Valley Rock, Concord *Also Called: Carone & Company Inc* ***(P-2215)***

ALPHABETIC

Diablo Vly College Foundation (PA)..B...... 925 685-1230
321 Golf Club Rd Pleasant Hill (94523) *(P-13267)*

Diageno Chateau & Estate Wines, Napa *Also Called: Diageo North America Inc* *(P-6794)*

Diageo North America Inc ....D...... 707 299-2600
555 Gateway Dr Napa (94558) *(P-6794)*

Diageo North America Inc ....C...... 707 939-6200
21468 8th St E Sonoma (95476) *(P-6795)*

Diagnostic Health Corporation ....C...... 310 665-7180
6801 Park Ter Los Angeles (90045) *(P-20345)*

Diagnostic Health Los Angeles, Los Angeles *Also Called: Diagnostic Health Corporation* *(P-20345)*

Diagnostic Labs & Rdlgy, Burbank *Also Called: Kan-Di-Ki LLC* *(P-16731)*

Diagnostic Medical Group, Monterey Park *Also Called: Chen Dvid MD Dgnstc Med Group* *(P-14679)*

Diagnstc Intrvntnal Srgcal CT ....D...... 310 574-0400
13160 Mindanao Way Ste 150 Marina Del Rey (90292) *(P-14730)*

Dial Communications, Camarillo *Also Called: Dial Security Inc* *(P-13106)*

Dial Security Inc (PA)..C...... 805 389-6700
760 W Ventura Blvd Camarillo (93010) *(P-13106)*

Diamond Contract Services Inc ....B...... 818 565-3554
11432 Vanowen St North Hollywood (91605) *(P-10889)*

Diamond Environmental Services, San Marcos *Also Called: Diamond Environmental Svcs LP* *(P-11028)*

Diamond Environmental Svcs LP ....D...... 760 744-7191
807 E Mission Rd San Marcos (92069) *(P-11028)*

Diamond Goldenwest Corporation (PA)....................................C...... 714 542-9000
15732 Tustin Village Way Tustin (92780) *(P-7550)*

Diamond Mountain Casino ....C...... 530 252-1100
900 Skyline Dr Susanville (96130) *(P-9741)*

Diamond Nghbrhood Fmly Hlth Ct, San Diego *Also Called: Family Hlth Ctrs San Diego Inc* *(P-17063)*

Diamond Peo LLC ....C...... 714 728-5186
27442 Calle Arroyo Ste A San Juan Capistrano (92675) *(P-11124)*

Diamond Resorts LLC ....D...... 760 866-1800
2800 S Palm Canyon Dr Palm Springs (92264) *(P-9742)*

Diamond Ridge Corporation ....C...... 909 949-0605
121 S Mountain Ave Upland (91786) *(P-8981)*

Diamond Vly Hlth Holdings LLC ....D...... 949 487-9500
29222 Rancho Viejo Rd Ste 127 San Juan Capistrano (92675) *(P-15425)*

Diamond W Floorcovering, City Of Industry *Also Called: W Diamond Supply Co* *(P-5143)*

Diamond Youth Shelter, San Francisco *Also Called: Larkin Street Youth Services* *(P-18039)*

Diamondrock San Dego Tnant LLC ....B...... 619 239-4500
400 W Broadway San Diego (92101) *(P-9743)*

Dianne Adair, Concord *Also Called: Dianne Adair Day Care Centers* *(P-18307)*

Dianne Adair Day Care Centers (PA)...D...... 925 580-9704
1862 Bailey Rd Concord (94521) *(P-18307)*

Diasorin Molecular LLC ....C...... 562 240-6500
11331 Valley View St Cypress (90630) *(P-2613)*

Diaz Plastering Inc ....D...... 661 244-8228
6013 Nathaniel Way Bakersfield (93313) *(P-1925)*

Diba Fashions Inc ....D...... 323 232-3775
472 N Bowling Green Way Los Angeles (90049) *(P-13268)*

Dibuduo Dfendis Insur Brks LLC (PA)...D...... 559 432-0222
6873 Nw Ave St 101 Fresno (93711) *(P-8545)*

Dicaperl Corporation (DH)..D...... 610 667-6640
23705 Crenshaw Blvd # 10 Torrance (90505) *(P-647)*

Dice Therapeutics Inc ....D...... 650 566-1402
400 E Jamie Ct Ste 300 South San Francisco (94080) *(P-19680)*

Dick Anderson & Sons Farming ....C...... 559 945-2511
15900 W Dorris Ave Huron (93234) *(P-175)*

Dick Dewese Chevrolet Inc ....C...... 909 793-2681
800 Alabama St Redlands (92374) *(P-7195)*

Dick James & Associates Inc ....C...... 916 332-7430
2990 Lava Ridge Ct Ste 240 Roseville (95661) *(P-8982)*

Dickson Testing Co Inc (DH) ....D...... 562 862-8378
11126 Palmer Ave South Gate (90280) *(P-19965)*

Didi Hirsch Psychiatric Svc (PA)...C...... 310 390-6612
4760 Sepulveda Blvd Culver City (90230) *(P-17954)*

Didi Hrsch Cmnty Mntal Hlth Ct, Culver City *Also Called: Didi Hirsch Psychiatric Svc* *(P-17954)*

Diede Construction Inc ....D...... 209 369-8255
12393 N Highway 99 Lodi (95240) *(P-903)*

Diestel Turkey Ranch (PA)..C...... 209 532-4950
22200 Lyons Bald Mountain Rd Sonora (95370) *(P-227)*

Diez & Leis RE Group Inc ....A...... 916 487-4287
5120 Manzanita Ave Ste 120 Carmichael (95608) *(P-8983)*

Digirad Imaging Solutions Inc ....C...... 800 947-6134
13100 Gregg St Ste A Poway (92064) *(P-10990)*

Digit, San Carlos *Also Called: Hello Digit LLC* *(P-13311)*

Digital Domain, Venice *Also Called: Power Studios Inc* *(P-13881)*

Digital Domain 30 Inc (PA)..B...... 213 797-3100
12641 Beatrice St Los Angeles (90066) *(P-13838)*

Digital Domain Media Group Inc ....A
12641 Beatrice St Los Angeles (90066) *(P-10806)*

Digital Film Labs, Los Angeles *Also Called: Point360* *(P-13947)*

Digital Insight Corporation ....D...... 818 879-1010
5601 Lindero Canyon Rd Ste 100 Westlake Village (91362) *(P-12657)*

Digital Insight Corporation (HQ)...C...... 818 879-1010
1300 Seaport Blvd Ste 300 Redwood City (94063) *(P-12658)*

Digital Marketing, San Diego *Also Called: Stn Digital LLC* *(P-10676)*

Digital Media Management Inc ....D...... 323 378-6505
6555 Barton Ave Ste 200 Los Angeles (90038) *(P-20081)*

Digital Realty ....C...... 415 738-6500
365 Main St San Francisco (94105) *(P-8984)*

Digital Room Holdings Inc (HQ)...D...... 310 575-4440
8000 Haskell Ave Van Nuys (91406) *(P-2568)*

Digital Storm, Gilroy *Also Called: Hanaps Enterprises* *(P-2831)*

Digital Wireless Telecom Inc ....D...... 650 472-7064
482 Alvarado St Monterey (93940) *(P-13269)*

Digitalist USA Ltd ....A...... 949 278-1354
611 Gateway Blvd Ste 120 South San Francisco (94080) *(P-12447)*

Digitalmojo Inc ....D...... 800 413-5916
3111 Camino Del Rio N Ste 400 San Diego (92108) *(P-4268)*

Digitalthink Inc (DH) ....C...... 415 625-4000
601 Brannan St San Francisco (94107) *(P-20346)*

Digitaria, San Diego *Also Called: Mirum Inc* *(P-10814)*

Digitas Inc ....C...... 617 867-1000
13031 W Jefferson Blvd Ste 800 Los Angeles (90094) *(P-10608)*

Digitas Inc ....D...... 617 867-1000
350 Bush St Fl 18 San Francisco (94104) *(P-10609)*

Digitaslbi, Los Angeles *Also Called: Digitas Inc* *(P-10608)*

Digite Inc ....C...... 408 418-3834
21060 Homestead Rd Ste 220 Cupertino (95014) *(P-11541)*

Dignified Home Loans LLC ....D...... 818 421-7753
1 Baxter Way Ste 120 Westlake Village (91362) *(P-7955)*

Dignity Health ....C...... 916 983-7400
1650 Creekside Dr Folsom (95630) *(P-16041)*

Dignity Health ....B...... 805 739-3000
1400 E Church St Santa Maria (93454) *(P-16042)*

Dignity Health ....B...... 916 537-5151
6501 Coyle Ave Fl 6 Carmichael (95608) *(P-16043)*

Dignity Health ....C...... 916 379-2996
3400 Data Dr Rancho Cordova (95670) *(P-16044)*

Dignity Health ....C...... 209 467-6353
1800 N California St Stockton (95204) *(P-16045)*

Dignity Health ....B...... 805 988-2868
200 Oceangate Long Beach (90802) *(P-16046)*

Dignity Health ....A...... 818 885-8500
18300 Roscoe Blvd Northridge (91325) *(P-16047)*

Dignity Health ....B...... 562 491-9000
1050 Linden Ave Long Beach (90813) *(P-16048)*

Dignity Health (HQ)..C...... 415 438-5500
185 Berry St Ste 200 San Francisco (94107) *(P-16049)*

Dignity Health ....A...... 916 537-5000
6501 Coyle Ave Carmichael (95608) *(P-16050)*

Dignity Health ....C...... 916 423-5940
7500 Hospital Dr Sacramento (95823) *(P-16051)*

Dignity Health ....C...... 805 389-5800
2309 Antonio Ave Camarillo (93010) *(P-16052)*

Dignity Health ....A...... 805 988-2500
1600 N Rose Ave Oxnard (93030) *(P-16053)*

Dignity Health ....A...... 415 668-1000
450 Stanyan St San Francisco (94117) *(P-16054)*

ALPHABETIC SECTION — Disney Cruise Line

Dignity Health .... B 661 663-6000
  400 Old River Rd Bakersfield (93311) *(P-16055)*

Dignity Health Med Foundation (DH) .... C 916 851-2000
  3400 Data Dr Rancho Cordova (95670) *(P-16056)*

Dignity Health Medical Clinic, Folsom *Also Called: Mercy Medical Group (P-16262)*

Dignity Hlth Med Grp-Dominican, Rancho Cordova *Also Called: Dignity Health Med Foundation (P-16056)*

Dilbeck Inc (PA) .... D 818 790-6774
  1030 Foothill Blvd La Canada (91011) *(P-8985)*

Dilbeck Realtors, La Canada *Also Called: Dilbeck Inc (P-8985)*

Diligence Security Group .... C 510 710-5806
  66 Franklin St Ste 300 Oakland (94607) *(P-1721)*

Diligent Delivery Systems, Valencia *Also Called: Central States Logistics Inc (P-3381)*

Diligente Technologies LLC .... B 510 304-0852
  226 Airport Pkwy San Jose (95110) *(P-12448)*

Dillingham Construction NA .... A 925 249-8850
  1020 Serpentine Ln Ste 110 Pleasanton (94566) *(P-1295)*

Dimar Enterprises Inc .... C 949 492-1100
  26021 Pala Ste 150 Mission Viejo (92691) *(P-10890)*

Dimare Company, Newman *Also Called: Dimare Enterprises Inc (P-29)*

Dimare Enterprises Inc (PA) .... C 209 827-2900
  1406 N St Newman (95360) *(P-29)*

Dimension Data Cloud, Santa Clara *Also Called: Ntt Cloud Infrastructure Inc (P-11787)*

Dinah's Garden Hotel, Palo Alto *Also Called: Dinahs Garden Hotel Inc (P-7473)*

Dinahs Garden Hotel Inc .... D 650 493-2844
  4261 El Camino Real Palo Alto (94306) *(P-7473)*

Dine Brands Global, Pasadena *Also Called: Dine Brands Global Inc (P-7474)*

Dine Brands Global Inc (PA) .... B 818 240-6055
  10 W Walnut St Fl 5 Pasadena (91103) *(P-7474)*

Diocese Fresno Education Corp .... D 209 722-7496
  1400 E 27th St Merced (95340) *(P-18308)*

Diocese Stockton Eductl Off .... C 209 634-8578
  1250 Cooper Ave Ste 3 Turlock (95380) *(P-17708)*

Diplomatic Security Services, Rancho Cucamonga *Also Called: Harrison Iyke (P-13123)*

Diplomatic Security Svcs LLC .... D 909 463-8409
  7581 Etiwanda Ave Rancho Cucamonga (91739) *(P-12965)*

Direct Chassislink Inc .... A 657 216-5846
  7777 Center Ave Ste 325 Huntington Beach (92647) *(P-11029)*

Direct Flow Medical Inc .... C 707 576-0420
  3945 Freedom Cir Ste 560 Santa Clara (95054) *(P-17222)*

Direct Parcel Inc .... D 303 381-4099
  1768 Hardial Ct Yuba City (95993) *(P-3610)*

Direct Technology, Roseville *Also Called: Directapps Inc (P-12779)*

Directapps Inc (PA) .... C 916 787-2200
  3009 Douglas Blvd Ste 300 Roseville (95661) *(P-12779)*

Directed LLC .... C 800 876-0800
  1 Viper Way Ste 1 Vista (92081) *(P-4008)*

Directly Inc .... D 650 714-7334
  333 Bryant St Ste 250 San Francisco (94107) *(P-11542)*

Directors Guild America Inc (PA) .... C 310 289-2000
  7920 W Sunset Blvd Los Angeles (90046) *(P-13932)*

Directv 323 810-2032
  1655 W 110th Pl Los Angeles (90047) *(P-4497)*

Directv, El Segundo *Also Called: Directv Group Holdings LLC (P-4213)*

Directv, El Segundo *Also Called: Directv Group Inc (P-4503)*

Directv Inc .... B 888 388-4249
  2260 E Imperial Hwy El Segundo (90245) *(P-4498)*

Directv Enterprises LLC .... A 310 535-5000
  2230 E Imperial Hwy El Segundo (90245) *(P-4499)*

Directv Group Holdings LLC (HQ) .... C 310 964-5000
  2260 E Imperial Hwy El Segundo (90245) *(P-4213)*

Directv Group Holdings LLC .... C 760 375-8300
  140 Station Ave Ridgecrest (93555) *(P-4500)*

Directv Group Holdings LLC .... C 805 207-6675
  360 Cortez Cir Camarillo (93012) *(P-4501)*

Directv Group Holdings LLC .... C 661 632-6562
  715 E Avenue L8 Ste 101 Lancaster (93535) *(P-4502)*

Directv Group Inc (DH) .... C 310 964-5000
  2260 E Imperial Hwy El Segundo (90245) *(P-4503)*

Directv Holdings LLC (DH) .... D 310 964-5000
  2230 E Imperial Hwy El Segundo (90245) *(P-4504)*

Directv International Inc (DH) .... C 310 964-6460
  2230 E Imperial Hwy Fl 10 El Segundo (90245) *(P-4505)*

Directv Latin America LLC .... D 310 535-5000
  2230 E Imperial Hwy El Segundo (90245) *(P-4506)*

Disaster Rstrtion Prfssnals In .... D 310 301-8030
  1517 W 130th St Gardena (90249) *(P-673)*

Discord Inc .... C 650 389-2453
  444 De Haro St Ste 200 San Francisco (94107) *(P-11543)*

Discount Builders Supply .... D 415 285-2800
  1695 Mission St San Francisco (94103) *(P-5153)*

DISCOUNT TECH, San Francisco *Also Called: Techsoup Global (P-18915)*

Discount Tire, Union City *Also Called: Southern Cal Disc Tire Co Inc (P-7357)*

Discount Tire, Rancho Cordova *Also Called: Southern Cal Disc Tire Co Inc (P-7358)*

Discount Tire, Hemet *Also Called: Southern Cal Disc Tire Co Inc (P-7359)*

Discount Tire, Escondido *Also Called: Southern Cal Disc Tire Co Inc (P-7360)*

Discount Tire, Huntington Beach *Also Called: Southern Cal Disc Tire Co Inc (P-7361)*

Discount Tire, Glendora *Also Called: Southern Cal Disc Tire Co Inc (P-7362)*

Discount Tire, San Marcos *Also Called: Southern Cal Disc Tire Co Inc (P-7363)*

Discount Tire, Ventura *Also Called: Southern Cal Disc Tire Co Inc (P-7364)*

Discount Tire, Escondido *Also Called: Southern Cal Disc Tire Co Inc (P-7365)*

Discount Tire, Solana Beach *Also Called: Southern Cal Disc Tire Co Inc (P-7366)*

Discount Tire, Poway *Also Called: Southern Cal Disc Tire Co Inc (P-7367)*

Discount Tire, Oceanside *Also Called: Southern Cal Disc Tire Co Inc (P-7368)*

Discount Tire, Sacramento *Also Called: Southern Cal Disc Tire Co Inc (P-7369)*

Discount Tire, Redwood City *Also Called: Southern Cal Disc Tire Co Inc (P-7370)*

Discount Tire, Mountain View *Also Called: Southern Cal Disc Tire Co Inc (P-7371)*

Discount Tire, Encinitas *Also Called: Southern Cal Disc Tire Co Inc (P-7372)*

Discount Tire, Campbell *Also Called: Southern Cal Disc Tire Co Inc (P-7373)*

Discount Tire, San Jose *Also Called: Southern Cal Disc Tire Co Inc (P-7374)*

Discount Tire, San Diego *Also Called: Southern Cal Disc Tire Co Inc (P-7375)*

Discount Tire, Carson *Also Called: Southern Cal Disc Tire Co Inc (P-7376)*

Discount Tire Center 025, North Hollywood *Also Called: Akh Company Inc (P-13680)*

Discount Tire Center 038, Redlands *Also Called: Akh Company Inc (P-7339)*

Discount Tire Center 077, Moreno Valley *Also Called: Akh Company Inc (P-7340)*

Discovery Communications Inc (PA) .... B 310 975-5906
  10100 Santa Monica Blvd Ste 1500 Los Angeles (90067) *(P-4535)*

Discovery Foods Inc .... D
  2395 American Ave Hayward (94545) *(P-6419)*

Discovery Health Services .... B 858 459-0785
  5726 La Jolla Blvd Ste 104 La Jolla (92037) *(P-17223)*

DISCOVERY MEDICAL STAFFING, La Jolla *Also Called: Discovery Health Services (P-17223)*

Discovery Practice MGT Inc .... B 714 828-1800
  18401 Von Karman Ave Ste 500 Irvine (92612) *(P-17054)*

Discovery Scnce Ctr Ornge Cnty .... C 866 552-2823
  2500 N Main St Santa Ana (92705) *(P-18650)*

Discus Dental LLC (PA) .... C 310 845-8600
  12121 Bluff Creek Dr Ste 100 Los Angeles (90094) *(P-5411)*

Dish Wireless LLC .... C 559 515-6866
  1190 N Chestnut Ave Fresno (93702) *(P-4214)*

Disney, Burbank *Also Called: Disney Enterprises Inc (P-4375)*

Disney, Anaheim *Also Called: Disney Enterprises Inc (P-9744)*

Disney, Anaheim *Also Called: Disney Enterprises Inc (P-13839)*

Disney, Glendale *Also Called: Disney Enterprises Inc (P-13840)*

Disney, Anaheim *Also Called: Disney Enterprises Inc (P-13841)*

Disney, Burbank *Also Called: Disney Incorporated (P-13842)*

Disney, Burbank *Also Called: Walt Disney Music Company (P-13913)*

Disney, Glendale *Also Called: Walt Disney Pictures (P-13914)*

Disney, Burbank *Also Called: Walt Disney Records Direct (P-13915)*

Disney, Glendale *Also Called: Walt Dsney Imgnring RES Dev In (P-13960)*

Disney, Burbank *Also Called: Walt Disney Company (P-14316)*

Disney, Burbank *Also Called: Disney Regional Entrmt Inc (P-14513)*

Disney Cnsmr Pdts Intrctive MD .... C 818 263-1374
  1201 Flower St Glendale (91201) *(P-11544)*

Disney Construction, Burlingame *Also Called: Disney Construction Inc (P-1096)*

Disney Construction Inc .... D 650 689-5149
  533 Airport Blvd Ste 120 Burlingame (94010) *(P-1096)*

Disney Cruise Line, Burbank *Also Called: Dcl Maritime LLC (P-20075)*

Disney Enterprises Inc — ALPHABETIC SECTION

Disney Enterprises Inc (DH) .... A 818 560-1000
  500 S Buena Vista St Burbank (91521) *(P-4375)*

Disney Enterprises Inc .... A 714 778-6600
  1150 W Magic Way Anaheim (92802) *(P-9744)*

Disney Enterprises Inc .... C 714 781-1651
  700 W Ball Rd Anaheim (92802) *(P-13839)*

Disney Enterprises Inc .... C 818 553-4103
  1101 Flower St Glendale (91201) *(P-13840)*

Disney Enterprises Inc .... D 407 397-6000
  1313 S Harbor Blvd Anaheim (92802) *(P-13841)*

Disney Financial Services, Burbank *Also Called: Twdc Enterprises 18 Corp (P-4466)*

Disney Incorporated (DH) .... C 818 560-1000
  500 S Buena Vista St Burbank (91521) *(P-13842)*

Disney Interactive Studios, Burbank *Also Called: Disney Interactive Studios Inc (P-11546)*

Disney Interactive Studios Inc .... B 818 560-1000
  601 Circle Seven Dr Glendale (91201) *(P-11545)*

Disney Interactive Studios Inc .... B 818 553-5000
  681 W Buena Vista St Burbank (91521) *(P-11546)*

Disney Networks Group LLC .... D 310 369-5104
  10201 W Pico Blvd Ste 100/3132 Los Angeles (90064) *(P-4425)*

Disney Networks Group LLC (DH) .... D 310 369-1000
  10201 W Pico Blvd Bldg 101 Los Angeles (90064) *(P-4426)*

Disney Regional Entrmt Inc (DH) .... C 818 560-1000
  500 S Buena Vista St Burbank (91521) *(P-14513)*

Disney Research Pittsburgh .... C 412 623-1800
  532 Paula Ave Glendale (91201) *(P-19681)*

Disney Streaming Services LLC .... C 818 560-1000
  500 S Buena Vista St San Francisco (94105) *(P-4376)*

Disneyland, Anaheim *Also Called: Disneyland International (P-9745)*

Disneyland, Anaheim *Also Called: Disneyland International (P-14302)*

Disneyland International .... A 714 956-6746
  1580 S Disneyland Dr Anaheim (92802) *(P-9745)*

Disneyland International (DH) .... C 714 781-4565
  1313 S Harbor Blvd Anaheim (92802) *(P-14302)*

Disneyland Resort .... A 714 781-7560
  1020 W Ball Rd Anaheim (92802) *(P-4127)*

Disneyland Resort (DH) .... C 714 781-4000
  1313 S Harbor Blvd Anaheim (92802) *(P-9746)*

Disneys Grnd Clifornian Ht Spa, Anaheim *Also Called: Wco Hotels Inc (P-10355)*

Dispatch Office, Oakland *Also Called: First Transit Inc (P-3137)*

Dispatch Trucking LLC (PA) .... D 909 355-5531
  14032 Santa Ana Ave Fontana (92337) *(P-4009)*

Disqo Inc .... D 818 237-2186
  400 N Brand Blvd Ste 600 Glendale (91203) *(P-19808)*

Disruptive Visions LLC .... D 949 502-3800
  23456 Madero Ste 210 Mission Viejo (92691) *(P-20739)*

Distel Family Ranch, Sonora *Also Called: Diestel Turkey Ranch (P-227)*

Distillery, Manhattan Beach *Also Called: Distillery Tech Inc (P-11547)*

Distillery Tech Inc .... C 310 776-6234
  1500 Rosecrans Ave Ste 500 Manhattan Beach (90266) *(P-11547)*

Distinctive Corporation .... D 408 568-5598
  14413 Big Basin Way Saratoga (95070) *(P-13270)*

Distribution Alternatives Inc .... D 909 673-1000
  1990 S Cucamonga Ave Ontario (91761) *(P-3697)*

Distribution Alternatives Inc .... C 909 746-5600
  10621 6th St Rancho Cucamonga (91730) *(P-3698)*

Distribution Alternatives Inc .... D 909 770-8900
  1979 Renaissance Pkwy Rialto (92376) *(P-6105)*

District Attorney, Van Nuys *Also Called: County of Los Angeles (P-17417)*

District Attorney, Los Angeles *Also Called: County of Los Angeles (P-17418)*

District Attorney, Westminster *Also Called: County of Orange (P-17934)*

District Attorney, Lancaster *Also Called: County of Los Angeles (P-20931)*

District Attorney's Office, Riverside *Also Called: County of Riverside (P-20932)*

District Council DC (PA) .... D 510 638-7600
  2272 San Pablo Ave Oakland (94612) *(P-17955)*

Diva Hotel, San Francisco *Also Called: Personality Hotels Inc (P-10115)*

Divergent 3d, Torrance *Also Called: Divergent Technologies Inc (P-19200)*

Divergent Technologies Inc .... C 424 542-2158
  19601 Hamilton Ave Torrance (90502) *(P-19200)*

Diverscape Inc .... D 951 245-1686
  21730 Bundy Canyon Rd Wildomar (92595) *(P-485)*

Diverse Journeys Inc (PA) .... D 310 643-7403
  525 S Douglas St Ste 210 El Segundo (90245) *(P-17956)*

Diversfied Cmmnctions Svcs Inc .... D 714 888-2284
  1260 Pioneer St Brea (92821) *(P-4269)*

Diversfied Mrcury Cmmnctons LL .... D 508 598-3569
  11620 Wilshire Blvd Los Angeles (90025) *(P-10729)*

Diversified Direct, La Mirada *Also Called: Diversified Mailing Incorporated (P-10771)*

Diversified Landscape Co, Wildomar *Also Called: Diverscape Inc (P-485)*

Diversified Mailing Incorporated .... C 714 994-6245
  14407 Alondra Blvd La Mirada (90638) *(P-10771)*

Diversified Metal Works, Orange *Also Called: Rika Corporation (P-2198)*

Diversified Prj Svcs Intl Inc (PA) .... D 661 371-2800
  5351 Olive Dr Ste 100 Bakersfield (93308) *(P-19201)*

Diversified Utility Svcs Inc .... B 661 325-3212
  3105 Unicorn Rd Bakersfield (93308) *(P-1205)*

Diversity Bus Solutions Inc .... C 909 395-0243
  3532 Old Archibald Ranch Rd Ontario (91761) *(P-11125)*

Dividend Finance .... D 858 880-7710
  3661 Valley Centre Dr Ste 250 San Diego (92130) *(P-13271)*

Divine Home Care, Oakland *Also Called: Wild Karma Inc (P-15735)*

Divine Specialties, San Fernando *Also Called: World-Wide Foods (P-6415)*

Division 1, Los Angeles *Also Called: Los Angles Cnty Mtro Trnsp Aut (P-3154)*

Division 7, Venice *Also Called: Los Angles Cnty Mtro Trnsp Aut (P-3151)*

Dixie SC Dst Maint Dept, San Rafael *Also Called: Miller Creek School District (P-17729)*

Dixieline Lumber Company LLC .... A 951 224-8491
  2625 Durahart St Riverside (92507) *(P-6959)*

Djont Operations LLC .... C 650 342-4600
  150 Anza Blvd Burlingame (94010) *(P-9747)*

Djont Operations LLC .... C 408 942-0400
  901 E Calaveras Blvd Milpitas (95035) *(P-9748)*

Djont Operations LLC .... C 310 640-3600
  1440 E Imperial Ave El Segundo (90245) *(P-9749)*

Djont/Cmb Ssf Leasing LLC .... D 650 589-3400
  250 Gateway Blvd South San Francisco (94080) *(P-9750)*

Djont/Jpm Hsptlity Lsg Spe LLC .... C 805 984-2500
  2101 Mandalay Beach Rd Oxnard (93035) *(P-9751)*

DK Hotels LLC .... D 925 640-3616
  501 N Cherokee Ln Lodi (95240) *(P-9752)*

Dkd Property Management, San Jose *Also Called: Property Maintenance Company (P-10950)*

Dkn Hotel LLC (PA) .... B 714 427-4320
  42 Corporate Park Ste 200 Irvine (92606) *(P-9753)*

Dl Imaging, Santa Ana *Also Called: Dekra-Lite Industries Inc (P-13260)*

DL Long Landscaping Inc .... D 909 628-5531
  5475 G St Chino (91710) *(P-428)*

Dla Piper LLP (us) .... C 310 595-3000
  2000 Avenue Of The Stars Ste 400n Los Angeles (90067) *(P-17438)*

Dlf Logistics, Los Angeles *Also Called: Dlf Logistics LLC (P-3388)*

Dlf Logistics LLC .... D 626 387-3797
  1019 S Rimpau Blvd Los Angeles (90019) *(P-3388)*

Dlh Davinci LLC .... D 818 703-5100
  22135 Roscoe Blvd Ste 101 West Hills (91304) *(P-16770)*

Dlight Design Inc .... A 415 872-6136
  2100 Geng Rd Ste 210 Palo Alto (94303) *(P-1422)*

Dlr Group Inc (HQ) .... C 213 800-9400
  700 S Flower St Ste 2200 Los Angeles (90017) *(P-19466)*

Dma Claims Management Inc .... D 323 342-6800
  330 N Brand Blvd Ste 230 Glendale (91203) *(P-8546)*

DMC Construction Incorporated .... D 831 656-1600
  2110 Del Monte Ave Monterey (93940) *(P-904)*

Dmi, Rancho Cascades *Also Called: Desert Mechanical Inc (P-1421)*

DMS, Anaheim *Also Called: DMS Facility Services Inc (P-10892)*

DMS Facility Services Inc .... A 510 656-9400
  3137 Skyway Ct Fremont (94539) *(P-10891)*

DMS Facility Services Inc .... A 949 975-1366
  2861 E Coronado St Anaheim (92806) *(P-10892)*

DMS Facility Services LLC .... A 949 975-1366
  2861 E Coronado St Anaheim (92806) *(P-19202)*

DMS Facility Services LLC .... A 858 560-4191
  5735 Kearny Villa Rd Ste 108 San Diego (92123) *(P-19203)*

DMS Insurance, San Diego *Also Called: Ue Authority Co (P-10683)*

ALPHABETIC SECTION

DMS Ue Acqisition Holdings Inc .... D 800 466-4178
225 Broadway Ste 2200 San Diego (92101) *(P-9310)*

Dna Specialty Inc .... D 310 767-4070
200 W Artesia Blvd Compton (90220) *(P-5036)*

Dna Twopointo Inc .... D 650 853-8347
37950 Central Ct Newark (94560) *(P-19682)*

Dna2.0, Newark *Also Called: Dna Twopointo Inc (P-19682)*

DNC Parks & Resorts At Sequoia .... C 559 565-4070
64740 Wuksachi Way Ofc C Seq Natl Pk (93262) *(P-9754)*

DNC Prks Resorts At Tenaya Inc (DH) .... C 559 683-6555
1122 Highway 41 Fish Camp (93623) *(P-9755)*

DNC Prks Rsorts At Sequoia Inc .... D 559 565-4070
64740 Wuksachi Way Seq Natl Pk (93262) *(P-9756)*

DNC Prks Rsrts At Yosemite Inc .... A 209 372-1001
9001 Village Dr Yosemite Ntpk (95389) *(P-9757)*

Dneg North America Inc (PA) .... D 323 461-7887
5750 Hannum Ave Ste 100 Culver City (90230) *(P-13933)*

Do It Center, Simi Valley *Also Called: Lumber City Corp (P-7123)*

Docker Inc (PA) .... B 415 941-0376
3790 El Camino Real Ste 1052 Palo Alto (94303) *(P-11548)*

Dockside Machine & Ship Repair, Wilmington *Also Called: Marine Technical Services Inc (P-13363)*

Docmagic Inc .... D 800 649-1362
1800 W 213th St Torrance (90501) *(P-13272)*

Docphin, Sunnyvale *Also Called: Healthtap Inc (P-14770)*

Doctor Genius, Irvine *Also Called: Foundation Lead Group LLC (P-20385)*

Doctor On Demand Inc .... D 310 988-2882
9454 Wilshire Blvd Ste 803 Beverly Hills (90212) *(P-17224)*

Doctors Company Foundation .... A 800 421-2368
185 Greenwood Rd Napa (94558) *(P-8263)*

Doctors Company Insurance Svcs .... B 707 226-0100
185 Greenwood Rd Napa (94558) *(P-8431)*

Doctors Hospital Manteca Inc .... B 209 823-3111
1205 E North St Manteca (95336) *(P-16057)*

Doctors Hospital W Covina Inc .... C 626 338-8481
725 S Orange Ave West Covina (91790) *(P-16058)*

Doctors Insurance Agcy of Cal, Napa *Also Called: Doctors Company Insurance Svcs (P-8431)*

Doctors Management Company (HQ) .... C 707 226-0100
185 Greenwood Rd Napa (94558) *(P-8547)*

Doctors Med Ctr Modesto Inc (HQ) .... B 209 578-1211
1441 Florida Ave Modesto (95350) *(P-16059)*

Doctors Medical Center LLC .... A 510 970-5000
2000 Vale Rd San Pablo (94806) *(P-16060)*

Document Systems, Torrance *Also Called: Docmagic Inc (P-13272)*

Docupace Technologies LLC (PA) .... C 310 445-7722
400 Corporate Pointe Ste 300 Culver City (90230) *(P-11549)*

Docusign Inc (PA) .... B 415 489-4940
221 Main St Ste 1550 San Francisco (94105) *(P-12162)*

Docusource Inc .... D 562 447-2600
13100 Alondra Blvd Ste 108 Cerritos (90703) *(P-7578)*

Dodge & Cox .... C 415 981-1710
555 California St 40th Fl San Francisco (94104) *(P-9367)*

Dodge Ridge Corporation .... B 209 536-5300
1 Dodge Ridge Rd Pinecrest (95364) *(P-9758)*

Dodge Ridge Mtn Resort LLC .... C 209 965-3474
1 Dodge Ridge Rd Pinecrest (95364) *(P-9759)*

Dodge Ridge Winter Sports Area, Pinecrest *Also Called: Dodge Ridge Corporation (P-9758)*

Doheny Eye Institute (PA) .... D 323 342-7120
150 N Orange Grove Blvd Pasadena (91103) *(P-19879)*

Dokken Engineering (PA) .... D 916 858-0642
110 Blue Ravine Rd Ste 200 Folsom (95630) *(P-19204)*

Dolan Concrete Construction .... D 408 869-3250
3045 Alfred St Santa Clara (95054) *(P-2115)*

Dolby, San Francisco *Also Called: Dolby Laboratories Inc (P-2879)*

Dolby Laboratories Inc (PA) .... A 415 558-0200
1275 Market St Fl 15 San Francisco (94103) *(P-2879)*

Dolce International / NAPA LLC .... D 707 257-0200
1600 Atlas Peak Rd Napa (94558) *(P-9760)*

Dole, Monterey *Also Called: Dole Fresh Vegetables Inc (P-2434)*

Dole Fresh Vegetables Inc (HQ) .... C 831 422-8871
2959 Salinas Hwy Monterey (93940) *(P-2434)*

Dole Holding Company LLC .... A 818 879-6600
1 Dole Dr Westlake Village (91362) *(P-115)*

Dolphin Bay Hotel & Residences, Shell Beach *Also Called: Dolphin Bay Ht & Residence Inc (P-9761)*

Dolphin Bay Ht & Residence Inc .... D 805 773-4300
2727 Shell Beach Rd Shell Beach (93449) *(P-9761)*

Dolphin Hkg Ltd (PA) .... D 310 215-3356
1125 W Hillcrest Blvd Inglewood (90301) *(P-6900)*

Dolphin International, Inglewood *Also Called: Dolphin Hkg Ltd (P-6900)*

Domaine Carneros Ltd .... D 707 257-0101
1240 Duhig Rd Napa (94559) *(P-72)*

Domaine Chandon Inc (DH) .... D 707 944-8844
1 California Dr Yountville (94599) *(P-2379)*

Dome Construction Corporation (PA) .... C 650 416-5600
393 E Grand Ave South San Francisco (94080) *(P-905)*

Dominator Radiology Systems, San Diego *Also Called: DR Systems Inc (P-16716)*

Dominguez Landscape Svcs Inc .... D 916 381-8855
7945 14th Ave Sacramento (95826) *(P-486)*

Dominguez Law Group PC .... D 213 388-7788
3250 Wilshire Blvd Ste 1750 Los Angeles (90010) *(P-17439)*

Dominican Hospital Foundation (DH) .... C 831 462-7700
1555 Soquel Dr Santa Cruz (95065) *(P-16061)*

Dominican Hospital Foundation .... C 831 457-7057
610 Frederick St Santa Cruz (95062) *(P-18417)*

Dominican Oaks Corporation .... D 831 462-6257
3400 Paul Sweet Rd Ofc Santa Cruz (95065) *(P-8801)*

Dominican Rehab Services, Santa Cruz *Also Called: Dominican Hospital Foundation (P-18417)*

Domino Data Lab Inc (PA) .... C 415 570-2425
135 Townsend St San Francisco (94107) *(P-11550)*

Domino Foods Inc .... C 510 787-2121
830 Loring Ave Crockett (94525) *(P-6626)*

Domino Realty Management Co .... D 714 556-0466
3700 S Plaza Dr Ofc Santa Ana (92704) *(P-8802)*

Don Francisco Cheese, Modesto *Also Called: Rizo Lopez Foods Inc (P-2346)*

Don Turner and Associates, Fresno *Also Called: Turner Camera SEC Systems Inc (P-13152)*

Donaghey Sales Inc (PA) .... C 559 486-0901
2363 S Cedar Ave Fresno (93725) *(P-6761)*

Donahue Gallager Woods LLP .... D 415 381-4161
1999 Harrison St Ste 2500 Oakland (94612) *(P-17440)*

Donahue Schrber Rlty Group Inc (PA) .... D 714 545-1400
200 Baker St Ste 100 Costa Mesa (92626) *(P-8986)*

Donahue Schriber Rlty Group LP (PA) .... D 714 545-1400
200 Baker St Ste 100 Costa Mesa (92626) *(P-8716)*

Donald J Schefflers Cnstr, Azusa *Also Called: Heidi Corporation (P-2127)*

Donald T Sterling Corporation .... D 310 275-5575
10300 Wilshire Blvd Los Angeles (90024) *(P-9762)*

Donations With Care .... D 916 544-3080
6220 Winding Way Carmichael (95608) *(P-17957)*

Donor Network West (PA) .... C 925 480-3100
12667 Alcosta Blvd Ste 500 San Ramon (94583) *(P-17225)*

Dons Mobile Glass Inc (PA) .... D 209 548-7000
3800 Finch Rd Modesto (95357) *(P-7114)*

Doorking, Inglewood *Also Called: Doorking Inc (P-2957)*

Doorking Inc (PA) .... C 310 645-0023
120 S Glasgow Ave Inglewood (90301) *(P-2957)*

Doose Landscape Incorporated .... D 760 591-4500
785 E Mission Rd San Marcos (92069) *(P-487)*

Dorado Network Systems Corp .... C 650 227-7300
40 Pacifica Irvine (92618) *(P-12163)*

Dorado Software Inc .... D 916 673-1100
4805 Golden Foothill Pkwy El Dorado Hills (95762) *(P-11551)*

Dorean Enterprises Inc .... D 714 992-2900
212 Catalina Rd Fullerton (92835) *(P-10610)*

Doremus & Company .... D 415 273-7800
720 California St Fl 6 San Francisco (94108) *(P-10611)*

Dorfman Milano Company (HQ) .... C 209 982-1400
2615 Boeing Way Stockton (95206) *(P-6172)*

Dorfman Pacific, Stockton *Also Called: Dorfman Milano Company (P-6172)*

Dorothy Johnson Center, Chico *Also Called: Chico Area Recreation & Pk Dst (P-14506)*

Dorothy Sarkozy .... C 858 259-0555
3810 Valley Centre Dr Ste 906 San Diego (92130) *(P-8987)*

Dos Gringos, Vista *Also Called: Gringo Ventures LLC (P-6860)*

DOT Foods Inc .... C...... 209 581-9090
2200 Nickerson Dr Modesto (95358) *(P-6250)*

DOT Printer Inc .... D...... 714 335-7012
9700 Toledo Way Irvine (92618) *(P-3699)*

DOT Printer Warehouse, Irvine *Also Called: DOT Printer Inc (P-3699)*

Dotsolved Systems Inc .... C...... 925 218-6903
4900 Hopyard Rd Pleasanton (94588) *(P-11552)*

Doty Bros Equipment Co (HQ) .... D...... **562 864-6566**
11232 Firestone Blvd Norwalk (90650) *(P-1206)*

Double Diamond Dairy & Ranch .... D...... 209 722-8505
729 E Jefferson Rd El Nido (95317) *(P-215)*

Double Eagle Trnsp Corp .... C...... 760 956-3770
12135 Scarbrough Ct Oak Hills (92344) *(P-3466)*

Double Forte .... D...... 415 863-4900
351 California St Ste 450 San Francisco (94104) *(P-20347)*

Double Tree Past Acute, Sacramento *Also Called: Sacramento Operating Co LP (P-15648)*

Doubleco Incorporated .... D...... 909 481-0799
9444 9th St Rancho Cucamonga (91730) *(P-2749)*

Doubledutch Inc (DH) .... D...... **800 748-9024**
44 Tehama St Ste 504 San Francisco (94105) *(P-12164)*

Doubletree, Campbell *Also Called: Doubltree By Hlton Ht Campbell (P-9763)*

Doubletree By Hilton, Monrovia *Also Called: Doubltree By Hlton Ht Monrovia (P-9764)*

Doubletree By Hilton, San Diego *Also Called: Gringteam Inc (P-9824)*

Doubletree By Hilton, San Diego *Also Called: San Diego Lessee LLC (P-10196)*

Doubletree By Hilton Carson, Carson *Also Called: Carson Operating Company LLC (P-9682)*

Doubletree By Hilton San Jose, San Jose *Also Called: San Jose Lessee LLC (P-10201)*

Doubletree Golf Resort, San Diego *Also Called: Gringteam Inc (P-9822)*

Doubletree Hotel, Torrance *Also Called: Ctc Group Inc (P-9731)*

Doubletree Hotel, Santa Barbara *Also Called: Fess Prker-Red Lion Gen Partnr (P-9796)*

Doubletree Hotel, Modesto *Also Called: Gringteam Inc (P-9823)*

Doubletree Hotel, Burlingame *Also Called: Gringteam Inc (P-9825)*

Doubletree Hotel, Dana Point *Also Called: Gringteam Inc (P-9826)*

Doubletree Hotel, Irvine *Also Called: Spectrum Hotel Group LLC (P-10260)*

Doubletree Hotel, Commerce *Also Called: W2005 Wyn Hotels LP (P-10351)*

Doubletree Hotel Boston, Los Angeles *Also Called: L-O Bedford Operating LLC (P-9957)*

Doubletree Ht San Diego Dwntwn, San Diego *Also Called: Harbor View Hotel Ventures LLC (P-9836)*

Doubletree Rosemead Hotel, Rosemead *Also Called: Sunshine Inn A Cal Ltd Partnr (P-10285)*

Doubletree San Diego Del Mar, San Diego *Also Called: Swvp Del Mar Hotel LLC (P-10294)*

Doubltree By Hilton Ht Modesto, Modesto *Also Called: Modesto Hospitality LLC (P-10021)*

Doubltree By Hlton Ht Bkrsfeld, Bakersfield *Also Called: Gringteam Inc (P-9827)*

Doubltree By Hlton Ht Campbell .... D...... 408 559-4300
1995 S Bascom Ave Campbell (95008) *(P-9763)*

Doubltree By Hlton Ht Monrovia .... C...... 626 357-1900
924 W Huntington Dr Monrovia (91016) *(P-9764)*

Doubltree By Hlton Ht Snoma Wi, Rohnert Park *Also Called: Park US Lessee Holdings LLC (P-10106)*

Doubltree By Hlton Ontrio Arpr, Ontario *Also Called: Dt Ontrio Ht Prtners Lssee LLC (P-9766)*

Doubltree Ht Anhim-Orange Cnty, Orange *Also Called: Anaheim Ca LLC (P-9609)*

Doubltree Los Angeles Westside, Culver City *Also Called: Crp Centinela LP (P-9730)*

Doubltree Palm Sprng Golf Rsor, Cathedral City *Also Called: T Allance One - Palm Sprng LLC (P-14567)*

Doubltree Stes By Hlton Anheim, Anaheim *Also Called: Orangewood LLC (P-10070)*

Doubltree Stes By Hlton Snta M, Santa Monica *Also Called: Santa Monica Hotel Owner LLC (P-10208)*

Doudell Trucking Company (PA) .... D...... **408 263-7300**
1505 N 4th St San Jose (95112) *(P-3467)*

Doug Mockett & Company Inc .... D...... 310 318-2491
1915 Abalone Ave Torrance (90501) *(P-2487)*

Doug Veerkamp General Engineering Inc (PA) .... C...... **530 626-0825**
2585 Cold Springs Rd Placerville (95667) *(P-1097)*

Douglas Fir Holdings LLC .... C...... 714 842-5551
8382 Newman Ave Huntington Beach (92647) *(P-15426)*

Douglas Steel Supply Inc (PA) .... D...... **323 587-7676**
4804 Laurel Canyon Blvd Valley Village (91607) *(P-5488)*

DOUGLAS STEEL SUPPLY CO., Valley Village *Also Called: Douglas Steel Supply Inc (P-5488)*

Doulas By Bay LLC .... D...... 415 510-9736
1201 Liberty St El Cerrito (94530) *(P-17226)*

Doulas By The Bay, El Cerrito *Also Called: Doulas By Bay LLC (P-17226)*

Doval Industries Inc .... D...... 323 226-0335
3961 N Mission Rd Los Angeles (90031) *(P-2729)*

Doval Industries Co, Los Angeles *Also Called: Doval Industries Inc (P-2729)*

Dowell Schlumberger, Bakersfield *Also Called: Schlumberger Technology Corp (P-628)*

Dowling Advisory Group .... D...... 626 319-1369
3579 E Foothill Blvd Ste 651 Pasadena (91107) *(P-20348)*

Downey Brand LLP (PA) .... C...... **916 444-1000**
621 Capitol Mall Fl 18 Sacramento (95814) *(P-17441)*

Downey Care Center, Downey *Also Called: Ensign Group Inc (P-15451)*

Downey Civic Theatre, Downey *Also Called: City of Downey (P-14034)*

Downey Community Health Center .... C...... 562 862-6506
8425 Iowa St Downey (90241) *(P-15427)*

Downey Regional Medical Center, Downey *Also Called: Pih Health Hospital - Whitti (P-16326)*

Downtown Berkeley YMCA, Berkeley *Also Called: Young MNS Chrstn Assn of E Bay (P-18971)*

Downtown Diversion Inc .... D...... 213 612-5005
2424 E Olympic Blvd Los Angeles (90021) *(P-4883)*

Downtown Palo Alto Kindercare, Palo Alto *Also Called: Childrens Crative Lrng Ctr Inc (P-18291)*

Downtown Streets Inc .... D...... 650 462-1795
1671 The Alameda San Jose (95126) *(P-17958)*

DOWNTOWN STREETS TEAM, San Jose *Also Called: Downtown Streets Inc (P-17958)*

Doximity Inc (PA) .... A...... **650 549-4330**
500 3rd St Ste 510 San Francisco (94107) *(P-11553)*

Dozuki .... D...... 805 464-0573
1105 Higuera St Ste 100 San Luis Obispo (93401) *(P-12165)*

Dpi Specialty Foods, Ontario *Also Called: Dpi Specialty Foods West Inc (P-6251)*

Dpi Specialty Foods West Inc (DH) .... C...... **909 975-1019**
601 S Rockefeller Ave Ontario (91761) *(P-6251)*

Dpi Specialty Foods West Inc .... C...... 909 975-1019
930 S Rockefeller Ave Ontario (91761) *(P-6252)*

Dpi West, Ontario *Also Called: Dpi Specialty Foods West Inc (P-6252)*

Dpp Real Estate, Sierra Madre *Also Called: Deasy Penner Podley (P-8976)*

Dpr Construction, Redwood City *Also Called: Dpr Construction A Gen Partnr (P-911)*

Dpr Construction (PA) .... A...... **650 474-1450**
1450 Veterans Blvd Redwood City (94063) *(P-906)*

Dpr Construction A Gen Partnr .... C...... 408 370-2322
1510 S Winchester Blvd San Jose (95128) *(P-907)*

Dpr Construction A Gen Partnr .... C...... 916 568-3434
1801 J St Sacramento (95811) *(P-908)*

Dpr Construction A Gen Partnr .... C...... 626 463-1265
88 W Colorado Blvd Ste 301 Pasadena (91105) *(P-909)*

Dpr Construction A Gen Partnr 858 646-0757
5010 Shoreham Pl Ste 100 San Diego (92122) *(P-910)*

Dpr Construction A Gen Partnr (HQ) .... A...... **650 474-1450**
1450 Veterans Blvd Redwood City (94063) *(P-911)*

DR Horton Inc .... D...... 951 272-9000
2280 Wardlow Cir Ste 100 Corona (92878) *(P-789)*

Dr Pepper Snapple Group, Riverside *Also Called: American Bottling Company (P-2398)*

Dr Squatch LLC .... C...... 631 229-7068
4065 Glencoe Ave Apt 300b Marina Del Rey (90292) *(P-2627)*

DR Systems Inc .... C...... 858 625-3344
10140 Mesa Rim Rd San Diego (92121) *(P-16716)*

Draeger Construction Inc .... A
605 Commercial St San Jose (95112) *(P-912)*

Dragados USA, Elk Grove *Also Called: Dragados Usa Inc (P-1099)*

Dragados Usa Inc .... D...... 657 229-7800
3200 Park Center Dr Ste 600 Costa Mesa (92626) *(P-1098)*

Dragados Usa Inc .... C...... 916 738-9927
5050 Laguna Blvd Ste 112 Elk Grove (95758) *(P-1099)*

Dragon Trade Intl Corp .... C...... 619 816-6062
614 5th Ave Ste D San Diego (92101) *(P-5601)*

Dragonfly Investments Group, Hayward *Also Called: Veev Group Inc (P-8173)*

Drakaina Logistics .... D...... 559 765-1347
958 Ryan Ave Clovis (93611) *(P-4151)*

Drake Haglan & Associates, Rancho Cordova *Also Called: Dewberry Engineers Inc (P-19198)*

Dramm and Echter Inc .... D...... 760 436-0188
1150 Quail Gardens Dr Encinitas (92024) *(P-124)*

ALPHABETIC SECTION — Dual Diagnosis Trtmnt Ctr Inc

Drawbridge Inc .... D....... 650 513-2323
479 N Pastoria Ave Sunnyvale (94085) *(P-20349)*

Drd Hospitality Inc .... C....... 916 952-6552
179 Commerce Ave Manteca (95336) *(P-9765)*

Dream Corps .... D....... 510 663-6500
436 14th St Ste 920 Oakland (94612) *(P-19081)*

Dream Hollywood, Los Angeles *Also Called: 6417 Selma Hotel LLC (P-9595)*

Dream Home Care Inc .... D....... 562 595-9021
20695 S Western Ave Ste 132 Torrance (90501) *(P-18418)*

Dream Mortgage Group, Brea *Also Called: Emet Lending Group Inc (P-7959)*

Dreamcatchers Empowerment, Fairfield *Also Called: Dreamctchers Empwerment Netwrk (P-18227)*

Dreamctchers Empwerment Netwrk .... A....... 707 558-1775
1125 Missouri St Fairfield (94533) *(P-18227)*

Dreamhost.com, Los Angeles *Also Called: New Dream Network LLC (P-4319)*

Dreamhost.com, Brea *Also Called: New Dream Network LLC (P-12697)*

Dreamteam Logistics LLC .... D....... 818 300-7785
8605 Santa Monica Blvd West Hollywood (90069) *(P-4152)*

Dreamworks Animation Pubg LLC .... A....... 818 695-5000
1000 Flower St Glendale (91201) *(P-13843)*

Dreier's Nursing Care Center, Glendale *Also Called: Ksm Healthcare Inc (P-15532)*

Dreisbach Enterprises Inc .... D....... 510 533-6600
2530 E 11th St Oakland (94601) *(P-8883)*

Dresser/Areia Construction .... C....... 800 392-9891
3940 Valley Ave Pleasanton (94566) *(P-1207)*

Drew Chain Security Corp .... D....... 626 457-8626
55 S Raymond Ave Ste 303 Alhambra (91801) *(P-12966)*

Drew Child Dev Corp Inc (PA) .... D....... 323 249-2950
1770 E 118th St Los Angeles (90059) *(P-17959)*

Drew Child Dev Corp Inc .... D....... 310 638-8108
3737 Martin Luther King Jr Blvd Ste 201 Lynwood (90262) *(P-18309)*

Drew Ford .... C....... 619 464-7777
8970 La Mesa Blvd La Mesa (91942) *(P-7196)*

Drew Hyundai, La Mesa *Also Called: Drew Ford (P-7196)*

Dreyer Babich Buccola Wood CAM .... D....... 530 889-1800
195 Cherry Ave Auburn (95603) *(P-17442)*

Dreyers Grand Ice Cream Inc .... B....... 209 823-4343
1351 Dupont Ct Manteca (95336) *(P-6435)*

Dreyers Grnd Ice Cream Hldngs (DH) .... C....... 510 652-8187
5929 College Ave Oakland (94618) *(P-6436)*

Dri Commercial Corporation .... C....... 949 266-1900
2081 Business Center Dr Ste 195 Irvine (92612) *(P-2057)*

Dri Companies .... B....... 949 266-1900
2081 Business Center Dr Ste 195 Irvine (92612) *(P-2058)*

Driftwood Health Care Ctr, Torrance *Also Called: Mariner Health Care Inc (P-15560)*

Driftwood Healthcare Center, Hayward *Also Called: Mariner Health Care Inc (P-15574)*

Drill Tech Drilling & Shoring Inc (PA) .... D....... 925 978-2060
2200 Wymore Way Antioch (94509) *(P-1296)*

Drillmec Inc .... D....... 281 885-0777
8140 Rosecrans Ave Paramount (90723) *(P-599)*

Drip Hydration .... D....... 323 333-9634
11948 Gorham Ave Apt 3 Los Angeles (90049) *(P-17227)*

Driscolls Inc (PA) .... D....... 831 424-0506
345 Westridge Dr Watsonville (95076) *(P-6534)*

Driscolls Inc .... D....... 800 871-3333
150 Westridge Dr Watsonville (95076) *(P-6535)*

Drishti Technologies Inc .... C....... 214 748-3647
800 W El Camino Real Ste 180 Mountain View (94040) *(P-11554)*

Driveai Inc .... C....... 408 693-0765
365 Ravendale Dr Mountain View (94043) *(P-12166)*

Drivenbi LLC .... D....... 626 795-2088
1606 Camino Lindo South Pasadena (91030) *(P-11555)*

Driver Inc .... D....... 415 999-4960
438 Shotwell St San Francisco (94110) *(P-12167)*

Drivesavers Inc .... D....... 415 382-2000
400 Bel Marin Keys Blvd Novato (94949) *(P-12659)*

Drivesavers Data Recovery, Novato *Also Called: Drivesavers Inc (P-12659)*

Drobo, Sunnyvale *Also Called: Drobo Inc (P-5296)*

Drobo Inc .... D....... 408 454-4200
1289 Anvilwood Ave Sunnyvale (94089) *(P-5296)*

Drohan Trade Center, Rancho Cordova *Also Called: McKesson Corporation (P-6127)*

Droisys Inc (PA) .... D....... 408 874-8333
46540 Fremont Blvd Ste 516 Fremont (94538) *(P-12449)*

Droisys Inc .... C....... 408 329-1761
4657 Hedgewick Ave Fremont (94538) *(P-12780)*

Dronebase Inc (PA) .... D....... 310 684-3076
2800 Olympic Blvd Fl 2 Santa Monica (90404) *(P-10796)*

Dropbox, San Francisco *Also Called: Dropbox Inc (P-12168)*

Dropbox Inc (PA) .... A....... 415 857-6800
1800 Owens St Ste 200 San Francisco (94158) *(P-12168)*

Dropzone Waterpark .... C....... 951 210-1600
2165 Trumble Rd Perris (92571) *(P-14514)*

Drs Daylight Solutions, San Diego *Also Called: Daylight Solutions Inc (P-2916)*

Drs Network & Imaging Systems, Cypress *Also Called: Drs Ntwork Imaging Systems LLC (P-2917)*

Drs Ntwork Imaging Systems LLC .... D....... 714 220-3800
10600 Valley View St Cypress (90630) *(P-2917)*

Drug Abuse Alternatives Center .... C....... 707 571-2233
2403 Professional Dr Ste 103 Santa Rosa (95403) *(P-17055)*

Dryco Construction Inc (PA) .... C....... 510 438-6500
42745 Boscell Rd Fremont (94538) *(P-1100)*

Drymaster, Mission Viejo *Also Called: Dimar Enterprises Inc (P-10890)*

Ds Lakeshore, Costa Mesa *Also Called: Donahue Schriber Rlty Group LP (P-8716)*

Ds Lakeshore LP .... D....... 916 286-5231
200 Baker St Ste 100 Costa Mesa (92626) *(P-18852)*

Dsca, Long Beach *Also Called: Denso Pdts & Svcs Americas Inc (P-5035)*

Dsd Trucking Inc .... D....... 310 338-3395
2411 Santa Fe Ave Redondo Beach (90278) *(P-3891)*

DSI Process Systems LLC .... C....... 314 382-1525
7595 Reynolds Cir Huntington Beach (92647) *(P-5829)*

Dsl Laboratories, Salida *Also Called: Silliker Inc (P-20001)*

DSM Biomedical Inc .... C....... 510 841-8800
2810 7th St Berkeley (94710) *(P-19683)*

DSP Concepts Inc (PA) .... C....... 408 747-5200
3235 Kifer Rd Ste 100 Santa Clara (95051) *(P-19205)*

Dsp Group, San Jose *Also Called: Dsp Group Inc (P-2918)*

Dsp Group Inc (HQ) .... D....... 408 986-4300
2055 Gateway Pl Ste 480 San Jose (95110) *(P-2918)*

Dss, Calabasas *Also Called: David Shield Security Inc (P-12963)*

Dssv Inc .... B....... 415 216-8495
548 Market St Pmb 95237 San Francisco (94104) *(P-17228)*

DSV, Fontana *Also Called: DSV Solutions LLC (P-3790)*

DSV Solutions LLC .... C....... 909 829-5804
13032 Slover Ave Ste 200 Fontana (92337) *(P-3790)*

DSV Solutions LLC .... C....... 909 349-6100
13230 San Bernardino Ave Fontana (92335) *(P-4010)*

DSV Solutions LLC .... C....... 909 390-4563
1670 Etiwanda Ave Ste A Ontario (91761) *(P-4011)*

DSV Solutions LLC .... D....... 714 630-0110
3454 E Miraloma Ave Anaheim (92806) *(P-4012)*

Dt Club Hotel Santa Ana, Santa Ana *Also Called: Jhc Investment Inc (P-9919)*

Dt Ontrio Ht Prtners Lssee LLC .... D....... 909 937-0900
222 N Vineyard Ave Ontario (91764) *(P-9766)*

Dti Services Inc (PA) .... D....... 213 670-1100
601 S Figueroa St Ste 4300 Los Angeles (90017) *(P-12781)*

Dtiq Holdings Inc .... C....... 323 576-1400
1755 N Main St Los Angeles (90031) *(P-13107)*

DTL Transport Inc .... D....... 559 277-9075
4375 N Golden State Blvd Fresno (93722) *(P-4153)*

Dtrs Santa Monica LLC .... B....... 310 458-6700
1700 Ocean Ave Santa Monica (90401) *(P-9767)*

Dtrs St Francis LLC .... C....... 415 397-7000
335 Powell St San Francisco (94102) *(P-9768)*

Dts, Sacramento *Also Called: California Department Tech (P-12747)*

Dts Inc (DH) .... C....... 818 436-1000
5220 Las Virgenes Rd Calabasas (91302) *(P-13934)*

Dtt, Los Angeles *Also Called: Dtiq Holdings Inc (P-13107)*

Dtz, Westlake Village *Also Called: C&W Facility Services Inc (P-10868)*

Dual Diagnosis Trtmnt Ctr Inc (PA) .... C....... 949 276-5553
1211 Puerta Del Sol # 200 San Clemente (92673) *(P-17056)*

Dual Diagnosis Trtmnt Ctr Inc .... C...... 949 324-4531
69640 Highway 111 Rancho Mirage (92270) *(P-17229)*

Duane Morris LLP .... D...... 415 957-3000
1 Market Plz Ste 2200 San Francisco (94105) *(P-17443)*

Duarte Manor, Los Angeles *Also Called: Emp III Inc (P-9507)*

Duarte Nursery Inc .... B...... 209 887-3409
23456 E Flood Rd Linden (95236) *(P-125)*

Duarte Nursery Inc .... B...... 209 531-0351
1555 Baldwin Rd Hughson (95326) *(P-126)*

Duarte Properties, Hughson *Also Called: Duarte Nursery Inc (P-126)*

Dublin Dodge, Dublin *Also Called: Dublin Volkswagen (P-7197)*

Dublin Honda, Dublin *Also Called: Harvey & Madding Inc (P-7231)*

Dublin San Ramon Services Dst (PA) .... C...... 925 875-2276
7051 Dublin Blvd Dublin (94568) *(P-4785)*

Dublin Volkswagen .... D...... 925 829-0800
6085 Scarlett Ct Dublin (94568) *(P-7197)*

Dubnoff Ctr For Child Dev Edct (PA) .... D...... 818 755-4950
10526 Dubnoff Way North Hollywood (91606) *(P-17709)*

Ducey's On The Lake, Bass Lake *Also Called: Pines Resorts of California (P-7503)*

Duckor Mtzger Wynne A Prof Law .... D...... 619 209-3000
101 W Broadway Ste 1700 San Diego (92101) *(P-17444)*

Ducommun Labarge Tech Inc (HQ) .... C...... 310 513-7200
23301 Wilmington Ave Carson (90745) *(P-2990)*

Duda Mobile Inc 855 790-0003
577 College Ave Palo Alto (94306) *(P-12169)*

Dudek Inc (PA) .... D...... 760 942-5147
605 3rd St Encinitas (92024) *(P-19206)*

Duetto Research Inc .... C...... 415 968-9389
333 Bush St Ste 1200 San Francisco (94104) *(P-11556)*

Duggan & Associates Inc .... D...... 323 965-1502
1442 W 135th St Gardena (90249) *(P-1613)*

Duke Pacific Inc .... D...... 909 591-0191
13950 Monte Vista Ave Chino (91710) *(P-2059)*

Dunamis Center Inc .... D...... 530 338-0087
1465 Victor Ave Ste B Redding (96003) *(P-17057)*

Dunamis Ctr Cunseling Wellness, Redding *Also Called: Dunamis Center Inc (P-17057)*

Dunn & Berger Inc .... B...... 818 986-1234
5955 De Soto Ave Ste 160 Woodland Hills (91367) *(P-16855)*

Duplo, Santa Ana *Also Called: Duplo USA Corporation (P-5245)*

Duplo USA Corporation (PA) .... D...... 949 752-8222
3050 Daimler St Santa Ana (92705) *(P-5245)*

Dupont Displays Inc .... C...... 805 562-5400
600 Ward Dr Ste C Santa Barbara (93111) *(P-19684)*

Dura Freight Lines, Walnut *Also Called: Tropicana Manufacturing Co Inc (P-3771)*

Dura-Metrics Inc (PA) .... D...... 707 546-5138
2628 El Camino Ave Ste B1 Sacramento (95821) *(P-16771)*

Duracite, Fairfield *Also Called: Halabi Inc (P-2716)*

Durago, Rancho Dominguez *Also Called: Iap West Inc (P-5045)*

Durham School Services, Campbell *Also Called: Durham School Services L P (P-3330)*

Durham School Services, Grass Valley *Also Called: Durham School Services L P (P-3332)*

Durham School Services L P .... C...... 310 767-5820
723 S Alameda St Compton (90220) *(P-3325)*

Durham School Services L P .... C...... 562 408-1206
8555 Flower Ave Paramount (90723) *(P-3326)*

Durham School Services L P .... C...... 925 606-0871
379 Earhart Way Livermore (94551) *(P-3327)*

Durham School Services L P .... C...... 818 880-4257
4029 Las Virgenes Rd Calabasas (91302) *(P-3328)*

Durham School Services L P .... C...... 909 899-1809
12999 Victoria St Rancho Cucamonga (91739) *(P-3329)*

Durham School Services L P .... C...... 833 698-7474
1506 White Oaks Rd Campbell (95008) *(P-3330)*

Durham School Services L P .... C...... 805 483-6076
3151 W 5th St Ste A Oxnard (93030) *(P-3331)*

Durham School Services L P .... C...... 530 273-7282
10701 E Bennett Rd Grass Valley (95945) *(P-3332)*

Durham School Services L P .... A...... 626 573-3769
2713 River Ave Rosemead (91770) *(P-3333)*

Durham School Services L P .... C...... 949 376-0376
2003 Laguna Canyon Rd Laguna Beach (92651) *(P-3334)*

Durham School Services L P .... B...... 714 542-8989
2818 W 5th St Santa Ana (92703) *(P-3355)*

Durkee Drayage Company .... D...... 510 970-7550
539 Stone Rd Benicia (94510) *(P-3585)*

Dutra Dredging Company (HQ) .... D...... 415 721-2131
2350 Kerner Blvd Ste 200 San Rafael (94901) *(P-1297)*

Dutra Group (PA) .... D...... 415 258-6876
2350 Kerner Blvd Ste 200 San Rafael (94901) *(P-1298)*

Dutra Group, The, San Rafael *Also Called: Dutra Group (P-1298)*

Dutra Materials, San Rafael *Also Called: San Rafael Rock Quarry Inc (P-635)*

Dv Custom Farming LLC .... D...... 661 858-2888
2101 Mettler Frontage Rd E Bakersfield (93307) *(P-176)*

DVeal Corporation .... C...... 626 296-8900
2750 E Washington Blvd Ste 230 Pasadena (91107) *(P-18585)*

Dvm Insurance Agency, Brea *Also Called: Veterinary Pet Insurance Services Inc (P-8681)*

DW Morgan LLC .... D...... 925 460-2700
4185 Blackhawk Plaza Cir Ste 260 Danville (94506) *(P-4154)*

DWA, Palm Springs *Also Called: Desert Water Agency Fing Corp (P-4784)*

Dwa Holdings LLC (DH) .... D...... 818 695-5000
1000 Flower St Glendale (91201) *(P-13844)*

Dwa Media, San Francisco *Also Called: David Wood and Associates Inc (P-10709)*

Dwayne Nash Industries Inc .... C...... 916 253-1900
8825 Washington Blvd Ste 100 Roseville (95678) *(P-2060)*

Dy-Dee Service Pasadena Inc .... D...... 626 792-6183
40 E California Blvd Pasadena (91105) *(P-10485)*

Dynalectric Company .... B...... 619 328-4007
1111 Pioneer Way El Cajon (92020) *(P-1722)*

Dynamic Auto Images Inc .... B...... 714 771-3400
2860 Michelle Ste 140 Irvine (92606) *(P-13692)*

Dynamic Detail, Irvine *Also Called: Dynamic Auto Images Inc (P-13692)*

Dynamic Home Care, Sherman Oaks *Also Called: Dynamic Home Care Service Inc (P-16856)*

Dynamic Home Care Service Inc (PA) .... D...... 818 981-4446
14260 Ventura Blvd Ste 301 Sherman Oaks (91423) *(P-16856)*

Dynamic Plumbing Systems Inc .... B...... 951 343-1200
5920 Winterhaven Ave Riverside (92504) *(P-1423)*

Dynamic Staffing, Roseville *Also Called: Calabria Group Inc (P-11101)*

Dynamic Trades Inc .... D...... 530 701-8138
4617 Weed Patch Ct Greenwood (95635) *(P-6901)*

Dynapower Company LLC .... C...... 802 860-7200
2913 Whipple Rd Union City (94587) *(P-5830)*

Dynasty Marketplace Inc .... B...... 804 837-0119
716 Hampton Dr Venice (90291) *(P-11557)*

Dynavax Technologies Corp (PA) .... D...... 510 848-5100
2100 Powell St 7th Fl Emeryville (94608) *(P-2621)*

Dynegy, Moss Landing *Also Called: Dynegy Marketing & Trade LLC (P-4570)*

Dynegy Marketing & Trade LLC .... D...... 831 633-6700
Hwy 1 & Dolan Rd Moss Landing (95039) *(P-4570)*

Dynegy Moss Landing LLC .... D...... 831 633-6618
7301 Highway 1 Moss Landing (95039) *(P-4571)*

Dyntek Inc (PA) .... C...... 949 271-6700
5241 California Ave Ste 150 Irvine (92617) *(P-12782)*

Dzkicorp Inc 805 464-0573
762 Higuera St Ste 216 San Luis Obispo (93401) *(P-11558)*

E & B Marine, Watsonville *Also Called: E & B Marine Inc (P-7393)*

E & B Marine Inc (HQ) .... D...... 831 728-2700
500 Westridge Dr Watsonville (95076) *(P-7393)*

E & B Ntral Resources Mgt Corp (PA) .... D...... 661 679-1714
1608 Norris Rd Bakersfield (93308) *(P-600)*

E & C Fashion Inc .... B...... 323 262-0099
1420 Esperanza St Los Angeles (90023) *(P-13273)*

E & E Co Ltd (PA) .... C...... 510 490-9788
45875 Northport Loop E Fremont (94538) *(P-5115)*

E & J Gallo Winery (PA) .... A...... 209 341-3111
600 Yosemite Blvd Modesto (95354) *(P-2380)*

E & J Gallo Winery .... C...... 559 458-0807
5610 E Olive Ave Fresno (93727) *(P-2381)*

E & J Gallo Winery .... D...... 209 394-6200
18000 River Rd Livingston (95334) *(P-2382)*

E & S International Entps Inc (PA) .... C...... 818 887-0700
7801 Hayvenhurst Ave Van Nuys (91406) *(P-5602)*

ALPHABETIC SECTION

East Bay Mncpl Utlity Dst Wtr

E & S Ring Management Corp .... D....... 310 821-4916
  4600 Via Marina Apt 209 Marina Del Rey (90292) *(P-8988)*

E B Stone & Son Inc .... D....... 707 426-2500
  6111 Lambie Rd Suisun City (94585) *(P-6823)*

E C R M C, El Centro *Also Called: El Centro Rgnal Med Ctr Fndtio (P-16072)*

E C S-Elitegroup Cmpt Systems, Newark *Also Called: Elitegroup Computer Systems Ho (P-5297)*

E Center .... C....... 530 634-1200
  1506 Starr Dr Yuba City (95993) *(P-18310)*

E E G and E P, Chico *Also Called: Enloe Medical Center (P-16082)*

E Entertainment Television Inc .... A....... 323 954-2400
  5750 Wilshire Blvd # 500 Los Angeles (90036) *(P-4507)*

E Film Digital Labratories, Los Angeles *Also Called: Efilm LLC (P-13845)*

E G I A, Sacramento *Also Called: Electric & Gas Industries Association (P-18708)*

E H Summit Inc (PA) .... D....... 310 476-6571
  11461 W Sunset Blvd Los Angeles (90049) *(P-9769)*

E J Harrison & Sons Inc .... C....... 805 647-1414
  1589 Lirio Ave Ventura (93004) *(P-4884)*

E Jordan Brookes Co., Santa Fe Springs *Also Called: The E Jordan Brookes Co Inc (P-5524)*

E L S, Los Angeles *Also Called: J C Entertainment Ltg Svcs Inc (P-14041)*

E La Carte Inc .... D....... 650 468-0680
  985 Industrial Rd Ste 205 San Carlos (94070) *(P-7442)*

E M Tharp Inc (PA) .... D....... 559 782-5800
  15243 Road 192 Porterville (93257) *(P-5007)*

E Management Services LLC .... D....... 818 835-9525
  20010 Ventura Blvd Woodland Hills (91364) *(P-6106)*

E O C Health Services, San Luis Obispo *Also Called: Community Action Prtnr San Lui (P-17031)*

E O S International, Carlsbad *Also Called: Electronic Online Systems International (P-12451)*

E P, Union City *Also Called: Emerald Packaging Inc (P-6902)*

E P I, Irvine *Also Called: Asian European Products Inc (P-5024)*

E P I, San Diego *Also Called: Engineering Partners Inc (P-19215)*

E P U, Fresno *Also Called: Exceptnal Prents Unlimited Inc (P-17971)*

E R I T Inc (PA) .... D....... 760 433-6024
  251 Airport Rd Oceanside (92058) *(P-18419)*

E S 3, San Diego *Also Called: Enginring Sftwr Sys Sltons Inc (P-19216)*

E S I, San Dimas *Also Called: Edgebanding Services Inc (P-6698)*

E Z Services .... D....... 714 635-7599
  1101 W Lincoln Ave Ste 145 Anaheim (92805) *(P-7853)*

E Z Staffing Inc (PA) .... B....... 818 845-2500
  200 N Maryland Ave Ste 303 Glendale (91206) *(P-11126)*

E-Filliate Inc .... D....... 916 858-1000
  11321 White Rock Rd Rancho Cordova (95742) *(P-7560)*

E-Loan Inc (DH) .... A....... 925 847-6200
  6230 Stoneridge Mall Rd Pleasanton (94588) *(P-8039)*

E-Times Corporation (PA) .... B....... 213 452-6720
  601 S Figueroa St Ste 5000 Los Angeles (90017) *(P-12660)*

E. S. Babcock & Sons, Riverside *Also Called: Babcock Laboratories Inc (P-19952)*

E&S Financial Group Inc .... D....... 805 644-1621
  700 E Main St Ventura (93001) *(P-7956)*

E2 Consulting Engineers Inc .... D....... 510 652-1164
  2100 Powell St Ste 850 Emeryville (94608) *(P-19207)*

E2open Inc .... D....... 866 432-6736
  4100 E 3rd Ave Ste 400 Foster City (94404) *(P-11559)*

Ea, Redwood City *Also Called: Electronic Arts Inc (P-12179)*

Ea Mobile Inc .... D....... 310 754-7125
  5510 Lincoln Blvd Los Angeles (90094) *(P-4215)*

Each One Teach One Foundation .... D....... 916 428-5627
  1800 59th Ave Sacramento (95822) *(P-18853)*

Eacom Inc .... C....... 650 628-1500
  209 Redwood Shores Pkwy Redwood City (94065) *(P-11560)*

Eag Holdings LLC .... A....... 408 530-3500
  2710 Walsh Ave Santa Clara (95051) *(P-19966)*

Eagle Ambulance .... D....... 800 304-6985
  3251 Franklin Canyon Rd Rodeo (94572) *(P-3252)*

Eagle Glen Country Club LLC .... D....... 951 272-4653
  1800 Eagle Glen Pkwy Corona (92883) *(P-14258)*

Eagle Glen Golf Club, Corona *Also Called: Eagle Glen Country Club LLC (P-14258)*

Eagle Mountain Casino .... C....... 559 788-6220
  681 South Tule Reservation Road Porterville (93258) *(P-9770)*

Eagle Paving Company Inc .... D....... 858 486-6400
  13915 Danielson St Ste 201 Poway (92064) *(P-1101)*

Eagle Roofing Products, Stockton *Also Called: Burlingame Industries Inc (P-5220)*

Eagle Roofing Products, Rialto *Also Called: Burlingame Industries Inc (P-10414)*

Eagle Security Services Inc .... C....... 310 642-0656
  12903 S Normandie Ave Gardena (90249) *(P-12967)*

Eagle Systems Intl Inc .... B....... 510 259-1700
  28436 Satellite St Hayward (94545) *(P-1424)*

Eagle Topco LP .... A....... 949 585-4329
  18200 Von Karman Ave Irvine (92612) *(P-12170)*

Eagle Vnes Vnyrds Golf CLB LLC .... D....... 707 257-4470
  1733 S Anaheim Blvd Anaheim (92805) *(P-14259)*

Eaglerider Finance LLC .... D....... 310 321-3191
  11860 S La Cienega Blvd Hawthorne (90250) *(P-13274)*

Eah Elena Gardens LP .... C....... 415 295-8840
  2169 Francisco Blvd E Ste B San Rafael (94901) *(P-8803)*

Eah Housing, San Rafael *Also Called: Eah Inc (P-8877)*

Eah Inc (PA) .... D....... 415 258-1800
  22 Pelican Way San Rafael (94901) *(P-8877)*

EAM Enterprises Inc .... D....... 818 951-6464
  8307 Foothill Blvd Sunland (91040) *(P-8989)*

EAM Enterprises Inc (PA) .... D....... 818 248-9100
  4005 Foothill Blvd La Crescenta (91214) *(P-8990)*

Eandm .... D....... 707 473-3137
  126 Mill St Healdsburg (95448) *(P-13758)*

Eappraiseit LLC (PA) .... D....... 800 281-6200
  12395 First American Way Poway (92064) *(P-8991)*

Earl's Organic Produce, San Francisco *Also Called: Earls Organic Produce (P-6536)*

Earle M Jorgensen Company (HQ) .... C....... 323 567-1122
  10650 Alameda St Lynwood (90262) *(P-5489)*

Earle M Jorgensen Company .... C....... 510 487-2700
  31100 Wiegman Rd Hayward (94544) *(P-5490)*

Earle M Jorgensen Company .... D....... 323 567-1122
  350 S Grand Ave Ste 5100 Los Angeles (90071) *(P-5491)*

Earls Organic Produce .... D....... 415 824-7419
  2101 Jerrold Ave Ste 100 San Francisco (94124) *(P-6536)*

Early Childhood Education, La Quinta *Also Called: Desert Snds Unfied Schl Dst SC (P-18306)*

Early Learning Center, Los Angeles *Also Called: California Childrens Academy (P-18273)*

Earnest, San Francisco *Also Called: Earnest Operations LLC (P-8040)*

Earnest Operations LLC .... D....... 888 601-2801
  535 Mission St Ste 1663 San Francisco (94105) *(P-8040)*

Earth Island Institute Inc .... D....... 510 859-9100
  2150 Allston Way Ste 460 Berkeley (94704) *(P-19082)*

Earth Technology Corp USA .... D....... 213 593-8000
  300 S Grand Ave Ste 900 Los Angeles (90071) *(P-4885)*

Earthbound Farm LLC (PA) .... A....... 831 623-7880
  1721 San Juan Hwy San Juan Bautista (95045) *(P-263)*

Earthjustice (PA) .... D....... 415 217-2000
  50 California St Ste 500 San Francisco (94111) *(P-18854)*

Earthjustice Legal Def Fund, San Francisco *Also Called: Earthjustice (P-18854)*

Earthlite, Vista *Also Called: Earthlite LLC (P-2490)*

Earthlite LLC (DH) .... D....... 760 599-1112
  990 Joshua Way Vista (92081) *(P-2490)*

Earthquakes, San Jose *Also Called: Earthquakes Soccer LLC (P-14135)*

Earthquakes Soccer LLC .... D....... 408 556-7700
  1123 Coleman Ave San Jose (95110) *(P-14135)*

Ease Entertainment Services LP .... D....... 310 469-7300
  8383 Wilshire Blvd Ste 90 Beverly Hills (90211) *(P-14081)*

Easihair, Vista *Also Called: Jon Renau Collection Inc (P-6919)*

East Bay Agency For Children .... D....... 510 655-4896
  6117 Martin Luther King J Oakland (94609) *(P-18311)*

East Bay Asian Local Dev Corp .... C....... 510 267-1917
  1825 San Pablo Ave Ste 200 Oakland (94612) *(P-8804)*

East Bay Asian Youth Center .... D....... 510 533-1092
  2025 E 12th St Oakland (94606) *(P-17960)*

East Bay Innovations .... D....... 510 618-1580
  2450 Washington Ave Ste 240 San Leandro (94577) *(P-13275)*

East Bay Mncpl Utlity Dst Wstw .... C....... 209 772-8204
  15083 Camanche Pkwy S Valley Springs (95252) *(P-4786)*

East Bay Mncpl Utlity Dst Wtr (PA) .... A....... 866 403-2683
  375 11th St Oakland (94607) *(P-4787)*

Employee Codes: A=Over 500 employees, B=251-500
C=101-250, D=51-100, E=20-50, F=10-19, G=1-9

2024 Directory of California
WholeSalers and Service Companies

© Mergent Inc. 1-800-342-5647
1111

East Bay Municipl Utilty Distr | ALPHABETIC SECTION

East Bay Municipl Utilty Distr .... C...... 866 403-2683
   2020 Wake Ave Oakland (94607) *(P-4886)*

East Bay Regional Park District (PA).. C...... 888 327-2757
   2950 Peralta Oaks Ct Oakland (94605) *(P-14515)*

East Bay Regional Park Dst .... D...... 510 848-7373
   10 Golf Course Dr Berkeley (94708) *(P-13276)*

East Bay Regional Park Dst .... C...... 510 881-1833
   17930 Lake Chabot Rd Castro Valley (94546) *(P-14516)*

East Bay Restaurant Supply Inc (PA)... C...... 510 465-4300
   49 4th St Oakland (94607) *(P-5377)*

East Bay Rgnal Pk Pub Sfety De, Castro Valley *Also Called: East Bay Regional Park Dst (P-14516)*

East Los Angles Dctors Hosp In .... B
   4060 Whittier Blvd Los Angeles (90023) *(P-16062)*

East Los Angles Healthcare LLC (PA)... D...... 323 268-0106
   1016 S Record Ave Los Angeles (90023) *(P-15428)*

East Los Angles Rmrkble Ctzens .... D...... 323 223-3079
   3839 Selig Pl Los Angeles (90031) *(P-17961)*

East Palo Alto Hotel Dev Inc .... C...... 650 566-1200
   2050 University Ave East Palo Alto (94303) *(P-9771)*

East Side Msqito Abatement Dst, Modesto *Also Called: County of Stanislaus (P-4977)*

East Valley Cmnty Hlth Ctr Inc (PA)... D...... 626 919-3402
   420 S Glendora Ave West Covina (91790) *(P-17058)*

East Valley Glendora Hosp LLC .... B...... 626 852-5000
   150 W Route 66 Glendora (91740) *(P-16063)*

East Valley Tourist Dev Auth .... A...... 760 342-5000
   84245 Indio Springs Dr Indio (92203) *(P-14517)*

East Valley Water District .... D...... 909 889-9501
   31111 Greenspot Rd Highland (92346) *(P-4788)*

EAST WEST, Pasadena *Also Called: East West Bancorp Inc (P-7678)*

EAST WEST, Pasadena *Also Called: East West Bank (P-7679)*

East West Bancorp Inc (PA).. B...... 626 768-6000
   135 N Los Robles Ave Fl 7 Pasadena (91101) *(P-7678)*

East West Bank (HQ).. B...... 626 768-6000
   135 N Los Robles Ave Ste 100 Pasadena (91101) *(P-7679)*

East West Tea Company LLC .... C...... 310 275-9891
   1616 Preuss Rd Los Angeles (90035) *(P-2361)*

Eastbiz Corporation .... C...... 310 212-7134
   3501 Jack Northrop Ave Hawthorne (90250) *(P-14518)*

Easter Seal Soc Superior Cal (PA)... D...... 916 485-6711
   9812 Old Winery Pl Ste 21 Sacramento (95827) *(P-17230)*

Easter Seals Main Office, Sacramento *Also Called: Easter Seal Soc Superior Cal (P-17230)*

Eastern California Museum (PA)... B...... 760 878-0292
   155 N Grant St Independence (93526) *(P-18651)*

Eastern District Office, El Cajon *Also Called: San Diego Gas & Electric Co (P-4671)*

Eastern Goldfields Inc .... C...... 619 497-2555
   1660 Hotel Cir N Ste 207 San Diego (92108) *(P-20350)*

Eastern Los Angeles RE (PA)... C...... 626 299-4700
   1000 S Fremont Ave Unit 23 Alhambra (91803) *(P-17962)*

Eastern Municipal Water Dst (PA)... B...... 951 928-3777
   2270 Trumble Rd Perris (92572) *(P-4789)*

Eastern Municipal Water Dst .... C...... 951 657-7469
   19750 Evans Rd Perris (92571) *(P-4790)*

Eastern Plmas Hlth Care Fndtio (PA)... B...... 530 832-4277
   500 1st Ave Portola (96122) *(P-17231)*

Eastern Plumas Hospital, Portola *Also Called: Eastern Plmas Hlth Care Fndtio (P-17231)*

Eastern Rgnal Lndfill Mtl Rcve, Truckee *Also Called: Tahoe Truckee Disposal Co Inc (P-4943)*

Eastern Staffing LLC .... B...... 805 882-2200
   301 Mentor Dr # 210 Santa Barbara (93111) *(P-11127)*

Easterncctv (usa) LLC .... C...... 626 961-8999
   525 Parriott Pl W City Of Industry (91745) *(P-13108)*

Easton Diamond Sports LLC .... C...... 800 632-7866
   3500 Willow Ln Thousand Oaks (91361) *(P-5977)*

Eastridge Workforce Solutions, San Diego *Also Called: Eplica Corporate Services Inc (P-11132)*

Eastridge Workforce Solutions, San Diego *Also Called: Teg Staffing Inc (P-11244)*

Eastridge Workforce Solutions, San Diego *Also Called: Eplica Inc (P-11284)*

Eastside Management Co Inc .... C...... 209 578-9852
   1131 12th St Ste C Modesto (95354) *(P-373)*

Eastwestproto Inc .... B...... 888 535-5728
   6605 E Washington Blvd Commerce (90040) *(P-3253)*

Easy Care Mso LLC .... C...... 562 676-9600
   3780 Kilroy Airport Way Ste 530 Long Beach (90806) *(P-17232)*

Easy Fuel, Aliso Viejo *Also Called: Efuel LLC (P-6728)*

Easy Fuel Inc .... D...... 408 280-5235
   1346 E Taylor St San Jose (95133) *(P-6727)*

Eataly Inc .... D...... 213 310-8000
   10250 Santa Monica Blvd Los Angeles (90067) *(P-7475)*

Eaton Aerospace LLC .... B...... 818 409-0200
   4690 Colorado Blvd Los Angeles (90039) *(P-5554)*

Eb, Santa Rosa *Also Called: Exchange Bank (P-7748)*

Ebac Therapeutic Nursery Schl, Oakland *Also Called: East Bay Agency For Children (P-18311)*

Ebc Inc (PA).. D...... 310 753-6407
   219 Manhattan Beach Blvd Ste 3 Manhattan Beach (90266) *(P-674)*

EBEN-EZER CHILDREN'S DAY CARE CENTER, Baldwin Park *Also Called: Eben-Ezer Chld Day Care Ctr (P-18312)*

Eben-Ezer Chld Day Care Ctr .... D...... 626 960-7100
   3970 Maine Ave Bldg B Baldwin Park (91706) *(P-18312)*

Eberhard .... C...... 818 782-4604
   15220 Raymer St Van Nuys (91405) *(P-2061)*

Ebioscience Inc .... C...... 858 642-2058
   10255 Science Center Dr San Diego (92121) *(P-19685)*

Ebmud, Valley Springs *Also Called: East Bay Mncpl Utility Dst Wstw (P-4786)*

Ebmud, Oakland *Also Called: East Bay Mncpl Utility Dst Wtr (P-4787)*

Ebmud, Oakland *Also Called: East Bay Municipl Utilty Distr (P-4886)*

Ebs General Engineering Inc .... D...... 951 279-6869
   1345 Quarry St Ste 101 Corona (92879) *(P-1102)*

Ebs New Mexico, Pleasanton *Also Called: Excel Building Services LLC (P-10894)*

Ebsavvy, Fremont *Also Called: Droisys Inc (P-12449)*

EBSC LP .... D...... 510 547-2244
   3875 Telegraph Ave Oakland (94609) *(P-14731)*

EC Closing Corp .... D...... 800 546-1531
   525 E Main St El Cajon (92020) *(P-7957)*

EC Group Inc (PA).. D...... 310 815-2700
   5960 Bowcroft St Los Angeles (90016) *(P-5088)*

Ec2002 Inc .... A...... 925 217-5000
   380 Diablo Rd Danville (94526) *(P-8992)*

Ecamsecure (DH).. D...... 888 246-0556
   3400 E Airport Way Long Beach (90806) *(P-13109)*

Ecamsecure, Long Beach *Also Called: Ecamsecure (P-13109)*

ECB Corp (PA).. D...... 714 385-8900
   6400 Artesia Blvd Buena Park (90620) *(P-1425)*

Ecc, Burlingame *Also Called: Environmental Chemical Corp (P-19217)*

Ecc Capital Corporation (PA).. D...... 949 954-7060
   2600 E Coast Hwy Ste 250 Corona Del Mar (92625) *(P-7958)*

Eccu, Brea *Also Called: Adelfi Credit Union (P-7819)*

Ecg Management Consultant .... C...... 206 689-2200
   11512 El Camino Real Ste 200 San Diego (92130) *(P-20351)*

Echo, San Jose *Also Called: Labcyte Inc (P-19724)*

Echo Bridge Home Entertainment, Los Angeles *Also Called: Platinum Disc LLC (P-6048)*

Ecifm Solutions Inc .... C...... 925 830-1925
   3160 Crow Canyon Rd Ste 240 San Ramon (94583) *(P-12450)*

Eclipse Berry Farms LLC .... D...... 310 207-7879
   11812 San Vicente Blvd Ste 250 Los Angeles (90049) *(P-51)*

Ecmc-CA, Rancho Cordova *Also Called: Educational Credit MGT Corp (P-7864)*

Ecmm Services Inc .... C...... 714 988-9388
   1320 Valley Vista Dr # 204 Diamond Bar (91765) *(P-3097)*

Eco Bay Services Inc .... C...... 415 643-7777
   1501 Minnesota St San Francisco (94107) *(P-20740)*

Ecology Recycling Services LLC .... C...... 909 370-1318
   785 E M St Colton (92324) *(P-4887)*

Econco Broadcast Service, Woodland *Also Called: CPI Econco Division (P-13738)*

Econo Air, Placentia *Also Called: Mddr Inc (P-1498)*

Econosoft Inc .... D...... 408 442-3663
   2375 Zanker Rd Ste 250 San Jose (95131) *(P-11561)*

Econtactlive Inc .... D...... 209 548-4300
   6436 Oakdale Rd Riverbank (95367) *(P-13277)*

Ecosense Lighting Inc (PA)... D...... 855 632-6736
   837 N Spring St Ste 103 Los Angeles (90012) *(P-5555)*

Ecotech Rfrgn & Hvac Inc .... D...... 888 833-8100
   630 S Sunkist St Ste R Anaheim (92806) *(P-1426)*

ALPHABETIC SECTION — Edwards Theatres Circuit Inc

Ecrio Inc .... D....... 408 973-7290
   19925 Stevens Creek Blvd Ste 100 Cupertino (95014) *(P-12171)*

Ecs Refining Inc .... C....... 209 774-5000
   2222 S Sinclair Ave Stockton (95215) *(P-4888)*

Ecs-National City Head Start, National City *Also Called: Episcopal Community Services (P-17969)*

Ecullet Inc .... D....... 650 493-7300
   1 Vintage Ct Woodside (94062) *(P-4889)*

Ed Rocha Livestock Trnsp Inc .... D....... 209 538-1302
   2400 Nickerson Dr Modesto (95358) *(P-3468)*

Ed Sped Solutions Inc .... D....... 408 372-8280
   39159 Paseo Padre Pkwy Ste 205 Fremont (94538) *(P-15279)*

Ed Supports LLC .... D....... 201 478-8711
   1045 Willow St San Jose (95125) *(P-17059)*

Ed Supports LLC .... D....... 201 478-8711
   6001 Telegraph Ave Oakland (94609) *(P-17060)*

Ed Supports LLC .... D....... 201 478-8711
   1710 Prairie City Rd Ste 100 Folsom (95630) *(P-17963)*

Edata Solutions Inc .... A....... 510 574-5380
   2450 Peralta Blvd Ste 202 Fremont (94536) *(P-12566)*

Edaw Inc (HQ) .... C....... 415 955-2800
   300 California St Fl 5 San Francisco (94104) *(P-9251)*

Edco Disposal Corporation (PA) .... C....... 619 287-7555
   2755 California Ave Signal Hill (90755) *(P-4890)*

Edelman Financial Engines LLC (HQ) .... C....... 408 498-6000
   1050 Enterprise Way Ste 300 Sunnyvale (94089) *(P-20352)*

Edelman Productions, San Francisco *Also Called: New Paradigm Productions Inc (P-13869)*

Eden Area Rgnal Occptnal Prgra .... D....... 510 293-2900
   26316 Hesperian Blvd Hayward (94545) *(P-18228)*

Eden Area Rop School, Hayward *Also Called: Eden Area Rgnal Occptnal Prgra (P-18228)*

Eden Housing Inc (PA) .... D....... 510 582-1460
   22645 Grand St Hayward (94541) *(P-755)*

Eden Housing Resident Svcs Inc .... D....... 510 582-1460
   22645 Grand St Hayward (94541) *(P-8805)*

Eden Labs Med Group Inc .... C....... 510 537-1234
   20103 Lake Chabot Rd Castro Valley (94546) *(P-16064)*

Eden Medical Center, Castro Valley *Also Called: Eden Township Hospital District Inc (P-16065)*

Eden Medical Center, Castro Valley *Also Called: Sutter Health (P-16528)*

Eden Township Hospital District Inc .... A....... 510 538-2031
   20400 Lake Chabot Rd # 303 Castro Valley (94546) *(P-16065)*

Eden Villa, Redding *Also Called: Ku Kyoung (P-15533)*

Edf Renewables Inc (PA) .... C....... 858 521-3300
   15445 Innovation Dr San Diego (92128) *(P-4572)*

Edf Renewables Services Inc (HQ) .... D....... 858 521-3575
   15445 Innovation Dr San Diego (92128) *(P-13681)*

Edge Mortgage Advisory Co LLC .... D....... 714 564-5800
   2125 E Katella Ave Ste 350 Anaheim (92806) *(P-20741)*

Edgebanding Services Inc (PA) .... D....... 909 599-2336
   828 W Cienega Ave San Dimas (91773) *(P-6698)*

Edgecast Inc (HQ) .... D....... 310 396-7400
   13031 W Jefferson Blvd Ste 900 Los Angeles (90094) *(P-12783)*

Edgemine Inc .... C....... 323 267-8222
   1801 E 50th St Los Angeles (90058) *(P-6198)*

Edgewave Inc .... D....... 800 782-3762
   4225 Executive Sq # 1600 La Jolla (92037) *(P-12172)*

Edgewood Ctr For Chldren Fmlie (PA) .... C....... 415 681-3211
   1801 Vicente St San Francisco (94116) *(P-18420)*

Edgewood Partners Insur Ctr .... D....... 925 244-7700
   3000 Executive Pkwy Ste 325 San Ramon (94583) *(P-8548)*

Edgewood Partners Insur Ctr .... C....... 949 263-0606
   4675 Macarthur Ct Newport Beach (92660) *(P-8549)*

Edgewood Partners Insur Ctr .... C....... 925 244-7700
   3001 Executive Pkwy Ste 325 San Ramon (94583) *(P-8550)*

Edgewood Partners Insur Ctr (PA) .... D....... 415 365-8000
   1 California St Ste 400 San Francisco (94111) *(P-8551)*

Edgewood Partners Insur Ctr, San Ramon *Also Called: Edgewood Partners Insur Ctr (P-8550)*

Edgeworth Integration LLC .... D....... 805 915-0211
   2360 Shasta Way Ste F Simi Valley (93065) *(P-13110)*

Edinger Medical Group Inc .... D....... 714 965-2500
   18682 Beach Blvd Ste 150 Huntington Beach (92648) *(P-14732)*

Edison Capital .... C....... 909 594-3789
   18101 Von Karman Ave Ste 1700 Irvine (92612) *(P-4573)*

Edison Energy LLC .... C....... 949 491-1633
   2 Park Plz Ste 200 Irvine (92614) *(P-13278)*

Edison International (PA) .... A....... 626 302-2222
   2244 Walnut Grove Ave Rosemead (91770) *(P-4574)*

Edison Mission, Rosemead *Also Called: Edison Mission Energy (P-4575)*

Edison Mission Energy (PA) .... C....... 626 302-5778
   2244 Walnut Grove Ave Rosemead (91770) *(P-4575)*

Edison Mssion Midwest Holdings .... A....... 626 302-2222
   2244 Walnut Grove Ave Rosemead (91770) *(P-4576)*

Edje-Enterprises .... D....... 951 245-7070
   18500 Pasadena St Ste B Lake Elsinore (92530) *(P-2062)*

Edmunds Holding Company (PA) .... A....... 310 309-6300
   2401 Colorado Ave Santa Monica (90404) *(P-12661)*

Edmunds.com, Santa Monica *Also Called: Edmunds Holding Company (P-12661)*

Edmundscom Inc (HQ) .... A....... 310 309-6300
   2401 Colorado Ave Ste P1 Santa Monica (90404) *(P-10710)*

Edna H Pagel Inc .... D....... 323 234-2200
   2050 E 38th St Vernon (90058) *(P-817)*

Edo Communications and Countermeasures Systems Inc ... D....... 818 464-2475
   7821 Orion Ave Van Nuys (91406) *(P-3004)*

Edraki, Babak MD, Walnut Creek *Also Called: Womens Cancer Center (P-15212)*

Edriving Fleet LLC (DH) .... D....... 877 566-6323
   5760 Fleet St Ste 210 Carlsbad (92008) *(P-13279)*

Edsi .... D....... 760 731-3501
   700 Ammunition Rd Bldg 103 Fallbrook (92028) *(P-19208)*

Education Elements Inc .... D....... 650 440-7860
   101 Hickey Blvd Ste A # 526 South San Francisco (94080) *(P-12173)*

Educational Credit MGT Corp .... B....... 800 367-1590
   Rancho Cordova (95741) *(P-7864)*

Educational Employees Cr Un (PA) .... C....... 559 437-7700
   2222 W Shaw Ave Ste 100 Fresno (93711) *(P-7762)*

Educational Employees Cr Un .... D....... 559 896-0222
   3488 W Shaw Ave Fresno (93711) *(P-7763)*

Educational Media Foundation (PA) .... C....... 916 251-1600
   5700 West Oaks Blvd Rocklin (95765) *(P-4377)*

Edulastic, Fremont *Also Called: Snapwiz Inc (P-12356)*

Edward B Ward & Company Inc .... D....... 559 487-1860
   2345 Los Angeles St Fresno (93721) *(P-5767)*

Edward G Chester Adult Center, Compton *Also Called: Compton Unified School Dst (P-17705)*

Edward Thomas Companies .... C....... 714 782-7500
   640 W Katella Ave Anaheim (92802) *(P-9772)*

Edward Thomas Hospitality Corp .... B....... 310 458-0030
   1 Pico Blvd Santa Monica (90405) *(P-9773)*

Edward W Scott Electric Co Inc .... C....... 415 206-7120
   1555 Burke Ave Ste L San Francisco (94124) *(P-4577)*

Edwards Cinemas University, Irvine *Also Called: Edwards Theatres Circuit Inc (P-13996)*

Edwards Technologies Inc .... D....... 310 536-7070
   139 Maryland St El Segundo (90245) *(P-1723)*

Edwards Theatres Inc .... C....... 949 582-4078
   27741 Crown Valley Pkwy Ste 301 Mission Viejo (92691) *(P-13986)*

Edwards Theatres Inc (DH) .... C....... 949 640-4600
   300 Newport Center Dr Newport Beach (92660) *(P-13987)*

Edwards Theatres Inc .... D....... 844 462-7342
   4767 Commons Way Calabasas (91302) *(P-13988)*

Edwards Theatres Inc .... C....... 844 462-7342
   1950 Foothill Blvd La Verne (91750) *(P-13989)*

Edwards Theatres Circuit Inc .... D....... 949 425-3838
   26701 Aliso Creek Rd Aliso Viejo (92656) *(P-13990)*

Edwards Theatres Circuit Inc .... C....... 714 428-0962
   901 S Coast Dr Costa Mesa (92626) *(P-13991)*

Edwards Theatres Circuit Inc .... C....... 619 660-3460
   2951 Jamacha Rd El Cajon (92019) *(P-13992)*

Edwards Theatres Circuit Inc .... C....... 858 635-7716
   10733 Westview Pkwy San Diego (92126) *(P-13993)*

Edwards Theatres Circuit Inc .... D....... 707 432-2121
   1549 Gateway Blvd Fairfield (94533) *(P-13994)*

Edwards Theatres Circuit Inc .... C....... 951 296-0144
   40750 Winchester Rd Temecula (92591) *(P-13995)*

Edwards Theatres Circuit Inc .... C....... 949 854-8811
   4245 Campus Dr Irvine (92612) *(P-13996)*

Edwards Theatres Circuit, Inc., Newport Beach Also Called: Edwards Theatres Inc (P-13987)
- **Edys Grand Ice Cream** .... A 510 652-8187
  5929 College Ave Oakland (94618) (P-2349)

Eeco, Los Angeles Also Called: Elevator Equipment Corporation (P-5831)

Efax Corporate, Los Angeles Also Called: J2 Cloud Services LLC (P-4366)
- **Efilm LLC** .... C 323 463-7041
  1144 N Las Palmas Ave Los Angeles (90038) (P-13845)
- **Efinix Inc (PA)** .... C 408 789-6917
  20400 Stevens Creek Blvd Ste 200 Cupertino (95014) (P-12174)
- **Eforcity Corporation** .... D 626 442-3168
  18525 Railroad St City Of Industry (91748) (P-5647)
- **Efront Financial Solutions Inc** .... D 415 653-3239
  135 Main St Ste 1330 San Francisco (94105) (P-11562)
- **Efuel LLC** .... D 949 330-7145
  65 Enterprise 3rd Fl Aliso Viejo (92656) (P-6728)

Egain, Sunnyvale Also Called: Egain Corporation (P-12175)
- **Egain Corporation (PA)** .... B 408 636-4500
  1252 Borregas Ave Sunnyvale (94089) (P-12175)
- **Eggleston Youth Centers Inc (PA)** .... D 626 480-8107
  256 W Badillo St Covina (91723) (P-17964)
- **Egl Holdco Inc** .... A 800 678-7423
  18200 Von Karman Ave # 1000 Irvine (92612) (P-12176)
- **Ego Inc** .... C 626 447-0296
  180 Via Verde Ste 100 San Dimas (91773) (P-19568)
- **Egon Zehnder International** .... B 213 337-1500
  350 S Grand Ave Ste 3580 Los Angeles (90071) (P-20353)
- **Egremont Schools Inc** .... D 818 363-7803
  19850 Devonshire St Chatsworth (91311) (P-17710)
- **Egs Financial Care Inc (DH)** .... B 877 217-4423
  5 Park Plz Ste 1100 Irvine (92614) (P-10740)
- **Eharmony Inc (HQ)** .... C 424 258-1199
  10900 Wilshire Blvd Fl 17 Los Angeles (90024) (P-10543)

Eharmony.com, Los Angeles Also Called: Eharmony Inc (P-10543)

EHC LIFEBUILDERS, Milpitas Also Called: Homefrst Svcs Santa Clara Cnty (P-18005)
- **Ehdd** .... D 415 285-9193
  1 Pier Ste 2 San Francisco (94111) (P-18855)

EHEALTH, Santa Clara Also Called: Ehealth Inc (P-8552)

Ehealth, Santa Clara Also Called: Ehealthinsurance Services Inc (P-8553)
- **Ehealth Inc (PA)** .... C 650 584-2700
  2625 Augustine Dr Fl 2 Santa Clara (95054) (P-8552)

Ehealth Insurance.com, Gold River Also Called: Ehealthinsurance Services Inc (P-11563)
- **Ehealthinsurance Services Inc (HQ)** .... D 650 584-2700
  2625 Augustine Dr Ste 201 Santa Clara (95054) (P-8553)
- **Ehealthinsurance Services Inc** .... C 916 608-6101
  11919 Foundation Pl Ste 100 Gold River (95670) (P-11563)
- **Ehealthwirecom Inc** .... C 916 924-8092
  2450 Venture Oaks Way Ste 100 Sacramento (95833) (P-17233)

Ehp Administrators, Chatsworth Also Called: Electronic Health Plans Inc (P-17234)
- **Eichleay Inc** .... C 562 256-8600
  500 N State College Blvd # 1205 Orange (92868) (P-19209)
- **Eichleay Inc (PA)** .... C 925 689-7000
  1390 Willow Pass Rd Ste 600 Concord (94520) (P-19210)
- **Eichleay Engineers Inc** .... C 925 689-7000
  1390 Willow Pass Rd Ste 600 Concord (94520) (P-19211)
- **Eide Bailly LLP** .... B 909 466-4410
  10681 Foothill Blvd Ste 300 Rancho Cucamonga (91730) (P-19569)

Eight Star Equipment, El Centro Also Called: Noblesse Oblige Inc (P-252)
- **Eighteenth Meridian Inc** .... B 714 706-3643
  200 Spectrum Center Dr Ste 300 Irvine (92618) (P-11564)
- **Eightfold Ai Inc (PA)** .... C 650 265-7380
  2625 Augustine Dr 6th Fl Santa Clara (95054) (P-12177)
- **Einfochips Inc** .... D 949 527-6459
  2361 Campus Dr Ste 105 Irvine (92612) (P-11565)
- **Einfochips Inc (HQ)** .... D 408 496-1882
  2025 Gateway Pl Ste 238 San Jose (95110) (P-11566)

Einstein Dental, San Diego Also Called: Einstein Industries Inc (P-11567)
- **Einstein Industries Inc** .... C 858 459-1182
  6825 Flanders Dr San Diego (92121) (P-11567)
- **Eis Group Inc** .... C 415 402-2622
  4 Embarcadero Ctr San Francisco (94111) (P-12178)

Eisenberg Village, Reseda Also Called: Los Angles Jewish HM For Aging (P-15555)
- **Eisenberg Vlg of The Los Angle** .... D 818 774-3372
  18855 Victory Blvd Reseda (91335) (P-15429)

Eisenhower Health, Rancho Mirage Also Called: Eisenhower Medical Center (P-16068)

Eisenhower Health Services, Rancho Mirage Also Called: Eisenhower Medical Center (P-16857)
- **Eisenhower Medical Center** .... C 760 836-0232
  34450 Gateway Dr Palm Desert (92211) (P-14733)
- **Eisenhower Medical Center** .... D 760 228-9900
  57475 29 Palms Hwy Ste 104 Yucca Valley (92284) (P-14734)
- **Eisenhower Medical Center** .... C 760 610-7200
  45280 Seeley Dr La Quinta (92253) (P-16066)
- **Eisenhower Medical Center** .... C 760 325-6621
  555 E Tachevah Dr Palm Springs (92262) (P-16067)
- **Eisenhower Medical Center (PA)** .... A 760 340-3911
  39000 Bob Hope Dr Rancho Mirage (92270) (P-16068)
- **Eisenhower Medical Center** .... C 760 773-1364
  39000 Bob Hope Dr Frnt Rancho Mirage (92270) (P-16717)
- **Eisenhower Medical Center** .... C 760 773-1888
  39000 Bob Hope Dr Ste 102 Rancho Mirage (92270) (P-16857)

Eisenhower-Memory-Care-center, Palm Desert Also Called: Eisenhower Medical Center (P-14733)

EISNER PEDIATRIC & FAMILY MEDI, Los Angeles Also Called: Pediatric & Family Medical Ctr (P-14953)
- **Eisneramper LLP** .... C 415 974-6000
  1 Market Ste 620 San Francisco (94105) (P-19570)
- **Eisneramper LLP** .... C 916 563-7790
  3001 Douglas Blvd Ste 350 Roseville (95661) (P-19571)
- **Eitacies Inc** .... D 805 500-4366
  4701 Patrick Henry Dr Bldg 25 Santa Clara (95054) (P-11568)

Eiu of California, Bakersfield Also Called: Electrical & Instrumentation Unlimited of California Inc (P-1726)
- **Ek Health Services Inc (PA)** .... C 408 973-0888
  992 S De Anza Blvd Ste 101 San Jose (95129) (P-20354)
- **Ekc Enterprises Inc** .... D 559 438-0330
  4658 E Weathermaker Ave Fresno (93703) (P-7443)
- **Ekedal Concrete Inc** .... D 949 729-8082
  19600 Fairchild Ste 123 Irvine (92612) (P-2116)

Eko Devices, Emeryville Also Called: Eko Devices Inc (P-3075)
- **Eko Devices Inc** .... D 844 356-3384
  2100 Powell St Ste 300 Emeryville (94608) (P-3075)

EL ARCA, Los Angeles Also Called: East Los Angles Rmrkble Ctzens (P-17961)
- **El Aviso Magazine** .... D 323 586-9199
  4850 Gage Ave Bell (90201) (P-6841)
- **El Caballero Country Club** .... C 818 654-3000
  18300 Tarzana Dr Tarzana (91356) (P-14371)

El Cajon Ford, El Cajon Also Called: El Cajon Motors (P-13595)

El Cajon Medical Offices, El Cajon Also Called: Kaiser Foundation Hospitals (P-14829)
- **El Cajon Motors (PA)** .... D 619 579-8888
  1595 E Main St El Cajon (92021) (P-13595)

EL CAMINO HEALTH, Mountain View Also Called: El Camino Hospital (P-16069)

El Camino Health, Mountain View Also Called: Silicon Valley Medical Dev LLC (P-17326)
- **El Camino Hospital (PA)** .... A 650 940-7000
  2500 Grant Rd Mountain View (94040) (P-16069)
- **El Camino Hospital** .... C 650 940-7000
  2480 Grant Rd Mountain View (94040) (P-16070)
- **El Camino Hospital** .... C 650 988-4825
  1737 N 1st St Ste 220 San Jose (95112) (P-16680)
- **El Camino Hospital** .... D 650 940-7310
  2505 Hospital Dr Ste 1 Mountain View (94040) (P-16981)
- **El Camino Hospital** .... D 650 988-7444
  1503 Grant Rd Ste 120 Mountain View (94040) (P-17965)

El Camino Hospital, San Jose Also Called: Maternal Cnnctons El Cmino Hos (P-16251)
- **El Camino Hospital Auxiliary** .... A 650 940-7214
  2500 Grant Rd Mountain View (94040) (P-16858)
- **El Camino Hospital District RE** .... C 650 962-4360
  2660 Grant Rd Mountain View (94040) (P-14735)
- **El Camino Labor LLC** .... D 831 809-9537
  1082 Monterey St Soledad (93960) (P-364)
- **El Camino Surgery Center LLC** .... D 650 961-1200
  15046 Karl Ave Monte Sereno (95030) (P-16071)

El Camino YMCA, Mountain View *Also Called: Young MNS Chrstn Assn Slcon VI* **(P-19002)**

El Capitan Canyon, Santa Barbara *Also Called: El Capitan Canyon LLC* **(P-10417)**

El Capitan Canyon LLC .... D....... 805 685-3887
 11560 Calle Real Santa Barbara (93117) **(P-10417)**

El Centro Hospitality LLC .... C....... 760 353-2600
 503 E Danenberg Dr El Centro (92243) **(P-9774)**

El Centro Hospitality 2 LLC .... C....... 760 370-3800
 3003 S Dogwood Rd El Centro (92243) **(P-9775)**

El Centro Motors .... D....... 760 336-2100
 1520 Ford Dr El Centro (92243) **(P-7198)**

El Centro Rgnal Med Ctr Fndtio (PA)............................ A....... 760 339-7100
 1415 Ross Ave El Centro (92243) **(P-16072)**

EL CONCILIO, Stockton *Also Called: El Concilio California* **(P-17966)**

El Concilio California (PA)... C....... 209 644-2600
 445 N San Joaquin St Ste A Stockton (95202) **(P-17966)**

El Dorado Broadcasters LLC .... D....... 760 241-1313
 11920 Hesperia Rd Hesperia (92345) **(P-4378)**

El Dorado County Health Dept .... D....... 530 621-6100
 931 Spring St Placerville (95667) **(P-14736)**

El Dorado Enterprises Inc .... A....... 310 719-9800
 1000 W Redondo Beach Blvd Gardena (90247) **(P-9776)**

El Dorado Hills Cmnty Svcs Dst .... D....... 916 933-6624
 1021 Harvard Way El Dorado Hills (95762) **(P-14519)**

El Dorado Irrigation District .... B....... 530 622-4513
 2890 Mosquito Rd Placerville (95667) **(P-4791)**

El Encanto Inc .... D....... 805 845-5800
 800 Alvarado Pl Santa Barbara (93103) **(P-9777)**

El Guapo Spices Inc (PA)... D....... 213 312-1300
 6200 E Slauson Ave Commerce (90040) **(P-6627)**

El Guapo Spices and Herbs Pkg, Commerce *Also Called: El Guapo Spices Inc* **(P-6627)**

El Macero Country Club Inc .... D....... 530 753-3363
 44571 Clubhouse Dr El Macero (95618) **(P-14372)**

El Monte Automotive Group Inc .... C....... 626 580-6200
 3530 Peck Rd El Monte (91731) **(P-7199)**

El Monte Automotive Group LLC .... D....... 626 444-0321
 3464 Peck Rd El Monte (91731) **(P-7200)**

El Monte Convalescent Hospital .... D....... 626 442-1500
 4096 Easy St El Monte (91731) **(P-15430)**

El Monte Rents Inc (HQ).. C....... 562 404-9300
 12818 Firestone Blvd Santa Fe Springs (90670) **(P-13598)**

El Monte Rv, Santa Fe Springs *Also Called: El Monte Rents Inc* **(P-13598)**

El Nido Family Centers (PA)... C....... 818 830-3646
 10200 Sepulveda Blvd Ste 350 Mission Hills (91345) **(P-17967)**

El Pollo Loco, Cypress *Also Called: WKS Restaurant Corporation* **(P-7518)**

El Pollo Loco Holdings Inc (PA)................................... C....... 714 599-5000
 3535 Harbor Blvd Ste 100 Costa Mesa (92626) **(P-7476)**

El Prado Golf Course LP .... D....... 909 597-1751
 6555 Pine Ave Chino (91708) **(P-14260)**

El Primo Foods Inc .... C....... 626 289-5054
 608 Monterey Pass Rd Monterey Park (91754) **(P-6420)**

El Rancho Vista Hlth Care Ctr, Pico Rivera *Also Called: Mariner Health Care Inc* **(P-15561)**

El Segundo Energy Center, El Segundo *Also Called: NRG El Segundo Operations Inc* **(P-4595)**

El Torito Franchising Company, Cypress *Also Called: Real Mex Foods Inc* **(P-6281)**

El-Bethel Terrace, San Francisco *Also Called: Christian Church Homes* **(P-18394)**

Elation Health Inc (PA)... D....... 415 213-5164
 530 Divisadero St # 872 San Francisco (94117) **(P-12784)**

Elavon Inc .... B....... 865 403-7000
 700 S Western Ave Los Angeles (90005) **(P-12662)**

Elcor Electric Inc .... C....... 408 986-1320
 3310 Bassett St Santa Clara (95054) **(P-1724)**

Elder Care Alliance Camarillo .... D....... 510 769-2700
 2500 Ponderosa Dr N Camarillo (93010) **(P-15431)**

Elder Care Alliance San Mateo .... C....... 650 212-4400
 4000 S El Camino Real San Mateo (94403) **(P-15432)**

Eldorado Care Center LP .... B....... 619 440-1211
 510 E Washington Ave El Cajon (92020) **(P-15433)**

Eldorado Country Club .... C....... 760 346-8081
 46000 E Eldorado Dr Indian Wells (92210) **(P-14373)**

Eldorado Stone LLC .... A....... 951 601-3838
 24100 Orange Ave Perris (92570) **(P-5202)**

Elec-Tech Enterprises Inc .... D....... 562 602-1015
 3508 Stanbridge Ave Long Beach (90808) **(P-1725)**

Electra Owners Assoc .... C....... 619 236-3310
 700 W E St San Diego (92101) **(P-18707)**

Electric & Gas Industries Association (PA)................... D....... 916 609-5300
 3800 Watt Ave Ste 105 Sacramento (95821) **(P-18708)**

Electric Department, Santa Clara *Also Called: City of Santa Clara* **(P-4566)**

Electric Motor & Supply Co., Fresno *Also Called: Electric Motor Shop* **(P-5556)**

Electric Motor Shop .... C....... 559 233-1153
 250 Broadway St Fresno (93721) **(P-5556)**

Electric On Target Inc .... D....... 949 247-3842
 17691 Mitchell N Ste B Irvine (92614) **(P-1427)**

Electric Power RES Inst Inc (PA).................................. A....... 650 855-2000
 3420 Hillview Ave Palo Alto (94304) **(P-19880)**

Electric Tech, Concord *Also Called: Electric Tech Construction Inc* **(P-1208)**

Electric Tech Construction Inc .... D....... 925 849-5324
 1910 Mark Ct Ste 130 Concord (94520) **(P-1208)**

Electrical & Instrumentation Unlimited of California Inc C
 6950 District Blvd Bakersfield (93313) **(P-1726)**

Electrical Distributors Co, San Jose *Also Called: Chester C Lehmann Co Inc* **(P-5546)**

Electrnic Rcyclers Intl - Ind .... D....... 317 522-1414
 7815 N Palm Ave Ste 140 Fresno (93711) **(P-4891)**

Electromed Inc .... D....... 805 523-7500
 4590 Ish Dr Simi Valley (93063) **(P-5412)**

Electronic Arts Inc (PA)... B....... 650 628-1500
 209 Redwood Shores Pkwy Redwood City (94065) **(P-12179)**

Electronic Clearing House Inc (HQ).............................. D....... 805 419-8700
 730 Paseo Camarillo Camarillo (93010) **(P-12180)**

Electronic Commerce, Newport Beach *Also Called: Electronic Commerce LLC* **(P-7919)**

Electronic Commerce LLC .... D....... 800 770-5520
 4100 Newport Place Dr Ste 500 Newport Beach (92660) **(P-7919)**

Electronic Control Systems LLC .... C....... 858 513-1911
 12575 Kirkham Ct Ste 1 Poway (92064) **(P-1727)**

Electronic Health Plans Inc .... D....... 818 734-4700
 9131 Oakdale Ave Ste 150 Chatsworth (91311) **(P-17234)**

Electronic Medical Management (PA)........................... D....... 209 473-6555
 3116 W March Ln Ste 200 Stockton (95219) **(P-19572)**

Electronic Online Systems International .... D....... 760 431-8400
 2292 Faraday Ave Frnt Carlsbad (92008) **(P-12451)**

Electronic Recyclers, Fresno *Also Called: Electrnic Rcyclers Intl - Ind* **(P-4891)**

Electronic Recyclers Intl Inc (PA).................................. C....... 559 442-3960
 7815 N Palm Ave Ste 140 Fresno (93711) **(P-4892)**

Eleganza Tiles Inc (PA)... D....... 714 224-1700
 3125 E Coronado St Anaheim (92806) **(P-1980)**

Element Materials (DH)... D....... 714 892-1961
 15062 Bolsa Chica St Huntington Beach (92649) **(P-19967)**

Element Mtrls Tech HB Inc .... D....... 310 632-8500
 18100 S Wilmington Ave Compton (90220) **(P-19968)**

Element Rancho Dominguez, Compton *Also Called: Element Mtrls Tech HB Inc* **(P-19968)**

Element Science Inc .... D....... 415 872-6500
 200 Kansas St Ste 210 San Francisco (94103) **(P-19881)**

Elena Gardens Apartments, San Rafael *Also Called: Eah Elena Gardens LP* **(P-8803)**

Elevate Addiction Services, Aptos *Also Called: Enlighticare Inc* **(P-16681)**

Elevated Resources Inc (PA).. C....... 949 419-6632
 3990 Westerly Pl Ste 270 Newport Beach (92660) **(P-12567)**

Elevator Equipment Corporation (PA)........................... D....... 323 245-0147
 4035 Goodwin Ave Los Angeles (90039) **(P-5831)**

Eleven, San Francisco *Also Called: Eleven Inc* **(P-10612)**

Eleven Inc .... C....... 415 707-1111
 394 Pacific Ave San Francisco (94111) **(P-10612)**

Eleven Western Builders Inc (PA)................................. D....... 760 796-6346
 2862 Executive Pl Escondido (92029) **(P-675)**

Elijah Textiles Inc .... D....... 310 666-3443
 1251 E Olympic Blvd Ste 108 Los Angeles (90021) **(P-5116)**

Elim Bedding Town, Walnut *Also Called: Tae Sook Chung* **(P-5136)**

Elite, Culver City *Also Called: West Publishing Corporation* **(P-12544)**

Elite Craftsman (PA)... C....... 562 989-3511
 2763 Saint Louis Ave Long Beach (90755) **(P-10893)**

Elite Electric .... D....... 951 681-5811
 9415 Bellegrave Ave Riverside (92509) **(P-1728)**

ALPHABETIC SECTION

Elite Enfrcment SEC Sltons Inc .... C 866 354-8308
29970 Technology Dr Ste 117d Murrieta (92563) *(P-12968)*

Elite Gates, Los Angeles *Also Called: United Marketing Group Inc (P-2024)*

Elite Metal Finishing LLC (PA) .... C 805 983-4320
540 Spectrum Cir Oxnard (93030) *(P-2760)*

Elite Security Group, Bay Point *Also Called: Elite Security Group Inc (P-13111)*

Elite Security Group Inc .... D 925 597-8852
640 Bailey Rd 124 Bay Point (94565) *(P-13111)*

Elite Show Services Inc .... A 619 574-1589
2878 Camino Del Rio S Ste 260 San Diego (92108) *(P-12969)*

Elitecare Medical Staffing LLC .... D 559 438-7700
761 E Locust Ave Ste 103 Fresno (93720) *(P-11128)*

Elitegroup Computer Systems Ho .... C 510 794-2952
6851 Mowry Ave Newark (94560) *(P-5297)*

Elitra Pharmaceuticals 858 410-3030
3510 Dunhill St Ste A San Diego (92121) *(P-2585)*

Elizabeth Glaser Pedia .... B 310 231-0400
16130 Ventura Blvd Ste 250 Encino (91436) *(P-17235)*

Elizabeth Glser Pdtric Aids FN .... B 310 593-0047
2950 31st St Ste 125 Santa Monica (90405) *(P-18856)*

Elizabeth Hospice Inc (PA) .... C 760 737-2050
800 W Valley Pkwy Escondido (92025) *(P-16859)*

Elk Grove Unified School Dst .... D 916 686-7733
8421 Gerber Rd Sacramento (95828) *(P-3335)*

Elk Valley Casino Inc .... D 707 464-1020
2021 Elk Ranch Rd Crescent City (95531) *(P-9778)*

Elk Valley Rancheria Cal, Crescent City *Also Called: Elk Valley Casino Inc (P-9778)*

Elkay Plastics Co Inc (PA) .... D 323 722-7073
6000 Sheila St Commerce (90040) *(P-6699)*

Elkins Kalt Wntraub Rben Grtsi .... D 310 746-4431
10345 W Olympic Blvd Los Angeles (90064) *(P-17445)*

Elkor Properties, Santa Monica *Also Called: Roscoe Real Estate Ltd Partnr (P-10173)*

Ellation LLC (DH) .... C 415 796-3560
835 Market St Ste 700 San Francisco (94103) *(P-11569)*

Ellie Mae, Pleasanton *Also Called: Ice Mortgage Technology Inc (P-12227)*

Ellie Mae Inc .... B 818 223-2000
24025 Park Sorrento Ste 210 Calabasas (91302) *(P-11570)*

ELLIE MAE, INC., Calabasas *Also Called: Ellie Mae Inc (P-11570)*

Ellis Building Contractors, Manhattan Beach *Also Called: Ebc Inc (P-674)*

Ellis Grge Cpllone Obrien Anng .... D 310 274-7100
2121 Avenue Of The Stars Fl 30 Los Angeles (90067) *(P-17446)*

Ellison Institute LLC (PA) .... C 310 228-6400
12414 Exposition Blvd Los Angeles (90064) *(P-19969)*

Ellison Technologies Inc .... D 562 949-8311
9912 Pioneer Blvd Santa Fe Springs (90670) *(P-5832)*

Ellisson Institute Technology, Los Angeles *Also Called: Ellison Institute LLC (P-19969)*

Elljay Acoustics Inc .... D 714 961-1173
511 Cameron St Placentia (92870) *(P-1926)*

Elmco Sales Inc (PA) .... D 626 855-4831
15070 Proctor Ave City Of Industry (91746) *(P-5746)*

ELMWOOD CARE CENTER, Berkeley *Also Called: Shattuck Health Care Inc (P-15663)*

Elo Touch Solutions Inc (PA) .... B 408 597-8000
670 N Mccarthy Blvd Ste 100 Milpitas (95035) *(P-5298)*

Els Investments .... C 916 388-0308
2701 Citrus Rd Rancho Cordova (95742) *(P-429)*

Elsa Corp .... C 408 431-6735
139 Old Orchard Dr Los Gatos (95032) *(P-12452)*

Elsinore Vly Municpl Wtr Dst (PA) .... D 951 674-3146
31315 Chaney St Lake Elsinore (92530) *(P-4792)*

Elysium Jennings LLC .... C 661 679-1700
1600 Norris Rd Bakersfield (93308) *(P-592)*

Emanate Health .... C 626 912-5282
1722 Desire Ave Ste 206 Rowland Heights (91748) *(P-14737)*

Emanate Health .... B 626 857-3477
427 W Carroll Ave Glendora (91741) *(P-16073)*

Emanate Health, Rowland Heights *Also Called: Emanate Health (P-14737)*

Emanate Health, West Covina *Also Called: Emanate Health Medical Center (P-16074)*

Emanate Health Medical Center (PA) .... A 626 962-4011
1115 S Sunset Ave West Covina (91790) *(P-16074)*

Emanate Health Medical Center .... B 626 858-8515
140 W College St Covina (91723) *(P-16075)*

Emanate Health Medical Center .... B 626 963-8411
1115 S Sunset Ave West Covina (91790) *(P-16076)*

Emanate Health Medical Center .... A 626 331-7331
210 W San Bernardino Rd Covina (91723) *(P-16077)*

Emanate Health Medical Group (PA) .... A 626 331-7331
210 W San Bernardino Rd Covina (91723) *(P-16078)*

Emanate Hlth Fthill Prsbt Hosp (PA) .... D 626 857-3145
250 S Grand Ave Glendora (91741) *(P-16079)*

Emanate Hlth Intr-Cmmnity Hosp, Covina *Also Called: Emanate Health Medical Group (P-16078)*

Embarcadero, The, San Francisco *Also Called: Crunch LLC (P-14193)*

Embassy Investments LLC .... D 707 422-4111
1350 Holiday Ln Fairfield (94534) *(P-9779)*

Embassy Sites-So San Francisco, South San Francisco *Also Called: Djont/Cmb Ssf Leasing LLC (P-9750)*

Embassy Stes - Mlpts/Slcon Vly, Milpitas *Also Called: Djont Operations LLC (P-9748)*

Embassy Stes - Mndlay Bch Rsor, Oxnard *Also Called: Djont/Jpm Hsptlity Lsg Spe LLC (P-9751)*

Embassy Suites, Burlingame *Also Called: Djont Operations LLC (P-9747)*

Embassy Suites, Garden Grove *Also Called: Embassy Suites & Hotel (P-9780)*

Embassy Suites, San Rafael *Also Called: Hotel McInnis Marin LLC (P-9873)*

Embassy Suites, San Diego *Also Called: Sunstone Top Gun Lessee Inc (P-10291)*

Embassy Suites, Lompoc *Also Called: Windsor Capital Group Inc (P-10372)*

Embassy Suites, Brea *Also Called: Windsor Capital Group Inc (P-10373)*

Embassy Suites, Temecula *Also Called: Windsor Capital Group Inc (P-10374)*

Embassy Suites, Santa Ana *Also Called: Windsor Capital Group Inc (P-10375)*

Embassy Suites - Lax Airport S, El Segundo *Also Called: Djont Operations LLC (P-9749)*

Embassy Suites & Hotel .... C 714 539-3300
11767 Harbor Blvd Garden Grove (92840) *(P-9780)*

Embassy Suites Brea, Brea *Also Called: Park Hotels & Resorts Inc (P-10101)*

Embassy Suites- Santa Clara, Santa Clara *Also Called: Msr Hotels & Resorts Inc (P-9537)*

Embee Plating, Santa Ana *Also Called: Embee Processing LLC (P-19212)*

Embee Processing LLC .... B 714 546-9842
2158 S Hathaway St Santa Ana (92705) *(P-19212)*

EMC Health Inc (DH) .... A 209 667-4200
825 Delbon Ave Turlock (95382) *(P-16080)*

Emcor Services, San Jose *Also Called: Air Systems Inc (P-1340)*

Emcor Services Mesa Energy, Irvine *Also Called: Mesa Energy Systems Inc (P-1500)*

Emed Technologies Corporation .... D 775 232-3287
4814 Golden Foothill Pkwy El Dorado Hills (95762) *(P-3700)*

Emerald Acquisition LLC .... C 714 891-8752
6381 Industry Way Westminster (92683) *(P-1103)*

Emerald Cloud Lab Inc .... D 650 257-7554
844 Dubuque Ave South San Francisco (94080) *(P-19686)*

Emerald Connect LLC (HQ) .... D 800 233-2834
15050 Avenue Of Science Ste 200 San Diego (92128) *(P-12568)*

Emerald Health Services, El Segundo *Also Called: Tempus LLC (P-11247)*

Emerald Hlls Asssted Lving Fcl, Auburn *Also Called: Emeritus Corporation (P-15754)*

Emerald Landscape Services Inc .... D 714 844-2200
26415 Summit Cir Santa Clarita (91350) *(P-488)*

Emerald Packaging Inc .... C 510 429-5700
33050 Western Ave Union City (94587) *(P-6902)*

Emerald Paving Company, Westminster *Also Called: Emerald Acquisition LLC (P-1103)*

Emergency Ambulance Svc Inc .... D 714 990-1331
3200 E Birch St Ste A Brea (92821) *(P-3254)*

Emergency Dept Dignity Hlth, Arroyo Grande *Also Called: Arroyo Grande Community Hospital (P-15953)*

Emergency Groups Office, San Dimas *Also Called: Ego Inc (P-19568)*

Emergency Groups' Office, San Dimas *Also Called: Brault (P-19541)*

Emergency Housing Chld Program, Sacramento *Also Called: Sacramento Area Emerg Housing (P-18102)*

Emergency Technologies Inc .... D 818 765-4421
7345 Varna Ave North Hollywood (91605) *(P-13112)*

Emergent Medical Associates .... D 818 995-5350
16237 Ventura Blvd Encino (91436) *(P-14738)*

Emergncy Mdcine Spclist Ornge .... D 714 543-8911
1310 W Stewart Dr Ste 212 Orange (92868) *(P-11283)*

Emerik Hotel Corp .... D 213 748-1291
1020 S Figueroa St Los Angeles (90015) *(P-9781)*

Emeritus At Casa Glendale, Glendale Also Called: Emeritus Corporation (P-15442)
Emeritus At San Dimas, San Dimas Also Called: Emeritus Corporation (P-15436)
Emeritus At Villa Colima, Walnut Also Called: Emeritus Corporation (P-15443)
Emeritus Corporation .... C....... 805 239-1313
  1919 Creston Rd Ofc Paso Robles (93446) (P-8806)
Emeritus Corporation .... C....... 831 443-6467
  290 Regency Cir Salinas (93906) (P-15434)
Emeritus Corporation .... C....... 510 797-4011
  38035 Martha Ave Fremont (94536) (P-15435)
Emeritus Corporation .... C....... 909 394-0304
  1740 S San Dimas Ave San Dimas (91773) (P-15436)
Emeritus Corporation .... C....... 858 292-8044
  5219 Clairemont Mesa Blvd San Diego (92117) (P-15437)
Emeritus Corporation .... C....... 951 744-9861
  1001 N Lyon Ave Hemet (92545) (P-15438)
Emeritus Corporation .... C....... 707 552-3336
  2261 Tuolumne St Vallejo (94589) (P-15439)
Emeritus Corporation .... C....... 714 639-3590
  142 S Prospect St Orange (92869) (P-15440)
Emeritus Corporation .... C....... 760 741-3055
  1351 E Washington Ave Escondido (92027) (P-15441)
Emeritus Corporation .... C....... 818 246-7457
  426 Piedmont Ave Glendale (91206) (P-15442)
Emeritus Corporation .... C....... 909 595-5030
  19850 Colima Rd Walnut (91789) (P-15443)
Emeritus Corporation .... C....... 714 441-0644
  411 E Commonwealth Ave Fullerton (92832) (P-15444)
Emeritus Corporation .... C....... 909 420-0153
  22325 Barton Rd Grand Terrace (92313) (P-15445)
Emeritus Corporation .... C....... 530 653-1974
  11550 Education St Apt 212 Auburn (95602) (P-15754)
Emeritus Corporation .... C....... 707 996-7101
  800 Oregon St Sonoma (95476) (P-15755)
Emeritus Corporation .... C....... 707 324-7087
  300 Fountaingrove Pkwy Santa Rosa (95403) (P-15756)
Emerson Collective LLC (PA) .... D....... 650 422-2152
  555 Bryant St Ste 259 Palo Alto (94301) (P-17809)
Emery Financial Inc (PA) .... D....... 949 219-0640
  625 Kings Rd Newport Beach (92663) (P-8041)
Emery Marina, Emeryville Also Called: Young MNS Chrstn Assn of E Bay (P-18968)
Emet Lending Group Inc .... D....... 714 933-9800
  2601 Saturn St Ste 200 Brea (92821) (P-7959)
Emida Technologies, Foothill Ranch Also Called: Debisys Inc (P-7852)
Emids Tech Private Ltd Corp .... A....... 805 304-5986
  6320 Canoga Ave Woodland Hills (91367) (P-11571)
EMJ Corporate, Lynwood Also Called: Earle M Jorgensen Company (P-5489)
EMJ Hayward, Hayward Also Called: Earle M Jorgensen Company (P-5490)
Emmett A Larkin Company Inc (PA) .... D....... 415 986-2332
  22 Battery St Ste 806 San Francisco (94111) (P-8082)
Emmi, Stockton Also Called: Electronic Medical Management (P-19572)
Emp III Inc .... D....... 323 231-4174
  1755 Mrtn Lthr Kng Jr Blv Los Angeles (90058) (P-9507)
Empcc Inc .... B....... 888 278-8200
  1682 Langley Ave Fl 2 Irvine (92614) (P-1614)
Empi Inc .... D....... 714 446-9606
  301 E Orangethorpe Ave Anaheim (92801) (P-5037)
Empire Cinema, San Francisco Also Called: Century Theatres Inc (P-14021)
Empire Cls Wrldwide Chffred Sv, El Segundo Also Called: Cls Trnsprttion Los Angles LLC (P-3249)
Empire Community Painting, Irvine Also Called: D P S Inc (P-1612)
Empire Community Painting, Irvine Also Called: Empcc Inc (P-1614)
Empire Demolition Inc .... D....... 909 393-8300
  137 N Joy St Corona (92879) (P-2234)
Empire Home Loans Inc .... C....... 916 715-1974
  4401 Hazel Ave Ste 135 Fair Oaks (95628) (P-7960)
Empire Med Transportations LLC .... D....... 877 473-6029
  1433 W Linden St Ste M Riverside (92507) (P-4013)
Empire Oil Co .... C....... 909 877-0226
  2756 S Riverside Ave Bloomington (92316) (P-6729)
Empire Realty Associates, Inc., Danville Also Called: Ec2002 Inc (P-8992)

Empire Transportation Inc .... B....... 562 529-2676
  8800 Park St Bellflower (90706) (P-3311)
Empire West Solutions LLC .... C....... 831 783-1649
  340 El Camino Real S # 35b Salinas (93901) (P-6903)
Employers Training Resource, Bakersfield Also Called: County of Kern (P-20942)
Employment Intake Training Ctr, Los Angeles Also Called: Swissport Usa Inc (P-3915)
Employnet Inc .... A....... 831 233-9999
  838 S Main St Ste B Salinas (93901) (P-11129)
Employnet Inc .... A....... 909 458-0961
  123 E 9th St Ste 103 Upland (91786) (P-11130)
Empower Annuity Insur Co Amer .... D....... 818 409-0880
  500 N Central Ave Ste 220 Glendale (91203) (P-8264)
Empower Our Youth .... D....... 323 203-5436
  6767 W Sunset Blvd 8-188 Los Angeles (90028) (P-9414)
Empres Financial Services LLC .... A....... 707 643-2793
  1527 Springs Rd Vallejo (94591) (P-15446)
Empresas Del Bosque Inc .... B....... 209 364-6428
  51481 W Shields Ave Firebaugh (93622) (P-177)
Empyr Incorporated .... D....... 888 664-5669
  8910 University Center Ln Ste 400 San Diego (92122) (P-10544)
EMQ FAMILIESFIRST, Campbell Also Called: Uplift Family Services (P-18164)
EMR Cpr LLC .... B....... 408 471-6804
  32970 Alvarado Niles Rd Ste 736 Union City (94587) (P-12453)
Emser International LLC (PA) .... D....... 323 650-2000
  8431 Santa Monica Blvd Los Angeles (90069) (P-5203)
Emser Tile LLC .... D....... 909 974-1600
  5300 Shea Center Dr Ontario (91761) (P-1981)
Emser Tile LLC (PA) .... B....... 323 650-2000
  8431 Santa Monica Blvd Los Angeles (90069) (P-5204)
Emsoc, Orange Also Called: Emergncy Mdcine Spclist Ornge (P-11283)
Emtek Products, Irwindale Also Called: Assa Abloy Rsdential Group Inc (P-5721)
En Pointe Technologies Sls LLC .... C....... 310 337-6151
  200 N Pacific Coast Hwy Ste 1050 El Segundo (90245) (P-5299)
Enbio Corp .... C....... 818 953-9976
  150 E Olive Ave Ste 114 Burbank (91502) (P-20355)
Enbiz International, Lake Forest Also Called: Cloudradiant Corp (P-6897)
Enbiz International, San Jose Also Called: Cloudradiant Corp (P-6898)
Encina Pepper Tree Joint Ventr (PA) .... D....... 805 687-5511
  3850 State St Santa Barbara (93105) (P-9782)
Encina Pepper Tree Joint Ventr .... D....... 805 682-7277
  2220 Bath St Santa Barbara (93105) (P-9783)
Encinitas Ford, Encinitas Also Called: Wayne Gossett Ford Inc (P-7330)
Encinitas Memory Care Cmnty, Encinitas Also Called: Silverado Senior Living Inc (P-15671)
Encinitas Ranch Golf Course, San Diego Also Called: JC Resorts LLC (P-20120)
Encino Financial Center, Encino Also Called: Lowe Enterprises Rlty Svcs Inc (P-9077)
Encino Living LLC .... C....... 818 907-1343
  16710 Magnolia Blvd Encino (91436) (P-14196)
Enclarity Inc .... B....... 949 797-7160
  16815 Von Karman Ave Ste 125 Irvine (92606) (P-12569)
Encompass Community Services .... D....... 831 724-3885
  225 Westridge Dr Watsonville (95076) (P-17968)
Encompass Fmly Physcans Med Gr .... D....... 619 660-6212
  10225 Austin Dr Ste 103 Spring Valley (91978) (P-14739)
Encore, San Diego Also Called: Encore Capital Group Inc (P-7893)
Encore Capital Group Inc (PA) .... A....... 877 445-4581
  350 Camino De La Reina Ste 100 San Diego (92108) (P-7893)
Encore Events Rentals Inc .... D....... 707 431-3500
  1001 American Way Windsor (95492) (P-11030)
Encore Glass Inc .... D....... 707 745-4444
  2925 Cordelia Rd Fairfield (94534) (P-5900)
Encore Semi Inc .... D....... 858 225-4993
  7310 Miramar Rd Ste 410 San Diego (92126) (P-19213)
Encore Senior Living III LLC .... D....... 760 242-3188
  18524 Corwin Rd Apple Valley (92307) (P-8807)
Encore Senior Living III LLC .... D....... 951 360-1616
  6280 Clay St Riverside (92509) (P-8808)
Encore Senior Living III LLC .... D....... 760 243-2271
  13815 Rodeo Dr Ofc Victorville (92395) (P-15447)
Encore Senior Vlg At Riverside, Riverside Also Called: Encore Senior Living III (P-8808)
End To End Analytics LLC .... D....... 650 331-9659
  2595 E Bayshore Rd Ste 150 Palo Alto (94303) (P-20356)

Endeavor Group Holdings Inc

ALPHABETIC SECTION

Endeavor Group Holdings Inc (PA)..................D...... 310 285-9000
9601 Wilshire Blvd Fl 3 Beverly Hills (90210) *(P-14136)*

Endemol Shine North America ....D...... 747 529-8000
5161 Lankershim Blvd Ste 400 North Hollywood (91601) *(P-13846)*

Endicia, Sunnyvale *Also Called: PSI Systems Inc (P-11849)*

Endors Toi Pbc ....D...... 434 987-0919
600 F St Ste 3 Arcata (95521) *(P-20357)*

Endoscopic Technologies Inc ....D...... 925 866-7111
2603 Camino Ramon Ste 100 San Ramon (94583) *(P-5413)*

Endpak Packaging Inc ....D...... 562 801-0281
9101 Perkins St Pico Rivera (90660) *(P-2532)*

Endura Healthcare Inc ....C...... 949 487-9500
29222 Rancho Viejo Rd Ste 127 San Juan Capistrano (92675) *(P-15448)*

Energy Club, Pacoima *Also Called: Energy Club Inc (P-6460)*

Energy Club Inc ....D
12950 Pierce St Pacoima (91331) *(P-6460)*

Energy Concepts Entps Inc ....D...... 559 485-2504
1835 N Fine Ave Ste 106 Fresno (93727) *(P-1428)*

Energy Enterprises USA Inc (PA)......................D...... 424 339-0005
6842 Van Nuys Blvd Ste 800 Van Nuys (91405) *(P-1429)*

Energy Experts International ....D...... 925 242-0446
12657 Alcosta Blvd # 470 San Ramon (94583) *(P-20358)*

Energy Experts International ....D...... 559 449-1124
7111 N Fresno St Ste 260 Fresno (93720) *(P-20742)*

Energy Solutions, Oakland *Also Called: Cohen Ventures Inc (P-20731)*

Energy Watch ....D...... 661 324-0930
3555 Landco Dr Bakersfield (93308) *(P-1729)*

Enerpath Services Inc ....D...... 909 335-1699
1758 Orange Tree Ln Redlands (92374) *(P-1730)*

Enervee Corporation ....C...... 844 363-7833
11845 W Olympic Blvd Ste 1100w Los Angeles (90064) *(P-12570)*

Enexus Global Inc ....D...... 510 936-4044
39510 Paseo Padre Pkwy Ste 390 Fremont (94538) *(P-12785)*

Engage3 Inc ....D...... 530 231-5485
501 2nd St Davis (95616) *(P-20359)*

Engel & Voelkers Newport Beach ....D...... 949 207-3101
3636 E Coast Hwy Ste B Corona Del Mar (92625) *(P-8993)*

Engel Holdings Inc ....C...... 866 950-9862
14754 Ceres Ave Fontana (92335) *(P-913)*

Engeo Incorporated ....D...... 408 574-4900
6399 San Ignacio Ave Ste 150 San Jose (95119) *(P-19214)*

Engeo Incorporated ....D...... 661 257-4004
27742 Hancock Pkwy Valencia (91355) *(P-20885)*

Engineering Department, Los Angeles *Also Called: LADWP Metro Water Yard (P-1229)*

Engineering Division, Lancaster *Also Called: County of Los Angeles (P-19186)*

Engineering Partners Inc ....D...... 858 824-1761
10150 Meanley Dr Ste 200 San Diego (92131) *(P-19215)*

Engineering Public Works, Glendale *Also Called: City of Glendale (P-19178)*

Enginring Sftwr Sys Sltons Inc (PA)................D...... 619 338-0380
600 B St San Diego (92101) *(P-19216)*

Enginrng/Rmdtion Rsrces Group (PA)............D...... 925 839-2200
4585 Pacheco Blvd Ste 200 Martinez (94553) *(P-4979)*

Enginrng/Rmdtion Rsrces Group ....C...... 415 395-9974
456 Montgomery St Ste 900 San Francisco (94104) *(P-20653)*

Englewood Marketing Group Inc ....D...... 909 875-3649
127 W Jurupa Ave Bloomington (92316) *(P-20360)*

English Oaks Convalescent 209 577-1001
2633 W Rumble Rd Modesto (95350) *(P-15449)*

ENGLISH OAKS CONVALESCENT & RE, Modesto *Also Called: English Oaks Convalescent (P-15449)*

Engstrom Lipscomb and Lack A (PA).............D...... 310 552-3800
10100 Santa Monica Blvd Los Angeles (90067) *(P-17447)*

Enki Health and RES Systems ....D...... 626 961-8971
160 S 7th Ave La Puente (91746) *(P-14740)*

Enki Health and RES Systems ....D...... 626 227-7001
3208 Rosemead Blvd Ste 100 El Monte (91731) *(P-17061)*

Enki Health Care, La Puente *Also Called: Enki Health and RES Systems (P-14740)*

Enlighticare Inc ....D...... 831 750-3546
138 Victoria Ln Aptos (95003) *(P-16681)*

Enloe Cardiology Svcs Clinic ....D...... 530 332-4400
185 E 7th Ave Ste A Chico (95926) *(P-14741)*

Enloe Homecare Services, Chico *Also Called: Enloe Medical Center (P-16860)*

Enloe Hospice Program, Chico *Also Called: Enloe Medical Center (P-16085)*

Enloe Hospt-Phys Thrpy ....B...... 530 891-7300
1444 Magnolia Ave Chico (95926) *(P-16081)*

Enloe Medical Center ....D...... 530 891-7347
W 5th Av & Esplanade Chico (95926) *(P-3255)*

Enloe Medical Center ....B...... 530 332-6138
340 W East Ave Chico (95926) *(P-15280)*

Enloe Medical Center ....C...... 530 332-4111
560 Cohasset Rd Chico (95926) *(P-16082)*

Enloe Medical Center ....C...... 530 332-7522
175 W 5th Ave Chico (95926) *(P-16083)*

Enloe Medical Center (PA)..................................A...... 530 332-7300
1531 Esplanade Chico (95926) *(P-16084)*

Enloe Medical Center ....C...... 530 332-5520
1536 Arcadian Ave Chico (95926) *(P-16085)*

Enloe Medical Center ....C...... 530 332-6400
888 Lakeside Vlg Cmns Chico (95928) *(P-16086)*

Enloe Medical Center ....C...... 530 332-6000
1515 Springfield Dr Ste 175 Chico (95928) *(P-16087)*

Enloe Medical Center ....C...... 530 332-6050
1390 E Lassen Ave Chico (95973) *(P-16860)*

Enloe Outpatient Center, Chico *Also Called: Enloe Medical Center (P-16086)*

Enloe Rehabilitation Center, Chico *Also Called: Enloe Medical Center (P-15280)*

Enlyte, San Diego *Also Called: Mitchell International Inc (P-11753)*

Enpower Innovation, City Of Industry *Also Called: PC Club Inc (P-7448)*

Enpower Management Corp ....D...... 925 244-1100
2603 Camino Ramon Ste 263 San Ramon (94583) *(P-4578)*

Ens Security, City Of Industry *Also Called: Easterncctv (usa) LLC (P-13108)*

ENSIGN, Palm Springs *Also Called: Ensign Palm I LLC (P-15456)*

ENSIGN, Ukiah *Also Called: Ensign Pleasanton LLC (P-15457)*

ENSIGN, Whittier *Also Called: Ensign Whittier East LLC (P-15461)*

ENSIGN, San Diego *Also Called: La Jolla Skilled Inc (P-15534)*

ENSIGN, Upland *Also Called: Upland Community Care Inc (P-15712)*

Ensign Cloverdale LLC ....B...... 707 894-5201
300 Cherry Creek Rd Cloverdale (95425) *(P-15450)*

Ensign Group Inc ....C...... 562 923-9301
13007 Paramount Blvd Downey (90242) *(P-15451)*

Ensign Group Inc ....C...... 818 893-6385
9541 Van Nuys Blvd Panorama City (91402) *(P-15452)*

Ensign Group Inc ....C...... 562 947-7817
10426 Bogardus Ave Whittier (90603) *(P-15453)*

Ensign Group Inc ....C...... 707 525-1250
3751 Montgomery Dr Santa Rosa (95405) *(P-15454)*

Ensign Group Inc ....D...... 626 607-2400
4800 Delta Ave Rosemead (91770) *(P-15455)*

Ensign Group Inc ....C...... 805 925-8713
1405 E Main St Santa Maria (93454) *(P-18421)*

Ensign Palm I LLC ....C...... 760 323-2638
2990 E Ramon Rd Palm Springs (92264) *(P-15456)*

Ensign Pleasanton LLC ....C...... 707 462-8864
1349 S Dora St Ukiah (95482) *(P-15457)*

Ensign San Dimas LLC ....C...... 626 963-7531
1033 E Arrow Hwy Glendora (91740) *(P-15843)*

Ensign Services Inc ....D...... 949 487-9500
29222 Rancho Viejo Rd Ste 127 San Juan Capistrano (92675) *(P-15458)*

Ensign Sonoma LLC ....C...... 707 938-8406
1250 Broadway Sonoma (95476) *(P-15459)*

Ensign Southland LLC ....C...... 949 487-9500
29222 Rancho Viejo Rd Ste 127 San Juan Capistrano (92675) *(P-15460)*

Ensign US Drlg Cal Inc ....C...... 661 387-8400
3701 Fruitvale Ave Bakersfield (93308) *(P-1731)*

Ensign Whittier East LLC ....C...... 562 947-7817
10426 Bogardus Ave Whittier (90603) *(P-15461)*

Ensign Whittier West LLC ....C...... 949 487-9500
27101 Puerta Real Ste 450 Mission Viejo (92691) *(P-15462)*

Ensign Willits LLC ....C...... 707 459-5592
64 Northbrook Way Willits (95490) *(P-15463)*

Entco LLC ....A...... 312 580-9100
1140 Enterprise Way Sunnyvale (94089) *(P-12181)*

ALPHABETIC SECTION

Entegris Inc ....D....... 805 541-9299
   4175 Santa Fe Rd San Luis Obispo (93401) *(P-20082)*

Entercom Media Corp ....C....... 909 825-9525
   900 E Washington St Ste 315 Colton (92324) *(P-4379)*

Entercom Media Corp ....D....... 559 490-0106
   1071 W Shaw Ave Fresno (93711) *(P-4380)*

Entercom Media Corp ....C....... 415 765-4097
   865 Battery St Fl 3 San Francisco (94111) *(P-4381)*

Entercom Media Corp ....C....... 323 930-7317
   5670 Wilshire Blvd Ste 200 Los Angeles (90036) *(P-4382)*

Entercom Media Corp ....C....... 916 923-6800
   280 Commerce Cir Sacramento (95815) *(P-4383)*

Enterprise Bank & Trust ....C....... 858 432-7000
   11939 Rancho Bernardo Rd Ste 200 San Diego (92128) *(P-7680)*

Enterprise Bank & Trust ....C....... 562 345-9092
   17785 Center Court Dr N # 750 Cerritos (90703) *(P-7681)*

Enterprise Development Auth ....A....... 833 337-3473
   3317 Forty Mile Rd Wheatland (95692) *(P-9784)*

Enterprise Events Group Inc ....C....... 415 499-4444
   950 Northgate Dr Ste 100 San Rafael (94903) *(P-20361)*

Enterprise Ntwrking Sltons Inc C
   2860 Gold Tailings Ct Rancho Cordova (95670) *(P-12786)*

Enterprise Rent-A-Car, San Ramon Also Called: Enterprise Rent-A-Car Co of San Francisco LLC *(P-13579)*

Enterprise Rent-A-Car, Huntington Beach Also Called: Enterprise Rnt--car Boston LLC *(P-13580)*

Enterprise Rent-A-Car, Orange Also Called: Enterprise Rnt--car Los Angles *(P-13581)*

Enterprise Rent-A-Car, Sacramento Also Called: Enterprise Rnt--car Scrmnto LL *(P-13582)*

Enterprise Rent-A-Car, El Dorado Hills Also Called: Enterprise Rnt--car Scrmnto LL *(P-13583)*

Enterprise Rent-A-Car, Mcclellan Also Called: Enterprise Rnt--car Scrmnto LL *(P-13584)*

Enterprise Rent-A-Car, Redding Also Called: Enterprise Rnt--car Scrmnto LL *(P-13585)*

Enterprise Rent-A-Car Co of San Francisco LLC (DH) ....D....... 925 464-5100
   2633 Camino Ramon Ste 400 San Ramon (94583) *(P-13579)*

Enterprise Rnt--car Boston LLC ....D....... 714 841-4141
   17541 Beach Blvd Huntington Beach (92647) *(P-13580)*

Enterprise Rnt--car Los Angles (DH) ....D....... 657 221-4400
   333 City Blvd W Ste 1000 Orange (92868) *(P-13581)*

Enterprise Rnt--car Scrmnto LL ....C....... 916 576-3164
   6320 Mcnair Cir Sacramento (95837) *(P-13582)*

Enterprise Rnt--car Scrmnto LL ....C....... 916 934-0783
   7034 Rossmore Ln El Dorado Hills (95762) *(P-13583)*

Enterprise Rnt--car Scrmnto LL ....C....... 916 648-1725
   3216 Palm St Mcclellan (95652) *(P-13584)*

Enterprise Rnt--car Scrmnto LL ....C....... 530 223-0700
   217 E Cypress Ave Redding (96002) *(P-13585)*

Enterprise Roofing Service Inc ....D....... 925 689-8100
   2400 Bates Ave Concord (94520) *(P-2063)*

Enterprise Security Inc (PA) ....D....... 714 630-9100
   22860 Savi Ranch Pkwy Yorba Linda (92887) *(P-13113)*

Enterprise Security Solutions, Yorba Linda Also Called: Enterprise Security Inc *(P-13113)*

Enterprise Solutions Inc ....B....... 408 727-3627
   2855 Kifer Rd Santa Clara (95051) *(P-20743)*

Entertainment Partners Inc (PA) ....B....... 818 955-6000
   2950 N Hollywood Way Burbank (91505) *(P-19573)*

Entertinment Studios Media Inc (PA) ....D....... 310 277-3500
   1925 Century Park E Ste 1025 Los Angeles (90067) *(P-14082)*

Entravsion Communications Corp ....D....... 323 900-6100
   5700 Wilshire Blvd Ste 250 Los Angeles (90036) *(P-4427)*

Entravsion Communications Corp ....D....... 760 836-0466
   72920 Parkview Dr Palm Desert (92260) *(P-4428)*

Entravsion Communications Corp (PA) ....C....... 310 447-3870
   2425 Olympic Blvd Ste 6000w Santa Monica (90404) *(P-4429)*

Entrepreneurial Capital Corp ....C....... 949 809-3900
   4100 Newport Place Dr Ste 400 Newport Beach (92660) *(P-8717)*

Envent Corporation (PA) ....D....... 562 997-9465
   3220 E 29th St Long Beach (90806) *(P-20744)*

Envirnment Ntral Resources Div ....A....... 415 744-6491
   301 Howard St Ste 1050 San Francisco (94105) *(P-18857)*

Envirnmental Trnsp Specialists ....D....... 916 442-4971
   4343 Chiles Rd Davis (95618) *(P-7201)*

Envirnmental Htg A Slutions Inc ....D....... 916 990-2952
   8417 Washington Blvd Ste 170 Roseville (95678) *(P-1430)*

Envirnmntal Systems Inc Nthrn (PA) ....D....... 408 980-1711
   3353 De La Cruz Blvd Santa Clara (95054) *(P-1431)*

Enviro Safety Products, Visalia Also Called: Guardian Safety and Supply LLC *(P-7582)*

Enviro Tech Chemical Svcs Inc (DH) ....C....... 209 581-9576
   500 Winmoore Way Modesto (95358) *(P-6708)*

Envirogenics Systems Company ....D....... 818 573-9220
   9255 Telstar Ave El Monte (91731) *(P-1299)*

Environment Control, Visalia Also Called: Tim Hofer Inc *(P-10973)*

Environmental Chemical Corp (PA) ....D....... 650 347-1555
   1240 Bayshore Hwy Burlingame (94010) *(P-19217)*

Environmental Construction Inc ....D....... 818 449-8920
   21550 Oxnard St Ste 1060 Woodland Hills (91367) *(P-914)*

Environmental Industries, Fillmore Also Called: Brightview Tree Company *(P-567)*

Environmental Ldscp Solutions, Rancho Cordova Also Called: Els Investments *(P-429)*

Environmental Remedies Inc ....D....... 925 461-3285
   22390 Thunderbird Pl Hayward (94545) *(P-20886)*

Environmental Resolutions Inc ....B....... 949 457-8950
   25371 Commercentre Dr Ste 250 Lake Forest (92630) *(P-20745)*

Environmental Resources MGT, Walnut Creek Also Called: Erm-West Inc *(P-19220)*

Environmental Science Assoc (PA) ....D....... 415 896-5900
   575 Market St Ste 3700 San Francisco (94105) *(P-19687)*

Environmental Science Assoc ....C....... 213 599-4300
   626 Wilshire Blvd Ste 1100 Los Angeles (90017) *(P-19688)*

Environmental Science Assoc ....C....... 858 638-0900
   9191 Towne Centre Dr Ste 340 San Diego (92122) *(P-20746)*

Environmental Systems Research Institute Inc (PA) ....A....... 909 793-2853
   380 New York St Redlands (92373) *(P-5300)*

Environments For Learning Inc (PA) ....D....... 949 855-5630
   24291 Muirlands Blvd Lake Forest (92630) *(P-18313)*

Envise (HQ) ....C....... 800 613-6240
   12131 Western Ave Garden Grove (92841) *(P-1432)*

Envise ....D....... 714 901-5800
   12131 Western Ave Garden Grove (92841) *(P-1433)*

Envise, Garden Grove Also Called: Envise *(P-1432)*

Envivio Inc ....C....... 650 243-2700
   2795 Augustine Dr Santa Clara (95054) *(P-4270)*

Enxco, San Diego Also Called: Edf Renewables Services Inc *(P-13681)*

Eoc Resource Development, Fresno Also Called: Fresno Cnty Ecnmic Opprtnties *(P-17989)*

Eon Reality Inc (PA) ....D....... 949 460-2000
   18 Technology Dr Ste 110 Irvine (92618) *(P-5301)*

Eos It MGT Solutions Inc ....A....... 510 600-4188
   30826 Santana St Hayward (94544) *(P-20362)*

Eoy, Los Angeles Also Called: Empower Our Youth *(P-9414)*

Epic Creations Inc ....C....... 650 918-7327
   702 Marshall St Ste 280 Redwood City (94063) *(P-11572)*

Epic Jet Centre, San Luis Obispo Also Called: Aviation Consultants Inc *(P-20028)*

Epic Management LP (PA) ....D....... 909 799-1818
   1615 Orange Tree Ln Redlands (92374) *(P-20083)*

Epic Production Technologies (us Sales) Inc ....D
   1401 Maulhardt Ave Ste A Oxnard (93030) *(P-11031)*

Epic Sciences Inc ....D....... 858 356-6610
   9381 Judicial Dr Ste 200 San Diego (92121) *(P-16718)*

Epic War, Palo Alto Also Called: Machine Zone Inc *(P-11722)*

EPICENTRE, San Diego Also Called: Harmonium Inc *(P-18319)*

Epicurean Group ....B....... 650 947-6800
   111 Main St Ste 3 Los Altos (94022) *(P-7477)*

Epidaurus ....B....... 213 743-9075
   3745 S Grand Ave Los Angeles (90007) *(P-9425)*

Episcopal Communities & Servic ....D....... 310 544-2204
   5801 Crestridge Rd Pls Vrds Pnsl (90275) *(P-15464)*

Episcopal Community Services ....D....... 619 470-0720
   2432 E 18th St National City (91950) *(P-17969)*

Episource LLC ....A....... 714 452-1961
   500 W 190th St Ste 400 Gardena (90248) *(P-8554)*

Epitec Inc ....A....... 760 650-2515
   515 Olive Ave Vista (92083) *(P-11573)*

Eplica Inc ....D....... 562 977-4300
   17785 Center Court Dr N Cerritos (90703) *(P-11131)*

Eplica Inc (PA) ....C....... 619 260-2000
   2385 Northside Dr Ste 250 San Diego (92108) *(P-11284)*

Eplica Corporate Services Inc .... A...... 619 282-1400		Erepublic Inc (PA).. C...... 916 932-1300	
2385 Northside Dr Ste 250 San Diego (92108) *(P-11132)*		100 Blue Ravine Rd Folsom (95630) *(P-13281)*	
EPLP, San Mateo *Also Called: Essex Portfolio LP (P-8809)*		Erepublic LLC .... C...... 916 932-1300	
Epn Enterprises Inc .... D...... 888 788-5424		100 Blue Ravine Rd Folsom (95630) *(P-10711)*	
1900 Point West Way Ste 171 Sacramento (95815) *(P-11285)*		Ergomotion Inc .... D...... 888 550-3746	
Epoch.com, Santa Monica *Also Called: Epochcom LLC (P-12571)*		6790 Navigator Way Goleta (93117) *(P-11576)*	
Epochcom LLC .... C...... 310 664-5700		Eri, Fresno *Also Called: Electronic Recyclers Intl Inc (P-4892)*	
3110 Main St Ste 220 Santa Monica (90405) *(P-12571)*		Eric F Anderson Incorporated .... D...... 510 430-8404	
Epr Recruiting Inc .... D...... 213 607-2001		1066 Beecher St San Leandro (94577) *(P-915)*	
4000 Calle Tecate Ste 213 Camarillo (93012) *(P-11574)*		Eric F. Anderson, San Leandro *Also Called: Eric F Anderson Incorporated (P-915)*	
Epri, Palo Alto *Also Called: Epri International Inc (P-19689)*		Eric Stark Interiors Inc .... D...... 408 441-6136	
Epri International Inc (HQ)... D...... 650 855-2000		2284 Paragon Dr San Jose (95131) *(P-1927)*	
3420 Hillview Ave Palo Alto (94304) *(P-19689)*		Erickson-Hall Construction Co (PA).......................... D...... 760 796-7700	
Eps Corporate Holdings Inc .... D...... 714 635-3131		500 Corporate Dr Escondido (92029) *(P-916)*	
1235 S Lewis St Anaheim (92805) *(P-5747)*		Ericsson Inc .... A...... 408 750-5000	
Epsilon Electronics Inc (PA)....................................... D...... 323 722-3333		2755 Augustine Dr Santa Clara (95054) *(P-4271)*	
1550 S Maple Ave Montebello (90640) *(P-5603)*		Eriks North America Inc .... D...... 916 366-9340	
Epsilon Plastics Inc .... D...... 310 609-1320		10182 Croydon Way Sacramento (95827) *(P-5901)*	
3100 E Harcourt St Compton (90221) *(P-6904)*		Erm-West Inc (DH)... B...... 925 946-0455	
Epsilon Systems Sltons Mssion .... D...... 619 702-1700		1277 Treat Blvd Ste 500 Walnut Creek (94597) *(P-19220)*	
9242 Lightwave Ave Ste 100 San Diego (92123) *(P-19218)*		Ernest Packaging (PA)... C...... 800 233-7788	
Epsilon Systems Solutions Inc .... C...... 619 474-3252		5777 Smithway St Commerce (90040) *(P-6905)*	
2101 Haffley Ave # A National City (91950) *(P-18709)*		Ernest Packaging Solutions, Sacramento *Also Called: Calvey Incorporated (P-6895)*	
Epsilon Systems Solutions Inc (PA).......................... D...... 619 702-1700		Ernest Paper, Commerce *Also Called: Ernest Packaging (P-6905)*	
9444 Balboa Ave Ste 100 San Diego (92123) *(P-19219)*		Ernst & Young LLP .... A...... 213 977-3200	
Epstein Becker & Green PC .... D...... 415 398-3500		725 S Figueroa St Ste 200 Los Angeles (90017) *(P-19574)*	
655 Montgomery St Ste 1150 San Francisco (94111) *(P-17448)*		Ernst & Young LLP .... C...... 408 947-5500	
Epstein Becker & Green PC .... C...... 310 556-8861		303 Almaden Blvd Ste 1000 San Jose (95110) *(P-19575)*	
1875 Century Park E Ste 500 Los Angeles (90067) *(P-17449)*		Ernst & Young LLP .... B...... 949 794-2300	
Epstein White Rtrment Income S .... D...... 858 564-8036		18101 Von Karman Ave Ste 1700 Irvine (92612) *(P-19576)*	
9740 Appaloosa Rd Ste 150 San Diego (92131) *(P-8555)*		Eros Stx Global Corporation .... A...... 818 524-7000	
Equator LLC (HQ)... C...... 310 469-9500		3900 W Alameda Ave Fl 32 Burbank (91505) *(P-14024)*	
6060 Center Dr Ste 500 Los Angeles (90045) *(P-11575)*		Erp Integrated Solutions LLC .... D...... 562 425-7800	
Equator Business Solutions, Los Angeles *Also Called: Equator LLC (P-11575)*		5000 Airport Plaza Dr Ste 230 Long Beach (90815) *(P-11577)*	
Equilar Inc .... C...... 877 441-6090		Errg, Martinez *Also Called: Enginrng/Rmdtion Rsrces Group (P-4979)*	
1100 Marshall St Redwood City (94063) *(P-13280)*		Errg-Er J V, San Francisco *Also Called: Enginrng/Rmdtion Rsrces Group (P-20653)*	
Equinix, Redwood City *Also Called: Equinix Inc (P-9466)*		Ert Operating Company .... A...... 412 390-3000	
Equinix Inc (PA)... C...... 650 598-6000		5615 Scotts Valley Dr Ste 150 Scotts Valley (95066) *(P-11578)*	
1 Lagoon Dr Ste 400 Redwood City (94065) *(P-9466)*		Erwin Street Medical Offices, Woodland Hills *Also Called: Kaiser Foundation Hospitals (P-16177)*	
Equinox, San Francisco *Also Called: Equinox-76th Street Inc (P-14201)*		Es Engineering Services LLC .... D...... 949 988-3500	
Equinox Fitness Club, San Francisco *Also Called: Equinox Holdings Inc (P-14197)*		4 Park Plz Ste 790 Irvine (92614) *(P-19221)*	
Equinox Fitness Club, Irvine *Also Called: Equinox-76th Street Inc (P-14202)*		ESA, San Francisco *Also Called: Environmental Science Assoc (P-19687)*	
Equinox Fitness Club, Los Angeles *Also Called: Equinox-76th Street Inc (P-14203)*		ESA, Los Angeles *Also Called: Environmental Science Assoc (P-19688)*	
Equinox Holdings Inc .... D...... 415 243-0492		Esaloncom LLC .... D...... 866 550-2424	
747 Market St San Francisco (94103) *(P-14197)*		1910 E Maple Ave El Segundo (90245) *(P-10496)*	
Equinox Hotel Management Inc .... D...... 415 668-6887		Esau Concrete Inc .... D...... 209 357-7601	
2422 Lake St San Francisco (94121) *(P-9785)*		101 Business Park Way Atwater (95301) *(P-2117)*	
Equinox-76th Street Inc .... D...... 310 727-9543		Eschat .... D...... 805 541-5044	
5400 W Rosecrans Ave Ste Uppr Hawthorne (90250) *(P-14198)*		3450 Broad St Ste 106 San Luis Obispo (93401) *(P-4216)*	
Equinox-76th Street Inc .... D...... 805 367-3925		Escondido Medical Offices, Escondido *Also Called: Kaiser Foundation Hospitals (P-14830)*	
112 S Lakeview Canyon Rd Westlake Village (91362) *(P-14199)*		Escondido Memory Care Cmnty, Escondido *Also Called: Silverado Senior Living Inc (P-15670)*	
Equinox-76th Street Inc .... D...... 310 479-5200		Escondido Motors LLC .... D...... 760 745-5000	
1835 S Sepulveda Blvd Los Angeles (90025) *(P-14200)*		1101 W 9th Ave Escondido (92025) *(P-7202)*	
Equinox-76th Street Inc .... C...... 415 398-0747		Escondido Post Acute Rehab, Escondido *Also Called: Mek Escondido LLC (P-15582)*	
301 Pine St San Francisco (94104) *(P-14201)*		Escrow.com, San Francisco *Also Called: Internet Escrow Services Inc (P-9052)*	
Equinox-76th Street Inc .... D...... 949 296-1700		Eset LLC (HQ).. C...... 619 876-5400	
19540 Jamboree Rd Irvine (92612) *(P-14202)*		610 W Ash St Ste 1700 San Diego (92101) *(P-5302)*	
Equinox-76th Street Inc .... D...... 310 552-0420		Eset North America, San Diego *Also Called: Eset LLC (P-5302)*	
10250 Santa Monica Blvd Los Angeles (90067) *(P-14203)*		Eskaton (PA)... D...... 916 334-0296	
Equinox-76th Street Inc .... D...... 949 975-8400		5105 Manzanita Ave Ste D Carmichael (95608) *(P-8718)*	
1980 Main St Fl 4 Irvine (92614) *(P-15281)*		Eskaton .... C...... 916 395-1722	
Equipment Brokers Unlimited, Cerritos *Also Called: Docusource Inc (P-7578)*		5701 Falconer Way Sacramento (95824) *(P-8719)*	
Equipment Depot Inc .... C...... 562 949-1000		Eskaton .... C...... 916 536-3750	
12393 Slauson Ave Whittier (90606) *(P-5833)*		9722 Fair Oaks Blvd Ste A Fair Oaks (95628) *(P-16861)*	
Equity International Inc .... A...... 978 664-2712		Eskaton .... C...... 530 672-8900	
5541 Fermi Ct Carlsbad (92008) *(P-5648)*		3421 Palmer Dr Cameron Park (95682) *(P-18422)*	
Equity Smart Home Loans Inc .... D...... 626 864-8774		Eskaton .... C...... 916 852-7900	
1499 Huntington Dr Ste 500 South Pasadena (91030) *(P-7961)*		11390 Coloma Rd Ofc Gold River (95670) *(P-18423)*	
Equity Title Company (DH)... D...... 818 291-4400			
801 N Brand Blvd Ste 400 Glendale (91203) *(P-9228)*			

Eskaton Center of Greenhaven, Sacramento *Also Called: Eskaton Properties Inc (P-18428)*

Eskaton Properties Inc .... C....... 916 974-2060
3847 Walnut Ave Carmichael (95608) *(P-15465)*

Eskaton Properties Inc .... C....... 916 331-8513
5318 Manzanita Ave Carmichael (95608) *(P-15466)*

Eskaton Properties Inc .... C....... 916 334-0296
5105 Manzanita Ave Ste D Carmichael (95608) *(P-17970)*

Eskaton Properties Inc .... C....... 916 441-1015
3225 Freeport Blvd Ofc Sacramento (95818) *(P-18424)*

Eskaton Properties Inc .... C....... 530 677-5066
3421 Palmer Dr Cameron Park (95682) *(P-18425)*

Eskaton Properties Inc .... C....... 916 334-0810
1650 Eskaton Loop Roseville (95747) *(P-18426)*

Eskaton Properties Inc .... C....... 916 965-4663
11300 Fair Oaks Blvd Fair Oaks (95628) *(P-18427)*

Eskaton Properties Inc .... C....... 916 393-2550
455 Florin Rd Sacramento (95831) *(P-18428)*

Eskaton Properties Inc (PA) .... D....... 916 334-0810
5105 Manzanita Ave Ste A Carmichael (95608) *(P-18429)*

Eskaton Properties Inc .... C....... 916 974-2000
3939 Walnut Ave Unit 399 Carmichael (95608) *(P-18430)*

Eskaton Village Care Center, Carmichael *Also Called: Eskaton Properties Inc (P-15465)*

Eskaton Village Charmichael, Carmichael *Also Called: Eskaton Properties Inc (P-18430)*

Eskaton Village Roseville, Roseville *Also Called: Eskaton Properties Inc (P-18426)*

Esl, Burbank *Also Called: Esl Gaming America Inc (P-14083)*

Esl Gaming America Inc .... D....... 818 861-7315
1212 Chestnut St Burbank (91506) *(P-14083)*

Esl Technologies Inc .... B....... 916 677-4500
8875 Washington Blvd B Roseville (95678) *(P-12706)*

Esparza Enterprises Inc .... A....... 760 344-2031
251 W Main St Ste G&F Brawley (92227) *(P-374)*

Esparza Enterprises Inc .... A....... 661 631-0347
500 Workman St Bakersfield (93307) *(P-3469)*

Esparza Enterprises Inc .... A....... 760 398-0349
51335 Cesar Chavez St Ste 112 Coachella (92236) *(P-11133)*

Esparza Enterprises Inc .... A....... 661 631-0347
222 S Union Ave Bakersfield (93307) *(P-11134)*

Esperanto Technologies Inc (PA) .... D....... 650 319-7357
800 W El Camino Real Ste 410 Mountain View (94040) *(P-2919)*

Espressive Inc .... D....... 408 753-8766
5201 Great America Pkwy Ste 110 Santa Clara (95054) *(P-12182)*

Esri, Redlands *Also Called: Environmental Systems Research Institute Inc (P-5300)*

Ess LLC .... D....... 888 303-6424
5227 Dantes View Dr Agoura Hills (91301) *(P-1434)*

Essence Healthcare Cal Inc .... A....... 650 723-4000
300 Pasteur Dr Stanford (94305) *(P-16088)*

Essendant Co .... C....... 626 961-0011
918 S Stimson Ave City Of Industry (91745) *(P-6065)*

Essense .... A....... 323 202-4650
6300 Wilshire Blvd Ste 720 Los Angeles (90048) *(P-20887)*

Essential Access Health (PA) .... D....... 213 386-5614
3600 Wilshire Blvd Ste 600 Los Angeles (90010) *(P-18586)*

Essential Products Inc .... D....... 650 300-0000
380 Portage Ave Palo Alto (94306) *(P-11579)*

Essex National Securities LLC .... D....... 707 258-5000
550 Gateway Dr Ste 210 Napa (94558) *(P-20363)*

Essex Portfolio LP (HQ) .... B....... 650 655-7800
1100 Park Pl Ste 200 San Mateo (94403) *(P-8809)*

Essex Properties LLC .... D....... 949 798-8100
18012 Sky Park Cir Ste 100 Irvine (92614) *(P-8994)*

Essex Property Trust Inc (PA) .... B....... 650 655-7800
1100 Park Pl Ste 200 San Mateo (94403) *(P-8810)*

Essey LLC .... B....... 212 490-7400
140 Geary St San Francisco (94108) *(P-17450)*

Estancia Hotel LLC .... C....... 949 474-7368
9700 N Torrey Pines Rd La Jolla (92037) *(P-9786)*

Estancia La Jolla Hotel & Spa, La Jolla *Also Called: Estancia Hotel LLC (P-9786)*

Estate Investment Group, Dublin *Also Called: New Home Professionals (P-9108)*

Estates At Trump Nat Golf CLB .... C....... 310 265-5000
1 Trump National Dr Rancho Palos Verdes (90275) *(P-14261)*

Estech, San Ramon *Also Called: Endoscopic Technologies Inc (P-5413)*

Esterline Mason, Rancho Cascades *Also Called: Janco Corporation (P-2943)*

Estes, City Of Industry *Also Called: Estes Express Lines (P-3474)*

Estes, Fresno *Also Called: Estes Express Lines (P-3475)*

Estes Express Lines .... C....... 714 994-3770
14727 Alondra Blvd La Mirada (90638) *(P-3470)*

Estes Express Lines .... D....... 619 425-4040
120 Press Ln Chula Vista (91910) *(P-3471)*

Estes Express Lines .... C....... 510 635-0165
1750 Adams Ave San Leandro (94577) *(P-3472)*

Estes Express Lines .... C....... 909 427-9850
10736 Cherry Ave Fontana (92337) *(P-3473)*

Estes Express Lines .... D....... 626 333-9090
13327 Temple Ave City Of Industry (91746) *(P-3474)*

Estes Express Lines .... D....... 559 441-0915
4355 S Chestnut Ave Fresno (93725) *(P-3475)*

Estrella Inc .... C....... 562 925-6418
1340 Highland Ave # 12 Duarte (91010) *(P-15467)*

Estuate Inc .... D....... 408 946-0002
830 Hillview Ct Ste 280 Milpitas (95035) *(P-11580)*

Estudysite .... D....... 619 955-5246
752 Medical Center Ct Ste 304 Chula Vista (91911) *(P-19690)*

Esurance Insurance Svcs Inc (HQ) .... D....... 415 875-4500
650 Davis St San Francisco (94111) *(P-8556)*

Esys Energy Control Company .... D....... 661 833-1902
4520 Stine Rd Ste 7 Bakersfield (93313) *(P-1732)*

Et Whitehall Seascape LLC .... C....... 310 581-5533
1910 Ocean Way Santa Monica (90405) *(P-9787)*

Etap, Irvine *Also Called: Operation Technology Inc (P-11799)*

Etch Mobile Inc .... D....... 512 299-3514
835 Howard St # 3 San Francisco (94103) *(P-11581)*

Etchandy Farms LLC .... D....... 805 983-4700
4324 Vineyard Ave Oxnard (93036) *(P-52)*

Etech-360 Inc (PA) .... A....... 714 900-3486
555 California St San Francisco (94104) *(P-12183)*

Etekcity, Anaheim *Also Called: Etekcity Corporation (P-5604)*

Etekcity Corporation .... C....... 855 686-3835
1202 N Miller St Unit A Anaheim (92806) *(P-5604)*

Ethan Conrad Properties Inc (PA) .... D....... 916 779-1000
1300 National Dr Ste 100 Sacramento (95834) *(P-8995)*

Etherwan Systems Inc .... D....... 714 779-3800
2301 E Winston Rd Anaheim (92806) *(P-12787)*

Ethos Event Collective LLC .... D....... 415 762-9773
2269 Chestnut St Ste 260 San Francisco (94123) *(P-20364)*

Ethos Seafood Group LLC .... D....... 312 858-3474
18531 S Broadwick St Rancho Dominguez (90220) *(P-2420)*

Etiwanda Power Plant, Rancho Cucamonga *Also Called: NRG California South LP (P-4592)*

Etl Testing Laboratories .... C....... 650 463-2900
1365 Adams Ct Menlo Park (94025) *(P-19970)*

Etnies, Lake Forest *Also Called: Sole Technology Inc (P-2685)*

Etonien, Manhattan Beach *Also Called: Etonien LLC (P-20747)*

Etonien LLC (PA) .... D....... 310 321-5800
1230 Rosecrans Ave Ste 530 Manhattan Beach (90266) *(P-20747)*

Etouch, Newark *Also Called: Etouch Systems Corp (P-12788)*

Etouch Systems Corp .... A....... 510 795-4800
39899 Balentine Dr Ste 200 Newark (94560) *(P-12788)*

Ets-Esc Holdings LLC .... B....... 925 314-7100
2001 Crow Canyon Rd Ste 110 San Ramon (94583) *(P-9311)*

Ettore, Alameda *Also Called: Ettore Products Co (P-5938)*

Ettore Products Co .... D....... 510 748-4130
2100 N Loop Rd Alameda (94502) *(P-5938)*

Euclid Parking, Porterville *Also Called: Exeter Packers Inc (P-266)*

Eugene Harris .... D....... 916 776-3393
3351 Duckhorn Dr Sacramento (95834) *(P-13586)*

Eureka District Office, Eureka *Also Called: State Compensation Insur Fund (P-8416)*

EUREKA REHABILITATION & WELLNE, Eureka *Also Called: Eureka Rhbltition Wllness Ctr L (P-15468)*

Eureka Rhbltition Wllness Ctr L .... D....... 707 445-3261
2353 23rd St Eureka (95501) *(P-15468)*

Euroamerican Propagators LLC .... B....... 760 731-6029
32149 Aquaduct Rd Bonsall (92003) *(P-127)*

Eurodrip USA Inc .... D...... 559 674-2670
7545 Carroll Rd San Diego (92121) *(P-5808)*

Eurofins Discoverx Pdts LLC .... D...... 510 979-1415
42501 Albrae St Fremont (94538) *(P-19691)*

Eurofins Eag Engrg Science LLC (DH) .... D...... 408 588-0050
2710 Walsh Ave Santa Clara (95051) *(P-19971)*

Eurofins Eag Laboratories, Sunnyvale *Also Called: Eurofins Eag Mtls Science LLC (P-19972)*

Eurofins Eag Mtls Science LLC (DH) .... C...... 408 454-4600
810 Kifer Rd Sunnyvale (94086) *(P-19972)*

Eurofins Eaton Analytical LLC (DH) .... D...... 626 386-1100
750 Royal Oaks Dr Ste 100 Monrovia (91016) *(P-19973)*

Eurofins Emlab P&K Fairfax Co, Tustin *Also Called: Eurofins Epk Bilt Envmt Tstg L (P-19974)*

Eurofins Epk Bilt Envmt Tstg L (DH) .... D...... 330 497-9396
2841 Dow Ave Ste 300 Tustin (92780) *(P-19974)*

Eurofins Fd Chmstry Tstg Mdson .... A...... 609 452-4440
2441 Constitution Dr Livermore (94551) *(P-19975)*

Europa Auto Imports Inc .... C...... 858 569-6900
4750 Kearny Mesa Rd San Diego (92111) *(P-7203)*

Europcar, Los Angeles *Also Called: Fox Rent A Car Inc (P-13588)*

European Ht Invstors I I A Cal .... D...... 949 474-7368
2532 Dupont Dr Irvine (92612) *(P-9788)*

European Wholesale Counter .... C...... 619 562-0565
10051 Prospect Ave Santee (92071) *(P-2503)*

Eva Automation Inc .... B...... 650 513-6875
3945 Freedom Cir Ste 560 Santa Clara (95054) *(P-20365)*

Evans Analytical Group LLC .... D...... 408 454-4600
2710 Walsh Ave Santa Clara (95051) *(P-19976)*

Evans Industries Inc .... D...... 626 912-1688
17915 Railroad St City Of Industry (91748) *(P-2766)*

Evault Inc .... C...... 415 432-2200
6001 Shellmound St Emeryville (94608) *(P-12789)*

Even Responsible Finance Inc .... D...... 360 977-2475
1440 Bdwy Fl 5 Oakland (94612) *(P-13282)*

Event Intelligence Group .... D...... 310 237-5375
4140 Jackson Ave Culver City (90232) *(P-13114)*

Eventbrite, San Francisco *Also Called: Eventbrite Inc (P-12790)*

Eventbrite Inc (PA) .... B...... 415 692-7779
535 Mission St Fl 8 San Francisco (94105) *(P-12790)*

Events Management Inc .... B...... 415 487-9114
1798 Bryant St San Francisco (94110) *(P-7478)*

Ever Increasing Faith Ministry, Los Angeles *Also Called: Crenshaw Chrstn Ctr Ch Los Ang (P-19017)*

Everbridge Inc (PA) .... C...... 818 230-9700
155 N Lake Ave Ste 900 Pasadena (91101) *(P-12184)*

Everde Growers, Fallbrook *Also Called: Treesap Farms LLC (P-203)*

Everest Sonoma Management LLC .... D...... 213 272-0088
520 Newport Center Dr Fl 2 Newport Beach (92660) *(P-9789)*

Everest Wtrprfing Rstrtion Inc .... D...... 415 282-9800
1270 Missouri St San Francisco (94107) *(P-10545)*

Evergent, Sunnyvale *Also Called: Evergent Technologies Inc (P-11582)*

Evergent Technologies Inc .... B...... 877 897-1240
1250 Borregas Ave Sunnyvale (94089) *(P-11582)*

Evergreen Alliance Golf Ltd LP .... D...... 909 886-0669
3380 Little Mountain Dr San Bernardino (92405) *(P-14374)*

Evergreen At Lakeport LLC (PA) .... D...... 707 263-6382
1291 Craig Ave Lakeport (95453) *(P-15469)*

Evergreen At Lakeport LLC .... D...... 661 871-3133
6212 Tudor Way Bakersfield (93306) *(P-15470)*

Evergreen At Springs Road LLC .... D...... 360 892-6628
1527 Springs Rd Vallejo (94591) *(P-15471)*

Evergreen Dstntion Hldings LLC .... D...... 209 379-2606
33160 Evergreen Rd Groveland (95321) *(P-9790)*

Evergreen Envmtl Svcs Inc .... C...... 510 795-4400
6880 Smith Ave Newark (94560) *(P-4893)*

Evergreen Fullerton Healthcare, Fullerton *Also Called: Fullerton Hlthcare Wllness CNT (P-15485)*

Evergreen Health Care LLC .... A...... 661 854-4475
323 Campus Dr Arvin (93203) *(P-15472)*

Evergreen Healthcare Center, Bakersfield *Also Called: Evergreen At Lakeport LLC (P-15470)*

Evergreen Lkport Halthcare Ctr, Lakeport *Also Called: Evergreen At Lakeport LLC (P-15469)*

Evergreen Lodge, Groveland *Also Called: Evergreen Dstntion Hldings LLC (P-9790)*

Evergreen Packaging LLC .... C...... 209 664-3426
1500 W Main St Turlock (95380) *(P-6906)*

Evergreen Solar Services, Agoura Hills *Also Called: Ess LLC (P-1434)*

Everlaw Inc (PA) .... B...... 844 383-7529
2101 Webster St Ste 1500 Oakland (94612) *(P-17451)*

Evernote Corporation (PA) .... B...... 650 216-7700
12671 High Bluff Dr San Diego (92130) *(P-11583)*

Everpac .... D...... 951 774-3274
1499 Palmyrita Ave Riverside (92507) *(P-5787)*

Everpark Inc .... C...... 310 987-6922
3470 Wilshire Blvd Ste 940 Los Angeles (90010) *(P-13605)*

Evertek Computer Corporation .... D...... 951 252-8700
42301 Zevo Dr Ste A Temecula (92590) *(P-5303)*

Evertek Computer Products, Temecula *Also Called: Evertek Computer Corporation (P-5303)*

Everyone Counts Inc .... D
3945 Freedom Cir Ste 560 Santa Clara (95054) *(P-11584)*

Everypath Inc .... D...... 408 562-8000
101 University Ave # 100 Palo Alto (94301) *(P-12572)*

Evidation Health Inc .... C...... 650 389-2494
11 N Ellsworth Ave San Mateo (94401) *(P-11585)*

Evidentio Inc (HQ) .... D...... 855 933-1337
7901 Stoneridge Dr Ste 150 Pleasanton (94588) *(P-11586)*

Evocative Inc .... D...... 888 365-2656
600 W 7th St Ste 510 Los Angeles (90017) *(P-12185)*

Evolent Health Inc .... B...... 571 389-6000
1 Kearny St Ste 300 San Francisco (94108) *(P-17236)*

Evolution Film & Tape Inc .... D...... 818 260-0300
3310 W Vanowen St Burbank (91505) *(P-13847)*

Evolution Fresh Inc .... C...... 800 794-9986
11655 Jersey Blvd Ste A Rancho Cucamonga (91730) *(P-6537)*

Evolution Hospitality LLC (HQ) .... D...... 949 325-1350
1211 Puerta Del Sol Ste 170 San Clemente (92673) *(P-20084)*

Evolution Juice, Rancho Cucamonga *Also Called: Evolution Fresh Inc (P-6537)*

Evolution Media, Burbank *Also Called: Evolution Film & Tape Inc (P-13847)*

Evolution Robotics Inc .... C...... 626 993-3300
1055 E Colorado Blvd Ste 320 Pasadena (91106) *(P-12186)*

Evolv Surfaces Inc .... C...... 415 767-4600
825 Potter St Berkeley (94710) *(P-2506)*

Evolve Discovery, San Francisco *Also Called: Andatha International Inc (P-17364)*

Evolve Growth Initiatives LLC .... C...... 424 281-5000
820 Moraga Dr Los Angeles (90049) *(P-18431)*

Evolve Manufacturing Tech Inc .... D...... 510 690-8959
47300 Bayside Pkwy Fremont (94538) *(P-3051)*

Evolve Treatment Centers .... D...... 310 622-1420
600 N Sepulveda Blvd Los Angeles (90049) *(P-17062)*

Evolve Treatment Centers, Los Angeles *Also Called: Evolve Growth Initiatives LLC (P-18431)*

Evolveware Inc .... D...... 408 748-8301
4677 Old Ironsides Dr Ste 240 Santa Clara (95054) *(P-11587)*

Evoq Properties Inc .... D...... 213 988-8890
1318 E 7th St Ste 200 Los Angeles (90021) *(P-8996)*

Evr Lending Inc .... D...... 949 492-4868
1397 Calle Avanzado San Clemente (92673) *(P-8997)*

EVR LENDING INC, San Clemente *Also Called: Evr Lending Inc (P-8997)*

EW Scripps Company .... C...... 619 237-1010
4600 Air Way San Diego (92102) *(P-4430)*

Eworkplace Manufacturing Inc .... C...... 949 583-1646
9861 Irvine Center Dr Irvine (92618) *(P-5304)*

Exactax Inc (PA) .... D...... 714 284-4802
1100 E Orangethorpe Ave Ste 100 Anaheim (92801) *(P-10521)*

Exadel Inc (PA) .... A...... 925 363-9510
1340 Treat Blvd Ste 375 Walnut Creek (94597) *(P-12187)*

Exagen Diagnostics Inc .... C...... 505 272-7966
1221 Liberty Way Ste A Vista (92081) *(P-16719)*

Exagen Diagnostics, Inc., Vista *Also Called: Exagen Diagnostics Inc (P-16719)*

Examine Your Practice, San Diego *Also Called: Trendsource Inc (P-19853)*

Examone, San Diego *Also Called: Examone World Wide Inc (P-17237)*

Examone World Wide Inc .... D...... 619 299-3926
7480 Mission Valley Rd Ste 101 San Diego (92108) *(P-17237)*

Exar International Inc .... C...... 949 753-8108
48760 Kato Rd Fremont (94538) *(P-5649)*

ALPHABETIC SECTION — Ey-Parthenon

Excalibur Well Services Corp .... C 661 589-5338
22034 Rosedale Hwy Bakersfield (93314) *(P-593)*

Excel Auto Transporting Towing, Jurupa Valley *Also Called: Deluxe Auto Carriers Inc (P-3387)*

Excel Building Services LLC .... A 925 474-1080
1061 Serpentine Ln Ste H Pleasanton (94566) *(P-10894)*

Excel Contractors Inc .... D 661 942-6944
348 E Avenue K8 Ste B Lancaster (93535) *(P-676)*

Excel Garden Products .... C 925 948-4000
1340 Treat Blvd Ste 600 Walnut Creek (94597) *(P-6824)*

Excel Landscape Inc .... C 951 735-9650
710 Rimpau Ave Ste 108 Corona (92879) *(P-489)*

Excel Managed Care Disa .... C 916 944-7185
3840 Watt Ave Bldg C Sacramento (95821) *(P-20366)*

Excel Mdular Scaffold Lsg Corp .... A 760 598-0050
2555 Birch St Vista (92081) *(P-2273)*

Excel Paving Co, Long Beach *Also Called: Palp Inc (P-1151)*

Excel Trust Inc .... D 858 613-1800
17140 Bernardo Center Dr San Diego (92128) *(P-9467)*

Excell Staffing & SEC Svcs, El Cajon *Also Called: Xl Staffing Inc (P-11263)*

Exceptional Chld Foundation .... C 213 748-3556
1430 Venice Blvd Los Angeles (90006) *(P-18229)*

Exceptional Chld Foundation (PA) .... C 310 204-3300
5350 Machado Ln Culver City (90230) *(P-18230)*

Exceptional Chld Foundation .... C 310 915-6606
11124 Fairbanks Way Culver City (90230) *(P-18858)*

Exceptnal Prents Unlimited Inc .... C 559 229-2000
4440 N 1st St Fresno (93726) *(P-17971)*

Exchange Bank (PA) .... C 707 524-3000
545 4th St Santa Rosa (95401) *(P-7748)*

Excite Credit Union (PA) .... D 800 232-8669
265 Curtner Ave San Jose (95125) *(P-7764)*

Exclusive Lifestyles Inc (PA) .... D 702 996-3030
27762 Antonio Pkwy Ladera Ranch (92694) *(P-8998)*

Executive Car Leasing Company (PA) .... D 800 800-3932
7807 Santa Monica Blvd West Hollywood (90046) *(P-13596)*

Executive Committee, The, San Diego *Also Called: Vistage International Inc (P-20605)*

Executive Inn Inc .... D 408 245-5330
1217 Wildwood Ave Sunnyvale (94089) *(P-9791)*

Executive Landscape Inc .... C 760 731-9036
2131 Huffstatler St Fallbrook (92028) *(P-430)*

Executive Network Entps Inc .... A 310 457-8822
1224 21st St Apt E Santa Monica (90404) *(P-3256)*

Executive Network Entps Inc (PA) .... D 310 447-2759
13440 Beach Ave Marina Del Rey (90292) *(P-3257)*

Executive Personnel Services .... B 714 310-9506
1526 Brookhollow Dr Ste 83 Santa Ana (92705) *(P-11135)*

Exelixis Inc .... B 650 837-7000
1851 Harbor Bay Pkwy Alameda (94502) *(P-3022)*

Exer, Simi Valley *Also Called: Providnce Facey Med Foundation (P-15257)*

Exer Holding Company LLC .... C 818 287-0894
15503 Ventura Blvd Encino (91436) *(P-14742)*

Exertus Fncl Prtners Insur AGC .... D 408 458-8418
830 Hillview Ct Ste 140 Milpitas (95035) *(P-20367)*

Exeter Engineering Inc .... D 559 592-3161
109 W Pine St Exeter (93221) *(P-264)*

Exeter Packers Inc .... C 626 993-6245
1095 E Green St Pasadena (91106) *(P-98)*

Exeter Packers Inc (PA) .... C 559 592-5168
1250 E Myer Ave Exeter (93221) *(P-265)*

Exeter Packers Inc .... C 559 784-8820
23744 Avenue 181 Porterville (93257) *(P-266)*

Exeter Packers Inc .... C 661 399-0416
33374 Lerdo Hwy Bakersfield (93308) *(P-3654)*

Exeter-Ivanhoe Citrus Assn .... D 559 592-3141
901 Rocky Hill Dr Exeter (93221) *(P-267)*

Exigen (usa) Inc (PA) .... B 415 402-2600
345 California St Fl 22 San Francisco (94104) *(P-11588)*

Exigen Group, San Francisco *Also Called: Exigen (usa) Inc (P-11588)*

Exit Realty Consultants, Ceres *Also Called: Klair Real Estate Inc (P-9066)*

Exois Inc .... C 408 777-6630
2567 Ingleton Ave Carlsbad (92009) *(P-12791)*

Exp Realty .... D 213 308-2927
7100 Hillside Ave Apt 601 Los Angeles (90046) *(P-8999)*

Expak Logistics, Los Angeles *Also Called: Kxp Carrier Services LLC (P-3618)*

Expanse LLC .... C 415 590-0129
425 Market St Fl 8 San Francisco (94105) *(P-11589)*

Expeditors International, Hawthorne *Also Called: Expeditors Intl Wash Inc (P-4018)*

Expeditors Intl Ocean Inc .... D 310 343-6200
5200 W Century Blvd Fl 6 Los Angeles (90045) *(P-4014)*

Expeditors Intl Wash Inc .... B 310 343-6200
19701 Hamilton Ave Torrance (90502) *(P-4015)*

Expeditors Intl Wash Inc .... D 619 710-1900
1470 Exposition Way Ste 110 San Diego (92154) *(P-4016)*

Expeditors Intl Wash Inc .... D 323 781-1600
12200 Wilkie Ave Ste 100 Hawthorne (90250) *(P-4017)*

Expeditors Intl Wash Inc .... D 310 343-6200
12200 Wilkie Ave # 100 Hawthorne (90250) *(P-4018)*

Expensifyorg .... C 971 365-3939
88 Kearny St Ste 1600 San Francisco (94108) *(P-18587)*

Experian, Costa Mesa *Also Called: Experian Info Solutions Inc (P-10762)*

Experian Corporation .... D 714 830-7000
475 Anton Blvd Santa Ana (92704) *(P-10761)*

Experian Health Inc .... C 415 716-6633
2233 Watt Ave Ste 275 Sacramento (95825) *(P-12454)*

Experian Info Solutions Inc (DH) .... A 714 830-7000
475 Anton Blvd Costa Mesa (92626) *(P-10762)*

Experian Marketing, Costa Mesa *Also Called: Experian Mktg Solutions LLC (P-10763)*

Experian Mktg Solutions LLC .... A 714 830-7000
475 Anton Blvd Costa Mesa (92626) *(P-10763)*

Experian Qas, Costa Mesa *Also Called: Marigold Usa Inc (P-11733)*

Experior Laboratories Inc .... D 805 483-3400
1635 Ives Ave Oxnard (93033) *(P-4536)*

Expert Dry Wall Systems Inc .... D 408 271-5044
1141 Old Bayshore Hwy Ste 30ca San Jose (95112) *(P-5154)*

Expitrans Inc .... D 949 650-4600
22412 Gilberto Ste B Rcho Sta Marg (92688) *(P-20368)*

Exploding Kittens Inc .... D 919 738-8440
101 S La Brea Ave # A Los Angeles (90036) *(P-11590)*

Exploratorium .... B 415 528-4462
17 Pier Ste 100 San Francisco (94111) *(P-18652)*

Expo Builders Supply, San Diego *Also Called: Expo Industries Inc (P-5155)*

Expo Industries Inc .... D 858 566-3110
7455 Carroll Rd San Diego (92121) *(P-5155)*

Exponent Inc (PA) .... C 650 326-9400
149 Commonwealth Dr Menlo Park (94025) *(P-19222)*

Exponential Tech Group Inc .... D 408 414-1450
188 Martinvale Ln San Jose (95119) *(P-5650)*

Express Contractors Inc .... D 951 360-6500
3810 Wacker Dr Jurupa Valley (91752) *(P-10474)*

Express Group Incorporated (PA) .... D 310 474-5999
10801 National Blvd Ste 104 Los Angeles (90064) *(P-3611)*

Express Imaging Services Inc .... D 888 846-8804
1805 W 208th St Ste 202 Torrance (90501) *(P-3791)*

Express Personnel Services .... D 530 671-9202
870 W Onstott Frontage Rd Ste E Yuba City (95991) *(P-11136)*

Express Personnel Services, Yuba City *Also Called: Express Personnel Services (P-11136)*

Expressworks International LLC (PA) .... D 925 244-0900
2410 Camino Ramon Ste 167 San Ramon (94583) *(P-20369)*

Exquisite Dental Technology .... D 626 237-0107
4816 Temple City Blvd Temple City (91780) *(P-16720)*

Extended Care Hosp Westminster .... D 714 891-2769
206 Hospital Cir Westminster (92683) *(P-15473)*

Extension Services, Long Beach *Also Called: County of Los Angeles (P-9413)*

Extra, Los Angeles *Also Called: Aligned Company (P-12548)*

Extreme Ventures, El Segundo *Also Called: Motor Trend Group LLC (P-13942)*

Exult Inc .... A 949 856-8800
121 Innovation Dr Ste 200 Irvine (92617) *(P-20370)*

Ey, Los Angeles *Also Called: Ernst & Young LLP (P-19574)*

Ey, San Jose *Also Called: Ernst & Young LLP (P-19575)*

Ey, Irvine *Also Called: Ernst & Young LLP (P-19576)*

Ey-Parthenon .... C 415 486-3600
555 California St Lbby San Francisco (94104) *(P-20371)*

Eye Care Center, The   **ALPHABETIC SECTION**

Eye Care Center, The, Fullerton *Also Called: Marshall B Ketchum University (P-17766)*
Eye Care Institute .... D....... 707 546-9800
   1017 2nd St Santa Rosa (95404) *(P-14743)*
Eye Q Vision Care (PA) .... C....... 559 486-2000
   7075 N Sharon Ave Fresno (93720) *(P-14744)*
Eyeline Studios, Los Angeles *Also Called: Scanlinevfx La LLC (P-13890)*
Eyeshadow, Los Angeles *Also Called: Stony Apparel Corp (P-2457)*
EZ Electric, Roseville *Also Called: Vexillum Inc (P-4717)*
EZ Lube LLC .... C....... 310 821-2517
   13421 Washington Blvd Marina Del Rey (90292) *(P-13713)*
EZ Lube LLC .... C....... 714 966-1647
   3599 Harbor Blvd Costa Mesa (92626) *(P-13714)*
EZ Lube- Costco, Marina Del Rey *Also Called: EZ Lube LLC (P-13713)*
EZ Pedo, Loomis *Also Called: Sprig Oral Health Technologies (P-16777)*
EZ Texting, San Francisco *Also Called: Callfire Inc (P-11481)*
Ezcaretech Usa Inc .... B....... 424 558-3191
   21081 S Western Ave Ste 130 Torrance (90501) *(P-13283)*
Ezviz Inc .... C....... 855 693-9849
   18639 Railroad St City Of Industry (91748) *(P-13115)*
F & A Federal Credit Union .... D....... 213 268-1226
   2625 Corporate Pl Monterey Park (91754) *(P-7765)*
F & E Arcft Mint Los Angles LL .... B....... 310 338-0063
   531 Main St Ste 672 El Segundo (90245) *(P-3892)*
F & H Construction (PA) .... D....... 209 931-3738
   1115 E Lockeford St Lodi (95240) *(P-917)*
F & L Racing Fuel, Long Beach *Also Called: M O Dion & Sons Inc (P-6733)*
F C I, Anaheim *Also Called: Fci Lender Services Inc (P-10741)*
F E A, San Jose *Also Called: Kaga Fei America Inc (P-19292)*
F E E, Rcho Sta Marg *Also Called: Fakouri Electrical Engrg Inc (P-12707)*
F Korbel & Bros (PA) .... C....... 707 824-7000
   13250 River Rd Guerneville (95446) *(P-2383)*
F M Tarbell Co .... D....... 951 677-3565
   39028 Winchester Rd Ste 101 Murrieta (92563) *(P-9000)*
F M Tarbell Co (HQ) .... C....... 714 972-0988
   1403 N Tustin Ave Ste 380 Santa Ana (92705) *(P-9001)*
F O X, Los Angeles *Also Called: Fox Sports Inc (P-4433)*
F P I, Shafter *Also Called: Farm Pump & Irrigation Co Inc (P-5834)*
F R T International Inc .... D....... 310 329-5700
   14439 S Avalon Blvd Gardena (90248) *(P-3701)*
F R T International Inc (PA) .... D....... 310 604-8208
   1700 N Alameda St Compton (90222) *(P-3702)*
F R T International Inc .... D....... 909 390-4892
   2825 Jurupa St Ontario (91761) *(P-4019)*
F&M Bank, Long Beach *Also Called: Farmers Merchants Bnk Long Bch (P-7683)*
F2 Consulting (PA) .... D....... 415 844-0641
   849 Almar Ave Ste C Santa Cruz (95060) *(P-20372)*
F2 Strategy, Santa Cruz *Also Called: F2 Consulting (P-20372)*
F3 and Associates Inc (PA) .... D....... 707 748-4300
   701 E H St Benicia (94510) *(P-19524)*
F6s Network Limited .... D....... 619 818-4363
   16935 Encino Hills Dr Encino (91436) *(P-19692)*
FAA Beverly Hills Inc .... D....... 323 801-1430
   5070 Wilshire Blvd Los Angeles (90036) *(P-7204)*
FAA Concord T Inc .... D....... 925 682-7131
   1090 Concord Ave Concord (94520) *(P-7205)*
Fabritec Structures, Tustin *Also Called: Shade Structures Inc (P-2745)*
Facebook Park Tower .... A....... 949 725-8637
   250 Howard St San Francisco (94105) *(P-12663)*
Facey Medical Group, Santa Clarita *Also Called: Providnce Facey Med Foundation (P-17301)*
Facilities MGT & Coml RPS Svcs, Anaheim *Also Called: Branded Group Inc (P-20300)*
Facility Masters Inc (PA) .... C....... 408 436-9090
   1604 Kerley Dr San Jose (95112) *(P-10895)*
Facility Solutions Group Inc .... D....... 714 993-3966
   801 Richfield Rd Placentia (92870) *(P-5557)*
Facter Direct Ltd .... B....... 323 634-1999
   4751 Wilshire Blvd Ste 140 Los Angeles (90010) *(P-13284)*
Fahetas LLC .... D....... 949 280-1983
   1419 N Tustin St Ste A Orange (92867) *(P-7479)*
Fair Financial Corp (PA) .... D....... 800 584-5000
   1540 2nd St Ste 200 Santa Monica (90401) *(P-11591)*

Fair Isaac International Corp (HQ) .... A....... 415 446-6000
   200 Smith Ranch Rd San Rafael (94903) *(P-12188)*
Fair Price Carpets, Riverside *Also Called: Fairprice Enterprises Inc (P-7430)*
FAIR TRADE USA, Oakland *Also Called: Transfair USA (P-19922)*
Fairbanks Ranch Cntry CLB Inc .... C....... 858 259-8811
   15150 San Dieguito Rd Rancho Santa Fe (92067) *(P-14375)*
Fairchild Medical Center, Yreka *Also Called: Siskiyou Hospital Inc (P-16431)*
Fairfield Inn By Mrrott Ltd Prt .... C....... 714 772-6777
   1460 S Harbor Blvd Anaheim (92802) *(P-9792)*
Fairfield Inn By Mrrott Scrmnto, Sacramento *Also Called: Welcome Group Inc (P-10356)*
Fairfield Development Inc (PA) .... C....... 858 457-2123
   5355 Mira Sorrento Pl Ste 100 San Diego (92121) *(P-756)*
Fairfield Inn, El Centro *Also Called: El Centro Hospitality LLC (P-9774)*
Fairfield Inn, Rancho Cordova *Also Called: Presidio Hotel Group LLC (P-10127)*
Fairfield Inn and Suites, Tulare *Also Called: Tulare Lodging Associates LLC (P-10328)*
Fairfield Post-Acute Rehab, Fairfield *Also Called: Sagebrush Healthcare Inc (P-15649)*
Fairfield Properties, San Diego *Also Called: Ffrt Residential LLC (P-8812)*
Fairfield Stadium Cinema, Fairfield *Also Called: Edwards Theatres Circuit Inc (P-13994)*
Fairfield-Suisun Sewer Dst .... D....... 707 429-8930
   1010 Chadbourne Rd Fairfield (94534) *(P-4849)*
Fairmont Designs, Buena Park *Also Called: Cambium Business Group Inc (P-5081)*
Fairmont Hotel, San Francisco *Also Called: Accor Services US LLC (P-9598)*
Fairmont Hsptal- Rgstrtion Dep, San Leandro *Also Called: County of Alameda (P-16021)*
Fairmont Miramar Hotel, Santa Monica *Also Called: Ocean Avenue LLC (P-10056)*
Fairmont San Francisco, San Francisco *Also Called: Mason Street Opco LLC (P-10009)*
Fairmont Snoma Mission Inn Spa, Sonoma *Also Called: Sonoma Hotel Operator Inc (P-10253)*
Fairn & Swanson Inc .... C....... 510 533-8260
   400 Lancaster St Oakland (94601) *(P-6107)*
Fairplex Enterprises Inc .... C....... 909 623-3111
   1101 W Mckinley Ave Pomona (91768) *(P-14520)*
Fairplex Rv Park, Pomona *Also Called: Los Angeles County Fair Assn (P-14543)*
Fairprice Enterprises Inc .... D....... 951 684-8578
   1070 Center St Riverside (92507) *(P-7430)*
Fairview Developmental Center, Costa Mesa *Also Called: Califrnia Dept State Hospitals (P-16642)*
Fairview Developmental Center, Costa Mesa *Also Called: Califrnia Dept Dvlpmental Svcs (P-18215)*
Fairway Technologies LLC (PA) .... D....... 858 454-4471
   4370 La Jolla Village Dr Ste 500 San Diego (92122) *(P-20373)*
Fairwinds Woodward Park, Fresno *Also Called: Leisure Care LLC (P-18470)*
Fairwinds-West Hills, West Hills *Also Called: Leisure Care LLC (P-15770)*
Fairwood Apartments, Carmichael *Also Called: Fairwood Associates Apts (P-8811)*
Fairwood Associates Apts .... D....... 916 944-0152
   8893 Fair Oaks Blvd Ofc Carmichael (95608) *(P-8811)*
Faith Electric LLC .... C....... 909 767-2682
   1980 Orange Tree Ln Ste 106 Redlands (92374) *(P-1733)*
Faith Jones & Associates Inc (PA) .... D....... 619 297-9601
   7801 Mission Center Ct Ste 106 San Diego (92108) *(P-16862)*
Faith Quality Auto Body Inc .... D....... 951 698-8215
   41130 Nick Ln Murrieta (92562) *(P-13636)*
Fakouri Electrical Engrg Inc .... D....... 949 888-2400
   30001 Comercio Rcho Sta Marg (92688) *(P-12707)*
Falck Mobile Health Corp .... B....... 323 720-1578
   212 S Atlantic Blvd Ste 102 Los Angeles (90022) *(P-3258)*
Falck Mobile Health Corp .... B....... 714 828-7750
   8932 Katella Ave Ste 201 Anaheim (92804) *(P-3259)*
Falcon Aerospace Holdings LLC .... A....... 661 775-7200
   27727 Avenue Scott Valencia (91355) *(P-5957)*
Falcon Crtcal Care Trnspt A Nr .... C....... 510 223-1171
   3508 San Pablo Dam Rd El Sobrante (94803) *(P-17238)*
Falcon Crtical Care Trnspt LLC .... D....... 510 223-1171
   1600 S Main St Ste 215 Walnut Creek (94596) *(P-3260)*
Falcon Technologies Inc .... D....... 916 638-1221
   3233 Luyung Dr Rancho Cordova (95742) *(P-19223)*
Falconer House, Sacramento *Also Called: Eskaton (P-8719)*
Falken Tire, Rancho Cucamonga *Also Called: Sumitomo Rubber North Amer Inc (P-5073)*
Falken Tire Holdings Inc .... D....... 800 723-2553
   8656 Haven Ave Rancho Cucamonga (91730) *(P-5069)*

ALPHABETIC SECTION

Falken Tires, Rancho Cucamonga Also Called: Falken Tire Holdings Inc *(P-5069)*
Falkner Winery Inc .... D....... 951 676-6741
  40620 Calle Contento Temecula (92591) *(P-2384)*
Falkon Furniture, Novato Also Called: CK Imports Inc *(P-5083)*
Fallas Discount Stores, Gardena Also Called: J & M Sales Inc *(P-7407)*
Fallbrook Public Utility Dst .... D....... 760 728-1125
  990 E Mission Rd Fallbrook (92028) *(P-4793)*
Fam Ppe LLC .... C....... 323 888-7755
  5553-B Bandini Blvd B Bell (90201) *(P-6040)*
Famand Inc .... D....... 707 255-9295
  1604 Airport Blvd Santa Rosa (95403) *(P-1435)*
Fame Assistance Corporation .... D....... 323 373-7720
  2270 S Harvard Blvd Los Angeles (90018) *(P-20748)*
Families Chice HM Care Svcs In .... D....... 909 303-9377
  545 N Mountain Ave Ste 209 Upland (91786) *(P-17972)*
Family & Children Services .... D....... 650 326-6576
  375 Cambridge Ave Palo Alto (94306) *(P-17973)*
Family Assistance Program .... D....... 760 843-0701
  15075 Seventh St Victorville (92395) *(P-17974)*
Family Asssment Cnsling Edcat .... D....... 714 447-9024
  1651 E 4th St Ste 128 Santa Ana (92701) *(P-17975)*
Family Bridges Inc .... C....... 510 839-2270
  168 11th St Oakland (94607) *(P-17976)*
Family Care Center, Ventura Also Called: County of Ventura *(P-20917)*
Family Care Network Inc (PA) .... D....... 805 503-6240
  1255 Kendall Rd San Luis Obispo (93401) *(P-18314)*
Family Christian Stores, Santa Clara Also Called: Family Christian Stores LLC *(P-7546)*
Family Christian Stores LLC (PA) .... D....... 616 554-8700
  3945 Freedom Cir Ste 560 Santa Clara (95054) *(P-7546)*
Family Health Center San Diego, Spring Valley Also Called: Family Hlth Ctrs San Diego Inc *(P-14748)*
Family Health Services Clinic, Madera Also Called: Madera Community Hospital *(P-16242)*
Family Hlth Ctrs San Diego Inc .... B....... 619 515-2526
  1845 Logan Ave San Diego (92113) *(P-14745)*
Family Hlth Ctrs San Diego Inc .... B....... 619 515-2435
  2391 Island Ave San Diego (92102) *(P-14746)*
Family Hlth Ctrs San Diego Inc .... B....... 619 515-2400
  5379 El Cajon Blvd San Diego (92115) *(P-14747)*
Family Hlth Ctrs San Diego Inc .... B....... 619 515-2555
  8788 Jamacha Rd Spring Valley (91977) *(P-14748)*
Family Hlth Ctrs San Diego Inc .... B....... 619 515-2444
  3705 Mission Blvd San Diego (92109) *(P-14749)*
Family Hlth Ctrs San Diego Inc .... B....... 619 515-2300
  1809 National Ave San Diego (92113) *(P-15226)*
Family Hlth Ctrs San Diego Inc (PA) .... D....... 619 515-2303
  823 Gateway Center Way San Diego (92102) *(P-17063)*
Family Hlth Ctrs San Diego Inc .... B....... 619 515-2550
  7592 Broadway Lemon Grove (91945) *(P-17239)*
Family Mtters In-Home Care LLC .... D....... 408 824-1021
  2155 S Bascom Ave Campbell (95008) *(P-16863)*
Family Options LLC .... D....... 559 275-2323
  3245 W Figarden Dr Fresno (93711) *(P-17977)*
Family Service Agency, San Rafael Also Called: Family Svc Agcy of Marin Cnty *(P-17978)*
Family Svc Agcy of Marin Cnty (PA) .... D....... 415 491-5700
  555 Northgate Dr San Rafael (94903) *(P-17978)*
Family Svc Agcy San Francisco, San Francisco Also Called: Felton Institute *(P-11286)*
Family Svc Agcy Snta Brbara CN .... D....... 805 965-1001
  123 W Gutierrez St Santa Barbara (93101) *(P-17979)*
Family Ties Home Care LLC .... D....... 818 565-9147
  1350 Lafitte Dr Oak Park (91377) *(P-6960)*
Family Tree Produce Inc .... C....... 714 693-5688
  5510 E La Palma Ave Anaheim (92807) *(P-6538)*
Famous Software LLC .... D....... 559 431-8100
  8080 N Palm Ave Ste 210 Fresno (93711) *(P-11592)*
Famous Vineyards LLC .... D....... 661 392-5000
  20715 Ave 8 Richgrove (93261) *(P-6539)*
Fancy Life Enterprises LLC (PA) .... C....... 619 560-9890
  8030 La Mesa Blvd Pmb 3039 La Mesa (91942) *(P-13848)*
Fancy Life Studios, La Mesa Also Called: Fancy Life Enterprises LLC *(P-13848)*
Fandango Inc (HQ) .... D....... 310 954-0278
  12200 W Olympic Blvd Ste 400 Los Angeles (90064) *(P-14037)*

Fandangonow, Los Angeles Also Called: Fandango Inc *(P-14037)*
Faneuil Inc .... B....... 757 722-4095
  5012 Dudley Blvd Mcclellan (95652) *(P-11137)*
Faneuil, Inc., Mcclellan Also Called: Faneuil Inc *(P-11137)*
Fantasy Springs Resort Casino, Indio Also Called: East Valley Tourist Dev Auth *(P-14517)*
Fao ROC Holdings LLC .... C....... 949 900-6501
  7755 Irvine Center Dr Ste 100 Irvine (92618) *(P-5990)*
Fao Schwarz, Irvine Also Called: Fao ROC Holdings LLC *(P-5990)*
Far East National Bank .... B....... 213 687-1300
  977 N Broadway Ste 306 Los Angeles (90012) *(P-20085)*
FAR NORTHERN REGIONAL CENTER, Redding Also Called: Far Nrthern Crdnting Cncil On *(P-17981)*
Far Nrthern Crdnting Cncil On .... D....... 530 895-8633
  1377 E Lassen Ave Chico (95973) *(P-17980)*
Far Nrthern Crdnting Cncil On (PA) .... D....... 530 222-4791
  1900 Churn Creek Rd Ste 114 Redding (96002) *(P-17981)*
Far West Inc .... C....... 559 627-1241
  4444 W Meadow Ave Visalia (93277) *(P-15474)*
Far West Inc .... D....... 909 884-4781
  467 E Gilbert St San Bernardino (92404) *(P-15475)*
Far West Inc .... D....... 559 733-0901
  4525 W Tulare Ave Visalia (93277) *(P-15844)*
Far West Bond Services Cal Inc (PA) .... B....... 818 704-1111
  5230 Las Virgenes Rd Calabasas (91302) *(P-8432)*
Far Western Graphics Inc .... D....... 408 481-9777
  2642 Heritage Park Cir San Jose (95132) *(P-10788)*
Farallon Capital Partners LP (PA) .... D....... 415 421-2132
  1 Maritime Plz Ste 2100 San Francisco (94111) *(P-9368)*
Fargo Colonial LLC .... D....... 858 454-2181
  910 Prospect St La Jolla (92037) *(P-9793)*
Farm Fresh To You LLC (PA) .... C....... 916 303-7145
  3880 Seaport Blvd West Sacramento (95691) *(P-178)*
Farm Pump & Irrigation Co Inc (PA) .... D....... 661 589-6901
  535 N Shafter Ave Shafter (93263) *(P-5834)*
Farm Water Technological Services Inc .... D....... 760 344-8000
  1620 Jones St Brawley (92227) *(P-7579)*
Farmers & Merchants Bancorp (PA) .... B....... 209 367-2300
  111 W Pine St Lodi (95240) *(P-7682)*
Farmers Group Inc (HQ) .... A....... 323 932-3200
  6301 Owensmouth Ave Woodland Hills (91367) *(P-8557)*
Farmers Insur Group Fdral Cr U (PA) .... D....... 323 209-6000
  2255 N Ontario St Ste 320 Burbank (91504) *(P-7766)*
Farmers Insurance .... B....... 818 876-3400
  6303 Owensmouth Ave Fl 1 Woodland Hills (91367) *(P-8558)*
Farmers Insurance .... C....... 661 257-0844
  27433 Tourney Rd Ste 170 Valencia (91355) *(P-8559)*
Farmers Insurance .... C....... 951 681-1068
  3600 Lime St Ste 122 Riverside (92501) *(P-8560)*
Farmers Insurance .... C....... 626 288-0870
  113 Avondale Ave Monterey Park (91754) *(P-8561)*
FARMERS INSURANCE, Burbank Also Called: Farmers Insur Group Fdral Cr U *(P-7766)*
Farmers Insurance, Woodland Hills Also Called: Farmers Group Inc *(P-8557)*
Farmers Insurance, Woodland Hills Also Called: Farmers Insurance *(P-8558)*
Farmers Insurance, Los Angeles Also Called: Farmers Insurance Beeline *(P-8562)*
Farmers Insurance, Exeter Also Called: Farmers Insurance Exchange *(P-8564)*
Farmers Insurance, Woodland Hills Also Called: Farmers Insurance Exchange *(P-8565)*
Farmers Insurance Beeline .... D....... 909 997-4734
  4601 Wilshire Blvd Los Angeles (90010) *(P-8562)*
Farmers Insurance Exchange .... C....... 510 895-6000
  2344 Merced St San Leandro (94577) *(P-8563)*
Farmers Insurance Exchange .... C....... 559 594-4149
  411 E Pine St Ste A Exeter (93221) *(P-8564)*
Farmers Insurance Exchange (DH) .... A....... 888 327-6335
  6301 Owensmouth Ave Woodland Hills (91367) *(P-8565)*
Farmers Link Inc .... D....... 213 623-5242
  2858 E 26th St Vernon (90058) *(P-6540)*
Farmers Merchants Bnk Long Bch (HQ) .... C....... 562 437-0011
  302 Pine Ave Long Beach (90802) *(P-7683)*
Farmhill LLC .... D....... 831 726-1986
  1800 San Juan Rd Aromas (95004) *(P-53)*

ALPHABETIC SECTION

Farmhouse Inn & Restaurant LLC .... D...... 707 887-3300
7871 River Rd Forestville (95436) *(P-9794)*

Farmington Fresh, Stockton Also Called: Farmington Fresh Sales LLC *(P-105)*

Farmington Fresh Sales LLC .... C...... 209 983-9700
7735 S Highway 99 Stockton (95215) *(P-105)*

Farwest Corrosion Control Co (PA) .... D...... 310 532-9524
12029 Regentview Ave Downey (90241) *(P-2274)*

Farwest Insulation Contracting .... D...... 310 634-2800
2741 Yates Ave Commerce (90040) *(P-1928)*

Fashion Apparel Service Trnsp .... C...... 866 835-1112
6701 Koll Center Pkwy Ste 200 Pleasanton (94566) *(P-3703)*

Fashion Logistics Inc .... C...... 424 201-4100
20550 Denker Ave Torrance (90501) *(P-3704)*

Fashion Resources, Vernon Also Called: Tarrant Apparel Group *(P-6224)*

Fashion World Incorporated .... C...... 310 273-6544
420 N Rodeo Dr Beverly Hills (90210) *(P-6173)*

Fashiongo.com, Los Angeles Also Called: Nhn Global Inc *(P-6211)*

Fast Pro Inc .... D...... 408 566-0200
2555 Lafayette St Ste 103 Santa Clara (95050) *(P-5038)*

Fast Undercar, Santa Clara Also Called: Fast Pro Inc *(P-5038)*

Fast Undercar, Ventura Also Called: Parts Authority LLC *(P-5053)*

Fastclick Inc .... A...... 805 689-9839
530 E Montecito St Santa Barbara (93103) *(P-10730)*

Fastclick.com, Santa Barbara Also Called: Fastclick Inc *(P-10730)*

Fastcor, Anaheim Also Called: Bisco Industries Inc *(P-5632)*

Fastech, Buena Park Also Called: Fueling and Service Tech Inc *(P-5835)*

Fastener Source, Long Beach Also Called: Master Fasteners International LLC *(P-5910)*

Fastener Technology Corp .... C...... 818 764-6467
7415 Fulton Ave North Hollywood (91605) *(P-5902)*

Fastly Inc (PA) .... B...... 844 432-7859
475 Brannan St Ste 300 San Francisco (94107) *(P-11593)*

Fat Brands Inc (PA) .... B...... 310 319-1850
9720 Wilshire Blvd Ste 500 Beverly Hills (90212) *(P-7480)*

Faucetdirect.com, Chico Also Called: Buildcom Inc *(P-5742)*

Faze Clan Inc .... B...... 818 688-6373
720 N Cahuenga Blvd Los Angeles (90038) *(P-14521)*

Faze Holdings Inc (PA) .... B...... 818 688-6373
720 N Cahuenga Blvd Los Angeles (90038) *(P-14522)*

FB Corporation .... B...... 626 300-0880
1211 E Valley Blvd Alhambra (91801) *(P-7684)*

Fbd Vanguard Construction Inc .... C...... 925 245-1300
550 Greenville Rd Livermore (94550) *(P-2118)*

Fci Lender Services Inc .... C...... 800 931-2424
8180 E Kaiser Blvd Anaheim (92808) *(P-10741)*

Fcp Inc (PA) .... D...... 951 678-4571
23100 Wildomar Trl Wildomar (92595) *(P-2747)*

Fcs Software Solutions Limited .... D...... 408 324-1203
2375 Zanker Rd Ste 250 San Jose (95131) *(P-11594)*

Fcti Inc (PA) .... D...... 310 405-0022
11766 Wilshire Blvd Ste 300 Los Angeles (90025) *(P-7854)*

Fdi Collateral Management, Sacramento Also Called: Dealertrack Clltral MGT Svcs I *(P-11534)*

FDIC-San Frncisco Regional Off, San Francisco Also Called: Federal Deposit Insurance Corp *(P-8472)*

Fdsi Logistics, Valencia Also Called: Fdsi Logistics LLC *(P-20374)*

Fdsi Logistics LLC .... D...... 818 971-3300
27680 Avenue Mentry # 2 Valencia (91355) *(P-20374)*

Feather Falls Casino, Oroville Also Called: Mooretown Rancheria *(P-14298)*

Feather River Disposal Inc .... B...... 530 283-2065
1166 Industrial Way Quincy (95971) *(P-3389)*

Feather River Hospital .... A...... 530 877-9361
5974 Pentz Rd Paradise (95969) *(P-16089)*

Feather Rver Recreation Pk Dst .... D...... 530 533-2011
1875 Feather River Blvd Oroville (95965) *(P-14523)*

FEC Fture Contrs Engineers Inc .... D...... 949 328-9758
184 Technology Dr Ste 205 Irvine (92618) *(P-1104)*

Federal Deposit Insurance Corp .... C...... 415 546-0160
25 Jessie St At Ecker Sq Ste 300 San Francisco (94105) *(P-8472)*

Federal Dfenders San Diego Inc (PA) .... D...... 619 234-8467
225 Broadway Ste 900 San Diego (92101) *(P-17452)*

Federal Express Corporation .... C...... 800 463-3339
8455 Pardee Dr Oakland (94621) *(P-3853)*

Federal Express Corporation .... D...... 800 463-3339
2500 Kimberly Ave Fullerton (92831) *(P-3854)*

Federal Express Corporation .... D...... 800 463-3339
3333 S Grand Ave Los Angeles (90007) *(P-3855)*

Federal Hm Ln Bnk San Frncisco (PA) .... C...... 415 616-1000
333 Bush St Fl 27 San Francisco (94104) *(P-7865)*

Federal Home Loan Mrtg Corp .... A...... 213 337-4200
444 S Flower St Fl 44 Los Angeles (90071) *(P-7962)*

Federal Land Bnk Assn Nthrn CA .... D...... 530 895-8698
3435 Silverbell Rd Chico (95973) *(P-7731)*

Federal Rsrve Bnk San Frncisco .... A...... 213 683-2300
950 S Grand Ave Fl 1 Los Angeles (90015) *(P-7602)*

Federted Indans Grton Rncheria .... A...... 707 588-7100
630 Park Ct Rohnert Park (94928) *(P-9795)*

Fedex, Oakland Also Called: Federal Express Corporation *(P-3853)*

Fedex, Fullerton Also Called: Federal Express Corporation *(P-3854)*

Fedex, Los Angeles Also Called: Federal Express Corporation *(P-3855)*

Fedex Freight West Inc .... A...... 775 356-7600
6411 Guadalupe Mines Rd San Jose (95120) *(P-3476)*

Fedex Services .... D...... 323 881-3400
5391 Rickenbacker Rd Bell (90201) *(P-13285)*

Fee Munson Ebert Architects, San Francisco Also Called: Forge Architecture *(P-19467)*

Feedzai Inc .... B...... 650 649-9486
1875 S Grant St Ste 950 San Mateo (94402) *(P-11595)*

Fehr & Peers (PA) .... D...... 925 977-3200
100 Pringle Ave Ste 600 Walnut Creek (94596) *(P-19224)*

Fehr & Peers, Walnut Creek Also Called: Fehr & Peers *(P-19224)*

Feit Electric, Pico Rivera Also Called: Feit Electric Company Inc *(P-2872)*

Feit Electric Company Inc (PA) .... C...... 562 463-2852
4901 Gregg Rd Pico Rivera (90660) *(P-2872)*

Feld Care Therapy Inc .... D...... 818 926-9057
31248 Oak Crest Dr Ste 120 Westlake Village (91361) *(P-17064)*

Felix Chevrolet, Los Angeles Also Called: Felix Chevrolet LP *(P-7206)*

Felix Chevrolet LP (PA) .... C...... 213 748-6141
714 W Olympic Blvd Ste 1124 Los Angeles (90015) *(P-7206)*

Fellowship Homes Inc .... C...... 209 529-4950
1745 Eldena Way Modesto (95350) *(P-18432)*

Felson Companies Inc .... D...... 510 538-1150
1290 B St Ste 210 Hayward (94541) *(P-9002)*

Felt Bicycles, Rancho Santa Margari Also Called: Group Rossignol Usa Inc *(P-7542)*

Felt Racing LLC .... D...... 949 452-9050
30452 Esperanza Rcho Sta Marg (92688) *(P-7541)*

Felton Institute (PA) .... D...... 415 474-7310
1500 Franklin St San Francisco (94109) *(P-11286)*

Fencecorp Inc .... D...... 760 721-2101
3045 Industry St Oceanside (92054) *(P-2275)*

Fencecorp Inc .... D...... 916 388-0887
6837 Power Inn Rd Sacramento (95828) *(P-2276)*

Fencecorp Inc (HQ) .... C...... 951 686-3170
18440 Van Buren Blvd Riverside (92508) *(P-2277)*

Fenceworks Inc (PA) .... C...... 951 788-5620
870 Main St Riverside (92501) *(P-2278)*

Fender Digital LLC .... D...... 323 462-2198
1575 N Gower St Ste 170 Los Angeles (90028) *(P-11596)*

Fenderscape Incorporated .... C...... 562 988-2228
1446 E Hill St Signal Hill (90755) *(P-490)*

Fenix Marine Services Ltd (DH) .... D...... 310 548-8877
614 Terminal Way San Pedro (90731) *(P-11032)*

Fennel Inc .... D...... 951 284-2020
1169 Sherborn St Corona (92879) *(P-1998)*

Fennemore Craig PC .... C...... 209 576-8888
1500 J St Modesto (95354) *(P-17453)*

Fennemore Craig PC .... C...... 510 834-6600
1111 Broadway 24th Fl Oakland (94607) *(P-17454)*

Fennemore Wendel, Modesto Also Called: Fennemore Craig PC *(P-17453)*

Fennemore Wendel, Oakland Also Called: Fennemore Craig PC *(P-17454)*

Fenwick & West LLP (PA) .... B...... 650 988-8500
801 California St Mountain View (94041) *(P-17455)*

ALPHABETIC SECTION — Firma Plastic Co Inc

Fenwick & West LLP .... C...... 415 875-2300
　555 California St Fl 12 San Francisco (94104) *(P-17456)*
Fergadis Enterprises, Bell *Also Called: Perrin Bernard Supowitz LLC (P-6090)*
Ferguson Fire Fabrication Inc (DH).. D...... 909 517-3085
　2750 S Towne Ave Pomona (91766) *(P-5748)*
Ferguson Fire Fabrication Inc .... D...... 951 272-8803
　235 N Joy St Corona (92879) *(P-5749)*
Ferma Corporation .... C...... 510 794-0414
　6655 Smith Ave Ste A Newark (94560) *(P-2235)*
Ferrar-Crano Vnyrds Winery LLC (PA) .... C...... 707 433-6700
　8761 Dry Creek Rd Healdsburg (95448) *(P-2385)*
Ferrari-Carano Winery, Healdsburg *Also Called: Ferrar-Crano Vnyrds Winery LLC (P-2385)*
Ferreira Service Inc (PA) .... D...... 925 831-9330
　1811 Tortuga St Acton (93510) *(P-1436)*
Ferring Research Institute Inc .... D...... 858 657-1400
　4245 Sorrento Valley Blvd San Diego (92121) *(P-19693)*
Ferry International LLC .... D...... 888 866-3377
　6 Hutton Centre Dr Ste 700 Santa Ana (92707) *(P-20375)*
Fess Prker-Red Lion Gen Partnr .... C...... 805 564-4333
　633 E Cabrillo Blvd Santa Barbara (93103) *(P-9796)*
Festival Fun Parks LLC .... C...... 408 238-9900
　2333 S White Rd San Jose (95148) *(P-14303)*
Ffd II, San Diego *Also Called: Fairfield Development Inc (P-756)*
FFF Enterprises Inc (PA) .... B...... 951 296-2500
　44000 Winchester Rd Temecula (92590) *(P-6108)*
FFI, Irvine *Also Called: First Foundation Inc (P-7685)*
Ffrt Residential LLC .... C...... 858 457-2123
　5510 Morehouse Dr Ste 200 San Diego (92121) *(P-8812)*
Fh & Hf-Torrance I LLC .... D...... 310 320-4130
　22617 S Vermont Ave Torrance (90502) *(P-15476)*
Fiber Optic Technologies, Torrance *Also Called: ACS Communications Inc (P-1656)*
Fibres Internation Recycling, Novato *Also Called: Fibres International Inc (P-4894)*
Fibres International Inc .... D...... 425 455-9811
　88 Rowland Way Ste 300 Novato (94945) *(P-4894)*
Fico .... D...... 858 369-8000
　3661 Valley Centre Dr San Diego (92130) *(P-12573)*
Fictiv Inc .... C...... 415 580-2509
　168 Welsh St San Francisco (94107) *(P-11597)*
Fidelity Home Energy Inc .... C...... 858 220-7784
　2235 Polvorosa Ave Ste 230 San Leandro (94577) *(P-1437)*
Fidelity Nat HM Warranty Co .... C...... 925 356-0194
　1850 Gateway Blvd Ste 400 Concord (94520) *(P-9229)*
Fidelity Nat Title Insur Co NY .... A...... 805 370-1400
　950 Hampshire Rd Westlake Village (91361) *(P-9230)*
Fidelity National, Lancaster *Also Called: Fidelity National Title Co (P-8439)*
Fidelity National, Westlake Village *Also Called: Fidelity Nat Title Insur Co NY (P-9230)*
Fidelity National Title Co .... D...... 818 881-7800
　42544 10th St W Ste C Lancaster (93534) *(P-8439)*
Field Fresh Farms LLC .... D...... 831 722-1422
　320 Industrial Rd Watsonville (95076) *(P-6541)*
Field Fresh Foods Incorporated .... A...... 310 719-8422
　14805 S San Pedro St Gardena (90248) *(P-6542)*
Fieldstone Communities Inc (PA) .... C...... 949 790-5400
　16 Technology Dr Ste 125 Irvine (92618) *(P-790)*
Fiesta De Reyes, San Diego *Also Called: Old Town Fmly Hospitality Corp (P-10062)*
Fiesta Ford Inc .... C...... 760 775-7777
　79015 Avenue 40 Indio (92203) *(P-7207)*
Fiesta Ford Lincoln-Mercury, Indio *Also Called: Fiesta Ford Inc (P-7207)*
Fifth Sun, Chico *Also Called: Gonzales Park LLC (P-6175)*
Fig Holdings LLC .... D...... 209 524-4817
　1310 W Granger Ave Modesto (95350) *(P-15477)*
Figg, San Diego *Also Called: Empyr Incorporated (P-10544)*
Fightcamp, Costa Mesa *Also Called: Hykso Inc (P-20408)*
Figma Inc (PA) .... D...... 888 236-4310
　760 Market St Fl 10 San Francisco (94102) *(P-11598)*
Figueroa Hotel, Los Angeles *Also Called: New Figueroa Hotel Inc (P-10042)*
Figure, San Francisco *Also Called: Figure Lending LLC (P-8042)*
Figure Lending LLC .... B...... 888 819-6388
　650 California St Fl 2700 San Francisco (94108) *(P-8042)*
Figure Technologies Inc .... B...... 888 819-6388
　650 California St Fl 2700 San Francisco (94108) *(P-13286)*

Figureplant LLC .... D...... 503 289-2070
　2122 Bryant St San Francisco (94110) *(P-14038)*
Filanity Corporation .... D...... 714 475-3521
　17011 Beach Bvld Ste 1440 Huntington Beach (92647) *(P-4272)*
Filenet Corporation .... A...... 800 315-3638
　3565 Harbor Blvd Costa Mesa (92626) *(P-12455)*
Fillmore Center, The, San Francisco *Also Called: Laramar Group LLC (P-9071)*
Film Payroll Services Inc (PA) .... D...... 310 440-9600
　500 S Sepulveda Blvd Fl 4 Los Angeles (90049) *(P-19577)*
Film Roman Llc .... C...... 818 748-4000
　6320 Canoga Ave Ste 450 Woodland Hills (91367) *(P-13849)*
Filml.a, Los Angeles *Also Called: A Filml Inc (P-13924)*
Filyn Corporation .... C...... 714 632-0225
　2950 E La Jolla St Anaheim (92806) *(P-3261)*
Fin-West Group .... B...... 805 658-7435
　5740 Ralston St Ste 130 Ventura (93003) *(P-7963)*
Final Film .... D...... 323 467-0700
　3620 W Valhalla Dr Burbank (91505) *(P-10807)*
Finan Group, North Hollywood *Also Called: Financial Group Inc (P-8566)*
Financial Engines, Sunnyvale *Also Called: Edelman Financial Engines LLC (P-20352)*
Financial Group Inc .... C...... 818 308-8527
　12432 Oxnard St North Hollywood (91606) *(P-8566)*
Financial Group Inc .... C...... 805 646-7974
　1991 Country Pl Ojai (93023) *(P-20086)*
Financial Pacific Insurance Co .... C...... 916 630-5000
　3850 Atherton Rd Rocklin (95765) *(P-8567)*
Financial Partners Credit Un (PA) .... D...... 562 904-3000
　7800 Imperial Hwy Downey (90242) *(P-7767)*
Financial Partners Credit Un, Downey *Also Called: Financial Partners Credit Un (P-7767)*
Financial Statement Svcs Inc (PA) .... C...... 714 436-3326
　3300 S Fairview St Santa Ana (92704) *(P-10772)*
Financial Svc Ctrs Coop Inc .... D...... 909 753-1213
　924 Overland Ct San Dimas (91773) *(P-13287)*
Financial Tech Sltons Intl Inc .... C...... 818 241-9571
　406 E Huntington Dr Ste 100 Monrovia (91016) *(P-20376)*
Financialforcecom Inc (PA) .... A...... 866 743-2220
　60 S Market St Ste 750 San Jose (95113) *(P-11599)*
Finastra Merchant Services Inc (PA) .... D...... 415 277-9900
　333 Bush St Fl 26 San Francisco (94104) *(P-7855)*
Find It Parts Inc .... D...... 888 312-8812
　11858 La Grange Ave Los Angeles (90025) *(P-5039)*
Findem Inc .... C...... 925 212-7277
　1991 Broadway St Redwood City (94063) *(P-11600)*
Finditparts, Los Angeles *Also Called: Find It Parts Inc (P-5039)*
Fine Arts Mseums San Francisco, San Francisco *Also Called: Corportion of Fine Arts Mseums (P-18645)*
FINE ARTS MUSEUM, Santa Barbara *Also Called: Santa Barbara Museum of Art (P-18674)*
Fine Arts Museum San Francisco, San Francisco *Also Called: Corportion of Fine Arts Mseums (P-18646)*
Finish Carpentry, Escondido *Also Called: Taylor Trim & Supply Inc (P-2021)*
Finlink Inc (PA) .... C...... 888 999-5467
　241 Center St Ste B Healdsburg (95448) *(P-11601)*
Fintech Open Source Foundation .... B...... 650 665-9773
　1117 California Ave Palo Alto (94304) *(P-5305)*
Fire Insurance Exchange (PA) .... A...... 323 932-3200
　6301 Owensmouth Ave Woodland Hills (91367) *(P-8568)*
Fire Safe Systems Inc .... D...... 310 542-0585
　1312 Kingsdale Ave Redondo Beach (90278) *(P-1438)*
Fire Sprnklr Fire Alarm Dsgn, San Diego *Also Called: Symons Fire Protection Inc (P-13149)*
Fire Systems, Los Angeles *Also Called: First Fire Systems Inc (P-1734)*
Firefighters First Credit Un (PA) .... C...... 323 254-1700
　1520 W Colorado Blvd Pasadena (91105) *(P-7768)*
Firestone, Ontario *Also Called: Ramona Auto Services Inc (P-7355)*
Firestone Vineyard LP .... D...... 805 688-3940
　5000 Zaca Station Rd Los Olivos (93441) *(P-2386)*
Firewood Marketing Inc .... C...... 415 872-5132
　311 California St Ste 200 San Francisco (94104) *(P-20377)*
Firm McNamara Law .... C...... 925 939-5330
　3480 Buskirk Ave Ste 200 Pleasant Hill (94523) *(P-17457)*
Firma Plastic Co Inc .... C...... 323 567-7767
　9309 Rayo Ave South Gate (90280) *(P-6007)*

ALPHABETIC SECTION

First & La Realty Corp (PA)..D....... 805 581-0021
1301 E Los Angeles Ave Simi Valley (93065) *(P-9003)*

First 5 Alameda County ....D....... 510 227-6900
1115 Atlantic Ave Alameda (94501) *(P-20944)*

First 5 La ....C....... 213 482-5920
750 N Alameda St Ste 300 Los Angeles (90012) *(P-17982)*

First Alarm (PA)..C....... 831 476-1111
1111 Estates Dr Aptos (95003) *(P-13116)*

First Alarm SEC & Patrol Inc ....B....... 707 584-1110
1240 Briggs Ave Santa Rosa (95401) *(P-12970)*

First Alarm SEC & Patrol Inc ....B....... 209 473-1110
5250 Claremont Ave Stockton (95207) *(P-13117)*

First Alarm SEC & Patrol Inc ....B....... 925 295-1260
1801 Oakland Blvd Ste 315 Walnut Creek (94596) *(P-13118)*

First Alarm SEC & Patrol Inc (PA)..C....... 408 866-1111
1731 Technology Dr Ste 800 San Jose (95110) *(P-13119)*

First Allied, San Diego *Also Called: First Allied Securities Inc (P-8083)*

First Allied Holdings Inc ....D....... 800 499-5489
655 W Broadway Fl 11 San Diego (92101) *(P-20378)*

First Allied Securities Inc (HQ)..D....... 619 702-9600
655 W Broadway Fl 11 San Diego (92101) *(P-8083)*

First Amercn HM Warranty Corp ....B....... 818 781-5050
8521 Fallbrook Ave Ste 340 Canoga Park (91304) *(P-9231)*

First Amercn Prof RE Svcs Inc (HQ)....................................C....... 714 250-1400
200 Commerce Irvine (92602) *(P-9004)*

First American Data Co LLC ....D....... 714 250-6594
4 First American Way Santa Ana (92707) *(P-9005)*

First American Data Tree, Santa Ana *Also Called: First American Data Co LLC (P-9005)*

First American Financial Corp (PA)......................................A....... 714 250-3000
1 First American Way Santa Ana (92707) *(P-8440)*

First American Home Warranty ....D....... 707 596-5151
1244 Apollo Way Santa Rosa (95407) *(P-9232)*

First American Mortgage Svcs ....B....... 714 250-4210
3 First American Way Santa Ana (92707) *(P-8441)*

First American Mortgage Svcs, Santa Ana *Also Called: First American Title Insur Co (P-8443)*

First American Team Realty Inc (PA)....................................C....... 562 427-7765
2501 Cherry Ave Ste 100 Signal Hill (90755) *(P-9006)*

First American Title Company ....A....... 714 250-3109
1 First American Way Santa Ana (92707) *(P-9233)*

First American Title Insur Co ....D....... 831 426-6500
330 Soquel Ave Santa Cruz (95062) *(P-8442)*

First American Title Insur Co (HQ)..B....... 800 854-3643
1 First American Way Santa Ana (92707) *(P-8443)*

First Amrcn Appraisal Svcs Inc (DH)....................................D....... 619 938-7078
12395 First American Way Poway (92064) *(P-9234)*

First Amrcn Prprty Insur Cslty ....C....... 949 474-7500
114 E 5th St Santa Ana (92701) *(P-8569)*

First Assmbly of God Bkrsfield ....D....... 661 327-2227
4901 California Ave Bakersfield (93309) *(P-17711)*

First Bank and Trust ....D....... 562 595-8775
4040 Atlantic Ave Long Beach (90807) *(P-7624)*

First Bptst Ch of Los Altos Th ....D....... 650 948-3738
625 Magdalena Ave Los Altos Hills (94024) *(P-18315)*

First Call Staffing Inc ....D....... 310 264-9914
401 Wilshire Blvd Ste 1050 Santa Monica (90401) *(P-11138)*

First Capitol Consulting Inc ....D....... 213 382-1115
520 S Grand Ave Los Angeles (90071) *(P-20379)*

First Class Foods, Hawthorne *Also Called: Firstclass Foods - Trojan Inc (P-2339)*

First Community Bancorp ....D....... 858 756-3023
5900 La Place Ct Ste 200 Carlsbad (92008) *(P-7625)*

First Entertainment Credit Un (PA)..D....... 323 851-3673
6735 Forest Lawn Dr Ste 100 Los Angeles (90068) *(P-7769)*

First Financial Federal Cr Un ....C....... 800 537-8491
650 Sierra Madre Villa Ave Ste 300 Pasadena (91107) *(P-7770)*

First Fire Systems Inc (PA)..D....... 310 559-0900
5947 Burchard Ave Los Angeles (90034) *(P-1734)*

First Foundation Inc (PA)..C....... 949 202-4160
18101 Von Karman Ave Ste 700 Irvine (92612) *(P-7685)*

First Foundation Inc ....D....... 626 993-1300
301 N Lake Ave Ste 100 Pasadena (91101) *(P-7732)*

First Group, Inglewood *Also Called: First Transit Inc (P-3129)*

First Mortgage Corporation ....B....... 909 595-1996
1131 W 6th St Ste 300 Ontario (91762) *(P-7964)*

First National Bank ....B....... 858 756-3023
6110 El Tordo Rancho Santa Fe (92067) *(P-7626)*

First National Bank, Rancho Santa Fe *Also Called: First National Bank (P-7626)*

First National Bank, South San Francisco *Also Called: First National Bank of Northern California (P-7627)*

First National Bank of Northern California ....C....... 650 583-8450
975 El Camino Real South San Francisco (94080) *(P-7627)*

First Orleans Hotel Assoc LP ....C....... 415 397-5572
222 Kearny St Ste 200 San Francisco (94108) *(P-9797)*

First Page Sage LLC ....D....... 206 369-6516
2930 Domingo Ave Berkeley (94705) *(P-13288)*

First Priority Financial Inc ....B....... 707 432-1000
3700 Hilborn Rd Ste 700 Fairfield (94534) *(P-7965)*

First Reprographic, Los Angeles *Also Called: Lasr Inc (P-10790)*

First Repub Securities Co LLC ....D....... 877 348-5576
111 Pine St Fl 2 San Francisco (94111) *(P-7686)*

First Republic Trust Company ....C....... 415 392-1400
111 Pine St San Francisco (94111) *(P-7687)*

First Responder Ems Inc ....D....... 530 897-6345
333 Huss Dr Ste 100 Chico (95928) *(P-3262)*

First Round Capital LLC ....C....... 415 646-0072
595 Pacific Ave Fl 4 San Francisco (94133) *(P-9508)*

First Security Services, San Jose *Also Called: First Alarm SEC & Patrol Inc (P-13119)*

First Step Communities, Folsom *Also Called: First Step Housing (P-20749)*

First Step Housing ....D....... 916 769-8877
139 Blakeslee Way Folsom (95630) *(P-20749)*

First Student Inc ....C....... 626 448-9446
4337 Rowland Ave El Monte (91731) *(P-3128)*

First Student Inc ....C....... 510 237-6677
436 Parr Blvd Richmond (94801) *(P-3336)*

First Student Inc ....C....... 415 455-9098
59 Jordan St San Rafael (94901) *(P-3337)*

First Student Inc ....B....... 760 320-4659
5006 E Calle San Raphael Palm Springs (92264) *(P-3338)*

First Student Inc ....C....... 209 466-7737
2005 Navy Dr Stockton (95206) *(P-3339)*

First Student Inc ....C....... 559 268-4077
2805 Se Ave Fresno (93725) *(P-3340)*

First Student Inc ....C....... 415 647-9012
2270 Jerrold Ave San Francisco (94124) *(P-3341)*

First Student Inc ....C....... 408 971-3466
931 Remillard Ct San Jose (95122) *(P-3342)*

First Student Inc ....B....... 818 896-0333
11233 San Fernando Rd San Fernando (91340) *(P-3343)*

First Student Inc ....C....... 951 736-3234
300 S Buena Vista Ave Corona (92882) *(P-3356)*

First Student Inc ....A....... 310 769-2400
14800 S Avalon Blvd Gardena (90248) *(P-3344)*

First Team RE - Orange Cnty ....D....... 949 759-5747
4 Corporate Plaza Dr Ste 100 Newport Beach (92660) *(P-9007)*

First Team RE - Orange Cnty ....D....... 951 270-2800
200 S Main St Ste 100 Corona (92882) *(P-9008)*

First Team RE - Orange Cnty ....C....... 714 974-9191
8028 E Santa Ana Canyon Rd Anaheim (92808) *(P-9009)*

First Team RE - Orange Cnty ....C....... 949 389-0004
26711 Aliso Creek Rd Ste 200a Aliso Viejo (92656) *(P-9010)*

First Team RE - Orange Cnty ....B....... 562 596-9911
12501 Seal Beach Blvd Ste 100 Seal Beach (90740) *(P-9011)*

First Team RE - Orange Cnty (PA)..C....... 949 988-3000
108 Pacifica Ste 300 Irvine (92618) *(P-9012)*

First Team RE - Orange Cnty ....D....... 562 346-5088
42 64th Pl Long Beach (90803) *(P-9013)*

First Team RE - Orange Cnty ....B....... 949 240-7979
32451 Golden Lantern Ste 210 Laguna Niguel (92677) *(P-9014)*

First Team RE - Orange Cnty ....C....... 714 544-5456
17240 17th St Tustin (92780) *(P-9015)*

First Team Real Estate, Anaheim *Also Called: First Team RE - Orange Cnty (P-9009)*

First Team Real Estate, Aliso Viejo *Also Called: First Team RE - Orange Cnty (P-9010)*

First Team Security Inc ....D....... 310 709-4921
1038 Harrison Ave Venice (90291) *(P-12971)*

ALPHABETIC SECTION

Fleetup

First Team Walk-In Realty, Irvine *Also Called: First Team RE - Orange Cnty* **(P-9012)**
First Tech Federal Credit Un, San Jose *Also Called: First Technology Federal Cr Un* **(P-7772)**
First Technology Federal Cr Un .... D....... 408 863-6240
   19960 Stevens Creek Blvd Cupertino (95014) **(P-7771)**
First Technology Federal Cr Un (PA)... D....... 855 855-8805
   2702 Orchard Pkwy San Jose (95134) **(P-7772)**
First Technology Federal Cr Un 855 855-8805
   1011 Sunset Blvd Ste 210 Rocklin (95765) **(P-7773)**
First Transit Inc 310 216-9584
   1213 W Arbor Vitae St Inglewood (90301) **(P-3129)**
First Transit Inc .... D....... 909 948-3474
   9421 Feron Blvd Ste 101 Rancho Cucamonga (91730) **(P-3130)**
First Transit Inc .... D....... 714 644-9828
   1717 E Via Burton Anaheim (92806) **(P-3131)**
First Transit Inc .... D....... 949 857-7211
   6671 Marine Way Irvine (92618) **(P-3132)**
First Transit Inc .... C....... 831 460-9911
   117 Fern St Ste 100 Santa Cruz (95060) **(P-3133)**
First Transit Inc .... D....... 323 222-0010
   15730 S Figueroa St Gardena (90248) **(P-3134)**
First Transit Inc .... D....... 626 307-7842
   4337 Rowland Ave El Monte (91731) **(P-3135)**
First Transit Inc .... D....... 209 385-1226
   2047 Grogan Ave Merced (95341) **(P-3136)**
First Transit Inc .... C....... 510 437-8990
   407 High St Oakland (94601) **(P-3137)**
First Transit Inc .... C....... 805 544-2730
   29 Prado Rd San Luis Obispo (93401) **(P-3138)**
Firstat Nursing Services Inc .... C....... 619 220-7600
   411 Camino Del Rio S Ste 100 San Diego (92108) **(P-16864)**
Firstcall (PA)... C....... 415 781-4300
   1 Salmon St Ste 3500 San Francisco (94104) **(P-12972)**
Firstcall 415 781-4300
   1350 Treat Blvd Ste 250 Walnut Creek (94597) **(P-20380)**
Firstclass Foods - Trojan Inc 310 676-2500
   12500 Inglewood Ave Hawthorne (90250) **(P-2339)**
Firsthive Tech Corporation 408 368-3424
   333 W San Carlos St Ste 600 San Jose (95110) **(P-10613)**
Firstmed Ambulance Svcs Inc .... D....... 818 982-8333
   8630 Tamarack Ave Sun Valley (91352) **(P-3263)**
Firstsrvice Rsidential Cal Inc (DH).. D....... 909 981-4131
   9130 Anaheim Pl Ste 110 Rancho Cucamonga (91730) **(P-9016)**
Firstsrvice Rsidential Cal LLC (HQ).. C....... 949 448-6000
   15241 Laguna Canyon Rd Irvine (92618) **(P-9017)**
Firstsrvice Rsidential Cal LLC .... C....... 213 213-0886
   3415 S Sepulveda Blvd Ste 720 Los Angeles (90034) **(P-20087)**
Firstsrvice Rsidential Cal LLC .... D....... 760 834-2480
   43100 Cook St Ste 103 Palm Desert (92211) **(P-20088)**
Firstsrvice Rsidential Cal LLC .... D....... 916 293-4740
   12009 Foundation Pl Gold River (95670) **(P-20089)**
Firstup Inc (PA).. B....... 844 975-2533
   1 Montgomery St Ste 2150 San Francisco (94104) **(P-12189)**
Fischer Tile and Marble Inc .... C....... 916 452-1426
   1800 23rd St Sacramento (95816) **(P-1982)**
Fish & Richardson PC .... C....... 650 839-5070
   500 Arguello St Ste 500 Redwood City (94063) **(P-17458)**
Fish & Richardson PC .... C....... 858 678-5070
   12390 El Camino Real San Diego (92130) **(P-17459)**
Fish House Foods Inc .... B....... 760 597-1270
   1263 Linda Vista Dr San Marcos (92078) **(P-2421)**
Fish House Partners One LLC .... D....... 323 460-4170
   5955 Melrose Ave Los Angeles (90038) **(P-7481)**
Fishel Company .... C....... 858 658-0830
   5878 Autoport Mall San Diego (92121) **(P-1735)**
Fisher & Paykel Healthcare Inc 949 453-4000
   17400 Laguna Canyon Rd Ste 300 Irvine (92618) **(P-5414)**
Fisher & Phillips LLP .... D....... 949 851-2424
   2050 Main St Ste 1000 Irvine (92614) **(P-17460)**
Fisher Investments Inc .... C....... 888 823-9566
   13100 Skyline Blvd Woodside (94062) **(P-8198)**
Fisher Ranch LLC .... D....... 760 922-4151
   10610 Ice Plant Rd Blythe (92225) **(P-268)**

Fisheries Resource Vlntr Corps .... C....... 562 596-9261
   109 Stanford Ln Seal Beach (90740) **(P-20381)**
Fishers Nursery .... D....... 209 599-3412
   24081 S Austin Rd Ripon (95366) **(P-6858)**
Fisk Electric Company .... C....... 818 884-1166
   15870 Olden St Rancho Cascades (91342) **(P-1736)**
Fit Athletic Club .... D....... 858 592-2440
   12171 World Trade Dr San Diego (92128) **(P-14524)**
Fitstar Inc .... A....... 415 409-8348
   80 Langton St San Francisco (94103) **(P-12190)**
FIVE ACRES, Altadena *Also Called: Five Acres - The Bys Grls Aid* **(P-18433)**
Five Acres - The Bys Grls Aid .... B....... 626 798-6793
   760 Mountain View St Altadena (91001) **(P-18433)**
Five Prime, South San Francisco *Also Called: Five Prime Therapeutics Inc* **(P-2586)**
Five Prime Therapeutics Inc .... D....... 415 365-5600
   111 Oyster Point Blvd South San Francisco (94080) **(P-2586)**
Five Star Auto Repair and Wash, Rocklin *Also Called: Jkf Auto Service Inc* **(P-13695)**
Five Star Plastering Inc .... D....... 949 683-5091
   23022 La Cadena Dr Ste 200 Laguna Hills (92653) **(P-1929)**
Five Star Qulty Care-CA II LLC (DH)... D....... 805 492-2444
   93 W Avenida De Los Arboles Thousand Oaks (91360) **(P-15478)**
Five Star Qulty Care-CA II LLC 209 466-2066
   537 E Fulton St Stockton (95204) **(P-15479)**
Five Star Senior Living Inc .... C....... 858 673-6300
   16925 Hierba Dr San Diego (92128) **(P-15480)**
Five Stars Loyalty Inc .... C....... 860 578-2770
   60 Francisco St San Francisco (94133) **(P-20382)**
Five9 Inc (PA)... A....... 925 201-2000
   3001 Bishop Dr Ste 350 San Ramon (94583) **(P-12191)**
Fivesixtwo Inc, Long Beach *Also Called: Traffic Management Pdts Inc* **(P-12383)**
Fivetran Inc (PA)... A....... 415 805-2799
   405 14th St Ste 1100 Oakland (94612) **(P-12192)**
Fixd Construction Co., Ontario *Also Called: Nhs Western Division Inc* **(P-704)**
FJ Willert Contracting Co .... C....... 619 421-1980
   1869 Nirvana Ave Chula Vista (91911) **(P-918)**
Fjs Inc .... C....... 714 905-1050
   888 S Disneyland Dr Ste 400 Anaheim (92802) **(P-9798)**
Fkc-Lake Shore, Sylmar *Also Called: Frontier-Kemper Constructors Inc* **(P-1303)**
Flagship, San Jose *Also Called: Flagship Facility Services Inc* **(P-10898)**
Flagship Airport Services, San Jose *Also Called: Flagship Airport Services Inc* **(P-10896)**
Flagship Airport Services Inc (HQ)... C....... 408 977-0155
   1050 N 5th St Ste E San Jose (95112) **(P-10896)**
Flagship Airport Services Inc .... D....... 310 328-8221
   1830 W 208th St Torrance (90501) **(P-10897)**
Flagship Credit Acceptance LLC .... C....... 949 748-7172
   7525 Irvine Center Dr Irvine (92618) **(P-13289)**
Flagship Facility Services Inc (HQ).. B....... 408 977-0155
   1050 N 5th St Ste E San Jose (95112) **(P-10898)**
Flagship Facility Services Inc .... B....... 408 977-0155
   1050 N 5th St Ste E San Jose (95112) **(P-10899)**
Flaherty Brothers Cnstr Inc .... D....... 650 268-9779
   3470 Fostoria Way Ste D Danville (94526) **(P-2064)**
Flair Building Maintenance, Santa Clara *Also Called: Flair Building Services* **(P-10900)**
Flair Building Services .... D....... 408 987-4040
   3470 Edward Ave Santa Clara (95054) **(P-10900)**
Flamingo Resort Hotel, Santa Rosa *Also Called: Bavarian Lion Company Cal* **(P-9633)**
Flash Point Graphix, Burbank *Also Called: Final Film* **(P-10807)**
Flat White Economy Inv USA LLC .... C....... 949 344-5013
   5151 California Ave Ste 100 Costa Mesa (92626) **(P-4895)**
Flatiron Construction Corp .... C....... 707 742-6270
   1200 Concord Ave Concord (94520) **(P-20090)**
Flatiron West Inc .... C....... 707 742-6000
   1200 Concord Ave Concord (94520) **(P-1180)**
Flatiron West Inc .... C....... 909 597-8413
   16341 Chino Corona Rd Chino (91708) **(P-1181)**
Flawless Vape Whl & Dist Inc .... D....... 714 406-2933
   1021 E Orangethorpe Ave Anaheim (92801) **(P-6879)**
Fleet Maintenance Dept, Santa Cruz *Also Called: Santa Cruz Metro Trnst Dst* **(P-3209)**
Fleet Mangement Solutions, Irvine *Also Called: Teletrac Inc* **(P-4554)**
Fleetup, San Jose *Also Called: Truelite Trace Inc* **(P-12637)**

Fleetwood Aluminum Products Inc .... C....... 800 736-7363
  1 Fleetwood Way Corona (92879) *(P-5156)*

Fleetwood Homes, Riverside *Also Called: Fleetwood Motor Homes-Califinc (P-13770)*

Fleetwood Motor Homes-Califinc .... C....... 951 274-2000
  2350 Fleetwood Dr Riverside (92509) *(P-13770)*

Fleetwood Windows and Doors, Corona *Also Called: Fleetwood Aluminum Products Inc (P-5156)*

Flexcare LLC .... A....... 866 564-3589
  532 Gibson Dr Ste 100 Roseville (95678) *(P-11139)*

Flexcare Medical Staffing, Roseville *Also Called: Flexcare LLC (P-11139)*

Flexilis, San Francisco *Also Called: Lookout Inc (P-12481)*

Flexon Technologies Inc .... C....... 925 398-8280
  7901 Stoneridge Dr Ste 390 Pleasanton (94588) *(P-11602)*

Flexport Inc .... D....... 323 524-7132
  1420 N Mckinley Ave Los Angeles (90059) *(P-6907)*

Flexport Inc (PA) .... C....... 415 231-5252
  760 Market St Fl 8 San Francisco (94102) *(P-8570)*

Flight Centre Usa Inc .... D....... 310 458-3310
  888 W 6th St Ste 110 Los Angeles (90017) *(P-3930)*

Flightdocs II LLC .... D....... 800 747-4560
  6080 Center Dr Fl 6 Los Angeles (90045) *(P-3893)*

Flint Builders, Roseville *Also Called: Flint Builders Inc (P-919)*

Flint Builders Inc .... D....... 916 757-1000
  401 Derek Pl Roseville (95678) *(P-919)*

Flint Energy Services Inc .... C....... 213 593-8000
  1999 Avenue Of The Stars Ste 2600 Los Angeles (90067) *(P-19225)*

Flipboard Inc (PA) .... C....... 650 323-6547
  811 Hamilton St Redwood City (94063) *(P-12792)*

Flixbus Inc .... C....... 925 577-4164
  12575 Beatrice St Los Angeles (90066) *(P-3264)*

Flo Dynamics, Compton *Also Called: Norco Industries Inc (P-2800)*

Flo-CHI, Los Angeles *Also Called: Lindsey & Sons (P-13354)*

Floaties Swim School, Poway *Also Called: Floaties Swim School LLC (P-14525)*

Floaties Swim School LLC .... D....... 877 277-7946
  13180 Poway Rd Poway (92064) *(P-14525)*

Flock Freight Inc .... C....... 855 744-7585
  701 S Coast Highway 101 Encinitas (92024) *(P-4020)*

Floor & Decor Outlets Amer Inc .... D....... 510 394-9976
  1700 Fairway Dr San Leandro (94577) *(P-7431)*

Florence Crttnton Svcs Ornge C .... B....... 714 680-9000
  801 E Chapman Ave Ste 203 Fullerton (92831) *(P-18434)*

Florence Filter Corporation .... D....... 310 637-1137
  530 W Manville St Compton (90220) *(P-5768)*

Florence Villa Hotel .... C....... 415 397-7700
  225 Powell St San Francisco (94102) *(P-9799)*

Florence Wstn Med Clinic Inc .... C....... 818 896-2999
  13500 Van Nuys Blvd Pacoima (91331) *(P-14750)*

Flory Industries (PA) .... D....... 209 545-1167
  4737 Toomes Rd Salida (95368) *(P-2769)*

Flowspace Inc .... C....... 323 741-1325
  660 Baker St Ste B201 Costa Mesa (92626) *(P-3705)*

Floyd Johnston Cnstr Co Inc .... C....... 559 299-7373
  2301 Herndon Ave Clovis (93611) *(P-1209)*

Flt Inc .... C....... 916 355-1500
  12747 Folsom Blvd Folsom (95630) *(P-13662)*

Fluidmaster Inc (PA) .... C....... 949 728-2000
  30800 Rancho Viejo Rd San Juan Capistrano (92675) *(P-2672)*

Fluids Manufacturing Inc .... C....... 818 264-4657
  11941 Vose St North Hollywood (91605) *(P-6695)*

Fluor Corporation .... D....... 949 349-2000
  3 Polaris Way Aliso Viejo (92656) *(P-19226)*

Fluor Daniel, Aliso Viejo *Also Called: Fluor Plant Services Intl Inc (P-19229)*

Fluor Daniel Construction, Aliso Viejo *Also Called: Fluor Daniel Construction Co (P-1182)*

Fluor Daniel Construction Co (DH) .... B....... 949 349-2000
  3 Polaris Way Aliso Viejo (92656) *(P-1182)*

Fluor Enterprises Inc .... C....... 949 349-2000
  3 Polaris Way Aliso Viejo (92656) *(P-19227)*

Fluor Enterprises Inc .... D....... 925 307-1200
  611 Gateway Blvd Ste 950 South San Francisco (94080) *(P-19228)*

Fluor Facility & Plant Svcs .... C....... 408 256-1333
  124 Blossom Hill Rd Ste H # 1524 San Jose (95123) *(P-10901)*

Fluor Fltron Blfour Btty Drgdo .... D....... 949 420-5000
  5901 W Century Blvd Los Angeles (90045) *(P-4155)*

Fluor Plant Services Intl Inc .... D....... 949 349-2000
  1 Enterprise Aliso Viejo (92656) *(P-19229)*

Flux Power Holdings Inc (PA) .... C....... 877 505-3589
  2685 S Melrose Dr Vista (92081) *(P-2948)*

Fluxx, San Francisco *Also Called: Fluxx Labs Inc (P-11603)*

Fluxx Labs Inc .... D....... 415 851-2453
  2261 Market St Pmb 4060 San Francisco (94114) *(P-11603)*

Flyr Inc (PA) .... D....... 415 841-3597
  3205 Pico Blvd Santa Monica (90405) *(P-12574)*

FMC Financial Group (PA) .... D....... 949 225-9369
  4675 Macarthur Ct Ste 1250 Newport Beach (92660) *(P-8571)*

FMI International West 2, San Pedro *Also Called: Toll Global Fwdg Scs USA Inc (P-4108)*

Fmsinfoserv, Los Angeles *Also Called: Cdsnet LLC (P-20723)*

FN Logistics Llc .... A....... 213 625-5900
  12588 Florence Ave Santa Fe Springs (90670) *(P-3586)*

FNB Bancorp .... C....... 650 588-6800
  975 El Camino Real South San Francisco (94080) *(P-7688)*

Fni International Inc .... D....... 916 643-1400
  1300 Ethan Way Sacramento (95825) *(P-20383)*

FNS, Torrance *Also Called: Fns Inc (P-4021)*

Fns Inc (PA) .... D....... 661 615-2300
  1545 Francisco St Torrance (90501) *(P-4021)*

Fntech .... D....... 714 429-7833
  3000 W Segerstrom Ave Santa Ana (92704) *(P-13290)*

Foam Co, The, Van Nuys *Also Called: Grht Inc (P-6914)*

Foam Distributors Incorporated .... D....... 510 441-8377
  31009 San Antonio St Hayward (94544) *(P-6908)*

Foam Fabrication For Packaging, Hayward *Also Called: Foam Distributors Incorporated (P-6908)*

Foamex LP 323 774-5600
  19201 S Reyes Ave Compton (90221) *(P-3706)*

Foasberg Laundry and Clrs Inc (PA) .... D....... 562 426-7345
  640 E Wardlow Rd Long Beach (90807) *(P-10434)*

Focus Diagnostics, Cypress *Also Called: Focus Diagnostics Inc (P-16721)*

Focus Diagnostics Inc .... B....... 714 220-1900
  11331 Valley View St Ste 150 Cypress (90630) *(P-16721)*

Focus Features LLC (DH) .... D
  1540 2nd St Ste 200 Santa Monica (90401) *(P-13850)*

Focus Industries Inc .... D....... 949 830-1350
  25301 Commercentre Dr Lake Forest (92630) *(P-2874)*

Focus Landscape, Lake Forest *Also Called: Focus Industries Inc (P-2874)*

Folsom Ambulatory Surgery Ctr, Folsom *Also Called: Kaiser Foundation Hospitals (P-14848)*

Folsom Lake Appliance Inc .... D....... 916 985-3426
  8146 Greenback Ln Ste 102 Fair Oaks (95628) *(P-13740)*

Folsom Lake Toyota, Folsom *Also Called: Flt Inc (P-13662)*

Folsom Outpatient Surgery Ctr, Folsom *Also Called: Folsom Surgery Center Inc (P-14751)*

Folsom Surgery Center Inc .... D....... 916 673-1990
  1651 Creekside Dr Ste 100 Folsom (95630) *(P-14751)*

Fontana Water Company, El Monte *Also Called: San Gabriel Valley Water Co (P-4825)*

Food 4 Less, Paso Robles *Also Called: Paq Inc (P-7389)*

Food Collective, Irvine *Also Called: Artisan Bistro Foods Inc (P-6416)*

Food Sales West Inc .... D....... 714 966-2900
  235 Baker St Costa Mesa (92626) *(P-6253)*

Food Specialists Inc .... B....... 510 444-3456
  2 Broadway Oakland (94607) *(P-7482)*

Foothill / Estrn Trnsp Crrdor .... D....... 949 754-3400
  125 Pacifica Ste 100 Irvine (92618) *(P-1105)*

Foothill Child Dev Svcs Inc .... D....... 818 353-3772
  16946 Sherman Way # 100 Van Nuys (91406) *(P-18316)*

Foothill Electric Motors, Santa Clarita *Also Called: Wrights Supply Inc (P-13759)*

Foothill Family Service .... C....... 626 246-1240
  3629 Santa Anita Ave Ste 201 El Monte (91731) *(P-17983)*

Foothill Family Service .... C....... 626 795-6907
  2500 E Foothill Blvd Ste 300 Pasadena (91107) *(P-17984)*

Foothill Health Center Inc .... C....... 408 729-4290
  2670 S White Rd Ste 200 San Jose (95148) *(P-14752)*

Foothill Home Improvement Center Inc .... D....... 909 355-3655
  15825 Foothill Blvd Fontana (92335) *(P-7118)*

ALPHABETIC SECTION

Foothill Packing Inc .... B...... 805 925-7900
  2255 S Broadway Santa Maria (93454) *(P-6254)*

Foothill Presbyterian Hospital, Glendora *Also Called: Emanate Hlth Fthill Prsbt Hosp*
(P-16079)

Foothill Regional Medical Ctr .... C...... 310 943-4500
  14662 Newport Ave Tustin (92780) *(P-16090)*

Foothill Regional Medical Ctr, Tustin *Also Called: Alta Hospitals System LLC (P-15938)*

Foothill Transit West Covina, Arcadia *Also Called: Coach Usa Inc (P-3317)*

Foothll-De Anza Cmnty Cllege D .... D...... 650 949-7260
  12345 S El Monte Rd Ste 6202 Los Altos Hills (94022) *(P-4384)*

For Cali Productions LLC .... B...... 323 956-9500
  5555 Melrose Ave Bldg 213 Los Angeles (90038) *(P-13935)*

Force Protection Systems, Van Nuys *Also Called: Edo Communications and Countermeasures Systems Inc (P-3004)*

Force10 Networks Global Inc .... A...... 800 289-3355
  350 Holger Way San Jose (95134) *(P-12456)*

Ford, Santa Monica *Also Called: Ford of Santa Monica Inc (P-7209)*

Ford, Simi Valley *Also Called: Ford of Simi Valley Inc (P-7210)*

Ford, Upland *Also Called: Park Place Ford LLC (P-7275)*

Ford, Irvine *Also Called: Ford Motor Land Dev Corp (P-8720)*

Ford Wlker Haggerty Behar LLP (PA) .... D...... 562 983-2500
  1 World Trade Ctr Ste 2700 Long Beach (90831) *(P-17461)*

Ford Construction Company Inc .... D...... 209 333-1116
  300 W Pine St Lodi (95240) *(P-1300)*

Ford Future Inc .... C...... 916 786-3673
  650 Automall Dr Roseville (95661) *(P-7208)*

Ford Lincoln Fairfield, Fairfield *Also Called: Price-Simms Ford LLC (P-7282)*

Ford Lincoln Mercury, El Centro *Also Called: El Centro Motors (P-7198)*

Ford Motor Company .... C...... 209 824-6600
  1269 Phoenix Dr Manteca (95336) *(P-5040)*

Ford Motor Land Dev Corp .... C...... 949 242-6606
  3 Glen Bell Way Ste 100 Irvine (92618) *(P-8720)*

Ford of Santa Monica Inc .... D...... 310 451-1588
  1402 Santa Monica Blvd Santa Monica (90404) *(P-7209)*

Ford of Simi Valley Inc .... D...... 805 583-0333
  2440 1st St Simi Valley (93065) *(P-7210)*

Ford Store Morgan Hill Inc .... D...... 408 782-8201
  17045 Condit Rd Morgan Hill (95037) *(P-7211)*

Ford Store San Leandro, San Leandro *Also Called: Nicholas K Corporation (P-7265)*

Forefront Power LLC .... D...... 415 800-1604
  100 Montgomery St Ste 725 San Francisco (94104) *(P-1439)*

Foreign Trade Corporation .... C...... 805 823-8400
  685 Cochran St Ste 200 Simi Valley (93065) *(P-5651)*

Forensic Analytical, Carson *Also Called: Forensic Analytical Spc Inc (P-19977)*

Forensic Analytical Spc Inc .... D...... 310 763-2374
  20535 Belshaw Ave Carson (90746) *(P-19977)*

Forensic Toxicology Associates, Chatsworth *Also Called: Pacific Toxicology Labs (P-16739)*

Forescout, San Jose *Also Called: Forescout Technologies Inc (P-11604)*

Forescout Technologies Inc (PA) .... A...... 408 213-3191
  300 Santana Row Ste 400 San Jose (95128) *(P-11604)*

Forest Hill Manor, Pacific Grove *Also Called: Califrnia-Nevada Methdst Homes (P-8796)*

Forest Home Inc .... C...... 909 389-2300
  40000 Valley Of The Falls Dr Forest Falls (92339) *(P-10401)*

Forest Home Ministries, Forest Falls *Also Called: Forest Home Inc (P-10401)*

Forest Lawn Co .... C...... 818 241-4151
  1712 S Glendale Ave Glendale (91205) *(P-9286)*

Forest Lawn Mem Parks Mortuary, Glendale *Also Called: Forest Lawn Memorial-Park Assn*
(P-7566)

Forest Lawn Memorial-Park Assn (PA) .... B...... 323 254-3131
  1712 S Glendale Ave Glendale (91205) *(P-7566)*

Forest Lawn Mortuary .... B...... 760 329-8737
  66272 Pierson Blvd Desert Hot Springs (92240) *(P-10512)*

Forever 21 Logistics LLC .... B...... 888 494-3837
  110 E 9th St Ste C910 Los Angeles (90079) *(P-13291)*

Foreverlawn Pacific Coast, Lake Elsinore *Also Called: Kdk Pacific Coast Entps LLC (P-505)*

Forex Capital Markets LLC .... C...... 415 343-4874
  201 Mission St Ste 290 San Francisco (94105) *(P-8084)*

Forge Architecture .... D...... 415 434-0320
  500 Montgomery St San Francisco (94111) *(P-19467)*

Forge Trust Co .... D...... 650 591-3335
  3050 S Delaware St Ste 202 San Mateo (94403) *(P-9426)*

Forgerock, San Francisco *Also Called: Forgerock Inc (P-11605)*

Forgerock Inc (PA) .... C...... 415 599-1100
  201 Mission St Ste 2900 San Francisco (94105) *(P-11605)*

Forgerock Us Inc (HQ) .... D...... 415 599-1100
  201 Mission St Ste 2900 San Francisco (94105) *(P-12193)*

Foria International Inc .... C...... 626 912-8836
  18689 Arenth Ave City Of Industry (91748) *(P-6174)*

Form Energy Inc .... D...... 844 367-6462
  2810 7th St Berkeley (94710) *(P-19694)*

Forma LLC .... D...... 415 477-0700
  201 Filbert St San Francisco (94133) *(P-13292)*

Formagrid Inc (PA) .... B...... 415 200-2040
  799 Market St Fl 8 San Francisco (94103) *(P-4273)*

Former Nt Corp .... D...... 330 702-3070
  1054 S De Anza Blvd # 202 San Jose (95129) *(P-12194)*

Formerly Known As LLC .... D...... 310 551-3500
  40 E Verdugo Ave Burbank (91502) *(P-10614)*

Formerra LLC .... D...... 888 502-0951
  11400 Newport Dr Ste B Rancho Cucamonga (91730) *(P-13293)*

FORMERRA, LLC, Rancho Cucamonga *Also Called: Formerra LLC (P-13293)*

Formosa Together .... B...... 916 661-8835
  8430 Pine River Way Sacramento (95823) *(P-20947)*

Fornaca Inc (PA) .... C...... 866 308-9461
  2400 National City Blvd National City (91950) *(P-7347)*

Forrest Group LLC (PA) .... D...... 619 808-9798
  1422 N Curson Ave Apt 9 Los Angeles (90046) *(P-3139)*

Fort Hill Construction (PA) .... D...... 323 656-7425
  12711 Ventura Blvd Ste 390 Studio City (91604) *(P-677)*

Fort James Communications Pprs, Emeryville *Also Called: Fort James Corporation (P-20091)*

Fort James Corporation .... A...... 510 594-4900
  2000 Powell St Emeryville (94608) *(P-20091)*

Fort Wash Golf & Cntry CLB .... D...... 559 434-1702
  10272 N Millbrook Ave Fresno (93730) *(P-14376)*

FORT, THE, Fresno *Also Called: Fort Wash Golf & Cntry CLB (P-14376)*

Fortanasce & Associates, Murrieta *Also Called: Michael G Frtnsce Physcl Thrap (P-15296)*

Forte Enterprises Inc (PA) .... C...... 650 994-3200
  99 Escuela Dr Daly City (94015) *(P-20092)*

Fortezza Iridium Holdings Inc .... A...... 415 765-6500
  150 California St San Francisco (94111) *(P-12195)*

Fortiss LLC .... D...... 323 415-4900
  1100 S Flower St Ste 3100 Los Angeles (90015) *(P-14526)*

Fortitude Technology Inc .... D...... 858 974-5080
  8929 Complex Dr Ste A San Diego (92123) *(P-4274)*

Fortress Holding Group LLC .... D...... 714 202-8710
  5500 E Santa Ana Canyon Rd Ste 220 Anaheim (92807) *(P-9312)*

Fortron/Source Corporation .... D...... 510 440-0188
  4231 Business Center Dr Ste 7 Fremont (94538) *(P-5652)*

Fortuna BMC, Mcclellan *Also Called: Fortuna Bus MGT Consulting Inc (P-20384)*

Fortuna Bus MGT Consulting Inc .... A...... 916 458-0991
  4926 43rd St Ste 120 Mcclellan (95652) *(P-20384)*

Fortuna Enterprises LP .... B...... 310 410-4000
  5711 W Century Blvd Los Angeles (90045) *(P-9800)*

Fortune Dynamic Inc .... D...... 909 979-8318
  21923 Ferrero City Of Industry (91789) *(P-6232)*

Fortune Senior Enterprises .... C...... 916 560-9100
  6060 Sunrise Vista Dr Ste 1180 Citrus Heights (95610) *(P-16865)*

Forty Niners Football Co LLC .... D...... 408 562-4949
  4949 Marie P Debartolo Way Santa Clara (95054) *(P-14137)*

Forty-Niner Shops Inc .... A...... 562 985-5093
  6049 E 7th St Long Beach (90840) *(P-7547)*

Forum At Rancho San Antonio, Cupertino *Also Called: Rancho San Antnio Rtrment Hsin*
(P-18507)

Forusall Inc .... D...... 844 401-2253
  665 3rd St Ste 400 San Francisco (94107) *(P-13294)*

Forward Inc .... C...... 209 982-4298
  9999 S Austin Rd Manteca (95336) *(P-4896)*

Forward Advantage Inc .... D...... 559 447-1777
  7255 N 1st St Ste 106 Fresno (93720) *(P-11606)*

Forward Management LLC .... D...... 415 869-6300
  244 California St Ste 200 San Francisco (94111) *(P-8199)*

Forward Networks Inc .... D...... 844 393-6389
  2390 Mission College Blvd # 401 Santa Clara (95054) *(P-12196)*

Forward Slope Incorporated .... D...... 619 299-4400
2020 Camino Del Rio N Ste 400 San Diego (92108) *(P-19230)*

Forward Slope., San Diego *Also Called: Forward Slope Incorporated (P-19230)*

Foshay Electric Co Inc .... D...... 858 277-7676
950 Industrial Blvd Chula Vista (91911) *(P-1737)*

Foss Maritime Co Inc .... D...... 562 435-0171
Pier D Berth 35 Long Beach (90802) *(P-3797)*

Foster Dairy Farms (PA) .... A...... 209 576-3400
529 Kansas Ave Modesto (95351) *(P-6437)*

Foster Farms LLC (HQ) .... D...... 209 394-7901
1000 Davis St Livingston (95334) *(P-225)*

Foster Poultry Farms .... B...... 559 265-2000
900 W Belgravia Ave Fresno (93706) *(P-2344)*

Foster Poultry Farms .... D...... 559 457-6509
4107 Ave 360 Traver (93673) *(P-6825)*

FOSTER POULTRY FARMS, Fresno *Also Called: Foster Poultry Farms (P-2344)*

FOSTER POULTRY FARMS, Traver *Also Called: Foster Poultry Farms (P-6825)*

Foster Poultry Farms LLC .... B...... 209 394-7901
834 Davis St Livingston (95334) *(P-229)*

Foster Turkey Products .... B...... 209 394-7901
1000 Davis St Livingston (95334) *(P-228)*

Foto Kem Film & Video, Burbank *Also Called: Foto-Kem Industries Inc (P-13936)*

Foto-Kem Industries Inc (PA) .... C...... 818 846-3102
2801 W Alameda Ave Burbank (91505) *(P-13936)*

Found Health Inc .... D...... 415 854-3296
1 Letterman Dr Ste C3500 San Francisco (94129) *(P-19978)*

Foundation 9 Entertainment Inc (PA) .... C...... 949 698-1500
30211 Avenida De Las Bandera Ste 200 Rancho Santa Margari (92688) *(P-12197)*

Foundation Building Materials, Santa Ana *Also Called: Foundation Building Mtls Inc (P-5157)*

Foundation Building Mtls Inc (HQ) .... C...... 714 380-3127
2520 Redhill Ave Santa Ana (92705) *(P-5157)*

Foundation Constructors Inc (PA) .... D...... 925 754-6633
81 Big Break Rd Oakley (94561) *(P-1301)*

Foundation Laboratory, Pomona *Also Called: Latara Enterprise Inc (P-16732)*

Foundation Lead Group LLC .... D...... 877 477-2311
16800 Aston Ste 270 Irvine (92606) *(P-20385)*

Foundation Pile Inc .... D...... 909 350-1584
8375 Almeria Ave Fontana (92335) *(P-1302)*

Founders Management II Corp .... B...... 650 570-5700
1221 Chess Dr Foster City (94404) *(P-9801)*

Foundtion For Stdnts Rsing ABO .... D...... 415 333-4222
2 Embarcadero Ctr Fl 8 San Francisco (94111) *(P-18859)*

Fountain View Cnvalescent Hosp, Los Angeles *Also Called: Genesis Healthcare LLC (P-15847)*

Fountain Vly Rgnal Hosp Med CT .... A...... 714 966-7200
17100 Euclid St Fountain Valley (92708) *(P-16091)*

FOUNTAINGROVE CLUB, THE, Santa Rosa *Also Called: Fountaingrove Golf & Athc CLB (P-14262)*

Fountaingrove Golf & Athc CLB .... D...... 707 701-3050
1525 Fountaingrove Pkwy Santa Rosa (95403) *(P-14262)*

Fountains At The Carlotta, The, Palm Desert *Also Called: Watermark Rtrment Cmmnties Inc (P-15728)*

Fountains At The Sea Bluffs, Dana Point *Also Called: Watermark Rtrment Cmmnties Inc (P-8871)*

Fountains, The, Yuba City *Also Called: United Com-Serve (P-15710)*

Four CS Service Inc .... D...... 559 237-3990
1560 H St Fresno (93721) *(P-2065)*

Four Pnts By Shrton La Intl Ar, Los Angeles *Also Called: Irp Lax Hotel LLC (P-9914)*

Four Pnts By Shrton Scrmnto In, Sacramento *Also Called: G B Commercial LLC (P-9805)*

Four Points Bakersfield, Bakersfield *Also Called: Cni Thl Propco Fe LLC (P-9710)*

Four Points San Diego-Seaworld, San Diego *Also Called: Greenwood Holdings LLC (P-9821)*

Four Seasons General Mdse, Vernon *Also Called: BTG S CORP (P-6894)*

Four Seasons Hotel, Los Angeles *Also Called: Burton-Way House Ltd A CA (P-9669)*

Four Seasons Hotel, San Francisco *Also Called: Cb-1 Hotel (P-9686)*

Four Seasons Hotel Inc .... C...... 415 633-3441
735 Market St Fl 6 San Francisco (94103) *(P-9802)*

Four Seasons Hotel Silicon Vly, East Palo Alto *Also Called: East Palo Alto Hotel Dev Inc (P-9771)*

Four Seasons Hotels Limited, Los Angeles *Also Called: Burton Way Hotels LLC (P-9667)*

Four Seasons Ht Westlake Vlg, Westlake Village *Also Called: Burton Way Htels Ltd A Cal Ltd (P-9668)*

Four Sisters Inns .... D...... 707 939-1340
630 Broadway Sonoma (95476) *(P-9803)*

Four Sisters Inns .... D...... 949 661-1304
34343 Blue Lantern St Dana Point (92629) *(P-20093)*

Four Ssons Hotel-San Francisco, San Francisco *Also Called: Four Seasons Hotel Inc (P-9802)*

Four Ssons Rsort Santa Barbara, Santa Barbara *Also Called: 1260 Bb Property LLC (P-9585)*

Four Star Chemical, Vernon *Also Called: Starco Enterprises Inc (P-2791)*

Four Wheel Parts Wholesalers, Compton *Also Called: Transamerican Dissolution LLC (P-7381)*

Foursquare International, Los Angeles *Also Called: Interntnal Ch of Frsqare Gospl (P-19022)*

Fourthfloor Fashion Talent, Los Angeles *Also Called: Career Group Inc (P-11102)*

Foutains Executive Course, Escondido *Also Called: Welk Group Inc (P-14296)*

Fowler Packing, Fresno *Also Called: Fowler Packing Company Inc (P-269)*

Fowler Packing Company Inc (PA) .... C...... 559 834-5911
8570 S Cedar Ave Fresno (93725) *(P-269)*

Fox, Los Angeles *Also Called: Twentieth Cntury Fox Intl Corp (P-13968)*

Fox Inc (DH) .... A...... 310 369-1000
10201 W Pico Blvd Los Angeles (90064) *(P-4431)*

Fox Baseball Holdings Inc .... C...... 323 224-1500
1000 Vin Scully Ave Los Angeles (90012) *(P-14138)*

Fox Broadcasting Company LLC (HQ) .... C...... 310 369-1000
10201 W Pico Blvd Bldg 1003220 Los Angeles (90064) *(P-4432)*

Fox BSB Holdco Inc (HQ) .... B...... 323 224-1500
1000 Vin Scully Ave Los Angeles (90012) *(P-14139)*

Fox Family Channel, Burbank *Also Called: International Fmly Entrmt Inc (P-4512)*

Fox Films Entertainment, Los Angeles *Also Called: Twentieth Cntury Fox Film Corp (P-13904)*

Fox Head Inc (HQ) .... B...... 949 757-9500
16752 Armstrong Ave Irvine (92606) *(P-6199)*

Fox Hills Auto Inc (PA) .... C...... 310 649-3673
5880 W Centinela Ave Los Angeles (90045) *(P-7212)*

Fox Interactive Media Inc .... C...... 310 969-7000
6100 Center Dr Ste 800 Los Angeles (90045) *(P-4275)*

Fox Landing, Avalon *Also Called: Guided Discoveries Inc (P-10403)*

Fox Luggage Inc .... D...... 323 588-1688
221 N Orange Ave City Of Industry (91744) *(P-6041)*

Fox Marble & Granite, Berkeley *Also Called: Evolv Surfaces Inc (P-2506)*

Fox Net Inc .... A...... 310 369-1000
10201 W Pico Blvd Los Angeles (90064) *(P-13851)*

Fox Network Center, Los Angeles *Also Called: Disney Networks Group LLC (P-4426)*

Fox Racing, Irvine *Also Called: Fox Head Inc (P-6199)*

Fox Rent A Car Inc .... D...... 310 342-5155
325 Baker St Costa Mesa (92626) *(P-13587)*

Fox Rent A Car Inc .... C...... 310 342-5155
5500 W Century Blvd Los Angeles (90045) *(P-13588)*

Fox Rent A Car Inc .... D...... 909 635-6390
1776 E Holt Blvd Ontario (91761) *(P-13589)*

Fox Rent A Car Inc .... D...... 408 210-2208
7600 Earhart Rd Ste 9 # O Oakland (94621) *(P-13590)*

Fox Rent-A-Car & Truck, Oakland *Also Called: Fox Rent A Car Inc (P-13590)*

Fox Rothschild LLP .... D...... 415 539-3336
1 Sansome St Ste 2850 San Francisco (94104) *(P-17462)*

Fox Sports Inc (DH) .... C...... 310 369-1000
10201 W Pico Blvd Los Angeles (90064) *(P-4433)*

Fox Television Center, Los Angeles *Also Called: Fox Television Stations Inc (P-4434)*

Fox Television Stations Inc (HQ) .... B...... 310 584-2000
1999 S Bundy Dr Los Angeles (90025) *(P-4434)*

Fox Transportation Inc (PA) .... D...... 909 291-4646
8610 Helms Ave Rancho Cucamonga (91730) *(P-3390)*

Fox Transportation Inc .... C...... 310 971-0867
18408 S Laurel Park Rd Compton (90220) *(P-3587)*

Fox US Productions 27 Inc .... C...... 310 727-2550
1600 Rosecrans Ave Bldg 5a Manhattan Beach (90266) *(P-4435)*

FP, San Francisco *Also Called: Francisco Partners GP III LP (P-12457)*

Fpg Services LLC .... C...... 818 858-1080
15821 Ventura Blvd Ste 625 Encino (91436) *(P-20386)*

FPI Management Inc .... C...... 530 756-5332
1124 F St Davis (95616) *(P-9018)*

FPI Management Inc .... C...... 530 272-5274
131 Eureka St Ofc Grass Valley (95945) *(P-9019)*

ALPHABETIC SECTION — Fremont Surgery Center

Fpk Investigaions, Valencia *Also Called: Fpk Security Inc (P-12973)*
Fpk Security Inc .... B....... 661 702-9091
  28348 Constellation Rd Ste 880 Valencia (91355) *(P-12973)*
Fragile Handle With Care, San Diego *Also Called: Chandler Packaging A Transpak Company (P-4126)*
Franciscan Conv. Hospital, Merced *Also Called: Avalon Care Ctr - Mrced Frncsc (P-15342)*
Francisco Partners, San Francisco *Also Called: Francisco Partners MGT LP (P-9509)*
Francisco Partners GP III LP (HQ)... D....... 415 418-2900
  1 Letterman Dr Bldg C San Francisco (94129) *(P-12457)*
Francisco Partners MGT LP (PA).. C....... 415 418-2900
  1 Letterman Dr Ste 410 San Francisco (94129) *(P-9509)*
Francsco Prtners III Cayman LP .... D....... 415 418-2900
  1 Letterman Dr Bldg C San Francisco (94129) *(P-20750)*
Frank C Alegre Trucking Inc (PA).. C....... 209 334-2112
  5100 W Highway 12 Lodi (95242) *(P-3477)*
Frank Carson Ldscp & Maint Inc .... C....... 916 856-5400
  9530 Elder Creek Rd Sacramento (95829) *(P-431)*
FRANK D LANTERMAN REGIONAL CEN, Los Angeles *Also Called: Los Angles Cnty Dvlpmntal Svcs (P-17271)*
Frank Ghiglione Inc (PA).. D....... 510 483-7000
  1622 Moreland Dr Alameda (94501) *(P-3391)*
Frank Ghiglione Inc .... D....... 510 483-2063
  2972 Alvarado St Ste H San Leandro (94577) *(P-3392)*
Frank M Booth Inc .... D....... 530 742-7134
  5900 Hollis St Ste C Emeryville (94608) *(P-1440)*
Frank M Booth Inc .... D....... 650 871-8292
  251 Michelle Ct South San Francisco (94080) *(P-1441)*
Frank S Smith Masonry Inc .... D....... 909 468-0525
  2830 Pomona Blvd Pomona (91768) *(P-1882)*
Frank Toyata & Scion, National City *Also Called: Fornaca Inc (P-7347)*
Frank-Lin Distillers Pdts Ltd (PA)... C....... 408 259-8900
  2455 Huntington Dr Fairfield (94533) *(P-6796)*
FRANKLIN, San Mateo *Also Called: Franklin Resources Inc (P-8200)*
Franklin Advisers Inc .... A....... 650 312-2000
  1 Franklin Pkwy San Mateo (94403) *(P-9369)*
Franklin Elementary School, Merced *Also Called: Merced City School District (P-17727)*
Franklin Resources Inc (PA)... B....... 650 312-2000
  1 Franklin Pkwy San Mateo (94403) *(P-8200)*
Franklin Templeton Investment, Rancho Cordova *Also Called: Franklin Tmpleton Inv Svcs LLC (P-8085)*
Franklin Templeton Svcs LLC .... A....... 650 312-3000
  1 Franklin Pkwy Bldg 970 San Mateo (94403) *(P-9370)*
Franklin Tmpleton Inv Svcs LLC (DH).. A....... 916 463-1500
  3344 Quality Dr Rancho Cordova (95670) *(P-8085)*
Franklin Tmpleton Inv Svcs LLC .... C....... 925 875-2619
  5130 Hacienda Dr Fl 4 Dublin (94568) *(P-8201)*
Franklin Tmpleton Inv Svcs LLC .... B....... 650 312-4053
  3366 Quality Dr Fl 1 Rancho Cordova (95670) *(P-9371)*
Franklin Tmpleton Inv Svcs LLC .... C....... 650 312-2100
  1 Franklin Pkwy San Mateo (94403) *(P-9372)*
Frasco Inc (PA).. D....... 818 848-3888
  215 W Alameda Ave Burbank (91502) *(P-12974)*
Frasco Investigative Services, Burbank *Also Called: Frasco Inc (P-12974)*
Fraser Yachts, San Diego *Also Called: Fraser Yachts Florida Inc (P-13295)*
Fraser Yachts Florida Inc .... D....... 619 225-0588
  4960 N Harbor Dr Ste 100 San Diego (92106) *(P-13295)*
Frazee Industries Inc .... A....... 858 626-3600
  6625 Miramar Rd San Diego (92121) *(P-2635)*
Frazee Paint & Wallcovering, San Diego *Also Called: Frazee Industries Inc (P-2635)*
Frazier Management LLC .... C....... 650 325-5156
  70 Willow Rd Ste 200 Menlo Park (94025) *(P-17240)*
Fred Will and Bill Inc C
  211 S Hill Dr Fl 2 Brisbane (94005) *(P-1442)*
Fred Finch Youth Center (PA)... C....... 510 773-6669
  3800 Coolidge Ave Oakland (94602) *(P-14753)*
Fred M Boerner Motor Co (PA).. D....... 323 560-3882
  3620 E Florence Ave Huntington Park (90255) *(P-7348)*
Freddie Mac, Los Angeles *Also Called: Federal Home Loan Mrtg Corp (P-7962)*
Frederick Labs LLC .... C....... 646 738-8303
  535 Mission St San Francisco (94105) *(P-20387)*

Fredericka Manor Care Center, Chula Vista *Also Called: Front Porch Communities & Svcs (P-15484)*
FREDERICKA MANOR CARE CENTER, Glendale *Also Called: Front Prch Cmmnties Oprting Gr (P-15846)*
Free Conferencing Corporation .... C....... 562 437-1411
  4300 E Pacific Coast Hwy Long Beach (90804) *(P-4276)*
Freeconferencecall.com, Long Beach *Also Called: Free Conferencing Corporation (P-4276)*
Freedom Communications Inc .... A....... 714 796-7000
  625 N Grand Ave Santa Ana (92701) *(P-2537)*
Freedom Debt Relief, San Mateo *Also Called: Freedom Financial Network LLC (P-10546)*
Freedom Equity Group .... D....... 408 340-5672
  1500 E Hamilton Ave Ste 215 Campbell (95008) *(P-20388)*
Freedom Financial Network LLC (PA)....................................... C....... 650 393-6619
  1875 S Grant St Ste 400 San Mateo (94402) *(P-10546)*
Freedom Forever, Temecula *Also Called: Freedom Solar Services (P-1445)*
Freedom Forever LLC (PA)... D....... 888 557-6431
  43445 Business Park Dr Ste 104 Temecula (92590) *(P-1443)*
Freedom Forever LLC .... A....... 714 955-8735
  3322 Garfield Ave Commerce (90040) *(P-1444)*
Freedom Newspapers, Santa Ana *Also Called: Freedom Communications Inc (P-2537)*
Freedom Properties, Hemet *Also Called: Casa-Pacifica Inc (P-18389)*
Freedom Properties Village, Hemet *Also Called: Casa-Pacifica Inc (P-18390)*
Freedom Properties-Hemet LLC .... C....... 949 489-0430
  27122b Paseo Espada Ste 1024 San Juan Capistrano (92675) *(P-8721)*
Freedom Solar Services .... C....... 888 557-6431
  43445 Business Park Dr Ste 110 Temecula (92590) *(P-1445)*
Freedom Village Healthcare Ctr .... D....... 949 472-4733
  23442 El Toro Rd Bldg 2 Lake Forest (92630) *(P-15481)*
Freeman, Anaheim *Also Called: Freeman Expositions LLC (P-13296)*
Freeman Brown Sperry & D Aiuto, Stockton *Also Called: Freeman D Aiuto Prof Law Corp (P-17463)*
Freeman D Aiuto Prof Law Corp .... D....... 209 474-1818
  1818 Grand Canal Blvd Ste 4 Stockton (95207) *(P-17463)*
Freeman Expositions LLC .... C....... 714 254-3400
  2170 S Towne Centre Pl Ste 100 Anaheim (92806) *(P-13296)*
Freeman Motors Inc .... C....... 707 542-1791
  2875 Corby Ave Santa Rosa (95407) *(P-7213)*
Freeman Toyota Rent-A-Car, Santa Rosa *Also Called: Freeman Motors Inc (P-7213)*
Freemont Health Care Center, Fremont *Also Called: Mariner Health Care Inc (P-15563)*
Freemont Rideout Health Group .... A....... 530 751-4270
  726 4th St Marysville (95901) *(P-16092)*
Freestyle, Santa Fe Springs *Also Called: Freestyle Sales Co Ltd Partnr (P-7553)*
Freestyle Sales Co Ltd Partnr .... D....... 323 660-3460
  12231 Florence Ave Santa Fe Springs (90670) *(P-7553)*
Freeway Insurance (PA)... C....... 714 252-2500
  7711 Center Ave Ste 200 Huntington Beach (92647) *(P-8572)*
Freight Solution Providers, Sacramento *Also Called: Kls Air Express Inc (P-4043)*
Fremantle Media, Burbank *Also Called: Prdctions N Fremantle Amer Inc (P-14056)*
Fremont, San Francisco *Also Called: Fremont Realty Capital LP (P-8884)*
Fremont Ambltory Srgery Ctr LP .... D....... 510 456-4600
  39350 Civic Center Dr Ste 350 Fremont (94538) *(P-14754)*
Fremont Bank (HQ)... C....... 510 505-5226
  39150 Fremont Blvd Fremont (94538) *(P-7689)*
Fremont Bank .... D....... 510 512-1900
  1679 Industrial Pkwy W Hayward (94544) *(P-7690)*
Fremont Bank .... D....... 925 314-1420
  210 Railroad Ave Danville (94526) *(P-7691)*
Fremont Bhc Hospital Inc .... D....... 510 796-1100
  39001 Sundale Dr Fremont (94538) *(P-16093)*
Fremont Group Management LLC .... C....... 415 284-8500
  405 Howard St San Francisco (94105) *(P-8086)*
Fremont Hospital .... C....... 530 751-4000
  620 J St Marysville (95901) *(P-16094)*
Fremont Hospital, Mariposa *Also Called: John C Fremont Healthcare Dst (P-16141)*
Fremont Marriott Silicon Vly, Fremont *Also Called: Ashford Trs Fremont LLC (P-9617)*
Fremont Medical Center, Marysville *Also Called: Fremont Hospital (P-16094)*
Fremont Realty Capital LP .... D....... 415 284-8665
  199 Fremont St Fl 19 San Francisco (94105) *(P-8884)*
Fremont Surgery Center, Fremont *Also Called: Fremont Ambltory Srgery Ctr LP (P-14754)*

ALPHABETIC SECTION

Fremont Un High Schols Fndtion .... A...... 408 522-2200
589 W Fremont Ave Sunnyvale (94087) *(P-18588)*

Fremont-Rideout Health Group, Marysville *Also Called: Freemont Rideout Health Group (P-16092)*

Fremouw Environmental Svcs Inc .... D...... 707 448-3700
6940 Tremont Rd Dixon (95620) *(P-20751)*

French Hospital Medical Center (DH) .... B...... 805 543-5353
1911 Johnson Ave San Luis Obispo (93401) *(P-16095)*

Frequence Inc .... C...... 650 520-6114
155 E Dana St Mountain View (94041) *(P-18779)*

Fresenius Kidney Care Clovis, Clovis *Also Called: Fresenius Med Care Clovis LLC (P-16982)*

Fresenius Kidney Care Lynwood, Downey *Also Called: Rai Care Centers Lynwood LLC (P-16992)*

Fresenius Med Care Clovis LLC .... A...... 559 324-8023
2585 Alluvial Ave Clovis (93611) *(P-16982)*

Fresenius Med Care Slano Cnty .... D...... 707 678-6433
125 N Lincoln St Ste B Dixon (95620) *(P-16983)*

Fresenius Med Care Solano Cnty, Dixon *Also Called: Fresenius Med Care Slano Cnty (P-16983)*

Fresenius Med Care Wdlnd Cal L .... D...... 530 668-4503
35 W Main St Woodland (95695) *(P-16984)*

Fresenius Medical Care Wdlnd, Woodland *Also Called: Fresenius Med Care Wdlnd Cal L (P-16984)*

Fresgo LLC .... D...... 626 389-3500
219 S Fair Oaks Ave Pasadena (91105) *(P-3393)*

Fresh Air, South El Monte *Also Called: Fresh Air Envmtl Svcs Inc (P-2279)*

Fresh Air Envmtl Svcs Inc .... D...... 323 913-1965
10675 Rush St South El Monte (91733) *(P-2279)*

Fresh Grill LLC .... C...... 714 444-2126
111 E Garry Ave Santa Ana (92707) *(P-13297)*

Fresh Innovations Cal LLC .... C...... 209 983-9700
7735 S Highway 99 Stockton (95215) *(P-6543)*

Fresh Leaf Farms LLC .... C...... 831 796-3760
25867 Esperanza Rd Salinas (93907) *(P-30)*

Fresh Lifelines For Youth Inc .... D...... 408 263-2630
568 Valley Way Milpitas (95035) *(P-17985)*

Fresh Origins, San Marcos *Also Called: San Diego Farms LLC (P-197)*

Fresh Start Bakeries, Ontario *Also Called: Aspire Bakeries LLC (P-6605)*

Fresh Venture Farms LLC .... D...... 805 754-4449
1181 S Wolff Rd Oxnard (93033) *(P-31)*

Fresh Water Systems Inc .... D...... 619 933-8275
9265 Dowdy Dr Ste 202 San Diego (92126) *(P-13771)*

Freshdeals.co, Elk Grove *Also Called: Shine Logistics LLC (P-4094)*

Freshko Produce Services Inc .... C...... 559 497-7000
2155 E Muscat Ave Fresno (93725) *(P-6544)*

Freshpoint Inc .... C...... 626 855-1400
155 N Orange Ave City Of Industry (91744) *(P-6545)*

Freshpoint Central Cal Inc .... C...... 209 216-0200
5900 N Golden State Blvd Turlock (95382) *(P-4128)*

Freshpoint Central California, Turlock *Also Called: Freshpoint Central Cal Inc (P-4128)*

Freshpoint Las Vegas, City Of Industry *Also Called: Freshpoint Inc (P-6545)*

Freshpoint Southern Cal Inc .... C...... 626 855-1400
155 N Orange Ave City Of Industry (91744) *(P-6546)*

Freshpoint Southern California, City Of Industry *Also Called: Freshpoint Southern Cal Inc (P-6546)*

Freshway Farms LLC .... C...... 805 349-7170
2165 W Main St Santa Maria (93458) *(P-54)*

Freshworks, San Mateo *Also Called: Freshworks Inc (P-12198)*

Freshworks Inc (PA) .... C...... 650 513-0514
2950 S Delaware St Ste 201 San Mateo (94403) *(P-12198)*

Fresno Airport Hotels LLC .... D...... 559 252-3611
5090 E Clinton Way Fresno (93727) *(P-9804)*

Fresno Auto Dealers Auction .... A...... 559 268-8051
278 N Marks Ave Fresno (93706) *(P-5008)*

Fresno Beverage Company Inc .... C...... 559 650-1500
3525 S East Ave Fresno (93725) *(P-6762)*

Fresno Chrysler Ddge Jeep Ram, Fresno *Also Called: Fresno Chrysler Jeep Inc (P-7214)*

Fresno Chrysler Jeep Inc .... D...... 559 431-4000
6162 N Blackstone Ave Fresno (93710) *(P-7214)*

Fresno City College Bus Off, Fresno *Also Called: State Center Cmnty College Dst (P-17789)*

Fresno Cmnty Hosp & Med Ctr .... D...... 559 324-4000
2755 Herndon Ave Clovis (93611) *(P-14755)*

Fresno Cmnty Hosp & Med Ctr (HQ) .... A...... 559 459-3948
2823 Fresno St Fresno (93721) *(P-16096)*

Fresno Cmnty Hosp & Med Ctr .... A...... 559 459-6000
2130 E Illinois Avenue Fresno (93701) *(P-16097)*

Fresno Cnty Ecnmic Opprtnties .... D...... 559 486-6587
3120 W Nielsen Ave Fresno (93706) *(P-17986)*

Fresno Cnty Ecnmic Opprtnties .... D...... 559 263-1000
1900 Mariposa Mall Ste 300 Fresno (93721) *(P-17987)*

Fresno Cnty Ecnmic Opprtnties (PA) .... A...... 559 263-1010
1920 Mariposa Mall Ste 300 Fresno (93721) *(P-17988)*

Fresno Cnty Ecnmic Opprtnties .... D...... 559 263-1013
1920 Mariposa Mall Fresno (93721) *(P-17989)*

Fresno Cnty Sprntndent Schools .... C...... 559 644-1000
16644 S Elm Ave Caruthers (93609) *(P-3345)*

Fresno District Office, Fresno *Also Called: State Compensation Insur Fund (P-8413)*

Fresno Eoc, Fresno *Also Called: Fresno Cnty Ecnmic Opprtnties (P-17987)*

Fresno Eoc, Fresno *Also Called: Fresno Cnty Ecnmic Opprtnties (P-17988)*

Fresno Heart Hospital LLC .... B...... 559 433-8000
15 E Audubon Dr Fresno (93720) *(P-16098)*

Fresno Irrigation District .... D...... 559 233-7161
2907 S Maple Ave Fresno (93725) *(P-4987)*

Fresno Metro Flood Ctrl Dst .... D...... 559 456-3292
5469 E Olive Ave Fresno (93727) *(P-13298)*

Fresno Pace, Fresno *Also Called: Innovative Integrated Hlth Inc (P-18460)*

Fresno Plumbing & Heating Inc (PA) .... C...... 559 294-0200
2585 N Larkin Ave Fresno (93727) *(P-1446)*

Fresno Respite Companion Svcs, Fresno *Also Called: Maxim Healthcare Services Inc (P-16894)*

Fresno Roofing Co Inc .... D...... 559 255-8377
5950 E Olive Ave Fresno (93727) *(P-2066)*

Fresno Skilled Nursing .... D...... 559 268-5361
1665 M St Fresno (93721) *(P-15482)*

Fresno Sklled Nrsing Wllness C .... D...... 559 268-5361
1665 M St Fresno (93721) *(P-16682)*

Fresno Staffing, Fresno *Also Called: Maxim Healthcare Services Inc (P-11304)*

Fresno Surgery Center LP (PA) .... C...... 559 431-8000
6125 N Fresno St Fresno (93710) *(P-16099)*

Fresno Surgical Hospital, Fresno *Also Called: Fresno Surgery Center LP (P-16099)*

Fresno Truck Center .... D...... 559 486-4310
2727 E Central Ave Fresno (93725) *(P-5009)*

Fresno Truck Center .... C...... 209 983-2400
10182 S Harlan Rd French Camp (95231) *(P-5010)*

Fresno Truck Center (PA) .... C...... 559 486-4310
2727 E Central Ave Fresno (93725) *(P-7215)*

Fresno Unified School District .... C...... 559 457-3030
4498 N Brawley Ave Fresno (93722) *(P-3707)*

Fresno Valves & Castings Inc (PA) .... C...... 559 834-2511
7736 E Springfield Ave Selma (93662) *(P-4988)*

FRESNO'S CHAFFEE ZOO, Fresno *Also Called: Fresnos Chaffee Zoo Corp (P-18688)*

Fresnos Chaffee Zoo Corp .... C...... 559 498-5910
894 W Belmont Ave Fresno (93728) *(P-18688)*

Freund Baking, Commerce *Also Called: Oakhurst Industries Inc (P-2369)*

Freund Baking Co, Hayward *Also Called: Oakhurst Industries Inc (P-6273)*

Friant & Associates LLC (PA) .... D...... 510 535-5113
1980 W Avenue 140th San Leandro (94577) *(P-7533)*

Frick Paper Company LLC .... C...... 714 787-4900
2164 N Batavia St Orange (92865) *(P-6077)*

Friction Materials LLC .... C...... 248 362-3600
2525 W 190th St Torrance (90504) *(P-19231)*

Friedas Inc .... D...... 714 826-6100
4465 Corporate Center Dr Los Alamitos (90720) *(P-6547)*

Friedas Specialty Produce, Los Alamitos *Also Called: Friedas Inc (P-6547)*

Friendly Hlls Cntry CLB Fndtio .... C...... 562 698-0331
8500 Villaverde Dr Whittier (90605) *(P-14377)*

Friends Group Express Inc .... D...... 909 346-6814
14520 Village Dr Apt 1013 Fontana (92337) *(P-3478)*

Friends Long Bch Anmal Shelter .... D...... 562 988-7647
3815 Atlantic Ave Ste 4 Long Beach (90807) *(P-19083)*

ALPHABETIC SECTION — Full Throttle Films LLC

Friends of Cultural Center Inc .... D....... 760 346-6505
　73000 Fred Waring Dr Palm Desert (92260) *(P-14039)*

Friends Outside .... D....... 209 955-0701
　1148 W Fremont St Stockton (95203) *(P-17990)*

Friends Santa Cruz State Parks .... D....... 831 429-1840
　1543 Pacific Ave Ste 206 Santa Cruz (95060) *(P-18860)*

Frito-Lay, Rancho Cucamonga *Also Called: Frito-Lay North America Inc (P-6461)*

Frito-Lay, Bakersfield *Also Called: Frito-Lay North America Inc (P-6462)*

Frito-Lay North America Inc .... B....... 909 941-6214
　9535 Archibald Ave Rancho Cucamonga (91730) *(P-6461)*

Frito-Lay North America Inc .... C....... 661 328-6034
　28801 Highway 58 Bakersfield (93314) *(P-6462)*

Fritz Companies Inc .... A....... 650 635-2693
　550-1 Eccles Ave San Francisco (94101) *(P-4022)*

Frize Corporation .... D....... 800 834-2127
　16605 Gale Ave City Of Industry (91745) *(P-818)*

Front, San Francisco *Also Called: Frontapp Inc (P-12199)*

Front Line MGT Group Inc .... D....... 310 209-3100
　1100 Glendon Ave Ste 2000 Los Angeles (90024) *(P-20094)*

Front Porch Inc (PA) .... D....... 209 288-5500
　27 S Shepherd St Sonora (95370) *(P-11607)*

Front Porch Communities & Svcs .... C....... 858 454-2151
　849 Coast Blvd La Jolla (92037) *(P-8813)*

Front Porch Communities & Svcs .... C....... 760 729-4983
　2855 Carlsbad Blvd Carlsbad (92008) *(P-8814)*

Front Porch Communities & Svcs .... C....... 323 661-1128
　1055 N Kingsley Dr Los Angeles (90029) *(P-15483)*

Front Porch Communities & Svcs .... C....... 619 427-2777
　111 Third Ave Chula Vista (91910) *(P-15484)*

Front Porch Communities & Svcs .... C....... 805 687-0793
　3775 Modoc Rd Santa Barbara (93105) *(P-15845)*

Front Porch Communities & Svcs .... C....... 510 835-4700
　100 Bay Pl Ofc Oakland (94610) *(P-18435)*

Front Porch Communities & Svcs .... D....... 831 373-3111
　651 Sinex Ave Pacific Grove (93950) *(P-18436)*

Front Porch Communities & Svcs .... C....... 707 538-8400
　5555 Montgomery Dr Santa Rosa (95409) *(P-18437)*

Front Porch Communities & Svcs .... C....... 415 776-0500
　1661 Pine St Apt 911 San Francisco (94109) *(P-18438)*

Front Prch Cmmnties Oprting Gr .... C....... 800 233-3709
　800 N Brand Blvd Fl 19 Glendale (91203) *(P-15846)*

Front St Inc .... C....... 831 420-0120
　1201 Shaffer Rd Ste 1a Santa Cruz (95060) *(P-15757)*

Front St Residential Care, Santa Cruz *Also Called: Front St Inc (P-15757)*

Frontapp Inc .... D....... 415 680-3048
　300 Montgomery St San Francisco (94104) *(P-12199)*

Frontier California Inc .... B....... 818 365-0542
　510 Park Ave San Fernando (91340) *(P-4277)*

Frontier California Inc .... B....... 212 395-1000
　295 Parkshore Dr Folsom (95630) *(P-4278)*

Frontier California Inc .... B....... 805 372-6000
　1 Wellpoint Way Westlake Village (91362) *(P-4279)*

Frontier California Inc .... B....... 760 342-0500
　83793 Doctor Carreon Blvd Indio (92201) *(P-4280)*

Frontier California Inc .... B....... 714 375-6713
　7352 Slater Ave Huntington Beach (92647) *(P-4281)*

Frontier California Inc .... B....... 209 239-4128
　525 E Yosemite Ave Manteca (95336) *(P-4282)*

Frontier California Inc .... B....... 760 872-0812
　350 Lagoon St Bishop (93514) *(P-4283)*

Frontier California Inc .... B....... 805 925-0000
　200 W Church St Santa Maria (93458) *(P-4284)*

Frontier Ford (PA) .... C....... 408 241-1800
　3701 Stevens Creek Blvd Santa Clara (95051) *(P-7216)*

Frontier Logistics Services, Gardena *Also Called: F R T International Inc (P-3701)*

Frontier Logistics Services, Compton *Also Called: F R T International Inc (P-3702)*

Frontier Logistics Services, Ontario *Also Called: F R T International Inc (P-4019)*

Frontier Mechanical Inc .... D....... 661 589-6203
　6309 Seven Seas Ave Bakersfield (93308) *(P-1447)*

Frontier Plumbing, Bakersfield *Also Called: Frontier Mechanical Inc (P-1447)*

Frontier Rent-A-Car, Santa Clara *Also Called: Frontier Ford (P-7216)*

Frontier-Kemper Constructors Inc (HQ) .... D....... 818 362-2062
　15900 Olden St Sylmar (91342) *(P-1303)*

Frontrange Solutions Inc .... B....... 408 601-2800
　490 N Mccarthy Blvd Ste 100 Milpitas (95035) *(P-20389)*

Frontwave Credit Union (PA) .... C....... 760 430-7511
　1278 Rocky Point Dr Oceanside (92056) *(P-7774)*

Frozen Bakery, Lodi *Also Called: Cottage Bakery Inc (P-2367)*

Fruit Fillings LLC .... C....... 559 237-4715
　2531 E Edgar Ave Fresno (93706) *(P-6548)*

Fruit Growers Supply Company .... D....... 909 390-0190
　225 S Wineville Ave Ontario (91761) *(P-6549)*

Fruit Patch Inc .... B....... 559 591-6140
　38773 Road 48 Dinuba (93618) *(P-270)*

FRUITVALE HEALTHCARE CENTER, Oakland *Also Called: SSC Oakland Fruitvale Oper LP (P-15898)*

Fry Steel Company .... C....... 562 802-2721
　13325 Molette St Santa Fe Springs (90670) *(P-5492)*

Frye Construction Inc .... D....... 661 588-8870
　18807 Highway 65 Bakersfield (93308) *(P-1930)*

Fryman Management Inc .... D....... 949 481-5211
　18 Goodyear Ste 105 Irvine (92618) *(P-20752)*

FS Commercial Landscape Inc (PA) .... D....... 951 360-7070
　5151 Pedley Rd Riverside (92509) *(P-432)*

FSA Arlanza Child Dev Ctr .... D....... 951 353-0129
　8172 Magnolia Ave Riverside (92504) *(P-18317)*

Fssi, Santa Ana *Also Called: Financial Statement Svcs Inc (P-10772)*

Ft 2 Inc .... C....... 714 765-5555
　1211 N Miller St Anaheim (92806) *(P-6042)*

Ftdi West Inc .... D....... 909 473-1111
　3375 Enterprise Dr Bloomington (92316) *(P-3708)*

FTg Construction Mtls Inc .... D....... 209 334-4038
　5100 W Highway 12 Lodi (95242) *(P-3479)*

Fti Consulting Inc .... D....... 213 689-1200
　350 S Grand Ave Ste 3000 Los Angeles (90071) *(P-19232)*

Fti Consulting Inc .... D....... 415 283-4200
　50 California St Ste 1900 San Francisco (94111) *(P-20753)*

Ftsi, Monrovia *Also Called: Financial Tech Sltons Intl Inc (P-20376)*

Fuel Delivery Services Inc .... D....... 209 751-2185
　4895 S Airport Way Stockton (95206) *(P-3480)*

Fuel50 Inc .... D....... 833 844-1103
　30025 Alicia Pkwy # 20-23 Laguna Niguel (92677) *(P-11608)*

Fueling and Service Tech Inc .... D....... 714 523-0194
　7050 Village Dr Ste D Buena Park (90621) *(P-5835)*

Fugro USA Land, Walnut Creek *Also Called: Fugro William Lettis Assoc Inc (P-19233)*

Fugro William Lettis Assoc Inc (DH) .... D....... 925 256-6070
　1777 Botelho Dr Ste 262 Walnut Creek (94596) *(P-19233)*

Fuji Bank Ltd .... D....... 415 362-4740
　601 California St Ste 400 San Francisco (94108) *(P-7835)*

Fujifilm Dimatix Inc .... D....... 408 565-0670
　2230 Martin Ave Santa Clara (95050) *(P-19695)*

Fujitec America Inc .... C....... 310 464-8270
　12170 Mora Dr Ste 1 Santa Fe Springs (90670) *(P-20095)*

Fujitsu Computer Pdts Amer Inc, Sunnyvale *Also Called: PFU America Inc (P-12510)*

Fujitsu Glovia, Inc., El Segundo *Also Called: Crescentone Inc (P-11522)*

Fujitsu Management Services of America Inc .... C....... 408 746-6000
　1250 E Arques Ave Sunnyvale (94085) *(P-2829)*

Fujitsu North America Inc (HQ) .... D....... 408 746-6000
　350 Cobalt Way Sunnyvale (94085) *(P-12458)*

Fujitsu Research America Inc (PA) .... D....... 800 385-4878
　350 Cobalt Way Sunnyvale (94085) *(P-19696)*

Fujitsu Software, Sunnyvale *Also Called: Fujitsu Management Services of America Inc (P-2829)*

Fujitsu Ten Corp of America .... D....... 310 327-2151
　19600 S Vermont Ave Torrance (90502) *(P-5605)*

Fulgent Genetics Inc (PA) .... A....... 626 350-0537
　4399 Santa Anita Ave El Monte (91731) *(P-16722)*

Full Scale Logistics LLC .... D....... 805 279-6799
　2722 Rocky Point Ct Thousand Oaks (91362) *(P-4156)*

Full Stack Finance .... D....... 800 941-0356
　2701 Ocean Park Blvd Ste 210 Santa Monica (90405) *(P-9510)*

Full Throttle Films LLC (DH) .... D....... 818 956-1444
　757 W California Ave Glendale (91203) *(P-13937)*

Fullerton College Bookstore, Fullerton Also Called: North Ornge Cnty Cmnty Cllege *(P-7548)*
Fullerton Hlthcare Wllness CNT .... C....... 714 992-5701
   2222 N Harbor Blvd Fullerton (92835) *(P-15485)*
Fullerton Operations Plant 1, Fullerton Also Called: Howmet Globl Fstning Systems I *(P-5905)*
Fullmer Construction .... C....... 909 947-9467
   1725 S Grove Ave Ontario (91761) *(P-819)*
Fulwider and Patton LLP .... D....... 310 824-5555
   111 W Ocean Blvd Ste 1510 Long Beach (90802) *(P-17464)*
Fume-A-Pest & Termite Control, Encino Also Called: A-Able Inc *(P-10826)*
Functional Software Inc (PA) .... D....... 415 823-8009
   132 Hawthorne St San Francisco (94107) *(P-11609)*
Fungible Inc .... C....... 669 292-5522
   3201 Scott Blvd Santa Clara (95054) *(P-20754)*
Funimation Entertainment, Culver City Also Called: Crunchyroll LLC *(P-13834)*
Funnelcloudsales .... D....... 661 284-6032
   21758 Placeritos Blvd Santa Clarita (91321) *(P-3612)*
Funtopia Inc .... C....... 510 246-3098
   3700 Brookstone Dr Turlock (95382) *(P-14527)*
Furnace Creek Ranch & Inn, Death Valley Also Called: Xanterra Parks & Resorts Inc *(P-10385)*
Fuscoe Engineering Inc (PA) .... D....... 949 474-1960
   15535 Sand Canyon Ave Irvine (92618) *(P-19234)*
Fusd Central Warehouse, Fresno Also Called: Fresno Unified School District *(P-3707)*
Fuse Corps .... D....... 855 687-9905
   235 Montgomery St Ste 1110 San Francisco (94104) *(P-19084)*
Fuse Project LLC .... D....... 415 908-1492
   1401 16th St San Francisco (94103) *(P-20755)*
Fusefx, Van Nuys Also Called: Fusefx LLC *(P-13938)*
Fusefx LLC .... B....... 818 237-5052
   14823 Califa St Van Nuys (91411) *(P-13938)*
Fusion Growth Partners Inc .... D....... 916 448-3174
   1300 National Dr Ste 170 Sacramento (95834) *(P-9020)*
Fusion Real Estate Network, Sacramento Also Called: Fusion Growth Partners Inc *(P-9020)*
Fusionstorm, San Francisco Also Called: Computacenter US Inc *(P-12764)*
Futek Advanced Sensor Tech, Irvine Also Called: Futek Advanced Sensor Tech Inc *(P-3016)*
Futek Advanced Sensor Tech Inc .... C....... 949 465-0900
   10 Thomas Irvine (92618) *(P-3016)*
Future Dial Incorporated (PA) .... D....... 408 245-8880
   392 Potrero Ave Sunnyvale (94085) *(P-11610)*
Future Energy Corporation .... D....... 760 477-9700
   4120 Avenida De La Plata Oceanside (92056) *(P-1931)*
Future Energy Corporation (PA) .... D....... 800 985-0733
   8980 Grant Line Rd Elk Grove (95624) *(P-1932)*
Future Energy Corporation .... D....... 916 685-4200
   9701 Elk Grove Florin Rd Elk Grove (95624) *(P-19235)*
Future Energy Savers, Elk Grove Also Called: Future Energy Corporation *(P-1932)*
Future Fast Inc .... D....... 559 813-0113
   5081 W Brown Ave Fresno (93722) *(P-13299)*
Future Ford Lincon, Roseville Also Called: Ford Future Inc *(P-7208)*
Future Ford Lncoln Mrcury Cnco, Concord Also Called: Future Ford of Concord LLC *(P-7217)*
Future Ford of Concord LLC .... D....... 925 686-5000
   2285 Diamond Blvd Concord (94520) *(P-7217)*
Future State .... C....... 925 956-4200
   415 Mission St Ste 3300 San Francisco (94105) *(P-12793)*
Futuredial K.K., Sunnyvale Also Called: Future Dial Incorporated *(P-11610)*
Futures Explored .... C....... 925 332-7183
   2150 John Glenn Dr Ste 300 Concord (94520) *(P-17991)*
Futurewei Technologies Inc .... C....... 469 277-5700
   2330 Central Expy Santa Clara (95050) *(P-4285)*
Futurewei Technologies Inc (HQ) .... C....... 469 277-5700
   2220 Central Expy Santa Clara (95050) *(P-20756)*
Fuze Inc (PA) .... C....... 800 890-1553
   675 Creekside Way Campbell (95008) *(P-4286)*
Fuzzy Pet Health Inc .... D....... 415 692-1875
   1355 Market St Ste 488 San Francisco (94103) *(P-19979)*
Fx Networks LLC .... C....... 310 369-1000
   10201 W Pico Blvd Bldg 103 Los Angeles (90064) *(P-4508)*
G & G Construction Co, Atwater Also Called: Gino/Giuseppe Inc *(P-2120)*
G B Commercial LLC .... D....... 916 263-9000
   4900 Duckhorn Dr Sacramento (95834) *(P-9805)*
G B Group Inc (PA) .... D....... 408 848-8118
   780 Jarvis Dr Morgan Hill (95037) *(P-757)*
G D B, San Rafael Also Called: Guide Dogs For Blind Inc *(P-362)*
G F I, Vernon Also Called: Good Fellas Industries Inc *(P-7438)*
G M I, San Diego Also Called: Guard Management Inc *(P-12981)*
G M S, Rancho Cucamonga Also Called: General Micro Systems Inc *(P-5308)*
G P H Medical Services, Beverly Hills Also Called: GPh Medical & Legal Services *(P-15500)*
G P Resources, Compton Also Called: General Petroleum LLC *(P-6730)*
G P S, Taft Also Called: General Production Svc Cal Inc *(P-1211)*
G S N, Santa Monica Also Called: Game Show Network Music LLC *(P-4509)*
G S T, Cerritos Also Called: Golden Star Technology Inc *(P-7444)*
G W Surfaces (PA) .... D....... 805 642-5004
   2432 Palma Dr Ventura (93003) *(P-2280)*
G/M Business Interiors, San Diego Also Called: Goforth & Marti *(P-5089)*
G&L Penasquitos Inc .... A....... 858 538-0802
   10584 Rancho Carmel Dr San Diego (92128) *(P-17992)*
G2 Secure Staff .... C....... 310 486-8155
   5757 W Century Blvd Ste 518 Los Angeles (90045) *(P-11140)*
G2 Software Systems Inc .... C....... 619 222-8025
   4025 Hancock St Ste 105 San Diego (92110) *(P-11611)*
G3 Enterprises Inc (PA) .... A....... 209 341-7515
   502 E Whitmore Ave Modesto (95358) *(P-6909)*
G3 Enterprises Inc .... D....... 209 341-5265
   2612 Crows Landing Rd Modesto (95358) *(P-10808)*
GA Gertmenian and Sons LLC (PA) .... C....... 213 250-7777
   300 W Avenue 33 Los Angeles (90031) *(P-5117)*
Gable House Inc .... D....... 310 378-2265
   1611 S Pacific Coast Hwy Redondo Beach (90277) *(P-14115)*
Gable House Bowl, Redondo Beach Also Called: Gable House Inc *(P-14115)*
Gachina Landscape MGT Inc .... B....... 650 853-0400
   1130 Obrien Dr Menlo Park (94025) *(P-433)*
GAF Energy LLC .... D....... 510 330-6870
   125 Mitchell Blvd San Rafael (94903) *(P-1448)*
GAF Materials, Shafter Also Called: Standard Industries Inc *(P-5225)*
Gafcon Inc (PA) .... D....... 858 875-0010
   10301 Meanley Dr # 225 San Diego (92131) *(P-20096)*
Gaia Interactive Inc C
   5201 Great America Pkwy Ste 320 Santa Clara (95054) *(P-4287)*
Gaia Online, Santa Clara Also Called: Gaia Interactive Inc *(P-4287)*
Gaigaew Inc .... D....... 805 545-5996
   1002 George St San Luis Obispo (93401) *(P-7483)*
Gainsight Inc (PA) .... B....... 888 623-8562
   350 Bay St Ste 100 San Francisco (94133) *(P-12200)*
Gaju Market Corporation .... C....... 213 382-9444
   450 S Western Ave Los Angeles (90020) *(P-6910)*
Galasso's Bakery, Jurupa Valley Also Called: Galassos Bakery *(P-6628)*
Galassos Bakery (PA) .... C....... 951 360-1211
   10820 San Sevaine Way Jurupa Valley (91752) *(P-6628)*
Gale/Triangle Inc (PA) .... D....... 562 741-1300
   12816 Shoemaker Ave Santa Fe Springs (90670) *(P-3394)*
Galkos Construction Inc .... D....... 714 373-8545
   15262 Pipeline Ln Huntington Beach (92649) *(P-920)*
Galkos Construction Inc (PA) .... D....... 714 373-8545
   15262 Pipeline Ln Huntington Beach (92649) *(P-10547)*
Gallegos United, Huntington Beach Also Called: Grupo Gallegos *(P-10621)*
Galleher, Santa Fe Springs Also Called: Galleher LLC *(P-5118)*
Galleher LLC (PA) .... C....... 562 944-8885
   9303 Greenleaf Ave Santa Fe Springs (90670) *(P-5118)*
Galleher LLC .... D....... 408 850-1990
   1741 Junction Ave San Jose (95112) *(P-5119)*
Galleria Park Associates LLC .... D....... 415 781-3060
   191 Sutter St San Francisco (94104) *(P-9806)*
Galleria Park Hotel, San Francisco Also Called: Galleria Park Associates LLC *(P-9806)*
Galli Produce Company .... D....... 408 436-6100
   1650 Old Bayshore Hwy San Jose (95112) *(P-6550)*
Galpin Ford, North Hills Also Called: Galpin Motors Inc *(P-7218)*
Galpin Motors Inc (PA) .... B....... 818 787-3800
   15505 Roscoe Blvd North Hills (91343) *(P-7218)*
Galpin Motors Inc .... D....... 323 957-3333
   1763 Ivar Ave Los Angeles (90028) *(P-13591)*

ALPHABETIC SECTION

Gama Contracting Services Inc .... C....... 626 442-7200
  1835 Floradale Ave South El Monte (91733) *(P-5788)*
Gambrell Bondie .... D....... 310 641-8408
  5855 W Centinela Ave Los Angeles (90045) *(P-10902)*
Game Play Network Inc .... D....... 844 462-7768
  10866 Wilshire Blvd Ste 700 Los Angeles (90024) *(P-11612)*
Game Show Network Music LLC (DH) .... C....... 310 255-6800
  2150 Colorado Ave Ste 100 Santa Monica (90404) *(P-4509)*
Gamevil Com2us USA, El Segundo *Also Called: Com2us Usa Inc (P-11505)*
Gameworks Entertainment LLC (PA) .... A....... 206 521-0952
  9737 Lurline Ave Chatsworth (91311) *(P-7484)*
Gan Limited .... B....... 702 964-5777
  400 Spectrum Center Dr Ste 1900 Irvine (92618) *(P-11613)*
Ganahl Lumber Company .... D....... 951 278-4000
  150 W Blaine St Corona (92878) *(P-6961)*
Ganahl Lumber Company .... D....... 714 522-2864
  6586 Beach Blvd Buena Park (90621) *(P-7119)*
Ganahl Lumber Company .... D....... 562 346-2100
  10742 Los Alamitos Blvd Los Alamitos (90720) *(P-7120)*
Ganahl Lumber Company .... D....... 949 830-3600
  23132 Orange Ave Lake Forest (92630) *(P-7121)*
Ganda, Kentfield *Also Called: Kleinfelder Inc (P-19295)*
Ganda, San Anselmo *Also Called: Garcia and Associates (P-20757)*
GANG ALTERNATIVES PROGRAM, Wilmington *Also Called: Harbor Area Gang Altrntves Prg (P-18592)*
Gano Excel (usa) Inc .... D....... 626 338-8081
  8652 Kimball Ave Chino (91708) *(P-6629)*
Ganz USA LLC .... C....... 818 901-0077
  16525 Sherman Way Ste C5 Van Nuys (91406) *(P-20390)*
Gar Bennett LLC (PA) .... C....... 559 638-6311
  8246 Crawford Ave Reedley (93654) *(P-20097)*
Gar Enterprises (PA) .... D....... 626 574-1175
  418 E Live Oak Ave Arcadia (91006) *(P-5306)*
Garage Team Mazda, Costa Mesa *Also Called: Team Garage LLC (P-10679)*
Garcia and Associates .... C....... 415 458-5803
  1 Saunders Ave San Anselmo (94960) *(P-20757)*
Garda CL West Inc (HQ) .... B....... 213 383-3611
  1612 W Pico Blvd Los Angeles (90015) *(P-12975)*
Garda World Security Corp .... C....... 909 468-2229
  20325 E Walnut Dr N City Of Industry (91789) *(P-12976)*
GARDA WORLD SECURITY CORP, City Of Industry *Also Called: Garda World Security Corp (P-12976)*
Garden City Inc .... A....... 408 244-3333
  1887 Matrix Blvd San Jose (95110) *(P-9807)*
Garden City Casino & Rest, San Jose *Also Called: Garden City Inc (P-9807)*
Garden City Healthcare Center, Modesto *Also Called: Fig Holdings LLC (P-15477)*
Garden Crest Cnvlscent Hosp In .... D....... 323 663-8281
  909 Lucile Ave Los Angeles (90026) *(P-15486)*
GARDEN CREST RETIREMENT RESIDE, Los Angeles *Also Called: Garden Crest Cnvlscent Hosp In (P-15486)*
Garden Grove Advanced Imaging .... C....... 310 445-2800
  1510 Cotner Ave Los Angeles (90025) *(P-14756)*
Garden Grove Hospital, Garden Grove *Also Called: Kenneth Corp (P-16203)*
Garden Grove Medical Investors (HQ) .... D....... 714 534-1041
  12332 Garden Grove Blvd Garden Grove (92843) *(P-15487)*
Garden Grove Rehabilitation, Garden Grove *Also Called: Garden Grove Medical Investors (P-15487)*
Garden Grove Unified Schl Dst .... D....... 714 663-6437
  8371 Orangewood Ave Garden Grove (92841) *(P-18318)*
Gardena Convalescent Center, Santa Fe Springs *Also Called: B & E Convalescent Center Inc (P-15815)*
Gardena Honda, Gardena *Also Called: DCH Gardena Honda (P-7194)*
Gardena Hospital LP .... A....... 310 532-4200
  1145 W Redondo Beach Blvd Gardena (90247) *(P-16100)*
Gardena Medical Offices, Gardena *Also Called: Kaiser Foundation Hospitals (P-16176)*
Gardena Retirement Center Inc .... C....... 310 327-4091
  14741 S Vermont Ave Gardena (90247) *(P-15488)*
Gardeners Guild Inc .... C....... 415 457-0400
  2780 Goodrick Ave Richmond (94801) *(P-491)*
Gardens Regional Hosp Med Ctr, Hawaiian Gardens *Also Called: Gardens Regional Hospital and Medical Center Incorporated (P-16101)*

Gardens Regional Hospital and Medical Center Incorporated .... B....... 877 877-1104
  21530 Pioneer Blvd Hawaiian Gardens (90716) *(P-16101)*
Gardner Family Hlth Netwrk Inc .... C....... 408 254-5197
  3030 Alum Rock Ave San Jose (95127) *(P-14757)*
Gardner Family Hlth Netwrk Inc .... C....... 408 457-7100
  1621 Gold St Alviso (95002) *(P-14758)*
Gardner Logistics, Chino *Also Called: CRST Expedited Inc (P-3461)*
Garfield Imaging Center Inc .... C....... 626 572-0912
  555 N Garfield Ave Monterey Park (91754) *(P-14759)*
Garfield Medical Center, Monterey Park *Also Called: Ahmc Garfield Medical Ctr LP (P-15318)*
Garfield Nursing Home Inc .... D....... 510 582-7676
  1100 Marina Village Pkwy Ste 100 Alameda (94501) *(P-15489)*
Garich Inc (PA) .... B....... 858 453-1331
  6050 Santo Rd Ste 200 San Diego (92124) *(P-11141)*
Garich Inc .... B....... 951 302-4750
  504 E Alvarado St Ste 201 Fallbrook (92028) *(P-11142)*
Garlic Company .... C....... 661 393-4212
  18602 Zerker Rd Shafter (93263) *(P-12)*
Garrad Hassan America Inc (DH) .... D....... 858 836-3370
  9665 Chesapeake Dr Ste 435 San Diego (92123) *(P-20758)*
Garrett J Gentry Gen Engrg Inc .... D....... 909 693-3391
  1297 W 9th St Upland (91786) *(P-19236)*
Garrett Motion Inc .... C....... 310 512-5424
  2525 W 190th St Torrance (90504) *(P-19697)*
Garris Plastering, Orange *Also Called: Padilla Construction Company (P-1954)*
Garrison Family Med Group Inc .... D....... 661 947-7100
  41210 11th St W Ste K Palmdale (93551) *(P-14760)*
Garrison Family Medical Group, Palmdale *Also Called: Garrison Family Med Group Inc (P-14760)*
Garton Tractor Inc (PA) .... D....... 209 632-3931
  2400 N Golden State Blvd Turlock (95382) *(P-7580)*
Garvey Nut & Candy, Pico Rivera *Also Called: Genesis Foods Corporation (P-2374)*
Garwood Laboratories Inc .... D....... 562 949-2727
  143 Calle Iglesia San Clemente (92672) *(P-19980)*
Garwood Labs, San Clemente *Also Called: Garwood Laboratories Inc (P-19980)*
Gary Cardiff Enterprises Inc .... D....... 760 568-1403
  75255 Sheryl Ave Palm Desert (92211) *(P-3265)*
Gary Steel Division, Santa Fe Springs *Also Called: Kloeckner Metals Corporation (P-5501)*
Gas Company, The, Los Angeles *Also Called: Southern California Gas Co (P-4727)*
Gas Company, The, Downey *Also Called: Southern California Gas Co (P-4730)*
Gas Transmission Systems Inc (HQ) .... D....... 530 893-6711
  130 Amber Grove Dr Ste 134 Chico (95973) *(P-19237)*
Gastroenterology Division .... C....... 415 206-8823
  1001 Potrero Ave Ste 1e21 San Francisco (94110) *(P-14761)*
Gat - Arln Ground Support Inc .... C....... 818 847-9127
  2627 N Hollywood Way Burbank (91505) *(P-3894)*
Gat - Arln Ground Support Inc .... B....... 916 923-2349
  6701 Lindbergh Dr Sacramento (95837) *(P-3895)*
Gatc, Berkeley *Also Called: Pivot Bio Inc (P-19843)*
Gate City Beverage Distrs (PA) .... B....... 909 799-0281
  2505 Steele Rd San Bernardino (92408) *(P-6763)*
Gate of Heaven Cemetery, Los Altos *Also Called: Roman Cthlic Bishp of San Jose (P-9289)*
Gate Three Healthcare LLC .... C....... 949 587-9000
  24962 Calle Aragon Laguna Hills (92637) *(P-15490)*
Gateb Consulting Inc .... D....... 310 526-8323
  815 Hampton Dr Unit 1b Venice (90291) *(P-20759)*
Gates, David L & Associates, Walnut Creek *Also Called: David L Gates & Associates Inc (P-426)*
Gateway, Los Angeles *Also Called: County of Los Angeles (P-10802)*
Gateway Fresh LLC .... C....... 951 378-5439
  3660 Grand Ave Ste A Chino Hills (91709) *(P-9313)*
Gateway Home Realty, Brea *Also Called: American Financial Network Inc (P-7927)*
Gateway Landscape Cnstr Inc .... D....... 925 875-0000
  6735 Sierra Ct Ste A Dublin (94568) *(P-492)*
Gateway Logistics Tech LLC .... B....... 732 750-9000
  11400 W Olympic Blvd Los Angeles (90064) *(P-3395)*
Gateway Portfolio Holdings LLC .... D....... 626 578-0777
  601 Gateway Blvd Ste 930 South San Francisco (94080) *(P-9468)*
Gateway Post Acute, Porterville *Also Called: Valley Careidence Opco LLC (P-15715)*
Gateway US Retail Inc .... C....... 949 471-7000
  7565 Irvine Center Dr Irvine (92618) *(P-2804)*

Gateways Hosp Mental Hlth Ctr (PA) .... C 323 644-2000
   1891 Effie St Los Angeles (90026) *(P-16650)*

Gator Bio Inc .... D 650 800-7651
   2455 Faber Pl Palo Alto (94303) *(P-19809)*

Gatto Pope Walwick LLP .... D 619 282-7366
   3131 Camino Del Rio N Ste 1200 San Diego (92108) *(P-19578)*

Gavin De Becker & Assoc GP LLC .... C 818 505-0177
   350 N Glendale Ave Ste 517 Glendale (91206) *(P-20391)*

Gavin De Becker & Associates, Glendale *Also Called: Gavin De Becker & Assoc GP LLC (P-20391)*

Gazelle Transportation LLC .... C 661 322-8868
   34915 Gazelle Ct Bakersfield (93308) *(P-3396)*

Gazillion Inc .... B 650 393-6500
   475 Concar Dr San Mateo (94402) *(P-12201)*

Gbc Concrete Masnry Cnstr Inc .... C 951 245-2355
   561 Birch St Lake Elsinore (92530) *(P-1883)*

Gbm, Alhambra *Also Called: Gracing Brand Management Inc (P-2466)*

Gbr Holdings LLC .... D 702 283-6519
   6414 Cayenne Ln Carlsbad (92009) *(P-13300)*

GBS Linens Inc (PA) .... D 714 778-6448
   305 N Muller St Anaheim (92801) *(P-10435)*

GBS Party Linens, Anaheim *Also Called: GBS Linens Inc (P-10435)*

Gbt, South San Francisco *Also Called: Global Blood Therapeutics Inc (P-2587)*

GBT Inc .... C 626 854-9338
   17358 Railroad St City Of Industry (91748) *(P-5307)*

Gcc, Santa Rosa *Also Called: Ghilotti Construction Co Inc (P-1304)*

Gcc, Clovis *Also Called: Graham Concrete Cnstr Inc (P-2122)*

GCI Energy Products, Huntington Beach *Also Called: Galkos Construction Inc (P-10547)*

Gciu Employer Retirement Fund, City Of Industry *Also Called: Benefits Prgram Adminsitration (P-9421)*

Gcl W, Los Angeles *Also Called: Garda CL West Inc (P-12975)*

Gcm Holding Corporation .... B 510 475-0404
   1350 Atlantic St Union City (94587) *(P-9314)*

Gcorp Consulting .... C 619 587-3160
   2831 Camino Del Rio S Ste 311 San Diego (92108) *(P-20392)*

GD Heil Inc .... C 714 687-9100
   1031 Segovia Cir Placentia (92870) *(P-2236)*

GD Nielson Construction Inc .... D 707 253-8774
   147 Camino Oruga Napa (94558) *(P-1210)*

Gdln, Burlingame *Also Called: Guideline Inc (P-19814)*

Gdr Group Inc .... C 949 453-8818
   3 Park Plz Ste 1700 Irvine (92614) *(P-12794)*

GE, Walnut *Also Called: General Electric Company (P-3709)*

GE Digital LLC .... B 925 242-6200
   2700 Camino Ramon San Ramon (94583) *(P-12202)*

GE Energy, Diamond Bar *Also Called: Motech Americas LLC (P-19739)*

Gearbox Pubg San Francisco Inc .... D 650 590-7700
   100 Redwood Shores Pkwy Fl 2 Redwood City (94065) *(P-12203)*

Geary Darling Lessee Inc .... C 415 292-0100
   501 Geary St San Francisco (94102) *(P-9808)*

Gebbs Software Intl Inc .... D 201 227-0088
   4640 Admiralty Way Fl 9 Marina Del Rey (90292) *(P-12795)*

Geek Squad, Cerritos *Also Called: Geek Squad Inc (P-12796)*

Geek Squad Inc .... D 562 402-1555
   12989 Park Plaza Dr Cerritos (90703) *(P-12796)*

Gehr Group, Commerce *Also Called: Gehr Industries Inc (P-2725)*

Gehr Industries Inc (HQ) .... C 323 728-5558
   7400 E Slauson Ave Commerce (90040) *(P-2725)*

Gehry Partners LLP .... C 310 482-3000
   12541 Beatrice St Los Angeles (90066) *(P-19468)*

Gehry Technologies Inc .... D 310 862-1200
   12181 Bluff Creek Dr Los Angeles (90094) *(P-11614)*

Geico, Sacramento *Also Called: Geico General Insurance Co (P-8573)*

Geico, Poway *Also Called: Geico General Insurance Co (P-8574)*

Geico General Insurance Co .... B 916 923-5050
   5211 Madison Ave Sacramento (95841) *(P-8573)*

Geico General Insurance Co .... A 858 848-8200
   14111 Danielson St Poway (92064) *(P-8574)*

Geil Enterprises Inc .... A 559 495-3000
   1945 N Helm Ave Ste 102 Fresno (93727) *(P-12977)*

Gel-Pak LLC .... D 510 576-2220
   31398 Huntwood Ave Hayward (94544) *(P-10809)*

Gelfand Rennert & Feldman LLP (PA) .... C 310 553-1707
   1880 Century Park E Ste 1600 Los Angeles (90067) *(P-13301)*

Gels Logistics Inc (PA) .... D 626 340-6660
   437 Baldwin Park Blvd City Of Industry (91746) *(P-4023)*

Gem, Palmdale *Also Called: Golden Empire Mortgage Inc (P-7971)*

Gem Medical Management, Tustin *Also Called: Professnal Rgistry Netwrk Corp (P-11207)*

Gem Mortgage, Bakersfield *Also Called: Golden Empire Mortgage Inc (P-7969)*

Gem Software Inc .... C 650 924-1622
   1 Post St Fl 18 San Francisco (94104) *(P-11615)*

Gemalto Cogent Inc (HQ) .... D 626 325-9600
   2964 Bradley St Pasadena (91107) *(P-12459)*

Gemini Basketball LLC .... D 213 929-1300
   9100 Wilshire Blvd Ste 700e Beverly Hills (90212) *(P-14140)*

Gemini Solutions LLC .... C 650 329-8194
   814 Mission St Fl 5 Palo Alto (94306) *(P-12797)*

Gemmm Corporation (PA) .... D 805 496-0555
   2860 E Thousand Oaks Blvd Thousand Oaks (91362) *(P-9021)*

Gemological Institute Amer Inc (PA) .... A 760 603-4000
   5345 Armada Dr Carlsbad (92008) *(P-17795)*

Gemological Institute America, Carlsbad *Also Called: Gemological Institute Amer Inc (P-17795)*

Gemperle Enterprises .... D 209 667-2651
   10218 Lander Ave Turlock (95380) *(P-226)*

Gemperle Farms, Turlock *Also Called: Gemperle Enterprises (P-226)*

Gen Lending, Folsom *Also Called: Sierra Pacific Mortgage Co Inc (P-8021)*

Genea Energy Partners Inc .... C 714 694-0536
   19100 Von Karman Ave Ste 550 Irvine (92612) *(P-12460)*

Genencor International, Palo Alto *Also Called: Danisco US Inc (P-2612)*

Genentech Inc .... A 650 225-1000
   1 Dna Way Stop 35 South San Francisco (94080) *(P-19579)*

Genentech Inc .... A 650 225-1000
   611 Gateway Blvd South San Francisco (94080) *(P-19698)*

Genentech Inc (DH) .... A 650 225-1000
   1 Dna Way South San Francisco (94080) *(P-19882)*

Genentech Procurement Dept, South San Francisco *Also Called: Genentech Inc (P-19579)*

Geneo United LLC .... D 224 548-5854
   2077 Gateway Pl Ste 300 San Jose (95110) *(P-5415)*

Gener8 LLC (PA) .... D 650 940-9898
   2560 Junction Ave San Jose (95134) *(P-19238)*

General AC & Plbg, Thousand Palms *Also Called: 10x Hvac of Ca LLC (P-1326)*

General Acute Care Hospital, Downey *Also Called: Pih Health Downey Hospital (P-16324)*

General Acute Care Hospital, Whittier *Also Called: Pih Health Whittier Hospital (P-16327)*

General Air Conditioning & Htg, Thousand Palms *Also Called: Harrison Enterprises Inc (P-1455)*

General Atomics .... D 858 455-4141
   3483 Dunhill St San Diego (92121) *(P-19699)*

General Atomics .... D 858 676-7100
   16969 Mesamint St San Diego (92127) *(P-19700)*

General Atomics .... C 858 455-4000
   4949 Greencraig Ln San Diego (92123) *(P-19701)*

General Atomics (HQ) .... A 858 455-2810
   3550 General Atomics Ct San Diego (92121) *(P-19810)*

General Atomics Energy Pdts, San Diego *Also Called: General Atomics (P-19701)*

General Coatings Corporation .... D 909 204-4150
   9349 Feron Blvd Rancho Cucamonga (91730) *(P-1615)*

General Coatings Corporation .... D 858 587-1277
   600 W Freedom Ave Orange (92865) *(P-1616)*

General Coatings Corporation (PA) .... C 858 587-1277
   6711 Nancy Ridge Dr San Diego (92121) *(P-1617)*

General Coatings Corporation .... D 559 495-4004
   1220 E North Ave Fresno (93725) *(P-1618)*

General Cold Stg 4145, Bell Gardens *Also Called: US Foods Inc (P-6686)*

General Contractor, Irvine *Also Called: Uprite Construction Corp (P-853)*

General Contractor, Duarte *Also Called: Png Builders (P-994)*

General Dynamics Info Tech Inc .... D 619 881-8989
   1615 Murray Canyon Rd Ste 600 San Diego (92108) *(P-12798)*

General Dynmics Mssion Systems .... D 650 966-2000
   100 Ferguson Dr Mountain View (94043) *(P-2805)*

ALPHABETIC SECTION — Georgia-Pacific

General Electric Company .... D....... 909 869-7404
  20005 Business Pkwy Walnut (91789) *(P-3709)*

General Engineering Wstn Inc (PA).................................. D....... 714 630-3200
  1140 N Red Gum St Anaheim (92806) *(P-1449)*

General Hydroponics, Sebastopol *Also Called: General Hydroponics Inc (P-2639)*

General Hydroponics Inc ....D....... 707 824-9376
  3789 Vine Hill Rd Sebastopol (95472) *(P-2639)*

General Internal Medicine, San Francisco *Also Called: University Cal San Francisco (P-17775)*

General Lgstics Systems US Inc .... C....... 951 677-3972
  24305 Prielipp Rd Wildomar (92595) *(P-3397)*

General Lgstics Systems US Inc .... C....... 562 577-6037
  12300 Bell Ranch Dr Santa Fe Springs (90670) *(P-3398)*

General Lgstics Systems US Inc .... C....... 800 322-5555
  4601 Malat St Oakland (94601) *(P-3613)*

General Lgstics Systems US Inc .... C....... 559 651-1850
  827 N American St Visalia (93291) *(P-3614)*

General Lgstics Systems US Inc .... C....... 415 492-1112
  760 Cabin Dr Mill Valley (94941) *(P-3615)*

General Micro Systems Inc (PA).. D....... 909 980-4863
  8358 Maple Pl Rancho Cucamonga (91730) *(P-5308)*

General Monitors Inc (DH)... C....... 949 581-4464
  16782 Von Karman Ave Ste 14 Irvine (92606) *(P-2901)*

General Networks Corporation .... D....... 818 249-1962
  3524 Ocean View Blvd Glendale (91208) *(P-12799)*

General Pavement Management Inc .... D....... 805 933-0909
  850 Lawrence Dr Ste 100 Thousand Oaks (91320) *(P-2119)*

General Petroleum LLC (HQ).. C....... 562 983-7300
  19501 S Santa Fe Ave Compton (90221) *(P-6730)*

General Procurement Inc (PA)... D....... 949 679-7960
  1964 W Corporate Way Anaheim (92801) *(P-5309)*

General Prod A Cal Ltd Partnr (PA)................................... C....... 916 441-6431
  7625 Lone Tree Rd Sacramento (95837) *(P-6551)*

General Produce, Vernon *Also Called: V & L Produce Inc (P-6588)*

General Production Svc Cal Inc .... C....... 661 765-5330
  1333 Kern St Taft (93268) *(P-1211)*

General Services, Martinez *Also Called: County of Contra Costa (P-13661)*

General Tool Inc .... D....... 949 261-2322
  2025 Alton Pkwy Irvine (92606) *(P-5903)*

General Underground .... C....... 714 632-8646
  701 W Grove Ave Orange (92865) *(P-1450)*

Generate Life Sciences Co, Los Angeles *Also Called: California Cryobank LLC (P-17196)*

Generation Clovis LLC .... C....... 559 297-4900
  1650 Shaw Ave Clovis (93611) *(P-18439)*

Generation Construction Inc .... C....... 909 923-2077
  15650 El Prado Rd Chino (91710) *(P-678)*

Generation Home Mortgage, Irvine *Also Called: Genhome Mortgage Corporation (P-7966)*

Generational Properties Inc .... B....... 323 583-3163
  3141 E 44th St Vernon (90058) *(P-3710)*

Generis Holdings LP (PA).. B....... 661 366-7209
  7200 E Brundage Ln Bakersfield (93307) *(P-32)*

Genesis Foods Corporation .... D....... 323 890-5890
  8825 Mercury Ln Pico Rivera (90660) *(P-2374)*

Genesis Health Care, Orange *Also Called: Prospect Medical Systems Inc (P-20187)*

GENESIS HEALTHCARE CORPORATION, Los Angeles *Also Called: Sharon Care Center LLC (P-15662)*

Genesis Healthcare LLC .... B....... 310 370-3594
  20900 Earl St Ste 100 Torrance (90503) *(P-15491)*

Genesis Healthcare LLC .... B....... 209 478-6488
  9107 Davis Rd Stockton (95209) *(P-15492)*

Genesis Healthcare LLC .... A....... 805 922-3558
  425 Barcellus Ave Santa Maria (93454) *(P-15493)*

Genesis Healthcare LLC .... B....... 323 461-9961
  5310 Fountain Ave Los Angeles (90029) *(P-15847)*

Genesis Tech Partners LLC .... C....... 800 950-2647
  21540 Plummer St Ste A Chatsworth (91311) *(P-13772)*

Genesys Cloud Services Inc (HQ)...................................... B....... 650 466-1100
  1302 El Camino Real Ste 300 Menlo Park (94025) *(P-12204)*

Genesys Telecom Labs, Menlo Park *Also Called: Genesys Cloud Services Inc (P-12204)*

Genetic Dsase Screening Program, Richmond *Also Called: California Dept of Pub Hlth (P-14643)*

Genex (DH)... C....... 424 672-9500
  800 Corporate Pointe Ste 100 Culver City (90230) *(P-11616)*

Genhome Mortgage Corporation .... D....... 949 561-0412
  16815 Von Karman Ave Ste 200 Irvine (92606) *(P-7966)*

Genica Corporation .... B....... 855 433-5747
  43195 Business Park Dr Temecula (92590) *(P-5310)*

Genium Inc .... C....... 415 935-3593
  4 W 4th Ave Ste 600 San Mateo (94402) *(P-11617)*

Genius Products Inc .... C....... 310 453-1222
  3301 Exposition Blvd Ste 100 Santa Monica (90404) *(P-6043)*

Genlabs (PA).. C....... 909 591-8451
  5568 Schaefer Ave Chino (91710) *(P-2624)*

Genmark Automation (DH)... D....... 510 897-3400
  46723 Lakeview Blvd Fremont (94538) *(P-5836)*

Genomic Health, Redwood City *Also Called: Genomic Health Inc (P-16723)*

Genomic Health Inc (HQ).. A....... 650 556-9300
  301 Penobscot Dr Redwood City (94063) *(P-16723)*

Genomics Inst of Nvrtis RES FN .... D....... 858 812-1805
  10675 John J Hopkins Dr San Diego (92121) *(P-19702)*

Gensler, San Francisco *Also Called: M Arthur Gensler Jr Assoc Inc (P-19489)*

Gensler, Newport Beach *Also Called: M Arthur Gensler Jr Assoc Inc (P-19491)*

Gensler and Associates, Los Angeles *Also Called: M Arthur Gensler Jr Assoc Inc (P-19490)*

Gensler Asscts/Ntrnational Ltd (HQ)................................ D....... 415 433-3700
  220 Montgomery St San Francisco (94104) *(P-19469)*

Gentex Corporation .... D....... 909 481-7667
  9859 7th St Rancho Cucamonga (91730) *(P-19703)*

Gentle Dental .... A....... 650 341-8008
  853 Middlefield Rd Ste 1 Palo Alto (94301) *(P-15227)*

Gentle Dental Service Corp (DH)....................................... D....... 800 277-1112
  9800 S La Cienega Blvd Ste 800 Inglewood (90301) *(P-15228)*

Gentry Associates LLC .... D....... 619 291-0999
  525 Spruce St San Diego (92103) *(P-9809)*

Genuine Parts Distributors, Ontario *Also Called: Tracy Industries Inc (P-2768)*

Geo H Wilson Inc .... D....... 831 423-9522
  250 Harvey West Blvd Santa Cruz (95060) *(P-1451)*

Geo Sales-Courtesy Chevrolet, San Diego *Also Called: Courtesy Chevrolet Center (P-7187)*

Geo. H. Wilson, Santa Cruz *Also Called: Acco Engineered Systems Inc (P-1332)*

Geocon, San Diego *Also Called: Geocon Consultants Inc (P-20760)*

Geocon Consultants Inc (PA)... D....... 858 558-6900
  6960 Flanders Dr San Diego (92121) *(P-20760)*

Geocon Incorporated .... D....... 858 558-6900
  6960 Flanders Dr San Diego (92121) *(P-19239)*

Geographic Solutions Inc .... B....... 831 757-4400
  234 Capitol St Ste A Salinas (93901) *(P-20393)*

Geolinks, Camarillo *Also Called: California Internet LP (P-4260)*

Geologic Associates Inc .... D....... 530 272-2448
  143 Spring Hill Dr Ste E Grass Valley (95945) *(P-19240)*

Geologics Corporation .... C....... 661 259-5767
  25375 Orchard Village Rd Ste 102 Valencia (91355) *(P-20761)*

Georg Fischer LLC (DH)... D....... 714 731-8800
  9271 Jeronimo Rd Irvine (92618) *(P-5493)*

Georg Fischer Piping, Irvine *Also Called: Georg Fischer LLC (P-5493)*

George Brazil Plbg Htg & AC, Santa Ana *Also Called: Orange County Services Inc (P-1520)*

George Chevrolet ....D....... 562 925-2500
  17000 Lakewood Blvd Bellflower (90706) *(P-7219)*

George Chevrolet, Bellflower *Also Called: George Chevrolet (P-7219)*

George Chiala Farms Inc .... C....... 408 778-0562
  15500 Hill Rd Morgan Hill (95037) *(P-33)*

George E Masker Inc .... D....... 510 568-1206
  7699 Edgewater Dr Oakland (94621) *(P-1619)*

George Fischer Inc (HQ).. C....... 626 571-2770
  5462 Irwindale Ave Ste A Baldwin Park (91706) *(P-2852)*

George G Sharp Inc .... D....... 619 425-4211
  1065 Bay Blvd Ste D Chula Vista (91911) *(P-19241)*

GEORGE L MEE MEMORIAL HOSPITAL, King City *Also Called: Southern Mntrey Cnty Mem Hosp (P-16448)*

Georgetown Mortgage, Rancho Cucamonga *Also Called: Thrive Mortgage LLC (P-8024)*

Georgia Atkison Snf LLC .... D....... 626 444-2535
  3825 Durfee Ave El Monte (91732) *(P-15494)*

Georgia-Pacific, Santa Fe Springs *Also Called: Georgia-Pacific LLC (P-6078)*

Georgia-Pacific LLC .... D...... 559 674-4685
24600 Avenue 13 Madera (93637) *(P-2513)*

Georgia-Pacific LLC .... B...... 562 861-6226
9206 Santa Fe Springs Rd Santa Fe Springs (90670) *(P-6078)*

Geovera Specialty Insurance Co .... D...... 707 863-3700
1455 Oliver Rd Fairfield (94534) *(P-8383)*

Gerawan Farming LLC .... C...... 559 638-9281
1467 E Dinuba Ave Reedley (93654) *(P-106)*

Gerawan Farming Partners, Fresno *Also Called: Wawona Packing Co LLC (P-6595)*

Gerawan Ranches .... C...... 559 787-8780
10045 W Lincoln Ave Fresno (93706) *(P-107)*

Geri-Care Inc .... D...... 310 320-0961
21521 S Vermont Ave Torrance (90502) *(P-15495)*

Geri-Care II Inc .... D...... 310 328-0812
22035 S Vermont Ave Torrance (90502) *(P-15848)*

German Association Orange Cnty, Anaheim *Also Called: Phoenix CLB Grman Assn In Orng (P-7502)*

German Motors Corporation .... C...... 415 590-3773
1675 Howard St San Francisco (94103) *(P-7220)*

Gerson Bakar & Associates, Palo Alto *Also Called: Oak Creek Apartments (P-8848)*

Ges, Sacramento *Also Called: Granite Electrical Supply Inc (P-5558)*

Ges, Huntington Beach *Also Called: Global Exprnce Specialists Inc (P-13303)*

Get Heal Inc .... D...... 310 528-4957
528 Palisades Dr Ste 176 Pacific Palisades (90272) *(P-11287)*

Get More Math, Sonora *Also Called: Front Porch Inc (P-11607)*

Get-A-Lift Handicap Bus Trnsp, Bakersfield *Also Called: Golden Empire Transit District (P-3141)*

Getac Inc .... D...... 949 681-2900
15495 Sand Canyon Ave Ste 350 Irvine (92618) *(P-5311)*

Getac North America, Irvine *Also Called: Getac Inc (P-5311)*

Getfeedback Inc .... D...... 888 684-8821
1 Curiosity Way San Mateo (94403) *(P-11618)*

Getinsured.com, Mountain View *Also Called: Vimo Inc (P-20874)*

Getmedlegal, San Dimas *Also Called: Legal Solutions Holdings Inc (P-17543)*

Gettler-Ryan Inc (PA) .... D...... 925 551-7555
6805 Sierra Ct Ste G Dublin (94568) *(P-2281)*

Getty Center, Los Angeles *Also Called: Bon Appetit Management Co (P-20045)*

Getty Publications, Los Angeles *Also Called: The J Paul Getty Trust (P-18679)*

Gfi Energy Group, Los Angeles *Also Called: Oaktree Capital Management LP (P-9547)*

Gfk Etilize Inc .... D...... 888 608-1212
34145 Pacific Coast Hwy 636 Dana Point (92629) *(P-19811)*

GFS Capital Holdings .... B...... 714 720-3918
6499 Havenwood Cir Ste 720 Huntington Beach (92648) *(P-7967)*

Ggc Administration LLC .... A...... 415 983-2700
1 Embarcadero Ctr Fl 39 San Francisco (94111) *(P-9315)*

Ggg Demolition Inc (PA) .... D...... 714 699-9350
1130 W Trenton Ave Orange (92867) *(P-921)*

Gh Group Inc .... C...... 562 264-5078
3645 Long Beach Blvd Long Beach (90807) *(P-9316)*

Ghangor Cloud Inc .... D...... 408 713-3303
2001 Gateway Pl Ste 710 San Jose (95110) *(P-2958)*

Ghc of Pleasanton LLC .... D...... 925 462-2400
300 Neal St Pleasanton (94566) *(P-15496)*

Ghc of San Rafael LLC .... D...... 415 499-1000
1550 Silveira Pkwy San Rafael (94903) *(P-15497)*

Ghilotti Bros Inc .... B...... 415 454-7011
525 Jacoby St San Rafael (94901) *(P-2217)*

Ghilotti Construction Co Inc .... C...... 707 556-9145
600 S Napa Junction Rd American Canyon (94503) *(P-1106)*

Ghilotti Construction Co Inc (PA) .... C...... 707 585-1221
246 Ghillotti Ave Santa Rosa (95407) *(P-1304)*

Ghirardelli, San Leandro *Also Called: Ghirardelli Chocolate Company (P-7158)*

Ghirardelli Chocolate Company (DH) .... B...... 510 483-6970
1111 139th Ave San Leandro (94578) *(P-7158)*

Ghost Management Group LLC .... C...... 949 870-1400
41 Discovery Irvine (92618) *(P-10712)*

Ghp Management Corporation .... C...... 310 432-1441
270 N Canon Dr Beverly Hills (90210) *(P-20098)*

GI Partners LLC (PA) .... A...... 415 688-4800
4 Embarcadero Ctr Ste 3200 San Francisco (94111) *(P-20762)*

Giampolini & Co .... C...... 415 673-1236
1482 67th St Emeryville (94608) *(P-1620)*

Giampolini/Courtney, Emeryville *Also Called: Giampolini & Co (P-1620)*

Giant, San Francisco *Also Called: Giant Creative Strategy Llc (P-10615)*

Giant Creative Strategy Llc .... C...... 415 655-5200
1700 Montgomery St Ste 485 San Francisco (94111) *(P-10615)*

Giant Inland Empire Rv Ctr Inc (PA) .... C...... 909 981-0444
9150 Benson Ave Montclair (91763) *(P-7394)*

Giant Media Corporation .... D...... 310 526-6739
5792 W Jefferson Blvd Los Angeles (90016) *(P-10616)*

Giant Mgllan Tlscope Orgnztion, Pasadena *Also Called: Gmto Corporation (P-3036)*

Giant Rv, Montclair *Also Called: Giant Inland Empire Rv Ctr Inc (P-7394)*

Giant Sportz Paintball Park, Bellflower *Also Called: Hollywood Sports Park LLC (P-13317)*

Gibbs Giden Locher .... D...... 310 552-3400
1880 Century Park E Ste 1200 Los Angeles (90067) *(P-17465)*

Gibbs & Associates, Newbury Park *Also Called: Cimatron Gibbs LLC (P-11490)*

Gibraltar Cnvalescent Hosp Inc (PA) .... D...... 714 577-3880
3050 Saturn St Ste 201 Brea (92821) *(P-15849)*

Gibraltar Cnvalescent Hosp Inc .... D...... 626 443-9425
2720 Nevada Ave El Monte (91733) *(P-15850)*

Gibson Dunn & Crutcher Inc .... C...... 213 229-7000
333 S Grand Ave Los Angeles (90071) *(P-17466)*

Gibson Dunn & Crutcher LLP .... D...... 650 849-5300
1881 Page Mill Rd Palo Alto (94304) *(P-17467)*

Gibson Dunn & Crutcher LLP .... D...... 949 451-3800
3161 Michelson Dr Ste 1200 Irvine (92612) *(P-17468)*

Gibson Dunn & Crutcher LLP (PA) .... B...... 213 229-7000
333 S Grand Ave Ste 4600 Los Angeles (90071) *(P-17469)*

Gibson Dunn & Crutcher LLP .... D...... 310 552-8500
2029 Century Park E Ste 4000 Los Angeles (90002) *(P-17470)*

Gibson Dunn & Crutcher LLP .... D...... 415 393-8200
555 Mission St Ste 3000 San Francisco (94105) *(P-17471)*

Gibson Exhaust Systems, Corona *Also Called: Gibson Performance Corporation (P-2973)*

Gibson Homeware, Commerce *Also Called: Gibson Overseas Inc (P-5120)*

Gibson Overseas Inc (PA) .... B...... 323 832-8900
2410 Yates Ave Commerce (90040) *(P-5120)*

Gibson Overseas Inc .... C...... 323 832-8900
7776 Tippecanoe Ave San Bernardino (92410) *(P-20763)*

Gibson Performance Corporation .... D...... 951 372-1220
1270 Webb Cir Corona (92879) *(P-2973)*

Gic Real Estate Inc (DH) .... D...... 415 229-1800
1 Bush St Ste 1100 San Francisco (94104) *(P-9022)*

Giddyup Group Inc .... D...... 800 828-2785
20 N Oak St Ste B Ventura (93001) *(P-10617)*

Gifting Company LLC (PA) .... C...... 209 365-2300
6011 E Pine St Lodi (95240) *(P-6552)*

Gifting Group LLC .... D...... 951 296-0310
42210 Zevo Dr Temecula (92590) *(P-6911)*

Giga Omni Media Inc .... D...... 415 974-6355
1613a Lyon St San Francisco (94115) *(P-13157)*

Gigabyte Technology, City Of Industry *Also Called: GBT Inc (P-5307)*

Gigamon Inc (HQ) .... C...... 408 831-4000
3300 Olcott St Santa Clara (95054) *(P-2830)*

Gigatera Communications .... D...... 714 515-1100
1818 E Orangethorpe Ave Fullerton (92831) *(P-2942)*

Gigster Inc .... C...... 941 888-4447
301 Howard St Ste 1800 San Francisco (94105) *(P-11619)*

Gilardi & Co LLC .... D...... 415 798-5900
1 Mcinnis Pkwy San Rafael (94903) *(P-20099)*

Gilbane Building Company .... D...... 858 658-6700
2033 Gateway Pl Ste 450 San Jose (95110) *(P-758)*

Gilbane Federal (DH) .... C...... 925 946-3100
1220 Concord Ave Concord (94520) *(P-19242)*

Gilbane Federal Company, Concord *Also Called: Gilbane Federal (P-19242)*

Gilbert Associates Inc .... D...... 916 646-6464
2880 Gateway Oaks Dr Ste 100 Sacramento (95833) *(P-19580)*

Gilbert Klly Crwley Jnnett LLP (PA) .... D...... 213 615-7000
550 S Hope St Ste 2200 Los Angeles (90071) *(P-17472)*

Gillette Citrus Inc .... D...... 559 626-4236
10175 S Anchor Ave Dinuba (93618) *(P-271)*

ALPHABETIC SECTION

Gillies Trucking Inc .... D 209 948-6268
   3931 Newton Rd Stockton (95205) *(P-3399)*

Gillig LLC .... B 510 264-5000
   1100 Voyager St Livermore (94550) *(P-3481)*

Gillig LLC .... B 800 735-1500
   25972 Eden Landing Rd Hayward (94545) *(P-5041)*

Gillispie School .... D 858 459-3773
   7380 Girard Ave La Jolla (92037) *(P-17712)*

Gillson Trucking Inc .... C 925 400-9094
   1801 E Dr Martin Luther King Jr Blvd Stockton (95205) *(P-3482)*

Gilroy Gardens Family Theme Pk .... C 408 840-7100
   3050 Hecker Pass Rd Gilroy (95020) *(P-14304)*

Gilroy Health & Rehab Ctr, Gilroy *Also Called: Mariner Health Care Inc (P-15564)*

Gilroy Health Care, Gilroy *Also Called: Covenant Care California LLC (P-15406)*

Gils Distributing Service .... C 213 627-0539
   718 E 8th St Los Angeles (90021) *(P-10731)*

Gilton Solid Waste MGT Inc .... C 209 527-3781
   755 S Yosemite Ave Oakdale (95361) *(P-4897)*

Gingerio Inc .... D 408 455-0574
   116 New Montgomery St Ste 500 San Francisco (94105) *(P-11620)*

Gino Morena Enterprises LLC .... B 530 788-0053
   Bldg 2434 Marysville (95903) *(P-10511)*

Gino Rinaldi Inc .... D 831 761-0195
   51 Fremont St Royal Oaks (95076) *(P-1983)*

Gino/Giuseppe Inc .... C 209 358-0556
   700 Enterprise Ct Atwater (95301) *(P-2120)*

Ginsberg Holdco Inc .... B 408 831-4000
   3300 Olcott St Santa Clara (95054) *(P-12205)*

Gipson Hffman Pncone A Prof Co .... D 310 556-4660
   1901 Avenue Of The Stars Ste 1100 Los Angeles (90067) *(P-17473)*

Girardi Keese (PA) .... D 213 977-0211
   1126 Wilshire Blvd Los Angeles (90017) *(P-17474)*

GIRL SCOUTS, Sacramento *Also Called: Girl Scouts Heart Central Cal (P-18861)*

GIRL SCOUTS, Alameda *Also Called: Girl Scouts Northern Cal (P-18862)*

Girl Scouts Heart Central Cal .... C 916 452-9181
   6601 Elvas Ave Sacramento (95819) *(P-18861)*

Girl Scouts Northern Cal (PA) .... D 510 562-8470
   1650 Harbor Bay Pkwy Ste 100 Alameda (94502) *(P-18862)*

GIRL SCOUTS SAN DIEGO, San Diego *Also Called: Girl Scuts San Dg-Mprial Cncil (P-18864)*

Girl Scuts Greater Los Angeles (PA) .... C 626 677-2265
   423 N La Brea Ave Inglewood (90302) *(P-18863)*

Girl Scuts San Dg-Mprial Cncil .... D 619 610-0751
   1231 Upas St San Diego (92103) *(P-18864)*

GIRLS REPUBLIC, Chino Hills *Also Called: Boys Republic (P-18380)*

Giroux, Los Angeles *Also Called: Giroux Glass Inc (P-2202)*

Giroux Glass Inc (PA) .... C 213 747-7406
   850 W Washington Blvd Ste 200 Los Angeles (90015) *(P-2202)*

Gitsit Solutions LLC (PA) .... D 714 352-2038
   333 S Anita Dr Ste 400 Orange (92868) *(P-9511)*

Giumarra Agricom Intl LLC .... A 760 480-8502
   15651 Old Milky Way Escondido (92027) *(P-6553)*

Giumarra Bros Fruit Co Inc (PA) .... D 213 627-2900
   1601 E Olympic Blvd Ste 400 Los Angeles (90021) *(P-6554)*

Giumarra International Berry, Los Angeles *Also Called: Giumarra Bros Fruit Co Inc (P-6554)*

Giumarra Vineyards Corporation .... C 661 395-7071
   11220 Edison Hwy Bakersfield (93307) *(P-73)*

Giumarra Vineyards Corporation (PA) .... B 661 395-7000
   11220 Edison Hwy Edison (93220) *(P-74)*

Give ME Shelter, Camarillo *Also Called: Moms Place (P-15589)*

GK Management Co Inc (PA) .... C 310 204-2050
   5150 Overland Ave Culver City (90230) *(P-9023)*

Gkk Corporation .... D 619 398-0215
   1775 Hancock St San Diego (92110) *(P-19470)*

Gkk Corporation (PA) .... D 949 250-1500
   2355 Main St Ste 220 Irvine (92614) *(P-19471)*

Gkkworks, Irvine *Also Called: Gkk Corporation (P-19471)*

GKN Aerospace Chem-Tronics Inc (DH) .... A 619 258-5000
   1150 W Bradley Ave El Cajon (92020) *(P-2985)*

Gky Dental Arts Inc (PA) .... D 310 214-8007
   4212 Artesia Blvd Torrance (90504) *(P-16772)*

GL, San Diego *Also Called: Garrad Hassan America Inc (P-20758)*

GL Nemirow Inc .... D 818 562-9433
   2550 N Hollywood Way Ste 502 Burbank (91505) *(P-10618)*

GLad Entertainment Inc (PA) .... D 559 292-9000
   4055 N Chestnut Ave Fresno (93726) *(P-14528)*

Glad-A-Way Gardens Inc .... C 805 938-0569
   2669 E Clark Ave Santa Maria (93455) *(P-128)*

Gladiator Corporation .... B 650 233-2900
   2882 Sand Hill Rd Ste 280 Menlo Park (94025) *(P-12206)*

Gladly Software Inc .... D 650 387-8485
   423 Broadway # 503 Millbrae (94030) *(P-11621)*

Glamour Industries Co .... D 213 687-8600
   100 Wilshire Blvd Ste 700 Santa Monica (90401) *(P-5939)*

Glamour Industries Co (PA) .... B 323 728-2999
   2220 Gaspar Ave Commerce (90040) *(P-6109)*

Glare Technology Usa Inc .... C 909 437-6999
   30898 Wealth St Murrieta (92563) *(P-13120)*

Glaser Weil Fink Jacobs (PA) .... C 310 553-3000
   10250 Constellation Blvd Fl 19 Los Angeles (90067) *(P-17475)*

Glass Lewis & Co LLC (HQ) .... D 415 678-4110
   255 California St Ste 1100 San Francisco (94111) *(P-19812)*

Glass House Group, Long Beach *Also Called: Gh Group Inc (P-9316)*

Glassbeam Inc .... D 408 740-4600
   2033 Gateway Pl Ste 658 San Jose (95110) *(P-11622)*

Glassdoor Inc (HQ) .... D 415 275-7411
   50 Beale St Fl 16 San Francisco (94105) *(P-11143)*

Glassdoor.com, San Francisco *Also Called: Glassdoor Inc (P-11143)*

GLAZA, Los Angeles *Also Called: Greater Los Angeles Zoo Assn (P-18589)*

Glazier, Anaheim *Also Called: Artisan Glass and Design Inc (P-2256)*

Glen Annie Golf Club .... D 805 968-6400
   405 Glen Annie Rd Goleta (93117) *(P-14263)*

Glen Ivy Hot Springs .... D 951 277-3529
   25000 Glen Ivy Rd Temescal Valley (92883) *(P-10548)*

Glen Ivy Hot Springs .... C 714 990-2090
   1001 Brea Mall Brea (92821) *(P-10549)*

Glenborough LLC (PA) .... D 650 343-9300
   400 S El Camino Real Ste 1100 San Mateo (94402) *(P-9024)*

Glendale Adventist Medical Ctr (HQ) .... A 818 409-8000
   1509 Wilson Ter Glendale (91206) *(P-16102)*

Glendale Associates Ltd .... D 818 246-6737
   100 W Broadway Ste 100 Glendale (91210) *(P-8722)*

Glendale Eye Medical Group (PA) .... D 818 956-1010
   607 N Central Ave Ste 203 Glendale (91203) *(P-14762)*

Glendale Medical Offices, Glendale *Also Called: Kaiser Foundation Hospitals (P-14827)*

Glendale Mem Hlth Foundation .... B 818 502-2375
   1420 S Central Ave Glendale (91204) *(P-16103)*

Glendale Memorial Breast Ctr, Glendale *Also Called: Glendale Memorial Health Corp (P-16104)*

Glendale Memorial Center, Glendale *Also Called: Glendale Memorial Health Corporation (P-16105)*

Glendale Memorial Health Corp .... A 818 502-2323
   222 W Eulalia St Glendale (91204) *(P-16104)*

Glendale Memorial Health Corporation .... A 818 502-1900
   1420 S Central Ave Glendale (91204) *(P-16105)*

GLENDALE YMCA SWIM SCHOOL, Glendale *Also Called: Young MNS Chrstn Assn Glndale (P-18956)*

Glendale Chevrolet, Glendora *Also Called: Martin Automotive Inc (P-13667)*

Glendora Country Club .... D 626 335-4051
   2400 Country Club Drive Glendora (91741) *(P-14378)*

Glendora Oaks Bhvral Hlth Hosp, Glendora *Also Called: East Valley Glendora Hosp LLC (P-16063)*

Glenn A Rick Engrg & Dev Co (PA) .... C 619 291-0708
   5620 Friars Rd San Diego (92110) *(P-19243)*

Glenn Medical Center Inc .... D 530 934-4681
   1133 W Sycamore St Willows (95988) *(P-16106)*

Glenoaks Convalescent Hospital .... D 818 240-4300
   409 W Glenoaks Blvd Glendale (91202) *(P-16107)*

Glidewell Laboratories, Newport Beach *Also Called: James R Gldwell Dntl Crmics In (P-16773)*

Glint Inc .... D 650 817-7240
   1000 W Maude Ave Sunnyvale (94085) *(P-12575)*

Glo Yoga   **ALPHABETIC SECTION**

Glo Yoga .... D....... 310 801-9031
    18041 Blue Sail Dr Pacific Palisades (90272) *(P-14529)*

Global Bakeries, Pacoima *Also Called: Surge Globl Bkries Hldings LLC (P-6676)*

Global Bakeries Inc .... D....... 818 896-0525
    13336 Paxton St Pacoima (91331) *(P-6630)*

Global Blood Therapeutics Inc .... B....... 650 741-7700
    181 Oyster Point Blvd South San Francisco (94080) *(P-2587)*

Global Blue Dvbe Inc .... D....... 916 632-2583
    4470 Yankee Hill Rd Ste 160 Rocklin (95677) *(P-12695)*

Global Building Services Inc (PA) .... D....... 800 675-6643
    27433 Tourney Rd Ste 280 Valencia (91355) *(P-10903)*

Global Building Services Inc .... A....... 209 858-9501
    17618 Murphy Pkwy Lathrop (95330) *(P-20888)*

Global Care Travel, San Diego *Also Called: Customzed Svcs Admnstrtors Inc (P-8539)*

Global Cash Card Inc .... C....... 949 751-0360
    3972 Barranca Pkwy Ste J610 Irvine (92606) *(P-12207)*

Global Customer Services Inc .... D....... 760 995-7949
    17373 Lilac St Hesperia (92345) *(P-13302)*

Global Domains Intl Inc .... D....... 760 602-3000
    701 Palomar Airport Rd Carlsbad (92011) *(P-4288)*

Global Exprnce Specialists Inc .... C....... 619 498-6300
    18504 Beach Blvd Unit 511 Huntington Beach (92648) *(P-13303)*

Global Gaming League, Los Angeles *Also Called: Professnl Intrctive Entrmt In (P-14058)*

Global Industry Analysts Inc .... D....... 408 528-9966
    6150 Hellyer Ave Ste 100 San Jose (95138) *(P-19813)*

Global Infotech Corporation .... B....... 408 567-0600
    2890 Zanker Rd Ste 202 San Jose (95134) *(P-20764)*

Global Innovation Advisors, San Francisco *Also Called: GI Partners LLC (P-20762)*

Global Innovation Partner, Los Angeles *Also Called: Cbre Globl Value Investors LLC (P-8928)*

Global Integrated Logistics, Irvine *Also Called: Agility Logistics Corp (P-3979)*

Global Invstments Aricor Group .... B....... 415 735-9191
    667 Clay St San Francisco (94111) *(P-8087)*

Global Language Solutions LLC .... D....... 949 798-1400
    19800 Macarthur Blvd Irvine (92612) *(P-13304)*

Global Mail Inc .... C....... 310 735-0800
    921 W Artesia Blvd Compton (90220) *(P-4024)*

Global Motorsport Parts Inc .... C....... 408 778-0500
    15750 Vineyard Blvd Ste 100 Morgan Hill (95037) *(P-2995)*

Global Paratransit Inc .... B....... 310 715-7550
    400 W Compton Blvd Gardena (90248) *(P-3266)*

Global Pcci (gpc) (PA) .... C....... 757 637-9000
    2465 Campus Dr Ste 100 Irvine (92612) *(P-2751)*

Global Plastics Inc .... C....... 951 657-5466
    145 Malbert St Perris (92570) *(P-6008)*

Global Plumbing & Fire Supply .... C....... 818 550-8444
    723 Sonora Ave Glendale (91201) *(P-5750)*

Global Rental Co Inc .... C....... 909 469-5160
    1253 Price Ave Pomona (91767) *(P-10997)*

Global Risk MGT Solutions LLC .... D....... 949 759-8500
    5271 California Ave Ste 290 Irvine (92617) *(P-20394)*

Global Risk Solutions Inc .... D....... 888 981-9484
    2100 Geng Rd Ste 210 Palo Alto (94303) *(P-12978)*

Global Service Resources Inc .... D....... 800 679-7658
    711 S Victory Blvd Burbank (91502) *(P-11623)*

Global Solutions Integration .... D....... 949 307-1849
    26632 Towne Centre Dr Ste 300 Foothill Ranch (92610) *(P-19244)*

Global Touchpoints Inc .... D....... 916 878-5954
    3017 Douglas Blvd Ste 300 Roseville (95661) *(P-11624)*

Global Trade Alliance Inc .... C....... 562 944-6422
    13642 Orden Dr Santa Fe Springs (90670) *(P-7349)*

Global Trend Productions, Pacoima *Also Called: Global Trend Productions Inc (P-11033)*

Global Trend Productions Inc .... D....... 818 768-4950
    10537 Glenoaks Blvd Ste A Pacoima (91331) *(P-11033)*

Global-Dining Inc California .... D....... 310 576-9922
    1212 3rd Street Promenade Santa Monica (90401) *(P-20100)*

Globalfoundries, Santa Clara *Also Called: Globalfoundries Americas Inc (P-5653)*

Globalfoundries Americas Inc .... C....... 408 462-3900
    2600 Great America Way Santa Clara (95054) *(P-5653)*

Globallogic Inc (HQ) .... C....... 408 273-8900
    2535 Augustine Dr Fl 5 Santa Clara (95054) *(P-11625)*

Globe Shoes, Carson *Also Called: Osata Enterprises Inc (P-6233)*

Globecast America Incorporated .... C....... 310 845-3900
    10525 Washington Blvd Culver City (90232) *(P-4510)*

Glory Global Solutions Inc .... D....... 714 897-7545
    11135 Knott Ave Ste C Cypress (90630) *(P-11626)*

Glovis America Inc (HQ) .... C....... 714 427-0944
    17305 Von Karman Ave Ste 200 Irvine (92614) *(P-4025)*

GLS US Freight Inc (PA) .... D....... 209 823-2168
    6750 Longe St Ste 100 Stockton (95206) *(P-3483)*

Glu Mobile Inc (HQ) .... D....... 415 800-6100
    209 Redwood Shores Pkwy Redwood City (94065) *(P-11627)*

GMI Building Services Inc .... C....... 858 279-6262
    8001 Vickers St San Diego (92111) *(P-10904)*

Gmj Air Shuttle LLC .... D....... 916 884-2001
    5411 Luce Ave # 201 Mcclellan (95652) *(P-3140)*

Gms Landscapes Inc .... D....... 805 402-3925
    207 Camino Leon Camarillo (93012) *(P-2734)*

Gmto Corporation .... D....... 626 204-0500
    300 N Lake Ave Fl 14 Pasadena (91101) *(P-3036)*

Gmu Construction Management, Rcho Sta Marg *Also Called: Gmu Geotechnical Inc (P-20889)*

Gmu Geotechnical Inc .... D....... 949 888-6513
    30336 Esperanza Rcho Sta Marg (92688) *(P-20889)*

Gnet Agency .... D....... 323 951-9399
    5455 Wilshire Blvd Ste 2200 Los Angeles (90036) *(P-8575)*

Go Capital, Roseville *Also Called: Nations First Capital LLC (P-7922)*

Go Durkee Logistics, Benicia *Also Called: Durkee Drayage Company (P-3585)*

Go Get Em Inc .... D....... 702 985-5637
    45248 Trevor Ave Lancaster (93534) *(P-13121)*

Go-Staff Inc .... A....... 760 730-8520
    9878 Complex Dr Oceanside (92054) *(P-11144)*

Go-Staff Inc .... A....... 657 242-9350
    240 W Lincoln Ave Anaheim (92805) *(P-11145)*

Go/Links, San Jose *Also Called: Golinks Enterprises Inc (P-12208)*

Goal Financial LLC .... C....... 619 684-7600
    401 W A St Ste 1300 San Diego (92101) *(P-7968)*

Goalbook .... D....... 650 207-9388
    234 7th Ave Unit 200 San Mateo (94401) *(P-20765)*

Godfrey Dadich Partners LLC .... D....... 415 217-2800
    564 Pacific Ave San Francisco (94133) *(P-10619)*

Goetzman Group Inc .... D....... 818 595-1112
    21333 Oxnard St Ste 200 Woodland Hills (91367) *(P-20395)*

Goforth & Marti (PA) .... D....... 800 686-6583
    110 W A St Ste 140 San Diego (92101) *(P-5089)*

Goglanian, Santa Ana *Also Called: Goglanian Bakeries Inc (P-6631)*

Goglanian Bakeries Inc (HQ) .... B....... 714 338-1145
    3401 W Segerstrom Ave Santa Ana (92704) *(P-6631)*

Gogrid LLC .... C....... 415 869-7444
    150 S 1st St Ste 101 San Jose (95113) *(P-4289)*

Goguardian, El Segundo *Also Called: Liminex Inc (P-11710)*

Gold Coast Health Plan, Camarillo *Also Called: Ventura Cnty Md-Cal Mnged Care (P-17345)*

Gold Coast Tours, Brea *Also Called: Hot Dogger Tours Inc (P-3318)*

Gold Country Casino, Oroville *Also Called: Tyme Maidu Tribe-Berry Creek (P-10330)*

Gold Country Health Center, Placerville *Also Called: Gold Country Health Center Inc (P-15498)*

Gold Country Health Center Inc (PA) .... C....... 530 621-1100
    4301 Golden Center Dr Placerville (95667) *(P-15498)*

Gold Cross Ambulance, Los Angeles *Also Called: Schaefer Ambulance Service Inc (P-3295)*

Gold Parent LP .... A....... 310 954-0444
    11111 Santa Monica Blvd Los Angeles (90025) *(P-8088)*

Gold River Racquet Club, Gold River *Also Called: Spare-Time Inc (P-14462)*

Gold Standard Diagnostics Corp .... D....... 530 759-8000
    2795 2nd St Ste 300 Davis (95618) *(P-5416)*

Gold's Gym, West Hollywood *Also Called: Rsg Group USA Inc (P-9333)*

Goldberg and Solovy Foods Inc, Vernon *Also Called: Palisades Ranch Inc (P-6275)*

Goldco, Calabasas *Also Called: Goldco Direct LLC (P-6022)*

Goldco Direct LLC .... D....... 818 343-0186
    24025 Park Sorrento Ste 210 Calabasas (91302) *(P-6022)*

Golden 1 Credit Union .... D....... 916 732-2900
    7770 College Town Dr Sacramento (95826) *(P-7825)*

Golden 1 Credit Union (PA) .... B....... 916 732-2900
    8945 Cal Center Dr Sacramento (95826) *(P-7826)*

ALPHABETIC SECTION

Golden Acorn Casino & Trvl Ctr, Campo *Also Called: Campo Band Missions Indians* *(P-14297)*

Golden Age Nutrition Program, Watsonville *Also Called: Community Bridges* *(P-17891)*

Golden Bear Physcl Thrapy Spt .... D....... 209 622-1191
210 W Pine St Lodi (95240) *(P-15282)*

Golden Bear Physcl Thrapy Spt .... D....... 209 576-0888
4318 Spyres Way Modesto (95356) *(P-15283)*

Golden Bear Physical Therapy .... D....... 209 895-4206
1700 Keystone Pacific Pkwy Unit C2 Patterson (95363) *(P-15284)*

Golden Brands, Huntington Beach *Also Called: Harbor Distributing Llc (P-6765)*

Golden Brands, West Sacramento *Also Called: Harbor Distributing LLC (P-6766)*

Golden Brands, Santa Cruz *Also Called: Reyes Holdings LLC (P-6780)*

Golden By-Products Inc .... D....... 209 668-4855
13000 Newport Rd Ballico (95303) *(P-2789)*

Golden Care Inc .... D....... 818 763-6275
6120 Vineland Ave North Hollywood (91606) *(P-15851)*

Golden Coast Cnstr Restoration .... D....... 916 955-7461
4811 Chippendale Dr Ste 301 Sacramento (95841) *(P-679)*

Golden Door, San Marcos *Also Called: Golden Door Properties LLC (P-9810)*

Golden Door Properties LLC .... C....... 760 744-5777
777 Deer Springs Rd San Marcos (92069) *(P-9810)*

Golden Eagle, San Diego *Also Called: Golden Eagle Insurance Corp (P-8384)*

Golden Eagle Distributing Corp .... D....... 916 645-6600
1251 Tinker Rd Rocklin (95765) *(P-5837)*

Golden Eagle Insurance Corp (DH) .... C....... 619 744-6000
525 B St Ste 1300 San Diego (92101) *(P-8384)*

Golden Empire Con Pdts Inc .... D....... 661 833-4490
8261 Mccutchen Rd Bakersfield (93311) *(P-2704)*

Golden Empire Convalescent Hos .... C....... 530 273-1316
121 Dorsey Dr Grass Valley (95945) *(P-16108)*

Golden Empire Mortgage Inc (PA) .... D....... 661 328-1600
1200 Discovery Dr Ste 300 Bakersfield (93309) *(P-7969)*

Golden Empire Mortgage Inc (PA) .... D....... 661 328-1600
2130 Chester Ave Bakersfield (93301) *(P-7970)*

Golden Empire Mortgage Inc .... B....... 661 949-3388
41331 12th St W Ste 102 Palmdale (93551) *(P-7971)*

Golden Empire Transit District (PA) .... C....... 661 869-2438
1830 Golden State Ave Bakersfield (93301) *(P-3141)*

Golden Gate Brdge Hwy Trnsp Ds (PA) .... C....... 415 921-5858
Golden Gate Bridge Toll Plaza San Francisco (94129) *(P-4138)*

Golden Gate Brdge Hwy Trnsp Ds .... D....... 415 455-2000
101 E Sir Francis Drake Blvd Larkspur (94939) *(P-4139)*

Golden Gate Bridge High .... A....... 415 457-3110
1011 Andersen Dr San Rafael (94901) *(P-4140)*

Golden Gate Capital, San Francisco *Also Called: Ggc Administration LLC (P-9315)*

Golden Gate Capital, San Francisco *Also Called: Golden Gate Private Equity Inc (P-9512)*

Golden Gate Ferry, Larkspur *Also Called: Golden Gate Brdge Hwy Trnsp Ds (P-4139)*

Golden Gate Fields, Albany *Also Called: Pacific Racing Association (P-14166)*

Golden Gate Freightliner Inc (HQ) .... C....... 559 486-4310
8200 Baldwin St Oakland (94621) *(P-7221)*

Golden Gate Nat Prks Cnsrvancy .... C....... 415 933-6760
680 Point Lobos Ave San Francisco (94121) *(P-18865)*

Golden Gate Nat Prks Cnsrvancy .... D....... 415 785-4787
1600 Los Gamos Dr San Rafael (94903) *(P-20890)*

Golden Gate Nat Prks Cnsrvancy (PA) .... D....... 415 561-3000
201 Fort Mason San Francisco (94123) *(P-20891)*

Golden Gate Private Equity Inc (PA) .... D....... 415 983-2706
1 Embarcadero Ctr Fl 39 San Francisco (94111) *(P-9512)*

Golden Gate Regional Ctr Inc (PA) .... C....... 415 546-9222
1355 Market St Ste 220 San Francisco (94103) *(P-17993)*

Golden Gate Transit, San Rafael *Also Called: Golden Gate Bridge High (P-4140)*

Golden Gate Truck Center, Oakland *Also Called: Golden Gate Freightliner Inc (P-7221)*

Golden Gateidence Opco LLC .... C....... 415 922-5085
2121 Pine St San Francisco (94115) *(P-15758)*

Golden Hotels Ltd Partnership .... C....... 949 833-2770
18700 Macarthur Blvd Irvine (92612) *(P-9811)*

Golden Hour Data Systems Inc .... C....... 858 768-2500
10052 Mesa Ridge Ct Ste 200 San Diego (92121) *(P-4026)*

Golden International .... A....... 213 628-1388
424 S Los Angeles St Ste 2 Los Angeles (90013) *(P-9513)*

Golden Living Center - Chateau, Stockton *Also Called: Beaver Dam Health Care Center* *(P-15354)*

Golden N-Life Diamite Intl Inc (PA) .... D....... 510 651-0405
4555 Great America Pkwy Ste 220 Santa Clara (95054) *(P-6110)*

Golden Optical Corporation .... D....... 408 246-4500
2855 Stevens Creek Blvd Ste 1051 Santa Clara (95050) *(P-15263)*

Golden Peterbilt, Porterville *Also Called: E M Tharp Inc (P-5007)*

Golden Queen Mining Co LLC .... C....... 661 824-4300
2818 Silver Queen Rd Mojave (93501) *(P-573)*

Golden Rain Foundation (PA) .... D....... 925 988-7700
1001 Golden Rain Rd Walnut Creek (94595) *(P-9025)*

Golden Rain Foundation .... B....... 925 988-7800
800 Rockview Dr Walnut Creek (94595) *(P-18866)*

Golden Star Technology Inc (PA) .... D....... 562 345-8700
12881 166th St Cerritos (90703) *(P-7444)*

Golden State Bulb Growers Inc .... C....... 831 728-0500
3060 Hilltop Rd Moss Landing (95039) *(P-129)*

Golden State Care Center, Baldwin Park *Also Called: Golden State Habilitation Conv* *(P-15499)*

Golden State Donor Services, West Sacramento *Also Called: DCI Donor Services Inc* *(P-17220)*

Golden State Drilling Inc .... D....... 661 589-0730
3500 Fruitvale Ave Bakersfield (93308) *(P-594)*

Golden State Engineering Inc .... C....... 562 634-3125
15338 Garfield Ave Paramount (90723) *(P-2784)*

Golden State Fence Co., Riverside *Also Called: Fenceworks Inc (P-2278)*

Golden State Flooring, Livermore *Also Called: H - Investment Company (P-5161)*

Golden State Habilitation Conv (PA) .... C....... 626 962-3274
1758 Big Dalton Ave Baldwin Park (91706) *(P-15499)*

Golden State Health Ctrs Inc .... C....... 310 451-9706
1340 15th St Santa Monica (90404) *(P-15852)*

Golden State Lumber Inc .... C....... 510 229-5500
38801 Cherry St Newark (94560) *(P-5158)*

Golden State Lumber Inc .... D....... 209 234-7700
3033 S Airport Way Stockton (95206) *(P-5159)*

Golden State Medical Sup Inc .... C....... 805 477-9866
5187 Camino Ruiz Camarillo (93012) *(P-5417)*

Golden State Medical Supply .... C....... 805 477-8966
5247 Camino Ruiz Camarillo (93012) *(P-6044)*

Golden State Mutl Lf Insur Co (PA) .... D....... 713 526-4361
1999 W Adams Blvd Los Angeles (90018) *(P-8233)*

Golden State Warriors LLC .... D....... 415 388-0100
1 Warriors Way San Francisco (94158) *(P-14141)*

Golden State Water Company (HQ) .... D....... 909 394-3600
630 E Foothill Blvd San Dimas (91773) *(P-4794)*

Golden Temple, Los Angeles *Also Called: East West Tea Company LLC (P-2361)*

Golden Valley Health Centers (PA) .... C....... 209 383-1848
737 W Childs Ave Merced (95341) *(P-14763)*

Golden Valley Health Centers .... D....... 209 382-0253
1910 Customer Care Way Atwater (95301) *(P-14764)*

Golden Vly Occpational Therapy, Oroville *Also Called: Oroville Hospital (P-15298)*

Golden West Casino, Bakersfield *Also Called: Golden West Partners Inc (P-9812)*

Golden West K-9, Pacoima *Also Called: Golden West Security (P-12979)*

Golden West Partners Inc .... C....... 661 324-6936
1001 S Union Ave Bakersfield (93307) *(P-9812)*

Golden West Security .... C....... 818 897-5965
12502 Van Nuys Blvd Ste 215 Pacoima (91331) *(P-12979)*

Golden West Trading Inc .... C....... 323 581-3663
4401 S Downey Rd Vernon (90058) *(P-6421)*

Goldman Data LLC .... D....... 714 283-5889
2156 N Shaffer St Orange (92865) *(P-20766)*

Goldman Sachs, San Francisco *Also Called: Goldman Sachs & Co LLC (P-8089)*

Goldman Sachs, Los Angeles *Also Called: Goldman Sachs & Co LLC (P-8090)*

Goldman Sachs & Co LLC .... C....... 415 393-7500
555 California St Ste 4500 San Francisco (94104) *(P-8089)*

Goldman Sachs & Co LLC .... C....... 310 407-5700
2121 Avenue Of The Stars Ste 2600 Los Angeles (90067) *(P-8090)*

Goldrich & Kest Industries LLC (PA) .... A....... 310 204-2050
5150 Overland Ave Culver City (90230) *(P-9252)*

Goldrich Kest Hirsch Stern LLC (PA) .... C....... 310 204-2050
5150 Overland Ave Culver City (90230) *(P-9253)*

Golds Gym, Northridge Also Called: Musclebound Inc *(P-14220)*
Goldstar, Irvine Also Called: Spireon Inc *(P-11940)*
Goleta Valley Cottage Hosp Aux ....B...... 805 681-6468
351 S Patterson Ave Santa Barbara (93111) *(P-16109)*
Golf Management Operating LLC ....A...... 760 777-4839
50200 Avnida Vista Bonita La Quinta (92253) *(P-14264)*
Golf Pro Shop, Riverside Also Called: Canyon Crest Country Club Inc *(P-14355)*
Golfland Entrmt Ctrs Inc ....C...... 408 263-6855
1199 Jacklin Rd Milpitas (95035) *(P-14530)*
Golfland-Sunsplash, Roseville Also Called: Roseville Golfland Ltd Partnr *(P-14556)*
Golinks Enterprises Inc ....D...... 562 715-4848
2558 Forest Ave San Jose (95117) *(P-12208)*
Gonsalves & Santucci Inc ....B...... 909 350-0474
13052 Dahlia St Fontana (92337) *(P-2121)*
Gonzales Park LLC ....C...... 530 343-8725
495 Ryan Ave Chico (95973) *(P-6175)*
Gonzalez Management Co Inc ....D...... 818 485-0596
10147 San Fernando Rd Pacoima (91331) *(P-20101)*
Good Fellas Industries Inc ....D...... 323 924-9495
4400 Bandini Blvd Vernon (90058) *(P-7438)*
Good Health Inc ....C...... 714 961-7930
410 Cloverleaf Dr Baldwin Park (91706) *(P-17241)*
Good Life Construction Inc ....D...... 916 833-1379
7748 Firestone Way Antelope (95843) *(P-680)*
Good Samaritan Breastcare Ctr, Los Gatos Also Called: Good Samaritan Hospital LP *(P-16111)*
Good Samaritan Hospital, San Jose Also Called: Good Samaritan Hospital LP *(P-16110)*
Good Samaritan Hospital LP (DH) ....A...... 408 559-2011
2425 Samaritan Dr San Jose (95124) *(P-16110)*
Good Samaritan Hospital LP ....C...... 408 358-8414
15400 National Ave Ste 200 Los Gatos (95032) *(P-16111)*
Good Samaritan Hospital LP ....C...... 408 356-4111
15891 Los Gatos Almaden Rd Los Gatos (95032) *(P-16112)*
Good Samaritan Hospital Aux ....B...... 213 977-2121
1225 Wilshire Blvd Los Angeles (90017) *(P-14765)*
GOOD SAMARITAN REHAB AND CARE, Stockton Also Called: Stockton Edson Healthcare Corp *(P-15901)*
Good Shepherd Cemetery, Huntington Beach Also Called: Roman Cthlic Diocese of Orange *(P-9290)*
Good Shepherd Lutheran Ch Corp ....D...... 949 552-1967
4800 Irvine Center Dr Irvine (92604) *(P-19019)*
Good Shepherd Lutheran HM of W ....D...... 510 505-1244
1335 Mowry Ave Fremont (94538) *(P-18440)*
Good Shepherd Lutheran HM of W ....C...... 805 526-2482
2949 Alamo St Simi Valley (93063) *(P-18441)*
Good Shepherd Lutheran HM of W ....D...... 559 454-8514
1696 S Helm Ave Fresno (93727) *(P-18442)*
Good Shphard Lthran Ch Prschoo, Irvine Also Called: Good Shepherd Lutheran Ch Corp *(P-19019)*
Good Smrtan Hosp A Cal Ltd Prt ....B...... 661 903-9555
901 Olive Dr Bakersfield (93308) *(P-16113)*
Good Sports Plus Ltd ....B...... 310 671-4400
370 Amapola Ave Ste 208 Torrance (90501) *(P-11628)*
Good Technology Corporation (HQ) ....C...... 408 352-9102
3001 Bishop Dr Ste 400 San Ramon (94583) *(P-11629)*
Good Technology Software Inc ....A...... 408 212-7500
430 N Mary Ave Ste 200 Sunnyvale (94085) *(P-12209)*
Goodby Silverstein & Partners, San Francisco Also Called: Goodby Slverstein Partners Inc *(P-10620)*
Goodby Slverstein Partners Inc ....C...... 415 392-0669
720 California St San Francisco (94108) *(P-10620)*
Gooden Center ....D...... 626 356-0078
191 N El Molino Ave Pasadena (91101) *(P-16683)*
Goodfellow Bros California LLC ....B...... 925 245-2111
50 Contractors St Livermore (94551) *(P-1107)*
Goodfellow Corporation ....D...... 909 874-2700
590 Crane St Lake Elsinore (92530) *(P-5789)*
Goodleap, Irvine Also Called: Goodleap LLC *(P-7973)*
Goodleap LLC ....D...... 916 290-9999
4200 Douglas Blvd Granite Bay (95746) *(P-7972)*
Goodleap LLC ....D...... 916 290-9999
22 Executive Park Ste 100 Irvine (92614) *(P-7973)*

Goodleap LLC (PA) ....C...... 916 290-9999
8781 Sierra College Blvd Roseville (95661) *(P-7974)*
GOODRX, Santa Monica Also Called: Goodrx Holdings Inc *(P-12576)*
Goodrx Holdings Inc (PA) ....B...... 855 268-2822
2701 Olympic Blvd Santa Monica (90404) *(P-12576)*
Goodspeed Distributing, Hesperia Also Called: R E Goodspeed and Sons Distributing Inc *(P-6717)*
Goodtime.io, San Francisco Also Called: Etch Mobile Inc *(P-11581)*
Goodwage Therapy Assoc LLC ....D...... 559 434-1969
1189 E Brandywine Ln Ste 110 Fresno (93720) *(P-17065)*
Goodwill Central Coast (PA) ....C...... 831 423-8611
1566 Moffett St Salinas (93905) *(P-7534)*
Goodwill Central Coast ....D...... 831 755-8668
1045 N Main St Salinas (93906) *(P-7535)*
Goodwill Central Coast ....C...... 805 544-0542
880 Industrial Way San Luis Obispo (93401) *(P-7536)*
Goodwill Inds of Grter E Bay I (PA) ....D...... 510 698-7200
1301 30th Ave Oakland (94601) *(P-7537)*
Goodwill Inds of Rdwood Empire (PA) ....D...... 707 523-0550
651 Yolanda Ave Santa Rosa (95404) *(P-7538)*
Goodwill Inds Orange Cnty Cal ....C...... 714 881-3986
5880 Edinger Ave Huntington Beach (92649) *(P-18231)*
Goodwill Inds San Diego Cnty ....D...... 760 806-7670
3841 Plaza Dr Ste 902 Oceanside (92056) *(P-19085)*
Goodwill Inds San Jquin Vly FN (PA) ....D...... 209 466-2311
4533 Alitalia Way Stockton (95206) *(P-7539)*
Goodwill Inds San Luis Obispo, San Luis Obispo Also Called: Goodwill Central Coast *(P-7536)*
Goodwill Inds Southern Cal (PA) ....A...... 323 223-1211
342 N San Fernando Rd Los Angeles (90031) *(P-7137)*
Goodwill Industries, Huntington Beach Also Called: Goodwill Inds Orange Cnty Cal *(P-18231)*
Goodwill Industries, Oceanside Also Called: Goodwill Inds San Diego Cnty *(P-19085)*
Goodwill Industries 15, Salinas Also Called: Goodwill Central Coast *(P-7535)*
Goodwill of Silicon Valley (PA) ....D...... 408 998-5774
1080 N 7th St San Jose (95112) *(P-11288)*
Goodwill of the San Francisco (PA) ....B...... 415 575-2101
750 Post St San Francisco (94109) *(P-7540)*
Goodwill Srving The Pple Sther (PA) ....D...... 562 435-3411
800 W Pacific Coast Hwy Long Beach (90806) *(P-13305)*
Goodyear Coml Tire & Svc Ctrs ....B...... 479 788-6400
3085 W Capitol Ave West Sacramento (95691) *(P-7350)*
Goodyear Coml Tire & Svc Ctrs, West Sacramento Also Called: Goodyear Coml Tire & Svc Ctrs *(P-7350)*
Google, Mountain View Also Called: Google LLC *(P-12664)*
Google Checkout, Mountain View Also Called: Google Payment Corp *(P-13306)*
Google Fiber Inc (DH) ....D...... 650 253-0000
1600 Amphitheatre Pkwy Mountain View (94043) *(P-4290)*
Google International LLC (DH) ....D...... 650 253-0000
35018 Avenue D Yucaipa (92399) *(P-4291)*
Google LLC (HQ) ....C...... 650 253-0000
1600 Amphitheatre Pkwy Mountain View (94043) *(P-12664)*
Google Payment Corp ....C...... 888 986-7944
1600 Amphitheatre Pkwy Mountain View (94043) *(P-13306)*
Gopro, San Mateo Also Called: Gopro Inc *(P-3084)*
Gopro Inc (PA) ....B...... 650 332-7600
3025 Clearview Way San Mateo (94402) *(P-3084)*
Goproto, San Diego Also Called: Higgs Fletcher & Mack Llp *(P-17493)*
Gordian Medical Inc ....B...... 714 556-0200
17595 Cartwright Rd Irvine (92614) *(P-5418)*
Gordon & Rees, Oakland Also Called: Gordon Rees Scully Mansukhani *(P-17476)*
Gordon and Schwenkmeyer Inc ....C...... 916 569-1740
1860 Howe Ave Ste 300 Sacramento (95825) *(P-13307)*
Gordon Betty Moore Foundation ....D...... 650 213-3000
1661 Page Mill Rd Palo Alto (94304) *(P-18867)*
Gordon E Btty I More Fundation ....D...... 650 213-3000
1661 Page Mill Rd Palo Alto (94304) *(P-20767)*
Gordon Prill Inc ....D...... 408 745-7164
310 E Caribbean Dr Sunnyvale (94089) *(P-922)*
Gordon Rees Scully Mansukhani ....C...... 510 463-8600
1111 Broadway Ste 1700 Oakland (94607) *(P-17476)*

ALPHABETIC SECTION

Gordon Rees Scully Mansukhani .... C 213 576-5000
633 W 5th St 52nd Fl Los Angeles (90071) *(P-17477)*

Gordon Rees Scully Mansukhani .... C 619 696-6700
101 W Broadway Ste 1600 San Diego (92101) *(P-17478)*

Gordon Rees Scully Mansukhani (PA) .... B *415 986-5900*
275 Battery St Ste 2000 San Francisco (94111) *(P-17479)*

Gordon Turner Motors .... C 916 488-2400
2535 Arden Way Sacramento (95825) *(P-7222)*

Gores Group LLC (PA) .... D 310 209-3010
9800 Wilshire Blvd Beverly Hills (90212) *(P-8091)*

Gorgias Inc .... C 917 859-5689
180 Sansome St San Francisco (94104) *(P-11630)*

Gosch Ford Lincoln Mercury, Hemet *Also Called: Jack Gosch Ford Inc (P-7238)*

Gosecure Inc (PA) .... C 301 442-3432
13220 Evening Creek Dr S Ste 107 San Diego (92128) *(P-7445)*

Gothic Ground Management, Santa Clarita *Also Called: Gothic Landscaping Inc (P-493)*

Gothic Grounds Mgmt, Valencia *Also Called: Gothic Landscaping Inc (P-434)*

Gothic Landscaping Inc .... D 661 257-5085
27413 Tourney Rd Ste 200 Valencia (91355) *(P-434)*

Gothic Landscaping Inc (PA) .... C *661 678-1400*
27413 Tourney Rd Santa Clarita (91355) *(P-493)*

Gottstein Corporation .... C 661 322-8934
3500 Chester Ave Bakersfield (93301) *(P-5790)*

Goudy Honda, Alhambra *Also Called: Alhambra Motors Inc (P-7166)*

Gould Electric Inc .... C 858 486-1727
12975 Brookprinter Pl Ste 280 Poway (92064) *(P-1738)*

Gould Evans P C .... D 415 503-1411
156 S Park St San Francisco (94107) *(P-19472)*

Gourmet Foods Inc (PA) .... D 310 632-3300
2910 E Harcourt St Compton (90221) *(P-6255)*

Gourmet India Food Company LLC .... D 562 698-9763
12220 Rivera Rd Ste A Whittier (90606) *(P-6632)*

Gourmet Specialties Inc .... D 323 587-1734
2120 E 25th St Vernon (90058) *(P-6555)*

Government Technology, Folsom *Also Called: Erepublic Inc (P-13281)*

Governmentjobscom Inc .... C 310 426-6304
2120 Park Pl Ste 100 El Segundo (90245) *(P-12210)*

Gpc, Irvine *Also Called: Global Pcci (gpc) (P-2751)*

GPde Slva Spces Incrporation (PA) .... D *562 407-2643*
8531 Loch Lomond Dr Pico Rivera (90660) *(P-2435)*

GPh Medical & Legal Services (PA) .... C *213 207-2700*
468 N Camden Dr Beverly Hills (90210) *(P-15500)*

Gpi Ca-Niii Inc .... D 626 305-3000
1434 Buena Vista St Duarte (91010) *(P-7223)*

GPM, Thousand Oaks *Also Called: General Pavement Management Inc (P-2119)*

Gps Painting Wallcovering Inc .... C 714 730-8904
1307 E Saint Gertrude Pl Ste C Santa Ana (92705) *(P-1621)*

Gr8 Care Inc .... D 626 337-7229
14518 Los Angeles St Baldwin Park (91706) *(P-15501)*

Grace Logistics Inc .... B 209 730-9800
912 11th St Ste 201 Modesto (95354) *(P-4027)*

Grace Yokley Middle School .... D 909 947-6774
2947 S Turner Ave Ontario (91761) *(P-17713)*

Gracing Brand Management Inc .... B 626 297-2472
1108 W Valley Blvd Ste 660 Alhambra (91803) *(P-2466)*

Gradient Engineers Inc .... C 949 477-0555
17781 Cowan Ste 140 Irvine (92614) *(P-19245)*

Graham & James LLP .... A 415 954-0200
1 Maritime Plz Fl 3 San Francisco (94111) *(P-17480)*

Graham Concrete Cnstr Inc .... D 559 292-6571
1323 Dayton Ave Ste 103 Clovis (93612) *(P-2122)*

Grail LLC (HQ) .... D *833 694-2553*
1525a Obrien Dr Menlo Park (94025) *(P-2588)*

Grain To Green Inc .... C 760 845-6107
301 N El Camino Real San Clemente (92672) *(P-6692)*

Gramercy Productions LLC .... D 818 777-1677
100 Universal City Plz Bldg 2150 Universal City (91608) *(P-13964)*

Grammarly Inc (PA) .... C *888 318-6146*
548 Market St Ste 35410 San Francisco (94104) *(P-12461)*

Granada Hills Care Center, Granada Hills *Also Called: In Granada Hlls Cnvlscent Hosp (P-15522)*

Granada Hills Sr High School, Granada Hills *Also Called: Los Angeles Unified School Dst (P-17723)*

Granada Hotel, San Francisco *Also Called: Broadmoor Hotel (P-9664)*

Grancell Village, Reseda *Also Called: Los Angles Jewish HM For Aging (P-15554)*

Grand Avenue Hlth Holdings LLC .... D 949 487-9500
29222 Rancho Viejo Rd Ste 127 San Juan Capistrano (92675) *(P-15502)*

GRAND CENTRAL STATION, Livermore *Also Called: All Guard Alarm Systems Inc (P-1660)*

Grand Del Mar, San Diego *Also Called: Grand Del Mar Resort LP (P-9813)*

Grand Del Mar Resort LP .... A 858 314-2000
5300 Grand Del Mar Ct San Diego (92130) *(P-9813)*

Grand Hyatt San Francisco, San Francisco *Also Called: Hyatt Corporation (P-9885)*

Grand Lake Gardens, Oakland *Also Called: Humangood Norcal (P-18454)*

Grand Pacific Carlsbad Ht LP .... B 760 827-2400
5480 Grand Pacific Dr Carlsbad (92008) *(P-9814)*

Grand Pacific Resorts Inc (PA) .... C *760 431-8500*
5900 Pasteur Ct Ste 200 Carlsbad (92008) *(P-9026)*

Grand Pacific Resorts Inc .... A 760 431-8500
5900 Pasteur Ct Ste 200 Carlsbad (92008) *(P-9815)*

Grand Pacific Resorts Svcs LP .... C 760 431-8500
5900 Pasteur Ct Ste 200 Carlsbad (92008) *(P-9816)*

Grand Slam Tennis Program, Pacific Palisades *Also Called: Riviera Country Club Inc (P-14554)*

Grand Supercenter Inc .... D 562 318-3451
8550 Chetle Ave Ste B Whittier (90606) *(P-6256)*

Grand Vista Hotel, Simi Valley *Also Called: Simi West Inc (P-10240)*

Grandcare Health Services LLC (PA) .... C *866 554-2447*
3452 E Foothill Blvd Ste 700 Pasadena (91107) *(P-16866)*

Grande Colonial, La Jolla *Also Called: Fargo Colonial LLC (P-9793)*

Grani Installation Inc (PA) .... D *714 898-0441*
5411 Commercial Dr Huntington Beach (92649) *(P-923)*

Granite, Watsonville *Also Called: Granite Construction Inc (P-1183)*

Granite Cnstr Northeast Inc .... B 831 724-1011
585 W Beach St Watsonville (95076) *(P-1108)*

Granite Construction Company (HQ) .... C *831 724-1011*
585 W Beach St Watsonville (95076) *(P-1109)*

Granite Construction Company .... B 760 775-7500
38000 Monroe St Indio (92203) *(P-1110)*

Granite Construction Company .... C 209 982-4750
10500 S Harlan Rd French Camp (95231) *(P-1111)*

Granite Construction Company .... C 805 964-9951
5335 Debbie Rd Santa Barbara (93111) *(P-1112)*

Granite Construction Inc .... D 805 667-8210
213 Columbia Way Lancaster (93535) *(P-1113)*

Granite Construction Inc (PA) .... B *831 724-1011*
585 W Beach St Watsonville (95076) *(P-1183)*

Granite Electrical Supply Inc .... D 916 648-3900
1701 National Dr Ste 200 Sacramento (95834) *(P-5558)*

Granite Fabrication Facility, Santa Fe Springs *Also Called: Lauren Andrew Surfaces Inc (P-13351)*

Granite Hills Child Dev Ctr, Porterville *Also Called: Clemmie Gill Schl of Scnce Cns (P-18294)*

Granite Power Inc .... B 831 724-1011
580 W Beach St Watsonville (95076) *(P-20102)*

Granite Rick Co .... C 831 768-2000
5225 Hellyer Ave Ste 220 San Jose (95138) *(P-9514)*

Granite Rock Co (PA) .... D *831 768-2000*
350 Technology Dr Watsonville (95076) *(P-637)*

Granite Rock Co .... D 650 869-3370
355 Blomquist St Redwood City (94063) *(P-1114)*

Granite Rock Co .... D 650 482-3800
365 Blomquist St Redwood City (94063) *(P-2649)*

Granite Rock Co 831 471-3440
303 Coral St Santa Cruz (95060) *(P-5205)*

Granite Rock Co .... D 831 724-3847
540 W Beach St Watsonville (95076) *(P-5206)*

Granite Solutions Groupe Inc (PA) .... C *415 963-3999*
235 Montgomery St Ste 430 San Francisco (94104) *(P-11146)*

Granite Wellness Centers .... D 530 878-5166
180 Sierra College Dr Grass Valley (95945) *(P-17066)*

Granlbakken Ski Racquet Resort, Tahoe City *Also Called: Granlibakken Management Co Ltd (P-9817)*

Employee Codes: A=Over 500 employees, B=251-500
C=101-250, D=51-100, E=20-50, F=10-19, G=1-9

Granlibakken Management Co Ltd .... D 800 543-3221
725 Granlibakken Rd Tahoe City (96145) *(P-9817)*

Grant & Weber (PA) .... D 818 878-7700
26610 Agoura Rd Ste 209 Calabasas (91302) *(P-10742)*

Grant & Weber Travel, Calabasas Also Called: Grant & Weber *(P-10742)*

Grant Construction Inc .... D 661 588-4586
7702 Meany Ave Ste 103 Bakersfield (93308) *(P-1999)*

Grant-Cuesta Nursing Center, Mountain View Also Called: Covenant Care California LLC *(P-16033)*

Grant, Richard S, Los Angeles Also Called: Wolf Rfkin Shpiro Schlman Rbk *(P-17685)*

Granville Homes Inc .... D 559 268-2000
1306 W Herndon Ave Ste 101 Fresno (93711) *(P-681)*

Graphic Packaging Intl LLC .... D 949 250-0900
1600 Barranca Pkwy Irvine (92606) *(P-6912)*

Graphic Packaging Intl LLC .... C 559 651-3535
1600 Kelsey Rd Visalia (93291) *(P-6913)*

Graphics Department, La Jolla Also Called: University Cal San Diego *(P-10821)*

Graphiq LLC .... C 805 335-2433
101a Innovation Pl Santa Barbara (93108) *(P-2555)*

Grasshopper House Partners LLC .... C 310 589-2880
6428 Meadows Ct Malibu (90265) *(P-17994)*

Graton Resort & Casino 707 588-7100
288 Golf Course Dr Rohnert Park (94928) *(P-14531)*

Gray Lift Inc .... D 559 268-6621
4646 E Jensen Ave Fresno (93725) *(P-5838)*

Gray Wc, Anaheim Also Called: Gray West Construction Inc *(P-820)*

Gray West Construction Inc .... C 714 491-1317
421 E Cerritos Ave Anaheim (92805) *(P-820)*

Graybar, Diamond Bar Also Called: Graybar Electric Company Inc *(P-5559)*

Graybar Electric Company Inc .... C 909 451-4300
1370 Valley Vista Dr Ste 100 Diamond Bar (91765) *(P-5559)*

Graybar Electric Company Inc .... D 916 561-1900
1211 Fee Dr Sacramento (95815) *(P-5560)*

Graybar Electric Company Inc .... D 858 578-8606
8606 Miralani Dr San Diego (92126) *(P-5561)*

Graybar Electric Company Inc .... D 925 557-3000
3089 Whipple Rd Union City (94587) *(P-5562)*

Graybill Medical Group Inc (PA) .... C 866 228-2236
225 E 2nd Ave Escondido (92025) *(P-14766)*

Graybill Medical Group Inc .... D 760 728-2777
1035 S Main Ave Fallbrook (92028) *(P-14767)*

Grayline of San Francisco, Brisbane Also Called: Blue Bus Tours LLC *(P-3961)*

Grclt Condominium Inc .... D 530 542-8400
1001 Heavenly Village Way South Lake Tahoe (96150) *(P-9818)*

Great Amrcn Logistics Dist Inc .... D 562 229-3601
13565 Larwin Cir Santa Fe Springs (90670) *(P-3588)*

Great Atlantic News LLC .... C 770 863-9000
1575 N Main St Orange (92867) *(P-6842)*

Great Clips, San Jose Also Called: Buena Vista Business Svcs LP *(P-10495)*

Great Endvors Adult Day Hlth C, San Jose Also Called: Tupaz Day Care Services Inc *(P-18156)*

Great River Food, City Of Industry Also Called: Derek and Constance Lee Corp *(P-2342)*

Great Western Distributing Svc, Los Angeles Also Called: Gils Distributing Service *(P-10731)*

Great Western Sales Inc .... D 310 323-7900
8737 Dice Rd Santa Fe Springs (90670) *(P-5751)*

Great-West Healthcare, Glendale Also Called: Empower Annuity Insur Co Amer *(P-8264)*

Greatcall Inc .... A 800 733-6632
10945 Vista Sorrento Pkwy Ste 120 San Diego (92130) *(P-7581)*

Greater Alarm Company Inc (DH) .... D 949 474-0555
3750 Schaufele Ave Ste 200 Long Beach (90808) *(P-13122)*

Greater Bay Area Cncer Rgistry, Belvedere Tiburon Also Called: Cancer Prevention Inst Cal *(P-19873)*

Greater El Monte Cmnty Hosp, El Monte Also Called: Ahm Gemch Inc *(P-15928)*

Greater Los Angeles Zoo Assn .... D 323 644-4200
5333 Zoo Dr Los Angeles (90027) *(P-18589)*

Greater Los Angles Area Cncil (PA) .... D 213 413-4400
2333 Scout Way Los Angeles (90026) *(P-18868)*

Greater Los Angeles Cnty Vctor .... C 562 944-7976
12545 Florence Ave Santa Fe Springs (90670) *(P-20768)*

Greater Los Angeles Vtrans RES 310 312-1554
11301 Wilshire Blvd Bldg 114 Los Angeles (90073) *(P-9415)*

Greater Sacramento Sur .... D 916 929-7229
2288 Auburn Blvd Ste 201 Sacramento (95821) *(P-17067)*

Greater Sacramento Surgery Ctr, Sacramento Also Called: Greater Sacramento Sur *(P-17067)*

Greater San Diego AC Co Inc .... C 619 469-7818
3883 Ruffin Rd Ste C San Diego (92123) *(P-1452)*

Greater Vallejo Recreation Dst .... D 707 648-4600
395 Amador St Vallejo (94590) *(P-14532)*

Greater Valley Med Group Inc (PA) .... D 818 838-4500
11600 Indian Hills Rd 300 Mission Hills (91345) *(P-17068)*

Greater Valley Medical Group .... C 818 781-7097
14600 Sherman Way Ste 300 Van Nuys (91405) *(P-17069)*

Greatlink International Inc .... A 510 657-1667
44168 S Grimmer Blvd Fremont (94538) *(P-5563)*

Gree International Inc .... C 415 409-5200
275 Battery St Ste 1700 San Francisco (94111) *(P-11631)*

Gree International Entrmt Inc .... C 415 409-5200
185 Berry St Ste 590 San Francisco (94107) *(P-11632)*

Green Acres Lodge, Rosemead Also Called: Longwood Management Corp *(P-15551)*

Green Acres Nursery & Sup LLC (PA) .... D 916 673-9720
604 Sutter St Ste 350 Folsom (95630) *(P-5809)*

Green Acres Nursery and Supply, Sacramento Also Called: Matsudas By Green Acres LLC *(P-138)*

Green Energy Innovations, Buena Park Also Called: Sfadia Inc *(P-1838)*

Green Farms Inc .... D 858 831-7701
2652 Long Beach Ave Los Angeles (90058) *(P-6556)*

Green Hasson & Janks LLP .... C 310 873-1600
700 S Flower St Ste 3300 Los Angeles (90017) *(P-19581)*

Green Hills Retirement Center, Millbrae Also Called: Hillsdale Group LP *(P-15855)*

Green Hills Software, Santa Barbara Also Called: Green Hills Software LLC *(P-12211)*

Green Hills Software LLC (HQ) .... C 805 965-6044
30 W Sola St Santa Barbara (93101) *(P-12211)*

Green Leaf Produce, Brisbane Also Called: Dairyland Produce LLC *(P-6531)*

Green Line Rail Eqp Maint, Lawndale Also Called: Los Angles Cnty Mtro Tmsp Aut *(P-3148)*

Green Living Planet LLC .... D 415 715-4718
687 20th Ave San Francisco (94121) *(P-10905)*

Green River Golf Corporation .... D 714 970-8411
5215 Green River Rd Corona (92878) *(P-14265)*

Green River Golf Course, Corona Also Called: Green River Golf Corporation *(P-14265)*

Green Shutter Plaza, Hayward Also Called: Crown Management Services Inc *(P-9729)*

Green Thumb International Inc .... D 818 340-6400
21812 Sherman Way Canoga Park (91303) *(P-6859)*

Green Thumb International Inc .... D 661 259-1071
23734 Newhall Ave Newhall (91321) *(P-7126)*

Green Thumb Nurseries, Newhall Also Called: Green Thumb International Inc *(P-7126)*

Green Thumb Produce Inc .... C 951 849-4711
2648 W Ramsey St Banning (92220) *(P-6557)*

Green Tomato Grill, Orange Also Called: Fahetas LLC *(P-7479)*

Green Valley Corporation .... D 831 475-7100
740 Front St Ste 315 Santa Cruz (95060) *(P-924)*

Green Valley Country Club .... D 707 864-1101
35 Country Club Dr Fairfield (94534) *(P-14379)*

Green-N-Clean Ex Car Wash Inc .... D 949 749-4977
28622 Oso Pkwy Pmb C Rcho Sta Marg (92688) *(P-13693)*

Greenall, Suisun City Also Called: E B Stone & Son Inc *(P-6823)*

Greenberg Glsker Flds Clman Mc .... C 310 553-3610
2049 Century Park E Ste 2600 Los Angeles (90067) *(P-17481)*

Greenberg Traurig, East Palo Alto Also Called: Greenberg Traurig LLP *(P-17484)*

Greenberg Traurig, Irvine Also Called: Greenberg Traurig LLP *(P-17486)*

Greenberg Traurig LLP .... D 415 655-1300
101 2nd St Ste 2200 San Francisco (94105) *(P-17482)*

Greenberg Traurig LLP .... D 310 586-7708
1840 Century Park E Ste 1900 Los Angeles (90067) *(P-17483)*

Greenberg Traurig LLP .... D 650 328-8500
1900 University Ave Fl 5 East Palo Alto (94303) *(P-17484)*

Greenberg Traurig LLP .... C 916 442-1111
400 Capitol Mall Sacramento (95814) *(P-17485)*

Greenberg Traurig LLP .... D 949 732-6500
18565 Jamboree Rd Ste 500 Irvine (92612) *(P-17486)*

Greenbox, Los Angeles Also Called: Greenbox Loans Inc *(P-7743)*

ALPHABETIC SECTION

Greenbox Loans Inc ....D...... 800 919-1086
3250 Wilshire Blvd Ste 1900 Los Angeles (90010) *(P-7743)*

Greenbrea Care Center, Greenbrae Also Called: Ocadian Care Centers LLC *(P-15604)*

Greenbriar, Sacramento Also Called: Volunters Amer Nthrn Cal Nthrn *(P-18186)*

Greenbriar Homes Communities ....D...... 510 497-8200
4340 Stevens Creek Blvd Ste 240 San Jose (95129) *(P-791)*

Greenbriar Homes Community, Los Altos Hills Also Called: Greenbriar Management Company *(P-9027)*

Greenbriar Management Company ....D...... 510 497-8200
26969 Beaver Ln Los Altos Hills (94022) *(P-9027)*

Greenbrier Rail, San Bernardino Also Called: Meridian Rail Acquisition *(P-4167)*

Greenbrier Rail Services, San Bernardino Also Called: Gunderson Rail Services LLC *(P-4158)*

Greene Rdvsky Maloney Share LP ....D...... 415 981-1400
4 Embarcadero Ctr Ste 4000 San Francisco (94111) *(P-17487)*

Greenheart, Arroyo Grande Also Called: Greenheart Farms Inc *(P-179)*

Greenheart Farms Inc ....B...... 805 481-2234
902 Zenon Way Arroyo Grande (93420) *(P-179)*

Greenhedge Escrow ....C...... 310 640-3040
2015 Manhattan Beach Blvd Redondo Beach (90278) *(P-9235)*

Greenhouse Agency Inc ....C...... 949 752-7542
4100 Birch St Ste 500 Newport Beach (92660) *(P-20396)*

Greenleaf Hotel Inc ....D
515 S Figueroa St # 1850 Los Angeles (90071) *(P-9819)*

Greenliant Systems Inc ....C...... 408 217-7400
3970 Freedom Cir Ste 100 Santa Clara (95054) *(P-2920)*

Greenlots, Los Angeles Also Called: Zeco Systems Inc *(P-6720)*

Greenpath Recovery Recycl Svcs, Colton Also Called: Greenpath Recovery West Inc *(P-6009)*

Greenpath Recovery West Inc ....D...... 909 954-0686
330 W Citrus St Ste 250 Colton (92324) *(P-6009)*

Greenridge Senior Care ....C...... 510 758-9600
2150 Pyramid Dr El Sobrante (94803) *(P-18443)*

Greens Group Inc ....C...... 949 829-4902
16530 Bake Pkwy Ste 200 Irvine (92618) *(P-9820)*

Greensoft Technology Inc ....C...... 323 254-5961
155 S El Molino Ave Ste 100 Pasadena (91101) *(P-12577)*

Greenteam of San Jose, San Jose Also Called: Waste Connections Cal Inc *(P-4952)*

Greenwlds Atbody Frmeworks Inc ....D...... 619 477-2600
2850 Erie St San Diego (92117) *(P-13637)*

Greenwood & Hall, Los Angeles Also Called: Pcs Link Inc *(P-20826)*

Greenwood Hall Inc ....C...... 310 905-8300
6230 Wilshire Blvd Ste 136 Los Angeles (90048) *(P-17810)*

Greenwood Holdings LLC ....D...... 619 299-6633
3888 Greenwood St San Diego (92110) *(P-9821)*

Grefco Dicaperl, Torrance Also Called: Dicaperl Corporation *(P-647)*

Gregg Drilling LLC ....C...... 562 427-6899
2726 Walnut Ave Signal Hill (90755) *(P-2172)*

Gregg Drilling & Testing Inc (PA) ....D...... 562 427-6899
2726 Walnut Ave Signal Hill (90755) *(P-2282)*

Gregg Electric Inc ....C...... 909 983-1794
608 W Emporia St Ontario (91762) *(P-1739)*

Gregory Consulting Inc (PA) ....C...... 805 642-0111
6350 Leland St Ventura (93003) *(P-7224)*

Gremlin Inc ....D...... 408 214-9885
440 N Barranca Ave Ste 3101 Walnut (91789) *(P-12212)*

Greyhound Lines Inc ....D...... 213 629-8400
1716 E 7th St Los Angeles (90021) *(P-3357)*

Greystar, Newport Beach Also Called: Greystar Management Svcs LP *(P-9029)*

Greystar LP ....A...... 650 386-6438
2580 California St Mountain View (94040) *(P-8815)*

Greystar LP ....A...... 650 386-6438
821 W El Camino Real Mountain View (94040) *(P-20103)*

Greystar Management Svcs LP ....C...... 818 596-2180
6320 Canoga Ave Ste 1512 Woodland Hills (91367) *(P-9028)*

Greystar Management Svcs LP ....A...... 949 705-0010
620 Newport Center Dr 15th Fl Newport Beach (92660) *(P-9029)*

Grht Inc ....D...... 323 873-6393
14818 Raymer St Van Nuys (91405) *(P-6914)*

Grid Alternative ....B...... 510 731-1310
1171 Ocean Ave Ste 200 Emeryville (94608) *(P-1453)*

Grid Dynamics Intl LLC (HQ) ....C...... 650 523-5000
5000 Executive Pkwy Ste 520 San Ramon (94583) *(P-12800)*

Gridgain Systems Inc (PA) ....C...... 650 241-2281
1065 E Hillsdale Blvd Ste 410 Foster City (94404) *(P-12213)*

Gridiron Systems Inc ....C...... 201 502-0512
4555 Great America Pkwy # 150 Santa Clara (95054) *(P-11633)*

Griffin Group LLC ....C...... 415 892-4569
4 Rebelo Ln Ste D Novato (94947) *(P-20104)*

Griffith Company (PA) ....C...... 714 984-5500
3050 E Birch St Brea (92821) *(P-1115)*

Griffith Company ....B...... 661 392-6640
1128 Carrier Parkway Ave Bakersfield (93308) *(P-1116)*

Griffith Company ....D...... 562 929-1128
12200 Bloomfield Ave Santa Fe Springs (90670) *(P-1117)*

Griffith Park Healthcare Ctr, Glendale Also Called: Griffith Pk Rhbltation Ctr LLC *(P-15503)*

Griffith Pk Rhbltation Ctr LLC ....D...... 818 845-8507
201 Allen Ave Glendale (91201) *(P-15503)*

Grifols Bio Supplies Inc ....C...... 760 651-4042
980 Park Center Dr Ste F Vista (92081) *(P-17242)*

Grifols Usa LLC ....A...... 626 435-2600
13111 Temple Ave City Of Industry (91746) *(P-5419)*

Grifols Wrldwide Oprtons USA I ....C...... 626 435-2600
13111 Temple Ave City Of Industry (91746) *(P-17243)*

Grigsby Label LLC ....C...... 916 933-4991
4995 Hillsdale Cir El Dorado Hills (95762) *(P-8092)*

Griley Air Freight, Los Angeles Also Called: Southern Counties Terminals *(P-3424)*

Grimbleby Clman Crtif Pub Accn ....D...... 209 527-4220
200 W Roseburg Ave Modesto (95350) *(P-19582)*

Grimmway Enterprises Inc ....D...... 661 399-0844
6301 Zerker Rd Shafter (93263) *(P-180)*

Grimmway Enterprises Inc ....B...... 661 393-3320
6101 Zerker Rd Shafter (93263) *(P-272)*

Grimmway Enterprises Inc ....B...... 661 854-6250
830 Sycamore Rd Arvin (93203) *(P-273)*

Grimmway Enterprises Inc ....A...... 661 854-6200
11412 Malaga Rd Arvin (93203) *(P-274)*

Grimmway Enterprises Inc ....C...... 661 845-5200
6900 Mountain View Rd Bakersfield (93307) *(P-275)*

Grimmway Enterprises Inc ....C...... 661 854-6240
12020 Malaga Rd Arvin (93203) *(P-821)*

Grimmway Enterprises Inc ....D...... 307 302-0090
11646 Malaga Rd Arvin (93203) *(P-3400)*

Grimmway Enterprises Inc ....B...... 661 845-3758
12000 Main St Lamont (93241) *(P-6558)*

Grimmway Enterprises Inc ....D...... 661 854-6200
14141 Di Giorgio Rd Arvin (93203) *(P-20105)*

Grimmway Farms, Arvin Also Called: Grimmway Enterprises Inc *(P-274)*

Grimmway Farms, Bakersfield Also Called: Grimmway Enterprises Inc *(P-275)*

Grimmway Frozen Foods, Arvin Also Called: Grimmway Enterprises Inc *(P-273)*

Grindr LLC ....C...... 310 776-6680
750 N San Vicente Blvd West Hollywood (90069) *(P-11634)*

Gringo Ventures LLC ....B...... 760 477-7999
3260 Corporate Vw Vista (92081) *(P-6860)*

Gringteam Inc ....D...... 858 485-4145
800 W Ivy St Ste D San Diego (92101) *(P-9822)*

Gringteam Inc ....D...... 209 526-6000
1150 9th St Frnt Modesto (95354) *(P-9823)*

Gringteam Inc ....B...... 619 297-5466
7450 Hazard Center Dr San Diego (92108) *(P-9824)*

Gringteam Inc ....D...... 650 344-5500
835 Airport Blvd Burlingame (94010) *(P-9825)*

Gringteam Inc ....D...... 949 661-1100
34402 Pacific Coast Hwy Dana Point (92624) *(P-9826)*

Gringteam Inc ....D...... 661 426-7919
3100 Camino Del Rio Ct Bakersfield (93308) *(P-9827)*

Grio, San Francisco Also Called: Bitalign Inc *(P-11460)*

Gripp, Temecula Also Called: Bbk Performance Inc *(P-5029)*

Grit Management LLC ....D...... 949 220-7765
234 E 17th St Ste 212 Costa Mesa (92627) *(P-14204)*

Gritcycle, Costa Mesa Also Called: Grit Management LLC *(P-14204)*

Grm Information MGT Svcs Inc (PA) ....B...... 201 798-7100
41099 Boyce Rd Fremont (94538) *(P-3792)*

Grocery Outlet Holding Corp | **ALPHABETIC SECTION**

Grocery Outlet Holding Corp (PA).................................B....... 510 845-1999
   5650 Hollis St Emeryville (94608) *(P-7143)*

Grolink, Oxnard *Also Called: Grolink Plant Company Inc (P-6861)*

Grolink Plant Company Inc (PA)..............................C....... 805 984-7958
   4107 W Gonzales Rd Oxnard (93036) *(P-6861)*

Groove Labs Inc ....D....... 650 999-0200
   660 4th St # 684 San Francisco (94107) *(P-12214)*

Groq Inc ....C....... 650 521-9007
   400 Castro St Ste 600 Mountain View (94041) *(P-11635)*

Grosslight Insurance Inc ....D....... 310 473-9611
   21300 Victory Blvd Ste 700 Woodland Hills (91367) *(P-8576)*

Grossmont Home Hlth & Hospice, La Mesa *Also Called: Grossmont Hospital Corporation (P-16115)*

Grossmont Hospital Corporation (HQ).......................A....... 619 740-6000
   5555 Grossmont Center Dr La Mesa (91942) *(P-16114)*

Grossmont Hospital Corporation ....B....... 619 667-1900
   8881 Fletcher Pkwy Ste 105 La Mesa (91942) *(P-16115)*

Grosvenor House, San Francisco *Also Called: Grosvenor Properties Ltd (P-9030)*

Grosvenor Inv MGT US Inc ....D....... 415 773-0275
   155 Montgomery St Ste 611 San Francisco (94104) *(P-8577)*

Grosvenor Inv MGT US Inc ....D....... 310 265-0297
   2308 Chelsea Rd Palos Verdes Estates (90274) *(P-8578)*

Grosvenor Properties Ltd ....B....... 415 421-1899
   899 Pine St Apt 103 San Francisco (94108) *(P-9030)*

Grosvenor Properties Ltd ....C....... 650 873-3200
   380 S Airport Blvd South San Francisco (94080) *(P-9828)*

Ground Force One, Redondo Beach *Also Called: Cputer Inc (P-12769)*

Groundlvel - Ovraa Joint Ventr ....D....... 925 446-6084
   5013 Forni Dr Ste C Concord (94520) *(P-925)*

Groundwork Coffee, North Hollywood *Also Called: Groundwork Coffee Roasters LLC (P-2427)*

Groundwork Coffee Roasters LLC ....C....... 818 506-6020
   5457 Cleon Ave North Hollywood (91601) *(P-2427)*

Groundwork Open Source Inc ....D....... 415 992-4500
   23332 Mill Creek Dr Ste 155 Laguna Hills (92653) *(P-12665)*

Groundworks Inc ....D....... 925 513-0300
   2145 Elkins Way Ste C Brentwood (94513) *(P-2123)*

Group Delphi, Alameda *Also Called: Delphi Productions Inc (P-13261)*

Group Rossignol Usa Inc ....D....... 949 452-9050
   30161 Avenida De Las Bandera Ste A Rancho Santa Margari (92688) *(P-7542)*

Grove - Design District, The, San Francisco *Also Called: Ps24 Inc (P-20189)*

Grove Collaborative Inc ....C....... 800 231-8527
   1301 Sansome St San Francisco (94111) *(P-6709)*

Grove Diagnstc Imaging Ctr Inc ....B....... 909 982-8638
   8805 Haven Ave Ste 120 Rancho Cucamonga (91730) *(P-14768)*

Grove Lumber & Bldg Sups Inc (PA)...........................C....... 909 947-0277
   27126 Watson Rd Menifee (92585) *(P-5160)*

Grove Street, San Francisco *Also Called: Baker Places Inc (P-17845)*

Groves Capital Inc ....C....... 619 519-4453
   4025 Stonebridge Ln Rancho Santa Fe (92091) *(P-9515)*

Growers Company Inc ....D....... 831 424-3850
   21570 Potter Rd Salinas (93908) *(P-11147)*

Growers Transplanting Inc (HQ)..................................D....... 831 449-3440
   360 Espinosa Rd Salinas (93907) *(P-161)*

Grubb & Ellis Company ....A....... 714 667-8252
   1551 N Tustin Ave Ste 300 Santa Ana (92705) *(P-9031)*

Grubb & Ellis Management Services Inc ....A....... 412 201-8200
   1551 N Tustin Ave Ste 300 Santa Ana (92705) *(P-9032)*

Gruen Assoc Archtects Planners, Los Angeles *Also Called: Gruen Associates Inc (P-19473)*

Gruen Associates Inc ....D....... 323 937-4270
   6330 San Vicente Blvd Ste 200 Los Angeles (90048) *(P-19473)*

Grupe Commercial Company ....C....... 209 473-6000
   1203 N Grant St Stockton (95202) *(P-9254)*

Grupe Company (PA)...D....... 209 473-6000
   3255 W March Ln Ste 400 Stockton (95219) *(P-9033)*

Grupe Huber Company, Stockton *Also Called: Grupe Commercial Company (P-9254)*

Grupo Gallegos ....D....... 562 256-3600
   300 Pacific Coast Hwy Ste 200 Huntington Beach (92648) *(P-10621)*

Grupoex, La Mirada *Also Called: Mejico Express Inc (P-3857)*

Gryphon, Chula Vista *Also Called: Gryphon Marine LLC (P-19246)*

Gryphon Investors Inc (PA)..C....... 415 217-7400
   1 Maritime Plz Ste 2300 San Francisco (94111) *(P-9516)*

Gryphon Marine LLC ....D....... 619 407-4010
   694 Moss St Chula Vista (91911) *(P-19246)*

Gs Brothers Inc (PA)..C....... 310 833-1369
   20331 Main St Carson (90745) *(P-494)*

GS Levine Insurance Svcs Inc ....D....... 858 481-8692
   10505 Sorrento Valley Rd Ste 200 San Diego (92121) *(P-8579)*

Gsa Des Plaines LLC ....D....... 310 557-5100
   10100 Santa Monica Blvd Ste 2600 Los Angeles (90067) *(P-9517)*

Gsa Media, San Francisco *Also Called: Tm Holdco LLC (P-10721)*

GSC Logistics Inc ....D....... 510 740-3151
   555 Maritime St Oakland (94607) *(P-4028)*

GSe Construction Company Inc (PA)..........................C....... 925 447-0292
   7633 Southfront Rd Ste 160 Livermore (94551) *(P-1212)*

Gsg Protective Services CA Inc ....C....... 310 371-5300
   15901 Hawthorne Blvd Ste 324 Redondo Beach (90278) *(P-12980)*

Gsico, Foothill Ranch *Also Called: Global Solutions Integration (P-19244)*

Gsl Holdings Inc ....D....... 213 625-2588
   333 S Alameda St Ste 234 Los Angeles (90013) *(P-20397)*

Gt Diamond, Irvine *Also Called: General Tool Inc (P-5903)*

GTS, Chico *Also Called: Gas Transmission Systems Inc (P-19237)*

Gtt Communications (mp) Inc (DH).............................C....... 415 687-3870
   6700 Koll Center Pkwy Ste 330 Pleasanton (94566) *(P-4292)*

Guadalupe Cooling Company Inc ....D....... 805 343-2331
   2040 Guadalupe Rd Guadalupe (93434) *(P-276)*

Guadalupe Union School Dst (PA)...............................C....... 805 343-2114
   4465 9th St Guadalupe (93434) *(P-17714)*

Guarachi Wine Partners Inc ....D....... 818 225-5100
   27001 Agoura Rd Ste 285 Calabasas (91301) *(P-6797)*

Guarantee Mortgage Corporation ....C....... 415 441-5050
   505 Montgomery St Ste 1275 San Francisco (94111) *(P-8043)*

Guarantee Real Estate ....D....... 559 650-6030
   756 W Shaw Ave Fresno (93704) *(P-9034)*

Guarantee Records Management, Fremont *Also Called: Grm Information MGT Svcs Inc (P-3792)*

Guaranteed Rate Inc ....C....... 424 354-5344
   230 Commerce Irvine (92602) *(P-7975)*

Guaranteed Rate Inc ....C....... 805 550-6933
   1065 Higuera St Ste 100 San Luis Obispo (93401) *(P-7976)*

Guaranteed Rate Inc ....C....... 916 501-3919
   915 Highland Pointe Dr Roseville (95678) *(P-7977)*

Guaranteed Rate Inc ....C....... 760 310-6008
   1455 Frazee Rd Ste 500 San Diego (92108) *(P-7978)*

Guard Management Inc ....C....... 858 279-8282
   8001 Vickers St San Diego (92111) *(P-12981)*

Guard Systems District 1, Monterey Park *Also Called: Guard-Systems Inc (P-12983)*

Guard-Systems Inc ....A....... 909 947-5400
   1910 S Archibald Ave Ste M2 Ontario (91761) *(P-12982)*

Guard-Systems Inc ....A....... 323 881-6715
   1190 Monterey Pass Rd Monterey Park (91754) *(P-12983)*

Guardant, Palo Alto *Also Called: Guardant Health Inc (P-16724)*

Guardant Health Inc (PA)..B....... 855 698-8887
   3100 Hanover St Palo Alto (94304) *(P-16724)*

Guardian Integrated SEC Inc (PA)...............................C....... 800 400-3167
   21828 Lassen St Ste A Chatsworth (91311) *(P-1740)*

Guardian Intl Solutions ....D....... 323 528-6555
   3415 S Sepulveda Blvd Ste 1100 Los Angeles (90034) *(P-12984)*

Guardian Life Insur Co Amer ....D....... 626 792-1935
   975 San Pasqual St Pasadena (91106) *(P-8234)*

Guardian Life Insur Co Amer ....D....... 213 624-2002
   510 W 6th St Ste 815 Los Angeles (90014) *(P-8235)*

Guardian Safety and Supply LLC ....D....... 559 651-0919
   8248 W Doe Ave Visalia (93291) *(P-7582)*

Guardian Security Agency, Concord *Also Called: Delta Personnel Services Inc (P-12964)*

Guardian Solutions, Orange *Also Called: Lres Corporation (P-9079)*

Guardian Title Company ....D....... 949 495-9306
   300 Commerce Irvine (92602) *(P-9236)*

Guardsmark LLC (DH)..D....... 714 619-9700
   1551 N Tustin Ave Ste 650 Santa Ana (92705) *(P-12985)*

Guess, Los Angeles *Also Called: Guess Inc (P-2463)*

ALPHABETIC SECTION

Guess Inc (PA) .... A..... 213 765-3100
  1444 S Alameda St Los Angeles (90021) *(P-2463)*
Guesty Inc (PA) .... D..... 415 244-0277
  340 S Lemon Ave Walnut (91789) *(P-9829)*
GUGGENHEIM INVESTMENTS, Los Angeles *Also Called: Fox BSB Holdco Inc (P-14139)*
Guggenheim Prtners Inv MGT LLC .... C..... 310 576-1270
  100 Wilshire Blvd 5th Fl Santa Monica (90401) *(P-9373)*
Guidance Software Inc (HQ) .... C..... 626 229-9191
  1055 E Colorado Blvd Ste 400 Pasadena (91106) *(P-12215)*
Guide Dogs For Blind Inc (PA) .... C..... 415 499-4000
  350 Los Ranchitos Rd San Rafael (94903) *(P-362)*
Guided Discoveries Inc .... D..... 951 659-6062
  26800 Saunders Meadows Rd Idyllwild (92549) *(P-10402)*
Guided Discoveries Inc .... D..... 310 510-1622
  1 Toyon Bay Rd Avalon (90704) *(P-10403)*
Guideline Inc .... C..... 888 228-3491
  1412 Chapin Ave Burlingame (94010) *(P-19814)*
Guidewire, San Mateo *Also Called: Guidewire Software Inc (P-12216)*
Guidewire Software Inc (PA) .... A..... 650 357-9100
  970 Park Pl Ste 200 San Mateo (94403) *(P-12216)*
Guild Holdings Company (PA) .... B..... 858 560-6330
  5887 Copley Dr San Diego (92111) *(P-7979)*
Guild Mortgage, San Diego *Also Called: Guild Holdings Company (P-7979)*
Guild Mortgage, San Diego *Also Called: Guild Mortgage Company LLC (P-9427)*
Guild Mortgage Company LLC (HQ) .... C..... 800 365-4441
  5887 Copley Dr San Diego (92111) *(P-9427)*
Guinn Corporation .... D..... 661 325-6109
  6533 Rosedale Hwy Bakersfield (93308) *(P-2218)*
Gulf- California Broadcast Co .... D..... 760 773-0342
  31276 Dunham Way Thousand Palms (92276) *(P-4436)*
Gulfside Supply Inc .... C..... 530 241-1615
  5858 Westside Rd Redding (96001) *(P-5221)*
Gumbiner Savett Inc .... D..... 310 828-9798
  1723 Cloverfield Blvd Santa Monica (90404) *(P-8723)*
Gumbiner Svett Fnkel Fnglson R, Santa Monica *Also Called: Gumbiner Savett Inc (P-8723)*
Gunderson Dettmer, Redwood City *Also Called: Gunderson Dttmer Stugh Vllnuve (P-17488)*
Gunderson Dttmer Stugh Vllnuve (PA) .... C..... 650 321-2400
  550 Allerton St Redwood City (94063) *(P-17488)*
Gunderson LLC .... C..... 209 578-5154
  884 Codoni Ave Modesto (95357) *(P-4157)*
Gunderson Modesto, Modesto *Also Called: Gunderson LLC (P-4157)*
Gunderson Rail Services LLC .... C..... 909 478-0541
  1475 Cooley Ct San Bernardino (92408) *(P-4158)*
Gursey Schneider & Co LLC (PA) .... C..... 310 552-0960
  1888 Century Park E Ste 900 Los Angeles (90067) *(P-19583)*
Guru Denim LLC (DH) .... C..... 323 266-3072
  500 W 190th St Ste 300 Gardena (90248) *(P-7401)*
Gusto Inc (PA) .... C..... 800 936-0383
  525 20th St San Francisco (94107) *(P-12217)*
Guthy-Renker Direct, Santa Monica *Also Called: Guthy-Renker LLC (P-6045)*
Guthy-Renker LLC .... D..... 310 581-6250
  3340 Ocean Park Blvd Fl 2 Santa Monica (90405) *(P-6045)*
Guthy-Renker LLC (PA) .... D..... 760 773-9022
  100 N Pacific Coast Hwy Ste 1600 El Segundo (90245) *(P-7583)*
Guy Yocom Construction Inc .... C..... 951 284-3456
  10712 E Mariposa Rd Stockton (95215) *(P-2124)*
Guy Yocom Construction Inc (PA) .... C..... 951 284-3456
  3299 Horseless Carriage Rd Ste H Norco (92860) *(P-2125)*
Guzman Grading and Paving Inc .... D..... 909 428-5960
  14030 Rose Ave Fontana (92337) *(P-11034)*
Gv Visual, Fresno *Also Called: Granville Homes Inc (P-681)*
Gvs Italy .... D..... 424 382-4343
  8616 La Tijera Blvd Los Angeles (90045) *(P-5494)*
Gxo Logistics Supply Chain Inc .... A..... 336 309-6201
  3520 S Cactus Ave Bloomington (92316) *(P-3711)*
Gxo Logistics Supply Chain Inc .... D..... 951 512-1201
  2163 S Riverside Ave Colton (92324) *(P-3712)*
Gxo Logistics Supply Chain Inc .... D..... 909 838-5631
  7140 Cajon Blvd San Bernardino (92407) *(P-4029)*
Gxo Logistics Supply Chain Inc .... D..... 909 253-5356
  2615 E 3rd St San Bernardino (92415) *(P-4030)*

Gynecologic Oncology Assoc, Newport Beach *Also Called: Micha-Rettenmaier Partnership (P-14899)*
H - Investment Company .... C..... 925 245-4300
  6999 Southfront Rd Livermore (94551) *(P-5161)*
H & D Electric .... B..... 916 332-0794
  5237 Walnut Ave Ste 100 Sacramento (95841) *(P-1741)*
H & H Agency Inc (PA) .... D..... 949 260-8840
  1403 N Tustin Ave Ste 280 Santa Ana (92705) *(P-8580)*
H & H Transportation LLC .... D..... 951 817-2300
  300 El Sobrante Rd Corona (92879) *(P-3484)*
H & H Truck Terminal, Victorville *Also Called: Hartwick & Hand Inc (P-3402)*
H & N Fish Co., Vernon *Also Called: H & N Foods International Inc (P-6470)*
H & N Foods International Inc (HQ) .... C..... 323 586-9300
  5580 S Alameda St Vernon (90058) *(P-6470)*
H & R Accounts Inc .... C..... 619 819-8844
  3131 Camino Del Rio N Ste 1500 San Diego (92108) *(P-11636)*
H A Bowen Electric Inc .... D..... 510 483-0500
  2055 Williams St San Leandro (94577) *(P-1742)*
H and H Drug Stores Inc (PA) .... D..... 818 956-6691
  3604 San Fernando Rd Glendale (91204) *(P-5420)*
H and H Drug Stores Inc .... D..... 209 931-5200
  4692 E Waterloo Rd Stockton (95215) *(P-5421)*
H and H Drug Stores Inc .... D..... 909 890-9700
  114 E Airport Dr San Bernardino (92408) *(P-5422)*
H C I, Riverside *Also Called: Hci LLC (P-1213)*
H C Olsen Cnstr Co Inc .... D..... 626 359-8900
  710 Los Angeles Ave Monrovia (91016) *(P-822)*
H C V T, Los Angeles *Also Called: Holthouse Carlin Van Trigt LLP (P-19585)*
H D G Associates .... C..... 805 963-0744
  1111 E Cabrillo Blvd Santa Barbara (93103) *(P-9830)*
H D Smith LLC .... D..... 310 641-1885
  1370 E Victoria St Carson (90746) *(P-6111)*
H E C I, Fresno *Also Called: Howe Electric Construction Inc (P-1752)*
H G Group Inc .... B..... 805 486-6463
  4225 Saviers Rd Oxnard (93033) *(P-10522)*
H L Moe Co Inc (PA) .... C..... 818 572-2100
  526 Commercial St Glendale (91203) *(P-1454)*
H M C, Chula Vista *Also Called: Heartland Meat Company Inc (P-6494)*
H M E, Carlsbad *Also Called: HM Electronics Inc (P-5659)*
H O K, San Francisco *Also Called: Hellmuth Obata & Kassabaum Inc (P-19475)*
H Rauvel Inc .... C..... 562 989-3333
  501 W Walnut St Compton (90220) *(P-3485)*
H Rauvel Inc (PA) .... D..... 310 604-0060
  1710 E Sepulveda Blvd Carson (90745) *(P-3713)*
H T V, Studio City *Also Called: High Technology Video Inc (P-13854)*
H U S D Maintenance Operation .... D..... 510 784-2666
  24400 Amador St Hayward (94544) *(P-10906)*
H V Welker Co Inc .... D..... 408 263-4400
  970 S Milpitas Blvd Milpitas (95035) *(P-2032)*
H W Hunter Inc (PA) .... D..... 661 948-8411
  1130 Auto Mall Dr Lancaster (93534) *(P-7225)*
H&H Catering LP .... D..... 408 354-1964
  111 Pine St San Francisco (94111) *(P-20398)*
H&H Resolution LLC .... D..... 408 362-2293
  151 Bernal Rd Ste 6 San Jose (95119) *(P-10743)*
H2o Innovation USA Holding Inc .... D..... 760 639-4400
  1048 La Mirada Ct Vista (92081) *(P-5752)*
H2go Car Wash, Rcho Sta Marg *Also Called: Green-N-Clean Ex Car Wash Inc (P-13690)*
H2o Leak Pros, Orange *Also Called: Alan Smith Pool Plastering Inc (P-1899)*
H2o Plus LLC (PA) .... D..... 800 242-2284
  111 Sutter St Fl 22 San Francisco (94104) *(P-2628)*
H2o.ai, Mountain View *Also Called: H2oai Inc (P-11637)*
H2oai Inc .... C..... 650 429-8337
  2307 Leghorn St Mountain View (94043) *(P-11637)*
Haaker Equipment Company (PA) .... D..... 909 598-2706
  2070 N White Ave La Verne (91750) *(P-5940)*
Haas Jr Evelyn & Walter Fund .... D..... 415 856-1400
  114 Sansome St Fl 6 San Francisco (94104) *(P-19086)*
Haber Corp Crtif Pub Accntants 818 783-9200
  16830 Ventura Blvd # 501 Encino (91436) *(P-20106)*

Haberfelde Ford (PA) .... C...... 661 328-3600
  2001 Oak St Bakersfield (93301) *(P-7226)*

Haberfelde Ford .... D...... 661 837-6400
  5300 Gasoline Alley Dr Bakersfield (93313) *(P-7227)*

Habib, Sindy Dvm, Sherman Oaks *Also Called: Best Friends Animal Hospital (P-329)*

Habitat For Hmnity E By/Slcon (PA) .... D...... 866 450-4432
  2619 Broadway Oakland (94612) *(P-18590)*

Habitat For Hmnity Grter San F .... D...... 415 625-1000
  1 Embarcadero Ctr Ste Sl12 San Francisco (94111) *(P-18591)*

HABITAT FOR HUMANITY, San Francisco *Also Called: Habitat For Hmnity Grter San F (P-18591)*

HABITAT FOR HUMANITY EAST BAY, Oakland *Also Called: Habitat For Hmnity E By/Slcon (P-18590)*

Habitat Rstration Sciences Inc (PA) .... D...... 760 479-4210
  1217 Distribution Way Vista (92081) *(P-495)*

Hacienda Care Center Inc .... C...... 559 784-7375
  301 W Putnam Ave Porterville (93257) *(P-15504)*

Hacienda Golf Club .... D...... 562 694-1081
  718 East Rd La Habra Heights (90631) *(P-14380)*

Hacienda Health Care, Hanford *Also Called: Hacienda Post Acute Inc (P-15505)*

Hacienda Post Acute Inc .... C...... 559 582-9221
  361 E Grangeville Blvd Hanford (93230) *(P-15505)*

Hackerone Inc (PA) .... C...... 415 891-0777
  22 4th St Fl 5 San Francisco (94103) *(P-12801)*

Hackworth Imax Dome, San Jose *Also Called: Imax Corporation (P-13999)*

Hadley Date Gardens Inc .... D...... 760 347-3044
  47382 Madison St Indio (92201) *(P-116)*

Haea, Fountain Valley *Also Called: Hyundai Autoever America LLC (P-12708)*

Hagen Streiff Newton & Oshiro Accountants PC .... D...... 949 390-7647
  4667 Macarthur Blvd Ste 400 Newport Beach (92660) *(P-19584)*

Hagen-Renaker Inc (PA) .... D...... 909 599-2341
  914 W Cienega Ave San Dimas (91773) *(P-2699)*

Haggin Marketing LLC .... B...... 415 289-1110
  100 Shoreline Hwy A200 Mill Valley (94941) *(P-10622)*

Haggin Oaks Golf Shop, Sacramento *Also Called: Morton Golf Management LLC (P-14278)*

Haig Precision Mfg Corp .... D...... 408 378-4920
  3616 Snell Ave San Jose (95136) *(P-2853)*

Haight, Los Angeles *Also Called: Haight Brown & Bonesteel LLP (P-17489)*

Haight Brown & Bonesteel LLP (PA) .... D...... 213 542-8000
  555 S Flower St Ste 4500 Los Angeles (90071) *(P-17489)*

Hair Perfect, Pasadena *Also Called: Hair Perfect International (P-10497)*

Hair Perfect International .... D...... 626 304-9286
  135 W California Blvd Pasadena (91105) *(P-10497)*

Hakes Sash & Door Inc .... C...... 951 674-2414
  31945 Corydon St Lake Elsinore (92530) *(P-2000)*

Hal Hays Construction Inc (PA) .... C...... 951 788-0703
  4181 Latham St Riverside (92501) *(P-823)*

Halabi Inc (PA) .... C...... 707 402-1600
  4447 Green Valley Rd Fairfield (94534) *(P-2716)*

Hale Aloha Convalescent, Turlock *Also Called: Mark One Corporation (P-15875)*

Haley & Aldrich Inc .... D...... 619 280-9210
  5333 Mission Center Rd Ste 300 San Diego (92108) *(P-20769)*

Half Moon Bay Golf Links, Half Moon Bay *Also Called: Ocean Colony Partners LLC (P-9267)*

Hall Ambulance Service Inc .... D...... 661 322-8741
  2001 O St # O Bakersfield (93301) *(P-3267)*

Hall Ambulance Service Inc (PA) .... D...... 661 322-8741
  1001 21st St Bakersfield (93301) *(P-3268)*

Hall and Chambers Inc .... D...... 818 476-3000
  1625 W Glenoaks Blvd Glendale (91201) *(P-9035)*

Hall Capital Partners LLC (PA) .... D...... 415 288-0544
  1 Maritime Plz Fl 5 San Francisco (94111) *(P-9374)*

Hall Management Corp .... A...... 559 846-7382
  759 S Madera Ave Kerman (93630) *(P-20107)*

Hallmark Channel, Studio City *Also Called: Hallmark Media US LLC (P-4437)*

Hallmark Construction, Santa Clara *Also Called: L & S Hallmark Construction Inc (P-956)*

Hallmark Labs LLC .... C...... 424 210-3600
  3130 Wilshire Blvd Ste 400 Santa Monica (90403) *(P-7556)*

Hallmark Media US LLC (DH) .... D...... 818 755-2400
  12700 Ventura Blvd Ste 100 Studio City (91604) *(P-4437)*

Hallmark Rehabilitation GP LLC .... D...... 949 282-5900
  2 Park Plz Ste 225 Irvine (92614) *(P-17995)*

Halonus Inc .... B...... 714 345-0822
  6855 E Swarthmore Dr Anaheim (92807) *(P-3107)*

Halozyme Inc .... C...... 858 794-8889
  12390 El Camino Real San Diego (92130) *(P-19704)*

Halozyme Therapeutics, San Diego *Also Called: Halozyme Inc (P-19704)*

Halrec Inc .... C...... 408 984-1234
  4202 Stevens Creek Blvd San Jose (95129) *(P-7228)*

Halsen Healthcare LLC .... A...... 831 724-4741
  75 Neilson St Watsonville (95076) *(P-16116)*

Halstead Partnership .... D...... 916 830-8000
  2850 Gateway Oaks Dr Ste 450 Sacramento (95833) *(P-926)*

HAM Brokerage .... D...... 909 659-5392
  325 W Hospitality Ln Ste 102 San Bernardino (92408) *(P-4031)*

Hamann Construction .... D...... 619 440-7424
  1000 Pioneer Way El Cajon (92020) *(P-927)*

Hamblin's Auto & Body Shop, Riverside *Also Called: Hamblins Bdy Pnt Frame Sp Inc (P-13663)*

Hamblins Bdy Pnt Frame Sp Inc .... D...... 951 689-8440
  7590 Cypress Ave Riverside (92503) *(P-13663)*

Hamburger Home (PA) .... D...... 323 876-0550
  7120 Franklin Ave Los Angeles (90046) *(P-18444)*

Hamilton and Dillon Elc Inc .... D...... 209 529-6292
  1128 Reno Ave Modesto (95351) *(P-1743)*

Hamilton Brwart Insur Agcy LLC .... D...... 909 920-3250
  1282 W Arrow Hwy Upland (91786) *(P-8581)*

Hamilton Families .... D...... 415 409-2100
  1631 Hayes St San Francisco (94117) *(P-17996)*

Hammer Head Security Inc .... C...... 209 227-6566
  4551 S B St Stockton (95206) *(P-1744)*

HAMMER MUSEUM, Los Angeles *Also Called: Armand Hmmer Mseum of Art Cltr (P-18637)*

Hammonds Ranch Inc .... D...... 209 364-6185
  47375 W Dakota Ave Firebaugh (93622) *(P-235)*

Hampstead Lafayette Hotel LLC .... C...... 619 296-2101
  2223 El Cajon Blvd San Diego (92104) *(P-9831)*

Hampton Inn, San Diego *Also Called: Boykin Mgt Co Ltd Lblty Co (P-9655)*

Hampton Inn, Rohnert Park *Also Called: Inn Hampton & Suites (P-9909)*

Hampton Inn, Foothill Ranch *Also Called: Stonebridge Rlty Advisors Inc (P-10279)*

Hampton Inn, Woodland *Also Called: Sunrise Hospitality Inc (P-10283)*

Hampton Inn & Suites By Hilton, Redding *Also Called: Larkspur Group LLC (P-9966)*

Hampton Products Intl Corp (PA) .... D...... 949 472-4256
  50 Icon Foothill Ranch (92610) *(P-5728)*

Hana Commercial Finance LLC .... D...... 213 240-1234
  1000 Wilshire Blvd Ste 570 Los Angeles (90017) *(P-7894)*

Hana Financial Inc (PA) .... D...... 213 240-1234
  1000 Wilshire Blvd Ste 2000 Los Angeles (90017) *(P-11035)*

Hanaps Enterprises .... D...... 669 235-3810
  8100 Camino Arroyo Gilroy (95020) *(P-2831)*

Handlery Hotels, San Diego *Also Called: Handlery Hotels Inc (P-9833)*

Handlery Hotels Inc .... C...... 415 781-7800
  351 Geary St San Francisco (94102) *(P-9832)*

Handlery Hotels Inc .... C...... 415 781-4550
  950 Hotel Cir N San Diego (92108) *(P-9833)*

Handlery Union Square Hotel, San Francisco *Also Called: Handlery Hotels Inc (P-9832)*

Hands Working Virtually Inc .... D...... 760 459-8138
  74710 Highway 111 Ste 102 Palm Desert (92260) *(P-20108)*

Handshake, San Francisco *Also Called: Stryder Corp (P-12367)*

Hanergy Holding (america) LLC (HQ) .... D...... 650 288-3722
  1350 Bayshore Hwy Ste 825 Burlingame (94010) *(P-2921)*

Hanford Community Hospital (HQ) .... A...... 559 582-9000
  115 Mall Dr Hanford (93230) *(P-16117)*

Hanford Community Hospital .... B...... 559 891-1000
  1141 Rose Ave Selma (93662) *(P-16118)*

Hanford Community Medical Ctr, Hanford *Also Called: Hanford Community Hospital (P-16117)*

Hanford Dialysis LLC .... D...... 559 587-9014
  900 N Douty St Hanford (93230) *(P-16985)*

Hanford Home Dialysis Pd, Hanford *Also Called: Hanford Dialysis LLC (P-16985)*

Hanford Hotels Inc .... C...... 714 557-3000
  3131 Bristol St Costa Mesa (92626) *(P-9834)*

Hanford Post Acute, Hanford *Also Called: Hanfordidence Opco LLC (P-15759)*

ALPHABETIC SECTION — Harman Management Corporation

Hanford Truck Repair & Parts, Hanford *Also Called: Danell Bros Inc (P-248)*

Hanfordidence Opco LLC .... C....... 559 582-2871
1007 W Lacey Blvd Hanford (93230) *(P-15759)*

Hanjin Global Logistics, Gardena *Also Called: Hanjin Transportation Co Ltd (P-4032)*

Hanjin Shipping Co Ltd .... A....... 201 291-4600
301 Hanjin Rd Long Beach (90802) *(P-3826)*

Hanjin Transportation Co Ltd .... D....... 310 522-5030
15913 S Main St Gardena (90248) *(P-4032)*

Hank Fisher Properties Inc .... C....... 916 921-1970
641 Feature Dr Apt 233 Sacramento (95825) *(P-15853)*

Hanken Cono Assad & Co Inc .... C....... 619 575-3100
1504 Oro Vista Rd Apt 145 San Diego (92154) *(P-9036)*

Hankey Group, Los Angeles *Also Called: Nowcom LLC (P-12847)*

Hanks Inc .... D....... 909 350-8365
13866 Slover Ave Fontana (92337) *(P-3401)*

Hannam Chain Super 1 Market, Los Angeles *Also Called: Hannam Chain USA Inc (P-5378)*

Hannam Chain USA Inc (PA) .... C....... 213 382-2922
2740 W Olympic Blvd Los Angeles (90006) *(P-5378)*

Hansel - Prestige Inc .... C....... 707 578-4717
2925 Corby Ave Santa Rosa (95407) *(P-7229)*

Hansel BMW of Santa Rosa, Santa Rosa *Also Called: Hansel - Prestige Inc (P-7229)*

Hansen Bros Enterprises (PA) .... D....... 530 273-3100
11727 La Barr Meadows Rd Grass Valley (95949) *(P-638)*

Hansen Ranches LLC .... D....... 559 992-3111
7124 Whitley Ave Corcoran (93212) *(P-181)*

Hanson Bridgett, San Francisco *Also Called: Hanson Bridgett LLP (P-17490)*

Hanson Bridgett LLP (PA) .... B....... 415 543-2055
425 Market St Fl 26 San Francisco (94105) *(P-17490)*

Hanson Distributing Company (PA) .... C....... 626 224-9800
975 W 8th St Azusa (91702) *(P-5042)*

Hanson Distributing Company .... D....... 559 802-1198
7940 W Doe Ave Visalia (93291) *(P-5043)*

Hanson Distributing Company .... D....... 626 839-4026
19154 San Jose Ave Rowland Heights (91748) *(P-7351)*

Hanson Drywall, San Martin *Also Called: Hanson Drywall Inc (P-1933)*

Hanson Drywall Inc .... D....... 831 297-4581
635 W San Martin Ave San Martin (95046) *(P-1933)*

Hanu Reddy Realty .... D....... 949 450-8800
16251 Laguna Canyon Rd Ste 100 Irvine (92618) *(P-9037)*

Hanwa American Corp .... D....... 949 955-2780
18100 Von Karman Ave Ste 320 Irvine (92612) *(P-5495)*

Hanwa American Los Angeles BR, Irvine *Also Called: Hanwa American Corp (P-5495)*

Hanwha Q Cells USA Corp .... D....... 949 748-5996
300 Spectrum Center Dr Ste 1250 Irvine (92618) *(P-4579)*

Hapag-Lloyd (america) LLC .... C....... 562 435-0771
555 E Ocean Blvd Ste 300 Long Beach (90802) *(P-4033)*

Hapag-Lloyd (america) LLC .... C....... 510 286-1940
180 Grand Ave Ste 1535 Oakland (94612) *(P-20399)*

Happy Money, Costa Mesa *Also Called: Payoff Inc (P-7884)*

Happy Money Inc .... B....... 949 430-0630
21515 Hawthorne Blvd Ste 200 Torrance (90503) *(P-7856)*

Happy Planner, The, Cypress *Also Called: ME & My Big Ideas LLC (P-5991)*

Happyco Inc (PA) .... C....... 415 230-9832
5857 Owens Ave Ste 300 Carlsbad (92008) *(P-11638)*

Har-Bro LLC (HQ) .... D....... 562 528-8000
2750 Signal Pkwy Signal Hill (90755) *(P-928)*

Haralambos Beverage Co .... B....... 562 347-4300
26717 Palmetto Ave Redlands (92374) *(P-6764)*

Harbert Roofing Inc .... D....... 530 223-3251
19799 Hirsch Ct Anderson (96007) *(P-2067)*

Harbill Inc .... D....... 909 883-8833
909 W 21st St San Bernardino (92405) *(P-7230)*

Harbin Hot Springs, Middletown *Also Called: Heart Consciousness Church Inc (P-10420)*

Harbor Area Gang Altrntves Prg .... D....... 310 519-7233
309 W Opp St Wilmington (90744) *(P-18592)*

Harbor Bay Club Inc .... D....... 510 521-5414
200 Packet Landing Rd Alameda (94502) *(P-14205)*

Harbor Distributing LLc (HQ) .... C....... 714 933-2400
5901 Bolsa Ave Huntington Beach (92647) *(P-6765)*

Harbor Distributing LLC .... B....... 916 373-5700
3500 Carlin Dr West Sacramento (95691) *(P-6766)*

Harbor Distributing LLC .... D....... 530 691-5811
6450 Lockheed Dr Redding (96002) *(P-6767)*

Harbor Distributing LLC .... D....... 310 538-5483
16407 S Main St Gardena (90248) *(P-6768)*

Harbor Distributing Co, Gardena *Also Called: Harbor Distributing LLC (P-6768)*

Harbor Dvlpmntal Dsblties Fndt .... C....... 310 540-1711
21231 Hawthorne Blvd Torrance (90503) *(P-18593)*

Harbor Freight Tools, Calabasas *Also Called: Central Purchasing LLC (P-5894)*

Harbor Glen Care Center .... C....... 626 963-7531
1033 E Arrow Hwy Glendora (91740) *(P-15506)*

Harbor Health Care Inc .... C....... 562 866-7054
9461 Flower St Bellflower (90706) *(P-18445)*

Harbor Health Systems LLC .... C....... 949 273-7020
3501 Jamboree Rd Ste 540 Newport Beach (92660) *(P-17244)*

Harbor Industrial, Wilmington *Also Called: Harbor Industrial Svcs Corp (P-10998)*

Harbor Industrial Svcs Corp .... D....... 310 522-1193
211 N Marine Ave Wilmington (90744) *(P-10998)*

Harbor Industries Inc .... C....... 925 461-1366
74 W Neal St Ste 102 Pleasanton (94566) *(P-20400)*

Harbor Island Hotel Group LP .... D....... 805 650-7770
1080 Navigator Dr Ventura (93001) *(P-9835)*

Harbor Packaging, Poway *Also Called: Liberty Diversified Intl Inc (P-2519)*

Harbor Pipe and Steel Inc .... C....... 951 369-3990
1495 Columbia Ave Bldg 10 Riverside (92507) *(P-5496)*

Harbor Post Accute Care Center, Torrance *Also Called: Geri-Care Inc (P-15495)*

HARBOR REGIONAL CENTER, Torrance *Also Called: Harbor Dvlpmntal Dsblties Fndt (P-18593)*

Harbor Truck Bodies Inc .... D....... 714 996-0411
255 Voyager Ave Brea (92821) *(P-2968)*

Harbor Truck Body, Brea *Also Called: Harbor Truck Bodies Inc (P-2968)*

Harbor Ucla Med Foundation, Torrance *Also Called: Harbor-Ucla Med Foundation Inc (P-20109)*

Harbor View Hotel Ventures LLC .... D....... 619 239-6800
1646 Front St San Diego (92101) *(P-9836)*

Harbor View House, San Pedro *Also Called: Healthview Inc (P-18449)*

Harbor View Pre-School, Corona Del Mar *Also Called: Newport Mesa Unified Schl Dst (P-17736)*

Harbor-Ucla Med Foundation Inc .... B....... 310 533-0413
21602 S Vermont Ave Torrance (90502) *(P-16986)*

Harbor-Ucla Med Foundation Inc (PA) .... D....... 310 222-5015
21840 Normandie Ave Ste 100 Torrance (90502) *(P-20109)*

Hard Rock Cafe Intl Inc .... A....... 530 633-6938
3317 Forty Mile Rd Wheatland (95692) *(P-9837)*

Hard Rock Hotel, San Diego *Also Called: T-12 Three LLC (P-10301)*

Hard Rock Hotel Palm Springs, Palm Springs *Also Called: Kittridge Hotels & Resorts LLC (P-9949)*

Hard Rock Ht Csino Scrmnto At, Wheatland *Also Called: Enterprise Development Auth (P-9784)*

Hard Rock Ht Csino Scrmnto At, Wheatland *Also Called: Hard Rock Cafe Intl Inc (P-9837)*

Harding & Associates, San Jose *Also Called: Harding Mktg Cmmunications Inc (P-10810)*

Harding Mktg Cmmunications Inc (PA) .... D....... 408 345-4545
377 S Daniel Way San Jose (95128) *(P-10810)*

Hardwoods Specialty Pdts US LP .... D....... 408 275-1990
620 Quinn Ave San Jose (95112) *(P-5162)*

Hardy Diagnostics Inc (PA) .... B....... 805 346-2766
1430 W Mccoy Ln Santa Maria (93455) *(P-5423)*

Hardy Window Company (PA) .... C....... 714 996-1807
1639 E Miraloma Ave Placentia (92870) *(P-5163)*

Haringa Inc (PA) .... D....... 800 499-9991
14422 Best Ave Santa Fe Springs (90670) *(P-13308)*

Harkins Theatres Inc .... D....... 909 627-8010
3100 Chino Ave Chino Hills (91709) *(P-13997)*

Harkins Theatres Inc .... D....... 909 793-7993
27481 San Bernardino Ave Redlands (92374) *(P-13998)*

Harman Cnncted Svcs Holdg Corp (DH) .... C....... 650 623-9400
636 Ellis St Mountain View (94043) *(P-12462)*

Harman International Inds Inc .... A....... 818 893-8411
8500 Balboa Blvd Northridge (91329) *(P-5654)*

Harman Management Corporation (PA) .... C....... 650 941-5681
595 Millich Dr Ste 106 Campbell (95008) *(P-7485)*

Harman-Kardon, Northridge *Also Called: Harman-Kardon Incorporated (P-5606)*
Harman-Kardon Incorporated .... B....... 818 841-4600
   8500 Balboa Blvd Northridge (91329) *(P-5606)*
Harmonium Inc (PA) .... C....... 858 684-3080
   5440 Morehouse Dr Ste 1000 San Diego (92121) *(P-18319)*
Haro & Haro Enterprises Inc .... A....... 209 334-2035
   115 W Walnut St Ste 4 Lodi (95240) *(P-365)*
Harper Federal Cnstr LLC .... D....... 619 543-1296
   14130 Biscayne Pl Poway (92064) *(P-1118)*
Harpo Entertainment Group, Van Nuys *Also Called: Harpo Productions Inc (P-13852)*
Harpo Productions Inc .... C....... 312 633-1000
   7619 N Patriot Way Van Nuys (91405) *(P-13852)*
Harrah's, Valley Center *Also Called: Caesars Entrtnment Oprting Inc (P-14501)*
Harrah's Northern California, Ione *Also Called: Buena Vista Gaming Authority (P-9665)*
Harrahs Resort Southern Cal, Valley Center *Also Called: Hcal LLC (P-9844)*
Harrington Industrial Plas LLC (PA) .... D....... 909 597-8641
   14480 Yorba Ave Chino (91710) *(P-5753)*
Harris & Associates Inc (PA) .... C....... 925 827-4900
   1401 Willow Pass Rd Ste 500 Concord (94520) *(P-19247)*
Harris & Associates Cnstr MGT, Concord *Also Called: Harris & Associates Inc (P-19247)*
Harris & Ruth Painting Contg (PA) .... D....... 626 960-4004
   28408 Lorna Ave West Covina (91790) *(P-1622)*
Harris Construction, Fresno *Also Called: Harris Construction Co Inc (P-929)*
Harris Construction Co Inc .... C....... 559 251-0301
   5286 E Home Ave Fresno (93727) *(P-929)*
Harris Farms Inc .... B....... 559 935-0717
   24505 W Dorris Ave Coalinga (93210) *(P-182)*
Harris Farms Inc (PA) .... C....... 559 884-2435
   29475 Fresno Coalinga Rd Coalinga (93210) *(P-183)*
Harris Freeman & Co Inc (PA) .... B....... 714 765-7525
   3110 E Miraloma Ave Anaheim (92806) *(P-6633)*
Harris Mycfo Inc .... D....... 480 348-7725
   2200 Geng Rd Ste 100 Palo Alto (94303) *(P-20401)*
Harris Ranch Beef Co, Coalinga *Also Called: Harris Farms Inc (P-183)*
Harris Tea Company, Anaheim *Also Called: Harris Freeman & Co Inc (P-6633)*
Harris Woolf Cal Almonds LLC .... C....... 559 884-2147
   26060 Colusa Ave Coalinga (93210) *(P-277)*
Harris, Jeffery P, Santa Barbara *Also Called: Nasif Hicks Harris & Co LLP (P-19614)*
Harrison Iyke .... D....... 909 463-8409
   7611 Etiwanda Ave Rancho Cucamonga (91739) *(P-13123)*
Harrison Enterprises Inc .... D....... 760 343-7488
   31170 Reserve Dr Thousand Palms (92276) *(P-1455)*
Harrison, E J & Sons Recycling, Ventura *Also Called: E J Harrison & Sons Inc (P-4884)*
Harry McCune Sound Service Inc (PA) .... C....... 650 873-1111
   101 Utah Ave South San Francisco (94080) *(P-11036)*
Harry's Auto Collision, Los Angeles *Also Called: Harrys Auto Body Inc (P-13638)*
Harry's Berries, Oxnard *Also Called: Iwamoto & Gean Farm (P-35)*
Harrys Auto Body Inc .... D....... 323 933-4600
   1013 S La Brea Ave Los Angeles (90019) *(P-13638)*
Hart Chemicals Inc .... D....... 510 549-3535
   2424 4th St Berkeley (94710) *(P-6826)*
Hart Howerton Ltd (PA) .... D....... 415 439-2200
   1 Union St Fl 3 San Francisco (94111) *(P-435)*
Hart Knle Pntecost A Prof Corp .... D....... 714 432-8700
   4 Hutton Centre Dr Ste 900 Santa Ana (92707) *(P-17491)*
Hartford, San Francisco *Also Called: Hartford Casualty Insurance Co (P-8385)*
Hartford Casualty Insurance Co .... C....... 415 836-4800
   101 Montgomery St Ste 2700 San Francisco (94104) *(P-8385)*
Hartman Industries .... D....... 909 428-0114
   20229 E Lorencita Dr Covina (91724) *(P-5497)*
Hartmann Studios Inc .... C....... 510 232-5030
   1150 Brickyard Cove Rd Ste 202 Point Richmond (94801) *(P-13309)*
Hartwick & Hand Inc (PA) .... D....... 760 245-1666
   16953 N D St Victorville (92394) *(P-3402)*
Harvard Grand LP .... D....... 714 939-9700
   1730 S State College Blvd Anaheim (92806) *(P-9838)*
Harvest Farms Inc .... D....... 661 945-3636
   45000 Yucca Ave Lancaster (93534) *(P-2357)*
Harvest Food Distributors, National City *Also Called: Harvest Meat Company Inc (P-6493)*
Harvest Landscape Entps Inc (PA) .... C....... 714 693-8100
   8030 E Crystal Dr Anaheim (92807) *(P-436)*

Harvest Landscape Maintenance, Anaheim *Also Called: Harvest Landscape Entps Inc (P-436)*
Harvest Management Sub LLC .... A....... 805 543-0187
   1299 Briarwood Dr San Luis Obispo (93401) *(P-8816)*
Harvest Meat Company Inc .... D....... 619 477-0185
   1022 Bay Marina Dr Ste 106 National City (91950) *(P-6492)*
Harvest Meat Company Inc (HQ) .... D....... 619 477-0185
   1000 Bay Marina Dr National City (91950) *(P-6493)*
HARVEST MEAT COMPANY, INC., National City *Also Called: Harvest Meat Company Inc (P-6492)*
Harvest Technical Service Inc .... C....... 925 937-4874
   1839 Ygnacio Valley Rd Ste 390 Walnut Creek (94598) *(P-11148)*
Harvey Inc .... C....... 858 769-4000
   9455 Ridgehaven Ct Ste 200 San Diego (92123) *(P-930)*
Harvey & Madding Inc .... D....... 925 828-8030
   6300 Dublin Blvd Dublin (94568) *(P-7231)*
Harvey General Contracting, San Diego *Also Called: Harvey Inc (P-930)*
Hashi, San Francisco *Also Called: Hashicorp Inc (P-11639)*
Hashicorp Inc (PA) .... A....... 415 301-3250
   101 2nd St Ste 700 San Francisco (94105) *(P-11639)*
Haskel International LLC (HQ) .... C....... 818 843-4000
   100 E Graham Pl Burbank (91502) *(P-2793)*
Hassard Bonnington LLP (PA) .... D....... 415 288-9800
   111 Pine St San Francisco (94111) *(P-17492)*
Hasura Inc .... C....... 415 861-9195
   576 Folsom St Fl 3 San Francisco (94105) *(P-12463)*
Hatchbeauty, Los Angeles *Also Called: Hatchbeauty Products LLC (P-6112)*
Hatchbeauty Products LLC (PA) .... D....... 310 396-7070
   355 S Grand Ave Los Angeles (90071) *(P-6112)*
Hathaway Children and Family, Pacoima *Also Called: Hathawy-Sycmres Child Fmly Svc (P-17997)*
Hathaway Dinwiddie, San Francisco *Also Called: Hathaway Dinwiddie Cnstr Co (P-932)*
Hathaway Dinwiddie Cnstr Co .... D....... 415 986-2718
   565 Laurelwood Rd Santa Clara (95054) *(P-931)*
Hathaway Dinwiddie Cnstr Co .... B....... 415 986-2718
   275 Battery St Ste 300 San Francisco (94111) *(P-932)*
Hathaway Dinwiddie Cnstr Group (PA) .... D....... 415 986-2718
   275 Battery St Ste 300 San Francisco (94111) *(P-933)*
Hathawy-Sycmres Child Fmly Svc .... C....... 626 395-7100
   12502 Van Nuys Blvd Ste 120 Pacoima (91331) *(P-17997)*
Hathawy-Sycmres Child Fmly Svc .... C....... 323 733-0322
   3741 Stocker St Ste 101 View Park (90008) *(P-17998)*
Hathawy-Sycmres Child Fmly Svc .... C....... 323 257-9600
   840 N Avenue 66 Los Angeles (90042) *(P-18446)*
Hathawy-Sycmres Child Fmly Svc (PA) .... D....... 626 395-7100
   100 W Walnut St Ste 375 Pasadena (91103) *(P-18447)*
Haulaway Storage Cntrs Inc .... B....... 800 826-9040
   11292 Western Ave Stanton (90680) *(P-3714)*
Havas Edge LLC (DH) .... D....... 760 929-0041
   1525 Faraday Ave Ste 250 Carlsbad (92008) *(P-10623)*
Havas Formula LLC .... D....... 619 234-0345
   1215 Cushman Ave San Diego (92110) *(P-20634)*
Havasu Landing Casino (PA) .... D....... 760 858-5380
   1 Main St Needles (92363) *(P-9839)*
Hawaiian Gardens Casino .... A....... 562 860-5887
   11871 Carson St Hawaiian Gardens (90716) *(P-9840)*
Hawaiian Gardens Casino .... A....... 562 860-5887
   11871 Carson St Hawaiian Gardens (90716) *(P-14533)*
Hawaiian Hotels & Resorts Inc .... C....... 805 480-0052
   2830 Borchard Rd Newbury Park (91320) *(P-9841)*
Hawk, Fontana *Also Called: Hawk Transportation Inc (P-3486)*
Hawk Transportation Inc .... D....... 800 709-4295
   15238 Arrow Blvd Fontana (92335) *(P-3486)*
Hawke Media Ventures LLC (PA) .... C....... 310 451-7295
   2231 S Barrington Ave Los Angeles (90064) *(P-20402)*
Hawker Pacific Aerospace .... B....... 818 765-6201
   11240 Sherman Way Sun Valley (91352) *(P-13773)*
Hawkins Brown USA Inc .... B....... 310 600-2695
   8500 Steller Dr Ste 1 Culver City (90232) *(P-19474)*
Hawthorn Suites Fremont Newark, Newark *Also Called: Pacific Hotel Management LLC (P-10082)*
Hawthorne Cat, San Diego *Also Called: Hawthorne Machinery Co (P-10999)*

ALPHABETIC SECTION
Health Services, Dept of

Hawthorne Lift Systems, Coachella *Also Called: Naumann/Hobbs Mtl Hdlg Corp II* **(P-5795)**
Hawthorne Lowe's, Hawthorne *Also Called: Lowes Home Centers LLC* **(P-7064)**
Hawthorne Machinery Co (PA)..C....... 858 674-7000
  16945 Camino San Bernardo San Diego (92127) **(P-10999)**
Hawthorne Rent-It Service (HQ)..D....... 858 674-7000
  16945 Camino San Bernardo San Diego (92127) **(P-11000)**
Hay Group, Los Angeles *Also Called: Korn Ferry (us)* **(P-20426)**
Hay House Inc (PA)...D....... 760 431-7695
  2591 Pioneer Ave Ste A Vista (92081) **(P-6843)**
Hayday Farms Inc ....D....... 760 922-4713
  15500 S Commercial St Blythe (92225) **(P-13)**
Hayes Mansion Conference Ctr..C....... 408 226-3200
  200 Edenvale Ave San Jose (95136) **(P-9842)**
Hayes Protective Services Inc ....C....... 323 755-2282
  2930 W Imperial Hwy 200b Inglewood (90303) **(P-12986)**
Hayes Welding Inc (PA)...D....... 760 246-4878
  12522 Violet Rd Adelanto (92301) **(P-13751)**
Haynes Building Service LLC ....C....... 626 359-6100
  16027 Arrow Hwy Ste I Baldwin Park (91706) **(P-10907)**
Haynes Family Programs Inc ....C....... 909 593-2581
  233 Baseline Rd La Verne (91750) **(P-18448)**
Hayward Convalescent Hospital, Hayward *Also Called: Hillsdale Group LP* **(P-15856)**
Hayward Hills Health Care Ctr, Hayward *Also Called: Mariner Health Care Inc* **(P-15573)**
Hayward Sisters Hospital (HQ)..A....... 510 264-4000
  27200 Calaroga Ave Hayward (94545) **(P-16119)**
Hayward Unified School Dst ....D....... 510 723-3170
  1633 East Ave Hayward (94541) **(P-17715)**
Hazard Construction, Lakeside *Also Called: Hazard Construction Company* **(P-1184)**
Hazard Construction Company ....D....... 858 587-3600
  10529 Vine St Ste 1 Lakeside (92040) **(P-1184)**
Hazel Creek Assisted Living, Orangevale *Also Called: Summerville At Hazel Creek LLC* **(P-15684)**
Hazel Hawkins Memorial Hosp, Hollister *Also Called: San Benito Health Care Dst* **(P-16375)**
Hazel Hawkins North Side, Hollister *Also Called: San Benito Health Care Dst* **(P-16376)**
Hazelrigg Claims MGT Svcs Inc (HQ).....................................D....... 909 606-6373
  15345 Fairfield Ranch Rd Ste 250 Chino (91710) **(P-8582)**
Hazens Investment LLC ....B....... 310 642-1111
  6101 W Century Blvd Los Angeles (90045) **(P-9843)**
Hazmat Tsdf Inc (PA)..D....... 909 873-4141
  180 W Monte Ave Rialto (92376) **(P-4898)**
HB, San Francisco *Also Called: Hassard Bonnington LLP* **(P-17492)**
HB Parkco Construction Inc (PA)..B....... 714 567-4752
  24795 State Highway 74 Perris (92570) **(P-2126)**
Hba Incorporated ....D....... 714 635-8602
  512 E Vermont Ave Anaheim (92805) **(P-1884)**
Hba International, Santa Monica *Also Called: Hirsch/Bedner Intl Inc* **(P-13316)**
Hbe Rental, Grass Valley *Also Called: Hansen Bros Enterprises* **(P-638)**
Hcal LLC ....B....... 760 751-3100
  777 S Resort Dr Valley Center (92082) **(P-9844)**
HCC Surety Group, Los Angeles *Also Called: American Contrs Indemnity Co* **(P-8427)**
Hci, San Marcos *Also Called: Hughes Circuits Inc* **(P-2907)**
Hci LLC (HQ)...B....... 951 520-4200
  6830 Airport Dr Riverside (92504) **(P-1213)**
Hcl America Inc (DH)..C....... 408 733-0480
  2600 Great America Way Ste 101& Santa Clara (95054) **(P-12696)**
Hcl America Solutions Inc ....A....... 408 733-0480
  2600 Great America Way Santa Clara (95054) **(P-11640)**
Hco Holding I Corporation (HQ)...D....... 323 583-5000
  999 N Pacific Coast Hwy Ste 800 El Segundo (90245) **(P-9317)**
Hcr Manorcare Med Svcs Fla LLC ....C....... 949 587-9000
  24962 Calle Aragon Aliso Viejo (92653) **(P-15507)**
Hct Group, Santa Monica *Also Called: Hct Packaging Inc* **(P-13310)**
Hct Packaging Inc (PA)..C....... 310 260-7680
  2800 28th St Ste 240 Santa Monica (90405) **(P-13310)**
Hd Supply Distribution Services LLC ....A....... 949 643-4700
  26940 Aliso Viejo Pkwy Aliso Viejo (92656) **(P-5729)**
Hd Supply Facilities Maint Ltd ....D....... 909 594-3843
  21651 Baker Pkwy City Of Industry (91789) **(P-5941)**
Hd Supply Facilities Maint Ltd ....D....... 510 783-4019
  2754 W Winton Ave Hayward (94545) **(P-5942)**

Hdc, Tustin *Also Called: Healthcare Design & Cnstr LLC* **(P-934)**
Hdmc Holdings LLC ....C....... 760 366-3711
  6601 White Feather Rd Joshua Tree (92252) **(P-16120)**
Head Office Banking 1, Beverly Hills *Also Called: City National Bank* **(P-7620)**
HEAD START, Quincy *Also Called: Sierra Cscade Fmly Opprtnities* **(P-18352)**
Head Start Child Development Council Inc ....A
  5361 N Pershing Ave Ste A Stockton (95207) **(P-18320)**
Headstart, Watsonville *Also Called: Encompass Community Services* **(P-17968)**
Headstart Nursery Inc (PA)..D....... 408 842-3030
  4860 Monterey Rd Gilroy (95020) **(P-6862)**
Headstrong Corporation ....C....... 408 732-8700
  150 Mathilda Pl Ste 200 Sunnyvale (94086) **(P-12802)**
Headway Technologies Inc ....A....... 425 503-2131
  39639 Leslie St Apt 135 Fremont (94538) **(P-10498)**
Heal, Pacific Palisades *Also Called: Get Heal Inc* **(P-11287)**
Healdsburg District Hospital, Healdsburg *Also Called: North Sonoma County Hosp Dst* **(P-16283)**
Health & Human Services, San Diego *Also Called: County of San Diego* **(P-16649)**
Health & Human Services Dept, Oakland *Also Called: City of Oakland* **(P-17888)**
Health & Human Services- Aging, Santee *Also Called: County of San Diego* **(P-15396)**
Health & Human Svcs, San Diego *Also Called: County of San Diego* **(P-18404)**
Health Advocates, Chatsworth *Also Called: Health Advocates LLC* **(P-18594)**
Health Advocates LLC ....B....... 818 995-9500
  21540 Plummer St Ste B Chatsworth (91311) **(P-18594)**
Health and Human Service, Crescent City *Also Called: County of Del Norte* **(P-18581)**
Health Care Fund, Oakland *Also Called: County of Alameda* **(P-16849)**
Health Care Resource Group, Buena Park *Also Called: Vsa and Associates Inc* **(P-19432)**
Health Care Workers Union (PA)..D....... 510 251-1250
  560 Thomas L Berkley Way Oakland (94612) **(P-8724)**
Health Dept, Los Angeles *Also Called: County of Los Angeles* **(P-17036)**
Health Education, Oakland *Also Called: La Clinica De La Raza Inc* **(P-17267)**
Health Fitness America, Irvine *Also Called: Equinox-76th Street Inc* **(P-15281)**
Health Gorilla Inc ....C....... 844 446-7455
  800 W El Camino Real Ste 100 Mountain View (94040) **(P-12218)**
Health Humn Svcs Agcy NAPA CNT ....D....... 707 253-4306
  2361 Elm St Napa (94559) **(P-15760)**
Health Investment Corporation ....A....... 714 669-2085
  14642 Newport Ave Ste 388 Tustin (92780) **(P-16121)**
Health Iq ....D....... 917 770-2190
  2513 Charleston Rd # 102 Mountain View (94043) **(P-17245)**
Health Iq, Mountain View *Also Called: Hi-Q Inc* **(P-8265)**
Health Lf Orgnization Inc Halo ....D....... 916 428-3788
  3030 Explorer Dr Sacramento (95827) **(P-17246)**
Health Link ....D....... 415 664-5500
  868 Brannan St Ste 307 San Francisco (94103) **(P-17247)**
Health Net, Rancho Cordova *Also Called: Health Net Federal Svcs LLC* **(P-8300)**
Health Net, Rancho Cordova *Also Called: Health Net Pharmaceutical Svcs* **(P-8302)**
Health Net LLC (HQ)...C....... 818 676-6000
  21650 Oxnard St Woodland Hills (91367) **(P-8298)**
Health Net LLC ....C....... 661 321-3904
  6013 Niles St Bakersfield (93306) **(P-8299)**
Health Net Federal Svcs LLC (DH)...A....... 916 935-5000
  10730 International Dr Rancho Cordova (95670) **(P-8300)**
Health Net Inc ....A....... 818 676-6000
  21650 Oxnard St Fl 25 Woodland Hills (91367) **(P-8301)**
Health Net Pharmaceutical Svcs ....C....... 800 977-7532
  2868 Prospect Park Dr Rancho Cordova (95670) **(P-8302)**
Health Plan of San Joaquin ....C....... 209 942-6300
  7751 S Manthey Rd French Camp (95231) **(P-8303)**
Health Plan of San Mateo, South San Francisco *Also Called: San Mateo Health Commission* **(P-17320)**
Health Resources Corp ....B....... 714 754-5454
  2701 S Bristol St Santa Ana (92704) **(P-16122)**
Health Services Advisory Group ....C....... 818 409-9220
  700 N Brand Blvd Fl 1 Glendale (91203) **(P-17248)**
Health Services Dept, Palos Verdes Peninsu *Also Called: County of Los Angeles* **(P-16024)**
Health Services Dept, Los Angeles *Also Called: County of Los Angeles* **(P-16026)**
Health Services Research Ctr, San Diego *Also Called: University Cal San Diego* **(P-19929)**
Health Services, Dept of, Los Angeles *Also Called: County of Los Angeles* **(P-14709)**

Health Services, Dept of

Health Services, Dept of, La Puente *Also Called: County of Los Angeles (P-14711)*
Health Services, Dept of, Bellflower *Also Called: County of Los Angeles (P-14712)*
Health Services, Dept of, Azusa *Also Called: County of Los Angeles (P-14713)*
Health Services, Dept of, Los Angeles *Also Called: County of Los Angeles (P-16025)*
Health Services, Dept of, Acton *Also Called: County of Los Angeles (P-16676)*
Health Services, Dept of, Castaic *Also Called: County of Los Angeles (P-16677)*
Health Services, Dept of, Los Angeles *Also Called: County of Los Angeles (P-17038)*
Health Services, Dept of, Downey *Also Called: County of Los Angeles (P-17040)*
Health Services, Dept of, City Of Industry *Also Called: County of Los Angeles (P-17930)*
Health Smart Clinic, Long Beach *Also Called: Healthsmart Pacific Inc (P-14769)*
Health Svcs Bneft Admnstrtors (PA) .... D....... 925 833-7300
   4160 Dublin Blvd Ste 400 Dublin (94568) *(P-8461)*
Health System, San Mateo *Also Called: County of San Mateo (P-14718)*
Health System Medical Network, Beverly Hills *Also Called: Cedars-Sinai Medical Center (P-15983)*
Health Trust .... D....... 408 513-8700
   3180 Newberry Dr Ste 200 San Jose (95118) *(P-17999)*
Healthcare, Sunnyvale *Also Called: Body Fit Plus Inc (P-11096)*
Healthcare, Oxnard *Also Called: Amigo Baby Inc (P-17835)*
Healthcare Barton System (PA) .... A....... 530 541-3420
   2170 South Ave South Lake Tahoe (96150) *(P-16123)*
Healthcare Centre of Fresno, Fresno *Also Called: Fresno Skilled Nursing (P-15482)*
Healthcare Centre of Fresno, Fresno *Also Called: Fresno Sklled Nrsing Wllness C (P-16682)*
Healthcare Ctr of Downey LLC .... C....... 562 869-0978
   12023 Lakewood Blvd Downey (90242) *(P-15508)*
Healthcare Design & Cnstr LLC .... D....... 714 245-0144
   18302 Irvine Blvd Ste 120 Tustin (92780) *(P-934)*
Healthcare Finance Direct LLC .... D....... 661 616-4400
   1707 Eye St Ste 300 Bakersfield (93301) *(P-20403)*
Healthcare Investments Inc (PA) .... D....... 310 323-3194
   1140 W Rosecrans Ave Gardena (90247) *(P-15509)*
Healthcare Management Systems Inc .... C....... 619 521-9641
   900 Lane Ave Ste 190 Chula Vista (91914) *(P-15510)*
Healthcare Partners, Van Nuys *Also Called: Greater Valley Medical Group (P-17069)*
Healthcare Partners Med Group, El Segundo *Also Called: Optumcare Management LLC (P-14941)*
Healthcare Resource Group .... C....... 562 945-7224
   6571 Altura Blvd Ste 200 Buena Park (90620) *(P-11289)*
Healthcare Services, French Camp *Also Called: San Jquin Gen Hosp Fndtion A C (P-16384)*
Healthcare Services Group Inc .... A....... 562 494-7939
   5199 E Pacific Coast Hwy Ste 402 Long Beach (90804) *(P-20892)*
Healthcare Talent .... D....... 714 341-1197
   26090 Towne Centre Dr Foothill Ranch (92610) *(P-17249)*
Healthcomp LLC (PA) .... B....... 559 499-2450
   621 Santa Fe Ave Fresno (93721) *(P-8583)*
Healthcomp Administrators, Fresno *Also Called: Healthcomp LLC (P-8583)*
Healthpoint Capital LLC (PA) .... C....... 212 935-7780
   9920 Pacific Heights Blvd Ste 150 San Diego (92121) *(P-19883)*
Healthquest Clinical Lab Inc .... D....... 909 445-9727
   9805 Research Dr Irvine (92618) *(P-16725)*
Healthsmart Management Service .... D....... 714 947-8600
   10855 Business Center Dr Ste C Cypress (90630) *(P-8584)*
Healthsmart Pacific Inc .... B....... 562 595-1911
   2683 Pacific Ave Long Beach (90806) *(P-14769)*
Healthsmart Pacific Inc (PA) .... A....... 562 595-1911
   5150 E Pacific Coast Hwy Ste 200 Long Beach (90804) *(P-16124)*
HealthSouth, Oxnard *Also Called: N S C Channel Islands Inc (P-14914)*
HealthSouth, Sacramento *Also Called: HealthSouth Corporation (P-17070)*
HealthSouth Corporation .... D....... 916 929-9431
   75 Scripps Dr Sacramento (95825) *(P-17070)*
Healthsport Ltd A Ltd Partnr (PA) .... C....... 707 822-3488
   300 Dr Martin Luther King Jr Pkwy Arcata (95521) *(P-14206)*
Healthsport-Arcata, Arcata *Also Called: Healthsport Ltd A Ltd Partnr (P-14206)*
Healthtap Inc .... D....... 650 268-9806
   209 E Java Dr Unit 61987 Sunnyvale (94088) *(P-14770)*
Healthview Inc (PA) .... C....... 310 638-4113
   921 S Beacon St San Pedro (90731) *(P-18449)*
Healthy Medical Solutions Inc .... D....... 818 974-1980
   5943 Rhodes Ave Valley Village (91607) *(P-17250)*

Healtth Sanitation Services, Santa Maria *Also Called: Valley Garbage Rubbish Co Inc (P-4949)*
Hearsay Social, San Francisco *Also Called: Hearsay Systems Inc (P-12219)*
Hearsay Systems Inc (PA) .... C....... 888 399-2280
   600 Harrison St Ste 120 San Francisco (94107) *(P-12219)*
Hearst Stations Inc .... C....... 916 446-3333
   3 Television Cir Sacramento (95814) *(P-4438)*
Hearst Stations Inc .... C....... 831 758-8888
   238 John St Salinas (93901) *(P-4439)*
Heart Consciousness Church Inc (PA) .... C....... 707 987-2477
   18424 Harbin Springs Rd Middletown (95461) *(P-10420)*
Heart Group, The, Fresno *Also Called: Cardio Vascular Associates (P-14655)*
Heartflow Inc (PA) .... C....... 650 241-1221
   331 E Evelyn Ave Ste 100 Mountain View (94041) *(P-12464)*
Heartland Child & Family Svcs .... D....... 916 922-9868
   811 Grand Ave Ste D Sacramento (95838) *(P-18000)*
Heartland Express, Fontana *Also Called: Heartland Express Inc Iowa (P-3487)*
Heartland Express Inc Iowa .... A....... 319 626-3600
   10131 Redwood Ave Fontana (92335) *(P-3487)*
Heartland Hospice, Monterey *Also Called: Promedica Health System Inc (P-16915)*
Heartland Hospice, Capitola *Also Called: Promedica Health System Inc (P-16916)*
Heartland Hospice Services, San Rafael *Also Called: Promedica Health System Inc (P-15785)*
Heartland Meat Company Inc .... D....... 619 407-3668
   3461 Main St Chula Vista (91911) *(P-6494)*
Heat, San Francisco *Also Called: Hvsf Transition LLC (P-10626)*
Heat and Control Inc (PA) .... C....... 510 259-0500
   21121 Cabot Blvd Hayward (94545) *(P-2787)*
Heat Software, Newport Beach *Also Called: Heat Waves LLC (P-11641)*
Heat Software USA Inc .... B....... 408 601-2800
   490 N Mccarthy Blvd Ste 100 Milpitas (95035) *(P-12220)*
Heat Transfer Pdts Group LLC .... C....... 909 786-3669
   1933 S Vineyard Ave Ontario (91761) *(P-5769)*
Heat Waves LLC .... C....... 719 651-4942
   4201 Jamboree Rd Unit 518 Newport Beach (92660) *(P-11641)*
Heavenly Construction Inc .... D....... 408 723-4954
   370 Umbarger Rd Ste A San Jose (95111) *(P-437)*
Heavenly Greens, San Jose *Also Called: Heavenly Construction Inc (P-437)*
Heavenly Hands .... D....... 510 881-0480
   21071 Foothill Blvd Hayward (94541) *(P-10499)*
Heaviland Enterprises Inc .... C....... 858 412-1576
   8710 Miramar Pl San Diego (92121) *(P-496)*
Heaviland Enterprises Inc (PA) .... D....... 760 598-7065
   2180 La Mirada Dr Vista (92081) *(P-497)*
Heavy Load Transfer LLC .... D....... 310 816-0260
   18735 S Ferris Pl Rancho Dominguez (90220) *(P-3403)*
Heavyai Inc .... D....... 415 997-2814
   100 Montgomery St 5th Fl San Francisco (94104) *(P-12221)*
Hebrew Home For Aged Disabled .... A....... 415 334-2500
   302 Silver Ave San Francisco (94112) *(P-15511)*
Hec Asset Management Inc .... D....... 661 587-2250
   29341 Kimberlina Rd Wasco (93280) *(P-5379)*
Hec Inc .... B....... 818 879-7414
   30961 Agoura Rd Ste 311 Westlake Village (91361) *(P-5655)*
Heffernan Insurance Brokers (PA) .... B....... 925 934-8500
   1350 Carlback Ave Walnut Creek (94596) *(P-8585)*
HEI Hospitality LLC .... C....... 818 887-4800
   21850 Oxnard St Woodland Hills (91367) *(P-9845)*
HEI Long Beach LLC .... C....... 562 983-3400
   701 W Ocean Blvd Long Beach (90831) *(P-9846)*
Heidelberg Investment Group In .... C....... 213 884-7747
   4957 Onaknoll Ave Los Angeles (90043) *(P-20404)*
Heidi Corporation .... D....... 626 333-6317
   727 N Vernon Ave Azusa (91702) *(P-2127)*
Heil Construction Inc .... D....... 626 303-7141
   701 S Myrtle Ave Monrovia (91016) *(P-824)*
Heimark Distributing, Santa Fe Springs *Also Called: Triangle Distributing Co (P-6785)*
Heirloom, Fresno *Also Called: Counter Hospitality Group LLC (P-7469)*
Helios Healthcare LLC .... B....... 408 739-2383
   1002 W Fremont Ave Sunnyvale (94087) *(P-15512)*
Helios Healthcare LLC .... C....... 925 935-6630
   1911 Oak Park Blvd Pleasant Hill (94523) *(P-15513)*

ALPHABETIC SECTION

Helium 10, Irvine *Also Called: Pixel Labs LLC (P-19995)*
Helix Electric Inc .... A....... 562 941-7200
   13100 Alondra Blvd Ste 108 Cerritos (90703) *(P-1745)*
Helix Electric Inc (PA)... C....... 858 535-0505
   6795 Flanders Dr San Diego (92121) *(P-1746)*
Helix Healthcare Inc .... B....... 619 465-4411
   7050 Parkway Dr La Mesa (91942) *(P-17071)*
Helix Holdings I LLC .... D....... 415 805-3360
   1 Circle Star Way Fl 2 San Carlos (94070) *(P-19705)*
Helix Mechanical Inc .... C....... 619 440-1518
   1100 N Magnolia Ave Ste L El Cajon (92020) *(P-1456)*
Helix Opco LLC .... D....... 415 805-3360
   101 S Ellsworth Ave Ste 350 San Mateo (94401) *(P-19706)*
Helix Renewables, San Diego *Also Called: Helix Electric Inc (P-1746)*
Hellas Construction Inc .... B....... 760 891-8090
   5135 Avenida Encinas Ste A Carlsbad (92008) *(P-1305)*
Hellmuth Obata & Kassabaum Inc (DH)................................ C....... 415 243-0555
   1 Bush St Ste 200 San Francisco (94104) *(P-19475)*
Hellmuth Obata & Kassabaum Inc .... D....... 310 838-9555
   757 S Alameda St Los Angeles (90021) *(P-19476)*
Hello Digit LLC .... D....... 415 260-2684
   2 Circle Star Way San Carlos (94070) *(P-13311)*
Hellosign, San Francisco *Also Called: Jn Projects Inc (P-10558)*
Helloworld Travel Svcs USA Inc .... D....... 310 535-1005
   6171 W Century Blvd Ste 160 Los Angeles (90045) *(P-3931)*
Helm Management Co (PA)... D....... 619 589-6222
   4668 Nebo Dr Ste A La Mesa (91941) *(P-9038)*
Helm, The, La Mesa *Also Called: Helm Management Co (P-9038)*
Helmet House LLC (PA)... D....... 800 421-7247
   26855 Malibu Hills Rd Calabasas Hills (91301) *(P-6176)*
Help & Care LLC .... D....... 408 384-4412
   20 S Santa Cruz Ave Ste 300 Los Gatos (95030) *(P-16867)*
HELP & CARE LLC, Los Gatos *Also Called: Help & Care LLC (P-16867)*
Help At Home Senior Care .... D....... 877 404-6636
   255 Elm Ave Auburn (95603) *(P-16868)*
Help Children World Foundation .... B....... 818 706-9848
   26500 Agoura Rd Ste 657 Calabasas (91302) *(P-18001)*
Help Group West (PA).. C....... 818 781-0360
   13130 Burbank Blvd Sherman Oaks (91401) *(P-17072)*
Help Unlimited, Ojai *Also Called: Help Unlmted Personnel Svc Inc (P-16869)*
Help Unlmted Personnel Svc Inc .... A....... 805 962-4646
   3202 E Ojai Ave Ojai (93023) *(P-16869)*
Heluna Health, City Of Industry *Also Called: Public Hlth Fndation Entps Inc (P-18899)*
Hely & Weber Orthopedic, Santa Paula *Also Called: Weber Orthopedic LP (P-3064)*
Hemacare Corporation, Northridge *Also Called: Charles Rver Labs Cell Sltons (P-17204)*
Hemet Unified School District .... D....... 951 765-5100
   2075 W Acacia Ave Hemet (92545) *(P-17716)*
Hemet Unified School District .... D....... 951 765-6287
   985 N Cawston Ave Hemet (92545) *(P-17717)*
Hemet Valley Medical Center, Hemet *Also Called: Hemet Valley Medical Center-Education (P-16125)*
Hemet Valley Medical Center-Education .... A....... 951 652-2811
   1117 E Devonshire Ave Hemet (92543) *(P-16125)*
Hemington Landscape Svcs Inc .... D....... 530 677-9290
   4170 Business Dr Cameron Park (95682) *(P-438)*
Hemodialysis Inc .... D....... 626 792-0548
   806 S Fair Oaks Ave Pasadena (91105) *(P-3052)*
Hemodialysis Inc .... D....... 818 365-6961
   14901 Rinaldi St Ste 100 Mission Hills (91345) *(P-16987)*
Hendrick Automotive Group .... D....... 925 463-4700
   4355 Rosewood Dr Pleasanton (94588) *(P-7232)*
Hendrickson Truck Lines Inc .... C....... 916 387-9614
   7080 Florin Perkins Rd Sacramento (95828) *(P-3488)*
Hendrickson Trucking Inc .... B....... 916 387-9614
   7080 Florin Perkins Rd Sacramento (95828) *(P-3489)*
Hendrie Radio Inc .... D....... 818 259-8175
   2871 Instone Ct Westlake Village (91361) *(P-4385)*
Henkel Corporation .... C....... 707 731-4964
   405 Industrial Way Dixon (95620) *(P-13312)*
Henkel US Operations Corp .... D....... 424 308-0505
   5800 Bristol Pkwy Culver City (90230) *(P-6710)*
Henkel US Operations Corp .... C....... 925 458-8086
   2850 Willow Pass Rd Bay Point (94565) *(P-19248)*
Henkel US Operations Corp .... C....... 714 368-8000
   14000 Jamboree Rd Irvine (92606) *(P-19815)*
Henkels & McCoy Inc .... B....... 909 517-3011
   2840 Ficus St Pomona (91766) *(P-1214)*
Henry Avocado Corporation (HQ).. D....... 760 745-6632
   2208 Harmony Grove Rd Escondido (92029) *(P-117)*
Henry Call Inc .... C....... 805 734-2762
   Bldg 861 Clark And Arguello Vandenberg Afb (93437) *(P-20654)*
Henry Hibino Farms LLC .... D....... 831 757-3081
   106 Rico St Salinas (93907) *(P-34)*
Henry J Kaiser Fmly Foundation (PA).................................. C....... 650 854-9400
   185 Berry St Ste 2000 San Francisco (94107) *(P-19087)*
Henry Mayo Newhall Mem Hosp (PA).................................. A....... 661 253-8000
   23845 Mcbean Pkwy Valencia (91355) *(P-16126)*
Henry Mayo Nwhall Mem Hlth Fnd .... A....... 661 253-8000
   23845 Mcbean Pkwy Valencia (91355) *(P-16127)*
Henry Samueli School Engrg, Irvine *Also Called: University California Irvine (P-19793)*
Henry Wine Group LLC (HQ)... B....... 707 745-8500
   4301 Industrial Way Benicia (94510) *(P-6798)*
Henry Wine Group of C.A., The, Benicia *Also Called: Henry Wine Group LLC (P-6798)*
Henry's Pub, Berkeley *Also Called: Hotel Durant A Ltd Partnership (P-9871)*
Henrymayo Newhall Mem Hosp, Valencia *Also Called: Henry Mayo Nwhall Mem Hlth Fnd (P-16127)*
Hensel Phelps Construction Co .... C....... 408 452-1800
   4750 Willow Rd Ste 100 Pleasanton (94588) *(P-935)*
Hensly Event Resources, Brisbane *Also Called: Michaael S Hensley (P-10562)*
Hentrel Greathouse Foundation .... D....... 302 513-4056
   1861 E Main St Barstow (92311) *(P-18869)*
Heppner Hardwoods Inc .... D....... 626 969-7983
   555 W Danlee St Azusa (91702) *(P-5164)*
Herald Christian Health Center (PA).................................... D....... 626 286-8700
   3401 Aero Jet Ave El Monte (91731) *(P-14771)*
Herbert Malarkey Roofing Co .... D....... 562 806-8000
   9301 Garfield Ave South Gate (90280) *(P-2068)*
Heritage Auctions Inc .... D....... 310 300-8390
   9478 W Olympic Blvd Beverly Hills (90212) *(P-13313)*
Heritage Bank of Commerce (HQ)....................................... C....... 408 947-6900
   224 Airport Pkwy Ste 100 San Jose (95110) *(P-7692)*
Heritage California Aco, Northridge *Also Called: Regal Medical Group Inc (P-18758)*
Heritage Container Inc .... D....... 951 360-1900
   4777 Felspar St Riverside (92509) *(P-2514)*
Heritage Estates-Livermore, Livermore *Also Called: Leisure Care LLC (P-18467)*
Heritage Gardens Hlth Care Ctr, Loma Linda *Also Called: Heritage Health Care Inc (P-15514)*
Heritage Golf Group LLC .... D....... 949 369-6226
   990 Avenida Talega San Clemente (92673) *(P-14266)*
Heritage Golf Group LLC .... C....... 661 254-4401
   27330 Tourney Rd Valencia (91355) *(P-14267)*
Heritage Health Care, Lancaster *Also Called: High Dsert Med Corp A Med Grou (P-14772)*
Heritage Health Care Inc .... C....... 909 796-0216
   25271 Barton Rd Loma Linda (92354) *(P-15514)*
Heritage Interests LLC (PA).. D....... 916 481-5030
   4300 Jetway Ct North Highlands (95660) *(P-2001)*
Heritage Medical Group .... B....... 760 956-1286
   12370 Hesperia Rd Ste 6 Victorville (92395) *(P-17251)*
HERITAGE MEDICAL GROUP, Victorville *Also Called: Heritage Medical Group (P-17251)*
Heritage Oak Prvate Elmntary S, Yorba Linda *Also Called: Rgbx Inc (P-18351)*
Heritage Oaks Bancorp .... B....... 805 369-5200
   1222 Vine St Paso Robles (93446) *(P-7693)*
Heritage Oaks Bank .... C....... 805 239-5200
   1222 Vine St Paso Robles (93446) *(P-7694)*
Heritage One, North Highlands *Also Called: Heritage One Win Bldg Sltons L (P-5166)*
Heritage One Door, North Highlands *Also Called: Heritage One Door Crpentry LLC (P-5165)*
Heritage One Door & Carpentry, North Highlands *Also Called: Builders Firstsource Inc (P-5149)*
Heritage One Door Crpentry LLC .... D....... 916 481-5030
   4300 Jetway Ct North Highlands (95660) *(P-5165)*
Heritage One Win Bldg Sltons L .... C....... 916 481-5030
   4300 Jetway Ct North Highlands (95660) *(P-5166)*

Heritage Paper Co (HQ) .... D....... 714 540-9737
2400 S Grand Ave Santa Ana (92705) *(P-2515)*

Heritage Paper Co, Livermore *Also Called: Heritage Paper LLC (P-2516)*

Heritage Paper LLC (PA) .... C....... 925 449-1148
6850 Brisa St Livermore (94550) *(P-2516)*

Heritage Pointe, Rancho Cucamonga *Also Called: National Community Renaissance (P-8846)*

HERITAGE POINTE, Mission Viejo *Also Called: Jewish HM For The Aging Ornge (P-15526)*

Heritage Security Services, Temecula *Also Called: Richman Management Corporation (P-13029)*

HERITAGE, THE, San Francisco *Also Called: San Frncsco Ldies Prtction Rli (P-18519)*

Herman Produce Sales LLC .... D....... 559 661-8253
2370 W Cleveland Ave # 108 Madera (93637) *(P-7157)*

Herman Weissker Inc (HQ) .... C....... 951 826-8800
1645 Brown Ave Riverside (92509) *(P-1215)*

Herning Enterprises Inc .... C....... 510 782-5330
23144 Clawiter Rd Hayward (94545) *(P-5564)*

Herning Underground Supply, Hayward *Also Called: Herning Enterprises Inc (P-5564)*

Herrero Builders Incorporated (PA) .... C....... 415 824-7675
2100 Oakdale Ave San Francisco (94124) *(P-825)*

Herring Networks Inc .... C....... 858 270-6900
4757 Morena Blvd San Diego (92117) *(P-4440)*

Hertzbrg-Dvis Frnsic Scnce Ctr, Los Angeles *Also Called: County of Los Angeles (P-19961)*

Herzog & Company .... D....... 818 762-4640
4640 Lankershim Blvd Ste 400 North Hollywood (91602) *(P-13853)*

Herzog Contracting Corp .... C....... 562 595-7414
3760 Kilroy Airport Way Ste 120 Long Beach (90806) *(P-1306)*

Herzog Contracting Corp .... D....... 619 849-6990
2155 Hancock St San Diego (92110) *(P-2283)*

Hesperia Unified School Dst .... D....... 760 948-1051
11176 G Ave Hesperia (92345) *(P-2436)*

Hesperia Usd Food Service, Hesperia *Also Called: Hesperia Unified School Dst (P-2436)*

Hetherington Engineering (PA) .... C....... 760 931-1917
4333 Apache St Oceanside (92056) *(P-19249)*

Hewlett Foundation, Menlo Park *Also Called: Hewlett Wlliam Flora Fndation (P-19088)*

Hewlett Packard Enterprise Co .... A....... 408 914-2390
4555 Great America Pkwy Ste 201 Santa Clara (95054) *(P-12578)*

Hewlett Wlliam Flora Fndation .... D....... 650 234-4500
2121 Sand Hill Rd Menlo Park (94025) *(P-19088)*

Hexagon Agility Inc .... D....... 949 236-5520
3335 Susan St Ste 100 Costa Mesa (92626) *(P-588)*

HF Cox Inc .... B....... 323 587-2359
8330 Atlantic Ave Cudahy (90201) *(P-3404)*

HF Cox Inc (PA) .... D....... 661 366-3236
118 Cox Transportation Way Bakersfield (93307) *(P-3490)*

HG Fenton Company .... C....... 619 400-0120
7577 Mission Valley Rd Ste 200 San Diego (92108) *(P-8817)*

HG Fenton Property Company (PA) .... C....... 619 400-0120
7577 Mission Valley Rd Ste 200 San Diego (92108) *(P-8885)*

Hggc LLC (PA) .... B....... 650 321-4910
1950 University Ave Ste 350 East Palo Alto (94303) *(P-9518)*

Hh Global, San Francisco *Also Called: Hh Global Limited (P-13314)*

Hh Global Limited .... B....... 847 984-2448
14 Geary St 2nd Fl San Francisco (94108) *(P-13314)*

HHS Communications Inc .... D....... 909 230-5170
2042 S Grove Ave Ontario (91761) *(P-1747)*

HI Anaheim LLC .... D....... 714 533-1500
100 W Katella Ave Anaheim (92802) *(P-9847)*

HI LLC (PA) .... D....... 757 655-4113
10361 Jefferson Blvd Culver City (90232) *(P-19816)*

HI Lo Motel, Edgewood *Also Called: Siskiyou Development Company (P-10241)*

HI Pro Inc .... C....... 760 367-7734
4584 Adobe Rd Twentynine Palms (92277) *(P-3491)*

Hi-Desert Medical Center, Joshua Tree *Also Called: Hdmc Holdings LLC (P-16120)*

Hi-Q Inc .... B....... 800 549-1664
2513 Charleston Rd Mountain View (94043) *(P-8265)*

Hi-Temp Insulation Inc .... B....... 805 484-2774
4700 Calle Alto Camarillo (93012) *(P-1934)*

Hidden Villa Ranch, Fullerton *Also Called: Hidden Villa Ranch Produce Inc (P-6444)*

Hidden Villa Ranch Produce Inc (HQ) .... B....... 714 680-3447
310 N Harbor Blvd Ste 205 Fullerton (92832) *(P-6444)*

Hideaway .... C....... 760 777-7400
80440 Hideaway Club Ct La Quinta (92253) *(P-7486)*

Hideaway, La Quinta *Also Called: Hideaway Club (P-14381)*

Hideaway Club .... B....... 760 777-7400
80440 Hideaway Club Ct La Quinta (92253) *(P-14381)*

Higgs Fletcher & Mack Llp .... C....... 619 236-1551
401 W A St Ste 2600 San Diego (92101) *(P-17493)*

High Caliber Line, Irwindale *Also Called: Calibre International LLC (P-20632)*

High Dsert Med Corp A Med Grou (PA) .... C....... 661 945-5984
43839 15th St W Lancaster (93534) *(P-14772)*

High Dsert Prtnr In Acdmic Exc .... B....... 760 946-5414
17500 Mana Rd Apple Valley (92307) *(P-19817)*

High End Development Inc .... C....... 925 687-2540
665 Stone Rd Benicia (94510) *(P-2284)*

High Moon Studios LLC .... C....... 760 448-3000
2051 Palomar Airport Rd Ste 250 Carlsbad (92011) *(P-10550)*

High Performance Logistics LLC .... D....... 702 300-4880
7227 Central Ave Riverside (92504) *(P-3405)*

High Plains Ranch LLC (PA) .... C....... 559 583-1277
2911 Hanford Armona Rd Hanford (93230) *(P-216)*

High Tech Pet Products .... D....... 805 644-1797
2111 Portola Rd # A Ventura (93003) *(P-5656)*

High Technology Video Inc .... C....... 323 969-8822
10900 Ventura Blvd Studio City (91604) *(P-13854)*

High Times Productions Inc .... C....... 844 933-3287
10990 Wilshire Blvd Los Angeles (90024) *(P-13315)*

High-Light Electric Inc .... D....... 951 352-9646
1460 E Cooley Dr Ste 100 Colton (92324) *(P-1748)*

Highbury Defense Group .... D....... 619 316-7979
2725 Congress St Ste 1m San Diego (92110) *(P-19250)*

Highcom Security Services .... D....... 510 893-7600
1900 Webster St Ste B Oakland (94612) *(P-12987)*

Higher Ground Education Inc (PA) .... B....... 949 836-9401
10 Orchard Ste 200 Lake Forest (92630) *(P-20770)*

Higher One Payments Inc .... B....... 510 769-9888
80 Swan Way Ste 200 Oakland (94621) *(P-12222)*

Higher Talent, Los Angeles *Also Called: Creative Solutions Svcs LLC (P-11113)*

Highland Capital Partners LLC .... C....... 650 687-3800
537 Hamilton Ave Palo Alto (94301) *(P-9519)*

Highland Hlthcare Cmllia Grdns .... C....... 626 798-6777
1920 N Fair Oaks Ave Pasadena (91103) *(P-15515)*

Highland Hosp Hghland Wellness, Oakland *Also Called: Alameda Health System (P-18552)*

Highland Palms Healthcare Ctr, Highland *Also Called: Cedar Holdings LLC (P-15368)*

Highland Pk Sklled Nrsing Wlln .... D....... 323 254-6125
5125 Monte Vista St Los Angeles (90042) *(P-15516)*

Highland Wholesale Foods, Stockton *Also Called: Highland Wholesale Foods Inc (P-6257)*

Highland Wholesale Foods Inc .... D....... 209 933-0580
1604 Tillie Lewis Dr Stockton (95206) *(P-6257)*

Highlands Inn Inc .... D....... 831 620-1234
120 Highland Dr Carmel (93923) *(P-9848)*

Highlands Inn Investors II LP .... C....... 831 624-3801
120 Highland Dr Carmel (93923) *(P-9849)*

Highmark Capital MGT Inc .... D....... 800 582-4734
350 California St 12th Fl San Francisco (94104) *(P-8202)*

Hightail, Menlo Park *Also Called: Open Text Inc (P-11796)*

Hightail Inc .... D....... 408 879-9118
1919 S Bascom Ave Campbell (95008) *(P-4293)*

Hignell Incorporated .... D....... 530 345-1965
1836 Laburnum Ave Chico (95926) *(P-8818)*

Hignell Incorporated .... D....... 530 342-0707
1770 Humboldt Rd Chico (95928) *(P-9255)*

Hii Fleet Support Group LLC .... C....... 619 474-8820
131 W 33rd St Ste 100a National City (91950) *(P-19251)*

Hii Fleet Support Group LLC .... B....... 858 522-6319
9444 Balboa Ave Ste 400 San Diego (92123) *(P-19707)*

Hikvision USA Inc (HQ) .... C....... 909 895-0400
18639 Railroad St City Of Industry (91748) *(P-13124)*

Hilbers Inc .... D....... 530 673-2947
770 N Walton Ave Ste 100 Yuba City (95993) *(P-936)*

Hilbers Contractors & Engrg, Yuba City *Also Called: Hilbers Inc (P-936)*

Hill Brothers Chemical, Brea *Also Called: Hill Brothers Chemical Company (P-6711)*

ALPHABETIC SECTION

Hill Brothers Chemical Company (PA)..................................C....... 714 998-8800
  3000 E Birch St Ste 108 Brea (92821) *(P-6711)*
Hill Farrer & Burrill ....D....... 213 620-0460
  300 S Grand Ave Fl 37 Los Angeles (90071) *(P-17494)*
Hill Phoenix Inc ....D....... 909 592-8830
  14680 Monte Vista Ave Chino (91710) *(P-5778)*
Hill Physicians Med Group Inc (PA).................................B....... 800 445-5747
  2409 Camino Ramon San Ramon (94583) *(P-14773)*
HILLCREST, La Verne Also Called: Brethren Hillcrest Homes *(P-18381)*
Hillcrest Contracting Inc ....D....... 951 273-9600
  1467 Circle City Dr Corona (92879) *(P-1119)*
Hillcrest Country Club ....C....... 310 553-8911
  10000 W Pico Blvd Los Angeles (90064) *(P-14382)*
Hillcrest Manor Sanitarium, National City Also Called: Imaginative Horizons Inc *(P-15521)*
Hillcrest Senior Housing Corp ....B....... 650 757-1737
  35 Hillcrest Dr Daly City (94014) *(P-8819)*
Hills Flat Lumber Co (PA)...D....... 530 273-6171
  380 Railroad Ave Grass Valley (95945) *(P-7122)*
Hills Wldg & Engrg Contr Inc ....D....... 661 746-5400
  22038 Stockdale Hwy Bakersfield (93314) *(P-613)*
Hillsdale Group LP ....C....... 818 623-2170
  12750 Riverside Dr North Hollywood (91607) *(P-15854)*
Hillsdale Group LP ....C....... 650 742-9150
  1201 Broadway Ofc Millbrae (94030) *(P-15855)*
Hillsdale Group LP ....D....... 510 538-3866
  1832 B St Hayward (94541) *(P-15856)*
HILLSIDE ENTERPRISES - AR & C, Long Beach Also Called: Advocacy For Rspect Chice - Lo *(P-18203)*
Hillside House ....D....... 805 687-0788
  1235 Veronica Springs Rd Santa Barbara (93105) *(P-15761)*
Hillsides ....B....... 323 254-2274
  940 Avenue 64 Pasadena (91105) *(P-18002)*
Hilltop Estates, Grass Valley Also Called: FPI Management Inc *(P-9019)*
Hilltop Family YMCA, Richmond Also Called: Young MNS Chrstn Assn of E Bay *(P-18979)*
Hilltop Ranch Inc ....C....... 209 874-1875
  13890 Looney Rd Ballico (95303) *(P-278)*
Hilltop Trading, Ballico Also Called: Hilltop Ranch Inc *(P-278)*
Hilltown Packing Co Inc ....B....... 831 784-1931
  9 Harris Pl Ste A Salinas (93901) *(P-279)*
Hillview Mental Health Ctr Inc ....D....... 818 896-1161
  12450 Van Nuys Blvd Ste 200 Pacoima (91331) *(P-17073)*
Hilton, Los Angeles Also Called: Fortuna Enterprises LP *(P-9800)*
Hilton, San Diego Also Called: Hilton Dbltree San Dego Rgnal *(P-9850)*
Hilton, Gilroy Also Called: Hilton Garden Inns MGT LLC *(P-9851)*
Hilton, Carlsbad Also Called: Hilton Garden Inns MGT LLC *(P-9852)*
Hilton, San Francisco Also Called: Hilton San Francisco Fincl Dst *(P-9855)*
Hilton, Orange Also Called: Hit Portfolio II Trs LLC *(P-9859)*
Hilton, San Diego Also Called: Lho Mssion Bay Rsie Lessee Inc *(P-9976)*
Hilton, Anaheim Also Called: Makar Anaheim LLC *(P-9997)*
Hilton, Long Beach Also Called: Merritt Hospitality LLC *(P-10015)*
Hilton, Santa Clara Also Called: Ontario Airport Hotel Corp *(P-10069)*
Hilton, San Francisco Also Called: Parc 55 Lessee LLC *(P-10100)*
Hilton, Oakland Also Called: Park Hotels & Resorts Inc *(P-10102)*
Hilton, Beverly Hills Also Called: Park Hotels & Resorts Inc *(P-10104)*
Hilton, San Bernardino Also Called: San Bernardino Hilton *(P-10193)*
Hilton, La Jolla Also Called: Torreyana Grille *(P-10316)*
Hilton, Huntington Beach Also Called: Waterfront Hotel LLC *(P-10354)*
Hilton, San Jose Also Called: West Hotel Partners LP *(P-10361)*
Hilton, Redding Also Called: Win River Hotel Corporation *(P-10370)*
Hilton, San Diego Also Called: Ww San Diego Harbor Island LLC *(P-10383)*
Hilton Concord, Concord Also Called: Vwi Concord LLC *(P-10347)*
Hilton Dbltree San Dego Rgnal ....D....... 619 270-2600
  404 Camino Del Rio S San Diego (92108) *(P-9850)*
Hilton Garden Inn Calabasas, Calabasas Also Called: T M Mian & Associates Inc *(P-10300)*
Hilton Garden Inn Cupertino, Cupertino Also Called: Cupertino Hspitality Assoc LLC *(P-9732)*
Hilton Garden Inn Livermore, Livermore Also Called: Hilton Garden Inns MGT LLC *(P-9853)*
Hilton Garden Inn Roseville, Roseville Also Called: Inn Ventures Inc *(P-9910)*
Hilton Garden Inns MGT LLC ....C....... 408 840-7000
  6070 Monterey Rd Gilroy (95020) *(P-9851)*
Hilton Garden Inns MGT LLC ....B....... 760 476-0800
  6450 Carlsbad Blvd Carlsbad (92011) *(P-9852)*
Hilton Garden Inns MGT LLC ....B....... 925 292-2000
  2801 Constitution Dr 2nd Fl Livermore (94551) *(P-9853)*
Hilton Grdn Inn San Dego Dwntw, San Diego Also Called: M4dev LLC *(P-9995)*
Hilton Grdn Inn San Frncsco Ar, South San Francisco Also Called: Larkspur Hsptality Dev MGT LLC *(P-9968)*
Hilton Hotels, Long Beach Also Called: HEI Long Beach LLC *(P-9846)*
Hilton Los Angeles Culver City, Culver City Also Called: Woodbine Lgacy/Playa Owner LLC *(P-10378)*
Hilton Los Angles Universal Cy ....C....... 818 506-2500
  555 Universal Hollywood Dr Universal City (91608) *(P-9854)*
Hilton Los Angls/Nversal Cy Ht, Universal City Also Called: Sun Hill Properties Inc *(P-10282)*
Hilton Port Los Angls-San Pdro, San Pedro Also Called: Meristar San Pedro Hilton LLC *(P-10013)*
Hilton Resort In Palm Spring, Palm Springs Also Called: Walters Family Partnership *(P-10352)*
Hilton San Diego Airport/Hrbr, San Diego Also Called: Bartell Hotels *(P-9632)*
Hilton San Diego/Del Mar, Del Mar Also Called: Sunstone Durante LLC *(P-10286)*
Hilton San Francisco Fincl Dst ....D....... 415 433-6600
  750 Kearny St San Francisco (94108) *(P-9855)*
Hilton Santa Clara, Santa Clara Also Called: Stanford Hotels Corporation *(P-10267)*
Hilton Woodland Hills & Towers ....D....... 818 595-1000
  6360 Canoga Ave Woodland Hills (91367) *(P-9856)*
Hinds Hospice (PA)..C....... 559 674-0407
  2490 W Shaw Ave Ste 100a Fresno (93711) *(P-15762)*
Hines Growers Inc ....A....... 800 554-4065
  27368 Via Industria Ste 201 Temecula (92590) *(P-130)*
Hines Horticulture Inc (PA)...B....... 949 559-4444
  12621 Jeffery Rd Irvine (92620) *(P-131)*
Hines Interests Ltd Partnr ....C....... 650 518-6139
  1 Hacker Way Bldg 10 Menlo Park (94025) *(P-9039)*
Hines Nurseries, Irvine Also Called: Hines Horticulture Inc *(P-131)*
Hinge Health Inc (PA)..A....... 855 902-7777
  455 Market St Ste 700 San Francisco (94105) *(P-17252)*
Hino Motors Mfg USA Inc ....D....... 951 727-0286
  4550 Wineville Ave Jurupa Valley (91752) *(P-5044)*
Hinode, Woodland Also Called: Sunfoods LLC *(P-6395)*
Hipcamp Inc (PA)..C....... 242 377-8982
  965 Market St Ste 480 San Francisco (94103) *(P-3932)*
Hira Paris Inc ....C....... 909 634-3900
  3811 Schaefer Ave Ste B Chino (91710) *(P-2375)*
Hire Up Staffing Service ....B....... 559 579-1331
  575 E Locust Ave Ste 203 Fresno (93720) *(P-11149)*
Hireteammate Inc ....C....... 650 386-5017
  2513 Charleston Rd Ste 200 Mountain View (94043) *(P-11150)*
Hiretual, Mountain View Also Called: Hireteammate Inc *(P-11150)*
Hirsch Electronics LLC ....D....... 949 250-8888
  1900 Carnegie Ave Ste B Santa Ana (92705) *(P-5657)*
Hirsch/Bedner Intl Inc (PA)...D....... 310 829-9087
  3216 Nebraska Ave Santa Monica (90404) *(P-13316)*
Hirsch3667 Corp ....C....... 310 641-6690
  5700 Hannum Ave Ste 250 Culver City (90230) *(P-9318)*
Hisamitsu Pharmaceutical Co Inc ....A....... 760 931-1756
  2730 Loker Ave W Carlsbad (92010) *(P-19884)*
Historic Mission Inn Corp ....B....... 951 784-0300
  3649 Mission Inn Ave Riverside (92501) *(P-9857)*
Historical Properties Inc (PA)..D....... 619 230-8417
  311 Island Ave San Diego (92101) *(P-9858)*
Hit Portfolio II Trs LLC ....D....... 714 938-1111
  400 N State College Blvd Orange (92868) *(P-9859)*
Hitachi, Santa Clara Also Called: Hitachi America Ltd *(P-5839)*
Hitachi America Ltd (HQ)..C....... 914 332-5800
  2535 Augustine Dr Santa Clara (95054) *(P-5839)*
Hitachi Energy USA Inc ....D....... 415 527-2850
  60 Spear St San Francisco (94105) *(P-12223)*
Hitachi High-Tech America Inc ....D....... 925 218-2800
  5960 Inglewood Dr Ste 200 Pleasanton (94588) *(P-5658)*
Hitachi Transport System (america) Ltd ....B....... 310 787-3420
  21061 S Wstn Ave Ste 300 Torrance (90501) *(P-4034)*

Hitachi Vantara LLC (HQ)..C...... 858 225-2095
2535 Augustine Dr Santa Clara (95054) *(P-11642)*

Hitt Contracting Inc ....B...... 424 326-1042
3733 Motor Ave Ste 200 Los Angeles (90034) *(P-937)*

Hiv Neural Behavioral Center ....D...... 619 543-5000
150 W Washington St La Jolla (92093) *(P-14774)*

Hive, The, San Francisco *Also Called: Castle Global Inc (P-11485)*

HM Electronics Inc (PA)..B...... 858 535-6000
2848 Whiptail Loop Carlsbad (92010) *(P-5659)*

Hmb Investors LLC ....D...... 415 474-5400
1075 California St San Francisco (94108) *(P-9860)*

HMC Architects, Ontario *Also Called: HMC Group (P-19477)*

HMC Assets LLC ....C...... 310 535-9293
2015 Manhattan Beach Blvd Ste 200 Redondo Beach (90278) *(P-8386)*

HMC Group (HQ) ....C...... 909 989-9979
3546 Concours Ontario (91764) *(P-19477)*

Hmclause Inc (DH)..C...... 800 320-4672
260 Cousteau Pl Ste 210 Davis (95618) *(P-132)*

Hmh Builders, Sacramento *Also Called: Swinerton Builders Hc (P-1036)*

Hmi Cardinal, Livermore *Also Called: Hoskin & Muir Inc (P-5167)*

Hmi Industrial Contractors, Rancho Cordova *Also Called: Hmi Industrial Contractors Inc (P-2248)*

Hmi Industrial Contractors Inc..................................D...... 916 386-2586
3899 Security Park Dr Rancho Cordova (95742) *(P-2248)*

HMS, Vista *Also Called: HMS Construction Inc (P-19252)*

HMS Construction Inc (PA)..D...... 760 727-9808
2885 Scott St Vista (92081) *(P-19252)*

Hmt Electric Inc ....D...... 858 458-9771
2340 Meyers Ave Escondido (92029) *(P-1749)*

Hntb Corporation ....D...... 619 684-6586
401 B St Ste 510 San Diego (92101) *(P-19253)*

Hntb Corporation ....D...... 909 727-5600
3633 Inland Empire Blvd Ontario (91764) *(P-19254)*

Hntb Corporation ....C...... 408 451-7300
1732 N 1st St Ste 400 San Jose (95112) *(P-19255)*

Hntb Corporation ....C...... 714 460-1600
6 Hutton Centre Dr Ste 500 Santa Ana (92707) *(P-19256)*

Hntb Corporation ....C...... 510 208-4599
2101 Webster St Oakland (94612) *(P-19257)*

Hntb Gerwick Water Solutions ....C...... 714 460-1600
200 Sandpointe Ave Santa Ana (92707) *(P-19258)*

Hoag Clinic ....B...... 949 764-1888
1 Hoag Dr Newport Beach (92663) *(P-16128)*

HOAG CORPORATE HEALTH, Newport Beach *Also Called: Hoag Clinic (P-16128)*

Hoag Family Cancer Institute ....C...... 949 764-7777
1190 Baker St Costa Mesa (92626) *(P-16129)*

Hoag Hospital Foundation (HQ)..D...... 949 764-7217
330 Placentia Ave Ste 100 Newport Beach (92663) *(P-16130)*

Hoag Hospital Irvine ....D...... 949 764-4624
16200 Sand Canyon Ave Irvine (92618) *(P-16131)*

Hoag Memorial Hospital Presbt (PA)..A...... 949 764-4624
1 Hoag Dr Newport Beach (92663) *(P-16132)*

Hoag Orthopedic Institute LLC ....B...... 949 515-0708
22 Corporate Plaza Dr Ste 150 Newport Beach (92660) *(P-16133)*

Hoag Orthpd Inst Srgery Ctr -, Newport Beach *Also Called: Hoag Orthopedic Institute LLC (P-16133)*

Hob Entertainment LLC ....C...... 714 520-2310
400 W Disney Way Ste 337 Anaheim (92802) *(P-14084)*

Hob Entertainment LLC ....D...... 619 299-2583
1055 5th Ave San Diego (92101) *(P-14085)*

Hob Entertainment LLC (DH)..C...... 323 769-4600
7060 Hollywood Blvd Los Angeles (90028) *(P-14086)*

Hochiki, Buena Park *Also Called: Hochiki America Corporation (P-5565)*

Hochiki America Corporation (HQ)..D...... 714 522-2246
7051 Village Dr Ste 100 Buena Park (90621) *(P-5565)*

Hoehn Company Inc ....D...... 760 438-1818
5454 Paseo Del Norte Carlsbad (92008) *(P-7233)*

Hoehn Honda, Carlsbad *Also Called: Hoehn Company Inc (P-7233)*

Hoem & Associates Inc ....C...... 650 871-5194
951 Linden Ave South San Francisco (94080) *(P-2033)*

Hoffman Hospice, Bakersfield *Also Called: Hoffmann Hospice of Valley Inc (P-15763)*

Hoffman Medical Research Ctr, Los Angeles *Also Called: Keck School (P-16202)*

Hoffmann Hospice of Valley Inc ....D...... 661 410-1010
4325 Buena Vista Rd Bakersfield (93311) *(P-15763)*

Hogan Mfg Inc (PA)..C...... 209 838-7323
1638 Main St Escalon (95320) *(P-3108)*

Hok, Los Angeles *Also Called: Hok Group Inc (P-19478)*

Hok Group Inc ....D...... 310 838-9555
757 S Alameda St Los Angeles (90021) *(P-19478)*

Hokto Kinoko Company ....D...... 323 526-1155
130 S Myers St Los Angeles (90033) *(P-162)*

Holbrook Construction Inc ....D...... 714 523-1150
9814 Norwalk Blvd Ste 200 Santa Fe Springs (90670) *(P-938)*

Holiday Inn, Sacramento *Also Called: Atrium Finance I LP (P-9620)*

Holiday Inn, San Francisco *Also Called: Bhr Operations LLC (P-9649)*

Holiday Inn, Los Angeles *Also Called: Brisam Lax (de) LLC (P-9660)*

Holiday Inn, Carlsbad *Also Called: Carlsbad Properties Inc (P-9679)*

Holiday Inn, Ventura *Also Called: Harbor Island Hotel Group LP (P-9835)*

Holiday Inn, Simi Valley *Also Called: Holiday Inn Express (P-9861)*

Holiday Inn, Merced *Also Called: Holiday Inn Express Merced (P-9862)*

Holiday Inn, Willows *Also Called: Kumar Hotels Inc (P-9955)*

Holiday Inn, Union City *Also Called: Lotus Hotels - Union City LLC (P-9986)*

Holiday Inn, North Hollywood *Also Called: Marcus Hotels Inc (P-10000)*

Holiday Inn, Concord *Also Called: Montclair Hotels Mb LLC (P-10025)*

Holiday Inn, Bakersfield *Also Called: Newport Hospitality Group Inc (P-10043)*

Holiday Inn, Chula Vista *Also Called: Otay Hospitality Inc (P-10072)*

Holiday Inn, Newark *Also Called: Raps Hospitality Group (P-10140)*

Holiday Inn, Los Angeles *Also Called: Remington Hotel Corporation (P-10147)*

Holiday Inn, North Hollywood *Also Called: Rio Vista Development Co Inc (P-10160)*

Holiday Inn, Santa Ana *Also Called: S W K Properties LLC (P-10185)*

Holiday Inn, San Diego *Also Called: San Diego Farah Partners LP (P-10194)*

Holiday Inn, Los Angeles *Also Called: Seattle Arprt Hospitality LLC (P-10217)*

Holiday Inn, Redwood City *Also Called: Shiva Enterprises Inc (P-10231)*

Holiday Inn, Lebec *Also Called: Six Continents Hotels Inc (P-10243)*

Holiday Inn, San Francisco *Also Called: Six Continents Hotels Inc (P-10245)*

Holiday Inn, San Francisco *Also Called: Six Continents Hotels Inc (P-10246)*

Holiday Inn, Burlingame *Also Called: Trevi Partners A Calif LP (P-10320)*

Holiday Inn, Mill Valley *Also Called: Trevi Partners A Calif LP (P-10323)*

Holiday Inn, Buena Park *Also Called: Uniwell Corporation (P-10334)*

Holiday Inn, Torrance *Also Called: V Todays Inc (P-10338)*

Holiday Inn, Victorville *Also Called: Victorvlle Trsure Holdings LLC (P-10344)*

Holiday Inn, Los Angeles *Also Called: W&J Business Ventures LLC (P-10350)*

Holiday Inn, Long Beach *Also Called: Yhb Long Beach LLC (P-10387)*

Holiday Inn Express ....C...... 805 584-6006
2550 Erringer Rd Simi Valley (93065) *(P-9861)*

Holiday Inn Express, San Diego *Also Called: Win Time Ltd (P-10371)*

Holiday Inn Express Manteca, Manteca *Also Called: Drd Hospitality Inc (P-9765)*

Holiday Inn Express Merced ....D...... 209 383-0333
730 Motel Dr Merced (95341) *(P-9862)*

Holiday Inn Fresno Downtown, Fresno *Also Called: Brisan LLC (P-9661)*

Holiday Inn La Mirada, La Mirada *Also Called: Cha La Mirada LLC (P-9692)*

Holiday Inn Resort At Lodge, Big Bear Lake *Also Called: Pacific Snow Valley Resort LLC (P-10088)*

Holiday Manor Care Center, Upland *Also Called: Sela Healthcare Inc (P-15659)*

Holiday Manor Care Center, Canoga Park *Also Called: Sela Healthcare Inc (P-15660)*

Holiday Tree Farms Inc ....C...... 323 276-1900
329 Van Norman Rd Montebello (90640) *(P-569)*

Holistic Homecare, Clovis *Also Called: Well Being Senior Solutions (P-16974)*

Holland & Knight LLP ....D...... 213 896-2400
400 S Hope St Ste 800 Los Angeles (90071) *(P-17495)*

Hollandia Dairy Inc (PA)..C...... 760 744-3222
622 E Mission Rd San Marcos (92069) *(P-217)*

HOLLENBECK HOME FOR THE AGED, Newhall *Also Called: Hollenbeck Palms (P-18450)*

Hollenbeck Palms ....C...... 323 263-6195
24431 Lyons Ave Apt 336 Newhall (91321) *(P-18450)*

Holliday Trucking Inc (PA)..D...... 909 982-1553
1401 N Benson Ave Upland (91786) *(P-2710)*

ALPHABETIC SECTION — Home Depot USA Inc

Hollingshead Management, Los Angeles *Also Called: Proland Property Managment LLC (P-9145)*

Hollywood Bowl, Los Angeles *Also Called: Los Angeles Philharmonic Assn (P-14094)*

Hollywood Cmnty Hosp Hollywood, Los Angeles *Also Called: Hollywood Cmnty Hosp Med Ctr I (P-16134)*

Hollywood Cmnty Hosp Med Ctr I .... C....... 323 462-2271
6245 De Longpre Ave Los Angeles (90028) *(P-16134)*

Hollywood Medical Center LP .... A....... 213 413-3000
1300 N Vermont Ave Los Angeles (90027) *(P-16135)*

Hollywood Park Casino, Inglewood *Also Called: Century Gaming Management Inc (P-9690)*

Hollywood Park Casino Co Inc .... C....... 310 330-2800
3883 W Century Blvd Inglewood (90303) *(P-9863)*

Hollywood Partnership .... D....... 323 463-7171
5410 Hollywood Blvd Los Angeles (90027) *(P-9864)*

Hollywood Presbyterian Med Ctr, Los Angeles *Also Called: Hollywood Medical Center LP (P-16135)*

Hollywood Rntals Prod Svcs LLC (PA) .... D....... 818 407-7800
5300 Melrose Ave Los Angeles (90038) *(P-13939)*

Hollywood Roosevelt Hotel, Los Angeles *Also Called: Roosevelt Hotel LLC (P-10170)*

Hollywood Sports Park LLC .... D....... 562 867-9600
9030 Somerset Blvd Bellflower (90706) *(P-13317)*

Holman Family Counseling Inc (PA) .... D....... 818 704-1444
8511 Fallbrook Ave Ste 400 West Hills (91304) *(P-15285)*

Holman Group, The, West Hills *Also Called: Holman Family Counseling Inc (P-15285)*

Holmes & Narver Inc (HQ) .... C....... 714 567-2400
999 W Town And Country Rd Orange (92868) *(P-19259)*

Holmes Body Shop-Alhambra .... C....... 626 282-6173
1130 E Main St Alhambra (91801) *(P-13639)*

Holmes Body Shop-Alhambra Inc (PA) .... D....... 626 795-6447
466 Foothill Blvd La Canada Flintridge (91011) *(P-13640)*

Holt CA, Pleasant Grove *Also Called: Holt of California (P-5791)*

Holt of California (HQ) .... C....... 916 991-8200
7310 Pacific Ave Pleasant Grove (95668) *(P-5791)*

Holt of California .... C....... 916 373-4100
3850 Channel Dr West Sacramento (95691) *(P-5792)*

Holt of California .... C....... 209 466-6000
1521 W Charter Way Stockton (95206) *(P-5793)*

Holthouse Carlin Van Trigt LLP (PA) .... C....... 310 566-1900
11444 W Olympic Blvd Fl 11 Los Angeles (90064) *(P-19585)*

Holy Cross Cemetary, San Diego *Also Called: Roman Cthlic Bshp of San Diego (P-9171)*

Holy Cross Renal Center, Mission Hills *Also Called: Hemodialysis Inc (P-16987)*

Holy Sepulcher Cemetery, Orange *Also Called: Roman Cthlic Diocese of Orange (P-9291)*

Holzheus El Rancho Market Inc .... D....... 805 688-4300
2886 Mission Dr Solvang (93463) *(P-7144)*

Home Away Inc .... D....... 559 642-3121
54432 Road 432 Bass Lake (93604) *(P-9865)*

Home Carpet Investment Inc (PA) .... D....... 619 262-8040
730 Design Ct Ste 401 Chula Vista (91911) *(P-2034)*

Home Comfort USA, Anaheim *Also Called: Ken Starr Inc (P-1476)*

Home Depot USA Inc .... C....... 951 361-1235
11650 Venture Dr Jurupa Valley (91752) *(P-3715)*

Home Depot USA Inc .... C....... 909 483-8115
8535 Oakwood Pl Ste B Rancho Cucamonga (91730) *(P-3716)*

Home Depot USA Inc .... C....... 858 859-4143
13250 Gregg St Ste A2 Poway (92064) *(P-3717)*

Home Depot USA Inc .... D....... 714 522-8651
14659 Alondra Blvd Ste B La Mirada (90638) *(P-3718)*

Home Depot USA Inc .... C....... 209 855-7000
1400 E Pescadero Ave Tracy (95304) *(P-3719)*

Home Depot USA Inc .... C....... 916 726-0620
5859 Antelope Rd Sacramento (95842) *(P-6962)*

Home Depot USA Inc .... B....... 562 776-2200
7121 Firestone Blvd Downey (90241) *(P-6963)*

Home Depot USA Inc .... C....... 818 780-5448
16800 Roscoe Blvd Van Nuys (91406) *(P-6964)*

Home Depot USA Inc .... C....... 714 539-0319
10801 Garden Grove Blvd Garden Grove (92843) *(P-6965)*

Home Depot USA Inc .... C....... 951 358-1370
3323 Madison St Riverside (92504) *(P-6966)*

Home Depot USA Inc .... C....... 650 525-9743
2001 Chess Dr Foster City (94404) *(P-6967)*

Home Depot USA Inc .... C....... 916 787-0201
10001 Fairway Dr Roseville (95678) *(P-6968)*

Home Depot USA Inc .... C....... 714 259-1030
1750 E Edinger Ave Santa Ana (92705) *(P-6969)*

Home Depot USA Inc .... C....... 323 587-5520
3040 E Slauson Ave Huntington Park (90255) *(P-6970)*

Home Depot USA Inc .... C....... 310 677-1944
3363 W Century Blvd Inglewood (90303) *(P-6971)*

Home Depot USA Inc .... C....... 209 474-8285
5010 Feather River Dr Stockton (95219) *(P-6972)*

Home Depot USA Inc .... D....... 916 381-3181
8000 Folsom Blvd Sacramento (95826) *(P-6973)*

Home Depot USA Inc .... C....... 626 256-0580
1625 S Mountain Ave Monrovia (91016) *(P-6974)*

Home Depot USA Inc .... C....... 408 978-1099
635 W Capitol Expy San Jose (95136) *(P-6975)*

Home Depot USA Inc .... D....... 510 490-0191
43900 Ice House Ter Fremont (94538) *(P-6976)*

Home Depot USA Inc .... D....... 707 836-0377
6280 Hembree Ln Windsor (95492) *(P-6977)*

Home Depot USA Inc .... C....... 909 748-0505
1151 W Lugonia Ave Redlands (92374) *(P-6978)*

Home Depot USA Inc .... C....... 408 942-7301
1177 Great Mall Dr Milpitas (95035) *(P-6979)*

Home Depot USA Inc .... D....... 707 251-0162
225 Soscol Ave Napa (94559) *(P-6980)*

Home Depot USA Inc .... C....... 323 292-1397
1830 W Slauson Ave Los Angeles (90047) *(P-6981)*

Home Depot USA Inc .... C....... 510 887-8544
21787 Hesperian Blvd Hayward (94541) *(P-6982)*

Home Depot USA Inc .... C....... 805 389-9918
401 W Ventura Blvd Camarillo (93010) *(P-6983)*

Home Depot USA Inc .... D....... 949 831-3698
27401 La Paz Rd Laguna Niguel (92677) *(P-6984)*

Home Depot USA Inc .... C....... 925 243-1212
2500 Las Positas Rd Livermore (94551) *(P-6985)*

Home Depot USA Inc .... B....... 323 342-9495
2055 N Figueroa St Los Angeles (90065) *(P-6986)*

Home Depot USA Inc .... C....... 714 459-4909
625 S Placentia Ave Fullerton (92831) *(P-6987)*

Home Depot USA Inc .... C....... 559 431-9860
7150 N Abby St Fresno (93720) *(P-6988)*

Home Depot USA Inc .... C....... 562 272-8055
6400 Alondra Blvd Paramount (90723) *(P-6989)*

Home Depot USA Inc .... C....... 559 782-4611
750 S Jaye St Porterville (93257) *(P-6990)*

Home Depot USA Inc .... D....... 619 263-1533
355 Marketplace Ave San Diego (92113) *(P-6991)*

Home Depot USA Inc .... C....... 760 233-1285
1475 E Valley Pkwy Escondido (92027) *(P-6992)*

Home Depot USA Inc .... C....... 805 983-0653
401 W Esplanade Dr Oxnard (93036) *(P-6993)*

Home Depot USA Inc .... C....... 559 455-9124
4864 E Kings Canyon Rd Fresno (93727) *(P-6994)*

Home Depot USA Inc .... D....... 951 727-0324
6140 Hamner Ave Eastvale (91752) *(P-6995)*

Home Depot USA Inc .... C....... 760 375-4614
575 N China Lake Blvd Ridgecrest (93555) *(P-6996)*

Home Depot USA Inc .... D....... 510 245-9572
1625 Sycamore Ave Hercules (94547) *(P-6997)*

Home Depot USA Inc .... C....... 925 513-6060
5631 Lone Tree Way Brentwood (94513) *(P-6998)*

Home Depot USA Inc .... D....... 951 485-5400
15975 Perris Blvd Moreno Valley (92551) *(P-6999)*

Home Depot USA Inc .... C....... 559 675-0127
2155 N Schnoor Ave Madera (93637) *(P-7000)*

Home Depot USA Inc .... D....... 714 921-1215
1095 N Pullman St Anaheim (92807) *(P-7001)*

Home Depot USA Inc .... C....... 408 779-9755
860 E Dunne Ave Morgan Hill (95037) *(P-7002)*

Home Depot USA Inc .... D....... 707 462-3009
350 N Orchard Ave Ukiah (95482) *(P-7003)*

Home Depot USA Inc

Home Depot USA Inc .... C 619 421-0639
1320 Eastlake Pkwy Chula Vista (91915) *(P-7004)*

Home Depot USA Inc .... C 626 813-7131
3200 Puente Ave Baldwin Park (91706) *(P-7005)*

Home Depot USA Inc .... D 619 401-6610
298 Fletcher Pkwy El Cajon (92020) *(P-7006)*

Home Depot USA Inc .... D 562 690-6006
600 S Harbor Blvd La Habra (90631) *(P-7007)*

Home Depot USA Inc .... C 310 835-7547
110 E Sepulveda Blvd Carson (90745) *(P-7008)*

Home Depot USA Inc .... C 562 789-4121
12322 Washington Blvd Whittier (90606) *(P-7009)*

Home Depot USA Inc .... C 714 966-8551
3500 W Macarthur Blvd Santa Ana (92704) *(P-7010)*

Home Depot USA Inc .... C 310 644-9600
14603 Ocean Gate Ave Hawthorne (90250) *(P-7011)*

Home Depot USA Inc .... C 714 538-9600
435 W Katella Ave Orange (92867) *(P-7012)*

Home Depot USA Inc .... C 951 698-1555
25100 Madison Ave Murrieta (92562) *(P-7013)*

Home Depot USA Inc .... C 209 491-0200
1617 N Carpenter Rd Modesto (95351) *(P-7014)*

Home Depot USA Inc .... C 951 808-0327
1355 E Ontario Ave Corona (92881) *(P-7015)*

Home Depot USA Inc .... C 949 646-4220
2300 Harbor Blvd Ste F Costa Mesa (92626) *(P-7016)*

Home Depot USA Inc .... C 949 609-0221
20021 Lake Forest Dr Lake Forest (92630) *(P-7017)*

Home Depot USA Inc .... C 760 955-2999
15150 Bear Valley Rd Victorville (92395) *(P-7018)*

Home Depot USA Inc .... B 323 727-9600
7015 Telegraph Rd Commerce (90040) *(P-7019)*

Home Depot USA Inc .... C 310 822-3330
12975 W Jefferson Blvd Los Angeles (90066) *(P-7020)*

Home Depot USA Inc .... D 949 364-1900
27952 Hillcrest Mission Viejo (92692) *(P-7021)*

Home Depot USA Inc .... C 818 365-7662
12960 Foothill Blvd Sylmar (91342) *(P-7022)*

Home Depot USA Inc .... C 661 252-7800
20642 Golden Triangle Rd Santa Clarita (91351) *(P-7023)*

Home Depot USA Inc .... C 619 589-2999
7530 Broadway Lemon Grove (91945) *(P-7024)*

Home Depot USA Inc .... D 562 595-9200
2450 Cherry Ave Long Beach (90755) *(P-7025)*

Home Depot USA Inc .... C 909 393-5205
14549 Ramona Ave Chino (91710) *(P-7026)*

Home Depot USA Inc .... D 415 458-8675
111 Shoreline Pkwy San Rafael (94901) *(P-7027)*

Home Depot USA Inc .... C 909 948-9200
11884 Foothill Blvd Rancho Cucamonga (91730) *(P-7028)*

Home Depot, The, Jurupa Valley *Also Called: Home Depot USA Inc (P-3715)*
Home Depot, The, Rancho Cucamonga *Also Called: Home Depot USA Inc (P-3716)*
Home Depot, The, Poway *Also Called: Home Depot USA Inc (P-3717)*
Home Depot, The, La Mirada *Also Called: Home Depot USA Inc (P-3718)*
Home Depot, The, Tracy *Also Called: Home Depot USA Inc (P-3719)*
Home Depot, The, Sacramento *Also Called: Home Depot USA Inc (P-6962)*
Home Depot, The, Downey *Also Called: Home Depot USA Inc (P-6963)*
Home Depot, The, Van Nuys *Also Called: Home Depot USA Inc (P-6964)*
Home Depot, The, Garden Grove *Also Called: Home Depot USA Inc (P-6965)*
Home Depot, The, Riverside *Also Called: Home Depot USA Inc (P-6966)*
Home Depot, The, Foster City *Also Called: Home Depot USA Inc (P-6967)*
Home Depot, The, Roseville *Also Called: Home Depot USA Inc (P-6968)*
Home Depot, The, Santa Ana *Also Called: Home Depot USA Inc (P-6969)*
Home Depot, The, Huntington Park *Also Called: Home Depot USA Inc (P-6970)*
Home Depot, The, Inglewood *Also Called: Home Depot USA Inc (P-6971)*
Home Depot, The, Stockton *Also Called: Home Depot USA Inc (P-6972)*
Home Depot, The, Sacramento *Also Called: Home Depot USA Inc (P-6973)*
Home Depot, The, Monrovia *Also Called: Home Depot USA Inc (P-6974)*
Home Depot, The, San Jose *Also Called: Home Depot USA Inc (P-6975)*
Home Depot, The, Fremont *Also Called: Home Depot USA Inc (P-6976)*
Home Depot, The, Windsor *Also Called: Home Depot USA Inc (P-6977)*
Home Depot, The, Redlands *Also Called: Home Depot USA Inc (P-6978)*
Home Depot, The, Milpitas *Also Called: Home Depot USA Inc (P-6979)*
Home Depot, The, Napa *Also Called: Home Depot USA Inc (P-6980)*
Home Depot, The, Los Angeles *Also Called: Home Depot USA Inc (P-6981)*
Home Depot, The, Hayward *Also Called: Home Depot USA Inc (P-6982)*
Home Depot, The, Camarillo *Also Called: Home Depot USA Inc (P-6983)*
Home Depot, The, Laguna Niguel *Also Called: Home Depot USA Inc (P-6984)*
Home Depot, The, Livermore *Also Called: Home Depot USA Inc (P-6985)*
Home Depot, The, Los Angeles *Also Called: Home Depot USA Inc (P-6986)*
Home Depot, The, Fullerton *Also Called: Home Depot USA Inc (P-6987)*
Home Depot, The, Fresno *Also Called: Home Depot USA Inc (P-6988)*
Home Depot, The, Paramount *Also Called: Home Depot USA Inc (P-6989)*
Home Depot, The, Porterville *Also Called: Home Depot USA Inc (P-6990)*
Home Depot, The, San Diego *Also Called: Home Depot USA Inc (P-6991)*
Home Depot, The, Escondido *Also Called: Home Depot USA Inc (P-6992)*
Home Depot, The, Oxnard *Also Called: Home Depot USA Inc (P-6993)*
Home Depot, The, Fresno *Also Called: Home Depot USA Inc (P-6994)*
Home Depot, The, Eastvale *Also Called: Home Depot USA Inc (P-6995)*
Home Depot, The, Ridgecrest *Also Called: Home Depot USA Inc (P-6996)*
Home Depot, The, Hercules *Also Called: Home Depot USA Inc (P-6997)*
Home Depot, The, Brentwood *Also Called: Home Depot USA Inc (P-6998)*
Home Depot, The, Moreno Valley *Also Called: Home Depot USA Inc (P-6999)*
Home Depot, The, Madera *Also Called: Home Depot USA Inc (P-7000)*
Home Depot, The, Anaheim *Also Called: Home Depot USA Inc (P-7001)*
Home Depot, The, Morgan Hill *Also Called: Home Depot USA Inc (P-7002)*
Home Depot, The, Ukiah *Also Called: Home Depot USA Inc (P-7003)*
Home Depot, The, Chula Vista *Also Called: Home Depot USA Inc (P-7004)*
Home Depot, The, Baldwin Park *Also Called: Home Depot USA Inc (P-7005)*
Home Depot, The, El Cajon *Also Called: Home Depot USA Inc (P-7006)*
Home Depot, The, La Habra *Also Called: Home Depot USA Inc (P-7007)*
Home Depot, The, Carson *Also Called: Home Depot USA Inc (P-7008)*
Home Depot, The, Whittier *Also Called: Home Depot USA Inc (P-7009)*
Home Depot, The, Santa Ana *Also Called: Home Depot USA Inc (P-7010)*
Home Depot, The, Hawthorne *Also Called: Home Depot USA Inc (P-7011)*
Home Depot, The, Orange *Also Called: Home Depot USA Inc (P-7012)*
Home Depot, The, Murrieta *Also Called: Home Depot USA Inc (P-7013)*
Home Depot, The, Modesto *Also Called: Home Depot USA Inc (P-7014)*
Home Depot, The, Corona *Also Called: Home Depot USA Inc (P-7015)*
Home Depot, The, Costa Mesa *Also Called: Home Depot USA Inc (P-7016)*
Home Depot, The, Lake Forest *Also Called: Home Depot USA Inc (P-7017)*
Home Depot, The, Victorville *Also Called: Home Depot USA Inc (P-7018)*
Home Depot, The, Commerce *Also Called: Home Depot USA Inc (P-7019)*
Home Depot, The, Los Angeles *Also Called: Home Depot USA Inc (P-7020)*
Home Depot, The, Mission Viejo *Also Called: Home Depot USA Inc (P-7021)*
Home Depot, The, Sylmar *Also Called: Home Depot USA Inc (P-7022)*
Home Depot, The, Santa Clarita *Also Called: Home Depot USA Inc (P-7023)*
Home Depot, The, Lemon Grove *Also Called: Home Depot USA Inc (P-7024)*
Home Depot, The, Long Beach *Also Called: Home Depot USA Inc (P-7025)*
Home Depot, The, Chino *Also Called: Home Depot USA Inc (P-7026)*
Home Depot, The, San Rafael *Also Called: Home Depot USA Inc (P-7027)*
Home Depot, The, Rancho Cucamonga *Also Called: Home Depot USA Inc (P-7028)*

Home Dlysis Thrapies San Diego .... D 619 422-0003
2060 Otay Lakes Rd Ste 120 Chula Vista (91915) *(P-16988)*

Home Entertainment Div, Los Angeles *Also Called: Fox Inc (P-4431)*

Home Express Delivery Svc LLC .... A 949 715-9844
25361 Commercentre Dr Ste 250 Lake Forest (92630) *(P-4035)*

Home Guiding Hands Corporation (PA) .... B 619 938-2850
1908 Friendship Dr El Cajon (92020) *(P-18451)*

Home Health Care MGT Inc .... D 530 343-0727
1398 Ridgewood Dr Chico (95973) *(P-16870)*

Home Helpers of North County, Escondido *Also Called: Cox Enterprises LLC (P-16850)*

Home Instead Senior Care, Victorville *Also Called: Branlyn Prominence Inc (P-16825)*

ALPHABETIC SECTION

Home Instead Senior Care, Rancho Cucamonga *Also Called: Branlyn Prominence Inc* *(P-16826)*

Home Instead Senior Care, Long Beach *Also Called: Coastal Cmnty Senior Care LLC* *(P-16841)*

Home Instead Senior Care, Fresno *Also Called: P K B Investments Inc* *(P-20498)*

Home Junction Inc .... D....... 858 777-9533
1 Venture Ste 300 Irvine (92618) *(P-11643)*

Home Mrtg Aliance Corp Hmac (PA).................................... B....... 800 900-7040
4 Hutton Centre Dr Ste 500 Santa Ana (92707) *(P-7980)*

Home of Peace Cemetery, Colma *Also Called: Congregation Emanu-El (P-9284)*

Home Organizers Inc .... A....... 562 699-9945
3860 Capitol Ave City Of Industry (90601) *(P-2002)*

Home Security and HM Ctrl Svcs, Anaheim *Also Called: ADT LLC (P-13087)*

Home Street Operations LLC .... D....... 949 449-2500
114 Pacifica Ste 230 Irvine (92618) *(P-15764)*

Home2 Sites By Hilton Temecula, Temecula *Also Called: Temecula Hhg Hotel Dev LP* *(P-10307)*

Homebound Technologies Inc .... B....... 415 854-3296
1 Letterman Dr Ste 3500 San Francisco (94129) *(P-10551)*

Homeboy Bakery, Los Angeles *Also Called: Homeboy Industries (P-18003)*

Homeboy Industries (PA)... B....... 323 526-1254
130 Bruno St Los Angeles (90012) *(P-18003)*

Homebridge Inc .... B....... 415 255-2079
1035 Market St Ste L1 San Francisco (94103) *(P-18004)*

Homebridge Financial Svcs Inc .... A....... 818 981-0606
15301 Ventura Blvd Ste D300 Sherman Oaks (91403) *(P-8044)*

Homeenergy Inc .... D....... 707 200-3758
2930 Domingo Ave Berkeley (94705) *(P-1457)*

Homefinance.com, La Jolla *Also Called: Prospect Financial Group Inc (P-8217)*

Homefrst Svcs Santa Clara Cnty .... C....... 408 539-2100
507 Valley Way Milpitas (95035) *(P-18005)*

Homegaincom Inc .... D....... 925 983-2852
12667 Alcosta Blvd Ste 200 San Ramon (94583) *(P-9040)*

Homeguard Incorporated (PA).. D....... 855 331-1900
510 Madera Ave San Jose (95112) *(P-10837)*

Homeland Housewares LLC .... D....... 310 996-7200
10900 Wilshire Blvd Ste 900 Los Angeles (90024) *(P-5607)*

Homelegance Inc (PA)... D....... 510 933-6888
48200 Fremont Blvd Fremont (94538) *(P-5090)*

Homeowners Association, Helendale *Also Called: Silver Lakes Association (P-18911)*

Homeq Servicing Corporation (DH).................................... A....... 916 339-6192
4837 Watt Ave North Highlands (95660) *(P-7981)*

Homes Media Solutions LLC .... D....... 888 510-8795
5510 Morehouse Dr Ste 100 San Diego (92121) *(P-10624)*

Homesite Svcs Inc A Cal Corp (PA)..................................... D....... 925 237-3050
6611 Preston Ave Ste E Livermore (94551) *(P-7432)*

Homestar Systems Inc .... D....... 415 323-4008
251 Post St Ste 302 San Francisco (94108) *(P-12803)*

Homestead of Fair Oaks, Fair Oaks *Also Called: Eskaton Properties Inc (P-18427)*

Homestore Apartments & Rentals, Santa Clara *Also Called: Move Sales Inc (P-9105)*

Homewatch Caregivers, Carlsbad *Also Called: North Coast Home Care Inc (P-16900)*

Homewatch Caregivers, Los Angeles *Also Called: South Bay Senior Services Inc (P-16930)*

Homewood Care Center, San Jose *Also Called: Ocadian Care Centers LLC (P-15608)*

Homewood Stes Hltn Sfo Arprt, Brisbane *Also Called: Sage Hospitality Resources LLC* *(P-10189)*

Homewood Suites, Oakland *Also Called: Homewood Suites Management LLC (P-9866)*

Homewood Suites, Palm Desert *Also Called: Palm Desert Hospitality LLC (P-10095)*

Homewood Suites, San Diego *Also Called: SD Hotel Circle LLC (P-10212)*

Homewood Suites Management LLC .... D....... 510 663-2700
1103 Embarcadero Oakland (94606) *(P-9866)*

Homexpress Mortgage Corp .... C....... 714 944-3022
1936 E Deere Ave Ste 200 Santa Ana (92705) *(P-7982)*

Hon Hai Precision Industry, San Jose *Also Called: Nsg Technology Inc (P-13742)*

Honda, Torrance *Also Called: Honda R&D Americas LLC (P-19818)*

Honda R&D Americas LLC .... A....... 310 781-5500
1900 Harpers Way Torrance (90501) *(P-19818)*

Honda World Westminster .... C....... 714 890-8900
13600 Beach Blvd Westminster (92683) *(P-7234)*

Honey, Los Angeles *Also Called: Honey Science LLC (P-11644)*

Honey Science LLC .... C....... 949 795-1695
963 E 4th St Ste 100 Los Angeles (90013) *(P-11644)*

Honeydew Intimates, Chatsworth *Also Called: Paradise Lingerie Inc (P-6214)*

Honeymoon Real Estate LP .... D....... 310 277-5221
9400 W Olympic Blvd Beverly Hills (90212) *(P-9867)*

Honeyville Inc .... D....... 909 980-9500
11600 Dayton Dr Rancho Cucamonga (91730) *(P-3650)*

Honeywell Authorized Dealer, Fresno *Also Called: Linkus Enterprises LLC (P-1231)*

Honeywell Authorized Dealer, Riverside *Also Called: 20/20 Plumbing & Heating Inc (P-1327)*

Honeywell Authorized Dealer, Chatsworth *Also Called: All Tmperatures Controlled Inc* *(P-1346)*

Honeywell Authorized Dealer, San Diego *Also Called: Atlas Mechanical Inc (P-1367)*

HONEYWELL AUTHORIZED DEALER, Fullerton *Also Called: C & L Refrigeration Corp* *(P-1389)*

Honeywell Authorized Dealer, North Hollywood *Also Called: Circulating Air Inc (P-1397)*

Honeywell Authorized Dealer, Sacramento *Also Called: Clarke & Rush Mechanical Inc* *(P-1399)*

Honeywell Authorized Dealer, Anaheim *Also Called: Control Air Conditioning Corporation* *(P-1403)*

Honeywell Authorized Dealer, Santa Clara *Also Called: Envirnmntal Systems Inc Nthrn* *(P-1431)*

Honeywell Authorized Dealer, San Diego *Also Called: Greater San Diego AC Co Inc (P-1452)*

Honeywell Authorized Dealer, San Jose *Also Called: J & J Air Conditioning Inc (P-1470)*

Honeywell Authorized Dealer, Berkeley *Also Called: L J Kruse Co (P-1480)*

Honeywell Authorized Dealer, Corona *Also Called: LDI Mechanical Inc (P-1483)*

Honeywell Authorized Dealer, Corona *Also Called: Multi Mechanical Inc (P-1504)*

Honeywell Authorized Dealer, San Diego *Also Called: Pacific Rim Mech Contrs Inc (P-1523)*

Honeywell Authorized Dealer, Paramount *Also Called: Reliable Energy Management Inc* *(P-1547)*

Honeywell Authorized Dealer, Hollister *Also Called: San Benito Htg & Shtmtl Inc (P-1554)*

Honeywell Authorized Dealer, Santa Clarita *Also Called: Tri-Signal Integration Inc (P-1864)*

Honeywell Authorized Dealer, Rocklin *Also Called: Bmi Inc (P-2735)*

Honk Technologies Inc .... C....... 800 979-3162
2251 Barry Ave Los Angeles (90064) *(P-12579)*

Honor Rancho Station, Valencia *Also Called: Southern California Gas Co (P-4745)*

Honor Technology Inc (PA).. D....... 512 762-2195
400 S El Camino Real Ste 800 San Mateo (94402) *(P-11645)*

Hood & Strong LLP (PA).. D....... 415 781-0793
275 Battery St Ste 900 San Francisco (94111) *(P-19586)*

Hood Packaging Corporation .... C....... 559 585-2040
10801 Iona Ave Hanford (93230) *(P-6915)*

Hoopa Modular Building Entp .... C....... 530 625-4551
151 Cal Pac Rd Hoopa (95546) *(P-792)*

Hoover Containers Inc .... D....... 909 444-9454
19570 San Jose Ave City Of Industry (91748) *(P-2517)*

Hoover Institution .... C....... 650 723-1754
434 Galvez Mall Stanford (94305) *(P-13318)*

Hope Bancorp Inc (PA).. D....... 213 639-1700
3200 Wilshire Blvd Ste 1400 Los Angeles (90010) *(P-7628)*

Hope Contra Costa, Pittsburg *Also Called: Lincoln Child Center Inc (P-18472)*

Hope Cooperative, Sacramento *Also Called: Tlcs Inc (P-18151)*

Hope Family Wines .... D....... 805 238-6979
4280 Second Wind Way Paso Robles (93446) *(P-6799)*

Hope Hospice Inc .... B....... 925 829-8770
6377 Clark Ave Ste 100 Dublin (94568) *(P-10392)*

Hope Hse For Mltple Hndcpped I (PA)................................. D....... 626 443-1313
4215 Peck Rd El Monte (91732) *(P-18452)*

Hopkins & Carley A Law Corp (PA)..................................... D....... 408 286-9800
70 S 1st St San Jose (95113) *(P-17496)*

Hopland Band Pomo Indians Inc .... C....... 707 744-1395
13101 Nokomis Rd Hopland (95449) *(P-14534)*

Hopland Band Pomo Indians Inc (PA)................................. D....... 707 472-2100
3000 Shanel Rd Hopland (95449) *(P-19089)*

Horiba Automotive Test Systems, Irvine *Also Called: Horiba Instruments Inc (P-3030)*

Horiba Instruments Inc (DH).. C....... 949 250-4811
9755 Research Dr Irvine (92618) *(P-3030)*

Horiba Medical, Irvine *Also Called: Horibaabx Inc (P-5424)*

Horibaabx Inc .... C....... 949 453-0500
34 Bunsen Irvine (92618) *(P-5424)*

Horizon 3 Ai Inc — ALPHABETIC SECTION

Horizon 3 Ai Inc .... D 304 677-4102
683 Spruce St San Francisco (94118) *(P-11646)*

Horizon Beverage Company .... D 800 332-8358
8380 Pardee Dr Oakland (94621) *(P-6800)*

Horizon Communication, Irvine *Also Called: Horizon Communication Tech Inc (P-4537)*

Horizon Communication Tech Inc .... D 714 982-3900
13700 Alton Pkwy Ste 154-278 Irvine (92618) *(P-4537)*

Horizon Global Americas Inc .... D 559 266-9000
3181 S Willow Ave Ste 104 Fresno (93725) *(P-13715)*

Horizon Hobby LLC .... D 909 390-9595
4710 E Guasti Rd Ste A Ontario (91761) *(P-3090)*

Horizon Media Inc .... B 310 282-0909
1888 Century Park E Ste 700 Los Angeles (90067) *(P-10625)*

HORIZON MEDIA, INC., Los Angeles *Also Called: Horizon Media Inc (P-10625)*

Horizon Solar Power, Hemet *Also Called: Lpsh Holdings Inc (P-1491)*

Horizon Solar Power, Hemet *Also Called: Lpsh Holdings Inc (P-1492)*

Horizon West, Monterey *Also Called: Monterey Pines Sklld Nursg Fac (P-15591)*

Horizon West Healthcare Inc (HQ) .... D 916 624-6230
4020 Sierra College Blvd Ste 190 Rocklin (95677) *(P-15517)*

Horizon West Healthcare Inc .... D 916 786-3173
1015 Madden Ln Ofc Roseville (95661) *(P-15857)*

Hornblower Cruisers and Events, Newport Beach *Also Called: Hornblower Yachts LLC (P-3935)*

Hornblower Cruises & Events, San Diego *Also Called: Hornblower Yachts LLC (P-3808)*

Hornblower Group Inc (PA) .... B 415 635-2210
Pier 3 The Embarcadero San Francisco (94111) *(P-3933)*

Hornblower Yachts LLC .... D 619 686-8700
2825 5th Ave San Diego (92103) *(P-3808)*

Hornblower Yachts LLC (PA) .... C 415 424-4309
Pier 3 The Embarcadero San Francisco (94111) *(P-3934)*

Hornblower Yachts LLC .... A 949 650-2412
2527 W Coast Hwy Newport Beach (92663) *(P-3935)*

Horrigan Cole Enterprises, Murrieta *Also Called: National Mentor Holdings Inc (P-18492)*

Horrigan Enterprises Inc .... C 909 481-9663
7945 Cartilla Ave Rancho Cucamonga (91730) *(P-18006)*

Horsemen Inc .... D 714 847-4243
16911 Algonquin St Huntington Beach (92649) *(P-12988)*

Horton Grand Hotel, San Diego *Also Called: Historical Properties Inc (P-9858)*

Hortonworks, Santa Clara *Also Called: Hortonworks Inc (P-12224)*

Hortonworks Inc (DH) .... A 408 916-4121
5470 Great America Pkwy Santa Clara (95054) *(P-12224)*

Hoskin & Muir Inc .... D 925 373-1135
6611 Preston Ave Ste B Livermore (94551) *(P-5167)*

Hospice and Palliative Care .... D 925 945-8924
2849 Miranda Ave Alamo (94507) *(P-15765)*

HOSPICE CARING PROJECT, Scotts Valley *Also Called: Hospice of Santa Cruz County (P-16871)*

Hospice Caring Project, Watsonville *Also Called: Hospice of Santa Cruz County (P-16872)*

Hospice of Marin, Larkspur *Also Called: By The Bay Health (P-16831)*

Hospice of San Joaquin .... D 209 957-3888
3888 Pacific Ave Stockton (95204) *(P-15518)*

Hospice of Santa Cruz County (PA) .... C 831 430-3000
940 Disc Dr Scotts Valley (95066) *(P-16871)*

Hospice of Santa Cruz County .... D 831 430-3000
65 Neilson St Ste 121 Watsonville (95076) *(P-16872)*

Hospice of The East Bay, Alamo *Also Called: Hospice and Palliative Care (P-15765)*

Hospital Loading Dock, Fresno *Also Called: Fresno Cmnty Hosp & Med Ctr (P-16097)*

Hospital of Barstow Inc (DH) .... D 760 256-1761
820 E Mountain View St Barstow (92311) *(P-16136)*

Hospital of Community .... C 831 649-7700
2 Upper Ragsdale Dr Ste D100 Monterey (93940) *(P-16137)*

Hospitality Bennett Group LLC .... C 916 750-5150
1595 Eureka Rd Roseville (95661) *(P-18749)*

Hospitller Order of St John Go .... B 323 731-0641
2468 S St Andrews Pl Los Angeles (90018) *(P-19020)*

Host Healthcare Inc .... A 858 999-3579
4225 Executive Sq Ste 1500 La Jolla (92037) *(P-11290)*

Host Hotels & Resorts LP .... D 760 341-2211
74855 Country Club Dr Palm Desert (92260) *(P-9868)*

Hot Dogger Tours Inc .... C 714 988-4088
105 Gemini Ave Brea (92821) *(P-3318)*

Hot Line Construction Inc .... A 925 634-9333
9020 Brentwood Blvd Ste H Brentwood (94513) *(P-1750)*

Hotchkis Wiley Capitl MGT LLC (PA) .... C 213 430-1000
725 S Figueroa St Ste 3900 Los Angeles (90017) *(P-20110)*

Hotdoodle.com, Fremont *Also Called: Metabyte Inc (P-12837)*

Hotel, Mountain View *Also Called: Silicon Valley Club LLC (P-10237)*

Hotel Angeleno, Los Angeles *Also Called: Ascot Hotel LP (P-9616)*

Hotel Associates Palm Springs, La Quinta *Also Called: Msr Desert Resort LP (P-7498)*

Hotel Avante, Mountain View *Also Called: Joie De Vivre Hospitality LLC (P-9928)*

Hotel Bel-Air .... B 310 472-1211
701 Stone Canyon Rd Los Angeles (90077) *(P-9869)*

Hotel Bel-Air, Los Angeles *Also Called: Kava Holdings Inc (P-9936)*

Hotel Britton, San Francisco *Also Called: Reneson Hotels Inc (P-10154)*

Hotel California, San Francisco *Also Called: Jame Hotel Corporation (P-9918)*

Hotel Casa Del Mar, Santa Monica *Also Called: Et Whitehall Seascape LLC (P-9787)*

Hotel Circle Property LLC .... B 619 291-7131
500 Hotel Cir N San Diego (92108) *(P-9870)*

Hotel Company, El Segundo *Also Called: Uhg Lax Prop Llc (P-10331)*

Hotel Del Coronado, Coronado *Also Called: Ksl Resorts Hotel Del Coronado (P-9952)*

Hotel Del Sol, San Francisco *Also Called: Joie De Vivre Hospitality LLC (P-9926)*

Hotel Drisco, San Francisco *Also Called: Joie De Vivre Hospitality LLC (P-20124)*

Hotel Durant A Ltd Partnership .... C 510 845-8981
2600 Durant Ave Berkeley (94704) *(P-9871)*

Hotel Fullerton Anaheim, The, Fullerton *Also Called: Huoyen International Inc (P-9881)*

Hotel Hanford, The, Costa Mesa *Also Called: Hanford Hotels Inc (P-9834)*

Hotel Healdsburg LLC .... D 707 922-5399
317 Healdsburg Ave Healdsburg (95448) *(P-9872)*

Hotel Indigo Del Mar, Del Mar *Also Called: Pacifica Hosts Inc (P-10091)*

Hotel Indigo Los Angles Dwntwn, Los Angeles *Also Called: Metropolis Hotel MGT LLC (P-10017)*

Hotel June, The, Los Angeles *Also Called: Custom Hotel LLC (P-9734)*

Hotel Kabuki, San Francisco *Also Called: Bre/Japantown Owner LLC (P-9658)*

Hotel Managers Group, San Diego *Also Called: Hotel Managers Group Llc (P-20111)*

Hotel Managers Group Llc .... B 858 673-1534
11590 W Bernardo Ct Ste 211 San Diego (92127) *(P-20111)*

Hotel Marmonte, Santa Barbara *Also Called: H D G Associates (P-9830)*

Hotel Maya, Long Beach *Also Called: Queensbay Hotel LLC (P-10133)*

Hotel McInnis Marin LLC .... D 415 499-9222
101 Mcinnis Pkwy San Rafael (94903) *(P-9873)*

Hotel Moneco, San Francisco *Also Called: Kimpton Hotel & Rest Group LLC (P-9945)*

Hotel Nikko San Francisco Inc .... B 415 394-1111
222 Mason St San Francisco (94102) *(P-9874)*

Hotel Pacific, Monterey *Also Called: Columbia Hospitality Inc (P-9714)*

Hotel Palomar, Los Angeles *Also Called: Behringer Harvard Wilshire Blv (P-9637)*

Hotel Portofino, Redondo Beach *Also Called: Portofino Hotel Partners LP (P-10124)*

Hotel Republic San Diego, San Diego *Also Called: Rp Scs Wsd Hotel LLC (P-10178)*

Hotel Shattuck Plaza, Palo Alto *Also Called: Bpr Properties Berkeley LLC (P-8703)*

Hotel Solamar, San Diego *Also Called: Souldriver Lessee Inc (P-10255)*

Hotel Vitale, San Francisco *Also Called: Joie De Vivre Hospitality LLC (P-9922)*

Hotel Whitcomb .... D 415 626-8000
1231 Market St San Francisco (94103) *(P-9875)*

Hotta Liesenberg Saito LLP .... D 424 246-2000
970 W 190th St Ste 900 Torrance (90502) *(P-19587)*

Hotwire Inc .... C 415 343-8400
114 Sansome St Ste 400 San Francisco (94104) *(P-4294)*

Hotwire.com, San Francisco *Also Called: Hotwire Inc (P-4294)*

Houalla Enterprises Ltd .... D 949 515-4350
2610 Avon St Newport Beach (92663) *(P-939)*

Houdini Inc (PA) .... D 714 525-0325
4225 N Palm St Fullerton (92835) *(P-7557)*

Houlihan Lokey Inc (PA) .... B 310 788-5200
10250 Constellation Blvd Fl 5 Los Angeles (90067) *(P-8203)*

Hound Labs Inc .... D 408 893-2654
47000 Warm Springs Blvd Ste 290 Fremont (94539) *(P-19981)*

House Ear, Los Angeles *Also Called: House Ear Clinic Inc (P-14775)*

House Ear Clinic Inc (PA) .... D 213 483-9930
1245 Wilshire Blvd Ste 812 Los Angeles (90017) *(P-14775)*

House Modesto (PA) .... D 209 529-7346
1601 Coffee Rd Modesto (95355) *(P-19021)*

ALPHABETIC SECTION

House of Air LLC (PA) .... D....... 415 345-9675
  926 Mason St San Francisco (94129) *(P-14535)*
House of Blues, Los Angeles *Also Called: Hob Entertainment LLC (P-14086)*
House of Blues Anaheim, Anaheim *Also Called: Hob Entertainment LLC (P-14084)*
House of Blues Concerts Inc (DH) .... C....... 323 769-4977
  6255 W Sunset Blvd Fl 16 Los Angeles (90028) *(P-14087)*
House Research Institute .... C....... 213 353-7012
  2100 W 3rd St Ste 500 Los Angeles (90057) *(P-19885)*
House Seven Gables RE Inc .... D....... 714 282-0306
  5753 E Santa Ana Canyon Rd Ste P Anaheim (92807) *(P-9041)*
House Seven Gables RE Inc .... D....... 714 500-3300
  19440 Goldenwest St Huntington Beach (92648) *(P-9042)*
Housing Auth of The Cy Scrmnto, Sacramento *Also Called: Sacramnto Hsing Rdvlpment Agcy (P-9174)*
HOUSING AUTHORITY OF SACRAMENT, Sacramento *Also Called: Sacramento Housing Dev Corp (P-20843)*
Housing Matters .... D....... 831 458-6020
  115b Coral St Santa Cruz (95060) *(P-18007)*
Houwelings Camarillo Inc .... B....... 805 250-1600
  645 Laguna Rd Camarillo (93012) *(P-163)*
Howard Frank R Memorial Hosp, Willits *Also Called: Willits Hospital Inc (P-16629)*
Howard Hughes Medical Inst .... D....... 415 476-9668
  1550 4th St Rm 190 San Francisco (94143) *(P-19708)*
Howard Johnson, Anaheim *Also Called: Northwest Hotel Corporation (P-10051)*
Howard Johnson, National City *Also Called: Trigild International Inc (P-10327)*
Howard Roofing Company Inc .... D....... 909 622-5598
  245 N Mountain View Ave Pomona (91767) *(P-2069)*
Howards Mbs Inc .... D....... 202 570-4074
  23909 Sylvan St Woodland Hills (91367) *(P-8586)*
Howe Construction Co, Anaheim *Also Called: Burt L Howe & Associates (P-17396)*
Howe Electric Inc .... C....... 559 255-8992
  4682 E Olive Ave Fresno (93702) *(P-1751)*
Howe Electric Construction Inc .... C....... 559 255-8992
  4682 E Olive Ave Fresno (93702) *(P-1752)*
Howmet Fastening Systems, Simi Valley *Also Called: Howmet Globl Fstning Systems I (P-5904)*
Howmet Globl Fstning Systems I (HQ) .... C....... 805 426-2270
  3990a Heritage Oak Ct Simi Valley (93063) *(P-5904)*
Howmet Globl Fstning Systems I .... D....... 714 871-1550
  800 S State College Blvd Fullerton (92831) *(P-5905)*
Howmet Globl Fstning Systems I .... D....... 310 784-0700
  3000 Lomita Blvd Torrance (90505) *(P-5906)*
Hoya Optical Inc (PA) .... D....... 209 579-7739
  1400 Carpenter Ln Modesto (95351) *(P-3080)*
HP, Palo Alto *Also Called: HP Inc (P-2806)*
HP Capital LLC .... D....... 858 753-8486
  3111 Camino Del Rio N Ste 400 San Diego (92108) *(P-20405)*
HP Communications Inc (PA) .... D....... 951 572-1200
  13341 Temescal Canyon Rd Corona (92883) *(P-1216)*
HP Communications Inc .... D....... 951 579-8339
  15453 Olde Highway 80 El Cajon (92021) *(P-1217)*
HP Communications Inc .... D....... 951 457-0133
  1931 Mateo St Los Angeles (90021) *(P-1218)*
HP Inc (PA) .... A....... 650 857-1501
  1501 Page Mill Rd Palo Alto (94304) *(P-2806)*
HP Lq Investment LP .... C....... 760 564-4111
  49249 Eisenhower Dr La Quinta (92253) *(P-9876)*
HP Pavillion At San Jose, San Jose *Also Called: San Jose Sharks LLC (P-14158)*
Hpa-USA, Compton *Also Called: Hydroprocessing Associates LLC (P-13319)*
Hpe Enterprises LLC (HQ) .... C....... 650 857-5817
  6280 America Center Dr San Jose (95002) *(P-12225)*
Hpi Liquidations Inc .... C....... 858 391-7302
  13100 Danielson St Poway (92064) *(P-2518)*
Hpi Racing, Lake Forest *Also Called: SMC Products Inc (P-5997)*
HPM Incorporated .... D....... 510 353-0770
  850 Auburn Ct Fremont (94538) *(P-5312)*
Hpp Food Services, Wilmington *Also Called: Icpk Corporation (P-6258)*
Hps Mechanical Inc (PA) .... C....... 661 397-2121
  3100 E Belle Ter Bakersfield (93307) *(P-1458)*
Hqe Systems Inc .... D....... 800 967-3036
  27419 Via Industria Temecula (92590) *(P-20771)*

HR&a Advisors Inc .... D....... 310 581-0900
  700 S Flower St Ste 2995 Los Angeles (90017) *(P-20406)*
Hrc Consultants, Carlsbad *Also Called: Human Resource Capitl Cons Inc (P-20407)*
Hrd Aero Systems Inc (PA) .... C....... 661 295-0670
  25555 Avenue Stanford Valencia (91355) *(P-13774)*
Hrl Laboratories LLC .... A....... 310 317-5000
  3011 Malibu Canyon Rd Malibu (90265) *(P-19819)*
Hrn Services, Citrus Heights *Also Called: Accountble Hlthcare Stffing In (P-11073)*
Hrn Services, Campbell *Also Called: Accountble Hlthcare Stffing In (P-11074)*
Hrn Services Inc .... D....... 323 951-1450
  520 N Brand Blvd Ste 200 Glendale (91203) *(P-11151)*
Hronis Inc A California Corp (PA) .... C....... 661 725-2503
  10443 Hronis Rd Delano (93215) *(P-99)*
Hsa & Associates Inc .... D....... 626 521-9931
  1906 W Garvey Ave S Ste 200 West Covina (91790) *(P-19260)*
HSA BELL GARDENS LAUP, Bell *Also Called: Human Services Association (P-18008)*
Hsba, Dublin *Also Called: Health Svcs Bneft Admnstrtors (P-8461)*
Hsf Affiliates LLC (PA) .... D....... 949 794-7900
  18500 Von Karman Ave Ste 400 Irvine (92612) *(P-9043)*
Hsf Programme, San Francisco *Also Called: San Francisco Health Authority (P-18760)*
Hst Lessee Boston LLC .... D....... 619 692-2255
  1380 Harbor Island Dr San Diego (92101) *(P-9877)*
Hst Lessee Mission Hills LP .... D....... 760 328-5955
  71333 Dinah Shore Dr Rancho Mirage (92270) *(P-9878)*
Hsu Foundation, Arcata *Also Called: Humboldt State Univ Spnsred PR (P-20773)*
Htec Group Inc (PA) .... A....... 213 785-7824
  535 Mission St Fl 14 San Francisco (94105) *(P-11647)*
Htpghnl, Ontario *Also Called: Heat Transfer Pdts Group LLC (P-5769)*
Hub City, Fullerton *Also Called: Hub Group Los Angeles LLC (P-4036)*
Hub Distributing Inc (HQ) .... B....... 951 340-3149
  1260 Corona Pointe Ct Corona (92879) *(P-7402)*
Hub Group Los Angeles LLC .... D....... 714 449-6300
  1400 N Harbor Blvd # 300 Fullerton (92835) *(P-4036)*
Hub Group Trucking Inc .... B....... 909 770-8950
  13867 Valley Blvd Fontana (92335) *(P-3406)*
Hub Intrntional Insur Svcs Inc .... C....... 559 447-4600
  548 W Cromwell Ave Ste 101 Fresno (93711) *(P-8587)*
Hub Parking Technology USA Inc .... D....... 510 483-7275
  1631 Neptune Dr San Leandro (94577) *(P-2285)*
Hub Television Networks LLC .... D....... 818 531-3600
  2950 N Hollywood Way Ste 100 Burbank (91505) *(P-4441)*
Hub-Limited Workshop, Los Angeles *Also Called: Mid-Cities Association Inc (P-18235)*
Hubb Systems LLC .... D....... 510 865-9100
  12305 Crosthwaite Cir Poway (92064) *(P-12465)*
Hudson H Clude Cmplete Hlth Ct, Los Angeles *Also Called: County of Los Angeles (P-14710)*
Hudson Pacific Properties Inc (PA) .... D....... 310 445-5700
  11601 Wilshire Blvd Ste 1600 Los Angeles (90025) *(P-9469)*
Hueston Hennigan LLP .... D....... 213 788-4340
  523 W 6th St Ste 400 Los Angeles (90014) *(P-17497)*
Hughes Circuits Inc (PA) .... D....... 760 744-0300
  546 S Pacific St San Marcos (92078) *(P-2907)*
Hughes Research Laboratories, Malibu *Also Called: Hrl Laboratories LLC (P-19819)*
Huhtamaki Inc .... C....... 323 269-0151
  4209 Noakes St Commerce (90023) *(P-2664)*
Huhtamaki Inc .... D....... 916 688-4938
  8450 Gerber Rd Sacramento (95828) *(P-6916)*
Hulu LLC .... A....... 888 631-4858
  12312 W Olympic Blvd Los Angeles (90064) *(P-4295)*
Hulu LLC (HQ) .... C....... 310 571-4700
  2500 Broadway Ste 200 Santa Monica (90404) *(P-4296)*
Human Capital Select, LLC, San Diego *Also Called: Lotus Workforce LLC (P-20441)*
Human Resource Capitl Cons Inc .... C....... 760 518-8816
  6236 Paseo Colina Carlsbad (92009) *(P-20407)*
Human Resources Department, Covina *Also Called: Emanate Health Medical Center (P-16075)*
Human Resources Services, Los Angeles *Also Called: Los Angeles World Airports (P-3898)*
Human Services Association (PA) .... D....... 562 806-5400
  6800 Florence Ave Bell (90201) *(P-18008)*
Humanapi Inc .... D....... 650 542-9800
  951 Mariners Island Blvd Ste 300 San Mateo (94404) *(P-11648)*

Humane Inc

Humane Inc .... C...... 415 891-1900
969 Folsom St San Francisco (94107) *(P-12466)*

Humane Society Silicon Valley .... D...... 408 262-2133
901 Ames Ave Milpitas (95035) *(P-19090)*

Humangood (PA) .... C...... 602 906-4024
1900 Huntington Dr Duarte (91010) *(P-15858)*

HUMANGOOD, Duarte *Also Called: Bay Vista Senior Housing (P-8792)*

Humangood Norcal .... C...... 510 654-7172
110 41st St Ofc Oakland (94611) *(P-8820)*

Humangood Norcal (HQ) .... D...... 925 924-7100
1900 Huntington Dr Duarte (91010) *(P-8821)*

Humangood Norcal .... C...... 650 948-8291
373 Pine Ln Los Altos (94022) *(P-15859)*

Humangood Norcal .... C...... 661 834-0620
1401 New Stine Rd Bakersfield (93309) *(P-15860)*

Humangood Norcal .... C...... 909 793-1233
900 Salem Dr Redlands (92373) *(P-15861)*

Humangood Norcal .... C...... 408 357-1100
800 Blossom Hill Rd Ofc Los Gatos (95032) *(P-15862)*

Humangood Norcal .... C...... 559 439-4770
5555 N Fresno St Fresno (93710) *(P-18453)*

Humangood Norcal .... C...... 510 893-8897
401 Santa Clara Ave Apt 522 Oakland (94610) *(P-18454)*

Humangood Socal .... C...... 949 854-9500
19191 Harvard Ave Ofc Irvine (92612) *(P-8822)*

Humangood Socal .... C...... 818 244-7219
1230 E Windsor Rd Ofc Glendale (91205) *(P-8823)*

Humangood Socal .... C...... 626 357-1632
1763 Royal Oaks Dr Ofc Duarte (91010) *(P-8824)*

Humangood Socal .... C...... 858 454-4201
7450 Olivetas Ave Ofc La Jolla (92037) *(P-18455)*

Humangood Socal .... C...... 626 359-8141
802 Buena Vista St Duarte (91010) *(P-18456)*

Humangood Socal .... C...... 760 747-4306
710 W 13th Ave Escondido (92025) *(P-18457)*

Humano LLC .... D...... 844 448-6266
4231 Balboa Ave San Diego (92117) *(P-20772)*

Humboldt Bay Fire Jint Pwers A .... D...... 707 441-4000
533 C St Eureka (95501) *(P-18710)*

Humboldt Cmnty Access Rsrce CT .... D...... 707 443-7077
1707 E St Ste 2 Eureka (95501) *(P-18009)*

Humboldt Cmnty Access Rsrce CT .... D...... 707 441-8625
1001 Searles St Eureka (95501) *(P-18010)*

Humboldt Snior Rsource Ctr Inc (PA) .... D...... 707 443-9747
1910 California St Eureka (95501) *(P-18011)*

Humboldt State Univ Spnsred PR .... D...... 707 826-4189
1 Harpst St Rm 427 Arcata (95521) *(P-20773)*

Humnit Hotel At Lax LLC .... D...... 424 702-1234
6225 W Century Blvd Los Angeles (90045) *(P-9879)*

Humphrey Plumbing Inc .... D...... 209 634-4626
880 S Kilroy Rd Turlock (95380) *(P-1459)*

Hungry Heart Media Inc .... C...... 323 951-0010
5450 W Washington Blvd Los Angeles (90016) *(P-13855)*

Hunnington Dialysis Center, Pasadena *Also Called: Hemodialysis Inc (P-3052)*

Hunsaker & Assoc Irvine Inc .... B...... 951 352-7200
2900 Adams St Ste A15 Riverside (92504) *(P-19261)*

Hunsaker & Assoc Irvine Inc (PA) .... D...... 949 583-1010
3 Hughes Irvine (92618) *(P-19262)*

Hunsaker & Associates, Irvine *Also Called: Hunsaker & Assoc Irvine Inc (P-19262)*

Hunt Capital Partners Tax Crdt .... D...... 818 380-6100
15910 Ventura Blvd Ste 1100 Encino (91436) *(P-9375)*

Hunt Enterprises Inc .... D...... 310 530-3733
23200 Western Ave Ofc Harbor City (90710) *(P-8825)*

Hunt Enterprises Inc .... D...... 310 325-1496
2270 Sepulveda Blvd Apt 50 Torrance (90501) *(P-9044)*

Hunter, San Marcos *Also Called: Hunter Industries Incorporated (P-4989)*

Hunter Dodge Chrysler Jeep Ram, Lancaster *Also Called: H W Hunter Inc (P-7225)*

Hunter Easterday Corporation .... C...... 714 238-3400
1475 N Hundley St Anaheim (92806) *(P-10908)*

Hunter Industries Incorporated (PA) .... C...... 760 744-5240
1940 Diamond St San Marcos (92078) *(P-4989)*

Hunter Laboratories Inc .... C...... 408 341-8600
2605 Winchester Blvd Campbell (95008) *(P-16726)*

Huntington Bch Senior Hsing LP .... C...... 714 842-4006
18765 Florida St Huntington Beach (92648) *(P-8826)*

Huntington Beach Ford, Huntington Beach *Also Called: York Enterprises South Inc (P-7336)*

Huntington Beach Hospital, Huntington Beach *Also Called: Prime Hlthcare Hntngton Bch LL (P-16336)*

Huntington Beach Union High .... C...... 714 478-7684
7180 Yorktown Ave Huntington Beach (92648) *(P-11152)*

Huntington Care LLC .... C...... 877 405-6990
3452 E Foothill Blvd Ste 760 Pasadena (91107) *(P-16873)*

Huntington Extended Care Ctr, Pasadena *Also Called: Pasadena Hospital Assn Ltd (P-15621)*

Huntington Gardens, Huntington Beach *Also Called: Huntington Bch Senior Hsing LP (P-8826)*

Huntington Home Care, Pasadena *Also Called: Huntington Care LLC (P-16873)*

Huntington Hotel Company .... D...... 858 756-1131
5951 Linea Del Cielo Rancho Santa Fe (92067) *(P-9880)*

Huntington Lib Art Cllctons BT .... B...... 626 405-2100
1151 Oxford Rd San Marino (91108) *(P-17791)*

Huntington Medical Foundation .... D...... 626 795-4210
10 Congress St Ste 208 Pasadena (91105) *(P-14776)*

Huntington Medical Foundation .... C...... 626 792-3141
65 N Madison Ave Ste 800 Pasadena (91101) *(P-16138)*

Huntington Memorial Hospital, Pasadena *Also Called: Pasadena Hospital Assn Ltd (P-16319)*

Huntington Memory Care Cmnty, Alhambra *Also Called: Silverado Senior Living Inc (P-15669)*

Huntington Park Nursing Center, Huntington Park *Also Called: Covenant Care California LLC (P-15402)*

Huntington Radiology .... D...... 562 904-1111
11525 Brookshire Ave # 11 Downey (90241) *(P-14777)*

Huntington Vly Healthcare Ctr, Huntington Beach *Also Called: Douglas Fir Holdings LLC (P-15426)*

Huntley Hotel Santa Monica Bch, Santa Monica *Also Called: Second Street Corporation (P-10218)*

Hunton Andrews Kurth LLP .... D...... 415 975-3700
50 California St Ste 1700 San Francisco (94111) *(P-17498)*

Huntsman Architectural Group (PA) .... D...... 415 394-1212
50 California St 7th Fl San Francisco (94111) *(P-19479)*

Huoyen International Inc .... D...... 714 635-9000
1500 S Raymond Ave Fullerton (92831) *(P-9881)*

Hurley, Costa Mesa *Also Called: Hurley International LLC (P-2455)*

Hurley Construction Inc .... D...... 916 446-7599
1801 I St Ste 200 Sacramento (95811) *(P-759)*

Hurley International LLC (PA) .... C...... 949 548-9375
3080 Bristol St Costa Mesa (92626) *(P-2455)*

Hussmann Corporation .... B...... 909 590-4910
13770 Ramona Ave Chino (91710) *(P-2842)*

Hustle Inc .... C...... 415 851-4878
548 Market St Pmb 19841 San Francisco (94104) *(P-11649)*

Hustler Casino, Gardena *Also Called: El Dorado Enterprises Inc (P-9776)*

Hutchins Healthcare Inc .... D...... 949 487-9500
27101 Puerta Real Ste 450 Mission Viejo (92691) *(P-14778)*

HV Randall Foods LLC .... C...... 323 261-6565
2900 Ayers Ave Vernon (90058) *(P-6495)*

Hvac Installation and Repair, Los Angeles *Also Called: Precise Air Systems Inc (P-1533)*

Hvantage Technologies Inc (PA) .... D...... 818 661-6301
22048 Sherman Way Ste 306 Canoga Park (91303) *(P-11650)*

Hvr Software Usa Inc .... D...... 415 489-3427
44 Montgomery St Ste 3 San Francisco (94104) *(P-12226)*

Hvsf Transition LLC .... C...... 415 477-1999
555 Mission St Ste 1400 San Francisco (94105) *(P-10626)*

Hwe Mechanical, Bakersfield *Also Called: Hills Wldg & Engrg Contr Inc (P-613)*

Hwood Group .... D...... 310 859-1011
9229 W Sunset Blvd Ste 305 West Hollywood (90069) *(P-5091)*

Hy-Lond Hlth Care Cnter-Merced, Merced *Also Called: Avalon Care Cen (P-15339)*

Hy-Lond Hlth Care Cntr-Modesto, Modesto *Also Called: Avalon Care Center - Modesto (P-15340)*

Hy-Tech Tile Inc .... C...... 951 788-0550
1130 Palmyrita Ave Ste 350 Riverside (92507) *(P-2035)*

Hyatt Carmel Highlands, Carmel *Also Called: Highlands Inn Inc (P-9848)*

ALPHABETIC SECTION

Hyatt Corp As Agt Brcp Hef Ht .... C...... 760 603-6851
   7100 Aviara Resort Dr Carlsbad (92011) *(P-9882)*
Hyatt Corporation .... C...... 323 656-1234
   8401 W Sunset Blvd Los Angeles (90069) *(P-9883)*
Hyatt Corporation .... D...... 650 347-1234
   1333 Bayshore Hwy Burlingame (94010) *(P-9884)*
Hyatt Corporation .... B...... 415 848-6050
   345 Stockton St San Francisco (94108) *(P-9885)*
Hyatt Corporation .... A...... 415 788-1234
   50 Drumm Street San Francisco (94111) *(P-9886)*
Hyatt Corporation .... B...... 562 432-0161
   200 S Pine Ave Long Beach (90802) *(P-9887)*
Hyatt Corporation .... C...... 650 452-1234
   55 S Mcdonnell Rd San Francisco (94128) *(P-9888)*
Hyatt Corporation .... D...... 831 372-1234
   1 Old Golf Course Rd Monterey (93940) *(P-9889)*
Hyatt Corporation .... D...... 949 975-1234
   17900 Jamboree Rd Irvine (92614) *(P-9890)*
Hyatt Corporation .... B...... 949 729-1234
   1107 Jamboree Rd Newport Beach (92660) *(P-9891)*
Hyatt Corporation .... A...... 415 788-1234
   5 Embarcadero Ctr San Francisco (94111) *(P-9892)*
Hyatt Corporation .... B...... 312 750-1234
   6225 W Century Blvd Los Angeles (90045) *(P-9893)*
Hyatt Corporation .... B...... 925 743-1882
   2323 San Ramon Valley Blvd San Ramon (94583) *(P-9894)*
Hyatt Corporation .... C...... 858 453-0018
   3777 La Jolla Village Dr San Diego (92122) *(P-9895)*
Hyatt Corporation .... A...... 760 341-1000
   44600 Indian Wells Ln Indian Wells (92210) *(P-9896)*
Hyatt Corporation .... C...... 619 232-1234
   1 Market Pl San Diego (92101) *(P-9897)*
Hyatt Corporation .... C...... 619 849-1234
   600 F St San Diego (92101) *(P-9898)*
Hyatt Equities LLC .... D...... 562 436-1047
   285 Bay St Long Beach (90802) *(P-9899)*
Hyatt Fshrmans Wharf San Frncs, San Francisco *Also Called: Chsp Trs Fisherman Wharf LLC (P-9698)*
Hyatt Grand Champion Resort, Indian Wells *Also Called: Hyatt Corporation (P-9896)*
Hyatt Hotel, Monterey *Also Called: Classic Rsdence Mgt Ltd Partnr (P-9706)*
Hyatt Hotel, Carmel *Also Called: Highlands Inn Investors II LP (P-9849)*
Hyatt Hotel, Carlsbad *Also Called: Hyatt Corp As Agt Brcp Hef Ht (P-9882)*
Hyatt Hotel, Los Angeles *Also Called: Hyatt Corporation (P-9883)*
Hyatt Hotel, San Francisco *Also Called: Hyatt Corporation (P-9886)*
Hyatt Hotel, Long Beach *Also Called: Hyatt Corporation (P-9887)*
Hyatt Hotel, San Francisco *Also Called: Hyatt Corporation (P-9888)*
Hyatt Hotel, Irvine *Also Called: Hyatt Corporation (P-9890)*
Hyatt Hotel, Newport Beach *Also Called: Hyatt Corporation (P-9891)*
Hyatt Hotel, Long Beach *Also Called: Hyatt Equities LLC (P-9899)*
Hyatt Hotel, Palm Springs *Also Called: Hyatt Hotels Management Corp (P-9900)*
Hyatt Hotel, Santa Clara *Also Called: Hyatt Regency Santa Clara (P-9902)*
Hyatt Hotel, Westlake Village *Also Called: Sky Court USA Inc (P-10247)*
Hyatt Hotels Management Corp .... D...... 760 322-9000
   285 N Palm Canyon Dr Palm Springs (92262) *(P-9900)*
Hyatt House San Ramon, San Ramon *Also Called: Hyatt Corporation (P-9894)*
Hyatt Hse Emryvll/San Frncsco, Emeryville *Also Called: Select Hotels Group LLC (P-10219)*
Hyatt Hse San Dg/Sorrento Mesa, San Diego *Also Called: Select Hotels Group LLC (P-10220)*
Hyatt Los Angeles Airport, Los Angeles *Also Called: Hyatt Corporation (P-9893)*
Hyatt Place San Jose/Downtown, San Jose *Also Called: West San Crlos Ht Partners LLC (P-10362)*
Hyatt Regency Century Plaza .... A...... 310 228-1234
   2025 Avenue Of The Stars Los Angeles (90067) *(P-9901)*
Hyatt Regency Lajolla, San Diego *Also Called: Hyatt Corporation (P-9895)*
Hyatt Regency Monterey, Monterey *Also Called: Hyatt Corporation (P-9889)*
Hyatt Regency Sacramento, Sacramento *Also Called: Capitol Regency LLC (P-9678)*
Hyatt Regency San Francisco Ht, San Francisco *Also Called: Hyatt Corporation (P-9892)*
Hyatt Regency Santa Clara .... D...... 408 200-1234
   5101 Great America Pkwy Santa Clara (95054) *(P-9902)*

Hyatt Rgency Suites Palm Sprng, Palm Springs *Also Called: Rbd Hotel Palm Springs LLC (P-10141)*
Hyatt Rgncy San Frncisco Arprt, Burlingame *Also Called: Cchh Burlingame LLC (P-9687)*
Hyatt Rgncy San Frncisco Arprt, Burlingame *Also Called: Hyatt Corporation (P-9884)*
Hyatt Westlake, Westlake Village *Also Called: Swvp Westlake LLC (P-10295)*
Hybrid Promotions, Cypress *Also Called: Hybrid Promotions LLC (P-6177)*
Hybrid Promotions LLC (PA) .... C...... 714 952-3866
   10700 Valley View St Cypress (90630) *(P-6177)*
Hyde & Company Inc .... D...... 559 741-3636
   3330 W Mineral King Ave Ste F Visalia (93291) *(P-9045)*
Hyde Pk Rehabilitation Ctr LLC .... D...... 323 753-1354
   6520 West Blvd Los Angeles (90043) *(P-15519)*
Hydratech LLC (HQ) .... D...... 559 233-0876
   453 Pollasky Ave Ste 106 Clovis (93612) *(P-13775)*
Hydrite Chemical Co .... C...... 559 651-3450
   1603 Clancy Ct Visalia (93291) *(P-6712)*
Hydro Tek, Redlands *Also Called: Hydro Tek Systems Inc (P-5943)*
Hydro Tek Systems Inc .... D...... 909 799-9222
   2353 Almond Ave Redlands (92374) *(P-5943)*
Hydro-Dig Inc .... D...... 714 772-9947
   700 E Sycamore St Anaheim (92805) *(P-439)*
Hydro-Pressure Systems, North Hollywood *Also Called: Woods Maintenance Services Inc (P-2335)*
Hydrochempsc, Bakersfield *Also Called: PSC Industrial Outsourcing LP (P-627)*
Hydrochempsc, San Ardo *Also Called: PSC Industrial Outsourcing LP (P-3419)*
Hydroprocessing Associates LLC .... D...... 310 667-6456
   19122 S Santa Fe Ave Compton (90221) *(P-13319)*
Hydrotech Construction Group, Newport Beach *Also Called: Citivest Inc (P-8935)*
Hykso Inc .... D...... 213 785-3372
   936 W 17th St Costa Mesa (92627) *(P-20408)*
Hyperbaric Technologies Inc .... D...... 619 336-2022
   3224 Hoover Ave National City (91950) *(P-3076)*
Hypercel Corporation .... D...... 661 310-1000
   28385 Constellation Rd Valencia (91355) *(P-5660)*
Hypergrid Inc .... D...... 650 316-5524
   425 Tasso St Palo Alto (94301) *(P-11651)*
Hyperloop One, Los Angeles *Also Called: Hyperloop Technologies Inc (P-4159)*
Hyperloop Technologies Inc .... C...... 213 800-3270
   777 S Alameda St Ste 400 Los Angeles (90021) *(P-4159)*
Hyro Ai Inc .... D...... 313 942-4560
   440 N Barranca Ave Covina (91723) *(P-11652)*
Hyundai ABS Funding LLC .... C...... 949 732-2697
   3161 Michelson Dr Irvine (92612) *(P-8093)*
Hyundai Amer Technical Ctr Inc .... C...... 734 337-2500
   101 Peters Canyon Rd Irvine (92606) *(P-19263)*
Hyundai Amer Technical Ctr Inc .... C...... 909 627-3525
   12610 E End Ave Chino (91710) *(P-19982)*
Hyundai America/Tech Center, Chino *Also Called: Hyundai Amer Technical Ctr Inc (P-19982)*
Hyundai Autoever America LLC .... B...... 714 965-3000
   10550 Talbert Ave 3rd Fl Fountain Valley (92708) *(P-12708)*
Hyundai Motor America (HQ) .... B...... 714 965-3000
   10550 Talbert Ave Fountain Valley (92708) *(P-5011)*
Hyundai Protection Plan Inc .... B...... 949 468-4000
   3161 Michelson Dr Ste 1900 Irvine (92612) *(P-7875)*
Hyve Solutions Corporation (HQ) .... C...... 855 869-6873
   44201 Nobel Dr Fremont (94538) *(P-12580)*
I A C, Irvine *Also Called: Irvine APT Communities LP (P-8834)*
I B S, Roseville *Also Called: Iptor Supply Chain Systems USA (P-11678)*
I Brands LLC .... C...... 424 336-5216
   2617 N Sepulveda Blvd Manhattan Beach (90266) *(P-5810)*
I C C, Fullerton *Also Called: Interntnal Cnnctors Cable Corp (P-2886)*
I C Class Components Corp (PA) .... D...... 310 539-5500
   23605 Telo Ave Torrance (90505) *(P-5661)*
I C S, San Rafael *Also Called: Integrated Community Services (P-18018)*
I C W, San Diego *Also Called: Insurance Company of West (P-8590)*
I Cypress Company (PA) .... C...... 831 647-7500
   1700 17-Mile Dr Pebble Beach (93953) *(P-9903)*
I D Property Corporation .... C...... 213 625-0100
   1001 Wilshire Blvd Ste 100 Los Angeles (90017) *(P-9046)*
I Did Smthing Good Tday Fndtio .... C...... 888 491-0054
   527 W 7th St Ste 926 Los Angeles (90014) *(P-18595)*

I E S — ALPHABETIC SECTION

I E S, Turlock Also Called: Independent Electric Sup Inc (P-5567)
I I D, Imperial Also Called: Imperial Irrigation District (P-4580)
I J S, San Dimas Also Called: Industrial Janitor Service (P-10910)
I Joah, Los Angeles Also Called: Misope U S A Inc (P-6209)
I M S Electonics Recycling, Poway Also Called: IMS Electronics Recycling Inc (P-4899)
I M T, Burbank Also Called: Integrated Media Tech Inc (P-12814)
I N C Builders Inc .... B...... 760 352-4200
  1560 Ocotillo Dr Ste L El Centro (92243) (P-11291)
I N G, Compton Also Called: Newport Apparel Corporation (P-6210)
I P S, Mentone Also Called: International Paving Svcs Inc (P-1121)
I Pwlc Inc .... D...... 760 630-0231
  408 Olive Ave Vista (92083) (P-440)
I S A Contracting Svcs Inc .... A...... 559 659-1080
  958 O St Firebaugh (93622) (P-250)
I S D, Los Angeles Also Called: IDS Real Estate Group (P-9047)
I S E, Poway Also Called: ISE Corporation (P-19715)
I T P, Burbank Also Called: Information Tech Partners Inc (P-12810)
I V C, Irvine Also Called: International Vitamin Corporat (P-2591)
I2c Inc .... B...... 650 593-5400
  100 Redwood Shores Pkwy Redwood City (94065) (P-5313)
IA, San Francisco Also Called: Interior Architects Inc (P-19480)
IA Lodging NAPA Solano Trs LLC .... C...... 707 253-8600
  3425 Solano Ave Napa (94558) (P-9904)
Iaba, Culver City Also Called: Institute For Applied Bhvior A (P-15290)
Iaba, Camarillo Also Called: Institute For Applied Bhvior A (P-15291)
IAC Search & Media Inc (HQ) .... C...... 510 985-7400
  555 12th St Ste 500 Oakland (94607) (P-12666)
Iap West Inc .... D...... 310 667-9720
  20036 S Via Baron Rancho Dominguez (90220) (P-5045)
Iatse Affl Prprty Crftsprson L .... C...... 818 769-2500
  12021 Riverside Dr North Hollywood (91607) (P-18780)
Ibackup.com, Calabasas Also Called: Idrive Inc (P-12805)
IBAM INC .... D...... 530 343-5678
  1293 E 1st Ave Chico (95926) (P-14207)
Ibaset Federal Services LLC (PA) .... D...... 949 598-5200
  27442 Portola Pkwy Ste 300 Foothill Ranch (92610) (P-11653)
Ibftech Inc .... D...... 424 217-8010
  343 Main St El Segundo (90245) (P-11153)
IBM, San Francisco Also Called: International Bus Mchs Corp (P-5248)
IBM, San Jose Also Called: International Bus Mchs Corp (P-11677)
IBM, San Jose Also Called: International Bus Mchs Corp (P-19712)
IBM Watson Health, San Diego Also Called: Merge Healthcare Solutions Inc (P-12487)
Ibuypower, City Of Industry Also Called: American Future Tech Corp (P-5270)
Ic Sensors Inc .... D...... 510 498-1570
  45738 Northport Loop W Fremont (94538) (P-2922)
Icann, Los Angeles Also Called: Internet Corp For Assgned Nmes (P-12471)
Icann Inc .... D...... 408 432-8818
  933 Berryessa Rd Ste 10 San Jose (95133) (P-11654)
Icann Pharmaceutical, San Jose Also Called: Icann Inc (P-11654)
Icare Private Duty Inc .... D...... 858 634-1012
  5473 Kearny Villa Rd Ste 110b San Diego (92123) (P-15520)
ICC, Riverside Also Called: Inland Cc Inc (P-2128)
Ice Center of San Jose, San Jose Also Called: San Jose Arena Management LLC (P-14561)
Ice Currency Services USA, Los Angeles Also Called: Lenlyn Ltd Which Will Do Bus I (P-7857)
Ice Mortgage Technology Inc (HQ) .... B...... 855 224-8572
  4420 Rosewood Dr Ste 500 Pleasanton (94588) (P-12227)
Icf Jones & Stokes Inc .... D...... 949 333-6600
  1 Ada Ste 100 Irvine (92618) (P-20409)
Icf Jones & Stokes Inc .... C...... 858 578-8964
  525 B St Ste 1700 San Diego (92101) (P-20774)
Icom, San Jose Also Called: Icom Mechanical Inc (P-1460)
Icom Mechanical Inc .... C...... 408 292-4968
  477 Burke St San Jose (95112) (P-1460)
Icon Design and Display Inc .... D...... 707 284-3400
  645 4th St Ste 212 Santa Rosa (95404) (P-13320)
Icon Media Direct Inc (PA) .... D...... 818 995-6400
  5910 Lemona Ave Van Nuys (91411) (P-10627)

Icon West Inc .... D...... 213 385-0027
  520 S La Fayette Park Pl Ste 503 Los Angeles (90057) (P-940)
Iconma LLC .... C...... 888 451-2519
  4701 Patrick Henry Dr Bldg 6 Santa Clara (95054) (P-11292)
Icpk Corporation .... D...... 310 830-8020
  1130 W C St Wilmington (90744) (P-6258)
Ics Integrated Comm Systems .... D...... 408 491-6000
  6680 Via Del Oro San Jose (95119) (P-1753)
Ictv .... D...... 408 931-9200
  333 W San Carlos St Ste 900 San Jose (95110) (P-12467)
Icw Group Holdings Inc (PA) .... C...... 858 350-2400
  15025 Innovation Dr San Diego (92128) (P-8387)
Icw Valencia LLC .... C...... 858 350-2600
  11455 El Camino Real Ste 200 San Diego (92130) (P-8725)
ID Analytics LLC .... C...... 858 312-6200
  10089 Willow Creek Rd Ste 120 San Diego (92131) (P-11655)
ID Tech Camps, Campbell Also Called: Internal Drive (P-10404)
Idc Technologies Inc (PA) .... C...... 408 376-0212
  920 Hillview Ct Ste 250 Milpitas (95035) (P-11154)
Idea Solutions Inc .... B...... 408 436-3800
  2099 Gateway Pl Ste 340 San Jose (95110) (P-12804)
Ideal Program Services Inc .... D...... 323 296-2255
  3970 W Martin Luther King Jr Blvd Los Angeles (90008) (P-11155)
Idealab (HQ) .... D...... 626 356-3654
  130 W Union St Pasadena (91103) (P-7235)
Idealab Holdings LLC (PA) .... A...... 626 585-6900
  130 W Union St Pasadena (91103) (P-9520)
Idec Corporation (HQ) .... D...... 408 747-0550
  1175 Elko Dr Sunnyvale (94089) (P-5662)
Identity Intlligence Group LLC .... C...... 626 522-7993
  43454 Business Park Dr Temecula (92590) (P-13125)
Ideo, San Francisco Also Called: Precision Ideo Inc (P-13428)
Ideo LP (PA) .... C...... 415 615-5000
  2525 16th St Ste 200 San Francisco (94103) (P-10811)
Ideoorg .... D...... 415 426-7080
  320 Florida St San Francisco (94110) (P-18870)
Idex Global Services Inc .... C...... 415 482-4242
  2301 Kerner Blvd Ste D San Rafael (94901) (P-1754)
Idiq, Temecula Also Called: Identity Intlligence Group LLC (P-13125)
Idirect Home Loans, San Diego Also Called: Iserve Residential Lending LLC (P-7985)
Idrive Inc .... D...... 818 594-5972
  26115 Mureau Rd Ste A Calabasas (91302) (P-12805)
IDS Inc .... D...... 866 297-5757
  20300 Ventura Blvd Ste 200 Woodland Hills (91364) (P-3936)
IDS Real Estate Group (PA) .... D...... 213 627-9937
  515 S Figueroa St Ste 1600 Los Angeles (90071) (P-9047)
IDS Technology, Woodland Hills Also Called: IDS Inc (P-3936)
Idsgt Foundation, Los Angeles Also Called: I Did Smthing Good Tday Fndtio (P-18595)
IEC, Commerce Also Called: Interstate Electric Co Inc (P-5380)
Iecp, Oxnard Also Called: Inclusive Edcatn Cmnty Prtnr I (P-17718)
Ieee Computer Society, Los Alamitos Also Called: Institute of Elec Elec Engners (P-18711)
Iehp, Rancho Cucamonga Also Called: Inland Empire Health Plan (P-8266)
Ies, San Diego Also Called: Ies Commercial Inc (P-1120)
Ies, Irvine Also Called: Ies Commercial Inc (P-20775)
Ies Commercial Inc .... C...... 858 210-4900
  6885 Flanders Dr Ste A San Diego (92121) (P-1120)
Ies Commercial Inc .... D...... 713 860-1500
  1633 Maria St Burbank (91504) (P-1755)
Ies Commercial Inc .... D...... 949 222-0320
  9211 Irvine Blvd Irvine (92618) (P-20775)
Ies Engineering, Bakersfield Also Called: Innovative Engrg Systems Inc (P-19269)
Iest Family Farms .... D...... 559 674-9417
  14576 Avenue 14 Madera (93637) (P-218)
If Live LLC (PA) .... D...... 323 957-6868
  2254 S Sepulveda Blvd Los Angeles (90064) (P-13856)
Igel Technology Corporation .... C...... 845 589-5900
  594 Howard St Ste 200 San Francisco (94105) (P-20635)
Igm Biosciences Inc .... B...... 650 965-7873
  325 E Middlefield Rd Mountain View (94043) (P-2589)
Ignite Health LLC (PA) .... D...... 949 861-3200
  7535 Irvine Center Dr Ste 200 Irvine (92618) (P-10628)

ALPHABETIC SECTION

Ignite Visibility LLC .... D 619 752-1955
   5060 Shoreham Pl Ste 260 San Diego (92122) *(P-10629)*

Ignited LLC (PA) .... C 310 773-3100
   111 Penn St El Segundo (90245) *(P-10630)*

Ignitenet, Irvine *Also Called: SMC Networks Inc (P-5350)*

Ignition Creative LLC .... C 310 315-6300
   1201 W 5th St Ste T1100 Los Angeles (90017) *(P-13857)*

Igo Medical Group A Med Corp (PA) .... D 858 455-7520
   9339 Genesee Ave Ste 220 San Diego (92121) *(P-14779)*

Ihealth Manufacturing Inc .... D 216 785-0107
   15715 Arrow Hwy Irwindale (91706) *(P-5425)*

Iheartcommunications Inc .... D 559 230-4300
   83 E Shaw Ave Ste 150 Fresno (93710) *(P-4386)*

Iherb LLC (PA) .... A 951 616-3600
   22780 Harley Knox Blvd Unit 101 Perris (92570) *(P-7161)*

Iherb House Brands, Perris *Also Called: Iherb LLC (P-7161)*

Ihg Management (maryland) LLC .... D 310 642-7500
   5985 W Century Blvd Los Angeles (90045) *(P-9905)*

Ihg Management (maryland) LLC .... D 213 688-7777
   900 Wilshire Blvd Los Angeles (90017) *(P-9906)*

Ihms (sf) LLC .... C 415 781-5555
   340 Stockton St San Francisco (94108) *(P-9907)*

IHSS Consortium, The, San Francisco *Also Called: Homebridge Inc (P-18004)*

Ikano Communications Inc (PA) .... D 801 924-0900
   9221 Corbin Ave Ste 260 Northridge (91324) *(P-12581)*

IKEA Purchasing Svcs US Inc .... C 818 841-3500
   600 N San Fernando Blvd Burbank (91502) *(P-20112)*

Ikes Landscape Inc .... D 530 758-1698
   2700 Tiber Ave Davis (95616) *(P-498)*

IL Fornaio (america) LLC .... C 714 752-7052
   16932 Valley View Ave Ste A La Mirada (90638) *(P-7487)*

Illume Agriculture LLC .... C 661 587-5198
   9100 Ming Ave Ste 200 Bakersfield (93311) *(P-375)*

Illumination Entertainment .... C 626 298-1879
   2043 Colorado Ave Santa Monica (90404) *(P-14088)*

Illumio Inc (PA) .... B 669 800-5000
   920 De Guigne Dr Sunnyvale (94085) *(P-11656)*

Ilovetocreate, Fresno *Also Called: Paisley Crafts LLC (P-5994)*

Ilwu Federal Credit Union .... D 310 834-6411
   3447 Atlantic Ave Long Beach (90807) *(P-7775)*

Im-Logstics An Ingram McRo Div, Irvine *Also Called: Ingram Micro Inc (P-5314)*

Image Business Forms, El Segundo *Also Called: Ibftech Inc (P-11153)*

Image IV Systems Inc (PA) .... D 818 841-0756
   512 S Varney St Burbank (91502) *(P-5246)*

Image Options (PA) .... D 949 586-7665
   80 Icon Foothill Ranch (92610) *(P-10732)*

Image Options Painting & Dctg, Foothill Ranch *Also Called: Image Options (P-10732)*

Image Source Inc (PA) .... C 310 477-0700
   2110 Pontius Ave Los Angeles (90025) *(P-6066)*

Image Transfer, Valencia *Also Called: D C Shower Doors Inc (P-3463)*

Imaginative Horizons Inc .... D 619 477-1176
   1889 National City Blvd National City (91950) *(P-15521)*

Imaging Hlthcare Spcalists LLC .... C 619 229-2299
   6386 Alvarado Ct San Diego (92120) *(P-14780)*

Imax Corporation .... D 408 294-8324
   201 S Market St San Jose (95113) *(P-13999)*

IMC, Canoga Park *Also Called: Azimc Investments Inc (P-5027)*

IMC, Los Angeles *Also Called: International Medical Corps (P-18021)*

IMD Path, Berkeley *Also Called: Integrted Miclar Dgnstics Pthl (P-17256)*

Imeg Consultants Corp .... D 714 490-5555
   222 S Harbor Blvd Ste 800 Anaheim (92805) *(P-19264)*

Imerys Minerals California Inc (HQ) .... D 805 736-1221
   2500 San Miguelito Rd Lompoc (93436) *(P-648)*

Imerys Talc America Inc (DH) .... B
   1732 N 1st St Ste 450 San Jose (95112) *(P-2718)*

Imhoff & Associates PC .... D 310 691-2200
   12424 Wilshire Blvd Ste 770 Los Angeles (90025) *(P-17499)*

Immanuel Baptist Day School, Highland *Also Called: Immanuel Bptst Ch San Bnrdino (P-18321)*

Immanuel Bptst Ch San Brnrdino .... D 909 862-6641
   28355 Baseline St Highland (92346) *(P-18321)*

IMMDEF, Los Angeles *Also Called: Immigrant Defenders Law Center (P-17500)*

Immediate Nursing Services, San Jose *Also Called: American-Way Services Corp (P-15325)*

Immigrant Defenders Law Center .... D 213 634-0999
   634 S Spring St Fl 10 Los Angeles (90014) *(P-17500)*

Immortals LLC .... D 310 554-8267
   11460 W Washington Blvd Los Angeles (90066) *(P-14142)*

Immunalysis Corporation .... D 909 482-0840
   829 Towne Center Dr Pomona (91767) *(P-16727)*

Imp Foods Inc .... D 510 429-4600
   1650 Delta Ct Hayward (94544) *(P-6471)*

Impac Mortgage, Irvine *Also Called: Impac Mortgage Corp (P-7983)*

Impac Mortgage Corp .... B 949 475-3600
   19500 Jamboree Rd Ste 100 Irvine (92612) *(P-7983)*

Impac Secured Assets Corp .... D 949 475-3600
   19500 Jamboree Rd Irvine (92612) *(P-9428)*

Impact Business Service, Redwood City *Also Called: Abilitypath (P-17820)*

Impaq International LLC .... C 510 597-2400
   1333 Broadway Ste 300 Oakland (94612) *(P-19886)*

Impco, Santa Ana *Also Called: Impco Technologies Inc (P-2974)*

Impco Technologies Inc (HQ) .... C 714 656-1200
   3030 S Susan St Santa Ana (92704) *(P-2974)*

Impec Group Inc (PA) .... C 408 330-9350
   3350 Scott Blvd Bldg 8 Santa Clara (95054) *(P-10909)*

Imperial Bag & Paper Co LLC .... D 800 834-6248
   2825 Warner Ave Irvine (92606) *(P-6079)*

Imperial Capital Group LLC (PA) .... D 310 246-3700
   2000 Avenue Of The Stars Ste 900s Los Angeles (90067) *(P-9521)*

Imperial Capital LLC (PA) .... D 310 246-3700
   10100 Santa Monica Blvd Ste 2400 Los Angeles (90067) *(P-8094)*

Imperial Care Center, Studio City *Also Called: Longwood Management Corp (P-15871)*

Imperial Convalescent, La Mirada *Also Called: Life Care Centers America Inc (P-15540)*

Imperial County Mental Health, El Centro *Also Called: County of Imperial (P-17035)*

Imperial Crest Healthcare Ctr, Hawthorne *Also Called: Longwood Management Corp (P-15549)*

Imperial Irrigation District (PA) .... A 800 303-7756
   333 E Barioni Blvd Imperial (92251) *(P-4580)*

Imperial Irrigation District .... C 760 398-5811
   81600 58th Ave La Quinta (92253) *(P-4758)*

Imperial Parking (us) LLC .... A 415 495-3909
   1740 Cesar Chavez Fl 2 San Francisco (94124) *(P-13606)*

Imperial Parking Inds Inc .... D 310 276-9766
   9454 Wilshire Blvd Ste P1a Beverly Hills (90212) *(P-13607)*

Imperial Pipe & Supply, Shafter *Also Called: Bps Supply Group (P-5480)*

Imperial Rfrgn & Ice Mchs, Huntington Beach *Also Called: Aire-Rite AC & Rfrgn LLC (P-1344)*

Imperva Inc (HQ) .... C 650 345-9000
   1 Curiosity Way Ste 203 San Mateo (94403) *(P-11657)*

Imply, Burlingame *Also Called: Imply Data Inc (P-12228)*

Imply Data Inc (PA) .... C 415 685-8187
   1633 Bayshore Hwy Ste 232 Burlingame (94010) *(P-12228)*

Import Collection (PA) .... D 818 782-3060
   7885 Nelson Rd Panorama City (91402) *(P-6917)*

Import Direct, Van Nuys *Also Called: E & S International Entps Inc (P-5602)*

Impress Communications Inc .... D 818 701-8800
   9320 Lurline Ave Chatsworth (91311) *(P-2560)*

Imri, Aliso Viejo *Also Called: Information MGT Resources Inc (P-12468)*

IMS, Sacramento *Also Called: Innovative Maintenance Solutions Inc (P-1465)*

IMS, Newark *Also Called: IMS - Insurance Med Svcs Inc (P-19709)*

IMS - Insurance Med Svcs Inc .... C 510 490-6211
   37600 Central Ct Ste 201 Newark (94560) *(P-19709)*

IMS Electronics Recycling Inc .... C 858 679-1555
   12455 Kerran St Ste 300 Poway (92064) *(P-4899)*

IMS Recycling Services, San Diego *Also Called: IMS Recycling Services Inc (P-4900)*

IMS Recycling Services Inc (PA) .... D 619 231-2521
   2697 Main St San Diego (92113) *(P-4900)*

In Granada Hlls Cnvlscent Hosp .... D 818 891-1745
   16123 Chatsworth St Granada Hills (91344) *(P-15522)*

In Montrose Wtr Sstnblity Svcs .... D 949 988-3500
   4 Park Plz Ste 790 Irvine (92614) *(P-20776)*

In Shape Health Clubs, Stockton *Also Called: In Shape Management Company (P-14208)*

In Shape Management Company .... B 209 472-2231
  6 S El Dorado St Stockton (95202) *(P-14208)*
In Stepps Inc .... D 949 474-1493
  10 Skypark Circle, Suite 110 Irvine (92614) *(P-15286)*
In-Roads Creative Programs .... B 909 989-9944
  9057 Arrow Rte Ste 120 Rancho Cucamonga (91730) *(P-18012)*
In-Roads Creative Programs .... B 909 947-9142
  1951 E Saint Andrews Dr Ontario (91761) *(P-18013)*
INALLIANCE, Sacramento *Also Called: Northern California Inalliance (P-18065)*
Inalliance, Placerville *Also Called: Northern California Inalliance (P-18066)*
Inbody, Cerritos *Also Called: Biospace Inc (P-19664)*
Incedo Inc .... C 408 531-6040
  2350 Mission College Blvd Ste 246 Santa Clara (95054) *(P-12806)*
Inception Homes Inc .... D 760 726-4302
  1850 Hacienda Dr Ste 15 Vista (92081) *(P-9048)*
Inchcape Testing Services, Menlo Park *Also Called: Intertek Testing Svcs NA Inc (P-19983)*
Incircle LLC .... A 800 843-7477
  44000 Winchester Rd Temecula (92590) *(P-13321)*
Inclin Inc (PA) .... D 650 961-3422
  155 Bovet Rd Ste 660 San Mateo (94402) *(P-19820)*
Included Health Inc (PA) .... C 800 929-0926
  1 California St Ste 2300 San Francisco (94111) *(P-17253)*
Inclusion Services, Whittier *Also Called: Inclusion Services LLC (P-18014)*
Inclusion Services LLC .... C 562 945-2000
  7255 Greenleaf Ave Ste 20 Whittier (90602) *(P-18014)*
Inclusive Edcatn Cmnty Prtnr I .... B 805 985-4808
  2323 Roosevelt Blvd Apt 3 Oxnard (93035) *(P-17718)*
Incode Technologies Inc (PA) .... C 650 446-3444
  221 Main St Ste 520 San Francisco (94105) *(P-12807)*
Incom Mechanical Inc .... D 707 586-0511
  975 Transport Way Ste 5 Petaluma (94954) *(P-1461)*
Incomnet Communications Corp .... D 949 251-8000
  2801 Main St Irvine (92614) *(P-4297)*
Incotec, Mojave *Also Called: Innovative Coatings Technology Corporation (P-2763)*
Indemnity Company California (DH) .... D 949 263-3300
  17771 Cowan Ste 100 Irvine (92614) *(P-8588)*
Independent, San Francisco *Also Called: Independent Electric Sup Inc (P-5568)*
Independent Construction Co, Concord *Also Called: D A McCosker Construction Co (P-1093)*
Independent Dar Producers Inc .... B 209 667-6076
  21522 Geer Ave Hilmar (95324) *(P-6438)*
Independent Electric Sup Inc .... D 916 924-4848
  4351 Northgate Blvd Sacramento (95834) *(P-5566)*
Independent Electric Sup Inc .... D 209 667-2659
  1565 Venture Ln Turlock (95380) *(P-5567)*
Independent Electric Sup Inc .... D 415 734-4700
  1575 Burke Ave San Francisco (94124) *(P-5568)*
Independent Fincl Group Inc .... D 858 436-3180
  12636 High Bluff Dr Ste 100 San Diego (92130) *(P-8204)*
Independent Fincl Group LLC .... C 858 436-3180
  12671 High Bluff Dr Ste 200 San Diego (92130) *(P-20410)*
Independent Options Inc .... D 714 738-4991
  2625 Sherwood Ave Fullerton (92831) *(P-18458)*
Independent Options Inc .... D 858 598-5260
  5095 Murphy Canyon Rd San Diego (92123) *(P-18459)*
Indepndent Brkley Stdnt Pubg I .... C 510 548-8300
  2483 Hearst Ave Berkeley (94709) *(P-2538)*
Indepndnt Asstd Lvng & Memory, Arcadia *Also Called: Arcadia Gardens MGT Corp (P-15746)*
Indian Health Council Inc (PA) .... D 760 749-1410
  50100 Golsh Rd Valley Center (92082) *(P-14781)*
Indian Hlth Ctr Snta Clara Vly .... C 408 445-3400
  1333 Meridian Ave San Jose (95125) *(P-14782)*
Indian River Transport Co .... C 209 664-0456
  8444 W Doe Ave Visalia (93291) *(P-3492)*
Indian Springs Resort & Spa, Calistoga *Also Called: Resort At Indian Springs LLC (P-10156)*
Indian Wells Country Club Inc .... D 760 345-2561
  46000 Club Dr Indian Wells (92210) *(P-14383)*
Indian Wells Golf Resort, Indian Wells *Also Called: Troon Golf LLC (P-20235)*
Indian Wells Property LLC .... D 442 305-4500
  45000 Indian Wells Ln Indian Wells (92210) *(P-9908)*
Indie LLC .... C 949 608-0854
  32 Journey Ste 100 Aliso Viejo (92656) *(P-20777)*

Indiegogo Inc .... C 866 641-4646
  2261 Market St Ste 4731 San Francisco (94114) *(P-4298)*
Indigo America Inc .... D 650 857-1501
  1501 Page Mill Rd Palo Alto (94304) *(P-2807)*
Indio Products Inc (PA) .... C 323 720-1188
  12910 Mulberry Dr Unit A Whittier (90602) *(P-5466)*
Indium Software Inc .... D 408 501-8844
  19925 Stevens Creek Blvd Ste 100 Cupertino (95014) *(P-12229)*
Inductive Automation LLC .... D 800 266-7798
  90 Blue Ravine Rd Folsom (95630) *(P-20411)*
Indus Technology Inc .... C 619 299-2555
  2243 San Diego Ave Ste 200 San Diego (92110) *(P-19265)*
Industrial Automtn Group LLC .... D 209 579-7527
  4400 Sisk Rd Modesto (95356) *(P-19266)*
Industrial Coml Systems Inc .... C 760 300-4094
  1165 Joshua Way Vista (92081) *(P-1462)*
Industrial Electrical Co, Fresno *Also Called: Modesto Industrial Elec Co Inc (P-1780)*
Industrial Electrical Company, Modesto *Also Called: Modesto Industrial Electrical Co Inc (P-1781)*
Industrial Janitor Service .... D 818 782-5658
  221 N San Dimas Ave Ste 217 San Dimas (91773) *(P-10910)*
Industrial Medical Group 661 327-2225
  2501 G St Bakersfield (93301) *(P-14783)*
Industrial Medical Support Inc .... A 877 878-9185
  3320 E Airport Way Long Beach (90806) *(P-17254)*
Industrial Metal Supply Co, Sun Valley *Also Called: Norman Industrial Mtls Inc (P-5503)*
Industrial Metal Supply Co, Irvine *Also Called: Norman Industrial Mtls Inc (P-5504)*
Industrial Parts Depot LLC (HQ) .... D 310 530-1900
  1550 Charles Willard St Carson (90746) *(P-5840)*
Industrial Stitchtech Inc .... C 818 361-6319
  520 Library St San Fernando (91340) *(P-13322)*
Industrial Tctnics Brings Corp (DH) .... C 310 537-3750
  18301 S Santa Fe Ave E Rncho Dmngz (90221) *(P-2794)*
Industry Station, City Of Industry *Also Called: Southern California Gas Co (P-4735)*
Indyne Inc .... B 805 606-7225
  1036 California Blvd Bldg 11013 Vandenberg Afb (93437) *(P-20655)*
Inertech, Monterey Park *Also Called: Inertech Supply Inc (P-2654)*
Inertech Supply Inc .... D 626 282-2000
  641 Monterey Pass Rd Monterey Park (91754) *(P-2654)*
Infertlity Gynclogy Obstetrics, San Diego *Also Called: Igo Medical Group A Med Corp (P-14779)*
Infineon Raceway, Sonoma *Also Called: Speedway Sonoma LLC (P-14167)*
Infineon Tech Americas Corp .... A 310 726-8000
  222 Kansas St El Segundo (90245) *(P-19588)*
Infinera, San Jose *Also Called: Infinera Corporation (P-2885)*
Infinera Corporation (PA) .... B 408 572-5200
  6373 San Ignacio Ave San Jose (95119) *(P-2885)*
Infinite Home Health Inc .... D 818 888-7772
  22151 Ventura Blvd Ste 102 Woodland Hills (91364) *(P-16874)*
Infinite Technologies LLC .... C 786 408-7995
  1667 N Batavia St Orange (92867) *(P-11658)*
Infinity Drywall Contg Inc .... D 714 634-2255
  225 S Loara St Anaheim (92802) *(P-1935)*
Infinity Energy Cnstr Inc .... D 888 839-2937
  3825 Atherton Rd Ste 101 Rocklin (95765) *(P-1463)*
Infinity Plumbing Designs Inc .... B 951 737-4436
  9182 Stellar Ct Corona (92883) *(P-1464)*
Inflection Risk Solutions LLC .... C 650 618-9910
  555 Twin Dolphin Dr Ste 600 Redwood City (94065) *(P-12582)*
Inflectioncom Inc .... C 650 618-9910
  303 Twin Dolphin Dr Ste 600 Redwood City (94065) *(P-20778)*
Influxdata Inc .... C 415 295-1901
  548 Market St Pmb 77953 San Francisco (94104) *(P-11659)*
Infoblox Inc (HQ) .... B 408 986-4000
  2390 Mission College Blvd Ste 501 Santa Clara (95054) *(P-11660)*
Infogain Corporation (PA) .... C 408 355-6000
  485 Alberto Way Ste 100 Los Gatos (95032) *(P-12808)*
Infogen Labs Inc .... D 323 816-4813
  25350 Magic Mountain Pkwy Ste 300 Valencia (91355) *(P-12809)*
Infoimage, Brisbane *Also Called: Infoimage of California Inc (P-2569)*
Infoimage of California Inc (PA) .... D 650 473-6388
  175 S Hill Dr Brisbane (94005) *(P-2569)*

ALPHABETIC SECTION

Infomagnus LLC .... D...... 714 810-3430
   5882 Bolsa Ave Ste 210 Huntington Beach (92649) *(P-11661)*

Infonet Services Corporation (DH) .... A...... 310 335-2600
   2160 E Grand Ave El Segundo (90245) *(P-4299)*

Infor Public Sector Inc (DH) .... C...... 916 921-0883
   11092 Sun Center Dr Rancho Cordova (95670) *(P-12230)*

Informa Research Services Inc (HQ) .... C...... 818 880-8877
   26565 Agoura Rd Ste 300 Calabasas (91302) *(P-19821)*

Informatica, Redwood City *Also Called: Informatica Inc (P-12232)*

Informatica Holdco Inc .... A...... 650 385-5000
   2100 Seaport Blvd Redwood City (94063) *(P-12231)*

Informatica Inc .... A...... 650 385-5000
   2100 Seaport Blvd Redwood City (94063) *(P-12232)*

Informatica LLC (DH) .... B...... 650 385-5000
   2100 Seaport Blvd Redwood City (94063) *(P-12233)*

Informatica LLC of Delaware, Redwood City *Also Called: Informatica LLC (P-12233)*

Information MGT Resources Inc (PA) .... C...... 949 215-8889
   85 Argonaut Ste 215 Aliso Viejo (92656) *(P-12468)*

Information Services, Stockton *Also Called: Dignity Health (P-16045)*

Information Systems, Orange *Also Called: St Joseph Hospital of Orange (P-16471)*

Information Tech Partners Inc .... D...... 800 789-7487
   3003 N San Fernando Blvd Burbank (91504) *(P-12810)*

Informtion Rfrral Fdrtion of L .... D...... 626 350-1841
   526 W Las Tunas Dr San Gabriel (91776) *(P-10552)*

Infosend Inc (PA) .... D...... 714 993-2690
   4240 E La Palma Ave Anaheim (92807) *(P-19589)*

Infosoft Inc .... D...... 408 659-4326
   7891 Westwood Dr Ste 113 Gilroy (95020) *(P-20779)*

Infospan .... A...... 949 260-9990
   31878 Del Obispo St Ste 118 San Juan Capistrano (92675) *(P-20412)*

Infostride Inc .... D...... 415 360-1700
   3031 Tisch Way Ste 110 San Jose (95128) *(P-12811)*

Infoway Solutions LLC .... C...... 925 435-9672
   46520 Fremont Blvd Ste 614 Fremont (94538) *(P-11662)*

Infoworksio Inc .... C...... 408 899-4687
   490 California Ave Ste 200 Palo Alto (94306) *(P-11663)*

Infoworld, San Francisco *Also Called: Infoworld Media Group Inc (P-2545)*

Infoworld Media Group Inc (DH) .... D...... 415 243-4344
   501 2nd St Ste 500 San Francisco (94107) *(P-2545)*

Infrastructure Engrg Corp .... D...... 760 529-0795
   301 Mission Ave Ste 202 Oceanside (92054) *(P-19267)*

Infusion Care, Long Beach *Also Called: Long Beach Medical Center (P-16232)*

Ingardia Bros Produce Inc .... C...... 949 645-1365
   700 S Hathaway St Santa Ana (92705) *(P-6559)*

Ingenio Inc .... C...... 415 248-4000
   182 Howard St # 826 San Francisco (94105) *(P-4300)*

Ingenium Technologies Corp .... D...... 858 227-4422
   5665 Oberlin Dr Ste 202 San Diego (92121) *(P-19268)*

Ingenuity Studios Intl Inc .... C...... 323 460-6096
   941 N Highland Ave 2nd Fl Los Angeles (90038) *(P-13323)*

Inglewood Cmtry Mortuary Inc .... D...... 310 412-6811
   3801 W Manchester Blvd Inglewood (90305) *(P-10513)*

Inglewood Health Care Center, Inglewood *Also Called: Mariner Health Care Inc (P-15569)*

Inglewood Park Cemetery (PA) .... C...... 310 412-6500
   720 E Florence Ave Inglewood (90301) *(P-9287)*

Ingram Micro Inc (HQ) .... A...... 714 566-1000
   3351 Michelson Dr Ste 100 Irvine (92612) *(P-5314)*

Ingram Micro Services LLC .... D...... 714 566-1000
   3351 Michelson Dr Ste 100 Irvine (92612) *(P-5315)*

Ingrooves, San Francisco *Also Called: Isolation Network Inc (P-2880)*

Inharvest, Colusa *Also Called: Riviana Foods Inc (P-6694)*

Inhouseit Inc .... D...... 949 660-5655
   400 Exchange Ste 100 Irvine (92602) *(P-12709)*

Initiative Media North America, Los Angeles *Also Called: Mediabrands Worldwide Inc (P-10646)*

Inizio Interventions Inc .... D...... 818 937-0882
   17037 Chatsworth St Ste 206 Granada Hills (91344) *(P-17074)*

Inkling Systems Inc .... D...... 415 975-4420
   535 Mission St Fl 14 San Francisco (94105) *(P-20413)*

Inko Industrial Corporation .... D...... 408 830-1040
   695 Vaqueros Ave Sunnyvale (94085) *(P-12583)*

Inland Bhavioral Hlth Svcs Inc (PA) .... D...... 909 881-6146
   1963 N E St San Bernardino (92405) *(P-17255)*

Inland Business Machines, Sacramento *Also Called: Inland Business Machines Inc (P-13776)*

Inland Business Machines Inc (DH) .... D...... 916 928-0770
   1326 N Market Blvd Sacramento (95834) *(P-13776)*

Inland Cc Inc .... C...... 909 355-1318
   7010 Wyndham Hill Dr Riverside (92506) *(P-2128)*

Inland Chrstn HM Fundation Inc .... C...... 909 395-9322
   1950 S Mountain Ave Ofc Ontario (91762) *(P-15523)*

Inland Cnties Regional Ctr Inc (PA) .... C...... 909 890-3000
   1365 S Waterman Ave San Bernardino (92408) *(P-18015)*

Inland Cnties Regional Ctr Inc .... C...... 951 826-2600
   1500 Iowa Ave Ste 100 Riverside (92507) *(P-20113)*

Inland Empire 66ers Bsbal CLB .... C...... 909 888-9922
   280 Se St San Bernardino (92401) *(P-14143)*

Inland Empire Chptr-Ssction Cr .... D...... 512 478-9000
   2210 E Route 66 Glendora (91740) *(P-19091)*

Inland Empire Health Plan (PA) .... A...... 909 890-2000
   10801 6th St Ste 120 Rancho Cucamonga (91730) *(P-8266)*

Inland Empire Health Plan .... A...... 866 228-4347
   805 W 2nd St Ste C San Bernardino (92410) *(P-8304)*

Inland Empire Heart Institute, San Bernardino *Also Called: St Bernardine Med Ctr Au. Inc (P-16453)*

Inland Empire Therapy Provider (PA) .... D...... 909 985-7905
   1150 N Mountain Ave # 214 Upland (91786) *(P-15287)*

Inland Empire Utlties Agcy A M (PA) .... D...... 909 993-1600
   6075 Kimball Ave Chino (91708) *(P-4795)*

Inland Eye Inst Med Group Inc (PA) .... D...... 909 825-3425
   1900 E Washington St Colton (92324) *(P-14784)*

Inland Kenworth Inc (HQ) .... C...... 909 823-9955
   9730 Cherry Ave Fontana (92335) *(P-5012)*

Inland Regional Center, San Bernardino *Also Called: Inland Cnties Regional Ctr Inc (P-18015)*

Inland Regional Center, Riverside *Also Called: Inland Cnties Regional Ctr Inc (P-20113)*

Inland Star Dist Ctrs Inc (PA) .... D...... 559 237-2052
   3146 S Chestnut Ave Fresno (93725) *(P-3493)*

Inland Valley Care & Rehab Ctr, Pomona *Also Called: Inland Valley Partners LLC (P-15288)*

Inland Valley Hospice Co .... D...... 760 243-2501
   19167 Us Highway 18 Ste 6 Apple Valley (92307) *(P-15766)*

Inland Valley Partners LLC .... C...... 909 623-7100
   250 W Artesia St Pomona (91768) *(P-15288)*

Inland Vly DRG Alchol Rcvery S (PA) .... D...... 909 932-1069
   1260 E Arrow Hwy Upland (91786) *(P-17075)*

Inland Vly Rgional Med Ctr Inc .... B...... 951 677-1111
   36485 Inland Valley Dr Wildomar (92595) *(P-16139)*

Inlog Inc .... D...... 949 212-3867
   6765 Westminster Blvd Ste 424 Westminster (92683) *(P-4037)*

Inmage Systems Inc .... D...... 408 200-3840
   1065 La Avenida St Mountain View (94043) *(P-12234)*

Inmode Aesthetic Solutions, Irvine *Also Called: Invasix Inc (P-19713)*

Inmotion Entrmt Group LLC .... C...... 904 332-0459
   3225 N Harbor Dr San Diego (92101) *(P-14089)*

Inn At Mssion San Juan Cpstran, San Juan Capistrano *Also Called: Marriott International Inc (P-10005)*

Inn Hampton & Suites .... D...... 707 586-8700
   6248 Redwood Dr Rohnert Park (94928) *(P-9909)*

Inn Ventures Inc .... D...... 916 773-7171
   1951 Taylor Rd Roseville (95661) *(P-9910)*

Inner Circle Labs LLC .... D...... 415 684-9400
   333 1st St Ste A San Francisco (94105) *(P-19822)*

Innercare, El Centro *Also Called: Clinicas De Slud Del Peblo Inc (P-14691)*

Innercool Therapies, San Diego *Also Called: Philips North America LLC (P-5610)*

Innocean USA, Huntington Beach *Also Called: Innocean Wrldwide Americas LLC (P-10631)*

Innocean Wrldwide Americas LLC (HQ) .... C...... 714 861-5200
   180 5th St Ste 200 Huntington Beach (92648) *(P-10631)*

Innocor West LLC .... B...... 909 307-3737
   300 S Tippecanoe Ave 310 San Bernardino (92408) *(P-2657)*

Innopath, Sunnyvale *Also Called: Innopath Software Inc (P-11664)*

Innopath Software Inc .... C...... 408 962-9200
   333 W El Camino Real Ste 230 Sunnyvale (94087) *(P-11664)*

Innova Solutions Inc .... A...... 408 889-2020
   3211 Scott Blvd Ste 202 Santa Clara (95054) *(P-12812)*

ALPHABETIC SECTION

Innovaccer Inc (PA)..B...... 510 327-8900
101 Mission St Ste 1950 San Francisco (94105) *(P-11665)*

Innovasystems Intl LLC...C...... 619 955-5890
850 Beech St Unit 1006 San Diego (92101) *(P-11666)*

Innovated Packaging Co Inc..D...... 510 745-8180
520 Marburg Way San Jose (95133) *(P-4129)*

Innovation Specialties..C...... 888 827-2387
11869 Teale St Ste 302 Culver City (90230) *(P-13324)*

Innovations Building Svcs LLC...D...... 323 787-6068
402 S Orange Ave Apt D Monterey Park (91755) *(P-10911)*

Innovative Cleaning Svcs LLC...B...... 949 251-9188
44 Waterworks Way Irvine (92618) *(P-10912)*

Innovative Cnstr Solutions..C...... 714 893-6366
575 Anton Blvd Ste 850 Costa Mesa (92626) *(P-20656)*

Innovative Coatings Technology Corporation....................C...... 661 824-8101
1347 Poole St 106 Mojave (93501) *(P-2763)*

Innovative Dialysis Partners Inc..B...... 562 495-8075
1 World Trade Ctr Long Beach (90831) *(P-7584)*

Innovative Engrg Systems Inc (PA)....................................D...... 661 381-7800
8800 Crippen St Bakersfield (93311) *(P-19269)*

Innovative Integrated Hlth Inc (PA).....................................C...... 559 400-6420
2042 Kern St Fresno (93721) *(P-18460)*

Innovative Maintenance Solutions Inc................................C...... 916 568-1400
725 Del Paso Rd Sacramento (95834) *(P-1465)*

Innovative Placements Inc..C...... 800 322-9796
12400 High Bluff Dr Ste 100 San Diego (92130) *(P-11156)*

Innovative Silicon Inc...D...... 408 572-8700
4800 Great America Pkwy # 500 Santa Clara (95054) *(P-13325)*

Innovative Skin Care, Burbank *Also Called: Science of Skincare LLC (P-6143)*

Innovative Vhcl Solutions LLC...C...... 714 896-8267
5831 Research Dr Huntington Beach (92649) *(P-20780)*

Innovel Solutions Inc..A...... 707 748-1940
521 Stone Rd Benicia (94510) *(P-4038)*

Innovel Solutions Inc..A...... 619 497-1123
960 Sherman St San Diego (92110) *(P-4039)*

Innovel Solutions Inc..A...... 909 605-1446
5691 E Philadelphia St Ste 200 Ontario (91761) *(P-4040)*

Innovtive Artsts Tlent Ltrary (PA).......................................D...... 310 656-0400
1505 10th St Santa Monica (90401) *(P-14040)*

Innovtive Emplyee Slutions Inc (PA)..................................D...... 858 715-5100
2307 Fenton Pkwy 107-615 San Diego (92108) *(P-19590)*

Inns At Sonoma, Sonoma *Also Called: Four Sisters Inns (P-9803)*

Inns of Monterey, Monterey *Also Called: Columbia Hospitality Inc (P-9713)*

Innsuites Hotels, San Diego *Also Called: Hampstead Lafayette Hotel LLC (P-9831)*

Inogen Inc (PA)...C...... 805 562-0500
301 Coromar Dr Goleta (93117) *(P-3053)*

Inova Diagnostics Inc (HQ)...B...... 858 586-9900
9900 Old Grove Rd San Diego (92131) *(P-19710)*

Inoxpa Usa Inc..B...... 707 585-3900
6145 State Farm Dr Rohnert Park (94928) *(P-5841)*

Inpatient Consultants Ala Inc..D...... 888 447-2362
8511 Fallbrook Ave Ste 120 West Hills (91304) *(P-14785)*

Input 1 LLC..C...... 818 340-0030
6200 Canoga Ave Ste 400 Woodland Hills (91367) *(P-7895)*

Inquiring Systems Inc..D...... 707 939-3900
887 Sonoma Ave Apt 23 Santa Rosa (95404) *(P-20414)*

Insco Dico Group , The, Irvine *Also Called: Developers Surety Indemnity Co (P-8430)*

Insco Insurance Services Inc (DH)......................................D...... 949 263-3415
17771 Cowan Ste 100 Irvine (92614) *(P-8589)*

Inseego, San Diego *Also Called: Inseego Corp (P-11667)*

Inseego Corp (PA)..D...... 858 812-3400
9710 Scranton Rd Ste 200 San Diego (92121) *(P-11667)*

Inseego North America LLC (HQ)......................................D...... 541 685-9045
9605 Scranton Rd Ste 300 San Diego (92121) *(P-12469)*

Inside Real Estate..D...... 415 525-4913
580 4th St San Francisco (94107) *(P-9049)*

Insideview Technologies, San Francisco *Also Called: Insideview Technologies Inc (P-5316)*

Insideview Technologies Inc..C...... 415 728-9309
444 De Haro St Ste 210 San Francisco (94107) *(P-5316)*

Insight Global Inc..C...... 213 404-4140
725 S Figueroa St Ste 2800 Los Angeles (90017) *(P-11157)*

Insignia Environmental...D...... 650 321-6787
545 Middlefield Rd Ste 210 Menlo Park (94025) *(P-20781)*

Insignia/Esg Ht Partners Inc (DH).......................................B...... 310 765-2600
11150 Santa Monica Blvd Ste 220 Los Angeles (90025) *(P-8726)*

Insignia/Esg Ht Partners Inc..B...... 408 288-2900
225 W Santa Clara St Ste 250 San Jose (95113) *(P-9050)*

Insignia/Esg Ht Partners Inc..B...... 415 772-0123
101 California St San Francisco (94111) *(P-9051)*

Insitro Inc..C...... 650 730-7074
279 E Grand Ave Ste 200 South San Francisco (94080) *(P-19711)*

Insomniac, Calabasas *Also Called: Insomniac Inc (P-14090)*

Insomniac Inc..C...... 323 874-7020
5023 Parkway Calabasas Calabasas (91302) *(P-14090)*

Inspection Services, Berkeley *Also Called: ISI Inspection Services Inc (P-13331)*

Inspectorate America Corp..C...... 800 424-0099
3401 Jack Northrop Ave Hawthorne (90250) *(P-13326)*

INSPECTORATE AMERICA CORPORATION, Hawthorne *Also Called: Inspectorate America Corp (P-13326)*

Inspira Inc..C...... 408 247-9500
4125 Blackford Ave Ste 255 San Jose (95117) *(P-11668)*

Inspire Energy, Santa Monica *Also Called: Inspire Energy Holdings LLC (P-4581)*

Inspire Energy Holdings LLC...C...... 866 403-2620
3402 Pico Blvd Ste 300 Santa Monica (90405) *(P-4581)*

Inspiria Inc (PA)...D...... 949 206-0606
140 Technology Dr Ste 100 Irvine (92618) *(P-19270)*

Instabug Inc...D...... 650 422-9555
855 El Camino Real Ste 13a-111 Palo Alto (94301) *(P-11669)*

INSTACART, San Francisco *Also Called: Maplebear Inc (P-12592)*

Instagram, Menlo Park *Also Called: Instagram LLC (P-12667)*

Instagram LLC...C...... 650 543-4800
1601 Willow Rd Menlo Park (94025) *(P-12667)*

Instant Checkmate, San Diego *Also Called: Instant Checkmate LLC (P-10553)*

Instant Checkmate LLC..C...... 800 222-8985
375 Camino De La Reina Ste 400 San Diego (92108) *(P-10553)*

Instant Systems Inc...D...... 510 657-8100
447 King Ave Fremont (94536) *(P-11670)*

Instantly Inc...C...... 866 872-4006
16501 Ventura Blvd # 300 Encino (91436) *(P-19823)*

Instantsys, Fremont *Also Called: Instant Systems Inc (P-11670)*

Institute For Applied Bhvior A...D...... 818 341-1933
9221 Corbin Ave Northridge (91324) *(P-15289)*

Institute For Applied Bhvior A (PA)....................................C...... 310 649-0499
5601 W Slauson Ave Culver City (90230) *(P-15290)*

Institute For Applied Bhvior A...D...... 805 987-5886
2310 E Ponderosa Dr Ste 1 Camarillo (93010) *(P-15291)*

Institute For Bhvoral Hlth Inc...B...... 909 289-1041
1905 Business Center Dr Ste 100 San Bernardino (92408) *(P-17076)*

INSTITUTE FOR CAREER DEVELOPME, San Jose *Also Called: Goodwill of Silicon Valley (P-11288)*

Institute For Defense Analyses..C...... 858 622-5439
4320 Westerra Ct San Diego (92121) *(P-19887)*

Institute of Elec Elec Engners..D...... 714 821-8380
10662 Los Vaqueros Cir Los Alamitos (90720) *(P-18711)*

Institute On Aging..C...... 510 536-3377
2880 Zanker Rd San Jose (95134) *(P-15863)*

Institute On Aging..C...... 415 600-2690
3698 California St San Francisco (94118) *(P-18016)*

Institute On Aging (PA)..D...... 415 750-4101
3575 Geary Blvd San Francisco (94118) *(P-18017)*

Instride, Los Angeles *Also Called: Attainment Holdco LLC (P-18732)*

Instrumental Global Hq...D...... 650 681-9361
777 California Ave Ste 150 Palo Alto (94304) *(P-8727)*

Insulectro (PA)..D...... 949 587-3200
20362 Windrow Dr Lake Forest (92630) *(P-5663)*

Insurance Company of West..D...... 858 350-2400
11455 El Camino Real Ste 200 San Diego (92130) *(P-8388)*

Insurance Company of West (HQ)......................................D...... 858 350-2400
15025 Innovation Dr San Diego (92128) *(P-8590)*

Insurance Company of West..D...... 925 474-2800
6140 Stoneridge Mall Rd Ste 390 Pleasanton (94588) *(P-8591)*

Insurance Inc Southern Cal..D...... 951 300-9333
3400 Central Ave Ste 220 Riverside (92506) *(P-8592)*

ALPHABETIC SECTION

Insure Express Insurance Svc, Calabasas *Also Called: Cartel Marketing Inc (P-8522)*
Intapp, Palo Alto *Also Called: Intapp Us Inc (P-11671)*
Intapp Us Inc (HQ) ....C....... 650 852-0400
 3101 Park Blvd Palo Alto (94306) *(P-11671)*
Intech Mechanical Company Inc ....D....... 916 797-4900
 7501 Galilee Rd Roseville (95678) *(P-1466)*
Intech Mechanical Company LLC ....C....... 916 797-4900
 7501 Galilee Rd Roseville (95678) *(P-1467)*
Integral Senior Living, Carlsbad *Also Called: Isl Employees Inc (P-18461)*
Integral Senior Living LLC (PA) ....C....... 760 547-2863
 2333 State St Ste 300 Carlsbad (92008) *(P-8827)*
Integrated Associates Inc ....C....... 858 412-6189
 4010 Morena Blvd Ste 222 San Diego (92117) *(P-11158)*
Integrated Community Services ....D....... 415 455-8481
 523 4th St Ste 100 San Rafael (94901) *(P-18018)*
Integrated Energy Group LLC ....D....... 605 381-7859
 3929 E Guasti Rd Ste F Ontario (91761) *(P-1468)*
Integrated Health Concepts Inc ....D....... 866 239-3784
 720 Aerovista Pl Ste D San Luis Obispo (93401) *(P-6113)*
INTEGRATED HEALTHCARE DELIVERY, Los Angeles *Also Called: Pih Health Good Samaritan Hosp (P-16325)*
Integrated Intermodal Svcs Inc ....D....... 909 355-4100
 8600 Banana Ave Fontana (92335) *(P-12813)*
Integrated Media Tech Inc (PA) ....D....... 818 761-9770
 832 N Victory Blvd Burbank (91502) *(P-12814)*
Integrated Pain Man ....D....... 925 238-0020
 4053 Lone Tree Way Antioch (94531) *(P-20114)*
Integrated Pain Man ....D....... 925 666-8972
 4530 Balfour Rd Brentwood (94513) *(P-20115)*
Integrated Pain Managemen ....C....... 925 691-9806
 165 Lennon Ln Ste 100 Walnut Creek (94598) *(P-20116)*
Integrated Parcel Network ....B....... 714 278-6100
 11135 Rush St Ste A South El Monte (91733) *(P-3616)*
Integrated Procurement Tech (PA) ....D....... 805 682-0842
 7230 Hollister Ave Goleta (93117) *(P-5958)*
Integrity Hlthcare Sltions Inc ....D....... 760 432-9811
 5625 Ruffin Rd San Diego (92123) *(P-16875)*
Integrity Mortgage Group ....D....... 858 225-5000
 9747 Businesspark Ave San Diego (92131) *(P-7984)*
Integrity Rebar Placers ....C....... 951 696-6843
 1345 Nandina Ave Perris (92571) *(P-2183)*
Integrted Healthcare Dlvry Sys, Whittier *Also Called: Pih Health Inc (P-16323)*
Integrted Mlclar Dgnstics Pthl ....D....... 866 944-8050
 3017 Telegraph Ave Ste 102 Berkeley (94705) *(P-17256)*
Integrted Pain MGT Med Group I ....D....... 916 333-5800
 333 University Ave # 140 Sacramento (95825) *(P-20117)*
Integrus LLC ....D....... 949 538-9211
 14370 Myford Rd Ste 100 Irvine (92606) *(P-5247)*
Intel, Santa Clara *Also Called: Intel Corporation (P-2923)*
Intel Corporation (PA) ....A....... 408 765-8080
 2200 Mission College Blvd Santa Clara (95054) *(P-2923)*
Intel Media Inc ....B....... 408 765-0063
 2200 Mission College Blvd M Santa Clara (95054) *(P-4511)*
Intelex Systems Inc ....D....... 818 992-2969
 21900 Burbank Blvd Ste 3087 Woodland Hills (91367) *(P-11672)*
Intelicare Direct Llc ....D....... 858 299-3636
 8885 Rio San Diego Dr San Diego (92108) *(P-10554)*
Intelity Inc ....D....... 310 596-8160
 16501 Ventura Blvd Encino (91436) *(P-20415)*
Intelius, San Diego *Also Called: Intelius LLC (P-10555)*
Intelius LLC ....C....... 888 245-1655
 375 Camino De La Reina San Diego (92108) *(P-10555)*
Intell Detection Systems Inc ....D....... 530 644-1904
 3092 Sly Park Rd Pollock Pines (95726) *(P-7585)*
Intell Security Systems, Pollock Pines *Also Called: Intell Detection Systems Inc (P-7585)*
Intell Set, Long Beach *Also Called: Intelsat US LLC (P-4539)*
Intellective, Irvine *Also Called: Vegatek Corporation (P-12014)*
Intellectual Ventures, Palo Alto *Also Called: Intellectual Ventures LLC (P-20118)*
Intellectual Ventures LLC ....B....... 650 941-1330
 200 California Ave Ste 200 Palo Alto (94306) *(P-20118)*

Intellectyx, Pasadena *Also Called: Intellectyx Inc (P-12235)*
Intellectyx Inc ....D....... 720 256-7540
 680 E Colorado Blvd Ste 180 Pasadena (91101) *(P-12235)*
Intellicus, Los Gatos *Also Called: Intellicus Tech Pvt Ltd (P-11673)*
Intellicus Tech Pvt Ltd ....D....... 408 213-3314
 720 University Ave Ste 130 Los Gatos (95032) *(P-11673)*
Intelligent Photonics, San Francisco *Also Called: Invuity Inc (P-3055)*
Intelliloan, Costa Mesa *Also Called: Metropolitan Home Mortgage Inc (P-8001)*
Intellimize Inc ....D....... 415 760-5710
 341 Dwight Rd Burlingame (94010) *(P-12470)*
Intellipower Inc ....D....... 714 921-1580
 1746 N Saint Thomas Cir Orange (92865) *(P-5664)*
Intellipro Group Inc (PA) ....B....... 408 200-9891
 3120 Scott Blvd # 301 Santa Clara (95054) *(P-12815)*
Intelliswift Software Inc (PA) ....C....... 510 370-2600
 39600 Balentine Dr Ste 200 Newark (94560) *(P-11674)*
Intellisync Corporation ....B....... 650 625-2185
 313 Fairchild Dr Mountain View (94043) *(P-11675)*
Intelpeer Cloud Cmmnctions LLC (PA) ....C....... 650 525-9200
 155 Bovet Rd Ste 405 San Mateo (94402) *(P-4538)*
Intelsat US LLC ....C....... 310 525-5500
 1600 Forbes Way Long Beach (90810) *(P-4539)*
Inter Community Hospital, Covina *Also Called: Emanate Health Medical Center (P-16077)*
Inter Continental, Fresno *Also Called: Six Continents Hotels Inc (P-10244)*
Inter Valley Pool Supply Inc ....D....... 626 969-5657
 1415 E 3rd St Pomona (91766) *(P-5978)*
Inter-City Cleaners LLC ....D....... 650 875-9200
 438 S Airport Blvd South San Francisco (94080) *(P-10467)*
Inter-Con Security Systems Inc (PA) ....A....... 626 535-2200
 210 S De Lacey Ave Pasadena (91105) *(P-12989)*
Interactive Media Holdings Inc ....C....... 949 861-8888
 2722 Michelson Dr Ste 100 Irvine (92612) *(P-10632)*
Interactive Solutions Inc (DH) ....D....... 510 214-9002
 283 4th St Ste 301 Oakland (94607) *(P-12236)*
Intercare Holdings Insur Svcs, Rocklin *Also Called: Pacific Secured Equities Inc (P-20499)*
Intercare Therapy Inc ....C....... 323 866-1880
 4221 Wilshire Blvd Ste 300a Los Angeles (90010) *(P-15292)*
Intercntinental Hotels Resorts, San Francisco *Also Called: Intercntnntal Htels San Frncsc (P-9911)*
Intercntinental Hotels Resorts, San Francisco *Also Called: Intercntnntal Htels San Frncsc (P-9912)*
Intercntnntal Htels San Frncsc ....D....... 770 604-5000
 888 Howard St San Francisco (94103) *(P-9911)*
Intercntnntal Htels San Frncsc ....C....... 415 616-6500
 888 Howard St San Francisco (94103) *(P-9912)*
Intercntnntal Los Angles Dwntw, Los Angeles *Also Called: Ihg Management (maryland) LLC (P-9906)*
Intercom Inc ....B....... 831 920-7088
 55 2nd St Fl 4 San Francisco (94105) *(P-11676)*
Intercommunity Care Center, Long Beach *Also Called: Intercommunity Care Ctrs Inc (P-15524)*
Intercommunity Care Ctrs Inc ....C....... 562 427-8915
 2626 Grand Ave Long Beach (90815) *(P-15524)*
Intercontinental Mark Hopkins, San Francisco *Also Called: One Nob Hill Associates LLC (P-10068)*
Intercontinental San Diego, San Diego *Also Called: Lfs Development LLC (P-9973)*
Intercontinental San Francisco, San Francisco *Also Called: Cdc San Francisco LLC (P-9688)*
Interctive Med Specialists Inc ....D....... 415 472-4204
 252 Waterside Cir San Rafael (94903) *(P-11293)*
Interdent Service Corporation ....D....... 951 682-1720
 3630 Central Ave Riverside (92506) *(P-15229)*
Interdent Service Corporation ....D....... 707 528-7000
 1421 Guerneville Rd Ste 102 Santa Rosa (95403) *(P-15230)*
Interface Associates Inc ....C....... 949 448-7056
 27721 La Paz Rd Laguna Niguel (92677) *(P-3054)*
Interface Catheter Solutions, Laguna Niguel *Also Called: Interface Associates Inc (P-3054)*
INTERFACE CHILDREN FAMILY SERV, Camarillo *Also Called: Interface Community (P-18019)*
Interface Community (PA) ....D....... 805 485-6114
 4001 Mission Oaks Blvd Ste I Camarillo (93012) *(P-18019)*
Interface Rehab Inc ....A....... 714 646-8300
 774 S Placentia Ave Ste 200 Placentia (92870) *(P-15293)*

Interfaith Community Services   **ALPHABETIC SECTION**

Interfaith Community Services, Escondido *Also Called: Interfaith Community Svcs Inc* *(P-18020)*
   Interfaith Community Svcs Inc .... D...... 760 489-6380
   250 N Ash St Escondido (92027) *(P-18020)*

Interfocus Inc (PA) .... D...... 844 972-8728
440 N Wolfe Rd E089 Sunnyvale (94085) *(P-6200)*

Intergro Rehab Service .... D...... 714 901-4200
13211 Foothill Blvd Santa Ana (92705) *(P-15294)*

Interhealth Services Inc (HQ) .... C...... 562 698-0811
12401 Washington Blvd Whittier (90602) *(P-16876)*

Interim Inc .... D...... 831 758-9457
200 Casentini St Salinas (93907) *(P-11294)*

Interim Inc .... D...... 831 754-3838
339 Pajaro St Salinas (93901) *(P-20893)*

Interim Healthcare Inc .... C...... 209 577-5936
1521 N Carpenter Rd Ste D3 Modesto (95351) *(P-11295)*

Interim Healthcare Inc .... C...... 916 486-8181
2255 Watt Ave Ste 30 Sacramento (95825) *(P-16877)*

Interim Healthcare Inc .... C...... 951 684-6111
7000 Indiana Ave Ste 107 Riverside (92506) *(P-16878)*

Interim Healthcare of Jackson, Jackson *Also Called: K&B Pichette Enterprises Inc (P-16881)*

Interim Hlthcare Hspice - Scrm, Sacramento *Also Called: Oakland Hospice Inc (P-16903)*

Interim Hlthcare San Diego LLC .... B...... 858 576-9501
5625 Ruffin Rd Ste 225 San Diego (92123) *(P-16879)*

Interim Services, Salinas *Also Called: Interim Inc (P-11294)*

Interim Services, Modesto *Also Called: Interim Healthcare Inc (P-11295)*

Interim Services, Sacramento *Also Called: Interim Healthcare Inc (P-16877)*

Interim Services, Riverside *Also Called: Interim Healthcare Inc (P-16878)*

Interim Services, Salinas *Also Called: Interim Inc (P-20893)*

Interior Architects Inc (PA) .... D...... 415 434-3305
500 Sansome St Fl 8 San Francisco (94111) *(P-19480)*

Interior Electric Incorporated .... D...... 714 771-9098
747 N Main St Orange (92868) *(P-1756)*

Interior Experts Gen Bldrs Inc .... D...... 909 203-4922
4534 Carter Ct Chino (91710) *(P-1936)*

Interior Lgic Group Hldngs IV (PA) .... D...... 800 959-8333
10 Bunsen Irvine (92618) *(P-941)*

Interior Logic Group HM Rmdlg, Irvine *Also Called: Interior Specialists Inc (P-2036)*

Interior Rmoval Specialist Inc .... C...... 323 357-6900
8990 Atlantic Ave South Gate (90280) *(P-2237)*

Interior Specialists Inc .... B...... 800 959-8333
18565 Jamboree Rd Ste 125 Irvine (92612) *(P-2036)*

Interior Specialists Inc (HQ) .... D...... 760 929-6700
1630 Faraday Ave Carlsbad (92008) *(P-2037)*

Interior Specialists Inc .... B...... 909 983-5386
15822 Bernardo Center Dr Ste 1 San Diego (92127) *(P-13327)*

Interlink Securities Corp .... D...... 818 992-6700
20750 Ventura Blvd Ste 300 Woodland Hills (91364) *(P-8095)*

Intermdia Cloud Cmmnctions Inc .... A...... 650 641-4000
100 Mathilda Pl Ste 600 Sunnyvale (94086) *(P-12237)*

Intermountain Specialty Eqp, La Palma *Also Called: Isec Incorporated (P-2005)*

Intermune Inc (DH) .... C...... 415 466-4383
1 Dna Way South San Francisco (94080) *(P-2590)*

Internal Drive .... A...... 408 871-2227
910 E Hamilton Ave Ste 300 Campbell (95008) *(P-10404)*

Internal Revenue Service .... D...... 714 512-2818
2400 E Katella Ave Ste 800 Anaheim (92806) *(P-10523)*

Internal Revenue Service .... D...... 510 576-7589
2469 Arf Ave Hayward (94545) *(P-14786)*

Internal Revenue Service .... D...... 916 974-5678
9006 Morganfield Pl Elk Grove (95624) *(P-14787)*

Internal Services, Los Angeles *Also Called: County of Los Angeles (P-11519)*

Internal Services Department, Los Angeles *Also Called: County of Los Angeles (P-19556)*

Internal Services Department, Downey *Also Called: County of Los Angeles (P-20071)*

Internal Services Dept, Los Angeles *Also Called: County of Los Angeles (P-13247)*

International Bay Clubs LLC (PA) .... C...... 949 645-5000
1221 W Coast Hwy Ste 145 Newport Beach (92663) *(P-14384)*

International Building Inv Inc .... D...... 916 716-9565
6117 Grant Ave Carmichael (95608) *(P-760)*

International Bus Mchs Corp .... C...... 415 545-4747
425 Market St San Francisco (94105) *(P-5248)*

International Bus Mchs Corp .... A...... 408 463-2000
555 Bailey Ave San Jose (95141) *(P-11677)*

International Bus Mchs Corp .... B...... 408 927-1080
650 Harry Rd San Jose (95120) *(P-19712)*

INTERNATIONAL CHILD RESOURCE I, Berkeley *Also Called: Interntnal Child Rsrce Exch In (P-18596)*

INTERNATIONAL CHILDREN'S CHARI, Calabasas *Also Called: Help Children World Foundation (P-18001)*

International Coffee & Tea LLC (HQ) .... D...... 310 237-2326
5700 Wilshire Blvd Ste 120 Los Angeles (90036) *(P-7488)*

International Energy Services USA Inc .... C...... 310 257-8222
3445 Kashiwa St Torrance (90505) *(P-19271)*

International Energy Svcs Co, Torrance *Also Called: International Energy Services USA Inc (P-19271)*

International Fmly Entrmt Inc (DH) .... C...... 818 560-1000
3800 W Alameda Ave Burbank (91505) *(P-4512)*

International House .... C...... 510 642-9490
2299 Piedmont Ave Ste 535 Berkeley (94720) *(P-10393)*

International Iron Products, San Diego *Also Called: Price Industries Inc (P-2720)*

International Media Group Inc .... D...... 310 478-1818
1990 S Bundy Dr Ste 850 Los Angeles (90025) *(P-4442)*

International Medical Corps Inc .... A...... 310 826-7800
12400 Wilshire Blvd Ste 1500 Los Angeles (90025) *(P-18021)*

International Merchandising, Beverly Hills *Also Called: Wme Img LLC (P-14162)*

International Paper, Livermore *Also Called: Veritiv Operating Company (P-6093)*

International Paper, Visalia *Also Called: Graphic Packaging Intl LLC (P-6913)*

International Paving Svcs Inc .... D...... 909 794-2101
1199 Opal Ave Mentone (92359) *(P-1121)*

International Research Labs, Moorpark *Also Called: Lifetech Resources LLC (P-6121)*

International Trnsp Svc LLC (PA) .... C...... 562 435-7781
1281 Pier G Way Long Beach (90802) *(P-3810)*

International Vitamin Corporat (PA) .... D...... 949 664-5500
1 Park Plz Ste 800 Irvine (92614) *(P-2591)*

International Window Corp .... D...... 562 928-6411
1320 Performance Dr Stockton (95206) *(P-5168)*

Internet Archive .... C...... 415 561-6767
300 Funston Ave San Francisco (94118) *(P-12668)*

Internet Brands, El Segundo *Also Called: Mh Sub I LLC (P-10648)*

Internet Corp For Assgned Nmes (PA) .... C...... 310 823-9358
12025 Waterfront Dr Ste 300 Los Angeles (90094) *(P-12471)*

Internet Escrow Services Inc .... D...... 888 511-8600
180 Montgomery St Ste 650 San Francisco (94104) *(P-9052)*

Interntional Un Oper Engineers (PA) .... D...... 916 444-6880
1121 L St Ste 401 Sacramento (95814) *(P-18781)*

Interntional Un Oper Engineers .... A...... 619 295-3186
3935 Normal St San Diego (92103) *(P-18782)*

Interntional Un Oper Engineers .... A...... 909 307-8700
1647 W Lugonia Ave Redlands (92374) *(P-18783)*

Interntnal Brthd Elc Wkr Lcal (PA) .... D...... 707 452-2700
30 Orange Tree Cir Vacaville (95687) *(P-18784)*

Interntnal Ch of Frsqare Gospl (PA) .... D...... 714 701-1818
1910 W Sunset Blvd Los Angeles (90026) *(P-19022)*

Interntnal Child Rsrce Exch In (PA) .... C...... 510 644-1000
125 University Ave Ste 201 Berkeley (94710) *(P-18596)*

Interntnal Cnnctors Cable Corp .... C...... 888 275-4422
2100 E Valencia Dr Ste D Fullerton (92831) *(P-2886)*

Interntnal Fndtion For Krea Un .... B...... 213 550-2182
3435 Wilshire Blvd Ste 480 Los Angeles (90010) *(P-18597)*

Interntnal Hse At U C Berkeley, Berkeley *Also Called: International House (P-10393)*

Interntnal Un Oper Engners Lca .... B...... 510 748-7400
1620 S Loop Rd Alameda (94502) *(P-18785)*

Interpac Distribution Center, Woodland *Also Called: Interpac Technologies Inc (P-13328)*

Interpac Technologies Inc .... D...... 530 662-6363
260 N Pioneer Ave Woodland (95776) *(P-13328)*

Interpreting Services Intl LLC .... D...... 818 753-9181
700 N Brand Blvd Ste 950 Glendale (91203) *(P-13329)*

Interpublic Group of Companies, San Francisco *Also Called: McCann-Erickson Corporation (P-10645)*

Interstate Electric Co Inc .... D...... 800 225-5432
2240 Yates Ave Commerce (90040) *(P-5380)*

Interstate Foods Inc .... C...... 310 635-2442
310 S Long Beach Blvd Compton (90221) *(P-6445)*

ALPHABETIC SECTION
Iron Mechanical Inc

Interstate Hotels Resorts Inc .... D....... 805 966-2285
901 E Cabrillo Blvd Santa Barbara (93103) *(P-9913)*

Interstate Rhbltation Svcs LLC .... C....... 818 244-5656
333 E Glenoaks Blvd Ste 204 Glendale (91207) *(P-17077)*

Interstate Truck Center LLC (PA) .... D....... 209 944-5821
2110 S Sinclair Ave Stockton (95215) *(P-5013)*

Intertechsynco, Menlo Park *Also Called: Etl Testing Laboratories (P-19970)*

Intertek Pharmaceutical Svcs, San Diego *Also Called: Intertek USA Inc (P-19984)*

Intertek Testing Svcs NA Inc .... D....... 650 463-2900
1365 Adams Ct Menlo Park (94025) *(P-19983)*

Intertek USA Inc .... D....... 858 558-2599
10420 Wateridge Cir San Diego (92121) *(P-19984)*

Intertrend Communications Inc .... D....... 562 733-1888
228 E Broadway Long Beach (90802) *(P-10633)*

Interval House .... D....... 562 594-4555
6615 E Pacific Coast Hwy Ste 170 Long Beach (90803) *(P-18022)*

Intervalley Pools, Pomona *Also Called: Inter Valley Pool Supply Inc (P-5978)*

Intervest Property MGT Inc .... D....... 562 634-5672
5601 N Paramount Blvd Long Beach (90805) *(P-8828)*

Interviewing Service Amer LLC (PA) .... C....... 818 989-1044
15400 Sherman Way Ste 400 Van Nuys (91406) *(P-19824)*

Intervrsity Chrstn Fllwshp/Usa .... A....... 310 510-0015
Gallager&Apos;S Cove Avalon (90704) *(P-10405)*

Interwest Insurance Svcs LLC .... D....... 916 784-1008
5 Sierra Gate Plz 2nd Fl Roseville (95678) *(P-8593)*

Interwest Insurance Svcs LLC (PA) .... C....... 916 488-3100
8950 Cal Center Dr Bldg 3 # 200 Sacramento (95826) *(P-8594)*

Intex Properties S Bay Corp (PA) .... C....... 310 549-5400
4001 Via Oro Ave Ste 210 Long Beach (90810) *(P-5979)*

Intex Recreation Corp .... D....... 310 549-5400
4001 Via Oro Ave Long Beach (90810) *(P-5092)*

Intex Recreation Corp .... C....... 310 549-5400
1665 Hughes Way Long Beach (90810) *(P-8728)*

INTEX RECREATION CORP, Long Beach *Also Called: Intex Recreation Corp (P-8728)*

Intouch Health, Goleta *Also Called: Intouch Technologies Inc (P-18598)*

Intouch Technologies Inc (HQ) .... C....... 805 562-8686
7402 Hollister Ave Goleta (93117) *(P-18598)*

Intrado Interactive Svcs Corp .... D....... 888 527-5225
100 Enterprise Way Ste A300 Scotts Valley (95066) *(P-4365)*

Intravas Inc .... D....... 760 650-4040
6300 Yarrow Dr Carlsbad (92011) *(P-20416)*

Intrepid, San Rafael *Also Called: Pedersen Media Group Inc (P-20641)*

Intrepid Inv Bankers LLC .... A....... 310 478-9000
11755 Wilshire Blvd Ste 2200 Los Angeles (90025) *(P-9522)*

Intuit, Mountain View *Also Called: Intuit Inc (P-12238)*

Intuit Financial Services, Redwood City *Also Called: Digital Insight Corporation (P-12658)*

Intuit Inc (PA) .... D....... 650 944-6000
2700 Coast Ave Mountain View (94043) *(P-12238)*

Intuit Inc .... C....... 818 436-7800
21650 Oxnard St Ste 2200 Woodland Hills (91367) *(P-12239)*

Intuit Inc .... C....... 650 944-6000
2535 Garcia Ave Mountain View (94043) *(P-12240)*

Intuit Inc .... C....... 858 780-2846
7535 Torrey Santa Fe Rd San Diego (92129) *(P-12241)*

Intuit Inc .... B....... 858 215-8000
7545 Torrey Santa Fe Rd San Diego (92129) *(P-12242)*

Invasix Inc .... D....... 855 418-5306
17 Hughes Irvine (92618) *(P-19713)*

Inventure Capital Corporation (PA) .... A....... 213 262-6903
429 Santa Monica Blvd Ste 450 Santa Monica (90401) *(P-9523)*

Inveserve Corporation .... D....... 626 458-3435
812 W Las Tunas Dr San Gabriel (91776) *(P-9053)*

Investbank Corp .... D....... 858 225-7825
4231 Balboa Ave # 1077 San Diego (92117) *(P-7920)*

Investopedia LLC .... C....... 510 985-7400
555 12th St Ste 500 Oakland (94607) *(P-12243)*

Invision, Walnut Creek *Also Called: Invision Communications Inc (P-20417)*

Invision Communications Inc (PA) .... D....... 925 944-1211
1280 Civic Dr 3rd Fl Walnut Creek (94596) *(P-20417)*

Invision Networking LLC .... C....... 949 309-3441
333 City Blvd W Ste 1700 Orange (92868) *(P-12816)*

INVITAE, San Francisco *Also Called: Invitae Corporation (P-16728)*

Invitae Corporation (PA) .... A....... 415 374-7782
1400 16th St San Francisco (94103) *(P-16728)*

Invitation Homes Inc .... D....... 805 372-2900
680 E Colorado Blvd Pasadena (91101) *(P-9054)*

Invoice2go LLC (DH) .... C....... 650 300-5180
2317 Broadway St Fl 2 Redwood City (94063) *(P-12244)*

Invuity Inc .... C....... 415 665-2100
444 De Haro St Ste 110 San Francisco (94107) *(P-3055)*

Inxeption Corporation .... C....... 888 852-4783
20450 Stevens Creek Blvd Ste 150 Cupertino (95014) *(P-12817)*

Iogear, Irvine *Also Called: Aten Technology Inc (P-5276)*

Ione Primemed Clinic, Ione *Also Called: Lodi Memorial Hosp Assn Inc (P-16219)*

Ionis, Carlsbad *Also Called: Ionis Pharmaceuticals Inc (P-2592)*

Ionis Pharmaceuticals Inc (PA) .... B....... 760 931-9200
2855 Gazelle Ct Carlsbad (92010) *(P-2592)*

Ionpath Inc .... D....... 650 336-3058
1455 Adams Dr 1036 Menlo Park (94025) *(P-19888)*

Iota Biosciences Inc .... D....... 831 229-3524
1020 Atlantic Ave Alameda (94501) *(P-19714)*

Ipayment Inc .... B....... 213 387-1353
3325 Wilshire Blvd Ste 535 Los Angeles (90010) *(P-13330)*

IPC Healthcare Inc (DH) .... C....... 888 447-2362
4605 Lankershim Blvd Ste 617 North Hollywood (91602) *(P-14788)*

Ipd, Carson *Also Called: Industrial Parts Depot LLC (P-5840)*

Ipi Travel, San Diego *Also Called: Innovative Placements Inc (P-11156)*

Ipitek, Carlsbad *Also Called: Ipitek Inc (P-1757)*

Ipitek Inc .... C....... 760 438-1010
2461 Impala Dr Carlsbad (92010) *(P-1757)*

Ipolipo Inc .... D....... 408 916-5290
440 N Wolfe Rd Sunnyvale (94085) *(P-12245)*

Ipsos Otx Corporation (HQ) .... C....... 310 736-3400
300 Corporate Pointe Ste 500 Culver City (90230) *(P-19825)*

Ipt, Goleta *Also Called: Integrated Procurement Tech (P-5958)*

Iptor Supply Chain Systems USA (DH) .... C....... 916 542-2820
915 Highland Pointe Dr Roseville (95678) *(P-11678)*

Iqa Solutions Inc .... D....... 562 420-1000
4089 E Conant St Long Beach (90808) *(P-19272)*

Iqms LLC (DH) .... C....... 805 227-1122
2231 Wisteria Ln Paso Robles (93446) *(P-12246)*

Iqvia Inc .... D....... 415 692-9898
135 Main St Fl 22 San Francisco (94105) *(P-19826)*

Iqvia Inc (DH) .... D....... 866 267-4479
2601 Main St Ste 650 Irvine (92614) *(P-19827)*

Iraje, Pleasanton *Also Called: Iraje Inc (P-13126)*

Iraje Inc .... C....... 925 400-6558
6200 Stnrdge Mall Rd Ste Pleasanton (94588) *(P-13126)*

Irell & Manella LLP .... B....... 949 760-0991
840 Newport Center Dr Ste 400 Newport Beach (92660) *(P-17501)*

Irell & Manella LLP (PA) .... C....... 310 277-1010
1800 Avenue Of The Stars Ste 900 Los Angeles (90067) *(P-17502)*

Irene Swndlls Adult Day Care P, San Francisco *Also Called: Institute On Aging (P-18016)*

Iris Usa Inc .... C....... 209 982-9100
3021 Boeing Way Stockton (95206) *(P-6634)*

Irise (PA) .... D....... 800 556-0399
2381 Rosecrans Ave Ste 100 El Segundo (90245) *(P-11679)*

Irish Communication Company (DH) .... D....... 626 288-6170
2649 Stingle Ave Rosemead (91770) *(P-1219)*

Irish Communication Company .... C....... 916 383-9000
8449 Specialty Cir Sacramento (95828) *(P-1220)*

Irish Construction (HQ) .... C....... 626 288-8530
2641 River Ave Rosemead (91770) *(P-1221)*

Irish Construction Company, Sacramento *Also Called: Irish Communication Company (P-1220)*

Irish Interiors Inc (HQ) .... C....... 949 559-0930
5511 Skylab Rd Ste 101 Huntington Beach (92647) *(P-2991)*

Irisys Inc .... D....... 858 623-1520
6828 Nancy Ridge Dr Ste 100 San Diego (92121) *(P-6114)*

Iron Mechanical Inc (PA) .... D....... 916 341-3530
721 N B St Ste 100 Sacramento (95811) *(P-1469)*

ALPHABETIC SECTION

Iron Mountain Info MGT LLC .... D...... 818 848-9766
441 N Oak St Inglewood (90302) *(P-4041)*

Iron Systems Inc (PA) .... D...... **408 943-8000**
980 Mission Ct Fremont (94539) *(P-5317)*

Ironman Renewal LLC .... D...... 951 735-3710
2535 Anselmo Dr Corona (92879) *(P-13664)*

IRONWORKERS UNION, Pasadena Also Called: Ironwrker Emplyees Beneft Corp *(P-9429)*

Ironwrker Emplyees Beneft Corp .... D...... 626 792-7337
131 N El Molino Ave Ste 330 Pasadena (91101) *(P-9429)*

Irp Lax Hotel LLC .... C...... 310 645-4600
9750 Airport Blvd Los Angeles (90045) *(P-9914)*

Irriscape Construction Inc .... D...... 951 694-6936
20182 Carancho Rd Temecula (92590) *(P-499)*

Irvine APT Communities LP .... C...... 714 937-8900
299 N State College Blvd Orange (92868) *(P-8829)*

Irvine APT Communities LP .... C...... 310 255-1221
1221 Ocean Ave Santa Monica (90401) *(P-8830)*

Irvine APT Communities LP .... C...... 949 854-4942
146 Berkeley Irvine (92612) *(P-8831)*

Irvine APT Communities LP .... C...... 408 943-1595
39 Rio Robles E San Jose (95134) *(P-8832)*

Irvine APT Communities LP .... C...... 714 537-8500
13212 Magnolia St Ofc Garden Grove (92844) *(P-8833)*

Irvine APT Communities LP (HQ) .... C...... 949 720-5600
110 Innovation Dr Irvine (92617) *(P-8834)*

Irvine APT Communities LP .... B...... 714 505-7181
100 Robinson Dr Tustin (92782) *(P-8835)*

Irvine Company Office Property, Newport Beach Also Called: Irvine Eastgate Office II LLC *(P-9470)*

Irvine Eastgate Office II LLC .... A...... 949 720-2000
550 Newport Center Dr Newport Beach (92660) *(P-9470)*

Irvine Medical Center, Orange Also Called: University California Irvine *(P-16603)*

Irvine Ranch Water District (PA) .... C...... 949 453-5300
15600 Sand Canyon Ave Irvine (92618) *(P-4796)*

Irvine Ranch Water District .... C...... 949 453-5300
3512 Michelson Dr Irvine (92612) *(P-4797)*

Irvine Regional Hospital, Anaheim Also Called: Tenet Healthsystem Medical Inc *(P-16571)*

Irvine Technology Corporation .... C...... 714 445-2624
2850 Redhill Ave Ste 230 Santa Ana (92705) *(P-20782)*

Irwin Industries Inc .... A...... 704 457-5117
2301 Rosecrans Ave Ste 3185 El Segundo (90245) *(P-1307)*

Irwin International Inc (PA) .... D...... 951 372-9555
225 Airport Cir Corona (92878) *(P-7400)*

Irwindale 6000, Irwindale Also Called: Southern California Edison Co *(P-4686)*

ISA, Van Nuys Also Called: Interviewing Service Amer LLC *(P-19824)*

Isaac Fair Corporation .... D...... 858 369-8000
3661 Valley Centre Dr San Diego (92130) *(P-11680)*

Iscs Inc .... C...... 408 362-3000
100 Great Oaks Blvd Ste 100 San Jose (95119) *(P-11681)*

ISE Corporation .... C...... 858 413-1720
12302 Kerran St Poway (92064) *(P-19715)*

ISE Labs Inc (DH) .... C...... **510 687-2500**
46800 Bayside Pkwy Fremont (94538) *(P-19985)*

Isearch Media LLC .... C...... 415 358-0882
1710 S Amphlett Blvd Ste 320 San Mateo (94402) *(P-10634)*

Isec Incorporated .... C...... 858 279-9085
10105 Carroll Canyon Rd San Diego (92131) *(P-826)*

Isec Incorporated .... D...... 805 375-6957
2363 Teller Rd Ste 106 Newbury Park (91320) *(P-2003)*

Isec Incorporated .... C...... 707 693-6555
1855 N 1st St Unit D Dixon (95620) *(P-2004)*

Isec Incorporated .... C...... 714 761-5151
20 Centerpointe Dr Ste 140 La Palma (90623) *(P-2005)*

Iserve Residential Lending LLC .... C...... 858 486-4169
10920 Via Frontera Ste 520 San Diego (92127) *(P-7985)*

Ishares, San Francisco Also Called: Blackrock Instnl Tr Nat Assn *(P-9361)*

Isheriff Inc .... C...... 650 412-4300
555 Twin Dolphin Dr Redwood City (94065) *(P-11682)*

ISI, Santa Rosa Also Called: Inquiring Systems Inc *(P-20414)*

ISI Inspection Services Inc (PA) .... D...... 510 900-2101
1798 University Ave Berkeley (94703) *(P-13331)*

Isiqalo LLC .... B...... 714 683-2820
5610 Daniels St Chino (91710) *(P-2445)*

Isl Employees Inc .... D...... 760 547-2863
2333 State St Ste 300 Carlsbad (92008) *(P-18461)*

Island Global Holdings Inc .... D...... 301 742-0775
6100 Bandini Blvd Commerce (90040) *(P-20418)*

Island Hospitality MGT LLC 650 574-4700
2000 Winward Way San Mateo (94404) *(P-9915)*

Island Hospitality MGT LLC .... D...... 408 720-8893
1080 Stewart Dr Sunnyvale (94085) *(P-9916)*

Isolation Network Inc (PA) .... D...... 818 212-2600
55 Francisco St Ste 350 San Francisco (94133) *(P-2880)*

Isotis Orthobiologics Inc .... C...... 949 595-8710
2 Goodyear Ste A Irvine (92618) *(P-19716)*

Ispace Inc .... C...... 310 563-3800
840 Apollo St Ste 100 El Segundo (90245) *(P-12818)*

Isuzu North America Corp (HQ) .... C...... **714 935-9300**
1400 S Douglass Rd Ste 100 Anaheim (92806) *(P-7236)*

Isuzu Truck Services, Santa Ana Also Called: Toms Truck Center Inc *(P-7314)*

Isys Solutions Inc .... D...... 714 521-7656
2601 Saturn St Ste 302 Brea (92821) *(P-20419)*

It Division Inc .... C...... 678 648-2709
9170 Irvine Center Dr Ste 200 Irvine (92618) *(P-17792)*

It Is Written, Riverside Also Called: Adventist Media Center Inc *(P-14025)*

Italfoods Inc .... D...... 650 877-0724
205 Shaw Rd South San Francisco (94080) *(P-6259)*

Itc Nexus Holding Company, San Diego Also Called: Accriva Dgnostics Holdings Inc *(P-3046)*

Itc Srvice Group Acqsition LLC .... C...... 530 717-0485
108 N East St Woodland (95776) *(P-20783)*

Itco Solutions Inc .... B...... 650 367-0514
1003 Whitehall Ln Redwood City (94061) *(P-12819)*

ITD Arizona Inc .... D...... 323 722-8542
6737 E Washington Blvd Commerce (90040) *(P-5070)*

Itek Services Inc .... D...... 949 770-4835
25501 Arctic Ocean Dr Lake Forest (92630) *(P-12820)*

Ito Packing Co Inc .... C...... 559 638-2531
1592 11th St Ste H Reedley (93654) *(P-280)*

Itrex Group USA Corporation .... B...... 213 436-7785
120 Vantis Dr Ste 545 Aliso Viejo (92656) *(P-11683)*

Itron Networked Solutions Inc (HQ) .... B...... **669 770-4000**
230 W Tasman Dr San Jose (95134) *(P-4540)*

ITW Rippey, El Dorado Hills Also Called: Rippey Corporation *(P-5342)*

Iunlimited Incorporated .... C...... 916 218-6198
7801 Folsom Blvd Ste 203 Sacramento (95826) *(P-12990)*

Ivanhoe, Exeter Also Called: Exeter-Ivanhoe Citrus Assn *(P-267)*

Ivy Enterprises Inc .... B...... 323 887-8661
5564 E 61st St Commerce (90040) *(P-20784)*

Iwamoto & Gean Farm 805 659-4568
2064 Olga St Oxnard (93036) *(P-35)*

Iwc, Stockton Also Called: International Window Corp *(P-5168)*

Iwerks Entertainment Inc .... D...... 661 678-1800
25040 Avenue Tibbitts Ste F Valencia (91355) *(P-2959)*

Ix Systems, San Jose Also Called: Ixsystems Inc *(P-11684)*

Ixia (HQ) .... B...... **818 871-1800**
26601 Agoura Rd Calabasas (91302) *(P-3026)*

Ixia, Santa Clara Also Called: Net Optics Inc *(P-12282)*

Ixsystems Inc (PA) .... C...... **408 943-4100**
2490 Kruse Dr San Jose (95131) *(P-11684)*

Ixys Intgrted Crcits Div AV In .... A...... 949 831-4622
145 Columbia Aliso Viejo (92656) *(P-2924)*

Iyuno-Sdi Group, Los Angeles Also Called: SDI Media USA Inc *(P-13891)*

Izmocars, San Francisco Also Called: Homestar Systems Inc *(P-12803)*

J & D Meat Company .... C...... 559 445-1123
4671 E Edgar Ave Fresno (93725) *(P-6635)*

J & J Acoustics Inc .... C...... 408 275-9255
2260 De La Cruz Blvd Santa Clara (95050) *(P-1937)*

J & J Air Conditioning Inc .... D...... 408 920-0662
1086 N 11th St San Jose (95112) *(P-1470)*

J & J Snack Foods Corp Cal (HQ) .... C...... **323 581-0171**
5353 S Downey Rd Vernon (90058) *(P-2371)*

ALPHABETIC SECTION

J & L Collections Services Inc .... D....... 800 481-6006
  8220 Longleaf Dr # 400 Elk Grove (95758) *(P-10744)*

J & L Daycare .... D....... 909 796-2656
  24723 Redlands Blvd Ste A-C Loma Linda (92354) *(P-18462)*

J & L Vineyards .... D....... 559 268-1627
  1850 Ramada Dr Ste 3 Paso Robles (93446) *(P-75)*

J & M Sales Inc .... A....... 310 324-9962
  15001 S Figueroa St Gardena (90248) *(P-7407)*

J B, Chatsworth Also Called: J B Whl Roofg Bldg Sups Inc *(P-7029)*

J B Hunt Transport Inc .... C....... 209 235-1371
  2660 Loomis Rd Stockton (95205) *(P-3494)*

J B Hunt Transport Inc .... C....... 385 226-4538
  3305 S Chestnut Ave Fresno (93725) *(P-3495)*

J B Hunt Transport Inc .... C....... 866 759-1127
  3170 Crow Canyon Pl Ste 180 San Ramon (94583) *(P-3496)*

J B Oxford & Co, Beverly Hills Also Called: National Clearing Corporation *(P-20482)*

J B Whl Roofg Bldg Sups Inc (DH).. D....... 818 998-0440
  21524 Nordhoff St Chatsworth (91311) *(P-7029)*

J Baron Inc .... D....... 949 451-1200
  5299 Alton Pkwy Irvine (92604) *(P-9055)*

J C C, San Rafael Also Called: Bernard Osher Mrin Jwish Cmnty *(P-17851)*

J C Entertainment Ltg Svcs Inc .... C....... 818 252-7481
  5435 W San Fernando Rd Los Angeles (90039) *(P-14041)*

J C Sales, Vernon Also Called: Shims Bargain Inc *(P-6948)*

J Craig Venter Institute Inc (PA)... B....... 301 795-7000
  4120 Capricorn Ln La Jolla (92037) *(P-19889)*

J D Diffenbaugh Inc .... D....... 951 351-6865
  6865 Airport Dr Riverside (92504) *(P-942)*

J D L Motor Express .... D....... 619 232-6136
  1250 Delevan Dr San Diego (92102) *(P-3407)*

J D Pasquetti Engineering .... D....... 916 543-9401
  3032 Thunder Valley Ct Ste 200 Lincoln (95648) *(P-19273)*

J G Boswell Company .... B....... 661 327-7721
  21101 Bear Mountain Blvd Bakersfield (93311) *(P-3)*

J G Boswell Company .... D....... 559 992-5141
  28001 S Dairy Ave Corcoran (93212) *(P-4)*

J G Boswell Company .... B....... 661 764-9000
  36889 Hwy 58 Buttonwillow (93206) *(P-92)*

J G Boswell Company .... B....... 559 992-5011
  26073 Santa Fe Ave Corcoran (93212) *(P-211)*

J G Boswell Company .... D....... 559 992-2141
  710 Bainum Ave Corcoran (93212) *(P-281)*

J G Construction, Chino Also Called: J Grothe Enterprises Inc *(P-943)*

J Ginger Masonry LP (PA)... B....... 951 688-5050
  8188 Lincoln Ave Ste 100 Riverside (92504) *(P-1885)*

J Grothe Enterprises Inc .... D....... 909 993-9393
  15632 El Prado Rd Chino (91710) *(P-943)*

J H Snyder Company LLC .... D....... 323 857-5546
  5757 Wilshire Blvd Ph 30 Los Angeles (90036) *(P-9056)*

J I T Supply, Norco Also Called: JIT Corporation *(P-5666)*

J Kenneth Forester .... D....... 201 288-5040
  7400 Flightline Dr Santa Rosa (95403) *(P-3865)*

J L Fisher Inc .... D....... 818 846-8366
  1000 W Isabel St Burbank (91506) *(P-11037)*

J L Wingert Company .... D....... 714 379-5519
  1298 N Blue Gum St Anaheim (92806) *(P-2848)*

J M Carden Sprinkler Co Inc .... D....... 323 258-8300
  2909 Fletcher Dr Los Angeles (90065) *(P-1471)*

J M D Enterprises (PA)... D....... 925 935-4780
  1434 N Main St Walnut Creek (94596) *(P-10500)*

J M Equipment Company Inc (PA)....................................... D....... 209 522-3271
  321 Spreckels Ave Manteca (95336) *(P-11038)*

J M Fremont Motors LLC .... D....... 510 403-3700
  43191 Boscell Rd Fremont (94538) *(P-7237)*

J M V B Inc .... D....... 714 288-9797
  12118 Severn Way Riverside (92503) *(P-1623)*

J Marchini & Son Inc .... C....... 559 665-2944
  12000 Le Grand Rd Le Grand (95333) *(P-184)*

J P H Consulting Inc .... C....... 323 934-5660
  4515 Huntington Dr S Los Angeles (90032) *(P-15525)*

J R Roberts Corp (HQ).. D....... 916 729-5600
  7745 Greenback Ln Ste 300 Citrus Heights (95610) *(P-944)*

J R Roberts Enterprises Inc .... C....... 916 729-5600
  7745 Greenback Ln Ste 300 Citrus Heights (95610) *(P-945)*

J Robert Scott Inc (PA).. C
  722 N La Cienega Blvd West Hollywood (90069) *(P-6155)*

J S West Prokrane Gas, Modesto Also Called: The Sonora J S West & Co Inc *(P-7426)*

J W Floor Covering Inc (PA)... C....... 858 536-8565
  9881 Carroll Centre Rd San Diego (92126) *(P-2038)*

J W Mrrott Los Angles L A Live .... D....... 213 765-8600
  900 W Olympic Blvd Los Angeles (90015) *(P-9917)*

J Waters Inc .... D....... 866 424-1946
  75 San Miguel Ave Ste 5 Salinas (93901) *(P-12991)*

J-M Manufacturing Company Inc .... D....... 909 822-3009
  10990 Hemlock Ave Fontana (92337) *(P-2576)*

J. W. Floor Covering, San Diego Also Called: J W Floor Covering Inc *(P-2038)*

J.L. Haley, Rancho Cordova Also Called: Vander-Bend Manufacturing Inc *(P-2857)*

J&E Private Security Corp .... D....... 909 594-1111
  3227 Producer Way Ste 110 Pomona (91768) *(P-12992)*

J&G Berry Farms LLC .... C....... 831 750-9408
  720 Rosemary Rd Santa Maria (93454) *(P-55)*

J&G Industries Inc .... D....... 949 207-3505
  7545 Irvine Center Dr Ste 200 Irvine (92618) *(P-2238)*

J&L Teamworks, Elk Grove Also Called: J & L Collections Services Inc *(P-10744)*

J&M Keystone Inc .... C....... 619 466-9876
  2709 Via Orange Way Ste A Spring Valley (91978) *(P-2286)*

J&S Goodwin Inc (HQ)... D....... 714 956-4040
  5753 E Santa Ana Canyon Rd Ste G-355 Anaheim (92807) *(P-2778)*

J2 Cloud Services LLC (HQ).. D....... 323 860-9200
  700 S Flower St Fl 15 Los Angeles (90017) *(P-4366)*

Jabil Silver Creek Inc (HQ)... C....... 669 255-2900
  4050 Technology Pl Fremont (94538) *(P-13752)*

Jacada Autonomous Cx, Palo Alto Also Called: Jacada Inc *(P-12247)*

Jacada Inc .... D....... 770 352-1300
  1001 Page Mill Rd Ste 100 Palo Alto (94304) *(P-12247)*

Jack Gosch Ford Inc .... D....... 951 658-3181
  150 Carriage Cir Hemet (92545) *(P-7238)*

Jack In Box Inc (PA).. A....... 858 571-2121
  9357 Spectrum Center Blvd San Diego (92123) *(P-7489)*

Jack In The Box, San Diego Also Called: Jack In Box Inc *(P-7489)*

Jack In The Box, Fremont Also Called: Yadav Enterprises Inc *(P-7519)*

Jack Jones Trucking Inc .... D....... 909 456-2500
  1090 E Belmont St Ontario (91761) *(P-3497)*

Jack Nadel Inc (PA)... D....... 310 815-2600
  5820 Uplander Way Culver City (90230) *(P-20420)*

Jack Nadel International, Culver City Also Called: Jack Nadel Inc *(P-20420)*

Jack Neal & Son Inc .... C....... 707 963-7303
  360 Lafata St Saint Helena (94574) *(P-76)*

Jack Pwell Chrysler - Ddge Inc .... D....... 760 745-2880
  1625 Auto Park Way Escondido (92029) *(P-7239)*

Jack Pwell Chrysler Ddge Jeep, Escondido Also Called: Jack Pwell Chrysler - Ddge Inc *(P-7239)*

Jack's Disposal Inc, San Bernardino Also Called: Burrtec Waste Industries Inc *(P-4871)*

Jackie Robinson Family YMCA, San Diego Also Called: YMCA of San Diego County *(P-18947)*

Jackaway Tyrman Wrthmer Asten .... D....... 310 553-0305
  1925 Century Park E 2nd Fl Los Angeles (90067) *(P-17503)*

Jacks Candy, Los Angeles Also Called: Consolidated Svc Distrs Inc *(P-6459)*

Jacks Car Wash 3 .... D....... 559 408-8201
  6745 N West Ave Fresno (93711) *(P-13694)*

Jackson & Blanc .... C....... 858 831-7900
  7929 Arjons Dr San Diego (92126) *(P-1472)*

Jackson Family Wines Inc (PA).. D....... 707 544-4000
  425 Aviation Blvd Santa Rosa (95403) *(P-2387)*

Jackson Laboratory .... D....... 800 422-6423
  1650 Santa Ana Ave Sacramento (95838) *(P-19890)*

Jackson Shrub Supply Inc .... D....... 818 982-0100
  11505 Vanowen St North Hollywood (91605) *(P-13940)*

Jacksons Hardware Inc .... D....... 415 870-4083
  435 Du Bois St. At Andersen Dr San Rafael (94901) *(P-5730)*

Jacmar Companies, The, Alhambra Also Called: Pacific Ventures Ltd *(P-20172)*

Jacob's Farm, Santa Cruz Also Called: Jacobs Farm/Del Cabo Inc *(P-185)*

Jacobs Atcs Fema A Joint Ventr   **ALPHABETIC SECTION**

Jacobs Atcs Fema A Joint Ventr .... D 571 218-1115
   155 N Lake Ave Fl 5 Pasadena (91101) *(P-19274)*

Jacobs Civil Inc .... C 310 847-2500
   1500 Hughes Way Ste B400 Long Beach (90810) *(P-19275)*

Jacobs Engineering Company .... A 626 449-2171
   1111 S Arroyo Pkwy Pasadena (91105) *(P-19276)*

Jacobs Engineering Group Inc .... D 949 224-7500
   2600 Michelson Dr Ste 500 Irvine (92612) *(P-19277)*

Jacobs Engineering Group Inc .... D 408 436-4936
   1737 N 1st St Ste 300 San Jose (95112) *(P-19278)*

Jacobs Engineering Group Inc .... D 626 578-3500
   1111 S Arroyo Pkwy Pasadena (91105) *(P-19279)*

Jacobs Engineering Inc (DH) .... C **626 578-3500**
   155 N Lake Ave Pasadena (91101) *(P-19280)*

Jacobs Farm/Del Cabo Inc .... D 831 421-9171
   1751 Coast Rd Santa Cruz (95060) *(P-185)*

Jacobs Farm/Del Cabo Inc .... D 650 827-1133
   390 Swift Ave Ste 8 South San Francisco (94080) *(P-186)*

Jacobs Government Services Co .... C 949 224-7500
   2600 Michelson Dr Ste 500 Irvine (92612) *(P-19281)*

Jacobs International Ltd Inc .... B 626 578-3500
   155 N Lake Ave Ste 800 Pasadena (91101) *(P-19282)*

Jacobs Project Management Co .... D 949 224-7908
   4 Embarcadero Ctr Ste 3800 San Francisco (94111) *(P-19283)*

Jacobs Project Management Co .... D 949 224-7695
   2600 Michelson Dr Ste 500 Irvine (92612) *(P-19284)*

Jacobs Technology Inc .... D 650 604-3784
   Building 227 Room 117a Mountain View (94035) *(P-19285)*

Jacobsson Engrg Cnstr Inc .... D 760 345-8700
   72310 Varner Rd Thousand Palms (92276) *(P-1122)*

Jacoby & Meyers Attys LLP .... D 310 312-3300
   10900 Wilshire Blvd Ste 930 Los Angeles (90024) *(P-17504)*

Jacuzzi Products Co .... B 909 548-7732
   14525 Monte Vista Ave Chino (91710) *(P-2667)*

Jade Inc .... D 818 365-7137
   11126 Sepulveda Blvd Ste B Mission Hills (91345) *(P-1938)*

Jag Professional Services Inc .... C 310 945-5648
   2008 Walnut Ave Manhattan Beach (90266) *(P-20785)*

Jagpreet Enterprises LLC .... C 510 336-8376
   3374 Enterprise Ave Hayward (94545) *(P-6636)*

Jake Hey Incorporated .... C 323 856-5280
   257 S Lake St Burbank (91502) *(P-13160)*

Jakov Dulcich and Sons LLC .... C 661 792-6360
   31956 Peterson Rd Mc Farland (93250) *(P-77)*

Jam City Inc .... D 804 920-8760
   2255 N Ontario St Burbank (91504) *(P-12248)*

Jam Fire Protection Inc .... D 858 495-2335
   8254 Ronson Rd San Diego (92111) *(P-7586)*

Jamboor Medical Corporation .... D 760 241-8063
   12675 Hesperia Rd Victorville (92395) *(P-16989)*

Jamboree Management, Laguna Hills *Also Called: Jamboree Realty Corp (P-9057)*

Jamboree Realty Corp (PA) .... C **949 380-0300**
   22982 Mill Creek Dr Laguna Hills (92653) *(P-9057)*

Jame Hotel Corporation .... D 415 885-2500
   405 Taylor St San Francisco (94102) *(P-9918)*

Jameco Electronics, Belmont *Also Called: James Electronics Limited (P-7561)*

James Allison Estates & Homes .... C 866 463-5780
   1902 Wright Pl Carlsbad (92008) *(P-682)*

James C Jenkins Insur Svc Inc .... C 925 798-3334
   1390 Willow Pass Rd Ste 800 Concord (94520) *(P-8595)*

James E Roberts-Obayashi Corp .... C 925 820-0600
   20 Oak Ct Danville (94526) *(P-761)*

James Electronics Limited .... D 650 592-6718
   1355 Shoreway Rd Belmont (94002) *(P-7561)*

James G Parker Insurance Assoc (PA) .... D **559 222-7722**
   1753 E Fir Ave Fresno (93720) *(P-8596)*

James H Cowan & Associates Inc .... D 310 457-2574
   5126 Clareton Dr Ste 200 Agoura Hills (91301) *(P-500)*

James Hardie Building Pdts Inc .... C 909 355-6500
   10901 Elm Ave Fontana (92337) *(P-5169)*

James Metals, Riverside *Also Called: Harbor Pipe and Steel Inc (P-5496)*

James Nevada Properties, Roseville *Also Called: Dick James & Associates Inc (P-8982)*

James R Gldwell Dntl Crmics In (PA) .... A **949 440-2600**
   4141 Macarthur Blvd Newport Beach (92660) *(P-16773)*

James Rebecca Prouty Entps Inc .... D 951 292-9777
   43980 Margarita Rd Ste 102 Temecula (92592) *(P-16880)*

Jameson Inn, North Hollywood *Also Called: Park Management Group LLC (P-10105)*

Jamestown Community Center Inc .... D 415 647-4709
   2929 19th St San Francisco (94110) *(P-18871)*

Janco Corporation .... C 818 361-3366
   13955 Balboa Blvd Rancho Cascades (91342) *(P-2943)*

Jane Technologies Inc .... D 617 285-2466
   1347 Pacific Ave Ste 201 Santa Cruz (95060) *(P-5318)*

Janitek Cleaning Solutions, Stockton *Also Called: Wtmg Inc (P-10987)*

Jankovich Company LLC .... D 619 232-4939
   961 E Harbor Dr San Diego (92101) *(P-6731)*

Janpro Inc .... C 408 293-7679
   92 N Bascom Ave San Jose (95128) *(P-10913)*

Jans Towing Inc .... C 909 596-9060
   134 N Valencia Ave Glendora (91741) *(P-13716)*

Janssen Alzheimer Immunothera .... D 650 794-2500
   700 Gateway Blvd South San Francisco (94080) *(P-19717)*

Janus Corporation (PA) .... D **925 969-9200**
   1081 Shary Cir Concord (94518) *(P-2287)*

Janus Et Cie (PA) .... C 310 601-2958
   12310 Greenstone Ave Santa Fe Springs (90670) *(P-5093)*

Janus of Santa Cruz .... D 831 462-1060
   200 7th Ave Ste 150 Santa Cruz (95062) *(P-16684)*

Japanese Cmnty Youth Council (PA) .... D **415 202-7905**
   2012 Pine St San Francisco (94115) *(P-18599)*

Japanese Retirement Home, Los Angeles *Also Called: Senior Keiro Health Care (P-18520)*

Japonesque, San Ramon *Also Called: Japonesque LLC (P-6115)*

Japonesque LLC .... D 925 866-6670
   12647 Alcosta Blvd Ste 375 San Ramon (94583) *(P-6115)*

Jarrow Formulas Inc (PA) .... D **310 204-6936**
   15233 Ventura Blvd Fl 900 Sherman Oaks (91403) *(P-6116)*

Jasper Hall LLC .... D 415 872-5745
   420 Mason St San Francisco (94102) *(P-10556)*

Jasper Ridge Partners .... D 650 494-4800
   2885 Sand Hill Rd Ste 100 Menlo Park (94025) *(P-9401)*

Jaspersoft Corporation .... C 415 348-2300
   350 Rhode Island St # 250 San Francisco (94103) *(P-12584)*

Java City (HQ) .... D **916 565-5500**
   1300 Del Paso Rd Sacramento (95834) *(P-6637)*

Java City, Sacramento *Also Called: Cucina Holdings Inc (P-7471)*

Javelin Logistics Company Inc .... C 800 577-1060
   7025 Central Ave Newark (94560) *(P-4042)*

Jay Nolan Community Svcs Inc .... C 408 293-5002
   1190 S Bascom Ave Ste 240 San Jose (95128) *(P-18023)*

Jay's Catering, Garden Grove *Also Called: Mastroianni Family Entps Ltd (P-10561)*

Jayem Enterprises Inc .... D 310 329-2263
   14930 S San Pedro St Gardena (90248) *(P-5498)*

Jazzercise, Carlsbad *Also Called: Jazzercise Inc (P-14209)*

Jazzercise Inc (PA) .... D **760 476-1750**
   2460 Impala Dr Carlsbad (92010) *(P-14209)*

JB Bostick Company Inc (PA) .... D **714 238-2121**
   2870 E La Cresta Ave Anaheim (92806) *(P-1123)*

JB Dental Supply Co Inc (PA) .... C **310 202-8855**
   17000 Kingsview Ave Carson (90746) *(P-5426)*

JBa Consulting Engineers Inc .... D 949 419-3030
   163 Technology Dr Ste 100 Irvine (92618) *(P-19286)*

Jbi LLC (PA) .... C **310 886-8034**
   2650 E El Presidio St Long Beach (90810) *(P-2509)*

Jbi Interiors, Long Beach *Also Called: Jbi LLC (P-2509)*

JC Penney, San Bernardino *Also Called: Penney Opco LLC (P-3743)*

JC Penney, Sacramento *Also Called: Penney Opco LLC (P-7129)*

JC Penney, Arcadia *Also Called: Penney Opco LLC (P-7130)*

JC Penney, Thousand Oaks *Also Called: Penney Opco LLC (P-7131)*

JC Penney, Stockton *Also Called: Penney Opco LLC (P-7132)*

JC Penney, Chico *Also Called: Penney Opco LLC (P-7134)*

JC Penney 1505, West Covina *Also Called: Penney Opco LLC (P-7133)*

ALPHABETIC SECTION

JC Resorts LLC .... A....... 949 376-2779
  1555 S Coast Hwy Laguna Beach (92651) *(P-20119)*
JC Resorts LLC .... B....... 760 944-1936
  4154 Maryland St San Diego (92103) *(P-20120)*
JC Resorts LLC .... C....... 858 675-8500
  17550 Bernardo Oaks Dr San Diego (92128) *(P-20121)*
JC Sales, Commerce *Also Called: Shims Bargain Inc (P-842)*
JC Weight Loss Centres Inc (PA) .... C....... 760 696-4000
  5770 Fleet St Carlsbad (92008) *(P-10557)*
Jcm Engineering Corp .... D....... 909 923-3730
  2690 E Cedar St Ontario (91761) *(P-5959)*
JCP, Visalia *Also Called: Penney Opco LLC (P-7128)*
Jcyc .... D....... 415 921-5537
  2012 Pine St San Francisco (94115) *(P-17078)*
JD Food, Fresno *Also Called: J & D Meat Company (P-6635)*
JD Pasquetti Engineering, Lincoln *Also Called: J D Pasquetti Engineering (P-19273)*
JD Power and Associates Inc .... C....... 805 418-8000
  2625 Townsgate Rd Ste 100 Westlake Village (91361) *(P-19828)*
Jdi Distribution, Loma Linda *Also Called: Bakell LLC (P-805)*
JDM Deliveries Inc .... D....... 626 831-1876
  802 Cotter Ave Duarte (91010) *(P-4160)*
Jeanne Jugan, A Residence, San Pedro *Also Called: Little Ssters of The Poor Los (P-15546)*
Jeb Holdings Corp (PA) .... D....... 951 659-2183
  54125 Maranatha Dr Idyllwild (92549) *(P-5665)*
Jeep Chrysler Ddge Ram Ontario, Ontario *Also Called: Jeep Chrysler of Ontario (P-7240)*
Jeep Chrysler of Ontario .... D....... 909 390-9898
  1202 Auto Center Dr Ontario (91761) *(P-7240)*
Jeep Gear, Irvine *Also Called: Alcone Marketing Group Inc (P-10588)*
Jeeva Corporation .... D....... 909 238-4073
  750 E E St Unit B Ontario (91764) *(P-1758)*
Jeff Carpenter Inc .... D....... 951 657-5115
  1380 W Oleander Ave Perris (92571) *(P-2219)*
Jeffco Painting & Coating Inc .... D....... 707 562-1900
  1260 Railroad Ave Vallejo (94592) *(P-1624)*
Jeffer Mngels Btlr Mtchell LLP .... C....... 310 203-8080
  1900 Avenue Of The Stars Fl 7 Los Angeles (90067) *(P-17505)*
Jeffrey Court, Norco *Also Called: Jeffrey Court Inc (P-1984)*
Jeffrey Court Inc .... D....... 951 340-3383
  620 Parkridge Ave Norco (92860) *(P-1984)*
Jeffrey Rome & Associates .... D....... 949 760-3929
  1715 Port Charles Pl Newport Beach (92660) *(P-19481)*
Jeffries Global Inc .... D....... 888 255-3488
  8484 Wilshire Blvd Ste 605 Beverly Hills (90211) *(P-2288)*
Jeld-Wen Inc .... B....... 760 597-4201
  2760 Progress St Ste B Vista (92081) *(P-5170)*
Jeld-Wen Inc .... C....... 909 879-8700
  120 S Cedar Ave Rialto (92376) *(P-5171)*
Jeld-Wen Windows, Vista *Also Called: Jeld-Wen Inc (P-5170)*
Jelight Company Inc (PA) .... D....... 949 380-8774
  2 Mason Irvine (92618) *(P-5569)*
Jenco Productions Inc (PA) .... C....... 909 381-9453
  401 S J St San Bernardino (92410) *(P-13332)*
Jenny Craig, Carlsbad *Also Called: JC Weight Loss Centres Inc (P-10557)*
Jensen Corp Landscape Contr .... C....... 408 446-4881
  1983 Concourse Dr San Jose (95131) *(P-501)*
Jensen Corporate Holdings Inc .... C....... 707 527-6187
  960 Lakeville St Petaluma (94952) *(P-502)*
Jensen Corporate Holdings Inc (PA) .... C....... 408 446-1118
  1250 Ames Ave Milpitas (95035) *(P-503)*
Jensen Enterprises Inc .... B....... 909 357-7264
  14221 San Bernardino Ave Fontana (92335) *(P-2705)*
Jensen Enterprises Inc .... D....... 916 992-8301
  5400 Raley Blvd Sacramento (95838) *(P-5227)*
Jensen Meat Company Inc .... D....... 619 754-6400
  2550 Britannia Blvd Ste 101 San Diego (92154) *(P-6496)*
Jensen Precast, Fontana *Also Called: Jensen Enterprises Inc (P-2705)*
Jensen Precast, Sacramento *Also Called: Jensen Enterprises Inc (P-5227)*
Jeppesen Dataplan Inc .... A....... 408 961-2825
  225 W Santa Clara St Ste 1600 San Jose (95113) *(P-12669)*
Jerde Partnership Intl, Los Angeles *Also Called: The Jerde Partnership Inc (P-19514)*

Jeremiah Phillips LLC .... D....... 650 697-7733
  863 Malcolm Rd Burlingame (94010) *(P-3142)*
Jerry Bruckheimer Inc .... D....... 310 664-6260
  1631 10th St Santa Monica (90404) *(P-13858)*
Jerry Leigh Entertainment AP, Van Nuys *Also Called: Leigh Jerry California Inc (P-2465)*
Jerry Melton & Sons Cnstr, Taft *Also Called: Jerry Melton & Sons Cnstr Inc (P-614)*
Jerry Melton & Sons Cnstr Inc .... D....... 661 765-5546
  100 Jamison Ln Taft (93268) *(P-614)*
Jerry Thompson & Sons Pntg Inc .... C....... 415 454-1500
  3 Simms St San Rafael (94901) *(P-1625)*
Jerry Thtompson & Sons Pntg, San Rafael *Also Called: Jerry Thompson & Sons Pntg Inc (P-1625)*
Jesse Alexander Transport .... D....... 760 669-0379
  9338 Azurite Ave Hesperia (92344) *(P-4161)*
Jessica Cosmetics Intl Inc .... D....... 818 759-1050
  13209 Saticoy St North Hollywood (91605) *(P-6117)*
Jessica's Cosmetics, North Hollywood *Also Called: Jessica Cosmetics Intl Inc (P-6117)*
Jessup Transportation, Gilroy *Also Called: Bert E Jessup Transportation (P-3447)*
Jet Blue, Long Beach *Also Called: Jetblue Airways Inc (P-3834)*
Jet Delivery Inc (PA) .... D....... 800 716-7177
  2169 Wright Ave La Verne (91750) *(P-3617)*
Jet Propulsion Laboratory, Pasadena *Also Called: California Institute Tech (P-19872)*
Jet Sets, North Hollywood *Also Called: M Gaw Inc (P-2294)*
Jetblue Airways Inc .... D....... 562 394-4397
  4100 E Donald Douglas Dr Long Beach (90808) *(P-3834)*
Jetro Cash and Carry Entps LLC .... D....... 619 233-0200
  1709 Main St San Diego (92113) *(P-6497)*
Jetro Holdings LLC .... B....... 858 564-0466
  7466 Carroll Rd Ste 100 San Diego (92121) *(P-5381)*
Jetro Holdings LLC .... C....... 213 516-0301
  1611 E Washington Blvd Los Angeles (90021) *(P-5382)*
Jetstream Communications Inc .... D....... 408 361-7000
  5400 Hellyer Ave San Jose (95138) *(P-2887)*
Jetty Marketing LLC .... D....... 310 867-9911
  1137 57th Ave Oakland (94621) *(P-20421)*
Jewelry Exchange, The, Tustin *Also Called: Diamond Goldenwest Corporation (P-7550)*
Jewelscent Inc .... D....... 800 550-1762
  955 W Imperial Hwy Ste 120 Brea (92821) *(P-6918)*
Jewish Cmnty Ctr San Francisco (PA) .... C....... 415 292-1200
  3200 California St San Francisco (94118) *(P-17719)*
Jewish Cmnty Fdrtion of San Fr (PA) .... D....... 415 777-0411
  121 Steuart St San Francisco (94105) *(P-18600)*
Jewish Cmnty Fndtion Los Angle (PA) .... C....... 323 761-8700
  6505 Wilshire Blvd Ste 1150 Los Angeles (90048) *(P-18872)*
JEWISH COMMUNITY CENTER, Los Gatos *Also Called: Addisn-Pnzak Jwish Cmnty Ctr S (P-14170)*
Jewish Community Ctr Long Bch .... C....... 562 426-7601
  3801 E Willow St Long Beach (90815) *(P-18024)*
Jewish Family and Chld Svcs (PA) .... D....... 415 449-1200
  2150 Post St San Francisco (94115) *(P-18025)*
Jewish Family and Chld Svcs .... B....... 415 449-3862
  600 5th Ave San Rafael (94901) *(P-18026)*
Jewish Family Svc Los Angeles .... C....... 323 937-5900
  330 N Fairfax Ave Los Angeles (90036) *(P-18027)*
Jewish HM For The Aging Ornge .... C....... 949 364-9685
  27356 Bellogente Mission Viejo (92691) *(P-15526)*
JEWISH HOME FOR THE AGED, San Francisco *Also Called: Hebrew Home For Aged Disabled (P-15511)*
Jewish Senior Living Group .... D....... 415 334-2500
  302 Silver Ave San Francisco (94112) *(P-20122)*
Jewish Synagogue, Los Angeles *Also Called: Temple Israel of Hollywood (P-10517)*
Jewish Vctnal Creer Cnsling Sv .... D....... 415 391-3600
  5106 Camden St Oakland (94619) *(P-18232)*
Jezowski & Markel Contrs Inc .... C....... 714 978-2222
  749 N Poplar St Orange (92868) *(P-2129)*
JF Shea Construction Inc .... D....... 530 246-4292
  17400 Clear Creek Rd Redding (96001) *(P-683)*
JF Shea Construction Inc .... D....... 925 245-3660
  2580 Shea Center Dr Livermore (94551) *(P-684)*
JF Shea Construction Inc (HQ) .... C....... 909 594-9500
  655 Brea Canyon Rd Walnut (91789) *(P-685)*

Jfc International Inc   **ALPHABETIC SECTION**

Jfc International Inc (HQ) .... C....... 323 721-6100
7101 E Slauson Ave Commerce (90040) *(P-6638)*

Jfc International Inc .... C....... 323 721-6900
7140 Bandini Blvd Commerce (90040) *(P-6639)*

Jfe Shoji America Holdings Inc (DH) .... D....... 562 637-3500
301 E Ocean Blvd Ste 1750 Long Beach (90802) *(P-5499)*

JFK Memorial Hospital Inc .... C....... 760 347-6191
47111 Monroe St Indio (92201) *(P-16140)*

Jfp Painting .... D....... 951 736-6037
2078 2nd St Norco (92860) *(P-1626)*

Jhc Investment Inc .... D....... 714 751-2400
7 Hutton Centre Dr Santa Ana (92707) *(P-9919)*

Jiff Inc (DH) .... B....... 415 829-1400
150 Spear St Ste 400 San Francisco (94105) *(P-11685)*

Jiff Inc .... C....... 510 844-4139
1999 Harrison St Ste 2070 Oakland (94612) *(P-12670)*

Jifflenow, Sunnyvale *Also Called: Ipolipo Inc (P-12245)*

Jiffy Lube, Tustin *Also Called: Allied Lube Inc (P-13656)*

Jiffy Lube, Morgan Hill *Also Called: Allied Lube Inc (P-13707)*

Jilk Heavy Construction Inc .... D....... 310 830-6323
500 S Kraemer Blvd Ste 380 Brea (92821) *(P-1308)*

Jim Burke Ford, Bakersfield *Also Called: Haberfelde Ford (P-7226)*

Jim Burke Ford, Bakersfield *Also Called: Haberfelde Ford (P-7227)*

Jim Murphy & Associates, Santa Rosa *Also Called: Murphy-True Inc (P-973)*

Jim Rodda Pottery World Owner, Rocklin *Also Called: Pottery World Inc (P-7590)*

Jimenez Nursery Inc .... D....... 805 684-7955
3800 Via Real Carpinteria (93013) *(P-133)*

Jimenez Nursery and Landscapes, Carpinteria *Also Called: Jimenez Nursery Inc (P-133)*

Jims Supply Co Inc (PA) .... D....... 661 616-6977
3500 Buck Owens Blvd Bakersfield (93308) *(P-5500)*

Jimway Inc .... D....... 310 886-3718
20101 S Santa Fe Ave Compton (90221) *(P-2876)*

Jin Yi Enterprises Inc .... D....... 714 778-0350
915 S Disneyland Dr Anaheim (92802) *(P-9920)*

Jipc Management Inc .... A....... 949 916-2000
22342 Avenida Empresa Ste 220 Rancho Santa Margari (92688) *(P-20123)*

JIT Corporation .... D....... 805 238-5000
2790 Valley View Ave Norco (92860) *(P-5666)*

Jit Transportation Inc .... B....... 408 232-4800
1075 Montague Express Way Milpitas (95035) *(P-4162)*

Jitterbug, San Diego *Also Called: Greatcall Inc (P-7581)*

Jj Fisher Construction Inc .... D....... 805 723-5220
261 W Dana St Ste 100 Nipomo (93444) *(P-1124)*

JJ Mac Intyre Co Inc (PA) .... C....... 951 898-4300
4160 Temescal Canyon Rd Ste 601 Corona (92883) *(P-10745)*

JJR Enterprises Inc (HQ) .... D....... 916 363-2666
2431 Mercantile Dr Rancho Cordova (95742) *(P-13741)*

Jk Imaging Ltd .... D....... 310 755-6848
17239 S Main St Gardena (90248) *(P-5238)*

Jkf Auto Service Inc .... D....... 916 315-0555
6818 Five Star Blvd Rocklin (95677) *(P-13695)*

JL Haley Enterprises Inc .... C....... 916 631-6375
3510 Luyung Dr Rancho Cordova (95742) *(P-2854)*

Jla Home, Fremont *Also Called: E & E Co Ltd (P-5115)*

Jlabs, San Diego *Also Called: Johnson Johnson Innovation LLC (P-20786)*

Jlg Harvesting Inc .... B....... 831 422-7871
27 Zabala Rd Salinas (93908) *(P-282)*

Jlm & Mag Associates Inc .... D....... 562 869-3343
9204 Lakewood Blvd Downey (90240) *(P-10501)*

Jls Environmental Services Inc .... D....... 916 660-1525
3460 Swetzer Rd Loomis (95650) *(P-20657)*

JM Roofing Company Inc .... D....... 805 966-3696
534 E Ortega St Santa Barbara (93103) *(P-2070)*

JM Stitt Construction Inc .... D....... 951 271-3440
3165 Palisades Dr Corona (92878) *(P-946)*

Jmac Home Loans, Santa Ana *Also Called: Jmac Lending Inc (P-7986)*

Jmac Lending Inc .... D....... 949 345-1508
2510 Redhill Ave Santa Ana (92705) *(P-7986)*

JMB, South San Francisco *Also Called: JMB Construction Inc (P-947)*

JMB Construction Inc .... D....... 650 267-5300
132 S Maple Ave South San Francisco (94080) *(P-947)*

Jmbm, Los Angeles *Also Called: Jeffer Mngels Btlr Mtchell LLP (P-17505)*

Jme Inc (PA) .... D....... 201 896-8600
527 Park Ave San Fernando (91340) *(P-5570)*

Jmg Investments Inc .... D....... 818 519-0670
23041 Hatteras St Woodland Hills (91367) *(P-9524)*

Jmg Security Systems Inc .... D....... 714 545-8882
17150 Newhope St Ste 109 Fountain Valley (92708) *(P-1759)*

Jmh Engineering and Cnstr .... D....... 562 317-1700
2457 Brayton Ave Signal Hill (90755) *(P-686)*

JMJ Enterprises Inc .... C....... 818 343-5151
5973 Reseda Blvd Tarzana (91356) *(P-7490)*

Jmp Group LLC (HQ) .... D....... 415 835-8900
600 Montgomery St Ste 1100 San Francisco (94111) *(P-8096)*

JMS Interiors Inc .... D....... 619 749-5098
10735 Prospect Ave Santee (92071) *(P-13333)*

JMS Realtors Ltd (PA) .... C....... 559 490-1500
575 E Alluvial Ave Ste 101 Fresno (93720) *(P-9058)*

Jn Projects Inc .... D....... 415 766-0273
333 Brannan St San Francisco (94107) *(P-10558)*

Jnr Inc .... D....... 949 476-2788
19900 Macarthur Blvd Ste 700 Irvine (92612) *(P-20422)*

Job Options Incorporated .... A....... 909 890-4612
1110 S Washington Ave San Bernardino (92408) *(P-10486)*

Jobs Plus, San Ramon *Also Called: Plus Group Inc (P-11320)*

Joe & Mary Mottino YMCA, Encinitas *Also Called: YMCA of San Diego County (P-18951)*

Joe Heger Farms LLC .... C....... 760 353-5111
1625 Drew Rd El Centro (92243) *(P-187)*

Joe's Auto Parks, Los Angeles *Also Called: L and R Auto Parks Inc (P-13608)*

Joes Sweeping Inc .... D....... 562 929-4344
11914 Front St Norwalk (90650) *(P-4901)*

Joguru Inc .... D....... 855 526-4332
2600 El Camino Real Ste 416 Palo Alto (94306) *(P-3964)*

Johanson Technology Inc .... C....... 805 575-0124
4001 Calle Tecate Camarillo (93012) *(P-2937)*

John A Martin & Associates Inc .... D....... 213 483-6490
950 S Grand Ave Ste 400 Los Angeles (90015) *(P-19287)*

John Aguilar & Company Inc .... D....... 209 546-0171
1505 Navy Dr Stockton (95206) *(P-3408)*

John Alden Life Insurance Co .... C....... 818 595-7600
20950 Warner Center Ln Ste A Woodland Hills (91367) *(P-8236)*

John C Fremont Healthcare Dst .... B....... 209 966-3631
5189 Hospital Rd Mariposa (95338) *(P-16141)*

John Collins Co Inc .... D....... 818 227-2190
5155 Cedarwood Rd Bonita (91902) *(P-8836)*

John Deere Authorized Dealer, Colton *Also Called: A-Z Bus Sales Inc (P-4998)*

John Deere Authorized Dealer, Poway *Also Called: Bay City Equipment Inds Inc (P-5542)*

John Deere Authorized Dealer, Robbins *Also Called: Valley Truck and Tractor Inc (P-5815)*

John Deere Authorized Dealer, Fresno *Also Called: Vucovich Inc (P-5816)*

John Deere Authorized Dealer, City Of Industry *Also Called: Valley Power Systems Inc (P-5879)*

John Deere Authorized Dealer, Lakeside *Also Called: Rdo Construction Equipment Co (P-11005)*

John Deere Authorized Dealer, Manteca *Also Called: J M Equipment Company Inc (P-11038)*

John F Kennedy Mem Hosp Aux .... A....... 760 347-6191
47111 Monroe St Indio (92201) *(P-16142)*

John F Otto Inc .... C....... 916 441-6870
1717 2nd St Sacramento (95811) *(P-948)*

John H Jones Community Clinic, Davis *Also Called: Communicare Health Centers (P-14698)*

John Hancock, Los Angeles *Also Called: John Hancock Life Insur Co USA (P-8597)*

John Hancock, San Diego *Also Called: John Hancock Life Insur Co USA (P-8598)*

John Hancock Life Insur Co USA .... D....... 949 254-1440
5000 Birch St Ste 120 Newport Beach (92660) *(P-8237)*

John Hancock Life Insur Co USA (DH) .... A....... 213 689-0813
865 S Figueroa St Ste 3320 Los Angeles (90017) *(P-8597)*

John Hancock Life Insur Co USA .... C....... 858 292-1667
10180 Telesis Ct San Diego (92121) *(P-8598)*

John Jackson Masonry .... D....... 916 381-8021
5691 Power Inn Rd Ste B Sacramento (95824) *(P-1886)*

John Jory Corporation (PA) .... B....... 714 279-7901
2180 N Glassell St Orange (92865) *(P-1939)*

ALPHABETIC SECTION — Jordana Cosmetics

John L SIlivan Investments Inc (PA).................. C...... 916 969-5911
  6200 Northfront Rd Livermore (94551) *(P-7241)*

John L Sullivan Chevrolet Inc .... C...... 916 742-7663
  350 Automall Dr Roseville (95661) *(P-7242)*

John M Frank Construction Inc .... D...... 714 210-3600
  913 E 4th St Santa Ana (92701) *(P-949)*

John M Frank Service Group, Santa Ana *Also Called: John M Frank Construction Inc (P-949)*

John Muir .... D...... 510 922-9659
  3100 San Pablo Ave Berkeley (94702) *(P-17257)*

John Muir Health (HQ).. A...... 925 947-4449
  1601 Ygnacio Valley Rd Walnut Creek (94598) *(P-16143)*

John Muir Health .... A...... 925 939-3000
  1601 Ygnacio Valley Rd Walnut Creek (94598) *(P-16144)*

John Muir Medical Center, Walnut Creek *Also Called: John Muir Health (P-16144)*
John Muir Medical Center, Walnut Creek *Also Called: John Muir Physician Network (P-16145)*

John Muir Physician Network (PA)...................... A...... 925 296-9700
  1450 Treat Blvd Walnut Creek (94597) *(P-16145)*

John Stewart Company .... D...... 415 345-4400
  2451 Meadowview Rd Sacramento (95832) *(P-8837)*

John Stewart Company .... C...... 916 561-0323
  1796 Tribute Rd Ste 100 Sacramento (95815) *(P-9059)*

John Stewart Company .... C...... 831 438-5725
  104 Whispering Pines Dr Ste 200 Scotts Valley (95066) *(P-9060)*

John Stewart Company (PA)............................... D...... 415 345-4400
  1388 Sutter St Ste 1100 San Francisco (94109) *(P-9061)*

JOHN TILLMAN COMPANY (DH)........................ D...... 310 764-0110
  1300 W Artesia Blvd Compton (90220) *(P-5842)*

John Wayne Airport, Costa Mesa *Also Called: County of Orange (P-3888)*

John Wheeler Logging Inc .... C...... 530 527-2993
  13570 State Highway 36 E Red Bluff (96080) *(P-2474)*

John,Xxiii Snior Ntrtn Site Ct, San Jose *Also Called: Catholic Chrties Snta Clara CN (P-17867)*

John's Incredible Pizza Co, Rancho Santa Margari *Also Called: Jipc Management Inc (P-20123)*

Johnny Was LLC .... D...... 310 656-0600
  395 Santa Monica Blvd # 124 Santa Monica (90401) *(P-6201)*

Johnson Cntrls Fire Prtction L .... C...... 858 633-9100
  3568 Ruffin Rd San Diego (92123) *(P-2902)*

Johnson Cntrls SEC Sltions LLC .... D...... 561 988-3600
  3870 Murphy Canyon Rd Ste 140 San Diego (92123) *(P-13127)*

Johnson Contrls Authorized Dlr, Montebello *Also Called: Johnstone Supply Inc (P-7440)*

Johnson Controls .... C...... 562 405-3817
  12728 Shoemaker Ave Santa Fe Springs (90670) *(P-13128)*

Johnson Controls, Cypress *Also Called: Johnson Controls Inc (P-2497)*

Johnson Controls Inc .... C...... 562 594-3200
  5770 Warland Dr Ste A Cypress (90630) *(P-2497)*

Johnson Fain Inc .... D...... 323 224-6000
  1201 N Broadway Los Angeles (90012) *(P-19482)*

Johnson Ford (PA)... C...... 888 483-0454
  1155 Auto Mall Dr Lancaster (93534) *(P-7243)*

Johnson Johnson Innovation LLC .... D...... 858 242-1504
  3210 Merryfield Row San Diego (92121) *(P-20786)*

Johnson Laminating Coating Inc .... D...... 310 635-4929
  20631 Annalee Ave Carson (90746) *(P-2662)*

Johnson Machinery Co (PA)............................... C...... 951 686-4560
  800 E La Cadena Dr Riverside (92507) *(P-5794)*

Johnson Outdoors Inc .... C...... 619 402-1023
  1166 Fesler St Ste A El Cajon (92020) *(P-3092)*

Johnson Ranch Racquet Club, Roseville *Also Called: Spare-Time Inc (P-14461)*

Johnson Service Group Inc .... A...... 408 728-9510
  950 S Bascom Ave San Jose (95128) *(P-8729)*

Johnson Western Gunite Company .... D...... 510 568-8112
  940 Doolittle Dr San Leandro (94577) *(P-2130)*

Johnson-Peltier .... D...... 562 944-3408
  12021 Shoemaker Ave Santa Fe Springs (90670) *(P-1760)*

Johnson-Peltier, Santa Fe Springs *Also Called: Johnson-Peltier (P-1760)*

Johnston Farms Fmly Ltd Partnr .... D...... 661 366-3201
  13031 E Packinghouse Rd Edison (93220) *(P-100)*

Johnston Vacuum Tank Service, Taft *Also Called: Watkins Construction Co Inc (P-1280)*

Johnstone Supply Inc .... D...... 323 722-2859
  8040 Slauson Ave Montebello (90640) *(P-7440)*

Joie De Vivre Hospitality LLC .... D...... 408 335-1700
  210 E Main St Los Gatos (95030) *(P-9921)*

Joie De Vivre Hospitality LLC .... C...... 415 278-3700
  8 Mission St San Francisco (94105) *(P-9922)*

Joie De Vivre Hospitality LLC .... C...... 415 567-8467
  444 Presidio Ave San Francisco (94115) *(P-9923)*

Joie De Vivre Hospitality LLC .... D...... 415 380-0400
  555 Redwood Hwy Frontage Rd Mill Valley (94941) *(P-9924)*

Joie De Vivre Hospitality LLC .... D...... 415 441-2700
  580 Geary St San Francisco (94102) *(P-9925)*

Joie De Vivre Hospitality LLC .... D...... 415 921-5520
  3100 Webster St San Francisco (94123) *(P-9926)*

Joie De Vivre Hospitality LLC .... D...... 415 776-1380
  601 Eddy St San Francisco (94109) *(P-9927)*

Joie De Vivre Hospitality LLC .... C...... 650 940-1000
  860 E El Camino Real Mountain View (94040) *(P-9928)*

Joie De Vivre Hospitality LLC .... C...... 415 775-1755
  845 Bush St San Francisco (94108) *(P-9929)*

Joie De Vivre Hospitality LLC .... C...... 415 346-2880
  2901 Pacific Ave San Francisco (94115) *(P-20124)*

Joie De Vivre Hospitality LLC .... D...... 415 986-2000
  386 Geary St San Francisco (94102) *(P-20125)*

Joie De Vivre Hospitality LLC .... D...... 650 879-1100
  2001 Rossi Rd Pescadero (94060) *(P-20126)*

Joie De Vivre Hospitality LLC .... D...... 408 738-0500
  910 E Fremont Ave Sunnyvale (94087) *(P-20127)*

Joint Juice, Emeryville *Also Called: Premier Nutrition Company LLC (P-6660)*

Jolly Roger Games, Commerce *Also Called: Ultra Pro International LLC (P-6000)*

Jolly Roger Inn, Anaheim *Also Called: Edward Thomas Companies (P-9772)*

Jomar Table Linens Inc .... D...... 909 390-1444
  4000 E Airport Dr Ste A Ontario (91761) *(P-2470)*

Jon Brooks Inc (PA).. D...... 626 330-0631
  14400 Lomitas Ave City Of Industry (91746) *(P-2719)*

Jon K Takata Corporation (PA).......................... D...... 510 315-5400
  3090 Independence Dr Livermore (94551) *(P-18028)*

Jon Renau Collection Inc .... D...... 760 598-0067
  2640 Business Park Dr Vista (92081) *(P-6919)*

Jonathan Beach Club, Santa Monica *Also Called: Jonathan Club (P-14385)*

Jonathan Club .... D...... 310 393-9245
  850 Palisades Beach Rd Santa Monica (90403) *(P-14385)*

Jonathan Club (PA)... C...... 213 624-0881
  545 S Figueroa St Los Angeles (90071) *(P-18873)*

Jones Covey Group, Rancho Cucamonga *Also Called: Jones/Covey Group Incorporated (P-2289)*

Jones Day, Los Angeles *Also Called: Jones Day Limited Partnership (P-17506)*

Jones Day Limited Partnership .... C...... 213 489-3939
  555 S Flower St Fl 50 Los Angeles (90071) *(P-17506)*

Jones Day Limited Partnership .... D...... 858 314-1200
  4655 Executive Dr Ste 1500 San Diego (92121) *(P-17507)*

Jones It, San Francisco *Also Called: Jones It Consulting LLC (P-20787)*

Jones It Consulting LLC .... C...... 415 578-7111
  3435 Cesar Chavez Ste Ph San Francisco (94110) *(P-20787)*

Jones Lang La Salle .... D...... 213 239-6000
  515 S Flower St Fl 13 Los Angeles (90071) *(P-9062)*

Jones Rest HM Cnvalescent Hosp, San Leandro *Also Called: Sanhyd Inc (P-15896)*

Jones Signs Co Inc .... C...... 858 569-1400
  9025 Balboa Ave Ste 150 San Diego (92123) *(P-5383)*

Jones/Covey Group Incorporated .... D...... 888 972-7581
  9595 Lucas Ranch Rd Ste 100 Rancho Cucamonga (91730) *(P-2289)*

Joni and Friends Foundation (PA).................... D...... 818 707-5664
  30009 Ladyface Ct Agoura (91301) *(P-18029)*

Jonset LLC .... D...... 949 551-5151
  16251 Construction Cir W Irvine (92606) *(P-4980)*

Jopari Solutions Inc .... D...... 925 459-5200
  1850 Gateway Blvd Concord (94520) *(P-13334)*

Jordan - Link & Company (PA)......................... D...... 559 733-9696
  2300 W Whitendale Ave Visalia (93277) *(P-9063)*

Jordan Park Group LLC .... C...... 415 417-3000
  100 Pine St Ste 2600 San Francisco (94111) *(P-8205)*

Jordan Vineyard & Winery, Healdsburg *Also Called: Jvw Corporation (P-2388)*

Jordana Cosmetics, Vernon *Also Called: Jordana Cosmetics LLC (P-6118)*

Jordana Cosmetics LLC — ALPHABETIC SECTION

Jordana Cosmetics LLC .... D....... 310 730-4400
  2035 E 49th St Vernon (90058) *(P-6118)*

Jordano's Food Service, Santa Barbara *Also Called: Jordanos Inc (P-6769)*

Jordanos Inc (PA) .... C....... 805 964-0611
  550 S Patterson Ave Santa Barbara (93111) *(P-6769)*

Jose C Castillo DDS Inc 619 295-2288
  2918 5th Ave Ste 310 San Diego (92103) *(P-15231)*

Joseph J Albanese Inc .... A....... 408 727-5700
  851 Martin Ave Santa Clara (95050) *(P-2131)*

Josephine's Personnel Services, San Jose *Also Called: Josephines Prof Staffing Inc (P-11159)*

Josephines Prof Staffing Inc (PA) .... C....... 408 943-0111
  2158 Ringwood Ave San Jose (95131) *(P-11159)*

Joslyn Sunbank Company LLC .... B....... 805 238-2840
  1740 Commerce Way Paso Robles (93446) *(P-2938)*

Jotform Inc .... D....... 347 624-5569
  4 Embarcadero Ctr Ste 780 San Francisco (94111) *(P-11686)*

Joyable Inc .... A....... 914 552-6753
  11770 Snowpeak Way Truckee (96161) *(P-11687)*

Joyent Inc .... C....... 415 400-0600
  645 Clyde Ave Ste 502 Mountain View (94043) *(P-12821)*

JP Allen Extended Stay (PA) .... D....... 818 956-0202
  450 Pioneer Dr Glendale (91203) *(P-9930)*

JP Morgan & Co .... D....... 213 485-1234
  1999 Avenue Of The Stars Ste 2600 Los Angeles (90067) *(P-17508)*

Jpa Landscape & Cnstr Inc .... D....... 925 960-9602
  256 Boeing Ct Livermore (94551) *(P-504)*

Jpi Development Group Inc .... D....... 951 973-7680
  41205 Golden Gate Cir Murrieta (92562) *(P-1473)*

Jpl Management, Los Angeles *Also Called: Jpl Management LLC (P-20128)*

Jpl Management LLC .... D....... 310 844-3662
  6427 W Sunset Blvd # 101 Los Angeles (90028) *(P-20128)*

JR Construction Inc .... D....... 858 505-4760
  8123 Engineer Rd San Diego (92111) *(P-687)*

JR Filanc Cnstr Co Inc (PA) .... D....... 760 941-7130
  740 N Andreasen Dr Escondido (92029) *(P-1222)*

JR Perce Plbg Inc Sacramento .... C....... 916 434-9554
  3610 Cincinnati Ave Rocklin (95765) *(P-1474)*

JS Held LLC .... D....... 949 390-7647
  4667 Macarthur Blvd Ste 400 Newport Beach (92660) *(P-19591)*

JS Homen Trucking Inc .... D....... 209 723-9559
  4224 Turlock Rd Snelling (95369) *(P-3409)*

Jsl Foods Inc (PA) .... D....... 323 223-2484
  3550 Pasadena Ave Los Angeles (90031) *(P-2437)*

Jsl Technologies Inc .... B....... 805 985-7700
  1451 N Rice Ave Ste A Oxnard (93030) *(P-19288)*

Jt Resources Inc .... C....... 661 367-6827
  26372 Ruether Ave Santa Clarita (91350) *(P-11160)*

JT Wimsatt Contg Co Inc (PA) .... B....... 661 775-8090
  28064 Avenue Stanford Unit B Valencia (91355) *(P-2132)*

Jt2 Integrated Resources (PA) .... D....... 925 556-7012
  333 Hegenberger Rd # 650 Oakland (94621) *(P-20129)*

Jt3 LLC .... A....... 661 277-4900
  190 S Wolfe Ave Bldg 1260 Edwards (93524) *(P-19289)*

Jtb Americas Ltd (HQ) .... D....... 310 406-3121
  3625 Del Amo Blvd Ste 260 Torrance (90503) *(P-3937)*

Jti Elctrcal Instrmntation LLC .... D....... 661 393-5535
  3901 Fanucchi Way Unit 201 Shafter (93263) *(P-4582)*

Judson Enterprises Inc (PA) .... B....... 916 596-6721
  2440 Gold River Rd Ste 100 Rancho Cordova (95670) *(P-762)*

Julie's Hallmark, San Jose *Also Called: Yamato Enterprises Inc (P-4122)*

Jumpshot Inc (PA) .... D....... 415 212-9250
  333 Bryant St Ste 240 San Francisco (94107) *(P-11688)*

Jumpstart Automotive Media, San Francisco *Also Called: Jumpstart Digital Mktg Inc (P-20423)*

Jumpstart Digital Mktg Inc (DH) .... D....... 415 844-6336
  550 Kearny St Ste 500 San Francisco (94108) *(P-20423)*

June Group LLC .... D....... 858 450-4290
  9909 Mira Mesa Blvd Ste 240 San Diego (92131) *(P-11296)*

Juniper Hotel, Cupertino *Also Called: Cupertino Lessee LLC (P-9733)*

JUNIPER NETWORKS, Sunnyvale *Also Called: Juniper Networks Inc (P-2832)*

Juniper Networks, Pleasanton *Also Called: Trapeze Networks Inc (P-12536)*

Juniper Networks Inc (PA) .... B....... 408 745-2000
  1133 Innovation Way Sunnyvale (94089) *(P-2832)*

Juniper Networks Inc .... A....... 408 745-2000
  1137 Innovation Way Bldg B Sunnyvale (94089) *(P-12472)*

Juniper Networks Inc .... D....... 805 880-2000
  6868 Cortona Dr Ste C Goleta (93117) *(P-12473)*

Juniper Networks (us) Inc (HQ) .... D....... 408 745-2000
  1133 Innovation Way Sunnyvale (94089) *(P-12474)*

Juniper Square Inc .... B....... 415 841-2722
  555 Montgomery St Ste 1400 San Francisco (94111) *(P-5319)*

Junk King Frnchise Systems LLC .... C....... 888 888-5865
  1616 Gilbreth Rd Burlingame (94010) *(P-6010)*

Jupiter Bellflower Doctors Hospital .... B
  3699 Wilshire Blvd Ste 540 Los Angeles (90010) *(P-16146)*

Jupiter Intelligence Inc .... D....... 650 477-2117
  181 2nd Ave Ste 300 San Mateo (94401) *(P-11689)*

Jurupa Community Services Dst .... D....... 951 685-7073
  11201 Harrel St Riverside (92509) *(P-4798)*

Jurupa Hills Post Acute, Riverside *Also Called: Mt Rubidouxidence Opco LLC (P-15593)*

Just Desserts, Fairfield *Also Called: New Desserts Inc (P-6655)*

Just Wheels & Tires LLC .... D
  3172 Nasa St Brea (92821) *(P-5046)*

Justanswer LLC .... C....... 800 785-2305
  38 Keyes Ave Ste 150 San Francisco (94129) *(P-4301)*

Justice Dvrsity Ctr of The Bar .... D....... 415 575-3130
  1360 Mission St San Francisco (94103) *(P-17509)*

Justman Packaging & Display (PA) .... D....... 323 728-8888
  5819 Telegraph Rd Commerce (90040) *(P-5384)*

Juvenile Facilities, Oxnard *Also Called: County of Ventura (P-20925)*

Juvenile Justice Division Cal .... A....... 805 485-7951
  3100 Wright Rd Camarillo (93010) *(P-20130)*

Juvo Atism Bhavioral Hlth Svcs, San Jose *Also Called: Ed Supports LLC (P-17059)*

Juvo Atism Bhavioral Hlth Svcs, Oakland *Also Called: Ed Supports LLC (P-17060)*

Juvo Atism Bhavioral Hlth Svcs, Folsom *Also Called: Ed Supports LLC (P-17963)*

Jvac Inc .... D....... 559 584-5531
  1073 Cadillac Ln Hanford (93230) *(P-7244)*

Jvckenwood USA Corporation (HQ) .... C....... 310 639-9000
  4001 Worsham Ave Long Beach (90808) *(P-5667)*

Jvs Socal .... B....... 323 761-8879
  6505 Wilshire Blvd Los Angeles (90048) *(P-18030)*

Jvw Corporation .... D....... 707 431-5250
  1474 Alexander Valley Rd Healdsburg (95448) *(P-2388)*

JW Marriott Le Merigot, Santa Monica *Also Called: C W Hotels Ltd (P-9672)*

JW Marrott Dsert Sprng Rsort S, Palm Desert *Also Called: Host Hotels & Resorts LP (P-9868)*

Jwch Institute Inc .... C....... 562 867-7999
  14371 Clark Ave Bellflower (90706) *(P-17258)*

Jwch Institute Inc .... C....... 562 862-1000
  8530 Firestone Blvd Downey (90241) *(P-17259)*

Jwch Institute Inc .... C....... 310 223-1035
  3591 E Imperial Hwy Lynwood (90262) *(P-18031)*

Jwch Institute Inc .... C....... 323 562-5813
  6912 Ajax Ave Bell (90201) *(P-19891)*

Jwch Institute Inc .... C....... 562 281-0306
  12360 Firestone Blvd Norwalk (90650) *(P-19892)*

Jwch Medical Center, Lynwood *Also Called: Jwch Institute Inc (P-18031)*

K & P Janitorial Services .... D....... 310 540-8878
  412 S Pacific Coast Hwy Ste 200 Redondo Beach (90277) *(P-10914)*

K & S Air Conditioning Inc .... C....... 714 685-0077
  143 E Meats Ave Orange (92865) *(P-1475)*

K A R Construction Inc .... D....... 909 988-5054
  1306 Brooks St Ontario (91762) *(P-688)*

K C C, El Segundo *Also Called: Carson Kurtzman Consultants (P-17401)*

K E, Irvine *Also Called: Kite Electric Incorporated (P-1762)*

K E S, San Diego *Also Called: Koam Engineering Systems Inc (P-12475)*

K G O T V News Bureau .... D....... 510 451-4772
  520 3rd St Ste 200 Oakland (94607) *(P-4387)*

K Hovnnian Clfrnia Oprtons In (HQ) .... D....... 714 368-4500
  400 Exchange Ste 200 Irvine (92602) *(P-689)*

ALPHABETIC SECTION — Kaiser Foundation Hospitals

K Motors Inc .... C....... 619 270-3000
965 Arnele Ave El Cajon (92020) *(P-7338)*

K P B S, San Diego *Also Called: San Diego State University (P-17767)*

K S B W- T V, Salinas *Also Called: Hearst Stations Inc (P-4439)*

K S Fabrication & Machine Inc .... C....... 661 617-1700
6205 District Blvd Bakersfield (93313) *(P-1223)*

K S I, Bakersfield *Also Called: KS Industries LP (P-1228)*

K S S C - F M, Los Angeles *Also Called: Entravsion Communications Corp (P-4427)*

K T A Construction Inc .... D....... 619 562-9464
1920 Cordell Ct Ste 105 El Cajon (92020) *(P-1224)*

K T Lucky Co Inc .... C....... 626 579-7272
10925 Schmidt Rd El Monte (91733) *(P-6640)*

K W Emerson Inc .... D....... 209 754-3839
413 W Saint Charles St San Andreas (95249) *(P-1225)*

K Wave 1079 .... 714 918-6207
3000 W Macarthur Blvd Ste 500 Santa Ana (92704) *(P-4388)*

K X T V Channel 10, Sacramento *Also Called: Kxtv Inc (P-4451)*

K-Designers, Rancho Cordova *Also Called: Judson Enterprises Inc (P-762)*

K-LOVE RADIO NETWORK, Rocklin *Also Called: Educational Media Foundation (P-4377)*

K-Micro Inc .... D....... 310 442-3200
1618 Stanford St Santa Monica (90404) *(P-5320)*

K. Hovnanian Companies Cal Inc, Irvine *Also Called: K Hovnnian Clfrnia Oprtons In (P-689)*

K&B Electric LLC .... C....... 951 808-9501
290 Corporate Terrace Cir Ste 200 Corona (92879) *(P-19290)*

K&B Engineering .... C....... 951 808-9501
290 Corporate Terrace Cir Ste 200 Corona (92879) *(P-19291)*

K&B Engineering, Corona *Also Called: K&B Electric LLC (P-19290)*

K&B Pichette Enterprises Inc .... D....... 209 452-5999
11992 State Highway 88 Ste 2046 Jackson (95642) *(P-16881)*

K&L Gates LLP .... D....... 415 882-8200
4 Embarcadero Ctr Lbby 10 San Francisco (94111) *(P-17510)*

K&L Gates LLP .... D....... 310 552-5000
10100 Santa Monica Blvd Ste 700 Los Angeles (90067) *(P-17511)*

K&S, Orange *Also Called: K & S Air Conditioning Inc (P-1475)*

K12 Oer Collaborative, The, Menlo Park *Also Called: Open Up Resources (P-20496)*

K3 Dev LLC .... D....... 408 733-7950
725 S Fair Oaks Ave Sunnyvale (94086) *(P-9931)*

K3 Dev LLC .... D....... 408 733-7950
597 E El Camino Real Sunnyvale (94087) *(P-9932)*

Ka Management II Inc .... D....... 858 404-6080
5820 Oberlin Dr Ste 201 San Diego (92121) *(P-20131)*

Kabam Inc (HQ) .... A....... 604 256-0054
575 Market St Ste 2450 San Francisco (94105) *(P-11690)*

Kadiant LLC .... C....... 209 521-4791
155 Grand Ave Ste 500 Oakland (94612) *(P-20788)*

Kaef TV, Redding *Also Called: California Oregon Broadcasting (P-4414)*

Kag West, West Sacramento *Also Called: Kag West LLC (P-6732)*

Kag West LLC .... D....... 916 371-4581
4076 Seaport Blvd West Sacramento (95691) *(P-6732)*

Kaga Fei America Inc (DH) .... D
2349 Bering Dr San Jose (95131) *(P-19292)*

Kahana & Feld LLP .... D....... 949 812-4781
2603 Main St Ste 900 Irvine (92614) *(P-17512)*

Kahn Rennaissance LLC .... C....... 510 260-3161
640 Bailey Rd Ste 509 Bay Point (94565) *(P-10436)*

Kaidan Hospitality LP .... D....... 530 221-8700
1830 Hilltop Dr Redding (96002) *(P-9933)*

Kainos HM Trning Ctr For Dvlpm .... D....... 650 361-1355
2761 Fair Oaks Ave Ste A Redwood City (94063) *(P-18032)*

Kainos Work Activity Ctr, Redwood City *Also Called: Kainos HM Trning Ctr For Dvlpm (P-18032)*

Kair Harbor Express LLC (PA) .... D....... 562 432-6800
1129 Canal Ave Long Beach (90813) *(P-3720)*

Kaiser .... D....... 925 924-6930
4480 Hacienda Dr Bldg B-4 Pleasanton (94588) *(P-17260)*

Kaiser Family Foundation, San Francisco *Also Called: Henry J Kaiser Fmly Foundation (P-19087)*

Kaiser Fndtion Hlth Plan GA In .... B....... 951 270-1200
1850 California Ave Corona (92881) *(P-8305)*

Kaiser Fndtion Hosp Gift Shppe .... C....... 323 857-3290
6041 Cadillac Ave Los Angeles (90034) *(P-8306)*

Kaiser Fndtion Rhblitation Ctr, Vallejo *Also Called: Kaiser Foundation Hospitals (P-8315)*

Kaiser Foundation Health Plan, Elk Grove *Also Called: Kaiser Foundation Hospitals (P-8310)*

Kaiser Foundation Health Plan, Vallejo *Also Called: Kaiser Foundation Hospitals (P-8313)*

Kaiser Foundation Health Plan, Elk Grove *Also Called: Kaiser Foundation Hospitals (P-8314)*

Kaiser Foundation Health Plan, Walnut Creek *Also Called: Kaiser Foundation Hospitals (P-8320)*

Kaiser Foundation Health Plan, Clovis *Also Called: Kaiser Foundation Hospitals (P-8323)*

Kaiser Foundation Health Plan, Daly City *Also Called: Kaiser Foundation Hospitals (P-8324)*

Kaiser Foundation Health Plan, Rohnert Park *Also Called: Kaiser Foundation Hospitals (P-8325)*

Kaiser Foundation Health Plan, West Covina *Also Called: Kaiser Foundation Hospitals (P-8326)*

Kaiser Foundation Health Plan, Fontana *Also Called: Kaiser Foundation Hospitals (P-8327)*

Kaiser Foundation Health Plan, Downey *Also Called: Kaiser Foundation Hospitals (P-8328)*

Kaiser Foundation Health Plan, Sacramento *Also Called: Kaiser Foundation Hospitals (P-8329)*

Kaiser Foundation Health Plan, San Jose *Also Called: Kaiser Foundation Hospitals (P-8330)*

Kaiser Foundation Health Plan, North Hollywood *Also Called: Kaiser Foundation Hospitals (P-8331)*

Kaiser Foundation Health Plan, Gilroy *Also Called: Kaiser Foundation Hospitals (P-8332)*

Kaiser Foundation Health Plan, Fresno *Also Called: Kaiser Foundation Hospitals (P-8333)*

Kaiser Foundation Health Plan, Modesto *Also Called: Kaiser Foundation Hospitals (P-8335)*

Kaiser Foundation Health Plan, Pleasanton *Also Called: Kaiser Fundation Hlth Plan Inc (P-8336)*

Kaiser Foundation Health Plan, San Diego *Also Called: Southern Cal Prmnnte Med Group (P-8368)*

Kaiser Foundation Health Plan, San Francisco *Also Called: Kaiser Foundation Hospitals (P-14800)*

Kaiser Foundation Health Plan, Victorville *Also Called: Kaiser Foundation Hospitals (P-14811)*

Kaiser Foundation Health Plan, Oakland *Also Called: Kaiser Fundation Hlth Plan Inc (P-14855)*

Kaiser Foundation Health Plan, Vacaville *Also Called: Kaiser Foundation Hospitals (P-16149)*

Kaiser Foundation Health Plan, Corona *Also Called: Kaiser Foundation Hospitals (P-17261)*

Kaiser Foundation Hospitals .... D....... 510 752-6808
275 W Macarthur Blvd Oakland (94611) *(P-5427)*

Kaiser Foundation Hospitals .... C....... 888 750-0036
3750 Grand Ave Chino (91710) *(P-8307)*

Kaiser Foundation Hospitals .... D....... 559 448-4620
4785 N 1st St Fl 2 Fresno (93726) *(P-8308)*

Kaiser Foundation Hospitals .... D....... 408 972-6560
270 International Cir San Jose (95119) *(P-8309)*

Kaiser Foundation Hospitals .... C....... 916 478-5000
9201 Big Horn Blvd Elk Grove (95758) *(P-8310)*

Kaiser Foundation Hospitals .... A....... 626 851-1011
1011 Baldwin Park Blvd Baldwin Park (91706) *(P-8311)*

Kaiser Foundation Hospitals .... B....... 562 657-9000
9333 Imperial Hwy Downey (90242) *(P-8312)*

Kaiser Foundation Hospitals .... B....... 707 645-2720
1761 Broadway St Ste 210 Vallejo (94589) *(P-8313)*

Kaiser Foundation Hospitals .... D....... 916 544-6000
10305 Promenade Pkwy Elk Grove (95757) *(P-8314)*

Kaiser Foundation Hospitals .... C....... 707 651-1000
975 Sereno Dr Vallejo (94589) *(P-8315)*

Kaiser Foundation Hospitals .... C....... 619 528-5000
8080 Parkway Dr La Mesa (91942) *(P-8316)*

Kaiser Foundation Hospitals .... D....... 866 319-4269
1249 S Sunset Ave West Covina (91790) *(P-8317)*

Kaiser Foundation Hospitals .... C....... 415 899-7400
97 San Marin Dr Novato (94945) *(P-8318)*

Kaiser Foundation Hospitals .... B....... 510 891-3400
2000 Brdwy Oakland (94612) *(P-8319)*

Kaiser Foundation Hospitals .... D....... 925 926-3000
25 N Via Monte Walnut Creek (94598) *(P-8320)*

Kaiser Foundation Hospitals .... A....... 916 688-2000
6600 Bruceville Rd Sacramento (95823) *(P-8321)*

Kaiser Foundation Hospitals .... C....... 866 340-5974
12470 Whittier Blvd Whittier (90602) *(P-8322)*

Kaiser Foundation Hospitals .... C....... 559 324-5100
2071 Herndon Ave Clovis (93611) *(P-8323)*

Kaiser Foundation Hospitals .... D....... 650 301-5860
395 Hickey Blvd Daly City (94015) *(P-8324)*

Kaiser Foundation Hospitals — ALPHABETIC SECTION

Kaiser Foundation Hospitals .... D...... 707 206-3000
5900 State Farm Dr Ste 100 Rohnert Park (94928) *(P-8325)*

Kaiser Foundation Hospitals .... D...... 626 856-3045
1539 W Garvey Ave N West Covina (91790) *(P-8326)*

Kaiser Foundation Hospitals .... B...... 909 427-3910
9961 Sierra Ave Fontana (92335) *(P-8327)*

Kaiser Foundation Hospitals .... C...... 562 622-4190
12200 Bellflower Blvd Downey (90242) *(P-8328)*

Kaiser Foundation Hospitals .... C...... 916 973-5000
2345 Fair Oaks Blvd Sacramento (95825) *(P-8329)*

Kaiser Foundation Hospitals .... C...... 408 972-3376
5755 Cottle Rd San Jose (95123) *(P-8330)*

Kaiser Foundation Hospitals .... C...... 818 503-7082
11666 Sherman Way North Hollywood (91605) *(P-8331)*

Kaiser Foundation Hospitals .... B...... 408 848-4600
7520 Arroyo Cir Gilroy (95020) *(P-8332)*

Kaiser Foundation Hospitals .... A...... 559 448-4500
7300 N Fresno St Fresno (93720) *(P-8333)*

Kaiser Foundation Hospitals .... A...... 510 559-5362
1795 2nd St Berkeley (94710) *(P-8334)*

Kaiser Foundation Hospitals .... B...... 209 557-1000
1625 I St Modesto (95354) *(P-8335)*

Kaiser Foundation Hospitals .... A...... 619 528-5888
4647 Zion Ave San Diego (92120) *(P-9430)*

Kaiser Foundation Hospitals .... A...... 925 372-1000
200 Muir Rd Martinez (94553) *(P-9431)*

Kaiser Foundation Hospitals .... D...... 323 881-5516
5119 Pomona Blvd Los Angeles (90022) *(P-9432)*

Kaiser Foundation Hospitals .... D...... 951 601-6174
12815 Heacock St Moreno Valley (92553) *(P-9433)*

Kaiser Foundation Hospitals .... D...... 909 427-5521
789 E Cooley Dr Colton (92324) *(P-9434)*

Kaiser Foundation Hospitals .... B...... 949 932-5000
6640 Alton Pkwy Irvine (92618) *(P-9435)*

Kaiser Foundation Hospitals .... C...... 707 258-2500
3285 Claremont Way Napa (94558) *(P-9436)*

Kaiser Foundation Hospitals 951 353-3790
10800 Magnolia Ave Riverside (92505) *(P-14789)*

Kaiser Foundation Hospitals .... D...... 817 372-8201
9521 Dalen St Downey (90242) *(P-14790)*

Kaiser Foundation Hospitals .... C...... 323 783-7955
1550 N Edgemont St Los Angeles (90027) *(P-14791)*

Kaiser Foundation Hospitals .... C...... 714 562-3420
5 Centerpointe Dr La Palma (90623) *(P-14792)*

Kaiser Foundation Hospitals .... B...... 925 813-6500
4501 Sand Creek Rd Antioch (94531) *(P-14793)*

Kaiser Foundation Hospitals .... C...... 818 375-4023
13652 Cantara St Panorama City (91402) *(P-14794)*

Kaiser Foundation Hospitals .... C...... 714 279-4675
411 N Lakeview Ave Anaheim (92807) *(P-14795)*

Kaiser Foundation Hospitals .... D...... 949 425-3150
24502 Pacific Park Dr Aliso Viejo (92656) *(P-14796)*

Kaiser Foundation Hospitals .... A...... 707 393-4000
401 Bicentennial Way Santa Rosa (95403) *(P-14797)*

Kaiser Foundation Hospitals .... D...... 619 528-5000
780 Shadowridge Dr Vista (92083) *(P-14798)*

Kaiser Foundation Hospitals .... C...... 714 741-3448
12100 Euclid St Garden Grove (92840) *(P-14799)*

Kaiser Foundation Hospitals .... C...... 415 833-2616
2350 Geary Blvd Fl 2 San Francisco (94115) *(P-14800)*

Kaiser Foundation Hospitals .... D...... 925 295-4145
710 S Broadway Walnut Creek (94596) *(P-14801)*

Kaiser Foundation Hospitals .... A...... 510 752-1000
3600 Broadway Oakland (94611) *(P-14802)*

Kaiser Foundation Hospitals .... A...... 415 833-2000
2425 Geary Blvd San Francisco (94115) *(P-14803)*

Kaiser Foundation Hospitals .... B...... 415 833-2200
2200 Ofarrell St San Francisco (94115) *(P-14804)*

Kaiser Foundation Hospitals .... C...... 888 750-0036
1301 California St Redlands (92374) *(P-14805)*

Kaiser Foundation Hospitals .... D...... 714 672-5100
1900 E Lambert Rd Brea (92821) *(P-14806)*

Kaiser Foundation Hospitals .... A...... 415 444-2000
99 Montecillo Rd San Rafael (94903) *(P-14807)*

Kaiser Foundation Hospitals .... A...... 510 307-1500
901 Nevin Ave Richmond (94801) *(P-14808)*

Kaiser Foundation Hospitals .... A...... 323 857-2000
6041 Cadillac Ave Los Angeles (90034) *(P-14809)*

Kaiser Foundation Hospitals .... A...... 818 375-2000
13651 Willard St Panorama City (91402) *(P-14810)*

Kaiser Foundation Hospitals .... D...... 888 750-0036
14011 Park Ave Victorville (92392) *(P-14811)*

Kaiser Foundation Hospitals .... D...... 800 780-1230
18600 S Figueroa St Gardena (90248) *(P-14812)*

Kaiser Foundation Hospitals .... D...... 209 735-5000
4601 Dale Rd Modesto (95356) *(P-14813)*

Kaiser Foundation Hospitals .... C...... 909 724-5000
2295 S Vineyard Ave Ontario (91761) *(P-14814)*

Kaiser Foundation Hospitals .... C...... 510 454-1000
2500 Merced St San Leandro (94577) *(P-14815)*

Kaiser Foundation Hospitals .... D...... 510 752-1000
280 W Macarthur Blvd Oakland (94611) *(P-14816)*

Kaiser Foundation Hospitals .... A...... 408 972-7000
250 Hospital Pkwy San Jose (95119) *(P-14817)*

Kaiser Foundation Hospitals .... D...... 714 830-6500
3401 S Harbor Blvd Santa Ana (92704) *(P-14818)*

Kaiser Foundation Hospitals .... D...... 310 915-5000
12001 W Washington Blvd Los Angeles (90066) *(P-14819)*

Kaiser Foundation Hospitals .... A...... 650 299-2000
1100 Veterans Blvd Redwood City (94063) *(P-14820)*

Kaiser Foundation Hospitals .... A...... 925 295-4000
1425 S Main St Walnut Creek (94596) *(P-14821)*

Kaiser Foundation Hospitals .... A...... 310 325-5111
25825 Vermont Ave Harbor City (90710) *(P-14822)*

Kaiser Foundation Hospitals .... A...... 909 427-5000
9961 Sierra Ave Fontana (92335) *(P-14823)*

Kaiser Foundation Hospitals .... C...... 661 398-5011
3501 Stockdale Hwy Bakersfield (93309) *(P-14824)*

Kaiser Foundation Hospitals .... B...... 408 945-2900
770 E Calaveras Blvd Milpitas (95035) *(P-14825)*

Kaiser Foundation Hospitals 951 352-0292
3951 Van Buren Blvd Riverside (92503) *(P-14826)*

Kaiser Foundation Hospitals .... C...... 818 552-3000
444 W Glenoaks Blvd Glendale (91202) *(P-14827)*

Kaiser Foundation Hospitals .... C...... 626 440-5639
3280 E Foothill Blvd Pasadena (91107) *(P-14828)*

Kaiser Foundation Hospitals .... D...... 619 528-5000
250 Travelodge Dr El Cajon (92020) *(P-14829)*

Kaiser Foundation Hospitals .... C...... 619 528-5000
732 N Broadway Escondido (92025) *(P-14830)*

Kaiser Foundation Hospitals .... D...... 530 757-7100
1955 Cowell Blvd Davis (95618) *(P-14831)*

Kaiser Foundation Hospitals .... B...... 707 765-3900
3900 Lakeville Hwy Petaluma (94954) *(P-14832)*

Kaiser Foundation Hospitals .... A...... 510 678-4000
27400 Hesperian Blvd Hayward (94545) *(P-14833)*

Kaiser Foundation Hospitals .... D...... 916 784-4000
1001 Riverside Ave Roseville (95678) *(P-14834)*

Kaiser Foundation Hospitals .... C...... 415 833-3450
2241 Geary Blvd Ste 118 San Francisco (94115) *(P-14835)*

Kaiser Foundation Hospitals .... D...... 661 334-2020
5055 California Ave Ste 110 Bakersfield (93309) *(P-14836)*

Kaiser Foundation Hospitals .... A...... 650 742-2000
1200 El Camino Real South San Francisco (94080) *(P-14837)*

Kaiser Foundation Hospitals .... A...... 510 248-3000
39400 Paseo Padre Pkwy Fremont (94538) *(P-14838)*

Kaiser Foundation Hospitals .... D...... 661 222-2323
27107 Tourney Rd Santa Clarita (91355) *(P-14839)*

Kaiser Foundation Hospitals .... A...... 951 353-2000
10800 Magnolia Ave Riverside (92505) *(P-14840)*

Kaiser Foundation Hospitals .... A...... 209 825-3700
1777 W Yosemite Ave Manteca (95337) *(P-14841)*

Kaiser Foundation Hospitals .... A...... 415 833-2000
2425 Geary Blvd San Francisco (94115) *(P-14842)*

ALPHABETIC SECTION — Kaiser Mental Health Center

Kaiser Foundation Hospitals .... A 951 243-0811
27300 Iris Ave Moreno Valley (92555) *(P-14843)*

Kaiser Foundation Hospitals .... D 310 419-3303
110 N La Brea Ave Inglewood (90301) *(P-14844)*

Kaiser Foundation Hospitals .... C 925 432-6000
3000 Las Positas Rd Livermore (94551) *(P-14845)*

Kaiser Foundation Hospitals .... A 559 448-4500
7300 N Fresno St Fresno (93720) *(P-14846)*

Kaiser Foundation Hospitals .... C 714 967-4700
1900 E 4th St Santa Ana (92705) *(P-14847)*

Kaiser Foundation Hospitals .... D 916 986-4178
285 Palladio Pkwy Folsom (95630) *(P-14848)*

Kaiser Foundation Hospitals .... A 510 987-1000
1950 Franklin St Oakland (94612) *(P-14849)*

Kaiser Foundation Hospitals .... D 916 817-5200
2155 Iron Point Rd Folsom (95630) *(P-14850)*

Kaiser Foundation Hospitals .... B 323 783-8306
1515 N Vermont Ave Fl 3 Los Angeles (90027) *(P-14851)*

Kaiser Foundation Hospitals .... C 408 972-3000
250 Hospital Pkwy Bldg D San Jose (95119) *(P-14852)*

Kaiser Foundation Hospitals .... D 310 922-8916
1011 Baldwin Park Blvd Baldwin Park (91706) *(P-14853)*

Kaiser Foundation Hospitals .... C 323 857-2000
6041 Cadillac Ave Los Angeles (90034) *(P-14854)*

Kaiser Foundation Hospitals .... D 661 631-3045
1200 Discovery Dr Bakersfield (93309) *(P-16147)*

Kaiser Foundation Hospitals .... C 949 262-5780
6 Willard Irvine (92604) *(P-16148)*

Kaiser Foundation Hospitals .... A 707 624-4000
1 Quality Dr Fl A1 Vacaville (95688) *(P-16149)*

Kaiser Foundation Hospitals .... C 916 746-3937
1680 E Roseville Pkwy Roseville (95661) *(P-16150)*

Kaiser Foundation Hospitals .... C 925 556-4200
3100 Dublin Blvd Dublin (94568) *(P-16151)*

Kaiser Foundation Hospitals .... A 818 719-2000
5601 De Soto Ave Woodland Hills (91367) *(P-16152)*

Kaiser Foundation Hospitals .... C 951 353-4000
12620 Prescott Ave Tustin (92782) *(P-16153)*

Kaiser Foundation Hospitals .... C 661 412-6777
8800 Ming Ave Bakersfield (93311) *(P-16154)*

Kaiser Foundation Hospitals .... D 323 783-4011
4867 W Sunset Blvd Los Angeles (90027) *(P-16155)*

Kaiser Foundation Hospitals .... C 925 906-2380
320 Lennon Ln Walnut Creek (94598) *(P-16156)*

Kaiser Foundation Hospitals .... D 408 363-4801
5831 Cottle Rd San Jose (95123) *(P-16157)*

Kaiser Foundation Hospitals .... A 714 644-2000
3440 E La Palma Ave Anaheim (92806) *(P-16158)*

Kaiser Foundation Hospitals .... C 310 937-4311
400 S Sepulveda Blvd Manhattan Beach (90266) *(P-16159)*

Kaiser Foundation Hospitals (HQ) .... C 510 271-6611
1 Kaiser Plz Oakland (94612) *(P-16160)*

Kaiser Foundation Hospitals .... C 323 783-4011
4733 W Sunset Blvd Fl 2 Los Angeles (90027) *(P-16161)*

Kaiser Foundation Hospitals .... A 510 752-1000
280 W Macarthur Blvd Oakland (94611) *(P-16162)*

Kaiser Foundation Hospitals .... C 916 558-6520
501 J St Sacramento (95814) *(P-16163)*

Kaiser Foundation Hospitals .... C 909 394-2530
1255 W Arrow Hwy San Dimas (91773) *(P-16164)*

Kaiser Foundation Hospitals .... C 619 528-2583
4405 Vandever Ave Fl 5 San Diego (92120) *(P-16165)*

Kaiser Foundation Hospitals .... C 408 972-6010
280 Hospital Pkwy San Jose (95119) *(P-16166)*

Kaiser Foundation Hospitals .... D 661 949-5000
1600 W Avenue J Lancaster (93534) *(P-16167)*

Kaiser Foundation Hospitals .... C 925 598-2799
5820 Owens Dr Bldg E-2 Pleasanton (94588) *(P-16168)*

Kaiser Foundation Hospitals .... C 858 573-1504
9455 Clairemont Mesa Blvd San Diego (92123) *(P-16169)*

Kaiser Foundation Hospitals .... D 408 235-4005
3900 Freedom Cir Ste 201 Santa Clara (95054) *(P-16170)*

Kaiser Foundation Hospitals .... A 916 973-5000
1650 Response Rd Sacramento (95815) *(P-16171)*

Kaiser Foundation Hospitals .... D 619 641-4663
10990 San Diego Mission Rd San Diego (92108) *(P-16172)*

Kaiser Foundation Hospitals .... C 951 353-2000
36450 Inland Valley Dr Ste 204 Wildomar (92595) *(P-16173)*

Kaiser Foundation Hospitals .... C 619 528-5000
1630 E Main St El Cajon (92021) *(P-16174)*

Kaiser Foundation Hospitals .... C 323 562-6400
7825 Atlantic Ave Cudahy (90201) *(P-16175)*

Kaiser Foundation Hospitals .... C 310 517-2956
15446 S Western Ave Gardena (90249) *(P-16176)*

Kaiser Foundation Hospitals .... D 818 592-3100
5601 De Soto Ave Woodland Hills (91367) *(P-16177)*

Kaiser Foundation Hospitals .... B 916 631-3088
10725 International Dr Rancho Cordova (95670) *(P-16178)*

Kaiser Foundation Hospitals .... D 833 574-2273
20000 Rinaldi St Porter Ranch (91326) *(P-16179)*

Kaiser Foundation Hospitals .... D 415 833-4393
4131 Geary Blvd San Francisco (94118) *(P-16180)*

Kaiser Foundation Hospitals .... D 510 752-1000
3505 Broadway Oakland (94611) *(P-16181)*

Kaiser Foundation Hospitals .... B 925 906-2000
501 Lennon Ln Walnut Creek (94598) *(P-16182)*

Kaiser Foundation Hospitals .... A 925 847-5000
7601 Stoneridge Dr Pleasanton (94588) *(P-16183)*

Kaiser Foundation Hospitals .... A 707 651-1000
975 Sereno Dr Vallejo (94589) *(P-16184)*

Kaiser Foundation Hospitals .... C 408 972-6700
275 Hospital Pkwy Ste 765a San Jose (95119) *(P-16185)*

Kaiser Foundation Hospitals .... B 626 440-5659
1055 E Colorado Blvd Ste 100 Pasadena (91106) *(P-16186)*

Kaiser Foundation Hospitals .... D 510 434-5835
5800 Coliseum Way Oakland (94621) *(P-16187)*

Kaiser Foundation Hospitals .... A 916 784-4000
1600 Eureka Rd Roseville (95661) *(P-16188)*

Kaiser Foundation Hospitals .... D 888 750-0036
250 W San Jose Ave Claremont (91711) *(P-16189)*

Kaiser Foundation Hospitals .... C 916 525-6300
7300 Wyndham Dr Sacramento (95823) *(P-16190)*

Kaiser Foundation Hospitals .... A 209 476-3101
7373 West Ln Stockton (95210) *(P-16191)*

Kaiser Foundation Hospitals .... A 408 851-1000
710 Lawrence Expy Santa Clara (95051) *(P-16192)*

Kaiser Foundation Hospitals .... A 661 726-2500
43112 15th St W Lancaster (93534) *(P-16193)*

Kaiser Foundation Hospitals .... D 650 903-3000
555 Castro St Fl 3 Mountain View (94041) *(P-16194)*

Kaiser Foundation Hospitals .... C 213 580-7200
765 W College St Los Angeles (90012) *(P-16651)*

Kaiser Foundation Hospitals .... B 209 476-3646
7373 West Ln Stockton (95210) *(P-16729)*

Kaiser Foundation Hospitals .... D 916 817-5651
2155 Iron Point Rd Folsom (95630) *(P-16730)*

Kaiser Foundation Hospitals .... C 408 361-2100
50 Great Oaks Blvd San Jose (95119) *(P-16882)*

Kaiser Foundation Hospitals .... B 925 779-5000
3400 Delta Fair Blvd Antioch (94509) *(P-17079)*

Kaiser Foundation Hospitals .... C 310 513-6707
23621 Main St Carson (90745) *(P-17080)*

Kaiser Foundation Hospitals .... B 916 482-1132
2829 Watt Ave Ste 150 Sacramento (95821) *(P-17081)*

Kaiser Foundation Hospitals .... D 866 984-7483
2055 Kellogg Ave Corona (92879) *(P-17261)*

Kaiser Foundation Hospitals .... A 916 974-6211
3200 Arden Way Sacramento (95825) *(P-20935)*

Kaiser Fundation Hlth Plan Inc .... D 510 271-5800
4460 Hacienda Dr Pleasanton (94588) *(P-8336)*

Kaiser Fundation Hlth Plan Inc (PA) .... B 510 271-5800
1 Kaiser Plz Oakland (94612) *(P-14855)*

Kaiser Mental Health Center, Los Angeles *Also Called: Kaiser Foundation Hospitals (P-16651)*

Employee Codes: A=Over 500 employees, B=251-500
C=101-250, D=51-100, E=20-50, F=10-19, G=1-9

Kaiser Permanent

Kaiser Permanent .... D....... 415 492-6311
100 Smith Ranch Rd San Rafael (94903) *(P-16195)*

Kaiser Permanente .... D....... 323 298-3100
5105 W Goldleaf Cir Los Angeles (90056) *(P-8337)*

Kaiser Permanente .... C....... 909 427-3910
9985 Sierra Ave Fontana (92335) *(P-8338)*

Kaiser Permanente .... C....... 510 752-6198
3772 Howe St Oakland (94611) *(P-17262)*

Kaiser Permanente, Chino *Also Called: Kaiser Foundation Hospitals (P-8307)*
Kaiser Permanente, Baldwin Park *Also Called: Kaiser Foundation Hospitals (P-8311)*
Kaiser Permanente, West Covina *Also Called: Kaiser Foundation Hospitals (P-8317)*
Kaiser Permanente, Whittier *Also Called: Kaiser Foundation Hospitals (P-8322)*
Kaiser Permanente, Berkeley *Also Called: Kaiser Foundation Hospitals (P-8334)*
Kaiser Permanente, Pasadena *Also Called: Southern Cal Prmnnte Med Group (P-8369)*
Kaiser Permanente, San Diego *Also Called: Kaiser Foundation Hospitals (P-9430)*
Kaiser Permanente, Los Angeles *Also Called: Kaiser Foundation Hospitals (P-9432)*
Kaiser Permanente, Colton *Also Called: Kaiser Foundation Hospitals (P-9434)*
Kaiser Permanente, Napa *Also Called: Kaiser Foundation Hospitals (P-9436)*
Kaiser Permanente, Vista *Also Called: Kaiser Foundation Hospitals (P-14798)*
Kaiser Permanente, Garden Grove *Also Called: Kaiser Foundation Hospitals (P-14799)*
Kaiser Permanente, Walnut Creek *Also Called: Kaiser Foundation Hospitals (P-14801)*
Kaiser Permanente, San Francisco *Also Called: Kaiser Foundation Hospitals (P-14804)*
Kaiser Permanente, Redlands *Also Called: Kaiser Foundation Hospitals (P-14805)*
Kaiser Permanente, Brea *Also Called: Kaiser Foundation Hospitals (P-14806)*
Kaiser Permanente, San Rafael *Also Called: Kaiser Foundation Hospitals (P-14807)*
Kaiser Permanente, Richmond *Also Called: Kaiser Foundation Hospitals (P-14808)*
Kaiser Permanente, Panorama City *Also Called: Kaiser Foundation Hospitals (P-14810)*
Kaiser Permanente, San Jose *Also Called: Kaiser Foundation Hospitals (P-14817)*
Kaiser Permanente, Santa Ana *Also Called: Kaiser Foundation Hospitals (P-14818)*
Kaiser Permanente, Los Angeles *Also Called: Kaiser Foundation Hospitals (P-14819)*
Kaiser Permanente, Redwood City *Also Called: Kaiser Foundation Hospitals (P-14820)*
Kaiser Permanente, Walnut Creek *Also Called: Kaiser Foundation Hospitals (P-14821)*
Kaiser Permanente, Harbor City *Also Called: Kaiser Foundation Hospitals (P-14822)*
Kaiser Permanente, Fontana *Also Called: Kaiser Foundation Hospitals (P-14823)*
Kaiser Permanente, Riverside *Also Called: Kaiser Foundation Hospitals (P-14826)*
Kaiser Permanente, San Francisco *Also Called: Kaiser Foundation Hospitals (P-14835)*
Kaiser Permanente, Bakersfield *Also Called: Kaiser Foundation Hospitals (P-14836)*
Kaiser Permanente, South San Francisco *Also Called: Kaiser Foundation Hospitals (P-14837)*
Kaiser Permanente, Fremont *Also Called: Kaiser Foundation Hospitals (P-14838)*
Kaiser Permanente, Santa Clarita *Also Called: Kaiser Foundation Hospitals (P-14839)*
Kaiser Permanente, San Francisco *Also Called: Kaiser Foundation Hospitals (P-14842)*
Kaiser Permanente, Inglewood *Also Called: Kaiser Foundation Hospitals (P-14844)*
Kaiser Permanente, Fresno *Also Called: Kaiser Foundation Hospitals (P-14846)*
Kaiser Permanente, Santa Ana *Also Called: Kaiser Foundation Hospitals (P-14847)*
Kaiser Permanente, Los Angeles *Also Called: Kaiser Foundation Hospitals (P-14851)*
Kaiser Permanente, San Diego *Also Called: Southern Cal Prmnnte Med Group (P-15076)*
Kaiser Permanente, Woodland Hills *Also Called: Kaiser Foundation Hospitals (P-16152)*
Kaiser Permanente, Tustin *Also Called: Kaiser Foundation Hospitals (P-16153)*
Kaiser Permanente, Bakersfield *Also Called: Kaiser Foundation Hospitals (P-16154)*
Kaiser Permanente, Los Angeles *Also Called: Kaiser Foundation Hospitals (P-16155)*
Kaiser Permanente, Oakland *Also Called: Kaiser Foundation Hospitals (P-16160)*
Kaiser Permanente, Oakland *Also Called: Kaiser Foundation Hospitals (P-16162)*
Kaiser Permanente, Sacramento *Also Called: Kaiser Foundation Hospitals (P-16163)*
Kaiser Permanente, San Dimas *Also Called: Kaiser Foundation Hospitals (P-16164)*
Kaiser Permanente, San Diego *Also Called: Kaiser Foundation Hospitals (P-16165)*
Kaiser Permanente, San Diego *Also Called: Kaiser Foundation Hospitals (P-16169)*
Kaiser Permanente, Santa Clara *Also Called: Kaiser Foundation Hospitals (P-16170)*
Kaiser Permanente, Sacramento *Also Called: Kaiser Foundation Hospitals (P-16171)*
Kaiser Permanente, Walnut Creek *Also Called: Kaiser Foundation Hospitals (P-16182)*
Kaiser Permanente, Pleasanton *Also Called: Kaiser Foundation Hospitals (P-16183)*
Kaiser Permanente, Pasadena *Also Called: Kaiser Foundation Hospitals (P-16186)*
Kaiser Permanente, Roseville *Also Called: Kaiser Foundation Hospitals (P-16188)*
Kaiser Permanente, Claremont *Also Called: Kaiser Foundation Hospitals (P-16189)*
Kaiser Permanente, Stockton *Also Called: Kaiser Foundation Hospitals (P-16191)*
Kaiser Permanente, Lancaster *Also Called: Kaiser Foundation Hospitals (P-16193)*
Kaiser Permanente, Downey *Also Called: Southern Cal Prmnnte Med Group (P-16441)*
Kaiser Permanente, Stockton *Also Called: Kaiser Foundation Hospitals (P-16729)*
Kaiser Permanente, Folsom *Also Called: Kaiser Foundation Hospitals (P-16730)*
Kaiser Permanente, San Jose *Also Called: Kaiser Foundation Hospitals (P-16882)*
Kaiser Permanente, Antioch *Also Called: Kaiser Foundation Hospitals (P-17079)*
Kaiser Permanente, Carson *Also Called: Kaiser Foundation Hospitals (P-17080)*
Kaiser Permanente, Oakland *Also Called: Permanente Medical Group Inc (P-17296)*
Kaiser Permanente, Sacramento *Also Called: Permanente Medical Group Inc (P-17297)*
Kaiser Permanente Division RES, Oakland *Also Called: Kaiser Foundation Hospitals (P-8319)*
Kaiser Permanente Med Group, Oakland *Also Called: Kaiser Foundation Hospitals (P-16181)*
Kaiser Permanente Medical Ctr, San Francisco *Also Called: Kaiser Foundation Hospitals (P-16180)*
Kaiser Permanente San, San Francisco *Also Called: Kaiser Foundation Hospitals (P-14803)*

Kaiser Permanente Watts C .... D....... 323 564-7911
1465 E 103rd St Los Angeles (90002) *(P-16196)*

Kaiser Perminente, Folsom *Also Called: Kaiser Foundation Hospitals (P-14850)*
Kaiser Prmanente Internet Svcs, Pleasanton *Also Called: Kaiser Foundation Hospitals (P-16168)*

Kaiser Prmanente Un Cy Landing .... D....... 408 235-4005
30116 Eigenbrodt Way Union City (94587) *(P-14856)*

Kaiser Prmnente Downey Med Ctr, Downey *Also Called: Kaiser Foundation Hospitals (P-8312)*
Kaiser Prmnnte Advice Ctr - Al, Sacramento *Also Called: Kaiser Foundation Hospitals (P-16190)*
Kaiser Prmnnte Antioch Med Ctr, Antioch *Also Called: Kaiser Foundation Hospitals (P-14793)*
Kaiser Prmnnte Eye Svcs - Optm, Roseville *Also Called: Kaiser Foundation Hospitals (P-16150)*
Kaiser Prmnnte Hayward Med Ctr, Hayward *Also Called: Kaiser Foundation Hospitals (P-14833)*
Kaiser Prmnnte Lvrmore Med Ctr, Livermore *Also Called: Kaiser Foundation Hospitals (P-14845)*
Kaiser Prmnnte Manteca Med Ctr, Manteca *Also Called: Kaiser Foundation Hospitals (P-14841)*
Kaiser Prmnnte Modesto Med Ctr, Modesto *Also Called: Permanente Medical Group Inc (P-14957)*
Kaiser Prmnnte Mreno Vly Med C, Moreno Valley *Also Called: Kaiser Foundation Hospitals (P-14843)*
Kaiser Prmnnte Oakland Med Ctr, Oakland *Also Called: Kaiser Foundation Hospitals (P-14816)*
Kaiser Prmnnte Ornge Cnty-Nhei, Anaheim *Also Called: Kaiser Foundation Hospitals (P-16158)*
Kaiser Prmnnte Psadena Med Off, Pasadena *Also Called: Kaiser Foundation Hospitals (P-14828)*
Kaiser Prmnnte S Scrmnto Med C, Sacramento *Also Called: Kaiser Foundation Hospitals (P-8321)*
Kaiser Prmnnte San Jose Med Ct, San Jose *Also Called: Kaiser Foundation Hospitals (P-14852)*
Kaiser Prmnnte San Jose Med Ct, San Jose *Also Called: Kaiser Foundation Hospitals (P-16185)*
Kaiser Prmnnte San Lndro Med C, San Leandro *Also Called: Kaiser Foundation Hospitals (P-14815)*

Kaiser Prmnnte Schl Anesthesia .... C....... 626 564-3016
100 S Los Robles Ste 501 Pasadena (91101) *(P-14857)*

Kaiser Prmnnte Snta Clara Med, Los Gatos *Also Called: Peter Castillo Md PA (P-14993)*
Kaiser Prmnnte Snta Clara Med, Santa Clara *Also Called: Kaiser Foundation Hospitals (P-16192)*
Kaiser Prmnnte Snta Rosa Med C, Santa Rosa *Also Called: Kaiser Foundation Hospitals (P-14797)*
Kaiser Prmnnte Vallejo Med Ctr, Vallejo *Also Called: Kaiser Foundation Hospitals (P-16184)*
Kaiser Prmnnte W Los Angles Me, Los Angeles *Also Called: Kaiser Foundation Hospitals (P-14809)*
Kaiserair, Oakland *Also Called: Kaiserair Inc (P-3866)*

Kaiserair Inc (PA) .... C....... 510 569-9622
8735 Earhart Rd Oakland (94621) *(P-3866)*

Kaiserair Inc .... D....... 707 528-7400
2240 Airport Blvd Santa Rosa (95403) *(P-3896)*

Kaizen Syndicate LLC .... C....... 858 309-2028
10413 Magical Waters Ct Spring Valley (91978) *(P-12822)*

ALPHABETIC SECTION
Keck Hospital of Usc

Kaleidioscope Stadium Cinema, Mission Viejo *Also Called: Edwards Theatres Inc (P-13986)*

Kaliocommerce Inc .... D....... 408 550-8040
19330 Stevens Creek Blvd Cupertino (95014) *(P-6641)*

Kallidus Inc 877 554-2176
555 Mission St Ste 1950 San Francisco (94105) *(P-11691)*

Kalway Inc .... D....... 800 303-0076
10156 Live Oak Ave Fontana (92335) *(P-3498)*

Kam Sang Company Inc .... D....... 714 523-2800
14419 Firestone Blvd La Mirada (90638) *(P-9934)*

Kamps Company .... C....... 209 823-8924
1915 Moffat Blvd Manteca (95336) *(P-11297)*

Kan-Di-Ki LLC (HQ) .... D....... 818 549-1880
2820 N Ontario St Burbank (91504) *(P-16731)*

Kana Pipeline Inc .... D....... 714 986-1400
12620 Magnolia Ave Riverside (92503) *(P-1226)*

Kane & Finkel LLC .... D....... 415 777-4990
534 4th St San Francisco (94107) *(P-10635)*

Kane Fnkle Hlthcare Cmmnctions, San Francisco *Also Called: Kane & Finkel LLC (P-10635)*

Kaney Foods, San Luis Obispo *Also Called: Amk Foodservices Inc (P-6239)*

Kang Family Partners LLC .... C....... 805 688-1000
555 Mcmurray Rd Buellton (93427) *(P-9935)*

Kap LP .... D....... 559 897-5132
10363 Davis Ave Kingsburg (93631) *(P-108)*

Kapor Center For Social Impact .... D....... 510 488-6600
2148 Broadway Oakland (94612) *(P-8238)*

Kapow Software, Irvine *Also Called: Kapow Technologies Inc (P-5321)*

Kapow Technologies Inc .... D....... 800 805-0828
15211 Laguna Canyon Rd Irvine (92618) *(P-5321)*

Karcher Environmental, San Leandro *Also Called: Karcher Environmental Inc (P-2290)*

Karcher Environmental Inc .... D....... 510 297-0180
1718 Fairway Dr San Leandro (94577) *(P-2290)*

Kare Klub .... C....... 858 538-5437
9995 Carmel Mountain Rd Ste B8 San Diego (92129) *(P-18322)*

Karen Kane Inc (PA) .... C....... 323 588-0000
2275 E 37th St Vernon (90058) *(P-6202)*

Kareo PM, Corona Del Mar *Also Called: Tebra Technologies Inc (P-11973)*

Kargo Global Inc .... C....... 212 979-9000
1437 4th St Ste 200 Santa Monica (90401) *(P-10713)*

Karius Inc .... C....... 866 452-7487
975 Island Dr Ste 100 Redwood City (94065) *(P-19718)*

Karl Storz Endscpy-America Inc (HQ) .... B....... 424 218-8100
2151 E Grand Ave El Segundo (90245) *(P-3056)*

Karma Inc .... C....... 209 239-1222
410 Eastwood Ave Manteca (95336) *(P-15527)*

Karman Topco LP (PA) .... D....... 949 797-2900
18100 Von Karman Ave Ste 1000 Irvine (92612) *(P-20789)*

Karsyn Construction Inc .... D....... 559 271-2900
4697 W Jacquelyn Ave Fresno (93722) *(P-950)*

Karthikeya Devireddy M D Inc .... D....... 209 826-2222
311 W I St Los Banos (93635) *(P-14858)*

Kartos Therapeutics Inc 650 542-0130
275 Shoreline Dr Ste 100 Redwood City (94065) *(P-19719)*

Kash Apparel LLC .... D....... 213 747-8885
1437 E 20th St Los Angeles (90011) *(P-6203)*

Kaspick & Co LLC (DH) .... D....... 650 585-4100
203 Redwood Shores Pkwy Ste 300 Redwood City (94065) *(P-8599)*

Katch Entertainment LLC .... D....... 650 380-0607
170 Wildwood Way Woodside (94062) *(P-14091)*

Katch LLC .... D....... 310 219-6200
2381 Rosecrans Ave Ste 400 El Segundo (90245) *(P-10636)*

Katella Properties .... D....... 562 704-8695
10140 Grayling Ave Whittier (90603) *(P-8730)*

Katella Properties .... D....... 562 596-5561
3902 Katella Ave Los Alamitos (90720) *(P-15428)*

Katerra .... D....... 720 449-3909
1950 W Corporate Way Anaheim (92801) *(P-690)*

Katerra Construction LLC .... A....... 720 449-3909
1950 W Corporate Way Anaheim (92801) *(P-691)*

Katten Muchin Rosenman LLP .... D....... 310 788-4400
2029 Century Park E Ste 2600 Los Angeles (90067) *(P-17513)*

Katzkin Leather Inc (PA) .... C....... 323 725-1243
6868 W Acco St Montebello (90640) *(P-6920)*

Kautz Ironstone Vineyards, Murphys *Also Called: Kautz Vineyards Inc (P-78)*

Kautz Vineyards Inc (PA) .... D....... 209 728-1251
1894 6 Mile Rd Murphys (95247) *(P-78)*

Kava Holdings Inc (DH) .... C....... 310 472-1211
701 Stone Canyon Rd Los Angeles (90077) *(P-9936)*

Kawahara Nursery Inc .... C....... 408 779-2400
698 Burnett Ave Morgan Hill (95037) *(P-134)*

Kawasaki Motors Corp USA (HQ) .... B....... 949 837-4683
26972 Burbank Foothill Ranch (92610) *(P-7397)*

KAWEAH DELTA HEALTH CARE DISTRICT, Exeter *Also Called: Kaweah Delta Health Care Dst (P-16197)*

KAWEAH DELTA HEALTH CARE DISTRICT, Visalia *Also Called: Kaweah Delta Health Care Dst (P-16198)*

KAWEAH DELTA HEALTH CARE DISTRICT, Dinuba *Also Called: Kaweah Delta Health Care Dst (P-16199)*

Kaweah Delta Health Care Dst .... D....... 559 592-7128
1014 San Juan Ave Exeter (93221) *(P-16197)*

Kaweah Delta Health Care Dst .... C....... 559 624-4800
1110 S Ben Maddox Way Visalia (93292) *(P-16198)*

Kaweah Delta Health Care Dst .... C....... 559 591-5513
355 Monte Vista Dr Dinuba (93618) *(P-16199)*

Kaweah Delta Medical Center, Visalia *Also Called: Kaweah Dlta Hlth Care Dst Gild (P-16200)*

Kaweah Dlta Hlth Care Dst Gild (PA) .... A....... 559 624-2000
400 W Mineral King Ave Visalia (93291) *(P-16200)*

Kaweah Dlta Hlth Care Dst Gild .... C....... 559 624-3300
1100 S Akers St Visalia (93277) *(P-16652)*

Kaweah Dlta Hlth Care Dst Gild .... C....... 559 624-3100
4945 W Cypress Ave Visalia (93277) *(P-17263)*

Kaydan Logistics LLC 951 961-9000
45562 Ponderosa Ct Temecula (92592) *(P-4163)*

Kayne Andrson Rdnick Inv MGT L .... D....... 310 229-9260
2000 Avenue Of The Stars Fl 11 Los Angeles (90067) *(P-9376)*

Kazan McClain Sttrley Grnwood .... C....... 877 995-6372
55 Harrison St Ste 400 Oakland (94607) *(P-17514)*

KB Home (PA) .... D....... 310 231-4000
10990 Wilshire Blvd Fl 7 Los Angeles (90024) *(P-793)*

KB Home Grater Los Angeles Inc (HQ) .... D....... 310 231-4000
10990 Wilshire Blvd # 700 Los Angeles (90024) *(P-692)*

KB Home Grater Los Angeles Inc .... C....... 951 691-5300
36310 Inland Valley Dr Wildomar (92595) *(P-693)*

KB Home South Bay Inc .... C....... 925 983-2500
5000 Executive Pkwy Ste 125 San Ramon (94583) *(P-763)*

Kbkg Inc .... C....... 626 449-4225
225 S Lake Ave Ste 400 Pasadena (91101) *(P-19592)*

Kbm Building Services, San Diego *Also Called: Kbm Fclity Sltons Holdings LLC (P-10915)*

Kbm Fclity Sltons Holdings LLC .... B....... 858 467-0202
7976 Engineer Rd Ste 200 San Diego (92111) *(P-10915)*

Kc Services, Anaheim *Also Called: Korean Community Services Inc (P-16685)*

KCAO, Hanford *Also Called: Kings Cmnty Action Orgnztion I (P-18034)*

Kcb Towers Inc .... D....... 909 862-0322
27260 Meines St Highland (92346) *(P-2184)*

Kcctech LLC .... C....... 628 400-2420
1630 N Main St Ste 305 Walnut Creek (94596) *(P-20790)*

Kcra, Sacramento *Also Called: Hearst Stations Inc (P-4438)*

KCS West Inc .... D....... 323 269-0020
250 E 1st St Ste 700 Los Angeles (90012) *(P-827)*

Kdc Construction, West Sacramento *Also Called: Cirks Construction Inc (P-894)*

Kdc Inc (HQ) .... C....... 714 828-7000
4462 Corporate Center Dr Los Alamitos (90720) *(P-1761)*

Kdc Systems, Los Alamitos *Also Called: Kdc Inc (P-1761)*

Kdg Construction Consulting, Glendale *Also Called: Kennard Development Group (P-764)*

Kdk Pacific Coast Entps LLC .... D....... 330 715-3143
18650 Collier Ave Ste B Lake Elsinore (92530) *(P-505)*

Kearney Agricultural Center, Parlier *Also Called: University Cal Rvrside Almni A (P-19928)*

Keating Dental Arts Inc .... C....... 949 955-2100
16881 Hale Ave Ste A Irvine (92606) *(P-16774)*

Keating Dental Lab, Irvine *Also Called: Keating Dental Arts Inc (P-16774)*

Kec Engineering .... C....... 951 734-3010
26320 Lester Cir Corona (92883) *(P-1125)*

Keck Hospital of Usc .... A....... 800 872-2273
1500 San Pablo St Los Angeles (90033) *(P-16201)*

ALPHABETIC SECTION

Keck Medical Center of Usc .... D....... 323 371-9535
1520 San Pablo St Los Angeles (90033) *(P-14859)*

Keck School .... D....... 323 442-1179
2011 Zonal Ave Los Angeles (90089) *(P-16202)*

Kedren Acute Psychtric Hosp Cm, Los Angeles Also Called: Kedren Community Hlth Ctr Inc *(P-16653)*

Kedren Community Hlth Ctr Inc (PA) .... B....... 323 233-0425
4211 Avalon Blvd Los Angeles (90011) *(P-16653)*

Kedren Community Hlth Ctr Inc .... C....... 323 524-0634
3800 S Figueroa St Los Angeles (90037) *(P-18033)*

Keefe Plumbing Services, Glendale Also Called: H L Moe Co Inc *(P-1454)*

Keenan & Associates .... D....... 510 986-6750
1111 Broadway Ste 2000 Oakland (94607) *(P-8600)*

Keenan & Associates (HQ) .... B....... 310 212-3344
2355 Crenshaw Blvd Ste 200 Torrance (90501) *(P-8601)*

Keenan Farms Inc .... D....... 559 945-1400
31510 Plymouth Ave Kettleman City (93239) *(P-93)*

Keenan Hpkins Sder Stwell Cntr (PA) .... D....... 714 695-3670
5109 E La Palma Ave Ste A Anaheim (92807) *(P-1940)*

Keesal Young Logan A Prof Corp (PA) .... D....... 562 436-2000
400 Oceangate Long Beach (90802) *(P-17515)*

KEIRO SENIOR HEALTH CARE, Los Angeles Also Called: Keiro Services *(P-20132)*

Keiro Services .... B....... 213 873-5700
420 E 3rd St Ste 1000 Los Angeles (90013) *(P-20132)*

Keiwit Infrastructure West Co, Fairfield Also Called: Kiewit Corporation *(P-1126)*

Keker Van Nest & Peters LLP .... D....... 415 391-5400
633 Battery St Bsmt 91 San Francisco (94111) *(P-17516)*

Keller Canyon Landfill Company .... C....... 925 458-9800
901 Bailey Rd Bay Point (94565) *(P-4902)*

Keller Lincoln Ford, Hanford Also Called: Jvac Inc *(P-7244)*

Keller North America Inc .... D....... 805 933-1331
1780 E Lemonwood Dr Santa Paula (93060) *(P-2291)*

Keller Williams Realtors, Beverly Hills Also Called: Keller Wllams Rlty Bvrly Hills *(P-9064)*

Keller Williams Realtors, Corona Also Called: Pro Group Inc *(P-9139)*

Keller Wllams Rlty Bvrly Hills .... D....... 310 432-6400
439 N Canon Dr Ste 300 Beverly Hills (90210) *(P-9064)*

Kelleyamerit Fleet Services, Walnut Creek Also Called: Kelleyamerit Holdings Inc *(P-20133)*

Kelleyamerit Holdings Inc (PA) .... D....... 877 512-6374
1331 N California Blvd Ste 150 Walnut Creek (94596) *(P-20133)*

Kellog, Woodland Hills Also Called: Kellogg Andlson Accntancy Corp *(P-19593)*

Kellogg Andlson Accntancy Corp (PA) .... D....... 818 971-5100
21700 Oxnard St Ste 800 Woodland Hills (91367) *(P-19593)*

Kellogg Garden Product, Lockeford Also Called: Kellogg Supply Inc *(P-2637)*

Kellogg Supply Inc .... C....... 209 727-3130
12686 Locke Rd Lockeford (95237) *(P-2637)*

Kelly Services, Costa Mesa Also Called: Southern Home Care Svcs Inc *(P-11338)*

Kelly Spicers Inc (HQ) .... C....... 562 698-1199
12310 Slauson Ave Santa Fe Springs (90670) *(P-6060)*

Kelly Spicers Packaging North, Santa Fe Springs Also Called: Kelly Spicers Inc *(P-6060)*

Kelly Thomas MD Ucsd Hlth Care .... C....... 619 543-2885
200 W Arbor Dr San Diego (92103) *(P-17264)*

Kelly Toys, Vernon Also Called: Kelly Toys Holdings LLC *(P-9319)*

Kelly Toys Holdings LLC .... D....... 323 923-1300
4811 S Alameda St Vernon (90058) *(P-9319)*

Kemper Insurance, Sacramento Also Called: Interwest Insurance Svcs LLC *(P-8594)*

Kemper Insurance, Kingsburg Also Called: Van Beurden Insurance Svcs Inc *(P-8680)*

Ken Blanchard Companies, The, Escondido Also Called: Blanchard Training and Dev Inc *(P-20298)*

Ken Grody Ford, Carlsbad Also Called: Ted Ford Jones Inc *(P-7309)*

Ken Grody Ford, Buena Park Also Called: Ted Ford Jones Inc *(P-13677)*

Ken Grody Ford - Redlands, Redlands Also Called: Ken Grody Redlands LLC *(P-7245)*

Ken Grody Redlands LLC .... D....... 909 793-3211
1121 W Colton Ave Redlands (92374) *(P-7245)*

Ken Real Estate Lease Ltd .... D....... 714 778-1700
900 S Disneyland Dr Anaheim (92802) *(P-9937)*

Ken Small Construction Inc .... D....... 661 617-1700
6205 District Blvd Bakersfield (93313) *(P-1227)*

Ken Starr Inc .... D....... 714 632-8789
1120 N Tustin Ave Anaheim (92807) *(P-1476)*

Kenai Drilling Limited .... C....... 661 587-0117
2651 Patton Way Bakersfield (93308) *(P-2173)*

Kendal At Snoma A Zen Inspred .... D....... 707 756-5036
1801 Boxheart Dr Healdsburg (95448) *(P-15529)*

Kendal Floral Supply LLC (PA) .... D....... 888 828-9875
1960 Kellogg Ave Carlsbad (92008) *(P-6863)*

Kendal North Bouquet Co, Carlsbad Also Called: Kendal Floral Supply LLC *(P-6863)*

Kendall-Jackson Wine Center .... C....... 707 571-7500
5007 Fulton Rd Fulton (95439) *(P-376)*

Kenna Security Inc .... C....... 855 474-7546
170 W Tasman Dr San Jose (95134) *(P-12823)*

Kennard Development Group .... D....... 818 241-0800
1025 N Brand Blvd Ste 300 Glendale (91202) *(P-764)*

Kennedy Jenks, San Francisco Also Called: Kennedy/Jenks Consultants Inc *(P-19293)*

Kennedy Team Inc .... D....... 619 921-5582
600 W Broadway Ste 1400 San Diego (92101) *(P-19010)*

Kennedy-Wilson Inc (PA) .... C....... 310 887-6400
151 El Camino Dr Beverly Hills (90212) *(P-9065)*

Kennedy/Jenks Consultants Inc (PA) .... D....... 415 243-2150
303 2nd St Ste 300s San Francisco (94107) *(P-19293)*

Kenneth Brdwick Intr Dsgns Inc .... D....... 310 274-9999
1615 Westwood Blvd Ste 202 Los Angeles (90024) *(P-13335)*

Kenneth Corp .... A....... 714 537-5160
12601 Garden Grove Blvd Garden Grove (92843) *(P-16203)*

KENNETH NORRIS CANCER HOSPITAL, Los Angeles Also Called: Tenet Health Systems Norris *(P-16570)*

Kensington At Sierra Madre, Sierra Madre Also Called: Kensington Sierra Madre LP *(P-18463)*

Kensington Sierra Madre LP .... D....... 626 355-5700
245 W Sierra Madre Blvd Sierra Madre (91024) *(P-18463)*

Kentfield Rehabilitation Hosp, Kentfield Also Called: 1125 Sir Frncis Drake Blvd Ope *(P-15914)*

Kentina, Temecula Also Called: Sft Realty Galway Downs LLC *(P-9177)*

Kenwood Vineyards, Kenwood Also Called: Pernod Ricard Usa LLC *(P-2390)*

Kenyon Construction Inc .... D....... 209 462-4060
1286 N Broadway Ave Stockton (95205) *(P-1941)*

Kenyon Plastering, Stockton Also Called: Kenyon Construction Inc *(P-1941)*

Keolis Transit America Inc .... C....... 818 616-5254
14663 Keswick St Van Nuys (91405) *(P-3143)*

Keolis Transit America Inc .... D....... 661 341-3910
660 W Avenue L Lancaster (93534) *(P-3144)*

Kerlan-Jobe Orthopedic Clinic (PA) .... D....... 310 665-7200
6801 Park Ter Ste 500 Los Angeles (90045) *(P-14860)*

Kern County Hospital Authority (PA) .... A....... 661 326-2102
1700 Mount Vernon Ave Bakersfield (93306) *(P-16204)*

Kern County Hospital Authority .... B....... 661 843-7980
1902 B St Bakersfield (93301) *(P-17082)*

Kern Direct Marketing, Woodland Hills Also Called: Kern Organization Inc *(P-10637)*

Kern Family Helathcare, Bakersfield Also Called: Kern Health Systems Inc *(P-14861)*

Kern Federal Credit Union .... D....... 661 327-9461
1717 Truxtun Ave Bakersfield (93301) *(P-7776)*

Kern Health Systems Inc .... D....... 661 664-5000
2900 Buck Owens Blvd Bakersfield (93308) *(P-14861)*

Kern Organization Inc .... D....... 818 703-8775
20955 Warner Center Ln Woodland Hills (91367) *(P-10637)*

Kern Rdlgy Imaging Systems Inc (PA) .... D....... 661 326-9600
2301 Bahamas Dr Bakersfield (93309) *(P-14862)*

Kern Rdlgy Imaging Systems Inc .... D....... 661 322-9958
4100 Truxtun Ave Ste 306 Bakersfield (93309) *(P-14863)*

Kern Regional Center (PA) .... C....... 661 327-8531
3200 N Sillect Ave Bakersfield (93308) *(P-18601)*

Kern Ridge Growers LLC .... B....... 661 854-3141
25429 Barbara St Arvin (93203) *(P-283)*

KERN RIVER HEALTH CENTER, Bakersfield Also Called: Clinica Sierra Vista *(P-14689)*

Kern River Transitional Care, Bakersfield Also Called: Bakersfieldidence Opco LLC *(P-15348)*

Kern Security Corporation .... D....... 661 363-6874
2701 Fruitvale Ave Bakersfield (93308) *(P-13129)*

Kern Security Systems, Bakersfield Also Called: Kern Security Corporation *(P-13129)*

Kern Valley Hosp Foundation (PA) .... B....... 760 379-2681
6412 Laurel Ave Lake Isabella (93240) *(P-7525)*

ALPHABETIC SECTION — Kimpton Hotel & Rest Group LLC

KERN VALLEY HOSPITAL, Lake Isabella Also Called: Kern Valley Hosp Foundation *(P-7525)*

Kern Valleyidence Opco LLC .... C....... 661 323-2894
3601 San Dimas St Bakersfield (93301) *(P-15767)*

Kernel, Culver City Also Called: HI LLC *(P-19816)*

Kernen Construction .... D....... 707 826-8686
2350 Glendale Dr Mckinleyville (95519) *(P-828)*

Kernridge Division, Mc Kittrick Also Called: Aera Energy LLC *(P-580)*

Kesq TV, Thousand Palms Also Called: Gulf- California Broadcast Co *(P-4436)*

Ketchum Incorporated .... D....... 415 984-6100
600 California St Fl 1 San Francisco (94108) *(P-20636)*

KETCHUM INCORPORATED, San Francisco Also Called: Ketchum Incorporated *(P-20636)*

Kettenburg Marine Corporation .... C....... 619 224-8211
2810 Carleton St San Diego (92106) *(P-5960)*

Kettmann Machining Inc .... C....... 408 727-5538
3590 Snell Ave Ste 10 San Jose (95136) *(P-13777)*

Kevcon Inc .... D....... 760 432-0307
10679 Westview Pkwy San Diego (92126) *(P-829)*

Keweier Nano Technologies Inc .... C....... 415 948-4335
41222 Malcolmson St Apt 20 Fremont (94538) *(P-13336)*

Key Air Cnditioning Contrs Inc .... D....... 562 941-2233
10905 Laurel Ave Santa Fe Springs (90670) *(P-1477)*

Key Environmental Services, Los Angeles Also Called: The Teecor Group Inc *(P-2321)*

Keyes Lexus, Van Nuys Also Called: Keylex Inc *(P-7247)*

Keyes Motors Inc (PA) .... D....... 818 782-0122
5855 Van Nuys Blvd Van Nuys (91401) *(P-7246)*

Keyes Toyota, Van Nuys Also Called: Keyes Motors Inc *(P-7246)*

Keylex Inc (PA) .... D....... 818 379-4000
5905 Van Nuys Blvd Van Nuys (91401) *(P-7247)*

Keynote LLC .... B....... 650 376-3033
777 Mariners Island Blvd San Mateo (94404) *(P-12585)*

Keynote Systems, San Mateo Also Called: Keynote LLC *(P-12585)*

KEYPOINT CREDIT SERVICES LLC .... B....... 800 745-7400
378 W Calaveras Blvd Milpitas (95035) *(P-10764)*

Keypoint Credit Union (PA) .... C....... 408 731-4100
2150 Trade Zone Blvd Ste 200 San Jose (95131) *(P-7777)*

Keysight Technologies Inc (PA) .... A....... 800 829-4444
1400 Fountaingrove Pkwy Santa Rosa (95403) *(P-3017)*

Keystone Automotive Warehouse .... D....... 951 277-5237
15640 Cantu Galleano Ranch Rd Eastvale (91752) *(P-5047)*

KEYSTONE AUTOMOTIVE WAREHOUSE, Eastvale Also Called: Keystone Automotive Warehouse *(P-5047)*

Keystone Educatn & Youth Svcs, Riverside Also Called: Keystone NPS LLC *(P-18603)*

Keystone Ford Inc (PA) .... C....... 562 868-0825
12000 Firestone Blvd Norwalk (90650) *(P-7248)*

Keystone NPS LLC (DH) .... D....... 909 633-6354
11980 Mount Vernon Ave Grand Terrace (92313) *(P-18602)*

Keystone NPS LLC .... C....... 951 785-0504
9994 County Farm Rd Riverside (92503) *(P-18603)*

Keystone Schools-Ramona, Grand Terrace Also Called: Keystone NPS LLC *(P-18602)*

Keystone Strategy LLC .... D....... 877 419-2623
150 Spear St Ste 1750 San Francisco (94105) *(P-20791)*

KEYSTONE STRATEGY, LLC, San Francisco Also Called: Keystone Strategy LLC *(P-20791)*

Keyt Television, Santa Barbara Also Called: Smith Broadcasting Group Inc *(P-4462)*

Kezar Life Sciences Inc (PA) .... D....... 650 822-5600
4000 Shoreline Ct Ste 300 South San Francisco (94080) *(P-2593)*

Kfjc FM, Los Altos Hills Also Called: Foothll-De Anza Cmnty Cllege D *(P-4384)*

Kfsn Television LLC .... C....... 559 442-1170
1777 G St Fresno (93706) *(P-4443)*

Kgo 810am, San Francisco Also Called: San Francisco Radio Assets LLC *(P-4403)*

Kgs Electronics, Arcadia Also Called: Gar Enterprises *(P-5306)*

Kgtv, San Diego Also Called: EW Scripps Company *(P-4430)*

Khaira Logistics, Sacramento Also Called: Khaira Logistics Inc *(P-4164)*

Khaira Logistics Inc .... D....... 916 308-4740
4451 Gateway Park Blvd Sacramento (95834) *(P-4164)*

Khamishon, Ilya MD, Folsom Also Called: University California Davis *(P-15153)*

Khan Academy Inc .... D....... 650 336-5426
1200 Villa St Ste 200 Mountain View (94041) *(P-12249)*

Khp V Carmel Trs LLC .... C....... 831 624-1841
3665 Rio Rd Carmel (93923) *(P-9938)*

Khs & S Contractors, Anaheim Also Called: Keenan Hpkins Sder Stwell Cntr *(P-1940)*

Khsl TV, Chico Also Called: Catamunt Brdcstg Chc-Rdding In *(P-4415)*

Khw Enterprises Inc .... D....... 562 236-8440
8550 Chetle Ave Ste A Whittier (90606) *(P-6921)*

Kia Design Center America, Irvine Also Called: Hyundai Amer Technical Ctr Inc *(P-19263)*

Kiavi Inc (PA) .... B....... 844 415-4663
2 Allegheny Ctr Ste 200 San Francisco (94105) *(P-9471)*

Kidango Inc .... D....... 408 258-9129
1824 Daytona Dr San Jose (95122) *(P-18323)*

Kidango Inc (PA) .... D....... 510 897-6900
44000 Old Warm Springs Blvd Fremont (94538) *(P-18324)*

Kidango Inc .... D....... 408 353-0473
3720 E Hills Dr Rm M1 San Jose (95127) *(P-18325)*

Kidango Inc .... D....... 510 494-9601
4700 Calaveras Ave Fremont (94538) *(P-18326)*

Kids Empire USA LLC .... D....... 424 527-1039
8605 Santa Monica Blvd West Hollywood (90069) *(P-14536)*

Kids Haven .... C....... 408 274-8766
6056 Montgomery Bnd San Jose (95135) *(P-18327)*

Kids Overcoming LLC .... D....... 415 748-8052
40029 St Ste 204 Oakland (94609) *(P-16883)*

Kids' Club YMCA Oxford School, Berkeley Also Called: Young MNS Chrstn Assn of E Bay *(P-18973)*

KIDSPACE, Pasadena Also Called: Kidspce A Prticipatory Museum *(P-18653)*

Kidspce A Prticipatory Museum .... D....... 626 449-9144
480 N Arroyo Blvd Pasadena (91103) *(P-18653)*

Kidztopros Inc .... C....... 408 421-0584
1584 Fulton Pl Fremont (94539) *(P-10406)*

Kiewit Corporation .... D....... 858 208-4285
12700 Stowe Dr Ste 180 Poway (92064) *(P-951)*

Kiewit Corporation .... D....... 707 439-7300
4650 Business Center Dr Fairfield (94534) *(P-1126)*

Kiewit Infrastructure West Co .... C....... 562 946-1816
10704 Shoemaker Ave Santa Fe Springs (90670) *(P-1127)*

Kifm Smooth Jazz 981 Inc .... C....... 619 297-3698
1615 Murray Canyon Rd San Diego (92108) *(P-4389)*

Kijiji Classifieds LLC .... D....... 669 213-9255
2125 Hamilton Ave San Jose (95125) *(P-4302)*

Kijiji Classifieds LLC .... D....... 408 376-4952
99 Fremont St San Francisco (94105) *(P-4303)*

Kijiji Classifieds LLC (HQ) .... D....... 408 376-4952
2065 Hamilton Ave San Jose (95125) *(P-4304)*

Kik Pool Additives Inc .... C....... 909 390-9912
5160 E Airport Dr Ontario (91761) *(P-2644)*

Kika Tech Inc .... C....... 650 229-3673
211 Westhill Dr Los Gatos (95032) *(P-11692)*

Kilam, Fremont Also Called: Kilam Inc *(P-6178)*

Kilam Inc .... C....... 510 943-4040
47685 Lakeview Blvd Fremont (94538) *(P-6178)*

Kilpatrick Twnsend Stckton LLP .... D....... 415 576-0200
2 Embarcadero Ctr Ste 1900 San Francisco (94111) *(P-17517)*

Kilroy Realty Corporation (PA) .... D....... 310 481-8400
12200 W Olympic Blvd Ste 200 Los Angeles (90064) *(P-9472)*

Klma W Medical Center .... C....... 530 625-4114
535 Airport Rd Hoopa (95546) *(P-17083)*

Kimball Tirey & St John LLP (PA) .... D....... 619 234-1690
7676 Hazard Center Dr Ste 900 San Diego (92108) *(P-17518)*

Kimco Services, Ontario Also Called: Kimco Staffing Services Inc *(P-11163)*

Kimco Staffing Services Inc .... A....... 951 686-3800
1770 Iowa Ave Ste 160 Riverside (92507) *(P-11161)*

Kimco Staffing Services Inc .... A....... 310 622-1616
3415 S Sepulveda Blvd Ste 1100 Los Angeles (90034) *(P-11162)*

Kimco Staffing Services Inc .... A....... 909 390-9881
4295 Jurupa St Ste 107 Ontario (91761) *(P-11163)*

Kimco Staffing Services Inc .... A....... 925 945-1444
1801 Oakland Blvd Ste 220 Walnut Creek (94596) *(P-17265)*

Kimco Staffing Solutions, Riverside Also Called: Kimco Staffing Services Inc *(P-11161)*

Kimpton Hotel, San Francisco Also Called: Kimpton Hotel & Rest Group LLC *(P-9941)*

Kimpton Hotel & Rest Group LLC .... B....... 415 885-2500
405 Taylor St San Francisco (94102) *(P-9939)*

Kimpton Hotel & Rest Group LLC .... C....... 323 852-6000
6317 Wilshire Blvd Los Angeles (90048) *(P-9940)*

Kimpton Hotel & Rest Group LLC   **ALPHABETIC SECTION**

Kimpton Hotel & Rest Group LLC (HQ) .... D 415 397-5572
   222 Kearny St Ste 200 San Francisco (94108) *(P-9941)*

Kimpton Hotel & Rest Group LLC .... C 415 561-1100
   425 N Point St San Francisco (94133) *(P-9942)*

Kimpton Hotel & Rest Group LLC .... C 415 392-8800
   127 Ellis St San Francisco (94102) *(P-9943)*

Kimpton Hotel & Rest Group LLC .... C 415 561-1111
   2455 Mason St San Francisco (94133) *(P-9944)*

Kimpton Hotel & Rest Group LLC .... C 415 292-0100
   501 Geary St San Francisco (94102) *(P-9945)*

Kincaid Industries Inc .... D 760 343-5457
   31065 Plantation Dr Thousand Palms (92276) *(P-1478)*

Kind Homecare Inc .... D 888 885-5463
   3705 Haven Ave Ste 104 Menlo Park (94025) *(P-16884)*

Kind Lending, Santa Ana Also Called: Solutions Inc *(P-20559)*

Kinder Mrgan Tank Stor Trmnals .... D 713 369-9000
   2000 E Sepulveda Blvd Carson (90810) *(P-3793)*

Kindred Healthcare Oper LLC .... B 510 357-8300
   2800 Benedict Dr San Leandro (94577) *(P-16205)*

Kindred Hospital, San Leandro Also Called: Kindred Healthcare Oper LLC *(P-16205)*

Kindred Hospital - Rancho, Rancho Cucamonga Also Called: Knd Development 55 LLC *(P-16206)*

Kindred Hospital La Mirata, West Covina Also Called: Southern Cal Spcialty Care Inc *(P-16443)*

Kindred Hospital Santa Ana, Santa Ana Also Called: Southern Cal Spcialty Care Inc *(P-16442)*

Kinecta, Manhattan Beach Also Called: Kinecta Federal Credit Union *(P-7778)*

Kinecta Federal Credit Union (PA) .... C 310 643-5400
   1440 Rosecrans Ave Manhattan Beach (90266) *(P-7778)*

Kinema Fitness Inc .... D 610 909-9331
   11601 Wilshire Blvd Ste 500 Los Angeles (90025) *(P-14537)*

Kinesis North, Escondido Also Called: Mental Health Systems Inc *(P-17090)*

Kinesso LLC .... C 415 262-5900
   600 Battery St San Francisco (94111) *(P-10638)*

Kineticom Inc (PA) .... D 619 330-3100
   333 H St Chula Vista (91910) *(P-11164)*

Kinetics Mechanical Svc Inc .... D 925 245-6200
   6336 Patterson Pass Rd Ste H Livermore (94550) *(P-1479)*

King & Spalding LLP .... C 650 422-6700
   601 California Ave Palo Alto (94304) *(P-17519)*

King & Spalding LLP .... C 415 318-1200
   50 California St Ste 3300 San Francisco (94111) *(P-17520)*

King Bros Enterprises LLC .... C 661 257-3262
   29101 The Old Rd Valencia (91355) *(P-2668)*

King City Child Dev Ctr, King City Also Called: Catalyst Family Inc *(P-18277)*

King Equipment LLC .... D 909 986-5300
   1690 Ashley Way Colton (92324) *(P-11001)*

King Holding Corporation .... A 586 254-3900
   360 N Crescent Dr Beverly Hills (90210) *(P-2750)*

King Relocation Services, Santa Fe Springs Also Called: Van King & Storage Inc *(P-3561)*

King Supply Company LLC .... D 714 670-8980
   6340 Valley View St Buena Park (90620) *(P-2292)*

King Ventures .... C 805 544-4444
   285 Bridge St San Luis Obispo (93401) *(P-9256)*

King World, Los Angeles Also Called: King World Productions Inc *(P-4444)*

King World Productions Inc .... C 310 264-3549
   1575 N Gower St Ste 100 Los Angeles (90028) *(P-4444)*

King-Reynolds Ventures LLC .... D 650 879-2136
   2001 Rossi Rd Pescadero (94060) *(P-13337)*

Kingfish Group Inc .... D 650 980-0200
   601 California St Ste 1250 San Francisco (94108) *(P-9525)*

Kings Arena Ltd Partnership .... D 916 928-0000
   1 Sports Pkwy Sacramento (95834) *(P-14144)*

Kings Card Club .... C 209 267-4567
   6111 West Ln Stockton (95210) *(P-14538)*

Kings Cmnty Action Orgnztion I (PA) .... D 559 582-4386
   1130 N 11th Ave Ca Hanford (93230) *(P-18034)*

Kings County Truck Lines (HQ) .... C 559 686-2857
   754 S Blackstone St Tulare (93274) *(P-3499)*

Kings Garden LLC .... C 760 275-4969
   3540 N Anza Rd Palm Springs (92262) *(P-20424)*

Kings Garden Royal Deliveries, Palm Springs Also Called: Kings Garden LLC *(P-20424)*

Kings Seafood Company LLC .... A 714 793-1177
   7691 Edinger Ave Huntington Beach (92647) *(P-6472)*

Kingsburg Center, Kingsburg Also Called: Sunbridge Care Entps W LLC *(P-15688)*

Kingsley Manor, Los Angeles Also Called: Front Porch Communities & Svcs *(P-15483)*

Kingston Technology Company Inc (PA) .... A 714 435-2600
   17600 Newhope St Fountain Valley (92708) *(P-5322)*

Kingsview Corp .... C 209 533-6245
   2 S Green St Sonora (95370) *(P-17084)*

Kingswood Capital MGT LP .... C 424 744-8238
   11111 Santa Monica Blvd Ste 1700 Los Angeles (90025) *(P-9402)*

Kinkisharyo International .... C 661 265-1647
   2825 E Avenue P Palmdale (93550) *(P-20792)*

Kinnate Biopharma Inc (PA) .... D 858 299-4699
   103 Montgomery St Ste 150 San Francisco (94129) *(P-2594)*

Kinsa Inc .... D 347 405-4315
   535 Mission St Fl 18 San Francisco (94105) *(P-16885)*

Kinsale Holdings Inc (PA) .... C 415 400-2600
   388 Market St Ste 860 San Francisco (94111) *(P-20425)*

Kinsbursky Bros Supply Inc (PA) .... D 714 738-8516
   125 E Commercial St Ste A Anaheim (92801) *(P-6011)*

Kinsbursky Brothers, Anaheim Also Called: Kinsbursky Bros Supply Inc *(P-6011)*

Kinsta Inc .... D 310 736-9306
   8605 Santa Monica Blvd # 92581 West Hollywood (90069) *(P-11693)*

Kintetsu Enterprises Co Amer (HQ) .... C 310 782-9300
   21241 S Western Ave Ste 100 Torrance (90501) *(P-9946)*

Kintetsu Enterprises Co Amer, Torrance Also Called: Kintetsu Enterprises Co Amer *(P-9946)*

Kio Networks, San Diego Also Called: Castle Access Inc *(P-4262)*

Kipp Foundation .... C 415 399-1556
   135 Main St Ste 1875 San Francisco (94105) *(P-18604)*

Kirkland & Ellis LLP .... B 650 859-7000
   3330 Hillview Ave Palo Alto (94304) *(P-17521)*

Kirkland & Ellis LLP .... C 310 552-4200
   2049 Century Park E Ste 3700 Los Angeles (90067) *(P-17522)*

Kirkland & Ellis LLP .... C 213 680-8400
   555 S Flower St Ste 3700 Los Angeles (90071) *(P-17523)*

Kirkland & Ellis LLP .... C 415 439-1400
   555 California St Ste 2700 San Francisco (94104) *(P-17524)*

Kirkland & Ellis LLP .... B 213 680-8400
   333 S Hope St Ste 3000 Los Angeles (90071) *(P-17525)*

Kirkwood Collection, Beverly Hills Also Called: Kirkwood Collection Inc *(P-9947)*

Kirkwood Collection Inc .... D 424 532-1160
   301 N Canon Dr Ste 302 Beverly Hills (90210) *(P-9947)*

Kirkwood Mountain Resorts LLC .... D 209 258-6000
   1501 Kirkwood Meadows Dr Kirkwood (95646) *(P-9948)*

Kirkwood Resort Company, Kirkwood Also Called: Kirkwood Mountain Resorts LLC *(P-9948)*

Kirschenman Enterprises Inc .... D 661 366-5736
   10100 Digiorgio Rd Bakersfield (93307) *(P-188)*

Kirschenman Enterprises Sls LP .... C 661 366-5736
   12826 Edison Hwy Edison (93220) *(P-13338)*

Kisco Senior Living LLC .... D 949 888-2250
   21952 Buena Suerte Rcho Sta Marg (92688) *(P-8838)*

Kisco Senior Living LLC .... C 714 997-5355
   620 S Glassell St Orange (92866) *(P-8839)*

Kisco Senior Living LLC .... D 707 585-1800
   1350 Oak View Cir Rohnert Park (94928) *(P-8840)*

Kisco Senior Living LLC .... D 650 948-7337
   1174 Los Altos Ave Ofc Los Altos (94022) *(P-8841)*

Kitchell Corporation .... C 916 648-9700
   2450 Venture Oaks Way Ste 500 Sacramento (95833) *(P-952)*

Kitchen Plus, Yuba City Also Called: R4k3 LLC *(P-2310)*

Kitchen United, Pasadena Also Called: Fresgo LLC *(P-3393)*

Kite Electric Incorporated .... C 949 380-7471
   2 Thomas Irvine (92618) *(P-1762)*

Kite Pharma Inc (HQ) .... D 310 824-9999
   2400 Broadway Ste 100 Santa Monica (90404) *(P-19720)*

Kite, A Gilead Company, Santa Monica Also Called: Kite Pharma Inc *(P-19720)*

Kitson Landscape MGT Inc .... D 805 681-9460
   5787 Thornwood Dr Goleta (93117) *(P-506)*

Kittridge Hotels & Resorts LLC .... D 760 325-9676
   150 S Indian Canyon Dr Palm Springs (92262) *(P-9949)*

ALPHABETIC SECTION — Korean Air

Kixeye .... D....... 415 400-8280
333 Bush St Fl 19 San Francisco (94104) *(P-10812)*

Kixie, Santa Monica *Also Called: Kixie Online Inc (P-11694)*

Kixie Online Inc .... D....... 424 800-3330
406 Wilshire Blvd Santa Monica (90401) *(P-11694)*

Kkw Trucking Inc (PA) .... A....... 909 869-1200
3100 Pomona Blvd Pomona (91768) *(P-3721)*

KLA, Milpitas *Also Called: KLA Corporation (P-3037)*

KLA Corporation (PA) .... B....... 408 875-3000
1 Technology Dr Milpitas (95035) *(P-3037)*

Klair Real Estate Inc .... C....... 209 484-8075
3018 E Service Rd Ste 104& Ceres (95307) *(P-9066)*

Klax Radio Station, Los Angeles *Also Called: Spanish Brdcstg Sys of Cal (P-4405)*

Kleary Masonry Inc .... C....... 916 869-6835
4612 Auburn Blvd Ste 2 Sacramento (95841) *(P-1887)*

Klein Denatale Goldner (PA) .... D....... 661 485-2100
10000 Stockdale Hwy Ste 200 Bakersfield (93311) *(P-17526)*

Klein Dntale Gldner Cper Rsnli, Bakersfield *Also Called: Klein Denatale Goldner (P-17526)*

Klein Foods Inc .... D....... 707 431-1533
11455 Old Redwood Hwy Healdsburg (95448) *(P-79)*

Kleinfelder, San Diego *Also Called: Kleinfelder Inc (P-19294)*

Kleinfelder Inc (HQ) .... C....... 619 831-4600
770 1st Ave Ste 400 San Diego (92101) *(P-19294)*

Kleinfelder Inc .... C....... 415 458-5803
63 Hermit Ln Kentfield (94904) *(P-19295)*

Kleinfelder Associates .... D....... 619 831-4600
550 W C St Ste 1200 San Diego (92101) *(P-19296)*

Kleinfelder Group Inc (PA) .... C....... 619 831-4600
770 1st Ave Ste 400 San Diego (92101) *(P-19297)*

Klientboost LLC .... C....... 657 203-7866
2787 Bristol St Ste 100 Costa Mesa (92626) *(P-10639)*

Klingstubbins Inc .... D....... 415 356-2040
160 Spear St Ste 330 San Francisco (94105) *(P-20894)*

Klink Citrus Association .... C....... 559 798-1881
32921 Road 159 Ivanhoe (93235) *(P-284)*

Klink Citrus Exchange, Ivanhoe *Also Called: Klink Citrus Association (P-284)*

Klm Laboratories Inc .... D....... 661 295-2600
28280 Alta Vista Ave Valencia (91355) *(P-5428)*

Klm Management Company .... D....... 626 330-3479
14120 Valley Blvd City Of Industry (91746) *(P-6439)*

Klm Orthotic, Valencia *Also Called: Klm Laboratories Inc (P-5428)*

Kloeckner Metals Corporation .... D....... 562 906-2020
9804 Norwalk Blvd # A Santa Fe Springs (90670) *(P-5501)*

Kloudgin, Sunnyvale *Also Called: Kloudgin Inc (P-12250)*

Kloudgin Inc .... C....... 877 256-8303
440 N Wolfe Rd Sunnyvale (94085) *(P-12250)*

Kloudspot Inc .... D....... 800 709-2211
1285 Oakmead Pkwy Sunnyvale (94085) *(P-12251)*

Kls Air Express Inc .... D
400 Capitol Mall Ste 2200 Sacramento (95814) *(P-4043)*

Klx LLC .... D....... 559 684-1037
1351 Charles Willard St Carson (90746) *(P-3500)*

Kmax TV, West Sacramento *Also Called: Sacramento Television Stns Inc (P-4460)*

Kmph Fox 26 .... C....... 559 255-2600
5111 E Mckinley Ave Fresno (93727) *(P-4445)*

Kms Financial Services Inc .... D....... 360 770-5117
251 Coon Heights Rd Ben Lomond (95005) *(P-13339)*

KMW Communications, Fullerton *Also Called: Gigatera Communications (P-2942)*

Knd Development 55 LLC .... C....... 909 581-6400
10841 White Oak Ave Rancho Cucamonga (91730) *(P-16206)*

Knight Law Group LLP .... D....... 424 355-1155
10250 Constellation Blvd Ste 2500 Los Angeles (90067) *(P-17527)*

Knight Transportation Inc .... D....... 559 685-9838
4450 S Blackstone St Tulare (93274) *(P-3410)*

Kno Inc .... D....... 408 844-8120
2200 Mission College Blvd Santa Clara (95054) *(P-12252)*

Knobbe Martens Olson Bear LLP ..... D....... 858 707-4000
12790 El Camino Real Ste 100 San Diego (92130) *(P-17528)*

Knobbe Martens Olson Bear LLP (PA) .... B....... 949 760-0404
2040 Main St Fl 14 Irvine (92614) *(P-17529)*

Knolls Convalescent Hosp Inc (PA) ... C....... 760 245-5361
16890 Green Tree Blvd Victorville (92395) *(P-15530)*

Knolls West Enterprise .... C....... 760 245-0107
16890 Green Tree Blvd Victorville (92395) *(P-15531)*

Knolls West Residential Care, Victorville *Also Called: Knolls West Enterprise (P-15531)*

Knott's Berry Farm, Buena Park *Also Called: Knotts Berry Farm LLC (P-14305)*

Knott's Berry Farm Hotel, Buena Park *Also Called: Knotts Berry Farm LLC (P-9950)*

Knotts Berry Farm LLC .... D....... 714 995-1111
7675 Crescent Ave Buena Park (90620) *(P-9950)*

Knotts Berry Farm LLC (HQ) .... B....... 714 827-1776
8039 Beach Blvd Buena Park (90620) *(P-14305)*

Knowledge Networks Inc .... A....... 650 289-2000
2100 Geng Rd Ste 210 Palo Alto (94303) *(P-19829)*

Knox Attorney Service Inc (PA) .... C....... 619 233-9700
1550 Hotel Cir N Ste 440 San Diego (92108) *(P-10789)*

Knox Services, San Diego *Also Called: Knox Attorney Service Inc (P-10789)*

Koam Engineering Systems Inc .... C....... 858 292-0922
7807 Convoy Ct Ste 200 San Diego (92111) *(P-12475)*

Kobert & Company Inc .... D....... 323 725-1000
6131 Garfield Ave Commerce (90040) *(P-5571)*

Kochergen Farms Composting .... D....... 559 266-2650
2365 E North Ave Fresno (93725) *(P-4903)*

KOCHERGEN FARMS COMPOSTING INC, Fresno *Also Called: Kochergen Farms Composting (P-4903)*

Kodella LLC .... C....... 844 563-3552
17922 Fitch Ste 200 Irvine (92614) *(P-12824)*

KODIAK, Palo Alto *Also Called: Kodiak Sciences Inc (P-2595)*

Kodiak Robotics Inc .... D....... 781 626-2729
1049 Terra Bella Ave Mountain View (94043) *(P-19298)*

Kodiak Roofing & Waterproofing, Roseville *Also Called: Dwayne Nash Industries Inc (P-2060)*

Kodiak Sciences Inc (PA) .... D....... 650 281-0850
1200 Page Mill Rd Palo Alto (94304) *(P-2595)*

Kofax Inc (PA) .... B....... 949 783-1000
15211 Laguna Canyon Rd Irvine (92618) *(P-11695)*

Koffler Elec Mech Apprtus Repr .... D....... 510 567-0630
527 Whitney St San Leandro (94577) *(P-5572)*

Koffler Electrical Mechanical, San Leandro *Also Called: Koffler Elec Mech Apprtus Repr (P-5572)*

Koi Cbd LLC .... D....... 562 650-4673
14631 Best Ave Norwalk (90650) *(P-6119)*

Kole Imports .... D....... 310 834-0004
24600 Main St Carson (90745) *(P-6922)*

Koll Construction LP .... D....... 949 833-3030
4343 Von Karman Ave Ste 150 Newport Beach (92660) *(P-953)*

Kona Bay Hotel, Manhattan Beach *Also Called: Oka & Oka Hawaii LLC (P-10061)*

Kona Kai Resort Hotel, San Diego *Also Called: Westgroup Kona Kai LLC (P-14483)*

Kone Inc .... D....... 510 351-5141
15021 Wicks Blvd San Leandro (94577) *(P-13778)*

Konica Minolta Laboratory USA Inc .. D....... 650 522-9619
2855 Campus Dr Ste 100 San Mateo (94403) *(P-19721)*

Konocti Vista Casino (PA) .... C....... 707 262-1900
2755 Mission Rancheria Rd Lakeport (95453) *(P-14539)*

Konoike-E Street Inc .... D....... 310 233-7300
901 E E St Wilmington (90744) *(P-5779)*

Konsus Inc .... C....... 415 659-9852
470 Ramona St Palo Alto (94301) *(P-11696)*

Kontron America Incorporated .... D....... 800 822-7522
9477 Waples St Ste 150 San Diego (92121) *(P-2808)*

Koos Manufacturing Inc .... A....... 323 249-1000
2741 Seminole Ave South Gate (90280) *(P-13340)*

Kopy Kat Attorney Service, Brea *Also Called: V A Anderson Enterprises Inc (P-13537)*

Korbel Champagne Cellers, Guerneville *Also Called: F Korbel & Bros (P-2383)*

Kore1 Inc .... D....... 949 706-6990
530 Technology Dr Ste 150 Irvine (92618) *(P-12825)*

Kore1 LLC .... C....... 949 706-6990
530 Technology Dr Ste 150 Irvine (92618) *(P-11165)*

Korea Trade and Inv Prom Agcy .... C....... 408 432-5000
3003 N 1st St San Jose (95134) *(P-12476)*

Korean Air, Los Angeles *Also Called: Korean Air Lines Co Ltd (P-3835)*

Korean Air, Los Angeles *Also Called: Korean Airlines Co Ltd (P-3837)*
Korean Air, Los Angeles *Also Called: Korean Airlines Co Ltd (P-3972)*
   Korean Air Lines Co Ltd .... C...... 310 646-4866
     380 World Way Ste S4 Los Angeles (90045) *(P-3835)*
   Korean Airlines Co Ltd .... C...... 310 410-2000
     6101 W Imperial Hwy Los Angeles (90045) *(P-3836)*
   Korean Airlines Co Ltd .... B...... 213 484-5700
     900 Wilshire Blvd Ste 1100 Los Angeles (90017) *(P-3972)*
   Korean Airlines Co Ltd .... D...... 213 484-1900
     1813 Wilshire Blvd Ste 400 Los Angeles (90057) *(P-3837)*
Korean Arln Crgo Reservations, Los Angeles *Also Called: Korean Airlines Co Ltd (P-3836)*
Korean Community Services Inc .... C...... 714 527-6561
   451 W Lincoln Ave Ste 100 Anaheim (92805) *(P-16685)*
Korn Ferry (PA) .... C...... 310 552-1834
   1900 Avenue Of The Stars Ste 1500 Los Angeles (90067) *(P-11166)*
Korn Ferry, Los Angeles *Also Called: Korn Ferry (P-11166)*
Korn Ferry (us) (HQ) .... C...... 310 552-1834
   1900 Avenue Of The Stars Ste 2600 Los Angeles (90067) *(P-20426)*
Kortz Gregg Dvm Dplomate Acvim, Los Angeles *Also Called: Animal Specialty Group (P-326)*
Korvalabs Inc .... C...... 888 702-9042
   1000 Coddingtown Ctr Santa Rosa (95401) *(P-13341)*
Kosan Biosciences Incorporated .... D...... 650 995-7356
   3832 Bay Center Pl Hayward (94545) *(P-2596)*
Kositch Enterprises Inc .... D...... 510 657-4460
   5700 Boscell Common Fremont (94538) *(P-1763)*
Kota Construction LLC .... D...... 855 800-5682
   1200 Lawrence Dr Ste 180 Newbury Park (91320) *(P-694)*
Kotobuki-Ya Inc .... D...... 650 344-7955
   720 Woodside Way San Mateo (94401) *(P-3145)*
Kotra, San Jose *Also Called: Korea Trade and Inv Prom Agcy (P-12476)*
Kp International, Oakland *Also Called: Permanente Kaiser Intl (P-8352)*
Kp LLC (PA) .... D...... 510 346-0729
   13951 Washington Ave San Leandro (94578) *(P-2561)*
Kpc Global Medical Centers Inc (DH) .... C...... 714 953-3500
   1117 E Devonshire Ave Hemet (92543) *(P-16207)*
Kpc Group Inc (PA) .... C...... 951 782-8812
   9 Kpc Pkwy # 301 Corona (92879) *(P-20427)*
KPC HEALTH, Santa Ana *Also Called: Orange Cnty Globl Med Ctr Inc (P-16296)*
Kpff Inc .... D...... 949 252-1022
   18500 Von Karman Ave Ste 1000 Irvine (92612) *(P-19299)*
Kpff Inc .... D...... 415 989-1004
   45 Fremont St Fl 28 San Francisco (94105) *(P-19300)*
Kpff Consulting Engineers, San Francisco *Also Called: Kpff Inc (P-19300)*
Kpit Infosystems Inc .... D...... 916 985-0300
   111 Woodmere Rd Ste 200 Folsom (95630) *(P-11697)*
Kpmg LLP .... D...... 703 286-8175
   4464 Jasmine Ave Culver City (90232) *(P-19594)*
Kpmg LLP .... C...... 949 885-5400
   20 Pacifica Ste 700 Irvine (92618) *(P-19595)*
Kprs, Brea *Also Called: Kprs Construction Services Inc (P-954)*
Kprs Construction Services Inc (PA) .... D...... 714 672-0800
   2850 Saturn St Ste 110 Brea (92821) *(P-954)*
Kptm-TV Channel 42, Visalia *Also Called: Pappas Telecasting of The Midlands LP (P-4456)*
Kpwr Radio LLC .... C...... 562 745-2300
   9550 Firestone Blvd Ste 105 Downey (90241) *(P-13342)*
Kqed Inc (PA) .... B...... 415 864-2000
   2601 Mariposa St San Francisco (94110) *(P-4446)*
KQED PUBLIC MEDIA, San Francisco *Also Called: Kqed Inc (P-4446)*
Kraco Enterprises LLC .... C...... 310 639-0666
   505 E Euclid Ave Compton (90222) *(P-7352)*
Kramer Lvin Nftlis Frankel LLP .... D...... 650 752-1700
   990 Marsh Rd Menlo Park (94025) *(P-17530)*
Kramer Media LLC .... D...... 415 439-4601
   201 Mission St Fl 9 San Francisco (94105) *(P-4541)*
Kramer Rgm Inc .... D...... 925 671-7717
   3230 Monument Way Concord (94518) *(P-955)*
Kramer-Wilson Company Inc (PA) .... C...... 818 760-0880
   340 N Westlake Blvd Ste 210 Westlake Village (91362) *(P-8389)*
Kranem, San Jose *Also Called: Kranem Corporation (P-12253)*
Kranem Corporation .... C...... 650 319-6743
   560 S Winchester Blvd Ste 500 San Jose (95128) *(P-12253)*

Kratos, San Diego *Also Called: Kratos Def & SEC Solutions Inc (P-2998)*
Kratos Def & SEC Solutions Inc (PA) .... C...... 858 812-7300
   10680 Treena St Ste 600 San Diego (92131) *(P-2998)*
Kratos Public Safety & Security Solutions Inc .... D...... 858 812-7300
   4820 Eastgate Mall Ste 200 San Diego (92121) *(P-13130)*
Kratos Tech Trning Sltions Inc (HQ) .... D...... 858 812-7300
   10680 Treena St Ste 600 San Diego (92131) *(P-19301)*
Kratos Unmnned Arial Systems I (HQ) .... C...... 916 431-7977
   5381 Raley Blvd Sacramento (95838) *(P-19302)*
Krazan & Associates (PA) .... D...... 559 348-2200
   215 W Dakota Ave Clovis (93612) *(P-20793)*
KRC Los Altos, Los Altos *Also Called: Kisco Senior Living LLC (P-8841)*
KRC Orange, Orange *Also Called: Kisco Senior Living LLC (P-8839)*
KRC Santa Margarita, Rcho Sta Marg *Also Called: Kisco Senior Living LLC (P-8838)*
Krca License LLC .... C...... 818 840-1400
   1845 W Empire Ave Burbank (91504) *(P-4390)*
Kreger Inc .... A...... 559 884-2585
   3520 W Howard Ave Visalia (93277) *(P-366)*
Kretek International Inc (DH) .... D...... 805 531-8888
   5449 Endeavour Ct Moorpark (93021) *(P-6880)*
Krg Technologies Inc (PA) .... B...... 661 257-9967
   25000 Avenue Stanford Ste 243 Valencia (91355) *(P-11698)*
Krikorian Premiere Theatre LLC .... D...... 714 826-7469
   8290 La Palma Ave Buena Park (90620) *(P-14000)*
Krikorian Premiere Theatre LLC .... D...... 760 945-7469
   25 Main St Vista (92083) *(P-14001)*
Krikorian Premiere Theatre LLC .... D...... 562 205-3456
   8540 Whittier Blvd Pico Rivera (90660) *(P-14002)*
Kroeker Inc .... C...... 559 237-3764
   4627 S Chestnut Ave Fresno (93725) *(P-2239)*
Kroger Co .... B...... 859 630-6959
   2201 S Wilmington Ave Compton (90220) *(P-3722)*
Kron-TV, San Francisco *Also Called: Chronicle Broadcasting Co (P-4421)*
Kron-TV, San Francisco *Also Called: Young Brdcstg of San Francisco (P-4471)*
Kronick Mskvitz Tdmann Grard A (PA) .... D...... 916 321-4500
   1331 Garden Hwy Ste 350 Sacramento (95833) *(P-17531)*
Kros-Wise .... C...... 619 607-2899
   435 E Carmel St San Marcos (92078) *(P-20794)*
Krost (PA) .... C...... 626 449-4225
   225 S Lake Ave Ste 400 Pasadena (91101) *(P-19596)*
Krost Bumgarten Kniss Guerrero, Pasadena *Also Called: Krost (P-19596)*
Kruze Consulting Inc .... D...... 415 601-6967
   3561 Jackson St San Francisco (94118) *(P-20795)*
Krzr 103 7 FM, Fresno *Also Called: Iheartcommunications Inc (P-4386)*
KS Fabrication & Machine, Bakersfield *Also Called: K S Fabrication & Machine Inc (P-1223)*
KS Industries LP (PA) .... A...... 661 617-1700
   6205 District Blvd Bakersfield (93313) *(P-1228)*
KS Trans Services Co .... D...... 559 264-5650
   3190 S Elm Ave Fresno (93706) *(P-3501)*
Ksby Communications LLC .... C...... 805 541-6666
   1772 Calle Joaquin San Luis Obispo (93405) *(P-4447)*
Kseg-FM, Roseville *Also Called: Audacy Inc (P-4373)*
Ksfcu, Bakersfield *Also Called: Valley Strong Credit Union (P-7817)*
Ksl Rancho Mirage Operating Co Inc .... B...... 760 568-2727
   41000 Bob Hope Dr Rancho Mirage (92270) *(P-9951)*
Ksl Recreation Management Operations LLC .... A...... 760 564-8000
   50905 Avenida Bermudas La Quinta (92253) *(P-14268)*
Ksl Resorts Hotel Del Coronado .... C...... 619 435-6611
   1500 Orange Ave Coronado (92118) *(P-9952)*
Ksm Healthcare Inc .... D...... 818 242-1183
   1400 W Glenoaks Blvd Glendale (91201) *(P-15532)*
Kssf Enterprises Ltd .... C...... 415 817-7840
   181 3rd St San Francisco (94103) *(P-9953)*
Kt Hotels LLC .... C...... 949 715-5000
   3 Ada Ste 100 Irvine (92618) *(P-9954)*
Ktb Software LLC .... D...... 213 935-0902
   11101 W Olympic Blvd Los Angeles (90064) *(P-11699)*
Ktgy Architecture Planning, Irvine *Also Called: Ktgy Group Inc (P-19483)*
Ktgy Group Inc (PA) .... D...... 949 851-2133
   17911 Von Karman Ave Ste 200 Irvine (92614) *(P-19483)*

ALPHABETIC SECTION

Ktsf Channel 26 .... D....... 415 467-6397
  100 Valley Dr Brisbane (94005) *(P-4448)*

Ktvu Partnership Inc .... C....... 510 834-1212
  2 Jack London Sq Oakland (94607) *(P-4449)*

Ktvu Television Fox 2, Oakland *Also Called: Ktvu Partnership Inc (P-4449)*

Ktxl-Fox 40, Sacramento *Also Called: Channel 40 Inc (P-4420)*

Ku Kyoung .... C....... 510 582-2765
  #unknown Redding (96003) *(P-15533)*

Kubota Authorized Dealer, Turlock *Also Called: Garton Tractor Inc (P-7580)*

Kubota Industrial Equipment .... C....... 817 756-1171
  3401 Del Amo Blvd Torrance (90503) *(P-5385)*

Kuehne + Nagel Inc .... C....... 415 656-4100
  150 W Hill Pl Brisbane (94005) *(P-4044)*

Kuehne + Nagel Inc .... C....... 310 641-5500
  20000 S Western Ave Torrance (90501) *(P-4045)*

Kugga Inc .... D....... 925 639-0721
  1841 Sunnyvale Ave Walnut Creek (94597) *(P-11700)*

Kuic Inc .... C....... 707 446-0200
  555 Mason St Ste 245 Vacaville (95688) *(P-4391)*

Kuic-FM, Vacaville *Also Called: Kuic Inc (P-4391)*

Kumar Hotels Inc (PA).. C....... **530 934-8900**
  545 N Humboldt Ave Willows (95988) *(P-9955)*

Kush Supply Co LLC .... D....... 714 243-4023
  7375 Chapman Ave Garden Grove (92841) *(P-6120)*

Kut From The Kloth, City Of Industry *Also Called: Swatfame Inc (P-6223)*

Kval Inc .... C....... 707 762-4363
  825 Petaluma Blvd S Petaluma (94952) *(P-2786)*

Kval Machinery Co, Petaluma *Also Called: Kval Inc (P-2786)*

Kvc Group LLC .... D....... 855 438-0377
  1551 N Tustin Ave Ste 550 Santa Ana (92705) *(P-20428)*

Kvcr, TV & FM, San Bernardino *Also Called: San Brnrdino Cmnty College Dst (P-4402)*

Kvie Inc (PA).. D....... **916 929-5843**
  2030 W El Camino Ave Ste 100 Sacramento (95833) *(P-4450)*

KVIE CHANNEL 6, Sacramento *Also Called: Kvie Inc (P-4450)*

Kw International Inc .... D....... 213 703-6914
  18724 S Broadwick St Rancho Dominguez (90220) *(P-3794)*

Kw International Inc .... D....... 310 354-6944
  1457 Glenn Curtiss St Carson (90746) *(P-4046)*

Kw International Inc .... D....... 310 747-1380
  18511 S Broadwick St Rancho Dominguez (90220) *(P-4047)*

Kwan Wo Ironworks Inc .... C....... 415 822-9628
  31628 Hayman St Hayward (94544) *(P-2185)*

KWPH Enterprises .... A....... 559 443-5900
  2911 E Tulare St Fresno (93721) *(P-3269)*

Kxp Carrier Services LLC .... C....... 424 320-5300
  11777 San Vicente Blvd Los Angeles (90049) *(P-3618)*

Kxtv Inc .... C....... 916 441-2345
  400 Broadway Sacramento (95818) *(P-4451)*

Kyo Autism Therapy LLC .... C....... 877 264-6747
  1155 Broadway St Ste 218 Redwood City (94063) *(P-20429)*

Kyo Autism Therapy LLC .... C....... 877 264-6747
  121 Paul Dr San Rafael (94903) *(P-20430)*

Kyocera Dcment Solutions W LLC .... C....... 800 996-9591
  14101 Alton Pkwy Irvine (92618) *(P-5249)*

Kyocera International Inc (HQ).. D....... **858 492-1456**
  8611 Balboa Ave San Diego (92123) *(P-2925)*

Kyoto Grand Hotel and Gardens, Los Angeles *Also Called: Crestline Hotels & Resorts Inc (P-9728)*

Kyte, San Francisco *Also Called: Decentral TV Corporation (P-4267)*

Kyue TV, Palm Desert *Also Called: Entravsion Communications Corp (P-4428)*

L & A Care Corporation .... C....... 310 202-7693
  5000 Overland Ave Ste 101 Culver City (90230) *(P-15768)*

L & L Distributors, Los Angeles *Also Called: L&L Manufacturing Co Inc (P-2459)*

L & L Nursery Supply Inc (HQ).. C....... **909 591-0461**
  2552 Shenandoah Way San Bernardino (92407) *(P-6827)*

L & O Aliso Viejo LLC .... C....... 949 643-6700
  50 Enterprise Aliso Viejo (92656) *(P-9956)*

L & R Distributors Inc .... B....... 909 980-3807
  9292 9th St Rancho Cucamonga (91730) *(P-6156)*

L & S Hallmark Construction Inc .... C....... 408 727-4422
  3360 De La Cruz Blvd Santa Clara (95054) *(P-956)*

L & T Meat Co .... D....... 323 262-2815
  3050 E 11th St Los Angeles (90023) *(P-6498)*

L A Air Inc .... C....... 310 215-8245
  5933 W Century Blvd 500 Los Angeles (90045) *(P-3838)*

L A Girl, Ontario *Also Called: Beauty 21 Cosmetics Inc (P-6097)*

L A H S A, Los Angeles *Also Called: Los Angeles Homeless Svcs Auth (P-18045)*

L A Hearne Company (PA)... D....... **831 385-5441**
  512 Metz Rd King City (93930) *(P-6828)*

L A Lighting, El Monte *Also Called: Los Angeles Ltg Mfg Co Inc (P-5575)*

L A P F C U, Van Nuys *Also Called: Los Angeles Police Credit Un (P-7828)*

L A Party Rents Inc .... D....... 818 989-4300
  13520 Saticoy St Van Nuys (91402) *(P-11039)*

L A PHILHARMONIC, Los Angeles *Also Called: Los Angeles Philharmonic Assn (P-14093)*

L A U S D, Pico Rivera *Also Called: Los Angeles Unified School Dst (P-13358)*

L and R Auto Parks Inc .... C....... 213 784-3018
  707 Wilshire Blvd Ste 4300 Los Angeles (90017) *(P-13608)*

L B Construction, Roseville *Also Called: Lancaster Burns Cnstr Inc (P-1942)*

L E Cooke Co .... C....... 559 732-9146
  26333 Road 140 Visalia (93292) *(P-135)*

L E Coppersmith Inc (PA).. D....... **310 607-8000**
  525 S Douglas St Ste 100 El Segundo (90245) *(P-4048)*

L J B, San Diego *Also Called: Tanvex Biopharma Usa Inc (P-19780)*

L J E Enterprises, Manteca *Also Called: Lee Jennings Target Ex Inc (P-4049)*

L J Kruse Co .... D....... 510 644-0260
  920 Pardee St Berkeley (94710) *(P-1480)*

L M I, Ontario *Also Called: Larry Mthvin Installations Inc (P-2694)*

L M S, Irvine *Also Called: Ovation Tech Inc (P-12852)*

L S A, Irvine *Also Called: Lsa Associates Inc (P-20800)*

L Tech Network Services Inc .... D....... 562 222-1121
  3424 Garfield Ave # A Commerce (90040) *(P-1764)*

L-O Bedford Operating LLC .... D....... 781 275-5500
  11755 Wilshire Blvd Ste 1350 Los Angeles (90025) *(P-9957)*

L-O Coronado Hotel Inc .... D....... 619 435-6611
  1500 Orange Ave Coronado (92118) *(P-9958)*

L-O Soma Hotel Inc .... A....... 415 974-6400
  50 3rd St San Francisco (94103) *(P-9959)*

L.A. Care Health Plan, Los Angeles *Also Called: Local Inttive Hlth Auth For Lo (P-8341)*

L.A. Cold Storage, Los Angeles *Also Called: Standard-Southern Corporation (P-3660)*

L.A. GAY & LESBIAN CENTER, Los Angeles *Also Called: Los Angeles Lgbt Center (P-18608)*

L.A. Inflight Service Company, Gardena *Also Called: World Svc Wst/La Inflght Svc L (P-3922)*

L.A.cO., Whittier *Also Called: Los Angeles Cnty Snttion Dstrct (P-4981)*

L.H. Dottie Co, Commerce *Also Called: Kobert & Company Inc (P-5571)*

L'Auberge Del Mar, Del Mar *Also Called: Lhoberge Lessee Inc (P-9977)*

L'Ermitage Hotel, Beverly Hills *Also Called: Raffles Lrmitage Beverly Hills (P-10137)*

L&L Foods Holdings LLC .... C....... 714 254-1430
  333 N Euclid Way Anaheim (92801) *(P-4130)*

L&L Manufacturing Co Inc .... B
  12400 Wilshire Blvd # 360 Los Angeles (90025) *(P-2459)*

L&T Staffing Inc .... B....... 323 727-9056
  2122 W Whittier Blvd Montebello (90640) *(P-11167)*

L&T Staffing Inc (PA).. D....... **714 558-1821**
  950 W 17th St Ste E Santa Ana (92706) *(P-11168)*

L3 Applied Technologies Inc .... C....... 510 577-7100
  2700 Merced St San Leandro (94577) *(P-19722)*

L3 Maripro Inc .... D....... 805 683-3881
  1522 Cook Pl Goleta (93117) *(P-19303)*

L3harris Interstate Elec Corp .... D....... 858 552-9500
  3033 Science Park Rd San Diego (92121) *(P-3027)*

L3harris Interstate Elec Corp .... D....... 714 758-0500
  707 E Vermont Ave A Anaheim (92805) *(P-5668)*

La 1000 Santa Fe LLC .... C....... 213 205-1000
  1000 S Santa Fe Ave Los Angeles (90021) *(P-20134)*

La Asccion Ncnal Pro Prsnas My .... A....... 213 202-5900
  1452 W Temple St Ste 100 Los Angeles (90026) *(P-18035)*

La Belle Days Spas and Salons, Palo Alto *Also Called: Beauty Bazar Inc (P-10492)*

LA BIOMED, Torrance *Also Called: Lundquist Institute For Biomedical Innovation At Harbor-Ucla Medical Center (P-19894)*

La Bonne Vie Inc .... D....... 805 773-5003
  2723 Shell Beach Rd Shell Beach (93449) *(P-14210)*

La Boulange, San Francisco *Also Called: Bay Bread LLC* **(P-6609)**
La Boxing Franchise Corp .... B...... 714 668-0911
   1241 E Dyer Rd Ste 100 Santa Ana (92705) **(P-14211)**
La Canada Flintridge Cntry CLB .... D...... 818 790-0611
   5500 Godbey Dr La Canada (91011) **(P-14386)**
La Capital, Los Angeles *Also Called: Los Angeles Capital MGT LLC* **(P-9377)**
La Casa Mhrc, Long Beach *Also Called: Telecare Corporation* **(P-17143)**
La Cienega Associates .... D...... 310 854-0071
   8500 Beverly Blvd Ste 501 Los Angeles (90048) **(P-9067)**
La Clinica De La Raza Inc .... B...... 510 535-6300
   1515 Fruitvale Ave Oakland (94601) **(P-14864)**
La Clinica De La Raza Inc .... C...... 707 556-8100
   243 Georgia St Vallejo (94590) **(P-14865)**
La Clinica De La Raza Inc .... B...... 510 535-4110
   1450 Fruitvale Ave # B Oakland (94601) **(P-14866)**
La Clinica De La Raza Inc .... C...... 510 535-4700
   3050 E 16th St Oakland (94601) **(P-14867)**
La Clinica De La Raza Inc .... C...... 510 535-6200
   1601 Fruitvale Ave Oakland (94601) **(P-14868)**
La Clinica De La Raza Inc .... C...... 925 431-1250
   337 E Leland Rd Pittsburg (94565) **(P-14869)**
La Clinica De La Raza Inc .... B...... 510 535-3500
   3451 E 12th St Oakland (94601) **(P-17266)**
La Clinica De La Raza Inc .... C...... 510 535-4130
   1537 Fruitvale Ave Oakland (94601) **(P-17267)**
La Clippers LLC .... C...... 213 742-7500
   1212 S Flower St Fl 5 Los Angeles (90015) **(P-14145)**
La Costa Glen, Carlsbad *Also Called: Continuing Lf Communities LLC* **(P-11112)**
La Costa Resort & Spa, Carlsbad *Also Called: Lc Trs Inc* **(P-9971)**
La Costa Urgent Care, Carlsbad *Also Called: Carbon Health Technologies Inc* **(P-15256)**
La County .... D...... 310 417-5184
   5530 W 83rd St Los Angeles (90045) **(P-8731)**
La County .... D...... 626 569-6459
   9320 Telstar Ave Ste 226 El Monte (91731) **(P-18036)**
La County Museum of Art, Los Angeles *Also Called: Museum Associates* **(P-18658)**
La County Probation, Whittier *Also Called: County of Los Angeles* **(P-17917)**
La County Sheriff PDC No .... C...... 661 294-6312
   211 W Temple St Los Angeles (90012) **(P-18874)**
La Cumbre Country Club .... D...... 805 687-2421
   4015 Via Laguna Santa Barbara (93110) **(P-14387)**
La Familia Counseling Ctr Inc .... D...... 916 452-3601
   5523 34th St Sacramento (95820) **(P-18037)**
La Folette Johnson Dehass Sesl .... D...... 213 426-3600
   865 S Figueroa St # 3200 Los Angeles (90017) **(P-17532)**
La Folltte Jhnson De Haas Fsle (PA) .... C...... 213 426-3600
   701 N Brand Blvd Ste 600 Glendale (91203) **(P-17533)**
LA Hydro-Jet Rooter Svc Inc .... D...... 818 768-4225
   10639 Wixom St Sun Valley (91352) **(P-13779)**
La Hydrojet, Sun Valley *Also Called: LA Hydro-Jet Rooter Svc Inc* **(P-13779)**
La Jolla Bch & Tennis CLB Inc .... B...... 858 459-8271
   8110 Camino Del Oro La Jolla (92037) **(P-9960)**
La Jolla Bch & Tennis CLB Inc (PA) .... C...... 858 454-7126
   2000 Spindrift Dr La Jolla (92037) **(P-14388)**
La Jolla Country Club Inc .... D...... 858 454-9601
   7301 High Ave La Jolla (92037) **(P-14389)**
La Jolla Cove Ht Mtl Aprtmnts .... D...... 858 459-2621
   1155 Coast Blvd La Jolla (92037) **(P-9961)**
La Jolla Cove Motel, La Jolla *Also Called: La Jolla Cove Ht Mtl Aprtmnts* **(P-9961)**
La Jolla Group Inc (PA) .... B...... 949 428-2800
   14350 Myford Rd Irvine (92606) **(P-13343)**
La Jolla Inst For Allrgy Immnl, La Jolla *Also Called: La Jolla Inst For Immunology* **(P-19893)**
La Jolla Inst For Immunology .... B...... 858 752-6500
   9420 Athena Cir La Jolla (92037) **(P-19893)**
La Jolla Nrsing Rhbltation Ctr, La Jolla *Also Called: Covenant Care La Jolla LLC* **(P-15408)**
La Jolla Orthpdic Srgery Ctr L .... D...... 858 657-0055
   4120 La Jolla Village Dr La Jolla (92037) **(P-14870)**
LA JOLLA PLAYHOUSE, La Jolla *Also Called: Theater Arts Fndtion San Dego* **(P-18917)**
La Jolla Skilled Inc .... C...... 858 625-8700
   3884 Nobel Dr San Diego (92122) **(P-15534)**
La Jolla Station, Anaheim *Also Called: Southern California Gas Co* **(P-4737)**

La Jolla YMCA, La Jolla *Also Called: YMCA of San Diego County* **(P-18938)**
LA MAESTRA COMMUNITY HEALTH CE, San Diego *Also Called: La Maestra Family Clinic Inc* **(P-14871)**
La Maestra Family Clinic Inc (PA) .... C...... 619 584-1612
   4060 Fairmount Ave San Diego (92105) **(P-14871)**
La Mancha Development, Los Angeles *Also Called: A M S Partnership* **(P-9243)**
La Mesa Disposal, Signal Hill *Also Called: Edco Disposal Corporation* **(P-4890)**
La Mesa Medical Offices, La Mesa *Also Called: Kaiser Foundation Hospitals* **(P-8316)**
La Mesa R V Center Inc (PA) .... C...... 858 874-8000
   7430 Copley Park Pl San Diego (92111) **(P-7395)**
LA Metropolitan Medical Center .... A...... 323 730-7300
   2231 Southwest Dr Los Angeles (90043) **(P-16208)**
La Palma Hospital Medical Center .... B...... 714 670-7400
   7901 Walker St La Palma (90623) **(P-16209)**
La Palma Intercommunity Hosp, La Palma *Also Called: La Palma Hospital Medical Center* **(P-16209)**
La Palma Medical Offices, La Palma *Also Called: Kaiser Foundation Hospitals* **(P-14792)**
La Peer Health Systems, Beverly Hills *Also Called: La Peer Surgery Center LLC* **(P-14872)**
La Peer Surgery Center LLC .... D...... 310 360-9119
   8920 Wilshire Blvd Ste 101 Beverly Hills (90211) **(P-14872)**
La Provence Inc .... D...... 760 736-3299
   1370 W San Marcos Blvd Ste 130 San Marcos (92078) **(P-6642)**
La Provence Bakery, San Marcos *Also Called: La Provence Inc* **(P-6642)**
La Quinta Inn .... D...... 510 632-8900
   8465 Enterprise Way Oakland (94621) **(P-9962)**
La Quinta Inn, Oakland *Also Called: La Quinta Inn* **(P-9962)**
La Quinta Inn, Los Angeles *Also Called: Lq Management LLC* **(P-9989)**
La Quinta Inn, San Francisco *Also Called: Mile Post Properties LLC* **(P-10020)**
La Quinta Resort & Club, La Quinta *Also Called: HP Lq Investment LP* **(P-9876)**
La Quinta Resort & Club, La Quinta *Also Called: Lqr Property LLC* **(P-9990)**
La Rams Football Club, Los Angeles *Also Called: Los Angeles Rams LLC* **(P-20144)**
La Rinconada Country Club Inc .... C...... 408 395-4181
   17405 Zena Ave Monte Sereno (95030) **(P-14390)**
La Rocque Better Roofs Inc .... D...... 909 476-2699
   9077 Arrow Rte Ste 100 Rancho Cucamonga (91730) **(P-2071)**
La Sierra Care Center, Merced *Also Called: CF Merced La Sierra LLC* **(P-15371)**
LA SOLAR GROUP, San Fernando *Also Called: La Solar Group Inc* **(P-1481)**
La Solar Group Inc .... D...... 818 373-0077
   560 Library St San Fernando (91340) **(P-1481)**
LA Spas Inc .... C...... 714 630-1150
   1325 N Blue Gum St Anaheim (92806) **(P-3109)**
LA Specialty Produce Co (PA) .... B...... 562 741-2200
   13527 Orden Dr Santa Fe Springs (90670) **(P-6560)**
La Sports Arena, Los Angeles *Also Called: Los Angeles Mem Coliseum Comm* **(P-19092)**
LA Sports Properties Inc .... C...... 213 742-7500
   1212 S Flower St Fl 5 Los Angeles (90015) **(P-14146)**
La Terra Fina Usa LLC .... C...... 510 404-5888
   1300 Atlantic St Union City (94587) **(P-830)**
La Tortilla Factory Inc (PA) .... B...... 707 586-4000
   3300 Westwind Blvd Santa Rosa (95403) **(P-6643)**
La Ventana Treatment Programs .... D...... 805 644-5745
   1408 E Thousand Oaks Blvd Thousand Oaks (91362) **(P-17085)**
La Verne Cinema 12, La Verne *Also Called: Edwards Theatres Inc* **(P-13989)**
La Verne Nursery Inc .... D...... 805 521-0111
   3653 Center St Piru (93040) **(P-136)**
La Workout Inc .... C...... 805 482-8884
   500 Paseo Camarillo Camarillo (93010) **(P-14212)**
La Workout Camarillo West, Camarillo *Also Called: La Workout Inc* **(P-14212)**
Laaco Ltd (HQ) .... C...... 213 622-1254
   4469 Admiralty Way Marina Del Rey (90292) **(P-8886)**
Lab-Gistics LLC .... C...... 650 309-2627
   885 Pacific Ave San Jose (95126) **(P-19723)**
Labcon North America .... C...... 707 766-2163
   3200 Lakeville Hwy Petaluma (94954) **(P-5429)**
Labcyte Inc .... D...... 408 747-2000
   170 Rose Orchard Way Ste 200 San Jose (95134) **(P-19724)**
Label Division, Modesto *Also Called: G3 Enterprises Inc* **(P-10808)**
Labelbox Inc .... C...... 415 294-0791
   510 Treat Ave San Francisco (94110) **(P-12254)**

ALPHABETIC SECTION

Laborers Fnds Admnstrtive Offi (PA)..................................D....... 707 864-2800
   5672 Stoneridge Dr Ste 100 Pleasanton (94588) *(P-18786)*

Laborers Trust Funds Nthrn Cal, Pleasanton *Also Called: Laborers Fnds Admnstrtive Offi (P-18786)*

Labratory, San Francisco *Also Called: Permanente Medical Group Inc (P-14965)*

Labs.dental, Santa Ana *Also Called: Chromium Dental II LLC (P-15220)*

Lac & Usc Medical Center ....D....... 323 409-2345
   2051 Marengo St Los Angeles (90033) *(P-14873)*

Lac Usc County Hospital ....D....... 323 226-2622
   2051 Marengo St Los Angeles (90033) *(P-16210)*

Lac Usc Medical Center C
   1200 N State St Rm 5250 Los Angeles (90089) *(P-16211)*

Lacba Counsel For Justice ....D....... 951 489-2919
   200 S Spring St Los Angeles (90012) *(P-18038)*

Lacera, Pasadena *Also Called: Los Angles Cnty Emplyees Rtrme (P-8463)*

Laclinica, Pittsburg *Also Called: La Clinica De La Raza Inc (P-14869)*

Lacma, Los Angeles *Also Called: Los Angles Cnty Mseum of Art (P-18655)*

Lacmta, Los Angeles *Also Called: Los Angles Cnty Mtro Trnsp Aut (P-3150)*

Ladera-Fox Hills Self Storage, Los Angeles *Also Called: Gambrell Bondie (P-10902)*

Ladwp, Independence *Also Called: Los Angeles Dept Wtr & Pwr (P-4806)*

Ladwp, Los Angeles *Also Called: Los Angeles Dept Wtr & Pwr (P-4807)*

LADWP Metro Water Yard ....D....... 213 367-6665
   433 E Temple St Los Angeles (90012) *(P-1229)*

Lady Shaw Activity Center, San Francisco *Also Called: Self-Help For Elderly (P-14564)*

Lafc Partners Lllp ....B....... 213 334-4239
   818 W 7th St Ste 1200 Los Angeles (90017) *(P-14391)*

Lafc Sports LLC ....D....... 323 549-4350
   4751 Wilshire Blvd Fl 3 Los Angeles (90010) *(P-14147)*

LAg and Associates LLC ....D....... 909 242-4394
   1514 E Adams Park Dr Covina (91724) *(P-13344)*

Laguna Blanca School (PA)...D....... 805 687-2461
   4125 Paloma Dr Santa Barbara (93110) *(P-17720)*

Laguna Clay Company, City Of Industry *Also Called: Jon Brooks Inc (P-2719)*

Laguna Creek Racquet Club, Elk Grove *Also Called: Spare-Time Inc (P-14463)*

Laguna Hills Surgery Center, Laguna Hills *Also Called: Cirrus Health II LP (P-14686)*

Laguna Home Health Svcs LLC ....C....... 949 707-5023
   25411 Cabot Rd Ste 205 Laguna Hills (92653) *(P-16886)*

Laguna Playhouse (PA)..C....... 949 497-2787
   606 Laguna Canyon Rd Laguna Beach (92651) *(P-14042)*

Laguna Sapphire LLC ....D....... 949 715-3300
   1200 S Coast Hwy Ste 105b Laguna Beach (92651) *(P-20796)*

Laguna Woods Village ....A....... 949 597-4267
   24351 El Toro Rd Laguna Woods (92637) *(P-9068)*

Lahontan Golf Club ....C....... 530 550-2400
   12700 Lodgetrail Dr Truckee (96161) *(P-14392)*

Lahontan Golf Club, Truckee *Also Called: Lahontan LLC (P-9257)*

Lahontan LLC ....D....... 530 550-2990
   11253 Brockway Rd Ste 201 Truckee (96161) *(P-9257)*

Laidlaw Educational Services, Palm Springs *Also Called: First Student Inc (P-3338)*

Laidlaw Transit Services, Santa Cruz *Also Called: First Transit Inc (P-3133)*

Laird Construction Co Inc ....D....... 909 989-5595
   9460 Lucas Ranch Rd Rancho Cucamonga (91730) *(P-1128)*

Lake Arrwhead Rsort Oprtor Inc (HQ)...................................C....... 909 336-1511
   27984 Hwy 189 Lake Arrowhead (92352) *(P-9963)*

Lake Chabot Golf Course, Oakland *Also Called: City of Oakland (P-14251)*

Lake Chevrolet ....C....... 951 674-3116
   31201 Auto Center Dr Lake Elsinore (92530) *(P-7249)*

Lake Cnty Trbal Hlth Cnsrtium ....D....... 707 263-8382
   925 Bevins Ct Lakeport (95453) *(P-15232)*

Lake Frest No Ii Mstr Hmwners ....D....... 949 586-0860
   24752 Toledo Ln Lake Forest (92630) *(P-18875)*

Lake Merced Golf Club ....D....... 650 755-2233
   2300 Junipero Serra Blvd Daly City (94015) *(P-14393)*

Lake Mission Viejo Association ....D....... 949 770-1313
   22555 Olympiad Rd Mission Viejo (92692) *(P-18876)*

Lake Mrritt Healthcare Ctr LLC ....D....... 510 227-1806
   309 Macarthur Blvd Oakland (94610) *(P-20135)*

Lake Natoma Inn, Folsom *Also Called: Lake Natoma Lodging LP (P-9964)*

Lake Natoma Lodging LP ....D....... 916 351-1500
   702 Gold Lake Dr Folsom (95630) *(P-9964)*

Lake Park Retirement Residence, Oakland *Also Called: Califrnia-Nevada Methdst Homes (P-15827)*

Lake Tahoe Resort Hotel, South Lake Tahoe *Also Called: Roppong-Thoe LP A Cal Ltd Prtn (P-10171)*

Lake Wildwood Association ....C....... 530 432-1152
   11255 Cottontail Way Penn Valley (95946) *(P-18877)*

LAKE WILDWOOD GOLF COURSE., Penn Valley *Also Called: Lake Wildwood Association (P-18877)*

Lakeport Post Acute, Lakeport *Also Called: Lakeport Post Acute LLC (P-15769)*

Lakeport Post Acute LLC ....D....... 707 263-6382
   1291 Craig Ave Lakeport (95453) *(P-15769)*

Lakes Country Club Assn Inc (PA).......................................C....... 760 568-4321
   161 Old Ranch Rd Palm Desert (92211) *(P-14394)*

Lakes Country Club, The, Palm Desert *Also Called: Lakes Country Club Assn Inc (P-14394)*

Lakeside Clubhouse, Daly City *Also Called: Olympic Club (P-18888)*

Lakeside Golf Club ....D....... 818 984-0601
   4500 W Lakeside Dr Burbank (91505) *(P-14269)*

Lakeside Medical Systems, Northridge *Also Called: Lakeside Systems Inc (P-20136)*

Lakeside Organic Gardens LLC (PA)...................................B....... 831 722-6266
   25 Sakata Ln Watsonville (95076) *(P-189)*

Lakeside Systems Inc ....A....... 866 654-3471
   8510 Balboa Blvd Ste 150 Northridge (91325) *(P-20136)*

Lakeside Tax & Financial Svcs ....D....... 619 561-2681
   9748 Los Coches Rd Ste 3 Lakeside (92040) *(P-13345)*

Lakeview Medical Offices, Anaheim *Also Called: Kaiser Foundation Hospitals (P-14795)*

Lakeview Senior Center, Irvine *Also Called: City of Irvine (P-17887)*

Lakewood Healthcare Center, Downey *Also Called: Healthcare Ctr of Downey LLC (P-15508)*

Lakewood Park Health Ctr Inc (PA)......................................B....... 562 869-0978
   12023 Lakewood Blvd Downey (90242) *(P-13346)*

Lakewood Regional Med Ctr Inc ....A....... 562 531-2550
   3700 South St Lakewood (90712) *(P-16212)*

Lakewood Regional Medical Ctr, Lakewood *Also Called: Tenet Healthsystem Medical Inc (P-15125)*

Lakewood Regional Medical Ctr, Lakewood *Also Called: Lakewood Regional Med Ctr Inc (P-16212)*

Lakin Tire of Calif, Santa Fe Springs *Also Called: Lakin Tire West Incorporated (P-5071)*

Lakin Tire West Incorporated (PA).......................................C....... 562 802-2752
   15305 Spring Ave Santa Fe Springs (90670) *(P-5071)*

Lakos, Fresno *Also Called: Lakos Corporation (P-5843)*

Lakos Corporation (HQ)...D....... 559 255-1601
   1365 N Clovis Ave Fresno (93727) *(P-5843)*

Lamar Jhnson Collaborative Inc ....C....... 424 361-3960
   8590 National Blvd Culver City (90232) *(P-19484)*

Lambda, San Jose *Also Called: Lambda Inc (P-11701)*

Lambda Inc ....C....... 650 741-0738
   2510 Zanker Rd San Jose (95131) *(P-11701)*

Lambdatest Inc ....C....... 866 430-7087
   1390 Market St Ste 200 San Francisco (94102) *(P-12477)*

Lamp Inc ....C....... 213 488-9559
   2116 Arlington Ave Lbby Los Angeles (90018) *(P-18464)*

Lamp Community, Los Angeles *Also Called: Lamp Inc (P-18464)*

Lamps Plus Inc ....D....... 909 801-5333
   9425 California St Redlands (92374) *(P-3723)*

Lanahan & Reilley LLP (PA)...C....... 415 856-4700
   600 Bicentennial Way # 300 Santa Rosa (95403) *(P-17534)*

Lancaster Burns Cnstr Inc ....C....... 916 624-8404
   8655 Washington Blvd Roseville (95678) *(P-1942)*

Lancaster Cmnty Svcs Fndtion I ....C....... 661 723-6230
   46008 7th St W Lancaster (93534) *(P-13665)*

Lancaster Crdlgy Med Group Inc (PA)..................................D....... 661 726-3058
   43847 Heaton Ave Ste B Lancaster (93534) *(P-14874)*

Lance Soll & Lunghard LLP ....D....... 714 672-0022
   203 N Brea Blvd Ste 203 Brea (92821) *(P-19597)*

Lance Rygg Dental Corp ....C....... 858 492-9300
   10405 Tierrasanta Blvd San Diego (92124) *(P-15233)*

Land & Personnel Management, Kerman *Also Called: Hall Management Corp (P-20107)*

Land Design Consultants Inc ....D....... 626 578-7000
   2700 E Foothill Blvd Ste 200 Pasadena (91107) *(P-20797)*

Land Disposition Company, Irvine *Also Called: NRLL LLC (P-9545)*

Land Gorilla LLC ....D....... 805 242-5847
   1241 Johnson Ave Ste 154 San Luis Obispo (93401) *(P-11702)*

Land Services Ldscp Contrs Inc .... D...... 510 656-8101
901 Brown Rd Fremont (94539) *(P-9258)*

Landcare Logic, San Diego *Also Called:* Shoreline Land Care Inc *(P-463)*

Landcare USA LLC .... D...... 949 559-7771
216 N Clara St Santa Ana (92703) *(P-507)*

Landcare USA LLC .... D...... 760 747-1174
770 Metcalf St Escondido (92025) *(P-508)*

Landcare USA LLC .... D...... 916 635-0936
3213 Fitzgerald Rd Rancho Cordova (95742) *(P-509)*

Landcare USA LLC .... C...... 858 453-1755
5248 Governor Dr San Diego (92122) *(P-510)*

Landcare USA LLC .... D...... 818 346-7552
7755 Deering Ave Canoga Park (91304) *(P-511)*

Landcare USA LLC .... C...... 925 462-2193
1064 Serpentine Ln Ste A Pleasanton (94566) *(P-512)*

Landcare USA LLC .... D...... 408 727-4099
85 Old Tully Rd San Jose (95111) *(P-513)*

Landesign Cnstr & Maint Inc .... D...... 707 578-2657
1328 Airport Blvd Santa Rosa (95403) *(P-514)*

Landesign Construction & Maint, Santa Rosa *Also Called:* Landesign Cnstr & Maint Inc *(P-514)*

Landforce Corporation .... C...... 760 843-7839
17201 N D St Victorville (92394) *(P-3502)*

Landjet (PA) .... C...... 909 873-4636
1090 Hall Ave Jurupa Valley (92509) *(P-3270)*

Landmark Distribution LLC .... D...... 805 965-3058
34 E Sola St Santa Barbara (93101) *(P-4165)*

Landmark Dividend, El Segundo *Also Called:* Landmark Dividend LLC *(P-9069)*

Landmark Dividend LLC (PA) .... D...... 323 306-2683
400 Continental Blvd Ste 500 El Segundo (90245) *(P-9069)*

Landmark Event Staffing .... A...... 714 293-4248
4790 Irvine Blvd Ste 105 Irvine (92620) *(P-12993)*

Landmark Health LLC .... B...... 657 237-2450
7755 Center Ave Ste 630 Huntington Beach (92647) *(P-16887)*

Landmark Healthcare Svcs Inc (DH) .... C...... 800 638-4557
1610 Arden Way Ste 280 Sacramento (95815) *(P-15262)*

Landmark Medical Center, Pomona *Also Called:* Landmark Medical Services Inc *(P-16654)*

Landmark Medical Services Inc .... D...... 909 593-2585
2030 N Garey Ave Pomona (91767) *(P-16654)*

Landmark Services Inc .... D...... 714 240-7913
410 N Fairview St Santa Ana (92703) *(P-10916)*

Landor & Fitch LLC (HQ) .... C...... 415 365-1700
360 3rd St San Francisco (94107) *(P-13347)*

Landor Associates, Irvine *Also Called:* Young & Rubicam LLC *(P-10691)*

Landor Associates, San Francisco *Also Called:* Landor & Fitch LLC *(P-13347)*

Landor Associates Intl Ltd (HQ) .... C...... 415 365-1700
360 3rd St # 5 San Francisco (94107) *(P-10813)*

Landsberg Los Angeles Div 1001, Montebello *Also Called:* Orora Packaging Solutions *(P-6085)*

Landscape & Tree Company, Inc., Roseville *Also Called:* Ltc Construction Inc *(P-441)*

Landscape Center, Riverside *Also Called:* B & B Nurseries Inc *(P-6850)*

Landscape Development Inc .... C...... 951 371-9370
1290 Carbide Dr Corona (92881) *(P-515)*

Landscape Development Inc (PA) .... B...... 661 295-1970
28447 Witherspoon Pkwy Valencia (91355) *(P-516)*

Landstar Global Logistics Inc .... D...... 909 266-0096
2313 E Philadelphia St Ste D Ontario (91761) *(P-3503)*

Lane Winpak Inc (HQ) .... D...... 909 386-1762
1365 N Ayala Dr Rialto (92376) *(P-6923)*

Langham Hotels International, Pasadena *Also Called:* Langham Hotels Pacific Corp *(P-9965)*

Langham Hotels Pacific Corp .... C...... 617 451-1900
1401 S Oak Knoll Ave Pasadena (91106) *(P-9965)*

Langham Huntington Hotel & Spa, Pasadena *Also Called:* Pacific Huntington Hotel Corp *(P-10086)*

Language Line Holdings Inc (HQ) .... B...... 831 648-5800
1 Lower Ragsdale Dr Bldg 2 Monterey (93940) *(P-13348)*

Languageline Solutions, Monterey *Also Called:* Language Line Holdings Inc *(P-13348)*

Lani, Irvine *Also Called:* Loan Administration Netwrk Inc *(P-11172)*

Lansing Farming Co, Fresno *Also Called:* Woolf Farming Co Cal Inc *(P-208)*

Lantz Security, Lancaster *Also Called:* Lantz Security Systems Inc *(P-12995)*

Lantz Security Systems Inc .... C...... 805 496-5775
101 N Westlake Blvd Ste 200 Westlake Village (91362) *(P-12994)*

Lantz Security Systems Inc (PA) .... D...... 661 949-3565
43440 Sahuayo St Lancaster (93535) *(P-12995)*

Lao-Hmong Security Agency Inc .... D...... 714 533-6776
10682 Trask Ave Garden Grove (92843) *(P-12996)*

Lapham Company Inc .... D...... 510 531-6000
4844 Telegraph Ave Oakland (94609) *(P-9070)*

Lapham Company Management, Oakland *Also Called:* Lapham Company Inc *(P-9070)*

Laramar Group LLC .... D...... 415 292-1800
1475 Fillmore St San Francisco (94115) *(P-9071)*

Largo Concrete Inc .... C...... 619 356-2142
591 Camino De La Reina Ste 620 San Diego (92108) *(P-695)*

Largo Concrete Inc .... B...... 909 981-7844
1690 W Foothill Blvd Ste B Upland (91786) *(P-2133)*

Largo Concrete Inc .... A...... 408 874-2500
891 W Hamilton Ave Campbell (95008) *(P-2134)*

Largo Concrete Inc (PA) .... D...... 714 731-3600
2741 Walnut Ave Ste 110 Tustin (92780) *(P-2135)*

Lark Ave Classic Car Wash, Los Gatos *Also Called:* Lark Avenue Car Wash *(P-13696)*

Lark Avenue Car Wash .... D...... 408 356-2525
16500 Lark Ave Los Gatos (95032) *(P-13696)*

Lark Avenue Car Wash .... D...... 408 371-2565
5005 Almaden Expy San Jose (95118) *(P-13697)*

Lark Avenue Car Wash .... D...... 408 377-2525
981 E Hamilton Ave Campbell (95008) *(P-13698)*

LARK Industries Inc (DH) .... D...... 714 701-4200
18565 Jamboree Rd Ste 125 Irvine (92612) *(P-13349)*

Larkin Street Youth Services .... D...... 415 567-1020
6324 Geary Blvd San Francisco (94121) *(P-18039)*

Larkspur Group LLC .... C...... 530 223-9344
2160 Larkspur Ln Redding (96002) *(P-9966)*

Larkspur Hsptality Dev MGT LLC .... D...... 650 827-1515
690 Gateway Blvd South San Francisco (94080) *(P-9967)*

Larkspur Hsptality Dev MGT LLC .... D...... 650 872-1515
670 Gateway Blvd South San Francisco (94080) *(P-9968)*

Larkspur Landing Home Sweet Ht, South San Francisco *Also Called:* Larkspur Hsptality Dev MGT LLC *(P-9967)*

Larry Hopkins Honda, Sunnyvale *Also Called:* Larry Hopkins Inc *(P-7250)*

Larry Hopkins Inc .... D...... 408 720-1888
1048 W El Camino Real Sunnyvale (94087) *(P-7250)*

Larry Jacinto Construction Inc .... D...... 909 794-2151
9555 N Wabash Ave Redlands (92374) *(P-1129)*

Larry Jacinto Farming Inc .... D...... 909 794-2276
9555 N Wabash Ave Redlands (92374) *(P-377)*

Larry Mthvin Installations Inc (HQ) .... D...... 909 563-1700
501 Kettering Dr Ontario (91761) *(P-2694)*

Larsen Supply Co (PA) .... D...... 562 698-0731
12055 Slauson Ave Santa Fe Springs (90670) *(P-5754)*

Larson AI Boat Shop .... D...... 310 514-4100
1046 S Seaside Ave San Pedro (90731) *(P-2994)*

Las Brisas, San Luis Obispo *Also Called:* Harvest Management Sub LLC *(P-8816)*

Las Brisas Hotel, Palm Springs *Also Called:* Robray Hotel Partnership LLP *(P-10168)*

Las Colinas Post Acute, Ontario *Also Called:* Ontarioidence Opco LLC *(P-15781)*

Las Posas Berry Farms LLC .... D...... 805 483-1000
730 S A St Oxnard (93030) *(P-56)*

Las Posas Country Club .... C...... 805 482-4518
955 Fairway Dr Camarillo (93010) *(P-14395)*

Las Vegas / LA Express Inc (PA) .... C...... 909 972-3100
1000 S Cucamonga Ave Ontario (91761) *(P-3504)*

Las Villas De Carlsbad, Oceanside *Also Called:* Villas De Crlsbad Ltd A Cal Lt *(P-18542)*

Las Villas Del Norte .... C...... 760 741-1047
1325 Las Villas Way Escondido (92026) *(P-18465)*

Las Virgenes Municipal Wtr Dst .... C...... 818 251-2100
4232 Las Virgenes Rd Lbby Calabasas (91302) *(P-4799)*

Lasalle Jones Lang .... D...... 415 388-4460
655 Redwood Hwy Frontage Rd Ste 177 Mill Valley (94941) *(P-9072)*

Lasaltte Hlth Rhbilitation Ctr, Stockton *Also Called:* Five Star Qulty Care-CA II LLC *(P-15479)*

Lasco, Santa Fe Springs *Also Called:* Larsen Supply Co *(P-5754)*

Laser Division, Milpitas *Also Called:* Spectra-Physics Inc *(P-2962)*

ALPHABETIC SECTION

Laser Electric Inc .... C....... 760 658-6626
   650 Opper St Escondido (92029) *(P-1765)*

Laserfiche Document Imaging, Long Beach *Also Called: Compulink Management Ctr Inc*
(P-11509)

Lash Construction Inc .... D....... 805 963-3553
   721 Carpinteria St Santa Barbara (93103) *(P-19304)*

Lash Group LLC .... C....... 800 788-9637
   999 Bayhill Dr Fl 3 San Bruno (94066) *(P-18605)*

Lash Group Healthcare Cons, San Bruno *Also Called: Lash Group LLC (P-18605)*

Lasher Wes ADI/ Ddg/Volkswagen, Sacramento *Also Called: Wesley B Lasher Inv Corp*
(P-7333)

Lasr Inc .... C....... 877 591-9979
   1517 Beverly Blvd Los Angeles (90026) *(P-10790)*

Lassen Canyon Nursery Inc (PA).. C....... 530 223-1075
   1300 Salmon Creek Rd Redding (96003) *(P-6260)*

Lastline Inc (PA) .... C....... 877 671-3239
   3401 Hillview Ave Palo Alto (94304) *(P-12255)*

Latara Enterprise Inc (PA) .... C....... 909 623-9301
   1716 W Holt Ave Pomona (91768) *(P-16732)*

Latentview Analytics Corp .... D....... 408 493-6653
   2540 N 1st St Ste 108 San Jose (95131) *(P-20431)*

Lateral Link Group Inc .... D....... 310 405-0092
   940 E 2nd St Apt 2 Los Angeles (90012) *(P-11169)*

Latham & Watkins LLP .... B....... 858 523-5400
   12670 High Bluff Dr Ste 100 San Diego (92130) *(P-17535)*

Latham & Watkins LLP (PA).. A....... 213 485-1234
   555 W 5th St Ste 300 Los Angeles (90013) *(P-17536)*

Latham & Watkins LLP .... B....... 213 891-7108
   555 W 5th St Ste 300 Los Angeles (90013) *(P-17537)*

Latham & Watkins LLP .... B....... 714 540-1235
   650 Town Center Dr Ste 2000 Costa Mesa (92626) *(P-17538)*

Latham & Watkins LLP .... C....... 415 391-0600
   505 Montgomery St Ste 2000 San Francisco (94111) *(P-17539)*

Lathrop Construction Assoc Inc (PA).................................... D....... 707 746-8000
   4001 Park Rd Benicia (94510) *(P-957)*

Latino Fmly Alchol DRG Abuse C, Los Angeles *Also Called: County of Los Angeles*
(P-17933)

Lattice Engines Inc (DH) .... C....... 877 460-0010
   1820 Gateway Dr Ste 200 San Mateo (94404) *(P-12478)*

LAuberge De Sonoma LLC .... C....... 707 938-2929
   29 E Macarthur St Sonoma (95476) *(P-9969)*

Laughlin Falbo Levy Moresi LLP (PA)................................... D....... 510 628-0496
   1001 Galaxy Way Ste 200 Concord (94520) *(P-17540)*

Launch Media Inc (HQ)... C....... 310 593-6152
   25 Taylor St San Francisco (94102) *(P-4305)*

Launchdarkly, Oakland *Also Called: Catamorphic Co (P-11486)*

Launchpad Communications, Anaheim *Also Called: Consumer Resource Network LLC*
(P-20325)

Laundry Design LLC .... C....... 323 933-2800
   4079 Redwood Ave Ste A Los Angeles (90066) *(P-13350)*

Lauras House .... D....... 949 361-3775
   33 Journey Ste 150 Aliso Viejo (92656) *(P-18040)*

Laurel Inn, San Francisco *Also Called: Joie De Vivre Hospitality LLC (P-9923)*

Lauren Andrew Surfaces Inc .... D....... 562 921-9549
   13220 Cambridge St Santa Fe Springs (90670) *(P-13351)*

Laurence-Hovenier Inc .... C....... 951 736-2990
   179 N Maple St Corona (92878) *(P-2006)*

Lav Hotel Corp .... C....... 858 454-0771
   1132 Prospect St La Jolla (92037) *(P-9970)*

Lava Scs LLC .... D....... 909 437-7881
   218 Machlin Ct Walnut (91789) *(P-3724)*

Law Offces Les Zeve A Prof Cor .... C....... 714 848-7920
   30 Corporate Park Ste 450 Irvine (92606) *(P-17541)*

Law Offices Juan J. Dominguez, Los Angeles *Also Called: Dominguez Law Group PC*
(P-17439)

Law Offices Michael Burgis PC .... D....... 818 994-9870
   5900 Sepulveda Blvd Ste 215 Sherman Oaks (91411) *(P-17542)*

Law School Financial Inc .... C....... 626 243-1800
   175 S Lake Ave Unit 200 Pasadena (91101) *(P-7866)*

Law School Loans, Pasadena *Also Called: Law School Financial Inc (P-7866)*

Lawrence Berkeley National Lab .... A....... 347 425-3735
   717 Potter St Berkeley (94710) *(P-16733)*

Lawrence Berkeley National Lab .... A....... 510 486-6954
   1 Cyclotron Rd # 90j0106 Berkeley (94720) *(P-19598)*

Lawrence Berkeley National Lab, Brea *Also Called: United Sttes Dept Enrgy Brkley (P-19923)*

Lawrence Berkeley National Lab, Albany *Also Called: United Sttes Dept Enrgy Brkley*
(P-19924)

Lawrence Berkeley National Lab, Berkeley *Also Called: United Sttes Dept Enrgy Brkley*
(P-19925)

Lawrence D. Sharpe M.D., Riverside *Also Called: Riverside Medical Clinic Inc (P-15026)*

Lawrence Fmly Jwish Cmnty Ctrs (PA)................................. C....... 858 362-1144
   4126 Executive Dr La Jolla (92037) *(P-18606)*

Lawrence Livermore Nat Lab, Livermore *Also Called: United Sttes Dept Enrgy Lvrmor*
(P-19791)

Lawrence Livermore Nat Lab, San Francisco *Also Called: United Sttes Dept Enrgy Lvrmor*
(P-19926)

Lawrence Livermore Nat Lab, San Jose *Also Called: United Sttes Dept Enrgy Lvrmor*
(P-19927)

Lawrence Livermore Nat SEC LLC .... B....... 925 453-3584
   2300 1st St Ste 204 Livermore (94550) *(P-13131)*

Lawrence Welk Desert Oasis, Cathedral City *Also Called: Whv Resort Group Inc (P-10368)*

Lawrys Restaurants II Inc .... C....... 323 664-0228
   2980 Los Feliz Blvd Los Angeles (90039) *(P-7491)*

Lawson Mechanical Contractors (PA).................................... D....... 916 381-5000
   6090 S Watt Ave Sacramento (95829) *(P-1482)*

Lawson Roofing Co Inc .... D....... 415 285-1661
   1495 Tennessee St San Francisco (94107) *(P-2072)*

Lawyers Title Escrow, Newport Beach *Also Called: Lawyers Title Insurance Corp (P-8446)*

Lawyers Title Insurance Corp .... B....... 805 484-2701
   2751 Park View Ct Oxnard (93036) *(P-8444)*

Lawyers Title Insurance Corp .... C....... 650 445-6300
   530 El Camino Real Ste A San Carlos (94070) *(P-8445)*

Lawyers Title Insurance Corp .... C....... 949 223-5575
   5000 Birch St Newport Beach (92660) *(P-8446)*

Lawyers Title Insurance Corp .... D....... 510 733-2250
   20630 Patio Dr Castro Valley (94546) *(P-8447)*

Lawyers Title Insurance Corp .... D....... 949 223-5575
   18551 Von Karman Ave Ste 100 Irvine (92612) *(P-8448)*

Layfield USA Corporation (DH).. D....... 619 562-1200
   10038 Marathon Pkwy Lakeside (92040) *(P-2293)*

Layline Automation .... D....... 415 758-0044
   1005 Northgate Dr San Rafael (94903) *(P-11703)*

Laz Karp Associates LLC .... C....... 323 464-4190
   1400 Ivar Ave Los Angeles (90028) *(P-13609)*

Lb3 Enterprises Inc .... D....... 619 579-6161
   12485 Highway 67 # 3 Lakeside (92040) *(P-1130)*

Lba Inc .... D....... 949 833-0400
   3333 Michelson Dr Ste 230 Irvine (92612) *(P-20432)*

Lba Realty, Irvine *Also Called: Lba Inc (P-20432)*

LBC Holdings USA Corporation (PA).................................... C....... 650 873-0750
   362 E Grand Ave South San Francisco (94080) *(P-3938)*

LBC Mundial Corporation (DH).. D....... 650 873-0750
   3563 Investment Blvd Ste 3 Hayward (94545) *(P-3856)*

LBC North America, Hayward *Also Called: LBC Mundial Corporation (P-3856)*

Lbct LLC .... D....... 562 951-6000
   1171 Pier F Ave Long Beach (90802) *(P-3811)*

Lbf Travel Inc .... B....... 858 429-7599
   4545 Murphy Canyon Rd Ste 210 San Diego (92123) *(P-3939)*

Lbi Media Holdings Inc .... B....... 714 554-5000
   3101 W 5th St Santa Ana (92703) *(P-4392)*

Lbn Leisure Care LLC .... D....... 916 604-3780
   1445 Expo Pkwy Sacramento (95815) *(P-18466)*

Lbs Financial Credit Union (PA)... C....... 562 598-9007
   5505 Garden Grove Blvd Ste 500 Westminster (92683) *(P-7827)*

Lc Trs Inc .... A....... 760 438-9111
   2100 Costa Del Mar Rd Carlsbad (92009) *(P-9971)*

Ld Acquisition Company 16 LLC .... D....... 310 294-8160
   400 Continental Blvd Ste 500 El Segundo (90245) *(P-9526)*

Ld Products Inc .... C....... 888 321-2552
   3700 Cover St Long Beach (90808) *(P-2510)*

LDI Mechanical Inc (PA).. C....... 951 340-9685
   1587 E Bentley Dr Corona (92879) *(P-1483)*

Ldla Clothing LLC .... D....... 323 312-2805
   13071 Temple Ave La Puente (91746) *(P-6204)*

Le Meridian Hotel — ALPHABETIC SECTION

Le Meridian Hotel, San Francisco *Also Called: Chesapeake Lodging Trust (P-9697)*
Le Montrose Hotel .... D...... 310 855-1115
    900 Hammond St Apt 434 West Hollywood (90069) *(P-9972)*
Le Montrose Suite Hotel, West Hollywood *Also Called: Le Montrose Hotel (P-9972)*
Le Parc Suite Hotel, West Hollywood *Also Called: Ols Hotels & Resorts LLC (P-10064)*
Le Vecke Corporation (PA) .... D...... 951 681-8600
    10810 Inland Ave Jurupa Valley (91752) *(P-6770)*
Le Vecke Group, Jurupa Valley *Also Called: Le Vecke Corporation (P-6770)*
Lea & Braze Engineering Inc (PA) .... D...... 510 887-4086
    2495 Industrial Pkwy W Hayward (94545) *(P-19305)*
Lead Genius .... D...... 415 969-2915
    2054 University Ave Berkeley (94704) *(P-10640)*
Lead Star Security Inc .... D...... 916 971-6218
    937 Enterprise Dr Sacramento (95825) *(P-12997)*
Leadcrunch Inc .... D...... 888 708-6649
    3830 Valley Centre Dr # 705-823 San Diego (92130) *(P-20433)*
Leader Drug Store, Torrance *Also Called: Little Company Mary Hospital (P-16215)*
Leader Emergency Vehicles, South El Monte *Also Called: Leader Industries Inc (P-3271)*
Leader Industries Inc .... C...... 626 575-0880
    10941 Weaver Ave South El Monte (91733) *(P-3271)*
Leading Edge Aviation Svcs Inc .... A...... 714 556-0576
    5251 California Ave # 170 Irvine (92617) *(P-1627)*
Leadiq Inc .... D...... 888 653-2347
    548 Market St Pmb 20317 San Francisco (94104) *(P-11704)*
Leadstack Inc .... D...... 628 200-3063
    611 Gateway Blvd Ste 120 South San Francisco (94080) *(P-11170)*
Leaf Communications LLC .... D...... 949 388-0192
    1000 Calle Cordillera San Clemente (92673) *(P-20798)*
Leaf Group, Santa Monica *Also Called: Leaf Group Ltd (P-12586)*
Leaf Group Ltd (HQ) .... C...... 310 394-6400
    1655 26th St Santa Monica (90404) *(P-12586)*
League of California Cities (PA) .... D...... 916 658-8200
    1400 K St Fl 4 Sacramento (95814) *(P-20637)*
Leal, Jennifer A, Pasadena *Also Called: Collins & Collins (P-8711)*
Leandata Inc .... C...... 669 600-5676
    2901 Patrick Henry Dr Santa Clara (95054) *(P-5323)*
Leanplum, San Francisco *Also Called: Leanplum Inc (P-12587)*
Leanplum Inc .... C...... 844 532-6758
    1550 Bryant St Ste 525 San Francisco (94103) *(P-12587)*
Lear Capital Inc .... D...... 310 571-0190
    1990 S Bundy Dr Ste 600 Los Angeles (90025) *(P-8097)*
Learfield Communications LLC .... D...... 949 823-1729
    5291 California Ave Ste 100 Irvine (92617) *(P-4393)*
Learning Tree Pre-School, Tujunga *Also Called: Crescenta-Canada YMCA (P-18849)*
Leasing Equipment, San Francisco *Also Called: Atel Capital Group (P-7916)*
Leather Factory LP .... D...... 559 297-7375
    788 W Shaw Ave Clovis (93612) *(P-13780)*
Leavitt United Insur Svcs Inc .... D...... 209 532-6951
    301 S Shepherd St Sonora (95370) *(P-8602)*
Ledcor CMI Inc .... D...... 602 595-3017
    6405 Mira Mesa Blvd Ste 100 San Diego (92121) *(P-831)*
Ledesma & Meyer Cnstr Co Inc .... D...... 909 297-1100
    9441 Haven Ave Rancho Cucamonga (91730) *(P-958)*
Ledra Brands Inc .... C...... 714 259-9959
    88 Maxwell Irvine (92618) *(P-5121)*
Lee Burkhart Liu Inc .... D...... 310 829-2249
    5510 Lincoln Blvd # 250 Playa Vista (90094) *(P-19485)*
Lee & Associates, Stockton *Also Called: Lee & Associates Central Vly (P-9073)*
Lee & Associates Central Vly .... D...... 209 983-1111
    241 Frank West Cir Ste 300 Stockton (95206) *(P-9073)*
Lee Bros Foodservices Inc (PA) .... D...... 408 275-0700
    660 E Gish Rd San Jose (95112) *(P-6261)*
Lee Financial Services, Fresno *Also Called: Fresno Truck Center (P-7215)*
Lee Industrial Catering, San Jose *Also Called: Lee Bros Foodservices Inc (P-6261)*
Lee Jennings Target Ex Inc .... D...... 209 823-0071
    815 Moffat Blvd Manteca (95336) *(P-4049)*
Lee Mar Aquarium & Pet Sups, Vista *Also Called: Lee-Mar Aquarium & Pet Sups (P-6924)*
Lee-Mar Aquarium & Pet Sups .... D...... 760 727-1300
    2459 Dogwood Way Vista (92081) *(P-6924)*
Leed Electric Inc .... C...... 562 270-9500
    13138 Arctic Cir Santa Fe Springs (90670) *(P-1766)*

Leekilpatrick Management Inc .... D...... 818 500-9631
    324 S Myrtle Ave Monrovia (91016) *(P-20434)*
Leemah Electronics Inc .... C...... 415 394-1288
    1080 Samson St San Francisco (94111) *(P-4583)*
Leena Ai Inc .... C...... 332 232-9740
    3260 Hillview Ave Palo Alto (94304) *(P-11705)*
Lees Maintenance Service Inc .... B...... 818 988-6644
    14740 Keswick St Van Nuys (91405) *(P-10917)*
Lefco, San Jose *Also Called: Lefco Inc (P-1484)*
Lefco Inc .... D...... 408 729-4800
    1650 Las Plumas Ave San Jose (95133) *(P-1484)*
Legacy and Nursing Rehab .... D...... 925 228-8383
    1790 Muir Rd Martinez (94553) *(P-15535)*
Legacy Farms LLC .... D...... 714 736-1800
    1765 W Penhall Way Anaheim (92801) *(P-6561)*
Legacy Global Logistics Svcs, San Jose *Also Called: Legacy Transportation Svcs Inc (P-3589)*
Legacy Healthcare Center LLC .... D...... 626 798-0558
    1570 N Fair Oaks Ave Pasadena (91103) *(P-17268)*
Legacy Marketing Group (PA) .... C...... 707 778-8638
    5341 Old Redwood Hwy Ste 400 Petaluma (94954) *(P-20435)*
Legacy Mech & Enrgy Svcs Inc .... D...... 925 820-6938
    3130 Crow Canyon Pl Ste 410 San Ramon (94583) *(P-1485)*
Legacy Mechanical, San Ramon *Also Called: Legacy Mech & Enrgy Svcs Inc (P-1485)*
Legacy Personnel Inc .... B...... 877 850-5132
    1680 Civic Center Dr Ste 230 Santa Clara (95050) *(P-11171)*
Legacy Prtners Residential Inc .... C...... 949 930-6600
    5141 California Ave Ste 100 Irvine (92617) *(P-20137)*
Legacy Prtners Residential Inc (PA) .... C...... 650 571-2250
    950 Tower Ln Ste 900 Foster City (94404) *(P-20138)*
Legacy Reinforcing Steel LLC .... D...... 619 646-0205
    1057 Tierra Del Rey Ste F Chula Vista (91910) *(P-2186)*
Legacy Transportation Svcs Inc (PA) .... C...... 408 294-9800
    935 Mclaughlin Ave San Jose (95122) *(P-3589)*
Legal Enterprise, Calabasas *Also Called: Litigtion Rsrces of America-CA (P-13355)*
Legal Solutions Holdings Inc .... C...... 800 244-3495
    955 Overland Ct Ste 200 San Dimas (91773) *(P-17543)*
LEGALZOOM, Glendale *Also Called: Legalzoomcom Inc (P-12588)*
Legalzoomcom Inc (PA) .... B...... 323 962-8600
    101 N Brand Blvd Fl 11 Glendale (91203) *(P-12588)*
Legend Films .... B...... 858 793-4420
    2200 Faraday Ave Ste 100 Carlsbad (92008) *(P-13941)*
Legendary Entertainment LLC .... D...... 818 688-7003
    2900 W Alameda Ave Unit 1500 Burbank (91505) *(P-13859)*
Legendary Pictures Films LLC .... C...... 818 688-7003
    2900 W Alameda Ave Burbank (91505) *(P-10641)*
Legion Technologies Inc .... C...... 408 605-2603
    3101 Park Blvd Palo Alto (94306) *(P-18878)*
Legoland California LLC .... B...... 760 450-3661
    1 Legoland Dr Carlsbad (92008) *(P-14306)*
Legoland California Resort, Carlsbad *Also Called: Legoland California LLC (P-14306)*
Lehar Sales Co .... D...... 510 465-3255
    477 Forbes Blvd South San Francisco (94080) *(P-6446)*
Lei AG Seattle, Los Angeles *Also Called: Lowe Enterprises Inc (P-9988)*
LEICHTAG ASSISTED LIVING, Encinitas *Also Called: San Diego Hebrew Homes (P-15651)*
Leidos Inc .... C...... 703 676-4300
    10260 Campus Point Dr Bldg C San Diego (92121) *(P-19725)*
Leidos Inc .... C...... 858 826-9090
    2985 Scott St Vista (92081) *(P-19726)*
Leidos Inc .... D...... 858 826-6000
    Naval Air Station San Diego (92135) *(P-19727)*
Leidos Inc .... C...... 858 826-9416
    4161 Campus Point Ct Stop Em3 San Diego (92121) *(P-19728)*
Leidos Engrg & Sciences LLC .... C...... 619 542-3130
    1330 30th St Ste A San Diego (92154) *(P-19729)*
Leidos Government Services Inc .... C...... 323 721-6979
    500 N Via Val Verde Montebello (90640) *(P-12826)*
Leigh Jerry California Inc (PA) .... B...... 818 909-6200
    7860 Nelson Rd Van Nuys (91402) *(P-2465)*
Leighton & Associates, Irvine *Also Called: Gradient Engineers Inc (P-19245)*
Leighton Group Inc .... C...... 760 776-4192
    75450 Gerald Ford Dr Ste 301 Palm Desert (92211) *(P-18750)*

Leiner Health Products, Carson Also Called: Leiner Health Products Inc (P-2597)
Leiner Health Products Inc (DH) .... C....... 631 200-2000
  901 E 233rd St Carson (90745) (P-2597)
Leisure Care LLC .... C....... 818 713-0900
  8138 Woodlake Ave West Hills (91304) (P-15770)
Leisure Care LLC .... D....... 925 371-2300
  800 E Stanley Blvd Livermore (94550) (P-18467)
Leisure Care LLC .... C....... 707 769-3300
  101 Ely Blvd S Petaluma (94954) (P-18468)
Leisure Care LLC .... C....... 714 974-1616
  380 S Anaheim Hills Rd Ofc Anaheim (92807) (P-18469)
Leisure Care LLC .... C....... 559 434-1237
  9525 N Fort Washington Rd Fresno (93730) (P-18470)
Leisure Care LLC .... C....... 626 447-0106
  601 Sunset Blvd Arcadia (91007) (P-18471)
Leisure Court Nursing Center, Anaheim Also Called: 1135 N Leisure Ct Inc (P-15314)
Leisure Gardens Retirement HM, Vacaville Also Called: Westlake Development Group LLC (P-15911)
Leisure Glen Convalescent Ctr, Glendale Also Called: Buena Ventura Care Center Inc (P-15824)
Leisure Vale Retirement Hotel, Glendale Also Called: BV General Inc (P-8793)
Leisure World Pharmacy, Seal Beach Also Called: Tenet Healthsystem Medical Inc (P-15124)
Leisure World Resales, Laguna Hills Also Called: Professional Cmnty MGT Cal Inc (P-9144)
Leland Stanford Junior Univ .... C....... 650 723-4000
  300 Pasteur Dr Stanford (94305) (P-16213)
Leland Stanford Junior Univ (PA) .... C....... 650 723-2300
  450 Jane Stanford Way Stanford (94305) (P-17762)
Leland Stanford Junior Univ .... A....... 650 935-5365
  505 Broadway St 4th Fl Redwood City (94063) (P-17763)
Leland Stanford Junior Univ .... C....... 650 721-2726
  1291 Welch Rd Stanford (94305) (P-17764)
Leland Stanford Junior Univ .... C....... 650 723-2021
  326 Galvez St Stanford (94305) (P-18879)
Lemo USA Inc .... D....... 707 206-3700
  635 Park Ct Rohnert Park (94928) (P-5669)
Lemon Grove Care Rhbltttion Ctr, Lemon Grove Also Called: Lemon Grove Health Assoc LLC (P-15536)
Lemon Grove Health Assoc LLC .... B....... 619 463-0294
  8351 Broadway Lemon Grove (91945) (P-15536)
Lemonlight .... D....... 310 801-6487
  4063 Glencoe Ave # A Marina Del Rey (90292) (P-4542)
Lemonlight Media Inc .... D....... 310 402-0275
  226 S Glasgow Ave Inglewood (90301) (P-13860)
Lemore Transportation Inc (PA) .... D....... 925 689-6444
  1420 Royal Industrial Way Concord (94520) (P-3505)
Lenders Investment Corp .... D....... 714 540-4747
  18101 Von Karman Ave Ste 400 Irvine (92612) (P-7987)
Lendingclub, San Francisco Also Called: Lendingclub Corporation (P-7876)
Lendingclub Asset MGT LLC .... D....... 415 632-5600
  71 Stevenson St Ste 300 San Francisco (94105) (P-8045)
Lendingclub Corporation (PA) .... B....... 415 632-5600
  595 Market St Fl 4 San Francisco (94105) (P-7876)
Lendingusa LLC .... D....... 800 994-6177
  15303 Ventura Blvd Ste 850 Sherman Oaks (91403) (P-13352)
Lendsure Mortgage Corp .... C....... 888 707-7811
  15253 Avenue Of Science San Diego (92128) (P-7988)
Lendus LLC .... A....... 925 295-9300
  3240 Stone Valley Rd W Alamo (94507) (P-7989)
Lenlyn Ltd Which Will Do Bus I (HQ) .... D....... 310 417-3432
  6151 W Century Blvd Ste 1108 Los Angeles (90045) (P-7857)
Lennar Builders, San Francisco Also Called: Lennar Homes California Inc (P-696)
Lennar Corporation .... D....... 949 349-8000
  15131 Alton Pkwy Ste 190 Irvine (92618) (P-794)
Lennar Homes California Inc (DH) .... C....... 949 349-8000
  1 California St Fl 27 San Francisco (94111) (P-696)
Lennar Mltfmily Cmmunities LLC .... B....... 415 975-4980
  492 9th St Ste 300 Oakland (94607) (P-795)
Lennar Multi Family Community, Aliso Viejo Also Called: LMC Hollywood Highland (P-961)
LENNAR MULTIFAMILY COMMUNITIES, LLC, Oakland Also Called: Lennar Mltfmily Cmmunities LLC (P-795)
Lenore John & Co (PA) .... C....... 619 232-6136
  1250 Delevan Dr San Diego (92102) (P-6644)

Lenox Financial Mortgage Corp .... B....... 949 428-5100
  200 Sandpointe Ave Ste 800 Santa Ana (92707) (P-7990)
Leo Hoffman Chevrolet Inc (PA) .... D....... 626 968-8411
  17300 E Gale Ave City Of Industry (91748) (P-7251)
Leo J Ryan Child Care Ctr, South San Francisco Also Called: Peninsula Family Service (P-18078)
Leonard Chaidez Inc .... D....... 714 279-8173
  2298 N Batavia St Orange (92865) (P-556)
Leonard Chaidez Tree Service, Orange Also Called: Leonard Chaidez Inc (P-556)
Leonard Green & Partners LP (PA) .... D....... 310 954-0444
  11111 Santa Monica Blvd Ste 2000 Los Angeles (90025) (P-8098)
Leonard Roofing Inc .... D....... 951 506-3811
  43280 Business Park Dr Ste 107 Temecula (92590) (P-2073)
Leonards Carpet Service Inc (PA) .... D....... 714 630-1930
  1121 N Red Gum St Anaheim (92806) (P-2504)
Leonid M Glsman DDS A Dntl Cor .... C....... 323 560-4514
  5021 Florence Ave Bell (90201) (P-15234)
Leport Educational Inst Inc .... B....... 914 374-8860
  1 Technology Dr Bldg A Irvine (92618) (P-18328)
Leport Schools .... D....... 714 377-6035
  1 Technology Dr Ste H100 Irvine (92618) (P-18329)
Leport Schools, Irvine Also Called: Leport Educational Inst Inc (P-18328)
Lereta LLC (PA) .... B....... 626 543-1765
  901 Corporate Center Dr Pomona (91768) (P-8099)
Lereta LLC .... C....... 626 332-1942
  10760 4th St Rancho Cucamonga (91730) (P-8732)
Lerexa Winery, Livingston Also Called: E & J Gallo Winery (P-2382)
LEROY HAYNES CENTER, La Verne Also Called: Haynes Family Programs Inc (P-18448)
Lescure Company Inc .... D....... 925 283-2528
  2301 Arnold Industrial Way Ste C Concord (94520) (P-1486)
Lesley Foundation .... D....... 650 726-4888
  701 Arnold Way Bldg A Half Moon Bay (94019) (P-20799)
Lestonnac Preschool, Tustin Also Called: Tustin Unified School District (P-17754)
Letner Roofing Company, Orange Also Called: Danny Letner Inc (P-2056)
Lets Talkcom Inc .... D....... 415 357-7600
  201 Mission St Ste 3000 San Francisco (94105) (P-4217)
Level 10 Construction LP (PA) .... C....... 408 747-5000
  1050 Enterprise Way Ste 250 Sunnyvale (94089) (P-959)
Level 5 Drywall Inc .... D....... 650 486-1657
  70 Glenn Way Ste 4 San Carlos (94070) (P-1943)
Level 99, Gardena Also Called: Phoenix Textile Inc (P-6159)
Level Ai, Mountain View Also Called: Ujwal Inc (P-12000)
Level Furnished Living, Los Angeles Also Called: Onni Properties LLC (P-20165)
Level-It Instlltions Group Inc .... D....... 604 942-2022
  3700 Yale Way Fremont (94538) (P-960)
Lever Inc .... D....... 415 458-2731
  939 Noe St San Francisco (94114) (P-11706)
Levine Lchtman Capitl Partners, Beverly Hills Also Called: Levine Lchtman Cpitl Prtners S (P-9453)
Levine Lchtman Cpitl Prtners S .... D....... 310 275-5335
  345 N Maple Dr Ste 300 Beverly Hills (90210) (P-9453)
Levity Live, Oxnard Also Called: Comedy Club Oxnard LLC (P-14361)
Levity of Brea LLC .... D....... 714 482-0700
  180 S Brea Blvd Brea (92821) (P-7520)
Levlad LLC .... C....... 818 882-2951
  9200 Mason Ave Chatsworth (91311) (P-5430)
Lewis & Taylor LLC .... C....... 415 781-3496
  440 Bryant St San Francisco (94107) (P-10918)
Lewis & Taylor Bldg Svc Contrs, San Francisco Also Called: Lewis & Taylor LLC (P-10918)
Lewis and Tibbitts Inc .... C....... 408 925-0220
  1470 Industrial Ave San Jose (95112) (P-1230)
Lewis Brsbois Bsgard Smith LLP (PA) .... A....... 213 250-1800
  633 W 5th St Ste 4000 Los Angeles (90071) (P-17544)
Lewis Brsbois Bsgard Smith LLP .... C....... 619 233-1006
  701 B St Ste 1900 San Diego (92101) (P-17545)
Lewis Brsbois Bsgard Smith LLP .... C....... 714 545-9200
  650 Town Center Dr Ste 1400 Costa Mesa (92626) (P-17546)
Lewis Brsbois Bsgard Smith LLP .... C....... 415 362-2580
  333 Bush St San Francisco (94104) (P-17547)
Lewis Brsbois Bsgard Smith LLP .... D....... 909 387-1130
  650 E Hospitality Ln Ste 600 San Bernardino (92408) (P-17548)

Lewis Center For Eductl RES, Apple Valley *Also Called: High Dsert Prtnr In Acdmic Exc* *(P-19817)*
Lewis Companies (PA) .... C....... 909 985-0971
   1156 N Mountain Ave Upland (91786) *(P-796)*
Lewis Lifetime Tools, Poway *Also Called: Richmond Engineering Co Inc* *(P-534)*
Lewis Management Corp .... C....... 909 985-0971
   1154 N Mountain Ave Upland (91786) *(P-20139)*
Lewisgoetz, Sacramento *Also Called: Valley Rubber & Gasket Company Inc* *(P-5934)*
Lexar Media Inc .... C....... 510 413-1200
   47300 Bayside Pkwy Fremont (94538) *(P-5324)*
Lexicon Marketing, Los Angeles *Also Called: Lexicon Marketing (usa) Inc* *(P-5467)*
Lexicon Marketing (usa) Inc (PA) .... D....... 323 782-8282
   640 S San Vicente Blvd Los Angeles (90048) *(P-5467)*
Lexington Group International .... C....... 562 428-4681
   260 E Market St Long Beach (90805) *(P-15864)*
Lexisnexis Examen Inc .... C....... 916 921-4300
   3831 N Freeway Blvd Ste 200 Sacramento (95834) *(P-12827)*
Lexisnexis Risk Assets Inc .... C....... 949 222-0028
   2112 Business Center Dr Ste 150 Irvine (92614) *(P-8603)*
Lexus of Cerritos, Cerritos *Also Called: Bargain Rent-A-Car* *(P-7170)*
Lexus of Roseville, Roseville *Also Called: RPM Luxury Auto Sales Inc* *(P-7292)*
Lexus Santa Monica, Santa Monica *Also Called: Volkswagen Santa Monica Inc* *(P-7326)*
Lexxiom Inc .... B....... 909 581-7313
   99 N San Antonio Ave Ste 330 Upland (91786) *(P-20140)*
LFC Corporate Services Inc .... D....... 949 640-4950
   17 Corporate Plaza Dr Ste 200 Newport Beach (92660) *(P-20141)*
Lfp Broadcasting LLC (PA) .... D....... 323 852-5020
   8484 Wilshire Blvd Ste 900 Beverly Hills (90211) *(P-13965)*
Lfp Ecommerce LLC .... D....... 314 428-5069
   210 N Sunset Ave West Covina (91790) *(P-13353)*
Lfs Development LLC .... C....... 619 501-5400
   901 Bayfront Ct Ste 1 San Diego (92101) *(P-9973)*
Lg, San Francisco *Also Called: Little Giant Bldg Maint Inc* *(P-10920)*
Lg Display America Inc (HQ) .... D....... 408 350-0190
   2540 N 1st St Ste 400 San Jose (95131) *(P-5670)*
Lge Electrical Sales Inc .... C....... 408 992-4145
   755 E Evelyn Ave Sunnyvale (94086) *(P-5573)*
LGS RECREATION, Los Gatos *Also Called: Los Gatos Saratoga Dept of Com* *(P-17811)*
Lgsrc, Los Gatos *Also Called: Los Gatos Swim and Racquet CLB* *(P-14217)*
Lh Indian Wells Operating LLC .... C....... 760 341-2200
   4500 Indian Wells Ln Indian Wells (92210) *(P-9974)*
Lh Universal Operating LLC .... B....... 818 980-1212
   333 Universal Hollywood Dr Universal City (91608) *(P-9975)*
Lho Mssion Bay Rsie Lessee Inc .... B....... 619 276-4010
   1775 E Mission Bay Dr San Diego (92109) *(P-9976)*
Lhoberge Lessee Inc .... C....... 858 259-1515
   1540 Camino Del Mar Del Mar (92014) *(P-9977)*
Liberman Broadcasting Inc (PA) .... D....... 818 729-5300
   1845 W Empire Ave Burbank (91504) *(P-4394)*
LIBERTY, Tahoe Vista *Also Called: Liberty Utlties Clpeco Elc LLC* *(P-4584)*
Liberty ADM Support Svcs, Orange *Also Called: Liberty Debt Relief LLC* *(P-10559)*
Liberty Ambulance LLC .... C....... 562 741-6230
   9441 Washburn Rd Downey (90242) *(P-3272)*
Liberty American Mortgage Corp (PA) .... D....... 916 780-3000
   193 Blue Ravine Rd # 240 Folsom (95630) *(P-8046)*
Liberty Debt Relief LLC .... D....... 800 756-8447
   333 City Blvd W Fl 17 Orange (92868) *(P-10559)*
Liberty Dental Plan Cal Inc .... B....... 949 223-0007
   340 Commerce Ste 100 Irvine (92602) *(P-8339)*
Liberty Dental Plan Corp (PA) .... D....... 888 703-6999
   340 Commerce Ste 100 Irvine (92602) *(P-8340)*
Liberty Diversified Intl Inc .... C....... 858 391-7302
   13100 Danielson St Poway (92064) *(P-2519)*
Liberty Healthcare Cal Inc .... D....... 610 668-8800
   2251 San Diego Ave Ste B110 San Diego (92110) *(P-16888)*
Liberty Landscaping Inc (PA) .... C....... 951 683-2999
   5212 El Rivino Rd Riverside (92509) *(P-517)*
Liberty Linehaul West Inc .... D....... 323 728-8900
   1501 Chapin Rd Montebello (90640) *(P-3506)*
Liberty Packing Company LLC (PA) .... D....... 209 826-7100
   724 Main St Woodland (95695) *(P-6562)*

Liberty Residential Svcs Inc .... D....... 858 500-0852
   12700 Stowe Dr Ste 110 Poway (92064) *(P-16889)*
Liberty Utilities Pk Wtr Corp (DH) .... D....... 562 923-0711
   9750 Washburn Rd Downey (90241) *(P-4800)*
Liberty Utlties Clpeco Elc LLC .... D....... 800 782-2506
   701 National Ave Tahoe Vista (96148) *(P-4584)*
Lick Wilmerding High School, San Francisco *Also Called: California School of Mech Arts* *(P-17697)*
Lidlaw Educational Services, Rancho Cucamonga *Also Called: Durham School Services L P* *(P-3329)*
Lieff Cbrser Hmann Brnstein LL (PA) .... C....... 415 788-0245
   275 Battery St 29th Fl San Francisco (94111) *(P-17549)*
Life Alert, Encino *Also Called: Life Alert Emrgncy Rsponse Inc* *(P-13132)*
Life Alert Emrgncy Rsponse Inc .... C....... 800 247-0000
   16027 Ventura Blvd Ste 400 Encino (91436) *(P-13132)*
Life Care Center of La Habra, La Habra *Also Called: Life Care Centers America Inc* *(P-15537)*
Life Care Center of Norwalk, Norwalk *Also Called: Life Care Centers America Inc* *(P-15542)*
Life Care Centers America Inc .... C....... 562 690-0852
   1233 W La Habra Blvd La Habra (90631) *(P-15537)*
Life Care Centers America Inc .... C....... 562 947-8691
   12200 La Mirada Blvd La Mirada (90638) *(P-15538)*
Life Care Centers America Inc .... C....... 760 741-6109
   1980 Felicita Rd Escondido (92025) *(P-15539)*
Life Care Centers America Inc .... C....... 562 943-7156
   11926 La Mirada Blvd La Mirada (90638) *(P-15540)*
Life Care Centers America Inc .... C....... 562 867-1761
   16910 Woodruff Ave Bellflower (90706) *(P-15541)*
Life Care Centers America Inc .... D....... 562 921-6624
   12350 Rosecrans Ave Norwalk (90650) *(P-15542)*
Life Care Centers America Inc .... C....... 760 252-2515
   27555 Rimrock Rd Barstow (92311) *(P-15543)*
Life Care Centers America Inc .... C....... 760 724-8222
   304 N Melrose Dr Vista (92083) *(P-15865)*
Life Care Centers of Escondido, Escondido *Also Called: Life Care Centers America Inc* *(P-15539)*
Life Cycle Engineering Inc .... C....... 619 785-5990
   7510 Airway Rd Ste 2 San Diego (92154) *(P-10919)*
Life Enchancing Therapies, Upland *Also Called: Inland Empire Therapy Provider* *(P-15287)*
Life Gnerations Healthcare LLC .... D....... 619 460-2330
   7800 Parkway Dr La Mesa (91942) *(P-15544)*
Life Plans, Irvine *Also Called: Burnham Bnefits Insur Svcs LLC* *(P-8516)*
Life Science Angels Inc .... D....... 408 541-1152
   1230 Bordeaux Dr Sunnyvale (94089) *(P-9527)*
Life Steps Foundation Inc .... D....... 805 349-9810
   2255 S Depot St Santa Maria (93455) *(P-18041)*
Life Steps Foundation Inc .... D....... 562 436-0751
   500 E 4th St Long Beach (90802) *(P-18042)*
Life Steps Foundation Inc .... D....... 805 549-0150
   1107 Johnson Ave San Luis Obispo (93401) *(P-18043)*
Life Time Inc .... D....... 949 492-1515
   111 Avenida Vista Montana San Clemente (92672) *(P-14213)*
Life Time Inc .... C....... 916 472-2000
   1435 E Roseville Pkwy Roseville (95661) *(P-14214)*
Life Time Inc .... D....... 858 459-0281
   1055 Wall St La Jolla (92037) *(P-14215)*
Life Time Fitness, San Clemente *Also Called: Life Time Inc* *(P-14213)*
Life Time Fitness Inc .... C....... 949 238-2700
   28221 Crown Valley Pkwy Laguna Niguel (92677) *(P-17269)*
LIFE TIME FITNESS, INC., Laguna Niguel *Also Called: Life Time Fitness Inc* *(P-17269)*
Lifecare Assurance Company .... C....... 818 887-4436
   21600 Oxnard St Fl 16 Woodland Hills (91367) *(P-8267)*
Lifecare Assurance Company, Woodland Hills *Also Called: 21st Century Lf & Hlth Co Inc* *(P-8254)*
Lifehouse Inc (PA) .... D....... 415 472-2373
   18 Professional Center Pkwy Fl 2 San Rafael (94903) *(P-18044)*
Lifeline Ambulance, Commerce *Also Called: Eastwestproto Inc* *(P-3253)*
LIFERAY, Diamond Bar *Also Called: Liferay Inc* *(P-12479)*
Liferay Inc (PA) .... A....... 877 543-3729
   1400 Montefino Ave Ste 100 Diamond Bar (91765) *(P-12479)*
Lifescript, Newport Beach *Also Called: Lifescript Inc* *(P-12671)*

Lifescript Inc .... C....... 949 454-0422
 4000 Macarthur Blvd Ste 800 Newport Beach (92660) *(P-12671)*

Lifestar Response of Alabama .... D....... 800 449-4911
 1517 W Braden Ct Orange (92868) *(P-3273)*

Lifestream, San Bernardino *Also Called: Blood Bnk San Bmrdino Rvrside (P-17190)*

Lifestreet Corporation .... D....... 650 508-2220
 98 Battery St, St 504 San Carlos (94070) *(P-6925)*

Lifestreet Media, San Carlos *Also Called: Lifestreet Corporation (P-6925)*

Lifetech Resources LLC .... D....... 805 944-1199
 700 Science Dr Moorpark (93021) *(P-6121)*

Lifetime Entrmt Svcs LLC .... B....... 310 556-7500
 2049 Century Park E Ste 840 Los Angeles (90067) *(P-4452)*

Lifetime Tennis Inc .... D....... 925 931-3449
 6715 Corte Santa Maria Pleasanton (94566) *(P-14540)*

Lifetime TV Network, Los Angeles *Also Called: Lifetime Entrmt Svcs LLC (P-4452)*

Lift By Encore, Huntington Beach *Also Called: Irish Interiors Inc (P-2991)*

Liftoff, Redwood City *Also Called: Lmi Inc (P-11713)*

Lightbend Inc .... D....... 877 989-7372
 580 California St Ste 1231 San Francisco (94104) *(P-11707)*

Lightfiction, Redwood City *Also Called: Des Architects Engineers Inc (P-19465)*

Lighthouse Healthcare Ctr LLC .... D....... 323 564-4461
 2222 Santa Ana S Los Angeles (90059) *(P-15545)*

Lighting Technologies Intl LLC .... C....... 626 480-0755
 13700 Live Oak Ave Baldwin Park (91706) *(P-5574)*

Lightspeed Management Co LLC .... D....... 650 234-8300
 2200 Sand Hill Rd Ste 100 Menlo Park (94025) *(P-20436)*

Lightstone Dt La LLC .... B....... 310 669-9252
 1260 S Figueron St Los Angeles (90015) *(P-9978)*

Lightthipe Substation, Long Beach *Also Called: Southern California Edison Co (P-4692)*

Lightworks Optics Inc .... D....... 714 247-7100
 14192 Chambers Rd Tustin (92780) *(P-3038)*

Lightyear Corporation .... D....... 415 605-9050
 365 Fulton St Apt 225 San Francisco (94102) *(P-11708)*

Lilt Inc (PA) .... C....... 415 992-5088
 2200 Powell St Ste 900 Emeryville (94608) *(P-11709)*

Lime .... C....... 650 762-9697
 1 Sansome St San Francisco (94104) *(P-14541)*

Limebike, San Francisco *Also Called: Neutron Holdings Inc (P-11772)*

Liminex Inc (PA) .... C....... 888 310-0410
 2030 E Maple Ave Ste 100 El Segundo (90245) *(P-11710)*

Lina Gale (usa) Inc (PA) .... D....... 909 595-8898
 22067 Ferrero Walnut (91789) *(P-6122)*

Lincoln (PA) .... D....... 510 273-4700
 1266 14th St Oakland (94607) *(P-17086)*

Lincoln, Oakland *Also Called: Lincoln (P-17086)*

Lincoln Broadcasting Company, Brisbane *Also Called: Ktsf Channel 26 (P-4448)*

Lincoln Child Center Inc .... D....... 925 521-1270
 51 Marina Blvd Pittsburg (94565) *(P-18472)*

Lincoln Glen Manor LLC .... D....... 408 267-1492
 2671 Plummer Ave Ste A San Jose (95125) *(P-18473)*

Lincoln Glen Skilled Nursing, San Jose *Also Called: Lincoln Glen Manor LLC (P-18473)*

Lincoln Prprty No 2087 Ltd Prt .... C....... 214 740-3300
 7777 Center Ave Ste 150 Huntington Beach (92647) *(P-9259)*

LINCOLN TRAINING CENTER, South El Monte *Also Called: Lincoln Trning Ctr Rhblttion W (P-18233)*

Lincoln Trning Ctr Rhblttion W .... D....... 626 442-0621
 2643 Loma Ave South El Monte (91733) *(P-18233)*

Linda Loma Univ Hlth Care (PA) .... A....... 909 558-4729
 11175 Campus St A-1108 Loma Linda (92350) *(P-14875)*

Linda Loma Univ Hlth Care (HQ) .... C....... 909 558-2806
 11370 Anderson St Ste 3900 Loma Linda (92354) *(P-16214)*

Linda Terra Farms (PA) .... C....... 559 867-3473
 5494 W Mount Whitney Ave Riverdale (93656) *(P-212)*

LINDA VISTA HEALTH CARE CENTER, San Diego *Also Called: San Diego Family Care (P-15040)*

Linda Yorba Water District (PA) .... D....... 714 701-3000
 1717 E Miraloma Ave Placentia (92870) *(P-4801)*

Lindbergh Child Care Center, Lynwood *Also Called: Lynwood Unified School Dst (P-17725)*

Linden Lab, San Francisco *Also Called: Linden Research Inc (P-11711)*

Linden Nut, Stockton *Also Called: Pearl Crop Inc (P-299)*

Linden Research Inc .... B....... 415 243-9000
 945 Battery St San Francisco (94111) *(P-11711)*

Linden Unified School District .... D....... 209 946-0707
 100 N Jack Tone Rd Stockton (95215) *(P-17721)*

Lindsey & Sons .... D....... 657 306-5369
 1226 E 76th St Los Angeles (90001) *(P-13354)*

Line Hotel, The, Los Angeles *Also Called: Sydell Hotels LLC (P-10298)*

Linea Solutions Inc .... D....... 310 443-4191
 4551 Glencoe Ave Ste 140 Marina Del Rey (90292) *(P-20437)*

Linen Lovers, Ontario *Also Called: Jomar Table Linens Inc (P-2470)*

Liner Law, Los Angeles *Also Called: Liner LLP (P-17550)*

Liner LLP .... C....... 310 500-3500
 1100 Glendon Ave 14th Los Angeles (90024) *(P-17550)*

Linkedin Corporation (HQ) .... B....... 650 687-3600
 1000 W Maude Ave Sunnyvale (94085) *(P-12672)*

Links Sign Lngage Intrprting S, Long Beach *Also Called: Goodwill Srving The Pple Sther (P-13305)*

Linksys LLC .... C....... 408 526-4000
 120 Theory Irvine (92617) *(P-5671)*

Linksys LLC .... C....... 310 751-5100
 121 Theory Ste 150 Irvine (92617) *(P-5672)*

Linksys Usa Inc .... D....... 949 270-8500
 121 Theory Irvine (92617) *(P-5673)*

Linkus Enterprises LLC .... B....... 559 256-6600
 5595 W San Madele Ave Fresno (93722) *(P-1231)*

Linnco LLC .... A....... 661 616-3900
 5201 Truxtun Ave Bakersfield (93309) *(P-601)*

Linqia Inc .... D....... 415 913-7179
 965 Mission St San Francisco (94103) *(P-20438)*

Linquest Corporation (PA) .... C....... 323 924-1600
 5140 W Goldleaf Cir Ste 400 Los Angeles (90056) *(P-19306)*

Linwood Grdns Convalescent Ctr, Visalia *Also Called: Far West Inc (P-15474)*

Lion Brothers Farms-Newstone, Madera *Also Called: Lion Raisins Inc (P-190)*

Lion Creek Crossing V, Oakland *Also Called: Lion Creek Senior Housing Part (P-9074)*

Lion Creek Senior Housing Part .... D....... 510 878-9120
 6710 Lion Way Oakland (94621) *(P-9074)*

Lion Raisins Inc .... C....... 559 662-8686
 12555 Road 9 Madera (93637) *(P-190)*

Lion Trading Company LLC .... C....... 408 946-0888
 835 Sinclair Frontage Rd Milpitas (95035) *(P-5122)*

Lion-Vallen Ltd Partnership .... D....... 760 385-4885
 22 Area Aven A Bldg #2234 Camp Pendleton (92055) *(P-20142)*

Lionakis (PA) .... C....... 916 558-1901
 2025 19th St Sacramento (95818) *(P-19486)*

Lions Gate Films Inc .... C....... 310 449-9200
 2700 Colorado Ave Santa Monica (90404) *(P-13861)*

Lionsgate Ht & Conference Ctr .... D....... 916 643-6222
 3410 Westover St Mcclellan (95652) *(P-9979)*

Lionsgate Productions Inc .... B....... 310 255-3937
 2700 Colorado Ave Ste 200 Santa Monica (90404) *(P-13966)*

Lipman Insur Admnistrators Inc .... D....... 510 796-4676
 39420 Liberty St Ste 260 Fremont (94538) *(P-8462)*

Liquid Advertising Inc .... D....... 310 450-2653
 138 Eucalyptus Dr El Segundo (90245) *(P-10642)*

Liquid Investments Inc (PA) .... C....... 858 509-8510
 3840 Via De La Valle Ste 300 Del Mar (92014) *(P-6771)*

Liquid Thinking Inc .... D....... 415 869-3300
 548 4th St San Francisco (94107) *(P-12828)*

Listencom Inc .... D....... 415 934-2000
 2012 16th St San Francisco (94103) *(P-4306)*

Lite Solar, Long Beach *Also Called: Lite Solar Corp (P-1487)*

Lite Solar Corp .... C....... 562 256-1249
 3553 Atlantic Ave Long Beach (90807) *(P-1487)*

Lithia, Temecula *Also Called: DCH Acura of Temecula (P-7192)*

Lithia Ford Mzda Suzuki Fresno, Fresno *Also Called: Lithia Motors Inc (P-7252)*

Lithia Motors Inc .... C....... 559 435-8400
 195 E Auto Center Dr Fresno (93710) *(P-7252)*

Litigtion Rsrces of America-CA (PA) .... D....... 818 878-9227
 4232-1 Las Virgenes Rd Ste 100 Calabasas (91302) *(P-13355)*

Litmus Automation Inc (PA) .... D....... 765 418-7405
 2350 Mission College Blvd Ste 1020 Santa Clara (95054) *(P-5325)*

Little Brothers Bakery, Gardena Also Called: Little Brothers Bakery LLC (P-2368)
Little Brothers Bakery LLC .... D...... 310 225-3790
320 W Alondra Blvd Gardena (90248) (P-2368)
Little Co Mary- San Pedro Hosp, San Pedro Also Called: San Pedro Peninsula Hospital (P-16386)
Little Company Mary Hospital .... A...... 310 540-7676
4101 Torrance Blvd Torrance (90503) (P-16215)
Little Company Mary Svc Area, Torrance Also Called: Little Company of Mary Health Services (P-16216)
Little Company of Mary Health Services .... A...... 310 540-7676
4101 Torrance Blvd Torrance (90503) (P-16216)
Little Giant Bldg Maint Inc (PA) .... D...... 415 508-0282
1485 Bay Shore Blvd Ste 117 San Francisco (94124) (P-10920)
Little Giant Bldg Maint Inc .... C...... 415 508-0282
15 Brooks Pl Pacifica (94044) (P-10921)
Little River Inn Inc .... C...... 707 937-5942
7901 N Highway 1 Little River (95456) (P-9980)
Little River Inn and Golf Crse, Little River Also Called: Little River Inn Inc (P-9980)
Little Sister's Truck Wash, Fallbrook Also Called: Little Sisters Truck Wash Inc (P-13699)
Little Sisters Truck Wash Inc (PA) .... D...... 760 731-3170
25 Rolling View Ln Fallbrook (92028) (P-13699)
Little Ssters of The Poor Los 310 548-0625
2100 S Western Ave San Pedro (90732) (P-15546)
Little Ssters of The Poor Okla .... D...... 415 751-6510
300 Lake St San Francisco (94118) (P-18474)
Littler, San Francisco Also Called: Littler Mendelson PC (P-17551)
Littler Mendelson PC (PA) .... B...... 415 433-1940
333 Bush St Fl 34 San Francisco (94104) (P-17551)
Littlethings Inc .... D...... 917 364-9277
642 Harrison St Fl 3 San Francisco (94107) (P-12829)
Live Action General Engrg Inc 559 292-2900
2972 Larkin Ave Clovis (93612) (P-1488)
Live Nation, Beverly Hills Also Called: Live Nation Entertainment Inc (P-13356)
Live Nation Entertainment Inc (PA) .... C...... 310 867-7000
9348 Civic Center Dr Lbby Beverly Hills (90210) (P-13356)
Live Nation Worldwide Inc (HQ) .... A...... 310 867-7000
9348 Civic Center Dr Lbby Beverly Hills (90210) (P-14092)
Live Nation Worldwide Inc .... B...... 310 867-7000
325 N Maple Dr Beverly Hills (90210) (P-14148)
Live Oak Rehab, San Gabriel Also Called: Longwood Management Corp (P-15872)
Livefyre, San Francisco Also Called: Livefyre Inc (P-11712)
Livefyre Inc .... C...... 415 800-0900
360 3rd St Ste 700 San Francisco (94107) (P-11712)
Liveoffice LLC .... D...... 877 253-2793
900 Corporate Pointe Culver City (90230) (P-12256)
LIVERAMP, San Francisco Also Called: Liveramp Holdings Inc (P-12589)
Liveramp Inc (HQ) .... A...... 866 352-3267
225 Bush St Fl 17 San Francisco (94104) (P-20439)
Liveramp Holdings Inc (PA) .... B...... 888 987-6764
225 Bush St Fl 17 San Francisco (94104) (P-12589)
Livermoore Police Facility, Livermore Also Called: City of Livermore (P-20928)
Livermore Area Rcration Pk Dst (PA) .... B...... 925 373-5700
4444 East Ave Livermore (94550) (P-14542)
Livermore Pleasanton Fire Dept, Pleasanton Also Called: City of Pleasanton (P-20933)
Livermore Valley Athc CLB Inc .... D...... 925 443-7700
2000 Arroyo Rd Livermore (94550) (P-14149)
Liveuniverse Inc 310 492-2200
9255 W Sunset Blvd Ste 1010 West Hollywood (90069) (P-10714)
Livhome (PA) .... A...... 800 807-5854
5670 Wilshire Blvd Ste 500 Los Angeles (90036) (P-16890)
Living Centers, Vallejo Also Called: Empres Financial Services LLC (P-15446)
Living Colors Inc 818 893-5068
16034 Rayen St North Hills (91343) (P-1628)
Living Desert .... C...... 760 346-5694
47900 Portola Ave Palm Desert (92260) (P-18689)
Living Doll, La Puente Also Called: Ldla Clothing LLC (P-6204)
Living Spaces Furniture, San Leandro Also Called: Living Spaces Furniture LLC (P-7421)
Living Spaces Furniture LLC .... D...... 510 351-6783
250 Floresta Blvd San Leandro (94578) (P-7421)
Living Spaces Furniture LLC .... C...... 760 945-6805
1900 University Dr Vista (92083) (P-7422)

Living Spaces Furniture LLC (PA) .... C...... 714 523-2000
14501 Artesia Blvd La Mirada (90638) (P-7423)
Livingston Community Health (PA) .... D...... 209 394-7913
600 B St Bldg A Livingston (95334) (P-14876)
Livingston Health Center, Livingston Also Called: Livingston Community Health (P-14876)
Livingston Mem Vna Hlth Corp .... B...... 805 642-0239
1996 Eastman Ave Ste 101 Ventura (93003) (P-20143)
Livingston Mem Vsting Nrse Ass, Ventura Also Called: Livingston Mem Vna Hlth Corp (P-20143)
LJ Walch Co Inc .... D...... 925 449-9252
6600 Preston Ave Livermore (94551) (P-5961)
Ljg, Irvine Also Called: La Jolla Group Inc (P-13343)
LLC Bates White .... C...... 858 523-2150
322 8th St Del Mar (92014) (P-17552)
LLC Brewer Crane .... D...... 619 390-8252
12570 Highway 67 Lakeside (92040) (P-11002)
LLC Noble Rider (PA) .... D...... 209 566-7800
4300 Spyres Way Modesto (95356) (P-6179)
LLC Wilson Daniels .... D...... 707 963-9661
1300 Main St Ste 300 Napa (94559) (P-6801)
LLC Woodward West .... C...... 661 822-7900
28400 Stallion Springs Dr Tehachapi (93561) (P-10407)
Lloyd Staffing Inc .... A...... 631 777-7600
18000 Studebaker Rd Ste 700 Cerritos (90703) (P-11298)
LLP Mayer Brown .... D...... 650 331-2000
2 Palo Alto Sq Ste 300 Palo Alto (94306) (P-17553)
LLP Mayer Brown .... B...... 213 229-9500
350 S Grand Ave Ste 2500 Los Angeles (90071) (P-17554)
LLP Moss Adams .... D...... 916 503-8100
2882 Prospect Park Dr Ste 300 Rancho Cordova (95670) (P-19599)
LLP Moss Adams .... D...... 209 955-6100
3121 W March Ln Ste 100 Stockton (95219) (P-19600)
LLP Moss Adams .... D...... 415 956-1500
101 2nd St Ste 900 San Francisco (94105) (P-19601)
LLP Moss Adams .... D...... 408 369-2400
635 Campbell Technology Pkwy Ste 100 Campbell (95008) (P-19602)
LLP Moss Adams .... C...... 310 477-0450
21700 Oxnard St Ste 300 Woodland Hills (91367) (P-19603)
LLP Moss Adams .... C...... 949 221-4000
2040 Main St Ste 900 Irvine (92614) (P-19604)
LLP Moss Adams .... D...... 858 627-1400
4747 Executive Dr Ste 1300 San Diego (92121) (P-19605)
LLP Raines Feldman .... D...... 310 440-4100
1900 Avenue Of The Stars Los Angeles (90067) (P-17555)
LLUCH, Loma Linda Also Called: Loma Linda Univ Chld Hosp (P-9437)
LLUMC, Loma Linda Also Called: Loma Linda University Med Ctr (P-16226)
Lm Veterinary Enterprises Inc .... D...... 310 659-5287
8725 Santa Monica Blvd West Hollywood (90069) (P-335)
Lmb Opco LLC .... B...... 310 348-6800
12181 Bluff Creek Dr Ste 250 Playa Vista (90094) (P-8047)
LMC Hollywood Highland .... B...... 949 448-1600
95 Enterprise Ste 200 Aliso Viejo (92656) (P-961)
Lmi Inc (PA) .... D...... 650 453-8305
900 Middlefield Rd Fl 2 Redwood City (94063) (P-11713)
LMI Net .... D...... 510 843-6389
1700 Martin Luther King Jr Way Berkeley (94709) (P-4307)
Lmntrix LLC .... D...... 888 388-1879
333 City Blvd W Ste 1700 Orange (92868) (P-11714)
LMS Electric .... D...... 818 248-1165
2735 Honolulu Ave Montrose (91020) (P-1767)
LMS Electric, Montrose Also Called: LMS Electric (P-1767)
LN Curtis and Sons (PA) .... D...... 510 839-5111
185 Lennon Ln # 110 Walnut Creek (94598) (P-5944)
Load Delivered Logistics LLC .... C...... 310 822-0215
214 Main St Venice (90291) (P-3507)
Loan Administration Netwrk Inc .... D...... 949 752-5246
2082 Business Center Dr Ste 250 Irvine (92612) (P-11172)
Loan Factory, San Jose Also Called: Loan Factory Inc (P-7877)
Loan Factory Inc .... D...... 408 646-6662
2195 Tully Rd San Jose (95122) (P-7877)
Loan Signing System LLC .... D...... 619 878-3431
5694 Mission Center Rd San Diego (92108) (P-9075)

ALPHABETIC SECTION

Loandepot, Irvine *Also Called: Loandepot Inc (P-7992)*
Loandepot Inc .... B....... 209 323-7900
3555 Deer Park Dr Stockton (95219) *(P-7991)*
Loandepot Inc (PA) .... B....... 888 337-6888
6561 Irvine Center Dr Irvine (92618) *(P-7992)*
Loandepot Inc .... B....... 619 245-0115
2080 Otay Lakes Rd # 101 Chula Vista (91913) *(P-7993)*
Loandepot Inc .... B....... 949 470-6263
25500 Commercentre Dr Lake Forest (92630) *(P-7994)*
Loandepot Inc .... B....... 209 229-4120
3555 Deer Park Dr Ste 100 Stockton (95219) *(P-7995)*
Loandepotcom LLC .... A....... 209 846-6400
1020 15th St Ste 20 Modesto (95354) *(P-7996)*
Loandepotcom LLC 661 202-1700
42455 10th St W Ste 109 Lancaster (93534) *(P-7997)*
Loandepotcom LLC .... A....... 760 797-6000
901 N Palm Canyon Dr Ste 107 Palm Springs (92262) *(P-7998)*
Loandepotcom LLC (DH) .... A....... 888 337-6888
26642 Towne Centre Dr Foothill Ranch (92610) *(P-7999)*
Lobue Bros Inc (PA) .... D....... 559 562-2548
201 S Sweetbriar Ave Lindsay (93247) *(P-285)*
Lobue Citrus, Lindsay *Also Called: Lobue Bros Inc (P-285)*
Local 12, San Diego *Also Called: Interntional Un Oper Engineers (P-18782)*
Local 12, Redlands *Also Called: Interntional Un Oper Engineers (P-18783)*
Local 250 Health Care Wkrs Un, Oakland *Also Called: Health Care Workers Union (P-8724)*
Local Corporation (PA) .... D....... 949 784-0800
7555 Irvine Center Dr Irvine (92618) *(P-10643)*
Local Inttive Hlth Auth For Lo (PA) .... A....... 213 694-1250
1055 W 7th St Fl 10 Los Angeles (90017) *(P-8341)*
Local Lighthouse Corp .... D....... 888 370-8231
1525 Mesa Verde Dr E Ste 225 Costa Mesa (92626) *(P-4308)*
Local Media San Diego LLC .... D....... 858 888-7000
6160 Cornerstone Ct E Ste 150 San Diego (92121) *(P-4395)*
Local.com, Irvine *Also Called: Local Corporation (P-10643)*
Location Services LLC (PA) .... D....... 800 588-0097
2365 Iron Point Rd Ste 160 Folsom (95630) *(P-4166)*
Locator Services Inc .... C....... 619 229-6100
4616 Mission Gorge Pl San Diego (92120) *(P-12998)*
Lockheed Martin, San Jose *Also Called: Lockheed Martin Corporation (P-2893)*
Lockheed Martin, Chula Vista *Also Called: Lockheed Martin Services LLC (P-19307)*
Lockheed Martin Corporation .... D....... 408 473-3000
3130 Zanker Rd San Jose (95134) *(P-2893)*
Lockheed Martin Corporation .... C....... 760 386-2572
Bldg 821 South Loop Fort Irwin (92310) *(P-3725)*
Lockheed Martin Services LLC .... B....... 619 271-9831
645 Marsat Ct Ste D Chula Vista (91911) *(P-19307)*
Lockheed Martin Unmanned .... D....... 805 503-4340
125 Venture Dr Ste 110 San Luis Obispo (93401) *(P-12480)*
Lockheed Martin Unmndd, San Luis Obispo *Also Called: AME Unmanned Air Systems Inc (P-19137)*
Lockton Cmpnies LLC - PCF Srie (HQ) .... B....... 213 689-0500
777 S Figueroa St Ste 5200 Los Angeles (90017) *(P-8604)*
Lockton Insurance Brokers, Los Angeles *Also Called: Lockton Cmpnies LLC - PCF Srie (P-8604)*
Locums Unlimited LLC .... A....... 619 550-3763
4141 Jutland Dr Ste 305 San Diego (92117) *(P-15295)*
Loda Mem Hosp Occpational Hlth, Lodi *Also Called: Lodi Memorial Hosp Assn Inc (P-16217)*
Lodge At Tiburon, Belvedere Tiburon *Also Called: 1651 Tiburon Hotel LLC (P-9586)*
Lodgeworks LP .... D....... 707 690-9800
1230 1st St Napa (94559) *(P-9981)*
Lodging, San Diego *Also Called: Nomad Temporary Housing Inc (P-8847)*
Lodi Memorial Hosp Assn Inc .... D....... 209 339-7441
975 S Fairmont Ave Ste 8 Lodi (95240) *(P-16217)*
Lodi Memorial Hosp Assn Inc .... D....... 209 339-7583
1200 W Vine St Lodi (95240) *(P-16218)*
Lodi Memorial Hosp Assn Inc .... D....... 209 274-2183
395 Preston Ave Ione (95640) *(P-16219)*
Lodi Memorial Hosp Assn Inc (HQ) .... A....... 209 334-3411
975 S Fairmont Ave Lodi (95240) *(P-16220)*
Lodi Memorial Hospital .... C....... 209 204-5004
801 S Ham Ln Ste S Lodi (95242) *(P-14877)*

Lodi Regional Hlth Systems Inc .... B....... 209 948-0808
10200 Trinity Pkwy Ste 102 Stockton (95219) *(P-16221)*
Loeb & Loeb, Los Angeles *Also Called: Loeb & Loeb LLP (P-17556)*
Loeb & Loeb LLP (PA) .... C....... 310 282-2000
10100 Santa Monica Blvd Ste 2200 Los Angeles (90067) *(P-17556)*
Loews Coronado Bay Resort, Coronado *Also Called: 51st St & 8th Ave Corp (P-9593)*
Loews Hollywood Hotel LLC .... B....... 323 450-2235
1755 N Highland Ave Hollywood (90028) *(P-9982)*
Loews Regency San Francisco, San Francisco *Also Called: San Francisco Hotel Group LLC (P-10199)*
Loews Santa Monica Beach Hotel, Santa Monica *Also Called: Dtrs Santa Monica LLC (P-9767)*
Log(n) LLC .... D....... 323 839-4538
5651 Dreyer Pl Oakland (94619) *(P-2556)*
Logicmonitor Inc (PA) .... C....... 805 394-8632
820 State St Fl 5 Santa Barbara (93101) *(P-12673)*
Logigear Corporation (PA) .... A....... 650 572-1400
1730 S Amphlett Blvd Ste 110 San Mateo (94402) *(P-11715)*
Logik Systems Inc (HQ) .... D....... 844 363-3347
111 Sutter St San Francisco (94104) *(P-12674)*
Logikcull, San Francisco *Also Called: Logik Systems Inc (P-12674)*
Login Consulting Services Inc .... D....... 310 607-9091
300 Continental Blvd Ste 405 El Segundo (90245) *(P-12830)*
Loginext, Fremont *Also Called: Loginext Solutions Inc (P-12257)*
Loginext Solutions Inc .... C....... 510 894-6225
5002 Spring Crest Ter Fremont (94536) *(P-12257)*
Logistar LLC .... D....... 323 274-9651
448 S Hill St Ste 1101 Los Angeles (90013) *(P-5094)*
Logisteed America Inc .... D....... 323 263-8100
1000 Corporate Center Dr Ste 400 Monterey Park (91754) *(P-4050)*
Logisteed Monterey Park, Monterey Park *Also Called: Logisteed America Inc (P-4050)*
Logistical Support LLC .... C....... 818 341-3344
20409 Prairie St Chatsworth (91311) *(P-5962)*
Logistics, Bell *Also Called: De Well Container Shipping Inc (P-4003)*
Logix Federal Credit Union (PA) .... C....... 888 718-5328
2340 N Hollywood Way Burbank (91505) *(P-7779)*
Logix3, Irvine *Also Called: Data Council LLC (P-13258)*
Loglogic Inc .... C....... 408 215-5900
110 Rose Orchard Way Ste 200 San Jose (95134) *(P-11716)*
Logomark Inc .... C....... 714 675-6100
1201 Bell Ave Tustin (92780) *(P-6926)*
Lohika Systems Inc .... C....... 216 904-9751
1825 S Grant St Ste 400 San Mateo (94402) *(P-11717)*
Lois Lauer Realty (PA) .... C....... 909 748-7000
1998 Orange Tree Ln Redlands (92374) *(P-9076)*
Lollicup Franchising LLC .... C....... 626 965-8882
6185 Kimball Ave Chino (91708) *(P-20440)*
Loma Linda Catering Center, Loma Linda *Also Called: Loma Linda University Med Ctr (P-16227)*
Loma Linda Community Hospital, Loma Linda *Also Called: Loma Linda University Med Ctr (P-16225)*
Loma Linda Healthcare Sys 605, Loma Linda *Also Called: Veterans Health Administration (P-15190)*
Loma Linda Pharmacy, Loma Linda *Also Called: Loma Linda University Med Ctr (P-16224)*
Loma Linda Univ Chld Hosp .... C....... 909 558-8000
11234 Anderson St Loma Linda (92354) *(P-9437)*
Loma Linda University Med Ctr .... D....... 909 558-4000
1269 E San Bernardino Ave San Bernardino (92408) *(P-4051)*
Loma Linda University Med Ctr .... D....... 909 558-4000
26780 Barton Rd Redlands (92373) *(P-16222)*
Loma Linda University Med Ctr .... D....... 909 558-4385
11370 Anderson St Loma Linda (92354) *(P-16223)*
Loma Linda University Med Ctr .... C....... 909 558-4216
11223 Campus St Loma Linda (92354) *(P-16224)*
Loma Linda University Med Ctr .... C....... 909 796-0167
25333 Barton Rd Loma Linda (92350) *(P-16225)*
Loma Linda University Med Ctr (DH) .... A....... 909 558-4000
11234 Anderson St Loma Linda (92354) *(P-16226)*
Loma Linda University Med Ctr .... D....... 909 558-8244
11175 Campos St Loma Linda (92350) *(P-16227)*
Loma Linda University Med Ctr .... D....... 909 558-9275
1710 Barton Rd Redlands (92373) *(P-16228)*

Loma Linda University Med Ctr, Loma Linda Also Called: Loma Lnda - Inland Empire Cnsr (P-16229)
   Loma Lnda - Inland Empire Cnsr .... C 909 558-4000
     11234 Anderson St Loma Linda (92354) *(P-16229)*
   Loma Lnda Univ Fmly Med Group .... D 909 558-6600
     25455 Barton Rd Ste 204b Loma Linda (92354) *(P-14878)*
   Lombardy Holdings Inc (PA) .... **C 951 808-4550**
     151 Kalmus Dr Ste F6 Costa Mesa (92626) *(P-1232)*
LOMITA CARE CENTER, Lomita Also Called: Lomita Verde Inc (P-15866)
   Lomita Logistics LLC .... D 310 784-8485
     3541 Lomita Blvd Torrance (90505) *(P-10773)*
   Lomita Verde Inc .... D 310 325-1970
     1955 Lomita Blvd Lomita (90717) *(P-15866)*
Lompoc Family YMCA, Lompoc Also Called: Channel Islnds Yung MNS Chrstn (P-18835)
Lompoc Skilled Care Center, Lompoc Also Called: Lompoc Valley Medical Center (P-16231)
   Lompoc Valley Medical Center .... C 805 735-9229
     1111 E Ocean Ave Ste 2 Lompoc (93436) *(P-16230)*
   Lompoc Valley Medical Center (PA) .... B 805 737-3300
     1515 E Ocean Ave Lompoc (93436) *(P-16231)*
London Spitfire, Santa Monica Also Called: Cloud9 Esports Inc (P-20319)
   Lone Cypress Company LLC .... D 831 625-8563
     Stevenston & Spyglass Rd Pebble Beach (93953) *(P-9983)*
   Lone Cypress Company LLC (PA) .... C 831 647-7500
     2700 17 Mile Dr Pebble Beach (93953) *(P-14270)*
   Lone Cypress Company LLC .... D 831 625-8507
     1567 Cypress Dr Pebble Beach (93953) *(P-14396)*
   Lone Tree Cnvalescent Hosp Inc .... C 925 754-0470
     4001 Lone Tree Way Antioch (94509) *(P-15547)*
Lone Tree Post Acute, Antioch Also Called: Contra Loma Healthcare LLC (P-17209)
   Lonestar Sierra LLC .... C 866 575-5680
     1820 W Orangewood Ave Orange (92868) *(P-5907)*
Long Bch Dept Hlth & Humn Svcs, Long Beach Also Called: City of Long Beach (P-20937)
   Long Bch Museum Art Foundation .... D 562 439-2119
     2300 E Ocean Blvd Long Beach (90803) *(P-18654)*
Long Beach Airport, Long Beach Also Called: City of Long Beach (P-3882)
   Long Beach Care Center Inc .... C 562 426-6141
     2615 Grand Ave Long Beach (90815) *(P-15548)*
Long Beach Convention Center, Long Beach Also Called: Smg Holdings LLC (P-8762)
   Long Beach Golden Sails Inc .... D 562 596-1631
     23545 Crenshaw Blvd Ste 100 Torrance (90505) *(P-9984)*
Long Beach Hilton, The, Long Beach Also Called: World Trade Ctr Ht Assoc Ltd (P-10379)
Long Beach Marriott, Long Beach Also Called: Ruffin Hotel Corp of Cal (P-10182)
   Long Beach Medical Center .... C 562 933-7701
     450 E Spring St Ste 11 Long Beach (90806) *(P-16232)*
   Long Beach Medical Center (HQ) .... A 562 933-2000
     2801 Atlantic Ave Fl 2 Long Beach (90806) *(P-16233)*
   Long Beach Medical Center .... C 562 933-0085
     1720 Termino Ave Long Beach (90804) *(P-16234)*
Long Beach Medical Clinic, Long Beach Also Called: CB Tang MD Incorporated (P-14660)
   Long Beach Memorial Hospi .... D 562 933-2000
     24451 Health Center Dr Laguna Hills (92653) *(P-16235)*
   Long Beach Memorial Med Ctr .... C 562 933-0432
     1057 Pine Ave Long Beach (90813) *(P-16236)*
LONG BEACH MEMORIAL MEDICAL CENTER, Long Beach Also Called: Long Beach Memorial Med Ctr (P-16236)
Long Beach Pain Center, Long Beach Also Called: Healthsmart Pacific Inc (P-16124)
   Long Beach Public Trnsp Co (PA) .... A **562 599-8571**
     1963 E Anaheim St Long Beach (90813) *(P-3146)*
   Long Beach Public Trnsp Co .... D 562 591-2301
     1300 Gardenia Ave Long Beach (90804) *(P-3147)*
Long Beach Transit, Long Beach Also Called: Long Beach Public Trnsp Co (P-3146)
   Long Beach Unified School Dst .... C 562 426-6176
     2700 Pine Ave Long Beach (90806) *(P-3346)*
   Long Beach Unified School Dst .... D 562 426-5571
     3038 Delta Ave Long Beach (90810) *(P-17722)*
   Long Beach Yacht Club .... D 562 598-9401
     6201 E Appian Way Long Beach (90803) *(P-14397)*
   Long Point Development LLC .... A 310 265-2800
     100 Terranea Way Rancho Palos Verdes (90275) *(P-9985)*
   Longo Construction .... D 916 397-5869
     209 W Ascot Ave Rio Linda (95673) *(P-697)*

Longo Lexus, El Monte Also Called: El Monte Automotive Group Inc (P-7199)
Longo Scion, El Monte Also Called: D Longo Inc (P-7190)
Longs Drug Store, Patterson Also Called: Longs Drug Stores Cal LLC (P-3726)
   Longs Drug Stores Cal LLC .... A 209 895-7839
     2400 Keystone Pacific Pkwy Patterson (95363) *(P-3726)*
Longwood Management, San Dimas Also Called: San Dimas Retirement Center (P-8859)
   Longwood Management Corp .... C 310 679-1461
     11834 Inglewood Ave Hawthorne (90250) *(P-15549)*
   Longwood Management Corp .... D 818 360-1864
     17922 San Fernando Mission Blvd Granada Hills (91344) *(P-15550)*
   Longwood Management Corp .... C 626 280-2293
     8101 Hill Dr Rosemead (91770) *(P-15551)*
   Longwood Management Corp .... C 626 280-4820
     8035 Hill Dr Rosemead (91770) *(P-15552)*
   Longwood Management Corp .... C 323 933-1560
     1900 S Longwood Ave Los Angeles (90016) *(P-15553)*
   Longwood Management Corp .... D 323 735-5146
     2000 W Washington Blvd Los Angeles (90018) *(P-15867)*
   Longwood Management Corp .... D 818 246-7174
     605 W Broadway Glendale (91204) *(P-15868)*
   Longwood Management Corp .... D 323 737-7778
     2190 W Adams Blvd Los Angeles (90018) *(P-15869)*
   Longwood Management Corp .... C 213 382-8461
     1240 S Hoover St Los Angeles (90006) *(P-15870)*
   Longwood Management Corp .... C 818 980-8200
     11429 Ventura Blvd Studio City (91604) *(P-15871)*
   Longwood Management Corp .... C 626 289-3763
     537 W Live Oak St San Gabriel (91776) *(P-15872)*
   Longwood Management Corp .... C 562 432-5751
     1913 E 5th St Long Beach (90802) *(P-15873)*
   Longwood Management Corp .... D 562 693-5240
     7716 Pickering Ave Whittier (90602) *(P-16237)*
   Longwood Management Corp .... D 818 881-7414
     7836 Reseda Blvd Reseda (91335) *(P-16238)*
   Longwood Management Corp .... D 310 675-9163
     14110 Cordary Ave Hawthorne (90250) *(P-18475)*
   Lookout Inc (PA) .... C **650 241-2358**
     275 Battery St Ste 200 San Francisco (94111) *(P-12481)*
Loomworks Apparel, Irvine Also Called: Delta Galil USA Inc (P-6197)
   Loon LLC .... C 310 625-3449
     100 Mayfield Ave Mountain View (94043) *(P-13357)*
   Loon LLC (DH) .... D
     1600 Amphitheatre Pkwy Mountain View (94043) *(P-12675)*
   Looney Bins Inc (HQ) .... D **818 485-8200**
     12153 Montague St Pacoima (91331) *(P-4904)*
Loop, Mountain View Also Called: Samsung Pay Inc (P-13458)
Lopez & Associates Engineers, El Monte Also Called: R and L Lopez Associates Inc (P-19369)
   Lopezgarcia Group Inc (DH) .... C **415 796-8100**
     300 California St San Francisco (94104) *(P-19308)*
   Lorber Greenfield & Polito LLP (PA) .... D **858 486-6757**
     12975 Brookprinter Pl Ste 200 Poway (92064) *(P-17557)*
   Lord & Sons Inc .... D 562 529-2500
     10504 Pioneer Blvd Santa Fe Springs (90670) *(P-5908)*
Lorenzo USA, Solana Beach Also Called: Simon Golub & Sons Inc (P-6026)
Lorin Robinson Center, Redding Also Called: Shascade Community Svcs Inc (P-18130)
Loring Ward, San Jose Also Called: Bam Advisor Services LLC (P-8188)
Los Adobes De Maria, Santa Maria Also Called: Peoples Self-Help Housing Corp (P-20827)
   Los Alamitos Medical Ctr Inc (HQ) .... A **714 826-6400**
     3751 Katella Ave Los Alamitos (90720) *(P-16239)*
   Los Alamitos Race Course .... C 714 820-2800
     4961 Katella Ave Cypress (90720) *(P-7492)*
Los Altos, City Of Industry Also Called: Los Altos Food Products LLC (P-6440)
   Los Altos Food Products LLC .... C 626 330-6555
     450 Baldwin Park Blvd City Of Industry (91746) *(P-6440)*
   Los Altos Golf and Country CLB .... D 650 947-3100
     1560 Country Club Dr Los Altos (94024) *(P-14398)*
Los Altos Sb-Cute Rhbltition Ct, Los Altos Also Called: Covenant Care California LLC (P-15407)
Los Angeles Angels of Anaheim, Anaheim Also Called: Angels Baseball LP (P-14126)

ALPHABETIC SECTION

Los Angeles Athletic Club Inc .... C....... 213 625-2211
   431 W 7th St Los Angeles (90014) *(P-14216)*

Los Angeles Branch, Commerce *Also Called: Jfc International Inc* *(P-6639)*

Los Angeles Branch, Los Angeles *Also Called: Federal Rsrve Bnk San Frncisco* *(P-7602)*

Los Angeles Capital MGT LLC (PA)................................... D....... 310 479-9998
   11150 Santa Monica Blvd Ste 200 Los Angeles (90025) *(P-9377)*

Los Angeles Cardiology Assoc (HQ).................................. D....... 213 977-0419
   1245 Wilshire Blvd Ste 703 Los Angeles (90017) *(P-14879)*

Los Angeles Chargers, Costa Mesa *Also Called: Chargers Football Company LLC* *(P-14132)*

Los Angeles Church of Christ, Santa Monica *Also Called: Los Angeles Intl Ch Chrst* *(P-19023)*

Los Angeles City Hauling, Sun Valley *Also Called: USA Waste of California Inc* *(P-4948)*

Los Angeles Clippers, Los Angeles *Also Called: LA Sports Properties Inc* *(P-14146)*

Los Angeles Cnty Mseum of Art .... B....... 323 857-6000
   5905 Wilshire Blvd Los Angeles (90036) *(P-18655)*

Los Angeles Cold Storage, Los Angeles *Also Called: Standard-Southern Corporation* *(P-3661)*

Los Angeles Cold Storage Co, Los Angeles *Also Called: Standard-Southern Corporation* *(P-3659)*

LOS ANGELES COMMUNITY HOSPITAL, Los Angeles *Also Called: Paraclsus Los Angles Cmnty Hos* *(P-16315)*

Los Angeles Conven and Exh .... B....... 213 741-1151
   1201 S Figueroa St Los Angeles (90015) *(P-8733)*

Los Angeles Convention Center, Los Angeles *Also Called: AEG Management Lacc LLC* *(P-20013)*

Los Angeles Country Club .... C....... 310 276-6104
   10101 Wilshire Blvd Los Angeles (90024) *(P-14399)*

Los Angeles County Bar Assn (PA)................................... D....... 213 627-2727
   444 S Flower St Los Angeles (90071) *(P-18751)*

Los Angeles County Fair Assn (PA).................................. D....... 909 623-3111
   1101 W Mckinley Ave Pomona (91768) *(P-14543)*

Los Angeles County Hospital, Los Angeles *Also Called: Lac Usc Medical Center* *(P-16211)*

Los Angeles County Pub Works, South Gate *Also Called: County of Los Angeles* *(P-17214)*

Los Angeles Dept Convetion Tou, Los Angeles *Also Called: Los Angeles Conven and Exh* *(P-8733)*

Los Angeles Dept Wtr & Pwr .... A....... 310 524-8500
   12700 Vista Del Mar Playa Del Rey (90293) *(P-4759)*

Los Angeles Dept Wtr & Pwr .... A....... 760 873-0299
   300 Mandich St Bishop (93514) *(P-4802)*

Los Angeles Dept Wtr & Pwr .... A....... 323 256-8079
   4030 Crenshaw Blvd Los Angeles (90008) *(P-4803)*

Los Angeles Dept Wtr & Pwr .... A....... 213 367-1342
   11801 Sheldon St Sun Valley (91352) *(P-4804)*

Los Angeles Dept Wtr & Pwr .... A....... 213 367-4211
   1630 N Main St Los Angeles (90012) *(P-4805)*

Los Angeles Dept Wtr & Pwr .... A....... 760 878-2156
   201 S Webster St Independence (93526) *(P-4806)*

Los Angeles Dept Wtr & Pwr (HQ)..................................... A....... 213 367-1320
   111 N Hope St Los Angeles (90012) *(P-4807)*

Los Angeles Dept Wtr & Pwr .... A....... 213 367-5706
   1141 W 2nd St Bldg D Los Angeles (90012) *(P-4808)*

Los Angeles Education Partnr .... D....... 213 622-5237
   1541 Wilshire Blvd Ste 200 Los Angeles (90017) *(P-18607)*

Los Angeles Engineering Inc .... C....... 626 869-1400
   633 N Barranca Ave Covina (91723) *(P-19309)*

Los Angeles Federal Credit Un (PA)................................... D....... 818 242-8640
   300 S Glendale Ave Ste 100 Glendale (91205) *(P-7780)*

Los Angeles Federal Credit Un, Glendale *Also Called: Los Angeles Federal Credit Un* *(P-7780)*

Los Angeles Free Clinic .... C....... 323 653-1990
   5205 Melrose Ave Los Angeles (90038) *(P-14880)*

Los Angeles Free Clinic (PA).. D....... 323 653-8622
   8405 Beverly Blvd Los Angeles (90048) *(P-14881)*

Los Angeles Freightliner, Fontana *Also Called: Los Angeles Truck Centers LLC* *(P-5014)*

Los Angeles Homeless Svcs Auth .... A....... 213 683-3333
   707 Wilshire Blvd Ste 1000 Los Angeles (90017) *(P-18045)*

Los Angeles Intl Ch Chrst .... C....... 213 351-2300
   2716 Ocean Park Blvd Ste 2006 Santa Monica (90405) *(P-19023)*

Los Angeles Junction Rlwy Co .... C....... 323 277-2004
   4433 Exchange Ave Vernon (90058) *(P-3116)*

LOS ANGELES LAWYER MAGAZINE, Los Angeles *Also Called: Los Angeles County Bar Assn* *(P-18751)*

Los Angeles Lgbt Center (PA).. C....... 323 993-7618
   1625 Schrader Blvd Los Angeles (90028) *(P-18608)*

Los Angeles Ltg Mfg Co Inc .... D....... 626 454-8300
   10141 Olney St El Monte (91731) *(P-5575)*

Los Angeles Mem Coliseum Comm .... B....... 213 747-7111
   3911 S Figueroa St Los Angeles (90037) *(P-19092)*

Los Angeles Mission Inc (PA)... D....... 213 629-1227
   303 E 5th St Los Angeles (90013) *(P-18476)*

Los Angeles Opera Company .... B....... 213 972-7219
   135 N Grand Ave Ste 327 Los Angeles (90012) *(P-14043)*

Los Angeles Philharmonic Assn (PA)................................. C....... 213 972-7300
   151 S Grand Ave Los Angeles (90012) *(P-14093)*

Los Angeles Philharmonic Assn .... A....... 323 850-2060
   2301 N Highland Ave Los Angeles (90068) *(P-14094)*

Los Angeles Police Credit Un (PA)..................................... D....... 818 787-6520
   16150 Sherman Way Van Nuys (91406) *(P-7828)*

Los Angeles Rams LLC (PA).. D....... 314 982-7267
   29899 Agoura Rd Agoura Hills (91301) *(P-14150)*

Los Angeles Rams LLC .... C....... 310 277-4700
   10271 W Pico Blvd Los Angeles (90064) *(P-20144)*

Los Angeles Regional Food Bank .... C....... 323 234-3030
   1734 E 41st St Vernon (90058) *(P-18046)*

Los Angeles Residential Comm F .... D....... 661 296-8636
   29890 Bouquet Canyon Rd Santa Clarita (91390) *(P-18477)*

Los Angeles Sales Office, Northridge *Also Called: Harman International Inds Inc* *(P-5654)*

Los Angeles Sparks, Beverly Hills *Also Called: Gemini Basketball LLC* *(P-14140)*

Los Angeles Truck Centers LLC .... C....... 909 510-4000
   13800 Valley Blvd Fontana (92335) *(P-5014)*

Los Angeles Truck Centers LLC (PA)................................ D....... 562 447-1200
   2429 Peck Rd Whittier (90601) *(P-13666)*

Los Angeles Turf Club Inc (DH)... C....... 626 574-6330
   285 W Huntington Dr Arcadia (91007) *(P-14164)*

Los Angeles Unified School Dst .... D....... 310 808-1500
   17729 S Figueroa St Gardena (90248) *(P-10922)*

Los Angeles Unified School Dst .... C....... 562 654-9007
   8525 Rex Rd Pico Rivera (90660) *(P-13358)*

Los Angeles Unified School Dst .... D....... 818 360-2361
   10535 Zelzah Ave Granada Hills (91344) *(P-17723)*

Los Angeles Unified School Dst .... C....... 818 346-3540
   6200 Winnetka Ave Woodland Hills (91367) *(P-17724)*

Los Angeles Unified School Dst .... D....... 213 763-2900
   1240 Naomi Ave Los Angeles (90021) *(P-17765)*

Los Angeles World Airports (PA).. C....... 855 463-5252
   1 World Way Los Angeles (90045) *(P-3897)*

Los Angeles World Airports .... B....... 424 646-5900
   7301 World Way W Fl 5 Los Angeles (90045) *(P-3898)*

Los Angeles World Airports .... C....... 424 646-9118
   5312 W 99th Pl Los Angeles (90045) *(P-3899)*

Los Angles Arbrtum Fndtion Inc .... D....... 626 821-3222
   301 N Baldwin Ave Arcadia (91007) *(P-18690)*

Los Angles Area Chmber Cmmerce .... D....... 213 580-7500
   350 S Bixel St Los Angeles (90017) *(P-18712)*

Los Angles Cnty Cntl Jail Hosp, Los Angeles *Also Called: County of Los Angeles* *(P-16027)*

Los Angles Cnty Dept Mntal HLT .... D....... 213 738-4431
   3205 N Lakewood Blvd Long Beach (90808) *(P-17270)*

Los Angles Cnty Dept Mntal Hlt, Reseda *Also Called: County of Los Angeles* *(P-17911)*

Los Angles Cnty Dvlpmntal Svcs .... C....... 213 383-1300
   3303 Wilshire Blvd Ste 700 Los Angeles (90010) *(P-17271)*

Los Angles Cnty Employees Assn .... D....... 213 368-8660
   1545 Wilshire Blvd Los Angeles (90017) *(P-18787)*

Los Angles Cnty Emplyees Rtrme (PA)............................. C....... 626 564-6000
   300 N Lake Ave Ste 720 Pasadena (91101) *(P-8463)*

Los Angles Cnty Mseum Ntral Hs (PA).............................. C....... 213 763-3466
   900 Exposition Blvd Los Angeles (90007) *(P-20918)*

Los Angles Cnty Mtro Trnsp Aut .... B....... 310 643-3804
   14724 Aviation Blvd Lawndale (90260) *(P-3148)*

Los Angles Cnty Mtro Trnsp Aut (PA)............................... A....... 323 466-3876
   1 Gateway Plz Fl 25 Los Angeles (90012) *(P-3149)*

Los Angles Cnty Mtro Trnsp Aut .... A....... 213 922-5012
   470 Bauchet St Los Angeles (90012) *(P-3150)*

Los Angles Cnty Mtro Trnsp Aut .... A....... 310 392-8636
   100 Sunset Ave Venice (90291) *(P-3151)*

Los Angles Cnty Mtro Trnsp Aut — ALPHABETIC SECTION

Los Angles Cnty Mtro Trnsp Aut .... A....... 213 922-6308
 9201 Canoga Ave Chatsworth (91311) *(P-3152)*
Los Angles Cnty Mtro Trnsp Aut .... A....... 213 922-5887
 900 Lyon St Los Angeles (90012) *(P-3153)*
Los Angles Cnty Mtro Trnsp Aut .... B....... 213 922-6301
 1130 E 6th St Los Angeles (90021) *(P-3154)*
Los Angles Cnty Mtro Trnsp Aut .... B....... 213 922-6203
 630 W Avenue 28 Los Angeles (90065) *(P-3155)*
Los Angles Cnty Mtro Trnsp Aut .... A....... 213 922-6202
 1 Gateway Plaza Dr Los Angeles (90012) *(P-3156)*
Los Angles Cnty Mtro Trnsp Aut .... A....... 213 922-6207
 8800 Santa Monica Blvd Los Angeles (90069) *(P-3157)*
Los Angles Cnty Mtro Trnsp Aut .... A....... 213 922-6215
 11900 Branford St Sun Valley (91352) *(P-3158)*
Los Angles Cnty Mtro Trnsp Aut .... A....... 213 533-1506
 720 E 15th St Los Angeles (90021) *(P-3159)*
Los Angles Cnty Mtro Trnsp Aut .... A....... 213 244-6783
 818 W 7th St Ste 500 Los Angeles (90017) *(P-3160)*
Los Angles Cnty Mtro Trnsp Aut .... A....... 213 626-4455
 320 S Santa Fe Ave Los Angeles (90013) *(P-3161)*
Los Angles Cnty Rncho Los Amgo .... A....... 562 385-7111
 7601 Imperial Hwy Downey (90242) *(P-15771)*
Los Angles Cnty Snttion Dstrct (PA) .... A....... 562 699-7411
 1955 Workman Mill Rd Whittier (90601) *(P-4981)*
Los Angles Dst Off Policy Svcs, Monterey Park *Also Called: State Compensation Insur Fund (P-8420)*
Los Angles Fireman Relief Assn .... D....... 800 244-3439
 2900 W Temple St Los Angeles (90026) *(P-18047)*
Los Angles Jewish HM For Aging (PA) .... B....... 818 774-3000
 7150 Tampa Ave Reseda (91335) *(P-15554)*
Los Angles Jewish HM For Aging .... B....... 818 774-3000
 18855 Victory Blvd Reseda (91335) *(P-15555)*
Los Angles Ryal Vsta Golf Crse .... D....... 909 595-7441
 20055 Colima Rd Walnut (91789) *(P-14400)*
Los Angles Ryal Vsta Golf Crse, Walnut *Also Called: Los Angles Ryal Vsta Golf Crse (P-14400)*
Los Feliz Ford Inc (PA) .... D....... 818 502-1901
 1101 S Brand Blvd Glendale (91204) *(P-7253)*
Los Gatos Saratoga Dept of Com .... C....... 408 354-8700
 208 E Main St Los Gatos (95030) *(P-17811)*
Los Gatos Swim and Racquet CLB .... D....... 408 356-2136
 14700 Oka Rd Los Gatos (95032) *(P-14217)*
Los Palos Convalescent Hosp, San Pedro *Also Called: San Pedro Convalescent HM Inc (P-15653)*
Los Robles Hospital & Med Ctr, Thousand Oaks *Also Called: Los Robles Regional Med Ctr (P-16240)*
Los Robles Regional Med Ctr .... B....... 805 494-0880
 2200 Lynn Rd Thousand Oaks (91360) *(P-14882)*
Los Robles Regional Med Ctr .... B....... 805 370-4531
 150 Via Merida Westlake Village (91362) *(P-14883)*
Los Robles Regional Med Ctr (DH) .... A....... 805 497-2727
 215 W Janss Rd Thousand Oaks (91360) *(P-16240)*
Los Serranos Golf & Cntry CLB, Chino Hills *Also Called: Los Serranos Golf Club (P-14271)*
Los Serranos Golf Club .... C....... 909 597-1769
 15656 Yorba Ave Chino Hills (91709) *(P-14271)*
Loss and Risk Advisors, San Diego *Also Called: Barney & Barney Inc (P-8507)*
Lotus Clinical Research LLC .... D....... 626 381-9830
 100 W California Blvd Pasadena (91105) *(P-16734)*
Lotus Communications Corp (PA) .... D....... 323 512-2225
 3301 Barham Blvd Ste 200 Los Angeles (90068) *(P-4396)*
Lotus Hotels - Union City LLC .... D....... 510 475-0600
 31140 Alvarado Niles Rd Union City (94587) *(P-9986)*
Lotus Workforce LLC .... A....... 480 264-0773
 5930 Cornerstone Ct W Ste 300 San Diego (92121) *(P-20441)*
Louden Madelon, Vernon *Also Called: National Corset Supply House (P-2464)*
Louis F Mascola DDS .... C....... 310 986-2930
 3660 Lomita Blvd Torrance (90505) *(P-15235)*
Lounge Spa Inc .... D....... 310 745-1646
 4016 East Blvd Los Angeles (90066) *(P-14218)*
Loupe, San Francisco *Also Called: Plangrid Inc (P-12320)*
Lovazzano Mechanical Inc .... D....... 650 367-6216
 189 Constitution Dr Menlo Park (94025) *(P-1489)*

Lovco Construction, Signal Hill *Also Called: Lovco Construction Inc (P-2220)*
Lovco Construction Inc .... C....... 562 595-1601
 1300 E Burnett St Signal Hill (90755) *(P-2220)*
Love At First Bite Catering .... D....... 714 369-0561
 18281 Gothard St Ste 108 Huntington Beach (92648) *(P-7493)*
Lowe Enterprises .... D....... 530 581-6628
 400 Squaw Creek Rd Olympic Valley (96146) *(P-9987)*
Lowe Enterprises, Los Angeles *Also Called: Lowe Enterprises RE Group (P-9260)*
Lowe Enterprises Inc (PA) .... C....... 310 820-6661
 11777 San Vicente Blvd Ste 900 Los Angeles (90049) *(P-9988)*
Lowe Enterprises RE Group .... C....... 310 820-6661
 11777 San Vicente Blvd Ste 900 Los Angeles (90049) *(P-9260)*
Lowe Enterprises Rlty Svcs Inc .... A....... 818 990-9555
 16133 Ventura Blvd Ste 535 Encino (91436) *(P-9077)*
Lowe's, Perris *Also Called: Lowes Home Centers LLC (P-3727)*
Lowe's, Fresno *Also Called: Lowes Home Centers LLC (P-7030)*
Lowe's, Modesto *Also Called: Lowes Home Centers LLC (P-7031)*
Lowe's, Rancho Cucamonga *Also Called: Lowes Home Centers LLC (P-7032)*
Lowe's, Rancho Santa Margari *Also Called: Lowes Home Centers LLC (P-7033)*
Lowe's, San Diego *Also Called: Lowes Home Centers LLC (P-7034)*
Lowe's, Victorville *Also Called: Lowes Home Centers LLC (P-7035)*
Lowe's, Pacoima *Also Called: Lowes Home Centers LLC (P-7036)*
Lowe's, San Francisco *Also Called: Lowes Home Centers LLC (P-7037)*
Lowe's, Menifee *Also Called: Lowes Home Centers LLC (P-7038)*
Lowe's, Paso Robles *Also Called: Lowes Home Centers LLC (P-7039)*
Lowe's, Folsom *Also Called: Lowes Home Centers LLC (P-7040)*
Lowe's, San Clemente *Also Called: Lowes Home Centers LLC (P-7041)*
Lowe's, San Jose *Also Called: Lowes Home Centers LLC (P-7042)*
Lowe's, Riverside *Also Called: Lowes Home Centers LLC (P-7043)*
Lowe's, La Quinta *Also Called: Lowes Home Centers LLC (P-7044)*
Lowe's, Norwalk *Also Called: Lowes Home Centers LLC (P-7045)*
Lowe's, Fairfield *Also Called: Lowes Home Centers LLC (P-7046)*
Lowe's, Vacaville *Also Called: Lowes Home Centers LLC (P-7047)*
Lowe's, Antioch *Also Called: Lowes Home Centers LLC (P-7048)*
Lowe's, West Hills *Also Called: Lowes Home Centers LLC (P-7049)*
Lowe's, Upland *Also Called: Lowes Home Centers LLC (P-7050)*
Lowe's, Union City *Also Called: Lowes Home Centers LLC (P-7051)*
Lowe's, San Bruno *Also Called: Lowes Home Centers LLC (P-7052)*
Lowe's, Palm Springs *Also Called: Lowes Home Centers LLC (P-7053)*
Lowe's, Roseville *Also Called: Lowes Home Centers LLC (P-7054)*
Lowe's, Livermore *Also Called: Lowes Home Centers LLC (P-7055)*
Lowe's, Elk Grove *Also Called: Lowes Home Centers LLC (P-7056)*
Lowe's, Chico *Also Called: Lowes Home Centers LLC (P-7057)*
Lowe's, Burbank *Also Called: Lowes Home Centers LLC (P-7058)*
Lowe's, Anaheim *Also Called: Lowes Home Centers LLC (P-7059)*
Lowe's, Oceanside *Also Called: Lowes Home Centers LLC (P-7060)*
Lowe's, Stockton *Also Called: Lowes Home Centers LLC (P-7061)*
Lowe's, Murrieta *Also Called: Lowes Home Centers LLC (P-7062)*
Lowe's, Vista *Also Called: Lowes Home Centers LLC (P-7063)*
Lowe's, Pico Rivera *Also Called: Lowes Home Centers LLC (P-7065)*
Lowe's, Moreno Valley *Also Called: Lowes Home Centers LLC (P-7066)*
Lowe's, Gilroy *Also Called: Lowes Home Centers LLC (P-7067)*
Lowe's, Citrus Heights *Also Called: Lowes Home Centers LLC (P-7068)*
Lowe's, La Habra *Also Called: Lowes Home Centers LLC (P-7069)*
Lowe's, Palmdale *Also Called: Lowes Home Centers LLC (P-7070)*
Lowe's, Temecula *Also Called: Lowes Home Centers LLC (P-7071)*
Lowe's, Torrance *Also Called: Lowes Home Centers LLC (P-7072)*
Lowe's, Visalia *Also Called: Lowes Home Centers LLC (P-7073)*
Lowe's, Chula Vista *Also Called: Lowes Home Centers LLC (P-7074)*
Lowe's, Ventura *Also Called: Lowes Home Centers LLC (P-7075)*
Lowe's, Merced *Also Called: Lowes Home Centers LLC (P-7076)*
Lowe's, Fontana *Also Called: Lowes Home Centers LLC (P-7077)*
Lowe's, Clovis *Also Called: Lowes Home Centers LLC (P-7078)*
Lowe's, Corona *Also Called: Lowes Home Centers LLC (P-7079)*
Lowe's, Lodi *Also Called: Lowes Home Centers LLC (P-7080)*

Lowes Home Centers LLC

Lowe's, Hemet *Also Called: Lowes Home Centers LLC (P-7081)*
Lowe's, Santee *Also Called: Lowes Home Centers LLC (P-7082)*
Lowe's, Redlands *Also Called: Lowes Home Centers LLC (P-7083)*
Lowe's, Lancaster *Also Called: Lowes Home Centers LLC (P-7084)*
Lowe's, Fremont *Also Called: Lowes Home Centers LLC (P-7085)*
Lowe's, El Centro *Also Called: Lowes Home Centers LLC (P-7086)*
Lowe's, Apple Valley *Also Called: Lowes Home Centers LLC (P-7087)*
Lowe's, Lake Elsinore *Also Called: Lowes Home Centers LLC (P-7088)*
Lowe's, Simi Valley *Also Called: Lowes Home Centers LLC (P-7089)*
Lowe's, Northridge *Also Called: Lowes Home Centers LLC (P-7090)*
Lowe's, Cotati *Also Called: Lowes Home Centers LLC (P-7091)*
Lowe's, Jackson *Also Called: Lowes Home Centers LLC (P-7092)*
Lowe's, Sunnyvale *Also Called: Lowes Home Centers LLC (P-7093)*
Lowe's, Redding *Also Called: Lowes Home Centers LLC (P-7094)*
Lowe's, Ontario *Also Called: Lowes Home Centers LLC (P-7095)*
Lowe's, Tulare *Also Called: Lowes Home Centers LLC (P-7096)*
Lowe's, Escondido *Also Called: Lowes Home Centers LLC (P-7097)*
Lowe's, Yuba City *Also Called: Lowes Home Centers LLC (P-7098)*
Lowe's, Turlock *Also Called: Lowes Home Centers LLC (P-7099)*
Lowe's, Bakersfield *Also Called: Lowes Home Centers LLC (P-7100)*
Lowe's, City Of Industry *Also Called: Lowes Home Centers LLC (P-7101)*
Lowe's, Rancho Cordova *Also Called: Lowes Home Centers LLC (P-7102)*
Lowe's, Tustin *Also Called: Lowes Home Centers LLC (P-7103)*
Lowe's, Dublin *Also Called: Lowes Home Centers LLC (P-7104)*
Lowe's, Porterville *Also Called: Lowes Home Centers LLC (P-7105)*
Lowe's, Madera *Also Called: Lowes Home Centers LLC (P-7106)*
Lowe's, Chino Hills *Also Called: Lowes Home Centers LLC (P-7107)*
Lowe's, Santa Clarita *Also Called: Lowes Home Centers LLC (P-7108)*
Lowe's, Hanford *Also Called: Lowes Home Centers LLC (P-7109)*
Lowe's, Highland *Also Called: Lowes Home Centers LLC (P-7110)*
Lowe's, Concord *Also Called: Lowes Home Centers LLC (P-7111)*
Lowepro, Petaluma *Also Called: Daymen US Inc (P-5237)*

Lowermybills Inc .... C....... 310 348-6800
12181 Bluff Creek Dr Ste 250 Playa Vista (90094) *(P-12676)*
Lowermybills.com, Playa Vista *Also Called: Lmb Opco LLC (P-8047)*
Lowermybills.com, Playa Vista *Also Called: Lowermybills Inc (P-12676)*

Lowes Home Centers LLC .... C....... 951 443-2500
3984 Indian Ave Perris (92571) *(P-3727)*
Lowes Home Centers LLC .... C....... 559 436-6266
7651 N Blackstone Ave Fresno (93720) *(P-7030)*
Lowes Home Centers LLC .... C....... 209 545-7676
3801 Pelandale Ave Side Frnt Modesto (95356) *(P-7031)*
Lowes Home Centers LLC .... C....... 909 476-9697
11399 Foothill Blvd Rancho Cucamonga (91730) *(P-7032)*
Lowes Home Centers LLC .... D....... 949 589-5005
30481 Avenida De Las Flores Rancho Santa Margari (92688) *(P-7033)*
Lowes Home Centers LLC .... C....... 619 584-5500
2318 Northside Dr San Diego (92108) *(P-7034)*
Lowes Home Centers LLC .... D....... 760 949-9565
14333 Bear Valley Rd Victorville (92392) *(P-7035)*
Lowes Home Centers LLC .... D....... 818 686-4300
13500 Paxton St Pacoima (91331) *(P-7036)*
Lowes Home Centers LLC .... C....... 415 486-8611
491 Bay Shore Blvd San Francisco (94124) *(P-7037)*
Lowes Home Centers LLC .... C....... 951 723-1930
30472 Haun Rd Menifee (92584) *(P-7038)*
Lowes Home Centers LLC .... C....... 805 602-9051
2445 Golden Hill Rd Paso Robles (93446) *(P-7039)*
Lowes Home Centers LLC .... C....... 916 984-7979
800 E Bidwell St Folsom (95630) *(P-7040)*
Lowes Home Centers LLC .... C....... 949 369-4644
907 Avenida Pico San Clemente (92673) *(P-7041)*
Lowes Home Centers LLC .... D....... 408 518-4165
775 Ridder Park Dr San Jose (95131) *(P-7042)*
Lowes Home Centers LLC .... C....... 951 509-5500
9851 Magnolia Ave Riverside (92503) *(P-7043)*
Lowes Home Centers LLC .... C....... 760 771-5566
78865 Highway 111 La Quinta (92253) *(P-7044)*
Lowes Home Centers LLC .... D....... 562 926-0826
14873 Carmenita Rd Norwalk (90650) *(P-7045)*
Lowes Home Centers LLC .... C....... 707 207-2070
3400 N Texas St Fairfield (94533) *(P-7046)*
Lowes Home Centers LLC .... D....... 707 455-4400
1751 E Monte Vista Ave Vacaville (95688) *(P-7047)*
Lowes Home Centers LLC .... D....... 925 756-0370
1951 Auto Center Dr Antioch (94509) *(P-7048)*
Lowes Home Centers LLC .... C....... 818 610-1960
8383 Topanga Canyon Blvd West Hills (91304) *(P-7049)*
Lowes Home Centers LLC .... D....... 909 982-4795
1659 W Foothill Blvd Upland (91786) *(P-7050)*
Lowes Home Centers LLC .... D....... 510 476-0600
32040 Union Lndg Union City (94587) *(P-7051)*
Lowes Home Centers LLC .... C....... 650 616-7800
1340 El Camino Real San Bruno (94066) *(P-7052)*
Lowes Home Centers LLC .... C....... 760 866-1901
5201 E Ramon Rd Palm Springs (92264) *(P-7053)*
Lowes Home Centers LLC .... D....... 916 771-7111
10201 Fairway Dr Roseville (95678) *(P-7054)*
Lowes Home Centers LLC .... D....... 925 245-2440
4255 1st St Livermore (94551) *(P-7055)*
Lowes Home Centers LLC .... C....... 916 688-1922
8369 Power Inn Rd Elk Grove (95624) *(P-7056)*
Lowes Home Centers LLC .... D....... 530 895-5130
2350 Forest Ave Chico (95928) *(P-7057)*
Lowes Home Centers LLC .... C....... 818 557-2300
2000 W Empire Ave Burbank (91504) *(P-7058)*
Lowes Home Centers LLC .... D....... 714 447-6140
1500 N Lemon St Anaheim (92801) *(P-7059)*
Lowes Home Centers LLC .... C....... 760 966-7140
155 Old Grove Rd Oceanside (92057) *(P-7060)*
Lowes Home Centers LLC .... D....... 209 956-7200
3645 E Hammer Ln Stockton (95212) *(P-7061)*
Lowes Home Centers LLC .... C....... 951 461-8916
24701 Madison Ave Murrieta (92562) *(P-7062)*
Lowes Home Centers LLC .... C....... 760 631-6255
151 Vista Village Dr Vista (92083) *(P-7063)*
Lowes Home Centers LLC .... C....... 323 327-4000
2800 W 120th St Hawthorne (90250) *(P-7064)*
Lowes Home Centers LLC .... C....... 562 942-9909
8600 Washington Blvd Pico Rivera (90660) *(P-7065)*
Lowes Home Centers LLC .... D....... 951 656-1859
12400 Day St Moreno Valley (92553) *(P-7066)*
Lowes Home Centers LLC .... D....... 408 413-6000
7151 Camino Arroyo Gilroy (95020) *(P-7067)*
Lowes Home Centers LLC .... D....... 916 728-7800
7840 Greenback Ln Citrus Heights (95610) *(P-7068)*
Lowes Home Centers LLC .... C....... 562 690-5122
1380 S Beach Blvd La Habra (90631) *(P-7069)*
Lowes Home Centers LLC .... D....... 661 267-9888
39500 Lowes Dr Palmdale (93551) *(P-7070)*
Lowes Home Centers LLC .... C....... 951 296-1618
40390 Winchester Rd Temecula (92591) *(P-7071)*
Lowes Home Centers LLC .... C....... 310 787-1469
22255 S Western Ave Torrance (90501) *(P-7072)*
Lowes Home Centers LLC .... C....... 559 624-4300
4144 S Mooney Blvd Visalia (93277) *(P-7073)*
Lowes Home Centers LLC .... C....... 619 739-9060
2225 Otay Lakes Rd Chula Vista (91915) *(P-7074)*
Lowes Home Centers LLC .... D....... 805 675-8800
500 S Mills Rd Ventura (93003) *(P-7075)*
Lowes Home Centers LLC .... C....... 209 385-5000
1750 W Olive Ave Merced (95348) *(P-7076)*
Lowes Home Centers LLC .... C....... 909 350-7900
16851 Sierra Lakes Pkwy Fontana (92336) *(P-7077)*
Lowes Home Centers LLC .... C....... 559 322-3000
875 Shaw Ave Clovis (93612) *(P-7078)*
Lowes Home Centers LLC .... D....... 951 256-9004
1285 Magnolia Ave Corona (92879) *(P-7079)*
Lowes Home Centers LLC .... C....... 209 339-2600
1389 S Lower Sacramento Rd Lodi (95242) *(P-7080)*

Lowes Home Centers LLC | ALPHABETIC SECTION

Lowes Home Centers LLC .... D....... 951 492-7000
  350 S Sanderson Ave Hemet (92545) *(P-7081)*

Lowes Home Centers LLC .... C....... 619 212-4100
  9416 Mission Gorge Rd Santee (92071) *(P-7082)*

Lowes Home Centers LLC .... D....... 909 307-8883
  1725 W Redlands Blvd Redlands (92373) *(P-7083)*

Lowes Home Centers LLC .... D....... 661 341-9000
  730 W Avenue K Lancaster (93534) *(P-7084)*

Lowes Home Centers LLC .... D....... 510 344-4920
  43612 Pacific Commons Blvd Fremont (94538) *(P-7085)*

Lowes Home Centers LLC .... D....... 760 337-6700
  2053 N Imperial Ave El Centro (92243) *(P-7086)*

Lowes Home Centers LLC .... D....... 760 961-3000
  12189 Apple Valley Rd Apple Valley (92308) *(P-7087)*

Lowes Home Centers LLC .... C....... 951 253-6000
  29335 Central Ave Lake Elsinore (92532) *(P-7088)*

Lowes Home Centers LLC .... D....... 805 426-2780
  1275 Simi Town Center Way Simi Valley (93065) *(P-7089)*

Lowes Home Centers LLC .... D....... 818 477-9022
  19601 Nordhoff St Northridge (91324) *(P-7090)*

Lowes Home Centers LLC .... D....... 707 242-5000
  7921 Redwood Dr Cotati (94931) *(P-7091)*

Lowes Home Centers LLC .... D....... 209 223-6140
  12071 Industry Blvd Jackson (95642) *(P-7092)*

Lowes Home Centers LLC .... C....... 408 470-1680
  811 E Arques Ave Sunnyvale (94085) *(P-7093)*

Lowes Home Centers LLC .... D....... 530 351-0181
  1200 E Cypress Ave Redding (96002) *(P-7094)*

Lowes Home Centers LLC .... C....... 909 969-9053
  2390 S Grove Ave Ontario (91761) *(P-7095)*

Lowes Home Centers LLC .... D....... 559 366-5000
  1145 E Prosperity Ave Tulare (93274) *(P-7096)*

Lowes Home Centers LLC .... C....... 760 484-5113
  620 W Mission Ave Escondido (92025) *(P-7097)*

Lowes Home Centers LLC .... D....... 530 844-5000
  935 Tharp Rd Yuba City (95993) *(P-7098)*

Lowes Home Centers LLC .... D....... 209 656-3020
  3303 Entertainment Way Turlock (95380) *(P-7099)*

Lowes Home Centers LLC .... C....... 661 889-9000
  1601 Columbus St Bakersfield (93305) *(P-7100)*

Lowes Home Centers LLC .... D....... 626 217-1133
  17789 Castleton St City Of Industry (91748) *(P-7101)*

Lowes Home Centers LLC .... C....... 916 267-2850
  3251 Zinfandel Dr Rancho Cordova (95670) *(P-7102)*

Lowes Home Centers LLC .... C....... 714 913-2663
  2500 Park Ave Tustin (92782) *(P-7103)*

Lowes Home Centers LLC .... D....... 925 241-3082
  3750 Dublin Blvd Dublin (94568) *(P-7104)*

Lowes Home Centers LLC .... C....... 559 306-5000
  500 W Vandalia Ave Porterville (93257) *(P-7105)*

Lowes Home Centers LLC .... C....... 559 416-4000
  2100 W Cleveland Ave Madera (93637) *(P-7106)*

Lowes Home Centers LLC .... C....... 909 438-9000
  4777 Chino Hills Pkwy Chino Hills (91709) *(P-7107)*

Lowes Home Centers LLC .... C....... 661 678-4430
  19001 Golden Valley Rd Santa Clarita (91387) *(P-7108)*

Lowes Home Centers LLC .... C....... 559 410-9000
  1955 W Lacey Blvd Hanford (93230) *(P-7109)*

Lowes Home Centers LLC .... D....... 909 557-9010
  27847 Greenspot Rd Highland (92346) *(P-7110)*

Lowes Home Centers LLC .... D....... 925 566-9000
  1935 Arnold Industrial Way Concord (94520) *(P-7111)*

Lowrys Inc .... D....... 818 768-4661
  8501 Telfair Ave Sun Valley (91352) *(P-5909)*

Loyal3, San Francisco *Also Called: Loyal3 Holdings Inc (P-13359)*

Loyal3 Holdings Inc .... C....... 415 981-0700
  150 California St Ste 400 San Francisco (94111) *(P-13359)*

Loyda Yu Real Estate Inc .... C....... 619 475-7777
  860 Kuhn Dr Ste 200 Chula Vista (91914) *(P-9078)*

Lozano Car Wash, Mountain View *Also Called: Lozano Inc (P-13700)*

Lozano Caseworks Inc .... D....... 909 783-7530
  242 W Hanna St Colton (92324) *(P-2007)*

Lozano Inc .... C....... 650 941-0590
  2690 W El Camino Real Mountain View (94040) *(P-13700)*

Lozano Plumbing Services Inc .... C....... 951 683-4840
  3615 Presley Ave Riverside (92507) *(P-1490)*

Lozano Smith LLP .... C....... 559 431-5600
  7404 N Spalding Ave Fresno (93720) *(P-17558)*

LPA Inc (PA) .... C....... **949 261-1001**
  5301 California Ave Ste 100 Irvine (92617) *(P-19487)*

Lpa Insurance Agency Inc .... C....... 916 286-7850
  3800 Watt Ave Ste 147 Sacramento (95821) *(P-12258)*

Lpas Inc .... D....... 916 443-0335
  723 S St Sacramento (95811) *(P-19488)*

LPC Commercial Services Inc .... C....... 213 362-9080
  915 Wilshire Blvd Ste 250 Los Angeles (90017) *(P-9261)*

LPC COMMERCIAL SERVICES, INC., Los Angeles *Also Called: LPC Commercial Services Inc (P-9261)*

Lpcc, Camarillo *Also Called: Las Posas Country Club (P-14395)*

Lpl Financial Holdings Inc (PA) .... B....... **800 877-7210**
  4707 Executive Dr San Diego (92121) *(P-8100)*

Lpl Holdings, San Diego *Also Called: Lpl Holdings Inc (P-20442)*

Lpl Holdings Inc (HQ) .... D....... **858 450-9606**
  4707 Executive Dr San Diego (92121) *(P-20442)*

Lplfh, San Diego *Also Called: Lpl Financial Holdings Inc (P-8100)*

Lpsh Holdings Inc (PA) .... D....... **855 647-5061**
  7100 W Florida Ave Hemet (92545) *(P-1491)*

Lpsh Holdings Inc .... B....... 951 926-1176
  3570 W Florida Ave Ste 168 Hemet (92545) *(P-1492)*

Lq Management LLC .... D....... 310 645-2200
  5249 W Century Blvd Los Angeles (90045) *(P-9989)*

Lqr Property LLC .... C....... 760 564-4111
  49499 Eisenhower Dr La Quinta (92253) *(P-9990)*

Lres Corporation (PA) .... D....... **714 520-5737**
  765 The City Dr S Orange (92868) *(P-9079)*

Lrw Group, Los Angeles *Also Called: Material Holdings LLC (P-19831)*

Ls9 Inc .... D....... 650 243-5400
  600 Gateway Blvd South San Francisco (94080) *(P-19730)*

Lsa Associates Inc (PA) .... C....... **949 553-0666**
  3210 El Camino Real Ste 100 Irvine (92602) *(P-20800)*

Lsf9 Cypress LP (PA) .... C....... **714 380-3127**
  2741 Walnut Ave Ste 200 Tustin (92780) *(P-5228)*

Lsf9 Cypress Parent 2 LLC .... A....... 714 380-3127
  2741 Walnut Ave Ste 200 Tustin (92780) *(P-5229)*

Lta Research & Exploration LLC (PA) .... D....... **408 396-0577**
  642 N Pastoria Ave Sunnyvale (94085) *(P-20443)*

Ltc Construction Inc (HQ) .... D....... **916 246-9987**
  93540 Viking Pl Roseville (95747) *(P-441)*

LTI Boyd .... A....... 800 554-0200
  600 S Mcclure Rd Modesto (95357) *(P-2785)*

Ltl Ex Inc .... D....... 951 255-1222
  11081 Cherry Ave Fontana (92337) *(P-4052)*

Ltl Pros Inc .... D....... 909 350-1600
  13610 S Archibald Ave Ontario (91761) *(P-3508)*

Lubin Olson & Niewiadomski LLP .... D....... 415 981-0550
  600 Montgomery St Fl 14 San Francisco (94111) *(P-17559)*

Lucas Digital Ltd (DH) .... B....... **415 258-2000**
  3155 Kerner Blvd San Rafael (94901) *(P-14044)*

Lucas Museum of Narrative Art .... D....... 831 566-9332
  700 S Flower St Ste 2400 Los Angeles (90017) *(P-18656)*

Lucasfilm Coml Productions, San Francisco *Also Called: Lucasfilm Ltd LLC (P-13862)*

Lucasfilm Ltd LLC (DH) .... C....... **415 623-1000**
  1110 Gorgas Ave Bldg C San Francisco (94129) *(P-13862)*

Lucero Dental Clinic .... D....... 714 557-0201
  2740 S Bristol St Ste 206 Santa Ana (92704) *(P-15236)*

Lucid Design Group Inc .... D....... 510 907-0400
  55 Harrison St Ste 200 Oakland (94607) *(P-12482)*

Lucid Motors, Newark *Also Called: Lucid Usa Inc (P-2966)*

Lucid Usa Inc (HQ) .... C....... **510 648-3553**
  7373 Gateway Blvd Newark (94560) *(P-2966)*

Lucidlink Corp .... D....... 650 517-0855
  58 West Portal Ave # 256 San Francisco (94127) *(P-11718)*

Lucidworks Inc (PA) .... C....... **415 329-6515**
  235 Montgomery St Ste 500 San Francisco (94104) *(P-12483)*

ALPHABETIC SECTION

LUCILE PACKARD CHILDREN'S HOSP, Palo Alto *Also Called: Packard Childrens Hlth Aliance (P-14947)*

Lucile Packard Childrens Hosp, Palo Alto *Also Called: Lucile Slter Pckard Chld Hosp (P-16686)*

Lucile Slter Pckard Chld Hosp (HQ) .... A....... 650 497-8000
　725 Welch Rd Palo Alto (94304) *(P-16686)*

Lucix, Camarillo *Also Called: Lucix Corporation (P-2944)*

Lucix Corporation (HQ) .... D....... 805 987-6645
　800 Avenida Acaso Ste E Camarillo (93012) *(P-2944)*

Lucky 7 Casino, Smith River *Also Called: Smith River Lucky 7 Casino (P-10249)*

Lucky Chances Inc .... A....... 650 758-2237
　1700 Hillside Blvd Colma (94014) *(P-9991)*

Lucky Chances Casino, Colma *Also Called: Lucky Chances Inc (P-9991)*

Lucky Farms Inc .... D....... 909 799-6688
　1194 E Brier Dr San Bernardino (92408) *(P-36)*

Lucky Stores II LLC 209 830-1977
　875 S Tracy Blvd Tracy (95376) *(P-7145)*

Lucky Strike Entertainment Inc .... B....... 213 542-4880
　800 W Olympic Blvd Ste 250 Los Angeles (90015) *(P-14116)*

Lucky Strike Entertainment LLC .... D....... 818 933-3752
　6801 Hollywood Blvd Ste 143 Los Angeles (90028) *(P-14117)*

Lucky Strike Entertainment LLC .... D....... 248 374-3420
　15260 Ventura Blvd Ste 1110 Sherman Oaks (91403) *(P-14118)*

Lucky Strike Entertainment LLC .... D....... 248 374-3420
　20 City Blvd W Ste G2 Orange (92868) *(P-14119)*

Lucky Strike Novi, Sherman Oaks *Also Called: Lucky Strike Entertainment LLC (P-14118)*

Lukes Local Inc .... D....... 415 742-4207
　960 Cole St San Francisco (94117) *(P-6262)*

Luma Pictures Inc .... C....... 310 888-8738
　1453 3rd Street Promenade Ste 400 Santa Monica (90401) *(P-13863)*

Lumber City Corp .... D....... 805 522-0533
　2695 Cochran St Simi Valley (93065) *(P-7123)*

Lumen Tech Gvrnment Sltons Inc .... A....... 916 781-7772
　2240 Douglas Blvd Ste 250 Roseville (95661) *(P-4309)*

Lumicity LLC .... D....... 213 262-2064
　7901 Santa Monica Blvd Ste 205 West Hollywood (90046) *(P-11173)*

Lumin Digital LLC .... D....... 727 561-2227
　3001 Bishop Dr Ste 110 San Ramon (94583) *(P-11719)*

Lumina Alliance .... D....... 805 781-6400
　51 Zaca Ln Ste 150 San Luis Obispo (93401) *(P-18048)*

Luminance, Rancho Cucamonga *Also Called: American De Rosa Lamparts LLC (P-804)*

Luminary Cloud Inc .... D....... 650 279-9579
　500 Arguello St Ste 105 Palo Alto (94305) *(P-11720)*

Luminary Group The, San Francisco *Also Called: Side Inc (P-9179)*

Luminous Computing Inc .... D....... 650 275-5950
　4750 Patrick Henry Dr Santa Clara (95054) *(P-12831)*

Lumiradx Inc .... C....... 951 201-9384
　444 S Cedros Ave Ste 101 Solana Beach (92075) *(P-11721)*

Lund Construction Co .... C....... 916 344-5800
　5302 Roseville Rd North Highlands (95660) *(P-19310)*

Lundberg Family Farms, Richvale *Also Called: Wehah-Lundberg Inc (P-2363)*

Lundquist Institute For Biomedical Innovation At Harbor-Ucla Medical Center 877 452-2674
　1124 W Carson St Torrance (90502) *(P-19894)*

Luppen and Hawley Inc .... C....... 916 456-7831
　6330 N Point Way Sacramento (95831) *(P-1493)*

Lupton Excavation Inc .... D....... 916 387-1104
　8467 Florin Rd Sacramento (95828) *(P-2221)*

Lusamerica Foods Inc (PA) .... D....... 408 778-7200
　16480 Railroad Ave Morgan Hill (95037) *(P-6473)*

Lusardi Construction Co .... C....... 925 829-1114
　6376 Clark Ave Dublin (94568) *(P-962)*

Lutema, San Diego *Also Called: MI Technologies Inc (P-2674)*

Luth Research Inc (PA) .... B....... 619 234-5884
　404 Camino Del Rio S Ste 505 San Diego (92108) *(P-19830)*

Luther Burbank Mem Foundation .... D....... 707 546-3600
　50 Mark West Springs Rd Santa Rosa (95403) *(P-14045)*

Luxe City Center, Los Angeles *Also Called: Emerik Hotel Corp (P-9781)*

Luxe Sunset Boulevard Hotel, Los Angeles *Also Called: E H Summit Inc (P-9769)*

Luxre Realty Inc .... D....... 949 498-3702
　222 Avenida Del Mar San Clemente (92672) *(P-9080)*

Luxury Presence Inc .... C....... 310 955-1077
　2805 W 233rd St Torrance (90505) *(P-12484)*

Lyell Immunopharma Inc .... D....... 650 383-5381
　401 E Jamie Ct South San Francisco (94080) *(P-19731)*

LYFT, San Francisco *Also Called: Lyft Inc (P-3274)*

Lyft Inc (PA) .... B....... 844 250-2773
　185 Berry St Ste 400 San Francisco (94107) *(P-3274)*

Lyle Company .... D....... 916 266-7000
　3140 Gold Camp Dr Ste 30 Rancho Cordova (95670) *(P-20801)*

Lymi Inc (PA) .... D....... 855 756-0560
　2744 E 11th St Los Angeles (90023) *(P-6205)*

Lynch Ambulance Service, Anaheim *Also Called: Filyn Corporation (P-3261)*

Lynwood Unified School Dst .... D....... 310 631-7308
　12120 Lindbergh Ave Lynwood (90262) *(P-17725)*

Lyon & Associates Realtors, Sacramento *Also Called: William L Lyon & Assoc Inc (P-9219)*

Lyon Realtors, Fair Oaks *Also Called: William L Lyon & Assoc Inc (P-9220)*

Lyon Realty .... C....... 530 295-4444
　4340 Golden Center Dr Ste A Placerville (95667) *(P-8887)*

Lyon Realty .... C....... 916 784-1500
　2220 Douglas Blvd Ste 100 Roseville (95661) *(P-9081)*

Lyon Realty .... C....... 916 481-3840
　2580 Fair Oaks Blvd Ste 20 Sacramento (95825) *(P-9082)*

Lyon Realty .... C....... 916 787-7700
　851 Pleasant Grove Blvd Ste 150 Roseville (95678) *(P-9083)*

Lyon Realty .... C....... 916 962-0111
　8814 Madison Ave Fair Oaks (95628) *(P-9084)*

Lyon Realty .... C....... 916 939-5300
　3900 Park Dr El Dorado Hills (95762) *(P-9085)*

Lyon Realty (PA) .... D....... 916 574-8800
　2280 Del Paso Rd Ste 100 Sacramento (95834) *(P-9086)*

Lyon Stahl Investment RE Inc .... D....... 310 425-9838
　239 Oregon St El Segundo (90245) *(P-9087)*

Lyra Administrative Services, Burlingame *Also Called: Lyra Health Inc (P-14884)*

Lyra Health Inc .... C....... 800 505-5972
　270 East Ln Burlingame (94010) *(P-14884)*

Lytton Rancheria .... A....... 510 215-7888
　13255 San Pablo Ave San Pablo (94806) *(P-9992)*

M & C, Los Angeles *Also Called: Murchison & Cumming LLP (P-17582)*

M & E Technical Services L L C .... D....... 256 964-6486
　3601 Bayview Dr Manhattan Beach (90266) *(P-20658)*

M & G Jewelers Inc .... C....... 909 989-2929
　10823 Edison Ct Rancho Cucamonga (91730) *(P-7551)*

M & H Realty Partners LP .... D....... 415 693-9000
　353 Sacramento St Fl 21 San Francisco (94111) *(P-9528)*

M & M Distributors, Los Angeles *Also Called: Wiemar Distributors Inc (P-6597)*

M & M Electric, Sacramento *Also Called: May-Han Electric Inc (P-1771)*

M & M Noori Dental Corp .... D....... 909 476-3000
　4323 Mills Cir Ste 101 Ontario (91764) *(P-15237)*

M & M Plumbing Inc .... D....... 951 354-5388
　6782 Columbus St Riverside (92504) *(P-1494)*

M & N Consulting Inc .... D....... 818 349-9400
　21358 Nordhoff St Chatsworth (91311) *(P-3619)*

M & R Joint Venture Electrical .... D....... 909 598-7700
　231 Benton Ct Walnut (91789) *(P-1768)*

M & S Acquisition Corporation (PA) .... C....... 213 385-1515
　707 Wilshire Blvd Ste 5200 Los Angeles (90017) *(P-9088)*

M & S Security Services Inc .... D....... 661 397-9616
　2900 L St Bakersfield (93301) *(P-12999)*

M & S Trading Inc .... D....... 714 241-7190
　15778 Gateway Cir Tustin (92780) *(P-6180)*

M A A C Project, Chula Vista *Also Called: Metropiltan Area Advsory Cmmtte (P-18234)*

M A C, Northridge *Also Called: Mikuni American Corporation (P-5050)*

M Arthur Gensler Jr Assoc Inc (PA) .... B....... 415 433-3700
　220 Montgomery St Ste 200 San Francisco (94104) *(P-19489)*

M Arthur Gensler Jr Assoc Inc .... C....... 213 927-3600
　500 S Figueroa St Los Angeles (90071) *(P-19490)*

M Arthur Gensler Jr Assoc Inc .... C....... 949 863-9434
　4675 Macarthur Ct Ste 100 Newport Beach (92660) *(P-19491)*

M B, San Jose *Also Called: Marquez Brothers Intl Inc (P-6264)*

M B M, Pleasanton *Also Called: McLane Foodservice Dist Inc (P-6423)*

ALPHABETIC SECTION

M Bar C Construction Inc .... D...... 760 744-4131
  1770 La Costa Meadows Dr San Marcos (92078) *(P-2187)*

M C, Los Angeles *Also Called: Muir-Chase Plumbing Co (P-1503)*

M C C, Brea *Also Called: Mercury Casualty Company (P-8390)*

M C C Equipment Rentals Inc .... D...... 909 795-9300
  32389 Dunlap Blvd Yucaipa (92399) *(P-1233)*

M Caratan Disc Inc .... C...... 661 725-2566
  33787 Cecil Ave Delano (93215) *(P-80)*

M D S I, Chowchilla *Also Called: Madera Disposal Systems Inc (P-4905)*

M E I, Santa Barbara *Also Called: Motion Engineering Inc (P-2834)*

M F Maher Inc .... D...... 707 552-2774
  490 Ryder St Vallejo (94590) *(P-2136)*

M F Salta Co Inc (PA) .... D...... 562 421-2512
  20 Executive Park Ste 150 Irvine (92614) *(P-20444)*

M Gaw Inc .... D...... 818 503-7997
  6910 Farmdale Ave North Hollywood (91605) *(P-2294)*

M H Deyoung Memorial, San Francisco *Also Called: Corportion of Fine Arts Mseums (P-18648)*

M I G, Berkeley *Also Called: Moore Iacofano Goltsman Inc (P-20806)*

M K Smith Chevrolet .... C...... 909 628-8961
  12845 Central Ave Chino (91710) *(P-7254)*

M L Stern & Co LLC (DH) .... C...... 323 658-4400
  8350 Wilshire Blvd Ste 300 Beverly Hills (90211) *(P-8101)*

M M C, Covina *Also Called: Davita Magan Management Inc (P-14722)*

M M Fab Inc .... D...... 310 763-3800
  2300 E Gladwick St Compton (90220) *(P-6157)*

M M P, Long Beach *Also Called: Maruhide Marine Products Inc (P-6474)*

M O Dion & Sons Inc (DH) .... D...... 562 432-3946
  1543 W 16th St Long Beach (90813) *(P-6733)*

M R I, Chatsworth *Also Called: Medical Research Institute (P-6130)*

M S International Inc (PA) .... B...... 714 685-7500
  2095 N Batavia St Orange (92865) *(P-5207)*

M Squared Consulting, San Francisco *Also Called: Collabrus Inc (P-19553)*

M T A, Sacramento *Also Called: MILES TREASTER & ASSOCIATES (P-7424)*

M T C, Fallbrook *Also Called: Maneri Traffic Control Inc (P-1133)*

M T C, San Francisco *Also Called: Metropolitan Trnsp Comm (P-3162)*

M T D, Santa Barbara *Also Called: Santa Barbara Metro Trnst Dst (P-3205)*

M T R, Newark *Also Called: Membrane Technology & RES Inc (P-19734)*

M Z J, Chino Hills *Also Called: Victory Intl Group LLC (P-6001)*

M Z T, Santa Ana *Also Called: Macro-Z-Technology Company (P-1131)*

M-7 Consolidation Inc .... C...... 310 898-3456
  475 W Apra St Compton (90220) *(P-4053)*

M-Aurora Worldwide (us) LP (PA) .... C...... 800 888-0808
  2222 Corinth Ave Los Angeles (90064) *(P-10394)*

M-N-Z Janitorial Services Inc .... C...... 323 851-4115
  2109 W Burbank Blvd Burbank (91506) *(P-10923)*

M&C Hotel Interests Inc .... B...... 310 399-9344
  530 Pico Blvd Santa Monica (90405) *(P-9993)*

M10 Dev LLC .... D...... 650 565-8100
  744 San Antonio Rd Palo Alto (94303) *(P-9994)*

M2 Automotive .... A...... 310 399-3887
  1100 Colorado Ave 2nd Fl Santa Monica (90401) *(P-13641)*

M4dev LLC .... D...... 619 696-6300
  2137 Pacific Hwy Ste A San Diego (92101) *(P-9995)*

MA Laboratories Inc (PA) .... B...... 408 941-0808
  2075 N Capitol Ave San Jose (95132) *(P-5326)*

MA Labs, San Jose *Also Called: MA Laboratories Inc (P-5326)*

MA Steiner Construction Inc .... D...... 916 988-6300
  8854 Greenback Ln Ste 1 Orangevale (95662) *(P-832)*

Maas Energy Works LLC .... C...... 530 710-8545
  1730 South St Redding (96001) *(P-4585)*

Mabie Marketing Group Inc .... C...... 858 279-5585
  8352 Clairemont Mesa Blvd San Diego (92111) *(P-13360)*

Mac Arthur Co .... C...... 510 251-2102
  2855 Mandela Pkwy Ste D Oakland (94608) *(P-5222)*

Mac Cal Company .... D...... 408 441-1435
  2520 Zanker Rd San Jose (95131) *(P-2744)*

Mac Cal Manufacturing, San Jose *Also Called: Mac Cal Company (P-2744)*

Macarthur Trnst Cmnty Prtners .... D...... 415 989-1111
  345 Spear St Ste 700 San Francisco (94105) *(P-698)*

Macaulay Brown Inc .... A...... 937 426-3421
  2933 Bunker Hill Ln Ste 220 Santa Clara (95054) *(P-19311)*

Macb, Santa Clara *Also Called: Macaulay Brown Inc (P-19311)*

MACERICH, Santa Monica *Also Called: Macerich Company (P-9473)*

Macerich Company (PA) .... D...... 310 394-6000
  401 Wilshire Blvd Ste 700 Santa Monica (90401) *(P-9473)*

Mach49 LLC .... D...... 415 939-1943
  130 Solana Rd Portola Valley (94028) *(P-13781)*

Machine Zone Inc .... D...... 650 320-1678
  1050 Page Mill Rd Palo Alto (94304) *(P-11722)*

Machinify Inc .... D...... 650 313-2932
  635 High St Palo Alto (94301) *(P-11723)*

Macias Gini & OConnell LLP .... C...... 213 408-8700
  700 S Flower St Ste 800 Los Angeles (90017) *(P-19606)*

Macias Gini & OConnell LLP .... C...... 323 653-8300
  2121 Avenue Of The Stars Ste 2200 Los Angeles (90067) *(P-19607)*

Macias Gini & OConnell LLP (PA) .... D...... 310 277-3373
  500 Capitol Mall Ste 2200 Sacramento (95814) *(P-19608)*

Macias Gini & OConnell LLP .... C...... 916 928-4600
  2121 Avenue Of The Stars Ste 2200 Los Angeles (90067) *(P-19609)*

Mackay Smps Cvil Engineers Inc (PA) .... D...... 925 416-1790
  5142 Franklin Dr Ste C Pleasanton (94588) *(P-19312)*

Mackevision LLC .... C...... 248 656-6566
  1255 Treat Blvd Ste 250 Walnut Creek (94597) *(P-12485)*

Mackin Consultancy LLC .... C...... 828 755-4073
  2880 Zanker Rd Ste 203 San Jose (95134) *(P-20802)*

Mackin Talent, San Jose *Also Called: Mackin Consultancy LLC (P-20802)*

Macmurray Pacific, San Francisco *Also Called: Wildenradt-Mcmurray Inc (P-5738)*

Macqurie Arcft Lsg Svcs US Inc .... D...... 415 829-6600
  2 Embarcadero Ctr Ste 200 San Francisco (94111) *(P-11040)*

Macro-Pro Inc (PA) .... C...... 562 595-0900
  2400 Grand Ave Long Beach (90815) *(P-13361)*

Macro-Z-Technology Company (PA) .... D...... 714 564-1130
  841 E Washington Ave Santa Ana (92701) *(P-1131)*

Macs Equipment Inc .... D...... 559 846-6668
  187 S Madera Ave Kerman (93630) *(P-13782)*

Mad Dog Express Inc (PA) .... D...... 650 588-1900
  299 Lawrence Ave South San Francisco (94080) *(P-3411)*

Mad Engine Global LLC .... B...... 858 558-5270
  6740 Cobra Way Ste 100 San Diego (92121) *(P-6206)*

Mad River Community Hospital, Arcata *Also Called: American Hospital Mgt Corp (P-15942)*

Madden Corporation .... C...... 714 922-1670
  2301 E Pacifica Pl Compton (90220) *(P-3620)*

Maddox Dairy LLC .... D...... 559 866-5308
  12863 W Kamm Ave Spc 2 Riverdale (93656) *(P-219)*

Maddox Dairy A Ltd Partnership (PA) .... D...... 559 867-3545
  12863 W Kamm Ave Spc 2 Riverdale (93656) *(P-220)*

Made Renovation, San Francisco *Also Called: Untitled Labs Inc (P-735)*

Mader News Inc .... D...... 818 551-5000
  508 S Varney St Burbank (91502) *(P-6844)*

Madera Chevy, Olds, Toyota, Madera *Also Called: Valley Auto Sales & Lsg LLC (P-7322)*

Madera Cmnty Hosp Foundation .... D...... 559 673-5101
  1250 E Almond Ave Madera (93637) *(P-16241)*

Madera Community Hospital .... C...... 559 675-5530
  1210 E Almond Ave Ste A Madera (93637) *(P-16242)*

Madera Community Hospital (PA) .... A...... 559 675-5555
  1250 E Almond Ave Madera (93637) *(P-16243)*

Madera Convalescent Hosp Inc (PA) .... C...... 559 673-9228
  517 S A St Madera (93638) *(P-15556)*

Madera Disposal Systems Inc (DH) .... D...... 559 665-3099
  21739 Road 19 Chowchilla (93610) *(P-4905)*

Maderas Golf Club .... D...... 858 451-8100
  17750 Old Coach Rd Poway (92064) *(P-14272)*

Madisn/Grham Clor Graphics Inc .... B...... 323 261-7171
  150 N Myers St Los Angeles (90033) *(P-2562)*

Madison Inc of Oklahoma .... D...... 918 224-6990
  18000 Studebaker Rd Cerritos (90703) *(P-2736)*

Madison Club Owners Assn .... C...... 760 777-9320
  53035 Meriwether Way La Quinta (92253) *(P-14273)*

Madison Club, The, La Quinta *Also Called: Madison Club Owners Assn (P-14273)*

Madonna Inn Inc .... C...... 805 543-3000
  100 Madonna Rd San Luis Obispo (93405) *(P-7159)*

ALPHABETIC SECTION — Maleko Personnel Inc

Maersk Whsng Dist Svcs USA LLC .... C 801 301-1732
1651 California St Ste A Redlands (92374) *(P-4054)*

Maersk Whsng Dist Svcs USA LLC (HQ) .... C 562 345-2200
2240 E Maple Ave El Segundo (90245) *(P-4055)*

Maf Industries Inc (HQ) .... D 559 897-2905
36470 Highway 99 Traver (93673) *(P-2798)*

Mafab Inc (PA) .... D 714 893-0551
1925 Century Park E Ste 650 Los Angeles (90067) *(P-9320)*

Magagnini, Newark *Also Called: Intelliswift Software Inc (P-11674)*

Magdalena Ecke Family YMCA, Encinitas *Also Called: YMCA of San Diego County (P-18944)*

MAGELLAN, San Diego *Also Called: Aurora - San Diego LLC (P-16636)*

Magento, San Jose *Also Called: Xcommerce Inc (P-12909)*

Maggiora and Ghilotti Inc .... D 415 459-8640
555 Du Bois St San Rafael (94901) *(P-2222)*

Magic 92.5, San Diego *Also Called: Local Media San Diego LLC (P-4395)*

Magic Acquisition Corp .... B 661 382-4700
23920 Creekside Rd Valencia (91355) *(P-7255)*

Magic Bullet, Los Angeles *Also Called: Homeland Housewares LLC (P-5607)*

Magic Castles Inc .... D 323 851-3313
7001 Franklin Ave Los Angeles (90028) *(P-7494)*

Magic International, Santa Monica *Also Called: Mens Apparel Guild In Cal Inc (P-18713)*

Magic Labs Inc .... D 707 653-5739
548 Market St San Francisco (94104) *(P-11724)*

Magic Mountain LLC .... C 661 255-4100
26101 Magic Mountain Pkwy Valencia (91355) *(P-14046)*

Magic Workforce Solutions LLC .... A 310 246-6153
9100 Wilshire Blvd Ste 700e Beverly Hills (90212) *(P-20638)*

Magical Cruise Company Limited .... D 800 742-8939
500 S Buena Vista St Burbank (91521) *(P-3940)*

Magiclinks Inc .... D 626 808-2215
361 Vernon Ave Ste 6 Venice (90291) *(P-20445)*

Magicom Inc .... D 415 404-6094
1375 55th St Emeryville (94608) *(P-12832)*

Magma Consulting Group LLC .... D 415 315-9364
830 Traction Ave 3a Los Angeles (90013) *(P-12833)*

Magma Design Automation Inc (HQ) .... B 408 565-7500
1650 Technology Dr Ste 100 San Jose (95110) *(P-11725)*

Magma Design Automation Inc .... D 408 432-7288
2880 Zanker Rd Ste 203 San Jose (95134) *(P-11726)*

Magmalabs, Los Angeles *Also Called: Magma Consulting Group LLC (P-12833)*

Magnell Associate Inc (DH) .... C 800 685-3471
17560 Rowland St City Of Industry (91748) *(P-5327)*

Magnetika Inc (PA) .... D 310 527-8100
2041 W 139th St Gardena (90249) *(P-5576)*

Magnit LLC (PA) .... C 516 437-3300
2635 Iron Point Rd Ste 270 Folsom (95630) *(P-12259)*

Magnit Rs Inc .... D 800 660-9544
9 Executive Cir Ste 290 Irvine (92614) *(P-11299)*

Magnolia Convalescent Hospital, Riverside *Also Called: Magnolia Rhbltion Nursing Ctr (P-15874)*

Magnolia Grdns Convalescent HM, Granada Hills *Also Called: Longwood Management Corp (P-15550)*

Magnolia Holdings LLC .... C 530 365-0025
3300 Franklin St Anderson (96007) *(P-15557)*

Magnolia of Millbrae Inc .... D 650 697-7700
201 Chadbourne Ave Millbrae (94030) *(P-18478)*

Magnolia Rhbltion Nursing Ctr .... C 951 688-4321
8133 Magnolia Ave Riverside (92504) *(P-15874)*

Magnum Drywall Inc .... D 510 979-0420
2030 Fortune Dr Ste 200 San Jose (95131) *(P-1944)*

Mahana Therapeutics Inc (PA) .... D 650 483-4720
201 Mission St Ste 1200 San Francisco (94105) *(P-3057)*

Maher M F Concrete Cnstr, Vallejo *Also Called: M F Maher Inc (P-2136)*

Mahindra Bristlecone, San Jose *Also Called: Bristlecone Incorporated (P-11476)*

MAI Construction Inc .... D 408 434-9880
50 Bonaventura Dr San Jose (95134) *(P-699)*

Mail Boxes Etc, San Diego *Also Called: UPS Store Inc (P-13535)*

Mail Handling Group Inc .... C 952 975-5000
2840 Madonna Dr Fullerton (92835) *(P-2563)*

Mail Handling Services, Fullerton *Also Called: Mail Handling Group Inc (P-2563)*

Mailcentro Inc .... C 916 985-4445
715 Sutter St Ste B Folsom (95630) *(P-4310)*

Mailers Software, Rcho Sta Marg *Also Called: Melissa Data Corporation (P-11740)*

Maimone Liquidating Corp (PA) .... D 626 286-5691
1390 E Palm St Altadena (91001) *(P-13642)*

Main Electric Supply Co LLC (PA) .... D 949 833-3052
3600 W Segerstrom Ave Santa Ana (92704) *(P-5577)*

Main Electric Supply Company, Santa Ana *Also Called: Main Electric Supply Co LLC (P-5577)*

Main Street Fibers Inc .... D 909 986-6310
608 E Main St Ontario (91761) *(P-4906)*

Main Street Management LLC (PA) .... D 310 640-3100
2015 Manhattan Beach Blvd Ste 100 Redondo Beach (90278) *(P-9089)*

Mainfreight Inc (HQ) .... D 310 900-1974
1400 Glenn Curtiss St Carson (90746) *(P-4056)*

Mainplace Senior Living, Orange *Also Called: Pennant Group Inc (P-15626)*

MainStay Medical Limited .... D 619 261-9144
2159 India St Ste 200 San Diego (92101) *(P-14885)*

Mainstream Energy Corporation .... B 805 528-9705
775 Fiero Ln Ste 200 San Luis Obispo (93401) *(P-1495)*

Mainstreet Realtors .... D 909 373-3821
8577 Haven Ave Ste 101 Rancho Cucamonga (91730) *(P-9090)*

Maintech Incorporated .... C 714 921-8000
2401 N Glassell St Orange (92865) *(P-11727)*

Maintenace Operations Svc Ctr, National City *Also Called: National School District (P-17734)*

Maintenance & Operation Dept, Montebello *Also Called: Montebello Unified School Dst (P-10932)*

Maintenance Department, Berkeley *Also Called: Berkeley Unified School Dst (P-10861)*

Maintenance Dept, Santa Cruz *Also Called: Santa Cruz Metro Trnst Dst (P-3208)*

Maintenance Dept, Gardena *Also Called: Los Angeles Unified School Dst (P-10922)*

Maintenance Dept, Port Hueneme *Also Called: NAVY UNITED STATES DEPARTMENT (P-13786)*

Maintenance Office, San Jose *Also Called: San Jose Unified School Dst (P-10957)*

Maintenancenet LLC .... C 408 526-4000
170 W Tasman Dr San Jose (95134) *(P-12590)*

Maintex Inc .... D 858 513-8286
13575 Gregg St Poway (92064) *(P-5945)*

Maintex Inc (PA) .... C 800 446-1888
13300 Nelson Ave City Of Industry (91746) *(P-2625)*

Maintnnce Repr For Rsdntial Hm, San Francisco *Also Called: Super Home Inc (P-18529)*

Majestic Industry Hills LLC .... A 626 810-4455
1 Industry Hills Pkwy City Of Industry (91744) *(P-9996)*

Majestic Management Co., City Of Industry *Also Called: Majestic Realty Co (P-9091)*

Majestic Realty Co (PA) .... C 562 692-9581
13191 Crossroads Pkwy N Ste 600 City Of Industry (91746) *(P-9091)*

Major Market Inc .... C 760 723-0857
845 S Main Ave Fallbrook (92028) *(P-7146)*

Major Market-Ftd Florist, Fallbrook *Also Called: Major Market Inc (P-7146)*

Makallon La Jolla Properties, Newport Beach *Also Called: Makar Properties LLC (P-9262)*

Makar Anaheim LLC .... A 714 740-4431
777 W Convention Way Anaheim (92802) *(P-9997)*

Makar Properties LLC (PA) .... D 949 255-1100
4100 Macarthur Blvd Ste 150 Newport Beach (92660) *(P-9262)*

Makena Capital Management LLC .... D 650 926-0510
2755 Sand Hill Rd Ste 200 Menlo Park (94025) *(P-9529)*

Maker Studios LLC (DH) .... C 310 606-2182
3515 Eastham Dr Culver City (90232) *(P-14095)*

Makespace Labs Inc .... C 800 920-9440
3526 Hayden Ave Culver City (90232) *(P-3728)*

Making Sense LLC .... D 210 364-0050
228 Hamilton Ave Ste 300 Palo Alto (94301) *(P-11728)*

Makita, La Mirada *Also Called: Makita USA Inc (P-5731)*

Makita USA Inc (HQ) .... C 714 522-8088
14930 Northam St La Mirada (90638) *(P-5731)*

Malcolm & Cisneros A Law Corp .... C 949 252-9400
2112 Business Center Dr Ste 100 Irvine (92612) *(P-17560)*

Malcolm Cisneros, Irvine *Also Called: Malcolm & Cisneros A Law Corp (P-17560)*

Malcolm Drilling Company Inc (PA) .... D 415 901-4400
92 Natoma St Ste 400 San Francisco (94105) *(P-2295)*

Maleko Personnel Inc .... D 480 405-2905
24301 Southland Dr Ste 400 Hayward (94545) *(P-11174)*

Malema — ALPHABETIC SECTION

Malema .... D 408 970-3419
2329 Zanker Rd San Jose (95131) *(P-19313)*

Malibu Conference Center Inc .... B 818 889-6440
327 Latigo Canyon Rd Malibu (90265) *(P-8734)*

Malibu Leather Inc .... C 310 985-0707
510 W 6th St Ste 1002 Los Angeles (90014) *(P-2686)*

Malibu Limousine Service, Marina Del Rey *Also Called: Executive Network Entps Inc (P-3257)*

Malk Partners .... D 858 914-1125
7911 Herschel Ave Ste 400 La Jolla (92037) *(P-9378)*

Maloney Vision Institute, Los Angeles *Also Called: Robert K Maloney Md Inc (P-15028)*

Maloof Sport Entertainment, Sacramento *Also Called: Kings Arena Ltd Partnership (P-14144)*

Malwarebytes, Santa Clara *Also Called: Malwarebytes Inc (P-12260)*

Malwarebytes Inc (PA) .... A 408 852-4336
3979 Freedom Cir Fl 12 Santa Clara (95054) *(P-12260)*

Malys of California Inc .... B 661 295-8317
28145 Harrison Pkwy Valencia (91355) *(P-5946)*

Mamba Logistics Inc .... D 661 234-8050
23749 Fitzgerald St West Hills (91304) *(P-3412)*

Mamco Inc (PA) .... C 951 776-9300
764 Ramona Expy Ste C Perris (92571) *(P-1132)*

Mammography Center, Lompoc *Also Called: Lompoc Valley Medical Center (P-16230)*

Mammoth Biosciences Inc .... D 770 655-1937
1000 Marina Blvd. Ste 600 Brisbane (94005) *(P-19732)*

MAMMOTH HOSPITAL, Mammoth Lakes *Also Called: Southern Mono Healthcare Dst (P-16449)*

Mammoth Mountain Inn, Mammoth Lakes *Also Called: Mammoth Mountain Ski Area LLC (P-9998)*

Mammoth Mountain Ski Area LLC (DH) .... B 760 934-2571
10001 Minaret Rd Mammoth Lakes (93546) *(P-9998)*

Mamolos Cntntl Bailey Bakeries .... C 805 496-0045
2734 Townsgate Rd Westlake Village (91361) *(P-7160)*

Mamone James M, Roseville *Also Called: Sutter Health (P-16519)*

Man Theateres, Westlake Village *Also Called: Weststar Cinemas Inc (P-14009)*

Managed Dental Care .... C 818 598-6599
6200 Canoga Ave Ste 100 Woodland Hills (91367) *(P-8342)*

Managed Dental Care California, Woodland Hills *Also Called: Managed Dental Care (P-8342)*

Managed Health, Huntington Beach *Also Called: Managed Health Network (P-8343)*

Managed Health, Mountain View *Also Called: Managed Health Network (P-8344)*

Managed Health, San Rafael *Also Called: Managed Health Network (P-8345)*

Managed Health Network .... B 714 934-5519
7755 Center Ave Ste 700 Huntington Beach (92647) *(P-8343)*

Managed Health Network .... C 650 988-4842
625 Ellis St Ste 100 Mountain View (94043) *(P-8344)*

Managed Health Network (DH) .... B 415 460-8168
2370 Kerner Blvd San Rafael (94901) *(P-8345)*

Manageengine, Pleasanton *Also Called: Zoho Corporation (P-19447)*

Management 360 .... D 310 272-7000
9111 Wilshire Blvd Beverly Hills (90210) *(P-14047)*

Management Applied Prgrm Inc (PA) .... D 562 463-5000
13191 Crossroads Pkwy N Ste 205 City Of Industry (91746) *(P-12591)*

Management Associates, Saint Helena *Also Called: Silverado Orchards LLC (P-8861)*

Management Success, Monrovia *Also Called: Leekilpatrick Management Inc (P-20434)*

Management Trust Assn Inc .... C 562 926-3372
12607 Hiddencreek Way Ste R Cerritos (90703) *(P-20446)*

Manatt Phelps & Phillips LLP (PA) .... B 310 312-4000
2049 Century Park E Ste 1700 Los Angeles (90067) *(P-17561)*

Manchester Grand Resorts LP .... C 619 232-1234
1 Market Pl Fl 33 San Diego (92101) *(P-9999)*

Manchster Grnd Hyatt San Diego, San Diego *Also Called: Hyatt Corporation (P-9897)*

Manchster Grnd Hyatt San Diego, San Diego *Also Called: Manchester Grand Resorts LP (P-9999)*

Manchester Mnor Cnvlescent Hosp .... D 323 753-1789
837 W Manchester Ave Los Angeles (90044) *(P-15558)*

Mandala, Carlsbad *Also Called: Oceanside Glasstile Company (P-2698)*

Mandalay Generating Station, Oxnard *Also Called: NRG California South LP (P-4594)*

Maneri Traffic Control Inc .... D 951 695-5104
4949 2nd St Fallbrook (92028) *(P-1133)*

Mangan Inc (PA) .... D 310 835-8080
3901 Via Oro Ave Long Beach (90810) *(P-19314)*

Mango Technologies Inc (PA) .... A 888 625-4258
350 10th Ave Ste 500 San Diego (92101) *(P-11729)*

Mangold Property MGT Inc .... D 831 372-1338
575 Calle Principal Monterey (93940) *(P-9092)*

Manhattan Bancorp .... C 310 606-8000
2141 Rosecrans Ave # 1100 El Segundo (90245) *(P-7629)*

Manhattan Country Club, Manhattan Beach *Also Called: 1334 Partners LP (P-14318)*

Manhattan Fruitier, Lodi *Also Called: Gifting Company LLC (P-6552)*

Manifold, San Francisco *Also Called: Manifold LLC (P-20447)*

Manifold LLC .... D 415 978-9500
531 Howard St Fl 3 San Francisco (94105) *(P-20447)*

Mann Packing Co Inc (DH) .... B 831 422-5341
49 Katherine St Gonzales (93926) *(P-286)*

Mann Packing Co Inc .... D 831 796-2670
1347 Harkins Rd Salinas (93901) *(P-4131)*

Mann Packing Pea Plant, Salinas *Also Called: Mann Packing Co Inc (P-4131)*

Manning Gardens Care Ctr Inc .... D 559 834-2586
2113 E Manning Ave Fresno (93725) *(P-15559)*

Manning Kass Ellrod Rmrez Trst (PA) .... C 213 624-6900
801 S Figueroa St 15th Fl Los Angeles (90017) *(P-17562)*

MANOR AT SANTA TERESITA HOSPIT, Duarte *Also Called: Santa Teresita Inc (P-16395)*

Manorcare Health Services, Aliso Viejo *Also Called: Hcr Manorcare Med Svcs Fla LLC (P-15507)*

Manske Dental Corporation .... D 213 907-4027
1418 7th St Apt 102 Santa Monica (90401) *(P-15238)*

Manson Construction Co .... D 562 983-2340
340 Golden Shore Ste 310 Long Beach (90802) *(P-1309)*

Manson Construction Co .... D 510 232-6319
1401 Marina Way S # F Richmond (94804) *(P-1310)*

Manteca Bulletin, Manteca *Also Called: Morris Newspaper Corp Cal (P-2540)*

Manticore Games Inc (PA) .... D 650 257-8177
1800 Gateway Dr Ste 250 San Mateo (94404) *(P-11730)*

Manuel Bros Inc .... D 530 272-4213
908 Taylorville Rd Ste 104 Grass Valley (95949) *(P-1234)*

Manufactured Packaging Pdts .... D 510 487-1211
33463 Western Ave Union City (94587) *(P-6927)*

Manufacturers Bank (DH) .... C 213 489-6200
515 S Figueroa St 4th Fl Los Angeles (90071) *(P-7695)*

Many LLC .... D 310 399-1515
17575 Pacific Coast Hwy Pacific Palisades (90272) *(P-10644)*

MAOF, Montebello *Also Called: Mexican Amrcn Oprtnty Fndation (P-18053)*

Maof Commerce, Commerce *Also Called: Mexican Amrcn Oprtnty Fndation (P-18054)*

Map Energy LLC .... D 650 324-9095
988 Howard Ave Burlingame (94010) *(P-8102)*

Mapcargo Global Logistics (PA) .... D 310 297-8300
2501 Santa Fe Ave Redondo Beach (90278) *(P-4057)*

Maple Dairy, Bakersfield *Also Called: Maple Dairy LP (P-221)*

Maple Dairy LP .... D 661 396-9600
15857 Bear Mountain Blvd Bakersfield (93311) *(P-221)*

Maplebear Inc (PA) .... C 888 246-7822
50 Beale St Ste 600 San Francisco (94105) *(P-12592)*

Maplelabs Inc .... C 408 743-4414
1248 Reamwood Ave Sunnyvale (94089) *(P-11731)*

Mapp Digital Us LLC .... B 619 342-4340
4660 La Jolla Village Dr Ste 100 San Diego (92122) *(P-20448)*

Marathon Construction Corp .... D 619 276-4401
10108 Riverford Rd Lakeside (92040) *(P-1311)*

Marathon General Inc .... D 760 738-9714
1728 Mission Rd Escondido (92029) *(P-1134)*

Marathon Industries Inc .... C 661 286-1520
25597 Springbrook Ave Santa Clarita (91350) *(P-5015)*

Marathon Land Inc .... C 805 488-3585
2599 E Hueneme Rd Oxnard (93033) *(P-137)*

Marathon Staffing Solutions .... D 978 649-6230
2950 Beacon Blvd Ste 45 West Sacramento (95691) *(P-11175)*

Marathon Truck Bodies, Santa Clarita *Also Called: Marathon Industries Inc (P-5015)*

Maravai Lf Scnces Holdings LLC (HQ) .... C 650 697-3600
10770 Wateridge Cir Ste 100 San Diego (92121) *(P-19733)*

Maravilla Foundation (PA) .... C 323 721-4162
5729 Union Pacific Ave Commerce (90022) *(P-18880)*

ALPHABETIC SECTION — Mariner Health Care Inc

Marborg Industries (PA) .... C 805 963-1852
728 E Yanonali St Santa Barbara (93103) *(P-4907)*

Marborg Recovery LP .... C 805 963-1852
14470 Calle Real Goleta (93117) *(P-4908)*

March For Our Lves Action Fund .... D 801 815-1989
16130 Ventura Blvd Ste 320 Encino (91436) *(P-18609)*

Marco's Auto Body, Altadena *Also Called: Maimone Liquidating Corp (P-13642)*

Marcus & Millichap, Calabasas *Also Called: Marcus & Millichap Inc (P-9093)*

Marcus & Millichap Inc (PA) .... C 818 212-2250
23975 Park Sorrento Ste 400 Calabasas (91302) *(P-9093)*

Marcus Evans Inc .... D 858 679-1275
13520 Evening Creek Dr N Ste 370 San Diego (92128) *(P-20449)*

Marcus Hotels Inc .... C 818 980-8000
4222 Vineland Ave North Hollywood (91602) *(P-10000)*

Marcus Millichap Corp RE Svcs (HQ) .... D 650 391-1700
2626 Hanover St Palo Alto (94304) *(P-9094)*

Marelich Mechanical Co Inc (HQ) .... D 510 785-5500
24041 Amador St Hayward (94544) *(P-1496)*

Marfred Industries .... B
12708 Branford St Sun Valley (91353) *(P-2520)*

Margartville Resort Palm Sprng, Palm Springs *Also Called: Margartvlle Rsort Orlndo Rsort (P-10001)*

Margartvlle Rsort Orlndo Rsort .... C 760 327-8311
1600 N Indian Canyon Dr Palm Springs (92262) *(P-10001)*

Maria Aleen Villarin Balce Inc .... D 408 320-2684
2897 Forbes Ave Santa Clara (95051) *(P-13362)*

Mariak Industries Inc .... B 310 661-4400
879 W 190th St Ste 1050 Gardena (90248) *(P-5123)*

Mariak Window Fashion, Gardena *Also Called: Mariak Industries Inc (P-5123)*

Marian Community Clinic .... D 805 739-3867
117 W Bunny Ave Santa Maria (93458) *(P-16244)*

Marian Medical Center .... A 805 739-3000
1400 E Church St Santa Maria (93454) *(P-16245)*

Marian Regional Medical Center, Santa Maria *Also Called: Dignity Health (P-16042)*

Marian Regional Medical Center, Santa Maria *Also Called: Marian Medical Center (P-16245)*

Mariani Packing Co Inc (PA) .... B 707 452-2800
500 Crocker Dr Vacaville (95688) *(P-287)*

Marie Cllender Wholesalers Inc .... A 951 737-6760
170 E Rincon St Corona (92879) *(P-6422)*

Marigold .... A 888 533-8098
631 Howard St Fl 5 San Francisco (94105) *(P-11732)*

Marigold Usa Inc .... C 617 385-6786
475 Anton Blvd Costa Mesa (92626) *(P-11733)*

Marika LLC .... D 323 888-7755
5553 Bandini Blvd B Bell (90201) *(P-2460)*

Marin Acura, Corte Madera *Also Called: Ted Stevens Inc (P-7310)*

Marin Clean Energy .... D 415 464-6028
1125 Tamalpais Ave San Rafael (94901) *(P-4586)*

Marin Community Clinic .... D 415 448-1500
9 Commercial Blvd Ste 100 Novato (94949) *(P-14886)*

MARIN COMMUNITY CLINICS, Novato *Also Called: Marin Community Clinic (P-14886)*

Marin Country Club Inc .... D 415 382-6700
500 Country Club Dr Novato (94949) *(P-14401)*

Marin County Office Education (PA) .... B 415 472-4110
1111 Las Gallinas Ave San Rafael (94903) *(P-17726)*

Marin General Hospital .... A 415 925-7000
250 Bon Air Rd Kentfield (94904) *(P-16246)*

Marin Healthcare District (PA) .... C 415 464-2090
100b Drakes Landing Rd Ste 250 Greenbrae (94904) *(P-16247)*

Marin Humane Society .... D 415 883-4621
171 Bel Marin Keys Blvd Novato (94949) *(P-19093)*

Marin Industrial Distributors, San Rafael *Also Called: Jacksons Hardware Inc (P-5730)*

Marin Municipal Water District (PA) .... C 415 945-1455
220 Nellen Ave Corte Madera (94925) *(P-4990)*

Marin Post Acute, San Rafael *Also Called: Marinidence Opco LLC (P-15578)*

Marin Resource Recovery Center, San Rafael *Also Called: Marin Sanitary Service (P-4909)*

Marin Sanitary Service (PA) .... D 415 456-2601
1050 Andersen Dr San Rafael (94901) *(P-4909)*

Marin Sanitary Service .... D 415 485-5646
565 Jacoby St San Rafael (94901) *(P-4910)*

MARIN SOFTWARE, San Francisco *Also Called: Marin Software Incorporated (P-12593)*

Marin Software Incorporated (PA) .... D 415 399-2580
149 New Montgomery St Fl 4 San Francisco (94105) *(P-12593)*

Marin Terrace, Mill Valley *Also Called: Cliff View Terrace Inc (P-18396)*

Marina, Orange *Also Called: Marina Landscape Inc (P-518)*

Marina Breeze, San Leandro *Also Called: Vasona Management Inc (P-8867)*

Marina City Club LP A Cali .... C 310 822-0611
4333 Admiralty Way Marina Del Rey (90292) *(P-8842)*

Marina Landscape Inc .... B 714 939-6600
3707 W Garden Grove Blvd Orange (92868) *(P-518)*

Marina Landscape Maint Inc, Anaheim *Also Called: Marina Maintenance Group Inc (P-442)*

Marina Maintenance Group Inc .... B 714 939-6600
1900 S Lewis St Anaheim (92805) *(P-442)*

Marina Security Services Inc .... B 415 773-2300
465 California St Ste 626 San Francisco (94104) *(P-13000)*

Marina Village, San Diego *Also Called: Southern Cal Pipe Trades ADM (P-9182)*

Marine Aviation Logistics, Oceanside *Also Called: United States Marine Corps (P-5970)*

Marine Corps United States .... D 760 725-3092
Traffic Management Office Camp Pendleton (92055) *(P-4058)*

Marine Corps United States .... A 760 725-1304
Camp Pendleton Oceanside (92055) *(P-16687)*

Marine Corps Cmnty Svcs Dept, San Diego *Also Called: Marine Corps Community Svcs (P-14544)*

Marine Corps Community Svcs .... B 858 577-1061
2273 Elrod Ave San Diego (92145) *(P-14544)*

Marine Corps Community Svcs .... C 760 725-6195
Acs Mccs Attn Semper Fi Box 555020 Marine Corp Base Camp Pendleton (92055) *(P-14545)*

Marine Corps Community Svcs .... C 760 725-5187
Camp Pendleton Marine Corps Base Oceanside (92055) *(P-15239)*

Marine Corps Community Svcs .... C 760 725-2817
202860 San Jacinto Rd Oceanside (92054) *(P-18330)*

Marine Corps Community Svcs .... C 760 725-7311
Basilone Rd Bldg 51080 Camp Pendleton (92055) *(P-18331)*

Marine Group Boat Works, Chula Vista *Also Called: Marine Group Boat Works LLC (P-13783)*

Marine Group Boat Works LLC .... C 619 427-6767
997 G St Chula Vista (91910) *(P-13783)*

Marine Room Restaurant, La Jolla *Also Called: La Jolla Bch & Tennis CLB Inc (P-14388)*

Marine Technical Services Inc .... D 310 549-8030
211 N Marine Ave Wilmington (90744) *(P-13363)*

Marine Terminals Corporation .... B 310 519-2300
389 Terminal Way San Pedro (90731) *(P-3812)*

Marine World Foundation .... B 707 644-4000
Marine World Pkwy Vallejo (94589) *(P-14307)*

Marine World/Africa USA, Vallejo *Also Called: Marine World Foundation (P-14307)*

Mariner Health Care Inc .... C 310 371-4628
4109 Emerald St Torrance (90503) *(P-15560)*

Mariner Health Care Inc .... D 562 942-7019
8925 Mines Ave Pico Rivera (90660) *(P-15561)*

Mariner Health Care Inc .... D 916 481-5500
3400 Alta Arden Expy Sacramento (95825) *(P-15562)*

Mariner Health Care Inc .... C 510 792-3743
39022 Presidio Way Fremont (94538) *(P-15563)*

Mariner Health Care Inc .... D 408 842-9311
8170 Murray Ave Gilroy (95020) *(P-15564)*

Mariner Health Care Inc .... C 408 298-3950
2065 Forest Ave San Jose (95128) *(P-15565)*

Mariner Health Care Inc .... C 510 783-8150
27350 Tampa Ave Hayward (94544) *(P-15566)*

Mariner Health Care Inc .... B 510 232-5945
13484 San Pablo Ave San Pablo (94806) *(P-15567)*

Mariner Health Care Inc .... C 760 776-7700
44610 Monterey Ave Palm Desert (92260) *(P-15568)*

Mariner Health Care Inc .... D 310 677-9114
100 S Hillcrest Blvd Inglewood (90301) *(P-15569)*

Mariner Health Care Inc .... D 323 665-1185
3032 Rowena Ave Los Angeles (90039) *(P-15570)*

Mariner Health Care Inc .... D 818 246-5677
430 N Glendale Ave Glendale (91206) *(P-15571)*

Mariner Health Care Inc .... D 831 475-6323
675 24th Ave Santa Cruz (95062) *(P-15572)*

Mariner Health Care Inc .... C....... 510 538-4424
　1768 B St Hayward (94541) *(P-15573)*

Mariner Health Care Inc .... C....... 510 785-2880
　19700 Hesperian Blvd Hayward (94541) *(P-15574)*

Mariner Health Care Inc .... C....... 415 479-3610
　45 Professional Center Pkwy San Rafael (94903) *(P-15575)*

Mariner Health Care Inc .... D....... 408 377-9275
　2065 Los Gatos Almaden Rd San Jose (95124) *(P-15576)*

Mariner Health Care Inc .... D....... 818 957-0850
　3050 Montrose Ave La Crescenta (91214) *(P-15577)*

Mariner Health Care Inc .... C....... 760 327-8541
　277 S Sunrise Way Palm Springs (92262) *(P-20145)*

Mariner's Village, Marina Del Rey *Also Called: E & S Ring Management Corp (P-8988)*

Marinidence Opco LLC .... C....... 415 479-3450
　234 N San Pedro Rd San Rafael (94903) *(P-15578)*

Mariposa Horticultural Entps, Irwindale *Also Called: Mariposa Landscapes Inc (P-519)*

Mariposa Landscapes Inc (PA) .... D....... 626 960-0196
　6232 Santos Diaz St Irwindale (91702) *(P-519)*

Mark & Fred Enterprises .... C....... 714 821-1993
　645 S Beach Blvd Anaheim (92804) *(P-15579)*

Mark 1 Restoration Service LLC .... C....... 714 283-9990
　3360 E La Palma Ave Anaheim (92806) *(P-18049)*

Mark Clemons .... C....... 760 361-1531
　4584 Adobe Rd Twentynine Palms (92277) *(P-3509)*

Mark Company, Orange *Also Called: Santa Ana Creek Development Company (P-2155)*

Mark E Jacobson M D .... D....... 707 571-4022
　1260 N Dutton Ave Ste 230 Santa Rosa (95401) *(P-14887)*

Mark III Construction Inc (PA) .... D....... 916 381-8080
　5101 Florin Perkins Rd Sacramento (95826) *(P-1769)*

Mark III Dvlpers Dsgn/Builders, Sacramento *Also Called: Mark III Construction Inc (P-1769)*

Mark Land Electric Inc .... C....... 818 883-5110
　7876 Deering Ave Canoga Park (91304) *(P-1770)*

Mark One Corporation .... C....... 209 667-2484
　812 W Main St Turlock (95380) *(P-15875)*

Mark Roberts, Santa Ana *Also Called: Celmol Inc (P-6896)*

Mark Scott Construction Inc .... D....... 707 864-8880
　2250 Boynton Ave Fairfield (94533) *(P-765)*

Mark Twain Medical Center (DH) .... C....... 209 754-3521
　768 Mountain Ranch Rd San Andreas (95249) *(P-16248)*

Mark Twain St Joseph's Hospital, San Andreas *Also Called: Mark Twain Medical Center (P-16248)*

Markel Corp .... B....... 818 595-0600
　21600 Oxnard St Ste 900 Woodland Hills (91367) *(P-8605)*

Marker Hotel, The, San Francisco *Also Called: Geary Darling Lessee Inc (P-9808)*

Market Hall Foods, Oakland *Also Called: Pasta Shop (P-6656)*

Market Scan, Camarillo *Also Called: Market Scan Info Systems Inc (P-11734)*

Market Scan Info Systems Inc .... D....... 800 658-7226
　815 Camarillo Springs Rd Camarillo (93012) *(P-11734)*

Marketbridge Corp .... D....... 240 752-1800
　601 Montgomery St Ste 650 San Francisco (94111) *(P-20450)*

MARKETBRIDGE CORP., San Francisco *Also Called: Marketbridge Corp (P-20450)*

Marketerhire LLC .... C....... 312 870-0008
　660 4th St San Francisco (94107) *(P-20451)*

Marketing Design Group, San Diego *Also Called: Phase Ten Strategic Corp (P-9132)*

Marketing Practice Inc .... D....... 415 793-8370
　101 Broadway Oakland (94607) *(P-20452)*

Marketo Inc (HQ) .... B....... 650 376-2303
　901 Mariners Island Blvd Ste 200 San Mateo (94404) *(P-11735)*

Marketshare Inc (PA) .... D....... 408 262-0677
　2001 Tarob Ct Milpitas (95035) *(P-3100)*

Marklogic Corporation (HQ) .... C....... 650 655-2300
　333 Twin Dolphin Dr Ste 380 Redwood City (94065) *(P-11736)*

Markstein Bev Co Sacramento .... C....... 916 920-3911
　60 Main Ave Sacramento (95838) *(P-6772)*

Markstein Beverage Co .... C....... 760 744-9100
　845 Rio Claro Ct Oceanside (92057) *(P-6773)*

Markstein Beverage Co, Antioch *Also Called: Markstein Sales Company (P-6774)*

Markstein Beverage Company, Sacramento *Also Called: Markstein Bev Co Sacramento (P-6772)*

Markstein Sales Company .... C....... 925 755-1919
　1645 Drive In Way Antioch (94509) *(P-6774)*

Marksys LLC .... D....... 916 745-4883
　3725 Cincinnati Ave Ste 200 Rocklin (95765) *(P-20453)*

Marksys Holdings LLC .... D....... 916 745-4883
　3725 Cincinnati Ave Ste 200 Rocklin (95765) *(P-20454)*

Markwins Beauty Brands, Walnut *Also Called: Lina Gale (usa) Inc (P-6122)*

Markwins Beauty Brands Inc (PA) .... C....... 909 595-8898
　22067 Ferrero City Of Industry (91789) *(P-6123)*

Markwins Beauty Products Inc .... D....... 909 595-8898
　22067 Ferrero City Of Industry (91789) *(P-6124)*

Marlin Equity Partners LLC (PA) .... D....... 310 364-0100
　1301 Manhattan Ave Hermosa Beach (90254) *(P-8206)*

Marlin Equity Partners III LP (PA) .... C....... 310 364-0100
　1301 Manhattan Ave Hermosa Beach (90254) *(P-9530)*

Marlinda Imperial Hospital, Pasadena *Also Called: Two Palms Nursing Center Inc (P-15905)*

Marlinda Management Inc (PA) .... C....... 310 631-6122
　3351 E Imperial Hwy Lynwood (90262) *(P-15876)*

Marlora Investments LLC .... D....... 562 494-3311
　3801 E Anaheim St Long Beach (90804) *(P-15580)*

Marlora Post Accute Rhblttion, Long Beach *Also Called: Marlora Investments LLC (P-15580)*

Marmol Rdzner An Archtctral Co .... D....... 310 826-6222
　12210 Nebraska Ave Los Angeles (90025) *(P-19492)*

Marna Health Services Inc .... D....... 909 882-2965
　4280 Cypress Dr San Bernardino (92407) *(P-15877)*

Marqeta Inc (PA) .... B....... 888 462-7738
　180 Grand Ave Ste 600 Oakland (94612) *(P-12261)*

Marques Gen Engrg Inc A Cal Co .... B....... 916 923-3434
　7225 26th St Rio Linda (95673) *(P-19315)*

Marquez Brothers Entps Inc .... C....... 626 330-3310
　15480 Valley Blvd City Of Industry (91746) *(P-6263)*

Marquez Brothers Intl Inc (PA) .... C....... 408 960-2700
　5801 Rue Ferrari San Jose (95138) *(P-6264)*

Marriott, Bakersfield *Also Called: Bakersfield Inn Inc (P-9629)*

Marriott, Anaheim *Also Called: Fairfield Inn By Mrrott Ltd Prt (P-9792)*

Marriott, Woodland Hills *Also Called: HEI Hospitality LLC (P-9845)*

Marriott, Lake Arrowhead *Also Called: Lake Arrwhead Rsort Oprtor Inc (P-9963)*

Marriott, San Jose *Also Called: Marriott Hotel Services Inc (P-10002)*

Marriott, Los Angeles *Also Called: Marriott International Inc (P-10003)*

Marriott, Irvine *Also Called: Marriott International Inc (P-10004)*

Marriott, La Jolla *Also Called: Marriott International Inc (P-10006)*

Marriott, Palm Desert *Also Called: Marriott Vacation Club Intl (P-10008)*

Marriott, Fullerton *Also Called: Merritt Hospitality LLC (P-10016)*

Marriott, Baldwin Park *Also Called: Ols Hotels & Resorts LLC (P-10063)*

Marriott, Los Angeles *Also Called: Renaissance Hotel Operating Co (P-10149)*

Marriott, San Francisco *Also Called: Renaissance Hotel Operating Co (P-10151)*

Marriott, Visalia *Also Called: Welcome Group Management LLC (P-10357)*

Marriott, Newport Beach *Also Called: Wj Newport LLC (P-10377)*

Marriott, Palm Desert *Also Called: Desert Willow Golf Resort (P-14256)*

Marriott Grnd Rsdnce CLB - Lk, South Lake Tahoe *Also Called: Grclt Condominium Inc (P-9818)*

Marriott Hotel Services Inc .... B....... 408 280-1300
　301 S Market St San Jose (95113) *(P-10002)*

Marriott International, Coronado *Also Called: Sanci Marriott Hotels (P-10204)*

Marriott International Inc .... A....... 310 641-5700
　5855 W Century Blvd Los Angeles (90045) *(P-10003)*

Marriott International Inc .... B....... 949 724-3606
　18000 Von Karman Ave Irvine (92612) *(P-10004)*

Marriott International Inc .... D....... 949 503-5700
　31692 El Camino Real San Juan Capistrano (92675) *(P-10005)*

Marriott International Inc .... B....... 858 587-1414
　4240 La Jolla Village Dr La Jolla (92037) *(P-10006)*

Marriott Intl Hotels Inc .... D....... 805 975-0660
　1601 State St Santa Barbara (93101) *(P-10007)*

Marriott San Dego Gslamp Qrter, San Diego *Also Called: San Diego Hotel Company LLC (P-10195)*

Marriott Vacation Club Intl .... D....... 760 674-2927
　9001 Shadow Ridge Rd Palm Desert (92211) *(P-10008)*

Marriott Vacatlon Club Pulse, San Francisco *Also Called: PHF Ruby LLC (P-10117)*

Mars & Co Consulting LLC .... C....... 415 288-6970
　600 Montgomery St Ste 1500 San Francisco (94111) *(P-20455)*

ALPHABETIC SECTION

Marsh, San Diego *Also Called: Marsh & McLennan Agency LLC* **(P-8606)**
Marsh & McLennan Agency LLC .... C....... 858 457-3414
  9171 Towne Centre Dr Ste 500 San Diego (92122) **(P-8606)**
Marsh Consulting Group .... D....... 239 433-5500
  2626 Summer Ranch Rd Paso Robles (93446) **(P-20803)**
Marsh Risk & Insurance Svcs .... A....... 213 624-5555
  633 W 5th St Ste 1200 Los Angeles (90071) **(P-8607)**
Marshall B Ketchum University (PA) .... C....... 714 463-7567
  2575 Yorba Linda Blvd Fullerton (92831) **(P-17766)**
MARSHALL HOSPITAL, Placerville *Also Called: Marshall Medical Center* **(P-16249)**
Marshall Medical Center (PA) .... A....... 530 622-1441
  1100 Marshall Way Placerville (95667) **(P-16249)**
Marshall Reddick RE Netwrk, Newport Beach *Also Called: Marshall Reddick Realty Inc* **(P-9095)**
Marshall Reddick Realty Inc .... C....... 949 885-8180
  4299 Macarthur Blvd Ste 102 Newport Beach (92660) **(P-9095)**
Marshall S Ezralow & Assoc, Calabasas *Also Called: MSE Enterprises Inc* **(P-9106)**
Marshall, Spector MD, San Gabriel *Also Called: Providnce Facey Med Foundation* **(P-17302)**
Marthas Village and Kitchen .... D....... 760 347-4741
  83791 Date Ave Indio (92201) **(P-18050)**
Martin AC Partners Inc .... C....... 213 683-1900
  444 S Flower St Ste 1200 Los Angeles (90071) **(P-19493)**
Martin Associates Group Inc (PA) .... D....... 213 483-6490
  950 S Grand Ave Fl 4 Los Angeles (90015) **(P-19316)**
Martin ATI-AC Inc (PA) .... D....... 925 648-8800
  4305 Hacienda Dr Ste 500 Pleasanton (94588) **(P-19494)**
Martin Automotive Inc .... D....... 909 394-9899
  1959 Auto Centre Dr Glendora (91740) **(P-13667)**
Martin Bros/Marcowall Inc (PA) .... C....... 310 532-5335
  17104 S Figueroa St Gardena (90248) **(P-1945)**
Martin Brothers Cnstr LLC (PA) .... D....... 916 386-1600
  8801 Folsom Blvd Ste 260 Sacramento (95826) **(P-1135)**
Martin Chevrolet .... D....... 323 772-6494
  23505 Hawthorne Blvd Torrance (90505) **(P-7256)**
Martin Lther King Jr Cmnty Hos, Los Angeles *Also Called: Martin Lther King Jr-Los Angle* **(P-17272)**
Martin Lther King Jr-Los Angle .... B....... 424 338-8000
  1680 E 120th St Los Angeles (90059) **(P-17272)**
Martin-Brower Company LLC .... B....... 209 466-2980
  4704 Fite Ct Stockton (95215) **(P-6265)**
Martin, John A & Associates, Los Angeles *Also Called: Martin Associates Group Inc* **(P-19316)**
Martin, Steve DDS, Santa Rosa *Also Called: Interdent Service Corporation* **(P-15230)**
Martina Landscape Inc .... D....... 408 871-8800
  811 Camden Ave Campbell (95008) **(P-520)**
Martinez Medical Offices, Martinez *Also Called: Kaiser Foundation Hospitals* **(P-9431)**
Martinez Outpatient Clinic, Martinez *Also Called: Veterans Health Administration* **(P-15192)**
Martinez Steel Corporation .... C....... 909 946-0686
  1500 S Haven Ave Ste 150 Ontario (91761) **(P-2188)**
Martinez Steel Inc .... D....... 909 946-0686
  8920 Vernon Ave Ste 128 Montclair (91763) **(P-2189)**
Martis Camp Club .... B....... 530 550-6000
  7951 Fleur Du Lac Ct Truckee (96161) **(P-18051)**
Maruchan Inc .... C....... 949 789-2300
  1902 Deere Ave Irvine (92606) **(P-2429)**
Maruhide Marine Products Inc .... D....... 562 435-6509
  2145 W 17th St Long Beach (90813) **(P-6474)**
Marvel Studios LLC (HQ) .... D....... 310 727-2700
  500 S Buena Vista St Burbank (91521) **(P-10490)**
Marvin Engineering Co Inc (PA) .... A....... 310 674-5030
  261 W Beach Ave Inglewood (90302) **(P-19317)**
Marvin Group, The, Inglewood *Also Called: Marvin Engineering Co Inc* **(P-19317)**
Mary Grahams Childrens Shelter, French Camp *Also Called: County of San Joaquin* **(P-17939)**
Mary Hlth of Sick Cnvlscent Nr .... D....... 805 498-3644
  2929 Theresa Dr Newbury Park (91320) **(P-15581)**
Marycrest Manor .... D....... 310 838-2778
  10664 Saint James Dr Culver City (90230) **(P-15878)**
Marymount Villa LLC .... D....... 510 895-5007
  345 Davis St Ofc San Leandro (94577) **(P-15772)**
Marysville Post-Acute, Marysville *Also Called: Melon Holdings LLC* **(P-15583)**

Maryvale .... C....... 626 280-6510
  7600 Graves Ave Rosemead (91770) **(P-18479)**
Maryvale Day Care Center .... C....... 626 357-1514
  2502 Huntington Dr Duarte (91010) **(P-18332)**
Maryvale Edcatn Fmly Rsrce Ctr, Duarte *Also Called: Maryvale Day Care Center* **(P-18332)**
MASADA HOMES, Gardena *Also Called: Counseling and Research Assoc* **(P-18401)**
Masco, San Jose *Also Called: Topbuild Services Group Corp* **(P-2322)**
MASCOLA, LOUIS F DDS, Torrance *Also Called: Louis F Mascola DDS* **(P-15235)**
Masergy Cloud Cmmnications Inc .... D....... 310 921-7000
  3663 Greve Dr Rancho Palos Verdes (90275) **(P-13364)**
Mashburn Trnsp Svcs Inc .... C....... 661 763-5724
  1423 Kern St Taft (93268) **(P-3510)**
Masker Painting, Oakland *Also Called: George E Masker Inc* **(P-1619)**
Mason Group .... D....... 818 707-8989
  638 Lindero Canyon Rd Oak Park (91377) **(P-1888)**
Mason McDuffie Mortgage Corp (PA) .... D....... 925 242-4400
  12647 Alcosta Blvd Ste 300 San Ramon (94583) **(P-8000)**
Mason Street Opco LLC .... A....... 415 772-5000
  950 Mason St San Francisco (94108) **(P-10009)**
Masonic Home For Adults, Union City *Also Called: Masonic Homes of California* **(P-18481)**
Masonic Homes of California (PA) .... B....... 415 776-7000
  1111 California St San Francisco (94108) **(P-18480)**
Masonic Homes of California .... B....... 510 441-3700
  34400 Mission Blvd Union City (94587) **(P-18481)**
Masonry Concepts Inc .... D....... 562 802-3700
  15408 Cornet St Santa Fe Springs (90670) **(P-1889)**
Masonry Group Nevada Inc .... D....... 951 509-5300
  8188 Lincoln Ave Ste 99 Riverside (92504) **(P-1890)**
Mass Precision Inc .... D....... 408 786-0378
  2070 Oakland Rd San Jose (95131) **(P-2074)**
Massachusetts Electric Company .... D....... 909 962-6001
  1925 Wright Ave Ste C La Verne (91750) **(P-20146)**
Massachusetts Mutl Lf Insur Co .... C....... 323 965-6339
  8383 Wilshire Blvd Ste 600 Beverly Hills (90211) **(P-8239)**
Massage Envy .... D....... 510 456-3689
  39016 Paseo Padre Pkwy Fremont (94538) **(P-10560)**
Massmutual, Beverly Hills *Also Called: Massachusetts Mutl Lf Insur Co* **(P-8239)**
Massmutual Pacific .... C....... 916 437-1713
  1435 River Park Dr Ste 410 Sacramento (95815) **(P-8240)**
MASSMUTUAL PACIFIC, Sacramento *Also Called: Massmutual Pacific* **(P-8240)**
Master Fasteners International LLC .... D....... 562 279-0150
  724 W Cowles St Long Beach (90813) **(P-5910)**
Master Lightning SEC Solutions .... D....... 626 337-2915
  545 N Mountain Ave Ste 207 Upland (91786) **(P-13001)**
Master Lightning SEC Solutions, Upland *Also Called: Master Lightning SEC Solutions* **(P-13001)**
Master Rent, Fresno *Also Called: Automatic Leasing Inc* **(P-10461)**
Master-Chef's Linen Rental, Los Angeles *Also Called: American Textile Maint Co* **(P-10428)**
Masterclass, San Francisco *Also Called: Yanka Industries Inc* **(P-14112)**
Mastroianni Family Entps Ltd .... B....... 310 952-1700
  10581 Garden Grove Blvd Garden Grove (92843) **(P-10561)**
Masuta National Inc .... C....... 916 520-0904
  65 Quinta Ct Ste C Sacramento (95823) **(P-3511)**
Matagrano Inc .... C....... 650 829-4829
  25858 Clawiter Rd Hayward (94545) **(P-6775)**
Mater Misericordiae Hospital (PA) .... A....... 209 564-5000
  333 Mercy Ave Merced (95340) **(P-16250)**
Materals MGT At St Mary Med Ct, Apple Valley *Also Called: St Mary Medical Center LLC* **(P-16482)**
Material Handling Supply Inc (HQ) .... D....... 562 921-7715
  12900 Firestone Blvd Santa Fe Springs (90670) **(P-5844)**
Material Holdings LLC (PA) .... C....... 310 553-0550
  1900 Avenue Of The Stars Ste 1600 Los Angeles (90067) **(P-19831)**
Material Security Inc .... D....... 408 649-9882
  1003 Main St Redwood City (94063) **(P-12262)**
Maternal Cnnctons El Cmino Hos .... D....... 650 988-8287
  2110 Forest Ave Ste B San Jose (95128) **(P-16251)**
Matesta Corporation .... C....... 949 874-6052
  5620 Knott Ave Buena Park (90621) **(P-6207)**
Math Holdings Inc (PA) .... C....... 909 517-2200
  15820 Euclid Ave Chino (91708) **(P-13365)**

Employee Codes: A=Over 500 employees, B=251-500
C=101-250, D=51-100, E=20-50, F=10-19, G=1-9

2024 Directory of California
WholeSalers and Service Companies

© Mergent Inc. 1-800-342-5647

Mathematica Inc .... C....... 510 830-3700
505 14th St Ste 800 Oakland (94612) *(P-19832)*

Matheny Sars Linkert Jaime LLP .... D....... 916 978-3434
3638 American River Dr Sacramento (95864) *(P-17563)*

Matheson Fast Freight Inc .... B....... 209 342-0184
9785 Goethe Rd Sacramento (95827) *(P-3512)*

Matheson Fast Freight Inc (HQ) .... **D....... 916 686-4600**
9780 Dino Dr Elk Grove (95624) *(P-3513)*

Matich Corporation (PA) .... **D....... 909 382-7400**
1596 E Harry Shepard Blvd San Bernardino (92408) *(P-1136)*

Matrix Absence Management Inc .... D....... 408 330-0754
3979 Freedom Cir Santa Clara (95054) *(P-20147)*

Matrix Absence Management Inc .... D....... 916 773-5737
1420 Rocky Ridge Dr Ste 270 Roseville (95661) *(P-20148)*

Matrix Aviation Services Inc .... C....... 310 337-3037
6171 W Century Blvd Ste 100 Los Angeles (90045) *(P-3973)*

Matrix Direct Insurance Svcs, San Diego *Also Called: AIG Direct Insurance Svcs Inc (P-8481)*

Matrix Environmental Inc .... D....... 562 236-2704
2330 E Cherry Industrial Cir Long Beach (90805) *(P-2296)*

Matrix Hg Inc .... C....... 925 459-9200
115 Mason Cir Ste B Concord (94520) *(P-1497)*

Matrix Surfaces Inc .... D....... 714 696-5449
5449 E La Palma Ave Anaheim (92807) *(P-1985)*

Matrixx Software, Foster City *Also Called: Matrixx Software Inc (P-12486)*

Matrixx Software Inc (PA) .... **D....... 669 267-6333**
1098 Foster City Blvd Ste 106 # 836 Foster City (94404) *(P-12486)*

Matson Alarm Co Inc .... D....... 559 438-8000
2005 W Ashland Ave Ste A Visalia (93277) *(P-13133)*

Matsudas By Green Acres LLC .... C....... 916 673-9290
10600 Florin Rd Sacramento (95830) *(P-138)*

Matsui Nursery Inc (PA) .... **D....... 831 422-6433**
1645 Old Stage Rd Salinas (93908) *(P-139)*

Matsushita International Corp (PA) .... **D....... 949 498-1000**
1141 Via Callejon San Clemente (92673) *(P-9531)*

Matt Construction Corporation (PA) .... **C....... 562 903-2277**
9814 Norwalk Blvd Ste 100 Santa Fe Springs (90670) *(P-20456)*

Mattermost Inc (PA) .... **C....... 650 667-8512**
530 Lytton Ave Palo Alto (94301) *(P-11737)*

MATTERPORT, Sunnyvale *Also Called: Matterport Inc (P-12263)*

Matterport Inc (PA) .... **C....... 650 641-2241**
352 E Java Dr Sunnyvale (94089) *(P-12263)*

Matterport Operating LLC (HQ) .... **C....... 650 641-2241**
352 E Java Dr Sunnyvale (94089) *(P-5328)*

Mattson, Foster City *Also Called: Peter H Mattson & Co Inc (P-19757)*

Maubertidence Opco LLC .... C....... 510 481-3200
15731 Maubert Ave San Leandro (94578) *(P-15773)*

Maud Booth Family Center, North Hollywood *Also Called: Volunteers of Amer Los Angeles (P-18181)*

Maury Microwave Inc (PA) .... **C....... 909 987-4715**
2900 Inland Empire Blvd Ontario (91764) *(P-5674)*

Mavenir International Holdings Inc .... D....... 408 855-2900
2890 Zanker Rd Ste 207 San Jose (95134) *(P-11738)*

Maverick Hospitality Inc .... D....... 714 730-7717
17662 Irvine Blvd Ste 4 Tustin (92780) *(P-10010)*

Maxar Space LLC .... A....... 650 852-4000
1140 Hamilton Ct Menlo Park (94025) *(P-3729)*

Maxar Space LLC (HQ) .... **D....... 650 852-4000**
3875 Fabian Way Palo Alto (94303) *(P-4543)*

Maxar Space Robotics LLC .... D....... 626 296-1373
1250 Lincoln Ave Ste 100 Pasadena (91103) *(P-19318)*

Maxim Healthcare Services Inc .... D....... 661 964-6350
28470 Avenue Stanford Ste 250 Valencia (91355) *(P-11300)*

Maxim Healthcare Services Inc .... C....... 310 329-9115
1515 W 190th St Gardena (90248) *(P-11301)*

Maxim Healthcare Services Inc .... D....... 916 614-9539
1651 Response Rd Ste 200 Sacramento (95815) *(P-11302)*

Maxim Healthcare Services Inc .... D....... 510 873-0700
2100 Powell St Emeryville (94608) *(P-11303)*

Maxim Healthcare Services Inc .... C....... 559 224-0299
5066 N Fresno St Ste 103 Fresno (93710) *(P-11304)*

Maxim Healthcare Services Inc .... C....... 916 771-7444
151 N Sunrise Ave Ste 905 Roseville (95661) *(P-11305)*

Maxim Healthcare Services Inc .... D....... 410 910-1500
1101 S Winchester Blvd Ste F164 San Mateo (94403) *(P-11306)*

Maxim Healthcare Services Inc .... C....... 951 694-0100
27555 Ynez Rd Temecula (92591) *(P-11307)*

Maxim Healthcare Services Inc .... D....... 951 684-4148
1845 Business Center Dr Ste 112 San Bernardino (92408) *(P-11308)*

Maxim Healthcare Services Inc .... D....... 661 322-3039
5201 California Ave Ste 200 Bakersfield (93309) *(P-11309)*

Maxim Healthcare Services Inc .... D....... 626 962-6453
801 Corporate Center Dr Ste 210 Pomona (91768) *(P-11310)*

Maxim Healthcare Services Inc .... C....... 408 914-7478
631 River Oaks Pkwy San Jose (95134) *(P-16891)*

Maxim Healthcare Services Inc .... B....... 866 465-5678
3580 Wilshire Blvd Ste 1000 Los Angeles (90010) *(P-16892)*

Maxim Healthcare Services Inc .... B....... 619 299-9350
3111 Camino Del Rio N Ste 1200 San Diego (92108) *(P-16893)*

Maxim Healthcare Services Inc .... C....... 559 227-2250
6051 N Fresno St Ste 102 Fresno (93710) *(P-16894)*

Maxim Healthcare Services Inc .... C....... 760 243-3377
560 E Hospitality Ln Ste 400 San Bernardino (92408) *(P-16895)*

Maxim Lighting, City Of Industry *Also Called: Maxim Lighting Intl Inc (P-5578)*

Maxim Lighting Intl Inc (PA) .... **C....... 626 956-4200**
253 Vineland Ave City Of Industry (91746) *(P-5578)*

Maximus Real Estate Partners .... D....... 415 584-4832
1 Maritime Plz Ste 1900 San Francisco (94111) *(P-8888)*

Maximus Tree Works LLC .... D....... 480 822-8050
1410 Beltline Rd Ste 1 Redding (96003) *(P-557)*

Maxin, Tustin *Also Called: Core Holdings Inc (P-16848)*

Maxon Lift Corp (PA) .... **C....... 562 464-0099**
11921 Slauson Ave Santa Fe Springs (90670) *(P-5845)*

Maxonic Inc .... D....... 408 739-4900
2542 S Bascom Ave Ste 190 Campbell (95008) *(P-12834)*

Maxplore Technologies Inc .... D....... 925 621-1400
4450 Rosewood Dr Ste 200 Pleasanton (94588) *(P-11739)*

Maxpreps, El Dorado Hills *Also Called: CBS Maxpreps Inc (P-4263)*

Maxus USA, Los Angeles *Also Called: Essense (P-20887)*

Maxwell Hotel, The, San Francisco *Also Called: Joie De Vivre Hospitality LLC (P-20125)*

May-Han Electric Inc .... D....... 916 929-0150
1600 Auburn Blvd Sacramento (95815) *(P-1771)*

Mayacama, Santa Rosa *Also Called: Mayacama Golf Club LLC (P-14402)*

Mayacama Golf Club LLC .... C....... 707 569-2900
1240 Mayacama Club Dr Santa Rosa (95403) *(P-14402)*

Mayer Brown & Platt, Los Angeles *Also Called: LLP Mayer Brown (P-17554)*

MAYWOOD ACRES HEALTHCARE, Oxnard *Also Called: Milwood Healthcare Inc (P-8736)*

Maze & Assoc Accounting Corp .... D....... 925 930-0902
3478 Buskirk Ave Pleasant Hill (94523) *(P-19610)*

MB Coatings Inc .... D....... 714 625-2118
1540 S Lewis St Anaheim (92805) *(P-13366)*

MB Herzog Electric Inc .... C....... 562 531-2002
15709 Illinois Ave Paramount (90723) *(P-1772)*

MBA Polymers Inc .... D....... 510 231-9031
500 W Ohio Ave Richmond (94804) *(P-4911)*

Mbanq, Healdsburg *Also Called: Finlink Inc (P-11601)*

Mbari, Moss Landing *Also Called: Monterey Bay Aquarium RES Inst (P-19898)*

MBC Systems, Santa Ana *Also Called: Medical Network Inc (P-20149)*

Mbe, Pasadena *Also Called: Ttg Engineers (P-19421)*

Mbh Arch, Alameda *Also Called: Mbh Architects Inc (P-19495)*

Mbh Architects Inc .... C....... 510 865-8663
960 Atlantic Ave Ste 100 Alameda (94501) *(P-19495)*

MBI, Stockton *Also Called: Midstate Barrier Inc (P-1139)*

Mbit Wireless Inc (PA) .... **C....... 949 205-4559**
4340 Von Karman Ave Ste 140 Newport Beach (92660) *(P-4218)*

Mbm, Ontario *Also Called: McLane Foodservice Dist Inc (P-7565)*

Mbp Land LLC .... A....... 619 291-5720
595 Hotel Cir S San Diego (92108) *(P-10011)*

Mc Graw Commercial Insur Svc (PA) .... **D....... 650 780-4800**
3601 Haven Ave Menlo Park (94025) *(P-8608)*

Mc Namara Ddge Ney Batt Sltter (PA) .... **D....... 925 939-5330**
3480 Buskirk Ave Ste 250 Pleasant Hill (94523) *(P-17564)*

Mc-40 (PA) .... **C....... 323 225-4111**
777 N Georgia Ave Azusa (91702) *(P-10924)*

ALPHABETIC SECTION

McAfee, San Jose *Also Called: McAfee Corp (P-12265)*
McAfee LLC (DH) .... C....... 888 847-8766
  6220 America Ctr Dr San Jose (95002) *(P-12264)*
McAfee Corp (HQ) .... C....... 866 622-3911
  6220 America Center Dr San Jose (95002) *(P-12265)*
McAfee Finance 2 LLC .... A....... 888 847-8766
  2821 Mission College Blvd Santa Clara (95054) *(P-12266)*
MCASD, San Diego *Also Called: Museum Cntmprary Art San Diego (P-18659)*
McC Pipeline, Yucaipa *Also Called: M C C Equipment Rentals Inc (P-1233)*
McCalls Catering, San Francisco *Also Called: Events Management Inc (P-7478)*
McCallum Theatre, Palm Desert *Also Called: Friends of Cultural Center Inc (P-14039)*
McCampbell Analytical Inc .... D....... 925 252-9262
  1534 Willow Pass Rd Pittsburg (94565) *(P-19986)*
McCann-Erickson Corporation (HQ) .... D....... 415 348-5600
  135 Main St 21st Fl San Francisco (94105) *(P-10645)*
McCarthy Bldg Companies Inc .... B....... 408 908-7005
  3975 Freedom Cir Ste 950 Santa Clara (95054) *(P-963)*
McCarthy Bldg Companies Inc .... D....... 949 851-8383
  20401 Sw Birch St Ste 300 Newport Beach (92660) *(P-964)*
McCarthy Bldg Companies Inc .... D....... 949 851-8383
  1113 Bush Orange (92868) *(P-965)*
McCarthy Bldg Companies Inc .... D....... 949 851-8383
  6363 Regent St Huntington Park (90255) *(P-966)*
McCarthy Bldg Companies Inc .... D....... 949 851-8383
  18943 Airport Way Santa Ana (92707) *(P-967)*
McCarthy Bldg Companies Inc .... B....... 949 851-8383
  20401 Sw Birch St Ste 200 Newport Beach (92660) *(P-968)*
McCarthy Bldg Companies Inc .... A....... 530 665-4774
  1460 Churchill Downs Ave Woodland (95776) *(P-969)*
McClatchy Newspapers Inc (DH) .... A....... 916 321-1855
  1601 Alhambra Blvd Ste 100 Sacramento (95816) *(P-2539)*
McClellan Business Park LLC .... D....... 916 965-7100
  3140 Peacekeeper Way Mcclellan (95652) *(P-20457)*
McClone Construction Company .... C....... 559 431-9411
  4340 Product Dr Cameron Park (95682) *(P-700)*
McClone Construction Company .... C....... 916 358-5495
  3880 El Dorado Hills Blvd El Dorado Hills (95762) *(P-2137)*
McCollisters Trnsp Group Inc .... D....... 909 428-5700
  10672 Jasmine St Fontana (92337) *(P-3514)*
McCormick Barstow, Fresno *Also Called: McCormick Brstow Shppard Wyte (P-17565)*
McCormick Brstow Shppard Wyte (PA) .... C....... 559 433-1300
  7647 N Fresno St Fresno (93720) *(P-17565)*
McCune Audio Visual Video Ltg, South San Francisco *Also Called: Harry McCune Sound Service Inc (P-11036)*
McDonald Packaging Inc C
  2601 S Garnsey St Santa Ana (92707) *(P-2521)*
McDonald's, Reseda *Also Called: Valley Management Associates (P-7515)*
McE, San Rafael *Also Called: Marin Clean Energy (P-4586)*
McE Corporation (PA) .... D....... 925 803-4111
  4000 Industrial Way Concord (94520) *(P-1137)*
McGrath Rentcorp (PA) .... C....... 925 606-9200
  5700 Las Positas Rd Livermore (94551) *(P-5846)*
McGuire and Hester (PA) .... B....... 510 632-7676
  2810 Harbor Bay Pkwy Alameda (94502) *(P-1235)*
MCH, Madera *Also Called: Madera Community Hospital (P-16243)*
Mch Electric Inc (PA) .... D....... 925 453-5041
  7693 Longard Rd Livermore (94551) *(P-1773)*
MCHC, Ukiah *Also Called: Mendocino Cmnty Hlth Clnic Inc (P-14895)*
McHenry Medical Group Inc .... D....... 209 577-3388
  1541 Florida Ave Ste 200 Modesto (95350) *(P-14888)*
McIntyre .... D....... 510 614-5890
  14680 Wicks Blvd San Leandro (94577) *(P-20458)*
McKee and Company Electric .... D....... 415 724-2738
  594 Monterey Blvd San Francisco (94127) *(P-1774)*
McKesson, Ontario *Also Called: McKesson Mdcl-Srgcal Mdmart In (P-6128)*
McKesson, San Francisco *Also Called: McKesson Property Company Inc (P-6129)*
McKesson Corporation .... D....... 510 666-0854
  3000 Colby St Berkeley (94705) *(P-6125)*
McKesson Corporation .... C....... 562 463-2100
  9501 Norwalk Blvd Santa Fe Springs (90670) *(P-6126)*
McKesson Corporation .... D....... 916 636-8700
  11000 Trade Center Dr Rancho Cordova (95670) *(P-6127)*
McKesson Drug Company, Santa Fe Springs *Also Called: McKesson Corporation (P-6126)*
McKesson Mdcl-Srgcal Mdmart In .... D....... 800 755-2090
  2800 E Philadelphia St Ontario (91761) *(P-6128)*
McKesson Mdcl-Srgcal Top Hldng .... B....... 800 300-4350
  1938 W Malvern Ave Fullerton (92833) *(P-5431)*
McKesson Property Company Inc .... C....... 415 983-8300
  1 Post St San Francisco (94104) *(P-6129)*
MCKINLEY CHILD DEVELOPMENT CENTER, Long Beach *Also Called: McKinley Child Development Ctr (P-18333)*
McKinley Child Development Ctr .... C....... 562 531-6182
  6822 N Paramount Blvd Long Beach (90805) *(P-18333)*
McKinley Childrens Center Inc (PA) .... C....... 909 599-1227
  180 Via Verde Ste 200 San Dimas (91773) *(P-18482)*
McKinnon Publishing Company .... A....... 858 571-5151
  4575 Viewridge Ave San Diego (92123) *(P-4453)*
McKinsey & Company Inc .... B....... 415 981-0250
  555 California St Ste 4700 San Francisco (94104) *(P-20459)*
McL Fresh, Commerce *Also Called: 4 Earth Farms LLC (P-6511)*
McLane, Merced *Also Called: McLane/Pacific Inc (P-6267)*
McLane Foodservice Inc .... C....... 951 867-3555
  14813 Meridian Pkwy Riverside (92518) *(P-6266)*
McLane Foodservice Dist Inc .... D....... 252 985-7200
  5675 Sunol Blvd Pleasanton (94566) *(P-6423)*
McLane Foodservice Dist Inc .... C....... 252 955-9547
  1051 Wineville Ave Ste 100 Ontario (91764) *(P-7565)*
McLane/Pacific Inc .... B....... 209 725-2500
  3876 E Childs Ave Merced (95341) *(P-6267)*
McLaren Strategic Solutions .... D....... 310 564-6754
  1 Park Plz Ste 600 Irvine (92614) *(P-12835)*
MCM Construction Inc (PA) .... D....... 916 334-1221
  6413 32nd St North Highlands (95660) *(P-1185)*
MCM Construction Inc .... D....... 909 875-0533
  19010 Slover Ave Bloomington (92316) *(P-1186)*
MCM Harvesters Inc .... B....... 805 659-6833
  1585 Lirio Ave Ventura (93004) *(P-11176)*
McMahon Steel Company Inc .... C....... 619 671-9700
  1880 Nirvana Ave Chula Vista (91911) *(P-2730)*
McMaster-Carr Supply Company .... B....... 562 692-5911
  9630 Norwalk Blvd Santa Fe Springs (90670) *(P-5911)*
McMillan Electric .... B....... 415 826-5100
  1480 Folsom St San Francisco (94103) *(P-1775)*
McMillin Communities Inc .... A....... 951 506-3303
  41687 Temeku Dr Temecula (92591) *(P-14274)*
McMillin Companies LLC (PA) .... D....... 619 477-4117
  2750 Womble Rd Ste 102 San Diego (92106) *(P-9532)*
McMillin Homes, San Diego *Also Called: McMillin Management Svcs LP (P-9379)*
McMillin Homes, San Diego *Also Called: McMillin Companies LLC (P-9532)*
McMillin Management Svcs LP (HQ) .... D....... 619 477-4117
  2750 Womble Rd Ste 102 San Diego (92106) *(P-9379)*
McMorgan & Company LLC (HQ) .... D....... 415 788-9300
  1 Front St Ste 500 San Francisco (94111) *(P-8207)*
McQ, Burbank *Also Called: Silver Saddle Ranch & Club Inc (P-9274)*
MCR Printing and Packg Corp .... C....... 619 488-3012
  8830 Siempre Viva Rd San Diego (92154) *(P-3730)*
McWhirter Steel Inc .... D....... 661 951-8998
  42211 7th St E Lancaster (93535) *(P-2737)*
MD Care Inc .... D....... 562 344-3400
  1640 E Hill St Signal Hill (90755) *(P-8268)*
MD Care Healthplan, Signal Hill *Also Called: MD Care Inc (P-8268)*
MD Imaging Inc A Prof Med Corp .... D....... 530 243-1249
  2020 Court St Redding (96001) *(P-14889)*
Md-Staff, Temecula *Also Called: Applied Statistics & MGT Inc (P-12094)*
Mddr Inc .... C....... 714 792-1993
  1921 Petra Ln Placentia (92870) *(P-1498)*
Mdh Network Inc .... C....... 562 945-4576
  7239 Washington Ave Whittier (90602) *(P-20460)*
Mdm Solutions LLC .... B....... 800 669-6361
  575 Anton Blvd Ste 300 Costa Mesa (92626) *(P-615)*
Mds Consulting (PA) .... D....... 949 251-8821
  17320 Red Hill Ave Ste 350 Irvine (92614) *(P-19319)*

Mdusd 1936 Carlotta Dr Concord (94519) *(P-17273)* .... D 925 682-8000

ME & My Big Ideas LLC 6261 Katella Ave Cypress (90630) *(P-5991)* .... C 240 348-5240

ME Fox & Company Inc 128 Component Dr San Jose (95131) *(P-6776)* .... C 408 435-8510

Meadow Club 1001 Bolinas Rd Fairfax (94930) *(P-14403)* .... D 415 453-3274

Meadow Glen Apartments, Sacramento Also Called: John Stewart Company *(P-8837)*

Meadow Lake Country Club, Escondido Also Called: Welk Group Inc *(P-14482)*

Meadowbrook Vlg Chrstn Rtrment 100 Holland Gln Escondido (92026) *(P-18483)* .... C 760 746-2500

Meadowlark Golf Course, Huntington Beach Also Called: City of Huntington Beach *(P-14250)*

Meadowood Assoc A Ltd Partnr (PA) 900 Meadowood Ln Saint Helena (94574) *(P-7495)* .... C 707 963-3646

Meadowood Nursing Center, Clearlake Also Called: Vindra Inc *(P-15724)*

Meadowood Resort and Cntry CLB, Saint Helena Also Called: Meadowood Assoc A Ltd Partnr *(P-7495)*

Meadows Nappa Valley Care Ctr, Napa Also Called: Califrnia Odd Fllows Hsing Nap *(P-8795)*

MEADOWS OF NAPA VALLEY, Napa Also Called: Califrnia Odd Fllows Hsing Nap *(P-8794)*

Meals On Wheels, San Jose Also Called: Health Trust *(P-17999)*

Mearsk, San Pedro Also Called: APM Terminals Pacific LLC *(P-3986)*

Measure of Excellence Cabinets, Poway Also Called: Kiewit Corporation *(P-951)*

Meathead Movers Inc (PA) 3600 S Higuera St San Luis Obispo (93401) *(P-3515)* .... D 805 544-6328

Mechanics Bank (DH) 1111 Civic Dr Ste 290 Walnut Creek (94596) *(P-7696)* .... C 800 797-6324

Med-Data Incorporated 3741 Douglas Blvd Roseville (95661) *(P-19611)* .... D 916 771-1362

Med-Legal LLC 955 Overland Ct Ste 200 San Dimas (91773) *(P-17566)* .... C 626 653-5160

Meda Cypress Ridge LP 2235 Meda Ave Santa Rosa (95404) *(P-9263)* .... C 707 526-9782

Medallia Inc (HQ) 6220 Stoneridge Mall Rd Fl 2 Pleasanton (94588) *(P-12267)* .... C 650 321-3000

Medallion Cnstr Clean-Up, Mountain View Also Called: Service By Medallion *(P-10964)*

Medallion Landscape MGT Inc (PA) 10 San Bruno Ave Morgan Hill (95037) *(P-443)* .... D 408 782-7500

Medamerica Inc (HQ) 2100 Powell St Ste 900 Emeryville (94608) *(P-20461)* .... D 510 350-2600

Medasend Biomedical Inc (PA) 1402 Daisy Ave Long Beach (90813) *(P-17274)* .... C 800 200-3581

Medholdings of Newnan LLC 1750 Vine St Los Angeles (90028) *(P-13367)* .... A 213 462-6252

Medi-Flight Northern Cal, Modesto Also Called: Sutter Central Vly Hospitals *(P-16514)*

Media Services, Los Angeles Also Called: Oberman Tivoli & Pickert Inc *(P-12507)*

Media Temple Inc 12655 W Jefferson Blvd # 400 Los Angeles (90066) *(P-4311)* 877 578-4000

Mediaalpha Inc (PA) 700 S Flower St Ste 640 Los Angeles (90017) *(P-10715)* .... D 213 316-6256

Mediabrands Worldwide Inc 1840 Century Park E Los Angeles (90067) *(P-10646)* .... B 323 370-8000

Mediatek USA Inc 10188 Telesis Ct Ste 500 San Diego (92121) *(P-5329)* .... C 858 731-9200

Medic Ambulance Service Inc (PA) 506 Couch St Vallejo (94590) *(P-3275)* .... C 707 644-1761

Medic-1 Ambulance Service Inc 1305 W Arrow Hwy Ste 206 San Dimas (91773) *(P-3276)* .... D 909 592-8840

Medical Anesthesia Cons Inc 100 N Wiget Ln Ste 160 Walnut Creek (94598) *(P-14890)* .... C 925 287-1505

Medical Billing Services, Monrovia Also Called: California Business Bureau Inc *(P-19546)*

Medical Center, San Bernardino Also Called: Far West Inc *(P-15475)*

Medical Center, San Diego Also Called: University Cal San Diego *(P-16590)*

Medical Center of Marin, Corte Madera Also Called: Brett V Crtis MD A Prof Corp I *(P-14637)*

Medical Centre, Sacramento Also Called: University California Davis *(P-16598)*

Medical Data Exchange, Anaheim Also Called: Cyber-Pro Systems Inc *(P-12562)*

Medical Device Technologies, San Diego Also Called: Miracor Diagnostics Inc *(P-16735)*

Medical Eye Services Inc 345 Baker St Costa Mesa (92626) *(P-8609)* .... D 714 619-4660

Medical Genetics, Los Angeles Also Called: Cedars-Sinai Medical Center *(P-15981)*

Medical Group, Fresno Also Called: Central Cal Fclty Med Group In *(P-14669)*

Medical Hill Healthcare Center, Oakland Also Called: Oaklandidence Opco LLC *(P-15779)*

Medical Hill Rehabilitation, Oakland Also Called: Ocadian Care Centers LLC *(P-15606)*

Medical Imging Ctr Sthern Cal 2811 Wilshire Blvd Ste 100 Santa Monica (90403) *(P-14891)* .... D 310 829-9788

Medical Insurance Exchange, Oakland Also Called: Medical Underwriters Cal Inc *(P-8610)*

Medical Insurance Exchange Cal 6250 Claremont Ave Oakland (94618) *(P-14892)* .... D 510 596-4935

Medical Linen Service Inc 290 S Maple Ave South San Francisco (94080) *(P-10437)* .... D 650 873-1221

Medical Management Cons Inc 6046 Cornerstone Ct W San Diego (92121) *(P-20462)* .... A 858 587-0609

Medical Network Inc 1809 E Dyer Rd Ste 311 Santa Ana (92705) *(P-20149)* .... D 949 863-0022

Medical Research Institute 21411 Prairie St Chatsworth (91311) *(P-6130)* .... C 818 739-6000

Medical Spc Managers Inc 1 City Blvd W Ste 1100 Orange (92868) *(P-20463)* .... C 714 571-5000

Medical Specialty Billing, Orange Also Called: Medical Spc Managers Inc *(P-20463)*

Medical Underwriters Cal Inc (PA) 6250 Claremont Ave Oakland (94618) *(P-8610)* .... D 510 428-9411

Medico Professional Linen Svc, Los Angeles Also Called: American Textile Maint Co *(P-10429)*

Medieval Times Entrmt Inc (HQ) 7662 Beach Blvd Buena Park (90620) *(P-10421)* .... A 714 523-1100

Medimpact Hlthcare Systems Inc (HQ) 10181 Scripps Gateway Ct San Diego (92131) *(P-18752)* .... C 858 566-2727

Medimpact Holdings Inc (PA) 10181 Scripps Gateway Ct San Diego (92131) *(P-9533)* .... A 858 566-2727

Medina Construction, Riverside Also Called: Bens Asphalt & Maint Co Inc *(P-1082)*

Mediscan Diagnostic Svcs LLC 21050 Califa St Ste 100 Woodland Hills (91367) *(P-11177)* .... D 818 758-4224

Mediscan Staffing Services, Woodland Hills Also Called: Mediscan Diagnostic Svcs LLC *(P-11177)*

Meditab Software Inc 8795 Folsom Blvd Ste 205 Sacramento (95826) *(P-12268)* .... D 510 201-0130

Medix Ambulance Service Inc (PA) 26021 Pala Mission Viejo (92691) *(P-3277)* .... C 949 470-8915

Medley Communications Inc (PA) 43015 Black Deer Loop Ste 203 Temecula (92590) *(P-1776)* .... C 951 245-5200

Medmark Trtmnt Ctrs - Scrmnto 7240 E Southgate Dr Ste G Sacramento (95823) *(P-17087)* .... D 916 391-4293

Medresponse LLC 9961 Baldwin Pl El Monte (91731) *(P-3278)* .... D 877 311-5555

Medric, Burlingame Also Called: Acumen LLC *(P-12415)*

Medrio Inc (PA) 345 California St Ste 325 San Francisco (94104) *(P-12269)* .... D 415 963-3700

Medstar LLC 20 Business Park Way Ste 100 Sacramento (95828) *(P-3279)* .... D 916 669-0550

Medterra Cbd LLC 18500 Von Karman Ave Irvine (92612) *(P-14)* .... D 800 971-1288

Medtrans Inc 345 S Woods Ave Los Angeles (90022) *(P-3280)* 323 780-9500

Medusind Solutions Inc (PA) 31103 Rancho Viejo Rd Ste 2150 San Juan Capistrano (92675) *(P-13368)* .... D 949 240-8895

Meebo Inc 1600 Amphitheatre Pkwy Mountain View (94043) *(P-4312)* .... D 650 253-0000

Meek's, South Lake Tahoe Also Called: Cha-Dor Realty LLC *(P-7116)*

Meeting Services Inc 1125 Joshua Way Vista (92081) *(P-11041)* .... D 858 348-0100

Mega Appraisers Inc 14724 Ventura Blvd Ste 800 Sherman Oaks (91403) *(P-13369)* .... A 818 246-7370

Mega Western Sales, Santa Fe Springs Also Called: Great Western Sales Inc *(P-5751)*

Megachips LSI USA Corporation 910 E Hamilton Ave Ste 120 Campbell (95008) *(P-2926)* .... D 408 570-0555

Megapath, Pleasanton Also Called: Gtt Communications (mp) Inc *(P-4292)*

Megapath Inc 6800 Koll Center Pkwy Ste 200 Pleasanton (94566) *(P-4313)* .... A 877 611-6342

Meggitt (orange County) Inc 355 N Pastoria Ave Sunnyvale (94085) *(P-3005)* .... D 408 739-3533

Meggitt Aerospace, Sunnyvale *Also Called: Meggitt (orange County) Inc* *(P-3005)*
Meggitt Ctrl Systms-Vntura Cnt, Simi Valley *Also Called: Meggitt Safety Systems Inc* *(P-2960)*
Meggitt Safety Systems Inc (DH)..C....... 805 584-4100
 1785 Voyager Ave Simi Valley (93063) *(P-2960)*
Mejico Express Inc (PA)..C....... 714 690-8300
 14849 Firestone Blvd Fl 1 La Mirada (90638) *(P-3857)*
Mek Enterprises Inc ....D....... 619 527-0957
 3517 Camino Del Rio S Ste 215 San Diego (92108) *(P-4132)*
Mek Escondido LLC ....C....... 760 747-0430
 421 E Mission Ave Escondido (92025) *(P-15582)*
Mek Industries Inc ....C....... 858 610-9601
 3517 Camino Del Rio S Ste 215 San Diego (92108) *(P-11311)*
Mel Bernie and Company Inc (PA)..C....... 818 841-1928
 3000 W Empire Ave Burbank (91504) *(P-6023)*
Mel Rapton Inc ....C....... 916 514-4050
 2329 Fulton Ave Sacramento (95825) *(P-7257)*
Mel Rapton Honda, Sacramento *Also Called: Mel Rapton Inc* *(P-7257)*
Melan Inc ....D....... 818 489-1745
 13700 Alton Pkwy Ste 154-2 Irvine (92618) *(P-13784)*
Melano Enterprises, Oceanside *Also Called: Mellano & Co* *(P-6864)*
Melin Enterprises Inc ....D....... 209 726-9182
 812 W 18th St Merced (95340) *(P-10925)*
Melissa Data Corporation (PA)...D....... 949 858-3000
 22382 Avenida Empresa Rcho Sta Marg (92688) *(P-11740)*
Melissas World Variety Produce, Vernon *Also Called: World Variety Produce Inc* *(P-6598)*
Melita Group, The, San Jose *Also Called: Melita-Mcdonald Insur Svcs Inc* *(P-8611)*
Melita-Mcdonald Insur Svcs Inc ....D....... 408 882-0800
 75 E Santa Clara St Ste 1200 San Jose (95113) *(P-8611)*
Mellano & Co ....C....... 760 433-9550
 734 Wilshire Rd Oceanside (92057) *(P-6864)*
Mellano & Company (PA)...D....... 213 622-0796
 766 Wall St Los Angeles (90014) *(P-6865)*
Mellano Enterprises, Los Angeles *Also Called: Mellano & Company* *(P-6865)*
Mellmo Inc ....C....... 858 847-3272
 131 Aberdeen Dr Cardiff By The Sea (92007) *(P-11741)*
Mellon, Los Angeles *Also Called: Bny Mellon National Assn* *(P-7609)*
Mellon, Newport Beach *Also Called: Bny Mellon National Assn* *(P-7662)*
Mellon Capital Management, San Francisco *Also Called: Mellon Global Oprtnty Fund LLC* *(P-9380)*
Mellon Global Oprtnty Fund LLC ....D....... 415 546-6056
 50 Fremont St Ste 3900 San Francisco (94105) *(P-9380)*
Melon Holdings LLC ....D....... 530 742-7311
 1617 Ramirez St Marysville (95901) *(P-15583)*
Membrane Technology & RES Inc (PA).......................................D....... 650 328-2228
 39630 Eureka Dr Newark (94560) *(P-19734)*
Memco Holdings Inc ....C....... 310 277-0057
 10390 Santa Monica Blvd # 210 Los Angeles (90025) *(P-9096)*
Memeged Tevuot Shemesh (PA)...C....... 866 575-1211
 5550 Topanga Canyon Blvd Ste 280 Woodland Hills (91367) *(P-1499)*
Memora Health Inc ....D....... 415 874-9390
 38 Bluxome St San Francisco (94107) *(P-17275)*
Memorex Products Inc ....C....... 562 653-2800
 17777 Center Court Dr N Ste 800 Cerritos (90703) *(P-5608)*
Memorial Care Medical Centers, Fountain Valley *Also Called: Memorial Health Services* *(P-16252)*
Memorial Center, Bakersfield *Also Called: Bakersfield Memorial Hospital* *(P-15956)*
Memorial Crdolgy Med Group Inc ....D....... 562 988-2995
 2898 Linden Ave Long Beach (90806) *(P-14893)*
Memorial Health Services (PA)...B....... 714 377-2900
 17360 Brookhurst St Ste 160 Fountain Valley (92708) *(P-16252)*
Memorial Healthtec Labratories ....A....... 714 962-4677
 9920 Talbert Ave Fountain Valley (92708) *(P-19735)*
Memorial Hlth Svcs - Univ Cal (PA)..A....... 562 933-2000
 2801 Atlantic Ave Long Beach (90806) *(P-16253)*
Memorial Hospital Los Banos ....C....... 209 826-0591
 520 W I St Los Banos (93635) *(P-16254)*
Memorial Hospital of Gardena ....B....... 323 268-5514
 4060 Woody Blvd Los Angeles (90023) *(P-16255)*
Memorial Hospital of Gardena, Gardena *Also Called: Gardena Hospital LP* *(P-16100)*

Memorial Medical Center, Modesto *Also Called: Sutter Central Vly Hospitals* *(P-16512)*
Memorial Medical Center, Modesto *Also Called: Sutter Central Vly Hospitals* *(P-16513)*
Memorial Medical Center Foundation ....A....... 562 933-2273
 2801 Atlantic Ave Long Beach (90806) *(P-19094)*
Memorial Orthpdic Srgcal Group ....D....... 562 424-6666
 2760 Atlantic Ave Long Beach (90806) *(P-14894)*
Memorialcare Medical Group ....D....... 714 378-7000
 18111 Brookhurst St Fountain Valley (92708) *(P-16256)*
Memorlcare Heart Vascular Inst, Laguna Hills *Also Called: Saddleback Memorial Med Ctr* *(P-16367)*
Memorlcare Srgcal Ctr At Ornge ....D....... 714 369-1100
 18111 Brookhurst St Ste 3200 Fountain Valley (92708) *(P-16257)*
MEMORY AND AGING CENTER, San Francisco *Also Called: University of California* *(P-20599)*
Memverge Inc ....D....... 408 605-0841
 1525 Mccarthy Blvd Ste 218 Milpitas (95035) *(P-11742)*
Men Tking Over Rfrming Soc Inc ....D....... 323 338-6633
 6630 Crenshaw Blvd Los Angeles (90043) *(P-18052)*
Men's Wearhouse, Fremont *Also Called: Twin Hill Acquisition Co Inc* *(P-6191)*
Mendel Biotechnology Inc ....D....... 510 264-0280
 3935 Point Eden Way Hayward (94545) *(P-19736)*
Mendocino Cmnty Hlth Clinic Inc (PA)..C....... 707 468-1010
 333 Laws Ave Ukiah (95482) *(P-14895)*
Mendocino Cmnty Hlth Clinic Inc ....C....... 707 456-9600
 45 Hazel St Willits (95490) *(P-14896)*
MENDOCINO COAST CLINICS, Fort Bragg *Also Called: Mendocino Coast Clinics Inc* *(P-17088)*
Mendocino Coast Clinics Inc ....D....... 707 964-1251
 205 South St Fort Bragg (95437) *(P-17088)*
Mendocino Coast District Hosp (PA)...B....... 707 961-1234
 700 River Dr Fort Bragg (95437) *(P-16258)*
Mendocino Forest Pdts Co LLC ....C....... 707 468-1431
 850 Kunzler Ranch Rd Ukiah (95482) *(P-5172)*
Mendocino Hotel & Grdn Suites, Mendocino *Also Called: Mendocino Hotel & Resort Corp* *(P-10012)*
Mendocino Hotel & Resort Corp ....D....... 707 937-0511
 45080 Main St Mendocino (95460) *(P-10012)*
Menlo Circus Club ....D....... 650 322-4616
 190 Park Ln Atherton (94027) *(P-14404)*
Menlo Gateway Inc ....D....... 650 356-2900
 303 Vintage Park Dr Ste 250 Foster City (94404) *(P-8878)*
Menlo Med Clinic A Med Corp ....C....... 650 498-6500
 1300 Crane St Menlo Park (94025) *(P-14897)*
Menlo Park Surgical Hospital, Burlingame *Also Called: Suttercare Corporation* *(P-16565)*
Menlo Worldwide Expedite, Redwood City *Also Called: Menlo Worldwide Forwarding Inc* *(P-3858)*
Menlo Worldwide Forwarding Inc ....A....... 650 596-9600
 1 Lagoon Dr Ste 400 Redwood City (94065) *(P-3858)*
Mens Apparel Guild In Cal Inc ....C....... 310 857-7500
 2901 28th St Ste 100 Santa Monica (90405) *(P-18713)*
Mental Health Department, Oakland *Also Called: La Clinica De La Raza Inc* *(P-14868)*
Mental Health Dept of, Artesia *Also Called: County of Los Angeles* *(P-17037)*
Mental Health Services, Stockton *Also Called: County of San Joaquin* *(P-17041)*
Mental Health Systems Inc (PA)...D....... 858 573-2600
 9465 Farnham St San Diego (92123) *(P-17089)*
Mental Health Systems Inc ....D....... 760 737-7125
 474 W Vermont Ave Ste 101 Escondido (92025) *(P-17090)*
Mental Hlth Assn San Francisco ....D....... 415 421-2926
 870 Market St Ste 928 San Francisco (94102) *(P-17091)*
Mentor California, Bakersfield *Also Called: Alliance Childrens Services* *(P-18372)*
Mentor Mdia USA Sup Chain MGT ....D....... 909 930-0800
 865 S Washington Ave San Bernardino (92408) *(P-20150)*
Mentor Worldwide LLC ....B....... 805 681-6000
 5425 Hollister Ave Santa Barbara (93111) *(P-5432)*
Menzies Aviation (texas) Inc ....D....... 909 937-3998
 1049 S Vineyard Ave Ontario (91761) *(P-3900)*
Meow Logistics, Walnut *Also Called: Straight Forwarding Inc* *(P-4102)*
Merakey USA ....D....... 916 923-9823
 3336 Bradshaw Rd Ste 175 Sacramento (95827) *(P-15584)*
Meraki Inc ....C....... 415 632-5800
 500 Terry A Francois Blvd San Francisco (94158) *(P-11743)*

Meraki LLC — ALPHABETIC SECTION

Meraki LLC (HQ) .... C 415 632-5800
500 Terry A Francois Blvd Ste 400 San Francisco (94158) *(P-12836)*

Mercado Latino Inc .... D 310 537-1062
1420 W Walnut St Compton (90220) *(P-3110)*

Mercado Latino Inc (PA) .... D 626 333-6862
245 Baldwin Park Blvd City Of Industry (91746) *(P-6268)*

Mercado Latino Inc .... D 510 475-5500
33430 Western Ave Union City (94587) *(P-6269)*

Mercari Inc .... B 855 464-7482
1530 Page Mill Rd Ste 100 Palo Alto (94304) *(P-11744)*

Mercari App, Palo Alto *Also Called: Mercari Inc (P-11744)*

Merced City School District .... D 209 385-6364
2736 Franklin Rd Merced (95348) *(P-17727)*

Merced Transportation Company .... D 209 384-2575
300 Grogan Ave Merced (95341) *(P-3347)*

Mercedes Benz of Bakersfield, Bakersfield *Also Called: Sangera Buick Inc (P-13674)*

Mercedes Benz of Escondido, Escondido *Also Called: Escondido Motors LLC (P-7202)*

Mercedes Benz of Riverside, Riverside *Also Called: Walters Auto Sales and Svc Inc (P-7329)*

Mercedes Benz of San Diego, San Diego *Also Called: Europa Auto Imports Inc (P-7203)*

Mercedes Diaz Homes Inc .... D 562 945-4576
7239 Washington Ave Ste 100 Whittier (90602) *(P-18484)*

Mercer (us) Inc .... D 949 222-1300
17901 Von Karman Ave Ste 1100 Irvine (92614) *(P-20464)*

Mercer Global Securities, Santa Barbara *Also Called: Mercer Global Securities LLC (P-8208)*

Mercer Global Securities LLC .... D 805 565-1681
1801 E Cabrillo Blvd Ste A Santa Barbara (93108) *(P-8208)*

Merchant of Tennis Inc .... A 909 923-3388
1625 Proforma Ave Ontario (91761) *(P-13370)*

Merchant Services, Irvine *Also Called: Universal Card Inc (P-13528)*

Merchant Services Inc (PA) .... B 817 725-0900
1 S Van Ness Ave Fl 5 San Francisco (94103) *(P-12594)*

Merchant Valley Corporation .... C 916 786-7227
1808 Avondale Dr Roseville (95747) *(P-18714)*

Merchants Bank California N A .... A 310 549-4350
1 Civic Plaza Dr Ste 100 Carson (90745) *(P-7697)*

Merchants Building Maint Co .... B 714 973-9272
1639 E Edinger Ave Ste C Santa Ana (92705) *(P-10926)*

Merchants Building Maint Co .... B 858 455-0163
9555 Distribution Ave Ste 102 San Diego (92121) *(P-10927)*

Merchants Building Maint Co .... A 909 622-8260
1995 W Holt Ave Pomona (91768) *(P-10928)*

Merchants Building Maint Co .... C 323 881-8902
606 Monterey Pass Rd Ste 202 Monterey Park (91754) *(P-10929)*

Merchants Building Maintenance, Santa Ana *Also Called: Merchants Building Maint Co (P-10926)*

Merchants Building Maintenance, Pomona *Also Called: Merchants Building Maint Co (P-10928)*

Merchants Landscape Services .... D 909 981-1022
8748 Industrial Ln # 1 Rancho Cucamonga (91730) *(P-444)*

Merchants Landscape Services .... D 619 778-6239
2865 Main St Ste A Chula Vista (91911) *(P-521)*

Merchsource LLC (DH) .... C 800 374-2744
7755 Irvine Center Dr Irvine (92618) *(P-5992)*

Mercury Casualty Company (HQ) .... A 323 937-1060
555 W Imperial Hwy Brea (92821) *(P-8390)*

Mercury Defense Systems Inc .... D 714 898-8200
10855 Business Center Dr Ste A Cypress (90630) *(P-12595)*

Mercury General, Los Angeles *Also Called: Mercury General Corporation (P-8391)*

Mercury General Corporation (PA) .... A 323 937-1060
4484 Wilshire Blvd Los Angeles (90010) *(P-8391)*

Mercury Insurance Broker, Santa Monica *Also Called: Mercury Insurance Company (P-8394)*

Mercury Insurance Company .... D 714 671-6700
555 W Imperial Hwy Brea (92821) *(P-8392)*

Mercury Insurance Company .... A 916 353-4859
104 Woodmere Rd Folsom (95630) *(P-8393)*

Mercury Insurance Company .... B 310 451-4943
1433 Santa Monica Blvd Santa Monica (90404) *(P-8394)*

Mercury Insurance Company .... A 714 255-5000
1700 Greenbriar Ln Brea (92821) *(P-8395)*

Mercury Insurance Company (HQ) .... C 323 937-1060
4484 Wilshire Blvd Los Angeles (90010) *(P-8396)*

Mercury Insurance Company .... A 858 694-4100
9635 Granite Ridge Dr Ste 200 San Diego (92123) *(P-8397)*

Mercury Insurance Company .... A 661 291-6470
27200 Tourney Rd Ste 400 Valencia (91355) *(P-8398)*

Mercury Insurance Group, Brea *Also Called: Mercury Insurance Company (P-8392)*

Mercury Insurance Group, Folsom *Also Called: Mercury Insurance Company (P-8393)*

Mercury Insurance Services LLC .... A 323 937-1060
4484 Wilshire Blvd Los Angeles (90010) *(P-8399)*

Mercury Media, Los Angeles *Also Called: Diversified Mrcury Cmmnctons LL (P-10729)*

Mercury Systems, Cypress *Also Called: Mercury Defense Systems Inc (P-12595)*

Mercury Systems Inc .... D 714 898-8200
10855 Business Center Dr Ste A Cypress (90630) *(P-12596)*

Mercury Technology Group Inc .... D 949 417-0260
6430 Oak Cyn Ste 100 Irvine (92618) *(P-12597)*

Mercy Air Tri-County LLC .... C 909 829-1051
1670 Miro Way Rialto (92376) *(P-13727)*

Mercy For Animals Inc .... C 347 839-6464
8033 W Sunset Blvd Ste 864 Los Angeles (90046) *(P-336)*

Mercy Healthcare Sacramento .... A 916 379-2871
3400 Data Dr Rancho Cordova (95670) *(P-16259)*

Mercy HM Svcs A Cal Ltd Partnr (DH) .... A 530 225-6000
2175 Rosaline Ave Ste A Redding (96001) *(P-16260)*

Mercy House Living Centers .... C 714 836-7188
807 N Garfield St Santa Ana (92701) *(P-18715)*

Mercy Hse Trnstnal Living Ctrs, Santa Ana *Also Called: Mercy House Living Centers (P-18715)*

Mercy Medical Center - Redding, Redding *Also Called: Mercy HM Svcs A Cal Ltd Partnr (P-16260)*

Mercy Medical Center Merced, Merced *Also Called: Mater Misericordiae Hospital (P-16250)*

Mercy Medical Group .... D 916 691-8500
9394 Big Horn Blvd Elk Grove (95758) *(P-16261)*

Mercy Medical Group .... D 916 351-4834
1700 Prairie City Rd Folsom (95630) *(P-16262)*

Mercy Medical Group .... D 916 933-4222
4987 Golden Foothill Pkwy El Dorado Hills (95762) *(P-16263)*

Mercy Medical Group .... D 916 681-6000
8120 Timberlake Way Ste 107 Sacramento (95823) *(P-16264)*

Mercy Medical Group .... D 916 536-2420
8001 Madison Ave Citrus Heights (95610) *(P-16265)*

Mercy Medical Group .... D 916 536-3600
6555 Coyle Ave Ste 110 Carmichael (95608) *(P-16266)*

Mercy Medical Group .... D 916 536-2500
2110 Professional Dr Ste 120 Roseville (95661) *(P-16267)*

Mercy Medical Group (DH) .... D 916 733-3333
3000 Q St Sacramento (95816) *(P-16268)*

Mercy Medical Group, A Service, Elk Grove *Also Called: Mercy Medical Group (P-16261)*

Mercy Medical Trnsp Inc .... C 760 739-8026
27350 Valley Center Rd Ste A Valley Center (92082) *(P-3281)*

Mercy Retirement and Care Ctr .... D 510 534-8540
3431 Foothill Blvd Oakland (94601) *(P-18485)*

Mercy San Juan Hospital, Rancho Cordova *Also Called: Mercy Healthcare Sacramento (P-16259)*

Mercy San Juan Med Lvel II Tru, Carmichael *Also Called: Dignity Health (P-16043)*

Mercy San Juan Medical Center .... C 916 773-1188
9241 Sierra College Blvd # 150 Roseville (95661) *(P-14898)*

Mercy San Juan Medical Center, Carmichael *Also Called: Dignity Health (P-16050)*

Mercy Surgery Center LP .... D 530 225-7400
2175 Rosaline Ave Ste A Redding (96001) *(P-16269)*

Meredith Baer & Associates, South Gate *Also Called: Meribear Productions Inc (P-13371)*

Merge Healthcare Solutions Inc .... D 858 625-3344
10140 Mesa Rim Rd San Diego (92121) *(P-12487)*

Merger Sub Gotham 2 LLC .... C 714 462-4603
6261 Katella Ave Ste 250 Cypress (90630) *(P-2673)*

Mergis Group, The, Irvine *Also Called: Randstad Professionals Us LLC (P-11321)*

Meribear Productions Inc .... D 310 204-5353
4100 Ardmore Ave South Gate (90280) *(P-13371)*

Merical LLC .... C 714 685-0977
447 W Freedom Ave Orange (92865) *(P-13372)*

Merical LLC .... B 714 283-9551
233 E Bristol Ln Orange (92865) *(P-13373)*

ALPHABETIC SECTION — Merrill Lynch Prce Fnner Smith

Merical LLC .... C....... 714 238-7225
  445 W Freedom Ave Orange (92865) *(P-13374)*

Merical/Vita-Pak, Orange *Also Called: Merical LLC (P-13373)*

Meridian, San Diego *Also Called: Meridian Rack & Pinion Inc (P-5048)*

Meridian, Folsom *Also Called: Meridian Knwldge Solutions LLC (P-20465)*

Meridian Gold Inc .... B....... 209 785-3222
  4461 Rock Creek Rd Copperopolis (95228) *(P-574)*

Meridian Knwldge Solutions LLC (DH) .... D....... 916 985-9625
  80 Iron Point Cir Ste 100 Folsom (95630) *(P-20465)*

Meridian Management Group .... C....... 415 434-9700
  1145 Bush St San Francisco (94109) *(P-9097)*

Meridian Project Systems Inc .... C....... 916 294-2000
  1720 Prairie City Rd Ste 120 Folsom (95630) *(P-12270)*

Meridian Rack & Pinion Inc .... C....... 888 875-0026
  9980 Huennekens St Ste 200 San Diego (92121) *(P-5048)*

Meridian Rail Acquisition .... C....... 909 478-0541
  1475 Cooley Ct San Bernardino (92408) *(P-4167)*

Meridian Systems, Folsom *Also Called: Meridian Project Systems Inc (P-12270)*

Mering Holdings (PA) .... D....... 916 441-0571
  1700 I St Ste 210 Sacramento (95811) *(P-10647)*

Meristar San Pedro Hilton LLC .... D....... 310 514-3344
  2800 Via Cabrillo Marina San Pedro (90731) *(P-10013)*

Merit Companies The, Irvine *Also Called: Firstsrvice Rsidential Cal LLC (P-9017)*

Merit Day Food Service, Pico Rivera *Also Called: Three Sons Inc (P-6506)*

Merit International Inc .... C....... 833 463-7487
  100 S Murphy Ave Sunnyvale (94086) *(P-11745)*

Meritage Group LP .... A....... 415 399-5330
  1 Ferry Building San Francisco (94111) *(P-20151)*

Meritage Medical Network .... C....... 415 884-1840
  4 Hamilton Landing Ste 100 Novato (94949) *(P-11312)*

Meritage Resort LLC .... B....... 707 251-1900
  875 Bordeaux Way Napa (94558) *(P-10014)*

Meritage Resort and Spa, The, Napa *Also Called: Meritage Resort LLC (P-10014)*

Meritek Electronics Corp (PA) .... D....... 626 373-1728
  5160 Rivergrade Rd Baldwin Park (91706) *(P-2790)*

Meriwest Credit Union (PA) .... C....... 408 363-3200
  5615 Chesbro Ave Ste 100 San Jose (95123) *(P-7781)*

Merli Concrete Pumping, Gardena *Also Called: Stefan Merli Plastering Co Inc (P-2161)*

Merlot Film Productions Inc .... C....... 323 575-2906
  7800 Beverly Blvd Los Angeles (90036) *(P-13864)*

Merrill Lynch, San Francisco *Also Called: Merrill Lynch Prce Fnner Smith (P-7630)*

Merrill Lynch, Beverly Hills *Also Called: Merrill Lynch Prce Fnner Smith (P-7631)*

Merrill Lynch, Woodland Hills *Also Called: Merrill Lynch Prce Fnner Smith (P-8104)*

Merrill Lynch, Costa Mesa *Also Called: Merrill Lynch Prce Fnner Smith (P-8105)*

Merrill Lynch, Redding *Also Called: Merrill Lynch Prce Fnner Smith (P-8106)*

Merill Lynch, Valencia *Also Called: Merrill Lynch Prce Fnner Smith (P-8107)*

Merrill Lynch, Indian Wells *Also Called: Merrill Lynch Prce Fnner Smith (P-8108)*

Merrill Lynch, Palo Alto *Also Called: Merrill Lynch Prce Fnner Smith (P-8109)*

Merrill Lynch, Newport Beach *Also Called: Merrill Lynch Prce Fnner Smith (P-8110)*

Merrill Lynch, Laguna Niguel *Also Called: Merrill Lynch Prce Fnner Smith (P-8111)*

Merrill Lynch, Santa Monica *Also Called: Merrill Lynch Prce Fnner Smith (P-8112)*

Merrill Lynch, San Francisco *Also Called: Merrill Lynch Prce Fnner Smith (P-8113)*

Merrill Lynch, San Diego *Also Called: Merrill Lynch Prce Fnner Smith (P-8114)*

Merrill Lynch, Ontario *Also Called: Merrill Lynch Prce Fnner Smith (P-8115)*

Merrill Lynch, Santa Barbara *Also Called: Merrill Lynch Prce Fnner Smith (P-8116)*

Merrill Lynch, Modesto *Also Called: Merrill Lynch Prce Fnner Smith (P-8117)*

Merrill Lynch, Roseville *Also Called: Merrill Lynch Prce Fnner Smith (P-8118)*

Merrill Lynch, San Jose *Also Called: Merrill Lynch Prce Fnner Smith (P-8119)*

Merrill Lynch, Rancho Santa Fe *Also Called: Merrill Lynch Prce Fnner Smith (P-8120)*

Merrill Lynch, Visalia *Also Called: Merrill Lynch Prce Fnner Smith (P-8122)*

Merrill Lynch, Pleasanton *Also Called: Merrill Lynch Prce Fnner Smith (P-8123)*

Merrill Lynch, Santa Barbara *Also Called: Merrill Lynch Prce Fnner Smith (P-8124)*

Merrill Lynch, Bakersfield *Also Called: Merrill Lynch Prce Fnner Smith (P-8125)*

Merrill Lynch, Brea *Also Called: Merrill Lynch Prce Fnner Smith (P-8126)*

Merrill Lynch, Stockton *Also Called: Merrill Lynch Prce Fnner Smith (P-8127)*

Merrill Lynch, Santa Rosa *Also Called: Merrill Lynch Prce Fnner Smith (P-8128)*

Merrill Lynch, El Segundo *Also Called: Merrill Lynch Prce Fnner Smith (P-8129)*

Merrill Lynch, Walnut Creek *Also Called: Merrill Lynch Prce Fnner Smith (P-8130)*

Merrill Lynch, Pasadena *Also Called: Merrill Lynch Prce Fnner Smith (P-8132)*

Merrill Lynch, Fresno *Also Called: Merrill Lynch Prce Fnner Smith (P-8133)*

Merrill Lynch, Monterey *Also Called: Merrill Lynch Prce Fnner Smith (P-8134)*

Merrill Lynch, Seal Beach *Also Called: Merrill Lynch Prce Fnner Smith (P-8135)*

Merrill Lynch, San Diego *Also Called: Merrill Lynch Prce Fnner Smith (P-8136)*

Merrill Lynch, San Mateo *Also Called: Merrill Lynch Prce Fnner Smith (P-8137)*

Merrill Lynch, Westlake Village *Also Called: Merrill Lynch Prce Fnner Smith (P-8138)*

Merrill Lynch, Mill Valley *Also Called: Merrill Lynch Prce Fnner Smith (P-8139)*

Merrill Lynch, La Jolla *Also Called: Merrill Lynch Prce Fnner Smith (P-8140)*

Merrill Lynch, San Diego *Also Called: Merrill Lynch Prce Fnner Smith (P-8141)*

Merrill Lynch, San Luis Obispo *Also Called: Merrill Lynch Prce Fnner Smith (P-8142)*

Merrill Lynch, Irvine *Also Called: Merrill Lynch Prce Fnner Smith (P-8143)*

Merrill Lynch Pierce Fenner .... D....... 408 260-6001
  560 S Winchester Blvd San Jose (95128) *(P-8103)*

Merrill Lynch Carlsbad Office, Carlsbad *Also Called: Merrill Lynch Prce Fnner Smith (P-8131)*

Merrill Lynch Prce Fnner Smith .... D....... 415 676-2500
  101 California St Fl 21 San Francisco (94111) *(P-7630)*

Merrill Lynch Prce Fnner Smith .... D....... 310 858-1500
  9595 Wilshire Blvd Beverly Hills (90212) *(P-7631)*

Merrill Lynch Prce Fnner Smith .... D....... 818 340-9500
  21215 Burbank Blvd Ste 600 Woodland Hills (91367) *(P-8104)*

Merrill Lynch Prce Fnner Smith .... D....... 714 429-2800
  650 Town Center Dr # 500 Costa Mesa (92626) *(P-8105)*

Merrill Lynch Prce Fnner Smith .... D....... 530 223-3005
  292 Hemsted Dr Ste 100 Redding (96002) *(P-8106)*

Merrill Lynch Prce Fnner Smith .... D....... 661 802-0764
  24200 Magic Mountain Pkwy Ste 115 Valencia (91355) *(P-8107)*

Merrill Lynch Prce Fnner Smith .... C....... 760 862-1400
  74800 Us Highway 111 Indian Wells (92210) *(P-8108)*

Merrill Lynch Prce Fnner Smith .... C....... 650 842-2440
  3075a Hansen Way Palo Alto (94304) *(P-8109)*

Merrill Lynch Prce Fnner Smith .... C....... 949 467-3760
  520 Newport Center Dr Ste 1900 Newport Beach (92660) *(P-8110)*

Merrill Lynch Prce Fnner Smith .... D....... 949 456-8082
  28202 Cabot Rd Laguna Niguel (92677) *(P-8111)*

Merrill Lynch Prce Fnner Smith .... D....... 310 477-3400
  100 Wilshire Blvd Ste 300 Santa Monica (90401) *(P-8112)*

Merrill Lynch Prce Fnner Smith .... C....... 415 955-3700
  555 California St Fl 9 San Francisco (94104) *(P-8113)*

Merrill Lynch Prce Fnner Smith .... C....... 619 699-3700
  701 B St Ste 2350 San Diego (92101) *(P-8114)*

Merrill Lynch Prce Fnner Smith .... C....... 909 476-5100
  901 Via Piemonte Ste 503 Ontario (91764) *(P-8115)*

Merrill Lynch Prce Fnner Smith .... D....... 805 695-7028
  1096 Coast Village Rd Santa Barbara (93108) *(P-8116)*

Merrill Lynch Prce Fnner Smith .... C....... 209 578-2600
  801 10th St Fl 7-1 Modesto (95354) *(P-8117)*

Merrill Lynch Prce Fnner Smith .... D....... 916 984-3200
  2998 Douglas Blvd Ste 290 Roseville (95661) *(P-8118)*

Merrill Lynch Prce Fnner Smith .... C....... 408 283-3000
  50 W San Fernando St Ste 1600 San Jose (95113) *(P-8119)*

Merrill Lynch Prce Fnner Smith .... D....... 800 403-8796
  5951 La Sendita A Rancho Santa Fe (92067) *(P-8120)*

Merrill Lynch Prce Fnner Smith .... D....... 916 648-6200
  555 Capitol Mall Ste 1400 Sacramento (95814) *(P-8121)*

Merrill Lynch Prce Fnner Smith .... D....... 559 741-9033
  212 E Main St Ste 101 Visalia (93291) *(P-8122)*

Merrill Lynch Prce Fnner Smith .... D....... 925 227-6600
  4900 Hopyard Rd Ste 140 Pleasanton (94588) *(P-8123)*

Merrill Lynch Prce Fnner Smith .... C....... 805 963-0333
  1424 State St Santa Barbara (93101) *(P-8124)*

Merrill Lynch Prce Fnner Smith .... C....... 661 326-7700
  5080 California Ave Ste 102 Bakersfield (93309) *(P-8125)*

Merrill Lynch Prce Fnner Smith .... C....... 714 257-4400
  145 S State College Blvd Ste 300 Brea (92821) *(P-8126)*

Merrill Lynch Prce Fnner Smith .... D....... 209 472-3500
  3255 W March Ln Ste 110 Stockton (95219) *(P-8127)*

Merrill Lynch Prce Fnner Smith .... D....... 707 575-6374
  90 S E St Frnt Santa Rosa (95404) *(P-8128)*

ALPHABETIC SECTION

Merrill Lynch Prce Fnner Smith .... D...... 310 536-1600
2301 Rosecrans Ave Ste 3150 El Segundo (90245) *(P-8129)*

Merrill Lynch Prce Fnner Smith .... D...... 925 945-4800
1331 N California Blvd Ste 400 Walnut Creek (94596) *(P-8130)*

Merrill Lynch Prce Fnner Smith .... D...... 760 930-3100
1000 Aviara Dr Ste 200 Carlsbad (92011) *(P-8131)*

Merrill Lynch Prce Fnner Smith .... C...... 800 637-7455
800 E Colorado Blvd Ste 400 Pasadena (91101) *(P-8132)*

Merrill Lynch Prce Fnner Smith .... D...... 559 436-0919
5260 N Palm Ave Ste 100 Fresno (93704) *(P-8133)*

Merrill Lynch Prce Fnner Smith .... C...... 831 625-2700
200 E Franklin St Monterey (93940) *(P-8134)*

Merrill Lynch Prce Fnner Smith .... D...... 562 493-1300
3010 Old Ranch Pkwy Ste 150 Seal Beach (90740) *(P-8135)*

Merrill Lynch Prce Fnner Smith .... D...... 858 673-6700
11811 Bernardo Plaza Ct San Diego (92128) *(P-8136)*

Merrill Lynch Prce Fnner Smith .... C...... 650 579-3050
101 S Ellsworth Ave Fl 4 San Mateo (94401) *(P-8137)*

Merrill Lynch Prce Fnner Smith .... D...... 805 381-2600
2815 Townsgate Rd Ste 300 Westlake Village (91361) *(P-8138)*

Merrill Lynch Prce Fnner Smith .... D...... 415 289-8800
2 Belvedere Pl Ste 100 Mill Valley (94941) *(P-8139)*

Merrill Lynch Prce Fnner Smith .... D...... 858 456-3600
7825 Fay Ave Ste 300 La Jolla (92037) *(P-8140)*

Merrill Lynch Prce Fnner Smith .... D...... 858 677-1300
12830 El Camino Real Ste 300 San Diego (92130) *(P-8141)*

Merrill Lynch Prce Fnner Smith .... D...... 805 596-2222
1020 Marsh St San Luis Obispo (93401) *(P-8142)*

Merrill Lynch Prce Fnner Smith .... D...... 949 235-5050
100 Spectrum Center Dr Irvine (92618) *(P-8143)*

Merrill Lynch Prce Fnner Smith, Sacramento *Also Called: Merrill Lynch Prce Fnner Smith* *(P-8121)*

Merrill Lynch Wealth MGT, San Jose *Also Called: Merrill Lynch Pierce Fenner* *(P-8103)*

Merritt Hawkins & Assoc LLC (HQ) .... C...... 858 792-0711
12400 High Bluff Dr Ste 100 San Diego (92130) *(P-11313)*

Merritt Hospitality LLC .... C...... 562 983-3400
701 W Ocean Blvd Long Beach (90831) *(P-10015)*

Merritt Hospitality LLC .... C...... 714 738-7800
2701 Nutwood Ave Fullerton (92831) *(P-10016)*

Meru Health Holding Inc .... D...... 760 841-8040
720 S B St San Mateo (94401) *(P-17092)*

Meruelo Enterprises Inc (PA) .... A...... 562 745-2300
9550 Firestone Blvd Ste 105 Downey (90241) *(P-970)*

Mesa Associates Inc .... D...... 909 979-6609
3670 W Temple Ave Ste 152 Pomona (91768) *(P-19320)*

Mesa Biotech Inc .... D...... 858 800-4929
6190 Cornerstone Ct E Ste 220 San Diego (92121) *(P-19737)*

Mesa Cnsld Wtr Dst Imprv Corp (PA) .... D...... 949 631-1200
1965 Placentia Ave Costa Mesa (92627) *(P-4809)*

Mesa Contracting Corporation C
22845 Savi Ranch Pkwy Ste D Yorba Linda (92887) *(P-1138)*

Mesa Distributing Co Inc (HQ) .... C...... 858 452-2300
3840 Via De La Valle Ste 300 Del Mar (92014) *(P-6777)*

Mesa Energy Systems Inc (HQ) .... C...... 949 460-0460
2 Cromwell Irvine (92618) *(P-1500)*

Mesa Insurance Solutions Inc .... C...... 805 308-6308
50 Castilian Dr Goleta (93117) *(P-8612)*

Mesa Management Inc .... D...... 949 851-0995
1451 Quail St Ste 201 Newport Beach (92660) *(P-9098)*

Mesa Pointe Stadium 12, Costa Mesa *Also Called: Edwards Theatres Circuit Inc* *(P-13991)*

Mesa Verde Country Club .... C...... 714 549-0377
3000 Club House Rd Costa Mesa (92626) *(P-14405)*

Mesa Verde Partners .... C...... 714 540-7500
1701 Golf Course Dr Costa Mesa (92626) *(P-14275)*

Mesa Verde Prosecute Care, Costa Mesa *Also Called: Mesa Vrde Cnvalescent Hosp Inc* *(P-15585)*

Mesa Vineyard Management Inc (PA) .... D...... 805 434-4100
110 Gibson Rd Templeton (93465) *(P-378)*

Mesa Vrde Cnvalescent Hosp Inc .... C...... 949 548-5584
661 Center St Costa Mesa (92627) *(P-15585)*

MESA WATER DISTRICT, Costa Mesa *Also Called: Mesa Cnsld Wtr Dst Imprv Corp* *(P-4809)*

Mesfin Enterprises .... B...... 310 615-0881
222 N Pacific Coast Hwy Ste 1570 El Segundo (90245) *(P-12488)*

Mesmerize LLC .... C...... 415 374-8298
350 Frank H Ogawa Plz Ste 310 Oakland (94612) *(P-20466)*

Messagesolution Inc .... D...... 925 833-8000
6690 Amador Plaza Rd Ste 255 Dublin (94568) *(P-7446)*

Messenger Express (PA) .... C...... 213 614-0475
5435 Cahuenga Blvd Ste C North Hollywood (91601) *(P-3621)*

Mestek Inc .... C...... 310 835-7500
1220 E Watson Center Rd Carson (90745) *(P-2843)*

Mesvision, Costa Mesa *Also Called: Medical Eye Services Inc* *(P-8609)*

Meta, Menlo Park *Also Called: Meta Platforms Inc* *(P-12677)*

Meta Platforms Inc (PA) .... A...... 650 543-4800
1601 Willow Rd Menlo Park (94025) *(P-12677)*

Metabase Inc .... D...... 415 767-0490
9740 Campo Rd Pmb 1029 Spring Valley (91977) *(P-12598)*

Metabiota Inc .... D...... 415 398-4712
425 California St Ste 1200 San Francisco (94104) *(P-19738)*

Metabyte Inc .... D...... 510 494-9700
43238 Christy St Fremont (94538) *(P-12837)*

Metagenics LLC (PA) .... C...... 949 366-0818
25 Enterprise Ste 200 Aliso Viejo (92656) *(P-6131)*

Metal Finishing Pntg Lab Tstg, Oxnard *Also Called: Elite Metal Finishing LLC* *(P-2760)*

Metal Supply LLC .... D...... 562 634-9940
11810 Center St South Gate (90280) *(P-2738)*

Metals USA, Brea *Also Called: Metals USA Building Pdts LP* *(P-2723)*

Metals USA Building Pdts LP (DH) .... A...... 713 946-9000
955 Columbia St Brea (92821) *(P-2723)*

Metaverse Mod Squad, Sacramento *Also Called: Modsquad Inc* *(P-20474)*

Methodist Hospital, Arcadia *Also Called: Usc Arcadia Hospital* *(P-16606)*

Methodist Hospital of S CA .... D...... 626 574-3755
300 W Huntington Dr Arcadia (91007) *(P-16270)*

Methodist Hospital Sacramento, Sacramento *Also Called: Dignity Health* *(P-16051)*

Metric Equipment Sales Inc .... D...... 510 264-0887
25841 Industrial Blvd Ste 200 Hayward (94545) *(P-5675)*

Metric Theory LLC .... D...... 415 659-8600
311 California St Ste 200 San Francisco (94104) *(P-20467)*

Metricom Networks .... D...... 480 522-0700
290 W Orange Show Rd Ste 101 San Bernardino (92408) *(P-1236)*

Metricstream Inc (PA) .... C...... 650 620-2955
6201 America Center Dr Ste 240 San Jose (95002) *(P-12271)*

Metro, Los Angeles *Also Called: Los Angles Cnty Mtro Trnsp Aut* *(P-3149)*

Metro, Sun Valley *Also Called: Los Angles Cnty Mtro Trnsp Aut* *(P-3158)*

Metro, Los Angeles *Also Called: Los Angles Cnty Mtro Trnsp Aut* *(P-3159)*

Metro Bldrs & Engineers Group, Newport Beach *Also Called: Houalla Enterprises Ltd* *(P-939)*

Metro Ports, Long Beach *Also Called: Suderman Contg Stevedores Inc* *(P-3819)*

Metro YMCA Leitch, Fremont *Also Called: Young MNS Chrstn Assn of E Bay* *(P-18984)*

Metro-Goldwyn-Mayer Inc (DH) .... B...... 310 449-3000
245 N Beverly Dr Beverly Hills (90210) *(P-13865)*

Metrolink, Los Angeles *Also Called: Southern Cal Rgional Rail Auth* *(P-3217)*

Metrolink Doc, Pomona *Also Called: Southern Cal Rgional Rail Auth* *(P-3216)*

Metromile, San Francisco *Also Called: Metromile Operating Company* *(P-8400)*

Metromile Operating Company (DH) .... D...... 888 244-1702
425 Market St Ste 700 San Francisco (94105) *(P-8400)*

Metroplitan Oakland Intl Arprt, Oakland *Also Called: Port Dept of The Cy Oakland* *(P-3906)*

Metropltan Area Advsory Cmmtte (PA) .... D...... 619 426-3595
1355 Third Ave Chula Vista (91911) *(P-18234)*

Metropltan Wtr Dst of Sthern C .... D...... 714 577-5031
3972 Valley View Ave Yorba Linda (92886) *(P-4810)*

Metropltan Wtr Dst of Sthern C .... B...... 909 593-7474
700 Moreno Ave La Verne (91750) *(P-4811)*

Metropolis Hotel MGT LLC .... C...... 213 683-4855
899 Francisco St Los Angeles (90017) *(P-10017)*

Metropolitan Automotive Warehouse .... A...... 909 885-2886
535 Tennis Court Ln San Bernardino (92408) *(P-5049)*

Metropolitan Club .... D...... 415 673-0600
640 Sutter St San Francisco (94102) *(P-14406)*

Metropolitan Education Dst (PA) .... D...... 408 723-6464
760 Hillsdale Ave Bldg 6 San Jose (95136) *(P-17728)*

Metropolitan Elec Cnstr Inc ..... C 415 642-3000
2400 3rd St San Francisco (94107) *(P-1777)*

Metropolitan Home Mortgage Inc ..... D 949 428-0161
3090 Bristol St Ste 600 Costa Mesa (92626) *(P-8001)*

Metropolitan Imports LLC ..... C 646 980-5343
16311 Ventura Blvd Encino (91436) *(P-13375)*

Metropolitan Realty MGT Inc ..... D 310 537-5441
11254 Atlantic Ave Ste 4 Lynwood (90262) *(P-9099)*

Metropolitan Theatres Corp ..... D 760 323-3221
789 E Tahquitz Canyon Way Palm Springs (92262) *(P-14003)*

Metropolitan Trnsp Comm (PA) ..... C 415 778-6700
375 Beale St Ste 800 San Francisco (94105) *(P-3162)*

Metropolitan Waste Disposal, Paramount Also Called: Calmet Inc *(P-4875)*

Metropolitan Water Lavern, La Verne Also Called: Metroplfan Wtr Dst of Sthern C *(P-4811)*

Metropro Road Services Inc ..... D 714 556-7600
957 W 17th St Costa Mesa (92627) *(P-13717)*

Metrostudy Inc ..... C 714 619-7800
4000 Macarthur Blvd Ste 40 Newport Beach (92660) *(P-20468)*

Mets//, Manhattan Beach Also Called: M & E Technical Services L L C *(P-20658)*

Metwest Total Return Bond Fund ..... D 800 241-4671
865 S Figueroa St Los Angeles (90017) *(P-9381)*

Meus, Cypress Also Called: Mitsubishi Electric Us Inc *(P-5676)*

Mexicali Inc ..... C 661 327-3861
631 18th St Bakersfield (93301) *(P-7496)*

Mexicali Restaurant, Bakersfield Also Called: Mexicali Inc *(P-7496)*

Mexican Amrcn Oprtnty Fndation (PA) ..... D 323 890-9600
401 N Garfield Ave Montebello (90640) *(P-18053)*

Mexican Amrcn Oprtnty Fndation ..... D 323 890-1555
5657 E Washington Blvd Commerce (90040) *(P-18054)*

Mexican Heritg Ctr Gallery Inc ..... D 209 969-9306
111 S Sutter St Stockton (95202) *(P-18657)*

Meyer Corporation US (HQ) ..... D 707 551-2800
1 Meyer Plz Vallejo (94590) *(P-2752)*

Meyer LLC ..... C 831 385-4047
102 Broadway St King City (93930) *(P-288)*

Meyer Tomatoes, King City Also Called: Meyer LLC *(P-288)*

Meyer Wines, Vallejo Also Called: Meyer Corporation US *(P-2752)*

Meyers Nave A Prof Corp (PA) ..... D 510 351-4300
1999 Harrison St Ste 900 Oakland (94612) *(P-17567)*

Mezmo Inc ..... C 408 471-9997
2059 Camden Ave # 297 San Jose (95124) *(P-12838)*

Mf Services Company LLC (HQ) ..... D 949 474-5800
4350 Von Karman Ave Ste 400 Newport Beach (92660) *(P-20469)*

MGA Entertainment Inc ..... A 800 222-4685
9220 Winnetka Ave Chatsworth (91311) *(P-5993)*

MGB Construction Inc ..... C 951 342-0303
91 Commercial Ave Riverside (92507) *(P-701)*

Mge Underground Inc ..... B 805 238-3510
2501 Golden Hill Rd Paso Robles (93446) *(P-2223)*

Mgh Corporation ..... D 323 754-1408
1202 W 101st St Los Angeles (90044) *(P-18486)*

Mgid Inc ..... D 424 322-8059
1149 3rd St Ste 210 Santa Monica (90403) *(P-20470)*

MGM, Beverly Hills Also Called: Metro-Goldwyn-Mayer Inc *(P-13865)*

MGM and Ua Services Company ..... A 310 449-3000
245 N Beverly Dr Beverly Hills (90210) *(P-20895)*

MGM Drywall Inc ..... D 408 292-4085
1050 Commercial St Ste 102 San Jose (95112) *(P-1946)*

Mgo, Sacramento Also Called: Macias Gini & OConnell LLP *(P-19608)*

Mgo, Los Angeles Also Called: Macias Gini & OConnell LLP *(P-19609)*

Mh Sub I LLC (PA) ..... B 310 280-4000
909 N Pacific Coast Hwy Fl 11 El Segundo (90245) *(P-10648)*

Mhf Mv Operating VI LLC ..... D 619 481-5881
595 Hotel Cir S San Diego (92108) *(P-10018)*

Mhh Holdings Inc ..... C 949 651-9903
5653 Alton Pkwy Irvine (92618) *(P-6645)*

Mhh Holdings Inc ..... C 626 744-9370
415 S Lake Ave Ste 108 Pasadena (91101) *(P-6646)*

Mhm Services Inc ..... C 707 652-2688
155 Glen Cove Marina Rd E # 200 Vallejo (94591) *(P-17093)*

Mhm Services Inc ..... C 805 904-6678
230 Station Way Arroyo Grande (93420) *(P-17094)*

Mhm Services Inc ..... C 559 412-8121
6041 N 1st St Fresno (93710) *(P-17095)*

Mhm Services Inc ..... C 707 623-9080
2380 Professional Dr Santa Rosa (95403) *(P-17096)*

Mhm Services Inc ..... C 415 416-6992
180 Redwood St San Francisco (94102) *(P-17097)*

Mhn Government Services LLC ..... B 916 294-4941
2370 Kerner Blvd San Rafael (94901) *(P-18055)*

MHRP Resort Inc ..... D 760 249-5808
24510 Highway 2 Wrightwood (92397) *(P-10019)*

MHS, San Diego Also Called: Mental Health Systems Inc *(P-17089)*

MHS Customer Services Inc ..... D 858 695-2151
7586 Trade St Ste C San Diego (92121) *(P-11178)*

MI Technologies Inc ..... A 619 710-2637
2215 Paseo De Las Americas Ste 30 San Diego (92154) *(P-2674)*

Mias Fashion Mfg Co Inc ..... B 562 906-1060
12623 Cisneros Ln Santa Fe Springs (90670) *(P-6208)*

Miasole, Santa Clara Also Called: Miasole Hi-Tech Corp *(P-2927)*

Miasole Hi-Tech Corp (DH) ..... C 408 919-5700
3211 Scott Blvd Ste 201 Santa Clara (95054) *(P-2927)*

Micha-Rettenmaier Partnership ..... D 714 280-1645
351 Hospital Rd Ste 507 Newport Beach (92663) *(P-14899)*

Michaael S Hensley ..... C 650 692-7007
180 W Hill Pl Brisbane (94005) *(P-10562)*

Michael Baker International Inc (DH) ..... B 949 472-3505
5 Hutton Centre Dr Ste 500 Santa Ana (92707) *(P-19321)*

Michael Dusi Trucking Inc ..... C 805 237-9499
4305 Second Wind Way Paso Robles (93446) *(P-3516)*

Michael G Frtnsce Physcl Thrap ..... C 626 446-7027
24630 Washington Ave Ste 200 Murrieta (92562) *(P-15296)*

Michael Levine Inc (PA) ..... D 213 622-6259
920 Maple Ave Los Angeles (90015) *(P-7559)*

Michael P Byko DDS A Prof Corp (PA) ..... D 909 888-7817
164 W Hospitality Ln Ste 14 San Bernardino (92408) *(P-15240)*

Michael Sullivan & Assoc LLP ..... C 310 337-4480
2401 E El Segundo Blvd El Segundo (90245) *(P-17568)*

Michaels Mngmnt-Affordable LLC ..... C 559 897-5885
333 Kern St Apt 101 Kingsburg (93631) *(P-8843)*

Michaels Trnsp Svc Inc ..... D 707 674-6013
140 Yolano Dr Vallejo (94589) *(P-3312)*

Michaelson Connor & Boul (PA) ..... D 714 230-3600
5312 Bolsa Ave Huntington Beach (92649) *(P-20471)*

Michels Pacific Energy Inc ..... C 920 924-8725
2200 Laurelwood Rd Santa Clara (95054) *(P-1237)*

Michelson Laboratories Inc (PA) ..... D 562 928-0553
6280 Chalet Dr Commerce (90040) *(P-19987)*

Micke Grove Park & Zoo, Lodi Also Called: County of San Joaquin *(P-20945)*

MICOP, Oxnard Also Called: Mixtec/Ndgena Cmnty Orgnzing P *(P-18056)*

Micro Focus, Pleasanton Also Called: Micro Focus LLC *(P-11746)*

Micro Focus LLC ..... D 925 784-3242
6701 Koll Center Pkwy # 300 Pleasanton (94566) *(P-11746)*

Micro Prcision Calibration Inc ..... C 714 901-5659
2165 N Glassell St Orange (92865) *(P-19988)*

Micro Precision, Orange Also Called: Micro Prcision Calibration Inc *(P-19988)*

Micro-Mode Products Inc ..... C 619 449-3844
1870 John Towers Ave El Cajon (92020) *(P-2894)*

Micro-Pro Microfilming Svcs, Long Beach Also Called: Macro-Pro Inc *(P-13361)*

Microfinancial Incorporated ..... C 805 367-8900
2801 Townsgate Rd Westlake Village (91361) *(P-11042)*

Microlease, Hayward Also Called: Metric Equipment Sales Inc *(P-5675)*

Microlease Inc (DH) ..... D 866 520-0200
6060 Sepulveda Blvd Van Nuys (91411) *(P-11043)*

Microsemi Frequency Time Corp (DH) ..... C 480 792-7200
3870 N 1st St San Jose (95134) *(P-2866)*

Microsemi Soc Corp (DH) ..... C 408 643-6000
3850 N 1st St San Jose (95134) *(P-2928)*

Microtek Lab Inc (HQ) ..... C 310 687-5823
13337 South St Cerritos (90703) *(P-5250)*

Mid State Steel Erection (PA) ..... D 209 464-9497
1916 Cherokee Rd Stockton (95205) *(P-2190)*

ALPHABETIC SECTION

Mid Valley Dairy, Turlock Also Called: Super Store Industries *(P-2350)*
Mid Valley Title and Escrow Co .... D....... 530 533-6680
2295 Feather River Blvd Ste A Oroville (95965) *(P-9237)*
Mid-Century Insurance Company .... C....... 323 932-7116
6303 Owensmouth Ave Fl 1 Woodland Hills (91367) *(P-8401)*
Mid-Cities Association Inc (PA) .... D....... 310 537-4510
14208 Towne Ave Los Angeles (90061) *(P-18235)*
Mid-Valley Y M C A, Van Nuys Also Called: Young MNS Chrstn Assn Mtro Los *(P-18958)*
Mida Industries Inc .... C....... 562 616-1020
6101 Obispo Ave Long Beach (90805) *(P-10930)*
Midas Express Los Angeles Inc .... C....... 310 609-0366
11854 Alameda St Lynwood (90262) *(P-3731)*
Middesk Inc .... D....... 408 306-2663
85 2nd St Ste 710 San Francisco (94105) *(P-11747)*
Midi Association, The, Aliso Viejo Also Called: Midi Manufacturers Assn Inc *(P-18716)*
Midi Manufacturers Assn Inc .... D....... 714 227-0068
85 Matisse Cir Aliso Viejo (92656) *(P-18716)*
Midland Credit Management, San Diego Also Called: Midland Credit Management Inc *(P-7896)*
Midland Credit Management Inc .... A....... 877 240-2377
350 Camino De La Reina Ste 100 San Diego (92108) *(P-7896)*
Midland Industries .... C....... 800 821-5725
659 E Ball Rd Anaheim (92805) *(P-5912)*
Midnight Mission (PA) .... D....... 213 624-9258
601 S San Pedro St Los Angeles (90014) *(P-18881)*
Midnight Oil Agency LLC .... B....... 818 295-6100
3800 W Vanowen St Ste 101 Burbank (91505) *(P-2564)*
Midnight Oil Agency, Inc., Burbank Also Called: Midnight Oil Agency LLC *(P-2564)*
Midnight Sun Enterprises Inc .... D....... 310 532-2427
19900 Normandie Ave Torrance (90502) *(P-20804)*
Midpen Housing, Foster City Also Called: Menlo Gateway Inc *(P-8878)*
Midpen Housing Corporation .... B....... 650 356-2900
303 Vintage Park Dr Ste 250 Foster City (94404) *(P-9264)*
Midpennsula Rgnal Open Space D .... D....... 650 691-1200
5050 El Camino Real Los Altos (94022) *(P-20896)*
Midstate Barrier Inc .... D....... 209 944-9565
3291 S Highway 99 Stockton (95215) *(P-1139)*
Midstate Construction Corp .... D....... 707 762-3200
1180 Holm Rd Ste A Petaluma (94954) *(P-702)*
Midway Car Rental, North Hollywood Also Called: Midway Rent A Car Inc *(P-13597)*
Midway International Inc .... D....... 800 826-2383
13131 166th St Cerritos (90703) *(P-6928)*
Midway Rent A Car Inc .... D....... 619 238-9600
2263 Pacific Hwy San Diego (92101) *(P-13592)*
Midway Rent A Car Inc .... D....... 818 985-9770
4201 Lankershim Blvd North Hollywood (91602) *(P-13597)*
Mig Management Services LLC .... D....... 949 474-5800
660 Newport Center Dr Ste 1300 Newport Beach (92660) *(P-20152)*
Mighty Leaf Tea .... D....... 415 491-2650
100 Smith Ranch Rd Ste 120 San Rafael (94903) *(P-6647)*
Mightyhive Inc (HQ) .... D....... **888 727-9742**
311 California St Ste 200 San Francisco (94104) *(P-11748)*
Migo Money Inc .... D....... 415 906-4040
3739 Balboa St Ste 1101 San Francisco (94121) *(P-13376)*
Mike Brown Electric Co .... C....... 707 792-8100
561a Mercantile Dr Cotati (94931) *(P-1778)*
Mike Campbell & Associates Ltd .... A....... 626 369-3981
10907 Downey Ave Ste 203 Downey (90241) *(P-3655)*
Mike Campbell Assoc Logictics, Downey Also Called: Mike Campbell & Associates Ltd *(P-3655)*
Mike Jensen Farms LLC .... C....... 559 897-4192
13138 S Bethel Ave Kingsburg (93631) *(P-109)*
Mike McCall Landscape Inc .... C....... 925 363-8100
4749 Clayton Rd Concord (94521) *(P-522)*
Mike Parker Landscape, Santa Ana Also Called: Mpl Enterprises Inc *(P-523)*
Mike Rovner Construction Inc .... C....... 408 453-6070
1758 Junction Ave Ste C San Jose (95112) *(P-703)*
Mike Rovner Construction Inc .... C....... 949 458-1562
22600 Lambert St Lake Forest (92630) *(P-20153)*
Miko, Pleasanton Also Called: Rn Chidakashi Technologies Inc *(P-5995)*
Mikuni American Corporation (HQ) .... D....... **310 676-0522**
8910 Mikuni Ave Northridge (91324) *(P-5050)*

Milani Cosmetics, Culver City Also Called: New Milani Group LLC *(P-6136)*
Milbank Global Securities, Los Angeles Also Called: Milbank Tweed Hdley McCloy LLP *(P-17569)*
Milbank Tweed Hdley McCloy LLP .... C....... 424 386-4000
2029 Century Park E Los Angeles (90002) *(P-17569)*
Mildara Blass Inc .... B....... 707 836-5000
205 Concourse Blvd Santa Rosa (95403) *(P-2389)*
Mile High Valet, Dana Point Also Called: Ciri - Stroup Inc *(P-10535)*
Mile Post Properties LLC .... D....... 415 673-4711
1050 Van Ness Ave San Francisco (94109) *(P-10020)*
Mile Square Golf Course .... C....... 714 962-5541
10401 Warner Ave Fountain Valley (92708) *(P-14276)*
MILES TREASTER & ASSOCIATES .... D....... 916 373-1800
1810 13th St Sacramento (95811) *(P-7424)*
Milestone Health Care Center, Costa Mesa Also Called: Costa Mesa Healthcare Inc *(P-15389)*
Milestone Holdco Inc .... A....... 650 376-2300
901 Mariners Island Blvd San Mateo (94404) *(P-9321)*
Milestone Rtrment Cmmnties LLC .... D....... 209 533-4822
20420 Rafferty Ct Soulsbyville (95372) *(P-18487)*
Milestone Technologies Inc (PA) .... A....... **510 651-2454**
3101 Skyway Ct Fremont (94539) *(P-12489)*
Milgard Manufacturing LLC .... B....... 480 763-6000
26879 Diaz Rd Temecula (92590) *(P-2675)*
Milgard Manufacturing LLC .... D....... 916 387-0700
6050 88th St Sacramento (95828) *(P-5173)*
Milgard Windows, Temecula Also Called: Milgard Manufacturing LLC *(P-2675)*
Milgard Windows, Sacramento Also Called: Milgard Manufacturing LLC *(P-5173)*
Military California Department .... B....... 562 795-2065
11300 Lexington Dr Bldg 1000 Los Alamitos (90720) *(P-20659)*
Milken Family Foundation .... C....... 310 570-4800
1250 4th St Fl 1 Santa Monica (90401) *(P-18882)*
Millard Group Inc .... C....... 530 899-7299
1950 E 20th St Chico (95928) *(P-10931)*
Millennia Stainless Inc .... D....... 562 946-3545
10016 Romandel Ave Santa Fe Springs (90670) *(P-5913)*
Millennial Home Lending, Chatsworth Also Called: Cake Mortgage Corp *(P-7939)*
Millennium Biltmore Hotel, Los Angeles Also Called: Whb Corporation *(P-10367)*
Millennium Health LLC .... B....... 877 451-3534
16981 Via Tazon Ste F San Diego (92127) *(P-19989)*
Millennium Management LLC .... A....... 415 844-4048
2 Embarcadero Ctr # 1640 San Francisco (94111) *(P-9403)*
Millennium Reinforcing Inc .... B....... 949 361-9730
1046 Calle Recodo San Clemente (92673) *(P-2191)*
Millenworks .... D....... 714 426-5500
1361 Valencia Ave Tustin (92780) *(P-2967)*
Miller and Associates, Los Angeles Also Called: Imhoff & Associates PC *(P-17499)*
Miller Automotive Group Inc (HQ) .... B....... **818 787-8400**
5425 Van Nuys Blvd Sherman Oaks (91401) *(P-7258)*
Miller Children's Hospital, Long Beach Also Called: Long Beach Medical Center *(P-16233)*
MILLER CHILDREN'S HOSPITAL, Long Beach Also Called: Memorial Medical Center Foundation *(P-19094)*
Miller Creek School District .... C....... 415 492-3776
121 Marinwood Ave San Rafael (94903) *(P-17729)*
Miller Environmental Inc .... C....... 714 385-0099
1130 W Trenton Ave Orange (92867) *(P-2240)*
Miller Kaplan Arase LLP (PA) .... C....... **818 769-2010**
4123 Lankershim Blvd North Hollywood (91602) *(P-19612)*
Miller Nissan, Sherman Oaks Also Called: Miller Automotive Group Inc *(P-7258)*
Miller Starr Rglia A Prof Law (PA) .... D....... **925 935-9400**
1331 N California Blvd Fl 5 Walnut Creek (94596) *(P-17570)*
Millerick Engineering Inc .... D....... 209 664-9111
735 E Main St Turlock (95380) *(P-19322)*
Millie and Severson Inc .... D....... 562 493-3611
3601 Serpentine Dr Los Alamitos (90720) *(P-833)*
Mills Corporation .... D....... 909 484-8300
1 Mills Cir Ste 1 Ontario (91764) *(P-8735)*
Mills Iron Works .... D....... 323 321-6520
14834 S Maple Ave Gardena (90248) *(P-5914)*
Mills-Peninsula Health Services .... A....... 650 696-5400
1501 Trousdale Dr Burlingame (94010) *(P-16271)*

ALPHABETIC SECTION — Mission Hills Mortgage Corp

Mills-Peninsula Hospitals, Burlingame *Also Called: Mills-Peninsula Health Services (P-16271)*

Millwood Inn, Millbrae *Also Called: Arvee Bros Inc (P-9615)*

Milpitas Golfland, Milpitas *Also Called: Golfland Entrmt Ctrs Inc (P-14530)*

Milpitas Medical Offices, Milpitas *Also Called: Kaiser Foundation Hospitals (P-14825)*

Milpitas Unified School Dst ....D...... 408 635-2686
250a Roswell Dr Milpitas (95035) *(P-17730)*

Milwood Healthcare Inc ....D...... 626 274-4345
2641 S C St Oxnard (93033) *(P-8736)*

Minaris Medical America Inc ....C....... 800 233-6278
630 Clyde Ct Mountain View (94043) *(P-3011)*

Mind Research Institute ....C....... 949 345-8700
5281 California Ave Ste 300 Irvine (92617) *(P-19895)*

Mindbody, San Luis Obispo *Also Called: Mindbody Inc (P-12599)*

Mindbody Inc (PA) ....C....... 877 755-4279
651 Tank Farm Rd San Luis Obispo (93401) *(P-12599)*

Mindgruve Holdings Inc ....C....... 619 757-1325
627 8th Ave Ste 300 San Diego (92101) *(P-10649)*

Mindlance Inc ....A....... 858 433-9298
10679 Westview Pkwy Fl 2 San Diego (92126) *(P-20472)*

MINDLANCE INC., San Diego *Also Called: Mindlance Inc (P-20472)*

Mindless Entertainment, North Hollywood *Also Called: 51 Minds Entertainment LLC (P-14075)*

Mindpath Health, Sacramento *Also Called: Community Psychiatry MGT LLC (P-15278)*

Mindspark Inc ....D...... 310 396-9292
21021 Ventura Blvd Ste 220 Woodland Hills (91364) *(P-11749)*

Mindwave Software, San Diego *Also Called: Isaac Fair Corporation (P-11680)*

Mine, Los Angeles *Also Called: Edgemine Inc (P-6198)*

Mineral Earth Sciences LLC ....D...... 650 532-9590
100 Mayfield Ave Mountain View (94043) *(P-2770)*

Minerva, San Jose *Also Called: Minerva Networks Inc (P-11750)*

Minerva Networks Inc (PA) ....D...... 800 806-9594
100 Century Center Ct Ste 800 San Jose (95112) *(P-11750)*

Mineta San Jose Intl Arprt, San Jose *Also Called: City of San Jose (P-3883)*

Ming Entertainment Group LLC ....D...... 949 679-2089
2082 Business Center Dr Ste 292 Irvine (92612) *(P-14096)*

Ming Tsuang Dr ....D...... 858 822-2464
9500 Gillman Dr Mc 0603 La Jolla (92093) *(P-14900)*

Miniluxe, Los Angeles *Also Called: Miniluxe Inc (P-10502)*

Miniluxe Inc ....D...... 424 442-1630
11965 San Vicente Blvd Los Angeles (90049) *(P-10502)*

Minio Inc ....D...... 833 696-3742
275 Shoreline Dr Ste 100 Redwood City (94065) *(P-11751)*

Ministry Services of The Daugh ....C....... 650 917-4500
26000 Altamont Rd Los Altos Hills (94022) *(P-9438)*

Minka Group, Corona *Also Called: Minka Lighting LLC (P-5579)*

Minka Lighting LLC (PA) ....D...... 951 735-9220
1151 Bradford Cir Corona (92882) *(P-5579)*

Minshew Brothers Stl Cnstr Inc C
12578 Vigilante Rd Lakeside (92040) *(P-834)*

Minted LLC (PA) ....C....... 415 399-1100
747 Front St Fl 2 San Francisco (94111) *(P-6067)*

Mintie Technologies, Azusa *Also Called: Mc-40 (P-10924)*

Minturn Huller Cooperative Inc ....D...... 559 665-1185
9080 S Minturn Rd Chowchilla (93610) *(P-6696)*

Mintz Levin Cohn Ferris GL ....D...... 858 314-1500
3580 Carmel Mountain Rd Ste 300 San Diego (92130) *(P-17571)*

MINTZ, LEVIN, COHN, FERRIS, GLOVSKY AND POPEO, P.C., San Diego *Also Called: Mintz Levin Cohn Ferris GL (P-17571)*

Mips Tech LLC ....D...... 408 530-5000
780 Montague Expy Ste 308 San Jose (95131) *(P-12839)*

Mir3 Inc ....D...... 858 724-1200
3398 Carmel Mountain Rd # 100 San Diego (92121) *(P-11752)*

Mira Loma Dry Depot, Jurupa Valley *Also Called: Costco Wholesale Corporation (P-3689)*

Mira Mesa Stadium 18, San Diego *Also Called: Edwards Theatres Circuit Inc (P-13993)*

Miracor Diagnostics Inc (PA) ....D...... 858 455-7127
9191 Towne Centre Dr Ste 400 San Diego (92122) *(P-16735)*

Mirada, Long Beach *Also Called: Motion Theory Inc (P-10815)*

Mirada Hlls Rehb Cnvlscent Hos, La Mirada *Also Called: Life Care Centers America Inc (P-15538)*

Mirama Enterprises Inc ....D...... 858 587-8866
6469 Flanders Dr San Diego (92121) *(P-5124)*

Miramar Acquisition Co LLC ....C....... 805 900-8338
1759 S Jameson Ln Santa Barbara (93108) *(P-9534)*

Miramar Ford Truck Sales Inc ....D...... 619 272-5340
6066 Miramar Rd San Diego (92121) *(P-5016)*

Miramar Hotel, Santa Barbara *Also Called: Morgans Hotel Group MGT LLC (P-10029)*

Miramar Transportation Inc 858 693-0071
9340 Cabot Dr Ste I San Diego (92126) *(P-4059)*

Miramax LLC ....D...... 310 409-4321
1901 Avenue Of The Stars Ste 2000 Los Angeles (90067) *(P-13866)*

Miramonte Enterprises LLC ....C....... 951 658-9441
275 N San Jacinto St Hemet (92543) *(P-15586)*

Mirati, San Diego *Also Called: Mirati Therapeutics Inc (P-2598)*

Mirati Therapeutics Inc (PA) ....A....... 858 332-3410
3545 Cray Ct San Diego (92121) *(P-2598)*

Mirda, Daniel P MD, Napa *Also Called: Redwood Rgnal Med Group DRG LL (P-15014)*

Miro Technologies Inc ....C....... 858 677-2100
5643 Copley Dr San Diego (92111) *(P-12490)*

Mirum Inc ....C....... 619 237-5552
350 10th Ave Ste 1200 San Diego (92101) *(P-10814)*

Mis Sciences Corp 818 847-0213
2550 N Hollywood Way Ste 404 Burbank (91505) *(P-4314)*

Misa Imports Inc ....D...... 562 281-6773
2343 Saybrook Ave Commerce (90040) *(P-6929)*

Misope U S A Inc ....D...... 213 746-0888
1100 S San Pedro St Ste A7 Los Angeles (90015) *(P-6209)*

MISSION, Oxnard *Also Called: Mission Produce Inc (P-289)*

Mission Ambulance Inc ....D...... 951 272-2300
400 Ramona Ave Corona (92879) *(P-3282)*

Mission Bargain Center, Oxnard *Also Called: Rescue Mission Alliance (P-19099)*

Mission Bay Aquatic Center, San Diego *Also Called: Mission Bay Youth Wtr Spt Camp (P-18883)*

Mission Bay Aquatic Center, San Diego *Also Called: Associated Stdnts San Dego State (P-19035)*

Mission Bay Youth Wtr Spt Camp ....D...... 858 539-2003
1001 Santa Clara Pl San Diego (92109) *(P-18883)*

Mission Bell Mfg Co Inc ....B....... 408 778-2036
16100 Jacqueline Ct Morgan Hill (95037) *(P-2008)*

Mission Bell Winery, Madera *Also Called: Constlltion Brnds US Oprtons I (P-6793)*

Mission Care Center, Rosemead *Also Called: Ensign Group Inc (P-15455)*

Mission Cloud Services Inc (PA) ....C....... 855 647-7466
9350 Wilshire Blvd Ste 203 Beverly Hills (90212) *(P-12840)*

Mission College, Santa Clara *Also Called: West Vlly-Mssion Cmnty Cllege (P-17790)*

Mission Community Bancorp ....C....... 805 782-5000
3380 S Higuera St San Luis Obispo (93401) *(P-7632)*

MISSION COMMUNITY HOSPITAL, Panorama City *Also Called: Deanco Healthcare LLC (P-16037)*

Mission Constructors Inc ....D...... 415 282-8453
195 Bay Shore Blvd San Francisco (94124) *(P-971)*

Mission Crmchael Hlthcare Ctr, Carmichael *Also Called: SSC Carmichael Operating Co LP (P-15679)*

Mission Economic Dev Agcy ....D...... 415 282-3334
2301 Mission St Ste 301 San Francisco (94110) *(P-18236)*

Mission Electric Company, Fremont *Also Called: Kositch Enterprises Inc (P-1763)*

Mission Federal Credit Union ....C....... 858 531-5106
4250 Clairemont Mesa Blvd Ste B San Diego (92117) *(P-7782)*

Mission Federal Credit Union (PA) ....D...... 858 546-2184
5785 Oberlin Dr Ste 312 San Diego (92121) *(P-7783)*

Mission Federal Services LLC (PA) ....C....... 858 524-2850
10325 Meanley Dr San Diego (92131) *(P-7784)*

Mission Healthcare, San Diego *Also Called: Mission HM Hlth San Diego LLC (P-16896)*

Mission Hills Country Club Inc ....C....... 760 324-9400
34600 Mission Hills Dr Rancho Mirage (92270) *(P-14407)*

Mission Hills Health Care Inc ....D...... 619 297-4086
726 Torrance St San Diego (92103) *(P-15587)*

Mission Hills Healthcare Ctr, San Diego *Also Called: Mission Hills Health Care Inc (P-15587)*

Mission Hills Mortgage Bankers, Irvine *Also Called: Mission Hills Mortgage Corp (P-8002)*

Mission Hills Mortgage Corp (HQ) ....C....... 714 972-3832
18500 Von Karman Ave Ste 1100 Irvine (92612) *(P-8002)*

Mission Hills Senior Living 34560 Bob Hope Dr Rancho Mirage (92270) *(P-18488)* .... D....... 760 770-7737

Mission HM Hlth San Diego LLC 2365 Northside Dr Ste 200 San Diego (92108) *(P-16896)* .... D....... 619 757-2700

Mission Hosp Regional Med Ctr (PA) 27700 Medical Center Rd Mission Viejo (92691) *(P-16272)* .... A....... 949 364-1400

Mission Hospice & HM Care Inc 66 Bovet Rd Ste 100 San Mateo (94402) *(P-15774)* .... C....... 650 554-1000

Mission Hospital, Mission Viejo *Also Called: Auxilary of Mssion Hosp Mssion (P-15954)*

Mission Hospital, Mission Viejo *Also Called: Mission Hosp Regional Med Ctr (P-16272)*

Mission Hspice Svcs San Dego L 2385 Northside Dr Ste 200 San Diego (92108) *(P-16897)* .... D....... 619 814-4020

Mission Inn Hotel and Spa, The, Riverside *Also Called: Historic Mission Inn Corp (P-9857)*

Mission Internal Med Group Inc 27882 Forbes Rd Ste 110 Laguna Niguel (92677) *(P-14901)* .... D....... 949 364-3605

Mission Internal Med Group Inc 26800 Crown Valley Pkwy Ste 103 Mission Viejo (92691) *(P-14902)* .... D....... 949 364-3570

Mission Ldscp Companies Inc 536 E Dyer Rd Santa Ana (92707) *(P-445)* .... C....... 714 545-9962

Mission Ldscp Companies Inc 16672 Millikan Ave Irvine (92606) *(P-446)* .... D....... 800 545-9963

Mission Linen, Salinas *Also Called: Mission Linen Supply (P-10440)*

Mission Linen & Unf Svc 178, Anaheim *Also Called: Mission Linen Supply (P-10438)*

Mission Linen & Uniform Svc, Lancaster *Also Called: Mission Linen Supply (P-10439)*

Mission Linen & Uniform Svc, Oceanside *Also Called: Mission Linen Supply (P-10441)*

Mission Linen & Uniform Svc, Sacramento *Also Called: Mission Linen Supply (P-10442)*

Mission Linen & Uniform Svc, Salinas *Also Called: Mission Linen Supply (P-10443)*

Mission Linen & Uniform Svc, Fresno *Also Called: Mission Linen Supply (P-10445)*

Mission Linen & Uniform Svc, Oxnard *Also Called: Mission Linen Supply (P-10446)*

Mission Linen & Uniform Svc, Chino *Also Called: Mission Linen Supply (P-10447)*

Mission Linen & Uniform Svc, Santa Barbara *Also Called: Mission Linen Supply (P-10449)*

Mission Linen & Uniform Svc, Chico *Also Called: Mission Linen Supply (P-10450)*

Mission Linen & Uniform Svc, Montebello *Also Called: Mission Linen Supply (P-10451)*

Mission Linen & Uniform Svc, Santa Maria *Also Called: Mission Linen Supply (P-10452)*

Mission Linen & Uniform Svc, Salinas *Also Called: Mission Linen Supply (P-10479)*

Mission Linen & Uniform Svc 4, Santa Barbara *Also Called: Mission Linen Supply (P-10448)*

Mission Linen Supply 520 E Mineral King Ave Visalia (93292) *(P-10424)* .... D....... 559 625-5423

Mission Linen Supply 1260 N Jefferson St Anaheim (92807) *(P-10438)* .... D....... 909 364-8752

Mission Linen Supply 619 W Avenue I Lancaster (93534) *(P-10439)* .... D....... 661 948-5052

Mission Linen Supply 435 W Market St Salinas (93901) *(P-10440)* .... D....... 831 423-1630

Mission Linen Supply 2727 Industry St Oceanside (92054) *(P-10441)* .... C....... 760 757-9099

Mission Linen Supply 7520 Reese Rd Sacramento (95828) *(P-10442)* .... C....... 916 423-3179

Mission Linen Supply 315 Kern St Salinas (93905) *(P-10443)* .... D....... 831 424-1707

Mission Linen Supply 1401 Summer St Eureka (95501) *(P-10444)* .... D....... 707 443-8681

Mission Linen Supply 2555 S Orange Ave Fresno (93725) *(P-10445)* .... D....... 559 268-0647

Mission Linen Supply 505 Maulhardt Ave Oxnard (93030) *(P-10446)* .... D....... 805 485-6794

Mission Linen Supply 5400 Alton Way Chino (91710) *(P-10447)* .... C....... 909 393-6857

Mission Linen Supply 725 E Montecito St Santa Barbara (93103) *(P-10448)* .... D....... 805 963-0414

Mission Linen Supply 712 E Montecito St Santa Barbara (93103) *(P-10449)* .... C....... 805 962-7687

Mission Linen Supply 1340 W 7th St Chico (95928) *(P-10450)* .... C....... 530 342-4110

Mission Linen Supply 721 Washington Blvd Montebello (90640) *(P-10451)* .... D....... 323 888-8971

Mission Linen Supply 602 S Western Ave Santa Maria (93458) *(P-10452)* .... D....... 805 922-3579

Mission Linen Supply 435 W Market St Salinas (93901) *(P-10479)* .... D....... 831 424-1753

Mission Linen Supply & Svcs, Eureka *Also Called: Mission Linen Supply (P-10444)*

Mission Medical Clinic, Pomona *Also Called: Western Univ Hlth Sciences (P-15205)*

Mission Neighborhood Hlth Ctr (PA) 240 Shotwell St San Francisco (94110) *(P-14903)* .... C....... 415 552-3870

Mission Neighborhood Hlth Ctr, San Francisco *Also Called: Mission Neighborhood Hlth Ctr (P-14903)*

Mission Oaks Hospital, Los Gatos *Also Called: Good Samaritan Hospital LP (P-16112)*

Mission Peak Orthopedics 5924 Stoneridge Dr Ste 200 Pleasanton (94588) *(P-14904)* .... D....... 510 797-3933

Mission Pets LLC 986 Mission St Fl 5 San Francisco (94103) *(P-6930)* .... D....... 415 904-9914

Mission Pets, Inc., San Francisco *Also Called: Mission Pets LLC (P-6930)*

Mission Pools of Escondido 22600 Lambert St Ste 1104 Lake Forest (92630) *(P-2297)* .... C....... 949 588-0100

Mission Pools of Lake Forest, Lake Forest *Also Called: Mission Pools of Escondido (P-2297)*

Mission Produce Inc (PA) 2710 Camino Del Sol Oxnard (93030) *(P-289)* .... C....... 805 981-3650

Mission Service Inc 1800 Avenue Of The Stars Ste 1400 Los Angeles (90067) *(P-13668)* .... A....... 323 266-2593

Mission Skilled Nursing Home, Santa Clara *Also Called: Covenant Care California LLC (P-15401)*

Mission Springs Conf Cntr, Scotts Valley *Also Called: Pacific Sthwest Cnfrnce of Eva (P-8742)*

Mission Terrace, Santa Barbara *Also Called: Cliff View Terrace Inc (P-18395)*

Mission Trail Wste Systems Inc 1060 Richard Ave Santa Clara (95050) *(P-3413)* .... D....... 408 727-5365

Mission Valley YMCA, San Diego *Also Called: YMCA of San Diego County (P-18950)*

Mission Viejo Country Club 26200 Country Club Dr Mission Viejo (92691) *(P-14408)* .... C....... 949 582-1550

Mission View Health Center, San Luis Obispo *Also Called: Compass Health Inc (P-15381)*

Mission Vly Cab / Counter Tech, Poway *Also Called: B Young Enterprises Inc (P-2479)*

Mission Vly Ford String Trcks, San Jose *Also Called: Mission Vly Ford Trck Sls Inc (P-7259)*

Mission Vly Ford Trck Sls Inc 780 E Brokaw Rd San Jose (95112) *(P-7259)* .... D....... 408 933-2300

Mission Volkswagen Inc 32922 Valle Rd San Juan Capistrano (92675) *(P-7260)* .... D....... 949 493-4511

Mission YMCA, San Francisco *Also Called: Young MNS Chrstn Assn San Frnc (P-18998)*

Mission-Bishop Real Estate Inc 39180 Liberty St Ste 205 Fremont (94538) *(P-9100)* .... D....... 510 796-2100

Mist, Cupertino *Also Called: Mist Systems Inc (P-12491)*

Mist Systems Inc 1601 S De Anza Blvd Ste 248 Cupertino (95014) *(P-12491)* .... C....... 408 326-0346

Mitchell International Inc (PA) 9771 Clairemont Mesa Blvd Ste A San Diego (92124) *(P-11753)* .... C....... 858 368-7000

Mitchell Silberberg Knupp LLP (PA) 2049 Century Park E Fl 18 Los Angeles (90067) *(P-17572)* .... C....... 310 312-2000

Mitchell Slbrberg Knupp Fndtio, Los Angeles *Also Called: Mitchell Silberberg Knupp LLP (P-17572)*

Mitchells Group Home, Los Angeles *Also Called: Mgh Corporation (P-18486)*

Mitek, San Diego *Also Called: Mitek Systems Inc (P-2833)*

Mitek Systems Inc (PA) 600 B St Ste 100 San Diego (92101) *(P-2833)* .... C....... 619 269-6800

Mitratech Holdings Inc 5900 Wilshire Blvd Ste 1500 Los Angeles (90036) *(P-12272)* .... C....... 323 964-0000

Mitre Corporation 3550 General Atomics Ct San Diego (92121) *(P-16898)* .... D....... 858 459-9701

Mitre Corporation 2401 E El Segundo Blvd Ste 400 El Segundo (90245) *(P-19896)* .... D....... 310 297-8350

Mitre Corporation 2756 Locust St San Diego (92106) *(P-19897)* .... D....... 619 758-7818

Mitsubishi Chemical Carbon Fiber and Composites, Inc., Irvine *Also Called: Mitsubishi Chemical Crbn Fbr (P-2643)*

Mitsubishi Chemical Crbn Fbr 1822 Reynolds Ave Irvine (92614) *(P-2643)* .... C....... 800 929-5471

Mitsubishi Electric Us Inc (DH) 5900 Katella Ave Ste A Cypress (90630) *(P-5676)* .... C....... 714 220-2500

Mitsubishi Motors Cr Amer Inc (DH) 6400 Katella Ave Cypress (90630) *(P-7878)* .... B....... 714 799-4730

Mittal Ram 100 E Hillcrest Blvd Inglewood (90301) *(P-5755)* .... D....... 310 769-6669

Miva Inc .... C....... 858 490-2570
16870 W Bernardo Dr Ste 100 San Diego (92127) *(P-12492)*

Miva Merchant, San Diego *Also Called: Miva Inc (P-12492)*

Mixtec/Ndgena Cmnty Orgnzing P .... D....... 805 483-1166
135 Magnolia Ave Oxnard (93030) *(P-18056)*

Mizuho Bank Ltd .... C....... 213 243-4500
350 S Grand Ave Ste 1500 Los Angeles (90071) *(P-7749)*

MIZUHO BANK LTD, Los Angeles *Also Called: Mizuho Bank Ltd (P-7749)*

Mka International Inc .... C....... 925 934-3235
100 Pringle Ave Ste 340 Walnut Creek (94596) *(P-19323)*

Mktg Inc .... B....... 310 972-7900
5800 Bristol Pkwy Ste 500 Culver City (90230) *(P-13377)*

MKTG, INC., Culver City *Also Called: Mktg Inc (P-13377)*

ML Kishigo Mfg Co LLC .... D....... 949 852-1963
11250 Slater Ave Fountain Valley (92708) *(P-2469)*

ML Mortgage, Rancho Cucamonga *Also Called: ML Mortgage Corp (P-8048)*

ML Mortgage Corp .... D....... 909 652-0780
8270 Aspen St Rancho Cucamonga (91730) *(P-8048)*

Mladen Buntich Cnstr Co Inc .... D....... 909 920-9977
1500 W 9th St Upland (91786) *(P-1238)*

Mlb Advanced Media LP .... A....... 559 625-0480
300 N Giddings St Visalia (93291) *(P-4513)*

Mlim Holdings LLC .... A....... 619 299-3131
350 Camino De La Reina San Diego (92108) *(P-9322)*

Mma Renewable Ventures LLC .... D....... 415 229-8817
44 Montgomery St Ste 2200 San Francisco (94104) *(P-5756)*

MMC, Los Angeles *Also Called: Marsh Risk & Insurance Svcs (P-8607)*

MMC, San Diego *Also Called: Medical Management Cons Inc (P-20462)*

Mmca, Cypress *Also Called: Mitsubishi Motors Cr Amer Inc (P-7878)*

Mmi Realty Services Inc .... D....... 415 288-6888
260 California St 4th Fl San Francisco (94111) *(P-8737)*

Mmi Services Inc .... C....... 661 589-9366
4042 Patton Way Bakersfield (93308) *(P-616)*

MNS Engineers Inc (PA) .... D....... 805 692-6921
201 N Calle Cesar Chavez Ste 300 Santa Barbara (93103) *(P-19324)*

Mob Scene LLC (PA) .... C....... 323 648-7200
8447 Wilshire Blvd Ste 100 Beverly Hills (90211) *(P-10650)*

Mob Scene Creative Productions, Beverly Hills *Also Called: Mob Scene LLC (P-10650)*

Mobica US Inc .... A....... 650 450-6654
2570 N 1st St 2nd Fl San Jose (95131) *(P-12493)*

Mobile Line Communications Corporation .... D
1402 Morgan Cir Tustin (92780) *(P-5677)*

Mobile Mdlar MGT Corp Prnce Gr, Livermore *Also Called: McGrath Rentcorp (P-5846)*

Mobile Modular Management Corp .... C....... 800 819-1084
11450 Mission Blvd Jurupa Valley (91752) *(P-2748)*

Mobilehome Communities America .... C....... 408 298-3230
2681 Monterey Hwy San Jose (95111) *(P-8880)*

Mobilenet Services Inc (PA) .... C....... 949 951-4444
18 Morgan Ste 200 Irvine (92618) *(P-19325)*

Mobileum Inc (PA) .... C....... 408 844-6600
20813 Stevens Creek Blvd Ste 200 Cupertino (95014) *(P-4544)*

Mobilitie Services, LLC, Irvine *Also Called: Boldyn Networks US Services LL (P-4255)*

Mobilityware, Irvine *Also Called: Upstanding LLC (P-12388)*

Mobillcash, San Francisco *Also Called: Boku Inc (P-11468)*

Mobis Parts America LLC (HQ) .... D....... 786 515-1101
10550 Talbert Ave 4th Fl Fountain Valley (92708) *(P-5051)*

Mobis Ventures Sv, Fountain Valley *Also Called: Mobis Parts America LLC (P-5051)*

Mobis Wholesale, Carpinteria *Also Called: Ocean Breeze International (P-143)*

Mobisystems Inc .... C....... 858 350-0315
4501 Mission Bay Dr Ste 3a San Diego (92109) *(P-12494)*

Mobitv Inc (PA) .... D....... 510 981-1303
345 California St Ste 2200 San Francisco (94104) *(P-4315)*

Mobiz, Redlands *Also Called: Mobiz It Inc (P-1779)*

Mobiz It Inc .... D....... 909 453-6700
1175 Idaho St Ste 103 Redlands (92374) *(P-1779)*

Moc Products Company Inc (PA) .... D....... 818 794-3500
12306 Montague St Pacoima (91331) *(P-2645)*

Mocean, Los Angeles *Also Called: Mocean LLC (P-12600)*

Mocean LLC .... C....... 310 481-0808
2440 S Sepulveda Blvd Ste 150 Los Angeles (90064) *(P-12600)*

Mode Media Corporation .... C....... 650 244-4000
1100 La Avenida St Mountain View (94043) *(P-10716)*

Model N, San Mateo *Also Called: N Model Inc (P-11762)*

Modera LLC .... D....... 408 946-2161
137 Ranch Dr Milpitas (95035) *(P-13378)*

Modern Air Mechanical .... D....... 209 722-1815
2200 Cooper Ave Merced (95348) *(P-1501)*

Modern Alloys Inc .... D....... 714 893-0551
11172 Western Ave Stanton (90680) *(P-5230)*

Modern Campus USA Inc (PA) .... D....... 805 484-9400
1320 Flynn Rd Ste 100 Camarillo (93012) *(P-11754)*

Modern Dev Co A Ltd Partnr .... D....... 949 646-6400
7900 All America City Way Paramount (90723) *(P-13379)*

Modern Gourmet Foods, Santa Ana *Also Called: Coastal Cocktails Inc (P-6615)*

Modern Health, San Francisco *Also Called: Modern Life Inc (P-17098)*

Modern Hr Inc .... D....... 877 842-4988
7590 N Glenoaks Blvd Burbank (91504) *(P-20473)*

Modern Life Inc (PA) .... D....... 617 980-9633
650 California St Fl 7 San Francisco (94108) *(P-17098)*

Modern Parking Inc .... C....... 818 783-3143
4955 Van Nuys Blvd Frnt Van Nuys (91403) *(P-13610)*

Modern Parking Inc .... C....... 310 271-1125
415 N Bedford Dr Beverly Hills (90210) *(P-13611)*

Modern Parking Inc .... C....... 310 821-1081
14110 Palawan Way Marina Del Rey (90292) *(P-13612)*

Modern Parking Inc .... C....... 619 233-0412
1025 W Laurel St Ste 105 San Diego (92101) *(P-13613)*

Modesto Christian School, Modesto *Also Called: Modestos Neighborhood Church (P-18334)*

Modesto Hospitality LLC .... C....... 209 526-6000
1150 9th St Modesto (95354) *(P-10021)*

Modesto Industrial Elec Co Inc .... D....... 559 292-4714
2516 N Sunnyside Ave Fresno (93727) *(P-1780)*

Modesto Industrial Electrical Co Inc (PA) .... D....... 209 527-2800
1417 Coldwell Ave Modesto (95350) *(P-1781)*

Modesto Irrigation District .... D....... 209 526-7373
929 Woodland Ave Modesto (95351) *(P-4587)*

Modesto Irrigation District .... D....... 209 526-7563
1231 11th St Modesto (95354) *(P-4588)*

Modesto Irrigation District (PA) .... C....... 209 526-7337
1231 11th St Modesto (95354) *(P-4589)*

Modesto Medical Offices, Modesto *Also Called: Kaiser Foundation Hospitals (P-14813)*

Modesto Scion World, Modesto *Also Called: Stinson Enterprises Inc (P-7305)*

Modestos Neighborhood Church .... C....... 209 529-5510
5921 Stoddard Rd Modesto (95356) *(P-18334)*

Modis, San Francisco *Also Called: Akkodis Inc (P-11392)*

Modis, San Jose *Also Called: Akkodis Inc (P-11393)*

Modis, Glendale *Also Called: Akkodis Inc (P-11394)*

Modivcare Solutions LLC .... C....... 714 503-6871
7441 Lincoln Way # 225 Garden Grove (92841) *(P-4060)*

Modoc Medial Center Hosp Aux .... C....... 530 233-3416
225 W Mcdowell Ave Alturas (96101) *(P-15588)*

Modoc Medical Center, Alturas *Also Called: Modoc Medical Center Hosp Aux (P-16273)*

Modoc Medical Center Hosp Aux (PA) .... D....... 530 708-8800
1111 N Nagle St Alturas (96101) *(P-16273)*

Modsquad Inc (PA) .... C....... 916 913-4465
1300 S St Ste B Sacramento (95811) *(P-20474)*

Modsy, San Francisco *Also Called: Pencil and Pixel Inc (P-11819)*

Modular Inc .... D....... 408 508-4539
228 Hamilton Ave Fl 3 Palo Alto (94301) *(P-11755)*

Modus LLC .... C....... 415 989-1102
240 Stockton St Fl 3 San Francisco (94108) *(P-11179)*

Modus Making It Move, San Francisco *Also Called: Modus LLC (P-11179)*

Moelis & Company LLC .... C....... 310 443-2300
1999 Avenue Of The Stars Ste 1900 Los Angeles (90067) *(P-9439)*

Moffatt & Nichol .... D....... 657 261-2699
555 Anton Blvd Ste 400 Costa Mesa (92626) *(P-19326)*

Moffatt & Nichol, Costa Mesa *Also Called: Moffatt & Nichol (P-19326)*

Mofo, San Francisco *Also Called: Morrison & Foerster LLP (P-17577)*

Mohawk Medical Group Inc .... D....... 661 324-4747
9500 Stockdale Hwy Ste 200 Bakersfield (93311) *(P-14905)*

Mojo Networks Inc (HQ) .... D...... 650 961-1111
   5453 Great America Pkwy Santa Clara (95054) *(P-12273)*
Molina Healthcare, Long Beach *Also Called: Molina Healthcare Inc (P-14906)*
Molina Healthcare Inc .... D...... 310 221-3031
   1500 Hughes Way Long Beach (90810) *(P-8346)*
Molina Healthcare Inc (PA) .... A...... 562 435-3666
   200 Oceangate Ste 100 Long Beach (90802) *(P-14906)*
Molina Healthcare Inc .... D...... 858 614-1580
   9275 Sky Park Ct Ste 190 San Diego (92123) *(P-17276)*
Molina Healthcare Inc .... C...... 562 435-3666
   1 Golden Shore Long Beach (90802) *(P-17277)*
Molina Healthcare California .... A...... 800 526-8196
   200 Oceangate Ste 100 Long Beach (90802) *(P-14907)*
Molina Healthcare New York Inc .... D...... 888 562-5442
   200 Oceangate Ste 100 Long Beach (90802) *(P-14908)*
Molina Hlthcare Cal Prtner Pla .... B...... 562 435-3666
   200 Oceangate Ste 100 Long Beach (90802) *(P-8269)*
Molina Pathways LLC .... B...... 562 491-5773
   200 Oceangate Ste 100 Long Beach (90802) *(P-14909)*
Molinas Pntg Wallcovering Inc .... D...... 925 228-7487
   4285 Pacheco Blvd Martinez (94553) *(P-1629)*
Moloco, Redwood City *Also Called: Moloco Inc (P-11756)*
Moloco Inc (PA) .... A...... 858 531-6550
   601 Marshall St Fl 5 Redwood City (94063) *(P-11756)*
Momentous Insurance Brkg Inc .... D...... 818 933-2700
   5990 Sepulveda Blvd Ste 550 Van Nuys (91411) *(P-8613)*
Momentum Work Inc (PA) .... D...... 805 566-9000
   5320 Carpinteria Ave Ste G Carpinteria (93013) *(P-18057)*
Moms Place .... D...... 805 383-6855
   30 La Patera Ct Camarillo (93010) *(P-15589)*
Monarch Beach Golf Links (HQ) .... D...... 949 240-8247
   50 Monarch Beach Resort N Dana Point (92629) *(P-14277)*
Monarch E & S Insurance Svcs .... D...... 559 226-0200
   2540 Foothill Blvd # 101 La Crescenta (91214) *(P-8614)*
Monarch Healthcare A Medical .... C...... 949 489-1960
   675 Camino De Los Mares Ste 300 San Clemente (92673) *(P-14910)*
Monarch Healthcare A Medical (HQ) .... D...... 949 923-3200
   11 Technology Dr Irvine (92618) *(P-14911)*
Monarch Hlthcare A Med Group I .... C...... 760 730-9448
   2562 State St Carlsbad (92008) *(P-17278)*
Monarch Ldscp Companies LLC .... D...... 213 797-5934
   550 S Hope St Ste 1675 Los Angeles (90071) *(P-447)*
Monarch Nut Company LLC .... C...... 661 725-6458
   786 Road 188 Delano (93215) *(P-290)*
Monarch Tractor, Livermore *Also Called: Zimeno Inc (P-20624)*
Monark LP .... D...... 310 769-6669
   2804 W El Segundo Blvd Gardena (90249) *(P-8844)*
Mondelez Global LLC .... D...... 909 605-0140
   5815 Clark St Ontario (91761) *(P-6648)*
Mondrian Holdings LLC .... B...... 323 848-6004
   8440 W Sunset Blvd West Hollywood (90069) *(P-10022)*
Mondrian Hotel, Los Angeles *Also Called: Morgans Hotel Group MGT LLC (P-10030)*
Monex, Newport Beach *Also Called: Monex Deposit A Cal Ltd Partnr (P-7552)*
Monex Deposit A Cal Ltd Partnr .... D...... 949 752-1400
   4910 Birch St Newport Beach (92660) *(P-7552)*
Monex Inc .... D...... 310 695-3059
   8383 Wilshire Blvd Ste 340 Beverly Hills (90211) *(P-13380)*
Moneyjet, San Diego *Also Called: National Funding Inc (P-7898)*
Monique Suraci .... D...... 951 677-8111
   41885 Ivy St Murrieta (92562) *(P-14219)*
Monkeybrains .... D...... 415 974-1313
   1611 17th St Oakland (94607) *(P-11757)*
Mono Wind Casino .... D...... 559 855-4350
   37302 Rancheria Ln Auberry (93602) *(P-10023)*
Monrovia Growes, Azusa *Also Called: Monrovia Nursery Company (P-140)*
MONROVIA MEMORIAL HOSPITAL, Monrovia *Also Called: Alakor Healthcare LLC (P-15935)*
Monrovia Nursery Company (PA) .... A...... 626 334-9321
   817 E Monrovia Pl Azusa (91702) *(P-140)*
Monrovia Ranch Market, Victorville *Also Called: Baja Fresh Supermarket (P-232)*
Monrovia Service Center, Monrovia *Also Called: Southern California Edison Co (P-4682)*

Monsieur Marcel, Los Angeles *Also Called: Strouk Group LLC (P-6504)*
Monsoon Commerce Inc .... C...... 510 594-4500
   1250 45th St Ste 100 Emeryville (94608) *(P-12841)*
MONSOON COMMERCE, INC., Emeryville *Also Called: Monsoon Commerce Inc (P-12841)*
Monster Inc (PA) .... B...... 415 840-2000
   601 Gateway Blvd Ste 900 South San Francisco (94080) *(P-6046)*
Monster Energy, Corona *Also Called: Monster Energy Company (P-6649)*
Monster Energy Company (HQ) .... B...... 866 322-4466
   1 Monster Way Corona (92879) *(P-6649)*
Monster Mep Inc .... D...... 408 727-8362
   1521 Terminal Ave San Jose (95112) *(P-1502)*
Monster Products, South San Francisco *Also Called: Monster Inc (P-6046)*
Montage Health (PA) .... A...... 831 625-4830
   23625 Holman Hwy Monterey (93940) *(P-18610)*
Montage Hotels & Resorts LLC (PA) .... A...... 949 715-5002
   3 Ada Ste 100 Irvine (92618) *(P-10024)*
Montage Hotels & Resorts LLC .... A...... 949 715-6000
   30801 Coast Hwy Laguna Beach (92651) *(P-20154)*
Montage Laguna Beach, Irvine *Also Called: Montage Hotels & Resorts LLC (P-10024)*
Montage Laguna Beach, Laguna Beach *Also Called: Montage Hotels & Resorts LLC (P-20154)*
Montage Medical Group .... C...... 831 241-9155
   23845 Holman Hwy Ste 203 Monterey (93940) *(P-14912)*
Montalvo Association .... D...... 408 961-5800
   15400 Montalvo Rd Saratoga (95070) *(P-18691)*
Montavista Software LLC (DH) .... D...... 408 572-8000
   2315 N 1st St 4th Fl San Jose (95131) *(P-12274)*
Montbleau & Associates Inc (PA) .... D...... 619 263-5550
   555 Raven St San Diego (92102) *(P-2496)*
Montclair Hospital Medical Center, Montclair *Also Called: Prime Hlthcare Srvcs-Mntclair (P-16338)*
Montclair Hotels Mb LLC .... B...... 925 687-5500
   1050 Burnett Ave Concord (94520) *(P-10025)*
Monte Vista Child Care Ctr Inc .... C...... 909 476-6780
   7976 Beechwood Dr Rancho Cucamonga (91701) *(P-18335)*
Monte Vista Grove Homes .... D...... 626 796-6135
   2889 San Pasqual St Pasadena (91107) *(P-18489)*
Montebello Unified School Dst .... D...... 323 887-2140
   500 Hendricks St 2nd Fl Montebello (90640) *(P-10932)*
Montebello Unified School Dst .... D...... 323 440-2899
   831 Perry Ave Montebello (90640) *(P-13381)*
Montecito Country Club Inc .... D...... 805 969-0800
   920 Summit Rd Santa Barbara (93108) *(P-14409)*
Montecito Family YMCA, Santa Barbara *Also Called: Channel Islnds Yung MNS Chrstn (P-18838)*
Montecito Retirement Assn .... B...... 805 969-8011
   300 Hot Springs Rd Santa Barbara (93108) *(P-15590)*
Monterey Bay Aqar Foundation (PA) .... B...... 831 648-4800
   886 Cannery Row Monterey (93940) *(P-18692)*
MONTEREY BAY AQUARIUM, Monterey *Also Called: Monterey Bay Aqar Foundation (P-18692)*
Monterey Bay Aquarium RES Inst .... C...... 831 775-1700
   7700 Sandholdt Rd Moss Landing (95039) *(P-19898)*
Monterey Bay Residental Care, Seaside *Also Called: Professional Health Care Inc (P-18506)*
Monterey Beach Hotel, Monterey *Also Called: Zhg Inc (P-10389)*
Monterey Collection Services, Oceanside *Also Called: Monterey Financial Svcs Inc (P-7879)*
Monterey County Sheriffs Dept, Salinas *Also Called: County of Monterey (P-19078)*
Monterey Financial Svcs Inc (PA) .... C...... 760 639-3500
   4095 Avenida De La Plata Oceanside (92056) *(P-7879)*
Monterey Palms Health Care Ctr, Palm Desert *Also Called: Mariner Health Care Inc (P-15568)*
Monterey Park Hospital .... C...... 626 570-9000
   900 S Atlantic Blvd Monterey Park (91754) *(P-16274)*
Monterey Park Hospital, Monterey Park *Also Called: Monterey Park Hospital (P-16274)*
Monterey Peninsula Country CLB .... C...... 831 373-1556
   3000 Club Rd Pebble Beach (93953) *(P-14410)*
Monterey Peninsula Engineering .... C...... 831 384-4081
   192 Healy Ave Marina (93933) *(P-1140)*
Monterey Pine Apartments .... C...... 510 215-1926
   680 S 37th St Richmond (94804) *(P-8845)*

ALPHABETIC SECTION — Morley Builders Inc

Monterey Pines Sklld Nursg Fac .... D....... 831 373-3716
  1501 Skyline Dr Monterey (93940) *(P-15591)*
Monterey Plaza Hotel & Spa, Monterey *Also Called: Monterey Plaza Ht Ltd Partnr (P-10026)*
Monterey Plaza Ht Ltd Partnr .... B....... 800 334-3999
  400 Cannery Row Monterey (93940) *(P-10026)*
Monterey Rgional Waste MGT Dst .... C....... 831 384-5313
  14201 Del Monte Blvd Marina (93933) *(P-4912)*
Monterey-Salinas Transit Corp .... C....... 831 754-2804
  1375 Burton Ave Salinas (93901) *(P-3308)*
MONTEREY-SALINAS TRANSIT CORPORATION, Salinas *Also Called: Monterey-Salinas Transit Corp (P-3308)*
Monterrey The Natural Choice, San Diego *Also Called: Mpci Holdings Inc (P-6499)*
Montesquieu Corp .... D....... 877 705-5669
  888 W E St San Diego (92101) *(P-6802)*
Montesquieu Vins & Domaines, San Diego *Also Called: Montesquieu Corp (P-6802)*
Montessori On The Lake, Lake Forest *Also Called: Environments For Learning Inc (P-18313)*
Montevina Winery, Plymouth *Also Called: Sierra Sunrise Vineyard Inc (P-2393)*
Montgomery Center, Santa Rosa *Also Called: St Joseph Hlth Nthrn Cal LLC (P-16459)*
Monticello Inn, San Francisco *Also Called: Kimpton Hotel & Rest Group LLC (P-9943)*
Montivista, Danville *Also Called: San Ramon Vly Unified Schl Dst (P-17748)*
Montrose Environmental Corp .... B....... 925 680-4300
  2825 Verne Roberts Cir Antioch (94509) *(P-20805)*
Monument Construction Inc .... D....... 408 778-1350
  18450 Technology Dr Ste E1 Morgan Hill (95037) *(P-448)*
Mony Life, Orange *Also Called: Mony Life Insurance Company (P-8615)*
Mony Life Insurance Company .... D....... 714 939-6669
  333 S Anita Dr Ste 750 Orange (92868) *(P-8615)*
Mood Media North America LLC .... D....... 858 362-2323
  3860 Calle Fortunada Ste 100 San Diego (92123) *(P-13382)*
Moog Inc .... B....... 310 533-1178
  1218 W Jon St Torrance (90502) *(P-2867)*
Moog Jon Street Warehouse, Torrance *Also Called: Moog Inc (P-2867)*
Moomoo Technologies Inc .... A....... 650 798-5700
  550 California Ave Ste 201 Palo Alto (94306) *(P-11758)*
Moonlight Companies, Reedley *Also Called: Moonlight Packing Corporation (P-6563)*
Moonlight Packing Corporation .... A....... 559 638-7799
  17770 E Huntsman Ave Reedley (93654) *(P-4133)*
Moonlight Packing Corporation .... A....... 559 638-7799
  1300 I St Reedley (93654) *(P-6424)*
Moonlight Packing Corporation (PA) .... C....... 559 638-7799
  17719 E Huntsman Ave Reedley (93654) *(P-6563)*
Moonrider Inn, Rowland Heights *Also Called: Moonrider LLC (P-10027)*
Moonrider LLC .... D....... 318 828-1375
  18559 Colima Rd Apt H Rowland Heights (91748) *(P-10027)*
Moonstone Bch Innvstors A Cal .... C....... 805 927-8661
  6700 Moonstone Beach Dr Cambria (93428) *(P-10028)*
Moonstone Hotel Properties, Cambria *Also Called: Moonstone Management Corp (P-9101)*
Moonstone Management Corp (PA) .... C....... 805 927-4200
  2905 Burton Dr Cambria (93428) *(P-9101)*
Moore Foundation, Palo Alto *Also Called: Gordon E Btty I More Fundation (P-20767)*
Moore Iacofano Goltsman Inc (PA) .... D....... 510 845-7549
  800 Hearst Ave Berkeley (94710) *(P-20806)*
Moore Industries, North Hills *Also Called: Moore Industries-International Inc (P-3018)*
Moore Industries-International Inc (PA) .... C....... 818 894-7111
  16650 Schoenborn St North Hills (91343) *(P-3018)*
Moore Law Group A Prof Corp .... D....... 714 431-2000
  3710 S Susan St Ste 210 Santa Ana (92704) *(P-17573)*
Moore Twining Associates Inc (PA) .... D....... 559 268-7021
  2527 Fresno St Fresno (93721) *(P-19990)*
Moorefield Construction Inc (PA) .... D....... 714 972-0700
  600 N Tustin Ave Ste 210 Santa Ana (92705) *(P-972)*
Mooretown Rancheria .... B....... 530 533-3885
  3 Alverda Dr Oroville (95966) *(P-14298)*
Moose, El Segundo *Also Called: Moose Toys LLC (P-3088)*
Moose Toys LLC .... D....... 310 341-4642
  737 Campus Sq W El Segundo (90245) *(P-3088)*
Morada Produce Company LP .... A....... 209 546-0426
  500 N Jack Tone Rd Stockton (95215) *(P-6564)*
Moraga Cntry CLB Hmowners Assn .... D....... 925 376-2200
  1600 Saint Andrews Dr Moraga (94556) *(P-14411)*

Moraga Country Club, Moraga *Also Called: Moraga Cntry CLB Hmowners Assn (P-14411)*
Moral Welfare and Recreation, Camp Pendleton *Also Called: Marine Corps Community Svcs (P-14545)*
MORE WORKSHOP, Placerville *Also Called: Mother Lode Rhblttion Entps In (P-18491)*
Moreno & Associates Inc .... D....... 408 924-0353
  782 Auzerais Ave San Jose (95126) *(P-10933)*
MORENO VALLEY FAMILY HEALTH CE, Moreno Valley *Also Called: Community Health Systems Inc (P-14701)*
Moreno Valley Heacock Med Offs, Moreno Valley *Also Called: Kaiser Foundation Hospitals (P-9433)*
Moreno Valley Snf LLC .... D....... 951 363-5434
  26940 E Hospital Rd Moreno Valley (92555) *(P-13383)*
Morgan Lewis & Bockius LLP .... A....... 415 442-1000
  One Market Spear St Tower San Francisco (94105) *(P-17574)*
Morgan Fabrics, Vernon *Also Called: Morgan Fabrics Corporation (P-6158)*
Morgan Fabrics Corporation (PA) .... D....... 323 583-9981
  4265 Exchange Ave Vernon (90058) *(P-6158)*
Morgan Linen Service, Los Angeles *Also Called: Morgan Services Inc (P-10453)*
Morgan Services Inc .... D....... 213 485-9666
  905 Yale St Los Angeles (90012) *(P-10453)*
Morgan Stanley Smith Barney, Laguna Niguel *Also Called: Morgan Stnley Smith Barney LLC (P-7699)*
Morgan Stanley Smith Barney, San Diego *Also Called: Morgan Stnley Smith Barney LLC (P-8155)*
Morgan Stnley Smith Barney LLC .... C....... 760 568-3500
  74199 El Paseo Ste 201 Palm Desert (92260) *(P-7698)*
Morgan Stnley Smith Barney LLC .... D....... 800 490-5412
  28202 Cabot Rd Ste 150 Laguna Niguel (92677) *(P-7699)*
Morgan Stnley Smith Barney LLC .... D....... 310 285-4800
  9665 Wilshire Blvd Ste 600 Beverly Hills (90212) *(P-7897)*
Morgan Stnley Smith Barney LLC .... C....... 650 316-6788
  650 Castro St Mountain View (94041) *(P-8144)*
Morgan Stnley Smith Barney LLC .... C....... 212 761-4000
  1225 Prospect St Ste 202 La Jolla (92037) *(P-8145)*
Morgan Stnley Smith Barney LLC .... C....... 951 682-1181
  3750 University Ave Ste 600 Riverside (92501) *(P-8146)*
Morgan Stnley Smith Barney LLC .... D....... 831 440-5200
  6004 La Madrona Dr Scotts Valley (95060) *(P-8147)*
Morgan Stnley Smith Barney LLC .... C....... 415 984-6500
  555 California St Fl 35 San Francisco (94104) *(P-8148)*
Morgan Stnley Smith Barney LLC .... C....... 213 891-3200
  444 S Flower St Ste 2700 Los Angeles (90071) *(P-8149)*
Morgan Stnley Smith Barney LLC .... C....... 818 715-1800
  21650 Oxnard St Ste 1800 Woodland Hills (91367) *(P-8150)*
Morgan Stnley Smith Barney LLC .... C....... 760 438-5100
  5796 Armada Dr Ste 200 Carlsbad (92008) *(P-8151)*
Morgan Stnley Smith Barney LLC .... C....... 714 674-4100
  10 Pointe Dr Ste 400 Brea (92821) *(P-8152)*
Morgan Stnley Smith Barney LLC .... C....... 408 346-0105
  225 W Santa Clara St Ste 900 San Jose (95113) *(P-8153)*
Morgan Stnley Smith Barney LLC .... C....... 805 963-3381
  1014 Santa Barbara St Santa Barbara (93101) *(P-8154)*
Morgan Stnley Smith Barney LLC .... C....... 619 238-1226
  101 W Broadway Ste 1800 San Diego (92101) *(P-8155)*
Morgan Stnley Smith Barney LLC .... D....... 707 443-3071
  2421 Buhne St Eureka (95501) *(P-8209)*
Morgans Hotel Group MGT LLC .... C....... 805 969-2203
  1555 S Jameson Ln Santa Barbara (93108) *(P-10029)*
Morgans Hotel Group MGT LLC .... C....... 323 650-8999
  8440 W Sunset Blvd Los Angeles (90069) *(P-10030)*
Morgans Hotel Group MGT LLC .... B....... 415 775-4700
  495 Geary St San Francisco (94102) *(P-10031)*
Morgenthaler Ventures, Menlo Park *Also Called: Morgenthler MGT Prtners VI LLC (P-9535)*
Morgenthler MGT Prtners VI LLC .... A....... 650 388-7600
  2710 Sand Hill Rd Ste 100 Menlo Park (94025) *(P-9535)*
Morgner Construction MGT, Los Angeles *Also Called: Morgner Technology Management (P-20155)*
Morgner Technology Management .... D....... 323 900-0030
  1880 Century Park E Ste 1402 Los Angeles (90067) *(P-20155)*
Morley Builders Inc (PA) .... C....... 310 399-1600
  3330 Ocean Park Blvd Santa Monica (90405) *(P-835)*

Morley Construction Company (HQ).................................. D...... 310 399-1600
   3330 Ocean Park Blvd Santa Monica (90405) *(P-2138)*

Morning Star Company The, Woodland *Also Called: Liberty Packing Company LLC (P-6562)*

Morningside Community Assn .... D...... 760 328-3323
   82 Mayfair Dr Rancho Mirage (92270) *(P-18884)*

Morningside of Fullerton, Fullerton *Also Called: Corecare I I I (P-18400)*

Morningstar of Mission Viejo, Mission Viejo *Also Called: Morningstar Senior MGT LLC (P-18490)*

Morningstar Senior MGT LLC .... C...... 949 298-3675
   28570 Marguerite Pkwy Mission Viejo (92692) *(P-18490)*

Morongo Band Mission Indians .... C...... 951 849-3080
   49500 Seminole Dr Cabazon (92230) *(P-14546)*

Morongo Casino Resort Spa, Cabazon *Also Called: Morongo Band Mission Indians (P-14546)*

Morphosis, Culver City *Also Called: Morphosis Architects (P-19496)*

Morphosis Architects .... D...... 310 453-2247
   3440 Wesley St Culver City (90232) *(P-19496)*

Morphotrak LLC (DH) .... C...... 714 238-2000
   5515 E La Palma Ave Ste 100 Anaheim (92807) *(P-12495)*

Morris & Willner Partners .... D...... 949 705-0682
   2151 Michelson Dr Ste 185 Irvine (92612) *(P-20475)*

Morris Distributing .... D...... 707 769-7294
   3800a Lakeville Hwy Petaluma (94954) *(P-6778)*

Morris Grritano Insur Agcy Inc .... D...... 805 543-6887
   1122 Laurel Ln San Luis Obispo (93401) *(P-8616)*

Morris Levin and Son .... C...... 559 686-8665
   1816 S K St Tulare (93274) *(P-7124)*

Morris Levin Rentl & Parts Ctr, Tulare *Also Called: Morris Levin and Son (P-7124)*

Morris Newspaper Corp Cal (HQ) .... D...... 209 249-3500
   531 E Yosemite Ave Manteca (95336) *(P-2540)*

Morris Polich & Purdy LLP (PA) .... D...... 213 891-9100
   1055 W 7th St Ste 2400 Los Angeles (90017) *(P-17575)*

Morrison & Foerster, Los Angeles *Also Called: Morrison & Foerster LLP (P-17576)*

Morrison & Foerster - Library, Palo Alto *Also Called: Morrison & Foerster LLP (P-17579)*

Morrison & Foerster LLP .... C...... 213 892-5200
   707 Wilshire Blvd Ste 6000 Los Angeles (90017) *(P-17576)*

Morrison & Foerster LLP (PA) .... B...... 415 268-7000
   425 Market St Fl 32 San Francisco (94105) *(P-17577)*

Morrison & Foerster LLP .... B...... 858 720-5100
   12531 High Bluff Dr Ste 100 San Diego (92130) *(P-17578)*

Morrison & Foerster LLP .... B...... 650 813-5600
   755 Page Mill Rd Palo Alto (94304) *(P-17579)*

Morrow-Meadows Corporation (PA) .... A...... 858 974-3650
   231 Benton Ct City Of Industry (91789) *(P-1782)*

Morrow-Meadows Corporation .... B...... 858 974-3650
   13000 Kirkham Way Ste 101 Poway (92064) *(P-1783)*

Mortech Manufacturing .... D...... 626 334-1471
   411 N Aerojet Dr Azusa (91702) *(P-2498)*

Mortgage Solutions Fcs Inc .... D...... 925 954-8364
   2700 Ygnacio Valley Rd Ste 255 Walnut Creek (94598) *(P-8003)*

Mortgage Works Financial, Redlands *Also Called: Mountain West Financial Inc (P-8004)*

Morton & Pitalo Inc (PA) .... D...... 916 984-7621
   600 Coolidge Dr Ste 140 Folsom (95630) *(P-19327)*

Morton Bakar Center, Alameda *Also Called: Garfield Nursing Home Inc (P-15489)*

Morton Golf Management LLC .... D...... 916 481-4653
   3645 Fulton Ave Sacramento (95821) *(P-14278)*

Mosaic Global Transportation, San Jose *Also Called: Rm Executive Transportation (P-3291)*

Moscone Center, San Francisco *Also Called: Smg Holdings LLC (P-13478)*

Moss & Company Inc (PA) .... D...... 310 453-0911
   15300 Ventura Blvd Ste 405 Sherman Oaks (91403) *(P-9102)*

Moss Landing Marine Labs .... D...... 831 771-4400
   8272 Moss Landing Rd Moss Landing (95039) *(P-16736)*

Moss Landing Power Plant, Moss Landing *Also Called: Dynegy Moss Landing LLC (P-4571)*

Moss Management Services Inc .... C...... 818 990-5999
   15300 Ventura Blvd # 405 Sherman Oaks (91403) *(P-9103)*

Moss Motors Ltd (PA) .... C...... 805 967-4546
   400 Rutherford St Goleta (93117) *(P-7353)*

Mosser Companies Inc .... D...... 415 284-9000
   308 Jessie St San Francisco (94103) *(P-10032)*

Mosser Vctrian Ht Arts Mus Inc .... C...... 415 777-1200
   68 4th St San Francisco (94103) *(P-7497)*

Mossy Automotive Group Inc (PA) .... D...... 858 581-4000
   4555 Mission Bay Dr San Diego (92109) *(P-7261)*

Mossy Ford Inc .... C...... 858 273-7500
   4570 Mission Bay Dr San Diego (92109) *(P-7262)*

Mossy Nissan Inc .... D...... 858 565-6608
   8118 Clairemont Mesa Blvd San Diego (92111) *(P-7263)*

Mossy Nissan Kearny Mesa, San Diego *Also Called: Mossy Nissan Inc (P-7263)*

Mossy Toyota, San Diego *Also Called: Mossy Automotive Group Inc (P-7261)*

Motech Americas LLC .... B...... 302 451-7500
   1300 Valley Vista Dr Ste 207 Diamond Bar (91765) *(P-19739)*

Moteng Inc .... D...... 858 715-2500
   12220 Parkway Centre Dr Poway (92064) *(P-6181)*

Mother Lode Holding Co .... D...... 916 624-8141
   9085 Foothills Blvd Roseville (95747) *(P-8449)*

Mother Lode Holding Co (HQ) .... C...... 530 887-2410
   189 Fulweiler Ave Auburn (95603) *(P-8450)*

Mother Lode Rhblttion Entps In .... C...... 530 622-4848
   399 Placerville Dr Placerville (95667) *(P-18491)*

Mother of Divine Grace Inc .... D...... 805 646-5818
   407 Bryant Cir Ste B Ojai (93023) *(P-17731)*

Motion Engineering Inc (DH) .... D...... 805 696-1200
   33 S La Patera Ln Santa Barbara (93117) *(P-2834)*

Motion Math, San Francisco *Also Called: Motion Math Inc (P-11759)*

Motion Math Inc .... A...... 415 590-2961
   582 Market St Ste 511 San Francisco (94104) *(P-11759)*

Motion Pcture Indust Pnsion Hl .... C...... 818 769-0007
   11365 Ventura Blvd Ste 300 Studio City (91604) *(P-8464)*

Motion Picture and TV Fund (PA) .... A...... 818 876-1777
   23388 Mulholland Dr Ste 200 Woodland Hills (91364) *(P-16275)*

Motion Theory Inc .... C...... 310 396-9433
   444 W Ocean Blvd Ste 1400 Long Beach (90802) *(P-10815)*

Motiv, Foster City *Also Called: Motiv Power Systems Inc (P-19328)*

Motiv Power Systems Inc .... C...... 650 458-4804
   330 Hatch Dr Foster City (94404) *(P-19328)*

Motivational Systems Inc (PA) .... D...... 619 474-8246
   2200 Cleveland Ave National City (91950) *(P-10816)*

Motive Energy Inc (PA) .... D...... 714 888-2525
   17260 Newhope St Fountain Valley (92708) *(P-5580)*

Motive Nation, Downey *Also Called: Rockview Dairies Inc (P-6662)*

Motivo Engineering LLC (PA) .... D...... 844 668-4861
   17700 S Figueroa St Gardena (90248) *(P-19329)*

Motivtnal Flfllment Lgstics Sv, Chino *Also Called: Math Holdings Inc (P-13365)*

Motogistics, Upland *Also Called: Motogistics Logistics Inc (P-4168)*

Motogistics Logistics Inc .... D...... 626 975-6470
   1490 E Foothill Blvd Ste C Upland (91786) *(P-4168)*

Motolease Funding LLC .... D...... 310 601-4779
   10866 Wilshire Blvd Los Angeles (90024) *(P-7921)*

Motor Trend Group LLC (HQ) .... D...... 630 353-2505
   831 S Douglas St El Segundo (90245) *(P-13942)*

Motorola, San Diego *Also Called: Motorola Mobility LLC (P-5678)*

Motorola Good Technology Group .... D...... 408 327-6000
   101 Redwood Shores Pkwy Ste 400 Redwood City (94065) *(P-20476)*

Motorola Mobility LLC .... D...... 858 455-1500
   6450 Sequence Dr San Diego (92121) *(P-5678)*

Moulton Animal Hospital Inc .... D...... 949 831-7297
   27261 La Paz Rd Ste I Laguna Beach (92677) *(P-337)*

Moulton Logistics Management .... C...... 818 997-1800
   7855 Hayvenhurst Ave Van Nuys (91406) *(P-3732)*

Moulton Nguel Wtr Dst Pub Fclt .... D...... 949 831-2500
   26161 Gordon Rd Laguna Hills (92653) *(P-4812)*

MOULTON NIGUEL WATER DISTRICT, Laguna Hills *Also Called: Moulton Nguel Wtr Dst Pub Fclt (P-4812)*

Mount Hermon Association Inc (PA) .... D...... 831 335-4466
   37 Conference Dr Mount Hermon (95041) *(P-10408)*

Mount San Jcnto Winter Pk Corp .... D...... 760 325-1449
   1 Tramway Rd Palm Springs (92262) *(P-14547)*

Mount Shasta Resort, Mount Shasta *Also Called: Siskiyou Lake Golf Resort Inc (P-14289)*

Mount Woodson Country Club, Ramona *Also Called: Spe Go Holdings Inc (P-14290)*

Mountain Cmmnties Hlth Care Ds (PA) .... D...... 530 623-5541
   60 Easter Ave Weaverville (96093) *(P-16276)*

ALPHABETIC SECTION — Mt Sinai Mem Pk & Mortuary

Mountain G Engineering, Folsom *Also Called: Mountain G Enterprises Inc (P-1141)*

Mountain G Enterprises Inc .... C....... 866 464-6351
950 Iron Point Rd Ste 190 Folsom (95630) *(P-1141)*

Mountain Gear Corporation .... C....... 626 851-2488
4889 4th St Irwindale (91706) *(P-6182)*

Mountain High Ski Resort, Wrightwood *Also Called: MHRP Resort Inc (P-10019)*

Mountain House Cmnty Svcs Dst ....D....... 209 831-2300
251 E Main St Mountain House (95391) *(P-18717)*

Mountain Meadow Mushrooms Inc .... D....... 760 749-1201
26948 N Broadway Escondido (92026) *(P-164)*

MOUNTAIN SHADOWS COMMUNITY HOM, Escondido *Also Called: Mountain Shadows Support Group (P-15775)*

Mountain Shadows Support Group (PA)..............................D....... 760 743-3714
2067 W El Norte Pkwy Escondido (92026) *(P-15775)*

Mountain Terrace, The, Woodside *Also Called: Skywood Events Corporation (P-10576)*

Mountain View Child Care Inc (PA)....................................B....... 909 796-6915
1720 Mountain View Ave Loma Linda (92354) *(P-16277)*

Mountain View Child Care Inc .... C....... 818 252-5863
10716 La Tuna Canyon Rd Sun Valley (91352) *(P-18336)*

Mountain View Children'c Ctr, El Monte *Also Called: Mountain View Elmntary Schl Ds (P-17732)*

Mountain View Elmntary Schl Ds ....D....... 626 652-4250
2109 Burkett Rd El Monte (91733) *(P-17732)*

MOUNTAIN VIEW HEALTHCARE CENTE, Mountain View *Also Called: Balboa Enterprises Inc (P-15349)*

Mountain View Schl Dist Grace, Ontario *Also Called: Grace Yokley Middle School (P-17713)*

Mountain View Transportation, Oxnard *Also Called: AG Rx (P-6820)*

Mountain Vista Golf Course At .... D....... 760 200-2200
38180 Del Webb Blvd Palm Desert (92211) *(P-14548)*

Mountain Vly Child Fmly Svcs I .... C....... 530 265-9057
24077 St Hwy 49 Nevada City (95959) *(P-15776)*

Mountain West Financial Inc (PA).......................................B....... 909 793-1500
31 W Stuart Ave Redlands (92374) *(P-8004)*

Mountains Community Hosp Fndtn .... C....... 909 336-3651
29101 Hospital Rd Lake Arrowhead (92352) *(P-16278)*

Mountains Community Hospital, Lake Arrowhead *Also Called: Mountains Community Hosp Fndtn (P-16278)*

Move Inc (HQ)...B....... 408 558-7100
3315 Scott Blvd Santa Clara (95054) *(P-9104)*

Move Sales Inc (DH)...D....... 805 557-2300
3315 Scott Blvd Santa Clara (95054) *(P-9105)*

Movella Technologies NA Inc .... D....... 310 481-1800
101 N Pacific Coast Hwy Ste 306 El Segundo (90245) *(P-13867)*

Movers and Shakers LLC .... D....... 310 893-7051
1217 Wilshire Blvd Santa Monica (90403) *(P-10651)*

Moveworks Inc (PA).. C....... 408 435-5100
1277 Terra Bella Ave Mountain View (94043) *(P-12275)*

Movieclips.com, Los Angeles *Also Called: Zefr Inc (P-19858)*

Moving Solutions Inc .... C....... 408 920-0110
7093 Central Ave Newark (94560) *(P-3590)*

Mowery Thomason Inc .... C....... 714 666-1717
1225 N Red Gum St Anaheim (92806) *(P-1947)*

Moxy AC Ht Dwntwn Los Angeles, Los Angeles *Also Called: Lightstone Dt La LLC (P-9978)*

Moyles Health Care Inc .... A....... 559 686-1601
604 E Merritt Ave Tulare (93274) *(P-15879)*

Mozilla Corp .... C....... 650 903-0800
149 New Montgomery St San Francisco (94105) *(P-12496)*

Mozilla Foundation (PA)... B....... 650 903-0800
149 New Montgomery St San Francisco (94105) *(P-11760)*

Mp Aero LLC .... D....... 818 901-9828
7701 Woodley Ave Van Nuys (91406) *(P-2298)*

MP Environmental Svcs Inc (PA).. C....... 800 458-3036
3400 Manor St Bakersfield (93308) *(P-4913)*

Mp Holdings, Mcclellan *Also Called: McClellan Business Park LLC (P-20457)*

Mp Mine Operations LLC .... C....... 702 277-0848
67750 Bailey Rd Mountain Pass (92366) *(P-646)*

Mp Nexlevel California Inc .... B....... 650 486-1359
266 Industrial Rd Ste B San Carlos (94070) *(P-1239)*

Mp3com Inc .... D....... 858 623-7000
4790 Eastgate Mall San Diego (92121) *(P-4316)*

Mpc Productions LLC .... D....... 310 418-8115
12035 Killion St Sherman Oaks (91401) *(P-14097)*

Mpcc, Pebble Beach *Also Called: Monterey Peninsula Country CLB (P-14410)*

Mpci Holdings Inc .... C....... 619 294-2222
7850 Waterville Rd San Diego (92154) *(P-6499)*

Mpg Office Trust Inc ....D....... 213 626-3300
355 S Grand Ave Ste 3300 Los Angeles (90071) *(P-9474)*

Mpl Enterprises Inc .... D....... 714 545-1717
2302 S Susan St Santa Ana (92704) *(P-523)*

Mpo Videotronics Inc (PA).. D....... 805 499-8513
5069 Maureen Ln Moorpark (93021) *(P-3085)*

Mpower Electronics Inc .... D....... 408 320-1266
2910 Scott Blvd Santa Clara (95054) *(P-5581)*

Mpower Holding Corporation (HQ).....................................D....... 866 699-8242
515 S Flower St Fl 36 Los Angeles (90071) *(P-4317)*

MPS Security, Murrieta *Also Called: National Bus Invstigations Inc (P-13389)*

Mpulse Mobile Inc (PA)... D....... 888 678-5735
21255 Burbank Blvd Woodland Hills (91367) *(P-4318)*

Mq Power, Cypress *Also Called: Multiquip Inc (P-5582)*

Mr Bug, Anaheim *Also Called: Reels Inc (P-5056)*

Mr Clean Maintenance Systems, Bloomington *Also Called: Chiro Inc (P-5936)*

Mr Copy Inc (DH)... D....... 858 573-6300
5657 Copley Dr San Diego (92111) *(P-5251)*

Mrc, Smart Tech Solutions, San Diego *Also Called: Mr Copy Inc (P-5251)*

Msblous LLC ....D....... 909 929-9689
11671 Dayton Dr Rancho Cucamonga (91730) *(P-3733)*

MSC Metalworking, City Of Industry *Also Called: Rutland Tool & Supply Co (P-5923)*

Msci Barra, Berkeley *Also Called: Barra LLC (P-12110)*

Msci Inc .... D....... 510 548-5442
2100 Milvia St Berkeley (94704) *(P-13384)*

Mscsoftware Corporation (HQ)... C....... 714 540-8900
5161 California Ave Ste 200 Irvine (92617) *(P-12276)*

MSE Enterprises Inc (PA).. D....... 818 223-3500
23622 Calabasas Rd Ste 200 Calabasas (91302) *(P-9106)*

MSI Computer Corp (HQ).. D....... 626 913-0828
901 Canada Ct City Of Industry (91748) *(P-5330)*

MSI Hvac, Fontana *Also Called: AC Pro Inc (P-5765)*

MSI Orange Showroom & Dist Ctr, Orange *Also Called: M S International Inc (P-5207)*

MSI Production Services, Vista *Also Called: Meeting Services Inc (P-11041)*

Msl Electric Inc .... D....... 714 693-4837
2918 E La Jolla St Anaheim (92806) *(P-1784)*

Msla Management LLC .... A....... 626 824-6020
1294 E Colorado Blvd Pasadena (91106) *(P-20807)*

Msr Desert Resort LP .... A....... 760 564-5730
49499 Eisenhower Dr La Quinta (92253) *(P-7498)*

Msr Hotels & Resorts Inc ....C....... 661 325-9700
5101 California Ave Ste 204 Bakersfield (93309) *(P-9536)*

Msr Hotels & Resorts Inc ....C....... 408 496-6400
2885 Lakeside Dr Santa Clara (95054) *(P-9537)*

Msr Hotels & Resorts Inc ....C....... 310 543-4566
3701 Torrance Blvd Torrance (90503) *(P-10033)*

Msr Hotels & Resorts Inc ....C....... 408 745-6000
1100 N Mathilda Ave Sunnyvale (94089) *(P-10034)*

Msr Resort Lodging Tenant LLC .... A....... 760 564-4111
49499 Eisenhower Dr La Quinta (92253) *(P-10035)*

MSRS INC .... C....... 310 952-9000
945 E Church St Riverside (92507) *(P-5125)*

Mssp, San Francisco *Also Called: Institute On Aging (P-18017)*

Mt Dblo Resource Recovery LLC .... B....... 925 682-9113
4080 Mallard Dr Concord (94520) *(P-3414)*

Mt Diablo Adult Education, Concord *Also Called: Mt Diablo Unified School Dst (P-17733)*

Mt Diablo Unified School Dst .... D....... 925 685-7340
1266 San Carlos Ave Concord (94518) *(P-17733)*

Mt Diblo Ctr Adult Day Hlth Ca, Pleasant Hill *Also Called: Choice In Aging (P-17027)*

Mt Miquel Covenant Village .... C....... 619 479-4790
325 Kempton St Spring Valley (91977) *(P-15592)*

Mt Rubidoux Convalescent Hosp, San Bernardino *Also Called: Waterman Convalescent Hosp Inc (P-15727)*

Mt Rubidouxidence Opco LLC .... C....... 951 681-2200
6401 33rd St Riverside (92509) *(P-15593)*

Mt Sinai Mem Pk & Mortuary, Los Angeles *Also Called: Sinai Temple (P-10516)*

Mt Sinai Mem Pk & Mortuary, Los Angeles *Also Called: Sinai Temple (P-19027)*

Mtc Financial Inc — ALPHABETIC SECTION

Mtc Financial Inc .... D....... 949 252-8300
17100 Gillette Ave Irvine (92614) *(P-20156)*

Mtc Transportation, Twentynine Palms *Also Called: Mark Clemons (P-3509)*

Mtc Worldwide Corp .... D....... 626 839-6800
17837 Rowland St City Of Industry (91748) *(P-5331)*

Mtd Kitchen Inc .... D....... 818 764-2254
13213 Sherman Way North Hollywood (91605) *(P-2478)*

Mtv Networks, Los Angeles *Also Called: Viacom Networks (P-13909)*

Mudflap Inc .... D....... 888 885-3835
400 Hamilton Ave Ste 410 Palo Alto (94301) *(P-11761)*

Muehlhan Marine, Fairfield *Also Called: Sipco Surface Protection Inc (P-1642)*

Mufg Americas Holdings Corp .... B....... 212 782-5911
1221 Broadway Fl 8 Oakland (94612) *(P-7633)*

Mufg Americas Leasing Corp (DH) .... D....... 213 488-3700
445 S Figueroa St Ste 2700 Los Angeles (90071) *(P-11044)*

Mufg Union Bank Foundation .... A....... 213 236-5000
445 S Figueroa St Los Angeles (90071) *(P-7634)*

Muir Elementary School, Long Beach *Also Called: Long Beach Unified School Dst (P-17722)*

Muir Orthopedic Specialists .... C....... 925 939-8585
2405 Shadelands Dr Ste 210 Walnut Creek (94598) *(P-14913)*

Muir WD Adolescent & Fmly Svcs, San Rafael *Also Called: Muir Wood LLC (P-17279)*

Muir Wood LLC .... D....... 310 903-1155
55 Shaver St Ste 200 San Rafael (94901) *(P-17279)*

Muir-Chase Plumbing Co Inc .... D....... 818 500-1940
4530 Brazil St Ste 1 Los Angeles (90039) *(P-1503)*

Mulen, Seal Beach *Also Called: P2f Holdings (P-6933)*

Mulholland Brand, Canoga Park *Also Called: Mulholland Security Ctrs LLC (P-13003)*

Mulholland SEC & Patrol Inc .... B....... 818 755-0202
11454 San Vicente Blvd Los Angeles (90049) *(P-13002)*

Mulholland Security Ctrs LLC .... D....... 818 983-9206
21260 Deering Ct Canoga Park (91304) *(P-13003)*

Mullenlowe US Inc .... C....... 424 738-6500
2121 Park Pl Ste 150 El Segundo (90245) *(P-10652)*

Mullenlowe US Inc .... C....... 424 738-6600
12130 Millennium Los Angeles (90094) *(P-10653)*

Muller Ranch LLC .... D....... 530 662-0105
15810 County Road 95 Woodland (95695) *(P-1)*

Mullin TBG Insur Agcy Svcs LLC (DH) C
3333 Michelson Dr Ste 820 Irvine (92612) *(P-8617)*

Mullintbg, Irvine *Also Called: Mullin TBG Insur Agcy Svcs LLC (P-8617)*

Mulroses Usa Inc .... D....... 213 489-1761
741 S San Pedro St Los Angeles (90014) *(P-141)*

Multi Mechanical Inc .... D....... 714 632-7404
469 Blaine St Corona (92879) *(P-1504)*

Multi Specialty Group Practice, Yuba City *Also Called: Sutter North Med Foundation (P-15115)*

Multi Specialty Medical Svc, Visalia *Also Called: Visalia Medical Clinic Inc (P-15195)*

Multi- Services, San Francisco *Also Called: Walden House Inc (P-18544)*

Multi-Pak Corporation .... D....... 818 709-0508
20131 Bahama St Chatsworth (91311) *(P-13385)*

Multicultural Rdo Brdcstg Inc .... D....... 626 844-8882
747 E Green St Pasadena (91101) *(P-4397)*

Multifamily Utility Co Inc .... D....... 858 442-7873
4891 Pacific Hwy Ste 102 San Diego (92110) *(P-20808)*

Multipak, Chatsworth *Also Called: Multi-Pak Corporation (P-13385)*

Multiplier .... D....... 415 421-3774
981 Mission St San Francisco (94103) *(P-20809)*

Multiquip Inc (DH) .... B....... 310 537-3700
6141 Katella Ave Ste 200 Cypress (90630) *(P-5582)*

Multivest, San Dimas *Also Called: Webmetro (P-12395)*

Multivision Inc (DH) .... D....... 510 740-5600
66 Franklin St 3rd Fl Oakland (94607) *(P-13386)*

Munger Tolles & Olson LLP .... B....... 213 683-9100
350 S Grand Ave Fl 50 Los Angeles (90071) *(P-17580)*

Munger Bros LLC .... A....... 661 721-0390
786 Road 188 Delano (93215) *(P-118)*

Munger Farm, Delano *Also Called: Munger Bros LLC (P-118)*

Munger Farms, Delano *Also Called: Monarch Nut Company LLC (P-290)*

Munger Tolles Olson Foundation (PA) .... B....... 213 683-9100
350 S Grand Ave Fl 50 Los Angeles (90071) *(P-17581)*

Muniservices LLC (DH) .... C....... 800 800-8181
7625 N Palm Ave Ste 108 Fresno (93711) *(P-20477)*

Murad LLC (HQ) .... C....... 310 726-0600
2121 Park Pl Fl 1 El Segundo (90245) *(P-2599)*

Murad LLC .... C....... 310 726-3300
1340 Storm Pkwy Torrance (90501) *(P-6132)*

Murad LLC .... C....... 310 726-0470
2141 Rosecrans Ave Ste 1151 El Segundo (90245) *(P-10503)*

Murad Spa, El Segundo *Also Called: Murad LLC (P-10503)*

Muranaka Farm .... C....... 805 529-0201
11018 W Los Angeles Ave Moorpark (93021) *(P-191)*

Murchison & Cumming LLP (PA) .... D....... 213 623-7400
801 S Grand Ave Ste 900 Los Angeles (90017) *(P-17582)*

Murcor Inc .... C....... 909 623-4001
740 Corporate Center Dr Ste 100 Pomona (91768) *(P-9107)*

Muriel Siebert & Co Inc .... D....... 800 993-2015
9378 Wilshire Blvd Ste 300 Beverly Hills (90212) *(P-8156)*

Murj Inc .... D....... 831 588-4462
3912 Portola Dr Ste 9 Santa Cruz (95062) *(P-20810)*

Murphy Murphy & Murphy Inc .... D....... 562 594-6678
6261 Katella Ave Cypress (90630) *(P-19613)*

Murphy & Beane Inc .... D....... 310 649-4470
5901 Green Valley Cir Ste 145 Culver City (90230) *(P-17583)*

Murphy-True Inc .... D....... 707 576-7337
464 Kenwood Ct Ste B Santa Rosa (95407) *(P-973)*

Murray Company, E Rncho Dmngz *Also Called: Murray Plumbing and Htg Corp (P-1505)*

Murray Plumbing and Htg Corp (PA) .... B....... 310 637-1500
18414 S Santa Fe Ave E Rncho Dmngz (90221) *(P-1505)*

Murrays Iron Works Inc (PA) .... C....... 323 521-1100
7355 E Slauson Ave Commerce (90040) *(P-2491)*

Murrieta Day Spa, Murrieta *Also Called: Monique Suraci (P-14219)*

Murrieta Development Company Inc .... C....... 951 719-1680
42540 Rio Nedo Temecula (92590) *(P-1240)*

Murrietta Circuits .... C....... 714 970-2430
5000 E Landon Dr Anaheim (92807) *(P-2908)*

Mursion Inc .... C....... 415 746-9631
2443 Fillmore St Pmb 515 San Francisco (94115) *(P-12277)*

Murtaugh Myer Nlson Trglia LLP .... D....... 949 794-4000
2603 Main St Ste 900 Irvine (92614) *(P-17584)*

Musclebound Inc .... B....... 818 349-0123
19835 Nordhoff St Northridge (91324) *(P-14220)*

Muse Concrete Contractors Inc .... D....... 530 226-5151
8599 Commercial Way Redding (96002) *(P-1142)*

Museum Associates .... B....... 323 857-6172
5905 Wilshire Blvd Los Angeles (90036) *(P-18658)*

Museum Cntmprary Art San Diego (PA) .... D....... 858 454-3541
1100 Kettner Blvd San Diego (92101) *(P-18659)*

Museum of Contemporary Art (PA) .... C....... 213 626-6222
250 S Grand Ave Los Angeles (90012) *(P-18660)*

Music Academy of West .... D....... 805 969-4726
1070 Fairway Rd Santa Barbara (93108) *(P-17812)*

Music Center, Los Angeles *Also Called: Performing Arts Ctr Los Angles (P-14054)*

Music Circus, Sacramento *Also Called: Broadway Sacramento (P-14030)*

Music Express Inc (PA) .... C....... 818 845-1502
2601 W Empire Ave Burbank (91504) *(P-3283)*

Music Intllgnce Neuro Dev Inst, Irvine *Also Called: Mind Research Institute (P-19895)*

Musick Peeler & Garrett LLP (PA) .... C....... 213 629-7600
624 S Grand Ave Ste 2000 Los Angeles (90023) *(P-17585)*

Musicmatch Inc .... C....... 858 485-4300
16935 W Bernardo Dr Ste 270 San Diego (92127) *(P-12278)*

Mutesix Group Inc .... C....... 800 935-6856
5800 Bristol Pkwy Ste 500 Culver City (90230) *(P-10654)*

Mutesix, An Iprospect Company, Culver City *Also Called: Mutesix Group Inc (P-10654)*

Muth Machine Works .... D....... 951 685-1521
4510 Rutile St Riverside (92509) *(P-20478)*

Mutual Trading Co Inc (DH) .... C....... 213 626-9458
4200 Shirley Ave El Monte (91731) *(P-6650)*

Mutual Trading Co Inc .... D....... 213 229-9393
843 E 4th St Los Angeles (90013) *(P-6931)*

Mv Medical Management .... D....... 323 257-7637
1860 Colorado Blvd Ste 200 Los Angeles (90041) *(P-20479)*

Mv Transit, Union City Also Called: Mv Transportation Inc (P-3168)
Mv Transportation, Newbury Park Also Called: Mv Transportation Inc (P-3173)
Mv Transportation Inc .... C 323 666-0856
  13690 Vaughn St San Fernando (91340) (P-3163)
Mv Transportation Inc .... C 510 351-1603
  1944 Williams St San Leandro (94577) (P-3164)
Mv Transportation Inc .... C 818 409-3387
  1242 Los Angeles St Glendale (91204) (P-3165)
Mv Transportation Inc .... C 209 547-7879
  1250 S Wilson Way Ste A1 Stockton (95205) (P-3166)
Mv Transportation Inc .... C 209 339-1972
  24 S Sacramento St Lodi (95240) (P-3167)
Mv Transportation Inc .... C 510 441-0698
  34650 7th St Union City (94587) (P-3168)
Mv Transportation Inc .... C 562 943-6776
  15677 Phoebe Ave La Mirada (90638) (P-3169)
Mv Transportation Inc .... C 916 788-3000
  501 Giuseppe Ct Ste F Roseville (95678) (P-3170)
Mv Transportation Inc .... C 805 557-7372
  265 S Rancho Rd Thousand Oaks (91361) (P-3171)
Mv Transportation Inc .... C 323 936-9783
  5420 W Jefferson Blvd Los Angeles (90016) (P-3172)
Mv Transportation Inc .... C 805 375-5467
  670 Lawrence Dr Newbury Park (91320) (P-3173)
Mv Transportation Inc .... B 310 638-0556
  14011 S Central Ave Los Angeles (90059) (P-3174)
Mv Transportation Inc .... C 760 400-0300
  303 Via Del Norte Oceanside (92058) (P-3175)
Mv Transportation Inc .... C 760 520-0118
  755 Norlak Ave Escondido (92025) (P-3176)
Mv Transportation Inc .... B 818 374-9145
  16738 Stagg St Van Nuys (91406) (P-3177)
Mv Transportation Inc .... B 415 206-7386
  3550 3rd St San Francisco (94124) (P-3178)
Mv Transportation Inc .... C 760 255-3330
  1612 State St Barstow (92311) (P-3179)
Mv Transportation Inc .... D 562 259-9911
  7231 Rosecrans Ave Paramount (90723) (P-3180)
Mv Transportation Inc .... B 916 854-2638
  10170 Croydon Way Ste A Sacramento (95827) (P-3181)
Mv Transportation Inc .... C 707 546-1999
  3250 Dutton Ave Santa Rosa (95407) (P-3182)
Mventix, Woodland Hills Also Called: Mventix Inc (P-13387)
Mventix Inc (PA) .... D 818 337-3747
  21600 Oxnard St Ste 1700 Woodland Hills (91367) (P-13387)
Mw Partners, Irvine Also Called: Morris & Willner Partners (P-20475)
Mwd, Los Angeles Also Called: The Metropolitan Water District of Southern California (P-4841)
Mwss, Irvine Also Called: In Montrose Wtr Sstnblity Svcs (P-20776)
My Ally Inc .... D 650 387-9118
  1000 Elwell Ct Ste 105 Palo Alto (94303) (P-12497)
MY DAY COUNTS, Anaheim Also Called: Orange Cnty Adult Achvment Ctr (P-18072)
My Eye Media LLC .... D 818 559-7200
  2211 N Hollywood Way Burbank (91505) (P-12279)
My Kids Dentist .... B 951 600-1062
  24635 Madison Ave Ste E Murrieta (92562) (P-15241)
My Network TV, Los Angeles Also Called: Twentieth Television Inc (P-13905)
My Office Inc .... D 858 549-6700
  8333 Arjons Dr Ste D San Diego (92126) (P-2299)
My Points.com, San Francisco Also Called: Mypointscom LLC (P-10655)
My True Image Mfg Inc .... D 510 970-7990
  999 Marina Way S Richmond (94804) (P-5433)
Mycase, San Diego Also Called: Appfolio Inc (P-12091)
Myers & Sons Construction LLC .... C 916 283-9950
  45 Morrison Ave Sacramento (95838) (P-1241)
Myers & Sons Construction LP .... C 424 227-3285
  5777 W Century Blvd Ste 600 Los Angeles (90045) (P-1143)
Myers & Sons Construction LP (HQ) .... C 916 283-9950
  45 Morrison Ave Sacramento (95838) (P-1144)
Myers Fdservice Eqp Sup Design, Santa Rosa Also Called: Myers Restaurant Supply LLC (P-5386)
Myers Restaurant Supply LLC .... C 707 570-1200
  1599 Cleveland Ave Santa Rosa (95401) (P-5386)
Myers-Briggs Company (PA) .... D 650 969-8901
  185 N Wolfe Rd Sunnyvale (94086) (P-20480)
Myhealthteams Inc .... D 415 860-7878
  1 Post St Ste 2250 San Francisco (94104) (P-10563)
Myhhbs Inc .... D 888 969-4427
  237 N Central Ave Ste A Glendale (91203) (P-18058)
Myles Stevens Architecture .... D 415 397-6500
  855 Sansome St Ste 200 San Francisco (94111) (P-19497)
Myotek Industries Incorporated (DH) .... D 949 502-3776
  1278 Glenneyre St Ste 431 Laguna Beach (92651) (P-2951)
Mypointscom LLC (HQ) .... D 415 615-1100
  44 Montgomery St Ste 1050 San Francisco (94104) (P-10655)
Myriad Womens Health Inc .... B 888 268-6795
  180 Kimball Way South San Francisco (94080) (P-16737)
Myst Therapeutics Inc .... D 415 516-8450
  570 Westwood Plz Bldg 114 Los Angeles (90095) (P-19740)
Mythic Inc .... D 734 707-7339
  333 Twin Dolphin Dr Ste 300 Redwood City (94065) (P-20481)
Myyogaworks, Culver City Also Called: Yogaworks Inc (P-14589)
N & S Tractor Co (PA) .... D 209 383-5888
  600 S Highway 59 Merced (95341) (P-13785)
N G I, Brea Also Called: Nevell Group Inc (P-976)
N H A, San Diego Also Called: Neighborhood House Association (P-18059)
N I D, Grass Valley Also Called: Nevada Irrigation District (P-4991)
N Model Inc (PA) .... B 650 610-4600
  777 Mariners Island Blvd Ste 300 San Mateo (94404) (P-11762)
N Qiagen Amercn Holdings Inc (HQ) .... C 800 426-8157
  27220 Turnberry Ln Ste 200 Valencia (91355) (P-6133)
N S C Channel Islands Inc .... B 805 485-1908
  2300 Wankel Way Oxnard (93030) (P-14914)
N T S, Woodland Hills Also Called: Network Telephone Services Inc (P-13391)
N Trans/Sub Regional Office, Valencia Also Called: Southern California Edison Co (P-4689)
N V B, Redding Also Called: North Valley Bank (P-7701)
N V H, Concord Also Called: N V Heathorn Inc (P-1506)
N V Heathorn Inc .... D 510 569-9100
  1980 Olivera Rd Ste C Concord (94520) (P-1506)
N-U Enterprise, Irvine Also Called: Ancca Corporation (P-1905)
N2 Acquisition Company Inc .... D 714 942-3563
  14440 Myford Rd Irvine (92606) (P-9323)
N2 Imaging Systems, Irvine Also Called: N2 Acquisition Company Inc (P-9323)
Nabiekim Enterprises Inc .... D 646 645-1958
  3039 E Campus Pointe Dr Fresno (93710) (P-13388)
Nabisco, Ontario Also Called: Mondelez Global LLC (P-6648)
Nabors Well Services Co .... D 805 648-2731
  2567 N Ventura Ave # C Ventura (93001) (P-617)
Nabors Well Services Co .... C 661 588-6140
  1025 Earthmover Ct Bakersfield (93314) (P-618)
Nabors Well Services Co .... D 310 639-7074
  19431 S Santa Fe Ave Compton (90221) (P-619)
Nabors Well Services Co .... C 661 392-7668
  1954 James Rd Bakersfield (93308) (P-620)
Nabors Well Services Co .... B 661 589-3970
  7515 Rosedale Hwy Bakersfield (93308) (P-621)
Nadco Inc .... D 310 623-7776
  360 S Elm Dr Apt 3 Beverly Hills (90212) (P-338)
Naf, Tustin Also Called: New American Funding LLC (P-7881)
Nafees Memon .... D 818 997-1666
  6819 Sepulveda Blvd Ste 312 Van Nuys (91405) (P-13004)
Nafees Mmon Cmmand Intl SEC Sv, Van Nuys Also Called: Nafees Memon (P-13004)
NAFTA Distributors .... C 800 956-2382
  5120 Santa Ana St Ontario (91761) (P-6270)
Nagarro Inc (PA) .... C 408 436-6170
  1737 N 1st St Ste 590 San Jose (95112) (P-12842)
Nagra, San Francisco Also Called: Opentv Inc (P-12304)
Nai BT Commercial, San Francisco Also Called: Cushman & Wakefield Inc (P-8956)
Nail Alliance - North Amer Inc .... D 714 449-1568
  4100 Bonita Pl Fullerton (92835) (P-10504)
Nakase Brothers Whl Nurs LP (PA) .... D 949 855-4388
  9441 Krepp Dr Huntington Beach (92646) (P-6866)

Nakase Brothers Wholesale Nurs .... C...... 949 855-4388
20621 Lake Forest Dr Lake Forest (92630) *(P-6867)*

NAKASE BROTHERS WHOLESALE NURSERY, Lake Forest *Also Called: Nakase Brothers Wholesale Nurs (P-6867)*

Nallatech, Camarillo *Also Called: Nallatech Inc (P-5679)*

Nallatech Inc .... D...... 805 383-8997
741 Flynn Rd Camarillo (93012) *(P-5679)*

Nalu Medical Inc .... C...... 760 603-8466
2320 Faraday Ave Ste 100 Carlsbad (92008) *(P-17280)*

NAMM, Carlsbad *Also Called: National Assn Mus Mrchnts Inc (P-18718)*

Namvars Inc .... D...... 858 792-5461
11815 Sorrento Valley Rd Ste A San Diego (92121) *(P-524)*

Nan Fang, San Leandro *Also Called: Nan Fang Dist Group Inc (P-5847)*

Nan Fang Dist Group Inc .... D...... 510 297-5382
2100 Williams St San Leandro (94577) *(P-5847)*

Nana Enterprises .... C...... 415 383-0340
707 Redwood Hwy Frontage Rd Mill Valley (94941) *(P-10036)*

Nanocomposix LLC .... D...... 858 565-4227
4878 Ronson Ct Ste J San Diego (92111) *(P-19899)*

Nanosolar Inc .... B
2434 Rock St Apt 14 Mountain View (94043) *(P-5757)*

Nantbioscience Inc .... D...... 310 883-1300
9920 Jefferson Blvd Culver City (90232) *(P-5434)*

Nantcell Inc .... B...... 562 397-3639
9920 Jefferson Blvd Culver City (90232) *(P-19741)*

Nantcell Inc .... C...... 310 883-1300
2040 E Mariposa Ave El Segundo (90245) *(P-19900)*

Nantenergy LLC .... D...... 310 905-4866
2040 E Mariposa Ave El Segundo (90245) *(P-2863)*

Nantworks LLC (PA) .... D...... 310 883-1300
9920 Jefferson Blvd Culver City (90232) *(P-12498)*

NAPA Golf Associates LLC .... D...... 707 257-1900
2555 Jameson Canyon Rd Napa (94558) *(P-14412)*

NAPA Golf Course At Kennedy Pk, Napa *Also Called: Courseco Inc (P-14254)*

NAPA Post Acute, Napa *Also Called: Napaidence Opco LLC (P-15594)*

NAPA Solano Cmnty Blood Ctr, Fairfield *Also Called: Vitalant Research Institute (P-17349)*

NAPA State Hospital, Napa *Also Called: Califrnia Dept State Hospitals (P-16643)*

NAPA Valley Country Club .... D...... 707 252-1111
3385 Hagen Rd Napa (94558) *(P-14413)*

NAPA Valley Lodge LP .... D...... 707 875-3525
103 Coast Highway 1 Bodega Bay (94923) *(P-10037)*

NAPA Valley Marriott, Napa *Also Called: IA Lodging NAPA Solano Trs LLC (P-9904)*

NAPA Valley PSI Inc .... D...... 707 255-0177
651 Trabajo Ln Napa (94559) *(P-18237)*

NAPA Valley Railroad Co, Napa *Also Called: NAPA Valley Wine Train LLC (P-14549)*

NAPA Valley Wine Train LLC (HQ) .... C...... 707 253-2160
1275 Mckinstry St Napa (94559) *(P-14549)*

Napaidence Opco LLC .... C...... 707 255-6060
705 Trancas St Napa (94558) *(P-15594)*

Napca Foundation .... A...... 800 799-4640
2600 W Olive Ave Ste 500 Burbank (91505) *(P-17813)*

Napd, Bakersfield *Also Called: New Advnces For Pple With Dsbl (P-18611)*

Napoleon Perdis Cosmetics Inc .... D...... 323 817-3611
16825 Saticoy St Van Nuys (91406) *(P-7587)*

Narus Inc .... C...... 408 215-4300
329 Bernardo Ave Mountain View (94043) *(P-11763)*

Narven Enterprises Inc .... D...... 619 239-2261
1430 7th Ave Ste B San Diego (92101) *(P-10038)*

Nasif Hicks Harris & Co LLP .... D...... 805 966-1521
104 W Anapamu St Ste B Santa Barbara (93101) *(P-19614)*

Nasser Company Inc (PA) .... D...... 714 279-2100
22720 Savi Ranch Pkwy Yorba Linda (92887) *(P-6271)*

Nasser Company of Arizona, Yorba Linda *Also Called: Nasser Company Inc (P-6271)*

Nastec International Inc .... D...... 818 222-0355
23875 Ventura Blvd Ste 204 Calabasas (91302) *(P-13005)*

Nat Geo TV, Los Angeles *Also Called: Disney Networks Group LLC (P-4425)*

National 9 Motels Inc .... D...... 530 622-3884
1500 Broadway Placerville (95667) *(P-10039)*

National Air Inc .... C...... 619 299-2500
2053 Kurtz St San Diego (92110) *(P-1507)*

National Air and Energy, San Diego *Also Called: National Air Inc (P-1507)*

National Assn For Hispanic, Los Angeles *Also Called: La Asccion Ncnal Pro Prsnas My (P-18035)*

National Assn Mus Mrchants Inc .... D...... 760 438-8001
5790 Armada Dr Carlsbad (92008) *(P-18718)*

National Attny Collection Svcs .... B...... 818 547-9760
700 N Brand Blvd Fl 2 Glendale (91203) *(P-17586)*

National Beverage Corp .... D...... 510 783-3200
26901 Industrial Blvd Hayward (94545) *(P-6651)*

National Bus Invstigations Inc .... D...... 951 677-3500
25020 Las Brisas Rd Ste A Murrieta (92562) *(P-13389)*

National Clearing Corporation (PA) .... D...... 310 385-2165
9665 Wilshire Blvd Beverly Hills (90212) *(P-20482)*

National Cmnty Renaissance Cal .... C...... 619 223-9222
8265 Aspen St Ste 100 Rancho Cucamonga (91730) *(P-9265)*

National Cmnty Renaissance Cal (PA) .... D...... 909 483-2444
9692 Haven Ave Ste 100 Rancho Cucamonga (91730) *(P-9266)*

National Cnstr Rentals Inc (HQ) .... D...... 818 221-6000
15319 Chatsworth St Mission Hills (91345) *(P-11045)*

National Community Renaissance .... C...... 909 948-7579
8590 Malven Ave Rancho Cucamonga (91730) *(P-8846)*

National Corset Supply House (PA) .... D...... 323 261-0265
3240 E 26th St Vernon (90058) *(P-2464)*

National Crmic Tile Stone Corp .... D...... 916 776-8715
9980 Horn Rd Ste 100 Sacramento (95827) *(P-1986)*

National Custom Packing Inc .... B...... 831 724-2026
13526 Blackie Rd Castroville (95012) *(P-291)*

National Distribution Agcy Inc (HQ) .... D...... 510 487-6226
7025 Central Ave Newark (94560) *(P-3734)*

National Express LLC .... A...... 209 201-9345
880 Thornton Rd Merced (95341) *(P-3284)*

National Financial Svcs LLC .... A...... 949 476-0157
19200 Von Karman Ave Ste 400 Irvine (92612) *(P-8157)*

National Financial Svcs LLC .... A...... 415 912-2805
44 Montgomery St Ste 1900 San Francisco (94104) *(P-8210)*

National Financial Svcs LLC .... A...... 650 343-6775
1411 Chapin Ave Burlingame (94010) *(P-9538)*

National Fitness Testing, Los Angeles *Also Called: Young MNS Chrstn Assn Mtro Los (P-18962)*

National Flooring Products Inc .... D...... 877 238-3225
5003 Ontario Mills Pkwy Ontario (91764) *(P-5126)*

National Food Laboratory LLC .... D...... 925 828-1440
365 N Canyons Pkwy Ste 201 Livermore (94551) *(P-19901)*

National Freight Inc .... D...... 909 348-5464
179 Grand Ave City Of Industry (91789) *(P-13562)*

National Funding Inc (PA) .... C...... 888 733-2383
9530 Towne Centre Dr Ste 120 San Diego (92121) *(P-7898)*

National Genetics Institute .... C...... 310 996-6610
2440 S Sepulveda Blvd Ste 235 Los Angeles (90064) *(P-19991)*

National Hot Rod Association (PA) .... C...... 626 914-4761
140 Via Verde Ste 100 San Dimas (91773) *(P-14165)*

National Insurance Crime Bur .... D...... 818 895-2867
15545 Devonshire St Ste 309 Mission Hills (91345) *(P-8618)*

National Link Incorporated .... D...... 909 670-1900
2235 Auto Centre Dr Glendora (91740) *(P-5252)*

National Med Assn Cmprhnsive H .... D...... 619 231-9300
3177 Ocean View Blvd San Diego (92113) *(P-17099)*

National Mentor Holdings Inc .... B...... 951 677-1453
30033 Technology Dr Murrieta (92563) *(P-18492)*

National Monitoring Center, Lake Forest *Also Called: Advanced Protection Inds LLC (P-13093)*

National Notary Association .... C...... 800 876-6827
9350 De Soto Ave Chatsworth (91311) *(P-18753)*

National Nurses United, Oakland *Also Called: California Nurses Association (P-18739)*

National Opinion Research Ctr .... C...... 415 315-2000
50 California St Ste 1500 San Francisco (94111) *(P-19833)*

National Opinion Research Ctr .... C...... 415 315-3800
1250 Borregas Ave Sunnyvale (94089) *(P-19834)*

National Paving Company Inc .... D...... 951 369-1332
4361 Fort Dr Riverside (92509) *(P-1145)*

National Planning Corporation .... C...... 800 881-7174
100 N Pacific Coast Hwy Ste 1800 El Segundo (90245) *(P-7880)*

National Raisin Company, Fowler Also Called: Sunshine Raisin Corporation *(P-307)*
National Rent A Fence Co., Mission Hills Also Called: National Cnstr Rentals Inc *(P-11045)*
National Research Group, Los Angeles Also Called: National Research Group Inc *(P-19835)*
National Research Group Inc .... B...... 323 406-6200
  12101 Bluff Creek Dr Los Angeles (90094) *(P-19835)*
National Retail Trnsp Inc .... D...... 951 243-6110
  400 Harley Knox Blvd Perris (92571) *(P-3517)*
National Retail Trnsp Inc .... D...... 310 605-3777
  355 W Carob St Compton (90220) *(P-3518)*
National School District .... C...... 619 336-7770
  1400 N Ave National City (91950) *(P-17734)*
National Security Industries .... B...... 831 425-2052
  501 Mission St Ste 1a Santa Cruz (95060) *(P-13006)*
National Security Santa Cruz, Santa Cruz Also Called: National Security Industries *(P-13006)*
National Security Tech LLC .... B...... 805 681-2432
  5520 Ekwill St Ste B Goleta (93111) *(P-19330)*
National Security Tech LLC .... A...... 925 960-2500
  161 S Vasco Rd Ste A Livermore (94551) *(P-19331)*
National Teleconsultants Inc .... C...... 818 265-4400
  550 N Brand Blvd Fl 17 Glendale (91203) *(P-19332)*
National Therapeutic Svcs Inc (PA) .... D...... 866 311-0003
  3822 Campus Dr Ste 100 Newport Beach (92660) *(P-17100)*
National Trench Safety LLC .... C...... 562 602-1642
  13217 Laureldale Ave Downey (90242) *(P-11046)*
National Tube & Steel, Mission Hills Also Called: The National Bus Group Inc *(P-11008)*
National Veterinary Assoc Inc (HQ) .... D...... 805 777-7722
  1 Baxter Way Westlake Village (91362) *(P-339)*
National Wire and Cable, Los Angeles Also Called: National Wire and Cable Corporation *(P-2721)*
National Wire and Cable Corporation .... C...... 323 225-5611
  136 N San Fernando Rd Los Angeles (90031) *(P-2721)*
NationaLease, San Diego Also Called: Miramar Ford Truck Sales Inc *(P-5016)*
Nationbuilder, Los Angeles Also Called: 3dna Corp *(P-11367)*
Nations First Capital LLC .... D...... 855 396-3600
  516 Gibson Dr Ste 160 Roseville (95678) *(P-7922)*
Nationsbenefits LLC .... D...... 877 439-2665
  1540 Scenic Ave Costa Mesa (92626) *(P-20483)*
Nationwide, Santa Ana Also Called: Turnkey Foundation Inc *(P-8025)*
Nationwide, San Mateo Also Called: Abd Insurance & Fincl Svcs Inc *(P-8476)*
Nationwide, Glendale Also Called: Arthur J Gallagher & Co *(P-8493)*
Nationwide, Visalia Also Called: Arthur J Gallagher & Co *(P-8494)*
Nationwide, Glendale Also Called: Arthur J Gallagher Risk Mgmt *(P-8495)*
Nationwide, San Diego Also Called: Atlas General Insur Svcs LLC *(P-8500)*
Nationwide, Cerritos Also Called: Auto Insurance Specialists LLC *(P-8501)*
Nationwide, Pasadena Also Called: B&C Liquidating Corp *(P-8506)*
Nationwide, San Francisco Also Called: Cal Insurance and Assoc Inc *(P-8517)*
Nationwide, Fresno Also Called: Dibuduo Dfendis Insur Brks LLC *(P-8545)*
Nationwide, San Ramon Also Called: Edgewood Partners Insur Ctr *(P-8548)*
Nationwide, Newport Beach Also Called: Edgewood Partners Insur Ctr *(P-8549)*
Nationwide, San Francisco Also Called: Edgewood Partners Insur Ctr *(P-8551)*
Nationwide, Woodland Hills Also Called: Grosslight Insurance Inc *(P-8576)*
Nationwide, Walnut Creek Also Called: Heffernan Insurance Brokers *(P-8585)*
Nationwide, Riverside Also Called: Insurance Inc Southern Cal *(P-8592)*
Nationwide, Roseville Also Called: Interwest Insurance Svcs LLC *(P-8593)*
Nationwide, Fresno Also Called: James G Parker Insurance Assoc *(P-8596)*
Nationwide, San Luis Obispo Also Called: Morris Grritano Insur Agcy Inc *(P-8616)*
Nationwide, Roseville Also Called: Networked Insurance Agents LLC *(P-8621)*
Nationwide, Cypress Also Called: Pacific Pioneer Insur Group *(P-8635)*
Nationwide, San Francisco Also Called: Pennbrook Insurance Service *(P-8638)*
Nationwide, Cerritos Also Called: Poliseek Ais Insur Sltions Inc *(P-8641)*
Nationwide, San Francisco Also Called: Symphony Risk Sltons Insur Svc *(P-8667)*
Nationwide, La Mesa Also Called: Teague Insurance Agency Inc *(P-8670)*
Nationwide, Pasadena Also Called: United Agencies Inc *(P-8678)*
Nationwide, San Diego Also Called: Wateridge Insurance Svcs Inc *(P-8683)*
Nationwide, Turlock Also Called: Winton-Ireland Insur Agcy Inc *(P-8688)*
Nationwide, Tustin Also Called: Wood Gutmann Bogart Insur Brkg *(P-8691)*
Nationwide, San Francisco Also Called: Woodruff-Sawyer & Co *(P-8693)*

Nationwide, San Francisco Also Called: Alliant Insurance Services Inc *(P-20016)*
Nationwide, Irvine Also Called: Sullivncrtsmnroe Insur Svcs LL *(P-20571)*
Nationwide, Irvine Also Called: Alliant Insurance Services Inc *(P-20684)*
Nationwide, San Diego Also Called: Alliant Insurance Services Inc *(P-20685)*
Nationwide Environmental Svcs, Norwalk Also Called: Joes Sweeping Inc *(P-4901)*
Nationwide Guard Services Inc .... B...... 909 608-1112
  9327 Fairway View Pl Ste 200 Rancho Cucamonga (91730) *(P-13007)*
Nationwide Legal LLC .... D...... 916 443-4400
  716 10th St Ste 102 Sacramento (95814) *(P-17587)*
Nationwide Theatres Corp (HQ) .... D...... 310 657-8420
  120 N Robertson Blvd Fl 3 Los Angeles (90048) *(P-14023)*
Nationwide Theatres Corp .... A...... 562 421-8448
  2500 Carson St Lakewood (90712) *(P-14120)*
Nationwide Trans Inc (PA) .... D...... 909 355-3211
  11727 Eastend Ave Chino (91710) *(P-4061)*
Native American Health Ctr Inc (PA) .... D...... 510 535-4400
  2950 International Blvd Oakland (94601) *(P-14915)*
Natividad Medical Center .... A...... 831 755-4111
  1441 Constitution Blvd Ste 200 Salinas (93906) *(P-16279)*
Natomas Marketplace 16, Sacramento Also Called: Regal Cinemas Inc *(P-14007)*
Natomas Racquet Club, Sacramento Also Called: Spare-Time Inc *(P-14233)*
Natren Inc .... D...... 805 371-4737
  3105 Willow Ln Thousand Oaks (91361) *(P-2438)*
Natron Energy Inc .... D...... 408 498-5828
  3542 Bassett St Santa Clara (95054) *(P-2949)*
Natura Holdings LLC .... D...... 916 209-0038
  8280 Elder Creek Rd Sacramento (95828) *(P-15)*
Natura Lifescience, Sacramento Also Called: Natura Holdings LLC *(P-15)*
Natural Balance Pet Foods LLC (PA) .... D...... 800 829-4493
  2358 University Ave Ste 2280 San Diego (92104) *(P-2364)*
Natural Balance Pet Foods Inc .... D...... 415 247-3020
  50 Elsie St San Francisco (94110) *(P-6652)*
Natural Balance Pet Foods, Inc., San Francisco Also Called: Natural Balance Pet Foods Inc *(P-6652)*
Natural Gas Corp California .... B...... 415 973-7000
  77 Beale St Fl 32 San Francisco (94105) *(P-4590)*
Natural Orange Inc .... D...... 408 963-6868
  434 Park Ave San Jose (95110) *(P-10838)*
Naturalife Eco Vite Labs .... D...... 310 370-1563
  20433 Earl St Torrance (90503) *(P-2348)*
Nature Conservancy .... D...... 415 777-0487
  201 Mission St Ste 400 San Francisco (94105) *(P-18885)*
Nature Expeditions Africa, Sacramento Also Called: Accent Hospitality Group LLC *(P-3957)*
Natures Best .... B...... 714 255-4600
  6 Pointe Dr Ste 300 Brea (92821) *(P-6653)*
Natures Image Inc .... D...... 949 680-4400
  20361 Hermana Cir Lake Forest (92630) *(P-449)*
Natures Produce .... C...... 323 235-4343
  3305 Bandini Blvd Vernon (90058) *(P-6565)*
Natures Products Inc (DH) .... C...... 954 233-3300
  1221 Broadway Oakland (94612) *(P-6134)*
Natureware Inc .... D...... 714 251-4510
  6590 Darin Way Cypress (90630) *(P-6135)*
Nau Country Insurance Company .... C...... 530 662-7466
  120 Main St Woodland (95695) *(P-8619)*
Nau Country Insurance Company .... C...... 559 252-7400
  7485 N Palm Ave Ste 105 Fresno (93711) *(P-8620)*
Naumann/Hobbs Mtl Hdlg Corp II .... C...... 866 266-2244
  86998 Avenue 52 Coachella (92236) *(P-5795)*
Nautilus Biotechnology, San Carlos Also Called: Nautilus Biotechnology Inc *(P-19742)*
Nautilus Biotechnology Inc .... C...... 206 333-2001
  835 Industrial Rd Ste 200 San Carlos (94070) *(P-19742)*
Nautilus Intl Holdg Corp .... B...... 209 465-5713
  413 Luce Ave Stockton (95203) *(P-3735)*
Navagis Inc (PA) .... D...... 800 819-7872
  50 California St Ste 1500 San Francisco (94111) *(P-11764)*
Naval Coating Inc .... C...... 619 234-8366
  2080 Cambridge Ave Cardiff By The Sea (92007) *(P-2300)*
Naval Facilities Engineer Comm .... D...... 619 532-1158
  1220 Pacific Hwy San Diego (92132) *(P-19333)*

ALPHABETIC SECTION

Naval Health Researc, San Diego *Also Called: NAVY UNITED STATES DEPARTMENT (P-19744)*

Naval Hosp Twntynine Plms Gfeb, Twentynine Palms *Also Called: NAVY UNITED STATES DEPARTMENT (P-17281)*

Naval Medical Center, San Diego *Also Called: NAVY UNITED STATES DEPARTMENT (P-16280)*

Naval Station Child Dev Ctr, San Diego *Also Called: Navy Exchange Service Command (P-18337)*

    Navan Inc (PA) .... C...... 888 505-8747
    3045 Park Blvd Palo Alto (94306) *(P-3941)*

    Navcom Technology Inc (HQ) .... D...... 310 381-2000
    20780 Madrona Ave Torrance (90503) *(P-2895)*

    Navigage Foundation (PA) .... D...... 818 790-2522
    849 Foothill Blvd Ste 8 La Canada (91011) *(P-15595)*

    Navigate Biopharma Svcs Inc .... C...... 866 992-4939
    1890 Rutherford Rd Carlsbad (92008) *(P-19743)*

    Navigators Management Co Inc .... C...... 949 255-4860
    19100 Von Karman Ave Irvine (92612) *(P-20157)*

    Navis Corporation (PA) .... D...... 510 267-5000
    32980 Alvarado Niles Rd Union City (94587) *(P-20811)*

    Navis LP (PA) .... C...... 510 267-5000
    55 Harrison St Ste 600 Oakland (94607) *(P-12280)*

    Navitas Semiconductor Corp (PA) .... C...... 901 685-2865
    3520 Challenger St Torrance (90503) *(P-9539)*

    Navtrak LLC .... D...... 410 548-2337
    20 Enterprise Ste 100 Aliso Viejo (92656) *(P-13134)*

    Navy Exchange Service Command .... D...... 909 517-2640
    4250 Eucalyptus Ave Chino (91710) *(P-3736)*

    Navy Exchange Service Command .... D...... 619 556-7466
    2375 Recreation Way San Diego (92136) *(P-18337)*

    NAVY UNITED STATES DEPARTMENT .... C...... 805 989-1328
    311 Navy Base Ventura County Port Hueneme (93042) *(P-13786)*

    NAVY UNITED STATES DEPARTMENT .... B...... 858 577-9849
    19871 Mitscher Way San Diego (92145) *(P-14916)*

    NAVY UNITED STATES DEPARTMENT .... A...... 619 532-6400
    34800 Bob Wilson Dr San Diego (92134) *(P-16280)*

    NAVY UNITED STATES DEPARTMENT .... D...... 760 830-2124
    1145 Sturgis Rd Twentynine Palms (92278) *(P-17281)*

    NAVY UNITED STATES DEPARTMENT .... D...... 619 524-6727
    Naval Training Ctr Bldg 287 San Diego (92133) *(P-19744)*

Naztech, Valencia *Also Called: Hypercel Corporation (P-5660)*

    Nazzareno Electric Co Inc .... D...... 714 712-4744
    1250 E Gene Autry Way Anaheim (92805) *(P-1785)*

    Nb Baker Electric Inc .... D...... 760 546-6030
    2120 Harmony Grove Rd Escondido (92029) *(P-1786)*

NBC, Universal City *Also Called: NBC Subsidiary (knbc-Tv) LLC (P-4454)*

NBC, Universal City *Also Called: NBC Studios Inc (P-14048)*

NBC 7/Channel 39, San Diego *Also Called: Station Venture Operations LP (P-4463)*

    NBC Consulting Inc .... D...... 310 798-5000
    2110 Artesia Blvd Ste 323 Redondo Beach (90278) *(P-20484)*

    NBC Studios Inc .... A...... 818 777-1000
    100 Universal City Plz Fl 3 Universal City (91608) *(P-14048)*

    NBC Subsidiary (knbc-Tv) LLC .... C...... 818 684-5746
    100 Universal City Plz Bldg 2120 Universal City (91608) *(P-4454)*

    NBC Universal Inc .... A
    100 Universal City Plz Universal City (91608) *(P-13868)*

    Nbcuniversal Media LLC .... A...... 818 777-1000
    100 Universal City Plz Bldg 2160 Universal City (91608) *(P-4398)*

    NC Interactive LLC .... D...... 512 623-8700
    660 Newport Center Dr Ste 800 Newport Beach (92660) *(P-12843)*

    Nc4 Soltra LLC .... C...... 408 489-5579
    21515 Hawthorne Blvd # 52 Torrance (90503) *(P-12281)*

    Ncc Group Inc (HQ) .... D...... 415 268-9300
    123 Mission St Ste 1020 San Francisco (94105) *(P-12844)*

NCCRC, Oakland *Also Called: Northern Cal Crpnters Rgnal CN (P-18788)*

Ncircle, San Francisco *Also Called: Ncircle Network Security Inc (P-11765)*

    Ncircle Network Security Inc .... D...... 415 625-5900
    101 2nd St Ste 400 San Francisco (94105) *(P-11765)*

NCIRE, San Francisco *Also Called: Northern Cal Inst For RES Edca (P-18613)*

    Ncn Management LLC .... C...... 800 275-3243
    5838 Edison Pl Ste 100 Carlsbad (92008) *(P-20158)*

Ncompass International, Hawthorne *Also Called: Ncompass International LLC (P-20485)*

    Ncompass International LLC .... C...... 323 785-1700
    12101 Crenshaw Blvd Ste 800 Hawthorne (90250) *(P-20485)*

Ncpa, Roseville *Also Called: Northern California Power Agcy (P-4591)*

Ncsoft, Newport Beach *Also Called: NC Interactive LLC (P-12843)*

Nctd, Oceanside *Also Called: North County Transit District (P-3183)*

Ndga, Irvine *Also Called: Bandai Namco Entrmt Amer Inc (P-5986)*

    Nds Americas Inc (DH) .... D...... 714 434-2100
    3500 Hyland Ave Costa Mesa (92626) *(P-4514)*

Ndti, Ridgecrest *Also Called: New Directions Tech Inc (P-12501)*

    Neal Electric Corp (HQ) .... D...... 858 513-2525
    2790 Business Park Dr Vista (92081) *(P-1787)*

    Neal Trucking Inc .... D...... 951 685-5048
    9749 Bellegrave Ave Riverside (92509) *(P-3415)*

    Near Intelligence Inc .... B...... 628 889-7680
    100 W Walnut St Ste A-4 Pasadena (91124) *(P-12601)*

    Neardata Inc .... D...... 818 249-2469
    3730 Park Pl Montrose (91020) *(P-20486)*

Neardata Systems, Montrose *Also Called: Neardata Inc (P-20486)*

    Neatly Technologies Inc .... D...... 415 509-1274
    3397 Silver Springs Ct Lafayette (94549) *(P-11180)*

    Nebula Inc .... D...... 650 539-9900
    1100 La Avenida St Mountain View (94043) *(P-19745)*

Nebula Systems, Mountain View *Also Called: Nebula Inc (P-19745)*

Nec Logistics America, Rancho Dominguez *Also Called: Nippon Ex Nec Lgstics Amer Inc (P-3416)*

    Ned L Webster Concrete Cnstr .... D...... 805 529-4900
    8800 Grimes Canyon Rd Moorpark (93021) *(P-2139)*

    Neeva Inc .... D...... 408 220-9086
    450 Concar Dr San Mateo (94402) *(P-12678)*

Nefab, Newark *Also Called: Nefab Packaging West LLC (P-13390)*

    Nefab Packaging Inc .... D...... 408 678-2500
    8477 Central Ave Newark (94560) *(P-2482)*

    Nefab Packaging West LLC .... D...... 408 678-2516
    8477 Central Ave Newark (94560) *(P-13390)*

    Neff Construction Inc .... D...... 909 947-3768
    1701 S Bon View Ave Unit 104 Ontario (91761) *(P-974)*

    Nehemiah Rebar Services Inc .... C...... 530 676-6310
    4110 Business Dr Ste B Cameron Park (95682) *(P-2192)*

    Neighborhood Church Castro Vly .... D...... 510 537-4690
    20600 John Dr Castro Valley (94546) *(P-19024)*

    Neighborhood Healthcare .... D...... 619 440-2751
    855 E Madison Ave El Cajon (92020) *(P-14917)*

    Neighborhood Healthcare .... C...... 760 737-2000
    460 N Elm St Escondido (92025) *(P-14918)*

    Neighborhood Healthcare .... C...... 760 737-6903
    401 E Valley Pkwy Escondido (92025) *(P-17282)*

    Neighborhood House Association (PA) .... B...... 858 715-2642
    5660 Copley Dr San Diego (92111) *(P-18059)*

    Neighborhood House Association .... D...... 619 263-7761
    841 S 41st St San Diego (92113) *(P-18060)*

Neighbrhood Hse Assn Fmly Svc, San Diego *Also Called: Neighborhood House Association (P-18060)*

Neillo Audi, Sacramento *Also Called: Niello Imports II Inc (P-7267)*

    Nelson & Associates Inc .... D...... 562 921-4423
    12816 Leffingwell Ave Santa Fe Springs (90670) *(P-5583)*

    Nelson Bros Property MGT Inc .... C...... 949 916-7300
    16b Journey Ste 200 Aliso Viejo (92656) *(P-20159)*

Nelson Brothers Property MGT, Aliso Viejo *Also Called: Nelson Bros Property MGT Inc (P-20159)*

Nelson Honda, El Monte *Also Called: El Monte Automotive Group LLC (P-7200)*

    Nelson Stud Welding Inc .... C...... 256 353-1931
    630 E Lambert Rd Brea (92821) *(P-5915)*

Neo Tech, Chatsworth *Also Called: Oncore Manufacturing LLC (P-19340)*

Neogov, El Segundo *Also Called: Governmentjobscom Inc (P-12210)*

    Neonroots LLC .... C...... 310 907-9210
    8560 W Sunset Blvd Ste 500 West Hollywood (90069) *(P-11766)*

    Neovia Logistics Dist LP .... D...... 909 657-4900
    5750 E Francis St Ontario (91761) *(P-3737)*

    Nep Bexel Inc (HQ) .... D...... 818 565-4399
    7850 Ruffner Ave Ste B Van Nuys (91406) *(P-13943)*

Nephrology, Los Angeles *Also Called: Cedars-Sinai Medical Center (P-15970)*

Ner Precious Metals Inc .... D....... 310 367-3179
640 St Hill St Ste 450 Los Angeles (90014) *(P-6024)*

Nerys Logistics Inc .... C....... 619 616-2124
9925 Airway Rd San Diego (92154) *(P-4169)*

Nes Health Care Group .... D....... 415 435-4591
39 Main St Belvedere Tiburon (94920) *(P-14919)*

Nest Labs Inc .... D....... 855 469-6378
3400 Hillview Ave Palo Alto (94304) *(P-5680)*

Nest Parent Inc .... A....... 310 551-0101
2125 E Katella Ave Ste 250 Anaheim (92806) *(P-19334)*

Nestle Dsd - Manteca DC, Manteca *Also Called: Dreyers Grand Ice Cream Inc (P-6435)*

Nestle Ice Cream Company .... A....... 661 398-3500
7301 District Blvd Bakersfield (93313) *(P-6441)*

Net Optics Inc .... D....... 408 737-7777
5301 Stevens Creek Blvd Santa Clara (95051) *(P-12282)*

Netafim Irrigation Inc (HQ) .... B....... 559 453-6800
5470 E Home Ave Fresno (93727) *(P-5811)*

Netafim USA, Fresno *Also Called: Netafim Irrigation Inc (P-5811)*

Netapp, San Jose *Also Called: Netapp Inc (P-2817)*

Netapp Inc (PA) .... A....... 408 822-6000
3060 Olsen Dr San Jose (95128) *(P-2817)*

Netapp Inc .... C....... 818 227-5025
6320 Canoga Ave Ste 1500 Woodland Hills (91367) *(P-12499)*

Netapp Capital Solutions Inc .... D....... 408 822-6000
3060 Olsen Dr San Jose (95128) *(P-9404)*

Netbase Quid, Santa Clara *Also Called: Netbase Solutions Inc (P-11767)*

Netbase Solutions Inc (PA) .... C....... 650 810-2100
3945 Freedom Cir Ste 730 Santa Clara (95054) *(P-11767)*

Netease Information Tech Corp .... D....... 919 579-3051
790 E Colorado Blvd Ste 280 Pasadena (91101) *(P-11768)*

Netflix, Los Gatos *Also Called: Netflix Inc (P-4515)*

Netflix Inc (PA) .... C....... 408 540-3700
121 Albright Way Los Gatos (95032) *(P-4515)*

Netfortris Acquisition Co Inc .... D....... 877 366-2548
11954 S La Cienega Blvd Hawthorne (90250) *(P-20812)*

Netfortris Acquisition Co Inc .... D....... 310 861-4300
200 Corporate Pointe Ste 300 Culver City (90230) *(P-20813)*

Netgear Inc (PA) .... C....... 408 907-8000
350 E Plumeria Dr San Jose (95134) *(P-2888)*

Netlinx Publishing Solutions, Sacramento *Also Called: System Integrators Inc (P-12531)*

Netpace Inc .... C....... 925 543-7760
5000 Executive Pkwy Ste 530 San Ramon (94583) *(P-11181)*

Netpolarity, Los Gatos *Also Called: Netpolarity Inc (P-11182)*

Netpolarity Inc .... C....... 408 971-1100
16301 Lavender Ln Los Gatos (95032) *(P-11182)*

Netronix Integration Inc (HQ) .... D....... 800 600-3939
2365 Paragon Dr Ste D San Jose (95131) *(P-1788)*

Netskope Inc (PA) .... A....... 800 979-6988
2445 Augustine Dr 3rd Fl Santa Clara (95054) *(P-12283)*

Netsol, Encino *Also Called: Netsol Technologies Inc (P-12284)*

Netsol Technologies Inc (PA) .... D....... 818 222-9197
16000 Ventura Blvd Ste 770 Encino (91436) *(P-12284)*

Netsuite Inc (DH) .... A....... 650 627-1000
2955 Campus Dr Ste 100 San Mateo (94403) *(P-12285)*

Network Capital, Irvine *Also Called: Network Capital Funding Corp (P-8005)*

Network Capital Funding Corp (PA) .... B....... 949 442-0060
7700 Irvine Center Dr Fl 3 Irvine (92618) *(P-8005)*

Network Intgrtion Partners Inc .... D....... 909 919-2800
11981 Jack Benny Dr Ste 103 Rancho Cucamonga (91739) *(P-12500)*

Network Management Group Inc (PA) .... C....... 323 263-2632
1100 S Flower St Ste 3110 Los Angeles (90015) *(P-20160)*

Network Medical Management Inc .... C....... 626 282-0288
1668 S Garfield Ave Ste 100 Alhambra (91801) *(P-20161)*

Network Real Estate, Grass Valley *Also Called: Papola Enterprises Inc (P-9126)*

Network Telephone Services Inc (PA) .... D....... 800 742-5687
21135 Erwin St Woodland Hills (91367) *(P-13391)*

Networked Insurance Agents LLC .... C....... 800 682-8476
1410 Rocky Ridge Dr Roseville (95661) *(P-8621)*

Neubloc LLC (PA) .... D....... 858 674-8701
10803 Thornmint Rd Ste 200 San Diego (92127) *(P-11769)*

Neudesic LLC (HQ) .... C....... 949 754-4500
200 Spectrum Center Dr Ste 2000 Irvine (92618) *(P-11770)*

Neuintel LLC (PA) .... D....... 949 625-6117
20 Pacifica Ste 1000 Irvine (92618) *(P-11771)*

Neuro Drinks, Sherman Oaks *Also Called: Neurobrands LLC (P-6654)*

Neurobrands LLC .... C....... 310 393-6444
15303 Ventura Blvd Ste 675 Sherman Oaks (91403) *(P-6654)*

Neuron Esb, Irvine *Also Called: Neudesic LLC (P-11770)*

Neuroscience Gamma Knife Ctr, Thousand Oaks *Also Called: Los Robles Regional Med Ctr (P-14882)*

Neurosurgery, Eureka *Also Called: St Joseph Hospital (P-16467)*

NeutonAI Inc .... C....... 925 399-6400
6200 Stoneridge Mall Rd Ste 300 Pleasanton (94588) *(P-12845)*

Neutron Holdings Inc (PA) .... A....... 888 546-3345
85 2nd St Ste 100 San Francisco (94105) *(P-11772)*

Nevada Irrigation District (PA) .... C....... 530 273-6185
1036 W Main St Grass Valley (95945) *(P-4991)*

Nevell Group Inc .... B....... 714 579-7501
179 Mason Cir Concord (94520) *(P-975)*

Nevell Group Inc (PA) .... C....... 714 579-7501
3001 Enterprise St Ste 200 Brea (92821) *(P-976)*

Nevell Group Inc .... B....... 760 598-3501
3284 Grey Hawk Ct Carlsbad (92010) *(P-977)*

Nevell Group Inc San Diego, Carlsbad *Also Called: Nevell Group Inc (P-977)*

Nevins Adams Properties, Santa Barbara *Also Called: Nevins/Adams Properties Inc (P-8738)*

Nevins/Adams Properties Inc (PA) .... C....... 805 963-2884
920 Garden St Ste A Santa Barbara (93101) *(P-8738)*

New Advnces For Pple With Dsbl .... C....... 661 322-9735
4032 Jewett Ave Bakersfield (93301) *(P-18611)*

New Advnces For Pple With Dsbl .... D....... 661 327-0188
1120 21st St Bakersfield (93301) *(P-18612)*

New Age Electric Inc .... D....... 408 279-8787
1085 N 11th St San Jose (95112) *(P-1789)*

New Age Electronics Inc .... C....... 310 549-0000
21950 Arnold Center Rd Carson (90810) *(P-5253)*

New Age Lamirada Inn, La Mirada *Also Called: Kam Sang Company Inc (P-9934)*

New Alternatives Incorporated .... A....... 619 863-5855
8755 Aero Dr Ste 230 San Diego (92123) *(P-18061)*

New America Funding LLC .... D....... 818 235-0640
19300 Rinaldi St Ste M Porter Ranch (91326) *(P-7899)*

New America Funding LLC .... D....... 408 429-2085
55 S Market St Ste 1600 San Jose (95113) *(P-7900)*

New America Funding LLC .... D....... 951 637-2300
11820 Pierce St Riverside (92505) *(P-13392)*

New America Funding LLC .... D....... 707 392-4254
3558 Round Barn Blvd Ste 200 Santa Rosa (95403) *(P-20487)*

NEW AMERICA FUNDING, LLC, Riverside *Also Called: New America Funding LLC (P-13392)*

New American Funding, Porter Ranch *Also Called: New America Funding LLC (P-7899)*

New American Funding, San Jose *Also Called: New America Funding LLC (P-7900)*

New American Funding, Santa Rosa *Also Called: New America Funding LLC (P-20487)*

New American Funding LLC (PA) .... A....... 949 430-7029
14511 Myford Rd Ste 100 Tustin (92780) *(P-7881)*

New Amsterdam Spirits, Modesto *Also Called: E & J Gallo Winery (P-2380)*

New Aster Enterprises Inc .... C....... 213 747-7566
2901 S Flower St Los Angeles (90007) *(P-10040)*

New Bi US Gaming LLC .... D....... 858 592-2472
10920 Via Frontera Ste 420 San Diego (92127) *(P-12286)*

New Bridge Foundation Inc .... D....... 510 548-7270
2323 Hearst Ave Berkeley (94709) *(P-17101)*

New CAM Commerce Solutions LLC .... C....... 714 338-0200
5555 Garden Grove Blvd Ste 100 Westminster (92683) *(P-11773)*

New Century Mortgage, Irvine *Also Called: New Century Mortgage Corp (P-8006)*

New Century Mortgage Corp .... A....... 949 440-7030
18400 Von Karman Ave Ste 1000 Irvine (92612) *(P-8006)*

New Chef Fashion Inc .... D....... 323 581-0300
3223 E 46th St Vernon (90058) *(P-2449)*

New Childrens Museum .... D....... 619 233-8792
200 W Island Ave San Diego (92101) *(P-18661)*

New Cingular Wireless Svcs Inc .... D....... 619 238-3638
252 Broadway San Diego (92101) *(P-4219)*

New Cingular Wireless Svcs Inc

New Cingular Wireless Svcs Inc .... D....... 707 535-0891
2166 Santa Rosa Ave Santa Rosa (95407) *(P-4220)*

New Colusa Indian Bingo .... B....... 530 458-8844
3770 State Highway 45 Colusa (95932) *(P-10041)*

New Crew Production Corp .... C....... 323 234-8880
1100 W 135th St Gardena (90247) *(P-13393)*

New Desserts Inc .... D....... 415 780-6860
5000 Fulton Dr Fairfield (94534) *(P-6655)*

New Directions Inc (PA) .... D....... 310 914-4045
11303 Wilshire Blvd Bldg 116 Los Angeles (90025) *(P-18062)*

New Directions For Veterans, Los Angeles *Also Called: New Directions Inc (P-18062)*

New Directions Tech Inc (PA) .... D....... 760 384-2444
137 W Drummond Ave Ste A Ridgecrest (93555) *(P-12501)*

New Dream Network LLC .... C....... 323 375-3842
707 Wilshire Blvd Ste 5050 Los Angeles (90017) *(P-4319)*

New Dream Network LLC (PA) .... D....... 626 644-9466
417 S Associated Rd Pmb 257 Brea (92821) *(P-12697)*

New England Shtmtl & Mech Co .... C....... 559 268-7375
2731 S Cherry Ave Fresno (93706) *(P-1508)*

New Figueroa Hotel Inc .... C....... 213 627-8971
1000 S Hope St Apt 201 Los Angeles (90015) *(P-10042)*

New First Fincl Resources LLC .... C....... 949 223-2160
100 Spectrum Center Dr Ste 400 Irvine (92618) *(P-8241)*

New Home Professionals .... D....... 925 556-1555
6500 Dublin Blvd Ste 201 Dublin (94568) *(P-9108)*

New Hope Harvesting LLC .... D....... 805 478-4469
918 Nita Ct Santa Maria (93454) *(P-251)*

New Legend Inc .... B....... 530 674-3100
1235 Oswald Rd Yuba City (95991) *(P-3519)*

New Legend Inc .... C....... 855 210-2300
8613 Etiwanda Ave Rancho Cucamonga (91739) *(P-3520)*

New Legend Logistics, Yuba City *Also Called: New Legend Inc (P-3519)*

New Milani Group LLC .... D....... 323 582-9404
10000 Washington Blvd Ste 210 Culver City (90232) *(P-6136)*

New Orange Hills, Orange *Also Called: Orange Coast Care Inc (P-15611)*

New Paradigm Productions Inc (PA) .... D....... 415 924-8000
39 Mesa St Ste 212 San Francisco (94129) *(P-13869)*

New Parrott & Co .... C....... 925 456-2286
5565 Tesla Rd Livermore (94550) *(P-6803)*

New Path Landscape Svcs Inc .... D....... 408 310-8476
16170 Vineyard Blvd Ste 180 Morgan Hill (95037) *(P-450)*

New Power Inc .... D....... 800 980-9825
887 Marlborough Ave Riverside (92507) *(P-1509)*

New Printing, Van Nuys *Also Called: Digital Room Holdings Inc (P-2568)*

New Pvcc Inc .... D....... 760 742-1230
15835 Pauma Valley Dr Pauma Valley (92061) *(P-14414)*

New Regency Productions Inc (PA) .... D....... 424 446-4092
10201 W Pico Blvd Bldg 12 Los Angeles (90064) *(P-13870)*

New Relic Inc (PA) .... A....... 650 777-7600
188 Spear St Fl 11 San Francisco (94105) *(P-12287)*

New Schools Venture Fund .... D....... 415 615-6860
1616 Franklin St # 2 Oakland (94612) *(P-13394)*

New Start Rcvery Solutions Inc .... D....... 530 854-4119
2167 Montgomery St Ste A Oroville (95965) *(P-16688)*

New Start Recovery Solutions, Sacramento *Also Called: Sierra Hlth Wellness Group LLC (P-17126)*

New Talco Enterprises LLC .... D....... 310 280-0755
2300 W Empire Ave Burbank (91504) *(P-19615)*

New Tangram LLC .... C....... 562 365-5000
9200 Sorensen Ave Santa Fe Springs (90670) *(P-5095)*

New Vista Behavioral Hlth LLC .... D....... 949 284-0095
3 Park Plz Ste 550 Irvine (92614) *(P-15777)*

New Vista Health Services .... C....... 310 477-5501
1516 Sawtelle Blvd Los Angeles (90025) *(P-15880)*

New Vista Health Services .... C....... 818 352-1421
8647 Fenwick St Sunland (91040) *(P-15881)*

New Vsta Nrsing Rhbltation Ctr, Sunland *Also Called: New Vista Health Services (P-15881)*

New Vsta Post Acute Care Ctr W, Los Angeles *Also Called: New Vista Health Services (P-15880)*

New Wave Electric, Oceanside *Also Called: Nwec Nevada Inc (P-1791)*

New Wave Entertainment, Burbank *Also Called: NW Entertainment Inc (P-13871)*

New Way Landscape & Tree Svcs .... C....... 858 505-8300
7485 Ronson Rd San Diego (92111) *(P-525)*

New West Partitions .... C....... 916 456-8365
2550 Sutterville Rd Sacramento (95820) *(P-1948)*

New York Life, San Francisco *Also Called: New York Life RE Investors (P-8622)*

New York Life RE Investors .... D....... 415 402-4117
50 California St San Francisco (94111) *(P-8622)*

Neway Packaging Corp (PA) .... D....... 602 454-9000
1973 E Via Arado Rancho Dominguez (90220) *(P-6080)*

Newberry Technical Services, Bakersfield *Also Called: Nts Inc (P-1246)*

Newco Auto Leasing, West Hollywood *Also Called: Executive Car Leasing Company (P-13596)*

Newco Distributors Inc .... D....... 909 291-2240
9060 Rochester Ave Rancho Cucamonga (91730) *(P-6829)*

Newfield Wireless Inc (DH) .... D....... 510 848-8248
2855 Telegraph Ave Ste 200 Berkeley (94705) *(P-20814)*

Newman Flange & Fitting Co, Newman *Also Called: Titan Newman Inc (P-5931)*

Newman Garrison + Partners Inc .... C....... 949 756-0818
3100 Bristol St Ste 400 Costa Mesa (92626) *(P-19498)*

Newmeyer & Dillion LLP (PA) .... C....... 949 854-7000
895 Dove St Ste 500 Newport Beach (92660) *(P-17588)*

Newport Apparel Corporation (PA) .... D....... 310 605-1900
1215 W Walnut St Compton (90220) *(P-6210)*

Newport Beach Country Club, Newport Beach *Also Called: Newport Beach Country Club Inc (P-14415)*

Newport Beach Country Club Inc .... D....... 949 644-9550
1 Clubhouse Dr Newport Beach (92660) *(P-14415)*

Newport Beach Surgery Ctr LLC .... C....... 949 631-0988
361 Hospital Rd Ste 124 Newport Beach (92663) *(P-14920)*

Newport Diversified Inc .... C....... 619 448-4111
1286 Fletcher Pkwy El Cajon (92020) *(P-13395)*

Newport Diversified Inc .... C....... 562 921-4359
13963 Alondra Blvd Santa Fe Springs (90670) *(P-13396)*

Newport Group Inc .... B....... 925 328-4540
35 Iron Point Cir Ste 300 Folsom (95630) *(P-8623)*

Newport Group Inc (HQ) .... C....... 925 328-4540
35 Iron Point Cir Ste 300 Folsom (95630) *(P-8624)*

Newport Hospitality Group Inc .... D....... 661 323-1900
801 Truxtun Ave Bakersfield (93301) *(P-10043)*

Newport Meat Company, Irvine *Also Called: Newport Meat Southern Cal Inc (P-6500)*

Newport Meat Southern Cal Inc .... C....... 949 399-4200
16691 Hale Ave Irvine (92606) *(P-6500)*

Newport Mesa Inn LLC .... D....... 949 650-3020
2642 Newport Blvd Costa Mesa (92627) *(P-10044)*

Newport Mesa Memory Care Cmnty, Costa Mesa *Also Called: Silverado Senior Living Inc (P-15668)*

Newport Mesa Unified Schl Dst .... D....... 714 424-5090
2985 Barrish St Bldg E Costa Mesa (92626) *(P-17735)*

Newport Mesa Unified Schl Dst .... D....... 949 515-6940
900 Goldenrod Ave Corona Del Mar (92625) *(P-17736)*

Newport Retirement Services, Folsom *Also Called: Newport Group Inc (P-8624)*

NEWPORT SPECIALTY HOSPITAL, Tustin *Also Called: Foothill Regional Medical Ctr (P-16090)*

Newport Specialty Hospital, Los Angeles *Also Called: Tustin Hospital and Medical Center (P-16583)*

Newport Television LLC .... A....... 661 283-1700
2120 L St Bakersfield (93301) *(P-4455)*

Newport Television LLC .... B....... 559 761-0243
4880 N 1st St Fresno (93726) *(P-14049)*

News Corp - Fox, Los Angeles *Also Called: Twentieth Cntury Fox Japan Inc (P-10820)*

News Group, The, Orange *Also Called: Great Atlantic News LLC (P-6842)*

Newshire Investment, Los Angeles *Also Called: Otts Asia Moorer Devon (P-9548)*

Newstar Fresh Foods LLC .... A....... 831 758-7800
126 Sun St Salinas (93901) *(P-292)*

Newstar Fresh Foods LLC (PA) .... C....... 888 782-7220
850 Work St Ste 101 Salinas (93901) *(P-6566)*

Newton Heat Treating Co Inc .... D....... 626 964-6528
19235 E Walnut Dr N City Of Industry (91748) *(P-2728)*

Nex Group LLC .... D....... 209 317-6677
9018 Rancho Viejo Dr Bakersfield (93314) *(P-4062)*

Nexcoil Incorporated .... D....... 619 671-9247
8753 Kerns St San Diego (92154) *(P-5502)*

Nexcoil San Diego Coil Center, San Diego Also Called: Nexcoil Incorporated *(P-5502)*
Nexem Staffing, Santa Barbara Also Called: Partners Prsnnel - MGT Svcs LL *(P-11195)*
Nexgen AC & Htg LLC .... D....... 760 616-5870
  700 N Valley St Ste K Anaheim (92801) *(P-1510)*
Nexgen Air Conditioning & Plbg, Anaheim Also Called: Nexgen AC & Htg LLC *(P-1510)*
Nexgen Air Heating and Plbg, Northridge Also Called: Nexgen Air Los Angeles *(P-1511)*
Nexgen Air Los Angeles .... C....... 818 900-2525
  19205 Parthenia St Northridge (91324) *(P-1511)*
Nexgenix Inc (PA) .... B....... 714 665-6240
  2 Peters Canyon Rd # 200 Irvine (92606) *(P-11774)*
Nexgrill Industries, Chino Also Called: Nexgrill Industries Inc *(P-5127)*
Nexgrill Industries Inc (PA) .... D....... 909 598-8799
  14050 Laurelwood Pl Chino (91710) *(P-5127)*
Nexstar Digital LLC .... D....... 310 971-9300
  12777 W Jefferson Blvd Ste B100 Los Angeles (90066) *(P-10656)*
Next Insurance Inc .... C....... 855 222-5919
  490 California Ave Ste 300 Palo Alto (94306) *(P-8625)*
Next Issue Media LLC .... D....... 650 521-5151
  1 Apple Park Way Cupertino (95014) *(P-13397)*
Next Trucking Inc .... C....... 213 444-2250
  301 E Ocean Blvd Ste 1950 Long Beach (90802) *(P-4063)*
Nextdoor, San Francisco Also Called: Nextdoorcom Inc *(P-12679)*
Nextdoorcom Inc (PA) .... D....... 415 236-0000
  875 Stevenson St Ste 100 San Francisco (94103) *(P-12679)*
Nextel, Irvine Also Called: Nextel Communications Inc *(P-4221)*
Nextel Communications Inc .... C....... 714 368-4509
  330 Commerce Irvine (92602) *(P-4221)*
Nextgen Healthcare, Irvine Also Called: Nextgen Hlthcare Info Systems *(P-11775)*
Nextgen Healthcare Inc (PA) .... B....... 949 255-2600
  18111 Von Karman Ave Ste 600 Irvine (92612) *(P-12288)*
Nextgen Hlthcare Info Systems (HQ) .... D....... 949 255-2600
  18111 Von Karman Ave Ste 700 Irvine (92612) *(P-11775)*
Nextpoint Inc (PA) .... D....... 310 360-5904
  8750 Wilshire Blvd Ste 200 Beverly Hills (90211) *(P-4320)*
Nextracker LLC (HQ) .... B....... 510 270-2500
  6200 Paseo Padre Pkwy Fremont (94555) *(P-12289)*
Nextroll Inc (PA) .... A....... 415 236-3956
  201 California St Ste 500 San Francisco (94111) *(P-12290)*
Nexus Capital Management LP .... A....... 424 330-8820
  11100 Santa Monica Blvd Los Angeles (90025) *(P-9540)*
Nexus Is Inc .... B....... 704 969-2200
  27202 Turnberry Ln Ste 100 Valencia (91355) *(P-4545)*
Nexxen Group LLC (PA) .... C....... 425 279-1222
  535 Mission St Fl 14 San Francisco (94105) *(P-4321)*
Nfi, Chino Also Called: Nfi Industries *(P-4064)*
Nfi Industries .... D....... 909 393-4471
  15750 Mountain Ave Chino (91708) *(P-4064)*
Nfi Transportation, City Of Industry Also Called: National Freight Inc *(P-13562)*
Nfl Network, Culver City Also Called: Nfl Properties LLC *(P-14151)*
Nfl Properties LLC .... D....... 310 840-4635
  10950 Washington Blvd Ste 100 Culver City (90232) *(P-14151)*
Nga 911 LLC .... D....... 877 899-8337
  8383 Wilshire Blvd Ste 800 Beverly Hills (90211) *(P-11776)*
Ngp Motors Inc .... C....... 818 980-9800
  5500 Lankershim Blvd North Hollywood (91601) *(P-7264)*
Ngrok Inc .... D....... 415 323-4184
  548 Market St Pmb 26741 San Francisco (94104) *(P-12291)*
Nhca Inc .... C....... 310 519-8200
  2330 Grand Ave Long Beach (90815) *(P-10045)*
Nhn Global Inc (HQ) .... C....... 424 672-1177
  2250 Maple Ave Los Angeles (90011) *(P-6211)*
Nhra, San Dimas Also Called: National Hot Rod Association *(P-14165)*
Nhs Western Division Inc .... D....... 909 947-9931
  115 S Palm Ave Ontario (91762) *(P-704)*
Niacc-Avitech Technologies Inc (PA) .... D....... 559 291-2500
  245 W Dakota Ave Clovis (93612) *(P-13787)*
Niantic Inc (PA) .... D....... 415 570-8671
  1 Ferry Building Ste 200 San Francisco (94111) *(P-11777)*
Nibbelink Masonry, Lancaster Also Called: Nibbelink Masonry Cnstr Corp *(P-1891)*
Nibbelink Masonry Cnstr Corp .... D....... 661 948-7859
  1120 W Avenue L8 Lancaster (93534) *(P-1891)*

Nibbi Bros Associates Inc .... C....... 415 863-1820
  1000 Brannan St Ste 102 San Francisco (94103) *(P-766)*
Nibbi Bros Concrete, San Francisco Also Called: Nibbi Bros Associates Inc *(P-766)*
Nibbi Bros Inc .... C....... 415 863-1820
  1000 Brannan St Ste 102 San Francisco (94103) *(P-978)*
Nibr, San Diego Also Called: Novartis Inst For Fnctnal Gnmi *(P-19747)*
Nic Partners, Rancho Cucamonga Also Called: Network Intgrtion Partners Inc *(P-12500)*
Nicholas K Corporation .... C....... 510 352-2000
  1111 Marina Blvd San Leandro (94577) *(P-7265)*
Nicholas W Rotas, D.D.S., Roseville Also Called: Mercy San Juan Medical Center *(P-14898)*
Nichols Inst Reference Labs (DH) .... A....... 949 728-4000
  33608 Ortega Hwy San Juan Capistrano (92675) *(P-16738)*
Nichols Lumber & Hardware Co .... D....... 626 960-4802
  13470 Dalewood St Baldwin Park (91706) *(P-5174)*
Nichols Research, Fremont Also Called: AMS Ventures Inc *(P-20274)*
Nick Alexander Imports .... C....... 800 800-6425
  6333 S Alameda St Los Angeles (90001) *(P-7266)*
Nick Sadek Sothebys Intl Rlty .... D....... 916 257-3229
  9217 Sierra College Blvd Roseville (95661) *(P-9109)*
Nick's Cove, Marshall Also Called: Nicks Cove Inc *(P-10046)*
Nicks Cove Inc .... D....... 415 663-1033
  23240 Ca-1 Marshall (94940) *(P-10046)*
Niello Imports II Inc .... C....... 916 480-2800
  2350 Auburn Blvd Sacramento (95821) *(P-7267)*
Nielsen Mobile, San Francisco Also Called: Nielsen Mobile LLC *(P-19836)*
Nielsen Mobile LLC (DH) .... C....... 917 435-9301
  1010 Battery St San Francisco (94111) *(P-19836)*
Nieves Landscape Inc .... C....... 714 835-7332
  1629 E Edinger Ave Santa Ana (92705) *(P-451)*
Nightdragon Acquisition Corp (PA) .... D....... 510 306-7780
  101 2nd St Ste 1275 San Francisco (94105) *(P-9541)*
Nightingale Nursing, San Leandro Also Called: RES-Care Inc *(P-16919)*
Nigro Krlin Sgal Fldstein Blno .... B....... 415 463-1300
  1 Embarcadero Ctr Ste 3840 San Francisco (94111) *(P-19616)*
Nihon Kohden America LLC (HQ) .... C....... 949 580-1555
  15353 Barranca Pkwy Irvine (92618) *(P-5435)*
Nihon Kohden America, Inc., Irvine Also Called: Nihon Kohden America LLC *(P-5435)*
Nijjar Realty Inc (PA) .... D....... 626 575-0062
  4900 Santa Anita Ave Ste 2c El Monte (91731) *(P-9110)*
Nike Usa Inc .... A....... 310 670-6770
  222 E Redondo Beach Blvd Ste C Gardena (90248) *(P-14152)*
Nikken Global Inc (HQ) .... C....... 949 789-2000
  18301 Von Karman Ave Ste 120 Irvine (92612) *(P-5947)*
Nikon Precision Inc (DH) .... C....... 650 508-4674
  1399 Shoreway Rd Belmont (94002) *(P-5848)*
Niles Audio Corporation .... D....... 760 710-0992
  1690 Corporate Cir Petaluma (94954) *(P-5681)*
Nimble Robotics Inc .... D....... 267 864-6879
  488 8th St San Francisco (94103) *(P-11778)*
Ninjio Llc .... D....... 805 864-1992
  880 Hampshire Rd Ste B Westlake Village (91361) *(P-20815)*
Ninos Latino Unidos FSA .... D....... 562 801-5454
  10016 Pioneer Blvd # 123 Santa Fe Springs (90670) *(P-18493)*
Ninthdecimal, San Francisco Also Called: Ninthdecimal Inc *(P-11779)*
Ninthdecimal Inc (PA) .... D....... 415 264-1849
  150 Post St Ste 500 San Francisco (94108) *(P-11779)*
Ninyo More Gtchncal Envmtl Scn (PA) .... D....... 858 576-1000
  5710 Ruffin Rd San Diego (92123) *(P-20816)*
Nippon Cargo Airlines Co Ltd .... D....... 310 417-0801
  6501 W Imperial Hwy Hngr 8 Los Angeles (90045) *(P-3839)*
Nippon Ex Nec Lgstics Amer Inc .... D....... 310 604-6100
  18615 S Ferris Pl Rancho Dominguez (90220) *(P-3416)*
Nippon Express .... C....... 310 782-3000
  21250 Hawthorne Blvd Fl 2 Torrance (90503) *(P-4065)*
Nippon Express USA Inc .... D....... 310 527-4237
  19500 S Vermont Ave Torrance (90502) *(P-4066)*
Nippon Travel Agency Amer Inc .... D....... 310 768-1817
  1411 W 190th St Ste 650 Gardena (90248) *(P-3942)*
Nippon Travel Agency PCF Inc (DH) .... D....... 310 768-0017
  1411 W 190th St Ste 650 Gardena (90248) *(P-3943)*

Nirvana Tech Inc .... D....... 617 800-6650
595 Market St Fl 10 San Francisco (94105) *(P-13398)*

Niscayah Inc .... D....... 626 683-8167
751 N Todd Ave Azusa (91702) *(P-5682)*

Nishiba Industries Corporation .... D....... 619 661-8866
2360 Marconi Ct San Diego (92154) *(P-2676)*

Nissan North America Inc .... C....... 714 433-3700
1683 Sunflower Ave Costa Mesa (92626) *(P-5017)*

Nissan of Tustin .... C....... 714 669-8282
30 Auto Center Dr Tustin (92782) *(P-7268)*

Nissho of California Inc .... B....... 760 727-9719
89055 64th Ave Thermal (92274) *(P-110)*

Nissho of California Inc (PA) .... C....... 760 727-9719
1902 S Santa Fe Ave Vista (92083) *(P-452)*

Nisum Technologies Inc .... A....... 714 619-7989
71 Stevenson St Ste 446 San Francisco (94105) *(P-11780)*

Nisum Technologies Inc .... A....... 714 579-7979
46231 Landing Pkwy Fremont (94538) *(P-11781)*

Nitro, San Francisco Also Called: *Nitro Software Inc* (P-11782)

Nitro Software Inc (HQ) .... C....... 415 632-4894
447 Sutter St San Francisco (94108) *(P-11782)*

Nitto, Oceanside Also Called: *Nitto Denko Technical Corp* (P-19837)

Nitto Avecia Pharma Svcs Inc .... D....... 949 951-4425
6 Vanderbilt Irvine (92618) *(P-13399)*

Nitto Denko America Inc .... D....... 510 445-5400
48500 Fremont Blvd Fremont (94538) *(P-5683)*

Nitto Denko Technical Corp .... D....... 760 435-7011
501 Via Del Monte Oceanside (92058) *(P-19837)*

Nitto Tyres, Cypress Also Called: *Toyo Tire USA Corp* (P-5075)

Nix Healthcare System, Los Angeles Also Called: *Nix Hospitals System LLC* (P-16281)

Nix Hospitals System LLC (HQ) .... C....... 210 271-1800
3415 S Sepulveda Blvd # 900 Los Angeles (90034) *(P-16281)*

Nixon Inc (PA) .... C....... 888 455-9200
2810 Whiptail Loop Ste 1 Carlsbad (92010) *(P-6025)*

Nixon Watches, Carlsbad Also Called: *Nixon Inc* (P-6025)

Nliven, San Diego Also Called: *Defenseweb Technologies Inc* (P-12776)

Nlyte Software Americas Ltd .... D....... 866 386-5983
1380 El Cajon Blvd Ste 220 El Cajon (92020) *(P-11783)*

Nmi Holdings Inc (PA) .... D....... 855 530-6642
2100 Powell St 12th Fl Emeryville (94608) *(P-8433)*

Nmi Industrial, Sacramento Also Called: *Nmi Industrial Holdings Inc* (P-2301)

Nmi Industrial Holdings Inc .... D....... 916 635-7030
8503 Weyand Ave Sacramento (95828) *(P-2301)*

Nms Management Inc .... D....... 619 425-0440
155 W 35th St Ste A National City (91950) *(P-10934)*

Nms Properties Inc .... D....... 310 656-2700
10960 Wilshire Blvd Los Angeles (90024) *(P-9111)*

Nna Insurance Services, Chatsworth Also Called: *National Notary Association* (P-18753)

Nna Insurance Services LLC .... C....... 818 739-4071
9350 De Soto Ave Chatsworth (91311) *(P-8626)*

Nnn Realty Investors LLC .... B....... 714 667-8252
19700 Fairchild Ste 300 Irvine (92612) *(P-9542)*

No Ordinary Moments Inc .... D....... 714 848-3800
16742 Gothard St Ste 115 Huntington Beach (92647) *(P-16899)*

Noah Concrete, Gilroy Also Called: *Noah Concrete Corporation* (P-2140)

Noah Concrete Corporation .... D....... 408 842-7211
5900 Rossi Ln Gilroy (95020) *(P-2140)*

Noarus Investments Inc .... D....... 310 649-2440
5850 W Centinela Ave Los Angeles (90045) *(P-7269)*

Noarus Tgg .... D....... 714 895-5595
9444 Trask Ave Garden Grove (92844) *(P-7270)*

Noatum Logistics Usa LLC .... C....... 310 527-2104
1100 W Walnut St Compton (90220) *(P-4067)*

Nob Hill Properties Inc .... B....... 415 474-5400
1075 California St San Francisco (94108) *(P-10047)*

Nobel Biocare Usa LLC .... B....... 714 282-4800
22715 Savi Ranch Pkwy Yorba Linda (92887) *(P-16775)*

Noble Credit Union .... D....... 559 252-5000
2580 W Shaw Ln Frnt Fresno (93711) *(P-7785)*

Noble Energy, Seal Beach Also Called: *Samedan Oil Corporation* (P-604)

Noble Investment Group LLC .... C....... 562 436-3000
333 E Ocean Blvd Long Beach (90802) *(P-10048)*

Noble Outfitters, Modesto Also Called: *LLC Noble Rider* (P-6179)

Noble Rents Inc .... D....... 855 767-4424
8314 Slauson Ave Pico Rivera (90660) *(P-11003)*

Noble/Utah Long Beach LLC .... C....... 562 436-3000
333 E Ocean Blvd Long Beach (90802) *(P-10049)*

Noblesse Oblige Inc .... C....... 760 353-3336
2015 Silsbee Rd El Centro (92243) *(P-252)*

Nogales Investors LLC .... B....... 310 276-7439
9229 W Sunset Blvd Ste 900 Los Angeles (90069) *(P-9543)*

Nohl Ranch Inn, Anaheim Also Called: *Leisure Care LLC* (P-18469)

Noia Residential Services Inc .... D....... 559 485-5555
606 E Belmont Ave Ste 101 Fresno (93701) *(P-18494)*

Noiro West LLC .... D....... 619 819-6620
701 A St San Diego (92101) *(P-10050)*

Nokia Inc .... A....... 408 530-7600
200 S Mathilda Ave Sunnyvale (94086) *(P-2896)*

Nolo .... C....... 510 549-1976
6801 Koll Center Pkwy Ste 300 Pleasanton (94566) *(P-2549)*

Nolte Associates, Sacramento Also Called: *Nv5 Inc* (P-19336)

Nolte, George S & Associates, San Diego Also Called: *Nv5 Inc* (P-19337)

Nomad Temporary Housing Inc (PA) .... D....... 619 313-4300
16835 W Bernardo Dr Ste 100 San Diego (92127) *(P-8847)*

Nominum Inc .... C....... 650 381-6000
3355 Scott Blvd Fl 3 Santa Clara (95054) *(P-12292)*

Nomis Solutions Inc (PA) .... D....... 650 588-9800
611 Gateway Blvd Ste 120 South San Francisco (94080) *(P-7447)*

Nongshim, Rancho Cucamonga Also Called: *Nongshim America Inc* (P-6272)

Nongshim America Inc (HQ) .... C....... 909 481-3698
12155 6th St Rancho Cucamonga (91730) *(P-6272)*

Noodle Analytics Inc .... D....... 415 412-2139
115 Sansome St Fl 8 San Francisco (94104) *(P-11784)*

Noodle.ai, San Francisco Also Called: *Noodle Analytics Inc* (P-11784)

Noosphere Venture Partners LP (PA) .... C....... 650 605-5684
800 W El Camino Real Ste 180 Mountain View (94040) *(P-9405)*

Nor-Cal Beverage Co Inc (PA) .... B....... 916 372-0600
2150 Stone Blvd West Sacramento (95691) *(P-6779)*

Nor-Cal Beverage Co Inc .... D....... 714 526-8600
1226 N Olive St Anaheim (92801) *(P-13400)*

Nor-Cal Controls Es Inc .... D....... 916 836-0800
4790 Golden Foothill Pkwy Ste 110 El Dorado Hills (95762) *(P-4760)*

Nor-Cal Moving Services (PA) .... C....... 510 371-4942
3129 Corporate Pl Hayward (94545) *(P-3591)*

Nor-Cal Pipeline Services .... D....... 916 442-5400
983 Reserve Dr Roseville (95678) *(P-1242)*

Nor-Cal Produce Inc .... C....... 916 373-0830
2995 Oates St West Sacramento (95691) *(P-6567)*

Nora Lighting Inc .... C....... 323 767-2600
6505 Gayhart St Commerce (90040) *(P-5584)*

Norac Pharma, Azusa Also Called: *S&B Pharma Inc* (P-2577)

Norcal, San Francisco Also Called: *Norcal Insurance Company* (P-8627)

Norcal Inc .... C....... 714 224-3949
1400 Moonstone Brea (92821) *(P-2009)*

Norcal Beverage Co, Anaheim Also Called: *Nor-Cal Beverage Co Inc* (P-13400)

Norcal Care Centers Inc .... D....... 925 757-8787
1210 A St Antioch (94509) *(P-15882)*

Norcal Harvesting LLC (PA) .... D....... 831 443-4999
27 Quail Run Cir Salinas (93907) *(P-57)*

Norcal Insurance Company (HQ) .... B....... 415 735-2000
575 Market St Fl 10 San Francisco (94105) *(P-8627)*

Norcal Pottery Products Inc .... C....... 909 390-3745
5700 E Airport Dr Ontario (91761) *(P-5128)*

Norcal Waste Services Inc .... D....... 626 357-8666
3514 Emery St Los Angeles (90023) *(P-4914)*

Norco Industries Inc (PA) .... C....... 310 639-4000
365 W Victoria St Compton (90220) *(P-2800)*

Norco Ranch Inc (DH) .... B....... 951 737-6735
720 S Stockton Ave Ripon (95366) *(P-236)*

Nordic Industries Inc .... D....... 530 742-7124
1437 Furneaux Rd Olivehurst (95961) *(P-1312)*

ALPHABETIC SECTION — Northbound LLC

Nordstrom, Ontario *Also Called: Nordstrom Inc (P-3738)*
Nordstrom, Newark *Also Called: Nordstrom Inc (P-3739)*
Nordstrom, Walnut Creek *Also Called: Nordstrom Inc (P-7408)*

Nordstrom Inc .... B 909 390-1040
1600 S Milliken Ave Ontario (91761) *(P-3738)*

Nordstrom Inc .... C 510 794-5440
37599 Filbert St Newark (94560) *(P-3739)*

Nordstrom Inc .... C 925 930-7959
1200 Broadway Plz Walnut Creek (94596) *(P-7408)*

Noredink Corp .... D 844 667-3346
442 N Barranca Ave Ste 153 Covina (91723) *(P-11785)*

Noritsu-America Corporation (HQ) .... C **714 521-9040**
6900 Noritsu Ave Buena Park (90620) *(P-5239)*

Norland Group Inc .... C 408 855-8255
3350 Scott Blvd Ste 6501 Santa Clara (95054) *(P-12846)*

Norman Charter, La Palma *Also Called: Norman International Inc (P-5129)*

Norman Industrial Mtls Inc (PA) .... C **818 729-3333**
8300 San Fernando Rd Sun Valley (91352) *(P-5503)*

Norman Industrial Mtls Inc .... D 949 250-3343
2481 Alton Pkwy Irvine (92606) *(P-5504)*

Norman International Inc .... D 562 946-0420
28 Centerpointe Dr Ste 120 La Palma (90623) *(P-5129)*

Norman S Wrght Mech Eqp Crprtn (PA) .... D **415 467-7600**
99 S Hill Dr Ste A Brisbane (94005) *(P-5770)*

Norman Y Mnt-San Jose Intl Arp .... C 408 392-3600
1701 Airport Blvd San Jose (95110) *(P-3901)*

Norman's, Linden *Also Called: Normans Nursery Inc (P-6870)*
Norman's Nursery, Carpinteria *Also Called: Normans Nursery Inc (P-142)*
Norman's Nursery, Baldwin Park *Also Called: Normans Nursery Inc (P-6869)*

Normans Nursery Inc .... C 805 684-1411
5770 Casitas Pass Rd Carpinteria (93013) *(P-142)*

Normans Nursery Inc .... C 805 684-5442
5800 Via Real Carpinteria (93013) *(P-6868)*

Normans Nursery Inc .... C 626 285-9795
20500 Ramona Blvd Baldwin Park (91706) *(P-6869)*

Normans Nursery Inc .... C 209 887-2033
6250 N Escalon Bellota Rd Linden (95236) *(P-6870)*

Norogachi Construction Inc/CA .... D 916 236-4201
600 Industrial Dr Ste 100 Galt (95632) *(P-1949)*

Nortech, Nevada City *Also Called: Nortech Waste LLC (P-4915)*

Nortech Waste LLC .... C 916 645-5230
219 Reward St Nevada City (95959) *(P-4915)*

North Amercn Science Assoc Inc .... D 949 951-3110
9 Morgan Irvine (92618) *(P-19992)*

North American Acceptance Corp .... C 714 868-3195
3191 Red Hill Ave Ste 100 Costa Mesa (92626) *(P-7882)*

North American Cinemas Inc .... C 707 571-1412
409 Aviation Blvd Santa Rosa (95403) *(P-14004)*

North American Cinemas Inc .... C 707 539-6773
551 Summerfield Rd Santa Rosa (95405) *(P-14005)*

North American Client Svcs Inc (PA) .... C **949 240-2423**
25910 Acero Ste 350 Mission Viejo (92691) *(P-20162)*

North American Med MGT Cal Inc (DH) .... D **909 605-8000**
3990 Concours Ste 500 Ontario (91764) *(P-20163)*

North American Van Lines, Newark *Also Called: Moving Solutions Inc (P-3590)*

North Amrcn SEC Investigations .... D 323 634-1911
550 E Carson Plaza Dr Ste 222 Carson (90746) *(P-13008)*

North Amrcn Staffing Group Inc .... D 714 599-8399
3 Pointe Dr Ste 100 Brea (92821) *(P-11183)*

North Anaheim Surgery Center, Anaheim *Also Called: Vanguard Health Systems Inc (P-15178)*

NORTH AREA COMMUNITY MENTAL HE, Sacramento *Also Called: Heartland Child & Family Svcs (P-18000)*

North Bay Auto Auction, Fairfield *Also Called: Wind River Enterprises Inc (P-5019)*

North Bay Construction Inc .... D 707 283-0093
431 Payran St Petaluma (94952) *(P-1146)*

North Bay Distribution Inc (PA) .... D **707 452-9984**
2050 Cessna Dr Vacaville (95688) *(P-3740)*

North Bay Dvlpmntal Dsblties S (PA) .... D **707 256-1224**
10 Exec Ct Ste A Napa (94558) *(P-18238)*

North Bay Fire .... D 707 823-1084
4500 Hessel Rd Sebastopol (95472) *(P-20936)*

NORTH BAY INDUSTRIES, Rohnert Park *Also Called: North Bay Rhblitation Svcs Inc (P-2472)*

NORTH BAY REGIONAL CENTER, Napa *Also Called: North Bay Dvlpmntal Dsblties S (P-18238)*

North Bay Regional Water, Fairfield *Also Called: City of Fairfield (P-4771)*

North Bay Rhblitation Svcs Inc (PA) .... C **707 585-1991**
649 Martin Ave Rohnert Park (94928) *(P-2472)*

North Cast Srgery Ctr Ltd A CA .... D 760 940-0997
3903 Waring Rd Oceanside (92056) *(P-14921)*

North Coast Fmly Med Group Inc .... D 760 942-0118
477 N El Camino Real Ste A306 Encinitas (92024) *(P-14922)*

North Coast Home Care Inc .... D 760 260-8700
5927 Balfour Ct Ste 111 Carlsbad (92008) *(P-16900)*

North County GMC, Vista *Also Called: County Ford North Inc (P-7186)*

North County Health Prj Inc (PA) .... C **760 736-6755**
150 Valpreda Rd Frnt San Marcos (92069) *(P-14923)*

North County Health Prj Inc .... C 760 736-6767
1130 2nd St Encinitas (92024) *(P-14924)*

North County Health Prj Inc .... D 760 757-4566
605 Crouch St Bldg C Oceanside (92054) *(P-14925)*

North County Services, San Marcos *Also Called: North County Health Prj Inc (P-14923)*

North County Transit District (PA) .... D **760 966-6500**
810 Mission Ave Oceanside (92054) *(P-3183)*

North East Medical Services (PA) .... D **415 391-9686**
1520 Stockton St San Francisco (94133) *(P-14926)*

North Island Credit Union, San Diego *Also Called: North Island Financial Credit Union (P-7829)*

North Island Financial Credit Union .... B 619 656-6525
5898 Copley Dr Ste 100 San Diego (92111) *(P-7829)*

North Kern S Tulare Hosp Dst .... C 661 720-2126
1509 Tokay St Delano (93215) *(P-16282)*

North La County Regional Ctr (PA) .... B **818 778-1900**
9200 Oakdale Ave Ste 100 Chatsworth (91311) *(P-20817)*

North Orange County Svc Ctr, Fullerton *Also Called: Southern California Edison Co (P-4701)*

North Ornge Cnty Cmnty Cllege .... B 714 992-7008
330 E Chapman Ave Fullerton (92832) *(P-7548)*

North Pt Hlth Wellness Ctr LLC .... C 559 320-2200
668 E Bullard Ave Fresno (93710) *(P-15596)*

North Pt Mrgers Acqsitions Inc .... D 415 358-3500
580 California St Ste 2000 San Francisco (94104) *(P-8158)*

North Ranch Country Club .... C 818 889-3531
4761 Valley Spring Dr Westlake Village (91362) *(P-14416)*

North Ranch Management Corp .... D 800 410-2153
9754 Deering Ave Chatsworth (91311) *(P-7439)*

North Ridge Country Club .... C 916 967-5717
7600 Madison Ave Fair Oaks (95628) *(P-14417)*

North San Jose Job Center, San Jose *Also Called: Work2future Foundation (P-18264)*

North Shore Investment Inc .... D 707 464-6151
1280 Marshall St Crescent City (95531) *(P-15597)*

North Sonoma County Hosp Dst .... C 707 431-6500
1375 University St Healdsburg (95448) *(P-16283)*

North State Elec Contrs Inc .... D 916 572-0571
11101 White Rock Rd Ste 100 Rancho Cordova (95670) *(P-1790)*

North Valley Bancorp .... B 530 226-2900
300 Park Marina Cir Redding (96001) *(P-7700)*

North Valley Bank .... C 530 226-2920
1327 South St Redding (96001) *(P-7701)*

North Wind Cnstr Svcs LLC .... D 916 333-3015
730 Howe Ave Ste 700 Sacramento (95825) *(P-705)*

Northbay Healthcare Corp (PA) .... C **707 646-5000**
1200 B Gale Wilson Blvd Fairfield (94533) *(P-16284)*

Northbay Healthcare Group (HQ) .... A **707 646-5000**
1200 B Gale Wilson Blvd Fairfield (94533) *(P-16285)*

Northbay Healthcare Group .... B 707 446-4000
1000 Nut Tree Rd Vacaville (95687) *(P-16286)*

Northbay Healthcare System, Fairfield *Also Called: Northbay Healthcare Corp (P-16284)*

NORTHBAY HEALTHCARE SYSTEM, Fairfield *Also Called: Northbay Healthcare Group (P-16285)*

Northbound LLC .... C 408 333-9780
961 E Arques Ave Sunnyvale (94085) *(P-20488)*

Northbound Treatment Services — ALPHABETIC SECTION

Northbound Treatment Services, Newport Beach Also Called: National Therapeutic Svcs Inc (P-17100)

Northbrook Healthcare Center, Willits Also Called: Ensign Willits LLC (P-15463)

Northeast Valley Health Corp .... D....... 818 896-0531
12756 Van Nuys Blvd Pacoima (91331) (P-14927)

Northeast Valley Health Corp (PA) .... D....... 818 898-1388
1172 N Maclay Ave San Fernando (91340) (P-18063)

Northeastern Rur Hlth Clinics (PA) .... D....... 530 251-5000
1850 Spring Ridge Dr Susanville (96130) (P-14928)

Northern CA Retiredd Ofcrs .... C....... 707 432-1200
2600 Estates Dr Fairfield (94533) (P-18495)

Northern Cal Cngrgtnal Rtrment .... C....... 831 624-1281
8545 Carmel Valley Rd Carmel (93923) (P-15883)

Northern Cal Crpnters Rgnal CN .... D....... 510 568-4788
265 Hegenberger Rd Ste 200 Oakland (94621) (P-18788)

Northern Cal Inst For RES Edca .... B....... 415 750-6954
4150 Clement St San Francisco (94121) (P-18613)

Northern Cal Rehabilitation, Redding Also Called: Ocadian Care Centers LLC (P-15605)

Northern Cal Rhbltion Hosp LL .... D....... 530 246-9000
2801 Eureka Way Redding (96001) (P-16287)

Northern California Inalliance .... D....... 530 633-9695
411 4th St Wheatland (95692) (P-18064)

Northern California Inalliance (PA) .... C....... 916 381-1300
6950 21st Ave Sacramento (95820) (P-18065)

Northern California Inalliance .... D....... 530 344-1244
660 Main St Placerville (95667) (P-18066)

Northern California Power Agcy (PA) .... D....... 916 781-3636
651 Commerce Dr Roseville (95678) (P-4591)

Northern California Presbyteri 415 922-9700
1400 Geary Blvd San Francisco (94109) (P-15598)

Northern California Presbyteri .... C....... 650 851-1501
501 Portola Rd Ste 500 Portola Valley (94028) (P-18496)

Northern Hydro, Big Creek Also Called: Southern California Edison Co (P-4681)

Northern Inyo Healthcare Dst .... B....... 760 873-5811
150 Pioneer Ln Bishop (93514) (P-16288)

Northern Inyo Hospital, Bishop Also Called: Northern Inyo Healthcare Dst (P-16288)

Northern Ornge Cnty Ent Mdcl .... D....... 213 252-0036
520 S Virgil Ave Ste 206 Los Angeles (90020) (P-17283)

Northern Reg. Sub Base, Bakersfield Also Called: Southern California Gas Co (P-4731)

Northern Rfrigerated Trnsp Inc (PA) .... C....... 209 664-3800
2700 W Main St Turlock (95380) (P-3521)

Northern Trust, Pasadena Also Called: Northern Trust of California (inc) (P-7635)

Northern Trust of California (inc) .... B
201 S Lake Ave Ste 600 Pasadena (91101) (P-7635)

Northern Vly Cthlic Scial Svc .... C....... 530 241-0552
2400 Washington Ave Redding (96001) (P-18067)

Northern Vly Indian Hlth Inc .... D....... 530 529-2567
2500 Main St Red Bluff (96080) (P-15242)

Northern Vly Indian Hlth Inc .... D....... 530 896-9400
845 W East Ave Chico (95926) (P-15243)

Northern Vly Indian Hlth Inc .... D....... 530 661-4400
175 W Court St Woodland (95695) (P-16655)

Northfield Medical Inc .... D....... 248 268-2500
13631 Pawnee Rd Apple Valley (92308) (P-13788)

Northgate Gonzalez Inc .... B....... 323 262-0595
425 S Soto St Los Angeles (90033) (P-20489)

NORTHPOINT DAY TREATMENT SCH, Northridge Also Called: Child and Family Guidance Ctr (P-17025)

NORTHPOINTE HEALTHCARE CENTRE, Fresno Also Called: North Pt Hlth Wellness Ctr LLC (P-15596)

Northridge Hosp Foundation Aux .... D....... 818 885-5341
18300 Roscoe Blvd Northridge (91325) (P-16289)

Northridge Hospital Med Ctr, Northridge Also Called: Dignity Health (P-16047)

Northridge Nursing Center, Reseda Also Called: Longwood Management Corp (P-16238)

Northrop Grmman Def Mssion Sys, San Diego Also Called: Northrop Grumman Systems Corp (P-3006)

Northrop Grmmn Spce & Mssn Sys .... B....... 310 812-4321
2501 Santa Fe Ave Redondo Beach (90278) (P-2975)

Northrop Grmmn Spce & Mssn Sys .... C....... 909 382-6800
862 E Hospitality Ln San Bernardino (92408) (P-19746)

Northrop Grumman Federal Cr Un (PA) ..... D....... 310 808-4000
879 W 190th St Ste 800 Gardena (90248) (P-7786)

Northrop Grumman Space & Mission Systems Corp ..... A..... 703 280-2900
6379 San Ignacio Ave San Jose (95119) (P-12502)

Northrop Grumman Systems Corp .... B....... 310 812-1089
1 Space Park Blvd Redondo Beach (90278) (P-2982)

Northrop Grumman Systems Corp .... A....... 410 765-5589
9326 Spectrum Center Blvd San Diego (92123) (P-3006)

Northrop Grumman Systems Corp .... B....... 858 592-4518
15120 Innovation Dr San Diego (92128) (P-3007)

Northrop Grumman Systems Corp .... C....... 858 618-4349
17066 Goldentop Rd San Diego (92127) (P-3008)

Northstar, Irvine Also Called: Custom Business Solutions Inc (P-5244)

Northstar, West Hollywood Also Called: Watt Inc (P-12036)

Northstar Contg Group Inc .... D....... 714 639-7600
13320 Cambridge St Santa Fe Springs (90670) (P-2241)

Northstar Contg Group Inc .... D....... 510 491-1330
2616 Barrington Ct Hayward (94545) (P-2302)

Northstar Dem & Remediation LP (DH) ...... C....... 714 672-3500
404 N Berry St Brea (92821) (P-2242)

Northstar Memorial Group LLC .... C....... 800 323-1342
2562 State St Carlsbad (92008) (P-10514)

Northstar Senior Living Inc .... A....... 530 242-8300
2334 Washington Ave Ste A Redding (96001) (P-20164)

Northstar-At-Tahoe, Truckee Also Called: Trimont Land Company (P-9198)

Northwest Administrators Inc .... D....... 650 570-7300
1000 Marina Blvd Ste 400 Brisbane (94005) (P-8628)

Northwest Excavating Inc .... D....... 818 349-5861
18201 Napa St Northridge (91325) (P-11004)

Northwest Exteriors Inc .... D....... 559 456-1632
4404 N Knoll Ave Fresno (93722) (P-2010)

Northwest Hotel Corporation (PA) .... D....... 714 776-6120
1380 S Harbor Blvd Anaheim (92802) (P-10051)

Northwest Recycler Core, Riverside Also Called: Recycler Core Company Inc (P-4930)

Northwest Stffing Rsources Inc .... A....... 916 960-2668
100 Howe Ave Sacramento (95825) (P-11184)

Northwestern Mutl Fincl Netwrk (PA) .... D....... 619 234-3111
4225 Executive Sq Ste 1250 La Jolla (92037) (P-8242)

Northwestern Mutl Inv MGT LLC .... B....... 949 759-5555
610 Newport Center Dr Ste 850 Newport Beach (92660) (P-8629)

Northwestern Mutual Investment, Newport Beach Also Called: Northwestern Mutl Inv MGT LLC (P-8629)

Norton Smon Mseum Art At Psden .... D....... 626 449-6840
411 W Colorado Blvd Pasadena (91105) (P-18662)

Norwalk Meadows Nursing Center, Norwalk Also Called: Norwalk Meadows Nursing Ctr LP (P-15599)

Norwalk Meadows Nursing Ctr LP .... D....... 562 864-2541
10625 Leffingwell Rd Norwalk (90650) (P-15599)

Norwalk Unified School Dst, Norwalk Also Called: Assoction Mxcan Amrcn Edcators (P-18731)

Norwest Venture Partners VI LP .... D....... 650 289-2243
525 University Ave Ste 800 Palo Alto (94301) (P-9544)

Nossaman LLP (PA) .... D....... 213 612-7800
777 S Figueroa St Ste 3400 Los Angeles (90017) (P-17589)

Nossaman LLP .... D....... 415 398-3600
50 California St Ste 3400 San Francisco (94111) (P-17590)

Nossaman LLP .... D....... 949 833-7800
18101 Von Karman Ave Ste 1800 Irvine (92612) (P-17591)

Not Your Daughters Jeans, Vernon Also Called: Nydj Apparel LLC (P-6212)

Nourish Inc .... D....... 917 572-6691
2170 Martin Ave Santa Clara (95050) (P-18068)

Nova Commercial Company Inc (PA) .... D....... 510 728-7000
24683 Oneil Ave Hayward (94544) (P-10935)

Nova Container Freight Station, Carson Also Called: H Rauvel Inc (P-3713)

Nova Development, Calabasas Also Called: Avanquest North America LLC (P-11440)

Nova Group Inc (HQ) .... D....... 707 265-1100
185 Devlin Rd Napa (94558) (P-1243)

Nova Skilled Home Health Inc .... C....... 323 658-6232
3300 N San Fernando Blvd Burbank (91504) (P-17284)

Nova Transportation Services, Compton Also Called: H Rauvel Inc (P-3485)

Nova/Tic Gvrnment Prjcts A Jin .... C....... 707 257-3200
185 Devlin Rd Napa (94558) (P-1244)

Novacap LLC .... B....... 661 295-5920
25111 Anza Dr Valencia (91355) (P-5684)

ALPHABETIC SECTION

Novalogic Inc (PA) .... D....... 818 880-1997
   27489 Agoura Rd Ste 300 Agoura Hills (91301) *(P-11786)*

Novariant Inc .... D....... 510 933-4800
   46610 Landing Pkwy Fremont (94538) *(P-19335)*

Novartis Inst For Fnctnal Gnmi .... A....... 858 812-1500
   10675 John J Hopkins Dr San Diego (92121) *(P-19747)*

Novatime Technology Inc (DH) .... D....... 909 895-8100
   9680 Haven Ave Ste 200 Rancho Cucamonga (91730) *(P-11185)*

Novato Community Hospital, Novato *Also Called: Sutter West Bay Hospitals (P-16563)*

Novato Fire Protection Dst .... D....... 415 878-2690
   95 Rowland Way Novato (94945) *(P-13401)*

NOVATO HEALTHCARE CENTER, Novato *Also Called: Novato Healthcare Center LLC (P-15600)*

Novato Healthcare Center LLC .... C....... 415 897-6161
   1565 Hill Rd Novato (94947) *(P-15600)*

Novato Medical Offices, Novato *Also Called: Kaiser Foundation Hospitals (P-8318)*

Novo Construction Inc (PA) .... D....... 650 701-1500
   1460 Obrien Dr Menlo Park (94025) *(P-979)*

Novo Distribution LLC .... D....... 951 742-5273
   31 Heron Ln Riverside (92507) *(P-5175)*

Novo Nordisk Biotech, Davis *Also Called: Novozymes Inc (P-19838)*

Novogradac & Company LLP (PA) .... C....... 415 356-8000
   1160 Battery St Ste 225 San Francisco (94111) *(P-19617)*

Novozymes Inc (DH) .... C....... 530 757-8100
   1445 Drew Ave Davis (95618) *(P-19838)*

Now Casting Inc .... C....... 818 588-3732
   211 N Victory Blvd Burbank (91502) *(P-14098)*

Nowcom LLC .... C....... 323 746-6888
   4751 Wilshire Blvd Ste 205 Los Angeles (90010) *(P-12847)*

Noymed Corp .... C....... 800 224-2090
   1101 N Pacific Ave Ste 303 Glendale (91202) *(P-19748)*

Noyo Technologies Inc .... D....... 347 721-2816
   735 Montgomery St Ste 250 San Francisco (94111) *(P-12503)*

Nozomi Networks Inc (HQ) .... D....... 800 314-6114
   575 Market St Ste 3650 San Francisco (94105) *(P-13135)*

NP Mechanical Inc .... B....... 951 667-4220
   9129 Stellar Ct Corona (92883) *(P-1512)*

NRC Environmental Services Inc (DH) .... D....... 510 749-1390
   1605 Ferry Pt Alameda (94501) *(P-4982)*

Nrci Telecom .... D....... 530 878-3970
   265 Applegate School Rd Applegate (95703) *(P-1245)*

Nrea-TRC 711 LLC .... C....... 213 488-3500
   711 S Hope St Los Angeles (90017) *(P-10052)*

Nreach Online Services Inc .... B....... 425 301-9168
   303 Twin Dolphin Dr Ste 6080 Redwood City (94065) *(P-12293)*

NRG California South LP .... C....... 909 899-7241
   8996 Etiwanda Ave Rancho Cucamonga (91739) *(P-4592)*

NRG California South LP .... C....... 760 254-5241
   37000 E Santa Fe St Daggett (92327) *(P-4593)*

NRG California South LP .... C....... 805 984-5241
   393 Harbor Blvd Oxnard (93035) *(P-4594)*

NRG El Segundo Operations Inc .... D....... 310 615-6344
   301 Vista Del Mar El Segundo (90245) *(P-4595)*

NRG Health & Fitness LLC .... D....... 310 570-5436
   79 Promesa Ave Rancho Mission Viejo (92694) *(P-14221)*

NRG Solar LLC .... C....... 760 710-2140
   5790 Fleet St Carlsbad (92008) *(P-4596)*

Nri Distribution, Los Angeles *Also Called: Nri Usa LLC (P-4068)*

Nri Usa LLC (PA) .... D....... 323 345-6456
   13200 S Broadway Los Angeles (90061) *(P-4068)*

NRLL LLC .... B....... 949 768-7777
   1 Mauchly Irvine (92618) *(P-9545)*

Nrp Holding Co Inc (PA) .... C....... 949 583-1000
   1 Mauchly Irvine (92618) *(P-9324)*

Nsbn, Los Angeles *Also Called: Cliftonlarsonallen LLP (P-19552)*

Nsg Technology Inc .... B....... 408 547-8770
   1705 Junction Ct Ste 200 San Jose (95112) *(P-13742)*

NSK Prcsion Amer Snta Fe Sprng, Cerritos *Also Called: NSK Precision America Inc (P-5916)*

NSK Precision America Inc .... D....... 562 968-1000
   13921 Bettencourt St Cerritos (90703) *(P-5916)*

Nsv International Corp .... D....... 562 438-3836
   1250 E 29th St Signal Hill (90755) *(P-5052)*

Nta America, Gardena *Also Called: Nippon Travel Agency Amer Inc (P-3942)*

Nta Pacific, Gardena *Also Called: Nippon Travel Agency PCF Inc (P-3943)*

NTD Architects .... D....... 858 565-4440
   9665 Chesapeake Dr # 365 San Diego (92123) *(P-19499)*

NTD Architecture, San Diego *Also Called: NTD Architects (P-19499)*

Ntrust Infotech Inc .... D....... 562 207-1600
   230 Commerce Ste 180 Irvine (92602) *(P-12294)*

Nts Inc .... B....... 661 588-8514
   8200 Stockdale Hwy Ste M10306 Bakersfield (93311) *(P-1246)*

Ntt Cloud Infrastructure Inc (HQ) .... D....... 408 567-2000
   5201 Great America Pkwy Ste 122 Santa Clara (95054) *(P-11787)*

Ntt Glbal Data Ctrs Amrcas Inc (DH) .... B....... 916 286-3000
   1625 National Dr Sacramento (95834) *(P-12698)*

Nu Forest Products Inc .... D....... 707 433-3313
   280 Asti Rd Cloverdale (95425) *(P-5176)*

Nuage Networks .... D....... 415 439-9420
   200 S Mathilda Ave Ste 5 Sunnyvale (94086) *(P-12504)*

Nucleushealth LLC .... D....... 858 251-3400
   13280 Evening Creek Dr S Ste 110 San Diego (92128) *(P-11788)*

Nucor Bldg Systems Utah LLC .... D....... 209 608-7701
   1100 Pinot Noir Dr Lodi (95240) *(P-13402)*

Nuera Communications Inc (DH) .... D....... 858 625-2400
   9890 Towne Centre Dr Ste 150 San Diego (92121) *(P-4322)*

Nuevacare LLC .... D....... 650 396-3596
   2100 Geng Rd Ste 210 Palo Alto (94303) *(P-16901)*

Nugget Market Inc .... C....... 530 662-5479
   157 Main St Woodland (95695) *(P-3741)*

Nugget Mkts Pharmacy, Woodland *Also Called: Nugget Market Inc (P-3741)*

Nulaid Foods Inc (PA) .... D....... 209 599-2121
   200 W 5th St Ripon (95366) *(P-6447)*

Number Holdings Inc (PA) .... C....... 323 980-8145
   4000 Union Pacific Ave Commerce (90023) *(P-7138)*

Numerical Technologies Inc .... C....... 408 919-1910
   70 W Plumeria Dr San Jose (95134) *(P-12295)*

Nuna Health, San Francisco *Also Called: Nuna Incorporated (P-11789)*

Nuna Incorporated .... D....... 415 942-5200
   370 Townsend St San Francisco (94107) *(P-11789)*

Nurix, San Francisco *Also Called: Nurix Therapeutics Inc (P-19749)*

Nurix Therapeutics Inc (PA) .... D....... 415 660-5320
   1700 Owens St Ste 205 San Francisco (94158) *(P-19749)*

Nurlogic Design Inc (DH) .... D....... 858 455-7570
   5580 Morehouse Dr San Diego (92121) *(P-12505)*

Nursechoice .... D....... 866 557-6050
   12400 High Bluff Dr San Diego (92130) *(P-11186)*

Nursecore Management Svcs LLC .... A....... 805 938-7660
   1010 S Broadway Ste A Santa Maria (93454) *(P-18497)*

Nursefinders, Los Angeles *Also Called: Nursefinders Inc (P-11187)*

Nursefinders, San Bernardino *Also Called: Nursefinders LLC (P-11188)*

Nursefinders, San Diego *Also Called: Nursefinders LLC (P-11189)*

Nursefinders Inc .... D....... 925 660-1153
   5120 W Goldleaf Cir Ste 100 Los Angeles (90056) *(P-11187)*

Nursefinders LLC .... C....... 909 890-2286
   1832 Commercenter Cir B San Bernardino (92408) *(P-11188)*

Nursefinders LLC (HQ) .... C....... 858 314-7427
   12400 High Bluff Dr San Diego (92130) *(P-11189)*

Nursefly Inc .... D....... 760 641-5940
   645 Harrison St Ste 200 San Francisco (94107) *(P-12296)*

Nurturing Tots Inc .... D....... 818 996-1602
   535 Avenue B # A Redondo Beach (90277) *(P-18338)*

Nutanix, San Jose *Also Called: Nutanix Inc (P-12297)*

Nutanix Inc (PA) .... A....... 408 216-8360
   1740 Technology Dr Ste 150 San Jose (95110) *(P-12297)*

Nutra-Blend LLC .... B....... 559 661-6161
   2140 W Industrial Ave Madera (93637) *(P-2365)*

Nutrilite, Buena Park *Also Called: Access Business Group LLC (P-6702)*

Nutrition Services, San Bernardino *Also Called: San Brnrdino Cy Unified Schl Ds (P-17318)*

Nutrition Services, Hemet *Also Called: Hemet Unified School District (P-17716)*

Nutrition Services Department, Costa Mesa *Also Called: Newport Mesa Unified Schl Dst (P-17735)*

Nuvia Water Technologies Inc .... D....... 951 734-7400
   108 Business Center Dr Corona (92878) *(P-13403)*

Nuvision Fincl Federal Cr Un (PA)..C....... 714 375-8000
7812 Edinger Ave Ste 100 Huntington Beach (92647) *(P-7787)*

Nuvoton Technology Corp Amer ....D....... 408 544-1718
2727 N 1st St San Jose (95134) *(P-5685)*

Nuzuna Corporation ....D....... 949 335-7790
1451 Quail St Ste 104 Newport Beach (92660) *(P-14222)*

Nuzuna Fitness, Newport Beach *Also Called: Nuzuna Corporation (P-14222)*

Nv5 Inc (DH) ....D....... 916 641-9100
2525 Natomas Park Dr Ste 300 Sacramento (95833) *(P-19336)*

Nv5 Inc ....C....... 858 385-0500
15092 Avenue Of Science # 200 San Diego (92128) *(P-19337)*

NVE Inc ....D....... 323 512-8400
912 N La Cienega Blvd 2nd Fl Los Angeles (90069) *(P-20490)*

Nvent Thermal LLC (DH) ....B....... 650 474-7414
899 Broadway St Redwood City (94063) *(P-3014)*

NW Entertainment Inc (PA) ....C....... 818 295-5000
2660 W Olive Ave Burbank (91505) *(P-13871)*

NW Packaging, Pomona *Also Called: NW Packaging LLC (P-6932)*

NW Packaging LLC (PA) ....D....... 909 706-3627
1201 E Lexington Ave Pomona (91766) *(P-6932)*

Nwec Nevada Inc ....D....... 760 757-0187
2612 Temple Heights Dr Oceanside (92056) *(P-1791)*

Nwp Services Corporation (DH) ....C....... 949 253-2500
535 Anton Blvd Ste 1100 Costa Mesa (92626) *(P-12298)*

Nxs Holding Corp ....C....... 408 791-3300
2025 Gateway Pl Ste 160 San Jose (95110) *(P-9325)*

NY Transport Inc ....D....... 909 355-9832
10191 Redwood Ave Fontana (92335) *(P-3522)*

Nydj Apparel LLC ....C....... 323 581-9040
5401 S Soto St Vernon (90058) *(P-6212)*

Nyse Arca Inc ....C....... 415 393-4000
115 Sansome St San Francisco (94104) *(P-8181)*

Nyx Cosmetics, Torrance *Also Called: Nyx Los Angeles Inc (P-2629)*

Nyx Los Angeles Inc ....C....... 323 869-9420
588 Crenshaw Blvd Torrance (90503) *(P-2629)*

Nzxt Inc (PA) ....B....... 800 228-9395
15736 E Valley Blvd City Of Industry (91744) *(P-12848)*

O & K Inc (PA) ....C....... 323 846-5700
2121 E 37th St Vernon (90058) *(P-6213)*

O & M Industries (PA) ....D....... 707 822-8800
5901 Ericson Way Arcata (95521) *(P-1513)*

O & M South, Arcata *Also Called: O & M Industries (P-1513)*

O C Jones & Sons Inc (PA) ....C....... 510 526-3424
1520 4th St Berkeley (94710) *(P-1147)*

O C Jones & Sons Inc ....D....... 510 663-6911
155 Filbert St Ste 209 Oakland (94607) *(P-20818)*

O C McDonald Co Inc ....C....... 408 295-2182
1150 W San Carlos St San Jose (95126) *(P-1514)*

O H I, Irvine *Also Called: European Ht Invstors I I A Cal (P-9788)*

O M Y A, Lucerne Valley *Also Called: Omya California Inc (P-2574)*

O.H. Kruse Grain and Milling, Goshen *Also Called: Western Milling LLC (P-9580)*

O'Connell Landscape Maint, Carson *Also Called: OConnell Landscape Maint Inc (P-526)*

O'Conner Wound Care Clinic, San Jose *Also Called: OConnor Hospital (P-14931)*

O'Connor Hosp Pdtric Ctr For L, San Jose *Also Called: OConnor Hospital (P-16291)*

O'Connor Hospital, San Jose *Also Called: Verity Health System Cal Inc (P-16617)*

O'Connor Woods, Stockton *Also Called: OConnor Woods Housing Corp (P-8850)*

O'Connor Wound Care Clinic, San Jose *Also Called: OConnor Hospital (P-16292)*

O'Neill Vintners & Distillers, Parlier *Also Called: ONeill Beverages Co LLC (P-81)*

O'Neill Vintners & Distillers, Larkspur *Also Called: ONeill Beverages Co LLC (P-82)*

O'Neill Wetsuits, Santa Cruz *Also Called: ONeill Wetsuits LLC (P-2658)*

O1 Communications, El Dorado Hills *Also Called: O1 Communications Inc (P-4323)*

O1 Communications Inc (PA) ....D....... 888 444-1111
4359 Town Center Blvd Ste 217 El Dorado Hills (95762) *(P-4323)*

O2 Micro Inc ....D....... 408 987-5920
3118 Patrick Henry Dr Santa Clara (95054) *(P-12506)*

Oak Creek Apartments ....C....... 650 327-1600
1600 Sand Hill Rd Palo Alto (94304) *(P-8848)*

Oak Grove Center, Murrieta *Also Called: Oak Grove Inst Foundation Inc (P-14929)*

Oak Grove Inst Foundation Inc (PA) ....C....... 951 677-5599
24275 Jefferson Ave Murrieta (92562) *(P-14929)*

Oak Grove Inst Foundation Inc ....C....... 951 238-6022
1251 N A St Perris (92570) *(P-18069)*

Oak Hill Capital MGT LLC ....A....... 650 234-0500
3000 Sand Hill Rd Bldg 2 Menlo Park (94025) *(P-9546)*

Oak Hill Capital Partners, Menlo Park *Also Called: Oak Hill Capital MGT LLC (P-9546)*

Oak Hill Capital Partners LP ....A....... 650 234-0500
3000 Sand Hill Rd Ste 2-160 Menlo Park (94025) *(P-16902)*

Oak Paper Products Co Inc (PA) ....C....... 323 268-0507
3686 E Olympic Blvd Los Angeles (90023) *(P-6081)*

Oak River Insurance Company ....C....... 800 661-6029
1 California St Ste 600 San Francisco (94111) *(P-8630)*

Oak River Rehabilitation, Anderson *Also Called: Magnolia Holdings LLC (P-15557)*

Oak Springs Nursery Inc ....D....... 818 367-5832
13761 Eldridge Ave Sylmar (91342) *(P-4992)*

Oak Valley Hospital District (PA) ....B....... 209 847-3011
350 S Oak Ave Oakdale (95361) *(P-16290)*

Oak Valley Hotel LLC ....D....... 619 297-1101
2270 Hotel Cir N San Diego (92108) *(P-10053)*

Oak View Snoma Hlls Apartments, Rohnert Park *Also Called: Kisco Senior Living LLC (P-8840)*

Oakdale Memorial Park (PA) ....D....... 626 335-0281
1401 S Grand Ave Glendora (91740) *(P-9288)*

Oakhurst Country Club, Clayton *Also Called: American Golf Corporation (P-14322)*

Oakhurst Healthcare Center LLC ....D....... 559 683-2244
40131 Highway 49 Oakhurst (93644) *(P-15778)*

Oakhurst Hlthcare Wllness Cntr, Oakhurst *Also Called: Oakhurst Skiled Nrsing Wllness (P-15601)*

Oakhurst Industries Inc (PA) ....C....... 323 724-3000
2050 S Tubeway Ave Commerce (90040) *(P-2369)*

Oakhurst Industries Inc ....C....... 510 265-2400
3265 Investment Blvd Hayward (94545) *(P-6273)*

Oakhurst Skiled Nrsing Wllness ....D....... 559 683-2244
40131 Highway 49 Oakhurst (93644) *(P-15601)*

Oakland Athletics, Oakland *Also Called: Athletics Investment Group LLC (P-14127)*

Oakland Healthcare & Wellness ....C....... 323 330-6572
3030 Webster St Oakland (94609) *(P-15602)*

Oakland Hospice Inc ....C....... 916 779-0811
2233 Watt Ave Ste 330 Sacramento (95825) *(P-16903)*

Oakland Medical Center, Oakland *Also Called: Kaiser Foundation Hospitals (P-14802)*

Oakland Mrriott Hotels Resorts, Oakland *Also Called: Oakland Renaissance Associates (P-10054)*

Oakland Museum of California ....D....... 510 318-8400
1000 Oak St Oakland (94607) *(P-18663)*

Oakland Packaging and Supply, Richmond *Also Called: Oakland Paper & Supply Incorporated (P-6082)*

Oakland Pallet Company Inc (PA) ....C....... 510 278-1291
2500 Grant Ave San Lorenzo (94580) *(P-5177)*

Oakland Paper & Supply Incorporated (PA) ....C....... 510 307-4242
3200 Regatta Blvd Ste F Richmond (94804) *(P-6082)*

Oakland Promise ....D....... 510 836-8900
484 9th St Oakland (94607) *(P-9416)*

Oakland Public Education Fund ....D....... 510 221-6968
520 3rd St Ste 109 Oakland (94607) *(P-9417)*

Oakland Renaissance Associates ....B....... 510 451-4000
1001 Broadway Oakland (94607) *(P-10054)*

Oakland Shops/Annex, Oakland *Also Called: San Francisco Bay Area Rapid (P-3198)*

OAKLAND ZOO IN KNOWLAND PARK, Oakland *Also Called: Conservation Society Cal (P-18687)*

Oaklandidence Opco LLC ....D....... 510 832-3222
475 29th St Oakland (94609) *(P-15779)*

Oakley Union School District ....D....... 925 625-5060
1100 Ohara Ave Oakley (94561) *(P-18886)*

Oakmont Country Club ....D....... 818 542-4260
3100 Country Club Dr Glendale (91208) *(P-14418)*

Oakmont Golf Club Inc ....D....... 707 538-2454
7025 Oakmont Dr Santa Rosa (95409) *(P-14279)*

Oakridge Landscape Inc (PA) ....D....... 661 295-7228
28042 Avenue Stanford Unit E Valencia (91355) *(P-242)*

Oaks Diagnostics Inc (PA) ....D....... 310 855-0035
6310 San Vicente Blvd Los Angeles (90048) *(P-14930)*

Oaktree Capital Management LP (DH) ....C....... 213 830-6300
333 S Grand Ave Fl 28 Los Angeles (90071) *(P-8211)*

Oaktree Capital Management LP .... D....... 310 442-0542
11611 San Vicente Blvd Ste 710 Los Angeles (90049) *(P-9547)*

Oaktree Holdings Inc .... A....... 213 830-6300
333 S Grand Ave Fl 28 Los Angeles (90071) *(P-9382)*

Oaktree Real Estate Opprtnties .... A....... 213 830-6300
333 S Grand Ave Fl 28 Los Angeles (90071) *(P-9383)*

Oaktree Strategic Income LLC .... A....... 213 830-6300
333 S Grand Ave Fl 28 Los Angeles (90071) *(P-9384)*

Oakwood Athletic Club, Lafayette *Also Called: Clubsport San Ramon LLC (P-14189)*

Oakwood Corporate Housing Inc .... C....... 909 922-8272
7922 Day Creek Blvd Rancho Cucamonga (91739) *(P-10395)*

Oakwood Temporary Housing, Long Beach *Also Called: Worldwide Corporate Housing LP (P-10396)*

Oasis Brands Inc .... D....... 540 658-2830
100 S Anaheim Blvd Ste 280 Anaheim (92805) *(P-6083)*

Oasis Materials Company LLC .... C....... 858 842-1338
4130 Citrus Ave Ste 17 Rocklin (95677) *(P-19338)*

Oasis Precision, Rocklin *Also Called: Oasis Materials Company LLC (P-19338)*

Oasis Systems LLC .... C....... 805 644-2191
4125 Market St Ste 12 Ventura (93003) *(P-19339)*

Oasis West Realty LLC .... A....... 310 274-8066
1800 Century Park E Ste 500 Los Angeles (90067) *(P-9406)*

Oasis West Realty LLC .... C....... 310 860-6666
9850 Wilshire Blvd Beverly Hills (90210) *(P-10055)*

Oberman Tivoli & Pickert Inc .... C....... 310 440-9600
500 S Sepulveda Blvd Ste 500 Los Angeles (90049) *(P-12507)*

Oberon Media Inc (PA) .... B....... 646 367-2020
1100 La Avenida St Ste A Mountain View (94043) *(P-11790)*

OBryant Electric Inc (PA) .... C....... 818 407-1986
9314 Eton Ave Chatsworth (91311) *(P-1792)*

Observatories of The Carnegie, Pasadena *Also Called: Carnegie Institution Wash (P-19874)*

Observatory, The, Beverly Hills *Also Called: Live Nation Worldwide Inc (P-14092)*

Obsidian Security Inc .... D....... 949 520-2866
500 Arguello St Fl 2 Redwood City (94063) *(P-1793)*

Oc 405 Partners Joint Venture .... D....... 858 251-2200
3100 W Lake Center Dr Ste 200 Santa Ana (92704) *(P-1187)*

Oc Acquisition LLC (HQ) .... C....... 650 506-7000
500 Oracle Pkwy Redwood City (94065) *(P-11791)*

OC Communications Inc .... A....... 916 686-3700
2204 Kausen Dr Ste 100 Elk Grove (95758) *(P-4516)*

OC FOOD BANK, Garden Grove *Also Called: Community Action Prtnr Ornge C (P-17890)*

Ocadian Care Centers LLC .... B....... 510 204-5801
2450 Ashby Ave Berkeley (94705) *(P-15603)*

Ocadian Care Centers LLC .... B....... 415 461-9700
1220 S Eliseo Dr Greenbrae (94904) *(P-15604)*

Ocadian Care Centers LLC .... A....... 530 246-9000
2801 Eureka Way Redding (96001) *(P-15605)*

Ocadian Care Centers LLC .... A....... 510 832-3222
475 29th St Oakland (94609) *(P-15606)*

Ocadian Care Centers LLC .... B....... 415 499-1000
1550 Silveira Pkwy San Rafael (94903) *(P-15607)*

Ocadian Care Centers LLC .... B....... 408 295-2665
75 N 13th St San Jose (95112) *(P-15608)*

Ocbang Inc .... D....... 650 625-7908
2550 N 1st St Ste 100 San Jose (95131) *(P-10564)*

Occidental Petroleum Corporation of California .... A
10889 Wilshire Blvd Fl 10 Los Angeles (90024) *(P-584)*

Occidental Petroleum Investment Co Inc .... A....... 310 208-8800
10889 Wilshire Blvd Fl 10 Los Angeles (90024) *(P-602)*

Occupational Health Clinic, San Francisco *Also Called: University Cal San Francisco (P-16597)*

Occupational Health Services, San Jose *Also Called: El Camino Hospital (P-16680)*

OCCUPATIONAL MEDICINE, Salinas *Also Called: Natividad Medical Center (P-16279)*

Occupational Therapy .... D....... 310 323-6887
19401 S Vermont Ave Ste A200 Torrance (90502) *(P-15297)*

Occupational Therapy Training, Torrance *Also Called: Special Service For Groups Inc (P-18628)*

Ocean Avenue LLC .... B....... 310 576-7777
101 Wilshire Blvd Santa Monica (90401) *(P-10056)*

Ocean Blue, Long Beach *Also Called: Ocean Blue Envmtl Svcs Inc (P-3417)*

Ocean Blue Envmtl Svcs Inc (PA) .... D....... 562 624-4120
925 W Esther St Long Beach (90813) *(P-3417)*

Ocean Breeze International .... D....... 805 684-1747
3910 Via Real Carpinteria (93013) *(P-143)*

Ocean Colony Partners LLC .... C....... 650 726-5764
2450 Cabrillo Hwy S Ste 200 Half Moon Bay (94019) *(P-9267)*

Ocean Direct LLC (HQ) .... C....... 424 266-9300
13771 Gramercy Pl Gardena (90249) *(P-2422)*

Ocean Fresh Fish Seafood Mktg, Los Angeles *Also Called: Ocean Group Inc (P-6475)*

Ocean Group Inc (PA) .... D....... 213 622-3677
1100 S Santa Fe Ave Los Angeles (90021) *(P-6475)*

Ocean Mist Farming Company (PA) .... C....... 831 633-2144
10855 Ocean Mist Pkwy Castroville (95012) *(P-37)*

Ocean Mist Farms, Castroville *Also Called: Ocean Mist Farming Company (P-37)*

Ocean Mist Farms, Castroville *Also Called: Califmia Artchoke Vgtble Grwe (P-171)*

Ocean Park Community Center .... C....... 310 828-6717
1447 16th St Santa Monica (90404) *(P-20819)*

Ocean Park Hotels-Hit Inc .... B....... 805 544-0812
9777 Blue Larkspur Ln Ste 102 Monterey (93940) *(P-10057)*

Ocean Park Optometry .... D....... 310 452-1039
2605 Lincoln Blvd Santa Monica (90405) *(P-15264)*

Ocean Service, San Diego *Also Called: Overseas Service Corporation (P-20898)*

Ocean Technology Systems, Santa Ana *Also Called: Undersea Systems Intl Inc (P-2964)*

Ocean View Convelesent Hosp, Santa Monica *Also Called: Golden State Health Ctrs Inc (P-15852)*

Ocean's Eleven, Oceanside *Also Called: Oceans Eleven Casino (P-10058)*

Oceans Eleven Casino .... B....... 760 439-6988
121 Brooks St Oceanside (92054) *(P-10058)*

Oceanside Auto Country Inc (PA) .... C....... 760 438-2000
6030 Avenida Encinas Ste 200 Carlsbad (92011) *(P-7271)*

Oceanside Glasstile Company (PA) .... B....... 760 929-4000
5858 Edison Pl Carlsbad (92008) *(P-2698)*

Oceanside Harbor Holdings LLC .... C....... 760 331-3177
645 S Beach Blvd Anaheim (92804) *(P-15609)*

Oceanx LLC (PA) .... D....... 310 774-4088
100 N Pacific Coast Hwy Ste 1500 El Segundo (90245) *(P-13404)*

Ocelot Engineering Inc .... C....... 800 841-2960
555 S H St San Bernardino (92410) *(P-7398)*

Ocm Real Estate Opprtnties Fun .... A....... 213 830-6300
333 S Grand Ave Fl 28 Los Angeles (90071) *(P-9385)*

Ocmban, Irvine *Also Called: Ocmbc Inc (P-8007)*

Ocmbc Inc .... B....... 949 679-7400
19000 Macarthur Blvd Ste 200 Irvine (92612) *(P-8007)*

OConnell Landscape Maint Inc .... A....... 800 339-1106
860 E Watson Center Rd Carson (90745) *(P-526)*

OConner Woods A California .... C....... 209 956-3400
3400 Wagner Heights Rd Ofc Stockton (95209) *(P-8849)*

OConnor Hospital .... C....... 408 947-2804
2105 Forest Ave 125 San Jose (95128) *(P-14931)*

OConnor Hospital .... C....... 408 947-2929
2039 Forest Ave San Jose (95128) *(P-16291)*

OConnor Hospital (HQ) .... A....... 408 947-2500
2105 Forest Ave San Jose (95128) *(P-16292)*

OConnor Woods Housing Corp .... D....... 209 956-3400
3400 Wagner Heights Rd Stockton (95209) *(P-8850)*

Octa, Orange *Also Called: Orange Cnty Trnsp Auth Schlrsh (P-3188)*

Octagon Inc .... C....... 310 967-2473
1840 Century Park E Ste 200 Los Angeles (90067) *(P-20491)*

Octave Health Group Inc .... D....... 415 360-3833
625 Market St Fl 15 San Francisco (94105) *(P-17102)*

OCWD, Fountain Valley *Also Called: Orange County Water District (P-4814)*

Odd Fellow-Rebekah Chld HM Cal (PA) .... C....... 408 846-2100
290 I O O F Ave Gilroy (95020) *(P-18498)*

Odd Fellows Home California .... B....... 408 741-7100
14500 Fruitvale Ave Bldg 1000 Saratoga (95070) *(P-18499)*

Odeh Engineers, Irvine *Also Called: Wsp USA Inc (P-19445)*

Odme Solutions LLC .... D....... 619 227-0059
1963 Christy Ln Del Mar (92014) *(P-20492)*

Odyssey Environmental Services, Lodi *Also Called: Odyssey Landscaping Co Inc (P-2141)*

Odyssey Landscaping Co Inc .... D....... 209 369-6197
5400 W Highway 12 Lodi (95242) *(P-2141)*

Oeg Inc .... D....... 408 909-9399
41458 Christy St Fremont (94538) *(P-1794)*

Oeoe Corp .... C....... 213 387-0933
  927 S Grand View St # 10 Los Angeles (90006) *(P-13405)*

Off Duty Officers Inc .... A....... 888 408-5900
  2365 La Mirada Dr Vista (92081) *(P-13009)*

Office Master Inc .... D....... 909 392-5678
  1110 Mildred St Ontario (91761) *(P-5096)*

Office of Inspector General, Los Angeles *Also Called: Los Angles Cnty Mtro Trnsp Aut*
(P-3160)

Office of Technology, Rancho Cordova *Also Called: California Department Tech (P-12746)*

Office of The Sheriff, Martinez *Also Called: County of Contra Costa (P-20929)*

Office On Aging Adrc Rvrside C, Riverside *Also Called: County of Riverside (P-17936)*

Office Star Products, Ontario *Also Called: Blumenthal Distributing Inc (P-5080)*

OfficeMax, Modesto *Also Called: OfficeMax North America Inc (P-6068)*

OfficeMax, Clovis *Also Called: OfficeMax North America Inc (P-10791)*

OfficeMax, Downey *Also Called: OfficeMax North America Inc (P-10792)*

OfficeMax North America Inc .... C....... 209 551-9700
  1800 Oakdale Rd Ste B Modesto (95355) *(P-6068)*

OfficeMax North America Inc .... C....... 559 298-0164
  1465 Shaw Ave Clovis (93611) *(P-10791)*

OfficeMax North America Inc .... C....... 562 927-6444
  7075 Firestone Blvd Downey (90241) *(P-10792)*

Officeworks Inc .... D....... 510 444-2161
  300 Frank H Ste 269 Oakland (94612) *(P-11190)*

Officeworks Inc .... D....... 951 784-2534
  11801 Pierce St Fl 2 Riverside (92505) *(P-11191)*

Ogilvy Group LLC .... D....... 310 280-2200
  2425 Olympic Blvd Ste 2200w Santa Monica (90404) *(P-10657)*

Ogilvy Pub Rlations World Wide .... C....... 650 324-7015
  800 El Camino Real Menlo Park (94025) *(P-20639)*

OGrady Paving Inc .... C....... 650 966-1926
  2513 Wyandotte St Mountain View (94043) *(P-1148)*

OH So Original Inc .... B....... 818 841-4770
  150 E Angeleno Ave Burbank (91502) *(P-10059)*

OHagins Inc .... D....... 707 303-3660
  210 Classic Ct Ste 100 Rohnert Park (94928) *(P-1515)*

Ohana Partners Inc (PA) .... D....... **408 856-3232**
  454 S Abbott Ave Milpitas (95035) *(P-11047)*

Ohi Resort Hotels LLC .... D....... 714 867-5555
  12021 Harbor Blvd Garden Grove (92840) *(P-10060)*

Ohmconnect, Oakland *Also Called: Ohmconnect Inc (P-4597)*

Ohmconnect Inc .... D....... 404 881-8659
  371 3rd St 2nd Fl Oakland (94607) *(P-4597)*

Oil Field Services, Santa Maria *Also Called: Pacific Petroleum California Inc (P-625)*

Oil Well Service, Santa Paula *Also Called: Oil Well Service Company (P-624)*

Oil Well Service Company .... D....... 661 746-4809
  10255 Enos Ln Shafter (93263) *(P-622)*

Oil Well Service Company (PA) .... C....... **562 612-0600**
  1241 E Burnett St Signal Hill (90755) *(P-623)*

Oil Well Service Company .... D....... 805 525-2103
  1015 Mission Rock Rd Santa Paula (93060) *(P-624)*

Oilfield Electric & Motor, Ventura *Also Called: Oilfield Electric Company (P-1795)*

Oilfield Electric Company .... D....... 805 648-3131
  1801 N Ventura Ave Ventura (93001) *(P-1795)*

Oj Insulation LP (PA) .... C....... **800 707-9278**
  600 S Vincent Ave Azusa (91702) *(P-1950)*

Ojai Health & Rehabilitation, Ojai *Also Called: Ojai Healthidence Opco LLC (P-15780)*

Ojai Healthidence Opco LLC .... C....... 805 646-8124
  601 N Montgomery St Ojai (93023) *(P-15780)*

Ojai Valley Community Hospital, Ojai *Also Called: Community Memorial Health Sys (P-16707)*

Ojai Valley Inn & Spa, Ojai *Also Called: Ovis LLC (P-10074)*

Ojai Valley School (PA) .... D....... **805 646-1423**
  723 El Paseo Rd Ojai (93023) *(P-17737)*

Ojai Vly Fmly Medicine Group .... D....... 805 646-7246
  117 Pirie Rd Ste D Ojai (93023) *(P-14932)*

OK Produce, Fresno *Also Called: Charles Matoian Entps Inc (P-3684)*

Oka & Oka Hawaii LLC .... C....... 808 329-1393
  1756 Ruhland Ave Manhattan Beach (90266) *(P-10061)*

Okcoin USA Inc .... C....... 415 991-2033
  115 Sansome St San Francisco (94104) *(P-7858)*

Okta, San Francisco *Also Called: Okta Inc (P-12299)*

Okta Inc (PA) .... A....... **888 722-7871**
  100 1st St Ste 600 San Francisco (94105) *(P-12299)*

Okx, San Francisco *Also Called: Okcoin USA Inc (P-7858)*

Ol Old Company .... D....... 800 492-6864
  404 E Commercial St Pomona (91767) *(P-5849)*

Olam Americas LLC (DH) .... A....... **559 447-1390**
  205 E River Park Cir Ste 310 Fresno (93720) *(P-293)*

Olam Americas Inc .... B....... 408 846-3200
  1350 Pacheco Pass Hwy Gilroy (95020) *(P-294)*

OLAM AMERICAS INC, Gilroy *Also Called: Olam Americas Inc (P-294)*

Olam Edible Nuts, Fresno *Also Called: Olam Americas LLC (P-293)*

Olam Farming Inc .... B....... 559 446-6446
  205 E River Park Cir Ste 310 Fresno (93720) *(P-192)*

Olam Spices & Vegetables, Firebaugh *Also Called: Olam West Coast Inc (P-296)*

Olam Spices & Vegetables Inc .... C....... 209 364-2132
  47641 W Nees Ave Firebaugh (93622) *(P-295)*

Olam West Coast Inc .... C....... 209 364-6164
  47641 W Nees Ave Firebaugh (93622) *(P-296)*

Olam West Coast Inc .... C....... 559 447-1390
  1350 Pacheco Pass Hwy Gilroy (95020) *(P-297)*

Olam West Coast Inc .... C....... 559 447-1390
  6401 Automall Pkwy Gilroy (95020) *(P-298)*

Old Connected Camps .... D....... 323 287-5580
  3913 Spad Pl Culver City (90232) *(P-10409)*

Old Globe, San Diego *Also Called: Old Globe Theatre (P-14050)*

Old Globe Theatre .... B....... 619 234-5623
  1363 Old Globe Way San Diego (92101) *(P-14050)*

Old Guys Rule, Ventura *Also Called: Streamline Dsign Slkscreen Inc (P-2456)*

Old Republic, Stockton *Also Called: Old Republic Title Company (P-8451)*

Old Republic, Stockton *Also Called: Old Republic Title Holdg Inc (P-8452)*

Old Republic, Fresno *Also Called: Old Republic Title Holdg Inc (P-8453)*

Old Republic, Pasadena *Also Called: Bitco Cnstr Insur Agcy Inc (P-8513)*

Old Republic, San Ramon *Also Called: Old Republic HM Protection Inc (P-8631)*

Old Republic HM Protection Inc .... B....... 925 866-1500
  2 Annabel Ln Ste 112 San Ramon (94583) *(P-8631)*

Old Republic Title Company .... D....... 209 951-9460
  3425 Brookside Rd Ste C Stockton (95219) *(P-8451)*

Old Republic Title Holdg Inc .... D....... 209 956-7663
  3558 Deer Park Dr Stockton (95219) *(P-8452)*

Old Republic Title Holdg Inc .... C....... 559 440-9249
  7451 N Remington Ave Ste 102 Fresno (93711) *(P-8453)*

Old Rpblic Title Info Concepts .... B....... 916 781-4100
  524 Gibson Dr Roseville (95678) *(P-8454)*

Old Spagetti Factory, San Marcos *Also Called: Osf International Inc (P-7500)*

Old Town Fmly Hospitality Corp .... C....... 619 246-8010
  2754 Calhoun St San Diego (92110) *(P-10062)*

Ole Health .... D....... 707 254-1770
  1141 Pear Tree Ln Ste 100 Napa (94558) *(P-14933)*

Oleander Holdings LLC .... D....... 916 331-4590
  5255 Hemlock St Sacramento (95841) *(P-15610)*

Olen Commercial Realty Corp .... B....... 949 644-6536
  7 Corporate Plaza Dr Newport Beach (92660) *(P-8739)*

Olen Companies, The, Newport Beach *Also Called: Olen Residential Realty Corp (P-767)*

Olen Residential Realty, Newport Beach *Also Called: Olen Commercial Realty Corp (P-8739)*

Olen Residential Realty Corp (HQ) .... D....... **949 644-6536**
  7 Corporate Plaza Dr Newport Beach (92660) *(P-767)*

OLinn Security Incorporated .... C....... 760 320-5303
  1027 S Palm Canyon Dr Palm Springs (92264) *(P-13010)*

Olivarez Honey Bees Inc .... D....... 530 865-0298
  6398 County Road 20 Orland (95963) *(P-231)*

Olive Avenue Productions LLC .... B....... 770 214-7052
  4000 Warner Blvd Burbank (91522) *(P-13944)*

Olive Crest (PA) .... B....... **714 543-5437**
  2130 E 4th St Ste 200 Santa Ana (92705) *(P-18500)*

Olive Crest, Santa Ana *Also Called: Olive Crest (P-18500)*

Olive Hill Greenhouses Inc .... D....... 760 728-4596
  3508 Olive Hill Rd Fallbrook (92028) *(P-144)*

Olive View-Ucla Medical Center (PA) .... D....... **818 364-1555**
  14445 Olive View Dr Sylmar (91342) *(P-14934)*

Olivenhain Municipal Water Dst .... D....... 760 753-6466
  1966 Olivenhain Rd Encinitas (92024) *(P-4813)*

ALPHABETIC SECTION

Oliver & Company Inc .... D....... 510 412-9090
  1300 S 51st St Richmond (94804) *(P-980)*

Oliver Healthcare Packaging Co .... D....... 714 864-3500
  1145 N Ocean Cir Anaheim (92806) *(P-5850)*

Olivera Egg Ranch LLC .... D....... 408 258-8074
  3315 Sierra Rd San Jose (95132) *(P-2345)*

Olivera Foods, San Jose *Also Called: Olivera Egg Ranch LLC (P-2345)*

Olivet International Inc (PA) .... D....... 951 681-8888
  11015 Hopkins St Jurupa Valley (91752) *(P-6047)*

Ols Hotels & Resorts LLC .... A....... 626 962-6000
  14635 Baldwin Park Towne Ctr Baldwin Park (91706) *(P-10063)*

Ols Hotels & Resorts LLC .... A....... 310 855-1115
  733 N West Knoll Dr West Hollywood (90069) *(P-10064)*

Olson Company LLC (PA) .... D....... 562 596-4770
  3010 Old Ranch Pkwy Ste 100 Seal Beach (90740) *(P-9268)*

Olson Company, The, Seal Beach *Also Called: Olson Urban Housing LLC (P-9269)*

Olson Homes, Seal Beach *Also Called: Olson Company LLC (P-9268)*

Olson Urban Housing LLC .... D....... 562 596-4770
  3010 Old Ranch Pkwy Ste 100 Seal Beach (90740) *(P-9269)*

Oltmans Construction Co .... B....... 805 495-9553
  270 Conejo Ridge Ave Ste 210 Thousand Oaks (91361) *(P-836)*

Oltmans Construction Co (PA) .... D....... 562 948-4242
  10005 Mission Mill Rd Whittier (90601) *(P-837)*

Olympia Convalescent Hospital .... C....... 213 487-3000
  1100 S Alvarado St Los Angeles (90006) *(P-15884)*

Olympia Health Care LLC .... A....... 323 938-3161
  5900 W Olympic Blvd Los Angeles (90036) *(P-16293)*

Olympia Medical Center, Los Angeles *Also Called: Olympia Health Care LLC (P-16293)*

Olympic Club .... D....... 415 676-1412
  665 Sutter St San Francisco (94102) *(P-14419)*

Olympic Club (PA) .... C....... 415 345-5100
  524 Post St San Francisco (94102) *(P-18887)*

Olympic Club .... D....... 415 404-4300
  599 Skyline Dr Daly City (94015) *(P-18888)*

Olympix Fitness LLC .... D....... 562 366-4600
  4101 E Olympic Plz Long Beach (90803) *(P-14223)*

Olympus Building Services Inc .... A....... 760 750-4629
  441 La Moree Rd San Marcos (92078) *(P-20660)*

OLYMPUS BUILDING SERVICES INC, San Marcos *Also Called: Olympus Building Services Inc (P-20660)*

Olympus Property .... B....... 661 393-1700
  3411 State Rd Bakersfield (93308) *(P-8889)*

Om Smart Seating, Ontario *Also Called: Office Master Inc (P-5096)*

Omada Health Inc .... B....... 888 987-8337
  500 Sansome St Ste 200 San Francisco (94111) *(P-16904)*

Ombudsman Patients Advocate, Modesto *Also Called: Catholic Chrties Of The Dcese (P-17865)*

Omega, Bell *Also Called: Omega Moulding West LLC (P-5130)*

Omega Accounting Solutions Inc .... D....... 949 348-2433
  15101 Alton Pkwy Ste 450 Irvine (92618) *(P-19618)*

Omega Management Services, Corning *Also Called: Omega Waste Management Inc (P-20493)*

Omega Moulding West LLC .... C....... 323 261-3510
  5500 Lindbergh Ln Bell (90201) *(P-5130)*

Omega Waste Management Inc .... D....... 530 824-1890
  957 Colusa St Corning (96021) *(P-20493)*

Omega/Cinema Props Inc .... D....... 323 466-8201
  1515 E 15th St Los Angeles (90021) *(P-13945)*

OMelveny & Myers LLP .... D....... 310 553-6700
  1999 Avenue Of The Stars Fl 8 Los Angeles (90067) *(P-17592)*

OMelveny & Myers LLP (PA) .... A....... 213 430-6000
  400 S Hope St 18th Fl Los Angeles (90071) *(P-17593)*

Omni Family Health (PA) .... D....... 661 459-1900
  4900 California Ave Ste 400b Bakersfield (93309) *(P-14935)*

Omni Hotels, Rancho Mirage *Also Called: Omni Hotels Corporation (P-10065)*

Omni Hotels Corporation .... B....... 760 568-2727
  41000 Bob Hope Dr Rancho Mirage (92270) *(P-10065)*

Omni La Costa Resort & Spa LLC .... C....... 760 438-9711
  2100 Costa Del Mar Rd Carlsbad (92009) *(P-10066)*

Omni La Costa Resort & Spa LLC (DH) .... C....... 760 438-9711
  2100 Costa Del Mar Rd Carlsbad (92009) *(P-10067)*

Omnia Italian Design LLC .... C....... 909 393-4400
  4900 Edison Ave Chino (91710) *(P-5097)*

Omniab Inc (PA) .... D....... 510 250-7800
  5980 Horton St Ste 600 Emeryville (94608) *(P-19750)*

Omnicell Inc .... C....... 650 251-6100
  1201 Charleston Rd Mountain View (94043) *(P-11792)*

Omniduct, Buena Park *Also Called: ECB Corp (P-1425)*

Omniome Inc .... D....... 510 935-3021
  1600 Adams Dr Ste 230 Menlo Park (94025) *(P-19751)*

Omniome North, Menlo Park *Also Called: Omniome Inc (P-19751)*

Omniteam Inc .... C....... 562 923-9660
  4380 Ayers Ave Vernon (90058) *(P-5780)*

Omnitrans (PA) .... C....... 909 379-7100
  1700 W 5th St San Bernardino (92411) *(P-3184)*

Omnitrans .... C....... 909 379-7100
  4748 Arrow Hwy Montclair (91763) *(P-3185)*

Omnitrans .... C....... 909 383-1680
  234 S I St San Bernardino (92410) *(P-18501)*

Omnitrans Access, San Bernardino *Also Called: Omnitrans (P-18501)*

Omnitron Systems Tech Inc .... D....... 949 250-6510
  38 Tesla Irvine (92618) *(P-5686)*

Omron Delta Tau, Chatsworth *Also Called: Delta Tau Data Systems Inc Cal (P-2799)*

Omron Robotics Safety Tech Inc (HQ) .... C....... 925 245-3400
  4225 Hacienda Dr Pleasanton (94588) *(P-2775)*

Omron STI Machine Services Inc .... D....... 714 693-1041
  6550 Dumbarton Cir Fremont (94555) *(P-20820)*

Omya California Inc .... D....... 760 248-7306
  7299 Crystal Creek Rd Lucerne Valley (92356) *(P-2574)*

Omya Inc .... D....... 760 248-5200
  7299 Crystal Creek Rd Lucerne Valley (92356) *(P-2575)*

On Assignment Healthcare .... D....... 818 878-0683
  26745 Malibu Hills Rd Agoura Hills (91301) *(P-17285)*

On Central Realty Inc .... B....... 323 543-8500
  1648 Colorado Blvd Los Angeles (90041) *(P-9112)*

On Lok Inc .... D....... 415 292-8888
  1333 Bush St San Francisco (94109) *(P-14936)*

On Lok Lifeways, San Francisco *Also Called: On Lok Senior Health Services (P-8347)*

On Lok Senior Health Services (PA) .... A....... 415 292-8888
  1333 Bush St San Francisco (94109) *(P-8347)*

On My Own Community Services .... C....... 916 726-0792
  6060 Sunrise Vista Dr Ste 2400 Citrus Heights (95610) *(P-15885)*

On My Own Ils Omo Omo Ils On M, Citrus Heights *Also Called: On My Own Ind Living Svcs (P-18070)*

On My Own Ind Living Svcs .... D....... 916 726-0792
  6939 Sunrise Blvd Ste 215 Citrus Heights (95610) *(P-18070)*

On The Rise Inc .... D....... 760 964-7473
  305 E Buena Vista St Barstow (92311) *(P-18614)*

On Trac .... D....... 916 921-6016
  1635 Main Ave Ste 3 Sacramento (95838) *(P-3622)*

On-Tech Enterprises C
  Fremont (94538) *(P-9326)*

On-Time AC & Htg LLC .... D....... 925 566-2422
  261 Arthur Rd Martinez (94553) *(P-1516)*

On-Time AC & Htg LLC .... D....... 925 800-5804
  96 Rickenbacker Cir Livermore (94551) *(P-1517)*

On-Time AC & Htg LLC (HQ) .... D....... 925 598-1911
  7020 Commerce Dr Pleasanton (94588) *(P-1518)*

On24 Inc (PA) .... B....... 415 369-8000
  50 Beale St Fl 8 San Francisco (94105) *(P-12300)*

Oncology Care Systems Group, Concord *Also Called: Siemens Med Solutions USA Inc (P-3077)*

Oncore Manufacturing LLC .... D....... 510 516-5488
  6600 Stevenson Blvd Fremont (94538) *(P-2909)*

Oncore Manufacturing LLC (HQ) .... A....... 818 734-6500
  9340 Owensmouth Ave Chatsworth (91311) *(P-19340)*

One Inc Software Corporation (PA) .... B....... 866 343-6940
  620 Coolidge Dr Ste 200 Folsom (95630) *(P-11793)*

One & All Inc (HQ) C
  2 N Lake Ave Ste 600 Pasadena (91101) *(P-10658)*

One California Plaza, Los Angeles *Also Called: Hill Farrer & Burrill (P-17494)*

One Call Plumber Goleta .... D....... 805 284-0441
  140 Nectarine Ave Apt 4 Goleta (93117) *(P-10565)*

ALPHABETIC SECTION

One Call Plumber Santa Barbara .... D...... 805 364-6337
　1016 Cliff Dr Apt 309 Santa Barbara (93109) *(P-1519)*

One Clothing, Vernon *Also Called: O & K Inc (P-6213)*

One Convergence, San Jose *Also Called: One Convergence Inc (P-11794)*

One Convergence Inc .... D...... 669 292-5251
　99 Almaden Blvd Ste 600 San Jose (95113) *(P-11794)*

One Diversified LLC .... D...... 408 969-1972
　3275 Edward Ave Santa Clara (95054) *(P-20821)*

One Events Inc .... D...... 310 498-5471
　8581 Santa Monica Blvd West Hollywood (90069) *(P-10566)*

One H.E.A.R.T., San Diego *Also Called: One Heart Worldwide (P-20494)*

One Heart Worldwide .... D...... 415 379-4762
　8141 El Extenso Ct San Diego (92119) *(P-20494)*

One Lambda Inc (HQ) .... D...... 747 494-1000
　22801 Roscoe Blvd West Hills (91304) *(P-19752)*

One LLP .... D...... 310 866-5157
　9301 Wilshire Blvd Ph 2 Beverly Hills (90210) *(P-17594)*

One Medical, San Francisco *Also Called: 1life Healthcare Inc (P-14591)*

One Medical, San Francisco *Also Called: One Medical Group Inc (P-14937)*

One Medical Group Inc (HQ) .... D...... 415 578-3100
　1 Embarcadero Ctr Ste 1900 San Francisco (94111) *(P-14937)*

One Nob Hill Associates LLC .... D...... 415 392-3434
　999 California St San Francisco (94108) *(P-10068)*

One Planet Ops Inc (PA) .... C...... 925 983-2800
　1820 Bonanza St Ste 200 Walnut Creek (94596) *(P-10659)*

One Silver Serve LLC .... D...... 818 995-6444
　16601 Ventura Blvd Fl 4 Encino (91436) *(P-10936)*

One Sun Power Inc .... A...... 844 360-9600
　3451 Via Montebello Ste 511 Carlsbad (92009) *(P-19341)*

One Workplace, Santa Clara *Also Called: One Workplace L Ferrari LLC (P-5098)*

One Workplace L Ferrari LLC (PA) .... C...... 669 800-2500
　2500 De La Cruz Blvd Santa Clara (95050) *(P-5098)*

Onebody Inc .... D...... 510 285-2000
　2000 Powell St Ste 555 Emeryville (94608) *(P-16905)*

Onegeneration (PA) .... D...... 818 708-6625
　17400 Victory Blvd Van Nuys (91406) *(P-18339)*

Onegenrtion Adult Dycare Chldc, Van Nuys *Also Called: Onegeneration (P-18339)*

Onehealth Solutions Inc .... C...... 858 947-6333
　420 Stevens Ave Ste 200 Solana Beach (92075) *(P-12849)*

ONeil Data Systems LLC .... C...... 310 448-6400
　12655 Beatrice St Los Angeles (90066) *(P-5851)*

ONeil Digital Solutions LLC .... C...... 310 448-6407
　12655 Beatrice St Los Angeles (90066) *(P-13406)*

ONeill Beverages Co LLC .... C...... 559 638-3544
　8418 S Lac Jac Ave Parlier (93648) *(P-81)*

ONeill Beverages Co LLC (PA) .... D...... 559 638-3544
　101 Larkspur Landing Cir Ste 350 Larkspur (94939) *(P-82)*

ONeill Wetsuits LLC (PA) .... D...... 831 475-7500
　1071 41st Ave Santa Cruz (95062) *(P-2658)*

Onelegacy (PA) .... D
　1303 W Optical Dr Irwindale (91702) *(P-17286)*

Onelink Corporation .... D...... 415 293-8277
　1 Market Plz San Francisco (94105) *(P-3944)*

Onelogin Inc (DH) .... C...... 415 645-6830
　848 Battery St San Francisco (94111) *(P-12301)*

Onerent Inc .... D...... 408 675-5490
　3031 Tisch Way Ste 110pw San Jose (95128) *(P-9113)*

Onesignal, San Mateo *Also Called: Onesignal Inc (P-12302)*

Onesignal Inc (PA) .... C...... 408 506-0701
　201 S B St Ste 200 San Mateo (94401) *(P-12302)*

Onewest Bank Group LLC .... A...... 626 535-4870
　888 E Walnut St Pasadena (91101) *(P-7744)*

Onfleet Inc .... D...... 650 283-7547
　703 Market St Fl 20 San Francisco (94103) *(P-11795)*

Online Capital, Newport Beach *Also Called: RMR Financial LLC (P-8054)*

Online Marketing Group LLC .... C...... 888 737-9635
　530 Technology Dr Ste 100 Irvine (92618) *(P-20495)*

Onni Properties LLC .... C...... 213 568-0278
　888 S Olive St Los Angeles (90014) *(P-20165)*

Onrad Inc .... D...... 800 848-5876
　1770 Iowa Ave Ste 280 Riverside (92507) *(P-14938)*

Onrad Medical Group, Riverside *Also Called: Onrad Inc (P-14938)*

Onriva Travel, San Mateo *Also Called: Alinor Holdings Inc (P-11396)*

Onsite Health Inc .... D...... 888 411-2290
　6610 Goodyear Rd Benicia (94510) *(P-17287)*

Ontario Airport Hotel Corp .... C...... 408 562-6709
　4949 Great America Pkwy Santa Clara (95054) *(P-10069)*

Ontario Automotive LLC .... C...... 909 974-3800
　1401 Auto Center Dr Ontario (91761) *(P-7272)*

Ontario Convention Center Corp .... B...... 909 937-3000
　2000 E Convention Center Way Ontario (91764) *(P-13407)*

Ontario Mills Shopping Center, Ontario *Also Called: Mills Corporation (P-8735)*

Ontario Vineyard Medical Offs, Ontario *Also Called: Kaiser Foundation Hospitals (P-14814)*

Ontario/Montclair YMCA, Ontario *Also Called: West End Yung MNS Christn Assn (P-18929)*

Ontarioidence Opco LLC .... B...... 909 984-8629
　800 E 5th St Ontario (91764) *(P-15781)*

Ontel Security Services Inc .... D...... 209 521-0200
　2125 Wylie Dr Ste 11 Modesto (95355) *(P-13011)*

Ontic Engineering and Mfg Inc (PA) .... D...... 818 678-6555
　20400 Plummer St Chatsworth (91311) *(P-5963)*

Ontrac Logistics Inc .... D...... 714 776-0363
　1745 W Penhall Way Anaheim (92801) *(P-3623)*

Ontrac Logistics Inc .... D...... 818 504-9043
　11085 Olinda St Sun Valley (91352) *(P-3624)*

Ontrac Logistics Inc .... C...... 804 334-5000
　9774 Calabash Ave Fontana (92335) *(P-3625)*

Ontrac Logistics Inc .... D...... 707 773-1564
　3830 Cypress Dr Petaluma (94954) *(P-7543)*

Ontraport Inc .... C...... 805 568-1424
　2040 Alameda Padre Serra Ste 220 Santa Barbara (93103) *(P-20166)*

Onvantage Inc .... D...... 408 562-3388
　3290 Freedom Cir 200 Santa Clara (95054) *(P-12303)*

Onyx Pharmaceuticals Inc .... A...... 650 266-0000
　1 Amgen Center Dr Newbury Park (91320) *(P-2600)*

Ooma, Sunnyvale *Also Called: Ooma Inc (P-12602)*

Ooma Inc (PA) .... D...... 650 566-6600
　525 Almanor Ave Ste 200 Sunnyvale (94085) *(P-12602)*

Op Bancorp (PA) .... C...... 213 892-9999
　1000 Wilshire Blvd Ste 500 Los Angeles (90017) *(P-7702)*

Opal Concepts Inc (PA) .... D...... 714 779-0545
　6401 E Nohl Ranch Rd Apt 10 Anaheim (92807) *(P-10505)*

OPEN America Inc .... C...... 562 428-9210
　4300 Long Beach Blvd Ste 450 Long Beach (90807) *(P-10937)*

Open Door Community Hlth Ctrs (PA) .... D...... 707 826-8642
　1275 8th St Arcata (95521) *(P-17103)*

Open Philanthropy Project .... D...... 415 429-0423
　182 Howard St Ste 225 San Francisco (94105) *(P-19095)*

Open Text Inc (HQ) .... C...... 650 645-3000
　2440 Sand Hill Rd Ste 302 Menlo Park (94025) *(P-11796)*

Open Text Inc .... D...... 949 784-8000
　8717 Research Dr Ste 100 Irvine (92618) *(P-11797)*

Open Up Resources .... D...... 650 450-3445
　1600 El Camino Real Ste 155 Menlo Park (94025) *(P-20496)*

Openai Inc (PA) .... C...... 650 387-6701
　3180 18th St Ste 100 San Francisco (94110) *(P-11798)*

Opendoor Labs Inc .... C...... 888 352-7075
　8880 Cal Center Dr Ste 400 Sacramento (95826) *(P-9114)*

Opendoor Property, Sacramento *Also Called: Opendoor Labs Inc (P-9114)*

Opengate Capital Group LLC .... D...... 310 432-7000
　10250 Constellation Blvd Fl 17 Los Angeles (90067) *(P-9407)*

Openpopcom Inc (PA) .... D...... 714 249-7044
　12539 Carson St Hawaiian Gardens (90716) *(P-20822)*

Opentable Inc (HQ) .... C...... 415 344-4200
　1 Montgomery St Ste 500 San Francisco (94104) *(P-13408)*

Opentv Inc .... B...... 415 962-5000
　275 Sacramento St San Francisco (94111) *(P-12304)*

Openworks, Long Beach *Also Called: OPEN America Inc (P-10937)*

Operam Inc .... D...... 855 673-7261
　1041 N Formosa Ave 500 West Hollywood (90046) *(P-20497)*

Operating Engineers Funds Inc (PA) .... C...... 866 400-5200
　100 Corson St Pasadena (91103) *(P-9440)*

Operating Engineers Loca .... C...... 408 782-9803
　325 Digital Dr Morgan Hill (95037) *(P-19342)*

ALPHABETIC SECTION — Orange County Water District

Operating Engners Lcal Un No 3, Alameda *Also Called: Interntnal Un Oper Engners Lca (P-18785)*

Operation Samahan Inc .... C...... 619 477-4451
10737 Camino Ruiz Ste 235138 San Diego (92126) *(P-14939)*

Operation Technology Inc .... D...... 949 462-0100
17 Goodyear Ste 100 Irvine (92618) *(P-11799)*

Operational Technical Svcs LLC .... D...... 424 203-6352
10250 Constellation Blvd Ste 3-115 Los Angeles (90067) *(P-11314)*

Oportun, San Carlos *Also Called: Oportun Financial Corporation (P-7883)*

Oportun Financial Corporation (PA) .... A...... 650 810-8823
2 Circle Star Way San Carlos (94070) *(P-7883)*

Oppenheim Group Inc .... D...... 310 927-7048
8606 W Sunset Blvd West Hollywood (90069) *(P-9115)*

Oppenheim Group Real Estate, West Hollywood *Also Called: Oppenheim Group Inc (P-9115)*

Oprah Winfrey Network, Burbank *Also Called: Own LLC (P-4517)*

Opsec Specialized Protection .... D...... 661 942-3999
44262 Division St Ste A Lancaster (93535) *(P-13012)*

Optim, Pleasanton *Also Called: Unchained Labs (P-16757)*

Optima Building Services, Santa Rosa *Also Called: Optima Building Services Inc (P-10938)*

Optima Building Services Inc .... D...... 707 586-6640
210 Mountain View Ave Santa Rosa (95407) *(P-10938)*

Optima Family Services Inc .... C...... 323 300-6066
253 N San Gabriel Blvd Pasadena (91107) *(P-18071)*

Optima Office Inc .... D...... 858 361-0481
5120 Shoreham Pl Ste 285 San Diego (92122) *(P-19619)*

Optima Protection Plan, Santa Ana *Also Called: Optima Tax Relief LLC (P-10524)*

Optima Tax Relief LLC .... C...... 714 361-4636
3100 S Harbor Blvd Ste 250 Santa Ana (92704) *(P-10524)*

Optio Solutions LLC .... B...... 800 360-2827
1444 N Mcdowell Blvd Petaluma (94954) *(P-10746)*

Options For All Inc .... B...... 858 565-9870
5050 Murphy Canyon Rd Ste 220 San Diego (92123) *(P-18239)*

Options Recovery Services .... D...... 510 666-9552
1835 Allston Way Berkeley (94703) *(P-17104)*

Optivus Proton Therapy Inc .... D...... 909 799-8300
1475 Victoria Ct San Bernardino (92408) *(P-3043)*

Optoplex Corporation .... B...... 510 490-9930
48500 Kato Rd Fremont (94538) *(P-2889)*

Optum, Ontario *Also Called: North American Med MGT Cal Inc (P-20163)*

Optumcare Management LLC .... C...... 562 988-7000
2600 Redondo Ave Ste 405 Long Beach (90806) *(P-14940)*

Optumcare Management LLC (HQ) .... A...... 310 354-4200
2175 Park Pl El Segundo (90245) *(P-14941)*

Optumcare Management LLC .... D...... 310 316-0811
502 Torrance Blvd Redondo Beach (90277) *(P-14942)*

Optumcare Management LLC .... D...... 714 964-6229
3501 S Harbor Blvd Santa Ana (92704) *(P-17288)*

Optumcare Management LLC .... D...... 714 968-0068
19066 Magnolia St Huntington Beach (92646) *(P-17289)*

Optumcare Management LLC .... D...... 714 835-8501
901 W Civic Center Dr Ste 120 Santa Ana (92703) *(P-17290)*

Optumcare Medical Group .... D...... 949 364-9112
800 Corporate Dr Ste 100 Ladera Ranch (92694) *(P-17291)*

Optumrx Inc .... B...... 760 804-2399
2858 Loker Ave E Ste 100 Carlsbad (92010) *(P-8348)*

Optumrx Inc (DH) .... B...... 714 825-3600
2300 Main St Irvine (92614) *(P-8349)*

Optumrx PBM Administrator Cal, Irvine *Also Called: Optumrx Inc (P-8349)*

Opus Bank .... A...... 949 250-9800
19900 Macarthur Blvd Ste 1200 Irvine (92612) *(P-7733)*

Oracle, San Francisco *Also Called: Oracle Corporation (P-11800)*

Oracle, Monte Sereno *Also Called: Oracle Systems Corporation (P-11801)*

Oracle, San Mateo *Also Called: Netsuite Inc (P-12285)*

Oracle, Mission Viejo *Also Called: Oracle Corporation (P-12306)*

Oracle, Rocklin *Also Called: Oracle Corporation (P-12307)*

Oracle America Inc (HQ) .... A...... 650 506-7000
500 Oracle Pkwy Redwood City (94065) *(P-2809)*

Oracle America Inc .... C...... 408 276-3331
4120 Network Cir Santa Clara (95054) *(P-12305)*

Oracle Corporation .... C...... 415 541-9462
75 Hawthorne St Ste 2000 San Francisco (94105) *(P-11800)*

Oracle Corporation .... B...... 626 315-7513
1 Bolero Mission Viejo (92692) *(P-12306)*

Oracle Corporation .... B...... 916 315-3500
1001 Sunset Blvd Rocklin (95765) *(P-12307)*

Oracle Systems Corporation .... D...... 650 506-4060
17527 Via Sereno Monte Sereno (95030) *(P-11801)*

Oracle Systems Corporation (HQ) .... A...... 650 506-7000
500 Oracle Pkwy Redwood City (94065) *(P-12850)*

Oracle Taleo LLC (HQ) .... D...... 925 452-3000
4140 Dublin Blvd Ste 400 Dublin (94568) *(P-12308)*

Oracle Usa Inc .... A...... 650 506-7000
500 Oracle Pkwy Redwood City (94065) *(P-12309)*

Orange Bakery Inc .... C...... 949 454-1247
75 Parker Irvine (92618) *(P-8740)*

Orange Belt Adventures, Visalia *Also Called: Orange Belt Stages (P-3319)*

Orange Belt Stages (PA) .... D...... 559 733-4408
2134 E Mineral King Ave Visalia (93292) *(P-3319)*

Orange Cast Mem Care Brast Ctr .... D...... 714 378-7955
9900 Talbert Ave Ste 102 Fountain Valley (92708) *(P-16294)*

Orange Cnty Adult Achvment Ctr .... C...... 714 744-5301
225 W Carl Karcher Way Anaheim (92801) *(P-18072)*

Orange Cnty Cncil Boy Scuts AM (PA) .... D...... 714 546-4990
2 Irvine Park Rd Orange (92869) *(P-18889)*

Orange Cnty George M Raymond N, Orange *Also Called: Raymond Group (P-20191)*

Orange Cnty Globl Med Ctr Aux (DH) .... C...... 714 835-3555
1301 N Tustin Ave Santa Ana (92705) *(P-16295)*

Orange Cnty Globl Med Ctr Inc .... D...... 714 953-3500
1001 N Tustin Ave Santa Ana (92705) *(P-16296)*

Orange Cnty Hlth Auth A Pub AG .... B...... 714 246-8500
505 City Pkwy W Orange (92868) *(P-18754)*

Orange Cnty Ryale Cnvlscent Ho (PA) .... B...... 714 546-6450
1030 W Warner Ave Santa Ana (92707) *(P-15886)*

Orange Cnty Trnsp Auth Schlrsh .... D...... 714 560-6282
11790 Cardinal Cir Garden Grove (92843) *(P-3186)*

Orange Cnty Trnsp Auth Schlrsh (PA) .... B...... 714 636-7433
550 S Main St Orange (92868) *(P-3187)*

Orange Cnty Trnsp Auth Schlrsh .... A...... 714 999-1726
600 S Main St Ste 910 Orange (92868) *(P-3188)*

Orange Coast Care Inc .... D...... 714 997-7090
5017 E Chapman Ave Orange (92869) *(P-15611)*

Orange Coast Ctr For Surgl Cr, Fountain Valley *Also Called: Memorlcare Srgcal Ctr At Ornge (P-16257)*

Orange Coast Medical Center, Fountain Valley *Also Called: Memorialcare Medical Group (P-16256)*

Orange Coast Memorial Med Ctr (HQ) .... A...... 714 378-7000
9920 Talbert Ave Fountain Valley (92708) *(P-16297)*

Orange Coast Service Center, Westminster *Also Called: Southern California Edison Co (P-4693)*

Orange Coast Title Company (PA) .... D...... 714 558-2836
1551 N Tustin Ave Ste 300 Santa Ana (92705) *(P-13409)*

Orange Coast Wns Med Group Inc .... D...... 949 829-5522
1031 Avenida Pico Ste 204 San Clemente (92673) *(P-14943)*

Orange County Head Start Inc (PA) .... D...... 714 241-8920
2501 Pullman St Santa Ana (92705) *(P-18340)*

Orange County Health Authority, Orange *Also Called: Orange Cnty Hlth Auth A Pub AG (P-18754)*

Orange County Health Care Agcy .... D...... 714 568-5683
405 W 5th St Ste 700 Santa Ana (92701) *(P-18755)*

Orange County Plst Co Inc .... C...... 714 957-1971
3191 Airport Loop Dr Ste B1 Costa Mesa (92626) *(P-1951)*

Orange County Produce LLC .... D...... 949 451-0880
210 W Walnut Ave Fullerton (92832) *(P-58)*

Orange County Sanitation (PA) .... B...... 714 962-2411
10844 Ellis Ave Fountain Valley (92708) *(P-4916)*

Orange County Service Center, San Clemente *Also Called: San Diego Gas & Electric Co (P-4753)*

Orange County Services Inc .... D...... 714 541-9753
3022 N Hesperian St Santa Ana (92706) *(P-1520)*

Orange County Trnsp Auth, Orange *Also Called: Orange Cnty Trnsp Auth Schlrsh (P-3187)*

Orange County Water District (PA) .... D...... 714 378-3200
18700 Ward St Fountain Valley (92708) *(P-4814)*

Orange County-Irvine Med Ctr, Irvine *Also Called: Kaiser Foundation Hospitals (P-9435)*

Orange Countys Credit Union (PA) .... C **714 755-5900**
1721 E Saint Andrew Pl Santa Ana (92705) *(P-7788)*

Orange Courier Inc .... B **714 384-3600**
15300 Desman Rd La Mirada (90638) *(P-13410)*

Orange Hlthcare Wllness Cntre .... C **714 633-3568**
920 W La Veta Ave Orange (92868) *(P-15612)*

Orange Labs, San Francisco *Also Called: Orange Silicon Valley LLC (P-19839)*

Orange Silicon Valley LLC .... D **415 284-9765**
60 Spear St Ste 1100 San Francisco (94105) *(P-19839)*

Orange Treeidence Opco LLC .... B **951 785-6060**
4000 Harrison St Riverside (92503) *(P-15782)*

Orangepeople LLC .... D **949 535-1308**
300 Spectrum Center Dr Ste 400 Irvine (92618) *(P-20897)*

Orangewood Foundation .... D **714 619-0200**
1575 E 17th St Santa Ana (92705) *(P-18073)*

Orangewood LLC .... C **714 750-3000**
2085 S Harbor Blvd Anaheim (92802) *(P-10070)*

Orangtree Cnvalescent Hosp Inc .... C **951 785-6060**
4000 Harrison St Riverside (92503) *(P-16298)*

Orba Financial & Inter SEC, Rancho Cordova *Also Called: Orba Insurance Services Inc (P-8632)*

Orba Insurance Services Inc .... D **916 858-1222**
2339 Gold Meadow Way Ste 200 Rancho Cordova (95670) *(P-8632)*

Orbit Industries Inc .... D **213 745-8884**
7533 Garfield Ave Bell Gardens (90201) *(P-5585)*

Orca Arms, San Diego *Also Called: Orca Arms LLC (P-3093)*

Orca Arms LLC .... D **858 586-0503**
9825 Carroll Centre Rd Ste 100 San Diego (92126) *(P-3093)*

Orca Biosystems Inc .... D **916 822-4235**
3400 Business Dr Ste 140 Sacramento (95820) *(P-19753)*

Orchard - Post Acute Care Ctr .... D **562 693-7701**
12385 Washington Blvd Whittier (90606) *(P-15613)*

Orchard Holdings Group Inc .... D **949 502-8300**
1 Venture Ste 300 Irvine (92618) *(P-9116)*

Orchard Hospital .... C **530 846-9000**
240 Spruce St Gridley (95948) *(P-16299)*

Orchem Division, Temecula *Also Called: Oreq Corporation (P-20167)*

Orchid Court Inc .... D **951 766-7840**
650 Camino Real Cir Hemet (92543) *(P-13411)*

Ordermark Inc .... C **833 673-3762**
12045 Waterfront Dr Ste 400 # 3 Playa Vista (90094) *(P-12603)*

Oregon PCF Bldg Pdts Calif Inc .... D **916 381-8051**
8185 Signal Ct Ste A Sacramento (95824) *(P-5178)*

Oregon PCF Bldg Pdts Maple Inc .... D **909 627-4043**
2401 E Philadelphia St Ontario (91761) *(P-5179)*

Orepac Building Products, Sacramento *Also Called: Oregon PCF Bldg Pdts Calif Inc (P-5178)*

Orepac Millwork Products, Ontario *Also Called: Oregon PCF Bldg Pdts Maple Inc (P-5179)*

Oreq Corporation .... D **951 296-5076**
42306 Remington Ave Temecula (92590) *(P-20167)*

Organicgirl LLC .... A **831 758-7800**
900 Work St Salinas (93901) *(P-2439)*

Oriental Motor USA Corporation (DH) .... D **310 715-3300**
570 Alaska Ave Ste A Torrance (90503) *(P-5586)*

Original Mels Inc (PA) .... D **916 458-6014**
3941 Park Dr Ste 20-369 El Dorado Hills (95762) *(P-7499)*

Original Mels Diner, El Dorado Hills *Also Called: Original Mels Inc (P-7499)*

Original Mowbrays Tree Svc Inc (PA) .... C **909 383-7009**
686 E Mill St San Bernardino (92408) *(P-558)*

Original Mowbrays Tree Svc Inc .... D **559 798-0530**
17332 Millwood Dr Visalia (93292) *(P-559)*

Original Sid Blackman Plbg Inc .... D **760 352-3632**
1160 S 2nd St El Centro (92243) *(P-1521)*

Orinda Country Club .... D **925 254-4313**
315 Camino Sobrante Orinda (94563) *(P-14420)*

Orion Construction Corporation .... D **760 597-9660**
2185 La Mirada Dr Vista (92081) *(P-1247)*

Orion Group World LLC .... C **415 602-5233**
143 Seminary Dr Apt Q Mill Valley (94941) *(P-13412)*

Orion Indemnity Company .... D **213 742-8700**
714 W Olympic Blvd Ste 800 Los Angeles (90015) *(P-8402)*

Orion Pictures Corporation .... A **310 449-3000**
245 N Beverly Dr Beverly Hills (90210) *(P-13872)*

Orion Security Patrol, San Jose *Also Called: Orion Security Patrol Inc (P-13013)*

Orion Security Patrol Inc .... B **408 287-4411**
675 E Gish Rd San Jose (95112) *(P-13013)*

Orion Solidified Inc (PA) .... D **818 483-0100**
10232 Arroyo Ave Hesperia (92345) *(P-11802)*

Orlando Wilshire Investments .... D **323 658-6600**
8384 W 3rd St Los Angeles (90048) *(P-10071)*

Orlando, The, Los Angeles *Also Called: Orlando Wilshire Investments (P-10071)*

Ormond Beach LP .... D **805 496-4948**
1259 E Thousand Oaks Blvd Thousand Oaks (91362) *(P-8741)*

Orohealth Corporation .... A **530 534-9183**
900 Oro Dam Blvd E Oroville (95965) *(P-14944)*

Orora North America, Buena Park *Also Called: Orora Packaging Solutions (P-6084)*

Orora Packaging Solutions (HQ) .... D **714 562-6000**
6600 Valley View St Buena Park (90620) *(P-6084)*

Orora Packaging Solutions .... C **323 832-2000**
1640 S Greenwood Ave Montebello (90640) *(P-6085)*

Orora Packaging Solutions .... D **916 645-8100**
1221 Tara Ct Rocklin (95765) *(P-6086)*

Orora Packaging Solutions .... C **714 562-6002**
6200 Caballero Blvd Buena Park (90620) *(P-6087)*

Oroville Hospital .... B **530 538-8700**
2353 Myers St Ste B Oroville (95966) *(P-15298)*

Oroville Hospital (PA) .... A **530 533-8500**
2767 Olive Hwy Oroville (95966) *(P-16300)*

Oroville Hospital .... B **530 532-8697**
2170 Bird St Oroville (95965) *(P-16301)*

Oroville Hospital, Oroville *Also Called: Orohealth Corporation (P-14944)*

Oroville Hospital Post Acute Center, Oroville *Also Called: 1000 Executive Parkway LLC (P-15313)*

Orphan Medical Inc .... D **650 496-3777**
3180 Porter Dr Palo Alto (94304) *(P-2601)*

Orrick Hrringtn Sut Foundtn .... D **916 329-7928**
400 Capitol Mall Ste 3000 Sacramento (95814) *(P-17595)*

Orrick Hrrington Sutcliffe LLP (PA) .... A **415 773-5700**
405 Howard St San Francisco (94105) *(P-17596)*

Orrick Hrrington Sutcliffe LLP .... C **650 614-7400**
1000 Marsh Rd Menlo Park (94025) *(P-17597)*

Orrick, Herrington & Sutcliffe, San Francisco *Also Called: Orrick Hrrington Sutcliffe LLP (P-17596)*

Orthalliance Inc .... A **310 792-1300**
21535 Hawthorne Blvd Ste 200 Torrance (90503) *(P-18615)*

Orthalliances, Torrance *Also Called: Orthalliance Inc (P-18615)*

Ortho Organizers Inc .... C **760 448-8600**
1822 Aston Ave Carlsbad (92008) *(P-3068)*

Orthocad, San Jose *Also Called: Cadent Inc (P-12429)*

Orthopaedic Hospital (PA) .... C **213 742-1000**
403 W Adams Blvd Los Angeles (90007) *(P-16302)*

Orthopaedic Inst For Children, Los Angeles *Also Called: Orthopaedic Hospital (P-16302)*

Orthopedics Department, Los Angeles *Also Called: Southern Cal Prmnnte Med Group (P-15094)*

Orthowest, Laguna Hills *Also Called: South Cnty Orthpd Spclsts A ME (P-15068)*

Os4labor LLC .... C **626 838-6745**
120 N Fairway Ln Ste A West Covina (91791) *(P-11192)*

Osata Enterprises Inc .... D **888 445-6237**
18105 Bishop Ave Carson (90746) *(P-6233)*

Osf International Inc .... D **760 471-0155**
111 N Twin Oaks Valley Rd San Marcos (92069) *(P-7500)*

Osher Ctr For Intgrtive Mdcine, San Francisco *Also Called: University Cal San Francisco (P-17774)*

Oshman Family Jewish Cmnty Ctr .... C **650 223-8700**
3921 Fabian Way Palo Alto (94303) *(P-18074)*

Oshyn Inc .... D **213 483-1770**
100 W Broadway Ste 330 Long Beach (90802) *(P-11803)*

OSI Engineering Inc .... C **408 550-2800**
901 Campisi Way Ste 160 Campbell (95008) *(P-19343)*

OSI Software, San Leandro *Also Called: Osisoft LLC (P-11804)*

OSI Staffing Inc .... D **562 261-5753**
10913 La Reina Ave Ste B Downey (90241) *(P-11193)*

ALPHABETIC SECTION

Osisoft LLC (DH) .... B 510 297-5800
 1600 Alvarado St San Leandro (94577) *(P-11804)*

Osram Sylvania Inc .... D 909 923-3003
 1651 S Archibald Ave Ontario (91761) *(P-3742)*

Osso Vr Inc .... C 310 709-8289
 2806 San Ardo Way Belmont (94002) *(P-11805)*

Ost Crane Service, Ventura *Also Called: Ost Trucks and Cranes Inc (P-13413)*

Ost Trucks and Cranes Inc .... D 805 643-9963
 2951 N Ventura Ave Ventura (93001) *(P-13413)*

OTasty Foods Inc .... D 626 330-1229
 160 S Hacienda Blvd City Of Industry (91745) *(P-6274)*

Otay Hospitality Inc .... D 619 422-2600
 4450 Main St Chula Vista (91911) *(P-10072)*

Otay River Constructors LLC .... C 619 397-7500
 860 Harold Pl Chula Vista (91914) *(P-1149)*

Otay Water District 619 670-2222
 2554 Sweetwater Springs Blvd Spring Valley (91978) *(P-4815)*

Otb Acquisition LLC .... C 520 458-0540
 770 S Brea Blvd Ste 227 Brea (92821) *(P-10073)*

Otis Elevator Company .... C 408 727-1231
 470 Lakeside Dr Ste D Sunnyvale (94085) *(P-5852)*

Otis Elevator Company 818 241-2828
 512 Paula Ave Ste A Glendale (91201) *(P-5853)*

Otis Elevator Company .... C 714 758-9593
 711 E Ball Rd Ste 200 Anaheim (92805) *(P-5854)*

Otis Elevator Company .... C 415 546-0880
 444 Spear St Ste 100 San Francisco (94105) *(P-5855)*

Oto Analytics Inc .... B 310 683-0000
 548 Market St Ste 73871 San Francisco (94104) *(P-12508)*

Otr Global Holdings II Inc .... C 415 675-7660
 155 Montgomery St Ste 501 San Francisco (94104) *(P-19840)*

Otto Construction, Sacramento *Also Called: John F Otto Inc (P-948)*

Otts Asia Moorer Devon .... C 323 603-6959
 10015 Baring Cross St Los Angeles (90044) *(P-9548)*

Our Alchemy LLC .... D 310 893-6289
 5900 Wilshire Blvd Fl 18 Los Angeles (90036) *(P-13976)*

OUR HOUSE, Victorville *Also Called: Family Assistance Program (P-17974)*

Our Lady Fatima Villa Inc .... D 408 741-2950
 20400 Saratoga Los Gatos Rd Saratoga (95070) *(P-15614)*

Our Lady of Mercy Pre-School, Merced *Also Called: Diocese Fresno Education Corp (P-18308)*

Outback Contractors Inc .... C 530 528-2225
 13670 State Highway 36 E Red Bluff (96080) *(P-1150)*

Outcast Agency LLC .... C 415 392-8282
 100 Montgomery St Ste 1200 San Francisco (94104) *(P-20640)*

Outlook Amusements Inc .... C 818 433-3800
 3746 Foothill Blvd La Crescenta (91214) *(P-12851)*

OUTREACH, San Jose *Also Called: Outreach & Escort Inc (P-18075)*

Outreach & Escort Inc (PA) .... D 408 678-8585
 2221 Oakland Rd Ste 200 San Jose (95131) *(P-18075)*

Outreach Corporation .... B 888 938-7356
 600 California St Fl 7 San Francisco (94108) *(P-12310)*

Outright Inc .... D 918 926-6578
 100 Mathilda Pl Ste 100 Sunnyvale (94086) *(P-11806)*

Outsource Utility Contr Corp .... C 714 238-9263
 8015 E Crystal Dr Anaheim (92807) *(P-4598)*

Outward Inc .... D 408 828-5492
 10444 Berkshire Dr Los Altos Hills (94024) *(P-11807)*

Ovation Fertility, Encino *Also Called: Fpg Services LLC (P-20386)*

Ovation Home Loans, Irvine *Also Called: Carnegie Mortgage LLC (P-8031)*

Ovation Tech Inc .... C 949 271-0054
 17551 Von Karman Ave Irvine (92614) *(P-12852)*

Overaa Construction, Richmond *Also Called: C Overaa & Co (P-885)*

Overland Storage Inc (HQ) .... B 408 283-4700
 2633 Camino Ramon Ste 325 San Ramon (94583) *(P-2818)*

Overland-Tandberg, San Ramon *Also Called: Overland Storage Inc (P-2818)*

Overseas Service Corporation .... C 858 408-0751
 8221 Arjons Dr Ste B2 San Diego (92126) *(P-20898)*

Overton Security Services Inc .... C 510 791-7380
 39300 Civic Center Dr Ste 370 Fremont (94538) *(P-13014)*

Ovis LLC .... A 805 646-5511
 905 Country Club Rd Ojai (93023) *(P-10074)*

OVS, Ojai *Also Called: Ojai Valley School (P-17737)*

Owens & Minor Distribution Inc .... A 805 524-0243
 452 Sespe Ave Fillmore (93015) *(P-5436)*

Owens Corning, Compton *Also Called: Owens Corning Sales LLC (P-2651)*

Owens Corning Sales LLC .... C 310 631-1062
 1501 N Tamarind Ave Compton (90222) *(P-2651)*

Owl Education and Training Inc .... B 949 797-2000
 2465 Campus Dr Irvine (92612) *(P-18240)*

Own LLC .... C 323 602-5500
 4000 Warner Blvd Burbank (91522) *(P-4517)*

Oxford Palace Hotel LLC .... D 213 382-7756
 745 S Oxford Ave Los Angeles (90005) *(P-10075)*

Oxnard City Hall, Oxnard *Also Called: City of Oxnard (P-20317)*

Oxnard Police Department .... B 805 385-8300
 251 S C St Oxnard (93030) *(P-18890)*

OXY, Los Angeles *Also Called: Occidental Petroleum Corporation of California (P-584)*

OXY Inc .... C 310 824-1315
 10889 Wilshire Blvd Los Angeles (90024) *(P-3945)*

OXY-World Travel, Los Angeles *Also Called: OXY Inc (P-3945)*

Oxyheal Health Group Inc .... C 619 336-2022
 3224 Hoover Ave National City (91950) *(P-13789)*

Oz North Coast Y M C A, Oceanside *Also Called: YMCA of San Diego County (P-18952)*

Ozark Trucking Inc (PA) .... C 916 561-5400
 4916 Dudley Blvd Mcclellan (95652) *(P-3523)*

P & R Paper Supply Co Inc (HQ) .... D 909 389-1807
 1898 E Colton Ave Redlands (92374) *(P-6088)*

P A C E, Los Angeles *Also Called: Pacific Asian Cnsrtium In Empl (P-18242)*

P A Motorcars LLC .... A 877 433-3517
 2016 E Garvey Ave S West Covina (91791) *(P-7273)*

P C A, Livermore *Also Called: Pen-Cal Administrators Inc (P-20174)*

P C M, Banning *Also Called: Professional Cmnty MGT Cal Inc (P-9141)*

P C S, Concord *Also Called: Patriot Contract Services LLC (P-3798)*

P D S, Irvine *Also Called: Pacific Dental Services LLC (P-15245)*

P H I, South San Francisco *Also Called: Peking Handicraft Inc (P-5131)*

P H S, Northridge *Also Called: Progressive Health Care System (P-14999)*

P J J Enterprises Inc .... D 619 232-6136
 1250 Delevan Dr San Diego (92102) *(P-11048)*

P J'S Construction Supplies, Fremont *Also Called: PJs Lumber Inc (P-5181)*

P K B Investments Inc .... C 559 243-1224
 745 E Locust Ave Ste 105 Fresno (93720) *(P-20498)*

P M D Holding Corp .... B 949 595-4777
 26672 Towne Centre Dr Ste 310 El Toro (92610) *(P-5437)*

P M I, Pittsburg *Also Called: Performance Mechanical Inc (P-839)*

P Monterey LP .... D 831 250-6159
 47 Via Cimarron Monterey (93940) *(P-8851)*

P Murphy & Associates Inc .... C 818 841-2002
 39600 Balentine Dr Newark (94560) *(P-11808)*

P P I, Santa Fe Springs *Also Called: Premiere Packaging Inds Inc (P-6937)*

P R P, Santa Ana *Also Called: Profit Recovery Partners LLC (P-20831)*

P W C, San Dimas *Also Called: Pacific W Space Cmmnctions Inc (P-1248)*

P.J.'s Rebar, Turlock *Also Called: PJs Lumber Inc (P-2193)*

P&O Stg-Carson 4150, Carson *Also Called: US Foods Inc (P-6689)*

P2f Holdings .... D 562 296-1055
 1760 Apollo Ct Seal Beach (90740) *(P-6933)*

P2s Inc 562 497-2999
 4660 La Jolla Village Dr San Diego (92122) *(P-19344)*

Paamco, Newport Beach *Also Called: Pacific Altrntive Asset MGT LL (P-8212)*

Paar Hospitality Inc .... D 510 828-3585
 500 W A St Hayward (94541) *(P-10076)*

Paat & Kimmel Development Inc .... D 909 315-8074
 600 N Mountain Ave Upland (91786) *(P-981)*

Pac West Land Care Inc .... C 760 630-0231
 408 Olive Ave Vista (92083) *(P-453)*

PAC-12, San Ramon *Also Called: Pac-12 Entepises LLC (P-10717)*

Pac-12 Entepises LLC .... C 415 580-4200
 12647 Alcosta Blvd San Ramon (94583) *(P-10717)*

Pac-West Telecomm Inc .... D 877 626-4325
 4210 Coronado Ave Stockton (95204) *(P-4324)*

Pacbell, San Francisco *Also Called: Pacific Bell Telephone Company (P-4325)*

Pacc, Canyon Country Also Called: Pure Autism Counseling Ctr Inc **(P-17115)**
PACE, Santa Clara Also Called: Pacific Autism Ctr For Educatn **(P-17814)**
Pace Engineering Inc .... D........ 530 244-0202
5155 Venture Pkwy Redding (96002) **(P-19345)**
Pace Solano .... D........ 707 426-6932
1955 W Texas St Fairfield (94533) **(P-18241)**
Pace Supply Corp (PA) .... D........ 707 755-2499
6000 State Farm Dr Ste 200 Rohnert Park (94928) **(P-5758)**
Pacer, Commerce Also Called: Xpo Cartage Inc **(P-3440)**
Pachulski Stang Zehl Jones LLP (PA) .... D........ 310 277-6910
10100 Santa Monica Blvd Ste 1100 Los Angeles (90067) **(P-17598)**
Pacifcare Hlth Plan Admnstrtor (DH) .... B........ 714 825-5200
3120 W Lake Center Dr Santa Ana (92704) **(P-8350)**
Pacific Advnced Cvil Engrg Inc (PA) .... D........ 714 481-7300
17520 Newhope St Ste 200 Fountain Valley (92708) **(P-19346)**
Pacific Aerospace Resources & Technologies LLC .... D
18284 Readiness St Victorville (92394) **(P-5964)**
Pacific Altrntive Asset MGT LL (HQ) .... D........ 949 261-4900
660 Newport Center Dr Ste 930 Newport Beach (92660) **(P-8212)**
Pacific American Fish Co Inc (PA) .... C........ 323 319-1551
5525 S Santa Fe Ave Vernon (90058) **(P-2417)**
Pacific American Income Shares, Pasadena Also Called: Western Assets Management Co **(P-9410)**
Pacific Aquascape Inc .... D........ 714 843-5734
17520 Newhope St Ste 120 Fountain Valley (92708) **(P-2303)**
Pacific Asian Cnsrtium In Empl (PA) .... C........ 213 353-3982
1055 Wilshire Blvd Ste 1475 Los Angeles (90017) **(P-18242)**
Pacific Asset Holding LLC .... C........ 949 219-3011
700 Newport Center Dr Newport Beach (92660) **(P-8243)**
Pacific Athletic Club, San Francisco Also Called: Bay Club America Inc **(P-14328)**
Pacific Autism Ctr For Educatn .... C........ 408 245-3400
1880 Pruneridge Ave Santa Clara (95050) **(P-17814)**
Pacific Ave Cpitl Partners LLC (PA) .... B........ 424 254-9774
2447 Pacific Coast Hwy Ste 101 Hermosa Beach (90254) **(P-9408)**
Pacific Aviation Corporation .... A........ 650 821-1190
San Francisco (94125) **(P-3902)**
Pacific Aviation Corporation (PA) .... C........ 310 646-4015
201 Continental Blvd Ste 220 El Segundo (90245) **(P-3903)**
Pacific Bay Lending Group .... D........ 714 367-5125
15020 La Mirada Blvd La Mirada (90638) **(P-8049)**
Pacific Bell Telephone Company .... A........ 650 572-6807
262 19th Ave San Mateo (94403) **(P-4222)**
Pacific Bell Telephone Company .... A........ 310 515-2898
3847 Cardiff Ave Culver City (90232) **(P-4223)**
Pacific Bell Telephone Company .... A........ 415 978-0881
2040 Polk St 267 San Francisco (94109) **(P-4224)**
Pacific Bell Telephone Company (HQ) .... A........ 415 542-9000
430 Bush St Fl 3 San Francisco (94108) **(P-4325)**
Pacific Biolabs Inc .... D........ 510 964-9000
551 Linus Pauling Dr Hercules (94547) **(P-19993)**
Pacific Building Group (PA) .... D........ 858 552-0600
9752 Aspen Creek Ct Ste 100 San Diego (92126) **(P-982)**
Pacific Building Group .... D........ 858 552-0600
13541 Stoney Creek Rd San Diego (92129) **(P-1952)**
Pacific Cambria Inc .... D........ 805 927-6114
2905 Burton Dr Cambria (93428) **(P-10077)**
Pacific Catalina Hotel Inc .... B........ 310 510-9255
888 Country Club Dr Avalon (90704) **(P-10078)**
Pacific Cheese Co Inc (PA) .... C........ 510 784-8800
21090 Cabot Blvd Hayward (94545) **(P-6442)**
Pacific Chemical, Buena Park Also Called: Pacific Chemical Dist Corp **(P-3795)**
Pacific Chemical Dist Corp (HQ) .... D........ 714 521-7161
6250 Caballero Blvd Buena Park (90620) **(P-3795)**
Pacific Child and Family Assoc, Glendale Also Called: Verdugo Hlls Psychthrapy Ctr A **(P-15185)**
Pacific City Hotel LLC .... B........ 714 698-6100
21080 Pacific Coast Hwy Huntington Beach (92648) **(P-10079)**
Pacific Clay Products Inc .... C........ 661 857-1401
14741 Lake St Lake Elsinore (92530) **(P-5208)**
Pacific Clinics Head Start .... C........ 626 254-5000
171 N Altadena Dr Pasadena (91107) **(P-18341)**

Pacific Clnics Psdena Calworks .... C........ 626 419-3228
2550 E Foothill Blvd Pasadena (91107) **(P-17105)**
Pacific Coast Bankers Bank .... D........ 415 399-1900
1676 N California Blvd Ste 300 Walnut Creek (94596) **(P-7703)**
Pacific Coast Building Products Inc (PA) .... C........ 916 631-6500
10600 White Rock Rd Ste 100 Rancho Cordova (95670) **(P-2715)**
Pacific Coast Chemicals Co., Berkeley Also Called: Hart Chemicals Inc **(P-6826)**
Pacific Coast Companies Inc .... C........ 916 631-6500
10811 International Dr Rancho Cordova (95670) **(P-13414)**
Pacific Coast Elevator Corp .... D........ 323 345-2550
3041 Roswell St Los Angeles (90065) **(P-13790)**
Pacific Coast Lacquer, Los Angeles Also Called: Berg Lacquer Co **(P-6883)**
Pacific Coast Ldscp MGT Inc .... D........ 925 513-2310
3960 Holway Dr Byron (94514) **(P-454)**
Pacific Coast Manor, Capitola Also Called: Covenant Care LLC **(P-15397)**
Pacific Coast Post Acute, Salinas Also Called: Salinasidence Opco LLC **(P-15793)**
Pacific Coast Producers .... C........ 209 365-9982
650 S Guild Ave Lodi (95240) **(P-13415)**
Pacific Coast Sales & Service Inc (PA) .... D........ 408 481-3600
310 Soquel Way Sunnyvale (94085) **(P-13728)**
Pacific Coast Services Inc .... D........ 209 956-2532
3202 W March Ln Ste D Stockton (95219) **(P-16906)**
Pacific Coast Sightseeing Tour .... C........ 714 507-1157
2001 S Manchester Ave Anaheim (92802) **(P-3965)**
Pacific Coast Supply LLC .... D........ 209 521-2466
1155 N Emerald Ave Modesto (95351) **(P-5223)**
Pacific Coast Trane Service Co, Sunnyvale Also Called: Pacific Coast Sales & Service Inc **(P-13728)**
Pacific Coast Tree Experts .... C........ 805 506-1211
21525 Strathern St Canoga Park (91304) **(P-560)**
Pacific Coast Warehouse Co, Newark Also Called: National Distribution Agcy Inc **(P-3734)**
Pacific Commerce Bank .... D........ 213 617-0082
420 E 3rd St Ste 100 Los Angeles (90013) **(P-7704)**
Pacific Compensation Insur Co .... C........ 818 575-8500
3011 Townsgate Rd Ste 120 Westlake Village (91361) **(P-8633)**
Pacific Concept Laundry, Los Angeles Also Called: E & C Fashion Inc **(P-13273)**
Pacific Consolidated Inds LLC .... C........ 951 479-0860
12201 Magnolia Ave Riverside (92503) **(P-2801)**
Pacific Contours Corporation .... D........ 714 693-1260
5340 E Hunter Ave Anaheim (92807) **(P-2992)**
Pacific Couriers, South El Monte Also Called: Integrated Parcel Network **(P-3616)**
Pacific Dental Services LLC (PA) .... B........ 714 845-8500
17000 Red Hill Ave Irvine (92614) **(P-15244)**
Pacific Dental Services LLC .... D........ 714 845-8500
17000 Red Hill Ave Irvine (92614) **(P-15245)**
Pacific Dntl Svcs Holdg Co Inc .... C........ 714 845-8500
17000 Red Hill Ave Irvine (92614) **(P-15246)**
Pacific Drayage Services LLC .... C........ 833 334-4622
550 W Artesia Blvd Compton (90220) **(P-3524)**
Pacific Echo Inc .... D........ 310 539-1822
23540 Telo Ave Torrance (90505) **(P-5917)**
Pacific Energy Fuels Company .... A........ 415 973-8200
77 Beale St Ste 100 San Francisco (94105) **(P-4599)**
Pacific Erth Rsrces Ltd A Cal (PA) .... D........ 805 986-8277
305 Hueneme Rd Camarillo (93012) **(P-145)**
Pacific Erth Rsrces Ltd A Cal .... D........ 209 892-3000
315 Hueneme Rd Camarillo (93012) **(P-146)**
Pacific Event Productions Inc .... C........ 858 458-9908
6989 Corte Santa Fe San Diego (92121) **(P-10567)**
Pacific Farms, Gerber Also Called: Pacific Farms and Orchards Inc **(P-111)**
Pacific Farms and Orchards Inc .... D........ 530 385-1475
22880 Gerber Rd Gerber (96035) **(P-111)**
Pacific Fire Safety, Pomona Also Called: Ferguson Fire Fabrication Inc **(P-5748)**
Pacific Fresh Seafood, Sacramento Also Called: Pacific Sfood - Sacramento LLC **(P-6425)**
Pacific Gardens, Santa Clara Also Called: Community Home Partners LLC **(P-15750)**
Pacific Gardens Med Ctr LLC .... C........ 562 860-0401
21530 Pioneer Blvd Hawaiian Gardens (90716) **(P-20168)**
Pacific Gas and Electric Co .... D........ 707 743-1197
16001 Powerhouse Rd Potter Valley (95469) **(P-4600)**
Pacific Gas and Electric Co .... C........ 916 275-2763
5555 Florin Perkins Rd Sacramento (95826) **(P-4601)**

ALPHABETIC SECTION

Pacific Hotel Management LLC

Pacific Gas and Electric Co .... B....... 925 779-7745
2111 Hillcrest Ave Antioch (94509) *(P-4602)*

Pacific Gas and Electric Co (HQ) .... A....... 415 973-7000
300 Lakeside Dr Oakland (94612) *(P-4603)*

Pacific Gas and Electric Co .... C....... 510 437-2222
6537 Foothill Blvd Oakland (94605) *(P-4604)*

Pacific Gas and Electric Co .... A....... 559 263-7361
650 O St Fresno (93721) *(P-4605)*

Pacific Gas and Electric Co .... B....... 209 942-1787
3136 Boeing Way # 2447a Stockton (95206) *(P-4606)*

Pacific Gas and Electric Co .... B....... 415 695-3513
2180 Harrison St San Francisco (94110) *(P-4607)*

Pacific Gas and Electric Co .... C....... 415 973-7000
425 Beck Ave Fairfield (94533) *(P-4608)*

Pacific Gas and Electric Co .... B....... 916 375-5005
885 Embarcadero Dr West Sacramento (95605) *(P-4609)*

Pacific Gas and Electric Co .... C....... 209 932-6550
Stockton (95201) *(P-4610)*

Pacific Gas and Electric Co .... A....... 209 726-7650
8 E River Park Pl W Fresno (93720) *(P-4611)*

Pacific Gas and Electric Co .... C....... 530 258-6215
350 Salem St Chico (95928) *(P-4612)*

Pacific Gas and Electric Co .... B....... 916 923-7007
2740 Gateway Oaks Dr Sacramento (95833) *(P-4613)*

Pacific Gas and Electric Co .... B....... 510 450-5744
4525 Hollis St Oakland (94608) *(P-4614)*

Pacific Gas and Electric Co .... D....... 650 592-9411
1970 Industrial Way Belmont (94002) *(P-4615)*

Pacific Gas and Electric Co .... D....... 707 579-6337
3965 Occidental Rd Santa Rosa (95401) *(P-4616)*

Pacific Gas and Electric Co .... C....... 650 513-0700
3400 Crow Canyon Rd San Ramon (94583) *(P-4617)*

Pacific Gas and Electric Co .... D....... 925 757-2000
777 Railroad Ave Pittsburg (94565) *(P-4618)*

Pacific Gas and Electric Co .... C....... 805 545-4562
4340 Old Santa Fe Rd San Luis Obispo (93401) *(P-4619)*

Pacific Gas and Electric Co .... C....... 800 743-5000
1220 Andersen Dr San Rafael (94901) *(P-4620)*

Pacific Gas and Electric Co .... D....... 209 942-5142
3955 Arch Rd Ste 100 Stockton (95215) *(P-4621)*

Pacific Gas and Electric Co .... C....... 707 765-5118
210 Corona Rd Petaluma (94954) *(P-4622)*

Pacific Gas and Electric Co .... C....... 530 229-4164
631 N Colusa St Willows (95988) *(P-4623)*

Pacific Gas and Electric Co .... B....... 800 756-7243
111 Stony Cir Santa Rosa (95401) *(P-4624)*

Pacific Gas and Electric Co .... C....... 925 676-0948
4690 Evora Rd Concord (94520) *(P-4625)*

Pacific Gas and Electric Co .... D....... 800 684-4648
3050 Geneva Ave Daly City (94014) *(P-4626)*

Pacific Gas and Electric Co .... D....... 800 684-4648
390 E Alisal St Salinas (93901) *(P-4627)*

Pacific Gas and Electric Co .... D....... 925 818-7082
1850 Gateway Blvd Fl 7 Concord (94520) *(P-4628)*

Pacific Gas and Electric Co .... D....... 559 891-2143
1745 2nd St Selma (93662) *(P-4629)*

Pacific Gas and Electric Co .... C....... 530 621-7237
4636 Missouri Flat Rd Placerville (95667) *(P-4630)*

Pacific Gas and Electric Co .... D....... 530 532-4093
1567 Huntoon St Oroville (95965) *(P-4631)*

Pacific Gas and Electric Co .... A....... 805 506-5280
9 Mi Nw Of Avila Bch Avila Beach (93424) *(P-4632)*

Pacific Gas and Electric Co .... D....... 530 389-2202
33995 Alta Bonny Nook Rd Alta (95701) *(P-4633)*

Pacific Gas and Electric Co .... A....... 530 365-7672
3600 Meadow View Dr Redding (96002) *(P-4634)*

Pacific Gas and Electric Co .... D....... 530 474-3333
31295 Manton Viola Rd Manton (96059) *(P-4635)*

Pacific Gas and Electric Co .... D....... 707 577-7283
3395 Mcmaude Pl Santa Rosa (95407) *(P-4636)*

Pacific Gas and Electric Co .... A....... 530 889-3102
12840 Bill Clark Way Auburn (95602) *(P-4637)*

Pacific Gas and Electric Co .... D....... 530 327-7633
202 Pearson Rd Paradise (95969) *(P-4638)*

Pacific Gas and Electric Co .... A....... 209 942-1523
4040 West Ln Stockton (95204) *(P-4639)*

Pacific Gas and Electric Co .... C....... 831 648-3231
2311 Garden Rd Monterey (93940) *(P-4640)*

Pacific Gas and Electric Co .... B....... 510 770-2025
42105 Boyce Rd Fremont (94538) *(P-4641)*

Pacific Gas and Electric Co .... B....... 707 444-0700
1000 King Salmon Ave Eureka (95503) *(P-4642)*

Pacific Gas and Electric Co .... C....... 559 855-6112
33755 Old Mill Rd Auberry (93602) *(P-4643)*

Pacific Gas and Electric Co .... D....... 209 826-5131
1028 6th St Los Banos (93635) *(P-4644)*

Pacific Gas and Electric Co .... C....... 760 253-2925
35863 Fairview Rd Hinkley (92347) *(P-4645)*

Pacific Gas and Electric Co .... B....... 209 576-6636
1524 N Carpenter Rd Modesto (95351) *(P-4646)*

Pacific Gas and Electric Co .... D....... 800 743-5000
811 W J St Oakdale (95361) *(P-4647)*

Pacific Gas and Electric Co .... C....... 530 896-4318
11239 Midway Chico (95928) *(P-4648)*

Pacific Gas and Electric Co .... B....... 559 263-7152
2221 S Orange Ave Fresno (93725) *(P-4649)*

Pacific Gas and Electric Co .... D....... 559 263-5438
502 E Grant Line Rd Tracy (95376) *(P-4650)*

Pacific Gas and Electric Co .... C....... 707 452-1983
5221 Quinn Rd Vacaville (95688) *(P-4651)*

Pacific Gas and Electric Co .... C....... 805 546-5267
800 Price Canyon Rd Pismo Beach (93449) *(P-4652)*

Pacific Gas and Electric Co .... C....... 925 373-2623
3797 1st St Livermore (94551) *(P-4653)*

Pacific Gas and Electric Co .... A....... 530 757-5803
316 L St Davis (95616) *(P-4654)*

Pacific Gas and Electric Co .... C....... 760 326-2615
145453 National Trails Hway Needles (92363) *(P-4655)*

Pacific Gas and Electric Co .... C....... 408 945-6215
66 Ranch Dr Milpitas (95035) *(P-4656)*

Pacific Gas and Electric Co .... C....... 209 295-2651
28570 Tiger Creek Rd Pioneer (95666) *(P-4657)*

Pacific Gas and Electric Co .... C....... 661 398-5918
4201 Arrow St Bakersfield (93308) *(P-4658)*

Pacific Gas and Electric Co .... D....... 805 434-4418
160 Cow Meadow Pl Templeton (93465) *(P-4659)*

Pacific Gas and Electric Co .... A....... 510 784-3253
24300 Clawiter Rd Hayward (94545) *(P-4723)*

Pacific Gas and Electric Co .... D....... 530 894-4739
460 Rio Lindo Ave Chico (95926) *(P-4724)*

Pacific Golf & Country Club .... D....... 949 498-6604
200 Avenida La Pata San Clemente (92673) *(P-14421)*

Pacific Grain & Foods LLC (PA) .... D....... 559 276-2580
4067 W Shaw Ave Ste 116 Fresno (93722) *(P-6693)*

Pacific Grain and Foods, Fresno *Also Called: Pacific Grain & Foods LLC (P-6693)*

Pacific Grdns Nrsing Rhblttion, Fresno *Also Called: Covenant Care California LLC (P-15403)*

Pacific Green Landscape Inc (PA) .... C....... 619 390-1546
8834 Winter Gardens Blvd Lakeside (92040) *(P-455)*

Pacific Groservice Inc .... B....... 408 727-4826
567 Cinnabar St San Jose (95110) *(P-6881)*

Pacific Gtwy Wrkfrce Prtnr Inc .... D....... 562 570-3700
4811 Airport Plaza Dr Ste 200 Long Beach (90815) *(P-11194)*

Pacific Haven Convalescent HM .... D....... 714 534-1942
12072 Trask Ave Garden Grove (92843) *(P-15887)*

Pacific Health and Wellness, Redondo Beach *Also Called: NBC Consulting Inc (P-20484)*

Pacific Health Corporation .... A....... 714 838-9600
14642 Newport Ave Tustin (92780) *(P-16303)*

Pacific Hmtlogy Oncology Assoc .... D....... 415 923-3012
2100 Webster St Ste 225 San Francisco (94115) *(P-14945)*

Pacific Homecare Services, Stockton *Also Called: Pacific Coast Services Inc (P-16906)*

Pacific Hotel Dev Ventr LP .... C....... 650 347-8250
625 El Camino Real Palo Alto (94301) *(P-10080)*

Pacific Hotel Management LLC .... C....... 510 547-7888
1603 Powell St Emeryville (94608) *(P-10081)*

Pacific Hotel Management LLC

ALPHABETIC SECTION

Pacific Hotel Management LLC .... C 510 791-7700
   39270 Cedar Blvd Newark (94560) *(P-10082)*

Pacific Hotel Management LLC .... C 510 262-0700
   3150 Garrity Way Richmond (94806) *(P-10083)*

Pacific Hotel Management LLC .... C 650 328-2800
   625 El Camino Real Palo Alto (94301) *(P-10084)*

Pacific Hotel Management Inc .... C 949 608-1091
   4545 Macarthur Blvd Newport Beach (92660) *(P-10085)*

Pacific Housing Group LLC .... D 559 651-1133
   1356 S Buttonwillow Ave Reedley (93654) *(P-7127)*

Pacific Housing Management (PA) .... D **714 508-1777**
   945 Katella St Laguna Beach (92651) *(P-9117)*

Pacific Huntington Hotel Corp .... A 626 568-3900
   1401 S Oak Knoll Ave Pasadena (91106) *(P-10086)*

Pacific Hydrotech Corporation .... C 951 943-8803
   314 E 3rd St Perris (92570) *(P-19347)*

Pacific Indemnity Company .... B 213 622-2334
   555 S Flower St Ste 300 Los Angeles (90071) *(P-8634)*

Pacific Industrial Electric, Brea *Also Called: Pacific Intl Elc Co Inc (P-1796)*

Pacific Insulation, Commerce *Also Called: Farwest Insulation Contracting (P-1928)*

Pacific Intl Elc Co Inc .... D 714 990-9280
   230 N Orange Ave Brea (92821) *(P-1796)*

Pacific Investment MGT Co LLC (DH) .... C **949 720-6000**
   650 Newport Center Dr Newport Beach (92660) *(P-9386)*

Pacific Life & Annuity Company .... A 949 219-3011
   700 Newport Center Dr Newport Beach (92660) *(P-8244)*

Pacific Life Fund Advisors LLC .... C 949 260-9000
   700 Newport Center Dr Newport Beach (92660) *(P-20169)*

Pacific Life Global Funding .... D 949 219-3011
   700 Newport Center Dr Newport Beach (92660) *(P-7901)*

Pacific Lodge Boy's Home, Woodland Hills *Also Called: Pacific Lodge Youth Svcs Inc (P-18502)*

Pacific Lodge Youth Svcs Inc .... C 818 347-1577
   4900 Serrania Ave Woodland Hills (91364) *(P-18502)*

Pacific Logistics Corp (PA) .... C **562 478-4700**
   7255 Rosemead Blvd Pico Rivera (90660) *(P-4069)*

Pacific Maritime Freight Inc .... D 562 590-8188
   1512 Pier C St Long Beach (90813) *(P-3823)*

PACIFIC MARITIME FREIGHT, INC., Long Beach *Also Called: Pacific Maritime Freight Inc (P-3823)*

Pacific Med Prsthtics Orthtics, Tracy *Also Called: Pacific Medical Inc (P-13416)*

Pacific Medical Inc (PA) .... D **800 726-9180**
   1700 N Chrisman Rd Tracy (95304) *(P-13416)*

Pacific Medical Group Inc .... D 949 493-1030
   212 Avenida Fabricante San Clemente (92672) *(P-5438)*

Pacific Metrics LLC .... C 831 646-6400
   1 Lower Ragsdale Dr Ste 150 Monterey (93940) *(P-20823)*

Pacific Metro Electric Inc .... D 209 939-3222
   3150 E Fremont St Stockton (95205) *(P-1797)*

Pacific Metro LLC (PA) .... B **408 201-5000**
   18715 Madrone Pkwy Morgan Hill (95037) *(P-18664)*

Pacific Mfg & Design LLC (PA) .... D **813 784-9958**
   13860 Stowe Dr Poway (92064) *(P-838)*

Pacific Monarch Resorts Inc (PA) .... D **949 609-2400**
   4000 Macarthur Blvd Ste 600 Newport Beach (92660) *(P-9118)*

Pacific Monarch Resorts Inc .... D 949 248-2944
   34630 Pacific Coast Hwy Capistrano Beach (92624) *(P-10087)*

Pacific Mortgage Resources, Walnut Creek *Also Called: Diablo Realty (P-8980)*

Pacific National Security Inc .... C 310 842-7073
   3719 Robertson Blvd Culver City (90232) *(P-13015)*

Pacific Natural Spices, Commerce *Also Called: Pacific Spice Company Inc (P-2440)*

Pacific Neuroscience Inst LLC .... D 310 829-8271
   2125 Arizona Ave Santa Monica (90404) *(P-18891)*

Pacific Outdoor Living, Sun Valley *Also Called: Pacific Pavingstone Inc (P-2142)*

Pacific Palms Healthcare LLC .... D 562 433-6791
   1020 Termino Ave Long Beach (90804) *(P-15615)*

Pacific Park, Santa Monica *Also Called: Santa Monica Amusements LLC (P-14313)*

Pacific Park Management .... D 415 440-4840
   1300 Fillmore St San Francisco (94115) *(P-20170)*

PACIFIC PARK MANAGEMENT, San Francisco *Also Called: Pacific Park Management (P-20170)*

Pacific Park Management Inc .... D 510 836-7730
   989 Franklin St Oakland (94607) *(P-13614)*

Pacific Partners MGT Svcs Inc .... D 650 358-5804
   1051 E Hillsdale Blvd Ste 750 Foster City (94404) *(P-20171)*

Pacific Partners MSI, Foster City *Also Called: Pacific Partners MGT Svcs Inc (P-20171)*

Pacific Parts International, Canoga Park *Also Called: Richard Huetter Inc (P-5057)*

Pacific Pavingstone Inc .... C 818 244-4000
   8309 Tujunga Ave Unit 201 Sun Valley (91352) *(P-2142)*

Pacific Petroleum California Inc .... B 805 925-1947
   1615 E Betteravia Rd Ste A Santa Maria (93454) *(P-625)*

Pacific Pioneer Insur Group (PA) .... D **714 228-7888**
   6363 Katella Ave Cypress (90630) *(P-8635)*

Pacific Place Retirement, Oceanside *Also Called: S L Start and Associates LLC (P-18517)*

Pacific Plms Conference Resort, City Of Industry *Also Called: Majestic Industry Hills LLC (P-9996)*

Pacific Precision Metals Inc .... C 951 226-1500
   1100 E Orangethorpe Ave Ste 253 Anaheim (92801) *(P-2753)*

Pacific Premier Bancorp Inc .... C 951 274-2400
   3403 10th St Ste 100 Riverside (92501) *(P-7705)*

Pacific Premier Bancorp Inc (PA) .... C **949 864-8000**
   17901 Von Karman Ave Ste 1200 Irvine (92614) *(P-7706)*

Pacific Premier Bank .... D 213 626-0085
   333 S Grand Ave Ste 3580 Los Angeles (90071) *(P-7707)*

Pacific Press, Anaheim *Also Called: Wasser Filtration Inc (P-2802)*

Pacific Process Systems Inc (PA) .... D **661 321-9681**
   7401 Rosedale Hwy Bakersfield (93308) *(P-626)*

Pacific Pulmonary Services Co, Petaluma *Also Called: Braden Prtners LP A Cal Ltd PR (P-5406)*

Pacific Racing Association .... C 510 559-7300
   1100 Eastshore Hwy Albany (94710) *(P-14166)*

Pacific Rebar Inc .... D 909 984-7199
   501 S Oaks Ave Ontario (91762) *(P-5505)*

Pacific Retirement Svcs Inc .... A 530 753-1450
   1515 Shasta Dr Ofc Davis (95616) *(P-18503)*

Pacific Rim Mech Contrs Inc .... C 714 285-2600
   1701 E Edinger Ave Ste F2 Santa Ana (92705) *(P-1522)*

Pacific Rim Mech Contrs Inc (PA) .... B **858 974-6500**
   9125 Rehco Rd San Diego (92121) *(P-1523)*

Pacific Sd/Pcfic Arbor Nrsries, Camarillo *Also Called: Pacific Erth Rsrces Ltd A Cal (P-145)*

Pacific Secured Equities Inc .... B 916 677-2500
   6020 West Oaks Blvd Ste 100 Rocklin (95765) *(P-20499)*

Pacific Select Distrs Inc .... D 949 219-3011
   700 Newport Center Dr Fl 4 Newport Beach (92660) *(P-8159)*

Pacific Service Credit Union (PA) .... D **888 858-6878**
   1355 Willow Way Ste 200 Concord (94520) *(P-7789)*

Pacific Sfood - Sacramento LLC .... C 916 419-5500
   1420 National Dr Sacramento (95834) *(P-6425)*

Pacific Shores Med Group Inc (HQ) .... D **562 590-0345**
   1043 Elm Ave Ste 104 Long Beach (90813) *(P-14946)*

Pacific Snow Valley Resort LLC .... D 909 866-3121
   40650 Village Dr Big Bear Lake (92315) *(P-10088)*

Pacific Sod, Camarillo *Also Called: Pacific Erth Rsrces Ltd A Cal (P-146)*

Pacific Spice Company Inc .... C 323 726-9190
   6430 E Slauson Ave Commerce (90040) *(P-2440)*

Pacific Steel Group .... B 858 449-7219
   2755 S Willow Ave Bloomington (92316) *(P-5506)*

Pacific Steel Group .... B 707 297-8922
   Bldg 411 Gilmore Ave Stockton (95203) *(P-5507)*

Pacific Sthwest Cnfrnce of Eva .... C 831 335-9133
   1050 Lockhart Gulch Rd Scotts Valley (95066) *(P-8742)*

Pacific Sthwest Structures Inc .... C 619 469-2323
   7845 Lemon Grove Way Ste A Lemon Grove (91945) *(P-2143)*

Pacific Strucframe LLC .... D 951 405-8536
   1600 Chicago Ave Ste R11 Riverside (92507) *(P-2075)*

Pacific Structures, Venice *Also Called: Pacific Structures Sc Inc (P-2144)*

Pacific Structures Sc Inc (PA) .... C **415 970-5434**
   1212 Abbot Kinney Blvd Apt A Venice (90291) *(P-2144)*

Pacific Suites Hotel, Santa Monica *Also Called: Windsor Capital Group Inc (P-10376)*

Pacific Supply, Orange *Also Called: Beacon Pacific Inc (P-5219)*

Pacific Supply, Modesto *Also Called: Pacific Coast Supply LLC (P-5223)*

ALPHABETIC SECTION — Pali Camp

Pacific Symphony .... D....... 714 755-5788
  17620 Fitch Ave Ste 100 Irvine (92614) *(P-14099)*

Pacific Systems Interiors Inc .... C....... 310 436-6820
  190 E Arrow Hwy Ste D San Dimas (91773) *(P-1953)*

Pacific Tech Solutions LLC .... C....... 949 830-1623
  15530 Rockfield Blvd Ste B4 Irvine (92618) *(P-11809)*

Pacific Towing, Stockton *Also Called: Covey Auto Express Inc (P-13712)*

Pacific Toxicology Labs .... D....... 818 598-3110
  9348 De Soto Ave Chatsworth (91311) *(P-16739)*

Pacific Trellis Fruit LLC (PA) .... C....... 323 859-9600
  2301 E 7th St Ste C200 Los Angeles (90023) *(P-6568)*

Pacific Trust Bank .... C....... 949 236-5211
  18500 Von Karman Ave Ste 1100 Irvine (92612) *(P-7745)*

Pacific Union Co .... D....... 415 789-8686
  1550 Tiburon Blvd Ste U Belvedere (94920) *(P-9119)*

Pacific Union Co .... D....... 415 474-6600
  1699 Van Ness Ave San Francisco (94109) *(P-9120)*

Pacific Union Co .... D....... 925 258-0090
  51 Moraga Way Ste 1 Orinda (94563) *(P-9121)*

Pacific Union Homes Inc (PA) .... D....... 925 314-3800
  675 Hartz Ave Ste 300 Danville (94526) *(P-9270)*

Pacific Union RE Group (DH) .... D....... 415 929-7100
  1699 Van Ness Ave # 2 San Francisco (94109) *(P-9122)*

Pacific Union Residential Brkg, Orinda *Also Called: Pacific Union Co (P-9121)*

Pacific Urethanes, Ontario *Also Called: Pacific Urethanes LLC (P-2471)*

Pacific Urethanes LLC .... C....... 909 390-8400
  1671 Champagne Ave Ste A Ontario (91761) *(P-2471)*

Pacific Utility Instllation Inc .... D....... 714 970-6430
  510 Malloy Ct Corona (92878) *(P-1798)*

Pacific Ventures Ltd .... C....... 626 576-0737
  2200 W Valley Blvd Alhambra (91803) *(P-20172)*

Pacific W Space Cmmnctions Inc .... D....... 909 592-4321
  900 W Gladstone St San Dimas (91773) *(P-1248)*

Pacific West Security Inc .... D....... 801 748-1034
  1587 Schallenberger Rd San Jose (95131) *(P-13136)*

Pacific West Tree Service, Vista *Also Called: Pac West Land Care Inc (P-453)*

Pacific Western Bank .... B....... 858 756-3023
  6110 El Tordo Rancho Santa Fe (92067) *(P-7636)*

Pacific World Corporation (PA) .... D....... 949 598-2400
  100 Technology Dr Ste 200 Irvine (92618) *(P-2630)*

Pacific Ygnacio Corporation .... C....... 925 939-3275
  201 California St Ste 500 San Francisco (94111) *(P-8890)*

Pacifica Companies, San Diego *Also Called: Pacifica Companies LLC (P-9475)*

Pacifica Companies LLC (PA) .... D....... 619 296-9000
  1775 Hancock St Ste 200 San Diego (92110) *(P-9475)*

Pacifica Emergency Med Assoc, Encino *Also Called: Emergent Medical Associates (P-14738)*

Pacifica Foods LLC .... C....... 951 371-3123
  1851 N Delilah St Corona (92879) *(P-2355)*

PACIFICA HOSPITAL OF THE VALLE, Sun Valley *Also Called: Pacifica of Valley Corporation (P-16304)*

Pacifica Hosts Inc .... D....... 310 670-9000
  6225 W Century Blvd Los Angeles (90045) *(P-10089)*

Pacifica Hosts Inc .... C....... 619 296-9000
  700 16th St Sacramento (95814) *(P-10090)*

Pacifica Hosts Inc .... C....... 858 755-1501
  710 Camino Del Mar Del Mar (92014) *(P-10091)*

Pacifica Hosts Inc .... D....... 858 792-8200
  717 S Highway 101 Solana Beach (92075) *(P-10092)*

Pacifica of Valley Corporation .... A....... 818 767-3310
  9449 San Fernando Rd Sun Valley (91352) *(P-16304)*

Pacifica Senior Living MGT LLC .... D....... 619 296-9000
  1775 Hancock St Ste 200 San Diego (92110) *(P-8852)*

Pacifica Services Inc .... D....... 626 405-0131
  106 S Mentor Ave Ste 200 Pasadena (91106) *(P-19348)*

Pacificare, Santa Ana *Also Called: Pacifcare Hlth Plan Admnstrtor (P-8350)*

Pacificare Health Systems, Cypress *Also Called: Uhc of California (P-8370)*

Pacificare Health Systems, Cypress *Also Called: Pacificare Health Systems LLC (P-16907)*

Pacificare Health Systems LLC (HQ) .... A....... 714 952-1121
  5995 Plaza Dr Cypress (90630) *(P-16907)*

Packaging Innovators LLC .... D....... 925 371-2000
  6850 Brisa St Livermore (94550) *(P-6089)*

Packard Childrens Hlth Aliance .... D....... 650 497-8000
  725 Welch Rd Palo Alto (94304) *(P-14947)*

Packeteer Inc .... B....... 408 220-2200
  420 N Mary Ave Sunnyvale (94085) *(P-12509)*

Paclo, Pico Rivera *Also Called: Pacific Logistics Corp (P-4069)*

Pacnet Services Usa Inc .... C....... 415 287-2500
  435 Harriet St Fl 2 San Francisco (94103) *(P-4326)*

Pactiv LLC .... C....... 562 693-1451
  12500 Slauson Ave Ste H1 Santa Fe Springs (90670) *(P-6934)*

Pactrack Inc .... D....... 213 201-5856
  11135 Rush St Ste A South El Monte (91733) *(P-4070)*

Pacwest Bancorp (PA) .... C....... 310 887-8500
  9701 Wilshire Blvd Ste 700 Beverly Hills (90212) *(P-7637)*

Pacwest Security Services .... C....... 909 948-0279
  2990 Inland Empire Blvd Ontario (91764) *(P-13016)*

Pacwest Security Services .... C....... 213 413-3500
  1545 Wilshire Blvd Ste 302 Los Angeles (90017) *(P-13017)*

PACWEST SECURITY SERVICES, Ontario *Also Called: Pacwest Security Services (P-13016)*

PACWEST SECURITY SERVICES, Los Angeles *Also Called: Pacwest Security Services (P-13017)*

Padi, Rcho Sta Marg *Also Called: Padi Americas Inc (P-18756)*

Padi Americas Inc .... C....... 949 858-7234
  30151 Tomas Rcho Sta Marg (92688) *(P-18756)*

Padilla Construction Company .... C....... 714 685-8500
  1620 N Brian St Orange (92867) *(P-1954)*

Padilla, David A MD, Roseville *Also Called: Sutter Valley Med Foundation (P-20222)*

Padre Dam Municipal Water Dst (PA) .... D....... 619 258-4617
  9300 Fanita Pkwy Santee (92071) *(P-4816)*

Padre Dam Municipal Water Dst .... D....... 619 258-4662
  9120 Carlton Oaks Dr Santee (92071) *(P-4817)*

Padres LP .... A....... 619 795-5000
  100 Park Blvd Petco Park San Diego (92101) *(P-14153)*

Pae Consulting Engineers Inc .... D....... 503 226-2921
  444 Spear St San Francisco (94105) *(P-19349)*

Pafco, Vernon *Also Called: Pacific American Fish Co Inc (P-2417)*

Paganini Companies, San Francisco *Also Called: Paganini Electric Corporation (P-1799)*

Paganini Electric Corporation .... C....... 415 575-3900
  190 Hubbell St Ste 200 San Francisco (94107) *(P-1799)*

Page Private School .... D....... 323 272-3429
  419 S Robertson Blvd Beverly Hills (90211) *(P-17738)*

Pagerduty, San Francisco *Also Called: Pagerduty Inc (P-12311)*

Pagerduty Inc (PA) .... A....... 844 800-3889
  600 Townsend St Ste 200 San Francisco (94103) *(P-12311)*

Paisley Crafts LLC .... C....... 559 291-4444
  5673 E Shields Ave Fresno (93727) *(P-5994)*

Paiute Palace Casino, Bishop *Also Called: Bishop Paiute Gaming Corp (P-9652)*

Pakedge Device & Software Inc .... C....... 714 880-4511
  17011 Beach Blvd Ste 600 Huntington Beach (92647) *(P-12312)*

Paklab, Chino *Also Called: Universal Packg Systems Inc (P-2633)*

Paklab, Chino *Also Called: Universal Packg Systems Inc (P-3776)*

PAKSN MANAGEMENT SERVICES, Manteca *Also Called: Karma Inc (P-15527)*

Pala Casino, Pala *Also Called: Pala Casino Spa & Resort (P-10093)*

Pala Casino Spa & Resort .... A....... 760 510-5100
  11154 Highway 76 Pala (92059) *(P-10093)*

Pala Mesa Limited Partnership .... C....... 760 728-5881
  2001 Old Highway 395 Fallbrook (92028) *(P-10094)*

Pala Mesa Resort, Fallbrook *Also Called: Pala Mesa Limited Partnership (P-10094)*

Palace of The Legion Honor, San Francisco *Also Called: Corportion of Fine Arts Mseums (P-18647)*

Paladin Private Security, Sacramento *Also Called: Paladin Prtction Spcalists Inc (P-13018)*

Paladin Prtction Spcalists Inc .... C....... 916 331-3175
  320 Commerce Cir Sacramento (95815) *(P-13018)*

Palanging International Inc .... C....... 619 948-2459
  861 Anchorage Pl Chula Vista (91914) *(P-9123)*

Palecek, Richmond *Also Called: Palecek Imports Inc (P-5099)*

Palecek Imports Inc (PA) .... D....... 510 236-7730
  601 Parr Blvd Richmond (94801) *(P-5099)*

Pali Adventures, Running Springs *Also Called: Pali Camp (P-10410)*

Pali Camp .... C....... 909 867-5743
  30778 Hwy 18 Running Springs (92382) *(P-10410)*

Palisades Group LLC   **ALPHABETIC SECTION**

Palisades Group LLC .... C...... 424 280-7560
   11755 Wilshire Blvd Ste 1700 Los Angeles (90025) *(P-8160)*
Palisades Ranch Inc .... B...... 323 581-6161
   5925 Alcoa Ave Vernon (90058) *(P-6275)*
Pall Fortebio LLC .... D...... 650 322-1360
   47661 Fremont Blvd Fremont (94538) *(P-19754)*
Palladium Valley Global Inc .... D...... 949 723-9613
   3857 Birch St Ste 9017 Newport Beach (92660) *(P-19841)*
Palm Canyon Resort & Spa, Palm Springs *Also Called: Diamond Resorts LLC (P-9742)*
Palm Desert Community Assn, Palm Desert *Also Called: Sun City Palm Dsert Cmnty Assn (P-18912)*
Palm Desert Greens Association .... D...... 760 346-8005
   73750 Country Club Dr Palm Desert (92260) *(P-18892)*
Palm Desert Hospitality LLC .... B...... 760 568-1600
   36999 Cook St Palm Desert (92211) *(P-10095)*
Palm Drive Healthcare District, Sebastopol *Also Called: County of Sonoma (P-16031)*
Palm Dsert Rcrtl Fclities Corp .... D...... 760 346-0015
   38995 Desert Willow Dr Palm Desert (92260) *(P-14280)*
PALM GROVE HEALTHCARE, Beaumont *Also Called: David-Kleis II LLC (P-17218)*
Palm Haven Care Center, Modesto *Also Called: Palm Haven Nursing & Rehab LLC (P-15616)*
Palm Haven Nursing & Rehab LLC .... C...... 209 823-1788
   4104 Fern Grove Ct Modesto (95356) *(P-15616)*
Palm Realty Boutique Inc .... D...... 310 545-2490
   401 Manhattan Beach Blvd Ste B Manhattan Beach (90266) *(P-9124)*
Palm Springs Art Museum Inc .... D...... 760 322-4800
   101 N Museum Dr Palm Springs (92262) *(P-18665)*
Palm Springs Convention Center, Palm Springs *Also Called: Smg Holdings LLC (P-20555)*
Palm Springs Disposal Services .... D...... 760 327-1351
   4690 E Mesquite Ave Palm Springs (92264) *(P-4917)*
Palm Springs Health Care Ctr, Palm Springs *Also Called: Mariner Health Care Inc (P-20145)*
Palm Springs Motors Inc .... C...... 760 699-6695
   69-200a Highway 111 Cathedral City (92234) *(P-7274)*
Palm Springs Renaissance, Palm Springs *Also Called: Remington Hotel Corporation (P-10148)*
Palm Sprng Ford Lncoln Mercury, Cathedral City *Also Called: Palm Springs Motors Inc (P-7274)*
Palm Ter Hlthcare Rhblttion Ct, Laguna Hills *Also Called: Gate Three Healthcare LLC (P-15490)*
Palm Valley School .... D...... 760 328-0861
   35525 Da Vall Dr Rancho Mirage (92270) *(P-17739)*
Palmcrest Grand Care Ctr Inc .... D...... 562 595-4551
   3501 Cedar Ave Long Beach (90807) *(P-15617)*
Palmcrest Medallion Convalesc .... D...... 562 595-4336
   3355 Pacific Pl Long Beach (90806) *(P-15618)*
Palmdale Water District .... D...... 661 947-4111
   2029 E Avenue Q Palmdale (93550) *(P-4818)*
Palmieri Tyler Wner Wlhelm Wld .... D...... 949 851-9400
   1900 Main St Ste 700 Irvine (92614) *(P-17599)*
Palo Alto Clinic, Palo Alto *Also Called: Sutter Bay Medical Foundation (P-15110)*
Palo Alto Community Child Care .... D...... 650 855-9828
   890 Escondido Rd Stanford (94305) *(P-18342)*
Palo Alto Hlls Golf Cntry CLB .... D...... 650 948-1800
   3000 Alexis Dr Palo Alto (94304) *(P-10568)*
Palo Alto Med Fndtion For Hlth, Santa Cruz *Also Called: Visiting Nrse Assn of Snta Cru (P-16964)*
Palo Alto Med Fndtion STA Cruz .... D...... 831 458-5670
   2025 Soquel Ave Santa Cruz (95062) *(P-14948)*
Palo Alto Medical Foundation .... A...... 650 321-4121
   795 El Camino Real Palo Alto (94301) *(P-14949)*
Palo Alto Medical Foundation, Palo Alto *Also Called: Chattopadhyay Runi MD (P-14678)*
Palo Alto Networks Inc (PA).. B...... 408 753-4000
   3000 Tannery Way Santa Clara (95054) *(P-2835)*
Palo Alto Nursing Center, Palo Alto *Also Called: Covenant Care California LLC (P-15400)*
Palo Alto Research Center Inc .... C...... 650 812-4000
   3333 Coyote Hill Rd Palo Alto (94304) *(P-19755)*
Palo Alto VA Medical Center, Palo Alto *Also Called: Veterans Health Administration (P-15188)*
Palo Alto Vineyard MGT LLC .... D...... 707 996-7725
   50 Adobe Canyon Rd Kenwood (95452) *(P-367)*
Palo Alto Vterans Inst For RES .... C...... 650 858-3970
   3801 Miranda Ave Bldg 101 Palo Alto (94304) *(P-19902)*

Palo Verde Health Care Dst .... C...... 760 922-4115
   250 N 1st St Blythe (92225) *(P-16305)*
Palo Verde Hospital, Blythe *Also Called: Palo Verde Health Care Dst (P-16305)*
Palo Verde Hospital Assn .... C...... 760 922-4115
   250 N 1st St Blythe (92225) *(P-16306)*
Palo Verde Irrigation District .... D...... 760 922-3144
   180 W 14th Ave Blythe (92225) *(P-4993)*
Palomar Health .... B...... 858 675-5218
   152255 Innovation Dr San Diego (92128) *(P-16307)*
Palomar Health (PA).. C...... 442 281-5000
   2125 Citracado Pkwy Ste 300 Escondido (92029) *(P-16308)*
Palomar Health .... A...... 760 739-3000
   15615 Pomerado Rd Poway (92064) *(P-16309)*
Palomar Health .... C...... 858 613-4000
   15615 Pomerado Rd Poway (92064) *(P-16310)*
Palomar Health .... C...... 760 740-6311
   800 W Valley Pkwy Ste 201 Escondido (92025) *(P-16689)*
Palomar Health Medical Group (HQ)... C...... 858 675-3100
   15611 Pomerado Rd Ste 575 Poway (92064) *(P-16311)*
Palomar Health Technology Inc .... C...... 442 281-5000
   2140 Enterprise St Escondido (92029) *(P-16312)*
Palomar Hlth Rhblttion Inst LL .... C...... 442 277-6100
   2181 Citracado Pkwy Escondido (92029) *(P-18076)*
Palomar Medical Center .... B...... 858 613-4000
   15615 Pomerado Rd Poway (92064) *(P-16313)*
Palomar Medical Center, Escondido *Also Called: Palomar Health (P-16308)*
Palomar Medical Center, Poway *Also Called: Palomar Health (P-16309)*
Palos Verdes Golf & Cntry CLB, Palos Verdes Estates *Also Called: Palos Verdes Golf Club (P-7521)*
Palos Verdes Golf Club .... D...... 310 375-2759
   3301 Via Campesina Palos Verdes Estates (90274) *(P-7521)*
Palp Inc .... C...... 562 599-5841
   2230 Lemon Ave Long Beach (90806) *(P-1151)*
Pam's Delivery Svc & Nat Msgnr, Compton *Also Called: Madden Corporation (P-3620)*
Pamc Ltd (PA) .... A...... 213 624-8411
   531 W College St Los Angeles (90012) *(P-16314)*
Pamc Health Foundation, Los Angeles *Also Called: Pamc Ltd (P-16314)*
Pamf - PA Division, Santa Clara *Also Called: Sutter Bay Medical Foundation (P-15108)*
Pampa Regional Medical Center, Ontario *Also Called: Prime Hlthcare Svcs - Pmpa LLC (P-16340)*
Pan American Bank Fsb .... B...... 949 224-1917
   18191 Von Karman Ave Ste 300 Irvine (92612) *(P-7746)*
Pan Pacific Petroleum Co Inc (PA).. D...... 562 928-0100
   9302 Garfield Ave South Gate (90280) *(P-3525)*
Pan Pacific Petroleum Co Inc .... D...... 661 589-3200
   1850 Coffee Rd Bakersfield (93308) *(P-3526)*
Pan Pacific San Diego, San Diego *Also Called: Pan Pcfic Htels Rsrts Amer Inc (P-10096)*
Pan Pcfic Htels Rsrts Amer Inc .... C...... 619 239-4500
   400 W Broadway San Diego (92101) *(P-10096)*
Pan-Pacific Mechanical, Fountain Valley *Also Called: Pan-Pacific Mechanical LLC (P-1524)*
Pan-Pacific Mechanical LLC (PA).. C...... 949 474-9170
   18250 Euclid St Fountain Valley (92708) *(P-1524)*
Pan-Pacific Mechanical LLC .... B...... 650 561-8810
   48363 Fremont Blvd Fremont (94538) *(P-1525)*
Pan-Pacific Mechanical LLC .... B...... 858 764-2464
   11622 El Camino Real Ste 100 San Diego (92130) *(P-1526)*
Pan-Pacific Plumbing & Mech, San Diego *Also Called: Pan-Pacific Mechanical LLC (P-1526)*
Pana-Pacific, Fresno *Also Called: Brix Group Inc (P-5635)*
Panalpina Inc .... D...... 310 819-4060
   19900 S Vermont Ave Ste A Torrance (90502) *(P-4071)*
Panamas Bar & Cafe, Chico *Also Called: 3-Downtown Bars Inc (P-10527)*
Panaroma Gardens, Panorama City *Also Called: Ensign Group Inc (P-15452)*
Panasas Inc (PA).. D...... 408 215-6800
   2680 N 1st St Ste 150 San Jose (95134) *(P-11810)*
Panasonic Avionics Corporation (DH).. B...... 949 672-2000
   3347 Michelson Dr Ste 100 Irvine (92612) *(P-19350)*
Panattoni Development Co Inc (PA).. D...... 916 381-1561
   2442 Dupont Dr Irvine (92612) *(P-9271)*
Panavision Group, Woodland Hills *Also Called: Panavision Inc (P-11049)*
Panavision Inc (PA).. A...... 818 316-1000
   6101 Variel Ave Woodland Hills (91367) *(P-11049)*

ALPHABETIC SECTION — Parc Waterworld LLC

Pancan, Manhattan Beach *Also Called: Pancrtic Cncer Action Ntwrk In (P-17292)*
Pancrtic Cncer Action Ntwrk In (PA) .... D 310 725-0025
  1500 Rosecrans Ave Ste 200 Manhattan Beach (90266) *(P-17292)*
Panda Express, South Pasadena *Also Called: Citadel Panda Express Inc (P-7467)*
Panda Express, Rosemead *Also Called: Panda Systems Inc (P-7501)*
Panda Systems Inc .... C 626 799-9898
  1683 Walnut Grove Ave Rosemead (91770) *(P-7501)*
Pandemic Studios LLC .... B 310 450-5199
  5510 Lincoln Blvd Los Angeles (90094) *(P-11811)*
Pandora, Oakland *Also Called: Pandora Media LLC (P-4400)*
Pandora Marketing LLC .... D 800 705-6856
  26970 Aliso Viejo Pkwy Ste 150 Aliso Viejo (92656) *(P-20500)*
Pandora Media LLC .... C 424 653-6803
  3000 Ocean Park Blvd Ste 3050 Santa Monica (90405) *(P-4399)*
Pandora Media LLC (DH) .... B 510 451-4100
  2100 Franklin St Ste 700 Oakland (94612) *(P-4400)*
Pango Group Inc .... D 818 502-0400
  6100 San Fernando Rd Glendale (91201) *(P-9125)*
Panoramic Doors LLC .... C 760 722-1300
  3265 Production Ave Ste A Oceanside (92058) *(P-5180)*
Pantheon Systems Inc (PA) .... D 855 927-9387
  717 California St San Francisco (94108) *(P-11812)*
Pantheon Ventures (us) LP .... C 415 249-6200
  555 California St Ste 3450 San Francisco (94104) *(P-8213)*
Pape Material Handling Inc .... D 562 692-9311
  2600 Peck Rd City Of Industry (90601) *(P-2779)*
Pape Material Handling Inc .... C 562 463-8000
  2615 Pellissier Pl City Of Industry (90601) *(P-5856)*
Pape Material Handling Inc .... D 510 659-4100
  47132 Kato Rd Fremont (94538) *(P-5857)*
Pape Trucks Inc .... D 559 268-4344
  2892 E Jensen Ave Fresno (93706) *(P-13669)*
Pape' Kenworth, Fresno *Also Called: Pape Trucks Inc (P-13669)*
Paper Company, The, Irvine *Also Called: Imperial Bag & Paper Co LLC (P-6079)*
Paper Mart Indus & Ret Packg, Orange *Also Called: Frick Paper Company LLC (P-6077)*
Papich Construction Co Inc (PA) .... D 805 473-3016
  398 Sunrise Ter Arroyo Grande (93420) *(P-706)*
Papola Enterprises Inc .... D 530 272-8885
  167 S Auburn St Grass Valley (95945) *(P-9126)*
Pappas & Co Inc .... C 559 233-1203
  181 Naples St Mendota (93640) *(P-193)*
Pappas Telecasting Company, Fresno *Also Called: Kmph Fox 26 (P-4445)*
Pappas Telecasting of The Midlands LP .... B 559 733-7800
  500 S Chinowth St Ste C Visalia (93277) *(P-4456)*
Paq Inc .... D 805 227-1660
  1465 Creston Rd Paso Robles (93446) *(P-7389)*
PAR Consulting LLC .... D 949 461-1140
  4500 Campus Dr Ste 380 Newport Beach (92660) *(P-7902)*
Par Services, Los Angeles *Also Called: Exceptional Chld Foundation (P-18229)*
PAR SERVICES, Culver City *Also Called: Exceptional Chld Foundation (P-18230)*
Par Western Line Contrs LLC .... A 760 737-0925
  11276 5th St Ste 100 Rancho Cucamonga (91730) *(P-13417)*
Para Sempre Inc .... D 310 444-0555
  11322 Idaho Ave Ste 202 Los Angeles (90025) *(P-20501)*
Paraccel Inc .... D 858 309-4733
  500 Arguello St Ste 200 Redwood City (94063) *(P-11813)*
Paraclsus Los Angles Cmnty Hos .... C 323 267-0477
  4081 E Olympic Blvd Los Angeles (90023) *(P-16315)*
Paracosma Inc .... D 650 924-9896
  2081 Norris Rd Walnut Creek (94596) *(P-11814)*
Parade Technologies Inc .... D 408 329-5540
  2720 Orchard Pkwy San Jose (95134) *(P-5687)*
Paradigm, Beverly Hills *Also Called: Paradigm Music LLC (P-14051)*
Paradigm Hotels Group LLC .... D 415 534-6500
  250 4th St San Francisco (94103) *(P-10097)*
Paradigm Industries Inc .... D 310 965-1900
  2522 E 37th St Vernon (90058) *(P-13418)*
Paradigm Music LLC (PA) .... D 310 288-8000
  360 N Crescent Dr Beverly Hills (90210) *(P-14051)*
Paradigm Talent Agency LLC .... D 310 288-8000
  6725 W Sunset Blvd Los Angeles (90028) *(P-14052)*

Paradise Ambulance Service, Chico *Also Called: First Responder Ems Inc (P-3262)*
Paradise Electric Inc .... B 619 449-4141
  697 Greenfield Dr El Cajon (92021) *(P-1800)*
Paradise Hotel Inc .... D 805 687-6444
  2819 State St Santa Barbara (93105) *(P-10098)*
Paradise Lessee Inc .... B 858 274-4630
  1404 Vacation Rd San Diego (92109) *(P-10099)*
Paradise Lingerie Inc .... D 818 717-9717
  20830 Dearborn St Chatsworth (91311) *(P-6214)*
Paradise Point Resort, San Diego *Also Called: Westgroup San Diego Associates (P-10363)*
Paradise Point Resort & Spa, San Diego *Also Called: Paradise Lessee Inc (P-10099)*
Paradise Ridge Fmly Resources, Chico *Also Called: Youth For Change (P-18197)*
PARADISE VALLEY ESTATES, Fairfield *Also Called: Northern CA Retiredd Ofcrs (P-18495)*
Paradise Valley Hospital (PA) .... A 619 470-4100
  2400 E 4th St National City (91950) *(P-16316)*
Paradise Valley Hospital .... B 619 472-7474
  180 Otay Lakes Rd Ste 100 Bonita (91902) *(P-16317)*
Paradise Valley Manor, National City *Also Called: Sterling Care Inc (P-15681)*
Parafin Inc .... D 646 919-0669
  301 Howard St Ste 1500 San Francisco (94105) *(P-11815)*
Paragon Biomedical Inc .... D 949 224-2800
  9685 Research Dr Irvine (92618) *(P-19842)*
Paragon Industries Inc .... D 714 778-1800
  1515 E Winston Rd Anaheim (92805) *(P-7112)*
Paragon Laboratories, Torrance *Also Called: Naturalife Eco Vite Labs (P-2348)*
Paragon Legal, San Francisco *Also Called: Paragon Legal Group LLC (P-17600)*
Paragon Legal Group LLC .... C 415 738-7870
  601 Montgomery St Ste 2030 San Francisco (94111) *(P-17600)*
Paragon Mechanical Inc .... C 408 727-7303
  16160 Caputo Dr Morgan Hill (95037) *(P-1527)*
Paragon Partners Cons Inc (PA) .... D 714 379-3376
  5660 Katella Ave Ste 100 Cypress (90630) *(P-20824)*
Paragon Services Engineering, San Diego *Also Called: San Diego Services LLC (P-19382)*
Paragon Textiles Inc .... D 310 323-7500
  13003 S Figueroa St Los Angeles (90061) *(P-6215)*
Parakeet Logistics Inc .... C 209 353-1818
  1112 N Main St # 417 Manteca (95336) *(P-4072)*
Parallel Domain Inc .... D 585 943-8571
  44 Montgomery St Ste 300 San Francisco (94104) *(P-11816)*
Paramount Citrus, Delano *Also Called: Wonderful Company LLC (P-103)*
Paramount Citrus Packing Co, Delano *Also Called: Wonderful Citrus Packing LLC (P-316)*
Paramount Equity, Roseville *Also Called: Goodleap LLC (P-7974)*
Paramount Home Care Inc .... D 714 994-1250
  12235 Beach Blvd Ste 102 Stanton (90680) *(P-16908)*
Paramount Investigations, San Jose *Also Called: Yosh Enterprises Inc (P-13080)*
Paramount Pictures, Los Angeles *Also Called: Paramount Television Service (P-13874)*
Paramount Pictures Corporation (HQ) .... A 323 956-5000
  5555 Melrose Ave Los Angeles (90038) *(P-13873)*
Paramount Properties, Beverly Hills *Also Called: Rodeo Realty Inc (P-9170)*
Paramount Studios, Los Angeles *Also Called: Paramount Pictures Corporation (P-13873)*
Paramount Swap Meet, Paramount *Also Called: Modern Dev Co A Ltd Partnr (P-13379)*
Paramount Television Service .... A 323 956-5000
  5555 Melrose Ave Rm 204 Los Angeles (90038) *(P-13874)*
Paramount Theatre of Arts Inc .... D 510 893-2300
  2025 Broadway Oakland (94612) *(P-14053)*
Paramout Farms, Lost Hills *Also Called: Roll Properties Intl Inc (P-9556)*
Paramunt Ovrseas Prdctions Inc .... A 323 956-5225
  5515 Melrose Ave Los Angeles (90038) *(P-13875)*
Paratransit Incorporated (PA) .... C 916 429-2009
  2501 Florin Rd Sacramento (95822) *(P-3285)*
Parc, Palo Alto *Also Called: Palo Alto Research Center Inc (P-19755)*
Parc 55 Hotel, San Francisco *Also Called: Rp/Kinetic Parc 55 Owner LLC (P-10179)*
Parc 55 Lessee LLC .... D 415 392-8000
  55 Cyril Magnin St San Francisco (94102) *(P-10100)*
Parc Management LLC .... C 925 609-1364
  1950 Waterworld Pkwy Concord (94520) *(P-14550)*
Parc Specialty Contractors .... D 916 992-5405
  1400 Vinci Ave Sacramento (95838) *(P-2304)*
Parc Waterworld LLC .... C 925 609-1364
  1950 Waterworld Pkwy Concord (94520) *(P-14308)*

Pardee Tree Nursery .... D....... 760 630-5400
  30970 Via Puerta Del Sol Oceanside (92057) *(P-6871)*

Parent Is Sitecore USA Holding, San Francisco *Also Called: Sitecore Usa Inc (P-12351)*

Parentals Place Parent Educatn, San Rafael *Also Called: Jewish Family and Chld Svcs (P-18026)*

Parentsquare Inc .... D....... 888 496-3168
  6144 Calle Real Ste 200a Goleta (93117) *(P-12313)*

Pareto Networks Inc .... B....... 877 727-8020
  1183 Bordeaux Dr Ste 22 Sunnyvale (94089) *(P-4327)*

Parexel International Corp .... C....... 818 254-7076
  1560 E Chevy Chase Dr Ste 140 Glendale (91206) *(P-19756)*

PAREXEL INTERNATIONAL CORPORATION, Glendale *Also Called: Parexel International Corp (P-19756)*

Paribas Asset Management Inc .... C....... 415 772-1300
  1 Front St 23rd Fl San Francisco (94111) *(P-7836)*

Parisa Lingerie & Swim Wear, Calabasas *Also Called: Afr Apparel International Inc (P-2462)*

Park Central Ht San Francisco, San Francisco *Also Called: Viva Soma Lessee Inc (P-20246)*

Park Cleaners Inc (PA) .... D....... 626 281-5942
  419 Mcgroarty St San Gabriel (91776) *(P-10454)*

Park Hotels & Resorts Inc .... D....... 714 990-6000
  900 E Birch St Brea (92821) *(P-10101)*

Park Hotels & Resorts Inc .... C....... 510 635-5000
  1 Hegenberger Rd Oakland (94621) *(P-10102)*

Park Hotels & Resorts Inc .... D....... 415 771-1400
  333 Ofarrell St San Francisco (94102) *(P-10103)*

Park Hotels & Resorts Inc .... C....... 310 415-3340
  9876 Wilshire Blvd Beverly Hills (90210) *(P-10104)*

Park Kngsburg Snior Apartments, Kingsburg *Also Called: Michaels Mngmnt-Affordable LLC (P-8843)*

Park Landscape Maint 1-2-3-4, Rcho Sta Marg *Also Called: Park West Landscape Maint Inc (P-528)*

Park Lane, The, Monterey *Also Called: P Monterey LP (P-8851)*

Park Management Corp .... C....... 707 643-6722
  1001 Fairgrounds Dr Vallejo (94589) *(P-14309)*

Park Management Group LLC .... A....... 404 350-9990
  1825 Gillespie Wy Ste 101 North Hollywood (91601) *(P-10105)*

Park Manor Suites, San Diego *Also Called: Gentry Associates LLC (P-9809)*

Park Marino Convalescent Ctr .... C....... 626 463-4105
  2585 E Washington Blvd Pasadena (91107) *(P-15888)*

Park Newport Apartments, Newport Beach *Also Called: Park Newport Ltd (P-8853)*

Park Newport Ltd (PA) .... D....... 949 644-1900
  1 Park Newport Newport Beach (92660) *(P-8853)*

Park Place Ford LLC .... D....... 909 946-5555
  555 W Foothill Blvd Upland (91786) *(P-7275)*

Park Regency Inc .... D....... 818 363-6116
  10146 Balboa Blvd Granada Hills (91344) *(P-9127)*

Park Regency Club Apts, Downey *Also Called: PRC Multi-Family LLC (P-8854)*

Park Shadelands Medical Offs, Walnut Creek *Also Called: Kaiser Foundation Hospitals (P-16156)*

Park Uniform Rentals, San Gabriel *Also Called: Park Cleaners Inc (P-10454)*

Park US Lessee Holdings LLC .... D....... 707 887-7838
  1 Doubletree Dr Rohnert Park (94928) *(P-10106)*

Park View Gardens, Santa Rosa *Also Called: Ensign Group Inc (P-15454)*

Park Vista At Morningside, Fullerton *Also Called: Corecare V A Cal Ltd Partnr (P-15388)*

Park West Landscape Inc .... D....... 310 363-4100
  13105 Crenshaw Blvd Hawthorne (90250) *(P-527)*

Park West Landscape Maint Inc (PA) .... B....... 949 546-8300
  22421 Gilberto Ste A Rcho Sta Marg (92688) *(P-528)*

Parkco Building Company .... D....... 714 444-1441
  24795 State Highway 74 Perris (92570) *(P-983)*

Parker Mllken Clark Ohara Smli .... D....... 818 784-8087
  555 S Flower St 30th Fl Los Angeles (90071) *(P-17601)*

Parker Palm Springs LLC .... D....... 760 770-5000
  4200 E Palm Canyon Dr Palm Springs (92264) *(P-10107)*

Parker Stanbury LLP (PA) .... D....... 619 528-1259
  444 S Flower St Ste 1900 Los Angeles (90071) *(P-17602)*

Parker Station, Calabasas *Also Called: Guarachi Wine Partners Inc (P-6797)*

Parker-Hannifin Corporation .... C....... 949 465-4519
  14300 Alton Pkwy Irvine (92618) *(P-5858)*

Parkhouse Tire, Bell Gardens *Also Called: Parkhouse Tire Service Inc (P-7354)*

Parkhouse Tire Service Inc (PA) .... D....... 562 928-0421
  6006 Shull St Bell Gardens (90201) *(P-7354)*

Parkhurst Terrace .... D....... 831 685-0800
  100 Parkhurst Cir Aptos (95003) *(P-768)*

Parking Company of America .... D....... 562 862-2118
  3165 Garfield Ave Commerce (90040) *(P-13615)*

Parking Concepts Inc .... D....... 626 577-8963
  33 E Green St Pasadena (91105) *(P-13616)*

Parking Concepts Inc .... D....... 714 543-5725
  1020 W Civic Center Dr Santa Ana (92703) *(P-13617)*

Parking Concepts Inc .... D....... 925 944-1964
  2999 Oak Rd Walnut Creek (94597) *(P-13618)*

Parking Concepts Inc .... D....... 415 553-6883
  25 Division St Ste 107 San Francisco (94103) *(P-13619)*

Parking Concepts Inc .... D....... 310 208-1611
  1036 Broxton Ave Los Angeles (90024) *(P-13620)*

Parking Concepts Inc .... C....... 213 746-5764
  1801 Georgia St Los Angeles (90015) *(P-13621)*

Parking Concepts Inc .... D....... 310 821-1081
  14110 Palawan Way Venice (90292) *(P-13622)*

Parking Concepts Inc .... D....... 213 623-2661
  800 Wilshire Blvd Los Angeles (90017) *(P-13623)*

Parking Concepts Inc .... D....... 310 322-5008
  12001 Vista Del Mar Playa Del Rey (90293) *(P-13624)*

Parking Network Inc .... C....... 213 613-1500
  1625 W Olympic Blvd Los Angeles (90015) *(P-2305)*

Parking Spot, The, Los Angeles *Also Called: Tps Parking Management LLC (P-13629)*

Parkinsons Institute .... D....... 650 770-0201
  2500 Hospital Dr Bldg 10 Mountain View (94040) *(P-19903)*

Parkmerced Apartment Community, San Francisco *Also Called: Parkmerced Management Corp (P-9128)*

Parkmerced Management Corp .... D....... 415 405-4600
  3711 19th Ave San Francisco (94132) *(P-9128)*

Parks & Recreation Dept, Canoga Park *Also Called: County of Los Angeles (P-10400)*

Parks and Recreation Dept, Pomona *Also Called: County of Los Angeles (P-14253)*

Parks and Recreation Dept, Citrus Heights *Also Called: County of Sacramento (P-18846)*

Parkside Health & Wellness Ctr, El Cajon *Also Called: Parkside Healthcare Inc (P-15783)*

Parkside Healthcare Inc .... D....... 619 442-7744
  444 W Lexington Ave El Cajon (92020) *(P-15783)*

Parkside Lending LLC .... D....... 415 771-3700
  180 Redwood St Ste 250 San Francisco (94102) *(P-8008)*

PARKTREE COMMUNITY HEALTH CENT, Pomona *Also Called: Pomona Community Health Center (P-18757)*

Parkview Cmnty Hosp Med Ctr .... A....... 951 354-7404
  3865 Jackson St Riverside (92503) *(P-16318)*

Parkview Healthcare Center, Hayward *Also Called: Mariner Health Care Inc (P-15566)*

Parkview Jlian Cnvlescent Hosp .... C....... 661 831-9150
  1801 Julian Ave Bakersfield (93304) *(P-15619)*

Parkview Julian LLC .... C....... 661 831-9150
  1801 Julian Ave Bakersfield (93304) *(P-15620)*

Parkview Julian Healthcare Ctr, Bakersfield *Also Called: Parkview Julian LLC (P-15620)*

Parkway Bowl, El Cajon *Also Called: Newport Diversified Inc (P-13395)*

Parkwood Landscape Maint Inc .... D....... 818 988-9677
  16443 Hart St Van Nuys (91406) *(P-529)*

Parron Hall Office Interiors, San Diego *Also Called: Parron-Hall Corporation (P-5100)*

Parron-Hall Corporation .... D....... 858 268-1212
  9655 Granite Ridge Dr Ste 100 San Diego (92123) *(P-5100)*

Parrott & Co, Livermore *Also Called: New Parrott & Co (P-6803)*

PARSONS, Pasadena *Also Called: Parsons Constructors Inc (P-20173)*

Parsons Constructors Inc .... A....... 626 440-2000
  100 W Walnut St Pasadena (91103) *(P-20173)*

Parsons Engrg Science Inc (DH) .... B....... 626 440-2000
  100 W Walnut St Pasadena (91103) *(P-19351)*

Parsons Government Svcs Inc .... B....... 619 685-0085
  525 B St Ste 1600 San Diego (92101) *(P-19352)*

Parsons Intl Cayman Islands .... A....... 626 440-6000
  100 W Walnut St Pasadena (91124) *(P-19353)*

Parsons Service Corporation .... A....... 626 440-2000
  100 W Walnut St Pasadena (91124) *(P-19354)*

Parsons Wtr Infrastructure Inc .... D....... 626 440-7000
  100 W Walnut St Pasadena (91124) *(P-19355)*

ALPHABETIC SECTION — Paul Ryan Associates

Parter Medical Products Inc .... C....... 310 327-4417
17015 Kingsview Ave Carson (90746) *(P-5439)*

Parthenon Capital LLC .... A....... 415 913-3900
4 Embarcadero Ctr Ste 2500 San Francisco (94111) *(P-9549)*

Parthenon-Ey .... D....... 617 478-2550
555 California St Ste 4375 San Francisco (94104) *(P-8743)*

Participant Channel Inc .... D....... 310 550-7715
331 Foothill Rd Fl 3 Beverly Hills (90210) *(P-4457)*

Partner Printing, Glendale *Also Called: Colour Concepts Inc (P-2559)*

Partners Capital Group, Santa Ana *Also Called: Partners Capital Group Inc (P-13419)*

Partners Capital Group Inc (PA) .... D....... 949 916-3900
201 Sandpointe Ave Ste 500 Santa Ana (92707) *(P-13419)*

Partners Federal Credit Union (PA) .... D....... 800 948-6677
100 N First St Ste 400 Burbank (91502) *(P-7790)*

Partners Information Tech (HQ) .... D....... 714 736-4487
888 S Disneyland Dr Ste 500 Anaheim (92802) *(P-12853)*

Partners Prsnnel - MGT Svcs LL .... A....... 805 689-8191
3820 State St Ste B Santa Barbara (93105) *(P-11195)*

Partnership Health Plan Cal .... B....... 707 863-4100
4665 Business Center Dr Fairfield (94534) *(P-8351)*

Partnership Staffing Solutions, Santa Clarita *Also Called: Partnership Staffing Svcs Inc (P-11196)*

Partnership Staffing Svcs Inc .... A....... 661 542-7074
19431 Soledad Canyon Rd A3 Santa Clarita (91351) *(P-11196)*

Partnerstack Inc .... C....... 619 648-4388
1049 El Monte Ave Ste C # 512 Mountain View (94040) *(P-11817)*

Parts Authority LLC .... C....... 805 676-3410
4277 Transport St Ventura (93003) *(P-5053)*

Pasadena Center Operating Co .... C....... 626 795-9311
300 E Green St Pasadena (91101) *(P-13420)*

Pasadena Convention Center, Pasadena *Also Called: Pasadena Center Operating Co (P-13420)*

Pasadena Hospital Assn Ltd .... B....... 626 397-3322
716 S Fair Oaks Ave Pasadena (91105) *(P-15621)*

Pasadena Hospital Assn Ltd (PA) .... A....... 626 397-5000
100 W California Blvd Pasadena (91105) *(P-16319)*

Pasadena Hotel Dev Ventr LP .... D....... 626 449-4000
303 Cordova St Pasadena (91101) *(P-10108)*

Pasadena Humane Society .... D....... 626 792-7151
361 S Raymond Ave Pasadena (91105) *(P-19096)*

Pasadena Madows Nursing Ctr LP .... D....... 626 796-1103
150 Bellefontaine St Pasadena (91105) *(P-15622)*

Pasadena Newspapers Inc (PA) .... C....... 626 578-6300
605 E Huntington Dr Ste 100 Monrovia (91016) *(P-2541)*

Pasadena Star-News, Monrovia *Also Called: Pasadena Newspapers Inc (P-2541)*

Pasadera Club Oc LLC .... D....... 831 647-2400
100 Pasadera Dr Monterey (93940) *(P-14422)*

Pasco Scientific (PA) .... C....... 916 786-3800
10101 Foothills Blvd Roseville (95747) *(P-3031)*

Pasco Scientific, Roseville *Also Called: Pasco Scientific (P-3031)*

Pasea Hotel & Spa, Huntington Beach *Also Called: Pacific City Hotel LLC (P-10079)*

Pasha Freight, San Rafael *Also Called: Pasha Group (P-4073)*

Pasha Group (PA) .... B....... 415 927-6400
4040 Civic Center Dr Ste 350 San Rafael (94903) *(P-4073)*

Pasha Hawaii Trnspt Lines LLC .... D....... 510 271-1400
1425 Maritime St Oakland (94607) *(P-3799)*

Paskenta Band Nomlaki Indians .... B....... 530 670-1750
22580 Olivewood Rd Corning (96021) *(P-20927)*

Passages, Malibu *Also Called: Grasshopper House Partners LLC (P-17994)*

Passages Malibu .... D....... 888 777-8525
6428 Meadows Ct Malibu (90265) *(P-17106)*

Passages Mlibu DRG Rhab Alchol, Malibu *Also Called: Passages Malibu (P-17106)*

Passport To Learning Inc .... D....... 661 538-9200
41319 12th St W Palmdale (93551) *(P-5440)*

PASSPORT TO LEARNING INCORPORATED, Palmdale *Also Called: Passport To Learning Inc (P-5440)*

Pasta Shop (PA) .... D....... 510 250-6005
5655 College Ave Ste 201 Oakland (94618) *(P-6656)*

Patelco Credit Union (PA) .... C....... 800 358-8228
3 Park Pl Dublin (94568) *(P-7791)*

Patent and Trademark Office US .... B....... 831 332-7127
26 S 4th St San Jose (95112) *(P-7734)*

Pater Dignitas Inc .... D....... 831 624-1875
23795 Holman Hwy Monterey (93940) *(P-15623)*

Path .... A....... 323 644-2216
340 N Madison Ave Los Angeles (90004) *(P-18077)*

Pathfinder Services, Folsom *Also Called: Location Services LLC (P-4166)*

Pathlab, Salinas *Also Called: Unilab Corporation (P-16765)*

Pathnostics, Irvine *Also Called: Cap Diagnostics LLC (P-16708)*

Pathology Associates .... D....... 559 326-2800
305 Park Creek Dr Clovis (93611) *(P-16690)*

Pathology Inc .... B....... 310 769-0561
19951 Mariner Ave Ste 150 Torrance (90503) *(P-20502)*

Pathpoint Inc .... D....... 914 500-7154
548 Market St San Francisco (94104) *(P-8636)*

Pathpoint Insurance Services, San Francisco *Also Called: Pathpoint Inc (P-8636)*

Pathstone Family Office LLC .... D....... 888 750-7284
1900 Avenue Of The Stars Ste 970 Los Angeles (90067) *(P-9129)*

Pathstone Federal Street, Los Angeles *Also Called: Pathstone Family Office LLC (P-9129)*

Pathways Home Health .... D....... 650 634-0133
395 Oyster Point Blvd Ste 128 South San Francisco (94080) *(P-17293)*

Patient Accounting, Sunnyvale *Also Called: Sutter Bay Medical Foundation (P-15107)*

Patient Business Services, San Diego *Also Called: Palomar Health (P-16307)*

Patient Home Monitoring Inc .... C....... 415 693-9690
550 Kearny St Ste 300 San Francisco (94108) *(P-16909)*

Patients Hospital .... D....... 530 225-8700
2900 Eureka Way Redding (96001) *(P-16320)*

Patpat, Sunnyvale *Also Called: Interfocus Inc (P-6200)*

Patra Corporation (PA) .... D....... 415 595-9987
1107 Investment Blvd Ste 100 El Dorado Hills (95762) *(P-8245)*

Patreon Inc (PA) .... C....... 415 967-2735
600 Townsend St Ste 500 San Francisco (94103) *(P-11818)*

Patric Communications Inc (PA) .... D....... 619 579-2898
15215 Alton Pkwy Ste 200 Irvine (92618) *(P-1801)*

Patrick K Willis and Co Inc .... B....... 800 398-6480
5118 Robert J Mathews Pkwy El Dorado Hills (95762) *(P-13421)*

Patricks Construction Clean-Up .... D....... 916 452-5495
7851 14th Ave Sacramento (95826) *(P-1313)*

Patriot Brokerage Inc .... D....... 910 227-4142
7840 Foothill Blvd Ste H Sunland (91040) *(P-4074)*

Patriot Contract Services LLC .... B....... 925 296-2000
1320 Willow Pass Rd Ste 485 Concord (94520) *(P-3798)*

Patriot Logistics Services LLC .... D....... 443 994-9660
1520 Independence Way Vista (92084) *(P-4170)*

Patriot Memory, Fremont *Also Called: Patriot Memory Inc (P-2929)*

Patriot Memory Inc (PA) .... C....... 510 979-1021
47027 Benicia St Fremont (94538) *(P-2929)*

Patriot Wastewater LLC .... C....... 714 921-4545
314 W Freedom Ave Orange (92865) *(P-20825)*

Patrol and Security Services, Los Angeles *Also Called: Guardian Intl Solutions (P-12984)*

Patrol Black Knight Inc .... D....... 213 985-6499
505 S Pacific Ave Unit 201 San Pedro (90731) *(P-13019)*

Patrol Solutions LLC .... C....... 916 919-6079
6060 Sunrise Vista Dr Ste 1500 Citrus Heights (95610) *(P-13020)*

Patron Solutions LLC .... C....... 949 823-1700
5171 California Ave Ste 200 Irvine (92617) *(P-12314)*

Patton State Hospital, Patton *Also Called: Califrnia Dept State Hospitals (P-16644)*

Pauba Valley Elem. School, Temecula *Also Called: Temecula Vly Unified Schl Dst (P-17753)*

Paul Graham Drilling, Rio Vista *Also Called: Paul Graham Drilling & Svc Co (P-595)*

Paul Graham Drilling & Svc Co .... C....... 707 374-5123
2500 Airport Rd Rio Vista (94571) *(P-595)*

Paul Hastings LLP (PA) .... A....... 213 683-6000
515 S Flower St Fl 25 Los Angeles (90071) *(P-17603)*

Paul Hastings LLP .... D....... 858 458-3000
4747 Executive Dr Ste 1200 San Diego (92121) *(P-17604)*

Paul Hastings LLP .... D....... 415 856-7000
101 California St San Francisco (94111) *(P-17605)*

Paul Mitchell, Santa Clarita *Also Called: Paul Mitchell John Systems (P-6137)*

Paul Mitchell John Systems (PA) .... D....... 800 793-8790
20705 Centre Pointe Pkwy Santa Clarita (91350) *(P-6137)*

Paul Ryan Associates .... D....... 415 861-3085
200 Gate 5 Rd Ste 113 Sausalito (94965) *(P-707)*

Pauls Tv LLC .... D....... 949 596-8800
900 Glenneyre St Laguna Beach (92651) *(P-5609)*

Paulus Engineering Inc .... D....... 714 632-3322
2871 E Coronado St Anaheim (92806) *(P-1249)*

Pauma Band of Mission Indians .... B....... 760 742-2177
777 Pauma Reservation Rd Pauma Valley (92061) *(P-10109)*

Pave, San Francisco *Also Called: Trove Information Tech Inc (P-11990)*

Pavement Coatings Co .... C....... 805 647-0693
736 Mission Rock Rd Santa Paula (93060) *(P-4918)*

Pavement Coatings Co, Santa Paula *Also Called: Pavement Coatings Co (P-4918)*

Pavement Recycling Systems Inc .... D....... 661 948-5599
48028 90th St W Lancaster (93536) *(P-2650)*

Pavement Recycling Systems Inc (PA) .... C....... 951 682-1091
10240 San Sevaine Way Jurupa Valley (91752) *(P-6012)*

Pavex Construction Company, Redwood City *Also Called: Granite Rock Co (P-1114)*

Pavilion At Ocean Point, The, San Diego *Also Called: Point Loma Rhblitation Ctr LLC (P-15631)*

Pavilion Surgery Center, Orange *Also Called: Pavilion Surgery Center LLC (P-14950)*

Pavilion Surgery Center LLC .... D....... 714 744-8850
1140 W La Veta Ave Ste 300 Orange (92868) *(P-14950)*

PAVIR, Palo Alto *Also Called: Palo Alto Vterans Inst For RES (P-19902)*

Pavletich Elc Cmmnications Inc (PA) .... D....... 661 589-9473
6308 Seven Seas Ave Bakersfield (93308) *(P-1802)*

Pavletich Electric, Bakersfield *Also Called: Pavletich Elc Cmmnications Inc (P-1802)*

Paw, Chatsworth *Also Called: Performance Automotive Whl Inc (P-7563)*

Pax Labs Inc .... D....... 415 829-2336
660 Alabama St Ste 2 San Francisco (94110) *(P-16)*

Paxata Inc .... D....... 650 542-7897
1800 Seaport Blvd # 1 Redwood City (94063) *(P-12315)*

Paychex Inc .... D....... 916 983-0303
50 Iron Point Cir Ste 200 Folsom (95630) *(P-19620)*

Paychex Benefit Tech Inc .... C....... 800 322-7292
2385 Northside Dr Ste 100 San Diego (92108) *(P-4328)*

Paydarfar Industries Inc .... D....... 949 481-3267
26054 Acero Mission Viejo (92691) *(P-5332)*

Payden & Rygel (PA) .... C....... 213 625-1900
333 S Grand Ave Ste 4000 Los Angeles (90071) *(P-8214)*

Paylocity Holding Corporation .... A....... 847 956-4850
2107 Livingston St Oakland (94606) *(P-12316)*

Payment Cloud LLC .... D....... 800 988-2215
16501 Ventura Blvd Ste 300 Encino (91436) *(P-12604)*

Paymentcloud, Encino *Also Called: Payment Cloud LLC (P-12604)*

Payoff, Torrance *Also Called: Happy Money Inc (P-7856)*

Payoff Inc .... D....... 949 430-0630
3200 Park Center Dr Ste 800 Costa Mesa (92626) *(P-7884)*

Paypal, San Jose *Also Called: Paypal Inc (P-13422)*

Paypal, San Jose *Also Called: Paypal Holdings Inc (P-13423)*

Paypal Inc (HQ) .... B....... 877 981-2163
2211 N 1st St San Jose (95131) *(P-13422)*

Paypal Global Holdings Inc .... D....... 408 967-1000
303 Bryant St Mountain View (94041) *(P-12605)*

Paypal Holdings Inc (PA) .... A....... 408 967-1000
2211 N 1st St San Jose (95131) *(P-13423)*

Payroll Dept., Chico *Also Called: Enloe Medical Center (P-16083)*

Paysafe Partners LP .... D....... 949 788-1010
2600 Michelson Dr Ste 1600 Irvine (92612) *(P-13424)*

Pazlo Education Foundation .... D....... 323 817-6550
1309 N Wilton Pl Fl 3 Los Angeles (90028) *(P-18893)*

Pb Fasteners, Gardena *Also Called: SPS Technologies LLC (P-5929)*

Pbc Companies, Anaheim *Also Called: Peterson Brothers Cnstr Inc (P-2148)*

Pbc Pavers Inc .... D....... 714 278-0488
2929 E White Star Ave Anaheim (92806) *(P-1630)*

Pbi, Calabasas *Also Called: Picore Bristain Initiative Inc (P-13022)*

Pbo Advisory Group, San Diego *Also Called: Pro Back Office LLC (P-19624)*

Pbs Paymaster Sales & Service, Santa Rosa *Also Called: Probusiness Holdings Inc (P-12609)*

PC Club Inc (HQ) .... D....... 626 839-8080
18537 Gale Ave City Of Industry (91748) *(P-7448)*

PC Specialists Inc (DH) .... C....... 858 566-1900
10620 Treena St Ste 300 San Diego (92131) *(P-5333)*

PC Vaughan Mfg Corp .... D....... 805 278-2555
1278 Mercantile St Oxnard (93030) *(P-2677)*

Pcam LLC .... D....... 562 862-2118
3165 Garfield Ave Commerce (90040) *(P-13625)*

Pcamp, Commerce *Also Called: Parking Company of America (P-13615)*

Pcb Bancorp (PA) .... C....... 213 210-2000
3701 Wilshire Blvd Ste 100 Los Angeles (90010) *(P-7708)*

PCB BANK (HQ) .... C....... 213 210-2000
3701 Wilshire Blvd Ste 900 Los Angeles (90010) *(P-7709)*

Pcg Technology Solutions LLC .... C....... 916 565-8090
2150 River Plaza Dr Ste 380 Sacramento (95833) *(P-12854)*

PCI, Riverside *Also Called: Pacific Consolidated Inds LLC (P-2801)*

PCI, San Diego *Also Called: Project Concern International (P-18087)*

PCI, Rancho Cordova *Also Called: Power Constructors Inc (P-19361)*

PCI Care Venture I .... D....... 661 949-2177
43454 30th St W Ofc Lancaster (93536) *(P-15624)*

PCI Care Venture I .... D....... 559 735-0828
3120 W Caldwell Ave Visalia (93277) *(P-15625)*

PCL Construction Services Inc .... C....... 818 246-3481
655 N Central Ave Ste 1600 Glendale (91203) *(P-984)*

PCL Construction Services Inc .... D....... 818 509-7816
100 Universal City Plz North Hollywood (91608) *(P-985)*

PCL Construction Services Inc .... C....... 858 657-3400
4690 Executive Dr Ste 100 San Diego (92121) *(P-986)*

PCL Industrial Services Inc .... B....... 661 832-3995
1500 S Union Ave Bakersfield (93307) *(P-987)*

Pcm, Laguna Woods *Also Called: Professional Cmnty MGT Cal Inc (P-9142)*

Pcm, Aliso Viejo *Also Called: Professional Community MGT Cal (P-20185)*

Pcm Inc (HQ) .... A....... 310 354-5600
200 N Pacific Coast Hwy Ste 1050 El Segundo (90245) *(P-7562)*

Pcs Concrete & Masonry, Atwater *Also Called: Esau Concrete Inc (P-2117)*

Pcs Link Inc .... B....... 949 655-5000
12424 Wilshire Blvd Ste 1030 Los Angeles (90025) *(P-20826)*

Pcs Mobile Solutions LLC .... D....... 323 567-2490
3534 Tweedy Blvd South Gate (90280) *(P-4329)*

Pcs Property Managment LLC .... C....... 310 231-1000
11859 Wilshire Blvd Ste 600 Los Angeles (90025) *(P-9130)*

Pcv Murcor Real Estate Svcs, Pomona *Also Called: Murcor Inc (P-9107)*

Pcwc, Ontario *Also Called: Chino-Pacific Warehouse Corp (P-3685)*

PDC A Bowman Company, San Diego *Also Called: Project Design Consultants LLC (P-20832)*

Pdc-Identicard, Valencia *Also Called: Precision Dynamics Corporation (P-2528)*

Pdf Solutions, Santa Clara *Also Called: Pdf Solutions Inc (P-12317)*

Pdf Solutions Inc (PA) .... C....... 408 280-7900
2858 De La Cruz Blvd Santa Clara (95050) *(P-12317)*

PDM Steel Service Centers Inc (HQ) .... D....... 209 943-0555
3535 E Myrtle St Stockton (95205) *(P-5508)*

PDM Steel Service Centers Inc .... C....... 916 513-4548
9245 Laguna Springs Dr # 350 Elk Grove (95758) *(P-5509)*

PDQ Automatic Transm Parts Inc .... D....... 916 681-7701
8380 Tiogawoods Dr Sacramento (95828) *(P-13653)*

Pdrfc, Palm Desert *Also Called: Palm Dsert Rcrtl Fclities Corp (P-14280)*

Pds, Compton *Also Called: Pacific Drayage Services LLC (P-3524)*

Pds, Irvine *Also Called: Pacific Dental Services LLC (P-15244)*

Pds Defense Inc .... C....... 408 916-4848
1798 Technology Dr Ste 130 San Jose (95110) *(P-11197)*

Pds Defense Inc .... C....... 214 647-9600
3100 S Harbor Blvd Ste 135 Santa Ana (92704) *(P-11198)*

Pds Tech, San Jose *Also Called: Pds Defense Inc (P-11197)*

Pe Facility Solutions LLC (PA) .... D....... 858 467-0202
4217 Ponderosa Ave Ste A San Diego (92123) *(P-10939)*

Pea Soup Andersen's Restaurant, Buellton *Also Called: Carpenters Southwest ADM Corp (P-7464)*

Peach Inc .... C....... 323 654-2333
1311 N Highland Ave Los Angeles (90028) *(P-3626)*

Peach Tree Healthcare .... D....... 530 749-3242
5730 Packard Ave Ste 500 Marysville (95901) *(P-14951)*

Peachwood Med Group Clovis Inc .... D....... 559 324-6200
275 W Herndon Ave Clovis (93612) *(P-14952)*

Peak Technical Services Inc .... B....... 855 650-7325
2150 Trade Zone Blvd Ste 100 San Jose (95131) *(P-11199)*

ALPHABETIC SECTION

Pearl Automation Inc .... D....... 831 316-5207
    100 Enterprise Way A101 Scotts Valley (95066) *(P-19356)*
Pearl Crop Inc (PA) .... D....... 209 808-7575
    1550 Industrial Dr Stockton (95206) *(P-299)*
Pearlman Brown & Wax LLP (PA) .... D....... 818 501-4343
    15910 Ventura Blvd Fl 18 Encino (91436) *(P-17606)*
Pearson Dental Supplies Inc (PA) .... C....... 818 362-2600
    13161 Telfair Ave Sylmar (91342) *(P-5441)*
Pearson Ford Co (PA) .... C....... 877 743-0421
    5900 Sycamore Canyon Blvd Riverside (92507) *(P-7276)*
Pearson Surgical Supply Co, Sylmar *Also Called: Pearson Dental Supplies Inc (P-5441)*
Pebble Bch Rsort DBA Lone Cypr .... C....... 831 624-3811
    17 Mile Dr Pebble Beach (93953) *(P-10110)*
Pebble Bch Rsort DBA Lone Cypr .... B....... 831 625-8480
    2136 Sunset Dr Pacific Grove (93950) *(P-10111)*
Pebble Beach Co / Rdc Whse, Pacific Grove *Also Called: Pebble Bch Rsort DBA Lone Cypr (P-10111)*
Pebble Beach Co A Ltd Partnr .... B....... 800 877-0597
    1518 Cypress Dr Pebble Beach (93953) *(P-10112)*
Pebble Beach Co A Ltd Partnr .... B....... 831 624-0348
    4005 Sunridge Rd Pebble Beach (93953) *(P-13682)*
Pebble Beach Company, Pebble Beach *Also Called: I Cypress Company (P-9903)*
Pebble Beach Company, The, Pebble Beach *Also Called: Tap Room At Lodge (P-10305)*
Pechanga Development Corp .... A....... 951 695-4655
    45000 Pechanga Pkwy Temecula (92592) *(P-10113)*
Pechanga Resort & Casino, Temecula *Also Called: Pechanga Development Corp (P-10113)*
Peck & Hiller Company .... D....... 707 258-8800
    870 Napa Valley Corporate Way Ste A Napa (94558) *(P-2145)*
Pecs, Rancho Cucamonga *Also Called: Professnl Elec Cnstr Svcs Inc (P-1812)*
Pedersen Media Group Inc .... C....... 415 512-9800
    1115 3rd St San Rafael (94901) *(P-20641)*
Pedi Center, Bakersfield *Also Called: Dignity Health (P-16055)*
Pediatric & Family Medical Ctr .... C....... 213 342-3325
    1530 S Olive St Los Angeles (90015) *(P-14953)*
Pediatric Cancer Research, Orange *Also Called: Childrens Healthcare Cal (P-14681)*
Pediatric Cardiology Med Grp .... D....... 707 863-8190
    5030 Business Center Dr Ste 230 Fairfield (94534) *(P-17294)*
Pediatric Nrology Therapeutics .... D....... 858 304-6440
    7090 Miratech Dr San Diego (92121) *(P-14954)*
Pediatric Therapy Network .... C....... 310 328-0276
    1815 W 213th St Ste 100 Torrance (90501) *(P-17107)*
Peerigon Medical Distribution, El Toro *Also Called: P M D Holding Corp (P-5437)*
Peerles Coffee and Tea, Oakland *Also Called: Peerless Coffee Company Inc (P-2428)*
Peerless Building Maint Co, Chatsworth *Also Called: Tuttle Family Enterprises Inc (P-10975)*
Peerless Coffee Company Inc .... D....... 510 763-1763
    260 Oak St Oakland (94607) *(P-2428)*
Peerless Maintenance Svc Inc .... B....... 714 871-3380
    1100 S Euclid St La Habra (90631) *(P-10940)*
Peet's Coffee, Emeryville *Also Called: Peets Coffee Inc (P-7162)*
Peets Coffee Inc (DH) .... D....... 510 594-2100
    1400 Park Ave Emeryville (94608) *(P-7162)*
Pegasus Building Svcs Co Inc .... B....... 858 444-2290
    7966 Arjons Dr Ste A San Diego (92126) *(P-10941)*
Pegasus Elite Aviation Inc .... C....... 818 742-6666
    7943 Woodley Ave Van Nuys (91406) *(P-3867)*
Pegasus HM Hlth Care A Cal Cor .... D....... 818 551-1932
    505 N Brand Blvd Ste 1000 Glendale (91203) *(P-16910)*
Pegasus Home Health Services, Glendale *Also Called: Pegasus HM Hlth Care A Cal Cor (P-16910)*
Pegasus Maritime Inc .... D....... 714 728-8565
    505 N Brand Blvd Ste 210 Glendale (91203) *(P-4075)*
Pegasus One, Fullerton *Also Called: Aspirez Inc (P-11430)*
Pegasus Risk Management Inc (PA) .... D....... 209 574-2800
    642 Galaxy Way Modesto (95356) *(P-8637)*
Pegasus Squire Inc .... D....... 866 208-6837
    12021 Wilshire Blvd Ste 770 Los Angeles (90025) *(P-12855)*
Pegasus Transit Inc .... D....... 805 988-1540
    210 Beedy St Oxnard (93036) *(P-3313)*
Peggs Company Inc (PA) .... D....... 253 584-9548
    4851 Felspar St Riverside (92509) *(P-13791)*

Peggy S Lane Inc .... D....... 510 483-1202
    2701 Merced St San Leandro (94577) *(P-2669)*
Peking Handicraft Inc (PA) .... C....... 650 871-3788
    1388 San Mateo Ave South San Francisco (94080) *(P-5131)*
Pelco, Fresno *Also Called: Pelco Inc (P-13137)*
Pelco By Schneider Electric, Chino *Also Called: Schneider Electric Usa Inc (P-3752)*
Pelco Inc (HQ) .... A....... 559 292-1981
    625 W Alluvial Ave Fresno (93711) *(P-13137)*
Pelomar Family YMCA, Encinitas *Also Called: YMCA of San Diego County (P-18941)*
Pen-Cal Administrators Inc .... D....... 925 251-3400
    7633 Southfront Rd Ste 120 Livermore (94551) *(P-20174)*
Pena's Recycling Center, Cutler *Also Called: Penas Disposal Inc (P-4919)*
Penas Disposal Inc .... D....... 559 528-3909
    12094 Avenue 408 Cutler (93615) *(P-4919)*
Pencil and Pixel Inc .... C....... 510 422-5036
    340 Brannan St Ste 500 San Francisco (94107) *(P-11819)*
Pendry San Diego, San Diego *Also Called: Rgc Gaslamp LLC (P-10159)*
Pendry, The, Irvine *Also Called: Kt Hotels LLC (P-9954)*
Penfield & Smith, Santa Barbara *Also Called: Penfield & Smith Engineers Inc (P-19357)*
Penfield & Smith Engineers Inc .... D....... 805 963-9532
    111 E Victoria St Santa Barbara (93101) *(P-19357)*
Penguin Computing Inc (DH) .... D....... 415 954-2800
    45800 Northport Loop W Fremont (94538) *(P-5334)*
Penhall Company .... D....... 510 357-8810
    13750 Catalina St San Leandro (94577) *(P-2146)*
Penhall Holding Company .... C....... 714 772-6450
    1801 W Penhall Way Anaheim (92801) *(P-2147)*
Penhall San Leandro 153, San Leandro *Also Called: Penhall Company (P-2146)*
Peninou French Ldry & Clrs Inc (PA) .... D....... 800 392-2532
    101 S Maple Ave South San Francisco (94080) *(P-10487)*
Peninsula Beverly Hill's, Beverly Hills *Also Called: Belvedere Hotel Partnership (P-9638)*
Peninsula Beverly Hills, The, Beverly Hills *Also Called: Belvedere Partnership (P-9639)*
Peninsula Crrdor Jint Pwers Bd .... C....... 650 508-6200
    1250 San Carlos Ave San Carlos (94070) *(P-3189)*
Peninsula Custom Homes Inc .... D....... 650 574-0241
    1401 Old County Rd San Carlos (94070) *(P-708)*
Peninsula Family Service .... C....... 650 952-6848
    1200 Miller Ave South San Francisco (94080) *(P-18078)*
Peninsula Family Service (PA) .... D....... 650 403-4300
    24 2nd Ave San Mateo (94401) *(P-18343)*
Peninsula Family YMCA Sunshine, San Diego *Also Called: YMCA of San Diego County (P-18946)*
Peninsula Golf & Country Club .... D....... 650 638-2200
    701 Madera Dr San Mateo (94403) *(P-14423)*
Peninsula Humane Soc & Spca .... D....... 650 340-7022
    1450 Rollins Rd Burlingame (94010) *(P-19097)*
Peninsula Jewish Community Ctr .... D....... 650 212-7522
    800 Foster City Blvd Foster City (94404) *(P-18079)*
Peninsula Parking Inc .... D....... 650 596-5728
    541 Taylor Way Ste 12 San Carlos (94070) *(P-10569)*
Peninsula Power Tool, Santa Clara *Also Called: C B Tool & Supply Inc (P-7115)*
Peninsula Regent, The, San Mateo *Also Called: Bay Area Senior Services Inc (P-17848)*
Peninsula YMCA, San Mateo *Also Called: Young MNS Chrstn Assn San Frnc (P-18993)*
Penitencia Water Trtmnt Plant, San Jose *Also Called: Santa Clara Vly Wtr Dst Pub Fc (P-4830)*
Pennant Group Inc .... B....... 714 978-2534
    1800 W Culver Ave Orange (92868) *(P-15626)*
Pennbrook Insurance Service .... D....... 415 820-2200
    300 Montgomery St Ste 450 San Francisco (94104) *(P-8638)*
Penney Lawn Service Inc .... D....... 661 587-4788
    4000 Allen Rd Bakersfield (93314) *(P-530)*
Penney Opco LLC .... D....... 972 431-2618
    5959 Palm Ave San Bernardino (92407) *(P-3743)*
Penney Opco LLC .... D....... 559 732-4171
    2115 S Mooney Blvd Visalia (93277) *(P-7128)*
Penney Opco LLC .... C....... 916 564-0315
    1695 Arden Way Sacramento (95815) *(P-7129)*
Penney Opco LLC .... C....... 626 445-6454
    400 S Baldwin Ave Lowr Arcadia (91007) *(P-7130)*
Penney Opco LLC .... C....... 805 497-6811
    280 W Hillcrest Dr Thousand Oaks (91360) *(P-7131)*

Penney Opco LLC .... C...... 209 951-1110
  4915 Claremont Ave Stockton (95207) *(P-7132)*
Penney Opco LLC .... C...... 626 960-3711
  1203 Plaza Dr West Covina (91790) *(P-7133)*
Penney Opco LLC .... C...... 530 899-8160
  1932 E 20th St Chico (95928) *(P-7134)*
Penny Lane Centers (PA) .... B...... 818 892-3423
  15305 Rayen St North Hills (91343) *(P-18616)*
Penny Lawn Service, Bakersfield Also Called: Penney Lawn Service Inc *(P-530)*
Pennymac, Westlake Village Also Called: Pennymac Financial Svcs Inc *(P-8010)*
Pennymac, Agoura Hills Also Called: Private Nat Mrtg Accptance LLC *(P-8012)*
Pennymac Broker Direct .... D...... 614 288-5126
  112 S Lakeview Canyon Rd Ste 130 Thousand Oaks (91362) *(P-8009)*
Pennymac Corp .... B...... 818 878-8416
  27001 Agoura Rd Agoura Hills (91301) *(P-8050)*
Pennymac Financial Svcs Inc (PA) .... D...... 818 224-7442
  3043 Townsgate Rd Westlake Village (91361) *(P-8010)*
Pensinmark Rtirement Group LLC .... C...... 805 456-6260
  24 E Cota St Ste 200 Santa Barbara (93101) *(P-20503)*
Penske, West Covina Also Called: Penske Motor Group LLC *(P-13564)*
Penske Corporation .... C...... 805 983-3788
  6551 Ventura Blvd Ventura (93003) *(P-13563)*
Penske Ford Chula Vista, Chula Vista Also Called: Rp Automotive II Inc *(P-13567)*
Penske Honda Ontario, Ontario Also Called: Ontario Automotive LLC *(P-7272)*
Penske Motor Group LLC .... B...... 626 859-1200
  2010 E Garvey Ave S West Covina (91791) *(P-13564)*
Penske Motorcars, West Covina Also Called: P A Motorcars LLC *(P-7273)*
Penske Transportation MGT LLC .... D...... 844 847-9518
  2280 Wardlow Cir Corona (92878) *(P-13565)*
Pentacon Inc .... B...... 818 727-8000
  21123 Nordhoff St Chatsworth (91311) *(P-5918)*
Pentair Equipment Protection, San Diego Also Called: Schroff Inc *(P-13743)*
Pentel of America Ltd (HQ) .... C...... 310 320-3831
  2715 Columbia St Torrance (90503) *(P-6069)*
Penwal Industries Inc .... D...... 909 466-1555
  10611 Acacia St Rancho Cucamonga (91730) *(P-988)*
People Pets and Vets LLC .... C...... 909 453-4213
  10986 Sierra Ave Ste 400 Fontana (92337) *(P-340)*
People Pets and Vets LLC .... C...... 909 329-2860
  16055 Sierra Lakes Pkwy Ste 100 Fontana (92336) *(P-341)*
People Concern .... C...... 310 883-1222
  1751 Cloverfield Blvd Santa Monica (90404) *(P-18080)*
People Concern .... C...... 310 450-0650
  1751 Cloverfield Blvd Santa Monica (90404) *(P-18081)*
People Connect, San Diego Also Called: Control Group Media Co LLC *(P-10600)*
People Creating Success Inc .... D...... 805 644-9480
  380 Arneill Rd Camarillo (93010) *(P-14955)*
People Creating Success Inc .... D...... 661 225-9700
  1607 E Palmdale Blvd Ste H Palmdale (93550) *(P-18082)*
People Creating Success Inc .... C...... 805 692-5290
  5350 Hollister Ave Ste I Santa Barbara (93111) *(P-18083)*
People Data Labs Inc .... D...... 415 568-8415
  455 Market St Ste 1670 San Francisco (94105) *(P-12606)*
PEOPLE'S CARE INC., Victorville Also Called: Peoples Care Inc *(P-16911)*
PEOPLE'S CARE INC., Santa Fe Springs Also Called: Peoples Care Inc *(P-18344)*
People's Place, Torrance Also Called: Topwin Corporation *(P-6189)*
Peopleai Inc .... D...... 888 997-3675
  303 Twin Dolphin Dr Fl 6 Redwood City (94065) *(P-11820)*
Peoples Care Inc .... C...... 760 962-1900
  13901 Amargosa Rd Ste 101 Victorville (92392) *(P-16911)*
Peoples Care Inc .... C...... 562 320-0174
  12215 Telegraph Rd Ste 208 Santa Fe Springs (90670) *(P-18344)*
Peoples Self-Help Housing Corp .... D...... 805 349-9341
  1026 W Boone St Santa Maria (93458) *(P-20827)*
Peopleshores Pbc .... D...... 408 431-4686
  2033 Gateway Pl Ste 500 San Jose (95110) *(P-20828)*
Pep Creations, San Diego Also Called: Pacific Event Productions Inc *(P-10567)*
Pepitastore, El Segundo Also Called: Scalefast Inc *(P-4336)*
Pepper Tree Inn .... D...... 530 583-3711
  645 N Lake Blvd Tahoe City (96145) *(P-10114)*

Peppermint Ridge (PA) .... D...... 951 273-7320
  825 Magnolia Ave Corona (92879) *(P-18504)*
Pepsi-Cola, Buena Park Also Called: Pepsi-Cola Metro Btlg Co Inc *(P-2406)*
Pepsi-Cola, Carson Also Called: Pepsi-Cola Metro Btlg Co Inc *(P-2407)*
Pepsi-Cola Metro Btlg Co Inc .... C...... 714 522-9635
  6261 Caballero Blvd Buena Park (90620) *(P-2406)*
Pepsi-Cola Metro Btlg Co Inc .... B...... 310 327-4222
  19700 Figueroa St Carson (90745) *(P-2407)*
Perceptioneering Inc .... D...... 805 962-4550
  808 State St Santa Barbara (93101) *(P-10660)*
Perennial Construction Corp .... D...... 212 727-1807
  1682 Langley Ave Irvine (92614) *(P-989)*
Perfect Bar LLC .... C...... 866 628-8548
  3931 Sorrento Valley Blvd Ste 100 San Diego (92121) *(P-6657)*
Perfect Snacks, San Diego Also Called: Perfect Bar LLC *(P-6657)*
Perfect World Entrmt Inc .... C...... 650 590-7700
  100 Redwood Shores Pkwy # 200 Redwood City (94065) *(P-11821)*
Perfict Global Inc .... C...... 949 945-8956
  1800 Sutter St Ste 870 Concord (94520) *(P-12856)*
Performance Automotive Whl Inc (PA) .... D...... 805 499-8973
  20235 Nordhoff St Chatsworth (91311) *(P-7563)*
Performance Building Services .... C...... 949 364-4364
  22642 Lambert St Ste 409 Lake Forest (92630) *(P-10942)*
Performance Chevrolet Inc .... C...... 916 338-7300
  8757 Auburn Folsom Rd Granite Bay (95746) *(P-7277)*
Performance Cleanroom Services, Lake Forest Also Called: Performance Building Services *(P-10942)*
Performance Contracting Inc .... D...... 913 310-7120
  4955 E Landon Dr Anaheim (92807) *(P-2249)*
Performance Designed Pdts LLC (PA) .... D...... 800 331-3844
  9179 Aero Dr San Diego (92123) *(P-5688)*
Performance Food Group Inc .... B...... 804 287-8097
  7587 Las Positas Rd Livermore (94551) *(P-6276)*
Performance Food Group Inc .... C...... 831 462-4400
  1047 17th Ave Santa Cruz (95062) *(P-6277)*
Performance Health Med Group .... C...... 714 740-1778
  13252 Garden Grove Blvd # 112 Garden Grove (92843) *(P-17295)*
Performance Mechanical Inc (HQ) .... A...... 925 432-4080
  701 Willow Pass Rd Ste 2 Pittsburg (94565) *(P-839)*
Performance Nissan, Duarte Also Called: Gpi Ca-Niii Inc *(P-7223)*
Performance Sheets LLC .... C...... 626 333-0195
  440 Baldwin Park Blvd City Of Industry (91746) *(P-2076)*
Performance Team, El Segundo Also Called: Maersk Whsng Dist Svcs USA LLC *(P-4055)*
Performance Tech Partners LLC .... C...... 800 787-4143
  500 Capitol Mall Ste 2350 Sacramento (95814) *(P-12857)*
Performant Financial Corp (PA) .... B...... 925 960-4800
  333 N Canyons Pkwy Ste 100 Livermore (94551) *(P-12680)*
Performant Recovery Inc 209 858-3500
  17080 S Harlan Rd Lathrop (95330) *(P-10747)*
Performant Recovery Inc (HQ) .... C...... 209 858-3994
  333 N Canyons Pkwy Ste 100 Livermore (94551) *(P-10748)*
Performing Arts Ctr Los Angles .... C...... 213 972-7512
  135 N Grand Ave Ste 314 Los Angeles (90012) *(P-14054)*
Performnce Foodservice-Ledyard, Santa Cruz Also Called: Performance Food Group Inc *(P-6277)*
Perkins & Will, San Francisco Also Called: Perkins + Will Inc *(P-19500)*
Perkins + Will Inc .... D...... 415 856-3000
  2 Bryant St Ste 300 San Francisco (94105) *(P-19500)*
Perkowitz & Ruth Architects, Long Beach Also Called: Rdc-S111 Inc *(P-19501)*
Perlman Clinic .... C...... 858 554-1212
  3900 5th Ave Ste 110 San Diego (92103) *(P-14956)*
Permanente Federation LLC .... D...... 510 625-6920
  1 Kaiser Plz 27th Fl Oakland (94612) *(P-20504)*
Permanente Kaiser Intl (HQ) .... B...... 510 271-5910
  1 Kaiser Plz Oakland (94612) *(P-8352)*
Permanente Medical Group, Mountain View Also Called: Kaiser Foundation Hospitals *(P-16194)*
Permanente Medical Group Inc .... B...... 650 827-6500
  220 Oyster Point Blvd South San Francisco (94080) *(P-8353)*
Permanente Medical Group Inc .... A...... 650 598-2852
  900 Veterans Blvd Ste 400 Redwood City (94063) *(P-8354)*

ALPHABETIC SECTION

Permanente Medical Group Inc .... A...... 510 559-5119
1725 Eastshore Hwy Berkeley (94710) *(P-8355)*

Permanente Medical Group Inc .... A...... 510 675-4010
3555 Whipple Rd Union City (94587) *(P-8356)*

Permanente Medical Group Inc .... A...... 209 735-5000
4601 Dale Rd Modesto (95356) *(P-14957)*

Permanente Medical Group Inc .... A...... 415 899-7400
97 San Marin Dr Novato (94945) *(P-14958)*

Permanente Medical Group Inc .... A...... 650 301-5800
395 Hickey Blvd Fl 2 Daly City (94015) *(P-14959)*

Permanente Medical Group Inc .... A...... 707 765-3930
1617 Broadway St Vallejo (94590) *(P-14960)*

Permanente Medical Group Inc .... A...... 510 625-6262
1800 Harrison St 7th Fl Oakland (94612) *(P-14961)*

Permanente Medical Group Inc .... A...... 559 448-4500
7300 N Fresno St Fresno (93720) *(P-14962)*

Permanente Medical Group Inc .... A...... 650 742-2100
901 El Camino Real San Bruno (94066) *(P-14963)*

Permanente Medical Group Inc .... A...... 707 393-4000
3558 Round Barn Blvd Santa Rosa (95403) *(P-14964)*

Permanente Medical Group Inc .... A...... 415 833-2000
2425 Geary Blvd San Francisco (94115) *(P-14965)*

Permanente Medical Group Inc .... B...... 408 972-6883
275 Hospital Pkwy Ste 470 San Jose (95119) *(P-14966)*

Permanente Medical Group Inc .... B...... 925 372-1000
200 Muir Rd Martinez (94553) *(P-14967)*

Permanente Medical Group Inc .... B...... 510 752-1000
3779 Piedmont Ave Oakland (94611) *(P-14968)*

Permanente Medical Group Inc .... A...... 510 248-3000
39400 Paseo Padre Pkwy Fremont (94538) *(P-14969)*

Permanente Medical Group Inc .... A...... 510 752-1190
235 W Macarthur Blvd Oakland (94611) *(P-14970)*

Permanente Medical Group Inc .... B...... 408 945-2900
770 E Calaveras Blvd Milpitas (95035) *(P-14971)*

Permanente Medical Group Inc .... A...... 925 813-6149
4501 Sand Creek Rd Antioch (94531) *(P-14972)*

Permanente Medical Group Inc .... A...... 650 299-2000
1150 Veterans Blvd Redwood City (94063) *(P-14973)*

Permanente Medical Group Inc .... A...... 650 299-2015
910 Marshall St Redwood City (94063) *(P-14974)*

Permanente Medical Group Inc .... A...... 510 231-5406
914 Marina Way S Richmond (94804) *(P-14975)*

Permanente Medical Group Inc .... B...... 916 486-5686
3184 Arden Way Sacramento (95825) *(P-14976)*

Permanente Medical Group Inc .... A...... 510 454-1000
2500 Merced St San Leandro (94577) *(P-14977)*

Permanente Medical Group Inc .... B...... 415 444-2000
99 Montecillo Rd San Rafael (94903) *(P-14978)*

Permanente Medical Group Inc .... A...... 925 906-2000
320 Lennon Ln Walnut Creek (94598) *(P-14979)*

Permanente Medical Group Inc .... B...... 415 209-2444
100 Rowland Way Ste 125 Novato (94945) *(P-14980)*

Permanente Medical Group Inc .... A...... 916 784-4000
1600 Eureka Rd Roseville (95661) *(P-14981)*

Permanente Medical Group Inc .... A...... 209 476-3737
7373 West Ln Stockton (95210) *(P-14982)*

Permanente Medical Group Inc .... A...... 415 833-2000
2238 Geary Blvd San Francisco (94115) *(P-14983)*

Permanente Medical Group Inc .... A...... 510 559-5338
1750 2nd St Berkeley (94710) *(P-14984)*

Permanente Medical Group Inc .... A...... 209 476-2000
1305 Tommydon St Stockton (95210) *(P-14985)*

Permanente Medical Group Inc .... A...... 310 325-5111
25825 Vermont Ave Harbor City (90710) *(P-14986)*

Permanente Medical Group Inc .... A...... 925 243-2600
3000 Las Positas Rd Livermore (94551) *(P-14987)*

Permanente Medical Group Inc .... A...... 650 358-7000
1000 Franklin Pkwy San Mateo (94403) *(P-14988)*

Permanente Medical Group Inc .... A...... 707 765-3900
3900 Lakeville Hwy Petaluma (94954) *(P-14989)*

Permanente Medical Group Inc .... B...... 916 631-3000
10725 International Dr Rancho Cordova (95670) *(P-14990)*

Permanente Medical Group Inc .... A...... 916 688-2055
6600 Bruceville Rd Sacramento (95823) *(P-14991)*

Permanente Medical Group Inc .... B...... 707 427-4000
1550 Gateway Blvd Fairfield (94533) *(P-16321)*

Permanente Medical Group Inc (DH) .... B...... 866 858-2226
1950 Franklin St 7th Fl Oakland (94612) *(P-17296)*

Permanente Medical Group Inc .... B...... 916 973-5175
4537 Valmonte Dr Sacramento (95864) *(P-17297)*

Permanentee Medical Group, Roseville *Also Called: Kaiser Foundation Hospitals (P-14834)*

Permira Advisers LLC .... A...... 650 681-4701
3000 Sand Hill Rd Ste 1-170 Menlo Park (94025) *(P-8215)*

Pernixdata Inc .... D...... 408 724-8413
1740 Technology Dr Ste 150 San Jose (95110) *(P-11822)*

Pernod Ricard Usa LLC .... D...... 707 833-5891
9592 Sonoma Hwy Kenwood (95452) *(P-2390)*

Perrin Bernard Supowitz LLC (HQ) .... C...... 323 981-2800
5496 Lindbergh Ln Bell (90201) *(P-6090)*

Perris Disposal Company, Perris *Also Called: CR&r Incorporated (P-4882)*

Perris Valley Cmnty Hosp LLC .... C...... 909 581-6400
10841 White Oak Ave Rancho Cucamonga (91730) *(P-16322)*

Perry Coast Construction Inc .... C...... 951 774-0677
3811 Wacker Dr Jurupa Valley (91752) *(P-990)*

Perry Ford, Poway *Also Called: Perry Ford of Poway LLC (P-7278)*

Perry Ford of Poway LLC .... D...... 858 748-1400
12740 Poway Rd Poway (92064) *(P-7278)*

Perryman Mechanical Inc .... D...... 916 371-8888
514 Glide Ave West Sacramento (95691) *(P-5231)*

Persistent Systems Inc (HQ) .... D...... 408 216-7010
2055 Laurelwood Rd Ste 210 Santa Clara (95054) *(P-11823)*

Persona Identities Inc (PA) .... C...... 415 355-4050
201 Post St San Francisco (94108) *(P-20175)*

Personal .... D...... 321 219-9161
914 Sanchez St San Francisco (94114) *(P-9131)*

Personal Energy Finance Inc .... D...... 877 858-3855
16870 W Bernardo Dr Ste 408 San Diego (92127) *(P-11200)*

Personal Protective Svcs Inc (PA) .... D...... 650 344-3302
398 Beach Rd 2nd Fl Burlingame (94010) *(P-13021)*

Personalis Inc (PA) .... C...... 650 752-1300
6600 Dumbarton Cir Fremont (94555) *(P-16740)*

Personality Hotels Inc .... C...... 415 885-0200
440 Geary St San Francisco (94102) *(P-10115)*

Personnel Concepts, Ontario *Also Called: Aio Acquisition Inc (P-2552)*

Personnel Plus Inc .... C...... 562 712-5490
12052 Imperial Hwy Ste 200 Norwalk (90650) *(P-11315)*

Perspectium Corp .... D...... 858 530-8093
10301 Meanley Dr Ste 250 San Diego (92131) *(P-11824)*

Pescatore, San Francisco *Also Called: Kimpton Hotel & Rest Group LLC (P-9944)*

Pet Pourri, Milpitas *Also Called: Humane Society Silicon Valley (P-19090)*

Petalon Landscape MGT Inc .... D...... 408 453-3998
1766 Rogers Ave San Jose (95112) *(P-456)*

PETALUMA HEALTH CENTER, Petaluma *Also Called: Petaluma Health Center Inc (P-14992)*

Petaluma Health Center Inc .... B...... 707 559-7500
1179 N Mcdowell Blvd Ste A Petaluma (94954) *(P-14992)*

Petaluma Medical Offices, Petaluma *Also Called: Kaiser Foundation Hospitals (P-14832)*

Petaluma Valley Hospital, Petaluma *Also Called: Srm Alliance Hospital Services (P-16452)*

Petalumaidence Opco LLC .... C...... 707 763-4109
101 Monroe St Petaluma (94954) *(P-2391)*

Petco, San Diego *Also Called: Petco Animal Supplies Inc (P-4134)*

Petco Animal Supplies Inc (DH) .... B...... 858 453-7845
10850 Via Frontera San Diego (92127) *(P-4134)*

Petco Health & Wellness Co Inc .... A...... 858 453-7845
10850 Via Frontera San Diego (92127) *(P-7588)*

Petco Park, San Diego *Also Called: City of San Diego (P-14133)*

Petdesk .... D...... 202 431-3045
2044 1st Ave Ste 200 San Diego (92101) *(P-11825)*

Pete Moffat Construction .... D...... 650 656-9720
250 Lowell Ave Palo Alto (94301) *(P-709)*

Peter Brasseler Holdings LLC .... D...... 805 650-5209
4837 Mcgrath St Ste J Ventura (93003) *(P-5442)*

Peter Castillo Md PA .... A...... 408 236-6400
15215 National Ave Ste 104 Los Gatos (95032) *(P-14993)*

Peter H Mattson & Co Inc .... D 650 356-2500
  343 Hatch Dr Foster City (94404) *(P-19757)*

Peter Rabbit Farms, Coachella *Also Called: Amazing Coachella Inc (P-19)*

Peter Wylan DDS .... D 562 925-3765
  10318 Rosecrans Ave Bellflower (90706) *(P-15247)*

Petersen-Dean Commercial Inc .... C 707 469-7470
  1705 Enterprise Dr Fairfield (94533) *(P-2077)*

Petersendean, Fairfield *Also Called: Petersen-Dean Commercial Inc (P-2077)*

Peterson Bros Construction, Anaheim *Also Called: Pbc Pavers Inc (P-1630)*

Peterson Brothers Cnstr Inc .... A 714 278-0488
  2929 E White Star Ave Anaheim (92806) *(P-2148)*

Peterson Cat, San Leandro *Also Called: Peterson Holding Company (P-5796)*

Peterson Cat, Redding *Also Called: Peterson Machinery Co (P-5797)*

Peterson Family Inc .... D 559 897-5064
  38694 Road 16 Kingsburg (93631) *(P-112)*

Peterson Holding Company (PA) .... D 510 357-6200
  955 Marina Blvd San Leandro (94577) *(P-5796)*

Peterson Machinery Co .... A 530 243-5410
  5100 Caterpillar Rd Redding (96003) *(P-5797)*

Peterson Mechanical Inc .... D 707 938-8481
  21819 8th St E Sonoma (95476) *(P-1528)*

Peterson Painting Inc .... B 925 455-5864
  5750 La Ribera St Livermore (94550) *(P-1631)*

Peterson-Chase General Engineering Construction Inc .... D 949 252-0441
  16351 Construction Cir W Irvine (92606) *(P-1152)*

Peterson's Spices, Pico Rivera *Also Called: GPde Slva Spces Incrporation (P-2435)*

Petes Road Service Inc .... D 714 545-5818
  120 W Warner Ave Santa Ana (92707) *(P-5072)*

Petit Ermitage, West Hollywood *Also Called: Valadon Hotel LLC (P-10340)*

Petra Risk Solutions .... D 800 466-8951
  5927 Priestly Dr Ste 102 Carlsbad (92008) *(P-8639)*

Petrelli Electric Inc .... D 661 268-7312
  11615 Davenport Rd Agua Dulce (91390) *(P-1803)*

Petro-Chem Industries Inc .... D 707 644-7455
  2300 Clayton Rd Concord (94520) *(P-1955)*

Petro-Chem Insulation, Concord *Also Called: Petro-Chem Industries Inc (P-1955)*

Petrochem, Long Beach *Also Called: Petrochem Insulation Inc (P-1956)*

Petrochem Insulation Inc .... D 310 638-6663
  3117 E South St Long Beach (90805) *(P-1956)*

Petrol Advertising Inc .... D 323 644-3720
  443 N Varney St Burbank (91502) *(P-10661)*

Petroleum Sales Inc (PA) .... C 415 256-1600
  1475 2nd St San Rafael (94901) *(P-13701)*

Petrosian Esthetic Entps LLC .... C 818 391-8231
  2919 W Burbank Blvd Burbank (91505) *(P-10506)*

Petti Kohn Ingrassia & L PR Co .... D 310 649-5772
  11622 El Camino Real Ste 300 San Diego (92130) *(P-17607)*

Pettit Kohn Ingrassia & Lutz, San Diego *Also Called: Petti Kohn Ingrassia & L PR Co (P-17607)*

PFC Management LLC .... D 310 401-1926
  10880 Wilshire Blvd Los Angeles (90024) *(P-20176)*

Pff Bancorp Inc (PA) .... A 213 683-6393
  2058 N Mills Ave Ste 139 Claremont (91711) *(P-7747)*

Pfitech, Huntington Beach *Also Called: Precise Fit Limited One LLC (P-11203)*

PFU America Inc (HQ) .... B 800 626-4686
  1250 E Arques Ave Sunnyvale (94085) *(P-12510)*

Pg Trucking Inc .... D 661 301-4942
  7216 Cafe Rouge Dr Bakersfield (93312) *(P-3418)*

Pg Usa LLC .... D 310 954-1040
  5150 W Goldleaf Cir Los Angeles (90056) *(P-7139)*

PG&e, San Francisco *Also Called: Pacific Energy Fuels Company (P-4599)*
PG&e, Potter Valley *Also Called: Pacific Gas and Electric Co (P-4600)*
PG&e, Sacramento *Also Called: Pacific Gas and Electric Co (P-4601)*
PG&e, Antioch *Also Called: Pacific Gas and Electric Co (P-4602)*
PG&E, Oakland *Also Called: Pacific Gas and Electric Co (P-4603)*
PG&e, Oakland *Also Called: Pacific Gas and Electric Co (P-4604)*
PG&e, Fresno *Also Called: Pacific Gas and Electric Co (P-4605)*
PG&e, Stockton *Also Called: Pacific Gas and Electric Co (P-4606)*
PG&e, San Francisco *Also Called: Pacific Gas and Electric Co (P-4607)*
PG&e, Fairfield *Also Called: Pacific Gas and Electric Co (P-4608)*
PG&e, West Sacramento *Also Called: Pacific Gas and Electric Co (P-4609)*
PG&e, Stockton *Also Called: Pacific Gas and Electric Co (P-4610)*
PG&e, Fresno *Also Called: Pacific Gas and Electric Co (P-4611)*
PG&e, Chico *Also Called: Pacific Gas and Electric Co (P-4612)*
PG&e, Sacramento *Also Called: Pacific Gas and Electric Co (P-4613)*
PG&e, Santa Rosa *Also Called: Pacific Gas and Electric Co (P-4616)*
PG&e, Pittsburg *Also Called: Pacific Gas and Electric Co (P-4618)*
PG&e, San Luis Obispo *Also Called: Pacific Gas and Electric Co (P-4619)*
PG&e, San Rafael *Also Called: Pacific Gas and Electric Co (P-4620)*
PG&e, Stockton *Also Called: Pacific Gas and Electric Co (P-4621)*
PG&e, Petaluma *Also Called: Pacific Gas and Electric Co (P-4622)*
PG&e, Willows *Also Called: Pacific Gas and Electric Co (P-4623)*
PG&e, Concord *Also Called: Pacific Gas and Electric Co (P-4625)*
PG&e, Daly City *Also Called: Pacific Gas and Electric Co (P-4626)*
PG&e, Salinas *Also Called: Pacific Gas and Electric Co (P-4627)*
PG&e, Concord *Also Called: Pacific Gas and Electric Co (P-4628)*
PG&e, Selma *Also Called: Pacific Gas and Electric Co (P-4629)*
PG&e, Placerville *Also Called: Pacific Gas and Electric Co (P-4630)*
PG&e, Oroville *Also Called: Pacific Gas and Electric Co (P-4631)*
PG&e, Avila Beach *Also Called: Pacific Gas and Electric Co (P-4632)*
PG&e, Alta *Also Called: Pacific Gas and Electric Co (P-4633)*
PG&e, Redding *Also Called: Pacific Gas and Electric Co (P-4634)*
PG&e, Manton *Also Called: Pacific Gas and Electric Co (P-4635)*
PG&e, Santa Rosa *Also Called: Pacific Gas and Electric Co (P-4636)*
PG&e, Auburn *Also Called: Pacific Gas and Electric Co (P-4637)*
PG&e, Paradise *Also Called: Pacific Gas and Electric Co (P-4638)*
PG&e, Stockton *Also Called: Pacific Gas and Electric Co (P-4639)*
PG&e, Monterey *Also Called: Pacific Gas and Electric Co (P-4640)*
PG&e, Fremont *Also Called: Pacific Gas and Electric Co (P-4641)*
PG&e, Eureka *Also Called: Pacific Gas and Electric Co (P-4642)*
PG&e, Auberry *Also Called: Pacific Gas and Electric Co (P-4643)*
PG&e, Los Banos *Also Called: Pacific Gas and Electric Co (P-4644)*
PG&e, Hinkley *Also Called: Pacific Gas and Electric Co (P-4645)*
PG&e, Modesto *Also Called: Pacific Gas and Electric Co (P-4646)*
PG&e, Oakdale *Also Called: Pacific Gas and Electric Co (P-4647)*
PG&e, Chico *Also Called: Pacific Gas and Electric Co (P-4648)*
PG&e, Fresno *Also Called: Pacific Gas and Electric Co (P-4649)*
PG&e, Tracy *Also Called: Pacific Gas and Electric Co (P-4650)*
PG&e, Vacaville *Also Called: Pacific Gas and Electric Co (P-4651)*
PG&e, Pismo Beach *Also Called: Pacific Gas and Electric Co (P-4652)*
PG&e, Livermore *Also Called: Pacific Gas and Electric Co (P-4653)*
PG&e, Davis *Also Called: Pacific Gas and Electric Co (P-4654)*
PG&e, Needles *Also Called: Pacific Gas and Electric Co (P-4655)*
PG&e, Milpitas *Also Called: Pacific Gas and Electric Co (P-4656)*
PG&e, Pioneer *Also Called: Pacific Gas and Electric Co (P-4657)*
PG&e, Bakersfield *Also Called: Pacific Gas and Electric Co (P-4658)*
PG&e, Templeton *Also Called: Pacific Gas and Electric Co (P-4659)*
PG&e, Hayward *Also Called: Pacific Gas and Electric Co (P-4723)*
PG&e, Chico *Also Called: Pacific Gas and Electric Co (P-4724)*

Pga West By Wldorf Astoria MGT, La Quinta *Also Called: Msr Resort Lodging Tenant LLC (P-10035)*

Pgs 360, City Of Industry *Also Called: Prime Global Solutions Inc (P-4078)*

Phamatech Incorporated .... C 888 635-5840
  15175 Innovation Dr San Diego (92128) *(P-19994)*

Pharmacy At Cares, The, Sacramento *Also Called: Cares Community Health (P-14659)*

Pharmaron Inc .... A 949 788-0586
  6 Venture Ste 250 Irvine (92618) *(P-19758)*

Pharmron San Dego Lab Svcs LLC .... D 858 560-9000
  7901 Vickers St San Diego (92111) *(P-19759)*

Phase 3 Communications, San Jose *Also Called: Phase 3 Communications Inc (P-1804)*

Phase 3 Communications Inc (PA) .... D 408 946-9011
  1355 Felipe Ave San Jose (95122) *(P-1804)*

Phase Ten Strategic Corp .... D 619 298-1445
  2445 5th Ave Ste 450 San Diego (92101) *(P-9132)*

ALPHABETIC SECTION

PHD Marketing Inc .... D....... 909 620-1000
1373 Ridgeway St Pomona (91768) *(P-6935)*

Phenomenon Mktg & Entrmt LLC (PA)..D....... 323 648-4000
5900 Wilshire Blvd Fl 28 Los Angeles (90036) *(P-20505)*

PHF II Burbank LLC .... C....... 818 843-6000
2500 N Hollywood Way Burbank (91505) *(P-10116)*

PHF Ruby LLC .... C....... 415 885-4700
2620 Jones St San Francisco (94133) *(P-10117)*

Phg Engineering Services LLC .... D....... 714 283-8288
27481 Ganso Mission Viejo (92691) *(P-19358)*

PHH, Hemet *Also Called: Kpc Global Medical Centers Inc (P-16207)*

Philips North America LLC .... D....... 858 677-6390
3721 Valley Centre Dr San Diego (92130) *(P-5610)*

Philmont Management Inc .... D....... 213 380-0159
3450 Wilshire Blvd Ste 850 Los Angeles (90010) *(P-991)*

Phoenix American Incorporated (PA).....................................D....... 415 485-4500
125 E Sir Francis Drake Blvd Ste 301 Larkspur (94939) *(P-20506)*

Phoenix CLB Grman Assn In Orng .... D....... 714 224-0194
1340 S Sanderson Ave Anaheim (92806) *(P-7502)*

Phoenix Engineering Co Inc .... D....... 310 532-1134
2480 Armacost Ave Los Angeles (90064) *(P-11316)*

Phoenix Engineering Tech LLC .... D....... 714 918-0630
17117 Leal Ave Cerritos (90703) *(P-19359)*

Phoenix Hotel, San Francisco *Also Called: Joie De Vivre Hospitality LLC (P-9927)*

PHOENIX HOUSE, Lake View Terrace *Also Called: Phoenix Houses Los Angeles Inc (P-18505)*

Phoenix Houses Los Angeles Inc .... D....... 818 686-3000
11600 Eldridge Ave Lake View Terrace (91342) *(P-18505)*

Phoenix Marketing Services Inc .... D....... 909 399-4000
651 Wharton Dr Claremont (91711) *(P-2565)*

Phoenix Personnel, Los Angeles *Also Called: Phoenix Engineering Co Inc (P-11316)*

Phoenix Technologies Inc .... C....... 408 570-1000
2105 S Bascom Ave Ste 316 Campbell (95008) *(P-11826)*

Phoenix Textile Inc (PA)..D....... 310 715-7090
14600 S Broadway Gardena (90248) *(P-6159)*

Phone Check Solutions LLC .... B....... 310 365-1855
16027 Ventura Blvd Ste 605 Encino (91436) *(P-11827)*

Phone Ware Inc .... B....... 858 530-8550
8902 Activity Rd Ste A San Diego (92126) *(P-13425)*

Phonecom Inc .... D....... 973 577-6380
14288 Danielson St Poway (92064) *(P-4330)*

Phonepower, Northridge *Also Called: Quality Speaks LLC (P-4332)*

Photon Research Associates Inc .... C....... 858 455-9741
9985 Pacific Heights Blvd Ste 200 San Diego (92121) *(P-19360)*

Phs / Mwa .... C....... 951 695-1008
42374 Avenida Alvarado # A Temecula (92590) *(P-3904)*

Phs Staffing, Seal Beach *Also Called: Premier Healthcare Svcs LLC (P-16912)*

Phs/Mwa Aviation Services, Temecula *Also Called: Phs / Mwa (P-3904)*

Physical Rhbltation Netwrk LLC (PA).....................................D....... 760 931-8310
2035 Corte Del Nogal Ste 200 Carlsbad (92011) *(P-15299)*

Physician Office Support Svcs, Torrance *Also Called: Torrance Health Assn Inc (P-16575)*

Physician Sales & Service, Fullerton *Also Called: McKesson Mdcl-Srgcal Top Hldng (P-5431)*

Physician Support Systems Inc (DH).....................................B....... 717 653-5340
1131 W 6th St Ste 300 Ontario (91762) *(P-19621)*

Physicians Automated Lab Inc (DH)......................................D....... 661 325-0744
820 34th St Ste 102 Bakersfield (93301) *(P-16741)*

Physicians Choice LLC .... D....... 818 340-9988
21860 Burbank Blvd Ste 120 Woodland Hills (91367) *(P-19622)*

Physicians Clinical Lab, Sacramento *Also Called: Unilab Corporation (P-16759)*

Physicians Datatrust Inc .... C....... 562 860-8771
17215 Studebaker Rd Ste 220 Cerritos (90703) *(P-20507)*

Physicians Hearing Services, Fresno *Also Called: Central Cal Ear Nose Throat ME (P-14666)*

Physicians Referral Service, Lancaster *Also Called: Lancaster Crdlgy Med Group Inc (P-14874)*

Piano Disc, Sacramento *Also Called: Burgett Incorporated (P-6031)*

Piazza Trucking, South Gate *Also Called: Samuel J Piazza & Son Inc (P-3594)*

Piccadilly Hospitality LLC .... D....... 559 348-5520
2305 W Shaw Ave Fresno (93711) *(P-10118)*

Piccadilly Inn Airport, Fresno *Also Called: Art Piccadilly Shaw LLC (P-9613)*

Piccadilly Inn Shaw, Fresno *Also Called: Piccadilly Hospitality LLC (P-10118)*

Pick Pull Auto Dismantling Inc .... D....... 916 689-1446
7600 Stockton Blvd Sacramento (95823) *(P-6013)*

Pickwick Hotel The, San Francisco *Also Called: Yhb San Francisco LLC (P-10388)*

Picnic Time Inc .... D....... 805 529-7400
5131 Maureen Ln Moorpark (93021) *(P-3111)*

Pico Cleaners Inc (PA)..D....... 310 274-2431
9150 W Pico Blvd Los Angeles (90035) *(P-10468)*

Pico Party Rents, Simi Valley *Also Called: Pico Rents Inc (P-11050)*

Pico Rents Inc .... D....... 310 275-9431
4646 E Los Angeles Ave Simi Valley (93063) *(P-11050)*

Picore Bristain Initiative Inc .... D....... 818 888-3659
23679 Calabasas Rd # 215 Calabasas (91302) *(P-13022)*

Picture Shop LLC .... D....... 323 785-1550
1017 N Las Palmas Ave Fl 3 Los Angeles (90038) *(P-13876)*

Pie Town Productions Inc .... C....... 818 255-9300
5433 Laurel Canyon Blvd North Hollywood (91607) *(P-13877)*

Piedmont Airlines Inc .... C....... 562 421-1806
4100 E Donald Douglas Dr Long Beach (90808) *(P-3840)*

Piedmont Airlines Inc .... C....... 559 269-5694
5175 E Clinton Way Fresno (93727) *(P-3841)*

Piedmont Gardens, Oakland *Also Called: Humangood Norcal (P-8820)*

Piege Co (PA)...D....... 818 727-9100
20120 Plummer St Chatsworth (91311) *(P-6216)*

Piehl, Joel J DDS, Hawthorne *Also Called: Schnierow Dental Care (P-15249)*

Pier 39 Limited Partnership (PA)..D....... 415 705-5500
Beach & Embarcadero Level 3 San Francisco (94133) *(P-8744)*

Pier Restaurant, San Francisco *Also Called: Blue and Gold Fleet (P-3805)*

Pierce Brothers (DH)...D....... 818 763-9121
10621 Victory Blvd North Hollywood (91606) *(P-10515)*

Piercey North Inc .... C....... 408 240-1400
525 E Bayshore Rd Redwood City (94063) *(P-7279)*

Piercey Toyota, Redwood City *Also Called: Piercey North Inc (P-7279)*

Pierre Landscape Inc .... C....... 626 587-2121
5455 2nd St Irwindale (91706) *(P-457)*

Pih Health Inc (PA)..A....... 562 698-0811
12401 Washington Blvd Whittier (90602) *(P-16323)*

Pih Health Downey Hospital (HQ)..B....... 562 698-0811
11500 Brookshire Ave Downey (90241) *(P-16324)*

Pih Health Good Samaritan Hosp (HQ)..................................A....... 213 977-2121
1225 Wilshire Blvd Los Angeles (90017) *(P-16325)*

Pih Health Hospital - Whitti .... A....... 562 904-5482
11500 Brookshire Ave Downey (90241) *(P-16326)*

Pih Health Whittier Hospital (HQ)...A....... 562 698-0811
12401 Washington Blvd Whittier (90602) *(P-16327)*

Pilgrim Haven, Los Altos *Also Called: Humangood Norcal (P-15859)*

Pilgrim Operations LLC .... B....... 818 478-4500
12020 Chandler Blvd Ste 200 North Hollywood (91607) *(P-5240)*

Pilgrim Place In Claremont (PA)...C....... 909 399-5500
625 Mayflower Rd Claremont (91711) *(P-15889)*

Pilgrim Studios Inc .... D....... 818 728-8800
12020 Chandler Blvd Ste 200 North Hollywood (91607) *(P-13161)*

Pillsbury, Los Angeles *Also Called: Pillsbury Wnthrop Shaw Pttman (P-17611)*

Pillsbury Winthrop Shaw .... C....... 415 983-1000
4 Embarcadero Ctr Fl 22 San Francisco (94111) *(P-17608)*

Pillsbury Winthrop Shaw .... B....... 415 983-1075
50 Fremont St Fl 5 San Francisco (94105) *(P-17609)*

Pillsbury Wnthrop Shaw Pttman .... D....... 916 329-4700
500 Capitol Mall Ste 1800 Sacramento (95814) *(P-17610)*

Pillsbury Wnthrop Shaw Pttman .... C....... 213 488-7100
725 S Figueroa St Ste 2800 Los Angeles (90017) *(P-17611)*

Pillsbury Wnthrop Shaw Pttman .... D....... 650 233-4500
2550 Hanover St Palo Alto (94304) *(P-17612)*

Pilot Freight Services, San Diego *Also Called: Miramar Transportation Inc (P-4059)*

Pilot Painting & Construction, Cypress *Also Called: Power Maintenance Services Inc (P-1632)*

Pimco, Newport Beach *Also Called: Pacific Investment MGT Co LLC (P-9386)*

Pimco Cyman Trst Pmco Cyman GL .... C....... 949 720-6000
650 Newport Center Dr Newport Beach (92660) *(P-9387)*

Pindler, Moorpark *Also Called: Pindler & Pindler Inc (P-6160)*

Pindler & Pindler Inc (PA)...D....... 805 531-9090
11910 Poindexter Ave Moorpark (93021) *(P-6160)*

Pine & Powell Partners LLC .... D....... 415 989-3500
905 California St San Francisco (94108) *(P-10119)*

Pine Grove Hospital Corp .... C 818 348-0500
9449 San Fernando Rd Sun Valley (91352) *(P-16656)*

Pine Mountain Lake, Groveland *Also Called: Pine Mountain Lake Association (P-18894)*

Pine Mountain Lake Association (PA) .... C 209 962-4080
19228 Pine Mountain Dr Groveland (95321) *(P-18894)*

Pine Park Health Inc .... D 925 594-3533
2144 65th Ave Ste F Oakland (94621) *(P-14994)*

Pine View Center, Paradise *Also Called: Sunbrdge Prdise Rhbltiton Ctr (P-15687)*

Pinedridge Care Ctr, San Rafael *Also Called: Mariner Health Care Inc (P-15575)*

Piner's Medical Supply, Napa *Also Called: Piners Nursing Home Inc (P-15627)*

Piners Nursing Home Inc .... D 707 224-7925
1800 Pueblo Ave Napa (94558) *(P-15627)*

Pinery LLC .... D 858 675-3575
13701 Highland Valley Rd Escondido (92025) *(P-570)*

Pines Resorts of California (PA) .... C 559 642-3121
54449 Road 432 Bass Lake (93604) *(P-7503)*

Pingcap (us) Inc .... D 650 382-9973
1250 Borregas Ave Sunnyvale (94089) *(P-11828)*

PINNACLE COMMUNICATION SERVICE, Glendale *Also Called: Pinnacle Networking Svcs Inc (P-1805)*

Pinnacle Escrow Company, Northridge *Also Called: Pinnacle Estate Properties (P-9133)*

Pinnacle Estate Properties (PA) .... C 818 993-4707
9137 Reseda Blvd Northridge (91324) *(P-9133)*

Pinnacle Hotels Usa Inc .... D 858 974-8201
8369 Vickers St Ste 101 San Diego (92111) *(P-10120)*

Pinnacle Networking Svcs Inc .... C 818 241-6009
730 Fairmont Ave Glendale (91203) *(P-1805)*

Pinnacle Rvrside Hspitality LP .... C 951 784-8000
3400 Market St Riverside (92501) *(P-10121)*

Pinnacle Travel Services LLC .... C 310 414-1787
390 N Pacific Coast Hwy El Segundo (90245) *(P-3946)*

Pinnacle Veterinary Center, Santa Clarita *Also Called: Delphic Enterprises Inc (P-334)*

Pinsetters Inc .... D 916 488-7545
2600 Watt Ave Sacramento (95821) *(P-14121)*

Pinterest, San Francisco *Also Called: Pinterest Inc (P-12607)*

Pinterest Inc (PA) .... B 415 762-7100
651 Brannan St San Francisco (94107) *(P-12607)*

Pioneer, Woodland *Also Called: Pioneer Hi-Bred Intl Inc (P-6830)*

Pioneer Healthcare Svcs LLC .... B 800 683-1209
6255 Ferris Sq # F San Diego (92121) *(P-11201)*

Pioneer Hi-Bred Intl Inc .... D 530 666-1084
18285 County Road 96 Woodland (95695) *(P-6830)*

Pioneer House, Sacramento *Also Called: Cathedral Pioneer Church Homes (P-15367)*

Pioneer Theatres Inc .... C 310 532-8183
2500 Redondo Beach Blvd Torrance (90504) *(P-13426)*

Pioneers Mem Healthcare Dst (PA) .... A 760 351-3333
207 W Legion Rd Brawley (92227) *(P-16328)*

PIONEERS MEMORIAL HOSPITAL, Brawley *Also Called: Pioneers Mem Healthcare Dst (P-16328)*

Pipeline Group LLC .... C 949 296-8375
2850 Redhill Ave Ste 110 Santa Ana (92705) *(P-20177)*

Pipeline Health LLC (PA) .... C 310 379-2134
898 N Pacific Coast Hwy Ste 700 El Segundo (90245) *(P-16329)*

Pipline, Oxnard *Also Called: West Coast Wldg & Piping Inc (P-13756)*

Pircher Nichols & Meeks (PA) .... D 310 201-0132
1925 Century Park E Ste 1700 Los Angeles (90067) *(P-17613)*

Pismo Coast Village Inc .... D 805 773-1811
165 S Dolliver St Pismo Beach (93449) *(P-10122)*

Pitco Foods, San Jose *Also Called: Pacific Groservice Inc (P-6881)*

Pitts & Bachmann Realtors Inc .... D 805 969-5005
1482 E Valley Rd Ste 44 Santa Barbara (93108) *(P-9134)*

Pitts & Bachmann Realtors Inc .... D 805 963-1391
1436 State St Santa Barbara (93101) *(P-9135)*

Pittsburgh Health Center, Pittsburg *Also Called: CC Co Health Cntr Information (P-14661)*

Piveg Inc .... C 858 436-3070
3525 Del Mar Heights Rd Ste 1069 San Diego (92130) *(P-6278)*

Pivot Bio Inc .... B 515 436-4762
2910 7th St Ste 100 Berkeley (94710) *(P-19843)*

Pivot Health Technologies Inc .... D 650 216-9680
1010 Commercial St Ste C San Carlos (94070) *(P-11829)*

Pivot Interiors Inc .... D 949 988-5400
3200 Park Center Dr Ste 100 Costa Mesa (92626) *(P-1806)*

Pivot Interiors Inc (PA) .... C 408 432-5600
3355 Scott Blvd Ste 110 Santa Clara (95054) *(P-7425)*

Pivot3 Inc .... C 512 807-2666
614 Lighthouse Ave Ste C Pacific Grove (93950) *(P-12318)*

Pivotal Labs, San Francisco *Also Called: Pivotal Software Inc (P-11830)*

Pivotal Software Inc (HQ) .... C 415 777-4868
875 Howard St Fl 5 San Francisco (94103) *(P-11830)*

Pixar .... C 707 364-7854
1215 45th St Emeryville (94608) *(P-10696)*

Pixar .... C 510 922-4075
500 N Buena Vista St Burbank (91505) *(P-13427)*

Pixar (DH) .... B 510 922-3000
1200 Park Ave Emeryville (94608) *(P-13878)*

Pixar Animation Studios, Emeryville *Also Called: Pixar (P-10696)*

Pixar Animation Studios, Emeryville *Also Called: Pixar (P-13878)*

Pixel Labs LLC .... D 512 560-5961
500 Technology Dr Ste 450 Irvine (92618) *(P-19995)*

Pixi Inc .... D 310 670-7767
10351 Santa Monica Blvd Ste 410 Los Angeles (90025) *(P-6138)*

Pixi Beauty, Los Angeles *Also Called: Pixi Inc (P-6138)*

Pixlee Turnto Inc .... C 718 753-5307
2443 Fillmore St San Francisco (94115) *(P-11831)*

Pixomondo LLC .... A 310 394-0555
2055 S Barrington Ave Los Angeles (90025) *(P-13946)*

Pixverse, Emeryville *Also Called: Magicom Inc (P-12832)*

Pjbs Holdings Inc (PA) .... D 661 822-5273
1401 Goodrick Dr Tehachapi (93561) *(P-4920)*

Pjcc .... D 650 212-7522
800 Foster City Blvd Foster City (94404) *(P-18617)*

PJs Lumber Inc .... D 209 850-9444
250 D St Turlock (95380) *(P-2193)*

PJs Lumber Inc .... C 510 743-5300
45055 Fremont Blvd Fremont (94538) *(P-5181)*

Pjs Rebar Inc .... D 510 490-0321
45055 Fremont Blvd Fremont (94538) *(P-5510)*

Pk1 Inc (HQ) .... D 559 662-1910
401 S Granada Dr Madera (93637) *(P-2522)*

Pkl Services Inc .... C 858 679-1755
14265 Danielson St Poway (92064) *(P-13792)*

Place Asian Amrcn Rcovery Svcs, San Jose *Also Called: Asian Amercn Recovery Svcs Inc (P-16662)*

Placentia Linda Hospital, Placentia *Also Called: Tenet Healthsystem Medical Inc (P-16699)*

Placer County Water Agency .... D 530 367-6701
24625 Harrison St Foresthill (95631) *(P-4660)*

Placer County Water Agency (PA) .... D 530 823-4850
144 Ferguson Rd Auburn (95603) *(P-4661)*

Placer County Water Agency, Auburn *Also Called: Placer County Water Agency (P-4661)*

Placer Drmtlogy Skin Care Ctr .... D 916 797-6261
9624 Wexford Cir Granite Bay (95746) *(P-14995)*

Placer Labs Inc .... B 415 228-2444
440 N Barranca Ave Pmb 1277 Covina (91723) *(P-11832)*

Placer.ai, Covina *Also Called: Placer Labs Inc (P-11832)*

Plaid Inc (PA) .... D 415 799-1354
1098 Harrison St San Francisco (94103) *(P-12681)*

Plan Member Financial Corp .... C 800 874-6910
6187 Carpinteria Ave Carpinteria (93013) *(P-8216)*

Planada Family Health Center, Atwater *Also Called: Golden Valley Health Centers (P-14764)*

Planet, San Francisco *Also Called: Planet Labs Inc (P-12608)*

Planet Green, Chatsworth *Also Called: Planet Green Cartridges Inc (P-3098)*

Planet Green Cartridges Inc .... D 818 725-2596
20724 Lassen St Chatsworth (91311) *(P-3098)*

Planet Labs Inc (HQ) .... B 415 829-3313
645 Harrison St Fl 4 San Francisco (94107) *(P-12608)*

Planet Orange, San Jose *Also Called: Natural Orange Inc (P-10838)*

Planetscale Inc .... D 415 706-2184
535 Mission St Fl 14 San Francisco (94105) *(P-11833)*

Planful Inc (HQ) .... C 650 249-7100
555 Twin Dolphin Dr Ste 400 Redwood City (94065) *(P-12319)*

ALPHABETIC SECTION — PMC Capital Partners LLC

Plangrid Inc (HQ) .... D....... 800 646-0796
2111 Mission St Ste 400 San Francisco (94110) *(P-12320)*

Planmember Services, Carpinteria *Also Called: Plan Member Financial Corp (P-8216)*

Planned Parenthood Los Angeles (PA) .... D....... 213 284-3200
400 W 30th St Los Angeles (90007) *(P-17108)*

Planned Prnthood Mar Monte Inc .... C....... 408 287-7532
1746 The Alameda San Jose (95126) *(P-17109)*

Planned Prnthood of PCF Sthwes (PA) .... D....... 619 881-4500
1075 Camino Del Rio S Ste 100 San Diego (92108) *(P-17110)*

Planned Prnthood of PCF Sthwes .... D....... 619 881-4500
1964 Via Ctr Vista (92081) *(P-17111)*

Planned Prnthood of PCF Sthwes .... D....... 619 881-4652
4501 Mission Bay Dr Ste 1c San Diego (92109) *(P-17112)*

Planning In A Box, Milpitas *Also Called: Pluto7 Consulting Inc (P-20829)*

Planprescriber Inc .... C....... 650 584-2700
440 E Middlefield Rd Mountain View (94043) *(P-8640)*

Plant 04, Reedley *Also Called: Moonlight Packing Corporation (P-4133)*

Plant 16, Van Nuys *Also Called: Weststar Cinemas Inc (P-14008)*

Plant Construction Company LP .... B....... 415 285-0500
300 Newhall St San Francisco (94124) *(P-992)*

Plant Maintenance Inc .... D....... 925 228-3285
1330 Arnold Dr Ste 147 Martinez (94553) *(P-11317)*

Plantel Nurseries Inc .... B....... 805 934-4300
3990 Foxen Canyon Rd Santa Maria (93454) *(P-147)*

Platform Science Inc .... C....... 844 475-8724
9560 Towne Centre Dr # 200 San Diego (92121) *(P-11834)*

Platform9 Systems Inc .... D....... 650 898-7369
800 W El Camino Real Ste 180 Mountain View (94040) *(P-11835)*

Platinum Capital Group (PA) .... D....... 310 406-3505
3500 N Sepulveda Blvd Ste E Manhattan Beach (90266) *(P-8051)*

Platinum Clg Indianapolis LLC .... B....... 310 584-8000
1522 2nd St Santa Monica (90401) *(P-10943)*

Platinum Construction Inc .... D....... 714 527-0700
865 S East St Anaheim (92805) *(P-993)*

Platinum Disc LLC .... D....... 608 784-6620
10203 Santa Monica Blvd Fl 5 Los Angeles (90067) *(P-6048)*

Platinum Empire Group Inc .... C....... 310 821-5888
2430 Amsler St Ste B Torrance (90505) *(P-11318)*

Platinum Group Companies Inc (PA) .... C....... 818 721-3800
22560 La Quilla Dr Chatsworth (91311) *(P-9327)*

Platinum Healthcare Staffing, Torrance *Also Called: Platinum Empire Group Inc (P-11318)*

Platinum Landscape Inc .... C....... 760 200-3673
42575 Melanie Pl Ste C Palm Desert (92211) *(P-458)*

Platinum Performance Inc .... D....... 800 553-2400
760 Mcmurray Rd Buellton (93427) *(P-13643)*

Platinum Roofing Inc .... D....... 408 280-5028
11500 W Olympic Blvd Ste 530 Los Angeles (90064) *(P-2078)*

Platinum Visual Systems, Corona *Also Called: ABC School Equipment Inc (P-5464)*

Plaxo Inc .... D....... 408 900-8701
1050 Enterprise Way # 200 Sunnyvale (94089) *(P-4518)*

Play Versus Inc .... D....... 949 636-4193
2236 S Barrington Ave Ste A Los Angeles (90064) *(P-19098)*

Playa Proper Jv LLC .... D....... 310 645-0400
8639 Lincoln Blvd Los Angeles (90045) *(P-10123)*

Playboy, Los Angeles *Also Called: Playboy Enterprises Inc (P-7589)*

Playboy Enterprises Inc (HQ) .... D....... 310 424-1800
10960 Wilshire Blvd Fl 22 Los Angeles (90024) *(P-7589)*

Playboy Entrmt Group Inc (DH) .... C....... 323 276-4000
2300 W Empire Ave Burbank (91504) *(P-13879)*

Playhaven LLC .... C....... 310 308-9668
1447 2nd St Ste 200 Santa Monica (90401) *(P-11836)*

Playphone Inc .... D....... 408 261-6200
3031 Tisch Way Ste 110pw San Jose (95128) *(P-11837)*

Playvox, Sunnyvale *Also Called: Arcaris Inc (P-12097)*

Playvs, Los Angeles *Also Called: Play Versus Inc (P-19098)*

Playwrights Foundation Inc .... D....... 415 626-2176
1616 16th St Ste 350 San Francisco (94103) *(P-14055)*

Plaza Bank .... D....... 949 502-4300
18200 Von Kaman Ave Ste 5 Irvine (92612) *(P-7735)*

Plaza De La Raza Child Dev Svc (PA) .... D....... 562 776-1301
13300 Crossroads Pkwy N Ste 440 La Puente (91746) *(P-18345)*

Plaza De La Raza Child Develop .... D....... 323 224-1788
225 N Avenue 25 Los Angeles (90031) *(P-18346)*

Plaza De La Raza Child Develop .... D....... 562 695-1070
6411 Norwalk Blvd Whittier (90606) *(P-18347)*

Plaza Home Mortgage Inc .... C....... 858 346-1208
9808 Scranton Rd San Diego (92121) *(P-8161)*

Plaza Suites, The, Santa Clara *Also Called: Sierra Lodgings Inc (P-10234)*

Plaza Tower 1, Costa Mesa *Also Called: Regus Business Centre LLC (P-13443)*

PLD Enterprises Inc .... D....... 213 626-4444
440 Stanford Ave Los Angeles (90013) *(P-6476)*

Pleasant Hawaiian Holiday, Westlake Village *Also Called: Pleasant Holidays LLC (P-3947)*

Pleasant Hill Post Acute, Pleasant Hill *Also Called: Pleasant Hillidence Opco LLC (P-15628)*

Pleasant Hillidence Opco LLC .... C....... 925 935-5222
1625 Oak Park Blvd Pleasant Hill (94523) *(P-15628)*

Pleasant Holidays LLC (HQ) .... B....... 818 991-3390
2404 Townsgate Rd Westlake Village (91361) *(P-3947)*

Pleasanton Hilton Hotel, Pleasanton *Also Called: American Property Management (P-9605)*

Pleasanton Nursing & Rehab Ctr, Pleasanton *Also Called: Ghc of Pleasanton LLC (P-15496)*

Pleasanton Truck & Eqp RPS Inc .... C....... 916 387-5288
8844 Elder Creek Rd Ste A Sacramento (95828) *(P-13670)*

Plenty Unlimited Inc (PA) .... D....... 650 735-3737
570 Eccles Ave South San Francisco (94080) *(P-194)*

Plg Estates .... D....... 310 788-0700
9877 Santa Monica Blvd Beverly Hills (90212) *(P-9136)*

Plg Law Group, Encino *Also Called: Price Law Group A Prof Corp (P-17615)*

Plott Family Care Centers, Riverside *Also Called: Orangtree Cnvalescent Hosp Inc (P-16298)*

Plug Connection Inc .... D....... 760 631-0992
2627 Ramona Dr Vista (92084) *(P-148)*

Plug Connection LLC .... C....... 760 631-0992
3742 Blue Bird Canyon Rd Vista (92084) *(P-20508)*

Plum Healthcare Group LLC .... C....... 760 471-0388
100 E San Marcos Blvd Ste 200 San Marcos (92069) *(P-15629)*

Plumas Hospital District (PA) .... C....... 530 283-2121
1065 Bucks Lake Rd Quincy (95971) *(P-16330)*

Plumbing Master, Riverside *Also Called: Lozano Plumbing Services Inc (P-1490)*

Plumbing Piping & Cnstr Inc .... D....... 714 821-0490
5950 Lakeshore Dr Cypress (90630) *(P-1529)*

Plumbing Solution Specialist .... D....... 714 326-1064
28202 Cabot Rd Ste 300 Laguna Niguel (92677) *(P-1530)*

Plumbing Systems West Inc .... D....... 909 794-3823
31491 Outer Highway 10 Redlands (92373) *(P-1531)*

Plumbing World, Long Beach *Also Called: Columbia Specialty Company Inc (P-5896)*

Plumpjack The, Olympic Valley *Also Called: Cncml A California Ltd Partnr (P-9709)*

Pluris Inc .... C....... 408 863-9920
10455 Bandley Dr Cupertino (95014) *(P-12511)*

Plus Group Inc .... A....... 209 342-9022
3300 Tully Rd Ste B1 Modesto (95350) *(P-11319)*

Plus Group Inc .... C....... 925 831-8551
2551 San Ramon Valley Blvd Ste 201 San Ramon (94583) *(P-11320)*

Plusai Inc .... D....... 408 508-4758
3315 Scott Blvd Santa Clara (95054) *(P-12321)*

Plushcare Inc .... D....... 415 231-5333
101 Mission St Ste 800 San Francisco (94105) *(P-14996)*

Pluto7 Consulting Inc .... D....... 408 824-9213
174 Hobbs Ct Milpitas (95035) *(P-20829)*

Plx Technology, San Jose *Also Called: Plx Technology Inc (P-12322)*

Plx Technology Inc (DH) C
1320 Ridder Park Dr San Jose (95131) *(P-12322)*

Plymouth Tower, Riverside *Also Called: Rhf Plymouth Tower (P-15637)*

Plymouth Village, Redlands *Also Called: Humangood Norcal (P-15861)*

Plz Corp .... D....... 951 683-2912
2321 3rd St Riverside (92507) *(P-2631)*

PM Realty Group LP .... A....... 949 390-5500
3 Park Plz Ste 450 Irvine (92614) *(P-8745)*

PM Realty Group LP .... D....... 949 553-8246
4680 Macarthur Ct Newport Beach (92660) *(P-9137)*

Pmb Motorcars LLC .... A....... 626 384-3600
1829 E Garvey Ave N West Covina (91791) *(P-7280)*

PMC Capital Partners LLC .... A....... 818 896-1101
12243 Branford St Sun Valley (91352) *(P-9550)*

PMC Leaders In Chemicals Inc   **ALPHABETIC SECTION**

PMC Leaders In Chemicals Inc (HQ)..C...... 818 896-1101
   12243 Branford St Sun Valley (91352) *(P-2665)*
PMC Southwest LLC, Jurupa Valley *Also Called: Arcticom Group Rfrgn LLC (P-13723)*
Pmcs Group Inc ....D...... 562 498-0808
   2600 E Pacific Coast Hwy Ste 160 Long Beach (90804) *(P-20509)*
Pmn Design Electric Inc ....D...... 925 846-0650
   39 Wyoming St Pleasanton (94566) *(P-1807)*
Pmt Crdit Risk Trnsf Tr 2015-1 ....D...... 818 224-7028
   3043 Townsgate Rd Westlake Village (91361) *(P-9441)*
Pmt Crdit Risk Trnsf Tr 2015-2 ....C...... 818 224-7442
   3043 Townsgate Rd Westlake Village (91361) *(P-9442)*
Pmt Crdit Risk Trnsf Tr 2019-2 ....D...... 818 224-7028
   3043 Townsgate Rd Westlake Village (91361) *(P-9443)*
Pmt Crdit Risk Trnsf Tr 2020-1 ....D...... 818 224-7028
   3043 Townsgate Rd Westlake Village (91361) *(P-9444)*
PNC, San Francisco *Also Called: Esurance Insurance Svcs Inc (P-8556)*
Png Builders ....D...... 626 256-9539
   2392 S Bateman Ave Duarte (91010) *(P-994)*
Pnmac Gmsr Issuer Trust ....A...... 818 746-2271
   3043 Townsgate Rd Westlake Village (91361) *(P-9445)*
Pnmac Holdings Inc (HQ) ....D...... 818 224-7442
   3043 Townsgate Rd Westlake Village (91361) *(P-8011)*
Poindexter Nut Company Inc ....B...... 559 834-1555
   5414 E Floral Ave Selma (93662) *(P-6463)*
Point, Palo Alto *Also Called: Point Digital Finance Inc (P-8162)*
Point Digital Finance Inc ....C...... 888 764-6823
   444 High St Fl 4 Palo Alto (94301) *(P-8162)*
Point Loma Convalescent Hosp ....D...... 619 224-4141
   3202 Duke St San Diego (92110) *(P-15630)*
Point Loma Rhbltation Ctr LLC ....C...... 619 308-3200
   3202 Duke St San Diego (92110) *(P-15631)*
Point One Elec Systems Inc ....D...... 925 667-2935
   6751 Southfront Rd Livermore (94551) *(P-1808)*
Point Reyes Bird Observatory ....D...... 707 781-2555
   3820 Cypress Dr Ste 11 Petaluma (94954) *(P-19904)*
Point360 ....D...... 818 556-5700
   1133 N Hollywood Way Burbank (91505) *(P-13880)*
Point360 (PA)..D...... 818 565-1400
   2701 Media Center Dr Los Angeles (90065) *(P-13947)*
Pointdirect Transport Inc ....D...... 909 371-0837
   19083 Mermack Ave Lake Elsinore (92532) *(P-3527)*
Pointe At Lantern Crest, The, Santee *Also Called: Santee Senior Retirement Com (P-18118)*
Pokeworks, Irvine *Also Called: Beyond Franchise Group Inc (P-7460)*
Polagram, Los Angeles *Also Called: Wellmade Inc (P-20610)*
Polar Air Cargo LP ....B...... 310 568-4551
   100 Oceangate Fl 15 Long Beach (90802) *(P-3842)*
Polar Tankers Inc ....C...... 310 519-8260
   60 Berth San Pedro (90731) *(P-3800)*
Polar Tankers Inc (DH)..D...... 562 388-1400
   300 Oceangate Long Beach (90802) *(P-3801)*
Polarion Software Inc ....D...... 877 572-4005
   1001 Marina Village Pkwy Ste 403 Alameda (94501) *(P-12323)*
Polaris Building Maint Inc ....D...... 650 964-9400
   2580 Wyandotte St Ste E Mountain View (94043) *(P-10944)*
Polaris Global Mobility, San Mateo *Also Called: Topia Mobility Inc (P-20585)*
Polaris Networks, San Jose *Also Called: Polaris Networks Incorporated (P-11838)*
Polaris Networks Incorporated ....D...... 408 625-7273
   14856 Holden Way San Jose (95124) *(P-11838)*
Police Credit Union of Cal (PA)...D...... 415 242-2142
   1250 Grundy Ln San Bruno (94066) *(P-7792)*
Poliseek Ais Insur Sltions Inc ....D...... 866 480-7335
   17785 Center Court Dr N Ste 250 Cerritos (90703) *(P-8641)*
Poll Everywhere Inc ....D...... 800 388-2039
   548 Market St Ste 17358 San Francisco (94104) *(P-18618)*
Polsinelli LLP, Los Angeles *Also Called: Polsinelli PC (P-17614)*
Polsinelli PC ....D...... 310 556-1801
   2049 Century Park E Ste 2300 Los Angeles (90067) *(P-17614)*
Polymer Logistics Inc ....D...... 951 567-2900
   1725 Sierra Ridge Dr Riverside (92507) *(P-2678)*
Polymer Technology Group, The, Berkeley *Also Called: DSM Biomedical Inc (P-19683)*

Polypeptide Labs San Diego LLC ....D...... 858 408-0808
   9395 Cabot Dr San Diego (92126) *(P-2602)*
Polytechnic School ....B...... 626 792-2147
   1030 E California Blvd Pasadena (91106) *(P-17740)*
Polyvore Inc ....D...... 650 968-1195
   701 First Ave Sunnyvale (94089) *(P-6936)*
Pom Medical LLC ....D...... 805 306-2105
   5456 Endeavour Ct Moorpark (93021) *(P-5443)*
Poma Holding Company Inc ....C...... 909 877-2441
   571 W Slover Ave Bloomington (92316) *(P-6734)*
Pomerado Hospital, Poway *Also Called: Palomar Health (P-16310)*
Pomerado Hospital, Poway *Also Called: Palomar Medical Center (P-16313)*
Pomerado Operations LLC ....D...... 858 487-6242
   12696 Monte Vista Rd Poway (92064) *(P-15632)*
Pomeroy Rcrtion Rhbltation Ctr (PA) ....C...... 415 665-4100
   207 Skyline Blvd San Francisco (94132) *(P-18084)*
Pomona Community Health Center ....D...... 909 630-7927
   1450 E Holt Ave Pomona (91767) *(P-18757)*
Pomona Valley Hospital Med Ctr (PA)................................A...... 909 865-9500
   1798 N Garey Ave Pomona (91767) *(P-16331)*
Pomwonderful LLC ....D...... 559 888-8500
   5286 S Del Rey Ave Del Rey (93616) *(P-5919)*
Pomwonderful LLC ....D...... 559 258-4834
   23154 Lerdo Hwy Buttonwillow (93206) *(P-6658)*
Pomwonderful LLC ....D...... 310 966-5800
   900 Airport Blvd Mendota (93640) *(P-6659)*
Ponderosa Electric Inc ....D...... 949 253-3100
   3911 E La Palma Ave Ste D Anaheim (92807) *(P-1809)*
Ponto Nursery ....D...... 760 724-6003
   2545 Ramona Dr Vista (92084) *(P-6872)*
Ponyai Inc ....B...... 510 906-8868
   3501 Gateway Blvd Fremont (94538) *(P-11839)*
Pope Mortgage & Associates Inc ....D...... 909 466-5380
   2980 Inland Empire Blvd Unit 100 Ontario (91764) *(P-8052)*
Poplar Homes, San Jose *Also Called: Onerent Inc (P-9113)*
Popout Inc (PA)..D...... 415 691-7447
   731 Market St Ste 200 San Francisco (94103) *(P-12324)*
Poppy Ridge Inc ....D...... 925 456-8229
   4280 Greenville Rd Livermore (94550) *(P-14281)*
Poppy Ridge Golf Course, Livermore *Also Called: Poppy Ridge Inc (P-14281)*
Poppy State Express Inc ....D...... 209 664-3950
   2700 W Main St Turlock (95380) *(P-3528)*
Popularmedia Inc ....D...... 415 928-5880
   1550 Bryant St Ste 220 San Francisco (94103) *(P-20830)*
Populus Financial Group Inc ....C...... 951 509-3506
   6302 Van Buren Blvd Riverside (92503) *(P-7859)*
Porchlight, San Diego *Also Called: San Diego Home Seller Inc (P-11900)*
Porrey Pines Bank Inc ....C...... 510 899-7500
   1951 Webster St Oakland (94612) *(P-7710)*
Port Dept City of Oakland (PA)...B...... 510 627-1100
   530 Water St 2nd Fl Oakland (94607) *(P-3813)*
Port Dept City of Oakland ....D...... 510 563-3697
   9532 Earhart Rd Ste 205 Oakland (94621) *(P-3905)*
Port Dept of The Cy Oakland ....D...... 510 563-3300
   1 Airport Dr Ste 45 Oakland (94621) *(P-3906)*
Port Logistics Group, Compton *Also Called: Transport Express Inc (P-3599)*
Port Logistics Group Inc ....B...... 310 669-2551
   19801 S Santa Fe Ave Compton (90221) *(P-4076)*
Port of Long Beach ....B...... 562 283-7000
   415 W Ocean Blvd Long Beach (90802) *(P-3814)*
Port of Los Angeles ....B...... 310 732-3508
   425 S Palos Verdes St San Pedro (90731) *(P-3815)*
Port of Oakland, Oakland *Also Called: Port Dept City of Oakland (P-3813)*
PORT OF SAN DIEGO, San Diego *Also Called: San Diego Unified Port Dst (P-3817)*
PORT OF STOCKTON, Stockton *Also Called: Stockton Port District (P-3818)*
Portco Inc ....D...... 415 771-5200
   496 Jefferson St San Francisco (94109) *(P-7504)*
Porteous Enterprises Inc (DH)..C...... 310 549-9180
   1040 E Watson Center Rd Carson (90745) *(P-5732)*
Porter Valley Catering, Northridge *Also Called: Porter Valley Country Club Inc (P-14424)*

ALPHABETIC SECTION
Precision Contracting

Porter Valley Country Club Inc .... C...... 818 360-1071
19216 Singing Hills Dr Northridge (91326) *(P-14424)*

Portermatt Electric Inc .... D...... 714 596-8788
5431 Production Dr Huntington Beach (92649) *(P-1810)*

Porterville Developmental Ctr, Porterville *Also Called: Califrnia Dept Dvlpmental Svcs* *(P-15362)*

Porterville Dialysis Center .... C...... 559 781-5551
385 Pearson Dr Porterville (93257) *(P-16990)*

Porterville Hemodialysis, Porterville *Also Called: Porterville Dialysis Center (P-16990)*

Portfolio Productions Inc .... D...... 510 434-1600
850 42nd Ave Oakland (94601) *(P-5101)*

Porto Inc .... D...... 760 709-3737
12 S San Gorgonio Ave Ste 204 Banning (92220) *(P-18085)*

Porto Vista Hotel, San Diego *Also Called: 1835 Columbia Street LP (P-9587)*

Portofino Hotel Partners LP .... C...... 310 379-8481
260 Portofino Way Redondo Beach (90277) *(P-10124)*

Portofino Inn & Suites Anaheim .... B...... 714 782-7600
1831 S Harbor Blvd Anaheim (92802) *(P-10125)*

Portola Hotel & Spa, Monterey *Also Called: Custom House Hotel LP (P-9735)*

Portola Pharmaceuticals Inc (DH) .... C...... 650 246-7300
270 E Grand Ave South San Francisco (94080) *(P-19760)*

Portworx, Mountain View *Also Called: Portworx Inc (P-11840)*

Portworx Inc .... D...... 650 386-0766
650 Castro St Ste 400 Mountain View (94041) *(P-11840)*

Posh'n Bae, Woodland Hills *Also Called: Conquistador International LLC (P-6103)*

Poshmark Inc (HQ) .... A...... 650 262-4771
203 Redwood Shores Pkwy Fl 8 Redwood City (94065) *(P-12325)*

Positioning Universal Inc .... D...... 619 639-0235
7071 Convoy Ct Ste 300 San Diego (92111) *(P-12858)*

Positive Behavior Steps, San Dimas *Also Called: Positive Behavior Steps Corp (P-17113)*

Positive Behavior Steps Corp .... D...... 626 940-5180
675 Cliffside Dr San Dimas (91773) *(P-17113)*

Post Alarm Systems (PA) .... D...... 626 446-7159
47 E Saint Joseph St Arcadia (91006) *(P-13138)*

Post Alarm Systems Patrol Svcs, Arcadia *Also Called: Post Alarm Systems (P-13138)*

Post Group Inc (PA) .... C...... 323 462-2300
1415 N Cahuenga Blvd Los Angeles (90028) *(P-13948)*

Post St Rnssnce Prtners A Cal .... B...... 415 563-0303
545 Post St San Francisco (94102) *(P-10126)*

Postaer Rubin and Associates .... C...... 312 644-3636
2525 Colorado Ave Ste 100 Santa Monica (90404) *(P-10662)*

Postalio Inc .... D...... 408 616-9284
75 Higuera St Ste 240 San Luis Obispo (93401) *(P-20510)*

Postman, San Francisco *Also Called: Postman Inc (P-11841)*

Postman Inc (PA) .... D...... 415 796-6470
201 Mission St Ste 2375 San Francisco (94105) *(P-11841)*

Postmates Inc (HQ) .... D...... 800 882-6106
950 23rd St San Francisco (94107) *(P-4171)*

Potawot Health Clinic, Arcata *Also Called: United Indian Health Svcs Inc (P-15143)*

Potential Industries Inc (PA) .... C...... 310 549-5901
720 East E St Wilmington (90744) *(P-4921)*

Pottery World Inc .... D...... 916 624-8080
4419 Granite Dr Rocklin (95677) *(P-7590)*

Poumtjack Hotels, Napa *Also Called: Carneros Inn LLC (P-9680)*

Poundex Associates Corporation .... D...... 909 444-5878
21490 Baker Pkwy City Of Industry (91789) *(P-5102)*

Poway Homecare, San Diego *Also Called: Maxim Healthcare Services Inc (P-16893)*

Poway Toyota, Poway *Also Called: Poway Toyota Scion Inc (P-7281)*

Poway Toyota Scion Inc .... C...... 858 486-2900
13631 Poway Rd Poway (92064) *(P-7281)*

Powell Works, La Puente *Also Called: Powell Works Inc (P-5859)*

Powell Works Inc .... B...... 909 861-6699
17807 Maclaren St Ste B La Puente (91744) *(P-5859)*

Powell, Matthew W, Sacramento *Also Called: Wilke Fleury Hoffelt Gould & Birney (P-17679)*

Power Acoustik Electronics, Montebello *Also Called: Epsilon Electronics Inc (P-5603)*

Power Automation Systems, Lathrop *Also Called: California Natural Products (P-2432)*

Power Constructors Inc .... D...... 916 858-8601
2934 Gold Pan Ct Ste 4 Rancho Cordova (95670) *(P-19361)*

Power Digital Marketing Inc (PA) .... B...... 619 501-1211
2251 San Diego Ave Ste A250 San Diego (92110) *(P-20511)*

Power Engineering Construction Company .... D...... 510 337-3800
1501 Viking St Ste 200 Alameda (94501) *(P-1314)*

Power Generation Entps Inc .... C...... 818 484-8550
26764 Oak Ave Canyon Country (91351) *(P-5860)*

Power Maintenance Services Inc .... D...... 714 229-5900
5555 Corporate Ave Cypress (90630) *(P-1632)*

Power Plant, Glendale *Also Called: City of Glendale (P-4564)*

Power Plus, Corona *Also Called: SRbray LLC (P-1849)*

Power Studios Inc .... C...... 310 314-2800
300 Rose Ave Venice (90291) *(P-13881)*

Power Systems Division, Foresthill *Also Called: Placer County Water Agency (P-4660)*

Powered By Fulfillment Inc .... D...... 626 825-9841
20880 Krameria Ave Riverside (92518) *(P-3656)*

Powerlight, Richmond *Also Called: Sunpower Corporation Systems (P-1576)*

Powers Park Healthcare Inc .... D...... 805 687-6651
3880 Via Lucero Santa Barbara (93110) *(P-15633)*

Powerschool .... B...... 877 873-1550
150 Parkshore Dr Folsom (95630) *(P-8746)*

Powerschool Group LLC (HQ) .... C...... 916 288-1588
150 Parkshore Dr Folsom (95630) *(P-12326)*

Powerschool Holdings Inc .... A...... 877 873-1550
150 Parkshore Dr Folsom (95630) *(P-12327)*

Powersource Talent LLC .... C...... 424 835-0878
12655 W Jefferson Blvd Ste 400 Los Angeles (90066) *(P-20512)*

Powertec Company Inc (PA) .... D...... 951 332-1198
1151 W Vermont Ave Anaheim (92802) *(P-1153)*

Ppc Enterprises Inc .... C...... 951 354-5402
5920 Rickenbacker Ave Riverside (92504) *(P-1532)*

Ppd Holding LLC (PA) .... D...... 310 733-2100
10119 Jefferson Blvd Culver City (90232) *(P-2451)*

Pphm Inc .... D...... 714 508-6100
14282 Franklin Ave Tustin (92780) *(P-6139)*

Ppmc, Corona *Also Called: Primary Provider MGT Co Inc (P-20181)*

Pponext West Inc .... B...... 888 446-6098
1501 Hughes Way Ste 400 Long Beach (90810) *(P-17298)*

Pps Parking Inc .... A...... 949 223-8707
1800 E Garry Ave Ste 107 Santa Ana (92705) *(P-10570)*

PR Construction Inc .... D...... 714 637-7848
1995 N Batavia St Orange (92865) *(P-995)*

Prager University Foundation .... D...... 833 772-4378
15021 Ventura Blvd Ste 552 Sherman Oaks (91403) *(P-13882)*

Prairie City Commons LLC .... D...... 916 458-0303
645 Willard Dr Folsom (95630) *(P-15784)*

Prairie City Landing, Folsom *Also Called: Prairie City Commons LLC (P-15784)*

Pramira Inc .... C...... 800 678-1169
404 N Berry St Brea (92821) *(P-12859)*

Prana, Carlsbad *Also Called: Prana Living LLC (P-6183)*

Prana Living LLC (HQ) .... D...... 866 915-6457
3209 Lionshead Ave Carlsbad (92010) *(P-6183)*

PRBO, Petaluma *Also Called: Point Reyes Bird Observatory (P-19904)*

PRC Multi-Family LLC 562 803-5000
10000 Imperial Hwy Downey (90242) *(P-8854)*

Prdctions N Fremantle Amer Inc (DH) .... D...... 818 748-1100
2900 W Alameda Ave Unit 800 Burbank (91505) *(P-14056)*

Pre-Employcom Inc 800 300-1821
3615 Meadow View Dr Redding (96002) *(P-11202)*

Precept Advisory Group LLC (DH) .... D...... 949 955-1430
130 Theory Ste 200 Irvine (92617) *(P-8642)*

Precept Group The, Irvine *Also Called: Precept Advisory Group LLC (P-8642)*

Precious Enterprises Inc .... D...... 408 265-2226
14130 Douglass Ln Saratoga (95070) *(P-18348)*

Precise Air Systems Inc .... D...... 818 646-9757
5467 W San Fernando Rd Los Angeles (90039) *(P-1533)*

Precise Fit Limited One LLC .... B...... 310 824-1800
17011 Beach Blvd Ste 900 Huntington Beach (92647) *(P-11203)*

Preciseq Inc .... D...... 310 709-6094
11601 Wilshire Blvd Fl 5 Los Angeles (90025) *(P-12860)*

Precision Cancer Medicine Bldg, San Francisco *Also Called: University Cal San Francisco (P-16700)*

Precision Contracting, Irvine *Also Called: Danny Ryan Precision Contg Inc (P-2233)*

Precision Dermatology Inc — ALPHABETIC SECTION

Precision Dermatology Inc .... D....... 415 202-1540
7064 Corline Ct Ste C Sebastopol (95472) *(P-14997)*

Precision Dynamics Corporation (HQ) .... C....... 818 897-1111
25124 Springfield Ct Ste 200 Valencia (91355) *(P-2528)*

Precision Effect Inc .... D....... 800 634-5315
3 Macarthur Pl Ste 700 Santa Ana (92707) *(P-10663)*

PRECISION EFFECT INC., Santa Ana Also Called: Precision Effect Inc *(P-10663)*

Precision Emprise Inc .... D....... 650 867-8657
335 Beach Rd Burlingame (94010) *(P-2149)*

Precision Energy Efficient Ltg, Yorba Linda Also Called: Precision Fluorescent West Inc *(P-5587)*

Precision Fluid Controls Inc .... D....... 916 626-3029
1751 Aviation Blvd Ste 200 Lincoln (95648) *(P-5920)*

Precision Fluorescent West Inc (DH) .... D....... 352 692-5900
23281 La Palma Ave Yorba Linda (92887) *(P-5587)*

Precision Ideo Inc .... B....... 650 688-3400
2525 16th St San Francisco (94103) *(P-13428)*

Precision Netwrk Solutions LLC .... D....... 562 318-4242
4259 Deeboyar Ave Lakewood (90712) *(P-12861)*

Precision Pipeline LLC .... B....... 909 229-6858
10400 Trademark St Rancho Cucamonga (91730) *(P-1250)*

Precision Silicones, Chino Also Called: Wacker Chemical Corporation *(P-2636)*

Precision Toxicology .... D....... 800 635-6901
4215 Sorrento Valley Blvd San Diego (92121) *(P-16742)*

Preferred Brokers Inc (PA) .... D....... 661 836-2345
9100 Ming Ave Ste 100 Bakersfield (93311) *(P-9138)*

Preferred Carrier California, Chino Also Called: Advanced Multimodal Dist Inc *(P-4142)*

Preferred Employers Insur Co .... D....... 619 688-3900
9797 Aero Dr Ste 200 San Diego (92123) *(P-8643)*

Preferred Frzr Svcs - Lbf LLC .... D....... 323 263-8811
4901 Bandini Blvd Vernon (90058) *(P-3657)*

Preferred Hlthcare Rgistry Inc .... C....... 800 787-6787
4909 Murphy Canyon Rd Ste 310 San Diego (92123) *(P-11204)*

Pregel America Inc .... C....... 909 598-8980
116 S Brent Cir Walnut (91789) *(P-18349)*

Premere Event Services, Huntington Beach Also Called: Love At First Bite Catering *(P-7493)*

Premier Ambulance, Brea Also Called: Premier Medical Transport Inc *(P-3286)*

Premier Amer Wealth MGT Group, Chatsworth Also Called: Premier America Credit Union *(P-7830)*

Premier America Credit Union (PA) .... C....... 818 772-4000
19867 Prairie St Lbby Chatsworth (91311) *(P-7830)*

Premier Cold Storage & Pkg LLC .... C....... 949 444-8859
1071 E 233rd St Carson (90745) *(P-3658)*

Premier Commercial Bancorp .... D....... 714 978-2400
2400 E Katella Ave Ste 125 Anaheim (92806) *(P-7711)*

Premier Dealer Services Inc .... D....... 858 810-1700
9449 Balboa Ave Ste 300 San Diego (92123) *(P-8644)*

Premier Dental Holdings Inc (PA) .... B....... 714 480-3000
530 S Main St Ste 600 Orange (92868) *(P-15248)*

Premier Disability Svcs LLC .... D....... 310 280-4000
909 N Pacific Coast Hwy Fl 11 El Segundo (90245) *(P-18619)*

Premier Food Services Inc .... B....... 760 843-8000
14359 Amargosa Rd Ste F Victorville (92392) *(P-6279)*

Premier Fuel Delivery Service, Riverside Also Called: Premier Fuel Distributors Inc *(P-6735)*

Premier Fuel Distributors Inc .... C....... 760 423-3610
156 E La Cadena Dr Riverside (92507) *(P-6735)*

Premier Healthcare Svcs LLC (DH) .... C....... 626 204-7930
3030 Old Ranch Pkwy Ste 100 Seal Beach (90740) *(P-16912)*

Premier Hlthcare Solutions Inc .... D....... 858 569-8629
12225 El Camino Real San Diego (92130) *(P-20178)*

Premier Home Loan Group, Visalia Also Called: Country Club Mortgage Inc *(P-7952)*

Premier IMS Insurance Services, San Diego Also Called: Premier Hlthcare Solutions Inc *(P-20178)*

Premier Infsion Hlthcare Svcs .... D....... 310 328-3897
19500 Normandie Ave Torrance (90502) *(P-16913)*

Premier Infusion Care, Torrance Also Called: Premier Infsion Hlthcare Svcs *(P-16913)*

Premier Meat Company, Vernon Also Called: Wayne Provision Co Inc *(P-6507)*

Premier Medical Transport Inc .... C....... 805 340-5191
260 N Palm St # 200 Brea (92821) *(P-3286)*

Premier Mushrooms LP .... C....... 530 458-2700
2847 Niagara Ave Colusa (95932) *(P-165)*

Premier Mushrooms LP (PA) .... D....... 530 458-2700
2880 Niagara Ave Colusa (95932) *(P-6569)*

Premier Nutrition Company LLC (HQ) .... C....... 415 814-9410
1222 67th St Ste 210 Emeryville (94608) *(P-6660)*

Premier Otptent Srgery Ctr Inc .... C....... 909 370-2190
900 E Washington St Ste 155 Colton (92324) *(P-14998)*

Premier Packaging/Assembly, Santa Fe Springs Also Called: Haringa Inc *(P-13308)*

Premier Pharmacy Service, Baldwin Park Also Called: Good Health Inc *(P-17241)*

Premier Plumbing Company, Riverside Also Called: Ppc Enterprises Inc *(P-1532)*

Premier Pool Service, Gold River Also Called: Premier Pools and Spas Lp *(P-2306)*

Premier Pools and Spas Lp (PA) .... D....... 916 852-0223
11250 Pyrites Way Gold River (95670) *(P-2306)*

Premier Pump and Supply, Rohnert Park Also Called: Pace Supply Corp *(P-5758)*

Premier Residential Svcs LLC .... D....... 760 773-4081
43100 Cook St Ste 101 Palm Desert (92211) *(P-10571)*

Premier Staffing Inc .... D....... 415 362-2211
3595 Mt Diablo Blvd Ste 340 Lafayette (94549) *(P-11205)*

Premier Talent Partners, Lafayette Also Called: Premier Staffing Inc *(P-11205)*

Premier Valley Bank .... C....... 559 438-2002
255 E River Park Cir Ste 180 Fresno (93720) *(P-7736)*

Premiere Credit North Amer LLC .... C....... 844 897-2901
17054 S Harlan Rd Lathrop (95330) *(P-10749)*

Premiere Customs Brokers Inc .... A....... 310 410-6825
5951 Skylab Rd Huntington Beach (92647) *(P-4077)*

Premiere Packaging Inds Inc .... D....... 562 799-9200
12202 Slauson Ave Santa Fe Springs (90670) *(P-6937)*

Premiere Packing, Shafter Also Called: Grimmway Enterprises Inc *(P-180)*

Premiere Rack Solutions Inc .... D....... 909 605-6300
4502 Brickell Privado St Ontario (91761) *(P-5103)*

Premiere Radio Network Inc (DH) .... C....... 818 377-5300
15260 Ventura Blvd Ste 400 Sherman Oaks (91403) *(P-14057)*

Premio Inc (PA) .... C....... 626 839-3100
918 Radecki Ct City Of Industry (91748) *(P-2810)*

Premium Outlet Partners LP .... D....... 805 445-8520
740 Ventura Blvd Camarillo (93010) *(P-8747)*

Premium Outlet Partners LP .... D....... 916 985-0312
13000 Folsom Blvd Ste 309 Folsom (95630) *(P-8748)*

Premium Outlet Partners LP .... D....... 707 448-3661
321 Nut Tree Rd Ste 2 Vacaville (95687) *(P-8749)*

Premium Outlet Partners LP .... D....... 760 804-9045
5620 Paseo Del Norte Ste 100 Carlsbad (92008) *(P-8750)*

Premium Outlet Partners LP .... D....... 408 842-3729
681 Leavesley Rd Gilroy (95020) *(P-8751)*

Premium Outlet Partners LP .... D....... 951 849-6641
48400 Seminole Dr Cabazon (92230) *(P-8752)*

Presbyterian Inter Cmnty Hosp, Whittier Also Called: Interhealth Services Inc *(P-16876)*

Prescott Hotel, The, San Francisco Also Called: Post St Rnssnce Prtners A Cal *(P-10126)*

Prescription Solutions, Carlsbad Also Called: Optumrx Inc *(P-8348)*

Presentation Products Inc (PA) .... D....... 714 367-2900
16751 Knott Ave La Mirada (90638) *(P-7591)*

Preserve Golf Club Inc .... D....... 831 620-6871
1 Rancho San Carlos Rd Carmel (93923) *(P-14282)*

President James Monroe Manor, Sacramento Also Called: Eskaton Properties Inc *(P-18424)*

Presidio Components Inc .... C....... 858 578-9390
7169 Construction Ct San Diego (92121) *(P-5689)*

Presidio Gate Apartments .... C....... 415 567-1050
2770 Lombard St San Francisco (94123) *(P-8855)*

Presidio Hill School .... D....... 415 213-8600
3839 Washington St San Francisco (94118) *(P-17741)*

Presidio Hotel Group LLC .... C....... 916 631-7500
10713 White Rock Rd Rancho Cordova (95670) *(P-10127)*

Presidio Trust .... C....... 415 561-5300
1750 Lincoln Blvd San Francisco (94129) *(P-20899)*

Presido YMCA, San Francisco Also Called: Young MNS Chrstn Assn San Frnc *(P-18992)*

Presort Center, The, Visalia Also Called: Central Valley Presort Inc *(P-10769)*

Prestige Animal Hospital North, Fontana Also Called: People Pets and Vets LLC *(P-341)*

Prestige Animal Hospital South, Fontana Also Called: People Pets and Vets LLC *(P-340)*

Prestige Asssted Lving At Lncs, Lancaster Also Called: PCI Care Venture I *(P-15624)*

Prestige Asssted Lving At Vsli, Visalia Also Called: PCI Care Venture I *(P-15625)*

ALPHABETIC SECTION — Priority Building Services LLC

Prestige Auto Collision Inc .... D 949 470-6031
23726 Via Fabricante Mission Viejo (92691) *(P-13644)*

Prestige Stations Inc (DH) .... C 714 670-5145
4 Centerpointe Dr La Palma (90623) *(P-7147)*

Preston Pipelines, Milpitas Also Called: Preston Pipelines Inc *(P-1251)*

Preston Pipelines Inc (PA) .... C 408 262-1418
133 Bothelo Ave Milpitas (95035) *(P-1251)*

Pretium Packaging, Chino Also Called: Pretium Packaging LLC *(P-2679)*

Pretium Packaging LLC .... C 714 777-9580
13980 Mountain Ave Chino (91710) *(P-2679)*

Prevedere Inc .... D 888 686-7746
440 N Wolfe Rd Sunnyvale (94085) *(P-11842)*

PRI Medical Technologies Inc .... D 818 394-2800
10939 Pendleton St Sun Valley (91352) *(P-5444)*

Pribuss Engineering Inc .... D 650 588-0447
523 Mayfair Ave South San Francisco (94080) *(P-13729)*

Price Industries Inc .... D 858 673-4451
10883 Thornmint Rd San Diego (92127) *(P-2720)*

Price Law Group A Prof Corp (PA) .... C 818 995-4540
15760 Ventura Blvd Ste 800 Encino (91436) *(P-17615)*

Price Postel and Parma LLP .... D 805 962-0011
200 E Carrillo St Ste 400 Santa Barbara (93101) *(P-17616)*

Price-Simms Inc (PA) .... D 408 245-6640
898 W El Camino Real Sunnyvale (94087) *(P-13671)*

Price-Simms Ford LLC .... D 707 421-3300
3050 Auto Mall Ct Fairfield (94534) *(P-7282)*

Pricegrabber.com, Los Angeles Also Called: Pg Usa LLC *(P-7139)*

Pricespider, Irvine Also Called: Neuintel LLC *(P-11771)*

Pricewaterhousecoopers LLP .... A 408 817-3700
488 Almaden Blvd Ste 1800 San Jose (95110) *(P-19623)*

Pride Auto Body, Van Nuys Also Called: Pride Collision Centers Inc *(P-13645)*

Pride Collision Centers Inc (HQ) .... D 818 909-0660
7950 Haskell Ave Van Nuys (91406) *(P-13645)*

Pride Industries (PA) .... C 916 788-2100
10030 Foothills Blvd Roseville (95747) *(P-3796)*

Pride Industries .... C 530 888-0331
13080 Earhart Ave Auburn (95602) *(P-18243)*

Primal Elements, Huntington Beach Also Called: Primal Elements Inc *(P-6140)*

Primal Elements Inc .... D 714 899-0757
18062 Redondo Cir Huntington Beach (92648) *(P-6140)*

Primary Care Assod Med Group I .... C 760 724-1033
3998 Vista Way Ste B Oceanside (92056) *(P-20179)*

Primary Care Assod Med Group I (PA) .... D 760 471-7505
1635 Lake San Marcos Dr Ste 201 San Marcos (92078) *(P-20180)*

Primary Diagnostics Inc .... C 619 356-3701
595 Pacific Ave Fl 4 San Francisco (94133) *(P-11843)*

Primary Provider MGT Co Inc (HQ) .... D 951 280-7700
2115 Compton Ave Ste 301 Corona (92881) *(P-20181)*

Primary School .... D 510 606-4563
2086 Clarke Ave East Palo Alto (94303) *(P-18895)*

Prime Administration LLC .... A 323 549-7155
357 S Curson Ave Los Angeles (90036) *(P-9476)*

Prime Electric, Dublin Also Called: AMS Electric Inc *(P-1665)*

Prime Electric Inc .... A 925 961-1600
1941 Ringwood Ave San Jose (95131) *(P-1811)*

Prime Electric, Inc., San Jose Also Called: Prime Electric Inc *(P-1811)*

Prime Focus World, Culver City Also Called: Dneg North America Inc *(P-13933)*

Prime Global Solutions Inc (PA) .... D 800 424-7746
15801 E Valley Blvd City Of Industry (91744) *(P-4078)*

Prime Group, Los Angeles Also Called: Prime Administration LLC *(P-9476)*

Prime Halthcare Foundation Inc (PA) .... C 909 235-4400
3480 E Guasti Rd Ontario (91761) *(P-16332)*

Prime Health Care .... C 909 394-2727
1350 W Covina Blvd San Dimas (91773) *(P-18350)*

Prime Healthcare Anaheim LLC .... A 714 827-3000
3033 W Orange Ave Anaheim (92804) *(P-16333)*

Prime Healthcare Centinela LLC .... A 310 673-4660
555 E Hardy St Inglewood (90301) *(P-16334)*

Prime Healthcare Services, Ontario Also Called: Bio-Med Services Inc *(P-15962)*

Prime Healthcare Services-Mont .... A 909 625-5411
5000 San Bernardino St Montclair (91763) *(P-16335)*

Prime Hlthcare Hntngton Bch LL .... B 714 843-5000
17772 Beach Blvd Huntington Beach (92647) *(P-16336)*

Prime Hlthcare Srvcs-Mntclair .... C 909 625-5411
5000 San Bernardino St Montclair (91763) *(P-16337)*

Prime Hlthcare Srvcs-Mntclair (DH) .... C 909 625-5411
5000 San Bernardino St Montclair (91763) *(P-16338)*

Prime Hlthcare Svcs - Encino H .... B 818 995-5000
16237 Ventura Blvd Encino (91436) *(P-16339)*

Prime Hlthcare Svcs - Pmpa LLC (DH) .... C 909 235-4400
3300 E Guasti Rd Ste 300 Ontario (91761) *(P-16340)*

Prime Hlthcare Svcs - San Dmas .... B 909 599-6811
1350 W Covina Blvd San Dimas (91773) *(P-16341)*

Prime Hlthcare Svcs - Shrman O .... B 818 981-7111
4929 Van Nuys Blvd Sherman Oaks (91403) *(P-16342)*

Prime Hlthcare Svcs - Shsta LL .... A 530 244-5400
1100 Butte St Redding (96001) *(P-16343)*

Prime Hlthcare Svcs - St John (DH) .... B 913 680-6000
3500 S 4th St Ontario (91761) *(P-16344)*

Prime Hospitality LLC .... D 909 975-5000
2200 E Holt Blvd Ontario (91761) *(P-10128)*

Prime Mso LLC .... D 818 937-9969
550 N Brand Blvd Ste 900 Glendale (91203) *(P-17114)*

Prime One Inc .... C 310 378-1944
22410 Hawthorne Blvd Ste 4 Torrance (90505) *(P-11206)*

Prime Tech Cabinets Inc .... C 949 757-4900
2215 S Standard Ave Santa Ana (92707) *(P-2011)*

Prime Time International, La Quinta Also Called: Sun and Sands Enterprises LLC *(P-6582)*

Prime Transport Inc .... D 909 972-1300
2404 S Grove Ave Ontario (91761) *(P-4172)*

Prime Wheel Corporation .... B 310 326-5080
23920 Vermont Ave Harbor City (90710) *(P-2976)*

Primeco .... D 760 967-8278
220 Oceanside Blvd Oceanside (92054) *(P-1633)*

Primed, San Ramon Also Called: Primed MGT Consulting Svcs Inc *(P-20182)*

Primed MGT Consulting Svcs Inc .... B 925 327-6710
2409 Camino Ramon San Ramon (94583) *(P-20182)*

Primeflight Aviation Svcs Inc .... C 650 877-1560
612 Mcdonald Rd Ste 100 San Francisco (94128) *(P-3907)*

Primerica, Modesto Also Called: Primerica Financial Services *(P-13429)*

Primerica Financial Services .... D 209 545-5887
1620 N Carpenter Rd Ste D47 Modesto (95351) *(P-13429)*

Primero Systems Incorporated .... D 866 426-0779
14123 Rasmussen Way San Diego (92129) *(P-11844)*

Primetime International Inc .... D 760 399-4166
47110 Washington St Ste 103 La Quinta (92253) *(P-6570)*

Primex Clinical Labs Inc (PA) .... D
16742 Stagg St Ste 120 Van Nuys (91406) *(P-16743)*

Primitive Logic Inc .... D 415 391-8080
130 Battery St Fl 3 San Francisco (94111) *(P-12862)*

Primoris Services Corporation .... C 949 598-9242
26000 Commercentre Dr Lake Forest (92630) *(P-1252)*

Prince Peace Lutheran Church .... D 510 797-8186
38451 Fremont Blvd Fremont (94536) *(P-17742)*

Prince Peace Lutheran School, Fremont Also Called: Prince Peace Lutheran Church *(P-17742)*

Princess Cruise Lines Ltd (HQ) .... A 661 753-0000
24305 Town Center Dr Santa Clarita (91355) *(P-3804)*

Princess Cruise Lines Ltd .... A 661 753-2197
24833 Anza Dr Santa Clarita (91355) *(P-3948)*

Princess Cruise Lines Ltd .... A 661 753-0000
24200 Magic Mountain Pkwy Santa Clarita (91355) *(P-3966)*

Princess Cruise Lines Ltd .... C 213 745-0314
1242 E 25th St Los Angeles (90011) *(P-6217)*

Princess Cruises, Santa Clarita Also Called: Princess Cruise Lines Ltd *(P-3804)*

Princess Cruises, Santa Clarita Also Called: Princess Cruise Lines Ltd *(P-3948)*

Principal Svc Solutions Inc .... C 209 408-1982
4285 Spyres Way Ste B Modesto (95356) *(P-19362)*

Prindle Decker & Amaro LLP (PA) .... D 562 436-3946
310 Golden Shore Fl 4 Long Beach (90802) *(P-17617)*

Priority Building Services LLC .... B 858 695-1326
7313 Carroll Rd Ste G San Diego (92121) *(P-10945)*

Priority Building Services LLC (PA) .... D....... 714 255-2963
  1524 W Mable St Anaheim (92802) *(P-10946)*
Priority Ctr Ending The Gnrtna .... D....... 714 543-4333
  1940 E Deere Ave Ste 100 Santa Ana (92705) *(P-18086)*
Priority Landscape Services, Anaheim *Also Called: Priority Building Services LLC (P-10946)*
Priority One Med Trnspt Inc (PA) .... D....... 909 948-4400
  9327 Fairway View Pl Ste 300 Rancho Cucamonga (91730) *(P-3287)*
Prismatik Dentalcraft Inc .... D....... 949 399-1930
  4141 Macarthur Blvd Newport Beach (92660) *(P-16776)*
Pristine Environments Inc (PA) .... D....... 703 245-4751
  3605 Ocean Ranch Blvd Ste 200 Oceanside (92056) *(P-20661)*
Privacera, Fremont *Also Called: Privacera Inc (P-11845)*
Privacera Inc .... D....... 510 413-7300
  39300 Civic Center Dr Ste 140 Fremont (94538) *(P-11845)*
Private Label, City Of Industry *Also Called: Private Label Pc LLC (P-5335)*
Private Label Pc LLC .... C....... 626 965-8686
  748 Epperson Dr City Of Industry (91748) *(P-5335)*
Private Medical-Care Inc .... A....... 562 924-8311
  12898 Towne Center Dr Cerritos (90703) *(P-8357)*
Private Nat Mrtg Accptance LLC (DH) .... A....... 818 224-7401
  6101 Condor Dr Agoura Hills (91301) *(P-8012)*
Private Suite Lax LLC .... C....... 310 907-9950
  6871 W Imperial Hwy Los Angeles (90045) *(P-3190)*
Privilege International Inc .... D....... 323 585-0777
  2323 Firestone Blvd South Gate (90280) *(P-5104)*
Prn Ambulance LLC .... B....... 818 810-3600
  8928 Sepulveda Blvd North Hills (91343) *(P-3288)*
Prn Radio Networks, Sherman Oaks *Also Called: Premiere Radio Network Inc (P-14057)*
Pro Act LLC .... D....... 831 655-4250
  40 Ragsdale Dr Ste 200 Monterey (93940) *(P-6571)*
Pro America Premium Tools, Baldwin Park *Also Called: American Kal Enterprises Inc (P-5720)*
Pro Back Office LLC .... D....... 858 622-1681
  3655 Nobel Dr Ste 520 San Diego (92122) *(P-19624)*
Pro Building Maintenance Inc (PA) .... C....... 951 279-3386
  149 N Maple St Ste H Corona (92878) *(P-10947)*
Pro Energy Services Group LLC .... B....... 760 789-7149
  2060 Aldergrove Ave Escondido (92029) *(P-20662)*
Pro Group Inc .... C....... 951 271-3000
  4160 Temescal Canyon Rd Ste 500 Corona (92883) *(P-9139)*
Pro Loaders Inc .... C....... 909 355-5531
  14032 Santa Ana Ave Fontana (92337) *(P-4079)*
Pro Pacific Fresh, Durham *Also Called: Chico Produce Inc (P-6525)*
Pro Safety & Rescue Inc .... D....... 888 269-5095
  3700 Pegasus Dr Ste 200 Bakersfield (93308) *(P-20513)*
Pro Safety Inc .... C....... 562 364-7450
  20503 Belshaw Ave Carson (90746) *(P-5861)*
Pro Specialties Group Inc .... D....... 858 541-1100
  8221 Arjons Dr Ste F San Diego (92126) *(P-6938)*
Pro Structural Inc .... D....... 951 526-2010
  29190 Riverside Dr Lake Elsinore (92530) *(P-1892)*
Pro Traffic Services Inc .... D....... 760 906-6961
  321 Hunter St Ramona (92065) *(P-1534)*
Pro-Clean Enterprises, San Jose *Also Called: Janpro Inc (P-10913)*
Pro-Craft Construction Inc .... C....... 909 790-5222
  500 Iowa St Ste 100 Redlands (92373) *(P-1535)*
Pro-Cuts, Anaheim *Also Called: Opal Concepts Inc (P-10505)*
Pro-Dex, Irvine *Also Called: Pro-Dex Inc (P-3058)*
Pro-Dex Inc (PA) .... C....... 949 769-3200
  2361 Mcgaw Ave Irvine (92614) *(P-3058)*
Pro-Form Manufacturing LLC .... B....... 707 752-9010
  521 Stone Rd Benicia (94510) *(P-3744)*
Pro-Form Manufacturing LLC .... B....... 707 752-9010
  4725 Industrial Way Benicia (94510) *(P-3745)*
Pro-Tech, Santa Fe Springs *Also Called: Pro-Tech Design & Mfg Inc (P-13430)*
Pro-Tech Design & Mfg Inc (PA) .... D....... 562 207-1680
  14561 Marquardt Ave Santa Fe Springs (90670) *(P-13430)*
Pro-Tech Fire Prtction Systems 916 388-0255
  8880 Cal Center Dr Ste 400 Sacramento (95826) *(P-1536)*
Pro-Tek Consulting (PA) .... C....... 805 807-5571
  21300 Victory Blvd Ste 240 Woodland Hills (91367) *(P-12863)*

Pro-Wash Inc .... D....... 323 756-6000
  9117 S Main St Los Angeles (90003) *(P-10464)*
Pro-Youth .... B....... 559 374-2030
  505 N Court St Visalia (93291) *(P-18896)*
Pro-Youth Heart, Visalia *Also Called: Pro-Youth (P-18896)*
Proactiv, El Segundo *Also Called: Guthy-Renker LLC (P-7583)*
Proactive Bus Solutions Inc .... C....... 510 302-0120
  1290 B St Ste 208 Hayward (94541) *(P-20183)*
Proactive Packg & Display LLC .... D....... 909 390-5624
  602 S Rockefeller Ave Ste A Ontario (91761) *(P-6939)*
Proactive Risk Management Inc .... D....... 213 840-8856
  22617 Hawthorne Blvd Torrance (90505) *(P-20184)*
Probation Department, Clovis *Also Called: County of Fresno (P-17903)*
Probation Department, Fresno *Also Called: County of Fresno (P-17904)*
Probation Department, Pasadena *Also Called: County of Los Angeles (P-17913)*
Probation Department, Lancaster *Also Called: County of Los Angeles (P-17914)*
Probation Department, Los Angeles *Also Called: County of Los Angeles (P-17919)*
Probation Department, Downey *Also Called: County of Los Angeles (P-17920)*
Probation Dept, Los Angeles *Also Called: County of Los Angeles (P-17916)*
Probation Dept, Santa Monica *Also Called: County of Los Angeles (P-17922)*
Probation Dept, Van Nuys *Also Called: County of Los Angeles (P-17923)*
Probation Dept, Los Angeles *Also Called: County of Los Angeles (P-17924)*
Probation Dept, Los Angeles *Also Called: County of Los Angeles (P-17925)*
Probation Dept, Compton *Also Called: County of Los Angeles (P-17926)*
Probation Dept, Pasadena *Also Called: County of Los Angeles (P-17927)*
Probation Dept, San Diego *Also Called: County of San Diego (P-17937)*
Probation Information Ctr Pic, Downey *Also Called: County of Los Angeles (P-17915)*
Probe Information Services Inc .... C....... 916 676-1826
  3835 N Freeway Blvd Ste 228 Sacramento (95834) *(P-13023)*
Prober & Raphael A Law Corp .... D....... 818 227-0100
  20750 Ventura Blvd Ste 100 Woodland Hills (91364) *(P-17618)*
Prober & Raphael, ALC, Woodland Hills *Also Called: Prober & Raphael A Law Corp (P-17618)*
Probusiness Holdings Inc .... D....... 845 354-5372
  3785 Brickway Blvd Ste 200 Santa Rosa (95403) *(P-12609)*
Process Cooling Intl Inc (PA) .... D....... 209 578-1000
  4812 Enterprise Way Modesto (95356) *(P-1537)*
Process Fab Inc .... C....... 562 921-1979
  13153 Lakeland Rd Santa Fe Springs (90670) *(P-2855)*
Processes Unlimited, Bakersfield *Also Called: Processes Unlimited International Inc (P-19363)*
Processes Unlimited International Inc .... B....... 661 396-3770
  5500 Ming Ave Ste 400 Bakersfield (93309) *(P-19363)*
Processing Office, Corcoran *Also Called: J G Boswell Company (P-281)*
Procida Landscape Inc .... C....... 916 387-5296
  8465 Specialty Cir Sacramento (95828) *(P-531)*
Procopio Cory Hargreaves & Savitch LLP (PA) .... C....... 619 238-1900
  530 B St Ste 2200 San Diego (92101) *(P-17619)*
Procore Technologies Inc (PA) .... A....... 866 477-6267
  6309 Carpinteria Ave Carpinteria (93013) *(P-11846)*
Proctoru Inc .... B....... 205 870-8122
  3687 Old Santa Rita Rd Ste 203 Pleasanton (94588) *(P-12682)*
Prodata Research, San Diego *Also Called: Soleil Communications LLC (P-19848)*
Prodege LLC (PA) .... D....... 310 294-9599
  2030 E Maple Ave Ste 200 El Segundo (90245) *(P-11847)*
Produce Exchange Incorporated (DH) .... D....... 925 454-8700
  7407 Southfront Rd Livermore (94551) *(P-6572)*
Producers Dairy Foods Inc (PA) .... C....... 559 264-6583
  250 E Belmont Ave Fresno (93701) *(P-6426)*
Producr-Wrters Gild Amer Pnsio .... D....... 818 846-1015
  2900 W Alameda Ave Unit 1100 Burbank (91505) *(P-8465)*
Product Development Corp .... A....... 831 333-1100
  30 Ragsdale Dr Ste 101 Monterey (93940) *(P-13431)*
Production Framing Systems Inc (PA) .... C....... 916 978-2888
  2000 Opportunity Dr Ste 140 Roseville (95678) *(P-2012)*
Productive Playhouse Inc (PA) .... B....... 323 250-3445
  25231 Paseo De Alicia Ste 205 Laguna Hills (92653) *(P-13432)*
Productos Chata, Chula Vista *Also Called: Culinary Hispanic Foods Inc (P-6623)*
Profes Nwfs Inc .... D....... 510 780-0202
  3559 Arden Rd Hayward (94545) *(P-4080)*
Professional Assessment & .... D....... 909 980-1000
  9330 Baseline Rd Ste 108 Rancho Cucamonga (91701) *(P-15300)*

ALPHABETIC SECTION

Professional Bureau of Collect ....C....... 916 685-3399
   9675 Elk Grove Florin Rd Elk Grove (95624) *(P-10750)*

Professional Cmnty MGT Cal Inc ....D....... 951 359-2840
   11860 Pierce St Ste 100 Riverside (92505) *(P-9140)*

Professional Cmnty MGT Cal Inc ....B....... 951 845-2191
   850 Country Club Dr Banning (92220) *(P-9141)*

Professional Cmnty MGT Cal Inc ....C....... 949 206-0580
   24351 El Toro Rd Laguna Woods (92637) *(P-9142)*

Professional Cmnty MGT Cal Inc ....D....... 760 918-8040
   906 Sycamore Ave Ste 210 Vista (92081) *(P-9143)*

Professional Cmnty MGT Cal Inc ....C....... 949 597-4200
   23522 Paseo De Valencia Laguna Hills (92653) *(P-9144)*

Professional Community MGT, Vista *Also Called: Professional Cmnty MGT Cal Inc (P-9143)*

Professional Community MGT Cal ....C....... 949 380-0725
   23081 Via Campo Verde Aliso Viejo (92656) *(P-20185)*

Professional Cr Reporting Inc ....B....... 714 556-1570
   3560 Hyland Ave Costa Mesa (92626) *(P-7885)*

Professional Health Care Inc ....D....... 831 899-2644
   555 Francis Ave Seaside (93955) *(P-18506)*

Professional Maint Systems, San Diego *Also Called: Professional Maint Systems Inc (P-10948)*

Professional Maint Systems Inc ....A....... 619 276-1150
   4912 Naples St San Diego (92110) *(P-10948)*

Professional Parking ....C....... 949 723-4027
   309 Palm St Newport Beach (92661) *(P-13626)*

Professional Produce ....D....... 323 277-1550
   2570 E 25th St Los Angeles (90058) *(P-6573)*

Professional Security Cons (PA) ....D....... 310 207-7729
   11454 San Vicente Blvd 2nd Fl Los Angeles (90049) *(P-13024)*

Professional Security Cons, Los Angeles *Also Called: Professional Security Cons (P-13024)*

Professional Services, San Francisco *Also Called: Quorum One LLC (P-20836)*

Professional Svcs Med Group, Huntington Park *Also Called: All Care Medical Group Inc (P-14597)*

Professnal Elec Cnstr Svcs Inc ....C....... 909 373-4100
   9112 Santa Anita Ave Rancho Cucamonga (91730) *(P-1812)*

Professnal Intrctve Entrmt In ....D....... 310 823-4445
   6080 Center Dr Ste 600 Los Angeles (90045) *(P-14058)*

Professnal Rgistry Netwrk Corp ....D....... 714 832-5776
   17592 17th St Ste 225 Tustin (92780) *(P-11207)*

Professnal Tchncal SEC Svcs In ....B....... 510 645-9200
   1970 Broadway Ste 840 Oakland (94612) *(P-13025)*

Professional Tele Answering Svc, Chatsworth *Also Called: Seven One Inc (P-13471)*

Profit Recovery Partners LLC ....D....... 949 851-2777
   3501 W Sunflower Ave Ste 100 Santa Ana (92704) *(P-20831)*

Proform Inc ....D....... 707 752-9010
   1140 S Rockefeller Ave Ontario (91761) *(P-16744)*

Proform Interior Cnstr Inc ....D....... 619 881-0041
   663 33rd St Ste C San Diego (92102) *(P-2307)*

Proform Labs, Ontario *Also Called: Proform Inc (P-16744)*

Progistics Distribution Inc ....A....... 415 369-8845
   480 Roland Way Ste 103 Oakland (94621) *(P-4081)*

Program Plg Professionals Inc ....C....... 415 692-5870
   71 Stevenson St Ste 825 San Francisco (94105) *(P-13433)*

Progress Glass Co Inc (PA) ....C....... 415 824-7040
   25 Patterson St San Francisco (94124) *(P-2203)*

Progress Software Corporation ....D....... 650 341-7733
   800 W El Camino Real Mountain View (94040) *(P-12328)*

Progression Drywall, Lancaster *Also Called: Excel Contractors Inc (P-676)*

Progressive Health Care System ....D....... 818 707-9603
   8510 Balboa Blvd Ste 150 Northridge (91325) *(P-14999)*

Progressive Management Systems, West Covina *Also Called: RM Galicia Inc (P-10751)*

Progressive Sub-Acute Care ....D....... 408 378-8875
   13425 Sousa Ln Saratoga (95070) *(P-16345)*

Progressive Transportation Inc ....D....... 310 684-2100
   1210 E 223rd St Ste 328 Carson (90745) *(P-3529)*

PROGRESSIVE TRANSPORTATION, INC., Carson *Also Called: Progressive Transportation Inc (P-3529)*

Proguard Security Services Inc ....D....... 415 672-0786
   300 Montgomery St San Francisco (94104) *(P-13139)*

Prohealth Home Care Inc (PA) ....D....... 408 451-9055
   2700 Zanker Rd Ste 180 San Jose (95134) *(P-16914)*

Project Concern International (PA) ....C....... 858 279-9690
   5151 Murphy Canyon Rd Ste 320 San Diego (92123) *(P-18087)*

Project Design Consultants LLC ....D....... 619 235-6471
   701 B St Ste 800 San Diego (92101) *(P-20832)*

Project Fortress Parent LLC ....A....... 415 599-1100
   201 Mission St Ste 2900 San Francisco (94105) *(P-9328)*

Project Frog Inc ....D....... 415 814-8500
   114 Sansome St Ste 1320 San Francisco (94104) *(P-769)*

Project Fusion LLC ....C....... 530 343-8725
   495 Ryan Ave Chico (95973) *(P-6940)*

Project Open Hand (PA) ....D....... 415 292-3400
   730 Polk St Fl 3 San Francisco (94109) *(P-18088)*

Project Skyline Intermediate H ....A....... 310 712-1850
   360 N Crescent Dr Bldg S Beverly Hills (90210) *(P-9329)*

Project Y, Mountain View *Also Called: Mode Media Corporation (P-10716)*

Projistics, San Jose *Also Called: Nagarro Inc (P-12842)*

Proland Property Managment LLC (PA) ....D....... 213 738-8175
   2510 W 7th St 2nd Fl Los Angeles (90057) *(P-9145)*

Prologic Rdmption Slutions Inc (PA) ....A....... 310 322-7774
   2121 Rosecrans Ave El Segundo (90245) *(P-13434)*

PROLOGIS, San Francisco *Also Called: Prologis Inc (P-9477)*

PROLOGIS, San Francisco *Also Called: Prologis LP (P-9478)*

Prologis Inc (PA) ....B....... 415 394-9000
   Pier 1 Bay 1 San Francisco (94111) *(P-9477)*

Prologis LP (HQ) ....B....... 415 394-9000
   Pier 1 Bay 1 San Francisco (94111) *(P-9478)*

Promab Biotechnologies Inc ....D....... 510 860-4615
   2600 Hilltop Dr San Pablo (94806) *(P-19761)*

Promedica Health System Inc ....C....... 415 472-2637
   1050 Northgate Dr Ste 400 San Rafael (94903) *(P-15785)*

Promedica Health System Inc ....C....... 831 373-8442
   2511 Garden Rd Ste A250 Monterey (93940) *(P-16915)*

Promedica Health System Inc ....C....... 831 476-2158
   824 Bay Ave Ste 40 Capitola (95010) *(P-16916)*

Prometheus Laboratories Inc ....B....... 858 824-0895
   9410 Carroll Park Dr San Diego (92121) *(P-2603)*

Prometheus RE Group Inc (PA) ....C....... 650 931-3400
   1900 S Norfolk St Ste 150 San Mateo (94403) *(P-9146)*

Promise Technology Inc ....D....... 408 645-3499
   39889 Eureka Dr Newark (94560) *(P-5336)*

Promote Media LP ....D....... 323 433-7950
   9200 W Sunset Blvd Ste 950 West Hollywood (90069) *(P-20514)*

Promotonal Design Concepts Inc ....D....... 626 579-4454
   9872 Rush St South El Monte (91733) *(P-2659)*

Promoveo Health LLC ....A....... 760 931-4794
   701 Palomar Airport Rd Carlsbad (92011) *(P-10664)*

Prompt Delivery Inc ....D....... 858 549-8000
   5757 Wilshire Blvd Ph 3 Los Angeles (90036) *(P-13435)*

Pronto Janitorial Svcs Inc ....D....... 562 273-5997
   12561 Persing Dr Whittier (90606) *(P-10949)*

Proof of Concept Poc Lab, Sunnyvale *Also Called: Juniper Networks Inc (P-12472)*

Proofpoint, Sunnyvale *Also Called: Proofpoint Inc (P-12610)*

Proofpoint Inc (HQ) ....C....... 408 517-4710
   925 W Maude Ave Sunnyvale (94085) *(P-12610)*

Propel Inc ....D....... 510 733-1700
   14824 Wicks Blvd San Leandro (94577) *(P-8856)*

Propel Software Solutions ....D....... 408 755-3780
   451 El Camino Real Santa Clara (95050) *(P-11848)*

Propeller Health, San Diego *Also Called: Reciprocal Labs Corp (P-11867)*

Proper Hospitality LLC ....C....... 310 277-5221
   73 Market St Venice (90291) *(P-10129)*

Property I D, Los Angeles *Also Called: I D Property Corporation (P-9046)*

Property Insight LLC ....A....... 877 747-2537
   2510 Redhill Ave Santa Ana (92705) *(P-9238)*

Property Maintenance Company (PA) ....C....... 408 297-7849
   2025 Gateway Pl San Jose (95110) *(P-10950)*

Property Management Assoc Inc (PA) ....C....... 323 295-2000
   6011 Bristol Pkwy Culver City (90230) *(P-9147)*

Property Shop La At Berkshire ....D....... 310 497-3654
   1714 Hillhurst Ave Los Angeles (90027) *(P-8753)*

Proplus Design Solutions Inc (PA) ....C....... 408 459-6128
   2025 Gateway Pl Ste 130 San Jose (95110) *(P-13436)*

Proponent — ALPHABETIC SECTION

Proponent, Brea *Also Called: Proponent Inc (P-5965)*
  Proponent Inc (PA) .... C 714 223-5400
    3120 Enterprise St Brea (92821) *(P-5965)*
Propulsion Controls Engrg (PA) .... D 619 235-0961
  1620 Rigel St San Diego (92113) *(P-13793)*
Proscape Landscape, Signal Hill *Also Called: Fenderscape Incorporated (P-490)*
Prosciento Inc (PA) .... C 619 427-1300
  855 Third Ave Ste 3340 Chula Vista (91911) *(P-19762)*
Prosearch Strategies LLC .... C 877 447-7291
  3250 Wilshire Blvd Ste 301 Los Angeles (90010) *(P-19844)*
Prosites Inc .... C 888 932-3644
  38977 Sky Canyon Dr Ste 200 Murrieta (92563) *(P-12864)*
Prosoft Technology Inc (HQ) .... C 661 716-5100
  9201 Camino Media Ste 200 Bakersfield (93311) *(P-4546)*
Prospect Enterprises Inc (PA) .... C 213 599-5700
  625 Kohler St Los Angeles (90021) *(P-6477)*
Prospect Financial Group Inc .... D 858 605-0952
  7825 Fay Ave Ste 160 La Jolla (92037) *(P-8217)*
Prospect Medical Group Inc (HQ) .... B 714 796-5900
  1920 E 17th St Ste 200 Santa Ana (92705) *(P-20186)*
Prospect Medical Holdings Inc (PA) .... C 310 943-4500
  3415 S Sepulveda Blvd Fl 9 Los Angeles (90034) *(P-15000)*
Prospect Medical Systems Inc (HQ) .... C 714 667-8156
  600 City Pkwy W Ste 800 Orange (92868) *(P-20187)*
Prospect Mortgage LLC .... A
  Sherman Oaks (91403) *(P-9330)*
Prosper Marketplace Inc (PA) .... C 415 593-5400
  221 Main St Fl 3 San Francisco (94105) *(P-8053)*
Protagonist Therapeutics, Newark *Also Called: Protagonist Therapeutics Inc (P-2604)*
Protagonist Therapeutics Inc (PA) .... D 510 474-0170
  7707 Gateway Blvd Ste 140 Newark (94560) *(P-2604)*
Protec Association Services (PA) .... C 858 569-1080
  10180 Willow Creek Rd San Diego (92131) *(P-10951)*
Protec Building Services, San Diego *Also Called: Protec Association Services (P-10951)*
Protect-US .... C 714 721-8127
  3505 Cadillac Ave Costa Mesa (92626) *(P-13026)*
Protection One, Riverside *Also Called: ADT LLC (P-13092)*
Protein Research, Livermore *Also Called: Berkeley Nutritional Mfg Corp (P-19800)*
Proterial America Ltd .... C 408 467-8900
  880 N Mccarthy Blvd Ste 200 Milpitas (95035) *(P-5511)*
PROTERIAL AMERICA, LTD, Milpitas *Also Called: Proterial America Ltd (P-5511)*
Protiviti Inc (HQ) .... D 650 234-6000
  2884 Sand Hill Rd Ste 200 Menlo Park (94025) *(P-20515)*
Prototypes, Los Angeles *Also Called: Prototypes Centers For Innov (P-18089)*
Prototypes Centers For Innov 213 542-3838
  1000 N Alameda St Ste 390 Los Angeles (90012) *(P-18089)*
Protransport-1, Cotati *Also Called: Protransport-1 LLC (P-3289)*
Protransport-1 LLC (HQ) .... C 707 975-2386
  720 Portal St Cotati (94931) *(P-3289)*
Protravel International LLC .... D 310 271-9566
  345 N Maple Dr Beverly Hills (90210) *(P-3949)*
Provenza Floors Inc (PA) .... D 949 788-0900
  15541 Mosher Ave Tustin (92780) *(P-7433)*
Providence, Mission Hills *Also Called: Providence Holy Cross Medical (P-16349)*
Providence Health & Svcs - Ore .... B 510 444-0839
  540 23rd St Oakland (94612) *(P-16346)*
Providence Health & Svcs - Ore .... A 818 365-8051
  15031 Rinaldi St Mission Hills (91345) *(P-16347)*
Providence Health System .... A 818 843-5111
  501 S Buena Vista St Burbank (91505) *(P-16348)*
Providence Holy Cross Med Ctr, Mission Hills *Also Called: Providence Health & Svcs - Ore (P-16347)*
Providence Holy Cross Medical (PA) .... B 818 365-8051
  15031 Rinaldi St Mission Hills (91345) *(P-16349)*
PROVIDENCE HOME HEALTH ORANGE, Anaheim *Also Called: Providence Medical Foundation (P-16350)*
Providence Medical Foundation (DH) .... C 714 712-3308
  200 W Center Street Promenade Ste 800 Anaheim (92805) *(P-16350)*
Providence Rest Partners LLC .... D 323 460-4170
  5955 Melrose Ave Los Angeles (90038) *(P-9551)*

Providence Santa Rosa Mem Hosp, Santa Rosa *Also Called: St Joseph Hlth Nthrn Cal LLC (P-16461)*
Providence St Johns Hlth Ctr .... B 971 268-7643
  2121 Santa Monica Blvd Santa Monica (90404) *(P-16351)*
Providence St Josephs Home Cr .... D 818 953-4494
  3413 W Pacific Ave Burbank (91505) *(P-17299)*
Providence Tarzana Medical Ctr .... A 818 881-0800
  18321 Clark St Tarzana (91356) *(P-16352)*
Provident, Walnut Creek *Also Called: Provident Lf Accident Insur Co (P-8246)*
Provident Care Inc .... C 209 578-1210
  1025 14th St Modesto (95354) *(P-16917)*
Provident Credit Union (PA) .... C 650 508-0300
  303 Twin Dolphin Dr Redwood City (94065) *(P-7831)*
Provident Financial Management .... D 310 282-0477
  3130 Wilshire Blvd Ste 600 Santa Monica (90403) *(P-20188)*
Provident Funding Assoc LP .... D 707 568-2420
  1235 N Dutton Ave Ste A Santa Rosa (95401) *(P-8013)*
Provident Lf Accident Insur Co .... D 925 944-4700
  1277 Treat Blvd Ste 300 Walnut Creek (94597) *(P-8246)*
Providnce Facey Med Foundation (PA) .... C 818 365-9531
  15451 San Fernando Mission Blvd Mission Hills (91345) *(P-15001)*
Providnce Facey Med Foundation .... D 661 513-2100
  27924 Seco Canyon Rd Santa Clarita (91350) *(P-15002)*
Providnce Facey Med Foundation .... C 818 365-9531
  11165 Sepulveda Blvd Mission Hills (91345) *(P-15003)*
Providnce Facey Med Foundation 805 206-2000
  2655 1st St Simi Valley (93065) *(P-15257)*
Providnce Facey Med Foundation .... D 818 861-7831
  191 S Buena Vista St Burbank (91505) *(P-15258)*
Providnce Facey Med Foundation .... C 818 837-5677
  11211 Sepulveda Blvd Mission Hills (91345) *(P-17300)*
Providnce Facey Med Foundation .... C 661 250-5225
  17909 Soledad Canyon Rd Santa Clarita (91387) *(P-17301)*
Providnce Facey Med Foundation .... D 626 576-0800
  1237 E Main St San Gabriel (91776) *(P-17302)*
Providnce Hlth Svcs Fndtn/San .... A 818 843-5111
  501 S Buena Vista St Burbank (91505) *(P-16353)*
Providnce Holy Cross Fundation, Burbank *Also Called: Providnce Hlth Svcs Fndtn/San (P-16353)*
Provost & Pritchard Engineering Group Inc (PA) ...... C 559 449-2700
  286 W Cromwell Ave Fresno (93711) *(P-19364)*
Provost and Pritchard, Fresno *Also Called: Provost & Pritchard Engineering Group Inc (P-19364)*
Prowall Lath and Plaster .... D 760 480-9001
  360 S Spruce St Escondido (92025) *(P-1957)*
Prsi, Jurupa Valley *Also Called: Pavement Recycling Systems Inc (P-6012)*
Prudential, Thousand Oaks *Also Called: Gemmm Corporation (P-9021)*
Prudential, Irvine *Also Called: Hsf Affiliates LLC (P-9043)*
Prudential, Irvine *Also Called: Brer Affiliates LLC (P-9452)*
Prudential Cleanroom Services, Irvine *Also Called: Prudential Overall Supply (P-10480)*
Prudential Norcal Realty, Carmichael *Also Called: Diez & Leis RE Group Inc (P-8983)*
Prudential Overall Supply (PA) .... D 949 250-4855
  1661 Alton Pkwy Irvine (92606) *(P-10480)*
Prutel Joint Venture .... A 949 240-5064
  1 Ritz Carlton Dr Dana Point (92629) *(P-10130)*
PS, Los Angeles *Also Called: Private Suite Lax LLC (P-3190)*
Ps2 (PA) .... D 310 243-2980
  17903 S Hobart Blvd Gardena (90248) *(P-1634)*
Ps2, Gardena *Also Called: Ps2 (P-1634)*
Ps24 Inc .... D 415 834-5105
  690 Mission St San Francisco (94105) *(P-20189)*
Psav Holdings LLC (PA) .... C 562 366-0138
  111 W Ocean Blvd Ste 1110 Long Beach (90802) *(P-11051)*
Psb .... D 949 465-0772
  26012 Atlantic Ocean Dr Lake Forest (92630) *(P-10665)*
PSC Industrial Outsourcing LP .... D 661 833-9991
  200 Old Yard Dr Bakersfield (93307) *(P-627)*
PSC Industrial Outsourcing LP .... C 831 627-2595
  62117 Railroad St San Ardo (93450) *(P-3419)*
Pse Holding LLC (DH) .... B 248 377-0165
  360 N Crescent Dr Beverly Hills (90210) *(P-14154)*

ALPHABETIC SECTION — Purpose Funding Inc

PSG Fencing Corporation .... D....... 951 275-9252
330 Main St Riverside (92501) *(P-2308)*

Psg Global Solutions LLC (HQ) .... D....... 310 405-0340
4551 Glencoe Ave Ste 150 Marina Del Rey (90292) *(P-11208)*

PSI, Glendale *Also Called: PSI Services LLC (P-20833)*

PSI Services LLC (PA) .... D....... 818 847-6180
611 N Brand Blvd Ste 10 Glendale (91203) *(P-20833)*

PSI Systems Inc .... C....... 650 321-2640
323 N Mathilda Ave Sunnyvale (94085) *(P-11849)*

Psomas .... C....... 714 751-7373
5 Hutton Centre Dr Ste 300 Santa Ana (92707) *(P-19525)*

Psomas (PA) .... C....... 213 223-1400
865 S Figueroa St Los Angeles (90017) *(P-19526)*

Psychemedics Corporation .... D....... 310 216-7776
5750 Hannum Ave Ste 100 Culver City (90230) *(P-19996)*

Psychic Eye Book Shops Inc (PA) .... D....... 818 906-8263
13435 Ventura Blvd Sherman Oaks (91423) *(P-7549)*

Psychnp Consultants Inc .... D....... 800 205-6107
7880 Alta Valley Dr # 107 Sacramento (95823) *(P-16691)*

Psychrom Inc .... D....... 760 366-9811
56310 Pima Trl Ste C Yucca Valley (92284) *(P-13437)*

PSYCHROM INC, Yucca Valley *Also Called: Psychrom Inc (P-13437)*

Psychtric Ctrs At San Dego Inc (HQ) .... D....... 619 528-4600
4542 Ruffner St Ste 200 San Diego (92111) *(P-15004)*

Psyonix LLC .... D....... 619 622-8772
401 W A St Ste 2400 San Diego (92101) *(P-11850)*

Pszyjw, Los Angeles *Also Called: Pachulski Stang Zehl Jones LLP (P-17598)*

Pt Gaming LLC .... A....... 323 260-5060
235 Oregon St El Segundo (90245) *(P-10131)*

Pta Clfrnia Cngress Prnts Tche, Oakley *Also Called: Oakley Union School District (P-18886)*

PTEC Solutions Inc (PA) .... C....... 510 358-3578
48633 Warm Springs Blvd Fremont (94539) *(P-19365)*

Pts, Tustin *Also Called: Pts Advance (P-11209)*

Pts Advance .... C....... 949 268-4000
1775 Flight Way Ste 100 Tustin (92782) *(P-11209)*

Pts Diagnostics California Inc .... C....... 877 870-5610
510 Oakmead Pkwy Sunnyvale (94085) *(P-16745)*

Ptsi Managed Services Inc .... D....... 626 440-3118
100 W Walnut St Pasadena (91124) *(P-19366)*

Ptw America Inc .... D....... 424 289-0347
1042 Princeton Dr Ste B Marina Del Rey (90292) *(P-13438)*

Public Authority .... D....... 619 731-3705
401 Mile Of Cars Way Ste 200 National City (91950) *(P-4819)*

Public Communications Svcs Inc .... C....... 310 231-1000
11859 Wilshire Blvd Ste 600 Los Angeles (90025) *(P-4331)*

Public Counsel .... D....... 213 385-2977
610 S Ardmore Ave Los Angeles (90005) *(P-17620)*

Public Defender Administration, Los Angeles *Also Called: County of Los Angeles (P-17416)*

Public Defender- Main Office, Riverside *Also Called: County of Riverside (P-17419)*

Public Defender, Alternate, San Diego *Also Called: County of San Diego (P-17420)*

Public Defender's Office, Clovis *Also Called: County of Fresno (P-17415)*

Public Employees Retirement .... B....... 916 795-3400
400 Q St Sacramento (95811) *(P-8466)*

Public Health Institute (PA) .... D....... 510 285-5500
555 12th St Ste 600 Oakland (94607) *(P-19905)*

Public Hlth Fndation Entps Inc .... C....... 323 261-6388
3648 E Olympic Blvd Los Angeles (90023) *(P-17303)*

Public Hlth Fndation Entps Inc .... C....... 562 801-2323
8666 Whittier Blvd Pico Rivera (90660) *(P-17304)*

Public Hlth Fndation Entps Inc .... C....... 323 733-9381
1649 W Washington Blvd Los Angeles (90007) *(P-17305)*

Public Hlth Fndation Entps Inc .... C....... 310 518-2835
125 E Anaheim St Wilmington (90744) *(P-17306)*

Public Hlth Fndation Entps Inc .... C....... 626 856-6618
12781 Shama Rd El Monte (91732) *(P-17307)*

Public Hlth Fndation Entps Inc .... C....... 626 856-6600
13181 Crossroads Pkwy N City Of Industry (91746) *(P-18090)*

Public Hlth Fndation Entps Inc .... C....... 323 263-0262
277 S Atlantic Blvd Los Angeles (90022) *(P-18897)*

Public Hlth Fndation Entps Inc .... C....... 310 320-5215
1640 W Carson St Ste G Torrance (90501) *(P-18898)*

Public Hlth Fndation Entps Inc (PA) .... C....... 800 201-7320
13300 Crossroads Pkwy N Ste 450 City Of Industry (91746) *(P-18899)*

Public Mdia Group Southern Cal (PA) .... D....... 714 241-4100
2900 W Alameda Ave Unit 600 Burbank (91505) *(P-4458)*

Public Nurse Office, Indio *Also Called: County of Riverside (P-17216)*

Public Service Yard, Glendale *Also Called: City of Glendale (P-4773)*

Public Services, Coronado *Also Called: City of Coronado (P-4750)*

Public Social Services, Moreno Valley *Also Called: County of Riverside (P-14714)*

Public Social Services, Norwalk *Also Called: County of Los Angeles (P-17905)*

Public Storage (PA) .... B....... 818 244-8080
701 Western Ave Glendale (91201) *(P-9479)*

Public Utilities, Riverside *Also Called: City of Riverside (P-4774)*

Public Works, San Diego *Also Called: County of San Diego (P-13248)*

Public Works and Planning, Fresno *Also Called: County of Fresno (P-19185)*

Public Works Association, Stockton *Also Called: City of Stockton (P-18842)*

Public Works Dept, Hayward *Also Called: County of Alameda (P-1091)*

Public Works Dept, Auburn *Also Called: County of Placer (P-19188)*

Public Works Equipment, Burbank *Also Called: City of Burbank (P-13660)*

Public Works Water Department, Ukiah *Also Called: City of Ukiah (P-4775)*

Public Works-Garage, Santa Rosa *Also Called: Santa Rosa City of (P-13675)*

Public Works, Dept of, Los Angeles *Also Called: County of Los Angeles (P-1092)*

Public Works, Dept of, Los Angeles *Also Called: County of Los Angeles (P-3690)*

Public Works, Dept of, Lancaster *Also Called: County of Los Angeles (P-4848)*

Publicis Collective, San Francisco *Also Called: Digitas Inc (P-10609)*

Pubmatic, Redwood City *Also Called: Pubmatic Inc (P-11851)*

Pubmatic Inc (PA) .... B....... 650 331-3485
601 Marshall St Redwood City (94063) *(P-11851)*

Puente Hills Chevrolet, City Of Industry *Also Called: Leo Hoffman Chevrolet Inc (P-7251)*

Puff Candy,, San Diego *Also Called: Puff Global Inc (P-13439)*

Puff Global Inc .... D....... 619 520-3499
402 W Broadway Ste 400 San Diego (92101) *(P-13439)*

Pulmonary Prctice At Parnassus, San Francisco *Also Called: University Cal San Francisco (P-17780)*

Pulmonary Sleep Disorders Ctr, Fresno *Also Called: Central Cal Fclty Med Group In (P-14668)*

Pulmuone USA Inc .... B....... 714 361-0806
5755 Rossi Ln Gilroy (95020) *(P-6661)*

Pulp Studio Incorporated .... D....... 310 815-4999
2100 W 139th St Gardena (90249) *(P-10817)*

Pulse Secure LLC (DH) .... D....... 408 372-9600
2700 Zanker Rd Ste 200 San Jose (95134) *(P-11852)*

Pulse Systems Inc (DH) .... D....... 316 636-5900
438 Listowe Dr Folsom (95630) *(P-11853)*

Pulsepoint Inc .... C....... 415 937-8208
115 Sansome St Ste 1002 San Francisco (94104) *(P-20516)*

Pulsora Inc .... C....... 650 575-5255
3321 Octavia St San Francisco (94123) *(P-11854)*

Punch Studio LLC (PA) .... C....... 310 390-9900
6025 W Slauson Ave Culver City (90230) *(P-6070)*

Pupil Transportation, Whittier *Also Called: County of Los Angeles (P-3324)*

Purcell-Murray Company Inc (PA) .... D....... 415 468-6620
235 Kansas St Fl 1 San Francisco (94103) *(P-5611)*

Purchasing Department, Ventura *Also Called: Community Mem Hosp San Bnvntur (P-16015)*

Pure Autism Counseling Ctr Inc .... D....... 661 360-7730
17702 Sierra Hwy Canyon Country (91351) *(P-17115)*

Pure Luxury Limousine Service .... C....... 800 626-5466
4246 Petaluma Blvd N Petaluma (94952) *(P-3290)*

Pure Luxury Worldwide Trnsp, Petaluma *Also Called: Pure Luxury Limousine Service (P-3290)*

PURE STORAGE, Santa Clara *Also Called: Pure Storage Inc (P-12329)*

Pure Storage Inc (PA) .... A....... 800 379-7873
2555 Augustine Dr Santa Clara (95054) *(P-12329)*

Pure Wafer Inc .... C....... 408 945-8112
2240 Ringwood Ave San Jose (95131) *(P-2930)*

Puregear, Irwindale *Also Called: Superior Communications Inc (P-5703)*

Purple Language Services Co .... C....... 916 435-8216
595 Menlo Dr Rocklin (95765) *(P-13883)*

Purpose Funding Inc .... D....... 949 456-7899
27651 La Paz Rd # 200 Laguna Niguel (92677) *(P-7903)*

Pusan Pipe America Inc .... B...... 949 655-8000
2100 Main St Ste 100 Irvine (92614) *(P-5512)*
Putnam Lexus, Redwood City *Also Called: Putnam Motors Inc (P-7283)*
Putnam Motors Inc .... D...... 650 381-3152
390 Convention Way Redwood City (94063) *(P-7283)*
Pvhmc, Pomona *Also Called: Pomona Valley Hospital Med Ctr (P-16331)*
Pw Fund B LP .... D...... 916 379-3852
555 Capitol Mall Sacramento (95814) *(P-9388)*
PWC STRategy& (us) LLC .... C...... 415 498-5000
3 Embarcadero Ctr Ste 1150 San Francisco (94111) *(P-20517)*
PWC STRategy& (us) LLC .... C...... 213 356-6000
601 S Figueroa St Ste 900 Los Angeles (90017) *(P-20518)*
Pyramid Flowers Inc .... C...... 805 382-8070
3813 Doris Ave Oxnard (93030) *(P-149)*
Pyramid Peak Corporation .... D...... 949 769-8600
1401 Avocado Ave Ste 709 Newport Beach (92660) *(P-9552)*
Pyro, Irvine *Also Called: Pyro-Comm Systems Inc (P-1813)*
Pyro-Comm Systems Inc (PA) .... C...... 714 902-8000
15215 Alton Pkwy Irvine (92618) *(P-1813)*
Q Analysts LLC (PA) .... D...... 408 907-8500
4320 Stevens Creek Blvd Ste 130 San Jose (95129) *(P-20519)*
Q Microwave Inc .... D...... 619 258-7322
1591 Pioneer Way El Cajon (92020) *(P-2945)*
Q S I, South San Francisco *Also Called: Quality Systems Instlltons Ltd (P-2309)*
Q Tech Corporation .... C...... 310 836-7900
6161 Chip Ave Cypress (90630) *(P-5690)*
Qad, Santa Barbara *Also Called: Qad Inc (P-12330)*
Qad Inc (HQ) .... C...... 805 566-6000
101 Innovation Pl Santa Barbara (93108) *(P-12330)*
Qantas Vctons Nwmans Vacations, Los Angeles *Also Called: Helloworld Travel Svcs USA Inc (P-3931)*
Qatalyst Partners LP .... D...... 415 844-7700
1 Maritime Plz Ste 2400 San Francisco (94111) *(P-9553)*
Qb3 LLC .... D...... 415 515-3595
29 Hunter Crk Fairfax (94930) *(P-20520)*
Qct LLC, San Jose *Also Called: Quanta Cloud Tech USA LLC (P-5337)*
Qdoba Mexican Grill, San Diego *Also Called: Qdoba Restaurant Corporation (P-7505)*
Qdoba Restaurant Corporation (HQ) .... C...... 858 766-4900
350 Camino De La Reina Fl 4 San Diego (92108) *(P-7505)*
Qf Liquidation Inc (PA) .... C...... 949 930-3400
25242 Arctic Ocean Dr Lake Forest (92630) *(P-2977)*
Qlm Inc .... C...... 408 265-0904
94 Umbarger Rd San Jose (95111) *(P-19367)*
Qmetry Inc .... C...... 408 727-1101
3200 Patrick Henry Dr Ste 250 Santa Clara (95054) *(P-20834)*
Qology Direct LLC .... C...... 310 341-4420
12130 Millennium Ste 600 Los Angeles (90094) *(P-13440)*
Qolsys, Campbell *Also Called: Qolsys Inc (P-12512)*
Qolsys Inc (HQ) .... C...... 855 476-5797
1919 S Bascom Ave Ste 600 Campbell (95008) *(P-12512)*
Qre Operating LLC .... D...... 213 225-5900
707 Wilshire Blvd Ste 4600 Los Angeles (90017) *(P-603)*
Qrs Corporation (DH) .... D...... 510 215-5000
1400 Marina Way S Richmond (94804) *(P-11855)*
Qsolv Inc .... C...... 408 429-0918
440 N Wolfe Rd Ste 26 Sunnyvale (94085) *(P-12513)*
Qtc Management Inc (DH) .... D...... 800 682-9701
924 Overland Ct San Dimas (91773) *(P-17308)*
Qtc Mdcal Group Inc A Med Corp .... A...... 800 260-1515
924 Overland Ct San Dimas (91773) *(P-17309)*
Qtc Medical Group, San Dimas *Also Called: Qtc Mdcal Group Inc A Med Corp (P-17309)*
Quad-C Jh Holdings Inc .... C...... 502 741-0421
1055 E Discovery Ln Anaheim (92801) *(P-5445)*
Quad-C Jh Holdings Inc .... C...... 800 966-6662
4593 Ish Dr Ste 320 Simi Valley (93063) *(P-5446)*
Quadriga Inc .... D...... 650 270-6326
1 Sansome St Ste 3500 San Francisco (94104) *(P-11856)*
Quagga Corporation .... D...... 916 357-5129
90 Blue Ravine Rd 200a Folsom (95630) *(P-1253)*
Quail H Farms LLC .... D...... 209 394-8001
5301 Robin Ave Livingston (95334) *(P-17)*

Quail Lodge Inc .... C...... 831 624-1581
8205 Valley Greens Dr Carmel (93923) *(P-10132)*
Quail Park Retirement Village, Visalia *Also Called: Quail Park Retirement Vlg LLC (P-15786)*
Quail Park Retirement Vlg LLC .... D...... 559 624-3500
4520 W Cypress Ave Visalia (93277) *(P-15786)*
Quake City Caps, Los Angeles *Also Called: Quake City Casuals Inc (P-6184)*
Quake City Casuals Inc .... C...... 213 746-0540
1800 S Flower St Los Angeles (90015) *(P-6184)*
QUAKER GARDENS, Stanton *Also Called: California Friends Homes (P-18383)*
Quaker Pet Group Inc .... D...... 415 721-7400
160 Mitchell Blvd San Rafael (94903) *(P-6941)*
Qualcomm, San Diego *Also Called: Qualcomm Incorporated (P-2897)*
Qualcomm, San Diego *Also Called: Qualcomm International Inc (P-9454)*
Qualcomm Atheros Inc (HQ) .... A...... 408 773-5200
1700 Technology Dr San Jose (95110) *(P-2931)*
Qualcomm Incorporated (PA) .... A...... 858 587-1121
5775 Morehouse Dr San Diego (92121) *(P-2897)*
Qualcomm International Inc (HQ) .... A...... 858 587-1121
5775 Morehouse Dr San Diego (92121) *(P-9454)*
Qualcomm Technologies Inc (HQ) .... B...... 858 587-1121
5775 Morehouse Dr San Diego (92121) *(P-2932)*
Qualia Collection Services, Petaluma *Also Called: Optio Solutions LLC (P-10746)*
Qualia Labs Inc .... C...... 440 477-5625
50 Fremont St Fl 36 San Francisco (94105) *(P-20835)*
Qualia Software, San Francisco *Also Called: Qualia Labs Inc (P-20835)*
Qualis Automotive LLC .... D...... 859 689-7772
21046 Figueroa St Carson (90745) *(P-13672)*
Qualitas Insurance Company .... D...... 619 876-4355
4545 Murphy Canyon Rd Fl 3 San Diego (92123) *(P-8645)*
Qualitas Premier Insur Svcs, San Diego *Also Called: Qualitas Insurance Company (P-8645)*
Quality Claims Management Corp .... D...... 619 450-8600
2763 Camino Del Rio S San Diego (92108) *(P-8646)*
Quality Erectors & Cnstr Co, Benicia *Also Called: Quality Erectors Cnstr Co Inc (P-2194)*
Quality Erectors Cnstr Co Inc .... D...... 707 746-1233
3130 Bayshore Rd Benicia (94510) *(P-2194)*
Quality First Woodworks Inc .... C...... 714 632-0480
1264 N Lakeview Ave Anaheim (92807) *(P-2486)*
Quality Group Homes Inc .... C...... 559 252-6844
4928 E Clinton Way Ste 108 Fresno (93727) *(P-710)*
Quality Inn, Sunnyvale *Also Called: Silicon Valley Inns Inc (P-10238)*
Quality Loan Service Corp .... B...... 619 645-7711
2763 Camino Del Rio S San Diego (92108) *(P-9446)*
Quality Management, Stanford *Also Called: Stanford Health Care (P-16493)*
Quality Marine, Los Angeles *Also Called: Allaquaria LLC (P-6887)*
Quality Production Svcs Inc .... D...... 310 406-3350
18711 S Broadwick St Compton (90220) *(P-1958)*
Quality Reimbursement Services .... D...... 626 445-5092
150 N Santa Anita Ave Ste 570a Arcadia (91006) *(P-19625)*
Quality Reinforcing Inc .... D...... 858 748-8400
13275 Gregg St Poway (92064) *(P-2195)*
Quality Speaks LLC (PA) .... D...... 818 264-4400
9221 Corbin Ave Ste 260 Northridge (91324) *(P-4332)*
Quality Systems Instlltons Ltd 650 875-9000
105 Associated Rd South San Francisco (94080) *(P-2309)*
Quality Techniques Engrg Cnstr, Rocklin *Also Called: Quality Telecom Cons Inc (P-1254)*
Quality Telecom Cons Inc (PA) .... D...... 916 315-0500
3740 Cincinnati Ave Rocklin (95765) *(P-1254)*
Quality Temp Staffing, Granada Hills *Also Called: Siracusa Enterprises Inc (P-11230)*
Qualitylogic Inc .... C...... 208 424-1905
2245 1st St Ste 103 Simi Valley (93065) *(P-2836)*
Qualstaff Resources, San Diego *Also Called: June Group LLC (P-11296)*
Qualy Pak Specialty Foods Inc .... D...... 310 541-3023
2208 Signal Pl San Pedro (90731) *(P-6478)*
Qualys, Foster City *Also Called: Qualys Inc (P-11857)*
Qualys Inc (PA) .... A...... 650 801-6100
919 E Hillsdale Blvd Ste 400 Foster City (94404) *(P-11857)*
Quanta Cloud Tech USA LLC 510 270-6111
1010 Rincon Cir San Jose (95131) *(P-5337)*
Quantos Payroll, Los Angeles *Also Called: Film Payroll Services Inc (P-19577)*

Quantum Bhvioral Solutions Inc (PA) .... D....... 626 531-6999
  445 S Figueroa St Ste 3100 Los Angeles (90071) *(P-15301)*
Quantum Bhvioral Solutions Inc .... D....... 626 531-6999
  2400 E Katella Ave Ste 800 Anaheim (92806) *(P-15302)*
Quantum Technologies, Lake Forest *Also Called: Qf Liquidation Inc (P-2977)*
Quantum World Technologies Inc .... B....... 805 834-0532
  4281 Katella Ave Ste 102 Los Alamitos (90720) *(P-11210)*
Quarry At La Quinta Inc (PA) .... D....... 760 777-1100
  41865 Boardwalk Ste 214 Palm Desert (92211) *(P-14283)*
Quartus Engineering Inc (PA) .... C....... 858 875-6000
  9689 Towne Centre Dr San Diego (92121) *(P-19368)*
Quartz Logistics Inc .... D....... 626 606-2001
  780 Nogales St Ste D City Of Industry (91748) *(P-4082)*
Quechan Gaming Commission, Winterhaven *Also Called: Quechan Indian Tribe (P-14551)*
Quechan Indian Tribe .... C....... 760 572-2413
  450 Quechan Rd Winterhaven (92283) *(P-14551)*
Queen Mary Hotel, Long Beach *Also Called: RMS Foundation Inc (P-10167)*
Queen Mary, The, Long Beach *Also Called: Urban Commons Queensway LLC (P-10335)*
Queen of The Valley Campus, West Covina *Also Called: Citrus Vly Hlth Partners Inc (P-16001)*
Queen of The Valley Hospital, West Covina *Also Called: Emanate Health Medical Center (P-16076)*
Queen of The Valley Hospital, Napa *Also Called: Work Health (P-20616)*
Queen of Vly Med Ctr Fundation (DH) .... A....... 707 252-4411
  1000 Trancas St Napa (94558) *(P-16354)*
Queen of Vly Med Ctr Fundation .... B....... 707 251-2000
  3448 Villa Ln Ste 102 Napa (94558) *(P-16355)*
Queensbay Hotel LLC .... D....... 562 481-3910
  700 Queensway Dr Long Beach (90802) *(P-10133)*
Queenscare Fmly Clnics - Estsi, Los Angeles *Also Called: Queenscare Health Centers (P-15005)*
Queenscare Health Centers .... D....... 323 780-4510
  4816 E 3rd St Los Angeles (90022) *(P-15005)*
Queenscare Health Centers .... D....... 323 644-6180
  4618 Fountain Ave Los Angeles (90029) *(P-15006)*
Quest, Roseville *Also Called: Quest Media & Supplies Inc (P-12865)*
Quest Dgnstics Nchols Inst Vln, Valencia *Also Called: Specialty Laboratories Inc (P-16753)*
Quest Diagnostics, San Juan Capistrano *Also Called: Quest Diagnostics Nichols Inst (P-3032)*
Quest Diagnostics, Roseville *Also Called: Unilab Corporation (P-16762)*
Quest Diagnostics, West Hills *Also Called: Unilab Corporation (P-16763)*
Quest Diagnostics Nichols Inst (HQ) .... A....... 949 728-4000
  33608 Ortega Hwy San Juan Capistrano (92675) *(P-3032)*
Quest International, Irvine *Also Called: Quest Intl Monitor Svc Inc (P-12710)*
Quest Intl Monitor Svc Inc (PA) .... D....... 949 581-9900
  60 Parker 65 Irvine (92618) *(P-12710)*
Quest Media & Supplies Inc (PA) .... D....... 916 338-7070
  9000 Foothills Blvd Ste 100 Roseville (95747) *(P-12865)*
Quest Software Inc .... D....... 949 754-8000
  20 Enterprise Aliso Viejo (92656) *(P-12331)*
Quest Software Inc (PA) .... A....... 949 754-8000
  20 Enterprise Ste 100 Aliso Viejo (92656) *(P-12514)*
Quick Box LLC .... C....... 310 436-6444
  13838 S Figueroa St Los Angeles (90061) *(P-3746)*
Quick Lane, Stockton *Also Called: Big Valley Ford Inc (P-7172)*
Quick Lane, San Diego *Also Called: Mossy Ford Inc (P-7262)*
Quick Lane, Riverside *Also Called: Raceway Ford Inc (P-7285)*
Quick Lane, Hawthorne *Also Called: South Bay Ford Inc (P-7299)*
Quick Lane, Fontana *Also Called: Sunrise Ford (P-7307)*
Quick Mount Pv, Walnut Creek *Also Called: Wencon Development Inc (P-1595)*
Quick-N-Ezee Indian Foods, Hayward *Also Called: Jagpreet Enterprises LLC (P-6636)*
Quicken Inc .... C....... 650 564-3399
  3760 Haven Ave Ste C Menlo Park (94025) *(P-11858)*
Quid LLC (PA) .... C....... 415 813-5300
  3960 Freedom Cir Ste 200 Santa Clara (95054) *(P-11859)*
Quidel Cardiovascular Inc .... D....... 858 552-1100
  9975 Summers Ridge Rd San Diego (92121) *(P-13441)*
Quigley-Simpson & Hepplewhite, Los Angeles *Also Called: Quigly-Simpson Heppelwhite Inc (P-10666)*
Quigly-Simpson Heppelwhite Inc .... C....... 310 996-5800
  11601 Wilshire Blvd Ste 710 Los Angeles (90025) *(P-10666)*

Quik Pick Express LLC .... C....... 310 763-3000
  23610 Banning Blvd Carson (90745) *(P-4083)*
Quiksilver, Huntington Beach *Also Called: Boardriders Wholesale LLC (P-6167)*
Quill Distribution Center, Ontario *Also Called: Quill LLC (P-3747)*
Quill LLC .... C....... 909 390-0600
  1500 S Dupont Ave Ontario (91761) *(P-3747)*
Quinn Company .... D....... 559 992-2193
  510 Pickerell Ave Corcoran (93212) *(P-5798)*
Quinn Company .... D....... 831 758-8461
  1300 Abbott St Salinas (93901) *(P-5799)*
Quinn Company .... D....... 661 393-5800
  2200 Pegasus Dr Bakersfield (93308) *(P-5800)*
Quinn Company .... D....... 805 485-2171
  801 Del Norte Blvd Oxnard (93030) *(P-5801)*
Quinn Company .... D....... 805 925-8611
  1655 Carlotti Dr Santa Maria (93454) *(P-5802)*
Quinn Emmanuel Trial Lawyers, Los Angeles *Also Called: Quinn Emnuel Urqhart Sllvan LL (P-17621)*
Quinn Emnuel Urqhart Sllvan LL (PA) .... B....... 213 443-3000
  865 S Figueroa St Fl 10 Los Angeles (90017) *(P-17621)*
Quinn Shepherd Machinery .... B....... 562 463-6000
  10006 Rose Hills Rd City Of Industry (90601) *(P-5803)*
Quinstar Technology Inc .... D....... 310 320-1111
  24085 Garnier St Torrance (90505) *(P-5691)*
Quintiles Pacific Incorporated .... B....... 858 552-3400
  10201 Wateridge Cir Ste 300 San Diego (92121) *(P-19845)*
Quiring Corporation .... D....... 559 432-2800
  5118 E Clinton Way Ste 201 Fresno (93727) *(P-996)*
Quiring General LLC .... D....... 559 432-2800
  5118 E Clinton Way Ste 201 Fresno (93727) *(P-997)*
Quoc Viet Foods Inc .... D....... 714 283-3663
  12221 Monarch St Garden Grove (92841) *(P-2441)*
Quorum One LLC .... D....... 760 786-7861
  5758 Geary Blvd Ste 141 San Francisco (94121) *(P-20836)*
Quotit Corporation .... C....... 714 564-5000
  721 S Parker St Ste 330 Orange (92868) *(P-12515)*
Quova Inc .... D....... 650 965-2898
  401 Castro St Fl 3 Mountain View (94041) *(P-20837)*
Qventus Inc .... C....... 585 690-9638
  2261 Market St Pmb 5023 San Francisco (94114) *(P-5338)*
Qwest, Burbank *Also Called: Qwest Cybersolutions LLC (P-4333)*
Qwest Cybersolutions LLC .... C....... 818 729-2100
  3015 Winona Ave Burbank (91504) *(P-4333)*
Qxv Software LLC .... D....... 626 219-0522
  215 N Marengo Ave Pasadena (91101) *(P-11860)*
Qy Research Inc .... D....... 626 295-2442
  17890 Castleton St City Of Industry (91748) *(P-19846)*
Qyk Brands LLC .... C....... 949 312-7119
  12821 Western Ave Garden Grove (92841) *(P-6141)*
R & A Painting Inc .... D....... 916 688-3955
  11730 Sheldon Lake Dr Elk Grove (95624) *(P-1635)*
R & B Reinforcing Steel Corp .... D....... 909 591-1726
  13581 5th St Chino (91710) *(P-2196)*
R & B Wholesale Distrs Inc (PA) .... D....... 909 230-5400
  2350 S Milliken Ave Ontario (91761) *(P-5612)*
R & D Fasteners, Rancho Cucamonga *Also Called: Doubleco Incorporated (P-2749)*
R & D Partners, San Diego *Also Called: R&D Consulting Group Inc (P-11211)*
R & J Hospitality LLC .... D....... 213 388-0301
  101 N Virgil Ave Los Angeles (90004) *(P-10134)*
R & L Brosamer Inc .... B....... 559 739-8215
  2916 W Main St Visalia (93291) *(P-998)*
R & R Industries, San Clemente *Also Called: Rosen & Rosen Industries Inc (P-3094)*
R & R Mechanical Contractors Inc .... D....... 619 449-9900
  1400 N Johnson Ave # 114 El Cajon (92020) *(P-1538)*
R & S Supply, Redding *Also Called: Gulfside Supply Inc (P-5221)*
R and L Lopez Associates Inc (PA) .... D....... 626 330-5296
  3649 Tyler Ave El Monte (91731) *(P-19369)*
R and R Labor Inc .... B....... 831 638-0290
  710 Kirkpatric Ct Ste A Hollister (95023) *(P-368)*
R C Furniture Inc .... D....... 626 964-4100
  1111 Jellick Ave City Of Industry (91748) *(P-2489)*

R C H ALPHABETIC SECTION

R C H, San Francisco *Also Called: Pomeroy Rcrtion Rhbltation Ctr (P-18084)*

R C Roberts & Co (PA) .... C....... 415 456-8600
801 A St San Rafael (94901) *(P-8881)*

R D Abbott Co Inc .... D....... 562 944-5354
11958 Monarch St Garden Grove (92841) *(P-6713)*

R E Barber-Ford .... C....... 805 656-4259
3440 E Main St Ventura (93003) *(P-7284)*

R E Goodspeed and Sons Distributing Inc .... D....... 760 949-3356
11211 G Ave Hesperia (92345) *(P-6717)*

R E Maher Inc .... D....... 707 642-3907
4545 Hess Rd American Canyon (94503) *(P-2150)*

R F Macdonald Co (PA) .... D....... 510 784-0110
25920 Eden Landing Rd Hayward (94545) *(P-5862)*

R G Canning Enterprises Inc .... C....... 323 560-7469
4515 E 59th Pl Maywood (90270) *(P-13442)*

R H A, Fresno *Also Called: Richard Heath & Associates Inc (P-20841)*

R H D, Corona *Also Called: Ranch House Doors Inc (P-2013)*

R H Strasbaugh (PA) .... D....... 805 541-6424
825 Buckley Rd San Luis Obispo (93401) *(P-2781)*

R J Lanthier Company Inc .... D....... 760 738-9798
485 Corporate Dr Escondido (92029) *(P-999)*

R Joy Inc .... D....... 530 832-5760
1584 Wolf Meadows Ln Portola (96122) *(P-19370)*

R K Properties, Long Beach *Also Called: Rance King Properties Inc (P-8857)*

R L Jones-San Diego Inc (PA) .... D....... 760 357-3177
1778 Zinetta Rd Ste A Calexico (92231) *(P-4084)*

R L T, Redding *Also Called: Redding Lumber Transport Inc (P-3592)*

R Lang Company .... D....... 559 651-0701
8240 W Doe Ave Visalia (93291) *(P-2741)*

R M Harris Company Inc .... D....... 925 335-3000
1000 Howe Rd Ste 200 Martinez (94553) *(P-1188)*

R Mc Closkey Insurance Agency .... C....... 949 223-8100
4001 Macarthur Blvd Ste 300 Newport Beach (92660) *(P-8647)*

R N D Enterprises, Lancaster *Also Called: BDR Industries Inc (P-4474)*

R P Direct, Santa Monica *Also Called: Rubin Postaer and Associates (P-10671)*

R P S Resort Corp .... B....... 760 327-8311
1600 N Indian Canyon Dr Palm Springs (92262) *(P-10135)*

R Planet Earth LLC .... C....... 213 320-0601
3200 Fruitland Ave Vernon (90058) *(P-4922)*

R Q Construction Inc .... C....... 760 631-7707
1620 Faraday Ave Carlsbad (92008) *(P-1000)*

R Ranch Market .... C....... 714 573-1182
1112 Walnut Ave Tustin (92780) *(P-237)*

R S D, Lake Forest *Also Called: Refrigeration Supplies Distributor (P-5781)*

R S Software India Limited .... D....... 408 382-1200
1900 Mccarthy Blvd Ste 103 Milpitas (95035) *(P-12866)*

R Software Inc (PA) .... D....... 650 575-7633
85 2nd St Ste 400 San Francisco (94105) *(P-11861)*

R Systems Inc .... C....... 916 939-9696
5000 Windplay Dr Ste 5 El Dorado Hills (95762) *(P-12516)*

R T A, Riverside *Also Called: Riverside Transit Agency (P-3192)*

R T I, Sunnyvale *Also Called: Real-Time Innovations Inc (P-11865)*

R W Smith & Co (HQ) .... D....... 858 530-1800
10101 Old Grove Rd San Diego (92131) *(P-5132)*

R W Smith & Co .... D....... 858 530-1800
10101 Old Grove Rd San Diego (92131) *(P-5387)*

R-Cold Inc .... D....... 951 436-5476
1221 S G St Perris (92570) *(P-2844)*

R.P. Barton Ranch, Escalon *Also Called: Barton Ranch Inc (P-233)*

R/GA Media Group Inc .... D....... 415 624-2000
45 Fremont St San Francisco (94105) *(P-12611)*

R/GA Media Group Inc .... D....... 415 913-7531
35 Park St San Francisco (94110) *(P-20642)*

R&C Motor Corporation .... C....... 909 625-1500
601 Auto Center Dr Claremont (91711) *(P-13673)*

R&D Consulting Group Inc .... D....... 415 697-2585
8910 University Center Ln Ste 400 San Diego (92122) *(P-11211)*

R&M USA Inc (DH) .... D....... 408 945-6626
840 Yosemite Way Milpitas (95035) *(P-5692)*

R2g Enterprises Inc .... D....... 510 489-6218
31154 San Benito St Hayward (94544) *(P-2079)*

R3 Strategic Support Group Inc .... D....... 800 418-2040
1050 B Ave Ste A Coronado (92118) *(P-20521)*

R4k3 LLC .... D....... 425 462-0375
1961 Taylor St Yuba City (95993) *(P-2310)*

RA Snyder Properties Inc (PA) .... C....... 619 297-0274
2399 Camino Del Rio S Ste 200 San Diego (92108) *(P-9148)*

RABBIT HAVEN THE, Scotts Valley *Also Called: Ava The Rabbit Haven Inc (P-20696)*

Rabobank National Association ....A
915 Highland Pointe Dr Roseville (95678) *(P-7712)*

Rabobank North America, Roseville *Also Called: Rabobank National Association (P-7712)*

RAC, Corcoran *Also Called: Recreational Assn Corcoran (P-18901)*

RAC & Associates .... D....... 858 694-5800
9541 Ridgehaven Ct San Diego (92123) *(P-10991)*

Race Street Partners Inc (PA) .... D....... 408 294-6161
967 W Hedding St San Jose (95126) *(P-6448)*

Race Telecommunications LLC (PA) .... D....... 650 246-8900
601 Gateway Blvd Ste 280 South San Francisco (94080) *(P-4334)*

Raceway Ford Inc .... C....... 951 571-9300
5900 Sycamore Canyon Blvd Riverside (92507) *(P-7285)*

Rachas Inc .... D....... 714 290-0636
135 N Beach Blvd Anaheim (92801) *(P-14224)*

Rackspace Hosting Inc .... C....... 201 792-1918
650 Castro St Ste 270 Mountain View (94041) *(P-12612)*

Rackspace Hosting Inc .... B....... 201 792-1918
150 S 1st St Ste 289 San Jose (95113) *(P-12613)*

RAD Diversified Reit Inc .... D....... 813 723-7348
3110 E Guasti Rd Ste 300 Ontario (91761) *(P-9149)*

Radford Studio Center LLC .... B....... 818 655-5000
4024 Radford Ave Studio City (91604) *(P-14059)*

Radial, Rialto *Also Called: Radial South LP (P-3748)*

Radial South LP .... B....... 610 491-7000
2225 Alder Ave Rialto (92377) *(P-3748)*

Radiant Health Centers .... D....... 949 809-5700
17982 Sky Park Cir Ste J Irvine (92614) *(P-18091)*

Radiant Services Corp (PA) .... C....... 310 327-6300
651 W Knox St Gardena (90248) *(P-10425)*

Radiation Onclogy - Cdrs-Snai, Los Angeles *Also Called: Cedars-Sinai Medical Center (P-14664)*

Radio Disney Group LLC .... D....... 818 569-5000
3800 W Alameda Ave Ste 1150 Burbank (91505) *(P-4401)*

Radio Time, San Francisco *Also Called: Tunein Inc (P-4407)*

Radiologic Health Branch, San Diego *Also Called: Department of Public Health (P-14724)*

Radiological Assoc Sacramento, Sacramento *Also Called: Radiological Associates of Sacramento Medical Group Inc (P-16746)*

Radiological Associates of Sacramento Medical Group Inc ....A....... 916 646-8300
1500 Expo Pkwy Sacramento (95815) *(P-16746)*

Radiology Partners Inc (HQ) .... B....... 424 290-8004
2101 E El Segundo Blvd Ste 401 El Segundo (90245) *(P-15007)*

Radiology Prtners Holdings LLC (PA) .... C....... 424 290-8004
2330 Utah Ave Ste 200 El Segundo (90245) *(P-15008)*

Radison Hotel Newport Beach, Newport Beach *Also Called: Pacific Hotel Management Inc (P-10085)*

Radisson Inn, Berkeley *Also Called: Boykin Mgt Co Ltd Lblty Co (P-9656)*

Radisson Inn, Los Angeles *Also Called: Pacifica Hosts Inc (P-10089)*

Radisson Inn, Ontario *Also Called: Prime Hospitality LLC (P-10128)*

Radisson Inn, Los Angeles *Also Called: Radlax Gateway Hotel LLC (P-10136)*

Radiumone Inc .... C....... 415 418-2840
601 Montgomery St Fl 16 San Francisco (94111) *(P-20643)*

Radius Product Development Inc .... B....... 408 361-6000
6375 San Ignacio Ave San Jose (95119) *(P-19371)*

Radix, Los Angeles *Also Called: Radix Textile Inc (P-6161)*

Radix Textile Inc .... D....... 323 234-1667
600 E Washington Blvd Ste C2 Los Angeles (90015) *(P-6161)*

Radlax Gateway Hotel LLC .... A....... 310 670-9000
6225 W Century Blvd Los Angeles (90045) *(P-10136)*

Radnet Inc (PA) .... A....... 310 478-7808
1510 Cotner Ave Los Angeles (90025) *(P-16747)*

Radnet Management, Lancaster *Also Called: Radnet Management I Inc (P-15009)*

Radnet Management I Inc .... C....... 661 945-5855
44725 10th St W Ste 150 Lancaster (93534) *(P-15009)*

Rady Childrens Hosp & Hlth Ctr (PA) .... A 858 576-1700
  3020 Childrens Way San Diego (92123) *(P-16356)*

Rady Childrens Specialists .... D 858 966-8197
  7920 Frost St Ste 200 San Diego (92123) *(P-15010)*

Rady Chld Hospital-San Diego (HQ) .... A 858 576-1700
  3020 Childrens Way San Diego (92123) *(P-16357)*

Rafael Convalescent Hospital .... D 415 479-3450
  234 N San Pedro Rd San Rafael (94903) *(P-15890)*

Rafco Products Brickform, Rancho Cucamonga *Also Called: Rafco-Brickform LLC (P-2782)*

Rafco-Brickform LLC (PA) .... D 909 484-3399
  11061 Jersey Blvd Rancho Cucamonga (91730) *(P-2782)*

Raffles Lrmitage Beverly Hills .... C 310 278-3344
  9291 Burton Way Beverly Hills (90210) *(P-10137)*

Raging Waters, San Dimas *Also Called: Raging Waters Group Inc (P-14310)*

Raging Waters Group Inc .... A 909 802-2200
  111 Raging Waters Dr San Dimas (91773) *(P-14310)*

Raging Waters San Jose 704, San Jose *Also Called: Festival Fun Parks LLC (P-14303)*

Raging Wire, Sacramento *Also Called: Ntt Glbal Data Ctrs Amrcas Inc (P-12698)*

Rahi Systems Holdings, Fremont *Also Called: Rahi Systems Inc (P-12867)*

Rahi Systems Inc (HQ) .... D 510 651-2205
  48303 Fremont Blvd Fremont (94538) *(P-12867)*

Rai Care Centers Colton LLC .... C 909 430-0930
  1275 W C St Colton (92324) *(P-16991)*

Rai Care Centers Lynwood LLC .... C 562 401-0155
  7700 Imperial Hwy Ste R Downey (90242) *(P-16992)*

Rai Care Ctrs Sthern Cal II LL .... C 619 442-4122
  858 Fletcher Pkwy El Cajon (92020) *(P-16993)*

Rai Care Ctrs Sthern Cal II LL .... C 619 229-1070
  7007 Mission Gorge Rd San Diego (92120) *(P-16994)*

Rai Care Ctrs Sthern Cal II LL .... C 310 673-6865
  1416 Centinela Ave Inglewood (90302) *(P-16995)*

Rai Care Ctrs Sthern Cal II LL .... C 760 346-7588
  41501 Corporate Way Palm Desert (92260) *(P-16996)*

Rai Centinela Inglewood, Inglewood *Also Called: Rai Care Ctrs Sthern Cal II LL (P-16995)*

Rai Corporate Way Palm Desert, Palm Desert *Also Called: Rai Care Ctrs Sthern Cal II LL (P-16996)*

Rai West C Colton, Colton *Also Called: Rai Care Centers Colton LLC (P-16991)*

Rai-Fletcher Parkway-El Cajon, El Cajon *Also Called: Rai Care Ctrs Sthern Cal II LL (P-16993)*

Rain Bird Corporation .... D 619 661-4493
  2475 Paseo De Las Americas Ste A # 1318 San Diego (92154) *(P-4994)*

Rain For Rent, Bakersfield *Also Called: Western Oilfields Supply Co (P-11063)*

Rain For Rent, Bakersfield *Also Called: Western Oilfields Supply Co (P-11064)*

Rainbow - Brite Indus Svcs LLC .... A 559 925-2580
  463 E Salmon River Dr Fresno (93730) *(P-10952)*

Rainbow Disposal Co Inc (HQ) .... C 714 847-3581
  17121 Nichols Ln Huntington Beach (92647) *(P-4923)*

Rainbow Refuse Recycling, Huntington Beach *Also Called: Rainbow Disposal Co Inc (P-4923)*

Rainbow Vending & Distributing, San Diego *Also Called: Canteen Vending - San Diego (P-6457)*

Rainbow Wtrprofing Restoration .... C 415 641-1578
  600 Treat Ave San Francisco (94110) *(P-2311)*

Raindrop Agency Inc .... D 661 724-6237
  8276 Ronson Rd San Diego (92111) *(P-20522)*

Rainmaker Systems Inc .... C 408 659-1800
  1821 S Bascom Ave Ste 385 Campbell (95008) *(P-20190)*

Raintree Systems Inc .... C 951 252-9400
  30650 Rancho California Rd Ste 406 Temecula (92591) *(P-11862)*

Rakuten Usa Inc .... C 650 383-1328
  800 Concar Dr Ste 175 San Mateo (94402) *(P-4335)*

Rakworx Inc .... C 949 215-1362
  1 Mason Irvine (92618) *(P-12711)*

Ralco Holdings Inc (DH) .... C 949 440-5500
  13861 Rosecrans Ave Santa Fe Springs (90670) *(P-5054)*

Raleigh Enterprises Inc (PA) .... C 310 899-8900
  5300 Melrose Ave Los Angeles (90038) *(P-10138)*

Raleigh Holdings, Los Angeles *Also Called: Raleigh Enterprises Inc (P-10138)*

Ralis, Orange *Also Called: Ralis Services Corp (P-20523)*

Ralis Services Corp .... C 844 347-2547
  1 City Blvd W Ste 600 Orange (92868) *(P-20523)*

Rally Health Inc .... C 408 821-5414
  665 3rd St Ste 200 San Francisco (94107) *(P-17310)*

Rally Holdings LLC .... A 817 919-6833
  17771 Mitchell N Irvine (92614) *(P-5055)*

Ralph Brennan Rest Group LLC .... C 714 776-5200
  1590 S Disneyland Dr Anaheim (92802) *(P-20524)*

Ralphs Logistics - Compton DC, Compton *Also Called: Kroger Co (P-3722)*

Ram Mechanical Inc .... D 209 531-9155
  3506 Moore Rd Ceres (95307) *(P-1539)*

Ram Plumbing .... D 800 487-5812
  14745 Addison St Sherman Oaks (91403) *(P-1540)*

Ramada By Wyndham, Irvine *Also Called: Western National Securities (P-9216)*

Ramada Inn, El Monte *Also Called: Amenities Development Co (P-9603)*

Ramada Inn, Hawthorne *Also Called: Calhot Illinios LLC (P-9675)*

Ramada Inn, San Diego *Also Called: Royal Hospitality Inc (P-10177)*

Ramada Inn, Costa Mesa *Also Called: Trigild International Inc (P-10325)*

Ramada Inn, El Cajon *Also Called: W Lodging Inc (P-10348)*

Ramada Inn Silicon Valley, Sunnyvale *Also Called: Executive Inn Inc (P-9791)*

Rambus, San Jose *Also Called: Rambus Inc (P-2933)*

Rambus Inc (PA) .... B 408 462-8000
  4453 N 1st St Ste 100 San Jose (95134) *(P-2933)*

Ramco Employment Services, Oxnard *Also Called: Ramco Enterprises LP (P-300)*

Ramco Enterprises LP .... B 805 486-9328
  520 E 3rd St Ste B Oxnard (93030) *(P-300)*

Ramco Enterprises LP .... B 831 722-3370
  585 Auto Center Dr Watsonville (95076) *(P-11212)*

Ramco Enterprises LP .... B 805 922-9888
  325 Plaza Dr Ste 1 Santa Maria (93454) *(P-11213)*

Ramona Auto Services Inc .... D 909 986-1785
  2451 S Euclid Ave Ontario (91762) *(P-7355)*

Ramona Care Inc .... C 626 442-5721
  11900 Ramona Blvd El Monte (91732) *(P-15634)*

Ramona Community Services Corp (HQ) .... C 951 658-9288
  890 W Stetson Ave Ste A Hemet (92543) *(P-16918)*

Ramona Nrsing Rhbilitation Ctr, El Monte *Also Called: Ramona Care Inc (P-15634)*

Ramona Rhblttion Post Acute CA .... C 951 652-0011
  485 W Johnston Ave Hemet (92543) *(P-16358)*

Ramona Rhblttion Post Acute Ca, Hemet *Also Called: Ramona Rhblttion Post Acute CA (P-16358)*

Ramona Vna & Hospice, Hemet *Also Called: Ramona Community Services Corp (P-16918)*

Ramos Oil Co Inc (PA) .... D 916 371-2570
  1515 S River Rd West Sacramento (95691) *(P-7390)*

Ramy Infotech Inc .... C 408 317-9256
  5201 Great America Pkwy Ste 320 Santa Clara (95054) *(P-11863)*

Rance King Properties Inc (PA) .... C 562 240-1000
  3737 E Broadway Long Beach (90803) *(P-8857)*

Ranch At Little Hills, The, Red Bluff *Also Called: Concessionaires Urban Park (P-14509)*

Ranch House Doors Inc .... D 951 278-2884
  1527 Pomona Rd Corona (92878) *(P-2013)*

Ranching Shop, Corcoran *Also Called: J G Boswell Company (P-4)*

Rancho, Temecula *Also Called: Rancho Ford Inc (P-7286)*

Rancho Bellagio Post Acute, Moreno Valley *Also Called: Moreno Valley Snf LLC (P-13383)*

Rancho Bernardo Golf Club .... D 858 487-1134
  17550 Bernardo Oaks Dr San Diego (92128) *(P-14552)*

Rancho Bernardo Inn, San Diego *Also Called: JC Resorts LLC (P-20121)*

Rancho California Water Dst (PA) .... C 951 296-6900
  42135 Winchester Rd Temecula (92590) *(P-4820)*

Rancho Cordova Medical Offices, Rancho Cordova *Also Called: Kaiser Foundation Hospitals (P-16178)*

Rancho Del Oro Ldscp Maint Inc .... D 760 726-0215
  4167 Avenida De La Plata Ste 109 Oceanside (92056) *(P-459)*

Rancho Foods Inc .... D 323 585-0503
  2528 E 37th St Vernon (90058) *(P-6501)*

Rancho Ford Inc .... C 951 699-1302
  26895 Ynez Rd Temecula (92591) *(P-7286)*

Rancho La Puerta Inc .... D 858 764-5500
  11722 Sorrento Valley Rd Ste G San Diego (92121) *(P-14225)*

Rancho Laguna Farms LLC .... D 805 925-7805
  2410 W Main St Santa Maria (93458) *(P-195)*

Rancho Las Palmas Resort & Spa, Rancho Mirage Also Called: Ksl Rancho Mirage Operating Co Inc *(P-9951)*

Rancho Mission Viejo LLC .... D....... 949 240-3363
28811 Ortega Hwy San Juan Capistrano (92675) *(P-9150)*

Rancho Monterey Apartments, Tustin Also Called: Irvine APT Communities LP *(P-8835)*

Rancho Murieta Country Club .... D....... 916 354-2400
7000 Alameda Dr Rancho Murieta (95683) *(P-14425)*

Rancho Physical Therapy, San Marcos Also Called: Rancho Physical Therapy Inc *(P-15303)*

Rancho Physical Therapy Inc .... C....... 760 752-1011
277 Rancheros Dr San Marcos (92069) *(P-15303)*

Rancho Physical Therapy Inc (PA) .... D....... 951 696-9353
24630 Washington Ave Ste 200 Murrieta (92562) *(P-15304)*

Rancho Pino Verdi, Lucerne Valley Also Called: Casa Clina Hosp Ctrs For Hlthc *(P-17862)*

Rancho Research Institute .... C....... 562 401-8111
7601 Imperial Hwy Downey (90242) *(P-19906)*

Rancho San Antnio Rtrment Hsin .... B....... 650 265-2637
23500 Cristo Rey Dr Cupertino (95014) *(P-18507)*

Rancho San Antonio Boys HM Inc (PA) .... D....... 818 882-6400
21000 Plummer St Chatsworth (91311) *(P-18508)*

Rancho San Carlos Partnership LP .... C....... 831 626-8200
1 Rancho San Carlos Rd Carmel (93923) *(P-9272)*

Rancho San Diego Cinema 16, El Cajon Also Called: Edwards Theatres Circuit Inc *(P-13992)*

Rancho Santa Ana Botanic Grdn .... D....... 909 625-8767
1500 N College Ave Claremont (91711) *(P-18693)*

Rancho Santa Fe, Rancho Santa Fe Also Called: Pacific Western Bank *(P-7636)*

Rancho Santa Fe Association .... D....... 858 756-1182
5827 Viadelacumere Rancho Santa Fe (92067) *(P-14426)*

Rancho Santa Fe Technology Inc (PA) .... D....... 858 565-7224
5961 Kearny Villa Rd San Diego (92123) *(P-1001)*

Rancho Sante Fe Golf Club, Rancho Santa Fe Also Called: Rancho Santa Fe Association *(P-14426)*

Rancho Springs Medical Center, Murrieta Also Called: Southwest Healthcare Sys Aux *(P-16451)*

Rancho Vista, Vista Also Called: Rancho Vista Health Center *(P-15787)*

Rancho Vista Development Co .... D....... 661 272-9082
3905 Club Rancho Dr Palmdale (93551) *(P-14284)*

Rancho Vista Golf Course, Palmdale Also Called: Rancho Vista Development Co *(P-14284)*

Rancho Vista Health Center .... C....... 760 941-1480
200 Grapevine Rd Apt 15 Vista (92083) *(P-15787)*

Rancho VIncia Rsort Prtners LL .... B....... 858 756-1123
5921 Valencia Cir Rancho Santa Fe (92067) *(P-10139)*

Ranchwood Contractors Inc .... D....... 209 826-6200
923 E Pacheco Blvd Los Banos (93635) *(P-1002)*

Rand, Santa Monica Also Called: The Rand Corporation *(P-19920)*

Randall - McAnany Company .... D....... 310 822-3344
1528 W 178th St Gardena (90248) *(P-1636)*

Randall Farms, Vernon Also Called: Sydney & Anne Bloom Farms Inc *(P-6505)*

Randstad Engineering, El Segundo Also Called: Randstad Professionals Us LLC *(P-11322)*

Randstad Finance & Accounting, Burlingame Also Called: Randstad Professionals Us LLC *(P-11214)*

Randstad Finance & Accounting, Cerritos Also Called: Randstad Professionals Us LLC *(P-11216)*

Randstad Professionals Us LLC .... C....... 650 343-5111
111 Anza Blvd Ste 202 Burlingame (94010) *(P-11214)*

Randstad Professionals Us LLC .... D....... 408 573-1111
2033 Gateway Pl Ste 120 San Jose (95110) *(P-11215)*

Randstad Professionals Us LLC .... D....... 562 468-0111
17777 Center Court Dr N Ste 225 Cerritos (90703) *(P-11216)*

Randstad Professionals Us LLC .... D....... 781 213-1500
3333 Michelson Dr Ste 210 Irvine (92612) *(P-11321)*

Randstad Professionals Us LLC .... D....... 424 246-4400
2321 Rosecrans Ave Ste 2215 El Segundo (90245) *(P-11322)*

Ranger Pipelines Incorporated .... C....... 415 822-3700
1790 Yosemite Ave San Francisco (94124) *(P-1255)*

Rantec Power Systems Inc (HQ) .... D....... 805 596-6000
1173 Los Olivos Ave Los Osos (93402) *(P-5693)*

RAPHAEL HOUSE, San Francisco Also Called: Raphael Hse San Francisco Inc *(P-18092)*

Raphael Hse San Francisco Inc .... D....... 415 345-7200
1065 Sutter St San Francisco (94109) *(P-18092)*

Raphaels Party Rentals Inc (PA) .... C....... 858 444-1692
8606 Miramar Rd San Diego (92126) *(P-11052)*

Rapid Response Force LLC .... D....... 408 612-8984
15105 Concord Cir Ste 210 Morgan Hill (95037) *(P-18093)*

Rapid Robotics Inc .... D....... 972 741-2627
100 Hooper St Ste 15 San Francisco (94107) *(P-5339)*

Rapidapi, San Francisco Also Called: R Software Inc *(P-11861)*

Rapp, Los Angeles Also Called: Rapp Worldwide Inc *(P-10668)*

Rapp Worldwide California Inc .... C....... 415 248-7983
55 Union St Fl 1 San Francisco (94102) *(P-10667)*

Rapp Worldwide Inc .... C....... 310 563-7200
12777 W Jefferson Blvd Bldg C Los Angeles (90066) *(P-10668)*

Raps Hospitality Group .... C....... 510 795-7995
5977 Mowry Ave Newark (94560) *(P-10140)*

RAPT THERAPEUTICS, South San Francisco Also Called: Rapt Therapeutics Inc *(P-2605)*

Rapt Therapeutics Inc .... D....... 650 489-9000
561 Eccles Ave South San Francisco (94080) *(P-2605)*

Rashman Corporation .... D....... 818 993-3030
8600 Wilbur Ave Northridge (91324) *(P-5447)*

RAVENSWOOD FAMILY HEALTH CENTE, East Palo Alto Also Called: South Cnty Cmnty Hlth Ctr Inc *(P-15067)*

Ravenswood Solutions Inc (HQ) .... D....... 650 241-3661
48371 Fremont Blvd Ste 105 Fremont (94538) *(P-12517)*

Ravi Patel MD Inc .... C....... 661 862-7113
6501 Truxtun Ave Bakersfield (93309) *(P-15011)*

Ravig Inc .... D....... 925 526-1234
510 Garcia Ave Ste E Pittsburg (94565) *(P-5340)*

Ravine Waterpark LLC .... C....... 805 237-8500
2301 Airport Rd Paso Robles (93446) *(P-14311)*

Ravine Waterpark, The, Paso Robles Also Called: Ravine Waterpark LLC *(P-14311)*

Rawlings Mechanical Corp (PA) .... D....... 323 875-2040
11615 Pendleton St Sun Valley (91352) *(P-1541)*

Rax Alar Products, Poway Also Called: Moteng Inc *(P-6181)*

Raxium Inc .... D....... 510 296-9935
1250 Reliance Way Fremont (94539) *(P-19372)*

Ray Gaskin Service .... D....... 916 682-5155
8553 Weyand Ave Sacramento (95828) *(P-13646)*

Ray L Hellwig Mechanical Co Inc .... D....... 408 727-5080
1309 Laurelwood Rd Santa Clara (95054) *(P-1542)*

Ray L Hellwig Plumbing & Heating Inc .... B....... 408 727-5612
1301 Laurelwood Rd Santa Clara (95054) *(P-1543)*

Raymond Group (PA) .... D....... 714 771-7670
520 W Walnut Ave Orange (92868) *(P-20191)*

Raymond Handling Concepts Corp (DH) .... D....... 510 745-7500
41400 Boyce Rd Fremont (94538) *(P-13794)*

Raymond Handling Solutions Inc (DH) .... C....... 562 944-8067
9939 Norwalk Blvd Santa Fe Springs (90670) *(P-5863)*

Raytheon, El Segundo Also Called: Raytheon Company *(P-3009)*

Raytheon, Goleta Also Called: Raytheon Company *(P-3010)*

Raytheon, El Segundo Also Called: Raytheon Secure Information Systems LLC *(P-19373)*

Raytheon Applied Sgnal Tech In .... D....... 310 436-7000
2000 E El Segundo Blvd El Segundo (90245) *(P-2898)*

Raytheon Cmmand Ctrl Sltons LL (DH) .... A....... 714 446-3118
1801 Hughes Dr Fullerton (92833) *(P-5694)*

Raytheon Company .... D....... 310 647-1000
1921 E Mariposa Ave El Segundo (90245) *(P-3009)*

Raytheon Company .... D....... 805 562-4611
75 Coromar Dr Goleta (93117) *(P-3010)*

Raytheon Lgstics Spport Trning .... B....... 310 647-9438
2000 E El Segundo Blvd El Segundo (90245) *(P-5966)*

Raytheon Secure Information Systems LLC .... C....... 310 647-9438
2000 E El Segundo Blvd El Segundo (90245) *(P-19373)*

Rayzebio Inc .... D....... 619 937-2754
5505 Morehouse Dr Ste 300 San Diego (92121) *(P-2606)*

Rba Builders Inc .... D....... 714 895-9000
16490 Harbor Blvd Ste A Fountain Valley (92708) *(P-1003)*

Rbc Transport Dynamics Corp .... C....... 203 267-7001
3131 W Segerstrom Ave Santa Ana (92704) *(P-5921)*

Rbd Hotel Palm Springs LLC .... D....... 760 322-9000
285 N Palm Canyon Dr Palm Springs (92262) *(P-10141)*

Rbz LLP .... C....... 310 478-4148
11766 Wilshire Blvd Fl 9 Los Angeles (90025) *(P-19626)*

RC Construction Services, Redlands Also Called: Robert Clapper Cnstr Svcs Inc *(P-1009)*

ALPHABETIC SECTION — Recology Sunset Scavenger

RC Maintenance Holdings Inc .... C....... 951 903-6303
569 Bateman Cir Corona (92878) *(P-1544)*

RC Wendt Painting Inc .... C....... 714 960-2700
21612 Surveyor Cir Huntington Beach (92646) *(P-1637)*

Rcac, West Sacramento *Also Called: Rural Cmnty Assistance Corp* *(P-18101)*

Rcb Corporation (PA) .... D....... 916 567-2600
2480 Natomas Park Dr Sacramento (95833) *(P-7713)*

RCEB, San Leandro *Also Called: Regional Center of E Bay Inc* *(P-18096)*

Rceb, Concord *Also Called: Regional Center of E Bay Inc* *(P-18097)*

Rcg Auto Logistics, Sacramento *Also Called: Rcg Logistics LLC* *(P-3530)*

Rcg Logistics LLC .... D....... 916 999-1234
9300 Tech Center Dr Ste 190 Sacramento (95826) *(P-3530)*

Rci General Engineering .... D....... 530 533-3918
5015 Feather River Blvd Oroville (95965) *(P-1189)*

RCWD, Temecula *Also Called: Rancho California Water Dst* *(P-4820)*

RD Olson Construction Inc .... C....... 949 474-2001
400 Spectrum Center Dr Ste 1200 Irvine (92618) *(P-1004)*

Rdc-S111 Inc (PA) .... D....... 562 628-8000
245 E 3rd St Long Beach (90802) *(P-19501)*

Rdl Reference Laboratory, Beverly Hills *Also Called: Rheumatology Diagnostics Lab* *(P-16750)*

RDM Express Inc .... D....... 415 642-4916
2000 Mckinnon Ave San Francisco (94124) *(P-6280)*

Rdo Construction Equipment Co .... D....... 619 443-3758
10108 Riverford Rd Lakeside (92040) *(P-11005)*

Rdr Builders LP .... D....... 209 368-7561
1333 E Kettleman Ln Lodi (95240) *(P-770)*

Rdr Production Builders, Lodi *Also Called: Rdr Builders LP* *(P-770)*

RDS Logistics Group (PA) .... D....... 909 355-4100
8600 Banana Ave Fontana (92335) *(P-3420)*

RE La Mesa LLC .... D....... 415 675-1500
300 California St Fl 8 San Francisco (94104) *(P-1315)*

Re/Max .... C....... 310 205-0050
9454 Wilshire Blvd Ste 150 Beverly Hills (90212) *(P-9151)*

Re/Max, San Leandro *Also Called: Propel Inc* *(P-8856)*

Re/Max, Los Alamitos *Also Called: College Park Realty Inc* *(P-8946)*

Re/Max, Upland *Also Called: Diamond Ridge Corporation* *(P-8981)*

Re/Max, Irvine *Also Called: J Baron Inc* *(P-9055)*

Re/Max, Beverly Hills *Also Called: Re/Max* *(P-9151)*

Re/Max, Modesto *Also Called: Re/Max Executive* *(P-9152)*

Re/Max, Santa Clarita *Also Called: RE/Max of Valencia Inc* *(P-9153)*

Re/Max, Los Angeles *Also Called: Remax 100* *(P-9160)*

Re/Max, Torrance *Also Called: Remax Exec King Harbor* *(P-9161)*

Re/Max, Northridge *Also Called: Remax Olson & Associates Inc* *(P-9162)*

Re/Max, Ventura *Also Called: Rgc Services Inc* *(P-9167)*

Re/Max, Camarillo *Also Called: Rgc Services Inc* *(P-9168)*

Re/Max Executive .... D....... 209 499-7772
220 Standiford Ave Ste A Modesto (95350) *(P-9152)*

RE/Max of Valencia Inc (PA) .... C....... 661 255-2650
25101 The Old Rd Santa Clarita (91381) *(P-9153)*

Reach Adult Development Inc .... D....... 916 203-6246
3280 Ramos Cir Sacramento (95827) *(P-20838)*

Reach Out West End .... D....... 909 982-8641
1126 W Foothill Blvd Ste 250 Upland (91786) *(P-18620)*

Reachlocal, Woodland Hills *Also Called: Reachlocal Inc* *(P-10669)*

Reachlocal Inc (DH) .... C....... 818 274-0260
21700 Oxnard St Ste 1600 Woodland Hills (91367) *(P-10669)*

Reading and Beyond .... D....... 559 840-1068
4670 E Butler Ave Fresno (93702) *(P-18900)*

Reading Entertainment Inc (HQ) .... D....... 213 235-2226
500 Citadel Dr Ste 300 Commerce (90040) *(P-14006)*

Reading Partners .... D....... 408 945-5720
600 Valley Way Milpitas (95035) *(P-18094)*

Ready Pac Foods, Irwindale *Also Called: Ready Pac Produce Inc* *(P-6575)*

Ready Pac Foods Inc (HQ) .... A....... 626 856-8686
4401 Foxdale St Irwindale (91706) *(P-2442)*

Ready Pac Foods Inc .... D....... 925 552-0400
125 Railroad Ave Ste 203 Danville (94526) *(P-6574)*

Ready Pac Produce Inc (DH) .... C....... 800 800-4088
4401 Foxdale St Irwindale (91706) *(P-6575)*

Ready Price LLC .... A....... 408 357-0931
5671 Santa Teresa Blvd San Jose (95123) *(P-11864)*

Readylink Inc .... D....... 760 343-7000
72030 Metroplex Dr Thousand Palms (92276) *(P-11217)*

Readylink Healthcare .... D....... 760 343-7000
72030 Metroplex Dr Thousand Palms (92276) *(P-11218)*

Real Estate & Mortgage Broker, Fresno *Also Called: Xander Mortgage & Real Estate* *(P-8028)*

Real Estate Equity Exchange .... D....... 415 992-4200
650 California St Fl 1800 San Francisco (94108) *(P-8014)*

Real Estate Image Inc (PA) .... C....... 714 502-3900
1415 S Acacia Ave Fullerton (92831) *(P-10774)*

Real Mex Foods Inc .... D....... 714 523-0031
5660 Katella Ave Ste 200 Cypress (90630) *(P-6281)*

Real-Time Innovations Inc (PA) .... D....... 408 990-7400
232 E Java Dr Sunnyvale (94089) *(P-11865)*

Realm, Milpitas *Also Called: R&M USA Inc* *(P-5692)*

Realm, Palo Alto *Also Called: Tightdb Inc* *(P-11980)*

Realmanage LLC .... D....... 415 444-1600
1701 Novato Blvd Ste 209 Novato (94947) *(P-9154)*

Realselect Inc .... C....... 661 803-5188
3063 W Chapman Ave Apt 6207 Orange (92868) *(P-9155)*

Realsuite SM, Santa Clara *Also Called: Move Inc* *(P-9104)*

Realty Concepts, Fresno *Also Called: JMS Realtors Ltd* *(P-9058)*

Realty Group San Diego, Carlsbad *Also Called: Richard Realty Group Inc* *(P-9169)*

Realty Income, San Diego *Also Called: Realty Income Corporation* *(P-8754)*

Realty Income Corporation (PA) .... D....... 858 284-5000
11995 El Camino Real San Diego (92130) *(P-8754)*

Realty One Group Inc .... D....... 951 565-8105
19322 Jesse Ln Riverside (92508) *(P-9156)*

Realty One Group BMC Assoc .... D....... 925 230-0700
2355 San Ramon Valley Blvd San Ramon (94583) *(P-9157)*

Reapplications Inc .... D....... 619 230-0209
8910 University Center Ln Ste 300 San Diego (92122) *(P-11866)*

Rebar Engineering Inc .... C....... 562 946-2461
10706 Painter Ave Santa Fe Springs (90670) *(P-2197)*

Rebas Inc .... C....... 562 941-4155
12907 Imperial Hwy Santa Fe Springs (90670) *(P-5864)*

Rebco Communities Inc .... B....... 714 557-5511
3090 Pullman St Costa Mesa (92626) *(P-771)*

Rebekah Children's Services, Gilroy *Also Called: Odd Fellow-Rebekah Chld HM Cal* *(P-18498)*

Rec Solar, San Luis Obispo *Also Called: Mainstream Energy Corporation* *(P-1495)*

Rec Solar, San Luis Obispo *Also Called: Rec Solar Commercial Corp* *(P-1545)*

Rec Solar Commercial Corp .... C....... 844 732-7652
3450 Broad St Ste 105 San Luis Obispo (93401) *(P-1545)*

Rec Van, San Diego *Also Called: La Mesa R V Center Inc* *(P-7395)*

Recall Masters Inc .... D....... 650 434-5211
740 Tunbridge Rd Danville (94526) *(P-10775)*

RECHE CANYON REGIONAL REHAB CE, Colton *Also Called: Cambridge Sierra Holdings LLC* *(P-15365)*

Recipro, San Francisco *Also Called: Riskoptics Inc* *(P-11883)*

Reciprocal Labs Corp .... D....... 608 251-0470
9001 Spectrum Center Blvd San Diego (92123) *(P-11867)*

Recology, San Francisco *Also Called: Recology Inc* *(P-4924)*

Recology, Sun Valley *Also Called: Recology Los Angeles* *(P-4926)*

Recology Blssom Vly Orgnics - .... D....... 209 545-4401
6224 Stoddard Rd Modesto (95356) *(P-150)*

Recology Inc (PA) .... D....... 415 875-1000
50 California St Ste 2400 San Francisco (94111) *(P-4924)*

Recology Inc .... D....... 916 379-3300
245 N 1st St Dixon (95620) *(P-4925)*

Recology King County Inc .... C....... 415 348-9700
250 Executive Park Blvd Ste 2100 San Francisco (94134) *(P-10953)*

Recology Los Angeles .... B....... 818 767-0675
9189 De Garmo Ave Sun Valley (91352) *(P-4926)*

Recology Sonoma Marin .... B....... 707 586-8261
3400 Standish Ave Santa Rosa (95407) *(P-4927)*

Recology South Valley (HQ) .... D....... 408 842-3358
1351 Pacheco Pass Hwy Gilroy (95020) *(P-4928)*

Recology Sunset Scavenger, San Francisco *Also Called: Sunset Scavenger Company* *(P-4942)*

Recology Yuba-Sutter   **ALPHABETIC SECTION**

Recology Yuba-Sutter .... D...... 530 743-6933
   300 4th St Marysville (95901) *(P-4929)*
Recon, San Diego *Also Called: Recon Environmental Inc (P-20839)*
Recon Environmental Inc (PA)... D...... 619 308-9333
   3111 Camino Del Rio N Ste 600 San Diego (92108) *(P-20839)*
Recovery Solutions Santa Ana, Santa Ana *Also Called: CRC Health Corporate (P-17046)*
Recp/Wndsor Scramento Ventr LP .... D...... 916 455-6800
   4422 Y St Sacramento (95817) *(P-10142)*
Recreational Assn Corcoran .... D...... 559 992-5171
   900 Dairy Ave Corcoran (93212) *(P-18901)*
Recruit 360 .... C...... 949 250-4420
   457 Ogle St Costa Mesa (92627) *(P-11219)*
Recruit Bobby, San Diego *Also Called: Kennedy Team Inc (P-19010)*
Recruitment Service, Sacramento *Also Called: Sutter Hlth Scrmnto Sierra Reg (P-16548)*
Recurly Inc (PA).. D...... 844 732-8759
   201 Spear St San Francisco (94105) *(P-19627)*
Recycle Waste, Santa Clara *Also Called: Mission Trail Wste Systems Inc (P-3413)*
Recycler Core Company Inc .... D...... 951 276-1687
   2727 Kansas Ave Riverside (92507) *(P-4930)*
Recycling Industries Inc .... D...... 916 452-3961
   4741 Watt Ave North Highlands (95660) *(P-4931)*
Red Blossom Farms, Salinas *Also Called: Red Blossom Sales Inc (P-196)*
Red Blossom Farms Inc .... D...... 805 686-4747
   1389 W Main St Santa Maria (93458) *(P-59)*
Red Blossom Sales Inc .... A...... 805 349-9404
   865 Black Rd Santa Maria (93458) *(P-60)*
Red Blossom Sales Inc .... B...... 831 751-9169
   9 Harris Pl Salinas (93901) *(P-196)*
Red Bull North America Inc (HQ)..................................... D...... 310 460-5356
   1630 Stewart St Santa Monica (90404) *(P-14100)*
Red Bull TV, Santa Monica *Also Called: Red Bull North America Inc (P-14100)*
Red Carpet Car Wash, Clovis *Also Called: Bowie Enterprises (P-13688)*
Red Chamber Co (PA)... B...... 323 234-9000
   1912 E Vernon Ave Vernon (90058) *(P-6479)*
Red Condor Inc .... C...... 707 569-7419
   1300 Valley House Dr Ste 115 Rohnert Park (94928) *(P-11868)*
Red Cross, Los Angeles *Also Called: American National Red Cross (P-17832)*
Red Earth Casino .... C...... 760 395-1200
   3089 Norm Niver Rd Thermal (92274) *(P-10143)*
Red Fish Grill, Anaheim *Also Called: Ralph Brennan Rest Group LLC (P-20524)*
Red Hawk Casino, Placerville *Also Called: Shingle Sprng Trbal Gming Auth (P-10230)*
Red Hill Country Club .... D...... 909 982-1358
   8358 Red Hill Country Club Dr Rancho Cucamonga (91730) *(P-14427)*
Red Lion Hotel Redding, Redding *Also Called: Kaidan Hospitality LP (P-9933)*
Red Peak Group LLC .... D...... 818 222-7762
   23975 Park Sorrento # 410 Calabasas (91302) *(P-20525)*
Red Pocket Inc .... D...... 888 993-3888
   2060d E Avenida De Los Arboles Ste 288 Thousand Oaks (91362) *(P-4225)*
Red Pocket Mobile, Thousand Oaks *Also Called: Red Pocket Inc (P-4225)*
Red Pointe Roofing LP (PA)... D...... 714 685-0010
   1814 N Neville St Orange (92865) *(P-2080)*
Red Robin, San Diego *Also Called: Red Robin International Inc (P-7506)*
Red Robin International Inc .... D...... 858 202-1651
   4545 La Jolla Village Dr San Diego (92122) *(P-7506)*
Red Storm, San Francisco *Also Called: Ubisoft Holdings Inc (P-11999)*
Red Tail Residential LLC (PA)... D...... 949 399-2510
   2082 Michelson Dr Fl 4 Irvine (92612) *(P-9158)*
Red Top Electric, Livermore *Also Called: Red Top Electric Co-Emeryville Inc (P-1814)*
Red Top Electric Co-Emeryville Inc .... D...... 925 667-2900
   6751 Southfront Rd Livermore (94551) *(P-1814)*
Red Zone Technologies, San Francisco *Also Called: Wilbur-Ellis Company LLC (P-6838)*
Redbarn Pet Products Inc (PA).. C...... 562 495-7315
   3229 E Spring St Ste 310 Long Beach (90806) *(P-6942)*
Redbarn Premium Pet Products, Long Beach *Also Called: Redbarn Pet Products Inc (P-6942)*
Redding Aero Enterprises Inc .... D...... 530 224-2300
   3775 Flight Ave Ste 100 Redding (96002) *(P-3191)*
Redding Jet Center, Redding *Also Called: Redding Aero Enterprises Inc (P-3191)*
Redding Lumber Transport Inc .... D...... 530 241-8193
   4301 Eastside Rd Redding (96001) *(P-3592)*

Redding Pathologists Lab (PA).. C...... 530 225-8000
   1725 Gold St Redding (96001) *(P-15012)*
Redding Rancheria (PA)... D...... 530 225-8979
   2000 Redding Rancheria Rd Redding (96001) *(P-10144)*
Redding Rnchria Ecnmic Dev Cor .... B...... 530 243-3377
   2100 Redding Rancheria Rd Redding (96001) *(P-10145)*
Redding Tree Growers Corp .... D...... 559 594-9299
   18985 Avenue 256 Apt A Exeter (93221) *(P-572)*
Redfish Labs Inc .... C...... 415 935-4249
   548 Market St Pmb 24776 San Francisco (94104) *(P-12868)*
Redhorse Constructors Inc .... D...... 415 492-2020
   36 Professional Center Pkwy San Rafael (94903) *(P-1005)*
Redica Systems Inc .... D...... 844 332-3320
   6700 Koll Center Pkwy Ste 140 Pleasanton (94566) *(P-12614)*
Redis Inc .... B...... 415 930-9666
   700 E El Camino Real Ste 250 Mountain View (94040) *(P-11869)*
Redlands Community Hospital (PA)............................... D...... 909 335-5500
   350 Terracina Blvd Redlands (92373) *(P-16359)*
REDLANDS COMMUNITY HOSPITAL, Redlands *Also Called: RHS Corp (P-20195)*
Redlands Country Club .... D...... 909 793-2661
   1749 Garden St Redlands (92373) *(P-14428)*
Redlands Employment Services .... B...... 951 688-0083
   4295 Jurupa St Ste 110 Ontario (91761) *(P-11220)*
Redlands Ford Inc .... D...... 909 793-3211
   1121 W Colton Ave Redlands (92374) *(P-13647)*
Redlands Healthcare Center, Redlands *Also Called: Ash Holdings LLC (P-15334)*
Redlands Staffing Services, Ontario *Also Called: Redlands Employment Services (P-11220)*
Redrocks Fumigation, San Jose *Also Called: Homeguard Incorporated (P-10837)*
Redseal Inc .... C...... 408 641-2200
   1300 El Camino Real Ste 300 Menlo Park (94025) *(P-12332)*
Redstone Print & Mail Inc .... D...... 916 318-6450
   910 Riverside Pkwy Ste 40 West Sacramento (95605) *(P-20526)*
Redtail Technology Inc .... D...... 800 206-5030
   3131 Fite Cir Sacramento (95827) *(P-11870)*
Redwood, Culver City *Also Called: Wovexx Holdings Inc (P-4559)*
Redwood Coast Petroleum Inc .... D...... 707 546-0766
   444 Yolanda Ave Ste A Santa Rosa (95404) *(P-6736)*
Redwood Community Services Inc .... D...... 707 472-2922
   350 E Gobbi St Ukiah (95482) *(P-18095)*
Redwood Credit Union (PA).. C...... 707 545-4000
   3033 Cleveland Ave Ste 100 Santa Rosa (95403) *(P-7793)*
Redwood Credit Union .... D...... 415 861-7928
   100 Van Ness Ave 10th Fl San Francisco (94102) *(P-7794)*
Redwood Elderlink & Homelink, Escondido *Also Called: Redwood Elderlink Scph (P-18509)*
Redwood Elderlink Scph .... B...... 760 480-1030
   710 W 13th Ave Escondido (92025) *(P-18509)*
Redwood Electric Group Inc (PA).................................... A...... 707 451-7348
   2775 Northwestern Pkwy Santa Clara (95051) *(P-1815)*
Redwood Empire Addctons Prgram, Santa Rosa *Also Called: Drug Abuse Alternatives Center (P-17055)*
Redwood Empire Ice Oprtons LLC (PA)......................... D...... 707 546-7147
   1667 W Steele Ln Santa Rosa (95403) *(P-14553)*
Redwood Empire Vinyrd MGT Inc .... D...... 707 857-3401
   22000 Geyserville Ave Geyserville (95441) *(P-379)*
Redwood Family Care Netwrk Inc .... A...... 909 942-0218
   13920 City Center Dr Chino Hills (91709) *(P-15013)*
Redwood Forest Foundation Inc .... D...... 510 459-1131
   2979 Santos Ln Walnut Creek (94597) *(P-18902)*
Redwood Health Club (PA).. D...... 707 468-0441
   3101 S State St Ukiah (95482) *(P-14226)*
Redwood Landfill Inc .... C...... 415 892-2851
   8950 Redwood Hwy Novato (94945) *(P-4932)*
Redwood Memorial Hosp Fortuna (PA)........................... C...... 707 725-7327
   3300 Renner Dr Fortuna (95540) *(P-16360)*
Redwood Painting Co Inc .... D...... 925 432-4500
   620 W 10th St Pittsburg (94565) *(P-1638)*
Redwood Regional Oncology Ctr, Santa Rosa *Also Called: Redwood Rgnal Med Group DRG LL (P-16748)*
Redwood Rgnal Med Group DRG LL .... D...... 707 253-7161
   1100 Trancas St Ste 256 Napa (94558) *(P-15014)*
Redwood Rgnal Med Group DRG LL (PA).................... D...... 707 525-4080
   990 Sonoma Ave Ste 15 Santa Rosa (95404) *(P-16748)*

ALPHABETIC SECTION

Redwood Senior Homes & Svcs, Escondido *Also Called: Humangood Socal (P-18457)*
Redwood Support Group Inc .... D....... 650 815-8933
50 Woodside Plz Redwood City (94061) *(P-13140)*
Redwood Toxicology Lab Inc ....C....... 707 577-7958
3650 Westwind Blvd Santa Rosa (95403) *(P-16749)*
Redwoods, The, Mill Valley *Also Called: The Redwoods A Cmnty Seniors (P-18531)*
Ree Medical Inc .... D....... 760 641-4359
3472 Calle Margarita Encinitas (92024) *(P-17311)*
Reed Smith LLP ....C....... 213 457-8000
355 S Grand Ave Ste 2900 Los Angeles (90071) *(P-17622)*
Reed Smith LLP ....C....... 415 543-8700
101 2nd St Ste 1800 San Francisco (94105) *(P-17623)*
Reed Thomas Company Inc .... D....... 714 558-7691
1025 Santiago St Santa Ana (92701) *(P-2224)*
Reedley Community Hospital .... D....... 559 638-8155
372 W Cypress Ave Reedley (93654) *(P-16361)*
Reef, Carlsbad *Also Called: South Cone Inc (P-6234)*
Reel Security California Inc .... D....... 818 928-4737
15303 Ventura Blvd Ste 1080 Sherman Oaks (91403) *(P-13027)*
Reels Inc .... D....... 714 446-9606
301 E Orangethorpe Ave Anaheim (92801) *(P-5056)*
Reeve Trucking Company, Stockton *Also Called: Reeve Trucking Company Inc (P-3531)*
Reeve Trucking Company Inc (PA) .... D....... 209 948-4061
5050 Carpenter Rd Stockton (95215) *(P-3531)*
Reeve-Knight Construction Inc .... D....... 916 786-5112
128 Ascot Dr Roseville (95661) *(P-1006)*
Refinery, The, Sherman Oaks *Also Called: Waldberg Inc (P-10723)*
Reflektive Inc (DH) ....C....... 203 886-9240
123 Townsend St Ste 300 San Francisco (94107) *(P-11871)*
Reformation, The, Los Angeles *Also Called: Lymi Inc (P-6205)*
Refrigeration Solutions LLC .... D....... 916 281-2000
1166 National Dr Ste 10 Sacramento (95834) *(P-1546)*
Refrigeration Supplies Distributor (PA) .... D....... 949 380-7878
26021 Atlantic Ocean Dr Lake Forest (92630) *(P-5781)*
Regal Cinemas Inc .... D....... 916 419-0205
3561 Truxel Rd Sacramento (95834) *(P-14007)*
Regal III LLC ....C....... 707 836-2100
421 Aviation Blvd Santa Rosa (95403) *(P-6804)*
Regal Medical Group Inc (PA) ....C....... 818 654-3400
8510 Balboa Blvd Ste 275 Northridge (91325) *(P-18758)*
Regal Technology Partners Inc .... D....... 714 835-1162
2921 Daimler St Santa Ana (92705) *(P-5341)*
Regal Wine Co, Santa Rosa *Also Called: Regal III LLC (P-6804)*
Regan Roofing Inc .... D....... 855 652-4050
2420 Industry St Ste B Oceanside (92054) *(P-2081)*
Regency Enterprises, Los Angeles *Also Called: New Regency Productions Inc (P-13870)*
Regency Enterprises Inc (PA) .... B....... 818 901-0255
9261 Jordan Ave Chatsworth (91311) *(P-5588)*
Regency Group, Pasadena *Also Called: One & All Inc (P-10658)*
REGENCY HEALTH SERVICES, Covina *Also Called: Covina Rehabilitation Center (P-15412)*
Regency Inn, Costa Mesa *Also Called: US Hotel and Resort MGT Inc (P-10337)*
Regency Real Estate Brks Inc ....C....... 949 707-4400
25950 Acero Ste 100 Mission Viejo (92691) *(P-9159)*
Regency Real Estate Brokers, Mission Viejo *Also Called: Regency Real Estate Brks Inc (P-9159)*
Regency Supply, Chatsworth *Also Called: Regency Enterprises Inc (P-5588)*
Regent, Valencia *Also Called: Regent Aerospace Corporation (P-5967)*
Regent LP (PA) .... D....... 310 299-4100
9720 Wilshire Blvd Fl 6 Beverly Hills (90212) *(P-9554)*
Regent Aerospace Corporation (PA) ....C....... 661 257-3000
28110 Harrison Pkwy Valencia (91355) *(P-5967)*
Regent Assisted Living Inc .... D....... 626 332-3344
150 S Grand Ave Ofc West Covina (91791) *(P-18510)*
Regent Assisted Living Inc ....C....... 831 459-8400
80 Front St Santa Cruz (95060) *(P-18511)*
Regent Senior Living W Covina, West Covina *Also Called: Regent Assisted Living Inc (P-18510)*
Regents of The University Cal .... D....... 310 267-9308
1250 16th St Santa Monica (90404) *(P-17312)*
Regents Point, Irvine *Also Called: Humangood Socal (P-8822)*

Regional Center, Chico *Also Called: Far Nrthern Crdnting Cncil On (P-17980)*
Regional Center of E Bay Inc (PA) ....C....... 510 618-6100
500 Davis St Ste 100 San Leandro (94577) *(P-18096)*
Regional Center of E Bay Inc .... D....... 925 691-2300
1320 Willow Pass Rd Ste 300 Concord (94520) *(P-18097)*
Regional Ctr Orange Cnty Inc (PA) .... B....... 714 796-5100
1525 N Tustin Ave Santa Ana (92705) *(P-20940)*
Regional Medical Ctr San Jose, San Jose *Also Called: San Jose Healthcare System LP (P-16383)*
Regional Office, Redlands *Also Called: Southern California Gas Co (P-4734)*
Regional Transportation Comm, San Diego *Also Called: San Diego Assn Governments (P-18720)*
Regis Contractors LP .... B....... 949 253-0455
18825 Bardeen Ave Irvine (92612) *(P-772)*
Regulus Therapeutics Inc .... D....... 858 202-6300
4224 Campus Point Ct Ste 210 San Diego (92121) *(P-19907)*
Regus Business Centre LLC ....C....... 714 371-4000
600 Anton Blvd Ste 1100 Costa Mesa (92626) *(P-13443)*
Regus Equity Business Ctrs LLC .... D....... 415 293-8000
One Market 35th And 36th Floors San Francisco (94105) *(P-13444)*
Reh Company ....C....... 619 238-1818
1055 2nd Ave San Diego (92101) *(P-10146)*
Rehab Alliance .... D....... 949 707-5555
22995 Mill Creek Dr Ste A Laguna Hills (92653) *(P-17116)*
Rehababilities Inc ....C....... 310 473-4448
11835 W Olympic Blvd Ste 1090e Los Angeles (90064) *(P-11221)*
Rehabilitation Ctr Bakersfield, Bakersfield *Also Called: Bakersfeld Hlthcare Wllness CN (P-15347)*
REHABILITATION INSTITUTE OF OR, Santa Ana *Also Called: Reimagine Network (P-17117)*
Rehabltion Cntre of Bvrly Hlls ....C....... 323 782-1500
580 S San Vicente Blvd Los Angeles (90048) *(P-15635)*
Rehabltition Ctr At San Jquin G, French Camp *Also Called: County of San Joaquin (P-17042)*
Rehabltition Ctr of Ornge Cnty ....C....... 714 826-2330
9021 Knott Ave Buena Park (90620) *(P-15636)*
Rehabltition Inst Sthern Cal Ri, Santa Ana *Also Called: Rio (P-17120)*
REHABWORKS AT FREEDOM VILLAGE, Lake Forest *Also Called: Freedom Village Healthcare Ctr (P-15481)*
Reichardt Duck Farm Inc .... D....... 707 762-6314
3770 Middle Two Rock Rd Petaluma (94952) *(P-230)*
Reimagine Network (PA) ....C....... 714 633-7400
1601 E Saint Andrew Pl Santa Ana (92705) *(P-17117)*
Reiter Affl Companies LLC ....C....... 805 925-8577
124 Carmen Ln Ste A Santa Maria (93458) *(P-61)*
Reiter Affl Companies LLC ....C....... 831 786-4244
140 Westridge Dr Watsonville (95076) *(P-62)*
Reiter Affl Companies LLC ....C....... 831 761-1424
411 Walker St Watsonville (95076) *(P-63)*
Reiter Berry Watsonville, Watsonville *Also Called: Reiter Affl Companies LLC (P-62)*
Related Management Corporation .... D....... 408 272-0356
303 Checkers Dr San Jose (95133) *(P-20192)*
Related Technologies Inc .... D....... 916 357-5900
81 Blue Ravine Rd Ste 230 Folsom (95630) *(P-12869)*
Relation Insurance Inc (PA) .... D....... 925 937-5858
1277 Treat Blvd Ste 400 Walnut Creek (94597) *(P-8648)*
Relation Insurance Services, Walnut Creek *Also Called: Relation Insurance Inc (P-8648)*
Relationalai Inc .... D....... 650 307-8776
2120 University Ave Berkeley (94704) *(P-12333)*
Relationedge LLC ....C....... 858 451-4665
10120 Pacific Heights Blvd Ste 110 San Diego (92121) *(P-12683)*
Releasepoint, Claremont *Also Called: Western Feld Invstigations Inc (P-12687)*
Reliable Container Corporation .... B....... 562 861-6226
9206 Santa Fe Springs Rd Santa Fe Springs (90670) *(P-2523)*
Reliable Energy Management Inc .... D....... 562 984-5511
6829 Walthall Way Paramount (90723) *(P-1547)*
Reliable Pntiac Cdllac Bick GM, Roseville *Also Called: Westrup-Sadler Inc (P-7334)*
Reliable Robotics Corporation .... D....... 650 336-0608
950 N Rengstorff Ave Ste E Mountain View (94043) *(P-5865)*
Reliable Service Company, Riverside *Also Called: Rsvc Company (P-1159)*
Reliable Wholesale Lumber Inc (PA) .... D....... 714 848-8222
7600 Redondo Cir Huntington Beach (92648) *(P-5182)*

ALPHABETIC SECTION

Reliance Communications LLC .... D..... 408 827-4726
100 Enterprise Way Ste A3 Scotts Valley (95066) *(P-4367)*

Reliance Company, Los Angeles *Also Called: Zastrow Construction Inc (P-786)*

Reliance Intermodal Inc .... D..... 209 946-0200
1919 Martin Luther King Ste A And B Stockton (95210) *(P-3532)*

Reliance Steel & Aluminum Co .... D..... 510 476-4400
33201 Western Ave Union City (94587) *(P-5513)*

Reliance Steel & Aluminum Co .... C..... 714 736-4800
15090 Northam St La Mirada (90638) *(P-5514)*

Reliance Steel & Aluminum Co .... C..... 323 583-6111
2537 E 27th St Vernon (90058) *(P-5515)*

Reliance Steel & Aluminum Co .... D..... 562 944-3322
12034 Greenstone Ave Santa Fe Springs (90670) *(P-5516)*

Reliance Steel Company, Vernon *Also Called: Reliance Steel & Aluminum Co (P-5515)*

Reliant Funding Group, San Diego *Also Called: Reliant Services Group LLC (P-7904)*

Reliant Services Group LLC .... C..... 877 850-0998
9540 Towne Centre Dr Ste 100 San Diego (92121) *(P-7904)*

Religion of Sports Hq .... D..... 214 557-1766
3310 Airport Ave Santa Monica (90405) *(P-4547)*

Relocity Inc .... C..... 323 207-9160
10250 Constellation Blvd Ste 100 Los Angeles (90067) *(P-20193)*

Reltio Inc (PA) .... B..... 855 360-3282
100 Marine Pkwy Ste 275 Redwood City (94065) *(P-11872)*

Relyance Ai, San Mateo *Also Called: Relyance Inc (P-11873)*

Relyance Inc 866 735-9623
1900 S Norfolk St Ste 350 San Mateo (94403) *(P-11873)*

REM Eye Wear, Sun Valley *Also Called: REM Optical Company Inc (P-5468)*

REM Optical Company Inc .... C..... 818 504-3950
10941 La Tuna Canyon Rd Sun Valley (91352) *(P-5468)*

Remax 100 .... D..... 323 933-4567
4311 Wilshire Blvd Ste 110 Los Angeles (90010) *(P-9160)*

Remax Accord, Pleasanton *Also Called: S&J Stadtler Inc (P-9173)*

Remax Exec King Harbor .... D..... 310 378-9889
23740 Hawthorne Blvd Torrance (90505) *(P-9161)*

Remax Olson & Associates Inc .... C..... 818 366-3300
11141 Tampa Ave Northridge (91326) *(P-9162)*

Remedy Intelligent Staffing, Aliso Viejo *Also Called: Remedytemp Inc (P-11323)*

Remedytemp Inc (DH) .... C..... 949 425-7600
101 Enterprise Ste 100 Aliso Viejo (92656) *(P-11323)*

Remi Vista Inc .... D..... 707 464-4349
370 9th St Crescent City (95531) *(P-18512)*

Remington Club I & II, San Diego *Also Called: Five Star Senior Living Inc (P-15480)*

Remington Hotel Corporation .... D..... 310 553-6561
1150 S Beverly Dr Los Angeles (90035) *(P-10147)*

Remington Hotel Corporation .... D..... 760 322-6000
888 E Tahquitz Canyon Way Palm Springs (92262) *(P-10148)*

Remix Software, San Francisco *Also Called: Remix Software Inc (P-11874)*

Remix Software Inc .... D..... 415 900-4332
1128 Howard St San Francisco (94103) *(P-11874)*

Remn Inc 951 697-8135
3400 Central Ave Ste 330 Riverside (92506) *(P-9163)*

Renaissance, Indian Wells *Also Called: Renaissnce Esmralda Resort Spa (P-10152)*

Renaissance Construction, Grass Valley *Also Called: Manuel Bros Inc (P-1234)*

Renaissance Hollywood Ht & Spa, Los Angeles *Also Called: Cim/H & H Hotel LP (P-9701)*

Renaissance Hotel Clubsport, Aliso Viejo *Also Called: L & O Aliso Viejo LLC (P-9956)*

Renaissance Hotel Operating Co .... B..... 310 337-2800
9620 Airport Blvd Los Angeles (90045) *(P-10149)*

Renaissance Hotel Operating Co .... A..... 760 773-4444
44400 Indian Wells Ln Indian Wells (92210) *(P-10150)*

Renaissance Hotel Operating Co .... B..... 415 989-3500
905 California St San Francisco (94108) *(P-10151)*

Renaissance Indian Wells, Indian Wells *Also Called: Renaissance Hotel Operating Co (P-10150)*

Renaissnce Esmralda Resort Spa .... D..... 760 773-4444
44400 Indian Wells Ln Indian Wells (92210) *(P-10152)*

Renal Center, Orange *Also Called: St Joseph Hospital of Orange (P-16474)*

Renesas Electronics America Inc .... A..... 408 588-6000
2801 Scott Blvd Santa Clara (95050) *(P-5695)*

Reneson Hotels Inc (PA) .... D..... 650 449-5353
2700 Junipero Serra Blvd Daly City (94015) *(P-10153)*

Reneson Hotels Inc .... C..... 415 621-7001
112 7th St San Francisco (94103) *(P-10154)*

Renew Financial Corp II .... C..... 610 433-7486
555 12th St Ste 1650 Oakland (94607) *(P-8015)*

Renew Medical Group Inc .... D..... 310 929-9790
1125 S Beverly Dr Ste 720 Los Angeles (90035) *(P-15015)*

Renewcare of Scottsdale Inc .... D..... 949 487-9500
27101 Puerta Real Ste 450 Mission Viejo (92691) *(P-9555)*

Renn Transportation Inc .... D..... 408 842-3545
8845 Forest St Gilroy (95020) *(P-3533)*

Reno Tenco, Boron *Also Called: Rio Tinto Minerals Inc (P-577)*

Renovate America Financing, San Diego *Also Called: Personal Energy Finance Inc (P-11200)*

Renovo Solutions LLC (PA) .... B..... 714 599-7969
4 Executive Cir Ste 185 Irvine (92614) *(P-20194)*

Rentex Incorporated .... D..... 833 737-6839
2915 Whipple Rd Union City (94587) *(P-12700)*

Rentokil North America Inc .... D..... 858 689-9161
165 Vallecitos De Oro San Marcos (92069) *(P-532)*

Rentokil North America Inc .... D..... 714 517-9000
1160 Sandhill Ave Carson (90746) *(P-10839)*

Rentokil North America Inc .... D..... 408 293-6032
1155 Mabury Rd San Jose (95133) *(P-10840)*

Rentokil North America Inc .... D..... 714 563-2450
311 N Crescent Way Anaheim (92801) *(P-10841)*

Rentokil North America Inc .... D..... 650 579-6565
3481 Arden Rd Hayward (94545) *(P-10842)*

Rentokil North America Inc .... D..... 562 802-2238
15415 Marquardt Ave Santa Fe Springs (90670) *(P-10843)*

Rentpayment.com, Walnut Creek *Also Called: Yapstone Inc (P-13559)*

Replanet LLC .... A..... 951 520-1700
800 N Haven Ave Ste 120 Ontario (91764) *(P-5866)*

Replicant Solutions Inc .... C..... 415 854-3296
1 Letterman Dr # 3500 San Francisco (94129) *(P-12334)*

Replicated Inc .... D..... 424 672-6624
8605 Santa Monica Blvd # 66909 West Hollywood (90069) *(P-11875)*

Reprints Desk Inc .... D..... 310 477-0354
15821 Ventura Blvd Ste 165 Encino (91436) *(P-12684)*

Reproductive Science Center .... D..... 925 867-1800
100 Park Pl Ste 200 San Ramon (94583) *(P-15016)*

Reproductive Science Ctr Bay, San Ramon *Also Called: Reproductive Science Center (P-15016)*

Republic Electric Inc .... C..... 916 294-0140
3820 Happy Ln Sacramento (95827) *(P-1816)*

Republic Electric West Inc .... D..... 916 294-0140
3820 Happy Ln Sacramento (95827) *(P-1817)*

Republic Floor, Montebello *Also Called: Reu Distribution LLC (P-5133)*

Republic Indemnity Co Amer .... D..... 415 981-3200
100 Pine St Fl 14 San Francisco (94111) *(P-8403)*

Republic Indemnity Co Amer (DH) .... C..... 818 990-9860
4500 Park Granada Ste 300 Calabasas (91302) *(P-8404)*

Republic Indemnity Company Cal .... C..... 818 990-9860
15821 Ventura Blvd Ste 370 Encino (91436) *(P-8405)*

Republic Master Chefs Textile, Long Beach *Also Called: American Textile Maint Co (P-10427)*

Republic Nat Distrg Co LLC (PA) .... C..... 714 368-4615
14402 Franklin Ave Tustin (92780) *(P-6805)*

Republic Services, Salinas *Also Called: BFI Waste Systems N Amer Inc (P-4866)*

Republic Uniform, Long Beach *Also Called: American Textile Maint Co (P-10426)*

Reputationcom Inc (PA) .... B..... 800 888-0924
6111 Bollinger Canyon Rd Ste 580 San Ramon (94583) *(P-12335)*

RES-Care Inc .... D..... 209 473-1202
5250 Claremont Ave Stockton (95207) *(P-15788)*

RES-Care Inc .... D..... 916 567-1244
1485 Response Rd Sacramento (95815) *(P-15789)*

RES-Care Inc .... D..... 760 775-2887
45691 Monroe St Ste 6 Indio (92201) *(P-15790)*

RES-Care Inc .... D..... 951 653-1311
22635 Alessandro Blvd Moreno Valley (92553) *(P-15791)*

RES-Care Inc .... D..... 909 596-5360
2120 Foothill Blvd Ste 205 La Verne (91750) *(P-15792)*

RES-Care Inc .... D..... 510 357-4222
101 Callan Ave Ste 208 San Leandro (94577) *(P-16919)*

ALPHABETIC SECTION

RES-Care Inc .... D....... 714 662-3075
   3187 Red Hill Ave Ste 115 Costa Mesa (92626) *(P-16920)*

RES-Care Inc .... D....... 818 637-7727
   611 S Central Ave Glendale (91204) *(P-18513)*

Res.net, Foothill Ranch *Also Called: US Real Estate Services Inc (P-9205)*

Rescue Agency Pub Benefit LLC (PA)......................... D....... 619 231-7555
   2437 Morena Blvd San Diego (92110) *(P-10670)*

Rescue Concrete Inc 916 852-2400
   9275 Beatty Dr Sacramento (95826) *(P-2151)*

Rescue Mission Alliance .... D....... 805 201-4341
   125 S Harrison Ave Oxnard (93030) *(P-17313)*

Rescue Mission Alliance (PA)..................................... D....... 805 487-1234
   315 N A St Oxnard (93030) *(P-19099)*

Rescue Rooter Bay East, Hayward *Also Called: American Rsdntial Svcs Ind Inc (P-1354)*

Research Affiliates, Newport Beach *Also Called: Research Affiliates Capital LP (P-8218)*

Research Affiliates, Newport Beach *Also Called: Research Affiliates MGT LLC (P-8219)*

Research Affiliates Capital LP .... D....... 949 325-8700
   620 Newport Center Dr Ste 900 Newport Beach (92660) *(P-8218)*

Research Affiliates MGT LLC .... D....... 949 325-8700
   620 Newport Center Dr Ste 900 Newport Beach (92660) *(P-8219)*

Research America Inc .... C....... 916 443-4722
   1232 Q St Ste 100 Sacramento (95811) *(P-12615)*

Reseda Dodge Sales Inc .... D....... 805 581-9090
   4470 Winnetka Ave Woodland Hills (91364) *(P-7287)*

Reserve Club .... D....... 760 674-2222
   49400 Desert Butte Trl Indian Wells (92210) *(P-14429)*

Residence Inn By Marriott, Los Angeles *Also Called: 901 West Olympic Blvd Ltd Prtn (P-9597)*

Residence Inn By Marriott, San Mateo *Also Called: Island Hospitality MGT LLC (P-9915)*

Residence Inn By Marriott, Torrance *Also Called: Msr Hotels & Resorts Inc (P-10033)*

Residence Inn By Marriott, San Diego *Also Called: Residence Inn By Marriott LLC (P-10155)*

Residence Inn By Marriott, Los Angeles *Also Called: Sunstone Hotel Properties Inc (P-10287)*

Residence Inn By Marriott, Manhattan Beach *Also Called: Sunstone Hotel Properties Inc (P-10288)*

Residence Inn By Marriott, Aliso Viejo *Also Called: Sunstone Hotel Properties Inc (P-10289)*

Residence Inn By Marriott LLC .... D....... 858 740-2200
   12011 Scripps Highlands Dr San Diego (92131) *(P-10155)*

Residence Inn Palm Desert, Palm Desert *Also Called: Ashford Trs Seven LLC (P-9618)*

Resident Group Services Inc (PA)............................... C....... 714 630-5300
   1156 N Grove St Anaheim (92806) *(P-533)*

Residential Design Services, Irvine *Also Called: LARK Industries Inc (P-13349)*

Residential Fire Systems Inc .... D....... 714 666-8450
   8085 E Crystal Dr Anaheim (92807) *(P-1548)*

Residential Framer, Riverside *Also Called: Silverado Framing & Cnstr (P-725)*

Residential Plumbing, San Jose *Also Called: Aqualine Piping Inc (P-1362)*

Residnce Inn By Mrriot Brkeley, Berkeley *Also Called: Berkeley Downtown Ht Owner LLC (P-9642)*

Residnce Inn By Mrriot Lx/Cntu, Los Angeles *Also Called: Svi Lax LLC (P-10293)*

Residncy Prgram Natividad Hosp, Salinas *Also Called: County of Monterey (P-16028)*

Resmed, San Diego *Also Called: Resmed Inc (P-3059)*

Resmed Inc (PA) .... A....... 858 836-5000
   9001 Spectrum Center Blvd San Diego (92123) *(P-3059)*

Resolve Systems LLC (PA).. D....... 949 325-0120
   300 Orchard City Dr Ste 110 Campbell (95008) *(P-11876)*

Resonate I Inc (PA)... C....... 408 545-5500
   90 Great Oaks Blvd Ste 205 San Jose (95119) *(P-11877)*

Resort At Indian Springs LLC .... C....... 707 709-2434
   1712 Lincoln Ave Calistoga (94515) *(P-10156)*

Resort At Pelican Hill LLC .... B....... 949 467-6800
   22701 Pelican Hill Rd S Newport Coast (92657) *(P-10157)*

Resort At Squaw Creek, Alpine Meadows *Also Called: Squaw Creek Associates LLC (P-10264)*

Resort Campground Intl, Lytle Creek *Also Called: Burlingame Industries Inc (P-10415)*

Resort Parking Services Inc .... C....... 760 328-4041
   39755 Berkey Dr # B Palm Desert (92211) *(P-13627)*

Resortcomm International .... D....... 619 683-2470
   404 Camino Del Rio S Fl 4 San Diego (92108) *(P-10458)*

Resortime.com, Carlsbad *Also Called: Grand Pacific Resorts Inc (P-9815)*

Resource Connection of Amador .... D....... 209 223-7685
   430 Sutter Hill Rd Sutter Creek (95685) *(P-18098)*

Resource Environmental Inc .... D....... 562 408-7000
   13100 Alondra Blvd Ste 108 Cerritos (90703) *(P-1007)*

Resource Innovations Inc (DH).................................. D....... 415 369-1000
   719 Main St Ste A Half Moon Bay (94019) *(P-20840)*

Resource Staffing Group, Sacramento *Also Called: Northwest Stffing Rsources Inc (P-11184)*

Resources Connection Inc (PA).................................. C....... 714 430-6400
   17101 Armstrong Ave Ste 100 Irvine (92614) *(P-20527)*

Resources Connection LLC (HQ)................................ D....... 714 430-6400
   17101 Armstrong Ave Ste 100 Irvine (92614) *(P-11222)*

Resources Global Professionals, Irvine *Also Called: Resources Connection LLC (P-11222)*

Resources Global Professionals, Irvine *Also Called: Resources Connection Inc (P-20527)*

Respawn Entertainment LLC .... C....... 818 960-4400
   20131 Prairie St Chatsworth (91311) *(P-13884)*

Restaurant Depot, San Diego *Also Called: Jetro Cash and Carry Entps LLC (P-6497)*

Restaurant Investment, Los Angeles *Also Called: Providence Rest Partners LLC (P-9551)*

Restaurants Bars & Food Svcs, Los Angeles *Also Called: Fish House Partners One LLC (P-7481)*

Restec Contractors Inc .... D....... 510 670-0100
   22955 Kidder St Hayward (94545) *(P-2312)*

Restoration Management Company, Livermore *Also Called: Jon K Takata Corporation (P-18028)*

Restorixhealth, Irvine *Also Called: Gordian Medical Inc (P-5418)*

Restpadd Health Corp .... D....... 530 727-9390
   925 Walnut St Red Bluff (96080) *(P-17314)*

Result Group Inc .... D....... 480 777-7130
   2603 Main St Ste 710 Irvine (92614) *(P-12518)*

Retail Realm Distribution Inc (PA)............................. D....... 707 996-5400
   454 W Napa St # B Sonoma (95476) *(P-6282)*

Retail Zipline Inc (PA)... D....... 510 390-4904
   2370 Market St Ste 436 San Francisco (94114) *(P-12336)*

Retailnext Inc (PA).. C....... 408 884-2162
   60 S Market St Ste 310 San Jose (95113) *(P-11878)*

Retina Communications, San Carlos *Also Called: Transiris Corporation (P-20590)*

Retirement Housing, Long Beach *Also Called: Retirement Housing Foundation (P-9164)*

Retirement Housing Foundation (PA)......................... D....... 562 257-5100
   911 N Studebaker Rd Ste 100 Long Beach (90815) *(P-9164)*

Retirment Fnding Solutions Inc .... D....... 802 238-4216
   3131 Camino Del Rio N Ste 190 San Diego (92108) *(P-7905)*

Reu Distribution LLC .... A....... 323 201-4200
   7227 Telegraph Rd Montebello (90640) *(P-5133)*

Reuben H Fleet Science Center .... C....... 619 238-1233
   1875 El Prado San Diego (92101) *(P-18666)*

Reunify LLC .... D....... 310 893-1736
   12121 Wilshire Blvd Ste 214 Los Angeles (90025) *(P-10572)*

Reutlinger Community .... C....... 925 964-2062
   4000 Camino Tassajara Danville (94506) *(P-18099)*

REUTLINGER COMMUNITY FOR JEWIS, Danville *Also Called: Reutlinger Community (P-18099)*

Revchem Composites Inc (PA).................................... D....... 909 877-8477
   2720 S Willow Ave # B Bloomington (92316) *(P-5224)*

Revchem Plastics, Bloomington *Also Called: Revchem Composites Inc (P-5224)*

Reveal Imaging, Vista *Also Called: Leidos Inc (P-19726)*

Revenue Solutions Inc .... B....... 916 780-8741
   2990 Lava Ridge Ct Ste 200 Roseville (95661) *(P-12616)*

Review Boost, Carlsbad *Also Called: Intravas Inc (P-20416)*

Review Wave .... D....... 800 563-0469
   16531 Scientific Irvine (92618) *(P-12519)*

Revinate LLC .... C....... 415 671-4703
   2345 Yale St Fl 1 Palo Alto (94306) *(P-11879)*

REVIVALS THRIFT STORES, Palm Springs *Also Called: Desert Aids Project (P-17951)*

Revjet Corporation .... C....... 650 508-2215
   981 Industrial Rd Ste D San Carlos (94070) *(P-12337)*

Revolt, Los Angeles *Also Called: Revolt Media and Tv LLC (P-4459)*

Revolt Media and Tv LLC .... C....... 323 645-3000
   9200 W Sunset Blvd Fl 3 Los Angeles (90069) *(P-4459)*

Revoltion Cnsmr Sltions CA LLC (DH)........................ C....... 323 980-0918
   3840 E 26th St Vernon (90058) *(P-6943)*

Rew, Riverside *Also Called: Roy E Whitehead Inc (P-2016)*

Rex Moore, Sacramento *Also Called: Rex Moore Group Inc (P-1818)*

Rex Moore Group Inc .... B....... 916 372-1300
   6001 Outfall Cir Sacramento (95828) *(P-1818)*

Rex More Elec Cntrs Engners In (PA) .... B 916 372-1300
   6001 Outfall Cir Sacramento (95828) *(P-1819)*

Rex More Elec Cntrs Engners In .... C 559 294-1300
   5803 E Harvard Ave Fresno (93727) *(P-1820)*

Rexford Industrial LLC .... D 858 536-8914
   9340 Cabot Dr San Diego (92126) *(P-9165)*

Rexford Industrial LLC .... D 909 987-2174
   10860 6th St Rancho Cucamonga (91730) *(P-9166)*

Rexford Industries, Rancho Cucamonga *Also Called: Rexford Industrial LLC (P-9166)*

REY Engineers Inc .... D 916 366-3040
   905 Sutter St Ste 200 Folsom (95630) *(P-19374)*

Rey-Crest Roofg Waterproofing .... D 323 257-9329
   3065 Verdugo Rd Los Angeles (90065) *(P-2313)*

Rey-Crest Roofg Waterproofing, Los Angeles *Also Called: Rey-Crest Roofg Waterproofing (P-2313)*

Reyes Coca-Cola Bottling LLC .... D 562 803-8100
   8729 Cleta St Downey (90241) *(P-2408)*

Reyes Coca-Cola Bottling LLC .... B 909 980-3121
   10670 6th St Rancho Cucamonga (91730) *(P-2409)*

Reyes Coca-Cola Bottling LLC .... B 619 266-6300
   5255 Federal Blvd San Diego (92105) *(P-2410)*

Reyes Holdings LLC .... C 831 761-6400
   1729 Seabright Ave Ste A Santa Cruz (95062) *(P-6780)*

Reynen & Bardis Cnstr LLC (PA) .... C 916 366-3665
   10630 Mather Blvd Mather (95655) *(P-711)*

Rfid Corporation .... C 925 473-9978
   701 Willow Pass Rd Ste 10 Pittsburg (94565) *(P-10455)*

Rfid Textile Services Inc .... D 408 840-7504
   8190 Murray Ave Gilroy (95020) *(P-10481)*

RFJ Corporation .... D 415 824-6890
   930 Innes Ave San Francisco (94124) *(P-1959)*

Rfj Meiswinkel, San Francisco *Also Called: RFJ Corporation (P-1959)*

Rfmw, San Jose *Also Called: Exponential Tech Group Inc (P-5650)*

Rfmw, San Jose *Also Called: Rfmw Ltd (P-5696)*

Rfmw Ltd .... D 408 414-1450
   188 Martinvale Ln San Jose (95119) *(P-5696)*

RGA Electric Inc .... D 562 941-6380
   10207 Freeman Ave Santa Fe Springs (90670) *(P-1821)*

Rgbx Inc .... C 714 524-1350
   16971 Imperial Hwy Yorba Linda (92886) *(P-18351)*

Rgc Gaslamp LLC .... C 619 738-7000
   550 J St San Diego (92101) *(P-10159)*

Rgc Services Inc (PA) .... C 805 644-1242
   5720 Ralston St Ste 100 Ventura (93003) *(P-9167)*

Rgc Services Inc .... C 805 484-1600
   601 E Daily Dr Ste 102 Camarillo (93010) *(P-9168)*

Rggd Inc (PA) .... D 323 581-6617
   4950 S Santa Fe Ave Vernon (90058) *(P-6049)*

Rgis LLC .... C 714 938-0663
   1937 W Chapman Ave Orange (92868) *(P-13445)*

Rgis LLC .... D 951 369-7131
   6529 Riverside Ave Ste 215 Riverside (92506) *(P-13446)*

Rgis LLC .... C 760 736-9241
   365 S Rancho Santa Fe Rd Ste 103 San Marcos (92078) *(P-13447)*

Rgis, Llc, Orange *Also Called: Rgis LLC (P-13445)*

Rgis, Llc, Riverside *Also Called: Rgis LLC (P-13446)*

Rgis, Llc, San Marcos *Also Called: Rgis LLC (P-13447)*

Rgn-San Diego I LLC .... C 619 344-2500
   350 10th Ave Ste 1000 San Diego (92101) *(P-13448)*

Rgn-San Francisco IV LLC .... C 415 882-6300
   75 Broadway Ste 202 San Francisco (94111) *(P-13449)*

Rgs Services, Anaheim *Also Called: Resident Group Services Inc (P-533)*

Rgw Construction Inc .... C 925 606-2400
   550 Greenville Rd Livermore (94550) *(P-1154)*

Rh Community Builders LP .... D 559 492-1373
   2550 W Clinton Ave B-142 Fresno (93705) *(P-18719)*

Rhcc, Fremont *Also Called: Raymond Handling Concepts Corp (P-13794)*

Rheumatology Diagnostics Lab .... D 310 253-5455
   324 S Beverly Dr Beverly Hills (90212) *(P-16750)*

Rhf Plymouth Tower .... D 951 248-0456
   3401 Lemon St Ofc Riverside (92501) *(P-15637)*

Rhi Inc (PA) .... D 818 508-3800
   5841 Lankershim Blvd North Hollywood (91601) *(P-7288)*

Rhino Building Services Inc .... C 858 455-1440
   6650 Flanders Dr Ste K San Diego (92121) *(P-10954)*

RHODA GOLDMAN PLAZA, San Francisco *Also Called: Scott St Snior Hsing Cmplex In (P-15656)*

Rhombus Systems Inc .... C 877 746-6797
   1920 20th St Sacramento (95811) *(P-11880)*

RHS Corp .... A 909 335-5500
   350 Terracina Blvd Redlands (92373) *(P-20195)*

Rhythm & Hues Studios, El Segundo *Also Called: Rhythm and Hues Inc (P-13885)*

Rhythm and Hues Inc (PA) .... C 310 448-7500
   2100 E Grand Ave Ste A El Segundo (90245) *(P-13885)*

Rhythm Newmedia Inc .... D 650 961-9024
   800 W El Camino Real Ste 100 Mountain View (94040) *(P-11881)*

Ria Financial Service, Buena Park *Also Called: Continental Exch Solutions Inc (P-7846)*

Ria Financial Services, Buena Park *Also Called: Continental Exch Solutions Inc (P-13244)*

Rialto Bioenergy Facility LLC .... C 760 436-8870
   5780 Fleet St Ste 310 Carlsbad (92008) *(P-19375)*

Rica, Calabasas *Also Called: Republic Indemnity Co Amer (P-8404)*

Rich Harvest Inc .... D 559 252-8000
   3515 N Sabre Dr Fresno (93727) *(P-113)*

Richard Bagdasarian Inc .... D 760 396-2168
   65500 Lincoln St Mecca (92254) *(P-83)*

Richard Brady & Associates Inc .... D 657 204-9124
   18837 Brookhurst St # 103 Fountain Valley (92708) *(P-19376)*

Richard H Vila, El Sobrante *Also Called: Vila Construction Co (P-1052)*

Richard Heath & Associates Inc (PA) .... D 559 447-7000
   590 W Locust Ave Ste 103 Fresno (93650) *(P-20841)*

Richard Huetter Inc .... D 818 700-8001
   21050 Osborne St Canoga Park (91304) *(P-5057)*

Richard Iest Dairy, Madera *Also Called: Iest Family Farms (P-218)*

Richard Iest Dairy Inc .... D 559 673-2635
   13507 Road 17 Madera (93637) *(P-18)*

Richard Joy Engineering, Portola *Also Called: R Joy Inc (P-19370)*

Richard Realty Group Inc .... D 760 603-8377
   5946 Priestly Dr Carlsbad (92008) *(P-9169)*

Richard Wilson Wellington .... D 626 812-7881
   1025 N Todd Ave Azusa (91702) *(P-151)*

Richards Wtson Grshon A Prof C (PA) .... C 213 626-8484
   355 S Grand Ave 40th Fl Los Angeles (90071) *(P-17624)*

Richman Management Corporation .... B 760 832-8520
   35400 Bob Hope Dr Ste 107 Rancho Mirage (92270) *(P-13028)*

Richman Management Corporation .... B 909 296-6189
   41743 Entp Cir N Ste 209 Temecula (92590) *(P-13029)*

Richmond Area Mlt-Services Inc .... D 415 579-3021
   1282 Market St San Francisco (94102) *(P-17118)*

Richmond Area Mlt-Services Inc (PA) .... D 415 800-0699
   4355 Geary Blvd San Francisco (94118) *(P-17119)*

Richmond Engineering Co Inc .... C 800 589-7058
   15472 Markar Rd Poway (92064) *(P-534)*

Richmond Sanitary Service Inc (HQ) .... C 510 262-7100
   3260 Blume Dr Ste 100 Richmond (94806) *(P-13795)*

Richwood Meat Company Inc .... D 209 722-8171
   2751 N Santa Fe Ave Merced (95348) *(P-2340)*

Rick Berry, Sanger *Also Called: Cal Custom Tile (P-1975)*

Rick Engineering Company, San Diego *Also Called: Glenn A Rick Engrg & Dev Co (P-19243)*

Rick Hamm Construction Inc .... D 714 532-0815
   201 W Carleton Ave Orange (92867) *(P-1155)*

Rick Solomon Enterprises Inc (PA) .... D 310 280-3700
   8460 Higuera St Culver City (90232) *(P-6185)*

Rico Corporation (HQ) .... C 818 394-2700
   8484 San Fernando Rd Sun Valley (91352) *(P-3087)*

Rico Products, Sun Valley *Also Called: Rico Corporation (P-3087)*

Ricoh Electronics Inc .... D 714 566-2500
   1920 W Base Line Rd Rialto (92376) *(P-5254)*

Ride At Home Care, Corona *Also Called: Bmb 1 LLC (P-15820)*

Ride On Transportation, San Luis Obispo *Also Called: United Crbral Plsy Assn San Lu (P-18161)*

Rideout Memorial Hospital (HQ) .... A 530 749-4416
   726 4th St Marysville (95901) *(P-16362)*

ALPHABETIC SECTION

Ridge, Corona *Also Called: Peppermint Ridge (P-18504)*
Ridgecrest Healthcare Inc .... D....... 760 446-3591
   5808 Monterey Rd Los Angeles (90042) *(P-15638)*
Ridgecrest Regional Hospital (PA) .... B....... 760 446-3551
   1081 N China Lake Blvd Ridgecrest (93555) *(P-16363)*
Ridgecrest Service Center, Ridgecrest *Also Called: Southern California Edison Co (P-4694)*
Riebes's Auto Parts, Rocklin *Also Called: Bi Warehousing Inc (P-7345)*
Riekes Ctr For Humn Enhncement .... D....... 650 364-2509
   3455 Edison Way Menlo Park (94025) *(P-14227)*
Rigel Pharmaceuticals Inc (PA) .... C....... 650 624-1100
   611 Gateway Blvd Ste 900 South San Francisco (94080) *(P-2607)*
Rigetti & Co LLC (PA) .... C....... 510 210-5550
   775 Heinz Ave Berkeley (94710) *(P-11882)*
Rigetti Quantum Computing, Berkeley *Also Called: Rigetti & Co LLC (P-11882)*
Rightpaq, Santa Ana *Also Called: McDonald Packaging Inc (P-2521)*
Rightsourcing, Inc., Irvine *Also Called: Magnit Rs Inc (P-11299)*
Rika Corporation .... D....... 949 830-9050
   332 W Brenna Ln Orange (92867) *(P-2198)*
Rim, San Ramon *Also Called: Blackberry Corporation (P-12118)*
Rim Corporation .... A....... 209 523-8331
   915 17th St Modesto (95354) *(P-20196)*
Rim Hospitality, Modesto *Also Called: Rim Corporation (P-20196)*
Rim of World Unified Schl Dst .... D....... 909 336-0330
   27614 Hwy 18 Across Building I Lake Arrowhead (92352) *(P-3348)*
Rinaldi Tile & Marble, Royal Oaks *Also Called: Gino Rinaldi Inc (P-1983)*
Rincon Consultants Inc .... C....... 805 547-0900
   1530 Monterey St Ste D San Luis Obispo (93401) *(P-20842)*
Rincon Pacific LLC .... D....... 805 986-8806
   1312 Del Norte Rd Camarillo (93010) *(P-64)*
Ring LLC (HQ) .... B....... 310 929-7085
   12515 Cerise Ave Hawthorne (90250) *(P-2859)*
Ringcentral, Belmont *Also Called: Ringcentral Inc (P-12617)*
Ringcentral Inc (PA) .... D....... 650 472-4100
   20 Davis Dr Belmont (94002) *(P-12617)*
Rinks Anaheim Ice, The, Anaheim *Also Called: Anaheim Ice (P-14489)*
Rio .... C....... 714 633-7400
   1601 E Saint Andrew Pl Santa Ana (92705) *(P-17120)*
Rio Del Oro Racquet Club, Sacramento *Also Called: Spare-Time Inc (P-14234)*
Rio Tinto Minerals Inc .... C....... 760 762-7121
   14486 Borax Rd Boron (93516) *(P-577)*
Rio Vista Development Co Inc (PA) .... C....... 818 980-8000
   4222 Vineland Ave North Hollywood (91602) *(P-10160)*
Riolo Transportation Inc .... B....... 760 729-4405
   2725 Jefferson St Ste 2d Carlsbad (92008) *(P-4173)*
Riot Creative Imaging .... D....... 213 516-3160
   934 Venice Blvd Los Angeles (90015) *(P-10793)*
Ripcord Inc .... C....... 408 838-7446
   30955 Huntwood Ave Hayward (94544) *(P-19377)*
Ripe Digital Entertainment Inc .... D....... 323 463-7070
   729 Seward St Los Angeles (90038) *(P-13886)*
Rippey Corporation .... D....... 916 939-4332
   5000 Hillsdale Cir El Dorado Hills (95762) *(P-5342)*
Ripple Foods Pbc .... D....... 510 269-2563
   901 Gilman St Ste A Berkeley (94710) *(P-19763)*
Risk Management Solutions Inc (HQ) .... C....... 510 505-2500
   7575 Gateway Blvd Ste 300 Newark (94560) *(P-9455)*
Riskoptics Inc .... C....... 415 851-8667
   548 Market St 73905 San Francisco (94104) *(P-11883)*
Rite-Way Meat Packers Inc .... D....... 323 826-2144
   5151 Alcoa Ave Vernon (90058) *(P-6502)*
Ritz Carlton Rancho Mirage, Rancho Mirage *Also Called: Ritz-Carlton Hotel Company LLC (P-10164)*
Ritz-Carlton, Dana Point *Also Called: Ritz-Carlton Hotel Company LLC (P-10161)*
Ritz-Carlton, Santa Barbara *Also Called: Ritz-Carlton Hotel Company LLC (P-10162)*
Ritz-Carlton Hotel Company LLC .... B....... 949 240-5020
   1 Ritz Carlton Dr Dana Point (92629) *(P-10161)*
Ritz-Carlton Hotel Company LLC .... A....... 805 968-0100
   8301 Hollister Ave Santa Barbara (93117) *(P-10162)*
Ritz-Carlton Hotel Company LLC .... B....... 415 773-6168
   600 Stockton St San Francisco (94108) *(P-10163)*

Ritz-Carlton Hotel Company LLC .... B....... 760 321-8282
   68900 Frank Sinatra Dr Rancho Mirage (92270) *(P-10164)*
Ritz-Carlton Laguna Niguel, Dana Point *Also Called: Prutel Joint Venture (P-10130)*
Ritz-Carlton Lake Tahoe, The, Truckee *Also Called: Bhr Trs Tahoe LLC (P-9651)*
Ritz-Carlton San Francisco, San Francisco *Also Called: Ritz-Carlton Hotel Company LLC (P-10163)*
River Bend Holdings LLC .... C....... 916 371-1890
   2215 Oakmont Way West Sacramento (95691) *(P-15639)*
River Bend Nursing Center, West Sacramento *Also Called: River Bend Holdings LLC (P-15639)*
River City Auto Recovery Inc .... D....... 916 851-1100
   3401 Fitzgerald Rd Rancho Cordova (95742) *(P-13450)*
River City Bank (HQ) .... D....... 916 567-2600
   2480 Natomas Park Dr Ste 100 Sacramento (95833) *(P-7714)*
RIVER CITY BANK, Sacramento *Also Called: Rcb Corporation (P-7713)*
RIVER CITY BANK, Sacramento *Also Called: River City Bank (P-7714)*
River City Staffing Inc .... C....... 916 485-1588
   7777 Greenback Ln Citrus Heights (95610) *(P-11223)*
River Oak Center For Children (PA) .... C....... 916 609-5100
   5445 Laurel Hills Dr Sacramento (95841) *(P-17121)*
River Ranch Fresh Foods LLC (PA) .... B....... 831 758-1390
   911 Blanco Cir Ste B Salinas (93901) *(P-6576)*
River Ridge Farms Inc .... D....... 805 647-6880
   3135 Los Angeles Ave Oxnard (93036) *(P-152)*
River Rock Casino, Geyserville *Also Called: River Rock Entertainment Auth (P-10165)*
River Rock Entertainment Auth .... A....... 707 857-2777
   3250 Highway 128 Geyserville (95441) *(P-10165)*
Rivera Sanatarium Inc .... D....... 562 949-2591
   7246 Rosemead Blvd Pico Rivera (90660) *(P-15640)*
Riverbed Technology LLC (HQ) .... D....... 415 247-8800
   680 Folsom St Ste 600 San Francisco (94107) *(P-5343)*
Riversd-San Brnrdino Cnty Indi (PA) .... C....... 909 864-1097
   11980 Mount Vernon Ave Grand Terrace (92313) *(P-15017)*
Riversd-San Brnrdino Cnty Indi .... C....... 951 654-0803
   607 Donna Way San Jacinto (92583) *(P-15018)*
Riverside Auto Auction, Anaheim *Also Called: Califrnia Auto Dalers Exch LLC (P-5006)*
Riverside Care Inc .... C....... 951 683-7111
   4301 Caroline Ct Riverside (92506) *(P-15641)*
Riverside Cmnty Hlth Systems (DH) .... A....... 951 788-3000
   4445 Magnolia Ave 6th Fl Riverside (92501) *(P-16364)*
Riverside Cnty Flood Ctrl Wtr .... C....... 951 955-1200
   1995 Market St Riverside (92501) *(P-20900)*
Riverside Cnty Rgional Med Ctr, Riverside *Also Called: Riverside Univ Hlth Sys Fndtio (P-16365)*
Riverside Cnvalescent Hosp Inc .... D....... 530 343-5595
   375 Cohasset Rd Chico (95926) *(P-15891)*
Riverside Community Hospital, Riverside *Also Called: Riverside Cmnty Hlth Systems (P-16364)*
Riverside Companion Services, San Bernardino *Also Called: Maxim Healthcare Services Inc (P-11308)*
Riverside Construction Company Inc .... C....... 951 682-8308
   4225 Garner Rd Riverside (92501) *(P-1156)*
RIVERSIDE CONVALESCENT HOSPIT, Chico *Also Called: Riverside Cnvalescent Hosp Inc (P-15891)*
Riverside Crona Rsrce Cnsrvtio, Riverside *Also Called: County of Riverside (P-18845)*
Riverside District Office, Riverside *Also Called: State Compensation Insur Fund (P-8418)*
Riverside Equities LLC .... B....... 951 688-2222
   8487 Magnolia Ave Riverside (92504) *(P-15642)*
Riverside Health Care Corp (PA) .... D....... 530 897-5100
   1469 Humboldt Rd Ste 175 Chico (95928) *(P-15892)*
Riverside Marriott, Riverside *Also Called: Pinnacle Rvrside Hspitality LP (P-10121)*
Riverside Med Clinic Cyn Sprng, Riverside *Also Called: Riverside Medical Clinic Inc (P-15022)*
Riverside Med Clnic Ptient Ctr, Riverside *Also Called: Riverside Medical Clinic Inc (P-15024)*
Riverside Medical Center, Riverside *Also Called: Kaiser Foundation Hospitals (P-14840)*
Riverside Medical Clinic, Riverside *Also Called: Riverside Medical Clinic Inc (P-15019)*
Riverside Medical Clinic Inc .... D....... 951 683-6370
   7117 Brockton Ave Riverside (92506) *(P-15019)*
Riverside Medical Clinic Inc .... D....... 951 360-5250
   6250 Clay St Riverside (92509) *(P-15020)*

ALPHABETIC SECTION

Riverside Medical Clinic Inc .... D....... 951 782-3614
   7117 Brockton Ave Fl 3 Riverside (92506) *(P-15021)*

Riverside Medical Clinic Inc .... D....... 951 683-6370
   6405 Day St Riverside (92507) *(P-15022)*

Riverside Medical Clinic Inc .... D....... 626 388-2392
   12742 Limonite Ave Eastvale (92880) *(P-15023)*

Riverside Medical Clinic Inc (PA) .... D....... 951 683-6370
   3660 Arlington Ave Riverside (92506) *(P-15024)*

Riverside Medical Clinic Inc .... D....... 951 782-3615
   7117 Brockton Ave Fl 2 Riverside (92506) *(P-15025)*

Riverside Medical Clinic Inc .... D....... 951 782-3684
   7117 Brockton Ave Riverside (92506) *(P-15026)*

Riverside Medical Clinic Inc .... D....... 951 782-3846
   7160 Brockton Ave Riverside (92506) *(P-15027)*

Riverside Medical Clinic Inc .... D....... 951 277-0000
   21634 Retreat Pkwy Corona (92883) *(P-17315)*

Riverside Transit Agency (PA) .... B....... 951 565-5000
   1825 3rd St Riverside (92507) *(P-3192)*

Riverside Univ Hlth Sys Fndtio (PA) .... B....... 951 358-5000
   4065 County Circle Dr Riverside (92503) *(P-16365)*

Riverside University Health .... B....... 951 486-4000
   26520 Cactus Ave Moreno Valley (92555) *(P-16366)*

Riverside-San Bernardino .... C....... 951 849-4761
   11555 1/2 Potrero Rd Banning (92220) *(P-17122)*

Riverview Golf and Country CLB .... D....... 530 224-2254
   4200 Bechelli Ln Redding (96002) *(P-14430)*

Riverview Intl Trcks LLC (PA) .... D....... 916 372-8541
   2445 Evergreen Ave West Sacramento (95691) *(P-7289)*

Riverwalk Post Acute, Riverside *Also Called: Orange Treeidence Opco LLC (P-15782)*

Riverwalk PST-Cute Rhblitation, Mission Viejo *Also Called: Rock Canyon Healthcare Inc (P-16921)*

Riviana Foods Inc .... D....... 530 458-8512
   2870 Niagara Rd Colusa (95932) *(P-6694)*

Riviera Country Club Inc .... C....... 310 454-6591
   1250 Capri Dr Pacific Palisades (90272) *(P-14554)*

Riviera Data Corp .... C....... 805 456-7082
   735 State St Ste 600 Santa Barbara (93101) *(P-20528)*

Riviera Finance of Texas Inc .... D....... 562 777-1300
   10430 Pioneer Blvd Ste 1 Santa Fe Springs (90670) *(P-7906)*

Riviera Health Care Center, Pico Rivera *Also Called: Riviera Nursing & Conva (P-15643)*

Riviera Nursing & Conva .... C....... 562 806-2576
   8203 Telegraph Rd Pico Rivera (90660) *(P-15643)*

Riviera Palm Sprng A Trbute PR .... C....... 760 327-8311
   1600 N Indian Canyon Dr Palm Springs (92262) *(P-10166)*

Riviera Shores, Capistrano Beach *Also Called: Pacific Monarch Resorts Inc (P-10087)*

Rizo Lopez Foods Inc .... B....... 800 626-5587
   201 S Mcclure Rd Modesto (95357) *(P-2346)*

RJ Allen Inc .... D....... 714 539-1022
   10392 Stanford Ave Garden Grove (92840) *(P-11006)*

RJ Noble Company (PA) .... C....... 714 637-1550
   15505 E Lincoln Ave Orange (92865) *(P-1157)*

Rjms Corporation .... C....... 831 757-1091
   773 Vertin Ave Salinas (93901) *(P-5867)*

Rjms Corporation (PA) .... D....... 510 675-0500
   6999 Southfront Rd Livermore (94551) *(P-7290)*

Rjn Investigations Inc .... D....... 951 686-7638
   360 E 1st St Ste 696 Tustin (92780) *(P-13030)*

Rjp Framing Inc .... C....... 916 941-3934
   1139 Sibley St Ste 100 Folsom (95630) *(P-2014)*

RJS & Associates Inc .... C....... 510 670-9111
   1675 Sabre St Hayward (94545) *(P-2152)*

RK Electric Inc .... C....... 510 772-4125
   49211 Milmont Dr Fremont (94538) *(P-1822)*

Rk Logistics, Fremont *Also Called: Rk Logistics Group Inc (P-20529)*

Rk Logistics Group Inc .... C....... 510 298-5128
   44951 Industrial Dr Fremont (94538) *(P-4085)*

Rk Logistics Group Inc (PA) .... D....... 408 942-8107
   41707 Christy St Fremont (94538) *(P-20529)*

RL Surgener Inc .... C....... 661 322-0153
   4201 Armour Ave Bakersfield (93308) *(P-5868)*

Rlh Fire Protection Inc (PA) .... D....... 661 322-9344
   4300 Stine Rd Ste 800 Bakersfield (93313) *(P-1549)*

Rls Industries, Bakersfield *Also Called: RL Surgener Inc (P-5868)*

Rm Esop Inc .... C....... 831 789-8300
   340 El Cmino Real S Ste 3 Salinas (93901) *(P-2524)*

Rm Executive Transportation .... C....... 650 260-1240
   525 Sunol St San Jose (95126) *(P-3291)*

RM Galicia Inc .... C....... 626 813-6200
   1521 W Cameron Ave Ste 100 West Covina (91790) *(P-10751)*

RMA Land Construction Inc .... D....... 714 985-2888
   2707 Saturn St Brea (92821) *(P-535)*

RMC Pacific Materials LLC (PA) C
   6601 Koll Center Pkwy Ste 300 Pleasanton (94566) *(P-2697)*

Rmd Group Inc .... B....... 562 866-9288
   2311 E South St Long Beach (90805) *(P-20530)*

Rmd Group LLC .... C....... 619 955-5750
   614 5th Ave Ste A San Diego (92101) *(P-11884)*

Rmkr, Campbell *Also Called: Rainmaker Systems Inc (P-20190)*

RMR Construction Company .... C....... 415 647-0884
   2424 Oakdale Ave San Francisco (94124) *(P-1008)*

RMR Financial LLC (DH) .... D....... 408 355-2000
   610 Newport Center Dr Newport Beach (92660) *(P-8054)*

RMS, Newark *Also Called: Risk Management Solutions Inc (P-9455)*

RMS Foundation Inc .... A....... 562 435-3511
   1126 Queens Hwy Long Beach (90802) *(P-10167)*

Rn Chidakashi Technologies Inc .... C....... 415 687-6145
   6200 Stoneridge Mall Rd Ste 300 Pleasanton (94588) *(P-5995)*

RNA Ann Arbor Incorporated .... C....... 877 762-7511
   508 S Smith Ave Ste A202 Corona (92882) *(P-10955)*

Rnc Capital Management LLC .... D....... 310 477-6543
   11601 Wilshire Blvd Los Angeles (90025) *(P-8220)*

Rnc Genter Capital Management, Los Angeles *Also Called: Rnc Capital Management LLC (P-8220)*

Rndc, Tustin *Also Called: Republic Nat Distrg Co LLC (P-6805)*

Rnl Design, Los Angeles *Also Called: Stantec Architecture Inc (P-13485)*

Ro Rocket Design Inc .... C....... 415 289-0830
   1306 Bridgeway Fl 2 Sausalito (94965) *(P-19502)*

Road Safety Inc .... C....... 916 543-4600
   4335 Pacific St Ste A Rocklin (95677) *(P-13451)*

Roadex America Inc .... D....... 310 878-9800
   2132 E Dominguez St Ste B Long Beach (90810) *(P-3749)*

Roadium Open Air Market, Torrance *Also Called: Pioneer Theatres Inc (P-13426)*

Roadrunner Shuttle, Camarillo *Also Called: Airport Connection Inc (P-3121)*

Roadster Inc .... A....... 833 568-5968
   250 Holger Way San Jose (95134) *(P-11885)*

Roadway Engineering Works Inc .... D....... 209 541-0920
   3442 6th St Ceres (95307) *(P-1823)*

Roadzen Inc .... B....... 347 745-6448
   111 Anza Blvd Ste 109 Burlingame (94010) *(P-12338)*

Roambi, Cardiff By The Sea *Also Called: Mellmo Inc (P-11741)*

Robar Enterprises Inc (PA) .... C....... 760 244-5456
   17671 Bear Valley Rd Hesperia (92345) *(P-2711)*

Robbins Geller Rudman Dowd LLP (PA) .... B....... 619 231-1058
   655 W Broadway Ste 1900 San Diego (92101) *(P-17625)*

Robert A Bothman Inc (PA) .... D....... 408 279-2277
   2690 Scott Blvd Santa Clara (95050) *(P-2153)*

Robert B Diemer Trtmnt Plant, Yorba Linda *Also Called: Metropltan Wtr Dst of Sthern C (P-4810)*

Robert Ballard Rehab Hospital (HQ) .... D....... 909 473-1200
   1760 W 16th St San Bernardino (92411) *(P-15305)*

Robert Bosch Healthcare Systems Inc .... C....... 650 690-9100
   2400 Geng Rd Ste 200 Palo Alto (94303) *(P-11886)*

Robert Clapper Cnstr Svcs Inc .... D....... 909 829-3688
   700 New York St Redlands (92374) *(P-1009)*

Robert Half Inc (PA) .... D....... 650 234-6000
   2884 Sand Hill Rd Ste 200 Menlo Park (94025) *(P-11324)*

Robert K Maloney Md Inc .... D....... 310 208-3937
   10921 Wilshire Blvd Ste 900 Los Angeles (90024) *(P-15028)*

Robert Kinsella Inc .... D....... 949 453-9533
   15375 Barranca Pkwy Ste G107 Irvine (92618) *(P-6283)*

Robert Moreno Insurance Svcs .... C....... 714 578-3318
   3110 E Guasti Rd Ste 500 Ontario (91761) *(P-8649)*

Robertson Honda, North Hollywood *Also Called: Rhi Inc (P-7288)*

ALPHABETIC SECTION

Robertson's, Corona *Also Called: Robertsons Rdymx Ltd A Cal Ltd (P-2712)*
Robertsons Rdymx Ltd A Cal Ltd (HQ)..................D....... 951 493-6500
200 S Main St Ste 200 Corona (92882) *(P-2712)*
Robertsons Ready Mix Ltd ....D....... 702 798-0568
16952 S D St Victorville (92395) *(P-5209)*
Robin Healthcare LLC ....C....... 310 601-6899
1845 Berkeley Way Berkeley (94703) *(P-17316)*
Robin Red Breast Inc ....D....... 323 466-7800
6616 Lexington Ave Los Angeles (90038) *(P-15029)*
Robin.ly, Milpitas *Also Called: Crosscircles Inc (P-11114)*
Robinhood, Menlo Park *Also Called: Robinhood Markets Inc (P-8163)*
Robinhood Markets Inc (PA)........................A....... 844 428-5411
85 Willow Rd Menlo Park (94025) *(P-8163)*
Robinson Calcagnie Inc ....D....... 619 338-4060
620 Newport Ctr Dr Ste 700 San Diego (92101) *(P-17626)*
Robinson Enterprises Investment Co Inc ....D....... 530 265-5844
293 Lower Grass Valley Rd Ste 201 Nevada City (95959) *(P-2475)*
Robinson Pharma Inc ....C....... 714 241-0235
3701 W Warner Ave Santa Ana (92704) *(P-2608)*
Robinson Timber, Nevada City *Also Called: Robinson Enterprises Investment Co Inc (P-2475)*
Roblox, San Mateo *Also Called: Roblox Corporation (P-12339)*
Roblox Corporation (PA)............................A....... 888 858-2569
970 Park Pl San Mateo (94403) *(P-12339)*
Robray Hotel Partnership LLP ....D....... 760 325-4372
222 S Indian Canyon Dr Palm Springs (92262) *(P-10168)*
ROC Nation LLC (HQ)................................D....... 310 975-6854
9348 Civic Center Dr Beverly Hills (90210) *(P-14101)*
Rocha Transportation, Modesto *Also Called: Ed Rocha Livestock Trnsp Inc (P-3468)*
Roche Molecular Solutions, Pleasanton *Also Called: Roche Molecular Systems Inc (P-19764)*
Roche Molecular Systems Inc (DH)..................B....... 925 730-8000
4300 Hacienda Dr Pleasanton (94588) *(P-19764)*
Roche Molecular Systems Inc ....C....... 408 217-5400
2801 Scott Blvd Santa Clara (95050) *(P-20531)*
Roche Nimblegen Inc ....C....... 608 316-3890
4300 Hacienda Dr Pleasanton (94588) *(P-19765)*
Rock Canyon Healthcare Inc ....C....... 719 404-1000
27101 Puerta Real Ste 450 Mission Viejo (92691) *(P-16921)*
Rock-It Cargo USA LLC ....C....... 310 410-0935
5343 W Imperial Hwy Ste 900 Los Angeles (90045) *(P-4086)*
Rockblue ....D....... 703 314-0208
601 Foothill Rd Ojai (93023) *(P-18759)*
Rocket, Lafayette *Also Called: Neatly Technologies Inc (P-11180)*
Rocket Fuel, San Francisco *Also Called: Sizmek Dsp Inc (P-10675)*
Rocket League, San Diego *Also Called: Psyonix LLC (P-11850)*
Rockin Jump Holdings LLC ....B....... 661 233-9907
1301 W Rancho Vista Blvd Ste B Palmdale (93551) *(P-14555)*
Rockin' Jump Trampoline, Palmdale *Also Called: Rockin Jump Holdings LLC (P-14555)*
Rockport ADM Svcs LLC (PA)........................D....... 323 330-6500
5900 Wilshire Blvd Ste 1600 Los Angeles (90036) *(P-20197)*
Rockport Healthcare Services, Los Angeles *Also Called: Rockport ADM Svcs LLC (P-20197)*
Rockstar San Diego Inc ....D....... 760 929-0700
2200 Faraday Ave Ste 200 Carlsbad (92008) *(P-12618)*
Rockview Dairies Inc (PA)..........................C....... 562 927-5511
7011 Stewart And Gray Rd Downey (90241) *(P-6662)*
Rocky Coast Builders Inc ....D....... 760 489-7770
135 Market Pl Escondido (92029) *(P-2015)*
Rocky Point Investments LLC (HQ)..................C....... 310 482-6500
6601 Center Dr W Ste 400 Los Angeles (90045) *(P-20532)*
Rodax Distributors ....D....... 818 765-6400
7230 Coldwater Canyon Ave North Hollywood (91605) *(P-13887)*
Rodda Electric Inc (PA)............................C....... 925 240-6024
380 Carrol Ct Ste L Brentwood (94513) *(P-1824)*
Rodeo Realty Inc (PA)..............................D....... 818 349-9997
9171 Wilshire Blvd Ste 321 Beverly Hills (90210) *(P-9170)*
Rodeway Inn, San Diego *Also Called: Narven Enterprises Inc (P-10038)*
Rodgers Trucking Co, Alameda *Also Called: Frank Ghiglione Inc (P-3391)*
Rodgz Farm Labor Contg LLC ....D....... 530 329-8403
4422 College Way Olivehurst (95961) *(P-369)*
Rodney Strong Vineyards, Healdsburg *Also Called: Klein Foods Inc (P-79)*
Rodolo Inc ....D
212 Industrial Dr Stockton (95206) *(P-9331)*

Roebbelen Construction Inc ....D....... 916 939-4000
1241 Hawks Flight Ct El Dorado Hills (95762) *(P-1010)*
Roebbelen Contracting Inc ....B....... 916 939-4000
1241 Hawks Flight Ct El Dorado Hills (95762) *(P-1011)*
Rof Ferrari Lending 1 LLC ....C....... 510 351-5520
14234 Catalina St San Leandro (94577) *(P-7148)*
Rogers Helicopters Inc ....D....... 559 299-4903
5508 E Aircorp Way Fresno (93727) *(P-3868)*
Rogers Poultry Co (PA)............................D....... 323 585-0802
5050 S Santa Fe Ave Vernon (90058) *(P-6449)*
Rogers Poultry Co ....D....... 800 585-0802
2020 E 67th St Los Angeles (90001) *(P-6450)*
Rogers Trucking, San Leandro *Also Called: Frank Ghiglione Inc (P-3392)*
Rohrback Cosasco Systems Inc (DH)................D....... 562 949-0123
11841 Smith Ave Santa Fe Springs (90670) *(P-3019)*
Roi Dna Inc ....D....... 831 238-2514
156 Cascade Dr Fairfax (94930) *(P-10718)*
Rok Hardware & Cabinets, Irvine *Also Called: Rok Inc (P-5733)*
Rok Inc ....D....... 714 322-8563
10 Lakeview Irvine (92604) *(P-5733)*
ROKU, San Jose *Also Called: Roku Inc (P-4519)*
Roku Inc (PA)......................................C....... 408 556-9040
1155 Coleman Ave San Jose (95110) *(P-4519)*
Roland Corporation US (HQ)........................C....... 323 890-3700
5100 S Eastern Ave Los Angeles (90040) *(P-6050)*
Roll Properties Intl Inc ....C....... 661 797-6500
13646 Highway 33 Lost Hills (93249) *(P-9556)*
Rolling Hills Casino ....C....... 530 528-3500
2655 Everett Freeman Way Corning (96021) *(P-10169)*
Rolling Hills Clinic ....D....... 530 690-2334
2540 Sister Mary Columba Dr Red Bluff (96080) *(P-17317)*
Rolling Hills Country Club ....D....... 424 903-0000
1 Chandler Ranch Rd Palos Verdes Estates (90274) *(P-14431)*
Rolling Hls Cntry CLB Golf Sp, Palos Verdes Estates *Also Called: Rolling Hills Country Club (P-14431)*
Rolling Oaks Radiology Inc ....D....... 805 778-1513
415 Rolling Oaks Dr Thousand Oaks (91361) *(P-15030)*
Rollins Leasing LLC ....D....... 626 913-7186
18305 Arenth Ave City Of Industry (91748) *(P-13566)*
Rollins Truck Rental-Leasing, City Of Industry *Also Called: Rollins Leasing LLC (P-13566)*
Romac, Yorba Linda *Also Called: Romac Supply Co Inc (P-2861)*
Romac Supply Co Inc ....D....... 323 721-5810
17722 Neff Ranch Rd Yorba Linda (92886) *(P-2861)*
Romak Iron Works ....D....... 707 751-2420
380 Industrial Ct Benicia (94510) *(P-2199)*
Roman Cathlic Bishp Sacramento ....C....... 707 556-9317
125 Corporate Pl Vallejo (94590) *(P-19025)*
Roman Catholic Bishp of Fresno ....D....... 559 561-4499
43816 Sierra Dr Three Rivers (93271) *(P-10411)*
Roman Cthlic Archbshop of San ....D....... 415 924-0501
120 King St Larkspur (94939) *(P-17743)*
Roman Cthlic Bishp of San Jose ....D....... 833 304-0763
22555 Cristo Rey Dr Los Altos (94024) *(P-9289)*
Roman Cthlic Bshp of San Diego ....D....... 619 264-3127
4470 Hilltop Dr San Diego (92102) *(P-9171)*
Roman Cthlic Diocese of Orange ....D....... 714 847-8546
8301 Talbert Ave Huntington Beach (92646) *(P-9290)*
Roman Cthlic Diocese of Orange ....C....... 714 532-6551
7845 E Santiago Canyon Rd Orange (92869) *(P-9291)*
Roman Cthlic Diocese of Orange ....C....... 714 544-1533
1311 Sycamore Ave Tustin (92780) *(P-17744)*
Roman Cthlic Diocese of Orange ....C....... 714 528-1794
801 N Bradford Ave Placentia (92870) *(P-17745)*
Romeo Power Technology, Cypress *Also Called: Romeo Systems Inc (P-2961)*
Romeo Systems Inc ....C....... 323 675-2180
5560 Katella Ave Cypress (90630) *(P-2961)*
Romero Construction, Escondido *Also Called: Romero General Cnstr Corp (P-1158)*
Romero General Cnstr Corp ....C....... 760 715-0154
8320 Nelson Way Escondido (92026) *(P-712)*
Romero General Cnstr Corp (PA)....................D....... 760 489-8412
2150 N Centre City Pkwy Ste I Escondido (92026) *(P-1158)*

Ron Nurss Inc .... D....... 916 631-9761
11290 Sunrise Park Dr Ste B Rancho Cordova (95742) *(P-2154)*

Ron Rick Holdings Montana LLC .... D....... 406 493-5606
80795 Vista Bonita Trl La Quinta (92253) *(P-9332)*

Ron's Pharmacy Services, San Diego *Also Called: Belville Enterprises Inc (P-14632)*

Ronald Reagan Building, Los Angeles *Also Called: Ucla Health (P-16585)*

Ronald Reagan Ucla Medical Ctr, Los Angeles *Also Called: University Cal Los Angeles (P-16589)*

Ronald Rgan Prsdntial Fndtion .... D....... 805 522-2977
40 Presidential Dr Ste 200 Simi Valley (93065) *(P-18667)*

Ronald Rgan Prsdntial Lib Fndt, Simi Valley *Also Called: Ronald Rgan Prsdntial Fndtion (P-18667)*

Ronsin Ltgtion Spport Svcs Inc (PA) .... D....... 909 594-5995
215 Lemon Creek Dr Walnut (91789) *(P-13452)*

Roo Veterinary Inc .... D....... 917 805-5220
595 Pacific Ave Fl 4 San Francisco (94133) *(P-11887)*

Roochi Traders Incorporated .... D....... 323 722-5592
6393 E Washington Blvd Commerce (90040) *(P-6186)*

Roofing Constructors Inc .... C....... 415 648-6472
15002 Wicks Blvd San Leandro (94577) *(P-2082)*

Roofstock Inc (PA) .... C....... 510 269-9400
2001 Broadway 4th Fl Oakland (94612) *(P-20533)*

Roosevelt Hotel LLC .... C....... 323 466-7000
7000 Hollywood Blvd Los Angeles (90028) *(P-10170)*

Rootstrap Inc .... C....... 310 907-9210
8306 Wilshire Blvd Ste 249 Beverly Hills (90211) *(P-11888)*

Rope Partner Inc .... D....... 831 460-9448
125 Mcpherson St Ste B Santa Cruz (95060) *(P-5922)*

Ropers Majeski A Prof Corp (PA) .... D....... 650 364-8200
535 Middlefield Rd Ste 245 Menlo Park (94025) *(P-17627)*

Ropers Majeski A Prof Corp .... C....... 213 312-2000
445 S Figueroa St Ste 3000 Los Angeles (90071) *(P-17628)*

Ropes & Gray LLP .... D....... 650 617-4000
1900 University Ave East Palo Alto (94303) *(P-17629)*

Roplast Industries Inc .... C....... 530 532-9500
3155 S 5th Ave Oroville (95965) *(P-2530)*

Roppong-Thoe LP A Cal Ltd Prtn .... C....... 530 544-5400
4130 Lake Tahoe Blvd South Lake Tahoe (96150) *(P-10171)*

Rosanna Inc .... C....... 714 751-5100
3350 Avenue Of The Arts Costa Mesa (92626) *(P-10172)*

Roscoe Real Estate Ltd Partnr .... D....... 310 260-7500
1819 Ocean Ave Santa Monica (90401) *(P-10173)*

Rose & Shore Inc .... B....... 323 826-2144
5151 Alcoa Ave Vernon (90058) *(P-13453)*

Rose Bowl Aquatics Center .... D....... 626 564-0330
360 N Arroyo Blvd Pasadena (91103) *(P-14432)*

Rose Brand Wipers Inc .... D....... 818 505-6290
11440 Sheldon St Sun Valley (91352) *(P-14060)*

Rose Child Development Center, Milpitas *Also Called: Milpitas Unified School Dst (P-17730)*

Rose Fmly Crtive Empwrment Ctr .... D....... 916 376-7916
7000 Franklin Blvd Ste 1000 Sacramento (95823) *(P-18903)*

Rose Hills Company (DH) .... A....... 562 699-0921
3888 Workman Mill Rd Whittier (90601) *(P-9292)*

Rose Hills Holdings Corp (HQ) .... B....... 562 699-0921
3888 Workman Mill Rd Whittier (90601) *(P-9293)*

Rose Hills Mem Pk & Mortuary, Whittier *Also Called: Rose Hills Company (P-9292)*

Rose Hills Mem Pk & Mortuary, Whittier *Also Called: Rose Hills Holdings Corp (P-9293)*

Rose Villa Healthcare Center, Bellflower *Also Called: Bell Villa Care Associates LLC (P-15356)*

Roseburg Forest Products Co .... D....... 530 938-2721
98 Mill St Weed (96094) *(P-5183)*

Rosecrans Care Center, Gardena *Also Called: Healthcare Investments Inc (P-15509)*

Rosecrans Villa, Hawthorne *Also Called: Longwood Management Corp (P-18475)*

Rosemary Childrens Services (PA) .... C....... 626 844-3033
36 S Kinneloa Ave # 200 Pasadena (91107) *(P-18514)*

Rosen & Rosen Industries Inc .... D....... 949 361-9238
204 Avenida Fabricante San Clemente (92672) *(P-3094)*

Rosen Electronics, Ontario *Also Called: Rosen Electronics LLC (P-6051)*

Rosen Electronics LLC .... D....... 951 898-9808
2500 E Francis St Ontario (91761) *(P-6051)*

Rosendin Electric, San Jose *Also Called: Rosendin Electric Inc (P-1825)*

Rosendin Electric Inc (PA) .... A....... 408 286-2800
880 Mabury Rd San Jose (95133) *(P-1825)*

Rosendin Electric Inc .... A....... 714 739-1334
1730 S Anaheim Way Anaheim (92805) *(P-1826)*

Rosendin Electric Inc .... A....... 408 321-2200
2777 Orchard Pkwy San Jose (95134) *(P-1827)*

Rosenthal Group, The, Venice *Also Called: Trg Inc (P-9197)*

Roseryan Inc .... D....... 510 456-3056
1999 S Bascom Ave Ste 700 Campbell (95008) *(P-20534)*

Roseville Care Center, Roseville *Also Called: Crocus Holdings LLC (P-15418)*

Roseville Golfland Ltd Partnr .... D....... 916 784-1273
1893 Taylor Rd Roseville (95661) *(P-14556)*

Roseville Home Healthcare, Roseville *Also Called: Maxim Healthcare Services Inc (P-11305)*

Roseville Toyota, Livermore *Also Called: John L Sllivan Investments Inc (P-7241)*

Rosewill Inc .... A....... 800 575-9885
17560 Rowland St City Of Industry (91748) *(P-2811)*

Rosewood Care Center, Pleasant Hill *Also Called: Helios Healthcare LLC (P-15513)*

Rosewood Court, Fullerton *Also Called: Emeritus Corporation (P-15444)*

Rosewood Gardens, Livermore *Also Called: Watermark Rtrment Cmmnties Inc (P-8870)*

Rosewood Hotels & Resorts LLC .... C....... 650 561-1580
2825 Sand Hill Rd Menlo Park (94025) *(P-10174)*

Rosewood Hotels & Resorts LLC (PA) .... D....... 650 561-1500
2825 Sand Hill Rd Menlo Park (94025) *(P-10175)*

Rosewood Miramar Bch Montecito, Santa Barbara *Also Called: Miramar Acquisition Co LLC (P-9534)*

Rosewood Mmory Care Asssted Lv, Duarte *Also Called: Humangood Norcal (P-8821)*

Rosewood Retirement Community, Bakersfield *Also Called: Humangood Norcal (P-15860)*

Rosewood Sand Hill Hotel, Menlo Park *Also Called: Rosewood Hotels & Resorts LLC (P-10175)*

Ross Baker Towing Inc .... D....... 818 886-7411
8750 Vanalden Ave Northridge (91324) *(P-13718)*

Ross Baker Towing Service, Northridge *Also Called: Ross Baker Towing Inc (P-13718)*

Ross Hospital .... C....... 415 258-6900
1111 Sir Francis Dr Kentfield (94904) *(P-16692)*

Ross Valley Homes Inc .... D....... 415 461-2300
501 Via Casitas Greenbrae (94904) *(P-18515)*

Rossin Steel Inc .... C....... 619 656-9200
9102 Birch St Spring Valley (91977) *(P-5517)*

Rossmoor, Walnut Creek *Also Called: Golden Rain Foundation (P-9025)*

Rostar Filters, Oxnard *Also Called: PC Vaughan Mfg Corp (P-2677)*

Rotary and Miission Systems, Fort Irwin *Also Called: Lockheed Martin Corporation (P-3725)*

Roth Capital Partners LLC (PA) .... D....... 800 678-9147
888 San Clemente Dr Newport Beach (92660) *(P-8164)*

Roth Mkm, Newport Beach *Also Called: Roth Capital Partners LLC (P-8164)*

Roth Staffing Companies LP (PA) .... D....... 714 939-8600
450 N State College Blvd Orange (92868) *(P-11325)*

Roto-Rooter, Valencia *Also Called: Russell-Warner Inc (P-13796)*

Rotolo Chevrolet Inc .... C....... 866 756-9776
16666 S Highland Ave Fontana (92336) *(P-7291)*

Rotorcraft Support Inc .... D....... 818 997-7667
67 D St Fillmore (93015) *(P-3908)*

Round Hill Country Club .... D....... 925 934-8211
3169 Roundhill Rd Alamo (94507) *(P-14433)*

Round Table Pizza, Concord *Also Called: Round Table Pizza Inc (P-7507)*

Round Table Pizza Inc (DH) .... D....... 800 866-5866
1390 Willow Pass Rd Ste 300 Concord (94520) *(P-7507)*

Roundabout Entertainment Inc .... D....... 818 842-9300
217 S Lake St Burbank (91502) *(P-13888)*

Rountree Plumbing and Htg Inc .... D....... 650 298-0300
1624 Santa Clara Dr Ste 130 Roseville (95661) *(P-1550)*

Rouse Services LLC .... D....... 310 360-9200
8383 Wilshire Blvd Ste 900 Beverly Hills (90211) *(P-10573)*

Rove Engineering Inc .... D....... 760 425-0001
398 E Aurora Dr El Centro (92243) *(P-19378)*

Row Hotel, The, San Jose *Also Called: Stay Cal San Jose LLC (P-10277)*

Row House, Irvine *Also Called: Row House Franchise LLC (P-14228)*

Row House Franchise LLC .... C....... 949 341-5585
17877 Von Karman Ave Ste 100 Irvine (92614) *(P-14228)*

Row Management Ltd Inc .... B....... 310 887-3671
499 N Canon Dr Beverly Hills (90210) *(P-9172)*

ALPHABETIC SECTION

Rowan Incorporated .... D....... 760 692-0700
   2778 Loker Ave W Carlsbad (92010) *(P-1828)*
Rowan Electric, Carlsbad *Also Called: Rowan Incorporated (P-1828)*
Rowi Usa Inc .... D....... 805 356-3372
   3155 Old Conejo Rd Thousand Oaks (91320) *(P-18100)*
Rowland Convalescent Hosp Inc .... D....... 626 967-2741
   330 W Rowland St Covina (91723) *(P-15644)*
ROWLAND, THE, Covina *Also Called: Rowland Convalescent Hosp Inc (P-15644)*
Roy E Whitehead Inc .... D....... 951 682-1490
   2245 Via Cerro Riverside (92509) *(P-2016)*
Roy Miller Freight Lines LLC (PA) .... D....... 714 632-5511
   3165 E Coronado St Anaheim (92806) *(P-3421)*
Royal Ambulance Inc .... C....... 877 995-6161
   14472 Wicks Blvd San Leandro (94577) *(P-3292)*
Royal Coach Tours (PA) .... D....... 408 279-4801
   630 Stockton Ave San Jose (95126) *(P-3320)*
Royal Crown Enterprises Inc .... C....... 626 854-8080
   780 Epperson Dr City Of Industry (91748) *(P-6663)*
Royal Electric Co, Sacramento *Also Called: Vellutini Corporation (P-1871)*
Royal Equestrian Apartments, Burbank *Also Called: Alliance Residential LLC (P-8699)*
Royal Express Inc (PA) .... C....... 559 272-3500
   3545 E Date Ave Fresno (93725) *(P-3593)*
Royal Glass Company Inc .... D....... 408 969-0444
   3200 De La Cruz Blvd Santa Clara (95054) *(P-2204)*
Royal Gorge Nordic Ski Resort .... C....... 530 426-3871
   9411 Hillside Rd Soda Springs (95728) *(P-10176)*
Royal Grge Cross Cntry Ski Rso, Soda Springs *Also Called: Royal Gorge Nordic Ski Resort (P-10176)*
Royal Hospitality Inc .... D....... 858 278-0800
   5550 Kearny Mesa Rd San Diego (92111) *(P-10177)*
Royal Imex Inc .... D....... 562 777-9787
   12605 Clark St Santa Fe Springs (90670) *(P-6944)*
Royal Laundry, South San Francisco *Also Called: American Etc Inc (P-10422)*
Royal Mountain King, Copperopolis *Also Called: Meridian Gold Inc (P-574)*
Royal Oaks, Duarte *Also Called: Humangood Socal (P-8824)*
Royal Paper Box Co California (PA) .... C....... 323 728-7041
   1105 S Maple Ave Montebello (90640) *(P-6945)*
Royal Plywood Company LLC .... D....... 916 426-3292
   6003 88th St Ste 100 Sacramento (95828) *(P-5184)*
Royal Plywood Company LLC (PA) .... D....... 562 404-2989
   14171 Park Pl Cerritos (90703) *(P-5185)*
Royal Poultry, Vernon *Also Called: Golden West Trading Inc (P-6421)*
Royal Specialty Undwrt Inc .... C....... 818 922-6700
   15303 Ventura Blvd Ste 500 Sherman Oaks (91403) *(P-8406)*
Royal Terrace Healthcare LLC .... D....... 626 256-4654
   1340 Highland Ave Duarte (91010) *(P-15645)*
Royal Trucking, Concord *Also Called: Lemore Transportation Inc (P-3505)*
Royal West Drywall Inc .... D....... 951 271-4600
   2008 2nd St Norco (92860) *(P-1960)*
Royal Westlake Roofing LLC .... C....... 760 967-0827
   3093 Industry St Ste A Oceanside (92054) *(P-2083)*
Royale Convalescent Hospital, Santa Ana *Also Called: Orange Cnty Ryale Cnvlscent Ho (P-15886)*
Roze Room Hospice, Culver City *Also Called: L & A Care Corporation (P-15768)*
Rp Automotive II Inc .... D....... 619 656-2500
   560 Auto Park Dr Chula Vista (91911) *(P-13567)*
Rp Construction Services LLC .... C....... 855 428-3000
   305 Dela Vina Ave Monterey (93940) *(P-2200)*
Rp Scs Wsd Hotel LLC .... D....... 619 398-3020
   421 W B St San Diego (92101) *(P-10178)*
Rp/Kinetic Parc 55 Owner LLC .... C....... 415 392-8000
   55 Cyril Magnin St San Francisco (94102) *(P-10179)*
RPC Old Town Jffrson Owner LLC .... C....... 619 725-4221
   2435 Jefferson St San Diego (92110) *(P-10180)*
Rpd Hotels 18 LLC (PA) .... A....... 213 746-1531
   1801 S La Cienega Blvd Ste 301 Los Angeles (90035) *(P-10181)*
RPM Consolidated Services Inc (HQ) .... D....... 714 388-3500
   1901 Raymer Ave Fullerton (92833) *(P-3750)*
RPM Luxury Auto Sales Inc .... C....... 916 783-9111
   300 Automall Dr Roseville (95661) *(P-7292)*

RPM Mortgage Inc .... C....... 925 295-9300
   3240 Stone Valley Rd W Alamo (94507) *(P-8016)*
RPM Services, Fresno *Also Called: Westco Equities Inc (P-9213)*
RPM Transportation Inc (DH) .... C....... 714 388-3500
   11660 Arroyo Ave Santa Ana (92705) *(P-3534)*
Rpx, San Francisco *Also Called: Rpx Corporation (P-9456)*
Rpx Corporation (HQ) .... D....... 866 779-7641
   4 Embarcadero Ctr Ste 4000 San Francisco (94111) *(P-9456)*
Rq Construction LLC .... C....... 760 631-7707
   1620 Faraday Ave Carlsbad (92008) *(P-840)*
Rreef, San Francisco *Also Called: The Rromeo Corporation (P-8224)*
Rreef Management Company .... C....... 415 781-3300
   101 California St # 2400 San Francisco (94111) *(P-8467)*
Rrf Tree Service, Morgan Hill *Also Called: Rapid Response Force LLC (P-18093)*
RRI, Downey *Also Called: Rancho Research Institute (P-19906)*
Rri Energy Coolwater Inc .... D....... 760 254-5290
   37000 E Santa Fe St Daggett (92327) *(P-4662)*
Rrm Design Group (PA) .... D....... 805 439-0442
   3765 S Higuera St Ste 102 San Luis Obispo (93401) *(P-19503)*
Rrt Enterprises LP (PA) .... C....... 310 397-2372
   3966 Marcasel Ave Los Angeles (90066) *(P-15646)*
Rrt Enterprises LP .... C....... 323 653-1521
   855 N Fairfax Ave Los Angeles (90046) *(P-15647)*
RRT ENTERPRISES LP, Los Angeles *Also Called: Rrt Enterprises LP (P-15647)*
Rs Investment Management LP .... C....... 415 591-2700
   1 Bush St Ste 900 San Francisco (94104) *(P-9389)*
Rse, Sacramento *Also Called: Runyon Saltzman Inc (P-10672)*
Rsg Group North America LP .... C....... 714 609-0572
   7007 Romaine St Ste 101 West Hollywood (90038) *(P-14229)*
Rsg Group USA Inc .... A....... 214 574-4653
   7007 Romaine St Ste 101 West Hollywood (90038) *(P-9333)*
RSI, Sacramento *Also Called: Refrigeration Solutions LLC (P-1546)*
RSI Home Products Inc .... D....... 949 720-1116
   620 Newport Center Dr Ste 1030 Newport Beach (92660) *(P-2492)*
RSI Leasing LLC .... D....... 626 966-6129
   1314 E Puente Ave West Covina (91790) *(P-11053)*
RSM US LLP .... D....... 408 572-4440
   100 W San Fernando St San Jose (95113) *(P-19628)*
Rsui Group, Sherman Oaks *Also Called: Royal Specialty Undwrt Inc (P-8406)*
Rsvc Company .... C....... 951 684-6578
   3051 Myers St Ste B Riverside (92503) *(P-1159)*
Rte Enterprises Inc .... D....... 818 999-5300
   21530 Roscoe Blvd Canoga Park (91304) *(P-1639)*
Rti Services Inc .... D....... 323 725-6370
   2836 Vail Ave Commerce (90040) *(P-13454)*
Rti Systems Inc .... D....... 213 599-8470
   7635 N San Fernando Rd Burbank (91505) *(P-13141)*
Ruan .... C....... 209 634-4928
   830 W Glenwood Ave Turlock (95380) *(P-3535)*
Ruan Transport Corporation .... D....... 209 599-5000
   830 W Glenwood Ave Turlock (95380) *(P-3536)*
Rubicon Programs Incorporated (PA) .... D....... 510 235-1516
   2500 Bissell Ave Richmond (94804) *(P-10956)*
Rubidoux Family Care Center, Riverside *Also Called: County of Riverside (P-14716)*
Rubin Postaer and Associates (PA) .... C....... 310 394-4000
   2525 Colorado Ave Ste 100 Santa Monica (90404) *(P-10671)*
Rubio Arts Corporation .... C....... 407 849-1643
   1313 S Harbor Blvd Anaheim (92802) *(P-20901)*
Rubrik Inc (PA) .... A....... 650 300-5862
   3495 Deer Creek Rd Palo Alto (94304) *(P-12619)*
Ruby Hill Golf Club LLC .... D....... 925 417-5840
   3400 W Ruby Hill Dr Pleasanton (94566) *(P-14285)*
Rudolph and Sletten Inc (HQ) .... D....... 650 216-3600
   120 Constitution Dr Menlo Park (94025) *(P-1012)*
Rudolph and Sletten Inc .... C....... 209 941-1040
   3614 Zephyr Ct Stockton (95206) *(P-1013)*
Rudolph and Sletten Inc .... C....... 916 781-8001
   1504 Eureka Rd Ste 200 Roseville (95661) *(P-1014)*
Rudolph and Sletten Inc .... C....... 949 252-1919
   2855 Michelle Ste 350 Irvine (92606) *(P-1015)*

Ruffin Hotel Corp of Cal   **ALPHABETIC SECTION**

Ruffin Hotel Corp of Cal .... B 562 425-5210
    4700 Airport Plaza Dr Long Beach (90815) *(P-10182)*

Rugby Laboratories Inc (DH) .... D **951 270-1400**
    311 Bonnie Cir Corona (92878) *(P-6142)*

Rugged Systems Inc .... C 858 391-1006
    13000 Danielson St Ste Q Poway (92064) *(P-2812)*

Ruggeri Marble and Granite Inc .... D 310 513-2155
    25028 Vermont Ave Harbor City (90710) *(P-2717)*

Ruhs-Emergency Department, Moreno Valley *Also Called: Riverside University Health*
(P-16366)

Ruiteng Internet Technology Co .... C 302 597-7438
    1344 W Foothill Blvd D Azusa (91702) *(P-12620)*

Run Roadlines Inc .... D 209 681-3640
    1326 Como Dr Manteca (95337) *(P-4087)*

Running Creek Casino .... C 707 275-9209
    635 E State Highway 20 Upper Lake (95485) *(P-10183)*

Runway Inc .... D 310 636-2000
    1330 Vine St Los Angeles (90028) *(P-13949)*

Runyon Saltzman Inc .... D 916 446-9900
    2020 L St Ste 100 Sacramento (95811) *(P-10672)*

Rural Cmnty Assistance Corp (PA) .... D 916 447-2854
    3120 Freeboard Dr Ste 201 West Sacramento (95691) *(P-18101)*

Rushmore Crrspndent Lnding Svc, Irvine *Also Called: Rushmore Loan MGT Svcs LLC*
(P-8017)

Rushmore Loan MGT Svcs LLC (PA) .... A **949 727-4798**
    15480 Laguna Canyon Rd Ste 100 Irvine (92618) *(P-8017)*

Russ August & Kabat LLP .... D 310 826-7474
    12424 Wilshire Blvd Ste 1200 Los Angeles (90025) *(P-17630)*

Russell Hobbs Inc .... D 909 792-8257
    2301 W San Bernardino Ave Redlands (92374) *(P-841)*

Russell Mechanical Inc .... D 916 635-2522
    3251 Monier Cir Ste A Rancho Cordova (95742) *(P-1551)*

Russell-Warner Inc .... C 661 257-9200
    24971 Avenue Stanford Valencia (91355) *(P-13796)*

Rustic Canyon Group LLC .... D 310 998-8000
    1025 Westwood Blvd Los Angeles (90024) *(P-9557)*

Rustic Canyon Partners, Los Angeles *Also Called: Rustic Canyon Group LLC (P-9557)*

Rutan & Tucker LLP (PA) .... B **714 641-5100**
    18575 Jamboree Rd Ste 900 Irvine (92612) *(P-17631)*

Rutherford Co Inc (PA) .... D 323 666-5284
    2107 Crystal St Los Angeles (90039) *(P-1961)*

Rutland Tool & Supply Co (HQ) .... C 562 566-5000
    2225 Workman Mill Rd City Of Industry (90601) *(P-5923)*

Rvl Packaging Inc .... C 818 735-5000
    31330 Oak Crest Dr Westlake Village (91361) *(P-13455)*

Rvm Davis Housing Corporation .... C 530 747-7095
    1501 Shasta Dr Davis (95616) *(P-18516)*

RW Zant LLC (DH) .... D 323 980-5457
    1470 E 4th St Los Angeles (90033) *(P-6503)*

RW&g, Los Angeles *Also Called: Richards Wtson Grshon A Prof C (P-17624)*

Rx Pro Health LLC .... A 858 369-4050
    12400 High Bluff Dr Ste 100 San Diego (92130) *(P-11326)*

Rxo Cstoms Clrnce Slutions LLC .... C 650 589-8150
    400 Oyster Point Blvd Ste 307 South San Francisco (94080) *(P-4088)*

Rxo Cstoms Clrnce Slutions LLC .... C 620 266-6315
    2200 Claremont Ct 2nd Fl Hayward (94545) *(P-4089)*

Rxo Freight Forwarding Inc .... A 630 795-1300
    32970 Alvarado Niles Rd Union City (94587) *(P-4090)*

Ryan Associates, Sausalito *Also Called: Paul Ryan Associates (P-707)*

Ryan Herco Flow Solutions, Burbank *Also Called: Ryan Herco Products Corp (P-5759)*

Ryan Herco Products Corp (DH) .... D 818 841-1141
    3010 N San Fernando Blvd Burbank (91504) *(P-5759)*

Ryan's Express, Torrance *Also Called: Ryans Express Trnsp Svcs Inc (P-3293)*

Ryans Express Trnsp Svcs Inc (PA) .... D 310 219-2960
    19500 Mariner Ave Torrance (90503) *(P-3293)*

Rydell Chevrolet-Northridge, Northridge *Also Called: San Fernando Valley Auto LLC (P-7294)*

Rye Electric Inc .... D 949 441-0545
    28202 Cabot Rd Ste 300 Laguna Niguel (92677) *(P-1829)*

Rynoclad Technologies Inc .... C 951 264-3441
    780 E Francis St Ste M Ontario (91761) *(P-2205)*

Rysun Labs Inc .... C 855 527-7890
    1525 Mccarthy Blvd Ste 212 Milpitas (95035) *(P-11889)*

Ryzlink Corp .... D 510 296-5433
    2855 Kifer Rd Ste 135 Santa Clara (95051) *(P-11890)*

S & M Moving Systems .... D 510 497-2300
    48551 Warm Springs Blvd Fremont (94539) *(P-3537)*

S & M Moving Systems, Santa Fe Springs *Also Called: Van Torrance & Storage Company (P-3602)*

S & S Construction Co, Beverly Hills *Also Called: Shapell Industries LLC (P-9273)*

S & S Drywall Inc (PA) .... C **408 294-4393**
    202 N 27th St San Jose (95116) *(P-1962)*

S & S Ranch Inc .... D 559 655-3491
    904 S Lyon Ave Mendota (93640) *(P-243)*

S & S Supplies and Solutions, Fairfield *Also Called: S & S Tool & Supply Inc (P-5924)*

S & S Tool & Supply Inc (HQ) .... D **800 430-8665**
    2700 Maxwell Way Fairfield (94534) *(P-5924)*

S A S, Concord *Also Called: Bay Alarm Company (P-1674)*

S B H Hotel Corporation .... A 909 889-0133
    285 E Hospitality Ln San Bernardino (92408) *(P-10184)*

S B M, Mcclellan *Also Called: Sbm Site Services LLC (P-10960)*

S C A, Victorville *Also Called: Comav Technical Services LLC (P-3887)*

S C A G, Los Angeles *Also Called: Cal Southern Assn Governments (P-20715)*

S C I R E, Long Beach *Also Called: Southern Cal Inst For RES Edca (P-19914)*

S C P M G, San Dimas *Also Called: Southern Cal Prmnnte Med Group (P-8366)*

S C P M G, Harbor City *Also Called: Permanente Medical Group Inc (P-14986)*

S C P M G, Anaheim *Also Called: Southern Cal Prmnnte Med Group (P-15074)*

S C P M G, Colton *Also Called: Southern Cal Prmnnte Med Group (P-15080)*

S C P M G, Culver City *Also Called: Southern Cal Prmnnte Med Group (P-15081)*

S C P M G, Inglewood *Also Called: Southern Cal Prmnnte Med Group (P-15082)*

S C P M G, El Cajon *Also Called: Southern Cal Prmnnte Med Group (P-15084)*

S C P M G, San Juan Capistrano *Also Called: Southern Cal Prmnnte Med Group (P-15085)*

S C P M G, San Diego *Also Called: Southern Cal Prmnnte Med Group (P-15086)*

S C P M G, Escondido *Also Called: Southern Cal Prmnnte Med Group (P-15087)*

S C P M G, Cudahy *Also Called: Southern Cal Prmnnte Med Group (P-15088)*

S C P M G, Woodland Hills *Also Called: Southern Cal Prmnnte Med Group (P-15089)*

S C P M G, Santa Clarita *Also Called: Southern Cal Prmnnte Med Group (P-15090)*

S C P M G, Santa Ana *Also Called: Southern Cal Prmnnte Med Group (P-15093)*

S C P M G, Fontana *Also Called: Southern Cal Prmnnte Med Group (P-16440)*

S C R, Costa Mesa *Also Called: South Coast Repertory Inc (P-14069)*

S C S, North Highlands *Also Called: Security Contractor Svcs Inc (P-5232)*

S C Valley Engineering Inc .... D 619 444-2366
    656 Front St El Cajon (92020) *(P-1256)*

S C Village, Bellflower *Also Called: S J S Enterprise Inc (P-14557)*

S D I, Lakeside *Also Called: Standard Drywall Inc (P-1965)*

S E C C Corporation (PA) .... D 909 393-5419
    502 N Sheridan St Corona (92878) *(P-1257)*

S E Labs, Santa Clara *Also Called: SE Laboratories Inc (P-19998)*

S E O P Inc .... C 949 682-7906
    1621 Alton Pkwy Ste 150 Irvine (92606) *(P-20535)*

S E Pipe Line Construction Co .... D 562 868-9771
    11832 Bloomfield Ave Santa Fe Springs (90670) *(P-1258)*

S G S Produce, Los Angeles *Also Called: Shapiro-Gilman-Shandler Co (P-6580)*

S J Amoroso Cnstr Co LLC (PA) .... B **650 654-1900**
    390 Bridge Pkwy Redwood City (94065) *(P-1016)*

S J Amoroso Cnstr Co LLC .... D 650 654-1900
    275 Baker St Ste B Costa Mesa (92626) *(P-1017)*

S J S Enterprise Inc .... C 949 489-9000
    9030 Somerset Blvd Bellflower (90706) *(P-14557)*

S J W, San Jose *Also Called: San Jose Water Company (P-4827)*

S L Start and Associates LLC .... D 760 414-9411
    3500 Lake Blvd Oceanside (92056) *(P-18517)*

S M U D, Sacramento *Also Called: Sacramento Municpl Utility Dst (P-4663)*

S P S Inc .... D 650 685-5913
    245 Medio Ave Half Moon Bay (94019) *(P-20536)*

S R C Devices Inccustomer .... B 866 772-8668
    6295 Ferris Sq Ste D San Diego (92121) *(P-2868)*

S S 8, Milpitas *Also Called: Ss8 Networks Inc (P-4553)*

S S F, South San Francisco *Also Called: Ssf Imported Auto Parts LLC (P-5063)*

S S I, Camarillo *Also Called: Synectic Solutions Inc (P-12886)*

ALPHABETIC SECTION

S S W Mechanical Cnstr Inc .... C....... 760 327-1481
670 S Oleander Rd Palm Springs (92264) *(P-1552)*

S Stamoules Inc .... A....... 559 655-9777
904 S Lyon Ave Mendota (93640) *(P-301)*

S T L, Sacramento *Also Called: Sacramento Theatrical Ltg Ltd* *(P-14062)*

S W K Properties LLC .... C....... 714 481-6300
2726 S Grand Ave Lbby Santa Ana (92705) *(P-10185)*

S W K Properties LLC (PA) .... D....... 213 383-9204
3807 Wilshire Blvd Ste 1226 Los Angeles (90010) *(P-10186)*

S-Mart, Modesto *Also Called: Save Mart Supermarkets LLC* *(P-7151)*

S&B Pharma Inc .... D....... 626 334-2908
405 S Motor Ave Azusa (91702) *(P-2577)*

S&B Surgery Center II, Rllng Hls Est *Also Called: Spalding Srgcal Ctr Bvrly Hlls* *(P-15096)*

S&E Gourmet Cuts Inc .... C....... 909 370-0155
1055 E Cooley Ave San Bernardino (92408) *(P-6464)*

S&J Stadtler Inc .... B....... 925 847-8900
5980 Stoneridge Dr Ste 122 Pleasanton (94588) *(P-9173)*

SA Camp Pump and Drilling Co, Bakersfield *Also Called: SA Camp Pump Company* *(P-13797)*

SA Camp Pump Company .... D....... 661 399-2976
17876 Zerker Rd Bakersfield (93308) *(P-13797)*

SA Recycling, Orange *Also Called: SA Recycling LLC* *(P-4933)*

SA Recycling LLC (PA) .... C....... 714 632-2000
2411 N Glassell St Orange (92865) *(P-4933)*

Sa-Tech, Oxnard *Also Called: Systems Application & Tech Inc* *(P-19403)*

Saalex Corp .... A....... 951 543-9259
27525 Enterprise Cir W Ste 101a Temecula (92590) *(P-11891)*

Saalex Corp (PA) .... C....... 805 482-1070
811 Camarillo Springs Rd Ste A Camarillo (93012) *(P-19379)*

Saalex Solutions, Camarillo *Also Called: Saalex Corp* *(P-19379)*

Saama, Campbell *Also Called: Saama Technologies Inc* *(P-11892)*

Saama Technologies Inc (PA) .... C....... 408 371-1900
900 E Hamilton Ave Ste 200 Campbell (95008) *(P-11892)*

Saarman Construction Ltd .... C....... 415 749-2700
1900 N Loop Rd Alameda (94502) *(P-773)*

Saatchi & Saatchi N Amer LLC .... C....... 310 437-2500
3501 Sepulveda Blvd Torrance (90505) *(P-10673)*

Saba Software Inc (DH) .... D....... 877 722-2101
4120 Dublin Blvd Ste 200 Dublin (94568) *(P-12340)*

Sabal Capital Partners LLC .... C....... 949 255-1007
680 E Colorado Blvd Ste 350 Pasadena (91101) *(P-9558)*

Saban Brands LLC (HQ) .... D....... 310 557-5230
10100 Santa Monica Blvd Ste 500 Los Angeles (90067) *(P-20537)*

Saban Capital Group LLC .... D....... 310 557-5100
11301 W Olympic Blvd Ste 121601 Los Angeles (90064) *(P-9334)*

Saban Community Clinic, Los Angeles *Also Called: Los Angeles Free Clinic* *(P-14881)*

Saban Research Institute, The, Los Angeles *Also Called: Childrens Hospital Los Angeles* *(P-15995)*

Saber, Paramount *Also Called: South Coast Piering Inc* *(P-1031)*

Sabre Systems Inc .... D....... 619 528-2226
3111 Camino Del Rio N Ste 400 San Diego (92108) *(P-19380)*

Sabsaf LLC .... D....... 951 266-6676
17192 Murphy Ave Unit 18641 Irvine (92623) *(P-3627)*

Sabsaf Logistics, Irvine *Also Called: Sabsaf LLC* *(P-3627)*

Sac International Steel Inc (PA) .... D....... 323 232-2467
6130 Avalon Blvd Los Angeles (90003) *(P-5518)*

Saca Technologies Inc .... D....... 888 603-9030
5101 E La Palma Ave Ste 200 Anaheim (92807) *(P-12870)*

Saccani Distributing Company .... D....... 916 441-0213
2600 5th St Sacramento (95818) *(P-6781)*

Sacramento, Sacramento *Also Called: Nationwide Legal LLC* *(P-17587)*

Sacramento 49er, Sacramento *Also Called: Sacramento 49er Travel Plaza* *(P-10187)*

Sacramento 49er Travel Plaza .... C....... 916 927-4774
2828 El Centro Rd Sacramento (95833) *(P-10187)*

Sacramento A-1 Door .... C....... 916 481-5030
4300 Jetway Ct North Highlands (95660) *(P-5186)*

Sacramento Area Emerg Housing .... D....... 916 455-2160
4516 Parker Ave Sacramento (95820) *(P-18102)*

Sacramento Bee, Sacramento *Also Called: McClatchy Newspapers Inc* *(P-2539)*

Sacramento Childrens Home (PA) .... C....... 916 452-3981
2750 Sutterville Rd Sacramento (95820) *(P-18518)*

Sacramento Community Clinic, Sacramento *Also Called: Health Lf Orgnization Inc Halo* *(P-17246)*

Sacramento Credit Union (PA) .... D....... 916 444-6070
800 H St Sacramento (95814) *(P-7832)*

Sacramento District Office, Sacramento *Also Called: State Compensation Insur Fund* *(P-8415)*

Sacramento Drive In, Sacramento *Also Called: Century Theatres Inc* *(P-14022)*

Sacramento Housing Dev Corp (PA) .... D....... 916 440-1333
801 12th St Sacramento (95814) *(P-20843)*

Sacramento Intl Jet Ctr Inc .... D....... 916 428-8292
6133 Freeport Blvd Sacramento (95822) *(P-6737)*

Sacramento Job Corp .... D....... 916 391-1016
3100 Meadowview Rd Sacramento (95832) *(P-18244)*

Sacramento Municpl Utility Dst (PA) .... A....... 916 452-3211
6201 S St Sacramento (95817) *(P-4663)*

Sacramento Municpl Utility Dst .... C....... 916 452-3211
6201 S St Sacramento (95817) *(P-4664)*

Sacramento Municpl Utility Dst .... D....... 916 732-5155
6301 S St Sacramento (95817) *(P-4665)*

Sacramento Municpl Utility Dst .... A....... 916 732-5616
6201 S St Sacramento (95817) *(P-4666)*

Sacramento Municpl Utility Dst .... C....... 916 732-5743
14295 Clay East Rd Herald (95638) *(P-13456)*

Sacramento Operating Co LP .... C....... 916 422-4825
7400 24th St Sacramento (95822) *(P-15648)*

Sacramento Post-Acute, Sacramento *Also Called: Oleander Holdings LLC* *(P-15610)*

Sacramento Reg Co Sanit Dist .... B....... 916 875-9000
8521 Laguna Station Rd Elk Grove (95758) *(P-4850)*

Sacramento Regional Trnst Dist (PA) .... A....... 916 726-2877
1400 29th St Sacramento (95816) *(P-3193)*

Sacramento Republic Fc, Sacramento *Also Called: Sacramnto Rpub Football CLB LLC* *(P-14155)*

Sacramento Staffing, Sacramento *Also Called: Maxim Healthcare Services Inc* *(P-11302)*

Sacramento State Sponsored RES, Sacramento *Also Called: University Enterprises Inc* *(P-17818)*

Sacramento Television Stns Inc (HQ) .... C....... 916 374-1452
2713 Kovr Dr West Sacramento (95605) *(P-4460)*

Sacramento Theatre Company .... D....... 916 446-7501
1419 H St Sacramento (95814) *(P-14061)*

Sacramento Theatrical Ltg Ltd .... D....... 916 447-3258
410 N 10th St Sacramento (95811) *(P-14062)*

Sacramnto Bhvral Hlthcare Hosp .... C....... 916 437-6410
1400 Expo Pkwy Sacramento (95815) *(P-15031)*

Sacramnto Chnese Cmnty Svc Ctr .... D....... 916 442-4228
420 I St Ste 5 Sacramento (95814) *(P-18103)*

Sacramnto Emplyment Trning AGC .... C....... 916 263-3800
925 Del Paso Blvd Ste 100 Sacramento (95815) *(P-18245)*

Sacramnto Emplyment Trning AGC (PA) .... C....... 916 263-3800
925 Del Paso Blvd Ste 100 Sacramento (95815) *(P-18246)*

Sacramnto Hsing Rdvlpment Agcy .... B....... 916 440-1376
630 I St Fl 3 Sacramento (95814) *(P-8650)*

Sacramnto Hsing Rdvlpment Agcy .... D....... 916 440-1399
801 12th St Sacramento (95814) *(P-9174)*

Sacramnto Mtro A Qulty MGT Dst .... D....... 916 874-4800
777 12th St Ste 300 Sacramento (95814) *(P-20844)*

Sacramnto Ntiv Amercn Hlth Ctr .... C....... 916 341-0575
2020 J St Sacramento (95811) *(P-15032)*

Sacramnto Rgnal Cnty Snttion D (PA) .... C....... 916 876-6000
10060 Goethe Rd Sacramento (95827) *(P-4983)*

Sacramnto Rpub Fotball CLB LLC .... D....... 916 307-6100
2421 117th St Sacramento (95818) *(P-14155)*

Sacramnto Soc For The Prvntion .... D....... 916 383-7387
6201 Florin Perkins Rd Sacramento (95828) *(P-19100)*

Sacramnto Subn Wtr Dst Fing Co .... D....... 916 972-7171
3701 Marconi Ave Ste 100 Sacramento (95821) *(P-4821)*

Sacred Heart Pre-School, Turlock *Also Called: Diocese Stockton Eductl Off* *(P-17708)*

Sada, North Hollywood *Also Called: Sada Systems Inc* *(P-12871)*

Sada Systems Inc (PA) .... C....... 818 766-2400
5250 Lankershim Blvd Ste 720 North Hollywood (91601) *(P-12871)*

Sadaf Foods, Vernon *Also Called: Soofer Co Inc* *(P-6669)*

Saddle Back Valley YMCA, Mission Viejo *Also Called: Young MNS Chrstn Assn Ornge CN* *(P-18990)*

Saddleback Memorial Med Ctr — ALPHABETIC SECTION

Saddleback Memorial Med Ctr (HQ) .... A 949 837-4500
24451 Health Center Dr Fl 1 Laguna Hills (92653) *(P-16367)*

Saddleback Valley Service Ctr, Irvine *Also Called: Southern California Edison Co (P-4691)*

Saddleback Vly .... D 949 586-1234
25631 Peter A Hartman Way Mission Viejo (92691) *(P-14434)*

Saddlemen, Compton *Also Called: Saddlemen Corporation (P-5058)*

Saddlemen Corporation .... C 310 638-1222
17801 S Susana Rd Compton (90221) *(P-5058)*

Safe & Sound Security .... D 925 942-0795
2125 Oak Grove Rd Ste 128 Walnut Creek (94598) *(P-13142)*

Safe Credit Union (PA) .... C 916 979-7233
2295 Iron Point Rd Ste 100 Folsom (95630) *(P-7795)*

Safe Harbor Home Care, San Diego *Also Called: Icare Private Duty Inc (P-15520)*

Safe Hbr Marina Bay Yacht Hbr, Richmond *Also Called: Shm Mbyh LLC (P-3825)*

Safe Refuge .... D 562 987-5722
1041 Redondo Ave Long Beach (90804) *(P-17123)*

Safe Securities Inc (PA) .... C 650 398-3669
3000 El Camino Real Bldg 4 Palo Alto (94306) *(P-11893)*

Safeco Door & Hardware Inc .... D 510 429-4768
31054 San Antonio St Hayward (94544) *(P-2206)*

Safeco Glass, Hayward *Also Called: Safeco Door & Hardware Inc (P-2206)*

Safeco Insurance Company Amer .... C 818 956-4250
330 N Brand Blvd Ste 680 Glendale (91203) *(P-8651)*

Safeguard Health Entps Inc (HQ) .... B 800 880-1800
95 Enterprise Ste 100 Aliso Viejo (92656) *(P-8358)*

Safeguard On Demand Inc .... C 800 640-2327
11037 Warner Ave # 297 Fountain Valley (92708) *(P-13031)*

Safelyyou, San Francisco *Also Called: Safelyyou Inc (P-12520)*

Safelyyou Inc .... D 713 822-6924
36 Clyde St San Francisco (94107) *(P-12520)*

Safety Network Inc (PA) .... D 559 291-8000
1345 N Rabe Ave Fresno (93727) *(P-7592)*

Safran, Anaheim *Also Called: Morphotrak LLC (P-12495)*

Safran Pass Innovations LLC (HQ) .... D 714 854-8600
3151 E Imperial Hwy Brea (92821) *(P-11894)*

Saga Kapital Group Inc .... D 714 294-4132
108 Saybrook Irvine (92620) *(P-20198)*

Sage, San Francisco *Also Called: Sage Project Inc (P-18104)*

Sage Apartment Communities Inc .... D 949 440-2300
18006 Sky Park Cir Irvine (92614) *(P-8858)*

Sage Group .... D 415 512-8200
33 Falmouth St San Francisco (94107) *(P-11224)*

Sage Hospitality Resources LLC .... C 626 357-5211
700 W Huntington Dr Monrovia (91016) *(P-10188)*

Sage Hospitality Resources LLC .... C 650 589-1600
2000 Shoreline Ct Brisbane (94005) *(P-10189)*

Sage Project Inc .... D 415 905-5050
68 12th St San Francisco (94103) *(P-18104)*

Sage Software Holdings Inc (HQ) .... B 866 530-7243
6561 Irvine Center Dr Irvine (92618) *(P-12341)*

Sage Staffing, Valencia *Also Called: Sage Staffing Consultants Inc (P-11327)*

Sage Staffing Consultants Inc (PA) .... C 661 254-4026
27441 Tourney Rd Ste 150 Valencia (91355) *(P-11327)*

Sage Veterinary Centers LP .... B 925 288-4856
1410 Monument Blvd Concord (94520) *(P-342)*

Sagebrush Healthcare Inc .... D 707 425-0623
1255 Travis Blvd Fairfield (94533) *(P-15649)*

Sago Mini Inc .... D 416 731-8586
5880 W Jefferson Blvd Ste A Los Angeles (90016) *(P-11895)*

Saguaro Palm Springs, The, Palm Springs *Also Called: Sydell Palm Springs LLC (P-10299)*

Sahargun Mechanical, Stockton *Also Called: Sahargun Plumbing Inc (P-1553)*

Sahargun Plumbing Inc .... D 209 474-2611
2216 Stewart St Stockton (95205) *(P-1553)*

SAI Management Co Inc .... D 714 772-5050
1600 S Harbor Blvd Anaheim (92802) *(P-10190)*

Saia Inc .... C 916 483-8331
1508 Wyant Way Sacramento (95864) *(P-3538)*

Saia Motor Freight Line LLC .... D 909 356-2808
14731 Santa Ana Ave Fontana (92337) *(P-3539)*

Saia Motor Freight Line LLC .... D 916 690-8417
9119 Elkmont Dr Elk Grove (95624) *(P-3540)*

Saia Motor Freight Line LLC .... D 323 277-2880
2550 E 28th St Vernon (90058) *(P-3541)*

Saia S Reno Barbara K, Sacramento *Also Called: Saia Inc (P-3538)*

Saic, San Diego *Also Called: Science Applications Intl Corp (P-12523)*

Saic, San Diego *Also Called: Leidos Inc (P-19725)*

Saic, San Diego *Also Called: Leidos Inc (P-19727)*

Saic Government Solutions, San Diego *Also Called: Science Applications Intl Corp (P-12873)*

Sails Washington Inc .... B 425 333-4114
13920 City Center Dr Ste 290 Chino Hills (91709) *(P-16922)*

Saint Agnes Medical Center (HQ) .... A 559 450-3000
1303 E Herndon Ave Fresno (93720) *(P-16368)*

Saint Anthony Retreat, Three Rivers *Also Called: Roman Catholic Bishp of Fresno (P-10411)*

SAINT BARNABAS SENIOR SERVICES, Los Angeles *Also Called: St Brnbas Snior Ctr Los Angle (P-18138)*

Saint Cecilia School, Tustin *Also Called: Roman Cthlic Diocese of Orange (P-17744)*

Saint Claires Nursing Ctr LLC .... C 916 392-4440
6248 66th Ave Sacramento (95823) *(P-15650)*

Saint Francis Memorial Hosp (DH) .... A 415 353-6000
900 Hyde St San Francisco (94109) *(P-16369)*

Saint Jhns Hlth Ctr Foundation .... C 310 315-6111
2200 Santa Monica Blvd Santa Monica (90404) *(P-15033)*

Saint John's Health Center, Santa Monica *Also Called: Saint Johns Health Center Foundation (P-16370)*

Saint John's Hospital X Ray, Long Beach *Also Called: Dignity Health (P-16046)*

Saint Johns Health Center Foundation (DH) .... A 310 829-5511
2121 Santa Monica Blvd Santa Monica (90404) *(P-16370)*

SAINT JOSEPH CENTER VOLUNTEER, Venice *Also Called: St Joseph Center (P-18139)*

Saint Joseph Hlth Sys Hospice, Anaheim *Also Called: St Joseph Hospice (P-18140)*

Saint Lise Rgnal Hosp Fndation .... B 408 848-4931
9400 N Name Uno Gilroy (95020) *(P-16371)*

Saint Louise Hospital .... B 408 848-2000
9400 N Name Uno Gilroy (95020) *(P-16372)*

Saint Mary Medical Center, Long Beach *Also Called: Dignity Health (P-16048)*

Saint-Gobain Performance Plas, San Diego *Also Called: Saint-Gobain Solar Gard LLC (P-2661)*

Saint-Gobain Solar Gard LLC (DH) .... D 866 300-2674
4540 Viewridge Ave San Diego (92123) *(P-2661)*

Saints Management LLC (PA) .... A 415 773-2080
475 Sansome St Ste 1850 San Francisco (94111) *(P-9559)*

Sajahtera Inc .... A 310 276-2251
9641 Sunset Blvd Beverly Hills (90210) *(P-10191)*

Sak Brand Group .... D 415 486-1200
400 Alabama St San Francisco (94110) *(P-6218)*

Sakata Seed America Inc (HQ) .... D 408 778-7758
18095 Serene Dr Morgan Hill (95037) *(P-6831)*

Sakura Finetek USA Inc (HQ) .... C 310 972-7800
1750 W 214th St Torrance (90501) *(P-5448)*

Salad Time Farms, Baldwin Park *Also Called: Tanimura Antle Fresh Foods Inc (P-309)*

Saladino's Foodservice, Fresno *Also Called: Saladinos Inc (P-6284)*

Saladinos Inc (PA) .... C 559 271-3700
3325 W Figarden Dr Fresno (93711) *(P-6284)*

Sales & Marketing, San Francisco *Also Called: Outreach Corporation (P-12310)*

Sales Advantage Group, Corona *Also Called: Temps Plus Inc (P-11246)*

Sales Mkt Mfg Smart Dining Sys, San Carlos *Also Called: E La Carte Inc (P-7442)*

Salesforce .... D 650 327-0110
117 University Ave Palo Alto (94301) *(P-12342)*

Salesforce, San Francisco *Also Called: Salesforce Inc (P-12343)*

Salesforce Inc (PA) .... A 415 901-7000
415 Mission St Fl 3 San Francisco (94105) *(P-12343)*

Salesforcecom/Foundation .... C 800 667-6389
The Landmark @ One Market Ste 300 San Francisco (94105) *(P-18105)*

Salesforceorg LLC .... A 415 901-7000
1 Market St San Francisco (94105) *(P-12344)*

Salient Global Technologies, Pittsburg *Also Called: Ravig Inc (P-5340)*

Salinas Golf and Cntry CLB Inc .... D 831 449-6617
475 San Juan Grade Rd Salinas (93906) *(P-14435)*

Salinas Land Company (PA) .... C 805 648-3363
44557 Teague Ave Greenfield (93927) *(P-38)*

Salinas Valley Health (PA) .... A 831 757-4333
450 E Romie Ln Salinas (93901) *(P-16373)*

ALPHABETIC SECTION
San Diego Assn Governments

Salinas Valley Medical Clinic .... D 831 424-7389
   236 San Jose St Salinas (93901) *(P-15034)*
Salinas Valley Memorial Hosp, Salinas *Also Called: Salinas Valley Health (P-16373)*
Salinasidence Opco LLC .... C 831 424-8072
   720 E Romie Ln Salinas (93901) *(P-15793)*
SALK INSTITUTE, THE, La Jolla *Also Called: The Salk Institute For Biological Studies San Diego California (P-19784)*
Salson Logistics Inc .... C 973 986-0200
   1331 Torrance Blvd Torrance (90501) *(P-4091)*
Salt Lake Hotel Associates LP (PA) .... C 415 397-5572
   222 Kearny St Ste 200 San Francisco (94108) *(P-10192)*
Salt Security Inc .... D 650 254-6580
   3921 Fabian Way Palo Alto (94303) *(P-11896)*
Salud Para La Gente .... C 831 728-0222
   195 Aviation Way Ste 200 Watsonville (95076) *(P-15035)*
SALUD PARA LA GENTE HEALTH CLI, Watsonville *Also Called: Salud Para La Gente (P-15035)*
Salvation Army (HQ) .... C 562 264-3600
   30840 Hawthorne Blvd Rancho Palos Verdes (90275) *(P-18106)*
Salvation Army .... D 714 832-7100
   10200 Pioneer Rd Tustin (92782) *(P-18107)*
Salvation Army, San Diego *Also Called: Salvation Army Ray & Joan (P-14230)*
Salvation Army, Tustin *Also Called: Salvation Army (P-18107)*
Salvation Army Ray & Joan .... B 619 287-5762
   6845 University Ave San Diego (92115) *(P-14230)*
Salvation Army Western Ttry, Rancho Palos Verdes *Also Called: Salvation Army (P-18106)*
Sam Sung Fixtures, Los Angeles *Also Called: Trust 1 Sales Inc (P-5393)*
Sam Trans, South San Francisco *Also Called: San Mateo County Transit Dst (P-3204)*
Sam Trans, San Carlos *Also Called: San Mateo County Transit Dst (P-3358)*
Samaritan Imaging Center .... A 213 977-2140
   1245 Wilshire Blvd Ste 205 Los Angeles (90017) *(P-16751)*
Samaritan Village Inc .... C 209 883-3212
   7700 Fox Rd Hughson (95326) *(P-18108)*
Sambanova Systems Inc (PA) .... B 650 263-1153
   2200 Geng Rd Ste 100 Palo Alto (94303) *(P-11897)*
Sambazon, San Clemente *Also Called: Sambazon Inc (P-6577)*
Sambazon Inc (PA) .... D 877 726-2296
   209 Avenida Fabricante Ste 200 San Clemente (92672) *(P-6577)*
Same Swim LLC .... D 323 582-2588
   2333 E 49th St Vernon (90058) *(P-6219)*
Samedan Oil Corporation .... B 661 319-5038
   1360 Landing Ave Seal Beach (90740) *(P-604)*
Sameday Health, Venice *Also Called: Sameday Technologies Inc (P-11898)*
Sameday Technologies Inc .... C 310 697-8126
   523 Victoria Ave Venice (90291) *(P-11898)*
Samepage Labs Inc .... B 408 628-0393
   307 Orchard City Dr Campbell (95008) *(P-11899)*
Samesky Health Inc .... D 855 735-6726
   5250 Lankershim Blvd North Hollywood (91601) *(P-13457)*
Samiyatex, Los Angeles *Also Called: Paragon Textiles Inc (P-6215)*
Samsara Inc (PA) .... A 415 985-2400
   1 De Haro St San Francisco (94103) *(P-12521)*
Samsung, San Jose *Also Called: Samsung Semiconductor Inc (P-5698)*
Samsung Electronics, Mountain View *Also Called: Samsung Electronics Amer Inc (P-5697)*
Samsung Electronics Amer Inc .... C 646 651-2309
   645 Clyde Ave Mountain View (94043) *(P-5344)*
Samsung Electronics Amer Inc .... C 323 374-6300
   5601 E Slauson Ave Ste 200 Commerce (90040) *(P-5613)*
Samsung Electronics Amer Inc .... A 650 210-1000
   665 Clyde Ave Mountain View (94043) *(P-5697)*
Samsung Pay Inc .... D 617 279-0520
   665 Clyde Ave Mountain View (94043) *(P-13458)*
Samsung Research America Inc .... B 949 468-1143
   18500 Von Karman Ave Ste 700 Irvine (92612) *(P-5345)*
Samsung Research America Inc (DH) .... C 650 210-1001
   665 Clyde Ave Mountain View (94043) *(P-19766)*
Samsung Semiconductor Inc (DH) .... C 408 544-4000
   3655 N 1st St San Jose (95134) *(P-5698)*
SAMTRANS, San Carlos *Also Called: San Mateo County Transit Dst (P-3203)*
Samuel Hale, Folsom *Also Called: Samuel Hale LLC (P-11225)*

Samuel Hale LLC .... A 916 235-1477
   2365 Iron Point Rd Ste 190 Folsom (95630) *(P-11225)*
Samuel J Piazza & Son Inc (PA) .... D 323 357-1999
   9001 Rayo Ave South Gate (90280) *(P-3594)*
Samy's Digital Imaging, Los Angeles *Also Called: Samys Camera Inc (P-7554)*
Samys Camera Inc (PA) .... C 310 591-2100
   12636 Beatrice St Los Angeles (90066) *(P-7554)*
San Andreas Regional Center (PA) .... C 408 374-9960
   6203 San Ignacio Ave Ste 200 San Jose (95119) *(P-18109)*
San Antnio Ambltory Srgcal Ctr .... D 909 579-1500
   901 San Bernardino Rd 2nd Fl Upland (91786) *(P-15036)*
San Antonio Gift Shop, Los Angeles *Also Called: San Antonio Winery Inc (P-2392)*
San Antonio Regional Hospital (PA) .... A 909 985-2811
   999 San Bernardino Rd Upland (91786) *(P-16374)*
San Antonio Winery Inc (PA) .... C 323 223-1401
   737 Lamar St Los Angeles (90031) *(P-2392)*
San Benito Health Care Dst (PA) .... B
   911 Sunset Dr Hollister (95023) *(P-16375)*
San Benito Health Care Dst .... C 831 635-1106
   900 Sunset Dr Hollister (95023) *(P-16376)*
San Benito Htg & Shtmtl Inc .... D 831 637-1112
   1771 San Felipe Rd Hollister (95023) *(P-1554)*
San Benito Supply (PA) .... C 831 637-5526
   1060 Nash Rd Hollister (95023) *(P-2706)*
San Bernabe Vineyards .... D 831 385-4897
   53001 Oasis Rd King City (93930) *(P-84)*
San Bernardino Care Company .... C 909 884-4781
   467 E Gilbert St San Bernardino (92404) *(P-15893)*
San Bernardino Cnty Trnsp Auth .... C 909 884-8276
   1170 W 3rd St Fl 2 San Bernardino (92410) *(P-3194)*
San Bernardino Family YMCA, San Bernardino *Also Called: YMCA of East Valley (P-18935)*
San Bernardino Fics, San Bernardino *Also Called: Victor Cmnty Support Svcs Inc (P-17157)*
San Bernardino Hilton (HQ) .... C 909 889-0133
   285 E Hospitality Ln San Bernardino (92408) *(P-10193)*
San Brnrdino Cmnty College Dst .... C 909 384-4444
   701 S Mount Vernon Ave San Bernardino (92410) *(P-4402)*
San Brnrdino Cnty Prbtion Offc .... B 909 887-2544
   4370 Hallmark Pkwy Ste 105 San Bernardino (92407) *(P-18110)*
San Brnrdino Cnty Rgonal Parks .... D 909 387-2583
   777 E Rialto Ave San Bernardino (92415) *(P-14558)*
San Brnrdino Cy Unfied Schl Ds .... D 909 881-8000
   1257 Northpark Blvd San Bernardino (92407) *(P-17318)*
San Bruno Skilled Nursing, San Bruno *Also Called: San Brunoidence Opco LLC (P-16377)*
San Brunoidence Opco LLC .... D 650 583-7768
   890 El Camino Real San Bruno (94066) *(P-16377)*
San Dego Chrstn Foundation Inc .... D 858 273-1306
   4282 Balboa Ave Ofc San Diego (92117) *(P-19026)*
San Dego Cnty Rgnal Arprt Auth (PA) .... C 619 400-2400
   3225 N Harbor Dr Fl 3 San Diego (92101) *(P-3909)*
San Dego Cnty Rgnal Arprt Auth .... D 619 400-2404
   2320 Stillwater Rd San Diego (92101) *(P-3910)*
San Dego Cnvntion Ctr Corp Inc (PA) .... B 619 782-4388
   111 W Harbor Dr San Diego (92101) *(P-13459)*
San Dego Ctr For Chldren Fndti (PA) .... D 858 277-9550
   3002 Armstrong St San Diego (92111) *(P-15894)*
San Dego Pthlgsts Med Group In .... C 619 297-4012
   7592 Metropolitan Dr Ste 406 San Diego (92108) *(P-15037)*
San Dego Repertory Theatre Inc .... D 619 231-3586
   79 Horton Plz San Diego (92101) *(P-14063)*
San Dego Soc of Ntural History .... D 619 232-3821
   1788 El Prado San Diego (92101) *(P-18668)*
San Dego Spt Mdcine Fmly Hlth .... D 619 229-3909
   6699 Alvarado Rd Ste 2100 San Diego (92120) *(P-15038)*
San Dego Symphony Orchestra Ass .... C 619 235-0800
   1245 7th Ave San Diego (92101) *(P-14102)*
San Dg-Mprial Cnties Dvlpmntal (PA) .... B 858 576-2996
   4355 Ruffin Rd Ste 220 San Diego (92123) *(P-18111)*
San Diego Air & Space Museum .... D 619 234-8291
   2001 Pan American Plz San Diego (92101) *(P-18669)*
San Diego Assn Governments (PA) .... C 619 699-1900
   401 B St Ste 800 San Diego (92101) *(P-18720)*

San Diego Blood Bank — ALPHABETIC SECTION

San Diego Blood Bank (PA) .... C...... 619 400-8132
3636 Gateway Center Ave Ste 100 San Diego (92102) *(P-17319)*

San Diego Blood Bnk Foundation, San Diego *Also Called: San Diego Blood Bank (P-17319)*

San Diego Cash Register Co Inc .... D....... 858 790-7327
7940 Arjons Dr San Diego (92126) *(P-5255)*

San Diego City College, San Diego *Also Called: San Diego Cmnty College Dst (P-17786)*

San Diego Cmnty College Dst .... C...... 619 388-4850
1960 National Ave San Diego (92113) *(P-17746)*

San Diego Cmnty College Dst .... D...... 619 388-3453
1313 Twelfth Ave San Diego (92101) *(P-17786)*

San Diego Cmnty College Dst .... A...... 619 388-2600
7250 Mesa College Dr San Diego (92111) *(P-17787)*

San Diego Composites Inc .... D...... 858 751-0450
9220 Activity Rd Ste 100 San Diego (92126) *(P-19381)*

San Diego Country Club Inc .... C...... 619 422-8895
88 L St Chula Vista (91911) *(P-14436)*

San Diego Country Estates Assn .... C...... 760 789-3788
24157 San Vicente Rd Ramona (92065) *(P-18904)*

San Diego County Credit Union (PA) .... C...... 877 732-2848
6545 Sequence Dr San Diego (92121) *(P-7796)*

San Diego County Water Auth (PA) .... D...... 858 522-6600
4677 Overland Ave San Diego (92123) *(P-4822)*

San Diego County Water Auth .... C...... 760 480-1991
610 W 5th Ave Escondido (92025) *(P-4823)*

San Diego Daily Transcript .... D...... 619 232-4381
34 Emerald Gln Laguna Niguel (92677) *(P-2511)*

San Diego Data Processing Corporation Inc .... A...... 858 581-9600
202 C St 3rd Fl San Diego (92101) *(P-12621)*

San Diego District Office, San Diego *Also Called: State Compensation Insur Fund (P-8412)*

San Diego Elec Training Tr .... D...... 858 569-6633
4675 Viewridge Ave San Diego (92123) *(P-17796)*

SAN DIEGO ELECTRICAL JATC, San Diego *Also Called: San Diego Elec Training Tr (P-17796)*

San Diego Family Care .... D...... 858 279-9676
4388 Thorn St San Diego (92105) *(P-15039)*

San Diego Family Care (PA) .... D...... 858 279-0925
6973 Linda Vista Rd San Diego (92111) *(P-15040)*

San Diego Family Care .... D...... 619 563-0250
4290 Polk Ave San Diego (92105) *(P-15041)*

San Diego Farah Partners LP .... D...... 619 239-2261
1430 7th Ave Ste B San Diego (92101) *(P-10194)*

San Diego Farms LLC .... C...... 760 736-4072
570 Quarry Rd San Marcos (92069) *(P-197)*

San Diego Gas & Electric Co .... C...... 858 547-2086
6875c Consolidated Way San Diego (92121) *(P-3751)*

San Diego Gas & Electric Co .... B...... 760 432-2508
2300 Haveson Pl Escondido (92029) *(P-4667)*

San Diego Gas & Electric Co .... B...... 858 654-6377
5488 Overland Ave San Diego (92123) *(P-4668)*

San Diego Gas & Electric Co .... C...... 858 613-3216
10975 Technology Pl San Diego (92127) *(P-4669)*

San Diego Gas & Electric Co .... D...... 858 654-1289
8306 Century Park Ct # Cp42c San Diego (92123) *(P-4670)*

San Diego Gas & Electric Co .... B...... 619 441-3834
104 N Johnson Ave El Cajon (92020) *(P-4671)*

San Diego Gas & Electric Co .... C...... 619 696-2000
1801 S Atlantic Blvd Monterey Park (91754) *(P-4672)*

San Diego Gas & Electric Co .... C...... 619 699-1018
701 33rd St San Diego (92102) *(P-4673)*

San Diego Gas & Electric Co .... C...... 858 541-5920
5488 Overland Ave San Diego (92123) *(P-4674)*

San Diego Gas & Electric Co .... D...... 800 411-7343
990 Bay Blvd Chula Vista (91911) *(P-4720)*

San Diego Gas & Electric Co .... C...... 951 243-2241
14601 Virginia St Moreno Valley (92555) *(P-4725)*

San Diego Gas & Electric Co (DH) .... B...... 619 696-2000
8330 Century Park Ct San Diego (92123) *(P-4751)*

San Diego Gas & Electric Co .... C...... 866 616-5565
8315 Century Park Ct Ste Cp-21d San Diego (92123) *(P-4752)*

San Diego Gas & Electric Co .... C...... 949 361-8090
662 Camino De Los Mares San Clemente (92673) *(P-4753)*

San Diego Gas & Electric Co .... C...... 760 438-6200
5016 Carlsbad Blvd Carlsbad (92008) *(P-4761)*

San Diego Gas & Electric Co .... C...... 858 654-1135
436 H St Chula Vista (91910) *(P-4762)*

San Diego Gulls Hockey CLB LLC .... D...... 619 359-4700
7676 Hazard Center Dr Ste 1075 San Diego (92108) *(P-14559)*

San Diego Hebrew Homes (PA) .... C...... 760 942-2695
211 Saxony Rd Encinitas (92024) *(P-15651)*

San Diego Home Seller Inc .... D...... 619 909-6345
4304 Ridgeway Dr San Diego (92116) *(P-11900)*

San Diego Hospice & Palliative, San Diego *Also Called: San Diego Hospice & Palliative Care Corporation (P-16923)*

San Diego Hospice & Palliative Care Corporation .... A...... 619 688-1600
4311 3rd Ave San Diego (92103) *(P-16923)*

San Diego Hotel Company LLC .... C...... 619 696-0234
660 K St San Diego (92101) *(P-10195)*

San Diego Humane Soc & Spca .... D...... 619 299-7012
5500 Gaines St San Diego (92110) *(P-19101)*

San Diego Lessee LLC .... D...... 619 297-5466
7450 Hazard Center Dr San Diego (92108) *(P-10196)*

San Diego Marriott Mission Vly, San Diego *Also Called: Ws Mmv Hotel LLC (P-10382)*

San Diego Mesa College, San Diego *Also Called: San Diego Cmnty College Dst (P-17787)*

San Diego Metro Trnst Sys .... A...... 619 231-1466
1255 Imperial Ave Ste 1000 San Diego (92101) *(P-3195)*

San Diego Metro Trnst Sys, San Diego *Also Called: San Diego Transit Corporation (P-3196)*

San Diego Mission Bay Resorts .... D...... 619 677-1161
1775 E Mission Bay Dr San Diego (92109) *(P-10197)*

San Diego Museum of Art .... D...... 619 696-1909
1450 El Prado San Diego (92101) *(P-18670)*

SAN DIEGO NATURAL HISTORY MUSE, San Diego *Also Called: San Dego Soc of Ntural History (P-18668)*

San Diego of San Diego .... D...... 760 710-2242
2251 Las Palmas Dr Carlsbad (92011) *(P-13460)*

San Diego Opera Association .... C...... 619 232-5911
3074 Commercial St San Diego (92113) *(P-14064)*

San Diego Opera Association .... C...... 619 232-5911
3064 Commercial St San Diego (92113) *(P-14065)*

San Diego Padres, San Diego *Also Called: California Sportservice Inc (P-14131)*

San Diego Padres, San Diego *Also Called: Padres LP (P-14153)*

San Diego Pro Staffing .... D...... 858 731-3116
591 Camino De La Reina Ste 1020 San Diego (92108) *(P-11328)*

San Diego Psychiatric Hospital, San Diego *Also Called: Choices (P-17028)*

San Diego Rescue Mission Inc (PA) .... D...... 619 819-1880
299 17th St San Diego (92101) *(P-18621)*

San Diego Saturn Retailers Inc .... D...... 858 373-3001
9985 Huennekens St San Diego (92121) *(P-13648)*

San Diego Services LLC .... C...... 858 654-0102
5415 Oberlin Dr San Diego (92121) *(P-19382)*

San Diego Sheraton Corporation .... C...... 619 291-6400
1590 Harbor Island Dr San Diego (92101) *(P-10198)*

San Diego State Aztecs, San Diego *Also Called: San Diego State University (P-14437)*

San Diego State University .... C...... 619 594-4263
5302 55th St San Diego (92182) *(P-14437)*

San Diego State University .... D...... 619 594-1515
5200 Campanile Dr San Diego (92182) *(P-17767)*

San Diego Supercomputer Center, La Jolla *Also Called: University Cal San Diego (P-12639)*

San Diego Symphony Foundation .... C...... 619 235-0800
1245 7th Ave San Diego (92101) *(P-14103)*

San Diego Theatres Inc .... C...... 619 615-4007
233 A St Ste 900 San Diego (92101) *(P-8755)*

San Diego Transit Corporation (PA) .... A...... 619 238-0100
100 16th St San Diego (92101) *(P-3196)*

San Diego Trolley Inc .... B...... 619 595-4933
1341 Commercial St San Diego (92113) *(P-3197)*

SAN DIEGO TROLLEY INC, San Diego *Also Called: San Diego Trolley Inc (P-3197)*

San Diego Unified Hbr Police, San Diego *Also Called: San Diego Unified Port Dst (P-20930)*

San Diego Unified Port Dst .... C...... 619 686-6200
1400 Tidelands Ave National City (91950) *(P-3816)*

San Diego Unified Port Dst (PA) .... C...... 619 686-6200
3165 Pacific Hwy San Diego (92101) *(P-3817)*

ALPHABETIC SECTION — San Joaquin Country Club

San Diego Unified Port Dst .... C....... 619 686-6585
  3380 N Harbor Dr San Diego (92101) *(P-20930)*
San Diego Union Tribune, The, San Diego *Also Called: San Diego Union-Tribune LLC* *(P-2542)*
San Diego Union-Tribune LLC *(PA)* .... A....... 619 299-3131
  600 B St Ste 1201 San Diego (92101) *(P-2542)*
San Diego V Inc *(PA)* .... D....... 888 308-2260
  5350 Kearny Mesa Rd San Diego (92111) *(P-7293)*
San Diego Volvo, San Diego *Also Called: San Diego V Inc (P-7293)*
San Diego Wild Animal Park, Escondido *Also Called: Zoological Society San Diego (P-18696)*
San Diego Zoo, San Diego *Also Called: Zoological Society San Diego (P-18695)*
San Diego Zoo, San Diego *Also Called: Zoological Society San Diego (P-18697)*
San Diego Zoo Wildlife Aliance, San Diego *Also Called: Zoological Society San Diego* *(P-18698)*
San Dimas Community Hospital, San Dimas *Also Called: Prime Hlthcare Svcs - San Dmas* *(P-16341)*
San Dimas Community Hospital, San Dimas *Also Called: Prime Health Care (P-18350)*
San Dimas Medical Group Inc .... D....... 661 663-4800
  100 Old River Rd Bakersfield (93311) *(P-15042)*
San Dimas Retirement Center *(PA)* .... D....... 909 599-8441
  834 W Arrow Hwy San Dimas (91773) *(P-8859)*
San Fernando City of Inc .... D....... 818 832-2400
  10605 Balboa Blvd Ste 100 Granada Hills (91344) *(P-17124)*
San Fernando Juvenile Hall, Sylmar *Also Called: County of Los Angeles (P-18403)*
San Fernando Valley Auto LLC .... C....... 818 832-1600
  18600 Devonshire St Northridge (91325) *(P-7294)*
San Francisco 49ers, Santa Clara *Also Called: Forty Niners Football Co LLC (P-14137)*
San Francisco Aids Foundation *(PA)* .... D....... 415 487-3000
  1035 Market St Ste 400 San Francisco (94103) *(P-18112)*
San Francisco Art Institute Inc .... C....... 415 771-7020
  800 Chestnut St San Francisco (94133) *(P-17768)*
San Francisco Ballet, San Francisco *Also Called: San Francisco Ballet Assn (P-14066)*
San Francisco Ballet Assn .... C....... 415 865-2000
  455 Franklin St San Francisco (94102) *(P-14066)*
San Francisco Baseball Associates LLC *(PA)* .... A....... 415 972-2000
  24 Willie Mays Plz San Francisco (94107) *(P-14156)*
San Francisco Bay Area Rapid .... A....... 510 286-2893
  601 E 8th St Oakland (94606) *(P-3198)*
San Francisco Federal Cr Un *(PA)* .... D....... 415 775-5377
  770 Golden Gate Ave San Francisco (94102) *(P-7797)*
San Francisco Food Bank .... D....... 415 282-1900
  900 Pennsylvania Ave San Francisco (94107) *(P-18113)*
San Francisco Forty Niners *(PA)* .... C....... 408 562-4949
  4949 Marie P Debartolo Way Santa Clara (95054) *(P-14157)*
San Francisco Foundation .... D....... 415 733-8500
  1 Embarcadero Ctr Ste 1400 San Francisco (94111) *(P-13461)*
San Francisco General Hospital, San Francisco *Also Called: Gastroenterology Division* *(P-14761)*
San Francisco General Hospital, San Francisco *Also Called: City & County San Francisco* *(P-16002)*
San Francisco General Hospital, San Francisco *Also Called: University Cal San Francisco* *(P-16660)*
San Francisco Giants, San Francisco *Also Called: San Francisco Baseball Associates LLC* *(P-14156)*
San Francisco Health Authority *(PA)* .... D....... 415 615-4407
  50 Beale St Fl 12 San Francisco (94105) *(P-18760)*
San Francisco Herb & Natural Food Co Inc .... D....... 510 770-1215
  47444 Kato Rd Fremont (94538) *(P-6664)*
San Francisco Herb Tea & Spice, Fremont *Also Called: San Francisco Herb & Natural Food Co Inc (P-6664)*
San Francisco Hilton & Towers, San Francisco *Also Called: Park Hotels & Resorts Inc* *(P-10103)*
San Francisco Hotel Group LLC .... D....... 415 276-9888
  222 Sansome St San Francisco (94104) *(P-10199)*
San Francisco Museum Modrn Art *(PA)* .... B....... 415 357-4035
  151 3rd St San Francisco (94103) *(P-18671)*
San Francisco Opera Assn .... A....... 415 861-4008
  301 Van Ness Ave San Francisco (94102) *(P-14067)*
San Francisco Parking Inc .... A....... 415 495-3909
  325 5th St San Francisco (94107) *(P-13628)*
San Francisco Post Acute, San Francisco *Also Called: San Franciscoidence Opco LLC* *(P-15895)*
San Francisco Radio Assets LLC (DH) .... C....... 415 216-1300
  750 Battery St Fl 2 San Francisco (94111) *(P-4403)*
SAN FRANCISCO RESIDENTIAL CARE, San Francisco *Also Called: Self-Help For Elderly* *(P-18122)*
San Francisco Spca .... D....... 415 554-3000
  2500 26th Ave San Francisco (94116) *(P-19102)*
SAN FRANCISCO SPCA, San Francisco *Also Called: San Frncsco Soc For The Prvnti* *(P-19103)*
San Francisco Sport and Spine .... C....... 415 861-1856
  2191 Market St Ste C San Francisco (94114) *(P-15306)*
San Francisco Symphony *(PA)* .... C....... 415 552-8000
  201 Van Ness Ave San Francisco (94103) *(P-14104)*
San Francisco Travel Assn .... D....... 415 974-6900
  1 Front St Ste 2900 San Francisco (94111) *(P-13462)*
San Francisco Unified Schl Dst *(PA)* .... C....... 415 241-6000
  555 Franklin St San Francisco (94102) *(P-17747)*
San Francisco Vamc, San Francisco *Also Called: Veterans Health Administration (P-15189)*
San Francisco Zoo, San Francisco *Also Called: San Francisco Zoological Soc (P-14560)*
San Francisco Zoological Soc .... C....... 415 753-7080
  1 Zoo Rd San Francisco (94132) *(P-14560)*
San Franciscoidence Opco LLC .... D....... 415 584-3294
  5767 Mission St San Francisco (94112) *(P-15895)*
San Frncisco Staffing Staffing, Emeryville *Also Called: Maxim Healthcare Services Inc* *(P-11303)*
San Frncsco Bay Area Rpid Trns *(PA)* .... B....... 510 464-6000
  2150 Webster St Oakland (94612) *(P-3199)*
San Frncsco Bay Cmpssnate Cmnt, San Francisco *Also Called: Charolais Care V Inc* *(P-16839)*
San Frncsco Cmnty Clnic Cnsrti .... D....... 415 355-2222
  170c Capp St San Francisco (94110) *(P-20199)*
San Frncsco Cnservatory of Mus *(PA)* .... C....... 415 864-7326
  50 Oak St San Francisco (94102) *(P-17815)*
San Frncsco Ldies Prtction Rli .... C....... 415 931-3136
  3400 Laguna St San Francisco (94123) *(P-18519)*
San Frncsco Prtclar Cncil of T .... D....... 415 255-3525
  525 5th St San Francisco (94107) *(P-18114)*
San Frncsco Soc For The Prvnti .... C....... 415 554-3000
  201 Alabama St San Francisco (94103) *(P-19103)*
San Gabriel Convalescent Ctr, Rosemead *Also Called: Longwood Management Corp* *(P-15552)*
San Gabriel Country Club .... D....... 626 287-9671
  350 E Hermosa Dr San Gabriel (91775) *(P-14438)*
San Gabriel Transit Inc *(PA)* .... C....... 626 258-1310
  3650 Rockwell Ave El Monte (91731) *(P-3200)*
San Gabriel Valley Cab Co, El Monte *Also Called: San Gabriel Transit Inc (P-3200)*
San Gabriel Valley Medical Ctr .... A....... 626 289-5454
  438 W Las Tunas Dr San Gabriel (91776) *(P-16378)*
San Gabriel Valley Water Assn .... D....... 626 815-1305
  725 N Azusa Ave Azusa (91702) *(P-4824)*
San Gabriel Valley Water Co *(PA)* .... C....... 626 448-6183
  11142 Garvey Ave El Monte (91733) *(P-4825)*
San Gabriel Valley Water Co .... C....... 909 822-2201
  8440 Nuevo Ave Fontana (92335) *(P-4826)*
SAN GABRIEL/POMONA REGIONAL CE, Pomona *Also Called: San Gbrl/Pmona Vlleys Dvlpmnta (P-18115)*
San Gbriel Ambltory Srgery Ctr .... C....... 626 300-5300
  207 S Santa Anita St Ste G16 San Gabriel (91776) *(P-15043)*
San Gbrl/Pmona Vlleys Dvlpmnta .... B....... 909 620-7722
  75 Rancho Camino Dr Pomona (91766) *(P-18115)*
San Gorgonio Memorial Hospital .... A....... 951 845-1121
  600 N Highland Springs Ave Banning (92220) *(P-16379)*
San Grgnio Mem Hosp Foundation *(PA)* .... C....... 951 845-1121
  600 N Highland Springs Ave Banning (92220) *(P-16380)*
San Jacinto Healthcare, Hemet *Also Called: Miramonte Enterprises LLC (P-15586)*
San Jerardo Migrant, Salinas *Also Called: Community Action Prtnr San Lui (P-18296)*
San Joaquin Cnty Aging & Commu .... C....... 209 468-9455
  102 S San Joaquin St Stockton (95202) *(P-18116)*
San Joaquin Community Hospital *(PA)* .... A....... 661 395-3000
  2615 Chester Ave Bakersfield (93301) *(P-16381)*
San Joaquin Country Club .... D....... 559 439-3483
  3484 W Bluff Ave Fresno (93711) *(P-14439)*

Employee Codes: A=Over 500 employees, B=251-500
C=101-250, D=51-100, E=20-50, F=10-19, G=1-9

San Joaquin Gardens, Fresno *Also Called: Humangood Norcal* *(P-18453)*
  San Joaquin General Hospital .... B....... 209 468-6000
  500 W Hospital Rd French Camp (95231) *(P-16382)*
  San Joaquin Regional Trnst Dst .... C....... 209 948-5566
  421 E Weber Ave Stockton (95202) *(P-3201)*
SAN JOAQUIN VALLEY REHABILITATION HOSPITAL, A DELAWARE LIMITED PARTNERSHIP, Oakhurst *Also Called: San Jquin Vly Rhbltion Hosp A (P-15307)*
  San Jose Arena Management LLC .... D....... 408 279-6000
  1500 S 10th St San Jose (95112) *(P-14561)*
  San Jose Arena Management LLC .... D....... 408 287-7070
  44388 Old Warm Springs Blvd Fremont (94538) *(P-20200)*
  San Jose Bluprt Svc & Sup Co .... C....... 408 295-5770
  821 Martin Ave Santa Clara (95050) *(P-7593)*
  San Jose Chld Discovery Museum 408 298-5437
  180 Woz Way San Jose (95110) *(P-18672)*
  San Jose Conservation Corps .... D....... 408 283-7171
  2650 Senter Rd San Jose (95111) *(P-18247)*
  San Jose Construction Co Inc .... D....... 408 986-8711
  1210 Coleman Ave Santa Clara (95050) *(P-1018)*
  San Jose Country Club .... D....... 408 258-4901
  15571 Alum Rock Ave San Jose (95127) *(P-14440)*
San Jose District Office, Sacramento *Also Called: State Compensation Insur Fund (P-8411)*
SAN JOSE EARTHQUAKES, Santa Clara *Also Called: San Jose Earthquakes MGT LLC (P-20201)*
  San Jose Earthquakes MGT LLC .... C....... 408 556-7700
  451 El Camino Real Ste 220 Santa Clara (95050) *(P-20201)*
  San Jose Fairmont Lessee LLC .... B....... 408 998-1900
  170 S Market St Lbby San Jose (95113) *(P-10200)*
San Jose Fthill Fmly Cmnty Cln, San Jose *Also Called: Foothill Health Center Inc (P-14752)*
  San Jose Healthcare System LP .... A....... 408 259-5000
  225 N Jackson Ave San Jose (95116) *(P-16383)*
  San Jose Lessee LLC .... D....... 408 453-4000
  2050 Gateway Pl San Jose (95110) *(P-10201)*
San Jose Medical Group / MGT, Woodland Hills *Also Called: Verity Medical Foundation (P-15186)*
San Jose Mini Golf Course, San Jose *Also Called: City of San Jose (P-14252)*
  San Jose Museum of Art Assn .... D....... 408 271-6840
  110 S Market St San Jose (95113) *(P-18673)*
San Jose Office, Santa Clara *Also Called: McCarthy Bldg Companies Inc (P-963)*
  San Jose Redevelopment Agency .... C....... 408 535-8500
  200 E Santa Clara St 14th Fl San Jose (95113) *(P-20845)*
  San Jose Sharks LLC (PA) .... C....... 408 999-6810
  525 W Santa Clara St San Jose (95113) *(P-14158)*
  San Jose Unified School Dst .... D....... 408 535-6200
  2222 Unified Way San Jose (95125) *(P-10957)*
  San Jose Water Company (HQ) .... C....... 408 288-5314
  110 W Taylor St San Jose (95110) *(P-4827)*
  San Jose Water Company .... C....... 408 298-0364
  1221 S Bascom Ave San Jose (95128) *(P-4828)*
  San Jquin Gen Hosp Fndtion A C .... A....... 209 468-6000
  500 W Hospital Rd French Camp (95231) *(P-16384)*
San Jquin Nrsing Rhblttion Ctr, Bakersfield *Also Called: Kern Valleyidence Opco LLC (P-15767)*
  San Jquin Vly Rhbltion Hosp A .... C....... 559 658-6490
  40232 Junction Dr Oakhurst (93644) *(P-15307)*
  San Jquin Vly Rhbltion Hosp A (HQ) .... B....... 559 436-3600
  7173 N Sharon Ave Fresno (93720) *(P-17125)*
  San Jquin Vly Unfied A Plition (PA) .... C....... 559 230-6000
  1990 E Gettysburg Ave Fresno (93726) *(P-20846)*
  San Juan Oaks LLC .... D....... 831 636-6113
  3825 Union Rd Hollister (95023) *(P-14286)*
San Juan Oaks Golf Club, Hollister *Also Called: San Juan Oaks LLC (P-14286)*
San Leandro Healthcare Center, San Leandro *Also Called: San Leandro Hlth Care Ctr Inc (P-15652)*
  San Leandro Hlth Care Ctr Inc .... D....... 510 357-4015
  368 Juana Ave San Leandro (94577) *(P-15652)*
  San Leandro Hospital LP .... B....... 510 357-6500
  13855 E 14th St San Leandro (94578) *(P-16385)*
San Lorenzo Village Shopg Ctr, San Mateo *Also Called: David D Bohannon Organization (P-8714)*
  San Luis Ambulance Service Inc .... C....... 805 543-2626
  3546 S Higuera St San Luis Obispo (93401) *(P-3294)*

San Luis Care Center, Newman *Also Called: Avalon Care Ctr - Newman LLC (P-15343)*
  San Luis Obispo County YMCA .... D....... 805 544-7225
  5785 Los Ranchos Rd San Luis Obispo (93401) *(P-18905)*
  San Luis Obispo Golf Cntry CLB .... C....... 805 543-3400
  255 Country Club Dr San Luis Obispo (93401) *(P-14441)*
  San Luis Obspo Rgnal Trnst Aut .... D....... 805 781-4465
  253 Elks Ln San Luis Obispo (93401) *(P-3202)*
  San Manuel Entertainment Auth (PA) .... A....... 909 864-5050
  777 San Manuel Blvd Highland (92346) *(P-14562)*
San Manuel Fire Dept, Highland *Also Called: San Mnuel Band Mission Indians (P-13463)*
San Marcos Mechanical, Vista *Also Called: Industrial Coml Systems Inc (P-1462)*
  San Mateo County Transit Dst (PA) .... C....... 650 508-6200
  1250 San Carlos Ave San Carlos (94070) *(P-3203)*
  San Mateo County Transit Dst .... B....... 650 588-4860
  301 N Access Rd South San Francisco (94080) *(P-3204)*
  San Mateo County Transit Dst .... C....... 650 508-6412
  501 Pico Blvd San Carlos (94070) *(P-3358)*
  San Mateo Credit Union .... D....... 650 363-1725
  525 Middlefield Rd Redwood City (94063) *(P-7798)*
  San Mateo Credit Union .... C....... 650 363-1725
  1515 S El Camino Real Ste 100 San Mateo (94402) *(P-7799)*
  San Mateo Health Commission .... C....... 650 616-0050
  801 Gateway Blvd Ste 100 South San Francisco (94080) *(P-17320)*
San Mateo Marriott, San Mateo *Also Called: Atrium Plaza LLC (P-9621)*
San Mateo Medical Center, San Mateo *Also Called: County of San Mateo (P-14717)*
San Mateo Staffing, San Mateo *Also Called: Maxim Healthcare Services Inc (P-11306)*
  San Miguel Produce Inc .... B....... 805 488-0981
  600 E Hueneme Rd Oxnard (93033) *(P-39)*
San Miguel Villa, Concord *Also Called: Tranquility Incorporated (P-15904)*
  San Mnuel Band Mission Indians .... C....... 909 425-4682
  101 Pure Water Ln Highland (92346) *(P-7860)*
  San Mnuel Band Mission Indians .... C....... 909 864-6928
  26540 Indian Service Rd Highland (92346) *(P-13463)*
San Onofre Child Care Center, Camp Pendleton *Also Called: Marine Corps Community Svcs (P-18331)*
  San Pedro Convalescent HM Inc .... D....... 310 832-6431
  1430 W 6th St San Pedro (90732) *(P-15653)*
  San Pedro Peninsula Hospital .... A....... 310 832-3311
  1300 W 7th St San Pedro (90732) *(P-16386)*
  San Psqual Band Mssion Indians .... C....... 760 291-5500
  16300 Nyemii Pass Rd Valley Center (92082) *(P-10202)*
  San Psqual Band Mssion Indians (PA) .... D....... 760 749-3200
  16400 Kumeyaay Way Valley Center (92082) *(P-20919)*
  San Rafael Rock Quarry Inc (HQ) .... D....... 415 459-7740
  2350 Kerner Blvd Ste 200 San Rafael (94901) *(P-635)*
  San Ramon Regional Med Ctr LLC .... A....... 925 275-9200
  6001 Norris Canyon Rd San Ramon (94583) *(P-16387)*
  San Ramon Vly Unified Schl Dst .... D....... 925 552-2880
  3131 Stone Valley Rd Danville (94526) *(P-17748)*
SAN TOMAS CONVALESCENT HOSPITA, San Jose *Also Called: Aquinas Corporation (P-15330)*
San Val Alarm System, Thousand Palms *Also Called: San Val Corp (P-460)*
  San Val Corp (PA) .... B....... 760 346-3999
  72203 Adelaid St Thousand Palms (92276) *(P-460)*
SAN VICENTE INN & GOLF CLUB, Ramona *Also Called: San Diego Country Estates Assn (P-18904)*
  San Ysidro Bb Property LLC .... C....... 805 368-6788
  900 San Ysidro Ln Santa Barbara (93108) *(P-10203)*
San Ysidro Health, San Diego *Also Called: Centro De Salud De La Comuni (P-17024)*
  San-Mar Construction Co Inc .... C....... 714 693-5400
  4875 E La Palma Ave Ste 602 Anaheim (92807) *(P-1019)*
SANBAG, San Bernardino *Also Called: San Bernardino Cnty Trnsp Auth (P-3194)*
  Sanborn Chevrolet Inc .... D....... 209 334-5000
  1210 S Cherokee Ln Lodi (95240) *(P-7295)*
Sanborn Collison Center, Lodi *Also Called: Sanborn Chevrolet Inc (P-7295)*
  Sanci Marriott Hotels .... D....... 619 435-3000
  2000 2nd St Coronado (92118) *(P-10204)*
Sanctuary Spa, San Diego *Also Called: Bay Clubs Company LLC (P-14334)*
Sanctuary, The, Redwood City *Also Called: Bay Clubs Company LLC (P-14179)*
  Sand Canyon Corporation (HQ) .... D....... 949 727-9425
  7595 Irvine Center Dr Ste 120 Irvine (92618) *(P-8055)*

ALPHABETIC SECTION — SANTA CLARA, COUNTY OF

Sandbox Vr Mission Valley LLC .... D....... 323 207-0840
   4695 Chabot Dr Ste 200 Pleasanton (94588) *(P-11901)*

Sander Langston LP .... C....... 949 863-9200
   17962 Cowan Irvine (92614) *(P-1020)*

Sanderlings, Aptos *Also Called: Seascape Rsort Ltd A Cal Ltd P (P-10215)*

Sanders & Wohrman Corporation .... C....... 714 919-0446
   709 N Poplar St Orange (92868) *(P-1640)*

Sanders Contracting Inc .... D....... 925 308-7305
   Byron (94514) *(P-1021)*

Sandis, Campbell *Also Called: Sandis Cvil Engners Srvyors Pl (P-19527)*

Sandis Cvil Engners Srvyors Pl (PA) .... D....... 408 636-0900
   1700 Winchester Blvd Ste 200 Campbell (95008) *(P-19527)*

Sandm San Diego Mrriott Del Mar .... A....... 858 523-1700
   11966 El Camino Real San Diego (92130) *(P-10205)*

Sands Rv Resort, San Rafael *Also Called: R C Roberts & Co (P-8881)*

Sanford Brnham Prbys Med Dscve (PA) .... A....... 858 795-5000
   10901 N Torrey Pines Rd La Jolla (92037) *(P-19908)*

Sangera Buick Inc .... D....... 661 833-5200
   5600 Gasoline Alley Dr Bakersfield (93313) *(P-13674)*

Sanhyd Inc .... D....... 510 483-6200
   524 Callan Ave San Leandro (94577) *(P-15896)*

Sanitec Industries Inc .... D....... 818 523-1942
   10700 Sherman Way Burbank (91505) *(P-4934)*

Sanittion Dstrcts Los Angles C .... A....... 562 908-4288
   1955 Workman Mill Rd Whittier (90601) *(P-4935)*

Sano, San Francisco *Also Called: Sano Intelligence Inc (P-11902)*

Sano Intelligence Inc .... C....... 408 483-6518
   1155 Bryant St San Francisco (94103) *(P-11902)*

Sansei Gardens Inc .... C....... 510 226-9191
   3250 Darby Cmn Fremont (94539) *(P-536)*

Sansum Clinic .... D....... 805 681-7500
   215 Pesetas Ln Santa Barbara (93110) *(P-7526)*

Sansum Clinic (PA) .... D....... 805 681-7700
   470 S Patterson Ave Santa Barbara (93111) *(P-15044)*

Santa Ana Country Club .... D....... 714 556-3000
   20382 Newport Blvd Santa Ana (92707) *(P-14442)*

Santa Ana Creek Development Company .... D....... 714 685-3462
   2288 N Batavia St Orange (92865) *(P-2155)*

Santa Ana District Office, Santa Ana *Also Called: State Compensation Insur Fund (P-8409)*

Santa Ana Job Training Program, Santa Ana *Also Called: City of Santa Ana (P-18221)*

Santa Anita Associates (PA) .... D....... 626 447-2764
   405 S Santa Anita Ave Arcadia (91006) *(P-14287)*

Santa Anita Cnvlscent Hosp Rtr .... C....... 626 579-0310
   5522 Gracewood Ave Temple City (91780) *(P-15654)*

Santa Anita Golf Course, Arcadia *Also Called: Santa Anita Associates (P-14287)*

Santa Anita Park, Arcadia *Also Called: Los Angeles Turf Club Inc (P-14164)*

Santa Barbara City of .... D....... 805 962-6464
   1100 Anacapa St Dept 3 Santa Barbara (93101) *(P-3967)*

Santa Barbara Adventure Co .... D....... 805 884-9283
   32 E Haley St Santa Barbara (93101) *(P-3968)*

Santa Barbara Airbus .... D....... 805 964-7759
   750 Technology Dr Goleta (93117) *(P-13593)*

Santa Barbara Cnty Social Svcs, Santa Maria *Also Called: Santa Brbara Cttage Hosp Fndti (P-16390)*

Santa Barbara Cottage Hospital .... B....... 805 569-7367
   400 W Pueblo St Santa Barbara (93105) *(P-16388)*

Santa Barbara Family YMCA, Santa Barbara *Also Called: Channel Islnds Yung MNS Chrstn (P-18837)*

Santa Barbara Farms LLC (PA) .... D....... 805 736-9776
   1200 Union Sugar Ave Lompoc (93436) *(P-40)*

Santa Barbara Farms LLC .... C....... 805 736-5608
   1105 Union Sugar Ave Lompoc (93436) *(P-41)*

Santa Barbara Group, Santa Barbara *Also Called: Tecolote Research Inc (P-20580)*

Santa Barbara Inn, Santa Barbara *Also Called: Interstate Hotels Resorts Inc (P-9913)*

Santa Barbara Metro Trnst Dst (PA) .... D....... 805 963-3364
   550 Olive St Santa Barbara (93101) *(P-3205)*

Santa Barbara Museum of Art (PA) .... D....... 805 963-4364
   1130 State St Santa Barbara (93101) *(P-18674)*

Santa Barbara Transportation, Visalia *Also Called: Santa Barbara Trnsp Corp (P-3350)*

Santa Barbara Trnsp Corp .... D....... 661 259-7285
   26501 Ruether Ave Santa Clarita (91350) *(P-3309)*

Santa Barbara Trnsp Corp .... C....... 661 510-0566
   42138 7th St W Lancaster (93534) *(P-3349)*

Santa Barbara Trnsp Corp .... C....... 559 738-5780
   1131 E Houston Ave Visalia (93292) *(P-3350)*

Santa Barbara Trnsp Corp .... C....... 760 746-0850
   520 Gannon Pl Escondido (92025) *(P-3351)*

Santa Barbara Trnsp Corp .... C....... 805 928-0402
   6500 Hollister Ave Ste 100 Goleta (93117) *(P-3352)*

Santa Barbara Wine Cntry Tours, Santa Barbara *Also Called: Santa Barbara Adventure Co (P-3968)*

SANTA BARBARA ZOO, Santa Barbara *Also Called: Santa Brbara Zlgcal Foundation (P-18694)*

Santa Brbara Artfl Kdney Ctr L .... D....... 805 682-9942
   1704 State St Santa Barbara (93101) *(P-16997)*

Santa Brbara Cmnty College Dst .... B....... 805 683-4191
   525 Anacapa St Santa Barbara (93101) *(P-17788)*

Santa Brbara Cnty Pub Hlth Dep .... D....... 805 739-8718
   220 S Palisade Dr Ste 104 Santa Maria (93454) *(P-15045)*

Santa Brbara Cttage Hosp Fndti .... B....... 805 569-7224
   400 W Pueblo St Santa Barbara (93105) *(P-16389)*

Santa Brbara Cttage Hosp Fndti .... B....... 805 346-7135
   2125 Centerpointe Pkwy Santa Maria (93455) *(P-16390)*

Santa Brbara Cttage Hosp Fndti (HQ) .... C....... 805 682-7111
   400 W Pueblo St Santa Barbara (93105) *(P-16391)*

Santa Brbara Med Fndtion Clnic, Santa Barbara *Also Called: Sansum Clinic (P-7526)*

Santa Brbara Mseum Ntral Hstor .... D....... 805 682-4711
   2559 Puesta Del Sol Santa Barbara (93105) *(P-18675)*

Santa Brbara San Luis Obspo RG .... C....... 800 421-2560
   4050 Calle Real Santa Barbara (93110) *(P-8270)*

Santa Brbara Zlgcal Foundation .... C....... 805 962-1673
   500 Ninos Dr Santa Barbara (93103) *(P-18694)*

Santa Catalina Island Company (PA) .... C....... 310 510-2000
   4 Park Plz Ste 420 Irvine (92614) *(P-3969)*

Santa Clara County of .... D....... 408 793-6410
   2325 Enborg Ln San Jose (95128) *(P-13464)*

Santa Clara County of .... C....... 408 848-2000
   9400 No Name Uno Gilroy (95020) *(P-16392)*

Santa Clara County of .... C....... 408 362-9817
   6201 San Ignacio Ave San Jose (95119) *(P-17321)*

Santa Clara Cnty Frgrnds MGT C .... D....... 408 494-3100
   344 Tully Rd San Jose (95111) *(P-14563)*

Santa Clara Convention Center .... D....... 408 748-7000
   5001 Great America Pkwy Santa Clara (95054) *(P-13465)*

SANTA CLARA COUNTY FMC, San Jose *Also Called: Santa Clara Cnty Frgrnds MGT C (P-14563)*

Santa Clara Family Health, San Jose *Also Called: Santa Clara County of (P-17321)*

Santa Clara Travelodge .... D....... 408 984-3364
   3477 El Camino Real Santa Clara (95051) *(P-10206)*

Santa Clara Valley Corporation .... D....... 408 947-1100
   715 N 1st St Ste 27 San Jose (95112) *(P-10958)*

Santa Clara Valley Medical Ctr .... A....... 408 885-6300
   2400 Moorpark Ave San Jose (95128) *(P-15046)*

Santa Clara Valley Medical Ctr .... A....... 408 792-5586
   976 Lenzen Ave San Jose (95126) *(P-15047)*

Santa Clara Valley Medical Ctr .... A....... 408 885-5730
   2220 Moorpark Ave San Jose (95128) *(P-17322)*

Santa Clara Valley Trnsp Auth (PA) .... A....... 408 321-2300
   3331 N 1st St San Jose (95134) *(P-3206)*

Santa Clara Valley Trnsp Auth .... C....... 408 321-5559
   3331 N 1st St Bldg B San Jose (95134) *(P-3207)*

Santa Clara Valley Water Dst, San Jose *Also Called: Santa Clara Vly Wtr Dst Pub Fc (P-4829)*

Santa Clara Vly Hlth Hosp Syst, San Jose *Also Called: County of Santa Clara (P-16030)*

Santa Clara Vly Hlth Hosp Syst, San Jose *Also Called: County of Santa Clara (P-19558)*

Santa Clara Vly Wtr Dst Pub Fc (PA) .... C....... 408 265-2600
   5750 Almaden Expy San Jose (95118) *(P-4829)*

Santa Clara Vly Wtr Dst Pub Fc .... C....... 408 630-2560
   3959 Whitman Way San Jose (95132) *(P-4830)*

Santa Clara Vly Wtr Dst Pub Fc .... C....... 408 395-8121
   400 More Ave Los Gatos (95032) *(P-4831)*

Santa Clara Vta, San Jose *Also Called: Santa Clara Valley Trnsp Auth (P-3206)*

SANTA CLARA, COUNTY OF, San Jose *Also Called: Santa Clara County of (P-13464)*

SANTA CLARITA VALLEY SENIOR CE

SANTA CLARITA VALLEY SENIOR CE, Santa Clarita Also Called: Santa Clrita Vly Cmmttee On AG *(P-18117)*
Santa Clarita Valley Wtr Agcy .... C....... 661 259-2737
   26521 Summit Cir Santa Clarita (91350) *(P-4832)*
Santa Clarita Water Division, Santa Clarita Also Called: Santa Clarita Valley Wtr Agcy *(P-4832)*
Santa Clrita Hlth Care Assn In (PA) .... D....... 661 253-8000
   23845 Mcbean Pkwy Santa Clarita (91355) *(P-20202)*
Santa Clrita Vly Cmmttee On AG .... D....... 661 259-9444
   22900 Market St Santa Clarita (91321) *(P-18117)*
Santa Clrita Vly Wtr Agcy Fing .... C....... 661 259-2737
   27234 Bouquet Canyon Rd Santa Clarita (91350) *(P-4833)*
Santa Cruz Beach Boardwalk, Santa Cruz Also Called: Santa Cruz Seaside Company *(P-14312)*
Santa Cruz Medical Foundation (HQ) .... D....... 831 458-5537
   2025 Soquel Ave Santa Cruz (95062) *(P-15048)*
Santa Cruz Medical Foundation .... A....... 831 477-2325
   2900 Chanticleer Ave Santa Cruz (95065) *(P-15049)*
Santa Cruz Medical Foundation .... A....... 831 477-2375
   2915 Chanticleer Ave Santa Cruz (95065) *(P-16393)*
Santa Cruz Metro Trnst Dst .... C....... 831 429-5455
   138 Golf Club Dr Santa Cruz (95060) *(P-3208)*
Santa Cruz Metro Trnst Dst .... D....... 831 469-1954
   110 Vernon St Ste B Santa Cruz (95060) *(P-3209)*
Santa Cruz Metro Trnst Dst .... D....... 831 426-6080
   135 Aviation Way Ste 2 Watsonville (95076) *(P-3210)*
Santa Cruz Seaside Company .... A....... 831 427-3400
   201 W Cliff Dr Santa Cruz (95060) *(P-10207)*
Santa Cruz Seaside Company (PA) .... B....... 831 423-5590
   400 Beach St Santa Cruz (95060) *(P-14312)*
Santa Cruz Warriors .... D....... 831 466-3200
   903 Pacific Ave Ste 101 Santa Cruz (95060) *(P-14159)*
Santa Fe Middle School, Hemet Also Called: Hemet Unified School District *(P-17617)*
Santa Lucia Preserve, Carmel Also Called: Rancho San Carlos Partnership LP *(P-9272)*
Santa Lucia Preserve Company .... D....... 831 620-6760
   1 Rancho San Carlos Rd Carmel (93923) *(P-14443)*
Santa Margarita Water District .... C....... 949 459-6400
   26101 Antonio Pkwy Rcho Sta Marg (92688) *(P-4834)*
Santa Maria Tire Inc (PA) .... D....... 805 347-4793
   2170 Hutton Rd Bldg A Nipomo (93444) *(P-7356)*
Santa Maria Wisdom Center, Santa Maria Also Called: Life Steps Foundation Inc *(P-18041)*
Santa Monica City of .... B....... 310 458-1975
   1685 Main St Santa Monica (90401) *(P-3310)*
Santa Monica Amusements LLC .... B....... 310 451-9641
   380 Santa Monica Pier Santa Monica (90401) *(P-14313)*
Santa Monica Bay Physicians He (PA) .... D....... 310 417-5900
   5767 W Century Blvd Los Angeles (90045) *(P-15050)*
Santa Monica Hotel Owner LLC .... C....... 310 395-3332
   1707 4th St Santa Monica (90401) *(P-10208)*
Santa Monica Proper Hotel, Santa Monica Also Called: Santa Monica Proper Jv LLC *(P-10209)*
Santa Monica Proper Jv LLC .... C....... 310 620-9990
   700 Wilshire Blvd Santa Monica (90401) *(P-10209)*
Santa Monica Seafood, Rancho Dominguez Also Called: Santa Monica Seafood Company *(P-2423)*
Santa Monica Seafood Company (PA) .... D....... 310 886-7900
   18531 S Broadwick St Rancho Dominguez (90220) *(P-2423)*
Santa Monica Ucla Medical Ctr, Santa Monica Also Called: Regents of The University Cal *(P-17312)*
Santa Paula Hospital, Santa Paula Also Called: Ventura County Medical Center *(P-15182)*
Santa Rosa City of .... D....... 707 543-3882
   55 Stony Point Rd Santa Rosa (95401) *(P-13675)*
Santa Rosa Berry Farms LLC .... B....... 805 981-3060
   3500 Camino Ave Ste 250 Oxnard (93030) *(P-65)*
Santa Rosa District Office, Santa Rosa Also Called: State Compensation Insur Fund *(P-8414)*
Santa Rosa Indian Cmnty of Snt, Fresno Also Called: Rainbow - Brite Indus Svcs LLC *(P-10952)*
Santa Rosa Jet Center, Santa Rosa Also Called: Kaiserair Inc *(P-3896)*
Santa Rosa Memorial Hospital, Santa Rosa Also Called: St Joseph Hlth Nthrn Cal LLC *(P-16462)*
Santa Rosa Post Acute, Santa Rosa Also Called: Santa Rosaidence Opco LLC *(P-15655)*

ALPHABETIC SECTION

Santa Rosa Surgery Center LP .... D....... 707 575-5831
   1111 Sonoma Ave Ste 214 Santa Rosa (95405) *(P-16394)*
Santa Rosaidence Opco LLC .... C....... 707 546-0471
   4650 Hoen Ave Santa Rosa (95405) *(P-15655)*
Santa Teresita Inc (PA) .... B....... 626 359-3243
   819 Buena Vista St Duarte (91010) *(P-16395)*
Santa Ynez Valley Marriott, Buellton Also Called: Kang Family Partners LLC *(P-9935)*
Santa Ynez Vly Cttage Hosp Inc .... D....... 805 688-6431
   2050 Viborg Rd Solvang (93463) *(P-16396)*
Santaluz Club Inc .... C....... 858 759-3120
   8170 Caminito Santaluz E San Diego (92127) *(P-14444)*
Santana Row Hotel Partners LP .... C....... 408 551-0010
   355 Santana Row Ste 1010 San Jose (95128) *(P-10210)*
Sante Community Physicians, Fresno Also Called: Sante Health System Inc *(P-8271)*
Sante Health System Inc (PA) .... D....... 559 228-5400
   7370 N Palm Ave Ste 101 Fresno (93711) *(P-8271)*
Santee Senior Retirement Com .... C....... 619 955-0901
   400 Lantern Crest Way Santee (92071) *(P-18118)*
Santen Incorporated .... D....... 415 268-9100
   6401 Hollis St Ste 125 Emeryville (94608) *(P-15265)*
Santos Legacy Builders LLC .... C....... 916 439-2777
   2829 Watt Ave # 101 Sacramento (95821) *(P-8652)*
Sanyo Fisher Company, San Diego Also Called: Sanyo North America Corp *(P-20847)*
Sanyo North America Corp .... B....... 619 661-1134
   2055 Sanyo Ave San Diego (92154) *(P-20847)*
Sap America Inc Newtown Sq PA, San Mateo Also Called: Successfactors Inc *(P-12368)*
Sap Labs LLC (DH) .... B....... 650 849-4000
   3410 Hillview Ave Palo Alto (94304) *(P-12345)*
Sapphire Clean Rooms LLC .... C....... 714 316-5036
   2810 E Coronado St Anaheim (92806) *(P-5469)*
Sapphire Softech Solutions LLC .... D....... 888 357-5222
   123 E 9th St Ste 323 Upland (91786) *(P-12872)*
Saputo Cheese USA Inc .... D....... 562 862-7686
   5611 Imperial Hwy South Gate (90280) *(P-2347)*
Saratech, Mission Viejo Also Called: Paydarfar Industries Inc *(P-5332)*
Saratoga Country Club Inc .... D....... 408 253-0340
   21990 Prospect Rd Saratoga (95070) *(P-14445)*
SARATOGA RETIREMENT COMMUNITY, Saratoga Also Called: Odd Fellows Home California *(P-18499)*
Saritasa LLC (PA) .... D....... 949 200-6839
   20411 Sw Birch St Ste 330 Newport Beach (92660) *(P-12622)*
Sas Textiles Inc .... D....... 323 277-5555
   3100 E 44th St Vernon (90058) *(P-2446)*
Sasco Electric Inc .... B....... 408 970-8300
   598 Gibraltar Dr Milpitas (95035) *(P-1830)*
Sasco Valley Electric, Milpitas Also Called: Sasco Electric Inc *(P-1830)*
Sasol Wax, Hayward Also Called: Sasol Wax North America Corporation *(P-6738)*
Sasol Wax North America Corporation .... D....... 510 783-9295
   3563 Inv Blvd Ste 2 Hayward (94545) *(P-6738)*
Sat, Sacramento Also Called: Lpa Insurance Agency Inc *(P-12258)*
SATELLITE DIALYSIS CENTERS, San Jose Also Called: Satellite Healthcare Inc *(P-16998)*
Satellite Healthcare Inc (PA) .... D....... 650 404-3600
   300 Santana Row Ste 300 San Jose (95128) *(P-16998)*
Satellite Management Co (PA) .... C....... 714 558-2411
   1010 E Chestnut Ave Santa Ana (92701) *(P-9175)*
Satellite Pros, Ontario Also Called: Jeeva Corporation *(P-1758)*
Saticoy Country Club .... D....... 805 647-1153
   4450 Clubhouse Dr Somis (93066) *(P-14446)*
Saticoy Fruit Exchange, Ventura Also Called: Saticoy Lemon Association *(P-101)*
Saticoy Fruit Exchange, Santa Paula Also Called: Saticoy Lemon Association *(P-302)*
Saticoy Lemon Association .... D....... 805 654-6500
   7560 Bristol Rd Ventura (93003) *(P-101)*
Saticoy Lemon Association (PA) .... D....... 805 654-6500
   103 N Peck Rd Santa Paula (93060) *(P-302)*
Saticoy Lemon Association .... D....... 805 654-6543
   600 E 3rd St Oxnard (93030) *(P-18721)*
Satmetrix Systems Inc .... C....... 650 227-8300
   555 Twin Dolphin Dr Ste 365 Redwood City (94065) *(P-11903)*
Saturn Fasteners Inc .... C....... 818 973-1807
   425 S Varney St Burbank (91502) *(P-2731)*

ALPHABETIC SECTION — Schneider Electric Usa Inc

Saul Ewing Arnstein & Lehr LLP .... D....... 310 398-6100
   1888 Century Park E Fl 19 Los Angeles (90067) *(P-17632)*

Saul Ewing Arnstein & Lehr LLP, Los Angeles *Also Called: Saul Ewing Arnstein & Lehr LLP* *(P-17632)*

SAVA SENIOR CARE, San Jose *Also Called: SSC San Jose Operating Co LP (P-15680)*

SAVA SENIOR CARE, Pittsburg *Also Called: SSC Pittsburg Operating Co LP (P-15899)*

Savage Services Corporation .... D....... 562 400-2044
   8636 Sorensen Ave Santa Fe Springs (90670) *(P-3422)*

Save Mart, Tracy *Also Called: Lucky Stores II LLC (P-7145)*

Save Mart, Fresno *Also Called: Save Mart Supermarkets Disc (P-7149)*

Save Mart, Riverbank *Also Called: Save Mart Supermarkets Disc (P-7150)*

Save Mart Supermarkets Disc .... D....... 559 261-4123
   6797 N Milburn Ave Fresno (93722) *(P-7149)*

Save Mart Supermarkets Disc .... D....... 209 863-1480
   2237 Claribel Rd Riverbank (95367) *(P-7150)*

Save Mart Supermarkets LLC (PA) .... C....... 209 577-1600
   1800 Standiford Ave Modesto (95350) *(P-7151)*

Savice Inc .... D....... 949 888-2444
   30052 Tomas Rcho Sta Marg (92688) *(P-18906)*

Savings Bank Mendocino County (PA) .... C....... 707 462-6613
   200 N School St Ukiah (95482) *(P-7715)*

Saviynt Inc (PA) .... C....... 310 641-1664
   1301 E El Segundo Blvd Ste D El Segundo (90245) *(P-20538)*

Savvion Inc .... C....... 408 330-3400
   5104 Old Ironsides Dr Ste 205 Santa Clara (95054) *(P-5346)*

Savvymoney Inc .... D....... 415 684-7261
   4160 Dublin Blvd Ste 250 Dublin (94568) *(P-7886)*

Sawmill, Ukiah *Also Called: Mendocino Forest Pdts Co LLC (P-5172)*

Saxco-Demptos Inc .... C....... 707 422-9999
   1855 Gateway Blvd Ste 400 Concord (94520) *(P-6946)*

Sb Waterman Holdings Inc (PA) .... C....... 909 883-8611
   1700 N Waterman Ave San Bernardino (92404) *(P-15051)*

Sbb Roofing Inc (PA) .... C....... 323 254-2888
   3310 Verdugo Rd Los Angeles (90065) *(P-2084)*

SBCI INC (PA) .... C....... 408 379-5500
   1711 Dell Ave Campbell (95008) *(P-774)*

Sbcs Corporation .... C....... 619 420-3620
   430 F St Chula Vista (91910) *(P-18119)*

SBE, Los Angeles *Also Called: Stockbridge/Sbe Holdings LLC (P-10278)*

SBE Electrical Contracting Inc .... C....... 714 544-5066
   2817 Mcgaw Ave Irvine (92614) *(P-1831)*

SBE Entertainment Group LLC (HQ) .... D....... 323 655-8000
   2535 Las Vegas Blvd S Los Angeles (90036) *(P-7522)*

SBE Hotel Group LLC .... D....... 323 655-8000
   8000 Beverly Blvd Los Angeles (90048) *(P-10211)*

Sbhis .... D....... 619 427-2689
   740 Bay Blvd Chula Vista (91910) *(P-775)*

Sbi Landscape Materials, Fulton *Also Called: Shear Builders Inc (P-722)*

Sbm Management Services, Mcclellan *Also Called: Sbm Management Services LP (P-10959)*

Sbm Management Services LP .... B....... 866 855-2211
   5241 Arnold Ave Mcclellan (95652) *(P-10959)*

Sbm Site Services LLC (PA) .... D....... 916 922-7600
   5241 Arnold Ave Mcclellan (95652) *(P-10960)*

Sbmc, Ukiah *Also Called: Savings Bank Mendocino County (P-7715)*

SBP, La Jolla *Also Called: Sanford Brnham Prbys Med Dscve (P-19908)*

Sbrm Inc (PA) .... D....... 760 480-0208
   2342 Meyers Ave Escondido (92029) *(P-10961)*

Sbsa, Redwood City *Also Called: Silicon Valley Clean Water (P-4851)*

Sbsbtc, National City *Also Called: South Bay Sand Blstg Tank Clg (P-13800)*

SC Builders Inc .... D....... 415 757-0405
   190 5th St San Francisco (94103) *(P-713)*

SC Fuels, Orange *Also Called: Southern Counties Oil Co (P-6719)*

SC Wright Construction Inc .... B....... 619 698-6909
   3838 Camino Del Rio N Ste 370 San Diego (92108) *(P-19383)*

Sca Enterprises Inc (PA) .... D....... 818 845-7621
   3817 W Magnolia Blvd Burbank (91505) *(P-13466)*

Scale LLP .... D....... 415 735-5933
   315 Montgomery St Fl 10 San Francisco (94104) *(P-17633)*

Scaled Composites LLC .... B....... 661 824-4541
   1624 Flight Line Mojave (93501) *(P-2983)*

Scalefast Inc (PA) .... C....... 310 595-4040
   2100 E Grand Ave El Segundo (90245) *(P-4336)*

Scaleflux Inc .... D....... 408 628-2291
   900 N Mccarthy Blvd Ste 200 Milpitas (95035) *(P-12522)*

Scalia Farms .... D....... 559 651-2711
   1001 N Demaree St Visalia (93291) *(P-198)*

Scan Group (PA) .... B....... 562 308-2733
   3800 Kilroy Airport Way Ste 100 Long Beach (90806) *(P-8359)*

Scan Health Plan, Long Beach *Also Called: Senior Care (P-8360)*

Scan-Vino LLC (PA) .... D....... 209 931-3570
   5463 Cherokee Rd Stockton (95215) *(P-3542)*

Scanline Vfx Inc .... A....... 310 827-1555
   6087 W Sunset Blvd Los Angeles (90028) *(P-13889)*

Scanlinevfx La LLC .... C....... 310 827-1555
   6087 W Sunset Blvd Los Angeles (90028) *(P-13890)*

Scantibodies Laboratory Inc (PA) .... C....... 619 258-9300
   9336 Abraham Way Santee (92071) *(P-19997)*

Scarborough Farms Inc .... C....... 805 483-9113
   731 Pacific Ave Oxnard (93030) *(P-199)*

Scat Enterprises Inc .... D....... 310 370-5501
   1400 Kingsdale Ave Redondo Beach (90278) *(P-5059)*

Scattergood Generation Plant, Playa Del Rey *Also Called: Los Angeles Dept Wtr & Pwr (P-4759)*

SCC Open Space Authority, San Jose *Also Called: County of Santa Clara (P-20946)*

Scci, Orcutt *Also Called: Spiess Construction Co Inc (P-1266)*

Sccr Properties Inc .... A....... 707 257-0200
   1600 Atlas Peak Rd Napa (94558) *(P-14447)*

Scdrg Inc .... D....... 818 874-0830
   473 S Carnegie Dr San Bernardino (92408) *(P-10674)*

Scds, Santa Rosa *Also Called: Sonoma Country Day School (P-17750)*

SCE, Rosemead *Also Called: Southern California Edison Co (P-4703)*

SCE FCU, Baldwin Park *Also Called: SCE Federal Credit Union (P-7800)*

SCE Federal Credit Union (PA) .... D....... 626 960-6888
   12701 Schabarum Ave Baldwin Park (91706) *(P-7800)*

Scenario Cockram USA Inc .... C....... 407 613-2949
   605 8th St San Fernando (91340) *(P-714)*

Scenic Oaks Funding Inc .... D....... 209 572-2301
   1156 Scenic Dr Modesto (95350) *(P-8018)*

Scenic Studio, San Diego *Also Called: San Diego Opera Association (P-14065)*

Schaefer Ambulance Service Inc .... B....... 323 468-1642
   4627 Beverly Blvd Los Angeles (90004) *(P-3295)*

Schaper Co, San Jose *Also Called: Schaper Construction Inc (P-1641)*

Schaper Construction Inc (PA) .... D....... 408 437-0337
   1177 N 15th St San Jose (95112) *(P-1641)*

Scheid Family Wines, Salinas *Also Called: Scheid Vineyards Inc (P-86)*

Scheid Vineyards Inc .... C....... 831 386-5022
   1972 Hobson Ave Greenfield (93927) *(P-85)*

Scheid Vineyards Inc (PA) .... D....... 831 455-9990
   305 Hilltown Rd Salinas (93908) *(P-86)*

Scherzer International Corp (PA) .... D....... 818 227-2770
   21650 Oxnard St Ste 300 Woodland Hills (91367) *(P-13467)*

Schetter Electric Inc (PA) .... D....... 916 446-2521
   471 Bannon St Sacramento (95811) *(P-1832)*

Schetter Electric Inc .... C....... 925 228-2424
   737 Arnold Dr Ste D Martinez (94553) *(P-1833)*

Schetter Electric LLC .... D....... 916 446-2521
   471 Bannon St Sacramento (95811) *(P-1834)*

Schick Moving & Storage Co (PA) .... D....... 714 731-5500
   2721 Michelle Dr Tustin (92780) *(P-3595)*

Schilling Paradise Corp .... C....... 619 449-4141
   697 Greenfield Dr El Cajon (92021) *(P-1259)*

Schindler Elevator Corporation .... C....... 818 336-3000
   16450 Foothill Blvd Ste 200 Sylmar (91342) *(P-13798)*

Schlumberger Technology Corp .... D....... 661 864-4721
   6120 Snow Rd Bakersfield (93308) *(P-628)*

Schmidt Fire Protection Co Inc .... D....... 858 279-6122
   4760 Murphy Canyon Rd Ste 100 San Diego (92123) *(P-1555)*

Schmitt House, El Monte *Also Called: Hope Hse For Mltple Hndcpped I (P-18452)*

Schneider Electric Usa Inc .... D....... 909 438-2295
   14725 Monte Vista Ave Chino (91710) *(P-3752)*

Schnierow Dental Care .... D...... 310 377-6453
  13450 Hawthorne Blvd Hawthorne (90250) *(P-15249)*
Schnitzer Fresno Inc .... D...... 559 233-3211
  2727 S Chestnut Ave Fresno (93725) *(P-6014)*
Scholls, Ontario Also Called: *Distribution Alternatives Inc (P-3697)*
School & College Legal Svcs, Santa Rosa Also Called: *Sonoma County Office Education (P-17660)*
School Messenger, Scotts Valley Also Called: *Reliance Communications LLC (P-4367)*
School of Veterinary Medicine, Davis Also Called: *University California Davis (P-17782)*
School-Link Technologies Inc .... D...... 310 434-2700
  1437 6th St Santa Monica (90401) *(P-11904)*
Schools Financial Credit Union (PA) .... C...... 916 569-5400
  1485 Response Rd Ste 126 Sacramento (95815) *(P-7801)*
Schoolsfirst Federal Credit Un .... D...... 800 462-8328
  10910 Foothill Blvd Ste 100 Rancho Cucamonga (91730) *(P-238)*
Schoolsfirst Federal Credit Un (PA) .... B...... 714 258-4000
  2115 N Broadway Santa Ana (92706) *(P-7802)*
Schoolsfirst Federal Credit Un .... D...... 480 777-5995
  15442 Del Amo Ave Tustin (92780) *(P-7803)*
Schroff Inc .... A...... 858 740-2400
  7328 Trade St San Diego (92121) *(P-6947)*
Schroff Inc .... C...... 858 740-2400
  7328 Trade St San Diego (92121) *(P-13743)*
Schwab Prvate Clent Inv Advsor .... A...... 415 667-0820
  211 Main St San Francisco (94105) *(P-8165)*
Schwager Davis Inc .... D...... 408 281-9300
  198 Hillsdale Ave San Jose (95136) *(P-1316)*
SCI, Lake Elsinore Also Called: *Sci Inc (P-2156)*
SCI, North Hollywood Also Called: *Pierce Brothers (P-10515)*
Sci Inc .... D...... 951 245-7511
  18501 Collier Ave Ste B106 Lake Elsinore (92530) *(P-2156)*
Scico, Irvine Also Called: *Santa Catalina Island Company (P-3969)*
Science 37 Inc .... D...... 984 377-3737
  12121 Bluff Creek Dr Ste 100 Los Angeles (90094) *(P-11905)*
Science Applications Intl Corp .... A...... 858 826-3061
  4015 Hancock St San Diego (92110) *(P-12523)*
Science Applications Intl Corp .... D...... 703 676-4300
  4065 Hancock St San Diego (92110) *(P-12873)*
Science of Skincare LLC .... D...... 818 254-7961
  3333 N San Fernando Blvd Burbank (91504) *(P-6143)*
Scihp, Santa Rosa Also Called: *Sonoma Cnty Indian Hlth Prj In (P-15064)*
Scilex Inc (HQ) .... D...... 650 516-4310
  960 San Antonio Rd Palo Alto (94303) *(P-6144)*
Scion Lending, Santa Ana Also Called: *Home Mrtg Aliance Corp Hmac (P-7980)*
Scis Air Security Corporation .... D...... 310 645-1216
  1006 W Hillcrest Blvd Inglewood (90301) *(P-13032)*
SCLARC, Los Angeles Also Called: *South Cntl Los Angles Rgnal CT (P-18623)*
SCMG, San Diego Also Called: *Sharp Community Medical Group (P-18761)*
Scmh, Whittier Also Called: *Southern California Material Handling Inc (P-5869)*
Scope Packaging Inc .... D...... 714 998-4411
  13400 Nelson Ave City Of Industry (91746) *(P-2525)*
Scopely Inc (DH) .... C...... 323 400-6618
  3530 Hayden Ave Ste A Culver City (90232) *(P-12346)*
Scorpion Design LLC (PA) .... A...... 661 702-0100
  27750 Entertainment Dr Valencia (91355) *(P-20539)*
Scott A Porter Prof Corp .... D...... 916 929-1481
  350 University Ave Ste 200 Sacramento (95825) *(P-17634)*
Scott St Snior Hsing Cmplex In .... C...... 415 345-5083
  2180 Post St San Francisco (94115) *(P-15656)*
Scott's Seafood Grill & Bar, Oakland Also Called: *Food Specialists Inc (P-7482)*
Scottel Voice & Data Inc .... C...... 310 737-7300
  6100 Center Dr Ste 720 Los Angeles (90045) *(P-13744)*
Scp Horton Owner 1 LLC .... D...... 310 693-4400
  10850 Wilshire Blvd Ste 1050 Los Angeles (90024) *(P-8756)*
Scq Construction, Cupertino Also Called: *Stevens Creek Quarry Inc (P-1165)*
Scrap Tire Company, Ballico Also Called: *Golden By-Products Inc (P-2789)*
Scratch Financial Inc .... D...... 855 727-2395
  225 S Lake Ave Ste 208 Pasadena (91101) *(P-13468)*
Scratchpay, Pasadena Also Called: *Scratch Financial Inc (P-13468)*
Screamline Investment Corp .... C...... 323 201-0114
  2130 S Tubeway Ave Commerce (90040) *(P-3970)*

Screen Actors Guild - American .... D...... 818 954-9400
  3601 W Olive Ave Fl 2 Burbank (91505) *(P-8468)*
Screen Actors Guild-Producers, Burbank Also Called: *Screen Actors Guild - American (P-8468)*
Screenworks LLC .... A...... 951 279-8877
  1900 Compton Ave Ste 101 Corona (92881) *(P-10818)*
Screenworks Nep, Corona Also Called: *Screenworks LLC (P-10818)*
Scribeamerica LLC .... B...... 877 819-5900
  840 Apollo St Ste 231 El Segundo (90245) *(P-17323)*
Scribemd LLC .... D...... 714 543-8911
  1310 W Stewart Dr Ste 212 Orange (92868) *(P-15052)*
Scripps Ambulatory Surgery Ctr, Encinitas Also Called: *Scripps Health (P-16398)*
Scripps Clinic .... C...... 858 794-1250
  12395 El Camino Real Ste 112 San Diego (92130) *(P-16397)*
Scripps Clinic Med Group Inc .... C...... 858 554-9000
  12395 El Camino Real Ste 112 San Diego (92130) *(P-20203)*
Scripps Clinic Medical Group .... D...... 858 554-9606
  10666 N Torrey Pines Rd La Jolla (92037) *(P-15053)*
Scripps Green Hospital, La Jolla Also Called: *Scripps Health (P-16404)*
Scripps Health .... D...... 760 753-8413
  320 Santa Fe Dr Ste 310 Encinitas (92024) *(P-16398)*
Scripps Health .... C...... 619 294-8111
  4077 5th Ave San Diego (92103) *(P-16399)*
Scripps Health .... D...... 858 271-9770
  15004 Innovation Dr San Diego (92128) *(P-16400)*
Scripps Health .... C...... 760 753-6501
  354 Santa Fe Dr Encinitas (92024) *(P-16401)*
Scripps Health .... C...... 619 691-7000
  435 H St Chula Vista (91910) *(P-16402)*
Scripps Health (PA) .... A...... 800 727-4777
  10140 Campus Point Dr San Diego (92121) *(P-16403)*
Scripps Health .... B...... 858 455-9100
  10666 N Torrey Pines Rd La Jolla (92037) *(P-16404)*
Scripps Health .... C...... 619 294-8111
  4077 5th Ave San Diego (92103) *(P-16405)*
Scripps Health .... D...... 800 727-4777
  10666 N Torrey Pines Rd La Jolla (92037) *(P-16406)*
Scripps Health .... B...... 858 626-6150
  9888 Genesee Ave La Jolla (92037) *(P-16407)*
Scripps Health, La Jolla Also Called: *Scripps Mmral-Ximed Med Ctr LP (P-16409)*
Scripps Mem Hosp - Encinatas, Encinitas Also Called: *Scripps Health (P-16401)*
Scripps Mem Hospital-La Jolla, La Jolla Also Called: *Scripps Health (P-16407)*
Scripps Mercy Hospital .... D...... 619 294-8111
  4077 5th Ave # Mer35 San Diego (92103) *(P-16408)*
Scripps Mercy Hospital, San Diego Also Called: *Scripps Health (P-16399)*
Scripps Mercy Hospital, San Diego Also Called: *Scripps Health (P-16405)*
Scripps Mercy Hospitals, Chula Vista Also Called: *Scripps Health (P-16402)*
Scripps Mmral-Ximed Med Ctr LP .... D...... 858 882-8350
  9850 Genesee Ave Ste 900 La Jolla (92037) *(P-16409)*
Scripps Rancho Bernardo, San Diego Also Called: *Scripps Health (P-16400)*
Scripps Research Institute .... D...... 858 242-1000
  11119 N Torrey Pines Rd Ste 100 La Jolla (92037) *(P-19909)*
Scripps Research Institute (PA) .... D...... 858 784-1000
  10550 N Torrey Pines Rd La Jolla (92037) *(P-19910)*
Scripps Torrey Pines, La Jolla Also Called: *Scripps Health (P-16406)*
Scs Engineers, Long Beach Also Called: *Stearns Conrad and Schmidt Consulting Engineers Inc (P-19399)*
Scully Leather Wear, Oxnard Also Called: *Scully Sportswear Inc (P-2468)*
Scully Sportswear Inc (PA) .... D...... 805 483-6339
  1701 Pacific Ave Oxnard (93033) *(P-2468)*
Scv, Santa Fe Springs Also Called: *Southern California Valve Inc (P-5927)*
Scv Facilities Services Inc .... D...... 310 803-4588
  1907 W 75th St Los Angeles (90047) *(P-10962)*
Scw Contracting Corporation .... D...... 760 728-1308
  2525 Old Highway 395 Fallbrook (92028) *(P-1260)*
SD Deacon Corp California .... D...... 916 969-0900
  7745 Greenback Ln Ste 250 Citrus Heights (95610) *(P-1022)*
SD Hotel Circle LLC .... D...... 619 881-6800
  2201 Hotel Cir S San Diego (92108) *(P-10212)*
SD&a Teleservices Inc (HQ) .... B
  5757 W Century Blvd Ste 300 Los Angeles (90045) *(P-13469)*

ALPHABETIC SECTION — Security and Patrol Services

Sdccu, San Diego *Also Called: San Diego County Credit Union (P-7796)*
Sdcda .... C....... 619 459-9632
  2125 Park Blvd San Diego (92101) *(P-17635)*
Sdcr, San Diego *Also Called: San Diego Cash Register Co Inc (P-5255)*
Sdcraa, San Diego *Also Called: San Dego Cnty Rgnal Arprt Auth (P-3909)*
Sdg Enterprises .... D....... 805 777-7978
  822 Hampshire Rd Ste H Westlake Village (91361) *(P-1556)*
SDG&e, Escondido *Also Called: San Diego Gas & Electric Co (P-4667)*
SDG&e, San Diego *Also Called: San Diego Gas & Electric Co (P-4668)*
SDG&e, San Diego *Also Called: San Diego Gas & Electric Co (P-4669)*
SDG&e, San Diego *Also Called: San Diego Gas & Electric Co (P-4670)*
SDG&e, Monterey Park *Also Called: San Diego Gas & Electric Co (P-4672)*
SDG&e, Moreno Valley *Also Called: San Diego Gas & Electric Co (P-4725)*
SDG&E, San Diego *Also Called: San Diego Gas & Electric Co (P-4751)*
SDG&e, Chula Vista *Also Called: San Diego Gas & Electric Co (P-4762)*
SDG&ec, San Diego *Also Called: San Diego Gas & Electric Co (P-4674)*
Sdhael Cajon Treatment Center, El Cajon *Also Called: CRC Health Group Inc (P-17048)*
Sdi Industries Inc (DH) .... C....... 818 890-6002
  24307 Magic Mountain Pkwy # 443 Valencia (91355) *(P-2776)*
SDI Media USA Inc (HQ) .... D....... 310 388-8800
  6060 Center Dr Ste 100 Los Angeles (90045) *(P-13891)*
Sdmv Hotel Partners LP .... D....... 949 516-0088
  520 Newport Center Dr # 2 Newport Beach (92660) *(P-8757)*
SE Laboratories Inc .... D....... 408 727-3286
  1065 Comstock St Santa Clara (95054) *(P-19998)*
SE Scher Corporation .... A....... 916 632-1363
  6731 Five Star Blvd Ste C Rocklin (95677) *(P-11226)*
SE Scher Corporation .... A....... 858 546-8300
  2525 Camino Del Rio S Ste 200 San Diego (92108) *(P-11227)*
SE Scher Corporation .... A....... 408 844-0772
  1585 The Alameda San Jose (95126) *(P-11329)*
Sea & Sand Inn, Santa Cruz *Also Called: Santa Cruz Seaside Company (P-10207)*
Sea Breeze Collision, Tustin *Also Called: Sterling Collision LLC (P-13649)*
Sea Breeze Financial Svcs Inc .... C....... 949 223-9700
  18191 Von Karman Ave Ste 150 Irvine (92612) *(P-8019)*
Sea Breeze Health Care Inc .... C....... 714 847-9671
  7781 Garfield Ave Huntington Beach (92648) *(P-15657)*
Sea Breeze Mortgage Services, Irvine *Also Called: Sea Breeze Financial Svcs Inc (P-8019)*
Sea Dwelling Creatures Inc .... D....... 310 676-9697
  5515 W 104th St Los Angeles (90045) *(P-7594)*
Sea-Logix Llc .... D....... 510 271-1400
  1425 Maritime St Oakland (94607) *(P-3543)*
Seabreeze Management Co Inc (PA) .... D....... 949 855-1800
  26840 Aliso Viejo Pkwy Ste 100 Aliso Viejo (92656) *(P-20204)*
Seachrome, Long Beach *Also Called: Seachrome Corporation (P-2733)*
Seachrome Corporation .... C....... 310 427-8010
  1906 E Dominguez St Long Beach (90810) *(P-2733)*
Seacliff Inn Inc .... D....... 831 661-4671
  7500 Old Dominion Ct Aptos (95003) *(P-10213)*
Seacoast Cmmerce Banc Holdings .... C....... 858 432-7000
  11939 Rancho Bernardo Rd San Diego (92128) *(P-7716)*
Seacrest Convalescent Hosp Inc .... D....... 310 833-3526
  1416 W 6th St San Pedro (90732) *(P-15658)*
Seafood Family Partners LP .... C....... 310 761-1500
  1123 Cory Ave West Hollywood (90069) *(P-6480)*
Seah Steel America, Irvine *Also Called: Pusan Pipe America Inc (P-5512)*
Seai Elk Grove LLC .... D....... 949 281-7897
  1170 N Gilbert St Anaheim (92801) *(P-1557)*
Seal Electric Inc .... C....... 619 449-7323
  1162 Greenfield Dr El Cajon (92021) *(P-1835)*
Seal Methods Inc (PA) .... D....... 562 944-0291
  11915 Shoemaker Ave Santa Fe Springs (90670) *(P-2529)*
Seaman Nurseries Inc .... D....... 559 665-1860
  336 Robertson Blvd Ste A Chowchilla (93610) *(P-244)*
Sears, West Covina *Also Called: Sears Home Imprv Pdts Inc (P-715)*
Sears, Redwood City *Also Called: Sears Home Imprv Pdts Inc (P-716)*
Sears, Hollister *Also Called: Sears Home Imprv Pdts Inc (P-717)*
Sears, Long Beach *Also Called: Sears Home Imprv Pdts Inc (P-718)*
Sears, Temple City *Also Called: Sears Home Imprv Pdts Inc (P-719)*

Sears, Benicia *Also Called: Innovel Solutions Inc (P-4038)*
Sears, San Diego *Also Called: Innovel Solutions Inc (P-4039)*
Sears, Ontario *Also Called: Innovel Solutions Inc (P-4040)*
Sears Home Imprv Pdts Inc .... C....... 626 671-1892
  730 S Orange Ave West Covina (91790) *(P-715)*
Sears Home Imprv Pdts Inc .... C....... 650 645-9974
  1155 Veterans Blvd Redwood City (94063) *(P-716)*
Sears Home Imprv Pdts Inc .... C....... 831 245-0062
  491 Tres Pinos Rd Hollister (95023) *(P-717)*
Sears Home Imprv Pdts Inc .... C....... 562 485-4904
  2900 N Bellflower Blvd Long Beach (90815) *(P-718)*
Sears Home Imprv Pdts Inc .... C....... 626 988-9134
  5665 Rosemead Blvd Temple City (91780) *(P-719)*
Seascape Resort Owners Assn .... D....... 831 688-6800
  1 Seascape Resort Dr Aptos (95003) *(P-10214)*
Seascape Rsort Ltd A Cal Ltd P .... D....... 831 662-7120
  19 Seascape Vlg Aptos (95003) *(P-10215)*
Seasholtz John .... C....... 559 659-3805
  1355 M St Firebaugh (93622) *(P-42)*
SEASHOLTZ, JOHN, Firebaugh *Also Called: Seasholtz John (P-42)*
Seaside Hospitality LP .... C....... 831 394-5335
  1400 Del Monte Blvd Seaside (93955) *(P-10216)*
Season Produce Co Inc .... B....... 213 689-0008
  1601 E Olympic Blvd Ste 315 Los Angeles (90021) *(P-6578)*
Seat Planners LLC .... D....... 619 237-9434
  311 4th Ave Apt 509 San Diego (92101) *(P-3950)*
Seattle Arprt Hospitality LLC .... D....... 310 476-6411
  170 N Church Ln Los Angeles (90049) *(P-10217)*
Seattle Tnnel Prtners A Jint V .... B....... 206 971-8701
  555 Anton Blvd Ste 1000 Costa Mesa (92626) *(P-720)*
Seaworld Global Logistics .... B....... 310 579-9164
  9350 Wilshire Blvd Ste 203 Beverly Hills (90212) *(P-4092)*
Seaworld Parks & Entrmt LLC .... D....... 619 226-3910
  1660 S Shores Rd San Diego (92109) *(P-14314)*
Second Hrvest Fd Bnk Ornge CNT .... D....... 949 653-2900
  8014 Marine Way Irvine (92618) *(P-18120)*
Second Image National LLC (PA) .... C....... 800 229-7477
  170 E Arrow Hwy San Dimas (91773) *(P-10794)*
Second Spectrum Inc .... C....... 213 995-6860
  312 E 1st St Los Angeles (90012) *(P-11906)*
Second Street Corporation .... C....... 310 394-5454
  1111 2nd St Santa Monica (90403) *(P-10218)*
Sectran Armored Truck Service, Pico Rivera *Also Called: Sectran Security Incorporated (P-13033)*
Sectran Security Incorporated (PA) .... C....... 562 948-1446
  7633 Industry Ave Pico Rivera (90660) *(P-13033)*
Secure Choice Lending .... D....... 951 733-8925
  1650 Spruce St Ste 100 Riverside (92507) *(P-7923)*
Secure Net Alliance .... D....... 818 848-4900
  601 S Glenoaks Blvd Ste 409 Burbank (91502) *(P-13034)*
Secure One Data Solutions LLC .... D....... 562 924-7056
  11090 Artesia Blvd Ste D Cerritos (90703) *(P-12623)*
Secure Transportation Co Inc .... D....... 858 790-3958
  8304 Clairemont Mesa Blvd Ste 202 San Diego (92111) *(P-4174)*
Secure-Dmz, Irvine *Also Called: Eighteenth Meridian Inc (P-11564)*
Secureauth Corporation (PA) .... C....... 949 777-6959
  49 Discovery Irvine (92618) *(P-11907)*
Securecom Inc .... D....... 916 638-2855
  4822 Golden Foothill Pkwy Unit 4 El Dorado Hills (95762) *(P-1836)*
Secured Funding Corporation .... A....... 714 689-6749
  2955 Red Hill Ave Costa Mesa (92626) *(P-8056)*
Securelion Security, Tracy *Also Called: Courtesy Security Inc (P-12954)*
Securitas SEC Svcs USA Inc .... B....... 818 706-6800
  4330 Park Terrace Dr Westlake Village (91361) *(P-13035)*
Securitas Technology Corp .... D....... 858 812-7349
  7002 Convoy Ct San Diego (92111) *(P-13143)*
Securitech Security Svcs Inc .... C....... 213 387-5050
  2733 N San Fernando Rd Los Angeles (90065) *(P-13036)*
Securiti Inc (PA) .... C....... 408 401-1160
  3031 Tisch Way Ste 502 San Jose (95128) *(P-11908)*
Security and Patrol Services, Fountain Valley *Also Called: Safeguard On Demand Inc (P-13031)*

Employee Codes: A=Over 500 employees, B=251-500
C=101-250, D=51-100, E=20-50, F=10-19, G=1-9

Security Company — ALPHABETIC SECTION

Security Company, Burbank *Also Called: Secure Net Alliance (P-13034)*
Security Contractor Svcs Inc (PA)..................D....... 916 338-4200
  5339 Jackson St North Highlands (95660) *(P-5232)*
Security First Loan, San Francisco *Also Called: Guarantee Mortgage Corporation (P-8043)*
Security Front Desk, Mc Kittrick *Also Called: Aera Energy Services Company (P-590)*
Security Indust Spcialists Inc ....A....... 408 247-0100
  2880 Stevens Creek Blvd San Jose (95128) *(P-13037)*
Security Indust Spcialists Inc (PA)................C....... 310 215-5100
  6071 Bristol Pkwy Culver City (90230) *(P-13038)*
Security Indust Spcialists Inc ....A....... 323 924-9147
  477 N Oak St Inglewood (90302) *(P-13039)*
Security Nat Mstr Holdg Co LLC (PA)..........C....... 707 442-2818
  323 5th St Eureka (95501) *(P-8020)*
Security Paving Company Inc (PA)................D....... 818 362-9200
  3075 Townsgate Rd Ste 210 # 200 Westlake Village (91361) *(P-1160)*
Secuto Music, Burbank *Also Called: Roundabout Entertainment Inc (P-13888)*
Sedgwick, Oakland *Also Called: Sedgwick Claims MGT Svcs Inc (P-8653)*
Sedgwick, Sacramento *Also Called: Sedgwick Claims MGT Svcs Inc (P-8654)*
Sedgwick, Ontario *Also Called: Sedgwick CMS Holdings Inc (P-8655)*
Sedgwick, San Francisco *Also Called: Sedgwick LLP (P-17636)*
Sedgwick Claims MGT Svcs Inc ....D....... 510 302-3000
  2101 Webster St Oakland (94612) *(P-8653)*
Sedgwick Claims MGT Svcs Inc ....D....... 916 568-7394
  1851 Heritage Ln Sacramento (95815) *(P-8654)*
Sedgwick CMS Holdings Inc ....B....... 909 477-5500
  3633 Inland Empire Blvd Ontario (91764) *(P-8655)*
Sedgwick LLP ....A....... 415 781-7900
  333 Bush St Fl 30 San Francisco (94104) *(P-17636)*
Seeds of Change Inc ....C....... 310 764-7700
  31 Mountain Laurel Trabuco Canyon (92679) *(P-6832)*
Seek Capital LLC ....D....... 855 978-6106
  6420 Wilshire Blvd Los Angeles (90048) *(P-20540)*
Seeley Brothers, Brea *Also Called: Norcal Inc (P-2009)*
Seer, Redwood City *Also Called: Seer Inc (P-3033)*
Seer Inc (PA) ....C....... 650 453-0000
  3800 Bridge Pkwy Ste 102 Redwood City (94065) *(P-3033)*
Sefnco Communications Inc ....D....... 925 271-2943
  8615 Elder Creek Rd Sacramento (95828) *(P-4548)*
Sega Entertainment USA Inc ....A....... 310 217-9500
  600 N Brand Blvd 5th Fl Glendale (91203) *(P-14299)*
Sega Holdings USA Inc ....A....... 415 701-6000
  9737 Lurline Ave Chatsworth (91311) *(P-3112)*
Sega of America Inc ....B....... 747 477-3708
  250 E Olive Ave Ste 200 Burbank (91502) *(P-5996)*
Sega of America Inc ....C....... 415 701-6000
  350 Rhode Island St Ste 300 San Francisco (94103) *(P-5347)*
Seidner-Miller Inc ....C....... 909 305-2000
  1949 Auto Centre Dr Glendora (91740) *(P-7296)*
Seiler LLP (PA) ....C....... 650 365-4646
  3 Lagoon Dr Ste 400 Redwood City (94065) *(P-19629)*
Seiu Local 2015 (PA) ....D....... 213 985-0384
  2910 Beverly Blvd Los Angeles (90057) *(P-18789)*
Seiu Local 2015 ....C....... 213 985-0419
  681 W Capitol Ave West Sacramento (95605) *(P-18790)*
Seiu Local 521 ....D....... 650 801-3500
  2302 Zanker Rd San Jose (95131) *(P-18791)*
Seiu Local 721 ....C....... 213 368-8660
  1545 Wilshire Blvd Ste 100 Los Angeles (90017) *(P-18792)*
Seiu Uhw-West, Commerce *Also Called: Seiu Untd Hlthcare Wrkrs-West (P-18794)*
Seiu United Healthcare Workers (PA)..........C....... 510 251-1250
  560 Thomas L Berkley Way Oakland (94612) *(P-18793)*
Seiu Untd Hlthcare Wrkrs-West ....D....... 323 734-8399
  5480 Ferguson Dr Commerce (90022) *(P-18794)*
Sela Healthcare Inc (PA)............................C....... 909 985-1981
  867 E 11th St Upland (91786) *(P-15659)*
Sela Healthcare Inc ....B....... 818 341-9800
  20554 Roscoe Blvd Canoga Park (91306) *(P-15660)*
Selane Products Inc (PA)............................D....... 818 998-7460
  9129 Lurline Ave Chatsworth (91311) *(P-3069)*
Select Aircargo Services Inc ....D....... 310 851-8500
  12801 S Figueroa St Los Angeles (90061) *(P-4093)*

Select Data, Anaheim *Also Called: Select Data Inc (P-11909)*
Select Data Inc ....C....... 714 577-1000
  4175 E La Palma Ave Ste 205 Anaheim (92807) *(P-11909)*
Select Home Care ....D....... 805 777-3855
  2393 Townsgate Rd Ste 100 Westlake Village (91361) *(P-16924)*
Select Home Warranty Ca Inc ....B....... 732 835-0110
  222 W 6th St Ste 400 San Pedro (90731) *(P-8434)*
Select Hotels Group LLC ....D....... 510 601-5880
  5800 Shellmound St Emeryville (94608) *(P-10219)*
Select Hotels Group LLC ....D....... 858 597-0500
  10044 Pacific Mesa Blvd San Diego (92121) *(P-10220)*
SELECT MEDICAL, Los Angeles *Also Called: Califrnia Rhblitation Inst LLC (P-15965)*
Select Personnel Services, Santa Barbara *Also Called: Select Temporaries LLC (P-11228)*
Select Staffing, Santa Barbara *Also Called: Eastern Staffing LLC (P-11127)*
Select Temporaries LLC (DH)......................D....... 805 882-2200
  3820 State St Santa Barbara (93105) *(P-11228)*
Selecta Products Inc (PA)............................D....... 661 823-7050
  1200 E Tehachapi Blvd Tehachapi (93561) *(P-5589)*
Selecta Switch, Tehachapi *Also Called: Selecta Products Inc (P-5589)*
Selectforce, Irvine *Also Called: Accurate Background LLC (P-12649)*
Selectqote Auto HM Insur Svcs ....A....... 415 977-1300
  595 Market St Fl 10 San Francisco (94105) *(P-8656)*
Selex Inc ....D....... 707 836-8836
  930 Shiloh Rd Windsor (95492) *(P-2314)*
Self Serve Auto Dismantlers (PA)................C....... 714 630-8901
  3200 E Frontera St Anaheim (92806) *(P-6015)*
Self-Help For Elderly ....D....... 415 677-7581
  1483 Mason St San Francisco (94133) *(P-14564)*
Self-Help For Elderly ....D....... 415 391-3843
  777 Stockton St Ste 110 San Francisco (94108) *(P-18121)*
Self-Help For Elderly (PA)............................C....... 415 677-7600
  731 Sansome St Ste 100 San Francisco (94111) *(P-18122)*
Self-Help For Elderly ....A....... 415 677-7556
  408 22nd Ave San Francisco (94121) *(P-18123)*
Selman Chevrolet Company ....C....... 714 633-3521
  1800 E Chapman Ave Orange (92867) *(P-7297)*
Selman Lchnger Edson Hsu Nwman ....D....... 310 445-0800
  11766 Wilshire Blvd Los Angeles (90025) *(P-17637)*
Seltzer - Doren MGT Co Inc ....D....... 818 709-5210
  20201 Sherman Way Ste 209 Canoga Park (91306) *(P-8860)*
Seltzer Cplan McMhon Vtek A La (PA)........C....... 619 685-3003
  750 B St Ste 2100 San Diego (92101) *(P-17638)*
Seltzer-Doren Company, Canoga Park *Also Called: Seltzer - Doren MGT Co Inc (P-8860)*
Sema, Diamond Bar *Also Called: Specialty Equipment Mkt Assn (P-18724)*
Sema LLC (PA)..D....... 949 830-1400
  4 Mason Ste A Irvine (92618) *(P-19630)*
Sema Construction Inc ....D....... 949 470-0500
  320 Goddard Ste 150 Irvine (92618) *(P-1161)*
Semi (PA)..C....... 408 943-6900
  673 S Milpitas Blvd Milpitas (95035) *(P-18722)*
Semiconductor Technologies Inc ....B....... 408 240-7000
  3901 N 1st St San Jose (95134) *(P-19999)*
Semiconductor Tooling Services LLC ....D....... 408 776-6646
  6781 Via Del Oro San Jose (95119) *(P-19384)*
Semifreddi's Bakery, Alameda *Also Called: Semifreddis Inc (P-6665)*
Semifreddis Inc (PA)....................................C....... 510 596-9930
  1980 N Loop Rd Alameda (94502) *(P-6665)*
Seminis, Oxnard *Also Called: Seminis Vegetable Seeds Inc (P-6833)*
Seminis Inc (DH)..B....... 805 485-7317
  2700 Camino Del Sol Oxnard (93030) *(P-19767)*
Seminis Vegetable Seeds Inc (DH) ....A....... 855 733-3834
  2700 Camino Del Sol Oxnard (93030) *(P-6833)*
Sempra (PA)..A....... 619 696-2000
  488 8th Ave San Diego (92101) *(P-4756)*
Sempra Energy ....A....... 619 696-2000
  9305 Lightwave Ave San Diego (92123) *(P-4675)*
Sempra Energy, San Diego *Also Called: Sempra Energy (P-4675)*
Sempra Energy Global Entps ....A....... 619 696-2000
  101 Ash St San Diego (92101) *(P-4676)*
Sempra Energy International ....A....... 619 696-2000
  101 Ash St San Diego (92101) *(P-4677)*

ALPHABETIC SECTION — Service Champions

Sempra Energy Utilities, San Diego *Also Called: Sempra Energy International (P-4677)*
Sempra LNG International LLC .... D...... 661 399-2077
  488 8th Ave San Diego (92101) *(P-1261)*
Semprius, Mountain View *Also Called: Semprius Inc (P-19768)*
Semprius Inc .... D...... 919 433-9980
  1100 La Avenida St Ste A Mountain View (94043) *(P-19768)*
Senclub LLC .... D...... 626 317-8073
  788 Mountain Shadows Dr Corona (92881) *(P-14068)*
Sendlane Inc .... D...... 301 520-3812
  10620 Treena St Ste 250 San Diego (92131) *(P-20541)*
Sendmail Inc .... C...... 510 594-5400
  892 Ross Dr Sunnyvale (94089) *(P-4337)*
Seneca Center, Oakland *Also Called: Seneca Family of Agencies (P-18125)*
Seneca Family of Agencies .... C...... 714 881-8600
  1801 Park Court Pl Bldg H Santa Ana (92701) *(P-8657)*
Seneca Family of Agencies .... C...... 805 278-0355
  2130 N Ventura Rd Oxnard (93036) *(P-18124)*
Seneca Family of Agencies .... C...... 510 317-1444
  8945 Golf Links Rd Oakland (94605) *(P-18125)*
Seneca Family of Agencies .... C...... 707 429-4440
  1234 Empire St Fairfield (94533) *(P-18126)*
Seneca Family of Agencies .... C...... 510 434-7990
  3695 High St Oakland (94619) *(P-18127)*
Seneca Healthcare District (PA) .... C...... 530 258-2151
  130 Brentwood Dr Chester (96020) *(P-16410)*
Senegence International, Foothill Ranch *Also Called: Sgii Inc (P-6145)*
Senior Asssted Lving Cmnty Cht, Pleasant Hill *Also Called: Carlton Senior Living Inc (P-18385)*
Senior Care (PA) .... A...... 562 989-5100
  3800 Kilroy Airport Way Long Beach (90806) *(P-8360)*
Senior Garden APT, San Diego *Also Called: Barker Management Incorporated (P-8791)*
Senior Health and Activity Ctr, Los Angeles *Also Called: Altamed Health Services Corp (P-14607)*
Senior Keiro Health Care .... D...... 323 263-9651
  325 S Boyle Ave Los Angeles (90033) *(P-18520)*
Senior Living Solutions LLC .... C...... 408 385-1835
  1725 S Bascom Ave Apt 105 Campbell (95008) *(P-15794)*
Senior Nutrition Program, Los Angeles *Also Called: Jewish Family Svc Los Angeles (P-18027)*
Senior Prdcrs In Rtrmnt TV .... D...... 760 773-9525
  75895 Altamira Dr Indian Wells (92210) *(P-13892)*
Senior TV, Indian Wells *Also Called: Senior Prdcrs In Rtrmnt TV (P-13892)*
Senor Sisig .... D...... 415 608-5048
  2277 Shafter Ave San Francisco (94124) *(P-14565)*
Sensata Technologies Inc .... D...... 805 716-0322
  1461 Lawrence Dr Thousand Oaks (91320) *(P-12874)*
Sense Spa, Menlo Park *Also Called: Rosewood Hotels & Resorts LLC (P-10174)*
Sensei Wellness Holdings Inc .... D...... 602 499-9862
  1119 Colorado Ave Ste 18 Santa Monica (90401) *(P-17324)*
Sentek Consulting Inc .... C...... 619 543-9550
  2811 Nimitz Blvd Ste G San Diego (92106) *(P-12875)*
Sentek Global, San Diego *Also Called: Sentek Consulting Inc (P-12875)*
Senti Biosciences Inc (PA) .... D...... 650 382-3281
  2 Corporate Dr Fl 1 South San Francisco (94080) *(P-2622)*
Sentinel Monitoring Corp (HQ) .... D...... 949 453-1550
  220 Technology Dr Ste 200 Irvine (92618) *(P-13144)*
Sentinel Offender Services LLC (PA) .... D...... 949 453-1550
  1290 N Hancock St Ste 103 Anaheim (92807) *(P-13145)*
Sentinel Peak Rsources Cal LLC .... D...... 661 395-5214
  1200 Discovery Dr Ste 100 Bakersfield (93309) *(P-605)*
Sentinel Peak Rsources Cal LLC .... D...... 323 298-2200
  5640 S Fairfax Ave Los Angeles (90056) *(P-606)*
Sentinelone, Mountain View *Also Called: Sentinelone Inc (P-12347)*
Sentinelone Inc (PA) .... A...... 855 868-3733
  444 Castro St Ste 400 Mountain View (94041) *(P-12347)*
Sentry, San Francisco *Also Called: Functional Software Inc (P-11609)*
Sentry Life Insurance Company .... C...... 925 370-7339
  535 Main St Fl 2 Martinez (94553) *(P-8658)*
Sentry Life Insurance Company .... C...... 661 274-4018
  4720 Aliso Way Oceanside (92057) *(P-8659)*

Sequenom Inc (HQ) .... D...... 858 202-9000
  3595 John Hopkins Ct San Diego (92121) *(P-19769)*
Sequenom Ctr For Mlclar Mdcine .... B...... 858 202-9051
  3595 John Hopkins Ct San Diego (92121) *(P-16752)*
Sequenom Laboratories, San Diego *Also Called: Sequenom Ctr For Mlclar Mdcine (P-16752)*
Sequoia Benefits, San Mateo *Also Called: Sequoia Bnefits Insur Svcs LLC (P-8660)*
Sequoia Beverage Company LP .... C...... 559 651-2444
  2122 N Plaza Dr Visalia (93291) *(P-6782)*
Sequoia Bnefits Insur Svcs LLC (PA) .... D...... 650 369-0200
  1850 Gateway Dr Ste 600 San Mateo (94404) *(P-8660)*
Sequoia Capital, Menlo Park *Also Called: Sequoia Capital Operations LLC (P-9560)*
Sequoia Capital Operations LLC (PA) .... D...... 650 854-3927
  2800 Sand Hill Rd Ste 101 Menlo Park (94025) *(P-9560)*
Sequoia Concepts Inc .... D...... 818 409-6000
  28632 Roadside Dr Ste 110 Agoura Hills (91301) *(P-10752)*
Sequoia Environmental Svcs Inc .... D...... 949 480-4742
  1 University Dr Aliso Viejo (92656) *(P-461)*
Sequoia Financial Services, Agoura Hills *Also Called: Sequoia Concepts Inc (P-10752)*
Sequoia Health Services (DH) .... B...... 650 369-5811
  170 Alameda De Las Pulgas Redwood City (94062) *(P-16411)*
Sequoia Health Services .... A...... 650 367-5544
  2900 Whipple Ave Ste 110 Redwood City (94062) *(P-16412)*
Sequoia Hospital, Redwood City *Also Called: Sequoia Health Services (P-16411)*
Sequoia Living Inc .... C...... 415 464-1767
  501 Via Casitas Ofc Greenbrae (94904) *(P-15897)*
Sequoia National Park, Seq Natl Pk *Also Called: DNC Prks Rsorts At Sequoia Inc (P-9756)*
Sequoia Residential Funding .... D...... 415 389-7373
  1 Belvedere Pl Ste 330 Mill Valley (94941) *(P-7907)*
Sequoia Senior Solutions Inc .... D...... 707 621-9235
  205 W Clay St Ukiah (95482) *(P-16925)*
Sequoias, The, Portola Valley *Also Called: Northern California Presbyteri (P-18496)*
Sequos-San Frncsco Residential, San Francisco *Also Called: Northern California Presbyteri (P-15598)*
Sequoyah Country Club .... C...... 510 632-2900
  4550 Heafey Rd Oakland (94605) *(P-7544)*
SEQUOYAH GOLF SHOP, Oakland *Also Called: Sequoyah Country Club (P-7544)*
Ser-Jobs For Prgress Inc - San (PA) .... D...... 559 452-0881
  255 N Fulton St Ste 106 Fresno (93701) *(P-18128)*
Serco Inc .... C...... 858 569-8979
  9350 Waxie Way Ste 400 San Diego (92123) *(P-19385)*
Serent Capital LLC .... D...... 415 343-1050
  44 Montgomery St Ste 3450 San Francisco (94104) *(P-9561)*
Serfin Funds Transfer (PA) .... D...... 626 457-3070
  1000 S Fremont Ave Bldg A-O Alhambra (91803) *(P-7861)*
Serra Community Med Clinic Inc .... C...... 818 768-3000
  9375 San Fernando Rd Sun Valley (91352) *(P-15054)*
Serra Community Medical Clinic, Sun Valley *Also Called: Serra Community Med Clinic Inc (P-15054)*
Serrano Associates LLC .... C...... 916 939-3333
  5005 Serrano Pkwy El Dorado Hills (95762) *(P-14448)*
Serrano Country Club .... C...... 916 933-5005
  5005 Serrano Pkwy # P El Dorado Hills (95762) *(P-14449)*
Serrano Country Club, El Dorado Hills *Also Called: Serrano Associates LLC (P-14448)*
Serrano Electric Inc .... D...... 408 986-1570
  15920 Concord Cir Morgan Hill (95037) *(P-1837)*
Serrano Hotel, San Francisco *Also Called: Kimpton Hotel & Rest Group LLC (P-9939)*
Serve People Inc .... D...... 714 352-2911
  1206 E 17th St Ste 101 Santa Ana (92701) *(P-19104)*
SERVE THE PEOPLE COMMUNITY HEA, Santa Ana *Also Called: Serve People Inc (P-19104)*
Servers Direct LLC .... C...... 800 576-7931
  20480 Business Pkwy Walnut (91789) *(P-5348)*
Servexo .... B...... 323 527-9994
  1411 W 190th St Ste 475 Gardena (90248) *(P-13040)*
Servexo Protective Service, Gardena *Also Called: Servexo (P-13040)*
Servi-Tek Inc .... B...... 858 638-7735
  8765 Sparren Way San Diego (92129) *(P-10963)*
Servi-Tek Janitorial Services, San Diego *Also Called: Servi-Tek Inc (P-10963)*
Service By Medallion .... A...... 650 625-1010
  455 National Ave Mountain View (94043) *(P-10964)*
Service Champions, Martinez *Also Called: On-Time AC & Htg LLC (P-1516)*

Service Champions | ALPHABETIC SECTION

Service Champions, Livermore Also Called: On-Time AC & Htg LLC *(P-1517)*

Service Champions, Pleasanton Also Called: On-Time AC & Htg LLC *(P-1518)*

Service Employee Intl Un, Los Angeles Also Called: Los Angles Cnty Employees Assn *(P-18787)*

Service Genius Los Angeles Inc .... D 818 200-3379
8925 Fullbright Ave Chatsworth (91311) *(P-1558)*

Service Hospitality LLC .... D 925 566-8820
1050 Burnett Ave Concord (94520) *(P-10221)*

Service Master By ARS, Gardena Also Called: Disaster Rstrtion Prfssnals In *(P-673)*

Service Mstr Rcvery By C2c Rst, Oceanside Also Called: Vnh Enterprises Inc *(P-10986)*

ServiceMaster, Merced Also Called: Melin Enterprises Inc *(P-10925)*

ServiceMaster By Best Pros Inc .... D 951 515-9051
6474 Western Ave Riverside (92505) *(P-10965)*

Servicemax Inc (HQ) .... C 800 756-4960
4450 Rosewood Dr Ste 200 Pleasanton (94588) *(P-11910)*

Servicetitan Inc (PA) .... D 855 899-0970
801 N Brand Blvd Ste 700 Glendale (91203) *(P-11911)*

Servicing Solutions LLC .... D 844 907-6583
1 City Blvd W Ste 200 Orange (92868) *(P-13470)*

Servicmster Cmplete Rstoration, Escondido Also Called: Sbrm Inc *(P-10961)*

Servicon Systems Inc .... A 310 970-0700
3329 Jack Northrop Ave Hawthorne (90250) *(P-2157)*

Serviz Inc .... D 818 381-4826
15303 Ventura Blvd Ste 1600 Sherman Oaks (91403) *(P-10574)*

SERVPRO Encino/Sherman Oaks, Encino Also Called: One Silver Serve LLC *(P-10936)*

SERVPRO Jeffries Global, Beverly Hills Also Called: Jeffries Global Inc *(P-2288)*

SERVPRO of Beverly Hills, Beverly Hills Also Called: D&A Endeavors Inc *(P-2271)*

Sesloc Federal Credit Union (PA) .... D 805 543-1816
3855 Broad St San Luis Obispo (93401) *(P-7804)*

Set A Head Start Westside, Sacramento Also Called: Sacramnto Emplyment Trning AGC *(P-18245)*

Seta, Sacramento Also Called: Sacramnto Emplyment Trning AGC *(P-18246)*

Setarehshenas Dental Corp .... C 805 583-5700
1197 E Los Angeles Ave Simi Valley (93065) *(P-15250)*

Sethi Management Inc .... C 760 692-5288
6156 Innovation Way Carlsbad (92009) *(P-20205)*

Seti Institute .... C 650 961-6633
339 Bernardo Ave Ste 200 Mountain View (94043) *(P-19911)*

Seti Institute, The, Mountain View Also Called: Seti Institute *(P-19911)*

Seton Medical Center Coastside, Moss Beach Also Called: Ahmc Seton Medical Center LLC *(P-15933)*

Seton Medical Ctr Foundation .... A 650 991-6464
1900 Sullivan Ave Daly City (94015) *(P-16413)*

Setschedule LLC .... C 888 222-0011
100 Spectrum Center Dr Fl 9 Irvine (92618) *(P-11912)*

Sev Lasers, Burbank Also Called: Petrosian Esthetic Entps LLC *(P-10506)*

Seven California Med Diagnstc, Glendale Also Called: Advanced Prof Imging Med Group *(P-14593)*

Seven Licensing Company LLC .... C 323 780-8250
801 S Figueroa St Ste 2500 Los Angeles (90017) *(P-6220)*

Seven Oaks Country Club .... C 661 664-6404
2000 Grand Lakes Ave Bakersfield (93311) *(P-14450)*

Seven One Inc (PA) .... D 818 904-3435
21540 Prairie St Ste E Chatsworth (91311) *(P-13471)*

Seven Sisters of New Orleans, Whittier Also Called: Indio Products Inc *(P-5466)*

Seven Up Btlg Co San Francisco (HQ) .... C 925 938-8777
2875 Prune Ave Fremont (94539) *(P-2411)*

Seven Up Btlg Co San Francisco .... C 916 929-7777
2670 Land Ave Sacramento (95815) *(P-2412)*

Seven-Up Bottling, Fremont Also Called: Seven Up Btlg Co San Francisco *(P-2411)*

Seven-Up Bottling, Sacramento Also Called: Seven Up Btlg Co San Francisco *(P-2412)*

Seven7 Brands, Los Angeles Also Called: Seven Licensing Company LLC *(P-6220)*

Severson & Werson A Prof Corp (PA) .... C 415 398-3344
595 Market St Ste 2600 San Francisco (94105) *(P-17639)*

Severson Group LLC .... C 760 550-9976
950 Boardwalk Ste 202 San Marcos (92078) *(P-7508)*

Severson Group Incorporated (PA) .... D 562 493-3611
3601 Serpentine Dr Los Alamitos (90720) *(P-1023)*

Severson Group, The, San Marcos Also Called: Severson Group LLC *(P-7508)*

Seville Classics Inc (PA) .... C 310 533-3800
19401 Harborgate Way Torrance (90501) *(P-5734)*

Sewer Maintenance, Stockton Also Called: County of San Joaquin *(P-20916)*

Sewing Collection Inc .... D 323 264-2223
3113 E 26th St Vernon (90058) *(P-2655)*

Sexual Recovery Institute Inc .... B 310 360-0130
1964 Westwood Blvd Ste 400 Los Angeles (90025) *(P-18129)*

Seyfarth Shaw LLP .... C 916 448-0159
400 Capitol Mall Ste 2350 Sacramento (95814) *(P-17640)*

Seyfarth Shaw LLP .... D 213 270-9600
601 S Figueroa St Ste 3300 Los Angeles (90017) *(P-17641)*

Seyfarth Shaw LLP .... C 310 277-7200
2029 Century Park E Ste 3300 Los Angeles (90002) *(P-17642)*

Seyfarth Shaw LLP .... D 415 397-2823
560 Mission St Fl 31 San Francisco (94105) *(P-17643)*

SF Broadcasting Wisconsin Inc .... C 310 586-2410
2425 Olympic Blvd Santa Monica (90404) *(P-4461)*

SF Marriott Marquis .... C 415 896-1600
780 Mission St San Francisco (94103) *(P-10222)*

SF Outsd Stg 4117, Livermore Also Called: US Foods Inc *(P-6688)*

SF-MARIN FOOD BANK, San Francisco Also Called: San Francisco Food Bank *(P-18113)*

Sfadia Inc .... D 323 622-1930
8485 Artesia Blvd Ste A Buena Park (90621) *(P-1838)*

Sfai, San Francisco Also Called: San Francisco Art Institute Inc *(P-17768)*

Sfccc, San Francisco Also Called: San Frncsco Cmnty Clnic Cnsrti *(P-20199)*

Sfcm, San Francisco Also Called: San Frncsco Cnservatory of Mus *(P-17815)*

SFCU, Palo Alto Also Called: Stanford Federal Credit Union *(P-7807)*

Sfd Partners LLC .... C 415 392-7755
450 Powell St San Francisco (94102) *(P-10223)*

Sff, Sacramento Also Called: Sierra Forever Families *(P-18133)*

Sffi Company Inc (PA) .... D 323 586-0000
11020 White Rock Rd Ste 100 Rancho Cordova (95670) *(P-6579)*

Sfii Fos Hldngs 1333 Brdway LL .... C 925 771-8198
260 California St # 1100 San Francisco (94111) *(P-9176)*

Sfiii Lake LLC .... D 415 395-9701
260 California St # 1100 San Francisco (94111) *(P-9562)*

SFMC, Lynwood Also Called: St Francis Medical Center *(P-16456)*

SFMOMA MUSEUM STORE, San Francisco Also Called: San Francisco Museum Modrn Art *(P-18671)*

Sfn Group Inc .... A 858 458-9200
4660 La Jolla Village Dr Ste 910 San Diego (92122) *(P-11330)*

Sfn Group Inc .... A 949 727-8500
114 Pacifica Ste 210 Irvine (92618) *(P-11331)*

Sfn Group Inc .... A 650 348-4967
919 E Hillsdale Blvd Foster City (94404) *(P-11332)*

Sfn Group Inc .... A 408 526-0115
401 River Oaks Pkwy San Jose (95134) *(P-11333)*

Sfn Group Inc .... A 530 222-3434
3050 Victor Ave Ste A Redding (96002) *(P-11334)*

Sfn Group Inc .... A 925 847-8500
3825 Hopyard Rd Ste 270 Pleasanton (94588) *(P-11335)*

Sfn Group Inc .... A 408 452-4845
2150 N 1st St Ste 230 San Jose (95131) *(P-11336)*

Sfn Group Inc .... A 707 551-2719
1 Meyer Plz Vallejo (94590) *(P-11337)*

Sfo Airporter Inc (PA) .... D 650 246-2734
1535 S 10th St San Jose (95112) *(P-3211)*

Sfo Airporter Inc .... D 415 495-3909
325 5th St San Francisco (94107) *(P-3212)*

Sfo Shuttle Bus Company, San Francisco Also Called: San Francisco Parking Inc *(P-13628)*

Sfpp LP (DH) .... C 714 560-4400
1100 W Town And Country Rd Ste 600 Orange (92868) *(P-3923)*

Sft Realty Galway Downs LLC .... D 951 232-1880
38801 Los Corralitos Rd Temecula (92592) *(P-9177)*

Sggh LLC .... A 805 435-1255
15301 Ventura Blvd Ste 400 Sherman Oaks (91403) *(P-5590)*

Sgi Environmental, Pleasant Hill Also Called: The Source Group Inc *(P-20865)*

Sgii Inc (PA) .... C 949 521-6161
19651 Alter Foothill Ranch (92610) *(P-6145)*

Sgws of CA, Union City Also Called: Southern Glzers Wine Sprits LL *(P-6807)*

ALPHABETIC SECTION

Shade Hotel Employs 7 .... D...... 310 546-4995
  1221 N Valley Dr Manhattan Beach (90266) *(P-10224)*

Shade Structures Inc .... D...... 714 427-6980
  115 E,2nd St Ste 101 Tustin (92780) *(P-2745)*

Shadow Hills Convalescent Home, Sunland *Also Called: Arcadia Convalescent Hosp Inc (P-15332)*

Shadow Hlls Cnvlscent Hosp Inc .... D...... 818 352-4438
  10158 Sunland Blvd Sunland (91040) *(P-15661)*

Shadow Mtn Rsort Rcquet CLB Tn, Palm Desert *Also Called: Destination Residences LLC (P-9740)*

Shady Canyon Golf Club Inc .... C...... 949 856-7000
  100 Shady Canyon Dr Irvine (92603) *(P-14451)*

Shamrock Capital Advisors LLC .... B...... 310 974-6600
  1100 Glendon Ave Ste 1600 Los Angeles (90024) *(P-9390)*

Shamrock Foods Company .... B...... 602 819-1654
  856 National Dr Sacramento (95834) *(P-6666)*

Shamrock Foods Company .... A...... 951 685-6314
  12400 Riverside Dr Eastvale (91752) *(P-6667)*

Shamrock Holdings Inc (PA) .... D...... 818 845-4444
  4444 W Lakeside Dr Ste 150 Burbank (91505) *(P-8221)*

Shamrock Holdings California, Burbank *Also Called: Shamrock Holdings Inc (P-8221)*

Shandin Hills Golf Club, San Bernardino *Also Called: Evergreen Alliance Golf Ltd LP (P-14374)*

Shanghai Anc Electronic Tech, Moorpark *Also Called: Anc Technology Inc (P-2905)*

Shannon Ranches Inc .... C...... 707 998-9656
  12601 E Highway 20 Clearlake Oaks (95423) *(P-20542)*

Shapell Industries LLC (HQ) .... D...... 323 655-7330
  8383 Wilshire Blvd Ste 700 Beverly Hills (90211) *(P-9273)*

Shapiro-Gilman-Shandler Co .... C...... 213 593-1200
  739 Decatur St Los Angeles (90021) *(P-6580)*

Shapp International Trdg Inc .... C...... 818 348-3000
  6000 Reseda Blvd Tarzana (91356) *(P-5187)*

Shapp Internatioonal, Tarzana *Also Called: Shapp International Trdg Inc (P-5187)*

Sharks Sports & Entrmt LLC .... A...... 408 287-7070
  525 W Santa Clara St San Jose (95113) *(P-14160)*

Sharon Care Center LLC .... D...... 323 655-2023
  8167 W 3rd St Los Angeles (90048) *(P-15662)*

Sharp Chula Vista Medical Ctr .... A...... 619 502-5800
  751 Medical Center Ct Chula Vista (91911) *(P-16414)*

Sharp Chula Vista Medical Ctr .... D...... 858 499-5150
  8695 Spectrum Center Blvd San Diego (92123) *(P-16415)*

Sharp Chula Vista Medical Ctr, Chula Vista *Also Called: Sharp Chula Vista Medical Ctr (P-16414)*

Sharp Community Medical Group .... C...... 858 499-4525
  8695 Spectrum Center Blvd San Diego (92123) *(P-18761)*

Sharp Coronado Hospital & Healthcare Center .... A...... 619 522-3600
  250 Prospect Pl Coronado (92118) *(P-16416)*

Sharp Fabric, Los Angeles *Also Called: Elijah Textiles Inc (P-5116)*

Sharp Grssmont Hosp Emrgncy Ca, La Mesa *Also Called: Team Health Holdings Inc (P-16568)*

Sharp Health Care, San Diego *Also Called: Sharp Healthcare Aco LLC (P-16421)*

Sharp Health Plan .... D...... 858 499-8300
  8520 Tech Way Ste 200 San Diego (92123) *(P-8361)*

Sharp Healthcare .... D...... 619 397-3088
  1400 E Palomar St Chula Vista (91913) *(P-239)*

Sharp Healthcare (PA) .... A...... 858 499-4000
  8695 Spectrum Center Blvd San Diego (92123) *(P-7527)*

Sharp Healthcare .... D...... 619 460-6200
  8860 Center Dr Ste 450 La Mesa (91942) *(P-15055)*

Sharp Healthcare .... D...... 858 621-4090
  10670 Wexford St San Diego (92131) *(P-15056)*

Sharp Healthcare .... C...... 858 939-5434
  8008 Frost St Ste 106 San Diego (92123) *(P-16417)*

Sharp Healthcare 858 499-2000
  751 Medical Center Ct Chula Vista (91911) *(P-16418)*

Sharp Healthcare Aco LLC .... D...... 619 688-3543
  2929 Health Center Dr San Diego (92123) *(P-7528)*

Sharp Healthcare Aco LLC .... D...... 619 398-2988
  7910 Frost St Ste 280 San Diego (92123) *(P-16419)*

Sharp Healthcare Aco LLC .... C...... 619 446-1575
  300 Fir St San Diego (92101) *(P-16420)*

Sharp Healthcare Aco LLC .... A...... 858 627-5152
  3554 Ruffin Rd Ste Soca San Diego (92123) *(P-16421)*

Sharp Healthcare Aco LLC .... D...... 858 541-4850
  8080 Dagget St Ste 200 San Diego (92111) *(P-16926)*

SHARP HEALTHCARE ACO, LLC, San Diego *Also Called: Sharp Healthcare Aco LLC (P-16419)*

Sharp Healthcare Foundation .... C...... 858 499-4800
  8695 Spectrum Center Blvd San Diego (92123) *(P-18622)*

Sharp Home Care, San Diego *Also Called: Sharp Healthcare Aco LLC (P-16926)*

Sharp Mary Birch H .... D...... 858 939-3400
  3003 Health Center Dr San Diego (92123) *(P-16422)*

Sharp McDonald Center .... A...... 858 637-6920
  7989 Linda Vista Rd San Diego (92111) *(P-16693)*

Sharp Memorial Hospital (HQ) .... **A...... 858 939-3636**
  7901 Frost St San Diego (92123) *(P-16423)*

Sharp Memorial Hospital .... C...... 858 278-4110
  7850 Vista Hill Ave San Diego (92123) *(P-16657)*

Sharp Mesa Vista Hospital, San Diego *Also Called: Sharp Memorial Hospital (P-16657)*

Sharp Rees-Stealy, San Diego *Also Called: Sharp Healthcare (P-16417)*

Sharp Rees-Stealy Div, San Diego *Also Called: Sharp Healthcare Aco LLC (P-16420)*

Sharp Rees-Stealy Med Group, Chula Vista *Also Called: Sharp Healthcare (P-239)*

Sharp Rees-Stealy Pharmacy, San Diego *Also Called: Sharp Healthcare Aco LLC (P-7528)*

Sharp RES-Stealy Med Group Inc .... C...... 619 644-6405
  7862 El Cajon Blvd Ste C La Mesa (91942) *(P-15057)*

Sharp RES-Stealy Med Group Inc .... C...... 619 221-9547
  3555 Kenyon St Ste 200 San Diego (92110) *(P-15058)*

Shartsis Friese LLP .... C...... 415 421-6500
  1 Maritime Plz Fl 18 San Francisco (94111) *(P-17644)*

Shascade Community Svcs Inc .... D...... 530 247-8324
  900 Twin View Blvd Redding (96003) *(P-18130)*

Shascade Community Svcs Inc .... D...... 530 243-1653
  1319 Sacramento St Redding (96001) *(P-18131)*

Shasta Beverages, Hayward *Also Called: National Beverage Corp (P-6651)*

Shasta Beverages Inc .... D...... 714 523-2280
  14405 Artesia Blvd La Mirada (90638) *(P-2413)*

Shasta Blood Center, San Francisco *Also Called: Vitalant Research Institute (P-17348)*

Shasta Family YMCA, Redding *Also Called: County of Shasta (P-17941)*

Shasta Landscaping Inc .... D...... 760 744-6551
  1340 Descanso Ave San Marcos (92069) *(P-462)*

Shasta Point Retirement Cmnty, Davis *Also Called: Rvm Davis Housing Corporation (P-18516)*

Shasta Regional Medical Center (SRMC), Redding *Also Called: Prime Hlthcare Svcs - Shsta LL (P-16343)*

Shasta-Siskiyou Transport .... D...... 530 241-1167
  2370 Wyndham Ln Redding (96001) *(P-6718)*

Shattuck Health Care Inc .... D...... 510 665-2800
  2829 Shattuck Ave Berkeley (94705) *(P-15663)*

Shaw Bakers LLC .... C...... 650 273-1440
  14490 Catalina St San Leandro (94577) *(P-6668)*

Shawmut Design and Cnstr, Los Angeles *Also Called: Shawmut Woodworking & Sup Inc (P-1024)*

Shawmut Woodworking & Sup Inc .... C...... 323 602-1000
  11390 W Olympic Blvd Fl 2 Los Angeles (90064) *(P-1024)*

Shawnan, Downey *Also Called: Sialic Contractors Corporation (P-1162)*

Shaxon Industries Inc .... D...... 714 779-1140
  337 W Freedom Ave Orange (92865) *(P-2819)*

Shc Reference Laboratory, Palo Alto *Also Called: Stanford Health Care (P-16491)*

SHD, Chester *Also Called: Seneca Healthcare District (P-16410)*

SHe Manages Properties Inc (PA) .... **D...... 619 291-6300**
  9340 Hazard Way Ste B2 San Diego (92123) *(P-9178)*

Shea Convalescent Hospital, Whittier *Also Called: Longwood Management Corp (P-16237)*

Shea Homes, Livermore *Also Called: JF Shea Construction Inc (P-684)*

Shea Homes, Walnut *Also Called: Shea Homes Vantis LLC (P-776)*

Shea Homes, Walnut *Also Called: Shea La Quinta LLC (P-8758)*

Shea Homes At Montage LLC .... C...... 909 594-9500
  655 Brea Canyon Rd Walnut (91789) *(P-721)*

Shea Homes For Active Adults, Walnut *Also Called: JF Shea Construction Inc (P-685)*

Shea Homes Ltd Prtnrshp, Walnut *Also Called: Vistancia Marketing LLC (P-20606)*

Shea Homes Vantis LLC .... D...... 909 594-9500
  655 Brea Canyon Rd Walnut (91789) *(P-776)*

Shea La Quinta LLC .... D....... 909 594-9500
655 Brea Canyon Rd Walnut (91789) *(P-8758)*

Shea Properties, Aliso Viejo *Also Called: Shea Properties MGT Co Inc (P-8759)*

Shea Properties MGT Co Inc .... B....... 949 389-7000
130 Vantis Dr Ste 200 Aliso Viejo (92656) *(P-8759)*

Shear Builders Inc .... D....... 707 284-8989
1000 River Rd Fulton (95439) *(P-722)*

Shed Media US Inc .... C....... 323 904-4680
3800 Barham Blvd Ste 410 Los Angeles (90068) *(P-10719)*

Sheedy Drayage Co (PA) .... D....... 415 648-7171
1215 Michigan St San Francisco (94107) *(P-11007)*

Shein Technology LLC (PA) .... B....... 213 628-4008
777 S Alameda St Fl 2 Los Angeles (90021) *(P-20543)*

Sheldon Mechanical Corporation .... D....... 661 286-1361
26015 Avenue Hall Santa Clarita (91355) *(P-1559)*

Shell, Stockton *Also Called: Van De Pol Enterprises Inc (P-6746)*

Shell, Anaheim *Also Called: Shell Oil Company (P-20544)*

Shell Oil Company .... C....... 714 991-9200
511 N Brookhurst St Anaheim (92801) *(P-20544)*

Shelter Pointe Hotel & Marina, San Diego *Also Called: Shelter Pointe LLC (P-3824)*

Shelter Pointe LLC .... C....... 619 221-8000
1551 Shelter Island Dr San Diego (92106) *(P-3824)*

Shelter Solano Inc .... D....... 925 957-7576
1333 Willow Pass Rd Ste 206 Concord (94520) *(P-18132)*

Shen Zhen New World II LLC .... D....... 818 980-1212
333 Universal Hollywood Dr Universal City (91608) *(P-10225)*

Shepard Bros Inc (PA) .... C....... 562 697-1366
503 S Cypress St La Habra (90631) *(P-2849)*

Sheppard Mllin Rchter Hmpton L .... D....... 619 338-6500
501 W Broadway Fl 19 San Diego (92101) *(P-17645)*

Sheppard Mllin Rchter Hmpton L (PA) .... B....... 213 620-1780
333 S Hope St Fl 43 Los Angeles (90071) *(P-17646)*

Sheppard Mllin Rchter Hmpton L .... D....... 858 720-8900
12275 El Camino Real Ste 100 San Diego (92130) *(P-17647)*

Sheppard Mllin Rchter Hmpton L .... D....... 415 434-9100
4 Embarcadero Ctr Ste 1700 San Francisco (94111) *(P-17648)*

Sheppard Mllin Rchter Hmpton L .... D....... 310 228-3700
1901 Avenue Of The Stars Ste 1600 Los Angeles (90067) *(P-17649)*

Sheppard Mllin Rchter Hmpton L .... D....... 714 513-5100
650 Town Center Dr Fl 10 Costa Mesa (92626) *(P-17650)*

Sheppard Mullin, Los Angeles *Also Called: Sheppard Mllin Rchter Hmpton L (P-17646)*

Sheraton, San Diego *Also Called: Ssd Management LLC (P-7558)*

Sheraton, San Diego *Also Called: 8110 Aero Holding LLC (P-9596)*

Sheraton, Anaheim *Also Called: Anaheim - 1855 S Hbr Blvd Owne (P-9608)*

Sheraton, Los Angeles *Also Called: Hazens Investment LLC (P-9843)*

Sheraton, San Diego *Also Called: Hst Lessee Boston LLC (P-9877)*

Sheraton, Universal City *Also Called: Lh Universal Operating LLC (P-9975)*

Sheraton, Sunnyvale *Also Called: Msr Hotels & Resorts Inc (P-10034)*

Sheraton, San Diego *Also Called: Noiro West LLC (P-10050)*

Sheraton, Los Angeles *Also Called: Nrea-TRC 711 LLC (P-10052)*

Sheraton, Emeryville *Also Called: Pacific Hotel Management LLC (P-10081)*

Sheraton, Palo Alto *Also Called: Pacific Hotel Management LLC (P-10084)*

Sheraton, Los Angeles *Also Called: S W K Properties LLC (P-10186)*

Sheraton, Universal City *Also Called: Shen Zhen New World II LLC (P-10225)*

Sheraton, Los Angeles *Also Called: Sheraton LLC (P-10227)*

Sheraton, Redding *Also Called: Sheraton Rdding Ht At Sndial B (P-10228)*

Sheraton, Pomona *Also Called: Starwood Htels Rsrts Wrldwide (P-10275)*

Sheraton Carlsbad Resort & Spa, Carlsbad *Also Called: Grand Pacific Carlsbad Ht LP (P-9814)*

Sheraton Ht San Dego Mssion Vl .... D....... 619 321-4602
1433 Camino Del Rio S San Diego (92108) *(P-10226)*

Sheraton Inn Bakersfield, Bakersfield *Also Called: Msr Hotels & Resorts Inc (P-9536)*

Sheraton LLC .... D....... 310 642-1111
6101 W Century Blvd Los Angeles (90045) *(P-10227)*

Sheraton Palo Alto, Palo Alto *Also Called: Pacific Hotel Dev Ventr LP (P-10080)*

Sheraton Pasadena, Pasadena *Also Called: Pasadena Hotel Dev Ventr LP (P-10108)*

Sheraton Pk Ht At Anheim Rsort, Anaheim *Also Called: 1855 S Hbr Blvd Drv Hldngs LLC (P-9588)*

Sheraton Rdding Ht At Sndial B .... D....... 530 364-2800
820 Sundial Bridge Dr Redding (96001) *(P-10228)*

Sheraton San Diego Mission Vly, San Diego *Also Called: Sheraton Ht San Dego Mssion Vl (P-10226)*

Sheraton Sonoma Cnty Petaluma, Petaluma *Also Called: Sonoma Hotel Partners LP (P-10254)*

SHERMAN OAKS, Sherman Oaks *Also Called: Sherman Oaks Health System (P-16424)*

Sherman Oaks Health System .... D....... 818 981-7111
4929 Van Nuys Blvd Sherman Oaks (91403) *(P-16424)*

Sherman Oaks Hospital, Sherman Oaks *Also Called: Prime Hlthcare Svcs - Shrman O (P-16342)*

Sherman Village Hlth Care Ctr, North Hollywood *Also Called: Coldwater Care Center LLC (P-15378)*

Sherman Village Hlth Care Ctr, North Hollywood *Also Called: Hillsdale Group LP (P-15854)*

Shermn-Lehr Cstm Tile Wrks Inc .... D....... 916 386-0417
5691 Power Inn Rd Ste A Sacramento (95824) *(P-1987)*

Sherpa Clinical Packaging LLC .... D....... 858 997-1493
6920 Carroll Rd San Diego (92121) *(P-13472)*

Sherwood Country Club .... C....... 805 496-3036
320 W Stafford Rd Thousand Oaks (91361) *(P-14452)*

Sherwood Guest Home, Lynwood *Also Called: Marlinda Management Inc (P-15876)*

Sherwood Mechanical Inc .... D....... 858 679-3000
6630 Top Gun St San Diego (92121) *(P-1560)*

Sherwood Oaks Enterprises Inc .... D....... 707 964-6333
130 Dana St Fort Bragg (95437) *(P-15664)*

Sherwood Oaks Health Center, Fort Bragg *Also Called: Sherwood Oaks Enterprises Inc (P-15664)*

Sherwood Oaks Post Acute, Thousand Oaks *Also Called: Westlake Oaks Healthcare LLC (P-17353)*

Sherwood Valley Rancheria .... D....... 707 459-7330
100 Kawi Pl Willits (95490) *(P-10229)*

Sherwood Vlley Rnchria Casino, Willits *Also Called: Sherwood Valley Rancheria (P-10229)*

Shibui Apartments, Torrance *Also Called: Hunt Enterprises Inc (P-9044)*

Shield Healthcare, Valencia *Also Called: Shield-Denver Health Care Ctr (P-5449)*

Shield Security Inc (DH) .... B....... 714 210-1501
1551 N Tustin Ave Ste 650 Santa Ana (92705) *(P-13041)*

Shield Security Inc .... C....... 818 239-5800
21110 Vanowen St Canoga Park (91303) *(P-13042)*

Shield Security Inc .... B....... 562 283-1100
150 E Wardlow Rd Long Beach (90807) *(P-13043)*

Shield Security Inc .... B....... 909 920-1173
265 N Euclid Ave Upland (91786) *(P-13044)*

Shield-Denver Health Care Ctr (HQ) .... C....... 661 294-4200
27911 Franklin Pkwy Valencia (91355) *(P-5449)*

Shields, Hercules *Also Called: Shields Nursing Centers Inc (P-15665)*

SHIELDS, Los Angeles *Also Called: Shields For Families (P-16694)*

Shields For Families (PA) .... D....... 323 242-5000
11601 S Western Ave Los Angeles (90047) *(P-16694)*

Shields Nursing Centers Inc (PA) C
606 Alfred Nobel Dr Hercules (94547) *(P-15665)*

Shift Network .... D....... 415 223-7560
101 San Antonio Rd Petaluma (94952) *(P-4549)*

Shih Yu-Lang Central YMCA, San Francisco *Also Called: Young MNS Chrstn Assn San Fmc (P-18996)*

Shimadzu Medical Systems USA, Long Beach *Also Called: Shimadzu Precision Instrs Inc (P-5968)*

Shimadzu Precision Instrs Inc .... D....... 310 217-8855
20101 S Vermont Ave Torrance (90502) *(P-5450)*

Shimadzu Precision Instrs Inc (DH) .... D....... 562 420-6226
3645 N Lakewood Blvd Long Beach (90808) *(P-5968)*

Shimano North Amer Holdg Inc (HQ) .... C....... 949 951-5003
1 Holland Irvine (92618) *(P-5980)*

Shimano North America Bicycle, Irvine *Also Called: Shimano North Amer Holdg Inc (P-5980)*

Shimmick Construction Co Inc .... C....... 510 777-5000
16481 Scientific Bldg 2 Irvine (92618) *(P-723)*

Shimmick Construction Co Inc .... C....... 707 419-5434
1 Harbor Ctr Suisun City (94585) *(P-1317)*

Shimmick Construction Co Inc (HQ) .... C....... 949 591-5922
530 Technology Dr Ste 300 Irvine (92618) *(P-1318)*

Shimmick Nicholson Cnstr JV .... A....... 510 777-5000
8201 Edgewater Dr Ste 202 Oakland (94621) *(P-1025)*

ALPHABETIC SECTION — Sierra International McHy LLC

Shims Bargain Inc .... C....... 323 726-8800
  7030 E Slauson Ave Commerce (90040) *(P-842)*
Shims Bargain Inc (PA).. D....... 323 881-0099
  2600 S Soto St Vernon (90058) *(P-6948)*
Shine Facility Services, San Francisco *Also Called: Green Living Planet LLC (P-10905)*
Shine Logistics LLC .... C....... 844 850-3391
  9245 Laguna Springs Dr Ste 200 Elk Grove (95758) *(P-4094)*
Shingle Sprng Trbal Gming Auth .... A....... 530 677-7000
  1 Red Hawk Pkwy Placerville (95667) *(P-10230)*
Shining Ocean Inc .... C....... 253 826-3700
  10888 7th St Rancho Cucamonga (91730) *(P-6481)*
Shinwoo P&C Usa Inc (HQ)... B....... 619 407-7164
  2177 Britannia Blvd Ste 203 San Diego (92154) *(P-13473)*
Ship Services, San Pedro *Also Called: So Cal Ship Services (P-3809)*
Shiperp, Long Beach *Also Called: Erp Integrated Solutions LLC (P-11577)*
Shiphawk .... D....... 805 335-2432
  3463 State St Ste 245 Santa Barbara (93105) *(P-11913)*
Shipping and Receiving, San Diego *Also Called: General Atomics (P-19699)*
Shipping Department, Anaheim *Also Called: Disneyland Resort (P-4127)*
Shippo, San Francisco *Also Called: Popout Inc (P-12324)*
Shipt .... A....... 408 592-1029
  701 Pine St Apt 43 San Francisco (94108) *(P-12624)*
Shiva Enterprises Inc .... C....... 650 366-2000
  2834 El Camino Real Redwood City (94061) *(P-10231)*
Shivay Hospitality Inc .... D....... 323 702-7103
  1738 N Las Palmas Ave Los Angeles (90028) *(P-10232)*
Shm Mbyh LLC .... D....... 510 236-1013
  1340 Marina Way S Richmond (94804) *(P-3825)*
Shn Cnslting Engners Glgsts In (PA).. D....... 707 441-8855
  812 W Wabash Ave Eureka (95501) *(P-19386)*
Shoei Foods (usa) Inc .... D....... 530 742-7866
  1900 Feather River Blvd Olivehurst (95961) *(P-6285)*
Shoffeitt Pipeline Inc .... D....... 949 581-1600
  15801 Rockfield Blvd Ste L Irvine (92618) *(P-1262)*
Shogun Labs Inc (PA).. C....... 317 676-2719
  340 S Lemon Ave # 1085 Walnut (91789) *(P-20000)*
Shondaland Inc .... D....... 323 468-8109
  2029 Century Park E Ste 1500 Los Angeles (90002) *(P-4550)*
Shook & Waller Cnstr Inc .... D....... 707 578-3933
  7677 Bell Rd Ste 101 Windsor (95492) *(P-2017)*
Shook Hardy & Bacon LLP .... C....... 415 544-1900
  1 Montgomery St Ste 2700 San Francisco (94104) *(P-17651)*
Shook Hardy & Bacon LLP .... C....... 949 475-1500
  5 Park Plz Ste 1600 Irvine (92614) *(P-17652)*
Shopper Inc .... B....... 805 527-6700
  2655 Park Center Dr Ste B Simi Valley (93065) *(P-5388)*
Shoppingcom Inc .... C....... 650 616-6500
  199 Fremont St Fl 4 San Francisco (94105) *(P-12625)*
Shopzilla.com, Santa Monica *Also Called: Connexity Inc (P-4266)*
Shorecliff Properties, Pismo Beach *Also Called: Tic Hotels Inc (P-10311)*
Shoreline Biosciences Inc .... D....... 619 890-0383
  11555 Sorrento Valley Rd Ste 101 San Diego (92121) *(P-19770)*
Shoreline Land Care Inc (PA).. D....... 858 560-8555
  4925 Market St San Diego (92102) *(P-463)*
Shorenstein Properties LLC (PA).. C....... 415 772-7000
  235 Montgomery St Fl 16 San Francisco (94104) *(P-8760)*
Shores Restaurant, La Jolla *Also Called: La Jolla Bch & Tennis CLB Inc (P-9960)*
Shoring & Excavating, Santa Fe Springs *Also Called: Shoring Engineers (P-2315)*
Shoring Engineers .... D....... 562 944-9331
  12645 Clark St Santa Fe Springs (90670) *(P-2315)*
Short Sale Agent Finder, San Diego *Also Called: Verseio Inc (P-12020)*
Showershapes, Ventura *Also Called: G W Surfaces (P-2280)*
Showroom Interiors LLC .... C....... 323 348-1551
  8905 Rex Rd Pico Rivera (90660) *(P-11054)*
Shrin LLC .... D....... 714 850-0303
  900 E Arlee Pl Anaheim (92805) *(P-5060)*
Shriner's Hospital, Pasadena *Also Called: Shriners Hspitals For Children (P-16696)*
Shriners Hspitals For Children .... B....... 916 453-2050
  2425 Stockton Blvd Sacramento (95817) *(P-16425)*
Shriners Hspitals For Children .... B....... 213 368-3302
  3160 Genieva St Montrose (91020) *(P-16695)*
Shriners Hspitals For Children .... B....... 626 389-9300
  909 S Fair Oaks Ave Pasadena (91105) *(P-16696)*
Shriners Hspitals For Children, Pasadena *Also Called: Shriners International (P-18907)*
Shriners International .... C....... 626 389-9300
  909 S Fair Oaks Ave Pasadena (91105) *(P-18907)*
Shryne Group Inc .... A....... 323 614-4558
  728 E Commercial St Los Angeles (90012) *(P-9335)*
Shums Coda Associates Inc .... D....... 925 463-0651
  5776 Stoneridge Mall Rd Ste 150 Pleasanton (94588) *(P-19387)*
Shutterfly LLC (HQ).. C....... 650 610-5200
  2800 Bridge Pkwy Ste 100 Redwood City (94065) *(P-13162)*
Shutters On The Beach, Santa Monica *Also Called: By The Blue Sea LLC (P-9670)*
Shutters On The Beach, Santa Monica *Also Called: Edward Thomas Hospitality Corp (P-9773)*
Shuttle Smart Inc .... C....... 310 338-9466
  6150 W 96th St Los Angeles (90045) *(P-3213)*
Sia Engineering (usa) Inc .... C....... 310 957-2928
  7001 W Imperial Hwy Los Angeles (90045) *(P-19388)*
Sialic Contractors Corporation .... D....... 562 803-9977
  12240 Woodruff Ave Downey (90241) *(P-1162)*
SICK CHILD CARE CENTER, THE, San Jose *Also Called: Sjb Child Development Centers (P-18353)*
Sicor Inc (HQ).. A....... 949 455-4700
  19 Hughes Irvine (92618) *(P-2609)*
Sid Rubin Preschool, San Diego *Also Called: Congrgtion Beth Israel San Deg (P-19016)*
Side Inc .... C....... 415 525-4913
  580 4th St San Francisco (94107) *(P-9179)*
Sideman & Bancroft LLP .... D....... 415 392-1960
  1 Embarcadero Ctr Fl 22 San Francisco (94111) *(P-17653)*
Sidley Austin LLP .... C....... 650 565-7000
  1001 Page Mill Rd Bldg 1 Palo Alto (94304) *(P-17654)*
Siege Media LLC .... D....... 858 751-4439
  624 Broadway Ste 301 San Diego (92101) *(P-4551)*
Siemens Energy Inc .... D....... 916 391-2993
  3215 47th Ave Sacramento (95824) *(P-4678)*
Siemens Industry Inc .... C....... 916 681-3000
  7464 French Rd Sacramento (95828) *(P-3015)*
Siemens Industry Inc .... D....... 714 761-2200
  6141 Katella Ave Cypress (90630) *(P-5591)*
Siemens Med Solutions USA Inc .... A....... 925 246-8200
  4040 Nelson Ave Concord (94520) *(P-3077)*
Siemens Mobility Inc .... D....... 916 621-2700
  5301 Price Ave Mcclellan (95652) *(P-13676)*
Sierra Agricultural Trnsp Inc .... D....... 559 738-5448
  1316 W Center Ave Visalia (93291) *(P-3544)*
Sierra At Tahoe Ski Resorts .... C....... 530 659-7519
  1111 Sierra At Tahoe Rd Twin Bridges (95735) *(P-10233)*
Sierra Canyon Inc .... D....... 818 882-8121
  11052 Independence Ave Chatsworth (91311) *(P-17749)*
Sierra Canyon Day Camp, Chatsworth *Also Called: Sierra Canyon Inc (P-17749)*
Sierra Central Credit Union (PA).. D....... 530 671-3009
  1351 Harter Pkwy Yuba City (95993) *(P-7805)*
Sierra Club (PA)... C....... 415 977-5500
  2101 Webster St Ste 1300 Oakland (94612) *(P-18908)*
SIERRA CLUB BOOKS, Oakland *Also Called: Sierra Club (P-18908)*
Sierra Cscade Fmly Opprtnities (PA).. D....... 530 283-1242
  424 N Mill Creek Rd Quincy (95971) *(P-18352)*
Sierra Disposal Service, South Lake Tahoe *Also Called: South Tahoe Refuse Co (P-4939)*
Sierra Eye Tissue Donor, West Sacramento *Also Called: DCI Donor Services Inc (P-17219)*
Sierra Forest Products .... C....... 559 535-4893
  9000 Road 234 Terra Bella (93270) *(P-5188)*
Sierra Forever Families .... D....... 916 368-5114
  8912 Volunteer Ln Sacramento (95826) *(P-18133)*
Sierra Frest Pdts Holdings Inc .... C....... 559 535-4893
  9000 Road 234 Terra Bella (93270) *(P-571)*
Sierra Gold Nurseries Inc .... D....... 530 674-1145
  5320 Garden Hwy Yuba City (95991) *(P-153)*
Sierra Hlth Wellness Ctrs LLC .... D....... 530 854-4119
  2167 Montgomery St Ste A Oroville (95965) *(P-17325)*
Sierra Hlth Wellness Group LLC .... C....... 530 854-4119
  9985 Folsom Blvd Sacramento (95827) *(P-17126)*
Sierra International McHy LLC .... D....... 661 327-7073
  1620 E Brundage Ln Frnt Bakersfield (93307) *(P-6016)*

Sierra Intrnal Mdcine Med Grou .... D...... 209 536-3738
  680 Guzzi Ln Ste 201 Sonora (95370) (P-15059)
Sierra Kings District Hospital .... B...... 559 638-8155
  372 W Cypress Ave Reedley (93654) (P-16426)
Sierra Lathing Company Inc .... C...... 909 421-0211
  1189 Leiske Dr Rialto (92376) (P-1963)
Sierra Lodgings Inc .... D...... 408 748-9800
  3100 Lakeside Dr Santa Clara (95054) (P-10234)
Sierra Manor Apts, Chico Also Called: Hignell Incorporated (P-8818)
Sierra Medical Group, Palmdale Also Called: Sierra Prmry Care Med Group A (P-15061)
Sierra Mountain, Sonora Also Called: Sierra Mountain Cnstr Inc (P-18134)
Sierra Mountain Cnstr Inc .... D...... 209 928-1900
  13919 Mono Way Sonora (95370) (P-18134)
Sierra Nevada Home Care, Grass Valley Also Called: Sierra Nevada Mem HM Care Inc (P-16927)
Sierra Nevada Mem HM Care Inc .... D...... 530 274-6350
  1020 Mccourtney Rd Ste A Grass Valley (95949) (P-16927)
Sierra Pacific Constrs Inc .... D...... 747 888-5000
  22212 Ventura Blvd Ste 300 Woodland Hills (91364) (P-1026)
Sierra Pacific Constructors, Woodland Hills Also Called: Sierra Pacific Constrs Inc (P-1026)
Sierra Pacific Engrg & Pdts, Long Beach Also Called: SPEP Acquisition Corp (P-2732)
Sierra Pacific Farms Inc (PA) .... D...... 951 699-9980
  43406 Business Park Dr Temecula (92590) (P-380)
Sierra Pacific Htg & Air-Solar, Rancho Cordova Also Called: Sierra PCF HM & Comfort Inc (P-5771)
Sierra Pacific Industries .... C...... 530 283-2820
  1538 Lee Rd Quincy (95971) (P-2476)
SIERRA PACIFIC INDUSTRIES, Quincy Also Called: Sierra Pacific Industries (P-2476)
Sierra Pacific Materials, Arroyo Grande Also Called: Papich Construction Co Inc (P-706)
Sierra Pacific Mortgage Co Inc (PA) .... A...... 916 932-1700
  950 Glenn Dr Folsom (95630) (P-8021)
Sierra PCF HM & Comfort Inc .... D...... 916 638-0543
  2550 Mercantile Dr Ste D Rancho Cordova (95742) (P-5771)
Sierra PCF Orthpdic Ctr Med Gr .... C...... 559 256-5200
  1630 E Herndon Ave Fresno (93720) (P-15060)
Sierra Precast Inc .... D...... 408 779-1000
  1 Live Oak Ave Morgan Hill (95037) (P-2707)
Sierra Prmry Care Med Group A .... D...... 661 273-0100
  38636 Medical Center Dr Ste C Palmdale (93551) (P-15061)
Sierra Regency, The, Roseville Also Called: Horizon West Healthcare Inc (P-15857)
Sierra Select, North Highlands Also Called: Sierra Select Distributors Inc (P-5614)
Sierra Select Distributors Inc .... D...... 916 483-9295
  4320 Roseville Rd North Highlands (95660) (P-5614)
Sierra Springs Apartments, San Bernardino Also Called: Woodman Realty Inc (P-9222)
Sierra Summit Inc .... A...... 559 233-2500
  59265 Hwy 168 Lakeshore (93634) (P-10235)
Sierra Sunrise Vineyard Inc .... D...... 209 245-6942
  20680 Shenandoah School Rd Plymouth (95669) (P-2393)
Sierra Telephone Company Inc .... C...... 559 683-4611
  49150 Road 426 Oakhurst (93644) (P-4338)
Sierra Traffic Markings Inc .... D...... 916 784-0430
  9725 Del Rd Ste B Roseville (95747) (P-1163)
Sierra Valley Rehab Center, Porterville Also Called: Hacienda Care Center Inc (P-15504)
SIERRA VIEW, Roseville Also Called: Sierra View Country Club (P-14453)
Sierra View Country Club .... D...... 916 782-3741
  105 Alta Vista Ave Roseville (95678) (P-14453)
Sierra View District Hospital, Porterville Also Called: Sierra View Local Hospital Dst (P-16427)
Sierra View Dst Hosp Leag Inc (PA) .... B...... 559 784-1110
  465 W Putnam Ave Porterville (93257) (P-15062)
Sierra View Hmes Rsdntial Care, Reedley Also Called: Sierra View Homes (P-15666)
Sierra View Homes .... C...... 559 637-2256
  1155 E Springfield Ave Reedley (93654) (P-15666)
Sierra View Local Hospital Dst .... C...... 559 781-7877
  283 Pearson Dr Porterville (93257) (P-16427)
Sierra View Medical Center, Porterville Also Called: Sierra View Dst Hosp Leag Inc (P-15062)
Sierra Vista, Victorville Also Called: Encore Senior Living III LLC (P-15447)
Sierra Vista Extended Stay, Brea Also Called: Otb Acquisition LLC (P-10073)
Sierra Vista Hospital, Sacramento Also Called: Willow Springs LLC (P-15210)
Sierra Vista Hospital Inc (HQ) .... A...... 805 546-7600
  1010 Murray Ave San Luis Obispo (93405) (P-16428)

Sierra Vista Regional Med Ctr, San Luis Obispo Also Called: Sierra Vista Hospital Inc (P-16428)
Sierra-Cascade Nursery Inc (PA) .... B...... 530 254-6867
  472-715 Johnson Rd Susanville (96130) (P-154)
Sierra-Kings Health Care Dst, Reedley Also Called: Sierra Kings District Hospital (P-16426)
Sift, San Francisco Also Called: Sift Science Inc (P-11914)
Sift Science Inc (PA) .... C...... 415 882-7709
  525 Market St Fl 6 San Francisco (94105) (P-11914)
Sight Machine Inc .... D...... 888 461-5739
  243 Vallejo St San Francisco (94111) (P-12348)
Sigmaways Inc .... D...... 510 573-4208
  39737 Paseo Padre Pkwy Fremont (94538) (P-20545)
Sign Lnguage Interpreting Svcs, San Diego Also Called: Deaf Cmnty Svcs San Diego Inc (P-17950)
Signal 88, Ontario Also Called: Signal 88 LLC (P-13045)
Signal 88 LLC .... A...... 714 713-5306
  821 S Rockefeller Ave Ontario (91761) (P-13045)
Signal Products Inc (PA) .... D...... 213 748-0990
  5600 W Adams Blvd Ste 200 Los Angeles (90016) (P-6221)
Signal Products/Guess Handbags, Los Angeles Also Called: Signal Products Inc (P-6221)
Signalwire Inc .... D...... 650 382-0000
  228 Hamilton Ave Fl 3 Palo Alto (94301) (P-11915)
Signature Analytics LLC .... D...... 888 284-3842
  10120 Pacific Heights Blvd Ste 110 San Diego (92121) (P-19631)
Signature Building Maint Inc .... D...... 408 377-8066
  4005 Clipper Ct Fremont (94538) (P-10966)
Signature Facilities Services, Fremont Also Called: Signature Building Maint Inc (P-10966)
Signature Homes Inc .... D...... 925 463-1122
  4670 Willow Rd Ste 200 Pleasanton (94588) (P-724)
Signature Parking LLC .... D...... 805 969-7275
  924 Chapala St Ste B Santa Barbara (93101) (P-10575)
Signature Select Personnel LLC .... D...... 626 940-3351
  138 W Bonita Ave Ste 207 San Dimas (91773) (P-11229)
Signet Testing Labs Inc .... D...... 916 374-0754
  498 N 3rd St Sacramento (95811) (P-13474)
Significant Cleaning Svcs LLC .... C...... 408 559-5959
  148 E Virginia St Ste 1 San Jose (95112) (P-10967)
Signifyd Inc .... B...... 866 220-1415
  99 Almaden Blvd Ste 400 San Jose (95113) (P-12349)
Signtech, San Diego Also Called: Signtech Electrical Advg Inc (P-3101)
Signtech Electrical Advg Inc .... C...... 619 527-6100
  4444 Federal Blvd San Diego (92102) (P-3101)
Sigue, Sylmar Also Called: Sigue Corporation (P-13475)
Sigue Corporation (PA) .... D...... 818 837-5939
  13190 Telfair Ave Sylmar (91342) (P-13475)
Silent Valley Club Inc .... D...... 951 849-4501
  46305 Poppet Flats Rd Banning (92220) (P-10236)
Silicon Graphics Intl Corp (HQ) .... C...... 669 900-8000
  940 N Mccarthy Blvd Milpitas (95035) (P-2837)
Silicon Processing and Trading Inc .... D...... 805 388-8683
  322 N Aviador St Camarillo (93010) (P-4936)
Silicon Valley Clean Water .... D...... 650 591-7121
  1400 Radio Rd Redwood City (94065) (P-4851)
Silicon Valley Club LLC (PA) .... D...... 408 202-9424
  579 Clyde Ave Ste 340 Mountain View (94043) (P-10237)
Silicon Valley Commerce LLC .... D...... 888 507-8266
  16 Jessie St San Francisco (94105) (P-11916)
Silicon Valley Country Club, San Jose Also Called: Silver Creek Vly Cntry CLB Inc (P-14454)
Silicon Valley Inns Inc .... D...... 408 734-3742
  940 W Weddell Dr Sunnyvale (94089) (P-10238)
Silicon Valley Mechanical Inc .... C...... 408 943-0380
  2115 Ringwood Ave San Jose (95131) (P-1561)
Silicon Valley Medical Dev LLC .... D...... 408 866-4000
  2500 Grant Rd Mountain View (94040) (P-17326)
Silicon Valley Power, Santa Clara Also Called: City of Santa Clara (P-4565)
Silicon Vly Cmnty Foundation (PA) .... C...... 650 450-5400
  444 Castro St Mountain View (94041) (P-18909)
Silicon Vly Cmnty Foundation .... C...... 650 458-2660
  1300 S El Camino Real San Mateo (94402) (P-18910)
Silicon Vly SEC & Patrol Inc (PA) .... C...... 408 267-1539
  1131 Luchessi Dr Ste 2 San Jose (95118) (P-13046)

Siliconsage Construction Inc .... C....... 408 916-3205
560 S Mathilda Ave Sunnyvale (94086) *(P-777)*

Silla Automotive LLC .... C....... 800 624-1499
1217 W Artesia Blvd Compton (90220) *(P-5061)*

Silla Cooling Systems, Compton *Also Called: Silla Automotive LLC (P-5061)*

Sillcrest Nursing Home, San Bernardino *Also Called: Marna Health Services Inc (P-15877)*

Silliker Inc .... D....... 209 549-7508
5262 Pirrone Ct Salida (95368) *(P-20001)*

Silman Construction, San Leandro *Also Called: Silman Venture Corporation (P-1027)*

Silman Venture Corporation (PA) .... C....... 510 347-4800
1600 Factor Ave San Leandro (94577) *(P-1027)*

Silva Farms LLC (PA) .... D....... 831 675-2327
111 Alpine Dr Gonzales (93926) *(P-43)*

Silver Creek Industries LLC .... C....... 951 943-5393
2830 Barrett Ave Perris (92571) *(P-1028)*

Silver Creek Vly Cntry CLB Inc .... D....... 408 239-5775
5460 Country Club Pkwy San Jose (95138) *(P-14454)*

Silver Hawk Freight Inc .... D....... 562 404-0226
16410 Bloomfield Ave Cerritos (90703) *(P-4095)*

Silver Lake Medical Center, Los Angeles *Also Called: Success Healthcare 1 LLC (P-16937)*

Silver Lake Partners Vii LP .... C....... 650 233-8120
2775 Sand Hill Rd Ste 100 Menlo Park (94025) *(P-9409)*

Silver Lakes Association .... D....... 760 245-1606
15273 Orchard Hill Ln Helendale (92342) *(P-18911)*

Silver Rock Resort Golf Club .... D....... 760 777-8884
79179 Ahmanson Ln La Quinta (92253) *(P-14288)*

Silver Saddle Ranch & Club Inc .... D....... 818 768-8808
7635 N San Fernando Rd Burbank (91505) *(P-9274)*

Silver Star Distribution, Irvine *Also Called: Str Worldwide Inc (P-6187)*

Silver Terrace Nurseries Inc .... D....... 650 879-2110
501 North St Pescadero (94060) *(P-155)*

Silverado Framing & Cnstr .... D....... 951 352-1100
3091 E La Cadena Dr Riverside (92507) *(P-725)*

Silverado Orchards LLC (PA) .... D....... 707 963-1461
601 Pope St Ofc Saint Helena (94574) *(P-8861)*

Silverado Resort, Napa *Also Called: Silverado Rsort Svcs Group LLC (P-10239)*

SILVERADO RESORT AND SPA, Napa *Also Called: Sccr Properties Inc (P-14447)*

Silverado Rsort Svcs Group LLC .... B....... 707 257-0200
1600 Atlas Peak Rd Napa (94558) *(P-10239)*

Silverado Senior Living Inc (PA) .... D....... 949 240-7200
6400 Oak Cyn Ste 200 Irvine (92618) *(P-15667)*

Silverado Senior Living Inc .... D....... 949 945-0189
350 W Bay St Costa Mesa (92627) *(P-15668)*

Silverado Senior Living Inc .... D....... 626 872-3941
1118 N Stoneman Ave Alhambra (91801) *(P-15669)*

Silverado Senior Living Inc .... D....... 760 456-5137
1500 Borden Rd Escondido (92026) *(P-15670)*

Silverado Senior Living Inc .... D....... 760 270-9917
335 Saxony Rd Encinitas (92024) *(P-15671)*

Silverado Senior Living Inc .... D....... 818 746-2583
25100 Calabasas Rd Calabasas (91302) *(P-15672)*

Silverado Senior Living Inc .... D....... 323 984-7313
330 N Hayworth Ave Los Angeles (90048) *(P-15673)*

Silverado Snior Lving Hldngs .... A....... 949 240-7200
6400 Oak Cyn Ste 200 Irvine (92618) *(P-18521)*

Silvergate San Marcos, San Marcos *Also Called: Americare Hlth Retirement Inc (P-8701)*

Silverlake Motel, Los Angeles *Also Called: New Aster Enterprises Inc (P-10040)*

Silverrest, Fullerton *Also Called: Brentwood Home LLC (P-2493)*

Silverton Business Center, San Diego *Also Called: HG Fenton Property Company (P-8885)*

Simas Floor Co Inc (PA) .... C....... 916 452-4933
3550 Power Inn Rd Sacramento (95826) *(P-2039)*

Simas Floor Co Design Center, Sacramento *Also Called: Simas Floor Co Inc (P-2039)*

Simbol Inc .... D....... 925 226-7400
6920 Koll Center Pkwy Ste 216 Pleasanton (94566) *(P-19771)*

Simbol Materials, Pleasanton *Also Called: Simbol Inc (P-19771)*

Simco Electronics (PA) .... D....... 408 734-9750
3131 Jay St Ste 100 Santa Clara (95054) *(P-13745)*

Simco Electronics, Santa Clara *Also Called: Simco Electronics (P-13745)*

Simco Foods Inc .... D....... 415 982-5872
39 Pier Ste A202 San Francisco (94133) *(P-6286)*

Simex-Iwerks, Valencia *Also Called: Iwerks Entertainment Inc (P-2959)*

Simi Valley Chrysler, Woodland Hills *Also Called: Reseda Dodge Sales Inc (P-7287)*

Simi Valley Family YMCA, Simi Valley *Also Called: Young MNS Chrstn Assn Sthast V (P-14590)*

Simi Vly Care & Rehabilitation, Simi Valley *Also Called: Chase Group Llc (P-19804)*

Simi Vly Hosp & Hlth Care Svcs .... A....... 805 955-6000
2750 Sycamore Dr Simi Valley (93065) *(P-16429)*

Simi Vly Hosp & Hlth Care Svcs (HQ) .... C....... 805 955-6000
2975 Sycamore Dr Simi Valley (93065) *(P-16430)*

Simi Vly Hosp & Hlth Care Svcs, Simi Valley *Also Called: Simi Vly Hosp & Hlth Care Svcs (P-16430)*

Simi West Inc .... C....... 760 346-5502
999 Enchanted Way Simi Valley (93065) *(P-10240)*

Simility LLC .... D....... 650 351-7592
2211 N 1st St San Jose (95131) *(P-12876)*

Simon and Gladstone A Prof, Irvine *Also Called: Berger Kahn A Law Corporation (P-17384)*

Simon Golub & Sons Inc (DH) .... D
514 Via De La Valle Ste 210 Solana Beach (92075) *(P-6026)*

Simonian Brothers Inc .... D....... 559 655-4722
3580 S Newcomb Ave Mendota (93640) *(P-87)*

Simonian Brothers Inc (PA) .... D....... 559 834-5921
511 N 7th St Fowler (93625) *(P-303)*

Simonian Brothers Inc .... D....... 559 834-5921
350 N 7th St Fowler (93625) *(P-304)*

Simonian Farming Co, Mendota *Also Called: Simonian Brothers Inc (P-87)*

Simonian Fruit, Fowler *Also Called: Simonian Brothers Inc (P-303)*

Simonian Fruit Company, Fowler *Also Called: Simonian Brothers Inc (P-304)*

Simplelegal Inc .... D....... 949 887-2900
488 Ellis St Mountain View (94043) *(P-20546)*

Simplexgrinnell, San Diego *Also Called: Johnson Cntrls Fire Prtction L (P-2902)*

Simplicontract Tech Inc .... D....... 403 833-5556
6387 Alvord Way Pleasanton (94588) *(P-13476)*

Simply Fresh Fruit, Rancho Cordova *Also Called: Sffi Company Inc (P-6579)*

Simply Fresh Fruit Inc .... D....... 323 586-0000
11020 White Rock Rd # 100 Rancho Cordova (95670) *(P-6581)*

Simply Solar .... D....... 707 285-7037
1740 Corporate Cir Petaluma (94954) *(P-1562)*

Simpplr Inc (PA) .... C....... 650 396-2646
3 Twin Dolphin Dr Ste 160 Redwood City (94065) *(P-12350)*

Simpson Automotive Inc .... D....... 714 690-6200
6600 Auto Center Dr Buena Park (90621) *(P-7298)*

Simpson Buick Pontiac GMC, Buena Park *Also Called: Simpson Automotive Inc (P-7298)*

Simpson Smpson MGT Cnslting In .... D....... 626 282-4000
718 S Date Ave Ste A1 Alhambra (91803) *(P-20547)*

Sims Group USA Corporation (DH) .... D....... 510 412-5300
600 S 4th St Richmond (94804) *(P-6017)*

Simsmetal America, Richmond *Also Called: Sims Group USA Corporation (P-6017)*

Simulstat Incorporated .... D....... 858 546-4337
440 Stevens Ave Ste 200 Solana Beach (92075) *(P-12877)*

Sinai Temple .... C....... 323 469-6000
5950 Forest Lawn Dr Los Angeles (90068) *(P-10516)*

Sinai Temple (PA) .... B....... 310 474-1518
10400 Wilshire Blvd Los Angeles (90024) *(P-19027)*

Sinanian, Tarzana *Also Called: Sinanian Development Inc (P-1029)*

Sinanian Development Inc .... D....... 818 996-9666
18980 Ventura Blvd Ste 200 Tarzana (91356) *(P-1029)*

Sinclair & Valentine, Watsonville *Also Called: Sv Labs Corporation (P-6146)*

Sinclair Concrete .... D....... 916 663-0303
7205 Church St Penryn (95663) *(P-2158)*

Sinecera Inc .... D....... 626 962-1087
5397 3rd St Irwindale (91706) *(P-13477)*

Singapore Airlines Limited .... C....... 310 647-1922
222 N Pacific Coast Hwy Ste 1600 El Segundo (90245) *(P-3843)*

Singer Vehicle Design LLC (PA) .... C....... 213 592-2728
19500 S Vermont Ave Torrance (90502) *(P-13719)*

Singerlewak, Los Angeles *Also Called: Singerlewak LLP (P-19632)*

Singerlewak LLP (PA) .... C....... 310 477-3924
10960 Wilshire Blvd Fl 7 Los Angeles (90024) *(P-19632)*

Singulex, Alameda *Also Called: Singulex Inc (P-19912)*

Singulex Inc .... B....... 510 995-9000
1701 Harbor Bay Pkwy Ste 200 Alameda (94502) *(P-19912)*

Sintex Security Services Inc .... D...... 209 543-9044
501 Bangs Ave Ste D Modesto (95356) *(P-13047)*

Sipco Surface Protection Inc (DH) .... D...... **707 639-4414**
2320 Cordelia Rd Fairfield (94534) *(P-1642)*

Sir Francis Drake Hotel, San Francisco *Also Called: Sfd Partners LLC (P-10223)*

Siracusa Enterprises Inc .... D...... 818 831-1130
17737 Chatsworth St Ste 200 Granada Hills (91344) *(P-11230)*

Sirius XM Radio Inc .... C...... 323 802-1100
953 N Sycamore Ave Los Angeles (90038) *(P-4404)*

SIS, Culver City *Also Called: Security Indust Spcialists Inc (P-13038)*

Sisa, Mountain View *Also Called: Samsung Research America Inc (P-19766)*

Siskiyou Development Company .... D...... 530 938-2731
88 S Weed Blvd Edgewood (96094) *(P-10241)*

Siskiyou Hospital Inc .... A...... 530 842-4121
444 Bruce St Yreka (96097) *(P-16431)*

Siskiyou Lake Golf Resort Inc .... D...... 530 926-3030
1000 Siskiyou Lake Blvd Mount Shasta (96067) *(P-14289)*

Siskiyou Opportunity Center (PA) .... D...... **530 926-4698**
1516 S Mount Shasta Blvd Mount Shasta (96067) *(P-18248)*

Sisters of Nzareth Los Angeles .... D...... 310 839-2361
3333 Manning Ave Los Angeles (90064) *(P-18522)*

SISTERS OF ST JOSEPH OF ORANGE, Eureka *Also Called: Sisters of St Joseph Orange (P-16929)*

Sisters of St Joseph Orange .... A...... 707 431-1135
205 East St Healdsburg (95448) *(P-16432)*

Sisters of St Joseph Orange .... A...... 747 206-9124
111 Sonoma Ave Ste 308 Santa Rosa (95405) *(P-16928)*

Sisters of St Joseph Orange .... A...... 707 443-9332
2127 Harrison Ave Ste 3 Eureka (95501) *(P-16929)*

Sisters of St Joseph Orange .... A...... 562 430-4638
240 Ocean Ave Seal Beach (90740) *(P-19028)*

Sisu Data Inc .... D...... 415 795-8250
548 Market St San Francisco (94104) *(P-11917)*

Sita Ram LLC .... D...... 209 223-0211
200 S State Highway 49 Jackson (95642) *(P-10242)*

Sitcom, Oakland *Also Called: Portfolio Productions Inc (P-5101)*

Site 204, Manteca *Also Called: Forward Inc (P-4896)*

Site 211, Martinez *Also Called: Browning-Ferris Inds Cal Inc (P-4868)*

Site 212, Bay Point *Also Called: Keller Canyon Landfill Company (P-4902)*

Site 906, Sun Valley *Also Called: BFI Waste Systems N Amer Inc (P-4867)*

Site 915, Milpitas *Also Called: BFI Waste Systems N Amer Inc (P-3373)*

Site 916, Fremont *Also Called: BFI Waste Systems N Amer Inc (P-4865)*

Site Crew Inc .... B...... 714 668-0100
3185 Airway Ave Ste G Costa Mesa (92626) *(P-10968)*

Site Helpers LLC .... D...... 877 217-5395
25232 Steinbeck Ave Stevenson Ranch (91381) *(P-20548)*

Site L71, Half Moon Bay *Also Called: Browning-Ferris Inds Cal Inc (P-4869)*

Site Sltions Cnstr Integration, Riverside *Also Called: Sitesol (P-19389)*

Sitecore Usa Inc (DH) .... C...... **415 380-0600**
101 California St Fl 16 San Francisco (94111) *(P-12351)*

Siteone Landscape Supply LLC (DH) .... D...... **770 255-2100**
10291 Ophir Rd Newcastle (95658) *(P-5592)*

Sitesol .... D...... 562 746-5884
7372 Sycamore Canyon Blvd Riverside (92508) *(P-19389)*

Siteworks Landscape Inc .... D...... 510 843-0409
5327 Jacuzzi St Ste 1b Richmond (94804) *(P-464)*

Sitonit Seating Inc .... D...... 714 995-4800
6415 Katella Ave Cypress (90630) *(P-5105)*

Sitrick Brincko Group LLC .... D...... 310 788-2850
1840 Century Park E # 800 Los Angeles (90067) *(P-20549)*

Six Continents Hotels Inc .... C...... 661 343-3316
612 Wainwight Ct Lebec (93243) *(P-10243)*

Six Continents Hotels Inc .... D...... 559 272-7840
2819 E Hamilton Ave Fresno (93721) *(P-10244)*

Six Continents Hotels Inc .... C...... 415 626-6103
50 8th St San Francisco (94103) *(P-10245)*

Six Continents Hotels Inc .... D...... 415 771-9000
495 Bay St San Francisco (94133) *(P-10246)*

Six Flags Magic Mountain, Valencia *Also Called: Magic Mountain LLC (P-14046)*

Six Flags Magic Mountain Inc .... D...... 661 255-4100
26101 Magic Mountain Pkwy Valencia (91355) *(P-14315)*

Six3 Advanced Systems Inc .... C...... 408 878-4920
2933 Bunker Hill Ln Santa Clara (95054) *(P-19390)*

Sizmek Dsp Inc .... C...... 415 757-2300
1455 Market St Ste 2100 San Francisco (94103) *(P-10675)*

Sizmek Dsp Inc (PA) .... C...... **650 595-1300**
2000 Seaport Blvd Ste 400 Redwood City (94063) *(P-12878)*

SJ Distributors LLC (PA) .... D...... **888 988-2328**
625 Vista Way Milpitas (95035) *(P-6482)*

Sj Lighting, West Sacramento *Also Called: All Phase Security Inc (P-12921)*

Sjb Child Development Centers (PA) .... D...... **408 538-0200**
1400 Parkmoor Ave Ste 220 San Jose (95126) *(P-18353)*

Sjrtd, Stockton *Also Called: San Joaquin Regional Trnst Dst (P-3201)*

SJW Group (PA) .... B...... **408 279-7800**
110 W Taylor St San Jose (95110) *(P-4835)*

Sk Hynix America Inc (HQ) .... D...... **408 232-8000**
3101 N 1st St San Jose (95134) *(P-5349)*

SK&a, Irvine *Also Called: Iqvia Inc (P-19827)*

Skadden Arps Slate Meagher & F .... C...... 213 687-5000
300 S Grand Ave Ste 3400 Los Angeles (90071) *(P-17655)*

Skadden Arps Slate Mgher Flom .... C...... 650 470-4500
525 University Ave Ste A100 Palo Alto (94301) *(P-17656)*

Skael Inc .... D...... 415 653-9433
535 Mission St Fl 14 San Francisco (94105) *(P-12626)*

Skanska Rocky Mountain Dst, Riverside *Also Called: Skanska USA Cvil W Rcky Mtn Ds (P-1319)*

Skanska USA Cvil W Cal Dst Inc (DH) .... A...... **951 684-5360**
1995 Agua Mansa Rd Riverside (92509) *(P-1164)*

Skanska USA Cvil W Rcky Mtn Ds (DH) .... D...... **970 565-8000**
1995 Agua Mansa Rd Riverside (92509) *(P-1319)*

Skava, San Francisco *Also Called: Kallidus Inc (P-11691)*

Skeffington Enterprises Inc .... D...... 714 540-1700
2200 S Yale St Santa Ana (92704) *(P-9336)*

Skid Row Housing Trust, Los Angeles *Also Called: Srht Property Holding LLC (P-9185)*

Skidmore Owings & Merrill LLP .... C...... 415 981-1555
1 Maritime Plz Fl 5 San Francisco (94111) *(P-19504)*

Skilled Healthcare LLC (DH) .... C...... **949 282-5800**
27442 Portola Pkwy Ste 200 Foothill Ranch (92610) *(P-15674)*

Skilled Nursing Facility, Oakhurst *Also Called: Oakhurst Healthcare Center LLC (P-15778)*

Skilled Nursing Facility, Oakland *Also Called: Summit Medical Center (P-16501)*

Skillsets Online Corporation .... C...... 925 964-0531
2010 Crow Canyon Pl Ste 200 San Ramon (94583) *(P-18249)*

Skillz Inc (PA) .... A...... **415 762-0511**
1061 Market St Fl 6 San Francisco (94103) *(P-11918)*

Skin Laundry Holdings Inc .... B...... 424 220-8826
130 Lomita St El Segundo (90245) *(P-20550)*

Skirball Cultural Center .... C...... 310 440-4500
2701 N Sepulveda Blvd Los Angeles (90049) *(P-18676)*

SKIRBALL CULTURAL CENTER, Los Angeles *Also Called: Skirball Cultural Center (P-18676)*

Skookum, Santa Clara *Also Called: Globallogic Inc (P-11625)*

Sky Court USA Inc .... C...... 805 497-9991
880 S Westlake Blvd Westlake Village (91361) *(P-10247)*

Skybox Security Inc (PA) .... D...... **408 441-8060**
2077 Gateway Pl Ste 200 San Jose (95110) *(P-11919)*

Skydive San Diego, Jamul *Also Called: TAC Air California Inc (P-14568)*

Skyhigh Networks Inc (DH) .... D...... **408 564-0278**
900 E Hamilton Ave Ste 400 Campbell (95008) *(P-13146)*

Skyhill Financial Inc .... D...... 714 657-3938
5762 Bolsa Ave Ste 110 Huntington Beach (92649) *(P-9180)*

Skylawn Memorial Park, Redwood City *Also Called: Chapel of Chimes (P-9283)*

Skyline Health Care Center, San Jose *Also Called: Mariner Health Care Inc (P-15565)*

Skyline Health Care Ctr, Los Angeles *Also Called: Mariner Health Care Inc (P-15570)*

SKYLINE HEALTHCARE CENTER, Los Angeles *Also Called: Skyline Hlthcare Wllness Ctr L (P-15675)*

Skyline Hlthcare Wllness Ctr L .... D...... 323 665-1185
3032 Rowena Ave Los Angeles (90039) *(P-15675)*

Skyline Scaffold Inc .... D...... 916 391-8929
3131 52nd Ave Sacramento (95823) *(P-2316)*

Skylink Travel Inc .... C...... 212 380-2438
18000 Studebaker Rd Ste 330 Cerritos (90703) *(P-3951)*

Skylite Networks .... D...... 408 934-9349
761 Mabury Rd Ste 75 San Jose (95133) *(P-11920)*

ALPHABETIC SECTION — Smart & Final Stores Inc

Skypark At Santa's Village, Skyforest Also Called: Spsv Entertainment LLC (P-14106)

Skype Inc .... D...... 650 493-7900
  One Microsoft Way, Redmond Palo Alto (94304) (P-4339)

Skypower Holdings LLC .... C...... 323 860-4900
  4700 Wilshire Blvd Los Angeles (90010) (P-1563)

Skytech Gaming, Ontario Also Called: Brainstorm Corporation (P-5282)

Skyview Capital LLC .... D...... 310 273-6000
  2000 Avenue Of The Stars Ste 810 Los Angeles (90067) (P-7908)

Skywalker Properties Ltd LLC .... D...... 415 746-5296
  1110 Gorgas Ave San Francisco (94129) (P-8761)

Skywalker Sound .... C...... 415 662-1000
  1110 Gorgas Ave San Francisco (94129) (P-1839)

Skywest Airlines Inc .... B...... 650 827-7000
  585 Mcdonnell Rd San Francisco (94128) (P-3844)

Skywest Airlines Inc .... C...... 559 252-3400
  Fresno Air Terminal Fresno (93727) (P-3845)

Skywood Events Corporation .... D...... 650 851-1606
  17285 Skyline Blvd Woodside (94062) (P-10576)

SL Blue Garden Corp .... C...... 626 633-2672
  3790 Keri Way Fallbrook (92028) (P-20551)

SL Power Electronics Corp (HQ) .... D...... 800 235-5929
  27001 Agoura Rd Ste 325 Calabasas (91301) (P-5699)

Slack, San Francisco Also Called: Slack Technologies Inc (P-12352)

Slack Technologies Inc (HQ) .... C...... 970 299-4848
  500 Howard St Ste 100 San Francisco (94105) (P-12352)

Slade Gorton & Co Inc .... D...... 714 676-4200
  1 Centerpointe Dr Ste 311 La Palma (90623) (P-6483)

Slakey Brothers Inc (PA) .... D...... 916 478-2000
  2215 Kausen Dr Ste 1 Elk Grove (95758) (P-5772)

Slalom LLC .... B...... 415 593-3450
  100 Pine St Ste 2500 San Francisco (94111) (P-20552)

Slalom LLC .... C...... 949 450-1100
  300 Spectrum Center Dr Ste 1500 Irvine (92618) (P-20848)

SLALOM, LLC, San Francisco Also Called: Slalom LLC (P-20552)

SLALOM, LLC, Irvine Also Called: Slalom LLC (P-20848)

Slashsupport Inc .... D...... 650 385-2000
  3175 Spring St Redwood City (94063) (P-4340)

SLASHSUPPORT, INC., Redwood City Also Called: Slashsupport Inc (P-4340)

Slater Inc .... D...... 909 822-6800
  11045 Rose Ave Fontana (92337) (P-1320)

Slauson Plaza Med Group, Pico Rivera Also Called: Altamed Health Services Corp (P-17173)

Sleep Data Services LLC .... D...... 619 299-6299
  5471 Kearny Villa Rd Ste 200 San Diego (92123) (P-15063)

Sleepio, San Francisco Also Called: Big Health Inc (P-15747)

SLI Systems Inc .... D...... 408 255-2487
  333 W San Carlos St Ste 1250 San Jose (95110) (P-11921)

Sliderule Labs Inc (PA) .... C...... 646 748-0378
  22 Battery St Ste 1100 San Francisco (94111) (P-11922)

Sling Media LLC .... C...... 650 293-8000
  1051 E Hillsdale Blvd Ste 500 Foster City (94404) (P-4226)

Slingshot Connections LLC .... D...... 408 247-8233
  840 The Alameda San Jose (95126) (P-11231)

Slipgatte Ironworks, San Mateo Also Called: Gazillion Inc (P-12201)

SLM Services, Simi Valley Also Called: Specialized Ldscp MGT Svcs Inc (P-466)

SLO TRANSITIONS, San Luis Obispo Also Called: Transitions - Mental Hlth Assn (P-17144)

Slogcc, San Luis Obispo Also Called: San Luis Obispo Golf Cntry CLB (P-14441)

Slorta, San Luis Obispo Also Called: San Luis Obspo Rgnal Trnst Aut (P-3202)

Slr International Corporation .... A...... 949 553-8417
  20 Corporate Park Ste 200 Irvine (92606) (P-20849)

Sls Hotel At Beverly Hills .... C...... 310 247-0400
  465 S La Cienega Blvd Los Angeles (90048) (P-10248)

SM International, Fremont Also Called: S & M Moving Systems (P-3537)

SM Tire, Nipomo Also Called: Santa Maria Tire Inc (P-7356)

SMA America, Rocklin Also Called: SMA Solar Technology Amer LLC (P-1564)

SMA Solar Technology Amer LLC .... C...... 916 625-0870
  3925 Atherton Rd Rocklin (95765) (P-1564)

Smachines, Santa Clara Also Called: Soft Machines Inc (P-12524)

Smarsh Inc .... C...... 650 631-6300
  900 Veterans Blvd Ste 500 Redwood City (94063) (P-12353)

Smart & Final, Los Angeles Also Called: Smart & Final Stores LLC (P-6321)
Smart & Final, Pacoima Also Called: Smart & Final Stores LLC (P-6328)
Smart & Final, Burbank Also Called: Smart & Final Stores LLC (P-6330)
Smart & Final, Bishop Also Called: Smart & Final Stores LLC (P-6331)
Smart & Final, Vallejo Also Called: Smart & Final Stores LLC (P-6332)
Smart & Final, El Toro Also Called: Smart & Final Stores LLC (P-6334)
Smart & Final, Delano Also Called: Smart & Final Stores LLC (P-6335)
Smart & Final, North Hollywood Also Called: Smart & Final Stores LLC (P-6336)
Smart & Final, Huntington Beach Also Called: Smart & Final Stores LLC (P-6337)
Smart & Final, Glendale Also Called: Smart & Final Stores LLC (P-6338)
Smart & Final, El Monte Also Called: Smart & Final Stores LLC (P-6339)
Smart & Final, La Quinta Also Called: Smart & Final Stores LLC (P-6340)
Smart & Final, San Diego Also Called: Smart & Final Stores LLC (P-6341)
Smart & Final, Ventura Also Called: Smart & Final Stores LLC (P-6346)
Smart & Final, Orange Also Called: Smart & Final Stores LLC (P-6350)
Smart & Final, Visalia Also Called: Smart & Final Stores LLC (P-6352)
Smart & Final, Lynwood Also Called: Smart & Final Stores LLC (P-6353)
Smart & Final, Corona Also Called: Smart & Final Stores LLC (P-6355)
Smart & Final, Los Angeles Also Called: Smart & Final Stores LLC (P-6356)
Smart & Final, Los Angeles Also Called: Smart & Final Stores LLC (P-6357)
Smart & Final, Los Angeles Also Called: Smart & Final Stores LLC (P-6358)
Smart & Final, Salinas Also Called: Smart & Final Stores LLC (P-6359)
Smart & Final, Los Angeles Also Called: Smart & Final Stores LLC (P-6360)
Smart & Final, Los Angeles Also Called: Smart & Final Stores LLC (P-6362)
Smart & Final, Fresno Also Called: Smart & Final Stores LLC (P-6363)
Smart & Final, Escondido Also Called: Smart & Final Stores LLC (P-6364)
Smart & Final, Buena Park Also Called: Smart & Final Stores LLC (P-6365)
Smart & Final, San Diego Also Called: Smart & Final Stores LLC (P-6370)
Smart & Final, Bell Also Called: Smart & Final Stores LLC (P-6371)
Smart & Final, Commerce Also Called: Smart & Final Stores LLC (P-6372)
Smart & Final, Los Angeles Also Called: Smart & Final Stores LLC (P-6373)
Smart & Final, Alhambra Also Called: Smart & Final Stores LLC (P-6374)
Smart & Final, El Cajon Also Called: Smart & Final Stores LLC (P-6376)
Smart & Final, El Centro Also Called: Smart & Final Stores LLC (P-6379)
Smart & Final, Simi Valley Also Called: Smart & Final Stores LLC (P-6380)
Smart & Final, Encino Also Called: Smart & Final Stores LLC (P-6383)
Smart & Final, Newhall Also Called: Smart & Final Stores LLC (P-6385)
Smart & Final, Tujunga Also Called: Smart & Final Stores LLC (P-6386)
Smart & Final, Covina Also Called: Smart & Final Stores LLC (P-6389)
Smart & Final, Commerce Also Called: Smart Stores Operations LLC (P-6391)
Smart & Final, Norwalk Also Called: Smart & Final Stores LLC (P-7141)
Smart & Final, Bakersfield Also Called: Smart & Final Stores LLC (P-7152)
Smart & Final 306, Rancho Palos Verdes Also Called: Smart & Final Stores LLC (P-6388)
Smart & Final 341, Los Angeles Also Called: Smart & Final Stores LLC (P-6361)
Smart & Final 355, San Diego Also Called: Smart & Final Stores LLC (P-6369)
Smart & Final 389, Costa Mesa Also Called: Smart & Final Stores LLC (P-6387)
Smart & Final 463, Chula Vista Also Called: Smart & Final Stores LLC (P-6378)
Smart & Final 508, Bakersfield Also Called: Smart & Final Stores LLC (P-6325)

Smart & Final Stores Inc .... B...... 619 449-2396
  9870 N Magnolia Ave Santee (92071) (P-6287)

Smart & Final Stores Inc .... C...... 323 549-9586
  4550 W Pico Blvd Los Angeles (90019) (P-6288)

Smart & Final Stores Inc .... B...... 909 592-2190
  1005 W Arrow Hwy San Dimas (91773) (P-6289)

Smart & Final Stores Inc .... C...... 909 773-1813
  13346 Limonite Ave Eastvale (92880) (P-6290)

Smart & Final Stores Inc .... C...... 619 522-2014
  150 B Ave Coronado (92118) (P-6291)

Smart & Final Stores Inc .... B...... 916 486-6315
  7223 Fair Oaks Blvd Carmichael (95608) (P-6292)

Smart & Final Stores Inc .... B...... 805 566-2174
  850 Linden Ave Carpinteria (93013) (P-6293)

Smart & Final Stores Inc .... B...... 714 549-2362
  1308 W Edinger Ave Santa Ana (92704) (P-6294)

Smart & Final Stores Inc .... B...... 619 390-1738
  13439 Camino Canada El Cajon (92021) (P-6295)

Smart & Final Stores Inc

ALPHABETIC SECTION

Smart & Final Stores Inc .... B...... 626 330-2495
15427 Amar Rd La Puente (91744) *(P-6296)*

Smart & Final Stores Inc .... B...... 818 368-6409
18555 Devonshire St Northridge (91324) *(P-6297)*

Smart & Final Stores Inc .... C...... 408 251-0109
1180 S King Rd San Jose (95122) *(P-6298)*

Smart & Final Stores Inc .... C...... 562 438-0450
644 Redondo Ave Long Beach (90814) *(P-6299)*

Smart & Final Stores Inc .... B...... 760 732-1480
1845 W Vista Way Vista (92083) *(P-6300)*

Smart & Final Stores Inc .... B...... 805 237-0323
2121 Spring St Paso Robles (93446) *(P-6301)*

Smart & Final Stores Inc .... C...... 760 434-2449
955 Carlsbad Village Dr Carlsbad (92008) *(P-6302)*

Smart & Final Stores Inc .... B...... 619 668-9039
933 Sweetwater Rd Spring Valley (91977) *(P-6303)*

Smart & Final Stores Inc .... B...... 949 581-1212
26911 Trabuco Rd Mission Viejo (92691) *(P-6304)*

Smart & Final Stores Inc .... B...... 530 823-1205
2825 Grass Valley Hwy Auburn (95603) *(P-6305)*

Smart & Final Stores Inc .... B...... 619 291-1842
2235 University Ave San Diego (92104) *(P-6306)*

Smart & Final Stores Inc .... C...... 323 497-8528
615 N Pacific Coast Hwy Redondo Beach (90277) *(P-6307)*

Smart & Final Stores Inc .... C...... 323 855-8434
240 S Diamond Bar Blvd Diamond Bar (91765) *(P-6308)*

Smart & Final Stores Inc .... C...... 818 954-8631
3830 W Verdugo Ave Burbank (91505) *(P-6309)*

Smart & Final Stores Inc .... B...... 661 722-6210
5038 W Avenue N Palmdale (93551) *(P-6310)*

Smart & Final Stores Inc .... C...... 818 889-8253
5770 Lindero Canyon Rd Westlake Village (91362) *(P-6311)*

Smart & Final Stores Inc .... B...... 805 647-4276
7800 Telegraph Rd Ventura (93004) *(P-6312)*

Smart & Final Stores Inc .... B...... 619 589-7000
2800 Fletcher Pkwy El Cajon (92020) *(P-6313)*

Smart & Final Stores Inc .... B...... 858 578-7343
10740 Westview Pkwy San Diego (92126) *(P-6314)*

Smart & Final Stores Inc .... B...... 562 907-7037
13003 Whittier Blvd Whittier (90602) *(P-6315)*

Smart & Final Stores Inc .... C...... 626 334-5189
303 E Foothill Blvd Azusa (91702) *(P-6316)*

Smart & Final Stores Inc .... B...... 559 229-2944
2425 N Blackstone Avenue Fresno (93703) *(P-6317)*

Smart & Final Stores Inc .... B...... 408 941-9642
401 Jacklin Rd Milpitas (95035) *(P-6318)*

Smart & Final Stores Inc .... C...... 805 520-6035
5135 E Los Angeles Ave Simi Valley (93063) *(P-6319)*

Smart & Final Stores Inc .... B...... 559 297-9376
790 W Shaw Ave Clovis (93612) *(P-6320)*

Smart & Final Stores LLC .... C...... 323 725-0791
5500 Sheila St Commerce (90040) *(P-3753)*

Smart & Final Stores LLC .... D...... 323 939-0946
5555 Wilshire Blvd Los Angeles (90036) *(P-6321)*

Smart & Final Stores LLC .... D...... 415 751-9951
350 7th Ave San Francisco (94118) *(P-6322)*

Smart & Final Stores LLC .... D...... 209 952-1030
744 W Hammer Ln Stockton (95210) *(P-6323)*

Smart & Final Stores LLC .... D...... 323 539-2400
2511 Daly St Los Angeles (90031) *(P-6324)*

Smart & Final Stores LLC .... D...... 661 589-2579
2749 Calloway Dr Ste 500 Bakersfield (93312) *(P-6325)*

Smart & Final Stores LLC .... D...... 760 439-3489
1737 Oceanside Blvd Oceanside (92054) *(P-6326)*

Smart & Final Stores LLC .... D...... 562 920-6268
15930 Bellflower Blvd Bellflower (90706) *(P-6327)*

Smart & Final Stores LLC .... D...... 818 896-6212
10893 San Fernando Rd Pacoima (91331) *(P-6328)*

Smart & Final Stores LLC .... D...... 760 322-8639
5001 E Ramon Rd Bldg 4 Palm Springs (92264) *(P-6329)*

Smart & Final Stores LLC .... D...... 818 562-3234
3708 W Burbank Blvd Burbank (91505) *(P-6330)*

Smart & Final Stores LLC .... D...... 760 873-7181
1180 N Main St Ste 101c Bishop (93514) *(P-6331)*

Smart & Final Stores LLC .... D...... 707 644-4281
3901 Sonoma Blvd Vallejo (94589) *(P-6332)*

Smart & Final Stores LLC .... D...... 714 441-1069
2475 E Chapman Ave Fullerton (92831) *(P-6333)*

Smart & Final Stores LLC .... D...... 949 770-8281
23631a El Toro Rd El Toro (92630) *(P-6334)*

Smart & Final Stores LLC .... D...... 661 721-2163
1804 Girard St Delano (93215) *(P-6335)*

Smart & Final Stores LLC .... D...... 818 982-6202
6601 Laurel Canyon Blvd North Hollywood (91606) *(P-6336)*

Smart & Final Stores LLC .... D...... 714 842-4637
6882 Edinger Ave Huntington Beach (92647) *(P-6337)*

Smart & Final Stores LLC .... D...... 818 243-4239
210 N Verdugo Rd Glendale (91206) *(P-6338)*

Smart & Final Stores LLC .... D...... 626 443-1381
11110 Ramona Blvd El Monte (91731) *(P-6339)*

Smart & Final Stores LLC .... D...... 760 342-1646
79770 Highway 111 La Quinta (92253) *(P-6340)*

Smart & Final Stores LLC .... D...... 619 239-3377
720 15th St San Diego (92101) *(P-6341)*

Smart & Final Stores LLC .... D...... 408 296-3293
2065 El Camino Real Santa Clara (95050) *(P-6342)*

Smart & Final Stores LLC .... D...... 650 345-1335
1840 S Norfolk St San Mateo (94403) *(P-6343)*

Smart & Final Stores LLC .... D...... 408 517-8803
5281 Prospect Rd San Jose (95129) *(P-6344)*

Smart & Final Stores LLC .... D...... 925 552-8153
480 Diablo Rd Danville (94526) *(P-6345)*

Smart & Final Stores LLC .... D...... 805 643-5556
2750 E Main St Ventura (93003) *(P-6346)*

Smart & Final Stores LLC .... D...... 951 341-8230
3310 Vine St Riverside (92507) *(P-6347)*

Smart & Final Stores LLC .... D...... 310 540-6157
1516 S Pacific Coast Hwy Redondo Beach (90277) *(P-6348)*

Smart & Final Stores LLC .... D...... 805 485-2051
2021 N Oxnard Blvd Oxnard (93036) *(P-6349)*

Smart & Final Stores LLC .... D...... 714 771-1470
1401 E Katella Ave Orange (92867) *(P-6350)*

Smart & Final Stores LLC .... D...... 323 219-6352
2795 S Paradise Ave Ste 170 Tracy (95304) *(P-6351)*

Smart & Final Stores LLC .... D...... 559 625-9044
600 W Center St Visalia (93291) *(P-6352)*

Smart & Final Stores LLC .... D...... 310 631-8639
10833 Long Beach Blvd Lynwood (90262) *(P-6353)*

Smart & Final Stores LLC .... D...... 909 622-3321
160 W Willow St Pomona (91768) *(P-6354)*

Smart & Final Stores LLC .... D...... 951 737-4151
760 N Main St Corona (92878) *(P-6355)*

Smart & Final Stores LLC .... C...... 310 559-1722
10113 Venice Blvd Los Angeles (90034) *(P-6356)*

Smart & Final Stores LLC .... D...... 323 732-9101
2949 W Pico Blvd Los Angeles (90006) *(P-6357)*

Smart & Final Stores LLC .... D...... 323 466-9289
939 N Western Ave Los Angeles (90029) *(P-6358)*

Smart & Final Stores LLC .... D...... 831 754-1068
319 E Market St Salinas (93901) *(P-6359)*

Smart & Final Stores LLC .... D...... 323 758-5734
8137 S Vermont Ave Los Angeles (90044) *(P-6360)*

Smart & Final Stores LLC .... D...... 323 569-7148
1125 E El Segundo Blvd Los Angeles (90059) *(P-6361)*

Smart & Final Stores LLC .... C...... 310 207-8688
12210 Santa Monica Blvd Los Angeles (90025) *(P-6362)*

Smart & Final Stores LLC .... C...... 559 439-5954
5700 N Blackstone Ave Fresno (93710) *(P-6363)*

Smart & Final Stores LLC .... D...... 760 746-5490
395 N Escondido Blvd Escondido (92025) *(P-6364)*

Smart & Final Stores LLC .... D...... 714 521-3680
7930 Valley View St Buena Park (90620) *(P-6365)*

Smart & Final Stores LLC .... D...... 661 326-7945
1725 Golden State Ave Bakersfield (93301) *(P-6366)*

ALPHABETIC SECTION

Smart & Final Stores LLC .... D....... 951 849-5658
  2971 W Ramsey St Banning (92220) *(P-6367)*
Smart & Final Stores LLC .... D....... 310 328-3023
  21600 S Vermont Ave Torrance (90502) *(P-6368)*
Smart & Final Stores LLC .... D....... 619 286-0688
  6235 El Cajon Blvd San Diego (92115) *(P-6369)*
Smart & Final Stores LLC .... D....... 858 541-2090
  5195 Clairemont Mesa Blvd San Diego (92117) *(P-6370)*
Smart & Final Stores LLC .... D....... 323 562-3421
  5029 Florence Ave Bell (90201) *(P-6371)*
Smart & Final Stores LLC (DH) .... D....... 323 869-7500
  600 Citadel Dr Commerce (90040) *(P-6372)*
Smart & Final Stores LLC .... C....... 323 268-9179
  2308 E 4th St Los Angeles (90033) *(P-6373)*
Smart & Final Stores LLC .... D....... 626 281-2049
  725 E Main St Alhambra (91801) *(P-6374)*
Smart & Final Stores LLC .... D....... 213 747-6697
  1216 Compton Ave Los Angeles (90021) *(P-6375)*
Smart & Final Stores LLC .... D....... 619 562-4151
  1090 Fletcher Pkwy El Cajon (92020) *(P-6376)*
Smart & Final Stores LLC .... D....... 951 352-5715
  4039 Tyler St Riverside (92503) *(P-6377)*
Smart & Final Stores LLC .... D....... 619 427-0202
  3141 Main St Chula Vista (91911) *(P-6378)*
Smart & Final Stores LLC .... D....... 760 352-0811
  1290 N Imperial Ave El Centro (92243) *(P-6379)*
Smart & Final Stores LLC .... D....... 805 582-9231
  1856 Erringer Rd Simi Valley (93065) *(P-6380)*
Smart & Final Stores LLC .... D....... 661 775-1416
  28207 Newhall Ranch Rd Valencia (91355) *(P-6381)*
Smart & Final Stores LLC .... D....... 408 846-7020
  250 E 10th St # 589 Gilroy (95020) *(P-6382)*
Smart & Final Stores LLC .... D....... 818 789-0242
  16847 Ventura Blvd Encino (91436) *(P-6383)*
Smart & Final Stores LLC .... D....... 510 536-7494
  1243 42nd Ave Oakland (94601) *(P-6384)*
Smart & Final Stores LLC .... D....... 661 255-9822
  23640 Lyons Ave Newhall (91321) *(P-6385)*
Smart & Final Stores LLC .... D....... 818 352-9399
  6555 Foothill Blvd Tujunga (91042) *(P-6386)*
Smart & Final Stores LLC .... D....... 949 548-8473
  707 W 19th St Costa Mesa (92627) *(P-6387)*
Smart & Final Stores LLC .... D....... 310 832-4179
  28500 S Western Ave Rancho Palos Verdes (90275) *(P-6388)*
Smart & Final Stores LLC .... D....... 626 915-6619
  114 N Azusa Ave Covina (91722) *(P-6389)*
Smart & Final Stores LLC .... D....... 562 868-0794
  10935 Firestone Blvd Norwalk (90650) *(P-7141)*
Smart & Final Stores LLC .... D....... 661 832-4540
  3400 White Ln Bakersfield (93309) *(P-7152)*
SMART & FINAL STORES, INC., Santee *Also Called: Smart & Final Stores Inc (P-6287)*
SMART & FINAL STORES, INC., Los Angeles *Also Called: Smart & Final Stores Inc (P-6288)*
SMART & FINAL STORES, INC., San Dimas *Also Called: Smart & Final Stores Inc (P-6289)*
SMART & FINAL STORES, INC., Eastvale *Also Called: Smart & Final Stores Inc (P-6290)*
SMART & FINAL STORES, INC., Coronado *Also Called: Smart & Final Stores Inc (P-6291)*
SMART & FINAL STORES, INC., Carmichael *Also Called: Smart & Final Stores Inc (P-6292)*
SMART & FINAL STORES, INC., Carpinteria *Also Called: Smart & Final Stores Inc (P-6293)*
SMART & FINAL STORES, INC., Santa Ana *Also Called: Smart & Final Stores Inc (P-6294)*
SMART & FINAL STORES, INC., El Cajon *Also Called: Smart & Final Stores Inc (P-6295)*
SMART & FINAL STORES, INC., La Puente *Also Called: Smart & Final Stores Inc (P-6296)*
SMART & FINAL STORES, INC., Northridge *Also Called: Smart & Final Stores Inc (P-6297)*
SMART & FINAL STORES, INC., San Jose *Also Called: Smart & Final Stores Inc (P-6298)*
SMART & FINAL STORES, INC., Long Beach *Also Called: Smart & Final Stores Inc (P-6299)*
SMART & FINAL STORES, INC., Vista *Also Called: Smart & Final Stores Inc (P-6300)*
SMART & FINAL STORES, INC., Paso Robles *Also Called: Smart & Final Stores Inc (P-6301)*
SMART & FINAL STORES, INC., Carlsbad *Also Called: Smart & Final Stores Inc (P-6302)*
SMART & FINAL STORES, INC., Spring Valley *Also Called: Smart & Final Stores Inc (P-6303)*
SMART & FINAL STORES, INC., Mission Viejo *Also Called: Smart & Final Stores Inc (P-6304)*
SMART & FINAL STORES, INC., Auburn *Also Called: Smart & Final Stores Inc (P-6305)*
SMART & FINAL STORES, INC., San Diego *Also Called: Smart & Final Stores Inc (P-6306)*
SMART & FINAL STORES, INC., Redondo Beach *Also Called: Smart & Final Stores Inc (P-6307)*
SMART & FINAL STORES, INC., Diamond Bar *Also Called: Smart & Final Stores Inc (P-6308)*
SMART & FINAL STORES, INC., Burbank *Also Called: Smart & Final Stores Inc (P-6309)*
SMART & FINAL STORES, INC., Palmdale *Also Called: Smart & Final Stores Inc (P-6310)*
SMART & FINAL STORES, INC., Westlake Village *Also Called: Smart & Final Stores Inc (P-6311)*
SMART & FINAL STORES, INC., Ventura *Also Called: Smart & Final Stores Inc (P-6312)*
SMART & FINAL STORES, INC., El Cajon *Also Called: Smart & Final Stores Inc (P-6313)*
SMART & FINAL STORES, INC., San Diego *Also Called: Smart & Final Stores Inc (P-6314)*
SMART & FINAL STORES, INC., Whittier *Also Called: Smart & Final Stores Inc (P-6315)*
SMART & FINAL STORES, INC., Azusa *Also Called: Smart & Final Stores Inc (P-6316)*
SMART & FINAL STORES, INC., Fresno *Also Called: Smart & Final Stores Inc (P-6317)*
SMART & FINAL STORES, INC., Milpitas *Also Called: Smart & Final Stores Inc (P-6318)*
SMART & FINAL STORES, INC., Simi Valley *Also Called: Smart & Final Stores Inc (P-6319)*
SMART & FINAL STORES, INC., Clovis *Also Called: Smart & Final Stores Inc (P-6320)*
Smart and Final Stores, Danville *Also Called: Smart & Final Stores LLC (P-6345)*
Smart Circle International LLC (PA) .... D....... 949 587-9207
  4490 Von Karman Ave Newport Beach (92660) *(P-20553)*
Smart Circle, The, Newport Beach *Also Called: Smart Circle International LLC (P-20553)*
Smart Energy Solar Inc .... C....... 800 405-1978
  1641 Comm St Corona (92880) *(P-1565)*
Smart Energy Systems Inc .... C....... 909 703-9609
  Michelson Dr Ste 3370 Irvine (92612) *(P-11923)*
Smart Energy USA, Corona *Also Called: Smart Energy Solar Inc (P-1565)*
Smart Energy Water, Irvine *Also Called: Smart Utility Systems Inc (P-11924)*
Smart Sftwr Tstg Solutions Inc .... D....... 833 778-7872
  11750 Dublin Blvd Ste 200 Dublin (94568) *(P-20850)*
Smart Stores Operations LLC .... C....... 858 748-0101
  12339 Poway Rd Poway (92064) *(P-6390)*
Smart Stores Operations LLC (DH) .... B....... 323 869-7500
  600 Citadel Dr Commerce (90040) *(P-6391)*
Smart Utility Systems Inc .... D....... 909 217-3344
  19900 Macarthur Blvd Ste 370 Irvine (92612) *(P-11924)*
Smartdrive Systems Inc (PA) .... D....... 858 225-5550
  9515 Towne Centre Dr San Diego (92121) *(P-11925)*
Smartek21 LLC .... B....... 650 617-3221
  530 Lytton Ave Fl 2 Palo Alto (94301) *(P-12879)*
Smartlogic, San Jose *Also Called: Smartlogic Semaphore Inc (P-12354)*
Smartlogic Semaphore Inc .... C....... 408 213-9500
  111 N Market St Ste 365 San Jose (95113) *(P-12354)*
Smartmatic USA Corp .... D....... 424 581-6604
  2450 Colorado Ave Santa Monica (90404) *(P-19913)*
Smartrecruiters Inc (PA) .... B....... 415 659-9130
  166 Geary St San Francisco (94108) *(P-11926)*
Smartrevenue, Santa Cruz *Also Called: Smartrevenuecom Inc (P-19847)*
Smartrevenuecom Inc .... B....... 203 733-9156
  101 Cooper St Ste 205 Santa Cruz (95060) *(P-19847)*
Smartstop Self Storage, Ladera Ranch *Also Called: Sst IV 8020 Las Vgas Blvd S LL (P-3757)*
Smartzip Analytics Inc .... D....... 855 661-1064
  6200 Stoneridge Mall Rd Ste 300 Pleasanton (94588) *(P-20554)*
Smbc Manubank, Los Angeles *Also Called: Manufacturers Bank (P-7695)*
SMC Networks Inc (HQ) .... D....... 949 679-8029
  20 Mason Irvine (92618) *(P-5350)*
SMC Products Inc .... D....... 949 753-1099
  22651 Lambert St Ste 105 Lake Forest (92630) *(P-5997)*
Smci, Costa Mesa *Also Called: Software Management Cons LLC (P-11931)*
Smci, Glendale *Also Called: Software Management Cons LLC (P-12880)*
SMD Logistics Inc .... C....... 831 758-5300
  26710 Encinal Rd Salinas (93908) *(P-4096)*
Smg .... B....... 209 937-7433
  3445 S El Dorado St Stockton (95206) *(P-20663)*
Smg Holdings LLC 562 499-7611
  300 E Ocean Blvd Long Beach (90802) *(P-8762)*
Smg Holdings LLC .... D....... 415 974-4040
  747 Howard St San Francisco (94103) *(P-13478)*
Smg Holdings LLC .... D....... 760 325-6611
  277 N Avenida Caballeros Palm Springs (92262) *(P-20555)*

Smg Management Facility, Ontario *Also Called: Ontario Convention Center Corp (P-13407)*
Smg Stockton, Stockton *Also Called: Smg (P-20663)*
Smile Brands Group Inc (PA).. D....... 714 668-1300
100 Spectrum Center Dr Ste 1500 Irvine (92618) *(P-20206)*
Smile Wide Dental, Irvine *Also Called: Universal Care Inc (P-17151)*
Smith Barney, San Jose *Also Called: Citigroup Global Markets Inc (P-8080)*
Smith Broadcasting Group Inc (PA).. C....... 805 965-0400
2315 Red Rose Way Santa Barbara (93109) *(P-20207)*
Smith Broadcasting Group Inc .... B....... 805 882-3933
730 Miramonte Dr Santa Barbara (93109) *(P-4462)*
Smith Electric Service, Santa Maria *Also Called: Smith McHncl-Lctrical-Plumbing (P-843)*
Smith McHncl-Lctrical-Plumbing .... C....... 805 621-5000
1340 W Betteravia Rd Santa Maria (93455) *(P-843)*
Smith Packing Inc .... C....... 805 348-1817
680 S Simas Rd Santa Maria (93455) *(P-6949)*
Smith Ranch Homes, San Rafael *Also Called: Smith Rnch Hmes Hmeowners Assn (P-8862)*
Smith Ranch Nursing Center, San Rafael *Also Called: Ghc of San Rafael LLC (P-15497)*
Smith River Lucky 7 Casino .... D....... 707 487-7777
350 N Indian Rd Smith River (95567) *(P-10249)*
Smith Rnch Hmes Hmeowners Assn 415 492-4900
500 Deer Valley Rd San Rafael (94903) *(P-8862)*
Smith-Emery International Inc (PA).. C....... 213 741-8500
791 E Washington Blvd Fl 3 Los Angeles (90021) *(P-20556)*
Smithgroup Inc .... C....... 313 442-8351
301 Battery St Fl 7 San Francisco (94111) *(P-19505)*
Smithgroupjjr, San Francisco *Also Called: Smithgroup Inc (P-19505)*
Sml Space Maintainers Labs, Chatsworth *Also Called: Selane Products Inc (P-3069)*
Smoke Tree Inc .... D....... 760 327-1221
1850 Smoke Tree Ln Palm Springs (92264) *(P-10250)*
Smoke Tree Ranch, Palm Springs *Also Called: Smoke Tree Inc (P-10250)*
SMS Transportation Inc .... D....... 310 527-9200
18516 S Broadway Gardena (90248) *(P-17657)*
SMS Transportation Svcs Inc .... C....... 213 489-5367
865 S Figueroa St Ste 2750 Los Angeles (90017) *(P-3214)*
Smud Energy Services, Sacramento *Also Called: Sacramento Municpl Utility Dst (P-4665)*
Smud Financing Authority, Herald *Also Called: Sacramento Municpl Utility Dst (P-13456)*
Sn Servicing Corporation .... D....... 707 445-9883
323 5th St Eureka (95501) *(P-8022)*
Snacknation, Los Angeles *Also Called: Awesome Office Inc (P-6455)*
Snackpass LLC .... D....... 203 684-5156
26 Ofarrell St Fl 8 San Francisco (94108) *(P-11927)*
Snap Inc (PA)... A....... 310 399-3339
3000 31st St Ste C Santa Monica (90405) *(P-11928)*
Snap Travel, San Francisco *Also Called: Snapcommerce Inc (P-3952)*
Snapchat, Santa Monica *Also Called: Snap Inc (P-11928)*
Snapcommerce Inc (PA)... D....... 917 704-4588
18 Bartol St San Francisco (94133) *(P-3952)*
Snapcomms Inc 805 715-0300
155 N Lake Ave Fl 9 Pasadena (91101) *(P-11929)*
Snaplogic Inc (PA)... C....... 888 494-1570
1825 S Grant St Ste 550 San Mateo (94402) *(P-12355)*
Snapwiz Inc .... C....... 510 328-3277
39300 Civic Center Dr Ste 310 Fremont (94538) *(P-12356)*
Snell & Wilmer, Costa Mesa *Also Called: Snell & Wilmer LLP (P-17658)*
Snell & Wilmer LLP .... D....... 714 427-7000
600 Anton Blvd Ste 1400 Costa Mesa (92626) *(P-17658)*
Snf Management .... D....... 310 385-1090
1901 Avenue Of The Stars Los Angeles (90067) *(P-20208)*
Snoopy's Galary and Gift Shop, Santa Rosa *Also Called: Redwood Empire Ice Oprtons LLC (P-14553)*
Snow Summit, Big Bear Lake *Also Called: Snow Summit Ski Corporation (P-10251)*
Snow Summit Ski Corporation (PA).. C....... 909 866-5766
880 Summit Blvd Big Bear Lake (92315) *(P-10251)*
Snow Valley Mountain Sports Pk, Running Springs *Also Called: Snow Valley Mtn Resort LLC (P-10412)*
Snow Valley Mtn Resort LLC .... D....... 909 867-2751
Hwy 18 Running Springs (92382) *(P-10412)*
Snow Well Service Inc .... D....... 661 765-7980
1150 Black Gold Rd Bakersfield (93308) *(P-13799)*

SNOWLINE HOSPICE, Diamond Springs *Also Called: Snowline Hspice El Dorado Cnty (P-15795)*
Snowline Hspice El Dorado Cnty .... C....... 530 621-7820
6520 Pleasant Valley Rd Diamond Springs (95619) *(P-15795)*
Snyder Langston, Irvine *Also Called: Sander Langston LP (P-1020)*
So Cal Land Maintenance Inc .... D....... 714 231-1454
3121 E La Palma Ave Ste K Anaheim (92806) *(P-10969)*
So Cal Sandbags Inc .... D....... 951 277-3404
12620 Bosley Ln Corona (92883) *(P-5925)*
So Cal Ship Services .... D....... 310 519-8411
971 S Seaside Ave San Pedro (90731) *(P-3809)*
Soboba Band Luiseno Indians .... A....... 951 665-1000
22777 Soboba Rd San Jacinto (92583) *(P-13479)*
Soboba Casino, San Jacinto *Also Called: Soboba Band Luiseno Indians (P-13479)*
Soboba Indian Health Clinic, San Jacinto *Also Called: Riversd-San Brnrdino Cnty Indi (P-15018)*
SOBRIETY HOUSE, Long Beach *Also Called: Safe Refuge (P-17123)*
Socal Sportsnet LLC .... A....... 619 795-5000
100 Park Blvd San Diego (92101) *(P-14161)*
Socalgas .... D....... 909 307-7022
1981 W Lugonia Ave Redlands (92374) *(P-4726)*
Socalgas, Northridge *Also Called: Southern California Gas Co (P-4728)*
Social Advctes For Yuth San De .... C....... 619 283-9624
4275 El Cajon Blvd Ste 101 San Diego (92105) *(P-18135)*
Social Finance Inc .... B....... 707 473-9889
375 Healdsburg Ave # 280 Healdsburg (95448) *(P-8057)*
Social Finance Inc (HQ).. C....... 415 930-4467
234 1st St San Francisco (94105) *(P-9295)*
SOCIAL FINANCE, INC, Healdsburg *Also Called: Social Finance Inc (P-8057)*
Social Intelligence, Santa Barbara *Also Called: Riviera Data Corp (P-20528)*
Social Interest Solutions, Sacramento *Also Called: Center To Prmote Hlthcare Acce (P-17202)*
Social Science Service Center .... D....... 909 421-7120
18612 Santa Ana Ave Bloomington (92316) *(P-16697)*
Social Sciences, Irvine *Also Called: University California Irvine (P-17783)*
Social Service Agency, San Jose *Also Called: County of Santa Clara (P-17940)*
Social Service Dept- Admin, City Of Industry *Also Called: County of Los Angeles (P-20070)*
Social Service Professionals, Los Angeles *Also Called: Rehababilities Inc (P-11221)*
Social Studies School Service .... D....... 310 839-2436
14401 S Main St Gardena (90248) *(P-5470)*
Social Talkie, Gardena *Also Called: Usfi Inc (P-6411)*
Socialcom Inc 310 289-4477
13468 Beach Ave Marina Del Rey (90292) *(P-20557)*
Socialite Clothing, Los Angeles *Also Called: Kash Apparel LLC (P-6203)*
Socialive .... D....... 978 821-4637
121 W Palm Ave Apt 3 El Segundo (90245) *(P-4552)*
Society of St Vncent De Paul A (PA).. D....... 510 638-7600
2272 San Pablo Ave Oakland (94612) *(P-19105)*
Society of St Vncent De Paul C (PA).. D....... 323 226-9645
210 N Avenue 21 Los Angeles (90031) *(P-19106)*
Society6, Santa Monica *Also Called: Society6 LLC (P-12627)*
Society6 LLC .... D....... 310 394-6400
1655 26th St Santa Monica (90404) *(P-12627)*
Soco Group Inc .... D....... 760 352-4683
350 E Main St El Centro (92243) *(P-6739)*
Soco Group Inc .... D....... 951 657-2350
240 E 1st St Perris (92570) *(P-6740)*
Soco Petroleum, El Centro *Also Called: Soco Group Inc (P-6739)*
Soco Petroleum Group, Perris *Also Called: Soco Group Inc (P-6740)*
Sodexo Management Inc .... A....... 925 325-9657
851 Howard St San Francisco (94103) *(P-20209)*
Sodexo Management Inc .... A....... 209 667-3634
1 University Cir Turlock (95382) *(P-20210)*
Sodexo Management Inc .... A....... 310 646-3738
450 World Way Los Angeles (90045) *(P-20558)*
Sofi, San Francisco *Also Called: Social Finance Inc (P-9295)*
Sofitel Los Angeles, Los Angeles *Also Called: Accor Corp (P-7454)*
Soft Machines Inc .... D....... 408 969-0215
3920 Freedom Cir Santa Clara (95054) *(P-12524)*
Softgear Technologies, San Mateo *Also Called: Logigear Corporation (P-11715)*

ALPHABETIC SECTION — Sonoma County Office Education

Softscript Inc .... A....... 310 451-2110
  2215 Campus Dr El Segundo (90245) *(P-10825)*
Softsol, Fremont Also Called: Softsol Resources Inc *(P-11930)*
Softsol Resources Inc (HQ) .... D....... 510 824-2000
  42840 Christy St Ste 231 Fremont (94538) *(P-11930)*
Software, Encino Also Called: Phone Check Solutions LLC *(P-11827)*
Software Dev Technical Support, San Diego Also Called: Adler Dev LLC *(P-11381)*
Software Dynamics Incorporated .... D....... 818 992-3299
  8501 Fallbrook Ave Ste 200 Canoga Park (91304) *(P-12525)*
Software Management Cons LLC .... C....... 714 662-1841
  959 S Coast Dr Ste 415 Costa Mesa (92626) *(P-11931)*
Software Management Cons LLC (HQ) .... B....... 818 240-3177
  500 N Brand Blvd Glendale (91203) *(P-12880)*
Soiree Valet Parking Service .... D....... 415 284-9700
  1470 Howard St San Francisco (94103) *(P-10577)*
Sol Nova Electric LLC .... C....... 833 765-6682
  330 Rancheros Dr Ste 116 San Marcos (92069) *(P-1840)*
Sol Republic Inc .... D....... 877 400-0310
  1000 Van Ness Ave San Francisco (94109) *(P-5700)*
Solag Disposal Co, San Juan Capistrano Also Called: Solag Incorporated *(P-4937)*
Solag Incorporated .... A....... 949 728-1206
  31641 Ortege Hwy San Juan Capistrano (92675) *(P-4937)*
Solana Labs Inc .... D....... 628 629-3265
  530 Divisadero St Pmb 722 San Francisco (94117) *(P-11932)*
Solano Cnty of Dept Rsrce MGT, Fairfield Also Called: County of Solano *(P-5485)*
SOLANO FAMILY & CHILDREN'S SER, Fairfield Also Called: Solano Fmly & Chld Council Inc *(P-18354)*
Solano Fmly & Chld Council Inc .... D....... 707 863-3950
  421 Executive Ct N Fairfield (94534) *(P-18354)*
Solano Irrigation District .... D....... 707 448-6847
  810 Vaca Valley Pkwy Ste 201 Vacaville (95688) *(P-4995)*
Solano Pacific Corporation .... D....... 707 745-6000
  900 1st St Benicia (94510) *(P-9181)*
Solar Company Inc .... D....... 510 888-9488
  20861 Wilbeam Ave Ste 1 Castro Valley (94546) *(P-1566)*
Solar Link International Inc .... C....... 909 605-7789
  4652 E Brickell St Ste A Ontario (91761) *(P-5926)*
Solar Spectrum LLC .... B....... 844 777-6527
  27368 Via Industria Ste 101 Temecula (92590) *(P-1567)*
Solari Enterprises Inc .... C....... 714 282-2520
  1507 W Yale Ave Orange (92867) *(P-8763)*
Solariant Capital LLC .... C....... 626 544-0279
  301 N Lake Ave Ste 950 Pasadena (91101) *(P-9337)*
Solarnet LLC .... C....... 707 992-3100
  1500 Valley House Dr Ste 210 Rohnert Park (94928) *(P-5760)*
Solarreserve Inc .... D....... 310 315-2200
  520 Broadway Fl 6 Santa Monica (90401) *(P-4679)*
Solarworld Americas LLC .... D....... 503 844-3400
  4650 Adohr Ln Camarillo (93012) *(P-5593)*
Solcius LLC .... C....... 951 772-0030
  12155 Magnolia Ave Ste 12b/C Riverside (92503) *(P-1568)*
SOLCIUS LLC, Riverside Also Called: Solcius LLC *(P-1568)*
Solcom Inc .... B....... 510 940-2490
  24801 Huntwood Ave Hayward (94544) *(P-1263)*
Solcom Communications Inc, Hayward Also Called: Solcom Inc *(P-1263)*
Solcom Group Inc .... D....... 510 940-2490
  28835 Mack St Hayward (94545) *(P-1264)*
Sole Technology Inc (PA) .... C....... 949 460-2020
  26921 Fuerte Dr Lake Forest (92630) *(P-2685)*
Solecon Industrial Contrs Inc .... D....... 209 572-7390
  1401 Mcwilliams Way Modesto (95351) *(P-1569)*
Soledad Cmnty Hlth Care Dst FN .... D....... 831 678-2462
  612 Main St Soledad (93960) *(P-15676)*
Soledad Medical Group, Soledad Also Called: Soledad Cmnty Hlth Care Dst FN *(P-15676)*
Soledad Migrant Headstart, Soledad Also Called: Community Action Prtnr San Lui *(P-18299)*
Soleil Communications LLC .... C....... 619 624-2888
  2655 Camino Del Rio N Ste 110 San Diego (92108) *(P-19848)*
Solex Contracting Inc .... C....... 951 308-1706
  42146 Remington Ave Temecula (92590) *(P-1265)*
Solheim Lutheran Home .... C....... 323 257-7518
  2236 Merton Ave Los Angeles (90041) *(P-18523)*

Solid Personnel Inc .... D....... 510 370-3550
  5175 Johnson Dr Pleasanton (94588) *(P-11232)*
Solid State Stor Tech USA Corp .... D....... 510 687-1800
  2610 Orchard Pkwy San Jose (95134) *(P-5351)*
Solidcore Systems Inc (DH) .... D....... 408 387-8400
  3965 Freedom Cir Santa Clara (95054) *(P-12357)*
Soligent Leasing LLC .... C....... 707 992-3100
  1500 Valley House Dr Rohnert Park (94928) *(P-5761)*
Solis Capital Partners LLC .... D....... 760 309-9436
  3371 Calle Tres Vistas Ste 100 Encinitas (92024) *(P-9563)*
Solis FL Owner, Los Angeles Also Called: Truamerica Multifamily LLC *(P-9575)*
Solix Technologies Inc (PA) .... D....... 408 654-6405
  4701 Patrick Henry Dr Ste 2001 Santa Clara (95054) *(P-11933)*
Sollis Health La PC A Med Corp .... D....... 415 233-9901
  1005 Van Ness Ave San Francisco (94109) *(P-16433)*
Solomon Ward Sdnwurm Smith LLP .... D....... 619 231-0303
  401 B St Ste 1200 San Diego (92101) *(P-17659)*
Solopower Inc .... C....... 503 388-3710
  5981 Optical Ct San Jose (95138) *(P-19772)*
Solpac Inc .... C....... 619 296-6247
  2424 Congress St San Diego (92110) *(P-1030)*
Solpac Construction Inc .... C....... 619 296-6247
  2424 Congress St San Diego (92110) *(P-20211)*
Soltek Pacific, San Diego Also Called: Solpac Inc *(P-1030)*
Soltek Pacific Construction Co, San Diego Also Called: Solpac Construction Inc *(P-20211)*
Solugenix, Brea Also Called: Solugenix Corporation *(P-12526)*
Solugenix Corporation (PA) .... C....... 866 749-7658
  601 Valencia Ave Ste 260 Brea (92823) *(P-12526)*
Solutions Inc .... C....... 949 899-0448
  4 Hutton Centre Dr Santa Ana (92707) *(P-20559)*
Solutionz Inc .... C....... 888 815-0322
  1029 Swarthmore Ave Pacific Palisades (90272) *(P-20560)*
Solv Energy LLC (HQ) .... C....... 858 251-4888
  16680 W Bernardo Dr San Diego (92127) *(P-4680)*
Solv Energy LLC .... B....... 858 622-4040
  16798 W Bernardo Dr San Diego (92128) *(P-12358)*
Solvang Lutheran Home Inc .... C....... 805 688-3263
  636 Atterdag Rd Solvang (93463) *(P-15677)*
Solve All Facility Services, Oceanside Also Called: Bergensons Property Svcs Inc *(P-10860)*
Someone's In The Kitchen, Tarzana Also Called: JMJ Enterprises Inc *(P-7490)*
Somis Pacific AG Management, Temecula Also Called: Sierra Pacific Farms Inc *(P-380)*
Sonance, San Clemente Also Called: Dana Innovations *(P-2878)*
Sonar Entertainment Inc (PA) .... D....... 424 230-7140
  2834 Colorado Ave Ste 300 Santa Monica (90404) *(P-13967)*
Sonata, Fremont Also Called: Sonata Software North Amer Inc *(P-11934)*
Sonata Software North Amer Inc (HQ) .... D....... 510 791-7220
  39300 Civic Center Dr Ste 270 Fremont (94538) *(P-11934)*
Sonata Solar LLC .... C....... 707 992-3100
  1500 Valley House Dr # 210 Rohnert Park (94928) *(P-5762)*
Sonatus Inc (PA) .... C....... 650 488-8500
  330 Gibraltar Dr Sunnyvale (94089) *(P-11935)*
Sonesta Intl Hotels Corp .... B....... 415 929-2393
  495 Geary St San Francisco (94102) *(P-10252)*
Sonia Corina Inc .... D....... 707 644-4491
  1100 Rose Dr Ste 140 Benicia (94510) *(P-17327)*
Sonic Industries Inc .... C....... 310 532-8382
  20030 Normandie Ave Torrance (90502) *(P-19391)*
Sonicwall Inc (PA) .... A....... 888 557-6642
  1033 Mccarthy Blvd Milpitas (95035) *(P-12527)*
Sonitrol, San Jose Also Called: Pacific West Security Inc *(P-13136)*
Sonoma Canopy Tours, Occidental Also Called: Alliance Rdwods Cnfrnce Grnds *(P-10398)*
Sonoma Cnty Indian Hlth Prj In (PA) .... C....... 707 521-4545
  144 Stony Point Rd Santa Rosa (95401) *(P-15064)*
Sonoma Cnty Scuritization Corp .... D....... 707 565-2241
  575 Administration Dr Rm 105a Santa Rosa (95403) *(P-3911)*
Sonoma Country Day School .... D....... 707 284-3200
  4400 Day School Pl Santa Rosa (95403) *(P-17750)*
Sonoma County Airport Ex Inc .... B....... 707 837-8700
  5807 Old Redwood Hwy Santa Rosa (95403) *(P-3215)*
Sonoma County Office Education .... D....... 707 524-2690
  5350 Skylane Blvd Santa Rosa (95403) *(P-17660)*

Employee Codes: A=Over 500 employees, B=251-500
C=101-250, D=51-100, E=20-50, F=10-19, G=1-9

Sonoma County Water Agency (PA) .... C 707 526-5370
  404 Aviation Blvd Santa Rosa (95403) *(P-4836)*
Sonoma Development Center, Eldridge *Also Called: Califrnia Dept Dvlpmental Svcs (P-16668)*
Sonoma Hotel Operator Inc .... C 707 938-9000
  100 Boyes Blvd Sonoma (95476) *(P-10253)*
Sonoma Hotel Partners LP .... D 707 283-2888
  745 Baywood Dr Petaluma (94954) *(P-10254)*
Sonoma Post Acute, Sonoma *Also Called: Sonomaidence Opco LLC (P-15796)*
Sonoma Technology Inc .... D 707 665-9900
  1450 N Mcdowell Blvd Ste 200 Petaluma (94954) *(P-20851)*
Sonoma Tilemakers Inc .... D 707 837-8177
  7890 Bell Rd Windsor (95492) *(P-3754)*
Sonoma Valley Health Care Dst (PA) .... B 707 935-5000
  347 Andrieux St Sonoma (95476) *(P-16434)*
Sonoma Valley Hospital, Sonoma *Also Called: Sonoma Valley Health Care Dst (P-16434)*
Sonoma West Medical Center .... C 707 823-8511
  501 Petaluma Ave Sebastopol (95472) *(P-16435)*
Sonomaidence Opco LLC .... D 707 938-1096
  678 2nd St W Sonoma (95476) *(P-15796)*
Sonora Community Hospital .... C 209 536-5012
  1000 Greenley Rd Sonora (95370) *(P-15065)*
Sonoran Roofing Inc .... D 916 624-1080
  4161 Citrus Ave Rocklin (95677) *(P-2085)*
Sonova USA Inc .... D 510 743-3900
  47257 Fremont Blvd Fremont (94538) *(P-13480)*
Sonrava, Orange *Also Called: Premier Dental Holdings Inc (P-15248)*
Sony Biotechnology Inc .... D 800 275-5963
  1730 N 1st St 2nd Fl San Jose (95112) *(P-12359)*
Sony Computer Entrmt Amer, Foster City *Also Called: Sony Interactive Entertainment America LLC (P-5998)*
Sony Corporation of America 650 655-8000
  2207 Bridgepointe Pkwy Foster City (94404) *(P-11936)*
Sony Electronics Inc (DH) .... A 858 942-2400
  16535 Via Esprillo 1 San Diego (92127) *(P-2881)*
Sony Interactive Entertainment, Foster City *Also Called: Sony Interactive Entrmt LLC (P-13481)*
Sony Interactive Entertainment America LLC .... A 650 655-8000
  2207 Bridgepointe Pkwy Foster City (94404) *(P-5998)*
Sony Interactive Entrmt LLC .... D 858 824-5501
  919 E Hillsdale Blvd Foster City (94404) *(P-13481)*
Sony Interactive Entrmt LLC .... C 650 655-8000
  2207 Bridgepointe Pkwy San Mateo (94404) *(P-14105)*
Sony Pctres Wrldwide Acqstons .... C 310 244-4000
  10202 Washington Blvd Culver City (90232) *(P-13893)*
Sony Pictures Entrmt Inc (DH) .... A 310 244-4000
  10202 Washington Blvd Culver City (90232) *(P-13894)*
Sony Pictures Imageworks Inc .... A 310 840-8000
  9050 Washington Blvd Culver City (90232) *(P-12628)*
Sony Pictures Studios, Culver City *Also Called: Sony Pictures Entrmt Inc (P-13894)*
Sony Pictures Studios Inc .... C 310 244-4000
  10202 Washington Blvd Culver City (90232) *(P-13895)*
Sony Pictures Television Inc (DH) .... B 310 244-7625
  10202 Washington Blvd Culver City (90232) *(P-13896)*
Soofer Co Inc .... D 323 234-6666
  2828 S Alameda St Vernon (90058) *(P-6669)*
SOS Security Incorporated .... C 310 392-9600
  3000 S Robertson Blvd Ste 100 Los Angeles (90034) *(P-13048)*
Soto Company Inc .... D 949 493-9403
  34275 Camino Capistrano Ste A Capistrano Beach (92624) *(P-537)*
Soto Food Service, City Of Industry *Also Called: Soto Provision Inc (P-5134)*
Soto Provision Inc .... D 626 458-4600
  488 Parriott Pl W City Of Industry (91745) *(P-5134)*
Soul Machines Inc .... D 649 283-0863
  44 Tehama St Ste 411 San Francisco (94105) *(P-12528)*
Souldriver Lessee Inc .... D 619 819-9500
  435 6th Ave San Diego (92101) *(P-10255)*
Sound Image, Escondido *Also Called: Cal Southern Sound Image Inc (P-5638)*
Sound Inpatient Physicians Inc .... D 650 257-3470
  702 Marshall St Redwood City (94063) *(P-1841)*
Sound Physicians, Redwood City *Also Called: Sound Inpatient Physicians Inc (P-1841)*
Sound River Corporation .... D 661 705-3700
  28238 Sonoma Avenue Crocker Valencia (91355) *(P-1842)*

Sound-Crete Contractors Inc .... D 760 291-1240
  530 Opper St Ste A Escondido (92029) *(P-5804)*
Source 44 LLC .... C 877 916-6337
  4660 La Jolla Village Dr Ste 100 San Diego (92122) *(P-20852)*
Source Intelligence, San Diego *Also Called: Source 44 LLC (P-20852)*
Source Logistics Center Corp .... D 323 887-3884
  812 Union St Montebello (90640) *(P-4097)*
Source One Staffing LLC .... A 626 337-0560
  5312 Irwindale Ave Ste 1h Baldwin Park (91706) *(P-11233)*
Sourceblue LLC .... C 510 267-8100
  100 Bush St Ste 510 San Francisco (94104) *(P-4098)*
Sourcecorp Bps Nthrn Cal Inc .... C 530 893-7900
  900 Fortress St Chico (95973) *(P-5256)*
Sourcewise .... D 408 350-3200
  3100 De La Cruz Blvd Ste 310 Santa Clara (95054) *(P-18136)*
SOUTH BAY CENTER FOR COMMUNITY, Wilmington *Also Called: South Bay Ctr For Counseling (P-18137)*
South Bay Construction Company, Campbell *Also Called: SBCI INC (P-774)*
South Bay Ctr For Counseling .... D 310 414-2090
  540 N Marine Ave Wilmington (90744) *(P-18137)*
South Bay Ford Inc (PA) .... C 310 644-0211
  5100 W Rosecrans Ave Hawthorne (90250) *(P-7299)*
South Bay Post Acute Care, Chula Vista *Also Called: Bayside Healthcare Inc (P-15352)*
South Bay Power Plant, Chula Vista *Also Called: San Diego Gas & Electric Co (P-4720)*
South Bay Sand Blstg Tank Clg .... D 619 238-8338
  326 W 30th St National City (91950) *(P-13800)*
South Bay Senior Services Inc .... D 310 338-8558
  8929 S Sepulveda Blvd Ste 314 Los Angeles (90045) *(P-16930)*
South Bay Toyota .... C 310 323-7800
  18416 S Western Ave Gardena (90248) *(P-7300)*
South Bay Wine Group LLC .... D 310 465-0551
  389 4th St E Sonoma (95476) *(P-6806)*
South Baylo Acupuncture Clinic, Los Angeles *Also Called: South Baylo University (P-17127)*
South Baylo University .... C 213 999-0297
  2727 W 6th St Los Angeles (90057) *(P-17127)*
South Cast A Qlty MGT Dst Bldg (PA) .... A 909 396-2000
  21865 Copley Dr Diamond Bar (91765) *(P-20853)*
South Central Family Hlth Ctr .... D 323 908-4200
  4425 S Central Ave Los Angeles (90011) *(P-15066)*
South Cntl Hlth Rhblttion Prgr .... D 310 667-4070
  2620 Industry Way Lynwood (90262) *(P-17128)*
South Cntl Los Angles Rgnal CT (PA) .... C 213 744-7000
  2500 S Western Ave Los Angeles (90018) *(P-18623)*
South Cntl Los Angles Rgnal CT .... C 231 744-8484
  650 W Adams Blvd Los Angeles (90007) *(P-18624)*
South Cnty Cmnty Hlth Ctr Inc (PA) .... D 650 330-7407
  1885 Bay Rd East Palo Alto (94303) *(P-15067)*
South Cnty Lxus At Mssion Vejo .... C 949 347-3400
  28242 Marguerite Pkwy Mission Viejo (92692) *(P-7301)*
South Cnty Orthpd Spclsts A ME .... D 949 586-3200
  24331 El Toro Rd Ste 200 Laguna Hills (92637) *(P-15068)*
South Coast Auto Insurance, Huntington Beach *Also Called: Freeway Insurance (P-8572)*
South Coast Behavioral Health .... D 714 312-5058
  2220 University Dr Newport Beach (92660) *(P-16931)*
South Coast Childrens Soc Inc .... C 909 478-3377
  24950 Redlands Blvd Loma Linda (92354) *(P-17129)*
South Coast Global Med Ctr Inc .... D 714 754-5454
  2701 S Bristol St Santa Ana (92704) *(P-15069)*
South Coast Mechanical Inc .... D 714 738-6644
  800 E Orangethorpe Ave Anaheim (92801) *(P-1570)*
South Coast Medical Center (PA) .... A 916 781-2000
  2100 Douglas Blvd Roseville (95661) *(P-16436)*
South Coast Piering Inc .... D 800 922-2488
  7301 Madison St Paramount (90723) *(P-1031)*
South Coast Plaza LLC .... C 714 435-2000
  3333 Bristol St Ofc Costa Mesa (92626) *(P-8764)*
South Coast Plaza Mall, Costa Mesa *Also Called: South Coast Plaza LLC (P-8764)*
South Coast Plaza Security .... C 714 435-2180
  695 Town Center Dr Ste 50 Costa Mesa (92626) *(P-20212)*
South Coast Repertory Inc .... D 714 708-5500
  655 Town Center Dr Costa Mesa (92626) *(P-14069)*

ALPHABETIC SECTION

Southern Cal Prmnnte Med Group

South Coast Trnsp & Dist Inc .... D....... 310 816-0280
1424 S Raymond Ave Fullerton (92831) *(P-3423)*

South Coast Westin Hotel Co .... D....... 714 540-2500
686 Anton Blvd Costa Mesa (92626) *(P-10256)*

South Coast YMCA, Laguna Niguel *Also Called: Young MNS Chrstn Assn Ornge CN*
(P-14485)

South Cone Inc .... C....... 760 431-2300
5935 Darwin Ct Carlsbad (92008) *(P-6234)*

South County Fire, Tracy *Also Called: South San Jquin Cnty Fire Auth (P-4837)*

South East Rio Vista YMCA, Maywood *Also Called: Young MNS Chrstn Assn Mtro Los*
(P-18959)

South Hills Country Club .... D....... 626 339-1231
2655 S Citrus St West Covina (91791) *(P-14455)*

South Park Commons LLC .... D....... 978 815-7723
27 S Park St Ste 101 San Francisco (94107) *(P-14456)*

South Plcer Fire Prtection Dst, Granite Bay *Also Called: County of Placer (P-20934)*

South Pninsula Hebrew Day Schl .... D....... 408 738-3060
1030 Astoria Dr Sunnyvale (94087) *(P-17751)*

South San Frncsco Scvenger Inc .... D....... 650 589-4020
500 E Jamie Ct South San Francisco (94080) *(P-4938)*

South San Jquin Cnty Fire Auth .... D....... 209 831-6702
835 N Central Ave Tracy (95376) *(P-4837)*

South San Jquin Irrigation Dst .... D....... 209 249-4600
11011 E Highway 120 Manteca (95336) *(P-4838)*

South Seas Imports, Compton *Also Called: M M Fab Inc (P-6157)*

South Sun Products Inc .... D....... 858 694-0910
8601 Aero Dr San Diego (92123) *(P-7405)*

South Tahoe Public Utility Dst .... C....... 530 544-6474
1275 Meadow Crest Dr South Lake Tahoe (96150) *(P-4852)*

South Tahoe Refuse Co .... D....... 530 541-5105
2140 Ruth Ave South Lake Tahoe (96150) *(P-4939)*

South Valley Almond Co LLC .... C....... 661 391-9000
15443 Beech Ave Wasco (93280) *(P-6697)*

South Valley Farms, Wasco *Also Called: South Valley Almond Co LLC (P-6697)*

Southbay BMW, Torrance *Also Called: Southbay European Inc (P-7302)*

Southbay European Inc .... D....... 310 939-7300
18800 Hawthorne Blvd Torrance (90504) *(P-7302)*

Southbourne Inc .... C....... 415 781-5555
340 Stockton St San Francisco (94108) *(P-10257)*

Southcoast Welding & Mfg LLC .... B....... 619 429-1337
2591 Faivre St Ste 1 Chula Vista (91911) *(P-13753)*

Southeast Fresno Rad LP .... C....... 559 443-8400
4430 E Hamilton Ave Fresno (93702) *(P-20854)*

SOUTHEAST INDUSTRIES, Downey *Also Called: ARC Los Angles Orange Counties (P-18206)*

Southeastern Westminster, Westminster *Also Called: Southern California Edison Co (P-4690)*

Southern Bptst Jnness Pk Encmp, Long Barn *Also Called: Califrnia Sthern Bptst Cnvntio*
(P-19012)

Southern CA Gastroenterology .... D....... 818 425-9761
50 Alessandro Pl Ste A30 Pasadena (91105) *(P-15070)*

Southern CA Hlth & Rhbltn Prg .... C....... 310 631-8004
2610 Industry Way Ste A Lynwood (90262) *(P-15071)*

Southern Cal Alchol DRG Prgram (PA) .... D....... 562 923-4545
11500 Paramount Blvd Downey (90241) *(P-17130)*

Southern Cal Appraisal Co, Burbank *Also Called: Sca Enterprises Inc (P-13466)*

Southern Cal Ctr For Spt Mdcin, Long Beach *Also Called: Memorial Orthpdic Srgcal Group*
(P-14894)

Southern Cal Dgnstc Imging Inc .... D....... 714 991-3367
1110 W La Palma Ave Anaheim (92801) *(P-15072)*

Southern Cal Disc Tire Co Inc .... C....... 510 429-1977
34734 Alvarado Niles Rd Union City (94587) *(P-7357)*

Southern Cal Disc Tire Co Inc .... D....... 916 638-2388
11127 Folsom Blvd Rancho Cordova (95670) *(P-7358)*

Southern Cal Disc Tire Co Inc .... C....... 951 929-2130
600 W Florida Ave Hemet (92543) *(P-7359)*

Southern Cal Disc Tire Co Inc .... C....... 760 741-9805
550 N Broadway Escondido (92025) *(P-7360)*

Southern Cal Disc Tire Co Inc .... C....... 714 901-8226
15672 Springdale St Huntington Beach (92649) *(P-7361)*

Southern Cal Disc Tire Co Inc .... D....... 626 335-2883
705 S Grand Ave Glendora (91740) *(P-7362)*

Southern Cal Disc Tire Co Inc .... D....... 760 744-3526
780 Grand Ave San Marcos (92078) *(P-7363)*

Southern Cal Disc Tire Co Inc .... D....... 805 639-0166
4640 Telephone Rd Ventura (93003) *(P-7364)*

Southern Cal Disc Tire Co Inc .... C....... 760 741-3801
209 S Escondido Blvd Escondido (92025) *(P-7365)*

Southern Cal Disc Tire Co Inc .... C....... 858 481-6387
685 San Rodolfo Dr Solana Beach (92075) *(P-7366)*

Southern Cal Disc Tire Co Inc .... C....... 858 486-3600
12651 Poway Rd Poway (92064) *(P-7367)*

Southern Cal Disc Tire Co Inc .... C....... 760 439-8539
1037 S Coast Hwy Oceanside (92054) *(P-7368)*

Southern Cal Disc Tire Co Inc .... C....... 916 427-1961
6434 Florin Rd Sacramento (95823) *(P-7369)*

Southern Cal Disc Tire Co Inc .... C....... 650 366-4003
1610 Broadway St Redwood City (94063) *(P-7370)*

Southern Cal Disc Tire Co Inc .... C....... 650 988-9611
32 W El Camino Real Mountain View (94040) *(P-7371)*

Southern Cal Disc Tire Co Inc .... C....... 760 634-2202
107 N El Camino Real Encinitas (92024) *(P-7372)*

Southern Cal Disc Tire Co Inc .... C....... 408 377-5010
980 E Hamilton Ave Campbell (95008) *(P-7373)*

Southern Cal Disc Tire Co Inc .... C....... 408 436-8274
536 E Brokaw Rd San Jose (95112) *(P-7374)*

Southern Cal Disc Tire Co Inc .... C....... 858 278-0661
3935 Convoy St San Diego (92111) *(P-7375)*

Southern Cal Disc Tire Co Inc .... C....... 310 324-2569
20741 Avalon Blvd Carson (90746) *(P-7376)*

Southern Cal Edson - Prvate Ch, Rosemead *Also Called: Southern California Edison Co*
(P-4702)

Southern Cal Fd Allergy Inst, Long Beach *Also Called: Transltnal Plmnary Immnlogy RE*
(P-15128)

Southern Cal Hlthcare Sys Inc .... B....... 310 836-7000
3828 Delmas Ter Culver City (90232) *(P-16437)*

Southern Cal Hlthcare Sys Inc (HQ) .... C....... 310 943-4500
3415 S Sepulveda Blvd 9th Fl Los Angeles (90034) *(P-16438)*

Southern Cal Hosp At Culver Cy, Culver City *Also Called: Brotman Medical Center Inc*
(P-15963)

Southern Cal Hosp At Culver Cy, Culver City *Also Called: Southern Cal Hlthcare Sys Inc*
(P-16437)

Southern Cal Ibw-Neca Hlth Tr .... D....... 323 221-5861
100 Corson St Ste 200 Pasadena (91103) *(P-18795)*

Southern Cal Inst For RES Edca .... D....... 562 826-8139
5901 E 7th St 151 Long Beach (90822) *(P-19914)*

Southern Cal Nursing Academy, Palm Desert *Also Called: Southern California Gas Co*
(P-4733)

Southern Cal Orthpd Inst LP (PA) .... C....... 818 901-6600
6815 Noble Ave Van Nuys (91405) *(P-15073)*

Southern Cal Pipe Trades ADM .... D....... 619 224-3125
1936 Quivira Way Bldg G San Diego (92109) *(P-9182)*

Southern Cal Pipe Trades ADM (PA) .... D....... 213 385-6161
501 Shatto Pl Ste 500 Los Angeles (90020) *(P-9447)*

Southern Cal Pipe Trades ADM, Los Angeles *Also Called: Southern Cal Pipe Trades ADM*
(P-9447)

Southern Cal Prmnnte Med Group .... B....... 800 272-3500
13652 Cantara St Panorama City (91402) *(P-8362)*

Southern Cal Prmnnte Med Group .... C....... 866 984-7483
10800 Magnolia Ave Riverside (92505) *(P-8363)*

Southern Cal Prmnnte Med Group .... B....... 626 960-4844
1511 W Garvey Ave N West Covina (91790) *(P-8364)*

Southern Cal Prmnnte Med Group .... C....... 714 734-4500
17542 17th St Ste 300 Tustin (92780) *(P-8365)*

Southern Cal Prmnnte Med Group .... C....... 909 394-2505
1255 W Arrow Hwy San Dimas (91773) *(P-8366)*

Southern Cal Prmnnte Med Group .... C....... 619 528-5000
6860 Avenida Encinas Carlsbad (92011) *(P-8367)*

Southern Cal Prmnnte Med Group .... B....... 858 974-1000
5855 Copley Dr Ste 250 San Diego (92111) *(P-8368)*

Southern Cal Prmnnte Med Group (HQ) .... D....... 626 405-5704
393 Walnut St Pasadena (91107) *(P-8369)*

Southern Cal Prmnnte Med Group .... C....... 714 279-4675
411 N Lakeview Ave Anaheim (92807) *(P-15074)*

Southern Cal Prmnnte Med Group .... C....... 661 398-5085
3501 Stockdale Hwy Bakersfield (93309) *(P-15075)*

Southern Cal Prmnnte Med Group

Southern Cal Prmnnte Med Group .... B....... 619 528-5000
 4647 Zion Ave San Diego (92120) *(P-15076)*
Southern Cal Prmnnte Med Group .... C....... 310 604-5700
 3830 Martin Luther King Jr Blvd Lynwood (90262) *(P-15077)*
Southern Cal Prmnnte Med Group .... C....... 800 780-1230
 25825 Vermont Ave Harbor City (90710) *(P-15078)*
Southern Cal Prmnnte Med Group .... C....... 323 783-5455
 4841 Hollywood Blvd Los Angeles (90027) *(P-15079)*
Southern Cal Prmnnte Med Group .... C....... 909 370-2501
 789 E Cooley Dr Colton (92324) *(P-15080)*
Southern Cal Prmnnte Med Group .... C....... 310 737-4900
 5620 Mesmer Ave Culver City (90230) *(P-15081)*
Southern Cal Prmnnte Med Group .... C....... 310 419-3306
 110 N La Brea Ave Inglewood (90301) *(P-15082)*
Southern Cal Prmnnte Med Group .... C....... 714 841-7293
 18081 Beach Blvd Huntington Beach (92648) *(P-15083)*
Southern Cal Prmnnte Med Group .... C....... 619 528-5000
 1630 E Main St El Cajon (92021) *(P-15084)*
Southern Cal Prmnnte Med Group .... C....... 949 234-2139
 30400 Camino Capistrano San Juan Capistrano (92675) *(P-15085)*
Southern Cal Prmnnte Med Group .... C....... 619 516-6000
 4405 Vandever Ave San Diego (92120) *(P-15086)*
Southern Cal Prmnnte Med Group .... C....... 760 839-7200
 732 N Broadway Escondido (92025) *(P-15087)*
Southern Cal Prmnnte Med Group .... C....... 323 562-6459
 7825 Atlantic Ave Cudahy (90201) *(P-15088)*
Southern Cal Prmnnte Med Group .... C....... 818 592-3038
 21263 Erwin St Woodland Hills (91367) *(P-15089)*
Southern Cal Prmnnte Med Group .... C....... 661 222-2150
 27107 Tourney Rd Santa Clarita (91355) *(P-15090)*
Southern Cal Prmnnte Med Group .... C....... 661 334-2020
 5055 California Ave Bakersfield (93309) *(P-15091)*
Southern Cal Prmnnte Med Group .... C....... 949 262-5780
 6 Willard Irvine (92604) *(P-15092)*
Southern Cal Prmnnte Med Group .... C....... 714 967-4760
 1900 E 4th St Santa Ana (92705) *(P-15093)*
Southern Cal Prmnnte Med Group .... C....... 323 783-4893
 4760 W Sunset Blvd Los Angeles (90027) *(P-15094)*
Southern Cal Prmnnte Med Group .... C....... 323 857-2000
 6041 Cadillac Ave Los Angeles (90034) *(P-15095)*
Southern Cal Prmnnte Med Group .... B....... 661 290-3100
 26415 Carl Boyer Dr Santa Clarita (91350) *(P-16439)*
Southern Cal Prmnnte Med Group .... B....... 909 427-5000
 9961 Sierra Ave Fontana (92335) *(P-16440)*
Southern Cal Prmnnte Med Group .... B....... 562 657-2200
 9353 Imperial Hwy Garden Medical Bldg Flr 3 Downey (90242) *(P-16441)*
Southern Cal Prmnnte Med Group .... C....... 949 376-8619
 23781 Maquina Mission Viejo (92691) *(P-17328)*
Southern Cal Prmnnte Med Group .... C....... 323 564-7911
 1465 E 103rd St Los Angeles (90002) *(P-17816)*
Southern Cal Rgional Rail Auth .... C....... 213 808-7043
 2704 N Garey Ave Pomona (91767) *(P-3216)*
Southern Cal Rgional Rail Auth (PA) .... C....... 213 452-0200
 900 Wilshire Blvd Ste 1500 Los Angeles (90017) *(P-3217)*
Southern Cal Spcialty Care Inc .... C....... 714 564-7800
 1901 College Ave Santa Ana (92706) *(P-16442)*
Southern Cal Spcialty Care Inc .... C....... 626 339-5451
 845 N Lark Ellen Ave West Covina (91791) *(P-16443)*
Southern Cal Spcialty Care Inc, La Mirada Also Called: *Southern Cal Spcialty Care LLC* *(P-16444)*
Southern Cal Spcialty Care LLC (DH) .... D....... 562 944-1900
 14900 Imperial Hwy La Mirada (90638) *(P-16444)*
Southern California Carriers, Heber Also Called: *C S Transport Inc* *(P-3376)*
Southern California Edison Co .... C....... 559 893-3611
 54205 Mt Poplar Ave Big Creek (93605) *(P-4681)*
Southern California Edison Co .... C....... 626 303-8480
 1440 S California Ave Monrovia (91016) *(P-4682)*
Southern California Edison Co .... D....... 805 496-3406
 3589 Foothill Dr Westlake Village (91361) *(P-4683)*
Southern California Edison Co .... A....... 909 274-1925
 2 Innovation Way Fl 1 Pomona (91768) *(P-4684)*
Southern California Edison Co .... D....... 818 999-1880
 3589 Foothill Dr Thousand Oaks (91361) *(P-4685)*
Southern California Edison Co .... D....... 626 815-7296
 6000 N Irwindale Ave Ste A Irwindale (91702) *(P-4686)*
Southern California Edison Co .... A....... 909 469-0251
 265 Ne End Ave Pomona (91767) *(P-4687)*
Southern California Edison Co .... B....... 310 608-5029
 1924 E Cashdan St Compton (90220) *(P-4688)*
Southern California Edison Co .... C....... 661 607-0207
 28250 Gateway Village Dr Valencia (91355) *(P-4689)*
Southern California Edison Co .... A....... 714 895-0420
 7300 Fenwick Ln Westminster (92683) *(P-4690)*
Southern California Edison Co .... C....... 949 587-5416
 14155 Bake Pkwy Irvine (92618) *(P-4691)*
Southern California Edison Co .... D....... 562 529-7301
 6900 Orange Ave Long Beach (90805) *(P-4692)*
Southern California Edison Co .... C....... 714 895-0163
 7333 Bolsa Ave Westminster (92683) *(P-4693)*
Southern California Edison Co .... C....... 760 375-1821
 510 S China Lake Blvd Ridgecrest (93555) *(P-4694)*
Southern California Edison Co .... B....... 626 814-4212
 13025 Los Angeles St Irwindale (91706) *(P-4695)*
Southern California Edison Co .... C....... 909 592-3757
 800 W Cienega Ave San Dimas (91773) *(P-4696)*
Southern California Edison Co .... B....... 562 903-3191
 9901 Geary Ave Santa Fe Springs (90670) *(P-4697)*
Southern California Edison Co .... C....... 626 812-7380
 6090 N Irwindale Ave Irwindale (91702) *(P-4698)*
Southern California Edison Co .... D....... 714 895-0119
 7400 Fenwick Ln Westminster (92683) *(P-4699)*
Southern California Edison Co .... C....... 559 893-2037
 55481 Mt Poplar Big Creek (93605) *(P-4700)*
Southern California Edison Co .... B....... 714 870-3225
 1851 W Valencia Dr Fullerton (92833) *(P-4701)*
Southern California Edison Co .... B....... 626 302-1212
 2131 Walnut Grove Ave Rosemead (91770) *(P-4702)*
Southern California Edison Co (HQ) .... **A....... 626 302-1212**
 2244 Walnut Grove Ave Rosemead (91770) *(P-4703)*
Southern California Edison Co .... D....... 626 543-8081
 4900 Rivergrade Rd Bldg 2b1 Irwindale (91706) *(P-4704)*
Southern California Edison Co .... C....... 760 873-0715
 4000 Bishop Creek Rd Bishop (93514) *(P-4705)*
Southern California Edison Co .... D....... 800 336-2822
 26125 Menifee Rd Romoland (92585) *(P-4706)*
Southern California Edison Co .... D....... 626 633-3070
 6042 N Irwindale Ave Ste A Irwindale (91702) *(P-4707)*
Southern California Edison Co .... C....... 562 491-3803
 125 Elm Ave Long Beach (90802) *(P-4708)*
Southern California Edison Co .... D....... 714 283-8568
 1900 E Taft Ave Orange (92865) *(P-4709)*
Southern California Edison Co .... A....... 626 308-6193
 501 S Marengo Ave Alhambra (91803) *(P-4710)*
Southern California Gas, Duarte Also Called: *Southern California Gas Co* *(P-4744)*
Southern California Gas Co .... B....... 818 701-2592
 9400 Oakdale Ave Chatsworth (91311) *(P-4721)*
Southern California Gas Co (HQ) .... **A....... 213 244-1200**
 555 W 5th St Ste 14h1 Los Angeles (90013) *(P-4727)*
Southern California Gas Co .... B....... 818 363-8542
 12801 Tampa Ave Northridge (91326) *(P-4728)*
Southern California Gas Co .... C....... 714 634-7221
 1 Liberty Aliso Viejo (92656) *(P-4729)*
Southern California Gas Co .... B....... 562 803-7500
 9240 Firestone Blvd Downey (90241) *(P-4730)*
Southern California Gas Co .... C....... 661 399-4431
 1510 N Chester Ave Bakersfield (93308) *(P-4731)*
Southern California Gas Co .... A....... 213 244-1200
 1801 S Atlantic Blvd Monterey Park (91754) *(P-4732)*
Southern California Gas Co .... D....... 714 262-0091
 73700 Dinah Shore Dr Ste 106 Palm Desert (92211) *(P-4733)*
Southern California Gas Co .... B....... 909 335-7802
 1981 W Lugonia Ave Redlands (92374) *(P-4734)*

ALPHABETIC SECTION

Southern California Gas Co .... C....... 213 244-1200
920 S Stimson Ave City Of Industry (91745) *(P-4735)*

Southern California Gas Co .... C....... 213 244-1200
25200 Trumble Rd Romoland (92585) *(P-4736)*

Southern California Gas Co .... C....... 213 244-1200
3050 E La Jolla St Anaheim (92806) *(P-4737)*

Southern California Gas Co .... C....... 323 881-3587
333 E Main St Ste J Alhambra (91801) *(P-4738)*

Southern California Gas Co .... D....... 562 803-3341
6738 Bright Ave Whittier (90601) *(P-4739)*

Southern California Gas Co .... B....... 310 823-7945
8141 Gulana Ave Venice (90293) *(P-4740)*

Southern California Gas Co .... C....... 909 335-7941
155 S G St San Bernardino (92410) *(P-4741)*

Southern California Gas Co .... C....... 213 244-1200
1600 Corporate Center Dr Monterey Park (91754) *(P-4742)*

Southern California Gas Co .... B....... 909 305-8297
1050 Overland Ct San Dimas (91773) *(P-4743)*

Southern California Gas Co .... D....... 626 358-4700
3318 Shadylawn Dr Duarte (91010) *(P-4744)*

Southern California Gas Co .... C....... 800 427-2200
23130 Valencia Blvd Valencia (91355) *(P-4745)*

Southern California Gas Tower .... A....... 213 244-1200
555 W 5th St Los Angeles (90013) *(P-4746)*

Southern California Material Handling Inc .... C....... 562 949-1006
12393 Slauson Ave Whittier (90606) *(P-5869)*

Southern California Messenger, Los Angeles *Also Called: Prompt Delivery Inc (P-13435)*

Southern California Mtl Hdlg, Whittier *Also Called: Equipment Depot Inc (P-5833)*

Southern California Permanente .... D....... 626 405-5722
393 E Walnut St Pasadena (91188) *(P-8661)*

Southern California Permanente Medical Group, Riverside *Also Called: Southern Cal Prmnnte Med Group (P-8363)*

SOUTHERN CALIFORNIA PERMANENTE MEDICAL GROUP, Carlsbad *Also Called: Southern Cal Prmnnte Med Group (P-8367)*

SOUTHERN CALIFORNIA PERMANENTE MEDICAL GROUP, Mission Viejo *Also Called: Southern Cal Prmnnte Med Group (P-17328)*

Southern California Physicia .... D....... 858 824-7000
6760 Top Gun St Ste 100 San Diego (92121) *(P-20213)*

Southern California Regional, Indio *Also Called: Granite Construction Company (P-1110)*

Southern California Valve Inc .... D....... 562 404-2246
13903 Maryton Ave Santa Fe Springs (90670) *(P-5927)*

Southern Contracting Company .... C....... 760 744-0760
559 N Twin Oaks Valley Rd San Marcos (92069) *(P-1843)*

Southern Counties Oil Co (DH) .... D....... 714 744-7140
1800 W Katella Ave Ste 210 Orange (92867) *(P-6719)*

Southern Counties Terminals .... D....... 310 642-0462
5341 W 104th St Los Angeles (90045) *(P-3424)*

Southern Glzers Wine Sprits Ca, Cerritos *Also Called: Southern Glzers Wine Sprits LL (P-6808)*

Southern Glzers Wine Sprits LL .... B....... 510 477-5500
33321 Dowe Ave Union City (94587) *(P-6807)*

Southern Glzers Wine Sprits LL .... B....... 562 926-2000
17101 Valley View Ave Cerritos (90703) *(P-6808)*

Southern Hmbldt Cmnty Dst Hosp .... D....... 707 923-3921
733 Cedar St Garberville (95542) *(P-16445)*

Southern Hmbldt Cmnty Hlth Car .... D....... 707 923-3921
733 Cedar St Garberville (95542) *(P-16446)*

Southern Home Care Svcs Inc .... D....... 714 979-7413
2900 Bristol St Ste D107 Costa Mesa (92626) *(P-11338)*

Southern Humboldt Cmnty Clinic, Garberville *Also Called: Southern Hmbldt Cmnty Dst Hosp (P-16445)*

Southern Implants Inc .... C....... 949 273-8505
5 Holland Ste 209 Irvine (92618) *(P-20214)*

Southern Indian Health Council (PA) .... D....... 619 445-1188
4058 Willows Rd Alpine (91901) *(P-17131)*

Southern Inyo Healthcare Dst .... C....... 760 876-5501
501 E Locust St Lone Pine (93545) *(P-16447)*

Southern Management Corp .... D....... 213 312-2268
808 S Olive St Los Angeles (90014) *(P-10970)*

Southern Mntrey Cnty Mem Hosp (PA) .... B....... 831 385-6000
300 Canal St King City (93930) *(P-16448)*

Southern Mono Healthcare Dst .... B....... 760 934-3311
85 Sierra Park Rd Mammoth Lakes (93546) *(P-16449)*

Southern Sierra Medical Clinic, Ridgecrest *Also Called: Ridgecrest Regional Hospital (P-16363)*

Southern Tire Mart LLC .... D....... 916 447-4220
1401 Richards Blvd Sacramento (95811) *(P-7377)*

Southland Box Company .... C....... 323 583-2231
4201 Fruitland Ave Vernon (90058) *(P-2526)*

Southland Care, San Juan Capistrano *Also Called: Ensign Southland LLC (P-15460)*

Southland Credit Union (PA) .... D....... 562 862-6831
10701 Los Alamitos Blvd Los Alamitos (90720) *(P-7806)*

Southland Integrated Svcs Inc (PA) .... D....... 714 558-6009
9862 Chapman Ave Garden Grove (92841) *(P-18625)*

Southland Paving Inc .... D....... 760 747-6895
361 N Hale Ave Escondido (92029) *(P-2159)*

Southland Rgnal Assn Rltors In (PA) .... D....... 818 786-2110
7232 Balboa Blvd Van Nuys (91406) *(P-18723)*

Southland Technology Inc .... D....... 858 694-0932
8053 Vickers St San Diego (92111) *(P-5352)*

Southland Transit Inc (PA) .... D....... 626 258-1310
3650 Rockwell Ave El Monte (91731) *(P-3218)*

Southwest Administrators Inc .... B
466 Foothill Blvd La Canada Flintridge (91011) *(P-8469)*

Southwest Airlines, Santa Ana *Also Called: Southwest Airlines Co (P-3846)*

Southwest Airlines Co .... D....... 949 252-5200
18601 Airport Way Ste 237 Santa Ana (92707) *(P-3846)*

Southwest Concrete Products .... C....... 909 983-9789
519 S Benson Ave Ontario (91762) *(P-2708)*

Southwest Construction Co Inc .... D....... 760 728-4460
2909 Rainbow Valley Blvd Fallbrook (92028) *(P-2160)*

Southwest Crpnters Trning Fund .... D....... 213 386-8590
533 S Fremont Ave Ste 700 Los Angeles (90071) *(P-18796)*

Southwest Dealer Services Inc .... C....... 925 753-0696
1001 G St Ste 113 Sacramento (95814) *(P-13482)*

Southwest Healthcare Sys Aux .... A....... 800 404-4627
38977 Sky Canyon Dr Ste 200 Murrieta (92563) *(P-16450)*

Southwest Healthcare Sys Aux (HQ) .... B....... 951 696-6000
25500 Medical Center Dr Murrieta (92562) *(P-16451)*

Southwest Landscape Inc .... D....... 714 545-1084
2205 S Standard Ave Santa Ana (92707) *(P-465)*

Southwest Material Hdlg Inc (PA) .... C....... 951 727-0477
3725 Nobel Ct Jurupa Valley (91752) *(P-7303)*

Southwest Patrol Inc .... D....... 909 861-1884
1800 E Lambert Rd Ste 155 Brea (92821) *(P-13049)*

Southwest Protective Svcs Inc .... C....... 760 996-1285
404 W Heil Ave El Centro (92243) *(P-13050)*

Southwest Rgnal Cncil Crpnters .... D....... 714 571-0449
7111 Firestone Blvd Buena Park (90621) *(P-18797)*

Southwest Security, El Centro *Also Called: Southwest Protective Svcs Inc (P-13050)*

Southwest Toyota Lift, Jurupa Valley *Also Called: Southwest Material Hdlg Inc (P-7303)*

Southwest Traders Incorporated .... D....... 209 462-1607
4747 Frontier Way Stockton (95215) *(P-6392)*

Southwest Traders Incorporated (PA) .... C....... 951 699-7800
27565 Diaz Rd Temecula (92590) *(P-6393)*

Southwest Transportation Agcy, Caruthers *Also Called: Fresno Cnty Sprntndent Schools (P-3345)*

Southwest YMCA, Saratoga *Also Called: Young MNS Chrstn Assn Slcon Vl (P-19122)*

Southwood Garden Apartments, Long Beach *Also Called: Intervest Property MGT Inc (P-8828)*

Souvenir Coffee Corporation .... D....... 510 450-0505
3084 Claremont Ave Berkeley (94705) *(P-6052)*

Sovena Usa Inc .... C....... 209 210-0388
705 E Whitmore Ave Modesto (95358) *(P-3755)*

Sovereign Health, Rancho Mirage *Also Called: Dual Diagnosis Trtmnt Ctr Inc (P-17229)*

Sovereign Health of California, San Clemente *Also Called: Dual Diagnosis Trtmnt Ctr Inc (P-17056)*

Sp, City Of Industry *Also Called: Scope Packaging Inc (P-2525)*

Sp Images Inc .... D....... 508 530-3225
6049 E Slauson Ave Commerce (90040) *(P-6950)*

Spa At Club Sport, San Ramon *Also Called: Clubsport San Ramon LLC (P-14190)*

Spa At Pebble Beach, The, Pebble Beach *Also Called: Pebble Beach Co A Ltd Partnr (P-10112)*

Spa Fitness Center   **ALPHABETIC SECTION**

Spa Fitness Center, Watsonville *Also Called: Spa Fitness Center Inc (P-14231)*
Spa Fitness Center Inc .... D....... 831 722-3895
  25 Penny Ln Watsonville (95076) *(P-14231)*
Spa Havens LP .... C....... 760 945-2055
  29402 Spa Haven Way Vista (92084) *(P-14232)*
Spa Resort Casino .... A....... 760 883-1034
  100 N Indian Canyon Dr Palm Springs (92262) *(P-10258)*
Spa Resort Casino (PA) .... D....... 888 999-1995
  401 E Amado Rd Palm Springs (92262) *(P-10259)*
Spa Resort Casino, Palm Springs *Also Called: Agua Clnte Band Chilla Indians (P-9600)*
Spacer.com, Pleasant Hill *Also Called: 500 Startups Management Co LLC (P-9481)*
Spalding Srgcal Ctr Bvrly Hlls .... D....... 949 863-0022
  27520 Hawthorne Blvd Ste 176 Rllng Hls Est (90274) *(P-15096)*
Span Construction, Madera *Also Called: Span Construction & Engrg Inc (P-1032)*
Span Construction & Engrg Inc (PA) .... D....... 559 661-1111
  3353 Yeager Rd Madera (93637) *(P-1032)*
Spanio Inc .... C....... 415 598-8578
  679 Bryant St San Francisco (94107) *(P-1844)*
Spanish Brdcstg Sys of Cal .... D....... 310 203-0900
  7007 Nw 77th Ave Los Angeles (90064) *(P-4405)*
Spanish Hills Club LLC .... D....... 805 388-5000
  999 Crestview Ave Camarillo (93010) *(P-14457)*
Spanish Hills Country Club (PA) .... C....... 805 389-1644
  999 Crestview Ave Camarillo (93010) *(P-14458)*
Spanish Spking Unity Cncil Alm .... C....... 510 836-0543
  1117 10th St Oakland (94607) *(P-18626)*
Spare-Time Inc .... C....... 916 649-0909
  2450 Natomas Park Dr Sacramento (95833) *(P-14233)*
Spare-Time Inc .... D....... 916 488-8100
  119 Scripps Dr Sacramento (95825) *(P-14234)*
Spare-Time Inc .... C....... 916 983-9180
  820 Halidon Way Folsom (95630) *(P-14459)*
Spare-Time Inc .... C....... 209 334-4897
  1900 S Hutchins St Lodi (95240) *(P-14460)*
Spare-Time Inc .... C....... 916 782-2600
  2501 Eureka Rd Roseville (95661) *(P-14461)*
Spare-Time Inc .... C....... 916 638-7001
  2201 Gold Rush Dr Gold River (95670) *(P-14462)*
Spare-Time Inc .... C....... 916 859-5910
  9570 Racquet Ct Elk Grove (95758) *(P-14463)*
Spark Compass, Los Angeles *Also Called: Total Cmmnicator Solutions Inc (P-12381)*
Spark Unlimited Inc .... D
  40 E Verdugo Ave # 2 Burbank (91502) *(P-11937)*
Spartan Inc .... D....... 661 327-1205
  3030 M St Bakersfield (93301) *(P-2739)*
Spc Building Services, Riverside *Also Called: J M V B Inc (P-1623)*
Spca, San Francisco *Also Called: Vh 10 Vh LP (P-353)*
Spe Go Holdings Inc .... D....... 858 638-0672
  16422 N Woodson Dr Ramona (92065) *(P-14290)*
Spear Tower, San Francisco *Also Called: Regus Equity Business Ctrs LLC (P-13444)*
Spearmint Rhino Cmpnies Wrldwi .... D....... 951 371-3788
  1875 Tandem Norco (92860) *(P-20215)*
Spearmint Rhino Gentlemens CLB, Torrance *Also Called: Midnight Sun Enterprises Inc (P-20804)*
Spears Manufacturing Co (PA) .... C....... 818 364-1611
  15853 Olden St Rancho Cascades (91342) *(P-5812)*
Spec Personnel LLC .... D....... 408 727-8000
  433 Airport Blvd Ste 310 Burlingame (94010) *(P-11234)*
Spec Personnel LLC .... D....... 408 727-8000
  1900 Lafayette St Ste 125 Santa Clara (95050) *(P-11235)*
Spec Services Inc .... B....... 714 963-8077
  10540 Talbert Ave Ste 100e Fountain Valley (92708) *(P-19392)*
Spec. Personnel, Burlingame *Also Called: Spec Personnel LLC (P-11234)*
Special Care, San Diego *Also Called: RAC & Associates (P-10991)*
Special Dispatch Cal Inc (PA) .... D....... 714 521-8200
  243 Newport Ave Long Beach (90803) *(P-3596)*
Special Service For Groups Inc (PA) .... D....... 213 368-1888
  905 E 8th St Los Angeles (90021) *(P-18250)*
Special Service For Groups Inc .... C....... 213 553-1800
  520 S La Fayette Park Pl # 30 Los Angeles (90057) *(P-18627)*
Special Service For Groups Inc .... C....... 310 323-6887
  19401 S Vermont Ave Ste A200 Torrance (90502) *(P-18628)*
Special Service For Groups Ssg, Los Angeles *Also Called: Special Service For Groups Inc (P-18250)*
Specialized Bicycle Components Holding Company Inc (PA) .... B....... 408 779-6229
  15130 Concord Cir Morgan Hill (95037) *(P-5981)*
Specilzed Ldscp MGT Svcs Inc .... D....... 805 520-7590
  4212 Peast Los Angeles Ave # 4211 Simi Valley (93063) *(P-466)*
Specialty A/C Products Inc (PA) .... D....... 408 481-3611
  310 Soquel Way Sunnyvale (94085) *(P-5773)*
Specialty Baking Inc .... D....... 408 298-6950
  3134 Capelaw Ct San Jose (95135) *(P-6670)*
Specialty Baking Co., San Jose *Also Called: Specialty Baking Inc (P-6670)*
Specialty Brands Incorporated .... A....... 909 477-4851
  4200 Concours Ste 100 Ontario (91764) *(P-2358)*
Specialty Clinic, Davis *Also Called: University California Davis (P-15154)*
Specialty Construction, San Carlos *Also Called: Level 5 Drywall Inc (P-1943)*
Specialty Construction Inc .... D....... 805 543-1706
  645 Clarion Ct San Luis Obispo (93401) *(P-1845)*
Specialty Equipment Mkt Assn (PA) .... D....... 909 396-0289
  1575 Valley Vista Dr Diamond Bar (91765) *(P-18724)*
Specialty Laboratories Inc (DH) .... A....... 661 799-6543
  27027 Tourney Rd Valencia (91355) *(P-16753)*
Specialty Restaurants Corp .... C....... 818 843-5013
  1250 E Harvard Rd Burbank (91501) *(P-7509)*
Specialty Solid Waste & Recycl, Santa Clara *Also Called: Bay Counties Waste Svcs Inc (P-4863)*
Specialty Steel Service, Stockton *Also Called: PDM Steel Service Centers Inc (P-5508)*
Specialty Sugical Ctr Encino, Encino *Also Called: Symbion Inc (P-15121)*
Specialty Surgical of Westlake, Westlake Village *Also Called: Symbion Inc (P-15120)*
Specialty Team Plastering Inc .... C....... 805 966-3858
  4652 Vintage Ranch Ln Santa Barbara (93110) *(P-1964)*
Specialty Textile Services LLC .... C....... 619 476-8750
  1333 30th St Ste A San Diego (92154) *(P-6162)*
Specilzed Foster Care Pasadena, Pasadena *Also Called: County of Los Angeles (P-17213)*
Specilzed Fster Care Chtsworth, Chatsworth *Also Called: County of Los Angeles (P-17215)*
Specimen Contracting, Sunland *Also Called: Brightview Tree Company (P-566)*
Spectra, Santa Clara *Also Called: Spec Personnel LLC (P-11235)*
Spectra Company .... C....... 909 599-0760
  2510 Supply St Pomona (91767) *(P-1893)*
Spectra Industrial Electric, Carson *Also Called: Spectra Industrial Svcs Inc (P-1846)*
Spectra Industrial Svcs Inc .... D....... 310 835-0808
  21818 S Wilmington Ave Ste 402 Carson (90810) *(P-1846)*
Spectra Laboratories Inc (DH) .... C....... 800 433-3773
  525 Sycamore Dr Milpitas (95035) *(P-16754)*
Spectra Premium (usa) Corp .... D....... 951 653-0640
  2220 Almond Ave Redlands (92374) *(P-5062)*
Spectra Services Acquisition L .... B....... 510 734-8394
  1646 N California Blvd Ste 342 Walnut Creek (94596) *(P-9564)*
Spectra USA, Chino *Also Called: Isiqalo LLC (P-2445)*
Spectra-Physics Inc (DH) .... D....... 877 835-9620
  1565 Barber Ln Milpitas (95035) *(P-2962)*
Spectrum Assembly Inc .... C....... 760 930-4000
  6300 Yarrow Dr Ste 100 Carlsbad (92011) *(P-2910)*
Spectrum Club, Los Angeles *Also Called: Bay Clubs Company LLC (P-14178)*
Spectrum Club Thousand Oaks, Chatsworth *Also Called: Bay Clubs Company LLC (P-14177)*
Spectrum Clubs Inc .... A....... 310 727-9300
  840 Apollo St Ste 100 El Segundo (90245) *(P-14235)*
Spectrum Cnstr Group Inc .... D....... 949 299-1400
  514 Via De La Valle Ste 210 Solana Beach (92075) *(P-844)*
Spectrum Electronics, Carlsbad *Also Called: Spectrum Assembly Inc (P-2910)*
Spectrum Equipment LLC .... D....... 760 599-8849
  2505 Commerce Way Vista (92081) *(P-6873)*
Spectrum Floral Service, Vista *Also Called: Spectrum Equipment LLC (P-6873)*
Spectrum Hotel Group LLC .... C....... 949 471-8888
  90 Pacifica Irvine (92618) *(P-10260)*
Spectrum Information Svcs LLC (PA) .... D....... 949 752-7070
  3323 Spectrum Irvine (92618) *(P-10776)*
Spectrum Labs Inc .... D....... 415 295-2752
  1990 N California Blvd Ste 800 Walnut Creek (94596) *(P-11938)*

ALPHABETIC SECTION — Spruce Technology Inc

Spectrum MGT Holdg Co LLC .... D....... 323 657-0899
3550 Wilshire Blvd Los Angeles (90010) *(P-4520)*

Spectrum MGT Holdg Co LLC .... D....... 858 695-3220
10450 Pacific Center Ct San Diego (92121) *(P-4521)*

Spectrum MGT Holdg Co LLC .... D....... 619 684-6106
5865 Friars Rd San Diego (92110) *(P-4522)*

Spectrum Security Services Inc (PA) .... C....... 619 669-6660
13967 Campo Rd Ste 101 Jamul (91935) *(P-13147)*

Spectrum Services Group Inc .... D....... 916 760-7913
3841 N Freeway Blvd Ste 120 Sacramento (95834) *(P-20855)*

Speedling Incorporated .... D....... 813 645-3221
2640 San Juan Hwy San Juan Bautista (95045) *(P-156)*

Speedway Sonoma LLC .... D....... 707 938-8448
Hwy 37 N Sonoma (95476) *(P-14167)*

Speedy Express LLC .... D....... 818 300-7785
4401 W Slauson Ave Ste A Los Angeles (90043) *(P-3628)*

Spencer Building Maintenance .... B....... 916 922-1900
10457 Old Placerville Rd # 100 Sacramento (95827) *(P-10971)*

Spencer Building Maintenance, Sacramento *Also Called: Spencer Building Maintenance (P-10971)*

SPEP Acquisition Corp (PA) .... D....... 310 608-0693
4041 Via Oro Ave Long Beach (90810) *(P-2732)*

Sperasoft Inc .... B....... 408 715-6615
2033 Gateway Pl Ste 500 San Jose (95110) *(P-11939)*

Sperber Ldscp Companies LLC (PA) .... C....... 818 437-1029
30700 Russell Ranch Rd Ste 120 Westlake Village (91362) *(P-467)*

Spf Capital Real Estate LLC .... D....... 310 519-8200
601 S Palos Verdes St San Pedro (90731) *(P-10261)*

Spg Solar Inc .... D....... 707 781-1000
1039 N Mcdowell Blvd Ste B Petaluma (94954) *(P-1847)*

SPHDS, Sunnyvale *Also Called: South Pninsula Hebrew Day Schl (P-17751)*

Sphere Institute .... B....... 650 558-3980
500 Airport Blvd Ste 340 Burlingame (94010) *(P-19849)*

Spherion Hr Consulting, San Jose *Also Called: Sfn Group Inc (P-11336)*

Spherion Prof Recruiting Group, San Diego *Also Called: Sfn Group Inc (P-11330)*

Spherion Staffing Group, Redding *Also Called: Sfn Group Inc (P-11334)*

Spherion Technology Svcs Group, Pleasanton *Also Called: Sfn Group Inc (P-11335)*

Spiess Construction Co Inc .... D....... 805 937-5859
201 S Broadway St Ste 140 Orcutt (93455) *(P-1266)*

Spilo Worldwide, Santa Monica *Also Called: Spilo Worldwide Inc (P-5948)*

Spilo Worldwide Inc .... D....... 213 687-8600
100 Wilshire Blvd Ste 700 Santa Monica (90401) *(P-5948)*

Spin Technology Inc .... D....... 888 883-2993
2100 Geng Rd Palo Alto (94303) *(P-5353)*

Spinergy Inc .... D....... 760 496-2121
1709 La Costa Meadows Dr San Marcos (92078) *(P-2996)*

Spiniello Companies .... C....... 909 629-1000
2650 Pomona Blvd Pomona (91768) *(P-1267)*

Spinitar, La Mirada *Also Called: Presentation Products Inc (P-7591)*

Spirent Calabasas, Calabasas *Also Called: Spirent Communications Inc (P-5354)*

Spirent Communications Inc (HQ) .... B....... 818 676-2300
27349 Agoura Rd Calabasas (91301) *(P-5354)*

Spireon Inc (PA) .... C....... 800 557-1449
18881 Von Karman Ave Ste 1500 Irvine (92612) *(P-11940)*

Split Software Inc (PA) .... C....... 650 399-0005
2317 Broadway St Fl 3 Redwood City (94063) *(P-12629)*

Splunk, San Francisco *Also Called: Splunk Inc (P-12360)*

Splunk Inc (PA) .... C....... 415 848-8400
270 Brannan St San Francisco (94107) *(P-12360)*

Spokeo Inc .... C....... 877 913-3088
556 S Fair Oaks Ave Ste 1 Pasadena (91105) *(P-4341)*

Sport Clips, San Diego *Also Called: Sport Clips Inc (P-10507)*

Sport Clips Inc .... A....... 858 273-9993
4839 Clairemont Dr Ste E San Diego (92117) *(P-10507)*

Sports Images, Commerce *Also Called: Sports Images Inc (P-6951)*

Sports Images Inc .... D....... 508 530-3225
6049 E Slauson Ave Commerce (90040) *(P-6951)*

Sportsmens Lodge Hotel LLC .... D....... 818 769-4700
12825 Ventura Blvd Studio City (91604) *(P-10262)*

Spotify USA Inc .... A....... 213 505-3040
555 Mateo St Los Angeles (90013) *(P-20561)*

Spotlight 29 Casino, Coachella *Also Called: 29 Palms Enterprises Corp (P-14486)*

Spotter Global Inc .... C....... 515 817-3726
8620 Thornton Ave Newark (94560) *(P-2754)*

Spoutable LLC .... C....... 609 743-7491
4150 Mission Blvd Ste 220 San Diego (92109) *(P-12630)*

Spr Op Co Inc .... C....... 510 232-5030
70 W Ohio Ave Ste H Richmond (94804) *(P-9338)*

Spreadtrum, San Diego *Also Called: Spreadtrum Cmmncations USA Inc (P-19773)*

Spreadtrum Cmmncations USA Inc .... D....... 858 546-0895
10180 Telesis Ct Ste 500 San Diego (92121) *(P-19773)*

Sprig Electric Co (HQ) .... C....... 408 298-3134
1860 S 10th St San Jose (95112) *(P-1848)*

Sprig Oral Health Technologies .... D....... 888 539-7336
6140 Horseshoe Bar Rd Ste L Loomis (95650) *(P-16777)*

Spring Bioscience Corp .... A....... 925 474-8463
4300 Hacienda Dr Pleasanton (94588) *(P-16755)*

Spring Creek Apartments, Santa Clara *Also Called: Acco Management Company (P-8895)*

Spring Mountain Hotel LLC .... D....... 530 304-5619
2850 Birkham Ct Fairfield (94534) *(P-10263)*

Spring Senior Assisted Living, Torrance *Also Called: Genesis Healthcare LLC (P-15491)*

Spring Valley Post Acute LLC .... C....... 760 245-6477
14973 Hesperia Rd Victorville (92395) *(P-15678)*

Springboard, San Francisco *Also Called: Sliderule Labs Inc (P-11922)*

Springfield Place, Petaluma *Also Called: Leisure Care LLC (P-18468)*

Springml, Pleasanton *Also Called: Springml Inc (P-12881)*

Springml Inc .... D....... 916 316-1566
6200 Stoneridge Mall Rd Ste 300 Pleasanton (94588) *(P-12881)*

Springs Club Inc .... D....... 760 328-0254
1 Duke Dr Rancho Mirage (92270) *(P-14464)*

SPRINGS COUNTRY CLUB, THE, Rancho Mirage *Also Called: Springs Club Inc (P-14464)*

SPRINGS ROAD HEALTHCARE, Vallejo *Also Called: Evergreen At Springs Road LLC (P-15471)*

Sprinkler Irrgtion Specialists, San Jose *Also Called: United Green Mark Inc (P-5814)*

Sprint, Temecula *Also Called: Sprint Communications Co LP (P-4228)*

Sprint, Los Angeles *Also Called: Sprint Corporation (P-4235)*

Sprint, South Gate *Also Called: Sprint Corporation (P-4236)*

Sprint, Garden Grove *Also Called: Sprint Communications Co LP (P-4342)*

Sprint Communications Co LP .... C....... 562 943-8907
15582 Whittwood Ln Whittier (90603) *(P-4227)*

Sprint Communications Co LP .... C....... 951 303-8501
31754 Temecula Pkwy Ste A Temecula (92592) *(P-4228)*

Sprint Communications Co LP .... C....... 310 216-9093
5381 W Centinela Ave Los Angeles (90045) *(P-4229)*

Sprint Communications Co LP .... C....... 760 941-4535
4225 Oceanside Blvd Oceanside (92056) *(P-4230)*

Sprint Communications Co LP .... C....... 951 461-9786
23865 Clinton Keith Rd Wildomar (92595) *(P-4231)*

Sprint Communications Co LP .... C....... 951 340-1924
3580 Grand Oaks Corona (92881) *(P-4232)*

Sprint Communications Co LP .... C....... 661 951-8927
44416 Valley Central Way Lancaster (93536) *(P-4233)*

Sprint Communications Co LP .... C....... 310 515-0293
1270 W Redondo Beach Blvd Gardena (90247) *(P-4234)*

Sprint Communications Co LP .... C....... 714 534-2107
12913 Harbor Blvd Ste Q4 Garden Grove (92840) *(P-4342)*

Sprint Communications Co LP .... C....... 626 339-0430
1316 N Azusa Ave Covina (91722) *(P-4343)*

Sprint Communications Co LP .... C....... 818 755-7100
111 Universal Hollywood Dr Universal City (91608) *(P-4344)*

Sprint Communications Co LP .... C....... 909 382-6030
1505 E Enterprise Dr San Bernardino (92408) *(P-4345)*

Sprint Corporation .... C....... 213 613-4200
432 S Broadway Los Angeles (90013) *(P-4235)*

Sprint Corporation .... C....... 323 357-0797
4707 Firestone Blvd South Gate (90280) *(P-4236)*

Sprouts Farmers Market Inc .... C....... 888 577-7688
280 De Berry St Colton (92324) *(P-3756)*

Sprouts Farmers Market Inc .... C....... 209 527-7575
1700 Mchenry Ave Modesto (95350) *(P-6394)*

Spruce Technology Inc .... C....... 925 415-8160
3516 Browntail Way San Ramon (94582) *(P-11941)*

SPS Holdings Inc .... D 310 532-7550
1702 W 134th St Gardena (90249) *(P-10456)*

SPS Technologies LLC .... B 949 474-6000
2541 White Rd Irvine (92614) *(P-5928)*

SPS Technologies LLC .... B 310 323-6222
1700 W 132nd St Gardena (90249) *(P-5929)*

SPS West LLC .... D 818 845-8050
1642 17th St Santa Monica (90404) *(P-13897)*

Spsv Entertainment LLC .... D 909 744-9373
28950 State Highway 18 Skyforest (92385) *(P-14106)*

Spus7 125 Cambridgepark LP .... C 213 683-4200
515 S Flower St Ste 3100 Los Angeles (90071) *(P-9183)*

Spus7 150 Cambridgepark LP .... C 213 683-4200
515 S Flower St Ste 3100 Los Angeles (90071) *(P-9184)*

Spy Inc (PA) .... D 760 804-8420
1896 Rutherford Rd Carlsbad (92008) *(P-3081)*

Spyglass Hill Golf Shop, Pebble Beach Also Called: Lone Cypress Company LLC *(P-9983)*

Sqa Services, Palos Verdes Estates Also Called: Sqa Services Inc *(P-20562)*

Sqa Services Inc .... B 800 333-6180
425 Via Corta Ste 203 Palos Verdes Estates (90274) *(P-20562)*

Square Enix Inc .... C 310 846-0400
999 N Pacific Coast Hwy Fl 3 El Segundo (90245) *(P-5355)*

Square H Brands Inc 323 267-4600
3615 E Vernon Ave Vernon (90058) *(P-845)*

Squaretrade Inc (DH) .... C 415 541-1000
2000 Sierra Point Pkwy Ste 300 Brisbane (94005) *(P-8473)*

Squaw Creek Associates LLC .... A 530 581-6624
400 Squaw Creek Rd Alpine Meadows (96146) *(P-10264)*

Squaw Creek Transportation, Olympic Valley Also Called: Lowe Enterprises *(P-9987)*

Squaw Valley Ski Holdings LLC .... B 800 403-0206
1960 Squaw Valley Rd Olympic Valley (96146) *(P-10265)*

Squires, Sanders and Dempsey, San Francisco Also Called: Graham & James LLP *(P-17480)*

SR Freeman Inc .... D 408 364-2200
2380 S Bascom Ave Ste 200 Campbell (95008) *(P-2018)*

Sr. Thea Bowman Manor, Oakland Also Called: Christian Church Homes *(P-8800)*

SRbray LLC .... D 951 898-3850
229 N Sherman Ave Corona (92882) *(P-1849)*

Srcsd, Sacramento Also Called: Sacramnto Rgnal Cnty Snttion D *(P-4983)*

Srd Engineering Inc .... D 714 630-2480
5300 Highland Ct Yorba Linda (92886) *(P-1268)*

Srg Holdings LLC (HQ) .... A 858 792-9300
500 Stevens Ave Ste 100 Solana Beach (92075) *(P-11055)*

Srht Property Holding LLC .... C 213 683-0522
1317 E 7th St Los Angeles (90021) *(P-9185)*

SRI International (PA) .... A 650 859-2000
333 Ravenswood Ave Menlo Park (94025) *(P-19915)*

Srm Alliance Hospital Services (PA) .... B 707 778-1111
400 N Mcdowell Blvd Petaluma (94954) *(P-16452)*

SRS, Camarillo Also Called: Silicon Processing and Trading Inc *(P-4936)*

SRS Consulting Inc (PA) .... B 510 252-0625
39465 Paseo Padre Pkwy Ste 3200 Fremont (94538) *(P-11942)*

SS Heritage Inn Ontario LLC .... D 909 937-5000
3595 E Guasti Rd Ontario (91761) *(P-10266)*

Ss Skikos Incorporated .... D 707 575-3000
1289 Sebastopol Rd Santa Rosa (95407) *(P-3597)*

Ss Travel, San Francisco Also Called: San Francisco Travel Assn *(P-13462)*

SS&c Advent, San Francisco Also Called: Advent Software Inc *(P-11384)*

Ss8 Networks Inc (PA) .... C 408 894-8400
750 Tasman Dr Milpitas (95035) *(P-4553)*

SSC Carmichael Operating Co LP .... A 916 485-4793
3630 Mission Ave Carmichael (95608) *(P-15679)*

SSC Construction Inc .... D 951 278-1177
4195 Chino Hills Pkwy Chino Hills (91709) *(P-19393)*

SSC Inc (HQ) .... D 510 477-0008
2910 Faber St Union City (94587) *(P-6484)*

SSC Oakland Fruitvale Oper LP .... D 510 261-5613
3020 E 15th St Oakland (94601) *(P-15898)*

SSC Pittsburg Operating Co LP .... B 925 427-4444
2351 Loveridge Rd Pittsburg (94565) *(P-15899)*

SSC San Jose Operating Co LP .... A 408 249-0344
340 Northlake Dr San Jose (95117) *(P-15680)*

Ssd Management LLC .... D 619 291-2900
1380 Harbor Island Dr San Diego (92101) *(P-7558)*

SSE Merchandise, San Jose Also Called: Sharks Sports & Entrmt LLC *(P-14160)*

Ssf Imported Auto Parts LLC (DH) .... D 800 203-9287
437 Rozzi Pl South San Francisco (94080) *(P-5063)*

Ssi, Stockton Also Called: Super Store Industries *(P-6675)*

Ssi, Valley Center Also Called: Survival Systems Intl Inc *(P-13802)*

Ssjid, Manteca Also Called: South San Jquin Irrigation Dst *(P-4838)*

SSPCA, Sacramento Also Called: Sacramnto Soc For The Prvntion *(P-19100)*

Sst IV 8020 Las Vgas Blvd S LL .... D 949 429-6600
10 Terrace Rd Ladera Ranch (92694) *(P-3757)*

Sst Oil, Redding Also Called: Shasta-Siskiyou Transport *(P-6718)*

Ssw, Palm Springs Also Called: S S W Mechanical Cnstr Inc *(P-1552)*

ST ANNE'S HOME, San Francisco Also Called: Little Ssters of The Poor Okla *(P-18474)*

St Annes Family Services .... C 213 381-2931
155 N Occidental Blvd Los Angeles (90026) *(P-18524)*

St Bernardine Med Ctr Aux Inc .... C 909 881-4320
2101 N Waterman Ave San Bernardino (92404) *(P-16453)*

St Bernardine Medical Center 909 883-8711
2101 N Waterman Ave San Bernardino (92404) *(P-16454)*

St Brnbas Snior Ctr Los Angle .... D 213 388-4444
675 S Carondelet St Los Angeles (90057) *(P-18138)*

St Elizabeth Community Hosp (DH) .... C 530 529-7760
2550 Sister Mary Columba Dr Red Bluff (96080) *(P-16455)*

St Francis Electric Inc .... C 510 639-0639
975 Carden St San Leandro (94577) *(P-1850)*

St Francis Electric LLC 510 639-0639
975 Carden St San Leandro (94577) *(P-1851)*

St Francis Medical Center (DH) .... B 310 900-8900
3630 E Imperial Hwy Lynwood (90262) *(P-16456)*

ST FRANCIS PAVILLION, Daly City Also Called: Forte Enterprises Inc *(P-20092)*

St Francis Yacht Club .... C 415 563-6363
700 Marina Blvd San Francisco (94123) *(P-14465)*

St George Auto Center Inc .... D 657 212-5042
13861 Harbor Blvd Garden Grove (92843) *(P-13683)*

St George Logistics, Compton Also Called: Tropicana Manufacturing Co Inc *(P-3772)*

ST HELENA HOSPITAL CLEARLAKE, Clearlake Also Called: Advintist Hlth Clearlake Hosp *(P-15927)*

St Helena Hospital (HQ) .... A 707 963-3611
10 Woodland Rd Saint Helena (94574) *(P-16457)*

St Helena Hospital Clearlake, Clearlake Also Called: Adventist Hlth Systm/West Corp *(P-15924)*

St Jhns Lthran Ch Bakersfield .... C 661 665-7815
4500 Buena Vista Rd Bakersfield (93311) *(P-19029)*

St Johns Lthran Schl Chldren C, Bakersfield Also Called: St Jhns Lthran Ch Bakersfield *(P-19029)*

St Johns Regional Medical Ctr, Oxnard Also Called: Dignity Health *(P-16053)*

St Johns Retirement Village .... C 530 662-9674
135 Woodland Ave Woodland (95695) *(P-15900)*

St Joseph Center .... D 310 396-6468
204 Hampton Dr Venice (90291) *(P-18139)*

St Joseph Health Per Care Svcs .... D 800 365-1110
1315 Corona Pointe Ct Ste 201 Corona (92879) *(P-16932)*

St Joseph Hlth Nthrn Cal LLC 707 547-2221
751 Lombardi Ct Santa Rosa (95407) *(P-16458)*

St Joseph Hlth Nthrn Cal LLC .... B 707 542-4704
1170 Montgomery Dr Santa Rosa (95405) *(P-16459)*

St Joseph Hlth Nthrn Cal LLC .... B 707 525-5300
2700 Dolbeer St Eureka (95501) *(P-16460)*

St Joseph Hlth Nthrn Cal LLC .... B 707 921-4717
151 Sotoyome St Santa Rosa (95405) *(P-16461)*

St Joseph Hlth Nthrn Cal LLC (PA) .... C 949 381-4000
1165 Montgomery Dr Santa Rosa (95405) *(P-16462)*

St Joseph Hlth Nthrn Cal LLC .... B 707 584-0672
1450 Medical Center Dr Rohnert Park (94928) *(P-17132)*

St Joseph Home Care Network (DH) .... D 714 712-9500
441 College Ave Santa Rosa (95401) *(P-16933)*

St Joseph Hospice .... B 714 712-7100
200 W Center Street Promenade Anaheim (92805) *(P-18140)*

St Joseph Hospital .... C 714 744-8601
1000 W La Veta Ave Orange (92868) *(P-16463)*

ALPHABETIC SECTION — Standard Insurance Company

St Joseph Hospital (PA) .... B 707 445-8121
  2700 Dolbeer St Eureka (95501) *(P-16464)*
St Joseph Hospital .... C 707 445-8121
  2700 Dolbeer St Eureka (95501) *(P-16465)*
St Joseph Hospital .... C 707 445-8121
  2700 Dolbeer St Eureka (95501) *(P-16466)*
St Joseph Hospital .... C 707 268-0190
  2752 Harrison Ave Ste A Eureka (95501) *(P-16467)*
St Joseph Hospital .... C 707 445-8121
  3645 E St Eureka (95503) *(P-16468)*
St Joseph Hospital of Eureka .... A 707 445-8121
  2700 Dolbeer St Eureka (95501) *(P-16469)*
St Joseph Hospital of Orange .... D 714 771-8222
  1310 W Stewart Dr Ste 203 Orange (92868) *(P-16470)*
St Joseph Hospital of Orange .... D 714 771-8006
  363 S Main St Ste 211 Orange (92868) *(P-16471)*
St Joseph Hospital of Orange (DH) .... A 714 633-9111
  1100 W Stewart Dr Orange (92868) *(P-16472)*
St Joseph Hospital of Orange .... C 714 568-5500
  3345 Michelson Dr Ste 100 Irvine (92612) *(P-16473)*
St Joseph Hospital of Orange .... D 714 771-8037
  1100 W Stewart Dr Orange (92868) *(P-16474)*
St Josephs Behavioral Hlth Ctr (DH) .... D 209 462-2826
  2510 N California St Stockton (95204) *(P-16475)*
St Josephs Med Ctr Stockton .... A 209 943-2000
  1800 N California St Stockton (95204) *(P-16476)*
St Josephs Medical Center Inc .... C 209 943-2000
  1800 N California St Stockton (95204) *(P-16477)*
St Josephs Physical Rehab Svcs, Orange *Also Called: St Joseph Hospital of Orange (P-16470)*
St Josephs School, Placentia *Also Called: Roman Cthlic Diocese of Orange (P-17745)*
St Josephs Surgery Center LP .... D 209 467-6316
  1800 N California St Ste 1 Stockton (95204) *(P-15097)*
St Jseph Heritg Med Group LLC (PA) .... C 714 633-1011
  2212 E 4th St Ste 201 Santa Ana (92705) *(P-15098)*
St Jseph Hlth Sys HM Care Svc .... A 714 712-9500
  200 W Center St Promenade Anaheim (92805) *(P-16934)*
St Jude Hospital (DH) .... A 714 871-3280
  101 E Valencia Mesa Dr Fullerton (92835) *(P-16478)*
St Jude Medical Center, Fullerton *Also Called: St Jude Hospital (P-16478)*
ST LOUIS RAMS, Agoura Hills *Also Called: Los Angeles Rams LLC (P-14150)*
St Lukes Health Care Center .... C 415 647-8600
  1580 Valencia St Ste 506 San Francisco (94110) *(P-16479)*
St Lukes Hospital .... A 415 600-3959
  2351 Clay St San Francisco (94115) *(P-16480)*
St Lukes Neighborhood Clinic, San Francisco *Also Called: St Lukes Health Care Center (P-16479)*
St Madeleine Sophies Center .... D 619 442-5129
  2119 E Madison Ave El Cajon (92019) *(P-18251)*
St Mary Medical Center (DH) .... A 562 491-9000
  1050 Linden Ave Long Beach (90813) *(P-16481)*
St Mary Medical Center LLC .... A 760 946-8767
  16000 Kasota Rd Apple Valley (92307) *(P-16482)*
St Mary Medical Center LLC (PA) .... A 760 242-2311
  18300 Us Highway 18 Apple Valley (92307) *(P-16483)*
St Mary's Medical Center, San Francisco *Also Called: Catholic Healthcare West (P-15968)*
ST MARY'S MEDICAL CENTER, Long Beach *Also Called: St Marys Medical Center (P-20563)*
St Mary's School of Nursing, Long Beach *Also Called: St Mary Medical Center (P-16481)*
St Marys Med Ctr Foundation .... C 415 668-1000
  450 Stanyan St San Francisco (94117) *(P-16484)*
St Marys Medical Center .... A 562 491-9230
  1050 Linden Ave Long Beach (90813) *(P-20563)*
St Marys Medical Center Inc .... A 415 668-1000
  450 Stanyan St San Francisco (94117) *(P-16485)*
St Matthews Episcopal Day Schl .... C 650 342-5436
  16 Baldwin Ave San Mateo (94401) *(P-17752)*
St Patricks School, Larkspur *Also Called: Roman Cthlic Archbshop of San (P-17743)*
St Paul's Villa, National City *Also Called: St Pauls Episcopal Home Inc (P-18526)*
St Pauls Episcopal Home Inc .... D 619 239-2097
  2635 2nd Ave Ofc San Diego (92103) *(P-18525)*
St Pauls Episcopal Home Inc .... D 619 232-2996
  2700 E 4th St National City (91950) *(P-18526)*

St Pauls Episcopal Home Inc .... D 619 239-8687
  235 Nutmeg St San Diego (92103) *(P-18527)*
St Vincent De Paul, Oakland *Also Called: District Council DC (P-17955)*
St Vincent De Paul Soc Los Ang, Los Angeles *Also Called: Society of St Vncent De Paul C (P-19106)*
St Vincent Health Care, Pasadena *Also Called: Vincent-Hayley Enterprises Inc (P-16621)*
St. John's Health Center, Santa Monica *Also Called: Providence St Johns Hlth Ctr (P-16351)*
St. Johns Pleasant Valley Hosp, Camarillo *Also Called: Dignity Health (P-16052)*
St. Joseph Dental, Santa Rosa *Also Called: St Joseph Hlth Nthrn Cal LLC (P-16458)*
St. Louise Regional Hospital, Gilroy *Also Called: Santa Clara County of (P-16392)*
St. Mary's Medical Center, San Francisco *Also Called: Dignity Health (P-16054)*
STA, Thousand Palms *Also Called: Sunline Transit Agency (P-3219)*
Staccato Communications Inc .... D 858 812-1000
  6195 Lusk Blvd Ste 200 San Diego (92121) *(P-13483)*
Stackla Inc .... D 415 789-3304
  548 Market St San Francisco (94104) *(P-12361)*
Staff Assistance, Thousand Oaks *Also Called: Staff Assistance Inc (P-16935)*
Staff Assistance Inc (PA) .... B 818 894-7879
  72 Moody Ct Ste 100 Thousand Oaks (91360) *(P-16935)*
Staff Assistance Inc .... B 805 371-9980
  72 Moody Ct Ste 100 Thousand Oaks (91360) *(P-11236)*
Staff Pro Inc .... A 619 544-1774
  675 Convention Way San Diego (92101) *(P-13051)*
Staff Pro Inc (PA) .... A 714 230-7200
  5455 Garden Grove Blvd Westminster (92683) *(P-13148)*
Staffing Solutions, Montebello *Also Called: L&T Staffing Inc (P-11167)*
Staffing Solutions, Santa Ana *Also Called: L&T Staffing Inc (P-11168)*
Staffing Solutions Inc .... D 408 980-9000
  2142 Bering Dr San Jose (95131) *(P-11237)*
Stage 4 Solutions Incorporated .... D 408 868-9739
  19200 Portos Dr Saratoga (95070) *(P-20564)*
Stagnaro Bros Seafood Inc .... D 831 423-1188
  320 Washington St Santa Cruz (95060) *(P-6485)*
Stainless Stl Fabricators Inc .... D 714 739-9904
  15120 Desman Rd La Mirada (90638) *(P-5870)*
Stallergenes Greer .... D 858 292-1060
  7203 Convoy Ct San Diego (92111) *(P-15099)*
Stamoules Produce Co, Mendota *Also Called: S Stamoules Inc (P-301)*
Stamoules Produce Company, Mendota *Also Called: S & S Ranch Inc (P-243)*
Stamps.com, El Segundo *Also Called: Stampscom Inc (P-10777)*
Stampscom Inc (PA) .... C 310 482-5800
  1990 E Grand Ave El Segundo (90245) *(P-10777)*
Stan Farm, Modesto *Also Called: Stanislaus Farm Supply Company (P-6834)*
Stance, San Clemente *Also Called: Stance Inc (P-6222)*
Stance Inc (PA) .... C 949 391-9030
  197 Avenida La Pata San Clemente (92673) *(P-6222)*
Stand 8 Technology Services, Seal Beach *Also Called: Talent & Acquisition LLC (P-11965)*
Stand For Fmlies Free Volence .... D 510 964-7109
  3220 Blume Dr San Pablo (94806) *(P-18141)*
STAND STRONG, San Luis Obispo *Also Called: Lumina Alliance (P-18048)*
Standard Biotools Inc (PA) .... B 650 266-6000
  2 Tower Pl Ste 2000 South San Francisco (94080) *(P-3034)*
Standard Calibrations Inc .... D 619 477-1668
  681 Anita St Ste 103 Chula Vista (91911) *(P-13746)*
Standard Cattle LLC .... D 559 693-1977
  8105a S Lassen Ave San Joaquin (93660) *(P-356)*
Standard Chartered Bank .... D 626 639-8000
  601 S Figueroa St Ste 2775 Los Angeles (90017) *(P-7717)*
Standard Chartered Bank .... C 408 629-3219
  9 Great Oaks Blvd San Jose (95119) *(P-7737)*
Standard Chartered Bank .... D 877 308-2182
  50 Fremont St Ste 2210 San Francisco (94105) *(P-7738)*
Standard Cognition Corp (PA) .... D 415 324-4156
  548 Market St # 96346 San Francisco (94104) *(P-12362)*
Standard Drywall Inc (HQ) .... B 619 443-7034
  9831 Channel Rd Lakeside (92040) *(P-1965)*
Standard Industries Inc .... D 661 387-1110
  6505 Zerker Rd Shafter (93263) *(P-5225)*
Standard Insurance Company .... D 925 947-3950
  1600 Riviera Ave Ste 150 Walnut Creek (94596) *(P-8662)*

Standard-Southern Corporation ALPHABETIC SECTION

Standard-Southern Corporation .... D...... 213 624-1831
  400 S Central Ave Los Angeles (90013) *(P-3659)*
Standard-Southern Corporation .... C...... 213 624-1831
  440 S Central Ave Los Angeles (90013) *(P-3660)*
Standard-Southern Corporation .... C...... 213 624-1831
  715 E 4th St Los Angeles (90013) *(P-3661)*
Standish Management, San Francisco *Also Called: Standish Management LLC (P-20216)*
Standish Management LLC .... C...... 925 300-3277
  750 Battery St Ste 600 San Francisco (94111) *(P-20216)*
Stanford Alumni Association, Stanford *Also Called: Leland Stanford Junior Univ (P-18879)*
Stanford Cancer Center, Palo Alto *Also Called: Stanford Health Care (P-18762)*
Stanford Cancer Center S Bay, San Jose *Also Called: Stanford Health Care (P-16494)*
Stanford Court Hotel, San Francisco *Also Called: Pine & Powell Partners LLC (P-10119)*
Stanford Federal Credit Union (PA) .... D...... 650 725-1000
  1860 Embarcadero Rd Palo Alto (94303) *(P-7807)*
Stanford Health Care .... C...... 650 723-5281
  801 Welch Rd Palo Alto (94304) *(P-15100)*
Stanford Health Care .... A...... 650 723-5171
  1000 Welch Rd Ste 300 Palo Alto (94304) *(P-16486)*
Stanford Health Care .... A...... 650 736-6661
  300 Pasteur Dr Stanford (94305) *(P-16487)*
Stanford Health Care .... A...... 650 497-8953
  725 Welch Rd Palo Alto (94304) *(P-16488)*
Stanford Health Care .... C...... 650 723-4000
  300 Pasteur Dr Stanford (94305) *(P-16489)*
Stanford Health Care .... B...... 650 723-8561
  500 Pasteur Dr Palo Alto (94304) *(P-16490)*
Stanford Health Care .... B...... 650 736-7844
  3375 Hillview Ave Palo Alto (94304) *(P-16491)*
Stanford Health Care .... B...... 650 213-8360
  1510 Page Mill Rd Ste 2 Palo Alto (94304) *(P-16492)*
Stanford Health Care .... A...... 650 723-4000
  300 Pasteur Dr Stanford (94305) *(P-16493)*
Stanford Health Care .... A...... 408 426-4900
  2589 Samaritan Dr San Jose (95124) *(P-16494)*
Stanford Health Care .... A...... 925 847-3000
  5555 W Las Positas Blvd Pleasanton (94588) *(P-16495)*
Stanford Health Care .... D...... 650 498-7489
  1300 Crane St Menlo Park (94025) *(P-16496)*
Stanford Health Care (HQ) .... A...... **650 723-4000**
  300 Pasteur Dr Stanford (94305) *(P-16497)*
Stanford Health Care .... C...... 650 723-4000
  1850 Embarcadero Rd Ste B Palo Alto (94303) *(P-16498)*
Stanford Health Care .... A...... 650 723-5256
  450 Broadway St Redwood City (94063) *(P-17329)*
Stanford Health Care .... D...... 650 723-4841
  866 Campus Dr Stanford (94305) *(P-17330)*
Stanford Health Care .... C...... 650 498-5032
  875 Blake Wilbur Dr Palo Alto (94304) *(P-18762)*
Stanford Health Care Advantage, Stanford *Also Called: Essence Healthcare Cal Inc (P-16088)*
Stanford Hlth Care - Vlleycare, Livermore *Also Called: Stanford Hlth Care Tri-Valley (P-16499)*
Stanford Hlth Care - Vlleycare, Livermore *Also Called: Stanford Hlth Care Tri-Valley (P-19107)*
Stanford Hlth Care Ctr For Edc, Palo Alto *Also Called: Stanford Health Care (P-16498)*
Stanford Hlth Care Tri-Valley .... C...... 925 373-4018
  1111 E Stanley Blvd Livermore (94550) *(P-15101)*
Stanford Hlth Care Tri-Valley .... C...... 925 447-7000
  1119 E Stanley Blvd Livermore (94550) *(P-16499)*
Stanford Hlth Care Tri-Valley .... C...... 925 416-3562
  5698 Stoneridge Dr Pleasanton (94588) *(P-16698)*
Stanford Hlth Care Tri-Valley .... C...... 925 447-1919
  2586 Regent Rd Livermore (94550) *(P-19107)*
Stanford Hlth Care Tri-Valley (DH) .... B...... **925 847-3000**
  5555 W Las Positas Blvd Pleasanton (94588) *(P-20217)*
Stanford Hospital, Palo Alto *Also Called: Stanford Health Care (P-16490)*
Stanford Hotels Corporation .... D...... 408 330-0001
  4949 Great America Pkwy Santa Clara (95054) *(P-10267)*
Stanford Law Schl Off Fncl Aid .... C...... 650 723-9247
  559 Nathan Abbott Way Rm 107 Stanford (94305) *(P-13484)*
Stanford Lthrop Mem HM For Frn, Sacramento *Also Called: Stanford Youth Solutions (P-18143)*
Stanford Medical Center, Stanford *Also Called: Stanford Health Care (P-16497)*
Stanford Medicine Partners, Newark *Also Called: University Healthcare Alliance (P-16958)*
Stanford Park Hotel .... C...... 650 322-1234
  100 El Camino Real Menlo Park (94025) *(P-10268)*
Stanford Schl Mdcine Jay McHae, Palo Alto *Also Called: Stanford Health Care (P-16486)*
Stanford School of Medicine, Stanford *Also Called: Leland Stanford Junior Univ (P-17764)*
Stanford Transportation Inc .... D...... 661 302-3288
  10201 Alondra Dr Bakersfield (93311) *(P-3425)*
Stanford Univ Frman Spgli Inst .... C...... 650 723-8681
  616 Jane Stanford Way Stanford (94305) *(P-19916)*
Stanford Univ Med Ctr Aux .... C...... 650 723-6636
  300 Pasteur Dr Stanford (94305) *(P-18142)*
Stanford University, Stanford *Also Called: Leland Stanford Junior Univ (P-17762)*
Stanford University - Et, Redwood City *Also Called: Leland Stanford Junior Univ (P-17763)*
Stanford University Medical, Stanford *Also Called: Leland Stanford Junior Univ (P-16213)*
Stanford Youth Solutions (PA) .... D...... 916 344-0199
  8912 Volunteer Ln Sacramento (95826) *(P-18143)*
Stanislaus Cnty Tobacco Fundng .... C...... 209 525-6376
  1010 10th St Ste 6400 Modesto (95354) *(P-7909)*
Stanislaus Distributing, Modesto *Also Called: Varni Brothers Corporation (P-6809)*
Stanislaus Distributing Co, Modesto *Also Called: Varni Brothers Corporation (P-6786)*
Stanislaus Farm Supply Company (PA) .... D...... 209 538-7070
  624 E Service Rd Modesto (95358) *(P-6834)*
Stanislaus Medical Center, Modesto *Also Called: County of Stanislaus (P-16032)*
Stanislaus Surgical Center, Modesto *Also Called: Stanislaus Surgical Hosp LLC (P-16500)*
Stanislaus Surgical Hosp LLC (PA) .... C...... **209 572-2700**
  1421 Oakdale Rd Modesto (95355) *(P-16500)*
Stanley G Alexander Inc (PA) .... C...... **714 731-1658**
  2942 Dow Ave Tustin (92780) *(P-3545)*
Stanley Steemer Carpet Cleaner, San Diego *Also Called: Colt Services Inc (P-10473)*
Stantec Architecture Inc .... B...... 213 955-9775
  801 S Figueroa St Ste 300 Los Angeles (90017) *(P-13485)*
Stantec Architecture Inc .... A...... 415 882-9500
  300 Montgomery St Ste 1200 San Francisco (94104) *(P-19394)*
Stantec Architecture Inc .... B...... 949 923-6000
  38 Technology Dr Ste 200 Irvine (92618) *(P-19506)*
Stantec Architecture Inc .... D...... 626 796-9141
  300 N Lake Ave Ste 400 Pasadena (91101) *(P-19507)*
Stantec Architecture Inc .... A...... 916 442-3230
  555 Capitol Mall Ste 650 Sacramento (95814) *(P-19508)*
Stantec Architecture Inc .... C...... 707 765-1660
  1383 N Mcdowell Blvd Ste 250 Petaluma (94954) *(P-19509)*
Stantec Consulting Svcs Inc .... D...... 916 924-8844
  3301 C St Ste 1900 Sacramento (95816) *(P-19395)*
Stantec Consulting Svcs Inc .... C...... 626 796-9141
  300 N Lake Ave Ste 400 Pasadena (91101) *(P-19396)*
Stantec Consulting Svcs Inc .... C...... 925 627-4500
  1340 Treat Blvd Ste 525 Walnut Creek (94597) *(P-19397)*
Stantec Consulting Svcs Inc .... C...... 949 923-6000
  38 Technology Dr Ste 100 Irvine (92618) *(P-19510)*
Stantec Holdings Del III Inc .... B...... 661 396-3770
  5500 Ming Ave Ste 300 Bakersfield (93309) *(P-9339)*
Stantec Oil and Gas, Bakersfield *Also Called: Stantec Holdings Del III Inc (P-9339)*
Stantru Reinforcing Steel, Fontana *Also Called: Stantru Resources Inc (P-846)*
Stantru Resources Inc .... D...... 909 587-1441
  11175 Redwood Ave Fontana (92337) *(P-846)*
Stapleton, Gridley *Also Called: Stapleton - Spence Packing Co (P-2353)*
Stapleton - Spence Packing Co (PA) .... D...... **408 297-8815**
  1900 State Highway 99 Gridley (95948) *(P-2353)*
Star Ford Lincoln Mercury, Glendale *Also Called: Los Feliz Ford Inc (P-7253)*
Star H-R .... A...... 707 894-4404
  105 E 1st St Cloverdale (95425) *(P-11238)*
Star H-R .... A...... 707 265-9911
  1822 Jefferson St Napa (94559) *(P-11239)*
Star Laundry Services Inc .... D...... 619 572-1009
  3410 Main St San Diego (92113) *(P-10488)*
Star of Ca LLC .... D...... 805 379-1401
  501 Marin St Thousand Oaks (91360) *(P-17331)*
Star of Ca LLC .... D...... 818 986-7827
  15260 Ventura Blvd Sherman Oaks (91403) *(P-17332)*

ALPHABETIC SECTION

Star of Ca LLC (HQ)..C....... 805 644-7827
4880 Market St Ventura (93003) *(P-17333)*

Star of California..D....... 805 466-1638
8834 Morro Rd Atascadero (93422) *(P-17334)*

STAR OF CALIFORNIA, A PROFESSIONAL PSYCHOLOGICAL CORPORATION, Atascadero
Also Called: Star of California *(P-17334)*

Star One Credit Union (PA)..................................C....... 408 543-5202
1306 Bordeaux Dr Sunnyvale (94089) *(P-7808)*

Star Pro Security Patrol Inc..................................C....... 714 617-5056
3303 Harbor Blvd Ste B3 Costa Mesa (92626) *(P-13052)*

Star Protection Agency CA, Oakland Also Called: Star Protection Agency LLC *(P-13053)*

Star Protection Agency LLC..................................D....... 510 635-1732
7901 Oakport St Ste 2000 Oakland (94621) *(P-13053)*

Star Scrap Metal Company Inc..............................D....... 562 921-5045
1509 S Bluff Rd Montebello (90640) *(P-4940)*

Star Services, San Diego Also Called: Star Laundry Services Inc *(P-10488)*

Star Shield Solutions LLC....................................D....... 866 662-4477
4315 Santa Ana St Ontario (91761) *(P-2680)*

Star Trac Fitness, Irvine Also Called: Star Trac Strength Inc *(P-3095)*

Star Trac Strength Inc...B....... 714 669-1660
14410 Myford Rd Irvine (92606) *(P-3095)*

Star Waggons LLC...D....... 818 367-5946
13334 Ralston Ave Sylmar (91342) *(P-13950)*

Starco Enterprises Inc (PA)..................................D....... 323 266-7111
3137 E 26th St Vernon (90058) *(P-2791)*

Starco Group Inc (PA)..D....... 909 989-9898
9160 Hyssop Dr Rancho Cucamonga (91730) *(P-13486)*

Stardust Studios Inc..D....... 310 399-6047
1823 Colorado Ave Santa Monica (90404) *(P-20565)*

Stargate Digital, South Pasadena Also Called: Stargate Films Inc *(P-13898)*

Stargate Films Inc..D....... 626 403-8403
1001 El Centro St South Pasadena (91030) *(P-13898)*

Stark Services...D....... 818 985-2003
12444 Victory Blvd Ste 300 North Hollywood (91606) *(P-12631)*

Starlight Educational Center, Westminster Also Called: Westview Services Inc *(P-18260)*

Starpint 1031 Property MGT LLC..........................C....... 310 247-0550
450 N Roxbury Dr Ste 1050 Beverly Hills (90210) *(P-9186)*

Stars, San Leandro Also Called: Subacute Trtmnt For Adlscent R *(P-17133)*

Starship Technologies Inc....................................C....... 844 445-5333
535 Mission St 19fl San Francisco (94105) *(P-11943)*

Startel Corporation (PA)..D....... 949 863-8700
16 Goodyear B-125 Irvine (92618) *(P-11944)*

Startengine Crowdfunding Inc..............................D....... 800 317-2200
750 N San Vicente Blvd Ste 800w West Hollywood (90069) *(P-7910)*

Startup Farms Intl LLC..B....... 510 440-0110
45690 Northport Loop E Fremont (94538) *(P-11945)*

Startx..D....... 408 230-3300
2627 Hanover St Palo Alto (94304) *(P-19108)*

Starvista..C....... 650 591-9623
610 Elm St Ste 212 San Carlos (94070) *(P-18144)*

Starwest Botanicals LLC (PA)..............................D....... 916 638-8100
161 Main Ave Sacramento (95838) *(P-6671)*

Starwood Inc...C....... 888 559-1749
402 W Broadway Ste 400 San Diego (92101) *(P-10269)*

Starwood Capital Group LLC................................D....... 415 247-1220
100 Pine St Ste 3000 San Francisco (94111) *(P-9565)*

Starwood Hotel...C....... 310 641-7740
5990 Green Valley Cir Culver City (90230) *(P-10270)*

Starwood Hotels & Resorts, San Diego Also Called: San Diego Sheraton Corporation *(P-10198)*

Starwood Hotels & Resorts, Costa Mesa Also Called: South Coast Westin Hotel Co *(P-10256)*

Starwood Hotels & Resorts, Culver City Also Called: Starwood Hotel *(P-10270)*

Starwood Hotels & Resorts, San Francisco Also Called: Starwood Htels Rsrts Wrldwide *(P-10271)*

Starwood Hotels & Resorts, Fresno Also Called: Starwood Htels Rsrts Wrldwide *(P-10272)*

Starwood Hotels & Resorts, San Francisco Also Called: Starwood Htels Rsrts Wrldwide *(P-10273)*

Starwood Hotels & Resorts, San Diego Also Called: Starwood Htels Rsrts Wrldwide *(P-10274)*

Starwood Htels Rsrts Wrldwide............................B....... 415 397-7000
335 Powell St San Francisco (94102) *(P-10271)*

Starwood Htels Rsrts Wrldwide............................C....... 559 230-8470
4 N Points By Sheraton 3737 Blac Ave Fresno (93726) *(P-10272)*

Starwood Htels Rsrts Wrldwide............................C....... 415 512-1111
2 New Montgomery St San Francisco (94105) *(P-10273)*

Starwood Htels Rsrts Wrldwide............................C....... 619 239-2200
910 Broadway Cir San Diego (92101) *(P-10274)*

Starwood Htels Rsrts Wrldwide............................C....... 909 622-2220
601 W Mckinley Ave Pomona (91768) *(P-10275)*

Stat Nursing Services Inc (PA).............................D....... 415 673-9791
2740 Van Ness Ave Ste 210 San Francisco (94109) *(P-11240)*

Stat Revenue Professional Corp...........................D....... 510 597-1800
2200 Powell St Emeryville (94608) *(P-20566)*

Statco, Huntington Beach Also Called: DSI Process Systems LLC *(P-5829)*

Statcomm Inc...D....... 650 988-9508
939 San Rafael Ave Ste C Mountain View (94043) *(P-19398)*

State Bar of California..D....... 213 765-1520
845 S Figueroa St Los Angeles (90017) *(P-18763)*

State Bar of California (PA)...................................B....... 415 538-2000
180 Howard St San Francisco (94105) *(P-18764)*

State Bar of California..C....... 805 544-7551
755 Santa Rosa St Ste 310 San Luis Obispo (93401) *(P-18765)*

State Center Cmnty College Dst...........................C....... 559 442-4600
1101 E University Ave Fresno (93704) *(P-17789)*

State Compensation Insur Fund...........................D....... 888 782-8338
2901 N Ventura Rd Ste 100 Oxnard (93036) *(P-8272)*

State Compensation Insur Fund (PA)...................D....... 888 782-8338
333 Bush St Ste 800 San Francisco (94104) *(P-8407)*

State Compensation Insur Fund...........................C....... 415 565-1222
1030 Vaquero Cir Vacaville (95688) *(P-8408)*

State Compensation Insur Fund...........................C....... 714 565-5000
1750 E 4th St Fl 3 Santa Ana (92705) *(P-8409)*

State Compensation Insur Fund...........................D....... 661 664-4000
9801 Camino Media Ste 101 Bakersfield (93311) *(P-8410)*

State Compensation Insur Fund...........................C....... 888 782-8338
2275 Gateway Oaks Dr Sacramento (95833) *(P-8411)*

State Compensation Insur Fund...........................C....... 888 782-8338
10105 Pacific Heights Blvd Ste 120 San Diego (92121) *(P-8412)*

State Compensation Insur Fund...........................C....... 559 433-2700
10 E River Park Pl E Ste 110 Fresno (93720) *(P-8413)*

State Compensation Insur Fund...........................B....... 888 782-8338
1450 Neotomas Ave Santa Rosa (95405) *(P-8414)*

State Compensation Insur Fund...........................C....... 916 924-5100
2275 Gateway Oaks Dr Sacramento (95833) *(P-8415)*

State Compensation Insur Fund...........................C....... 707 443-9721
800 W Harris St Ste 37 Eureka (95503) *(P-8416)*

State Compensation Insur Fund...........................A....... 818 888-4750
21300 Victory Blvd Ste 600 Woodland Hills (91367) *(P-8417)*

State Compensation Insur Fund...........................C....... 888 782-8338
6301 Day St Riverside (92507) *(P-8418)*

State Compensation Insur Fund...........................C....... 888 782-8338
5890 Owens Dr Pleasanton (94588) *(P-8419)*

State Compensation Insur Fund...........................C....... 323 266-5000
900 Corporate Center Dr Monterey Park (91754) *(P-8420)*

State Compensation Insur Fund...........................C....... 888 782-8338
5900 State Farm Dr Rohnert Park (94928) *(P-8421)*

State Contract Office, Rohnert Park Also Called: State Compensation Insur Fund *(P-8421)*

State Farm General Insur Co................................D....... 619 227-5777
945 Otay Lakes Rd Ste K Chula Vista (91913) *(P-8663)*

State Farm Insurance, Chula Vista Also Called: State Farm General Insur Co *(P-8663)*

State Farm Insurance, Bakersfield Also Called: State Farm Mutl Auto Insur Co *(P-8664)*

State Farm Mutl Auto Insur Co.............................D....... 309 766-2311
900 Old River Rd 400 Bakersfield (93311) *(P-8664)*

State Fish Co Inc..C....... 310 547-9530
624 W 9th St Ste 100 San Pedro (90731) *(P-2424)*

State Fund, San Francisco Also Called: State Compensation Insur Fund *(P-8407)*

State Roofing Systems Inc....................................D....... 510 317-1477
15444 Hesperian Blvd San Leandro (94578) *(P-2086)*

Stateline Travelodge Inc..D....... 530 544-6000
4011 Lake Tahoe Blvd South Lake Tahoe (96150) *(P-10276)*

States Drawer Box Spc LLC..................................D....... 714 744-4247
1482 N Batavia St Orange (92867) *(P-5189)*

States Logistics Services Inc

ALPHABETIC SECTION

States Logistics Services Inc (PA)...C....... 714 521-6520
  5650 Dolly Ave Buena Park (90621) *(P-4099)*
Station Venture Operations LP ....D....... 619 231-3939
  9680 Granite Ridge Dr San Diego (92123) *(P-4463)*
Statrad - Radconnect, San Diego *Also Called: Nucleushealth LLC (P-11788)*
Status Medical Management, Modesto *Also Called: Pegasus Risk Management Inc (P-8637)*
Staub Metals LLC ....D....... 562 602-2200
  7747 Rosecrans Ave Paramount (90723) *(P-5519)*
Stay Cal San Jose LLC ....C....... 408 275-2147
  2404 Stevens Creek Blvd San Jose (95128) *(P-10277)*
STC Netcom Inc (PA) ....D....... 951 685-8181
  11611 Industry Ave Fontana (92337) *(P-1852)*
Steadfast Companies, Irvine *Also Called: Steadfast Management Co Inc (P-9187)*
Steadfast Management Co Inc (PA) ....D....... 949 748-3000
  18100 Von Karman Ave Ste 500 Irvine (92612) *(P-9187)*
Steady Platform Inc ....D....... 678 792-8364
  5636 Fallsgrove St Los Angeles (90016) *(P-11946)*
Stearns Conrad and Schmidt Consulting Engineers Inc (PA).......D....... 562 426-9544
  3900 Kilroy Airport Way Ste 100 Long Beach (90806) *(P-19399)*
Stearns Holdings LLC ....C....... 916 358-9170
  2600 E Bidwell St Ste 160 Folsom (95630) *(P-8023)*
Steel Unlimited Inc ....D....... 909 873-1222
  3200 Myers St Riverside (92503) *(P-5520)*
Steele, San Francisco *Also Called: Steele Cis LLC (P-17661)*
Steele Cis LLC ....B....... 415 692-5000
  1 Sansome St Ste 3500 San Francisco (94104) *(P-17661)*
Steele Corp SEC Advisory Svcs, San Francisco *Also Called: Firstcall (P-12972)*
Steelhead, Los Angeles *Also Called: Deutsch La Inc (P-10606)*
Steelrver Infrstrcture Fund N (HQ)..C....... 415 291-2200
  1 Letterman Dr Bldg D San Francisco (94129) *(P-4747)*
Steelrver Infrstrcture Prtners (PA)..C....... 415 512-1515
  1 Harbor Dr Ste 101 Sausalito (94965) *(P-9340)*
Steelrver Infrstrcture Prtners, San Francisco *Also Called: Steelrver Infrstrcture Fund N (P-4747)*
Steelwave Inc (PA)...C....... 650 571-2200
  999 Baker Way Ste 200 San Mateo (94404) *(P-9275)*
Steelwave LLC ....A....... 310 821-1111
  4553 Glencoe Ave Ste 300 Marina Del Rey (90292) *(P-9276)*
Steelwave LLC ....A....... 408 564-7678
  333 W San Carlos St Ste 200 San Jose (95110) *(P-9277)*
Steelwedge Software Inc ....D....... 925 460-1700
  3875 Hopyard Rd Ste 300 Pleasanton (94588) *(P-12363)*
Stefan Merli Plastering Co Inc (PA)..D....... 310 323-0404
  1230 W 130th St Gardena (90247) *(P-2161)*
Steico, Oceanside *Also Called: Steico Industries Inc (P-2755)*
Steico Industries Inc ....C....... 760 438-8015
  1814 Ord Way Oceanside (92056) *(P-2755)*
Stein Sam & Rose Education Ctr, San Diego *Also Called: Vista Hill Foundation (P-17819)*
Steinberg Architects, Los Angeles *Also Called: Steinberg Hart (P-19511)*
Steinberg Hart (PA)..D....... 408 295-5446
  818 W 7th St Ste 1100 Los Angeles (90017) *(P-19511)*
Steiny and Company Inc ....C....... 707 552-6900
  27 Sheridan St Vallejo (94590) *(P-1853)*
Steiny and Company Inc ....B....... 213 382-2331
  221 N Ardmore Ave Los Angeles (90004) *(P-1854)*
Stella Technology Incorporated ....D....... 402 350-1681
  450 S Abel St Unit 360832 Milpitas (95035) *(P-12882)*
Stellar Cyber Inc ....D....... 408 548-0860
  2590 N 1st St Ste 360 San Jose (95131) *(P-12364)*
Stellar Distributing, Inc., Madera *Also Called: Catania Worldwide (P-6523)*
Stellartech Research Corp (PA)..C....... 408 331-3000
  560 Cottonwood Dr Milpitas (95035) *(P-19774)*
Stemconnector LLC ....D....... 424 543-4074
  1500 Rosecrans Ave Ste 500 Manhattan Beach (90266) *(P-12883)*
STEMCONNECTOR LLC, Manhattan Beach *Also Called: Stemconnector LLC (P-12883)*
Step, Sacramento *Also Called: Stratgies To Empwer People Inc (P-15797)*
Step Up On Second Street Inc (PA) ....D....... 310 394-6889
  1328 2nd St Ofc Santa Monica (90401) *(P-16936)*
Steppechange LLC ....D....... 415 279-7638
  900 Uccelli Dr Apt 9301 Redwood City (94063) *(P-11947)*

Steren Electronic Solutions, San Diego *Also Called: Steren Electronics Intl LLC (P-5701)*
Steren Electronics Intl LLC (PA) ....D....... 800 266-3333
  8445 Camino Santa Fe San Diego (92121) *(P-5701)*
Stereo D LLC ....D....... 818 861-3100
  3355 W Empire Ave 1st Fl Burbank (91504) *(P-13951)*
Stereod, Burbank *Also Called: Stereo D LLC (P-13951)*
Stereomax, Mill Valley *Also Called: Haggin Marketing LLC (P-10622)*
Sterling BMW, Newport Beach *Also Called: Sterling Motors Ltd (P-7304)*
Sterling Brand, San Francisco *Also Called: Sterling Consulting Group LLC (P-20567)*
Sterling Care Inc ....C....... 619 470-6700
  2575 E 8th St National City (91950) *(P-15681)*
Sterling Collision LLC (PA) ....D....... 714 259-1111
  1111 Bell Ave Ste A Tustin (92780) *(P-13649)*
Sterling Consulting Group LLC ....D....... 415 248-7900
  600 California St Fl 8 San Francisco (94108) *(P-20567)*
Sterling Healthcare Svcs LLC ....A....... 502 262-2914
  19925 Stevens Creek Blvd Ste 100 Cupertino (95014) *(P-20568)*
Sterling Hills Golf Club, Camarillo *Also Called: Sterling Hills LLC (P-14291)*
Sterling Hills LLC ....D....... 805 604-1234
  901 Sterling Hills Dr Camarillo (93010) *(P-14291)*
Sterling Management Systems, Glendale *Also Called: Wilson Emery Corporation (P-20615)*
Sterling Motors Ltd ....D....... 949 645-5900
  3000 W Coast Hwy Newport Beach (92663) *(P-7304)*
Sterling Plumbing Inc ....D....... 714 641-5480
  3111 W Central Ave Santa Ana (92704) *(P-1571)*
Sterling Vineyards Inc ....C....... 707 252-7410
  1105 Oak Knoll Ave Napa (94558) *(P-2394)*
STERLING VINEYARDS, INC., Napa *Also Called: Sterling Vineyards Inc (P-2394)*
Steve P Rados Inc ....C....... 619 328-1360
  1638 Pioneer Way El Cajon (92020) *(P-1190)*
Steve Thomas BMW, Camarillo *Also Called: Thomas Bavarian Mtr Works Inc (P-7312)*
Steven Engineering, South San Francisco *Also Called: Steven Engineering Inc (P-5594)*
Steven Engineering Inc (HQ)...D....... 650 588-9200
  230 Ryan Way South San Francisco (94080) *(P-5594)*
Steven Global Freight Services, Redondo Beach *Also Called: Stevens Global Logistics Inc (P-4100)*
Steven Label Corporation (PA) ....C....... 562 698-9971
  11926 Burke St Santa Fe Springs (90670) *(P-6163)*
Steven P Abelow MD ....D....... 530 544-8033
  2311 Lake Tahoe Blvd South Lake Tahoe (96150) *(P-15102)*
Stevens and Associates, San Francisco *Also Called: Myles Stevens Architecture (P-19497)*
Stevens Creek Quarry Inc (PA) ....D....... 408 253-2512
  21771 Stevens Creek Blvd Ste 100 Cupertino (95014) *(P-1165)*
Stevens Creek Toyota, San Jose *Also Called: Halrec Inc (P-7228)*
Stevens Global Logistics Inc (PA) ....D....... 800 229-7284
  3700 Redondo Beach Ave Redondo Beach (90278) *(P-4100)*
Stevens Transportation Inc ....C....... 661 366-3286
  7100 E Brundage Ln Bakersfield (93307) *(P-3546)*
Stevens Trucking, Bakersfield *Also Called: Stevens Transportation Inc (P-3546)*
Steves Plating Corporation ....C....... 818 842-2184
  3111 N San Fernando Blvd Burbank (91504) *(P-2507)*
Stewart & Jasper Marketing Inc (PA)...C....... 209 862-9600
  3500 Shiells Rd Newman (95360) *(P-2376)*
Stewart & Jasper Orchards, Newman *Also Called: Stewart & Jasper Marketing Inc (P-2376)*
Stewart Title California Inc (DH) ....C....... 619 692-1600
  7676 Hazard Center Dr Ste 1400 San Diego (92108) *(P-8455)*
Stewart Title California Inc ....C....... 818 502-2700
  525 N Brand Blvd Ste 200 Glendale (91203) *(P-9239)*
Stg Auto Group, Garden Grove *Also Called: St George Auto Center Inc (P-13683)*
Stg Logistics Inc ....D....... 323 869-6000
  5800 Sheila St Commerce (90040) *(P-4101)*
Stinson Enterprises Inc ....C....... 209 529-2933
  4513 Mchenry Ave Modesto (95356) *(P-7305)*
Stir Foods, Corona *Also Called: Pacifica Foods LLC (P-2355)*
Stjohn God Rtirement Care Ctr ....C....... 323 731-0641
  2468 S St Andrews Pl Los Angeles (90018) *(P-15682)*
Stn Digital LLC ....D....... 619 292-8683
  3033 Bunker Hill St San Diego (92109) *(P-10676)*
Stockbridge/Sbe Holdings LLC ....A....... 323 655-8000
  5900 Wilshire Blvd Ste 3100 Los Angeles (90036) *(P-10278)*

ALPHABETIC SECTION

Stockdale Christian School, Bakersfield Also Called: First Assmbly of God Bkrsfield **(P-17711)**
Stockdale Country Club .... D....... 661 832-0310
  7001 Stockdale Hwy Bakersfield (93309) **(P-14466)**
Stockdale Medical Offices, Bakersfield Also Called: Kaiser Foundation Hospitals **(P-14824)**
Stockham Construction Inc .... B....... 707 664-0945
  475 Portal St Cotati (94931) **(P-2019)**
Stockmar Industrial, Long Beach Also Called: Elite Craftsman **(P-10893)**
Stockton, French Camp Also Called: Granite Construction Company **(P-1111)**
Stockton Edson Healthcare Corp .... D....... 209 948-8762
  1630 N Edison St Stockton (95204) **(P-15901)**
Stockton Fics, Stockton Also Called: Victor Cmnty Support Svcs Inc **(P-17158)**
Stockton Golf and Country Club .... D....... 209 466-4313
  3800 Country Club Blvd Stockton (95204) **(P-14467)**
Stockton Port District .... D....... 209 946-0246
  2201 W Washington St Ste 13 Stockton (95203) **(P-3818)**
Stok LLC .... D....... 415 265-2366
  26 Ofarrell St Fl 2 San Francisco (94108) **(P-20856)**
Stoke, San Jose Also Called: Mavenir International Holdings Inc **(P-11738)**
STOLLWOOD CONVALESCENT HOSPITA, Woodland Also Called: St Johns Retirement Village **(P-15900)**
Stomper Company Inc .... D....... 510 574-0570
  3135 Diablo Ave Hayward (94545) **(P-2243)**
Stone Entertainment, Costa Mesa Also Called: Volcom LLC **(P-13547)**
Stone Land Company (PA) .... D....... 559 947-3185
  28521 Nevada Ave Stratford (93266) **(P-5)**
Stone Ranch, Stratford Also Called: Stone Land Company **(P-5)**
Stonebridge Rlty Advisors Inc .... A....... 949 597-8700
  27102 Towne Centre Dr Foothill Ranch (92610) **(P-10279)**
Stonebrook Convalescent Center .... C....... 925 689-7457
  4367 Concord Blvd Concord (94521) **(P-15683)**
Stonebrook Health Care Center, Concord Also Called: Stonebrook Convalescent Center **(P-15683)**
Stonecalibre LLC (PA) .... D....... 310 774-0014
  2049 Century Park E Ste 2550 Los Angeles (90067) **(P-9566)**
Stonehouse Restaurant, Santa Barbara Also Called: San Ysidro Bb Property LLC **(P-10203)**
Stoneland, North Hollywood Also Called: Arriaga Usa Inc **(P-1974)**
Stoneriver Inc .... D....... 714 705-8227
  770 The City Dr S Ste 5000 Orange (92868) **(P-11948)**
Stonesfair Financial Corp .... D....... 650 347-0442
  577 Airport Blvd Ste 700 Burlingame (94010) **(P-8863)**
Stony Apparel Corp (PA) .... C....... 323 981-9080
  1201 S Grand Ave Los Angeles (90015) **(P-2457)**
Stop 'n' Save Liquors, Modesto Also Called: C W Brower Inc **(P-7384)**
Stop Hop Center, Carson Also Called: Anschutz Sthern Cal Spt Cmplex **(P-14490)**
Storage West, Marina Del Rey Also Called: Laaco Ltd **(P-8886)**
Storagepro Inc .... D....... 510 900-5474
  1205 Franklin St Oakland (94612) **(P-3758)**
Storagepro Inc .... D....... 408 560-0511
  601 N King Rd San Jose (95133) **(P-3759)**
Storer Transportation Service (PA) .... B....... 209 521-8250
  3519 Mcdonald Ave Modesto (95358) **(P-3314)**
Storer Travel Service, Modesto Also Called: Storer Transportation Service **(P-3314)**
Storm, Torrance Also Called: Storm Industries Inc **(P-2771)**
Storm Industries Inc (PA) .... D....... 310 534-5232
  23223 Normandie Ave Torrance (90501) **(P-2771)**
Stormgeo (DH) .... C....... 408 731-8600
  140 Kifer Ct Sunnyvale (94086) **(P-20902)**
Str, Carlsbad Also Called: Systems & Technology RES LLC **(P-19402)**
Str Worldwide Inc .... A....... 949 276-5990
  17462 Von Karman Ave Irvine (92614) **(P-6187)**
Stradling Ycca Crlson Ruth A P (PA) .... C....... 949 725-4000
  660 Newport Center Dr Ste 1600 Newport Beach (92660) **(P-17662)**
Straight Forwarding Inc .... D....... 909 594-3400
  20275 Business Pkwy Walnut (91789) **(P-4102)**
Straight Talk Counseling Ctr, La Mirada Also Called: Straight Talk Inc **(P-18145)**
Straight Talk Inc .... D....... 562 943-0195
  13710 La Mirada Blvd La Mirada (90638) **(P-18145)**
Strand Hill Properties .... D....... 310 545-0707
  1131 Morningside Dr Manhattan Beach (90266) **(P-8765)**

Strasbaugh, San Luis Obispo Also Called: R H Strasbaugh **(P-2781)**
Strata Information Group Inc .... D....... 619 296-0170
  3935 Harney St Ste 203 San Diego (92110) **(P-12884)**
Stratacare, Irvine Also Called: Stratacare Llc **(P-11949)**
Stratacare Llc .... C....... 949 743-1200
  17838 Gillette Ave Ste D Irvine (92614) **(P-11949)**
Strategic Asset Services LLC .... D....... 949 713-0053
  27422 Portola Pkwy Ste 150 Foothill Ranch (92610) **(P-8766)**
Strategic Bus Insights Inc (PA) .... D....... 650 859-4600
  333 Ravenswood Ave Menlo Park (94025) **(P-20569)**
Strategic Command US .... D....... 858 603-8901
  9406 Stargaze Ave San Diego (92129) **(P-19400)**
Strategic Distribution L P .... C....... 818 671-2100
  9800 De Soto Ave Chatsworth (91311) **(P-2452)**
Strategic Materials, Commerce Also Called: Strategic Materials Inc **(P-4941)**
Strategic Materials Inc .... D....... 323 887-6831
  7000 Bandini Blvd Commerce (90040) **(P-4941)**
Strategic Mechanical Inc .... C....... 559 291-1952
  4661 E Commerce Ave Fresno (93725) **(P-1572)**
Strategic Operations Inc .... C....... 858 244-0559
  4705 Ruffin Rd San Diego (92123) **(P-13487)**
Strategic Property Management .... D....... 619 295-2211
  2055 3rd Ave Ste 200 San Diego (92101) **(P-9188)**
Strategy Companion Corp .... D....... 714 460-8398
  100 Pacifica Irvine (92618) **(P-12365)**
Strateos Inc (PA) .... D....... 650 763-8432
  930 Guinda St Palo Alto (94301) **(P-20570)**
Stratford School Inc .... B....... 408 973-7320
  1999 S Bascom Ave Ste 400 Campbell (95008) **(P-18355)**
Stratgic Hlthcare Programs LLC .... D....... 805 963-9446
  6500 Hollister Ave Ste 210 Goleta (93117) **(P-11950)**
Stratgies To Empwer People Inc (PA) .... D....... 916 679-1555
  2330 Glendale Ln Sacramento (95825) **(P-15797)**
Strathmoore Press Inc .... D....... 510 843-8888
  2550 9th St Ste 103 Berkeley (94710) **(P-13488)**
Stratus Real Estate Inc .... D....... 626 441-5549
  435 Garfield Ave South Pasadena (91030) **(P-8058)**
Stratus Real Estate Inc .... D....... 310 549-7028
  1100 N Banning Blvd Apt 111 Wilmington (90744) **(P-8059)**
Stratus Realestate, South Pasadena Also Called: Stratus Real Estate Inc **(P-8058)**
Straub Distributing Co Ltd (PA) .... C....... 714 779-4000
  4633 E La Palma Ave Anaheim (92807) **(P-6783)**
Streamelements Inc .... D....... 323 928-7848
  11400 W Olympic Blvd Los Angeles (90064) **(P-19850)**
Streamlabs LLC .... C....... 415 990-9187
  565 Commercial St Fl 3 San Francisco (94111) **(P-11951)**
Streamland Media LLC .... C....... 416 909-2103
  1117 W Isabel St Burbank (91506) **(P-20218)**
Streamline Design Slkscreen Inc (PA) .... D....... 805 884-1025
  1299 S Wells Rd Ventura (93004) **(P-2456)**
Streamline Finishes Inc .... D....... 949 600-8964
  26429 Rancho Pkwy S Ste 140 Lake Forest (92630) **(P-1033)**
Strength United .... D....... 818 787-9700
  14651 Oxnard St Van Nuys (91411) **(P-18146)**
Stretto Inc (PA) .... D....... 949 222-1212
  410 Exchange Ste 100 Irvine (92602) **(P-17663)**
Stria, Bakersfield Also Called: Technosocialworkcom LLC **(P-12635)**
Strikes Unlimited Inc .... D....... 916 626-3600
  5681 Lonetree Blvd Rocklin (95765) **(P-14122)**
Stripe, South San Francisco Also Called: Stripe Heavy Industries Inc **(P-12529)**
Stripe Inc (PA) .... C....... 888 963-8955
  354 Oyster Point Blvd South San Francisco (94080) **(P-13489)**
Stripe Heavy Industries Inc (HQ) .... C....... 877 887-7815
  354 Oyster Point Blvd South San Francisco (94080) **(P-12529)**
Stripe Payments Company, South San Francisco Also Called: Stripe Inc **(P-13489)**
Strivr Labs Inc .... C....... 650 656-9987
  3520 Thomas Rd Ste C Santa Clara (95054) **(P-11952)**
Strocal Inc .... B....... 209 948-4646
  4651 Quail Lakes Dr Stockton (95207) **(P-2201)**
Stromasys Inc .... D....... 919 239-8450
  871 Marlborough Ave Riverside (92507) **(P-12366)**

Stroock & Stroock & Lavan, Los Angeles Also Called: Stroock & Stroock & Lavan LLP (P-17664)

Stroock & Stroock & Lavan LLP .... C....... 310 556-5800
2029 Century Park E Ste 1800 Los Angeles (90002) *(P-17664)*

Strouk Group LLC .... C....... 323 939-7792
6333 W 3rd St Ste 150 Los Angeles (90036) *(P-6504)*

Structral Prsrvtion Systems LL .... B....... 714 891-9080
11800 Monarch St Garden Grove (92841) *(P-2162)*

Structurecast, Bakersfield Also Called: Golden Empire Con Pdts Inc (P-2704)

Stryder Corp (PA) .... D....... 415 981-8400
225 Bush St Fl 12 San Francisco (94104) *(P-12367)*

Stuart C. Gildred Family YMCA, Santa Ynez Also Called: Channel Islnds Yung MNS Chrstn (P-18840)

Stuart Event Rentals, Milpitas Also Called: Arena Event Services Inc (P-11020)

Stuart Rental Company, Milpitas Also Called: Ohana Partners Inc (P-11047)

Student Transportation America, Santa Clarita Also Called: Santa Barbara Trnsp Corp (P-3309)

Student Transportation America, Escondido Also Called: Santa Barbara Trnsp Corp (P-3351)

Student Transportation America, Goleta Also Called: Santa Barbara Trnsp Corp (P-3352)

Studio 71 LP .... C....... 323 370-1500
8383 Wilshire Blvd Ste 1050 Beverly Hills (90211) *(P-10720)*

Studio City .... D....... 818 557-7777
5161 Lankershim Blvd # 200 North Hollywood (91601) *(P-13899)*

Studio Distribution Svcs LLC .... C....... 818 954-6000
4000 Warner Blvd Burbank (91522) *(P-13900)*

Sturdy Oil Company .... D....... 831 970-9897
721 Vertin Ave Salinas (93901) *(P-6741)*

Sturgeon Son Grading & Pav Inc (PA) .... C....... 661 322-4408
3511 Gilmore Ave Bakersfield (93308) *(P-2225)*

Stussy, Irvine Also Called: Stussy Inc (P-6188)

Stussy Inc .... D....... 949 474-9255
17426 Daimler St Irvine (92614) *(P-6188)*

Stutman Treister Glatt Prof Co, Los Angeles Also Called: Stutman Trster Glatt Prof Corp (P-17665)

Stutman Trster Glatt Prof Corp .... D....... 310 228-5600
1901 Avenue Of The Stars Ste 200 Los Angeles (90067) *(P-17665)*

Stv Architects Inc .... C....... 213 482-9444
1055 W 7th St Ste 3150 Los Angeles (90017) *(P-19512)*

Stv Incorporated .... B....... 510 763-1313
505 14th St Ste 1060 Oakland (94612) *(P-19513)*

Stx Entertainment, Burbank Also Called: Stx Financing LLC (P-13901)

Stx Financing LLC .... D....... 310 742-2300
3900 W Alameda Ave Fl 32 Burbank (91505) *(P-13901)*

Style Network, Los Angeles Also Called: E Entertainment Television Inc (P-4507)

Styleseat Inc .... D....... 415 638-6658
218a Clara St San Francisco (94107) *(P-10508)*

Styra Inc .... D....... 650 980-4280
548 Market St San Francisco (94104) *(P-11953)*

Sub-Acute Saratoga Hospital, Saratoga Also Called: Progressive Sub-Acute Care (P-16345)

Subacute Trtmnt For Adlscent R (PA) .... D....... 510 352-9200
545 Estudillo Ave San Leandro (94577) *(P-17133)*

Subsidy of Be Aerospace, Fullerton Also Called: ADB Industries (P-2727)

Success Healthcare 1 LLC .... A....... 626 288-1160
7500 Hellman Ave Rosemead (91770) *(P-15103)*

Success Healthcare 1 LLC (PA) .... D....... 213 989-6100
1711 W Temple St Los Angeles (90026) *(P-16937)*

Success Strategies Inst Inc .... D....... 949 721-6808
6 Hutton Centre Dr Ste 700 Santa Ana (92707) *(P-18252)*

Successfactors Inc (DH) .... D
1500 Fashion Island Blvd San Mateo (94404) *(P-12368)*

Successful Altrntves For Addct .... D....... 510 247-8300
795 Fletcher Ln Hayward (94544) *(P-17134)*

Successor Agcy To Nrco Cmnty R, Norco Also Called: City of Norco (P-20728)

Suderman Contg Stevedores Inc (PA) .... D....... 409 762-8131
3806 Worsham Ave Long Beach (90808) *(P-3819)*

Sudwerk, Davis Also Called: Sudwerk Privatbrauerei Hubsch (P-7510)

Sudwerk Privatbrauerei Hubsch .... D....... 530 756-2739
2001 2nd St Davis (95618) *(P-7510)*

Suffolk Construction Co Inc .... B....... 415 848-0500
525 Market St Ste 2850 San Francisco (94105) *(P-726)*

Sufi, Fremont Also Called: Startup Farms Intl LLC (P-11945)

Sugar Bowl Corporation .... D....... 530 426-9000
629 Sugar Bowl Rd Norden (95724) *(P-10280)*

Sugar Bowl Resort, Norden Also Called: Sugar Bowl Corporation (P-10280)

Sugar Foods Corporation .... D....... 510 441-0311
33378 Transit Ave Union City (94587) *(P-6672)*

Sugar Foods Corporation .... C....... 818 768-7900
9500 El Dorado Ave Sun Valley (91352) *(P-13490)*

Sugarcrm Inc (PA) .... C....... 877 842-7276
10050 N Wolfe Rd Ste Sw2130 Cupertino (95014) *(P-11954)*

Sui Companies, Riverside Also Called: Steel Unlimited Inc (P-5520)

Suissa Miller Advertising LLC .... D....... 310 392-9666
8687 Melrose Ave West Hollywood (90069) *(P-10677)*

Sukut Construction LLC .... D....... 714 540-5351
4010 W Chandler Ave Santa Ana (92704) *(P-1269)*

Sukut Construction Inc .... C....... 714 540-5351
4010 W Chandler Ave Santa Ana (92704) *(P-2226)*

Sullivan, San Diego Also Called: Sullivan International Group Inc (P-4984)

Sullivan International Group Inc .... C....... 619 260-1432
2750 Womble Rd Ste 100 San Diego (92106) *(P-4984)*

Sullivncrtsmnroe Insur Svcs LL (PA) .... C....... 800 427-3253
1920 Main St Ste 600 Irvine (92614) *(P-20571)*

Sully Miller Contracting, Brea Also Called: United Rock Products Corp (P-1175)

Sully-Miller Contracting Co (DH) .... D....... 714 578-9600
135 S State College Blvd Ste 400 Brea (92821) *(P-1166)*

Sully-Miller Holding Corp .... C....... 714 578-9600
135 S State College Blvd Ste 400 Brea (92821) *(P-1167)*

Sulpizio Cardiovascular Center .... C....... 858 657-7000
9434 Medical Center Dr La Jolla (92037) *(P-15104)*

Sumaria Systems LLC .... D....... 805 606-4973
105 13th St Vandenberg Afb (93437) *(P-19401)*

Sumitomo Elc DVC Innvtons USA .... D....... 408 232-9500
2355 Zanker Rd San Jose (95131) *(P-5702)*

Sumitomo Elc Intrcnnect Pdts I .... D....... 760 761-0600
915 Armorlite Dr San Marcos (92069) *(P-5595)*

Sumitomo Mitsui Banking Corp .... C....... 213 452-7800
601 S Figueroa St Ste 1800 Los Angeles (90017) *(P-7739)*

Sumitomo Rubber North Amer Inc (HQ) .... C....... 909 466-1116
8656 Haven Ave Rancho Cucamonga (91730) *(P-5073)*

Summer Glen Apartments, Harbor City Also Called: Hunt Enterprises Inc (P-8825)

Summer Systems Inc .... D....... 661 257-4419
28942 Hancock Pkwy Valencia (91355) *(P-1034)*

Summerville At Hazel Creek LLC .... C....... 916 988-7901
6125 Hazel Ave Orangevale (95662) *(P-15684)*

Summit Building Services Inc .... D....... 925 827-9500
1128 Willow Pass Ct Concord (94520) *(P-10972)*

Summit Hotel Trs 115 LLC .... D....... 650 624-3700
264 S Airport Blvd South San Francisco (94080) *(P-10281)*

Summit Medical Center .... C....... 510 869-6758
3100 Summit St Oakland (94609) *(P-16501)*

Summit Medical Center (DH) .... A....... 510 655-4000
350 Hawthorne Ave Oakland (94609) *(P-16502)*

Summit Medical Group .... D....... 510 655-4000
350 Hawthorne Ave Oakland (94609) *(P-16503)*

Summit Trail Hlth Holdings LLC .... D....... 949 487-9500
29222 Rancho Viejo Rd Ste 127 San Juan Capistrano (92675) *(P-15685)*

Summitview Child & Family Svcs .... D....... 530 644-2412
670 Placerville Dr Ste 2 Placerville (95667) *(P-18147)*

Sumo Logic, Redwood City Also Called: Sumo Logic Inc (P-11955)

Sumo Logic Inc (PA) .... A....... 650 810-8700
305 Main St Redwood City (94063) *(P-11955)*

SUN & SAIL CLUB, Lake Forest Also Called: Lake Frest No II Mstr Hmwners (P-18875)

Sun Air Jets LLC .... C....... 805 389-9301
855 Aviation Dr Ste 200 Camarillo (93010) *(P-3869)*

Sun and Sands Enterprises LLC (PA) .... D....... 760 399-4166
47110 Washington St Ste 103 La Quinta (92253) *(P-6582)*

Sun City Palm Dsert Cmnty Assn (PA) .... D....... 760 200-2100
38180 Del Webb Blvd Palm Desert (92211) *(P-18912)*

Sun City Rsvlle Cmnty Assn Inc (PA) .... C....... 916 774-3880
7050 Del Webb Blvd Roseville (95747) *(P-14292)*

Sun Coast Merchandise Corp .... C....... 323 720-9700
6405 Randolph St Commerce (90040) *(P-6053)*

ALPHABETIC SECTION

Sunrise Hospitality Inc

Sun Community Federal Cr Un .... D....... 760 337-4200
  1001 E Us Highway 98 Calexico (92231) *(P-7809)*
Sun Deep Cosmetics, Hayward *Also Called: Sun Deep Inc (P-2632)*
Sun Deep Inc (PA)... D....... 510 441-2525
  31285 San Clemente St Hayward (94544) *(P-2632)*
Sun Deep Inc .... C....... 510 206-7405
  1900 Peters Ranch Rd Danville (94526) *(P-10509)*
Sun Diego Charter, National City *Also Called: Sureride Charter Inc (P-3321)*
Sun Electric LP .... D....... 714 210-3744
  2101 S Yale St Ste B Santa Ana (92704) *(P-1855)*
Sun Energy Construction, Rancho Cucamonga *Also Called: Calvin Dubois (P-1392)*
SUN EXPRESS, Fontana *Also Called: Hanks Inc (P-3401)*
Sun Healthcare Group Inc (DH)....................................... B
  27442 Portola Pkwy Ste 200 Foothill Ranch (92610) *(P-15105)*
Sun Hill Properties Inc .... B....... 818 506-2500
  555 Universal Hollywood Dr Universal City (91608) *(P-10282)*
Sun Light & Power .... D....... 510 845-2997
  1035 Folger Ave Berkeley (94710) *(P-13491)*
SUN MAR HEALTH CARE, Riverside *Also Called: Riverside Equities LLC (P-15642)*
Sun Microsystems, Redwood City *Also Called: Oracle America Inc (P-2809)*
Sun Oaks Tennis & Fitness, Redding *Also Called: Walsh Group Inc (P-14241)*
Sun Pacific Cold Storage, Bakersfield *Also Called: Exeter Packers Inc (P-3654)*
Sun Pacific Farming, Bakersfield *Also Called: 7th Standard Ranch Company (P-67)*
Sun Pacific Farming, Bakersfield *Also Called: Sun Pacific Marketing Coop Inc (P-6584)*
Sun Pacific Farming Coop Inc (PA).................................. B....... 559 592-7121
  1250 E Myer Ave Exeter (93221) *(P-381)*
Sun Pacific Farming Coop Inc .... D....... 661 399-0376
  33374 Lerdo Hwy Bakersfield (93308) *(P-382)*
Sun Pacific Farms, Bakersfield *Also Called: Sun Pacific Farming Coop Inc (P-382)*
Sun Pacific Marketing Coop Inc .... B....... 559 784-6845
  20715 Ave 8 Richgrove (93261) *(P-6583)*
Sun Pacific Marketing Coop Inc .... B....... 661 847-1015
  31452 Old River Rd Bakersfield (93311) *(P-6584)*
Sun Pacific Marketing Coop Inc .... B....... 213 612-9957
  33502 Lerdo Hwy Bakersfield (93308) *(P-20572)*
Sun Pacific Packers, Exeter *Also Called: Exeter Packers Inc (P-265)*
Sun Pacific Shippers, Pasadena *Also Called: Exeter Packers Inc (P-98)*
Sun Valley Group Inc (PA).. B....... 707 822-2885
  3160 Upper Bay Rd Arcata (95521) *(P-157)*
Sun Valley Packing, Reedley *Also Called: Walter L Jones Family Ltd (P-313)*
Sun World Inc .... A....... 805 833-6460
  5544 California Ave Ste 280 Bakersfield (93309) *(P-305)*
Sun World International Inc (PA) .... A....... 661 392-5000
  16351 Driver Rd Bakersfield (93308) *(P-306)*
Sun-Maid Growers California (PA)................................. A....... 559 896-8000
  6795 N Palm Ave Ste 200 Fresno (93704) *(P-6673)*
Suna Solutions Inc .... D....... 888 223-4788
  530 B St Ste 300 San Diego (92101) *(P-20219)*
SunAmerica, Los Angeles *Also Called: SunAmerica Inc (P-7838)*
SunAmerica, Los Angeles *Also Called: SunAmerica Life Insurance Company (P-8247)*
SunAmerica, Los Angeles *Also Called: SunAmerica Investments Inc (P-20220)*
SunAmerica Inc (HQ)... A....... 310 772-6000
  1 Sun America Ctr Fl 38 Los Angeles (90067) *(P-7838)*
SunAmerica Investments Inc (DH)................................ D....... 310 772-6000
  1 Sun America Ctr Fl 37 Los Angeles (90067) *(P-20220)*
SunAmerica Life Insurance Company .... C....... 310 772-6000
  1 Sun America Ctr Fl 36 Los Angeles (90067) *(P-8247)*
Sunbelt Controls Inc .... D....... 626 610-2340
  735 N Todd Ave Azusa (91702) *(P-1573)*
Sunbelt Towing Inc (PA).. D....... 619 297-8697
  4370 Pacific Hwy San Diego (92110) *(P-13720)*
Sunberry Growers, Salinas *Also Called: Sunberry Growers LLC (P-6585)*
Sunberry Growers LLC .... A....... 805 922-9888
  710 La Guardia St Ste A Salinas (93905) *(P-6585)*
Sunbrdge Brttany Rhbltttion Ctr .... A....... 916 484-1393
  3900 Garfield Ave Carmichael (95608) *(P-15686)*
Sunbrdge Prdise Rhbltttion Ctr .... A....... 530 872-3200
  8777 Skyway Paradise (95969) *(P-15687)*
Sunbridge Care Entps W LLC .... C....... 559 897-5881
  1101 Stroud Ave Kingsburg (93631) *(P-15688)*

Suncal, Santa Ana *Also Called: Argent Management LLC (P-8902)*
Sunco Liquidation Inc .... B....... 510 496-5500
  66 Franklin St Ste 310 Oakland (94607) *(P-1574)*
Sundale Fndtion For Stdnts Cmn .... D....... 559 688-3419
  13990 Avenue 240 Tulare (93274) *(P-18356)*
Sundale School, Tulare *Also Called: Sundale Fndtion For Stdnts Cmn (P-18356)*
Sundt Construction, Sacramento *Also Called: Halstead Partnership (P-926)*
Sunfood Corporation .... D....... 619 596-7979
  1830 Gillespie Way Ste 101 El Cajon (92020) *(P-6674)*
Sunfood Superfoods, El Cajon *Also Called: Sunfood Corporation (P-6674)*
Sunfoods LLC (HQ)... D....... 530 661-1923
  1620 E Kentucky Ave Woodland (95776) *(P-6395)*
Sungard, Calabasas *Also Called: Sungard Treasury Systems Inc (P-12369)*
Sungard Treasury Systems Inc .... C....... 818 223-2300
  23975 Park Sorrento Ste 100 Calabasas (91302) *(P-12369)*
Sungarden Company Inc .... D....... 916 379-9088
  4 Wayne Ct Ste 3 Sacramento (95829) *(P-538)*
Sungevity, Temecula *Also Called: Solar Spectrum LLC (P-1567)*
Sungevity, Oakland *Also Called: Sunco Liquidation Inc (P-1574)*
Suning Cmmerce R D Ctr USA Inc .... D....... 650 834-9800
  845 Page Mill Rd Palo Alto (94304) *(P-19851)*
Suning USA, Palo Alto *Also Called: Suning Cmmerce R D Ctr USA Inc (P-19851)*
Sunkist Enterprises .... D....... 650 347-3900
  1308 Rollins Rd Burlingame (94010) *(P-5735)*
Sunkist Growers Inc (PA).. C....... 661 290-8900
  27770 Entertainment Dr Valencia (91355) *(P-6586)*
Sunland, Fresno *Also Called: Sunland Insurance Agency (P-8665)*
Sunland Ford Inc .... D....... 760 241-7751
  15330 Palmdale Rd Victorville (92392) *(P-7306)*
Sunland Ford-Lincoln-Mercury, Victorville *Also Called: Sunland Ford Inc (P-7306)*
Sunland Insurance Agency .... C....... 559 251-7861
  4961 E Kings Canyon Rd Fresno (93727) *(P-8665)*
Sunland Scaffold .... D....... 951 595-9402
  24885 Whitewood Rd # 106 Murrieta (92563) *(P-2317)*
Sunland Shutters, Long Beach *Also Called: Ta Chen International Inc (P-5521)*
Sunline Transit Agency (PA)... C....... 760 343-3456
  32505 Harry Oliver Trl Thousand Palms (92276) *(P-3219)*
Sunline Transit Agency .... C....... 760 972-4059
  790 Vine Ave Coachella (92236) *(P-3296)*
Sunnova Energy Corporation .... A....... 877 757-7697
  6531 Irvine Center Dr Ste 200 Irvine (92618) *(P-4711)*
Sunny View Care Center, Los Angeles *Also Called: Longwood Management Corp (P-15867)*
SUNNYSIDE NURSING CENTER, Torrance *Also Called: Fh & Hf-Torrance I LLC (P-15476)*
Sunnyvale Health Care, Sunnyvale *Also Called: Sunnyvale Healthcare Center (P-15689)*
Sunnyvale Healthcare Center .... D....... 408 245-8070
  1291 S Bernardo Ave Sunnyvale (94087) *(P-15689)*
Sunnyvale Seafood, Union City *Also Called: SSC Inc (P-6484)*
Sunopta Grains and Foods Inc .... D....... 323 774-6000
  12128 Center St South Gate (90280) *(P-2359)*
Sunoptics Prismatic Skylights, Sacramento *Also Called: Washoe Equipment Inc (P-2873)*
Sunpower Corporation Systems .... D....... 661 758-2501
  23900 Mc Combs Rd Wasco (93280) *(P-1575)*
Sunpower Corporation Systems (DH).......................... D....... 510 260-8200
  1414 Harbour Way S Ste 1901 Richmond (94804) *(P-1576)*
Sunpro Solar Inc .... D....... 951 678-7733
  34859 Frederick St Ste 101 Wildomar (92595) *(P-1577)*
Sunridge Nurseries Inc .... D....... 661 363-8463
  441 Vineland Rd Bakersfield (93307) *(P-245)*
Sunrise At Bonita, Chula Vista *Also Called: Sunrise Senior Living LLC (P-15693)*
Sunrise At Canyon Crest, Riverside *Also Called: Sunrise Senior Living LLC (P-15691)*
Sunrise At Tustin, Santa Ana *Also Called: Sunrise Senior Living LLC (P-15697)*
Sunrise Farms LLC .... D....... 707 778-6450
  395 Liberty Rd Petaluma (94952) *(P-6451)*
Sunrise Ford .... C....... 909 822-4401
  16005 Valley Blvd Fontana (92335) *(P-7307)*
Sunrise Ford, North Hollywood *Also Called: Ngp Motors Inc (P-7264)*
Sunrise Growers Inc .... C....... 714 706-6090
  701 W Kimberly Ave # 210 Placentia (92870) *(P-6587)*
Sunrise Hospitality Inc .... C....... 916 419-4440
  2060 Freeway Dr Woodland (95776) *(P-10283)*

Employee Codes: A=Over 500 employees, B=251-500
C=101-250, D=51-100, E=20-50, F=10-19, G=1-9

ALPHABETIC SECTION

Sunrise of Claremont, Claremont Also Called: Sunrise Senior Living LLC *(P-15690)*

Sunrise of Fresno, Fresno Also Called: Sunrise Senior Living LLC *(P-15696)*

Sunrise of Mission Viejo, Mission Viejo Also Called: Sunrise Senior Living LLC *(P-15692)*

Sunrise of Monterey, Monterey Also Called: Sunrise Senior Living LLC *(P-15698)*

Sunrise of Sunnyvale, Sunnyvale Also Called: Sunrise Senior Living LLC *(P-15695)*

Sunrise of Woodland Hills, Encino Also Called: Sunrise Senior Living LLC *(P-15694)*

Sunrise Respiratory Care Inc .... C 949 398-6555
1881 Langley Ave Irvine (92614) *(P-5451)*

Sunrise Senior Living LLC .... D 909 398-4688
2053 N Towne Ave Claremont (91711) *(P-15690)*

Sunrise Senior Living LLC .... D 951 686-6075
5265 Chapala Dr Riverside (92507) *(P-15691)*

Sunrise Senior Living LLC .... D 949 582-2010
26151 Country Club Dr Mission Viejo (92691) *(P-15692)*

Sunrise Senior Living LLC .... D 619 470-2220
3302 Bonita Rd Chula Vista (91910) *(P-15693)*

Sunrise Senior Living LLC .... D 818 346-9046
5501 Newcastle Ave Apt 130 Encino (91316) *(P-15694)*

Sunrise Senior Living LLC .... D 408 749-8600
633 S Knickerbocker Dr Ste 263 Sunnyvale (94087) *(P-15695)*

Sunrise Senior Living LLC .... D 559 325-8170
7444 N Cedar Ave Fresno (93720) *(P-15696)*

Sunrise Senior Living LLC .... D 714 544-5959
12291 Newport Ave Santa Ana (92705) *(P-15697)*

Sunrise Senior Living LLC .... D 831 643-2400
1110 Cass St Monterey (93940) *(P-15698)*

Sunrise Senior Living MGT Inc .... C 760 720-9898
3140 El Camino Real Carlsbad (92008) *(P-15699)*

Sunrise Senior Living MGT Inc .... C 909 447-5259
120 W San Jose Ave Claremont (91711) *(P-18528)*

Sunroad Asset Management Inc .... C 858 362-8500
4445 Eastgate Mall Ste 400 San Diego (92121) *(P-20221)*

Sunrun Delphi Manager 2016 LLC .... D 415 536-6704
595 Market St San Francisco (94105) *(P-1578)*

Sunscape Eyewear Inc .... D 949 553-0590
17526 Von Karman Ave Ste A Irvine (92614) *(P-6054)*

Sunset Aviation LLC .... C 510 783-3584
7951 Earhart Rd Oakland (94621) *(P-3912)*

Sunset Development Company (PA) .... C 925 277-1700
2600 Camino Ramon Ste 201 San Ramon (94583) *(P-8767)*

Sunset Landscape Maintenance .... D 949 455-4636
27201 Burbank El Toro (92610) *(P-539)*

Sunset Manor Convalescent Hosp, El Monte Also Called: Gibraltar Cnvalescent Hosp Inc *(P-15850)*

Sunset Pacific Transportation Inc (PA) .... D 909 464-1677
14522 Yorba Ave Chino (91710) *(P-3547)*

Sunset Property Services, Irvine Also Called: Jonset LLC *(P-4980)*

Sunset Scavenger Company .... B 415 330-1300
250 Executive Park Blvd Ste 2100 San Francisco (94134) *(P-4942)*

Sunset Tower Hotel LLC .... D 323 654-7100
8358 W Sunset Blvd Los Angeles (90069) *(P-10284)*

Sunshine Communications SE Inc .... C 619 448-7600
350 Cypress Ln Ste D El Cajon (92020) *(P-1856)*

Sunshine Floral Inc .... D 805 684-1177
4595 Foothill Rd Carpinteria (93013) *(P-6874)*

Sunshine Floral LLC .... D 805 982-8822
1070 S Rice Ave Ste 1 Oxnard (93033) *(P-6875)*

Sunshine Inn A Cal Ltd Partnr .... D 323 722-8800
888 Montebello Blvd Rosemead (91770) *(P-10285)*

Sunshine Metal Clad Inc .... D 661 366-0575
7201 Edison Hwy Bakersfield (93307) *(P-1966)*

Sunshine Preschool, Cerritos Also Called: Cerritos Church of Nazarene *(P-19014)*

Sunshine Raisin Corporation (PA) .... C 559 834-5981
626 S 5th St Fowler (93625) *(P-307)*

Sunshine Villa Assisted Living, Santa Cruz Also Called: Regent Assisted Living Inc *(P-18511)*

Sunstone Durante LLC .... C 858 792-5200
15575 Jimmy Durante Blvd Del Mar (92014) *(P-10286)*

Sunstone Hotel Properties Inc .... C 310 228-4100
1177 S Beverly Dr Los Angeles (90035) *(P-10287)*

Sunstone Hotel Properties Inc .... C 310 546-7627
1700 N Sepulveda Blvd Manhattan Beach (90266) *(P-10288)*

Sunstone Hotel Properties Inc (DH) .... C 949 330-4000
120 Vantis Dr Ste 350 Aliso Viejo (92656) *(P-10289)*

Sunstone Hotel Properties Inc .... D 858 277-1199
3805 Murphy Canyon Rd San Diego (92123) *(P-10290)*

Sunstone Partners, San Mateo Also Called: Sunstone Partners LLC *(P-9567)*

Sunstone Partners, San Mateo Also Called: Sunstone Partners MGT LLC *(P-9568)*

Sunstone Partners LLC .... D 650 289-4400
400 S El Camino Real Ste 300 San Mateo (94402) *(P-9567)*

Sunstone Partners MGT LLC .... D 650 289-4400
400 S El Camino Real Ste 300 San Mateo (94402) *(P-9568)*

Sunstone Top Gun Lessee Inc .... C 949 330-4000
4550 La Jolla Village Dr San Diego (92122) *(P-10291)*

Sunsystem Technology LLC .... C 559 412-7870
2025 N Gateway Blvd Ste 112 Fresno (93727) *(P-19775)*

Suntreat, Lindsay Also Called: Suntreat Pkg Shipg A Ltd Prtnr *(P-4135)*

Suntreat Pkg Shipg A Ltd Prtnr .... C 559 562-4991
391 Oxford Ave Lindsay (93247) *(P-4135)*

Sunvair Aerospace Group Inc (PA) .... D 661 294-3777
29145 The Old Rd Valencia (91355) *(P-13801)*

Sunvalley, Fullerton Also Called: Sunvalleytek International Inc *(P-5356)*

Sunvalleytek International Inc .... D 888 456-8468
4260 N Harbor Blvd Fullerton (92835) *(P-5356)*

Sunwest Electric Inc .... C 714 630-8700
3064 E Mariloma Anaheim (92806) *(P-1857)*

Super 8 Anaheim Disneyland Drv, Anaheim Also Called: Jin Yi Enterprises Inc *(P-9920)*

Super 8 Motel, Goleta Also Called: Super 8 Motel Goleta *(P-10292)*

Super 8 Motel, Bakersfield Also Called: Tiburon Hospitality LLC *(P-10310)*

Super 8 Motel Goleta .... D 805 967-5591
6021 Hollister Ave, Us Hwy 101 Goleta (93117) *(P-10292)*

Super Center Concepts Inc .... C 323 562-8980
7300 Atlantic Ave Cudahy (90201) *(P-7153)*

Super Center Concepts Inc .... C 951 372-9485
1130 W 6th St Corona (92882) *(P-13492)*

Super Center Concepts Inc .... C 323 223-3878
133 W Avenue 45 Los Angeles (90065) *(P-13493)*

Super D Phantom Distribution, Irvine Also Called: C D Listening Bar Inc *(P-6032)*

Super Evil Mega Corp (PA) .... D 650 696-0608
119a S B St San Mateo (94401) *(P-11956)*

Super Home Inc .... D 844 997-8737
120 2nd St Ste 400 San Francisco (94105) *(P-18529)*

Super Micro Computer Inc (PA) .... A 408 503-8000
980 Rock Ave San Jose (95131) *(P-2813)*

Super Pallet Recycling Center, Elk Grove Also Called: Super Pallet Recycling Corp *(P-5190)*

Super Pallet Recycling Corp (PA) .... D 916 686-1700
10401 Grant Line Rd Elk Grove (95624) *(P-5190)*

Super Services, Anaheim Also Called: E Z Services *(P-7853)*

Super Store Industries .... D 209 668-2100
2600 Spengler Way Turlock (95380) *(P-2350)*

Super Store Industries .... B 209 858-3365
2800 W March Ln Ste 210 Stockton (95219) *(P-6675)*

Super Talent Technology Corp .... A 408 957-8133
2077 N Capitol Ave San Jose (95132) *(P-5357)*

Super7, San Francisco Also Called: Super7 Retail Inc *(P-5999)*

Super7 Retail Inc .... D 415 374-7190
777 Florida St Ste 202 San Francisco (94110) *(P-5999)*

Superbroward LLC .... C 650 348-4881
1222 Broadway Burlingame (94010) *(P-10510)*

Supercuts, Walnut Creek Also Called: J M D Enterprises *(P-10500)*

Supercuts, Downey Also Called: Jlm & Mag Associates Inc *(P-10501)*

Supercuts, Burlingame Also Called: Superbroward LLC *(P-10510)*

Superior Automatic Sprnklr Co .... D 408 946-7272
4378 Enterprise St Fremont (94538) *(P-1579)*

Superior Communications Inc (PA) .... C 877 522-4727
5027 Irwindale Ave Ste 900 Irwindale (91706) *(P-5703)*

Superior Construction Inc .... D 951 808-8780
265 N Joy St Corona (92879) *(P-727)*

Superior Elec Mech & Plbg Inc .... B 909 357-9400
8613 Helms Ave Rancho Cucamonga (91730) *(P-1858)*

Superior Electrical Advg Inc (PA) .... D 562 495-3808
1700 W Anaheim St Long Beach (90813) *(P-3102)*

ALPHABETIC SECTION

Superior Equipment Solutions .... D....... 323 722-7900
  1085 Bixby Dr Hacienda Heights (91745) *(P-2870)*
Superior Foods Inc .... D....... 831 728-3691
  275 Westgate Dr Watsonville (95076) *(P-6396)*
Superior Foods Companies, The, Watsonville *Also Called: Superior Foods Inc (P-6396)*
Superior Fruit LLC .... C....... 805 485-2519
  4324 E Vineyard Ave Oxnard (93036) *(P-66)*
Superior Grocers, Los Angeles *Also Called: Super Center Concepts Inc (P-13493)*
Superior Gunite (HQ) .... C....... 818 896-9199
  12306 Van Nuys Blvd Sylmar (91342) *(P-2163)*
Superior Masonry Walls Ltd .... D....... 909 370-1800
  300 W Olive St Ste A Colton (92324) *(P-1894)*
Superior Paving Company Inc .... D....... 951 739-9200
  1880 N Delilah St Corona (92879) *(P-1168)*
Superior Press, Santa Fe Springs *Also Called: Superior Printing Inc (P-2570)*
Superior Printing Inc .... D....... 888 590-7998
  9440 Norwalk Blvd Santa Fe Springs (90670) *(P-2570)*
Superior Ready Mix Concrete LP .... D....... 760 728-1128
  1564 Mission Rd Escondido (92029) *(P-2713)*
Superior Seafood Co, Los Angeles *Also Called: PLD Enterprises Inc (P-6476)*
Superior Sod I LP .... C....... 909 923-5068
  17821 17th St Ste 165 Tustin (92780) *(P-158)*
Superior Super Warehouse, Cudahy *Also Called: Super Center Concepts Inc (P-7153)*
Superior Tile Co, San Leandro *Also Called: TRM Corporation (P-1988)*
Superior Wall Systems Inc .... B....... 714 278-0000
  1232 E Orangethorpe Ave Fullerton (92831) *(P-1967)*
Supermedia LLC .... D....... 562 594-5101
  3131 Katella Ave Los Alamitos (90720) *(P-2557)*
Supermicro, San Jose *Also Called: Super Micro Computer Inc (P-2813)*
Supershuttle International Inc .... D....... 650 246-2786
  323 S Canal St South San Francisco (94080) *(P-3220)*
Supershuttle International Inc .... D....... 415 558-8500
  700 16th St San Francisco (94158) *(P-3221)*
Supershuttle International Inc .... D....... 650 246-2704
  160 S Linden Ave South San Francisco (94080) *(P-3297)*
Supherb Farms .... C....... 209 633-3600
  300 Dianne Dr Turlock (95380) *(P-2443)*
Supherb Farms, Turlock *Also Called: Supherb Farms (P-2443)*
Supplier Diversity, San Diego *Also Called: San Diego Gas & Electric Co (P-4752)*
Supply Change Services, Sacramento *Also Called: Sacramento Municpl Utility Dst (P-4666)*
Supplyshift (PA) .... D....... 831 824-4326
  217 River St Santa Cruz (95060) *(P-12370)*
Supplyworks .... D....... 408 954-1234
  650 Brennan St San Jose (95131) *(P-6055)*
Support Trtmnt Edcatn For Prnt, Irvine *Also Called: In Stepps Inc (P-15286)*
Supportlogic Inc (PA) .... D....... 408 471-4710
  356 Santana Row Ste 1000 San Jose (95128) *(P-18629)*
Supra National Express Inc .... C....... 310 549-7105
  1421 Charles Willard St Carson (90746) *(P-4103)*
Supreme Almonds California Inc .... D....... 661 746-6475
  16897 Highway 43 Wasco (93280) *(P-94)*
Supreme Security Services Inc .... D....... 760 415-7399
  3517 Cameo Dr Unit 84 Oceanside (92056) *(P-13054)*
Sureco Hlth Lf Insur Agcy Inc .... D....... 949 333-0263
  201 Sandpointe Ave Ste 600 Santa Ana (92707) *(P-8666)*
Surecraft Supply Inc C
  2875 Executive Pl Escondido (92029) *(P-2020)*
Surefox North America Inc .... C....... 650 665-1852
  655 3rd St San Francisco (94107) *(P-20857)*
Sureride Charter Inc .... C....... 619 336-9200
  522 W 8th St National City (91950) *(P-3321)*
Surf Sand Hotel, Laguna Beach *Also Called: JC Resorts LLC (P-20119)*
SURFSIDE RACE PLACE AT DEL MAR, Del Mar *Also Called: Del Mar Thoroughbred Club (P-14163)*
Surge Globl Bkries Hldings LLC (PA) .... D....... 818 896-0525
  13336 Paxton St Pacoima (91331) *(P-6676)*
SURGERY CENTER OF ALTA BATES S, Oakland *Also Called: Summit Medical Center (P-16502)*
Surgery Center of Health South, Oakland *Also Called: EBSC LP (P-14731)*
Surgery Ctr of Alta Btes Smmit (HQ) .... A....... 510 204-4444
  2450 Ashby Ave Berkeley (94705) *(P-16504)*

Surgery Department, San Francisco *Also Called: St Marys Medical Center Inc (P-16485)*
Surplus Line Association Cal .... C....... 415 434-4900
  12667 Alcosta Blvd Ste 450 San Ramon (94583) *(P-18725)*
Surprise Valley Hlth Care Dst .... D....... 530 279-6111
  741 Main St Cedarville (96104) *(P-16505)*
Survey Junkie, Glendale *Also Called: Disqo Inc (P-19808)*
Surveysavvy.com, San Diego *Also Called: Luth Research Inc (P-19830)*
Survival Systems Intl Inc (PA) .... D....... 760 749-6800
  34140 Valley Center Rd Valley Center (92082) *(P-13802)*
Susan J Harris Inc .... C....... 619 498-8450
  344 F St Ste 100 Chula Vista (91910) *(P-18530)*
Suss McRtec Phtnic Systems Inc .... D....... 951 817-3700
  2520 Palisades Dr Corona (92882) *(P-2963)*
Sustainable Agriculture, Trabuco Canyon *Also Called: Seeds of Change Inc (P-6832)*
Sutherland Digital Svcs Inc .... B....... 510 474-2616
  691 S Milpitas Blvd Milpitas (95035) *(P-12885)*
Sutter Amador Hospital, Jackson *Also Called: Sutter Valley Hospitals (P-16561)*
Sutter Amador Hospital Lab, Jackson *Also Called: Sutter Hlth Scrmnto Sierra Reg (P-16542)*
Sutter Amador Womens Services .... A....... 209 223-2034
  255 New York Ranch Rd Ste C Jackson (95642) *(P-16506)*
SUTTER AMADOR WOMENS SERVICES, Jackson *Also Called: Sutter Amador Womens Services (P-16506)*
Sutter Bay Hospitals .... D....... 415 600-2632
  3698 California St San Francisco (94118) *(P-15106)*
Sutter Bay Hospitals (HQ) .... A....... 415 600-6000
  475 Brannan St Ste 130 San Francisco (94107) *(P-16507)*
Sutter Bay Hospitals .... D....... 510 869-6199
  2420 Ashby Ave Berkeley (94705) *(P-16508)*
Sutter Bay Hospitals .... C....... 415 600-2403
  3801 Sacramento St Ste 61 San Francisco (94118) *(P-16509)*
Sutter Bay Hospitals .... C....... 510 655-4000
  350 Hawthorne Ave Oakland (94609) *(P-16510)*
Sutter Bay Hospitals .... D....... 831 423-4111
  2025 Soquel Ave Santa Cruz (95062) *(P-16511)*
Sutter Bay Medical Foundation .... C....... 408 730-4321
  535 Oakmead Pkwy Sunnyvale (94085) *(P-15107)*
Sutter Bay Medical Foundation .... D....... 650 812-3751
  2951 Gordon Ave Santa Clara (95051) *(P-15108)*
Sutter Bay Medical Foundation .... D....... 650 934-7956
  877 W Fremont Ave Ste N Sunnyvale (94087) *(P-15109)*
Sutter Bay Medical Foundation (HQ) .... A....... 650 321-4121
  795 El Camino Real Palo Alto (94301) *(P-15110)*
SUTTER C H S, San Francisco *Also Called: Sutter Bay Hospitals (P-16507)*
SUTTER C H S, Vallejo *Also Called: Sutter Solano Med Ctr Guild (P-16558)*
SUTTER C H S, Vallejo *Also Called: Sutter Solano Medical Center (P-16559)*
Sutter Care & Home .... D....... 650 685-2800
  700 S Claremont St Ste 220 San Mateo (94402) *(P-16938)*
Sutter Central Vly Hospitals .... A....... 209 572-5900
  1200 Scenic Dr Ste 200 Modesto (95350) *(P-16512)*
Sutter Central Vly Hospitals (HQ) .... C....... 209 526-4500
  1700 Coffee Rd Modesto (95355) *(P-16513)*
Sutter Central Vly Hospitals .... A....... 209 526-4500
  1700 Coffee Rd Modesto (95355) *(P-16514)*
Sutter Central Vly Hospitals .... A....... 209 572-8270
  1316 Celeste Dr Ste 104 Modesto (95355) *(P-16515)*
Sutter Central Vly Hospitals .... A....... 209 569-7544
  1800 Coffee Rd Ste 30 Modesto (95355) *(P-16516)*
Sutter Club .... D....... 916 442-0456
  1220 9th St Sacramento (95814) *(P-18913)*
Sutter Coast Hospital (HQ) .... C....... 707 464-8511
  800 E Washington Blvd Crescent City (95531) *(P-16517)*
Sutter Coast Hospital .... B....... 707 464-8741
  983 3rd St Ste D Crescent City (95531) *(P-16939)*
Sutter Connect LLC .... B....... 510 596-4700
  2000 Powell St Ste 100 Emeryville (94608) *(P-13494)*
SUTTER CONNECT, LLC, Emeryville *Also Called: Sutter Connect LLC (P-13494)*
Sutter Counseling Center, Sacramento *Also Called: Sutter Hlth Scrmnto Sierra Reg (P-15113)*
Sutter Delta Medical Center .... C....... 925 779-7200
  3901 Lone Tree Way Antioch (94509) *(P-16518)*
Sutter Elk Grove Surgery Ctr, Elk Grove *Also Called: Sutter Health (P-16526)*

Sutter Gould Med Foundation

Sutter Gould Med Foundation, Modesto *Also Called: Sutter Valley Med Foundation* *(P-15119)*

Sutter Health .... C....... 916 783-8114
  1680 E Roseville Pkwy Ste 100 Roseville (95661) *(P-15111)*

Sutter Health .... D....... 916 929-3393
  2 Scripps Dr Ste 110 Sacramento (95825) *(P-15112)*

Sutter Health .... D....... 916 454-8200
  3707 Schriever Ave Mather (95655) *(P-15700)*

Sutter Health .... D....... 510 618-5200
  1651 Alvarado St San Leandro (94577) *(P-15798)*

Sutter Health .... C....... 916 797-4725
  2 Medical Plaza Dr Roseville (95661) *(P-16519)*

Sutter Health .... D....... 415 600-7034
  2395 Sacramento St San Francisco (94115) *(P-16520)*

Sutter Health .... D....... 916 733-9588
  1020 29th St Ste 600 Sacramento (95816) *(P-16521)*

Sutter Health .... C....... 925 779-7273
  3901 Lone Tree Way Antioch (94509) *(P-16522)*

Sutter Health .... D....... 831 458-6310
  1301 Mission St Santa Cruz (95060) *(P-16523)*

Sutter Health .... C....... 415 600-1020
  2340 Clay St Rm 121 San Francisco (94115) *(P-16524)*

Sutter Health .... C....... 916 566-4819
  2880 Gateway Oaks Dr Ste 220 Sacramento (95833) *(P-16525)*

Sutter Health .... D....... 916 544-5423
  8200 Laguna Blvd Elk Grove (95758) *(P-16526)*

Sutter Health .... D....... 415 600-4280
  2015 Steiner St Fl 1 San Francisco (94115) *(P-16527)*

Sutter Health .... A....... 510 537-1234
  20103 Lake Chabot Rd Castro Valley (94546) *(P-16528)*

Sutter Health .... C....... 415 897-8495
  100 Rowland Way Ste 210 Novato (94945) *(P-16529)*

Sutter Health .... D....... 707 864-4660
  2700 Gateway Oaks Dr Sacramento (95833) *(P-16530)*

Sutter Health .... A....... 510 547-2244
  3875 Telegraph Ave Oakland (94609) *(P-16531)*

Sutter Health .... D....... 510 869-8777
  3000 Telegraph Ave Oakland (94609) *(P-16532)*

Sutter Health .... D....... 415 600-6000
  1101 Van Ness Ave San Francisco (94109) *(P-16533)*

Sutter Health (PA) .... A....... **916 733-8800**
  2200 River Plaza Dr Sacramento (95833) *(P-16534)*

Sutter Health .... D....... 650 262-4262
  50 S San Mateo Dr Ste 470 San Mateo (94401) *(P-16535)*

Sutter Health .... C....... 415 600-6000
  1580 Valencia St Ste 237 San Francisco (94110) *(P-16536)*

Sutter Health .... C....... 415 600-6000
  2333 Buchanan St San Francisco (94115) *(P-16537)*

Sutter Health .... D....... 650 934-7000
  701 E El Camino Real Mountain View (94040) *(P-16538)*

Sutter Health .... C....... 916 797-4700
  3 Medical Plaza Dr Ste 100 Roseville (95661) *(P-16539)*

Sutter Health .... C....... 916 220-1927
  1201 Alhambra Blvd Ste 210 Sacramento (95816) *(P-17135)*

Sutter Health .... D....... 925 371-3800
  2950 Collier Canyon Rd Livermore (94551) *(P-17335)*

Sutter Health, Santa Rosa *Also Called: Santa Rosa Surgery Center LP* *(P-16394)*

Sutter Health Sacsierra Region, Sacramento *Also Called: Sutter Health* *(P-16534)*

Sutter Hlth Rhabilitation Svcs .... D....... 916 733-3040
  2801 L St Fl 3 Sacramento (95816) *(P-16540)*

Sutter Hlth Scrmnto Sierra Reg .... B....... 916 386-3000
  7700 Folsom Blvd Sacramento (95826) *(P-15113)*

Sutter Hlth Scrmnto Sierra Reg .... C....... 530 747-5010
  2030 Sutter Pl Ste 2000 Davis (95616) *(P-15541)*

Sutter Hlth Scrmnto Sierra Reg .... B....... 209 223-7540
  100 Mission Blvd Jackson (95642) *(P-16542)*

Sutter Hlth Scrmnto Sierra Reg .... C....... 916 733-7080
  701 Howe Ave Ste F20 Sacramento (95825) *(P-16543)*

Sutter Hlth Scrmnto Sierra Reg (HQ) .... B....... **916 733-8800**
  2200 River Plaza Dr Sacramento (95833) *(P-16544)*

Sutter Hlth Scrmnto Sierra Reg .... B....... 916 373-3400
  1600 Cebrian St West Sacramento (95691) *(P-16545)*

Sutter Hlth Scrmnto Sierra Reg .... B....... 916 454-2222
  5151 F St Sacramento (95819) *(P-16546)*

Sutter Hlth Scrmnto Sierra Reg .... B....... 916 446-3100
  1234 U St Sacramento (95818) *(P-16547)*

Sutter Hlth Scrmnto Sierra Reg .... B....... 916 924-7666
  2700 Gateway Oaks Dr Sacramento (95833) *(P-16548)*

Sutter Hlth Scrmnto Sierra Reg .... B....... 707 554-4444
  300 Hospital Dr Vallejo (94589) *(P-16549)*

Sutter Hlth Scrmnto Sierra Reg .... A....... 916 733-3095
  2800 L St Sacramento (95816) *(P-16550)*

Sutter Hlth Scrmnto Sierra Reg .... C....... 530 406-5616
  475 Pioneer Ave Ste 100 Woodland (95776) *(P-16551)*

Sutter Home Winery Inc (PA) .... C....... **707 963-3104**
  100 St Helena Hwy (Hwy. 29) S Saint Helena (94574) *(P-2395)*

Sutter Lakeside Hospital .... B....... 707 262-5000
  5176 Hill Rd E Lakeport (95453) *(P-16552)*

Sutter Lakeside Hospital, Lakeport *Also Called: Sutter West Bay Hospitals* *(P-16564)*

Sutter Material Management, West Sacramento *Also Called: Sutter Hlth Scrmnto Sierra Reg* *(P-16545)*

Sutter Maternity & Surgery, Santa Cruz *Also Called: Sutter Bay Hospitals* *(P-16511)*

Sutter Med Group of Rdwods Inc .... C....... 707 546-2788
  3883 Airway Dr Ste 202 Santa Rosa (95403) *(P-15114)*

Sutter Medical Center .... D....... 916 887-0000
  2825 Capitol Ave Sacramento (95816) *(P-16553)*

Sutter Medical Center, Sacramento *Also Called: Sutter Hlth Scrmnto Sierra Reg* *(P-16550)*

Sutter Medical Center, Woodland *Also Called: Sutter Hlth Scrmnto Sierra Reg* *(P-16551)*

Sutter Medical Ctr Sacramento, Sacramento *Also Called: Sutter Hlth Rhabilitation Svcs* *(P-16540)*

Sutter Medical Gen Campus Phrm, Sacramento *Also Called: Sutter Medical Center* *(P-16553)*

Sutter Medical Plaza Roseville, Roseville *Also Called: Sutter Valley Med Foundation* *(P-15118)*

Sutter Memorial Hospital, Sacramento *Also Called: Sutter Hlth Scrmnto Sierra Reg* *(P-16544)*

Sutter Memorial Hospital, Sacramento *Also Called: Sutter Hlth Scrmnto Sierra Reg* *(P-16546)*

Sutter Mtrnty/Srgry Ctr-Snt Cr .... D....... 831 477-2200
  2900 Chanticleer Ave Santa Cruz (95065) *(P-16554)*

Sutter N Med Group A Prof Corp (PA) .... D....... **530 749-3661**
  969 Plumas St Ste 205 Yuba City (95991) *(P-16555)*

Sutter North Med Foundation (PA) .... C....... **530 741-1300**
  969 Plumas St Yuba City (95991) *(P-15115)*

Sutter Occupational Hlth Svcs, Roseville *Also Called: Sutter Health* *(P-16539)*

Sutter Physician Services (HQ) .... A....... **916 854-6600**
  10470 Old Placerville Rd Ste 100 Sacramento (95827) *(P-20573)*

Sutter Regional Med Foundation .... C....... 707 631-9423
  2720 Low Ct Fairfield (94534) *(P-15116)*

Sutter Regional Med Foundation .... C....... 707 454-5800
  770 Mason St Vacaville (95688) *(P-15117)*

Sutter Regional Med Foundation .... C....... 707 551-3616
  127 Hospital Dr Ste 102 Vallejo (94589) *(P-18914)*

Sutter Roseville Medical Ctr .... A....... 916 781-1000
  1 Medical Plaza Dr Roseville (95661) *(P-16556)*

Sutter Rsvlle Med Ctr Fndation .... B....... 916 781-1000
  1 Medical Plaza Dr Roseville (95661) *(P-16557)*

Sutter Securities Inc .... C....... 415 352-6300
  6 Venture Ste 395 Irvine (92618) *(P-8166)*

Sutter Senior Care, Sacramento *Also Called: Sutter Hlth Scrmnto Sierra Reg* *(P-16547)*

Sutter Solano Med Ctr Guild (HQ) .... D....... **707 554-4444**
  300 Hospital Dr Vallejo (94589) *(P-16558)*

Sutter Solano Medical Center .... A....... 707 554-4444
  300 Hospital Dr Vallejo (94589) *(P-16559)*

Sutter Valley Hospitals (HQ) .... B....... **916 733-8800**
  2200 River Plaza Dr Sacramento (95833) *(P-16560)*

Sutter Valley Hospitals .... B....... 209 223-7514
  200 Mission Blvd Jackson (95642) *(P-16561)*

Sutter Valley Med Foundation .... C....... 916 865-1140
  3100 Douglas Blvd Roseville (95661) *(P-15118)*

Sutter Valley Med Foundation .... C....... 209 524-1211
  600 Coffee Rd Modesto (95355) *(P-15119)*

Sutter Valley Med Foundation .... D....... 916 924-7764
  1625 Stockton Blvd Ste 110 Sacramento (95816) *(P-15308)*

Sutter Valley Med Foundation .... C....... 916 865-1140
  568 N Sunrise Ave Ste 250 Roseville (95661) *(P-20222)*

ALPHABETIC SECTION

SUTTER VISITING NURSE ASSOCIATION & HOSPICE, Modesto *Also Called: Sutter Vsting Nrse Assn Hspice (P-16942)*

Sutter Vsiting Nurse Assn Hosp, Concord *Also Called: Sutter Vsting Nrse Assn Hspice (P-16944)*

Sutter Vsting Nrse Assn Hspice .... C....... 510 618-5277
   1651 Alvarado St San Leandro (94577) *(P-15701)*

Sutter Vsting Nrse Assn Hspice .... C....... 415 600-6200
   1625 Van Ness Ave San Francisco (94109) *(P-16940)*

Sutter Vsting Nrse Assn Hspice .... C....... 510 895-4403
   2953 Teagarden St San Leandro (94577) *(P-16941)*

Sutter Vsting Nrse Assn Hspice .... C....... 209 342-4048
   1316 Celeste Dr Ste 140 Modesto (95355) *(P-16942)*

Sutter Vsting Nrse Assn Hspice .... C....... 831 455-8901
   19045 Portola Dr Ste B Salinas (93908) *(P-16943)*

Sutter Vsting Nrse Assn Hspice .... C....... 925 677-4250
   5099 Commercial Cir Ste 20594520 Concord (94520) *(P-16944)*

Sutter West Bay Hospitals .... C....... 415 492-4800
   100 Rowland Way Ste 310 Novato (94945) *(P-16562)*

Sutter West Bay Hospitals (HQ) .... **B....... 415 209-1300**
   180 Rowland Way Novato (94945) *(P-16563)*

Sutter West Bay Hospitals .... B....... 707 262-5000
   5176 Hill Rd E Lakeport (95453) *(P-16564)*

Sutter West Foundation, Davis *Also Called: Sutter Hlth Scrmnto Sierra Reg (P-16541)*

Sutter Yuba Mental Health Svcs, Yuba City *Also Called: County of Sutter (P-17044)*

Suttercare Corporation .... A....... 650 853-8500
   1501 Trousdale Dr Burlingame (94010) *(P-16565)*

Suttercare Corporation .... A....... 650 696-5363
   1601 Trousdale Dr Burlingame (94010) *(P-17136)*

Sutters Place Inc (PA) .... D....... 408 451-8888
   1801 Bering Dr San Jose (95112) *(P-7511)*

Suttles Plumbing & Mech Corp .... D....... 818 718-9779
   2267 Agate Ct Simi Valley (93065) *(P-1580)*

Sv Academy, San Francisco *Also Called: Be School Inc (P-12740)*

Sv Group, Morgan Hill *Also Called: Svg Contractors Inc (P-2244)*

Sv Labs Corporation (PA) .... D....... 831 722-9526
   480 Airport Blvd Watsonville (95076) *(P-6146)*

Svb Financial Group (PA) .... A....... 408 654-7400
   3003 Tasman Dr Santa Clara (95054) *(P-7718)*

Svb Securities LLC .... D....... 800 778-1164
   255 California St Fl 12 San Francisco (94111) *(P-8167)*

Svcf, Mountain View *Also Called: Silicon Vly Cmnty Foundation (P-18909)*

Svendsen Marine Distributing, Alameda *Also Called: Svendsens Boat Works Inc (P-5969)*

Svendsens Boat Works Inc .... D....... 510 522-2886
   2900 Main St Ste 1900 Alameda (94501) *(P-5969)*

Svg Contractors Inc .... D....... 408 218-0993
   155 E Main Ave Ste 110 Morgan Hill (95037) *(P-2244)*

Svi Lax LLC .... D....... 310 281-0300
   5933 W Century Blvd Los Angeles (90045) *(P-10293)*

Swa Group (PA) .... D....... 415 332-5100
   2200 Bridgeway Sausalito (94965) *(P-468)*

Swagbucks, El Segundo *Also Called: Prodege LLC (P-11847)*

Swander Pace Capital LLC (PA) .... A....... 415 477-8500
   101 Mission St Ste 1900 San Francisco (94105) *(P-9569)*

Swaner Hardwood Co Inc (PA) .... D....... 818 953-5350
   5 W Magnolia Blvd Burbank (91502) *(P-2481)*

Swann, Santa Fe Springs *Also Called: Swann Communications USA Inc (P-5704)*

Swann Communications USA Inc .... D....... 562 777-2551
   12636 Clark St Santa Fe Springs (90670) *(P-5704)*

Swarco McCain Inc (DH) .... C....... 760 727-8100
   2365 Oak Ridge Way Vista (92081) *(P-5871)*

Swatfame Inc (PA) .... B....... 626 961-7928
   16425 Gale Ave City Of Industry (91745) *(P-6223)*

Swds, Irvine *Also Called: Swds Holdings Inc (P-9341)*

Swds Holdings Inc .... B....... 800 395-5277
   8659 Research Dr Irvine (92618) *(P-9341)*

Sweatheory LLC .... D....... 310 956-2307
   1503 N Cahuenga Blvd Los Angeles (90028) *(P-14236)*

Sweatheory Wellness LLC .... D....... 310 844-3662
   6427 W Sunset Blvd # 106 Los Angeles (90028) *(P-17336)*

Sweda, City Of Industry *Also Called: Sweda Company LLC (P-6027)*

Sweda Company LLC .... B....... 626 357-9999
   17411 E Valley Blvd City Of Industry (91744) *(P-6027)*

Sweetener Products, Vernon *Also Called: Edna H Pagel Inc (P-817)*

Sweetgrace Home Hlth Svcs LLC .... D....... 909 463-7400
   6101 Cherry Ave Fontana (92336) *(P-17337)*

Sweetrush Inc .... C....... 415 647-1956
   363 Valencia St Apt 4 San Francisco (94103) *(P-12632)*

Sweetwter Auth Emplyees Cmmtte (PA) .... **C....... 619 420-1413**
   505 Garrett Ave Chula Vista (91910) *(P-4839)*

Sweis Inc (PA) .... **D....... 310 375-0558**
   20000 Mariner Ave Torrance (90503) *(P-5949)*

Swenson Developers and Contrs, San Jose *Also Called: Santa Clara Valley Corporation (P-10958)*

Swift Leasing Co LLC .... B....... 909 347-0500
   14392 Valley Blvd Fontana (92335) *(P-3548)*

Swift Media Entertainment Inc .... D....... 310 308-3694
   5340 Alla Rd Ste 101 Los Angeles (90066) *(P-13495)*

Swift Real Estate Partners LLC .... D....... 415 395-9701
   260 California St Ste 1100 San Francisco (94111) *(P-9570)*

Swinerton Builders (HQ) .... **D....... 925 602-6400**
   2001 Clayton Rd Ste 700 Concord (94520) *(P-847)*

Swinerton Builders .... D....... 858 622-4040
   16798 W Bernardo Dr San Diego (92128) *(P-1035)*

Swinerton Builders, San Diego *Also Called: Solv Energy LLC (P-12358)*

Swinerton Builders Hc .... C....... 916 383-4825
   15 Business Park Way Ste 101 Sacramento (95828) *(P-1036)*

Swinerton Incorporated (PA) .... **C....... 415 421-2980**
   2001 Clayton Rd Fl 7 San Francisco (94107) *(P-1037)*

Swinerton MGT & Consulting, Concord *Also Called: Swinerton Builders (P-847)*

Swinerton Renewable Energy .... C....... 858 622-4040
   16680 W Bernardo Dr San Diego (92127) *(P-20574)*

Swirl Inc .... D....... 415 276-8300
   650 California St Fl 30 San Francisco (94108) *(P-10678)*

Swirl McGarrybowen, San Francisco *Also Called: Swirl Inc (P-10678)*

Swiss Port Corp .... B....... 310 417-0258
   11001 Aviation Blvd Los Angeles (90045) *(P-20664)*

Swiss RE Solutions Holdg Corp 415 834-2200
   111 Sutter St Ste 400 San Francisco (94105) *(P-8422)*

Swissport, Los Angeles *Also Called: Swiss Port Corp (P-20664)*

Swissport Cargo Services LP .... D....... 703 742-4300
   5757 W Century Blvd Ste 860 Los Angeles (90045) *(P-3913)*

Swissport Cargo Services LP .... C....... 310 910-9541
   11001 Aviation Blvd Los Angeles (90045) *(P-3914)*

Swissport Usa Inc .... D....... 310 345-1986
   7025 W Imperial Hwy Los Angeles (90045) *(P-3915)*

Swissport Usa Inc .... D....... 650 821-6220
   San Francisco Intl Airport San Francisco (94128) *(P-3916)*

Swissport Usa Inc .... D....... 310 910-9560
   11001 Aviation Blvd Los Angeles (90045) *(P-3917)*

Swisstex California Inc (PA) .... **C....... 310 516-6800**
   13660 S Figueroa St Los Angeles (90061) *(P-13496)*

Switchfly LLC (PA) .... **D....... 415 541-9100**
   500 3rd St Ste 215 San Francisco (94107) *(P-5358)*

Sws, Fullerton *Also Called: Superior Wall Systems Inc (P-1967)*

Swt Stockton, Temecula *Also Called: Southwest Traders Incorporated (P-6393)*

Swvp Del Mar Hotel LLC .... D....... 858 481-5900
   11915 El Camino Real San Diego (92130) *(P-10294)*

Swvp Westlake LLC .... C....... 805 557-1234
   880 S Westlake Blvd Westlake Village (91361) *(P-10295)*

Swwc Utilities Inc (DH) C
   1325 N Grand Ave Ste 100 Covina (91724) *(P-4840)*

Sybase 365 LLC .... D....... 925 236-5000
   1 Sybase Dr Dublin (94568) *(P-11957)*

Sycamore Cc Inc .... D....... 760 451-3700
   39500 Robert Trent Jones Pkwy Murrieta (92563) *(P-14293)*

SYCAMORE COURT APT, Newport Beach *Also Called: 10632 Bolsa Avenue LP (P-8786)*

Sycamore Mineral Spring Resort .... D....... 805 595-7302
   1215 Avila Beach Dr San Luis Obispo (93405) *(P-10296)*

SYCAMORES, Pasadena *Also Called: Hathaway-Sycmres Child Fmly Svc (P-18447)*

Sycuan Casino .... A....... 619 445-6002
   5469 Casino Way El Cajon (92019) *(P-10297)*

Sycuan Casino (PA) .... C 619 445-6002
5459 Casino Way El Cajon (92019) *(P-14566)*

Sycuan Resort, El Cajon *Also Called: Sycuan Tribal Development (P-7512)*

Sycuan Resort and Casino, El Cajon *Also Called: Sycuan Casino (P-14566)*

Sycuan Tribal Development .... C 619 442-3425
1530 Hilton Head Rd Ste 210 El Cajon (92019) *(P-7512)*

Sydata Inc .... C 760 444-4368
6494 Weathers Pl Ste 100 San Diego (92121) *(P-4346)*

Sydell Hotels LLC .... C 213 381-7411
3515 Wilshire Blvd Los Angeles (90010) *(P-10298)*

Sydell Palm Springs LLC .... D 760 323-1711
1800 E Palm Canyon Dr Palm Springs (92264) *(P-10299)*

Sydney & Anne Bloom Farms Inc .... A 323 261-6565
2900 Ayers Ave Vernon (90058) *(P-6505)*

Sygma, Lancaster *Also Called: Sygma Network Inc (P-6397)*

Sygma, Stockton *Also Called: Sygma Network Inc (P-6398)*

Sygma Network Inc .... C 661 723-0405
46905 47th St W Lancaster (93536) *(P-6397)*

Sygma Network Inc .... C 209 932-5300
3741 Gold River Ln Stockton (95215) *(P-6398)*

Sygma Network, The, Sun Valley *Also Called: Sugar Foods Corporation (P-13490)*

Sylmark Group, Van Nuys *Also Called: Sylmark Inc (P-20223)*

Sylmark Inc (PA) .... D 818 217-2000
7821 Orion Ave Ste 200 Van Nuys (91406) *(P-20223)*

Symantec .... D 213 489-3262
1200 W 7th St Los Angeles (90017) *(P-12371)*

Symantec, Los Angeles *Also Called: Symantec (P-12371)*

Symbion Inc .... C 805 413-7920
696 Hampshire Rd Ste 100 Westlake Village (91361) *(P-15120)*

Symbion Inc .... C 818 501-1080
16501 Ventura Blvd Ste 103 Encino (91436) *(P-15121)*

Symes Cadillac Inc .... D 626 689-4386
3475 E Colorado Blvd Pasadena (91107) *(P-7308)*

Symes Cadillac of Pasadena, Pasadena *Also Called: Symes Cadillac Inc (P-7308)*

Symitar Systems Inc .... C 619 542-6700
8985 Balboa Ave San Diego (92123) *(P-11958)*

Symons Fire Protection Inc .... C 619 588-6364
9475 Chesapeake Dr Ste A San Diego (92123) *(P-13149)*

Symphony Comm Svcs LLC (PA) .... C 650 733-6660
640 W California Ave Ste 200 Sunnyvale (94086) *(P-20575)*

Symphony Risk Sltons Insur Svc .... D 415 957-0600
44 Montgomery St Ste 1700 San Francisco (94104) *(P-8667)*

Symphony Technology Group LLC (DH) .... A 650 935-9500
428 University Ave Palo Alto (94301) *(P-20858)*

Symyx Technologies Inc .... B 408 764-2000
2804 Mission College Blvd Santa Clara (95054) *(P-19776)*

SYNACK, Redwood City *Also Called: Synack Inc (P-11959)*

Synack Inc (PA) .... C 855 796-2251
303 Twin Dolphin Dr Fl 6 Redwood City (94065) *(P-11959)*

Synapse Design, Santa Clara *Also Called: Synapse Design Automation Inc (P-12530)*

Synapse Design Automation Inc (DH) .... D 408 850-9527
2200 Laurelwood Rd Santa Clara (95054) *(P-12530)*

SYNAPTICS, San Jose *Also Called: Synaptics Incorporated (P-2838)*

Synaptics Incorporated (PA) .... B 408 904-1100
1109 Mckay Dr San Jose (95131) *(P-2838)*

Synaptics Incorporated .... D 408 454-5100
3120 Scott Blvd Santa Clara (95054) *(P-4347)*

Synarc Inc (DH) .... C 415 817-8900
777 Mariners Island Blvd Ste 550 San Mateo (94404) *(P-11960)*

Sync Brokerage Inc .... D 818 770-3663
22020 Clarendon St Ste 200 Woodland Hills (91367) *(P-13497)*

Synchronoss Technologies Inc .... B 800 575-7606
60 S Market St Ste 700 San Jose (95113) *(P-1859)*

Syncreon America Inc .... D 909 610-4511
14780 Bar Harbor Rd Ste B Fontana (92336) *(P-4104)*

SYNCREON AMERICA INC., Fontana *Also Called: Syncreon America Inc (P-4104)*

Synctruck LLC .... D 415 425-0447
415 Darrell Rd Hillsborough (94010) *(P-3629)*

Synectic Solutions Inc (PA) .... D 805 483-4800
771 E Daily Dr Ste 200 Camarillo (93010) *(P-12886)*

Synergy Companies .... C 800 439-9610
2626 West Ln # 100 Stockton (95205) *(P-20859)*

Synergy Companies, Hayward *Also Called: Eagle Systems Intl Inc (P-1424)*

Synergy Health Companies Inc .... D 209 577-4625
1521 N Carpenter Rd Ste D1 Modesto (95351) *(P-17338)*

Synergy Orthpd Specialists Inc .... D 858 450-7118
4445 Eastgate Mall Ste 103 San Diego (92121) *(P-17339)*

Synerzip LLC .... D 510 579-9673
5924 Roxie Ter Fremont (94555) *(P-5359)*

Synophic Systems Inc .... B 408 459-7676
19925 Stevens Creek Blvd Cupertino (95014) *(P-11961)*

Synopsys, Sunnyvale *Also Called: Synopsys Inc (P-12372)*

Synopsys Inc (PA) .... B 650 584-5000
675 Almanor Ave Sunnyvale (94085) *(P-12372)*

Synopsys Foundation .... D 650 584-5000
675 Almanor Ave Sunnyvale (94085) *(P-19109)*

Synoptek LLC (PA) .... D 949 241-8600
19520 Jamboree Rd Ste 110 Irvine (92612) *(P-12887)*

Synplicity Inc (HQ) .... C 650 584-5000
690 E Middlefield Rd Mountain View (94043) *(P-12373)*

Syntron Bioresearch Inc .... B 760 930-2200
2774 Loker Ave W Carlsbad (92010) *(P-2614)*

Syrinx Consulting Corp .... D 781 487-7800
1919 S Bascom Ave Campbell (95008) *(P-11962)*

Sysco, Modesto *Also Called: Sysco Central California Inc (P-6399)*

Sysco, Walnut *Also Called: Sysco Los Angeles Inc (P-6400)*

Sysco, Pleasant Grove *Also Called: Sysco Sacramento Inc (P-6402)*

Sysco, Poway *Also Called: Sysco San Diego Inc (P-6403)*

Sysco, Fremont *Also Called: Sysco San Francisco Inc (P-6404)*

Sysco, Oxnard *Also Called: Sysco Ventura Inc (P-6405)*

Sysco Central California Inc .... B 209 527-7700
136 Mariposa Rd Modesto (95354) *(P-6399)*

Sysco Los Angeles Inc .... A 909 595-9595
20701 Currier Rd Walnut (91789) *(P-6400)*

Sysco Riverside Inc .... B 951 601-5300
15750 Meridian Pkwy Riverside (92518) *(P-6401)*

Sysco Sacramento Inc .... B 916 275-2714
7062 Pacific Ave Pleasant Grove (95668) *(P-6402)*

Sysco San Diego Inc .... B 858 513-7300
12180 Kirkham Rd Poway (92064) *(P-6403)*

Sysco San Francisco Inc .... A 510 226-3000
5900 Stewart Ave Fremont (94538) *(P-6404)*

Sysco Ventura Inc .... B 805 205-7000
3100 Sturgis Rd Oxnard (93030) *(P-6405)*

Sysdig Inc (PA) .... C 415 872-9473
135 Main St 21st Fl San Francisco (94105) *(P-11963)*

Syserco Inc .... D 707 664-8443
1425 N Mcdowell Blvd Ste 115 Petaluma (94954) *(P-1581)*

Syserco Inc (PA) .... D 510 498-1171
215 Fourier Ave Fremont (94539) *(P-1582)*

Syspro, Tustin *Also Called: Syspro Impact Software Inc (P-5360)*

Syspro Impact Software Inc .... C 714 437-1000
1775 Flight Way Ste 150 Tustin (92782) *(P-5360)*

Systech Integrators Inc .... C 408 441-2700
2050 Gateway Pl San Jose (95110) *(P-12888)*

Systech Solutions Inc (PA) .... D 818 550-9690
500 N Brand Blvd Ste 1900 Glendale (91203) *(P-11964)*

Systechs, Orange *Also Called: Cruz Modular Inc (P-3584)*

System Integrators Inc .... C 916 830-2400
1740 N Market Blvd Sacramento (95834) *(P-12531)*

System1 Inc (PA) .... B 310 924-6037
4235 Redwood Ave Los Angeles (90066) *(P-12374)*

Systems & Technology RES LLC .... D 844 204-0963
1808 Aston Ave Ste 180 Carlsbad (92008) *(P-19402)*

Systems America Public Sector, Pleasanton *Also Called: Tryfacta Inc (P-11995)*

Systems Application & Tech Inc .... D 805 487-7373
1000 Town Center Dr Ste 110 Oxnard (93036) *(P-19403)*

Systems Experience Inc .... D 310 215-9000
6033 W Century Blvd Ste 820 Los Angeles (90045) *(P-20860)*

Systems Paving Inc (PA) .... D 949 263-8301
1570 Brookhollow Dr Santa Ana (92705) *(P-1169)*

ALPHABETIC SECTION

Systems Tech Unlimited LLC .... D...... 310 341-5169
   7409 West Blv Inglewood (90305) *(P-13150)*

T - Y Nursery Inc .... C...... 760 742-2151
   15335 Highway 76 Pauma Valley (92061) *(P-6876)*

T & P Farms .... D...... 530 476-3038
   1241 Putnam Way Arbuckle (95912) *(P-2)*

T & T Trucking Inc (PA) .... C...... 800 692-3457
   11396 N Highway 99 Lodi (95240) *(P-3549)*

T Allance One - Palm Sprng LLC .... D...... 760 322-7000
   67967 Vista Chino Cathedral City (92234) *(P-14567)*

T and B Boots Inc .... D...... 805 434-9904
   72 S Main St B Templeton (93465) *(P-7411)*

T B Penick & Sons Inc .... C...... 858 558-1800
   15435 Innovation Dr Ste 200 San Diego (92128) *(P-848)*

T C Construction Company Inc .... C...... 619 448-4560
   10540 Prospect Ave Santee (92071) *(P-1270)*

T C P, Santa Monica *Also Called: Tennenbaum Capitl Partners LLC (P-9573)*

T D R, Turlock *Also Called: Tdr Development Inc (P-5813)*

T F Louderback Inc .... C...... 510 965-6120
   700 National Ct Richmond (94804) *(P-6784)*

T G T Enterprises Inc .... C...... 858 413-0300
   12650 Danielson Ct Poway (92064) *(P-20576)*

T L Fabrications LP .... D...... 562 802-3980
   2921 E Coronado St Anaheim (92806) *(P-13754)*

T M B, San Fernando *Also Called: Jme Inc (P-5570)*

T M I, San Diego *Also Called: Toward Maximum Independence (P-18153)*

T M Mian & Associates Inc .... D...... 818 591-2300
   24150 Park Sorrento Calabasas (91302) *(P-10300)*

t McGee Electric Inc .... D...... 909 591-6461
   2390 S Reservoir St Pomona (91766) *(P-1860)*

T R L, Rancho Cucamonga *Also Called: TRL Systems Incorporated (P-1866)*

T S W Alloy Wheels, Brea *Also Called: Just Wheels & Tires LLC (P-5046)*

T U D, Sonora *Also Called: Tuolumne Utilities District (P-4842)*

T Y Lin International (HQ) .... D...... 415 291-3700
   345 California St Fl 23 San Francisco (94104) *(P-19404)*

T-12 Three LLC .... B...... 619 702-3000
   207 5th Ave San Diego (92101) *(P-10301)*

T-Force, Newport Beach *Also Called: T-Force Inc (P-20861)*

T-Force Inc (PA) .... D...... 949 208-1527
   4695 Macarthur Ct Newport Beach (92660) *(P-20861)*

T.com Ontario Fc T-9479, Ontario *Also Called: Target Corporation (P-3762)*

T/O Printing, Westlake Village *Also Called: Thousand Oaks Prtg & Spc Inc (P-13509)*

T& R Bangis Argriculture Svcs .... A...... 661 725-1948
   375 Rd 200 Richgrove (93261) *(P-11241)*

T&C Roofing Inc .... D...... 925 513-8463
   2155 Elkins Way Ste H Brentwood (94513) *(P-2087)*

T3w Business Solutions Inc .... D...... 619 298-0888
   3921 Ampudia St San Diego (92110) *(P-20224)*

Ta Chen International Inc (HQ) .... C...... 562 808-8000
   5855 Obispo Ave Long Beach (90805) *(P-5521)*

Table Mountain, Friant *Also Called: Table Mountain Casino (P-10302)*

Table Mountain Casino .... A...... 559 822-7777
   8184 Table Mountain Rd Friant (93626) *(P-10302)*

Tabletops Unlimited, Carson *Also Called: Tabletops Unlimited Inc (P-5135)*

Tabletops Unlimited Inc (PA) .... D...... 310 549-6000
   23000 Avalon Blvd Carson (90745) *(P-5135)*

Tabula Inc .... D...... 408 986-9140
   1100 La Avenida St Mountain View (94043) *(P-5705)*

TAC Air California Inc .... D...... 619 216-8416
   13531 Otay Lakes Rd Jamul (91935) *(P-14568)*

Tacer, Van Nuys *Also Called: Town & Cntry Event Rentals Inc (P-11056)*

Tachi Palace Casino Resort .... A...... 559 924-7751
   17225 Jersey Ave Lemoore (93245) *(P-10303)*

Taco Bell, Irvine *Also Called: Taco Bell Corp (P-7513)*

Taco Bell Corp (HQ) .... A...... 949 863-4500
   1 Glen Bell Way Irvine (92618) *(P-7513)*

Tactical Engrg & Analis Inc (PA) .... D...... 858 573-9869
   6050 Santo Rd Ste 250 San Diego (92124) *(P-12889)*

Tactical Telesolutions Inc .... C...... 415 788-8808
   2121 N California Blvd Ste 290 Walnut Creek (94596) *(P-13498)*

Tad Group LLC .... C...... 949 476-3601
   5000 Birch St Ste 3000 Newport Beach (92660) *(P-13151)*

Tad Pgs Inc .... A...... 800 261-3779
   12062 Valley View St Ste 108 Garden Grove (92845) *(P-11339)*

Tad Pgs Inc .... A...... 571 451-2428
   10805 Holder St Ste 250 Cypress (90630) *(P-11340)*

Tadin Herb & Tea Co., Vernon *Also Called: Tadin Inc (P-6677)*

Tadin Inc .... D...... 213 406-8880
   3345 E Slauson Ave Vernon (90058) *(P-6677)*

Tae Life Sciences Us LLC (PA) .... D...... 949 344-6112
   19571 Pauling Foothill Ranch (92610) *(P-19777)*

Tae Sook Chung .... D...... 909 598-6255
   21080 Golden Springs Dr Walnut (91789) *(P-5136)*

Tae Technologies, Foothill Ranch *Also Called: Tae Technologies Inc (P-19778)*

Tae Technologies Inc (PA) .... C...... 949 830-2117
   19631 Pauling Foothill Ranch (92610) *(P-19778)*

Taft Electric Company (PA) .... C...... 805 642-0121
   1694 Eastman Ave Ventura (93003) *(P-1861)*

Taft Production Company .... D...... 661 765-7194
   950 Petroleum Club Rd Taft (93268) *(P-578)*

Tag Toys Inc .... C...... 310 639-4566
   1810 S Acacia Ave Compton (90220) *(P-3113)*

Taheem Johnson Inc .... D...... 818 835-3785
   1237 S Victoria Ave Oxnard (93035) *(P-12890)*

Tahoe Beach & Ski Club .... D...... 530 541-6220
   3601 Lake Tahoe Blvd South Lake Tahoe (96150) *(P-10304)*

Tahoe Forest Hospital District .... C...... 530 582-3277
   10956 Donner Pass Rd Ste 230 Truckee (96161) *(P-16566)*

Tahoe Forest Hospital District (PA) .... B...... 530 587-6011
   10121 Pine Ave Truckee (96161) *(P-16567)*

Tahoe Seasons Resort, South Lake Tahoe *Also Called: Tahoe Ssons Rsort Time Intrval (P-9189)*

Tahoe Ssons Rsort Time Intrval .... C...... 530 541-6700
   3901 Saddle Rd South Lake Tahoe (96150) *(P-9189)*

Tahoe Stag, Brea *Also Called: Griffith Company (P-1115)*

Tahoe Truckee Disposal Co Inc .... D...... 530 583-7825
   900 Cabin Creek Rd Truckee (96161) *(P-4943)*

Tahoe Workx, Truckee *Also Called: Tahoe Forest Hospital District (P-16566)*

Tai Capital Company, San Francisco *Also Called: Banc America Lsg & Capitl LLC (P-7604)*

Tailbroom Media Grop, North Hollywood *Also Called: Pilgrim Operations LLC (P-5240)*

Tailored Living, Napa *Also Called: Tailored Living Choices LLC (P-2318)*

Tailored Living Choices LLC .... C...... 707 259-0526
   1957 Sierra Ave Napa (94558) *(P-2318)*

Taisei Construction Corporation .... C...... 714 886-1530
   970 W 190th St Ste 920 Torrance (90502) *(P-849)*

Takane USA Inc .... C...... 909 923-5511
   2055 S Haven Ave Ontario (91761) *(P-3760)*

Takeda Dev Ctr Americas Inc (HQ) .... C...... 858 622-8528
   9625 Towne Centre Dr San Diego (92121) *(P-19917)*

Takken's Comfort Shoes, Templeton *Also Called: T and B Boots Inc (P-7411)*

Tala, Santa Monica *Also Called: Inventure Capital Corporation (P-9523)*

Talbert Medical Center, Santa Ana *Also Called: Optumcare Management LLC (P-17290)*

Talco Plastics Inc .... D...... 562 630-1224
   3270 E 70th St Long Beach (90805) *(P-2681)*

Talco Plastics Inc (PA) .... D...... 951 531-2000
   1000 W Rincon St Corona (92878) *(P-4944)*

Talega Golf Club, San Clemente *Also Called: Heritage Golf Group LLC (P-14266)*

Talent & Acquisition LLC .... C...... 888 970-9575
   3020 Old Ranch Pkwy Ste 300 Seal Beach (90740) *(P-11965)*

Talent Space Inc .... C...... 408 330-1900
   1650 The Alameda San Jose (95126) *(P-11242)*

Talentburst Inc .... D...... 415 813-4011
   575 Market St Ste 3025 San Francisco (94105) *(P-13499)*

Talis Lending, San Diego *Also Called: Lendsure Mortgage Corp (P-7988)*

Talkwalker Inc .... C...... 415 805-7240
   600 California St Fl 14 San Francisco (94108) *(P-12633)*

Taller Technologies, San Francisco *Also Called: Quadriga Inc (P-11856)*

Talley & Associates, Santa Fe Springs *Also Called: Talley Inc (P-5706)*

Talley Farms .... C...... 805 489-2508
   2900 Lopez Dr Arroyo Grande (93420) *(P-308)*

Talley Inc (PA) .... C 562 906-8000
12976 Sandoval St Santa Fe Springs (90670) *(P-5706)*

Talon Therapeutics Inc .... D 949 788-6700
18200 Von Karman Ave Ste 700 Irvine (92612) *(P-19779)*

Tam O'Shanter Inn, Los Angeles *Also Called: Lawrys Restaurants II Inc (P-7491)*

Tama Trading Company .... D 213 748-8262
1920 E 20th St Vernon (90058) *(P-6678)*

Tamal Pais, Greenbrae *Also Called: Sequoia Living Inc (P-15897)*

TAMALPAIS, Greenbrae *Also Called: Ross Valley Homes Inc (P-18515)*

Tanaka Farms .... D 949 653-2100
5380 University Dr Irvine (92612) *(P-6679)*

Tandy Leather 05, Clovis *Also Called: Leather Factory LP (P-13780)*

Tangible Play, Palo Alto *Also Called: Tangible Play Inc (P-11966)*

Tangible Play Inc (HQ) .... D 650 667-1693
195 Page Mill Rd Ste 105 Palo Alto (94306) *(P-11966)*

Tangoe-PI Inc C
9920 Pacific Heights Blvd Ste 200 San Diego (92121) *(P-20862)*

Tanimura & Antle, Salinas *Also Called: Tanimura Antle Fresh Foods Inc (P-44)*

Tanimura Antle Fresh Foods Inc (PA) .... D 831 455-2950
1 Harris Rd Salinas (93908) *(P-44)*

Tanimura Antle Fresh Foods Inc .... C 831 424-6100
4401 Foxdale St Baldwin Park (91706) *(P-309)*

Tanimura Antle Fresh Foods Inc .... C 805 483-2358
761 Commercial Ave Oxnard (93030) *(P-3761)*

Tanium Inc .... A 510 704-0202
2100 Powell St 3rd Fl Emeryville (94608) *(P-12375)*

Tanvex Biopharma Usa Inc (PA) .... C 858 210-4100
10394 Pacific Center Ct San Diego (92121) *(P-19780)*

Tao Digital Solutions Inc .... C 408 391-0930
4699 Old Ironsides Dr Ste 430 Santa Clara (95054) *(P-11967)*

Tao of Wllness Snta Mnica A PR .... D 626 397-1000
171 S Los Robles Ave Pasadena (91101) *(P-15309)*

Taoglas .... D 760 855-4580
2106 Orange Ave Escondido (92029) *(P-5707)*

Taos Mountain LLC .... D 888 826-7686
1 Market St 36th Fl San Francisco (94105) *(P-11341)*

Tap Room At Lodge .... C 831 624-3811
Seventeen Mile Dr Pebble Beach (93953) *(P-10305)*

Tap Worldwide LLC (HQ) .... C 310 900-5500
400 W Artesia Blvd Compton (90220) *(P-5064)*

Tapestry Solutions Inc (HQ) .... C 858 503-1990
6910 Carroll Rd San Diego (92121) *(P-11968)*

Tapetech Tool Company .... A 858 268-0656
7360 Convoy Ct San Diego (92111) *(P-9571)*

Tapetech Tool Company .... A 925 676-7002
2190 Meridian Park Blvd Concord (94520) *(P-20577)*

Tapetech Tool Company, San Diego *Also Called: Tapetech Tool Company (P-9571)*

Tapetech Tool Company, Concord *Also Called: Tapetech Tool Company (P-20577)*

Tapia Brothers Co, Maywood *Also Called: Tapia Enterprises Inc (P-6406)*

Tapia Enterprises Inc (PA) .... D 323 560-7415
6067 District Blvd Maywood (90270) *(P-6406)*

Tarbel Realtors, Murrieta *Also Called: F M Tarbell Co (P-9000)*

Tarbell Financial Corporation (PA) .... D 714 972-0988
1403 N Tustin Ave Ste 380 Santa Ana (92705) *(P-8060)*

Tarbell Realtors, Santa Ana *Also Called: F M Tarbell Co (P-9001)*

Target, Fontana *Also Called: Target Corporation (P-3763)*

Target, Woodland *Also Called: Target Corporation (P-3764)*

Target Corporation .... C 909 937-5500
1505 S Haven Ave Ontario (91761) *(P-3762)*

Target Corporation .... C 909 355-6000
14750 Miller Ave Fontana (92336) *(P-3763)*

Target Corporation .... D 530 666-3705
2050 E Beamer St Woodland (95776) *(P-3764)*

Target Specialty Products, San Jose *Also Called: Rentokil North America Inc (P-10840)*

Target Specialty Products, Santa Fe Springs *Also Called: Rentokil North America Inc (P-10843)*

Target Specialty Products Inc .... D 562 865-9541
15415 Marquardt Ave Santa Fe Springs (90670) *(P-6835)*

Targus, Anaheim *Also Called: Targus International LLC (P-6952)*

Targus International LLC (PA) .... C 714 765-5555
1211 N Miller St Anaheim (92806) *(P-6952)*

Tarra Landscape, San Leandro *Also Called: Tree Sculpture Group (P-541)*

Tarrant Apparel Group .... D 323 780-8250
5401 S Soto St Vernon (90058) *(P-6224)*

Tarrant Capital Ip LLC (PA) .... A 415 743-1500
345 California St Ste 3300 San Francisco (94104) *(P-8222)*

Tarsadia Hotels (DH) .... D 949 610-8000
620 Newport Center Dr Ste 1400 Newport Beach (92660) *(P-10306)*

Tarsadia Hotels, Newport Beach *Also Called: Uka LLC (P-10332)*

Tarsco Holdings LLC .... C 562 869-0200
11905 Regentview Ave Downey (90241) *(P-13803)*

Tarzana Treatment Centers Inc .... D 818 654-3815
320 E Palmdale Blvd Palmdale (93550) *(P-17137)*

Tarzana Treatment Centers Inc .... C 562 428-4111
5190 Atlantic Ave Lakewood (90805) *(P-17138)*

Tarzana Treatment Centers Inc .... C 562 218-1868
2101 Magnolia Ave Long Beach (90806) *(P-17139)*

Tarzana Treatment Centers Inc .... C 661 726-2630
44447 10th St W Lancaster (93534) *(P-17140)*

Tarzana Treatment Centers Inc (PA) .... C 818 996-1051
18646 Oxnard St Tarzana (91356) *(P-17141)*

Tarzana Treatment Ctr, Lancaster *Also Called: Tarzana Treatment Centers Inc (P-17140)*

Tarzana Trtmnt Ctrs LNG Bch O, Lakewood *Also Called: Tarzana Treatment Centers Inc (P-17138)*

Task Help LLC .... D 833 229-0726
1390 Market St Ste 200 San Francisco (94102) *(P-11969)*

Taslimi Construction Co Inc .... D 310 447-3000
1805 Colorado Ave Santa Monica (90404) *(P-1038)*

Tasteful Selections LLC .... C 661 854-3998
13003 Di Giorgio Rd Arvin (93203) *(P-9)*

Tata America Intl Corp .... D 408 569-5845
5201 Great America Pkwy Ste 522 Santa Clara (95054) *(P-12891)*

Tata America Intl Corp .... D 818 333-1650
500 N Brand Blvd Glendale (91203) *(P-12892)*

Tata Consultancy Services, Glendale *Also Called: Tata America Intl Corp (P-12892)*

Tata Consulting Services, Santa Clara *Also Called: Tata America Intl Corp (P-12891)*

Tatcha LLC .... C 650 239-9000
37 Estates Dr Millbrae (94030) *(P-15122)*

Tatum Management Company LLC .... D 559 577-4474
1781 E Fir Ave Ste 102 Fresno (93720) *(P-20225)*

Taulia, San Francisco *Also Called: Taulia LLC (P-11970)*

Taulia LLC (HQ) .... C 415 376-8280
95 3rd St Ste 284 San Francisco (94103) *(P-11970)*

Tavant Technologies Inc (PA) .... C 408 519-5400
3965 Freedom Cir Ste 750 Santa Clara (95054) *(P-11971)*

Tawa Supermarket Inc .... D 714 521-8899
6363 Regio Ave Buena Park (90620) *(P-850)*

Tax and Financial Group, Newport Beach *Also Called: R Mc Closkey Insurance Agency (P-8647)*

Tax Credit Co, The, Los Angeles *Also Called: The Tax Credit Company (P-10765)*

Taxaudit.com, Folsom *Also Called: Taxresources Inc (P-10526)*

Taxes Decoded Inc .... D 626 780-7076
4060 Glencoe Ave Apt 322 Marina Del Rey (90292) *(P-10525)*

Taxresources Inc (PA) .... C 877 369-7827
600 Coolidge Dr Ste 300 Folsom (95630) *(P-10526)*

Taylor Farms, San Juan Bautista *Also Called: Earthbound Farm LLC (P-263)*

Taylor Fresh Foods Inc (PA) .... C 831 676-9023
150 Main St Ste 400 Salinas (93901) *(P-310)*

Taylor Guitars, El Cajon *Also Called: Taylor-Listug Inc (P-6056)*

Taylor Trim & Supply Inc .... D 760 740-2000
2342 Meyers Ave Escondido (92029) *(P-2021)*

Taylor-Listug Inc (PA) .... C 619 258-1207
1980 Gillespie Way El Cajon (92020) *(P-6056)*

Taylored Fmi LLC .... D 909 510-4800
1495 E Locust St Ontario (91761) *(P-3765)*

Taylored Services, Ontario *Also Called: Taylored Services LLC (P-3766)*

Taylored Services, Ontario *Also Called: Taylored Services Holdings LLC (P-3767)*

Taylored Services LLC (DH) .... D 909 510-4800
1495 E Locust St Ontario (91761) *(P-3766)*

Taylored Services Holdings LLC (DH) .... D 909 510-4800
1495 E Locust St Ontario (91761) *(P-3767)*

ALPHABETIC SECTION — Techno Coatings Inc

Taylored Svcs Parent Co Inc (PA) .... D 909 510-4800
   1495 E Locust St Ontario (91761) *(P-4105)*

Taylored Transload LLC .... D 909 510-4800
   1495 E Locust St Ontario (91761) *(P-4175)*

Tbc Shared Services LLC .... A 707 829-9864
   742 S Main St Sebastopol (95472) *(P-7378)*

TBG Insurance Services Corp .... D 310 203-8770
   100 N Pacific Coast Hwy Ste 500 El Segundo (90245) *(P-8668)*

Tbs, Costa Mesa *Also Called: Transprttion Brkg Spclists Inc (P-3427)*

Tbwa Chiat/Day Inc .... B 310 305-5000
   5353 Grosvenor Blvd Los Angeles (90066) *(P-13500)*

Tc Construction Company, Santee *Also Called: T C Construction Company Inc (P-1270)*

Tcal, San Diego *Also Called: Takeda Dev Ctr Americas Inc (P-19917)*

Tcg Capital Management LP .... C 310 633-2900
   12180 Millennium Ste 500 Playa Vista (90094) *(P-9572)*

Tcg Software Services Inc .... B 714 665-6200
   320 Commerce Ste 200 Irvine (92602) *(P-11972)*

TCI Aluminum/North Inc .... D 510 786-3750
   2353 Davis Ave Hayward (94545) *(P-5522)*

TCI Transportation Services .... C 909 355-8545
   14561 Merrill Ave Bldg B Fontana (92335) *(P-3550)*

Tcl Electronics, Irvine *Also Called: Tte Technology Inc (P-5615)*

Tcp Global Corporation .... D 858 909-2110
   6695 Rasha St San Diego (92121) *(P-6884)*

Tcr SC Construc 1 Ltd Ptr, Costa Mesa *Also Called: Trammell Crow Residential Co (P-8865)*

Tct Mobile Inc .... D 949 892-2990
   189 Technology Dr Irvine (92618) *(P-20226)*

Tcw Absolute Return Credit LLC .... D 213 244-0000
   865 S Figueroa St Ste 2100 Los Angeles (90017) *(P-9391)*

Tcw Funds Management Inc .... D 213 244-0000
   865 S Figueroa St Ste 2100 Los Angeles (90017) *(P-9392)*

Tcw Group Inc (PA) .... B 213 244-0000
   865 S Figueroa St Ste 1800 Los Angeles (90017) *(P-8223)*

Tcwglobal, San Diego *Also Called: Wmbe Payrolling Inc (P-11258)*

Td Synnex, Fremont *Also Called: Td Synnex Corporation (P-7449)*

Td Synnex Corporation (PA) .... C 510 656-3333
   44201 Nobel Dr Fremont (94538) *(P-7449)*

Td Synnex Corporation .... D 510 688-3507
   44131 Nobel Dr. Fremont (94538) *(P-13501)*

Tdic, Sacramento *Also Called: Dentists Insurance Company (P-8297)*

Tdk-Lambda Americas Inc .... C 619 575-4400
   401 Mile Of Cars Way Ste 325 National City (91950) *(P-5708)*

Tdr Development Inc .... D 209 667-6455
   1819 S Walnut Rd Turlock (95380) *(P-5813)*

Teachers Pension & Insur Svcs .... D 800 474-1440
   213 S Sierra Ave Oakdale (95361) *(P-8669)*

Teachorg Which Will Do Bus In .... D 650 575-5277
   174 Hermann St San Francisco (94102) *(P-15259)*

Teague Insurance Agency Inc .... C 619 464-6851
   4700 Spring St Ste 400 La Mesa (91942) *(P-8670)*

Tealium Inc (PA) .... A 858 779-1344
   11095 Torreyana Rd Fl 2 San Diego (92121) *(P-12634)*

Team Beachbody, El Segundo *Also Called: Beachbody LLC (P-10703)*

Team Bruin LLC .... D 310 206-6784
   1 Ironsides St Apt 4 Marina Del Rey (90292) *(P-14468)*

Team C Construction .... D 619 579-6572
   1272 Greenfield Dr El Cajon (92021) *(P-2164)*

Team Companies LLC (PA) .... D 818 558-3261
   2300 W Empire Ave Ste 500 Burbank (91504) *(P-19633)*

Team Dykspra (PA) .... D 951 898-6482
   2315 California Ave Corona (92881) *(P-13702)*

Team Finish Inc .... D 714 671-9190
   155 Arovista Cir Ste A Brea (92821) *(P-2165)*

Team Garage LLC .... D 714 913-9900
   3200 Bristol St Ste 300 Costa Mesa (92626) *(P-10679)*

Team Group LLC .... D 951 688-8593
   4076 Flat Rock Dr Riverside (92505) *(P-20227)*

Team Health Holdings Inc .... B 619 740-4401
   5555 Grossmont Center Dr La Mesa (91942) *(P-16568)*

Team Logic If La W Hollywood .... D 310 292-0063
   751 N Formosa Ave Los Angeles (90046) *(P-18148)*

Team Post-Op, Irvine *Also Called: Team Post-Op Inc (P-5452)*

Team Post-Op Inc .... C 949 253-5500
   17256 Red Hill Ave Irvine (92614) *(P-5452)*

Team Power Forklift, Fair Oaks *Also Called: Clarklift-West Inc (P-5826)*

Team Risk MGT Strategies LLC .... A 877 767-8728
   3131 Camino Del Rio N Ste 650 San Diego (92108) *(P-20863)*

Team Rubicon USA .... D 310 906-1636
   300 Continental Blvd Ste 100 El Segundo (90245) *(P-19110)*

Team San Jose .... A 408 295-9600
   408 Almaden Blvd San Jose (95110) *(P-13502)*

Team Services, Burbank *Also Called: Team Companies LLC (P-19633)*

Team West Contracting Corp .... D 951 340-3426
   2733 S Vista Ave Bloomington (92316) *(P-2319)*

Team-One Staffing Services Inc .... A 951 616-3515
   16030 Ventura Blvd Ste 430 Encino (91436) *(P-11243)*

Teamone Employment, Encino *Also Called: Team-One Staffing Services Inc (P-11243)*

Tebra Technologies Inc (PA) .... C 888 775-2736
   1111 Bayside Dr Ste 150 Corona Del Mar (92625) *(P-11973)*

Tecan, Morgan Hill *Also Called: Tecan Systems Inc (P-3012)*

Tecan Sp Inc .... D 626 962-0010
   14180 Live Oak Ave Baldwin Park (91706) *(P-5471)*

Tecan Systems Inc .... D 408 953-3100
   18635 Sutter Blvd Morgan Hill (95037) *(P-3012)*

TECH, San Jose *Also Called: Tech Interactive (P-18677)*

Tech Interactive (PA) .... C 408 795-6116
   201 S Market St San Jose (95113) *(P-18677)*

Tech Interactive .... D 408 795-6168
   145 W San Carlos St San Jose (95113) *(P-18678)*

Tech Knowledge Associates LLC .... D 714 735-3810
   1 Centerpointe Dr Ste 200 La Palma (90623) *(P-13804)*

Tech Mahindra Cerium Systems .... D 408 623-0787
   1735 Technology Dr Ste 575 San Jose (95110) *(P-12893)*

Tech Systems Inc .... C 714 523-5404
   7372 Walnut Ave Ste J Buena Park (90620) *(P-5709)*

Techcon, Morgan Hill *Also Called: Monument Construction Inc (P-448)*

Techflow Inc (PA) .... C 858 412-8000
   9889 Willow Creek Rd Ste 100 San Diego (92131) *(P-20665)*

Techflow Scntfc A Div Tchflow, San Diego *Also Called: Techflow Inc (P-20665)*

Technclor Crative Svcs USA Inc .... B 818 260-1214
   8921 Lindblade St Culver City (90232) *(P-13952)*

Technclor Vdocassette Mich Inc (DH) .... B 805 445-1122
   3601 Calle Tecate Ste 120 Camarillo (93012) *(P-13953)*

Technet Partners, Carlsbad *Also Called: Technet Partners Inc (P-12532)*

Technet Partners Inc .... D 760 683-8393
   6116 Innovation Way Carlsbad (92009) *(P-12532)*

Techni-Tools, Moorpark *Also Called: Testequity LLC (P-13748)*

Technicolor, Calexico *Also Called: Vantiva Sup Chain Slutions Inc (P-13958)*

Technicolor Inc .... B 818 260-4577
   2255 N Ontario St Ste 180 Burbank (91504) *(P-13163)*

Technicolor Creative Studios, Culver City *Also Called: Technclor Crative Svcs USA Inc (P-13952)*

Technicolor Disc Services Corp (HQ) .... C 805 445-1122
   3601 Calle Tecate Ste 120 Camarillo (93012) *(P-2953)*

Technicolor Entertainment Svcs, Burbank *Also Called: Technicolor Thomson Group Inc (P-13954)*

Technicolor Lab, Burbank *Also Called: Technicolor Inc (P-13163)*

Technicolor Thomson Group Inc (HQ) .... B
   2233 N Ontario St Ste 300 Burbank (91504) *(P-13954)*

Technicolor Video Service, Camarillo *Also Called: Technclor Vdocassette Mich Inc (P-13953)*

Technicolor Video Services, Camarillo *Also Called: Vantiva Sup Chain Slutions Inc (P-13959)*

Technicon Design Corporation .... C 949 218-1300
   30011 Ivy Glenn Dr Ste 115 Laguna Niguel (92677) *(P-13503)*

Technip Usa Inc .... B 909 447-3600
   555 W Arrow Hwy Claremont (91711) *(P-19405)*

Techno Coatings Inc .... D 714 774-4671
   785 E Debra Ln Anaheim (92805) *(P-1039)*

Techno Coatings Inc .... D 714 774-4671
   795 E Debra Ln Anaheim (92805) *(P-1040)*

Techno Coatings Inc (PA) .... C 714 635-1130
   1391 S Allec St Anaheim (92805) *(P-1041)*

Techno West

ALPHABETIC SECTION

Techno West, Anaheim Also Called: Techno Coatings Inc *(P-1041)*

Technocel, Simi Valley Also Called: Foreign Trade Corporation *(P-5651)*

Technologent, Irvine Also Called: Thomas Gallaway Corporation *(P-11976)*

Technology Associates EC Inc .... D....... 760 765-5275
3129 Tiger Run Ct Ste 206 Carlsbad (92010) *(P-20578)*

Technology Credit Union (PA) .... C....... 408 451-9111
2010 N 1st St Ste 200 San Jose (95131) *(P-7810)*

Technology Integration Group, San Diego Also Called: PC Specialists Inc *(P-5333)*

Technosocialworkcom LLC .... D....... 661 617-6601
4300 Resnik Ct Unit 103 Bakersfield (93313) *(P-12635)*

Techprose, San Francisco Also Called: Future State *(P-12793)*

Techsoup Global (PA) .... C....... 800 659-3579
435 Brannan St Ste 100 San Francisco (94107) *(P-18915)*

Techworkers, Walnut Creek Also Called: Bay Area Techworkers *(P-11093)*

Tecma Group LLC .... A....... 619 918-7371
6020 Progressive Ave San Diego (92154) *(P-13504)*

Teco Diagnostics .... D....... 714 693-7788
1268 N Lakeview Ave Anaheim (92807) *(P-2615)*

Tecolote Research Inc .... D....... 310 640-4700
2120 E Grand Ave Ste 200 El Segundo (90245) *(P-20579)*

Tecolote Research Inc .... C....... 805 964-6963
5266 Hollister Ave Ste 301 Santa Barbara (93111) *(P-20580)*

Tecom Industries Incorporated 805 267-0100
375 Conejo Ridge Ave Thousand Oaks (91361) *(P-5710)*

Tecta America Southern Cal Inc .... D....... 714 973-6233
1217 E Wakeham Ave Santa Ana (92705) *(P-2088)*

Ted Ford Jones Inc .... C....... 760 438-9171
5555 Paseo Del Norte Carlsbad (92008) *(P-7309)*

Ted Ford Jones Inc (PA) .... C....... 714 521-3110
6211 Beach Blvd Buena Park (90621) *(P-13677)*

Ted Levine Drum Co (PA) .... D....... 626 579-1084
1817 Chico Ave South El Monte (91733) *(P-13805)*

Ted Stevens Inc 415 927-5664
5860 Paradise Dr Corte Madera (94925) *(P-7310)*

Teecom .... C....... 510 337-2800
50 California St Ste 1500 San Francisco (94111) *(P-19406)*

Teecom, Inc., San Francisco Also Called: Teecom *(P-19406)*

Teeko LLC .... D....... 415 652-3380
500 Hazel Ave Millbrae (94030) *(P-13505)*

Teg Staffing Inc .... A....... 800 918-1678
2385 Northside Dr Ste 250 San Diego (92108) *(P-11244)*

Tegile Systems Inc .... C....... 510 791-7900
7999 Gateway Blvd Ste 120 Newark (94560) *(P-19781)*

Tegra118 Wealth Solutions Inc (HQ) .... C....... 888 800-0188
700 N San Vicente Blvd Ste G605 West Hollywood (90069) *(P-12636)*

Tegtmeier Associates Inc .... D....... 650 847-1639
14 Mansion Ct Menlo Park (94025) *(P-8768)*

Teichert Inc .... D....... 530 587-3811
13879 Butterfield Dr Truckee (96161) *(P-639)*

Teichert Inc .... D....... 209 832-4150
36314 S Bird Rd Tracy (95304) *(P-640)*

Teichert Inc .... C....... 530 885-4244
2601 State Highway 49 Cool (95614) *(P-641)*

Teichert Inc .... D....... 530 749-1230
3331 Walnut Ave Marysville (95901) *(P-642)*

Teichert Inc .... C....... 530 743-6111
4249 Hammonton Smartville Rd Marysville (95901) *(P-643)*

Teichert Inc .... D....... 916 351-0123
3417 Grant Line Rd Rancho Cordova (95742) *(P-644)*

Teichert Inc .... C....... 916 386-6900
8760 Kiefer Blvd Sacramento (95826) *(P-645)*

Teichert Inc .... D....... 209 983-2300
265 Val Dervin Pkwy Stockton (95206) *(P-1170)*

Teichert Inc .... C....... 530 406-4200
24207 County Road 100a Davis (95616) *(P-1171)*

Teichert Inc .... D....... 916 645-4800
4401 Duluth Ave Roseville (95678) *(P-1172)*

Teichert Inc .... C....... 559 813-3100
5771 Toyota Pl Fresno (93725) *(P-1173)*

Teichert Inc (PA) .... C....... 916 484-3011
5200 Franklin Dr Ste 115 Pleasanton (94588) *(P-2714)*

Teichert Aggregates, Truckee Also Called: Teichert Inc *(P-639)*

Teichert Aggregates, Tracy Also Called: Teichert Inc *(P-640)*

Teichert Aggregates, Cool Also Called: Teichert Inc *(P-641)*

Teichert Aggregates, Marysville Also Called: Teichert Inc *(P-642)*

Teichert Aggregates, Marysville Also Called: Teichert Inc *(P-643)*

Teichert Aggregates, Rancho Cordova Also Called: Teichert Inc *(P-644)*

Teichert Aggregates, Sacramento Also Called: Teichert Inc *(P-645)*

Teichert Construction, Stockton Also Called: Teichert Inc *(P-1170)*

Teichert Construction, Davis Also Called: Teichert Inc *(P-1171)*

Teichert Construction, Roseville Also Called: Teichert Inc *(P-1172)*

Teichert Construction, Fresno Also Called: Teichert Inc *(P-1173)*

Teichert Enrgy Utlties Group l .... D....... 916 484-3011
3780 Kilroy Airport Way Long Beach (90806) *(P-20228)*

Teixeira and Sons, Los Banos Also Called: Teixeira and Sons LLC *(P-6)*

Teixeira and Sons LLC .... C....... 209 827-9800
22759 S Mercey Springs Rd Los Banos (93635) *(P-6)*

Teixeira Farms Desert Inc .... D....... 805 928-3801
2600 Bonita Lateral Rd Santa Maria (93458) *(P-45)*

Tekberry Inc .... B....... 707 313-5345
3763 Shillingford Pl Santa Rosa (95404) *(P-11245)*

Teknova, Hollister Also Called: Alpha Teknova Inc *(P-19862)*

Tekworks Inc .... D....... 877 835-9675
12742 Knott St Garden Grove (92841) *(P-4348)*

Tele-Direct Communications Inc .... D....... 916 348-2170
4741 Madison Ave Ste 200 Sacramento (95841) *(P-13506)*

Telecare, Norwalk Also Called: Telecare Act 7 *(P-17142)*

Telecare Act 7 .... D....... 562 929-6688
12440 Firestone Blvd Ste 3025 Norwalk (90650) *(P-17142)*

Telecare Corporation .... D....... 213 533-1050
1005 S Central Ave Los Angeles (90021) *(P-16658)*

Telecare Corporation (PA) .... C....... 510 337-7950
1080 Marina Village Pkwy Ste 100 Alameda (94501) *(P-16659)*

Telecare Corporation .... C....... 562 630-8672
6060 N Paramount Blvd Long Beach (90805) *(P-17143)*

Telecom Inc .... D....... 510 873-8283
2201 Broadway Ste 103 Oakland (94612) *(P-13507)*

Telecommunication, Beverly Hills Also Called: Nga 911 LLC *(P-11776)*

Telecontact Resource Services, Riverbank Also Called: Econtactlive Inc *(P-13277)*

Teledyne Controls, El Segundo Also Called: Teledyne Technologies Inc *(P-2946)*

Teledyne Judson Technologies, Camarillo Also Called: Teledyne Scentific Imaging LLC *(P-19782)*

Teledyne Scentific Imaging LLC .... D....... 805 373-4979
5212 Verdugo Way Camarillo (93012) *(P-19782)*

Teledyne Scentific Imaging LLC (HQ) .... C....... 805 373-4545
1049 Camino Dos Rios Thousand Oaks (91360) *(P-19783)*

Teledyne Scientific Company, Thousand Oaks Also Called: Teledyne Scentific Imaging LLC *(P-19783)*

Teledyne Technologies Inc .... B....... 310 765-3600
501 Continental Blvd El Segundo (90245) *(P-2946)*

Teleflora, Los Angeles Also Called: The Wonderful Company LLC *(P-312)*

Telenet, El Segundo Also Called: Telenet Voip Inc *(P-13747)*

Telenet Voip Inc .... D....... 310 253-9000
850 N Park View Dr El Segundo (90245) *(P-13747)*

Teleperformance, Pasadena Also Called: Tpusa - Fhcs Inc *(P-12699)*

Teleplan Service Solutions Inc .... D....... 916 677-4500
151 N Sunrise Ave Ste 1008 Roseville (95661) *(P-12712)*

Telescape, Los Angeles Also Called: Truconnect Communications Inc *(P-4352)*

Telesector Resources Group Inc .... B....... 626 813-4538
5010 Azusa Canyon Rd Baldwin Park (91706) *(P-20581)*

Telesis Community Credit Union (PA) .... D....... 818 885-1226
9301 Winnetka Ave Chatsworth (91311) *(P-7811)*

Telesis Onion Co .... C....... 559 884-2441
21484 S Colusa Five Points (93624) *(P-311)*

TELESIS ONION CO., Five Points Also Called: Telesis Onion Co *(P-311)*

Telestream LLC (PA) .... D....... 530 470-1300
848 Gold Flat Rd Nevada City (95959) *(P-11974)*

Teletrac Inc (PA) .... C....... 714 897-0877
310 Commerce Ste 100 Irvine (92602) *(P-4554)*

Telisimo International Corp .... B....... 619 325-1593
2330 Shelter Island Dr Ste 210a San Diego (92106) *(P-4349)*

ALPHABETIC SECTION

Telit Wireless Solutions Inc .... C....... 949 461-7150
   7700 Irvine Center Dr Irvine (92618) *(P-5711)*

Tell Steel Inc .... D....... 562 435-4826
   2345 W 17th St Long Beach (90813) *(P-5523)*

Telles Ranch Inc .... C....... 209 364-6262
   44328 W Nees Ave Firebaugh (93622) *(P-200)*

Tellme Networks Inc .... B....... 650 693-1009
   1065 La Avenida St Mountain View (94043) *(P-2558)*

Telshare, San Francisco *Also Called: Alpine Invstors Cnfrnce Call H (P-9486)*

Telus Health (us) Ltd Inc .... D....... 888 577-3784
   27715 Jefferson Ave Ste 103 Temecula (92590) *(P-20582)*

Temalpakh Inc .... D....... 760 770-5778
   73750 Spyder Cir Palm Desert (92211) *(P-1042)*

Temarry Recycling Inc .... D....... 619 270-9453
   476 Tecate Rd Tecate (91980) *(P-4945)*

Temco, Pomona *Also Called: C & B Delivery Service (P-3679)*

Temco Logistics, Lake Forest *Also Called: Home Express Delivery Svc LLC (P-4035)*

Temecula Hhg Hotel Dev LP .... D....... 951 331-3622
   28400 Rancho California Rd Temecula (92590) *(P-10307)*

Temecula Homecare, Temecula *Also Called: Maxim Healthcare Services Inc (P-11307)*

Temecula Stadium Cinemas 15, Temecula *Also Called: Edwards Theatres Circuit Inc (P-13995)*

Temecula Valley Drywall Inc .... D....... 951 600-1742
   41228 Raintree Ct Murrieta (92562) *(P-1968)*

Temecula Vly Unified Schl Dst .... D....... 951 302-5140
   33125 Regina Dr Temecula (92592) *(P-17753)*

Temeku Hills, Temecula *Also Called: McMillin Communities Inc (P-14274)*

Tempest, Santa Barbara *Also Called: Tempest Telecom Solutions LLC (P-20864)*

Tempest Telecom Solutions LLC (HQ) .... D....... 805 879-4800
   136 W Canon Perdido St Ste 100 Santa Barbara (93101) *(P-20864)*

Temple Community Hospital, Los Angeles *Also Called: Temple Hospital Corporation (P-16569)*

Temple Hospital Corporation .... B....... 213 355-3200
   242 N Hoover St Los Angeles (90004) *(P-16569)*

Temple Israel of Hollywood (PA) .... D....... 323 876-8330
   7300 Hollywood Blvd Los Angeles (90046) *(P-10517)*

Temple Jdea of W San Frnndo Vl .... D....... 818 758-3800
   5429 Lindley Ave Tarzana (91356) *(P-18357)*

Temple Judea Nursery School, Tarzana *Also Called: Temple Jdea of W San Frnndo Vl (P-18357)*

Temple Pk Cnvalescent Hosp Inc .... D....... 213 380-2035
   2411 W Temple St Los Angeles (90026) *(P-15902)*

Tempo Communications Inc (PA) .... D....... 800 642-2155
   1390 Aspen Way Vista (92081) *(P-4350)*

Temporary Plant Cleaners, Martinez *Also Called: Plant Maintenance Inc (P-11317)*

Temporary Staffing Union .... A....... 714 728-5186
   19800 Macarthur Blvd Ste 300 Irvine (92612) *(P-18798)*

Temps Plus Inc .... C....... 951 549-8309
   268 N Lincoln Ave Ste 12 Corona (92882) *(P-11246)*

Tempus LLC .... D....... 800 917-5055
   2041 Rosecrans Ave Ste 245 El Segundo (90245) *(P-11247)*

Ten 15 Inc .... D....... 415 431-1200
   1015 Folsom St San Francisco (94103) *(P-7523)*

Ten Days Manufacturing .... C....... 888 222-1575
   1615 Yeager Ave La Verne (91750) *(P-5930)*

Ten Publishing Media LLC (PA) .... C....... 310 531-9900
   831 S Douglas St El Segundo (90245) *(P-13955)*

Ten Stone Wbster Prcess Tech .... B....... 909 447-3600
   555 W Arrow Hwy Claremont (91711) *(P-19407)*

Ten-X, San Mateo *Also Called: Auctioncom LLC (P-8907)*

Ten-X, Irvine *Also Called: Ten-X Finance Inc (P-9191)*

Ten-X LLC .... C....... 800 793-6107
   1301 Shoreway Rd Ste 425 Belmont (94002) *(P-9190)*

Ten-X Finance Inc .... C....... 949 465-8523
   15295 Alton Pkwy Irvine (92618) *(P-9191)*

TEN-X, LLC, Belmont *Also Called: Ten-X LLC (P-9190)*

Tenaya Lodge, Fish Camp *Also Called: DNC Prks Resorts At Tenaya Inc (P-9755)*

Tencate Advanced Composite .... C....... 707 359-3400
   2450 Cordelia Rd Fairfield (94534) *(P-6836)*

TenCate Advanced Composites USA, Inc., Fairfield *Also Called: Tencate Advanced Composite (P-6836)*

Tenderloin Housing Clinic Inc (PA) .... D....... 415 771-9850
   126 Hyde St San Francisco (94102) *(P-9192)*

Tenderloin Housing Clinic Inc .... C....... 415 771-2427
   488 Ellis St San Francisco (94102) *(P-17340)*

Tenergy Corporation .... D....... 510 687-0388
   436 Kato Ter Fremont (94539) *(P-2950)*

Tenet, Palm Springs *Also Called: Desert Regional Med Ctr Inc (P-16038)*

Tenet, Palm Springs *Also Called: Desert Regional Med Ctr Inc (P-16039)*

Tenet Health Systems Norris .... B....... 323 865-3000
   1441 Eastlake Ave Los Angeles (90089) *(P-16570)*

Tenet Healthsystem Medical Inc .... B....... 805 546-7698
   3751 Katella Ave Los Alamitos (90720) *(P-15123)*

Tenet Healthsystem Medical Inc .... C....... 562 493-9581
   1661 Golden Rain Rd Seal Beach (90740) *(P-15124)*

Tenet Healthsystem Medical Inc .... A....... 562 531-2550
   3700 South St Lakewood (90712) *(P-15125)*

Tenet Healthsystem Medical Inc .... C....... 714 428-6800
   1400 S Douglass Rd Ste 250 Anaheim (92806) *(P-16571)*

Tenet Healthsystem Medical Inc .... B....... 408 378-6131
   815 Pollard Rd Los Gatos (95032) *(P-16572)*

Tenet Healthsystem Medical Inc .... B....... 714 993-2000
   1301 N Rose Dr Placentia (92870) *(P-16699)*

Tenet Healthsystem Medical Inc .... D....... 310 673-4660
   555 E Hardy St Inglewood (90301) *(P-18358)*

Tennenbaum Capitl Partners LLC (HQ) .... D....... 310 566-1000
   2951 28th St Ste 1000 Santa Monica (90405) *(P-9573)*

Tennessee Hospitalists Inc .... D....... 888 447-2362
   4605 Lankershim Blvd Ste 617 North Hollywood (91602) *(P-16573)*

Tennis Channel Inc (HQ) .... D....... 310 392-1920
   3003 Exposition Blvd Santa Monica (90404) *(P-14070)*

Tensilica Inc (HQ) .... D....... 408 986-8000
   3393 Octavius Dr Santa Clara (95054) *(P-9457)*

Tensoriot Inc .... D....... 909 342-2459
   625 The City Dr S Ste 485 Orange (92868) *(P-12894)*

Terabase Energy Inc .... D....... 415 763-7181
   2222 Harold Way Berkeley (94704) *(P-4712)*

Teradata, San Diego *Also Called: Teradata Corporation (P-12376)*

Teradata Corporation (PA) .... A....... 866 548-8348
   17095 Via Del Campo San Diego (92127) *(P-12376)*

Teradata Operations Inc (HQ) .... D....... 937 242-4030
   17095 Via Del Campo San Diego (92127) *(P-2814)*

Terawave Communication Inc .... D....... 510 429-5300
   30680 Huntwood Ave Hayward (94544) *(P-19408)*

TERI COMMON GROUNDS CAFE & COF, Oceanside *Also Called: E R I T Inc (P-18419)*

Terix Computer Service, Santa Clara *Also Called: Tusa Inc (P-12713)*

Terminal SEC Solutions Inc .... D....... 877 858-3855
   3806 Worsham Ave Long Beach (90808) *(P-1862)*

Terra Bella Nursery, San Diego *Also Called: Bella Terra Nursery Inc (P-6852)*

Terra Nova Counseling (PA) .... D....... 916 344-0249
   5750 Sunrise Blvd Ste 100 Citrus Heights (95610) *(P-18149)*

Terra Nova Technologies Inc .... D....... 619 596-7400
   10770 Rockville St Ste A Santee (92071) *(P-2777)*

Terra Pacific Landscape (HQ) .... D....... 714 567-0177
   12891 Nelson St Garden Grove (92840) *(P-469)*

Terra Universal Inc .... C....... 714 526-0100
   800 S Raymond Ave Fullerton (92831) *(P-2796)*

Terra Vista Management, San Diego *Also Called: Terra Vista Management Inc (P-9193)*

Terra Vista Management Inc .... B....... 858 581-4200
   2211 Pacific Beach Dr San Diego (92109) *(P-9193)*

Terrace, The, Grand Terrace *Also Called: Emeritus Corporation (P-15445)*

Terraces At Squaw Peak, Duarte *Also Called: Humangood (P-15858)*

Terraces of Los Gatos Agei, Los Gatos *Also Called: Humangood Norcal (P-15862)*

Terraces of Roseville, The, Roseville *Also Called: Westmont Living Inc (P-18547)*

Terranea Resort, Rancho Palos Verdes *Also Called: Long Point Development LLC (P-9985)*

Terre Du Soleil Ltd .... B....... 707 963-1211
   180 Rutherford Hill Road Rutherford (94573) *(P-10308)*

Terry Hines & Assoc, Burbank *Also Called: GL Nemirow Inc (P-10618)*

Terry Town Corporation .... D....... 619 421-5354
   8851 Kerns St Ste 100 San Diego (92154) *(P-2467)*

Terry Tuell Concrete Inc .... D....... 559 431-0812
   287 W Fallbrook Ave Ste 105 Fresno (93711) *(P-2166)*

ALPHABETIC SECTION

Tesancia La Jlla Ht Spa Resort, La Jolla *Also Called: Destination Residences LLC (P-10542)*
Teserra (PA)..B....... 760 340-9000
   86100 Avenue 54 Coachella (92236) *(P-2320)*
Tesla Energy Operations Inc (HQ)..................................A....... 888 765-2489
   3055 Clearview Way San Mateo (94402) *(P-1583)*
Tesoro Refining & Mktg Co LLC....................................C....... 877 837-6762
   2101 E Pacific Coast Hwy Wilmington (90744) *(P-6742)*
Tessera Technologies Inc (DH)......................................C....... 408 321-6000
   3025 Orchard Pkwy San Jose (95134) *(P-2934)*
Tessie Clvland Cmnty Svcs Corp...................................D....... 310 965-9759
   18220 S Broadway Gardena (90248) *(P-18150)*
Tessitura Network Inc..C....... 888 643-5778
   2295 Fletcher Pkwy Ste 101 El Cajon (92020) *(P-12377)*
Test-Rite Products Corp (DH)...D....... 909 605-9899
   1900 Burgundy Pl Ontario (91761) *(P-5137)*
Testequity, Moorpark *Also Called: Testequity Inc (P-5872)*
Testequity Inc...D....... 805 498-9933
   6100 Condor Dr Moorpark (93021) *(P-5872)*
Testequity LLC (PA)..C....... 805 498-9933
   6100 Condor Dr Moorpark (93021) *(P-13748)*
Testronic Inc...C....... 818 845-3223
   111 N First St Ste 204 Burbank (91502) *(P-13956)*
Testronic Labs, Burbank *Also Called: Testronic Inc (P-13956)*
Teton Healthcare Inc...D....... 949 487-9500
   27101 Puerta Real Ste 450 Mission Viejo (92691) *(P-15702)*
Tetra Tech, Pasadena *Also Called: Tetra Tech Inc (P-19409)*
Tetra Tech Inc (PA)..C....... 626 351-4664
   3475 E Foothill Blvd Pasadena (91107) *(P-19409)*
Tetra Tech Inc..D....... 949 263-0846
   17885 Von Karman Ave Ste 500 Irvine (92614) *(P-19410)*
Tetra Tech Bas Inc (HQ)..D....... 909 860-7777
   21700 Copley Dr Ste 200 Diamond Bar (91765) *(P-19411)*
Tetra Tech Em Inc..C....... 415 265-3715
   135 Main St Ste 1800 San Francisco (94105) *(P-19412)*
Tetra Tech Executive Svcs Inc.......................................C....... 626 470-2400
   3475 E Foothill Blvd Pasadena (91107) *(P-11248)*
Tetra Tech Nus Inc..C....... 412 921-7090
   3475 E Foothill Blvd Pasadena (91107) *(P-19413)*
Texaco, San Ramon *Also Called: Texaco Inc (P-7391)*
Texaco Inc (HQ)..A....... 925 842-1000
   6001 Bollinger Canyon Rd San Ramon (94583) *(P-7391)*
Texas Home Health America LP (PA)..........................D....... 972 201-3800
   1455 Auto Center Dr Ste 200 Ontario (91761) *(P-16945)*
Texas Home Health of America, Ontario *Also Called: Texas Home Health America LP (P-16945)*
Tg Art Inc...D....... 510 525-0070
   1109 Washington Ave Albany (94706) *(P-14569)*
Tga Franchise Spt Holdings LLC...................................D....... 310 333-0622
   1960 E Grand Ave Ste 811 El Segundo (90245) *(P-14469)*
Tga Premier Sports, El Segundo *Also Called: Tga Franchise Spt Holdings LLC (P-14469)*
Tgcon Inc (DH)..D....... 925 449-5764
   50 Contractors St Livermore (94551) *(P-19414)*
Tgg Accounting..D....... 760 697-1033
   10188 Telesis Ct Ste 130 San Diego (92121) *(P-19634)*
Thaihot Investment Co US Ltd..A....... 949 242-5300
   18201 Von Karman Ave Ste 600 Irvine (92612) *(P-16756)*
Thales Esecurity Inc (HQ)..D....... 408 433-6000
   2125 Zanker Rd San Jose (95131) *(P-12895)*
Tharpe & Howell (PA)..D....... 818 205-9955
   15250 Ventura Blvd Fl 9 Sherman Oaks (91403) *(P-17666)*
Thats No Moon Entrmt Inc...D....... 310 795-8282
   5419 Mcconnell Ave Los Angeles (90066) *(P-13508)*
The Aerospace Corporation (PA)...................................A....... 310 336-5000
   2310 E El Segundo Blvd El Segundo (90245) *(P-19918)*
THE BERRY MAN, INC, San Luis Obispo *Also Called: Berry Man Inc (P-6515)*
The Broadmoore, San Francisco *Also Called: Broadmoor Hotel (P-9662)*
THE CANCER CENTER OF SANTA BARBARA, Santa Barbara *Also Called: Cancer Center of Santa Barbara (P-14650)*
The Clear Group Inc, Los Angeles *Also Called: Clear Group Inc (P-9707)*
The Coding Source LLC...C....... 866 235-7553
   3415 S Sepulveda Blvd Ste 900 Los Angeles (90034) *(P-17797)*

The Copley Press Inc...A....... 858 454-0411
   7776 Ivanhoe Ave La Jolla (92037) *(P-13158)*
The David Lcile Pckard Fndtion......................................D....... 650 917-7167
   300 2nd St Los Altos (94022) *(P-19111)*
The Doctors Company..A....... 707 226-0289
   185 Greenwood Rd Napa (94558) *(P-5453)*
The E Jordan Brookes Co Inc...D....... 562 968-2100
   10634 Shoemaker Ave Santa Fe Springs (90670) *(P-5524)*
The Eberly Company, Beverly Hills *Also Called: Charles & Cynthia Eberly Inc (P-8798)*
The Gersh Agency LLC (PA)..D....... 310 274-6611
   9465 Wilshire Blvd Fl 6 Beverly Hills (90212) *(P-14071)*
The Golf Club of California, Murrieta *Also Called: Sycamore Cc Inc (P-14293)*
THE GROWERS COMPANY, INC, Salinas *Also Called: Growers Company Inc (P-11147)*
The Hsptal Cmmttee For Lvrmr-P, Pleasanton *Also Called: Stanford Hlth Care Tri-Valley (P-20217)*
The J David Gladstone Institutes...................................B....... 415 734-2000
   1650 Owens St San Francisco (94158) *(P-19919)*
The J Paul Getty Trust (PA)..A....... 310 440-7300
   1200 Getty Center Dr Ste 500 Los Angeles (90049) *(P-18679)*
The Jerde Partnership Inc..D....... 310 399-1987
   601 W 5th St Ste 500 Los Angeles (90071) *(P-19514)*
The Linux Foundation (PA)...D....... 415 723-9709
   548 Market St Pmb 57274 San Francisco (94104) *(P-18916)*
The Lodge At Torrey Pines Partnership L P...................B
   998 W Mission Bay Dr San Diego (92109) *(P-10309)*
The Marketing Practice Inc, Oakland *Also Called: Marketing Practice Inc (P-20452)*
The Metropolitan Water District of Southern California (PA).....................A....... 213 217-6000
   700 N Alameda St Los Angeles (90012) *(P-4841)*
The Morning Star Company (PA)...................................D....... 530 666-6600
   724 Main St Ste 202 Woodland (95695) *(P-11342)*
The National Bus Group Inc..D....... 818 221-6000
   15319 Chatsworth St Mission Hills (91345) *(P-11008)*
The Origin Project Inc...D....... 415 601-2409
   2121 Vallejo St San Francisco (94123) *(P-18680)*
The Orthopedic Institute of...A....... 213 977-2010
   616 Witmer St Los Angeles (90017) *(P-15126)*
The Ortiz Corporation..D....... 619 434-7925
   2000 Mckinley Ave National City (91950) *(P-1271)*
The Palace of Auburn Hills, Beverly Hills *Also Called: Pse Holding LLC (P-14154)*
The Pines Ltd...C....... 619 447-1880
   1423 E Washington Ave El Cajon (92019) *(P-8864)*
The Pr-Mplycom Fmly Cmpnies In, Redding *Also Called: Pre-Employcom Inc (P-11202)*
The Rand Corporation (PA)..A....... 310 393-0411
   1776 Main St Santa Monica (90401) *(P-19920)*
The Redwoods A Cmnty Seniors....................................C....... 415 383-2741
   40 Camino Alto Ofc Mill Valley (94941) *(P-18531)*
THE RK LOGISTICS GROUP, INC, Fremont *Also Called: Rk Logistics Group Inc (P-4085)*
The Roman Catholic Archbishop of San Francisco (PA)...........C....... 415 614-5500
   1 Peter Yorke Way 1 San Francisco (94109) *(P-17817)*
The Rromeo Corporation..C....... 415 781-3300
   101 California St Fl 24 San Francisco (94111) *(P-8224)*
The Rule Group, Newport Beach *Also Called: Trg Insurance Services (P-8676)*
The Rutter Group, North Hollywood *Also Called: West Publishing Corporation (P-2551)*
The Ryland Group Inc...A....... 805 367-3800
   3011 Townsgate Rd Ste 200 Westlake Village (91361) *(P-797)*
The Salk Institute For Biological Studies San Diego California.......A....... 858 453-4100
   10010 N Torrey Pines Rd La Jolla (92037) *(P-19784)*
The San Diego Yacht Club..C....... 619 221-8400
   1011 Anchorage Ln San Diego (92106) *(P-14470)*
The Sonora J S West & Co Inc.......................................B....... 209 577-3221
   501 9th St Modesto (95354) *(P-7426)*
The Source Group Inc..D....... 925 944-2856
   3478 Buskirk Ave Ste 100 Pleasant Hill (94523) *(P-20865)*
The Strand Energy Company..B....... 213 225-5900
   515 S Flower St Ste 4800 Los Angeles (90071) *(P-585)*
The Sweet Life Enterprises Inc......................................C....... 949 261-7400
   2350 Pullman St Santa Ana (92705) *(P-2360)*
The Tax Credit Company..D....... 323 927-0750
   6464 W Sunset Blvd # 1150 Los Angeles (90028) *(P-10765)*
The Teecor Group Inc...D....... 213 632-2350
   1450 S Burlington Ave Los Angeles (90006) *(P-2321)*

ALPHABETIC SECTION

The Tristaff Group, San Diego *Also Called: Garich Inc (P-11141)*
The Villa Florence Hotel, San Francisco *Also Called: Florence Villa Hotel (P-9799)*
The White Sheet, Palm Desert *Also Called: Associated Desert Shoppers Inc (P-2553)*
The Wonderful Company LLC (PA) .... C 310 966-5700
   11444 W Olympic Blvd Ste 210 Los Angeles (90064) *(P-312)*
The Woodbridge Golf Cntry CLB .... D 209 369-2371
   800 E Woodbridge Rd Woodbridge (95258) *(P-14471)*
Theater Arts Fndtion San Dego .... E 858 623-3366
   2910 La Jolla Village Dr La Jolla (92093) *(P-18917)*
Theatre Department, Fresno *Also Called: California State Univ Long Bch (P-17805)*
Thebouqs.com, Marina Del Rey *Also Called: Bouqs Company (P-6853)*
Thekey LLC .... D 707 492-8411
   1802 Soscol Ave Napa (94559) *(P-16946)*
Thekey LLC .... D 408 356-0127
   15734 Los Gatos Blvd Los Gatos (95032) *(P-16947)*
Thekey LLC .... D 858 842-1346
   1330 Orange Ave Ste 300 Coronado (92118) *(P-16948)*
Thekey LLC .... D 916 358-3801
   2222 Francisco Dr Ste 610 El Dorado Hills (95762) *(P-16949)*
Thekey LLC .... D 650 462-6900
   480 California Ave Ste 100 Palo Alto (94306) *(P-16950)*
Theodore Robins Inc .... D 949 642-0010
   2060 Harbor Blvd Costa Mesa (92627) *(P-7311)*
Theodore Robins Ford, Costa Mesa *Also Called: Theodore Robins Inc (P-7311)*
Theraex Rehab Services .... C 510 239-9614
   1511 Sycamore Ave Ste M258 Hercules (94547) *(P-16951)*
Therapak LLC (DH) .... D 909 267-2000
   651 Wharton Dr Claremont (91711) *(P-5454)*
Therapy Specialist, Chula Vista *Also Called: Susan J Harris Inc (P-18530)*
Therapytravelers LLC .... D 888 223-8002
   355 Redondo Ave Long Beach (90814) *(P-15310)*
Therma, San Jose *Also Called: Therma Holdings LLC (P-1863)*
Therma Holdings LLC (PA) .... C 408 347-3400
   1601 Las Plumas Ave San Jose (95133) *(P-1863)*
Thermal Air, Anaheim *Also Called: General Engineering Wstn Inc (P-1449)*
Thermal Engineering, Cerritos *Also Called: Thermal Engrg Intl USA Inc (P-19415)*
Thermal Engrg Intl USA Inc (HQ) .... D 323 726-0641
   18000 Studebaker Rd Ste 400 Cerritos (90703) *(P-19415)*
Thermal Mechanical .... D 408 988-8744
   425 Aldo Ave Santa Clara (95054) *(P-1584)*
Thermalair Inc (HQ) .... D 714 630-3200
   1140 N Red Gum St Anaheim (92806) *(P-1585)*
Thermionics Laboratory Inc .... D 510 786-0680
   3118 Depot Rd Hayward (94545) *(P-2761)*
Thermocraft .... D 619 813-2985
   2554 Commercial St San Diego (92113) *(P-2845)*
THETRADEDESK, Ventura *Also Called: Trade Desk Inc (P-11985)*
Thi Inc .... D 714 444-4643
   1525 E Edinger Ave Santa Ana (92705) *(P-3060)*
Thi Holdings (delaware) Inc .... B 661 266-7423
   2140 E Palmdale Blvd Ste O Palmdale (93550) *(P-8671)*
Think Together .... B 562 236-3835
   12016 Telegraph Rd Santa Fe Springs (90670) *(P-14237)*
Think Together .... B 909 723-1400
   202 E Airport Dr Ste 200 San Bernardino (92408) *(P-18359)*
Think Together .... B 626 373-2311
   800 S Barranca Ave Ste 120 Covina (91723) *(P-18360)*
Think Together .... B 951 571-9944
   22620 Goldencrest Dr Ste 104 Moreno Valley (92553) *(P-18361)*
Think Together .... B 760 269-1230
   17270 Bear Valley Rd Ste 103 Victorville (92395) *(P-19112)*
Thinkbasic Inc .... C 858 755-6922
   350 10th Ave San Diego (92101) *(P-10819)*
Thinkom Solutions Inc .... C 310 371-5486
   4881 W 145th St Hawthorne (90250) *(P-4555)*
Thirdlove, San Francisco *Also Called: Thirdlove Inc (P-6225)*
Thirdlove Inc .... C 415 692-0089
   555 Market St Fl 13 San Francisco (94105) *(P-6225)*
Thismoment Inc .... C 415 200-4730
   690 Market St Unit 1101 San Francisco (94104) *(P-11975)*

Thomas Bavarian Mtr Works Inc .... D 805 482-8878
   411 E Daily Dr Camarillo (93010) *(P-7312)*
Thomas Doll & Company, Walnut Creek *Also Called: Thomas Wirig Doll & Co Cpas (P-19635)*
Thomas Gallaway Corporation (PA) .... D 949 517-9500
   100 Spectrum Center Dr Ste 700 Irvine (92618) *(P-11976)*
Thomas James Capital Inc .... C 949 481-7026
   26940 Aliso Viejo Pkwy Ste 100 Aliso Viejo (92656) *(P-8225)*
Thomas James Homes Inc .... C 949 424-2356
   26880 Aliso Viejo Pkwy Ste 100 Aliso Viejo (92656) *(P-9194)*
Thomas Kinkade Company, The, Morgan Hill *Also Called: Pacific Metro LLC (P-18664)*
Thomas Products, Madera *Also Called: Nutra-Blend LLC (P-2365)*
Thomas Properties Group Inc .... C 213 613-1900
   515 S Flower St Fl 6 Los Angeles (90071) *(P-9195)*
Thomas St John Inc .... D 424 273-1172
   10877 Wilshire Blvd Ste 1550 Los Angeles (90024) *(P-20583)*
Thomas Weisel Partners LLC (DH) .... B 415 364-2500
   1 Montgomery St Ste 3700 San Francisco (94104) *(P-8168)*
Thomas Wirig Doll & Co Cpas .... D 925 939-2500
   165 Lennon Ln Ste 200 Walnut Creek (94598) *(P-19635)*
Thompson Builders, Novato *Also Called: Thompson Builders Corporation (P-778)*
Thompson Builders Corporation .... C 415 456-8972
   5400 Hanna Ranch Rd Novato (94945) *(P-778)*
Thompson Building Materials, Fontana *Also Called: Valori Sand & Gravel Company (P-5212)*
Thompson Cnstr Sup Door Frame, Corona *Also Called: Fennel Inc (P-1998)*
Thoro--Packaging (DH) .... C 951 278-2100
   1467 Davril Cir Corona (92878) *(P-6953)*
Thorpe Design Inc .... D 925 634-0787
   410 Beatrice Ct Ste A Brentwood (94513) *(P-1586)*
Thorsnes Bartolotta & McGuire .... D 619 236-9363
   2550 5th Ave Ste 1100 San Diego (92103) *(P-17667)*
Thoughtful Asia Limited, Sherman Oaks *Also Called: Adactive Media Ca Inc (P-10699)*
Thoughtspot Inc (PA) .... B 800 508-7008
   444 Castro St Ste 1000 Mountain View (94041) *(P-12378)*
THOUSAND OAKS HEALTH CARE CENTER, Thousand Oaks *Also Called: Five Star Qulty Care-CA II LLC (P-15478)*
Thousand Oaks Prtg & Spc Inc .... C 818 706-8330
   5334 Sterling Center Dr Westlake Village (91361) *(P-13509)*
Thousand Oaks Service Center, Thousand Oaks *Also Called: Southern California Edison Co (P-4685)*
Thousand Oaks Surgical Hosp LP .... D 805 777-7750
   401 Rolling Oaks Dr Thousand Oaks (91361) *(P-16574)*
Thousandeyes LLC (HQ) .... D 415 513-4526
   500 Terry A Francois Blvd San Francisco (94158) *(P-12379)*
Thq Inc .... A 818 591-1310
   21900 Burbank Blvd Woodland Hills (91367) *(P-12380)*
Thq San Diego, Woodland Hills *Also Called: Thq Inc (P-12380)*
Threatmetrix Inc (DH) .... C 408 200-5700
   160 W Santa Clara St Ste 1400 San Jose (95113) *(P-11977)*
Three Sons Inc .... D 562 801-4100
   5201 Industry Ave Pico Rivera (90660) *(P-6506)*
Three Way, Fremont *Also Called: Three Way Logistics Inc (P-4106)*
Three Way Inc .... C 408 748-6902
   2940 Mead Ave Santa Clara (95051) *(P-3598)*
Three Way Logistics Inc (PA) .... D 408 748-3929
   42505 Christy St Fremont (94538) *(P-4106)*
Three-Way Chevrolet Co (PA) .... C 661 847-6400
   4501 Wible Rd Bakersfield (93313) *(P-7313)*
Threesixty Group, Irvine *Also Called: Merchsource LLC (P-5992)*
Thrive Mortgage LLC .... D 909 527-3736
   9587 Foothill Blvd Rancho Cucamonga (91730) *(P-8024)*
Thriving Seniors LLC .... D 707 317-1740
   479 Mason St Ste 109 Vacaville (95688) *(P-16952)*
Thums Long Beach Company .... C 562 624-3400
   111 W Ocean Blvd Ste 800 Long Beach (90802) *(P-586)*
Thunder Industries .... D 415 228-0861
   313 Sheridan Ave Palo Alto (94306) *(P-10680)*
Thunderbird Country Club .... D 760 328-2161
   70737 Country Club Dr Rancho Mirage (92270) *(P-14472)*
Thunderhead One Inc .... D 877 838-8945
   6220 Stoneridge Mall Rd Pleasanton (94588) *(P-5361)*

Thunkable Inc   **ALPHABETIC SECTION**

Thunkable Inc .... C....... 415 200-3736
   605 Market St Ste 700 San Francisco (94105) *(P-11978)*

Thurgood Mrshall Erly Head Sta, Oakland *Also Called: Spanish Spking Unity Cncil Alm (P-18626)*

Thyde Inc (PA) .... C....... 951 817-2300
   300 El Sobrante Rd Corona (92879) *(P-13510)*

Thyme Holdings LLC .... D....... 559 733-0901
   4525 W Tulare Ave Visalia (93277) *(P-9342)*

Thyssenkrupp Indus Svcs NA Inc .... C....... 209 395-9111
   201 Discovery Dr Livermore (94551) *(P-5525)*

THYSSENKRUPP INDUSTRIAL SERVICES NA, INC., Livermore *Also Called: Thyssenkrupp Indus Svcs NA Inc (P-5525)*

Tiburon Community Snf LLC .... D....... 415 435-4554
   30 Hacienda Dr Belvedere Tiburon (94920) *(P-15703)*

Tiburon Hills Care Center, Belvedere Tiburon *Also Called: Tiburon Community Snf LLC (P-15703)*

Tiburon Hospitality LLC .... C....... 661 322-1012
   901 Real Rd Bakersfield (93309) *(P-10310)*

Tic, Panorama City *Also Called: Import Collection (P-6917)*

Tic Hotels Inc .... D....... 805 773-4671
   2555 Price St Pismo Beach (93449) *(P-10311)*

Tic Hotels Inc .... D....... 619 238-7577
   555 W Ash St San Diego (92101) *(P-10312)*

Ticketmanager .... D....... 818 698-3616
   26635 Agoura Rd Ste 200 Calabasas (91302) *(P-11979)*

Ticketmaster, Los Angeles *Also Called: Ticketmaster Corporation (P-14570)*

Ticketmaster, Los Angeles *Also Called: Ticketmaster Group Inc (P-14572)*

Ticketmaster, Beverly Hills *Also Called: Ticketmster New Vntres Hldngs (P-14573)*

Ticketmaster Corporation .... A....... 323 769-4600
   7060 Hollywood Blvd Ste 2 Los Angeles (90028) *(P-14570)*

Ticketmaster Entertainment LLC .... A....... 800 653-8000
   8800 W Sunset Blvd West Hollywood (90069) *(P-14571)*

Ticketmaster Group Inc .... A....... 800 745-3000
   3701 Wilshire Blvd Fl 9 Los Angeles (90010) *(P-14572)*

Ticketmster New Vntres Hldngs (HQ) .... C....... 800 653-8000
   325 N Maple Dr Beverly Hills (90210) *(P-14573)*

Tides Inc (PA) .... D....... 415 561-6400
   1012 Torney Ave San Francisco (94129) *(P-18630)*

Tides Center .... C....... 415 359-9401
   124 Turk St San Francisco (94102) *(P-10313)*

TIDES SHARED SPACES, San Francisco *Also Called: Tides Inc (P-18630)*

Tidwell Excav Acquisition Inc .... D....... 805 647-4707
   1691 Los Angeles Ave Ventura (93004) *(P-2227)*

Tidwell Excavating, Ventura *Also Called: Tidwell Excav Acquisition Inc (P-2227)*

Tierra Del Sol Foundation .... D....... 909 626-8301
   250 W 1st St Ste 120 Claremont (91711) *(P-14574)*

Tierra Del Sol Foundation (PA) .... D....... 818 352-1419
   9919 Sunland Blvd Sunland (91040) *(P-18532)*

Tierra Del Soul, Claremont *Also Called: Tierra Del Sol Foundation (P-14574)*

Tiffany Dale Inc (PA) .... D....... 714 739-2700
   14765 Firestone Blvd La Mirada (90638) *(P-5138)*

Tiffany Homecare Inc (PA) .... B....... 818 886-1602
   9700 Reseda Blvd Ste 105 Northridge (91324) *(P-16953)*

Tiger Lines LLC (HQ) .... D....... 209 334-4100
   927 Black Diamond Way Lodi (95240) *(P-3551)*

Tiger Woods Learning Center .... D....... 714 765-8040
   1 Tiger Woods Way Anaheim (92801) *(P-18362)*

Tigerconnect Inc (PA) .... D....... 310 401-1820
   2054 Broadway Santa Monica (90404) *(P-12896)*

Tightdb Inc .... C....... 415 766-2020
   100 Forest Ave Palo Alto (94301) *(P-11980)*

Tilden Park, Berkeley *Also Called: East Bay Regional Park Dst (P-13276)*

Tile Inc (HQ) .... C....... 650 274-0676
   1900 S Norfolk St Ste 310 San Mateo (94403) *(P-5712)*

Tiller Constructors, Orange *Also Called: Tiller Constructors Partnr Inc (P-1043)*

Tiller Constructors Partnr Inc .... D....... 714 771-5600
   306 W Katella Ave Ste A Orange (92867) *(P-1043)*

Tilton Pacific Cnstr Inc .... D....... 408 551-0492
   2216 The Alameda Santa Clara (95050) *(P-20229)*

Tim Hofer Inc .... C....... 559 732-6676
   148 N Akers St Visalia (93291) *(P-10973)*

TIMBER CREEK GOLF COURSE, Roseville *Also Called: Sun City Rsvlle Cmnty Assn Inc (P-14292)*

Timberlake Corporation .... D....... 916 423-2198
   8322 Ferguson Ave Sacramento (95828) *(P-7595)*

Timberlake Medical Gas Supply, Sacramento *Also Called: Timberlake Corporation (P-7595)*

Timberlake Painting, Murrieta *Also Called: Temecula Valley Drywall Inc (P-1968)*

Time Motion Tools Inc .... D....... 858 679-0303
   12778 Brookprinter Pl Poway (92064) *(P-5736)*

Time Warner, Los Angeles *Also Called: Spectrum MGT Holdg Co LLC (P-4520)*

Time Warner, San Diego *Also Called: Spectrum MGT Holdg Co LLC (P-4522)*

Time Warner, Burbank *Also Called: Time Warner Cable Entps LLC (P-4523)*

Time Warner, Burbank *Also Called: Time Warner Cable Entps LLC (P-4524)*

Time Warner, Santa Monica *Also Called: Time Warner Companies Inc (P-4525)*

Time Warner Cable Entps LLC .... D....... 818 972-0808
   3500 W Olive Ave Ste 1000 Burbank (91505) *(P-4523)*

Time Warner Cable Entps LLC .... D....... 818 977-7840
   4000 Warner Blvd Burbank (91526) *(P-4524)*

Time Warner Companies Inc .... A....... 310 315-4437
   2939 Nebraska Ave Santa Monica (90404) *(P-4525)*

Timec, Benicia *Also Called: Timec Companies Inc (P-1322)*

Timec, E Rncho Dmngz *Also Called: Timec Companies Inc (P-1323)*

Timec Acquisitions Inc (DH) .... A....... 707 642-2222
   155 Corporate Pl Vallejo (94590) *(P-1321)*

Timec Companies Inc (DH) .... B....... 707 642-2222
   473 E Channel Rd Benicia (94510) *(P-1322)*

Timec Companies Inc .... C....... 310 885-4710
   2997 E Maria St E Rncho Dmngz (90221) *(P-1323)*

Timeshare Compliance, Aliso Viejo *Also Called: Pandora Marketing LLC (P-20500)*

Timmerman Starlite Trckg Inc .... D....... 209 538-1706
   3955 Starlite Dr Ceres (95307) *(P-3552)*

Timmons Volkswagen, Long Beach *Also Called: Walter Timmons Enterprises Inc (P-7328)*

Tinco Sheet Metal Inc .... C....... 323 263-0511
   958 N Eastern Ave Los Angeles (90063) *(P-2089)*

Tintri, Mountain View *Also Called: Tintri Inc (P-12685)*

Tintri Inc .... B....... 650 810-8200
   303 Ravendale Dr Mountain View (94043) *(P-12685)*

Tiny Pictures Inc .... D....... 415 513-5998
   454 Natoma St San Francisco (94103) *(P-10578)*

Tinyco Inc .... C....... 415 644-8101
   225 Bush St Ste 1900 San Francisco (94104) *(P-7450)*

Tire Pros, Simi Valley *Also Called: Am-Pac Tire Dist Inc (P-7341)*

Tireco Inc (PA) .... C....... 310 767-7990
   500 W 190th St Ste 600 Gardena (90248) *(P-5074)*

Tires Warehouse LLC .... B....... 714 432-8851
   18203 Mount Baldy Cir Fountain Valley (92708) *(P-7379)*

Tissue-Grown Corporation .... D....... 805 525-1975
   15245 W Telegraph Rd Santa Paula (93060) *(P-19785)*

Titan Led .... D....... 805 523-7500
   11959 Discovery Ct Moorpark (93021) *(P-8769)*

Titan Mfg & Distrg Inc .... D....... 559 475-0882
   480 E North Ave Ste 101 Fresno (93706) *(P-5982)*

Titan Newman Inc .... D....... 209 862-2977
   1649 L St Newman (95360) *(P-5931)*

Titan Oilfield Services, Bakersfield *Also Called: Titan Oilfield Services Inc (P-629)*

Titan Oilfield Services Inc .... D....... 661 861-1630
   21535 Kratzmeyer Rd Bakersfield (93314) *(P-629)*

Titan Solar, Woodland Hills *Also Called: Memeged Tevuot Shemesh (P-1499)*

Titan Tank Lines, Sanger *Also Called: D & D Cahill Inc (P-13255)*

Titan Wolrdwide, Cerritos *Also Called: Silver Hawk Freight Inc (P-4095)*

Titanum Health Care .... D....... 213 765-8123
   1414 S Grand Ave Los Angeles (90015) *(P-20584)*

Title Resource Group LLC .... D....... 818 291-4400
   801 N Brand Blvd Glendale (91203) *(P-9240)*

TITLE RESOURCE GROUP LLC, Glendale *Also Called: Title Resource Group LLC (P-9240)*

Tivo, San Jose *Also Called: Tivo Corporation (P-9458)*

Tivo Corporation (HQ) .... D....... 408 519-9100
   2160 Gold St San Jose (95002) *(P-9458)*

Tjd LLC .... C....... 209 357-3420
   1685 Shaffer Rd Atwater (95301) *(P-15903)*

ALPHABETIC SECTION

Tk Elevator Corporation .... D....... 916 376-8700
  940 Riverside Pkwy Ste 20 West Sacramento (95605) *(P-2250)*
Tk Elevator Corporation .... C....... 510 476-1900
  14400 Catalina St San Leandro (94577) *(P-5873)*
Tk Elevator Corporation .... C....... 619 596-7220
  1965 Gillespie Way Ste 101 El Cajon (92020) *(P-5874)*
Tk1sc .... C....... 949 751-5800
  15231 Laguna Canyon Rd Ste 100 Irvine (92618) *(P-19416)*
Tka, La Palma *Also Called: Tech Knowledge Associates LLC (P-13804)*
Tks Wireless Inc .... C....... 510 227-6440
  3320 Foothill Blvd Oakland (94601) *(P-4237)*
TL Montgomery & Associates Inc .... C....... 323 583-1645
  2833 Leonis Blvd Ste 205 Vernon (90058) *(P-6680)*
TLC of Bay Area Inc .... D....... 408 988-7667
  991 Clyde Ave Santa Clara (95054) *(P-15704)*
Tlcs Inc .... C....... 916 441-0123
  650 Howe Ave Ste 400-A Sacramento (95825) *(P-18151)*
Tld Acquisition Co LLC C
  505 S 7th Ave City Of Industry (91746) *(P-6681)*
Tld Distribution Co, City Of Industry *Also Called: Tld Acquisition Co LLC (P-6681)*
Tm Claims Service Inc .... D....... 626 568-7800
  800 E Colorado Blvd Pasadena (91101) *(P-8672)*
Tm Highland Insurance Services, South Pasadena *Also Called: Tokio Marine Highland Insurance Services Inc (P-8673)*
Tm Holdco LLC (PA) C
  50 1st St Ste 600 San Francisco (94105) *(P-10721)*
Tm Sleeves LLC .... C....... 415 374-8210
  475 14th St Ste 200 Oakland (94612) *(P-10681)*
TMC Financing .... D....... 415 989-8855
  1611 Telegraph Ave Oakland (94612) *(P-13511)*
Tms Health Solutions .... D....... 844 867-8444
  360 Post St Ste 500 San Francisco (94108) *(P-17341)*
TMT Industries Inc .... D....... 909 493-3441
  14774 Jurupa Ave Fontana (92337) *(P-3553)*
Tmt Intrntonal Observatory LLC .... D....... 626 395-1651
  100 W Walnut St Ste 300 Pasadena (91124) *(P-19921)*
Tmx Aerospace .... C....... 562 215-4410
  12821 Carmenita Rd Unit F Santa Fe Springs (90670) *(P-5526)*
Tmz Productions Inc (HQ) .... D....... 818 972-8000
  8033 W Sunset Blvd Los Angeles (90046) *(P-4464)*
Tmz TV, Los Angeles *Also Called: Chm Productions Inc (P-13828)*
Tnhc Realty and Cnstr Inc .... C....... 925 244-0700
  1990 N California Blvd Ste 650 Walnut Creek (94596) *(P-728)*
Tnk Therapeutics Inc (HQ) .... C....... 858 210-3700
  9380 Judicial Dr San Diego (92121) *(P-19786)*
TO HELP EVERYONE HEALTH AND WE, Los Angeles *Also Called: Clinic Inc (P-14688)*
Toan D Nguyen DDS Inc .... D....... 909 599-3398
  213 N San Dimas Ave San Dimas (91773) *(P-15251)*
TOAN D NGUYEN DDS INC, San Dimas *Also Called: Toan D Nguyen DDS Inc (P-15251)*
Toaster LLC .... D....... 917 655-6440
  7083 Hollywood Blvd Fl 5 Los Angeles (90028) *(P-19852)*
Tobin Lucks, West Hills *Also Called: Tobin Lucks A Prof Corp (P-17668)*
Tobin Lucks A Prof Corp (PA) .... D....... 818 226-3400
  8511 Fallbrook Ave Ste 400 West Hills (91304) *(P-17668)*
Toby Wells YMCA, San Diego *Also Called: YMCA of San Diego County (P-18937)*
Todays IV .... A....... 213 835-4016
  404 S Figueroa St Ste 516 Los Angeles (90071) *(P-10314)*
Todd Plumbing, Visalia *Also Called: Todd Plumbing Inc (P-13806)*
Todd Plumbing Inc .... C....... 559 651-5820
  1701 Clancy Ct Visalia (93291) *(P-13806)*
Together Labs Inc .... C....... 650 231-4688
  901 Marshall St # 200 Redwood City (94063) *(P-4351)*
Toiyabe Indian Health Prj Inc (PA) .... D....... 760 873-8461
  250 N See Vee Ln Bishop (93514) *(P-15252)*
Tokio Marine Highland Insurance Services Inc (DH) .. D....... 626 463-6486
  899 El Centro St South Pasadena (91030) *(P-8673)*
Tokio Marine Michido, Pasadena *Also Called: Tm Claims Service Inc (P-8672)*
Tokyopop Inc (PA) .... D....... 323 920-5967
  4136 Del Rey Ave Marina Del Rey (90292) *(P-2550)*
TOLL GLOBAL FORWARDING SCS (USA) INC., Jurupa Valley *Also Called: Toll Global Fwdg Scs Inc (P-4107)*

Toll Global Fwdg Scs USA Inc .... D....... 951 360-8310
  3355 Dulles Dr Jurupa Valley (91752) *(P-4107)*
Toll Global Fwdg Scs USA Inc .... C....... 732 750-9000
  400 Westmont Dr 450 San Pedro (90731) *(P-4108)*
Tollhouse Hotel, Los Gatos *Also Called: Trevi Partners A Calif LP (P-10324)*
Tom Bell Chevrolet, Redlands *Also Called: Dick Dewese Chevrolet Inc (P-7195)*
Tom Dreher Sales Inc .... D....... 562 355-4074
  2021 W 17th St Long Beach (90813) *(P-5389)*
Tom Ferry Coaching, Santa Ana *Also Called: Ferry International LLC (P-20375)*
Tom Ferry Your Coach, Santa Ana *Also Called: Success Strategies Inst Inc (P-18252)*
Tomarco Contractor Spc Inc (PA) .... D....... 714 523-1771
  14848 Northam St La Mirada (90638) *(P-5737)*
Tomarco Fastening Systems, La Mirada *Also Called: Tomarco Contractor Spc Inc (P-5737)*
Tomas Jewelry, Arcata *Also Called: Toucan Inc (P-6028)*
Tommie's Home Health Care, Baldwin Park *Also Called: Tommies Medical Ctr Phrm Inc (P-7529)*
Tommies Medical Ctr Phrm Inc .... D....... 714 961-7930
  410 Cloverleaf Dr Baldwin Park (91706) *(P-7529)*
Tommy Gun Plastering Inc .... D....... 909 795-9966
  944 4th St Calimesa (92320) *(P-1969)*
Toms Truck Center Inc .... C....... 714 835-1978
  1008 E 4th St Santa Ana (92701) *(P-7314)*
Tonal Systems Inc .... D....... 855 698-6625
  617 Bryant St San Francisco (94107) *(P-14575)*
Tonomi Inc .... B....... 650 523-5000
  4600 Bohannon Dr Ste 220 Menlo Park (94025) *(P-11981)*
Tony Lrssas Anmal Rscue Fndtio .... D....... 925 256-1273
  2890 Mitchell Dr Walnut Creek (94598) *(P-343)*
Tonys Express Inc (PA) .... C....... 909 427-8700
  10613 Jasmine St Fontana (92337) *(P-3768)*
Tonys Fine Foods (HQ) .... B....... 916 374-4000
  3575 Reed Ave West Sacramento (95605) *(P-6443)*
Toolworks Inc .... B....... 510 649-1322
  3075 Adeline St Ste 230 Berkeley (94703) *(P-18152)*
Toolworks Inc (PA) .... D....... 415 733-0990
  25 Kearny St Ste 400 San Francisco (94108) *(P-18253)*
Toor Farming LLC .... D....... 559 500-1331
  27725 Road 92 Visalia (93277) *(P-201)*
Top Finance Company, Chatsworth *Also Called: Platinum Group Companies Inc (P-9327)*
Top Priority Couriers Inc (PA) .... D....... 951 781-1000
  1257 Columbia Ave Ste D1 Riverside (92507) *(P-3630)*
Topa Insurance Company (HQ) .... D....... 310 201-0451
  1800 Avenue Of The Stars Ste 1200 Los Angeles (90067) *(P-8674)*
Topa Property Group Inc (HQ) .... C....... 310 203-9199
  1800 Avenue Of The Stars Ste 1400 Los Angeles (90067) *(P-8770)*
Topbuild Services Group Corp .... A....... 408 882-0411
  1341 Oakland Rd San Jose (95112) *(P-2322)*
Topco Sales, Simi Valley *Also Called: Wsm Investments LLC (P-9460)*
Topcon, Livermore *Also Called: Topcon Positioning Systems Inc (P-3044)*
Topcon Positioning Systems Inc (DH) .... C....... 925 245-8300
  7400 National Dr Livermore (94550) *(P-3044)*
Topgolf Callaway Brands Corp (PA) .... B....... 760 931-1771
  2180 Rutherford Rd Carlsbad (92008) *(P-3096)*
Topia Mobility Inc (PA) .... D....... 415 666-2130
  1900 S Norfolk St Ste 350 San Mateo (94403) *(P-20585)*
Topmark Funding LLC .... D....... 866 627-6644
  516 Gibson Dr Ste 160 Roseville (95678) *(P-7911)*
Topson Downs, Culver City *Also Called: Topson Downs California Inc (P-7404)*
Topson Downs California Inc (PA) .... C....... 310 558-0300
  3840 Watseka Ave Culver City (90232) *(P-7404)*
Toptal LLC .... B....... 888 604-3188
  548 Market St Ste 36879 San Francisco (94104) *(P-12897)*
Topwin Corporation (PA) .... D....... 310 325-2255
  1808 Abalone Ave Torrance (90501) *(P-6189)*
Torch Leadership Labs, San Francisco *Also Called: Redfish Labs Inc (P-12868)*
Toro Enterprises Inc .... D....... 805 483-4515
  2101 Ventura Blvd Oxnard (93036) *(P-1174)*
Torrance Care Center West Inc .... C....... 310 370-4561
  4333 Torrance Blvd Torrance (90503) *(P-15705)*
Torrance Cultural Art Center, Torrance *Also Called: City of Torrance (P-20915)*

Torrance Health Assn Inc — ALPHABETIC SECTION

Torrance Health Assn Inc (PA) .... A 310 325-9110
   3330 Lomita Blvd Torrance (90505) *(P-16575)*

Torrance Marriott Hotel, Torrance *Also Called: Xld Group LLC (P-10386)*

Torrance Memorial Breast Diagn, Manhattan Beach *Also Called: Torrance Memorial Medical Ctr (P-16577)*

Torrance Memorial Medical Ctr .... B 310 784-6316
   3333 Skypark Dr Ste 200 Torrance (90505) *(P-16576)*

Torrance Memorial Medical Ctr .... B 310 939-7847
   855 Manhattan Beach Blvd Ste 208 Manhattan Beach (90266) *(P-16577)*

Torrance Memorial Medical Ctr .... B 310 784-3740
   22411 Hawthorne Blvd Torrance (90505) *(P-16578)*

Torrance Memorial Medical Ctr (HQ) .... A 310 325-9110
   3330 Lomita Blvd Torrance (90505) *(P-16579)*

Torrey Point Group LLC .... D 408 734-1500
   1350 Dell Ave Ste 206 Campbell (95008) *(P-11982)*

Torrey Suites LP .... D 858 720-9500
   3939 Ocean Bluff Ave San Diego (92130) *(P-10315)*

Torreyana Grille .... D 858 558-1500
   10950 N Torrey Pines Rd La Jolla (92037) *(P-10316)*

Torreypoint, Campbell *Also Called: Torrey Point Group LLC (P-11982)*

Torrid Merchandising Inc .... B 626 667-1002
   18501 San Jose Ave City Of Industry (91748) *(P-20586)*

Toscana Country Club Inc .... C 760 404-1444
   76009 Via Club Villa Indian Wells (92210) *(P-14473)*

Toshiba, Irvine *Also Called: Toshiba Amer Elctrnic Cmpnnts (P-2882)*

Toshiba, South San Francisco *Also Called: Toshiba America Mri Inc (P-3078)*

Toshiba, Lake Forest *Also Called: Toshiba Amer Bus Solutions Inc (P-5257)*

Toshiba Amer Bus Solutions Inc (DH) .... B 949 462-6000
   25530 Commercentre Dr Lake Forest (92630) *(P-5257)*

Toshiba Amer Elctrnic Cmpnnts (DH) .... B 949 462-7700
   5231 California Ave Irvine (92617) *(P-2882)*

Toshiba America Inc .... A 212 596-0600
   5241 California Ave Ste 200 Irvine (92617) *(P-2883)*

Toshiba America Mri Inc .... C 650 737-6686
   280 Utah Ave Ste 200 South San Francisco (94080) *(P-3078)*

Tosoh Bioscience Inc .... D 650 615-4970
   6000 Shoreline Ct Ste 101 South San Francisco (94080) *(P-5455)*

Tosoh USA, South San Francisco *Also Called: Tosoh Bioscience Inc (P-5455)*

Total Airport Services LLC .... C 650 358-0144
   3537 Branson Dr San Mateo (94403) *(P-3918)*

Total Clean, La Verne *Also Called: Haaker Equipment Company (P-5940)*

Total Cmmnicator Solutions Inc .... D 619 277-1488
   11150 Sta Monica Ste 600 Los Angeles (90025) *(P-12381)*

Total Debt Management, Irvine *Also Called: Egs Financial Care Inc (P-10740)*

Total Garments, Westlake Village *Also Called: Hec Inc (P-5655)*

Total Logistics Online LLC .... D 714 526-3559
   628 N Gilbert St Fullerton (92833) *(P-4109)*

Total Quality Maintenance Inc .... C 650 846-4700
   895 Commercial St Palo Alto (94303) *(P-10974)*

Total Recon Solutions Inc .... D 949 584-8417
   27 Oakbrook Trabuco Canyon (92679) *(P-20587)*

Total Telco Specialists Inc .... D 805 541-2232
   602 W Southern Ave Orange (92865) *(P-13749)*

Total Vision LLC .... C 949 652-7242
   27271 Las Ramblas Ste 200a Mission Viejo (92691) *(P-15266)*

Total Warehouse Inc .... C 480 582-3954
   2895 E Miraloma Ave Anaheim (92806) *(P-3769)*

Totally Kids Rhbilitation Hosp, Loma Linda *Also Called: Mountain View Child Care Inc (P-16277)*

Totally Kids Spcalty Hlth Care, Sun Valley *Also Called: Mountain View Child Care Inc (P-18336)*

Totex Manufacturing Inc .... D 310 326-2028
   3050 Lomita Blvd Torrance (90505) *(P-2682)*

Totten Tubes Inc (PA) .... D 626 812-0220
   500 W Danlee St Azusa (91702) *(P-5527)*

Toucan Inc (PA) .... D 707 822-6662
   824 L St Ste 6 Arcata (95521) *(P-6028)*

Touchofmodern Inc .... C 888 868-1232
   30063 Ahern Ave Union City (94587) *(P-13512)*

Touchpint Rest Innovations Inc .... C 800 992-9540
   263 California Ave Palo Alto (94306) *(P-11983)*

Touchpoint Rest Innovations, Palo Alto *Also Called: Touchpint Rest Innovations Inc (P-11983)*

Tour Master, Calabasas Hills *Also Called: Helmet House LLC (P-6176)*

Tourcoach Transportation, Commerce *Also Called: Screamline Investment Corp (P-3970)*

Tourdates.com, San Francisco *Also Called: Launch Media Inc (P-4305)*

Toward Maximum Independence (PA) .... C 858 467-0600
   4740 Murphy Canyon Rd Ste 300 San Diego (92123) *(P-18153)*

Tower Glass Inc .... D 619 596-6199
   9570 Pathway St Ste A Santee (92071) *(P-2207)*

Tower Hmtlogy Oncology Med Grou .... D 310 888-8680
   9090 Wilshire Blvd Ste 200 Beverly Hills (90211) *(P-15127)*

Town & Cntry Event Rentals Inc (PA) .... B 818 908-4211
   7725 Airport Business Pkwy Van Nuys (91406) *(P-11056)*

Town & Cntry Event Rentals Inc .... B 805 770-5729
   1 N Calle Cesar Chavez Santa Barbara (93103) *(P-11057)*

Town & Country Roofing, Brentwood *Also Called: T&C Roofing Inc (P-2087)*

Town and Country, San Diego *Also Called: Atlas Hotels Inc (P-9619)*

Town and Country Hotel, San Diego *Also Called: Hotel Circle Property LLC (P-9870)*

Town Cntry Mnor of Chrstn Mssn .... C 714 547-7581
   555 E Memory Ln Side Santa Ana (92706) *(P-15706)*

Town of Danville .... D 925 314-3400
   420 Front St Danville (94526) *(P-14576)*

Towne Drywall Inc .... D 619 334-3750
   10612 Prospect Ave Ste 105 Santee (92071) *(P-1970)*

Towne Ford Sales, Redwood City *Also Called: Towne Motor Company (P-7315)*

Towne Motor Company .... C 650 366-5744
   1 Bair Island Rd Redwood City (94063) *(P-7315)*

TownePlace Stes Anaheim Mingate, Anaheim *Also Called: Harvard Grand LP (P-9838)*

TownePlace Suites El Centro, El Centro *Also Called: El Centro Hospitality 2 LLC (P-9775)*

Toyo Tire USA Corp (DH) .... D 714 236-2080
   5665 Plaza Dr Ste 300 Cypress (90630) *(P-5075)*

Toyon Research Corporation (PA) .... C 805 968-6787
   6800 Cortona Dr Goleta (93117) *(P-19417)*

Toyota Arena .... D 909 244-5500
   4000 E Ontario Center Pkwy Ontario (91764) *(P-14577)*

Toyota Carlsbad, Carlsbad *Also Called: Oceanside Auto Country Inc (P-7271)*

Toyota Downtown La .... C 213 342-3646
   714 W Olympic Blvd Ste 1131 Los Angeles (90015) *(P-7380)*

Toyota Material Hdlg Nthrn CA, Salinas *Also Called: Rjms Corporation (P-5867)*

Toyota Material Hdlg Nthrn Cal, Livermore *Also Called: Rjms Corporation (P-7290)*

Toyota Material Hdlg Solutions, Santa Fe Springs *Also Called: Rebas Inc (P-5864)*

Toyota of Downtown L.A., Los Angeles *Also Called: Toyota Downtown La (P-7380)*

Toyota of El Cajon, El Cajon *Also Called: K Motors Inc (P-7338)*

Toyota of Glendora, Glendora *Also Called: Seidner-Miller Inc (P-7296)*

Toyota of Orange Inc .... C 714 639-6750
   1400 N Tustin St Orange (92867) *(P-7316)*

Toyota of Oxnard, Oxnard *Also Called: DCH California Motors Inc (P-7193)*

Toyota of Riverside Inc .... C 951 687-1622
   7870 Indiana Ave Riverside (92504) *(P-7317)*

Toyota of Santa Cruz, Capitola *Also Called: Capitola Imports Inc (P-7179)*

Toyota Scion Place, Garden Grove *Also Called: Noarus Tgg (P-7270)*

TP USA, Claremont *Also Called: Technip Usa Inc (P-19405)*

Tp-Link USA Corporation .... D 562 528-7700
   3760 Kilroy Airport Way Ste 600 Long Beach (90806) *(P-5362)*

Tpg Growth, San Francisco *Also Called: Tarrant Capital Ip LLC (P-8222)*

Tps Aviation Inc (PA) .... D 510 475-1010
   1515 Crocker Ave Hayward (94544) *(P-5713)*

Tps Parking Management LLC .... D 310 846-4747
   9101 S Sepulveda Blvd Los Angeles (90045) *(P-13629)*

Tpusa - Fhcs Inc (DH) .... C 213 873-5100
   215 N Marengo Ave Ste 160 Pasadena (91101) *(P-12699)*

Tpx Communications, Los Angeles *Also Called: Mpower Holding Corporation (P-4317)*

Tq Logistics Inc .... D 408 565-0188
   700 Laurelwood Rd Santa Clara (95054) *(P-3554)*

Trace3, Irvine *Also Called: Trace3 LLC (P-12533)*

Trace3, San Diego *Also Called: Trace3 LLC (P-20589)*

Trace3 Inc .... D 310 220-0164
   2120 E Grand Ave Ste 145 El Segundo (90245) *(P-20588)*

Trace3 LLC (HQ) .... C 949 333-2300
   7505 Irvine Center Dr Ste 100 Irvine (92618) *(P-12533)*

ALPHABETIC SECTION — Transtech Engineers Inc

Trace3 LLC .... D....... 858 345-2650
  12636 High Bluff Dr Ste 300 San Diego (92130) *(P-20589)*
TRACE3, INC., El Segundo *Also Called: Trace3 Inc (P-20588)*
Trackonomy Systems Inc (PA) .... B....... 833 872-2566
  214 Devcon Dr San Jose (95112) *(P-12382)*
Trackr Inc .... D....... 855 981-1690
  7410 Hollister Ave Santa Barbara (93117) *(P-11984)*
Tracpatch Health Inc .... D....... 916 355-7123
  2020 L St Ste 220 Sacramento (95811) *(P-5456)*
Tracy Auto LP .... D....... 209 834-1111
  2895 Naglee Rd Tracy (95304) *(P-7318)*
Tracy Dlta Solid Waste Mgt Inc .... D....... 209 835-0601
  30703 S Macarthur Dr Tracy (95377) *(P-4946)*
Tracy Industries Inc .... C....... 562 692-9034
  3200 E Guasti Rd Ste 100 Ontario (91761) *(P-2768)*
Tracy Ryder Landscape Inc .... D....... 949 858-7017
  22421 Gilberto Ste A Rcho Sta Marg (92688) *(P-540)*
Tracy Ryder Landscape Cnstr, Rcho Sta Marg *Also Called: Tracy Ryder Landscape Inc (P-540)*
Tracy Sutter Community Hosp .... B....... 209 835-1500
  1420 N Tracy Blvd Tracy (95376) *(P-16580)*
Tracy Toyota, Tracy *Also Called: Tracy Auto LP (P-7318)*
Trade Desk Inc (PA) .... B....... 805 585-3434
  42 N Chestnut St Ventura (93001) *(P-11985)*
Tradeshift Holdings Inc (PA) .... D....... 800 381-3585
  221 Main St Ste 250 San Francisco (94105) *(P-9343)*
Tradesmen International, Cypress *Also Called: Tradesmen International LLC (P-20230)*
Tradesmen International LLC .... D....... 949 588-3280
  11145 Knott Ave Ste G Cypress (90630) *(P-20230)*
Tradewinds Lodge (PA) .... D....... 707 964-4761
  400 S Main St Fort Bragg (95437) *(P-10317)*
Tradition Golf Club, La Quinta *Also Called: Chapman Golf Development LLC (P-14248)*
Tradition Golf Club Associates .... D....... 760 564-3355
  78505 Avenue 52 La Quinta (92253) *(P-14474)*
Traditions Golf LLC .... D....... 408 323-5200
  23600 Mckean Rd San Jose (95141) *(P-14294)*
Traffic Control Service Inc C
  4695 Macarthur Ct Ste 1100 Newport Beach (92660) *(P-11058)*
Traffic Management (PA) .... C....... 562 595-4278
  4900 Airport Plaza Dr Ste 300 Long Beach (90815) *(P-13513)*
Traffic Management Pdts Inc .... A....... 800 763-3999
  4900 Airport Plaza Dr Ste 300 Long Beach (90815) *(P-12383)*
Trail Lines Inc .... D....... 562 758-6980
  9415 Sorensen Ave Santa Fe Springs (90670) *(P-3426)*
Trailer Park Inc (PA) .... D....... 310 845-3000
  6922 Hollywood Blvd Fl 12 Los Angeles (90028) *(P-10682)*
Traina Dried Fruit Inc .... C....... 209 892-5472
  280 S 1st St Patterson (95363) *(P-6682)*
Traina Dried Fruit Inc (PA) .... D....... 209 892-5472
  337 Lemon Ave Patterson (95363) *(P-6683)*
Traina Foods, Patterson *Also Called: Traina Dried Fruit Inc (P-6682)*
Traina Foods, Patterson *Also Called: Traina Dried Fruit Inc (P-6683)*
Trammell Crow Centl Texas Ltd .... D....... 310 765-2600
  2221 Rosecrans Ave El Segundo (90245) *(P-9196)*
Trammell Crow Residential Co .... D....... 714 966-9355
  949 S Coast Dr Ste 400 Costa Mesa (92626) *(P-8865)*
Trams Inc (DH) .... D....... 310 641-8726
  7 Lower Blackwater Cyn Rd Rolling Hills (90274) *(P-12534)*
Trane, Sunnyvale *Also Called: Specialty A/C Products Inc (P-5773)*
Trane, Rocklin *Also Called: Trane US Inc (P-5774)*
Trane US Inc .... D....... 916 577-1100
  4145 Delmar Ave Ste 2 Rocklin (95677) *(P-5774)*
Tranquility Incorporated .... C....... 925 825-4280
  1050 San Miguel Rd Concord (94518) *(P-15904)*
Trans AM Travel, Los Angeles *Also Called: Trans-American Travel (P-3953)*
Trans Western Polymers Inc .... B....... 925 449-7800
  7539 Las Positas Rd Livermore (94551) *(P-2531)*
Trans-American Travel .... D....... 310 670-2111
  4929 Wilshire Blvd Ste 310 Los Angeles (90010) *(P-3953)*
Trans-Pak Incorporated .... C....... 310 618-6937
  2601 S Garnsey St Santa Ana (92707) *(P-13514)*

Trans-West Services Inc .... B....... 661 381-2900
  8503 Crippen St Bakersfield (93311) *(P-13055)*
Transamerica Corporation .... D....... 415 392-9742
  600 Montgomery St Fl 16 San Francisco (94111) *(P-8248)*
Transamerica Finance Corp (DH) .... C....... 415 983-4000
  600 Montgomery St Fl 16 San Francisco (94111) *(P-8249)*
Transamerica Occidental Life Insurance Company .... A....... 213 742-2111
  1150 S Olive St Fl 23 Los Angeles (90015) *(P-8250)*
Transamerican, Escondido *Also Called: Transamerican Direct Inc (P-10778)*
Transamerican Direct Inc .... D....... 760 745-5343
  355 State Pl Escondido (92029) *(P-10778)*
Transamerican Dissolution LLC (HQ) .... C....... 310 900-5500
  400 W Artesia Blvd Compton (90220) *(P-7381)*
Transcentra Inc .... A....... 310 603-0105
  20500 Belshaw Ave Carson (90746) *(P-12535)*
Transcosmos Omniconnect LLC .... D....... 310 630-0072
  879 W 190th St Ste 1050 Gardena (90248) *(P-20231)*
Transdev Services Inc .... B....... 530 342-6851
  326 Huss Dr Chico (95928) *(P-3222)*
Transdev Services Inc .... A....... 626 357-7912
  5640 Peck Rd Arcadia (91006) *(P-3298)*
Transdev Services Inc .... C....... 619 401-4503
  544 Vernon Way El Cajon (92020) *(P-3299)*
Transdev Services Inc .... C....... 408 282-4706
  2361 Airport Blvd San Jose (95110) *(P-3300)*
Transfair USA .... C....... 510 663-5260
  360 Grand Ave Unit 311 Oakland (94610) *(P-19922)*
Transglobal Holding Company .... D....... 626 447-7888
  1045 W Huntington Dr Ste 200 Arcadia (91007) *(P-8061)*
Transiris Corporation .... D....... 650 303-3495
  530 Sycamore St San Carlos (94070) *(P-20590)*
Transit Air Cargo Inc .... D....... 714 571-0393
  2204 E 4th St Santa Ana (92705) *(P-4110)*
Transitamerica Services Inc .... C....... 408 961-4350
  93 Cahill St San Jose (95110) *(P-3223)*
Transitions - Mental Hlth Assn (PA) .... D....... 805 540-6500
  784 High St San Luis Obispo (93401) *(P-17144)*
Translations LLC .... D....... 415 373-7396
  3255 Broderick St San Francisco (94123) *(P-13515)*
Transltnal Plmnary Immnlogy RE .... D....... 562 490-9900
  701 E 28th St Ste 419 Long Beach (90806) *(P-15128)*
Transnational Computer Tech, El Segundo *Also Called: Mesfin Enterprises (P-12488)*
Transom Capital Group LLC (PA) .... D....... 424 293-2818
  10990 Wilshire Blvd Ste 440 Los Angeles (90024) *(P-9574)*
Transom Post Midco LLC .... C....... 312 254-3300
  100 N Pacific Coast Hwy # 17 El Segundo (90245) *(P-9344)*
Transon Media LLC .... D....... 415 621-9830
  548 Market St Ste 41895 San Francisco (94104) *(P-4556)*
Transpac Inc .... D....... 707 452-0600
  1050 Aviator Dr Vacaville (95688) *(P-5139)*
Transpak Los Angeles, Santa Ana *Also Called: Trans-Pak Incorporated (P-13514)*
Transport Express Inc .... D....... 310 898-2000
  19801 S Santa Fe Ave Compton (90221) *(P-3599)*
Transportation, Lake Arrowhead *Also Called: Rim of World Unified Schl Dst (P-3348)*
Transportation Corridor Agency, Irvine *Also Called: Foothill / Estrn Trnsp Crrdor (P-1105)*
Transportation Department, Sacramento *Also Called: Elk Grove Unified School Dst (P-3335)*
Transportation Department, Long Beach *Also Called: Long Beach Unified School Dst (P-3346)*
Transportation Department, Culver City *Also Called: City of Culver City (P-20913)*
Transportation Service Dept, Davis *Also Called: University California Davis (P-3921)*
Transportation Services, Davis *Also Called: University California Davis (P-3353)*
Transprttion Brkg Spclists Inc .... B....... 714 754-4236
  3151 Airway Ave Ste F208 Costa Mesa (92626) *(P-3427)*
Transprttion Oprtion MGT Sltion .... C....... 858 391-0260
  1917 Palomar Oaks Way Ste 110 Carlsbad (92008) *(P-13516)*
Transprttion Oprtons MGT Sltion, Irvine *Also Called: Shimmick Construction Co Inc (P-1318)*
Transtar Metals Corp .... B....... 562 630-1400
  14001 Orange Ave Paramount (90723) *(P-5528)*
Transtech Engineers Inc (PA) .... D....... 909 595-8599
  13367 Benson Ave Chino (91710) *(P-19418)*

Transwest Truck Center LLC — 10150 Cherry Ave Fontana (92335) *(P-7319)* — D — 909 770-5170

Trantor, Menlo Park Also Called: Trantor Inc *(P-11986)*

Trantor Inc — 3723 Haven Ave Menlo Park (94025) *(P-11986)* — A — 650 777-5480

Trapeze Networks Inc — 5753 W Las Positas Blvd Pleasanton (94588) *(P-12536)* — C — 925 474-2200

Travel Store (PA) — 11601 Wilshire Blvd Ste 300 Los Angeles (90025) *(P-3954)* — D — 310 575-5540

Travel Wizard LLC — 100 Smith Ranch Rd Ste 110 San Rafael (94903) *(P-3955)* — 415 446-5252

Travelerhelpdesk.com, San Diego Also Called: Lbf Travel Inc *(P-3939)*

Travelers Insurance, Walnut Creek Also Called: Travelers Property Cslty Corp *(P-8675)*

Travelers Property Cslty Corp — 401 Lennon Ln Walnut Creek (94598) *(P-8675)* — C — 925 945-4000

Travelodge, Santa Ana Also Called: Chen & Huang Partners LP *(P-9696)*

Travelodge, Mill Valley Also Called: Nana Enterprises *(P-10036)*

Travelodge, Santa Clara Also Called: Santa Clara Travelodge *(P-10206)*

Travelodge, South Lake Tahoe Also Called: Stateline Travelodge Inc *(P-10276)*

Travelodge Downtown — 345 Marsh St San Luis Obispo (93401) *(P-10318)* — D — 805 543-6443

Travelodge Hotels Inc — 3327 Del Mar Ave Rosemead (91770) *(P-10319)* — C — 800 257-2297

Travelstore, Los Angeles Also Called: Travel Store *(P-3954)*

Travelzoo Inc — 800 W El Camino Real Mountain View (94040) *(P-10722)* — D — 650 316-6956

TRAVERE, San Diego Also Called: Travere Therapeutics Inc *(P-2610)*

Travere Therapeutics Inc (PA) — 3611 Valley Centre Dr Ste 300 San Diego (92130) *(P-2610)* — C — 888 969-7879

Travis Credit Union (PA) — 1 Travis Way Vacaville (95687) *(P-7812)* — B — 707 449-4000

Travis Flight Service Inc — 2112 Adams Ave San Leandro (94577) *(P-3919)* — D — 707 437-4900

Travis James Watts — 646 Willowgreen Cir Galt (95632) *(P-202)* — C — 209 810-6159

Traxero North America LLC — 1730 E Holly Ave Ste 740 El Segundo (90245) *(P-12384)* — D — 423 497-1164

TRC Solutions — 10680 White Rock Rd Ste 100 Rancho Cordova (95670) *(P-20866)* — C — 916 962-7001

TRC Solutions Inc (HQ) — 9685 Research Dr Ste 100 Irvine (92618) *(P-20867)* — C — 949 753-0101

Tre Venezie Inc — 4100 Cahuenga Blvd Toluca Lake (91602) *(P-7514)* — D — 818 985-4669

Treasure Data Inc (HQ) — 800 W El Camino Real Ste 180 Mountain View (94040) *(P-11987)* — D — 866 899-5386

Treasury Chateau & Estates — 10300 Chalk Hill Rd Healdsburg (95448) *(P-2396)* — C — 707 299-2600

Treasury Prime Inc — 2261 Market St # 4037 San Francisco (94114) *(P-13517)* — D — 415 439-0241

TREDC, Porterville Also Called: Tule River Economic Dev *(P-20868)*

Tree Sculpture Group — 642 Mccormick St San Leandro (94577) *(P-541)* — D — 510 562-4000

Tree Services, Redding Also Called: Maximus Tree Works LLC *(P-557)*

Treebeard Landscape Inc — 9917 Campo Rd Spring Valley (91977) *(P-470)* — D — 619 697-8302

Treeland Farms, Woodland Hills Also Called: Boething Treeland Farms Inc *(P-564)*

Treering Corporation — 217 S B St Ste 5 San Mateo (94401) *(P-12898)* — D — 650 385-8733

Treesap Farms LLC — 2500 Rainbow Valley Blvd Fallbrook (92028) *(P-203)* — D — 760 990-7770

Treivush Industries Inc — 940 W Washington Blvd Los Angeles (90015) *(P-2461)* — D — 213 745-7774

Trellisware Technologies Inc (HQ) — 10641 Scripps Summit Ct Ste 100 San Diego (92131) *(P-4238)* — C — 858 753-1600

Trench Plate Rental, Downey Also Called: National Trench Safety LLC *(P-11046)*

Trend Micro Incorporated — 3031 Tisch Way San Jose (95128) *(P-5363)* — D — 408 257-1500

Trend Micro Incorporated — 10101 N De Anza Blvd Cupertino (95014) *(P-5364)* — D — 408 257-1500

Trendsource Inc — 4891 Pacific Hwy Ste 200 San Diego (92110) *(P-19853)* — D — 619 718-7467

Trevi Partners A Calif LP — 1250 Bayshore Hwy Burlingame (94010) *(P-10320)* — D — 650 347-2381

Trevi Partners A Calif LP — 3665 Rio Rd Carmel (93923) *(P-10321)* — D — 831 624-1841

Trevi Partners A Calif LP (PA) — 5955 Coronado Ln Pleasanton (94588) *(P-10322)* — C — 925 225-4000

Trevi Partners A Calif LP — 160 Shoreline Hwy Mill Valley (94941) *(P-10323)* — D — 415 332-5700

Trevi Partners A Calif LP — 140 S Santa Cruz Ave Los Gatos (95030) *(P-10324)* — D — 408 395-7070

Trey Arch LLC — 3420 Ocean Park Blvd Ste 2000 Santa Monica (90405) *(P-5365)* — B — 310 581-4700

Trg Inc — 1350 Abbot Kinney Blvd # 101 Venice (90291) *(P-9197)* — D — 310 396-6750

Trg Insurance Services — 4675 Macarthur Ct Newport Beach (92660) *(P-8676)* — C — 949 474-1550

Tri City Mental Health Center, Pomona Also Called: Tri-City Mental Health Auth *(P-17145)*

Tri Counties Bank (HQ) — 63 Constitution Dr Chico (95973) *(P-7740)* — D — 530 898-0300

Tri Counties Bank — 975 El Camino Real South San Francisco (94080) *(P-7741)* — C — 650 583-8450

Tri Pointe, Irvine Also Called: Tri Pointe Homes Inc *(P-781)*

Tri Pointe Homes Inc — 57 Furlong Irvine (92602) *(P-779)* — C — 714 389-5933

Tri Pointe Homes Inc — 2700 Camino Ramon Ste 130 San Ramon (94583) *(P-780)* — C — 925 804-2220

Tri Pointe Homes Inc (HQ) — 3161 Michelson Dr Ste 1500 Irvine (92612) *(P-781)* — D — 949 438-1400

Tri Pointe Homes Inc — 5 Peters Canyon Rd Ste 100 Irvine (92606) *(P-798)* — C — 949 478-8600

Tri Star Engineering Inc — 6774 Calle De Linea Ste 106 San Diego (92154) *(P-19419)* — D — 619 710-8038

Tri Star Spt Entrmt Group Inc — 9255 W Sunset Blvd Fl 2 West Hollywood (90069) *(P-14107)* — D — 615 309-0969

Tri Tool Inc (HQ) — 3041 Sunrise Blvd Rancho Cordova (95742) *(P-5875)* — C — 916 288-6100

Tri-Ad — 221 W Crest St Ste 300 Escondido (92025) *(P-8677)* — D — 760 743-7555

Tri-Ad, Escondido Also Called: Tri-Ad Actuaries Inc *(P-20591)*

Tri-Ad Actuaries Inc — 221 W Crest St Ste 300 Escondido (92025) *(P-20591)* — C — 760 743-7555

Tri-City Hospital District — 6250 El Camino Real Carlsbad (92009) *(P-14238)* — B — 760 931-3171

Tri-City Hospital District (PA) — 4002 Vista Way Oceanside (92056) *(P-16581)* — A — 760 724-8411

Tri-City Medical Center, Oceanside Also Called: Tri-City Hospital District *(P-16581)*

Tri-City Mental Health Auth (PA) — 2008 N Garey Ave Pomona (91767) *(P-17145)* — D — 909 623-6131

Tri-City Wellness Center, Carlsbad Also Called: Tri-City Hospital District *(P-14238)*

Tri-Cnties Assn For Dvlpmntlly (PA) — 520 E Montecito St Santa Barbara (93103) *(P-18154)* — D — 805 962-7881

Tri-Cnties Assn For Dvlpmntlly — 1146 Farmhouse Ln San Luis Obispo (93401) *(P-18155)* — C — 805 543-2833

TRI-COUNTIES REGIONAL CENTER, Santa Barbara Also Called: Tri-Cnties Assn For Dvlpmntlly *(P-18154)*

Tri-Counties Regional Center, San Luis Obispo Also Called: Tri-Cnties Assn For Dvlpmntlly *(P-18155)*

Tri-Marine Fish Company LLC — 220 Cannery St San Pedro (90731) *(P-6486)* — D — 310 547-1144

Tri-Modal Dist Svcs Inc — 22560 Lucerne St Carson (90745) *(P-3770)* — D — 310 522-1844

Tri-Mountain, Irwindale Also Called: Mountain Gear Corporation *(P-6182)*

Tri-Signal Integration Inc (PA) — 28110 Avenue Stanford Unit D Santa Clarita (91355) *(P-1864)* — D — 818 566-8558

Tri-Signal Integration Inc — 5007 Windplay Dr Ste 1 El Dorado Hills (95762) *(P-1865)* — C — 916 933-3155

Tri-Tech Logistics LLC — 1370 Brea Blvd Ste 200 Fullerton (92835) *(P-4111)* — C — 855 373-7049

Tri-Tech Restoration Co Inc — 3301 N San Fernando Blvd Burbank (91504) *(P-851)* — D — 818 565-3900

Tri-Union Seafoods LLC (DH) — 2150 E Grand Ave El Segundo (90245) *(P-6487)* — D — 424 397-8556

ALPHABETIC SECTION — Troon Golf LLC

Tri-Valley YMCA, Pleasanton *Also Called: Young MNS Chrstn Assn of E Bay (P-18980)*

Tri-West Ltd (PA) .... C...... 562 692-9166
  12005 Pike St Santa Fe Springs (90670) *(P-5140)*

Triad Broadcasting, Monterey *Also Called: Triad Broadcasting Company (P-4406)*

Triad Broadcasting Company (PA) .... C...... 831 655-6350
  2511 Garden Rd Ste A104 Monterey (93940) *(P-4406)*

Triad Properties .... D...... 805 648-5008
  995 Riverside St Ventura (93001) *(P-8771)*

Triage Entertainment LLC .... D...... 310 417-4800
  6701 Center Dr W Ste 300 Los Angeles (90045) *(P-13902)*

Triangle Distributing Co .... B...... 562 699-3424
  12065 Pike St Santa Fe Springs (90670) *(P-6785)*

Triangle Rock Product Inc .... B...... 209 826-5066
  22101 W Sunset Ave Los Banos (93635) *(P-5210)*

Triangle Rock Products, Los Banos *Also Called: Triangle Rock Product Inc (P-5210)*

Triangle Rock Products LLC .... B...... 818 553-8820
  500 N Brand Blvd Ste 500 Glendale (91203) *(P-636)*

Triangle West, Santa Fe Springs *Also Called: Gale/Triangle Inc (P-3394)*

Tribridge Holdings LLC .... A...... 813 287-8887
  523 W 6th St Ste 830 Los Angeles (90014) *(P-11988)*

Tribute Portfolio Hotels, Palm Springs *Also Called: Riviera Palm Sprng A Trbute PR (P-10166)*

Tricap International LLC .... D...... 509 703-8780
  19067 S Reyes Ave Compton (90221) *(P-4112)*

Trico Bancshares (PA) .... C...... 530 898-0300
  63 Constitution Dr Chico (95973) *(P-7719)*

Tricom Management Inc .... C...... 714 630-2029
  4025 E La Palma Ave Ste 101 Anaheim (92807) *(P-20232)*

Tricon American Homes LLC .... C...... 844 874-2661
  15771 Red Hill Ave Tustin (92780) *(P-729)*

Trident Consulting .... D...... 925 352-3885
  6101 Bollinger Canyon Rd Ste 330 San Ramon (94583) *(P-20903)*

Trident Dental Labratories, Hawthorne *Also Called: Trident Labs LLC (P-16778)*

Trident Labs LLC .... C...... 310 915-9121
  12000 Aviation Blvd Hawthorne (90250) *(P-16778)*

Trifecta Nutrition Inc .... D...... 530 564-8388
  428 J St Ste 800 Sacramento (95814) *(P-7163)*

Trigild International Inc .... D...... 949 645-2221
  1680 Superior Ave Costa Mesa (92627) *(P-10325)*

Trigild International Inc .... D...... 760 944-0260
  133 Encinitas Blvd Encinitas (92024) *(P-10326)*

Trigild International Inc .... D...... 619 474-6517
  521 Roosevelt Ave National City (91950) *(P-10327)*

Trilar Management Group .... C...... 951 925-2021
  1025 S Gilbert St Hemet (92543) *(P-20233)*

Trilink Biotechnologies LLC .... C...... 800 863-6801
  10770 Wateridge Cir Ste 200 San Diego (92121) *(P-19787)*

Trilliant Networks Inc (PA) .... D...... 650 204-5050
  1100 Island Dr Ste 201 Redwood City (94065) *(P-13518)*

Trilogy At Rio Vista Mstr Assn .... D...... 707 374-6871
  1200 Clubhouse Dr Rio Vista (94571) *(P-730)*

Trilogy Golf At La Quinta .... B...... 760 771-0707
  60151 Trilogy Pkwy La Quinta (92253) *(P-14295)*

Trilogy Plumbing Inc .... C...... 714 441-2952
  1525 S Sinclair St Anaheim (92806) *(P-1587)*

Trimark Erf Inc (PA) .... D...... 415 626-5611
  1200 7th St San Francisco (94107) *(P-5390)*

Trimark Orange County, Irvine *Also Called: Trimark Raygal LLC (P-5391)*

Trimark R. W. Smith & Co., San Diego *Also Called: R W Smith & Co (P-5387)*

Trimark R.W. Smith, San Diego *Also Called: R W Smith & Co (P-5132)*

Trimark Raygal LLC .... C...... 949 474-1000
  210 Commerce Irvine (92602) *(P-5391)*

Trimco Finish Inc .... C...... 714 708-0300
  3130 W Harvard St Santa Ana (92704) *(P-2022)*

Trimont Land Company (DH) .... B...... 530 562-1010
  5001 Northstar Dr Truckee (96161) *(P-9198)*

Trinamix Inc (PA) .... B...... 408 507-3583
  35 Amoret Dr Irvine (92602) *(P-20592)*

Trinchero Family Estates, Saint Helena *Also Called: Sutter Home Winery Inc (P-2395)*

Trine Integrated Services Inc .... D...... 209 521-1590
  241 E 10th St Ste A Tracy (95376) *(P-13056)*

Trinet, Dublin *Also Called: Trinet Group Inc (P-20593)*

Trinet Group Inc (PA) .... A...... 510 352-5000
  1 Park Pl Ste 600 Dublin (94568) *(P-20593)*

Trinet Zenefits, San Francisco *Also Called: Yourpeople Inc (P-12406)*

Trinidad/Benham Corp .... D...... 626 723-2300
  12400 Wilshire Blvd Ste 1180 Los Angeles (90025) *(P-6684)*

Trinity Brdcstg Netwrk Inc .... C...... 714 665-3619
  2442 Michelle Dr Tustin (92780) *(P-4465)*

Trinity Capital Corporation .... D...... 415 956-5174
  475 Sansome St Fl 19 San Francisco (94111) *(P-7924)*

Trinity Christn Ctr Santa Ana, Tustin *Also Called: Trinity Brdcstg Netwrk Inc (P-4465)*

Trinity Equipment Inc .... D...... 951 790-1652
  2650 S La Cadena Dr Colton (92324) *(P-5392)*

Trinity Fresh Distribution Llc .... D...... 916 714-7368
  8200 Berry Ave Ste 140 Sacramento (95828) *(P-6685)*

Trinity Health Systems (PA) .... D...... 626 960-1971
  14318 Ohio St Baldwin Park (91706) *(P-15707)*

Trinity Hospital, Weaverville *Also Called: Mountain Cmmnties Hlth Care Ds (P-16276)*

Trinity Packing Company Inc (PA) .... B...... 559 433-3785
  18700 E South Ave Reedley (93654) *(P-13519)*

Trinity Packing Company Inc .... B...... 559 743-3913
  7612 S Reed Ave Reedley (93654) *(P-13520)*

Trinity River Lumber Company (PA) .... C...... 530 623-5561
  1375 Main St Weaverville (96093) *(P-5191)*

Trinity Technology Group Inc .... D...... 916 779-0201
  2015 J St Ste 105 Sacramento (95811) *(P-12537)*

Trinity Youth Services (PA) .... D...... 909 825-5588
  201 N Indian Hill Blvd Ste 201 Claremont (91711) *(P-18533)*

Trion Worlds Inc .... B...... 650 631-9800
  2400 Bridge Pkwy 100 Redwood City (94065) *(P-12385)*

Tripalink Corp .... C...... 323 717-9139
  600 Wilshire Blvd Ste 1540 Los Angeles (90005) *(P-20234)*

Triple E Produce LP .... C...... 209 835-5123
  8690 W Linne Rd Tracy (95304) *(P-46)*

Triple R Transportation Inc .... D...... 661 725-6494
  978 Rd 192 Delano (93215) *(P-3301)*

Triple-E Machinery Moving Inc .... D...... 626 444-1137
  3301 Gilman Rd El Monte (91732) *(P-3555)*

Tripod Inc .... D...... 805 585-2273
  1545 W 5th St Ste 200 Oxnard (93030) *(P-11343)*

Tristaff Group, Fallbrook *Also Called: Garich Inc (P-11142)*

Tristar Industrial LLC .... D...... 562 634-6425
  5875 Obispo Ave Long Beach (90805) *(P-5932)*

Tristar Insurance Group Inc (PA) .... A...... 562 495-6600
  100 Oceangate Ste 700 Long Beach (90802) *(P-8423)*

Tristar Risk Management, Long Beach *Also Called: Tristar Insurance Group Inc (P-8423)*

Triton Logistics Corporation .... D...... 619 822-8832
  706 Steffy Rd Ramona (92065) *(P-4113)*

Triton Structural Concrete Inc .... C...... 858 866-2450
  15435 Innovation Dr Ste 225 San Diego (92128) *(P-1044)*

Triumph Protection Group Inc .... B...... 800 224-0286
  853 Cotting Ct Ste D Vacaville (95688) *(P-13057)*

Trius Trucking Inc .... D...... 559 834-4000
  4692 E Lincoln Ave Fowler (93625) *(P-3556)*

Trivad Inc .... C...... 650 286-1086
  880 Mitten Rd Ste 107 Burlingame (94010) *(P-5366)*

Triways Inc .... D...... 951 361-4840
  11201 Iberia St Ste B Jurupa Valley (91752) *(P-3557)*

Triyar Sv LLC (PA) .... B...... 310 234-2888
  10850 Wilshire Blvd Ste 1050 Los Angeles (90024) *(P-9199)*

TRL Systems Incorporated .... D...... 909 390-8392
  9531 Milliken Ave Rancho Cucamonga (91730) *(P-1866)*

Trlggc Services LLC .... B...... 323 266-3072
  1888 Rosecrans Ave Manhattan Beach (90266) *(P-6190)*

TRM Corporation (PA) .... D...... 510 895-2700
  2378 Polvorosa Ave San Leandro (94577) *(P-1988)*

Trojan Professional Svcs Inc .... D...... 714 816-7169
  11075 Knott Ave Ste A Cypress (90630) *(P-12686)*

Trona Railway Company .... A...... 760 372-2312
  13068 Main St Trona (93562) *(P-3117)*

Troon Golf LLC .... C...... 760 346-4653
  44500 Indian Wells Ln Indian Wells (92210) *(P-20235)*

Troop Real Estate Inc — 4165 E Thousand Oaks Blvd Ste 100 Westlake Village (91362) *(P-9200)* .... C 805 402-3028

Troop Real Estate Inc (PA) — 1308 Madera Rd Ste 8 Simi Valley (93065) *(P-9201)* .... D 805 581-3200

Troop Real Estate Inc — 586 W Main St Santa Paula (93060) *(P-9202)* .... C 805 921-0030

Troop Real Estate Inc — 236 W Ojai Ave Ste 100 Ojai (93023) *(P-9203)* .... C 805 640-1440

Tropical Plaza Nursery Inc — 9642 Santiago Blvd Villa Park (92867) *(P-542)* .... D 714 998-4100

Tropicana Manufacturing Co Inc — 525 S Lemon Ave Walnut (91789) *(P-3771)* .... D 909 444-1025

Tropicana Manufacturing Co Inc — 1650 S Central Ave Compton (90220) *(P-3772)* .... D 310 764-4395

Troutman Ppper Hmlton Snders L — 5 Park Plz Ste 1400 Irvine (92614) *(P-17669)* .... D 949 622-2700

Troutman Sanders, Irvine Also Called: Troutman Ppper Hmlton Snders L *(P-17669)*

Trovata, Solana Beach Also Called: Trovata Inc *(P-11989)*

Trovata Inc (PA) — 312 S Cedros Ave Ste 312 Solana Beach (92075) *(P-11989)* .... D 312 914-8106

Trove Information Tech Inc (PA) — 1 Montgomery St Ste 700 San Francisco (94104) *(P-11990)* .... C 610 945-6533

Trove Recommerce Inc — 240 Valley Dr Brisbane (94005) *(P-20594)* .... C 925 726-3316

Troy Lee Designs LLC (DH) — 155 E Rincon St Corona (92879) *(P-5983)* .... D 951 371-5219

Troygould PC — 1801 Century Park E Ste 1600 Los Angeles (90067) *(P-17670)* .... D 310 553-4441

Trs Rentelco, Jurupa Valley Also Called: Mobile Modular Management Corp *(P-2748)*

Trs Staffing Solutions, Aliso Viejo Also Called: Fluor Corporation *(P-19226)*

Truamerica Multifamily LLC — 10100 Santa Monica Blvd Ste 400 Los Angeles (90067) *(P-9575)* .... D 424 325-2750

Truck Terminal, Bakersfield Also Called: Pan Pacific Petroleum Co Inc *(P-3526)*

Truck Underwriters Association — 6303 Owensmouth Ave Fl 1 Woodland Hills (91367) *(P-8251)* .... A 323 932-3200

Truck Underwriters Association (DH) — 4680 Wilshire Blvd Los Angeles (90010) *(P-18766)* .... A 323 932-3200

Truckee Dnner Pub Utlty Dst F — 11570 Donner Pass Rd Truckee (96161) *(P-4713)* .... D 530 587-3896

Truckee Dnner Rcreation Pk Dst — 10981 Truckee Way Truckee (96161) *(P-14578)* .... D 530 582-7720

TRUCKEE DONNER PUD, Truckee Also Called: Truckee Dnner Pub Utlty Dst F *(P-4713)*

Trucking Jobs Technologies Inc — 19925 Stevns Crk Blvd # 100 Cupertino (95014) *(P-11991)* .... C 202 918-2404

Truconnect Communications Inc (PA) — 1149 S Hill St Ste 400 Los Angeles (90015) *(P-4352)* .... C 512 919-2641

True Air Mechanical Inc — 4 Faraday Irvine (92618) *(P-1588)* .... C 888 316-0642

True Home Heating and AC, Irvine Also Called: True Air Mechanical Inc *(P-1588)*

True North America Inc — 8 Cadiz Cir Redwood City (94065) *(P-11992)* .... D 877 525-8783

True Religion Apparel, Gardena Also Called: Guru Denim LLC *(P-7401)*

True Wrld Fods San Frncsco LLC — 1815 Williams St San Leandro (94577) *(P-6488)* .... D 510 352-8140

Truelite Trace Inc — 675 N 1st St Ste 1100 San Jose (95112) *(P-12637)* .... D 833 663-5338

Truenorth, Redwood City Also Called: True North America Inc *(P-11992)*

Truepic Inc — 402 W Broadway Ste 400 Pmb 5021 San Diego (92101) *(P-13521)* .... D 619 848-3632

Truework — 325 Pacific Ave Fl 2 San Francisco (94111) *(P-11993)* .... C 833 878-3967

Truframe, Visalia Also Called: R Lang Company *(P-2741)*

Trugreen, Santa Ana Also Called: Landcare USA LLC *(P-507)*

Trugreen, Escondido Also Called: Landcare USA LLC *(P-508)*

Trugreen, Rancho Cordova Also Called: Landcare USA LLC *(P-509)*

Trugreen, San Diego Also Called: Landcare USA LLC *(P-510)*

Trugreen, Canoga Park Also Called: Landcare USA LLC *(P-511)*

Trugreen, San Jose Also Called: Landcare USA LLC *(P-513)*

Truitt Oilfield Maint Corp — 1051 James Rd Bakersfield (93308) *(P-630)* .... B 661 871-4099

Trulia Inc — 116 New Montgomery St San Francisco (94105) *(P-8866)* .... A 415 648-4358

Trulia Inc (HQ) — 535 Mission St Ste 700 San Francisco (94105) *(P-12638)* .... B 415 648-4358

Truline Realty — 714 W Olympic Blvd Ste 622 Los Angeles (90015) *(P-9204)* .... D 323 389-5432

Trump Nat Golf CLB Los Angeles, Rancho Palos Verdes Also Called: Estates At Trump Nat Golf CLB *(P-14261)*

Truog-Ryding Company Inc — 2659 Townsgate Rd Ste 101 Westlake Village (91361) *(P-20595)* .... D 805 371-9222

Trusaic, Los Angeles Also Called: First Capitol Consulting Inc *(P-20379)*

Truss, San Francisco Also Called: Trussworks Inc *(P-11994)*

Trussworks Inc — 548 Market St # 97444 San Francisco (94104) *(P-11994)* .... C 415 891-0828

Trussworks International Inc — 1275 E Franklin Ave Pomona (91766) *(P-2740)* .... D 714 630-2772

Trust 1 Sales Inc — 1737 S Vermont Ave Los Angeles (90006) *(P-5393)* .... D 323 732-3300

Trust Automation Inc — 125 Venture Dr Ste 110 San Luis Obispo (93401) *(P-19420)* .... D 805 544-0761

Trust Company of West — 865 S Figueroa St Ste 1800 Los Angeles (90017) *(P-8169)* .... A 213 244-0000

Trust Employee ADM & MGT, San Diego Also Called: Team Risk MGT Strategies LLC *(P-20863)*

Trust Safety, Redwood City Also Called: Inflection Risk Solutions LLC *(P-12582)*

Trust Will — 961 W Laurel St San Diego (92101) *(P-9448)* .... D 415 246-4503

Trustee Corps, Irvine Also Called: Mtc Financial Inc *(P-20156)*

Truu Inc — 2350 Mission College Blvd Ste 380 Santa Clara (95054) *(P-12899)* .... D 888 498-0107

Truvian Sciences Inc — 10300 Campus Point Dr Ste 190 San Diego (92121) *(P-19788)* .... D 858 251-3646

Truvida Recovery — 45 Timberland Aliso Viejo (92656) *(P-17146)* .... D 949 283-4679

Trux Transport — 237 Harbor Way South San Francisco (94080) *(P-3920)* .... D 650 244-0200

Truxtun Radiology Med Group LP — 20960 Sage Ln Ste B Tehachapi (93561) *(P-15129)* .... D 661 822-6619

Truxtun Radiology Med Group LP — 3940 San Dimas St Bakersfield (93301) *(P-15130)* .... C 661 325-6200

Truxtun Radiology Med Group LP — 1917 Truxtun Ave Bakersfield (93301) *(P-15131)* .... D 661 616-1201

Truxtun Radiology Med Group LP — 11622 Harrington St Bakersfield (93311) *(P-15132)* .... D 661 205-6567

TRY VALLEY MONTESSORI SCHOOL, Livermore Also Called: Valley Montessori School *(P-17755)*

Tryad Service Corporation — 5900 E Lerdo Hwy Shafter (93263) *(P-631)* .... D 661 391-1524

Tryfacta Inc — 4637 Chabot Dr Ste 100 Pleasanton (94588) *(P-11995)* .... B 408 419-9200

TSC Auto ID Technology America (HQ) — 3040 Saturn St Ste 200 Brea (92821) *(P-5933)* .... C 909 468-0100

Tsia — 17065 Camino San Bernardo Ste 200 San Diego (92127) *(P-18767)* .... D 858 674-5491

Tsmc North America (HQ) — 2851 Junction Ave San Jose (95134) *(P-20596)* .... B 408 382-8000

Tst Inc (PA) — 13428 Benson Ave Chino (91710) *(P-2722)* .... B 951 685-2155

TT Electronics, Brea Also Called: Bi Technologies Corporation *(P-2940)*

TT Trucking Services, Victorville Also Called: TT Trucking Services LLC *(P-3428)*

TT Trucking Services LLC — 12745 Jade Rd Victorville (92392) *(P-3428)* .... D 323 790-3408

Tte Technology Inc — 189 Technology Dr Irvine (92618) *(P-5615)* .... C 877 300-8837

Ttg Engineers — 300 N Lake Ave Fl 14 Pasadena (91101) *(P-19421)* .... B 626 463-2800

TTI Technologies, Exeter Also Called: Exeter Engineering Inc *(P-264)*

Tts, Orange Also Called: Total Telco Specialists Inc *(P-13749)*

Tty-Deaf Hndcppd-Cmmnction Ctr, Chico Also Called: Enloe Medical Center *(P-3255)*

Tubemogul Inc — 1250 53rd St Ste 1 Emeryville (94608) *(P-12386)* .... A 510 653-0126

ALPHABETIC SECTION

Tubing Seal Cap Co, Anaheim *Also Called: Pacific Precision Metals Inc (P-2753)*
Tubular Labs Inc (HQ)..C...... 650 260-8823
  153 Castro St Ste 300 Mountain View (94041) *(P-20597)*
Tuitionio Inc ....D...... 855 353-9395
  10960 Wilshire Blvd Ste 1420 Los Angeles (90024) *(P-7867)*
Tuksy, Irvine *Also Called: Arbitech LLC (P-5273)*
TULARE DISTRICT HOSPITAL, Tulare *Also Called: Tulare Local Health Care Dst (P-16582)*
Tulare Local Health Care Dst ....A...... 559 685-3462
  869 N Cherry St Tulare (93274) *(P-16582)*
Tulare Lodging Associates LLC ....D...... 559 686-4700
  1225 Hillman St Tulare (93274) *(P-10328)*
Tule River Alcoholism Program ....D...... 559 781-8797
  1010 N Reservation Rd Porterville (93257) *(P-18534)*
Tule River Economic Dev ....D...... 559 781-4271
  31071 Highway 190 Porterville (93257) *(P-20868)*
Tule River Indian Hlth Ctr Inc ....D...... 559 784-2316
  380 N Reservation Rd Porterville (93257) *(P-17147)*
Tule River Tibal Council, Porterville *Also Called: Tule River Alcoholism Program (P-18534)*
Tully-Wihr Company ....C...... 530 346-2649
  148 Whitcomb Ave Colfax (95713) *(P-2566)*
Tumbleweed Day Camp, Los Angeles *Also Called: Tumbleweed Eductl Entps Inc (P-14579)*
Tumbleweed Eductl Entps Inc ....C...... 310 444-3232
  1024 Hanley Ave Los Angeles (90049) *(P-14579)*
Tunein Inc ....C...... 650 319-7100
  475 Brannan St Ste 320 San Francisco (94107) *(P-4407)*
Tuolomne Cnty Bhvral Hlth Rcve, Sonora *Also Called: Kingsview Corp (P-17084)*
Tuolumne M-Wuk Indian Hlth Ctr ....D...... 209 928-5400
  18880 Cherry Valley Blvd Tuolumne (95379) *(P-15133)*
Tuolumne Mewuk Indian Health, Tuolumne *Also Called: Tuolumne M-Wuk Indian Hlth Ctr (P-15133)*
Tuolumne Utilities District ....D...... 209 532-5536
  18885 Nugget Blvd Sonora (95370) *(P-4842)*
Tupaz Day Care Services Inc ....D...... 408 377-1622
  3015 Union Ave San Jose (95124) *(P-18156)*
Tupaz Homes LLC ....D...... 408 377-1622
  2038 Biarritz Pl San Jose (95138) *(P-731)*
Turbotax, San Diego *Also Called: Intuit Inc (P-12242)*
Turing Video ....D...... 877 730-8222
  1730 S El Camino Real Ste 480 San Mateo (94402) *(P-11996)*
Turlock Hospitality LLC ....D...... 209 250-1501
  1000 Powers Ct Turlock (95380) *(P-10329)*
Turlock Irrgtion Dst Emplyees (PA)..C...... 209 883-8222
  333 E Canal Dr Turlock (95380) *(P-4714)*
Turlock Nrsing Rhabilation Ctr, Turlock *Also Called: Covenant Care California LLC (P-15405)*
Turlock Plant, Turlock *Also Called: Evergreen Packaging LLC (P-6906)*
Turn Around Communications Inc ....C...... 626 443-2400
  100 N Barranca St Ste 260 West Covina (91791) *(P-1272)*
Turn Key Scaffold LLC ....C...... 619 642-0880
  410 W 30th St National City (91950) *(P-2323)*
Turner Camera SEC Systems Inc ....C...... 559 486-3466
  120 W Shields Ave Fresno (93705) *(P-13152)*
Turner Construction Company ....B...... 714 940-9000
  1900 S State College Blvd Ste 200 Anaheim (92806) *(P-1045)*
Turner Construction Company ....D...... 916 444-4421
  2500 Venture Oaks Way Ste 200 Sacramento (95833) *(P-1046)*
Turner Dockworth, San Francisco *Also Called: Destination Moon LP (P-10805)*
Turner Volvo, Sacramento *Also Called: Gordon Turner Motors (P-7222)*
Turning Point Central Cal Inc ....D...... 559 627-1490
  711 N Court St Visalia (93291) *(P-18157)*
Turning Point Cmnty Programs (PA)..D...... 916 364-8395
  10850 Gold Center Dr Ste 325 Rancho Cordova (95670) *(P-17148)*
TURNING POINT COUNSELING, Fullerton *Also Called: Turning Point Ministries (P-18159)*
Turning Point For God ....D...... 619 258-3600
  San Diego (92163) *(P-18158)*
Turning Point Ministries ....D...... 800 998-6329
  1370 Brea Blvd Ste 245 Fullerton (92835) *(P-18159)*
Turning Point Therapeutics Inc ....D...... 858 926-5251
  10300 Campus Point Dr San Diego (92121) *(P-19789)*
Turnkey Foundation Inc ....D...... 949 557-6203
  1805 E Garry Ave Ste 130 Santa Ana (92705) *(P-8025)*

Turo Inc (PA)..C...... 866 735-2901
  111 Sutter St Ste 600 San Francisco (94104) *(P-13594)*
Turtle Beach, San Diego *Also Called: Voyetra Turtle Beach Inc (P-2840)*
Turtle Rock Cdc, Irvine *Also Called: Child Development Incorporated (P-18285)*
Tusa Inc (PA)..C...... 888 848-3749
  986 Walsh Ave Santa Clara (95050) *(P-12713)*
Tuscan Inn, San Francisco *Also Called: Kimpton Hotel & Rest Group LLC (P-9942)*
Tusimple, San Diego *Also Called: Tusimple Holdings Inc (P-12538)*
Tusimple Holdings Inc (PA)..B...... 619 916-3144
  9191 Towne Centre Dr Ste 600 San Diego (92122) *(P-12538)*
Tustin Executive Center, Tustin *Also Called: Southern Cal Prmnnte Med Group (P-8365)*
Tustin Hospital, Tustin *Also Called: Pacific Health Corporation (P-16303)*
Tustin Hospital and Medical Center ....B...... 714 619-7700
  3699 Wilshire Blvd # 540 Los Angeles (90010) *(P-16583)*
Tustin Ranch Golf Club, Tustin *Also Called: Crown Golf Properties LP (P-20336)*
Tustin Saab, Tustin *Also Called: Nissan of Tustin (P-7268)*
Tustin Unified School District ....D...... 714 542-4271
  16791 E Main St Tustin (92780) *(P-17754)*
Tutor Perini, Rancho Cascades *Also Called: Tutor Perini Corporation (P-1047)*
Tutor Perini Corporation (PA)...C...... 818 362-8391
  15901 Olden St Rancho Cascades (91342) *(P-1047)*
Tutor Time Learning Ctrs LLC ....C...... 818 710-1677
  5855 De Soto Ave Woodland Hills (91367) *(P-18363)*
Tutor Time Learning Ctrs LLC ....C...... 714 484-1000
  5805 Corporate Ave Cypress (90630) *(P-18364)*
Tutor-Saliba Corporation (HQ)..D...... 818 362-8391
  15901 Olden St Rancho Cascades (91342) *(P-1048)*
Tutor-Saliba Perini ....A...... 818 362-8391
  15901 Olden St Sylmar (91342) *(P-1049)*
Tuttle Click Ford, Irvine *Also Called: Tuttle-Click Ford Inc (P-7320)*
Tuttle Family Enterprises Inc ....B...... 818 534-2566
  9510 Topanga Canyon Blvd Chatsworth (91311) *(P-10975)*
Tuttle-Click Ford Inc ....C...... 949 855-1704
  43 Auto Center Dr Irvine (92618) *(P-7320)*
TV Guide Entrmt Group LLC ....D...... 310 360-1441
  2700 Colorado Ave Ste 200 Santa Monica (90404) *(P-5616)*
Tvgla, Culver City *Also Called: Visionaire Group Inc (P-20604)*
TW Holdings Inc ....A...... 858 217-8750
  10805 Rancho Bernardo Rd Ste 120 San Diego (92127) *(P-14239)*
TW Security Corp (DH)...C...... 949 932-1000
  5 Park Plz Ste 400 Irvine (92614) *(P-5367)*
TW Services Inc ....B...... 714 441-2400
  1801 W Romneya Dr Ste 601 Anaheim (92801) *(P-4176)*
Twdc Enterprises 18 Corp (HQ)..A...... 818 560-1000
  500 S Buena Vista St Burbank (91521) *(P-4466)*
Twe Logistics, Pleasanton *Also Called: Fashion Apparel Service Trnsp (P-3703)*
Twenteth Cntury Fox HM Entrmt (PA)..A...... 310 369-1000
  10201 W Pico Blvd Los Angeles (90064) *(P-13903)*
Twenteth Cntury Fox Intl TV In ....A...... 310 369-1000
  10201 W Pico Blvd Los Angeles (90064) *(P-4467)*
Twenteth Cntury Fox Film Corp (DH)...D
  10201 W Pico Blvd Los Angeles (90064) *(P-13904)*
Twentieth Cntury Fox Intl Corp (HQ)..C...... 310 369-1000
  10201 W Pico Blvd Bldg 1 Los Angeles (90064) *(P-13968)*
Twentieth Cntury Fox Japan Inc ....A...... 310 369-4636
  10201 W Pico Blvd Los Angeles (90064) *(P-10820)*
Twentieth Television Inc ....D...... 310 584-2000
  1999 S Bundy Dr Los Angeles (90025) *(P-4468)*
Twentieth Television Inc (DH)...D...... 310 369-1000
  10201 W Pico Blvd Los Angeles (90064) *(P-13905)*
Twenty Mile Productions LLC ....C...... 412 251-0767
  11833 Mississippi Ave Ste 101 Los Angeles (90025) *(P-14108)*
Twenty4seven Hotels Corp ....B...... 949 734-6400
  520 Newport Center Dr Ste 520 Newport Beach (92660) *(P-20236)*
Twilight Hven A Cal Nn-Prfit C ....D...... 559 251-8417
  1717 S Winery Ave Fresno (93727) *(P-15708)*
Twilio Segment ....C...... 415 603-6900
  100 California St Ste 700 San Francisco (94111) *(P-11997)*
Twin Arbors Athletic Club, Lodi *Also Called: Spare-Time Inc (P-14460)*
Twin Cities Community Hosp Inc ....B...... 805 434-3500
  1100 Las Tablas Rd Templeton (93465) *(P-15134)*

ALPHABETIC SECTION

Twin Hill Acquisition Co Inc .... D...... 281 776-7000
  6100 Stevenson Blvd Fremont (94538) *(P-6191)*
Twin Med Inc .... B
  5900 Wilshire Blvd Los Angeles (90036) *(P-5457)*
Twin Oaks Power LP (HQ) .... D...... 619 696-2034
  101 Ash St Hq10b San Diego (92101) *(P-4715)*
Twin Pine Casino & Hotel .... D...... 707 987-0197
  22223 Rancheria Rd Hwy 29 Middletown (95461) *(P-7524)*
Twining Inc (PA) .... D...... 562 426-3355
  2883 E Spring St Ste 300 Long Beach (90806) *(P-20002)*
Twining Laboratories, Long Beach *Also Called: Twining Inc (P-20002)*
Twist Bioscience Corporation (PA) .... B...... 800 719-0671
  681 Gateway Blvd South San Francisco (94080) *(P-19790)*
Two Bit Circus, Los Angeles *Also Called: Two Bit Circus Dtla LLC (P-14109)*
Two Bit Circus Dtla LLC .... D...... 323 438-9808
  634 Mateo St Los Angeles (90021) *(P-14109)*
Two Jinn Inc (PA) .... D...... 760 431-9911
  1000 Aviara Dr Ste 300 Carlsbad (92011) *(P-13522)*
Two Palms Nursing Center Inc .... C...... 626 796-1103
  150 Bellefontaine St Pasadena (91105) *(P-15905)*
Twomagnets Inc .... A...... 408 837-0116
  440 N Barranca Ave Ste 5028 Covina (91723) *(P-11249)*
TWR Enterprises Inc .... C...... 951 279-2000
  1661 Railroad St Corona (92878) *(P-2023)*
Txtmequickcom .... C...... 703 596-8989
  44 Montgomery St Fl 6 San Francisco (94104) *(P-4557)*
Tydg Enterprises Inc .... D...... 562 903-9030
  10232 Palm Dr Santa Fe Springs (90670) *(P-9345)*
TYlin Intl Group Ltd (PA) .... C...... 415 291-3700
  345 California St Fl 23 San Francisco (94104) *(P-19422)*
Tyme Maidu Tribe-Berry Creek .... A...... 530 538-4560
  4020 Olive Hwy Oroville (95966) *(P-10330)*
Tyson, San Diego *Also Called: Tyson & Mendes (P-17671)*
Tyson & Mendes .... D...... 858 459-1476
  12520 High Bluff Dr Ste 360 San Diego (92130) *(P-17671)*
U C I Distribution Plus, Pasadena *Also Called: United Couriers Inc (P-3848)*
U C L Incorporated (PA) .... D...... 323 235-0099
  620 S Hacienda Blvd City Of Industry (91745) *(P-3558)*
U C S D Medical Center, San Diego *Also Called: University Cal San Diego (P-16592)*
U C S F Medical Center, San Francisco *Also Called: Devron H Char MD (P-14729)*
U C San Diego Foundation .... C...... 858 534-1032
  9500 Gilman Dr La Jolla (92093) *(P-19113)*
U C San Francisco Gynecology .... D...... 415 885-7788
  2356 Sutter St San Francisco (94115) *(P-15135)*
U F C Pension Trust Fund, Cypress *Also Called: Cal Southern United Food (P-8457)*
U Gym LLC (PA) .... D...... 714 668-0911
  1501 Quail St Ste 100 Newport Beach (92660) *(P-14240)*
U P C Inc .... C...... 650 462-2010
  165 Channing Ave Palo Alto (94301) *(P-10579)*
U P S, San Francisco *Also Called: Fritz Companies Inc (P-4022)*
U S C, Glendale *Also Called: Usc Vrdugo Hlls Hosp Fundation (P-16608)*
U S Cold Storage, Mcclellan *Also Called: United States Cold Storage Inc (P-3665)*
U S Trust Company NA .... B...... 213 861-5000
  515 S Flower St Ste 2700 Los Angeles (90071) *(P-8226)*
U S Weatherford L P .... C...... 661 589-9483
  2815 Fruitvale Ave Bakersfield (93308) *(P-632)*
U S Xpress Inc .... B...... 760 768-6707
  363 Nina Lee Rd Calexico (92231) *(P-3559)*
U T L A, Los Angeles *Also Called: United Teachers-Los Angeles (P-18806)*
U W G Southern California Div, Los Angeles *Also Called: Unified Grocers Inc (P-3773)*
U-Haul, Sacramento *Also Called: U-Haul Business Consultants (P-13568)*
U-Haul, Corona *Also Called: U-Haul Business Consultants (P-13569)*
U-Haul, Fremont *Also Called: U-Haul Co of California (P-13570)*
U-Haul, Moreno Valley *Also Called: U-Haul Leasing & Sales Co (P-13571)*
U-Haul, Fremont *Also Called: U-Haul Neighborhood Dealer (P-13599)*
U-Haul Business Consultants .... C...... 916 331-7601
  5220 Auburn Blvd Sacramento (95841) *(P-13568)*
U-Haul Business Consultants .... C...... 951 736-7811
  314 E 6th St Corona (92879) *(P-13569)*

U-Haul Co of California (DH) .... C...... 602 287-7830
  44511 S Grimmer Blvd Fremont (94538) *(P-13570)*
U-Haul Leasing & Sales Co .... B...... 951 485-2003
  23730 Sunnymead Blvd Moreno Valley (92553) *(P-13571)*
U-Haul Neighborhood Dealer .... D...... 510 371-0122
  300 Mowry Ave Fremont (94536) *(P-13599)*
U-Tech Media Usa LLC .... C...... 408 597-1600
  1105 Montague Expy Milpitas (95035) *(P-2954)*
U. S. Grant Hotel, San Diego *Also Called: American Prprty-Mnagement Corp (P-9606)*
U.C.S.d Plastic Surgery, San Diego *Also Called: University Cal San Diego (P-15146)*
U.S. Airconditioning Distrs, City Of Industry *Also Called: US Airconditioning Distributors Inc (P-5775)*
U.S. Concrete Precast Group, Morgan Hill *Also Called: Sierra Precast Inc (P-2707)*
U.S. Foodservice 4114, Stockton *Also Called: US Foods Inc (P-6690)*
U.S. Healthworks Medical Group, Valencia *Also Called: US Healthworks Inc (P-15172)*
Ua Local 342 Jatc .... C...... 925 686-0730
  2450 Whitman Rd Concord (94518) *(P-18799)*
UA Local 38 Pension Tr Fund .... D...... 415 626-2000
  1625 Market St San Francisco (94103) *(P-18800)*
UAS, Los Angeles *Also Called: Cal State La Univ Aux Svcs Inc (P-20050)*
Ubeo West LLC (HQ) .... C...... 530 343-6065
  3131 Esplanade Chico (95973) *(P-5258)*
Uber .... D...... 866 440-6700
  101 Jefferson Dr Menlo Park (94025) *(P-3956)*
Uber, San Francisco *Also Called: Uber Technologies Inc (P-13523)*
Uber Technologies Inc (PA) .... A...... 415 612-8582
  1515 3rd St San Francisco (94158) *(P-13523)*
Ubicom Inc .... D...... 415 547-4000
  625 3rd St Fl 3 San Francisco (94107) *(P-14110)*
Ubics Inc .... C...... 415 289-1400
  1050 Bridgeway Sausalito (94965) *(P-11998)*
Ubiquiti Networks Inc .... C...... 408 942-3085
  91 E Tasman Dr San Jose (95134) *(P-12539)*
Ubiquity, San Francisco *Also Called: Decimal Inc (P-13259)*
Ubisoft Holdings Inc .... C...... 415 547-4000
  625 3rd St Fl 3 San Francisco (94107) *(P-11999)*
UBS Americas Inc .... C...... 619 557-2400
  600 W Broadway Ste 2800 San Diego (92101) *(P-8170)*
Uc Berkeley Comm Network Svcs, Berkeley *Also Called: University California Berkeley (P-12902)*
Uc Davis Children's Hospital, Sacramento *Also Called: University California Davis (P-15161)*
Uc Davis Medical Center, Sacramento *Also Called: University California Davis (P-16599)*
Uc Hastings Foundation .... C...... 415 565-4704
  200 Mcallister St San Francisco (94102) *(P-19114)*
Uc Innovation Inc .... D...... 949 415-8246
  2855 Michelle Ste 190 Irvine (92606) *(P-12900)*
Uc Irvine Health .... D...... 714 456-6191
  200 S Manchester Ave Ste 400 Orange (92868) *(P-17342)*
Uc Irvine Health Mktg Dept .... D...... 714 456-6726
  333 City Blvd W Ste 1250 Orange (92868) *(P-16584)*
Uc Irvine Hlth Rgonal Burn Ctr, Orange *Also Called: University California Irvine (P-15163)*
Uc Irvine Medical Center, Orange *Also Called: University California Irvine (P-16602)*
Uc Riverside RES Economic Dev, Riverside *Also Called: University Cal Riverside (P-19854)*
UC SAN DIEGO, La Jolla *Also Called: U C San Diego Foundation (P-19113)*
Ucertify LLC .... D...... 800 796-3062
  1684 Decoto Rd Union City (94587) *(P-10580)*
UCI Cancer Center, Orange *Also Called: University California Irvine (P-16601)*
UCI Construction Inc .... D...... 661 587-0192
  3900 Fruitvale Ave Bakersfield (93308) *(P-19423)*
UCI Construction Inc (PA) .... D...... 925 370-9808
  167 Grobric Ct Fairfield (94534) *(P-1324)*
UCI Division Plastic Surgery, Orange *Also Called: University California Irvine (P-19637)*
UCI Family Health Center, Santa Ana *Also Called: University California Irvine (P-15164)*
UCI Health Blood Donor Center, Irvine *Also Called: University California Irvine (P-17344)*
UCI Westminster Medical Center, Westminster *Also Called: University California Irvine (P-16604)*
Ucla Dept of Design Media, Los Angeles *Also Called: Associated Students UCLA (P-17761)*
Ucla Foundation .... B...... 310 794-3193
  10889 Wilshire Blvd Ste 1100 Los Angeles (90024) *(P-9418)*

ALPHABETIC SECTION

Ucla Hbr Dlysis Ctr Med Fndtio, Torrance *Also Called: Harbor-Ucla Med Foundation Inc* *(P-16986)*

Ucla Health .... D....... 310 825-9111
 757 Westwood Plz Los Angeles (90095) *(P-16585)*

Ucla Health Auxiliary .... A....... 310 267-4327
 10920 Wilshire Blvd Ste 400 Los Angeles (90024) *(P-16954)*

Ucla Healthcare .... D....... 310 319-4560
 1821 Wilshire Blvd Fl 6 Santa Monica (90403) *(P-16586)*

Ucla Mdcn SC Phrmclgy, Los Angeles *Also Called: Associated Students UCLA* *(P-14620)*

Ucla Snta Mnica Gstrenterology .... D....... 310 582-6240
 1223 16th St Ste 3100 Santa Monica (90404) *(P-15136)*

Ucp, San Jose *Also Called: Ucp Inc* *(P-732)*

Ucp Inc .... C....... 408 207-9499
 99 Almaden Blvd Ste 400 San Jose (95113) *(P-732)*

Ucp of Orange County, Santa Ana *Also Called: United Crbral Plsy Assn Ornge* *(P-18160)*

Ucsd, La Jolla *Also Called: Ming Tsuang Dr* *(P-14900)*

Ucsd, San Diego *Also Called: Kelly Thomas MD Ucsd Hlth Care* *(P-17264)*

Ucsd Fac & Design, La Jolla *Also Called: University Cal San Diego* *(P-19515)*

Ucsd Neuroscience Center .... D....... 619 287-7661
 6645 Alvarado Rd San Diego (92120) *(P-15137)*

Ucsd Thornton Hospital, La Jolla *Also Called: University Cal San Diego* *(P-16591)*

Ucsf Benioff Childrens Hosp .... D....... 925 979-4000
 2401 Shadelands Dr Ste 120 Walnut Creek (94598) *(P-15138)*

Ucsf Benioff Chld Hosp Oakland, Oakland *Also Called: Childrens Hosp RES Ctr At Okla* *(P-15994)*

Ucsf Benioff Chld Physicians .... D....... 415 476-4977
 6425 Christie Ave Ste 220 Emeryville (94608) *(P-15139)*

Ucsf Btty Irene Moore Wns Hosp (HQ) .... D....... 415 476-1000
 1855 4th St San Francisco (94143) *(P-15709)*

Ucsf Center On Deafness, San Francisco *Also Called: University Cal San Frncsco Fnd* *(P-18535)*

Ucsf Dental Center-Buchanan, San Francisco *Also Called: University Cal San Francisco* *(P-15253)*

Ucsf Design Construction, San Francisco *Also Called: University Cal San Francisco* *(P-17772)*

Ucsf Medical Center .... C....... 415 353-9229
 150 Executive Park Blvd Ste 150c San Francisco (94134) *(P-15140)*

Ucsf Medical Center, San Francisco *Also Called: Ucsf Btty Irene Moore Wns Hosp* *(P-15709)*

Ucsf Medical Center At Mt Zion, San Francisco *Also Called: University Cal San Francisco* *(P-16596)*

Ucsf Mmory Clnic Alzhimers Ctr, San Francisco *Also Called: University Cal San Francisco* *(P-17776)*

Ucsf Mount Zion Cancer Center, San Francisco *Also Called: University Cal San Francisco* *(P-17781)*

Ucsf Neuro Epidemiology Lab, San Francisco *Also Called: University Cal San Francisco* *(P-19931)*

Ucsf Orthpdic Srgery Fclty Prc, San Francisco *Also Called: University Cal San Francisco* *(P-15150)*

Ucsf Otlrynglogy - Head Neck S, San Francisco *Also Called: University Cal San Francisco* *(P-17771)*

Ucsf Plstic Rcnstrctive Srgery, San Francisco *Also Called: University Cal San Francisco* *(P-17779)*

Ucsf Sports Medicine Center, San Francisco *Also Called: University Cal San Francisco* *(P-15151)*

Ucsf Ward 86, San Francisco *Also Called: University Cal San Francisco* *(P-19930)*

Ucsf/Div Behv & Dev Pediatrics, San Francisco *Also Called: University Cal San Francisco* *(P-15152)*

Ucsf/Mz Neurosurgery Abic, San Francisco *Also Called: University Cal San Francisco* *(P-17777)*

Ucsf/Obgyn Oncology, San Francisco *Also Called: University Cal San Francisco* *(P-17778)*

UDC, Anaheim *Also Called: Universal Dust Cllctr Mfg Sup* *(P-852)*

Ue Authority Co .... D....... 800 466-4178
 225 Broadway Ste 2200 San Diego (92101) *(P-10683)*

Uesugi Farms Incorporated C
 1020 State Highway 25 Gilroy (95020) *(P-47)*

Ufc Gym, Newport Beach *Also Called: U Gym LLC* *(P-14240)*

Ufcw & Employers Trust LLC (PA) .... C....... 800 552-2400
 1000 Burnett Ave Ste 110 Concord (94520) *(P-9449)*

Ufcw Local 770, Los Angeles *Also Called: United Food and Commercial* *(P-18804)*

Ugm Citatah Inc (PA) .... C....... 562 921-9549
 13220 Cambridge St Santa Fe Springs (90670) *(P-5211)*

Ugmc, Santa Fe Springs *Also Called: Ugm Citatah Inc* *(P-5211)*

Uhc of California (DH) .... A....... 952 936-6615
 5995 Plaza Dr Cypress (90630) *(P-8370)*

Uhg Lax Prop Llc .... C....... 310 322-0999
 1985 E Grand Ave El Segundo (90245) *(P-10331)*

Uhp Healthcare, Inglewood *Also Called: Watts Health Foundation Inc* *(P-15805)*

UHS, Chino *Also Called: Canyon Ridge Hospital Inc* *(P-16646)*

UHS Surgical Services, Sun Valley *Also Called: PRI Medical Technologies Inc* *(P-5444)*

Uhs-Corona Inc (HQ) .... A....... 951 737-4343
 800 S Main St Corona (92882) *(P-16587)*

Uhs-Corona Inc .... C....... 951 736-7200
 730 Magnolia Ave Corona (92879) *(P-17149)*

UIC, Orange *Also Called: University California Irvine* *(P-15167)*

Ujwal Inc .... D....... 503 708-4410
 148 Castro St Unit 2a Mountain View (94041) *(P-12000)*

Uka LLC .... B....... 949 610-8000
 620 Newport Center Dr Ste 1400 Newport Beach (92660) *(P-10332)*

Ukiah Adventist Hospital (HQ) .... B....... 707 462-3111
 275 Hospital Dr Ukiah (95482) *(P-16588)*

Ukiah Valley Medical Center, Ukiah *Also Called: Ukiah Adventist Hospital* *(P-16588)*

Uls Express Inc .... C....... 310 631-0800
 2850 E Del Amo Blvd Compton (90221) *(P-3429)*

Ultimate, Long Beach *Also Called: Altamed Health Services Corp* *(P-14601)*

Ultimate Builders Inc .... D....... 818 481-2627
 23679 Calabasas Rd Calabasas (91302) *(P-733)*

ULTIMATE BUILDERS INC, Calabasas *Also Called: Ultimate Builders Inc* *(P-733)*

Ultimate Demo, Pomona *Also Called: Ultimate Removal Inc* *(P-734)*

Ultimate Landscaping MGT .... D....... 714 502-9711
 700 E Sycamore St Anaheim (92805) *(P-543)*

Ultimate Removal Inc .... C....... 909 524-0800
 2168 Pomona Blvd Pomona (91768) *(P-734)*

Ultimate Staffing Services, Orange *Also Called: Roth Staffing Companies LP* *(P-11325)*

Ultimo Software Solutions Inc .... C....... 408 943-1490
 33268 Central Ave # 2 Union City (94587) *(P-12001)*

Ultisat Inc .... A....... 240 243-5107
 11839 Sorrento Valley Rd San Diego (92121) *(P-12540)*

Ultra Mobile, Costa Mesa *Also Called: Uvnv Inc* *(P-4354)*

Ultra Pro International LLC .... C....... 323 890-2100
 6049 E Slauson Ave Commerce (90040) *(P-6000)*

Ultracare Services LLC .... D....... 818 266-9668
 1117 W Manchester Blvd Ste B Inglewood (90301) *(P-16955)*

Ultramet .... D....... 818 899-0236
 12173 Montague St Pacoima (91331) *(P-2762)*

Ultrasigns Electrical Advg, San Diego *Also Called: Jones Signs Co Inc* *(P-5383)*

Ultura, Long Beach *Also Called: Ultura Inc* *(P-20666)*

Ultura Inc .... C....... 562 661-4999
 3605 Long Beach Blvd Ste 201 Long Beach (90807) *(P-20666)*

Uma Enterprises Inc (PA) .... D....... 310 631-1166
 350 W Apra St Compton (90220) *(P-5141)*

Uma Home Decor, Compton *Also Called: Uma Enterprises Inc* *(P-5141)*

Umc, Sunnyvale *Also Called: Umc Group (usa)* *(P-2935)*

Umc Group (usa) .... D....... 408 523-7800
 488 De Guigne Dr Sunnyvale (94085) *(P-2935)*

Ums Banking, Glendale *Also Called: United Merchant Svcs Cal Inc* *(P-5259)*

Umspe, Fresno *Also Called: University Cal San Francisco* *(P-8891)*

Unac/Uhcp, San Dimas *Also Called: Alliance Health Care Unions* *(P-18770)*

Unbroken Studios LLC .... D....... 310 741-2670
 2120 Park Pl Ste 110 El Segundo (90245) *(P-12387)*

Unchained Labs (PA) .... C....... 925 587-9800
 4747 Willow Rd Pleasanton (94588) *(P-16757)*

Underground Cnstr Co Inc .... C....... 707 746-8800
 5145 Industrial Way Benicia (94510) *(P-4754)*

Undersea Systems Intl Inc .... D....... 714 754-7848
 3133 W Harvard St Santa Ana (92704) *(P-2964)*

Unfi, Rocklin *Also Called: United Natural Foods West Inc* *(P-3775)*

Unfold Agency Inc .... D....... 818 679-4837
 4841 Cherryvale Ave Soquel (95073) *(P-10684)*

Unger Construction Co .... D....... 916 325-5500
 910 X St Sacramento (95818) *(P-1050)*

UNI Care Home Health Inc .... D....... 760 510-0055
   1510 S Escondido Blvd Escondido (92025) *(P-16956)*

UNI Hosiery Co Inc (PA) .... C....... 213 228-0100
   1911 E Olympic Blvd Los Angeles (90021) *(P-6192)*

Unibal-Rodamco-Westfield Group .... C....... 310 478-4456
   2049 Century Park E 41st Fl Los Angeles (90067) *(P-8772)*

Unicare Medical Transportation, Riverside *Also Called: Empire Med Transportations LLC*
(P-4013)

Unicolors Inc .... D....... 323 307-9878
   3251 E 26th St Vernon (90058) *(P-6164)*

Unified Aircraft Services Inc (PA) .... D....... 909 877-0535
   1571 S Lilac Ave Bloomington (92316) *(P-4136)*

Unified Grocers Inc .... C....... 559 268-8454
   1888 S East Ave Fresno (93721) *(P-3662)*

Unified Grocers Inc .... D....... 323 232-6124
   457 E Martin Luther King Jr Blvd Los Angeles (90011) *(P-3773)*

Unified Grocers Inc .... C....... 209 832-6200
   800 E Pescadero Ave Tracy (95304) *(P-6407)*

Unified Grocers, Inc., Tracy *Also Called: Unified Grocers Inc (P-6407)*

Unified Protective Svcs Inc .... D....... 310 350-1755
   4431 W Rosecrans Ave Ste 300 Hawthorne (90250) *(P-13058)*

Unifirst, Ontario *Also Called: Unifirst Corporation (P-10482)*

Unifirst Corporation .... C....... 909 390-8670
   700 Etiwanda Ave Ste C Ontario (91761) *(P-10482)*

Unifirst Mortgage Lending, San Ramon *Also Called: Mason McDuffie Mortgage Corp (P-8000)*

Uniform Accessories, Northridge *Also Called: Rashman Corporation (P-5447)*

Unify Fincl Cr Un Prof Corp (PA) .... D....... 877 254-9328
   2305b W 190th St Torrance (90504) *(P-7813)*

Unigro, San Bernardino *Also Called: L & L Nursery Supply Inc (P-6827)*

Unilab Corporation .... A....... 510 444-5213
   470 27th St Oakland (94612) *(P-16758)*

Unilab Corporation .... A....... 916 733-3330
   3160 Folsom Blvd Sacramento (95816) *(P-16759)*

Unilab Corporation .... A....... 559 225-5076
   5325 N Fresno St Ste 106 Fresno (93710) *(P-16760)*

Unilab Corporation .... A....... 916 927-9900
   3714 Northgate Blvd Sacramento (95834) *(P-16761)*

Unilab Corporation .... A....... 916 781-3031
   51 N Sunrise Ave Ste 515 Roseville (95661) *(P-16762)*

Unilab Corporation (HQ) .... B....... 818 737-6000
   8401 Fallbrook Ave West Hills (91304) *(P-16763)*

Unilab Corporation .... A....... 408 927-8331
   6475 Camden Ave Ste 104 San Jose (95120) *(P-16764)*

Unilab Corporation .... A....... 831 424-3858
   1328 Natividad Rd Salinas (93906) *(P-16765)*

Unilever United States Inc .... B....... 209 466-9580
   1400 Waterloo Rd Stockton (95205) *(P-204)*

Union Building Maintenance, Commerce *Also Called: Uniserve Facilities Svcs Corp (P-10976)*

Union Editorial LLC .... D....... 310 481-2200
   12200 W Olympic Blvd Ste 140 Los Angeles (90064) *(P-20904)*

Union Pacific Lines, Long Beach *Also Called: Union Pacific Railroad Company (P-3118)*

Union Pacific Railroad Company .... B....... 562 490-7000
   2401 E Sepulveda Blvd Long Beach (90810) *(P-3118)*

Union Sanitary District .... C....... 510 477-7500
   5072 Benson Rd Union City (94587) *(P-4853)*

Union Sup Comsy Solutions Inc .... B....... 785 357-5005
   2301 E Pacifica Pl Rancho Dominguez (90220) *(P-6408)*

Unionbancal Mortgage Corp .... D....... 415 705-7350
   400 California St San Francisco (94104) *(P-7638)*

Uniper Care Inc .... D....... 888 471-7623
   3415 S Sepulveda Blvd Los Angeles (90034) *(P-18365)*

Unique Protective Services, Santa Clarita *Also Called: Cottrell Paul Enterprises LLC*
(P-12953)

Unique Scaffold .... D....... 925 457-3379
   2501 Annalisa Dr Concord (94520) *(P-2324)*

Unis LLC .... D....... 310 747-7388
   19914 S Via Baron Rancho Dominguez (90220) *(P-3774)*

Unis LLC (PA) .... C....... 909 839-2600
   218 Machlin Ct Ste A Walnut (91789) *(P-4114)*

Unis Transportation LLC .... D....... 626 271-9800
   218 Machlin Ct Ste A Walnut (91789) *(P-3430)*

Uniserve Facilities Svcs Corp (PA) .... B....... 213 533-1000
   2363 S Atlantic Blvd Commerce (90040) *(P-10976)*

Uniserve Facilities Svcs Corp .... B....... 310 440-6747
   1200 Getty Center Dr Los Angeles (90049) *(P-10977)*

Unison, San Francisco *Also Called: Real Estate Equity Exchange (P-8014)*

Unisource Packaging Inc .... C....... 925 227-6000
   4225 Hacienda Dr Ste A Pleasanton (94588) *(P-6091)*

Unisource Solutions Inc (PA) .... C....... 562 654-3500
   8350 Rex Rd Pico Rivera (90660) *(P-5106)*

Unisys Corporation .... C....... 949 380-5000
   9701 Jeronimo Rd Ste 100 Irvine (92618) *(P-12002)*

Unitas Insurance Services, Rocklin *Also Called: Builders Trdsmens Insur Svcs I (P-8514)*

Unite Eurotherapy Inc .... D....... 760 585-1800
   2870 Whiptail Loop Ste 100 Carlsbad (92010) *(P-6147)*

Unite Hair .... D....... 760 585-1800
   2870 Whiptail Loop Ste 100 Carlsbad (92010) *(P-18801)*

United Access LLC .... D....... 623 879-0800
   4797 Ruffner St San Diego (92111) *(P-7596)*

United Administrative Services, San Jose *Also Called: Chelbay Schuler & Chelbay (P-8460)*

United Agencies Inc (PA) .... D....... 818 952-8818
   301 E Colorado Blvd Ste 200 Pasadena (91101) *(P-8678)*

United Airlines Inc .... D....... 310 258-3319
   7300 World Way W Rm 144 Los Angeles (90045) *(P-3847)*

United Amrcn Indian Invlvment (PA) .... C....... 213 202-3970
   1125 W 6th St Ste 103 Los Angeles (90017) *(P-17150)*

United Artist Releasing, Beverly Hills *Also Called: United Artists Films Company (P-13970)*

United Artists Corporation .... C....... 310 449-3000
   10250 Constellation Blvd Fl 19 Los Angeles (90067) *(P-13969)*

United Artists Films Company (DH) .... C....... 310 449-3000
   245 N Beverly Dr Beverly Hills (90210) *(P-13970)*

United Artists Productions Inc .... C....... 310 449-3000
   10250 Constellation Blvd Fl 19 Los Angeles (90067) *(P-13971)*

United Artists Television Corp .... B....... 310 449-3000
   10250 Constellation Blvd Fl 27 Los Angeles (90067) *(P-13972)*

United Behavioral Health (HQ) .... C....... 415 547-1403
   595 Market St San Francisco (94105) *(P-20237)*

United Blood Svcs Centl Coast, Ventura *Also Called: Vitalant (P-17347)*

United Brothers Concrete Inc .... C....... 760 346-1013
   41905 Boardwalk Ste K Palm Desert (92211) *(P-2167)*

United Building Maint Inc .... C....... 916 772-8101
   1143 N Market Blvd Ste 3 Sacramento (95834) *(P-10978)*

United Building Maintenance, Sacramento *Also Called: United Building Maint Inc (P-10978)*

United Bys Grls Clubs Snta BRB .... D....... 805 967-1612
   5701 Hollister Ave Goleta (93117) *(P-18918)*

United California Glass & Door .... D....... 415 824-8500
   745 Cesar Chavez San Francisco (94124) *(P-13807)*

United Cargo, San Francisco *Also Called: Skywest Airlines Inc (P-3844)*

United Cargo Logistics, City Of Industry *Also Called: U C L Incorporated (P-3558)*

United Cerebral Palsy Assoc (PA) .... C....... 209 956-0290
   333 W Benjamin Holt Dr Ste 1 Stockton (95207) *(P-18768)*

United Chrisitan Schools, Stockton *Also Called: Christian Brookside Schools (P-18293)*

United Com-Serve .... D....... 530 790-3000
   1260 Williams Way Yuba City (95991) *(P-15710)*

United Convalescent Facilities .... D....... 213 748-0491
   230 E Adams Blvd Los Angeles (90011) *(P-15906)*

United Couriers Inc (DH) .... C....... 213 383-3611
   3280 E Foothill Blvd Pasadena (91107) *(P-3848)*

Unitas Crbral Plsy Assn Ornge .... B....... 949 333-6400
   1251 E Dyer Rd Ste 150 Santa Ana (92705) *(P-18160)*

United Crbral Plsy Assn San Jq .... D....... 209 239-3066
   134 S Pacific Rd Manteca (95337) *(P-18631)*

United Crbral Plsy Assn San Lu .... D....... 805 543-2039
   3620 Sacramento Dr Ste 201 San Luis Obispo (93401) *(P-18161)*

United El Segundo Inc (PA) .... D....... 310 323-3992
   4130 Cover St Long Beach (90808) *(P-7392)*

United Fabricare Supply Inc (PA) .... D....... 310 537-2096
   1237 W Walnut St Compton (90220) *(P-5950)*

United Facility Solutions Inc .... B....... 310 743-3000
   19208 S Vermont Ave Ste 200 Gardena (90248) *(P-13059)*

United Farm Workers America (PA) .... C....... 661 822-5571
   29700 Woodford Tehachapi Rd Keene (93531) *(P-18802)*

ALPHABETIC SECTION

United Fmly Care Inc A Med Cor .... C....... 909 874-1679
8110 Mango Ave Ste 104 Fontana (92335) *(P-15141)*

United Food & Commercl Workers (PA)................................... D....... 714 995-4601
8530 Stanton Ave Buena Park (90620) *(P-18803)*

United Food and Commercial (PA).. D....... 213 487-7070
630 Shatto Pl Ste 300 Los Angeles (90005) *(P-18804)*

United Frfghters Los Angles Cy .... D....... 213 489-1300
1571 Beverly Blvd Los Angeles (90026) *(P-18805)*

United Gastroenterologists, Murrieta *Also Called: United Medical Doctors (P-15144)*

United Green Mark Inc .... D....... 408 295-3376
1145 N 13th St San Jose (95112) *(P-5814)*

United Guard Security Inc .... C....... 714 242-4051
1100 W Town And Country Rd Ste 1250 Orange (92868) *(P-13060)*

United Guard Security Inc .... C....... 909 402-0754
473 E Carnegie Dr Ste 200 San Bernardino (92408) *(P-13061)*

United Health Systems Inc .... C....... 530 662-9161
124 Walnut St Woodland (95695) *(P-15711)*

United Hlth Ctrs of San Jquin (PA)... D....... 559 646-6618
3875 W Beechwood Ave Fresno (93711) *(P-15142)*

United Imaging, Woodland Hills *Also Called: United Ribbon Company Inc (P-5260)*

United Indian Health Svcs Inc (PA)... C....... 707 825-5000
1600 Weeot Way Arcata (95521) *(P-15143)*

United Innovation Services Inc .... D....... 831 334-0673
950 Tower Ln Foster City (94404) *(P-20598)*

United International, Novato *Also Called: Cellmark Inc (P-6034)*

United Irrigation Inc .... D....... 760 347-6161
44907 Golf Center Pkwy Ste 3 Indio (92201) *(P-4996)*

United Lab Services Inc .... D....... 951 444-0467
2479 S Vicentia Ave Corona (92882) *(P-16766)*

United Marble & Granite Inc .... D....... 408 347-3300
2163 Martin Ave Santa Clara (95050) *(P-2325)*

United Marketing Group Inc .... D....... 323 778-4283
5957 S St Andrews Pl Los Angeles (90047) *(P-2024)*

United Material Handling Inc .... D....... 951 657-4900
4160 Temescal Canyon Rd Corona (92883) *(P-5876)*

United Mechanical, San Jose *Also Called: California United Mech Inc (P-1391)*

United Medical Doctors .... D....... 951 566-5229
28078 Baxter Rd Ste 530 Murrieta (92563) *(P-15144)*

United Medical Imaging (PA).. D....... 310 943-8400
1762 Westwood Blvd Ste 230 Los Angeles (90024) *(P-15145)*

United Medical Management Inc .... C....... 909 886-5291
1680 N Waterman Ave San Bernardino (92404) *(P-15907)*

United Merchant Svcs Cal Inc .... D....... 818 246-6767
750 Fairmont Ave Ste 201 Glendale (91203) *(P-5259)*

United Mfg Assembly Inc .... D....... 510 490-4680
44169 Fremont Blvd Fremont (94538) *(P-20003)*

United Natural Foods West Inc (HQ).. B....... 916 625-4100
1101 Sunset Blvd Rocklin (95765) *(P-3775)*

United Network Info Svcs, Walnut *Also Called: Unis LLC (P-4114)*

United Oil, Long Beach *Also Called: United El Segundo Inc (P-7392)*

United Online Advg Netwrk Inc .... D....... 818 287-3000
21301 Burbank Blvd Woodland Hills (91367) *(P-10685)*

United Owners Services, Anaheim *Also Called: Tricom Management Inc (P-20232)*

United Pacific Designs, Vernon *Also Called: UPD INC (P-3089)*

United Pacific Hotel Group LP .... C....... 650 295-6103
1221 Chess Dr Foster City (94404) *(P-10333)*

United Pacific Industries Inc .... D....... 562 421-3888
3788 E Conant St Long Beach (90808) *(P-5065)*

United Pacific Waste .... D....... 562 699-7600
4334 San Gabriel River Pkwy Pico Rivera (90660) *(P-4947)*

United Pallet Services Inc .... C....... 209 538-5844
4043 Crows Landing Rd Modesto (95358) *(P-2484)*

United Paradyne Corporation .... D....... 805 734-4734
Bldg 7525, Utah & 10th St Lompoc (93437) *(P-20238)*

United Parcel Service Inc .... D....... 559 442-2950
1601 W Mckinley Ave Fresno (93728) *(P-3431)*

United Parcel Service Inc .... C....... 530 623-3938
716 Main St 1 Weaverville (96093) *(P-3631)*

United Parcel Service Inc .... B....... 510 262-2338
1601 Atlas Rd Richmond (94806) *(P-3632)*

United Parcel Service Inc .... B....... 916 373-4076
1380 Shore St West Sacramento (95691) *(P-3633)*

United Parcel Service Inc .... A....... 949 643-6634
22 Brookline Aliso Viejo (92656) *(P-3634)*

United Parcel Service Inc .... C....... 310 217-2646
17115 S Western Ave Gardena (90247) *(P-3635)*

United Parcel Service Inc .... A....... 909 974-7212
3140 Jurupa St Ontario (91761) *(P-3636)*

United Parcel Service Inc .... D....... 408 291-2942
1999 S 7th St San Jose (95112) *(P-3637)*

United Parcel Service Inc .... A....... 415 252-4564
2222 17th St San Francisco (94103) *(P-3638)*

United Parcel Service Inc .... B....... 404 828-6000
16000 Arminta St Van Nuys (91406) *(P-3639)*

United Parcel Service Inc .... A....... 909 279-5111
7925 Ronson Rd San Diego (92111) *(P-3640)*

United Parcel Service Inc .... A....... 510 813-5662
8400 Pardee Dr Oakland (94621) *(P-3641)*

United Parcel Service Inc .... B....... 562 404-3236
13233 Moore St Cerritos (90703) *(P-3642)*

United Parcel Service Inc .... D....... 805 375-1832
1501 Rancho Conejo Blvd Newbury Park (91320) *(P-3643)*

United Parcel Service Inc .... C....... 619 482-8119
2300 Boswell Ct Chula Vista (91914) *(P-3644)*

United Parcel Service Inc .... B....... 626 814-6216
1100 Baldwin Park Blvd Baldwin Park (91706) *(P-3645)*

United Parcel Service Inc .... C....... 800 742-5877
1457 E Victoria Ave San Bernardino (92408) *(P-3849)*

United Parcel Service Inc .... C....... 510 264-8880
26557 Danti Ct 1st Fl Hayward (94545) *(P-3850)*

United Parcel Service Inc .... C....... 909 605-7740
3110 Jurupa St Ontario (91761) *(P-3851)*

United Parcel Service Inc .... C....... 323 260-8957
3333 S Downey Rd Vernon (90058) *(P-3859)*

United Paving Company, Corona *Also Called: Superior Paving Company Inc (P-1168)*

United Pumping Service Inc .... D....... 626 961-9326
14000 Valley Blvd City Of Industry (91746) *(P-3432)*

United Ribbon Company Inc .... D....... 818 716-1515
21201 Oxnard St Woodland Hills (91367) *(P-5260)*

United Riggers & Erectors Inc (PA).. D....... 909 978-0400
4188 Valley Blvd Walnut (91789) *(P-2251)*

United Rock Products Corp .... C....... 714 578-9600
135 S State College Blvd Ste 400 Brea (92821) *(P-1175)*

United SEC Specialists Inc .... C....... 408 878-5120
2010 El Camino Real Santa Clara (95050) *(P-13062)*

United Site Services Cal Inc .... C....... 408 295-2263
3408 Hillcap Ave San Jose (95136) *(P-11059)*

United Site Services Cal Inc .... D....... 805 933-2793
411 S Beckwith Rd Santa Paula (93060) *(P-11060)*

United States Cold Storage Cal, Bakersfield *Also Called: United States Cold Storage Inc (P-3664)*

United States Cold Storage Inc .... D....... 209 668-1636
3500 W Canal Dr Turlock (95380) *(P-3663)*

United States Cold Storage Inc .... D....... 661 832-2653
6501 District Blvd Bakersfield (93313) *(P-3664)*

United States Cold Storage Inc .... D....... 916 392-9160
3936 Dudley Blvd Mcclellan (95652) *(P-3665)*

United States Cold Storage Inc .... D....... 209 835-2653
1400 N Macarthur Dr Ste A Tracy (95376) *(P-3666)*

United States Enrgy Foundation .... D....... 415 561-6700
55 2nd St San Francisco (94105) *(P-19115)*

United States Luggage Co LLC .... D....... 562 293-4400
13300 Carmenita Rd Santa Fe Springs (90670) *(P-6057)*

United States Marine Corps .... D....... 760 725-3564
Marine Corps Air Stn Bldg 23122 (Camp Pendleton) Oceanside (92049) *(P-5970)*

United States Technical Svcs .... C....... 714 374-6300
16541 Gothard St Ste 214 Huntington Beach (92647) *(P-12901)*

United Stationers, City Of Industry *Also Called: Essendant Co (P-6065)*

United Sttes Dept Enrgy Brkley .... C....... 510 486-7089
555 W Imperial Hwy Brea (92821) *(P-19923)*

United Sttes Dept Enrgy Brkley .... C....... 510 701-1089
1226 Cornell Ave Albany (94706) *(P-19924)*

United Sttes Dept Enrgy Brkley .... C....... 510 486-4033
419 Latimer Hall Berkeley (94720) *(P-19925)*

ALPHABETIC SECTION

United Sttes Dept Enrgy Lvrmor .... A....... 925 423-1521
   741 S H St Livermore (94550) *(P-19791)*

United Sttes Dept Enrgy Lvrmor .... A....... 415 648-3878
   539 Peralta Ave San Francisco (94110) *(P-19926)*

United Sttes Dept Enrgy Lvrmor .... A....... 408 267-1413
   1413 Willowtree Ct San Jose (95118) *(P-19927)*

United Studios Self Def Inc .... C....... 858 486-8773
   13331 Poway Rd Poway (92064) *(P-14580)*

United Studios Self Def Inc .... C....... 949 293-1391
   28251 Marguerite Pkwy Ste J Mission Viejo (92692) *(P-14581)*

United Support Services Inc .... C....... 858 373-9500
   3252 Holiday Ct Ste 110 La Jolla (92037) *(P-12003)*

United Svcs Amer Federal Cr Un (PA) .... D....... 858 831-8100
   9999 Willow Creek Rd San Diego (92131) *(P-7814)*

United Talent Agency LLC .... C....... 310 776-8160
   9336 Civic Center Dr Beverly Hills (90210) *(P-13524)*

United Talent Agency, LLC, Beverly Hills Also Called: United Talent Agency LLC *(P-13524)*

United Teachers-Los Angeles .... D....... 213 487-5560
   3303 Wilshire Blvd Fl 10 Los Angeles (90010) *(P-18806)*

United Technologies, Anaheim Also Called: Otis Elevator Company *(P-5854)*

United Terminal Leasing LLC .... B....... 510 302-3900
   3 Embarcadero Ctr Ste 550 San Francisco (94111) *(P-11061)*

United Textile Inc .... D....... 510 276-2288
   1025 98th Ave Bldg A Oakland (94603) *(P-13525)*

United Van Lines, Fontana Also Called: McCollisters Trnsp Group Inc *(P-3514)*

United Vision Financial Inc .... C....... 818 285-0211
   16027 Ventura Blvd # 200 Encino (91436) *(P-8062)*

United Way Inc (PA) .... D....... **213 808-6220**
   1150 S Olive St Ste T-500 Los Angeles (90015) *(P-18632)*

United Way Greater Los Angeles, Los Angeles Also Called: United Way Inc *(P-18632)*

UNItogether Inc .... D....... 707 208-7602
   1253 Gray Hawk Ln Suisun City (94585) *(P-19116)*

Unitrin Direct Insurance Co (HQ) .... D....... 760 603-3276
   80 Blue Ravine Rd Ste 200 Folsom (95630) *(P-8474)*

Unity Care Group .... D....... 408 971-9822
   1400 Parkmoor Ave Ste 115 San Jose (95126) *(P-18162)*

Unity Courier Service Inc (DH) .... C....... **323 255-9800**
   3231 Fletcher Dr Los Angeles (90065) *(P-3646)*

Unity Courier Service Inc .... C....... 510 568-8890
   1132 Beecher St San Leandro (94577) *(P-3647)*

Unity Courier Service Inc .... C....... 209 239-5400
   955 W Center St Manteca (95337) *(P-13526)*

Unity Courier Service Inc .... C....... 916 246-0390
   1645 Parkway Blvd Ste A West Sacramento (95691) *(P-13527)*

Unity Software Inc (PA) .... B....... **415 539-3162**
   30 3rd St San Francisco (94103) *(P-12004)*

Univar Solutions USA Inc .... C....... 323 727-7005
   2600 Garfield Ave Commerce (90040) *(P-6714)*

Universal, Richmond Also Called: Universal Bldg Svcs & Sup Co *(P-10980)*

Universal American Mrtg Co Cal .... A....... 916 773-2722
   1420 Rocky Ridge Dr Ste 320 Roseville (95661) *(P-8026)*

Universal Bldg Svcs & Sup Co .... C....... 707 781-7434
   1318 Ross St Petaluma (94954) *(P-10979)*

Universal Bldg Svcs & Sup Co (PA) .... C....... **510 527-1078**
   3120 Pierce St Richmond (94804) *(P-10980)*

Universal Bldg Svcs & Sup Co .... D....... 925 934-5533
   421 N Buchanan Cir Ste 3 Pacheco (94553) *(P-10981)*

Universal Bldg Svcs & Sup Co .... D....... 408 995-5111
   430 Roberson Ln San Jose (95112) *(P-10982)*

Universal Building Svc & Sup, Petaluma Also Called: Universal Bldg Svcs & Sup Co *(P-10979)*

Universal Card Inc .... B....... 949 861-4000
   9012 Research Dr Ste 200 Irvine (92618) *(P-13528)*

Universal Care Inc (HQ) .... B....... **562 424-6200**
   19762 Macarthur Blvd Ste 100 Irvine (92612) *(P-17151)*

Universal Charter Services, Sacramento Also Called: Universal Limousine & Trnsp Co *(P-3302)*

Universal City Studios Lllp .... A....... 818 622-8477
   100 Universal City Plz Universal City (91608) *(P-13906)*

Universal Custom Courier, San Fernando Also Called: Universal Mail Delivery Svc *(P-10779)*

Universal Dust Cllctr Mfg Sup (PA) .... D....... **714 630-8588**
   1041 N Kraemer Pl Anaheim (92806) *(P-852)*

Universal Home Care Inc .... C....... 323 653-9222
   151 N San Vicente Blvd Ste 200 Beverly Hills (90211) *(P-16957)*

Universal Limousine & Trnsp Co .... D....... 916 361-5466
   9944 Mills Station Rd Ste C Sacramento (95827) *(P-3302)*

Universal Mail Delivery Svc (PA) .... D....... **818 365-3144**
   501 S Brand Blvd # 104 San Fernando (91340) *(P-10779)*

Universal Mus Group Dist Corp .... D....... 818 508-9550
   111 Universal Hollywood Dr Ste 1420 Universal City (91608) *(P-13529)*

Universal Mus Investments Inc (HQ) .... D....... **888 583-7176**
   2220 Colorado Ave Santa Monica (90404) *(P-13530)*

Universal Music Group Inc (HQ) .... D....... 310 865-0770
   2220 Colorado Ave Santa Monica (90404) *(P-13531)*

Universal Packg Systems Inc (PA) .... A....... **909 517-2442**
   14570 Monte Vista Ave Chino (91710) *(P-2633)*

Universal Packg Systems Inc .... C....... 909 517-2442
   14570 Monte Vista Ave Chino (91710) *(P-3776)*

Universal Pctres HM Entrmt LLC (DH) .... D....... **818 777-1000**
   100 Universal City Plz Bldg 1440/7 Universal City (91608) *(P-13907)*

Universal Pictures Intl, Universal City Also Called: Nbcuniversal Media LLC *(P-4398)*

Universal Protection Svc LP (HQ) .... D....... **866 877-1965**
   545 Sansome St San Francisco (94111) *(P-13063)*

Universal Prtction SEC Systems (DH) .... D....... **714 923-3700**
   1815 E Wilshire Ave Ste 910 Santa Ana (92705) *(P-13064)*

Universal Robots USA Inc .... D....... 949 230-3642
   101 Pacifica Ste 350 Irvine (92618) *(P-5877)*

Universal Services America LP .... A....... 714 923-3700
   1815 E Wilshire Ave Ste 912 Santa Ana (92705) *(P-10983)*

Universal Services America LP .... A....... 760 200-2865
   77725 Enfield Ln Palm Desert (92211) *(P-13065)*

Universal Services America LP (HQ) .... D....... **866 877-1965**
   450 Exchange Irvine (92602) *(P-13066)*

Universal Services America LP .... A....... 408 993-1965
   777 N 1st St Ste 150 San Jose (95112) *(P-13067)*

Universal Shopping Plaza A CA .... C....... 714 521-8899
   6281 Regio Ave Buena Park (90620) *(P-8773)*

Universal Site Services Inc (PA) .... D....... **800 647-9337**
   760 E Capitol Ave Milpitas (95035) *(P-10984)*

Universal Stdios Licensing LLC .... C....... 818 695-1273
   100 Universal City Plz Universal City (91608) *(P-9459)*

Universal Studios, Universal City Also Called: Creative Park Productions LLC *(P-13833)*

Universal Studios, Universal City Also Called: Universal City Studios Lllp *(P-13906)*

Universal Studios Company LLC (DH) .... A....... **818 777-1000**
   100 Universal City Plz North Hollywood (91608) *(P-13908)*

Universal Technical Inst Inc .... C....... 909 484-1929
   9494 Haven Ave Rancho Cucamonga (91730) *(P-17798)*

UNIVERSITY BOOKSTORE, Long Beach Also Called: Forty-Niner Shops Inc *(P-7547)*

University Business Ctr Assoc .... D....... 601 354-3555
   5383 Hollister Ave Ste 120 Santa Barbara (93111) *(P-8774)*

University Cal Los Angeles .... A....... 310 825-9111
   757 Westwood Plz Los Angeles (90095) *(P-16589)*

University Cal Los Angeles .... C....... 310 825-7852
   420 Westwood Plz Rm 7702 Los Angeles (90095) *(P-17769)*

University Cal Riverside .... C....... 951 027-4801
   1160 University Ave Riverside (92507) *(P-19854)*

University Cal Rvrside Almni A .... D....... 559 646-6500
   9240 S Riverbend Ave Parlier (93648) *(P-19928)*

University Cal San Diego .... B....... 858 534-2377
   9500 Gilman Dr Dept 908 La Jolla (92093) *(P-10821)*

University Cal San Diego .... B....... 858 534-5000
   10100 Hopkins Dr La Jolla (92093) *(P-12639)*

University Cal San Diego .... D....... 619 294-3746
   4520 Executive Dr Ste 101 San Diego (92121) *(P-15146)*

University Cal San Diego .... A....... 619 543-6654
   200 W Arbor Dr.Frnt San Diego (92103) *(P-16590)*

University Cal San Diego .... A....... 858 657-7000
   9300 Campus Point Dr La Jolla (92037) *(P-16591)*

University Cal San Diego .... C....... 619 543-6170
   402 Dickinson St Ste 380 San Diego (92103) *(P-16592)*

University Cal San Diego .... D....... 619 471-9393
   200 W Arbor Dr San Diego (92103) *(P-16593)*

University Cal San Diego .... D....... 858 534-2177
   10280 N Torrey Pines Rd Ste 470 La Jolla (92037) *(P-19515)*

ALPHABETIC SECTION — University Honda

University Cal San Diego .... D 858 622-1771
5440 Morehouse Dr Ste 2600 San Diego (92121) *(P-19929)*

University Cal San Francisco .... D 510 987-0700
616 Forbes Blvd South San Francisco (94080) *(P-3777)*

University Cal San Francisco .... D 559 251-3033
2120 N Winery Ave Ste 102 Fresno (93703) *(P-8891)*

University Cal San Francisco .... C 415 989-5339
311 California St Ste 410 San Francisco (94104) *(P-15147)*

University Cal San Francisco .... D 415 353-2383
400 Parnassus Ave San Francisco (94143) *(P-15148)*

University Cal San Francisco .... C 415 353-7900
1545 Divisadero St San Francisco (94143) *(P-15149)*

University Cal San Francisco .... C 415 353-1915
1500 Owens St San Francisco (94158) *(P-15150)*

University Cal San Francisco .... D 415 353-7576
1701 Divisadero St Ste 240 San Francisco (94115) *(P-15151)*

University Cal San Francisco .... D 415 476-4575
400 Parnassus Ave Fl 2 San Francisco (94143) *(P-15152)*

University Cal San Francisco .... D 415 476-5608
100 Buchanan St San Francisco (94102) *(P-15253)*

University Cal San Francisco .... C 415 476-7000
401 Parnassus Ave San Francisco (94143) *(P-16594)*

University Cal San Francisco .... D 415 476-1611
400 Parnassus Ave Ste A633 San Francisco (94143) *(P-16595)*

University Cal San Francisco .... C 415 567-6600
1600 Divisadero St San Francisco (94143) *(P-16596)*

University Cal San Francisco .... D 415 206-8812
2550 23rd St Bldg 9 San Francisco (94110) *(P-16597)*

University Cal San Francisco .... D 415 206-8430
1001 Potrero Ave Ste 7m San Francisco (94110) *(P-16660)*

University Cal San Francisco .... D 415 502-8516
1825 4th St San Francisco (94143) *(P-16700)*

University Cal San Francisco .... D 415 597-8047
982 Mission St San Francisco (94103) *(P-17152)*

University Cal San Francisco .... D 415 476-2695
513 Parnassus Ave # 0556 San Francisco (94143) *(P-17770)*

University Cal San Francisco .... D 415 353-2757
2380 Sutter St Fl 3 San Francisco (94115) *(P-17771)*

University Cal San Francisco .... D 415 885-7257
1100 Van Ness Ave San Francisco (94109) *(P-17772)*

University Cal San Francisco .... C 415 476-3016
521 Parnassus Ave Rm C152 San Francisco (94143) *(P-17773)*

University Cal San Francisco .... C 415 353-7700
1545 Divisadero St Fl 4 San Francisco (94143) *(P-17774)*

University Cal San Francisco .... D 415 353-7300
1701 Divisadero St San Francisco (94115) *(P-17775)*

University Cal San Francisco .... D 415 885-3668
1500 Owens St Ste 320 San Francisco (94158) *(P-17776)*

University Cal San Francisco .... D 415 885-7495
2233 Post St Ste 303 San Francisco (94115) *(P-17777)*

University Cal San Francisco .... D 415 885-3610
2356 Sutter St Fl 3 San Francisco (94115) *(P-17778)*

University Cal San Francisco .... D 415 476-3061
350 Parnassus Ave Ste 509 San Francisco (94117) *(P-17779)*

University Cal San Francisco .... D 415 353-2961
400 Parnassus Ave Fl 5 San Francisco (94143) *(P-17780)*

University Cal San Francisco .... D 415 885-7478
2356 Sutter St San Francisco (94115) *(P-17781)*

University Cal San Francisco .... D 628 206-2400
995 Potrero Ave San Francisco (94110) *(P-19930)*

University Cal San Francisco .... D 415 476-9323
1450 3rd St San Francisco (94143) *(P-19931)*

UNIVERSITY CAL SAN FRANCISCO, San Francisco *Also Called: University Cal San Francisco (P-15147)*

University Cal San Frncsco Fnd .... D 415 775-2111
3333 California St Ste 10 San Francisco (94118) *(P-18535)*

University California Davis .... C 530 752-8277
1 Shields Ave Davis (95616) *(P-3353)*

University California Davis .... D 530 752-5435
1 Shields Ave Davis (95616) *(P-3921)*

University California Davis .... D 916 985-9300
251 Turn Pike Dr Folsom (95630) *(P-15153)*

University California Davis .... D 530 747-3000
2660 W Covell Blvd Davis (95616) *(P-15154)*

University California Davis .... D 530 885-5618
3200 Bell Rd Auburn (95603) *(P-15155)*

University California Davis .... D 916 734-8514
4150 V St Sacramento (95817) *(P-15156)*

University California Davis .... C 530 752-4167
Rm Tb 128 Old Davis Rd Davis (95616) *(P-15157)*

University California Davis .... D 916 734-3588
4860 Y St Sacramento (95817) *(P-15158)*

University California Davis .... D 916 295-5700
550 W Ranch View Dr Ste 2005 Rocklin (95765) *(P-15159)*

University California Davis .... D 916 442-1011
500 University Ave Ste 220 Sacramento (95825) *(P-15160)*

University California Davis .... C 916 734-2846
2315 Stockton Blvd Rm 6309 Sacramento (95817) *(P-15161)*

University California Davis .... D 916 734-3141
4400 V St Sacramento (95817) *(P-16598)*

University California Davis .... C 916 734-2011
2315 Stockton Blvd Sacramento (95817) *(P-16599)*

University California Davis .... D 916 734-5113
4150 V St Ste 1200 Sacramento (95817) *(P-16600)*

University California Davis .... D 530 752-2314
1 Shields Ave Davis (95616) *(P-16767)*

University California Davis .... D 530 752-1653
4112a Tupper Hall Davis (95616) *(P-17782)*

University California Davis .... C 530 750-1313
2801 2nd St Davis (95618) *(P-19792)*

University California Irvine .... C 949 824-6483
1001 Health Sciences Rd Irvine (92617) *(P-13532)*

University California Irvine .... D 949 644-5245
43 Cambria Dr Corona Del Mar (92625) *(P-15162)*

University California Irvine .... A 714 456-6170
101 The City Dr S Bldg 1a Orange (92868) *(P-15163)*

University California Irvine .... B 714 480-2443
800 N Main St Santa Ana (92701) *(P-15164)*

University California Irvine .... C 714 456-7890
101 The City Dr S Orange (92868) *(P-15165)*

University California Irvine .... D 949 646-2267
1640 Newport Blvd Ste 340 Costa Mesa (92627) *(P-15166)*

University California Irvine .... D 714 456-6966
101 The City Dr S Ste 313 Orange (92868) *(P-15167)*

University California Irvine .... B 714 456-8000
101 The City Dr S Orange (92868) *(P-16601)*

University California Irvine .... A 714 456-6011
101 The City Dr S Orange (92868) *(P-16602)*

University California Irvine .... C 714 456-5558
200 S Manchester Ave 400 Orange (92868) *(P-16603)*

University California Irvine .... C 714 775-3066
15355 Brookhurst St Ste 102 Westminster (92683) *(P-16604)*

University California Irvine .... D 949 939-7106
31865 Circle Dr Laguna Beach (92651) *(P-17343)*

University California Irvine .... D 949 824-2662
106 B Student Ctr Irvine (92697) *(P-17344)*

University California Irvine .... C 949 824-7725
3151 Social Science Plz Irvine (92697) *(P-17783)*

University California Irvine .... D 949 824-6828
120 Theory Ste 200 Irvine (92617) *(P-19636)*

University California Irvine .... D 714 456-6655
200 S Manchester Ave Ste 650 Orange (92868) *(P-19637)*

University California Irvine .... A 949 824-2819
2220 Engineering Gtwy Irvine (92697) *(P-19793)*

University California Berkeley .... D 510 642-6000
2195 Hearst Ave Ste 250 Berkeley (94720) *(P-12902)*

University Credit Union .... C 310 477-6628
1500 S Sepulveda Blvd Los Angeles (90025) *(P-7815)*

University Enterprises Inc .... A 916 278-7001
6000 J St Sacramento (95819) *(P-17818)*

University Healthcare Alliance .... C 510 974-8281
7999 Gateway Blvd Ste 200 Newark (94560) *(P-16958)*

University Honda, Davis *Also Called: Envirnmental Trnsp Specialists (P-7201)*

University Marelich Mech Inc .... D...... 714 632-2600
1000 N Kraemer Pl Anaheim (92806) *(P-1589)*

University of California .... C...... 530 752-0503
1 Shields Ave Davis (95616) *(P-20239)*

University of California .... C...... 415 353-2057
1500 Owens St Ste 320 San Francisco (94158) *(P-20599)*

University Park Healthcare Ctr, Los Angeles Also Called: United Convalescent Facilities *(P-15906)*

University Retirement Cmnty, Davis Also Called: Pacific Retirement Svcs Inc *(P-18503)*

University Southern California .... D...... 323 865-3050
1441 Eastlake Ave Los Angeles (90089) *(P-15168)*

University Southern California .... A...... 323 442-8500
1500 San Pablo St Los Angeles (90033) *(P-16605)*

University Surgical Associates, Fresno Also Called: Central Cal Fclty Med Group In *(P-14667)*

Univision Radio Inc .... D...... 619 744-4370
600 W Broadway Ste 2150 San Diego (92101) *(P-4408)*

Uniwell Corporation .... C...... 559 268-1000
2233 Ventura St Fresno (93721) *(P-9278)*

Uniwell Corporation .... C...... 714 522-7000
7000 Beach Blvd Buena Park (90620) *(P-10334)*

Unix Packaging LLC .... B...... 213 627-5050
5361 Alexander St Commerce (90040) *(P-6954)*

Unravel Data Systems Inc .... D...... 650 741-3442
801 High St Palo Alto (94301) *(P-12005)*

Unspoken Language Services Inc .... B...... 626 532-8096
1370 Valley Vista Dr Ste 200 Diamond Bar (91765) *(P-13533)*

Untitled Labs Inc .... D...... 415 858-7078
One Market Spear Tower 36th Fl San Francisco (94105) *(P-735)*

UPD INC .... D...... 323 588-8811
4507 S Maywood Ave Vernon (90058) *(P-3089)*

Upland Community Care Inc .... C...... 909 985-1903
1221 E Arrow Hwy Upland (91786) *(P-15712)*

Upland Highlanders High Ptsa .... D...... 909 949-7880
565 W 11th St Upland (91786) *(P-18919)*

Uplift Inc .... C...... 408 396-3374
440 N Wolfe Rd Sunnyvale (94085) *(P-13534)*

Uplift Family Services .... D...... 626 287-2988
9353 E Valley Blvd Ste C Rosemead (91770) *(P-15169)*

Uplift Family Services .... A...... 626 254-5000
800 S Santa Anita Ave Arcadia (91006) *(P-18163)*

Uplift Family Services (PA) .... D...... **408 379-3790**
251 Llewellyn Ave Campbell (95008) *(P-18164)*

Uplift Travel Services, Sunnyvale Also Called: Uplift Inc *(P-13534)*

Uprite Construction Corp .... D...... 949 877-8877
2211 Michelson Dr Ste 500 Irvine (92612) *(P-853)*

UPS, Fresno Also Called: United Parcel Service Inc *(P-3431)*
UPS, Weaverville Also Called: United Parcel Service Inc *(P-3631)*
UPS, Richmond Also Called: United Parcel Service Inc *(P-3632)*
UPS, West Sacramento Also Called: United Parcel Service Inc *(P-3633)*
UPS, Aliso Viejo Also Called: United Parcel Service Inc *(P-3634)*
UPS, Gardena Also Called: United Parcel Service Inc *(P-3635)*
UPS, Ontario Also Called: United Parcel Service Inc *(P-3636)*
UPS, San Jose Also Called: United Parcel Service Inc *(P-3637)*
UPS, Van Nuys Also Called: United Parcel Service Inc *(P-3639)*
UPS, San Diego Also Called: United Parcel Service Inc *(P-3640)*
UPS, Oakland Also Called: United Parcel Service Inc *(P-3641)*
UPS, Cerritos Also Called: United Parcel Service Inc *(P-3642)*
UPS, Newbury Park Also Called: United Parcel Service Inc *(P-3643)*
UPS, Chula Vista Also Called: United Parcel Service Inc *(P-3644)*
UPS, Baldwin Park Also Called: United Parcel Service Inc *(P-3645)*
UPS, San Leandro Also Called: UPS Expedited Mail Svcs Inc *(P-3648)*
UPS, San Bernardino Also Called: United Parcel Service Inc *(P-3849)*
UPS, Hayward Also Called: United Parcel Service Inc *(P-3850)*
UPS, Ontario Also Called: United Parcel Service Inc *(P-3851)*
UPS, Vernon Also Called: United Parcel Service Inc *(P-3859)*
UPS, Union City Also Called: UPS Worldwide Logistics Inc *(P-4115)*

UPS Expedited Mail Svcs Inc .... B...... 510 297-4600
14390 Washington Ave San Leandro (94578) *(P-3648)*

UPS Expedited Mail Svcs Inc .... B...... 510 297-5029
14500 Washington Ave San Leandro (94578) *(P-3649)*

UPS Freight .... C...... 408 727-0703
751 Nuttman St Santa Clara (95054) *(P-4177)*

UPS Store Inc (HQ) .... B...... **858 455-8800**
6060 Cornerstone Ct W San Diego (92121) *(P-13535)*

UPS Worldwide Logistics Inc .... D...... 510 476-4000
30336 Whipple Rd Union City (94587) *(P-4115)*

Upstanding LLC .... C...... 949 788-9900
440 Exchange Ste 100 Irvine (92602) *(P-12388)*

Upstart, San Mateo Also Called: Upstart Network Inc *(P-7887)*

Upstart Network Inc .... C...... 650 204-1000
2950 S Delaware St Ste 300 San Mateo (94403) *(P-7887)*

Upstrem Inc .... D...... 858 229-2979
1253 University Ave Ste 1003 San Diego (92103) *(P-20600)*

Upwind Blade Solutions Inc .... B...... 866 927-3142
2869 Historic Decatur Rd Ste 100 San Diego (92106) *(P-13808)*

Upwork Inc (PA) .... C...... **650 316-7500**
2625 Augustine Dr Ste 601 Santa Clara (95054) *(P-11250)*

Urata & Sons Concrete Inc .... C...... 916 638-5364
3430 Luyung Dr Rancho Cordova (95742) *(P-2168)*

Urata & Sons Concrete LLC .... D...... 916 638-5364
3430 Luyung Dr Rancho Cordova (95742) *(P-2169)*

Urban Alchemy .... D...... 415 757-0896
1035 Market St Ste 150 San Francisco (94103) *(P-18165)*

Urban Commons Queensway LLC .... A...... 562 499-1611
1126 Queens Hwy Long Beach (90802) *(P-10335)*

Urban Corps San Diego County .... C...... 619 235-6884
3127 Jefferson St San Diego (92110) *(P-18920)*

Urban Decay, Newport Beach Also Called: Urban Decay Cosmetics LLC *(P-6148)*

Urban Decay Cosmetics LLC .... B...... 949 631-4504
833 W 16th St Newport Beach (92663) *(P-6148)*

Urban Painting Inc .... D...... 415 485-1130
630 Las Gallinas Ave San Rafael (94903) *(P-1643)*

Urban Services Eastlake YMCA, Oakland Also Called: Young MNS Chrstn Assn of E Bay *(P-18981)*

Urban Services YMCA, Oakland Also Called: Young MNS Chrstn Assn of E Bay *(P-18963)*

Urgent Care Center, Livermore Also Called: Stanford Hlth Care Tri-Valley *(P-15101)*

Urgent Care Center, Montclair Also Called: Prime Hlthcare Srvcs-Mntclair *(P-16337)*

Urology Associates Central Cal .... D...... 559 321-2800
7014 N Whitney Ave Ste A Fresno (93720) *(P-15170)*

URS, Long Beach Also Called: URS Group Inc *(P-19424)*
URS, Oakland Also Called: URS Group Inc *(P-19425)*
URS, Oakland Also Called: URS Group Inc *(P-19426)*
URS, San Jose Also Called: URS Group Inc *(P-19427)*
URS, Fresno Also Called: URS Group Inc *(P-19428)*
URS, Chico Also Called: URS Group Inc *(P-19932)*

URS Global Holdings Inc .... D...... 415 774-2700
600 Montgomery St Fl 28 San Francisco (94111) *(P-19516)*

URS Group Inc .... D...... 562 420-2933
3995 Via Oro Ave Long Beach (90810) *(P-19424)*

URS Group Inc .... A...... 510 893-3600
300 Lakeside Dr Ste 400 Oakland (94612) *(P-19425)*

URS Group Inc .... D...... 925 446-3800
300 Lakeside Dr Ste 400 Oakland (94612) *(P-19426)*

URS Group Inc .... D...... 408 297-9585
4 N 2nd St San Jose (95113) *(P-19427)*

URS Group Inc .... D...... 559 255-2541
1360 E Spruce Ave Ste 101 Fresno (93720) *(P-19428)*

URS Group Inc .... D...... 530 893-9675
1550 Humboldt Rd Ste 2 Chico (95928) *(P-19932)*

URS Holdings Inc (DH) .... B...... **415 774-2700**
600 Montgomery St Fl 25 San Francisco (94111) *(P-19429)*

Ursus It Staffing and Services .... D...... 877 668-7787
600 California St San Francisco (94108) *(P-11251)*

US Airconditioning Distributors Inc (PA) .... C...... **626 854-4500**
16900 Chestnut St City Of Industry (91748) *(P-5775)*

US Bank, Larkspur Also Called: US Bank Equipment Finance *(P-7720)*

US Bank Equipment Finance .... D...... 415 461-4600
801 Larkspur Landing Cir Larkspur (94939) *(P-7720)*

ALPHABETIC SECTION

US Bankcard Services Inc .... D...... 888 888-8872
　17171 Gale Ave Ste 110 City Of Industry (91745) *(P-13536)*
US Best Repair Service Inc .... C...... 888 750-2378
　1652 Edinger Ave Ste E Tustin (92780) *(P-736)*
US Best Repairs, Tustin *Also Called: US Best Repair Service Inc (P-736)*
US Business Funding, Newport Beach *Also Called: PAR Consulting LLC (P-7902)*
US Carenet Services LLC .... C...... 408 871-9860
　901 Campisi Way Ste 205 Campbell (95008) *(P-16959)*
US Carenet Services LLC .... C...... 408 378-6131
　815 Pollard Rd Los Gatos (95032) *(P-16960)*
US Carenet Services LLC .... C...... 661 945-7350
　42225 10th St W Ste 2b Lancaster (93534) *(P-16961)*
US Data Management LLC (PA) .... D...... 888 231-0816
　535 Chapala St Santa Barbara (93101) *(P-12903)*
US Dermatology Medical Management Inc .... D...... 817 962-2157
　1401 N Batavia St Ste 204 Orange (92867) *(P-15171)*
US Foods Inc .... B...... 925 606-3525
　300 Lawrence Dr Frnt Livermore (94551) *(P-6409)*
US Foods Inc .... C...... 714 670-3500
　15155 Northam St La Mirada (90638) *(P-6410)*
US Foods Inc .... C...... 562 806-2445
　8457 Eastern Ave Bell Gardens (90201) *(P-6686)*
US Foods Inc .... C...... 213 623-4150
　636 Stanford Ave Los Angeles (90021) *(P-6687)*
US Foods Inc .... C...... 925 606-1919
　4671 Las Positas Rd Ste B Livermore (94551) *(P-6688)*
US Foods Inc .... C...... 310 632-6265
　1610 E Sepulveda Blvd Carson (90745) *(P-6689)*
US Foods Inc .... C...... 209 948-0793
　1320 W Weber Ave Stockton (95203) *(P-6690)*
US Grant Hotel Ventures LLC .... D...... 619 744-2007
　326 Broadway San Diego (92101) *(P-10336)*
US Healthworks Inc (DH) .... D...... 661 678-2300
　28035 Avenue Stanford Valencia (91355) *(P-15172)*
US Hotel and Resort MGT Inc .... C...... 949 650-2988
　2544 Newport Blvd Costa Mesa (92627) *(P-10337)*
US Interactive Delaware .... C...... 408 863-7500
　1270 Oakmead Pkwy Ste 318 Sunnyvale (94085) *(P-10686)*
US Lines, Newport Beach *Also Called: US Lines LLC (P-4116)*
US Lines LLC (DH) .... D...... 714 751-3333
　3501 Jamboree Rd Ste 300 Newport Beach (92660) *(P-4116)*
US Real Estate Services Inc .... D...... 949 598-9920
　27442 Portola Pkwy Ste 300 Foothill Ranch (92610) *(P-9205)*
US Security Associates, Burbank *Also Called: US Security Associates Inc (P-13068)*
US Security Associates Inc .... B...... 818 697-1809
　455 N Moss St Burbank (91502) *(P-13068)*
US Security Associates Inc .... B...... 714 352-0773
　2275 W 190th St Ste 100 Torrance (90504) *(P-13069)*
US Skillserve Inc .... A...... 909 621-4751
　9620 Fremont Ave Montclair (91763) *(P-15713)*
US Solid Surfaces .... D...... 510 300-8980
　23481 Connecticut St Hayward (94545) *(P-2326)*
US Trust, Los Angeles *Also Called: U S Trust Company NA (P-8226)*
US Venture Partners .... D...... 650 854-9080
　1460 El Camino Real Ste 100 Menlo Park (94025) *(P-8171)*
USA Enterprise Inc .... B...... 310 750-4246
　9777 Wilshire Blvd Ste 400 Beverly Hills (90212) *(P-9576)*
USA Federal Credit Union, San Diego *Also Called: United Svcs Amer Federal Cr Un (P-7814)*
USA Multifamily Management Inc .... C...... 916 773-6060
　3200 Douglas Blvd Ste 200 Roseville (95661) *(P-9206)*
USA Seller Co LLC .... A...... 209 656-7085
　2840 Countryside Dr Turlock (95380) *(P-7597)*
USA Staffing Inc .... D...... 805 269-2677
　505 Higuera St San Luis Obispo (93401) *(P-11344)*
USA Travel Services LLC .... A...... 207 899-8803
　714 Washington Blvd Marina Del Rey (90292) *(P-19117)*
USA Waste of California Inc .... D...... 818 252-3112
　9081 Tujunga Ave Sun Valley (91352) *(P-4948)*
Usamp, Encino *Also Called: Instantly Inc (P-19823)*
USB Slrcity Mstr Tnant 2009 LL .... D...... 650 963-5693
　393 Vintage Park Dr Ste 140 Foster City (94404) *(P-9346)*

Usc Arcadia Hospital (PA) .... A...... 626 898-8000
　300 W Huntington Dr Arcadia (91007) *(P-16606)*
Usc Information Sciences Inst .... C...... 310 448-9438
　4676 Admiralty Way Ste 1001 Marina Del Rey (90292) *(P-19933)*
Usc Keck School of Medicine .... D...... 949 474-5730
　330 Old Newport Blvd Newport Beach (92663) *(P-15173)*
Usc Keck School of Medicine .... D...... 949 474-5720
　300 Old Newport Blvd Newport Beach (92663) *(P-15174)*
Usc Keck School of Medicine .... D...... 949 646-6441
　330 Old Newport Blvd Newport Beach (92663) *(P-15175)*
Usc Onclgy/Hmtlogy Infsion Ctr, Newport Beach *Also Called: Usc Keck School of Medicine (P-15175)*
Usc Oncology/Hematology, Newport Beach *Also Called: Usc Keck School of Medicine (P-15173)*
Usc Oncology/Hematology, Newport Beach *Also Called: Usc Keck School of Medicine (P-15174)*
Usc University Hospital, Los Angeles *Also Called: University Southern California (P-16605)*
Usc Verdugo Hills Hospital LLC .... A...... 818 790-7100
　1812 Verdugo Blvd Glendale (91208) *(P-16607)*
Usc Vrdugo Hlls Hosp Fundation (HQ) .... B...... 800 872-2273
　1812 Verdugo Blvd Glendale (91208) *(P-16608)*
Usc/Radiation Onocology, Los Angeles *Also Called: University Southern California (P-15168)*
Uscb Inc (PA) .... C...... 213 985-2111
　355 S Grand Ave Ste 3200 Los Angeles (90071) *(P-10753)*
Uscb America, Los Angeles *Also Called: Uscb Inc (P-10753)*
Uscf Advisers LLC .... B...... 510 522-9600
　1999 Harrison St Ste 1530 Oakland (94612) *(P-8227)*
Usd, Union City *Also Called: Union Sanitary District (P-4853)*
Usdm Life Science, Santa Barbara *Also Called: US Data Management LLC (P-12903)*
Used Cardboard Boxes Inc .... C...... 323 724-2500
　4032 Wilshire Blvd Ste 402 Los Angeles (90010) *(P-6092)*
Usertesting Technologies Inc .... D...... 888 877-1882
　1484 Pollard Rd # 271 Los Gatos (95032) *(P-12006)*
Usfi Inc .... D...... 424 260-9210
　108 W Walnut St Ste 221 Gardena (90248) *(P-6411)*
USG, Stockton *Also Called: USG Interiors LLC (P-5192)*
USG Interiors LLC .... B...... 209 466-4636
　2575 Loomis Rd Stockton (95205) *(P-5192)*
Ushio America Inc (HQ) .... D...... 714 236-8600
　5440 Cerritos Ave Cypress (90630) *(P-5596)*
Ushur Inc (PA) .... C...... 408 744-6802
　3975 Freedom Cir Santa Clara (95054) *(P-12007)*
Usko Express Inc .... D...... 916 515-8065
　11290 Point East Dr Ste 200 Rancho Cordova (95742) *(P-3667)*
Usoc Bio-Medical Services, Irvine *Also Called: Usoc Medical LLC (P-7598)*
Usoc Medical LLC .... D...... 949 243-9109
　20 Morgan Irvine (92618) *(P-7598)*
USS Cal Builders Inc .... C...... 714 828-4882
　8031 Main St Stanton (90680) *(P-1051)*
USS Hornet Museum .... D...... 510 521-8448
　94 Chatham Pt Alameda (94502) *(P-18681)*
UST, Aliso Viejo *Also Called: UST Global Inc (P-12008)*
UST Global Inc (HQ) .... D...... 949 716-8757
　5 Polaris Way Aliso Viejo (92656) *(P-12008)*
Ustream Inc .... D...... 415 489-9400
　410 Townsend St Fl 4 San Francisco (94107) *(P-4353)*
Usts, Huntington Beach *Also Called: United States Technical Svcs (P-12901)*
Utbbb Inc .... D...... 562 594-4411
　10711 Bloomfield St Los Alamitos (90720) *(P-2372)*
Utc, Mas, Costa Mesa *Also Called: Carrier Fire SEC Americas Corp (P-2900)*
Uti, Rancho Cucamonga *Also Called: Universal Technical Inst Inc (P-17798)*
Utility Line MGT Svcs Inc .... D...... 909 920-0812
　2315 W Foothill Blvd Ste 4 Upland (91786) *(P-20240)*
Utility Partners America LLC .... D...... 864 269-2302
　508 Enos Ln Bakersfield (93314) *(P-1273)*
Utility Traffic Services LLC .... B...... 562 264-2355
　2845 E Spring St Long Beach (90806) *(P-19430)*
Utility Trailer Mfg Co .... C...... 909 594-6026
　17295 Railroad St Ste A City Of Industry (91748) *(P-2980)*
Utility Trlr Sls Sthern Cal LL (PA) .... D...... 877 275-4887
　15567 Valley Blvd Fontana (92335) *(P-5018)*

Uvnv Inc (HQ) .... D....... 888 777-0446
1550 Scenic Ave Ste 100 Costa Mesa (92626) *(P-4354)*

V & L Produce Inc .... C....... 323 589-3125
2550 E 25th St Vernon (90058) *(P-6588)*

V A Anderson Enterprises Inc (PA) .... D....... 714 990-6100
400 Atlas St Brea (92821) *(P-13537)*

V A Desert PCF Federal Cr Un .... D....... 562 498-1250
5901 E 7th St Long Beach (90822) *(P-7816)*

V B Z, Richgrove Also Called: Vincent B Zaninovich Sons Inc *(P-88)*

V C A Central Animal Hospital .... D....... 909 981-2855
281 N Central Ave Upland (91786) *(P-344)*

V M S, Glendora Also Called: Venue Management Systems Inc *(P-13070)*

V N A & Hospice Southern Calif, San Bernardino Also Called: Vnacare *(P-16970)*

V P H, Van Nuys Also Called: Valley Presbyterian Hospital *(P-16614)*

V S S, West Sacramento Also Called: Vss International Inc *(P-1176)*

V Todays Inc .... C....... 310 781-9100
19800 S Vermont Ave Torrance (90502) *(P-10338)*

V Troth Inc .... D....... 661 948-4646
1801 W Avenue K Ste 101 Lancaster (93534) *(P-9207)*

V Vcc Havens, Vista Also Called: Vista Valley Country Club *(P-14481)*

V.O.I.C.E., Loma Linda Also Called: J & L Daycare *(P-18462)*

V&H Performance LLC .... D....... 562 921-7461
13861 Rosecrans Ave Santa Fe Springs (90670) *(P-2997)*

V2solutions Inc .... D....... 408 981-3075
7150 Rainbow Dr Apt 18 San Jose (95129) *(P-12009)*

V3 Electric Inc .... C....... 916 597-2627
4925 Robert J Mathews Pkwy Ste 100 El Dorado Hills (95762) *(P-4716)*

VA Palo Alto Healthcare System, Palo Alto Also Called: Veterans Health Administration *(P-20244)*

Vaca Valley Hospital, Vacaville Also Called: Northbay Healthcare Group *(P-16286)*

Vacation Bay Hotel Prpts Inc .... D....... 949 494-8566
647 S Coast Hwy Laguna Beach (92651) *(P-10339)*

Vacation Interval Realty, Newport Beach Also Called: Pacific Monarch Resorts Inc *(P-9118)*

Vacation Village Hotel, Laguna Beach Also Called: Vacation Bay Hotel Prpts Inc *(P-10339)*

Vacaville Healthcare Inc .... C....... 707 449-8000
585 Nut Tree Ct Vacaville (95687) *(P-11345)*

Vacavlle Cnvalescent Rehab Ctr .... C....... 707 449-8000
585 Nut Tree Ct Vacaville (95687) *(P-15908)*

Vacuum Process Engineering Inc .... D....... 916 925-6100
150 Commerce Cir Sacramento (95815) *(P-19794)*

Vadnais Trenchless Svcs Inc .... D....... 858 550-1460
11858 Bernardo Plaza Ct Ste 100 San Diego (92128) *(P-1274)*

Vagabond Inns, Los Angeles Also Called: Rpd Hotels 18 LLC *(P-10181)*

Vagaro, Pleasanton Also Called: Vagaro Inc *(P-12010)*

Vagaro Inc .... C....... 800 919-0157
4430 Rosewood Dr # 500 Pleasanton (94588) *(P-12010)*

Vahe Enterprises Inc .... D....... 323 235-6657
750 E Slauson Ave Los Angeles (90011) *(P-2969)*

Vahi Toyota Inc (PA) .... C....... 760 241-6484
14612 Valley Center Dr Victorville (92395) *(P-7321)*

Val-Pro Inc .... D....... 213 689-0844
1661 Mcgarry St Los Angeles (90021) *(P-6589)*

Val-Pro Inc (PA) .... C....... 213 627-8736
1601 E Olympic Blvd Ste 300 Los Angeles (90021) *(P-6590)*

Valadon Hotel LLC .... D....... 310 854-1114
8822 Cynthia St West Hollywood (90069) *(P-10340)*

Valassis Direct Mail Inc .... D....... 916 923-2398
1601 Response Rd Sacramento (95815) *(P-10780)*

Vale Healthcare Center, San Pablo Also Called: Mariner Health Care Inc *(P-15567)*

Vale Healthcare Center, San Pablo Also Called: Vale Operating Company LP *(P-15714)*

Vale Operating Company LP .... A....... 510 232-5945
13484 San Pablo Ave San Pablo (94806) *(P-15714)*

Valeant Biomedicals Inc (DH) .... D....... 949 461-6000
1 Enterprise Aliso Viejo (92656) *(P-6715)*

Valencia Country Club, Valencia Also Called: Heritage Golf Group LLC *(P-14267)*

Valencia Gardens Health Care Center, Riverside Also Called: Riverside Care Inc *(P-15641)*

Valencia Group LLC .... C....... 949 379-6489
94 Mayfair Irvine (92620) *(P-10341)*

Valet Parking Service, Los Angeles Also Called: Valet Parking Svc A Cal Partnr *(P-13630)*

Valet Parking Svc A Cal Partnr (PA) .... A....... 323 465-5873
6933 Hollywood Blvd Los Angeles (90028) *(P-13630)*

Valet Services, Bell Gardens Also Called: Anitsa Inc *(P-10423)*

Valew Welding & Fabrication, Adelanto Also Called: Hayes Welding Inc *(P-13751)*

Valey Farm, Dixon Also Called: Waveco Inc *(P-3437)*

Valgenesis Inc (PA) .... D....... 510 445-0505
5201 Great America Pkwy Ste 354 Santa Clara (95054) *(P-12011)*

Validant, San Francisco Also Called: Kinsale Holdings Inc *(P-20425)*

Valin, San Jose Also Called: Valin Corporation *(P-5878)*

Valin Corporation (PA) .... D....... 408 730-9850
5225 Hellyer Ave Ste 250 San Jose (95138) *(P-5878)*

Valle Vsta Cnvlescent Hosp Inc .... D....... 760 745-1288
1025 W 2nd Ave Escondido (92025) *(P-15909)*

Vallecitos Water District, San Marcos Also Called: Vallecitos Water District Financing Corporation *(P-4843)*

Vallecitos Water District Financing Corporation (HQ) ... D....... 760 744-0460
201 Vallecitos De Oro San Marcos (92069) *(P-4843)*

Vallejo Flood & Wastewater Dst .... D....... 707 644-8949
450 Ryder St Vallejo (94590) *(P-20869)*

Vallejo Flood Wstwter Dst Fing .... D....... 707 644-8949
450 Ryder St Vallejo (94590) *(P-20870)*

Valley Agricultural Sftwr Inc .... B....... 559 686-9496
220 S Akers St Ste E Visalia (93291) *(P-12012)*

Valley Air District, Fresno Also Called: San Jquin Vly Unified A Plltion *(P-20846)*

Valley Animal Medical Center .... A....... 760 342-4711
46920 Jefferson St Indio (92201) *(P-345)*

Valley Auto Sales & Lsg LLC .... D....... 559 674-9000
1300 Country Club Dr Madera (93638) *(P-7322)*

Valley Base Materials, Westlake Village Also Called: Security Paving Company Inc *(P-1160)*

Valley Bulk Inc .... D....... 760 843-0574
17649 Turner Rd Victorville (92394) *(P-3560)*

Valley Business Bank .... D....... 559 622-9000
701 W Main St Visalia (93291) *(P-7721)*

Valley Care Center, Porterville Also Called: Wescordon Incorporated *(P-15729)*

Valley Care Olive View Med Ctr, Sylmar Also Called: Olive View-Ucla Medical Center *(P-14934)*

Valley Careidence Opco LLC .... D....... 559 784-8371
661 W Poplar Ave Porterville (93257) *(P-15715)*

Valley Center Municpl Wtr Dst .... D....... 760 735-4500
29300 Valley Center Rd Valley Center (92082) *(P-4854)*

Valley Childrens Hospital .... C....... 559 353-6425
9300 Valley Childrens Pl Madera (93636) *(P-16609)*

Valley Childrens Hospital (PA) .... A....... 559 353-3000
9300 Valley Childrens Pl Madera (93636) *(P-16610)*

Valley Childrens Hospital .... C....... 559 353-7442
5085 E Mckinley Ave Fresno (93727) *(P-16611)*

Valley Chld Hlthcare Fundation .... A....... 559 353-3000
9300 Valley Childrens Pl Madera (93636) *(P-15176)*

Valley Commerce Bancorp .... D....... 559 622-9000
701 W Main St Visalia (93291) *(P-7722)*

Valley Communications Inc (PA) .... D....... 916 349-7300
6921 Roseville Rd Sacramento (95842) *(P-1867)*

Valley Community Healthcare .... B....... 818 763-8836
6801 Coldwater Canyon Ave Ste 1b North Hollywood (91605) *(P-15177)*

Valley Couriers Inc .... D....... 909 605-2999
181 S Wineville Ave Ste O Ontario (91761) *(P-3433)*

Valley Crest Residential, Apple Valley Also Called: Encore Senior Living III LLC *(P-8807)*

Valley Ctr Mncpl Wtr Dst Fclti .... D....... 760 735-4500
29300 Valley Center Rd Valley Center (92082) *(P-4844)*

Valley Detriot Diesel, Bakersfield Also Called: Valley Power Systems Inc *(P-5880)*

Valley Fabrication Inc .... D....... 831 757-5151
1056 Pellet Ave Salinas (93901) *(P-2772)*

Valley Fruit & Produce Co, Los Angeles Also Called: Val-Pro Inc *(P-6590)*

Valley Garbage Rubbish Co Inc .... C....... 805 614-1131
1850 W Betteravia Rd Santa Maria (93455) *(P-4949)*

Valley Health Care Systems Inc .... C....... 916 505-4112
1300 National Dr Ste 140 Sacramento (95834) *(P-11252)*

Valley Health Plan .... A....... 408 885-4760
2480 N 1st St Ste 160 San Jose (95131) *(P-8371)*

Valley Healthcare, San Bernardino Also Called: United Medical Management Inc *(P-15907)*

ALPHABETIC SECTION

Valley Healthcare Center, Fresno *Also Called: Valley Healthcare Center LLC (P-15716)*
Valley Healthcare Center LLC .... D....... 559 251-7161
   4840 E Tulare Ave Fresno (93727) *(P-15716)*
Valley Healthcare Staffing, Sacramento *Also Called: Valley Health Care Systems Inc (P-11252)*
Valley Hospital Medical Center Foundation .... A....... 818 885-8500
   18300 Roscoe Blvd Northridge (91325) *(P-16612)*
Valley House Care Center, Santa Clara *Also Called: TLC of Bay Area Inc (P-15704)*
Valley Hunt Club .... D....... 626 793-7134
   520 S Orange Grove Blvd Pasadena (91105) *(P-18921)*
Valley Insurance Service Inc .... A....... 949 707-4080
   23181 Verdugo Dr Ste 100b Laguna Hills (92653) *(P-8679)*
Valley Iron Inc (PA) .... D....... **559 485-3900**
   3114 S Cherry Ave Fresno (93706) *(P-5529)*
Valley Landscaping & Maint Inc .... C....... 209 334-3659
   12900 N Lower Sacramento Rd Lodi (95242) *(P-544)*
Valley Lght Ctr For Scial Advn .... D....... 626 337-6200
   109 W 6th St Azusa (91702) *(P-18254)*
VALLEY LIGHT INDUSTRIES, Azusa *Also Called: Valley Lght Ctr For Scial Advn (P-18254)*
Valley Management Associates (PA) .... D....... **818 881-6801**
   18747 Sherman Way Frnt Reseda (91335) *(P-7515)*
Valley Manor Convalescent Hosp, North Hollywood *Also Called: Golden Care Inc (P-15851)*
Valley Med Ctr Billing Dept, San Jose *Also Called: County of Santa Clara (P-19557)*
Valley Med Group Lompoc Inc .... D....... 805 736-1253
   136 N 3rd St Lompoc (93436) *(P-16613)*
Valley Milk LLC .... D....... 209 410-6701
   400 N Washington Rd Turlock (95380) *(P-222)*
Valley Montessori School .... D....... 925 455-8021
   1273 N Livermore Ave Livermore (94551) *(P-17755)*
Valley Northamerican, West Sacramento *Also Called: Valley Rlction Stor Nthrn Cal (P-3600)*
Valley Northamerican, Milpitas *Also Called: Valley Rlction Stor Nthm Cal (P-3601)*
Valley of Sun Cosmetics LLC .... C....... 310 327-9062
   535 Patrice Pl Gardena (90248) *(P-6149)*
Valley of The Sun Labs, Gardena *Also Called: Valley of Sun Cosmetics LLC (P-6149)*
Valley Pacific, Stockton *Also Called: Valley Pacific Petro Svcs Inc (P-6744)*
Valley Pacific Petro Svcs Inc .... D....... 209 461-3635
   1083 Madison Ln Salinas (93907) *(P-6743)*
Valley Pacific Petro Svcs Inc (PA) .... D....... **209 948-9412**
   152 Frank West Cir Ste 100 Stockton (95206) *(P-6744)*
Valley Pacific Petro Svcs Inc .... D....... 661 746-7737
   9521 Enos Ln Bakersfield (93314) *(P-6745)*
Valley Peterbilt, Stockton *Also Called: Interstate Truck Center LLC (P-5013)*
Valley Pnte Nrsing Rhbltion C, Castro Valley *Also Called: Valley Pointeidence Opco LLC (P-15799)*
Valley Pointeidence Opco LLC .... D....... 510 538-8464
   20090 Stanton Ave Castro Valley (94546) *(P-15799)*
Valley Power Systems Inc (PA) .... D....... **626 333-1243**
   425 S Hacienda Blvd City Of Industry (91745) *(P-5879)*
Valley Power Systems Inc .... D....... 661 325-9001
   4000 Rosedale Hwy Bakersfield (93308) *(P-5880)*
Valley Presbyterian Hospital .... A....... 818 782-6600
   15107 Vanowen St Van Nuys (91405) *(P-16614)*
Valley Pride Inc (PA) .... B....... **831 633-5883**
   10855 Ocean Mist Pkwy D Castroville (95012) *(P-370)*
Valley Rlction Stor Nthrn Cal .... D....... 916 375-0001
   3230 Reed Ave West Sacramento (95605) *(P-3600)*
Valley Rlction Stor Nthrn Cal .... D....... 408 938-3672
   835 Sinclair Frontage Rd Milpitas (95035) *(P-3601)*
Valley Rubber & Gasket, Sacramento *Also Called: Eriks North America Inc (P-5901)*
Valley Rubber & Gasket Company Inc .... D....... 916 369-8885
   10182 Croydon Way Sacramento (95827) *(P-5934)*
Valley Sheet Metal, South San Francisco *Also Called: Frank M Booth Inc (P-1441)*
Valley Strong Credit Union (PA) .... D....... **661 833-7900**
   11500 Bolthouse Dr Bakersfield (93311) *(P-7817)*
Valley Substation, Romoland *Also Called: Southern California Edison Co (P-4706)*
Valley Teen Ranch .... D....... 559 437-1144
   2610 W Shaw Ln Ste 105 Fresno (93711) *(P-18536)*
Valley Tool and Machine Co Inc .... D....... 909 595-2205
   111 Explorer St Pomona (91768) *(P-2856)*
Valley Truck and Tractor Inc .... D....... 530 738-4421
   Hwy 113 Robbins (95676) *(P-5815)*

Valley Unique Electric Inc .... D....... 559 237-4795
   75 Park Creek Dr Ste 101 Clovis (93611) *(P-1868)*
Valley View Casino, Valley Center *Also Called: San Psqual Band Mssion Indians (P-10202)*
Valley Village .... C....... 818 446-0366
   8727 Fenwick St Sunland (91040) *(P-15800)*
Valley Village (PA) .... D....... **818 587-9450**
   20830 Sherman Way Winnetka (91306) *(P-18166)*
Valley Vsta Nrsing Trnstnal CA .... C....... 818 763-6275
   6120 Vineland Ave North Hollywood (91606) *(P-15717)*
Valley Vsta Nrsing Trnstnal Ca, North Hollywood *Also Called: Valley Vsta Nrsing Trnstnal CA (P-15717)*
Valley Waterproofing Inc .... D....... 408 985-7701
   825 Civic Center Dr Ste 6 Santa Clara (95050) *(P-2327)*
Valley Wholesale Drug, Stockton *Also Called: Valley Wholesale Drug Co LLC (P-6150)*
Valley Wholesale Drug Co LLC .... D....... 209 466-0131
   1401 W Fremont St Stockton (95203) *(P-6150)*
Valley Wide Beverage Company, Fresno *Also Called: Fresno Beverage Company Inc (P-6762)*
Valley-HI Country Club .... D....... 916 684-2120
   9595 Franklin Blvd Elk Grove (95758) *(P-14475)*
Valley-HI Toyota Honda, Victorville *Also Called: Vahi Toyota Inc (P-7321)*
Valley-Mntain Regional Ctr Inc (PA) .... C....... **209 473-0951**
   702 N Aurora St Stockton (95202) *(P-18167)*
Valley-Mntain Regional Ctr Inc .... D....... 209 955-3207
   Cummins Drive Modesto (95350) *(P-18168)*
Valley-Mntain Regional Ctr Inc .... D....... 209 529-2626
   1620 Cummins Dr Modesto (95358) *(P-18537)*
Valleycare Recovery Center, Pleasanton *Also Called: Stanford Hlth Care Tri-Valley (P-16698)*
Valleycrest Productions Ltd .... D....... 818 560-5391
   500 S Buena Vista St Burbank (91521) *(P-4469)*
Valmetal Tulare Inc .... D....... 559 685-0340
   2955 S K St Tulare (93274) *(P-2773)*
Valori Sand & Gravel Company .... C....... 909 350-3000
   11027 Cherry Ave Fontana (92337) *(P-5212)*
Vals Plumbing and Heating Inc .... D....... 831 424-1633
   413 Front St Salinas (93901) *(P-1590)*
Valtron Technologies Inc .... D....... 805 257-0333
   28309 Avenue Crocker Santa Clarita (91355) *(P-12714)*
Valueoptions of California Inc, Cerritos *Also Called: Carelon Bhaviroal Hlth Cal Inc (P-8520)*
Valumark, Tustin *Also Called: Logomark Inc (P-6926)*
Valverde Construction Inc .... C....... 562 906-1826
   10936 Shoemaker Ave Santa Fe Springs (90670) *(P-1275)*
Valvoline Instant Oil Change, Costa Mesa *Also Called: EZ Lube LLC (P-13714)*
Valvoline Instant Oil Change, Santa Fe Springs *Also Called: Valvoline Instant Oil Chnge Fr (P-13721)*
Valvoline Instant Oil Chnge Fr .... D....... 562 906-6200
   9520 John St Santa Fe Springs (90670) *(P-13721)*
Van Acker Cnstr Assoc Inc .... C....... 415 383-5589
   1060 Redwood Hwy Frontage Rd Mill Valley (94941) *(P-737)*
Van Acker Construction, Mill Valley *Also Called: Van Acker Cnstr Assoc Inc (P-737)*
Van Beurden Insurance Svcs Inc (PA) .... D....... **559 634-7125**
   1600 Draper St Kingsburg (93631) *(P-8680)*
Van Daele Development Corp .... C....... 951 354-6800
   2900 Adams St Ste C25 Riverside (92504) *(P-799)*
Van Daele Homes, Riverside *Also Called: Van Daele Development Corp (P-799)*
Van Daele Homes Inc .... D....... 951 354-2121
   2900 Adams St Ste C25 Riverside (92504) *(P-782)*
Van De Pol Enterprises Inc (PA) .... D....... **209 465-3421**
   4895 S Airport Way Stockton (95206) *(P-6746)*
Van Groningen & Sons Inc (PA) .... B....... **209 982-5248**
   15100 Jack Tone Rd Manteca (95336) *(P-205)*
Van King & Storage Inc .... D....... 562 921-0555
   13535 Larwin Cir Santa Fe Springs (90670) *(P-3561)*
Van Ness Hotel Inc .... D....... 415 673-4711
   1050 Van Ness Ave San Francisco (94109) *(P-10342)*
Van Torrance & Storage Company (PA) .... D
   12128 Burke St Santa Fe Springs (90670) *(P-3602)*
Vance & Hines, Santa Fe Springs *Also Called: V&H Performance LLC (P-2997)*
Vance Brown Builders, Palo Alto *Also Called: Vance Brown Inc (P-854)*
Vance Brown Inc (PA) .... D....... **650 849-9900**
   2585 E Bayshore Rd Palo Alto (94303) *(P-854)*

Vance Executive Protection, Los Angeles Also Called: Andrews International Inc *(P-12930)*

Vander-Bend Manufacturing Inc .... C....... 916 631-6375
3510 Luyung Dr Rancho Cordova (95742) *(P-2857)*

Vanderra Resources LLC .... B....... 817 439-2220
1801 Century Park E Ste 2400 Los Angeles (90067) *(P-633)*

Vanguard Health Systems Inc .... B....... 714 635-6272
1154 N Euclid St Anaheim (92801) *(P-15178)*

Vanguard Lgistics Svcs USA Inc (HQ) .... D....... 310 847-3000
5000 Airport Plaza Dr Ste 200 Long Beach (90815) *(P-4117)*

Vanguard Space Tech Inc .... C....... 858 587-4210
4398 Corporate Center Dr Los Alamitos (90720) *(P-19431)*

Vanguard Univ Southern Cal .... C....... 714 668-6163
55 Fair Dr Costa Mesa (92626) *(P-17784)*

Vanir Construction MGT Inc (PA) .... D....... 916 444-3700
4540 Duckhorn Dr Ste 300 Sacramento (95834) *(P-20241)*

Vann Brothers .... C....... 530 473-2607
365 Ruggieri Way Williams (95987) *(P-48)*

Vann Family LLC .... C....... 530 473-3317
6141 Abel Rd Williams (95987) *(P-114)*

Vann Family Orchard, Williams Also Called: Vann Family LLC *(P-114)*

Vanpike Inc (PA) .... D....... 858 453-1331
6336 Greenwich Dr Ste 100 San Diego (92122) *(P-11346)*

Vantage Apparel, Santa Ana Also Called: Vantage Custom Classics Inc *(P-6193)*

Vantage Associates Inc .... D....... 562 968-1400
12333 Los Nietos Rd Santa Fe Springs (90670) *(P-2683)*

Vantage Custom Classics Inc .... C....... 714 755-1133
3321 S Susan St Santa Ana (92704) *(P-6193)*

Vantage Elevation LLC .... D....... 916 426-2347
6201 Warehouse Way Sacramento (95826) *(P-5881)*

Vantage Elevation- Sacramento, Sacramento Also Called: Vantage Elevation LLC *(P-5881)*

Vantagepoint Capital Partners, Santa Barbara Also Called: Vantagepoint Management Inc *(P-9577)*

Vantagepoint Management Inc (PA) .... D....... 650 866-3100
1505 E Valley Rd Ste E Santa Barbara (93108) *(P-9577)*

Vantiva Sup Chain Slutions Inc .... C....... 909 974-2016
5491 E Philadelphia St Ontario (91761) *(P-13957)*

Vantiva Sup Chain Slutions Inc .... D....... 760 357-3372
461 Rood Rd Ste A Calexico (92231) *(P-13958)*

Vantiva Sup Chain Slutions Inc (HQ) .... B....... 805 445-1122
3601 Calle Tecate Ste 120 Camarillo (93012) *(P-13959)*

Vaquero Farms Inc .... D....... 559 659-2790
43405 W Panoche Rd Firebaugh (93622) *(P-206)*

Varian, Palo Alto Also Called: Varian Medical Systems Inc *(P-3079)*

Varian Medical Systems Inc (DH) .... A....... 650 493-4000
3100 Hansen Way Palo Alto (94304) *(P-3079)*

Variations In Stone Inc 949 438-8337
360 La Perle Pl Costa Mesa (92627) *(P-1895)*

Varis LLC .... D....... 916 294-0860
9245 Sierra College Blvd # 100 Roseville (95661) *(P-20601)*

Varner Bros Inc .... C....... 661 399-2944
1808 Roberts Ln Bakersfield (93308) *(P-4950)*

Varner Family Ltd Partnership (PA) .... D....... 661 399-1163
5900 E Lerdo Hwy Shafter (93263) *(P-9450)*

Varni Brothers Corporation (PA) .... D....... 209 521-1777
400 Hosmer Ave Modesto (95351) *(P-6786)*

Varni Brothers Corporation .... D....... 209 526-5513
416 Hosmer Ave Modesto (95351) *(P-6809)*

Varsity Contractors Inc .... C....... 949 586-8283
24155 Laguna Hills Mall Laguna Hills (92653) *(P-10985)*

Vascular and Varicose Vein Ctr, Roseville Also Called: Sutter Health *(P-15111)*

Vasinda Investments Inc .... D....... 661 324-4277
5353 Truckston Ave Bakersfield (93309) *(P-11347)*

Vasko Electric Inc 916 568-7700
4300 Astoria St Sacramento (95838) *(P-1869)*

Vasona Management Inc .... C....... 510 413-0091
37390 Central Mont Place Fremont (94536) *(P-738)*

Vasona Management Inc .... C....... 510 352-8728
13949 Doolittle Dr San Leandro (94577) *(P-8867)*

Vasonic Construction, Fremont Also Called: Vasona Management Inc *(P-738)*

Vasquez & Company LLP (PA) .... D....... 213 873-1700
655 N Central Ave Ste 1550 Glendale (91203) *(P-19638)*

Vastek Inc .... C....... 925 948-5701
1230 Columbia St Ste 1180 San Diego (92101) *(P-13538)*

Vasto Valle Farms, Huron Also Called: Dick Anderson & Sons Farming *(P-175)*

Vaya Workforce Solutions .... C....... 866 687-7390
5930 Cornerstone Ct W Ste 300 San Diego (92121) *(P-11348)*

Vbp Orange, San Francisco Also Called: Venables/Bell & Partners LLC *(P-10687)*

VCA, Los Angeles Also Called: VCA Inc *(P-7599)*

VCA Animal Hospitals Inc .... D....... 818 883-8387
22123 Ventura Blvd Woodland Hills (91364) *(P-346)*

VCA Animal Hospitals Inc .... D....... 858 560-8006
5610 Kearny Mesa Rd Ste B San Diego (92111) *(P-347)*

VCA Animal Hospitals Inc .... D....... 310 473-2951
1900 S Sepulveda Blvd Los Angeles (90025) *(P-348)*

VCA Inc (DH) .... C....... 310 571-6500
12401 W Olympic Blvd Los Angeles (90064) *(P-7599)*

VCA Prfessional Animal Lab Inc 310 571-6500
12401 W Olympic Blvd Los Angeles (90064) *(P-349)*

VCA Vtrnary Specialists of Vly, Woodland Hills Also Called: VCA Animal Hospitals Inc *(P-346)*

VCA West Los Angles Anmal Hosp, Los Angeles Also Called: VCA Animal Hospitals Inc *(P-348)*

Vci Construction LLC (HQ) .... D....... 909 946-0905
1921 W 11th St Ste A Upland (91786) *(P-1276)*

Vci Event Technology Inc .... C....... 714 772-2002
25172 Arctic Ocean Dr Ste 102 Lake Forest (92630) *(P-11062)*

Vcomply Technologies Inc .... D....... 650 319-8842
75 E Santa Clara St Fl 6 San Jose (95113) *(P-12013)*

Vcore Technology Partners LLC (PA) .... D....... 877 348-7714
5185 Foxglove Dr Huntington Beach (92649) *(P-12541)*

Vector Capital Management LP (PA) .... D....... 415 293-5000
1 Market St Ste 2300 San Francisco (94105) *(P-8172)*

Vector Resources Inc (PA) .... C....... 310 436-1000
20917 Higgins Ct Torrance (90501) *(P-1870)*

Vectorusa, Torrance Also Called: Vector Resources Inc *(P-1870)*

Veev Group Inc .... C....... 650 292-0752
2701 W Winton Ave Hayward (94545) *(P-8173)*

Veeva, Pleasanton Also Called: Veeva Systems Inc *(P-12389)*

Veeva Systems Inc (PA) .... B....... 925 452-6500
4280 Hacienda Dr Pleasanton (94588) *(P-12389)*

Veg Fresh, Corona Also Called: Veg-Fresh Farms LLC *(P-6591)*

Veg Fresh Logistics LLC .... C....... 714 446-8800
1400 W Rincon St Corona (92878) *(P-4118)*

Veg-Fresh Farms LLC (PA) .... C....... 800 422-5535
1400 W Rincon St Corona (92878) *(P-6591)*

Vegatek Corporation .... D....... 949 502-0090
470 Wald Irvine (92618) *(P-12014)*

Vege - Kurl Inc .... D....... 818 956-5582
412 W Cypress St Glendale (91204) *(P-2634)*

Vege-Mist Inc 310 353-2300
407 E Redondo Beach Blvd Gardena (90248) *(P-2846)*

Vege-Tech Company, Glendale Also Called: Vege - Kurl Inc *(P-2634)*

Vegiworks Inc .... D....... 415 643-8686
6 Viewmont Ter South San Francisco (94080) *(P-6592)*

Velaro Incorporated .... D....... 800 983-5276
1234 N La Brea Ave West Hollywood (90038) *(P-7451)*

Vellutini Corporation .... C....... 916 226-2100
8481 Carbide Ct Sacramento (95828) *(P-1871)*

Velocity Vehicle Group, Whittier Also Called: Los Angeles Truck Centers LLC *(P-13666)*

Velodyne Labs, Alameda Also Called: Velodyne Lidar Inc *(P-19795)*

Velodyne Lidar Inc 510 522-2351
1210 Marina Village Pkwy Alameda (94501) *(P-19795)*

Venables/Bell & Partners LLC .... C....... 415 288-3300
201 Post St Fl 2 San Francisco (94108) *(P-10687)*

Venco Western Inc .... C....... 805 981-2400
2400 Eastman Ave Oxnard (93030) *(P-545)*

Vendo LLC .... D....... 310 300-2810
11601 Wilshire Blvd Ste 1818 Los Angeles (90025) *(P-20242)*

Vendor Direct Solutions LLC (PA) .... C....... 213 362-5622
515 S Figueroa St Ste 1900 Los Angeles (90071) *(P-12015)*

Vengroff Williams & Assoc Inc .... C....... 714 889-6200
2099 S State College Blvd Ste 600 Anaheim (92806) *(P-10754)*

ALPHABETIC SECTION — Verizon Wireless

Venice Family Clinic .... D 310 392-8636
  2509 Pico Blvd Santa Monica (90405) *(P-15179)*
VENICE FAMILY CLINIC, Santa Monica *Also Called: Venice Family Clinic (P-15179)*
Venice Fmly Clinic Foundation (PA) .... D 310 664-7703
  604 Rose Ave Venice (90291) *(P-15180)*
Venice Team, The, Alamo *Also Called: Lendus LLC (P-7989)*
Venida Packing Company .... C 559 592-2816
  19823 Avenue 300 Exeter (93221) *(P-6955)*
Ventana Inn & Spa, Big Sur *Also Called: 48123 CA Investors LLC (P-9592)*
Ventegra Inc A Cal Beneft Corp .... D 858 551-8111
  450 N Brand Blvd Ste 600 Glendale (91203) *(P-20871)*
Ventura Cnty Md-Cal Mnged Care .... D 888 301-1228
  711 E Daily Dr Ste 106 Camarillo (93010) *(P-17345)*
Ventura Cnty Obstet Gynclgic M .... D 805 643-8695
  2795 Loma Vista Rd Ventura (93003) *(P-15181)*
Ventura County Credit Union (PA) .... D 805 477-4000
  2575 Vista Del Mar Dr Ste 100 Ventura (93001) *(P-7818)*
Ventura County Lemon Coop .... D 805 385-3345
  2620 Sakioka Dr Oxnard (93030) *(P-6593)*
Ventura County Medical Center .... C 805 933-8600
  845 N 10th St Ste 3 Santa Paula (93060) *(P-15182)*
Ventura County Medical Center .... C 805 652-6201
  3291 Loma Vista Rd Bldg 343 Ventura (93003) *(P-15183)*
Ventura County Medical Center .... C 805 652-6729
  300 Hillmont Ave Ventura (93003) *(P-15311)*
Ventura County Medical Center .... D 805 677-5184
  825 N 10th St Santa Paula (93060) *(P-20602)*
Ventura Family YMCA, Ventura *Also Called: Channel Islnds Yung MNS Chrstn (P-18839)*
Ventura Hsptality Partners LLC .... C 805 648-2100
  450 Harbor Blvd Ventura (93001) *(P-10343)*
Ventura Medical Management LLC .... B 805 477-6220
  2601 E Main St Ventura (93003) *(P-20243)*
Ventura Pacific Co, Oxnard *Also Called: Ventura County Lemon Coop (P-6593)*
Ventura Transfer Company (PA) .... D 310 549-1660
  2418 E 223rd St Long Beach (90810) *(P-3562)*
Ventura Yuth Crrctional Fcilty, Camarillo *Also Called: Juvenile Justice Division Cal (P-20130)*
Venture Design Services Inc .... D 510 744-3770
  6737 Mowry Ave Newark (94560) *(P-5368)*
Venture Design Services Inc .... D 707 524-8368
  451 Aviation Blvd Ste 215 Santa Rosa (95403) *(P-13539)*
Venue Management Systems Inc .... A 626 445-6000
  2041 E Gladstone St Ste A Glendora (91740) *(P-13070)*
Venus Concept Inc .... D 408 489-4925
  1800 Bering Dr San Jose (95112) *(P-3061)*
Venus Group Inc (PA) .... D 949 609-1299
  25861 Wright St Foothill Ranch (92610) *(P-5142)*
Venus Textiles, Foothill Ranch *Also Called: Venus Group Inc (P-5142)*
Vep Healthcare Inc .... C 925 482-2839
  1001 Galaxy Way Ste 400 Concord (94520) *(P-15184)*
Vep-Ohec, Concord *Also Called: Vep Healthcare Inc (P-15184)*
Ver, Glendale *Also Called: Full Throttle Films LLC (P-13937)*
VERACYTE, South San Francisco *Also Called: Veracyte Inc (P-16768)*
Veracyte Inc (PA) .... D 650 243-6300
  6000 Shoreline Ct Ste 300 South San Francisco (94080) *(P-16768)*
Verana Health Inc .... C 888 774-0077
  360 3rd St Ste 425 San Francisco (94107) *(P-12390)*
Verance Corporation .... D 858 202-2800
  6046 Cornerstone Ct W Ste 216 San Diego (92121) *(P-19855)*
Veranda Luxe Cinema, Concord *Also Called: Concord Veranda Cinema LLC (P-13831)*
Veratex, Chatsworth *Also Called: Avitex Inc (P-2444)*
Verdugo Hills Hospital Inc .... C 818 790-7100
  1812 Verdugo Blvd Glendale (91208) *(P-16615)*
Verdugo Hlls Psychthrapy Ctr A (PA) .... C 818 241-6780
  410 Arden Ave Ste 201 Glendale (91203) *(P-15185)*
Verdugo Vista Healthcare Ctr, La Crescenta *Also Called: Mariner Health Care Inc (P-15577)*
Veridiam Allied Swiss .... D 760 941-1702
  4645 North Ave Oceanside (92056) *(P-20872)*
Verifi Inc .... D 323 655-5789
  8391 Beverly Blvd Ste 310 Los Angeles (90048) *(P-20603)*
Veritas, Santa Clara *Also Called: Veritas Technologies LLC (P-12016)*

Veritas Health Services Inc .... A 909 464-8600
  5451 Walnut Ave Chino (91710) *(P-16616)*
Veritas Technologies LLC (DH) .... C 866 837-4827
  2625 Augustine Dr Santa Clara (95054) *(P-12016)*
Veritas Technologies LLC .... C 310 202-0757
  16501 Ventura Blvd Ste 400 Encino (91436) *(P-12017)*
Veritas US Inc .... C 650 933-1000
  2625 Augustine Dr Santa Clara (95054) *(P-12018)*
Veritiv Operating Company .... C 925 245-6060
  7337 Las Positas Rd Livermore (94551) *(P-6093)*
Verity Health System Cal Inc .... A 408 947-2500
  2105 Forest Ave San Jose (95128) *(P-16617)*
Verity Medical Foundation (PA) .... D 408 278-3000
  6300 Canoga Ave Ste 1500 Woodland Hills (91367) *(P-15186)*
Verizon, Los Alamitos *Also Called: Supermedia LLC (P-2557)*
Verizon, Livermore *Also Called: Cellco Partnership (P-4187)*
Verizon, Capitola *Also Called: Cellco Partnership (P-4193)*
Verizon, Brea *Also Called: Cellco Partnership (P-4194)*
Verizon, Covina *Also Called: Verizon Communications Inc (P-4242)*
Verizon, Santa Monica *Also Called: Verizon Services Corp (P-4243)*
Verizon, Goleta *Also Called: Verizon South Inc (P-4244)*
Verizon, San Fernando *Also Called: Frontier California Inc (P-4277)*
Verizon, Folsom *Also Called: Frontier California Inc (P-4278)*
Verizon, Westlake Village *Also Called: Frontier California Inc (P-4279)*
Verizon, Indio *Also Called: Frontier California Inc (P-4280)*
Verizon, Huntington Beach *Also Called: Frontier California Inc (P-4281)*
Verizon, Manteca *Also Called: Frontier California Inc (P-4282)*
Verizon, Bishop *Also Called: Frontier California Inc (P-4283)*
Verizon, Santa Maria *Also Called: Frontier California Inc (P-4284)*
Verizon, Baldwin Park *Also Called: Telesector Resources Group Inc (P-20581)*
Verizon Bus Netwrk Svcs LLC .... C 916 779-5600
  11080 White Rock Rd Ste 100 Rancho Cordova (95670) *(P-4239)*
Verizon Bus Netwrk Svcs LLC .... C 916 569-5999
  1740 Creekside Oaks Dr Ste 200 Sacramento (95833) *(P-4240)*
Verizon Bus Netwrk Svcs LLC .... C 510 497-2500
  4340 Solar Way Fremont (94538) *(P-4241)*
Verizon Bus Netwrk Svcs LLC .... C 925 934-3030
  2175 N California Blvd Ste 700 Walnut Creek (94596) *(P-4355)*
Verizon Business, Rancho Cordova *Also Called: Verizon Bus Netwrk Svcs LLC (P-4239)*
Verizon Business, Sacramento *Also Called: Verizon Bus Netwrk Svcs LLC (P-4240)*
Verizon Business, Fremont *Also Called: Verizon Bus Netwrk Svcs LLC (P-4241)*
Verizon Business, Walnut Creek *Also Called: Verizon Bus Netwrk Svcs LLC (P-4355)*
Verizon Communications Inc .... D 626 858-1739
  176 E Badillo St Covina (91723) *(P-4242)*
Verizon Connect Telo Inc (DH) .... C 844 617-1100
  15505 Sand Canyon Ave Irvine (92618) *(P-12640)*
Verizon Media Inc .... A 310 907-3016
  701 First Ave Sunnyvale (94089) *(P-20905)*
Verizon Services Corp .... B 310 315-1100
  2530 Wilshire Blvd Fl 1 Santa Monica (90403) *(P-4243)*
Verizon South Inc .... C 805 681-8527
  424 S Patterson Ave Goleta (93111) *(P-4244)*
Verizon Wireless, Laguna Beach *Also Called: 4g Wireless Inc (P-4181)*
Verizon Wireless, Grass Valley *Also Called: Cellco Partnership (P-4188)*
Verizon Wireless, Sacramento *Also Called: Cellco Partnership (P-4189)*
Verizon Wireless, Orange *Also Called: Cellco Partnership (P-4190)*
Verizon Wireless, Compton *Also Called: Cellco Partnership (P-4191)*
Verizon Wireless, Clovis *Also Called: Cellco Partnership (P-4192)*
Verizon Wireless, Encinitas *Also Called: Cellco Partnership (P-4195)*
Verizon Wireless, Santa Clarita *Also Called: Cellco Partnership (P-4196)*
Verizon Wireless, Taft *Also Called: Cellco Partnership (P-4197)*
Verizon Wireless, Orange *Also Called: Cellco Partnership (P-4198)*
Verizon Wireless, Los Angeles *Also Called: Cellco Partnership (P-4199)*
Verizon Wireless, Gilroy *Also Called: Cellco Partnership (P-4200)*
Verizon Wireless, Rancho Mirage *Also Called: Cellco Partnership (P-4201)*
Verizon Wireless, Lake Forest *Also Called: Cellco Partnership (P-4202)*
Verizon Wireless, Tustin *Also Called: Cellco Partnership (P-4203)*

Verizon Wireless, Stockton Also Called: Cellco Partnership *(P-4204)*
Verizon Wireless, Norwalk Also Called: Cellco Partnership *(P-4205)*
Verizon Wireless, Hesperia Also Called: Cellco Partnership *(P-4206)*
Verizon Wireless, Chino Also Called: Cellco Partnership *(P-4207)*
Verizon Wireless, Riverside Also Called: Your Wireless Retailer Inc *(P-4245)*
Verkada Inc (PA) .... A....... 650 514-2500
   406 E 3rd Ave San Mateo (94401) *(P-13153)*
Vermont Care Center, Torrance Also Called: Geri-Care II Inc *(P-15848)*
Vernon Central Warehouse Inc .... C....... 323 234-2200
   2050 E 38th St Vernon (90058) *(P-3603)*
Vernon Transportation Company, Stockton Also Called: John Aguilar & Company Inc *(P-3408)*
Vernon Warehouse Co, Vernon Also Called: Vernon Central Warehouse Inc *(P-3603)*
Versa Networks Inc (PA) .... C....... 408 385-7660
   2550 Great America Way Ste 350 Santa Clara (95054) *(P-12019)*
Versailles On The Lake, Santa Ana Also Called: Domino Realty Management Co *(P-8802)*
Verseio Inc .... D....... 888 373-9942
   550 W B St Fl 4 San Diego (92101) *(P-12020)*
Vertex Coatings Inc .... D....... 909 923-5795
   1291 W State St Ontario (91762) *(P-1644)*
Vertical Communication (HQ) .... D....... 408 969-9600
   3979 Freedom Cir Ste 400 Santa Clara (95054) *(P-4558)*
Vertisystem Inc .... C....... 510 794-8099
   39300 Civic Center Dr Ste 160 Fremont (94538) *(P-12542)*
Verve Group Inc .... C....... 760 536-8350
   350 Marine Pkwy Ste 220 Redwood City (94065) *(P-19856)*
Very Good Security Inc .... C....... 844 847-0232
   548 Market St San Francisco (94104) *(P-1872)*
Verys, Santa Ana Also Called: Verys LLC *(P-12904)*
Verys LLC .... C....... 949 423-3295
   1251 E Dyer Rd Ste 210 Santa Ana (92705) *(P-12904)*
Vescom Corporation (PA) .... A....... 207 945-5051
   1125 W 190th St Gardena (90248) *(P-13071)*
Vessels Club Restaurant, Cypress Also Called: Los Alamitos Race Course *(P-7492)*
Vesta Foodservice, Santa Fe Springs Also Called: LA Specialty Produce Co *(P-6560)*
Vesta Luxury Home Staging, Pico Rivera Also Called: Showroom Interiors LLC *(P-11054)*
Vestis Corporation .... D....... 818 973-3700
   115 N First St Burbank (91502) *(P-10457)*
Vestis Corporation .... C....... 559 291-6631
   3333 N Sabre Dr Fresno (93727) *(P-10458)*
Veterans Affairs Palo Alto Hea, Pleasanton Also Called: David Howard *(P-17050)*
Veterans EZ Info, San Diego Also Called: Veterans EZ Info Inc *(P-20873)*
Veterans EZ Info Inc .... C....... 866 839-1329
   1901 1st Ave Ste 192 San Diego (92101) *(P-20873)*
Veterans Health Administration .... A....... 559 225-6100
   2615 E Clinton Ave Fresno (93703) *(P-15187)*
Veterans Health Administration 650 493-5000
   3801 Miranda Ave Bldg 101 Palo Alto (94304) *(P-15188)*
Veterans Health Administration .... A....... 415 750-2009
   4150 Clement St Bldg 6 San Francisco (94121) *(P-15189)*
Veterans Health Administration 909 825-7084
   11201 Benton St Loma Linda (92357) *(P-15190)*
Veterans Health Administration 310 478-3711
   11301 Wilshire Blvd Los Angeles (90073) *(P-15191)*
Veterans Health Administration 925 372-2000
   150 Muir Rd Martinez (94553) *(P-15192)*
Veterans Health Administration .... C....... 650 493-5000
   3801 Miranda Ave Palo Alto (94304) *(P-20244)*
Veterans Med RES Fndtion San D .... C....... 858 642-3080
   3350 La Jolla Village Dr Ste 151a San Diego (92161) *(P-18922)*
Veterans of Foreign Wars of US .... D....... 951 202-3792
   1525 W Oakland Ave Hemet (92543) *(P-18923)*
Veterans of Foreign Wars of US .... D....... 909 797-1898
   12235 California St Yucaipa (92399) *(P-18924)*
Veterans of Foreign Wars of US 916 786-7757
   9136 Elk Grove Blvd # 100 Elk Grove (95624) *(P-18925)*
Veterans of Foreign Wars of US .... D....... 530 241-9168
   1251 Oregon St Redding (96001) *(P-18926)*
VETERANS VILLAGE OF SAN DIEGO, San Diego Also Called: Vietnam Veterans of San Diego *(P-18927)*

Veterinary Centers America VCA, Los Angeles Also Called: Vicar Operating Inc *(P-354)*
Veterinary Genetics Laboratory, Davis Also Called: University California Davis *(P-16767)*
Veterinary Pet Insurance Services Inc .... B....... 714 989-0555
   1800 E Imperial Hwy Ste 145 Brea (92821) *(P-8681)*
Veterinary Pet Services Inc .... C....... 714 989-0555
   3060 Saturn St Brea (92821) *(P-8682)*
Veterinary Practice Assoc Inc .... C....... 949 833-9020
   10435 Sorrento Valley Rd San Diego (92121) *(P-350)*
Veterinary Service Inc .... D....... 559 651-1633
   1607 N Plaza Dr Visalia (93291) *(P-5458)*
Veterinary Specialty Hosp .... C....... 858 875-7500
   10435 Sorrento Valley Rd San Diego (92121) *(P-351)*
Veterinary Specialty Hospital, San Diego Also Called: Veterinary Practice Assoc Inc *(P-350)*
Veterinary Specialty Hospital, San Diego Also Called: Veterinary Specialty Hosp *(P-351)*
Veternary Srgcal Spclsts A VTR .... D....... 949 936-0055
   2965 Edinger Ave Tustin (92780) *(P-352)*
Veterinary Surgical Specialists, Tustin Also Called: Veternary Srgcal Spclsts A VTR *(P-352)*
Vets Securing America Inc .... A....... 310 645-6200
   1125 W 190th St Gardena (90248) *(P-13072)*
Vexillum Inc .... D....... 916 218-3815
   10636 Industrial Ave Roseville (95678) *(P-4717)*
Vezina Industries Inc .... D....... 559 479-8287
   33543 Avenue 9 Madera (93636) *(P-1971)*
Vfs Fire Protection Services, Orange Also Called: Bernel Inc *(P-1376)*
Vgp Holdings LLC .... B....... 562 906-6200
   9520 John St Santa Fe Springs (90670) *(P-5066)*
Vh 10 Vh LP .... D....... 415 554-3000
   2343 Fillmore St San Francisco (94115) *(P-353)*
Via Care Cmnty Hlth Ctr Inc .... D....... 323 268-9191
   507 S Atlantic Blvd Los Angeles (90022) *(P-15193)*
Viacom Networks .... D....... 310 752-8000
   1575 N Gower St Ste 100 Los Angeles (90028) *(P-13909)*
Viant, Irvine Also Called: Interactive Media Holdings Inc *(P-10632)*
Viasat, Carlsbad Also Called: Viasat Inc *(P-2899)*
Viasat Inc (PA) .... A....... 760 476-2200
   6155 El Camino Real Carlsbad (92009) *(P-2899)*
Vibiana, Los Angeles Also Called: Vibiana Events LLC *(P-10581)*
Vibiana Events LLC .... D....... 213 626-1507
   214 S Main St Los Angeles (90012) *(P-10581)*
Vibra Healthcare LLC .... C....... 530 246-9000
   2801 Eureka Way Redding (96001) *(P-16618)*
Vibra Healthcare LLC .... C....... 619 260-8300
   555 Washington St San Diego (92103) *(P-16619)*
Vibra Hospital Northern Cal, Redding Also Called: Vibra Healthcare LLC *(P-16618)*
Vibra Hospital of San Diego, San Diego Also Called: Vibra Healthcare LLC *(P-16619)*
Vibra Hospital Sacramento LLC .... C....... 916 351-9151
   330 Montrose Dr Folsom (95630) *(P-16620)*
Vibrant Planet, Truckee Also Called: Vibrant Planet Pbc *(P-13540)*
Vibrant Planet Pbc .... D....... 530 208-9839
   11025 Pioneer Trl Truckee (96161) *(P-13540)*
Vicar Operating Inc (DH) .... D....... 310 571-6500
   12401 W Olympic Blvd Los Angeles (90064) *(P-354)*
Victims Services Center, Madera Also Called: Community Action Prtnr Mdera C *(P-18577)*
Victor Cmnty Support Svcs Inc .... C....... 760 987-8225
   15095 Amargosa Rd Ste 201 Victorville (92394) *(P-17153)*
Victor Cmnty Support Svcs Inc 530 273-2244
   900 E Main St Ste 201 Grass Valley (95945) *(P-17154)*
Victor Cmnty Support Svcs Inc .... C....... 951 212-1770
   1105 E Florida Ave Hemet (92543) *(P-17155)*
Victor Cmnty Support Svcs Inc .... C....... 760 245-4695
   14360 St Andrews Dr Ste 11 Victorville (92395) *(P-17156)*
Victor Cmnty Support Svcs Inc .... C....... 909 890-5930
   1908 Business Center Dr Ste 109 San Bernardino (92408) *(P-17157)*
Victor Cmnty Support Svcs Inc .... C....... 209 465-1080
   2495 W March Ln Ste 125 Stockton (95207) *(P-17158)*
Victor Cmnty Support Svcs Inc .... D....... 530 267-1710
   1360 E Lassen Ave Chico (95973) *(P-17159)*
Victor Rane Group Inc .... D....... 424 248-3623
   2337 Buckingham Ln Los Angeles (90077) *(P-13541)*
Victor Treatment Centers, Lodi Also Called: Victor Treatment Centers Inc *(P-17756)*

ALPHABETIC SECTION — Vincent Scaffolding

Victor Treatment Centers, San Bernardino *Also Called: Victor Treatment Centers Inc* *(P-18538)*

Victor Treatment Centers Inc .... D...... 209 465-1080
12755 N Highway 88 Lodi (95240) *(P-17756)*

Victor Treatment Centers Inc .... D...... 951 436-5200
1053 N D St San Bernardino (92410) *(P-18538)*

Victor Treatment Centers Inc .... C...... 707 360-1509
341 Irwin Ln Santa Rosa (95401) *(P-18539)*

Victoria Care Center .... D...... 805 642-1736
5445 Everglades St Ventura (93003) *(P-15718)*

Victoria Care Center, Ventura *Also Called: Victoria Vntura Healthcare LLC* *(P-15720)*

Victoria Club .... C...... 951 683-5323
2521 Arroyo Dr Riverside (92506) *(P-14476)*

Victoria Place Community Assn .... D...... 909 981-4131
195 N Euclid Ave Upland (91786) *(P-19118)*

Victoria Vntura Asssted Lving .... D...... 805 642-1736
27101 Puerta Real Ste 450 Mission Viejo (92691) *(P-15719)*

Victoria Vntura Healthcare LLC .... B...... 805 642-1736
5445 Everglades St Ventura (93003) *(P-15720)*

Victorian Post Acute, San Francisco *Also Called: Golden Gateidence Opco LLC* *(P-15758)*

Victorville Homecare, San Bernardino *Also Called: Maxim Healthcare Services Inc* *(P-16895)*

Victorville Speedwash Inc .... D...... 760 998-2482
13311 Main St Hesperia (92345) *(P-13703)*

Victorville Speedwash Inc .... D...... 760 388-0112
15200 Palmdale Rd Victorville (92392) *(P-13704)*

Victorville Speedwash Inc .... D...... 760 388-0113
12875 Bear Valley Rd Victorville (92392) *(P-13705)*

Victorvlle Trsure Holdings LLC .... D...... 760 245-6565
15494 Palmdale Rd Victorville (92392) *(P-10344)*

Victory Foam Inc (PA) .... D...... 949 474-0690
3 Holland Irvine (92618) *(P-6956)*

Victory Intl Group LLC .... C...... 949 407-5888
14748 Pipeline Ave Ste B Chino Hills (91709) *(P-6001)*

Victory Studio, Burbank *Also Called: Warner Bros Entertainment Inc* *(P-13916)*

Vid, Vista *Also Called: Vista Irrigation District* *(P-4997)*

Vida Health Inc .... D...... 415 989-1017
100 Montgomery St Ste 750 San Francisco (94104) *(P-12021)*

Vident .... D...... 714 221-6700
22705 Savi Ranch Pkwy Yorba Linda (92887) *(P-5459)*

Video Products Distributors, Folsom *Also Called: VPD IV Inc* *(P-13973)*

Video Sensing Division, Tustin *Also Called: Canon Medical Systems USA Inc* *(P-5408)*

Video Vice Data Communications (PA) .... C...... 714 897-6300
7391 Lincoln Way Garden Grove (92841) *(P-4526)*

Videoamp Inc (PA) .... D...... 424 272-7774
2229 S Carmelina Ave Los Angeles (90064) *(P-12391)*

Videocam, Lake Forest *Also Called: Vci Event Technology Inc* *(P-11062)*

Videojeeves Inc .... C...... 877 958-8129
45333 Fremont Blvd Ste 5 Fremont (94538) *(P-12022)*

Viele & Sons Inc (PA) .... D...... 714 447-3663
1820 E Valencia Dr Fullerton (92831) *(P-6412)*

Viele & Sons Instnl Groc, Fullerton *Also Called: Viele & Sons Inc* *(P-6412)*

Vienna Convalescent Hosp Inc .... C...... 209 368-7141
800 S Ham Ln Lodi (95242) *(P-15721)*

Vienna Nrsing Rhbilitation Ctr, Lodi *Also Called: Vienna Convalescent Hosp Inc* *(P-15721)*

Vietnam Veterans of San Diego (PA) .... D...... 619 497-0142
4141 Pacific Hwy San Diego (92110) *(P-18927)*

VIETNAMESE COMMUNITY OF ORANGE, Garden Grove *Also Called: Southland Integrated Svcs Inc* *(P-18625)*

Vietnumber, Huntington Beach *Also Called: Filanity Corporation* *(P-4272)*

View Heights Convalescent Hosp, Los Angeles *Also Called: Amada Enterprises Inc* *(P-15323)*

View Park Convalescent Center, Los Angeles *Also Called: Burlington Convalescent Hosp* *(P-15360)*

View Park Convalescent Center, Los Angeles *Also Called: Burlington Convalescent Hosp* *(P-15361)*

Viewray Technologies Inc .... D...... 650 252-0920
815 E Middlefield Rd Mountain View (94043) *(P-5460)*

Viewsonic, Brea *Also Called: Viewsonic Corporation* *(P-2839)*

Viewsonic Corporation (PA) .... C...... 909 444-8888
10 Pointe Dr Ste 200 Brea (92821) *(P-2839)*

Vigilant Private Security .... D...... 559 800-7233
2100 N Winery Ave Ste 102 Fresno (93703) *(P-13073)*

Vigilant Private Security, Fresno *Also Called: Vigilant Private Security* *(P-13073)*

Vignolo Farms Inc .... C...... 661 746-2148
33342 Dresser Ave Bakersfield (93308) *(P-7)*

Viking Industrial, Pittsburg *Also Called: Viking Industrial Corporation* *(P-5530)*

Viking Industrial Corporation .... C...... 925 427-2518
620 Clark Ave Pittsburg (94565) *(P-5530)*

Viking Office Products Inc (DH) .... B...... 562 490-1000
3366 E Willow St Signal Hill (90755) *(P-6071)*

Viktor Benes Bakeries, Westlake Village *Also Called: Mamolos Cntntl Bailey Bakeries* *(P-7160)*

Vila Construction Co .... D...... 510 236-9111
5371 Heavenly Ridge Ln El Sobrante (94803) *(P-1052)*

Villa At San Mateo, San Mateo *Also Called: Elder Care Alliance San Mateo* *(P-15432)*

Villa Convalescent Hosp Inc .... D...... 951 689-5788
8965 Magnolia Ave Riverside (92503) *(P-15722)*

VILLA CONVALESCENT HOSPITAL, Riverside *Also Called: Villa Convalescent Hosp Inc* *(P-15722)*

Villa De La Mar Inc .... C...... 562 494-5001
5001 E Anaheim St Long Beach (90804) *(P-15910)*

Villa Del Rey Retirement Inn, Escondido *Also Called: Emeritus Corporation* *(P-15441)*

Villa Ford Inc .... C...... 714 637-8222
2550 N Tustin St Orange (92865) *(P-7323)*

Villa Maria Care Center, Baldwin Park *Also Called: Trinity Health Systems* *(P-15707)*

Villa Marin Homeowners Assn .... C...... 415 499-8711
100 Thorndale Dr San Rafael (94903) *(P-18928)*

VILLA MONTALVO, Saratoga *Also Called: Montalvo Association* *(P-18691)*

Villa Mrin Rtrement Residences, San Rafael *Also Called: Villa Marin Homeowners Assn* *(P-18928)*

Villa Park Substation, Orange *Also Called: Southern California Edison Co* *(P-4709)*

Villa Serena Healthcare Center .... D...... 562 437-2797
723 E 9th St Long Beach (90813) *(P-15723)*

Villa Siena .... D...... 650 961-6484
1855 Miramonte Ave # 117 Mountain View (94040) *(P-18540)*

Villa Venetia .... B...... 714 540-1800
2775 Mesa Verde Dr E Costa Mesa (92626) *(P-8063)*

Village At Northridge .... C...... 818 514-4497
9222 Corbin Ave Northridge (91324) *(P-18541)*

Village Management Svcs Inc .... D...... 949 597-4360
24351 El Toro Rd Laguna Woods (92637) *(P-20245)*

Village Nurseries Whl LLC .... B...... 916 993-2292
6901 Bradshaw Rd Sacramento (95829) *(P-6877)*

Village Nurseries Whl LLC .... B...... 951 657-3940
20099 Santa Rosa Mine Rd Perris (92570) *(P-6878)*

Village Road Show Pictures USA .... D...... 310 385-4300
10100 Santa Monica Blvd Ste 200 Los Angeles (90067) *(P-13910)*

Village The, San Juan Capistrano *Also Called: Freedom Properties-Hemet LLC* *(P-8721)*

Village West Health Center, Riverside *Also Called: Air Force Village West Inc* *(P-15319)*

Village West Interiors, Stockton *Also Called: Grupe Company* *(P-9033)*

Villages Golf and Country Club .... C...... 408 274-4400
5000 Cribari Ln San Jose (95135) *(P-14477)*

Villages, The, San Jose *Also Called: Villages Golf and Country Club* *(P-14477)*

Villara Corporation (PA) .... B...... 916 646-2700
4700 Lang Ave Mcclellan (95652) *(P-1591)*

Villas De Crlsbad Ltd A Cal Lt .... D...... 760 434-7116
3500 Lake Blvd Oceanside (92056) *(P-18542)*

Vim Inc .... C...... 910 727-1834
548 Market St Pmb 84904 San Francisco (94104) *(P-12023)*

Vimark Inc .... D...... 707 857-3588
19500 Geyserville Ave Geyserville (95441) *(P-383)*

Vimark Vineyards, Geyserville *Also Called: Vimark Inc* *(P-383)*

Vimo Inc (PA) .... D...... 650 618-4600
1305 Terra Bella Ave Mountain View (94043) *(P-20874)*

Vin Di Bona Productions, Los Angeles *Also Called: Cara Communications LLC* *(P-13928)*

Vincent B Zaninovich Sons Inc .... A...... 661 720-9031
20715 Ave 8 Richgrove (93261) *(P-88)*

Vincent Contractors Inc .... B...... 714 660-0165
4501 E La Palma Ave Ste 200 Anaheim (92807) *(P-1896)*

Vincent Scaffolding, Anaheim *Also Called: Vincent Contractors Inc* *(P-1896)*

Vincent-Hayley Enterprises Inc

ALPHABETIC SECTION

Vincent-Hayley Enterprises Inc .... D....... 626 398-8182
1810 N Fair Oaks Ave Pasadena (91103) *(P-16621)*

Vinculums, Irvine *Also Called: Vinculums Services LLC (P-20875)*

Vinculums Services LLC .... C....... 949 783-3552
10 Pasteur Ste 100 Irvine (92618) *(P-20875)*

Vindicia Inc .... C....... 650 264-4700
1000 Sansome St Ste 200 San Francisco (94111) *(P-12392)*

Vindra Inc .... D....... 707 994-7738
3805 Dexter Ln Clearlake (95422) *(P-15724)*

Vineyard Post Acute, Petaluma *Also Called: Petalumaidence Opco LLC (P-2391)*

Vineyards of Monterey, Santa Rosa *Also Called: Jackson Family Wines Inc (P-2387)*

Vinh - Sanh Trading Corp .... D....... 626 968-6888
13500 Nelson Ave City Of Industry (91746) *(P-6691)*

Vino Farms Inc .... C....... 916 775-4095
51375 S Netherlands Rd Clarksburg (95612) *(P-207)*

Vino Farms Inc .... C....... 707 433-8241
10651 Eastside Rd Healdsburg (95448) *(P-384)*

Vino Farms LLC .... B....... 209 334-6975
1377 E Lodi Ave Lodi (95240) *(P-6810)*

Vinson & Elkins LLP .... C....... 650 617-8400
1841 Page Mill Rd Fl 2 Palo Alto (94304) *(P-17672)*

Vintage, Sonoma *Also Called: Vintage Senior Management Inc (P-8868)*

Vintage Associates Inc .... C....... 760 772-3673
78755 Darby Rd Bermuda Dunes (92203) *(P-546)*

Vintage Club .... D....... 760 340-0500
75001 Vintage Dr W Indian Wells (92210) *(P-14478)*

Vintage Design LLC (HQ) .... D....... 949 900-5400
25200 Commercentre Dr Lake Forest (92630) *(P-2040)*

Vintage Design LLC .... D....... 858 695-9544
8310 Juniper Creek Ln San Diego (92126) *(P-13542)*

Vintage Fire Nrsing Rhbltion C, Modesto *Also Called: Covenant Care California LLC (P-15834)*

Vintage Nursery, Bermuda Dunes *Also Called: Vintage Associates Inc (P-546)*

Vintage Production California, Santa Clarita *Also Called: California Resources Prod Corp (P-583)*

Vintage Senior Management Inc .... A....... 707 595-0009
91 Napa Rd Sonoma (95476) *(P-8868)*

Vintage Senior Management Inc .... A....... 818 954-9500
2721 W Willow St Burbank (91505) *(P-18169)*

VINTAGE SENIOR MANAGEMENT, INC., Burbank *Also Called: Vintage Senior Management Inc (P-18169)*

Vintners Inn .... D....... 707 575-7350
4350 Barnes Rd Santa Rosa (95403) *(P-10345)*

Vinyl Technology Inc (PA) .... C....... 626 443-5257
200 Railroad Ave Monrovia (91016) *(P-2527)*

Violin Memory Inc (PA) .... C....... 650 396-1500
4555 Great America Pkwy Ste 150 Santa Clara (95054) *(P-2820)*

VIP, Folsom *Also Called: Visionary Intgrtion Prfssnals (P-9347)*

VIP Tours of California Inc .... D....... 310 216-7507
1419 E Maple Ave El Segundo (90245) *(P-3971)*

Vir Biotechnology Inc (PA) .... C....... 415 906-4324
1800 Owens St Fl 11 San Francisco (94158) *(P-19796)*

Virco Inc (HQ) .... C....... 310 533-0474
2027 Harpers Way Torrance (90501) *(P-5107)*

Virga Investment Property .... C....... 530 755-4409
430 S George Wash Blvd Yuba City (95993) *(P-8775)*

Virgin Fish Inc (PA) .... C....... 310 391-6161
1000 Corporate Pointe Ste 150 Culver City (90230) *(P-3303)*

Virginia Cntry CLB of Long Bch .... C....... 562 427-0924
4602 N Virginia Rd Long Beach (90807) *(P-14479)*

Virident Systems Inc .... C....... 408 573-5000
1745 Tech Dr Ste 700 San Jose (95110) *(P-19797)*

Viridos Inc .... C....... 858 754-2900
250 W Schrimpf Rd Calipatria (92233) *(P-19798)*

Virtium LLC .... D....... 949 888-2444
30052 Tomas Rcho Sta Marg (92688) *(P-5369)*

Virtunet LLC .... D....... 650 847-8633
1900 S Norfolk St Ste 300 San Mateo (94403) *(P-12024)*

Virtunet Systems, San Mateo *Also Called: Virtunet LLC (P-12024)*

Visa, Foster City *Also Called: Visa Inc (P-13543)*

Visa, Foster City *Also Called: Visa International Svc Assn (P-13544)*

Visa Inc .... D....... 415 805-4000
1 Market St Ste 600 San Francisco (94105) *(P-10582)*

Visa Inc (PA) .... A....... 650 432-3200
900 Metro Center Blvd Foster City (94404) *(P-13543)*

Visa International Svc Assn (HQ) .... C....... 650 432-3200
900 Metro Center Blvd Foster City (94404) *(P-13544)*

Visa USA Inc (HQ) .... D....... 650 432-3200
900 Metro Center Blvd Foster City (94404) *(P-13545)*

Visage Imaging Inc .... D....... 858 345-4410
12625 High Bluff Dr Ste 205 San Diego (92130) *(P-10583)*

Visalia Country Club .... D....... 559 734-3733
625 N Ranch St Visalia (93291) *(P-14480)*

Visalia Medical Clinic .... D....... 559 562-1361
839 Sequoia Ave Lindsay (93247) *(P-15194)*

Visalia Medical Clinic Inc (PA) .... B....... 559 733-5222
5400 W Hillsdale Ave Visalia (93291) *(P-15195)*

Visalia Rawhide, Visalia *Also Called: Mlb Advanced Media LP (P-4513)*

Visalia Youth Services, Visalia *Also Called: Turning Point Central Cal Inc (P-18157)*

Vish Consulting Services Inc .... D....... 916 800-3762
9655 Granite Ridge Dr Ste 200 San Diego (92123) *(P-11253)*

Vision Care Center Central Cal, Fresno *Also Called: Vision Care Ctr A Med Group In (P-15196)*

Vision Care Ctr A Med Group In (PA) .... D....... 559 486-2000
7075 N Sharon Ave Fresno (93720) *(P-15196)*

Vision Legal Inc .... D....... 310 469-4966
4712 E 2nd St Ste 840 Long Beach (90803) *(P-17673)*

Vision Realty Managements, Beverly Hills *Also Called: Starpint 1031 Property MGT LLC (P-9186)*

Vision Service Plan (PA) .... A....... 916 851-5000
3333 Quality Dr Rancho Cordova (95670) *(P-8372)*

Vision Solutions Inc (HQ) .... D....... 949 253-6500
15300 Barranca Pkwy Irvine (92618) *(P-12025)*

Visionaire Group Inc .... D....... 310 823-1800
400 Corporate Pointe Ste 700 Culver City (90230) *(P-20604)*

Visionary Intgrtion Prfssnals (PA) .... C....... 916 985-9625
80 Iron Point Cir Ste 100 Folsom (95630) *(P-9347)*

Visionary Intgrtion Prfssnals (HQ) .... D....... 916 985-9625
80 Iron Point Cir Ste 100 Folsom (95630) *(P-12905)*

Visionary Intgrtion Prfssonals, Folsom *Also Called: Visionary Intgrtion Prfssnals (P-12905)*

Visionary Nutrition LLC .... C....... 510 567-1200
9957 Medford Ave Ste 4 Oakland (94603) *(P-855)*

Visions Unlimited .... C....... 916 394-0800
8766 Williamson Dr Elk Grove (95624) *(P-17160)*

Visiquate Inc .... C....... 707 546-4377
520 3rd St Ste 300 Santa Rosa (95401) *(P-12026)*

Visiting Angels .... C....... 800 365-4189
73700 Dinah Shore Dr Ste 105 Palm Desert (92211) *(P-16962)*

Visiting Angels, Chino *Also Called: Angels In Motion LLC (P-16808)*

Visiting Nrse Assn of Inland C (PA) .... A....... 951 413-1200
600 W Santa Ana Blvd Ste 114 Santa Ana (92701) *(P-16963)*

Visiting Nrse Assn of Snta Cru (DH) .... D....... 831 477-2600
2880 Soquel Ave Ste 10 Santa Cruz (95062) *(P-16964)*

Visiting Nurse & Hospice .... C....... 805 965-5555
512 E Gutierrez St Santa Barbara (93103) *(P-16965)*

Visiting Nurse & Hospice Care (PA) .... C....... 805 965-5555
509 E Montecito St Ste 200 Santa Barbara (93103) *(P-16966)*

VISITING NURSE & HOSPICE CARE, Santa Barbara *Also Called: Visiting Nurse & Hospice Care (P-16966)*

Visitor Services & Facilities, San Jose *Also Called: City of San Jose (P-18686)*

Visiworks Software, El Dorado Hills *Also Called: Dorado Software Inc (P-11551)*

Vista Care Group LLC (PA) .... D....... 760 295-3900
1863 Devon Pl Vista (92084) *(P-18170)*

Vista Community Clinic (PA) .... B....... 760 631-5000
1000 Vale Terrace Dr Vista (92084) *(P-15260)*

Vista Del Campo, Irvine *Also Called: American Cmpus Communities Inc (P-10391)*

Vista Del Mar Child Fmly Svcs (PA) .... B....... 310 836-1223
3200 Motor Ave Los Angeles (90034) *(P-17757)*

Vista Del Mar Child Fmly Svcs .... C....... 310 836-1223
1533 Euclid St Santa Monica (90404) *(P-18543)*

Vista Del Mar Health Centers, Vista *Also Called: Life Care Centers America Inc (P-15865)*

Vista Equity Partners Fund III, San Francisco *Also Called: Amber Holdings Inc (P-11402)*

ALPHABETIC SECTION — Volt Management Corp

Vista Ford Inc .... D....... 805 983-6511
   1501 Auto Center Dr Oxnard (93036) *(P-7324)*

Vista Ford of Oxnard, Oxnard *Also Called: Vista Ford Inc (P-7324)*

Vista Gardens, Vista *Also Called: Vista Care Group LLC (P-18170)*

Vista Hill Foundation .... D....... 619 281-5511
   6145 Decena Dr San Diego (92120) *(P-17819)*

Vista Hill Foundation .... D....... 619 266-0166
   4125 Alpha St San Diego (92113) *(P-18171)*

Vista Hospital Riverside, Rancho Cucamonga *Also Called: Perris Valley Cmnty Hosp LLC (P-16322)*

Vista Hospital San Gabriel Vly, Baldwin Park *Also Called: Vista Spclty Hosp Sthern Cal L (P-16622)*

Vista Irrigation District .... D....... 760 597-3100
   1391 Engineer St Vista (92081) *(P-4997)*

Vista JV Partners LLC .... B....... 214 738-2771
   2035 Corte Del Nogal Ste 200 Carlsbad (92011) *(P-15312)*

Vista Knoll Spclzed Care Fclty, Vista *Also Called: Vista Woods Health Assoc LLC (P-15726)*

Vista Pacifica Center, Jurupa Valley *Also Called: Vista Pacifica Enterprises Inc (P-15725)*

Vista Pacifica Enterprises Inc (PA) .... C....... 951 682-4833
   3674 Pacific Ave Jurupa Valley (92509) *(P-15725)*

Vista Spclty Hosp Sthern Cal L .... D....... 626 388-2700
   14148 Francisquito Ave Baldwin Park (91706) *(P-16622)*

Vista Valley Country Club .... D....... 760 758-2800
   29354 Vista Valley Dr Vista (92084) *(P-14481)*

Vista Woods Health Assoc LLC .... C....... 760 630-2273
   2000 Westwood Rd Vista (92083) *(P-15726)*

Vistage International Inc (PA) .... D....... 858 523-6800
   4840 Eastgate Mall San Diego (92121) *(P-20605)*

Vistancia Marketing LLC .... C....... 909 594-9500
   655 Brea Canyon Rd Walnut (91789) *(P-20606)*

Vistar Northern California, Livermore *Also Called: Performance Food Group Inc (P-6276)*

Visterra Credit Union .... C....... 951 656-4411
   23520 Cactus Ave Moreno Valley (92553) *(P-7833)*

Visual Concepts Entertainment .... B....... 415 479-3634
   10 Hamilton Landing Novato (94949) *(P-12027)*

Visual Pak San Diego LLC .... C....... 847 689-1000
   2320 Paseo De Las Americas Ste 201 San Diego (92154) *(P-13546)*

Visual Supply Company (PA) .... D....... 847 721-9285
   1500 Broadway Ste 300 Oakland (94612) *(P-12028)*

Vita North America, Yorba Linda *Also Called: Vident (P-5459)*

Vital Health Sciences Inc .... D....... 619 675-5521
   San Diego (92191) *(P-17346)*

Vitalant .... D....... 805 654-1603
   2223 Eastman Ave Ste A Ventura (93003) *(P-17347)*

Vitalant Research Institute (PA) .... C....... 415 923-5771
   360 Spear St Ste 200 San Francisco (94105) *(P-17348)*

Vitalant Research Institute .... D....... 707 428-6001
   1325 Gateway Blvd Ste C1 Fairfield (94533) *(P-17349)*

Vitalant Research Institute .... D....... 530 221-0600
   2680 Larkspur Ln Redding (96002) *(P-17350)*

VITAMIN ANGEL, Goleta *Also Called: Vitamin Angel Alliance Inc (P-19119)*

Vitamin Angel Alliance Inc .... D....... 805 564-8400
   6500 Hollister Ave Ste 130 Goleta (93117) *(P-19119)*

Vitas Healthcare Corporation .... D....... 858 805-6254
   9106 Pulsar Ct Ste D Corona (92883) *(P-15801)*

Vitas Healthcare Corporation .... D....... 415 874-4400
   670 N Mccarthy Blvd Ste 220 Milpitas (95035) *(P-15802)*

Vitas Healthcare Corporation .... D....... 805 437-2100
   333 N Lantana St Ste 124 Camarillo (93010) *(P-15803)*

Vitco Distributors Inc .... C....... 909 355-1300
   715 E California St Ontario (91761) *(P-6413)*

Vitco Food Service, Ontario *Also Called: Vitco Distributors Inc (P-6413)*

Vitesse LLC .... A....... 650 543-4800
   1601 Willow Rd Menlo Park (94025) *(P-12641)*

Vito Trucking LLC .... D....... 209 342-5104
   2812 Nathan Ave Modesto (95354) *(P-3563)*

Vitro, San Diego *Also Called: Vitrorobertson LLC (P-10688)*

Vitrorobertson LLC .... D....... 619 234-0408
   225 Broadway San Diego (92101) *(P-10688)*

Vituity, Emeryville *Also Called: Cep America LLC (P-14675)*

Viva Life Science Inc .... C....... 949 645-6100
   350 Paularino Ave Costa Mesa (92626) *(P-6151)*

Viva Soma Lessee Inc .... A....... 415 974-6400
   50 3rd St San Francisco (94103) *(P-20246)*

Vivalon .... D....... 415 454-0964
   930 Tamalpais Ave San Rafael (94901) *(P-18172)*

Vivian Health Inc .... D....... 415 851-1168
   150 Spear St Ste 725 San Francisco (94105) *(P-16967)*

Vivid Digital .... D....... 818 908-0481
   1933 N Bronson Ave Apt 209 Los Angeles (90068) *(P-12029)*

Vivid Interactive, Los Angeles *Also Called: Vivid Digital (P-12029)*

Vivint Solar Developer, Stockton *Also Called: Vivint Solar Developer LLC (P-1592)*

Vivint Solar Developer LLC .... D....... 209 942-2040
   614 Wilshire Ave Ste A Stockton (95203) *(P-1592)*

Vivio Health Inc .... D....... 925 365-6600
   1933 Davis St Ste 274 San Leandro (94577) *(P-8373)*

Viz Media LLC .... C....... 415 546-7073
   1355 Market St Ste 200 San Francisco (94103) *(P-2546)*

Viz Media Music, San Francisco *Also Called: Viz Media LLC (P-2546)*

Vly Air Cond & RPR .... D....... 559 237-2123
   825 S Topeka Ave Fresno (93721) *(P-13730)*

Vm International, Riverside *Also Called: MSRS INC (P-5125)*

Vm Services Inc (DH) .... C....... 510 744-3720
   1621 Barber Ln Milpitas (95035) *(P-12030)*

Vm Services Inc .... D....... 510 744-3720
   6723 Mowry Ave Newark (94560) *(P-12031)*

Vmware, Palo Alto *Also Called: Vmware Inc (P-12393)*

Vmware Inc (PA) .... A....... 650 427-5000
   3401 Hillview Ave Palo Alto (94304) *(P-12393)*

Vna of Greater Los Angeles Inc .... D....... 951 252-5314
   17682 Mitchell N Ste 100 Irvine (92614) *(P-16968)*

Vna Private Duty Care, San Bernardino *Also Called: Vnacare (P-16971)*

Vnacare .... D....... 760 946-4730
   16147 Kamana Rd Apple Valley (92307) *(P-16969)*

Vnacare .... D....... 909 384-0737
   412 E Vanderbilt Way San Bernardino (92408) *(P-16970)*

Vnacare (PA) .... D....... 909 624-3574
   412 E Vanderbilt Way Ste 100 San Bernardino (92408) *(P-16971)*

Vnaic, Santa Ana *Also Called: Visiting Nrse Assn of Inland C (P-16963)*

Vnh Enterprises Inc .... D....... 877 468-3566
   2636 Vista Pacific Dr Oceanside (92056) *(P-10986)*

Voa, Los Angeles *Also Called: Volunteers of Amer Los Angeles (P-18182)*

Voa Plainview Head Start, Tujunga *Also Called: Volunteers of Amer Los Angeles (P-18178)*

Vocation Plus Inc .... C....... 559 221-8019
   3985 N Fresno St Ste 106 Fresno (93726) *(P-18255)*

Vocational Imprv Program Inc (PA) .... D....... 909 483-5924
   9210 Rochester Ave Rancho Cucamonga (91730) *(P-18256)*

Vocational Visions .... C....... 949 837-7280
   26041 Pala Mission Viejo (92691) *(P-18257)*

Voipment, Tustin *Also Called: Xbp Inc (P-12052)*

Voit Real Estate Services LLC .... C....... 949 851-5100
   2020 Main St Irvine (92614) *(P-9279)*

Volcano Communications Company (PA) .... D....... 209 296-7502
   20000 State Highway 88 Pine Grove (95665) *(P-4356)*

Volcano Telephone Company, Pine Grove *Also Called: Volcano Communications Company (P-4356)*

Volcom LLC (HQ) .... C....... 949 646-2175
   1740 Monrovia Ave Costa Mesa (92627) *(P-13547)*

Volkswagen of Van Nuys Inc .... D....... 323 873-3311
   300 Hitchcock Way Santa Barbara (93105) *(P-7325)*

Volkswagen Santa Monica Inc (PA) .... C....... 310 829-1888
   2440 Santa Monica Blvd Santa Monica (90404) *(P-7326)*

Voloagri Inc .... C....... 805 547-9391
   41970 E Main St Woodland (95776) *(P-6837)*

Volt Management Corp .... D....... 707 547-1660
   3700 Old Redwood Hwy Ste 105 Santa Rosa (95403) *(P-11254)*

Volt Management Corp .... D....... 805 237-0882
   715 6th St Paso Robles (93446) *(P-11349)*

Volt Management Corp .... D....... 831 975-4374
   635 Sanborn Pl Salinas (93901) *(P-11350)*

Volt Management Corp .... D...... 951 789-8133
1650 Iowa Ave Ste 140 Riverside (92507) *(P-11351)*

Volt Management Corp .... D...... 805 485-0506
1701 Solar Dr Ste 145 Oxnard (93030) *(P-11352)*

Volt Management Corp .... D...... 310 316-8523
19191 S Vermont Ave Ste 950 Torrance (90502) *(P-11353)*

Volt Management Corp .... B...... 800 654-2624
2411 N Glassell St Orange (92865) *(P-11354)*

Volt Management Corp .... D...... 626 931-1437
100 N Citrus St Ste 150 West Covina (91791) *(P-11355)*

Volt Management Corp .... D...... 714 879-9330
1400 N Harbor Blvd Ste 103 Fullerton (92835) *(P-11356)*

Volt Management Corp .... D...... 858 576-3140
7676 Hazard Center Dr Ste 1000 San Diego (92108) *(P-11357)*

Volt Management Corp .... D...... 805 560-8658
1300 Santa Barbara St Ste A Santa Barbara (93101) *(P-11358)*

Volt Management Corp .... D...... 559 435-1255
7330 N Palm Ave Ste 105 Fresno (93711) *(P-11359)*

Volt Management Corp .... D...... 916 923-0454
1544 Eureka Rd Ste 100 Roseville (95661) *(P-11360)*

Volt Management Corp .... D...... 209 952-5627
3558 Deer Park Dr # 2 Stockton (95219) *(P-11361)*

Volt Telecom Group, Corona *Also Called: Volt Telecom Group Inc (P-20876)*

Volt Telecom Group Inc .... B...... 951 493-8900
218 Helicopter Cir Corona (92878) *(P-20876)*

Volt Temporary Services, Orange *Also Called: Volt Management Corp (P-11354)*

Volt Workforce Solutions, Santa Rosa *Also Called: Volt Management Corp (P-11254)*

Volt Workforce Solutions, Paso Robles *Also Called: Volt Management Corp (P-11349)*

Volt Workforce Solutions, Salinas *Also Called: Volt Management Corp (P-11350)*

Volt Workforce Solutions, Riverside *Also Called: Volt Management Corp (P-11351)*

Volt Workforce Solutions, Oxnard *Also Called: Volt Management Corp (P-11352)*

Volt Workforce Solutions, Torrance *Also Called: Volt Management Corp (P-11353)*

Volt Workforce Solutions, West Covina *Also Called: Volt Management Corp (P-11355)*

Volt Workforce Solutions, Fullerton *Also Called: Volt Management Corp (P-11356)*

Volt Workforce Solutions, San Diego *Also Called: Volt Management Corp (P-11357)*

Volt Workforce Solutions, Santa Barbara *Also Called: Volt Management Corp (P-11358)*

Volt Workforce Solutions, Fresno *Also Called: Volt Management Corp (P-11359)*

Volt Workforce Solutions, Roseville *Also Called: Volt Management Corp (P-11360)*

Volt Workforce Solutions, Stockton *Also Called: Volt Management Corp (P-11361)*

Volta Charging LLC .... D...... 415 735-5169
155 De Haro St San Francisco (94103) *(P-10697)*

Voltage Security LLC .... D...... 408 886-3200
20400 Stevens Creek Blvd Ste 500 Cupertino (95014) *(P-13154)*

Volume Services Inc .... B...... 415 972-1500
24 Willie Mays Plz San Francisco (94107) *(P-14582)*

Volume Services Inc .... B...... 323 644-6038
5333 Zoo Dr Los Angeles (90027) *(P-14583)*

Volume Services Inc .... B...... 619 525-5800
111 W Harbor Dr San Diego (92101) *(P-14584)*

Volunteers America Head Start, San Fernando *Also Called: Child Care Resource Center Inc (P-18282)*

Volunteers of Amer Los Angeles .... C...... 213 749-0362
1032 W 18th St Los Angeles (90015) *(P-18173)*

Volunteers of Amer Los Angeles .... D...... 818 834-9097
10896 Lehigh Ave Pacoima (91331) *(P-18174)*

Volunteers of Amer Los Angeles .... C...... 323 780-3770
522 N Dangler Ave Los Angeles (90022) *(P-18175)*

Volunteers of Amer Los Angeles .... C...... 626 337-9878
1760 W Cameron Ave Ste 104 West Covina (91790) *(P-18176)*

Volunteers of Amer Los Angeles .... D...... 661 290-2829
25141 Avenida Rondel Valencia (91355) *(P-18177)*

Volunteers of Amer Los Angeles .... C...... 818 352-5974
10819 Plainview Ave Tujunga (91042) *(P-18178)*

Volunteers of Amer Los Angeles .... D...... 714 426-9834
2100 N Broadway Ste 300 Santa Ana (92706) *(P-18179)*

Volunteers of Amer Los Angeles .... C...... 818 769-3617
6724 Tujunga Ave North Hollywood (91606) *(P-18180)*

Volunteers of Amer Los Angeles .... C...... 818 506-0597
11243 Kittridge St North Hollywood (91606) *(P-18181)*

Volunteers of Amer Los Angeles .... C...... 213 627-8002
515 E 6th St Fl 9 Los Angeles (90021) *(P-18182)*

Volunteers of Amer Los Angeles .... D...... 818 834-8957
12550 Van Nuys Blvd Pacoima (91331) *(P-18183)*

Volunteers of Amer Los Angeles .... C...... 310 830-3404
334 Figueroa St Wilmington (90744) *(P-18184)*

Volunteers of America, Los Angeles *Also Called: Volunteers of Amer Los Angeles (P-18173)*
Volunteers of America, Pacoima *Also Called: Volunteers of Amer Los Angeles (P-18174)*
Volunteers of America, Los Angeles *Also Called: Volunteers of Amer Los Angeles (P-18175)*
Volunteers of America, West Covina *Also Called: Volunteers of Amer Los Angeles (P-18176)*
Volunteers of America, Valencia *Also Called: Volunteers of Amer Los Angeles (P-18177)*
Volunteers of America, Santa Ana *Also Called: Volunteers of Amer Los Angeles (P-18179)*
Volunteers of America, North Hollywood *Also Called: Volunteers of Amer Los Angeles (P-18180)*
Volunteers of America, Pacoima *Also Called: Volunteers of Amer Los Angeles (P-18183)*
Volunteers of America, Wilmington *Also Called: Volunteers of Amer Los Angeles (P-18184)*
Volunteers of America, Oakland *Also Called: Volunters Amer Nthrn Cal Nthm (P-18185)*

Volunters Amer Nthrn Cal Nthrn .... D...... 510 419-0360
624 14th St Oakland (94612) *(P-18185)*

Volunters Amer Nthrn Cal Nthrn .... D...... 916 488-0171
2844 Wright St Sacramento (95821) *(P-18186)*

Volvo, Stockton *Also Called: Berberian Bros Inc (P-7171)*
Volvo, Chico *Also Called: Courtesy Motors Auto Ctr Inc (P-7188)*
Vomela, Santa Fe Springs *Also Called: Vomela Specialty Company (P-2567)*

Vomela Specialty Company .... C...... 562 944-3853
9810 Bell Ranch Dr Santa Fe Springs (90670) *(P-2567)*

Vons 2407, Brawley *Also Called: Vons Companies Inc (P-7154)*

Vons Companies Inc .... C...... 760 351-3002
475 W Main St Brawley (92227) *(P-7154)*

Voter Prcnct Vter Rgstrtion Of, Norwalk *Also Called: County of Los Angeles (P-12560)*

Vox Network Solutions Inc .... C...... 650 989-1000
130 Produce Ave Ste C South San Francisco (94080) *(P-2890)*

Voyage Auto Inc .... D...... 917 588-1249
333 Brannan St San Francisco (94107) *(P-3304)*

Voyetra Turtle Beach Inc (DH) .... D...... 914 345-2255
11011 Via Frontera Ste A San Diego (92127) *(P-2840)*

Vpb Operating Co LLC .... D...... 805 773-1011
147 Stimson Ave Pismo Beach (93449) *(P-10346)*

VPD IV Inc .... B...... 916 605-1500
150 Parkshore Dr Folsom (95630) *(P-13973)*

Vpm Management Inc .... C...... 949 863-1500
2400 Main St Ste 201 Irvine (92614) *(P-20247)*

Vroom Automotive Finance Corp (HQ) .... B...... 949 224-1226
1071 Camelback St Ste 100 Newport Beach (92660) *(P-13678)*

Vrp Consulting Inc .... A...... 415 225-6466
268 Bush St 3836 San Francisco (94104) *(P-12032)*

Vsa and Associates Inc .... D...... 562 698-2468
6571 Altura Blvd Ste 100 Buena Park (90620) *(P-19432)*

VSC Sports Inc .... D...... 415 820-3525
750 Folsom St San Francisco (94107) *(P-20877)*

Vsco, Oakland *Also Called: Visual Supply Company (P-12028)*

Vss International Inc (HQ) .... D...... 916 373-1500
3785 Channel Dr West Sacramento (95691) *(P-1176)*

VT Milcom Inc .... D...... 619 424-9024
1660 Logan Ave Ste 2 San Diego (92113) *(P-19433)*

Vta .... D...... 408 546-7777
787 Regent Park Dr San Jose (95123) *(P-3224)*

Vta Telephone Information .... B...... 408 321-7127
3331 N 1st St San Jose (95134) *(P-4357)*

Vtc Enterprises (PA) .... D...... 805 928-5000
2445 A St Santa Maria (93455) *(P-18258)*

Vu Holdings LLC .... D...... 661 808-4004
55 Fair Dr Costa Mesa (92626) *(P-17351)*

Vubiquity, Sherman Oaks *Also Called: Vubiquity Holdings Inc (P-4527)*

Vubiquity Holdings Inc (DH) .... C...... 818 526-5000
15301 Ventura Blvd Ste 3000 Sherman Oaks (91403) *(P-4527)*

Vucovich Inc (PA) .... D...... 559 486-8020
4288 S Bagley Ave Fresno (93725) *(P-5816)*

Vulcan Cyber Inc .... D...... 415 429-4311
2345 Yale St Fl 1 Palo Alto (94306) *(P-20607)*

Vulcan Materials, Glendale *Also Called: Calmat Co (P-2648)*

ALPHABETIC SECTION
Walton Electric Corporation

Vumedi, Oakland *Also Called: Vumedi Inc (P-13911)*
Vumedi Inc (PA)..D....... 650 450-2603
555 12th St Ste 1775 Oakland (94607) *(P-13911)*

Vungle, San Francisco *Also Called: Vungle Inc (P-10689)*
Vungle Inc (PA)..D....... 415 800-1400
1255 Battery St Ste 500 San Francisco (94111) *(P-10689)*

Vvd Communications, Garden Grove *Also Called: Video Vice Data Communications (P-4526)*
Vwi Concord LLC...C....... 925 827-2000
1970 Diamond Blvd Concord (94520) *(P-10347)*

Vwise Inc...D....... 949 716-1276
85 Enterprise Ste 320 Aliso Viejo (92656) *(P-12033)*

Vxi Global Solutions, Los Angeles *Also Called: Vxi Global Solutions LLC (P-13548)*
Vxi Global Solutions LLC (PA)..A....... 213 739-4720
220 W 1st St Fl 3 Los Angeles (90012) *(P-13548)*

Vynca Inc..D....... 650 427-0573
548 Market St Ste 83340 San Francisco (94104) *(P-16972)*

Vyond..D....... 888 360-9639
204 2nd Ave Ste 638 San Mateo (94401) *(P-13912)*

W A Rasic Cnstr Co Inc (PA)...C....... 562 928-6111
4150 Long Beach Blvd Long Beach (90807) *(P-1277)*

W B Starr Inc..D....... 949 770-8835
20602 Canada Rd Lake Forest (92630) *(P-547)*

W C Q, Fremont *Also Called: West Coast Quartz Corporation (P-2689)*
W Diamond Supply Co (DH)...D....... 909 859-8939
19321 E Walnut Dr N City Of Industry (91748) *(P-5143)*

W E O'Neil Construction, Rancho Cucamonga *Also Called: WE Oneil Construction Co Cal (P-1053)*

W G A, Irvine *Also Called: Western Growers Association (P-18726)*

W I C, Sutter Creek *Also Called: Resource Connection of Amador (P-18098)*

W L Hickey Sons Inc..C....... 408 736-4938
1960 Hartog Dr Ste 10 San Jose (95131) *(P-1593)*

W Lodging Inc...A....... 619 258-6565
1825 Gillespie Way Ste 10 El Cajon (92020) *(P-10348)*

W Los Angeles..B....... 310 208-8765
930 Hilgard Ave Los Angeles (90024) *(P-10349)*

W M Lyles Co..C....... 951 296-2354
42142 Roick Dr Temecula (92590) *(P-1278)*

W M Lyles Co..C....... 916 375-1833
3925 Progress Dr Rocklin (95765) *(P-1279)*

W M Lyles Co..C....... 661 387-1600
2810 Unicorn Rd Bakersfield (93308) *(P-19434)*

W N G Construction Jv Inc (PA)......................................D....... 714 524-7100
4175 E La Palma Ave Ste 125 Anaheim (92807) *(P-856)*

W O R K, Carpinteria *Also Called: Momentum Work Inc (P-18057)*

W R Hambrecht Co Inc (PA)...D....... 415 551-8600
Pier 1, Bay 3 San Francisco (94111) *(P-8174)*

W Why W Enterprises Inc...D....... 626 969-4292
2671 Pomona Blvd Pomona (91768) *(P-3604)*

W&J Business Ventures LLC..D....... 310 645-7700
8620 Airport Blvd Los Angeles (90045) *(P-10350)*

W2005 Wyn Hotels LP...D....... 323 887-8100
5757 Telegraph Rd Commerce (90040) *(P-10351)*

Wacker Chemical Corporation.......................................D....... 909 590-8822
13910 Oaks Ave Chino (91710) *(P-2636)*

Wade Casey..D....... 916 395-9996
1648 Kathleen Ave Ste A Sacramento (95815) *(P-13074)*

Wafer Reclaim Services LLC..C....... 408 945-8112
2240 Ringwood Ave San Jose (95131) *(P-2936)*

Waggl Inc (PA)..D....... 415 399-9949
1750 Bridgeway Ste B103 Sausalito (94965) *(P-12394)*

Wagner Hts Nrsng Rhblttion Ct, Stockton *Also Called: Covenant Care California LLC (P-15399)*

Waldberg Inc...D....... 818 843-0004
15301 Ventura Blvd Ste 300 Sherman Oaks (91403) *(P-10723)*

Walden House Inc..C....... 415 554-1131
1735 Mission St San Francisco (94103) *(P-18544)*

Walden House Inc..C....... 626 258-0300
845 E Arrow Hwy Pomona (91767) *(P-18545)*

Walden House Inc..C....... 415 554-1480
214 Haight St San Francisco (94102) *(P-18546)*

Walden House Adolescent, San Francisco *Also Called: Walden House Inc (P-18546)*

Waldorf Astoria Beverly Hills, Beverly Hills *Also Called: Oasis West Realty LLC (P-10055)*
Waldorf Astria Mnrc Bch Rsort, Dana Point *Also Called: Cph Monarch Hotel LLC (P-9727)*
Walk Through Video, Mcclellan *Also Called: Villara Corporation (P-1591)*
Walker & Dunlop Inc..D....... 301 215-5500
12100 Wilshire Blvd Ste 300 Los Angeles (90025) *(P-8027)*

Walker & Zanger, North Hills *Also Called: Walker & Zanger LLC (P-5213)*
Walker & Zanger LLC (HQ)...D....... 818 280-8300
16719 Schoenborn St North Hills (91343) *(P-5213)*

Walking Company Holdings Inc (PA).............................C....... 805 963-8727
1800 Avenue Of The Stars Ste 300 Los Angeles (90067) *(P-7409)*

Wallace-Kuhl Investments LLC (PA)..............................D....... 916 372-1434
3050 Industrial Blvd West Sacramento (95691) *(P-19435)*

Wally Parking, Los Angeles *Also Called: All Star Parking (P-13602)*
Walmart, Riverside *Also Called: Walmart Inc (P-3778)*
Walmart, Red Bluff *Also Called: Walmart Inc (P-3779)*
Walmart, Hanford *Also Called: Walmart Inc (P-3780)*
Walmart, Rialto *Also Called: Walmart Inc (P-7135)*
Walmart Inc...C....... 951 320-5722
1001 Columbia Ave Riverside (92507) *(P-3778)*

Walmart Inc...A....... 530 529-0916
10815 State Highway 99w Red Bluff (96080) *(P-3779)*

Walmart Inc...C....... 559 583-6071
13231 11th Ave Hanford (93230) *(P-3780)*

Walmart Inc...C....... 909 820-9912
1366 S Riverside Ave Rialto (92376) *(P-7135)*

Walnut Country, Concord *Also Called: Cowell Homeowners Assn Inc (P-18847)*
Walnut Creek Associates 2 Inc......................................D....... 925 934-0530
1707 N Main St Walnut Creek (94596) *(P-7327)*

Walnut Creek Honda, Walnut Creek *Also Called: Walnut Creek Associates 2 Inc (P-7327)*
Walnut Investment Corp..A....... 714 238-9240
2940 E White Star Ave Anaheim (92806) *(P-5193)*

Walsh Group Inc...D....... 530 221-4405
3135 Agassi Ln Redding (96002) *(P-14241)*

Walsh Vineyards Management Inc.................................C....... 707 258-1500
1125 Golden Gate Dr Napa (94558) *(P-9208)*

Walt Disney Company...D....... 818 560-4665
7131 Tujunga Ave North Hollywood (91605) *(P-4470)*

Walt Disney Company (PA)...A....... 818 560-1000
500 S Buena Vista St Burbank (91521) *(P-14316)*

Walt Disney Family Museum..D....... 415 345-6800
104 Montgomery St San Francisco (94129) *(P-18682)*

Walt Disney Music Company (DH).................................A....... 818 560-1000
500 S Buena Vista St Burbank (91521) *(P-13913)*

Walt Disney Pictures...B....... 818 409-2200
811 Sonora Ave Glendale (91201) *(P-13914)*

Walt Disney Records Direct (DH)...................................A....... 818 560-1000
500 S Buena Vista St Burbank (91521) *(P-13915)*

Walt Dsney Imgnring RES Dev In (DH)..........................A....... 818 544-6500
1401 Flower St Glendale (91201) *(P-13960)*

Walter & Wolf, Fremont *Also Called: Walters & Wolf Glass Company (P-2208)*
Walter Anderson Plumbing Inc.......................................C....... 619 449-7646
1830 John Towers Ave El Cajon (92020) *(P-1594)*

Walter L Jones Family Ltd...D....... 559 591-1515
7381 Avenue 432 Reedley (93654) *(P-313)*

Walter Timmons Enterprises Inc....................................D....... 562 595-4601
3940 Cherry Ave Long Beach (90807) *(P-7328)*

Walters & Wolf Glass Company (PA).............................C....... 510 490-1115
41450 Boscell Rd Fremont (94538) *(P-2208)*

Walters & Wolf Glass Company......................................D....... 909 392-1961
1975 Puddingstone Dr La Verne (91750) *(P-2209)*

Walters & Wolf Interiors (PA)..D....... 415 243-9400
41450 Boscell Rd Fremont (94538) *(P-2025)*

Walters Auto Sales and Svc Inc......................................C....... 888 316-4097
3213 Adams St Riverside (92504) *(P-7329)*

Walters Family Partnership...C....... 760 320-6868
400 E Tahquitz Canyon Way Palm Springs (92262) *(P-10352)*

Walton Construction Inc..D....... 909 267-7777
358 E Foothill Blvd Ste 100 San Dimas (91773) *(P-783)*

Walton Construction Services, San Dimas *Also Called: Walton Construction Inc (P-783)*
Walton Electric Corporation..C....... 909 981-5051
755 N Central Ave Ste A Upland (91786) *(P-2903)*

Walton Engineering Inc — 3900 Commerce Dr West Sacramento (95691) *(P-2328)* — D — 916 372-1888

Wamc Company Inc — 7420 Clairemont Mesa Blvd San Diego (92111) *(P-8869)* — D — 858 454-2753

Wanclouds Inc — 2811 Mission College Blvd Fl 7 Santa Clara (95054) *(P-12034)* — D — 408 663-6753

Wand Topco Inc — 4774 W Adams Blvd Los Angeles (90016) *(P-13650)* — A — 323 734-3333

Wand Topco Inc — 123 California Dr Burlingame (94010) *(P-13651)* — A — 650 375-0600

Wand Topco Inc — 331 Bangs Ave Modesto (95356) *(P-13652)* — A — 209 524-6824

Warbritton & Assoc Impairment — 24301 Southland Dr Hayward (94545) *(P-15197)* — D — 510 781-0211

Wardlow 2 LP (PA) — 333 S Grand Ave Ste 4070 Los Angeles (90071) *(P-13809)* — D — 562 432-8066

Wardrobe and Bath Specialties, Modesto Also Called: Dons Mobile Glass Inc *(P-7114)*

Ware Disposal Inc — 1451 Manhattan Ave Fullerton (92831) *(P-4951)* — C — 714 834-0234

Ware Malcomb (PA) — 10 Edelman Irvine (92618) *(P-19517)* — C — 949 660-9128

Warehouse, Redlands Also Called: Lamps Plus Inc *(P-3723)*

Warehouse, Laguna Beach Also Called: Pauls Tv LLC *(P-5609)*

Warehouse and Distribution, Jurupa Valley Also Called: Triways Inc *(P-3557)*

Warehouse and Receiving Center, San Bernardino Also Called: Loma Linda University Med Ctr *(P-4051)*

Warehouse Specialists LLC — 2743 Thompson Creek Rd Pomona (91767) *(P-3781)* — D — 909 596-2566

Warehouse Sys, Fresno Also Called: Gray Lift Inc *(P-5838)*

Warmington, Costa Mesa Also Called: Warmington Mr 14 Assoc LLC *(P-20248)*

Warmington Homes (PA) — 3090 Pullman St Costa Mesa (92626) *(P-800)* — C — 714 434-4435

Warmington Homes — 15615 Alton Pkwy Ste 150 Irvine (92618) *(P-801)* — C — 949 679-3100

Warmington Homes — 4160 Dublin Blvd Ste 130 Dublin (94568) *(P-802)* — C — 925 866-6700

Warmington Homes California, Costa Mesa Also Called: Rebco Communities Inc *(P-771)*

Warmington Mr 14 Assoc LLC — 3090 Pullman St Costa Mesa (92626) *(P-20248)* — D — 714 557-5511

Warmington Residental, Dublin Also Called: Warmington Homes *(P-802)*

Warmington Residential Cal Inc — 3090 Pullman St Costa Mesa (92626) *(P-739)* — C — 714 557-5511

Warner Bros, Burbank Also Called: Warner Bros Transatlantic Inc *(P-13975)*

Warner Bros Consumer Pdts Inc (DH) — 4001 W Olive Ave Burbank (91505) *(P-20878)* — C — 818 954-7980

Warner Bros Distributing Inc — 4000 Warner Blvd Bldg 154 Burbank (91522) *(P-20249)* — B — 818 954-6000

Warner Bros Entertainment Inc (DH) — 4000 Warner Blvd Burbank (91522) *(P-13916)* — C — 818 954-6000

Warner Bros Entertainment Inc — 3500 W Olive Ave Ste 200 Burbank (91505) *(P-13917)* — C — 818 954-2209

Warner Bros Home Entrmt Group (DH) — 4000 Warner Blvd Burbank (91522) *(P-14111)* — D — 818 954-6000

Warner Bros Home Entrmt Inc (DH) — 4000 Warner Blvd Bldg 160 Burbank (91522) *(P-13918)* — D — 818 954-6000

Warner Bros Intl TV Dist Inc — 4000 Warner Blvd Burbank (91522) *(P-13919)* — 818 954-6000

Warner Bros Records Inc (DH) — 777 S Santa Fe Ave Los Angeles (90021) *(P-13549)* — B — 818 846-9090

Warner Bros Studio Facilities, Burbank Also Called: Warner Bros Entertainment Inc *(P-13917)*

Warner Bros Transatlantic Inc — 4001 W Olive Ave Burbank (91505) *(P-13974)* — B — 818 954-5990

Warner Bros Transatlantic Inc — 3300 W Olive Ave Ste 200 Burbank (91505) *(P-13975)* — B — 818 977-6384

Warner Food Management Co Inc — 4917 Genesta Ave Encino (91316) *(P-7516)* — C — 818 285-2160

Warnerview Skilled Nursing, Alturas Also Called: Modoc Medial Center Hosp Aux *(P-15588)*

Warren E & P, Long Beach Also Called: Warren E&P Inc *(P-607)*

Warren E&P Inc — 400 Oceangate Ste 200 Long Beach (90802) *(P-607)* — D — 214 393-9688

Warwick California Corporation — 490 Geary St San Francisco (94102) *(P-10353)* — D — 415 992-3809

Warwick Hotel San Francisco, San Francisco Also Called: Warwick California Corporation *(P-10353)*

Warwick, Mal & Associates, Berkeley Also Called: Strathmoore Press Inc *(P-13488)*

Wasco Medical Plaza, Wasco Also Called: Adventist Health Delano *(P-9420)*

Wash Mltfmily Ldry Systems LLC (PA) — 2200 195th St Torrance (90501) *(P-10465)* — C — 800 421-6897

Washington C3 Center, San Diego Also Called: Mitre Corporation *(P-19897)*

Washington Center LLC — 14766 Washington Ave San Leandro (94578) *(P-16623)* — D — 510 352-2211

Washington Hosp Healthcare Sys — 2000 Mowry Ave Fremont (94538) *(P-16624)* — A — 510 797-3342

Washington Hospital, Fremont Also Called: Washington On Wheels *(P-16625)*

Washington Inventory Service — 9265 Sky Park Ct Ste 100 San Diego (92123) *(P-13550)* — A — 858 565-8111

Washington Iron Works, Gardena Also Called: Washington Orna Ir Works Inc *(P-2329)*

Washington On Wheels — 2000 Mowry Ave Fremont (94538) *(P-16625)* — C — 510 494-7053

Washington Orna Ir Works Inc (PA) — 17926 S Broadway Gardena (90248) *(P-2329)* — C — 310 327-8660

Washington Otptent Srgery Ctr — 2299 Mowry Ave Fl 1 Fremont (94538) *(P-15198)* — D — 510 791-5374

Washington Otptent Surgery Ctr, Fremont Also Called: Washington Otptent Srgery Ctr *(P-15198)*

Washoe Equipment Inc — 6201 27th St Sacramento (95822) *(P-2873)* — A — 916 395-4700

Wassco — 12778 Brookprinter Pl Poway (92064) *(P-5882)* — C — 858 679-0444

Wassco Sales, Poway Also Called: Wassco *(P-5882)*

Wasser Filtration Inc (PA) — 1215 N Fee Ana St Anaheim (92807) *(P-2802)* — D — 714 696-6450

Wasserman, Los Angeles Also Called: Wasserman Media Group LLC *(P-20608)*

Wasserman Comden & Casselman (PA) — 5567 Reseda Blvd Ste 330 Tarzana (91356) *(P-17674)* — D — 323 872-0995

Wasserman Media Group LLC (PA) — 10900 Wilshire Blvd Ste 1200 Los Angeles (90024) *(P-20608)* — C — 310 407-0200

Waste Connections Cal Inc (DH) — 1333 Oakland Rd San Jose (95112) *(P-4952)* — C — 408 282-4400

Waste Management, Sun Valley Also Called: Waste Management Recycling *(P-3434)*

Waste Management, Walnut Creek Also Called: Waste MGT Collectn Recycl Inc *(P-3435)*

Waste Management, Kettleman City Also Called: Chemical Waste Management Inc *(P-4877)*

Waste Management, Los Angeles Also Called: Downtown Diversion Inc *(P-4883)*

Waste Management, Sun Valley Also Called: Waste Management Cal Inc *(P-4953)*

Waste Management, Oceanside Also Called: Waste Management Cal Inc *(P-4954)*

Waste Management, Corona Also Called: Waste Management Cal Inc *(P-4955)*

Waste Management, Palmdale Also Called: Waste Management Cal Inc *(P-4956)*

Waste Management, El Cajon Also Called: Waste Management Cal Inc *(P-4957)*

Waste Management, Simi Valley Also Called: Waste Management Cal Inc *(P-4958)*

Waste Management, Oakland Also Called: Waste MGT Alameda Cnty Inc *(P-4960)*

Waste Management, Fort Bragg Also Called: Waste MGT Collectn Recycl Inc *(P-4961)*

Waste Management, Woodland Also Called: Waste MGT Collectn Recycl Inc *(P-4962)*

Waste Management, Gardena Also Called: Waste MGT Collectn Recycl Inc *(P-4963)*

Waste Management, Watsonville Also Called: Waste MGT Collectn Recycl Inc *(P-4964)*

Waste Management, Ukiah Also Called: Waste MGT Collectn Recycl Inc *(P-4965)*

Waste Management, Baldwin Park Also Called: Waste MGT Collectn Recycl Inc *(P-4966)*

Waste Management, Moreno Valley Also Called: Waste MGT Collectn Recycl Inc *(P-4967)*

Waste Management, Irvine Also Called: Waste MGT Collectn Recycl Inc *(P-4968)*

Waste Management Cal Inc (HQ) — 9081 Tujunga Ave Sun Valley (91352) *(P-4953)* — C — 877 836-6526

Waste Management Cal Inc — 2141 Oceanside Blvd Oceanside (92054) *(P-4954)* — C — 760 439-2824

Waste Management Cal Inc — 10910 Dawson Canyon Rd Corona (92883) *(P-4955)* — C — 951 277-1740

Waste Management Cal Inc — 1200 W City Ranch Rd Palmdale (93551) *(P-4956)* — C — 661 947-7197

Waste Management Cal Inc — 1001 W Bradley Ave El Cajon (92020) *(P-4957)* — C — 619 596-5100

ALPHABETIC SECTION

Waste Management Cal Inc .... C....... 805 522-7023
  2801 N Madera Rd Simi Valley (93065) *(P-4958)*

Waste Management Cal Inc .... D....... 408 779-2206
  910 Coyote Creek Golf Dr Morgan Hill (95037) *(P-4959)*

Waste Management Recycling .... D....... 818 767-6180
  9227 Tujunga Ave Sun Valley (91352) *(P-3434)*

Waste MGT Alameda Cnty Inc (HQ) .... A....... 510 613-8710
  172 98th Ave Oakland (94603) *(P-4960)*

Waste MGT Collectn Recycl Inc .... D....... 925 935-8900
  2658 N Main St Walnut Creek (94597) *(P-3435)*

Waste MGT Collectn Recycl Inc .... D....... 707 964-9172
  219 Pudding Creek Rd Fort Bragg (95437) *(P-4961)*

Waste MGT Collectn Recycl Inc .... C....... 530 662-8748
  1324 Paddock Pl Woodland (95776) *(P-4962)*

Waste MGT Collectn Recycl Inc .... C....... 310 532-6511
  1449 W Rosecrans Ave Gardena (90249) *(P-4963)*

Waste MGT Collectn Recycl Inc .... C....... 831 768-9505
  1340 W Beach St Watsonville (95076) *(P-4964)*

Waste MGT Collectn Recycl Inc .... D....... 707 462-0210
  450 Orr Springs Rd Ukiah (95482) *(P-4965)*

Waste MGT Collectn Recycl Inc .... D....... 626 960-7551
  13940 Live Oak Ave Baldwin Park (91706) *(P-4966)*

Waste MGT Collectn Recycl Inc .... C....... 951 242-0421
  17700 Indian St Moreno Valley (92551) *(P-4967)*

Waste MGT Collectn Recycl Inc .... C....... 949 451-2600
  16122 Construction Cir E Irvine (92606) *(P-4968)*

Watchpoint Logistics Inc (PA) .... C....... 800 486-8326
  700 Airport Blvd Ste 380 Burlingame (94010) *(P-4119)*

Water & Power Department, Long Beach *Also Called: County of Los Angeles (P-4780)*

Water Division, Fresno *Also Called: City of Fresno (P-4772)*

Water Supply, Vacaville *Also Called: County of Solano (P-4782)*

Water Tech, Brawley *Also Called: Farm Water Technological Services Inc (P-7579)*

Wateranywhere, Vista *Also Called: Applied Membranes Inc (P-2847)*

Watercourse Way, Palo Alto *Also Called: U P C Inc (P-10579)*

Waterfront Hotel LLC .... B....... 714 845-8000
  21100 Pacific Coast Hwy Huntington Beach (92648) *(P-10354)*

Waterhouse Management Corp .... C....... 916 772-4918
  500 Giuseppe Ct Ste 2 Roseville (95678) *(P-8882)*

Wateridge Insurance Svcs Inc .... D....... 858 452-2200
  9655 Granite Ridge Dr San Diego (92123) *(P-8683)*

Waterman Canyon Post Acute, San Bernardino *Also Called: Watermanidence Opco LLC (P-15804)*

Waterman Convalescent Hosp Inc (PA) .... C....... 909 882-1215
  1850 N Waterman Ave San Bernardino (92404) *(P-15727)*

Watermanidence Opco LLC .... B....... 909 882-1215
  1850 N Waterman Ave San Bernardino (92404) *(P-15804)*

Watermark Rtrment Cmmnties Inc .... D....... 925 344-5661
  35 Fenton St Livermore (94550) *(P-8870)*

Watermark Rtrment Cmmnties Inc .... D....... 949 443-9543
  25411 Sea Bluffs Dr Dana Point (92629) *(P-8871)*

Watermark Rtrment Cmmnties Inc .... D....... 760 346-5420
  41505 Carlotta Dr Palm Desert (92211) *(P-15728)*

Waterprfing Rofg Solutions Inc .... D....... 310 571-0892
  11041 Santa Monica Blvd Ste 306 Los Angeles (90025) *(P-2330)*

WATERPROOFING ASSOCIATES, Santa Clara *Also Called: Waterproofing Associates Inc (P-2090)*

Waterproofing Associates Inc .... D....... 650 937-1299
  1295 Norman Ave Santa Clara (95054) *(P-2090)*

Waters Moving & Storage Inc .... D....... 925 372-0914
  37 Bridgehead Rd Martinez (94553) *(P-3436)*

Watsafe Swim School, Los Alamitos *Also Called: Watsafe Swim School Inc (P-14585)*

Watsafe Swim School Inc .... D....... 562 596-8608
  3686 Cerritos Ave Los Alamitos (90720) *(P-14585)*

Waterstone Faucets, Murrieta *Also Called: Waterstone Faucets LLC (P-5763)*

Waterstone Faucets LLC .... C....... 951 304-0520
  41180 Raintree Ct Murrieta (92562) *(P-5763)*

Waterwiseone .... D....... 866 758-4393
  23411 Aliso Viejo Pkwy Aliso Viejo (92656) *(P-12035)*

Waterworks Park, Redding *Also Called: Yanaco Inc (P-14317)*

Waterworld California, Concord *Also Called: Parc Waterworld LLC (P-14308)*

Waterworld USA, Concord *Also Called: Parc Management LLC (P-14550)*

Watg, Irvine *Also Called: Wimberly Allison Tong Goo NA In (P-19520)*

Watkins Construction Co Inc .... D....... 661 763-5395
  112 E Cedar St Taft (93268) *(P-1280)*

Watlow, San Jose *Also Called: Semiconductor Tooling Services LLC (P-19384)*

Watlow Electric Mfg Co .... D....... 408 776-6646
  6781 Via Del Oro San Jose (95119) *(P-19436)*

Watson Cogeneration Co Inc .... D....... 310 816-8100
  22850 Wilmington Ave Carson (90745) *(P-4718)*

Watsonville Coast Produce Inc .... D....... 831 722-3851
  275 Kearney Ext Frnt Watsonville (95076) *(P-6594)*

Watsonville Community Hospital, Watsonville *Also Called: Halsen Healthcare LLC (P-16116)*

Watt Commercial Properties, Santa Monica *Also Called: Watt Properties Inc (P-8776)*

Watt Inc .... D....... 310 896-8197
  8605 Santa Monica Blvd Pmb 65044 West Hollywood (90069) *(P-12036)*

Watt Properties Inc (PA) .... D....... 310 314-2430
  2716 Ocean Park Blvd Ste 2025 Santa Monica (90405) *(P-8776)*

WATTS HEALTH, Los Angeles *Also Called: Watts Healthcare Corporation (P-15199)*

Watts Health Center, Los Angeles *Also Called: Watts Health Foundation Inc (P-9451)*

Watts Health Foundation Inc .... D....... 323 357-6688
  10300 Compton Ave Los Angeles (90002) *(P-9451)*

Watts Health Foundation Inc (HQ) .... B....... 310 424-2220
  3405 W Imperial Hwy Ste 304 Inglewood (90303) *(P-15805)*

Watts Health Systems Inc (PA) .... A....... 310 424-2220
  3405 W Imperial Hwy Inglewood (90303) *(P-20609)*

Watts Healthcare Corporation (PA) .... C....... 323 564-4331
  10300 Compton Ave Los Angeles (90002) *(P-15199)*

Watts Labor Community Action .... C....... 323 563-5639
  4142 Palmwood Dr Apt 11 Los Angeles (90008) *(P-18187)*

Wave Plastic Surgery Ctr Inc .... D....... 626 964-7788
  18433 Colima Rd La Puente (91748) *(P-15200)*

Wave Plastic Surgery Ctr Inc .... D....... 626 898-9711
  400 N Santa Anita Ave Arcadia (91006) *(P-16626)*

Wave Plstic Srgery Ctr Arcadia, Arcadia *Also Called: Wave Plastic Surgery Ctr Inc (P-16626)*

Waveco Inc (PA) .... D....... 707 678-4404
  8656 Sparling Ln Dixon (95620) *(P-3437)*

Wavelabs Technologies Inc .... D....... 408 203-7670
  691 S Milpitas Blvd Ste 217 Milpitas (95035) *(P-13551)*

Wavestream Corporation (HQ) .... C....... 909 599-9080
  545 W Terrace Dr San Dimas (91773) *(P-2947)*

Wavestrong Inc .... D....... 844 299-8264
  2000 Crow Canyon Pl Ste 150 San Ramon (94583) *(P-12543)*

Wawona Packing Co LLC .... A
  7700 N Palm Ave Ste 206 Fresno (93711) *(P-6595)*

Waxie, Ontario *Also Called: Waxies Enterprises LLC (P-5951)*

Waxie Sanitary Supply, San Diego *Also Called: Waxies Enterprises LLC (P-5952)*

Waxie Sanitary Supply, Santa Ana *Also Called: Waxies Enterprises LLC (P-7600)*

Waxies Enterprises LLC .... D....... 909 942-3100
  905 Wineville Ave Ontario (91764) *(P-5951)*

Waxies Enterprises LLC .... D....... 714 545-8441
  3220 S Fairview St Santa Ana (92704) *(P-7600)*

Waxies Enterprises LLC (DH) .... C....... 800 995-4466
  9353 Waxie Way San Diego (92123) *(P-5952)*

Waymakers (PA) .... D....... 714 492-1010
  440 Exchange Irvine (92602) *(P-18188)*

Wayne E Swisher Cem Contr Inc .... D....... 925 757-3660
  2620 E 18th St Antioch (94509) *(P-2170)*

Wayne Gossett Ford Inc .... D....... 760 753-6286
  1424 Encinitas Blvd Encinitas (92024) *(P-7330)*

Wayne Perry Inc (PA) .... C....... 714 826-0352
  8281 Commonwealth Ave Buena Park (90621) *(P-2331)*

Wayne Provision Co Inc (PA) .... D....... 323 277-5888
  5030 Gifford Ave Vernon (90058) *(P-6507)*

Waypoint Real Estate Group LLC .... D....... 510 250-2200
  1999 Harrison St Fl 24 Oakland (94612) *(P-9209)*

Wayve Technologies Inc .... C....... 832 651-4438
  709 N Shoreline Blvd Mountain View (94043) *(P-12037)*

Wazuh Inc (PA) .... C....... 844 349-2984
  1021 Lenor Way San Jose (95128) *(P-12906)*

Wb Electric Inc .... D....... 408 842-7911
  6790 Monterey Rd Gilroy (95020) *(P-1873)*

ALPHABETIC SECTION

Wc AG Services Inc .... A 209 538-3131
800 E Keyes Rd Ceres (95307) *(P-385)*

Wcchd, San Pablo *Also Called: West Contra Costa Healthcare District (P-16975)*

Wcct Global Inc .... D 714 252-0700
5630 Cerritos Ave Cypress (90630) *(P-19799)*

Wcct Global Inc (PA) .... D 714 668-1500
5630 Cerritos Ave Cypress (90630) *(P-19934)*

Wcf Select Insurance Company .... C 415 899-2000
1465 N Mcdowell Blvd Ste 100 Petaluma (94954) *(P-8252)*

Wcirb, Oakland *Also Called: Workers Cmpnstion Insur Rting (P-8695)*

Wco Hotels Inc .... A 714 635-2300
1600 S Disneyland Dr Anaheim (92802) *(P-10355)*

Wdm Group, San Diego *Also Called: White Digital Media Inc (P-6845)*

We Care Services For Children .... D 925 685-0207
1450 Civic Ct Ste 200 Concord (94520) *(P-18366)*

WE Oneil Construction Co Cal .... C 909 466-5300
9485 Haven Ave Ste 101 Rancho Cucamonga (91730) *(P-1053)*

We Pack It All LLC .... C 626 301-9214
2745 Huntington Dr Duarte (91010) *(P-13552)*

We See Dragons LLC .... C 310 361-5700
1100 Glendon Ave Ste 1700 Los Angeles (90024) *(P-12907)*

Weapon X Security Inc .... D 818 818-9950
297 Country Club Dr Simi Valley (93065) *(P-20906)*

Weatherford BMW, Concord *Also Called: Weatherford Motors Inc (P-7331)*

Weatherford Motors Inc .... C 510 654-8280
1967 Market St Concord (94520) *(P-7331)*

Weave Inc (PA) .... D 916 448-2321
1900 K St Ste 200 Sacramento (95811) *(P-11362)*

Web Traffic School, Oakland *Also Called: Interactive Solutions Inc (P-12236)*

Webasto Charging Systems Inc (DH) .... D 626 415-4000
1333 S Mayflower Ave Ste 100 Monrovia (91016) *(P-5067)*

Webb, Riverside *Also Called: Albert A Webb Associates (P-19134)*

Webb Del California Corp (DH) .... B 760 772-5300
39755 Berkey Dr Palm Desert (92211) *(P-9280)*

Webcor Builders, San Diego *Also Called: Webcor Construction LP (P-1055)*

Webcor Builders, Oakland *Also Called: Webcor Construction LP (P-1056)*

Webcor Builders, Los Angeles *Also Called: Webcor Construction LP (P-1057)*

Webcor Builders, Alameda *Also Called: Webcor Construction LP (P-1058)*

Webcor Builders, San Francisco *Also Called: Webcor Construction LP (P-1059)*

Webcor Construction LP .... C 408 277-0311
1 Almaden Blvd Ste 460 San Jose (95113) *(P-1054)*

Webcor Construction LP .... C 619 798-3891
2150 W Washington St Ste 308 San Diego (92110) *(P-1055)*

Webcor Construction LP .... C 510 748-7950
7801 Capwell Dr Oakland (94621) *(P-1056)*

Webcor Construction LP .... C 213 239-2800
333 S Grand Ave Ste 4400 Los Angeles (90071) *(P-1057)*

Webcor Construction LP .... C 510 748-1900
2320 Blanding Ave Ste 200 Alameda (94501) *(P-1058)*

Webcor Construction LP (DH) .... D 415 978-1000
207 King St Ste 300 San Francisco (94107) *(P-1059)*

Weber Distribution LLC (PA) .... D 855 469-3237
13530 Rosecrans Ave Santa Fe Springs (90670) *(P-3668)*

Weber Logistics, Santa Fe Springs *Also Called: Weber Distribution LLC (P-3668)*

Weber Motors Fresno Inc .... D 559 447-6700
7171 N Palm Ave Fresno (93650) *(P-7332)*

Weber Orthopedic LP (PA) .... D 800 221-5465
1185 E Main St Santa Paula (93060) *(P-3064)*

Webers Quality Meats Inc .... C 510 635-9892
990 Carden St San Leandro (94577) *(P-6508)*

Webex.com, San Jose *Also Called: Cisco Webex LLC (P-13233)*

Webflow Inc (PA) .... B 916 607-8280
398 11th St Fl 2 San Francisco (94103) *(P-12642)*

Webmetro .... D 909 599-8885
160 Via Verde Ste 1 San Dimas (91773) *(P-12395)*

Webpass Inc .... D 415 233-4100
267 8th St San Francisco (94103) *(P-4358)*

Webster Investment Management, San Francisco *Also Called: Forward Management LLC (P-8199)*

Webtyme Design & Hosting, San Mateo *Also Called: D E M Enterprises Inc (P-12564)*

Weck Anlytical Envmtl Svcs Inc .... D 626 336-2139
14859 Clark Ave City Of Industry (91745) *(P-20004)*

Weck Laboratories, City Of Industry *Also Called: Weck Anlytical Envmtl Svcs Inc (P-20004)*

Weco, Woodland *Also Called: Woodside Electronics Corp (P-13812)*

Wedbush Securities Inc (HQ) .... B 213 688-8000
1000 Wilshire Blvd Ste 900 Los Angeles (90017) *(P-8175)*

Wedgewood Inc (PA) .... D 310 640-3070
2015 Manhattan Beach Blvd Ste 100 Redondo Beach (90278) *(P-9578)*

Wehah-Lundberg Inc .... C 530 882-4551
5311 Midway Richvale (95974) *(P-2363)*

WEI-Chuan USA Inc (PA) .... C 626 225-7168
13031 Temple Ave City Of Industry (91746) *(P-6427)*

Weider Health and Fitness .... B 818 884-6800
21100 Erwin St Woodland Hills (91367) *(P-2416)*

Weil Gotshal & Manges LLP .... C 650 802-3000
201 Redwood Shores Pkwy Ste 400 Redwood City (94065) *(P-17675)*

Weinberg Rger Rsnfeld A Prof C (PA) .... D 510 337-1001
1001 Marina Village Pkwy Ste 200 Alameda (94501) *(P-17676)*

Weingart Center Association .... C 213 622-6359
566 S San Pedro St Los Angeles (90013) *(P-18189)*

Weingart Center For Homeless, Los Angeles *Also Called: Weingart Center Association (P-18189)*

Welbe Health LLC .... C 209 800-0621
582 E Harding Way Stockton (95204) *(P-16973)*

Welbe Health LLC .... C 559 777-6722
1649 Van Ness Ave Fresno (93721) *(P-18190)*

Welbe Health LLC, Fresno *Also Called: Welbe Health LLC (P-18190)*

Welbehealth Sierra Pace, Stockton *Also Called: Welbe Health LLC (P-16973)*

WELCOME BABY, Santa Ana *Also Called: Priority Ctr Ending The Gnrtna (P-18086)*

Welcome Group Inc .... C 916 920-5300
1780 Tribute Rd Sacramento (95815) *(P-10356)*

Welcome Group Management LLC .... D 310 378-6666
300 S Court St Visalia (93291) *(P-10357)*

Welcometech LLC .... D 408 582-7998
105 Serra Way # 145 Milpitas (95035) *(P-11255)*

Weldlogic Inc .... D 805 375-1670
2651 Lavery Ct Newbury Park (91320) *(P-13755)*

Weldlogic Gas & Supply, Newbury Park *Also Called: Weldlogic Inc (P-13755)*

Weldmac Manufacturing Company .... C 619 440-2300
1451 N Johnson Ave El Cajon (92020) *(P-2858)*

Welk Group Inc .... B 760 749-3000
8860 Lawrence Welk Dr Escondido (92026) *(P-10358)*

Welk Group Inc (PA) .... B 760 749-3000
11400 W Olympic Blvd Ste 760 Los Angeles (90064) *(P-10359)*

Welk Group Inc .... C 760 749-3225
8860 Lawrence Welk Dr Escondido (92026) *(P-14296)*

Welk Group Inc .... C 760 749-0983
10333 Meadow Glen Way E Escondido (92026) *(P-14482)*

Welk Music Group, Los Angeles *Also Called: Welk Group Inc (P-10359)*

Welk Resort Center, San Marcos *Also Called: Whv Resort Group Inc (P-9218)*

Welk Resort Center, Escondido *Also Called: Welk Group Inc (P-10358)*

Welker Bros, Milpitas *Also Called: H V Welker Co Inc (P-2032)*

Well Being Senior Solutions .... D 559 321-8295
55 Shaw Ave Ste 220 Clovis (93612) *(P-16974)*

Wella Operations US LLC .... B 818 999-5112
4500 Park Granada Ste 100 Calabasas (91302) *(P-6152)*

Wellington Crt Asssted Lving C, Arcadia *Also Called: Leisure Care LLC (P-18471)*

Wellmade Inc .... D 213 221-1123
800 E 12th St Los Angeles (90021) *(P-20610)*

Wellmade Products, Merced *Also Called: WLMD (P-2334)*

Wellness Together .... C 877 412-8031
1382 Blue Oaks Blvd Ste 213 Roseville (95678) *(P-18191)*

Wellnest .... D 323 766-2345
3787 S Vermont Ave Los Angeles (90007) *(P-8777)*

Wellnest Emtonal Hlth Wellness (PA) .... C 323 373-2400
3031 S Vermont Ave Los Angeles (90007) *(P-18192)*

Wells & Bennett Inc (PA) .... D 510 531-7000
1451 Leimert Blvd Oakland (94602) *(P-9210)*

Wells Fargo, San Francisco *Also Called: Wells Fargo & Company (P-7639)*

Wells Fargo, San Francisco *Also Called: Wells Fargo Bank National Assn (P-7643)*

ALPHABETIC SECTION

Wells Fargo, San Francisco *Also Called: Wells Fargo Financing Corporation (P-7723)*
Wells Fargo & Company (PA) .... A...... 866 249-3302
420 Montgomery St San Francisco (94104) *(P-7639)*
Wells Fargo Bank Ltd .... D...... 213 253-6227
333 S Grand Ave Ste 500 Los Angeles (90071) *(P-7640)*
Wells Fargo Bank National Assn .... D...... 925 463-1983
5798 Stone Ridge Mall Pleasanton (94588) *(P-7641)*
Wells Fargo Bank National Assn .... D...... 510 530-3095
2220 Mountain Blvd Ste 160 Oakland (94611) *(P-7642)*
Wells Fargo Bank National Assn (HQ) .... C...... 605 575-6900
420 Montgomery St Frnt San San Francisco (94104) *(P-7643)*
Wells Fargo Capital Fin LLC (DH) .... D...... 310 453-7300
2450 Colorado Ave Ste 3000w Santa Monica (90404) *(P-7925)*
Wells Fargo Capital Finance Inc .... C...... 310 453-7300
2450 Colo Ave 3000w 3rd Fl Santa Monica (90404) *(P-13553)*
Wells Fargo Center For Arts .... D...... 707 527-7006
50 Mark West Springs Rd Ofc Santa Rosa (95403) *(P-7644)*
Wells Fargo Coml Dist Fin LLC .... C...... 916 636-2020
3100 Zinfandel Dr Ste 255 Rancho Cordova (95670) *(P-7912)*
Wells Fargo Financing Corporation .... A...... 415 222-4292
420 Montgomery St Frnt San Francisco (94104) *(P-7723)*
Wells Fargo Investments LLC .... D...... 310 546-4235
603 14th St Manhattan Beach (90266) *(P-7645)*
Wells Fargo Investments LLC .... D...... 619 702-6949
401 B St Ste 101 San Diego (92101) *(P-7646)*
Wells Fargo Investments LLC .... D...... 707 521-1232
3550 Round Barn Blvd Ste 307 Santa Rosa (95403) *(P-8176)*
Wells Fargo Prime Services LLC .... D...... 415 848-0269
45 Fremont St Ste 3000 San Francisco (94105) *(P-8177)*
Wells Fargo Securities LLC .... A...... 310 479-3500
1800 Century Park E Ste 1100 Los Angeles (90067) *(P-7647)*
Wells Frgo Bnk NA As Trstee Fo .... D...... 925 765-6316
1330 N Broadway Ste C Walnut Creek (94596) *(P-7648)*
Wells Frgo Insur Svcs Minn Inc .... C...... 909 481-3802
4141 Inland Empire Blvd Ontario (91764) *(P-8684)*
Wellspace Womens Health Center .... D...... 916 313-8462
7601 Hospital Dr Ste 200 Sacramento (95823) *(P-15201)*
Welltower Om Group LLC .... C...... 626 254-0552
301 W Huntington Dr Ste 5 Arcadia (91007) *(P-8778)*
Wems Inc (PA) .... D...... 310 644-0251
4650 W Rosecrans Ave Hawthorne (90250) *(P-2797)*
Wems Electronics, Hawthorne *Also Called: Wems Inc (P-2797)*
Wencon Development Inc .... D...... 925 478-8269
2700 Mitchell Dr Ste 2 Walnut Creek (94598) *(P-1595)*
Wente Bros (PA) .... D...... 925 456-2300
5565 Tesla Rd Livermore (94550) *(P-20611)*
Wente Vineyards, Livermore *Also Called: Wente Bros (P-20611)*
Wenzlau Engineering Inc .... D...... 310 604-3400
2950 E Harcourt St E Rncho Dmngz (90221) *(P-5714)*
Werfen, San Diego *Also Called: Inova Diagnostics Inc (P-19710)*
Weride Corp .... C...... 408 645-7118
2630 Orchard Pkwy San Jose (95134) *(P-12038)*
Wermers, San Diego *Also Called: Wermers Multi-Family Corp (P-784)*
Wermers Multi-Family Corp .... C...... 858 535-1475
5120 Shoreham Pl Ste 150 San Diego (92122) *(P-784)*
Wesco Aircraft, Valencia *Also Called: Falcon Aerospace Holdings LLC (P-5957)*
Wesco Aircraft Hardware Corp .... B...... 661 775-7200
27727 Avenue Scott Valencia (91355) *(P-5971)*
Wescom Central Credit Union (PA) .... B...... 888 493-7266
123 S Marengo Ave Pasadena (91101) *(P-7834)*
Wescordon Incorporated .... C...... 559 784-8371
661 W Poplar Ave Porterville (93257) *(P-15729)*
Weslar Inc .... D...... 661 702-1362
28310 Constellation Rd Valencia (91355) *(P-2026)*
Weslend Financial, Santa Ana *Also Called: Lenox Financial Mortgage Corp (P-7990)*
Wesley B Lasher Inv Corp (PA) .... D...... 916 290-8500
5800 Florin Rd Sacramento (95823) *(P-7333)*
West Air Inc .... D...... 559 454-7843
5005 E Andersen Ave Fresno (93727) *(P-3860)*
West Anaheim Care Center, Anaheim *Also Called: Mark & Fred Enterprises (P-15579)*
West Anaheim Medical Center, Anaheim *Also Called: Prime Healthcare Anaheim LLC (P-16333)*
West Angeles Ch God In Chrst .... C...... 323 731-2567
3010 Crenshaw Blvd Los Angeles (90016) *(P-17758)*
West Angeles Christian Academy, Los Angeles *Also Called: West Angeles Ch God In Chrst (P-17758)*
West Central Food Service, Norwalk *Also Called: West Central Produce Inc (P-6596)*
West Central Produce Inc .... B...... 213 629-3600
12840 Leyva St Norwalk (90650) *(P-6596)*
West Cntinela Vly Care Ctr Inc .... D...... 310 674-3216
950 S Flower St Inglewood (90301) *(P-15730)*
West Coast AC Co Inc .... C...... 619 561-8000
1155 Pioneer Way Ste 101 El Cajon (92020) *(P-1596)*
West Coast Arborists Inc .... C...... 408 855-8660
3625 Stevenson Ave Stockton (95205) *(P-548)*
West Coast Arborists Inc .... C...... 805 671-5092
11405 Nardo St Ventura (93004) *(P-561)*
West Coast Arborists Inc .... C...... 909 783-6544
21718 Walnut Ave Grand Terrace (92313) *(P-562)*
West Coast Arborists Inc .... C...... 559 275-2086
5424 N Barcus Ave Fresno (93722) *(P-563)*
West Coast Arborists Inc .... C...... 858 566-4204
8163 Commercial St La Mesa (91942) *(P-740)*
West Coast Arborists Inc (PA) .... D...... 714 991-1900
2200 E Via Burton Anaheim (92806) *(P-549)*
West Coast Beauty Supply Co .... A...... 707 748-4800
5001 Industrial Way Benicia (94510) *(P-5953)*
West Coast Construction, Jurupa Valley *Also Called: Perry Coast Construction Inc (P-990)*
West Coast Consulting LLC .... C...... 949 250-4102
9233 Research Dr Ste 200 Irvine (92618) *(P-12396)*
West Coast Countertops Inc .... D...... 951 719-3670
1200 Marlborough Ave Ste B Riverside (92507) *(P-2332)*
West Coast Dental Labs LLC .... B...... 855 220-5600
12002 Aviation Blvd Hawthorne (90250) *(P-16779)*
West Coast Distribution Inc .... D...... 323 588-6508
4440 E 26th St Vernon (90058) *(P-857)*
West Coast Drywall & Co Inc .... B...... 951 778-3592
1610 W Linden St Riverside (92507) *(P-1972)*
West Coast Drywall & Paint, Riverside *Also Called: West Coast Drywall & Co Inc (P-1972)*
West Coast Electric & Pwr Inc .... D...... 562 447-3254
741 E Ball Rd Ste 206 Anaheim (92805) *(P-4719)*
West Coast Firestopping Inc .... D...... 714 935-1104
1130 W Trenton Ave Orange (92867) *(P-2333)*
West Coast Gasket Co .... D...... 714 869-0123
300 Ranger Ave Brea (92821) *(P-2656)*
West Coast Interiors Inc .... A...... 951 778-3592
1610 W Linden St Riverside (92507) *(P-1645)*
West Coast Iron Inc .... D...... 619 464-8456
9302 Jamacha Rd Spring Valley (91977) *(P-2252)*
West Coast Ltg & Enrgy Inc .... D...... 951 296-0680
18550 Minthorn St Lake Elsinore (92530) *(P-1874)*
West Coast Materials, Buena Park *Also Called: West Coast Sand and Gravel Inc (P-5214)*
West Coast Milling, Lancaster *Also Called: Pavement Recycling Systems Inc (P-2650)*
West Coast Office & Dist Ctr, Rancho Cordova *Also Called: E-Filliate Inc (P-7560)*
West Coast Painting, Riverside *Also Called: West Coast Interiors Inc (P-1645)*
West Coast Physical Therapy, Laguna Niguel *Also Called: Mission Internal Med Group Inc (P-14901)*
West Coast Quartz Corporation (HQ) .... D...... 510 249-2160
1000 Corporate Way Fremont (94539) *(P-2689)*
West Coast Sand and Gravel Inc (PA) .... D...... 714 522-0282
7282 Orangethorpe Ave Buena Park (90621) *(P-5214)*
West Coast Switchgear (DH) .... D...... 562 802-3441
13837 Bettencourt St Cerritos (90703) *(P-2862)*
West Coast Wldg & Piping Inc .... D...... 805 246-5841
750 W Hueneme Rd Oxnard (93033) *(P-13756)*
West Contra Costa Healthcare District .... A...... 510 970-5102
2000 Vale Rd San Pablo (94806) *(P-16975)*
West Contra Costa YMCA, Richmond *Also Called: Young MNS Chrstn Assn of E Bay (P-18977)*
West County Health Centers Inc (PA) .... D...... 707 869-1594
16312 3rd St Guerneville (95446) *(P-15202)*
West County Trnsp Agcy .... C...... 707 206-9988
367 W Robles Ave Santa Rosa (95407) *(P-3225)*

ALPHABETIC SECTION

West Covina Foster Family Agcy .... D...... 626 814-9085
527 E Rowland St Ste 100 Covina (91723) *(P-8685)*

West Covina Medical Clinic Inc (PA) .... C...... 626 960-8614
1500 W West Covina Pkwy Ste 100 West Covina (91790) *(P-15203)*

WEST COVINA PHYSICAL THERAPY, West Covina Also Called: Doctors Hospital W Covina Inc *(P-16058)*

West Dermatology, Newport Beach Also Called: West Dermatology Med MGT Inc *(P-15204)*

West Dermatology Med MGT Inc (PA) .... A...... 909 793-3000
680 Newport Center Dr Ste 150 Newport Beach (92660) *(P-15204)*

West Edge, Chula Vista Also Called: West Edge Inc *(P-9211)*

West Edge Inc .... D...... 619 475-4095
1061 Tierra Del Rey Chula Vista (91910) *(P-9211)*

West End Yung MNS Christn Assn .... C...... 909 477-2780
1257 E D St Ontario (91764) *(P-18929)*

West End Yung MNS Christn Assn .... C...... 909 597-7445
5665 Edison Ave Chino (91710) *(P-18930)*

West Health Care, Bonita Also Called: Paradise Valley Hospital *(P-16317)*

West Health Incubator Inc .... D...... 858 535-7000
10350 N Torrey Pines Rd La Jolla (92037) *(P-17352)*

West Hollywood Edition .... D...... 310 795-7103
9040 W Sunset Blvd West Hollywood (90069) *(P-10360)*

West Hotel Partners LP .... C...... 408 947-4450
300 Almaden Blvd San Jose (95110) *(P-10361)*

West Los Angeles V A Med Ctr, Los Angeles Also Called: Veterans Health Administration *(P-15191)*

West Pacific Medical Lab, Santa Fe Springs Also Called: California Lab Sciences LLC *(P-19953)*

West Pacific Services Inc .... C...... 888 401-0188
4445 Eastgate Mall Ste 200 San Diego (92121) *(P-1060)*

West Pak Avocado Inc (PA) .... C...... 951 296-5757
38655 Sky Canyon Dr Murrieta (92563) *(P-314)*

West Pico Foods Inc .... C...... 323 586-9050
5201 S Downey Rd Vernon (90058) *(P-6428)*

West Publishing Corporation .... B...... 800 747-3161
5161 Lankershim Blvd North Hollywood (91601) *(P-2551)*

West Publishing Corporation .... A...... 424 243-2100
800 Crprate Pinte Ste 150 Culver City (90230) *(P-12544)*

West San Crlos Ht Partners LLC .... D...... 408 998-0400
282 Almaden Blvd San Jose (95113) *(P-10362)*

West Shores Realty Inc .... C...... 310 541-8000
449 Silver Spur Rd Pls Vrds Pnsl (90274) *(P-9212)*

West Side Rehab Corporation .... C...... 323 231-4174
1755 E Martin Luther King Jr Blvd Los Angeles (90069) *(P-8779)*

West Tech Contracting Inc .... D...... 760 233-2570
568 N Tulip St Escondido (92025) *(P-1281)*

West Valley Cnstr Co Inc (PA) .... C...... 408 371-5510
603 Campbell Technology Pkwy Campbell (95008) *(P-1282)*

West Valley Construction, Campbell Also Called: West Valley Cnstr Co Inc *(P-1282)*

West Valley Engineering Inc (PA) .... A...... 408 735-1420
390 Potrero Ave Sunnyvale (94085) *(P-11363)*

West Valley Occupational Ctr, Woodland Hills Also Called: Los Angeles Unified School Dst *(P-17724)*

West Valley Post Acute, West Hills Also Called: West Valleyidence Opco LLC *(P-15806)*

West Valley Staffing Group, Sunnyvale Also Called: West Valley Engineering Inc *(P-11363)*

West Valleyidence Opco LLC .... C...... 818 348-8422
7057 Shoup Ave West Hills (91307) *(P-15806)*

West Vlly-Mssion Cmnty Cllege .... B...... 408 988-2200
3000 Mission College Blvd Santa Clara (95054) *(P-17790)*

West Yost & Associates Inc (PA) .... D...... 530 756-5905
2020 Research Park Dr Ste 100 Davis (95618) *(P-19437)*

Westair Gases & Equipment, Bakersfield Also Called: Westair Gases & Equipment Inc *(P-5883)*

Westair Gases & Equipment Inc .... C...... 661 387-6800
3901 Buck Owens Blvd Bakersfield (93308) *(P-5883)*

Westamerica Bancorporation (PA) .... D...... 707 863-6000
1108 5th Ave San Rafael (94901) *(P-7724)*

Westamerica Communications Inc .... D...... 949 340-8942
26012 Atlantic Ocean Dr Lake Forest (92630) *(P-20907)*

Westar Marine Services, San Francisco Also Called: Cross Link Inc *(P-3822)*

Westates Mechanical Corp Inc .... D...... 510 635-9830
2566 Barrington Ct Hayward (94545) *(P-1597)*

Westbrook Ops LLC .... D...... 818 832-2300
24151 Ventura Blvd Ste 200 Calabasas (91302) *(P-13920)*

Westco Equities Inc (PA) .... D...... 559 228-6788
1625 E Shaw Ave Ste 116 Fresno (93710) *(P-9213)*

Westcoast Childrens Clinic .... C...... 510 269-9030
3301 E 12th St Ste 259 Oakland (94601) *(P-17161)*

Westcoast Iron, Spring Valley Also Called: West Coast Iron Inc *(P-2252)*

Westcoe Escrow Division, Riverside Also Called: Westcoe Realtors Inc *(P-9214)*

Westcoe Realtors Inc .... D...... 951 784-2500
7191 Magnolia Ave Riverside (92504) *(P-9214)*

Westcor Construction of Cal .... D...... 909 796-8900
2351 W Lugonia Ave Ste D Redlands (92374) *(P-741)*

Westcore Croydon, San Diego Also Called: Westcore Delta Venture LLC *(P-9579)*

Westcore Delta Venture LLC .... D...... 858 625-4100
4350 La Jolla Village Dr Ste 900 San Diego (92122) *(P-9579)*

Westech Systems Inc .... D...... 559 455-1720
827 Jefferson Ave Clovis (93612) *(P-1875)*

Wested .... D...... 510 302-4200
300 Lakeside Dr 25th Fl Oakland (94612) *(P-19935)*

Wested .... D...... 415 289-2300
180 Harbor Dr Ste 112 Sausalito (94965) *(P-19936)*

Wested (PA) .... C...... 415 565-3000
730 Harrison St San Francisco (94107) *(P-19937)*

Westerlay Orchids, Carpinteria Also Called: Westerlay Orchids LP *(P-159)*

Westerlay Orchids LP .... C...... 805 684-5411
3504 Via Real Carpinteria (93013) *(P-159)*

Western AG Incorporated .... D...... 530 713-7901
686 King Ave Yuba City (95991) *(P-4178)*

Western Alliance Bank .... D...... 408 423-8500
55 Almaden Blvd Ste 200 San Jose (95113) *(P-7725)*

Western Alliance Bank, Oakland Also Called: Porrey Pines Bank Inc *(P-7710)*

Western Allied Mechanical Inc .... C...... 650 326-0750
33210 Central Ave Union City (94587) *(P-19438)*

Western Asset Core Plus Bond P .... C...... 626 844-9400
385 E Colorado Blvd Pasadena (91101) *(P-9393)*

Western Asset Mrtg Capitl Corp .... A...... 626 844-9400
385 E Colorado Blvd Pasadena (91101) *(P-9480)*

Western Assets Management Co .... D...... 626 844-9400
385 E Colorado Blvd Pasadena (91101) *(P-9410)*

Western Athletic Clubs Inc .... B...... 415 781-1874
1 Lombard St San Francisco (94111) *(P-14242)*

Western Attorney Services, San Francisco Also Called: Western Messenger Service Inc *(P-3438)*

Western Building Materials Co (PA) .... D...... 559 454-8500
4620 E Olive Ave Fresno (93702) *(P-7113)*

Western City Magazine, Sacramento Also Called: League of California Cities *(P-20637)*

Western Convelescence, Los Angeles Also Called: Longwood Management Corp *(P-15869)*

Western Dental & Orthodontics, Orange Also Called: Western Dental Services Inc *(P-15254)*

Western Dental Services Inc (HQ) .... B...... 714 480-3000
530 S Main St Ste 600 Orange (92868) *(P-15254)*

Western Division Regional Off, Long Beach Also Called: Southern California Edison Co *(P-4708)*

Western Drug, Glendale Also Called: H and H Drug Stores Inc *(P-5420)*

Western Drug Medical Supply, Stockton Also Called: H and H Drug Stores Inc *(P-5421)*

Western Drug Medical Supply, San Bernardino Also Called: H and H Drug Stores Inc *(P-5422)*

Western Drywall Inc .... D...... 209 543-9361
4971 Salida Blvd Salida (95368) *(P-1973)*

Western Energy Services Corp .... C...... 403 984-5916
3430 Getty St Bakersfield (93308) *(P-11009)*

Western Engineering Contractors Inc .... C...... 916 652-3990
3171 Rippey Rd Loomis (95650) *(P-1177)*

Western Feld Invstigations Inc (PA) .... D...... 800 999-9589
405 W Foothill Blvd Ste 204 Claremont (91711) *(P-12687)*

Western Fire Protection Inc (PA) .... D...... 858 513-4949
13630 Danielson St Poway (92064) *(P-1598)*

Western Flower Company, Arcata Also Called: Endors Toi Pbc *(P-20357)*

Western General Insurance Co .... C...... 818 880-9070
5230 Las Virgenes Rd Ste 100 Calabasas (91302) *(P-8424)*

Western Growers Association (PA) .... C...... 949 863-1000
6501 Irvine Center Dr Irvine (92618) *(P-18726)*

Western Health Advantage ....D....... 916 567-1950
  2349 Gateway Oaks Dr Ste 100 Sacramento (95833) *(P-8273)*
Western Health Resources ....C....... 707 459-1818
  100 San Hedrin Cir Willits (95490) *(P-20612)*
Western Medical Center Aux, Santa Ana *Also Called: Orange Cnty Globl Med Ctr Aux*
(P-16295)
Western Messenger Service Inc ....C....... 415 487-4229
  75 Columbia Sq San Francisco (94103) *(P-3438)*
Western Milling LLC (HQ) ....C....... 559 302-1000
  31120 West St Goshen (93227) *(P-9580)*
Western Mutual Insurance Co ....D....... 818 879-2142
  27489 Agoura Rd Agoura Hills (91301) *(P-8425)*
Western National Contractors ....D....... 949 862-6200
  8 Executive Cir Irvine (92614) *(P-20250)*
Western National Group LP ....D....... 949 862-6200
  8 Executive Cir Irvine (92614) *(P-9215)*
Western National Life Insur Co ....C....... 925 946-5100
  1395 Creekside Dr Walnut Creek (94596) *(P-8253)*
Western National Prpts LLC (PA) ....C....... 949 862-6200
  8 Executive Cir Irvine (92614) *(P-785)*
Western National Securities (PA) ....C....... 949 862-6200
  8 Executive Cir Irvine (92614) *(P-9216)*
Western Nevada Supply Co ....D....... 530 582-5009
  10990 Industrial Way Ste A Truckee (96161) *(P-5764)*
Western Oilfields Supply Co ....D....... 480 895-9225
  5101 Office Park Dr Ste 100 Bakersfield (93309) *(P-11063)*
Western Oilfields Supply Co (PA) ....C....... 661 399-9124
  3404 State Rd Bakersfield (93308) *(P-11064)*
Western Operations, Rancho Cucamonga *Also Called: Gentex Corporation (P-19703)*
Western Operations Center, Westlake Village *Also Called: Securitas SEC Svcs USA Inc*
(P-13035)
Western Pacific Distrg LLC ....C....... 714 974-6837
  341 W Meats Ave Orange (92865) *(P-5215)*
Western Pacific Roofing Corp ....C....... 661 273-1336
  3462 E La Campana Way Palm Springs (92262) *(P-2091)*
Western Penn AAA Insur Agcy ....B....... 805 682-5811
  3712 State St Santa Barbara (93105) *(P-8686)*
Western Refining Inc ....D....... 602 286-1400
  2619 S East Ave Fresno (93706) *(P-5884)*
Western Refining Inc ....D....... 714 708-2200
  1201 Baker St Costa Mesa (92626) *(P-5885)*
Western Region, Milpitas *Also Called: Xcerra Corporation (P-5717)*
Western Rim Pipeline, Lakeside *Also Called: A M Ortega Construction Inc (P-1649)*
Western Roofing Service, San Leandro *Also Called: Roofing Constructors Inc (P-2082)*
Western States Info Netwrk Inc ....D....... 916 263-1188
  1825 Bell St Ste 205 Sacramento (95825) *(P-19938)*
Western States Wholesale Inc (PA) ....D....... 909 947-0028
  1420 S Bon View Ave Ontario (91761) *(P-2700)*
Western Towing, San Diego *Also Called: Sunbelt Towing Inc (P-13720)*
Western Univ Hlth Sciences ....D....... 909 865-2565
  360 E Mission Blvd Pomona (91766) *(P-15205)*
Western Wine Services Inc (PA) ....D....... 800 999-8463
  880 Hanna Dr American Canyon (94503) *(P-3782)*
Westervelt Company ....C....... 916 646-3644
  3636 American River Dr Sacramento (95864) *(P-20879)*
Westfield LLC (DH) ....B....... 310 478-4456
  2049 Century Park E 41st Fl Los Angeles (90067) *(P-8780)*
Westfield America Inc (HQ) ....C....... 310 478-4456
  2049 Century Park E 41st Fl Los Angeles (90067) *(P-8781)*
Westfield America Ltd Partnr ....B....... 310 277-3898
  2049 Century Park E Ste 4100 Los Angeles (90067) *(P-8782)*
Westgage Grdn Convalescent Ctr, Visalia *Also Called: Far West Inc (P-15844)*
Westgate Cnstr & Maint Inc ....D....... 707 208-5763
  5045 Fulton Dr Ste D Fairfield (94534) *(P-1061)*
Westgate Gardens Care Center, Visalia *Also Called: Thyme Holdings LLC (P-9342)*
Westgate Gardens Care Ctr Inc ....C....... 916 624-6230
  4020 Sierra College Blvd Ste 190 Rocklin (95677) *(P-15731)*
Westgate Hotel, San Diego *Also Called: Reh Company (P-10146)*
Westgate Manufacturing, Vernon *Also Called: Westgate Mfg Inc (P-2965)*
Westgate Mfg Inc ....D....... 323 826-9490
  2462 E 28th St Vernon (90058) *(P-2965)*

Westgroup Kona Kai LLC ....D....... 619 221-8000
  1551 Shelter Island Dr San Diego (92106) *(P-14483)*
Westgroup San Diego Associates ....C....... 858 274-4630
  1404 Vacation Rd San Diego (92109) *(P-10363)*
Westin, Anaheim *Also Called: Westin Anaheim Resort (P-10364)*
Westin Anaheim Resort ....D....... 657 279-9786
  1030 W Katella Ave Anaheim (92802) *(P-10364)*
Westin Bonaventure Ht & Suites, Los Angeles *Also Called: Todays IV (P-10314)*
Westin Long Beach Hotel, The, Long Beach *Also Called: Noble Investment Group LLC*
(P-10048)
Westin Long Beach Hotel, The, Long Beach *Also Called: Noble/Utah Long Beach LLC*
(P-10049)
Westin Rncho Mrage Golf Rsort, Rancho Mirage *Also Called: Hst Lessee Mission Hills LP*
(P-9878)
Westin San Diego, San Diego *Also Called: Diamondrock San Dego Tnant LLC (P-9743)*
Westin St. Francis, The, San Francisco *Also Called: Dtrs St Francis LLC (P-9768)*
Westlake Development Group LLC (PA) ....D....... 650 579-1010
  520 S El Camino Real Ste 900 San Mateo (94402) *(P-8783)*
Westlake Development Group LLC ....D....... 408 251-2746
  2155 Lanai Ave Apt 60 San Jose (95122) *(P-8872)*
Westlake Development Group LLC ....D....... 707 447-7496
  799 Yellowstone Dr Ofc Vacaville (95687) *(P-15911)*
Westlake Development Group LLC ....C....... 650 579-1010
  520 El Camino Real Fl 9 Belmont (94002) *(P-20251)*
Westlake Diagnostic Center, Thousand Oaks *Also Called: Rolling Oaks Radiology Inc*
(P-15030)
Westlake Financial Services, Los Angeles *Also Called: Westlake Services LLC (P-7926)*
Westlake Health Care Center ....B....... 805 494-1233
  1101 Crenshaw Blvd Los Angeles (90019) *(P-15732)*
Westlake Oaks Healthcare LLC ....B....... 805 494-1233
  250 Fairview Rd Thousand Oaks (91361) *(P-17353)*
Westlake Properties Inc ....C....... 818 889-0230
  31943 Agoura Rd Westlake Village (91361) *(P-10365)*
Westlake Realty, San Mateo *Also Called: Westlake Realty Group Inc (P-9217)*
Westlake Realty Group Inc (PA) ....D....... 650 579-1010
  520 S El Camino Real Ste 900 San Mateo (94402) *(P-9217)*
Westlake Royal Stone LLC ....A....... 770 645-4539
  3817 Ocean Ranch Blvd Ste 114 Oceanside (92056) *(P-5216)*
Westlake Services LLC (HQ) ....C....... 323 692-8800
  4751 Wilshire Blvd Ste 100 Los Angeles (90010) *(P-7926)*
Westlake Village Inn, Westlake Village *Also Called: Westlake Properties Inc (P-10365)*
Westmed Ambulance Inc ....C....... 310 456-3830
  3872 Las Flores Canyon Rd Malibu (90265) *(P-3305)*
Westmed Ambulance Inc ....C....... 310 219-1779
  2537 Old San Pasqual Rd Escondido (92027) *(P-3306)*
WESTMED AMBULANCE, INC, Malibu *Also Called: Westmed Ambulance Inc (P-3305)*
WESTMED AMBULANCE, INC, Escondido *Also Called: Westmed Ambulance Inc (P-3306)*
Westmont Living Inc ....C....... 916 786-3277
  707 Sunrise Ave Roseville (95661) *(P-18547)*
Westmont Living Inc (PA) ....D....... 858 456-1233
  7660 Fay Ave Ste N La Jolla (92037) *(P-18548)*
Westpac Labs Inc ....B....... 562 906-5227
  10200 Pioneer Blvd # 500 Santa Fe Springs (90670) *(P-20005)*
Westpac Materials, Orange *Also Called: Western Pacific Distrg LLC (P-5215)*
Westport Capital Partners LLC ....D....... 310 294-1234
  2121 Rosecrans Ave Ste 4325 El Segundo (90245) *(P-9581)*
Westrec Properties Inc ....B....... 818 907-0400
  16633 Ventura Blvd Fl 6 Encino (91436) *(P-20252)*
Westrup-Sadler Inc ....D....... 916 783-2077
  400 Automall Dr Roseville (95661) *(P-7334)*
Westrux International Inc (PA) ....D....... 562 404-1020
  15555 Valley View Ave Santa Fe Springs (90670) *(P-7335)*
Westside Crdvsclar Med Group I ....C....... 310 289-9955
  99 N La Cienega Blvd Ste 203 Beverly Hills (90211) *(P-15206)*
Westside Jewish Cmnty Ctr Inc (PA) ....C....... 323 938-2531
  5870 W Olympic Blvd Los Angeles (90036) *(P-18633)*
Westside Security Patrol, Bakersfield *Also Called: M & S Security Services Inc (P-12999)*
Weststar Cinemas Inc ....D....... 818 779-0323
  7876 Van Nuys Blvd Van Nuys (91402) *(P-14008)*
Weststar Cinemas Inc ....C....... 805 379-8966
  180 Promenade Way Ste R Westlake Village (91362) *(P-14009)*

ALPHABETIC SECTION

Weststar Cinemas Inc .... D 805 658-6544
   1440 Eastman Ave Ventura (93003) *(P-14010)*

Weststar Cinemas Inc .... D 818 707-9987
   29045 Agoura Rd Agoura Hills (91301) *(P-14011)*

Weststar Cinemas Inc .... C 661 723-9392
   742 W Lancaster Blvd Lancaster (93534) *(P-14072)*

Westveiw Vo Ser, Anaheim *Also Called: Westview Services Inc (P-18262)*

Westview Cmnty Arts Program, Anaheim *Also Called: Westview Services Inc (P-15733)*

Westview Services Inc .... D 714 956-4199
   1701 S Euclid St Ste E Anaheim (92802) *(P-15733)*

Westview Services Inc .... D 626 962-0956
   1515 W Cameron Ave Ste 310 West Covina (91790) *(P-18259)*

Westview Services Inc .... D 714 418-2090
   9421 Edinger Ave Westminster (92683) *(P-18260)*

Westview Services Inc .... D 951 699-0047
   27576 Commerce Center Dr Ste 103 Temecula (92590) *(P-18261)*

Westview Services Inc .... D 714 530-2703
   9776 Katella Ave Anaheim (92804) *(P-18262)*

Westview Services Inc .... D 714 635-2444
   1655 S Euclid St Ste A Anaheim (92802) *(P-18263)*

Westview Services Inc .... D 951 343-2356
   1650 Spruce St Riverside (92507) *(P-20908)*

Westview Vocational Services, Temecula *Also Called: Westview Services Inc (P-18261)*

Westview Vocational Services, Anaheim *Also Called: Westview Services Inc (P-18263)*

Westwind Engineering Inc .... C 310 831-3454
   625 Esplanade Unit 70 Redondo Beach (90277) *(P-19439)*

Westwind Equity Investors, Newport Beach *Also Called: Windjmmer Cpitl Invstors III L (P-9582)*

Westwood Express Messenger Svc, Los Angeles *Also Called: Express Group Incorporated (P-3611)*

WESTWOOD FAMILY PRACTICE, Susanville *Also Called: Northeastern Rur Hlth Clinics (P-14928)*

Westwood Healthcare Center LP .... D 310 826-0821
   12121 Santa Monica Blvd Los Angeles (90025) *(P-15734)*

Westwood Insurance Agency LLC (HQ) .... D 818 990-9715
   6320 Canoga Ave Woodland Hills (91367) *(P-8687)*

Westwood Marquis Hotel & Grdns, Los Angeles *Also Called: W Los Angeles (P-10349)*

Wet (PA) .... C 818 769-6200
   10847 Sherman Way Sun Valley (91352) *(P-13554)*

Wet Design, Sun Valley *Also Called: Wet (P-13554)*

Wet N Wild Los Angeles, City Of Industry *Also Called: Markwins Beauty Products Inc (P-6124)*

Wetherby Asset Management LLC .... D 415 399-9159
   580 California St Fl 8 San Francisco (94104) *(P-8228)*

Wetmore Cutting Tools, Chino *Also Called: Wetmore Tool and Engrg Co (P-2783)*

Wetmore Tool and Engrg Co .... D 909 364-1000
   5091 G St Chino (91710) *(P-2783)*

Wetzel & Sons Mvg & Stor Inc .... D 818 890-0992
   12400 Osborne St Pacoima (91331) *(P-3439)*

Wetzel Trucking, Pacoima *Also Called: Wetzel & Sons Mvg & Stor Inc (P-3439)*

Wexler Corporation .... A 818 846-9381
   1111 S Victory Blvd Burbank (91502) *(P-5715)*

Wexler Video, Burbank *Also Called: Wexler Corporation (P-5715)*

Weyerhaeuser Company .... D 714 523-3330
   11100 Hope St Cypress (90630) *(P-5194)*

Wfc Holdings LLC (HQ) .... C 415 396-7392
   420 Montgomery St San Francisco (94104) *(P-7649)*

Wfcf Technology E2040-030, Santa Monica *Also Called: Wells Fargo Capital Finance Inc (P-13553)*

Wfg National Title Insur Co (PA) .... D 818 476-4000
   700 N Brand Blvd Ste 1100 Glendale (91203) *(P-9241)*

Wfi Equipment Inc .... D 661 327-4900
   2200 E Brundage Ln Bakersfield (93307) *(P-6747)*

Wha, Newport Beach *Also Called: William Hzmlhlch Archtects Inc (P-19519)*

Whaling Bar & Grill, La Jolla *Also Called: Lav Hotel Corp (P-9970)*

Whatever It Takes Inc .... D 760 329-6000
   10805 Palm Dr Desert Hot Springs (92240) *(P-10366)*

Whb Corporation .... A 213 624-1011
   506 S Grand Ave Los Angeles (90071) *(P-10367)*

Wheeler Auto Group Inc .... D 530 673-3765
   350 Colusa Ave Yuba City (95991) *(P-7382)*

Wheeler Chevrolet, Yuba City *Also Called: Wheeler Auto Group Inc (P-7382)*

Whelan Security Co .... C 310 343-8628
   400 Continental Blvd El Segundo (90245) *(P-13075)*

Whi Solutions Inc .... C 661 257-2120
   28470 Avenue Stanford Ste 200 Valencia (91355) *(P-5370)*

Whi Solutions Inc (HQ) .... D 914 697-9301
   2145 Hamilton Ave San Jose (95125) *(P-12039)*

Whiskey Girl .... C 619 236-1616
   702 5th Ave San Diego (92101) *(P-20253)*

Whistlestop, San Rafael *Also Called: Vivalon (P-18172)*

White & Case LLP .... C 213 620-7724
   555 S Flower St Ste 2700 Los Angeles (90071) *(P-17677)*

White & Case LLP .... D 650 213-0300
   3000 El Camino Real Ste 2-900 # & Palo Alto (94306) *(P-17678)*

White Cap 301, Santa Clarita *Also Called: White Cap Supply Group Inc (P-5233)*

White Cap Supply Group Inc .... A 661 294-7737
   28255 Kelly Johnson Pkwy Santa Clarita (91355) *(P-5233)*

White Crane, Indio *Also Called: Whites Crane Service Inc (P-11010)*

White Digital Media Inc .... C 760 827-7800
   3394 Carmel Mountain Rd Ste 250 San Diego (92121) *(P-6845)*

White House Sales, Sacramento *Also Called: Chem Quip Inc (P-5974)*

White House Sanitation Inc .... D 951 943-1550
   18916 Seaton Ave Perris (92570) *(P-13810)*

White Mem Cmnty Hlth Ctr A Cal 323 987-1222
   1828 E Cesar E Chavez Ave Ste 6100 Los Angeles (90033) *(P-15207)*

White Memorial Med Group Inc (PA) .... D 323 987-1300
   1701 E Cesar E Chavez Ave Ste 510 Los Angeles (90033) *(P-15208)*

White Memorial Medical Center .... A 323 260-5739
   1720 E Cesar E Chavez Ave Los Angeles (90033) *(P-15209)*

White Memorial Medical Center (HQ) .... A 323 268-5000
   1720 E Cesar E Chavez Ave Los Angeles (90033) *(P-16627)*

White Rabbit Partners Inc .... C 310 975-1450
   9000 W Sunset Blvd Ste 1500 West Hollywood (90069) *(P-18549)*

White Sands of La Jolla Clinic, La Jolla *Also Called: Humangood Socal (P-18455)*

White Swan Inn, The, San Francisco *Also Called: Joie De Vivre Hospitality LLC (P-9929)*

Whiterabbitai Inc .... D 408 215-8876
   3930 Freedom Cir Ste 101 Santa Clara (95054) *(P-12040)*

Whites Crane Service Inc .... D 760 347-3401
   45524 Towne St Indio (92201) *(P-11010)*

Whiting Door Mfg Corp .... D 909 877-0120
   301 S Milliken Ave Ontario (91761) *(P-13811)*

Whiting-Turner Contracting Co .... B 949 863-0800
   250 Commerce Ste 150 Irvine (92602) *(P-1062)*

Whiting-Turner Contracting Co .... C 916 355-1355
   800 R St Sacramento (95811) *(P-1063)*

Whitmire Distribution, Valencia *Also Called: Cardinal Health Inc (P-6100)*

Whittier Hills Health Care Ctr, Whittier *Also Called: Ensign Group Inc (P-15453)*

Whittier Hospital Med Ctr Inc .... C 562 945-3561
   9080 Colima Rd Whittier (90605) *(P-16628)*

Whittier Inst For Diabetes .... D 877 944-8843
   10140 Campus Point Dr San Diego (92121) *(P-19939)*

Whittier Service Center, Santa Fe Springs *Also Called: Southern California Edison Co (P-4697)*

Whittier Union High Schl Dist .... C 562 693-8826
   7200 Greenleaf Ave Ste 170 Whittier (90602) *(P-17759)*

Who Dat Nation Trnsp LLC .... D 760 403-7237
   13186 Rincon Rd Apple Valley (92308) *(P-4179)*

Wholesale, Norwalk *Also Called: Koi Cbd LLC (P-6119)*

Whv Resort Group Inc (HQ) .... C 760 652-4913
   300 Rancheros Dr Ste 310 San Marcos (92069) *(P-9218)*

Whv Resort Group Inc .... A 760 770-9755
   34567 Cathedral Canyon Dr Cathedral City (92234) *(P-10368)*

Whv Resort Properties Inc .... D 760 481-7739
   300 Rancheros Dr Ste 310 San Marcos (92069) *(P-10369)*

Wic, San Jose *Also Called: Gardner Family Hlth Netwrk Inc (P-14757)*

Wic, Oakland *Also Called: La Clinica De La Raza Inc (P-14866)*

Wic, El Monte *Also Called: Public Hlth Fndation Entps Inc (P-17307)*

Wic, Torrance *Also Called: Public Hlth Fndation Entps Inc (P-18898)*

Wicks Solar Inc .... D 805 546-9056
   2170 Hutton Rd Bldg A Nipomo (93444) *(P-2092)*

ALPHABETIC SECTION

Wideorbit, San Francisco *Also Called: Wideorbit LLC (P-12041)*
Wideorbit LLC (PA) .... D....... 415 675-6700
1160 Battery St Ste 300 San Francisco (94111) *(P-12041)*
Wider Circle Inc .... D....... 650 924-2491
50 Woodside Plz Ste 743 Redwood City (94061) *(P-18550)*
Widly Inc .... C....... 951 279-0900
785 E Harrison St Ste 100 Corona (92879) *(P-2494)*
Widows Orphans Dsbled Frmens F, Los Angeles *Also Called: Los Angles Fireman Relief Assn (P-18047)*
Wieland Brookes, Ontario *Also Called: Wieland Metal Services LLC (P-5531)*
Wieland Metal Services LLC .... D....... 562 968-2100
5100 S Archibald Ave Ontario (91762) *(P-5531)*
Wiemar Distributors Inc .... D....... 213 747-7036
1953 S Alameda St Los Angeles (90058) *(P-6597)*
Wiggins Lift Co Inc .... D....... 805 485-7821
2571 Cortez St Oxnard (93036) *(P-5886)*
Wikimedia Foundation Inc .... B....... 415 839-6885
1 Montgomery St Ste 1600 San Francisco (94104) *(P-19120)*
Wilbur Curtis Co Inc .... B....... 800 421-6150
6913 W Acco St Montebello (90640) *(P-9348)*
Wilbur Packing Company Inc .... D....... 530 671-4911
1500 Eager Rd Live Oak (95953) *(P-315)*
Wilbur-Ellis Company LLC (DH) .... B....... 415 772-4000
345 California St Fl 27 San Francisco (94104) *(P-6838)*
Wilbur-Ellis Holdings II Inc (HQ) .... D....... 415 772-4000
345 California St Fl 27 San Francisco (94104) *(P-7601)*
Wild Karma Inc .... B....... 510 639-9088
5275 Broadway Oakland (94618) *(P-15735)*
Wild Palms Hotel, The, Sunnyvale *Also Called: Joie De Vivre Hospitality LLC (P-20127)*
Wildenradt-Mcmurray Inc .... D....... 510 835-5500
568 7th St San Francisco (94103) *(P-5738)*
Wildfire Interactive Inc .... C....... 650 253-0000
1600 Amphitheatre Pkwy Mountain View (94043) *(P-12397)*
Wildflour Bakery, Woodland Hills *Also Called: Coolish Holdings LLC (P-2366)*
Wildlife Health Center, Davis *Also Called: University California Davis (P-15157)*
Wildlife International, Santa Clara *Also Called: Evans Analytical Group LLC (P-19976)*
Wildomar Medical Offices, Wildomar *Also Called: Kaiser Foundation Hospitals (P-16173)*
Wilke Fleury Hoffelt Gould & Birney .... D....... 916 441-2430
400 Capitol Mall Ste 2200 Sacramento (95814) *(P-17679)*
Will Perkins Inc .... D....... 213 270-8400
617 W 7th St Fl 12 Los Angeles (90017) *(P-19518)*
Willamette Valley Trtmnt Ctr, Cupertino *Also Called: CRC Health Corporate (P-17045)*
Willdan Engineering .... D....... 916 661-3520
9281 Office Park Cir Ste 100 Elk Grove (95758) *(P-19440)*
Willdan Engineering .... D....... 916 924-7000
2240 Douglas Blvd Ste 270 Roseville (95661) *(P-19441)*
Willdan Engineering .... D....... 805 653-6597
374 Poli St Ste 101 Ventura (93001) *(P-19442)*
Willdan Group Inc (PA) .... C....... 800 424-9144
2401 E Katella Ave Ste 300 Anaheim (92806) *(P-19443)*
William Hzmlhlch Archtects Inc .... D....... 949 250-0607
680 Newport Center Dr Ste 300 Newport Beach (92660) *(P-19519)*
William L Lyon & Assoc Inc .... B....... 916 447-7878
2801 J St Sacramento (95816) *(P-9219)*
William L Lyon & Assoc Inc .... B....... 916 535-0356
8814 Madison Ave Fair Oaks (95628) *(P-9220)*
William Morris Consulting, Beverly Hills *Also Called: William Mrris Endvor Entrmt LL (P-14074)*
William Mrris Endvor Entrmt FN (DH) .... C....... 310 285-9000
9601 Wilshire Blvd Fl 3 Beverly Hills (90210) *(P-14073)*
William Mrris Endvor Entrmt LL (DH) .... C....... 212 586-5100
9601 Wilshire Blvd Beverly Hills (90210) *(P-11256)*
William Mrris Endvor Entrmt LL .... B....... 310 285-9000
9601 Wilshire Blvd Fl 3 Beverly Hills (90210) *(P-14074)*
William Oneil & Co Inc (PA) .... C....... 310 448-6800
12655 Beatrice St Los Angeles (90066) *(P-8178)*
William Warren Properties Inc .... D....... 310 454-1500
201 Wilshire Blvd Ste 102 Santa Monica (90401) *(P-8873)*
Williams Scotsman Inc .... C....... 559 441-8181
2829 S Chestnut Ave Fresno (93725) *(P-5234)*
Williams Scotsman Inc .... C....... 619 710-8468
14015 Kirkham Way Poway (92064) *(P-10733)*

Williams Scotsman - Fresno, Fresno *Also Called: Williams Scotsman Inc (P-5234)*
Williams Tank Lines (PA) .... D....... 209 944-5613
1477 Tillie Lewis Dr Stockton (95206) *(P-3564)*
Williams Tank Lines .... D....... 661 634-9755
2148 Bricyn Ln Bakersfield (93308) *(P-3565)*
Willis Construction Co Inc .... C....... 831 623-2900
2261 San Juan Hwy San Juan Bautista (95045) *(P-2709)*
Willis Insurance Services Cal, Irvine *Also Called: Willis North America Inc (P-20613)*
Willis North America Inc .... C....... 909 476-3300
18101 Von Karman Ave Ste 600 Irvine (92612) *(P-20613)*
Willis, Burton F MD, Huntington Beach *Also Called: Edinger Medical Group Inc (P-14732)*
Willits Hospital Inc .... B....... 707 459-6801
1 Marcela Dr Willits (95490) *(P-16629)*
Wilmark Cmmnties Univ Vlg Inc (PA) .... D....... 858 271-0582
9948 Hibert St Ste 210 San Diego (92131) *(P-8874)*
Willow Creek Healthcare Ctr LLC .... C....... 559 323-6200
650 W Alluvial Ave Clovis (93611) *(P-15736)*
Willow Creek Healthcare Center, Clovis *Also Called: Willow Creek Healthcare Ctr LLC (P-15736)*
Willow Creek Treatment Center, Santa Rosa *Also Called: Victor Treatment Centers Inc (P-18539)*
Willow Pass Hlth Care Ctr Inc .... D....... 925 689-9222
3318 Willow Pass Rd Concord (94519) *(P-16976)*
Willow Pavillion, Mountain View *Also Called: El Camino Hospital (P-16070)*
Willow Springs LLC .... A....... 916 288-0300
8001 Bruceville Rd Sacramento (95823) *(P-15210)*
Willow Springs LLC .... A....... 510 796-1100
39001 Sundale Dr Fremont (94538) *(P-15211)*
Willow Springs LLC .... A....... 916 489-3336
4250 Auburn Blvd Sacramento (95841) *(P-16630)*
Wilmark Development, San Diego *Also Called: Wilmark Management Svcs Inc (P-9221)*
Wilmark Management Svcs Inc (PA) .... D....... 858 271-0583
9948 Hibert St Ste 210 San Diego (92131) *(P-9221)*
Wilsey Foods Inc .... A....... 714 257-3700
40 Pointe Dr Brea (92821) *(P-2377)*
Wilshire 2015 Fund .... D....... 310 451-3051
1299 Ocean Ave Ste 700 Santa Monica (90401) *(P-9394)*
Wilshire Advisors LLC (PA) .... C....... 310 451-3051
1299 Ocean Ave Ste 700 Santa Monica (90401) *(P-20614)*
Wilshire Bancorp Inc .... A....... 213 387-3200
3200 Wilshire Blvd Los Angeles (90010) *(P-7726)*
Wilshire Bank .... B....... 213 427-1000
3200 Wilshire Blvd Fl 10 Los Angeles (90010) *(P-7727)*
Wilshire Boulevard Temple .... D....... 310 457-7861
11495 Pacific Coast Hwy Malibu (90265) *(P-10413)*
Wilshire Boulevard Temple .... D....... 323 261-6135
4334 Whittier Blvd Los Angeles (90023) *(P-19030)*
Wilshire Country Club .... D....... 323 934-6050
301 N Rossmore Ave Los Angeles (90004) *(P-14484)*
Wilshire Income Opportunities .... D....... 310 451-3051
1299 Ocean Ave Ste 700 Santa Monica (90401) *(P-9395)*
Wilshire Kingsley Inc .... D....... 213 382-6677
3575 Wilshire Blvd Los Angeles (90010) *(P-8784)*
Wilshire State Bank, Los Angeles *Also Called: Wilshire Bank (P-7727)*
Wilson & Hampton Pntg Contrs .... D....... 714 772-5091
1524 W Mable St Anaheim (92802) *(P-1646)*
Wilson Creek Winery, Temecula *Also Called: Wilson Creek Wnery Vnyards Inc (P-2397)*
Wilson Creek Wnery Vnyards Inc .... C....... 951 699-9463
35960 Rancho California Rd Temecula (92591) *(P-2397)*
Wilson Elser Mskwitz Edlman DC .... D....... 213 443-5100
555 S Flower St Ste 2900 Los Angeles (90071) *(P-17680)*
Wilson Emery Corporation .... D....... 818 245-6387
350 Arden Ave Ste 200 Glendale (91203) *(P-20615)*
Wilson Snsini Gdrich Rsati Pro (PA) .... A....... 650 493-9300
650 Page Mill Rd Palo Alto (94304) *(P-17681)*
Wimberly Allson Tong Goo NA In .... D....... 949 574-8500
300 Spectrum Center Dr Ste 500 Irvine (92618) *(P-19520)*
Win River Hotel Corporation .... A....... 530 226-5111
5050 Bechelli Ln Redding (96002) *(P-10370)*
Win River Mini Mart, Redding *Also Called: Redding Rancheria (P-10144)*
Win Telecom Global Corporation .... D....... 408 477-5672
1735 Independence Blvd Apt #101 Salinas (93906) *(P-4368)*

Employee Codes: A=Over 500 employees, B=251-500
C=101-250, D=51-100, E=20-50, F=10-19, G=1-9

Win Time Ltd   **ALPHABETIC SECTION**

Win Time Ltd (PA) .... C...... 858 695-2300
   9335 Kearny Mesa Rd San Diego (92126) *(P-10371)*

Win-Dor Inc (PA) .... C...... 714 576-2030
   450 Delta Ave Brea (92821) *(P-2027)*

Win-River Casino, Redding *Also Called: Redding Rnchria Ecnmic Dev Cor (P-10145)*

Winbond Electronics Corp Amer .... D...... 408 943-6666
   2727 N 1st St San Jose (95134) *(P-5716)*

Winchester Mystery House, San Jose *Also Called: Winchester Mystery House LLC (P-14586)*

Winchester Mystery House LLC .... D...... 408 247-2101
   525 S Winchester Blvd San Jose (95128) *(P-14586)*

Winchster Intrcnnect CM CA Inc .... C...... 800 848-4257
   1873 Diamond St San Marcos (92078) *(P-2726)*

Winco Foods LLC .... C...... 209 556-6040
   4400 Crows Landing Rd Modesto (95358) *(P-3783)*

Wind River, Alameda *Also Called: Wind River Systems Inc (P-12398)*

Wind River Enterprises Inc .... D...... 707 864-1040
   250 Dittmer Rd Fairfield (94534) *(P-5019)*

Wind River Systems Inc (HQ) .... A...... 510 748-4100
   500 Wind River Way Alameda (94501) *(P-12398)*

Windermere RE Coachella Vly, Indian Wells *Also Called: Bennion Deville Fine Homes Inc (P-8910)*

Windes Inc (PA) .... D...... 562 435-1191
   3780 Kilroy Airport Way Ste 600 Long Beach (90806) *(P-19639)*

Windjmmer Cpitl Invstors III L .... A...... 949 706-9989
   610 Newport Center Dr Ste 1100 Newport Beach (92660) *(P-9582)*

Windjmmer Cpitl Invstors IV LP .... B...... 919 706-9989
   610 Newport Center Dr Ste 1100 Newport Beach (92660) *(P-9583)*

Window Instlltion Insul Instll, Madera *Also Called: Vezina Industries Inc (P-1971)*

Windsor Anaheim Healthcare (PA) .... C...... 714 826-8950
   3415 W Ball Rd Anaheim (92804) *(P-15737)*

Windsor Capital Group Inc .... C...... 805 735-8311
   1117 N H St Lompoc (93436) *(P-10372)*

Windsor Capital Group Inc .... C...... 714 990-6000
   900 E Birch St Brea (92821) *(P-10373)*

Windsor Capital Group Inc .... A...... 951 676-5656
   29345 Rancho California Rd Temecula (92591) *(P-10374)*

Windsor Capital Group Inc .... C...... 714 241-3800
   1325 E Dyer Rd Santa Ana (92705) *(P-10375)*

Windsor Capital Group Inc .... C...... 310 566-1100
   2800 28th St Ste 385 Santa Monica (90405) *(P-10376)*

Windsor Capital Holet Group, Sacramento *Also Called: Recp/Wndsor Scramento Ventr LP (P-10142)*

Windsor Cnvlscent Rhblttion CT .... D...... 925 689-2266
   3806 Clayton Rd Concord (94521) *(P-15738)*

Windsor Cnvlscent Rhblttion CT .... D...... 510 793-7222
   2400 Parkside Dr Fremont (94536) *(P-15739)*

Windsor Cnvlscent Rhblttion CT .... D...... 831 424-0687
   637 E Romie Ln Salinas (93901) *(P-15740)*

Windsor Cypress Garden, Riverside *Also Called: Windsor Cypress Grdns Hlthcare (P-15912)*

Windsor Cypress Grdns Hlthcare .... A...... 951 688-3643
   9025 Colorado Ave Riverside (92503) *(P-15912)*

Windsor Foods, Ontario *Also Called: Ajinomoto Foods North Amer Inc (P-2356)*

Windsor Gardens Healthcare C .... C...... 510 582-4636
   1628 B St Hayward (94541) *(P-15913)*

Windsor Gardens Rehabilitation Center of Salinas, Salinas *Also Called: Windsor Cnvlscent Rhblttion CT (P-15740)*

Windsor Grdns Cnvlescent Ctr A, Anaheim *Also Called: Windsor Anaheim Healthcare (P-15737)*

Windsor Manor, Glendale *Also Called: Humangood Socal (P-8823)*

Windsor Manor Rehabilitation Center of Co, Concord *Also Called: Windsor Cnvlscent Rhblttion CT (P-15738)*

Windsor Palms Care Ctr Artesia, Artesia *Also Called: Windsor Twin Plms Hlthcare Ctr (P-15742)*

Windsor Park Care Center of Fremont, Fremont *Also Called: Windsor Cnvlscent Rhblttion CT (P-15739)*

Windsor Redding Care Ctr LLC .... D...... 530 246-0600
   2490 Court St Redding (96001) *(P-15741)*

Windsor Twin Plms Hlthcare Ctr .... C...... 562 865-0271
   11900 Artesia Blvd Artesia (90701) *(P-15742)*

Windsor Vineyards, Santa Rosa *Also Called: Mildara Blass Inc (P-2389)*

Windward Life Care, San Diego *Also Called: Buena Vista MGT Svcs LLC (P-16829)*

Windy City Express, Oakland *Also Called: Edys Grand Ice Cream (P-2349)*

Windy Cy Wire Cble Tech Pdts L .... C...... 510 284-3956
   8024 Central Ave Newark (94560) *(P-5597)*

Wine & Roses LLC .... C...... 209 334-6988
   2505 W Turner Rd Lodi (95242) *(P-7517)*

Wine & Roses Hotel and Rest, Lodi *Also Called: Wine & Roses LLC (P-7517)*

Wine Country Gift Baskets, Fullerton *Also Called: Houdini Inc (P-7557)*

Wine Country Party & Events, Torrance *Also Called: Bright Event Rentals LLC (P-11022)*

Wine Dept, Los Angeles *Also Called: Youngs Market Company LLC (P-6816)*

Wine Industry Network LLC .... D...... 707 953-9672
   155 Foss Creek Cir Healdsburg (95448) *(P-6811)*

Wine Warehouse, Richmond *Also Called: Breakthru Beverage Cal LLC (P-6788)*

Winebow, Benicia *Also Called: CENTRAL COAST WINE COMPANY (P-6791)*

Wing Aviation LLC .... C...... 650 224-1198
   1600 Amphitheatre Pkwy Mountain View (94043) *(P-3861)*

Wingert Grbing Brbker Jstkie L .... D...... 619 232-8151
   1230 Columbia St Ste 400 San Diego (92101) *(P-17682)*

Winners Only Inc .... C...... 760 599-0300
   1365 Park Center Dr Vista (92081) *(P-5108)*

Winpak, Rialto *Also Called: Lane Winpak Inc (P-6923)*

Winston & Strawn LLP .... D...... 415 591-1000
   101 California St Ste 3900 San Francisco (94111) *(P-17683)*

Wintergreen Apts, San Diego *Also Called: Hanken Cono Assad & Co Inc (P-9036)*

Winton-Ireland Insur Agcy Inc (PA) .... D...... 209 667-0995
   627 E Canal Dr Turlock (95380) *(P-8688)*

Wipeout Bar & Grill, San Francisco *Also Called: Simco Foods Inc (P-6286)*

Wipple Laboratories, Redwood City *Also Called: Sequoia Health Services (P-16412)*

Wired, San Francisco *Also Called: Wired Ventures Inc (P-2547)*

Wired Ventures Inc .... C...... 415 276-8400
   520 3rd St Ste 305 San Francisco (94107) *(P-2547)*

Wirtz Quality Installations .... D...... 858 569-3816
   7932 Armour St San Diego (92111) *(P-1897)*

Wis, San Diego *Also Called: Washington Inventory Service (P-13550)*

Wise & Healthy Aging .... D...... 818 876-1402
   23388 Mulholland Dr Stop 60 Woodland Hills (91364) *(P-18193)*

Wise Buys 9.98 or Less, Roseville *Also Called: Wise Buys Liquidators Inc (P-13555)*

Wise Buys Liquidators Inc .... D...... 916 773-3998
   1159 Roseville Sq Roseville (95678) *(P-13555)*

Wise Commerce Inc .... C...... 855 469-4737
   1730 S El Camino Real Ste 500 San Mateo (94402) *(P-12042)*

Wise Skulls LLC .... D...... 669 260-9005
   1812 W Burbank Blvd Burbank (91506) *(P-11257)*

Wiser Foods Inc .... D...... 310 895-0888
   5405 E Village Rd Unit 8219 Long Beach (90808) *(P-2414)*

Wisetack Inc .... C...... 415 918-2380
   460 Brannan St Unit 78384 San Francisco (94107) *(P-12043)*

Wismettac Asian Foods Inc (HQ) .... C...... 562 802-1900
   13409 Orden Dr Santa Fe Springs (90670) *(P-6414)*

Wismettac Fresh Fish, Santa Fe Springs *Also Called: Wismettac Asian Foods Inc (P-6414)*

Withers Bergman, San Diego *Also Called: Withers Bergman LLP (P-17684)*

Withers Bergman LLP .... B...... 203 974-0412
   12830 El Camino Real Ste 350 San Diego (92130) *(P-17684)*

Withrow Cattle .... D...... 916 780-0364
   5301 Pleasant Grove Rd Pleasant Grove (95668) *(P-223)*

Withrow Dairy, Pleasant Grove *Also Called: Withrow Cattle (P-223)*

Withumsmith+brown PC .... D...... 415 434-3744
   601 California St Ste 1800 San Francisco (94108) *(P-19640)*

Wj Newport LLC .... C...... 949 476-2001
   4500 Macarthur Blvd Newport Beach (92660) *(P-10377)*

Wjbradley Mortgage Capital, Newport Beach *Also Called: Emery Financial Inc (P-8041)*

WKS Restaurant Corporation (PA) .... C...... 562 425-1402
   5856 Corporate Ave Ste 200 Cypress (90630) *(P-7518)*

WL Butler Inc .... D...... 650 361-1270
   5666 La Ribera St Ste A Livermore (94550) *(P-742)*

WL Butler Inc .... C...... 650 361-1270
   1629 Main St Redwood City (94063) *(P-1064)*

Wlcac, Los Angeles *Also Called: Watts Labor Community Action (P-18187)*

WLMD 209 723-9120
   1715 Kibby Rd Merced (95341) *(P-2334)*

ALPHABETIC SECTION

Wm B Saleh Co .... D...... 559 255-2046
   1364 N Jackson Ave Fresno (93703) *(P-1647)*

Wm Bolthouse Farms Inc (HQ) .... A...... 661 366-7209
   7200 E Brundage Ln Bakersfield (93307) *(P-49)*

Wm Healthcare Solutions Inc .... D...... 713 328-7350
   3670 Enterprise Ave Hayward (94545) *(P-4969)*

Wm Healthcare Solutions Inc .... D...... 713 328-7350
   7010 Auto Mall Pkwy Fremont (94538) *(P-4970)*

Wm Healthcare Solutions Inc .... D...... 713 328-7350
   5337 Luce Ave Mcclellan (95652) *(P-4971)*

WM Klorman Construction Corp .... D...... 818 591-5969
   23047 Ventura Blvd Fl 2 Woodland Hills (91364) *(P-1065)*

Wm Michael Stemler Inc (PA) .... C...... 209 948-8483
   3244 Brookside Rd Ste 200 Stockton (95219) *(P-8689)*

Wm Michael Stemler Inc .... D...... 559 228-4144
   7110 N Fresno St Ste 350 Fresno (93720) *(P-8690)*

Wm Technology, Irvine *Also Called: Wm Technology Inc (P-12399)*

Wm Technology Inc .... B...... 844 933-3627
   41 Discovery Irvine (92618) *(P-12399)*

Wmbe Payrolling Inc .... C...... 858 810-3000
   3545 Aero Ct San Diego (92123) *(P-11258)*

Wme, Beverly Hills *Also Called: William Mrris Endvor Entrmt LL (P-11256)*

Wme Bi LLC .... D...... 877 592-2472
   17075 Camino San Diego (92127) *(P-12400)*

Wme Img LLC (DH) .... C...... 212 586-5100
   9601 Wilshire Blvd Beverly Hills (90210) *(P-14162)*

Wmhs Bay Area, Hayward *Also Called: Wm Healthcare Solutions Inc (P-4969)*

Wmhs Sacramento, Mcclellan *Also Called: Wm Healthcare Solutions Inc (P-4971)*

Wmhs Tri Cities, Fremont *Also Called: Wm Healthcare Solutions Inc (P-4970)*

Wng, Irvine *Also Called: Western National Group LP (P-9215)*

Wolf Rfkin Shpiro Schlman Rbk (PA) .... D...... 310 445-8817
   11400 W Olympic Blvd Ste 900 Los Angeles (90064) *(P-17685)*

Wolf & Raven LLC .... D...... 800 431-6471
   206 W 4th St Ste 439 Santa Ana (92701) *(P-20254)*

Wolf Firm, Santa Ana *Also Called: Wolf Firm A Law Corporation (P-17686)*

Wolf Firm A Law Corporation .... D...... 949 720-9200
   1651 E 4th St Ste 121 Santa Ana (92701) *(P-17686)*

Wolfsen Incorporated .... C...... 209 827-7700
   1269 W I St Los Banos (93635) *(P-8)*

Womanhaven .... D...... 760 353-6922
   510 W Main St Ste 106 El Centro (92243) *(P-18194)*

Womble Bond Dickinson (us) LLP .... C...... 310 207-3800
   12400 Wilshire Blvd Ste 600 Los Angeles (90025) *(P-17687)*

Women's Health Center, Colusa *Also Called: Colusa Regional Medical Center Inc (P-20061)*

Women's Imaging Center, Redding *Also Called: MD Imaging Inc A Prof Med Corp (P-14889)*

Womens Cancer Center .... D...... 925 627-3440
   1455 Montego Ste 100 Walnut Creek (94598) *(P-15212)*

Womens Cancer Center .... D...... 408 358-6500
   815 Pollard Rd Los Gatos (95032) *(P-16701)*

Womens Ctr - Youth & Fmly Svcs (PA) .... D...... 209 941-2611
   620 N San Joaquin St Stockton (95202) *(P-18195)*

Womens Health Specialists .... D...... 510 248-1470
   2299 Mowry Ave Ste 3c Fremont (94538) *(P-15213)*

Womens Rcvery Assn San Mteo CN .... C...... 650 348-6603
   2015 Pioneer Ct San Mateo (94403) *(P-18769)*

Womens Recovery Association, San Mateo *Also Called: Womens Rcvery Assn San Mteo CN (P-18769)*

Womply, San Francisco *Also Called: Oto Analytics Inc (P-12508)*

Wonderful Agency .... A...... 310 966-8600
   11444 W Olympic Blvd Ste 210 Los Angeles (90064) *(P-10690)*

Wonderful Citrus Cooperative .... A...... 661 720-2400
   5001 California Ave Ste 230 Bakersfield (93309) *(P-18727)*

Wonderful Citrus LLC (HQ) .... D...... 661 720-2400
   1701 S Lexington St Delano (93215) *(P-102)*

Wonderful Citrus Packing LLC (HQ) .... B...... 661 720-2400
   1901 S Lexington St Delano (93215) *(P-316)*

Wonderful Company LLC .... B...... 661 720-2400
   1901 S Lexington St Delano (93215) *(P-103)*

Wonderful Company LLC .... A...... 559 781-7438
   5001 California Ave Bakersfield (93309) *(P-317)*

Wonderful Company LLC .... A...... 661 399-4456
   6801 E Lerdo Hwy Shafter (93263) *(P-318)*

Wonderful Company LLC .... B...... 661 720-2609
   11444 W Olympic Blvd Ste 210 Los Angeles (90064) *(P-319)*

Wonderful Orchards LLC (HQ) .... C...... 661 399-4456
   6801 E Lerdo Hwy Shafter (93263) *(P-95)*

Wonderful Orchards LLC .... B...... 661 797-6400
   13646 Highway 33 Lost Hills (93249) *(P-96)*

Wonderful Orchards LLC .... D...... 661 797-2509
   21707 Lerdo Hwy Mc Kittrick (93251) *(P-97)*

Wonderfulpistachiosandalmonds, Lost Hills *Also Called: Wonderful Orchards LLC (P-96)*

Wonderware, Lake Forest *Also Called: Aveva Software LLC (P-12424)*

Wonderware Corporation (DH) .... B...... 949 727-3200
   26561 Rancho Pkwy S Lake Forest (92630) *(P-12401)*

Wondros, Los Angeles *Also Called: Hungry Heart Media Inc (P-13855)*

Wonolo Inc .... D...... 415 706-7692
   535 Mission St San Francisco (94105) *(P-11259)*

Woocommerce Inc .... B...... 650 388-0901
   60 29th St San Francisco (94110) *(P-12044)*

Wood Bros Inc .... D...... 559 924-7715
   14147 18th Ave Lemoore (93245) *(P-1325)*

Wood Gutmann Bogart Insur Brkg .... D...... 714 505-7000
   15901 Red Hill Ave Ste 100 Tustin (92780) *(P-8691)*

Wood Gutmann Bogart Insur Brks .... C...... 714 505-7000
   15901 Red Hill Ave Ste 100 Tustin (92780) *(P-8692)*

Wood Rodgers Inc (PA) .... C...... 916 341-7760
   3301 C St Ste 100b Sacramento (95816) *(P-19444)*

Woodbine Lgacy/Playa Owner LLC .... D...... 678 292-4962
   6161 W Centinela Ave Culver City (90230) *(P-10378)*

Woodbridge Glass Inc .... C...... 714 838-4444
   14321 Myford Rd Tustin (92780) *(P-2210)*

Woodbridge Village Association .... D...... 949 786-1800
   31 Creek Rd Irvine (92604) *(P-18931)*

Woodlake, The, Sacramento *Also Called: Lbn Leisure Care LLC (P-18466)*

Woodland Healthcare (DH) .... B...... 530 662-3961
   1325 Cottonwood St Woodland (95695) *(P-16631)*

Woodland Healthcare .... C...... 530 669-5680
   261 California St Woodland (95695) *(P-16632)*

Woodland Healthcare .... C...... 530 756-2364
   2660 W Covell Blvd Davis (95616) *(P-16633)*

Woodland Healthcare .... C...... 530 668-2600
   1207 Fairchild Ct Woodland (95695) *(P-16634)*

Woodland Healthcare Home Hlth, Woodland *Also Called: Woodland Healthcare (P-16632)*

Woodland Memorial Hospital .... C...... 916 851-2150
   3400 Data Dr Rancho Cordova (95670) *(P-13556)*

Woodman Realty Inc .... C...... 909 425-5324
   26030 Base Line St Apt 97 San Bernardino (92410) *(P-9222)*

Woodmont Realty Advisors Inc .... B...... 650 592-3960
   1050 Ralston Ave Belmont (94002) *(P-8470)*

Woodmont Senior Living, Redding *Also Called: Northstar Senior Living Inc (P-20164)*

Woodruff Spradlin & Smart .... D...... 714 558-7000
   555 Anton Blvd Ste 1200 Costa Mesa (92626) *(P-17688)*

Woodruff Convalescent Center, Duarte *Also Called: Estrella Inc (P-15467)*

Woodruff-Sawyer & Co (PA) .... C...... 415 391-2141
   50 California St Fl 12 San Francisco (94111) *(P-8693)*

Woods Bagot Architects PC .... C...... 415 277-3000
   128 Spear St Lbby San Francisco (94105) *(P-19521)*

Woods Maintenance Services Inc .... C...... 818 764-2515
   7250 Coldwater Canyon Ave North Hollywood (91605) *(P-2335)*

Woodside Electronics Corp .... D...... 530 666-9190
   1311 Blue Grass Pl Woodland (95776) *(P-13812)*

Woodward Duarte, Duarte *Also Called: Woodward Hrt Inc (P-2993)*

Woodward Hrt Inc .... C...... 626 359-9211
   1700 Business Center Dr Duarte (91010) *(P-2993)*

Woodway Healthcare Inc .... D...... 254 420-0056
   27101 Puerta Real Ste 450 Mission Viejo (92691) *(P-15743)*

Woolf Enterprises, Huron *Also Called: California Valley Land Co Inc (P-241)*

Woolf Farming Co Cal Inc .... A...... 559 945-9292
   7041 N Van Ness Blvd Fresno (93711) *(P-208)*

Wooltari Usa Inc .... D...... 310 933-8648
   17022 Montanero Ave Ste 2 Carson (90746) *(P-7155)*

Word & Brown Insurance Administrators Inc   **ALPHABETIC SECTION**

Word & Brown Insurance Administrators Inc (PA) .... B...... 714 835-5006
   721 S Parker St Ste 300 Orange (92868) *(P-8694)*

Wordsmart Corporation .... D
   10025 Mesa Rim Rd San Diego (92121) *(P-12402)*

Work Force Services Inc .... C...... 661 327-5019
   1811 Oak St Bakersfield (93301) *(P-11364)*

Work Force Staffing, Bakersfield *Also Called: Work Force Services Inc (P-11364)*

Work Health .... D...... 707 257-4084
   3421 Villa Ln Ste 2a Napa (94558) *(P-20616)*

Work Inc .... D...... 805 739-0451
   3070 Skyway Dr Ste 104 Santa Maria (93455) *(P-18196)*

Work Truck Solutions Inc .... D...... 855 987-4544
   2485 Notre Dame Blvd Ste 370e Chico (95928) *(P-12908)*

Work2fture - Yuth Training Ctr, San Jose *Also Called: Work2future Foundation (P-18265)*

Work2future - Gilroy Job Ctr, Gilroy *Also Called: Work2future Foundation (P-18266)*

Work2future Foundation .... C...... 408 216-6202
   1901 Zanker Rd San Jose (95112) *(P-18264)*

Work2future Foundation .... C...... 408 794-1234
   2072 Lucretia Ave San Jose (95122) *(P-18265)*

Work2future Foundation .... C...... 408 758-3477
   379 Tomkins Ct Gilroy (95020) *(P-18266)*

Workato Inc (PA) .... A...... 844 469-6752
   215 Castro St Fl 3 Mountain View (94041) *(P-12045)*

Workboard Inc (PA) .... C...... 650 294-4480
   487 Seaport Ct Ste 100 Redwood City (94063) *(P-12403)*

Workcare Inc .... C...... 714 978-7488
   300 S Harbor Blvd Ste 600 Anaheim (92805) *(P-20667)*

Workday, Pleasanton *Also Called: Workday Inc (P-12046)*

Workday Inc (PA) .... A...... 925 951-9000
   6110 Stoneridge Mall Rd Pleasanton (94588) *(P-12046)*

Workers Cmpnstion Insur Rting (PA) .... C...... 888 229-2472
   1901 Harrison St 17th Fl Oakland (94612) *(P-8695)*

Workforcelogic .... D...... 707 939-4300
   425 California St San Francisco (94104) *(P-12047)*

Working Alternatives Inc .... D...... 714 898-6400
   3465 Camino Del Rio S Ste 240 San Diego (92108) *(P-18551)*

Working Assets Long Distance, San Francisco *Also Called: Credo Mobile Inc (P-4210)*

Working With Autism Inc .... D...... 818 501-4240
   14724 Ventura Blvd Ste 1110 Sherman Oaks (91403) *(P-17162)*

Workrite Uniform Company Inc (DH) .... B...... 805 483-0175
   1701 Lombard St Ste 200 Oxnard (93030) *(P-10483)*

Works Floor & Wall, The, Palm Desert *Also Called: Temalpakh Inc (P-1042)*

Workspan .... D...... 650 223-4243
   3 Twin Dolphin Dr Ste 350 Redwood City (94065) *(P-12048)*

Workstream Technologies Inc .... D...... 415 767-1006
   521 7th St San Francisco (94103) *(P-12049)*

Workway Inc .... C...... 619 278-0012
   3111 Camino Del Rio N Ste 400 San Diego (92108) *(P-11260)*

Workway Inc .... C...... 949 553-8700
   19742 Macarthur Blvd Ste 235 Irvine (92612) *(P-11261)*

World Centric .... D...... 707 241-9190
   1500 Valley House Dr Ste 210 Rohnert Park (94928) *(P-2534)*

World Centric, Rohnert Park *Also Called: World Centric (P-2534)*

World Class Distribution Inc .... D...... 909 574-4140
   2121 Boeing Way Stockton (95206) *(P-3784)*

World Class Distribution Inc .... D...... 909 574-4140
   800 S Shamrock Ave Monrovia (91016) *(P-3785)*

World Class Distribution Inc .... D...... 909 574-4140
   343 S Lena Rd San Bernardino (92408) *(P-3786)*

World Gym Fitness Centers, Los Angeles *Also Called: World Gym International LLC (P-14243)*

World Gym International LLC .... C...... 310 557-8804
   1901 Avenue Of The Stars Ste 1100 Los Angeles (90067) *(P-14243)*

World Mvie Awrds Orgnztion Wma .... D...... 833 375-5857
   9171 Wilshire Blvd # 500a Beverly Hills (90210) *(P-18932)*

World Oil Corp .... C...... 562 928-0100
   9302 Garfield Ave South Gate (90280) *(P-587)*

World Oil Environmental Svcs, Compton *Also Called: Asbury Environmental Services (P-3370)*

World Private Security Inc .... C...... 818 894-1800
   16921 Parthenia St Ste 201 Northridge (91343) *(P-13076)*

World Svc Wst/La Inflght Svc L .... C...... 310 538-7000
   1812 W 135th St Gardena (90249) *(P-3922)*

World Trade Ctr Ht Assoc Ltd .... D...... 562 983-3400
   701 W Ocean Blvd Long Beach (90831) *(P-10379)*

World Variety Produce Inc .... B...... 800 588-0151
   5325 S Soto St Vernon (90058) *(P-6598)*

World Vision International (PA) .... C...... 626 303-8811
   800 W Chestnut Ave Monrovia (91016) *(P-19121)*

World Wind & Solar, Tehachapi *Also Called: World Wind Electrical Svcs Inc (P-1876)*

World Wind & Solar, Paso Robles *Also Called: Worldwind Services LLC (P-1877)*

World Wind Electrical Svcs Inc .... B...... 661 822-4877
   228 W Tehachapi Blvd Tehachapi (93561) *(P-1876)*

World Wine Estates .... C...... 707 257-5300
   1250 Cuttings Wharf Rd Napa (94559) *(P-6812)*

World-Wide Foods .... D...... 818 887-1338
   501 Library St San Fernando (91340) *(P-6415)*

Worldbridge Partners .... C...... 661 775-9999
   25000 Avenue Stanford Ste 250 Valencia (91355) *(P-11262)*

Worldlink East, Los Angeles *Also Called: Worldlink LLC (P-13557)*

Worldlink LLC (PA) .... D...... 323 866-5900
   6100 Wilshire Blvd Ste 1400 Los Angeles (90048) *(P-13557)*

Worldmark At Palm Springs, Palm Springs *Also Called: Worldmark Club (P-10381)*

Worldmark Club .... D...... 707 274-0118
   3927 E State Hwy 20 Nice (95464) *(P-10380)*

Worldmark Club .... D...... 760 416-4428
   1177 N Palm Canyon Dr Palm Springs (92262) *(P-10381)*

Worldsite.ws, Carlsbad *Also Called: Global Domains Intl Inc (P-4288)*

Worldwide Inc .... D...... 310 276-7171
   9601 Wilshire Blvd Beverly Hills (90210) *(P-9223)*

Worldwide Aeros Corp .... D...... 818 344-3999
   3971 Fredonia Dr Los Angeles (90068) *(P-2984)*

Worldwide Corporate Housing LP .... B...... 972 392-4747
   1 World Trade Ctr Ste 2400 Long Beach (90831) *(P-10396)*

Worldwide Holdings Inc (PA) .... D...... 213 236-4500
   725 S Figueroa St Ste 1900 Los Angeles (90017) *(P-8696)*

Worldwide Intgrted Rsurces Inc .... D...... 323 838-8938
   7171 Telegraph Rd Montebello (90640) *(P-5739)*

Worldwide Produce, Los Angeles *Also Called: Green Farms Inc (P-6556)*

Worldwide Security Assoc Inc (HQ) .... B...... 310 743-3000
   10311 S La Cienega Blvd Los Angeles (90045) *(P-13077)*

Worldwind Services LLC .... A...... 661 822-4877
   1222 Vine St Ste 301 Paso Robles (93446) *(P-1877)*

Worldwise Inc (DH) .... D...... 415 721-7400
   6 Hamilton Landing Ste 150 Novato (94949) *(P-6957)*

Woven By Toyota US Inc .... B...... 808 221-7117
   900 Arastradero Rd Palo Alto (94304) *(P-12050)*

Woven Planet North America Inc, Palo Alto *Also Called: Woven By Toyota US Inc (P-12050)*

Wovexx Holdings Inc (DH) .... D...... 310 424-2080
   10381 Jefferson Blvd Culver City (90232) *(P-4559)*

Wpromote LLC (PA) .... D...... 310 421-4844
   101 Continental Blvd El Segundo (90245) *(P-20617)*

Wrangler Topco LLC .... A...... 415 439-1400
   555 California St Ste 2900 San Francisco (94104) *(P-5371)*

Wrc Huntington, San Francisco *Also Called: Hmb Investors LLC (P-9860)*

Wright Finlay & Zak LLP .... D...... 949 477-5050
   4665 Macarthur Ct Ste 200 Newport Beach (92660) *(P-17689)*

Wright Celebrations .... D...... 916 773-2133
   8845 Washington Blvd Ste 140 Roseville (95678) *(P-11065)*

Wright Contracting EPA, Santa Rosa *Also Called: Wright Contracting LLC (P-1066)*

Wright Contracting LLC .... D...... 707 528-1172
   3020 Dutton Ave Santa Rosa (95407) *(P-1066)*

Wright Ford Young & Co .... D...... 949 910-2727
   16140 Sand Canyon Ave Irvine (92618) *(P-19641)*

Wrights Supply Inc .... D...... 661 254-8400
   25838 Springbrook Ave Santa Clarita (91350) *(P-13759)*

Writers Guild America West Inc .... C...... 323 951-4000
   7000 W 3rd St Los Angeles (90048) *(P-18807)*

Writing Company, Gardena *Also Called: Social Studies School Service (P-5470)*

Wrs Materials, San Jose *Also Called: Pure Wafer Inc (P-2930)*

Wrs Materials, San Jose *Also Called: Wafer Reclaim Services LLC (P-2936)*

ALPHABETIC SECTION

YMCA

Ws Mmv Hotel LLC .... D....... 619 692-3800
  8757 Rio San Diego Dr San Diego (92108) *(P-10382)*

Wsa Group Inc .... A....... 310 743-3000
  19208 S Vermont Ave # 200 Gardena (90248) *(P-13078)*

WSB & Associates Inc .... C....... 415 864-3510
  150 Executive Park Blvd Ste 4700 San Francisco (94134) *(P-13079)*

Wsi, Pomona Also Called: Warehouse Specialists LLC *(P-3781)*

Wsm Investments LLC .... C....... 818 332-4600
  3990b Heritage Oak Ct Simi Valley (93063) *(P-9460)*

Wsp USA Inc .... D....... 714 973-4880
  15231 Laguna Canyon Rd Irvine (92618) *(P-19445)*

Wti Distribution Inc .... D....... 909 597-8410
  5491 E Francis St Ontario (91761) *(P-3787)*

Wtmg Inc .... C....... 209 888-6600
  3225 Tomahawk Dr Stockton (95205) *(P-10987)*

Wun, Goleta Also Called: Yardi Kube Inc *(P-12405)*

Wurl Inc .... D....... 662 649-8825
  591 Lytton Ave Palo Alto (94301) *(P-20255)*

Wurms Janitorial Service Inc .... D....... 951 582-0003
  601 S Milliken Ave Ontario (91761) *(P-10988)*

Wurth Louis and Company (DH) .... D....... 714 529-1771
  895 Columbia St Brea (92821) *(P-5740)*

Ww San Diego Harbor Island LLC .... C....... 619 291-6700
  1960 Harbor Island Dr San Diego (92101) *(P-10383)*

Wyndcrest Dd Florida, Los Angeles Also Called: Digital Domain Media Group Inc *(P-10806)*

Wyndham Anaheim Garden Grove, Garden Grove Also Called: Ohi Resort Hotels LLC *(P-10060)*

Wyndham Cntrbury At San Frncsc, San Francisco Also Called: Canterbury Hotel Corp *(P-9677)*

Wyndham Garden Fresno Airport, Fresno Also Called: Fresno Airport Hotels LLC *(P-9804)*

Wyndham Hotels & Resorts, Fullerton Also Called: Anaheim Park Hotel *(P-9610)*

Wyndham Indio, Indio Also Called: Wyndham Resort Dev Corp *(P-10384)*

Wyndham Residence, Arroyo Grande Also Called: Compass Health Inc *(P-18399)*

Wyndham Resort Dev Corp .... D....... 760 342-1040
  42151 Worldmark Way Indio (92203) *(P-10384)*

Wyndham San Diego Bayside, San Diego Also Called: Bhr Operations LLC *(P-9650)*

Wyse Technology LLC (DH) .... C....... 800 438-9973
  5455 Great America Pkwy Santa Clara (95054) *(P-5372)*

X Corp .... A....... 415 222-9670
  1355 Market St Ste 900 San Francisco (94103) *(P-12688)*

X-Act Finish & Trim Inc .... D....... 951 582-9229
  248 Glider Cir Corona (92878) *(P-2028)*

X3 Management Services Inc .... D....... 760 597-9336
  700 La Terraza Blvd Ste 110 Escondido (92025) *(P-1878)*

Xactly Corporation (HQ) .... D....... 408 977-3132
  221 Los Gatos Saratoga Rd Los Gatos (95030) *(P-12051)*

Xander Mortgage & Real Estate .... D....... 855 905-2575
  2520 W Shaw Ln Ste 106 Fresno (93711) *(P-8028)*

Xanterra Parks & Resorts Inc .... C....... 760 786-2345
  Hwy 190 Death Valley (92328) *(P-10385)*

Xbp Inc .... D....... 888 895-7116
  333 El Camino Real Ste 201 Tustin (92780) *(P-12052)*

XCEL, Palo Alto Also Called: Xcelmobility Inc *(P-12404)*

XCEL Mechanical Systems Inc .... C....... 310 660-0090
  1710 W 130th St Gardena (90249) *(P-1599)*

Xcelmobility Inc .... D....... 650 320-1728
  2225 E Bayshore Rd Ste 200 Palo Alto (94303) *(P-12404)*

Xcerra Corporation .... C....... 408 635-4300
  880 N Mccarthy Blvd Ste 100 Milpitas (95035) *(P-5717)*

Xcom Labs Inc .... D....... 858 987-9266
  9450 Carroll Park Dr San Diego (92121) *(P-20006)*

Xcommerce Inc (HQ) .... D....... 310 954-8012
  345 Park Ave San Jose (95110) *(P-12909)*

Xdbs Corporation .... C....... 844 932-7356
  3501 Jack Northrop Ave Hawthorne (90250) *(P-19857)*

Xdbs Corporation .... D....... 415 513-0068
  2400 Broadway St Ste 130 Redwood City (94063) *(P-20618)*

Xdbsb2b, Hawthorne Also Called: Xdbs Corporation *(P-19857)*

Xerox Corporation .... D....... 650 813-7138
  3333 Coyote Hill Rd Palo Alto (94304) *(P-5261)*

Xerox Education Services LLC (DH) .... D....... 310 830-9847
  2277 E 220th St Long Beach (90810) *(P-5262)*

Xgrass Turf Direct, Anaheim Also Called: Leonards Carpet Service Inc *(P-2504)*

Xgrid Inc .... C....... 408 242-7937
  6598 Alleghany Ct San Jose (95120) *(P-12053)*

Xi Enterprise Inc .... D....... 661 266-3200
  2140 E Palmdale Blvd Palmdale (93550) *(P-14244)*

Xilinx, San Jose Also Called: Xilinx Inc *(P-2911)*

Xilinx Inc (HQ) .... A....... 408 559-7778
  2100 Logic Dr San Jose (95124) *(P-2911)*

XI Construction Corporation .... D....... 916 282-2900
  1810 13th St Ste 110 Sacramento (95811) *(P-743)*

XI Construction Corporation (PA) .... B....... 408 240-6000
  851 Buckeye Ct Milpitas (95035) *(P-1067)*

XI Specialty Insurance Company .... B....... 925 942-6142
  1340 Treat Blvd Walnut Creek (94597) *(P-8435)*

XI Staffing Inc .... C....... 619 579-0442
  826 Jackman St El Cajon (92020) *(P-11263)*

Xld Group LLC .... D....... 310 316-3636
  3635 Fashion Way Torrance (90503) *(P-10386)*

Xojet Sales LLC .... C....... 877 599-6538
  2000 Sierra Point Pkwy Ste 200 Brisbane (94005) *(P-9584)*

Xoom Corporation .... C....... 415 777-4800
  425 Market St Ste 1200 San Francisco (94105) *(P-7862)*

Xoriant, Sunnyvale Also Called: Xoriant Corporation *(P-12910)*

Xoriant Corporation (PA) .... C....... 408 743-4400
  1248 Reamwood Ave Sunnyvale (94089) *(P-12910)*

Xp Power LLC (DH) .... D....... 408 732-7777
  990 Benecia Ave Sunnyvale (94085) *(P-5718)*

Xpo, Torrance Also Called: Lomita Logistics LLC *(P-10773)*

Xpo Cartage Inc .... D....... 800 837-7584
  5800 Sheila St Commerce (90040) *(P-3440)*

Xpo Logistics Freight Inc .... D....... 858 569-8921
  4965 Convoy St San Diego (92111) *(P-3566)*

Xpo Logistics Freight Inc .... D....... 209 983-8285
  5475 S Airport Way Stockton (95206) *(P-3567)*

Xpo Logistics Freight Inc .... D....... 408 435-3876
  2171 Otoole Ave San Jose (95131) *(P-3568)*

Xpo Logistics Freight Inc .... C....... 559 485-1164
  4195 E Central Ave Fresno (93725) *(P-3569)*

Xpo Logistics Freight Inc .... D....... 714 282-7717
  2102 N Batavia St Orange (92865) *(P-3570)*

Xpo Logistics Freight Inc .... D....... 916 399-8291
  3516 Kiessig Ave Sacramento (95823) *(P-3571)*

Xpo Logistics Freight Inc .... D....... 949 581-9030
  20697 Prism Pl Lake Forest (92630) *(P-3572)*

Xpo Logistics Freight Inc .... C....... 213 744-0664
  1955 E Washington Blvd Los Angeles (90021) *(P-3573)*

Xpo Logistics Freight Inc .... D....... 510 785-6920
  2200 Claremont Ct Hayward (94545) *(P-3574)*

Xpo Logistics Freight Inc .... D....... 951 685-1244
  13364 Marlay Ave Fontana (92337) *(P-3575)*

Xpo Logistics Freight Inc .... D....... 562 946-8331
  12903 Lakeland Rd Santa Fe Springs (90670) *(P-3576)*

Xpo Logistics Supply Chain Inc .... C....... 909 390-9799
  5200b E Airport Dr Ontario (91761) *(P-4120)*

Xponential Fitness Inc (PA) .... B....... 949 346-3000
  17877 Von Karman Ave Ste 100 Irvine (92614) *(P-14245)*

Xport Forwarding LLC .... D....... 949 354-0609
  620 Newport Center Dr Ste 1100 Newport Beach (92660) *(P-4121)*

Xq Institute .... D....... 844 825-5297
  248 3rd St Ste 319 Oakland (94607) *(P-19940)*

Xse Group Inc .... C....... 888 272-8340
  92 Argonaut Ste 235 Aliso Viejo (92656) *(P-6072)*

Xsens North America Inc., El Segundo Also Called: Movella Technologies NA Inc *(P-13867)*

Xsolla, Sherman Oaks Also Called: Xsolla (usa) Inc *(P-4359)*

Xsolla (usa) Inc (PA) .... A....... 818 435-6613
  15260 Ventura Blvd Ste 2230 Sherman Oaks (91403) *(P-4359)*

Xx Artists LLC .... D....... 503 871-5298
  12045 Waterfront Dr Ste 460 Los Angeles (90094) *(P-10822)*

Y M C A, Berkeley Also Called: Young MNS Chrstn Assn of E Bay *(P-18975)*

Y M C A Metro Clinic, Berkeley *Also Called: Young MNS Chrstn Assn of E Bay (P-18969)*
Y, The, San Diego *Also Called: YMCA of San Diego County (P-18939)*
Y&R-Wcj Spectrum, Irvine *Also Called: Young & Rubicam LLC (P-10692)*
Yaamava Rsort Csino At San Mnu, Highland *Also Called: San Manuel Entertainment Auth (P-14562)*
Yadav Enterprises Inc .... D...... 510 792-3393
   3550 Mowry Ave Ste 301 Fremont (94538) *(P-7519)*
Yahoo Cv LLC (HQ) .... D...... 408 349-3300
   701 First Ave Sunnyvale (94089) *(P-12643)*
Yahoo Cv LLC .... C...... 408 349-3300
   11985 Bluff Creek Dr Playa Vista (90094) *(P-12644)*
Yahoo Inc .... D...... 408 248-3589
   950 Teal Dr Santa Clara (95051) *(P-13558)*
Yale/Chase Equipment and Services Inc .... C...... 562 463-8000
   2615 Pellissier Pl City Of Industry (90601) *(P-5887)*
Yamaha Corporation of America (HQ) .... B...... 714 522-9011
   6600 Orangethorpe Ave Buena Park (90620) *(P-6058)*
Yamaha Motor Corporation USA (HQ) .... B...... 714 761-7300
   6555 Katella Ave Cypress (90630) *(P-7399)*
Yamaha Music Corporation U S A, Buena Park *Also Called: Yamaha Corporation of America (P-6058)*
Yamamoto of Orient Inc (HQ) .... C...... 909 594-7356
   122 Voyager St Pomona (91768) *(P-8785)*
Yamamotoyama of America, Pomona *Also Called: Yamamoto of Orient Inc (P-8785)*
Yamato Enterprises Inc .... D...... 408 677-3554
   1773 Creek Dr San Jose (95125) *(P-4122)*
Yammer Inc .... C...... 415 796-7400
   410 Townsend St San Francisco (94107) *(P-12911)*
Yanaco Inc .... C...... 530 246-9550
   151 N Boulder Dr Redding (96003) *(P-14317)*
Yanka Industries Inc .... B...... 855 981-8208
   660 4th St Ste 443 San Francisco (94107) *(P-14112)*
Yapstone Inc (PA) .... D...... 866 289-5977
   2121 N California Blvd Ste 400 Walnut Creek (94596) *(P-13559)*
Yardi Kube Inc .... D...... 805 699-2040
   430 S Fairview Ave Goleta (93117) *(P-12405)*
Yardi Systems Inc (PA) .... B...... 805 699-2040
   430 S Fairview Ave Santa Barbara (93117) *(P-12054)*
Yardzen Co .... D...... 415 729-0115
   480 Gate 5 Rd Sausalito (94965) *(P-471)*
Yasheng Group .... A...... 650 363-8345
   251 Ginko Ter Sunnyvale (94086) *(P-2641)*
YC Cable Usa Inc (HQ) .... D...... 510 824-2788
   48010 Fremont Blvd Fremont (94538) *(P-13560)*
YCUSD, Yuba City *Also Called: Yuba Cy Unified Schl Dst Fing C (P-18634)*
Yee Yuen Laundry and Clrs Inc .... D...... 323 734-7205
   2575 S Normandie Ave Los Angeles (90007) *(P-10459)*
Yee Yuen Linen Service, Los Angeles *Also Called: Yee Yuen Laundry and Clrs Inc (P-10459)*
Yefllow Shttle Vtrans Sdan Svc, San Leandro *Also Called: A-Para Transit Corp (P-3119)*
Yellow Jacket Drlg Svcs LLC .... C...... 909 989-8563
   9460 Lucas Ranch Rd Rancho Cucamonga (91730) *(P-2174)*
Yellow Luxury, Calabasas *Also Called: Abbyson Living Corp (P-5077)*
Yellowbrick Data Inc (PA) .... C...... 877 492-3282
   660 W Dana St Mountain View (94041) *(P-12645)*
Yellowpagescom LLC (DH) .... B...... 818 937-5500
   611 N Brand Blvd Ste 500 Glendale (91203) *(P-13561)*
Yelp Inc (PA) .... D...... 415 908-3801
   350 Mission St Fl 10 San Francisco (94105) *(P-12689)*
Yes Videocom Inc (PA) .... D...... 408 907-7600
   2805 Bowers Ave Ste 230 Santa Clara (95051) *(P-13921)*
Yesco, Jurupa Valley *Also Called: Young Electric Sign Company (P-3103)*
Yf Art Holdings Gp LLC .... A...... 678 441-1400
   9130 W Sunset Blvd Los Angeles (90069) *(P-9349)*
Ygrene Energy Fund Inc .... B...... 916 444-9700
   2600 Capitol Ave Ste 100 Sacramento (95816) *(P-20880)*
Yhb Long Beach LLC .... D...... 562 597-4401
   2640 N Lakewood Blvd Long Beach (90815) *(P-10387)*
Yhb San Francisco LLC .... D...... 415 421-7500
   85 5th St San Francisco (94103) *(P-10388)*
Ylopo LLC .... C...... 818 915-9150
   4712 Admiralty Way 548 Marina Del Rey (90292) *(P-9224)*

Ymarketing LLC .... D...... 714 545-2550
   4000 Macarthur Blvd Ste 350 Newport Beach (92660) *(P-20619)*
YMCA, Watsonville *Also Called: Central Coast YMCA (P-18833)*
YMCA, Torrance *Also Called: Young MNS Chrstn Assn Mtro Los (P-18957)*
YMCA, Los Angeles *Also Called: Young MNS Chrstn Assn Mtro Los (P-18960)*
YMCA, Berkeley *Also Called: Young MNS Chrstn Assn of E Bay (P-18985)*
YMCA, Berkeley *Also Called: Young MNS Chrstn Assn of E Bay (P-18987)*
YMCA, Newport Beach *Also Called: Young MNS Chrstn Assn Ornge CN (P-18989)*
YMCA, San Francisco *Also Called: Young MNS Chrstn Assn San Frnc (P-18995)*
YMCA, Alhambra *Also Called: Young Men Chrstn Assoc W San G (P-19031)*
YMCA After School-Olinda, Richmond *Also Called: Young MNS Chrstn Assn of E Bay (P-18986)*
YMCA Camp Edwards, Angelus Oaks *Also Called: YMCA of East Valley (P-18934)*
YMCA Child Care Chadbourne, Fremont *Also Called: Young MNS Chrstn Assn of E Bay (P-18976)*
YMCA Child Care Resource Svcs, San Diego *Also Called: YMCA of San Diego County (P-18948)*
YMCA Crescenta-Canada, La Canada *Also Called: Crescenta-Canada YMCA (P-18848)*
YMCA Elementary School, Mountain View *Also Called: Young MNS Chrstn Assn of E Bay (P-18974)*
YMCA Head Start, Berkeley *Also Called: Young MNS Chrstn Assn of E Bay (P-18970)*
YMCA of East Bay, Oakland *Also Called: Young MNS Chrstn Assn of E Bay (P-18967)*
YMCA of East Valley (PA) .... C...... 909 798-9622
   500 E Citrus Ave Redlands (92373) *(P-18933)*
YMCA of East Valley .... C...... 909 794-1702
   42842 Jenks Lake Rd E Angelus Oaks (92305) *(P-18934)*
YMCA of East Valley .... C...... 909 881-9622
   808 E 21st St San Bernardino (92404) *(P-18935)*
YMCA of East Valley .... D...... 909 425-9622
   7793 Central Ave Highland (92346) *(P-18936)*
YMCA of Redwoods, Boulder Creek *Also Called: Young MNS Chrstn Assn Slcon Vl (P-19005)*
YMCA of San Diego County .... D...... 858 496-9622
   5105 Overland Ave San Diego (92123) *(P-18937)*
YMCA of San Diego County .... B...... 858 453-3483
   8355 Cliffridge Ave La Jolla (92037) *(P-18938)*
YMCA of San Diego County (PA) .... B...... 858 292-9622
   3708 Ruffin Rd San Diego (92123) *(P-18939)*
YMCA of San Diego County .... C...... 619 428-1168
   3085 Beyer Blvd Ste 105 San Diego (92154) *(P-18940)*
YMCA of San Diego County .... C...... 760 745-7490
   200 Saxony Rd Encinitas (92024) *(P-18941)*
YMCA of San Diego County .... C...... 619 464-1323
   8881 Dallas St La Mesa (91942) *(P-18942)*
YMCA of San Diego County .... B...... 619 280-9622
   5505 Friars Rd San Diego (92110) *(P-18943)*
YMCA of San Diego County .... B...... 858 292-4034
   200 Saxony Rd Encinitas (92024) *(P-18944)*
YMCA of San Diego County .... C...... 619 281-8313
   2927 Meade Ave San Diego (92116) *(P-18945)*
YMCA of San Diego County .... B...... 619 226-8888
   2150 Beryl St Ste 18 San Diego (92109) *(P-18946)*
YMCA of San Diego County .... C...... 619 264-0144
   5505 Friars Rd San Diego (92110) *(P-18947)*
YMCA of San Diego County .... C...... 619 521-3055
   3333 Camino Del Rio S Ste 400 San Diego (92108) *(P-18948)*
YMCA of San Diego County .... C...... 760 765-0642
   4761 Pine Hills Rd Julian (92036) *(P-18949)*
YMCA of San Diego County .... B...... 619 298-3576
   5505 Friars Rd San Diego (92110) *(P-18950)*
YMCA of San Diego County .... C...... 760 758-0808
   200 Saxony Rd Encinitas (92024) *(P-18951)*
YMCA of San Diego County .... C...... 760 721-8930
   215 Barnes St Oceanside (92054) *(P-18952)*
YMCA of Santa Clara Valley, San Jose *Also Called: Young MNS Chrstn Assn Slcon Vl (P-19003)*
YMCA of Santa Clara Valley, San Jose *Also Called: Young MNS Chrstn Assn Slcon Vl (P-19004)*
YMCA OF THE FOOTHILLS, La Canada *Also Called: Young MNS Chrstn Assn of Fthll (P-18988)*
YMCA of Westchester, Los Angeles *Also Called: Young MNS Chrstn Assn Mtro Los (P-18961)*

ALPHABETIC SECTION

Young MNS Chrstn Assn of E Bay

YMCA Overnight Camp, Julian *Also Called: YMCA of San Diego County (P-18949)*

YMCA Pre School Hillview, Richmond *Also Called: Young MNS Chrstn Assn of E Bay (P-18972)*

YMCA Pt Bnita Otdoor Cnfrnce C, Sausalito *Also Called: Young MNS Chrstn Assn San Frnc (P-18997)*

YMCA San Benito County, Hollister *Also Called: Central Coast YMCA (P-18832)*

YMCA Sch Age Pgrm Durham, Fremont *Also Called: Young MNS Chrstn Assn of E Bay (P-18983)*

YMCA Youth & Family Services, San Diego *Also Called: YMCA of San Diego County (P-18945)*

Ymcasf, San Rafael *Also Called: Young MNS Chrstn Assn San Frnc (P-18991)*

Yoga Shelter, Studio City *Also Called: Yoga Shelter LLC (P-14587)*

Yoga Shelter LLC ....D....... 818 691-3000
  12408 Ventura Blvd Studio City (91604) *(P-14587)*

Yoga Source Partners LLC ....D....... 408 402-9642
  16185 Los Gatos Blvd Los Gatos (95032) *(P-14588)*

Yogasource, Los Gatos *Also Called: Yoga Source Partners LLC (P-14588)*

Yogaworks Inc (HQ) ....D....... 310 664-6470
  5780 Uplander Way Culver City (90230) *(P-14589)*

Yokohama Corp North America (HQ) ....C....... 540 389-5426
  1 Macarthur Pl Santa Ana (92707) *(P-2653)*

Yokohama Tire, Santa Ana *Also Called: Yokohama Corp North America (P-2653)*

Yokohama Tire Corporation (DH) ....C....... 714 870-3800
  1 Macarthur Pl Ste 800 Santa Ana (92707) *(P-5076)*

Yokohama Tire USA, Santa Ana *Also Called: Yokohama Tire Corporation (P-5076)*

Yolo County Trnsp Dist, Woodland *Also Called: County of Yolo (P-4000)*

Yorba Bena Ice Skting Bowl Ctr, San Francisco *Also Called: VSC Sports Inc (P-20877)*

Yorba Park Medical Group, Santa Ana *Also Called: St Jseph Heritg Med Group LLC (P-15098)*

York Enterprises South Inc ....D....... 714 842-6611
  18255 Beach Blvd Huntington Beach (92648) *(P-7336)*

Yosemite Concession Services, Yosemite Ntpk *Also Called: DNC Prks Rsrts At Yosemite Inc (P-9757)*

Yosemite Farm Credit Aca (PA) ....D....... 209 667-2366
  806 W Monte Vista Ave Turlock (95382) *(P-7868)*

Yosemite Foods Inc ....C....... 209 990-5400
  4221 E Mariposa Rd Stockton (95215) *(P-6509)*

Yosemite Lakes Owners Assn ....D....... 559 658-7466
  30250 Yosemite Springs Pkwy Unit A Coarsegold (93614) *(P-18953)*

Yosemite Meat Company Inc ....D....... 209 524-5117
  601 Zeff Rd Modesto (95351) *(P-6510)*

Yosemite Technologies Inc ....D....... 559 449-8181
  7435 N Ingram Ave Fresno (93711) *(P-12055)*

Yosh Enterprises Inc (PA) ....C....... 408 287-4411
  675 E Gish Rd San Jose (95112) *(P-13080)*

Yoshimura RES & Dev Amer Inc ....D....... 909 628-4722
  5420 Daniels St Ste A Chino (91710) *(P-5068)*

You ME and Sciences Inc ....D....... 310 406-7350
  202 W Manchester Ave Playa Del Rey (90293) *(P-14113)*

Yougov & Polimetrix Co, Redwood City *Also Called: Yougov America Inc (P-19528)*

Yougov America Inc ....B....... 650 462-8000
  999 Main St Ste 101 Redwood City (94063) *(P-19528)*

Young & Rubicam LLC ....C....... 949 754-2100
  7535 Irvine Center Dr Irvine (92618) *(P-10691)*

Young & Rubicam LLC ....B....... 949 754-2000
  7535 Irvine Center Dr Irvine (92618) *(P-10692)*

Young & Rubicam LLC ....C....... 213 930-5000
  4751 Wilshire Blvd Ste 201 Los Angeles (90010) *(P-10693)*

Young & Rubicam LLC ....C....... 415 365-1700
  1001 Front St San Francisco (94111) *(P-10823)*

Young & Rubicam LLC ....B....... 949 224-6300
  1735 Irvine Center Dr Irvine (92618) *(P-20620)*

Young & Rubicam LLC ....C....... 650 287-4000
  100 Pine St Ste 2300 San Francisco (94111) *(P-20644)*

Young Brdcstg of San Francisco ....D....... 415 441-4444
  900 Front St San Francisco (94111) *(P-4471)*

Young Communications, San Francisco *Also Called: Young Electric Co (P-1879)*

Young Electric Co ....C....... 415 648-3355
  195 Erie St San Francisco (94103) *(P-1879)*

Young Electric Sign Company ....C....... 909 923-7668
  10235 Bellegrave Ave Jurupa Valley (91752) *(P-3103)*

Young Men Chrstn Assoc W San G (PA) ....D....... 626 576-0226
  401 Corto St Alhambra (91801) *(P-19031)*

Young Men's Christian Assoc, Thousand Oaks *Also Called: Young MNS Chrstn Assn Sthast V (P-19006)*

Young Mens Christian Association of The East Bay ....A....... 510 451-8039
  2350 Broadway Oakland (94612) *(P-18954)*

Young Mens Christn Assocation, Highland *Also Called: YMCA of East Valley (P-18936)*

Young Mens Christn Assocation, La Mesa *Also Called: YMCA of San Diego County (P-18942)*

Young Mens Christn Assocation, San Jose *Also Called: Young MNS Chrstn Assn Slcon Vl (P-19000)*

Young MNS Chrstn Assn Brbank C (PA) ....D....... 818 845-8551
  321 E Magnolia Blvd Burbank (91502) *(P-18955)*

Young MNS Chrstn Assn Glndale ....D....... 818 484-8256
  140 N Louise St Glendale (91206) *(P-18956)*

Young MNS Chrstn Assn Mtro Los ....D....... 310 325-5885
  2900 Sepulveda Blvd Torrance (90505) *(P-18957)*

Young MNS Chrstn Assn Mtro Los ....D....... 818 989-3800
  6901 Lennox Ave Van Nuys (91405) *(P-18958)*

Young MNS Chrstn Assn Mtro Los ....D....... 323 588-2256
  4801 E 58th St Maywood (90270) *(P-18959)*

Young MNS Chrstn Assn Mtro Los (PA) ....D....... 213 380-6448
  625 S New Hampshire Ave Los Angeles (90005) *(P-18960)*

Young MNS Chrstn Assn Mtro Los ....D....... 310 216-9036
  8015 S Sepulveda Blvd Los Angeles (90045) *(P-18961)*

Young MNS Chrstn Assn Mtro Los ....C....... 323 467-4161
  1553 Schrader Blvd Los Angeles (90028) *(P-18962)*

Young MNS Chrstn Assn of E Bay ....B....... 510 654-9622
  3265 Market St Oakland (94608) *(P-18963)*

Young MNS Chrstn Assn of E Bay ....C....... 510 412-5644
  200 Lake Ave Rodeo (94572) *(P-18964)*

Young MNS Chrstn Assn of E Bay ....B....... 510 412-5640
  1250 23rd St Richmond (94804) *(P-18965)*

Young MNS Chrstn Assn of E Bay ....C....... 925 609-7971
  1705 Thornwood Dr Concord (94521) *(P-18966)*

Young MNS Chrstn Assn of E Bay ....A....... 510 451-8039
  2350 Broadway Oakland (94612) *(P-18967)*

Young MNS Chrstn Assn of E Bay ....B....... 510 601-8674
  4727 San Pablo Ave Emeryville (94608) *(P-18968)*

Young MNS Chrstn Assn of E Bay ....B....... 510 486-8400
  2111 Martin Luther King Jr Way Berkeley (94704) *(P-18969)*

Young MNS Chrstn Assn of E Bay ....B....... 510 848-9092
  2009 10th St Berkeley (94710) *(P-18970)*

Young MNS Chrstn Assn of E Bay ....A....... 510 848-9622
  2001 Allston Way Berkeley (94704) *(P-18971)*

Young MNS Chrstn Assn of E Bay ....C....... 510 223-7070
  3800 Clark Rd Richmond (94803) *(P-18972)*

Young MNS Chrstn Assn of E Bay ....B....... 510 526-2146
  1130 Oxford St Berkeley (94707) *(P-18973)*

Young MNS Chrstn Assn of E Bay ....B....... 650 526-3500
  505 Escuela Ave Mountain View (94040) *(P-18974)*

Young MNS Chrstn Assn of E Bay ....C....... 510 644-6290
  2241 Russell St Berkeley (94705) *(P-18975)*

Young MNS Chrstn Assn of E Bay ....B....... 510 656-7243
  801 Plymouth Ave Fremont (94539) *(P-18976)*

Young MNS Chrstn Assn of E Bay ....A....... 510 222-9622
  4300 Lakeside Dr Ste 150 Richmond (94806) *(P-18977)*

Young MNS Chrstn Assn of E Bay ....A....... 510 412-5647
  263 S 20th St Richmond (94804) *(P-18978)*

Young MNS Chrstn Assn of E Bay ....B....... 510 222-9622
  4300 Lakeside Dr Richmond (94806) *(P-18979)*

Young MNS Chrstn Assn of E Bay ....B....... 925 475-6100
  5000 Pleasanton Ave Ste 200 Pleasanton (94566) *(P-18980)*

Young MNS Chrstn Assn of E Bay ....B....... 510 534-7441
  1612 45th Ave Oakland (94601) *(P-18981)*

Young MNS Chrstn Assn of E Bay ....B....... 510 683-9165
  41811 Blacow Rd Fremont (94538) *(P-18982)*

Young MNS Chrstn Assn of E Bay ....C....... 510 683-9107
  40292 Leslie St 402 Fremont (94538) *(P-18983)*

Young MNS Chrstn Assn of E Bay ....C....... 510 683-9147
  47100 Fernald St 471 Fremont (94539) *(P-18984)*

Young MNS Chrstn Assn of E Bay ....C....... 510 848-6800
  2001 Allston Way Berkeley (94704) *(P-18985)*

Employee Codes: A=Over 500 employees, B=251-500
C=101-250, D=51-100, E=20-50, F=10-19, G=1-9

Young MNS Chrstn Assn of E Bay .... C...... 510 262-6588
5855 Olinda Rd Richmond (94803) *(P-18986)*

Young MNS Chrstn Assn of E Bay .... B...... 510 559-2090
1422 San Pablo Ave Berkeley (94702) *(P-18987)*

Young MNS Chrstn Assn of Fthll .... D...... 818 790-0123
1930 Foothill Blvd La Canada (91011) *(P-18988)*

Young MNS Chrstn Assn Ornge CN .... D...... 949 495-9622
29831 Crown Valley Pkwy Laguna Niguel (92677) *(P-14485)*

Young MNS Chrstn Assn Ornge CN .... D...... 949 642-9990
2300 University Dr Newport Beach (92660) *(P-18989)*

Young MNS Chrstn Assn Ornge CN .... D...... 949 859-9622
27341 Trabuco Cir Mission Viejo (92692) *(P-18990)*

Young MNS Chrstn Assn San Frnc .... D...... 415 492-9622
1500 Los Gamos Dr San Rafael (94903) *(P-18991)*

Young MNS Chrstn Assn San Frnc .... D...... 415 447-9622
63 Funston Ave San Francisco (94129) *(P-18992)*

Young MNS Chrstn Assn San Frnc .... C...... 650 286-9622
1877 S Grant St San Mateo (94402) *(P-18993)*

Young MNS Chrstn Assn San Frnc .... C...... 650 747-1200
11000 Pescadero Rd La Honda (94020) *(P-18994)*

Young MNS Chrstn Assn San Frnc .... C...... 415 957-9622
169 Steuart St San Francisco (94105) *(P-18995)*

Young MNS Chrstn Assn San Frnc .... D...... 415 885-0460
246 Eddy St San Francisco (94102) *(P-18996)*

Young MNS Chrstn Assn San Frnc .... C...... 415 331-9622
981 Fort Barry Sausalito (94965) *(P-18997)*

Young MNS Chrstn Assn San Frnc .... C...... 415 586-6900
4080 Mission St San Francisco (94112) *(P-18998)*

Young MNS Chrstn Assn Slcon VI (PA) .... D...... 408 351-6400
80 Saratoga Ave Santa Clara (95051) *(P-18999)*

Young MNS Chrstn Assn Slcon VI .... D...... 650 493-9622
1922 The Alameda Ste 300 San Jose (95126) *(P-19000)*

Young MNS Chrstn Assn Slcon VI .... C...... 408 298-1717
1717 The Alameda San Jose (95126) *(P-19001)*

Young MNS Chrstn Assn Slcon VI .... C...... 650 969-9622
2400 Grant Rd Mountain View (94040) *(P-19002)*

Young MNS Chrstn Assn Slcon VI .... C...... 408 226-9622
5632 Santa Teresa Blvd San Jose (95123) *(P-19003)*

Young MNS Chrstn Assn Slcon VI .... D...... 408 729-4223
1855 Majestic Way San Jose (95132) *(P-19004)*

Young MNS Chrstn Assn Slcon VI .... B...... 831 338-2128
16275 Highway 9 Boulder Creek (95006) *(P-19005)*

Young MNS Chrstn Assn Slcon VI .... C...... 408 370-1877
13500 Quito Rd Saratoga (95070) *(P-19122)*

Young MNS Chrstn Assn Sthast V .... D...... 805 583-5338
3200 Cochran St Simi Valley (93065) *(P-14590)*

Young MNS Chrstn Assn Sthast V .... D...... 805 523-7613
4031 N Moorpark Rd Thousand Oaks (91360) *(P-19006)*

Young Wns Chrstn Assn Grter Lo .... C...... 323 295-4280
2501 W Vernon Ave Los Angeles (90008) *(P-19007)*

Young Wns Chrstn Assn Grter Lo .... C...... 323 295-4288
2519 W Vernon Ave Los Angeles (90008) *(P-19008)*

Youngdahl Consulting Group Inc .... D...... 916 933-0633
1234 Glenhaven Ct El Dorado Hills (95762) *(P-19446)*

Youngs Holdings Inc (PA) .... D...... 714 368-4615
15 Enterprise Ste 100 Aliso Viejo (92656) *(P-6813)*

Youngs Market Company LLC (HQ) .... B...... 800 317-6150
14402 Franklin Ave Tustin (92780) *(P-6814)*

Youngs Market Company LLC .... C...... 408 782-3121
850 Jarvis Dr Morgan Hill (95037) *(P-6815)*

Youngs Market Company LLC .... B...... 213 629-3929
500 S Central Ave Los Angeles (90013) *(P-6816)*

Youngstown Grape Distrs Inc .... C...... 559 638-2271
1625 G St Reedley (93654) *(P-320)*

Your Practice Online LLC (PA) .... C...... 877 388-8569
4590 Macarthur Blvd Ste 500 Newport Beach (92660) *(P-20621)*

Your Way Fumigation Inc .... D...... 951 699-9116
1660 Chicago Ave Ste N9 Riverside (92507) *(P-10844)*

Your Wireless Retailer Inc .... D...... 310 293-3706
3540 Riverside Plaza Dr Ste 338 Riverside (92506) *(P-4245)*

Yourmechanic, Burlingame *Also Called: Yourmechanic Inc (P-13679)*

Yourmechanic Inc .... C...... 215 253-7941
520 San Antonio Rd Ste 110 Mountain View (94040) *(P-13722)*

Yourmechanic Inc .... D...... 800 701-6230
20 Park Rd Ste H Burlingame (94010) *(P-13679)*

Yourpeople Inc .... A...... 888 249-3263
50 Beale St Ste 1000 San Francisco (94105) *(P-12406)*

Youth For Change (PA) .... C...... 530 877-8187
260 Cohasset Rd Ste 120 Chico (95926) *(P-18197)*

Youth Services, Long Beach *Also Called: Altamed Health Services Corp (P-17174)*

Ytel Inc .... D...... 800 382-4913
26632 Towne Centre Dr Ste 300 Lake Forest (92610) *(P-4360)*

Yti, San Pedro *Also Called: Yusen Terminals LLC (P-3820)*

Yuba Cnty Prbtion Chldren Fmli, Marysville *Also Called: County of Yuba (P-17943)*

Yuba Community College Dst .... D...... 530 788-0973
2088 N Beale Rd Marysville (95901) *(P-18198)*

Yuba County Juvenile Hall, Marysville *Also Called: County of Yuba (P-18405)*

Yuba County Probation Dept, Marysville *Also Called: County of Yuba (P-17944)*

Yuba Cy Unfied Schl Dst Fing C .... A...... 530 822-7601
425 Plumas Blvd Yuba City (95991) *(P-18634)*

Yubico Inc .... B...... 408 774-4064
5201 Great America Pkwy Ste 122 Santa Clara (95054) *(P-5263)*

Yucaipa Companies LLC (PA) .... C...... 310 789-7200
9130 W Sunset Blvd Los Angeles (90069) *(P-20881)*

Yucaipa Disposal Inc .... D...... 909 429-4200
9890 Cherry Ave Fontana (92335) *(P-4972)*

Yue Feng Inc .... D...... 310 253-9795
145 S Fairfax Ave Los Angeles (90036) *(P-18199)*

Yugabytedb Inc (PA) .... B...... 408 663-6632
771 Vaqueros Ave Sunnyvale (94085) *(P-12056)*

Yuja Inc .... C...... 888 257-2278
84 W Santa Clara St Ste 400 San Jose (95113) *(P-12407)*

Yuma Lakes Resort, Earp *Also Called: Colorado River Adventures Inc (P-10416)*

Yume, San Francisco *Also Called: Yume Inc (P-10694)*

Yume Inc (HQ) .... B...... 650 591-9400
601 Montgomery St Ste 1600 San Francisco (94111) *(P-10694)*

Yuneec USA, Rancho Cucamonga *Also Called: Yuneec USA Inc (P-5719)*

Yuneec USA Inc .... D...... 855 284-8888
9227 Haven Ave Ste 210 Rancho Cucamonga (91730) *(P-5719)*

Yusen Logistics Americas Inc .... C...... 310 518-3008
2417 E Carson St Ste 100 Carson (90810) *(P-4123)*

Yusen Terminals LLC (DH) .... D...... 310 548-8000
701 New Dock St San Pedro (90731) *(P-3820)*

Yva.ai, Santa Clara *Also Called: Yvaai Inc (P-12057)*

Yvaai Inc .... D...... 650 704-5503
2445 Augustine Dr Ste 150 Santa Clara (95054) *(P-12057)*

YWCA, Martinez *Also Called: YWCA Contra Costa/Sacramento (P-18200)*

YWCA, Los Angeles *Also Called: Young Wns Chrstn Assn Grter Lo (P-19007)*

YWCA, San Jose *Also Called: YWCA Golden Gate Silicon Vly (P-19009)*

YWCA Contra Costa/Sacramento (PA) .... D...... 925 372-4213
1320 Arnold Dr Ste 170 Martinez (94553) *(P-18200)*

YWCA Golden Gate Silicon Vly .... D...... 408 295-4011
375 S 3rd St San Jose (95112) *(P-19009)*

Yyk Enterprises Operations LLC (PA) .... C...... 619 474-6229
3475 E St San Diego (92102) *(P-2336)*

Z Willing J A Henckels, Commerce *Also Called: Zwilling JA Henckels LLC (P-5144)*

Z-Best Concrete Inc .... D...... 951 774-1870
2575 Main St Riverside (92501) *(P-2171)*

Z57 Inc .... C...... 858 623-5577
2443 Impala Dr Ste B Carlsbad (92010) *(P-12646)*

Za Management .... D...... 310 271-2200
101 N Robertson Blvd Beverly Hills (90211) *(P-20256)*

Zabin Industries Inc (PA) .... D...... 213 749-1215
3957 S Hill St Ste A Los Angeles (90037) *(P-6165)*

Zacharias, Don M MD, Sacramento *Also Called: University California Davis (P-15160)*

Zadaonet .... D...... 650 556-6377
685 Scofield Ave Apt 22 East Palo Alto (94303) *(P-4361)*

Zambezi LLC .... D...... 310 450-6800
3522 Hayden Ave Culver City (90232) *(P-10724)*

Zanger Vineyards, Hollister *Also Called: CDF Parkway LLC (P-7156)*

Zantaz Inc .... B...... 925 598-3000
5758 W Las Positas Blvd Pleasanton (94588) *(P-12058)*

ALPHABETIC SECTION

Zaplabs LLC (DH) .... D
 2000 Powell St Ste 700 Emeryville (94608) *(P-9225)*

Zappos Ip Inc .... A...... 702 943-7725
 121 2nd St Fl 3 San Francisco (94105) *(P-12059)*

Zastrow Construction Inc .... D...... 323 478-1956
 3267 Verdugo Rd Los Angeles (90065) *(P-786)*

Zazmic Inc (PA) .... C...... 415 728-1621
 156 2nd St San Francisco (94105) *(P-12060)*

Zbs Law LLP .... D...... 714 848-7920
 30 Corporate Park Ste 450 Irvine (92606) *(P-17690)*

Zeco Systems Inc .... D...... 888 751-8560
 767 S Alameda St Ste 200 Los Angeles (90021) *(P-6720)*

Zef SCI, San Diego Also Called: Zef Scientific Inc *(P-13813)*

Zef Scientific Inc (PA) .... D...... 781 791-5799
 9920 Pacific Heights Blvd Ste 150 San Diego (92121) *(P-13813)*

Zefr Inc .... B...... 310 392-3555
 4101 Redwood Ave Los Angeles (90066) *(P-19858)*

Zelar Soft LLC .... C...... 510 262-2801
 595 Pacific Ave Fl 4 San Francisco (94133) *(P-12545)*

Zendesk, San Francisco Also Called: Zendesk Inc *(P-12408)*

Zendesk Inc (HQ) .... C...... 415 418-7506
 989 Market St San Francisco (94103) *(P-12408)*

Zenith A Fairfax Company, The, Woodland Hills Also Called: Zenith Insurance Company *(P-8426)*

Zenith Insurance Company (DH) .... B...... 818 713-1000
 21255 Califa St Woodland Hills (91367) *(P-8426)*

Zenlayer Inc .... B...... 909 718-3558
 21680 Gateway Center Dr Ste 350 Diamond Bar (91765) *(P-4362)*

Zenleads Inc .... B...... 415 640-9303
 440 N Barranca Ave # 4750 Covina (91723) *(P-20622)*

Zennify LLC .... D...... 208 739-2118
 1755 Creekside Oaks Dr Sacramento (95833) *(P-12061)*

Zeno Group Inc .... D...... 650 801-7950
 275 Shoreline Dr Ste 530 Redwood City (94065) *(P-20909)*

Zenput Inc .... D...... 800 537-0227
 548 Market St San Francisco (94104) *(P-12062)*

Zeons Inc .... B...... 323 302-8299
 291 S La Cienega Blvd Ste 102 Beverly Hills (90211) *(P-2690)*

Zep Inc .... C...... 877 428-9937
 1000 Railroad St Corona (92882) *(P-6716)*

Zephyr Realestate .... D...... 415 552-9500
 4040 24th St San Francisco (94114) *(P-9226)*

Zerep Management Corporation (PA) .... C...... 626 855-5522
 17445 Railroad St City Of Industry (91748) *(P-4973)*

Zero, Campbell Also Called: Zero Cognitive Systems Inc *(P-12063)*

Zero Cognitive Systems Inc .... D...... 650 720-2324
 1475 S Bascom Ave Ste 204 Campbell (95008) *(P-12063)*

Zero Energy Contracting Inc .... C...... 626 701-3180
 13850 Cerritos Corporate Dr Ste D Cerritos (90703) *(P-1600)*

Zero Energy Contracting LLC .... D...... 626 701-3180
 13850 Cerritos Corporate Dr Ste D Cerritos (90703) *(P-1601)*

Zero Gravity Consulting LLC .... A...... 310 989-7989
 458 N Doheny Dr West Hollywood (90069) *(P-20882)*

Zero Gravity Management .... D...... 310 656-9440
 11110 Ohio Ave Ste 100 Los Angeles (90025) *(P-20257)*

Zero Waste Solutions, Concord Also Called: Zero Waste Solutions Inc *(P-20668)*

Zero Waste Solutions Inc .... C...... 925 270-3339
 1850 Gateway Blvd Ste 1030 Concord (94520) *(P-20668)*

Zest Anchors LLC .... D...... 760 743-7744
 2230 Enterprise St Escondido (92029) *(P-5461)*

Zest Dental Solutions, Escondido Also Called: Zest Anchors LLC *(P-5461)*

Zest.ai, Burbank Also Called: Zestfinance Inc *(P-12064)*

Zestfinance Inc .... D...... 323 450-3000
 3900 W Alameda Ave Ste 1600 Burbank (91505) *(P-12064)*

Zetterlund, Patrik MD, Salinas Also Called: Central Cast Crdlgy A Med Corp *(P-14672)*

Zettler Components Inc (PA) .... C...... 949 831-5000
 75 Columbia Orange (92868) *(P-2904)*

Zeus, Valley Village Also Called: Zeus Networks LLC *(P-14114)*

Zeus Networks LLC .... D...... 323 910-4420
 11713 Riverside Dr Valley Village (91607) *(P-14114)*

Zhg Inc .... D...... 831 394-3321
 2600 Sand Dunes Dr Monterey (93940) *(P-10389)*

Zhoug Hong .... D...... 415 647-7742
 1 Harbor Dr Sausalito (94965) *(P-18201)*

Ziffren B B F G-L S&C Fnd .... C...... 310 552-3388
 1801 Century Park W Fl 7 Los Angeles (90067) *(P-17691)*

Zignal Labs Inc .... D...... 415 683-7871
 600 California St Fl 11 San Francisco (94108) *(P-12065)*

Zillow Inc .... D...... 877 215-8423
 535 Mission St San Francisco (94105) *(P-20623)*

Zim Industries Inc .... C...... 661 393-9661
 7212 Fruitvale Ave Bakersfield (93308) *(P-2175)*

Zim Industries Inc (PA) .... **D...... 559 834-1551**
 4532 E Jefferson Ave Fresno (93725) *(P-1283)*

Zimeno Inc .... C...... 833 247-4797
 203 Lawrence Dr Ste A Livermore (94551) *(P-20624)*

Zimmer Dental Inc .... B...... 800 854-7019
 1900 Aston Ave Carlsbad (92008) *(P-3065)*

Zimmer Gnsul Frsca Archtcts LL .... C...... 213 617-1901
 515 S Flower St Ste 3700 Los Angeles (90071) *(P-19522)*

Zimmer Gnsul Frsca Partnr Amer, Los Angeles Also Called: Zimmer Gnsul Frsca Archtcts LL *(P-19522)*

Zimmerman Roofing Inc .... D...... 916 454-3667
 3675 R St Sacramento (95816) *(P-2093)*

Zinier Inc .... C...... 787 504-4826
 3182 Campus Dr Ste 333 San Mateo (94403) *(P-12912)*

Zinio Systems Inc .... D...... 415 494-2700
 114 Sansome St 4th Fl San Francisco (94104) *(P-12409)*

Zions Bancorporation .... A...... 424 290-5123
 200 N Pacific Coast Hwy Ste 1850 El Segundo (90245) *(P-11264)*

Zions Bank, El Segundo Also Called: Zions Bancorporation *(P-11264)*

Zip-Chem Products, Morgan Hill Also Called: Andpak Inc *(P-13192)*

Zipline, South San Francisco Also Called: Zipline International Inc *(P-20625)*

Zipline International Inc .... C...... 508 340-3291
 333 Corey Way South San Francisco (94080) *(P-12066)*

Zipline International Inc .... C...... 408 475-8625
 333 Corey Way South San Francisco (94080) *(P-20625)*

ZIPRECRUITER, Santa Monica Also Called: Ziprecruiter Inc *(P-20626)*

Ziprecruiter Inc .... A...... 877 252-1062
 604 Arizona Ave Santa Monica (90401) *(P-20626)*

ZI Technologies Inc (PA) .... **D...... 408 240-8989**
 860 N Mccarthy Blvd Ste 100 Milpitas (95035) *(P-12067)*

Zocalo .... D...... 415 293-1600
 1551 Bancroft Ave 1508 San Francisco (94124) *(P-5109)*

Zodiac Inflight Innovations US, Brea Also Called: Safran Pass Innovations LLC *(P-11894)*

Zodiac Pool Systems LLC .... D...... 760 599-9600
 2611 Commerce Way Ste B Vista (92081) *(P-2337)*

Zoe Holding Company Inc .... C...... 415 421-4900
 44 Montgomery St San Francisco (94104) *(P-20910)*

Zoek, Irvine Also Called: Online Marketing Group LLC *(P-20495)*

Zoho Corporation .... B...... 925 924-9500
 4900 Hopyard Rd Ste 310 Pleasanton (94588) *(P-19447)*

Zoho Corporation .... B...... 925 924-9500
 4141 Hacienda Dr Pleasanton (94588) *(P-20627)*

Zoic Inc .... C...... 310 838-0770
 3582 Eastham Dr Culver City (90232) *(P-13922)*

Zoic Studios, Culver City Also Called: Zoic Inc *(P-13922)*

Zonare, Mountain View Also Called: Zonare Medical Systems Inc *(P-19941)*

Zonare Medical Systems Inc .... D...... 650 230-2800
 420 Bernardo Ave Mountain View (94043) *(P-19941)*

Zonda Intelligence, Newport Beach Also Called: Metrostudy Inc *(P-20468)*

Zoo, El Segundo Also Called: Zoo Digital Production LLC *(P-13923)*

Zoo Digital Production LLC .... C...... 310 220-3939
 2201 Park Pl Ste 100 El Segundo (90245) *(P-13923)*

Zoo Med Laboratories Inc .... C...... 805 542-9988
 3650 Sacramento Dr San Luis Obispo (93401) *(P-3114)*

Zoological Society San Diego .... D...... 619 718-3000
 123 Camino De La Reina Ste 100s San Diego (92108) *(P-6839)*

Zoological Society San Diego .... C...... 619 744-3325
 2920 Zoo Dr San Diego (92101) *(P-18695)*

Zoological Society San Diego .... C...... 760 747-8702
 15500 San Pasqual Valley Rd Escondido (92027) *(P-18696)*

Zoological Society San Diego .... C...... 619 231-1515
   10946 Willow Ct Ste 200 San Diego (92127) *(P-18697)*
Zoological Society San Diego (PA) .... A...... 619 231-1515
   2920 Zoo Dr San Diego (92101) *(P-18698)*
Zoom, San Jose *Also Called: Zoom Video Communications Inc (P-12068)*
Zoom Video Communications Inc (PA) .... A...... 888 799-9666
   55 Almaden Blvd Ste 600 San Jose (95113) *(P-12068)*
Zoominfo Technologies LLC .... A...... 360 783-6924
   Dept La 24789 Pasadena (91185) *(P-12690)*
Zscaler, San Jose *Also Called: Zscaler Inc (P-12069)*
Zscaler Inc (PA) .... A...... 408 533-0288
   120 Holger Way San Jose (95134) *(P-12069)*
Zspace Inc .... D...... 408 498-4050
   55 Nicholson Ln Ste 2 San Jose (95134) *(P-5598)*
Zultys Inc .... D...... 408 328-0450
   785 Lucerne Dr Sunnyvale (94085) *(P-12913)*
Zumwalt Construction Inc .... D...... 559 252-1000
   5520 E Lamona Ave Fresno (93727) *(P-1068)*
ZUORA, Redwood City *Also Called: Zuora Inc (P-12410)*
Zuora Inc (PA) .... B...... 800 425-1281
   101 Redwood Shores Pkwy Ste 100 Redwood City (94065) *(P-12410)*

Zuum Transportation Inc .... D...... 909 667-7478
   131 Innovation Dr Ste 100 Irvine (92617) *(P-12070)*
Zwicker & Associates PC .... D...... 925 689-7070
   1220 Concord Ave Concord (94520) *(P-17692)*
Zwift Inc (PA) .... B...... 855 469-9438
   111 W Ocean Blvd Ste 1800 Long Beach (90802) *(P-12411)*
Zwilling JA Henckels LLC .... C...... 323 597-1421
   100 Citadel Dr Ste 575 Commerce (90040) *(P-5144)*
Zyante Inc .... D...... 510 541-4434
   41 E Main St Los Gatos (95030) *(P-6846)*
Zybooks, Los Gatos *Also Called: Zyante Inc (P-6846)*
Zyme Solutions Inc (PA) .... D...... 650 585-2258
   240 Twin Dolphin Dr Ste D Redwood City (94065) *(P-12691)*
Zynga, San Mateo *Also Called: Zynga Inc (P-12647)*
Zynga Inc (HQ) .... C...... 855 449-9642
   1200 Park Pl Ste 100 San Mateo (94403) *(P-12647)*
Zyxel, Anaheim *Also Called: Zyxel Communications Inc (P-4363)*
Zyxel Communications Inc .... D...... 714 632-0882
   1130 N Miller St Anaheim (92806) *(P-4363)*

COUNTY/CITY CROSS-REFERENCE INDEX

Alameda
Alameda
Albany
Berkeley
Castro Valley
Dublin
Emeryville
Fremont
Hayward
Livermore
Newark
Oakland
Pleasanton
San Leandro
San Lorenzo
Sunol
Union City

Alpine
Kirkwood

Amador
Ione
Jackson
Pine Grove
Pioneer
Plymouth
Sutter Creek

Butte
Chico
Durham
Gridley
Oroville
Paradise
Richvale

Calaveras
Bear Valley
Copperopolis
Murphys
San Andreas
Valley Springs

Colusa
Arbuckle
Colusa
Williams

Contra Costa
Alamo
Antioch
Bay Point
Brentwood
Byron
Clayton
Concord
Crockett
Danville
El Cerrito
El Sobrante
Hercules
Lafayette
Martinez
Moraga
Oakley
Orinda
Pacheco
Pinole
Pittsburg
Pleasant Hill
Point Richmond
Richmond
Rodeo
San Pablo
San Ramon
Walnut Creek

Del Norte
Crescent City
Smith River

El Dorado
Cameron Park
Camino
Cool
Diamond Springs
El Dorado Hills
Garden Valley
Greenwood
Placerville
Pollock Pines
Shingle Springs
South Lake Tahoe
Twin Bridges

Fresno
Auberry
Big Creek
Caruthers
Clovis
Coalinga
Del Rey
Firebaugh
Five Points
Fowler
Fresno
Friant
Huron
Kerman
Kingsburg
Lakeshore
Mendota
Orange Cove
Parlier
Reedley
Riverdale
San Joaquin
Sanger
Selma

Glenn
Orland
Willows

Humboldt
Arcata
Blue Lake
Eureka
Fortuna
Garberville
Hoopa
Loleta
Mckinleyville
Trinidad

Imperial
Brawley
Calexico
Calipatria
El Centro
Heber
Imperial
Winterhaven

Inyo
Bishop
Death Valley
Independence
Little Lake
Lone Pine

Kern
Arvin
Bakersfield
Boron
Buttonwillow
Delano
Edison
Edwards
Keene
Lake Isabella
Lamont
Lebec
Lost Hills
Maricopa
Mc Farland
Mc Kittrick
Mojave
Ridgecrest
Shafter
Taft
Tehachapi
Wasco

Kings
Corcoran
Hanford
Kettleman City
Lemoore
Stratford

Lake
Clearlake
Clearlake Oaks
Kelseyville
Lakeport
Middletown
Nice
Upper Lake

Lassen
Susanville

Los Angeles
Acton
Agoura
Agoura Hills
Agua Dulce
Alhambra
Altadena
Arcadia
Artesia
Avalon
Azusa
Baldwin Park
Bell
Bell Gardens
Bellflower
Beverly Hills
Burbank
Calabasas
Calabasas Hills
Canoga Park
Canyon Country
Carson
Castaic
Cerritos
Chatsworth
City Of Industry
Claremont
Commerce
Compton
Covina
Cudahy
Culver City
Diamond Bar
Downey
Duarte
E Rncho Dmngz
El Monte
El Segundo
Encino
Gardena
Glendale
Glendora
Granada Hills
Hacienda Heights
Harbor City
Hawaiian Gardens
Hawthorne
Hermosa Beach
Hollywood
Huntington Park
Inglewood
Irwindale
La Canada
La Canada Flintridge
La Crescenta
La Mirada
La Puente
La Verne
Lake View Terrace
Lakewood
Lancaster
Lawndale
Lomita
Long Beach
Los Angeles
Lynwood
Malibu
Manhattan Beach
Marina Del Rey
Maywood
Mission Hills
Monrovia
Montebello
Monterey Park
Montrose
Newhall
North Hills
North Hollywood
Northridge
Norwalk
Pacific Palisades
Pacoima
Palmdale
Palos Verdes Estates
Palos Verdes Peninsu
Panorama City
Paramount
Pasadena
Pico Rivera
Playa Del Rey
Playa Vista
Pls Vrds Pnsl
Pomona
Porter Ranch
Rancho Cascades
Rancho Dominguez
Rancho Palos Verdes
Redondo Beach
Reseda
Rlng Hls Est
Rolling Hills
Rosemead
Rowland Heights
San Dimas
San Fernando
San Gabriel
San Marino
San Pedro
Santa Clarita
Santa Fe Springs
Santa Monica
Saugus
Sherman Oaks
Sierra Madre
Signal Hill
South El Monte
South Gate
South Pasadena
Stevenson Ranch
Studio City
Sun Valley
Sunland
Sylmar
Tarzana
Temple City
Toluca Lake
Torrance
Tujunga
Universal City
Valencia
Valley Village
Van Nuys
Venice
Vernon
View Park
Walnut
West Covina
West Hills
West Hollywood
Whittier
Wilmington
Winnetka
Woodland Hills

Madera
Bass Lake
Chowchilla
Coarsegold
Madera
Oakhurst

COUNTY/CITY CROSS-REFERENCE

Marin
Belvedere
Belvedere Tiburon
Corte Madera
Fairfax
Greenbrae
Kentfield
Larkspur
Marshall
Mill Valley
Novato
Ross
San Anselmo
San Rafael
Sausalito

Mariposa
Fish Camp
Mariposa
Yosemite Ntpk

Mendocino
Fort Bragg
Hopland
Little River
Mendocino
Potter Valley
Redwood Valley
Ukiah
Willits

Merced
Atwater
Ballico
El Nido
Hilmar
Le Grand
Livingston
Los Banos
Merced
Snelling
Winton

Modoc
Alturas
Cedarville

Mono
Mammoth Lakes

Monterey
Aromas
Big Sur
Carmel
Carmel Valley
Castroville
Chualar
Gonzales
Greenfield
King City
Marina
Monterey
Moss Landing
Pacific Grove
Pebble Beach
Salinas
San Ardo
Seaside
Soledad

Napa
American Canyon
Angwin
Calistoga
Napa
Rutherford
Saint Helena
Yountville

Nevada
Grass Valley
Nevada City
Norden
Penn Valley
Soda Springs
Truckee

Orange
Aliso Viejo
Anaheim
Brea
Buena Park
Capistrano Beach
Corona Del Mar
Costa Mesa
Cypress
Dana Point
El Toro
Foothill Ranch
Fountain Valley
Fullerton
Garden Grove
Huntington Beach
Irvine
La Habra
La Habra Heights
La Palma
Ladera Ranch
Laguna Beach
Laguna Hills
Laguna Niguel
Laguna Woods
Lake Forest
Los Alamitos
Mission Viejo
Newport Beach
Newport Coast
Orange
Placentia
Rancho Mission Viejo
Rancho Santa Margari
Rcho Sta Marg
San Clemente
San Juan Capistrano
Santa Ana
Seal Beach
Stanton
Trabuco Canyon
Tustin
Villa Park
Westminster
Yorba Linda

Placer
Alpine Meadows
Alta
Applegate
Auburn
Colfax
Foresthill
Granite Bay
Lincoln
Loomis
Newcastle
Olympic Valley
Penryn
Rocklin
Roseville
Tahoe City
Tahoe Vista

Plumas
Chester
Portola
Quincy

Riverside
Anza
Banning
Beaumont
Bermuda Dunes
Blythe
Cabazon
Calimesa
Canyon Lake
Cathedral City
Coachella
Corona
Desert Hot Springs
Eastvale
Hemet
Idyllwild
Indian Wells
Indio
Jurupa Valley
La Quinta
Lake Elsinore
Mecca
Menifee
Moreno Valley
Murrieta
Norco
Palm Desert
Palm Springs
Perris
Rancho Mirage
Riverside
Romoland
San Jacinto
Temecula
Temescal Valley
Thermal
Thousand Palms
Wildomar

Sacramento
Antelope
Carmichael
Citrus Heights
Elk Grove
Fair Oaks
Folsom
Galt
Gold River
Herald
Mather
Mcclellan
North Highlands
Orangevale
Rancho Cordova
Rancho Murieta
Rio Linda
Sacramento

San Benito
Hollister
San Juan Bautista

San Bernardino
Adelanto
Angelus Oaks
Apple Valley
Barstow
Big Bear Lake
Bloomington
Chino
Chino Hills
Colton
Daggett
Earp
Fontana
Forest Falls
Fort Irwin
Grand Terrace
Helendale
Hesperia
Highland
Hinkley
Joshua Tree
Lake Arrowhead
Loma Linda
Lucerne Valley
Lytle Creek
Mentone
Montclair
Mountain Pass
Needles
Oak Hills
Ontario
Patton
Rancho Cucamonga
Redlands
Rialto
Running Springs
San Bernardino
Skyforest
Trona
Twentynine Palms
Upland
Victorville
Wrightwood
Yucaipa
Yucca Valley

San Diego
Alpine
Bonita
Bonsall
Borrego Springs
Camp Pendleton
Campo
Cardiff By The Sea
Carlsbad
Chula Vista
Coronado
Del Mar
El Cajon
Encinitas
Escondido
Fallbrook
Imperial Beach
Jamul
Julian
La Jolla
La Mesa
Lakeside
Lemon Grove
National City
Oceanside
Pala
Pauma Valley
Poway
Ramona
Rancho Santa Fe
San Diego
San Marcos
Santee
Solana Beach
Spring Valley
Tecate
Valley Center
Vista

San Francisco
San Francisco

San Joaquin
Acampo
Escalon
Farmington
French Camp
Lathrop
Linden
Lockeford
Lodi
Manteca
Mountain House
Ripon
Stockton
Tracy
Woodbridge

San Luis Obispo
Arroyo Grande
Atascadero
Avila Beach
Cambria
Los Osos
Morro Bay
Nipomo
Paso Robles
Pismo Beach
San Luis Obispo
San Simeon
Shell Beach
Templeton

San Mateo
Atherton
Belmont
Brisbane
Burlingame
Colma
Daly City
Foster City
Half Moon Bay
Hillsborough
La Honda
Menlo Park
Millbrae
Moss Beach
Pacifica
Pescadero
Portola Valley
Redwood City
San Bruno
San Carlos
San Francisco
San Mateo
South San Francisco
Woodside

Santa Barbara
Buellton
Carpinteria

COUNTY/CITY CROSS-REFERENCE

Goleta
Guadalupe
Lompoc
Los Olivos
Orcutt
Santa Barbara
Santa Maria
Santa Ynez
Solvang
Vandenberg Afb

Santa Clara

Alviso
Campbell
Cupertino
East Palo Alto
Gilroy
Los Altos
Los Altos Hills
Los Gatos
Milpitas
Moffett Field
Monte Sereno
Morgan Hill
Mountain View
Palo Alto
San Jose
San Martin
Santa Clara
Saratoga
Stanford
Sunnyvale

Santa Cruz

Aptos
Ben Lomond
Boulder Creek
Capitola
Felton
Mount Hermon
Royal Oaks
Santa Cruz
Scotts Valley
Soquel
Watsonville

Shasta

Anderson
Redding

Siskiyou

Edgewood
Mount Shasta
Weed
Yreka

Solano

Benicia
Dixon
Fairfield
Rio Vista
Suisun City
Vacaville
Vallejo

Sonoma

Bodega Bay
Cloverdale
Cotati
Eldridge
Forestville
Fulton
Geyserville
Guerneville
Healdsburg
Kenwood
Occidental
Petaluma
Rohnert Park
Santa Rosa
Sebastopol
Sonoma
Windsor

Stanislaus

Ceres
Hughson
Modesto
Newman
Oakdale
Patterson
Riverbank
Salida
Turlock

Sutter

Live Oak
Meridian
Pleasant Grove
Robbins
Yuba City

Tehama

Corning
Gerber
Los Molinos
Manton
Red Bluff
Vina

Trinity

Weaverville

Tulare

Cutler
Dinuba
Exeter
Farmersville
Goshen
Ivanhoe
Lindsay
Pixley
Porterville
Richgrove
Seq Natl Pk
Terra Bella
Three Rivers
Tipton
Traver
Tulare
Visalia

Tuolumne

Groveland
Long Barn
Pinecrest
Sonora
Soulsbyville
Tuolumne

Ventura

Camarillo
Fillmore
Moorpark
Newbury Park
Oak Park
Ojai
Oxnard
Piru
Port Hueneme
Santa Paula
Simi Valley
Somis
Thousand Oaks
Ventura
Westlake Village

Yolo

Brooks
Capay
Clarksburg
Davis
El Macero
West Sacramento
Woodland

Yuba

Marysville
Olivehurst
Wheatland

GEOGRAPHIC SECTION

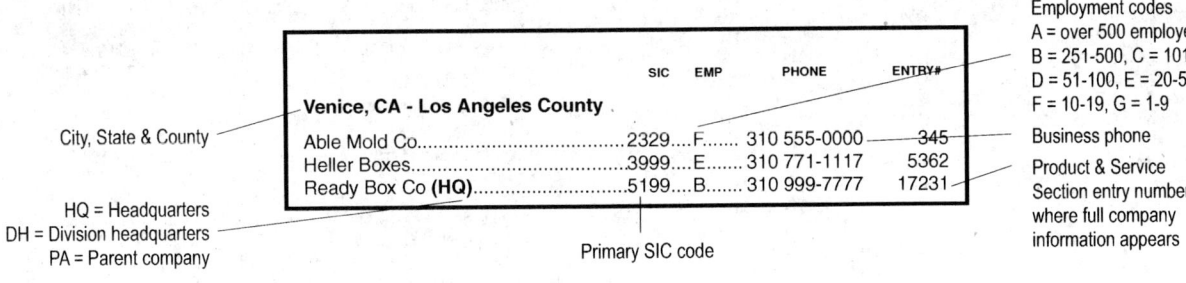

City, State & County — Venice, CA - Los Angeles County
Able Mold Co..............................2329....F......310 555-0000........345
Heller Boxes..............................3999....E......310 771-1117........5362
Ready Box Co **(HQ)**..................5199....B......310 999-7777........17231

HQ = Headquarters
DH = Division headquarters
PA = Parent company

Primary SIC code

Employment codes
A = over 500 employees
B = 251-500, C = 101-250
D = 51-100, E = 20-50
F = 10-19, G = 1-9
Business phone
Product & Service
Section entry number
where full company
information appears

- Listings in this section are sorted alphabetically by city.
- Listings within each city are sorted alphabetically by company name.

	SIC	EMP	PHONE	ENTRY#
ACAMPO, CA - San Joaquin County				
Constlltion Brnds US Oprtons I	5182	D	209 294-4110	6792
ACTON, CA - Los Angeles County				
Davis Construction Plbg Inc	1711	D	661 269-4325	1418
Ferreira Service Inc **(PA)**	1711	D	925 831-9330	1436
County of Los Angeles	8069	C	661 223-8700	16676
ADELANTO, CA - San Bernardino County				
Commercial Wood Products Company	1751	C	760 246-4530	1995
Apex Bulk Commodities Inc **(PA)**	4212	C	760 246-6077	3368
Hayes Welding Inc **(PA)**	7692	D	760 246-4878	13751
Amko Service Company	7699	D	760 246-3600	13763
AGOURA, CA - Los Angeles County				
Joni and Friends Foundation **(PA)**	8322	D	818 707-5664	18029
AGOURA HILLS, CA - Los Angeles County				
Brightview Golf Maint Inc **(DH)**	0781	D	818 223-8500	394
James H Cowan & Associates Inc	0782	D	310 457-2574	500
Ess LLC	1711	D	888 303-6424	1434
American Travel Solutions LLC **(PA)**	4724	D	818 359-6514	3927
Athas Capital Group Inc	6162	C	877 877-1477	7935
Private Nat Mrtg Accptance LLC **(DH)**	6162	A	818 224-7401	8012
Pennymac Corp	6163	B	818 878-8416	8050
Western Mutual Insurance Co	6331	C	818 879-2142	8425
Davidson Hotel Partners Lp	7011	A	818 707-1220	9739
Sequoia Concepts Inc	7322	D	818 409-6000	10752
Novalogic **(PA)**	7371	D	818 880-1997	11786
Weststar Cinemas Inc	7832	D	818 707-9987	14011
Los Angeles Rams LLC **(PA)**	7941	D	314 982-7267	14150
On Assignment Healthcare	8099	D	818 878-0683	17285
Albert & Mackenzie LLP **(PA)**	8111	D	818 575-9876	17359
Cydcor LLC **(PA)**	8742	D	805 277-5500	20337
AGUA DULCE, CA - Los Angeles County				
Petrelli Electric Inc	1731	D	661 268-7312	1803
ALAMEDA, CA - Alameda County				
Saarman Construction Ltd	1522	C	415 749-2700	773
Webcor Construction LP	1542	C	510 748-1900	1058
McGuire and Hester **(PA)**	1623	B	510 632-7676	1235
Power Engineering Construction Company	1629	B	510 337-3800	1314
Exelixis Inc	3824	B	650 837-7000	3022
Frank Ghiglione Inc **(PA)**	4212	D	510 483-7000	3391
Commodore Dining Cruises Inc	4489	D	510 337-9000	3807
Ballena Technologies	4841	B	510 521-0720	4473
Alameda Bureau Elec Imprv Corp **(HQ)**	4911	D	510 748-3902	4561
NRC Environmental Services Inc **(DH)**	4959	D	510 749-1390	4982
Abb/Con-Cise Optical Group LLC	5048	B	510 483-9400	5462
Ettore Products Co	5087	D	510 748-4130	5938
Svendsens Boat Works Inc	5088	D	510 522-2886	5969
Semifreddis Inc **(PA)**	5149	C	510 596-9930	6665
Alameda Alliance For Health	6324	C	510 747-4555	8276
Calidad Industries Inc	7349	D	510 698-7200	10871
Polarion Software Inc	7372	D	877 572-4005	12323
Wind River Systems Inc **(HQ)**	7372	A	510 748-4100	12398
Absolutdata Technologies Inc	7389	D	510 748-9922	13173
Delphi Productions Inc	7389	C	510 748-7494	13261
Bladium Inc **(PA)**	7991	D	510 814-4999	14180

	SIC	EMP	PHONE	ENTRY#
Harbor Bay Club Inc	7991	D	510 521-5414	14205
Alameda Hlthcare & Wellnss Ctr	8051	D	510 523-8857	15320
Bay View Rhbilitation Hosp LLC	8051	D	510 521-5600	15350
Garfield Nursing Home Inc	8051	D	510 582-7676	15489
City Alameda Health Care Corp	8062	A	510 522-3700	16003
Telecare Corporation **(PA)**	8063	C	510 337-7950	16659
Weinberg Rger Rsnfeld A Prof C **(PA)**	8111	D	510 337-1001	17676
Alameda Family Services	8351	D	510 629-6300	18267
Aircraft Crier Hrnet Fundation	8412	D	510 521-8448	18636
USS Hornet Museum	8412	D	510 521-8448	18681
Interntnal Un Oper Engners Lca	8631	B	510 748-7400	18785
Girl Scouts Northern Cal **(PA)**	8641	D	510 562-8470	18862
Mbh Architects Inc	8712	C	510 865-8663	19495
Iota Biosciences Inc	8731	D	831 229-3524	19714
Velodyne Lidar Inc	8731	C	510 522-2351	19795
Singulex Inc	8733	B	510 995-9000	19912
First 5 Alameda County	9441	D	510 227-6900	20944
ALAMO, CA - Contra Costa County				
Albert D Seeno Cnstr Co Inc	1521	D	925 671-7711	652
Lendus LLC	6162	A	925 295-9300	7989
RPM Mortgage Inc	6162	C	925 295-9300	8016
Round Hill Country Club	7997	D	925 934-8211	14433
Hospice and Palliative Care	8052	D	925 945-8924	15765
ALBANY, CA - Alameda County				
Albany Ford Inc **(PA)**	5511	D	510 528-1244	7165
Pacific Racing Association	7948	C	510 559-7300	14166
Tg Art Inc	7999	D	510 525-0070	14569
United Sttes Dept Enrgy Brkley	8733	C	510 701-1089	19924
ALHAMBRA, CA - Los Angeles County				
Gracing Brand Management Inc	2369	B	626 297-2472	2466
Southern California Edison Co	4911	A	626 308-6193	4710
Southern California Gas Co	4924	C	323 881-3587	4738
County of Los Angeles	4941	B	626 458-4000	4781
Smart & Final Stores LLC	5141	D	626 281-2049	6374
Alhambra Motors Inc	5511	C	626 576-1114	7166
FB Corporation	6022	B	626 300-0880	7684
Serfin Funds Transfer **(PA)**	6099	D	626 457-3070	7861
County of Los Angeles	6324	D	626 299-5300	8294
Drew Chain Security Corp	7381	D	626 457-8626	12966
Holmes Body Shop-Alhambra	7532	C	626 282-6173	13639
Ahmc Inc	8011	D	626 570-1606	14596
Atherton Baptist Homes	8051	C	626 863-1710	15336
Silverado Senior Living Inc	8051	D	626 872-3941	15669
Alhambra Hospital Med Ctr LP	8062	C	626 570-1606	15936
County of Los Angeles	8322	C	626 308-5542	17928
Eastern Los Angeles RE **(PA)**	8322	C	626 299-4700	17962
Chinatown Service Center	8331	D	213 808-1700	18219
Young Men Chrstn Assoc W San G **(PA)**	8661	D	626 576-0226	19031
Binoptics LLC	8711	D	607 257-3200	19153
Network Medical Management Inc	8741	C	626 282-0288	20161
Pacific Ventures Ltd	8741	C	626 576-0737	20172
Simpson Smpson MGT Cnslting In	8742	D	626 282-4000	20547
ALISO VIEJO, CA - Orange County				
Brightview Landscape Svcs Inc	0781	D	949 480-4187	414
Brightview Landscape Svcs Inc	0781	D	310 829-4707	417
Sequoia Environmental Svcs Inc	0781	D	949 480-4742	461

Employee Codes: A=Over 500 employees, B=251-500
C=101-250, D=51-100, E=20-50, F=10-19, G=1-9

2024 Directory of California
WholeSalers and Service Companies

© Mergent Inc. 1-800-342-5647
1389

ALISO VIEJO CA

	SIC	EMP	PHONE	ENTRY#
LMC Hollywood Highland	1542	B	949 448-1600	961
Fluor Daniel Construction Co (DH)	1622	B	949 349-2000	1182
Biovail Technologies Ltd	2834	D	703 995-2400	2581
Centon Electronics Inc (PA)	3572	D	949 855-9111	2816
Astronic	3672	C	949 454-1180	2906
Ixys Intgrted Crcits Div AV In	3674	A	949 831-4622	2924
United Parcel Service Inc	4215	A	949 643-6634	3634
Southern California Gas Co	4924	C	714 634-7221	4729
Datallegro Inc	5045	D	949 680-3000	5294
Hd Supply Distribution Services LLC	5072	A	949 643-4700	5729
Xse Group Inc	5112	C	888 272-8340	6072
Metagenics LLC (PA)	5122	C	949 366-0818	6131
Valeant Biomedicals Inc (DH)	5169	D	949 461-6000	6715
Efuel LLC	5172	D	949 330-7145	6728
Youngs Holdings Inc (PA)	5182	D	714 368-4615	6813
Clearedge Lending	6162	D	562 708-7706	7950
Thomas James Capital Inc	6282	C	949 481-7026	8225
Safeguard Health Entps Inc (HQ)	6324	B	800 880-1800	8358
Shea Properties MGT Co Inc	6512	B	949 389-7000	8759
First Team RE - Orange Cnty	6531	C	949 389-0004	9010
Thomas James Homes Inc	6531	C	949 424-2356	9194
L & O Aliso Viejo LLC	7011	C	949 643-6700	9956
Sunstone Hotel Properties Inc (DH)	7011	C	949 330-4000	10289
Cloudstaff LLC	7299	B	888 551-5339	10536
Adecco Employment Services	7361	C	949 586-2342	11076
Remedytemp Inc (DH)	7363	C	949 425-7600	11323
Itrex Group USA Corporation	7371	B	213 436-7785	11683
UST Global Inc (HQ)	7371	D	949 716-8757	12008
Vwise Inc	7371	D	949 716-1276	12033
Waterwiseone	7371	D	866 758-4393	12035
Quest Software Inc	7372	C	949 754-8000	12331
Information MGT Resources Inc (PA)	7373	C	949 215-8889	12468
Quest Software Inc (PA)	7373	A	949 754-8000	12514
Navtrak LLC	7382	D	410 548-2337	13134
Edwards Theatres Circuit Inc	7832	D	949 425-3838	13990
Kaiser Foundation Hospitals	8011	D	949 425-3150	14796
Covenant Care LLC (PA)	8051	B	949 349-1200	15409
Hcr Manorcare Med Svcs Fla LLC	8051	C	949 587-9000	15507
Truvida Recovery	8093	D	949 283-4679	17146
American Assn Crtcal Care Nrse	8299	C	949 362-2000	17799
Lauras House	8322	D	949 361-3775	18040
Midi Manufacturers Assn Inc	8611	D	714 227-0068	18716
Fluor Corporation	8711	D	949 349-2000	19226
Fluor Enterprises Inc	8711	D	949 349-2000	19227
Fluor Plant Services Intl Inc	8711	D	949 349-2000	19229
Clarient Diagnostic Svcs Inc	8734	C	888 443-3310	19957
Nelson Bros Property MGT Inc	8741	C	949 916-7300	20159
Professional Community MGT Cal	8741	C	949 380-0725	20185
Seabreeze Management Co Inc (PA)	8741	D	949 855-1800	20204
Basketball Marketing Co Inc	8742	C	610 249-2255	20291
Pandora Marketing LLC	8742	D	800 705-6856	20500
Channelwave Software Inc	8748	D	949 448-4500	20727
Indie LLC	8748	C	949 608-0854	20777

ALPINE, CA - San Diego County

	SIC	EMP	PHONE	ENTRY#
Abhe & Svoboda Inc	1542	D	619 659-1320	859
Alpine Convalescent Center Inc	8093	D	619 659-3120	17002
Southern Indian Health Council (PA)	8093	D	619 445-1188	17131

ALPINE MEADOWS, CA - Placer County

	SIC	EMP	PHONE	ENTRY#
Squaw Creek Associates LLC	7011	A	530 581-6624	10264

ALTA, CA - Placer County

	SIC	EMP	PHONE	ENTRY#
Pacific Gas and Electric Co	4911	D	530 389-2202	4633

ALTADENA, CA - Los Angeles County

	SIC	EMP	PHONE	ENTRY#
Anre Technologies Inc	7371	C	818 627-5433	11408
Maimone Liquidating Corp (PA)	7532	D	626 286-5691	13642
Altadena Town and Country Club	7997	D	626 345-9088	14321
Five Acres - The Bys Grls Aid	8361	B	626 798-6793	18433

ALTURAS, CA - Modoc County

	SIC	EMP	PHONE	ENTRY#
Atlas Operations Group	7381	D	844 414-2857	12936
Modoc Medial Center Hosp Aux	8051	D	530 233-3416	15588
Modoc Medical Center Hosp Aux (PA)	8062	D	530 708-8800	16273

ALVISO, CA - Santa Clara County

	SIC	EMP	PHONE	ENTRY#
Bayscape Management Inc	0781	D	408 288-2940	389
Acme Building Maint Co Inc (DH)	7349	D	408 263-5911	10848
Cpacket Networks Inc	7379	D	650 969-9500	12768
Gardner Family Hlth Netwrk Inc	8011	D	408 457-7100	14758

AMERICAN CANYON, CA - Napa County

	SIC	EMP	PHONE	ENTRY#
Ghilotti Construction Co Inc	1611	C	707 556-9145	1106
R E Maher Inc	1771	D	707 642-3907	2150
Western Wine Services Inc (PA)	4225	D	800 999-8463	3782
Bvk Gaming Inc	7999	D	707 644-8853	14500

ANAHEIM, CA - Orange County

	SIC	EMP	PHONE	ENTRY#
Brightview Landscape Svcs Inc	0781	D	714 215-7423	400
Harvest Landscape Entps Inc (PA)	0781	C	714 693-8100	436
Hydro-Dig Inc	0781	D	714 772-9947	439
Marina Maintenance Group Inc	0781	B	714 939-6600	442
Resident Group Services Inc (PA)	0782	C	714 630-5300	533
Ultimate Landscaping MGT	0782	D	714 502-9711	543
West Coast Arborists Inc (PA)	0782	D	714 991-1900	549
Capsule Manufacturing Inc	1389	D	949 245-4151	609
Brownco Construction Co Inc	1521	D	714 935-9600	663
Katerra	1521	D	720 449-3909	690
Katerra Construction LLC	1521	A	720 449-3909	691
Gray West Construction Inc	1541	D	714 491-1317	820
Universal Dust Cllctr Mfg Sup (PA)	1541	D	714 630-8588	852
W N G Construction Jv Inc (PA)	1541	D	714 524-7100	856
Platinum Construction Inc	1542	D	714 527-0700	993
San-Mar Construction Co Inc	1542	D	714 693-5400	1019
Techno Coatings Inc	1542	D	714 774-4671	1039
Techno Coatings Inc	1542	D	714 774-4671	1040
Techno Coatings Inc (PA)	1542	D	714 635-1130	1041
Turner Construction Company	1542	B	714 940-9000	1045
JB Bostick Company Inc (PA)	1611	D	714 238-2121	1123
Powertec Company Inc (PA)	1611	D	951 332-1198	1153
Paulus Engineering Inc	1623	D	714 632-3322	1249
Aldoc Inc	1711	D	714 836-8477	1345
Control Air Conditioning Corporation	1711	D	714 777-8600	1403
Ecotech Rfrgn & Hvac Inc	1711	D	888 833-8100	1426
General Engineering Wstn Inc (PA)	1711	D	714 630-3200	1449
Ken Starr Inc	1711	D	714 632-8789	1476
Nexgen AC & Htg LLC	1711	D	760 616-5870	1510
Residential Fire Systems Inc	1711	D	714 666-8450	1548
Seai Elk Grove LLC	1711	D	949 281-7897	1557
South Coast Mechanical Inc	1711	D	714 738-6644	1570
Thermalair Inc (HQ)	1711	D	714 630-3200	1585
Trilogy Plumbing Inc	1711	C	714 441-2952	1587
University Marelich Mech Inc	1711	D	714 632-2600	1589
Borbon Incorporated	1721	D	714 994-0170	1606
Pbc Pavers Inc	1721	D	714 278-0488	1630
Wilson & Hampton Pntg Contrs	1721	D	714 772-5091	1646
Msl Electric Inc	1731	D	714 693-4837	1784
Nazzareno Electric Co Inc	1731	D	714 712-4744	1785
Ponderosa Electric Inc	1731	D	949 253-3100	1809
Rosendin Electric Inc	1731	A	714 739-1334	1826
Sunwest Electric Inc	1731	C	714 630-8700	1857
Hba Incorporated	1741	D	714 635-8602	1884
Vincent Contractors Inc	1741	B	714 660-0165	1896
Best Interiors Inc (PA)	1742	C	714 490-7999	1910
Infinity Drywall Contg Inc	1742	D	714 634-2255	1935
Keenan Hpkins Sder Stwell Cntr (PA)	1742	C	714 695-3670	1940
Mowery Thomason Inc	1742	C	714 666-1717	1947
Eleganza Tiles Inc (PA)	1743	D	714 224-1700	1980
Matrix Surfaces Inc	1743	D	714 696-5449	1985
Arciero Brothers Inc	1771	C	714 238-6600	2095
Penhall Holding Company	1771	C	714 772-6450	2147
Peterson Brothers Cnstr Inc	1771	A	714 278-0488	2148
Performance Contracting Inc	1796	D	913 310-7120	2249
Artisan Glass and Design Inc	1799	D	714 542-0507	2256
ATI Restoration LLC (PA)	1799	C	714 283-9990	2259
Quality First Woodworks Inc	2499	C	714 632-0480	2486
Leonards Carpet Service Inc (PA)	2541	D	714 630-1930	2504
Teco Diagnostics	2835	D	714 693-7788	2615
Aquatic Co	3088	C	714 993-1220	2666
Pacific Precision Metals Inc	3469	C	951 226-5100	2753
J&S Goodwin Inc (HQ)	3537	D	714 956-4040	2778
Wasser Filtration Inc (PA)	3569	D	714 696-6450	2802
J L Wingert Company	3589	D	714 379-5519	2848
Murrietta Circuits	3672	C	714 970-2430	2908
Pacific Contours Corporation	3728	D	714 693-1260	2992
DG Performance Spc Inc	3799	D	714 961-8850	2999
Halonus Inc	3999	B	714 345-0822	3107
LA Spas Inc	3999	C	714 630-1150	3109
First Transit Inc	4111	D	714 644-9828	3131
Falck Mobile Health Corp	4119	B	714 828-7750	3259
Filyn Corporation	4119	C	714 632-0225	3261
Roy Miller Freight Lines LLC (PA)	4212	D	714 632-5511	3421
All Counties Courier Inc	4215	D	714 599-9300	3605
Di Overnite LLC	4215	D	877 997-7447	3609

GEOGRAPHIC SECTION

ANAHEIM CA

	SIC	EMP	PHONE	ENTRY#
Ontrac Logistics Inc	4215	D	714 776-0363	3623
Total Warehouse Inc	4225	C	480 582-3954	3769
Pacific Coast Sightseeing Tour	4725	C	714 507-1157	3965
DSV Solutions LLC	4731	D	714 630-0110	4012
Disneyland Resort	4783	A	714 781-7560	4127
L&L Foods Holdings LLC	4783	C	714 254-1430	4130
TW Services Inc	4789	B	714 441-2400	4176
AT&T Corp	4812	D	714 284-2878	4183
Zyxel Communications Inc	4813	D	714 632-0882	4363
Outsource Utility Contr Corp	4911	C	714 238-9263	4598
West Coast Electric & Pwr Inc	4911	D	562 447-3254	4719
Southern California Gas Co	4924	C	213 244-1200	4737
City of Anaheim	4971	D	714 254-0125	4986
Califrnia Auto Dalers Exch LLC	5012	B	714 996-2400	5006
Cal-State Auto Parts Inc (PA)	5013	C	714 630-5950	5031
Empi Inc	5013	D	714 446-9606	5037
Reels Inc	5013	D	714 446-9606	5056
Shrin LLC	5013	D	714 850-0303	5060
Atrium Door & Win Co Ariz Inc	5031	C	714 693-0601	5147
Walnut Investment Corp	5031	A	714 238-9240	5193
General Procurement Inc (PA)	5045	D	949 679-7960	5309
Quad-C Jh Holdings Inc	5047	C	502 741-0421	5445
Sapphire Clean Rooms LLC	5049	C	714 316-5036	5469
Etekcity Corporation	5064	C	855 686-3835	5604
Bisco Inc	5065	C	714 693-2901	5631
Bisco Industries Inc (HQ)	5065	D	800 323-1232	5632
L3harris Interstate Elec Corp	5065	C	714 758-0500	5668
B & B Specialties Inc	5072	B	714 985-3075	5723
Eps Corporate Holdings Inc	5074	C	714 635-3131	5747
Oliver Healthcare Packaging Co	5084	D	714 864-3500	5850
Otis Elevator Company	5084	C	714 758-9593	5854
Midland Industries	5085	D	800 821-5725	5912
American Sanitary Supply Inc	5087	B	714 632-3010	5935
Adams International Mtls Corp	5093	C	714 630-8901	6003
Kinsbursky Bros Supply Inc (PA)	5093	D	714 738-8516	6011
Self Serve Auto Dismantlers (PA)	5093	C	714 630-8901	6015
Ft 2 Inc	5099	D	714 765-5555	6042
5 Day Business Forms Mfg Inc	5112	C	714 632-8674	6061
Bunzl Distribution Cal LLC (DH)	5113	C	714 688-1900	6074
Oasis Brands Inc	5113	D	540 658-2830	6083
Alstyle AP & Activewear MGT Co (HQ)	5137	A	714 765-0400	6194
Advantage-Crown Sls & Mktg LLC (DH)	5141	A	714 780-3000	6237
A & R Wholesale Distrs Inc	5145	D	714 777-7742	6452
Bridgford Marketing Company (DH)	5147	C	714 526-5533	6490
Family Tree Produce Inc	5148	C	714 693-5688	6538
Legacy Farms LLC	5148	D	714 736-1800	6561
Harris Freeman & Co Inc (PA)	5149	B	714 765-7525	6633
Straub Distributing Co Ltd (PA)	5181	C	714 779-4000	6783
Flawless Vape Whl & Dist Inc	5194	D	714 406-2933	6879
Targus International LLC (PA)	5199	C	714 765-5555	6952
Home Depot USA Inc	5211	D	714 921-1215	7001
Lowes Home Centers LLC	5211	D	714 447-6140	7059
Paragon Industries Inc	5211	D	714 778-1800	7112
Isuzu North America Corp (HQ)	5511	C	714 935-9300	7236
Cintas Corporation	5699	D	714 646-2550	7413
Phoenix CLB Grman Assn In Orng	5812	D	714 224-0194	7502
Premier Commercial Bancorp	6022	D	714 978-2400	7711
Credit Union Southern Cal (PA)	6061	D	562 698-8326	7761
E Z Services	6099	D	714 635-7599	7853
Carrington Mrtg Holdings LLC	6162	C	888 267-0584	7943
Change Lending LLC (PA)	6162	D	949 423-6814	7947
City of Anaheim	6512	D	714 704-2400	8709
First Team RE - Orange Cnty	6531	C	714 974-9191	9009
House Seven Gables RE Inc	6531	D	714 282-0306	9041
Fortress Holding Group LLC	6719	D	714 202-8710	9312
1855 S Hbr Blvd Drv Hldngs LLC	7011	D	714 750-1811	9588
American Koyu Corporation	7011	C	626 793-0669	9604
Anaheim - 1855 S Hbr Blvd Owne	7011	D	714 750-1811	9608
Anaheim Plaza Hotel Inc	7011	C	714 772-5900	9611
Best Western Stovalls Inn (PA)	7011	D	714 956-4430	9645
Cinderella Motel	7011	D	559 432-0118	9703
Comfort California Inc	7011	C	714 750-3131	9717
Disney Enterprises Inc	7011	A	714 778-6600	9744
Disneyland International	7011	C	714 956-6746	9745
Disneyland Resort (DH)	7011	C	714 781-4000	9746
Edward Thomas Companies	7011	D	714 782-7500	9772
Fairfield Inn By Mrrott Ltd Prt	7011	D	714 772-6777	9792
Fjs Inc	7011	D	714 905-1050	9798
Harvard Grand LP	7011	D	714 939-9700	9838
HI Anaheim LLC	7011	D	714 533-1500	9847
Jin Yi Enterprises Inc	7011	D	714 778-0350	9920
Ken Real Estate Lease Ltd	7011	D	714 778-1700	9937
Makar Anaheim LLC	7011	A	714 740-4431	9997
Northwest Hotel Corporation (PA)	7011	D	714 776-6120	10051
Orangewood LLC	7011	C	714 750-3000	10070
Portofino Inn & Suites Anaheim	7011	B	714 782-7600	10125
SAI Management Co Inc	7011	D	714 772-5050	10190
Wco Hotels Inc	7011	A	714 635-2300	10355
Westin Anaheim Resort	7011	D	657 279-9786	10364
GBS Linens Inc (PA)	7213	C	714 778-6448	10435
Mission Linen Supply	7213	D	909 364-8752	10438
Opal Concepts Inc (PA)	7231	D	714 779-0545	10505
Exactax Inc (PA)	7291	D	714 284-4802	10521
Internal Revenue Service	7291	D	714 512-2818	10523
Fci Lender Services Inc	7322	C	800 931-2424	10741
Vengroff Williams & Assoc Inc	7322	D	714 889-6200	10754
Advantage Mailing LLC (PA)	7331	C	714 538-3881	10766
AST Sportswear Inc	7331	B	714 223-2030	10767
Rentokil North America Inc	7342	D	714 563-2450	10841
Coastal Building Services Inc	7349	B	714 775-2855	10876
DMS Facility Services Inc	7349	A	949 975-1366	10892
Hunter Easterday Corporation	7349	C	714 238-3400	10908
Priority Building Services LLC (PA)	7349	D	714 255-2963	10946
So Cal Land Maintenance Inc	7349	D	714 231-1454	10969
Go-Staff Inc	7361	A	657 242-9350	11145
Blaze Solutions Inc	7371	D	415 964-5689	11464
Bpo Management Services Inc (PA)	7371	D	714 972-2670	11471
Select Data Inc	7371	C	714 577-1000	11909
Bpoms/Hro Inc (HQ)	7372	D	714 974-2670	12125
Morphotrak LLC (DH)	7373	C	714 238-2000	12495
Cyber-Pro Systems Inc	7374	C	562 256-3800	12562
Bcp Systems Inc	7378	D	714 202-3900	12704
Etherwan Systems Inc	7379	D	714 779-3800	12787
Partners Information Tech (HQ)	7379	C	714 736-4487	12853
Saca Technologies Inc	7379	D	888 603-9030	12870
Access Control Security Inc	7381	D	714 826-3800	12918
Califrnia Suthland Private SEC	7381	C	714 367-4005	12943
ADT LLC	7382	C	714 450-6461	13085
ADT LLC	7382	D	626 593-1020	13087
Sentinel Offender Services LLC (PA)	7382	D	949 453-1550	13145
Freeman Expositions LLC	7389	C	714 254-3400	13296
MB Coatings Inc	7389	D	714 625-2118	13366
Nor-Cal Beverage Co Inc	7389	D	714 526-8600	13400
Alamo Rental (us) Inc	7514	D	714 748-7368	13572
Anaheim Hills Auto Body Inc	7532	C	714 632-8266	13631
Cablecom LLC	7629	D	714 666-2400	13735
T L Fabrications LP	7692	D	562 802-3980	13754
Disney Enterprises Inc	7812	C	714 781-1651	13839
Disney Enterprises Inc	7812	C	407 397-6000	13841
Hob Entertainment LLC	7929	C	714 520-2310	14084
Anaheim Arena Management LLC	7941	A	714 704-2400	14123
Anaheim Ducks Hockey Club LLC (PA)	7941	D	714 940-2900	14125
Angels Baseball LP (PA)	7941	A	714 940-2000	14126
Rachas Inc	7991	D	714 290-0636	14224
Eagle Vnes Vnyrds Golf CLB LLC	7992	D	707 257-4470	14259
Disneyland International (DH)	7996	C	714 781-4565	14302
Adventure City Inc	7999	D	714 821-3311	14487
Anaheim Ice	7999	D	714 535-7465	14489
Agile Occupational Medicine PC	8011	D	949 464-4036	14595
Altamed Health Services Corp	8011	D	714 635-0593	14603
Anaheim Urgent Care Inc	8011	D	714 533-2273	14612
Kaiser Foundation Hospitals	8011	C	714 279-4675	14795
Southern Cal Dgnstc Imging Inc	8011	D	714 991-3367	15072
Southern Cal Prmnnte Med Group	8011	C	714 279-4675	15074
Vanguard Health Systems Inc	8011	B	714 635-6272	15178
Quantum Bhvioral Solutions Inc	8049	D	626 531-6999	15302
1135 N Leisure Ct Inc	8051	D	714 772-1353	15314
Anaheim Healthcare Center LLC	8051	D	714 816-0540	15326
Coventry Court Health Center	8051	C	714 636-2800	15411
Mark & Fred Enterprises	8051	C	714 821-1993	15579
Oceanside Harbor Holdings LLC	8051	C	760 331-3177	15609
Westview Services Inc	8051	C	714 956-4199	15733
Windsor Anaheim Healthcare (PA)	8051	C	714 826-8950	15737
Ahmc Anheim Rgional Med Ctr LP	8062	A	714 774-1450	15929
Ahmc Anheim Rgional Med Ctr LP (PA)	8062	A	714 774-1450	15930
Anaheim Global Medical Center	8062	C	714 533-6220	15945
Anaheim Regional Medical Ctr	8062	A	714 774-1450	15946
Anaheim Regional Medical Ctr	8062	C	714 999-3847	15947
Kaiser Foundation Hospitals	8062	A	714 644-2000	16158
Prime Healthcare Anaheim LLC	8062	A	714 827-3000	16333
Providence Medical Foundation (DH)	8062	C	714 712-3308	16350
Tenet Healthsystem Medical Inc	8062	C	714 428-6800	16571
Korean Community Services Inc	8069	A	714 527-6551	16685
St Jseph Hlth Sys HM Care Svc	8082	C	714 712-9500	16934
Behavioral Health Works Inc	8093	D	800 249-1266	17012
Burt L Howe & Associates	8111	D	714 701-9180	17396

Employee Codes: A=Over 500 employees, B=251-500
C=101-250, D=51-100, E=20-50, F=10-19, G=1-9

2024 Directory of California
WholeSalers and Service Companies

© Mergent Inc. 1-800-342-5647
1391

ANAHEIM CA

	SIC	EMP	PHONE	ENTRY#
Mark 1 Restoration Service LLC	8322	D	714 283-9990	18049
Orange Cnty Adult Achvment Ctr	8322	C	714 744-5301	18072
St Joseph Hospice	8322	B	714 712-7100	18140
Westview Services Inc	8331	D	714 530-2703	18262
Westview Services Inc	8331	D	714 635-2444	18263
Tiger Woods Learning Center	8351	D	714 765-8040	18362
Leisure Care LLC	8361	C	714 974-1616	18469
Automobile Club Southern Cal	8699	D	714 774-2392	19043
Development Resource Cons Inc (PA)	8711	D	714 685-6860	19197
DMS Facility Services LLC	8711	A	949 975-1366	19202
Imeg Consultants Corp	8711	D	714 490-5555	19264
Nest Parent Inc	8711	A	310 551-0101	19334
Willdan Group Inc (PA)	8711	C	800 424-9144	19443
Infosend Inc (PA)	8721	D	714 993-2690	19589
Country Villa Service Corp (PA)	8741	C	310 574-3733	20066
Tricom Management Inc	8741	C	714 630-2029	20232
Branded Group Inc	8742	C	323 940-1444	20300
Consumer Resource Network LLC	8742	B	800 291-4794	20325
Ralph Brennan Rest Group LLC	8742	C	714 776-5200	20524
Shell Oil Company	8742	C	714 991-9200	20544
Workcare Inc	8744	C	714 978-7488	20667
Aliantel Inc	8748	D	714 829-1650	20683
C M E Corp	8748	C	714 632-6939	20714
Edge Mortgage Advisory Co LLC	8748	C	714 564-5800	20741
Rubio Arts Corporation	8999	C	407 849-1643	20901

ANDERSON, CA - Shasta County

	SIC	EMP	PHONE	ENTRY#
Harbert Roofing Inc	1761	D	530 223-3251	2067
Magnolia Holdings LLC	8051	C	530 365-0025	15557

ANGELUS OAKS, CA - San Bernardino County

	SIC	EMP	PHONE	ENTRY#
YMCA of East Valley	8641	C	909 794-1702	18934

ANGWIN, CA - Napa County

	SIC	EMP	PHONE	ENTRY#
Crestwood Behavioral Hlth Inc	8059	D	707 965-2461	15841

ANTELOPE, CA - Sacramento County

	SIC	EMP	PHONE	ENTRY#
Good Life Construction Inc	1521	D	916 833-1379	680
American Concrete Washouts Inc	1771	D	916 496-2798	2094

ANTIOCH, CA - Contra Costa County

	SIC	EMP	PHONE	ENTRY#
Drill Tech Drilling & Shoring Inc (PA)	1629	D	925 978-2060	1296
Banister Electrical Inc	1731	D	925 778-7801	1672
Black Diamond Electric Inc	1731	D	925 777-3440	1684
Wayne E Swisher Cem Contr Inc	1771	D	925 757-3660	2170
Bond Manufacturing Co Inc (PA)	3272	D	866 771-2663	2702
Allied Container Systems Inc	3448	C	925 944-7600	2746
Pacific Gas and Electric Co	4911	B	925 779-7745	4602
Delta Diablo Sanitation District	4959	D	925 756-1900	4978
Markstein Sales Company	5181	D	925 755-1919	6774
Lowes Home Centers LLC	5211	D	925 756-0370	7048
Kaiser Foundation Hospitals	8011	D	925 813-6500	14793
Permanente Medical Group Inc	8011	A	925 813-6149	14972
Antioch Dunes Healthcare LLC	8051	D	925 757-8787	15329
Lone Tree Cnvalescent Hosp Inc	8051	C	925 754-0470	15547
Norcal Care Centers Inc	8059	D	925 757-8787	15882
Sutter Delta Medical Center	8062	C	925 779-7200	16518
Sutter Health	8062	C	925 779-7273	16522
Kaiser Foundation Hospitals	8093	B	925 779-5000	17079
Contra Loma Healthcare LLC	8099	C	925 754-0470	17209
Integrated Pain Man	8741	D	925 238-0020	20114
Montrose Environmental Corp	8748	B	925 680-4300	20805

ANZA, CA - Riverside County

	SIC	EMP	PHONE	ENTRY#
Cahuilla Creek Rest & Casino	7999	C	951 763-1200	14502

APPLE VALLEY, CA - San Bernardino County

	SIC	EMP	PHONE	ENTRY#
Brightview Tree Company	0781	D	760 955-2560	419
Who Dat Nation Trnsp LLC	4789	C	760 403-7237	4179
Cco Holdings LLC	4841	C	760 810-4076	4487
Lowes Home Centers LLC	5211	D	760 961-3000	7087
Encore Senior Living III LLC	6513	D	760 242-3188	8807
Northfield Medical Inc	7699	D	248 268-2500	13788
Inland Valley Hospice Co	8052	D	760 243-2501	15766
St Mary Medical Center LLC	8062	A	760 946-8767	16482
St Mary Medical Center LLC (PA)	8062	A	760 242-2311	16483
Vnacare	8082	D	760 946-4730	16969
BEST Opportunities Inc	8331	C	760 628-0111	18212
High Dsert Prtnr In Acdmic Exc	8732	B	760 946-5414	19817

APPLEGATE, CA - Placer County

	SIC	EMP	PHONE	ENTRY#
Nrci Telecom	1623	D	530 878-3970	1245

APTOS, CA - Santa Cruz County

	SIC	EMP	PHONE	ENTRY#
Parkhurst Terrace	1522	D	831 685-0800	768
Seacliff Inn Inc	7011	D	831 661-4671	10213
Seascape Resort Owners Assn	7011	D	831 688-6800	10214
Seascape Rsort Ltd A Cal Ltd P	7011	D	831 662-7120	10215
First Alarm (PA)	7382	C	831 476-1111	13116
Enlighticare Inc	8069	D	831 750-3546	16681
Aegis Senior Communities LLC	8082	C	831 684-2700	16799
Cabrillo Cmnty Cllege Dst Fing (PA)	8222	A	831 479-6100	17785

ARBUCKLE, CA - Colusa County

	SIC	EMP	PHONE	ENTRY#
T & P Farms	0111	D	530 476-3038	2
California Family Foods LLC	2044	D	530 476-3326	2362
Alsco - Geyer Irrigation Inc	5083	D	530 476-2253	5805

ARCADIA, CA - Los Angeles County

	SIC	EMP	PHONE	ENTRY#
Transdev Services Inc	4119	A	626 357-7912	3298
Coach Usa Inc	4142	D	626 357-7912	3317
365 Delivery Inc	4212	D	818 815-5005	3359
Gar Enterprises (PA)	5045	D	626 574-1175	5306
Penney Opco LLC	5311	C	626 445-6454	7130
Burlington Coat Fctry Whse of	5651	C	626 447-8784	7406
Transglobal Holding Company	6163	D	626 447-7888	8061
Welltower Om Group LLC	6512	C	626 254-0552	8778
Coldwell Banker Residential RE	6531	C	626 445-5500	8941
Post Alarm Systems (PA)	7382	D	626 446-7159	13138
Los Angeles Turf Club Inc (DH)	7948	D	626 574-6330	14164
Santa Anita Associates (PA)	7992	D	626 447-2764	14287
Arcadia Eye Ctr	8011	D	626 445-4873	14615
Country Villa Service Corp	8051	C	626 445-2421	15394
Arcadia Gardens MGT Corp	8052	D	626 574-8571	15746
Arcadia Convalescent Hosp Inc (PA)	8059	C	626 445-2170	15813
Methodist Hospital of S CA	8062	B	626 574-3755	16270
Usc Arcadia Hospital (PA)	8062	A	626 898-8000	16606
Wave Plastic Surgery Ctr Inc	8062	D	626 898-9711	16626
Christian Arcadia School	8211	D	626 574-8229	17701
Uplift Family Services	8322	A	626 254-5000	18163
Leisure Care LLC	8361	C	626 447-0106	18471
Los Angles Arbrtum Fndtion Inc	8422	D	626 821-3222	18690
Quality Reimbursement Services	8721	D	626 445-5092	19625

ARCATA, CA - Humboldt County

	SIC	EMP	PHONE	ENTRY#
Sun Valley Group Inc (PA)	0181	B	707 822-2885	157
Danco Builders	1522	D	707 822-9000	754
O & M Industries (PA)	1711	D	707 822-8800	1513
Toucan Inc (PA)	5094	D	707 822-6662	6028
AMG Data Services	7374	D	707 822-4888	12550
Healthsport Ltd A Ltd Partnr (PA)	7991	C	707 822-3488	14206
United Indian Health Svcs Inc (PA)	8011	C	707 825-5000	15143
American Hospital Mgt Corp (PA)	8062	B	707 822-3621	15942
Open Door Community Hlth Ctrs (PA)	8093	D	707 826-8642	17103
Endors Toi Pbc	8742	D	434 987-0919	20357
Humboldt State Univ Spnsred PR	8748	D	707 826-4189	20773

AROMAS, CA - Monterey County

	SIC	EMP	PHONE	ENTRY#
Farmhill LLC	0171	D	831 726-1986	53

ARROYO GRANDE, CA - San Luis Obispo County

	SIC	EMP	PHONE	ENTRY#
Greenheart Farms Inc	0191	B	805 481-2234	179
Talley Farms	0723	C	805 489-2508	308
Papich Construction Co Inc (PA)	1521	D	805 473-3016	706
Anderson Burton Cnstr Inc (PA)	1542	C	805 481-5096	865
Cco Holdings LLC	4841	C	805 904-1047	4485
Ameri-Kleen	7349	C	805 546-0706	10853
Compass Health Inc	8051	C	805 489-8137	15383
Arroyo Grande Community Hospital	8062	B	805 473-7626	15953
Mhm Services Inc	8093	C	805 904-6678	17094
Community Action Partnership	8111	D	805 489-4026	17409
Compass Health Inc	8361	C	805 474-7260	18399

ARTESIA, CA - Los Angeles County

	SIC	EMP	PHONE	ENTRY#
Windsor Twin Plms Hlthcare Ctr	8051	C	562 865-0271	15742
Artesia Christian Home Inc	8059	C	562 865-5218	15814
County of Los Angeles	8093	D	562 402-0688	17037
Automobile Club Southern Cal	8699	D	562 924-6636	19067

ARVIN, CA - Kern County

	SIC	EMP	PHONE	ENTRY#
Tasteful Selections LLC	0134	C	661 854-3998	9
Grimmway Enterprises Inc	0723	B	661 854-6250	273
Grimmway Enterprises Inc	0723	A	661 854-6200	274
Kern Ridge Growers LLC	0723	B	661 854-3141	283
Grimmway Enterprises Inc	1541	C	661 854-6240	821
Grimmway Enterprises Inc	4212	D	307 302-0090	3400

GEOGRAPHIC SECTION

BAKERSFIELD CA

	SIC	EMP	PHONE	ENTRY#
Blue Beacon USA LP	7542	C	661 858-2090	13684
Evergreen Health Care LLC	8051	A	661 854-4475	15472
Grimmway Enterprises Inc.	8741	D	661 854-6200	20105

ATASCADERO, CA - San Luis Obispo County

	SIC	EMP	PHONE	ENTRY#
Central Coast Seafoods	5146	C	805 462-3474	6468
Compass Health Inc.	8051	C	805 466-9254	15384
Califrnia Dept State Hospitals	8063	A	805 468-2000	16645
Star of California	8099	C	805 466-1638	17334

ATHERTON, CA - San Mateo County

	SIC	EMP	PHONE	ENTRY#
Menlo Circus Club	7997	D	650 322-4616	14404

ATWATER, CA - Merced County

	SIC	EMP	PHONE	ENTRY#
Esau Concrete Inc.	1771	D	209 357-7601	2117
Gino/Giuseppe Inc.	1771	C	209 358-0556	2120
Golden Valley Health Centers	8011	D	209 382-0253	14764
Tjd LLC	8059	C	209 357-3420	15903
Central Counties	8734	D	209 356-0355	19955

AUBERRY, CA - Fresno County

	SIC	EMP	PHONE	ENTRY#
Pacific Gas and Electric Co.	4911	C	559 855-6112	4643
Mono Wind Casino	7011	D	559 855-4350	10023

AUBURN, CA - Placer County

	SIC	EMP	PHONE	ENTRY#
Decker Landscaping Inc.	0782	D	916 652-1780	483
Pacific Gas and Electric Co.	4911	A	530 889-3102	4637
Placer County Water Agency (PA)	4911	D	530 823-4850	4661
Smart & Final Stores Inc.	5141	D	530 823-1205	6305
Mother Lode Holding Co (HQ)	6361	C	530 887-2410	8450
Auburn Area Recreation Pk Dst	7999	D	530 537-2185	14494
Alpine Allrgy Asthma Assoc Inc	8011	D	530 888-1016	14599
Chapa-De Indian Hlth Prgram In (PA)	8011	D	530 887-2800	14677
University California Davis	8011	D	530 885-5618	15155
Auburn Oaks Care Center	8051	D	650 949-7777	15338
Emeritus Corporation	8052	C	530 653-1974	15754
Help At Home Senior Care	8082	D	877 404-6636	16868
Dreyer Babich Buccola Wood CAM	8111	D	530 889-1800	17442
Pride Industries	8331	C	530 888-0331	18243
California Envmtl Systems Inc	8711	D	530 820-3693	19167
County of Placer	8711	D	530 889-7500	19188

AVALON, CA - Los Angeles County

	SIC	EMP	PHONE	ENTRY#
Pacific Catalina Hotel Inc.	7011	B	310 510-9255	10078
Guided Discoveries Inc.	7032	D	310 510-1622	10403
Intervrsity Chrstn Fllwshp/Usa	7032	A	310 510-0015	10405

AVILA BEACH, CA - San Luis Obispo County

	SIC	EMP	PHONE	ENTRY#
Pacific Gas and Electric Co.	4911	A	805 506-5280	4632

AZUSA, CA - Los Angeles County

	SIC	EMP	PHONE	ENTRY#
Monrovia Nursery Company (PA)	0181	A	626 334-9321	140
Richard Wilson Wellington	0181	D	626 812-7881	151
Sunbelt Controls Inc.	1711	D	626 610-2340	1573
Berger Bros Inc	1742	B	626 334-2699	1908
Oj Insulation LP (PA)	1742	C	800 707-9278	1950
Heidi Corporation	1771	D	626 333-6317	2127
Mortech Manufacturing	2531	D	626 334-1471	2498
S&B Pharma Inc.	2833	D	626 334-2908	2577
Dhb Delivery LLC	4215	D	626 588-7562	3608
Cco Holdings LLC	4841	C	626 513-0204	4483
City of Azusa	4941	D	626 969-4408	4770
San Gabriel Valley Water Assn	4941	D	626 815-1305	4824
Hanson Distributing Company (PA)	5013	C	626 224-9800	5042
Heppner Hardwoods Inc.	5031	D	626 969-7983	5164
Cemex Cement Inc.	5032	C	626 969-1747	5197
Totten Tubes Inc (PA)	5051	D	626 812-0220	5527
Niscayah Inc.	5065	D	626 683-8167	5682
Smart & Final Stores Inc.	5141	C	626 334-5189	6316
Buena Vista Food Products Inc (DH)	5149	C	626 815-8859	6612
Mc-40 (PA)	7349	C	323 225-4111	10924
Ruiteng Internet Technology Co	7374	C	302 597-7438	12620
Artistic Entrmt Svcs LLC	7929	D	626 334-9388	14078
County of Los Angeles	8011	D	626 969-7885	14713
Casa Clina Hosp Ctrs For Hlthc	8049	D	626 334-8735	15271
Valley Lght Ctr For Scial Advn	8331	D	626 337-6200	18254
Amatel Inc (PA)	8748	D	323 801-0199	20687

BAKERSFIELD, CA - Kern County

	SIC	EMP	PHONE	ENTRY#
J G Boswell Company	0131	B	661 327-7721	3
Vignolo Farms Inc.	0131	C	661 746-2148	7
Bolthouse Farms	0161	A	661 366-7205	23
Generis Holdings LP (PA)	0161	B	661 366-7209	32
Wm Bolthouse Farms Inc (HQ)	0161	A	661 366-7209	49
7th Standard Ranch Company	0172	B	661 399-0416	67
Giumarra Vineyards Corporation	0172	C	661 395-7071	73
Crystal Organic Farms LLC	0191	C	661 845-5200	173
Dv Custom Farming LLC	0191	D	661 858-2888	176
Kirschenman Enterprises Inc	0191	C	661 366-5736	188
Maple Dairy LP	0241	D	661 396-9600	221
AC Irrigation Holdco LLC	0711	C	661 368-3550	240
Sunridge Nurseries Inc.	0721	B	661 363-8463	245
Grimmway Enterprises Inc.	0723	C	661 845-5200	275
Sun World Inc.	0723	A	805 833-6460	305
Sun World International Inc (PA)	0723	A	661 392-5000	306
Wonderful Company LLC	0723	A	559 781-7438	317
Ag-Wise Enterprises Inc (PA)	0762	C	661 325-1567	371
Illume Agriculture LLC.	0762	C	661 587-5198	375
Sun Pacific Farming Coop Inc	0762	D	661 399-0376	382
Penney Lawn Service Inc.	0782	C	661 587-4788	530
Aera Energy LLC	1311	A	661 665-5000	579
Aera Energy Services Company (HQ)	1381	A	661 665-5000	589
Elysium Jennings LLC.	1381	C	661 679-1700	592
Excalibur Well Services Corp.	1381	C	661 589-5338	593
Golden State Drilling Inc.	1381	D	661 589-0730	594
E & B Ntral Resources Mgt Corp (PA)	1382	D	661 679-1714	600
Linnco LLC.	1382	A	661 616-3900	601
Sentinel Peak Rsources Cal LLC	1382	C	661 395-5214	605
C&J Well Services LLC	1389	A	661 589-5220	608
CJ Berry Well Services MGT LLC	1389	A	661 589-5220	610
CL Knox Inc.	1389	D	661 837-0477	611
Hills Wldg & Engrg Contr Inc	1389	D	661 746-5400	613
Mmi Services Inc.	1389	C	661 589-9366	616
Nabors Well Services Co.	1389	C	661 588-6140	618
Nabors Well Services Co.	1389	C	661 392-7668	620
Nabors Well Services Co.	1389	B	661 589-3970	621
Pacific Process Systems Inc (PA)	1389	C	661 321-9681	626
PSC Industrial Outsourcing LP	1389	D	661 833-9991	627
Schlumberger Technology Corp	1389	C	661 864-4721	628
Titan Oilfield Services Inc.	1389	C	661 861-1630	629
Truitt Oilfield Maint Corp.	1389	B	661 871-4099	630
U S Weatherford L P	1389	C	661 589-9483	632
Colombo Construction Co Inc.	1542	C	661 316-0100	899
PCL Industrial Services Inc.	1542	B	661 832-3995	987
Griffith Company	1611	B	661 392-6640	1116
Diversified Utility Svcs Inc.	1623	B	661 325-3212	1205
K S Fabrication & Machine Inc.	1623	C	661 617-1700	1223
Ken Small Construction Inc.	1623	D	661 617-1700	1227
KS Industries LP (PA)	1623	A	661 617-1700	1228
Nts Inc.	1623	B	661 588-8514	1246
Utility Partners America LLC.	1623	D	864 269-2302	1273
Bland A/C & Heating Inc (PA)	1711	D	661 836-3880	1379
Frontier Mechanical Inc.	1711	D	661 589-6203	1447
Hps Mechanical Inc (PA)	1711	C	661 397-2121	1458
Rlh Fire Protection Inc (PA)	1711	D	661 322-9344	1549
Ardent Companies Inc.	1731	D	661 633-1465	1668
Contra Costa Electric Inc.	1731	C	661 322-4036	1708
Electrical & Instrumentation Unlimi	1731	C		1726
Energy Watch	1731	D	661 324-0930	1729
Ensign US Drlg Cal Inc.	1731	C	661 387-8400	1731
Esys Energy Control Company	1731	D	661 833-1902	1732
Pavletich Elc Cmmnications Inc (PA)	1731	C	661 589-9473	1802
Diaz Plastering Inc.	1742	D	661 244-8228	1925
Frye Construction Inc.	1742	D	661 588-8870	1930
Sunshine Metal Clad Inc.	1742	D	661 366-0575	1966
Grant Construction Inc.	1751	D	661 588-4586	1999
Baymarr Constructors Inc.	1771	C	661 395-1676	2097
Kenai Drilling Limited	1781	D	661 587-0117	2173
Zim Industries Inc.	1781	C	661 393-9661	2175
Guinn Corporation	1794	D	661 325-6109	2218
Sturgeon Son Grading & Pav Inc (PA)	1794	C	661 322-4408	2225
American Bottling Company	2086	D	661 323-7921	2399
Crystal Geyser Water Company	2086	D	661 323-6296	2405
Golden Empire Con Pdts Inc.	3272	D	661 833-4490	2704
Spartan Inc.	3441	D	661 327-1205	2739
Golden Empire Transit District (PA)	4111	C	661 869-2438	3141
Hall Ambulance Service Inc.	4119	C	661 322-8741	3267
Hall Ambulance Service Inc (PA)	4119	C	661 322-8741	3268
Gazelle Transportation LLC.	4212	C	661 322-8868	3396
Pg Trucking Inc.	4212	D	661 301-4942	3418
Stanford Transportation Inc.	4212	D	661 302-3288	3425
Esparza Enterprises Inc.	4213	A	661 631-0347	3469
HF Cox Inc (PA)	4213	D	661 366-3236	3490
Pan Pacific Petroleum Co Inc.	4213	C	661 589-3200	3526
Stevens Transportation Inc.	4213	C	661 366-3286	3546
Williams Tank Lines	4213	D	661 634-9755	3565

BAKERSFIELD CA

GEOGRAPHIC SECTION

	SIC	EMP	PHONE	ENTRY#
Exeter Packers Inc	4222	C	661 399-0416	3654
United States Cold Storage Inc	4222	D	661 832-2653	3664
Nex Group LLC	4731		209 317-6677	4062
AGM California Inc	4832	C	661 328-0118	4371
Newport Television LLC	4833	A	661 283-1700	4455
Prosoft Technology Inc (HQ)	4899	C	661 716-5100	4546
Pacific Gas and Electric Co	4911	C	661 398-5918	4658
Southern California Gas Co	4924	C	661 399-4431	4731
MP Environmental Svcs Inc (PA)	4953	C	800 458-3036	4913
Varner Bros Inc	4953	C	661 399-2944	4950
Bakersfield Shingles Wholesale Inc	5039	D	661 327-3727	5226
B & B Surplus Inc (PA)	5051	D	661 589-0381	5478
Jims Supply Co Inc (PA)	5051	D	661 616-6977	5500
Cameron West Coast Inc	5082	D		5784
Gottstein Corporation	5082	C	661 322-8934	5790
Quinn Company	5082	C	661 393-5800	5800
RL Surgener Inc	5084	C	661 322-0153	5868
Valley Power Systems Inc	5084	C	661 325-9001	5880
Westair Gases & Equipment Inc	5084	C	661 387-6800	5883
Sierra International McHy LLC	5093	D	661 327-7073	6016
Smart & Final Stores LLC	5141	D	661 589-2579	6325
Smart & Final Stores LLC	5141	D	661 326-7945	6366
Nestle Ice Cream Company	5143	A	661 398-3500	6441
Frito-Lay North America Inc	5145	C	661 328-6034	6462
Sun Pacific Marketing Coop Inc	5148	B	661 847-1015	6584
Aspire Bakeries LLC	5149	B	661 832-0409	6604
Core-Mark International Inc	5149	C	661 366-2673	6618
Valley Pacific Petro Svcs Inc	5172	D	661 746-7737	6745
Wfi Equipment Inc	5172	D	661 327-4900	6747
Advance Beverage Co Inc	5181	D	661 833-3783	6748
Lowes Home Centers LLC	5211	C	663 889-9000	7100
Smart & Final Stores LLC	5411	D	661 832-4540	7152
Cjm Automotive Group Inc	5511	D	661 832-3000	7185
Haberfelde Ford (PA)	5511	D	661 328-3600	7226
Haberfelde Ford	5511	D	661 837-6400	7227
Three-Way Chevrolet Co (PA)	5511	C	661 847-6400	7313
Mexicali Inc	5812	C	661 327-3861	7496
Kern Federal Credit Union	6061	D	661 327-9461	7776
Valley Strong Credit Union (PA)	6061	D	661 833-7900	7817
Golden Empire Mortgage Inc (PA)	6162	D	661 328-1600	7969
Golden Empire Mortgage Inc (PA)	6162	D	661 328-1600	7970
Merrill Lynch Prce Fnner Smith	6211	D	661 326-7700	8125
Health Net LLC	6324	C	661 321-3904	8299
State Compensation Insur Fund	6331	D	661 664-4000	8410
State Farm Mutl Auto Insur Co	6411	D	309 766-2311	8664
Olympus Property	6519	B	661 393-1700	8889
Bakersfield Westwind Corp	6531	C	661 327-2121	8908
Preferred Brokers Inc (PA)	6531	D	661 836-2345	9138
Stantec Holdings Del III Inc	6719	B	661 396-3770	9339
Msr Hotels & Resorts Inc	6799	C	661 325-9700	9536
Bakersfield Hospitality LLC	7011	D	661 393-1277	9628
Bakersfield Inn Inc	7011	D	661 323-1900	9629
Cni Thl Propco Fe LLC	7011	D	661 325-9700	9710
Golden West Partners Inc	7011	D	661 324-6936	9812
Gringteam Inc	7011	C	661 426-7919	9827
Newport Hospitality Group Inc	7011	D	661 323-1900	10043
Tiburon Hospitality LLC	7011	C	661 322-1012	10310
Banks Pest Control	7342	B	661 323-7858	10829
Western Energy Services Corp	7353	C	403 984-5916	11009
Western Oilfields Supply Co	7359	D	480 895-9225	11063
Western Oilfields Supply Co (PA)	7359	C	661 399-9124	11064
Century Hlth Staffing Svcs Inc	7361	C	661 322-0606	11111
Esparza Enterprises Inc	7361	A	661 631-0347	11134
Maxim Healthcare Services Inc	7363	D	661 322-3039	11309
Vasinda Investments Inc	7363	D	661 324-4277	11347
Work Force Services Inc	7363	D	661 327-5019	11364
Technosocialworkcom LLC	7374	D	661 617-6601	12635
M & S Security Services Inc	7381	D	661 397-9616	12999
Trans-West Services Inc	7381	B	661 381-2900	13055
Kern Security Corporation	7382	B	661 363-6874	13129
Arrival Communications Inc (DH)	7389	D	661 716-2100	13196
Califrnia Grnhse Frm II Ltd PR	7389	D	949 715-3987	13224
Sangera Buick Inc	7538	C	661 833-5200	13674
Car Wash Partners Inc	7542	C	661 377-1020	13690
Car Wash Partners Inc	7542	D	661 231-3689	13691
SA Camp Pump Company	7699	D	661 399-2976	13797
Snow Well Service Inc	7699	D	661 765-7980	13799
Bakersfield Country Club	7997	D	661 871-4000	14326
Seven Oaks Country Club	7997	C	661 664-6404	14450
Stockdale Country Club	7997	D	661 832-0310	14466
Bakersfield Family Medical Group Inc (PA)	8011	D	661 327-4411	14621
Central Cardiology Med Clinic	8011	D	661 395-0000	14671
Clinica Sierra Vista (PA)	8011	D	661 635-3050	14689

	SIC	EMP	PHONE	ENTRY#
Cns Inc	8011	D	661 872-3408	14692
Industrial Medical Group	8011	D	661 327-2225	14783
Kaiser Foundation Hospitals	8011	C	661 398-5011	14824
Kaiser Foundation Hospitals	8011	D	661 334-2020	14836
Kern Health Systems Inc	8011	D	661 664-5000	14861
Kern Rdlgy Imaging Systems Inc (PA)	8011	D	661 326-9600	14862
Kern Rdlgy Imaging Systems Inc	8011	D	661 322-9958	14863
Mohawk Medical Group Inc	8011	D	661 324-4747	14905
Omni Family Health (PA)	8011	D	661 459-1900	14935
Ravi Patel MD Inc	8011	D	661 862-7113	15011
San Dimas Medical Group Inc	8011	D	661 663-4800	15042
Southern Cal Prmnnte Med Group	8011	D	661 398-5085	15075
Southern Cal Prmnnte Med Group	8011	D	661 334-2020	15091
Truxtun Radiology Med Group LP	8011	D	661 325-6200	15130
Truxtun Radiology Med Group LP	8011	D	661 616-1201	15131
Truxtun Radiology Med Group LP	8011	D	661 205-6567	15132
Azad Professional Dental Corp	8021	D	661 558-0022	15217
Bakersfeld Hlthcare Wllness CN	8051	D	661 872-2121	15347
Bakersfieldidence Opco LLC	8051	C	661 399-2472	15348
Evergreen At Lakeport LLC	8051	D	661 871-3133	15470
Parkview Jlian Cnvlescent Hosp	8051	D	661 831-9150	15619
Parkview Julian LLC	8051	D	661 831-9150	15620
Hoffmann Hospice of Valley Inc	8052	D	661 410-1010	15763
Kern Valleyidence Opco LLC	8052	C	661 323-2894	15767
Crestwood Behavioral Hlth Inc	8059	D	661 363-8127	15842
Humangood Norcal	8059	C	661 834-0620	15860
Adventist Hlth Systm/West Corp	8062	B	661 316-6000	15923
Bakersfeld Mem Hosp Foundation	8062	D	661 327-4647	15955
Bakersfield Memorial Hospital	8062	A	661 327-1792	15956
County of Kern	8062	A	661 326-2054	16023
Dignity Health	8062	B	661 663-6000	16055
Good Smrtan Hosp A Cal Ltd Prt	8062	B	661 903-9555	16113
Kaiser Foundation Hospitals	8062	D	661 631-3045	16147
Kaiser Foundation Hospitals	8062	D	661 412-6777	16154
Kern County Hospital Authority (PA)	8062	A	661 326-2102	16204
San Joaquin Community Hospital (PA)	8062	A	661 395-3000	16381
Bakersfeld Bhvral Hlthcare Hos	8063	C	661 398-1800	16640
Physicians Automated Lab Inc (DH)	8071	D	661 325-0744	16741
Centre For Neuro Skills (PA)	8093	B	661 872-3408	17023
Kern County Hospital Authority	8093	D	661 843-7980	17082
Bakersfield Family Med Group	8099	D	661 846-3605	17183
Klein Denatale Goldner (PA)	8111	D	661 485-2100	17526
First Assmbly of God Bkrsfield	8211	D	661 327-2227	17711
City of Bakersfield	8322	D	661 852-7300	17886
Bakersfeld Assn For Rtrded Ctz	8331	D	661 834-2272	18210
Alliance Childrens Services	8361	D	661 863-0350	18372
Community Action Partnr Kern	8361	D	661 336-5300	18398
Community Action Partnr Kern	8399	D	661 835-5405	18575
Kern Regional Center (PA)	8399	D	661 327-8531	18601
New Advnces For Pple With Dsbl	8399	D	661 322-9735	18611
New Advnces For Pple With Dsbl	8399	D	661 327-0188	18612
Wonderful Citrus Cooperative	8611	A	661 720-2400	18727
Boys Girls Clubs of Kern Cnty	8641	B	661 325-3730	18822
St Jhns Lthran Ch Bakersfield	8661	D	661 665-7815	19029
Automobile Club Southern Cal	8699	D	661 327-4661	19046
A-C Electric Company	8711	B	661 633-5368	19123
Diversified Prj Svcs Intl Inc (PA)	8711	D	661 371-2800	19201
Innovative Engrg Systems Inc (PA)	8711	D	661 381-7800	19269
Processes Unlimited International Inc	8711	B	661 396-3770	19363
UCI Construction Inc	8711	D	661 587-0192	19423
W M Lyles Co	8711	D	661 387-1600	19434
Brown Armstrong Accntancy Corp	8721	D	661 324-4971	19542
Analytical Pace Services LLC	8734	C	800 878-4911	19948
Healthcare Finance Direct LLC	8742	D	661 616-4400	20403
Pro Safety & Rescue Inc	8742	D	888 269-5095	20513
Sun Pacific Marketing Coop Inc	8742	B	213 612-9957	20572
County of Kern	9441	C	661 336-6871	20942

BALDWIN PARK, CA - Los Angeles County

	SIC	EMP	PHONE	ENTRY#
Tanimura Antle Fresh Foods Inc	0723	C	831 424-6100	309
County of Los Angeles	0742	D	626 962-3577	332
Crosstown Elec & Data Inc	1731	D	626 813-6693	1712
Meritek Electronics Corp (PA)	3559	D	626 373-1728	2790
George Fischer Inc (HQ)	3599	C	626 571-2770	2852
United Parcel Service Inc	4215	B	626 814-6216	3645
Cedarwood-Young Company (PA)	4953	C	626 962-4447	4876
Waste MGT Collectn Recycl Inc	4953	D	626 960-7551	4966
Nichols Lumber & Hardware Co	5031	D	626 960-4802	5174
Tecan Sp Inc	5049	D	626 962-0010	5471
Lighting Technologies Intl LLC	5063	C	626 480-0755	5574
American Kal Enterprises Inc (PA)	5072	D	626 338-7308	5720
Normans Nursery Inc	5193	C	626 285-9795	6869
Home Depot USA Inc	5211	C	626 813-7131	7005

	SIC	EMP	PHONE	ENTRY#
Tommies Medical Ctr Phrm Inc	5912	D	714 961-7930	7529
SCE Federal Credit Union (PA)	6061	D	626 960-6888	7800
Kaiser Foundation Hospitals	6324	A	626 851-1011	8311
Baldwin Hospitality LLC	7011	D	626 446-2988	9630
Ols Hotels & Resorts LLC	7011	A	626 962-6000	10063
Haynes Building Service LLC	7349	C	626 359-6100	10907
Source One Staffing LLC	7361	A	626 337-0560	11233
Alphatech General Inc	7699	D	626 337-4640	13761
Kaiser Foundation Hospitals	8011	D	310 922-8916	14853
Golden State Habilitation Conv (PA)	8051	C	626 962-3274	15499
Gr8 Care Inc	8051	C	626 337-7229	15501
Trinity Health Systems (PA)	8051	D	626 960-1971	15707
Vista Spclty Hosp Sthern Cal L	8062	D	626 388-2700	16622
Good Health Inc	8099	D	714 961-7930	17241
Eben-Ezer Chld Day Care Ctr	8351	D	626 960-7100	18312
County of Los Angeles	8711	D	626 337-1277	19187
American Mzhou Dngpo Group Inc	8741	D	626 820-9239	20022
Telesector Resources Group Inc	8742	B	626 813-4538	20581

BALLICO, CA - Merced County

	SIC	EMP	PHONE	ENTRY#
Hilltop Ranch Inc	0723	C	209 874-1875	278
Golden By-Products Inc	3559	D	209 668-4855	2789

BANNING, CA - Riverside County

	SIC	EMP	PHONE	ENTRY#
Smart & Final Stores LLC	5141	D	951 849-5658	6367
Green Thumb Produce Inc	5148	C	951 849-4711	6557
Professional Cmnty MGT Cal Inc	6531	B	951 845-2191	9141
Silent Valley Club Inc	7011	D	951 849-4501	10236
San Gorgonio Memorial Hospital	8062	A	951 845-1121	16379
San Grgnio Mem Hosp Foundation (PA)	8062	C	951 845-1121	16380
Riverside-San Bernardino	8093	C	951 849-4761	17122
Porto Inc	8322	D	760 709-3737	18085

BARSTOW, CA - San Bernardino County

	SIC	EMP	PHONE	ENTRY#
Mv Transportation Inc	4111	C	760 255-3330	3179
Life Care Centers America Inc	8051	C	760 252-2515	15543
Hospital of Barstow Inc (DH)	8062	C	760 256-1761	16136
On The Rise Inc	8399	D	760 964-7473	18614
Hentrel Greathouse Foundation	8641	D	302 513-4056	18869

BASS LAKE, CA - Madera County

	SIC	EMP	PHONE	ENTRY#
Pines Resorts of California (PA)	5812	C	559 642-3121	7503
Home Away Inc	7011	D	559 642-3121	9865

BAY POINT, CA - Contra Costa County

	SIC	EMP	PHONE	ENTRY#
Keller Canyon Landfill Company	4953	C	925 458-9800	4902
Kahn Rennaissance LLC	7213	C	510 260-3161	10436
Elite Security Group Inc	7382	D	925 597-8852	13111
Henkel US Operations Corp	8711	D	925 458-8086	19248

BEAR VALLEY, CA - Calaveras County

	SIC	EMP	PHONE	ENTRY#
Bear Valley Ski Co	7999	B	209 753-2301	14497

BEAUMONT, CA - Riverside County

	SIC	EMP	PHONE	ENTRY#
David-Kleis II LLC	8099	D	951 845-3125	17218
Beaumont Unifed Schl Dst Pub F	8211	B	951 845-6580	17694
Childhelp Inc	8361	C	951 845-6737	18392

BELL, CA - Los Angeles County

	SIC	EMP	PHONE	ENTRY#
Marika LLC	2339	D	323 888-7755	2460
Custom Building Products LLC	2891	C	323 582-0846	2642
De Well Container Shipping Inc	4731	C	310 735-8600	4003
Omega Moulding West LLC	5023	C	323 261-3510	5130
Fam Ppe LLC	5099	C	323 888-7755	6040
Perrin Bernard Supowitz LLC (HQ)	5113	C	323 981-2800	6090
Smart & Final Stores LLC	5141	D	323 562-3421	6371
El Aviso Magazine	5192	D	323 586-9199	6841
Fedex Services	7389	D	323 881-3400	13285
Leonid M Glsman DDS A Dntl Cor	8021	D	323 560-4514	15234
Human Services Association (PA)	8322	D	562 806-5400	18008
Jwch Institute Inc	8733	D	323 562-5813	19891

BELL GARDENS, CA - Los Angeles County

	SIC	EMP	PHONE	ENTRY#
C T and F Inc	1731	D	562 927-2339	1690
Orbit Industries Inc	5063	D	213 745-8884	5585
US Foods Inc	5149	C	562 806-2445	6686
Parkhouse Tire Service Inc (PA)	5531	D	562 928-0421	7354
Anitsa Inc	7211	D	213 237-0533	10423
Bell Gardens Bicycle Club Inc	7999	A	562 806-4646	14498
Del Rio Sanitarium Inc	8051	C	562 927-6586	15422

BELLFLOWER, CA - Los Angeles County

	SIC	EMP	PHONE	ENTRY#
Cutting Edge Creative LLC	2542	D	562 907-7007	2505
Empire Transportation Inc	4141	B	562 529-2676	3311
Smart & Final Stores LLC	5141	D	562 920-6268	6327
George Chevrolet	5511	D	562 925-2500	7219
Hollywood Sports Park LLC	7389	D	562 867-9600	13317
S J S Enterprise Inc	7999	C	949 489-9000	14557
County of Los Angeles	8011	D	562 804-8111	14712
Peter Wylan DDS	8021	D	562 925-3765	15247
Bell Villa Care Associates LLC	8051	D	562 925-4252	15356
Life Care Centers America Inc	8051	C	562 867-1761	15541
Jwch Institute Inc	8099	D	562 867-7999	17258
Clara Shortridge Foltz	8111	D	562 925-3039	17404
Harbor Health Care Inc	8361	D	562 866-7054	18445

BELMONT, CA - San Mateo County

	SIC	EMP	PHONE	ENTRY#
Pacific Gas and Electric Co	4911	D	650 592-9411	4615
Nikon Precision Inc (DH)	5084	C	650 508-4674	5848
James Electronics Limited	5961	D	650 592-6718	7561
Woodmont Realty Advisors Inc	6371	B	650 592-3960	8470
Ten-X LLC	6531	C	800 793-6107	9190
Osso Vr Inc	7371	C	310 709-8289	11805
Ringcentral Inc (PA)	7374	C	650 472-4100	12617
Belmont Oaks Academy	8351	D	650 593-6175	18270
Westlake Development Group LLC	8741	C	650 579-1010	20251

BELVEDERE, CA - Marin County

	SIC	EMP	PHONE	ENTRY#
Pacific Union Co	6531	D	415 789-8686	9119

BELVEDERE TIBURON, CA - Marin County

	SIC	EMP	PHONE	ENTRY#
1651 Tiburon Hotel LLC	7011	D	401 946-4600	9586
Nes Health Care Group	8011	D	415 435-4591	14919
Tiburon Community Snf LLC	8051	D	415 435-4554	15703
Cancer Prevention Inst Cal (PA)	8733	C	510 608-5000	19873

BEN LOMOND, CA - Santa Cruz County

	SIC	EMP	PHONE	ENTRY#
Kms Financial Services Inc	7389	D	360 770-5117	13339

BENICIA, CA - Solano County

	SIC	EMP	PHONE	ENTRY#
Awt Construction Group Inc	1521	D	707 746-7500	657
Lathrop Construction Assoc Inc (PA)	1542	D	707 746-8000	957
American Cvil Cnstrs W Cast LL	1611	D	707 746-8028	1075
American Civil Cnstrs LLC	1629	D	707 746-8028	1284
Timec Companies Inc (DH)	1629	B	707 642-2222	1322
DC Solar Solutions Inc	1711	D	925 203-1088	1419
Delta Corey Inc	1711	C	707 747-7500	1420
Califrnia Erctors Bay Area Inc	1791	D	707 746-1990	2182
Quality Erectors Cnstr Co Inc	1791	D	707 746-1233	2194
Romak Iron Works	1791	D	707 751-2420	2199
C E Toland & Son	1799	D	707 747-1000	2262
High End Development Inc	1799	C	925 687-2540	2284
Durkee Drayage Company	4214	D	510 970-7550	3585
Pro-Form Manufacturing LLC	4225	D	707 752-9010	3744
Pro-Form Manufacturing LLC	4225	B	707 752-9010	3745
Innovel Solutions Inc	4731	A	707 748-1940	4038
Underground Cnstr Co Inc	4931	C	707 746-8800	4754
1-800 Radiator & A/C LLC (DH)	5013	D	707 747-7400	5020
Abb Inc	5063	D	808 497-7240	5532
West Coast Beauty Supply Co	5087	A	707 748-4800	5953
All-Points Petroleum LLC	5172	D	707 745-1116	6722
CENTRAL COAST WINE COMPANY	5182	C	707 745-8500	6791
Henry Wine Group LLC (HQ)	5182	B	707 745-8500	6798
Solano Pacific Corporation	6531	D	707 745-6000	9181
Onsite Health Inc	8099	D	888 411-2290	17287
Sonia Corina Inc	8099	D	707 644-4491	17327
F3 and Associates Inc (PA)	8713	D	707 748-4300	19524
Certifiedsafety Inc	8742	D	707 747-9400	20313
Clean Harbors Envmtl Svcs Inc	8748	D	707 747-6699	20729

BERKELEY, CA - Alameda County

	SIC	EMP	PHONE	ENTRY#
O C Jones & Sons Inc (PA)	1611	C	510 526-3424	1147
Homeenergy Inc	1711	D	707 200-3758	1457
L J Kruse Co	1711	D	510 644-0260	1480
Berkeley Cement Inc	1771	C	510 525-8175	2101
Evolv Surfaces Inc	2542	C	415 767-4600	2506
Indepndnt Brkley Stdnt Pubg I	2711	C	510 548-8300	2538
Backroads (PA)	4725	D	510 527-1555	3960
LMI Net	4813	D	510 843-6389	4307
Callisto Media Inc	4899	C	510 253-0500	4531
Terabase Energy Inc	4911	D	415 763-7181	4712
Cemex Corp	5032	C	800 992-3639	5199
Souvenir Coffee Corporation	5099	D	510 450-0505	6052
McKesson Corporation	5122	D	510 666-0854	6125
Annies Homegrown Inc	5149	D	510 558-7500	6600
Hart Chemicals Inc	5191	D	510 549-3535	6826

BERKELEY CA

GEOGRAPHIC SECTION

	SIC	EMP	PHONE	ENTRY#
Kaiser Foundation Hospitals	6324	A	510 559-5362	8334
Permanente Medical Group Inc	6324	A	510 559-5119	8355
Berkeley	7011	B	510 845-7300	9641
Berkeley Downtown Ht Owner LLC	7011	D	510 982-2100	9642
Boykin Mgt Co Ltd Lblty Co	7011	D	510 548-7920	9656
Claremont Hotel Properties LLC	7011	A	510 843-3000	9705
Hotel Durant A Ltd Partnership	7011	C	510 845-8981	9871
International House	7021	C	510 642-9490	10393
Berkeley Student Coop Inc	7041	D	510 848-1936	10418
Lead Genius	7311	D	415 969-2915	10640
Berkeley Unified School Dst	7349	D	510 644-6250	10861
Arris Composites Inc	7371	C	510 730-0067	11426
Rigetti & Co LLC (PA)	7371	C	510 210-5550	11882
Barra LLC (HQ)	7372	B	510 548-5442	12110
Relationalai Inc	7372	C	650 307-8776	12333
University California Berkeley	7379	D	510 642-6000	12902
C P Shades Inc	7389	B	510 647-9605	13219
East Bay Regional Park Dst	7389	D	510 848-7373	13276
First Page Sage LLC	7389	D	206 369-6516	13288
ISI Inspection Services Inc (PA)	7389	D	510 900-2101	13331
Msci Inc	7389	D	510 548-5442	13384
Strathmoore Press Inc	7389	D	510 843-8888	13488
Sun Light & Power	7389	D	510 845-2997	13491
Permanente Medical Group Inc	8011	A	510 559-5338	14984
Chaparral Foundation	8051	D	510 848-8774	15375
Ocadian Care Centers LLC	8051	D	510 204-5801	15603
Shattuck Health Care Inc	8051	D	510 665-2800	15663
Surgery Ctr of Alta Btes Smmit (HQ)	8062	A	510 204-4444	16504
Sutter Bay Hospitals	8062	D	510 869-6199	16508
Lawrence Berkeley National Lab	8071	A	347 425-3735	16733
Berkeley Community Health Prj	8082	D	510 548-2570	16819
New Bridge Foundation Inc	8093	D	510 548-7270	17101
Options Recovery Services	8093	D	510 666-9552	17104
Integrted Mlclar Dgnstics Pthl	8099	D	866 944-8050	17256
John Muir	8099	D	510 922-9659	17257
Robin Healthcare LLC	8099	C	310 601-6899	17316
Assocted Stdnts of The Univ CA (PA)	8299	C	510 642-5420	17801
Toolworks Inc	8322	B	510 649-1322	18152
Bay Area Hspano Inst For Advnc	8351	D	510 525-1463	18269
Interntnl Child Rsrce Exch In (PA)	8399	C	510 644-1000	18596
Young MNS Chrstn Assn of E Bay	8641	B	510 486-8400	18969
Young MNS Chrstn Assn of E Bay	8641	B	510 848-9092	18970
Young MNS Chrstn Assn of E Bay	8641	C	510 848-9622	18971
Young MNS Chrstn Assn of E Bay	8641	B	510 526-2146	18973
Young MNS Chrstn Assn of E Bay	8641	C	510 644-6290	18975
Young MNS Chrstn Assn of E Bay	8641	C	510 848-6800	18985
Young MNS Chrstn Assn of E Bay	8641	B	510 559-2090	18987
Earth Island Institute Inc	8699	D	510 859-9100	19082
Lawrence Berkeley National Lab	8721	A	510 486-6954	19598
Curtis & Tompkins Ltd	8731	D	510 486-0900	19676
DSM Biomedical Inc	8731	D	510 841-8800	19683
Form Energy Inc	8731	D	844 367-6462	19694
Ripple Foods Pbc	8731	D	510 269-2563	19763
Pivot Bio Inc	8732	B	515 436-4462	19843
United Sttes Dept Enrgy Brkley	8733	C	510 486-4033	19925
Moore Iacofano Goltsman Inc (PA)	8748	D	510 845-7549	20806
Newfield Wireless Inc (DH)	8748	D	510 848-8248	20814

BERMUDA DUNES, CA - Riverside County

	SIC	EMP	PHONE	ENTRY#
Vintage Associates Inc	0782	C	760 772-3673	546

BEVERLY HILLS, CA - Los Angeles County

	SIC	EMP	PHONE	ENTRY#
Nadco Inc	0742	D	310 623-7776	338
D&A Endeavors Inc	1799	D	310 390-7540	2271
Jeffries Global Inc	1799	D	888 255-3488	2288
Zeons Inc	3229	B	323 302-8299	2690
King Holding Corporation	3452	A	586 254-3900	2750
Protravel International LLC	4724	C	310 271-9566	3949
Seaworld Global Logistics	4731	B	310 579-9164	4092
Nextpoint Inc (PA)	4813	D	310 360-5904	4320
Participant Channel Inc	4833	D	310 550-7715	4457
Fashion World Incorporated	5136	C	310 273-6544	6173
BW Hotel LLC	5812	A	310 275-5200	7462
Fat Brands Inc (PA)	5812	B	310 319-1850	7480
City National Bank	6021	D	310 888-6150	7620
City National Securities LLC	6021	C	310 888-6393	7623
Merrill Lynch Prce Fnner Smith	6021	D	310 858-1500	7631
Pacwest Bancorp (PA)	6021	D	310 887-8500	7637
Morgan Stnley Smith Barney LLC	6153	D	310 285-4800	7897
Gores Group LLC (PA)	6211	D	310 209-3010	8091
M L Stern & Co LLC (DH)	6211	C	323 658-4400	8101
Muriel Siebert & Co Inc	6211	B	800 993-2015	8156
Massachusetts Mutl Lf Insur Co	6311	D	323 965-6339	8239
Charles & Cynthia Eberly Inc	6513	D	323 937-6468	8798
Compass	6531	D	818 629-9776	8950
Keller Wllams Rlty Bvrly Hills	6531	C	310 432-6400	9064
Kennedy-Wilson Inc (PA)	6531	C	310 887-6400	9065
Plg Estates	6531	D	310 788-0700	9136
Re/Max	6531	D	310 205-0050	9151
Rodeo Realty Inc (PA)	6531	D	818 349-9997	9170
Row Management Ltd Inc	6531	B	310 887-3671	9172
Starpint 1031 Property MGT LLC	6531	D	310 247-0550	9186
Worldwide Inc	6531	D	310 276-7171	9223
Century Pacific Realty Corp	6552	C	310 729-9922	9248
Shapell Industries LLC (HQ)	6552	D	323 655-7330	9273
Project Skyline Intermediate H	6719	A	310 712-1850	9329
Levine Lchtman Cpitl Prtners S	6794	D	310 275-5335	9453
Regent LP (PA)	6799	D	310 299-4100	9554
USA Enterprise Inc	6799	B	310 750-4246	9576
Belvedere Hotel Partnership	7011	B	310 551-2888	9638
Belvedere Partnership	7011	B	310 551-2888	9639
Beverly Hills Collection	7011	D	310 276-1022	9646
Honeymoon Real Estate LP	7011	D	310 277-5221	9867
Kirkwood Collection Inc	7011	D	424 532-1160	9947
Oasis West Realty LLC	7011	D	310 860-6666	10055
Park Hotels & Resorts Inc	7011	C	310 415-3340	10104
Raffles Lrmitage Beverly Hills	7011	D	310 278-3344	10137
Sajahtera Inc	7011	A	310 276-2251	10191
Rouse Services LLC	7299	D	310 360-9200	10573
Mob Scene LLC (PA)	7311	C	323 648-7200	10650
Studio 71 LP	7313	C	323 370-1500	10720
William Mrris Endvor Entrmt LL (DH)	7361	D	212 586-5100	11256
Anderson Assoc Staffing Corp (PA)	7363	C	323 930-3170	11272
Cedar Sinai	7363	D	310 285-7268	11279
Nga 911 LLC	7371	D	877 899-8337	11776
Rootstrap Inc	7371	C	310 907-9210	11888
Mission Cloud Services Inc (PA)	7379	C	855 647-7466	12840
American Health Connection	7389	A	424 226-0420	13190
Heritage Auctions Inc	7389	D	310 300-8390	13313
Live Nation Entertainment Inc (PA)	7389	C	310 867-7000	13356
Monex Inc	7389	D	310 695-3059	13380
United Talent Agency LLC	7389	C	310 776-8160	13524
Imperial Parking Inds Inc	7521	D	310 276-9766	13607
Modern Parking Inc	7521	C	310 271-1125	13611
Brillstein Entrmt Partners LLC (HQ)	7812	D	310 205-5100	13823
Metro-Goldwyn-Mayer Inc (DH)	7812	B	310 449-3000	13865
Orion Pictures Corporation	7812	A	310 449-3000	13872
Condor Productions LLC	7819	D	310 449-3000	13930
Lfp Broadcasting LLC (PA)	7822	D	323 852-5020	13965
United Artists Films Company (DH)	7822	A	310 449-3000	13970
Agency For Performing Arts Inc (PA)	7922	D	310 557-9049	14027
Circle Talent Agency LLC	7922	D	323 424-4970	14033
Management 360	7922	D	310 272-7000	14047
Paradigm Music LLC (PA)	7922	D	310 288-8000	14051
The Gersh Agency LLC (PA)	7922	D	310 274-6611	14071
William Mrris Endvor Entrmt FN (DH)	7922	C	310 285-9000	14073
William Mrris Endvor Entrmt LL	7922	B	310 285-9000	14074
Cznd Inc	7929	D	323 378-6505	14080
Ease Entertainment Services LP	7929	D	310 469-7300	14081
Live Nation Worldwide Inc (HQ)	7929	A	310 867-7000	14092
ROC Nation LLC (HQ)	7929	D	310 975-6854	14101
Endeavor Group Holdings Inc (PA)	7941	D	310 285-9000	14136
Gemini Basketball LLC	7941	B	213 929-1300	14140
Live Nation Worldwide Inc	7941	B	310 867-7000	14148
Pse Holding LLC (DH)	7941	B	248 377-0165	14154
Wme Img LLC (DH)	7941	C	212 586-5100	14162
Ba Sports Nutrition LLC	7991	D	718 357-7402	14172
Ticketmster New Vntres Hldngs (HQ)	7999	C	800 653-8000	14573
La Peer Surgery Center LLC	8011	C	310 360-9119	14872
Tower Hmtlogy Oncology Med Grou	8011	C	310 888-8680	15127
Westside Crdvsclar Med Group I	8011	C	310 289-9955	15206
GPh Medical & Legal Services (PA)	8051	C	213 207-2700	15500
Cedars-Sinai Medical Center	8062	D	310 967-1884	15979
Cedars-Sinai Medical Center	8062	A	310 385-3400	15983
Beverly Hlls Oncology Med Group	8069	D	310 432-8900	16667
Rheumatology Diagnostics Lab	8071	D	310 253-5455	16750
Universal Home Care Inc	8082	C	323 653-9222	16957
Doctor On Demand Inc	8099	D	310 988-2882	17224
BD&j PC	8111	D	855 906-3699	17382
One LLP	8111	D	310 866-5157	17594
Page Private School	8211	D	323 272-3429	17738
Academy Mpic Arts & Sciences (PA)	8621	D	310 247-3000	18728
World Mvie Awrds Orgnztion Wma	8641	D	833 375-5857	18932
Collective MGT Group LLC	8741	C	323 655-8585	20060
Ghp Management Corporation	8741	C	310 432-1441	20098
Za Management	8741	D	310 271-2200	20256

GEOGRAPHIC SECTION

BRENTWOOD CA

	SIC	EMP	PHONE	ENTRY#
National Clearing Corporation (PA)	8742	D	310 385-2165	20482
Magic Workforce Solutions LLC	8743	A	310 246-6153	20638
Boosted Ecommerce Inc	8748	D	310 721-6316	20709
MGM and Ua Services Company	8999	A	310 449-3000	20895

BIG BEAR LAKE, CA - San Bernardino County

Pacific Snow Valley Resort LLC	7011	D	909 866-3121	10088
Snow Summit Ski Corporation (PA)	7011	C	909 866-5766	10251
Bear Vly Cmnty Healthcare Dst (PA)	8062	C	909 866-6501	15960

BIG CREEK, CA - Fresno County

Southern California Edison Co	4911	C	559 893-3611	4681
Southern California Edison Co	4911	C	559 893-2037	4700

BIG SUR, CA - Monterey County

48123 CA Investors LLC	7011	C	831 667-2331	9592

BISHOP, CA - Inyo County

Frontier California Inc	4813	B	760 872-0812	4283
Southern California Edison Co	4911	C	760 873-0715	4705
Los Angeles Dept Wtr & Pwr	4941	A	760 873-0299	4802
Smart & Final Stores LLC	5141	D	760 873-7181	6331
Bishop Paiute Gaming Corp	7011	C	760 872-6005	9652
Toiyabe Indian Health Prj Inc (PA)	8021	D	760 873-8461	15252
Northern Inyo Healthcare Dst	8062	B	760 873-5811	16288

BLOOMINGTON, CA - San Bernardino County

MCM Construction Inc	1622	D	909 875-0533	1186
Team West Contracting Corp	1799	D	951 340-3426	2319
Ftdi West Inc	4225	D	909 473-1111	3708
Gxo Logistics Supply Chain Inc	4225	A	336 309-6201	3711
Unified Aircraft Services Inc (PA)	4783	D	909 877-0535	4136
Revchem Composites Inc (PA)	5033	D	909 877-8477	5224
Pacific Steel Group	5051	B	858 449-7219	5506
Chiro Inc (PA)	5087	C	909 879-1160	5936
Empire Oil Co	5172	C	909 877-0226	6729
Poma Holding Company Inc	5172	C	909 877-2441	6734
Social Science Service Center	8069	D	909 421-7120	16697
Englewood Marketing Group Inc	8742	D	909 875-3649	20360

BLUE LAKE, CA - Humboldt County

Blue Lake Casino	7011	D	707 668-5101	9653

BLYTHE, CA - Riverside County

Hayday Farms Inc	0139	D	760 922-4713	13
Fisher Ranch LLC	0723	D	760 922-4151	268
Palo Verde Irrigation District	4971	D	760 922-3144	4993
Palo Verde Health Care Dst	8062	C	760 922-4115	16305
Palo Verde Hospital Assn	8062	C	760 922-4115	16306

BODEGA BAY, CA - Sonoma County

NAPA Valley Lodge LP	7011	C	707 875-3525	10037
Bodega Harbour Homeowners Assn	8641	D	707 875-3519	18817

BONITA, CA - San Diego County

John Collins Co Inc	6513	D	818 227-2190	8836
Crockett & Coinc	7992	D	619 267-1103	14255
Paradise Valley Hospital	8062	B	619 472-7474	16317

BONSALL, CA - San Diego County

Euroamerican Propagators LLC	0181	B	760 731-6029	127

BORON, CA - Kern County

Rio Tinto Minerals Inc	1241	C	760 762-7121	577

BORREGO SPRINGS, CA - San Diego County

Borrego Cmnty Hlth Foundation (PA)	8011	C	855 436-1234	14633

BOULDER CREEK, CA - Santa Cruz County

Cortlandt Liquidating LLC	6531	C	831 338-4500	8953
Young MNS Chrstn Assn Slcon VI	8641	B	831 338-2128	19005

BRAWLEY, CA - Imperial County

Esparza Enterprises Inc	0762	A	760 344-2031	374
Border Valley Trading Ltd	5191	D	760 344-6700	6822
Vons Companies Inc	5411	C	760 351-3002	7154
Farm Water Technological Services Inc	5999	D	760 344-3068	7579
Pioneers Mem Healthcare Dst (PA)	8062	A	760 351-3333	16328
Brawley Union High School Dist (PA)	8211	D	760 312-6068	17696
City of Brawley (PA)	9111	D	760 344-8941	20911

BREA, CA - Orange County

RMA Land Construction Inc	0782	D	714 985-2888	535
Beazer Mortgage Corporation	1531	D	714 480-1635	787
Bergman Kprs LLC (PA)	1542	C	714 924-7000	872
Kprs Construction Services Inc (PA)	1542	D	714 672-0800	954
Nevell Group Inc (PA)	1542	C	714 579-7501	976
Griffith Company (PA)	1611	C	714 984-5500	1115
Sully-Miller Contracting Co (DH)	1611	D	714 578-9600	1166
Sully-Miller Holding Corp	1611	C	714 578-9600	1167
United Rock Products Corp	1611	C	714 578-9600	1175
Jilk Heavy Construction Inc	1629	D	310 830-6323	1308
Coolsys Coml Indus Sltions Inc (DH)	1711	D	714 510-9609	1407
Apollo Electric	1731	D	714 256-8414	1667
Pacific Intl Elc Co Inc	1731	D	714 990-9280	1796
Norcal Inc	1751	D	714 224-3949	2009
Win-Dor Inc (PA)	1751	C	714 576-2030	2027
Team Finish Inc	1771	D	714 671-9190	2165
Northstar Dem & Remediation LP (DH)	1795	C	714 672-3500	2242
Wilsey Foods Inc	2079	A	714 257-3700	2377
West Coast Gasket Co	3053	D	714 869-0123	2656
Metals USA Building Pdts LP (DH)	3355	A	713 946-9000	2723
Viewsonic Corporation (PA)	3577	C	909 444-8888	2839
Bi Technologies Corporation (HQ)	3679	B	714 447-2300	2940
Harbor Truck Bodies Inc	3713	D	714 996-0411	2968
Emergency Ambulance Svc Inc	4119	D	714 990-1331	3254
Premier Medical Transport Inc	4119	C	805 340-5191	3286
Hot Dogger Tours Inc	4142	C	714 988-4088	3318
Delivery Solutions Inc	4212	D	800 335-6557	3386
Cellco Partnership	4812	D	714 256-6015	4194
Diversfied Cmmnctions Svcs Inc	4813	D	714 888-2284	4269
Just Wheels & Tires LLC	5013			5046
Wurth Louis and Company (DH)	5072	D	714 529-1771	5740
Air Treatment Corporation (PA)	5075	D	909 869-7975	5766
Nelson Stud Welding Inc	5085	C	256 353-1931	5915
TSC Auto ID Technology America (HQ)	5085	C	909 468-0100	5933
Proponent Inc (PA)	5088	C	714 223-5400	5965
Acosta Inc	5141	C	714 988-1500	6235
Natures Best	5149	B	714 255-4600	6653
Hill Brothers Chemical Company (PA)	5169	C	714 998-8800	6711
Jewelscent Inc	5199	D	800 550-1762	6918
American Suzuki Motor Corporation	5511	B	714 996-7040	7169
Levity of Brea LLC	5813	C	714 482-0700	7520
Beverages & More Inc	5921	C	714 990-2060	7530
Capitalsource Bank	6022	D	714 989-4600	7668
American First Credit Union (PA)	6061	D	562 691-1112	7753
Adelfi Credit Union	6062	C	714 671-5700	7819
Amwest Funding Corp	6153	C	714 831-3333	7890
American Financial Network Inc (PA)	6162	C	714 831-4000	7927
Emet Lending Group Inc	6162	D	714 933-9800	7959
Merrill Lynch Prce Fnner Smith	6211	C	714 257-4400	8126
Morgan Stnley Smith Barney LLC	6211	C	714 674-4100	8152
Mercury Casualty Company (HQ)	6331	A	323 937-1060	8390
Mercury Insurance Company	6331	D	714 671-6700	8392
Mercury Insurance Company	6331	A	714 255-5000	8395
Veterinary Pet Insurance Services Inc	6411	B	714 989-0555	8681
Veterinary Pet Services Inc	6411	C	714 989-0555	8682
Otb Acquisition LLC	7011	D	520 458-0540	10073
Park Hotels & Resorts Inc	7011	D	714 990-6000	10101
Windsor Capital Group Inc	7011	C	714 990-6000	10373
Glen Ivy Hot Springs	7299	C	714 990-2090	10549
Cmre Financial Services Inc	7322	B	714 528-3200	10738
Contract Services Group Inc	7349	C	714 582-1800	10878
North Amrcn Staffing Group Inc	7361	C	714 599-8399	11183
Safran Pass Innovations LLC (HQ)	7371	C	714 854-8600	11894
Solugenix Corporation (PA)	7373	C	866 749-7658	12526
New Dream Network LLC (PA)	7376	D	626 644-9466	12697
Pramira Inc	7379	C	800 678-1169	12859
Southwest Patrol Inc	7381	D	909 861-1884	13049
V A Anderson Enterprises Inc (PA)	7389	D	714 990-6100	13537
Aer Technologies Inc	7699	B	714 871-7357	13760
Kaiser Foundation Hospitals	8011	A	714 672-5100	14806
Gibraltar Cnvalescent Hosp Inc (PA)	8059	D	714 577-3880	15849
Burns & McDonnell Inc	8711	D	714 256-1595	19164
Lance Soll & Lunghard LLP	8721	D	714 672-0022	19597
United Sttes Dept Enrgy Brkley	8733	C	510 486-7089	19923
Isys Solutions Inc	8742	D	714 521-7656	20419
Acepex Management Corporation	8744	C	909 625-6900	20645

BRENTWOOD, CA - Contra Costa County

Associted Vtrnary Practices Inc	0742	C	925 634-1177	328
Thorpe Design Inc	1711	D	925 634-0787	1586
Hot Line Construction Inc	1731	A	925 634-9333	1750
Rodda Electric Inc (PA)	1731	D	925 240-6024	1824
T&C Roofing Inc	1761	D	925 513-8463	2087
Groundworks Inc	1771	D	925 513-0300	2123

BRENTWOOD CA

GEOGRAPHIC SECTION

	SIC	EMP	PHONE	ENTRY#
Bay Standard Inc.	5085	D	925 634-1181	5891
Home Depot USA Inc.	5211	C	925 513-6060	6998
Del Webb Corporation	6552	D	925 513-2640	9250
Banyan Solutions Inc.	7363	D	650 766-9338	11275
Club Corp Incorporated	7991	D	925 240-2990	14187
Delta Valley Health Club	7991	D	925 240-2990	14195
Integrated Pain Man.	8741	D	925 666-8972	20115

BRISBANE, CA - San Mateo County

	SIC	EMP	PHONE	ENTRY#
Fred Will and Bill Inc.	1711	C		1442
Infoimage of California Inc (PA)	2759	D	650 473-6388	2569
Blue Bus Tours LLC	4725	C	415 353-5310	3961
Kuehne + Nagel Inc.	4731	C	415 656-4100	4044
Ktsf Channel 26	4833	D	415 467-6397	4448
Bear Communications Inc.	5065	C	415 656-2327	5630
Norman S Wrght Mech Eqp Crprtn (PA)	5075	D	415 467-7600	5770
Bi-Rite Restaurant Sup Co Inc.	5141	B	415 656-0187	6241
Dairyland Produce LLC	5148	C	415 647-2991	6531
Squaretrade Inc (DH)	6399	C	415 541-1000	8473
Northwest Administrators Inc.	6411	D	650 570-7300	8628
Xojet Sales LLC	6799	C	877 599-6538	9584
Sage Hospitality Resources LLC	7011	D	650 589-1600	10189
Michaael S Hensley.	7299	C	650 692-7007	10562
Childcare Careers LLC	7363	A	650 372-0211	11280
Covenant Aviation Security LLC	7381	A	650 219-3473	12955
Caredx Inc (PA)	8071	B	415 287-2300	16710
Mammoth Biosciences Inc.	8731	D	770 655-1937	19732
Trove Recommerce Inc.	8742	D	925 726-3116	20594

BROOKS, CA - Yolo County

	SIC	EMP	PHONE	ENTRY#
Cache Creek Casino Resort	7011	A	530 796-3118	9674

BUELLTON, CA - Santa Barbara County

	SIC	EMP	PHONE	ENTRY#
Carpenters Southwest ADM Corp	5812	C	805 688-5581	7464
Kang Family Partners LLC	7011	C	805 688-1000	9935
Platinum Performance Inc.	7532	B	800 553-2400	13643

BUENA PARK, CA - Orange County

	SIC	EMP	PHONE	ENTRY#
Tawa Supermarket Inc.	1541	D	714 521-8899	850
ECB Corp (PA)	1711	D	714 385-8900	1425
AAA Network Solutions Inc.	1731	D	714 484-2711	1653
Sfadia Inc.	1731	D	323 622-1930	1838
King Supply Company LLC	1799	D	714 670-8980	2292
Wayne Perry Inc (PA)	1799	C	714 826-0352	2331
Pepsi-Cola Metro Btlg Co Inc.	2086	D	714 522-9635	2406
Pacific Chemical Dist Corp (HQ)	4226	D	714 521-7161	3795
States Logistics Services Inc (PA)	4731	C	714 521-6520	4099
Communications Supply Corp.	4899	D	714 670-7711	4534
Cambium Business Group Inc (PA)	5021	D	714 670-1171	5081
West Coast Sand and Gravel Inc (PA)	5032	D	714 522-0282	5214
Noritsu-America Corporation (HQ)	5043	C	714 521-9040	5239
Hochiki America Corporation (HQ)	5063	D	714 522-2246	5565
Tech Systems Inc.	5065	C	714 523-5404	5709
Amada America Inc (HQ)	5084	D	714 739-2111	5818
Fueling and Service Tech Inc.	5084	D	714 523-0194	5835
Yamaha Corporation of America (HQ)	5099	B	714 522-9011	6058
Orora Packaging Solutions (HQ)	5113	D	714 562-6000	6084
Orora Packaging Solutions.	5113	D	714 562-6002	6087
Matesta Corporation.	5137	D	949 874-6052	6207
Smart & Final Stores LLC.	5141	D	714 521-3680	6365
Access Business Group LLC.	5169	B	714 562-6200	6701
Access Business Group LLC.	5169	D	714 562-7914	6702
Ganahl Lumber Company.	5251	D	714 522-2864	7119
Simpson Automotive Inc.	5511	D	714 690-6200	7298
Continental Exch Solutions Inc (HQ)	6099	D	714 522-7044	7846
Universal Shopping Plaza A CA.	6512	C	714 521-8899	8773
Knotts Berry Farm LLC.	7011	D	714 995-1111	9950
Uniwell Corporation.	7011	C	714 522-7000	10334
Medieval Times Entrmt Inc (HQ)	7041	A	714 523-1100	10421
Amada Capital Corporation.	7359	D	714 739-2111	11019
Healthcare Resource Group.	7363	C	562 945-7224	11289
A J Parent Company (PA).	7389	D	714 521-1100	13168
Continental Exch Solutions Inc.	7389	D	562 345-2100	13244
Ted Ford Jones Inc (PA).	7538	D	714 521-3110	13677
Krikorian Premiere Theatre LLC.	7832	D	714 826-7469	14000
Knotts Berry Farm LLC (HQ).	7996	B	714 827-1776	14305
Rehablttion Ctr of Ornge Cnty.	8051	D	714 826-2330	15636
Southwest Rgnal Cncil Crpnters.	8631	D	714 571-0449	18797
United Food & Commercl Workers (PA).	8631	D	714 995-4601	18803
Vsa and Associates Inc.	8711	D	562 698-2468	19432

BURBANK, CA - Los Angeles County

	SIC	EMP	PHONE	ENTRY#
Ace Industrial Supply Inc (PA)	1521	D	818 252-1981	651
716 Management Inc.	1522	D	818 471-4956	744
Tri-Tech Restoration Co Inc.	1541	D	818 565-3900	851
Ies Commercial Inc.	1731	D	713 860-1500	1755
Swaner Hardwood Co Inc (PA)	2435	D	818 953-5350	2481
Steves Plating Corporation.	2542	C	818 842-2184	2507
Midnight Oil Agency LLC.	2752	B	818 295-6100	2564
Saturn Fasteners Inc.	3429	C	818 973-1807	2731
Haskel International LLC (HQ)	3561	D	818 843-4000	2793
Music Express Inc (PA)	4119	C	818 845-1502	3283
Ardwin Inc.	4213	C	818 767-7777	3443
Ameriflight LLC.	4512	C	818 847-0000	3831
Avjet Corporation (DH)	4522	D	818 841-6190	3863
Gat - Arln Ground Support Inc.	4581	C	818 847-9127	3894
Magical Cruise Company Limited.	4724	D	800 742-8939	3940
Mis Sciences Corp.	4813	C	818 847-0213	4314
Qwest Cybersolutions LLC.	4813	C	818 729-2100	4333
Deluxe Encore Inc.	4822	C	323 466-7663	4364
ABC Cable Networks Group (HQ)	4832	C	818 460-7477	4369
Disney Enterprises Inc (DH)	4832	A	818 560-1000	4375
Krca License LLC.	4832	C	818 840-1400	4390
Liberman Broadcasting Inc (PA)	4832	D	818 729-5300	4394
Radio Disney Group LLC.	4832	D	818 569-5000	4401
ABC Signature Studios Inc.	4833	D	818 560-1000	4410
Cw Network LLC (HQ)	4833	C	818 977-2500	4424
Hub Television Networks LLC.	4833	D	818 531-3600	4441
Public Mdia Group Southern Cal (PA)	4833	D	714 241-4100	4458
Twdc Enterprises 18 Corp (HQ)	4833	A	818 560-1000	4466
Valleycrest Productions Ltd.	4833	D	818 560-5391	4469
International Fmly Entrmt Inc (DH)	4841	C	818 560-1000	4512
Own LLC.	4841	C	323 602-5500	4517
Time Warner Cable Entps LLC.	4841	D	818 972-0808	4523
Time Warner Cable Entps LLC.	4841	D	818 977-7840	4524
City of Burbank.	4931	B	818 238-3550	4749
Sanitec Industries Inc.	4953	D	818 523-1942	4934
Image IV Systems Inc (PA)	5044	D	818 841-0756	5246
Wexler Corporation.	5065	A	818 846-9381	5715
Ryan Herco Products Corp (DH)	5074	D	818 841-1141	5759
Sega of America Inc.	5092	B	747 477-3708	5996
Mel Bernie and Company Inc (PA)	5094	C	818 841-1928	6023
Science of Skincare LLC.	5122	D	818 254-7961	6143
Smart & Final Stores Inc.	5141	C	818 954-8631	6309
Smart & Final Stores LLC.	5141	D	818 562-3234	6330
Mader News Inc.	5192	D	818 551-5000	6844
Lowes Home Centers LLC.	5211	C	818 557-2300	7058
Specialty Restaurants Corp.	5812	C	818 843-5013	7509
Farmers Insur Group Fdral Cr U (PA)	6061	D	323 209-6000	7766
Logix Federal Credit Union (PA)	6061	C	888 718-5328	7779
Partners Federal Credit Union (PA)	6061	D	800 948-6677	7790
Shamrock Holdings Inc (PA)	6282	D	818 845-4444	8221
Allianz Globl Risks US Insur (DH)	6331	C		8375
Producr-Wrters Gild Amer Pnsio.	6371	D	818 846-1015	8465
Screen Actors Guild - American.	6371	D	818 954-9400	8468
Alliance Residential LLC.	6512	D	818 841-2441	8699
Silver Saddle Ranch & Club Inc.	6552	D	818 768-8808	9274
Anabelle Hotel Inc.	7011	D	818 845-7800	9607
OH So Original Inc.	7011	B	818 841-4770	10059
PHF II Burbank LLC.	7011	C	818 843-6000	10116
Vestis Corporation.	7213	D	818 973-3700	10457
Aramark Unf & Career AP LLC.	7218	A	818 973-3700	10478
Marvel Studios LLC (HQ)	7221	D	310 727-2700	10490
Petrosian Esthetic Entps LLC.	7231	C	818 391-8231	10506
Formerly Known As LLC.	7311	D	310 551-3500	10614
GL Nemirow Inc.	7311	D	818 562-9433	10618
Legendary Pictures Films LLC.	7311	C	818 688-7003	10641
Petrol Advertising Inc.	7311	D	323 644-3720	10661
Final Film.	7336	D	323 467-0700	10807
Come Land Maint Svc Co Inc.	7349	A	818 567-2455	10877
M-N-Z Janitorial Services Inc.	7349	C	323 851-4115	10923
J L Fisher Inc.	7359	D	818 846-8366	11037
Wise Skulls LLC.	7361	D	669 260-9005	11257
Blu Digital Group Inc (PA)	7371	C	818 527-2763	11465
Disney Interactive Studios Inc.	7371	B	818 553-5000	11546
Global Service Resources Inc.	7371	D	800 679-7658	11623
Spark Unlimited Inc.	7371	D		11937
Zestfinance Inc.	7371	D	323 450-3000	12064
Jam City Inc.	7372	D	804 920-8760	12248
My Eye Media LLC.	7372	D	818 559-7200	12279
Information Tech Partners Inc.	7379	D	800 789-7487	12810
Integrated Media Tech Inc (PA)	7379	D	818 761-9770	12814
Andrews International Inc (DH)	7381	A	818 487-4060	12931
Frasco Inc (PA)	7381	D	818 848-3888	12974
Secure Net Alliance.	7381	D	818 848-4900	13034
US Security Associates Inc (PA)	7381	B	818 697-1809	13068

GEOGRAPHIC SECTION

CALABASAS CA

	SIC	EMP	PHONE	ENTRY#
Rti Systems Inc	7382	D	213 599-8470	13141
Buena Vista Television (DH)	7383	C	818 560-1878	13155
Coloredge	7384	C	818 842-1121	13159
Jake Hey Incorporated	7384	C	323 856-5280	13160
Technicolor Inc	7384	B	818 260-4577	13163
Pixar	7389	C	510 922-4075	13427
Sca Enterprises Inc (PA)	7389	D	818 845-7621	13466
Alamo Rental (us) Inc	7514	D	818 953-5438	13574
City of Burbank	7538	D	818 238-3838	13660
ABC Family Worldwide Inc (HQ)	7812	B	818 560-1000	13814
Barnstorm Vfx Inc	7812	D	818 792-1899	13820
Buddy Stoopid Stoodios LLC	7812	C	818 333-8600	13824
Buena Vista International Inc	7812	C	818 295-5200	13825
Disney Incorporated (DH)	7812	C	818 560-1000	13842
Evolution Film & Tape Inc	7812	C	818 260-0300	13847
Legendary Entertainment LLC	7812	C	818 688-7003	13859
NW Entertainment Inc (PA)	7812	C	818 295-5000	13871
Playboy Entrmt Group Inc (DH)	7812	C	323 276-4000	13879
Point360	7812	C	818 556-5700	13880
Roundabout Entertainment Inc	7812	C	818 842-9300	13888
Studio Distribution Svcs LLC	7812	C	818 954-6000	13900
Stx Financing LLC	7812	C	310 742-2300	13901
Walt Disney Music Company (DH)	7812	C	818 560-1000	13913
Walt Disney Records Direct (DH)	7812	A	818 560-1000	13915
Warner Bros Entertainment Inc (DH)	7812	C	818 954-6000	13916
Warner Bros Entertainment Inc	7812	C	818 954-2209	13917
Warner Bros Home Entrmt Inc (DH)	7812	C	818 954-6000	13918
Warner Bros Intl TV Dist Inc	7812	C	818 954-6000	13919
Deluxe Media Inc (PA)	7819	C	818 565-3697	13931
Foto-Kem Industries Inc (PA)	7819	C	818 846-3102	13936
Olive Avenue Productions LLC	7819	B	770 214-7052	13944
Stereo D LLC	7819	C	818 861-3100	13951
Technicolor Thomson Group Inc (HQ)	7819	B		13954
Testronic Inc	7819	C	818 845-3223	13956
Warner Bros Transatlantic Inc	7822	B	818 954-5990	13974
Warner Bros Transatlantic Inc	7822	B	818 977-6384	13975
Eros Stx Global Corporation	7841	A	818 524-7000	14024
Prdctions N Fremantle Amer Inc (DH)	7922	D	818 748-1100	14056
Bang Zoom Entertainment Inc	7929	D	818 295-3939	14079
Esl Gaming America Inc	7929	C	818 861-7315	14083
Now Casting Inc	7929	C	818 588-3732	14098
Warner Bros Home Entrmt Group (DH)	7929	D	818 954-6000	14111
Lakeside Golf Club	7992	D	818 984-0601	14269
Walt Disney Company (PA)	7996	A	818 560-1000	14316
Disney Regional Entrmt Inc (DH)	7999	D	818 560-1000	14513
Providnce Facey Med Foundation	8031	D	818 861-7831	15258
A-1 Hospice Care Inc	8052	D	818 237-2700	15744
Providence Health System	8062	A	818 843-5111	16348
Providnce Hlth Svcs Fndtn/San	8062	A	818 843-5111	16353
Kan-Di-Ki LLC (HQ)	8071	D	818 549-1880	16731
Burbank Dental Laboratory Inc	8072	C	818 841-2256	16769
Nova Skilled Home Health Inc	8099	C	323 658-6232	17284
Providence St Josephs Home Cr	8099	D	818 953-4494	17299
Napca Foundation	8299	A	800 799-4640	17813
Vintage Senior Management Inc	8322	A	818 954-9500	18169
American Fdrtion Mscans Lcal 4	8631	D	323 462-2161	18771
Boys Grls CLB Brbank Grter E V	8641	D	818 842-9333	18823
Young MNS Chrstn Assn Brbank C (PA)	8641	D	818 845-8551	18955
Cast & Crew LLC (PA)	8721	C	818 570-6180	19549
Entertainment Partners Inc (PA)	8721	B	818 955-6000	19573
New Talco Enterprises LLC	8721	D	310 280-0755	19615
Team Companies LLC (PA)	8721	D	818 558-3261	19633
Certified Laboratories LLC	8734	A	818 845-0070	19956
Dcl Maritime LLC	8741	C	818 560-1000	20075
IKEA Purchasing Svcs US Inc	8741	D	818 841-3500	20112
Streamland Media LLC	8741	C	416 909-2103	20218
Warner Bros Distributing Inc	8741	B	818 954-6000	20249
Enbio Corp	8742	C	818 953-9976	20355
Modern Hr Inc	8742	D	877 842-4988	20473
Warner Bros Consumer Pdts Inc (DH)	8748	C	818 954-7980	20878

BURLINGAME, CA - San Mateo County

	SIC	EMP	PHONE	ENTRY#
Brightview Landscape Svcs Inc	0781	D	650 289-9324	408
Disney Construction Inc	1611	D	650 689-5149	1096
Allen Drywall & Associates	1742	D	650 579-0664	1904
Precision Emprise Inc	1771	D	650 867-8657	2149
Hanergy Holding (america) LLC (HQ)	3674	D	650 288-3722	2921
Jeremiah Phillips LLC	4111	D	650 697-7733	3142
Watchpoint Logistics Inc (PA)	4731	C	800 486-8326	4119
Trivad Inc	5045	C	650 286-1086	5366
Color Health Inc	5047	A	650 651-7116	5409
Abx Engineering Inc	5065	D	650 552-2300	5617
Sunkist Enterprises	5072	D	650 347-3900	5735
Junk King Frnchise Systems LLC	5093	C	888 888-5865	6010
City National Bank	6021	D	650 696-6404	7619
Blackstone Technology Group (PA)	6211	D	415 837-1400	8067
Map Energy LLC	6211	D	650 324-9095	8102
Stonesfair Financial Corp	6513	D	650 347-0442	8863
National Financial Svcs LLC	6799	A	650 343-6775	9538
Airport Blvd Hotels LLC	7011	C	650 342-9200	9601
Cchh Burlingame LLC	7011	C	650 696-2607	9687
Djont Operations LLC	7011	C	650 342-4600	9747
Gringteam Inc	7011	D	650 344-5500	9825
Hyatt Corporation	7011	D	650 347-1234	9884
Trevi Partners A Calif LP	7011	C	650 347-2381	10320
Coit Services Inc (PA)	7216	C	650 697-5471	10466
Superbroward LLC	7231	C	650 348-4881	10510
Randstad Professionals Us LLC	7361	C	650 343-5111	11214
Spec Personnel LLC	7361	D	408 727-8000	11234
Imply Data Inc (PA)	7372	C	415 685-8187	12228
Roadzen Inc	7372	B	347 745-6448	12338
Acumen LLC	7373	C	650 558-8882	12415
Intellimize Inc	7373	D	415 760-5710	12470
Allied Universal	7381	C	650 223-3221	12923
Personal Protective Svcs Inc (PA)	7381	D	650 344-3302	13021
Wand Topco Inc	7532	A	650 375-0600	13651
Yourmechanic Inc	7538	D	800 701-6230	13679
Lyra Health Inc	8011	C	800 505-5972	14884
Mills-Peninsula Health Services	8062	A	650 696-5400	16271
Suttercare Corporation	8062	A	650 853-8500	16565
Suttercare Corporation	8093	A	650 696-5363	17136
Carr McClellan PC (PA)	8111	C	650 342-9600	17399
California Teachers Assn (PA)	8621	C	650 697-1400	18741
Peninsula Humane Soc & Spca	8699	D	650 340-7022	19097
Environmental Chemical Corp (PA)	8711	D	650 347-1555	19217
Guideline Inc	8732	C	888 228-3491	19814
Sphere Institute	8732	B	650 558-3980	19849

BUTTONWILLOW, CA - Kern County

	SIC	EMP	PHONE	ENTRY#
J G Boswell Company	0173	B	661 764-9000	92
Pomwonderful LLC	5149	D	559 258-4834	6658

BYRON, CA - Contra Costa County

	SIC	EMP	PHONE	ENTRY#
Pacific Coast Ldscp MGT Inc	0781	D	925 513-2310	454
Sanders Contracting Inc	1542	D	925 308-7305	1021

CABAZON, CA - Riverside County

	SIC	EMP	PHONE	ENTRY#
Premium Outlet Partners LP	6512	D	951 849-6641	8752
Morongo Band Mission Indians	7999	C	951 849-3080	14546

CALABASAS, CA - Los Angeles County

	SIC	EMP	PHONE	ENTRY#
Ultimate Builders Inc	1521	D	818 481-2627	733
Brightview Companies LLC (DH)	1629	C	818 223-8500	1290
Afr Apparel International Inc	2341	D	818 773-5000	2462
Ixia (HQ)	3825	B	818 871-1800	3026
Durham School Services L P	4151	C	818 880-4257	3328
Amawaterways LLC (PA)	4724	C	800 626-0126	3926
Las Virgenes Municipal Wtr Dst	4941	C	818 251-2100	4799
Abbyson Living Corp	5021	C	805 465-5500	5077
Spirent Communications Inc (HQ)	5045	B	818 676-2300	5354
SL Power Electronics Corp (HQ)	5065	D	800 235-5929	5699
Central Purchasing LLC (HQ)	5085	B	800 444-3353	5894
Goldco Direct LLC	5094	D	818 343-0186	6022
Wella Operations US LLC	5122	D	818 999-5112	6152
Guarachi Wine Partners Inc	5182	C	818 225-5100	6797
Arcs Commercial Mortgage Co LP (DH)	6162	C	818 676-3274	7934
Republic Indemnity Co Amer (DH)	6331	C	818 990-9860	8404
Western General Insurance Co	6331	C	818 880-9070	8424
Far West Bond Services Cal Inc (PA)	6351	B	818 704-1111	8432
Cartel Marketing Inc	6411	C	818 483-1130	8522
Alliant Asset MGT Co LLC (HQ)	6531	A	818 668-2805	8897
Dg Real Estate Inc	6531	D	818 591-8800	8979
Marcus & Millichap Inc (PA)	6531	C	818 212-2250	9093
MSE Enterprises Inc (PA)	6531	D	818 223-3500	9106
23627 Calabasas Road LLC	7011	D	818 222-5300	9589
T M Mian & Associates	7011	D	818 591-2300	10300
Grant & Weber (PA)	7322	D	818 878-7700	10742
Avanquest North America LLC (HQ)	7371	D	818 591-9600	11440
Ellie Mae Inc	7371	B	818 223-2000	11570
Ticketmanager	7371	D	818 698-3616	11979
Sungard Treasury Systems Inc	7372	C	818 223-2300	12369
Idrive Inc	7379	D	818 594-5972	12805
David Shield Security Inc	7381	C	310 849-4950	12963
Nastec International Inc	7381	D	818 222-0355	13005
Picore Bristain Initiative Inc	7381	C	818 888-3659	13022
Litigtion Rsrces of America-CA (PA)	7389	D	818 878-9227	13355

CALABASAS CA

	SIC	EMP	PHONE	ENTRY#
Able Cable Inc (PA)	7629	C	818 223-3600	13731
Westbrook Ops LLC	7812	D	818 832-2300	13920
Dts Inc (DH)	7819	D	818 436-1000	13934
Edwards Theatres Inc	7832	D	844 462-7342	13988
Insomniac Inc	7929	C	323 874-7020	14090
Silverado Senior Living Inc	8051	C	818 746-2583	15672
Help Children World Foundation	8322	B	818 706-9848	18001
Davis Research LLC	8732	C	818 591-2408	19807
Informa Research Services Inc (HQ)	8732	C	818 880-8877	19821
Center For Civic Education (PA)	8733	C	818 591-9321	19875
Red Peak Group LLC	8742	D	818 222-7762	20525

CALABASAS HILLS, CA - Los Angeles County

	SIC	EMP	PHONE	ENTRY#
Helmet House LLC (PA)	5136	D	800 421-7247	6176

CALEXICO, CA - Imperial County

	SIC	EMP	PHONE	ENTRY#
Cooper Lighting LLC	1731	C	760 357-4760	1709
U S Xpress Inc	4213	B	760 768-6707	3559
R L Jones-San Diego Inc (PA)	4731	C	760 357-3177	4084
Coppel Corporation	5021	D	760 357-3707	5086
Sun Community Federal Cr Un	6061	D	760 337-4200	7809
Vantiva Sup Chain Slutions Inc	7819	D	760 357-3372	13958

CALIMESA, CA - Riverside County

	SIC	EMP	PHONE	ENTRY#
Tommy Gun Plastering Inc	1742	D	909 795-9966	1969

CALIPATRIA, CA - Imperial County

	SIC	EMP	PHONE	ENTRY#
Calenergy LLC	1731	B	402 231-1527	1691
Viridos Inc	8731	D	858 754-2900	19798

CALISTOGA, CA - Napa County

	SIC	EMP	PHONE	ENTRY#
Resort At Indian Springs LLC	7011	C	707 709-2434	10156
Calistoga Spa Inc	7991	D	707 942-6269	14184

CAMARILLO, CA - Ventura County

	SIC	EMP	PHONE	ENTRY#
Boskovich Farms Inc	0161	C	805 987-1443	24
Rincon Pacific LLC	0171	D	805 986-8806	64
Pacific Erth Rsrces Ltd A Cal (PA)	0181	D	805 986-8277	145
Pacific Erth Rsrces Ltd A Cal	0181	D	209 892-3000	146
Houwelings Camarillo Inc	0182	B	805 250-1600	163
ABS	1731	D	805 453-9359	1654
Hi-Temp Insulation Inc	1742	B	805 484-2774	1934
Gms Landscapes Inc	3432	C	805 402-3925	2734
Johanson Technology Inc	3675	C	805 575-0124	2937
Lucix Corporation (HQ)	3679	D	805 987-6645	2944
Technicolor Disc Services Corp (HQ)	3695	C	805 445-1122	2953
Airborne Technologies Inc	3728	C	805 389-3700	2987
Airport Connection Inc	4111	C	805 389-8196	3121
Sun Air Jets LLC	4522	C	805 389-9301	3869
California Internet LP (PA)	4813	C	805 225-4638	4260
Directv Group Holdings LLC	4841	C	805 207-6675	4501
Silicon Processing and Trading Inc	4953	D	805 388-8683	4936
Data Exchange Corporation (PA)	5045	D	805 388-1711	5293
Golden State Medical Sup Inc	5047	C	805 477-9866	5417
Solarworld Americas LLC	5063	D	503 844-3400	5593
Nallatech Inc	5065	D	805 383-8997	5679
Arconix/Usa Inc	5085	C	805 388-2525	5890
Golden State Medical Supply	5099	D	805 477-8966	6044
Basso Distributing Coinc	5181	C	805 656-1946	6751
Home Depot USA Inc	5211	C	805 389-9918	6983
Thomas Bavarian Mtr Works Inc	5511	B	805 482-8878	7312
Al Hewitt Inc	6282	C	661 945-7050	8183
Premium Outlet Partners LP	6512	C	805 445-8520	8747
Cushman & Wakefield Cal Inc	6531	B	805 322-7244	8963
Rgc Services Inc	6531	C	805 484-1600	9168
Barrett Business Services Inc	7361	A	805 987-0331	11092
Applied Engineering MGT Corp	7371	C	805 484-1909	11415
Epr Recruiting Inc	7371	D	213 607-2001	11574
Market Scan Info Systems Inc	7371	C	800 658-7226	11734
Modern Campus USA Inc (PA)	7371	C	805 484-9400	11754
Electronic Clearing House Inc (HQ)	7372	D	805 419-8700	12180
Synectic Solutions Inc (PA)	7379	D	805 483-4800	12886
Dial Security Inc (PA)	7382	C	805 389-6700	13106
Technclor Vdocassette Mich Inc (DH)	7819	B	805 445-1122	13953
Vantiva Sup Chain Slutions Inc (HQ)	7819	B	805 445-1122	13959
Delicate Productions Inc (PA)	7922	D	415 484-1174	14036
La Workout Inc	7991	C	805 482-8884	14212
Sterling Hills LLC	7992	B	805 604-1234	14291
Las Posas Country Club	7997	C	805 482-4518	14395
Spanish Hills Club	7997	B	805 388-5000	14457
Spanish Hills Country Club (PA)	7997	B	805 389-1644	14458
People Creating Success Inc	8011	D	805 644-9480	14955
Institute For Applied Bhvior A	8049	D	805 987-5886	15291
Elder Care Alliance Camarillo	8051	D	510 769-2700	15431
Moms Place	8051	D	805 383-6855	15589
Vitas Healthcare Corporation	8052	C	805 437-2100	15803
Dignity Health	8062	C	805 389-5800	16052
Bio-Mdcal Applctons Cmrllo Inc	8092	C	805 388-2449	16978
Ventura Cnty Md-Cal Mnged Care	8099	D	888 301-1228	17345
Casa Pcfica Ctrs For Chldren F (PA)	8322	C	805 482-3260	17864
Interface Community (PA)	8322	B	805 485-6114	18019
Channel Islnds Yung MNS Chrstn	8641	B	805 484-0423	18836
Dex Corporation	8711	C	805 388-1711	19199
Saalex Corp (PA)	8711	C	805 482-1070	19379
Teledyne Scentific Imaging LLC	8731	C	805 373-4979	19782
Camarillo Healthcare Center	8741	C	805 482-9805	20051
Juvenile Justice Division Cal	8741	A	805 485-7951	20130
County of Ventura	9199	D	805 388-4341	20926

CAMBRIA, CA - San Luis Obispo County

	SIC	EMP	PHONE	ENTRY#
Moonstone Management Corp (PA)	6531	C	805 927-4200	9101
Moonstone Bch Innvstors A Cal	7011	C	805 927-8661	10028
Pacific Cambria Inc	7011	D	805 927-6114	10077

CAMERON PARK, CA - El Dorado County

	SIC	EMP	PHONE	ENTRY#
Hemington Landscape Svcs Inc	0781	D	530 677-9290	438
McClone Construction Company	1521	C	559 431-9411	700
Nehemiah Rebar Services Inc	1791	C	530 676-6310	2192
Cameron Park Country Club Inc	7997	C	530 672-9840	14354
Eskaton	8361	C	530 672-8900	18422
Eskaton Properties Inc	8361	C	530 677-5066	18425

CAMINO, CA - El Dorado County

	SIC	EMP	PHONE	ENTRY#
Coastal Mountain Timber Inc	0783	D	530 303-3378	554

CAMP PENDLETON, CA - San Diego County

	SIC	EMP	PHONE	ENTRY#
Marine Corps United States	4731	D	760 725-3092	4058
Marine Corps Community Svcs	7999	C	760 725-6195	14545
Marine Corps Community Svcs	8351	C	760 725-7311	18331
Lion-Vallen Ltd Partnership	8741	D	760 385-4885	20142

CAMPBELL, CA - Santa Clara County

	SIC	EMP	PHONE	ENTRY#
Martina Landscape Inc	0782	D	408 871-8800	520
SBCI INC (PA)	1522	C	408 379-5500	774
West Valley Cnstr Co Inc (PA)	1623	C	408 371-5510	1282
Agc Inc	1711	D	408 369-6305	1339
Daleys Drywall and Taping Inc	1742	B	408 378-9500	1923
SR Freeman Inc	1751	D	408 364-2200	2018
Largo Concrete Inc	1771	A	408 874-2500	2134
Megachips LSI USA Corporation	3674	D	408 570-0555	2926
Durham School Services L P	4151	C	833 698-7474	3330
8x8 Inc (PA)	4813	A	408 727-1885	4248
Fuze Inc (PA)	4813	C	800 890-1553	4286
Hightail Inc	4813	D	408 879-9118	4293
Bouton Construction Inc	5082	D	408 375-0829	5783
Southern Cal Disc Tire Co Inc	5531	C	408 377-5010	7373
Harman Management Corporation (PA)	5812	C	650 941-5681	7485
Chicago Title Insurance Co	6361	A	408 371-4100	8437
Barracuda Holdings LLC	6719	A	408 342-5400	9301
Doubltree By Hlton Ht Campbell	7011	B	408 559-4300	9763
Internal Drive	7032	A	408 871-2227	10404
Accountble Hlthcare Stffing In	7361	B	408 377-9960	11074
Bairesdev LLC	7371	A	847 796-1636	11446
Bitglass Inc	7371	C	408 337-0190	11461
Phoenix Technologies Inc	7371	C	408 570-1000	11826
Resolve Systems LLC (PA)	7371	D	949 325-0120	11876
Saama Technologies Inc (PA)	7371	C	408 371-1900	11892
Samepage Labs Inc	7371	B	408 628-0393	11899
Syrinx Consulting Corp	7371	C	781 487-7800	11962
Torrey Point Group LLC	7371	C	408 734-1500	11982
Zero Cognitive Systems Inc	7371	D	650 720-2324	12063
Barracuda Networks Inc (PA)	7372	A	408 342-5400	12111
Content Guru Inc	7373	B	408 559-3988	12439
Qolsys Inc (HQ)	7373	C	855 476-5797	12512
24 7ai Inc (PA)	7379	C	650 385-2247	12715
Aicent Inc	7379	B	408 324-1316	12724
Maxonic Inc	7379	C	408 739-4900	12834
Skyhigh Networks Inc (DH)	7382	D	408 564-0278	13146
Lark Avenue Car Wash	7542	C	408 377-2525	13698
Senior Living Solutions LLC	8052	C	408 385-1835	15794
Childrens Recovery Ctr 1 LLC	8069	C	408 558-3640	16672
Hunter Laboratories Inc	8071	C	408 341-8600	16726
Family Mtters In-Home Care LLC	8082	A	408 824-1021	16863
US Carenet Services Inc	8082	C	408 871-9860	16959
CRC Health Group Inc	8093	D	408 866-8167	17047
Campbell Christian School	8211	D	408 370-4900	17698

GEOGRAPHIC SECTION

CARLSBAD CA

	SIC	EMP	PHONE	ENTRY#
Uplift Family Services (PA)	8322	D	408 379-3790	18164
Stratford School Inc	8351	B	408 973-7320	18355
OSI Engineering Inc	8711	C	408 550-2800	19343
Sandis Cvil Engners Srvyors Pl (PA)	8713	D	408 636-0900	19527
LLP Moss Adams	8721	D	408 369-2400	19602
Rainmaker Systems Inc	8741	C	408 659-1800	20190
Freedom Equity Group	8742	D	408 340-5672	20388
Roseryan Inc	8742	D	510 456-3056	20534

CAMPO, CA - San Diego County

	SIC	EMP	PHONE	ENTRY#
Campo Band Missions Indians	7993	B	619 938-6000	14297

CANOGA PARK, CA - Los Angeles County

	SIC	EMP	PHONE	ENTRY#
American Landscape Inc	0781	C	818 999-2041	386
American Landscape MGT Inc (PA)	0781	C	818 999-2041	387
Landcare USA LLC	0782	D	818 346-7552	511
Pacific Coast Tree Experts	0783	D	805 506-1211	560
Rte Enterprises Inc	1721	D	818 999-5300	1639
Mark Land Electric Inc	1731	C	818 883-5110	1770
Azimc Investments Inc	5013	C	818 678-1200	5027
Richard Huetter Inc	5013	D	818 700-8001	5057
Alterntive Protective Svcs Inc	5063	D	818 456-0989	5534
Buyers Consultation Svc Inc (PA)	5065	D	818 341-4820	5637
Green Thumb International Inc	5193	D	818 340-6400	6859
Seltzer - Doren MGT Co Inc	6513	C	818 709-5210	8860
First Amercn HM Warranty Corp	6541	B	818 781-5050	9231
County of Los Angeles	7032	D	818 340-2633	10400
Computrition Inc (HQ)	7371	C	818 961-3999	11511
Hvantage Technologies Inc (PA)	7371	D	818 661-6301	11650
Software Dynamics Incorporated	7373	D	818 992-3299	12525
Mulholland Security Ctrs LLC	7381	D	818 983-9206	13003
Shield Security Inc	7381	C	818 239-5800	13042
Sela Healthcare Inc	8051	B	818 341-9800	15660
APn Business Resources Inc	8742	D	818 717-9980	20278

CANYON COUNTRY, CA - Los Angeles County

	SIC	EMP	PHONE	ENTRY#
Design Masonry Inc	1741	D	661 252-2784	1881
Power Generation Entps Inc	5084	C	818 484-8550	5860
Pure Autism Counseling Ctr Inc	8093	D	661 360-7730	17115

CANYON LAKE, CA - Riverside County

	SIC	EMP	PHONE	ENTRY#
Alexander Dennis Incorporated	5012	A	951 244-9429	5003
Cbabr Inc (PA)	6531	D	951 640-7056	8925

CAPAY, CA - Yolo County

	SIC	EMP	PHONE	ENTRY#
Capay Incorporated (PA)	5148	D	530 796-0730	6522

CAPISTRANO BEACH, CA - Orange County

	SIC	EMP	PHONE	ENTRY#
Soto Company Inc	0782	D	949 493-9403	537
Pacific Monarch Resorts Inc	7011	D	949 248-2944	10087

CAPITOLA, CA - Santa Cruz County

	SIC	EMP	PHONE	ENTRY#
Cellco Partnership	4812	D	831 475-3100	4193
Capitola Imports Inc	5511	C	831 462-4200	7179
Bay Federal Credit Union (PA)	6061	D	831 479-6000	7756
Change Lending LLC	6162	D	831 460-0202	7944
Covenant Care LLC	8051	B	831 476-0770	15397
Promedica Health System Inc	8082	C	831 476-2158	16916

CARDIFF BY THE SEA, CA - San Diego County

	SIC	EMP	PHONE	ENTRY#
Naval Coating Inc	1799	C	619 234-8366	2300
Mellmo Inc	7371	C	858 847-3272	11741

CARLSBAD, CA - San Diego County

	SIC	EMP	PHONE	ENTRY#
Brehm Communities (PA)	1521	D	760 448-2420	661
James Allison Estates & Homes	1521	C	866 463-5780	682
Rq Construction LLC	1541	C	760 631-7707	840
Bomel Construction Co Inc	1542	C	760 431-6360	875
Nevell Group Inc	1542	B	760 598-3501	977
R Q Construction Inc	1542	C	760 631-7707	1000
Hellas Construction Inc	1629	B	760 891-8090	1305
Bergelectric Corp (PA)	1731	D	760 638-2374	1675
Bergelectric Corp	1731	A	760 746-1003	1676
Ipitek Inc	1731	D	760 438-1010	1757
Rowan Incorporated	1731	D	760 692-0700	1828
Interior Specialists Inc (HQ)	1752	D	760 929-6700	2037
Akcea Therapeutics Inc (HQ)	2834	D	617 207-0202	2579
Ionis Pharmaceuticals Inc (PA)	2834	B	760 931-9200	2592
Syntron Bioresearch Inc	2835	B	760 930-2200	2614
Oceanside Glasstile Company (PA)	3253	B	760 929-4000	2698
Arlo Technologies Inc	3651	D	408 890-3900	2877
Viasat Inc (PA)	3663	A	760 476-2200	2899
Spectrum Assembly Inc	3672	C	760 930-4000	2910
Alphatec Spine Inc (HQ)	3842	C	760 431-9286	3062
Zimmer Dental Inc	3842	B	800 854-7019	3065
Ortho Organizers Inc	3843	C	760 448-8600	3068
Spy Inc (PA)	3851	D	760 804-8420	3081
Topgolf Callaway Brands Corp (PA)	3949	B	760 931-1771	3096
CAV Inc	4119	D	760 729-5199	3248
Riolo Transportation Inc	4789	B	760 729-4405	4173
Adicio Inc	4813	D	760 602-9502	4251
Global Domains Intl Inc	4813	D	760 602-3000	4288
Buzztime Inc	4833	C	760 476-1976	4413
NRG Solar LLC	4911	C	760 710-2140	4596
San Diego Gas & Electric Co	4939	C	760 438-6200	4761
Argonaut Mfg Svcs Inc	5047	D	888 834-8892	5399
Equity International Inc	5065	A	978 664-2712	5648
HM Electronics Inc (PA)	5065	B	858 535-6000	5659
Bikes Online Inc	5091	C	650 272-3378	5973
Nixon Inc (PA)	5094	C	888 455-9200	6025
Colorescience Inc	5122	C	866 426-5673	6102
Unite Eurotherapy Inc	5122	D	760 585-1800	6147
Prana Living LLC (HQ)	5136	C	866 915-6457	6183
South Cone Inc	5139	C	760 431-2300	6234
Smart & Final Stores Inc	5141	C	760 434-2449	6302
Kendal Floral Supply LLC (PA)	5193	D	888 828-9875	6863
Bob Baker Volkswagen	5511	D	760 438-2200	7173
Hoehn Company Inc	5511	C	760 438-1818	7233
Oceanside Auto Country Inc (PA)	5511	C	760 438-2000	7271
Ted Ford Jones Inc	5511	C	760 438-9171	7309
First Community Bancorp	6021	D	858 756-3023	7625
Merrill Lynch Prce Fnner Smith	6211	D	760 930-3100	8131
Morgan Stnley Smith Barney LLC	6211	C	760 438-5100	8151
Optumrx Inc	6324	B	760 804-2399	8348
Southern Cal Prmnnte Med Group	6324	C	619 528-5000	8367
Petra Risk Solutions	6411	D	800 466-8951	8639
Premium Outlet Partners LP	6512	D	760 804-9045	8750
Front Porch Communities & Svcs	6513	C	760 729-4983	8814
Integral Senior Living LLC (PA)	6513	C	760 547-2863	8827
Common Grounds Holdings LLC	6531	D	760 206-7861	8949
Grand Pacific Resorts Inc (PA)	6531	C	760 431-8500	9026
Richard Realty Group Inc	6531	D	760 603-8377	9169
Aviara Fsrc Associates Limited	7011	A	760 603-6800	9622
Carlsbad Properties Inc	7011	C	760 438-7880	9679
Grand Pacific Carlsbad Ht LP	7011	B	760 827-2400	9814
Grand Pacific Resorts Inc	7011	A	760 431-8500	9815
Grand Pacific Resorts Svcs LP	7011	C	760 431-8500	9816
Hilton Garden Inns MGT LLC	7011	B	760 476-0800	9852
Hyatt Corp As Agt Brcp Hef Ht	7011	C	760 603-6851	9882
Lc Trs Inc	7011	C	760 438-9111	9971
Omni La Costa Resort & Spa LLC	7011	C	760 438-9111	10066
Omni La Costa Resort & Spa LLC (DH)	7011	C	760 438-9111	10067
Northstar Memorial Group LLC	7261	C	800 323-1342	10514
High Moon Studios LLC	7299	C	760 448-3000	10550
JC Weight Loss Centres Inc (PA)	7299	C	760 696-4000	10557
Havas Edge LLC (DH)	7311	D	760 929-0041	10623
Promoveo Health LLC	7311	A	760 931-4794	10664
Basepoint Analytics LLC	7323	B	760 602-4515	10756
Continuing Lf Communities LLC (PA)	7361	D	760 704-6400	11112
Alogent Holdings Inc	7371	D	760 410-9000	11397
Aveva Software LLC	7371	D	760 268-7700	11441
Happyco Inc (PA)	7371	D	415 230-9832	11638
Aira Tech Corp	7372	D	800 835-1934	12083
Applied Biosystems LLC (DH)	7372	C		12093
Electronic Online Systems International	7373	D	760 431-8400	12451
Technet Partners Inc	7373	D	760 683-8393	12532
Cofa Media Group LLC	7374	D	877 293-2007	12558
Rockstar San Diego Inc	7374	D	760 929-0700	12618
Z57 Inc	7374	C	858 623-5577	12646
Alphabold	7379	D	949 637-7148	12729
Exois Inc	7379	D	408 777-6630	12791
Axim Geospatial LLC	7389	D	608 352-4180	13203
Edriving Fleet LLC (DH)	7389	D	877 566-6323	13279
Gbr Holdings LLC	7389	D	702 283-6519	13300
San Diego of San Diego	7389	D	760 710-2242	13460
Transprttion Oprtion MGT Slton	7389	C	858 391-0260	13516
Two Jinn Inc (PA)	7389	D	760 431-9911	13522
Legend Films	7819	B	858 793-4420	13941
24 Hour Fitness Usa LLC (HQ)	7991	C	925 543-3100	14168
24 Hour Fitness Worldwide Inc	7991	A	925 543-3100	14169
Chopra Global LLC	7991	D	760 494-1604	14185
Jazzercise Inc (PA)	7991	C	760 476-1750	14209
Tri-City Hospital District	7991	B	760 931-3171	14238
Legoland California LLC	7996	B	760 450-3661	14306
Carbon Health Technologies Inc	8031	C	760 603-3221	15256
Physical Rhbltation Netwrk LLC (PA)	8049	D	760 931-8310	15299

Employee Codes: A=Over 500 employees, B=251-500
C=101-250, D=51-100, E=20-50, F=10-19, G=1-9

CARLSBAD CA

	SIC	EMP	PHONE	ENTRY#
Vista JV Partners LLC	8049	B	214 738-2771	15312
Sunrise Senior Living MGT Inc	8051	D	760 720-9898	15699
North Coast Home Care Inc	8082	C	760 260-8700	16900
Che Behavioral Health Services	8099	C	760 300-3664	17205
Monarch Hlthcare A Med Group I	8099	C	760 730-9448	17278
Nalu Medical Inc	8099	C	760 603-8466	17280
Gemological Institute Amer Inc (PA)	8249	A	760 603-4000	17795
Buffini & Company (PA)	8331	C	760 827-2100	18213
Isl Employees Inc	8361	D	760 547-2863	18461
National Assn Mus Mrchants Inc	8611	D	760 438-8001	18718
Unite Hair	8631	D	760 585-1800	18801
Carlsbad Firefighters Assn	8699	D	760 729-3730	19076
One Sun Power Inc	8711	A	844 360-9600	19341
Rialto Bioenergy Facility LLC	8711	C	760 436-8870	19375
Systems & Technology RES LLC	8711	D	844 204-0963	19402
Navigate Biopharma Svcs Inc	8731	C	866 992-4939	19743
Hisamitsu Pharmaceutical Co Inc	8733	A	760 931-1756	19884
Ncn Management LLC	8741	C	800 275-3243	20158
Sethi Management Inc	8741	C	760 692-5288	20205
Corporate Visions Inc	8742	C	760 458-0914	20330
Human Resource Capitl Cons Inc	8742	C	760 518-8816	20407
Intravas Inc	8742	C	760 650-4040	20416
Technology Associates EC Inc	8742	D	760 765-5275	20578
Camston Wrather LLC	8744	C	858 525-9999	20651
3E Company Env Ec n Eng (PA)	8748	C	760 602-8700	20670
By Referral Only Inc	8748	D	760 707-1300	20713

CARMEL, CA - Monterey County

	SIC	EMP	PHONE	ENTRY#
Abbott Manco Inc	6531	D	831 250-7397	8892
Rancho San Carlos Partnership LP	6552	C	831 626-8200	9272
Cvr Hsge LLC	7011	C	831 625-9500	9736
Highlands Inn Inc	7011	C	831 620-1234	9848
Highlands Inn Investors II LP	7011	C	831 624-3801	9849
Khp V Carmel Trs LLC	7011	C	831 624-1841	9938
Quail Lodge Inc	7011	C	831 624-1581	10132
Trevi Partners A Calif LP	7011	C	831 624-1841	10321
Preserve Golf Club Inc	7992	C	831 620-6871	14282
Santa Lucia Preserve Company	7997	C	831 620-6760	14443
Northern Cal Cngrgtnal Rtrment	8059	C	831 624-1281	15883

CARMEL VALLEY, CA - Monterey County

	SIC	EMP	PHONE	ENTRY#
Carmel Rlty Carmel Vly Sls Off	6531	D	831 622-1000	8923

CARMICHAEL, CA - Sacramento County

	SIC	EMP	PHONE	ENTRY#
International Building Inv Inc	1522	D	916 716-9565	760
Smart & Final Stores Inc	5141	B	916 486-6315	6292
Blue Shield Cal Lf Hlth Insur	6324	A	800 660-3007	8283
Eskaton (PA)	6512	D	916 334-0296	8718
Fairwood Associates Apts	6513	D	916 944-0152	8811
Diez & Leis RE Group Inc	6531	A	916 487-4287	8983
Acct Holdings LLC	7389	A	916 971-1981	13175
Carmichael Rcrtion Pk Dst Fndt	7999	D	916 485-5322	14504
Capital Eye Medical Group	8011	D	916 241-9378	14651
Eskaton Properties Inc	8051	C	916 974-2060	15465
Eskaton Properties Inc	8051	C	916 331-8513	15466
SSC Carmichael Operating Co LP	8051	A	916 485-4793	15679
Sunbrdge Brttany Rhbltttion Ctr	8051	C	916 484-1393	15686
Dignity Health	8062	B	916 537-5151	16043
Dignity Health	8062	A	916 537-5000	16050
Mercy Medical Group	8062	A	916 536-3600	16266
Donations With Care	8322	C	916 544-3080	17957
Eskaton Properties Inc	8322	D	916 334-0296	17970
Eskaton Properties Inc (PA)	8361	D	916 334-0810	18429
Eskaton Properties Inc	8361	D	916 974-2000	18430

CARPINTERIA, CA - Santa Barbara County

	SIC	EMP	PHONE	ENTRY#
Jimenez Nursery Inc	0181	D	805 684-7955	133
Normans Nursery Inc	0181	C	805 684-1411	142
Ocean Breeze International	0181	D	805 684-1747	143
Westerlay Orchids LP	0181	D	805 684-5411	159
Dako North America Inc	5122	B	805 566-6655	6104
Smart & Final Stores Inc	5141	B	805 566-2174	6293
Applied Silicone Company LLC	5169	D	805 525-5657	6705
Normans Nursery Inc	5193	C	805 684-5442	6868
Sunshine Floral Inc	5193	D	805 684-1177	6874
Carls Jr Restaurants LLC	5812	B	805 684-6388	7463
Plan Member Financial Corp	6282	C	800 874-6910	8216
AGIA Inc (PA)	6411	C	805 566-9191	8480
Procore Technologies Inc (PA)	7371	A	866 477-6267	11846
Momentum Work Inc (PA)	8322	D	805 566-9000	18057

CARSON, CA - Los Angeles County

	SIC	EMP	PHONE	ENTRY#
Gs Brothers Inc (PA)	0782	C	310 833-1369	494
OConnell Landscape Maint Inc	0782	A	800 339-1106	526
Ampam Parks Mechanical Inc	1711	A	310 835-1532	1355
Clay Dunn Enterprises Inc	1711	C	310 549-1698	1400
Spectra Industrial Svcs Inc	1731	D	310 835-0808	1846
Pepsi-Cola Metro Btlg Co Inc	2086	B	310 327-4222	2407
Leiner Health Products Inc (DH)	2834	C	631 200-2000	2597
Johnson Laminating Coating Inc	3083	D	310 635-4929	2662
Avalon Glass & Mirror Company	3231	D	323 321-8806	2692
Mestek Inc	3585	C	310 835-7500	2843
Ducommun Labarge Tech Inc (HQ)	3728	C	310 513-7200	2990
Klx LLC	4213	D	559 684-1037	3500
Progressive Transportation Inc	4213	D	310 684-2100	3529
Premier Cold Storage & Pkg LLC	4222	D	949 444-8859	3658
Custom Goods LLC	4225	D	310 241-6700	3691
Custom Goods LLC	4225	D	310 241-6700	3692
H Rauvel Inc (PA)	4225	D	310 604-0060	3713
Tri-Modal Dist Svcs Inc	4225	D	310 522-1844	3770
Kinder Mrgan Tank Stor Trmnals	4226	D	713 369-9000	3793
Air Group Leasing Inc	4731	A	310 684-4095	3981
Kw International Inc	4731	D	310 354-6944	4046
Mainfreight Inc (HQ)	4731	D	310 900-1974	4056
Quik Pick Express LLC	4731	D	310 763-3000	4083
Supra National Express Inc	4731	C	310 549-7105	4103
Yusen Logistics Americas Inc	4731	C	310 518-3008	4123
Watson Cogeneration Co Inc	4911	D	310 816-8100	4718
Apw Knox-Seeman Warehouse Inc (HQ)	5013	D	310 604-4373	5023
Tabletops Unlimited Inc (PA)	5023	D	310 549-6000	5135
New Age Electronics Inc	5044	C	310 549-0000	5253
JB Dental Supply Co Inc (PA)	5047	D	310 202-8855	5426
Parter Medical Products Inc	5047	D	310 327-4417	5439
Porteous Enterprises Inc (DH)	5072	C	310 549-9180	5732
Industrial Parts Depot LLC (HQ)	5084	D	310 530-1900	5840
Pro Safety Inc	5084	D	562 364-7450	5861
H D Smith LLC	5122	C	310 641-1885	6111
Osata Enterprises Inc	5139	C	888 445-6237	6233
US Foods Inc	5149	C	310 632-6265	6689
Kole Imports	5199	C	310 834-0004	6922
Home Depot USA Inc	5211	D	310 835-7547	7008
Wooltari Usa Inc	5411	D	310 933-8648	7155
Southern Cal Disc Tire Co Inc	5531	C	310 324-2569	7376
Merchants Bank California N A	6022	C	310 549-4350	7697
Aldon Inc	6719	D		9296
Carson Operating Company LLC	7011	D	310 830-9200	9682
Rentokil North America Inc	7342	D	714 517-9000	10839
Transcentra Inc	7373	A	310 603-0105	12535
North Amrcn SEC Investigations	7381	D	323 634-1911	13008
Qualis Automotive LLC	7538	D	859 689-7772	13672
Anschutz Sthern Cal Spt Cmplex	7999	C	310 630-2000	14490
Kaiser Foundation Hospitals	8093	C	310 513-6707	17080
Forensic Analytical Spc Inc	8734	D	310 763-2374	19977

CARUTHERS, CA - Fresno County

	SIC	EMP	PHONE	ENTRY#
Batth Farms Inc	0173	D	559 864-9421	89
Campos Bros Farms	0173	B	559 864-9488	90
Caruthers Raisin Pkg Co Inc (PA)	2034	D	559 864-9448	2354
Fresno Cnty Sprntndent Schools	4151	C	559 644-1000	3345

CASTAIC, CA - Los Angeles County

	SIC	EMP	PHONE	ENTRY#
County of Los Angeles	0752	D	661 257-3191	361
County of Los Angeles	8069	D	661 223-8700	16677

CASTRO VALLEY, CA - Alameda County

	SIC	EMP	PHONE	ENTRY#
Solar Company Inc	1711	D	510 888-9488	1566
Lawyers Title Insurance Corp	6361	D	510 733-2250	8447
American Building Service Inc	7349	D	510 483-5120	10856
East Bay Regional Park Dst	7999	C	510 881-1833	14516
California Skin Institute	8011	D	510 881-7822	14647
Valley Pointeidence Opco LLC	8052	D	510 538-8464	15799
Eden Labs Med Group Inc	8062	D	510 537-1234	16064
Eden Township Hospital District Inc	8062	A	510 538-2031	16065
Sutter Health	8062	A	510 537-1234	16528
Baywood Court (PA)	8082	B	510 733-2102	16816
Neighborhood Church Castro Vly	8661	D	510 537-4690	19024

CASTROVILLE, CA - Monterey County

	SIC	EMP	PHONE	ENTRY#
Ocean Mist Farming Company (PA)	0161	C	831 633-2144	37
Califrnia Artchoke Vgtble Grwe	0191	C	831 633-2144	171
National Custom Packing Inc	0723	B	831 724-2026	291
Valley Pride Inc (PA)	0761	B	831 633-5883	370

CATHEDRAL CITY, CA - Riverside County

	SIC	EMP	PHONE	ENTRY#
Palm Springs Motors Inc	5511	C	760 699-6695	7274
Whv Resort Group Inc	7011	A	760 770-9755	10368

GEOGRAPHIC SECTION

CHICO CA

	SIC	EMP	PHONE	ENTRY#
Big Lgue Dreams Consulting LLC	7032	C	760 324-5600	10399
T Allance One - Palm Sprng LLC	7999	D	760 322-7000	14567
Califrnia Dept Dvlpmental Svcs	8099	B	760 770-6248	17197

CEDARVILLE, CA - Modoc County

	SIC	EMP	PHONE	ENTRY#
Surprise Valley Hlth Care Dst	8062	D	530 279-6111	16505

CERES, CA - Stanislaus County

	SIC	EMP	PHONE	ENTRY#
Dan Avila & Sons Farms Inc	0161	D	209 495-3899	27
Wc AG Services Inc	0762	A	209 538-3131	385
Ram Mechanical Inc	1711	D	209 531-9155	1539
Roadway Engineering Works Inc	1731	D	209 541-0920	1823
Timmerman Starlite Trckg Inc	4213	D	209 538-1706	3552
Bronco Wine Company **(PA)**	5182	C	209 538-3131	6789
Klair Real Estate Inc	6531	C	209 484-8075	9066

CERRITOS, CA - Los Angeles County

	SIC	EMP	PHONE	ENTRY#
Resource Environmental Inc	1542	D	562 468-7000	1007
Zero Energy Contracting Inc	1711	C	626 701-3180	1600
Zero Energy Contracting LLC	1711	C	626 701-3180	1601
Helix Electric Inc	1731	A	562 941-7200	1745
Madison Inc of Oklahoma	3441	D	918 224-6990	2736
West Coast Switchgear **(DH)**	3613	C	562 802-3441	2862
United Parcel Service Inc	4215	B	562 404-3236	3642
Skylink Travel Inc	4724	D	212 380-2438	3951
Silver Hawk Freight Inc	4731	D	562 404-0226	4095
Complete Office California Inc	5021	C	714 880-1222	5084
Royal Plywood Company LLC **(PA)**	5031	D	562 404-2989	5185
Microtek Lab Inc **(HQ)**	5044	C	310 687-5823	5250
Arjo Inc	5047	B	714 412-1170	5400
Memorex Products Inc	5064	C	562 653-2800	5608
Allied High Tech Products Inc	5085	D	310 635-2466	5888
NSK Precision America Inc	5085	C	562 968-1000	5916
Southern Glzers Wine Sprits LL	5182	B	562 926-2000	6808
Midway International Inc	5199	D	800 826-2383	6928
Bargain Rent-A-Car	5511	C	562 865-7447	7170
Golden Star Technology Inc **(PA)**	5734	D	562 345-8700	7444
Docusource Inc	5999	D	562 447-2600	7578
Enterprise Bank & Trust	6022	C	562 345-9092	7681
Caremore Health Plan **(HQ)**	6321	C	562 622-2950	8262
Private Medical-Care Inc	6324	A	562 924-8311	8357
Allstate Floral Inc	6411	C	562 926-2989	8484
Auto Insurance Specialists LLC **(DH)**	6411	C	562 345-6247	8501
Carelon Bhavioral Hlth Cal Inc	6411	A	800 228-1286	8520
Crest Financial Corporation **(DH)**	6411	D	562 733-6500	8535
Poliseek Ais Insur Sltions Inc	6411	D	866 480-7335	8641
Eplica Inc	7361	D	562 977-4300	11131
Randstad Professionals Us LLC	7361	D	562 468-0111	11216
Lloyd Staffing Inc	7363	A	631 777-7600	11298
Auditboard Inc **(PA)**	7371	D	877 769-5444	11433
Secure One Data Solutions LLC	7374	D	562 924-7056	12623
Amkotron Inc **(PA)**	7378	D	562 921-3330	12702
Apex Computer Systems Inc	7378	D	562 926-6820	12703
Geek Squad Inc	7379	D	562 402-1555	12796
Commercial Protective Svcs Inc	7381	A	310 515-5290	12945
College Hospital Inc **(PA)**	8063	B	562 924-9581	16648
Axelacare Holdings Inc	8082	C	714 522-8802	16813
Atkinson Andlson Loya Ruud Rom **(PA)**	8111	C	562 653-3200	17369
Cerritos Church of Nazarene	8661	D	562 809-4143	19014
Phoenix Engineering Tech LLC	8711	D	714 918-0630	19359
Thermal Engrg Intl USA Inc **(HQ)**	8711	D	323 726-0641	19415
Biospace Inc	8731	D	323 932-6503	19664
Caremore Medical Management Company	8741	A	562 741-4300	20053
Management Trust Assn Inc	8742	C	562 926-3372	20446
Physicians Datatrust Inc	8742	C	562 860-8771	20507
City of Cerritos	9111	C	562 916-8500	20912

CHATSWORTH, CA - Los Angeles County

	SIC	EMP	PHONE	ENTRY#
All Tmperatures Controlled Inc	1711	D	818 882-1478	1346
Service Genius Los Angeles Inc	1711	D	818 200-3379	1558
Comet Electric Inc	1731	C	818 340-0965	1702
Guardian Integrated SEC Inc **(PA)**	1731	C	800 400-3167	1740
OBryant Electric Inc **(PA)**	1731	C	818 407-1986	1792
Avitex Inc **(PA)**	2211	C	818 994-6487	2444
Strategic Distribution L P	2326	C	818 671-2100	2452
Impress Communications Inc	2752	D	818 701-8800	2560
Careismatic Brands Inc **(PA)**	3143	C	818 671-2100	2684
Delta Tau Data Systems Inc Cal **(HQ)**	3569	D	818 998-2095	2799
Selane Products Inc **(PA)**	3843	D	818 998-7460	3069
Planet Green Cartridges Inc	3955	D	818 725-2596	3098
Sega Holdings USA Inc	3999	A	415 701-6000	3112
Los Angles Cnty Mtro Trnsp Aut	4111	B	213 922-6308	3152
M & N Consulting Inc	4215	D	818 349-9400	3619

	SIC	EMP	PHONE	ENTRY#
Southern California Gas Co	4922	B	818 701-2592	4721
Allstate Imaging Inc **(PA)**	5044	D	818 678-4550	5242
Levlad LLC	5047	C	818 882-2951	5430
Regency Enterprises Inc **(PA)**	5063	B	818 901-0255	5588
Air Electro Inc **(PA)**	5065	D	818 407-5400	5623
Cbol Corporation	5065	C	818 704-8200	5640
Clover Envmtl Solutions LLC	5085	A	815 431-8100	5895
Pentacon Inc	5085	C	818 727-8000	5918
Logistical Support LLC	5088	C	818 341-3344	5962
Ontic Engineering and Mfg Inc **(PA)**	5088	B	818 678-6555	5963
MGA Entertainment Inc	5092	A	800 222-4685	5993
Medical Research Institute	5122	C	818 739-6000	6130
Paradise Lingerie Inc	5137	D	818 717-9717	6214
Piege Co **(PA)**	5137	D	818 727-9100	6216
J B Whl Roofg Bldg Sups Inc **(DH)**	5211	D	818 998-0440	7029
North Ranch Management Corp	5719	D	800 410-2153	7439
Gameworks Entertainment LLC **(PA)**	5812	A	206 521-0952	7484
Performance Automotive Whl Inc **(PA)**	5961	D	805 499-8973	7563
Cosmetic Laboratories of America LLC	5999	B	818 717-6140	7576
Telesis Community Credit Union	6061	D	818 885-1226	7811
Premier America Credit Union **(PA)**	6062	C	818 772-4000	7830
Cake Mortgage Corp	6162	D	818 812-5150	7939
Nna Insurance Services LLC	6411	D	818 739-4071	8626
Platinum Group Companies Inc	6719	C	818 721-3800	9327
Bellami Hair LLC	7231	D	844 235-5264	10494
101communications LLC **(HQ)**	7313	D	818 734-1520	10698
Tuttle Family Enterprises Inc	7349	B	818 534-2566	10975
Datadirect Networks Inc **(PA)**	7371	C	818 700-7600	11528
ADT LLC	7382	C	818 464-5001	13086
ADT LLC	7382	C	818 574-3809	13088
American Copak Corporation	7389	C	818 576-1000	13189
Multi-Pak Corporation	7389	D	818 709-0508	13385
Seven One Inc **(PA)**	7389	D	818 904-3435	13471
Genesis Tech Partners LLC	7699	C	800 950-2647	13772
Respawn Entertainment LLC	7812	C	818 960-4400	13884
Bay Clubs Company LLC	7991	B	805 778-0888	14177
Crunch Fitness	7991	D	805 522-5454	14194
Cpcc Inc	8059	D	818 882-3200	15835
Pacific Toxicology Labs	8071	B	818 598-3110	16739
County of Los Angeles	8099	A	818 717-4644	17215
Electronic Health Plans Inc	8099	B	818 734-4700	17234
Egremont Schools Inc	8211	D	818 363-7803	17710
Sierra Canyon Inc	8211	D	818 882-8121	17749
Child Care Resource Center Inc **(PA)**	8322	C	818 717-1000	17876
Rancho San Antonio Boys HM Inc **(PA)**	8361	D	818 882-6400	18508
Health Advocates LLC	8399	B	818 995-9500	18594
National Notary Association	8621	C	800 876-6827	18753
Oncore Manufacturing Inc **(HQ)**	8711	A	818 734-6500	19340
Color Design Laboratory Inc **(PA)**	8734	C	818 341-5100	19958
North La County Regional Ctr **(PA)**	8748	B	818 778-1900	20817

CHESTER, CA - Plumas County

	SIC	EMP	PHONE	ENTRY#
Seneca Healthcare District **(PA)**	8062	C	530 258-2151	16410

CHICO, CA - Butte County

	SIC	EMP	PHONE	ENTRY#
Chico Nut Company	0173	D	530 894-5441	91
BCM Construction Company Inc	1541	D	530 342-1722	806
Alternative Energy Systems Inc	1711	D	530 345-6980	1352
Chico Electric Inc	1731	D	530 891-1933	1696
Butte County Assn Governments	4111	D	530 809-4616	3124
Transdev Services Inc	4111	B	530 342-6851	3222
Enloe Medical Center	4119	D	530 891-7347	3255
First Responder Ems Inc	4119	D	530 897-6345	3262
11 Main Inc	4813	C	530 892-9191	4246
Catamunt Brdcstg Chc-Rdding In **(PA)**	4833	D	530 893-2424	4415
Pacific Gas and Electric Co	4911	C	530 258-6215	4612
Pacific Gas and Electric Co	4911	C	530 896-4318	4648
Pacific Gas and Electric Co	4924	D	530 894-4739	4724
Sourcecorp Bps Nthrn Cal Inc	5044	D	530 893-7900	5256
Ubeo West LLC **(HQ)**	5044	C	530 343-6065	5258
Buildcom Inc	5074	B	800 375-3403	5742
Gonzales Park LLC	5136	C	530 343-8725	6175
Project Fusion LLC	5199	C	530 343-8725	6940
Lowes Home Centers LLC	5211	D	530 895-5130	7057
Penney Opco LLC	5311	D	530 899-8160	7134
Courtesy Motors Auto Ctr Inc	5511	C	530 345-9444	7188
Assocted Stdnts Cal State Univ **(PA)**	5942	A	530 898-6815	7545
Trico Bancshares **(PA)**	6022	D	530 898-0300	7719
Federal Land Bnk Assn Nthrn CA	6029	D	530 895-8698	7731
Tri Counties Bank **(HQ)**	6029	D	530 898-0300	7740
Hignell Incorporated	6513	D	530 345-1965	8818
Hignell Incorporated	6552	D	530 342-0707	9255
Mission Linen Supply	7213	C	530 342-4110	10450

CHICO CA — GEOGRAPHIC SECTION

Company	SIC	EMP	PHONE	ENTRY#
3-Downtown Bars Inc	7299	D	530 898-9898	10527
Millard Group Inc	7349	C	530 899-7299	10931
Clock Shark LLC	7371	D	530 433-0981	11495
Work Truck Solutions Inc	7379	D	855 987-4544	12908
Armed Guard Private SEC Inc	7381	D	530 751-3218	12932
IBAM INC	7991	D	530 343-5678	14207
Chico Area Recreation & Pk Dst (PA)	7999	C	530 895-4711	14506
Enloe Cardiology Svcs Clinic	8011	D	530 332-4400	14741
Northern Vly Indian Hlth Inc	8021	D	530 896-9400	15243
Enloe Medical Center	8049	B	530 332-6138	15280
Arbor Post Acute LLC	8051	D	530 342-4885	15331
California Vocations Inc	8059	C	530 877-0937	15826
Riverside Cnvalescent Hosp Inc	8059	D	530 343-5595	15891
Riverside Health Care Corp (PA)	8059	D	530 897-5100	15892
Enloe Hospt-Phys Thrpy	8062	B	530 891-7300	16081
Enloe Medical Center	8062	C	530 332-4111	16082
Enloe Medical Center	8062	C	530 332-7522	16083
Enloe Medical Center (PA)	8062	A	530 332-7300	16084
Enloe Medical Center	8062	C	530 332-5520	16085
Enloe Medical Center	8062	C	530 332-6400	16086
Enloe Medical Center	8062	C	530 332-6000	16087
Addus Healthcare Inc	8082	C	530 566-0405	16795
Butte Home Health Inc	8082	D	530 895-0462	16830
Enloe Medical Center	8082	C	530 332-6050	16860
Home Health Care MGT Inc	8082	D	530 343-0727	16870
Victor Cmnty Support Svcs Inc	8093	D	530 267-1710	17159
Bloodsource Inc	8099	D	530 893-5433	17192
ARC of Butte County (PA)	8322	C	530 891-5865	17837
Far Nrthern Crdnting Cncil On	8322	D	530 895-8633	17980
Youth For Change (PA)	8322	C	530 877-8187	18197
Boys & Girls Clubs of N Vly	8641	D	530 899-0335	18819
Chico State Enterprises	8641	A	530 898-6811	18841
Gas Transmission Systems Inc (HQ)	8711	D	530 893-6711	19237
URS Group Inc	8733	D	530 893-9675	19932

CHINO, CA - San Bernardino County

Company	SIC	EMP	PHONE	ENTRY#
American Beef Packers Inc	0751	C	909 628-4888	355
DL Long Landscaping Inc	0781	D	909 628-5531	428
Generation Construction Inc	1521	C	909 923-2077	678
J Grothe Enterprises Inc	1542	D	909 993-9393	943
Flatiron West Inc	1622	C	909 597-8413	1181
Advantage Pntg Solutions Inc	1721	D	951 739-9204	1603
Campbell Painting Inc	1721	D	919 591-4300	1608
Interior Experts Gen Bldrs Inc	1742	D	909 203-4922	1936
Duke Pacific Inc	1761	D	909 591-0191	2059
R & B Reinforcing Steel Corp	1791	D	909 591-1726	2196
Hira Paris Inc	2064	C	909 634-3900	2375
Isiqalo LLC	2253	B	714 683-2820	2445
Genlabs (PA)	2842	C	909 591-8451	2624
Universal Packg Systems Inc (PA)	2844	A	909 517-2442	2633
Wacker Chemical Corporation	2869	D	909 590-8822	2636
Jacuzzi Products Co	3088	B	909 548-7732	2667
Pretium Packaging LLC	3089	C	714 777-9580	2679
Tst Inc (PA)	3341	B	951 685-2155	2722
Wetmore Tool and Engrg Co	3545	C	909 364-1000	2783
Hussmann Corporation	3585	B	909 590-4910	2842
CRST Expedited Inc	4213	D	909 563-5606	3461
Sunset Pacific Transportation Inc (PA)	4213	D	909 464-1677	3547
Navy Exchange Service Command	4225	C	909 517-2640	3736
Schneider Electric Usa Inc	4225	D	909 438-2295	3752
Universal Packg Systems Inc	4225	C	909 517-2442	3776
Aviation Maintenance Group Inc	4581	D	714 469-0515	3880
Nationwide Trans Inc (PA)	4731	D	909 355-3211	4061
Nfi Industries	4731	D	909 393-4471	4064
Advanced Multimodal Dist Inc	4789	C	800 838-3058	4142
Cellco Partnership	4812	D	909 591-9740	4207
Inland Empire Utlties Agcy A M (PA)	4941	D	909 993-1600	4795
Yoshimura RES & Dev Amer Inc	5013	D	909 628-4722	5068
Omnia Italian Design LLC	5021	C	909 393-4400	5097
Nexgrill Industries Inc (PA)	5023	D	909 598-8799	5127
A Plus International Inc (PA)	5047	D	909 591-5168	5394
Harrington Industrial Plas LLC (PA)	5074	D	909 597-8641	5753
Hill Phoenix Inc	5078	D	909 592-8830	5778
Gano Excel (usa) Inc	5149	D	626 338-8081	6629
Home Depot USA Inc	5211	C	909 393-5205	7026
M K Smith Chevrolet	5511	C	909 628-8961	7254
Kaiser Foundation Hospitals	6324	D	888 750-0036	8307
Hazelrigg Claims MGT Svcs Inc (HQ)	6411	D	909 606-6373	8582
Mission Linen Supply	7213	C	909 393-6857	10447
Baronhr LLC	7361	D	909 517-3800	11088
Math Holdings Inc (PA)	7389	D	909 517-2200	13365
El Prado Golf Course LP	7992	D	909 597-1751	14260
Chino Medical Group Inc	8011	D	909 591-6446	14684
Veritas Health Services Inc	8062	A	909 464-8600	16616
Canyon Ridge Hospital Inc	8063	B	909 590-3700	16646
Angels In Motion LLC	8082	C	909 590-9102	16808
West End Yung MNS Christn Assn	8641	C	909 597-7445	18930
Automobile Club Southern Cal	8699	C	909 591-9451	19057
Transtech Engineers Inc (PA)	8711	C	909 595-8599	19418
Hyundai Amer Technical Ctr Inc	8734	C	909 627-3525	19982
Lollicup Franchising LLC	8742	C	626 965-8882	20440

CHINO HILLS, CA - San Bernardino County

Company	SIC	EMP	PHONE	ENTRY#
Victory Intl Group LLC	5092	C	949 407-5888	6001
Lowes Home Centers LLC	5211	C	909 438-9000	7107
Crmls LLC	6512	C	909 859-2040	8713
Gateway Fresh LLC	6719	C	951 378-5439	9313
Harkins Theatres Inc	7832	D	909 627-8010	13997
Los Serranos Golf Club	7992	C	909 597-1769	14271
Redwood Family Care Netwrk Inc	8011	A	909 942-0218	15013
Sails Washington Inc	8082	B	425 333-4114	16922
Boys Republic (PA)	8361	C	909 902-6690	18380
SSC Construction Inc	8711	C	951 278-1177	19393

CHOWCHILLA, CA - Madera County

Company	SIC	EMP	PHONE	ENTRY#
Seaman Nurseries Inc	0721	D	559 665-1860	244
Madera Disposal Systems Inc (DH)	4953	D	559 665-3099	4905
Minturn Huller Cooperative Inc	5159	D	559 665-1185	6696
Avalon Care Ctr - Chwchlla LLC	8051	C	559 665-4826	15341

CHUALAR, CA - Monterey County

Company	SIC	EMP	PHONE	ENTRY#
C & G Farms Inc	0161	C	831 679-2978	25

CHULA VISTA, CA - San Diego County

Company	SIC	EMP	PHONE	ENTRY#
Sharp Healthcare	0291	D	619 397-3088	239
Merchants Landscape Services	0782	D	619 778-6239	521
Sbhis	1522	D	619 427-2689	775
FJ Willert Contracting Co	1542	C	619 421-1980	918
Otay River Constructors LLC	1611	C	619 397-7500	1149
Foshay Electric Co Inc	1731	D	858 277-7676	1737
Home Carpet Investment Inc (PA)	1752	D	619 262-8040	2034
Legacy Reinforcing Steel LLC	1791	D	619 646-0205	2186
McMahon Steel Company Inc	3429	C	619 671-9700	2730
Circor Naval Solutions LLC (HQ)	3561	D	413 436-7711	2792
Estes Express Lines	4213	D	619 425-4040	3471
United Parcel Service Inc	4215	C	619 482-8119	3644
San Diego Gas & Electric Co	4922	D	800 411-7343	4720
San Diego Gas & Electric Co	4939	C	858 654-1135	4762
Sweetwter Auth Emplyees Cmmtte (PA)	4941	C	619 420-1413	4839
Smart & Final Stores LLC	5141	D	619 427-0202	6378
Heartland Meat Company Inc	5147	D	619 407-3668	6494
California Baking Company	5149	B	619 591-8289	6613
Culinary Hispanic Foods Inc	5149	A	619 955-6101	6623
Home Depot USA Inc	5211	C	619 421-0639	7004
Lowes Home Centers LLC	5211	C	619 739-9060	7074
California Credit Union	6061	C	858 769-7369	7758
Amnet Esop Corporation	6162	C	877 354-1110	7931
Loandepot Inc	6162	B	619 245-0115	7993
State Farm General Insur Co	6411	D	619 227-5777	8663
Loyda Yu Real Estate Inc	6531	D	619 475-7777	9078
Palanging International Inc	6531	D	619 948-2459	9123
West Edge Inc	6531	D	619 475-4095	9211
Otay Hospitality Inc	7011	D	619 422-2600	10072
Kineticom Inc (PA)	7361	D	619 330-3100	11164
Ado Staffing Inc	7363	C	619 691-3659	11267
Rp Automotive II Inc	7513	D	619 656-2500	13567
Standard Calibrations Inc	7629	D	619 477-1668	13746
Southcoast Welding & Mfg LLC	7692	B	619 429-1337	13753
Marine Group Boat Works LLC	7699	D	619 427-6767	13783
San Diego Country Club Inc	7997	C	619 422-8895	14436
Community Health Group	8011	C	800 224-7766	14700
Bayside Healthcare Inc	8051	C	619 426-8611	15352
Front Porch Communities & Svcs	8051	C	619 427-2777	15484
Healthcare Management Systems Inc	8051	C	619 521-9641	15510
Sunrise Senior Living LLC	8051	C	619 470-2220	15693
Bayview Hosp Mntal Hlth System	8062	C	619 426-6310	15959
Scripps Health	8062	C	619 691-7000	16402
Sharp Chula Vista Medical Ctr	8062	A	619 502-5800	16414
Sharp Healthcare	8062	C	858 499-2000	16418
Home Dlysis Thrapies San Diego	8092	D	619 422-0003	16988
ARC of San Diego	8322	D	619 427-7524	17838
Sbcs Corporation	8322	D	619 420-3620	18119
Metropltan Area Advsory Cmmtte (PA)	8331	D	619 426-3595	18234
Child Development Assoc Inc	8351	C	619 422-7115	18283
Susan J Harris Inc	8361	C	619 498-8450	18530
CHG Foundation	8699	B	619 422-0422	19077

GEOGRAPHIC SECTION

CLEARLAKE CA

	SIC	EMP	PHONE	ENTRY#
George G Sharp Inc	8711	D	619 425-4211	19241
Gryphon Marine LLC	8711	D	619 407-4010	19246
Lockheed Martin Services LLC	8711	B	619 271-9831	19307
Armando C Ibrra CPA A Prof Cor	8721	D	619 422-1348	19530
Estudysite	8731	D	619 955-5246	19690
Prosciento Inc (PA)	8731	C	619 427-1300	19762

CITRUS HEIGHTS, CA - Sacramento County

	SIC	EMP	PHONE	ENTRY#
J R Roberts Corp (HQ)	1542	D	916 729-5600	944
J R Roberts Enterprises Inc	1542	C	916 729-5600	945
SD Deacon Corp California	1542	C	916 969-0900	1022
Lowes Home Centers LLC	5211	B	916 728-7800	7068
Accountble Hlthcare Stffing In	7361	C	916 286-7667	11073
Crossroads Diversfd Svcs Inc	7361	C	916 676-2540	11115
River City Staffing Inc	7361	C	916 485-1588	11223
Patrol Solutions LLC	7381	C	916 919-6079	13020
On My Own Community Services	8059	D	916 726-0792	15885
Mercy Medical Group	8062	D	916 536-2420	16265
Always Home Nursing Svcs Inc	8082	C	916 989-6420	16805
Fortune Senior Enterprises	8082	C	916 560-9100	16865
On My Own Ind Living Svcs	8322	D	916 726-0792	18070
Terra Nova Counseling (PA)	8322	D	916 344-0249	18149
County of Sacramento	8641	B	916 725-1585	18846

CITY OF INDUSTRY, CA - Los Angeles County

	SIC	EMP	PHONE	ENTRY#
Alta-Dena Certified Dairy LLC (DH)	0241	B	626 964-6401	213
Frize Corporation	1541	D	800 834-2127	818
Morrow-Meadows Corporation (PA)	1731	A	858 974-3650	1782
Closet World Inc	1751	D	626 855-0846	1993
Home Organizers Inc	1751	A	562 699-9945	2002
Performance Sheets LLC	1761	C	626 333-0195	2076
Closet World Inc	1799	D	800 576-7717	2267
Derek and Constance Lee Corp (PA)	2013	D	909 595-8831	2342
Berkeley Farms LLC	2026	B	510 265-8600	2351
Commercial Lbr & Pallet Co Inc (PA)	2448	C	626 968-0631	2483
R C Furniture Inc	2512	D	626 964-4100	2489
Hoover Containers Inc	2653	C	909 444-9454	2517
Scope Packaging Inc	2653	D	714 998-4411	2525
Maintex Inc (PA)	2842	C	800 446-1888	2625
Jon Brooks Inc (PA)	3295	D	626 330-0631	2719
Newton Heat Treating Co Inc	3398	D	626 964-6528	2728
Evans Industries Inc	3499	C	626 912-1688	2766
Pape Material Handling Inc	3537	D	562 692-9311	2779
Premio Inc (PA)	3571	C	626 839-3100	2810
Rosewill Inc	3571	A	800 575-9885	2811
Utility Trailer Mfg Co	3715	C	909 594-6026	2980
United Pumping Service Inc	4212	D	626 961-9326	3432
Estes Express Lines	4213	D	626 333-9090	3474
U C L Incorporated (PA)	4213	C	323 235-0099	3558
17400 Inc	4214	D	626 913-1800	3577
Gels Logistics Inc (PA)	4731	D	626 340-6660	4023
Prime Global Solutions Inc (PA)	4731	D	800 424-7746	4078
Quartz Logistics Inc	4731	C	626 606-2001	4082
Southern California Gas Co	4924	C	213 244-1200	4735
Arakelian Enterprises Inc	4953	B	626 336-3636	4857
Arakelian Enterprises Inc (PA)	4953	B	626 336-3636	4859
Zerep Management Corporation (PA)	4953	C	626 855-5522	4973
Poundex Associates Corporation	5021	D	909 444-5878	5102
Soto Provision Inc	5023	D	626 458-4600	5134
W Diamond Supply Co (DH)	5023	D	909 859-8939	5143
Carrara Marble Co Amer Inc (PA)	5032	D	626 961-6010	5196
American Future Tech Corp	5045	D	888 462-3899	5270
GBT Inc	5045	C	626 854-9338	5307
Magnell Associate Inc (DH)	5045	D	800 685-3471	5327
MSI Computer Corp (HQ)	5045	D	626 913-0828	5330
Mtc Worldwide Corp	5045	D	626 839-6800	5331
Private Label Pc LLC	5045	C	626 965-8686	5335
Grifols Usa LLC	5047	A	626 435-2600	5419
California Steel and Tube	5051	C	626 968-5511	5481
Maxim Lighting Intl Inc (PA)	5063	D	626 956-4200	5578
Eforcity Corporation	5065	D	626 442-3168	5647
Assa Abloy Rsdential Group Inc	5072	A	626 369-4718	5722
Elmco Sales Inc (PA)	5074	D	626 855-4831	5746
US Airconditioning Distributors Inc (PA)	5075	C	626 854-4500	5775
Quinn Shepherd Machinery	5082	B	562 463-6000	5803
Pape Material Handling Inc	5084	C	562 463-8000	5856
Valley Power Systems Inc (PA)	5084	D	626 333-1243	5879
Yale/Chase Equipment and Services Inc	5084	C	562 463-8000	5887
Rutland Tool & Supply Co (HQ)	5085	C	562 566-5000	5923
Hd Supply Facilities Maint Ltd	5087	D	909 594-3843	5941
Delta Creative Inc	5092	C	800 423-4135	5989
Sweda Company LLC	5094	B	626 357-9999	6027
Fox Luggage Inc	5099	D	323 588-1688	6041
Cenveo Worldwide Limited	5112	B	626 369-4921	6064
Essendant Co	5112	C	626 961-0011	6065
Markwins Beauty Brands Inc (PA)	5122	C	909 595-8898	6123
Markwins Beauty Products Inc	5122	C	909 595-8898	6124
Foria International Inc	5136	D	626 912-8836	6174
Swatfame Inc (PA)	5137	B	626 961-7928	6223
Fortune Dynamic Inc	5139	D	909 979-8318	6232
Marquez Brothers Entps Inc	5141	B	626 330-3310	6263
Mercado Latino Inc (PA)	5141	D	626 333-6862	6268
OTasty Foods Inc	5141	D	626 330-1229	6274
WEI-Chuan USA Inc (PA)	5142	C	626 225-7168	6427
Dfa Dairy Brands Fluid LLC	5143	D	800 395-7004	6434
Klm Management Company	5143	D	626 330-3479	6439
Los Altos Food Products LLC	5143	D	626 330-6555	6440
D&D Wholesale Distributors LLC	5148	D	626 333-2111	6530
Freshpoint Inc	5148	C	626 855-1400	6545
Freshpoint Southern Cal Inc	5148	C	626 855-1400	6546
Royal Crown Enterprises Inc	5149	C	626 854-8080	6663
Tld Acquisition Co LLC	5149	C		6681
Vinh - Sanh Trading Corp	5149	D	626 968-6888	6691
Classic Bev Southern Cal LLC	5181	C	626 934-3700	6756
American Paper & Plastics LLC	5199	C	626 444-0000	6888
Lowes Home Centers LLC	5211	D	626 217-1133	7101
Leo Hoffman Chevrolet Inc (PA)	5511	D	626 968-8411	7251
PC Club Inc (HQ)	5734	D	626 839-8080	7448
Citifinancial Credit Company	6141	D	626 712-8780	7874
Cubeworkcom Inc	6531	D	909 991-6669	8955
Majestic Realty Co (PA)	6531	D	562 692-9581	9091
Bethar Corporation	6719	C		9302
Benefits Prgram Adminsitration	6733	D	562 463-5000	9421
Majestic Industry Hills LLC	7011	A	626 810-4455	9996
CSC Serviceworks Inc	7215	D	626 389-0169	10463
Boiling Point Rest S CA Inc	7361	B	626 551-5181	11097
Management Applied Prgrm Inc (PA)	7374	D	562 463-5000	12591
Nzxt Inc (PA)	7379	D	800 228-9395	12848
Garda World Security Corp	7381	C	909 468-2229	12976
Easterncctv (usa) LLC	7382	D	626 961-8999	13108
Ezviz Inc	7382	C	855 693-9849	13115
Hikvision USA Inc (HQ)	7382	C	909 895-0400	13124
US Bankcard Services Inc	7389	D	888 888-8872	13536
National Freight Inc	7513	D	909 348-5464	13562
Rollins Leasing LLC	7513	D	626 913-7186	13566
Dacor	7629	D	626 961-2256	13739
Allied Entertainment Group Inc (PA)	7812	B	626 330-0600	13816
Grifols Wrldwide Oprtons USA I	8099	D	626 435-2600	17243
County of Los Angeles	8322	D	626 854-4987	17930
Public Hlth Fndation Entps Inc	8322	C	626 856-6600	18090
Public Hlth Fndation Entps Inc (PA)	8641	C	800 201-7320	18899
Qy Research Inc	8732	D	626 295-2442	19846
Weck Anlytical Envmtl Svcs Inc	8734	D	626 336-2139	20004
Cameron Energy Services Corp	8741	B	562 321-9183	20052
County of Los Angeles	8741	D	562 908-8400	20070
Torrid Merchandising Inc	8742	B	626 667-1002	20586

CLAREMONT, CA - Los Angeles County

	SIC	EMP	PHONE	ENTRY#
Atmc Incorporated (PA)	1731	D	909 390-0470	1670
Phoenix Marketing Services Inc	2752	D	909 399-4000	2565
Therapak LLC (DH)	5047	D	909 267-2000	5454
Pff Bancorp Inc (PA)	6035	A	213 683-6393	7747
Western Feld Invstigations Inc (PA)	7375	D	800 999-9589	12687
R&C Motor Corporation	7538	C	909 625-1500	13673
Claremont Tennis Club	7997	C	909 625-9515	14360
Tierra Del Sol Foundation	7999	D	909 626-8301	14574
Sunrise Senior Living LLC	8051	D	909 398-4688	15690
Pilgrim Place In Claremont (PA)	8059	D	909 399-5500	15889
Kaiser Foundation Hospitals	8062	D	888 750-0036	16189
Bluebridge Prof Svcs Inc	8082	D	909 625-6151	16824
Sunrise Senior Living MGT Inc	8361	C	909 447-5259	18528
Trinity Youth Services (PA)	8361	D	909 825-5588	18533
Rancho Santa Ana Botanic Grdn	8422	D	909 625-8767	18693
Technip Usa Inc	8711	B	909 447-3600	19405
Ten Stone Wbster Prcess Tech	8711	B	909 447-3600	19407
Bon Appetit Management Co	8741	C	909 607-2788	20042

CLARKSBURG, CA - Yolo County

	SIC	EMP	PHONE	ENTRY#
Vino Farms Inc	0191	C	916 775-4095	207

CLAYTON, CA - Contra Costa County

	SIC	EMP	PHONE	ENTRY#
American Golf Corporation	7997	D	925 672-9737	14322

CLEARLAKE, CA - Lake County

	SIC	EMP	PHONE	ENTRY#
Bayberry Inc	5999	D	707 995-1643	7573
Vindra Inc	8051	D	707 994-7738	15724

Employee Codes: A=Over 500 employees, B=251-500
C=101-250, D=51-100, E=20-50, F=10-19, G=1-9

2024 Directory of California
WholeSalers and Service Companies

© Mergent Inc. 1-800-342-5647

CLEARLAKE CA

CLEARLAKE CA

Company	SIC	EMP	PHONE	ENTRY#
Adventist Hlth Clrlake Hosp In	8062	C	707 994-6486	15920
Adventist Hlth Clrlake Hosp In (HQ)	8062	B	707 994-6486	15921
Adventist Hlth Systm/West Corp	8062	C	707 994-6486	15924
Advintist Hlth Clearlake Hosp	8062	C	707 994-6486	15927

CLEARLAKE OAKS, CA - Lake County

Company	SIC	EMP	PHONE	ENTRY#
Shannon Ranches Inc	8742	C	707 998-9656	20542

CLOVERDALE, CA - Sonoma County

Company	SIC	EMP	PHONE	ENTRY#
All-Coast Forest Products Inc (PA)	5031	D	707 894-4281	5145
Nu Forest Products Inc	5031	D	707 433-3313	5176
Star H-R	7361	A	707 894-4404	11238
Ensign Cloverdale LLC	8051	B	707 894-5201	15450

CLOVIS, CA - Fresno County

Company	SIC	EMP	PHONE	ENTRY#
Floyd Johnston Cnstr Co Inc	1623	D	559 299-7373	1209
Live Action General Engrg Inc	1711	C	559 292-2900	1488
Valley Unique Electric Inc	1731	D	559 237-4795	1868
Westech Systems Inc	1731	D	559 455-1720	1875
Graham Concrete Cnstr Inc	1771	D	559 292-6571	2122
Drakaina Logistics	4789	D	559 765-1347	4151
Cellco Partnership	4812	C	559 321-8116	4192
Smart & Final Stores	5141	B	559 297-9376	6320
Lowes Home Centers LLC	5211	C	559 322-3000	7078
C2 Financial Corporation	6282	C	559 824-2300	8193
Kaiser Foundation Hospitals	6324	C	559 324-5100	8323
OfficeMax North America Inc	7334	C	559 298-0164	10791
Conservis Corp	7371	D	612 424-6300	11513
Bowie Enterprises	7542	D	559 292-6565	13688
Hydratech LLC (HQ)	7699	D	559 233-0876	13775
Leather Factory LP	7699	D	559 297-7375	13780
Niacc-Avitech Technologies Inc (PA)	7699	D	559 291-2500	13787
Central Valley Indian Hlth Inc (PA)	8011	D	559 299-2578	14673
Fresno Cmnty Hosp & Med Ctr	8011	D	559 324-4000	14755
Peachwood Med Group Clovis Inc	8011	D	559 324-6200	14952
Willow Creek Hlthcare Ctr LLC	8051	D	559 323-6200	15736
Pathology Associates	8069	D	559 326-2800	16690
Well Being Senior Solutions	8082	D	559 321-8295	16974
Fresenius Med Care Clovis LLC	8092	A	559 324-8023	16982
County of Fresno	8111	D	559 600-3546	17415
County of Fresno	8322	D	559 600-5127	17903
Generation Clovis LLC	8361	C	559 297-4900	18439
Krazan & Associates (PA)	8748	D	559 348-2200	20793
County of Fresno	9199	C	559 299-6057	20923

COACHELLA, CA - Riverside County

Company	SIC	EMP	PHONE	ENTRY#
Amazing Coachella Inc	0161	D	760 398-0151	19
Anthony Vineyards Inc	0172	D	760 391-5488	68
Teserra (PA)	1799	B	760 340-9000	2320
Sunline Transit Agency	4119	C	760 972-4059	3296
Naumann/Hobbs Mtl Hdlg Corp II	5082	C	866 266-2244	5795
Desert Valley Date LLC	5149	D	760 398-0999	6625
Esparza Enterprises Inc	7361	A	760 398-0349	11133
Augustine Gaming MGT Corp	7371	D	760 391-9500	11434
29 Palms Enterprises Corp	7999	A	760 775-5566	14486

COALINGA, CA - Fresno County

Company	SIC	EMP	PHONE	ENTRY#
Harris Farms Inc (PA)	0191	B	559 935-0717	182
Harris Farms Inc	0191	C	559 884-2435	183
Coalinga Feed Yard Inc	0211	D	559 935-0836	209
Harris Woolf Cal Almonds LLC	0723	C	559 884-2147	277
Aera Energy Services Company	3533	C	559 935-7418	2774
Coalinga Regional Med Ctr Aux	8062	C	559 935-6400	16005
Califrnia Dept State Hospitals	8063	A	559 935-4300	16641

COARSEGOLD, CA - Madera County

Company	SIC	EMP	PHONE	ENTRY#
Chukchansi Gold Resort Casino	7011	A	866 794-6946	9699
Yosemite Lakes Owners Assn	8641	D	559 658-7466	18953

COLFAX, CA - Placer County

Company	SIC	EMP	PHONE	ENTRY#
Tully-Wihr Company	2752	C	530 346-2649	2566

COLMA, CA - San Mateo County

Company	SIC	EMP	PHONE	ENTRY#
Congregation Emanu-El	6553	C	650 755-4700	9284
Cypress Lawn Cemetery Assn	6553	D	650 755-0580	9285
Lucky Chances Inc	7011	A	650 758-2237	9991

COLTON, CA - San Bernardino County

Company	SIC	EMP	PHONE	ENTRY#
High-Light Electric Inc	1731	D	951 352-9646	1748
Superior Masonry Walls Ltd	1741	D	909 370-1800	1894
Lozano Caseworks Inc	1751	D	909 783-7530	2007
Gxo Logistics Supply Chain Inc	4225	D	951 512-1201	3712
Sprouts Farmers Market Inc	4225	C	888 577-7688	3756
Entercom Media Corp	4832	C	909 825-9525	4379
Ecology Recycling Services LLC	4953	C	909 370-1318	4887
A-Z Bus Sales Inc (PA)	5012	D	951 781-7188	4998
Trinity Equipment Inc	5046	D	951 790-1652	5392
Greenpath Recovery West Inc	5093	D	909 954-0686	6009
Kaiser Foundation Hospitals	6733	D	909 427-5521	9434
King Equipment LLC	7353	D	909 986-5300	11001
Inland Eye Inst Med Group Inc (PA)	8011	D	909 825-3425	14784
Premier Otptent Srgery Ctr Inc	8011	C	909 370-2190	14998
Southern Cal Prmnnte Med Group	8011	C	909 370-2501	15080
Cambridge Sierra Holdings LLC	8051	B	909 370-4411	15365
Charter Hospice Colton LLC	8052	C	909 825-2969	15749
Arrowhead Regional Medical Ctr	8062	A	909 580-1000	15952
Rai Care Centers Colton LLC	8092	C	909 430-0930	16991

COLUSA, CA - Colusa County

Company	SIC	EMP	PHONE	ENTRY#
Premier Mushrooms LP	0182	C	530 458-2700	165
Premier Mushrooms LP (PA)	5148	D	530 458-2700	6569
Riviana Foods Inc	5153	D	530 458-8512	6694
New Colusa Indian Bingo	7011	B	530 458-8844	10041
Colusa Indian Cmnty Council	8011	D	530 458-5787	14694
Colusa Indian Cmnty Council	8011	D	530 458-5501	14695
Colusa Indian Cmnty Council	8399	B	530 458-6572	18573
Colusa Regional Medical Center Inc	8741	C	530 458-5821	20061

COMMERCE, CA - Los Angeles County

Company	SIC	EMP	PHONE	ENTRY#
Shims Bargain Inc	1541	C	323 726-8800	842
Freedom Forever LLC	1711	A	714 955-8735	1444
L Tech Network Services Inc	1731	D	562 222-1121	1764
Farwest Insulation Contracting	1742	D	310 634-2800	1928
Oakhurst Industries Inc (PA)	2051	C	323 724-3000	2369
Chameleon Beverage Company Inc (PA)	2086	C	323 724-8223	2404
Caffe DAmore Inc	2095	C		2426
Pacific Spice Company Inc	2099	C	323 726-9190	2440
Murrays Iron Works Inc (PA)	2514	C	323 521-1100	2491
Huhtamaki Inc	3086	C	323 269-0151	2664
Century Wire & Cable Inc	3357	D	800 999-5566	2724
Gehr Industries Inc (HQ)	3357	C	323 728-5558	2725
Eastwestproto Inc	4119	B	888 535-5728	3253
Xpo Cartage Inc	4212	C	800 837-7584	3440
Dart International A Corp (HQ)	4225	C	323 264-8746	3695
Dart Warehouse Corporation (HQ)	4225	B	323 264-1011	3696
Smart & Final Stores LLC	4225	D	323 725-0791	3753
Screamline Investment Corp	4725	C	323 201-0114	3970
Stg Logistics Inc	4731	C	323 869-6000	4101
Strategic Materials Inc	4953	C	323 887-6831	4941
ITD Arizona Inc	5014	D	323 722-8542	5070
Gibson Overseas Inc (PA)	5023	B	323 832-8900	5120
Zwilling JA Henckels LLC	5023	C	323 597-1421	5144
Interstate Electric Co Inc	5046	D	800 225-5432	5380
Justman Packaging & Display (PA)	5046	D	323 728-8888	5384
Adj Products LLC (PA)	5063	C	323 582-2650	5533
Kobert & Company Inc	5063	D	323 725-1000	5571
Nora Lighting Inc	5063	C	323 767-2600	5584
Samsung Electronics Amer Inc	5064	D	323 374-6300	5613
Ultra Pro International LLC	5092	B	323 890-2100	6000
D J American Supply Inc	5099	C	323 582-2650	6039
Sun Coast Merchandise Corp	5099	C	323 720-9700	6053
Glamour Industries Co (PA)	5122	B	323 728-2999	6109
Charming Trim & Packaging	5131	A	415 302-7021	6153
Roochi Traders Incorporated	5136	D	323 722-5592	6186
BP Clothing LLC	5137	C		6195
Smart & Final Stores LLC (DH)	5141	D	323 869-7500	6372
Smart Stores Operations LLC (DH)	5141	B	323 869-7500	6391
Century Snacks LLC	5145	B	323 278-9578	6458
4 Earth Farms LLC (PA)	5148	C	323 201-5800	6511
Buy Fresh Produce Inc	5148	D	323 796-0127	6520
El Guapo Spices Inc (PA)	5149	D	213 312-1300	6627
Jfc International Inc (HQ)	5149	C	323 721-6100	6638
Jfc International Inc	5149	C	323 721-6900	6639
Elkay Plastics Co Inc (PA)	5162	D	323 722-7073	6699
Univar Solutions USA Inc	5169	C	323 727-7005	6714
Breakthru Beverage Cal LLC (HQ)	5182	B	800 331-2829	6787
99 Cents Only Stores LLC (HQ)	5199	C	323 980-8145	6885
Ernest Packaging (PA)	5199	C	800 233-7788	6905
Misa Imports Inc	5199	D	562 281-6773	6929
Sp Images Inc	5199	D	508 530-3225	6950
Sports Images Inc	5199	D	508 530-3225	6951
Unix Packaging LLC	5199	B	213 627-5050	6954
Home Depot USA Inc	5211	B	323 727-9600	7019
Number Holdings Inc (PA)	5331	C	323 980-8145	7138
California Commerce Club Inc	7011	A	323 721-2100	9676
W2005 Wyn Hotels LP	7011	D	323 887-8100	10351

GEOGRAPHIC SECTION

CONCORD CA

	SIC	EMP	PHONE	ENTRY#
Uniserve Facilities Svcs Corp (PA)	7349	B	213 533-1000	10976
Rti Services Inc	7389	D	323 725-6370	13454
Parking Company of America	7521	D	562 862-2118	13615
Pcam LLC	7521	D	562 862-2118	13625
Reading Entertainment Inc (HQ)	7832	D	213 235-2226	14006
Altamed Health Services Corp (PA)	8011	C	323 725-8751	14606
Alexandra Lzano Immgrtion Law	8111	D	323 524-9944	17361
County of Los Angeles	8322	B	323 889-3405	17908
Mexican Amrcn Oprtnty Fndation	8322	D	323 890-1555	18054
Seiu Untd Hlthcare Wrkrs-West	8631	C	323 734-8399	18794
Maravilla Foundation (PA)	8641	C	323 721-4162	18880
Michelson Laboratories Inc (PA)	8734	D	562 928-0553	19987
Island Global Holdings Inc	8742	D	301 742-0775	20418
Ivy Enterprises Inc	8748	B	323 887-8661	20784

COMPTON, CA - Los Angeles County

	SIC	EMP	PHONE	ENTRY#
Nabors Well Services Co	1389	D	310 639-7074	619
Quality Production Svcs Inc	1742	D	310 406-3350	1958
Crew Inc	1794	D	310 608-6860	2216
American Dawn Inc (PA)	2299	D	800 821-2221	2448
Owens Corning Sales LLC	2952	D	310 631-1062	2651
AAA Plating & Inspection Inc	3471	D	323 979-8930	2756
Norco Industries Inc (PA)	3569	C	310 639-4000	2800
Jimway Inc	3648	D	310 886-3718	2876
Mercado Latino Inc	3999	D	310 537-1062	3110
Tag Toys Inc	3999	D	310 639-4566	3113
Durham School Services L P	4151	C	310 767-5820	3325
Ajr Trucking Inc	4212	D	310 707-1120	3366
Asbury Environmental Services (PA)	4212	D	310 886-3400	3370
Uls Express Inc	4212	C	310 631-0800	3429
H Rauvel Inc	4213	C	562 989-3333	3485
National Retail Trnsp Inc	4213	C	310 605-3777	3518
Pacific Drayage Services LLC	4213	C	833 334-4622	3524
Fox Transportation Inc	4214	C	310 971-0867	3587
Transport Express Inc	4214	D	310 898-2000	3599
Madden Corporation	4215	D	714 922-1670	3620
F R T International Inc (PA)	4225	D	310 604-8208	3702
Foamex LP	4225	C	323 774-5600	3706
Kroger Co	4225	B	859 630-6959	3722
Tropicana Manufacturing Co Inc	4225	D	310 764-4395	3772
Apex Logistics Intl Inc (PA)	4731	C	310 665-0288	3985
Dhx-Dependable Hawaiian Ex Inc (PA)	4731	D	310 537-2000	4007
Global Mail Inc	4731	C	310 735-0800	4024
M-7 Consolidation Inc	4731	C	310 898-3456	4053
Noatum Logistics Usa LLC	4731	C	310 527-2104	4067
Port Logistics Group Inc	4731	B	310 669-2551	4076
Tricap International LLC	4731	D	509 703-8780	4112
Cellco Partnership	4812	D	310 603-0101	4191
Southern California Edison Co	4911	B	310 608-5029	4688
4 Wheel Parts Wholesalers LLC	5013	B	310 900-7725	5021
Dna Specialty Inc	5013	D	310 767-4070	5036
Saddlemen Corporation	5013	C	310 638-1222	5058
Silla Automotive LLC	5013	C	800 624-1499	5061
Tap Worldwide LLC (HQ)	5013	C	310 900-5500	5064
Uma Enterprises Inc (PA)	5023	D	310 631-1166	5141
Concrete Tie Industries Inc (PA)	5032	D	310 628-2328	5201
Cordelia Lighting Inc	5063	C	310 886-3490	5549
Florence Filter Corporation	5075	D	310 637-1137	5768
JOHN TILLMAN COMPANY (DH)	5084	D	310 764-0110	5842
United Fabricare Supply Inc (PA)	5087	D	310 537-2096	5950
M M Fab Inc	5131	D	310 763-3800	6157
Colosseum Athletics Corp	5136	D	310 667-8341	6171
Newport Apparel Corporation (PA)	5137	D	310 605-1900	6210
Gourmet Foods Inc (PA)	5141	D	310 632-3300	6255
Interstate Foods Inc	5144	C	310 635-2442	6445
General Petroleum LLC (HQ)	5172	C	562 983-7300	6730
Beauchamp Distributing Company	5181	D	310 639-5320	6752
Epsilon Plastics Inc	5199	D	310 609-1320	6904
Kraco Enterprises LLC	5531	C	310 639-0666	7352
Transamerican Dissolution LLC (HQ)	5531	C	310 900-5500	7381
Celebrity Casinos Inc	7011	B	310 631-3838	9689
Hydroprocessing Associates LLC	7389	D	310 667-6456	13319
Compton Unified School Dst	8211	D	310 898-6470	17705
Compton Unified School Dst	8211	D	310 639-4321	17706
County of Los Angeles	8322	D	310 603-7311	17926
Brinderson LLC (DH)	8711	C	714 466-7100	19160
Element Mtrls Tech HB Inc	8734	D	310 632-8500	19968
Beyondsoft Consulting Inc	8748	D	310 532-2822	20705

CONCORD, CA - Contra Costa County

	SIC	EMP	PHONE	ENTRY#
Sage Veterinary Centers LP	0742	B	925 288-4856	342
Mike McCall Landscape Inc	0782	C	925 363-8100	522
Aptim Federal Services LLC	1521	B	925 288-9898	655
Swinerton Builders (HQ)	1541	D	925 602-6400	847
Bayside Insulation & Cnstr Inc	1542	D	925 288-8960	871
Groundlvel - Ovraa Joint Ventr	1542	D	925 446-6084	925
Kramer Rgm Inc	1542	D	925 671-7717	955
Nevell Group Inc	1542	B	714 579-7501	975
Apco Paving Company	1611	D	925 827-9850	1078
D A McCosker Construction Co	1611	C	925 686-1780	1093
McE Corporation (PA)	1611	D	925 803-4111	1137
American Bridge/Fluor Enterprises Inc	1622	D	510 808-4623	1178
Flatiron West Inc	1622	C	707 742-6000	1180
Electric Tech Construction Inc	1623	D	925 849-5324	1208
Lescure Company Inc	1711	D	925 283-2528	1486
Matrix Hg Inc	1711	D	925 459-9200	1497
N V Heathorn Inc	1711	D	510 569-9100	1506
Bay Alarm Company (PA)	1731	D	925 935-1100	1674
Petro-Chem Industries Inc	1742	D	707 644-7455	1955
Enterprise Roofing Service Inc	1761	D	925 689-8100	2063
Conco Companies	1771	D	303 996-9841	2110
Bay Cities Pav & Grading Inc	1794	C	925 687-6666	2213
Carone & Company Inc	1794	D	925 602-8800	2215
Janus Corporation (PA)	1799	D	925 969-9200	2287
Unique Scaffold	1799	D	925 457-3379	2324
Siemens Med Solutions USA Inc	3845	A	925 246-8200	3077
Bay Medic Transportation Inc	4119	C	800 689-9511	3240
Mt Dblo Resource Recovery LLC	4212	B	925 682-9113	3414
Lemore Transportation Inc (PA)	4213	D	925 689-6444	3505
Patriot Contract Services LLC	4412	B	925 296-2000	3798
Pacific Gas and Electric Co	4911	C	925 676-0948	4625
Pacific Gas and Electric Co	4911	D	925 818-7082	4628
Contra Costa Water District (PA)	4941	D	925 688-8000	4778
Saxco-Demptos Inc	5199	C	707 422-9999	6946
Lowes Home Centers LLC	5211	B	925 566-9000	7111
FAA Concord T Inc	5511	D	925 682-7131	7205
Future Ford of Concord LLC	5511	D	925 686-5000	7217
Weatherford Motors Inc	5511	D	510 654-8280	7331
Round Table Pizza Inc (DH)	5812	D	800 866-5866	7507
Pacific Service Credit Union (PA)	6061	D	888 858-6878	7789
Aetna Health California Inc (DH)	6324	C	925 543-9223	8275
Athens Insurance Service Inc	6411	C	925 826-1000	8499
James C Jenkins Insur Svc Inc	6411	C	925 798-3334	8595
Coldwell Bnkr Residential Brkg (DH)	6531	C	925 275-3000	8942
Denova Home Sales Inc	6531	D	925 852-0545	8978
Fidelity Nat HM Warranty Co	6541	C	925 356-0194	9229
Ufcw & Employers Trust LLC (PA)	6733	C	800 552-2400	9449
Concord Hotel LLC	7011	D	925 521-3751	9719
Montclair Hotels Mb LLC	7011	B	925 687-5500	10025
Service Hospitality LLC	7011	D	925 566-8820	10221
Vwi Concord LLC	7011	C	925 827-2000	10347
Consumer Cr Cnsling Svc San Fr (PA)	7299	D	888 456-2227	10539
Dave Calhoun and Assoc LLC	7349	C	925 688-1234	10888
Summit Building Services Inc	7349	D	925 827-9500	10972
Perfict Global Inc	7379	C	949 945-8956	12856
Delta Personnel Services Inc	7381	D	925 356-3034	12964
Admiral Security Services Inc	7382	B	888 471-1128	13084
ADT LLC	7382	D	925 602-0500	13090
Compumail Information Svcs Inc	7389	C	925 689-7100	13241
Jopari Solutions Inc	7389	D	925 459-5200	13334
Concord Veranda Cinema LLC	7812	D	707 762-0990	13831
Brenden Theatre Corporation (PA)	7832	C	925 677-0462	13977
Parc Waterworld LLC	7996	C	925 609-1364	14308
Bay Area Seating Service Inc	7999	B	925 671-4000	14495
Parc Management LLC	7999	C	925 609-1364	14550
Vep Healthcare Inc	8011	C	925 482-2839	15184
Stonebrook Convalescent Center	8051	C	925 689-7457	15683
Windsor Cnvlscent Rhblttion CT	8051	D	925 689-2266	15738
Tranquility Incorporated	8059	C	925 825-4280	15904
Sutter Vsting Nrse Assn Hspice	8082	C	925 677-4250	16944
Willow Pass Hlth Care Ctr Inc	8082	D	925 689-9222	16976
Mdusd	8099	D	925 682-8000	17273
Laughlin Falbo Levy Moresi LLP (PA)	8111	D	510 628-0496	17540
Zwicker & Associates PC	8111	D	925 689-7070	17692
Mt Diablo Unified School Dst	8211	D	925 685-7340	17733
Futures Explored	8322	C	925 332-7183	17991
Regional Center of E Bay Inc	8322	C	925 691-2300	18097
Shelter Solano Inc	8322	D	925 957-7576	18132
Dianne Adair Day Care Centers (PA)	8351	D	925 580-9704	18307
We Care Services For Children	8351	D	925 685-0207	18366
Cocokids Inc	8399	C	925 676-5442	18572
Ua Local 342 Jatc	8631	C	925 686-0730	18799
Cowell Homeowners Assn Inc (PA)	8641	D	925 825-0250	18847
Young MNS Chrstn Assn of E Bay	8641	C	925 609-7971	18966
Aptim Corp	8711	C	925 288-9898	19142
Cooper Vali & Associates Inc (HQ)	8711	D	510 446-8301	19184

CONCORD CA

	SIC	EMP	PHONE	ENTRY#
Crown Energy Services Inc	8711	C	925 827-6299	19189
Eichleay Inc **(PA)**	8711	C	925 689-7000	19210
Eichleay Engineers Inc	8711	D	925 689-7000	19211
Gilbane Federal **(DH)**	8711	C	925 946-3100	19242
Harris & Associates Inc **(PA)**	8711	C	925 827-4900	19247
Flatiron Construction Corp	8741	C	707 742-6270	20090
Tapetech Tool Company	8742	A	925 676-7002	20577
Zero Waste Solutions Inc	8744	C	925 270-3339	20668
Aptim Corp	8748	C	925 288-9898	20692

COOL, CA - El Dorado County

	SIC	EMP	PHONE	ENTRY#
Teichert Inc	1442	C	530 885-4244	641

COPPEROPOLIS, CA - Calaveras County

	SIC	EMP	PHONE	ENTRY#
Meridian Gold Inc	1041	B	209 785-3222	574

CORCORAN, CA - Kings County

	SIC	EMP	PHONE	ENTRY#
J G Boswell Company	0131	D	559 992-5141	4
Hansen Ranches LLC	0191	D	559 992-3111	181
J G Boswell Company	0212	B	559 992-5011	211
J G Boswell Company	0723	D	559 992-2141	281
Quinn Company	5082	D	559 992-2193	5798
Corcoran District Hospital Foundation	8062	C	559 992-3300	16019
Recreational Assn Corcoran	8641	D	559 992-5171	18901

CORNING, CA - Tehama County

	SIC	EMP	PHONE	ENTRY#
Rolling Hills Casino	7011	C	530 528-3500	10169
Omega Waste Management Inc	8742	D	530 824-1890	20493
Paskenta Band Nomlaki Indians	9199	B	530 670-1750	20927

CORONA, CA - Riverside County

	SIC	EMP	PHONE	ENTRY#
Excel Landscape Inc	0782	C	951 735-9650	489
Landscape Development Inc	0782	C	951 371-9370	515
Champion Home Builders Inc	1521	D	951 256-4617	666
Superior Construction Inc	1521	D	951 808-8780	727
DR Horton Inc	1531	D	951 272-9000	789
AK Constructors Inc	1542	D	951 280-0269	862
JM Stitt Construction Inc	1542	D	951 271-3440	946
All American Asphalt **(PA)**	1611	C	951 736-7600	1071
All American Asphalt	1611	C	951 736-7617	1072
All American Asphalt	1611	C	951 736-7617	1073
Ebs General Engineering Inc	1611	C	951 279-6869	1102
Hillcrest Contracting Inc	1611	C	951 273-9600	1119
Kec Engineering	1611	C	951 734-3010	1125
Superior Paving Company Inc	1611	C	951 739-9200	1168
Arizona Pipeline Company	1623	C	951 270-3100	1195
Boudreau Pipeline Corporation	1623	B	951 493-6780	1198
HP Communications Inc **(PA)**	1623	C	951 572-1200	1216
S E C C Corporation **(PA)**	1623	D	909 393-5419	1257
Couts Heating & Cooling Inc	1711	C	951 278-5560	1411
Infinity Plumbing Designs Inc	1711	B	951 737-4436	1464
LDI Mechanical Inc **(PA)**	1711	C	951 340-9685	1483
Multi Mechanical Inc	1711	D	714 632-7404	1504
NP Mechanical Inc	1711	B	951 667-4220	1512
RC Maintenance Holdings Inc	1711	C	951 903-6303	1544
Smart Energy Solar Inc	1711	C	800 405-1978	1565
Pacific Utility Instllation Inc	1731	D	714 970-6430	1798
SRbray LLC	1731	D	951 898-3850	1849
Fennel Inc	1751	D	951 284-2020	1998
Laurence-Hovenier Inc	1751	C	951 759-2945	2006
Ranch House Doors Inc	1751	C	951 278-2884	2013
TWR Enterprises Inc	1751	C	951 279-2000	2023
X-Act Finish & Trim Inc	1751	D	951 582-9229	2028
Cornerstone Concrete Inc	1771	C	951 279-2221	2112
Empire Demolition Inc	1795	C	909 393-8300	2234
Pacifica Foods LLC	2035	C	951 371-3123	2355
Widly Inc	2515	C	951 279-0900	2494
Century Blinds Inc	2591	D	951 734-3762	2508
Robertsons Rdymx Ltd A Cal Ltd **(HQ)**	3273	D	951 493-6500	2712
Circor Aerospace Inc **(HQ)**	3491	D	951 270-6200	2764
Cremach Tech Inc **(PA)**	3541	D	951 735-3194	2780
Suss McRtec Phtnic Systems Inc	3699	D	951 817-3700	2963
Gibson Performance Corporation	3714	D	951 372-1220	2973
Developlus Inc	3999	D	951 738-8595	3106
Mission Ambulance Inc	4119	D	951 272-2300	3282
First Student Inc	4173	D	951 736-3234	3356
H & H Transportation LLC	4213	D	951 817-2300	3484
Veg Fresh Logistics LLC	4731	C	714 446-8800	4118
Sprint Communications Co LP	4812	C	951 340-1924	4232
Agile Sourcing Partners Inc	4939	C	951 279-4154	4757
Talco Plastics Inc **(PA)**	4953	D	951 531-2000	4944
Waste Management Cal Inc	4953	D	951 277-1740	4955
Fleetwood Aluminum Products Inc	5031	C	800 736-7363	5156
ABC School Equipment Inc	5049	D	951 817-2200	5464
American Electric Supply Inc **(PA)**	5063	D	951 734-7910	5535
Minka Lighting LLC **(PA)**	5063	D	951 735-9220	5579
Corona Clipper Inc	5072	C	951 737-6515	5727
Ferguson Fire Fabrication Inc	5074	D	951 272-8803	5749
United Material Handling Inc	5084	D	951 657-4900	5876
So Cal Sandbags Inc	5085	D	951 277-3404	5925
Troy Lee Designs LLC **(DH)**	5091	C	951 371-5219	5983
Amerisourceberg Drug Corp	5122	C	951 371-2000	6094
Rugby Laboratories Inc **(DH)**	5122	C	951 270-1400	6142
Smart & Final Stores LLC	5141	D	951 737-4151	6355
Marie Cllender Wholesalers Inc	5142	A	951 737-6760	6422
Veg-Fresh Farms LLC **(PA)**	5148	C	800 422-5535	6591
Monster Energy Company **(HQ)**	5149	B	866 322-4466	6649
Zep Inc	5169	C	877 428-9937	6716
Thoro--Packaging **(DH)**	5199	C	951 278-2100	6953
Ganahl Lumber Company	5211	D	951 278-4000	6961
Home Depot USA Inc	5211	C	951 808-0327	7015
Lowes Home Centers LLC	5211	D	951 256-9004	7079
Irwin International Inc **(PA)**	5599	D	951 372-9555	7400
Hub Distributing Inc **(HQ)**	5611	B	951 340-3149	7402
Aurelio Felix Barreto III	5699	D	951 354-9528	7412
Ames Construction Inc	5712	B	951 356-1275	7419
Kaiser Fndtion Hlth Plan GA In	6324	B	951 270-1200	8305
First Team RE - Orange Cnty	6531	D	951 270-2800	9008
Pro Group Inc	6531	C	951 271-3000	9139
Bellota US Corp	6722	C	951 737-6515	9358
JJ Mac Intyre Co Inc **(PA)**	7322	C	951 898-4300	10745
Screenworks LLC	7336	A	951 279-8877	10818
Pro Building Maintenance Inc **(PA)**	7349	C	951 279-3386	10947
RNA Ann Arbor Incorporated	7349	C	877 762-7511	10955
Temps Plus Inc	7361	C	951 549-8309	11246
American Power SEC Svc Inc	7381	D	866 974-9994	12927
Aztecs Telecom Inc	7389	D	714 373-1560	13204
Nuvia Water Technologies Inc	7389	D	951 734-7400	13403
Super Center Concepts Inc	7389	D	951 372-9485	13492
Thyde Inc **(PA)**	7389	D	951 817-2300	13510
Penske Transportation MGT LLC	7513	D	844 847-9518	13565
U-Haul Business Consultants	7513	D	951 736-7811	13569
Ironman Renewal LLC	7538	D	951 735-3710	13664
Team Dykspra **(PA)**	7542	D	951 898-6482	13702
Senclub LLC	7922	D	626 317-8073	14068
Eagle Glen Country Club LLC	7992	D	951 272-4653	14258
Green River Golf Corporation	7992	D	714 970-8411	14265
Corona Regional Med Ctr LLC	8011	C	951 737-4343	14708
Vitas Healthcare Corporation	8052	D	858 805-6254	15801
Bmb 1 LLC	8059	C	951 741-0663	15820
Uhs-Corona Inc **(HQ)**	8062	A	951 737-4343	16587
United Lab Services Inc	8071	D	951 444-0467	16766
St Joseph Health Per Care Svcs	8082	D	800 365-1110	16932
Uhs-Corona Inc	8093	C	951 736-7200	17149
Kaiser Foundation Hospitals	8099	D	866 984-7483	17261
Riverside Medical Clinic Inc	8099	D	951 277-0000	17315
Crossrads Chrstn Schols Corona	8299	C	951 278-3199	17808
Ability Counts Inc **(PA)**	8331	D	951 734-6595	18202
Peppermint Ridge **(PA)**	8361	C	951 273-7320	18504
Automobile Club Southern Cal	8699	D	951 808-9624	19064
K&B Electric LLC	8711	C	951 808-9501	19290
K&B Engineering	8711	C	951 808-9501	19291
Primary Provider MGT Co Inc **(HQ)**	8741	D	951 280-7700	20181
Kpc Group Inc **(PA)**	8742	C	951 782-8812	20427
Ae & Associates LLC	8748	C	951 278-3477	20676
Volt Telecom Group Inc	8748	B	951 493-8900	20876

CORONA DEL MAR, CA - Orange County

	SIC	EMP	PHONE	ENTRY#
Ecc Capital Corporation **(PA)**	6162	D	949 954-7060	7958
Best Life and Health Insur Co	6311	D	949 253-4080	8232
Engel & Voelkers Newport Beach	6531	D	949 207-3101	8993
Tebra Technologies Inc **(PA)**	7371	C	888 775-2736	11973
Anaheim Ducks Hockey Club LLC	7941	D	714 940-2900	14124
University California Irvine	8011	D	949 644-5245	15162
Newport Mesa Unified Schl Dst	8211	D	949 515-6940	17736

CORONADO, CA - San Diego County

	SIC	EMP	PHONE	ENTRY#
City of Coronado	4931	C	619 522-7380	4750
Smart & Final Stores Inc	5141	C	619 522-2014	6291
51st St & 8th Ave Corp	7011	C	619 424-4000	9593
Ksl Resorts Hotel Del Coronado	7011	C	619 435-6611	9952
L-O Coronado Hotel Inc	7011	D	619 435-6611	9958
Sanci Marriott Hotels	7011	D	619 435-3000	10204
Sharp Coronado Hospital & Healthcare Center	8062	A	619 522-3600	16416
Thekey LLC	8082	D	858 842-1346	16948
R3 Strategic Support Group Inc	8742	D	800 418-2040	20521

GEOGRAPHIC SECTION

COVINA CA

	SIC	EMP	PHONE	ENTRY#

CORTE MADERA, CA - Marin County

Company	SIC	EMP	PHONE	ENTRY#
Marin Municipal Water District (PA)	4971	C	415 945-1455	4990
Ted Stevens Inc	5511	D	415 927-5664	7310
Bay Clubs Company LLC	7997	B	415 945-3000	14333
Brett V Crtis MD A Prof Corp I	8011	D	415 924-4525	14637

COSTA MESA, CA - Orange County

Company	SIC	EMP	PHONE	ENTRY#
Hexagon Agility Inc	1321	D	949 236-5520	588
Mdm Solutions LLC	1389	B	800 669-6361	615
Brookfeld Sthland Holdings LLC	1521	C	714 427-6868	662
Seattle Tnnel Prtners A Jint V	1521	B	206 971-8701	720
Warmington Residential Cal Inc	1521	C	714 557-5511	739
Rebco Communities Inc	1522	B	714 557-5511	771
Warmington Homes (PA)	1531	C	714 434-4435	800
Andrew L Youngquist Cnstr Inc	1542	D	949 862-5611	866
S J Amoroso Cnstr Co LLC	1542	D	650 654-1900	1017
Adopt-A-Highway Maintenance	1611	C	800 200-0003	1070
Beador Construction Co Inc	1611	C	951 674-7352	1080
Dragados Usa Inc	1611	D	657 229-7800	1098
Lombardy Holdings Inc (PA)	1623	C	951 808-4550	1232
Pivot Interiors Inc	1731	D	949 988-5400	1806
Variations In Stone Inc	1741	C	949 438-8337	1895
Orange County Plst Co Inc	1742	C	714 957-1971	1951
Hurley International LLC (PA)	2329	C	949 548-9375	2455
Carrier Fire SEC Americas Corp	3669	C	949 737-7800	2900
Transprttion Brkg Spclists Inc	4212	B	714 754-4236	3427
Flowspace Inc	4225	D	323 741-1325	3705
County of Orange	4581	C	949 252-5006	3888
Local Lighthouse Corp	4813	D	888 370-8231	4308
Uvnv Inc (HQ)	4813	D	888 777-0446	4354
Nds Americas Inc (DH)	4841	D	714 434-2100	4514
Mesa Cnsld Wtr Dst Imprv Corp (PA)	4941	D	949 631-1200	4809
Flat White Economy Inv USA LLC	4953	C	949 344-5013	4895
ABC Bus Inc	5012	D	714 444-5888	4999
Nissan North America Inc	5012	C	714 433-3700	5017
Altametrics Hosting LLC	5045	C	800 676-1281	5268
Benq America Corp (HQ)	5045	D	714 559-4900	5280
Western Refining Inc	5084	C	714 708-2200	5885
Viva Life Science Inc	5122	C	949 645-6100	6151
Food Sales West Inc	5141	D	714 966-2900	6253
Smart & Final Stores LLC	5141	A	949 548-8473	6387
Home Depot USA Inc	5211	D	949 646-4220	7016
Theodore Robins Inc	5511	D	949 642-0010	7311
Annas Linens Inc	5719	A	714 850-0504	7434
El Pollo Loco Holdings Inc (PA)	5812	C	714 599-5000	7476
North American Acceptance Corp	6141	C	714 868-3195	7882
Payoff Inc	6141	D	949 430-0630	7884
Professional Cr Reporting Inc	6141	B	714 556-1570	7885
Balboa Capital Corporation (DH)	6153	C	949 756-9905	7891
Metropolitan Home Mortgage Inc	6162	D	949 428-0161	8001
Secured Funding Corporation	6163	A	714 689-6749	8056
Villa Venetia	6163	B	714 540-1800	8063
Merrill Lynch Prce Fnner Smith	6211	D	714 429-2800	8105
Auto Club Enterprises (PA)	6321	A	714 850-5111	8258
Automobile Club Southern Cal	6411	C	714 885-1343	8504
Medical Eye Services Inc	6411	D	714 619-4660	8609
Donahue Schriber Rlty Group LP (PA)	6512	D	714 545-1400	8716
South Coast Plaza Inc	6512	C	714 435-2000	8764
Trammell Crow Residential Co	6513	D	714 966-9355	8865
Donahue Schrber Rlty Group Inc (PA)	6531	D	714 545-1400	8986
Hanford Hotels Inc	7011	C	714 557-3000	9834
Newport Mesa Inn LLC	7011	D	949 650-3020	10044
Rosanna Inc	7011	C	714 751-5100	10172
South Coast Westin Hotel Co	7011	C	714 540-2500	10256
Trigild International Inc	7011	D	949 645-2221	10325
US Hotel and Resort MGT Inc	7011	C	949 650-2988	10337
Casanova Publicidad LLC	7311	D	949 271-6344	10597
Klientboost LLC	7311	C	657 203-7866	10639
Team Garage LLC	7311	D	714 913-9900	10679
Clarity Services Inc	7323	D	727 489-7266	10757
Experian Info Solutions Inc (DH)	7323	A	714 830-7000	10762
Experian Mktg Solutions LLC	7323	A	714 830-7000	10763
Crisp Enterprises Inc (PA)	7334	D	714 668-6955	10787
All-Rite Leasing Company Inc	7349	B	714 667-1822	10851
Site Crew Inc	7349	D	714 668-0100	10968
Career Strategies Tmpry Inc	7361	C	714 824-6840	11109
Recruit 360	7361	C	949 250-4420	11219
Southern Home Care Svcs Inc	7363	D	714 979-7413	11338
Marigold Usa Inc	7371	C	617 385-6786	11733
Software Management Cons LLC	7371	C	714 662-1841	11931
Nwp Services Corporation (DH)	7372	C	949 253-2500	12298
Filenet Corporation	7373	A	800 345-3638	12455
Protect-US	7381	C	714 721-8127	13026
Star Pro Security Patrol Inc	7381	C	714 617-5056	13052
Carecredit LLC	7389	C	800 300-3046	13227
Cliq Inc	7389	D	714 361-1900	13238
Creative Design Consultants (PA)	7389	D	714 641-4868	13249
Regus Business Centre LLC	7389	C	714 371-4000	13443
Volcom LLC (HQ)	7389	D	949 646-2175	13547
Fox Rent A Car Inc	7514	D	310 342-5155	13587
EZ Lube LLC	7549	D	714 966-1647	13714
Metropro Road Services Inc	7549	D	714 556-7600	13717
Edwards Theatres Circuit Inc	7832	C	714 428-0962	13991
South Coast Repertory Inc	7922	D	714 708-5500	14069
Chargers Football Company LLC (PA)	7941	C	619 280-2121	14132
Grit Management LLC	7991	D	949 220-7765	14204
Mesa Verde Partners	7992	C	714 540-7500	14275
Mesa Verde Country Club	7997	C	714 549-0377	14405
Amen Clinics Inc A Med Corp (PA)	8011	C	888 564-2700	14610
University California Irvine	8011	D	949 646-2267	15166
Beaver Dam Health Care Center	8051	D	949 642-0387	15353
Costa Mesa Healthcare Inc	8051	D	949 631-4282	15389
Mesa Vrde Cnvalescent Hosp Inc	8051	C	949 548-5584	15585
Silverado Senior Living Inc	8051	D	949 945-0189	15668
College Hospital Costa Mesa Mso Inc (HQ)	8062	D	949 642-2734	16007
Hoag Family Cancer Institute	8062	C	949 764-7777	16129
Califrnia Dept State Hospitals	8063	A	714 957-5000	16642
Accredited Nursing Services	8082	C	714 973-1234	16792
Competent Care Inc	8082	D	714 545-4818	16844
RES-Care Inc	8082	C	714 662-3075	16920
Vu Holdings LLC	8099	D	661 808-4004	17351
Baker & Hostetler LLP	8111	C	714 754-6600	17372
Cooksey Tlen Gage Dffy Woog A (PA)	8111	C	714 431-1100	17411
Latham & Watkins LLP	8111	B	714 540-1235	17538
Lewis Brsbois Bsgard Smith LLP	8111	C	714 545-9200	17546
Sheppard Mllin Rchter Hmpton L	8111	D	714 513-5100	17650
Snell & Wilmer LLP	8111	C	714 427-7000	17658
Woodruff Spradlin & Smart	8111	D	714 558-7000	17688
Newport Mesa Unified Schl Dst	8211	D	714 424-5090	17735
Vanguard Univ Southern Cal	8221	C	714 668-6163	17784
Califrnia Dept Dvlpmental Svcs	8331	A	714 957-5151	18215
Ds Lakeshore LP	8641	D	916 286-5231	18852
Moffatt & Nichol	8711	D	657 261-2699	19326
Newman Garrison + Partners Inc	8712	D	949 756-0818	19498
Deloitte & Touche LLP	8721	C	714 436-7419	19563
South Coast Plaza Security	8741	C	714 435-2180	20212
Warmington Mr 14 Assoc LLC	8741	D	714 557-5511	20248
Hykso Inc	8742	D	213 785-3372	20408
Nationsbenefits LLC	8742	D	877 439-2665	20483
Brand Amp LLC	8743	D	949 438-1060	20631
Innovative Cnstr Solutions	8744	C	714 893-6366	20656

COTATI, CA - Sonoma County

Company	SIC	EMP	PHONE	ENTRY#
Mike Brown Electric Co	1731	C	707 792-8100	1778
Stockham Construction Inc	1751	B	707 664-0945	2019
Ats Medical Services LLC	4119	A	815 963-5001	3238
Protransport-1 LLC (HQ)	4119	C	707 975-2386	3289
Lowes Home Centers LLC	5211	D	707 242-5000	7091
21st Century Health Club (PA)	8093	D	707 795-0400	16999

COVINA, CA - Los Angeles County

Company	SIC	EMP	PHONE	ENTRY#
Brutoco Engineering & Construction Inc	1611	C		1083
Verizon Communications Inc	4812	D	626 858-1739	4242
Sprint Communications Co LP	4813	D	626 339-0430	4343
Swwc Utilities Inc (DH)	4941	C		4840
Hartman Industries	5051	D	909 428-0114	5497
Smart & Final Stores LLC	5141	D	626 915-6619	6389
Continental Exch Solutions Inc	6099	D	626 969-4130	7851
West Covina Foster Family Agcy	6411	D	626 814-9085	8685
Briteworks Inc	7349	D	626 337-0099	10866
Twomagnets Inc	7361	A	408 837-0116	11249
Hyro Ai Inc	7371	D	313 942-4560	11652
Noredink Corp	7371	D	844 667-3346	11785
Placer Labs Inc	7371	B	415 228-2444	11832
LAg and Associates LLC	7389	D	909 242-4394	13344
Davita Magan Management Inc (DH)	8011	C	626 331-6411	14722
Covina Rehabilitation Center	8051	C	626 967-3874	15412
Rowland Convalescent Hosp Inc	8051	C	626 967-2741	15644
Emanate Health Medical Center	8062	A	626 858-8515	16075
Emanate Health Medical Center	8062	A	626 331-7331	16077
Emanate Health Medical Group (PA)	8062	A	626 331-7331	16078
Aurora Chrtr Oak - Los Angeles	8063	D	626 966-1632	16638
Charter Bhvral Hlth Sys S C/Ch	8063	C	626 966-1632	16647
Citrus Vly Hlth Partners Inc	8099	B	626 732-3100	17206
Eggleston Youth Centers Inc (PA)	8322	D	626 480-8107	17964
Think Together	8351	B	626 373-2311	18360

Employee Codes: A=Over 500 employees, B=251-500
C=101-250, D=51-100, E=20-50, F=10-19, G=1-9

COVINA CA

GEOGRAPHIC SECTION

	SIC	EMP	PHONE	ENTRY#
Los Angeles Engineering Inc	8711	C	626 869-1400	19309
Zenleads Inc	8742	B	415 640-9303	20622

CRESCENT CITY, CA - Del Norte County

	SIC	EMP	PHONE	ENTRY#
Elk Valley Casino Inc	7011	D	707 464-1020	9778
North Shore Investment Inc	8051	D	707 464-6151	15597
Sutter Coast Hospital (HQ)	8062	D	707 464-8511	16517
Sutter Coast Hospital	8082	B	707 464-8741	16939
Remi Vista Inc	8361	D	707 464-4349	18512
County of Del Norte	8399	D	707 464-3191	18581

CROCKETT, CA - Contra Costa County

	SIC	EMP	PHONE	ENTRY#
Domino Foods Inc	5149	C	510 787-2121	6626

CUDAHY, CA - Los Angeles County

	SIC	EMP	PHONE	ENTRY#
HF Cox Inc	4212	B	323 587-2359	3404
Super Center Concepts Inc	5411	C	323 562-8980	7153
Southern Cal Prmnnte Med Group	8011	C	323 562-6459	15088
Kaiser Foundation Hospitals	8062	C	323 562-6400	16175

CULVER CITY, CA - Los Angeles County

	SIC	EMP	PHONE	ENTRY#
Access Spclty Animal Hospitals	0742	D	310 558-6100	321
Advanced Crtcal Care Emrgncy S	0742	C	310 558-6111	324
Ppd Holding LLC (PA)	2326	D	310 733-2100	2451
Virgin Fish Inc (PA)	4119	C	310 391-6161	3303
Makespace Labs Inc	4225	C	800 920-9440	3728
Pacific Bell Telephone Company	4812	A	310 515-2898	4223
Globecast America Incorporated	4841	D	310 845-3900	4510
Wovexx Holdings Inc (DH)	4899	D	310 424-2080	4559
Nantbioscience Inc	5047	D	310 883-1300	5434
Punch Studio LLC (PA)	5112	C	310 390-9900	6070
New Milani Group LLC	5122	D	323 582-9404	6136
Rick Solomon Enterprises Inc (PA)	5136	C	310 280-3700	6185
Blowfish LLC	5139	C	310 566-5700	6230
Henkel US Operations Corp	5169	D	424 308-0505	6710
Topson Downs California Inc (PA)	5621	C	310 558-0300	7404
Charles David of California (PA)	5661	C	310 348-5050	7410
GK Management Co Inc (PA)	6531	C	310 204-2050	9023
Property Management Assoc Inc	6531	C	323 295-2000	9147
Goldrich & Kest Industries LLC (PA)	6552	A	310 204-2050	9252
Goldrich Kest Hirsch Stern LLC (PA)	6552	C	310 204-2050	9253
Hirsch3667 Corp	6719	C	310 641-6690	9318
Crp Centinela LP	7011	C	901 821-4117	9730
Starwood Hotel	7011	C	310 641-7740	10270
Woodbine Lgacy/Playa Owner LLC	7011	D	678 292-4962	10378
Old Connected Camps	7032	D	323 287-5580	10409
Clutter Inc (PA)	7299	C	800 805-4023	10537
Mutesix Group Inc	7311	C	800 935-6856	10654
Zambezi LLC	7313	C	310 450-6800	10724
Carat N Amer Dntsu Ageis Ntwrk	7319	C	310 255-1000	10726
Advanced Medical Reviews LLC	7363	C	310 575-0900	11268
Amazon Studios LLC	7371	C	818 804-0884	11401
Blur Studio Inc	7371	C	424 258-3145	11467
Docupace Technologies LLC (PA)	7371	C	310 445-7722	11549
Genex (DH)	7371	C	424 672-9500	11616
Liveoffice LLC	7372	D	877 253-2793	12256
Scopely Inc (DH)	7372	C	323 400-6618	12346
Nantworks LLC (PA)	7373	D	310 883-1300	12498
West Publishing Corporation	7373	A	424 243-2100	12544
Sony Pictures Imageworks Inc	7374	A	310 840-8000	12628
Aegis SEC & Investigations Inc	7381	C	310 838-2787	12919
Pacific National Security Inc	7381	C	310 842-7073	13015
Security Indust Spcialists Inc (PA)	7381	C	310 215-5100	13038
Event Intelligence Group	7382	D	310 237-5375	13114
Innovation Specialties	7389	C	888 827-2387	13324
Mktg Inc	7389	B	310 972-7900	13377
Anonymous Content LLC (PA)	7812	D	310 558-6000	13818
Columbia Pictures Inds Inc (DH)	7812	C	310 244-4000	13830
Crunchyroll LLC (DH)	7812	D	972 355-7300	13834
Sony Pctres Wrldwide Acqstons	7812	C	310 244-4000	13893
Sony Pictures Entrmt Inc (DH)	7812	A	310 244-4000	13894
Sony Pictures Studios Inc	7812	C	310 244-4000	13895
Sony Pictures Television Inc (DH)	7812	B	310 244-7625	13896
Zoic Inc	7812	C	310 838-0770	13922
Dneg North America Inc (PA)	7819	D	323 461-7887	13933
Technclor Crative Svcs USA Inc	7819	B	818 260-1214	13952
Maker Studios LLC (DH)	7929	C	310 606-2182	14095
Nfl Properties LLC	7941	C	310 840-4635	14151
Yogaworks Inc (HQ)	7999	D	310 664-6470	14589
Southern Cal Prmnnte Med Group	8011	C	310 737-4900	15081
Institute For Applied Bhvior A (PA)	8049	C	310 649-0499	15290
L & A Care Corporation	8052	C	310 202-7693	15768
Marycrest Manor	8059	D	310 838-2778	15878
Brotman Medical Center Inc	8062	B	310 836-7000	15963
Southern Cal Halthcare Sys Inc	8062	B	310 836-7000	16437
Alcott Ctr For Mntal Hlth Svcs	8093	D	310 785-2121	17001
Murphy & Beane Inc	8111	D	310 649-4470	17583
Didi Hirsch Psychiatric Svc (PA)	8322	C	310 390-6612	17954
Exceptional Chld Foundation (PA)	8331	C	310 204-3300	18230
Allies For Every Child Inc	8351	D	310 846-4100	18268
Exceptional Chld Foundation	8641	C	310 915-6606	18858
Hawkins Brown USA Inc	8712	B	310 600-2695	19474
Lamar Jhnson Collaborative Inc	8712	C	424 361-3960	19484
Morphosis Architects	8712	C	310 453-2247	19496
Kpmg LLP	8721	D	703 286-8175	19594
Altor Bscnce LLC An Indrect Wh	8731	D	310 733-7107	19654
Nantcell Inc	8731	B	562 397-3639	19741
HI LLC (PA)	8732	D	757 655-4113	19816
Ipsos Otx Corporation (HQ)	8732	C	310 736-3400	19825
Psychemedics Corporation	8734	D	310 216-7776	19996
Altruist Corp	8742	C	949 370-5096	20269
Jack Nadel Inc (PA)	8742	C	310 815-2600	20420
Visionaire Group Inc	8742	D	310 823-1800	20604
Netfortris Acquisition Co Inc	8748	C	310 861-4300	20813
City of Culver City	9111	D	310 253-6525	20913

CUPERTINO, CA - Santa Clara County

	SIC	EMP	PHONE	ENTRY#
Stevens Creek Quarry Inc (PA)	1611	D	408 253-2512	1165
Apple Inc (PA)	3663	A	408 996-1010	2891
Mobileum Inc	4899	C	408 844-6600	4544
Trend Micro Incorporated	5045	C	408 257-1500	5364
Kaliocommerce Inc	5149	C	408 550-8040	6641
First Technology Federal Cr Un	6061	D	408 863-6240	7771
Cupertino Hspitality Assoc LLC	7011	C	408 777-8787	9732
Cupertino Lessee LLC	7011	C	908 253-8900	9733
Claris International Inc (HQ)	7371	C	800 725-2747	11493
Digite Inc	7371	C	408 418-3834	11541
Sugarcrm Inc (PA)	7371	C	877 842-7276	11954
Synophic Systems Inc	7371	C	408 459-7676	11961
Trucking Jobs Technologies Inc	7371	C	202 918-2404	11991
Ecrio Inc	7372	C	408 973-7290	12171
Efinix Inc (PA)	7372	C	408 789-6917	12174
Indium Software Inc	7372	C	408 501-8844	12229
Mist Systems Inc	7373	C	408 326-0346	12491
Pluris Inc	7373	C	408 863-9920	12511
Inxeption Corporation	7379	C	888 852-4783	12817
Corinthian Intl Prkg Svcs Inc (PA)	7382	B	408 867-7275	13103
Voltage Security LLC	7382	D	408 886-3200	13154
Next Issue Media LLC	7389	D	650 521-5151	13397
Cupertino Hlthcare Wllness Ctr	8051	D	408 253-9034	15420
CRC Health LLC (DH)	8069	D	877 272-8668	16679
CRC Health Corporate (DH)	8093	D	408 367-0044	17045
Rancho San Antnio Rtrment Hsin	8361	B	650 265-2637	18507
Deepmind Foundation	8641	D	408 887-1605	18851
Sterling Healthcare Svcs LLC	8742	A	502 262-2914	20568

CUTLER, CA - Tulare County

	SIC	EMP	PHONE	ENTRY#
Penas Disposal Inc	4953	D	559 528-3909	4919

CYPRESS, CA - Orange County

	SIC	EMP	PHONE	ENTRY#
Plumbing Piping & Cnstr Inc	1711	D	714 821-0490	1529
Power Maintenance Services Inc	1721	D	714 229-5900	1632
Johnson Controls Inc	2531	C	562 594-3200	2497
Diasorin Molecular LLC	2835	C	562 240-6500	2613
Merger Sub Gotham 2 LLC	3089	C	714 462-4603	2673
Drs Ntwork Imaging Systems LLC	3674	D	714 220-3800	2917
Romeo Systems Inc	3699	C	323 675-2180	2961
Christie Digital Systems Inc (HQ)	3861	D	714 236-8610	3083
Contiki US Holdings Inc	4725	D	714 935-0808	3963
Toyo Tire USA Corp (DH)	5014	D	714 236-2080	5075
Sitonit Seating Inc	5021	D	714 995-4800	5105
Weyerhaeuser Company	5031	D	714 523-3330	5194
Christie Dgtal Systems USA Inc (HQ)	5043	D	714 236-8610	5236
Multiquip Inc (DH)	5063	B	310 537-3700	5582
Siemens Industry Inc	5063	C	714 761-2200	5591
Ushio America Inc (HQ)	5063	D	714 236-8600	5596
Mitsubishi Electric Us Inc (DH)	5065	C	714 220-2500	5676
Q Tech Corporation	5065	C	310 836-7900	5690
Beverages & More Inc	5078	C	714 891-1242	5776
ME & My Big Ideas LLC	5092	C	240 348-5240	5991
Natureware Inc	5122	C	714 251-4510	6135
Hybrid Promotions LLC (PA)	5136	C	714 952-3866	6177
Real Mex Foods Inc	5141	C	714 523-0031	6281
Yamaha Motor Corporation USA (HQ)	5571	B	714 761-7300	7399
Los Alamitos Race Course	5812	C	714 820-2800	7492
WKS Restaurant Corporation (PA)	5812	C	562 425-1402	7518

GEOGRAPHIC SECTION

DIAMOND SPRINGS CA

	SIC	EMP	PHONE	ENTRY#
Mitsubishi Motors Cr Amer Inc (DH)	6141	B	714 799-4730	7878
Uhc of California (DH)	6324	A	952 936-6615	8370
Cal Southern United Food	6371	C	714 220-2297	8457
Healthsmart Management Service	6411	D	714 947-8600	8584
Pacific Pioneer Insur Group (PA)	6411	D	714 228-7888	8635
DAndrea Graphic Corportion	7336	D	310 642-0260	10803
B2b Staffing Services Inc	7363	B	714 243-4104	11274
Tad Pgs Inc	7363	A	571 451-2428	11340
Glory Global Solutions Inc	7371	D	714 897-7545	11626
Mercury Defense Systems Inc	7374	D	714 898-8200	12595
Mercury Systems Inc	7374	D	714 898-8200	12596
Trojan Professional Svcs Inc	7375	D	714 816-7169	12686
Consoldted Med Bo-Analysis Inc (PA)	8071	D	714 657-7369	16712
Focus Diagnostics Inc	8071	B	714 220-1900	16721
Pacificare Health Systems LLC (HQ)	8082	A	714 952-1121	16907
Tutor Time Learning Ctrs LLC	8351	C	714 484-1000	18364
Murphy Murphy & Murphy Inc	8721	D	562 594-6678	19613
Applied Research Assoc Inc	8731	D	505 881-8074	19656
Wcct Global Inc	8731	D	714 252-0700	19799
Wcct Global Inc (PA)	8733	D	714 668-1500	19934
Tradesmen International LLC	8741	D	949 588-3280	20230
Paragon Partners Cons Inc (PA)	8748	D	714 379-3376	20824

DAGGETT, CA - San Bernardino County

	SIC	EMP	PHONE	ENTRY#
NRG California South LP	4911	C	760 254-5241	4593
Rri Energy Coolwater Inc	4911	D	760 254-5290	4662

DALY CITY, CA - San Mateo County

	SIC	EMP	PHONE	ENTRY#
Pacific Gas and Electric Co	4911	D	800 684-4648	4626
Kaiser Foundation Hospitals	6324	D	650 301-5860	8324
Hillcrest Senior Housing Corp	6513	B	650 757-1737	8819
Reneson Hotels Inc (PA)	7011	D	650 449-5353	10153
Lake Merced Golf Club	7997	D	650 755-2233	14393
Permanente Medical Group Inc	8011	A	650 301-5800	14959
Seton Medical Ctr Foundation	8062	A	650 991-6464	16413
Olympic Club	8641	D	415 404-4300	18888
Forte Enterprises Inc (PA)	8741	C	650 994-3200	20092

DANA POINT, CA - Orange County

	SIC	EMP	PHONE	ENTRY#
Watermark Rtrment Cmmnties Inc	6513	D	949 443-9543	8871
Cph Monarch Hotel LLC	7011	A	949 234-3200	9727
Gringteam Inc	7011	D	949 661-1100	9826
Prutel Joint Venture	7011	A	949 240-5064	10130
Ritz-Carlton Hotel Company LLC	7011	B	949 240-5020	10161
Ciri - Stroup Inc	7299	D	949 488-3104	10535
Monarch Beach Golf Links (HQ)	7992	D	949 240-8247	14277
Gfk Etilize Inc	8732	D	888 608-1212	19811
Alter Management LLC	8741	D	949 629-0214	20018
Four Sisters Inns	8741	D	949 661-1304	20093

DANVILLE, CA - Contra Costa County

	SIC	EMP	PHONE	ENTRY#
Clearkin Inc	0781	C	925 838-2551	422
James E Roberts-Obayashi Corp	1522	C	925 820-0600	761
Braddock Logan Ventr Group LP (PA)	1531	C	925 736-4000	788
Braddock & Logan Services Inc	1542	C	925 736-4000	878
Flaherty Brothers Cnstr Inc	1761	D	650 268-9779	2064
DW Morgan LLC	4789	D	925 460-2700	4154
Smart & Final Stores LLC	5141	D	925 552-8153	6345
Ready Pac Foods Inc	5148	D	925 552-0400	6574
Fremont Bank	6022	D	925 314-1420	7691
Ec2002 Inc	6531	A	925 217-5000	8992
Pacific Union Homes Inc (PA)	6552	D	925 314-3800	9270
Sun Deep Inc	7231	C	510 206-7405	10509
Recall Masters Inc	7331	D	650 434-5211	10775
Blackhawk Country Club	7997	C	925 736-6500	14347
Town of Danville	7999	D	925 314-3400	14576
Bay Valley Medical Group Inc (PA)	8011	D	510 785-5000	14627
Building Cnnctons Bhvoral Hlth	8099	D	925 743-1678	17194
San Ramon Vly Unified Schl Dst	8211	D	925 552-2880	17748
Reutlinger Community	8322	C	925 964-2062	18099
Community Presbt Ch Danville (PA)	8661	C	925 837-5525	19015

DAVIS, CA - Yolo County

	SIC	EMP	PHONE	ENTRY#
Hmclause Inc (DH)	0181	C	800 320-4672	132
Animal Rescue Squad Intl II	0742	A	530 761-6008	325
Ikes Landscape Inc	0782	D	530 758-1698	498
Teichert Inc	1611	C	530 406-4200	1171
University California Davis	4151	D	530 752-8277	3353
University California Davis	4581	D	530 752-5435	3921
Pacific Gas and Electric Co	4911	A	530 757-5803	4654
Gold Standard Diagnostics Corp	5047	D	530 759-8000	5416
Envinrnmental Trnsp Specialists	5511	D	916 442-4971	7201
Sudwerk Privatbrauerei Hubsch	5812	D	530 756-2739	7510
FPI Management Inc	6531	C	530 756-5332	9018
Cvf Capital Partners Inc	6799	C	530 757-7004	9505
Communicare Health Centers (PA)	8011	D	530 758-2060	14696
Communicare Health Centers	8011	D	530 758-2060	14698
Communicare Health Centers	8011	D	530 758-2060	14699
Kaiser Foundation Hospitals	8011	D	530 757-7100	14831
University California Davis	8011	D	530 747-3000	15154
University California Davis	8011	D	530 752-4167	15157
Sutter Hlth Scrmnto Sierra Reg	8062	D	530 747-5010	16541
Woodland Healthcare	8062	D	530 756-2364	16633
University California Davis	8071	D	530 752-2314	16767
University California Davis	8221	D	530 752-1653	17782
Pacific Retirement Svcs Inc	8361	A	530 753-1450	18503
Rvm Davis Housing Corporation	8361	D	530 747-7095	18516
West Yost & Associates Inc (PA)	8711	D	530 756-5905	19437
University California Davis	8731	D	530 750-1313	19792
Novozymes Inc (DH)	8732	D	530 757-8100	19838
University of California	8741	D	530 752-0503	20239
Engage3 Inc	8742	D	530 231-5485	20359

DEATH VALLEY, CA - Inyo County

	SIC	EMP	PHONE	ENTRY#
Xanterra Parks & Resorts Inc	7011	C	760 786-2345	10385

DEL MAR, CA - San Diego County

	SIC	EMP	PHONE	ENTRY#
Crest Beverage Company Inc	5181	C	858 452-2300	6758
Liquid Investments Inc (PA)	5181	D	858 509-8510	6771
Mesa Distributing Co Inc (HQ)	5181	C	858 452-2300	6777
Dayton Dmh Inc	6514	C	858 350-4400	8876
Lhoberge Lessee Inc	7011	C	858 259-1515	9977
Pacifica Hosts Inc	7011	D	858 755-1501	10091
Sunstone Durante LLC	7011	C	858 792-5200	10286
Del Mar Fairgrounds	7299	D	858 792-4288	10541
Culver Personnel Agencies Inc	7361	C	888 600-5733	11118
Del Mar Thoroughbred Club	7948	B	858 755-1141	14163
Casa Palmera LLC	8093	D	888 481-4481	17019
LLC Bates White	8111	C	858 523-2150	17552
Odme Solutions LLC	8742	D	619 227-0059	20492
California Dept Fd Agriculture	9641	A	858 755-1161	20949

DEL REY, CA - Fresno County

	SIC	EMP	PHONE	ENTRY#
Pomwonderful LLC	5085	D	559 888-8500	5919

DELANO, CA - Kern County

	SIC	EMP	PHONE	ENTRY#
M Caratan Disc Inc	0172	C	661 725-2566	80
Hronis Inc A California Corp (PA)	0174	C	661 725-2503	99
Wonderful Citrus LLC (HQ)	0174	C	661 720-2400	102
Wonderful Company LLC	0174	B	661 720-2400	103
Munger Bros LLC	0179	C	661 721-0390	118
Cal Treehouse Almonds LLC	0723	C	661 725-6334	260
Monarch Nut Company LLC	0723	C	661 725-6458	290
Wonderful Citrus Packing LLC (HQ)	0723	B	661 720-2400	316
Triple R Transportation Inc	4119	C	661 725-6494	3301
Smart & Final Stores LLC	5141	D	661 721-2163	6335
City of Delano	7992	D	661 721-3350	14249
Delano Dst Sklled Nrsing Fclty	8051	C	661 720-2100	15424
Adventist Health Delano (HQ)	8062	A	661 725-4800	15915
Adventist Health Delano	8062	C	661 721-5337	15916
North Kern S Tulare Hosp Dst	8062	C	661 720-2126	16282

DESERT HOT SPRINGS, CA - Riverside County

	SIC	EMP	PHONE	ENTRY#
Desert Hot Sprng Real Prpts In	6512	D	760 329-6000	8715
Whatever It Takes Inc	7011	D	760 329-6000	10366
Forest Lawn Mortuary	7261	B	760 329-8737	10512
Borrego Cmnty Hlth Foundation	8011	C	760 251-0044	14636

DIAMOND BAR, CA - Los Angeles County

	SIC	EMP	PHONE	ENTRY#
Ecmm Services Inc	3955	C	714 988-9388	3097
Zenlayer Inc	4813	B	909 718-3558	4362
Graybar Electric Company Inc	5063	C	909 451-4300	5559
Smart & Final Stores Inc	5141	C	323 855-8434	6308
24-Hour Med Staffing Svcs LLC	7361	C	909 895-8960	11066
Liferay Inc (PA)	7373	A	877 543-3729	12479
Unspoken Language Services Inc	7389	C	626 532-8096	13533
Central Health Plan Cal Inc	8082	C	626 938-7120	16838
Specialty Equipment Mkt Assn (PA)	8611	D	909 396-0289	18724
Tetra Tech Bas Inc (HQ)	8711	D	909 860-7777	19411
Motech Americas LLC	8731	C	302 451-7500	19739
South Cast A Qlty MGT Dst Bldg (PA)	8748	A	909 396-2000	20853

DIAMOND SPRINGS, CA - El Dorado County

	SIC	EMP	PHONE	ENTRY#
Snowline Hspice El Dorado Cnty	8052	C	530 621-7820	15795

DINUBA CA — GEOGRAPHIC SECTION

	SIC	EMP	PHONE	ENTRY#

DINUBA, CA - Tulare County

	SIC	EMP	PHONE	ENTRY#
Fruit Patch Inc.	0723	B	559 591-6140	270
Gillette Citrus Inc.	0723	D	559 626-4236	271
Adventist Health System.	8011	B	559 595-9890	14594
Kaweah Delta Health Care Dst.	8062	C	559 591-5513	16199

DIXON, CA - Solano County

	SIC	EMP	PHONE	ENTRY#
Isec Incorporated	1751	C	707 693-6555	2004
Waveco Inc (PA)	4212	D	707 678-4404	3437
Button Transportation Inc.	4213	C	707 678-7434	3450
Recology Inc.	4953	C	916 379-3300	4925
Henkel Corporation.	7389	D	707 731-4964	13312
Fresenius Med Care Slano Cnty.	8092	D	707 678-6433	16983
Fremouw Environmental Svcs Inc.	8748	D	707 448-3700	20751

DOWNEY, CA - Los Angeles County

	SIC	EMP	PHONE	ENTRY#
County of Los Angeles.	0752	D	562 658-2085	360
Meruelo Enterprises Inc (PA)	1542	A	562 745-2300	970
Sialic Contractors Corporation	1611	D	562 803-9977	1162
Farwest Corrosion Control Co (PA)	1799	D	310 532-9524	2274
Reyes Coca-Cola Bottling LLC	2086	D	562 803-8100	2408
Liberty Ambulance LLC	4119	C	562 741-6230	3272
Mike Campbell & Associates Ltd	4222	A	626 369-3981	3655
Southern California Gas Co.	4924	B	562 803-7500	4730
Liberty Utilities Pk Wtr Corp (DH)	4941	C	562 923-0711	4800
Rockview Dairies Inc (PA)	5149	C	562 927-5511	6662
Home Depot USA Inc.	5211	D	562 776-2200	6963
Financial Partners Credit Un (PA)	6061	D	562 904-3000	7767
Kaiser Foundation Hospitals.	6324	C	562 657-9000	8312
Kaiser Foundation Hospitals.	6324	C	562 622-4190	8328
PRC Multi-Family LLC.	6513	D	562 803-5000	8854
Jlm & Mag Associates Inc.	7231	D	562 869-3343	10501
OfficeMax North America Inc.	7334	C	562 927-6444	10792
National Trench Safety LLC	7359	D	562 602-1642	11046
OSI Staffing Inc.	7361	D	562 261-5753	11193
Biu Inc.	7389	D	909 556-1311	13214
Kpwr Radio LLC.	7389	C	562 745-2300	13342
Lakewood Park Health Ctr Inc (PA)	7389	D	562 869-0978	13346
Tarsco Holdings LLC.	7699	D	562 869-0200	13803
City of Downey.	7922	C	562 861-8211	14034
Huntington Radiology.	8011	D	562 904-1111	14777
Kaiser Foundation Hospitals.	8011	D	817 372-8201	14790
Downey Community Health Center.	8051	D	562 862-6506	15427
Ensign Group Inc.	8051	C	562 923-9301	15451
Healthcare Ctr of Downey LLC.	8051	C	562 869-0978	15508
Los Angles Cnty Rncho Los Amgo.	8052	A	562 385-7111	15771
Pih Health Downey Hospital (HQ)	8062	B	562 698-0811	16324
Pih Health Hospital - Whitti.	8062	A	562 904-5482	16326
Southern Cal Prmnnte Med Group.	8062	B	562 657-2200	16441
Rai Care Centers Lynwood LLC.	8092	C	562 401-0155	16992
County of Los Angeles.	8093	A	562 401-7088	17040
Southern Cal Alchol DRG Prgram (PA)	8093	D	562 923-4545	17130
Jwch Institute Inc.	8099	C	562 862-1000	17259
County of Los Angeles.	8322	D	562 940-2470	17915
County of Los Angeles.	8322	D	562 940-6856	17920
ARC Los Angles Orange Counties (PA)	8331	C	562 803-1556	18206
Automobile Club Southern Cal.	8699	C	562 904-5970	19048
Rancho Research Institute.	8733	C	562 401-8111	19906
County of Los Angeles.	8741	C	562 940-2907	20071

DUARTE, CA - Los Angeles County

	SIC	EMP	PHONE	ENTRY#
Png Builders.	1542	D	626 256-9539	994
Alcorn Fence Company (PA)	1799	D	818 983-0650	2254
Delafield Corporation (PA)	3599	C	626 303-0740	2851
Woodward Hrt Inc.	3728	C	626 359-9211	2993
JDM Deliveries Inc.	4789	D	626 831-1876	4160
Southern California Gas Co.	4924	D	626 358-4700	4744
Advantage Ford Lincoln Mercury.	5511	D	626 305-9188	7164
Gpi Ca-Niii Inc.	5511	D	626 305-3000	7223
Bay Vista Senior Housing.	6513	B	925 924-7100	8792
Humangood Norcal (HQ)	6513	D	925 924-7100	8821
Humangood Socal.	6513	D	626 357-1632	8824
Arecont Vision Costar LLC.	7382	D	818 937-0700	13096
We Pack It All LLC.	7389	C	626 301-9214	13552
Beckman RES Inst of The Cy Hop.	8011	C	626 359-8111	14631
Estrella Inc.	8051	C	562 925-6418	15467
Royal Terrace Healthcare LLC.	8051	A	626 256-4654	15645
Humangood (PA)	8059	C	602 906-4024	15858
City Hope National Medical Ctr (HQ)	8062	A	626 256-4673	16004
Santa Teresita Inc (PA)	8062	B	626 359-3243	16395
Maryvale Day Care Center.	8351	C	626 357-1514	18332
Humangood Socal.	8361	C	626 359-8141	18456
City of Hope.	8399	B	213 202-5735	18571
City of Hope (PA)	8741	B	626 256-4673	20057

DUBLIN, CA - Alameda County

	SIC	EMP	PHONE	ENTRY#
Gateway Landscape Cnstr Inc.	0782	D	925 875-0000	492
Warmington Homes.	1531	C	925 866-6700	802
Lusardi Construction Co.	1542	C	925 829-1114	962
Desilva Gates Construction LP (PA)	1611	D	925 361-1380	1095
AMS Electric Inc.	1731	D	925 961-1600	1665
Gettler-Ryan Inc (PA)	1799	D	925 551-7555	2281
Carl Ziss X-Ray Microscopy Inc.	3844	D	925 701-3600	3070
Dublin San Ramon Services Dst (PA)	4941	C	925 875-2276	4785
Lowes Home Centers LLC.	5211	D	925 241-3082	7104
Dublin Volkswagen.	5511	D	925 829-0800	7197
Harvey & Madding Inc.	5511	D	925 828-8030	7231
Messagesolution Inc.	5734	D	925 833-8000	7446
Patelco Credit Union (PA)	6061	C	800 358-8228	7791
Savvymoney Inc.	6141	D	415 684-7261	7886
Franklin Tmpleton Inv Svcs LLC.	6282	C	925 875-2619	8201
Health Svcs Bneft Admnstrtors (PA)	6371	D	925 833-7300	8461
New Home Professionals.	6531	D	925 556-1555	9108
Hope Hospice Inc.	7021	B	925 829-8770	10392
Astute Business Solutions.	7371	D	925 997-3267	11431
Sybase 365 LLC.	7371	D	925 236-5000	11957
Oracle Taleo LLC (HQ)	7372	D	925 452-3000	12308
Saba Software Inc (DH)	7372	D	877 722-2101	12340
Cooke & Associates Inc.	7381	B	408 842-0602	12950
Kaiser Foundation Hospitals.	8062	C	925 556-4200	16151
Care Options Management Plans.	8082	A	925 551-3227	16833
Trinet Group Inc (PA)	8742	A	510 352-5000	20593
Smart Sftwr Tstg Solutions Inc.	8748	D	833 778-7872	20850

DURHAM, CA - Butte County

	SIC	EMP	PHONE	ENTRY#
Chico Produce Inc (PA)	5148	C	530 893-0596	6525

E RNCHO DMNGZ, CA - Los Angeles County

	SIC	EMP	PHONE	ENTRY#
Timec Companies Inc.	1629	C	310 885-4710	1323
Murray Plumbing and Htg Corp (PA)	1711	B	310 637-1500	1505
Industrial Tctnics Brings Corp (DH)	3562	C	310 537-3750	2794
Dependable Global Express Inc (PA)	4731	C	310 537-2000	4004
Wenzlau Engineering Inc.	5065	D	310 604-3400	5714

EARP, CA - San Bernardino County

	SIC	EMP	PHONE	ENTRY#
Colorado River Adventures Inc (PA)	7033	C	760 663-3737	10416

EAST PALO ALTO, CA - Santa Clara County

	SIC	EMP	PHONE	ENTRY#
Zadaonet.	4813	D	650 556-6377	4361
Hggc LLC (PA)	6799	B	650 321-4910	9518
East Palo Alto Hotel Dev Inc.	7011	C	650 566-1200	9771
South Cnty Cmnty Hlth Ctr Inc (PA)	8011	B	650 330-7407	15067
Greenberg Traurig LLP.	8111	C	650 328-8500	17484
Ropes & Gray LLP.	8111	C	650 617-4000	17629
Primary School.	8641	B	510 606-4563	18895

EASTVALE, CA - Riverside County

	SIC	EMP	PHONE	ENTRY#
CJ Logistics America LLC.	4212	C	909 605-7233	3383
Keystone Automotive Warehouse.	5013	C	951 277-5237	5047
Smart & Final Stores LLC.	5141	C	909 773-1813	6290
Shamrock Foods Company.	5149	A	951 685-6314	6667
Home Depot USA Inc.	5211	D	951 727-0324	6995
Riverside Medical Clinic Inc.	8011	D	626 388-2392	15023

EDGEWOOD, CA - Siskiyou County

	SIC	EMP	PHONE	ENTRY#
Siskiyou Development Company.	7011	D	530 938-2731	10241

EDISON, CA - Kern County

	SIC	EMP	PHONE	ENTRY#
Giumarra Vineyards Corporation (PA)	0172	B	661 395-7000	74
Johnston Farms Fmly Ltd Partnr.	0174	D	661 366-3201	100
Kirschenman Enterprises Sls LP.	7389	C	661 366-5736	13338

EDWARDS, CA - Kern County

	SIC	EMP	PHONE	ENTRY#
Jt3 LLC.	8711	A	661 277-4900	19289

EL CAJON, CA - San Diego County

	SIC	EMP	PHONE	ENTRY#
California Shtmtl Works Inc.	1541	D	619 562-7010	809
Hamann Construction.	1542	D	619 440-7424	927
Steve P Rados Inc.	1622	C	619 328-1360	1190
Cass Construction Inc (PA)	1623	B	619 590-0929	1202
HP Communications Inc.	1623	D	951 579-8339	1217
K T A Construction Inc.	1623	C	619 562-9464	1224
S C Valley Engineering Inc.	1623	D	619 444-2366	1256
Schilling Paradise Corp.	1623	C	619 449-4141	1259
Alpha Mechanical Inc (PA)	1711	D	858 278-3500	1350
Astro Mechanical Contractors Inc.	1711	D	619 442-9686	1366

GEOGRAPHIC SECTION

EL SEGUNDO CA

	SIC	EMP	PHONE	ENTRY#
Countywide Mech Systems LLC	1711	C	619 449-9900	1410
Helix Mechanical Inc	1711	C	619 440-1518	1456
R & R Mechanical Contractors Inc	1711	D	619 449-9900	1538
Walter Anderson Plumbing Inc	1711	C	619 449-7646	1594
West Coast AC Co Inc	1711	C	619 561-8000	1596
City-Wide Electronic Systems Inc	1731	D	619 444-0219	1698
Dynalectric Company	1731	B	619 328-4007	1722
Paradise Electric Inc	1731	C	619 449-4141	1800
Seal Electric Inc	1731	C	619 449-7323	1835
Sunshine Communications SE Inc	1731	C	619 448-7600	1856
Team C Construction	1771	D	619 579-6572	2164
Artimex Iron Inc	1791	C	619 444-3155	2178
Weldmac Manufacturing Company	3599	C	619 440-2300	2858
Micro-Mode Products Inc	3663	C	619 449-3844	2894
Q Microwave Inc	3679	D	619 258-7322	2945
GKN Aerospace Chem-Tronics Inc (DH)	3724	A	619 258-5000	2985
Johnson Outdoors Inc	3949	C	619 402-1023	3092
California Neon Products	3993	D	619 283-2191	3099
Transdev Services Inc	4119	C	619 401-4503	3299
San Diego Gas & Electric Co	4911	B	619 441-3834	4671
Waste Management Cal Inc	4953	C	619 596-5100	4957
Denardi Machinery Inc	5082	C	619 749-0039	5786
Tk Elevator Corporation	5084	C	619 596-7220	5874
Taylor-Listug Inc (PA)	5099	C	619 258-1207	6056
Smart & Final Stores Inc	5141	B	619 390-1738	6295
Smart & Final Stores Inc	5141	B	619 589-7000	6313
Smart & Final Stores LLC	5141	C	619 562-4151	6376
Sunfood Corporation	5149	D	619 596-7979	6674
AJM Packaging Corporation	5199	C	619 448-4007	6886
Home Depot USA Inc	5211	D	619 401-6610	7006
K Motors Inc	5521	C	619 270-3000	7338
Sycuan Tribal Development	5812	C	619 442-3425	7512
EC Closing Corp	6162	D	800 546-1531	7957
The Pines Ltd	6513	C	619 447-1880	8864
Sycuan Casino	7011	A	619 445-6002	10297
W Lodging Inc	7011	A	619 258-6565	10348
Beauty Boutique Inc	7231	C	619 442-3407	10493
XI Staffing Inc	7361	C	619 579-0442	11263
Nlyte Software Americas Ltd	7371	D	866 386-5983	11783
Tessitura Network Inc	7372	C	888 643-5778	12377
Newport Diversified Inc	7389	C	619 448-4111	13395
El Cajon Motors (PA)	7515	D	619 579-8888	13595
Edwards Theatres Circuit Inc	7832	C	619 660-3460	13992
Sycuan Casino (PA)	7999	C	619 445-6002	14566
Kaiser Foundation Hospitals	8011	D	619 528-5000	14829
Neighborhood Healthcare	8011	C	619 440-2751	14917
Southern Cal Prmnnte Med Group	8011	D	619 528-5000	15084
Country Hills Health Care Inc	8051	C	619 441-8745	15390
Eldorado Care Center LP	8051	B	619 440-1211	15433
Parkside Healthcare Inc	8052	D	619 442-7744	15783
Bradley Court	8059	C	619 448-6633	15822
Kaiser Foundation Hospitals	8062	C	619 528-5000	16174
Apheresis Care Group Inc	8092	C	619 440-4612	16977
Rai Care Ctrs Sthern Cal II LL	8092	C	619 442-4122	16993
CRC Health Group Inc	8093	D	214 634-2722	17048
Christan Community Theatre	8299	D	619 588-0206	17806
St Madeleine Sophies Center	8331	B	619 442-5129	18251
Home Guiding Hands Corporation (PA)	8361	B	619 938-2850	18451
ARC of San Diego	8399	B	619 448-2415	18558

EL CENTRO, CA - Imperial County

	SIC	EMP	PHONE	ENTRY#
Braga Fresh Family Farms Inc	0191	C	760 353-1155	170
Joe Heger Farms LLC	0191	C	760 353-5111	187
Noblesse Oblige Inc	0722	C	760 353-3336	252
California Department Trnsp	1611	D	760 352-1129	1086
Original Sid Blackman Plbg Inc	1711	D	760 352-3632	1521
Smart & Final Stores LLC	5141	D	760 352-0811	6379
Soco Group Inc	5172	D	760 352-4683	6739
Lowes Home Centers LLC	5211	D	760 337-6700	7086
El Centro Motors	5511	C	760 336-2100	7198
El Centro Hospitality LLC	7011	C	760 353-2600	9774
El Centro Hospitality 2 LLC	7011	C	760 370-3800	9775
I N C Builders Inc	7363	B	760 352-4200	11291
Southwest Protective Svcs Inc	7381	C	760 996-1285	13050
Clinicas De Slud Del Peblo Inc (PA)	8011	D	760 344-9951	14691
El Centro Rgnal Med Ctr Fndtio (PA)	8062	A	760 339-7100	16072
Accentcare HM Hlth El Cntro In	8082	C	760 352-4022	16787
County of Imperial	8093	D	760 482-4120	17035
ARC - Imperial Valley (PA)	8322	C	760 352-0180	17836
Womanhaven	8322	B	760 353-6922	18194
Rove Engineering Inc	8711	D	760 425-0001	19378

EL CERRITO, CA - Contra Costa County

	SIC	EMP	PHONE	ENTRY#
Daiso California LLC	6531	D	510 679-5121	8974
Berkeley Country Club	7997	D	510 233-7550	14342
Doulas By Bay LLC	8099	D	415 510-9736	17226

EL DORADO HILLS, CA - El Dorado County

	SIC	EMP	PHONE	ENTRY#
Roebbelen Construction Inc	1542	B	916 939-4000	1010
Roebbelen Contracting Inc	1542	B	916 939-4000	1011
8minutenergy US Solar LLC	1711	C	916 608-9060	1329
Bayview Engrg & Cnstr Co Inc	1711	C	916 939-8986	1373
Securecom Inc	1731	D	916 638-2855	1836
Tri-Signal Integration Inc	1731	C	916 933-3155	1865
McClone Construction Company	1771	C	916 358-5495	2137
Emed Technologies Corporation	4225	D	775 232-3287	3700
CBS Maxpreps Inc	4813	D	530 676-6440	4263
O1 Communications Inc (PA)	4813	D	888 444-1111	4323
V3 Electric Inc	4911	D	916 597-2627	4716
Nor-Cal Controls Es Inc	4939	D	916 836-0800	4760
Rippey Corporation	5045	D	916 939-4332	5342
Original Mels Inc (PA)	5812	D	916 458-6014	7499
Grigsby Label LLC	6211	D	916 933-4991	8092
Patra Corporation (PA)	6311	D	415 595-9987	8245
Lyon Realty	6531	D	916 939-5300	9085
Dorado Software Inc	7371	D	916 673-1100	11551
R Systems Inc	7373	C	916 939-9696	12516
Patrick K Willis and Co Inc	7389	B	800 398-6480	13421
Enterprise Rnt--car Scrmnto LL	7514	D	916 934-0783	13583
Serrano Associates LLC	7997	D	916 939-3333	14448
Serrano Country Club	7997	D	916 933-5005	14449
El Dorado Hills Cmnty Svcs Dst	7999	D	916 933-6624	14519
Mercy Medical Group	8062	D	916 933-4222	16263
Thekey LLC	8082	D	916 358-3801	16949
Youngdahl Consulting Group Inc	8711	D	916 933-0633	19446

EL MACERO, CA - Yolo County

	SIC	EMP	PHONE	ENTRY#
El Macero Country Club Inc	7997	D	530 753-3363	14372

EL MONTE, CA - Los Angeles County

	SIC	EMP	PHONE	ENTRY#
Envirogenics Systems Company	1629	D	818 573-9220	1299
Andari Fashion Inc	2329	C	626 575-2759	2453
Access Services	4111	D	213 270-6000	3120
First Student Inc	4111	D	626 448-9446	3128
First Transit Inc	4111	C	626 307-7842	3135
San Gabriel Transit Inc (PA)	4111	C	626 258-1310	3200
Southland Transit Inc (PA)	4111	C	626 258-1310	3218
Medresponse LLC	4119	D	877 311-5555	3278
Triple-E Machinery Moving Inc	4213	C	626 444-1137	3555
San Gabriel Valley Water Co (PA)	4941	D	626 448-6183	4825
Los Angeles Ltg Mfg Co Inc	5063	D	626 454-8300	5575
Burke Engineering Co	5074	C	626 579-6763	5743
Bdi Inc	5085	C	626 442-8948	5892
Bangkit (usa) Inc	5112	C	626 672-0888	6062
Smart & Final Stores LLC	5141	D	626 443-1381	6339
K T Lucky Co Inc	5149	D	626 579-7272	6640
Mutual Trading Co Inc (DH)	5149	C	213 626-9458	6650
D Longo Inc	5511	B	626 580-6000	7190
El Monte Automotive Group Inc	5511	C	626 580-6200	7199
El Monte Automotive Group LLC	5511	D	626 444-0321	7200
Architectural Window Shades	5719	D	626 578-1936	7435
Cathay Capital Trust II	6022	D	213 625-4700	7670
Nijjar Realty Inc (PA)	6531	C	626 575-0062	9110
Amenities Development Co	7011	C	626 350-9588	9603
Herald Christian Health Center (PA)	8011	D	626 286-8700	14771
El Monte Convalescent Hospital	8051	D	626 442-1500	15430
Georgia Atkison Snf LLC	8051	D	626 444-2535	15494
Ramona Care Inc	8051	C	626 442-5721	15634
Gibraltar Cnvalescent Hosp Inc	8059	D	626 443-9425	15850
Ahm Gemch Inc	8062	C	626 579-7777	15928
Fulgent Genetics Inc (PA)	8071	A	626 350-0537	16722
Enki Health and RES Systems	8093	D	626 227-7001	17061
Altamed Health Services Corp	8099	C	626 453-8466	17175
Public Hlth Fndation Entps Inc	8099	D	626 856-6618	17307
Mountain View Elmntary Schl Ds	8211	D	626 652-4250	17732
Foothill Family Service	8322	D	626 246-1240	17983
La County	8322	D	626 569-6459	18036
Hope Hse For Mltple Hndcpped I (PA)	8361	D	626 443-1313	18452
R and L Lopez Associates Inc (PA)	8711	D	626 330-5296	19369

EL NIDO, CA - Merced County

	SIC	EMP	PHONE	ENTRY#
Double Diamond Dairy & Ranch	0241	D	209 722-8505	215

EL SEGUNDO, CA - Los Angeles County

	SIC	EMP	PHONE	ENTRY#
Irwin Industries Inc	1629	A	704 457-5117	1307

EL SEGUNDO CA

Company	SIC	EMP	PHONE	ENTRY#
Edwards Technologies Inc.	1731	D	310 536-7070	1723
Murad LLC (HQ)	2834	C	310 726-0600	2599
Belkin International Inc (DH)	3577	B	310 751-5100	2825
Nantenergy LLC	3621	D	310 905-4866	2863
Raytheon Applied Sgnal Tech In	3663	D	310 436-7000	2898
Teledyne Technologies Inc.	3679	B	310 765-3600	2946
Aerojet Rcketdyne Holdings Inc (HQ)	3812	D	310 252-8100	3000
Raytheon Company	3812	D	310 647-1000	3009
Karl Storz Endscpy-America Inc (HQ)	3841	B	424 218-8100	3056
Moose Toys LLC	3942	C	310 341-4642	3088
Cls Trnsprttion Los Angles LLC (HQ)	4119	C	310 414-8189	3249
Air New Zealand Limited	4512	D	310 648-7000	3828
Singapore Airlines Limited	4512	C	310 647-1922	3843
F & E Arcft Mint Los Angles LL	4581	B	310 338-0063	3892
Pacific Aviation Corporation (PA)	4581	C	310 646-4015	3903
Pinnacle Travel Services LLC	4724	C	310 414-1787	3946
VIP Tours of California Inc.	4725	D	310 216-7507	3971
Dfds International Corporation	4731	D	310 414-1516	4005
L E Coppersmith Inc (PA)	4731	D	310 607-8000	4048
Maersk Whsng Dist Svcs USA LLC (HQ)	4731	C	562 345-2200	4055
AT&T Corp	4812	D	303 596-8431	4184
Directv Group Holdings (HQ)	4812	D	310 964-5000	4213
Infonet Services Corporation (DH)	4813	A	310 335-2600	4299
Scalefast Inc (PA)	4813	C	310 595-4040	4336
Directv Inc.	4841	B	888 388-4249	4498
Directv Enterprises LLC	4841	A	310 535-5000	4499
Directv Group Inc (DH)	4841	C	310 964-5000	4503
Directv Holdings LLC (DH)	4841	D	310 964-5000	4504
Directv International Inc (DH)	4841	C	310 964-6460	4505
Directv Latin America LLC	4841	D	310 535-5000	4506
Socialive	4899	D	978 821-4637	4552
NRG El Segundo Operations Inc.	4911	C	310 615-6344	4595
En Pointe Technologies Sls LLC	5045	C	310 337-6151	5299
Square Enix Inc.	5045	C	310 846-0400	5355
Com Dev Usa LLC	5088	D	424 456-8000	5956
Raytheon Lgstics Spport Trning	5088	B	310 647-9438	5966
A-Mark Precious Metals Inc (PA)	5094	D	310 587-1477	6018
Tri-Union Seafoods LLC (DH)	5146	D	424 397-8556	6487
Chevron Corporation	5541	A	310 615-5000	7385
Cookingcom Inc.	5719	C	310 664-1283	7437
Pcm Inc (HQ)	5961	A	310 354-5600	7562
Guthy-Renker LLC (PA)	5999	D	760 773-9022	7583
Manhattan Bancorp	6021	C	310 606-8000	7629
Bank of Manhattan	6029	C	310 606-8000	7728
National Planning Corporation	6141	C	800 881-7174	7880
Charger Investment Partners LP	6211	D	310 372-5525	8075
Merrill Lynch Prce Fnner Smith	6211	D	310 536-1600	8129
Computershare Inc.	6289	C	800 522-6645	8230
Associated Third Party Administrators Inc.	6371	B		8456
TBG Insurance Services Corp.	6411	D	310 203-8770	8668
Landmark Dividend LLC (PA)	6531	D	323 306-2683	9069
Lyon Stahl Investment RE Inc.	6531	D	310 425-9838	9087
Trammell Crow Centl Texas Ltd	6531	D	310 765-2600	9196
American Academic Hlth Sys LLC	6719	A	310 414-7200	9299
Asp Henry Holdings Inc	6719	A	310 955-9200	9300
Hco Holding I Corporation (HQ)	6719	D	323 583-5000	9317
Transom Post Midco LLC	6719	D	312 254-3300	9344
Century Pk Capitl Partners LLC (PA)	6726	C	310 867-2210	9399
Ld Acquisition Company 16 LLC	6799	D	310 294-8160	9526
Westport Capital Partners LLC	6799	D	310 294-1234	9581
Djont Operations LLC	7011	C	310 640-3600	9749
Pt Gaming LLC	7011	A	323 260-5060	10131
Uhg Lax Prop Llc	7011	D	310 322-0999	10331
Esaloncom LLC	7231	D	866 550-2424	10496
Murad LLC	7231	C	310 726-0470	10503
David & Goliath LLC	7311	C	310 445-5200	10602
Ignited LLC (PA)	7311	D	310 773-3100	10630
Katch LLC	7311	D	310 219-6200	10636
Liquid Advertising Inc.	7311	D	310 450-2653	10642
Mh Sub I LLC (PA)	7311	B	310 280-4000	10648
Mullenlowe US Inc.	7311	C	424 738-6500	10652
Beachbody LLC	7313	D	310 883-9000	10703
Beachbody LLC (HQ)	7313	B	310 883-9000	10704
Stampscom Inc (PA)	7331	C	310 482-5800	10777
Softscript Inc.	7338	A	310 451-2110	10825
Ibftech Inc.	7361	D	424 217-8010	11153
Tempus LLC	7361	D	800 917-5055	11247
Zions Bancorporation	7361	A	424 290-5123	11264
Altech Services Inc.	7363	B	888 725-8324	11271
Randstad Professionals Us LLC	7363	D	424 246-4400	11322
Agent Image Inc.	7371	B	310 577-9222	11388
Artic Sentinel Inc.	7371	D	310 227-8230	11427
Com2us Usa Inc.	7371	D	310 416-1100	11505
Crescentone Inc (HQ)	7371	C	310 563-7000	11522
Irise (PA)	7371	D	800 556-0399	11679
Liminex Inc (PA)	7371	C	888 310-0410	11710
Prodege LLC (PA)	7371	D	310 294-9599	11847
Governmentjobscom Inc.	7372	C	310 426-6304	12210
Traxero North America LLC	7372	D	423 497-1164	12384
Unbroken Studios LLC	7372	D	310 741-2670	12387
Mesfin Enterprises	7373	B	310 615-0881	12488
Design People Inc.	7374	C	800 969-5799	12565
Crowdstrike Inc.	7379	C	888 512-8906	12772
Ispace Inc.	7379	C	310 563-3800	12818
Login Consulting Services Inc.	7379	D	310 607-9091	12830
Cornerstone Protective Svcs	7381	C	888 848-4791	12951
Whelan Security Co.	7381	D	310 343-8628	13075
Da Vinci Schools Fund	7389	C	310 725-5800	13256
Oceanx LLC (PA)	7389	D	310 774-4088	13404
Prologic Rdmption Slutions Inc (PA)	7389	A	310 322-7774	13434
Telenet Voip Inc.	7629	D	310 253-9000	13747
Crafty Apes LLC (PA)	7812	A	310 837-3900	13832
Movella Technologies NA Inc.	7812	D	310 481-1800	13867
Rhythm and Hues Inc (PA)	7812	D	310 448-7500	13885
Zoo Digital Production LLC	7812	D	310 220-3939	13923
Bear Nash Productions	7819	D	310 428-5167	13927
Motor Trend Group LLC (HQ)	7819	D	630 353-2505	13942
Ten Publishing Media LLC (PA)	7819	C	310 531-9900	13955
Spectrum Clubs Inc.	7991	A	310 727-9300	14235
American Golf Corporation (HQ)	7997	D	310 664-4000	14323
Tga Franchise Spt Holdings LLC	7997	D	310 333-0622	14469
Optumcare Management LLC (HQ)	8011	A	310 354-4200	14941
Radiology Partners Inc (HQ)	8011	B	424 290-8004	15007
Radiology Prtners Holdings LLC (PA)	8011	C	424 290-8004	15008
Pipeline Health LLC (PA)	8062	C	310 379-2134	16329
Scribeamerica LLC	8099	D	877 819-5900	17323
BMC Group Inc.	8111	D	310 321-5555	17389
Carson Kurtzman Consultants (DH)	8111	C	310 823-9000	17401
Michael Sullivan & Assoc LLP	8111	C	310 337-4480	17568
Diverse Journeys Inc (PA)	8322	D	310 643-7403	17956
Premier Disability Svcs LLC	8399	D	310 280-4000	18619
Team Rubicon USA	8699	D	310 906-1636	19110
Raytheon Secure Information Systems LLC	8711	C	310 647-9438	19373
Infineon Tech Americas Corp.	8721	A	310 726-8000	19588
Mitre Corporation	8733	D	310 297-8350	19896
Nantcell Inc.	8733	D	310 883-1300	19900
The Aerospace Corporation (PA)	8733	A	310 336-5000	19918
Bellwether Asset MGT Inc (PA)	8741	D	310 525-3022	20036
Avasant LLC (PA)	8742	D	310 643-3030	20284
Saviynt Inc (PA)	8742	C	310 641-1664	20538
Skin Laundry Holdings Inc.	8742	B	424 220-8826	20550
Tecolote Research Inc.	8742	D	310 640-4700	20579
Trace3 Inc.	8742	D	310 220-0164	20588
Wpromote LLC (PA)	8742	D	310 421-4844	20617
Clearesult Operating LLC	8748	D	508 836-9500	20730

EL SOBRANTE, CA - Contra Costa County

Company	SIC	EMP	PHONE	ENTRY#
Vila Construction Co.	1542	D	510 236-9111	1052
Falcon Crtcal Care Trnspt A Nr	8099	C	510 223-1171	17238
Greenridge Senior Care	8361	C	510 758-9600	18443

EL TORO, CA - Orange County

Company	SIC	EMP	PHONE	ENTRY#
Sunset Landscape Maintenance	0782	D	949 455-4636	539
P M D Holding Corp.	5047	B	949 595-4777	5437
Smart & Final Stores LLC	5141	D	949 770-8281	6334

ELDRIDGE, CA - Sonoma County

Company	SIC	EMP	PHONE	ENTRY#
Califrnia Dept Dvlpmental Svcs	8069	A	707 938-6000	16668

ELK GROVE, CA - Sacramento County

Company	SIC	EMP	PHONE	ENTRY#
Dragados Usa Inc.	1611	C	916 738-9927	1099
R & A Painting Inc.	1721	D	916 688-3955	1635
Future Energy Corporation (PA)	1742	D	800 985-0733	1932
Concrete North Inc.	1771	D	209 745-7400	2111
Matheson Fast Freight Inc (HQ)	4213	D	916 686-4600	3513
Saia Motor Freight Line LLC	4213	D	916 690-8417	3540
Shine Logistics LLC	4731	C	844 850-3391	4094
OC Communications Inc.	4841	A	916 686-3700	4516
Sacramento Reg Co Sanit Dist.	4952	B	916 875-9000	4850
Super Pallet Recycling Corp	5031	D	916 686-1700	5190
PDM Steel Service Centers Inc.	5051	D	916 513-4548	5509
Slakey Brothers Inc (PA)	5075	D	916 478-2000	5772
Cardinal Health Inc.	5122	B	916 372-9880	6099
Lowes Home Centers LLC	5211	D	916 688-1922	7056
Bel Air Mart	5411	D	916 714-6996	7142
Kaiser Foundation Hospitals	6324	C	916 478-5000	8310

GEOGRAPHIC SECTION

ESCONDIDO CA

	SIC	EMP	PHONE	ENTRY#
Kaiser Foundation Hospitals	6324	D	916 544-6000	8314
J & L Collections Services Inc	7322	D	800 481-6006	10744
Professional Bureau of Collect	7322	D	916 685-3399	10750
Alldata LLC	7372	B	916 684-5200	12088
Airborne Security Patrol Inc	7381	D	916 599-8120	12920
Comprehensive SEC Svcs Inc (PA)	7381	D	916 683-3605	12947
Century Theatres Inc	7833	B	916 683-5290	14012
Spare-Time Inc	7997	D	916 859-5910	14463
Valley-HI Country Club	7997	D	916 684-2120	14475
Cosumnes Community Svcs Dst	7999	B	916 405-7150	14510
Internal Revenue Service	8011	D	916 974-5678	14787
Mercy Medical Group	8062	D	916 691-8500	16261
Sutter Health	8062	D	916 544-5423	16526
Visions Unlimited	8093	C	916 394-0800	17160
Veterans of Foreign Wars of US	8641	D	916 786-7757	18925
Future Energy Corporation	8711	D	916 685-4200	19235
Willdan Engineering	8711	D	916 661-3520	19440
Apex Site Solutions Inc	8742	D	916 685-8619	20277

EMERYVILLE, CA - Alameda County

	SIC	EMP	PHONE	ENTRY#
Anvil Builders Inc	1611	C	415 285-5000	1077
Frank M Booth Inc	1711	D	530 742-7134	1440
Grid Alternative	1711	B	510 731-1310	1453
Armstrong Instlltion Svc A Cal	1721	D	408 777-1234	1605
Giampolini & Co	1721	C	415 673-1236	1620
Clif Bar & Company LLC (HQ)	2064	B	510 596-6300	2373
Dynavax Technologies Corp (PA)	2836	D	510 848-5100	2621
Bruker Cellular Analysis Inc (HQ)	3826	D	510 858-2855	3029
Eko Devices Inc	3845	D	844 356-3384	3075
Premier Nutrition Company LLC (HQ)	5149	C	415 814-9410	6660
Grocery Outlet Holding Corp (PA)	5411	B	510 845-1999	7143
Peets Coffee Inc (DH)	5499	D	510 594-2100	7162
Nmi Holdings Inc (PA)	6351	D	855 530-6642	8433
Zaplabs LLC (DH)	6531	D		9225
Broadmoor Hotel	7011	D	415 673-8445	9663
Pacific Hotel Management LLC	7011	C	510 547-7888	10081
Select Hotels Group LLC	7011	D	510 601-5880	10219
Pixar	7312	C	707 364-7854	10696
Maxim Healthcare Services Inc	7363	D	510 873-0700	11303
Lilt Inc (PA)	7371	C	415 992-5088	11709
Bigfix Inc	7372	C	510 652-6700	12114
Tanium Inc	7372	A	510 704-0202	12375
Tubemogul Inc	7372	A	510 653-0126	12386
Evault Inc	7379	C	415 432-2200	12789
Magicom Inc	7379	D	415 404-6094	12832
Monsoon Commerce Inc	7379	C	510 594-4500	12841
Sutter Connect LLC	7389	B	510 596-4700	13494
Pixar (DH)	7812	B	510 922-3000	13878
Cep America - Illinois LLP	8011	D	510 350-2777	14674
Cep America LLC	8011	D	510 350-2691	14675
Ucsf Benioff Chld Physicians	8011	D	415 476-4977	15139
Santen Incorporated	8042	D	415 268-9100	15265
Onebody Inc	8082	D	510 285-2000	16905
Barry Bishop	8111	D	510 596-0888	17380
Cep America-California (PA)	8621	D	510 350-2700	18744
Young MNS Chrstn Assn of E Bay	8641	B	510 601-8674	18968
E2 Consulting Engineers Inc	8711	D	510 652-1164	19207
4d Molecular Therapeutics Inc	8731	D	510 505-2680	19643
Omniab Inc (PA)	8731	D	510 250-7800	19750
Fort James Corporation	8741	A	510 594-4900	20091
Medamerica Inc (HQ)	8742	D	510 350-2600	20461
Stat Revenue Professional Corp	8742	D	510 597-1800	20566
Berkeley Research Group LLC (PA)	8748	C	510 285-3300	20703

ENCINITAS, CA - San Diego County

	SIC	EMP	PHONE	ENTRY#
Dramm and Echter Inc	0181	D	760 436-0188	124
Flock Freight Inc	4731	C	855 744-7585	4020
Cellco Partnership	4812	D	760 642-0430	4195
Olivenhain Municipal Water Dst	4941	D	760 753-6466	4813
Black Box Inc	5136	D	760 804-3300	6166
Wayne Gossett Ford Inc	5511	D	760 753-6286	7330
Southern Cal Disc Tire Co Inc	5531	C	760 634-2202	7372
Solis Capital Partners LLC	6799	D	760 309-9436	9563
Trigild International Inc	7011	D	760 944-0260	10326
North Coast Fmly Med Group Inc	8011	D	760 942-0118	14922
North County Health Prj Inc	8011	C	760 736-6767	14924
San Diego Hebrew Homes (PA)	8051	D	760 942-2695	15651
Silverado Senior Living Inc	8051	D	760 270-9917	15671
Scripps Health	8062	D	760 753-8413	16398
Scripps Health	8062	D	760 753-6501	16401
At Home Nursing Care Inc	8082	D	760 634-8000	16812
Ree Medical Inc	8099	D	760 641-4359	17311
YMCA of San Diego County	8641	C	760 745-7490	18941
YMCA of San Diego County	8641	B	858 292-4034	18944
YMCA of San Diego County	8641	C	760 758-0808	18951
Dudek Inc (PA)	8711	D	760 942-5147	19206

ENCINO, CA - Los Angeles County

	SIC	EMP	PHONE	ENTRY#
Smart & Final Stores LLC	5141	D	818 789-0242	6383
Benihana Inc	5812	D	818 788-7121	7459
Warner Food Management Co Inc	5812	D	818 285-2160	7516
United Vision Financial Inc	6163	D	818 285-0211	8062
Republic Indemnity Company Cal	6331	C	818 990-9860	8405
Lowe Enterprises Rlty Svcs Inc	6531	A	818 990-9555	9077
Hunt Capital Partners Tax Crdt	6722	D	818 380-6100	9375
A-Able Inc (PA)	7342	D	323 658-5779	10826
One Silver Serve LLC	7349	D	818 995-6444	10936
Team-One Staffing Services Inc	7361	A	951 616-3515	11243
Phone Check Solutions LLC	7371	B	310 365-1855	11827
Veritas Technologies LLC	7371	C	310 202-0757	12017
D3publisher of America Inc	7372	D	310 268-0820	12157
Netsol Technologies Inc (PA)	7372	D	818 222-9197	12284
Payment Cloud LLC	7374	D	800 988-2215	12604
Reprints Desk Inc	7375	D	310 477-0354	12684
Life Alert Emrgncy Rsponse Inc (PA)	7382	C	800 247-0000	13132
Answer Financial Inc (HQ)	7389	D	818 644-4000	13195
Metropolitan Imports LLC	7389	D	646 980-5343	13375
Encino Living LLC	7991	D	818 907-1343	14196
Emergent Medical Associates	8011	B	818 995-5350	14738
Exer Holding Company LLC	8011	C	818 287-0894	14742
Symbion Inc	8011	C	818 501-1080	15121
Sunrise Senior Living LLC	8051	D	818 346-9046	15694
Prime Hlthcare Svcs - Encino H	8062	B	818 995-5000	16339
Ascend Healthcare LLC	8093	D	747 247-2176	17005
Elizabeth Glaser Pedia	8099	B	310 231-0400	17235
Pearlman Brown & Wax LLP (PA)	8111	D	818 501-4343	17606
Price Law Group A Prof Corp (PA)	8111	D	818 995-4540	17615
March For Our Lves Action Fund	8399	D	801 815-1989	18609
Baker Tilly Us LLP	8721	B	818 981-2600	19534
F6s Network Limited	8731	D	619 818-4363	19692
Instantly Inc	8732	C	866 872-4006	19823
Haber Corp Crtif Pub Accntants	8741	D	818 783-9200	20106
Westrec Properties Inc	8741	B	818 907-0400	20252
Fpg Services LLC	8742	D	818 858-1080	20386
Intelity Inc	8742	D	310 596-8160	20415

ESCALON, CA - San Joaquin County

	SIC	EMP	PHONE	ENTRY#
Dan R Costa Incorporated	0191	C	209 234-2004	174
Barton Ranch Inc	0291	D	209 838-8930	233
Hogan Mfg Inc (PA)	3999	C	209 838-7323	3108

ESCONDIDO, CA - San Diego County

	SIC	EMP	PHONE	ENTRY#
Henry Avocado Corporation (HQ)	0179	D	760 745-6632	117
Mountain Meadow Mushrooms Inc	0182	D	760 749-1201	164
Landcare USA LLC	0782	D	760 747-1174	508
Pinery LLC	0811	D	858 675-3575	570
Eleven Western Builders Inc (PA)	1521	D	760 796-6346	675
Romero General Cnstr Corp	1521	C	760 715-0154	712
Erickson-Hall Construction Co (PA)	1542	D	760 796-7700	916
R J Lanthier Company Inc	1542	D	760 738-9798	999
Marathon General Inc	1611	D	760 738-9714	1134
Romero General Cnstr Corp (PA)	1611	D	760 489-8412	1158
JR Filanc Cnstr Co Inc (PA)	1623	D	760 941-7130	1222
West Tech Contracting Inc	1623	D	760 233-2570	1281
Associate Mech Contrs Inc	1711	C	760 294-3517	1365
Baker Electric & Renewables LLC	1731	A	760 745-2001	1671
Bergelectric Corp	1731	D	760 746-1003	1677
Bergelectric Corp	1731	D	760 291-8100	1678
Hmt Electric Inc	1731	D	858 458-9771	1749
Laser Electric Inc	1731	C	760 658-6626	1765
Nb Baker Electric Inc	1731	D	760 546-6030	1786
X3 Management Services Inc	1731	D	760 597-9336	1878
Prowall Lath and Plaster	1742	D	760 480-9001	1957
Rocky Coast Builders Inc	1751	D	760 489-7770	2015
Surecraft Supply Inc	1751	C		2020
Taylor Trim & Supply Inc	1751	D	760 740-2000	2021
Southland Paving Inc	1771	D	760 747-6895	2159
Dcc General Engrg Contrs Inc	3272	D	760 480-7400	2703
Superior Ready Mix Concrete LP	3273	D	760 728-1128	2713
Avr Global Technologies Inc (PA)	3679	C	949 391-1180	2939
Mv Transportation Inc	4111	C	760 520-0118	3176
Westmed Ambulance Inc	4119	C	310 219-1779	3306
Santa Barbara Trnsp Corp	4151	C	760 746-0850	3351
San Diego Gas & Electric Co	4911	B	760 432-2508	4667
San Diego County Water Auth	4941	C	760 480-1991	4823
Zest Anchors LLC	5047	D	760 743-7744	5461

ESCONDIDO CA

	SIC	EMP	PHONE	ENTRY#
Cal Southern Sound Image Inc (PA)	5065	D	760 737-3900	5638
Taoglas	5065	D	760 855-4580	5707
Sound-Crete Contractors Inc	5082	D	760 291-1240	5804
B J T C Inc	5083	D	760 737-2442	5806
Smart & Final Stores LLC	5141	D	760 746-5490	6364
Giumarra Agricom Intl LLC	5148	A	760 480-8502	6553
Home Depot USA Inc	5211	C	760 233-1285	6992
Lowes Home Centers LLC	5211	D	760 484-5113	7097
Brecht Enterprises Inc	5511	D	760 745-3000	7177
Escondido Motors LLC	5511	D	760 745-5000	7202
Jack Pwell Chrysler - Ddge Inc	5511	D	760 745-2880	7239
Southern Cal Disc Tire Co Inc	5531	C	760 741-9805	7360
Southern Cal Disc Tire Co Inc	5531	C	760 741-3801	7365
Acapulco Restaurants Inc	5812	C	562 346-1200	7453
Tri-Ad	6411	C	760 743-7555	8677
Welk Group Inc	7011	B	760 749-3000	10358
ARS National Services Inc (PA)	7322	C	800 456-5053	10735
Transamerican Direct Inc	7331	D	760 745-5343	10778
Sbrm Inc (PA)	7349	D	760 480-0208	10961
Controltec Inc	7379	D	760 975-9750	12765
Dane Karno Inc	7389	D	619 813-8585	13257
Welk Group Inc	7992	C	760 749-3225	14296
Castle Creek Country Club Inc	7997	D	760 749-2877	14356
Welk Group Inc	7997	C	760 749-0983	14482
Borrego Cmnty Hlth Foundation	8011	C	760 466-1080	14634
Graybill Medical Group (PA)	8011	C	866 228-2236	14766
Kaiser Foundation Hospitals	8011	C	619 528-5000	14830
Neighborhood Healthcare	8011	C	760 737-2000	14918
Southern Cal Prmnnte Med Group	8011	C	760 839-7200	15087
Emeritus Corporation	8051	C	760 741-3055	15441
Life Care Centers America Inc	8051	C	760 741-6109	15539
Mek Escondido LLC	8051	C	760 747-0430	15582
Silverado Senior Living Inc	8051	D	760 456-5137	15670
Mountain Shadows Support Group (PA)	8052	D	760 743-3714	15775
Valle Vsta Cnvlescent Hosp Inc	8059	D	760 745-1288	15909
Palomar Health (PA)	8062	A	442 281-5000	16308
Palomar Health Technology Inc	8062	A	442 281-5000	16312
Palomar Health	8069	C	760 740-6311	16689
Cox Enterprises LLC	8082	C	858 822-8587	16850
Elizabeth Hospice Inc (PA)	8082	C	760 737-2050	16859
UNI Care Home Health Inc	8082	D	760 510-0055	16956
Mental Health Systems Inc	8093	C	760 737-7125	17090
Neighborhood Healthcare	8099	D	760 737-6903	17282
Interfaith Community Svcs Inc	8322	D	760 489-6380	18020
Palomar Hlth Rhblttion Inst LL	8322	A	442 277-6100	18076
Atria Management Company LLC	8361	B	760 480-8155	18376
Humangood Socal	8361	C	760 747-4306	18457
Las Villas Del Norte	8361	C	760 741-1047	18465
Meadowbrook Vlg Chrstn Rtrment	8361	C	760 746-2500	18483
Redwood Elderlink Scph	8361	B	760 480-1030	18509
Califrnia Ctr For Arts Escndid	8412	C	760 839-4138	18640
Zoological Society San Diego	8422	C	760 747-8702	18696
Automobile Club Southern Cal	8699	C	760 745-2124	19058
Blanchard Training and Dev Inc (PA)	8742	C	760 489-5005	20298
Tri-Ad Actuaries Inc	8742	C	760 743-7555	20591
Pro Energy Services Group LLC	8744	B	760 789-7149	20662

EUREKA, CA - Humboldt County

	SIC	EMP	PHONE	ENTRY#
Pacific Gas and Electric Co	4911	B	707 444-0700	4642
Coast Central Credit Union (PA)	6061	D	707 445-8801	7759
Security Nat Mstr Holdg Co LLC (PA)	6162	C	707 442-2818	8020
Sn Servicing Corporation	6162	D	707 445-9883	8022
Morgan Stnley Smith Barney LLC	6282	C	707 443-3071	8209
State Compensation Insur Fund	6331	C	707 443-9721	8416
Mission Linen Supply	7213	C	707 443-8681	10444
Eureka Rhblttion Wllness Ctr L	8051	C	707 445-3261	15468
St Joseph Hlth Nthrn Cal LLC	8062	B	707 525-5300	16460
St Joseph Hospital (PA)	8062	B	707 445-8121	16464
St Joseph Hospital	8062	C	707 445-8121	16465
St Joseph Hospital	8062	C	707 445-8121	16466
St Joseph Hospital	8062	C	707 268-0190	16467
St Joseph Hospital	8062	C	707 445-8121	16468
St Joseph Hospital of Eureka	8062	A	707 445-8121	16469
Sisters of St Joseph Orange	8082	A	707 443-9332	16929
Humboldt Cmnty Access Rsrce CT	8322	D	707 443-7077	18009
Humboldt Cmnty Access Rsrce CT	8322	D	707 441-8625	18010
Humboldt Snior Rsource Ctr Inc (PA)	8322	D	707 443-9747	18011
Humboldt Bay Fire Jint Pwers A	8611	D	707 441-4000	18710
Shn Cnslting Engners Glgsts In (PA)	8711	D	707 441-8855	19386
California Department Trnsp	8748	C	707 445-6600	20716

EXETER, CA - Tulare County

	SIC	EMP	PHONE	ENTRY#
Exeter Engineering Inc	0723	D	559 592-3161	264
Exeter Packers Inc (PA)	0723	C	559 592-5168	265
Exeter-Ivanhoe Citrus Assn	0723	D	559 592-3141	267
Sun Pacific Farming Coop Inc (PA)	0762	B	559 592-7121	381
Redding Tree Growers Corp	0851	D	559 594-9299	572
Venida Packing Company	5199	C	559 592-2816	6955
Farmers Insurance Exchange	6411	C	559 594-4149	8564
Kaweah Delta Health Care Dst	8062	D	559 592-7128	16197

FAIR OAKS, CA - Sacramento County

	SIC	EMP	PHONE	ENTRY#
Clarklift-West Inc	5084	C	916 381-5674	5826
Empire Home Loans Inc	6162	C	916 715-1974	7960
Lyon Realty	6531	C	916 962-0111	9084
William L Lyon & Assoc Inc	6531	B	916 535-0356	9220
Folsom Lake Appliance Inc	7629	D	916 985-3426	13740
North Ridge Country Club	7997	D	916 967-5717	14417
Eskaton	8082	D	916 536-3750	16861
Eskaton Properties Inc	8361	C	916 965-4663	18427

FAIRFAX, CA - Marin County

	SIC	EMP	PHONE	ENTRY#
Roi Dna Inc	7313	D	831 238-2514	10718
Meadow Club	7997	D	415 453-3274	14403
Qb3 LLC	8742	D	415 515-3595	20520

FAIRFIELD, CA - Solano County

	SIC	EMP	PHONE	ENTRY#
Bcfs Health and Human Services	0752	B	707 422-8802	357
Mark Scott Construction Inc	1522	D	707 864-8880	765
Westgate Cnstr & Maint Inc	1542	D	707 208-5763	1061
California Department Trnsp	1611	C	707 428-2031	1084
Kiewit Corporation	1611	D	707 439-7300	1126
UCI Construction Inc (PA)	1629	D	925 370-9808	1324
Certified Coatings Company	1721	D	707 639-4414	1609
Sipco Surface Protection Inc (DH)	1721	D	707 639-4414	1642
Petersen-Dean Commercial Inc	1761	C	707 469-7470	2077
Halabi Inc (PA)	3281	C	707 402-1600	2716
Pacific Gas and Electric Co	4911	C	415 973-7000	4608
City of Fairfield	4941	C	707 428-7680	4771
Fairfield-Suisun Sewer Dst	4952	D	707 429-8930	4849
Wind River Enterprises Inc	5012	D	707 864-1040	5019
CMC Rebar West	5051	C	707 759-1400	5482
County of Solano	5051	C	707 421-6055	5485
Encore Glass Inc	5085	D	707 745-4444	5900
S & S Tool & Supply Inc (HQ)	5085	C	800 430-8665	5924
New Desserts Inc	5149	D	415 780-6860	6655
Frank-Lin Distillers Pdts Ltd (PA)	5182	C	408 259-8900	6796
Tencate Advanced Composite	5191	C	707 359-3400	6836
Lowes Home Centers LLC	5211	D	707 207-2070	7046
Price-Simms Ford LLC	5511	D	707 421-3300	7282
Caliber Home Loans Inc	6162	D	707 432-1000	7942
First Priority Financial Inc	6162	B	707 432-1000	7965
Partnership Health Plan Cal	6324	B	707 863-4100	8351
Geovera Specialty Insurance Co	6331	C	707 863-3700	8383
Embassy Investments Inc	7011	D	707 422-4111	9779
Spring Mountain Hotel LLC	7011	D	530 304-5619	10263
Edwards Theatres Circuit Inc	7832	D	707 432-2121	13994
Green Valley Country Club	7997	D	707 864-1101	14379
Sutter Regional Med Foundation	8011	D	707 631-9423	15116
Sagebrush Healthcare Inc	8051	D	707 425-0623	15649
Northbay Healthcare Corp (PA)	8062	D	707 646-5000	16284
Northbay Healthcare Group (HQ)	8062	A	707 646-5000	16285
Permanente Medical Group Inc	8062	B	707 427-4000	16321
Pediatric Cardiology Med Grp	8099	D	707 863-8190	17294
Vitalant Research Institute	8099	D	707 428-6001	17349
Seneca Family of Agencies	8322	C	707 429-4440	18126
Dreamctchers Empwerment Netwrk	8331	A	707 558-1775	18227
Pace Solano	8331	C	707 426-6932	18241
Solano Fmly & Chld Council Inc	8351	C	707 863-3950	18354
Northern CA Retiredd Ofcrs	8361	C	707 432-1200	18495

FALLBROOK, CA - San Diego County

	SIC	EMP	PHONE	ENTRY#
Olive Hill Greenhouses Inc	0181	D	760 728-4596	144
Treesap Farms LLC	0191	C	760 990-7770	203
Executive Landscape Inc	0781	C	760 731-9036	430
Maneri Traffic Control Inc	1611	D	951 695-5104	1133
Scw Contracting Corporation	1623	C	760 728-1308	1260
Southwest Construction Co Inc	1771	C	760 728-4460	2160
Fallbrook Public Utility Dst	4941	D	760 728-1125	4793
Altman Specialty Plants Inc	5193	B	800 348-4881	6849
Major Market Inc	5411	C	760 723-0857	7146
Pala Mesa Limited Partnership	7011	C	760 728-5881	10094
Garich Inc	7361	B	951 302-4750	11142
Little Sisters Truck Wash Inc (PA)	7542	D	760 731-3170	13699
Graybill Medical Group Inc	8011	D	760 728-2777	14767
Crestwood Behavioral Hlth Inc	8059	C	760 451-4165	15840

GEOGRAPHIC SECTION

FONTANA CA

	SIC	EMP	PHONE	ENTRY#
Boys Club of Fallbrook	8641	D	760 728-5871	18821
Edsi	8711	D	760 731-3501	19208
SL Blue Garden Corp	8742	C	626 633-2672	20551

FARMERSVILLE, CA - Tulare County

	SIC	EMP	PHONE	ENTRY#
AAA Quality Services Inc (PA)	7359	C	559 594-1128	11011

FARMINGTON, CA - San Joaquin County

	SIC	EMP	PHONE	ENTRY#
Brightview Tree Company	0781	D	209 886-5511	420

FELTON, CA - Santa Cruz County

	SIC	EMP	PHONE	ENTRY#
Cupertino Electric Inc	1731	A	408 808-8260	1716

FILLMORE, CA - Ventura County

	SIC	EMP	PHONE	ENTRY#
California Watercress Inc (PA)	0161	D	805 524-4808	26
Allied Avocados & Citrus Inc	0723	D	805 625-7155	253
Brightview Tree Company	0811	D	714 546-7975	567
Rotorcraft Support Inc	4581	D	818 997-7667	3908
Owens & Minor Distribution Inc	5047	A	805 524-0243	5436

FIREBAUGH, CA - Fresno County

	SIC	EMP	PHONE	ENTRY#
Seasholtz John	0161	C	559 659-3805	42
Empresas Del Bosque Inc	0191	B	209 364-6428	177
Telles Ranch Inc	0191	C	209 364-6262	200
Vaquero Farms Inc	0191	D	559 659-2790	206
Hammonds Ranch Inc	0291	D	209 364-6185	235
Bosque Joe L Del Jr	0722	B	209 364-6428	246
I S A Contracting Svcs Inc	0722	A	559 659-1080	250
Olam Spices & Vegetables Inc	0723	C	209 364-2132	295
Olam West Coast Inc	0723	C	209 364-6164	296

FISH CAMP, CA - Mariposa County

	SIC	EMP	PHONE	ENTRY#
DNC Prks Resorts At Tenaya Inc (DH)	7011	C	559 683-6555	9755

FIVE POINTS, CA - Fresno County

	SIC	EMP	PHONE	ENTRY#
Telesis Onion Co	0723	C	559 884-2441	311

FOLSOM, CA - Sacramento County

	SIC	EMP	PHONE	ENTRY#
Mountain G Enterprises Inc	1611	C	866 464-6351	1141
Quagga Corporation	1623	D	916 357-5129	1253
Rjp Framing Inc	1751	D	916 941-3934	2014
City of Folsom	4111	C	916 355-8395	3126
Location Services LLC (PA)	4789	D	800 588-0097	4166
Frontier California Inc	4813	B	212 395-1000	4278
Mailcentro Inc	4813	C	916 985-4445	4310
Califrnia Ind Sys Oprator Corp (PA)	4911	B	916 351-4400	4562
Green Acres Nursery & Sup LLC (PA)	5083	D	916 673-9720	5809
Lowes Home Centers LLC	5211	C	916 984-7979	7040
Safe Credit Union (PA)	6061	C	916 979-7233	7795
Sierra Pacific Mortgage Co Inc (PA)	6162	A	916 932-1700	8021
Stearns Holdings LLC	6162	C	916 358-9170	8023
Liberty American Mortgage Corp (PA)	6163	D	916 780-3000	8046
Mercury Insurance Company	6331	A	916 353-4859	8393
Unitrin Direct Insurance Co (HQ)	6399	D	760 603-3276	8474
Benefit & Risk Management Svcs	6411	C	888 326-2555	8508
Csac Excess Insurance Auth	6411	D	916 850-7300	8538
Newport Group Inc	6411	B	925 328-4540	8623
Newport Group Inc (HQ)	6411	C	925 328-4540	8624
Powerschool	6512	B	877 873-1550	8746
Premium Outlet Partners LP	6512	D	916 985-0312	8748
Altergy Systems	6719	D	916 458-8590	9297
Visionary Intgrtion Prfssnals (PA)	6719	C	916 985-9625	9347
Lake Natoma Lodging LP	7011	D	916 351-1500	9964
Taxresources Inc (PA)	7291	C	877 369-7827	10526
Erepublic LLC	7313	C	916 932-1300	10711
Samuel Hale LLC	7361	A	916 235-1477	11225
Kpit Infosystems Inc	7371	D	916 985-0300	11697
One Inc Software Corporation (PA)	7371	B	866 343-6940	11793
Pulse Systems Inc (DH)	7371	D	316 636-5900	11853
Magnit LLC (PA)	7372	C	516 437-3300	12259
Meridian Project Systems Inc	7372	C	916 294-2000	12270
Powerschool Group LLC (HQ)	7372	C	916 288-1588	12326
Powerschool Holdings Inc	7372	A	877 873-1550	12327
Related Technologies Inc	7379	D	916 357-5900	12869
Visionary Intgrtion Prfssnals (HQ)	7379	D	916 985-9625	12905
Erepublic Inc (PA)	7389	C	916 932-1300	13281
Flt Inc	7538	C	916 355-1500	13662
VPD IV Inc	7822	B	916 605-1500	13973
Spare-Time Inc	7997	C	916 983-9180	14459
Folsom Surgery Center Inc	8011	D	916 673-1990	14751
Kaiser Foundation Hospitals	8011	D	916 986-4178	14848
Kaiser Foundation Hospitals	8011	D	916 817-5200	14850
University California Davis	8011	D	916 985-9300	15153
Burger Physcl Therapy Svcs Inc (HQ)	8049	C	916 983-5900	15269
Burger Rhblitation Systems Inc (PA)	8049	C	800 900-8491	15270
Prairie City Commons LLC	8052	D	916 458-0303	15784
Dignity Health	8062	D	916 983-7400	16041
Mercy Medical Group	8062	D	916 351-4834	16262
Vibra Hospital Sacramento LLC	8062	C	916 351-9151	16620
Kaiser Foundation Hospitals	8071	D	916 817-5651	16730
Ed Supports LLC	8322	D	201 478-8711	17963
Dokken Engineering (PA)	8711	D	916 858-0642	19204
Morton & Pitalo Inc (PA)	8711	D	916 984-7621	19327
REY Engineers Inc	8711	D	916 366-3040	19374
Paychex Inc	8721	D	916 983-0303	19620
Inductive Automation LLC	8742	D	800 266-7798	20411
Meridian Knwldge Solutions LLC (DH)	8742	D	916 985-9625	20465
First Step Housing	8748	D	916 769-8877	20749

FONTANA, CA - San Bernardino County

	SIC	EMP	PHONE	ENTRY#
People Pets and Vets LLC	0742	C	909 453-4213	340
People Pets and Vets LLC	0742	C	909 329-2860	341
Brightview Landscape Svcs Inc	0781	D	909 946-3196	402
Stantru Resources Inc	1541	D	909 587-1441	846
Engel Holdings Inc	1542	C	866 950-9862	913
Cattrac Construction Inc	1629	D	909 355-1146	1292
Foundation Pile Inc	1629	D	909 350-1584	1302
Slater Inc	1629	D	909 822-6800	1320
STC Netcom Inc (PA)	1731	D	951 685-8181	1852
Gonsalves & Santucci Inc	1771	B	909 350-0474	2121
J-M Manufacturing Company Inc	2821	D	909 822-3009	2576
Avilas Garden Art (PA)	3272	C	909 350-4546	2701
Jensen Enterprises Inc	3272	B	909 357-7264	2705
American Security Products Co	3499	C	951 685-9680	2765
Cargo Solution Brokerage Inc	4212	C	909 350-1644	3378
Hanks Inc	4212	D	909 350-8365	3401
Hub Group Trucking Inc	4212	B	909 770-8950	3406
RDS Logistics Group (PA)	4212	D	909 355-4100	3420
Cargo Solution Express Inc (PA)	4213	D	909 350-1644	3452
Estes Express Lines	4213	C	909 427-9850	3473
Friends Group Express Inc	4213	D	909 346-6814	3478
Hawk Transportation Inc	4213	D	800 709-4295	3486
Heartland Express Inc Iowa	4213	A	319 626-3600	3487
Kalway Inc	4213	D	800 303-0076	3498
McCollisters Trnsp Group Inc	4213	D	909 428-5700	3514
NY Transport Inc	4213	D	909 355-9832	3522
Saia Motor Freight Line LLC	4213	D	909 356-2808	3539
Swift Leasing Co LLC	4213	B	909 347-0500	3548
TCI Transportation Services	4213	C	909 355-8545	3550
TMT Industries Inc	4213	D	909 493-3441	3553
Xpo Logistics Freight Inc	4213	D	951 685-1244	3575
Ontrac Logistics Inc	4215	D	804 334-5000	3625
Advanced Strlztion Pdts Svcs I	4225	B	909 350-6987	3670
Dalton Trucking Inc (PA)	4225	C	909 823-0663	3694
Target Corporation	4225	D	909 355-6000	3763
Tonys Express Inc (PA)	4225	D	909 427-8700	3768
DSV Solutions LLC	4226	D	909 829-5804	3790
Blackrock Logistics Inc	4731	C	909 259-5357	3990
Dispatch Trucking LLC (PA)	4731	D	909 355-5531	4009
DSV Solutions LLC	4731	D	909 349-6100	4010
Ltl Ex Inc	4731	D	951 255-1222	4052
Pro Loaders Inc	4731	C	909 355-5531	4079
Syncreon America Inc	4731	D	909 610-4511	4104
San Gabriel Valley Water Co	4941	C	909 822-2201	4826
Burrtec Waste Industries Inc (HQ)	4953	C	909 429-4200	4870
Yucaipa Disposal Inc	4953	D	909 429-4200	4972
Inland Kenworth Inc (HQ)	5012	C	909 823-9955	5012
Los Angeles Truck Centers LLC	5012	C	909 510-4000	5014
Utility Trlr Sls Sthern Cal LL (PA)	5012	C	877 275-4887	5018
Anfinson Lumber Sales Inc (PA)	5031	D	951 681-4707	5146
James Hardie Building Pdts Inc	5031	C	909 355-6500	5169
Valori Sand & Gravel Company	5032	C	909 350-3000	5212
Daniel Gerard Worldwide Inc	5051	D	951 361-1111	5487
AC Pro Inc (PA)	5075	C	951 360-7849	5765
Lowes Home Centers LLC	5211	D	909 350-7900	7077
Foothill Home Improvement Center Inc	5251	D	909 355-3655	7118
Rotolo Chevrolet Inc	5511	C	866 756-9776	7291
Sunrise Ford	5511	D	909 822-4401	7307
Transwest Truck Center LLC	5511	D	909 770-5170	7319
Kaiser Foundation Hospitals	6324	B	909 427-3910	8327
Kaiser Permanente	6324	C	909 427-3910	8338
Bragg Investment Company Inc	7353	C	909 350-3738	10994
Guzman Grading and Paving Corp	7359	D	909 428-5960	11034
Integrated Intermodal Svcs Inc	7379	D	909 355-4100	12813
Amerit Fleet Solutions Inc	7549	A	909 357-0100	13708
Kaiser Foundation Hospitals	8011	A	909 427-5000	14823

Employee Codes: A=Over 500 employees, B=251-500
C=101-250, D=51-100, E=20-50, F=10-19, G=1-9

FONTANA CA

	SIC	EMP	PHONE	ENTRY#
United Fmly Care Inc A Med Cor	8011	C	909 874-1679	15141
Southern Cal Prmnnte Med Group	8062	B	909 427-5000	16440
Sweetgrace Home Hlth Svcs LLC	8099	D	909 463-7400	17337

FOOTHILL RANCH, CA - Orange County

	SIC	EMP	PHONE	ENTRY#
Belshire Trnsp Svcs Inc	4212	C	949 460-5200	3372
Venus Group Inc (PA)	5023	D	949 609-1299	5142
Hampton Products Intl Corp (PA)	5072	D	949 472-4256	5728
Daiwa Corporation	5091	D	562 375-6800	5976
Sgii Inc (PA)	5122	C	949 521-6161	6145
Kawasaki Motors Corp USA (HQ)	5571	B	949 837-4683	7397
Debisys Inc (PA)	6099	D	949 699-1401	7852
Loandepotcom LLC (DH)	6162	A	888 337-6888	7999
Strategic Asset Services LLC	6512	D	949 713-0053	8766
US Real Estate Services Inc	6531	D	949 598-9920	9205
Stonebridge Rlty Advisors Inc	7011	A	949 597-8700	10279
Image Options (PA)	7319	D	949 586-7665	10732
Ibaset Federal Services LLC (PA)	7371	D	949 598-5200	11653
Sun Healthcare Group Inc (DH)	8011	B		15105
Skilled Healthcare LLC (DH)	8051	C	949 282-5800	15674
Healthcare Talent	8099	D	714 341-1197	17249
Global Solutions Integration	8711	D	949 307-1849	19244
Tae Life Sciences Us LLC (PA)	8731	D	949 344-6112	19777
Tae Technologies Inc (PA)	8731	C	949 830-2117	19778

FOREST FALLS, CA - San Bernardino County

	SIC	EMP	PHONE	ENTRY#
Forest Home Inc	7032	C	909 389-2300	10401

FORESTHILL, CA - Placer County

	SIC	EMP	PHONE	ENTRY#
Placer County Water Agency	4911	D	530 367-6701	4660

FORESTVILLE, CA - Sonoma County

	SIC	EMP	PHONE	ENTRY#
Farmhouse Inn & Restaurant LLC	7011	D	707 887-3300	9794

FORT BRAGG, CA - Mendocino County

	SIC	EMP	PHONE	ENTRY#
Anderson Logging Inc	2411	D	707 964-2770	2473
Waste MGT Collectn Recycl Inc	4953	D	707 964-9172	4961
Tradewinds Lodge (PA)	7011	C	707 964-4761	10317
Sherwood Oaks Enterprises Inc	8051	D	707 964-6333	15664
Mendocino Coast District Hosp (PA)	8062	B	707 961-1234	16258
Mendocino Coast Clinics Inc	8093	D	707 964-1251	17088
Cv Starr Community Center	8322	D	707 964-9446	17948

FORT IRWIN, CA - San Bernardino County

	SIC	EMP	PHONE	ENTRY#
Lockheed Martin Corporation	4225	C	760 386-2572	3725

FORTUNA, CA - Humboldt County

	SIC	EMP	PHONE	ENTRY#
Redwood Memorial Hosp Fortuna (PA)	8062	C	707 725-7327	16360

FOSTER CITY, CA - San Mateo County

	SIC	EMP	PHONE	ENTRY#
AC Square Inc	1731	B	650 293-2730	1655
Sling Media LLC	4812	C	650 293-8000	4226
Adchemy Inc	4813	D	650 581-4600	4250
Sony Interactive Entertainment America LLC	5092	A	650 655-8000	5998
Home Depot USA Inc	5211	C	650 525-9343	6967
Menlo Gateway Inc	6514	D	650 356-2900	8878
Midpen Housing Corporation	6552	B	650 356-2900	9264
USB Slrcity Mstr Tnant 2009 LL	6719	C	650 963-5693	9346
Founders Management II Corp	7011	B	650 570-5700	9801
United Pacific Hotel Group LP	7011	C	650 295-6103	10333
Sfn Group Inc	7363	A	650 348-4967	11332
E2open Inc	7371	D	866 432-6736	11559
Qualys Inc (PA)	7371	A	650 801-6100	11857
Sony Corporation of America	7371	C	650 655-8000	11936
Gridgain Systems Inc (PA)	7372	C	650 241-2281	12213
Matrixx Software Inc (PA)	7373	D	669 267-6333	12486
Cybersource Corporation (HQ)	7374	C	650 432-7350	12563
All Covered Inc	7379	B	650 486-5000	12727
Sony Interactive Entrmt LLC	7389	D	858 824-5501	13481
Visa Inc (PA)	7389	A	650 432-3200	13543
Visa International Svc Assn (HQ)	7389	A	650 432-3200	13544
Visa USA Inc (HQ)	7389	D	650 432-3200	13545
Peninsula Jewish Community Ctr	8322	D	650 212-7522	18079
Pjcc	8399	D	650 212-7522	18617
Motiv Power Systems Inc	8711	C	650 458-4804	19328
Peter H Mattson & Co Inc	8731	D	650 356-2500	19757
Legacy Prtners Residential Inc (PA)	8741	B	650 571-2250	20138
Pacific Partners MGT Svcs Inc	8741	D	650 358-5804	20171
United Innovation Services Inc	8742	D	831 334-0573	20598

FOUNTAIN VALLEY, CA - Orange County

	SIC	EMP	PHONE	ENTRY#
Brightview Companies LLC	0782	C	714 437-1586	477
Rba Builders Inc	1542	D	714 895-9000	1003
Pan-Pacific Mechanical LLC (PA)	1711	C	949 474-9170	1524
Jmg Security Systems Inc	1731	D	714 545-8882	1759
Pacific Aquascape Inc	1799	D	714 843-5734	2303
ML Kishigo Mfg Co LLC	2389	D	949 852-1963	2469
Orange County Water District (PA)	4941	D	714 378-3200	4814
Orange County Sanitation (PA)	4953	D	714 962-2411	4916
Hyundai Motor America (HQ)	5012	B	714 965-3000	5011
Mobis Parts America LLC (HQ)	5013	D	786 515-1101	5051
Kingston Technology Company Inc (PA)	5045	A	714 435-2600	5322
Custom Power LLC	5063	D	714 962-7600	5551
Motive Energy Inc (PA)	5063	D	714 888-2525	5580
Tires Warehouse LLC	5531	B	714 432-8851	7379
Ceridian Tax Service Inc	7291	B	714 963-1311	10520
Hyundai Autoever America LLC	7378	D	714 965-3000	12708
Safeguard On Demand Inc	7381	C	800 640-2327	13031
Mile Square Golf Course	7992	C	714 962-5541	14276
Fountain Vly Rgnal Hosp Med CT	8062	A	714 966-7200	16091
Memorial Health Services (PA)	8062	B	714 377-2900	16252
Memorialcare Medical Group	8062	D	714 378-7000	16256
Memorlcare Srgcal Ctr At Ornge	8062	D	714 369-1100	16257
Orange Cast Mem Care Brast Ctr	8062	D	714 378-7955	16294
Orange Coast Memorial Med Ctr (HQ)	8062	D	714 378-7000	16297
Boys Grls Clubs Huntington Vly (PA)	8641	D	714 531-2582	18826
Pacific Advnced Cvil Engrg Inc (PA)	8711	D	714 481-7300	19346
Richard Brady & Associates Inc	8711	D	657 204-9124	19376
Spec Services Inc	8711	D	714 963-8077	19392
Memorial Healthtec Labratories	8731	A	714 962-4677	19735
Ampm Systems Inc	8742	D	949 629-7800	20272

FOWLER, CA - Fresno County

	SIC	EMP	PHONE	ENTRY#
Bee Sweet Citrus Inc	0723	C	559 834-5345	256
Simonian Brothers Inc (PA)	0723	C	559 834-5921	303
Simonian Brothers Inc	0723	C	559 834-5921	304
Sunshine Raisin Corporation (PA)	0723	C	559 834-5981	307
Trius Trucking Inc	4213	D	559 834-4000	3556

FREMONT, CA - Alameda County

	SIC	EMP	PHONE	ENTRY#
Del Contes Landscaping Inc	0781	D	510 353-6030	427
Sansei Gardens Inc	0782	C	510 226-9191	536
Vasona Management Inc	1521	D	510 413-0091	738
Advance Construction Tech Inc	1522	D	510 876-8403	745
Bjork Construction Company Inc (PA)	1542	D	510 656-4688	873
Level-It Instlltions Group Inc	1542	D	604 942-2022	960
Chrisp Company (PA)	1611	D	510 656-2840	1088
Dryco Construction Inc (PA)	1611	D	510 438-6500	1100
Pan-Pacific Mechanical LLC	1711	B	650 561-8810	1525
Superior Automatic Sprnklr Co	1711	D	408 946-7272	1579
Syserco Inc (PA)	1711	D	510 498-1171	1582
Bergelectric Corp	1731	D	510 314-8590	1680
Kositch Enterprises Inc	1731	C	510 657-4460	1763
Oeg Inc	1731	D	408 909-9399	1794
RK Electric Inc	1731	C	510 772-4125	1822
Alcal Specialty Contg Inc	1742	D	510 477-9380	1901
Bayside Interiors Inc (PA)	1742	D	510 438-9171	1907
Walters & Wolf Interiors (PA)	1751	D	415 243-9400	2025
Walters & Wolf Glass Company (PA)	1793	C	510 490-1115	2208
Seven Up Btlg Co San Francisco (HQ)	2086	C	925 938-8777	2411
American Air Liquide Inc (DH)	2813	A	510 624-4000	2572
West Coast Quartz Corporation (HQ)	3229	D	510 249-2160	2689
3dconnexion Inc	3577	D	510 713-6000	2821
Colleen & Herb Enterprises Inc	3599	D	510 226-6083	2850
Optoplex Corporation	3661	B	510 490-9930	2889
Oncore Manufacturing LLC	3672	B	510 516-5488	2909
Ic Sensors Inc	3674	D	510 498-1570	2922
Patriot Memory Inc (PA)	3674	D	510 979-1021	2929
Compass Components Inc (PA)	3679	C	510 656-4700	2941
Tenergy Corporation	3691	D	510 687-0388	2950
Evolve Manufacturing Tech Inc	3841	D	510 690-8959	3051
S & M Moving Systems	4213	D	510 497-2300	3537
Grm Information MGT Svcs Inc (PA)	4226	B	201 798-7100	3792
Rk Logistics Group Inc	4731	C	510 298-5128	4085
Three Way Logistics Inc (PA)	4731	D	408 748-3929	4106
Alom Technologies Corporation	4783	D	510 360-3600	4125
Verizon Bus Netwrk Svcs LLC	4812	C	510 497-2500	4241
Axxcelera Brdband Wireless Inc	4899	C	510 573-4708	4529
Pacific Gas and Electric Co	4911	B	510 770-2025	4641
Alameda County Water District (PA)	4941	D	510 668-4200	4763
BFI Waste Systems N Amer Inc	4953	C	510 657-1350	4865
Wm Healthcare Solutions Inc	4953	D	713 328-7350	4970
Homelegance (PA)	5021	D	510 933-6888	5090
E & E Co Ltd (PA)	5023	C	510 490-9788	5115
PJs Lumber Inc	5031	C	510 743-5300	5181
Amax Engineering Corporation (PA)	5045	C	510 651-8886	5269

GEOGRAPHIC SECTION

FRESNO CA

Company	SIC	EMP	PHONE	ENTRY#
American Portwell Tech Inc (PA)	5045	D	510 403-3399	5271
Asus Computer International	5045	C	510 739-3777	5275
HPM Incorporated	5045	D	510 353-0770	5312
Iron Systems Inc (PA)	5045	D	408 943-8000	5317
Lexar Media Inc	5045	C	510 413-1200	5324
Penguin Computing Inc (DH)	5045	D	415 954-2800	5334
Synerzip LLC	5045	D	510 579-9673	5359
Pjs Rebar Inc	5051	D	510 490-0321	5510
Greatlink International Inc	5063	A	510 657-1667	5563
Atlas Sales and Rentals Inc	5064	D	510 713-3313	5599
Braemac (ca) LLC	5065	D	510 687-1000	5634
Delta America Ltd (HQ)	5065	C	510 668-5100	5646
Exar International Inc	5065	C	949 753-8108	5649
Fortron/Source Corporation	5065	D	510 440-0188	5652
Nitto Denko America Inc	5065	D	510 445-5400	5683
Genmark Automation (DH)	5084	C	510 897-3400	5836
Pape Material Handling Inc	5084	D	510 659-4100	5857
Cleansmart Solutions Inc (DH)	5111	D	510 413-4700	6059
Kilam Inc	5136	C	510 943-4040	6178
Twin Hill Acquisition Co Inc	5136	D	281 776-7000	6191
Sysco San Francisco Inc	5141	A	510 226-3000	6404
San Francisco Herb & Natural Food Co Inc	5149	C	510 770-1215	6664
Home Depot USA Inc	5211	D	510 490-0191	6976
Lowes Home Centers LLC	5211	D	510 344-4920	7085
J M Fremont Motors LLC	5511	D	510 403-3700	7237
Td Synnex Corporation (PA)	5734	C	510 656-3333	7449
Yadav Enterprises Inc	5812	C	510 792-3393	7519
Advantel Incorporated	5999	C	800 377-4911	7570
Fremont Bank (HQ)	6022	C	510 505-5226	7689
Cal Coast Financial Inc	6162	D	510 683-9850	7940
Lipman Insur Admnistrators Inc	6371	D	510 796-4676	8462
Ardenbrook Inc	6531	D	510 794-1020	8901
Mission-Bishop Real Estate Inc	6531	D	510 796-2100	9100
Land Services Ldscp Contrs Inc	6552	D	510 656-8101	9258
On-Tech Enterprises	6719	C		9326
Ashford Trs Fremont LLC	7011	D	510 413-3700	9617
Kidztopros Inc	7032	C	408 421-0584	10406
Headway Technologies Inc	7231	A	425 503-2131	10498
Massage Envy	7299	D	510 456-3689	10560
American Bldg Maint Co of Ill	7349	B	510 573-1618	10854
DMS Facility Services Inc	7349	A	510 656-9400	10891
Signature Building Maint Inc	7349	D	408 377-8066	10966
Abjayon Inc	7371	C	510 824-3260	11375
Actividentity Inc	7371	B	510 574-0100	11377
Bista Solutions Inc (PA)	7371	C	858 401-2332	11459
Cognitiveclouds Software Inc	7371	D	415 234-3611	11502
Cross Match Inc	7371	C	650 474-4000	11523
Dgn Technologies Inc (PA)	7371	D	510 252-0346	11540
Infoway Solutions LLC	7371	D	925 435-9672	11662
Instant Systems Inc	7371	D	510 657-8100	11670
Nisum Technologies Inc	7371	A	714 579-7979	11781
Ponyai Inc	7371	B	510 906-8868	11839
Privacera Inc	7371	C	510 413-7300	11845
Softsol Resources Inc (HQ)	7371	D	510 824-2000	11930
Sonata Software North Amer Inc (HQ)	7371	D	510 791-7220	11934
SRS Consulting Inc (PA)	7371	B	510 252-0625	11942
Startup Farms Intl LLC	7371	D	510 440-0110	11945
Videojeeves Inc	7371	C	877 958-8129	12022
Alertenterprise Inc (PA)	7372	C	510 440-0840	12087
Loginext Solutions Inc	7372	C	510 894-6225	12257
Nextracker LLC (HQ)	7372	B	510 270-2500	12289
Snapwiz Inc	7372	C	510 328-3277	12356
AVI-Spl LLC	7373	A	510 344-5618	12425
Azuga Inc (DH)	7373	B	866 497-2512	12426
Droisys Inc (PA)	7373	D	408 874-8333	12449
Milestone Technologies Inc (PA)	7373	A	510 651-2454	12489
Ravenswood Solutions Inc (HQ)	7373	D	650 241-3661	12517
Vertisystem Inc	7373	C	510 794-8099	12542
Actividentity Corporation	7374	C	510 574-0100	12547
Edata Solutions Inc	7374	A	510 574-5380	12566
Hyve Solutions Corporation (HQ)	7374	C	855 869-6873	12580
Basic Solutions Corp	7379	C	510 573-3658	12739
Covestic LLC	7379	D	425 803-9889	12766
Droisys Inc	7379	C	408 329-1761	12780
Enexus Global Inc	7379	D	510 936-4044	12785
Metabyte Inc	7379	D	510 494-9700	12837
Rahi Systems Inc (HQ)	7379	D	510 651-2205	12867
Overton Security Services Inc	7381	C	510 791-7380	13014
Concentrix Corporation (PA)	7389	A	800 747-0583	13242
Keweier Nano Technologies Inc	7389	C	415 948-4335	13336
Sonova USA Inc	7389	D	510 743-3900	13480
Td Synnex Corporation	7389	D	510 688-3507	13501
YC Cable Usa Inc (HQ)	7389	D	510 824-2788	13560
U-Haul Co of California (DH)	7513	C	602 287-7830	13570
U-Haul Neighborhood Dealer	7519	D	510 371-0122	13599
Jabil Silver Creek Inc (HQ)	7692	C	669 255-2900	13752
Raymond Handling Concepts Corp (DH)	7699	D	510 745-7500	13794
Bay Area Community Health (PA)	8011	C	510 770-8040	14623
Fremont Ambltory Srgery Ctr LP	8011	D	510 456-4600	14754
Kaiser Foundation Hospitals	8011	A	510 248-3000	14838
Permanente Medical Group Inc	8011	A	510 248-3000	14969
Washington Otptent Srgery Ctr	8011	D	510 791-5374	15198
Willow Springs LLC	8011	C	510 796-1100	15211
Womens Health Specialists	8011	D	510 248-1470	15213
Ed Sped Solutions Inc	8049	D	408 372-8280	15279
Crestwood Behavioral Hlth Inc	8051	B	510 651-1244	15415
Crestwood Behavioral Hlth Inc	8051	C	510 793-8383	15416
Emeritus Corporation	8051	C	510 797-4011	15435
Mariner Health Care Inc	8051	C	510 792-3743	15563
Windsor Cnvlscent Rhblttion CT	8051	C	510 793-7222	15739
Fremont Bhc Hospital Inc	8062	D	510 796-1100	16093
Washington Hosp Healthcare Sys	8062	A	510 797-3342	16624
Washington On Wheels	8062	D	510 494-7053	16625
Personalis Inc (PA)	8071	C	650 752-1300	16740
Aegis Senior Communities LLC	8082	D	510 739-0909	16798
Prince Peace Lutheran Church	8211	D	510 797-8186	17742
Bay Area Community Svcs Inc	8322	D	510 656-7742	17847
Kidango Inc (PA)	8351	A	510 897-6900	18324
Kidango Inc	8351	D	510 494-9601	18326
Aegis Asssted Living Prpts LLC	8361	C	510 739-1515	18368
Good Shepherd Lutheran HM of W	8361	D	510 505-1244	18440
American High Schl Booster CLB	8641	D	510 796-1776	18811
Young MNS Chrstn Assn of E Bay	8641	B	510 656-7243	18976
Young MNS Chrstn Assn of E Bay	8641	B	510 683-9165	18982
Young MNS Chrstn Assn of E Bay	8641	B	510 683-9107	18983
Young MNS Chrstn Assn of E Bay	8641	B	510 683-9147	18984
Novariant Inc	8711	D	510 933-4800	19335
PTEC Solutions Inc (PA)	8711	B	510 358-3578	19365
Raxium Inc	8711	D	510 296-9935	19372
Bis Research Inc	8731	C	510 404-8135	19665
Eurofins Discoverx Pdts LLC	8731	D	510 979-1415	19691
Pall Fortebio LLC	8731	D	650 322-1360	19754
Hound Labs Inc	8734	D	408 893-2654	19981
ISE Labs Inc (DH)	8734	C	510 687-2500	19985
United Mfg Assembly Inc	8734	D	510 490-4680	20003
Delta Electronics Americas Ltd (DH)	8741	D	510 668-5111	20076
San Jose Arena Management LLC	8741	C	408 287-7070	20200
Agama Solutions Inc	8742	C	510 796-9300	20264
AMS Ventures Inc	8742	B	301 980-5087	20274
Rk Logistics Group Inc (PA)	8742	D	408 942-8107	20529
Sigmaways Inc	8742	C	510 573-4208	20545
Omron STI Machine Services Inc	8748	D	714 693-1041	20820

FRENCH CAMP, CA - San Joaquin County

Company	SIC	EMP	PHONE	ENTRY#
Granite Construction Company	1611	C	209 982-4750	1111
Fresno Truck Center	5012	C	209 983-2400	5010
Health Plan of San Joaquin	6324	C	209 942-6300	8303
San Joaquin General Hospital	8062	B	209 468-6000	16382
San Jquin Gen Hosp Fndtion A C	8062	A	209 468-6000	16384
County of San Joaquin	8093	D	209 468-6280	17042
County of San Joaquin	8322	D	209 468-6966	17939

FRESNO, CA - Fresno County

Company	SIC	EMP	PHONE	ENTRY#
Baloian Packing Co Inc (PA)	0161	D	559 485-9200	21
Baloian Packing Co Inc	0161	D	559 441-7043	22
Gerawan Ranches	0175	C	559 787-8780	107
Rich Harvest Inc	0175	D	559 252-8000	113
Campos Family Farms LLC	0191	D	559 275-3000	172
Olam Farming Inc	0191	B	559 446-6446	192
Woolf Farming Co Cal Inc	0191	A	559 945-9292	208
Fowler Packing Company Inc (PA)	0723	C	559 834-5911	269
Olam Americas LLC (DH)	0723	A	559 447-1390	293
Champagne Landscape Nurs Inc	0782	D	559 277-8188	482
West Coast Arborists Inc	0783	C	559 275-2086	563
Cvc Construction Corp	1521	B	559 276-6050	669
Granville Homes Inc	1521	D	559 268-2000	681
Quality Group Homes Inc	1521	C	559 252-6844	710
Harris Construction Co Inc	1542	D	559 251-0301	929
Karsyn Construction Inc	1542	D	559 271-2900	950
Quiring Corporation	1542	C	559 432-2800	996
Quiring General LLC	1542	C	559 432-2800	997
Zumwalt Construction Inc	1542	D	559 252-1000	1068
Teichert Inc	1611	C	559 813-3100	1173
Linkus Enterprises LLC	1623	B	559 256-6600	1231
Zim Industries Inc (PA)	1623	D	559 834-1551	1283
Clark Bros Inc	1629	D	209 392-6144	1293

Employee Codes: A=Over 500 employees, B=251-500
C=101-250, D=51-100, E=20-50, F=10-19, G=1-9

FRESNO CA — GEOGRAPHIC SECTION

Company	SIC	EMP	PHONE	ENTRY#
California Coml Solar Inc	1711	C	559 667-9200	1390
Cosco Fire Protection Inc	1711	C	559 275-3795	1408
Energy Concepts Entps Inc	1711	D	559 485-2504	1428
Fresno Plumbing & Heating Inc (PA)	1711	C	559 294-0200	1446
New England Shtmtl & Mech Co	1711	C	559 268-7375	1508
Strategic Mechanical Inc	1711	C	559 291-1952	1572
General Coatings Corporation	1721	D	559 495-4004	1618
Wm B Saleh Co	1721	D	559 255-2046	1647
A-C Electric Company	1731	D	559 233-2208	1650
Bergelectric Corp	1731	C	559 860-2590	1679
Howe Electric Inc	1731	C	559 255-8992	1751
Howe Electric Construction Inc	1731	C	559 255-8992	1752
Modesto Industrial Elec Co Inc	1731	D	559 292-4714	1780
Rex More Elec Cntrs Engners In	1731	C	559 294-1300	1820
Bratton Masonry Inc (PA)	1741	D	559 291-9423	1880
Northwest Exteriors Inc	1751	D	559 456-1632	2010
Four CS Service Inc	1761	C	559 237-3990	2065
Fresno Roofing Co Inc	1761	C	559 255-8377	2066
Terry Tuell Concrete Inc	1771	D	559 431-0812	2166
A J Excavation Inc	1794	C	559 408-5908	2211
Kroeker Inc	1795	C	559 237-3764	2239
Foster Poultry Farms	2015	B	559 265-2000	2344
E & J Gallo Winery	2084	C	559 458-0807	2381
Brandt Consolidated Inc	2875	D	559 499-2100	2638
City of Fresno	4111	B	559 621-7433	3127
KWPH Enterprises	4119	A	559 443-5900	3269
First Student Inc	4151	C	559 268-4077	3340
United Parcel Service Inc	4212	D	559 442-2950	3431
Estes Express Lines	4213	D	559 441-0915	3475
Inland Star Dist Ctrs Inc (PA)	4213	D	559 237-2052	3493
J B Hunt Transport Inc	4213	C	385 226-4538	3495
KS Trans Services Co	4213	C	559 264-5650	3501
Xpo Logistics Freight Inc	4213	C	559 485-1164	3569
Royal Express Inc (PA)	4214	C	559 272-3500	3593
Unified Grocers Inc	4222	C	559 268-8454	3662
Charles Matoian Entps Inc (PA)	4225	C	559 445-8600	3684
Fresno Unified School District	4225	A	559 457-3030	3707
Piedmont Airlines Inc	4512	C	559 269-5694	3841
Skywest Airlines Inc	4512	C	559 252-3400	3845
West Air Inc	4513	C	559 454-7843	3860
Rogers Helicopters Inc	4522	D	559 299-4903	3868
Conner Logistics Inc	4731	D	888 939-4637	3999
DTL Transport Inc	4789	D	559 277-9075	4153
Dish Wireless LLC	4812	C	559 515-6866	4214
Entercom Media Corp	4832	D	559 490-0106	4380
Iheartcommunications Inc	4832	D	559 230-4300	4386
Kfsn Television LLC	4833	C	559 442-1170	4443
Kmph Fox 26	4833	C	559 255-2600	4445
Pacific Gas and Electric Co	4911	A	559 263-7361	4605
Pacific Gas and Electric Co	4911	A	209 726-7650	4611
Pacific Gas and Electric Co	4911	B	559 263-7152	4649
City of Fresno	4941	C	559 621-5300	4772
Aries Industries Inc	4952	C	559 291-0383	4845
Electric Rcyclers Intl - Ind	4953	D	317 522-1414	4891
Electronic Recyclers Intl Inc (PA)	4953	C	559 442-3960	4892
Kochergen Farms Composting	4953	D	559 266-2650	4903
Fresno Irrigation District	4971	D	559 233-7161	4987
Fresno Auto Dealers Auction	5012	A	559 268-8051	5008
Fresno Truck Center	5012	D	559 486-4310	5009
Contract Interiors San Diego	5021	D	559 276-0561	5085
Williams Scotsman Inc	5039	C	559 441-8181	5234
Valley Iron Inc (PA)	5051	D	559 485-3900	5529
Electric Motor Shop	5063	C	559 233-1471	5556
Brix Group Inc (PA)	5065	C	559 457-4700	5635
Charles McMurray Co (PA)	5072	D	559 292-5751	5725
Edward B Ward & Company Inc	5075	D	559 487-1860	5767
Netafim Irrigation Inc (HQ)	5083	B	559 453-6800	5811
Vucovich Inc (PA)	5083	D	559 486-8020	5816
Blue White Robotics US Inc (PA)	5084	C	559 731-2239	5822
Gray Lift Inc	5084	D	559 268-6621	5838
Lakos Corporation (HQ)	5084	D	559 255-1601	5843
Western Refining Inc	5084	D	602 286-1400	5884
Titan Mfg & Distrg Inc	5091	D	559 475-0882	5982
Paisley Crafts LLC	5092	C	559 291-4444	5994
Schnitzer Fresno Inc	5093	D	559 233-3211	6014
C&S Wholesale Grocers Inc	5141	C	559 442-4700	6243
Saladinos Inc (PA)	5141	C	559 271-3700	6284
Smart & Final Stores Inc	5141	B	559 229-2944	6317
Smart & Final Stores LLC	5141	C	559 439-5954	6363
Producers Dairy Foods Inc (PA)	5142	C	559 264-6583	6426
Freshko Produce Services Inc	5148	C	559 497-7000	6544
Fruit Fillings LLC	5148	C	559 237-4715	6548
Wawona Packing Co LLC	5148	A		6595
J & D Meat Company	5149	C	559 445-1123	6635
Sun-Maid Growers California (PA)	5149	A	559 896-8000	6673
Pacific Grain & Foods LLC (PA)	5153	D	559 276-2580	6693
Donaghy Sales Inc (PA)	5181	C	559 486-0901	6761
Fresno Beverage Company Inc	5181	C	559 650-1500	6762
Home Depot USA Inc	5211	C	559 431-9860	6988
Home Depot USA Inc	5211	C	559 455-9124	6994
Lowes Home Centers LLC	5211	C	559 436-6266	7030
Western Building Materials Co (PA)	5211	D	559 454-8500	7113
Save Mart Supermarkets Disc	5411	C	559 261-4123	7149
Central Valley Trlr Repr Inc	5511	D	559 233-8444	7181
Fresno Chrysler Jeep Inc	5511	D	559 431-4000	7214
Fresno Truck Center (PA)	5511	D	559 486-4310	7215
Lithia Motors Inc	5511	C	559 435-8400	7252
Weber Motors Fresno Inc	5511	D	559 447-6700	7332
Ekc Enterprises Inc	5734	D	559 438-0330	7443
Counter Hospitality Group LLC	5812	D	559 228-9735	7469
Safety Network Inc (PA)	5999	D	559 291-8000	7592
Chase Inc	6021	D	559 275-7331	7610
Central Valley Cmnty Bancorp (PA)	6022	C	559 298-1775	7672
Central Valley Community Bank (HQ)	6022	C	800 298-1775	7673
Premier Valley Bank	6029	C	559 438-2002	7736
Educational Employees Cr Un (PA)	6061	C	559 437-7700	7762
Educational Employees Cr Un	6061	D	559 896-0222	7763
Noble Credit Union	6061	C	559 252-5000	7785
Xander Mortgage & Real Estate	6162	D	855 905-2575	8028
Carrington Mortgage Svcs LLC	6211	C	559 261-1724	8071
Merrill Lynch Prce Fnner Smith	6211	D	559 436-0919	8133
Sante Health System Inc (PA)	6321	D	559 228-5400	8271
Anthem Insurance Companies Inc	6324	D	559 230-6200	8280
California Physicians Service	6324	D	559 440-4000	8290
Kaiser Foundation Hospitals	6324	D	559 448-4620	8308
Kaiser Foundation Hospitals	6324	A	559 448-4500	8333
State Compensation Insur Fund	6331	C	559 433-2700	8413
Old Republic Title Holdg Inc	6361	C	559 440-9249	8453
Acclamation Insurance Mgt Svcs	6411	D	559 227-9891	8477
Dibuduo Dfendis Insur Brks LLC (PA)	6411	D	559 432-0222	8545
Healthcomp LLC (PA)	6411	B	559 499-2450	8583
Hub Intrntional Insur Svcs Inc	6411	D	559 447-4600	8587
James G Parker Insurance Assoc (PA)	6411	D	559 222-7722	8596
Nau Country Insurance Company	6411	C	559 252-7400	8620
Sunland Insurance Agency	6411	D	559 251-7861	8665
Wm Michael Stemler Inc	6411	D	559 228-4144	8690
University Cal San Francisco	6519	D	559 251-3033	8891
Guarantee Real Estate	6531	D	559 650-6030	9034
JMS Realtors Ltd (PA)	6531	D	559 490-1500	9058
Westco Equities Inc (PA)	6531	D	559 228-6788	9213
Uniwell Corporation	6552	D	559 268-1000	9278
Art Piccadilly Shaw LLC	7011	C	559 375-7760	9613
Art Piccadilly Shaw LLC	7011	D	559 224-4200	9614
Brisan LLC	7011	C	559 233-6650	9661
Club One Casino Inc	7011	B	559 497-3000	9708
Fresno Airport Hotels LLC	7011	D	559 252-3611	9804
Piccadilly Hospitality LLC	7011	D	559 348-5520	10118
Six Continents Hotels Inc	7011	D	559 272-7840	10244
Starwood Htels Rsrts Wrldwide	7011	D	559 230-8470	10272
Mission Linen Supply	7213	D	559 268-0647	10445
Vestis Corporation	7213	C	559 291-6631	10458
Automatic Leasing Inc	7215	B	559 233-2444	10461
Ameripride Services Inc	7218	D	559 266-0627	10477
Buckingham Property Management	7299	D	559 322-1105	10531
Rainbow - Brite Indus Svcs LLC	7349	A	559 925-2580	10952
Elitecare Medical Staffing LLC	7361	D	559 438-7700	11128
Hire Up Staffing Service	7361	B	559 579-1331	11149
Maxim Healthcare Services Inc	7363	D	559 224-0299	11304
Volt Management Corp	7363	D	559 435-1255	11359
Famous Software LLC	7371	D	559 431-8100	11592
Forward Advantage Inc	7371	D	559 447-1777	11606
Yosemite Technologies Inc	7371	D	559 449-8181	12055
Geil Enterprises Inc	7381	A	559 495-3000	12977
Vigilant Private Security	7381	D	559 800-7233	13073
Pelco Inc (HQ)	7382	A	559 292-1981	13137
Turner Camera SEC Systems Inc	7382	D	559 486-3466	13152
Bradford Messenger Service	7389	C	559 252-0775	13217
California Hlth Collaborative (PA)	7389	D	559 221-6315	13221
Fresno Metro Flood Ctrl Dst	7389	D	559 456-3292	13298
Future Fast Inc	7389	D	559 813-0113	13299
Nabiekim Enterprises Inc	7389	D	646 645-1958	13388
Pape Trucks Inc	7538	D	559 268-4344	13669
Bowie Enterprises (PA)	7542	D	559 227-6221	13687
Jacks Car Wash 3	7542	D	559 438-8201	13694
Horizon Global Americas Inc	7549	D	559 266-9000	13715
Vly Air Cond & RPR	7623	D	559 237-2123	13730

GEOGRAPHIC SECTION

GARDEN GROVE CA

	SIC	EMP	PHONE	ENTRY#
Cablecom LLC	7629	D	559 412-8720	13734
Newport Television LLC	7922	B	559 761-0243	14049
Fort Wash Golf & Cntry CLB	7997	D	559 434-1702	14376
San Joaquin Country Club	7997	D	559 439-3483	14439
GLad Entertainment Inc (PA)	7999	D	559 292-9000	14528
California Eye Institute	8011	C	559 449-5000	14644
Cardio Vascular Associates	8011	D	559 439-6808	14655
Cardiovascular Consultants Hea	8011	D	559 432-4303	14657
Central Cal Ear Nose Throat ME	8011	D	559 432-3724	14666
Central Cal Fclty Med Group In	8011	D	559 435-6600	14667
Central Cal Fclty Med Group In	8011	D	559 435-4700	14668
Central Cal Fclty Med Group In (PA)	8011	D	559 453-5200	14669
Central Cal Fclty Med Group In	8011	D	559 320-1090	14670
Community Regional Medical Ctr	8011	D	559 459-2415	14704
Eye Q Vision Care (PA)	8011	C	559 486-2000	14744
Kaiser Foundation Hospitals	8011	A	559 448-4500	14846
Permanente Medical Group Inc	8011	A	559 448-4500	14962
Sierra PCF Orthpdic Ctr Med Gr	8011	C	559 256-5200	15060
United Hlth Ctrs of San Jquin (PA)	8011	D	559 646-6618	15142
Urology Associates Central Cal	8011	D	559 321-2800	15170
Veterans Health Administration	8011	A	559 225-6100	15187
Vision Care Ctr A Med Group In (PA)	8011	D	559 486-2000	15196
Covenant Care California LLC	8051	D	559 251-8463	15403
Fresno Skilled Nursing	8051	D	559 268-5361	15482
Manning Gardens Care Ctr Inc	8051	D	559 834-2586	15559
North Pt Hlth Wellness Ctr LLC	8051	D	559 320-2200	15596
Sunrise Senior Living	8051	D	559 325-8170	15696
Twilight Hven A Cal Nn-Prfit C	8051	D	559 251-8417	15708
Valley Healthcare Center LLC	8051	D	559 251-7161	15716
Hinds Hospice (PA)	8052	C	559 674-0407	15762
California HM For The Aged Inc	8059	C	559 251-8414	15825
Community Hospitals Centl Cal (PA)	8062	A	559 459-6000	16013
Community Hospitals Centl Cal	8062	A	559 459-6000	16014
Fresno Cmnty Hosp & Med Ctr (HQ)	8062	A	559 459-3948	16096
Fresno Cmnty Hosp & Med Ctr	8062	A	559 459-6000	16097
Fresno Heart Hospital LLC	8062	B	559 433-8000	16098
Fresno Surgery Center LP (PA)	8062	C	559 431-8000	16099
Saint Agnes Medical Center (HQ)	8062	A	559 450-3000	16368
Valley Childrens Hospital	8062	C	559 353-7442	16611
Fresno Sklled Nrsing Wllness C	8069	D	559 268-5361	16682
Unilab Corporation	8071	A	559 225-5076	16760
Maxim Healthcare Services Inc	8082	C	559 227-2250	16894
Goodwage Therapy Assoc LLC	8093	D	559 434-1969	17065
Mhm Services Inc	8093	C	559 412-8121	17095
San Jquin Vly Rhbltttion Hosp A (HQ)	8093	B	559 436-3600	17125
Central California Blood Ctr (PA)	8099	C	559 389-5433	17203
Aaron Dowling Incorporated	8111	D	559 432-4500	17355
Baker Manock & Jensen Pc	8111	C	559 432-5400	17376
Lozano Smith LLP	8111	C	559 431-5600	17558
McCormick Brstow Shppard Wyte (PA)	8111	C	559 433-1300	17565
State Center Cmnty College Dst	8222	C	559 442-4600	17789
California State Univ Long Bch	8299	C	559 278-2216	17805
California Autism Center	8322	D	559 475-7860	17857
County of Fresno	8322	C	559 600-2822	17904
Exceptnal Prents Unlimited Inc	8322	C	559 229-2000	17971
Family Options LLC	8322	C	559 275-2323	17977
Fresno Cnty Ecnmic Opprtnties	8322	D	559 486-6587	17986
Fresno Cnty Ecnmic Opprtnties	8322	D	559 263-1000	17987
Fresno Cnty Ecnmic Opprtnties (PA)	8322	A	559 263-1010	17988
Fresno Cnty Ecnmic Opprtnties	8322	D	559 263-1013	17989
Ser-Jobs For Prgress Inc - San (PA)	8322	D	559 452-0881	18128
Welbe Health LLC	8322	C	559 777-6722	18190
ARC Fresno/Madera Counties (PA)	8331	D	559 226-6268	18205
Vocation Plus Inc	8331	D	559 221-8019	18255
Good Shepherd Lutheran HM of W	8361	D	559 454-8514	18442
Humangood Norcal	8361	D	559 439-4770	18453
Innovative Integrated Hlth Inc (PA)	8361	C	559 400-6420	18460
Leisure Care LLC	8361	C	559 434-1237	18470
Noia Residential Services Inc	8361	D	559 485-5555	18494
Valley Teen Ranch	8361	D	559 437-1144	18536
Fresnos Chaffee Zoo Corp	8422	D	559 498-5910	18688
Rh Community Builders LP	8611	D	559 492-1373	18719
Reading and Beyond	8641	D	559 840-1068	18900
Calif Stat Univ Fres Foun	8699	D	559 278-0850	19072
BSK Associates	8711	D	559 497-2888	19163
County of Fresno	8711	D	559 600-4078	19185
Provost & Pritchard Engineering Group Inc (PA)	8711	C	559 449-2700	19364
URS Group Inc	8711	D	559 255-2541	19428
Darden Architects Inc	8712	D	559 448-8051	19463
Boos & Associates A Prof Corp	8721	C	559 449-7688	19539
Sunsystem Technology LLC	8731	D	559 412-7870	19775
Moore Twining Associates Inc (PA)	8734	D	559 268-7021	19990
Tatum Management Company LLC	8741	D	559 577-4474	20225

	SIC	EMP	PHONE	ENTRY#
Muniservices LLC (DH)	8742	C	800 800-8181	20477
P K B Investments Inc	8742	C	559 243-1224	20498
Biola Fresh Inc	8748	D	559 970-8881	20706
Energy Experts International	8748	D	559 449-1124	20742
Richard Heath & Associates Inc (PA)	8748	D	559 447-7000	20841
San Jquin Vly Unified A Plltion (PA)	8748	C	559 230-6000	20846
Southeast Fresno Rad LP	8748	C	559 443-8400	20854

FRIANT, CA - Fresno County

	SIC	EMP	PHONE	ENTRY#
Table Mountain Casino	7011	A	559 822-7777	10302

FULLERTON, CA - Orange County

	SIC	EMP	PHONE	ENTRY#
Orange County Produce LLC	0171	D	949 451-0880	58
AMS American Mech Svcs MD Inc	1711	C	714 888-6820	1356
Anderson Air Conditioning LP	1711	C	714 998-6850	1359
C & L Refrigeration Corp	1711	C	800 901-4822	1389
AJ Kirkwood & Associates Inc	1731	B	714 505-1977	1657
Superior Wall Systems Inc	1742	B	714 278-0000	1967
Charlies Specialties Inc	2052	C	724 346-2350	2370
Brentwood Home LLC (PA)	2515	C	562 949-3759	2493
Amtrend Corporation	2541	D	714 630-2070	2499
Mail Handling Group Inc	2752	C	952 975-5000	2563
ADB Industries	3398	B	310 679-9193	2727
Terra Universal Inc	3564	C	714 526-0100	2796
Interntnal Cnnctors Cable Corp	3661	D	888 275-4422	2886
Gigatera Communications	3679	C	714 515-1100	2942
South Coast Trnsp & Dist Inc	4212	C	310 816-0280	3423
RPM Consolidated Services Inc (HQ)	4225	D	714 388-3500	3750
Federal Express Corporation	4513	C	800 463-3339	3854
Adcom Express Inc	4731	C	714 870-7447	3976
Hub Group Los Angeles LLC	4731	C	714 449-6300	4036
Total Logistics Online LLC	4731	C	714 526-3559	4109
Tri-Tech Logistics LLC	4731	C	855 373-7049	4111
Southern California Edison Co	4911	B	714 870-3225	4701
Ware Disposal Inc	4953	C	714 834-0234	4951
Sunvalleytek International Inc	5045	C	888 456-8468	5356
McKesson Mdcl-Srgcal Top Hldng	5047	B	800 300-4350	5431
Raytheon Cmmand Ctrl Sltons LL (DH)	5065	A	714 446-3118	5694
Howmet Globl Fstning Systems I	5085	D	714 871-1550	5905
Smart & Final Stores LLC	5141	C	714 441-1069	6333
Viele & Sons Inc (PA)	5141	C	714 447-3663	6412
Hidden Villa Ranch Produce Inc (HQ)	5144	B	714 680-3447	6444
Bakery Ex Southern Cal LLC	5149	C	714 446-9470	6608
Home Depot USA Inc	5211	C	714 459-4909	6987
North Ornge Cnty Cmnty Cllege	5942	B	714 992-7008	7548
Houdini Inc (PA)	5947	C	714 525-0325	7557
Anaheim Park Hotel	7011	C	714 992-1700	9610
Huoyen International Inc	7011	D	714 635-9000	9881
Merritt Hospitality LLC	7011	C	714 738-7800	10016
Nail Alliance - North Amer Inc	7231	D	714 449-1568	10504
Dorean Enterprises Inc	7311	C	714 992-2900	10610
Real Estate Image Inc (PA)	7331	D	714 502-3900	10774
Volt Management Corp	7363	C	714 879-9330	11356
Aspirez Inc	7371	C	714 485-8104	11430
Corecare V A Cal Ltd Partnr	8051	C	714 256-1000	15388
Emeritus Corporation	8051	C	714 441-0644	15444
Fullerton Hlthcare Wllness CNT	8051	C	714 992-5701	15485
St Jude Hospital (DH)	8062	A	714 871-3280	16478
Marshall B Ketchum University (PA)	8221	C	714 871-7567	17766
Autism Spctrum Intrvntions Inc	8322	C	562 972-4846	17842
Turning Point Ministries	8322	D	800 998-6329	18159
Corecare I I I	8361	C	714 256-8000	18400
Florence Crttnton Svcs Ornge C	8361	B	714 680-9000	18434
Independent Options Inc	8361	C	714 738-4991	18458

FULTON, CA - Sonoma County

	SIC	EMP	PHONE	ENTRY#
Kendall-Jackson Wine Center	0762	C	707 571-7500	376
Shear Builders Inc	1521	D	707 284-8989	722

GALT, CA - Sacramento County

	SIC	EMP	PHONE	ENTRY#
Travis James Watts	0191	C	209 810-6159	202
Norogachi Construction Inc/CA	1742	D	916 236-4201	1949
Building Material Distrs Inc (PA)	5031	C	800 356-3001	5150

GARBERVILLE, CA - Humboldt County

	SIC	EMP	PHONE	ENTRY#
Benbow Valley Investments LLC	7011	D	707 923-2124	9640
Southern Hmbldt Cmnty Dst Hosp	8062	D	707 923-3921	16445
Southern Hmbldt Cmnty Hlth Car	8062	D	707 923-3921	16446

GARDEN GROVE, CA - Orange County

	SIC	EMP	PHONE	ENTRY#
Terra Pacific Landscape (HQ)	0781	D	714 567-0177	469
Envise (HQ)	1711	C	800 613-6240	1432
Envise	1711	D	714 901-5800	1433

GARDEN GROVE CA

GEOGRAPHIC SECTION

	SIC	EMP	PHONE	ENTRY#
Structral Prsrvtion Systems LL	1771	B	714 891-9080	2162
Quoc Viet Foods Inc	2099	D	714 283-3663	2441
Cham-Cal Engineering Co	3231	D	714 898-9721	2693
Orange Cnty Trnsp Auth Schlrsh	4111	D	714 560-6282	3186
Modivcare Solutions LLC	4731	C	714 503-6871	4060
Sprint Communications Co LP	4813	C	714 534-2107	4342
Tekworks Inc	4813	D	877 835-9675	4348
Video Vice Data Communications (PA)	4841	D	714 897-6300	4526
Battery Systems Inc	5013	C	714 667-9320	5028
Kush Supply Co LLC	5122	D	714 243-4023	6120
Qyk Brands LLC	5122	C	949 312-7119	6141
California Shirt Printer Inc	5136	D	714 898-9946	6169
R D Abbott Co Inc	5169	D	562 944-5354	6713
Home Depot USA Inc	5211	D	714 539-0319	6965
Noarus Tgg	5511	D	714 895-5595	7270
Continental Exch Solutions Inc	6099	D	714 530-3582	7845
Abbey-Properties LLC (PA)	6512	D	562 435-2100	8698
Irvine APT Communities LP	6513	C	714 537-8500	8833
Cushman & Wakefield Cal Inc	6531	B	714 591-0451	8960
Embassy Suites & Hotel	7011	C	714 539-3300	9780
Ohi Resort Hotels LLC	7011	D	714 867-5555	10060
Mastroianni Family Entps Ltd	7299	B	310 952-1700	10561
RJ Allen Inc	7353	D	714 539-1022	11006
Compass Group Usa Inc	7359	C	714 899-2520	11027
Tad Pgs Inc	7363	A	800 261-3779	11339
Brinks Incorporated	7381	C	714 903-9272	12942
Lao-Hmong Security Agency Inc	7381	D	714 533-6776	12996
Aaron Thomas Company Inc (PA)	7389	C	714 894-4468	13170
St George Auto Center Inc	7539	D	657 212-5042	13683
Kaiser Foundation Hospitals	8011	D	714 741-3448	14799
Garden Grove Medical Investors (HQ)	8051	D	714 534-1041	15487
Pacific Haven Convalescent HM	8059	D	714 534-1942	15887
Childrens Hospital Orange Cnty	8062	B	714 638-5990	15996
Kenneth Corp	8062	C	714 537-5160	16203
Performance Health Med Group	8099	C	714 740-1778	17295
Boys Grls Clubs Grdn Grove Inc (PA)	8299	C	714 530-0430	17803
Community Action Prtnr Ornge C	8322	C	714 897-6670	17890
Garden Grove Unified Schl Dst	8351	D	714 663-6437	18318
Southland Integrated Svcs Inc (PA)	8399	D	714 558-6009	18625
Crystal Cathedral Ministries (PA)	8661	C	714 622-2900	19018
Buffalo Spot MGT Group LLC	8741	C	949 354-0884	20048

GARDEN VALLEY, CA - El Dorado County

	SIC	EMP	PHONE	ENTRY#
Buckland Vineyard MGT Inc	8741	D	530 333-1534	20047

GARDENA, CA - Los Angeles County

	SIC	EMP	PHONE	ENTRY#
County of Los Angeles	0742	D	310 523-9566	331
Brightview Landscape Svcs Inc	0781	C	310 327-8700	416
Disaster Rstrtion Prfssnals In	1521	D	310 301-8030	673
Charles E Thomas Company Inc (PA)	1542	D	310 323-6730	892
AMG Construction Group	1611	D	800 310-2609	1076
Cooland Inc	1711	D	424 329-3550	1406
XCEL Mechanical Systems Inc	1711	D	310 660-0090	1599
Arena Painting Contractors Inc	1721	D	310 316-2446	1604
Duggan & Associates Inc	1721	D	323 945-1502	1613
Ps2 (PA)	1721	D	310 243-2980	1634
Randall - McAnany Company	1721	D	310 822-3344	1636
Martin Bros/Marcowall Inc (PA)	1742	D	310 532-5335	1945
Best Contracting Services Inc (PA)	1761	B	310 328-9176	2045
Claud Townsley Inc	1761	D	310 527-6770	2051
Stefan Merli Plastering Co Inc (PA)	1771	D	310 323-0404	2161
Anvil Steel Corporation	1791	D	310 329-5811	2177
Washington Orna Ir Works Inc (PA)	1799	C	310 327-8660	2329
Little Brothers Bakery LLC	2051	D	310 225-3790	2368
Ocean Direct LLC (HQ)	2092	C	424 266-9300	2422
Vege-Mist Inc	3585	D	310 353-2300	2846
First Transit Inc	4111	D	323 222-0010	3134
Global Paratransit Inc	4119	B	310 715-7550	3266
Administrative Svcs Coop Inc	4121	D	310 715-1968	3307
First Student Inc	4151	A	310 769-2400	3344
United Parcel Service Inc	4215	D	310 217-2646	3635
Carroll Shelby Licensing Inc	4225	D	310 914-1843	3681
F R T International Inc	4225	D	310 329-5700	3701
World Svc Wst/La Inflght Svc L	4581	D	310 538-7000	3922
Nippon Travel Agency Amer Inc	4724	D	310 768-1817	3942
Nippon Travel Agency PCF Inc (DH)	4724	D	310 768-0017	3943
Hanjin Transportation Co Ltd	4731	D	310 522-5030	4032
Comprehensive Dist Svcs Inc	4789	C	310 523-1546	4149
Sprint Communications Co LP	4812	C	310 515-0293	4234
California Waste Services LLC	4953	C	310 538-5998	4873
Waste MGT Collectn Recycl Inc	4953	C	310 532-6511	4963
Cleanstreet LLC	4959	C	800 225-7316	4975
Tireco Inc (PA)	5014	C	310 767-7990	5074
Mariak Industries Inc	5023	B	310 661-4400	5123
Jk Imaging Ltd	5043	D	310 755-6848	5238
Canon Business Solutions-West Inc	5044	B	310 217-3000	5243
Social Studies School Service	5049	D	310 839-2436	5470
Jayem Enterprises Inc	5051	D	310 329-2263	5498
Magnetika Inc (PA)	5063	D	310 527-8100	5576
Mills Iron Works	5085	D	323 321-6520	5914
SPS Technologies LLC	5085	B	310 323-6222	5929
California Supply Inc	5113	D	310 532-2500	6076
Valley of Sun Cosmetics LLC	5122	C	310 327-9062	6149
Phoenix Textile Inc (PA)	5131	D	310 715-7090	6159
Usfi Inc	5141	D	424 260-9210	6411
Field Fresh Foods Incorporated	5148	A	310 719-8422	6542
Harbor Distributing LLC	5181	D	310 538-5483	6768
DCH Gardena Honda	5511	C	310 515-5700	7194
South Bay Toyota	5511	D	310 323-7800	7300
Autozone Inc	5531	D	310 525-2333	7343
Guru Denim LLC (DH)	5611	C	323 266-3072	7401
J & M Sales Inc	5651	D	310 324-9962	7407
Northrop Grumman Federal Cr Un (PA)	6061	D	310 808-4000	7786
Episource LLC	6411	A	714 452-1961	8554
Monark LP	6513	D	310 769-6669	8844
El Dorado Enterprises Inc	7011	A	310 719-9800	9776
Radiant Services Corp (PA)	7211	D	310 327-6300	10425
SPS Holdings Inc	7213	D	310 532-7550	10456
CM Laundry LLC	7219	D	310 436-6170	10484
Pulp Studio Incorporated	7336	D	310 815-4999	10817
Los Angeles Unified School Dst	7349	D	310 808-1500	10922
Decton Inc	7361	D	310 838-7246	11122
Maxim Healthcare Services Inc	7363	D	310 329-9115	11301
American Guard Services Inc (PA)	7381	B	310 645-6200	12926
Construction Protective Services Inc (PA)	7381	D	800 257-5512	12948
Eagle Security Services Inc	7381	D	310 642-0656	12967
Servexo	7381	D	323 527-9994	13040
United Facility Solutions Inc	7381	D	310 743-3000	13059
Vescom Corporation (PA)	7381	D	207 945-5051	13071
Vets Securing America Inc	7381	D	310 645-6200	13072
Wsa Group Inc	7381	D	310 743-3000	13078
New Crew Production Corp	7389	C	323 234-8880	13393
Nike Usa Inc	7941	C	310 670-6770	14152
Kaiser Foundation Hospitals	8011	D	800 780-1230	14812
Gardena Retirement Center Inc	8051	D	310 327-4091	15488
Healthcare Investments Inc (PA)	8051	D	310 323-3194	15509
Clear View Sanitarium Inc	8059	D	310 538-2323	15831
Gardena Hospital LP	8062	A	310 532-4200	16100
Kaiser Foundation Hospitals	8062	A	310 517-2956	16176
SMS Transportation Inc	8111	D	310 527-9200	17657
Tessie Clvland Cmnty Svcs Corp	8322	D	310 965-9759	18150
Counseling and Research Assoc (PA)	8361	D	310 715-2020	18401
Motivo Engineering LLC (PA)	8711	D	844 668-4861	19329
Transcosmos Omniconnect LLC	8741	D	310 630-0072	20231

GERBER, CA - Tehama County

	SIC	EMP	PHONE	ENTRY#
Pacific Farms and Orchards Inc	0175	D	530 385-1475	111

GEYSERVILLE, CA - Sonoma County

	SIC	EMP	PHONE	ENTRY#
Redwood Empire Vinyrd MGT Inc	0762	D	707 857-3401	379
Vimark Inc	0762	D	707 857-3588	383
River Rock Entertainment Auth	7011	A	707 857-2777	10165

GILROY, CA - Santa Clara County

	SIC	EMP	PHONE	ENTRY#
Christopher Ranch LLC (PA)	0139	C	408 847-1100	11
Uesugi Farms Incorporated	0161	C		47
Olam Americas Inc	0723	B	408 846-3200	294
Olam West Coast Inc	0723	C	559 447-1390	297
Olam West Coast Inc	0723	C	559 447-1390	298
Wb Electric Inc	1731	D	408 842-7911	1873
Noah Concrete Corporation	1771	D	408 842-7211	2140
Hanaps Enterprises	3577	D	669 235-3810	2831
Bert E Jessup Transportation	4213	D	408 848-3390	3447
Renn Transportation Inc	4213	D	408 842-3545	3533
Cellco Partnership	4812	D	408 846-5170	4200
Cco Holdings LLC	4841	D	408 413-0317	4484
Recology South Valley (HQ)	4953	C	408 842-3358	4928
Smart & Final Stores LLC	5141	D	408 846-7020	6382
Pulmuone USA Inc	5149	B	714 361-0806	6661
Headstart Nursery Inc (PA)	5193	D	408 842-3030	6862
Lowes Home Centers LLC	5211	D	408 413-6000	7067
Kaiser Foundation Hospitals	6324	B	408 848-4600	8332
Premium Outlet Partners LP	6512	C	408 842-3729	8751
Hilton Garden Inns MGT Inc	7011	C	408 840-7000	9851
Crothall Services Group	7215	A	909 991-4887	10462
Rfid Textile Services Inc	7218	D	408 840-7504	10481

GEOGRAPHIC SECTION

GOLD RIVER CA

	SIC	EMP	PHONE	ENTRY#
Advance Services Inc.	7631	A	408 767-2797	13750
Gilroy Gardens Family Theme Pk	7996	C	408 840-7100	14304
Center For Social Dynamics LLC	8049	D	408 843-9350	15274
Covenant Care California LLC	8051	C	408 842-9311	15406
Mariner Health Care Inc	8051	D	408 842-9311	15564
Saint Lise Rgnal Hosp Fndation	8062	B	408 848-4931	16371
Saint Louise Hospital	8062	B	408 848-2000	16372
Santa Clara County of	8062	C	408 848-2000	16392
Community Sltons For Chldren F (PA)	8322	C	408 842-7138	17894
Work2future Foundation	8331	C	408 758-3477	18266
Odd Fellow-Rebekah Chld HM Cal (PA)	8361	C	408 846-2100	18498
Infosoft Inc	8748	D	408 659-4326	20779

GLENDALE, CA - Los Angeles County

	SIC	EMP	PHONE	ENTRY#
Triangle Rock Products LLC	1429	B	818 553-8820	636
Kennard Development Group	1522	D	818 241-0800	764
PCL Construction Services Inc	1542	C	818 246-3481	984
Caspian Commercial Plbg Inc	1711	D	818 649-2500	1394
H L Moe Co Inc (PA)	1711	C	818 572-2100	1454
Pinnacle Networking Svcs Inc	1731	C	818 241-6009	1805
Colour Concepts Inc	2752	C		2559
Vege - Kurl Inc	2844	D	818 956-5582	2634
Calmat Co (DH)	2951	C	818 553-8821	2648
Mv Transportation Inc	4111	C	818 409-3387	3165
Pegasus Maritime Inc	4731	D	714 728-8565	4075
Ambiance Transportation LLC	4789	D	818 955-5757	4143
American Transportation Co LLC	4789	D	818 660-2343	4144
City of Glendale	4911	D	818 548-3980	4564
City of Glendale	4941	D	818 548-2011	4773
United Merchant Svcs Cal Inc	5044	D	818 246-6767	5259
H and H Drug Stores Inc (PA)	5047	D	818 956-6691	5420
Global Plumbing & Fire Supply	5074	C	818 550-8444	5750
Otis Elevator Company	5084	C	818 241-2828	5853
Smart & Final Stores LLC	5141	D	818 243-4239	6338
Allen Gwynn Chevrolet Inc	5511	D	818 240-0000	7167
Los Feliz Ford Inc (PA)	5511	D	818 502-1901	7253
Chop Stop Inc	5812	D	818 369-7350	7466
Forest Lawn Memorial-Park Assn (PA)	5992	B	323 254-3131	7566
Los Angeles Federal Credit Un (PA)	6061	D	818 242-8640	7780
California Credit Union (PA)	6062	C	818 291-6700	7821
Associates First Capital Corp	6141	D	818 248-7055	7870
Countrywide Home Loans Inc	6162	A	818 550-8700	7954
Carelon Med Benefits MGT Inc	6321	A	847 310-0366	8261
Empower Annuity Insur Co Amer	6321	D	818 409-0880	8264
Cigna Behavioral Health of Cal	6324	B	800 753-0540	8292
Cigna Healthcare Cal Inc (DH)	6324	B	818 500-6262	8293
Arthur J Gallagher & Co	6411	D	818 539-2300	8493
Arthur J Gallagher Risk Mgmt	6411	D	818 539-2300	8495
Califrnia Insur Guarantee Assn	6411	C	818 844-4300	8519
Coaction Spclty Insur Group In	6411	D	818 230-8200	8528
Dedicted Dfned Benefit Svcs LLC	6411	C	415 931-1990	8543
Dma Claims Management Inc	6411	D	323 342-6800	8546
Safeco Insurance Company Amer	6411	D	818 956-4250	8651
Glendale Associates Ltd	6512	D	818 246-6737	8722
BV General Inc	6513	D	818 244-2323	8793
Humangood Socal	6513	C	818 247-7219	8823
Hall and Chambers Inc	6531	D	818 476-3000	9035
Pango Group Inc	6531	D	818 502-0400	9125
Equity Title Company (DH)	6541	D	818 291-4400	9228
Stewart Title California Inc	6541	C	818 502-2700	9239
Title Resource Group LLC	6541	D	818 291-4400	9240
Wfg National Title Insur Co (PA)	6541	D	818 476-4000	9241
Forest Lawn Co	6553	C	818 241-4151	9286
Public Storage (PA)	6798	B	818 244-8080	9479
JP Allen Extended Stay (PA)	7011	D	818 956-0202	9930
Asab Inc (DH)	7338	C	818 551-7300	10824
AppleOne Inc (HQ)	7361	C	818 240-8688	11082
AppleOne Inc	7361	C	818 240-8688	11083
E Z Staffing Inc (PA)	7361	B	818 845-2500	11126
Hrn Services Inc	7361	D	323 951-1450	11151
Akkodis Inc	7371	C	818 546-2848	11394
Britive Inc	7371	D	213 915-4142	11477
Disney Cnsmr Pdts Intrctive MD	7371	D	818 263-1374	11544
Disney Interactive Studios Inc	7371	B	818 560-1000	11545
Servicetitan Inc (PA)	7371	D	855 899-0970	11911
Systech Solutions Inc (PA)	7371	D	818 550-9690	11964
Legalzoomcom Inc (PA)	7374	B	323 962-8600	12588
Assign Corporation	7379	C	818 247-7100	12734
General Networks Corporation	7379	D	818 249-1962	12799
Software Management Cons LLC (HQ)	7379	B	818 240-3177	12880
Tata America Intl Corp	7379	D	818 333-1650	12892
2310 Catalina LLC	7389	D	818 696-2040	13165
Interpreting Services Intl LLC	7389	D	818 753-9181	13329
Yellowpagescom LLC (DH)	7389	B	818 937-5500	13561
Bunim-Murray Productions	7812	C	818 756-5100	13826
Disney Enterprises Inc	7812	B	818 553-4103	13840
Dreamworks Animation Pubg LLC	7812	A	818 695-5000	13843
Dwa Holdings LLC (DH)	7812	D	818 695-5000	13844
Walt Disney Pictures	7812	B	818 409-2200	13914
Full Throttle Films LLC (DH)	7819	D	818 956-1444	13937
Walt Dsney Imgnring RES Dev In (DH)	7819	A	818 544-6500	13960
Sega Entertainment USA Inc	7993	A	310 217-9500	14299
Oakmont Country Club	7997	C	818 542-4260	14418
Advanced Prof Imging Med Group	8011	C	818 244-4646	14593
Glendale Eye Medical Group (PA)	8011	D	818 956-1010	14762
Kaiser Foundation Hospitals	8011	C	818 552-3000	14827
Verdugo Hlls Psychthrapy Ctr A (PA)	8011	D	818 241-6780	15185
Country Villa Service Corp	8051	D	818 246-5516	15393
Emeritus Corporation	8051	C	818 246-7457	15442
Griffith Pk Rhbltation Ctr LLC	8051	D	818 845-8507	15503
Ksm Healthcare Inc	8051	D	818 242-1183	15532
Mariner Health Care Inc	8051	D	818 246-5677	15571
Buena Ventura Care Center Inc	8059	D	818 247-4476	15824
Front Prch Cmmnties Oprting Gr	8059	C	800 233-3709	15846
Longwood Management Corp	8059	B	818 246-7174	15868
American Hlthcare Systems Corp (PA)	8062	B	818 646-9933	15941
Glendale Adventist Medical Ctr (HQ)	8062	A	818 409-8000	16102
Glendale Mem Hlth Foundation	8062	B	818 502-2375	16103
Glendale Memorial Health Corp	8062	A	818 502-2323	16104
Glendale Memorial Health Corporation	8062	B	818 502-1900	16105
Glenoaks Convalescent Hospital	8062	D	818 240-4300	16107
Usc Verdugo Hills Hospital LLC	8062	A	818 790-7100	16607
Usc Vrdugo Hlls Hosp Fundation (HQ)	8062	B	800 872-2273	16608
Verdugo Hills Hospital Inc	8062	C	818 790-7100	16615
Pegasus HM Hlth Care A Cal Cor	8082	D	818 551-1932	16910
Interstate Rhbltation Svcs LLC	8093	C	818 244-5656	17077
Prime Mso LLC	8093	D	818 937-9969	17114
Health Services Advisory Group	8099	C	818 409-9220	17248
Christie Parker & Hale LLP (PA)	8111	C	626 795-9900	17403
La Folltte Jhnson De Haas Fsle (PA)	8111	C	213 426-3600	17533
National Attny Collection Svcs	8111	B	818 547-9760	17586
Myhhbs Inc	8322	D	888 969-4427	18058
RES-Care Inc	8361	D	818 637-7727	18513
Young MNS Chrstn Assn Glndale	8641	D	818 484-8256	18956
City of Glendale	8711	C	818 548-3945	19178
National Teleconsultants	8711	C	818 265-4400	19332
Vasquez & Company LLP (PA)	8721	D	213 873-1700	19638
Avery Corp	8731	C	626 304-2000	19661
Disney Research Pittsburgh	8731	C	412 623-1800	19681
Noymed Corp	8731	C	800 224-2900	19748
Parexel International Corp	8731	B	818 254-7076	19756
Disqo Inc	8732	D	818 237-2186	19808
Allzone Management Svcs Inc	8741	B	213 291-8879	20017
Amco Foods Inc	8742	C	818 247-4716	20271
Gavin De Becker & Assoc GP LLC	8742	C	818 505-0177	20391
Wilson Emery Corporation	8742	D	818 245-6387	20615
PSI Services LLC (PA)	8748	D	818 847-6180	20833
Ventegra Inc A Cal Benefit Corp	8748	D	858 551-8111	20871

GLENDORA, CA - Los Angeles County

	SIC	EMP	PHONE	ENTRY#
BR Building Resources Co	1542	C	626 963-4880	877
Calportland Company (DH)	3241	D	626 852-6200	2696
National Link Incorporated	5044	D	909 670-1900	5252
Seidner-Miller Inc	5511	C	909 305-2000	7296
Southern Cal Disc Tire Co Inc	5531	C	626 335-2883	7362
Americas Christian Credit Un (PA)	6061	D	626 208-5400	7754
Oakdale Memorial Park (PA)	6553	C	626 335-0281	9288
Venue Management Systems Inc	7381	A	626 445-6000	13070
Martin Automotive Inc	7538	D	909 394-9899	13667
Jans Towing Inc	7549	C	909 596-9060	13716
Glendora Country Club	7997	C	626 335-4051	14378
Harbor Glen Care Center	8051	C	626 963-7531	15506
Ensign San Dimas LLC	8059	C	626 963-7531	15843
East Valley Glendora Hosp LLC	8062	B	626 852-5000	16063
Emanate Health	8062	B	626 857-3477	16073
Emanate Hlth Fthill Prsbt Hosp (PA)	8062	B	626 857-3145	16079
Care Unlimited Health Svcs Inc	8082	D	626 332-3767	16834
Berkshire Hathaway Home Servic	8322	D	626 335-6001	17850
Automobile Club Southern Cal	8699	D	626 963-8531	19045
Inland Empire Chptr-Ssction Cr	8699	D	512 478-9000	19091

GOLD RIVER, CA - Sacramento County

	SIC	EMP	PHONE	ENTRY#
Premier Pools and Spas Lp (PA)	1799	D	916 852-0223	2306
Creative Recrtl Systems Inc	5091	D	916 638-5375	5975
Ehealthinsurance Services Inc	7371	C	916 608-6101	11563
Spare-Time Inc	7997	C	916 638-7001	14462

Employee Codes: A=Over 500 employees, B=251-500
C=101-250, D=51-100, E=20-50, F=10-19, G=1-9

2024 Directory of California
WholeSalers and Service Companies

© Mergent Inc. 1-800-342-5647

GOLD RIVER CA

	SIC	EMP	PHONE	ENTRY#
Eskaton	8361	C	916 852-7900	18423
Firstsrvice Rsidential Cal LLC	8741	D	916 293-4740	20089
Cretelligent Inc	8742	D	916 288-8177	20334

GOLETA, CA - Santa Barbara County

	SIC	EMP	PHONE	ENTRY#
Apeel Technology Inc (PA)	0723	B	805 203-0146	255
Kitson Landscape MGT Inc	0782	D	805 681-9460	506
Anderson Systems Inc	1711	D	805 683-6133	1360
Raytheon Company	3812	D	805 562-4611	3010
Inogen Inc (PA)	3841	C	805 562-0500	3053
Santa Barbara Trnsp Corp	4151	C	805 928-0402	3352
Verizon South Inc	4812	C	805 681-8527	4244
Marborg Recovery LP	4953	C	805 963-1852	4908
Integrated Procurement Tech (PA)	5088	D	805 682-0842	5958
Moss Motors Ltd (PA)	5531	C	805 967-4546	7353
CMC Rescue Inc	5999	D	805 562-9120	7575
Mesa Insurance Solutions Inc	6411	D	805 308-6308	8612
6500 Hllister Ave Partners LLC	6512	D	805 722-1362	8697
Super 8 Motel Goleta	7011	D	805 967-5591	10292
One Call Plumber Goleta	7299	D	805 284-0441	10565
Citrix Online LLC	7371	B	805 690-6400	11491
Ergomotion Inc	7371	D	888 550-3746	11576
Stratgic Hlthcare Programs LLC	7371	D	805 963-9446	11950
Parentsquare Inc	7372	D	888 496-3168	12313
Yardi Kube Inc	7372	D	805 699-2040	12405
Juniper Networks Inc	7373	D	805 880-2000	12473
Santa Barbara Airbus	7514	D	805 964-7759	13593
Glen Annie Golf Club	7992	D	805 968-6400	14263
Bay Clubs Company LLC	7997	B	805 964-0556	14329
Devereux Foundation	8093	A	805 968-2525	17053
Intouch Technologies Inc (HQ)	8399	C	805 562-8686	18598
United Bys Grls Clubs Snta BRB	8641	B	805 967-1612	18918
Vitamin Angel Alliance Inc	8699	B	805 564-8400	19119
L3 Maripro Inc	8711	B	805 683-3881	19303
National Security Tech LLC	8711	B	805 681-2432	19330
Toyon Research Corporation (PA)	8711	C	805 968-6787	19417

GONZALES, CA - Monterey County

	SIC	EMP	PHONE	ENTRY#
Silva Farms LLC (PA)	0161	D	831 675-2327	43
Mann Packing Co Inc (DH)	0723	B	831 422-5341	286
Braga Fresh Family Farms Inc	5148	C	831 675-2361	6519

GOSHEN, CA - Tulare County

	SIC	EMP	PHONE	ENTRY#
Western Milling LLC (HQ)	6799	C	559 302-1000	9580

GRANADA HILLS, CA - Los Angeles County

	SIC	EMP	PHONE	ENTRY#
Park Regency Inc	6531	D	818 363-6116	9127
Siracusa Enterprises Inc	7361	D	818 831-1130	11230
In Granada Hlls Cnvlscent Hosp	8051	D	818 891-1745	15522
Longwood Management Corp	8051	B	818 360-1864	15550
Aegis Senior Communities LLC	8082	C	818 363-3373	16802
Inizio Interventions Inc	8093	D	818 937-0882	17074
San Fernando City of Inc	8093	D	818 832-2400	17124
Los Angeles Unified School Dst	8211	D	818 360-2361	17723

GRAND TERRACE, CA - San Bernardino County

	SIC	EMP	PHONE	ENTRY#
West Coast Arborists Inc	0783	C	909 783-6544	562
Riversd-San Brnrdino Cnty Indi (PA)	8011	C	909 864-1097	15017
Emeritus Corporation	8051	D	909 420-0153	15445
Keystone NPS LLC (DH)	8399	D	909 633-6354	18602

GRANITE BAY, CA - Placer County

	SIC	EMP	PHONE	ENTRY#
Bushnell Gardens	5193	D	916 791-4199	6854
Performance Chevrolet Inc	5511	D	916 338-7300	7277
Goodleap LLC	6162	D	916 290-9999	7972
Placer Drmtlogy Skin Care Ctr	8011	D	916 797-6261	14995
County of Placer	9224	C	916 791-7059	20934

GRASS VALLEY, CA - Nevada County

	SIC	EMP	PHONE	ENTRY#
Hansen Bros Enterprises (PA)	1442	D	530 273-3100	638
Manuel Bros Inc	1623	D	530 272-4213	1234
Byers Enterprises Inc	1761	D	530 272-7777	2049
Durham School Services L P	4151	D	530 273-7282	3332
Cellco Partnership	4812	D	530 477-8042	4188
Nevada Irrigation District	4971	C	530 273-6185	4991
Hills Flat Lumber Co (PA)	5251	D	530 273-6171	7122
FPI Management Inc	6531	D	530 272-5274	9019
Papola Enterprises Inc	6531	D	530 272-8885	9126
Chapa-De Indian Hlth Prgram In	8021	D	530 477-8545	15219
Golden Empire Convalescent Hos	8062	D	530 273-1316	16108
Sierra Nevada Mem HM Care Inc	8082	D	530 274-6350	16927
Granite Wellness Centers	8093	D	530 878-5166	17066
Victor Cmnty Support Svcs Inc	8093	C	530 273-2244	17154

GREENBRAE, CA - Marin County

	SIC	EMP	PHONE	ENTRY#
Briarpatch Coop Nev Cnty Inc	8699	C	530 272-5333	19071
Geologic Associates Inc	8711	D	530 272-2448	19240
Coldwell Bnkr Rsdntial RE Svcs	6531	B	415 461-2020	8943
Califrnia Cncer Care A Med Gro	8011	D	415 925-5000	14648
Ocadian Care Centers LLC	8051	B	415 461-9700	15604
Sequoia Living Inc	8059	D	415 464-1767	15897
Marin Healthcare District (PA)	8062	C	415 464-2090	16247
Ross Valley Homes Inc	8361	D	415 461-2300	18515

GREENFIELD, CA - Monterey County

	SIC	EMP	PHONE	ENTRY#
Salinas Land Company (PA)	0161	C	805 648-3363	38
Scheid Vineyards Inc	0172	C	831 386-5022	85

GREENWOOD, CA - El Dorado County

	SIC	EMP	PHONE	ENTRY#
Dynamic Trades Inc	5199	D	530 701-8138	6901

GRIDLEY, CA - Butte County

	SIC	EMP	PHONE	ENTRY#
Stapleton - Spence Packing Co (PA)	2033	D	408 297-8815	2353
Orchard Hospital	8062	C	530 846-9000	16299

GROVELAND, CA - Tuolumne County

	SIC	EMP	PHONE	ENTRY#
Evergreen Dstntion Hldings LLC	7011	D	209 379-2606	9790
Pine Mountain Lake Association (PA)	8641	C	209 962-4080	18894

GUADALUPE, CA - Santa Barbara County

	SIC	EMP	PHONE	ENTRY#
Guadalupe Cooling Company Inc	0723	D	805 343-2331	276
Guadalupe Union School Dst (PA)	8211	C	805 343-2114	17714

GUERNEVILLE, CA - Sonoma County

	SIC	EMP	PHONE	ENTRY#
F Korbel & Bros (PA)	2084	C	707 824-7000	2383
West County Health Centers Inc (PA)	8011	D	707 869-1594	15202

HACIENDA HEIGHTS, CA - Los Angeles County

	SIC	EMP	PHONE	ENTRY#
Superior Equipment Solutions	3631	D	323 722-7900	2870
Baronhr LLC	8742	D	626 209-8888	20289

HALF MOON BAY, CA - San Mateo County

	SIC	EMP	PHONE	ENTRY#
Browning-Ferris Inds Cal Inc	4953	C	650 726-1819	4869
Ocean Colony Partners LLC	6552	C	650 726-5764	9267
S P S Inc	8742	D	650 685-5913	20536
Lesley Foundation	8748	D	650 726-4888	20799
Resource Innovations Inc (DH)	8748	D	415 369-1000	20840

HANFORD, CA - Kings County

	SIC	EMP	PHONE	ENTRY#
High Plains Ranch LLC (PA)	0241	C	559 583-1277	216
Danell Bros Inc	0722	D	559 582-1251	248
Danell Custom Harvesting LLC	0722	D	559 582-1251	249
Walmart Inc	4225	D	559 583-6071	3780
Hood Packaging Corporation	5199	C	559 585-2040	6915
Lowes Home Centers LLC	5211	C	559 410-9000	7109
Jvac Inc	5511	D	559 584-5531	7244
All Health Services Corp (PA)	7361	C	559 583-9101	11079
Hacienda Post Acute Inc	8051	D	559 582-9221	15505
Hanfordidence Opco LLC	8052	C	559 582-2871	15759
Adventist Med Center-Hanford (HQ)	8062	C	559 582-9000	15925
Adventist Med Center-Hanford	8062	C	559 537-1377	15926
Central Valley General Hosp (HQ)	8062	B	559 583-2100	15986
Hanford Community Hospital (HQ)	8062	A	559 582-9000	16117
Hanford Dialysis LLC	8092	D	559 587-9014	16985
Kings Cmnty Action Orgnztion I (PA)	8322	D	559 582-4386	18034

HARBOR CITY, CA - Los Angeles County

	SIC	EMP	PHONE	ENTRY#
Bennett Entps A Cal Ldscp Cntg	0781	D	310 534-3543	391
Ruggeri Marble and Granite Inc	3281	D	310 513-2155	2717
Prime Wheel Corporation	3714	B	310 326-5080	2976
Hunt Enterprises Inc	6513	D	310 530-3733	8825
Allied Protection Services Inc	7381	C	310 330-8314	12922
Kaiser Foundation Hospitals	8011	A	310 325-5111	14822
Permanente Medical Group Inc	8011	A	310 325-5111	14986
Southern Cal Prmnnte Med Group	8011	C	800 780-1230	15078

HAWAIIAN GARDENS, CA - Los Angeles County

	SIC	EMP	PHONE	ENTRY#
Hawaiian Gardens Casino	7011	A	562 860-5887	9840
Hawaiian Gardens Casino	7999	A	562 860-5887	14533
Gardens Regional Hospital and Medic	8062	B	877 877-1104	16101
Pacific Gardens Med Ctr LLC	8741	C	562 860-0401	20168
Openpopcom Inc (PA)	8748	D	714 249-7044	20822

HAWTHORNE, CA - Los Angeles County

	SIC	EMP	PHONE	ENTRY#
Park West Landscape Inc	0782	D	310 363-4100	527
Servicon Systems Inc	1771	A	310 970-0700	2157

GEOGRAPHIC SECTION

HELENDALE CA

	SIC	EMP	PHONE	ENTRY#
Firstclass Foods - Trojan Inc	2011	C	310 676-2500	2339
Wems Inc (PA)	3564	D	310 644-0251	2797
Ring LLC (HQ)	3612	B	310 929-7085	2859
Averitt Express Inc	4213	D	310 970-9520	3445
All Cartage Transportation Inc (PA)	4214	D	310 970-0600	3578
Advanced Air LLC	4522	C	310 644-3344	3862
Expeditors Intl Wash Inc	4731	D	323 781-1600	4017
Expeditors Intl Wash Inc	4731	D	310 343-6200	4018
Thinkom Solutions Inc	4899	C	310 371-5486	4555
Home Depot USA Inc	5211	C	310 644-9600	7011
Lowes Home Centers LLC	5211	C	323 327-4000	7064
South Bay Ford Inc (PA)	5511	C	310 644-0211	7299
Ayres Group	7011	C	310 220-6447	9626
Calhot Illinios LLC	7011	D	310 536-9800	9675
Unified Protective Svcs Inc	7381	D	310 350-1755	13058
Eaglerider Finance LLC	7389	D	310 321-3191	13274
Inspectorate America Corp	7389	C	800 424-0099	13326
Equinox-76th Street Inc	7991	D	310 727-9543	14198
Eastbiz Corporation	7999	C	310 212-7134	14518
Schnierow Dental Care	8021	C	310 377-6453	15249
Longwood Management Corp	8051	C	310 679-1461	15549
Trident Labs LLC	8072	C	310 915-9121	16778
West Coast Dental Labs LLC	8072	B	855 220-5600	16779
Longwood Management Corp	8361	D	310 675-9163	18475
Xdbs Corporation	8732	C	844 932-7356	19857
Analysts Inc	8734	C	800 424-0099	19947
Ncompass International LLC	8742	C	323 785-1700	20485
Netfortris Acquisition Co Inc	8748	D	877 366-2548	20812

HAYWARD, CA - Alameda County

	SIC	EMP	PHONE	ENTRY#
Brightview Landscape Svcs Inc	0781	D	510 487-4826	398
Arborwell Inc (PA)	0783	C	510 881-4260	552
Andrew Chekene Enterprises Inc	1521	C	650 588-1001	654
Axis Services Inc	1522	C	510 732-6111	746
Eden Housing Inc (PA)	1522	D	510 582-1460	755
American Asp Repr Rsrfcing Inc (PA)	1611	D	510 723-0280	1074
County of Alameda	1611	C	510 670-5455	1091
Solcom Inc	1623	B	510 940-2490	1263
Solcom Group Inc	1623	D	510 940-2490	1264
American Rsdntial Svcs Ind Inc	1711	B	650 409-1986	1354
Climate Pros LLC	1711	C	510 784-8990	1401
Control Air Enterprises LLC	1711	B	510 441-1800	1404
Control Air North Inc	1711	D	510 441-1800	1405
D W Nicholson Corporation (PA)	1711	C	510 887-0900	1415
Eagle Systems Intl Inc	1711	B	510 259-1700	1424
Marelich Mechanical Co Inc (HQ)	1711	D	510 785-5500	1496
Westates Mechanical Corp Inc	1711	D	510 635-9830	1597
Anning-Johnson Company	1742	C	510 670-0100	1906
Boyett Construction Inc (PA)	1742	D	510 264-9100	1911
Bigham Taylor Roofing Corp	1761	D	510 886-0197	2046
R2g Enterprises Inc	1761	D	510 489-6218	2079
Casey-Fogli Con Contrs Inc (PA)	1771	D	510 887-0837	2104
RJS & Associates Inc	1771	C	510 670-9111	2152
Kwan Wo Ironworks Inc	1791	C	415 822-9628	2185
Safeco Door & Hardware Inc	1793	D	510 429-4768	2206
Cleveland Wrecking Company	1795	A	510 674-2600	2232
Stomper Company Inc	1795	D	510 574-0570	2243
ATI Restoration LLC	1799	D	510 429-5000	2258
Northstar Contg Group Inc	1799	D	510 491-1330	2302
Restec Contractors Inc	1799	D	510 670-0100	2312
US Solid Surfaces	1799	D	510 300-8980	2326
Columbus Foods LLC	2011	B	510 921-3400	2338
Azuma Foods Intl Inc USA (HQ)	2092	D	510 782-1112	2418
Kosan Biosciences Incorporated	2834	D	650 995-7356	2596
Sun Deep Inc (PA)	2844	C	510 441-2525	2632
Thermionics Laboratory Inc	3471	D	510 786-0680	2761
Heat and Control Inc (PA)	3556	C	510 259-0500	2787
Xpo Logistics Freight Inc	4213	D	510 785-6920	3574
Nor-Cal Moving Services (PA)	4214	D	510 371-4942	3591
United Parcel Service Inc	4512	C	510 264-8880	3850
LBC Mundial Corporation (DH)	4513	D	650 873-0750	3856
Dhx-Dependable Hawaiian Ex Inc	4731	D	510 686-2600	4006
Profes Nwfs Inc	4731	D	510 780-0202	4080
Rxo Cstoms Clrnce Slutions LLC	4731	C	620 266-6315	4089
Pacific Gas and Electric Co	4924	A	510 784-3253	4723
County of Alameda	4941	D	510 670-6466	4779
Bay Area Concrete LLC	4953	D	510 294-0220	4862
Wm Healthcare Solutions Inc	4953	D	713 328-7350	4969
Gillig LLC	5013	B	800 735-1500	5041
Allmodular Systems Inc	5044	D	510 887-9000	5241
Earle M Jorgensen Company	5051	C	510 487-2700	5490
TCI Aluminum/North Inc	5051	D	510 786-3750	5522
Herning Enterprises Inc	5063	C	510 782-5330	5564
Cnet Technology Corporation	5065	C	408 392-9966	5642
Metric Equipment Sales Inc	5065	D	510 264-0887	5675
Tps Aviation Inc (PA)	5065	D	510 475-1010	5713
Cal-Steam Supply	5074	C	510 512-7700	5744
Big Joe California North Inc (PA)	5084	C	510 785-6900	5821
R F Macdonald Co (PA)	5084	D	510 784-0110	5862
Hd Supply Facilities Maint Ltd	5087	D	510 783-4019	5942
Oakhurst Industries Inc	5141	C	510 265-2400	6273
Discovery Foods Inc	5142	D		6419
Pacific Cheese Co Inc (PA)	5143	C	510 784-8800	6442
Imp Foods Inc	5146	D	510 429-4600	6471
Core-Mark International Inc	5149	C	510 487-3000	6621
Jagpreet Enterprises LLC	5149	C	510 336-8376	6636
National Beverage Corp	5149	D	510 783-3200	6651
Sasol Wax North America Corporation	5172	D	510 783-9295	6738
Matagrano Inc	5181	C	650 829-4829	6775
B2b Industrial Products LLC	5199	D	510 887-4586	6890
Foam Distributors Incorporated	5199	D	510 441-8377	6908
Home Depot USA Inc	5211	C	510 887-8544	6982
Fremont Bank	6022	D	510 512-1900	7690
Veev Group Inc	6211	C	650 292-0752	8173
Casa Sandoval LLC	6513	D	510 727-1700	8797
Eden Housing Resident Svcs Inc	6513	D	510 582-1460	8805
Felson Companies Inc	6531	D	510 538-1150	9002
Chapel of Chimes (DH)	6553	D	510 471-3363	9282
Crown Management Services Inc	7011	D	510 537-8470	9729
Paar Hospitality Inc	7011	D	828 203-3585	10076
Heavenly Hands	7231	D	510 881-0480	10499
Gel-Pak LLC	7336	D	510 576-2220	10809
Rentokil North America Inc	7342	D	650 579-6565	10842
Bms Catastrophe Inc	7349	D	877 730-1948	10864
H U S D Maintenance Operation	7349	D	510 784-2666	10906
Nova Commercial Company Inc (PA)	7349	D	510 728-7000	10935
Maleko Personnel Inc	7361	D	480 405-2905	11174
CPS Security Solutions Inc	7381	B	510 806-7227	12956
Best Choice LLC	7389	C	510 862-4989	13213
Compass Group Usa Inc	7389	C	510 259-0416	13240
Internal Revenue Service	8011	D	510 576-7589	14786
Kaiser Foundation Hospitals	8011	A	510 678-4000	14833
Warbritton & Assoc Impairment	8011	D	510 781-0211	15197
Mariner Health Care Inc	8051	C	510 783-8150	15566
Mariner Health Care Inc	8051	D	510 538-4424	15573
Mariner Health Care Inc	8051	C	510 785-2800	15574
Hillsdale Group LP	8059	D	510 538-3866	15856
Windsor Gardens Healthcare C	8059	C	510 582-4636	15913
Hayward Sisters Hospital (HQ)	8062	A	510 264-4000	16119
Coram Hlthcare Corp Nthrn Cal	8082	A	415 292-6811	16846
Crescent Healthcare Inc	8082	B	510 264-5454	16851
Successful Altrntves For Addct	8093	C	510 247-8300	17134
Bay Area Community Health	8099	B	510 770-8040	17185
Hayward Unified School Dst	8211	A	510 723-3170	17715
Eden Area Rgnal Occptnal Prgra	8331	D	510 293-2900	18228
Lea & Braze Engineering Inc (PA)	8711	C	510 887-4086	19305
Ripcord Inc	8711	C	408 838-7446	19377
Terawave Communication Inc	8711	D	510 429-5300	19408
Arcus Biosciences Inc (PA)	8731	D	510 694-6200	19659
Mendel Biotechnology Inc	8731	D	510 264-0280	19736
C3 Nano Inc	8732	D	510 259-9650	19802
Proactive Bus Solutions Inc	8741	D	510 302-0120	20183
Eos It MGT Solutions Inc	8742	A	510 600-4188	20362
Environmental Remedies Inc	8999	D	925 461-3285	20886

HEALDSBURG, CA - Sonoma County

	SIC	EMP	PHONE	ENTRY#
Klein Foods Inc	0172	D	707 431-1533	79
Vino Farms Inc	0762	C	707 433-8241	384
Ferrar-Crano Vnyrds Winery LLC (PA)	2084	C	707 433-6700	2385
Jvw Corporation	2084	D	707 431-5250	2388
Treasury Chateau & Estates	2084	D	707 299-2600	2396
Wine Industry Network LLC	5182	D	707 953-9672	6811
Social Finance Inc	6163	B	707 473-9889	8057
Hotel Healdsburg LLC	7011	D	707 922-5399	9872
Finlink Inc (PA)	7371	C	888 999-5467	11601
Eandm	7694	D	707 473-3137	13758
Alliance Medical Center Inc	8011	D	707 431-8234	14598
Kendal At Snoma A Zen Inspred	8051	D	707 756-5036	15529
North Sonoma County Hosp Dst	8062	C	707 431-6500	16283
Sisters of St Joseph Orange	8062	A	707 431-1135	16432

HEBER, CA - Imperial County

	SIC	EMP	PHONE	ENTRY#
C S Transport Inc	4212	D	760 666-5661	3376

HELENDALE, CA - San Bernardino County

	SIC	EMP	PHONE	ENTRY#
Silver Lakes Association	8641	D	760 245-1606	18911

HEMET CA — GEOGRAPHIC SECTION

	SIC	EMP	PHONE	ENTRY#
HEMET, CA - Riverside County				
Lpsh Holdings Inc (PA)	1711	D	855 647-5061	1491
Lpsh Holdings Inc	1711	B	951 926-1176	1492
Lowes Home Centers LLC	5211	D	951 492-7000	7081
Jack Gosch Ford Inc	5511	D	951 658-3181	7238
Southern Cal Disc Tire Co Inc	5531	C	951 929-2130	7359
Orchid Court Inc	7389	D	951 766-7840	13411
Emeritus Corporation	8051	D	951 744-9861	15438
Miramonte Enterprises LLC	8051	C	951 658-9441	15586
Hemet Valley Medical Center-Education	8062	A	951 652-2811	16125
Kpc Global Medical Centers Inc (DH)	8062	C	714 953-3500	16207
Ramona Rhblttion Post Acute CA	8062	C	951 652-0011	16358
Ramona Community Services Corp (HQ)	8082	C	951 658-9288	16918
Victor Cmnty Support Svcs Inc	8093	C	951 212-1770	17155
Hemet Unified School District	8211	D	951 765-5100	17716
Hemet Unified School District	8211	D	951 765-6287	17717
Casa-Pacifica Inc	8361	B	951 658-3369	18389
Casa-Pacifica Inc	8361	C	951 766-5116	18390
Veterans of Foreign Wars of US	8641	D	951 202-3792	18923
Automobile Club Southern Cal	8699	D	951 652-6202	19062
Trilar Management Group	8741	C	951 925-2021	20233
HERALD, CA - Sacramento County				
Sacramento Municpl Utility Dst	7389	C	916 732-5743	13456
HERCULES, CA - Contra Costa County				
Home Depot USA Inc	5211	D	510 245-9572	6997
City Mechanical Inc	7623	D	510 724-9088	13724
Shields Nursing Centers Inc (PA)	8051	C		15665
Blize Healthcare Cal Inc	8082	D	800 343-2549	16822
Theraex Rehab Services Inc	8082	C	510 239-9614	16951
Pacific Biolabs Inc	8734	D	510 964-9000	19993
HERMOSA BEACH, CA - Los Angeles County				
Marlin Equity Partners LLC (PA)	6282	C	310 364-0100	8206
Pacific Ave Cpitl Partners LLC (PA)	6726	B	424 254-9774	9408
Marlin Equity Partners III LP (PA)	6799	C	310 364-0100	9530
HESPERIA, CA - San Bernardino County				
Arizona Pipeline Company (PA)	1623	B	760 244-8212	1194
Hesperia Unified School Dst	2099	D	760 948-1051	2436
Robar Enterprises Inc (PA)	3273	C	760 244-5456	2711
Jesse Alexander Transport	4789	D	760 669-0379	4161
Cellco Partnership	4812	D	760 662-5914	4206
El Dorado Broadcasters LLC	4832	D	760 241-1313	4378
Best Way Disposal Co Inc	4953	C	760 244-9773	4864
R E Goodspeed and Sons Distributing Inc	5171	D	760 949-3356	6717
Orion Solidified Inc (PA)	7371	D	818 483-0100	11802
Global Customer Services Inc	7389	D	760 995-7949	13302
Caliber Bodyworks Texas Inc	7532	D	760 949-6269	13632
Victorville Speedwash Inc	7542	D	760 998-2482	13703
Davita Inc	8092	C	310 536-2406	16979
HIGHLAND, CA - San Bernardino County				
Kcb Towers Inc	1791	D	909 862-0322	2184
Cco Holdings LLC	4841	D	909 742-8273	4492
East Valley Water District	4941	D	909 889-9501	4788
Lowes Home Centers LLC	5211	D	909 557-9010	7110
San Mnuel Band Mission Indians	6099	C	909 425-4682	7860
San Manuel Band Mission Indians	7389	C	909 864-6293	13463
San Manuel Entertainment Auth (PA)	7999	A	909 864-5050	14562
Beaver Medical Group LP (HQ)	8011	C	909 425-3321	14630
Cedar Holdings LLC	8051	D	909 862-0611	15368
Immanuel Bptst Ch San Brnrdino	8351	D	909 862-6641	18321
YMCA of East Valley	8641	D	909 425-9622	18936
HILLSBOROUGH, CA - San Mateo County				
Synctruck LLC	4215	D	415 425-0447	3629
Burlingame Country Club	7997	D	650 696-8100	14352
HILMAR, CA - Merced County				
Americore Inc	3841	D	209 632-5679	3048
Independent Dar Producers Inc	5143	B	209 667-6076	6438
HINKLEY, CA - San Bernardino County				
Pacific Gas and Electric Co	4911	C	760 253-2925	4645
HOLLISTER, CA - San Benito County				
R and R Labor Inc	0761	B	831 638-0290	368
Sears Home Imprv Pdts Inc	1521	C	831 245-0062	717
San Benito Htg & Shtmtl Inc	1711	D	831 637-1112	1554
San Benito Supply (PA)	3272	C	831 637-5526	2706
CDF Parkway LLC (PA)	5431	C	408 842-7282	7156
San Juan Oaks LLC	7992	D	831 636-6113	14286
San Benito Health Care Dst (PA)	8062	B		16375
San Benito Health Care Dst	8062	C	831 635-1106	16376
Chamberlains Children Ctr Inc	8361	D	831 636-2121	18391
Central Coast YMCA	8641	C	831 637-8600	18832
Alpha Teknova Inc	8733	C	831 637-1100	19862
HOLLYWOOD, CA - Los Angeles County				
Loews Hollywood Hotel LLC	7011	B	323 450-2235	9982
HOOPA, CA - Humboldt County				
Hoopa Modular Building Entp	1531	B	530 625-4551	792
Klma W Medical Center	8093	D	530 625-4114	17083
HOPLAND, CA - Mendocino County				
Hopland Band Pomo Indians Inc	7999	C	707 744-1395	14534
Hopland Band Pomo Indians Inc (PA)	8699	D	707 472-2100	19089
HUGHSON, CA - Stanislaus County				
Duarte Nursery Inc	0181	B	209 531-0351	126
Samaritan Village Inc	8322	C	209 883-3212	18108
HUNTINGTON BEACH, CA - Orange County				
Coastline Cnstr & Awng Co Inc	1521	D	714 891-9798	667
Galkos Construction Inc	1542	D	714 373-8545	920
Grani Installation Inc (PA)	1542	D	714 898-0441	923
Aire-Rite AC & Rfrgn LLC	1711	D	714 895-2338	1344
Brymax Construction Svcs Inc	1711	C	949 200-9619	1388
Critchfeld Mech Inc Sthern Cal	1711	D	949 390-2900	1412
RC Wendt Painting Inc	1721	C	714 960-2700	1637
Portermatt Electric Inc	1731	D	714 596-8788	1810
California Closet Company Inc	1799	C	714 899-4905	2263
Boardriders Inc (HQ)	2329	A	714 889-5404	2454
Airtech International Inc (PA)	3728	C	714 899-8100	2988
Irish Interiors Inc (HQ)	3728	C	949 559-0930	2991
Americare Medservices Inc	4119	C	310 632-1141	3236
Premiere Customs Brokers Inc	4731	A	310 410-6825	4077
Filanity Corporation	4813	D	714 475-3521	4272
Frontier California Inc	4813	C	714 375-6713	4281
Rainbow Disposal Co Inc (HQ)	4953	C	714 847-3581	4923
Reliable Wholesale Lumber Inc (PA)	5031	D	714 848-8222	5182
Bartco Lighting Inc	5063	C	714 230-3200	5540
DSI Process Systems LLC	5084	C	314 382-1525	5829
Primal Elements Inc	5122	D	714 899-0757	6140
Boardriders Wholesale LLC (DH)	5136	C	714 889-2200	6167
Smart & Final Stores LLC	5141	D	714 842-4637	6337
Kings Seafood Company LLC	5146	A	714 793-1177	6472
Astra Oil Company Inc	5172	C	714 969-6569	6723
Harbor Distributing LLc (HQ)	5181	C	714 933-2400	6765
Nakase Brothers Whl Nurs LP (PA)	5193	D	949 855-4388	6866
York Enterprises South Inc	5511	C	714 842-6611	7336
Classic Camaro Inc	5531	C	714 847-6887	7346
Southern Cal Disc Tire Co Inc	5531	C	714 901-8226	7361
Boiling Crab Operations LLC	5812	C	714 636-4885	7461
Love At First Bite Catering	5812	B	714 369-0561	7493
Nuvision Fincl Federal Cr Un (PA)	6061	C	714 375-8000	7787
GFS Capital Holdings	6162	B	714 720-3918	7967
Managed Health Network	6324	B	714 934-5519	8343
Confie Holding II Co (PA)	6411	C	714 252-2500	8532
Freeway Insurance (PA)	6411	C	714 252-2500	8572
Huntington Bch Senior Hsing LP	6513	C	714 842-4006	8826
Burleigh Point LLC	6531	C	949 428-3200	8918
Child Development Incorporated	6531	B	714 842-4064	8932
House Seven Gables RE Inc	6531	D	714 500-3300	9042
Skyhill Financial Inc	6531	C	714 657-3938	9180
Lincoln Prprty No 2087 Ltd Prt	6552	D	214 740-3300	9259
Roman Cthlic Diocese of Orange	6553	D	714 847-8546	9290
Pacific City Hotel LLC	7011	B	714 698-6100	10079
Waterfront Hotel LLC	7011	B	714 845-8000	10354
Galkos Construction Inc (PA)	7299	D	714 373-8545	10547
Grupo Gallegos	7311	D	562 256-3600	10621
Innocean Wrldwide Americas LLC (HQ)	7311	C	714 861-5200	10631
Direct Chassislink Inc	7359	A	657 216-5846	11029
Huntington Beach Union High	7361	C	714 478-7684	11152
Precise Fit Limited One LLC	7361	B	310 824-1800	11203
Infomagnus LLC	7371	D	714 810-3430	11661
Pakedge Device & Software Inc	7372	C	714 880-4511	12312
Vcore Technology Partners LLC (PA)	7373	D	877 348-7714	12541
United States Technical Svcs	7379	C	714 374-6300	12901
Horsemen LLC	7381	D	714 847-4243	12988
Global Exprnce Specialists Inc	7389	C	619 498-6300	13303
Enterprise Rnt--car Boston LLC	7514	C	714 841-4141	13580
Century Theatres Inc	7832	C	714 373-4573	13982

GEOGRAPHIC SECTION

IRVINE CA

	SIC	EMP	PHONE	ENTRY#
City of Huntington Beach	7992	D	714 846-4450	14250
Covid Clinic Inc	8011	B	877 219-8378	14720
Edinger Medical Group Inc	8011	D	714 965-2500	14732
Southern Cal Prmnnte Med Group	8011	C	714 841-7293	15083
Douglas Fir Holdings LLC	8051	C	714 842-5551	15426
Sea Breeze Health Care Inc	8051	C	714 847-9671	15657
Prime Hlthcare Hntngton Bch LL	8062	D	714 843-5000	16336
Landmark Health LLC	8082	B	657 237-2450	16887
No Ordinary Moments Inc	8082	D	714 848-3800	16899
Optumcare Management LLC	8099	D	714 968-0068	17289
Careworks Health Services	8322	D	714 859-4700	17859
Goodwill Inds Orange Cnty Cal	8331	C	714 881-3986	18231
Element Materials (DH)	8734	D	714 892-1961	19967
BJs Restaurant Operations Co	8741	B	714 500-2440	20038
Michaelson Connor & Boul (PA)	8742	D	714 230-3600	20471
Innovative Vhcl Solutions LLC	8748	C	714 896-8267	20780

HUNTINGTON PARK, CA - Los Angeles County

	SIC	EMP	PHONE	ENTRY#
McCarthy Bldg Companies Inc	1542	D	949 851-8383	966
Home Depot USA Inc	5211	C	323 587-5520	6970
Fred M Boerner Motor Co (PA)	5531	D	323 560-3882	7348
Bancolmbia PR Intrnacional Inc	7389	D	323 582-2255	13208
All Care Medical Group Inc	8011	D	408 278-3550	14597
Altamed Health Services Corp	8011	A	323 277-7678	14604
Covenant Care California LLC	8051	C	323 589-5941	15402
Aircraft Xray Laboratories Inc	8734	D	323 587-4141	19944

HURON, CA - Fresno County

	SIC	EMP	PHONE	ENTRY#
Dick Anderson & Sons Farming	0191	C	559 945-2511	175
California Valley Land Co Inc (PA)	0721	D	559 945-9292	241

IDYLLWILD, CA - Riverside County

	SIC	EMP	PHONE	ENTRY#
Jeb Holdings Corp (PA)	5065	D	951 659-2183	5665
Guided Discoveries Inc	7032	D	951 659-6062	10402

IMPERIAL, CA - Imperial County

	SIC	EMP	PHONE	ENTRY#
Imperial Irrigation District (PA)	4911	A	800 303-7756	4580

IMPERIAL BEACH, CA - San Diego County

	SIC	EMP	PHONE	ENTRY#
Boys & Girls Clubs South Cnty	8641	D	619 424-2266	18820

INDEPENDENCE, CA - Inyo County

	SIC	EMP	PHONE	ENTRY#
Los Angeles Dept Wtr & Pwr	4941	A	760 878-2156	4806
Eastern California Museum (PA)	8412	B	760 878-0292	18651

INDIAN WELLS, CA - Riverside County

	SIC	EMP	PHONE	ENTRY#
Merrill Lynch Prce Fnner Smith	6211	C	760 862-1400	8108
Bennion Deville Fine Homes Inc	6531	B	760 674-3452	8910
Hyatt Corporation	7011	A	760 341-1000	9896
Indian Wells Property LLC	7011	D	442 305-4500	9908
Lh Indian Wells Operating LLC	7011	C	760 341-2200	9974
Renaissance Hotel Operating Co	7011	A	760 773-4444	10150
Renaissnce Esmralda Resort Spa	7011	D	760 773-4444	10152
Senior Prdcrs In Rtrmnt TV	7812	D	760 773-9525	13892
Dhccnp	7997	D	760 340-4646	14370
Eldorado Country Club	7997	C	760 346-8081	14373
Indian Wells Country Club Inc	7997	D	760 345-2561	14383
Reserve Club	7997	D	760 674-2222	14429
Toscana Country Club Inc	7997	D	760 404-1444	14473
Vintage Club	7997	D	760 340-0500	14478
Bjz LLC	8082	C	760 851-0740	16821
Troon Golf LLC	8741	C	760 346-4653	20235

INDIO, CA - Riverside County

	SIC	EMP	PHONE	ENTRY#
Hadley Date Gardens Inc	0179	D	760 347-3044	116
Valley Animal Medical Center	0742	A	760 342-4711	345
AK Landscaping Maint Inc	0782	D	760 347-9747	472
Granite Construction Company	1611	B	760 775-7500	1110
All Wall Inc	1742	D	760 600-5108	1903
Frontier California Inc	4813	B	760 342-0500	4280
United Irrigation Inc	4971	D	760 347-6161	4996
Commercial Lighting Inds Inc	5063	C	800 755-0155	5548
Fiesta Ford Inc	5511	C	760 775-7777	7207
Cabazon Band Mission Indians	7011	A	760 342-5000	9673
Wyndham Resort Dev Corp	7011	D	760 342-1040	10384
Whites Crane Service Inc	7353	D	760 347-3401	11010
East Valley Tourist Dev Auth	7999	A	760 342-5000	14517
RES-Care Inc	8052	D	760 775-2887	15790
JFK Memorial Hospital Inc	8062	C	760 347-6191	16140
John F Kennedy Mem Hosp Aux	8062	A	760 347-6191	16142
County of Riverside	8099	D	760 863-8450	17216
Marthas Village and Kitchen	8322	D	760 347-4741	18050

INGLEWOOD, CA - Los Angeles County

	SIC	EMP	PHONE	ENTRY#
Doorking Inc (PA)	3699	C	310 645-0023	2957
First Transit Inc	4111	D	310 216-9584	3129
Apollo Couriers Inc (PA)	4215	C	310 337-0377	3606
Air-Sea Forwarders Inc (PA)	4731	D	310 216-1616	3982
Iron Mountain Info MGT LLC	4731	D	818 848-9766	4041
Mittal Ram	5074	D	310 769-6669	5755
Dolphin Hkg Ltd (PA)	5199	D	310 215-3356	6900
Home Depot USA Inc	5211	C	310 677-1944	6971
Carpet USA Ltd (PA)	5713	D	310 390-8570	7428
Inglewood Park Cemetery (PA)	6553	C	310 412-6500	9287
Century Gaming Management Inc	7011	A	310 330-2800	9690
Hollywood Park Casino Co Inc	7011	A	310 330-2800	9863
Inglewood Cmtry Mortuary Inc	7261	D	310 412-6811	10513
After-Party2 Inc (DH)	7359	C	310 202-0011	11015
After-Party6 Inc	7359	C	310 966-4900	11016
Classic Party Rentals Inc	7359	C	310 966-4900	11025
American Egle Prtctive Svcs In	7381	C	310 412-0019	12925
Hayes Protective Services Inc	7381	C	323 755-2282	12986
Scis Air Security Corporation	7381	C	310 645-1216	13032
Security Indust Spcialists Inc	7381	C	323 924-9147	13039
Aero Port Services Inc (PA)	7382	C	310 623-8230	13094
Systems Tech Unlimited LLC	7382	D	310 341-5169	13150
Alamo Rental (us) Inc	7514	C	310 649-2242	13573
Lemonlight Media Inc	7812	D	310 402-0275	13860
Kaiser Foundation Hospitals	8011	D	310 419-3303	14844
Southern Cal Prmnnte Med Group	8011	D	310 419-3306	15082
Dedicated Dental Systems Inc	8021	D	661 397-5513	15225
Gentle Dental Service Corp (DH)	8021	D	800 277-1112	15228
Centinela Sklled Nrsing Wllnes	8051	D	310 674-3216	15370
Mariner Health Care Inc	8051	D	310 677-9114	15569
West Cntinela Vly Care Ctr Inc	8051	D	310 674-3216	15730
Watts Health Foundation Inc (HQ)	8052	B	310 424-2220	15805
Cfhs Holdings Inc	8062	A	310 673-4660	15990
Prime Healthcare Centinela LLC	8062	A	310 673-4660	16334
Ultracare Services LLC	8082	D	818 266-9668	16955
Rai Care Ctrs Sthern Cal II LL	8092	C	310 673-6865	16995
Tenet Healthsystem Medical Inc	8351	C	310 673-4660	18358
Girl Scuts Greater Los Angeles (PA)	8641	C	626 677-2265	18863
Automobile Club Southern Cal	8699	A	310 673-5170	19054
Marvin Engineering Co Inc (PA)	8711	A	310 674-5030	19317
Watts Health Systems Inc (PA)	8742	A	310 424-2220	20609

IONE, CA - Amador County

	SIC	EMP	PHONE	ENTRY#
Buena Vista Gaming Authority	7011	B	866 915-0777	9665
Concessionaires Urban Park	7999	C	209 763-5121	14508
Lodi Memorial Hosp Assn Inc	8062	D	209 274-2183	16219

IRVINE, CA - Orange County

	SIC	EMP	PHONE	ENTRY#
Medterra Cbd LLC	0139	D	800 971-1288	14
Hines Horticulture Inc (PA)	0181	B	949 559-4444	131
Mission Ldscp Companies Inc	0781	C	800 545-9963	446
A Clark/Mccarthy Joint Venture	1521	A	714 429-9779	649
K Hovnnian Clfrnia Oprtons In (HQ)	1521	D	714 368-4500	689
Shimmick Construction Co Inc	1521	C	510 777-5000	723
Regis Contractors LP	1522	B	949 253-0455	772
Tri Pointe Homes Inc	1522	D	714 389-5933	779
Tri Pointe Homes Inc (HQ)	1522	D	949 438-1400	781
Western National Prpts LLC (PA)	1522	D	949 862-6200	785
Fieldstone Communities Inc (PA)	1531	C	949 790-5400	790
Lennar Corporation	1531	D	949 349-8000	794
Tri Pointe Homes Inc	1531	D	949 478-8600	798
Warmington Homes	1531	D	949 679-3100	801
Clark Cnstr Group - Cal Inc	1541	B	714 754-0764	810
Uprite Construction Corp	1541	D	949 877-8877	853
Clark Cnstr Group - Cal LP	1542	A	714 429-9779	897
Interior Lgic Group Hldngs IV (PA)	1542	A	800 959-8333	941
Perennial Construction Corp	1542	D	212 727-1807	989
RD Olson Construction Inc	1542	C	949 474-2001	1004
Rudolph and Sletten Inc	1542	C	949 252-1919	1015
Sander Langston LP	1542	C	949 863-9200	1020
Whiting-Turner Contracting Co	1542	B	949 863-0800	1062
Atkinson Construction Inc	1611	B	303 410-2540	1079
FEC Fture Contrs Engineers Inc	1611	D	949 328-9758	1104
Foothill / Estrn Trnsp Crrdor	1611	D	949 754-3400	1105
Peterson-Chase General Engineering	1611	D	949 252-0441	1152
Sema Construction Inc	1611	D	949 470-0500	1161
A & H Communications Inc	1623	C	949 250-4555	1191
Shoffeitt Pipeline Inc	1623	D	949 581-1600	1262
Shimmick Construction Co Inc (HQ)	1629	C	949 591-5922	1318
Brightview Landscape Dev Inc	1711	C	714 546-7975	1385
Bromic Heating Pty Limited	1711	D	855 552-7432	1387
Cfp Fire Protection Inc	1711	D	949 727-3277	1395

Employee Codes: A=Over 500 employees, B=251-500
C=101-250, D=51-100, E=20-50, F=10-19, G=1-9

2024 Directory of California WholeSalers and Service Companies

© Mergent Inc. 1-800-342-5647

1427

IRVINE CA

	SIC	EMP	PHONE	ENTRY#
Electric On Target Inc.	1711	D	949 247-3842	1427
Mesa Energy Systems Inc (HQ)	1711	C	949 460-0460	1500
True Air Mechanical Inc.	1711	C	888 316-0642	1588
Cwpnc Inc.	1721	D	714 564-7904	1610
D P S Inc.	1721	D	888 278-8200	1612
Empcc Inc.	1721	B	888 278-8200	1614
Leading Edge Aviation Svcs Inc	1721	A	714 556-0576	1627
Anderson & Howard Electric Inc.	1731	C	949 250-4555	1666
Assi Security (PA)	1731	D	949 955-0244	1669
Kite Electric Incorporated.	1731	C	949 380-7471	1762
Patric Communications Inc (PA)	1731	D	619 579-2898	1801
Pyro-Comm Systems Inc (PA)	1731	C	714 902-8000	1813
SBE Electrical Contracting Inc.	1731	C	714 544-5066	1831
Ancca Corporation.	1742	D	949 553-0084	1905
Interior Specialists Inc.	1752	B	800 959-8333	2036
Dri Commercial Corporation.	1761	C	949 266-1900	2057
Dri Companies.	1761	B	949 266-1900	2058
Ekedal Concrete Inc.	1771	D	949 729-8082	2116
Danny Ryan Precision Contg Inc.	1795	D	949 642-6664	2233
J&G Industries Inc.	1795	D	949 207-3505	2238
Antis Roofg Waterproofing LLC	1799	D	949 461-9222	2255
Courtney Inc (PA)	1799	D	949 222-2050	2268
Maruchan Inc.	2098	C	949 789-2300	2429
Advanstar Communications Inc.	2721	D	714 513-8400	2543
International Vitamin Corporat (PA)	2834	D	949 664-5500	2591
Sicor Inc (HQ)	2834	A	949 455-4700	2609
Pacific World Corporation (PA)	2844	D	949 598-2400	2630
Mitsubishi Chemical Crbn Fbr.	2891	C	800 929-5471	2643
Global Pcci (gpc) (PA)	3469	C	757 637-9000	2751
Cummins Pacific LLC (HQ)	3519	D	949 253-6000	2767
Gateway US Retail Inc.	3571	C	949 471-7000	2804
Toshiba Amer Elctrnc Cmpnnts (DH)	3651	B	949 462-7700	2882
Toshiba America Inc.	3651	A	212 596-0600	2883
General Monitors Inc (DH)	3669	C	949 581-4464	2901
Futek Advanced Sensor Tech Inc.	3823	C	949 465-0900	3016
Horiba Instruments Inc (DH)	3826	C	949 250-4811	3030
Alcon Vision LLC.	3841	A	949 753-6488	3047
Pro-Dex Inc (PA)	3841	C	949 769-3200	3058
3M Company.	3843	B	949 863-1360	3066
Bien Air Usa Inc.	3843	D	949 477-6050	3067
Ampronix LLC.	3845	D	949 273-8000	3071
Star Trac Strength Inc.	3949	B	714 669-1660	3095
First Transit Inc.	4111	D	949 857-7211	3132
Sabsaf LLC.	4215	D	951 266-6676	3627
Albertsons LLC.	4225	D	949 855-2465	3672
DOT Printer Inc.	4225	D	714 335-7012	3699
Santa Catalina Island Company (PA)	4725	C	310 510-2000	3969
Agility Holdings Inc (DH)	4731	D	714 617-6300	3978
Agility Logistics Corp (DH)	4731	D	714 617-6300	3979
Glovis America Inc (HQ)	4731	C	714 427-0944	4025
Cofiroute Usa LLC.	4785	C	949 754-0198	4137
Nextel Communications Inc.	4812	C	714 368-4509	4221
Boldyn Networks US Services LL	4813	B	877 999-7070	4255
Boldyn Ntwrks US Oprations LLC.	4813	C	949 515-1500	4256
Incomnet Communications Corp.	4813	D	949 251-8000	4297
Learfield Communications LLC.	4832	D	949 823-1729	4393
Horizon Communication Tech Inc.	4899	D	714 982-3900	4537
Teletrac Inc (PA)	4899	D	714 897-0877	4554
Chestnut Ridge Energy Company.	4911	C		4563
Edison Capital.	4911	C	909 594-3789	4573
Hanwha Q Cells USA Corp.	4911	D	949 748-5996	4579
Southern California Edison Co.	4911	C	949 587-5416	4691
Sunnova Energy Corporation.	4911	A	877 757-7697	4711
Irvine Ranch Water District (PA)	4941	C	949 453-5300	4796
Irvine Ranch Water District.	4941	C	949 453-5300	4797
Waste MGT Collectn Recycl Inc.	4953	C	949 451-2600	4968
Ampco Contracting Inc.	4959	C	949 955-2255	4974
Jonset LLC.	4959	D	949 551-5151	4980
Asian European Products Inc.	5013	C	949 553-3900	5024
Rally Holdings LLC.	5013	A	817 919-6833	5055
Ledra Brands Inc.	5023	C	714 259-9959	5121
Canon USA Inc.	5043	B	949 753-4000	5235
Custom Business Solutions Inc (PA)	5044	D	949 380-7674	5244
Integrus LLC.	5044	D	949 538-9211	5247
Kyocera Dcment Solutions W LLC.	5044	C	800 996-9591	5249
Arbitech LLC.	5045	D	949 376-6650	5273
Aten Technology Inc.	5045	D	949 453-8782	5276
Axiom Memory Solutions Inc.	5045	D	949 581-1450	5278
D-Link Systems Incorporated.	5045	C	714 885-6000	5292
Eon Reality Inc (PA)	5045	C	949 460-2000	5301
Eworkplace Manufacturing Inc.	5045	D	949 583-1646	5304
Getac Inc.	5045	D	949 681-2900	5311
Ingram Micro Inc (HQ)	5045	A	714 566-1000	5314
Ingram Micro Services LLC.	5045	D	714 566-1000	5315
Kapow Technologies Inc.	5045	D	800 805-0828	5321
Samsung Research America Inc.	5045	B	949 468-1143	5345
SMC Networks Inc (HQ)	5045	D	949 679-8029	5350
TW Security Corp (DH)	5045	C	949 932-1000	5367
Trimark Raygal LLC.	5046	C	949 474-1000	5391
American Medical Tech Inc.	5047	D	949 553-0359	5397
Balt Usa LLC.	5047	D	949 788-1443	5402
Fisher & Paykel Healthcare Inc.	5047	C	949 453-4000	5414
Gordian Medical Inc.	5047	B	714 556-0200	5418
Horibaabx Inc.	5047	C	949 453-0500	5424
Nihon Kohden America LLC (HQ)	5047	D	949 580-1555	5435
Sunrise Respiratory Care Inc.	5047	D	949 398-6555	5451
Team Post-Op Inc.	5047	C	949 253-5500	5452
Georg Fischer LLC (DH)	5051	D	714 731-8800	5493
Hanwa American Corp.	5051	D	949 955-2780	5495
Norman Industrial Mtls Inc.	5051	C	949 250-3343	5504
Pusan Pipe America Inc.	5051	B	949 655-8000	5512
Jelight Company Inc (PA)	5063	D	949 380-8774	5569
Tte Technology Inc.	5064	C	877 300-8837	5615
Linksys LLC.	5065	C	408 526-4000	5671
Linksys LLC.	5065	C	310 751-5100	5672
Linksys Usa Inc.	5065	C	949 270-8500	5673
Omnitron Systems Tech Inc.	5065	C	949 250-6510	5686
Telit Wireless Solutions Inc.	5065	C	949 461-7150	5711
Rok Inc.	5072	C	714 322-8563	5733
Parker-Hannifin Corporation.	5084	C	949 465-4519	5858
Universal Robots USA Inc.	5084	D	949 230-3642	5877
General Tool Inc.	5085	D	949 261-2322	5903
SPS Technologies LLC.	5085	B	949 474-6000	5928
Nikken Global Inc (HQ)	5087	C	949 789-2000	5947
Shimano North Amer Holdg Inc (HQ)	5091	C	949 951-5003	5980
Bandai Namco Entrmt Amer Inc.	5092	C	408 235-2000	5986
Fao ROC Holdings LLC.	5092	C	949 900-6501	5990
Merchsource LLC (DH)	5092	C	800 374-2744	5992
C D Listening Bar Inc.	5099	A	949 225-1170	6032
Sunscape Eyewear Inc.	5099	D	949 553-0590	6054
Blue Sky The Clor Imgntion LLC.	5112	D	714 389-7700	6063
Imperial Bag & Paper Co LLC.	5113	D	800 834-6248	6079
Str Worldwide Inc.	5136	A	949 276-5990	6187
Stussy Inc.	5136	D	949 474-9255	6188
Delta Galil USA Inc.	5137	C	949 296-0380	6197
Fox Head Inc (HQ)	5137	B	949 757-9500	6199
Asics America Corporation (HQ)	5139	C	949 453-8888	6227
Robert Kinsella Inc.	5141	D	949 453-9533	6283
Artisan Bistro Foods Inc.	5142	C	949 797-0014	6416
Newport Meat Southern Cal Inc.	5147	C	949 399-4200	6500
Mhh Holdings Inc.	5149	C	949 651-9903	6645
Tanaka Farms.	5149	C	949 653-2100	6679
Graphic Packaging Intl LLC.	5199	D	949 250-0900	6912
Victory Foam Inc (PA)	5199	D	949 474-0690	6956
Tuttle-Click Ford Inc.	5511	C	949 855-1704	7320
Budget Blinds LLC (DH)	5719	D	949 404-1100	7436
Beyond Franchise Group Inc.	5812	C	949 398-7338	7460
Taco Bell Corp (HQ)	5812	A	949 863-4500	7513
Usoc Medical LLC.	5999	D	949 243-9109	7598
City National Bank.	6021	D	949 223-4000	7617
California Republic Bank.	6022	B	949 270-9700	7667
First Foundation Inc.	6022	C	949 202-4160	7685
Pacific Premier Bancorp Inc (PA)	6022	C	949 864-8000	7706
Opus Bank.	6029	A	949 250-9800	7733
Plaza Bank.	6029	D	949 502-4300	7735
Pacific Trust Bank.	6035	C	949 236-5211	7745
Pan American Bank Fsb.	6035	B	949 224-1917	7746
Cig Financial LLC.	6141	C	877 244-4442	7872
Hyundai Protection Plan Inc.	6141	B	949 468-4000	7875
Change Lending LLC.	6162	D	949 769-3526	7945
Genhome Mortgage Corporation.	6162	D	949 561-0412	7966
Goodleap LLC.	6162	D	916 290-9999	7973
Guaranteed Rate Inc.	6162	C	424 354-5344	7975
Impac Mortgage Corp.	6162	C	949 475-3600	7983
Lenders Investment Corp.	6162	C	714 540-4747	7987
Loandepot Inc (PA)	6162	B	888 337-6888	7992
Mission Hills Mortgage Corp (HQ)	6162	C	714 972-3832	8002
Network Capital Funding Corp (PA)	6162	B	949 442-0060	8005
New Century Mortgage Corp.	6162	A	949 440-7030	8006
Ocmbc Inc.	6162	D	949 679-7400	8007
Rushmore Loan MGT Svcs LLC (PA)	6162	A	949 727-4798	8017
Sea Breeze Financial Svcs Inc.	6162	C	949 223-9700	8019
5 Arches LLC.	6163	D	949 387-8092	8029
Carnegie Mortgage LLC.	6163	B	949 379-7000	8031
Clear Mortgage Capital Inc.	6163	D	866 239-8068	8034
Clearpath Lending.	6163	C	949 502-3577	8035

GEOGRAPHIC SECTION

IRVINE CA

Company	SIC	EMP	PHONE	ENTRY#
Dana Capital Group Inc **(PA)**	6163	D	949 789-0200	8038
Sand Canyon Corporation **(HQ)**	6163	D	949 727-9425	8055
Hyundai ABS Funding LLC	6211	C	949 732-2697	8093
Merrill Lynch Prce Fnner Smith	6211	D	949 235-5050	8143
National Financial Svcs LLC	6211	A	949 476-0157	8157
Sutter Securities Inc	6211	C	415 352-6300	8166
American Funds Service Company **(DH)**	6289	B	949 975-5000	8229
New First Fincl Resources LLC	6311	C	949 223-2160	8241
Liberty Dental Plan Cal Inc	6324	B	949 223-0007	8339
Liberty Dental Plan Corp **(PA)**	6324	D	888 703-6999	8340
Optumrx Inc **(DH)**	6324	B	714 825-3600	8349
Developers Surety Indemnity Co **(DH)**	6351	D	949 263-3300	8430
Lawyers Title Insurance Corp	6361	D	949 223-5575	8448
American Heritage Lf Insur Co	6411	D	800 753-9227	8486
Automobile Club Southern Cal	6411	C	714 973-1211	8502
Burnham Bnefits Insur Svcs LLC **(PA)**	6411	D	805 772-7965	8516
Indemnity Company California **(DH)**	6411	D	949 263-3300	8588
Insco Insurance Services Inc **(DH)**	6411	D	949 263-3415	8589
Lexisnexis Risk Assets Inc	6411	C	949 222-0028	8603
Mullin TBG Insur Agcy Svcs LLC **(DH)**	6411	C		8617
Precept Advisory Group LLC **(DH)**	6411	D	949 955-1430	8642
Ford Motor Land Dev Corp	6512	C	949 242-6606	8720
Orange Bakery Inc	6512	C	949 454-1247	8740
PM Realty Group LP	6512	D	949 390-5500	8745
Humangood Socal	6513	C	949 854-9500	8822
Irvine APT Communities LP	6513	C	949 854-4942	8831
Irvine APT Communities LP **(HQ)**	6513	C	949 720-5600	8834
Sage Apartment Communities LLC	6513	D	949 440-2300	8858
Action Property Management Inc **(PA)**	6514	D	949 450-0202	8875
Atlas Hospitality Group	6531	D	949 622-3400	8904
Auctioncom Inc	6531	C	800 499-6199	8905
Auctioncom LLC	6531	C	949 859-2777	8906
Cushman & Wakefield Cal Inc	6531	A	949 474-4004	8970
Essex Properties LLC	6531	D	949 798-8100	8994
First Amercn Prof RE Svcs Inc **(HQ)**	6531	C	714 250-1400	9004
First Team RE - Orange Cnty **(PA)**	6531	C	949 988-3000	9012
Firstsrvice Rsidential Cal LLC **(HQ)**	6531	C	949 448-6000	9017
Hanu Reddy Realty	6531	D	949 450-8800	9037
Hsf Affiliates LLC **(PA)**	6531	D	949 794-7900	9043
J Baron Inc	6531	D	949 451-1200	9055
Orchard Holdings Group Inc	6531	D	949 502-8300	9116
Red Tail Residential LLC **(PA)**	6531	D	949 399-2510	9158
Steadfast Management Co Inc **(PA)**	6531	D	949 748-3000	9187
Ten-X Finance Inc	6531	C	949 465-8523	9191
Western National Group LP	6531	D	949 862-6200	9215
Western National Securities **(PA)**	6531	C	949 862-6200	9216
Guardian Title Company	6541	D	949 495-9306	9236
Panattoni Development Co Inc **(PA)**	6552	D	916 381-1561	9271
Voit Real Estate Services LLC	6552	C	949 851-5100	9279
N2 Acquisition Company Inc	6719	D	714 942-3563	9323
Nrp Holding Co Inc **(PA)**	6719	C	949 583-1000	9324
Swds Holdings Inc	6719	B	800 395-5277	9341
Acorns Grow Incorporated **(PA)**	6726	B	949 251-0095	9396
Impac Secured Assets Corp	6733	B	949 475-3600	9428
Kaiser Foundation Hospitals	6733	B	949 932-5000	9435
Brer Affiliates LLC **(DH)**	6794	C	949 794-7900	9452
Centerline Mortgage Capitl Inc	6799	B	949 221-6685	9498
Nnn Realty Investors LLC	6799	B	714 667-8252	9542
NRLL LLC	6799	B	949 768-7777	9545
Courtyard Management Corp	7011	D	949 453-1033	9725
Dkn Hotel LLC **(PA)**	7011	B	714 427-4320	9753
European Ht Invstors I I A Cal	7011	D	949 474-7368	9788
Golden Hotels Ltd Partnership	7011	C	949 833-2770	9811
Greens Group Inc	7011	C	949 829-4902	9820
Hyatt Corporation	7011	D	949 975-1234	9890
Kt Hotels LLC	7011	C	949 715-5000	9954
Marriott International Inc	7011	B	949 724-3606	10004
Montage Hotels & Resorts LLC **(PA)**	7011	A	949 715-5002	10024
Spectrum Hotel Group LLC	7011	B	949 471-8888	10260
Valencia Group LLC	7011	C	949 379-6489	10341
American Cmpus Communities Inc	7021	D	949 854-0900	10391
Prudential Overall Supply **(PA)**	7218	D	949 250-4855	10480
Americor Funding Inc	7299	C	866 333-8686	10529
Alcone Marketing Group Inc **(HQ)**	7311	D	949 595-5322	10588
Ignite Health LLC **(PA)**	7311	D	949 861-3200	10628
Interactive Media Holdings Inc	7311	C	949 861-8888	10632
Local Corporation **(PA)**	7311	D	949 784-0800	10643
Young & Rubicam LLC	7311	C	949 754-2100	10691
Young & Rubicam LLC	7311	B	949 754-2000	10692
Ghost Management Group LLC	7313	C	949 870-1400	10712
Egs Financial Care Inc **(DH)**	7322	D	877 217-4423	10740
Corelogic Credco LLC **(DH)**	7323	C	800 255-0792	10759
Database Marketing Group Inc	7331	D	714 727-0800	10770
Spectrum Information Svcs LLC **(PA)**	7331	D	949 752-7070	10776
Bzya Corporation	7349	B	949 656-3220	10867
Calico Building Services Inc	7349	D	949 380-8707	10870
Creative Maintenance Systems	7349	D	949 852-2871	10880
Innovative Cleaning Svcs LLC	7349	B	949 251-9188	10912
Celtic Leasing Corp	7359	D	949 263-3880	11023
Ctpartners Exec Search Inc	7361	D	949 754-2821	11117
Cybercoders	7361	C	949 885-5151	11120
Cybercoders Staffing Svcs LLC	7361	C	949 885-5151	11121
Kore1 LLC	7361	C	949 706-6990	11165
Loan Administration Netwrk Inc	7361	D	949 752-5246	11172
Resources Connection LLC **(HQ)**	7361	C	714 430-6400	11222
Workway Inc	7361	C	949 553-8700	11261
Magnit Rs Inc	7363	D	800 660-9544	11299
Randstad Professionals Us Inc	7363	D	781 213-1500	11321
Sfn Group Inc	7363	A	949 727-8500	11331
Applied Computer Solutions **(DH)**	7371	D	714 861-2200	11414
Arcules Inc	7371	D	949 439-0053	11420
Avamar Technologies Inc	7371	D	949 743-5100	11439
Buddy Group Inc	7371	D	949 468-0042	11478
Codazen Inc	7371	D	949 916-6266	11498
Eighteenth Meridian Inc	7371	D	714 706-3643	11564
Einfochips Inc	7371	D	949 527-6459	11565
Gan Limited	7371	B	702 964-5777	11613
Home Junction Inc	7371	D	858 777-9533	11643
Kofax Inc **(PA)**	7371	B	949 783-1000	11695
Neudesic LLC **(HQ)**	7371	C	949 754-4500	11770
Neuintel LLC **(PA)**	7371	D	949 625-6117	11771
Nexgenix Inc **(PA)**	7371	B	714 665-6240	11774
Nextgen Hlthcare Info Systems **(HQ)**	7371	C	949 255-2600	11775
Open Text Inc	7371	D	949 784-8000	11797
Operation Technology Inc	7371	D	949 462-0100	11799
Pacific Tech Solutions LLC	7371	C	949 830-1623	11809
Secureauth Corporation **(PA)**	7371	C	949 777-6959	11907
Setschedule LLC	7371	C	888 222-0011	11912
Smart Energy Systems Inc	7371	C	909 703-9609	11923
Smart Utility Systems Inc	7371	C	909 217-3344	11924
Spireon Inc **(PA)**	7371	C	800 557-1449	11940
Startel Corporation **(PA)**	7371	C	949 863-8700	11944
Stratacare Llc	7371	C	949 743-1200	11949
Tcg Software Services Inc	7371	B	714 665-6200	11972
Thomas Gallaway Corporation **(PA)**	7371	C	949 517-9500	11976
Unisys Corporation	7371	C	949 380-5000	12002
Vegatek Corporation	7371	D	949 502-0090	12014
Vision Solutions Inc **(HQ)**	7371	D	949 253-6500	12025
Zuum Transportation Inc	7371	C	909 667-7478	12070
Activision Blizzard Inc	7372	C	949 955-1380	12074
Blizzard Entertainment Inc **(DH)**	7372	C	949 955-1380	12120
Calamp Corp **(PA)**	7372	C	949 600-5600	12130
Dorado Network Systems Corp	7372	C	650 227-7300	12163
Eagle Topco LP	7372	A	949 585-4329	12170
Egl Holdco Inc	7372	A	800 678-7423	12176
Global Cash Card Inc	7372	C	949 751-0360	12207
Mscsoftware Corporation **(HQ)**	7372	C	714 540-8900	12276
Nextgen Healthcare Inc **(PA)**	7372	C	949 255-2600	12288
Ntrust Infotech Inc	7372	D	562 207-1600	12294
Patron Solutions LLC	7372	C	949 823-1700	12314
Sage Software Holdings Inc **(HQ)**	7372	B	866 530-7243	12341
Strategy Companion Corp	7372	C	714 460-8398	12365
Upstanding LLC	7372	C	949 788-9900	12388
West Coast Consulting LLC	7372	C	949 250-4102	12396
Wm Technology Inc	7372	B	844 933-3627	12399
Computer Tech Resources Inc	7373	C	714 665-6507	12437
Genea Energy Partners Inc	7373	C	714 694-0536	12460
Result Group Inc	7373	D	480 777-7130	12518
Review Wave	7373	D	800 563-0469	12519
Trace3 LLC **(HQ)**	7373	C	949 333-2300	12533
Automatic Data Processing Inc	7374	C	949 751-0360	12551
Celestial-Saturn Parent Inc **(PA)**	7374	C	949 214-1000	12557
Enclarity Inc	7374	B	949 797-7160	12569
Mercury Technology Group Inc	7374	D	949 417-0260	12597
Verizon Connect Telo Inc **(DH)**	7374	C	844 617-1100	12640
Accurate Background LLC **(PA)**	7375	B	800 784-3911	12649
Inhouseit Inc	7378	C	949 660-5655	12709
Quest Intl Monitor Svc Inc **(PA)**	7378	D	949 581-9900	12710
Rakworx Inc	7378	C	949 215-1362	12711
Caylent Inc	7379	C	800 215-9100	12751
Crowdstrike Inc	7379	C	888 512-8906	12770
Crowdstrike Inc	7379	C	888 512-8906	12771
Dyntek Inc **(PA)**	7379	C	949 271-6700	12782
Gdr Group Inc	7379	D	949 453-8818	12794
Kodella LLC	7379	C	844 563-3552	12824
Kore1 Inc	7379	D	949 706-6990	12825

Employee Codes: A=Over 500 employees, B=251-500
C=101-250, D=51-100, E=20-50, F=10-19, G=1-9

IRVINE CA — GEOGRAPHIC SECTION

Company	SIC	EMP	PHONE	ENTRY#
McLaren Strategic Solutions	7379	D	310 564-6754	12835
Ovation Tech Inc	7379	C	949 271-0054	12852
Synoptek LLC (PA)	7379	D	949 241-8600	12887
Uc Innovation Inc	7379	D	949 415-8246	12900
ABM Onsite Services Inc	7381	A	949 863-9100	12917
Landmark Event Staffing	7381	A	714 293-4248	12993
Universal Services America LP (HQ)	7381	D	866 877-1965	13066
Sentinel Monitoring Corp (HQ)	7382	D	949 453-1550	13144
Alorica Customer Care Inc	7389	C	941 906-9000	13185
Alorica Inc (PA)	7389	D	866 256-7422	13186
Andrew Lauren Company Inc	7389	C	949 861-4222	13193
Baxalta US Inc	7389	C	949 474-6301	13212
Boost Mobile LLC	7389	A	949 451-1563	13216
Consoldted Fire Protection LLC (HQ)	7389	A	949 727-3277	13243
Data Council LLC	7389	D	904 512-3200	13258
Edison Energy LLC	7389	C	949 491-1633	13278
Flagship Credit Acceptance LLC	7389	C	949 748-7172	13289
Global Language Solutions LLC	7389	D	949 798-1400	13304
La Jolla Group Inc (PA)	7389	B	949 428-2800	13343
LARK Industries Inc (DH)	7389	D	714 701-4200	13349
Nitto Avecia Pharma Svcs Inc	7389	D	949 951-4425	13399
Paysafe Partners LP	7389	D	949 788-1010	13424
Universal Card Inc	7389	D	949 861-4000	13528
University California Irvine	7389	C	949 824-6483	13532
Ameripark LLC	7521	D	949 279-7525	13603
Dynamic Auto Images Inc	7542	B	714 771-3400	13692
Bsh Home Appliances Corp (DH)	7629	C	949 440-7100	13733
Melan Inc	7699	D	818 489-1745	13784
Edwards Theatres Circuit Inc	7832	C	949 854-8811	13996
Ming Entertainment Group LLC	7929	D	949 679-2089	14079
Pacific Symphony	7929	D	714 755-5788	14099
Equinox-76th Street Inc	7991	D	949 296-1700	14202
Row House Franchise LLC	7991	C	949 341-5585	14228
Xponential Fitness Inc (PA)	7991	B	949 346-3000	14245
Shady Canyon Golf Club Inc	7997	C	949 856-7000	14451
Beacon Park School	7999	D	949 936-8400	14496
Monarch Healthcare A Medical (HQ)	8011	D	949 923-3200	14911
Southern Cal Prmnnte Med Group	8011	C	949 262-5780	15092
Pacific Dental Services LLC (PA)	8021	B	714 845-8500	15244
Pacific Dental Services LLC	8021	D	714 845-8500	15245
Pacific Dntl Svcs Holdg Co Inc	8021	D	714 845-8500	15246
Equinox-76th Street Inc	8049	D	949 975-8400	15281
In Stepps Inc	8049	D	949 474-1493	15286
Silverado Senior Living Inc (PA)	8051	D	949 240-7200	15667
Home Street Operations LLC	8052	D	949 449-2500	15764
New Vista Behavioral Hlth LLC	8052	D	949 284-0095	15777
Childrens Hospital Orange Cnty	8062	C	949 387-2586	15999
Hoag Hospital Irvine	8062	D	949 764-4624	16131
Kaiser Foundation Hospitals	8062	C	949 262-5780	16148
St Joseph Hospital of Orange	8062	C	714 568-5500	16473
Alliance Healthcare Svcs Inc (DH)	8071	C	800 544-3215	16703
Cap Diagnostics LLC	8071	C	714 966-1221	16708
Healthquest Clinical Lab Inc	8071	D	909 445-9727	16725
Thaihot Investment Co US Ltd	8071	A	949 242-5300	16756
Keating Dental Arts Inc	8072	C	949 955-2100	16774
Vna of Greater Los Angeles Inc	8082	D	951 252-5314	16968
Davita Inc	8092	B	949 930-4400	16980
Discovery Practice MGT Inc	8093	B	714 828-1800	17054
Universal Care Inc (HQ)	8093	B	562 424-6200	17151
Ambitions Behavioral Hlth LLC	8099	D	408 373-6752	17176
University California Irvine	8099	A	949 824-2662	17344
Berger Kahn A Law Corporation (PA)	8111	D	949 474-1880	17384
Crowell & Moring LLP	8111	C	949 263-8400	17428
Fisher & Phillips LLP	8111	D	949 851-2424	17460
Gibson Dunn & Crutcher LLP	8111	D	949 451-3800	17468
Greenberg Traurig LLP	8111	D	949 732-6500	17486
Kahana & Feld LLP	8111	D	949 812-4781	17512
Knobbe Martens Olson Bear LLP (PA)	8111	B	949 760-0404	17529
Law Offces Les Zeve A Prof Cor	8111	C	714 848-7920	17541
Malcolm & Cisneros A Law Corp	8111	C	949 252-9400	17560
Murtaugh Myer Nlson Trglia LLP	8111	D	949 794-4000	17584
Nossaman LLP	8111	D	949 833-7800	17591
Palmieri Tyler Wner Wlhelm Wld	8111	D	949 851-9400	17599
Rutan & Tucker LLP (PA)	8111	B	714 641-5100	17631
Shook Hardy & Bacon LLP	8111	C	949 475-1500	17652
Stretto Inc (PA)	8111	D	949 222-1212	17663
Troutman Ppper Hmltn Snders L	8111	D	949 622-2700	17669
Zbs Law LLP	8111	D	714 848-7920	17690
University California Irvine	8221	C	949 824-7725	17783
It Division Inc	8243	C	678 648-2709	17792
City of Irvine	8322	D	949 724-6900	17887
Council On Aging - Sthern Cal	8322	D	714 479-0107	17899
Hallmark Rehabilitation GP LLC	8322	D	949 282-5900	17995
Radiant Health Centers	8322	D	949 809-5700	18091
Second Hrvest Fd Bnk Ornge CNT	8322	D	949 653-2900	18120
Waymakers	8322	D	714 492-1010	18188
Owl Education and Training Inc	8331	B	949 797-2000	18240
Child Development Incorporated	8351	B	949 854-5060	18285
Leport Educational Inst Inc	8351	D	914 374-8860	18328
Leport Schools	8351	D	714 377-6035	18329
Silverado Snior Lving Hldngs	8361	A	949 240-7200	18521
Western Growers Association (PA)	8611	C	949 863-1000	18726
Temporary Staffing Union	8631	A	714 728-5186	18798
Boys Grls Clubs Cntl Ornge Cas	8641	D	714 543-5540	18825
Woodbridge Village Association	8641	D	949 786-1800	18931
Good Shepherd Lutheran Ch Corp	8661	D	949 552-1967	19019
ABM Facility Services LLC	8711	A	949 330-1555	19124
ABS Consulting Inc	8711	D	714 734-4242	19125
Aria Group Incorporated	8711	D	949 475-2915	19143
Es Engineering Services LLC	8711	D	949 988-3500	19221
Fuscoe Engineering Inc (PA)	8711	D	949 474-1960	19234
Gradient Engineers Inc	8711	C	949 477-0555	19245
Hunsaker & Assoc Irvine Inc (PA)	8711	D	949 583-1010	19262
Hyundai Amer Technical Ctr Inc	8711	C	734 337-2500	19263
Inspiria Inc (PA)	8711	D	949 206-0606	19270
Jacobs Engineering Group Inc	8711	D	949 224-7500	19277
Jacobs Government Services Co	8711	D	949 224-7500	19281
Jacobs Project Management Co	8711	D	949 224-7695	19284
JBa Consulting Engineers Inc	8711	D	949 419-3030	19286
Kpff Inc	8711	D	949 252-1022	19299
Mds Consulting (PA)	8711	D	949 251-8821	19319
Mobilenet Services Inc (PA)	8711	D	949 951-4444	19325
Panasonic Avionics Corporation (DH)	8711	B	949 672-2000	19350
Tetra Tech Inc	8711	D	949 263-0846	19410
Tk1sc	8711	C	949 751-5800	19416
Wsp USA Inc	8711	D	714 973-4880	19445
Gkk Corporation (PA)	8712	B	949 250-1500	19471
Ktgy Group Inc (PA)	8712	D	949 851-2133	19483
LPA Inc (PA)	8712	D	949 261-1001	19487
Stantec Architecture Inc	8712	D	949 923-6000	19506
Stantec Consulting Svcs Inc	8712	D	949 923-6000	19510
Ware Malcomb (PA)	8712	C	949 660-9128	19517
Wimberly Allson Tong Goo NA In	8712	D	949 574-8500	19520
Baker Tilly Us LLP	8721	B	949 222-2999	19537
Ernst & Young LLP	8721	B	949 794-2300	19576
Kpmg LLP	8721	C	949 885-5400	19595
LLP Moss Adams	8721	C	949 221-4000	19604
Omega Accounting Solutions Inc	8721	D	949 348-2433	19618
Sema LLC (PA)	8721	D	949 830-1400	19630
University California Irvine	8721	D	949 824-6828	19636
Wright Ford Young & Co	8721	D	949 910-2727	19641
Agendia Inc	8731	C	949 540-6300	19647
Bioduro LLC	8731	B	858 529-6600	19662
Invasix Inc	8731	D	855 418-5306	19713
Isotis Orthobiologics Inc	8731	C	949 595-8710	19716
Pharmaron Inc	8731	A	949 788-0586	19758
Talon Therapeutics Inc	8731	D	949 788-6700	19779
University California Irvine	8731	A	949 824-2819	19793
Henkel US Operations Corp	8732	C	714 368-8000	19815
Iqvia Inc (DH)	8732	D	866 267-4479	19827
Paragon Biomedical Inc	8732	D	949 224-2800	19842
Mind Research Institute	8733	C	949 345-8700	19895
Aptim Corp	8734	A	949 261-6441	19949
Csa America Standards Inc	8734	D	949 733-4300	19963
Csa America Standards Inc	8734	D	949 733-4300	19964
North Amercn Science Assoc Inc	8734	D	949 951-3110	19992
Pixel Labs LLC	8734	D	512 560-5961	19995
D7 LLC	8741	D	808 630-9169	20073
Demandblue Inc	8741	D	909 402-3453	20077
Legacy Prtners Residential Inc	8741	C	949 930-6600	20137
Mtc Financial Inc	8741	D	949 252-8300	20156
Navigators Management Co Inc	8741	C	949 255-4860	20157
Renovo Solutions LLC (PA)	8741	B	714 599-7969	20194
Saga Kapital Group Inc	8741	D	714 294-4132	20198
Smile Brands Group Inc (PA)	8741	D	714 668-1300	20206
Southern Implants Inc	8741	C	949 273-8505	20214
Tct Mobile Inc	8741	D	949 892-2990	20226
Vpm Management Inc	8741	D	949 863-1500	20247
Western National Contractors	8741	D	949 862-6200	20250
Advantage Sales & Mktg Inc (DH)	8742	C	949 797-2900	20262
Advantage Sales & Mktg LLC (DH)	8742	C	949 797-2900	20263
Beacon Resources LLC	8742	C	949 955-1773	20292
Benefitcompass LLC	8742	D	949 289-9300	20293
Bridgwter Consulting Group Inc	8742	D	949 535-1755	20302
Brown and Streza LLP	8742	D	949 453-2900	20304
Caerus Marketing Group LLC	8742	D	877 627-2509	20305

GEOGRAPHIC SECTION

	SIC	EMP	PHONE	ENTRY#
City of Irvine	8742	C	949 724-7600	20316
Denken Solutions Inc	8742	C	949 630-5263	20343
Exult Inc	8742	A	949 856-8800	20370
Foundation Lead Group LLC	8742	D	877 477-2311	20385
Global Risk MGT Solutions LLC	8742	D	949 759-8500	20394
Icf Jones & Stokes Inc	8742	D	949 333-6600	20409
Jnr Inc	8742	D	949 476-2788	20422
Lba Inc	8742	D	949 833-0400	20432
M F Salta Co Inc (PA)	8742	D	562 421-2512	20444
Mercer (us) Inc	8742	D	949 222-1300	20464
Morris & Willner Partners	8742	D	949 705-0682	20475
Online Marketing Group LLC	8742	C	888 737-9635	20495
Resources Connection Inc (PA)	8742	C	714 430-6400	20527
S E O P Inc	8742	C	949 682-7906	20535
Sullivncrtsmnroe Insur Svcs LL (PA)	8742	C	800 427-3253	20571
Trinamix Inc (PA)	8742	B	408 507-3583	20592
Willis North America Inc	8742	C	909 476-3300	20613
Young & Rubicam LLC	8742	B	949 224-6300	20620
Alliant Insurance Services Inc (PA)	8748	C	949 756-0271	20684
Anchor Cnsling Edcatn Sltons L	8748	D	213 505-6322	20689
Aptim Corp	8748	D	949 261-6441	20691
Datatrace Title	8748	D	800 221-2056	20736
Fryman Management Inc	8748	D	949 481-5211	20752
Ies Commercial Inc	8748	D	949 222-0320	20775
In Montrose Wtr Sstnblity Svcs	8748	D	949 988-3500	20776
Karman Topco LP (PA)	8748	C	949 797-2900	20789
Lsa Associates Inc (PA)	8748	C	949 553-0666	20800
Slalom LLC	8748	C	949 450-1100	20848
Slr International Corporation	8748	A	949 553-8417	20849
TRC Solutions Inc (HQ)	8748	C	949 753-0101	20867
Vinculums Services LLC	8748	C	949 783-3552	20875
Orangepeople LLC	8999	C	949 535-1308	20897

IRWINDALE, CA - Los Angeles County

	SIC	EMP	PHONE	ENTRY#
Pierre Landscape Inc	0781	C	626 587-2121	457
Mariposa Landscapes Inc (PA)	0782	D	626 960-0196	519
Church & Larsen Inc	1742	C	626 303-8741	1921
Ready Pac Foods Inc (HQ)	2099	A	626 856-8686	2442
Best Overnite Express Inc (PA)	4213	D	626 256-6340	3448
Southern California Edison Co	4911	B	626 815-7296	4686
Southern California Edison Co	4911	B	626 814-4212	4695
Southern California Edison Co	4911	C	626 812-7380	4698
Southern California Edison Co	4911	D	626 543-8081	4704
Southern California Edison Co	4911	D	626 633-3070	4707
Ihealth Manufacturing Inc	5047	D	216 785-0107	5425
Superior Communications Inc (PA)	5065	C	877 522-4727	5703
Assa Abloy Rsdential Group Inc (HQ)	5072	C	626 961-0413	5721
Mountain Gear Corporation	5136	C	626 851-2488	6182
Ready Pac Produce Inc (DH)	5148	C	800 800-4088	6575
Sinecera Inc	7389	D	626 962-1087	13477
Onelegacy (PA)	8099	D		17286
Calibre International LLC (PA)	8743	C	626 969-4660	20632

IVANHOE, CA - Tulare County

	SIC	EMP	PHONE	ENTRY#
Klink Citrus Association	0723	C	559 798-1881	284

JACKSON, CA - Amador County

	SIC	EMP	PHONE	ENTRY#
Lowes Home Centers LLC	5211	D	209 223-6140	7092
Sita Ram LLC	7011	D	209 223-0211	10242
Sutter Amador Womens Services	8062	A	209 223-2034	16506
Sutter Hlth Scrmnto Sierra Reg	8062	D	209 223-7540	16542
Sutter Valley Hospitals	8062	B	209 223-7514	16561
K&B Pichette Enterprises Inc	8082	D	209 452-5999	16881
Amador Tlmne Cmnty Action Agcy (PA)	8399	D	209 296-2785	18554
American Lgion Post No 108 Amb	8641	D	209 223-2963	18812

JAMUL, CA - San Diego County

	SIC	EMP	PHONE	ENTRY#
Spectrum Security Services Inc (PA)	7382	C	619 669-6660	13147
TAC Air California Inc	7999	D	619 216-8416	14568

JOSHUA TREE, CA - San Bernardino County

	SIC	EMP	PHONE	ENTRY#
Hdmc Holdings LLC	8062	C	760 366-3711	16120

JULIAN, CA - San Diego County

	SIC	EMP	PHONE	ENTRY#
YMCA of San Diego County	8641	C	760 765-0642	18949

JURUPA VALLEY, CA - Riverside County

	SIC	EMP	PHONE	ENTRY#
Perry Coast Construction Inc	1542	C	951 774-0677	990
Christian Brothers Mechanical Services Inc	1711	C	951 361-2247	1396
Calpaco Papers Inc (PA)	2679	C	323 767-2800	2533
Mobile Modular Management Corp	3448	C	800 819-1084	2748
Young Electric Sign Company	3993	C	909 923-7668	3103
Landjet (PA)	4119	C	909 873-4636	3270
Deluxe Auto Carriers Inc	4212	D	909 746-0900	3387
Triways Inc	4213	D	951 361-4840	3557
Act Fulfillment Inc (PA)	4225	C	909 930-9083	3669
Costco Wholesale Corporation	4225	A	951 361-3606	3689
Home Depot USA Inc	4225	C	951 361-1235	3715
Toll Global Fwdg Scs USA Inc	4731	D	951 360-8310	4107
Hino Motors Mfg USA Inc	5013	C	951 727-0286	5044
Pavement Recycling Systems Inc (PA)	5093	C	951 682-1091	6012
Olivet International Inc (PA)	5099	B	951 681-8888	6047
Galassos Bakery (PA)	5149	C	951 360-1211	6628
Le Vecke Corporation (PA)	5181	C	951 681-8600	6770
Southwest Material Hdlg Inc (PA)	5511	C	951 727-0477	7303
Express Contractors Inc	7217	C	951 360-6500	10474
Arcticom Group Rfrgn LLC	7623	B	916 484-3190	13723
Vista Pacifica Enterprises Inc (PA)	8051	C	951 682-4833	15725

KEENE, CA - Kern County

	SIC	EMP	PHONE	ENTRY#
United Farm Workers America (PA)	8631	C	661 822-5571	18802

KELSEYVILLE, CA - Lake County

	SIC	EMP	PHONE	ENTRY#
AFLAC	6411	C	800 992-3522	8479

KENTFIELD, CA - Marin County

	SIC	EMP	PHONE	ENTRY#
1125 Sir Frncis Drake Blvd Ope	8062	C	415 456-9680	15914
Marin General Hospital	8062	A	415 925-7000	16246
Ross Hospital	8069	C	415 258-6900	16692
Kleinfelder Inc	8711	C	415 458-5803	19295
Crometrics	8742	D	415 482-8899	20335

KENWOOD, CA - Sonoma County

	SIC	EMP	PHONE	ENTRY#
Palo Alto Vineyard MGT LLC	0761	D	707 996-7725	367
Pernod Ricard Usa LLC	2084	D	707 833-5891	2390

KERMAN, CA - Fresno County

	SIC	EMP	PHONE	ENTRY#
Macs Equipment Inc	7699	D	559 846-6668	13782
Hall Management Corp	8741	A	559 846-7382	20107

KETTLEMAN CITY, CA - Kings County

	SIC	EMP	PHONE	ENTRY#
Keenan Farms Inc	0173	D	559 945-1400	93
Chemical Waste Management Inc	4953	C	559 386-9711	4877

KING CITY, CA - Monterey County

	SIC	EMP	PHONE	ENTRY#
San Bernabe Vineyards	0172	C	831 385-4897	84
Meyer LLC	0723	C	831 385-4047	288
L A Hearne Company (PA)	5191	D	831 385-5441	6828
Southern Mntrey Cnty Mem Hosp (PA)	8062	B	831 385-6000	16448
Catalyst Family Inc	8351	B	831 385-4005	18277

KINGSBURG, CA - Fresno County

	SIC	EMP	PHONE	ENTRY#
Kap LP	0175	D	559 897-5132	108
Mike Jensen Farms LLC	0175	C	559 897-4192	109
Peterson Family Inc	0175	C	559 897-5064	112
Cheema Logistics	4449	C	559 702-1444	3802
Van Beurden Insurance Svcs Inc (PA)	6411	D	559 634-7125	8680
Michaels Mngmnt-Affordable LLC	6513	C	559 897-5885	8843
Sunbridge Care Entps W LLC	8051	C	559 897-5881	15688
Crestwood Behavioral Hlth Inc	8059	D	559 238-6981	15836
Dfa of California	8741	D	559 233-7249	20079

KIRKWOOD, CA - Alpine County

	SIC	EMP	PHONE	ENTRY#
Kirkwood Mountain Resorts LLC	7011	D	209 258-6000	9948

LA CANADA, CA - Los Angeles County

	SIC	EMP	PHONE	ENTRY#
Descanso Gardens Guild Inc	5261	D	818 952-4408	7125
Dilbeck Inc (PA)	6531	D	818 790-6774	8985
La Canada Flintridge Cntry CLB	7997	D	818 790-0611	14386
Navigage Foundation (PA)	8051	D	818 790-2522	15595
Crescenta-Canada YMCA (PA)	8641	C	818 790-0123	18848
Young MNS Chrstn Assn of Fthll	8641	C	818 790-0123	18988

LA CANADA FLINTRIDGE, CA - Los Angeles County

	SIC	EMP	PHONE	ENTRY#
Allen Lund Company LLC (HQ)	4731	C	818 777-6142	3984
Cal Tech Emplyees Fderal Cr Un (PA)	6061	D	818 952-4444	7757
Southwest Administrators Inc	6371	B		8469
Holmes Body Shop-Alhambra Inc (PA)	7532	D	626 795-6447	13640

LA CRESCENTA, CA - Los Angeles County

	SIC	EMP	PHONE	ENTRY#
Monarch E & S Insurance Svcs	6411	D	559 226-0200	8614
EAM Enterprises Inc (PA)	6531	D	818 248-9100	8990
Outlook Amusements Inc	7379	C	818 433-3800	12851
Mariner Health Care Inc	8051	D	818 957-0850	15577

LA HABRA, CA - Orange County

Company	SIC	EMP	PHONE	ENTRY#
Albd Electric and Cable	1731	D	949 440-1216	1658
Shepard Bros Inc **(PA)**	3589	C	562 697-1366	2849
Home Depot USA Inc	5211	D	562 690-6006	7007
Lowes Home Centers LLC	5211	C	562 690-5122	7069
Peerless Maintenance Svc Inc	7349	B	714 871-3380	10940
Life Care Centers America Inc	8051	C	562 690-0852	15537

LA HABRA HEIGHTS, CA - Orange County

Company	SIC	EMP	PHONE	ENTRY#
Hacienda Golf Club	7997	D	562 694-1081	14380

LA HONDA, CA - San Mateo County

Company	SIC	EMP	PHONE	ENTRY#
Alesia Viticulture Svcs LLC	0761	D	650 333-5490	363
Young MNS Chrstn Assn San Frnc	8641	C	650 747-1200	18994

LA JOLLA, CA - San Diego County

Company	SIC	EMP	PHONE	ENTRY#
Merrill Lynch Prce Fnner Smith	6211	D	858 456-3600	8140
Morgan Stnley Smith Barney LLC	6211	C	212 761-4000	8145
Prospect Financial Group Inc	6282	D	858 605-0952	8217
Northwestern Mutl Fincl Netwrk **(PA)**	6311	D	619 234-3111	8242
Front Porch Communities & Svcs	6513	C	858 454-2151	8813
Malk Partners	6722	D	858 914-1125	9378
Estancia Hotel LLC	7011	C	949 474-7368	9786
Fargo Colonial LLC	7011	D	858 454-2181	9793
La Jolla Bch & Tennis CLB Inc	7011	B	858 459-8271	9960
La Jolla Cove Ht Mtl Aprtmnts	7011	D	858 459-2621	9961
Lav Hotel Corp	7011	C	858 454-0771	9970
Marriott International Inc	7011	B	858 587-1414	10006
Torreyana Grille	7011	D	858 558-1500	10316
Destination Residences LLC	7299	B	858 550-1000	10542
University Cal San Diego	7336	B	858 534-2377	10821
Host Healthcare Inc	7363	A	858 999-3579	11290
Abacus Data Systems Inc	7371	D	858 529-0020	11372
Altium Inc **(HQ)**	7371	D	858 864-1500	11400
United Support Services Inc	7371	C	858 373-9500	12003
Edgewave Inc	7372	D	800 782-3762	12172
University Cal San Diego	7374	B	858 534-5000	12639
The Copley Press Inc	7383	A	858 454-0411	13158
Life Time Inc	7991	D	858 459-0281	14215
La Jolla Bch & Tennis CLB Inc **(PA)**	7997	C	858 454-7126	14388
La Jolla Country Club Inc	7997	D	858 454-9601	14389
Balboa Nphrology Med Group Inc	8011	C	858 810-8000	14622
Hiv Neural Behavioral Center	8011	D	619 543-5000	14774
La Jolla Orthpdic Srgery Ctr L	8011	D	858 657-0055	14870
Ming Tsuang Dr	8011	D	858 822-2464	14900
Scripps Clinic Medical Group	8011	D	858 554-9606	15053
Sulpizio Cardiovascular Center	8011	C	858 657-7000	15104
Covenant Care La Jolla LLC	8051	C	858 453-5810	15408
Scripps Health	8062	B	858 455-9100	16404
Scripps Health	8062	D	800 727-4777	16406
Scripps Health	8062	B	858 626-6150	16407
Scripps Mmral-Ximed Med Ctr LP	8062	D	858 882-8350	16409
University Cal San Diego	8062	A	858 657-7000	16591
Discovery Health Services	8099	B	858 459-0785	17223
West Health Incubator Inc	8099	D	858 535-7000	17352
Gillispie School	8211	D	858 459-3773	17712
Humangood Socal	8361	C	858 454-4201	18455
Westmont Living Inc **(PA)**	8361	D	858 456-1233	18548
Lawrence Fmly Jwish Cmnty Ctrs **(PA)**	8399	C	858 362-1144	18606
Theater Arts Fndtion San Dego	8641	C	858 623-3366	18917
YMCA of San Diego County	8641	B	858 453-3483	18938
U C San Diego Foundation	8699	C	858 534-1032	19113
University Cal San Diego	8712	D	858 534-2177	19515
Agouron Pharmaceuticals Inc	8731	B	858 622-3000	19649
The Salk Institute For Biological S	8731	A	858 453-4100	19784
California Institute For Biomedical Research	8733	C	858 242-1000	19871
J Craig Venter Institute Inc **(PA)**	8733	B	301 795-7000	19889
La Jolla Inst For Immunology	8733	B	858 752-6500	19893
Sanford Brnham Prbys Med Dscve **(PA)**	8733	A	858 795-5000	19908
Scripps Research Institute	8733	D	858 242-1000	19909
Scripps Research Institute **(PA)**	8733	D	858 784-1000	19910

LA MESA, CA - San Diego County

Company	SIC	EMP	PHONE	ENTRY#
West Coast Arborists Inc	1521	C	858 566-4204	740
Crew Builders Inc	1542	C	619 587-2033	901
Brady Company/San Diego Inc	1742	B	619 462-2600	1912
Brady Socal Incorporated	1742	D	619 462-2600	1913
Bob Stall Chevrolet	5511	C	619 460-1311	7174
Drew Ford	5511	C	619 464-7777	7196
Kaiser Foundation Hospitals	6324	C	619 528-5000	8316
Teague Insurance Agency Inc	6411	D	619 464-6851	8670
Helm Management Co **(PA)**	6531	D	619 589-6222	9038
Fancy Life Enterprises LLC **(PA)**	7812	C	619 560-9890	13848
Sharp Healthcare	8011	D	619 460-6200	15055
Sharp RES-Stealy Med Group Inc	8011	C	619 644-6405	15057
Community Care Center	8051	D	619 465-0702	15379
Life Gnerations Healthcare LLC	8051	D	619 460-2330	15544
Grossmont Hospital Corporation **(HQ)**	8062	A	619 740-6000	16114
Grossmont Hospital Corporation	8062	B	619 667-1900	16115
Team Health Holdings Inc	8062	B	619 740-4401	16568
Bh-SD Opco LLC **(PA)**	8093	D	619 465-4411	17015
Brightqest Trtmnt Ctrs - San D	8093	D	619 466-0547	17017
Helix Healthcare Inc	8093	B	619 465-4411	17071
YMCA of San Diego County	8641	C	619 464-1323	18942

LA MIRADA, CA - Los Angeles County

Company	SIC	EMP	PHONE	ENTRY#
Shasta Beverages Inc	2086	D	714 523-2280	2413
Mv Transportation Inc	4111	C	562 943-6776	3169
Estes Express Lines	4213	C	714 994-3770	3470
Home Depot USA Inc	4225	D	714 522-8651	3718
Mejico Express Inc **(PA)**	4513	C	714 690-8300	3857
Tiffany Dale Inc **(PA)**	5023	D	714 739-2700	5138
Reliance Steel & Aluminum Co	5051	C	714 736-4800	5514
Makita USA Inc **(HQ)**	5072	C	714 522-8088	5731
Tomarco Contractor Spc Inc **(PA)**	5072	D	714 523-1771	5737
Stainless Stl Fabricators Inc	5084	D	714 739-9904	5870
US Foods Inc	5141	C	714 670-3500	6410
Living Spaces Furniture LLC **(PA)**	5712	C	714 523-2000	7423
IL Fornaio (america) LLC	5812	C	714 752-7052	7487
Presentation Products Inc **(PA)**	5999	D	714 367-2900	7591
Pacific Bay Lending Group	6163	D	714 367-5125	8049
Cha La Mirada LLC	7011	C	714 739-8500	9692
Kam Sang Company Inc	7011	D	714 523-2800	9934
Diversified Mailing Incorporated	7331	C	714 994-6245	10771
Bigge Group	7353	C	714 523-4092	10993
Orange Courier Inc	7389	B	714 384-3600	13410
Crothall Services Group	7699	A	714 562-9275	13769
Life Care Centers America Inc	8051	C	562 947-8691	15538
Life Care Centers America Inc	8051	C	562 943-7156	15540
Southern Cal Spcialty Care LLC **(DH)**	8062	D	562 944-1900	16444
Straight Talk Inc	8322	D	562 943-0195	18145

LA PALMA, CA - Orange County

Company	SIC	EMP	PHONE	ENTRY#
Isec Incorporated	1751	C	714 761-5151	2005
Norman International Inc	5023	D	562 946-0420	5129
Slade Gorton & Co Inc	5146	D	714 676-4200	6483
Prestige Stations Inc **(DH)**	5411	C	714 670-5145	7147
Atlantic Richfield Company **(DH)**	5541	A	800 333-3991	7383
Commercial Crrers Insur Agcy I	6411	D	562 404-4900	8530
Tech Knowledge Associates LLC	7699	D	714 735-3810	13804
Kaiser Foundation Hospitals	8011	C	714 562-3420	14792
La Palma Hospital Medical Center	8062	B	714 670-7400	16209
Applecare Medical MGT LLC	8741	C	714 443-4507	20024

LA PUENTE, CA - Los Angeles County

Company	SIC	EMP	PHONE	ENTRY#
AZ Construction Inc **(PA)**	1521	C	626 333-0727	658
Alert Insulation Company Inc	1742	D	626 961-9113	1902
Athens Disposal Company Inc **(PA)**	4953	B	626 336-3636	4860
Powell Works Inc	5084	B	909 861-6699	5859
Ldla Clothing LLC	5137	D	323 312-2805	6204
Smart & Final Stores Inc	5141	B	626 330-2495	6296
Cacique Distributors US	5143	C	626 961-3399	6430
Cacique Foods LLC	5143	C	626 961-3399	6431
Aperto Property Management Inc	6513	B	626 965-1961	8790
County of Los Angeles	8011	D	626 968-3711	14711
Enki Health and RES Systems	8011	D	626 961-8971	14740
Wave Plastic Surgery Ctr Inc	8011	D	626 964-7788	15200
Plaza De La Raza Child Dev Svc **(PA)**	8351	D	562 776-1301	18345
California Prof Engrg Inc	8711	D	626 810-1338	19169

LA QUINTA, CA - Riverside County

Company	SIC	EMP	PHONE	ENTRY#
Imperial Irrigation District	4939	C	760 398-5811	4758
Smart & Final Stores LLC	5141	D	760 342-1646	6340
Primetime International Inc	5148	D	760 399-4166	6570
Sun and Sands Enterprises LLC **(PA)**	5148	D	760 399-4166	6582
Lowes Home Centers LLC	5211	C	760 771-5566	7044
Hideaway	5812	C	760 777-7400	7486
Msr Desert Resort LP	5812	A	760 564-5730	7498
Ron Rick Holdings Montana LLC	6719	D	406 493-5606	9332
HP Lq Investment LP	7011	C	760 564-4111	9876
Lqr Property LLC	7011	C	760 564-4111	9990
Msr Resort Lodging Tenant LLC	7011	A	760 564-4111	10035
Career Strategies Tmpry Inc	7361	C	760 564-5959	11107
Chapman Golf Development LLC	7992	D	760 564-8723	14248
Golf Management Operating LLC	7992	A	760 777-4839	14264
Ksl Recreation Management Operations LLC	7992	A	760 564-8000	14268

GEOGRAPHIC SECTION

LAKE ISABELLA CA

	SIC	EMP	PHONE	ENTRY#
Madison Club Owners Assn	7992	C	760 777-9320	14273
Silver Rock Resort Golf Club	7992	D	760 777-8884	14288
Trilogy Golf At La Quinta	7992	B	760 771-0707	14295
Hideaway Club	7997	D	760 777-7400	14381
Tradition Golf Club Associates	7997	D	760 564-3355	14474
Eisenhower Medical Center	8062	C	760 610-7200	16066
Desert Snds Unfied Schl Dst SC	8351	D	760 777-4200	18306

LA VERNE, CA - Los Angeles County

	SIC	EMP	PHONE	ENTRY#
Andersen Commercial Plbg Inc	1711	C	909 599-5950	1357
Walters & Wolf Glass Company	1793	D	909 392-1961	2209
Jet Delivery Inc (PA)	4215	C	800 716-7177	3617
Metropltan Wtr Dst of Sthern C	4941	B	909 593-7474	4811
Ten Days Manufacturing	5085	C	888 222-1575	5930
Haaker Equipment Company (PA)	5087	D	909 598-2706	5940
Chases LLC	6029	D	909 596-6810	7729
Alquest Technologies Inc	7378	D	909 592-8708	12701
Edwards Theatres Inc	7832	C	844 462-7342	13989
RES-Care Inc	8052	D	909 596-5360	15792
Brethren Hillcrest Homes	8361	D	909 593-4917	18381
David and Margaret Home Inc	8361	D	909 596-5921	18414
Haynes Family Programs Inc	8361	D	909 593-2581	18448
Massachusetts Electric Company	8741	D	909 962-6001	20146

LADERA RANCH, CA - Orange County

	SIC	EMP	PHONE	ENTRY#
Sst IV 8020 Las Vgas Blvd S LL	4225	D	949 429-6600	3757
Exclusive Lifestyles Inc (PA)	6531	D	702 996-3030	8998
Optumcare Medical Group	8099	D	949 364-9112	17291

LAFAYETTE, CA - Contra Costa County

	SIC	EMP	PHONE	ENTRY#
Neatly Technologies Inc	7361	D	415 509-1274	11180
Premier Staffing Inc	7361	D	415 362-2211	11205
Civications Inc	7379	D	510 408-7510	12757
Clubsport San Ramon LLC	7991	D	925 283-4000	14189

LAGUNA BEACH, CA - Orange County

	SIC	EMP	PHONE	ENTRY#
Moulton Animal Hospital Inc	0742	D	949 831-7297	337
Myotek Industries Incorporated (DH)	3694	D	949 502-3776	2951
Durham School Services L P	4151	C	949 376-0376	3334
4g Wireless Inc (PA)	4812	D	949 748-6100	4181
Pauls Tv LLC	5064	D	949 596-8800	5609
Pacific Housing Management (PA)	6531	D	714 508-1777	9117
Vacation Bay Hotel Prpts Inc	7011	D	949 494-8566	10339
Laguna Playhouse (PA)	7922	C	949 497-2787	14042
University California Irvine	8099	D	949 939-7106	17343
JC Resorts LLC	8741	A	949 376-2779	20119
Montage Hotels & Resorts LLC	8741	A	949 715-6000	20154
Laguna Sapphire LLC	8748	D	949 715-3300	20796

LAGUNA HILLS, CA - Orange County

	SIC	EMP	PHONE	ENTRY#
Five Star Plastering Inc	1742	D	949 683-5091	1929
Moulton Nguel Wtr Dst Pub Fclt	4941	C	949 831-2500	4812
American Capital Group Inc	6159	D	949 271-5800	7914
Valley Insurance Service Inc	6411	A	949 707-4080	8679
Jamboree Realty Corp (PA)	6531	C	949 380-0300	9057
Professional Cmnty MGT Cal Inc	6531	C	949 597-4200	9144
Varsity Contractors Inc	7349	D	949 586-8283	10985
Groundwork Open Source Inc	7375	D	415 992-4500	12665
Altec Products Inc (PA)	7389	D	949 727-1248	13187
Productive Playhouse Inc (PA)	7389	B	323 250-3445	13432
Cirrus Health II LP	8011	D	949 855-0562	14686
South Cnty Orthpd Spclsts A ME	8011	D	949 586-3200	15068
Gate Three Healthcare LLC	8051	C	949 587-9000	15490
Long Beach Memorial Hospi	8062	A	562 933-2000	16235
Saddleback Memorial Med Ctr (HQ)	8062	A	949 837-4500	16367
Laguna Home Health Svcs LLC	8082	C	949 707-5023	16886
Rehab Alliance	8093	D	949 707-5555	17116
Automobile Club Southern Cal	8699	D	949 951-1400	19060

LAGUNA NIGUEL, CA - Orange County

	SIC	EMP	PHONE	ENTRY#
Plumbing Solution Specialist	1711	D	714 326-1064	1530
Rye Electric Inc	1731	D	949 441-0545	1829
Beverages & More Inc	2086	C	949 643-3020	2403
San Diego Daily Transcript	2621	D	619 232-4381	2511
Interface Associates Inc	3841	C	949 448-7056	3054
Home Depot USA Inc	5211	D	949 831-3698	6984
Morgan Stnley Smith Barney LLC	6022	D	800 490-5412	7699
Purpose Funding Inc	6153	D	949 456-7899	7903
Merrill Lynch Prce Fnner Smith	6211	D	949 456-8082	8111
First Team RE - Orange Cnty	6531	B	949 240-7979	9014
Fuel50 Inc	7371	D	833 844-1103	11608
Technicon Design Corporation	7389	C	949 218-1300	13503
Young MNS Chrstn Assn Ornge CN	7997	C	949 495-9622	14485

	SIC	EMP	PHONE	ENTRY#
Mission Internal Med Group Inc	8011	D	949 364-3605	14901
Life Time Fitness Inc	8099	C	949 238-2700	17269
Aegis Senior Communities LLC	8361	C	949 496-8080	18370

LAGUNA WOODS, CA - Orange County

	SIC	EMP	PHONE	ENTRY#
Laguna Woods Village	6531	A	949 597-4267	9068
Professional Cmnty MGT Cal Inc	6531	C	949 206-0580	9142
Countryside Inn-Corona LP	7011	D	949 588-0131	9721
Village Management Svcs Inc	8741	D	949 597-4360	20245

LAKE ARROWHEAD, CA - San Bernardino County

	SIC	EMP	PHONE	ENTRY#
Rim of World Unified Schl Dst	4151	D	909 336-0330	3348
Lake Arrwhead Rsort Oprtor Inc (HQ)	7011	C	909 336-1511	9963
Mountains Community Hosp Fndtn	8062	C	909 336-3651	16278

LAKE ELSINORE, CA - Riverside County

	SIC	EMP	PHONE	ENTRY#
Kdk Pacific Coast Entps LLC	0782	D	330 715-3143	505
Dalinghaus Construction Inc	1521	D	877 360-9227	670
West Coast Ltg & Enrgy Inc	1731	C	951 296-0680	1874
Gbc Concrete Masnry Cnstr Inc	1741	C	951 245-2355	1883
Pro Structural Inc	1741	D	951 526-2010	1892
Hakes Sash & Door Inc	1751	C	951 674-2414	2000
Edje-Enterprises	1761	D	951 245-7070	2062
Sci Inc	1771	C	951 245-7511	2156
Pointdirect Transport Inc	4213	D	909 371-0837	3527
Elsinore Vly Municpl Wtr Dst (PA)	4941	C	951 674-3146	4792
Pacific Clay Products Inc	5032	C	661 857-1401	5208
Goodfellow Corporation	5082	C	909 874-2700	5789
Lowes Home Centers LLC	5211	C	951 253-6000	7088
Lake Chevrolet	5511	C	951 674-3116	7249
AWI Management Corporation	8741	C	951 674-8200	20030

LAKE FOREST, CA - Orange County

	SIC	EMP	PHONE	ENTRY#
Natures Image Inc	0781	D	949 680-4400	449
W B Starr Inc	0782	D	949 770-8835	547
Streamline Finishes Inc	1542	D	949 600-8964	1033
Arb Inc (HQ)	1623	C	949 598-9242	1192
Primoris Services Corporation	1623	C	949 598-9242	1252
Cbr Electric Inc	1731	C	949 455-0331	1694
Vintage Design LLC (HQ)	1752	D	949 900-5400	2040
Mission Pools of Escondido	1799	C	949 588-0100	2297
Sole Technology Inc (PA)	3149	C	949 460-2020	2685
Focus Industries Inc	3646	D	949 830-1350	2874
Qf Liquidation Inc (PA)	3714	C	949 930-3400	2977
Aminco International USA Inc	3911	D	949 457-3261	3086
Xpo Logistics Freight Inc	4213	D	949 581-9030	3572
Home Express Delivery Svc LLC	4731	A	949 715-9844	4035
Cellco Partnership	4812	D	949 472-0700	4202
Ytel Inc	4813	D	800 382-4913	4360
Toshiba Amer Bus Solutions Inc (DH)	5044	B	949 462-6000	5257
Commercial Indus Design Co Inc	5045	D	949 273-6199	5286
Insulectro (PA)	5065	C	949 587-3200	5663
Refrigeration Supplies Distributor (PA)	5078	D	949 380-7878	5781
SMC Products Inc	5092	D	949 753-1099	5997
Nakase Brothers Wholesale Nurs	5193	C	949 855-4388	6867
Cloudradiant Corp (PA)	5199	D	408 256-1527	6897
Home Depot USA Inc	5211	C	949 609-0221	7017
Ganahl Lumber Company	5251	C	949 830-3600	7121
Del Taco Restaurants Inc (PA)	5812	C	949 462-9300	7472
Loandepot Inc	6162	B	949 470-6263	7994
Psb	7311	D	949 465-0772	10665
Performance Building Services	7349	C	949 364-4364	10942
Vci Event Technology Inc	7359	C	714 772-2002	11062
Wonderware Corporation (DH)	7372	B	949 727-3200	12401
Aveva Software LLC (DH)	7373	B	949 727-3200	12424
Avidex Industries LLC	7379	D	949 428-6333	12737
Itek Services Inc	7379	D	949 770-4835	12820
Advanced Protection Inds LLC	7382	C	800 662-1711	13093
Freedom Village Healthcare Ctr	8051	D	949 472-4733	15481
Environments For Learning Inc (PA)	8351	D	949 855-5630	18313
Lake Frest No II Mstr Hmwners	8641	D	949 586-0860	18875
Alcon Research LLC	8733	D	800 862-5266	19861
Alcon Vision LLC	8734	B	949 505-6890	19945
Beech Street Corporation (HQ)	8741	B	949 672-1000	20034
Mike Rovner Construction Inc	8741	C	949 458-1562	20153
Environmental Resolutions Inc	8748	B	949 457-8950	20745
Higher Ground Education Inc (PA)	8748	D	949 836-9401	20770
Westamerica Communications Inc	8999	D	949 340-8942	20907

LAKE ISABELLA, CA - Kern County

	SIC	EMP	PHONE	ENTRY#
Kern Valley Hosp Foundation (PA)	5912	B	760 379-2681	7525

LAKE VIEW TERRACE CA — GEOGRAPHIC SECTION

	SIC	EMP	PHONE	ENTRY#

LAKE VIEW TERRACE, CA - Los Angeles County
	SIC	EMP	PHONE	ENTRY#
Phoenix Houses Los Angeles Inc.	8361	D	818 686-3000	18505

LAKEPORT, CA - Lake County
	SIC	EMP	PHONE	ENTRY#
Konocti Vista Casino (PA)	7999	C	707 262-1900	14539
Lake Cnty Trbal Hlth Cnsrtium	8021	D	707 263-8382	15232
Evergreen At Lakeport LLC (PA)	8051	D	707 263-6382	15469
Lakeport Post Acute LLC	8052	D	707 263-6382	15769
Sutter Lakeside Hospital	8062	B	707 262-5000	16552
Sutter West Bay Hospitals	8062	B	707 262-5000	16564

LAKESHORE, CA - Fresno County
	SIC	EMP	PHONE	ENTRY#
Sierra Summit Inc.	7011	A	559 233-2500	10235

LAKESIDE, CA - San Diego County
	SIC	EMP	PHONE	ENTRY#
Pacific Green Landscape Inc (PA)	0781	C	619 390-1546	455
Minshew Brothers Stl Cnstr Inc.	1541	C		834
Lb3 Enterprises Inc.	1611	D	619 579-6161	1130
Hazard Construction Company	1622	D	858 587-3600	1184
Marathon Construction Corp.	1629	D	619 276-4401	1311
A M Ortega Construction Inc (PA)	1731	D	619 390-1988	1649
Standard Drywall Inc (HQ)	1742	B	619 443-7034	1965
Clauss Construction	1795	C	619 390-4440	2231
Layfield USA Corporation (DH)	1799	D	619 562-1200	2293
Christian Bros Flrg Intrors In.	5713	C	619 443-9500	7429
Barona Resort & Casino	7011	A	619 443-2300	9631
LLC Brewer Crane	7353	D	619 390-8252	11002
Rdo Construction Equipment Co.	7353	D	619 443-3758	11005
Lakeside Tax & Financial Svcs	7389	D	619 561-2681	13345

LAKEWOOD, CA - Los Angeles County
	SIC	EMP	PHONE	ENTRY#
Berkshire Hathaway Home Servic.	6331	D	562 809-1331	8378
Precision Netwrk Solutions LLC	7379	D	562 318-4242	12861
Nationwide Theatres Corp.	7933	A	562 421-8448	14120
Tenet Healthsystem Medical Inc.	8011	A	562 531-2550	15125
Lakewood Regional Med Ctr Inc.	8062	A	562 531-2550	16212
Center For Dscovery Adolescnt	8093	D	562 425-6404	17021
Tarzana Treatment Centers Inc.	8093	D	562 428-4111	17138
County of Los Angeles	8322	D	562 497-3500	17912

LAMONT, CA - Kern County
	SIC	EMP	PHONE	ENTRY#
Grimmway Enterprises Inc.	5148	B	661 845-3758	6558
Clinica Sierra Vista	8011	D	661 845-3717	14690

LANCASTER, CA - Los Angeles County
	SIC	EMP	PHONE	ENTRY#
Desert Haven Enterprises	0782	A	661 948-8402	484
Excel Contractors Inc.	1521	D	661 942-6944	676
Granite Construction Inc.	1611	D	805 667-8210	1113
Circulating Air Inc.	1711	D	661 942-2048	1398
Nibbelink Masonry Cnstr Corp.	1741	D	661 948-7859	1891
Harvest Farms Inc.	2038	D	661 945-3636	2357
Pavement Recycling Systems Inc.	2951	D	661 948-5599	2650
McWhirter Steel Inc.	3441	D	661 951-8998	2737
Keolis Transit America Inc.	4111	D	661 341-3910	3144
Antelope Vly Schl Trnsp Agcy	4151	C	661 952-3106	3322
Santa Barbara Trnsp Corp	4151	C	661 510-0566	3349
Avery Transport Inc.	4213	D	661 948-3627	3446
Sprint Communications Co LP	4812	C	661 951-8927	4233
BDR Industries Inc (PA)	4841	D	661 940-8554	4474
Directv Group Holdings LLC	4841	C	661 632-6562	4502
County of Los Angeles	4952	D	661 942-6042	4848
Sygma Network Inc	5141	D	661 723-0405	6397
Lowes Home Centers LLC	5211	D	661 341-9000	7084
H W Hunter Inc (PA)	5511	D	661 948-8411	7225
Johnson Ford (PA)	5511	C	888 483-0454	7243
Loandepotcom LLC	6162	A	661 202-1700	7997
Fidelity National Title Co.	6361	D	818 881-7800	8439
V Troth Inc.	6531	D	661 948-4646	9207
Mission Linen Supply	7213	D	661 948-5052	10439
Lantz Security Systems Inc (PA)	7381	D	661 949-3565	12995
Opsec Specialized Protection	7381	D	661 942-3999	13012
Go Get Em Inc.	7382	D	702 985-5637	13121
Lancaster Cmnty Svcs Fndtion I.	7538	C	661 723-6230	13665
Weststar Cinemas Inc.	7922	C	661 723-9392	14072
City of Lancaster	7996	C	661 723-6071	14301
Antelope Valley Hospital Inc.	8011	B	661 726-6180	14614
High Dsert Med Corp A Med Grou (PA)	8011	C	661 945-5936	14772
Lancaster Crdlgy Med Group Inc (PA)	8011	D	661 726-3058	14874
Radnet Management I Inc.	8011	C	661 945-5855	15009
Antelope Vly Retirement HM Inc.	8051	B	661 949-5584	15328
PCI Care Venture I.	8051	D	661 948-2177	15624
Antelope Vly Retirement HM Inc.	8059	D	661 948-7501	15809
Antelope Vly Retirement HM Inc.	8059	C	661 949-5524	15810
Antelope Valley Health Care Di (PA)	8062	A	661 949-5000	15948
Antelope Valley Hospital Inc.	8062	C	661 949-5936	15949
Antelope Valley Hospital Inc.	8062	C	661 949-5000	15950
Antelope Valley Hospital Inc.	8062	C	661 726-6050	15951
Kaiser Foundation Hospitals	8062	D	661 949-5000	16167
Kaiser Foundation Hospitals	8062	A	661 726-2500	16193
US Carenet Services LLC	8082	C	661 945-7350	16961
County of Los Angeles	8093	C	661 524-2005	17039
Tarzana Treatment Centers Inc.	8093	C	661 726-2630	17140
County of Los Angeles	8322	D	661 948-2320	17906
County of Los Angeles	8322	D	661 940-4181	17914
County of Los Angeles	8711	C	661 723-6088	19186
City of Lancaster	9199	D	661 723-6008	20922
County of Los Angeles	9222	D	661 974-7700	20931

LARKSPUR, CA - Marin County
	SIC	EMP	PHONE	ENTRY#
ONeill Beverages Co LLC (PA)	0172	D	559 638-3544	82
Golden Gate Brdge Hwy Trnsp Ds.	4785	C	415 455-2000	4139
Blackwater Cellular Corp.	4812	C	415 526-2200	4186
US Bank Equipment Finance	6022	D	415 461-4600	7720
By The Bay Health (PA)	8082	D	415 927-2273	16831
Roman Cthlic Archbshop of San.	8211	D	415 924-0501	17743
Phoenix American Incorporated (PA)	8742	D	415 485-4500	20506
Burkland Consulting Inc.	8748	D	415 944-8215	20711

LATHROP, CA - San Joaquin County
	SIC	EMP	PHONE	ENTRY#
Cen Cal Plastering Inc.	1742	B	209 981-5265	1920
California Natural Products	2099	B	209 858-2525	2432
Cunha Draying Inc.	4213	D	209 858-1400	3462
Capstone Logistics LLC	4789	C	209 858-1401	4147
Performant Recovery Inc.	7322	C	209 858-3500	10747
Premiere Credit North Amer LLC	7322	C	844 897-2901	10749
Global Building Services Inc.	8999	A	209 858-9501	20888

LAWNDALE, CA - Los Angeles County
	SIC	EMP	PHONE	ENTRY#
Los Angles Cnty Mtro Trnsp Aut.	4111	B	310 643-3804	3148
Automotive Aftermarket Inc.	5013	D	310 793-0046	5025
Burnham Benefits Insur Svcs	6411	D	310 370-5000	8515

LE GRAND, CA - Merced County
	SIC	EMP	PHONE	ENTRY#
J Marchini & Son Inc.	0191	C	559 665-2944	184

LEBEC, CA - Kern County
	SIC	EMP	PHONE	ENTRY#
Six Continents Hotels Inc.	7011	C	661 343-3316	10243

LEMON GROVE, CA - San Diego County
	SIC	EMP	PHONE	ENTRY#
Aztec Landscaping Inc (PA)	0782	C	619 464-3303	475
Condon-Johnson & Assoc Inc.	1522	B	858 530-9165	750
Pacific Sthwest Structures Inc.	1771	C	619 469-2323	2143
Home Depot USA Inc.	5211	C	619 589-2999	7024
Lemon Grove Health Assoc LLC	8051	B	619 463-0294	15536
Family Hlth Ctrs San Diego Inc.	8099	B	619 515-2550	17239
Develpmntal Svcs Continuum Inc.	8361	D	619 460-7333	18416

LEMOORE, CA - Kings County
	SIC	EMP	PHONE	ENTRY#
Wood Bros Inc.	1629	D	559 924-7715	1325
Tachi Palace Casino Resort	7011	A	559 924-7751	10303

LINCOLN, CA - Placer County
	SIC	EMP	PHONE	ENTRY#
Precision Fluid Controls Inc.	5085	D	916 626-3029	5920
Catta Verdera Country Club LLC.	7997	D	916 645-7200	14358
J D Pasquetti Engineering	8711	D	916 543-9401	19273

LINDEN, CA - San Joaquin County
	SIC	EMP	PHONE	ENTRY#
Duarte Nursery Inc.	0181	B	209 887-3409	125
Normans Nursery Inc.	5193	C	209 887-2033	6870

LINDSAY, CA - Tulare County
	SIC	EMP	PHONE	ENTRY#
Lobue Bros Inc (PA)	0723	D	559 562-2548	285
Suntreat Pkg Shipg A Ltd Prtnr.	4783	C	559 562-4991	4135
Visalia Medical Clinic	8011	D	559 562-1361	15194

LITTLE LAKE, CA - Inyo County
	SIC	EMP	PHONE	ENTRY#
Coso Operating Company LLC.	4911	D	760 764-1300	4567
Cgp Holdings LLC.	4961	D	760 764-1300	4985

LITTLE RIVER, CA - Mendocino County
	SIC	EMP	PHONE	ENTRY#
Little River Inn Inc.	7011	C	707 937-5942	9980

LIVE OAK, CA - Sutter County
	SIC	EMP	PHONE	ENTRY#
Wilbur Packing Company Inc.	0723	D	530 671-4911	315

GEOGRAPHIC SECTION

LOMPOC CA

	SIC	EMP	PHONE	ENTRY#

LIVERMORE, CA - Alameda County

	SIC	EMP	PHONE	ENTRY#
Brightview Landscape Svcs Inc	0781	D	925 243-0288	410
Aragon Commercial Ldscpg Inc	0782	C	408 998-0600	474
Jpa Landscape & Cnstr Inc	0782	D	925 960-9602	504
Davey Tree Surgery Company (HQ)	0783	A	925 443-1723	555
JF Shea Construction Inc	1521	D	925 245-3660	684
WL Butler Inc	1521	D	650 361-1270	742
Country Builders Inc	1522	C	925 373-1020	751
Goodfellow Bros California LLC	1611	B	925 245-2111	1107
Rgw Construction Inc	1611	C	925 606-2400	1154
GSe Construction Company Inc (PA)	1623	C	925 447-0292	1212
Kinetics Mechanical Svc Inc	1711	D	925 245-6200	1479
On-Time AC & Htg LLC	1711	D	925 800-5804	1517
Peterson Painting Inc	1721	D	925 455-5864	1631
All Guard Alarm Systems Inc (PA)	1731	D	800 255-4273	1660
Cosco Fire Protection Inc	1731	D	925 455-2751	1710
Mch Electric Inc (PA)	1731	D	925 453-5041	1773
Point One Elec Systems Inc	1731	D	925 667-2935	1808
Red Top Electric Co-Emeryville Inc	1731	D	925 667-2900	1814
Fbd Vanguard Construction Inc	1771	D	925 245-1300	2118
Califrnias Gnite Pool Plst Inc	1799	D	925 960-9500	2264
Csrw Inc	1799	D	925 724-2324	2270
Heritage Paper LLC (PA)	2653	C	925 449-1148	2516
Trans Western Polymers Inc	2673	B	925 449-7800	2531
Topcon Positioning Systems Inc (DH)	3829	D	925 245-8300	3044
Durham School Services L P	4151	C	925 606-0871	3327
Gillig LLC	4213	B	510 264-5000	3481
Cellco Partnership	4812	D	925 245-0494	4187
Clfrn/Clrd/Flrd/rgon I Comcast	4812	C	925 424-0273	4208
Pacific Gas and Electric Co	4911	C	925 373-2623	4653
H - Investment Company	5031	C	925 245-4300	5161
Hoskin & Muir Inc	5031	D	925 373-1135	5167
Architectural GL & Alum Co Inc (PA)	5051	C	925 583-2460	5475
Thyssenkrupp Indus Svcs NA Inc	5051	C	209 395-9111	5525
American Wholesale Ltg Inc	5063	D	510 252-1088	5536
Central Wholesale Electrical Distributors Inc	5063	D	925 245-9310	5545
McGrath Rentcorp (PA)	5084	C	925 606-9200	5846
LJ Walch Co Inc	5088	D	925 449-9252	5961
Packaging Innovators LLC	5113	D	925 371-2000	6089
Veritiv Operating Company	5113	C	925 245-6060	6093
Performance Food Group Inc	5141	B	804 287-8097	6276
US Foods Inc	5141	B	925 606-3525	6409
Produce Exchange Incorporated (DH)	5148	C	925 454-8700	6572
US Foods Inc	5149	D	925 606-1919	6688
New Parrott & Co	5182	C	925 456-2286	6803
Home Depot USA Inc	5211	D	925 243-1212	6985
Lowes Home Centers LLC	5211	B	925 245-2440	7055
John L Sllivan Investments Inc (PA)	5511	C	916 969-5911	7241
Rjms Corporation (PA)	5511	D	510 675-0500	7290
Homesite Svcs Inc A Cal Corp (PA)	5713	D	925 237-3050	7432
Watermark Rtrment Cmmnties Inc	6513	D	925 344-5661	8870
Hilton Garden Inns MGT LLC	7011	B	925 292-2000	9853
Cattlemens	7299	C	925 447-1224	10533
Performant Recovery Inc (HQ)	7322	C	209 858-3994	10748
Performant Financial Corp (PA)	7375	B	925 960-4800	12680
Lawrence Livermore Nat SEC LLC	7382	B	925 453-3584	13131
Livermore Valley Athc CLB Inc	7941	D	925 443-7700	14149
Poppy Ridge Inc	7992	D	925 456-8229	14281
Livermore Area Rcration Pk Dst (PA)	7999	B	925 373-5700	14542
Kaiser Foundation Hospitals	8011	C	925 432-6000	14845
Permanente Medical Group Inc	8011	A	925 243-2600	14987
Stanford Hlth Care Tri-Valley	8011	C	925 373-4018	15101
Stanford Hlth Care Tri-Valley	8062	C	925 447-7000	16499
Sutter Health	8099	D	925 371-3800	17335
Cape Inc	8211	D	925 443-3434	17699
Valley Montessori School	8211	D	925 455-8021	17755
Jon K Takata Corporation (PA)	8322	D	510 315-5400	18028
Leisure Care LLC	8361	D	925 371-2300	18467
Stanford Hlth Care Tri-Valley	8699	C	925 447-1919	19107
National Security Tech LLC	8711	A	925 960-2500	19331
Tgcon Inc (DH)	8711	D	925 449-5764	19414
United Sttes Dept Enrgy Lvrmor	8731	A	925 423-1521	19791
Berkeley Nutritional Mfg Corp (PA)	8732	D	925 243-6300	19800
National Food Laboratory LLC	8733	D	925 828-1440	19901
Eurofins Fd Chmstry Tstg Mdson	8734	A	609 452-4440	19975
Beets Hospitality Group	8741	D	925 294-8667	20035
Pen-Cal Administrators Inc	8741	B	925 251-3400	20174
Wente Bros (PA)	8742	D	925 456-2300	20611
Zimeno Inc	8742	C	833 247-4797	20624
City of Livermore	9221	D	925 371-4848	20928

LIVINGSTON, CA - Merced County

	SIC	EMP	PHONE	ENTRY#
Quail H Farms LLC	0139	D	209 394-8001	17
Foster Farms LLC (HQ)	0252	D	209 394-7901	225
Foster Turkey Products	0253	B	209 394-7901	228
Foster Poultry Farms LLC	0254	B	209 394-7901	229
E & J Gallo Winery	2084	D	209 394-6200	2382
Livingston Community Health (PA)	8011	D	209 394-7913	14876

LOCKEFORD, CA - San Joaquin County

	SIC	EMP	PHONE	ENTRY#
Kellogg Supply Inc	2873	C	209 727-3130	2637

LODI, CA - San Joaquin County

	SIC	EMP	PHONE	ENTRY#
Delu Vineyards Inc	0172	D	209 334-6660	71
Csn Winddown Inc	0181	D	209 369-3018	122
Haro & Haro Enterprises Inc	0761	A	209 334-2035	365
Valley Landscaping & Maint Inc	0782	C	209 334-3659	544
Boething Treeland Farms Inc	0811	D	209 727-3741	565
Rdr Builders LP	1522	D	209 368-7561	770
Diede Construction Inc	1542	D	209 369-8255	903
F & H Construction (PA)	1542	D	209 931-3738	917
Ford Construction Company Inc	1629	D	209 333-1116	1300
Odyssey Landscaping Co Inc	1771	D	209 369-6197	2141
Cottage Bakery Inc	2051	B	209 334-3616	2367
Mv Transportation Inc	4111	C	209 339-1972	3167
Frank C Alegre Trucking Inc (PA)	4213	C	209 334-2112	3477
FTg Construction Mtls Inc	4213	C	209 334-4038	3479
T & T Trucking Inc (PA)	4213	C	800 692-3457	3549
Tiger Lines LLC (HQ)	4213	C	209 334-4100	3551
Gifting Company LLC (PA)	5148	C	209 365-2300	6552
Vino Farms LLC	5182	B	209 334-6975	6810
Lowes Home Centers LLC	5211	B	209 339-2600	7080
Sanborn Chevrolet Inc	5511	D	209 334-5000	7295
Wine & Roses LLC	5812	C	209 334-6988	7517
Farmers & Merchants Bancorp (PA)	6022	B	209 367-2300	7682
DK Hotels LLC	7011	C	925 640-3616	9752
Clark Pest Ctrl Stockton Inc (HQ)	7342	D	209 368-7152	10832
Bart Manufacturing Inc	7389	C	408 250-4975	13211
City of Lodi (PA)	7389	D	209 333-6700	13234
Nucor Bldg Systems Utah LLC	7389	D	209 608-7701	13402
Pacific Coast Producers	7389	C	209 365-9982	13415
Spare-Time Inc	7997	C	209 334-4897	14460
Delta Radiology Medical Group	8011	C	209 334-4416	14723
Lodi Memorial Hospital	8011	C	209 204-5004	14877
Golden Bear Physcl Thrapy Spt	8049	C	209 622-1191	15282
Beaver Dam Health Care Center	8051	C	209 368-0693	15355
Chancellor Hlth Care of Cal IV	8051	B	209 367-8870	15374
Vienna Convalescent Hosp Inc	8051	C	209 368-7141	15721
Lodi Memorial Hosp Assn Inc	8062	C	209 339-7441	16217
Lodi Memorial Hosp Assn Inc	8062	C	209 339-7583	16218
Lodi Memorial Hosp Assn Inc (HQ)	8062	A	209 334-3411	16220
Victor Treatment Centers Inc	8211	D	209 465-1080	17756
Century Assembly Inc (PA)	8661	C	209 334-3230	19013
County of San Joaquin	9512	D	209 331-7270	20945

LOLETA, CA - Humboldt County

	SIC	EMP	PHONE	ENTRY#
Bear River Casino	7011	C	707 733-9644	9636

LOMA LINDA, CA - San Bernardino County

	SIC	EMP	PHONE	ENTRY#
Bakell LLC	1541	D	800 292-2137	805
Loma Linda Univ Chld Hosp	6733	C	909 558-8000	9437
ABI Document Support Svcs LLC	7389	D	909 793-0613	13172
Linda Loma Univ Hlth Care (PA)	8011	A	909 558-4729	14875
Loma Lnda Univ Fmly Med Group	8011	D	909 558-6600	14878
Veterans Health Administration	8011	A	909 825-7084	15190
Heritage Health Care Inc	8051	C	909 796-0216	15514
Linda Loma Univ Hlth Care (HQ)	8062	D	909 558-2806	16214
Loma Linda University Med Ctr	8062	D	909 558-4385	16223
Loma Linda University Med Ctr	8062	D	909 558-4216	16224
Loma Linda University Med Ctr	8062	D	909 796-0167	16225
Loma Linda University Med Ctr (DH)	8062	A	909 558-4000	16226
Loma Linda University Med Ctr	8062	D	909 558-8244	16227
Loma Lnda - Inland Empire Cnsr	8062	D	909 558-4000	16229
Mountain View Child Care Inc (PA)	8062	B	909 796-6915	16277
South Coast Childrens Soc Inc	8093	C	909 478-3377	17129
J & L Daycare	8361	D	909 796-2656	18462

LOMITA, CA - Los Angeles County

	SIC	EMP	PHONE	ENTRY#
Lomita Verde Inc	8059	D	310 325-1970	15866

LOMPOC, CA - Santa Barbara County

	SIC	EMP	PHONE	ENTRY#
Santa Barbara Farms LLC (PA)	0161	D	805 736-9776	40
Santa Barbara Farms LLC	0161	C	805 736-5608	41
Imerys Minerals California Inc (HQ)	1499	D	805 736-1221	648
Windsor Capital Group Inc	7011	C	805 735-8311	10372
Lompoc Valley Medical Center	8062	C	805 735-9229	16230

Employee Codes: A=Over 500 employees, B=251-500
C=101-250, D=51-100, E=20-50, F=10-19, G=1-9

LOMPOC CA

	SIC	EMP	PHONE	ENTRY#
Lompoc Valley Medical Center (PA)	8062	B	805 737-3300	16231
Valley Med Group Lompoc Inc	8062	D	805 736-1253	16613
Crestwood Behavioral Hlth Inc	8361	D	805 308-8720	18412
Channel Islnds Yung MNS Chrstn	8641	D	805 736-3483	18835
Automobile Club Southern Cal	8699	D	805 735-2731	19065
United Paradyne Corporation	8741	D	805 734-4734	20238

LONE PINE, CA - Inyo County

	SIC	EMP	PHONE	ENTRY#
Southern Inyo Healthcare Dst	8062	C	760 876-5501	16447

LONG BARN, CA - Tuolumne County

	SIC	EMP	PHONE	ENTRY#
Califrnia Sthern Bptst Cnvntio	8661	D	209 965-3735	19012

LONG BEACH, CA - Los Angeles County

	SIC	EMP	PHONE	ENTRY#
California Resources Corp (PA)	1311	D	888 848-4754	582
Thums Long Beach Company	1311	C	562 624-3400	586
Warren E&P Inc	1382	D	214 393-9688	607
Sears Home Imprv Pdts Inc	1521	C	562 485-4904	718
Palp Inc	1611	C	562 599-5841	1151
W A Rasic Cnstr Co Inc (PA)	1623	D	562 928-6111	1277
Curtin Maritime Corp	1629	B	562 983-7257	1294
Herzog Contracting Corp	1629	D	562 595-7414	1306
Manson Construction Co	1629	D	562 983-2340	1309
Lite Solar Corp	1711	D	562 256-1249	1487
Elec-Tech Enterprises Inc	1731	D	562 602-1015	1725
Terminal SEC Solutions Inc	1731	D	877 858-3855	1862
Petrochem Insulation Inc	1742	D	310 638-6663	1956
Matrix Environmental Inc	1799	D	562 236-2704	2296
Wiser Foods Inc	2086	D	310 895-0888	2414
Jbi LLC (PA)	2599	C	310 886-8034	2509
Ld Products Inc	2621	C	888 321-2552	2510
Talco Plastics Inc	3089	D	562 630-1224	2681
SPEP Acquisition Corp (PA)	3429	D	310 608-0693	2732
Seachrome Corporation	3431	C	310 427-8010	2733
Superior Electrical Advg Inc (PA)	3993	D	562 495-3808	3102
Union Pacific Railroad Company	4011	B	562 490-7000	3118
Long Beach Public Trnsp Co (PA)	4111	A	562 599-8571	3146
Long Beach Public Trnsp Co	4111	D	562 591-2301	3147
Atlantic Express Trnsp	4119	C	562 997-6868	3237
Long Beach Unified School Dst	4151	C	562 426-6176	3346
Ocean Blue Envmtl Svcs Inc (PA)	4212	D	562 624-4120	3417
Ventura Transfer Company	4213	D	310 549-1660	3562
Special Dispatch Cal Inc (PA)	4214	D	714 521-8200	3596
Kair Harbor Express LLC (PA)	4225	C	562 432-6800	3720
Roadex America Inc	4225	D	310 878-9800	3749
Foss Maritime Co Inc	4412	D	562 435-0171	3797
Polar Tankers Inc (DH)	4424	D	562 388-1400	3801
International Trnsp Svc LLC (PA)	4491	C	562 435-7781	3810
Lbct LLC	4491	D	562 951-6000	3811
Port of Long Beach	4491	B	562 283-7000	3814
Suderman Contg Stevedores Inc (PA)	4491	D	409 762-8131	3819
Pacific Maritime Freight Inc	4492	D	562 590-8188	3823
Hanjin Shipping Co Ltd	4499	A	201 291-4600	3826
Jetblue Airways Inc	4512	D	562 394-4397	3834
Piedmont Airlines Inc	4512	C	562 421-1806	3840
Polar Air Cargo LP	4512	B	310 568-4551	3842
City of Long Beach	4581	D	562 570-2600	3882
Cargomatic Inc (PA)	4731	C	866 513-2343	3993
Cfr Rinkens LLC (PA)	4731	D	310 639-7725	3997
Hapag-Lloyd (america) LLC	4731	C	562 435-0771	4033
Next Trucking Inc	4731	D	213 444-2250	4063
Vanguard Lgistics Svcs USA Inc (HQ)	4731	D	310 847-3000	4117
Free Conferencing Corporation	4813	C	562 437-1411	4276
California Broadcast Ctr LLC	4841	D	310 233-2425	4475
Cco Holdings LLC	4841	D	562 228-1262	4490
Intelsat US LLC	4899	C	310 525-5500	4539
AES Alamitos LLC	4911	D	562 493-7891	4560
Southern California Edison Co	4911	D	562 529-7301	4692
Southern California Edison Co	4911	D	562 491-3803	4708
County of Los Angeles	4941	D	213 367-3176	4780
Covanta Long Bch Rnwble Enrgy	4953	C	562 436-0636	4881
Denso Pdts & Svcs Americas Inc (DH)	5013	B	310 834-6352	5035
United Pacific Industries Inc	5013	D	562 421-3888	5065
Intex Recreation Corp	5021	D	310 549-5400	5092
ALI Roofg Mtls Long Bch Inc	5033	D	562 595-7377	5218
Xerox Education Services LLC (DH)	5044	D	310 830-9847	5262
Tp-Link USA Corporation	5045	D	562 528-7700	5362
Tom Dreher Sales Inc	5046	D	562 355-4074	5389
Jfe Shoji America Holdings Inc (DH)	5051	D	562 637-3500	5499
Ta Chen International Inc (HQ)	5051	D	562 808-8000	5521
Tell Steel Inc	5051	D	562 435-4826	5523
Jvckenwood USA Corporation (HQ)	5065	C	310 639-9000	5667
Clarendon Specialty Fas Inc	5072	D	714 842-2603	5726
Airgas Usa LLC	5084	A	562 497-1991	5817
Columbia Specialty Company Inc	5085	D	562 634-6425	5896
Master Fasteners International LLC	5085	D	562 279-0150	5910
Tristar Industrial LLC	5085	D	562 634-6425	5932
Shimadzu Precision Instrs Inc (DH)	5088	D	562 420-6226	5968
Intex Properties S Bay Corp (PA)	5091	C	310 549-5400	5979
Smart & Final Stores Inc	5141	C	562 438-0450	6299
Maruhide Marine Products Inc	5146	D	562 435-6509	6474
Casey Company (PA)	5172	C	562 436-9685	6724
M O Dion & Sons Inc (DH)	5172	D	562 432-3946	6733
Redbarn Pet Products Inc (PA)	5199	C	562 495-7315	6942
Home Depot USA Inc	5211	D	562 595-9200	7025
Cabe Brothers	5511	D	562 595-7411	7178
Walter Timmons Enterprises Inc	5511	D	562 595-4601	7328
United El Segundo Inc (PA)	5541	D	310 323-3992	7392
Forty-Niner Shops Inc	5942	A	562 985-5093	7547
Innovative Dialysis Partners Inc	5999	B	562 495-8075	7584
Citibank FSB	6021	D	562 999-3453	7614
First Bank and Trust	6021	D	562 595-8775	7624
Farmers Merchants Bnk Long Bch (HQ)	6022	C	562 437-0011	7683
Allied Halthcare Federal Cr Un	6061	D	562 933-0370	7751
Ilwu Federal Credit Union	6061	D	310 834-6411	7775
V A Desert PCF Federal Cr Un	6061	D	562 498-1255	7816
Molina Hlthcare Cal Prtner Pla	6321	B	562 435-3666	8269
California Physicians Service	6324	D	310 744-2668	8288
Molina Healthcare Inc	6324	D	310 221-3031	8346
Scan Group	6324	B	562 308-2733	8359
Senior Care (PA)	6324	A	562 989-5100	8360
Tristar Insurance Group Inc (PA)	6331	A	562 495-6600	8423
Intex Recreation Corp	6512	C	310 549-5400	8728
Smg Holdings LLC	6512	D	562 499-7611	8762
Intervest Property MGT Inc	6513	D	562 634-5672	8828
Rance King Properties Inc (PA)	6513	C	562 240-1000	8857
American Development Corp (PA)	6531	D	562 989-3730	8899
Coastal Alliance Holdings Inc	6531	C	562 370-1000	8936
Cushman & Wakefield Cal Inc	6531	C	562 276-1400	8969
First Team RE - Orange Cnty	6531	C	562 346-5088	9013
Retirement Housing Foundation (PA)	6531	C	562 257-5100	9164
Gh Group Inc	6719	C	562 264-5078	9316
County of Los Angeles	6732	D	562 985-4687	9413
HEI Long Beach LLC	7011	D	562 983-3400	9846
Hyatt Corporation	7011	D	562 432-0161	9887
Hyatt Equities LLC	7011	D	562 436-1047	9899
Merritt Hospitality LLC	7011	C	562 983-3400	10015
Nhca Inc	7011	D	310 519-8200	10045
Noble Investment Group LLC	7011	C	562 436-3000	10048
Noble/Utah Long Beach LLC	7011	C	562 436-3000	10049
Queensbay Hotel LLC	7011	D	562 481-3910	10133
RMS Foundation Inc	7011	A	562 435-3511	10167
Ruffin Hotel Corp of Cal	7011	B	562 425-5210	10182
Urban Commons Queensway LLC	7011	A	562 499-1611	10335
World Trade Ctr Ht Assoc Ltd	7011	D	562 983-3400	10379
Yhb Long Beach LLC	7011	C	562 597-4401	10387
Worldwide Corporate Housing LP	7021	B	972 392-4747	10396
American Textile Maint Co	7213	D	562 438-7656	10426
American Textile Maint Co	7213	D	562 438-1126	10427
Foasberg Laundry and Clrs Inc (PA)	7213	D	562 426-7345	10434
American Textile Maint Co	7218	D	562 424-1607	10476
Choura Venue Services	7299	D	562 426-0555	10534
Intertrend Communications Inc	7311	D	562 733-1888	10633
Apartment Seo LLC	7313	D	877 309-7363	10700
Continental Graphics Corp (HQ)	7336	C	714 503-4200	10801
Designory Inc (HQ)	7336	C	562 624-0200	10804
Motion Theory Inc	7336	C	310 396-9433	10815
Elite Craftsman (PA)	7349	C	562 989-3511	10893
Mida Industries Inc	7349	C	562 616-1020	10930
OPEN America Inc	7349	C	562 428-9210	10937
Bragg Investment Company Inc (PA)	7353	B	562 984-2400	10995
Psav Holdings LLC (PA)	7359	C	562 366-0138	11051
Pacific Gtwy Wrkfrce Prtnr Inc	7361	D	562 570-3700	11194
Compulink Management Ctr Inc (PA)	7371	C	562 988-1688	11509
Erp Integrated Solutions LLC	7371	D	562 425-7800	11577
Oshyn Inc	7371	D	213 483-1770	11803
Traffic Management Pdts Inc	7372	A	800 763-3999	12383
Zwift Inc (PA)	7372	B	855 469-9438	12411
Shield Security Inc	7381	B	562 283-1100	13043
Ecamsecure (DH)	7382	D	888 246-0556	13109
Greater Alarm Company Inc (DH)	7382	D	949 474-0555	13122
California Traffic Control	7389	D	562 595-7575	13222
Goodwill Srving The Pple Sther (PA)	7389	D	562 435-3411	13305
Macro-Pro Inc (PA)	7389	D	562 595-0900	13361
Traffic Management Inc (PA)	7389	C	562 595-4278	13513
Olympix Fitness LLC	7991	D	562 366-4600	14223

GEOGRAPHIC SECTION

LOS ANGELES CA

	SIC	EMP	PHONE	ENTRY#
Long Beach Yacht Club	7997	D	562 598-9401	14397
Virginia Cntry CLB of Long Bch	7997	C	562 427-0924	14479
Altamed Health Services Corp	8011	C	562 923-9414	14601
CB Tang MD Incorporated	8011	D	562 437-0831	14660
Childrens Clnic Srving Chldren	8011	B	562 264-4638	14680
Healthsmart Pacific Inc	8011	B	562 595-1911	14769
Memorial Crdolgy Med Group Inc	8011	D	562 988-2995	14893
Memorial Orthpdic Srgcal Group	8011	D	562 424-6666	14894
Molina Healthcare Inc (PA)	8011	A	562 435-3666	14906
Molina Healthcare California	8011	A	800 526-8196	14907
Molina Healthcare New York Inc	8011	D	888 562-5442	14908
Molina Pathways LLC	8011	B	562 491-5773	14909
Optumcare Management LLC	8011	C	562 988-7000	14940
Pacific Shores Med Group Inc (HQ)	8011	D	562 590-0345	14946
Transltnl Plmnary Immnlogy RE	8011	D	562 490-9900	15128
Therapytravelers LLC	8049	D	888 223-8002	15310
Alamitos-Belmont Rehab Inc	8051	C	562 434-8421	15321
Atlantic Mem Hlthcare Assoc In (HQ)	8051	C	562 424-8101	15337
Intercommunity Care Ctrs Inc	8051	C	562 427-8915	15524
Long Beach Care Center Inc	8051	C	562 426-6141	15548
Marlora Investments LLC	8051	C	562 494-3311	15580
Pacific Palms Healthcare LLC	8051	C	562 433-6791	15615
Palmcrest Grand Care Ctr Inc	8051	C	562 595-4551	15617
Palmcrest Medallion Convalesc	8051	C	562 595-4336	15618
Villa Serena Healthcare Center	8051	C	562 437-2797	15723
Blyth/Wndsor Cntry Pk Hlthcare	8052	B	310 385-1090	15748
Lexington Group International	8059	C	562 428-4681	15864
Longwood Management Corp	8059	C	562 432-5751	15873
Villa De La Mar Inc	8059	C	562 494-5001	15910
Catholic Hlthcare W Sthern Cal (HQ)	8062	C,	562 491-9000	15969
Community Hospital Long Beach	8062	A	562 494-0600	16011
Dignity Health	8062	B	805 988-2868	16046
Dignity Health	8062	B	562 491-9000	16048
Healthsmart Pacific Inc (PA)	8062	A	562 595-1911	16124
Long Beach Medical Center	8062	C	562 933-7701	16232
Long Beach Medical Center (HQ)	8062	A	562 933-2000	16233
Long Beach Medical Center	8062	C	562 933-0085	16234
Long Beach Memorial Med Ctr	8062	C	562 933-0432	16236
Memorial Hlth Svcs - Univ Cal (PA)	8062	A	562 933-2000	16253
St Mary Medical Center (DH)	8062	A	562 491-9000	16481
Coastal Cmnty Senior Care LLC	8082	C	562 596-4884	16841
Safe Refuge	8093	D	562 987-5722	17123
Tarzana Treatment Centers Inc	8093	C	562 218-1868	17139
Telecare Corporation	8093	C	562 630-8672	17143
Altamed Health Services Corp	8099	D	562 595-8040	17174
Easy Care Mso LLC	8099	C	562 676-9600	17232
Industrial Medical Support Inc	8099	A	877 878-9185	17254
Los Angeles Cnty Dept Mntal HLT	8099	D	213 738-4431	17270
Medasend Biomedical Inc (PA)	8099	C	800 200-3581	17274
Molina Healthcare Inc	8099	C	562 435-3666	17277
Pponext West Inc	8099	B	888 446-6098	17298
Ford Wlker Haggerty Behar LLP (PA)	8111	D	562 983-2500	17461
Fulwider and Patton LLP	8111	D	310 824-5555	17464
Keesal Young Logan A Prof Corp (PA)	8111	D	562 436-2000	17515
Prindle Decker & Amaro LLP (PA)	8111	D	562 436-3946	17617
Vision Legal Inc	8111	D	310 469-4966	17673
Long Beach Unified School Dst	8211	A	562 426-5571	17722
Arts and Svcs For Disabled Inc	8322	D	562 377-0302	17839
Childnet Youth & Fmly Svcs Inc (PA)	8322	C	562 498-5500	17880
Interval House	8322	D	562 594-4555	18022
Jewish Community Ctr Long Bch	8322	C	562 426-7601	18024
Life Steps Foundation Inc	8322	D	562 436-0751	18042
Advocacy For Rspect Chice - Lo (PA)	8331	D	562 597-7716	18203
Conservation Corps Long Beach	8331	C	562 986-1249	18224
McKinley Child Development Ctr	8351	D	562 531-6182	18333
Brittany House LLC	8361	C	562 421-4717	18382
Long Bch Museum Art Foundation	8412	D	562 439-2119	18654
Aquarium of Pacific (PA)	8422	C	562 590-3100	18683
Assocted Stdnts Cal State Univ	8641	D	562 985-4994	18815
Automobile Club Southern Cal	8699	D	562 425-8350	19066
Friends Long Bch Anmal Shelter	8699	D	562 988-7647	19083
Memorial Medical Center Foundation	8699	A	562 933-2273	19094
California Mfg Tech Consulting	8711	D	310 263-3060	19168
Capital Engineering LLC	8711	D	562 612-1302	19172
Iqa Solutions Inc	8711	D	562 420-1000	19272
Jacobs Civil Inc	8711	C	310 847-2500	19275
Mangan Inc (PA)	8711	D	310 835-8080	19314
Stearns Conrad and Schmidt Consulti (PA)	8711	D	562 426-9544	19399
URS Group Inc	8711	D	562 420-2933	19424
Utility Traffic Services LLC	8711	B	562 264-2355	19430
Rdc-S111 Inc (PA)	8712	D	562 628-8000	19501
California State Univ Long Bch	8721	C	562 985-1764	19547
Windes Inc (PA)	8721	D	562 435-1191	19639
Southern Cal Inst For RES Edca	8733	D	562 826-8139	19914
Twining Inc (PA)	8734	D	562 426-3355	20002
Advanced Medical MGT Inc	8741	D	562 766-2000	20012
Avsc Intllctual Prprty MGT Inc	8741	B	562 366-1924	20029
Country Villa Service Corp	8741	C	562 597-8817	20067
Teichert Enrgy Utlties Group I	8741	D	916 484-3011	20228
Pmcs Group Inc	8742	D	562 498-0808	20509
Rmd Group Inc	8742	B	562 866-9288	20530
St Marys Medical Center	8742	A	562 491-9230	20563
Argus Management Company LLC	8744	B	562 299-5200	20650
Ultura Inc	8744	C	562 661-4999	20666
Envent Corporation (PA)	8748	D	562 997-9465	20744
Healthcare Services Group Inc	8999	A	562 494-7939	20892
City of Long Beach	9431	D	562 570-4000	20937

LOOMIS, CA - Placer County

	SIC	EMP	PHONE	ENTRY#
Western Engineering Contractors Inc	1611	C	916 652-3990	1177
Applimotion Inc	5063	D	916 652-3118	5538
Sprig Oral Health Technologies	8072	D	888 539-7336	16777
Jls Environmental Services Inc	8744	D	916 660-1525	20657

LOS ALAMITOS, CA - Orange County

	SIC	EMP	PHONE	ENTRY#
Millie and Severson Inc	1541	D	562 493-3611	833
Severson Group Incorporated (PA)	1542	D	562 493-3611	1023
Carol Electric Company Inc	1731	D	562 431-1870	1692
Kdc Inc (HQ)	1731	C	714 828-7000	1761
Utbbb Inc	2052	D	562 594-4411	2372
Supermedia LLC	2741	D	562 594-5101	2557
Friedas Inc	5148	D	714 826-6100	6547
Ganahl Lumber Company	5251	D	562 346-2100	7120
Southland Credit Union (PA)	6061	D	562 862-6831	7806
College Park Realty Inc (PA)	6531	D	562 594-6753	8946
Quantum World Technologies Inc	7361	B	805 834-0532	11210
Watersafe Swim School Inc	7999	D	562 596-8608	14585
Tenet Healthsystem Medical Inc	8011	A	805 546-7698	15123
Katella Properties	8051	C	562 596-5561	15528
Los Alamitos Medical Ctr Inc (HQ)	8062	A	714 826-6400	16239
Institute of Elec Elec Engners	8611	D	714 821-8380	18711
Vanguard Space Tech Inc	8711	C	858 587-4210	19431
Military California Department	8744	D	562 795-2001	20659

LOS ALTOS, CA - Santa Clara County

	SIC	EMP	PHONE	ENTRY#
Adobe Animal Hospital	0742	D	650 948-9661	322
Epicurean Group	5812	B	650 947-6800	7477
Kisco Senior Living LLC	6513	D	650 948-7337	8841
Roman Cthlic Bishp of San Jose	6553	D	833 304-0763	9289
Cohesity Inc	6733	C	650 968-4470	9424
Comity Designs Inc	7379	D	415 967-1530	12763
Los Altos Golf and Country CLB	7997	D	650 947-3100	14398
Covenant Care California LLC	8051	C	650 941-5255	15407
Humangood Norcal	8059	C	650 948-8291	15859
Creative Lrng Ctr Preschool	8351	C	650 823-1496	18304
David Lcile Packard Foundation	8699	C	650 948-7658	19080
The David Lcile Pckard Fndtion	8699	D	650 917-7167	19111
Ahntech Inc (PA)	8711	D	650 861-3987	19132
Midpennsula Rgnal Open Space D	8999	C	650 691-1200	20896

LOS ALTOS HILLS, CA - Santa Clara County

	SIC	EMP	PHONE	ENTRY#
Foothll-De Anza Cmnty Cllege D	4832	C	650 949-7260	4384
Greenbriar Management Company	6531	D	510 497-8200	9027
Ministry Services of The Daugh	6733	C	650 917-4500	9438
Outward Inc	7371	D	408 828-5492	11807
First Bptst Ch of Los Altos Th	8351	D	650 948-3738	18315

LOS ANGELES, CA - Los Angeles County

	SIC	EMP	PHONE	ENTRY#
Eclipse Berry Farms LLC	0171	D	310 207-7879	51
Mulroses Usa Inc	0181	D	213 489-1761	141
Hokto Kinoko Company	0182	D	323 526-1155	162
The Wonderful Company LLC (PA)	0723	C	310 966-5700	312
Wonderful Company LLC	0723	B	661 720-2609	319
Animal Specialty Group	0742	D	818 244-7977	326
Mercy For Animals Inc	0742	C	347 839-6464	336
VCA Animal Hospitals Inc	0742	A	310 473-2951	348
VCA Prfessional Animal Lab Inc	0742	D	310 571-6500	349
Vicar Operating Inc (DH)	0742	A	310 571-6500	354
Camp Bow Wow Franchising Inc	0752	D	310 571-6500	358
Monarch Ldscp Companies LLC	0781	D	213 797-5934	447
Breitburn Energy Partners LP	1311	A	213 225-5900	581
Occidental Petroleum Corporation of California	1311	A		584
The Strand Energy Company	1311	B	213 225-5900	585
Occidental Petroleum Investment Co Inc	1382	A	310 208-8800	602
Qre Operating LLC	1382	D	213 225-5900	603
Sentinel Peak Rsources Cal LLC	1382	D	323 298-2200	606

Employee Codes: A=Over 500 employees, B=251-500
C=101-250, D=51-100, E=20-50, F=10-19, G=1-9

LOS ANGELES CA

GEOGRAPHIC SECTION

Company	SIC	EMP	PHONE	ENTRY#
Vanderra Resources LLC	1389	B	817 439-2220	633
KB Home Grater Los Angeles Inc (HQ)	1521	D	310 231-4000	692
Zastrow Construction Inc	1522	D	323 478-1956	786
KB Home (PA)	1531	D	310 231-4000	793
KCS West Inc	1541	D	323 269-0020	827
Austin Commercial LP	1542	C	310 421-0269	868
Hitt Contracting Inc	1542	B	424 326-1042	937
Icon West Inc	1542	D	213 385-0027	940
Philmont Management Inc	1542	D	213 380-0159	991
Shawmut Woodworking & Sup Inc	1542	C	323 602-1000	1024
Webcor Construction LP	1542	C	213 239-2800	1057
County of Los Angeles	1611	D	626 458-1700	1092
Myers & Sons Construction LP	1611	C	424 227-3285	1143
HP Communications Inc	1623	D	951 457-0133	1218
LADWP Metro Water Yard	1623	D	213 367-6665	1229
AD Receivables Corp (PA)	1711	D	323 296-8787	1336
Arrowhead Brass & Plumbing LLC	1711	D	800 332-4267	1363
J M Carden Sprinkler Co Inc	1711	D	323 258-8300	1471
Muir-Chase Plumbing Co Inc	1711	D	818 500-1940	1503
Precise Air Systems Inc	1711	D	818 646-9757	1533
Skypower Holdings LLC	1711	C	323 860-4900	1563
American Solar Direct Inc	1731	E	424 214-6700	1664
First Fire Systems Inc (PA)	1731	D	310 559-0900	1734
Steiny and Company Inc	1731	B	213 382-2331	1854
Capital Drywall LP	1742	C	909 599-6818	1918
Rutherford Co Inc (PA)	1742	C	323 666-5284	1961
United Marketing Group Inc	1751	D	323 778-4283	2024
Platinum Roofing Inc	1761	D	408 280-5028	2078
Sbb Roofing Inc (PA)	1761	C	323 254-2888	2084
Tinco Sheet Metal Inc	1761	C	323 263-0511	2089
Giroux Glass Inc (PA)	1793	C	213 747-7406	2202
Asbestos Instant Response Inc	1799	D	323 733-0508	2257
Closet Factory Inc (PA)	1799	C	310 516-7000	2266
Parking Network Inc	1799	D	213 613-1500	2305
Rey-Crest Roofg Waterproofing	1799	D	323 257-9329	2313
The Teecor Group Inc	1799	D	213 632-2350	2321
Waterprfing Rofg Solutions Inc	1799	D	310 571-0892	2330
Commodity Sales Co	2015	C	323 980-5463	2343
East West Tea Company LLC	2043	C	310 275-9891	2361
San Antonio Winery Inc (PA)	2084	C	323 223-1401	2392
Jsl Foods Inc (PA)	2099	D	323 223-2484	2437
Stony Apparel Corp (PA)	2331	C	323 981-9080	2457
Ambiance USA Inc (PA)	2339	D	323 587-0007	2458
L&L Manufacturing Co Inc	2339	B		2459
Treivush Industries Inc	2339	D	213 745-7774	2461
Guess Inc (PA)	2341	A	213 765-3100	2463
Daily Journal Corporation (PA)	2711	D	213 229-5300	2536
Madisn/Grham Clor Graphics Inc	2752	B	323 261-7171	2562
Malibu Leather Inc	3172	C	310 985-0707	2686
National Wire and Cable Corporation	3315	C	323 225-5611	2721
Doval Industries Inc	3429	D	323 226-0335	2729
Vahe Enterprises Inc	3713	D	323 235-6657	2969
Worldwide Aeros Corp	3721	D	818 344-3999	2984
Carolense Entrmt Group LLC	3861	D	405 493-1120	3082
Forrest Group LLC (PA)	4111	D	619 808-9798	3139
Los Angles Cnty Mtro Trnsp Aut (PA)	4111	A	323 466-3876	3149
Los Angles Cnty Mtro Trnsp Aut	4111	A	213 922-5012	3150
Los Angles Cnty Mtro Trnsp Aut	4111	A	213 922-5887	3153
Los Angles Cnty Mtro Trnsp Aut	4111	B	213 922-6301	3154
Los Angles Cnty Mtro Trnsp Aut	4111	B	213 922-6203	3155
Los Angles Cnty Mtro Trnsp Aut	4111	A	213 922-6202	3156
Los Angles Cnty Mtro Trnsp Aut	4111	A	213 922-6207	3157
Los Angles Cnty Mtro Trnsp Aut	4111	A	213 533-1506	3159
Los Angles Cnty Mtro Trnsp Aut	4111	A	213 244-6783	3160
Los Angles Cnty Mtro Trnsp Aut	4111	A	213 626-4455	3161
Mv Transportation Inc	4111	C	323 936-9783	3172
Mv Transportation Inc	4111	B	310 638-0556	3174
Private Suite Lax LLC	4111	C	310 907-9950	3190
Shuttle Smart Inc	4111	C	310 338-9466	3213
SMS Transportation Svcs Inc	4111	C	213 489-5367	3214
Southern Cal Rgional Rail Auth (PA)	4111	C	213 452-0200	3217
Bls Lmsine Svc Los Angeles Inc	4119	B	323 644-7166	3242
Falck Mobile Health Corp	4119	B	323 720-1578	3258
Flixbus Inc	4119	C	925 577-4164	3264
Medtrans Inc	4119	D	323 780-9500	3280
Schaefer Ambulance Service Inc	4119	B	323 468-1642	3295
Greyhound Lines Inc	4173	B	213 629-8400	3357
A & S Metal Recycling Inc (PA)	4212	D	213 623-9443	3360
Dlf Logistics LLC	4212	D	626 387-3797	3388
Gateway Logistics Tech LLC	4212	B	732 750-9000	3395
Southern Counties Terminals	4212	D	310 642-0462	3424
Dependable Companies	4213	C	800 548-8608	3464
Dependable Highway Express Inc (PA)	4213	B	323 526-2200	3465
Xpo Logistics Freight Inc	4213	C	213 744-0664	3573
City Moving Inc (PA)	4214	C	888 794-8808	3580
Express Group Incorporated (PA)	4215	D	310 474-5999	3611
Kxp Carrier Services LLC	4215	C	424 320-5300	3618
Peach Inc	4215	C	323 654-2333	3626
Speedy Express LLC	4215	D	818 300-7785	3628
Unity Courier Service Inc (DH)	4215	C	323 255-9800	3646
Standard-Southern Corporation	4222	D	213 624-1831	3659
Standard-Southern Corporation	4222	C	213 624-1831	3660
Standard-Southern Corporation	4222	C	213 624-1831	3661
County of Los Angeles	4225	D	626 458-1707	3690
Quick Box LLC	4225	C	310 436-6444	3746
Unified Grocers Inc	4225	D	323 232-6124	3773
Aerotransporte De Carge Union	4512	B	310 649-0069	3827
American Airlines Inc	4512	B	310 646-4553	3830
China Airlines Ltd	4512	C	310 484-1818	3832
China Airlines Ltd	4512	C	310 646-4293	3833
Korean Air Lines Co Ltd	4512	C	310 646-4866	3835
Korean Airlines Co Ltd	4512	C	310 410-2000	3836
Korean Airlines Co Ltd	4512	D	213 484-1900	3837
L A Air Inc	4512	C	310 215-8245	3838
Nippon Cargo Airlines Co Ltd	4512	D	310 417-0801	3839
United Airlines Inc	4512	D	310 258-3319	3847
Federal Express Corporation	4513	D	800 463-3339	3855
Airport Terminal MGT Inc	4581	B	310 988-1492	3872
Alliance Ground Intl LLC	4581	A	310 646-2446	3873
Department of Arprts of The Cy	4581	A	855 463-5252	3890
Flightdocs II LLC	4581	D	800 747-4560	3893
Los Angeles World Airports (PA)	4581	A	855 463-5252	3897
Los Angeles World Airports	4581	B	424 646-5900	3898
Los Angeles World Airports	4581	C	424 646-9118	3899
Swissport Cargo Services LP	4581	D	703 742-4300	3913
Swissport Cargo Services LP	4581	C	310 910-9541	3914
Swissport Usa Inc	4581	B	310 345-1986	3915
Swissport Usa Inc	4581	C	310 910-9560	3917
Altour International Inc (PA)	4724	A	310 571-6000	3924
Altour International Inc	4724	B	310 571-6000	3925
Americantours Intl LLC (HQ)	4724	C	310 641-9953	3928
Booking Com	4724	D	323 801-4200	3929
Flight Centre Usa Inc	4724	D	310 458-3310	3930
Helloworld Travel Svcs USA Inc	4724	D	310 535-1005	3931
OXY Inc	4724	C	310 824-1315	3945
Trans-American Travel	4724	D	310 670-2111	3953
Travel Store (PA)	4724	D	310 575-5540	3954
Antenna Audio Inc (PA)	4725	A	203 523-0320	3959
Korean Airlines Co Ltd	4729	B	213 484-5700	3972
Matrix Aviation Services Inc	4729	C	310 337-3037	3973
Able Freight Services LLC (PA)	4731	D	310 568-8883	3974
Expeditors Intl Ocean Inc	4731	C	310 343-6200	4014
Nri Usa LLC (PA)	4731	D	323 345-6456	4068
Rock-It Cargo USA LLC	4731	C	310 410-0935	4086
Select Aircargo Services Inc	4731	D	310 851-8500	4093
Fluor Fltron Blfour Btty Drgdo	4789	D	949 420-5000	4155
Hyperloop Technologies Inc	4789	C	213 800-3270	4159
Cellco Partnership	4812	D	323 662-0009	4199
Ea Mobile Inc	4812	D	310 754-7125	4215
Sprint Communications Co LP	4812	C	310 216-9093	4229
Sprint Corporation	4812	C	213 613-4200	4235
Fox Interactive Media Inc	4813	C	310 969-7000	4275
Hulu LLC	4813	A	888 631-4858	4295
Media Temple Inc	4813	C	877 578-4000	4311
Mpower Holding Corporation (HQ)	4813	D	866 699-8242	4317
New Dream Network LLC	4813	D	323 375-3842	4319
Public Communications Svcs Inc	4813	C	310 231-1000	4331
Truconnect Communications Inc (PA)	4813	C	512 919-2641	4352
J2 Cloud Services LLC (HQ)	4822	D	323 860-9200	4366
Dash Radio Inc	4832	D	310 456-9993	4374
Entercom Media Corp	4832	D	323 930-7317	4382
Lotus Communications Corp (PA)	4832	D	323 512-2225	4396
Sirius XM Radio Inc	4832	C	323 802-1100	4404
Spanish Brdcstg Sys of Cal	4832	D	310 203-0900	4405
Cnn America Inc	4833	C	323 993-5000	4422
Disney Networks Group LLC	4833	C	310 369-5104	4425
Disney Networks Group LLC (DH)	4833	D	310 369-1000	4426
Entravsion Communications Corp	4833	D	323 900-6100	4427
Fox Inc (DH)	4833	A	310 369-1000	4431
Fox Broadcasting Company LLC (HQ)	4833	C	310 369-1000	4432
Fox Sports Inc (DH)	4833	C	310 369-1000	4433
Fox Television Stations Inc (HQ)	4833	B	310 584-2000	4434
International Media Group Inc	4833	D	310 478-1818	4442
King World Productions Inc	4833	C	310 264-3549	4444
Lifetime Entrmt Svcs LLC	4833	B	310 556-7500	4452
Revolt Media and Tv LLC	4833	C	323 645-3000	4459

GEOGRAPHIC SECTION

LOS ANGELES CA

Company	SIC	EMP	PHONE	ENTRY#
Tmz Productions Inc (HQ)	4833	D	818 972-8000	4464
Twentieth Cntury Fox Intl TV In	4833	A	310 369-1000	4467
Twentieth Television Inc	4833	D	310 584-2000	4468
Directv	4841	D	323 810-2032	4497
E Entertainment Television Inc	4841	A	323 954-2400	4507
Fx Networks LLC	4841	C	310 369-1000	4508
Spectrum MGT Holdg Co LLC	4841	D	323 657-0899	4520
Discovery Communications Inc (PA)	4899	B	310 975-5906	4535
Shondaland Inc	4899	D	323 468-8109	4550
Southern California Gas Co (HQ)	4924	A	213 244-1200	4727
Southern California Gas Tower	4924	A	213 244-1200	4746
Los Angeles Dept Wtr & Pwr	4941	A	323 256-8079	4803
Los Angeles Dept Wtr & Pwr	4941	A	213 367-4211	4805
Los Angeles Dept Wtr & Pwr (HQ)	4941	A	213 367-1320	4807
Los Angeles Dept Wtr & Pwr	4941	A	213 367-5706	4808
The Metropolitan Water District of (PA)	4941	A	213 217-6000	4841
Downtown Diversion Inc	4953	D	213 612-5005	4883
Earth Technology Corp USA	4953	D	213 593-8000	4885
Norcal Waste Services Inc	4953	D	626 357-8666	4914
Club Assist North America Inc (DH)	5013	D	213 388-4333	5033
Find It Parts Inc	5013	D	888 312-8812	5039
EC Group Inc (PA)	5021	D	310 815-2700	5088
Logistar LLC	5021	D	323 274-9651	5094
Elijah Textiles Inc	5023	D	310 666-3443	5116
GA Gertmenian and Sons LLC (PA)	5023	C	213 250-7777	5117
Emser International LLC (PA)	5032	D	323 650-2000	5203
Emser Tile LLC (PA)	5032	B	323 650-2000	5204
Hannam Chain USA Inc (PA)	5046	C	213 382-2922	5378
Jetro Holdings LLC	5046	C	213 516-0301	5382
Trust 1 Sales Inc	5046	D	323 732-3300	5393
Discus Dental LLC (PA)	5047	C	310 845-8600	5411
Twin Med Inc	5047	B		5457
Lexicon Marketing (usa) Inc (PA)	5049	C	323 782-8282	5467
Alpert & Alpert Iron & Metal Inc (PA)	5051	D	323 265-4040	5472
Earle M Jorgensen Company	5051	C	323 567-1122	5491
Gvs Italy	5051	D	424 382-4343	5494
Sac International Steel Inc (PA)	5051	D	323 232-2467	5518
Eaton Aerospace LLC	5063	B	818 409-0200	5554
Ecosense Lighting Inc (PA)	5063	D	855 632-6736	5555
Automatic Leasing Inc (PA)	5064	D	213 746-4117	5600
Homeland Housewares LLC	5064	D	310 996-7200	5607
Bear Communications Inc	5065	D	310 854-2327	5629
CP Document Technologies LLC (PA)	5065	D	213 617-4040	5643
Elevator Equipment Corporation (PA)	5084	C	323 245-0147	5831
ONeil Data Systems LLC	5084	C	310 448-6400	5851
C&C Jewelry Mfg Inc	5094	C	213 623-6800	6020
Ner Precious Metals Inc	5094	D	310 367-3179	6024
Platinum Disc LLC	5099	D	608 784-6620	6048
Roland Corporation US (HQ)	5099	C	323 890-3700	6050
Image Source Inc (PA)	5112	C	310 477-0700	6066
Oak Paper Products Co Inc (PA)	5113	C	323 268-0507	6081
Used Cardboard Boxes Inc	5113	C	323 724-2500	6092
Hatchbeauty Products LLC (PA)	5122	D	310 396-7070	6112
Pixi Inc	5122	C	310 670-7767	6138
Design Collection Inc	5131	C	323 277-9200	6154
Radix Textile Inc	5131	D	323 234-1667	6161
Zabin Industries Inc (PA)	5131	D	213 749-1215	6165
Quake City Casuals Inc	5136	C	213 746-0540	6184
UNI Hosiery Co Inc (PA)	5136	C	213 228-0100	6192
California Rain Company Inc	5137	D	213 623-6061	6196
Edgemine Inc	5137	C	323 267-8222	6198
Kash Apparel LLC	5137	D	213 747-8885	6203
Lymi Inc (PA)	5137	D	855 756-0560	6205
Misope U S A Inc	5137	D	213 746-0888	6209
Nhn Global Inc (HQ)	5137	C	424 672-1177	6211
Paragon Textiles Inc	5137	C	310 323-7500	6215
Princess Cruise Lines Ltd	5137	C	213 745-0314	6217
Seven Licensing Company LLC	5137	C	323 780-8250	6220
Signal Products Inc (PA)	5137	C	213 748-0990	6221
Aci International (PA)	5139	D	310 889-3400	6226
Buffalo Market Inc	5141	C	650 337-0078	6242
Canton Food Co Inc	5141	C	213 688-7707	6244
Smart & Final Stores Inc	5141	C	323 549-9586	6288
Smart & Final Stores LLC	5141	D	323 939-0946	6321
Smart & Final Stores LLC	5141	D	323 539-2400	6324
Smart & Final Stores LLC	5141	C	310 559-1722	6356
Smart & Final Stores LLC	5141	D	323 732-9101	6357
Smart & Final Stores LLC	5141	D	323 466-9289	6358
Smart & Final Stores LLC	5141	D	323 758-5734	6360
Smart & Final Stores LLC	5141	D	323 569-7148	6361
Smart & Final Stores LLC	5141	C	310 207-8688	6362
Smart & Final Stores LLC	5141	C	323 268-9179	6373
Smart & Final Stores LLC	5141	D	213 747-6697	6375
Arya Ice Cream Distrg Co Inc	5143	D	323 234-2994	6429
Rogers Poultry Co	5144	D	800 585-0802	6450
American Trading Intl Inc	5145	D	310 445-2000	6454
Awesome Office Inc	5145	D	310 845-7750	6455
Consolidated Svc Distrs Inc	5145	D	908 687-5800	6459
Ocean Group Inc (PA)	5146	D	213 622-3677	6475
PLD Enterprises Inc	5146	D	213 626-4444	6476
Prospect Enterprises Inc (PA)	5146	D	213 599-5700	6477
L & T Meat Co	5147	D	323 262-2815	6498
RW Zant LLC (DH)	5147	D	323 980-5457	6503
Strouk Group LLC	5147	C	323 939-7792	6504
Borg Produce Sales LLC	5148	D	213 624-2674	6517
Coast Produce Company (PA)	5148	C	213 955-4900	6528
Davalan Sales Inc	5148	C	213 623-2500	6532
Giumarra Bros Fruit Co Inc (PA)	5148	D	213 627-2900	6554
Green Farms Inc	5148	C	858 831-7701	6556
Pacific Trellis Fruit LLC (PA)	5148	C	323 859-9600	6568
Professional Produce	5148	D	323 277-1550	6573
Season Produce Co Inc	5148	B	213 689-0008	6578
Shapiro-Gilman-Shandler Co	5148	D	213 593-1200	6580
Val-Pro Inc	5148	D	213 689-0844	6589
Val-Pro Inc (PA)	5148	C	213 627-8736	6590
Wiemar Distributors Inc	5148	D	213 747-7036	6597
App Wholesale LLC	5149	B	323 980-8315	6601
Trinidad/Benham Corp	5149	D	626 723-2300	6684
US Foods Inc	5149	C	213 623-4150	6687
Zeco Systems Inc	5171	D	888 751-8560	6720
Youngs Market Company LLC	5182	D	213 629-3929	6816
Delta Floral Distributors Inc	5193	D	323 751-8116	6857
Mellano & Company (PA)	5193	D	213 622-0796	6865
Berg Lacquer Co (PA)	5198	D	323 261-8114	6883
Allaquaria LLC	5199	D	310 645-1107	6887
Flexport Inc	5199	D	323 524-7132	6907
Gaju Market Corporation	5199	D	213 382-9444	6910
Mutual Trading Co Inc	5199	D	213 229-9393	6931
Home Depot USA Inc	5211	C	323 292-1397	6981
Home Depot USA Inc	5211	B	323 342-9495	6986
Home Depot USA Inc	5211	D	310 822-3330	7020
Goodwill Inds Southern Cal (PA)	5331	A	323 223-1211	7137
Pg Usa LLC	5331	D	310 954-1040	7139
FAA Beverly Hills Inc	5511	D	323 801-1430	7204
Felix Chevrolet LP (PA)	5511	C	213 748-6141	7206
Fox Hills Auto Inc (PA)	5511	C	310 649-3673	7212
Nick Alexander Imports	5511	C	800 800-6425	7266
Noarus Investments Inc	5511	C	310 649-2440	7269
Toyota Downtown La	5531	C	213 342-3646	7380
American Rag Compagnie	5621	C	323 935-3154	7403
Walking Company Holdings Inc (PA)	5651	C	805 963-8727	7409
ABC Home Furnishings Inc (PA)	5712	A	212 473-3000	7418
ABC Carpet Co Inc (PA)	5713	D	212 473-3000	7427
Accor Corp	5812	C	310 278-5444	7454
Eataly Inc	5812	D	213 310-8000	7475
Fish House Partners One LLC	5812	D	323 460-4170	7481
International Coffee & Tea LLC (HQ)	5812	D	310 237-2326	7488
Lawrys Restaurants II Inc	5812	C	323 664-0228	7491
Magic Castles Inc	5812	D	323 851-3313	7494
SBE Entertainment Group LLC (HQ)	5813	C	323 655-8000	7522
Samys Camera Inc (PA)	5946	C	310 591-2100	7554
Michael Levine Inc (PA)	5949	C	213 622-6259	7559
Avery Group Inc	5963	B	310 217-1070	7564
Playboy Enterprises Inc (HQ)	5999	D	310 424-1800	7589
Sea Dwelling Creatures Inc	5999	D	310 676-9697	7594
VCA Inc (DH)	5999	C	310 571-6500	7599
Federal Rsrve Bnk San Frncisco	6011	A	213 683-2300	7602
Bank of Hope (HQ)	6021	C	213 639-1700	7607
Bbcn Bank	6021	A	213 251-2222	7608
Bny Mellon National Assn	6021	C	310 551-7600	7609
City National Bank (DH)	6021	B	310 888-6000	7616
City National Bank	6021	C	310 888-6500	7621
City National Corporation	6021	A		7622
Hope Bancorp Inc (PA)	6021	C	213 639-1700	7628
Mufg Union Bank Foundation	6021	D	213 236-5000	7634
Wells Fargo Bank Ltd	6021	D	213 253-6227	7640
Wells Fargo Securities LLC	6021	A	310 479-3500	7647
1st Century Bancshares Inc	6022	D	310 270-9500	7650
Busa Servicing Inc (PA)	6022	C	310 203-3400	7664
Cathay Bank (HQ)	6022	C	626 279-3698	7669
Cathay General Bancorp (PA)	6022	C	213 625-4700	7671
Manufacturers Bank (DH)	6022	C	213 489-6200	7695
Op Bancorp (PA)	6022	C	213 892-9999	7702
Pacific Commerce Bank	6022	D	213 617-0082	7704
Pacific Premier Bank	6022	D	213 626-0085	7707
Pcb Bancorp (PA)	6022	C	213 210-2000	7708

Employee Codes: A=Over 500 employees, B=251-500
C=101-250, D=51-100, E=20-50, F=10-19, G=1-9

LOS ANGELES CA — GEOGRAPHIC SECTION

Company	SIC	EMP	PHONE	ENTRY#
PCB BANK (HQ)	6022	C	213 210-2000	7709
Standard Chartered Bank	6022	D	626 639-8000	7717
Wilshire Bancorp Inc	6022	A	213 387-3200	7726
Wilshire Bank	6022	B	213 427-1000	7727
Sumitomo Mitsui Banking Corp	6029	C	213 452-7800	7739
Greenbox Loans Inc	6035	D	800 919-1086	7743
Mizuho Bank Ltd	6036	C	213 243-4500	7749
First Entertainment Credit Un (PA)	6061	D	323 851-3673	7769
University Credit Union	6061	C	310 477-6628	7815
SunAmerica Inc (HQ)	6091	A	310 772-6000	7838
Fcti Inc (PA)	6099	D	310 405-0022	7854
Lenlyn Ltd Which Will Do Bus I (HQ)	6099	D	310 417-3432	7857
Deutsche Bank National Tr Co	6111	D	310 788-6200	7863
Tuitionio Inc	6111	D	855 353-9395	7867
Hana Commercial Finance LLC	6153	D	213 240-1234	7894
Skyview Capital LLC	6153	D	310 273-6000	7908
Capitalsource Inc	6159	A	213 443-7700	7917
Capnet Financial Services Inc (PA)	6159	D	877 980-0558	7918
Motolease Funding LLC	6159	D	310 601-4779	7921
Westlake Services LLC (HQ)	6159	C	323 692-8800	7926
Federal Home Loan Mrtg Corp	6162	A	213 337-4200	7962
Walker & Dunlop Inc	6162	D	301 215-5500	8027
Canyon Partners Incorporated (HQ)	6211	D	310 272-1000	8070
Charles Schwab Corporation	6211	D	800 435-4000	8077
Gold Parent LP	6211	A	310 954-0444	8088
Goldman Sachs & Co LLC	6211	C	310 407-5700	8090
Imperial Capital LLC (PA)	6211	D	310 246-3700	8094
Lear Capital Inc	6211	D	310 571-0190	8097
Leonard Green & Partners LP (PA)	6211	D	310 954-0444	8098
Morgan Stnley Smith Barney LLC	6211	C	213 891-3200	8149
Palisades Group LLC	6211	C	424 280-7560	8160
Trust Company of West	6211	A	213 244-0000	8169
Wedbush Securities Inc (HQ)	6211	B	213 688-8000	8175
William Oneil & Co Inc (PA)	6211	C	310 448-6800	8178
Adviceperiod	6282	D	424 281-3600	8182
Anderson Kayne Capital	6282	D	800 231-7414	8186
Atlas Capital Group LLC	6282	D	213 988-8890	8187
Bel Air Inv Advisors LLC	6282	D	310 229-1500	8190
Capital Group Companies Inc (PA)	6282	A	213 486-9200	8196
Capital Research and MGT Co (HQ)	6282	B	213 486-9200	8197
Houlihan Lokey Inc (PA)	6282	C	310 788-5200	8203
Oaktree Capital Management LP (DH)	6282	C	213 830-6300	8211
Payden & Rygel (PA)	6282	C	213 625-1900	8214
Rnc Capital Management LLC	6282	D	310 477-6543	8220
Tcw Group Inc (PA)	6282	B	213 244-0000	8223
U S Trust Company NA	6282	B	213 861-5000	8226
Golden State Mutl Lf Insur Co (PA)	6311	D	713 526-4361	8233
Guardian Life Insur Co Amer	6311	D	213 624-2002	8235
SunAmerica Life Insurance Company	6311	C	310 772-6000	8247
Transamerica Occidental Life Insura	6311	A	213 742-2111	8250
Kaiser Fndtion Hosp Gift Shppe	6324	C	323 857-3290	8306
Kaiser Permanente	6324	D	323 298-3100	8337
Local Inttive Hlth Auth For Lo (PA)	6324	A	213 694-1250	8341
Mercury General Corporation (PA)	6331	A	323 937-1060	8391
Mercury Insurance Company (HQ)	6331	C	323 937-1060	8396
Mercury Insurance Services LLC	6331	C	323 937-1060	8399
Orion Indemnity Company	6331	D	213 742-8700	8402
American Contrs Indemnity Co (DH)	6351	C	213 330-1309	8427
Cap-Mpt (PA)	6351	C	213 473-8600	8429
Allstate Financial Svcs LLC	6411	D	323 981-8520	8483
AON/Albert G Ruben Insur Svcs (DH)	6411	D	310 234-6800	8492
Automobile Club Southern Cal (PA)	6411	C	213 741-3686	8505
California Fair Plan Assn	6411	D	213 487-0111	8518
Farmers Insurance Beeline	6411	D	909 997-4734	8562
Gnet Agency	6411	D	323 951-9399	8575
John Hancock Life Insur Co USA (DH)	6411	A	213 689-0813	8597
Lockton Cmpnies LLC - PCF Srie (PA)	6411	B	213 689-0500	8604
Marsh Risk & Insurance Svcs	6411	A	213 624-5555	8607
Pacific Indemnity Company	6411	B	213 622-2334	8634
Topa Insurance Company (HQ)	6411	D	310 201-0451	8674
Worldwide Holdings Inc (PA)	6411	D	213 236-4500	8696
Arden Realty Inc	6512	B	310 966-2600	8702
CB Richard Ellis Strgc Prtners	6512	D	213 683-4200	8707
Cdcf III PCF Lndmark Scrmnto L	6512	D	310 552-7211	8708
Colony MB Partners LP	6512	D	310 282-8820	8712
Insignia/Esg Ht Partners Inc (DH)	6512	B	310 765-2600	8726
La County	6512	D	310 417-5184	8731
Los Angeles Conven and Exh	6512	B	213 741-1151	8733
Property Shop La At Berkshire	6512	D	310 497-3654	8753
Scp Horton Owner 1 LLC	6512	D	310 693-4400	8756
Topa Property Group Inc (HQ)	6512	C	310 203-9199	8770
Unibal-Rodamco-Westfield Group	6512	C	310 478-4456	8772
Wellnest	6512	D	323 766-2345	8777
West Side Rehab Corporation	6512	C	323 231-4174	8779
Westfield LLC (DH)	6512	B	310 478-4456	8780
Westfield America Inc (HQ)	6512	C	310 478-4456	8781
Westfield America Ltd Partnr	6512	B	310 277-3898	8782
Wilshire Kingsley Inc	6512	D	213 382-6677	8784
A Community of Friends	6513	D	213 480-0809	8788
Abode Communities LLC	6531	C	213 629-2702	8893
All California Title Escrow Co	6531	D	800 626-0106	8896
Bgk Equities Inc (HQ)	6531	D	505 982-2184	8914
Caruso MGT Ltd A Cal Ltd Prtnr (PA)	6531	D	323 900-8100	8924
Cbre Globl Value Investors LLC (DH)	6531	C	213 683-4200	8928
Charles Dunn RE Svcs Inc (PA)	6531	D	213 270-6200	8931
Commercial Property MGT Inc (PA)	6531	D	213 739-2000	8948
Cushman & Wakefield Cal Inc	6531	D	310 556-1805	8968
Cushman Realty Corporation	6531	C	213 627-4700	8973
Evoq Properties Inc	6531	D	213 988-8890	8996
Exp Realty	6531	D	213 308-2927	8999
I D Property Corporation	6531	C	213 625-0100	9046
IDS Real Estate Group (PA)	6531	D	213 627-9937	9047
J H Snyder Company LLC	6531	D	323 857-5546	9056
Jones Lang La Salle	6531	D	213 239-6000	9062
La Cienega Associates	6531	D	310 854-0071	9067
M & S Acquisition Corporation (PA)	6531	C	213 385-1515	9088
Memco Holdings Inc	6531	C	310 277-0057	9096
Nms Properties Inc	6531	C	310 656-2700	9111
On Central Realty Inc	6531	B	323 543-8500	9112
Pathstone Family Office LLC	6531	D	888 750-7284	9129
Pcs Property Managment LLC	6531	C	310 231-1000	9130
Proland Property Managment LLC (PA)	6531	D	213 738-8175	9145
Remax 100	6531	D	323 933-4567	9160
Spus7 125 Cambridgepark LP	6531	C	213 683-4200	9183
Spus7 150 Cambridgepark LP	6531	C	213 683-4200	9184
Srht Property Holding LLC	6531	D	213 683-0522	9185
Thomas Properties Group Inc	6531	C	213 613-1900	9195
Triyar Sv LLC (PA)	6531	B	310 234-2888	9199
Truline Realty	6531	D	323 389-5432	9204
A M S Partnership (PA)	6552	D	310 312-6698	9243
Lowe Enterprises RE Group	6552	D	310 820-6661	9260
LPC Commercial Services Inc	6552	C	213 362-9080	9261
Banamex USA Bancorp (DH)	6712	C	310 203-3440	9294
Mafab Inc (PA)	6719	D	714 893-0551	9320
Saban Capital Group LLC	6719	D	310 557-5100	9334
Shryne Group Inc	6719	A	323 614-4558	9335
Yf Art Holdings Gp LLC	6719	A	678 441-1400	9349
Alliancebernstein LP	6722	C	310 286-6000	9351
American Funds Distrs Inc (DH)	6722	C	213 486-9200	9352
American Mutual Fund	6722	C	213 486-9200	9353
Ares Management Corporation (PA)	6722	C	310 201-4100	9354
Ares Management LLC (HQ)	6722	C	310 201-4100	9355
Aristotle Credit Partners LLC	6722	D	310 478-4005	9356
Causeway Capital MGT LLC	6722	C	310 231-6100	9364
Kayne Andrson Rdnick Inv MGT L	6722	D	310 229-9260	9376
Los Angeles Capital MGT LLC (PA)	6722	D	310 479-9998	9377
Metwest Total Return Bond Fund	6722	D	800 241-4671	9381
Oaktree Holdings Inc	6722	A	213 830-6300	9382
Oaktree Real Estate Opprtnties	6722	A	213 830-6300	9383
Oaktree Strategic Income LLC	6722	A	213 830-6300	9384
Ocm Real Estate Opprtnties Fun	6722	A	213 830-6300	9385
Shamrock Capital Advisors LLC	6722	B	310 974-6600	9390
Tcw Absolute Return Credit LLC	6722	D	213 244-0000	9391
Tcw Funds Management Inc	6722	D	213 244-0000	9392
Kingswood Capital MGT LP	6726	C	424 744-8238	9402
Oasis West Realty LLC	6726	D	310 274-8066	9406
Opengate Capital Group LLC	6726	D	310 432-7000	9407
Empower Our Youth	6732	D	323 203-5436	9414
Greater Los Angles Vtrans RES	6732	D	310 312-1554	9415
Ucla Foundation	6732	B	310 794-3193	9418
Capital Guardian Trust Company (HQ)	6733	D	213 486-9200	9422
Epidaurus	6733	B	213 743-9075	9425
Kaiser Foundation Hospitals	6733	D	323 881-5516	9432
Moelis & Company LLC	6733	C	310 443-2300	9439
Southern Cal Pipe Trades ADM (PA)	6733	D	213 385-6161	9447
Watts Health Foundation Inc	6733	D	323 357-6688	9451
5525 E Pacific Coast Hwy Inc	6798	D	323 669-9090	9461
Coresite LLC	6798	B	213 327-1231	9465
Hudson Pacific Properties Inc (PA)	6798	D	310 445-5700	9469
Kilroy Realty Corporation (PA)	6798	D	310 481-8400	9472
Mpg Office Trust Inc	6798	D	213 626-3300	9474
Prime Administration LLC	6798	A	323 549-7155	9476
Broadreach Capitl Partners LLC	6799	A	310 601-5760	9492
Call To Action Partners Llc (PA)	6799	D	310 996-7200	9495
Capital Intl Investors	6799	D	213 486-9200	9496
Clearview Capital LLC	6799	A	310 806-9555	9501

GEOGRAPHIC SECTION
LOS ANGELES CA

	SIC	EMP	PHONE	ENTRY#
Corridor Capital LLC (PA)	6799	C	310 442-7000	9502
Emp III Inc	6799	D	323 231-4174	9507
Golden International	6799	A	213 628-1388	9513
Gsa Des Plaines LLC	6799	D	310 557-5100	9517
Imperial Capital Group LLC (PA)	6799	D	310 246-3700	9521
Intrepid Inv Bankers LLC	6799	A	310 478-9000	9522
Nexus Capital Management LP	6799	A	424 330-8820	9540
Nogales Investors LLC	6799	B	310 276-7439	9543
Oaktree Capital Management LP	6799	D	310 442-0542	9547
Otts Asia Moorer Devon	6799	C	323 603-6959	9548
Providence Rest Partners LLC	6799	D	323 460-4170	9551
Rustic Canyon Group LLC	6799	D	310 998-8000	9557
Stonecalibre LLC (PA)	6799	D	310 774-0014	9566
Transom Capital Group LLC (PA)	6799	C	424 293-2818	9574
Truamerica Multifamily LLC	6799	D	424 325-2750	9575
417 Stockton St LLC	7011	C	323 327-9656	9590
550 Flower St Operations LLC	7011	C	213 892-8080	9594
6417 Selma Hotel LLC	7011	C	323 844-6417	9595
901 West Olympic Blvd Ltd Prtn	7011	C	347 992-5707	9597
Andaz West Hollywood	7011	D	323 656-1234	9612
Ascot Hotel LP	7011	C	310 476-6411	9616
Behringer Harvard Wilshire Blv	7011	D	310 475-8711	9637
Beverly Hills Luxury Hotel LLC	7011	B	310 274-9999	9647
Brisam Lax (de) LLC	7011	D	310 649-5151	9660
Burton Way Hotels LLC	7011	D	310 273-2222	9667
Burton-Way House Ltd A CA	7011	C	310 273-2222	9669
Carpenters Southwest ADM Corp (PA)	7011	D	213 386-8590	9681
Cim Group LP (PA)	7011	C	323 860-4900	9700
Cim/H & H Hotel LP	7011	B	323 856-1200	9701
Clear Group Inc	7011	C	603 325-5600	9707
Core/Related Gala Retail LLC	7011	D	213 349-8585	9720
Courtyard By Marriott/Lax	7011	D	310 981-2350	9723
Courtyard La LLC	7011	D	917 913-8333	9724
Crestline Hotels & Resorts Inc (HQ)	7011	C	213 629-1200	9728
Custom Hotel LLC	7011	B	310 645-0400	9734
Donald T Sterling Corporation	7011	C	310 275-5575	9762
E H Summit Inc (PA)	7011	D	310 476-6571	9769
Emerik Hotel Corp	7011	D	213 748-1291	9781
Fortuna Enterprises LP	7011	B	310 410-4000	9800
Greenleaf Hotel Inc	7011	D		9819
Hazens Investment LLC	7011	B	310 642-1111	9843
Hollywood Partnership	7011	D	323 463-7171	9864
Hotel Bel-Air	7011	B	310 472-1211	9869
Humnit Hotel At Lax LLC	7011	D	424 702-1234	9879
Hyatt Corporation	7011	C	323 656-1234	9883
Hyatt Corporation	7011	B	312 750-1234	9893
Hyatt Regency Century Plaza	7011	A	310 228-1234	9901
Ihg Management (maryland) LLC	7011	D	310 642-7500	9905
Ihg Management (maryland) LLC	7011	D	213 688-7777	9906
Irp Lax Hotel LLC	7011	C	310 645-4600	9914
J W Mrrott Los Angles L A Live	7011	D	213 765-8600	9917
Kava Holdings Inc (DH)	7011	C	310 472-1211	9936
Kimpton Hotel & Rest Group LLC	7011	C	323 852-6000	9940
L-O Bedford Operating LLC	7011	C	781 275-5500	9957
Lightstone Dt La LLC	7011	B	310 669-9252	9978
Lowe Enterprises Inc (PA)	7011	C	310 820-6661	9988
Lq Management LLC	7011	D	310 645-2200	9989
Marriott International Inc	7011	A	310 641-5700	10003
Metropolis Hotel MGT LLC	7011	D	213 683-4855	10017
Morgans Hotel Group MGT LLC	7011	C	323 650-8999	10030
New Aster Enterprises Inc	7011	D	213 747-7566	10040
New Figueroa Hotel Inc	7011	D	213 627-8971	10042
Nrea-TRC 711 LLC	7011	C	213 488-3500	10052
Orlando Wilshire Investments	7011	D	323 658-6000	10071
Oxford Palace Hotel LLC	7011	D	213 382-7756	10075
Pacifica Hosts Inc	7011	D	310 670-9000	10089
Playa Proper Jv LLC	7011	D	310 645-0400	10123
R & J Hospitality LLC	7011	D	213 388-0301	10134
Radlax Gateway Hotel LLC	7011	A	310 670-9000	10136
Raleigh Enterprises Inc (PA)	7011	D	310 899-8900	10138
Remington Hotel Corporation	7011	D	310 553-6561	10147
Renaissance Hotel Operating Co	7011	B	310 337-2800	10149
Roosevelt Hotel LLC	7011	D	323 466-7000	10170
Rpd Hotels 18 LLC (PA)	7011	A	213 746-1531	10181
S W K Properties LLC (PA)	7011	D	213 383-9204	10186
SBE Hotel Group LLC	7011	D	323 655-8000	10211
Seattle Arprt Hospitality LLC	7011	C	310 476-6411	10217
Sheraton LLC	7011	D	310 642-1111	10227
Shivay Hospitality Inc	7011	D	323 702-7103	10232
Sls Hotel At Beverly Hills	7011	C	310 247-0400	10248
Stockbridge/Sbe Holdings LLC	7011	A	323 655-8000	10278
Sunset Tower Hotel LLC	7011	D	323 654-7100	10284
Sunstone Hotel Properties Inc	7011	C	310 228-4100	10287
Svi Lax LLC	7011	D	310 281-0300	10293
Sydell Hotels LLC	7011	C	213 381-7411	10298
Todays IV	7011	A	213 835-4016	10314
W Los Angeles	7011	B	310 208-8765	10349
W&J Business Ventures LLC	7011	D	310 645-7700	10350
Welk Group Inc (PA)	7011	B	760 749-3000	10359
Whb Corporation	7011	A	213 624-1011	10367
M-Aurora Worldwide (us) LP (PA)	7021	C	800 888-0808	10394
American Textile Maint Co	7213	C	323 735-1661	10428
American Textile Maint Co	7213	D	213 749-4433	10429
Morgan Services Inc	7213	D	213 485-9666	10453
Yee Yuen Laundry and Clrs Inc	7213	D	323 734-7205	10459
Pro-Wash Inc	7215	C	323 756-6000	10464
Pico Cleaners Inc (PA)	7216	D	310 274-2431	10468
Miniluxe Inc	7231	D	424 442-1630	10502
Sinai Temple	7261	C	323 469-6000	10516
Temple Israel of Hollywood (PA)	7261	D	323 876-8330	10517
Andersen Tax LLC	7291	C	213 593-2300	10519
Eharmony Inc (HQ)	7299	C	424 258-1199	10543
Reunify LLC	7299	C	310 893-1736	10572
Vibiana Events LLC	7299	D	213 626-1507	10581
180la LLC	7311	C	310 382-1400	10584
Big Token Inc	7311	D	310 569-6553	10592
Campbell-Ewald Company	7311	C	310 358-4800	10596
Cimarron Partner Associates LLC	7311	C	323 337-0300	10598
Collab Inc (PA)	7311	D	310 991-0062	10599
Daviselen Advertising Inc (PA)	7311	C	213 688-7000	10603
Deutsch La Inc	7311	C	310 862-3000	10606
Digitas Inc	7311	C	617 867-1000	10608
Giant Media Corporation	7311	C	310 526-6739	10616
Horizon Media Inc	7311	B	310 282-0909	10625
Mediabrands Worldwide Inc	7311	B	323 370-8000	10646
Mullenlowe US Inc	7311	C	424 738-6600	10653
Nexstar Digital LLC	7311	D	310 971-9300	10656
Quigly-Simpson Heppelwhite Inc	7311	C	310 996-5800	10666
Rapp Worldwide Inc	7311	C	310 563-7200	10668
Trailer Park Inc (PA)	7311	D	310 845-3000	10682
Wonderful Agency	7311	A	310 966-8600	10690
Young & Rubicam LLC	7311	C	213 930-5000	10693
Bamko Inc	7312	C	310 470-5859	10695
Attn Inc	7313	C	323 413-2878	10702
BLT Cmmnctions LLC A Ltd Lblty	7313	C	323 860-4000	10706
Breitbart News Network LLC	7313	C	424 371-0585	10707
Mediaalpha Inc (PA)	7313	D	213 316-6256	10715
Shed Media US Inc	7313	C	323 904-4680	10719
Diversfied Mrcury Cmmnctons LL	7319	D	508 598-3569	10729
Gils Distributing Service	7319	C	213 627-0539	10731
Uscb Inc (PA)	7322	D	213 985-2111	10753
The Tax Credit Company	7323	D	323 927-0750	10765
Lasr Inc	7334	C	877 591-9979	10790
Riot Creative Imaging	7334	D	213 516-3160	10793
BLT & Associates Inc	7336	C	323 860-4000	10798
Cinnabar	7336	D	818 842-8190	10799
Cinnabar California Inc	7336	D	818 842-8190	10800
County of Los Angeles	7336	C	213 922-6210	10802
Digital Domain Media Group Inc	7336	A		10806
Twentieth Cntury Fox Japan Inc	7336	A	310 369-4636	10820
Xx Artists LLC	7336	D	503 871-5298	10822
Aramark Facility Services LLC	7349	D	213 740-8968	10858
Crown Energy Services Inc	7349	A	213 765-7800	10886
Gambrell Bondie	7349	D	310 641-8408	10902
Scv Facilities Services Inc	7349	D	310 803-4588	10962
Southern Management Corp	7349	D	213 312-2268	10970
Uniserve Facilities Svcs Corp	7349	B	310 440-6747	10977
Aercap Global Aviation Trust (HQ)	7359	C	310 788-1999	11013
Air Lease Corporation (PA)	7359	D	310 553-0555	11017
Hana Financial Inc (PA)	7359	D	213 240-1234	11035
Mufg Americas Leasing Corp (DH)	7359	D	213 488-3700	11044
Attorney Network Services Inc	7361	D	213 430-0440	11086
Career Group Inc (PA)	7361	A	310 277-8188	11102
Creative Solutions Svcs LLC	7361	C	646 495-1558	11113
G2 Secure Staff	7361	C	310 486-8155	11140
Ideal Program Services Inc	7361	D	323 296-2255	11155
Insight Global Inc	7361	C	213 404-4140	11157
Kimco Staffing Services Inc	7361	A	310 622-1616	11162
Korn Ferry	7361	C	310 552-1834	11166
Lateral Link Group Inc	7361	D	310 405-0092	11169
Nursefinders Inc	7361	D	925 660-1153	11187
Rehababilities Inc	7361	C	310 473-4448	11221
Operational Technical Svcs LLC	7363	D	424 203-6531	11314
Phoenix Engineering Co Inc	7363	D	310 532-1134	11316
3dna Corp (PA)	7371	C	213 992-4809	11367
Adcolony Inc	7371	D	650 625-1262	11380

Employee Codes: A=Over 500 employees, B=251-500
C=101-250, D=51-100, E=20-50, F=10-19, G=1-9

LOS ANGELES CA — GEOGRAPHIC SECTION

Company	SIC	EMP	PHONE	ENTRY#
Aftershock La Studios Inc	7371	D	650 450-9660	11387
Automotus Inc	7371	D	805 504-5750	11437
Babyfirst Americas LLC	7371	D	310 442-9853	11444
Bahare	7371	C	516 472-1457	11445
County of Los Angeles	7371	A	562 940-4324	11519
Daz Systems LLC	7371	B	310 640-1300	11532
Deadline Hollywood Media LLC	7371	D	310 321-5000	11533
Deviation Games LLC	7371	D	310 873-5225	11539
Equator LLC (HQ)	7371	C	310 469-9500	11575
Exploding Kittens Inc	7371	D	919 738-8440	11590
Fender Digital LLC	7371	D	323 462-2198	11596
Game Play Network Inc	7371	D	844 462-7768	11612
Gehry Technologies Inc	7371	C	310 862-1200	11614
Honey Science LLC	7371	C	949 795-1695	11644
Ktb Software LLC	7371	D	213 935-0902	11699
Pandemic Studios LLC	7371	B	310 450-5199	11811
Sago Mini Inc	7371	D	416 731-8586	11895
Science 37 Inc	7371	D	984 377-3737	11905
Second Spectrum Inc	7371	C	213 995-6860	11906
Steady Platform Inc	7371	D	678 792-8364	11946
Tribridge Holdings LLC	7371	A	813 287-8887	11988
Vendor Direct Solutions LLC (PA)	7371	C	213 362-5622	12015
Vivid Digital	7371	D	818 908-0481	12029
Agencycom LLC	7372	B	415 817-3800	12079
Chrome River Technologies Inc	7372	C	888 781-0088	12135
Consensus Cloud Solutions Inc (PA)	7372	D	323 860-9200	12147
Dave Inc (PA)	7372	C	844 857-3283	12159
Evocative Inc	7372	C	888 365-2656	12185
Mitratech Holdings Inc	7372	D	323 964-0000	12272
Symantec	7372	C	213 489-3262	12371
System1 Inc (PA)	7372	B	310 924-6037	12374
Total Cmmnicator Solutions Inc	7372	D	619 277-1488	12381
Videoamp Inc (PA)	7372	D	424 272-7774	12391
Cordoba Corporation	7373	D	213 895-0224	12440
Internet Corp For Assgned Nmes (PA)	7373	D	310 823-9358	12471
Oberman Tivoli & Pickert Inc	7373	C	310 440-9600	12507
Aligned Company	7374	D	917 558-4565	12548
Enervee Corporation	7374	D	844 363-7833	12570
Honk Technologies Inc	7374	C	800 979-3162	12579
Mocean LLC	7374	C	310 481-0808	12600
County of Los Angeles	7375	C	213 974-0515	12656
E-Times Corporation (PA)	7375	B	213 452-6720	12660
Elavon Inc	7375	B	865 403-7000	12662
Adams Comm & Engrg Tech Inc	7379	D	301 861-5000	12721
Dti Services Inc (PA)	7379	D	213 670-1100	12781
Edgecast Inc (HQ)	7379	D	310 396-7400	12783
Magma Consulting Group LLC	7379	D	415 315-9364	12833
Nowcom LLC	7379	C	323 746-6888	12847
Pegasus Squire Inc	7379	D	866 208-6537	12855
Preciseq Inc	7379	D	310 709-6094	12860
We See Dragons LLC	7379	C	310 361-5700	12907
Andrews International Inc	7381	D	310 575-4844	12930
Garda CL West Inc (HQ)	7381	B	213 383-3611	12975
Guardian Intl Solutions	7381	D	323 528-6555	12984
Mulholland SEC & Patrol Inc	7381	B	818 755-0202	13002
Pacwest Security Services	7381	C	213 413-3500	13017
Professional Security Cons (PA)	7381	D	310 207-7729	13024
Securitech Security Svcs Inc	7381	C	213 387-5050	13036
SOS Security Incorporated	7381	D	310 392-9600	13048
Worldwide Security Assoc Inc (HQ)	7381	B	310 743-3000	13077
Dtiq Holdings Inc	7382	C	323 576-1400	13107
Assocted Ldscp Dsplay Group In	7389	D	714 558-6100	13198
B Riley Securities Inc	7389	C	310 966-1444	13205
County of Los Angeles	7389	D	323 267-2771	13247
Diba Fashions Inc	7389	D	323 232-3775	13268
E & C Fashion Inc	7389	B	323 262-0099	13273
Facter Direct Ltd	7389	B	323 634-1999	13284
Forever 21 Logistics LLC	7389	D	888 494-3837	13291
Gelfand Rennert & Feldman LLP (PA)	7389	C	310 553-1707	13301
High Times Productions Inc	7389	C	844 933-3287	13315
Ingenuity Studios Intl Inc	7389	C	323 460-6096	13323
Ipayment Inc	7389	B	213 387-1353	13330
Kenneth Brdwick Intr Dsgns Inc	7389	C	310 274-9999	13335
Laundry Design LLC	7389	C	323 933-2800	13350
Lindsey & Sons	7389	D	657 306-5369	13354
Medholdings of Newnan LLC	7389	A	213 462-6252	13367
Oeoe Corp	7389	C	213 387-0933	13405
ONeil Digital Solutions LLC	7389	C	310 448-6407	13406
Prompt Delivery Inc	7389	D	858 549-8000	13435
Qology Direct LLC	7389	C	310 341-4420	13440
SD&a Teleservices Inc (HQ)	7389	B		13469
Stantec Architecture Inc	7389	B	213 955-9775	13485
Super Center Concepts Inc	7389	C	323 223-3878	13493
Swift Media Entertainment Inc	7389	D	310 308-3694	13495
Swisstex California Inc (PA)	7389	C	310 516-6800	13496
Tbwa Chiat/Day Inc	7389	B	310 305-5000	13500
Thats No Moon Entrmt Inc	7389	D	310 795-8282	13508
Victor Rane Group Inc	7389	D	424 248-3623	13541
Vxi Global Solutions LLC (PA)	7389	A	213 739-4720	13548
Warner Bros Records Inc (DH)	7389	B	818 846-9090	13549
Worldlink LLC (PA)	7389	D	323 866-5900	13557
Fox Rent A Car Inc	7514	C	310 342-5155	13588
Galpin Motors Inc	7514	C	323 957-3333	13591
ABM Parking Services Inc	7521	A	213 284-7600	13600
All Star Parking	7521	C	310 337-1944	13602
Everpark Inc	7521	C	310 987-6922	13605
L and R Auto Parks Inc	7521	C	213 784-3018	13608
Laz Karp Associates LLC	7521	C	323 464-4190	13609
Parking Concepts Inc	7521	D	310 208-1611	13620
Parking Concepts Inc	7521	D	213 746-5764	13621
Parking Concepts Inc	7521	D	213 623-2661	13623
Tps Parking Management LLC	7521	D	310 846-4747	13629
Valet Parking Svc A Cal Partnr (PA)	7521	A	323 465-5873	13630
Caliber Holdings Corporation	7532	D	323 913-4000	13635
Harrys Auto Body Inc	7532	D	323 933-4600	13638
Wand Topco Inc	7532	A	323 734-3333	13650
Mission Service Inc	7538	A	323 266-2593	13668
Blue Beacon USA LP II	7542	D	213 477-1060	13685
Authorized Cellular Service	7629	D	310 466-4144	13732
Scottel Voice & Data Inc	7629	C	310 737-7300	13744
Pacific Coast Elevator Corp	7699	D	323 345-2550	13790
Wardlow 2 LP (PA)	7699	D	562 432-8066	13809
Advanced Digital Services Inc (PA)	7812	D	323 962-8585	13815
Chm Productions Inc	7812	D	818 972-8433	13828
Deluxe Media Services LLC	7812	D	323 462-6171	13837
Digital Domain 30 Inc (PA)	7812	B	213 797-3100	13838
Efilm LLC	7812	D	323 463-7041	13845
Fox Net Inc	7812	A	310 369-1000	13851
Hungry Heart Media Inc	7812	C	323 951-0010	13855
If Live LLC (PA)	7812	D	323 957-6868	13856
Ignition Creative LLC	7812	D	310 315-6300	13857
Merlot Film Productions Inc	7812	C	323 575-2906	13864
Miramax LLC	7812	D	310 409-4321	13866
New Regency Productions Inc (PA)	7812	D	424 446-4092	13870
Paramount Pictures Corporation (HQ)	7812	A	323 956-5000	13873
Paramount Television Service	7812	D	323 956-5000	13874
Paramunt Ovrseas Prdctions Inc	7812	A	323 956-5225	13875
Picture Shop LLC	7812	D	323 785-1550	13876
Ripe Digital Entertainment Inc	7812	D	323 463-7070	13886
Scanline Vfx Inc	7812	A	310 827-1555	13889
Scanlinevfx La LLC	7812	C	310 827-1555	13890
SDI Media USA Inc (HQ)	7812	D	310 388-8800	13891
Triage Entertainment LLC	7812	D	310 417-4800	13902
Twenteth Cntury Fox HM Entrmt (PA)	7812	A	310 369-1000	13903
Twentieth Cntury Fox Film Corp (DH)	7812	D		13904
Twentieth Television Inc (DH)	7812	D	310 369-1000	13905
Viacom Networks	7812	D	310 752-8000	13909
Village Road Show Pictures USA	7812	D	310 385-4300	13910
A Filml Inc	7819	D	213 977-8600	13924
Cara Communications LLC	7819	D	310 442-5600	13928
Directors Guild America Inc (PA)	7819	C	310 289-2000	13932
For Cali Productions LLC	7819	B	323 956-9500	13935
Hollywood Rntals Prod Svcs LLC (PA)	7819	D	818 407-7800	13939
Omega/Cinema Props LLC	7819	D	323 466-8201	13945
Pixomondo LLC	7819	A	310 394-0555	13946
Point360 (PA)	7819	D	818 565-1400	13947
Post Group Inc (PA)	7819	D	323 462-2300	13948
Runway Inc	7819	D	310 636-2000	13949
Twentieth Cntury Fox Intl Corp (HQ)	7822	C	310 369-1000	13968
United Artists Corporation	7822	C	310 449-3000	13969
United Artists Productions Inc	7822	C	310 449-3000	13971
United Artists Television Corp	7822	B	310 449-3000	13972
Our Alchemy LLC	7829	D	310 893-6289	13976
Decurion Corporation (PA)	7832	D	310 659-9432	13985
Nationwide Theatres Corp (HQ)	7833	D	310 657-8420	14023
AEG Presents LLC (DH)	7922	D	323 930-5700	14026
Center Thtre Group Los Angeles (PA)	7922	C	213 972-7344	14032
Creative Artsts Agcy Hldngs LL (PA)	7922	A	424 288-2000	14035
Fandango Inc (HQ)	7922	D	310 954-0278	14037
J C Entertainment Ltg Svcs Inc	7922	C	818 252-7481	14041
Los Angeles Opera Company	7922	B	213 972-7219	14043
Paradigm Talent Agency LLC	7922	D	310 288-8000	14052
Performing Arts Ctr Los Angles	7922	C	213 972-7512	14054
Professnal Intrctive Entrmt In	7922	D	310 823-4445	14058
Anschutz Entrmt Group Inc (HQ)	7929	C	213 763-7700	14076
Entertinment Studios Media Inc (PA)	7929	D	310 277-3500	14082

GEOGRAPHIC SECTION

LOS ANGELES CA

	SIC	EMP	PHONE	ENTRY#
Hob Entertainment LLC (DH)	7929	C	323 769-4600	14086
House of Blues Concerts Inc (DH)	7929	C	323 769-4977	14087
Los Angeles Philharmonic Assn (PA)	7929	C	213 972-7300	14093
Los Angeles Philharmonic Assn	7929	A	323 850-2060	14094
Twenty Mile Productions LLC	7929	C	412 251-0767	14108
Two Bit Circus Dtla LLC	7929	D	323 438-9808	14109
Lucky Strike Entertainment Inc	7933	B	213 542-4880	14116
Lucky Strike Entertainment LLC	7933	C	818 933-3752	14117
Fox Baseball Holdings Inc	7941	C	323 224-1500	14138
Fox BSB Holdco Inc (HQ)	7941	B	323 224-1500	14139
Immortals LLC	7941	D	310 554-8267	14142
La Clippers LLC	7941	C	213 742-7500	14145
LA Sports Properties Inc	7941	C	213 742-7500	14146
Lafc Sports LLC	7941	D	323 549-4350	14147
Barrys Bootcamp LLC (PA)	7991	D	323 452-0037	14174
Bay Clubs Company LLC	7991	B	310 216-3060	14178
Bliss World LLC	7991	D	323 500-0921	14181
Equinox-76th Street Inc	7991	D	310 479-5200	14200
Equinox-76th Street Inc	7991	D	310 552-0420	14203
Los Angeles Athletic Club Inc	7991	C	213 625-2211	14216
Lounge Spa Inc	7991	D	310 745-1646	14218
Sweatheory LLC	7991	D	310 956-2307	14236
World Gym International LLC	7991	C	310 557-8804	14243
Bel-Air Country Club	7997	D	310 472-9563	14340
Brentwood Country Club Los Angeles	7997	D	310 451-8011	14350
Hillcrest Country Club	7997	C	310 553-8911	14382
Lafc Partners Lllp	7997	B	213 334-4239	14391
Los Angeles Country Club	7997	C	310 276-6104	14399
Wilshire Country Club	7997	D	323 934-6050	14484
Aroma Spa & Sports LLC	7999	D	213 387-2111	14492
Faze Clan Inc	7999	B	818 688-6373	14521
Faze Holdings Inc (PA)	7999	C	818 688-6373	14522
Fortiss LLC	7999	D	323 415-4900	14526
Kinema Fitness Inc	7999	D	610 909-9331	14537
Ticketmaster Corporation	7999	A	323 769-4600	14570
Ticketmaster Group Inc	7999	A	800 745-3000	14572
Tumbleweed Eductl Entps Inc	7999	C	310 444-3232	14579
Volume Services Inc	7999	B	323 644-6038	14583
Altamed Health Services Corp	8011	C	323 980-4466	14600
Altamed Health Services Corp	8011	C	323 728-0411	14607
Altamed Health Services Corp	8011	C	323 269-0421	14608
Arroyo Vsta Frmly Hlth Fndation	8011	D	323 224-2188	14617
Associated Students UCLA	8011	D	310 825-9451	14620
Cedars-Sinai Medical Center	8011	B	310 423-3849	14662
Cedars-Sinai Medical Center	8011	D	310 423-7900	14663
Cedars-Sinai Medical Center	8011	D	310 423-4208	14664
Cha Health Systems Inc (PA)	8011	A	213 487-3211	14676
Clinic Inc	8011	D	323 730-1920	14688
Core Med Staff	8011	D	213 382-5550	14707
County of Los Angeles	8011	A	323 226-7131	14709
County of Los Angeles	8011	D	213 744-3919	14710
Garden Grove Advanced Imaging	8011	C	310 445-2800	14756
Good Samaritan Hospital Aux	8011	B	213 977-2121	14765
House Ear Clinic Inc (PA)	8011	D	213 483-9930	14775
Kaiser Foundation Hospitals	8011	C	323 783-7955	14791
Kaiser Foundation Hospitals	8011	A	323 857-2000	14809
Kaiser Foundation Hospitals	8011	D	310 915-5000	14819
Kaiser Foundation Hospitals	8011	B	323 783-8306	14851
Kaiser Foundation Hospitals	8011	C	323 857-2000	14854
Keck Medical Center of Usc	8011	D	323 371-9535	14859
Kerlan-Jobe Orthopedic Clinic (PA)	8011	D	310 665-7200	14860
Lac & Usc Medical Center	8011	D	323 409-2345	14873
Los Angeles Cardiology Assoc (HQ)	8011	D	213 977-0419	14879
Los Angeles Free Clinic	8011	C	323 653-1990	14880
Los Angeles Free Clinic (PA)	8011	D	323 653-8622	14881
Oaks Diagnostics Inc (PA)	8011	D	310 855-0035	14930
Pediatric & Family Medical Ctr	8011	C	213 342-3325	14953
Prospect Medical Holdings Inc (PA)	8011	C	310 943-4500	15000
Queenscare Health Centers	8011	D	323 780-4510	15005
Queenscare Health Centers	8011	D	323 644-6180	15006
Renew Medical Group Inc	8011	C	310 929-9790	15015
Robert K Maloney Md Inc	8011	D	310 208-3937	15028
Robin Red Breast Inc	8011	D	323 466-7800	15029
Santa Monica Bay Physicians He (PA)	8011	D	310 417-5900	15050
South Central Family Hlth Ctr	8011	D	323 908-4200	15066
Southern Cal Prmnnte Med Group	8011	C	323 783-5455	15079
Southern Cal Prmnnte Med Group	8011	C	323 783-4893	15094
Southern Cal Prmnnte Med Group	8011	C	323 857-2000	15095
The Orthopedic Institute of	8011	A	213 977-2010	15126
United Medical Imaging Inc (PA)	8011	D	310 943-8400	15145
University Southern California	8011	D	323 865-3050	15168
Veterans Health Administration	8011	A	310 478-3711	15191
Via Care Cmnty Hlth Ctr Inc	8011	D	323 268-9191	15193
Watts Healthcare Corporation (PA)	8011	C	323 564-4331	15199
White Mem Cmnty Hlth Ctr A Cal	8011	D	323 987-1222	15207
White Memorial Med Group Inc (PA)	8011	D	323 987-1300	15208
White Memorial Medical Center	8011	A	323 260-5739	15209
Che Snior Psychological Svcs PC	8049	C	888 307-0893	15277
Intercare Therapy Inc	8049	C	323 866-1880	15292
Quantum Bhvioral Solutions Inc (PA)	8049	D	626 531-6999	15301
Amada Enterprises Inc	8051	C	323 757-1881	15323
Beverly West Health Care Inc	8051	D	323 938-2451	15358
Burlington Convalescent Hosp (PA)	8051	D	213 381-5585	15360
Burlington Convalescent Hosp	8051	C	323 295-7737	15361
Cha Hollywood Medical Ctr LP	8051	A	213 413-3000	15373
Country Villa Nursing Ctr Inc	8051	C	213 484-9730	15392
Culver West Health Center LLC	8051	D	310 390-9506	15419
East Los Angeles Healthcare LLC (PA)	8051	D	323 268-0106	15428
Front Porch Communities & Svcs	8051	C	323 661-1128	15483
Garden Crest Cnvlscent Hosp In	8051	D	323 663-8281	15486
Highland Pk Sklled Nrsing Wlln	8051	D	323 254-6125	15516
Hyde Pk Rehabilitation Ctr LLC	8051	D	323 753-1354	15519
J P H Consulting Inc	8051	C	323 934-5660	15525
Lighthouse Healthcare Ctr LLC	8051	D	323 564-4461	15545
Longwood Management Corp	8051	C	323 933-1560	15553
Manchster Mnor Cnvlscent Hosp	8051	D	323 753-1789	15558
Mariner Health Care Inc	8051	D	323 665-1185	15570
Rehabltion Cntre of Bvrly Hlls	8051	D	323 782-1500	15635
Ridgecrest Healthcare Inc	8051	D	760 446-3591	15638
Rrt Enterprises LP (PA)	8051	C	310 397-2372	15646
Rrt Enterprises LP	8051	C	323 653-1521	15647
Sharon Care Center LLC	8051	D	323 655-2023	15662
Silverado Senior Living Inc	8051	D	323 984-7313	15673
Skyline Hlthcare Wllness Ctr L	8051	C	323 665-1185	15675
Stjohn God Rtirement Care Ctr	8051	C	323 731-0641	15682
Westlake Health Care Center	8051	B	805 494-1233	15732
Westwood Healthcare Center LP	8051	D	310 826-0821	15734
Amberwood Convalescent Hosp	8059	D	323 254-3407	15808
Ararat Home Los Angeles Inc	8059	C	323 256-8012	15811
Bonnie Brae Cnvlscent Hosp Inc (PA)	8059	D	213 483-8144	15821
Chase Care Center Inc	8059	D	323 935-8490	15830
Country Villa Terrace (PA)	8059	D	323 653-3980	15833
Genesis Healthcare LLC	8059	B	323 461-9961	15847
Longwood Management Corp	8059	D	323 735-5146	15867
Longwood Management Corp	8059	C	323 737-7778	15869
Longwood Management Corp	8059	D	213 382-8461	15870
New Vista Health Services	8059	C	310 477-5501	15880
Olympia Convalescent Hospital	8059	C	213 487-3000	15884
Temple Pk Cnvalescent Hosp Inc	8059	D	213 380-2035	15902
United Convalescent Facilities	8059	D	213 748-0491	15906
Alta Healthcare System LLC (HQ)	8062	C	323 267-0477	15937
Califrnia Hosp Med Ctr Fndtion	8062	A	213 742-5867	15964
Califrnia Rhblitation Inst LLC	8062	D	424 363-1003	15965
Cedars-Sinai Medical Center	8062	A	310 824-3664	15970
Cedars-Sinai Medical Center	8062	C	310 423-6451	15973
Cedars-Sinai Medical Center	8062	C	310 423-2587	15974
Cedars-Sinai Medical Center	8062	B	310 423-8965	15975
Cedars-Sinai Medical Center	8062	B	310 423-3277	15980
Cedars-Sinai Medical Center	8062	B	310 423-9520	15981
Childrens Hosp Los Angles Med (PA)	8062	D	323 361-2336	15992
Childrens Hospital Los Angeles	8062	B	323 361-2751	15995
County of Los Angeles	8062	B	310 668-4545	16025
County of Los Angeles	8062	C	323 226-6021	16026
County of Los Angeles	8062	C	213 473-6100	16027
East Los Angles Dctors Hosp In	8062	B		16062
Hollywood Cmnty Hosp Med Ctr I	8062	C	323 462-2271	16134
Hollywood Medical Center LP	8062	A	213 413-3000	16135
Jupiter Bellflower Doctors Hospital	8062	B		16146
Kaiser Foundation Hospitals	8062	D	323 783-4011	16155
Kaiser Foundation Hospitals	8062	D	323 783-4011	16161
Kaiser Permanente Watts C	8062	D	323 564-7911	16196
Keck Hospital of Usc	8062	A	800 872-2273	16201
Keck School	8062	D	323 442-1179	16202
LA Metropolitan Medical Center	8062	A	323 730-7300	16208
Lac Usc County Hospital	8062	D	323 226-2622	16210
Lac Usc Medical Center	8062	C		16211
Memorial Hospital of Gardena	8062	B	323 268-5514	16255
Nix Hospitals System LLC (HQ)	8062	C	210 271-1800	16281
Olympia Health Care LLC	8062	A	323 938-3161	16293
Orthopaedic Hospital (PA)	8062	A	213 742-1000	16302
Pamc Ltd (PA)	8062	A	213 624-8411	16314
Paraclsus Los Angeles Cmnty Hos	8062	C	323 267-0477	16315
Pih Health Good Samaritan Hosp (HQ)	8062	A	213 977-2121	16325
Southern Cal Hsalthcare Sys Inc (HQ)	8062	C	310 943-4500	16438
Temple Hospital Corporation	8062	B	213 355-3200	16569
Tenet Health Systems Norris	8062	B	323 865-3000	16570

Employee Codes: A=Over 500 employees, B=251-500
C=101-250, D=51-100, E=20-50, F=10-19, G=1-9

LOS ANGELES CA — GEOGRAPHIC SECTION

Name	SIC	EMP	PHONE	ENTRY#
Tustin Hospital and Medical Center	8062	B	714 619-7700	16583
Ucla Health	8062	D	310 825-9111	16585
University Cal Los Angeles	8062	A	310 825-9111	16589
University Southern California	8062	A	323 442-8500	16605
White Memorial Medical Center (HQ)	8062	A	323 268-5000	16627
Gateways Hosp Mental Hlth Ctr (PA)	8063	C	323 644-2000	16650
Kaiser Foundation Hospitals	8063	C	213 580-7200	16651
Kedren Community Hlth Ctr Inc (PA)	8063	B	323 233-0425	16653
Telecare Corporation	8063	D	213 533-1050	16658
Barlow Group (PA)	8069	C	213 250-4200	16663
Barlow Respiratory Hospital (PA)	8069	C	213 250-4200	16664
Childrens Hospital Los Angeles (PA)	8069	A	323 660-2450	16671
County of Los Angeles	8069	C	323 226-3468	16675
County of Los Angeles	8069	D	213 974-7284	16678
Shields For Families (PA)	8069	D	323 242-5000	16694
Radnet Inc (PA)	8071	A	310 478-7808	16747
Samaritan Imaging Center	8071		213 977-2140	16751
Clinics On Demand Inc	8082	D	310 709-7355	16840
Livhome Inc (PA)	8082	A	800 807-5854	16890
Maxim Healthcare Services Inc	8082	B	866 465-5678	16892
South Bay Senior Services Inc	8082	D	310 338-8558	16930
Success Healthcare 1 LLC (PA)	8082	D	213 989-6100	16937
Ucla Health Auxiliary	8082	A	310 267-4327	16954
Amanecer Cmnty Cnsling Svc A N	8093	D	213 481-7464	17003
Behavioral Learning Netwrk LLC	8093	D	310 871-6800	17013
Brand Therapy LLC	8093	D	415 336-6411	17016
Comprehensive Cancer Centers Inc	8093	C	323 966-3400	17033
County of Los Angeles	8093	B	323 897-6187	17036
County of Los Angeles	8093	D	323 769-7800	17038
Evolve Treatment Centers	8093	D	310 622-1420	17062
Planned Parenthood Los Angeles (PA)	8093	D	213 284-3200	17108
South Baylo University	8093	D	213 999-0297	17127
United Amrcn Indian Invlvment (PA)	8093	D	213 202-3970	17150
Altamed Health Services Corp	8099	D	323 307-0400	17171
Altamed Health Services Corp	8099	D	323 890-8767	17172
California Cryobank LLC (DH)	8099	D	310 496-5691	17196
Camden Center Inc	8099	D	310 526-3807	17200
Cope Health Solutions	8099	D	213 542-2250	17210
County of Los Angeles	8099	D	213 739-2360	17212
Drip Hydration	8099	D	323 333-9634	17227
Los Angles Cnty Dvlpmntal Svcs	8099	D	213 383-1300	17271
Martin Lther King Jr-Los Angle	8099	B	424 338-8000	17272
Northern Ornge Cnty Ent Mdcl	8099	D	213 252-0036	17283
Public Hlth Fndation Entps Inc	8099	C	323 261-6388	17303
Public Hlth Fndation Entps Inc	8099	C	323 733-9381	17305
Sweatheory Wellness LLC	8099	D	310 844-3662	17336
A Buchalter Professional Corp (PA)	8111	C	213 891-0700	17354
Abramson Labor Group	8111	D	213 493-6300	17356
Akerman LLP	8111	C	213 688-9500	17357
Akin Gump Struss Huer Feld LLP	8111	D	310 229-1000	17358
Allen Mtkins Leck Gmble Mllory (PA)	8111	C	213 622-5555	17362
Alston & Bird LLP	8111	C	213 576-1000	17363
Arnold Porter Kaye Scholer LLP	8111	D	213 243-4000	17368
Austin Sidley CA LLP	8111	C	213 896-6000	17370
Baker & Hostetler LLP	8111	D	310 820-8800	17371
Baker & McKenzie LLP	8111	C	310 201-4728	17374
Ballard Spahr LLP	8111	D	424 204-4400	17377
Barnes & Thornburg LLP	8111	C	310 284-3880	17378
Barnes Firm LC	8111	D	800 800-0000	17379
Bird Mrlla Bxer Wlpert Nssim	8111	D	310 201-2100	17386
Blakely Sokoloff Taylor & Zafman LLP	8111	C	310 207-3800	17387
Bonne Brdges Mller Okefe Nchol (PA)	8111	D	213 480-1900	17390
Burke Williams & Sorensen LLP (PA)	8111	D	213 236-0600	17394
County of Los Angeles	8111	D	213 974-2811	17416
County of Los Angeles	8111	D	213 974-3512	17418
Covington & Burling LLP	8111	C	424 332-4800	17424
Cox Castle & Nicholson LLP (PA)	8111	C	310 284-2200	17425
Crowell & Moring LLP	8111	C	213 622-4750	17427
Danning Gill Damnd Kollitz LLP	8111	D	310 277-0077	17429
Davis Wright Tremaine LLP	8111	C	213 633-6800	17433
De Castro W Chdrow Mndler Glck	8111	D	310 478-2541	17434
Dechert LLP	8111	D	949 442-6000	17435
Dentons US LLP	8111	D	213 623-9300	17437
Dla Piper LLP (us)	8111	D	310 595-3000	17438
Dominguez Law Group PC	8111	D	213 388-7788	17439
Elkins Kalt Wntraub Rben Grtsi	8111	D	310 746-4431	17445
Ellis Grge Cpllone Obrien Anng	8111	D	310 274-7100	17446
Engstrom Lipscomb and Lack A (PA)	8111	D	213 552-3800	17447
Epstein Becker & Green PC	8111	D	310 556-8861	17449
Gibbs Giden Locher	8111	D	310 552-3400	17465
Gibson Dunn & Crutcher Inc	8111	C	213 229-7000	17466
Gibson Dunn & Crutcher LLP (PA)	8111	B	213 229-7000	17469
Gibson Dunn & Crutcher LLP	8111	D	310 552-8500	17470
Gilbert Klly Crwley Jnnett LLP (PA)	8111	D	213 615-7000	17472
Gipson Hffman Pncone A Prof Co	8111	D	310 556-4660	17473
Girardi Keese (PA)	8111	D	213 977-0211	17474
Glaser Weil Fink Jacobs (PA)	8111	C	310 553-3000	17475
Gordon Rees Scully Mansukhani	8111	C	213 576-5000	17477
Greenberg Glsker Flds Clman Mc	8111	C	310 553-3610	17481
Greenberg Traurig LLP	8111	D	310 586-7708	17483
Haight Brown & Bonesteel LLP (PA)	8111	D	213 542-8000	17489
Hill Farrer & Burrill	8111	D	213 620-0460	17494
Holland & Knight LLP	8111	D	213 896-2400	17495
Hueston Hennigan LLP	8111	D	213 788-4340	17497
Imhoff & Associates PC	8111	D	310 691-2200	17499
Immigrant Defenders Law Center	8111	D	213 634-0999	17500
Irell & Manella LLP (PA)	8111	C	310 277-1010	17502
Jackoway Tyrman Wrthmer Asten	8111	D	310 553-0305	17503
Jacoby & Meyers Attys LLP	8111	D	310 312-3300	17504
Jeffer Mngels Btlr Mtchell LLP (PA)	8111	D	310 203-8080	17505
Jones Day Limited Partnership	8111	C	213 489-3939	17506
JP Morgan & Co	8111	D	213 485-1234	17508
K&L Gates LLP	8111	C	310 552-5000	17511
Katten Muchin Rosenman LLP	8111	C	310 788-4400	17513
Kirkland & Ellis LLP	8111	D	310 552-4200	17522
Kirkland & Ellis LLP	8111	C	213 680-8400	17523
Kirkland & Ellis LLP	8111	B	213 680-8400	17525
Knight Law Group LLP	8111	D	424 355-1155	17527
La Folette Johnson Dehass Sesl	8111	D	213 426-3600	17532
Latham & Watkins LLP (PA)	8111	A	213 485-1234	17536
Latham & Watkins LLP	8111	D	213 891-7108	17537
Lewis Brsbois Bsgard Smith LLP (PA)	8111	D	213 250-1800	17544
Liner LLP	8111	C	310 500-3500	17550
LLP Mayer Brown	8111	B	213 229-9500	17554
LLP Raines Feldman	8111	D	310 440-4100	17555
Loeb & Loeb LLP (PA)	8111	C	310 282-2000	17556
Manatt Phelps & Phillips LLP (PA)	8111	B	310 312-4000	17561
Manning Kass Ellrod Rmrez Trst (PA)	8111	C	213 624-6900	17562
Milbank Tweed Hdley McCloy LLP	8111	C	424 386-4000	17569
Mitchell Silberberg Knupp LLP (PA)	8111	C	310 312-2000	17572
Morris Polich & Purdy LLP (PA)	8111	D	213 891-9100	17575
Morrison & Foerster LLP	8111	C	213 892-5200	17576
Munger Tolles & Olson LLP	8111	B	213 683-9100	17580
Munger Tolles Olson Foundation (PA)	8111	B	213 683-9100	17581
Murchison & Cumming LLP (PA)	8111	D	213 623-7400	17582
Musick Peeler & Garrett LLP (PA)	8111	C	213 629-7600	17585
Nossaman LLP (PA)	8111	D	213 612-7800	17589
OMelveny & Myers LLP	8111	D	310 553-6700	17592
OMelveny & Myers LLP (PA)	8111	A	213 430-6000	17593
Pachulski Stang Zehl Jones LLP (PA)	8111	D	310 277-6910	17598
Parker Mllken Clark Ohara Smli	8111	D	818 784-8087	17601
Parker Stanbury LLP (PA)	8111	C	619 528-1259	17602
Paul Hastings LLP (PA)	8111	A	213 683-6000	17603
Pillsbury Wnthrop Shaw Pttman	8111	C	213 488-7100	17611
Pircher Nichols & Meeks (PA)	8111	D	310 201-0132	17613
Polsinelli PC	8111	D	310 556-1801	17614
Public Counsel	8111	D	213 385-2977	17620
Quinn Emnuel Urqhart Sllvan LL (PA)	8111	B	213 443-3000	17621
Reed Smith LLP	8111	D	213 457-8000	17622
Richards Wtson Grshon A Prof C (PA)	8111	C	213 626-8484	17624
Ropers Majeski A Prof Corp	8111	C	213 312-2000	17628
Russ August & Kabat LLP	8111	C	310 826-7474	17630
Saul Ewing Arnstein & Lehr LLP	8111	D	310 398-6100	17632
Selman Lchnger Edson Hsu Nwman	8111	D	310 445-0800	17637
Seyfarth Shaw LLP	8111	D	213 270-9600	17641
Seyfarth Shaw LLP	8111	C	310 277-7200	17642
Sheppard Mllin Rchter Hmpton L (PA)	8111	B	213 620-1780	17646
Sheppard Mllin Rchter Hmpton L	8111	D	310 228-3700	17649
Skadden Arps Slate Meagher & F	8111	C	213 687-5000	17655
Stroock & Stroock & Lavan LLP	8111	C	310 556-5800	17664
Stutman Trster Glatt Prof Corp	8111	D	310 228-5600	17665
Troygould PC	8111	D	310 553-4441	17670
White & Case LLP	8111	C	213 620-7724	17677
Wilson Elser Mskwitz Edlman DC	8111	D	213 443-5100	17680
Wolf Rfkin Shpiro Schlman Rbk (PA)	8111	D	310 445-8817	17685
Womble Bond Dickinson (us) LLP	8111	D	310 207-3800	17687
Ziffren B B F G-L S&C Fnd	8111	C	310 552-3388	17691
Berkeley Hall Schl Foundation	8211	D	310 476-6421	17695
Vista Del Mar Child Fmly Svcs (PA)	8211	B	310 836-1223	17757
West Angeles Ch God In Chrst	8211	D	323 731-2567	17758
Associated Students UCLA	8221	C	310 206-8282	17761
Los Angeles Unified School Dst	8221	D	213 763-2900	17765
University Cal Los Angeles	8221	C	310 825-7852	17769
The Coding Source LLC	8249	C	866 235-7553	17797
Greenwood Hall Inc	8299	C	310 905-8300	17810
Southern Cal Prmnnte Med Group	8299	C	323 564-7911	17816

Mergent email: customerrelations@mergent.com
2024 Directory of California WholeSalers and Service Companies
(P-0000) Products & Services Section entry number
(PA)=Parent Co (HQ)=Headquarters (DH)=Div Headquarters

GEOGRAPHIC SECTION — LOS ANGELES CA

Name	SIC	EMP	PHONE	ENTRY#
Advancment Thrugh Oprtnty Knwl	8322	D	323 730-9400	17823
Aids Project Los Angeles (PA)	8322	D	213 201-1600	17824
American National Red Cross	8322	C	310 445-9900	17832
American Red Cross Los Angles (PA)	8322	C	310 445-9900	17833
Aviva Family & Childrens Svcs (PA)	8322	D	323 876-0550	17843
Blc Residential Care Inc	8322	D	310 722-7541	17852
Braille Institute America Inc (PA)	8322	C	323 663-1111	17854
Childrens Bureau Southern Cal (PA)	8322	C	213 342-0100	17881
Childrens Inst Los Angeles	8322	A	213 383-2765	17883
Childrens Institute Inc (PA)	8322	C	213 385-5100	17884
Core Cmnty Orgnzed Rlief Effor	8322	B	323 934-4400	17898
County of Los Angeles	8322	D	213 351-7257	17907
County of Los Angeles	8322	D	213 351-5600	17910
County of Los Angeles	8322	D	213 974-9331	17916
County of Los Angeles	8322	D	323 235-7047	17918
County of Los Angeles	8322	D	323 226-8511	17919
County of Los Angeles	8322	C	323 780-2185	17924
County of Los Angeles	8322	C	323 586-6469	17925
County of Los Angeles	8322	D	323 551-7224	17931
County of Los Angeles	8322	D	323 722-4529	17933
Crystal Stairs Inc (PA)	8322	B	323 299-8998	17947
Drew Child Dev Corp Inc (PA)	8322	D	323 249-2950	17959
East Los Angles Rmrkble Ctzens	8322	D	323 223-3079	17961
First 5 La	8322	C	213 482-5920	17982
Homeboy Industries (PA)	8322	B	323 526-1254	18003
International Medical Corps (PA)	8322	A	310 826-7800	18021
Jewish Family Svc Los Angeles	8322	C	323 937-5900	18027
Jvs Socal	8322	B	323 761-8879	18030
Kedren Community Hlth Ctr Inc	8322	C	323 524-0634	18033
La Asccion Ncnal Pro Prsnas My	8322	A	213 202-5900	18035
Lacba Counsel For Justice	8322	D	951 489-2919	18038
Los Angeles Homeless Svcs Auth	8322	A	213 683-3333	18045
Los Angles Fireman Relief Assn	8322	D	800 244-3439	18047
Men Tking Over Rfrming Soc Inc	8322	D	323 338-6633	18052
New Directions Inc (PA)	8322	D	310 914-4045	18062
Path	8322	A	323 644-2216	18077
Prototypes Centers For Innov	8322	D	213 542-3838	18089
Sexual Recovery Institute Inc	8322	B	310 360-0130	18129
St Brnbas Snior Ctr Los Angle	8322	D	213 388-4444	18138
Team Logic If La W Hollywood	8322	D	310 292-0063	18148
Volunteers of Amer Los Angeles	8322	C	213 749-0362	18173
Volunteers of Amer Los Angeles	8322	C	323 780-3770	18175
Volunteers of Amer Los Angeles	8322	D	213 627-8002	18182
Watts Labor Community Action	8322	C	323 563-5639	18187
Weingart Center Association	8322	C	213 622-6359	18189
Wellnest Emtonal Hlth Wellness (PA)	8322	C	323 373-2400	18192
Yue Feng Inc	8322	D	310 253-9795	18199
Asian Rehabilitation Svc Inc	8331	D	213 680-3790	18209
Chinatown Service Center (PA)	8331	D	213 808-1701	18220
Exceptional Chld Foundation	8331	C	213 748-3556	18229
Mid-Cities Association Inc (PA)	8331	D	310 537-4510	18235
Pacific Asian Cnsrtium In Empl (PA)	8331	C	213 353-3982	18242
Special Service For Groups Inc (PA)	8331	D	213 368-1888	18250
California Childrens Academy	8351	C	323 263-3846	18273
Carousel Child Care Corp	8351	C	310 216-6641	18275
Plaza De La Raza Child Develop	8351	D	323 224-1788	18346
Uniper Care Inc	8351	D	888 471-7623	18365
County of Los Angeles	8361	D	323 226-8611	18402
Covenant House California	8361	C	323 461-3131	18406
Evolve Growth Initiatives LLC	8361	C	424 281-5000	18431
Hamburger Home (PA)	8361	D	323 876-0550	18444
Hathaway-Sycmres Child Fmly Svc	8361	D	323 257-9600	18446
Lamp Inc	8361	C	213 488-9559	18464
Los Angeles Mission Inc (PA)	8361	D	213 629-1227	18476
Mgh Corporation	8361	D	323 754-1408	18486
Senior Keiro Health Care	8361	D	323 263-9651	18520
Sisters of Nzareth Los Angeles	8361	D	310 839-2361	18522
Solheim Lutheran Home	8361	C	323 257-7518	18523
St Annes Family Services	8361	D	213 381-2931	18524
Anti-Recidivism Coalition	8399	D	213 955-5885	18556
Associated Students UCLA (PA)	8399	B	310 794-8836	18561
Associated Students UCLA	8399	C	310 794-0242	18562
California Endowment (PA)	8399	D	213 928-8800	18567
Community Partners (PA)	8399	D	213 346-3200	18580
Essential Access Health (PA)	8399	D	213 386-5614	18586
Greater Los Angeles Zoo Assn	8399	A	323 644-4200	18589
I Did Smthing Good Tday Fndtio	8399	D	888 491-0054	18595
Interntnal Fndtion For Krea Un	8399	B	213 550-2182	18597
Los Angeles Education Partnr	8399	D	213 622-5237	18607
Los Angeles Lgbt Center (PA)	8399	C	323 993-7618	18608
South Cntl Los Angles Rgnal CT (PA)	8399	C	213 744-7000	18623
South Cntl Los Angles Rgnal CT	8399	C	231 744-8484	18624
Special Service For Groups Inc	8399	C	213 553-1800	18627
United Way Inc (PA)	8399	D	213 808-6220	18632
Westside Jewish Cmnty Ctr Inc (PA)	8399	C	323 938-2531	18633
Academy Museum Motion Pictures	8412	D	310 247-3000	18635
Armand Hmmer Mseum of Art Cltr	8412	C	310 443-7000	18637
Autry Museum of American West	8412	C	323 667-2000	18639
Califrnia Scnce Ctr Foundation	8412	B	213 744-2545	18641
Los Angeles Cnty Mseum of Art	8412	B	323 857-6000	18655
Lucas Museum of Narrative Art	8412	D	831 566-9332	18656
Museum Associates	8412	B	323 857-6172	18658
Museum of Contemporary Art (PA)	8412	D	213 626-6222	18660
Skirball Cultural Center	8412	C	310 440-4500	18676
The J Paul Getty Trust (PA)	8412	A	310 440-7300	18679
California Assn Realtors Inc (PA)	8611	D	213 739-8200	18700
California RE Assn Inc	8611	D	213 739-8200	18702
Los Angles Area Chmber Cmmerce	8611	D	213 580-7500	18712
Attainment Holdco LLC	8621	C	310 954-1578	18732
Coopertive Amrcn Physcians Inc (PA)	8621	D	213 473-8600	18746
County of Los Angeles	8621	D	213 240-8412	18747
Los Angeles County Bar Assn (PA)	8621	D	213 627-2727	18751
State Bar of California	8621	D	213 765-1520	18763
Truck Underwriters Association (DH)	8621	A	323 932-3200	18766
Los Angles Cnty Employees Assn	8631	D	213 368-8660	18787
Seiu Local 2015 (PA)	8631	D	213 985-0384	18789
Seiu Local 721	8631	D	213 368-8660	18792
Southwest Crpnters Trning Fund	8631	D	213 386-8590	18796
United Food and Commercial (PA)	8631	D	213 487-7070	18804
United Frfghters Los Angles Cy	8631	D	213 489-1300	18805
United Teachers-Los Angeles	8631	D	213 487-5560	18806
Writers Guild America West Inc	8631	C	323 951-4000	18807
California Club	8641	C	213 622-1391	18828
Catholic Education Founda	8641	D	213 637-7475	18830
Greater Los Angles Area Cncil (PA)	8641	D	213 413-4400	18868
Jewish Cmnty Fndtion Los Angle (PA)	8641	C	323 761-8700	18872
Jonathan Club (PA)	8641	D	213 624-0881	18873
La County Sheriff PDC No	8641	C	661 294-6312	18874
Midnight Mission (PA)	8641	D	213 624-9258	18881
Pazlo Education Foundation	8641	D	323 817-6550	18893
Public Hlth Fndation Entps Inc	8641	C	323 263-0262	18897
Young MNS Chrstn Assn Mtro Los (PA)	8641	D	213 380-6448	18960
Young MNS Chrstn Assn Mtro Los	8641	D	310 216-9036	18961
Young MNS Chrstn Assn Mtro Los	8641	D	323 467-4161	18962
Young Wns Chrstn Assn Grter Lo	8641	C	323 295-4280	19007
Young Wns Chrstn Assn Grter Lo	8641	C	323 295-4288	19008
Crenshaw Chrstn Ctr Ch Los Ang (PA)	8661	B	323 758-3777	19017
Hospitller Order of St John Go	8661	B	323 731-0641	19020
Interntnal Ch of Frsqare Gospl (PA)	8661	D	714 701-1818	19022
Sinai Temple (PA)	8661	B	310 474-1518	19027
Wilshire Boulevard Temple	8661	D	323 261-6135	19030
Best Friends Animal Society	8699	C	818 643-3989	19070
Los Angeles Mem Coliseum Comm	8699	B	213 747-7111	19092
Play Versus Inc	8699	D	949 636-4193	19098
Society of St Vncent De Paul C (PA)	8699	D	323 226-9645	19106
Aecom Global II LLC (HQ)	8711	D	213 593-8100	19129
Arup North America Limited	8711	B	310 578-4182	19144
Flint Energy Services Inc	8711	C	213 593-8000	19225
Fti Consulting Inc	8711	D	213 689-1200	19232
John A Martin & Associates Inc	8711	D	213 483-6490	19287
Linquest Corporation (PA)	8711	C	323 924-1600	19306
Martin Associates Group Inc (PA)	8711	D	213 483-6490	19316
Sia Engineering (usa) Inc	8711	C	310 957-2928	19388
5 Design Inc	8712	D	323 308-3558	19448
Aecom Services Inc (HQ)	8712	D	213 593-8000	19449
Altoon Partners LLP (PA)	8712	D	213 225-1900	19450
Co Architects (PA)	8712	C	323 525-0500	19461
Dlr Group Inc (HQ)	8712	C	213 800-9400	19466
Gehry Partners LLP	8712	C	310 482-3000	19468
Gruen Associates Inc	8712	D	323 937-4270	19473
Hellmuth Obata & Kassabaum Inc	8712	D	310 838-9555	19476
Hok Group Inc	8712	D	310 838-9555	19478
Johnson Fain Inc	8712	D	323 224-6000	19482
M Arthur Gensler Jr Assoc Inc	8712	D	213 927-3600	19490
Marmol Rdzner An Archtctral Co	8712	D	310 826-6222	19492
Martin AC Partners Inc	8712	D	213 683-1900	19493
Steinberg Hart (PA)	8712	D	408 295-5446	19511
Stv Architects Inc	8712	D	213 482-9444	19512
The Jerde Partnership Inc	8712	D	310 399-1987	19514
Will Perkins Inc	8712	D	213 270-8400	19518
Zimmer Gnsul Frsca Archtcts LL	8712	C	213 617-1901	19522
Psomas (PA)	8713	D	213 223-1400	19526
Armanino LLP	8721	B	310 478-4148	19531
Baker Tilly Us LLP	8721	A	310 826-4474	19535
Cliftonlarsonallen LLP	8721	D	310 273-2501	19552
County of Los Angeles	8721	A	323 267-2136	19556

LOS ANGELES CA

	SIC	EMP	PHONE	ENTRY#
Deloitte & Touche LLP	8721	A	213 688-0800	19562
Deloitte Tax LLP	8721	C	404 885-6754	19565
Ernst & Young LLP	8721	A	213 977-3200	19574
Film Payroll Services Inc (PA)	8721	D	310 440-9600	19577
Green Hasson & Janks LLP	8721	C	310 873-1600	19581
Gursey Schneider & Co LLC (PA)	8721	C	310 552-0960	19583
Holthouse Carlin Van Trigt LLP (PA)	8721	C	310 566-1900	19585
Macias Gini & OConnell LLP	8721	C	213 408-8700	19606
Macias Gini & OConnell LLP	8721	C	323 653-8300	19607
Macias Gini & OConnell LLP	8721	C	916 928-4600	19609
Rbz LLP	8721	C	310 478-4148	19626
Singerlewak LLP (PA)	8721	C	310 477-3924	19632
Aerospace Corporation	8731	A	310 336-7270	19646
Environmental Science Assoc	8731	C	213 599-4300	19688
Myst Therapeutics Inc	8731	D	415 516-8450	19740
Cornerstone Research Inc	8732	D	213 553-2500	19806
Material Holdings LLC (PA)	8732	C	310 553-0550	19831
National Research Group Inc	8732	B	323 406-6200	19835
Prosearch Strategies LLC	8732	C	877 447-7291	19844
Streamelements Inc	8732	C	323 928-7848	19850
Toaster LLC	8732	D	917 655-6440	19852
Zefr Inc	8732	B	310 392-3555	19858
Brentwood Bmdical RES Inst Inc	8733	C	310 312-1554	19867
Childrens Inst Los Angeles (PA)	8733	C	213 385-5100	19877
House Research Institute	8733	C	213 353-7012	19885
County of Los Angeles	8734	C	323 267-6167	19961
Ellison Institute LLC (PA)	8734	C	310 228-6400	19969
National Genetics Institute	8734	C	310 996-6610	19991
AEG Management Lacc LLC	8741	C	213 741-1151	20013
Ajit Healthcare Inc	8741	D	213 484-0510	20014
Bon Appetit Management Co	8741	C	310 440-6052	20041
Bon Appetit Management Co	8741	C	310 440-6209	20045
Cal State La Univ Aux Svcs Inc	8741	A	323 343-2531	20050
Chan Family Partnership LP	8741	C	626 322-7132	20055
Country Villa Service Corp	8741	C	323 666-1544	20065
Country Villa Service Corp	8741	C	323 734-1101	20068
Country Villa Service Corp	8741	C	323 734-9122	20069
Digital Media Management Inc	8741	D	323 378-6505	20081
Far East National Bank	8741	B	213 687-1300	20085
Firstsrvice Rsidential Cal LLC	8741	C	213 213-0886	20087
Front Line MGT Group Inc	8741	C	310 209-3100	20094
Hotchkis Wiley Capitl MGT LLC (PA)	8741	C	213 430-1000	20110
Jpl Management LLC	8741	C	310 844-3662	20128
Keiro Services	8741	B	213 873-5700	20132
La 1000 Santa Fe LLC	8741	C	213 205-1000	20134
Los Angeles Rams LLC	8741	C	310 277-4700	20144
Morgner Technology Management	8741	D	323 900-0030	20155
Network Management Group Inc (PA)	8741	C	323 263-2632	20160
Onni Properties LLC	8741	C	213 568-0278	20165
PFC Management LLC	8741	C	310 401-1926	20176
Relocity Inc	8741	C	323 207-9160	20193
Rockport ADM Svcs LLC (PA)	8741	C	323 330-6500	20197
Snf Management	8741	C	310 385-1090	20208
SunAmerica Investments Inc (DH)	8741	D	310 772-6000	20220
Tripalink Corp	8741	C	323 717-9139	20234
Vendo LLC	8741	D	310 300-2810	20242
Zero Gravity Management	8741	D	310 656-9440	20257
Alvarez Mrsal Bus Cnslting LLC	8742	C	310 975-2600	20270
Bain & Company Inc	8742	D	310 229-3000	20287
Blackstone Consulting Inc (PA)	8742	C	310 826-4389	20297
Captain Marketing Inc	8742	D	310 402-9709	20308
Cashmere Agency Inc	8742	C	323 928-5080	20309
Catalyst Speech LLC	8742	B	213 346-9945	20311
Diagnostic Health Corporation	8742	C	310 665-7180	20345
Egon Zehnder International	8742	B	213 337-1500	20353
First Capitol Consulting Inc	8742	D	213 382-1115	20379
Gsl Holdings Inc	8742	D	213 625-2588	20397
Hawke Media Ventures LLC (PA)	8742	C	310 451-7295	20402
Heidelberg Investment Group In	8742	D	213 884-7747	20404
HR&a Advisors Inc	8742	D	310 581-0900	20406
Korn Ferry (us) (HQ)	8742	C	310 552-1834	20426
Mv Medical Management	8742	C	323 257-7637	20479
Northgate Gonzalez Inc	8742	B	323 262-0595	20489
NVE Inc	8742	D	323 512-8400	20490
Octagon Inc	8742	C	310 967-2473	20491
Para Sempre Inc	8742	D	310 444-0555	20501
Phenomenon Mktg & Entrmt LLC (PA)	8742	D	323 648-4000	20505
Powersource Talent LLC	8742	C	424 835-0878	20512
PWC STRategy& (us) LLC	8742	C	213 356-6000	20518
Rocky Point Investments LLC (HQ)	8742	D	310 482-6500	20532
Saban Brands LLC (HQ)	8742	C	310 557-5230	20537
Seek Capital LLC	8742	D	855 978-6106	20540
Shein Technology LLC (PA)	8742	B	213 628-4008	20543

	SIC	EMP	PHONE	ENTRY#
Sitrick Brincko Group LLC	8742	D	310 788-2850	20549
Smith-Emery International Inc (PA)	8742	C	213 741-8500	20556
Sodexo Management Inc	8742	D	310 646-3738	20558
Spotify USA Inc	8742	A	213 505-3040	20561
Thomas St John Inc	8742	D	424 273-1172	20583
Titanum Health Care	8742	D	213 765-8123	20584
Verifi Inc	8742	C	323 655-5789	20603
Wasserman Media Group LLC (PA)	8742	C	310 407-0200	20608
Wellmade Inc	8742	D	213 221-1123	20610
Swiss Port Corp	8744	B	310 417-0258	20664
Aecom Technical Services Inc (HQ)	8748	D	213 593-8100	20677
Aecom Usa Inc	8748	D	213 330-7200	20678
Aecom Usa Inc	8748	D	213 593-8000	20680
Ankura Consulting Group LLC	8748	C	213 223-2109	20690
Broadband Telecom Inc	8748	C	818 450-5714	20710
Cal Southern Assn Governments (PA)	8748	C	213 236-1800	20715
Cdsnet LLC	8748	B	310 981-9500	20723
CRA International Inc	8748	D	310 393-5530	20735
Deloitte Consulting LLP	8748	C	212 489-1600	20737
Fame Assistance Corporation	8748	D	323 373-7720	20748
Pcs Link Inc	8748	B	949 655-5000	20826
Systems Experience Inc	8748	D	310 215-9000	20860
Yucaipa Companies LLC (PA)	8748	C	310 789-7200	20881
Essense	8999	A	323 202-4650	20887
Union Editorial LLC	8999	D	310 481-2200	20904
Los Angles Cnty Mseum Ntral Hs (PA)	9111	C	213 763-3466	20918
County of Los Angeles	9431	C	213 738-4601	20938

LOS BANOS, CA - Merced County

	SIC	EMP	PHONE	ENTRY#
Teixeira and Sons LLC	0131	C	209 827-9800	6
Wolfsen Incorporated	0131	C	209 827-7700	8
Ranchwood Contractors Inc	1542	D	209 826-6200	1002
Pacific Gas and Electric Co	4911	D	209 826-5131	4644
Cemex Corp	5032	C	800 992-3639	5198
Triangle Rock Product Inc	5032	B	209 826-5066	5210
Karthikeya Devireddy M D Inc	8011	D	209 826-2222	14858
Memorial Hospital Los Banos	8062	C	209 826-0591	16254

LOS GATOS, CA - Santa Clara County

	SIC	EMP	PHONE	ENTRY#
Adobe Animal Hospital	0742	D	408 357-8000	323
Netflix Inc (PA)	4841	C	408 540-3700	4515
Santa Clara Vly Wtr Dst Pub Fc	4941	D	408 395-8121	4831
Zyante Inc	5192	D	510 541-4434	6846
Joie De Vivre Hospitality LLC	7011	D	408 335-1700	9921
Trevi Partners A Calif LP	7011	D	408 395-7070	10324
Arvato USA LLC	7334	D	408 402-3469	10784
Netpolarity Inc	7361	C	408 971-1100	11182
Intellicus Tech Pvt Ltd	7371	D	408 213-3314	11673
Kika Tech Inc	7371	C	650 229-3673	11692
Usertesting Technologies Inc	7371	D	888 877-1882	12006
Xactly Corporation (HQ)	7371	D	408 977-3132	12051
Elsa Corp	7373	C	408 431-6735	12452
Ciphertrace Inc	7379	D	650 996-2142	12756
Infogain Corporation (PA)	7379	C	408 355-6000	12808
Lark Avenue Car Wash	7542	D	408 356-2525	13696
Addisn-Pnzak Jwish Cmnty Ctr S	7991	C	408 358-3636	14170
Club At Los Gatos Inc	7991	D	408 354-4808	14186
Los Gatos Swim and Racquet CLB	7991	D	408 356-2136	14217
Courtside Tennis Club	7997	D	408 395-7111	14365
County of Santa Clara	7999	C	408 355-2200	14511
Yoga Source Partners LLC	7999	D	408 402-9642	14588
Peter Castillo Md PA	8011	A	408 236-6400	14993
Humangood Norcal	8059	C	408 357-1100	15862
Good Samaritan Hospital LP	8062	C	408 358-8414	16111
Good Samaritan Hospital LP	8062	C	408 356-4111	16112
Tenet Healthsystem Medical Inc	8062	B	408 378-6131	16572
Womens Cancer Center	8069	D	408 358-6500	16701
Associated Pathology Med Group	8071	D	408 399-5010	16704
Help & Care LLC	8082	D	408 384-4412	16867
Thekey LLC	8082	D	408 356-0127	16947
US Carenet Services LLC	8082	C	408 378-6131	16960
Los Gatos Saratoga Dept of Com	8299	C	408 354-8700	17811

LOS MOLINOS, CA - Tehama County

	SIC	EMP	PHONE	ENTRY#
Crain Walnut Shelling LP	1541	B	530 529-1585	814

LOS OLIVOS, CA - Santa Barbara County

	SIC	EMP	PHONE	ENTRY#
Firestone Vineyard LP	2084	D	805 688-3940	2386

LOS OSOS, CA - San Luis Obispo County

	SIC	EMP	PHONE	ENTRY#
Rantec Power Systems Inc (HQ)	5065	D	805 596-6000	5693

GEOGRAPHIC SECTION

MARIPOSA CA

	SIC	EMP	PHONE	ENTRY#

LOST HILLS, CA - Kern County

Wonderful Orchards LLC	0173	B	661 797-6400	96
Roll Properties Intl Inc	6799	C	661 797-6500	9556

LUCERNE VALLEY, CA - San Bernardino County

Omya California Inc	2819	D	760 248-7306	2574
Omya Inc	2819	D	760 248-5200	2575
Casa Clina Hosp Ctrs For Hlthc	8322	C	760 248-6245	17862

LYNWOOD, CA - Los Angeles County

Midas Express Los Angeles Inc	4225	C	310 609-0366	3731
Earle M Jorgensen Company (HQ)	5051	C	323 567-1122	5489
Smart & Final Stores LLC	5141	D	310 631-8639	6353
Metropolitan Realty MGT Inc	6531	D	310 537-5441	9099
Altamed Health Services Corp	8011	C	310 632-0415	14602
Southern CA Hlth & Rhbltn Prg	8011	C	310 631-8004	15071
Southern Cal Prmnnte Med Group	8011	C	310 604-5700	15077
Country Villa Service Corp	8051	C	310 537-2500	15395
Marlinda Management Inc (PA)	8059	C	310 631-6122	15876
St Francis Medical Center (DH)	8062	B	310 900-8900	16456
South Cntl Hlth Rhblttion Prgr	8093	D	310 667-4070	17128
Lynwood Unified School Dst	8211	D	310 631-7308	17725
Jwch Institute Inc	8322	C	310 223-1035	18031
Drew Child Dev Corp Inc	8351	D	310 638-8108	18309

LYTLE CREEK, CA - San Bernardino County

Burlingame Industries Inc	7033	C	909 887-7038	10415

MADERA, CA - Madera County

Richard Iest Dairy Inc	0139	D	559 673-2635	18
Lion Raisins Inc	0191	C	559 662-8686	190
Iest Family Farms	0241	C	559 674-9417	218
Span Construction & Engrg Inc (PA)	1542	D	559 661-1111	1032
Vezina Industries Inc	1742	C	559 479-8287	1971
Nutra-Blend LLC	2048	B	559 661-6161	2365
Georgia-Pacific LLC	2653	D	559 674-4685	2513
Pk1 Inc (HQ)	2653	D	559 662-1910	2522
B-K Lighting Inc	3645	C	559 438-5800	2871
Catania Worldwide	5148	B	559 664-8400	6523
Canandaigua Wine Company Inc	5182	D	559 673-7071	6790
Constlltion Brnds US Oprtons I	5182	A	559 485-0141	6793
Home Depot USA Inc	5211	C	559 675-0127	7000
Lowes Home Centers LLC	5211	D	559 416-4000	7106
Herman Produce Sales LLC	5431	D	559 661-8253	7157
Valley Auto Sales & Lsg LLC	5511	D	559 674-9000	7322
Camarena Health (PA)	8011	C	559 664-4000	14649
Valley Chld Hlthcare Fundation	8011	A	559 353-3000	15176
Madera Convalescent Hosp Inc (PA)	8051	C	559 673-9228	15556
Madera Cmnty Hosp Foundation	8062	C	559 673-5101	16241
Madera Community Hospital	8062	A	559 675-5530	16242
Madera Community Hospital (PA)	8062	A	559 675-5555	16243
Valley Childrens Hospital	8062	A	559 353-6425	16609
Valley Childrens Hospital (PA)	8062	A	559 353-3000	16610
Community Action Prtnr Mdera C (PA)	8351	C	559 673-9173	18295
Community Action Prtnr Mdera C	8399	C	559 661-1000	18577

MALIBU, CA - Los Angeles County

Westmed Ambulance Inc	4119	C	310 456-3830	3305
Cco Holdings LLC	4841	C	310 589-3008	4480
Malibu Conference Center Inc	6512	B	818 889-6440	8734
Wilshire Boulevard Temple	7032	D	310 457-7861	10413
Credibility Corp	7389	C	310 456-8271	13250
Passages Malibu	8093	D	888 777-8525	17106
Clarkson Law Firm PC	8111	D	213 788-4050	17405
Grasshopper House Partners LLC	8322	C	310 589-2880	17994
Hrl Laboratories LLC	8732	A	310 317-5000	19819

MAMMOTH LAKES, CA - Mono County

Mammoth Mountain Ski Area LLC (DH)	7011	B	760 934-2571	9998
Southern Mono Healthcare Dst	8062	B	760 934-3311	16449

MANHATTAN BEACH, CA - Los Angeles County

Ebc Inc (PA)	1521	D	310 753-6407	674
Fox US Productions 27 Inc	4833	C	310 727-2550	4435
I Brands LLC	5083	D	424 336-5216	5810
Trlggc Services LLC	5136	B	323 266-3072	6190
Wells Fargo Investments LLC	6021	D	310 546-4235	7645
Kinecta Federal Credit Union (PA)	6061	C	310 643-5400	7778
Platinum Capital Group (PA)	6163	D	310 406-3505	8051
Coverance Insur Solutions Inc	6411	C	310 856-9925	8533
Strand Hill Properties	6512	C	310 545-0707	8765
Palm Realty Boutique Inc	6531	D	310 545-2490	9124
B Capital Group US LLC	6799	D	310 698-1270	9489

Oka & Oka Hawaii LLC	7011	C	808 329-1393	10061
Shade Hotel Employs 7	7011	D	310 546-4995	10224
Sunstone Hotel Properties Inc	7011	D	310 546-7627	10288
Distillery Tech Inc	7371	C	310 776-6234	11547
Stemconnector LLC	7379	D	424 543-4074	12883
1334 Partners LP	7997	D	310 546-5656	14318
Kaiser Foundation Hospitals	8062	C	310 937-4311	16159
Torrance Memorial Medical Ctr	8062	B	310 939-7847	16577
Pancrtic Cncer Action Ntwrk In (PA)	8099	C	310 725-0025	17292
Automobile Club Southern Cal	8699	C	310 376-0521	19050
M & E Technical Services L L C	8744	C	256 964-6486	20658
Etonien LLC (PA)	8748	D	310 321-5800	20747
Jag Professional Services Inc	8748	C	310 945-5648	20785

MANTECA, CA - San Joaquin County

Van Groningen & Sons Inc (PA)	0191	B	209 982-5248	205
Cool Roofing Systems Inc	1761	D	209 825-0818	2054
Cal-West Concrete Cutting Inc	1771	C	209 823-2236	2103
American Modular Systems Inc	2452	C	209 825-1921	2485
Morris Newspaper Corp Cal (HQ)	2711	D	209 249-3500	2540
CRST Expedited Inc	4213	C	209 249-4403	3459
Lee Jennings Target Ex Inc	4731	D	209 823-0071	4049
Parakeet Logistics Inc	4731	C	209 353-1818	4072
Run Roadlines Inc	4731	C	209 681-3640	4087
Frontier California Inc	4813	C	209 239-4128	4282
South San Jquin Irrigation Dst	4941	C	209 249-4600	4838
Forward Inc	4953	C	209 982-4298	4896
Ford Motor Company	5013	C	209 824-6600	5040
B R Funsten & Co	5023	C	209 825-5375	5110
Dreyers Grand Ice Cream Inc	5143	B	209 823-4343	6435
Drd Hospitality Inc	7011	D	916 952-6552	9765
American Crane Rental Inc	7353	C	209 838-8815	10992
J M Equipment Company Inc (PA)	7359	C	209 522-3271	11038
Clearpath Workforce MGT Inc	7363	C	209 239-8700	11281
Kamps Company	7363	C	209 823-8924	11297
Unity Courier Service Inc	7389	C	209 239-5400	13526
Kaiser Foundation Hospitals	8011	A	209 825-3700	14841
Karma Inc	8051	D	209 239-1222	15527
Doctors Hospital Manteca Inc	8062	B	209 823-3111	16057
United Crbral Plsy Assn San Jq	8399	D	209 239-3066	18631

MANTON, CA - Tehama County

Pacific Gas and Electric Co	4911	D	530 474-3333	4635

MARICOPA, CA - Kern County

Aera Energy Services Company	1381	C	661 665-3200	591
Calmat Co	1422	C	661 858-2673	634

MARINA, CA - Monterey County

Monterey Peninsula Engineering	1611	C	831 384-4081	1140
Monterey Rgional Waste MGT Dst	4953	C	831 384-5313	4912

MARINA DEL REY, CA - Los Angeles County

Tokyopop Inc (PA)	2731	D	323 920-5967	2550
Dr Squatch LLC	2844	C	631 229-7068	2627
Executive Network Entps Inc (PA)	4119	C	310 447-2759	3257
Lemonlight	4899	D	310 801-6487	4542
Bouqs Company	5193	D	888 320-2687	6853
Marina City Club LP A Cali	6513	C	310 822-0611	8842
Laaco Ltd (HQ)	6519	C	213 622-1254	8886
E & S Ring Management Corp	6531	C	310 821-4916	8988
Ylopo LLC	6531	C	818 915-9150	9224
Steelwave LLC	6552	A	310 821-1111	9276
Taxes Decoded Inc	7291	D	626 780-7076	10525
Psg Global Solutions LLC (HQ)	7361	D	310 405-0340	11208
Gebbs Software Intl Inc	7379	D	201 227-0088	12795
Ptw America Inc	7389	D	424 289-0347	13438
Modern Parking Inc	7521	C	310 821-1081	13612
EZ Lube Inc	7549	D	310 821-2517	13713
Deluxe Nms Inc	7822	C	310 760-8500	13963
Team Bruin LLC	7997	C	310 206-6784	14468
Diagnstic Intrvntnal Srgcal CT	8011	D	310 574-0400	14730
Cfhs Holdings Inc	8062	A	310 823-8911	15988
Cfhs Holdings Inc	8062	A	310 448-7800	15989
Bail Project	8399	D	323 366-0799	18565
USA Travel Services LLC	8699	A	207 899-8803	19117
Usc Information Sciences Inst	8733	C	310 448-9438	19933
Linea Solutions Inc	8742	D	310 443-4191	20437
Socialcom Inc	8742	D	310 289-4477	20557

MARIPOSA, CA - Mariposa County

John C Fremont Healthcare Dst	8062	B	209 966-3631	16141

Employee Codes: A=Over 500 employees, B=251-500
C=101-250, D=51-100, E=20-50, F=10-19, G=1-9

MARSHALL CA

GEOGRAPHIC SECTION

	SIC	EMP	PHONE	ENTRY#

MARSHALL, CA - Marin County
	SIC	EMP	PHONE	ENTRY#
Nicks Cove Inc	7011	D	415 663-1033	10046

MARTINEZ, CA - Contra Costa County
	SIC	EMP	PHONE	ENTRY#
Brightview Landscape Svcs Inc	0781	C	925 957-8831	405
Cagwin & Dorward LLC	0782	D	415 892-7710	478
R M Harris Company Inc	1622	D	925 335-3000	1188
On-Time AC & Htg LLC	1711	D	925 566-2422	1516
Molinas Pntg Wallcovering Inc	1721	D	925 228-7487	1629
Contra Costa Electric Inc (DH)	1731	B	925 229-4250	1707
Schetter Electric Inc	1731	C	925 228-2424	1833
Baja Construction Co Inc (PA)	1791	D	925 229-0732	2179
Waters Moving & Storage Inc	4212	D	925 372-0914	3436
Contra Costa County	4812	B	925 313-1323	4209
Central Cntra Csta Sani Dst Em	4952	B	925 228-9500	4846
Central Contra Costa Sanitary Distr	4952	C	925 228-9500	4847
Browning-Ferris Inds Cal Inc	4953	D	925 313-8901	4868
Enginrng/Rmdtion Rsrces Group (PA)	4959	C	925 839-2200	4979
Sentry Life Insurance Company	6411	C	925 370-7339	8658
Kaiser Foundation Hospitals	6733	A	925 372-1000	9431
Plant Maintenance Inc	7363	D	925 228-3285	11317
County of Contra Costa	7538	D	510 313-7077	13661
Careonsite Inc	8011	B	562 437-0381	14658
Contra Csta Rgonal Med Ctr Aux	8011	C	925 370-5000	14706
Permanente Medical Group Inc	8011	B	925 372-1000	14967
Veterans Health Administration	8011	C	925 372-2000	15192
Legacy and Nursing Rehab	8051	D	925 228-8383	15535
County of Contra Costa	8062	C	925 370-5000	16022
YWCA Contra Costa/Sacramento (PA)	8322	D	925 372-4213	18200
County of Contra Costa	9221	D	925 655-0000	20929

MARYSVILLE, CA - Yuba County
	SIC	EMP	PHONE	ENTRY#
County of Yuba	0742	D	530 741-6478	333
Teichert Inc	1442	D	530 749-1230	642
Teichert Inc	1442	C	530 743-6111	643
Recology Yuba-Sutter	4953	D	530 743-6933	4929
Gino Morena Enterprises LLC	7241	B	530 788-0053	10511
Peach Tree Healthcare	8011	D	530 749-3242	14951
Melon Holdings LLC	8051	D	530 742-7311	15583
Freemont Rideout Health Group	8062	A	530 751-4270	16092
Fremont Hospital	8062	C	530 751-4000	16094
Rideout Memorial Hospital (HQ)	8062	A	530 749-4416	16362
County of Yuba	8322	D	530 741-6275	17943
County of Yuba	8322	C	530 749-7550	17944
Yuba Community College Dst	8322	D	530 788-0973	18198
County of Yuba	8361	D	530 741-6371	18405

MATHER, CA - Sacramento County
	SIC	EMP	PHONE	ENTRY#
Reynen & Bardis Cnstr LLC (PA)	1521	C	916 366-3665	711
Construction Innovations LLC	3699	C	855 725-9555	2955
Sutter Health	8051	D	916 454-8200	15700
Bloodsource Inc (PA)	8099	B	916 456-1500	17191

MAYWOOD, CA - Los Angeles County
	SIC	EMP	PHONE	ENTRY#
Tapia Enterprises Inc (PA)	5141	D	323 560-7415	6406
R G Canning Enterprises Inc	7389	C	323 560-7469	13442
Young MNS Chrstn Assn Mtro Los	8641	D	323 588-2256	18959

MC FARLAND, CA - Kern County
	SIC	EMP	PHONE	ENTRY#
Jakov Dulcich and Sons LLC	0172	C	661 792-6360	77
A G Hacienda Incorporated	4212	B	661 792-2418	3361

MC KITTRICK, CA - Kern County
	SIC	EMP	PHONE	ENTRY#
Wonderful Orchards LLC	0173	D	661 797-2509	97
Aera Energy LLC	1311	D	661 334-3100	580
Aera Energy Services Company	1381	C	661 665-4400	590

MCCLELLAN, CA - Sacramento County
	SIC	EMP	PHONE	ENTRY#
Villara Corporation (PA)	1711	B	916 646-2700	1591
Gmj Air Shuttle LLC	4111	D	916 884-2001	3140
Califrnia Shock Truma A Rescue (PA)	4119	B	916 921-4000	3244
Ozark Trucking Inc (PA)	4213	C	916 561-5400	3523
United States Cold Storage Inc	4222	D	916 392-9160	3665
Wm Healthcare Solutions Inc	4953	D	713 328-7350	4971
Lionsgate Ht & Conference Ctr	7011	D	916 643-6222	9979
Sbm Management Services LP	7349	B	866 855-2211	10959
Sbm Site Services LLC (PA)	7349	D	916 922-7600	10960
Faneuil Inc	7361	D	757 722-4095	11137
Enterprise Rnt--car Scrmnto LL	7514	C	916 648-1725	13584
Siemens Mobility Inc	7538	D	916 621-2700	13676
Cablecom LLC	7629	D	916 891-2400	13736
Fortuna Bus MGT Consulting Inc	8742	A	916 458-0991	20384
McClellan Business Park LLC	8742	D	916 965-7100	20457

MCKINLEYVILLE, CA - Humboldt County
	SIC	EMP	PHONE	ENTRY#
Kernen Construction	1541	D	707 826-8686	828

MECCA, CA - Riverside County
	SIC	EMP	PHONE	ENTRY#
Richard Bagdasarian Inc	0172	D	760 396-2168	83

MENDOCINO, CA - Mendocino County
	SIC	EMP	PHONE	ENTRY#
Mendocino Hotel & Resort Corp	7011	D	707 937-0511	10012

MENDOTA, CA - Fresno County
	SIC	EMP	PHONE	ENTRY#
Simonian Brothers Inc	0172	D	559 655-4722	87
Pappas & Co Inc	0191	C	559 233-1203	193
S & S Ranch Inc	0721	D	559 655-3491	243
S Stamoules Inc	0723	A	559 655-9777	301
Pomwonderful LLC	5149	D	310 966-5800	6659
Continental Exch Solutions Inc	6099	D	559 655-7583	7848

MENIFEE, CA - Riverside County
	SIC	EMP	PHONE	ENTRY#
Grove Lumber & Bldg Sups Inc (PA)	5031	C	909 947-0277	5160
Lowes Home Centers LLC	5211	C	951 723-1930	7038
City of Menifee	8741	D	951 672-6777	20058

MENLO PARK, CA - San Mateo County
	SIC	EMP	PHONE	ENTRY#
Gachina Landscape MGT Inc	0781	B	650 853-0400	433
Novo Construction Inc (PA)	1542	D	650 701-1500	979
Rudolph and Sletten Inc (HQ)	1542	D	650 216-3600	1012
Critchfield Mechanical Inc	1711	B	650 321-7801	1413
Lovazzano Mechanical Inc	1711	D	650 367-6216	1489
Grail LLC (HQ)	2834	D	833 694-2553	2588
Maxar Space LLC	4225	A	650 852-4000	3729
Uber	4724	D	866 440-6700	3956
Ah Capital Management LLC	6211	A	650 798-5800	8064
Robinhood Markets Inc (PA)	6211	A	844 428-5411	8163
US Venture Partners	6211	D	650 854-9080	8171
Permira Advisers LLC	6282	A	650 681-4701	8215
Mc Graw Commercial Insur Svc (PA)	6411	A	650 780-4800	8608
Tegtmeier Associates Inc	6512	C	650 847-1639	8768
Hines Interests Ltd Partnr	6531	C	650 518-6139	9039
Jasper Ridge Partners	6726	C	650 494-4800	9401
Silver Lake Partners Vii LP	6726	C	650 233-8120	9409
Accel-KKR Company LLC (PA)	6799	C	650 289-2460	9484
Ah Parallel Fund V LP	6799	B	650 798-3900	9485
Broadreach Capitl Partners LLC (PA)	6799	C	650 331-2500	9493
Century Pk Capitl Partners LLC	6799	C	650 324-1956	9499
Dcm Ventures LLC	6799	C	650 233-1400	9506
Makena Capital Management LLC	6799	C	650 926-0510	9529
Morgenthler MGT Prtners VI LLC	6799	A	650 388-7600	9535
Oak Hill Capital MGT LLC	6799	A	650 234-0500	9546
Sequoia Capital Operations LLC (PA)	6799	D	650 854-3927	9560
Rosewood Hotels & Resorts LLC	7011	C	650 561-1580	10174
Rosewood Hotels & Resorts LLC (PA)	7011	C	650 561-1500	10175
Stanford Park Hotel	7011	C	650 322-1234	10268
Robert Half Inc (PA)	7363	D	650 234-6000	11324
Betterworks Systems Inc	7371	D	650 656-9013	11455
Boomr LLC	7371	A	877 687-6228	11470
Cataphora Inc (PA)	7371	D	650 622-9840	11487
Open Text Inc (HQ)	7371	C	650 645-3000	11796
Quicken Inc	7371	C	650 564-3399	11858
Tonomi Inc	7371	B	650 523-5000	11981
Trantor Inc	7371	A	650 777-5480	11986
Aha Labs Inc	7372	C	650 515-1425	12082
Genesys Cloud Services Inc (HQ)	7372	B	650 466-1100	12204
Gladiator Corporation	7372	C	650 233-2900	12206
Redseal Inc	7372	C	408 641-2200	12332
Vitesse LLC	7374	A	650 543-4800	12641
Instagram LLC	7375	C	650 543-4800	12667
Meta Platforms Inc (PA)	7375	A	650 543-4800	12677
Riekes Ctr For Humn Enhncement	7991	D	650 364-2509	14227
Boys Girls Clubs of Peninsula	7997	D	650 322-6255	14348
Menlo Med Clinic A Med Corp	8011	C	650 498-6500	14897
Stanford Health Care	8062	D	650 498-7489	16496
Billiontoone Inc	8071	D	650 460-2551	16706
Kind Homecare Inc	8082	D	888 885-5463	16884
Oak Hill Capital Partners LP	8082	A	650 234-0500	16902
Frazier Management LLC	8099	D	650 325-5156	17240
Davis Polk & Wardwell LLP	8111	D	650 752-2000	17431
Kramer Lvin Nftlis Frankel LLP	8111	D	650 752-1700	17530
Orrick Hrrington Sutcliffe LLP	8111	C	650 614-7400	17597
Ropers Majeski A Prof Corp (PA)	8111	D	650 364-8200	17627
Hewlett Wlliam Flora Fndation	8699	D	650 234-4500	19088
Exponent Inc (PA)	8711	C	650 326-9400	19222
Burr Pilger Mayer Inc	8721	C	650 855-6800	19544
Deepcell Inc	8731	D	617 447-1067	19677

GEOGRAPHIC SECTION

	SIC	EMP	PHONE	ENTRY#
Omniome Inc.	8731	D	510 935-3021	19751
Centrak Inc.	8732	C	215 860-2928	19803
Ionpath Inc.	8733	D	650 336-3058	19888
SRI International (PA)	8733	A	650 859-2000	19915
Etl Testing Laboratories	8734	C	650 463-2900	19970
Intertek Testing Svcs NA Inc	8734	C	650 463-2900	19983
Andressen Hrwitz Lsv Fund II L	8742	A	650 798-5800	20276
Lightspeed Management Co LLC	8742	D	650 234-8300	20436
Open Up Resources	8742	D	650 450-3445	20496
Protiviti Inc (HQ)	8742	A	650 234-6000	20515
Strategic Bus Insights Inc (PA)	8742	D	650 859-4600	20569
Ogilvy Pub Rlations World Wide	8743	C	650 324-7015	20639
Cornerstone Research Inc (PA)	8748	D	650 853-1660	20734
Insignia Environmental	8748	D	650 321-6787	20781

MENTONE, CA - San Bernardino County

International Paving Svcs Inc	1611	D	909 794-2101	1121

MERCED, CA - Merced County

	SIC	EMP	PHONE	ENTRY#
Modern Air Mechanical	1711	D	209 722-1815	1501
WLMD	1799	C	209 723-9120	2334
Richwood Meat Company Inc	2011	D	209 722-8171	2340
First Transit Inc	4111	D	209 385-1226	3136
National Express LLC	4119	A	209 201-9345	3284
Merced Transportation Company	4151	D	209 384-2575	3347
Central Valley Concrete Inc (PA)	4212	C	209 723-8846	3382
McLane/Pacific Inc	5141	B	209 725-2500	6267
Lowes Home Centers LLC	5211	D	209 385-5000	7076
Holiday Inn Express Merced	7011	D	209 383-0333	9862
Melin Enterprises Inc	7349	D	209 726-9182	10925
N & S Tractor Co (PA)	7699	D	209 383-5888	13785
Golden Valley Health Centers (PA)	8011	C	209 383-1848	14763
Anberry Transitional Care LLC	8051	C	209 357-3420	15327
Avalon Care Cen	8051	C	209 723-1056	15339
Avalon Care Ctr - Mrced Frncsc	8051	D	209 722-6231	15342
CF Merced La Sierra LLC	8051	D	209 723-4224	15371
Mater Misericordiae Hospital (PA)	8062	A	209 564-5000	16250
Merced City School District	8211	D	209 385-6364	17727
Country Villa Service Corp	8322	C	209 723-2911	17901
Diocese Fresno Education Corp	8351	D	209 722-7496	18308

MERIDIAN, CA - Sutter County

Colusa Produce Corporation	5149	D	530 696-0121	6616

MIDDLETOWN, CA - Lake County

Twin Pine Casino & Hotel	5813	D	707 987-0197	7524
Heart Consciousness Church Inc (PA)	7041	C	707 987-2477	10420

MILL VALLEY, CA - Marin County

	SIC	EMP	PHONE	ENTRY#
Van Acker Cnstr Assoc Inc	1521	C	415 383-5589	737
General Lgstics Systems US Inc	4215	C	415 492-1112	3615
Sequoia Residential Funding	6153	D	415 389-7373	7907
Merrill Lynch Prce Fnner Smith	6211	D	415 289-8800	8139
Lasalle Jones Lang	6531	D	415 388-4460	9072
Joie De Vivre Hospitality LLC	7011	D	415 380-0400	9924
Nana Enterprises	7011	D	415 383-0340	10036
Trevi Partners A Calif LP	7011	D	415 332-5700	10323
Haggin Marketing LLC	7311	B	415 289-1110	10622
AOA Technology Partners	7371	D	888 828-6426	11411
Advantis Global Inc (PA)	7379	C	415 612-3338	12723
Orion Group World LLC	7389	D	415 602-5233	13412
Cliff View Terrace Inc	8361	D	415 388-9526	18396
The Redwoods A Cmnty Seniors	8361	C	415 383-2741	18531

MILLBRAE, CA - San Mateo County

Aloft Ht San Francisco Arprt	7011	D	650 443-5500	9602
Arvee Bros Inc	7011	D	650 583-3935	9615
Gladly Software Inc	7371	D	650 387-8485	11621
Teeko LLC	7389	D	415 652-3380	13505
Tatcha LLC	8011	C	650 239-9000	15122
Hillsdale Group LP	8059	C	650 742-9150	15855
Magnolia of Millbrae Inc	8361	D	650 697-7700	18478

MILPITAS, CA - Santa Clara County

Jensen Corporate Holdings Inc (PA)	0782	C	408 446-1118	503
Devcon Construction Inc (PA)	1542	B	408 942-8200	902
Xl Construction Corporation (PA)	1542	B	408 240-6000	1067
Preston Pipelines Inc (PA)	1623	C	408 262-1418	1251
Sasco Electric Inc	1731	B	408 970-8300	1830
Custom Drywall Inc	1742	D	408 263-1616	1922
B T Mancini Co Inc (PA)	1752	D	408 942-7900	2029
H V Welker Co Inc	1752	D	408 263-4400	2032
Blues Roofing Co	1761	D	408 240-0580	2048

	SIC	EMP	PHONE	ENTRY#
Silicon Graphics Intl Corp (HQ)	3577	C	669 900-8000	2837
Altigen Communications Inc	3661	C	408 597-9000	2884
U-Tech Media Usa LLC	3695	C	408 597-1600	2954
Spectra-Physics Inc (DH)	3699	D	877 835-9620	2962
KLA Corporation (PA)	3827	B	408 875-3000	3037
Marketshare Inc (PA)	3993	D	408 262-0677	3100
BFI Waste Systems N Amer Inc	4212	D	408 432-1234	3373
Valley Rlction Stor Nthrn Cal	4214	D	408 938-3672	3601
Jit Transportation Inc	4789	B	408 232-4800	4162
Casela Technologies USA	4899	D	650 892-8480	4533
Ss8 Networks Inc (PA)	4899	C	408 894-8400	4553
Pacific Gas and Electric Co	4911	C	408 945-6215	4656
Lion Trading Company LLC	5023	C	408 946-0888	5122
Creative Labs Inc (DH)	5045	C	408 428-6600	5288
Elo Touch Solutions Inc (PA)	5045	B	408 597-8000	5298
Proterial America Ltd	5051	C	408 467-8900	5511
R&M USA Inc (DH)	5065	C	408 945-6626	5692
Xcerra Corporation	5065	C	408 635-4300	5717
Smart & Final Stores Inc	5141	B	408 941-9642	6318
SJ Distributors LLC (PA)	5146	D	888 988-2328	6482
Bottomley Distributing Co Inc	5181	D	408 945-0660	6753
Home Depot USA Inc	5211	C	408 942-7301	6979
Arena Stuart Rentals Inc	5947	C	408 856-3232	7555
B H R Operations LLC	7011	A	408 321-9500	9627
Djont Operations LLC	7011	D	408 942-0400	9748
KEYPOINT CREDIT SERVICES LLC	7323	B	800 745-7400	10764
Universal Site Services Inc (PA)	7349	D	800 647-9337	10984
Arena Event Services Inc	7359	D	408 856-3232	11020
Ohana Partners Inc (PA)	7359	C	408 856-3232	11047
Crosscircles Inc	7361	D	626 341-8469	11114
Idc Technologies Inc (PA)	7361	C	408 376-0212	11154
Welcometech LLC	7361	D	408 582-7998	11255
3k Technologies LLC	7371	C	408 716-5900	11368
Abbyy USA Software House Inc (HQ)	7371	C	408 457-9777	11374
Advantech Corporation (HQ)	7371	B	408 519-3800	11382
Estuate Inc	7371	D	408 946-0002	11580
Memverge Inc	7371	D	408 605-0841	11742
Rysun Labs Inc	7371	C	855 527-7890	11889
Vm Services Inc (DH)	7371	C	510 744-3720	12030
ZI Technologies Inc (PA)	7371	D	408 240-8989	12067
Composite Software LLC (DH)	7372	D	800 553-6387	12144
Heat Software USA Inc	7372	B	408 601-2800	12220
At Road Inc	7373	A	510 668-1638	12420
Scaleflux Inc	7373	D	408 628-2291	12522
Sonicwall Inc (PA)	7373	A	888 557-6642	12527
Accrete Solutions LLC	7379	B	877 849-5838	12719
R S Software India Limited	7379	D	408 382-1200	12866
Stella Technology Incorporated	7379	D	402 350-1681	12882
Sutherland Digital Svcs Inc	7379	B	510 474-2616	12885
Modera LLC	7389	D	408 946-2161	13378
Wavelabs Technologies Inc	7389	D	408 203-7670	13551
Century Theatres Inc	7833	B	408 942-7441	14013
Golfland Entrmt Ctrs Inc	7999	C	408 263-6855	14530
Kaiser Foundation Hospitals	8011	B	408 945-2900	14825
Permanente Medical Group Inc	8011	B	408 945-2900	14971
Vitas Healthcare Corporation	8052	D	415 874-4400	15802
Spectra Laboratories Inc (DH)	8071	C	800 433-3773	16754
Milpitas Unified School Dst	8211	D	408 635-2686	17730
Fresh Lifelines For Youth Inc	8322	D	408 263-2630	17985
Homefrst Svcs Santa Clara Cnty	8322	C	408 539-2100	18005
Reading Partners	8322	D	408 945-5720	18094
Semi (PA)	8611	D	408 943-6900	18722
Cassy	8641	D	408 493-5289	18829
Humane Society Silicon Valley	8699	D	408 262-2133	19090
Stellartech Research Corp (PA)	8731	C	408 331-3000	19774
Exertus Fncl Prtners Insur AGC	8742	D	408 458-8418	20367
Frontrange Solutions Inc	8742	B	408 601-2800	20389
Cetecom Inc	8748	D	408 586-6200	20725
Pluto7 Consulting Inc	8748	D	408 824-9213	20829

MISSION HILLS, CA - Los Angeles County

Jade Inc	1742	D	818 365-7137	1938
National Insurance Crime Bur	6411	D	818 895-2867	8618
The National Bus Group Inc (PA)	7353	D	818 221-6000	11008
National Cnstr Rentals Inc (HQ)	7359	D	818 221-6000	11045
Providnce Facey Med Foundation (PA)	8011	C	818 365-9531	15001
Providnce Facey Med Foundation	8011	C	818 365-9531	15003
Ararat Home Los Angeles Inc	8059	C	818 837-1800	15812
Providence Health & Svcs - Ore	8062	A	818 365-8051	16347
Providence Holy Cross Medical (PA)	8062	B	818 365-8051	16349
Hemodialysis Inc	8092	D	818 365-6961	16987
Greater Valley Med Group Inc (PA)	8093	D	818 838-4500	17068
Providnce Facey Med Foundation	8099	C	818 837-5677	17300

Employee Codes: A=Over 500 employees, B=251-500
C=101-250, D=51-100, E=20-50, F=10-19, G=1-9

2024 Directory of California
WholeSalers and Service Companies

© Mergent Inc. 1-800-342-5647

MISSION HILLS CA

	SIC	EMP	PHONE	ENTRY#
El Nido Family Centers (PA)	8322	C	818 830-3646	17967

MISSION VIEJO, CA - Orange County

	SIC	EMP	PHONE	ENTRY#
Medix Ambulance Service Inc (PA)	4119	C	949 470-8915	3277
Black Dot Wireless LLC	4812	D	949 502-3800	4185
Paydarfar Industries Inc	5045	C	949 481-3267	5332
Advanced Mp Technology LLC (DH)	5065	C	800 492-3113	5620
Smart & Final Stores Inc	5141	B	949 581-1212	6304
Home Depot USA Inc	5211	D	949 364-1900	7021
South Cnty Lxus At Mssion Vejo	5511	C	949 347-3400	7301
Camden Development Inc	6531	C	949 427-4674	8921
Coldwell Banker Residential (DH)	6531	D	949 837-5700	8940
Coldwell Bnkr Rsdntial Rfrral (DH)	6531	B	949 367-1800	8944
Regency Real Estate Brks Inc	6531	C	949 707-4400	9159
Renewcare of Scottsdale Inc	6799	D	949 487-9500	9555
Ayres Group	7011	D	949 455-2545	9625
Dimar Enterprises Inc	7349	C	949 492-1100	10890
Oracle Corporation	7372	B	626 315-7513	12306
Auxilio Inc	7379	D	949 614-0731	12736
Prestige Auto Collision Inc	7532	D	949 470-6031	13644
Edwards Theatres Inc	7832	C	949 582-4078	13986
Mission Viejo Country Club	7997	C	949 582-1550	14408
Saddleback Vly	7997	D	949 586-1234	14434
United Studios Self Def Inc	7999	C	949 293-1391	14581
Community Orthpd Med Group Prt	8011	C	949 348-4000	14703
Hutchins Healthcare Inc	8011	D	949 487-9500	14778
Mission Internal Med Group Inc	8011	D	949 364-3570	14902
Total Vision LLC	8042	C	949 652-7242	15266
Bridgestone Living LLC	8051	D	949 487-9500	15359
Ensign Whittier West LLC	8051	C	949 487-9500	15462
Jewish HM For The Aging Ornge	8051	C	949 364-9685	15526
Sunrise Senior Living LLC	8051	D	949 582-2010	15692
Teton Healthcare Inc	8051	D	949 487-9500	15702
Victoria Vntura Asssted Lving	8051	A	805 642-1736	15719
Woodway Healthcare Inc	8051	D	254 420-0056	15743
Auxilary of Mssion Hosp Mssion	8062	A	949 364-1400	15954
Mission Hosp Regional Med Ctr (PA)	8062	A	949 364-1400	16272
Brightstar Care Lake Forest	8082	B	949 837-7000	16828
Rock Canyon Healthcare Inc	8082	C	719 404-1000	16921
Southern Cal Prmnnte Med Group	8099	C	949 376-8619	17328
American Justice Solutions Inc	8299	C	949 369-6210	17800
Vocational Visions	8331	C	949 837-7280	18257
Atria Assisted Living Group	8361	C	949 427-8191	18374
Morningstar Senior MGT LLC	8361	C	949 298-3675	18490
Lake Mission Viejo Association	8641	D	949 770-1313	18876
Young MNS Chrstn Assn Ornge CN	8641	D	949 859-9622	18990
Phg Engineering Services LLC	8711	D	714 283-8288	19358
North American Client Svcs Inc (PA)	8741	C	949 240-2423	20162
Disruptive Visions LLC	8748	D	949 502-3800	20739

MODESTO, CA - Stanislaus County

	SIC	EMP	PHONE	ENTRY#
Recology Blssom Vly Orgnics -	0181	D	209 545-4401	150
Blue Diamond Growers	0723	C	209 545-6221	258
Eastside Management Co Inc	0762	C	209 578-9852	373
Process Cooling Intl Inc (PA)	1711	D	209 578-1000	1537
Solecon Industrial Contrs Inc	1711	D	209 572-7390	1569
D C Vient Inc (PA)	1721	D	209 578-1224	1611
Hamilton and Dillon Elc Inc	1731	D	209 529-6292	1743
Modesto Industrial Electrical Co Inc (PA)	1731	D	209 527-2800	1781
Rizo Lopez Foods Inc	2022	B	800 626-5587	2346
E & J Gallo Winery (PA)	2084	A	209 341-3111	2380
United Pallet Services Inc	2448	D	209 538-5844	2484
Crown Painting Inc	2519	D	209 322-3275	2495
LTI Boyd	3549	A	800 554-0200	2785
Hoya Optical Inc (PA)	3851	D	209 579-7739	3080
Storer Transportation Service (PA)	4141	B	209 521-8250	3314
Ed Rocha Livestock Trnsp Inc	4213	D	209 538-1302	3468
Vito Trucking LLC	4213	D	209 342-5104	3563
Sovena Usa Inc	4225	D	209 210-0388	3755
Winco Foods LLC	4225	C	209 556-6040	3783
Grace Logistics Inc	4731	B	209 730-9800	4027
Gunderson LLC	4789	C	209 578-5154	4157
Modesto Irrigation District	4911	D	209 526-7373	4587
Modesto Irrigation District	4911	D	209 526-7563	4588
Modesto Irrigation District (PA)	4911	C	209 526-7337	4589
Pacific Gas and Electric Co	4911	B	209 576-6636	4646
County of Stanislaus	4959	D	209 522-4098	4977
Pacific Coast Supply LLC	5033	D	209 521-2466	5223
OfficeMax North America Inc	5112	C	209 551-9700	6068
LLC Noble Rider (PA)	5136	D	209 566-7800	6179
DOT Foods Inc	5141	D	209 581-9090	6250
Sprouts Farmers Market Inc	5141	C	209 527-7575	6394
Sysco Central California Inc	5141	B	209 527-7700	6399
Foster Dairy Farms (PA)	5143	A	209 576-3400	6437
Yosemite Meat Company Inc	5147	D	209 524-5117	6510
Enviro Tech Chemical Svcs Inc (DH)	5169	C	209 581-9576	6708
Delta Sierra Beverage LLC	5181	B	209 522-9011	6760
Varni Brothers Corporation (PA)	5181	D	209 521-1777	6786
Varni Brothers Corporation	5182	D	209 526-5513	6809
Stanislaus Farm Supply Company Inc	5191	D	209 538-7070	6834
G3 Enterprises Inc (PA)	5199	A	209 341-7515	6909
Home Depot USA Inc	5211	C	209 491-0200	7014
Lowes Home Centers LLC	5211	C	209 545-7676	7031
Dons Mobile Glass Inc (PA)	5231	C	209 548-7000	7114
Save Mart Supermarkets LLC (PA)	5411	C	209 577-1600	7151
Stinson Enterprises Inc	5511	C	209 529-2933	7305
C W Brower Inc (PA)	5541	C	209 523-1828	7384
The Sonora J S West & Co Inc	5712	B	209 577-3221	7426
Stanislaus Cnty Tobacco Fundng	6153	C	209 525-6376	7909
Loandepotcom LLC	6162	A	209 846-6400	7996
Scenic Oaks Funding Inc	6162	C	209 572-2301	8018
Merrill Lynch Prce Fnner Smith	6211	D	209 578-2600	8117
Kaiser Foundation Hospitals	6324	B	209 557-1000	8335
Pegasus Risk Management Inc (PA)	6411	D	209 574-2800	8637
Re/Max Executive	6531	D	209 499-7772	9152
Gringteam Inc	7011	D	209 526-6000	9823
Modesto Hospitality LLC	7011	C	209 526-6000	10021
C & S Draperies Inc	7217	C	209 466-5371	10470
G3 Enterprises Inc	7336	D	209 341-5265	10808
Clark Pest Ctrl Stockton Inc	7342	D	209 524-6384	10833
Interim Healthcare Inc	7363	C	209 577-5936	11295
Plus Group Inc	7363	A	209 342-9022	11319
Ontel Security Services Inc	7381	D	209 521-0200	13011
Sintex Security Services Inc	7381	D	209 543-9044	13047
Primerica Financial Services	7389	D	209 545-5887	13429
Wand Topco Inc	7532	A	209 524-6824	13652
Brenden Theatre Corporation	7832	D	209 491-7770	13979
Del Rio Golf & Country Club	7997	C	209 341-2414	14369
Community Trnstional Resources	8011	D	209 529-2200	14705
Kaiser Foundation Hospitals	8011	A	209 735-5000	14813
McHenry Medical Group Inc	8011	D	209 577-3388	14888
Permanente Medical Group Inc	8011	A	209 735-5000	14957
Sutter Valley Med Foundation	8011	C	209 524-1211	15119
Golden Bear Physcl Thrapy Spt	8049	D	209 576-0888	15283
Avalon Care Center - Modesto	8051	C	209 526-1775	15340
Crestwood Behavioral Hlth Inc	8051	B	209 526-8050	15413
English Oaks Convalescent	8051	D	209 577-1001	15449
Fig Holdings LLC	8051	D	209 524-4817	15477
Palm Haven Nursing & Rehab LLC	8051	C	209 823-1788	15616
Community Hospice Inc (PA)	8052	C	209 578-6300	15751
Covenant Care California LLC	8059	C	209 521-2094	15834
Central Vly Specialty Hosp Inc	8062	D	209 248-7700	15987
County of Stanislaus	8062	D	209 525-7000	16032
Doctors Med Ctr Modesto Inc (HQ)	8062	B	209 578-1211	16059
Stanislaus Surgical Hosp LLC (PA)	8062	C	209 572-2700	16500
Sutter Central Vly Hospitals	8062	A	209 572-5900	16512
Sutter Central Vly Hospitals (HQ)	8062	A	209 526-4500	16513
Sutter Central Vly Hospitals	8062	A	209 526-4500	16514
Sutter Central Vly Hospitals	8062	A	209 572-8270	16515
Sutter Central Vly Hospitals	8062	A	209 569-7544	16516
Addus Healthcare Inc	8082	C	209 526-8451	16794
Provident Care Inc	8082	C	209 578-1210	16917
Sutter Vsting Nrse Assn Hspice	8082	C	209 342-4048	16942
Synergy Health Companies Inc	8099	D	209 577-4625	17338
Fennemore Craig PC	8111	C	209 576-8888	17453
Catholic Chrties of The Dcese	8322	D	209 529-3784	17865
Center For Human Services (PA)	8322	C	209 526-1476	17870
Valley-Mntain Regional Ctr Inc	8322	D	209 955-3207	18168
County of Stanislaus	8331	D	209 558-2100	18226
Modestos Neighborhood Church	8351	D	209 529-5510	18334
Fellowship Homes Inc	8361	C	209 529-4950	18432
Valley-Mntain Regional Ctr Inc	8361	D	209 529-2626	18537
County of Stanislaus	8399	D	209 525-6225	18583
Big Vlley Grace Cmnty Ch Inc M (PA)	8661	D	209 577-1604	19011
House Modesto (PA)	8661	D	209 529-7346	19021
Industrial Automtn Group LLC	8711	D	209 579-7527	19266
Principal Svc Solutions Inc	8711	C	209 408-1982	19362
Grimbleby Clman Crtif Pub Accn	8721	D	209 527-4220	19582
Rim Corporation	8741	A	209 523-8331	20196

MOFFETT FIELD, CA - Santa Clara County

	SIC	EMP	PHONE	ENTRY#
Bay Area Envmtl Res Inst	8733	D	707 938-9387	19864

MOJAVE, CA - Kern County

	SIC	EMP	PHONE	ENTRY#
Golden Queen Mining Co LLC	1041	C	661 824-4300	573
Calportland Company	3241	C	661 824-2401	2695

GEOGRAPHIC SECTION   MORENO VALLEY CA

	SIC	EMP	PHONE	ENTRY#
Innovative Coatings Technology Corporation	3479	C	661 824-8101	2763
Scaled Composites LLC	3721	B	661 824-4541	2983

MONROVIA, CA - Los Angeles County

	SIC	EMP	PHONE	ENTRY#
H C Olsen Cnstr Co Inc	1541	D	626 359-8900	822
Heil Construction Inc	1541	D	626 303-7141	824
Air-Tro Incorporated	1711	D	626 357-3535	1342
Cell-Crete Corporation (PA)	1771	C	626 357-3500	2106
Vinyl Technology Inc (PA)	2671	C	626 443-5257	2527
Pasadena Newspapers Inc (PA)	2711	C	626 578-6300	2541
World Class Distribution Inc	4225	D	909 574-4140	3785
Southern California Edison Co	4911	C	626 303-8480	4682
Webasto Charging Systems Inc (DH)	5013	D	626 415-4000	5067
Home Depot USA Inc	5211	C	626 256-0580	6974
Doubltree By Hlton Ht Monrovia	7011	C	626 357-1900	9764
Sage Hospitality Resources LLC	7011	C	626 357-5211	10188
Ctour Holiday LLC	7999	B	323 261-8811	14512
Childrens Oncology Group	8011	C	626 447-0064	14682
Alakor Healthcare LLC	8062	C	626 408-9800	15935
Advanced Medical Analysis LLC	8071	D	626 301-0126	16702
Curative-Korva LLC	8071	D	424 645-7575	16714
California Cancer Specialists Medical Group Inc.	8621	B	626 775-3200	18735
World Vision International (PA)	8699	C	626 303-8811	19121
California Business Bureau Inc (PA)	8721	C	626 303-1515	19546
Eurofins Eaton Analytical LLC (DH)	8734	D	626 386-1100	19973
360 Support Services	8741	D	866 360-6468	20008
Country Villa Service Corp	8741	C	626 358-4547	20064
Curative Inc	8741	A	650 713-8928	20072
Financial Tech Sltons Intl Inc	8742	C	818 241-9571	20376
Leekilpatrick Management Inc	8742	D	818 500-9631	20434

MONTCLAIR, CA - San Bernardino County

	SIC	EMP	PHONE	ENTRY#
Cls Landscape Management Inc	0783	B	909 628-3005	553
Martinez Steel Inc	1791	D	909 946-0686	2189
Omnitrans	4111	C	909 379-7100	3185
Archipelago Lighting Inc	5063	D	909 627-5333	5539
Cascade Turf LLC	5083	D	909 626-8586	5807
Giant Inland Empire Rv Ctr Inc (PA)	5561	C	909 981-0444	7394
US Skillserve Inc	8051	A	909 621-4751	15713
Prime Healthcare Services-Mont	8062	A	909 625-5411	16335
Prime Hlthcare Srvcs-Mntclair	8062	C	909 625-5411	16337
Prime Hlthcare Srvcs-Mntclair (DH)	8062	C	909 625-5411	16338

MONTE SERENO, CA - Santa Clara County

	SIC	EMP	PHONE	ENTRY#
Oracle Systems Corporation	7371	D	650 506-4060	11801
La Rinconada Country Club Inc	7997	C	408 395-4181	14390
El Camino Surgery Center LLC	8062	D	650 961-1200	16071

MONTEBELLO, CA - Los Angeles County

	SIC	EMP	PHONE	ENTRY#
Holiday Tree Farms Inc	0811	C	323 276-1900	569
Cobe Chemical Co Inc	2844	D	877 691-3590	2626
Liberty Linehaul West Inc	4213	D	323 728-8900	3506
Source Logistics Center Corp	4731	D	323 887-3884	4097
Star Scrap Metal Company Inc	4953	D	562 921-5045	4940
Reu Distribution LLC	5023	A	323 201-4200	5133
Epsilon Electronics Inc (PA)	5064	C	323 722-3333	5603
Worldwide Intgrted Rsurces Inc	5072	D	323 838-8938	5739
Orora Packaging Solutions	5113	C	323 832-2000	6085
Katzkin Leather Inc (PA)	5199	C	323 725-1243	6920
Royal Paper Box Co California (PA)	5199	C	323 728-7041	6945
Costco Wholesale Corporation	5399	C	323 890-1904	7140
Johnstone Supply Inc	5722	D	323 722-2859	7440
Wilbur Curtis Co Inc	6719	B	800 421-6150	9348
Mission Linen Supply	7213	D	323 888-8971	10451
Montebello Unified School Dst	7349	D	323 887-2140	10932
L&T Staffing Inc	7361	B	323 727-9056	11167
Leidos Government Services Inc	7379	C	323 721-6979	12826
Montebello Unified School Dst	7389	D	323 440-2899	13381
Beverly Community Hosp Assn (PA)	8062	A	323 726-1222	15961
Mexican Amrcn Oprtnty Fndation (PA)	8322	D	323 890-9600	18053
Altura Management Services LLC	8741	B	323 768-2898	20019

MONTEREY, CA - Monterey County

	SIC	EMP	PHONE	ENTRY#
DMC Construction Incorporated	1542	D	831 656-1600	904
Rp Construction Services LLC	1791	C	855 428-3000	2200
Dole Fresh Vegetables Inc (HQ)	2099	C	831 422-8871	2434
Triad Broadcasting Company (PA)	4832	C	831 655-6350	4406
Pacific Gas and Electric Co	4911	D	831 648-3231	4640
Pro Act LLC	5148	D	831 655-4250	6571
Cox & Young Ventures LLC	5812	D	831 647-0114	7470
Merrill Lynch Prce Fnner Smith	6211	C	831 625-2700	8134
California Capital Insur Co (HQ)	6331	D	831 233-5500	8379
P Monterey LP	6513	D	831 250-6159	8851
Mangold Property MGT Inc	6531	D	831 372-1338	9092
Bayview Properties Inc (PA)	7011	D	831 394-3321	9634
Classic Rsdence Mgt Ltd Partnr	7011	D	831 373-0101	9706
Columbia Hospitality Inc	7011	A	831 646-8900	9713
Columbia Hospitality Inc	7011	A	831 373-5700	9714
Columbia Hospitality Inc	7011	B	630 366-2309	9715
Custom House Hotel LP	7011	C	831 649-4511	9735
Hyatt Corporation	7011	D	831 372-1234	9889
Monterey Plaza Ht Ltd Partnr	7011	B	800 334-3999	10026
Ocean Park Hotels-Hit Inc	7011	B	805 544-0812	10057
Zhg Inc	7011	D	831 394-3321	10389
Digital Wireless Telecom Inc	7389	D	650 472-7064	13269
Language Line Holdings Inc (HQ)	7389	B	831 648-5800	13348
Product Development Corp	7389	A	831 333-1100	13431
Pasadera Club Oc LLC	7997	D	831 647-2400	14422
Montage Medical Group	8011	C	831 241-9155	14912
Monterey Pines Sklld Nursg Fac	8051	D	831 373-3716	15591
Pater Dignitas Inc	8051	D	831 624-1875	15623
Sunrise Senior Living LLC	8051	D	831 643-2400	15698
Community Hosp Mntrey Pninsula	8062	C	831 625-4500	16009
Community Hospital Monterey	8062	C	831 625-4600	16012
Hospital of Community	8062	C	831 649-7700	16137
Community Hosp of Mntrey Pnnsu (HQ)	8069	A	831 624-5311	16674
Coastal Home Care Services Inc	8082	C	831 424-1344	16842
Promedica Health System Inc	8082	C	831 373-8442	16915
Childrens Crative Lrng Ctr Inc	8351	B	831 647-1880	18290
Montage Health	8399	A	831 625-4830	18610
Monterey Bay Aqar Foundation (PA)	8422	B	831 648-4800	18692
Pacific Metrics LLC	8748	C	831 646-6400	20823

MONTEREY PARK, CA - Los Angeles County

	SIC	EMP	PHONE	ENTRY#
Architectural Woodworking Co	2541	D	626 570-4125	2500
Inertech Supply Inc	3053	D	626 282-2000	2654
Carmichael International Svc (DH)	4731	D	213 353-0800	3994
Logisteed America Inc	4731	C	323 263-8100	4050
San Diego Gas & Electric Co	4911	C	619 696-2000	4672
Southern California Gas Co	4924	A	213 244-1200	4732
Southern California Gas Co	4924	C	213 244-1200	4742
El Primo Foods Inc	5142	C	626 289-5054	6420
F & A Federal Credit Union	6061	D	213 268-1226	7765
Care 1st Health Plan (PA)	6321	C	323 889-6638	8260
State Compensation Insur Fund	6331	C	323 266-5000	8420
Farmers Insurance	6411	C	626 288-0870	8561
Innovations Building Svcs LLC	7349	D	323 787-6068	10911
Merchants Building Maint Co	7349	C	323 881-8902	10929
Guard-Systems Inc	7381	A	323 881-6715	12983
Chen Dvid MD Dgnstc Med Group	8011	D	626 288-8029	14679
Garfield Imaging Center Inc	8011	C	626 572-0912	14759
Ahmc Garfield Medical Ctr LP	8051	C	626 573-2222	15318
Monterey Park Hospital	8062	C	626 570-9000	16274
Ahmc Healthcare Inc	8099	C	626 570-9000	17167
Childrens Law Center Cal (PA)	8111	C	323 980-8700	17402

MONTROSE, CA - Los Angeles County

	SIC	EMP	PHONE	ENTRY#
LMS Electric	1731	D	818 248-1165	1767
Shriners Hspitals For Children	8069	B	213 368-3302	16695
Neardata Inc	8742	D	818 249-2469	20486

MOORPARK, CA - Ventura County

	SIC	EMP	PHONE	ENTRY#
Muranaka Farm	0191	C	805 529-0201	191
Ned L Webster Concrete Cnstr	1771	D	805 529-4900	2139
Anc Technology Inc	3672	D	805 530-3958	2905
Mpo Videotronics Inc (PA)	3861	D	805 499-8513	3085
Picnic Time Inc	3999	D	805 529-7400	3111
Pom Medical LLC	5047	D	805 306-2105	5443
Testequity Inc	5084	D	805 498-9933	5872
Lifetech Resources LLC	5122	D	805 944-1199	6121
Pindler & Pindler Inc (PA)	5131	C	805 531-9090	6160
Kretek International Inc (DH)	5194	D	805 531-8888	6880
Titan Led	6512	D	805 523-7500	8769
Citrus North Venture LLC	7011	D	256 428-2000	9704
Cardservice International Inc (DH)	7389	B		13226
Testequity LLC (PA)	7629	C	805 498-9933	13748

MORAGA, CA - Contra Costa County

	SIC	EMP	PHONE	ENTRY#
Moraga Cntry CLB Hmowners Assn	7997	D	925 376-2200	14411
Aegis Senior Communities LLC	8361	C	925 377-7900	18371
Bergerson Group	8742	D	925 948-8110	20294

MORENO VALLEY, CA - Riverside County

	SIC	EMP	PHONE	ENTRY#
Cardinal Glass Industries Inc	3211	C	951 485-9007	2688
Access Info Holdings LLC	4226	A	909 459-1417	3788
Capstone Logistics LLC	4789	C	770 414-1929	4146

Employee Codes: A=Over 500 employees, B=251-500
C=101-250, D=51-100, E=20-50, F=10-19, G=1-9

MORENO VALLEY CA

GEOGRAPHIC SECTION

	SIC	EMP	PHONE	ENTRY#
San Diego Gas & Electric Co.	4924	C	951 243-2241	4725
Waste MGT Collectn Recycl Inc.	4953	C	951 242-0421	4967
Home Depot USA Inc.	5211	D	951 485-5400	6999
Lowes Home Centers LLC	5211	D	951 656-1859	7066
Akh Company Inc.	5531	C	951 924-5356	7340
Acapulco Restaurants Inc.	5812	D	951 653-8809	7452
Visterra Credit Union.	6062	C	951 656-4411	7833
Kaiser Foundation Hospitals.	6733	D	951 601-6174	9433
Butler America Holdings Inc.	7361	B	951 563-0020	11098
Moreno Valley Snf LLC.	7389	D	951 363-5434	13383
U-Haul Leasing & Sales Co.	7513	B	951 485-2003	13571
Community Health Systems Inc.	8011	C	951 571-2300	14701
County of Riverside.	8011	A	951 486-4000	14714
County of Riverside.	8011	A	951 486-4000	14715
Kaiser Foundation Hospitals.	8011	A	951 243-0811	14843
RES-Care Inc.	8052	D	951 653-1311	15791
Riverside University Health.	8062	B	951 486-4000	16366
Think Together.	8351	B	951 571-9944	18361

MORGAN HILL, CA - Santa Clara County

	SIC	EMP	PHONE	ENTRY#
George Chiala Farms Inc.	0161	C	408 778-0562	33
Kawahara Nursery Inc.	0181	C	408 779-2400	134
Medallion Landscape MGT Inc (PA)	0781	D	408 782-7500	443
Monument Construction Inc.	0781	D	408 778-1350	448
New Path Landscape Svcs Inc.	0781	D	408 310-8476	450
G B Group Inc (PA)	1522	D	408 848-8118	757
Paragon Mechanical Inc.	1711	D	408 727-7303	1527
Serrano Electric Inc.	1731	D	408 986-1570	1837
Mission Bell Mfg Co Inc.	1751	B	408 778-2036	2008
Svg Contractors Inc.	1795	D	408 218-0993	2244
Sierra Precast Inc.	3272	C	408 779-1000	2707
Global Motorsport Parts Inc.	3751	C	408 778-0500	2995
Tecan Systems Inc.	3821	D	408 953-3100	3012
Anritsu US Holding Inc (HQ)	3825	B	408 778-2000	3023
Waste Management Cal Inc.	4953	C	408 779-2206	4959
Custom Chrome Manufacturing.	5013	B	408 825-5000	5034
Anritsu Americas Sales Company.	5084	A	408 778-2000	5819
Specialized Bicycle Components Hold (PA)	5091	B	408 779-6229	5981
Del Monaco Foods Inc.	5141	D	408 500-4100	6248
Lusamerica Foods Inc (PA)	5146	D	408 778-7200	6473
Youngs Market Company LLC.	5182	C	408 782-3121	6815
Sakata Seed America Inc (HQ)	5191	D	408 778-7758	6831
Home Depot USA Inc.	5211	D	408 779-9755	7002
D & J Lumber Co Inc (PA)	5251	D	408 778-1550	7117
Ford Store Morgan Hill Inc.	5511	D	408 782-8201	7211
California Kit Cab Door Corp.	6512	C	408 776-1105	8706
Coyote Creek Consulting LLC	7379	D	408 383-9200	12767
Andpak Inc.	7389	D	408 776-1072	13192
Allied Lube Inc.	7549	D	408 779-8969	13707
Rapid Response Force LLC.	8322	D	408 612-8984	18093
Catalyst Family Inc (PA)	8351	D	408 556-7300	18276
Pacific Metro LLC (PA)	8412	D	408 201-5000	18664
Operating Engineers Loca.	8711	C	408 782-9803	19342

MORRO BAY, CA - San Luis Obispo County

	SIC	EMP	PHONE	ENTRY#
Compass Health Inc.	8051	C	805 772-7372	15382

MOSS BEACH, CA - San Mateo County

	SIC	EMP	PHONE	ENTRY#
Ahmc Seton Medical Center LLC.	8062	B	650 563-7100	15933

MOSS LANDING, CA - Monterey County

	SIC	EMP	PHONE	ENTRY#
Golden State Bulb Growers Inc.	0181	C	831 728-0500	129
Dynegy Marketing & Trade LLC.	4911	D	831 633-6700	4570
Dynegy Moss Landing LLC.	4911	D	831 633-6618	4571
Moss Landing Marine Labs.	8071	A	831 771-4400	16736
Monterey Bay Aquarium RES Inst.	8733	C	831 775-1700	19898

MOUNT HERMON, CA - Santa Cruz County

	SIC	EMP	PHONE	ENTRY#
Mount Hermon Association Inc (PA)	7032	D	831 335-4466	10408

MOUNT SHASTA, CA - Siskiyou County

	SIC	EMP	PHONE	ENTRY#
Siskiyou Lake Golf Resort Inc.	7992	D	530 926-3030	14289
Siskiyou Opportunity Center (PA)	8331	D	530 926-4698	18248

MOUNTAIN HOUSE, CA - San Joaquin County

	SIC	EMP	PHONE	ENTRY#
Mountain House Cmnty Svcs Dst.	8611	D	209 831-2300	18717

MOUNTAIN PASS, CA - San Bernardino County

	SIC	EMP	PHONE	ENTRY#
Chevron Mining Inc.	1221	C	760 856-7625	575
Mp Mine Operations LLC.	1481	C	702 277-0848	646

MOUNTAIN VIEW, CA - Santa Clara County

	SIC	EMP	PHONE	ENTRY#
Animus Inc.	0742	C	650 969-8555	327
Bcci Construction LLC.	1521	C	650 543-8900	659
OGrady Paving Inc.	1611	C	650 966-1926	1148
Tellme Networks Inc.	2741	B	650 693-1009	2558
Igm Biosciences Inc.	2834	B	650 965-7873	2589
Mineral Earth Sciences LLC	3523	D	650 532-9590	2770
General Dynmics Mssion Systems.	3571	D	650 966-2000	2805
Esperanto Technologies Inc (PA)	3674	D	650 319-7357	2919
Aeva Technologies Inc (PA)	3714	C	650 481-7070	2971
Asrc Aerospace Corp.	3812	B	650 604-5946	3001
Minaris Medical America Inc.	3821	D	800 233-6278	3011
Applied Physics Systems Inc (PA)	3829	C	650 965-0500	3041
Wing Aviation LLC.	4513	C	650 224-1198	3861
Channel Intelligence Inc.	4813	C	321 939-5600	4264
Google Fiber Inc (DH)	4813	D	650 253-0000	4290
Meebo Inc.	4813	D	650 253-0000	4312
Attivo Networks Inc.	5045	D	510 623-1000	5277
Samsung Electronics Amer Inc.	5045	C	646 651-2309	5344
Viewray Technologies Inc.	5047	D	650 252-0920	5460
Samsung Electronics Amer Inc.	5065	A	650 210-1000	5697
Tabula Inc.	5065	D	408 986-9140	5705
Nanosolar Inc.	5074	B		5757
Reliable Robotics Corporation.	5084	C	650 336-0608	5865
Bossa Nova Robotics Inc.	5099	C	415 234-5136	6030
Southern Cal Disc Tire Co Inc.	5531	C	650 988-9611	7371
Morgan Stnley Smith Barney LLC.	6211	C	650 316-6788	8144
Hi-Q Inc.	6321	B	800 549-1664	8265
Managed Health Network.	6324	C	650 988-4842	8344
Planprescriber Inc.	6411	C	650 584-2700	8640
Greystar LP.	6513	A	650 386-6438	8815
Noosphere Venture Partners LP (PA)	6726	C	650 605-5684	9405
Joie De Vivre Hospitality LLC	7011	C	650 940-1000	9928
Silicon Valley Club LLC (PA)	7011	D	408 202-9424	10237
Mode Media Corporation.	7313	D	650 244-4000	10716
Travelzoo Inc.	7313	D	650 316-6956	10722
Compex Legal Services LLC	7334	C	650 833-0460	10786
Polaris Building Maint Inc.	7349	D	650 964-9400	10944
Service By Medallion.	7349	A	650 625-1010	10964
Hireteammate Inc.	7361	C	650 386-5017	11150
Aera Technology Inc (PA)	7371	D	408 524-2222	11386
Alphabet Inc (PA)	7371	B	650 253-0000	11399
Apigee Corporation.	7371	B	408 343-7300	11412
Applied Intuition Inc (PA)	7371	D	630 935-8986	11416
Apteligent Inc.	7371	D	415 371-1402	11418
Aspect Development Inc (DH)	7371	B	650 428-2700	11429
Atrenta Inc (HQ)	7371	D	408 453-3333	11432
CSRA LLC.	7371	A	703 641-2000	11524
Drishti Technologies Inc.	7371	C	214 748-3647	11554
Groq Inc.	7371	C	650 521-9007	11635
H2oai Inc.	7371	C	650 429-8337	11637
Intellisync Corporation.	7371	B	650 625-2185	11675
Narus Inc.	7371	C	408 215-4300	11763
Oberon Media Inc (PA)	7371	B	646 367-2020	11790
Omnicell Inc.	7371	C	650 251-6100	11792
Partnerstack Inc.	7371	C	619 648-4388	11817
Platform9 Systems Inc.	7371	D	650 898-7369	11835
Portworx Inc.	7371	D	650 386-0766	11840
Redis Inc.	7371	C	415 930-9666	11869
Rhythm Newmedia Inc.	7371	D	650 961-9024	11881
Treasure Data Inc (HQ)	7371	D	866 899-5386	11987
Ujwal Inc.	7371	D	503 708-4410	12000
Wayve Technologies Inc.	7371	C	832 651-4438	12037
Workato Inc (PA)	7371	A	844 469-6752	12045
Agilepoint Inc (PA)	7372	D	650 968-6789	12080
Avast Software Inc (PA)	7372	D	844 340-9251	12108
Blackberry Corporation.	7372	D	650 564-0016	12117
Blue Coat LLC.	7372	A	408 220-2200	12121
Cloudsimple Inc.	7372	D	412 568-3487	12143
Confluent Inc (PA)	7372	A	800 439-3207	12146
Coursera Inc (PA)	7372	C	650 963-9884	12151
Cumulus Networks Inc (PA)	7372	C	650 383-6700	12152
Datavisor Inc.	7372	D	408 331-9886	12158
Driveai Inc.	7372	C	408 693-0765	12166
Health Gorilla Inc.	7372	C	844 446-7455	12218
Inmage Systems Inc.	7372	C	408 200-3840	12234
Intuit Inc (PA)	7372	D	650 944-6000	12238
Intuit Inc.	7372	C	650 944-6000	12240
Khan Academy Inc.	7372	C	650 336-5426	12249
Moveworks Inc (PA)	7372	C	408 435-5100	12275
Progress Software Corporation.	7372	D	650 341-7733	12328
Sentinelone Inc (PA)	7372	A	855 868-3733	12347
Synplicity Inc (HQ)	7372	C	650 584-5000	12373
Thoughtspot Inc (PA)	7372	B	800 508-7008	12378
Wildfire Interactive Inc.	7372	C	650 253-0000	12397

GEOGRAPHIC SECTION — NATIONAL CITY CA

Company	SIC	EMP	PHONE	ENTRY#
Aurora Operations Inc.	7373	D	888 583-9506	12422
Harman Cnncted Svcs Holdg Corp (DH)	7373	C	650 623-9400	12462
Heartflow Inc (PA)	7373	C	650 241-1221	12464
Paypal Global Holdings Inc	7374	D	408 967-1000	12605
Rackspace Hosting Inc	7374	C	201 792-1918	12612
Yellowbrick Data Inc (PA)	7374	C	877 492-3282	12645
Google LLC (HQ)	7375	D	650 253-0000	12664
Loon LLC (DH)	7375	D		12675
Tintri Inc.	7375	B	650 810-8200	12685
Joyent Inc.	7379	C	415 400-0600	12821
Chronicle LLC	7382	D	650 214-5199	13101
Google Payment Corp	7389	C	888 986-7944	13306
Loon LLC	7389	C	310 625-3449	13357
Samsung Pay Inc	7389	D	617 279-0520	13458
Lozano Inc.	7542	C	650 941-0590	13700
Yourmechanic Inc.	7549	C	215 253-7941	13722
Century Theatres Inc.	7833	B	650 961-3828	14019
El Camino Hospital District RE	8011	C	650 962-4360	14735
Balboa Enterprises Inc	8051	D	650 961-6161	15349
Covenant Care California LLC	8062	C	650 964-0543	16033
El Camino Hospital (PA)	8062	A	650 940-7000	16069
El Camino Hospital	8062	C	650 940-7000	16070
Kaiser Foundation Hospitals	8062	D	650 903-3000	16194
Sutter Health	8062	C	650 934-7000	16538
El Camino Hospital Auxiliary	8082	A	650 940-7214	16858
El Camino Hospital	8092	D	650 940-7310	16981
Health Iq	8099	D	917 770-2190	17245
Silicon Valley Medical Dev LLC	8099	C	408 866-4000	17326
Fenwick & West LLP (PA)	8111	B	650 988-8500	17455
El Camino Hospital	8322	D	650 988-7444	17965
Childrens Crative Lrng Ctr Inc	8351	B	650 968-2600	18289
Villa Siena	8361	D	650 961-6484	18540
Frequence Inc.	8631	C	650 520-6114	18779
Silicon Vly Cmnty Foundation (PA)	8641	C	650 450-5400	18909
Young MNS Chrstn Assn of E Bay	8641	B	650 526-3500	18974
Young MNS Chrstn Assn Slcon VI	8641	C	650 969-9622	19002
Jacobs Technology Inc.	8711	D	650 604-3784	19285
Kodiak Robotics Inc.	8711	D	781 626-2729	19298
Statcomm Inc.	8711	D	650 988-9508	19398
Nebula Inc.	8731	D	650 539-9900	19745
Samsung Research America Inc (DH)	8731	C	650 210-1001	19766
Semprius Inc.	8731	D	919 433-9980	19768
Parkinsons Institute	8733	D	650 770-0201	19903
Seti Institute	8733	C	650 961-6633	19911
Zonare Medical Systems Inc.	8733	D	650 230-2800	19941
Greystar LP	8741	A	650 386-6438	20103
Coda Project Inc.	8742	D	561 267-1403	20322
Simplelegal Inc.	8742	D	949 887-2900	20546
Tubular Labs Inc (HQ)	8742	C	650 260-8823	20597
Quova Inc.	8748	D	650 965-2898	20837
Vimo Inc (PA)	8748	D	650 618-4600	20874

MURPHYS, CA - Calaveras County

Company	SIC	EMP	PHONE	ENTRY#
Kautz Vineyards Inc (PA)	0172	D	209 728-1251	78

MURRIETA, CA - Riverside County

Company	SIC	EMP	PHONE	ENTRY#
West Pak Avocado Inc (PA)	0723	C	951 296-5757	314
Jpi Development Group Inc	1711	D	951 973-7680	1473
Temecula Valley Drywall Inc.	1742	D	951 600-1742	1968
Classic Installs Inc.	1796	D	951 678-9906	2247
Sunland Scaffold	1799	D	951 595-9402	2317
Battery Systems Inc.	5065	B	951 894-2960	5627
Waterstone Faucets LLC	5074	C	951 304-0520	5763
Home Depot USA Inc	5211	C	951 698-1555	7013
Lowes Home Centers LLC	5211	B	951 461-8916	7062
Carmax Inc.	5521	C	951 387-3887	7337
F M Tarbell Co	6531	D	951 677-3565	9000
ARC Document Solutions LLC	7334	A	951 445-4480	10783
Busy Bee LLC	7342	D	951 404-9900	10830
Prosites Inc.	7379	C	888 932-3644	12864
Elite Enfrcment SEC Sltons Inc	7381	C	866 354-8308	12968
Glare Technology Usa Inc.	7382	C	909 437-6999	13120
National Bus Invstigations Inc	7389	D	951 677-3500	13389
Faith Quality Auto Body Inc.	7532	D	951 698-8215	13636
Complete Coach Works	7549	C	800 300-3751	13711
Monique Suraci	7991	D	951 677-8111	14219
Sycamore Cc Inc.	7992	D	760 451-3700	14293
Oak Grove Inst Foundation Inc (PA)	8011	A	951 677-5599	14929
United Medical Doctors	8011	D	951 566-5229	15144
My Kids Dentist	8021	B	951 600-1062	15241
Michael G Frtnsce Physcl Thrap	8049	D	626 446-7027	15296
Rancho Physical Therapy Inc (PA)	8049	D	951 696-9353	15304
Southwest Healthcare Sys Aux	8062	A	800 404-6627	16450
Southwest Healthcare Sys Aux (HQ)	8062	B	951 696-6000	16451
National Mentor Holdings Inc	8361	B	951 677-1453	18492

NAPA, CA - Napa County

Company	SIC	EMP	PHONE	ENTRY#
Domaine Carneros Ltd.	0172	D	707 257-0101	72
CMC Rebar West	1541	C	707 863-3933	812
GD Nielson Construction Inc.	1623	D	707 253-8774	1210
Nova Group Inc (HQ)	1623	D	707 265-1100	1243
Nova/Tic Gvrnment Prjcts A Jin	1623	D	707 257-3200	1244
Bell Products Inc.	1711	D	707 255-1811	1375
Peck & Hiller Company	1771	D	707 258-8800	2145
Tailored Living Choices LLC	1799	C	707 259-0526	2318
Sterling Vineyards Inc.	2084	C	707 252-7410	2394
The Doctors Company	5047	A	707 226-0289	5453
Diageo North America Inc.	5182	D	707 299-2600	6794
LLC Wilson Daniels	5182	D	707 963-9661	6801
World Wine Estates	5182	D	707 257-5300	6812
Home Depot USA Inc	5211	D	707 251-0162	6980
Doctors Company Foundation	6321	A	800 421-2368	8263
Doctors Company Insurance Svcs	6351	B	707 226-0100	8431
Doctors Management Company (HQ)	6411	D	707 226-0100	8547
Califrnia Odd Fllows Hsing Nap (PA)	6513	D	707 257-7885	8794
Califrnia Odd Fllows Hsing Nap	6513	D	707 257-7885	8795
Walsh Vineyards Management Inc.	6531	C	707 258-1500	9208
Kaiser Foundation Hospitals	6733	C	707 258-2500	9436
Carneros Inn LLC	7011	B	707 299-4880	9680
Dolce International / NAPA LLC	7011	C	707 257-0200	9760
IA Lodging NAPA Solano Trs LLC	7011	C	707 253-8600	9904
Lodgeworks LP	7011	C	707 690-9800	9981
Meritage Resort LLC	7011	B	707 251-1900	10014
Silverado Rsort Svcs Group LLC	7011	B	707 257-0200	10239
Star H-R	7361	A	707 265-9911	11239
AUL Corp (DH)	7694	C	707 257-9700	13757
Courseco Inc.	7992	A	707 255-4333	14254
NAPA Golf Associates LLC	7997	B	707 251-1900	14412
NAPA Valley Country Club	7997	D	707 252-1111	14413
Sccr Properties Inc.	7997	C	707 257-0200	14447
NAPA Valley Wine Train LLC (HQ)	7999	C	707 253-2160	14549
Ole Health	8011	D	707 254-1770	14933
Redwood Rgnal Med Group DRG LL	8011	D	707 253-7161	15014
Napaidence Opco LLC	8051	C	707 255-6060	15594
Piners Nursing Home Inc.	8051	D	707 224-7925	15627
Health Humn Svcs Agcy NAPA CNT	8052	D	707 253-4306	15760
Queen of Vly Med Ctr Fundation (DH)	8062	A	707 252-4411	16354
Queen of Vly Med Ctr Fundation	8062	B	707 251-2000	16355
Califrnia Dept State Hospitals	8063	A	707 253-5000	16643
Collabria Care	8082	D	707 258-9080	16843
Thekey LLC	8082	D	707 492-8411	16946
Bass Medical Group	8099	D	707 346-5100	17184
NAPA Valley PSI Inc.	8331	C	707 255-0177	18237
North Bay Dvlpmntal Dsblties S (PA)	8331	A	707 256-1224	18238
Essex National Securities	8742	C	707 258-5000	20363
Work Health	8742	C	707 257-4084	20616
Cbr Group	8748	D	415 806-2323	20722

NATIONAL CITY, CA - San Diego County

Company	SIC	EMP	PHONE	ENTRY#
Brightview Landscape Svcs Inc.	0781	D	619 474-4478	406
The Ortiz Corporation	1623	D	619 434-7925	1271
Turn Key Scaffold LLC	1799	C	619 642-0880	2323
Hyperbaric Technologies Inc.	3845	D	619 336-2022	3076
Sureride Charter Inc.	4142	C	619 336-9200	3321
San Diego Unified Port Dst	4491	C	619 686-6200	3816
Public Authority	4941	C	619 731-3705	4819
Tdk-Lambda Americas Inc	5065	C	619 575-4400	5708
Del Mar Holding LLC	5147	A	313 659-7300	6491
Harvest Meat Company Inc.	5147	D	619 477-0185	6492
Harvest Meat Company Inc (HQ)	5147	D	619 477-0185	6493
Fornaca Inc (PA)	5531	C	866 308-9461	7347
Adventist Health System/West	6513	D	619 475-5040	8789
Trigild International Inc.	7011	D	619 474-6517	10327
Motivational Systems Inc (PA)	7336	D	619 474-8246	10816
Nms Management Inc.	7349	D	619 425-0440	10934
Oxyheal Health Group Inc.	7699	D	619 336-2022	13789
South Bay Sand Blstg Tank Clg	7699	D	619 238-8338	13800
Castle Manor Inc.	8051	D	619 791-7900	15366
Imaginative Horizons Inc.	8051	D	619 477-1176	15521
Sterling Care Inc.	8051	C	619 470-6700	15681
Paradise Valley Hospital (PA)	8062	A	619 470-4100	16316
National School District	8211	C	619 336-7770	17734
Episcopal Community Services	8322	C	619 470-0720	17969
St Pauls Episcopal Home Inc.	8361	D	619 232-2996	18526
Epsilon Systems Solutions Inc.	8611	C	619 474-3252	18709
Hii Fleet Support Group LLC	8711	C	619 474-8820	19251

Employee Codes: A=Over 500 employees, B=251-500
C=101-250, D=51-100, E=20-50, F=10-19, G=1-9

NEEDLES CA

GEOGRAPHIC SECTION

	SIC	EMP	PHONE	ENTRY#
NEEDLES, CA - San Bernardino County				
Pacific Gas and Electric Co.	4911	C	760 326-2615	4655
Havasu Landing Casino **(PA)**	7011	D	760 858-5380	9839
Community Hlthcare Partner Inc.	8011	D	760 326-4531	14702
NEVADA CITY, CA - Nevada County				
Robinson Enterprises Investment Co Inc.	2411	D	530 265-5844	2475
Nortech Waste LLC	4953	C	916 645-5230	4915
Telestream LLC **(PA)**	7371	D	530 470-1300	11974
Anderson Physical Therapy Inc.	8049	D	530 265-8100	15268
Mountain Vly Child Fmly Svcs I.	8052	D	530 265-9057	15776
NEWARK, CA - Alameda County				
Ferma Corporation.	1795	C	510 794-0414	2235
Nefab Packaging Inc.	2441	D	408 678-2500	2482
Protagonist Therapeutics Inc **(PA)**	2834	C	510 474-0170	2604
Spotter Global Inc.	3469	C	515 817-3726	2754
Lucid Usa Inc **(HQ)**	3711	C	510 648-3553	2966
Moving Solutions Inc.	4214	C	408 920-0110	3590
National Distribution Agcy Inc **(HQ)**	4225	D	510 487-6226	3734
Nordstrom Inc.	4225	D	510 794-5440	3739
Javelin Logistics Company Inc.	4731	C	800 577-1060	4042
Evergreen Envmtl Svcs Inc.	4953	C	510 795-4400	4893
Golden State Lumber Inc.	5031	C	510 229-5500	5158
Elitegroup Computer Systems Ho.	5045	C	510 794-2952	5297
Promise Technology Inc.	5045	D	408 645-3499	5336
Venture Design Services Inc.	5045	C	510 744-3770	5368
Windy Cy Wire Cble Tech Pdts L.	5063	C	510 284-3956	5597
Aspire Bakeries LLC	5149	B	510 494-1700	6606
Createme Technologies LLC	5699	C	646 880-8625	7417
Risk Management Solutions Inc **(HQ)**	6794	C	510 505-2500	9455
Pacific Hotel Management LLC	7011	C	510 791-7700	10082
Raps Hospitality Group.	7011	C	510 795-7995	10140
Intelliswift Software Inc **(PA)**	7371	C	510 370-2600	11674
P Murphy & Associates Inc.	7371	C	818 841-2002	11808
Vm Services Inc.	7371	D	510 744-3720	12031
Central Business Solutions Inc **(PA)**	7379	C	510 573-5500	12753
Cloudwick Technologies Inc **(PA)**	7379	D	650 346-5788	12761
Etouch Systems Corp.	7379	A	510 795-4800	12788
Nefab Packaging West LLC	7389	C	408 678-2516	13390
University Healthcare Alliance.	8082	C	510 974-8281	16958
Challenger Schools.	8351	D	510 770-1771	18280
Advanced Cell Diagnostics Inc.	8731	D	510 576-8800	19645
Allogene Therapeutics Inc.	8731	D	650 457-2700	19653
Dna Twopointo Inc.	8731	D	650 853-8347	19682
IMS - Insurance Med Svcs Inc.	8731	D	510 490-6211	19709
Membrane Technology & RES Inc **(PA)**	8731	D	650 328-2228	19734
Tegile Systems Inc.	8731	D	510 791-7900	19781
Dataknox Solutions Inc.	8742	D	510 673-7070	20338
NEWBURY PARK, CA - Ventura County				
Kota Construction LLC.	1521	D	855 800-5682	694
Isec Incorporated.	1751	D	805 375-6957	2003
Onyx Pharmaceuticals Inc.	2834	A	650 266-0000	2600
Mv Transportation Inc.	4111	D	805 375-5467	3173
United Parcel Service Inc.	4215	D	805 375-1832	3643
Carnegie Agency Inc.	6411	C	805 445-1470	8521
Carefree Communities Inc.	6515	C	805 498-2612	8879
Hawaiian Hotels & Resorts Inc.	7011	D	805 480-0052	9841
Cimatron Gibbs LLC.	7371	D	805 523-0004	11490
Compulink Business Systems Inc **(PA)**	7372	D	805 446-2050	12145
Weldlogic Inc.	7692	C	805 375-1670	13755
Mary Hlth of Sick Cnvlscent Nr.	8051	D	805 498-3644	15581
NEWCASTLE, CA - Placer County				
Siteone Landscape Supply LLC **(DH)**	5063	D	770 255-2100	5592
NEWHALL, CA - Los Angeles County				
Calex Engineering Inc.	1794	D	661 254-1866	2214
Smart & Final Stores LLC.	5141	D	661 255-9822	6385
Green Thumb International Inc.	5261	C	661 259-1071	7126
Hollenbeck Palms.	8361	C	323 263-6195	18450
NEWMAN, CA - Stanislaus County				
Dimare Enterprises Inc **(PA)**	0161	C	209 827-2900	29
Stewart & Jasper Marketing Inc **(PA)**	2068	C	209 862-9600	2376
Titan Newman Inc.	5085	D	209 862-2977	5931
Avalon Care Ctr - Newman LLC.	8051	D	209 862-2862	15343
NEWPORT BEACH, CA - Orange County				
Olen Residential Realty Corp **(HQ)**	1522	D	949 644-6536	767
Houalla Enterprises Ltd.	1542	D	949 515-4350	939
Koll Construction LP.	1542	D	949 833-3030	953
McCarthy Bldg Companies Inc.	1542	D	949 851-8383	964
McCarthy Bldg Companies Inc.	1542	B	949 851-8383	968
RSI Home Products Inc.	2514	D	949 720-1116	2492
Conexant Holdings Inc.	3674	A	415 983-2706	2915
Hornblower Yachts LLC	4724	A	949 650-2412	3935
US Lines LLC **(DH)**	4731	D	714 751-3333	4116
Xport Forwarding LLC.	4731	D	949 354-0609	4121
Mbit Wireless Inc **(PA)**	4812	C	949 205-4559	4218
Clean Energy.	4924	A	949 437-1000	4722
Clean Energy Fuels Corp **(PA)**	4932	D	949 437-1000	4755
Bitcentral Inc.	5065	D	949 253-9000	5633
Urban Decay Cosmetics LLC.	5122	B	949 631-4504	6148
Sterling Motors Ltd.	5511	D	949 645-5900	7304
Monex Deposit A Cal Ltd Partnr.	5944	D	949 752-1400	7552
American Security Bank.	6022	D	949 440-5200	7653
Bny-Mellon National Assn.	6022	A	877 420-6377	7662
Pacific Life Global Funding.	6153	D	949 219-3011	7901
PAR Consulting LLC.	6153	D	949 461-1140	7902
Electronic Commerce LLC	6159	D	800 770-5520	7919
Emery Financial Inc **(PA)**	6163	D	949 219-0640	8041
RMR Financial LLC **(DH)**	6163	D	408 355-2000	8054
Merrill Lynch Prce Fnner Smith.	6211	C	949 467-3760	8110
Pacific Select Distrs Inc.	6211	D	949 219-3011	8159
Roth Capital Partners LLC **(PA)**	6211	D	800 678-9147	8164
Allianz Global Investors of America LP.	6282	A	949 219-2200	8184
Pacific Altrntive Asset MGT LL **(HQ)**	6282	D	949 261-4900	8212
Research Affiliates Capital LP.	6282	D	949 325-8700	8218
Research Affiliates MGT LLC.	6282	D	949 325-8700	8219
John Hancock Life Insur Co USA.	6311	D	949 254-1440	8237
Pacific Asset Holding LLC.	6311	C	949 219-3011	8243
Pacific Life & Annuity Company.	6311	A	949 219-3011	8244
Lawyers Title Insurance Corp.	6361	C	949 223-5575	8446
Edgewood Partners Insur Ctr.	6411	D	949 263-0606	8549
FMC Financial Group **(PA)**	6411	D	949 225-9369	8571
Northwestern Mutl Inv MGT LLC.	6411	B	949 759-5555	8629
R Mc Closkey Insurance Agency.	6411	C	949 223-8100	8647
Trg Insurance Services.	6411	D	949 474-1550	8676
Entrepreneurial Capital Corp.	6512	C	949 809-3900	8717
Olen Commercial Realty Corp.	6512	B	949 644-6536	8739
Sdmv Hotel Partners LP.	6512	D	949 516-0088	8757
10632 Bolsa Avenue LP.	6513	D	949 673-1221	8786
Park Newport Ltd **(PA)**	6513	D	949 644-1900	8853
BKM Diablo 227 LLC.	6531	D	602 688-6409	8915
Buchanan Street Partners LP.	6531	D	949 721-1414	8917
C B Coast Newport Properties.	6531	A	949 644-1600	8919
Cbre Globl Value Investors LLC.	6531	C	949 725-8500	8929
Citivest Inc.	6531	D	949 705-0420	8935
Coldwell Bnkr Rsdntial Rfrral.	6531	A	949 673-8700	8945
Core Realty Holdings MGT Inc.	6531	D	949 863-1031	8952
Csl Berkshire Operating Co LLC.	6531	D	949 333-8580	8954
First Team RE - Orange Cnty.	6531	D	949 759-5747	9007
Greystar Management Svcs LP.	6531	A	949 705-0010	9029
Marshall Reddick Realty Inc.	6531	D	949 885-8180	9095
Mesa Management Inc.	6531	D	949 851-0995	9098
Pacific Monarch Resorts Inc **(PA)**	6531	D	949 609-2400	9118
PM Realty Group LP.	6531	D	949 553-8246	9137
Makar Properties LLC **(PA)**	6552	D	949 255-1100	9262
Absolute Return Portfolio.	6722	A	800 800-7646	9350
Pacific Investment MGT Co LLC **(DH)**	6722	C	949 720-6000	9386
Pimco Cyman Trst Pmco Cyman GL.	6722	C	949 720-6000	9387
Irvine Eastgate Office II LLC.	6798	A	949 720-2000	9470
Pyramid Peak Corporation.	6799	D	949 769-8600	9552
Windjmmer Cpitl Invstors III L.	6799	A	949 706-9989	9582
Windjmmer Cpitl Invstors IV LP.	6799	B	919 706-9989	9583
Everest Sonoma Management LLC.	7011	D	213 272-0088	9789
Hyatt Corporation.	7011	B	949 729-1234	9891
Pacific Hotel Management Inc.	7011	C	949 608-1091	10085
Tarsadia Hotels **(DH)**	7011	D	949 610-8000	10306
Uka LLC.	7011	D	949 610-8000	10332
Wj Newport LLC.	7011	C	949 476-2001	10377
Beauty Barrage LLC.	7231	C	949 771-3399	10491
Traffic Control Service Inc.	7359	C		11058
Arose Recruiting Co Inc.	7361	C	949 642-2696	11084
Heat Waves LLC.	7371	C	719 651-4942	11641
Conversionpoint Holdings Inc.	7372	D	888 706-6764	12148
Elevated Resources Inc **(PA)**	7374	C	949 419-6632	12567
Saritasa LLC **(PA)**	7374	D	949 200-6839	12622
Lifescript Inc.	7375	C	949 454-0422	12671
Ajilon LLC.	7379	C	949 955-0100	12725
Cognizant Trizetto.	7379	D	949 719-2200	12762
NC Interactive LLC.	7379	D	512 623-8700	12843
Tad Group LLC.	7382	C	949 476-3601	13151
Professional Parking.	7521	C	949 723-4027	13626

GEOGRAPHIC SECTION

NORTH HOLLYWOOD CA

	SIC	EMP	PHONE	ENTRY#
Vroom Automotive Finance Corp (HQ)	7538	B	949 224-1226	13678
Edwards Theatres Inc (DH)	7832	C	949 640-4600	13987
Nuzuna Corporation	7991	D	949 335-7790	14222
U Gym LLC (PA)	7991	D	714 668-0911	14240
Balboa Bay Club Inc (HQ)	7997	B	949 645-5000	14327
Big Canyon Country Club	7997	C	949 644-5404	14343
International Bay Clubs LLC (PA)	7997	C	949 645-5000	14384
Newport Beach Country Club Inc	7997	C	949 644-9550	14415
Micha-Rettenmaier Partnership	8011	D	714 280-1645	14899
Newport Beach Surgery Ctr LLC	8011	C	949 631-0988	14920
Usc Keck School of Medicine	8011	D	949 474-5730	15173
Usc Keck School of Medicine	8011	D	949 474-5720	15174
Usc Keck School of Medicine	8011	D	949 646-6441	15175
West Dermatology Med MGT Inc (PA)	8011	A	909 793-3000	15204
Ben Bennett Inc (PA)	8059	C	949 209-9712	15816
Hoag Clinic	8062	B	949 764-1888	16128
Hoag Hospital Foundation (HQ)	8062	D	949 764-7217	16130
Hoag Memorial Hospital Presbt (PA)	8062	A	949 764-4624	16132
Hoag Orthopedic Institute LLC	8062	B	949 515-7000	16133
Akua Behavioral Health Inc (PA)	8069	D	949 777-2283	16661
James R Gldwell Dntl Crmics In (PA)	8072	C	949 440-2600	16773
Prismatik Dentalcraft Inc	8072	C	949 399-1930	16776
South Coast Behavioral Health	8082	D	714 312-5058	16931
National Therapeutic Svcs Inc (PA)	8093	D	866 311-0003	17100
Harbor Health Systems LLC	8099	C	949 273-7020	17244
Irell & Manella LLP	8111	B	949 760-0991	17501
Newmeyer & Dillion LLP (PA)	8111	C	949 854-7000	17588
Stradling Ycca Crlson Ruth A P (PA)	8111	C	949 725-4000	17662
Wright Finlay & Zak LLP	8111	D	949 477-5050	17689
Childrens Hospital Orange Cnty	8351	C	949 631-2062	18292
Young MNS Chrstn Assn Ornge CN	8641	D	949 642-9990	18989
Automobile Club Southern Cal	8699	D	949 476-8880	19052
Bkf Engineers/Ags	8711	D	949 526-8400	19156
Concept Technology Inc (PA)	8711	D	949 854-7047	19179
Bassenian/Lagoni Architects	8712	D	949 553-9100	19455
Jeffrey Rome & Associates	8712	D	949 760-3929	19481
M Arthur Gensler Jr Assoc Inc	8712	D	949 863-9434	19491
William Hzmlhlch Archtects Inc	8712	D	949 250-0607	19519
Hagen Streiff Newton & Oshiro Accountants PC	8721	D	949 390-7647	19584
JS Held LLC	8721	D	949 390-7647	19591
Palladium Valley Global Inc	8732	D	949 723-9613	19841
Baypointe Management Inc	8741	D	813 503-5551	20032
LFC Corporate Services Inc	8741	D	949 640-4950	20141
Mig Management Services LLC	8741	D	949 474-5800	20152
Pacific Life Fund Advisors LLC	8741	C	949 260-9000	20169
Twenty4seven Hotels Corp	8741	B	949 734-6400	20236
Greenhouse Agency Inc	8742	C	949 752-7542	20396
Metrostudy Inc	8742	C	714 619-7800	20468
Mf Services Company LLC (HQ)	8742	D	949 474-5800	20469
Smart Circle International LLC (PA)	8742	D	949 587-9207	20553
Ymarketing LLC	8742	D	714 545-2550	20619
Your Practice Online LLC (PA)	8742	C	877 388-8569	20621
Capstone Partners	8748	D	949 660-1717	20718
T-Force Inc (PA)	8748	D	949 208-1527	20861

NEWPORT COAST, CA - Orange County

	SIC	EMP	PHONE	ENTRY#
Resort At Pelican Hill LLC	7011	B	949 467-6800	10157

NICE, CA - Lake County

	SIC	EMP	PHONE	ENTRY#
Worldmark Club	7011	D	707 274-0118	10380

NIPOMO, CA - San Luis Obispo County

	SIC	EMP	PHONE	ENTRY#
Jj Fisher Construction Inc	1611	D	805 723-5220	1124
Wicks Solar Inc	1761	D	805 546-9056	2092
Santa Maria Tire Inc (PA)	5531	D	805 347-4793	7356

NORCO, CA - Riverside County

	SIC	EMP	PHONE	ENTRY#
Cal-West Nurseries Inc	0782	C	951 270-0667	479
Cal West Underground Inc	1629	D	951 371-6775	1291
Jfp Painting	1721	D	951 736-6037	1626
Royal West Drywall Inc	1742	D	951 271-4600	1960
Jeffrey Court Inc	1743	D	951 340-3383	1984
Guy Yocom Construction Inc	1771	C	951 284-3456	2125
JIT Corporation	5065	D	805 238-5000	5666
Clima-Tech Inc	7623	D	909 613-5513	13725
Spearmint Rhino Cmpnies Wrldwi	8741	D	951 371-3788	20215
City of Norco	8748	D	951 270-5617	20728

NORDEN, CA - Nevada County

	SIC	EMP	PHONE	ENTRY#
Sugar Bowl Corporation	7011	D	530 426-9000	10280

NORTH HIGHLANDS, CA - Sacramento County

	SIC	EMP	PHONE	ENTRY#
MCM Construction Inc (PA)	1622	D	916 334-1221	1185
Capital City Drywall Inc	1742	D	916 331-9200	1917
Heritage Interests LLC (PA)	1751	D	916 481-5030	2001
Recycling Industries Inc	4953	D	916 452-3961	4931
Builders Firstsource Inc	5031	B	916 481-5030	5149
Heritage One Door Crpentry LLC	5031	D	916 481-5030	5165
Heritage One Win Bldg Sltons L	5031	C	916 481-5030	5166
Sacramento A-1 Door	5031	D	916 481-5030	5186
Security Contractor Svcs Inc (PA)	5039	D	916 338-4200	5232
Sierra Select Distributors Inc	5064	D	916 483-9295	5614
Homeq Servicing Corporation (DH)	6162	A	916 339-6192	7981
Child Abuse Prvntion Cncil SCR	8322	D	916 244-1900	17875
Lund Construction Co	8711	C	916 344-5800	19310
Construction Tstg & Engrg Inc	8734	B	916 331-6030	19959

NORTH HILLS, CA - Los Angeles County

	SIC	EMP	PHONE	ENTRY#
Living Colors Inc	1721	D	818 893-5068	1628
Moore Industries-International Inc (PA)	3823	C	818 894-7111	3018
Prn Ambulance LLC	4119	B	818 810-3600	3288
Walker & Zanger LLC (HQ)	5032	B	818 280-8300	5213
Battery Systems Inc	5063	D	818 474-1500	5541
Galpin Motors Inc (PA)	5511	D	818 787-3800	7218
Penny Lane Centers (PA)	8399	B	818 892-3423	18616

NORTH HOLLYWOOD, CA - Los Angeles County

	SIC	EMP	PHONE	ENTRY#
PCL Construction Services Inc	1542	D	818 509-7816	985
Circulating Air Inc (PA)	1711	D	818 764-0530	1397
Arriaga Usa Inc (PA)	1743	D	818 982-9559	1974
M Gaw Inc	1799	D	818 503-7997	2294
Woods Maintenance Services Inc	1799	C	818 764-2515	2335
Groundwork Coffee Roasters LLC	2095	C	818 506-6020	2427
Mtd Kitchen Inc	2431	D	818 764-2254	2478
West Publishing Corporation	2731	B	800 747-3161	2551
Ambulnz Health LLC	4119	B	877 311-5555	3227
Messenger Express (PA)	4215	C	213 614-0475	3621
Walt Disney Company	4833	D	818 560-4665	4470
Pilgrim Operations LLC	5043	D	818 478-4500	5240
Davis Wholesale Electric Inc	5063	D	818 392-2400	5553
Fastener Technology Corp	5085	C	818 764-6467	5902
Jessica Cosmetics Intl Inc	5122	D	818 759-1050	6117
Smart & Final Stores LLC	5141	D	818 982-6202	6336
Fluids Manufacturing Inc	5159	C	818 264-4657	6695
Century West LLC	5511	D	818 432-5800	7182
Ngp Motors Inc	5511	C	818 980-9800	7264
Rhi Inc (PA)	5511	D	818 508-3800	7288
Kaiser Foundation Hospitals	6324	C	818 503-7082	8331
Financial Group Inc	6411	D	818 308-8527	8566
Century National Properties (PA)	7011	D	818 760-0880	9691
Marcus Hotels Inc	7011	C	818 980-8000	10000
Park Management Group LLC	7011	A	404 350-9990	10105
Rio Vista Development Co Inc (PA)	7011	C	818 980-8000	10160
Pierce Brothers (DH)	7261	D	818 763-9121	10515
Cats USA Inc	7342	D	818 506-1000	10831
Diamond Contract Services Inc	7349	B	818 565-3554	10889
Core Bts Inc	7373	C	818 766-2400	12441
Stark Services	7374	D	818 985-2003	12631
Sada Systems Inc (PA)	7379	C	818 766-2400	12871
Babylon Security Services Inc	7381	D	818 766-8122	12937
Emergency Technologies Inc	7382	D	818 765-4421	13112
Pilgrim Studios Inc	7384	D	818 728-8800	13161
Samesky Health Inc	7389	D	855 735-6726	13457
Midway Rent A Car Inc	7515	D	818 985-9770	13597
Akh Company Inc	7539	D	818 691-1978	13680
Bento Box Entertainment LLC	7812	B	818 333-7700	13821
Endemol Shine North America	7812	D	747 529-8000	13846
Herzog & Company	7812	D	818 762-4640	13853
Pie Town Productions Inc	7812	C	818 255-9300	13877
Rodax Distributors	7812	D	818 765-6400	13887
Studio City	7812	D	818 557-7777	13899
Universal Studios Company LLC (DH)	7812	A	818 777-1000	13908
Aspect Ratio Inc (HQ)	7819	D	323 467-2121	13926
Chapmn/Lnard Stdio Eqp Cnada I (PA)	7819	C	323 877-5309	13929
Jackson Shrub Supply Inc	7819	D	818 982-0100	13940
Century Theatres Inc	7833	B	818 508-1943	14018
51 Minds Entertainment LLC	7929	D	818 643-8200	14075
IPC Healthcare Inc (DH)	8011	C	888 447-2362	14788
Valley Community Healthcare	8011	B	818 763-8836	15177
Coldwater Care Center LLC	8051	D	818 766-6105	15378
Valley Vsta Nrsing Trnstnal CA	8051	C	818 763-6275	15717
Golden Care Inc	8059	D	818 763-6275	15851
Hillsdale Group LP	8059	D	818 623-2170	15854
Tennessee Hospitalists Inc	8062	D	888 447-2362	16573
Dubnoff Ctr For Child Dev Edct (PA)	8211	D	818 755-4950	17709
Concorde Career Colleges Inc	8249	D	818 766-8151	17794

NORTH HOLLYWOOD CA

GEOGRAPHIC SECTION

	SIC	EMP	PHONE	ENTRY#
Volunteers of Amer Los Angeles	8322	C	818 769-3617	18180
Volunteers of Amer Los Angeles	8322	C	818 506-0597	18181
Cri-Help Inc (PA)	8361	D	818 985-8323	18413
Iatse Affl Prprty Crftsprson L	8631	C	818 769-2500	18780
Miller Kaplan Arase LLP (PA)	8721	C	818 769-2010	19612
Criterion Labs Inc	8734	D	818 506-8332	19962

NORTHRIDGE, CA - Los Angeles County

	SIC	EMP	PHONE	ENTRY#
Nexgen Air Los Angeles	1711	D	818 900-2525	1511
Quality Speaks LLC (PA)	4813	C	818 264-4400	4332
Southern California Gas Co	4924	B	818 363-8542	4728
Mikuni American Corporation (HQ)	5013	D	310 676-0522	5050
Rashman Corporation	5047	D	818 993-3030	5447
Harman-Kardon Incorporated	5064	B	818 841-4600	5606
Harman International Inds Inc	5065	A	818 893-8411	5654
Smart & Final Stores Inc	5141	B	818 368-6409	6297
Lowes Home Centers LLC	5211	D	818 477-9022	7090
San Fernando Valley Auto LLC	5511	C	818 832-1600	7294
Pinnacle Estate Properties (PA)	6531	C	818 993-4707	9133
Remax Olson & Associates Inc	6531	C	818 366-3300	9162
Northwest Excavating Inc	7353	D	818 349-5861	11004
Assisted Home Recovery Inc (PA)	7361	C	818 894-8117	11085
Ikano Communications Inc (PA)	7374	C	801 924-0900	12581
Contemporary Services Corp (PA)	7381	A	818 885-5150	12949
World Private Security Inc	7381	C	818 894-1800	13076
Ross Baker Towing Inc	7549	D	818 886-7411	13718
Musclebound Inc	7991	B	818 349-0123	14220
Porter Valley Country Club Inc	7997	C	818 360-1071	14424
Progressive Health Care System	8011	D	818 707-9603	14999
Institute For Applied Bhvior A	8049	D	818 341-1933	15289
Dignity Health	8062	A	818 885-8500	16047
Northridge Hosp Foundation Aux	8062	D	818 885-5341	16289
Valley Hospital Medical Center Foundation	8062	A	818 885-8500	16612
Tiffany Homecare Inc	8082	B	818 886-1602	16953
Child and Family Guidance Ctr (PA)	8093	C	818 739-5140	17025
Charles Rver Labs Cell Sltons (HQ)	8099	C	877 310-0717	17204
Village At Northridge	8361	C	818 514-4497	18541
Regal Medical Group Inc (PA)	8621	C	818 654-3400	18758
Automobile Club Southern Cal	8699	D	818 993-1616	19047
Lakeside Systems Inc	8741	A	866 654-3471	20136

NORWALK, CA - Los Angeles County

	SIC	EMP	PHONE	ENTRY#
Doty Bros Equipment Co (HQ)	1623	D	562 864-6566	1206
Cabinets 2000 LLC	2434	C	562 868-0909	2480
Cellco Partnership	4812	D	562 244-8814	4205
Cco Holdings LLC	4841	C	562 239-2761	4481
Joes Sweeping Inc	4953	D	562 929-4344	4901
Aquirecorps Norwalk Auto Auctn	5012	C	562 864-7464	5005
Di-Sep Systems Intl Inc (HQ)	5074	D	562 407-3432	5745
Koi Cbd LLC	5122	D	562 650-4673	6119
West Central Produce Inc	5148	B	213 629-3600	6596
Lowes Home Centers LLC	5211	D	562 926-0826	7045
Smart & Final Stores LLC	5399	D	562 868-0794	7141
Keystone Ford Inc (PA)	5511	C	562 868-0825	7248
Personnel Plus Inc	7363	C	562 712-5490	11315
County of Los Angeles	7374	D	562 462-2094	12560
Bally Total Fitness Corporation	7991	A	562 484-2000	14173
Life Care Centers America Inc	8051	D	562 921-6624	15542
Norwalk Meadows Nursing Ctr LP	8051	D	562 864-2541	15599
Coast Plz Dctors Hosp A Cal Lt (DH)	8062	D	562 868-3751	16006
Telecare Act 7	8093	D	562 929-6688	17142
County of Los Angeles	8322	D	562 807-7860	17905
Assoction Mxcan Amrcn Edcators	8621	D	562 868-0431	18731
Jwch Institute Inc	8733	C	562 281-0306	19892

NOVATO, CA - Marin County

	SIC	EMP	PHONE	ENTRY#
Comet Building Maintenance Inc	0781	D	415 382-1150	424
Thompson Builders Corporation	1522	C	415 456-8972	778
Fibres International Inc	4953	D	425 455-9811	4894
Redwood Landfill Inc	4953	C	415 892-2851	4932
CK Imports Inc	5021	D	915 225-5747	5083
2k Games Inc	5092	C		5984
Cellmark Inc (DH)	5099	D	415 927-1700	6034
Birkenstock Usa Lp	5139	C	415 884-3200	6229
Worldwise Inc (DH)	5199	D	415 721-7400	6957
Bank of Marin Bancorp (PA)	6022	C	415 763-4520	7655
Kaiser Foundation Hospitals	6324	C	415 899-7400	8318
Realmanage LLC	6531	D	415 444-1600	9154
Meritage Medical Network	7363	C	415 884-1840	11312
Visual Concepts Entertainment	7371	B	415 479-3634	12027
Drivesavers Inc	7375	D	415 382-2000	12659
Barbier Security Group	7381	C	415 747-8473	12938
Novato Fire Protection Dst	7389	D	415 878-2690	13401

	SIC	EMP	PHONE	ENTRY#
Marin Country Club Inc	7997	D	415 382-6700	14401
Marin Community Clinic	8011	D	415 448-1500	14886
Permanente Medical Group Inc	8011	A	415 899-7400	14958
Permanente Medical Group Inc	8011	B	415 209-2444	14980
Novato Healthcare Center LLC	8051	C	415 897-6161	15600
Sutter Health	8062	C	415 897-8495	16529
Sutter West Bay Hospitals	8062	C	415 492-4800	16562
Sutter West Bay Hospitals (HQ)	8062	B	415 209-1300	16563
Bear Flag Marketing Corp	8082	C	415 899-8466	16817
Buckelew Programs (PA)	8093	D	415 457-6964	17018
Brayton Purcell APC (PA)	8111	C	415 898-1555	17392
Marin Humane Society	8699	D	415 883-4621	19093
Buck Inst For RES On Aging (PA)	8733	C	415 209-2000	19868
Griffin Group LLC	8741	C	415 892-4569	20104
Advisorycloud Inc	8748	C	415 289-7115	20675

OAK HILLS, CA - San Bernardino County

	SIC	EMP	PHONE	ENTRY#
Double Eagle Trnsp Corp	4213	C	760 956-3770	3466

OAK PARK, CA - Ventura County

	SIC	EMP	PHONE	ENTRY#
Mason Group	1741	D	818 707-8989	1888
Family Ties Home Care LLC	5211	D	818 565-9147	6960

OAKDALE, CA - Stanislaus County

	SIC	EMP	PHONE	ENTRY#
Central Valley AG Trnspt LLC	0723	D	209 544-9246	261
Acosta and Sons Inc	1751	D	209 322-3181	1989
Pacific Gas and Electric Co	4911	D	800 743-5000	4647
Gilton Solid Waste MGT Inc	4953	C	209 527-3781	4897
A L Gilbert Company (PA)	5191	D	209 847-1721	6817
Teachers Pension & Insur Svcs	6411	D	800 474-1440	8669
Oak Valley Hospital District (PA)	8062	B	209 847-3011	16290

OAKHURST, CA - Madera County

	SIC	EMP	PHONE	ENTRY#
Sierra Telephone Company Inc	4813	C	559 683-4611	4338
San Jquin Vly Rhbltion Hosp A	8049	C	559 658-6490	15307
Oakhurst Sklled Nrsing Wllness	8051	D	559 683-2244	15601
Oakhurst Healthcare Center LLC	8052	D	559 683-2244	15778

OAKLAND, CA - Alameda County

	SIC	EMP	PHONE	ENTRY#
Lennar Mltfmily Cmmunities LLC	1531	B	415 975-4980	795
D-Line Constructors Inc	1541	D	510 251-6400	815
Visionary Nutrition LLC	1541	D	510 567-1200	855
Charles Pnkow Bldrs Ltd A Cal	1542	B	510 893-5170	893
Shimmick Nicholson Cnstr JV	1542	A	510 777-5000	1025
Webcor Construction LP	1542	C	510 748-7950	1056
Allied Fire Protection	1711	D	510 533-5516	1347
Broadway Mech - Contrs Inc	1711	C	510 746-4000	1386
Sunco Liquidation Inc	1711	C	510 496-5500	1574
George E Masker Inc	1721	D	510 568-1206	1619
Diligence Security Group	1731	C	510 710-5806	1721
Andrew M Jordan Inc	1794	D	510 999-6000	2212
Alarcon Bohm Corp	1795	D	510 893-4405	2228
Bayview Environmental Svcs Inc	1799	C	510 562-6181	2260
Edys Grand Ice Cream	2024	A	510 652-8187	2349
Peerless Coffee Company Inc	2095	C	510 763-1763	2428
Log(n) LLC	2741	D	323 839-4538	2556
Clorox Services Company (HQ)	2842	A	510 271-7000	2623
Brite Industries Inc	3999	D	510 250-9330	3105
Alameda-Contra Costa Trnst Dst (PA)	4111	C	510 891-4777	3122
First Transit Inc	4111	C	510 437-8990	3137
San Francisco Bay Area Rapid	4111	A	510 286-2893	3198
San Frncsco Bay Area Rpid Trns (PA)	4111	B	510 464-6000	3199
Alameda-Contra Costa Trnst Dst	4173	A	510 577-8816	3354
Sea-Logix Llc	4213	D	510 271-1400	3543
General Lgstics Systems US Inc	4215	D	800 322-5555	3613
United Parcel Service Inc	4215	A	510 813-5662	3641
Storagepro Inc	4225	D	510 900-5474	3758
Pasha Hawaii Trnspt Lines LLC	4424	D	510 271-1400	3799
Port Dept City of Oakland (PA)	4491	D	510 627-1100	3813
Federal Express Corporation	4513	C	800 463-3339	3853
Kaiserair Inc (PA)	4522	C	510 569-9622	3866
Port Dept City of Oakland	4581	D	510 563-3697	3905
Port Dept of The Cy Oakland	4581	D	510 563-3300	3906
Sunset Aviation LLC	4581	D	510 783-3584	3912
GSC Logistics Inc	4731	D	510 740-3151	4028
Progistics Distribution Inc	4731	A	415 369-8845	4081
Califrnia Dept Indus Relations	4789	D	510 286-7000	4145
Tks Wireless Inc	4812	C	510 227-6440	4237
Ask Media Group LLC	4813	D	212 524-8716	4254
K G O T V News Bureau	4832	D	510 451-4773	4387
Pandora Media LLC (DH)	4832	B	510 451-4100	4400
Ktvu Partnership Inc	4833	C	510 834-1212	4449
Cypress Communications Inc	4841	D	415 962-4500	4496

GEOGRAPHIC SECTION

OAKLAND CA

Company	SIC	EMP	PHONE	ENTRY#
Ohmconnect Inc.	4911	D	404 881-8659	4597
Pacific Gas and Electric Co (HQ)	4911	A	415 973-7000	4603
Pacific Gas and Electric Co.	4911	C	510 437-2222	4604
Pacific Gas and Electric Co.	4911	B	510 450-5744	4614
East Bay Mncpl Utility Dst Wtr (PA)	4941	A	866 403-2683	4787
Civicorps.	4953	C	510 992-7800	4879
East Bay Municipl Utility Distr.	4953	C	866 403-2683	4886
Waste MGT Alameda Cnty Inc (HQ)	4953	A	510 613-8710	4960
Portfolio Productions Inc.	5021	D	510 434-1600	5101
Mac Arthur Co.	5033	C	510 251-2102	5222
East Bay Restaurant Supply Inc (PA)	5046	C	510 465-4300	5377
Kaiser Foundation Hospitals.	5047	D	510 752-6808	5427
Brita Products Company.	5074	D	510 271-7000	5741
Cromer Inc.	5084	B	510 534-6566	5827
Cass Inc (PA)	5093	C	510 893-6476	6005
Fairn & Swanson Inc.	5122	C	510 533-8260	6107
Natures Products Inc (DH)	5122	C	954 233-3300	6134
Smart & Final Stores LLC.	5141	D	510 536-7494	6384
Dreyers Grnd Ice Cream Hldngs (DH)	5143	C	510 652-8187	6436
Creative Energy Foods Inc.	5149	D	510 638-8668	6622
Pasta Shop (PA).	5149	D	510 250-6005	6656
Horizon Beverage Company.	5182	D	800 332-8358	6800
Golden Gate Freightliner Inc (HQ)	5511	C	559 486-4310	7221
Bellevue Club.	5812	D	510 451-1000	7458
Food Specialists Inc.	5812	B	510 444-3456	7482
Goodwill Inds of Grter E Bay I (PA)	5932	C	510 698-7200	7537
Sequoyah Country Club.	5941	C	510 632-2900	7544
Mufg Americas Holdings Corp.	6021	B	212 782-5911	7633
Wells Fargo Bank National Assn.	6021	D	510 530-3095	7642
California Bancorp (PA)	6022	C	510 457-3737	7665
Porrey Pines Bank Inc.	6022	C	510 899-7500	7710
Renew Financial Corp II.	6162	C	610 433-7486	8015
Uscf Advisers LLC.	6282	B	510 522-9600	8227
Kapor Center For Social Impact.	6311	D	510 488-6600	8238
California Physicians Service (PA)	6324	A	510 607-2000	8286
Center For Elders Independence.	6324	C	510 433-1150	8291
Kaiser Foundation Hospitals.	6324	B	510 891-3400	8319
Permanente Kaiser Intl (HQ)	6324	B	510 271-5910	8352
Alameda Cnty Employees Rtrment.	6411	D	510 628-3000	8482
Dealey Renton and Associates.	6411	D	510 465-3090	8542
Keenan & Associates.	6411	D	510 986-6750	8600
Medical Underwriters Cal Inc (PA)	6411	D	510 428-9411	8610
Sedgwick Claims MGT Svcs Inc.	6411	D	510 302-3000	8653
Workers Cmpnstion Insur Rting (PA)	6411	C	888 229-2472	8695
Health Care Workers Union (PA)	6512	D	510 251-1250	8724
Christian Church Homes.	6513	D	510 420-8802	8800
East Bay Asian Local Dev Corp.	6513	C	510 267-1917	8804
Humangood Norcal.	6513	D	510 654-7172	8820
Dreisbach Enterprises Inc.	6519	D	510 533-6600	8883
Cushman & Wakefield Cal Inc.	6531	A	510 763-4900	8962
Lapham Company Inc.	6531	D	510 531-6000	9070
Lion Creek Senior Housing Part.	6531	D	510 878-9120	9074
Waypoint Real Estate Group LLC.	6531	D	510 250-2200	9209
Wells & Bennett Inc (PA)	6531	D	510 531-7000	9210
Oakland Promise.	6732	D	510 836-8900	9416
Oakland Public Education Fund.	6732	D	510 221-6968	9417
Carpenter Fnds Admnstrtive Off.	6733	D	510 633-0333	9423
Cim/Oakland City Center LLC.	7011	D	510 451-4000	9702
Homewood Suites Management LLC.	7011	D	510 663-2700	9866
La Quinta Inn.	7011	D	510 632-8900	9962
Oakland Renaissance Associates.	7011	B	510 451-4000	10054
Park Hotels & Resorts Inc.	7011	C	510 635-5000	10102
Tm Sleeves LLC.	7311	C	415 374-8210	10681
99designs Inc (PA)	7336	C	415 539-1088	10797
Officeworks Inc.	7361	D	510 444-2161	11190
Catamorphic Co (PA)	7371	C	415 579-3275	11486
Monkeybrains.	7371	D	415 974-1313	11757
Visual Supply Company (PA)	7371	D	847 721-9285	12028
Deem Inc (DH)	7372	D	415 590-8300	12160
Fivetran Inc (PA)	7372	A	415 805-2799	12192
Higher One Payments Inc.	7372	B	510 769-9888	12222
Interactive Solutions Inc (DH)	7372	D	510 214-9002	12236
Investopedia LLC.	7372	C	510 985-7400	12243
Marqeta Inc (PA)	7372	B	888 462-7738	12261
Navis LP (PA)	7372	C	510 267-5000	12280
Paylocity Holding Corporation.	7372	A	847 956-4850	12316
Lucid Design Group Inc.	7373	D	510 907-0400	12482
IAC Search & Media Inc (HQ)	7375	D	510 985-7400	12666
Jiff Inc.	7375	C	510 844-4139	12670
ABC Security Service Inc.	7381	C	510 436-0666	12916
Highcom Security Services.	7381	D	510 893-7600	12987
Professnl Tchncal SEC Svcs In.	7381	B	510 645-9200	13025
Star Protection Agency LLC.	7381	D	510 635-1732	13053
3vr Security Inc.	7382	D	415 513-4577	13082
Credit Karma LLC (HQ)	7389	C	415 510-5059	13252
Even Responsible Finance Inc.	7389	D	360 977-2475	13282
Multivision Inc (DH)	7389	D	510 740-5600	13386
New Schools Venture Fund.	7389	D	415 615-6860	13394
Telecom Inc.	7389	D	510 873-8283	13507
TMC Financing.	7389	D	415 989-8855	13511
United Textile Inc.	7389	D	510 276-2288	13525
Fox Rent A Car Inc.	7514	D	408 210-2208	13590
Pacific Park Management Inc.	7521	D	510 836-7730	13614
Vumedi Inc (PA)	7812	D	650 450-2603	13911
Paramount Theatre of Arts Inc.	7922	D	510 893-2300	14053
Athletics Investment Group LLC (PA)	7941	C	510 638-4900	14127
City of Oakland.	7992	D	510 351-5812	14251
Claremont Country Club.	7997	D	510 653-6789	14359
East Bay Regional Park District (PA)	7999	C	888 327-2757	14515
Asian Health Services (PA)	8011	C	510 986-6800	14618
Brown Tland Physcn Svcs Orgnzt (DH)	8011	C	415 972-4162	14641
EBSC LP.	8011	D	510 547-2244	14731
Fred Finch Youth Center (PA)	8011	C	510 773-6669	14753
Kaiser Foundation Hospitals.	8011	A	510 752-1000	14802
Kaiser Foundation Hospitals.	8011	A	510 752-1000	14816
Kaiser Foundation Hospitals.	8011	A	510 987-1000	14849
Kaiser Fundation Hlth Plan Inc (PA)	8011	B	510 271-5800	14855
La Clinica De La Raza Inc.	8011	C	510 535-6300	14864
La Clinica De La Raza Inc.	8011	B	510 535-4110	14866
La Clinica De La Raza Inc.	8011	D	510 535-4700	14867
La Clinica De La Raza Inc.	8011	C	510 535-6200	14868
Medical Insurance Exchange Cal.	8011	D	510 596-4935	14892
Native American Health Ctr Inc (PA)	8011	D	510 535-4400	14915
Permanente Medical Group Inc.	8011	A	510 625-6262	14961
Permanente Medical Group Inc.	8011	B	510 752-1000	14968
Permanente Medical Group Inc.	8011	A	510 752-1190	14970
Pine Park Health Inc.	8011	D	925 594-3533	14994
Oakland Healthcare & Wellness.	8051	C	323 330-6572	15602
Ocadian Care Centers LLC.	8051	A	510 832-3222	15606
Wild Karma Inc.	8051	B	510 639-9088	15735
Oaklandidence Opco LLC.	8052	D	510 832-3222	15779
Califrnia-Nevada Methdst Homes.	8059	C	510 835-5511	15827
SSC Oakland Fruitvale Oper LP.	8059	D	510 261-5613	15898
Carbon Health Technologies Inc.	8062	C	510 844-4097	15966
Childrens Hosp Okland Res Inst.	8062	D	510 450-7600	15993
Childrens Hosp RES Ctr At Okla (PA)	8062	A	510 428-3000	15994
Kaiser Foundation Hospitals (HQ)	8062	C	510 271-6611	16160
Kaiser Foundation Hospitals.	8062	A	510 752-1000	16162
Kaiser Foundation Hospitals.	8062	D	510 752-1000	16181
Kaiser Foundation Hospitals.	8062	D	510 434-5835	16187
Providence Health & Svcs - Ore.	8062	B	510 444-0839	16346
Summit Medical Center.	8062	C	510 869-6758	16501
Summit Medical Center (DH)	8062	A	510 655-4000	16502
Summit Medical Group.	8062	C	510 655-4000	16503
Sutter Bay Hospitals.	8062	C	510 655-4000	16510
Sutter Health.	8062	D	510 547-2244	16531
Sutter Health.	8062	D	510 869-8777	16532
Unilab Corporation.	8071	A	510 444-5213	16758
County of Alameda.	8082	D	510 437-4190	16849
Kids Overcoming LLC.	8082	D	415 748-8052	16883
Asian Community Mental Hlth Bd.	8093	D	510 869-6003	17006
Ed Supports LLC.	8093	D	201 478-8711	17060
Lincoln (PA).	8093	D	510 273-4700	17086
Westcoast Childrens Clinic.	8093	C	510 269-9030	17161
Kaiser Permanente.	8099	D	510 752-6198	17262
La Clinica De La Raza Inc.	8099	B	510 535-3500	17266
La Clinica De La Raza Inc.	8099	C	510 535-4130	17267
Permanente Medical Group Inc (DH)	8099	B	866 858-2226	17296
Burnham Brown A Prof Corp.	8111	C	510 444-6800	17395
Donahue Gallager Woods LLP (PA)	8111	D	415 381-4161	17440
Everlaw Inc (PA)	8111	B	844 383-7529	17451
Fennemore Craig PC.	8111	C	510 834-6600	17454
Gordon Rees Scully Mansukhani.	8111	C	510 463-8600	17476
Kazan McClain Sttrley Grnwood.	8111	C	877 995-6372	17514
Meyers Nave A Prof Corp (DH)	8111	D	510 351-4300	17567
Alameda Cnty Cmnty Fd Bnk Inc.	8322	D	510 635-3663	17825
American National Red Cross.	8322	C	510 594-5100	17830
Bay Area Community Svcs Inc.	8322	D	510 601-1074	17846
Bonita House Inc.	8322	D	510 923-0180	17853
Catholic Chrties of The Dcese (PA)	8322	D	510 768-3100	17866
City of Oakland.	8322	D	510 238-6796	17888
Crucible.	8322	D	510 444-0919	17946
District Council DC (PA)	8322	D	510 638-7600	17955
East Bay Asian Youth Center.	8322	D	510 533-1092	17960
Family Bridges Inc.	8322	D	510 839-2270	17976
Seneca Family of Agencies.	8322	C	510 317-1444	18125

Employee Codes: A=Over 500 employees, B=251-500
C=101-250, D=51-100, E=20-50, F=10-19, G=1-9

2024 Directory of California
WholeSalers and Service Companies

© Mergent Inc. 1-800-342-5647
1457

OAKLAND CA

	SIC	EMP	PHONE	ENTRY#
Seneca Family of Agencies	8322	C	510 434-7990	18127
Volunteers Amer Nthrn Cal Nthrn	8322	D	510 419-0360	18185
Jewish Vctnal Creer Cnsling Sv	8331	D	415 391-3600	18232
East Bay Agency For Children	8351	D	510 655-4896	18311
Front Porch Communities & Svcs	8361	C	510 835-4700	18435
Humangood Norcal	8361	D	510 893-8897	18454
Mercy Retirement and Care Ctr	8361	D	510 534-8540	18485
Alameda Health System (PA)	8399	D	510 437-4800	18552
Alegria Community Living	8399	C	510 287-8488	18553
Habitat For Hmnity E By/Slcon (PA)	8399	D	866 450-4432	18590
Spanish Spking Unity Cncil Alm	8399	C	510 836-0543	18626
Oakland Museum of California	8412	D	510 318-8400	18663
Conservation Society Cal	8422	C	510 632-9525	18687
California Nurses Association (PA)	8621	D	510 273-2200	18739
Northern Cal Crpnters Rgnal CN	8631	D	510 568-4788	18788
Seiu United Healthcare Workers (PA)	8631	C	510 251-1250	18793
Sierra Club (PA)	8641	C	415 977-5500	18908
Young Mens Christian Association of	8641	A	510 451-8039	18954
Young MNS Chrstn Assn of E Bay	8641	B	510 654-9622	18963
Young MNS Chrstn Assn of E Bay	8641	A	510 451-8039	18967
Young MNS Chrstn Assn of E Bay	8641	B	510 534-7441	18981
Asylum Access	8699	D	510 891-8700	19037
Dream Corps	8699	D	510 663-6500	19081
Society of St Vncent De Paul A (PA)	8699	D	510 638-7600	19105
Aecom-TSE Joint Venture	8711	D	510 285-6639	19130
Amec Geomatrix Inc	8711	B	510 663-4100	19138
B&C Transit Inc (HQ)	8711	D	510 483-3560	19150
Cygna Group Inc	8711	C	510 419-5000	19193
Hntb Corporation	8711	C	510 208-4599	19257
URS Group Inc	8711	A	510 893-3600	19425
URS Group Inc	8711	D	925 446-3800	19426
Carter & Burgess Inc	8712	D	510 457-0027	19459
Stv Incorporated	8712	B	510 763-1313	19513
Mathematica Inc	8732	D	510 830-3700	19832
Behavior Change Institute LLC	8733	D	866 273-2451	19865
Impaq International LLC	8733	D	510 597-2400	19886
Public Health Institute (PA)	8733	D	510 285-5500	19905
Transfair USA	8733	C	510 663-5260	19922
Wested	8733	D	510 302-4200	19935
Xq Institute	8733	D	844 825-5297	19940
Brightsource Construction Management Inc	8741	B	510 550-8161	20046
Jt2 Integrated Resources (PA)	8741	D	925 556-7012	20129
Lake Mrritt Healthcare Ctr LLC	8741	D	510 227-1806	20135
Altais Clinical Services (HQ)	8742	D	510 607-4000	20268
College Track	8742	C	510 834-3295	20324
Hapag-Lloyd (america) LLC	8742	C	510 286-1940	20399
Jetty Marketing LLC	8742	D	310 867-9911	20421
Marketing Practice Inc	8742	D	415 793-8370	20452
Mesmerize LLC	8742	C	415 374-8298	20466
Permanente Federation LLC	8742	C	510 625-6920	20504
Roofstock Inc (PA)	8742	C	510 269-9400	20533
Cohen Ventures Inc (PA)	8748	D	510 482-4420	20731
Kadiant LLC	8748	C	209 521-4791	20788
O C Jones & Sons Inc	8748	D	510 663-6911	20818

OAKLEY, CA - Contra Costa County

	SIC	EMP	PHONE	ENTRY#
Foundation Constructors Inc (PA)	1629	D	925 754-6633	1301
Oakley Union School District	8641	D	925 625-5060	18886

OCCIDENTAL, CA - Sonoma County

	SIC	EMP	PHONE	ENTRY#
Alliance Rdwods Cnfrnce Grunds	7032	C	707 874-3507	10398

OCEANSIDE, CA - San Diego County

	SIC	EMP	PHONE	ENTRY#
Rancho Del Oro Ldscp Maint Inc	0781	D	760 726-0215	459
Primeco	1721	D	760 967-8278	1633
Nwec Nevada Inc	1731	D	760 757-0187	1791
Future Energy Corporation	1742	D	760 477-9700	1931
Regan Roofing Inc	1761	D	855 652-4050	2081
Royal Westlake Roofing LLC	1761	C	760 967-0827	2083
Fencecorp Inc	1799	D	760 721-2101	2275
Steico Industries Inc	3469	C	760 438-8015	2755
Mv Transportation Inc	4111	C	760 400-0300	3175
North County Transit District (PA)	4111	D	760 966-6500	3183
Sprint Communications Co LP	4812	C	760 941-4535	4230
Waste Management Cal Inc	4953	C	760 439-2824	4954
Panoramic Doors LLC	5031	C	760 722-1300	5180
Westlake Royal Stone LLC	5032	A	770 645-4539	5216
United States Marine Corps	5088	D	760 725-3564	5970
Brixton	5136	D	866 264-4245	6168
Smart & Final Stores LLC	5141	D	760 439-3489	6326
Markstein Beverage Co	5181	C	760 744-9100	6773
Mellano & Co	5193	C	760 433-9550	6864
Pardee Tree Nursery	5193	D	760 630-5400	6871
Lowes Home Centers LLC	5211	C	760 966-7140	7060
Southern Cal Disc Tire Co Inc	5531	C	760 439-8539	7368
Frontwave Credit Union (PA)	6061	C	760 430-7511	7774
Monterey Financial Svcs Inc (PA)	6141	C	760 639-3500	7879
Sentry Life Insurance Company	6411	C	661 274-4018	8659
Oceans Eleven Casino	7011	B	760 439-6988	10058
Mission Linen Supply	7213	C	760 757-9099	10441
Bergensons Property Svcs Inc	7349	A	760 631-5111	10860
Vnh Enterprises Inc	7349	D	877 468-3566	10986
Go-Staff Inc	7361	A	760 730-8520	11144
Supreme Security Services Inc	7381	D	760 415-7399	13054
North Cast Srgery Ctr Ltd A CA	8011	D	760 940-0997	14921
North County Health Prj Inc	8011	D	760 757-4566	14925
Marine Corps Community Svcs	8021	C	760 725-5187	15239
Tri-City Hospital District (PA)	8062	A	760 724-8411	16581
Marine Corps United States	8069	A	760 725-1304	16687
Marine Corps Community Svcs	8351	C	760 725-2817	18330
Aegis Asssted Living Prpts LLC	8361	C	760 806-3600	18369
E R I T Inc (PA)	8361	D	760 433-6024	18419
S L Start and Associates LLC	8361	D	760 414-9411	18517
Villas De Crlsbad Ltd A Cal Lt	8361	D	760 434-7116	18542
YMCA of San Diego County	8641	D	760 721-8930	18952
Automobile Club Southern Cal	8699	D	760 433-6261	19049
Goodwill Inds San Diego Cnty	8699	D	760 806-7670	19085
Hetherington Engineering (PA)	8711	C	760 931-1917	19249
Infrastructure Engrg Corp	8711	D	760 529-0795	19267
Nitto Denko Technical Corp	8732	D	760 435-7011	19837
Primary Care Assod Med Group I	8741	C	760 724-1033	20179
Pristine Environments Inc (PA)	8744	D	703 245-4751	20661
Veridiam Allied Swiss	8748	D	760 941-1702	20872

OJAI, CA - Ventura County

	SIC	EMP	PHONE	ENTRY#
Troop Real Estate Inc	6531	C	805 640-1440	9203
Ovis LLC	7011	A	805 646-5511	10074
Ojai Vly Fmly Medicine Group	8011	D	805 646-7246	14932
Ojai Healthidence Opco LLC	8052	C	805 646-8124	15780
Community Memorial Health Sys	8062	C	805 646-1401	16017
Help Unlmted Personnel Svc Inc	8082	A	805 962-4646	16869
Mother of Divine Grace Inc	8211	D	805 646-5818	17731
Ojai Valley School (PA)	8211	D	805 646-1423	17737
Rockblue	8621	D	703 314-0208	18759
Financial Group Inc	8741	D	805 646-7974	20086

OLIVEHURST, CA - Yuba County

	SIC	EMP	PHONE	ENTRY#
Rodgz Farm Labor Contg LLC	0761	D	530 329-8403	369
Nordic Industries Inc	1629	D	530 742-7124	1312
Shoei Foods (usa) Inc	5141	D	530 742-7866	6285

OLYMPIC VALLEY, CA - Placer County

	SIC	EMP	PHONE	ENTRY#
Cncml A California Ltd Partnr	7011	D	530 583-1578	9709
Lowe Enterprises	7011	D	530 581-6628	9987
Squaw Valley Ski Holdings LLC	7011	B	800 403-0206	10265

ONTARIO, CA - San Bernardino County

	SIC	EMP	PHONE	ENTRY#
K A R Construction Inc	1521	D	909 988-5054	688
Nhs Western Division Inc	1521	D	909 947-9931	704
Fullmer Construction	1541	D	909 947-9467	819
Bomel Construction Co Inc	1542	D	909 923-3319	876
Neff Construction Inc	1542	D	909 947-3768	974
CA Station Management Inc	1623	C	909 245-6251	1200
Integrated Energy Group LLC	1711	D	605 381-7859	1468
Vertex Coatings Inc	1721	D	909 923-5795	1644
Communication Tech Svcs LLC	1731	B	508 382-2700	1704
Gregg Electric Inc	1731	C	909 983-1794	1739
HHS Communications Inc	1731	D	909 230-5170	1747
Jeeva Corporation	1731	D	909 238-4073	1758
Emser Tile LLC	1743	D	909 974-1600	1981
Martinez Steel Corporation	1791	C	909 946-0686	2188
Rynoclad Technologies Inc	1793	C	951 264-3441	2205
Ajinomoto Foods North Amer Inc	2038	C	909 477-4700	2356
Specialty Brands Incorporated	2038	A	909 477-4851	2358
Jomar Table Linens Inc	2392	D	909 390-1444	2470
Pacific Urethanes LLC	2392	D	909 390-8400	2471
Aio Acquisition Inc (HQ)	2741	D	800 333-3795	2552
Kik Pool Additives Inc	2899	C	909 390-9912	2644
Classic Containers Inc	3085	B	909 930-3610	2663
Star Shield Solutions LLC	3089	D	866 662-4477	2680
Larry Mthvin Installations Inc (HQ)	3231	C	909 563-1700	2694
Western States Wholesale Inc (PA)	3271	D	909 947-0028	2700
Southwest Concrete Products	3272	C	909 983-9789	2708
Tracy Industries Inc	3519	C	562 692-9034	2768
Horizon Hobby LLC	3944	D	909 390-9595	3090
A-1 Delivery Co	4212	D	909 444-1220	3362

GEOGRAPHIC SECTION

ORANGE CA

	SIC	EMP	PHONE	ENTRY#
C P S Express	4212	C	951 685-1041	3375
Valley Couriers Inc	4212	D	909 605-2999	3433
CRST Expedited Inc	4213	B	909 563-5606	3460
Jack Jones Trucking Inc	4213	D	909 456-2500	3497
Landstar Global Logistics Inc	4213	D	909 266-0096	3503
Las Vegas / LA Express Inc (PA)	4213	D	909 972-3100	3504
Ltl Pros Inc	4213	D	909 350-1600	3508
United Parcel Service Inc	4215	A	909 974-7212	3636
Americold Logistics LLC	4222	C	909 937-2200	3651
Americold Logistics LLC	4222	D	909 390-4950	3652
Chino-Pacific Warehouse Corp (PA)	4225	D	909 545-8100	3685
Coastal Pacific Fd Distrs Inc	4225	D	909 947-2066	3688
Distribution Alternatives Inc	4225	D	909 673-1000	3697
Neovia Logistics Dist LP	4225	C	909 657-4900	3737
Nordstrom Inc	4225	B	909 390-1040	3738
Osram Sylvania Inc	4225	C	909 923-3003	3742
Quill LLC	4225	C	909 390-0600	3747
Takane USA Inc	4225	C	909 923-5511	3760
Target Corporation	4225	D	909 937-5500	3762
Taylored Fmi LLC	4225	D	909 510-4800	3765
Taylored Services LLC (DH)	4225	D	909 510-4800	3766
Taylored Services Holdings LLC (DH)	4225	D	909 510-4800	3767
Wti Distribution Inc	4225	D	909 597-8410	3787
United Parcel Service Inc	4512	C	909 605-7740	3851
Menzies Aviation (texas) Inc	4581	D	909 937-3998	3900
DSV Solutions LLC	4731	C	909 390-4563	4011
F R T International Inc	4731	D	909 390-4892	4019
Innovel Solutions Inc	4731	A	909 605-1446	4040
Taylored Svcs Parent Co Inc (PA)	4731	D	909 510-4800	4105
Xpo Logistics Supply Chain Inc	4731	D	909 390-9799	4120
Prime Transport Inc	4789	D	909 972-1300	4172
Taylored Transload LLC	4789	D	909 510-4800	4175
Comcast Corporation	4841	D	909 890-0886	4493
Main Street Fibers Inc	4953	D	909 986-6310	4906
Blumenthal Distributing Inc (PA)	5021	C	909 930-2000	5080
Office Master Inc	5021	D	909 392-5678	5096
Premiere Rack Solutions Inc	5021	D	909 605-6300	5103
National Flooring Products Inc	5023	D	877 238-3225	5126
Norcal Pottery Products Inc	5023	C	909 390-3745	5128
Test-Rite Products Corp (DH)	5023	D	909 605-9899	5137
Oregon PCF Bldg Pdts Maple Inc	5031	C	909 627-4043	5179
Brainstorm Corporation	5045	C	888 370-8882	5282
Pacific Rebar Inc	5051	D	909 984-7199	5505
Wieland Metal Services LLC	5051	D	562 968-2100	5531
R & B Wholesale Distrs Inc (PA)	5064	C	909 230-5400	5612
Maury Microwave Inc (PA)	5065	C	909 987-4715	5674
Heat Transfer Pdts Group LLC	5075	C	909 786-3669	5769
Replanet LLC	5084	A	951 520-1700	5866
Solar Link International Inc	5085	C	909 605-7789	5926
Waxies Enterprises LLC	5087	D	909 942-3100	5951
Jcm Engineering Corp	5088	D	909 923-3730	5959
Rosen Electronics Inc	5099	D	951 898-9808	6051
Beauty 21 Cosmetics Inc	5122	C	909 945-2220	6097
McKesson Mdcl-Srgcal Mdmart In	5122	D	800 755-2090	6128
Concord Foods Inc (HQ)	5141	D	909 975-2000	6247
Dpi Specialty Foods West Inc (DH)	5141	C	909 975-1019	6251
Dpi Specialty Foods West Inc	5141	C	909 975-1019	6252
NAFTA Distributors	5141	D	800 956-2382	6270
Vitco Distributors Inc	5141	C	909 355-1300	6413
Fruit Growers Supply Company	5148	D	909 390-0190	6549
Aspire Bakeries LLC	5149	C	909 472-3500	6605
Mondelez Global LLC	5149	D	909 605-0140	6648
Proactive Packg & Display LLC	5199	D	909 390-5624	6939
Lowes Home Centers LLC	5211	C	909 969-9053	7095
Citrus Motors Ontario Inc (PA)	5511	C	909 390-0930	7184
Jeep Chrysler of Ontario	5511	D	909 390-9898	7240
Ontario Automotive LLC	5511	C	909 974-3800	7272
Ramona Auto Services Inc	5531	D	909 986-1785	7355
McLane Foodservice Dist Inc	5963	D	252 955-9547	7565
American Business Bank	6022	D	909 919-2040	7651
Citizens Business Bank (HQ)	6022	C	909 980-4030	7674
Cvb Financial Corp (PA)	6022	C	909 980-4030	7677
First Mortgage Corporation	6162	B	909 595-1996	7964
Pope Mortgage & Associates Inc	6163	D	909 466-5380	8052
Merrill Lynch Prce Fnner Smith	6211	D	909 476-5100	8115
Adminsure Inc	6411	C	909 718-1200	8478
Robert Moreno Insurance Svcs	6411	C	714 578-3318	8649
Sedgwick CMS Holdings Inc	6411	B	909 477-5500	8655
Wells Frgo Insur Svcs Minn Inc	6411	D	909 481-3802	8684
Mills Corporation	6512	D	909 484-8300	8735
Cushman & Wakefield Cal Inc	6531	D	909 483-0077	8965
Cushman & Wakefield Cal Inc	6531	B	909 980-3781	8966
RAD Diversified Reit Inc	6531	D	813 723-7348	9149

	SIC	EMP	PHONE	ENTRY#
Dt Ontrio Ht Prtners Lssee LLC	7011	D	909 937-0900	9766
Prime Hospitality LLC	7011	D	909 975-5000	10128
SS Heritage Inn Ontario LLC	7011	D	909 937-5000	10266
Unifirst Corporation	7218	C	909 390-8670	10482
Wurms Janitorial Service Inc	7349	D	951 582-0003	10988
Diversity Bus Solutions Inc	7361	C	909 395-0243	11125
Kimco Staffing Services Inc	7361	A	909 390-9881	11163
Redlands Employment Services	7361	B	951 688-0083	11220
Care Stffing Professionals Inc	7363	D	909 906-2060	11278
CU Direct Corporation (PA)	7371	C	833 908-0121	11525
Guard-Systems Inc	7381	C	909 947-5400	12982
Pacwest Security Services	7381	C	909 948-0279	13016
Signal 88 LLC	7381	A	714 713-5306	13045
Arvato USA LLC	7389	C	502 356-8063	13197
Merchant of Tennis Inc	7389	A	909 923-3388	13370
Ontario Convention Center Corp	7389	B	909 937-3000	13407
Alamo Rental (us) Inc	7514	D	888 826-6893	13575
Fox Rent A Car Inc	7514	D	909 635-6390	13589
Automotive Tstg & Dev Svcs Inc (PA)	7549	C	909 390-1100	13710
Whiting Door Mfg Corp	7699	D	909 877-0120	13811
Vantiva Sup Chain Slutions Inc	7819	C	909 974-2016	13957
Toyota Arena	7999	D	909 244-5500	14577
Kaiser Foundation Hospitals	8011	C	909 724-5000	14814
M & M Noori Dental Corp	8021	D	909 476-3000	15237
Inland Chrstn HM Fundation Inc	8051	C	909 395-9322	15523
Ontarioidence Opco LLC	8052	B	909 984-8629	15781
Bio-Med Services Inc	8062	C	909 235-4400	15962
Prime Halthcare Foundation Inc (PA)	8062	C	909 235-4400	16332
Prime Hlthcare Svcs - Pmpa LLC (DH)	8062	C	909 235-4400	16340
Prime Hlthcare Svcs - St John (DH)	8062	B	913 680-6400	16344
Proform Inc	8071	C	707 752-9010	16744
Accentcare Home Hlth Yuma Inc	8082	B	909 605-7000	16789
Texas Home Health America LP (PA)	8082	D	972 201-3800	16945
Grace Yokley Middle School	8211	D	909 947-6774	17713
In-Roads Creative Programs	8322	B	909 947-9142	18013
West End Yung MNS Chrstn Assn	8641	C	909 477-2780	18929
Hntb Corporation	8711	D	909 727-5600	19254
HMC Group (HQ)	8712	C	909 989-9979	19477
Physician Support Systems Inc (DH)	8721	D	717 653-5340	19621
North American Med MGT Cal Inc (DH)	8741	D	909 605-8000	20163
Aveta Health Solution Inc	8742	B	909 605-8000	20285

ORANGE, CA - Orange County

	SIC	EMP	PHONE	ENTRY#
Marina Landscape Inc	0782	B	714 939-6600	518
Leonard Chaidez Inc	0783	D	714 279-8173	556
Ggg Demolition Inc (PA)	1542	D	714 699-9350	921
McCarthy Bldg Companies Inc	1542	D	949 851-8383	965
PR Construction Inc	1542	D	714 637-7848	995
Tiller Constructors Partnr Inc	1542	D	714 771-5600	1043
Rick Hamm Construction Inc	1611	D	714 532-0815	1155
RJ Noble Company (PA)	1611	C	714 637-1550	1157
American Contractors Inc	1711	D	714 282-5700	1353
Bernel Inc	1711	D	714 778-6070	1376
General Underground	1711	D	714 632-8646	1450
K & S Air Conditioning Inc	1711	C	714 685-0077	1475
Cal/Pac Pntngs Ctngs Acqstion	1721	D	714 628-1514	1607
General Coatings Corporation	1721	D	858 587-1277	1616
Sanders & Wohrman Corporation	1721	D	714 919-0446	1640
Interior Electric Incorporated	1731	D	714 771-9098	1756
Alan Smith Pool Plastering Inc	1742	D	714 628-9494	1899
Calderon Drywall Contrs Inc	1742	D	714 696-2977	1915
John Jory Corporation (PA)	1742	B	714 279-7901	1939
Padilla Construction Company	1742	C	714 685-8500	1954
Cmf Inc	1761	D	714 637-2409	2052
Danny Letner Inc	1761	C	714 633-0030	2056
Red Pointe Roofing LP (PA)	1761	C	714 685-0010	2080
Jezowski & Markel Contrs Inc	1771	C	714 978-2222	2129
Santa Ana Creek Development Company	1771	C	714 685-3462	2155
Bapko Metal Inc	1791	D	714 639-9380	2180
Rika Corporation	1791	D	949 830-9050	2198
Miller Environmental Inc	1795	D	714 385-0099	2240
West Coast Firestopping Inc	1799	D	714 935-1104	2333
American Bottling Company	2086	C	714 974-8560	2401
Continuous Coating Corp (PA)	3471	D	714 637-4642	2759
Shaxon Industries Inc	3572	C	714 779-1140	2819
Zettler Components Inc (PA)	3669	C	949 831-5000	2904
Orange Cnty Trnsp Auth Schlrsh (PA)	4111	B	714 636-7433	3187
Orange Cnty Trnsp Auth Schlrsh	4111	A	714 999-1726	3188
Lifestar Response of Alabama	4119	D	800 449-4911	3273
Xpo Logistics Freight Inc	4213	D	714 282-7717	3570
Cruz Modular Inc (PA)	4214	D	714 283-2890	3584
Sfpp LP (DH)	4613	C	714 560-4400	3923
Cellco Partnership	4812	D	714 564-0050	4190

Employee Codes: A=Over 500 employees, B=251-500
C=101-250, D=51-100, E=20-50, F=10-19, G=1-9

2024 Directory of California
WholeSalers and Service Companies

© Mergent Inc. 1-800-342-5647

1459

ORANGE CA

	SIC	EMP	PHONE	ENTRY#
Cellco Partnership	4812	D	951 205-4170	4198
Cco Holdings LLC	4841	C	714 509-5861	4491
Southern California Edison Co	4911	D	714 283-8568	4709
SA Recycling LLC (PA)	4953	C	714 632-2000	4933
Custom Comfort Mattress Co Inc (PA)	5021	C	714 693-6161	5087
States Drawer Box Spc LLC	5031	D	714 744-4247	5189
M S International Inc (PA)	5032	B	714 685-7500	5207
Western Pacific Distrg LLC	5032	C	714 974-6837	5215
Beacon Pacific Inc	5033	C	714 288-1974	5219
County Whl Elc Co Los Angeles	5063	D	714 633-3801	5550
Intellipower Inc	5065	C	714 921-1580	5664
Lonestar Sierra LLC	5085	C	866 575-5680	5907
Frick Paper Company LLC	5113	C	714 787-4900	6077
Cencora Inc	5122	C	610 727-7000	6101
Smart & Final Stores LLC	5141	C	714 771-1470	6350
Bluetriton Brands Inc	5149	C	714 532-6220	6610
Southern Counties Oil Co (DH)	5171	C	714 744-7140	6719
Great Atlantic News LLC	5192	C	770 863-9000	6842
Home Depot USA Inc	5211	C	714 538-9600	7012
Selman Chevrolet Company	5511	C	714 633-3521	7297
Toyota of Orange Inc	5511	C	714 639-6750	7316
Villa Ford Inc	5511	C	714 637-8222	7323
Fahetas LLC	5812	D	949 280-1983	7479
Beverages & More Inc	5921	C	714 279-8131	7531
Cashcall Inc	6141	A	949 752-4600	7871
Alignment Health Plan	6324	D	323 728-7232	8277
Alignment Healthcare Inc (PA)	6324	C	844 310-2247	8278
Choic Admini Insur Servi	6411	B	714 542-4200	8526
Conexis Bnfits Admnstrators LP (HQ)	6411	C	714 835-5006	8531
Mony Life Insurance Company	6411	D	714 939-6669	8615
Word & Brown Insurance Administrato (PA)	6411	B	714 835-5006	8694
Solari Enterprises Inc	6512	C	714 282-2520	8763
Irvine APT Communities LP	6513	C	714 937-8900	8829
Kisco Senior Living LLC	6513	C	714 997-5355	8839
Absolutely Zero Corporation	6531	B	949 269-3300	8894
Lres Corporation (PA)	6531	D	714 520-5737	9079
Realselect Inc	6531	C	661 803-5188	9155
Roman Cthlic Diocese of Orange	6553	C	714 532-6551	9291
Gitsit Solutions LLC (PA)	6799	D	714 352-2038	9511
Anaheim Ca LLC	7011	C	714 634-4500	9609
Hit Portfolio II Trs LLC	7011	D	714 938-1111	9859
Liberty Debt Relief LLC	7299	D	800 756-8447	10559
Emergncy Mdcine Spclist Ornge	7363	D	714 543-8911	11283
Roth Staffing Companies LP (PA)	7363	D	714 939-8600	11325
Volt Management Corp	7363	B	800 654-2624	11354
Ashunya Inc	7371	D	714 385-1900	11428
Infinite Technologies LLC	7371	C	786 408-7995	11658
Lmntrix LLC	7371	D	888 388-1879	11714
Maintech Incorporated	7371	C	714 921-8000	11727
Stoneriver Inc	7371	C	714 705-8227	11948
Quotit Corporation	7373	C	714 564-5000	12515
Invision Networking LLC	7379	C	949 309-3441	12816
Tensoriot Inc	7379	D	909 342-2459	12894
United Guard Security Inc	7381	C	714 242-4051	13060
Merical Inc	7389	C	714 685-0977	13372
Merical LLC	7389	B	714 283-9551	13373
Merical LLC	7389	C	714 238-7225	13374
Rgis LLC	7389	C	714 938-0663	13445
Servicing Solutions LLC	7389	D	844 907-6583	13470
Enterprise Rnt--car Los Angles (DH)	7514	D	657 221-4400	13581
Total Telco Specialists Inc	7629	D	805 541-2232	13749
Lucky Strike Entertainment LLC	7933	D	248 374-3420	14119
Childrens Healthcare Cal	8011	B	714 997-3000	14681
Pavilion Surgery Center LLC	8011	D	714 744-8850	14950
Scribemd LLC	8011	D	714 543-8911	15052
University California Irvine	8011	A	714 456-6170	15163
University California Irvine	8011	C	714 456-7890	15165
University California Irvine	8011	C	714 456-6966	15167
US Dermatology Medical Management Inc	8011	D	817 962-2157	15171
Access Dental Plan (PA)	8021	D	916 922-5000	15214
Premier Dental Holdings Inc (PA)	8021	B	714 480-3000	15248
Western Dental Services Inc (HQ)	8021	C	714 480-3000	15254
Emeritus Corporation	8051	D	714 639-3590	15440
Orange Coast Care Inc	8051	D	714 997-7090	15611
Orange Hlthcare Wllness Cntre	8051	C	714 633-3568	15612
Pennant Group Inc	8051	B	714 978-2534	15626
Chapman Global Medical Ctr Inc	8062	D	714 633-0011	15991
Childrens Hospital Orange Cnty (PA)	8062	A	714 509-8300	15997
Childrens Hospital Orange Cnty	8062	B	949 365-2416	15998
St Joseph Hospital	8062	D	714 744-8601	16463
St Joseph Hospital of Orange	8062	D	714 771-8222	16470
St Joseph Hospital of Orange	8062	D	714 771-8006	16471
St Joseph Hospital of Orange (DH)	8062	A	714 633-9111	16472
St Joseph Hospital of Orange	8062	D	714 771-8037	16474
Uc Irvine Health Mktg Dept	8062	D	714 456-6726	16584
University California Irvine	8062	D	714 456-8000	16601
University California Irvine	8062	A	714 456-6011	16602
University California Irvine	8062	C	714 456-5558	16603
Chapman House Inc	8069	D	714 288-6100	16669
Childrens Healthcare Cal (PA)	8069	A	714 997-3000	16670
Accel Therapies Inc	8093	C	855 443-3822	17000
Arbormed Inc (PA)	8099	C	714 689-1500	17179
Astiva Health Inc	8099	C	858 707-5111	17180
Uc Irvine Health	8099	C	714 456-6191	17342
City Orange Police Assn Inc	8611	C	714 457-5340	18704
Orange Cnty Hlth Auth A Pub AG	8621	B	714 246-8500	18754
Aclu Fndation Southern Cal LLC	8641	D	213 977-9500	18809
Orange Cnty Cncil Boy Scuts AM (PA)	8641	D	714 546-4990	18889
Boyle Engineering Corporation	8711	B	949 476-3300	19158
Eichleay Inc	8711	C	562 256-8600	19209
Holmes & Narver Inc (HQ)	8711	C	714 567-2400	19259
Architects Orange Inc	8712	C	714 639-9860	19451
University California Irvine	8721	D	714 456-6655	19637
Micro Prcision Calibration Inc	8734	C	714 901-5659	19988
American Intgrted Rsources Inc	8741	D	714 921-4100	20020
Corvel Corporation	8741	C	714 385-8500	20063
Prospect Medical Systems Inc (HQ)	8741	C	714 667-8156	20187
Raymond Group (PA)	8741	D	714 771-7670	20191
Medical Spc Managers Inc	8742	C	714 571-5000	20463
Ralis Services Corp	8742	D	844 347-2547	20523
Aecom Usa Inc	8748	D	714 567-2501	20681
Goldman Data LLC	8748	D	714 283-5889	20766
Patriot Wastewater LLC	8748	D	714 921-4545	20825
California Dept of Pub Hlth	9199	D	714 567-2906	20920

ORANGE COVE, CA - Fresno County

	SIC	EMP	PHONE	ENTRY#
Booth Ranches LLC	0291	D	559 626-4472	234
Cecelia Packing Corporation	5148	C	559 626-5000	6524

ORANGEVALE, CA - Sacramento County

	SIC	EMP	PHONE	ENTRY#
MA Steiner Construction Inc	1541	D	916 988-6300	832
California Family Health LLC (PA)	7991	D	916 987-2030	14183
Summerville At Hazel Creek LLC	8051	D	916 988-7901	15684

ORCUTT, CA - Santa Barbara County

	SIC	EMP	PHONE	ENTRY#
Spiess Construction Co Inc	1623	D	805 937-5859	1266

ORINDA, CA - Contra Costa County

	SIC	EMP	PHONE	ENTRY#
Pacific Union Co	6531	D	925 258-0090	9121
Axa Rosenberg Inv MGT LLC	6722	C	925 253-3300	9357
California Shakespeare Theater (PA)	7922	D	510 548-3422	14031
Orinda Country Club	7997	D	925 254-4313	14420

ORLAND, CA - Glenn County

	SIC	EMP	PHONE	ENTRY#
Olivarez Honey Bees Inc	0279	D	530 865-0298	231

OROVILLE, CA - Butte County

	SIC	EMP	PHONE	ENTRY#
Rci General Engineering	1622	D	530 533-3918	1189
Roplast Industries Inc	2673	C	530 532-9500	2530
Pacific Gas and Electric Co	4911	D	530 532-4093	4631
Mid Valley Title and Escrow Co	6541	D	530 533-6680	9237
Tyme Maidu Tribe-Berry Creek	7011	A	530 538-4560	10330
County of Butte	7349	D	530 538-7407	10879
Mooretown Rancheria	7993	B	530 533-3885	14298
Feather Rver Recreation Pk Dst	7999	D	530 533-2011	14523
Orohealth Corporation	8011	A	530 534-9183	14944
Oroville Hospital	8049	B	530 538-8700	15298
1000 Executive Parkway LLC	8051	D	530 533-7335	15313
Oroville Hospital (PA)	8062	A	530 533-8500	16300
Oroville Hospital	8062	B	530 532-8697	16301
New Start Rcvery Solutions Inc	8069	D	530 854-4119	16688
Sierra Hlth Wellness Ctrs LLC	8099	D	530 854-4119	17325

OXNARD, CA - Ventura County

	SIC	EMP	PHONE	ENTRY#
Fresh Venture Farms LLC	0161	D	805 754-4449	31
Iwamoto & Gean Farm	0161	D	805 659-4568	35
San Miguel Produce Inc	0161	B	805 488-0981	39
Etchandy Farms LLC	0171	D	805 983-4700	52
Las Posas Berry Farms LLC	0171	D	805 483-1000	56
Santa Rosa Berry Farms LLC	0171	B	805 981-3060	65
Superior Fruit LLC	0171	C	805 485-2519	66
Marathon Land Inc	0181	C	805 488-3585	137
Pyramid Flowers Inc	0181	B	805 382-8070	149
River Ridge Farms Inc	0181	D	805 647-6880	152
Channel Islnds Vgtble Frms Inc (PA)	0182	D	805 984-1910	160
Scarborough Farms Inc	0191	C	805 483-9113	199

GEOGRAPHIC SECTION

PALM SPRINGS CA

	SIC	EMP	PHONE	ENTRY#
Boskovich Farms Inc (PA)	0723	C	805 487-2299	259
Mission Produce Inc (PA)	0723	C	805 981-3650	289
Ramco Enterprises LP	0723	B	805 486-9328	300
Venco Western Inc	0782	C	805 981-2400	545
Dcor LLC (PA)	1382	C	805 535-2000	598
Toro Enterprises Inc	1611	D	805 483-4515	1174
Blois Construction Inc	1623	C	805 485-0011	1197
Scully Sportswear Inc (PA)	2386	D	805 483-6339	2468
PC Vaughan Mfg Corp	3089	D	805 278-2555	2677
Elite Metal Finishing LLC (PA)	3471	C	805 983-4320	2760
Pegasus Transit Inc	4141	D	805 988-1540	3313
Durham School Services L P	4151	C	805 483-6076	3331
Tanimura Antle Fresh Foods Inc	4225	C	805 483-2358	3761
Experior Laboratories Inc	4899	D	805 483-3400	4536
NRG California South LP	4911	D	805 984-5241	4594
Bragg Investment Company Inc	5013	D	805 485-2106	5030
American Tooth Industries	5047	D	805 487-9868	5398
Aluminum Precision Pdts Inc	5051	C	805 488-4401	5473
Quinn Company	5082	D	805 485-2171	5801
Wiggins Lift Co Inc	5084	C	805 485-7821	5886
Smart & Final Stores LLC	5141	D	805 485-2051	6349
Sysco Ventura Inc	5141	B	805 205-7000	6405
Boskovich Fresh Cut LLC	5148	C	805 487-2299	6518
Ventura County Lemon Coop	5148	D	805 385-3345	6593
AG Rx (PA)	5191	C	805 487-0696	6820
Seminis Vegetable Seeds Inc (DH)	5191	A	855 733-3834	6833
Grolink Plant Company Inc (PA)	5193	C	805 984-7958	6861
Sunshine Floral LLC	5193	D	805 982-8822	6875
Adas Investment Holdings Inc	5198	D	805 483-2341	6882
Home Depot USA Inc	5211	C	805 983-0653	6993
DCH California Motors Inc	5511	D	805 988-7900	7193
Vista Ford Inc	5511	D	805 983-6511	7324
State Compensation Insur Fund	6321	D	888 782-8338	8272
Lawyers Title Insurance Corp	6361	B	805 484-2701	8444
Milwood Healthcare Inc	6512	D	626 274-4345	8736
Courtyard Oxnard	7011	C	805 988-3600	9726
Djont/Jpm Hsptlity Lsg Spe LLC	7011	C	805 984-2500	9751
Mission Linen Supply	7213	D	805 485-6794	10446
Workrite Uniform Company Inc (DH)	7218	B	805 483-0175	10483
H G Group Inc	7291	D	805 486-6463	10522
Epic Production Technologies (us Sales) Inc	7359	D		11031
Tripod Inc	7363	D	805 585-2273	11343
Volt Management Corp	7363	D	805 485-0506	11352
Taheem Johnson Inc	7379	D	818 835-3785	12890
Boyd and Associates	7381	D	805 988-8298	12940
West Coast Wldg & Piping Inc	7692	D	805 246-5841	13756
Comedy Club Oxnard LLC	7997	D	805 535-5400	14361
Arizona Channel Isla	7999	D	480 788-0755	14491
Cabrillo Crdolgy Med Group Inc	8011	D	805 983-0922	14642
N S C Channel Islands Inc	8011	B	805 485-1908	14914
Dignity Health	8062	A	805 988-2500	16053
Rescue Mission Alliance	8099	D	805 201-4341	17313
Inclusive Edcatn Cmnty Prtnr I	8211	B	805 985-4808	17718
Amigo Baby Inc	8322	D	805 901-1237	17835
Child Dev Rsrces of Vntura CNT (PA)	8322	C	805 485-7878	17878
Mixtec/Ndgena Cmnty Orgnzing P	8322	D	805 483-1166	18056
Seneca Family of Agencies	8322	D	805 278-0355	18124
Saticoy Lemon Association	8611	D	805 654-6543	18721
Oxnard Police Department	8641	B	805 385-8300	18890
Rescue Mission Alliance (PA)	8699	D	805 487-1234	19099
Jsl Technologies Inc	8711	B	805 985-7700	19288
Systems Application & Tech Inc	8711	D	805 487-7373	19403
Seminis Inc (DH)	8731	B	805 485-7317	19767
City of Oxnard (PA)	8742	C	805 385-7803	20317
Behavioral Science Technology Inc (PA)	8748	D	805 646-0166	20702
County of Ventura	9199	D	805 981-5521	20925

PACHECO, CA - Contra Costa County

	SIC	EMP	PHONE	ENTRY#
Biocare Medical LLC (PA)	2835	C	925 603-8000	2611
Universal Bldg Svcs & Sup Co	7349	D	925 934-5533	10981

PACIFIC GROVE, CA - Monterey County

	SIC	EMP	PHONE	ENTRY#
Califrnia-Nevada Methdst Homes	6513	C	831 657-5200	8796
Pebble Bch Rsort DBA Lone Cypr	7011	B	831 625-8480	10111
Pivot3 Inc	7372	C	512 807-2666	12318
Front Porch Communities & Svcs	8361	D	831 373-3111	18436

PACIFIC PALISADES, CA - Los Angeles County

	SIC	EMP	PHONE	ENTRY#
Many LLC	7311	D	310 399-1515	10644
Get Heal Inc	7363	D	310 528-4957	11287
Bel-Air Bay Club Ltd	7997	D	310 230-4700	14339
Glo Yoga	7999	D	310 801-9031	14529
Riviera Country Club Inc	7999	C	310 454-6591	14554
Atria Senior Living Inc	8361	D	310 573-9545	18378
Solutionz Inc	8742	C	888 815-0322	20560

PACIFICA, CA - San Mateo County

	SIC	EMP	PHONE	ENTRY#
Little Giant Bldg Maint Inc	7349	C	415 508-0282	10921

PACOIMA, CA - Los Angeles County

	SIC	EMP	PHONE	ENTRY#
Moc Products Company Inc (PA)	2899	D	818 794-3500	2645
Ultramet	3471	D	818 899-0236	2762
Wetzel & Sons Mvg & Stor Inc	4212	D	818 890-0992	3439
Looney Bins Inc (HQ)	4953	D	818 485-8200	4904
Smart & Final Stores LLC	5141	D	818 896-6212	6328
Energy Club Inc	5145	D		6460
Global Bakeries Inc	5149	D	818 896-0525	6630
Surge Globl Bkries Hldings LLC (PA)	5149	D	818 896-0525	6676
Lowes Home Centers LLC	5211	B	818 686-4300	7036
Global Trend Productions Inc	7359	D	818 768-4950	11033
Golden West Security	7381	C	818 897-5965	12979
Florence Wstn Med Clinic Inc	8011	D	818 896-2999	14750
Northeast Valley Health Corp	8011	B	818 896-0531	14927
Hillview Mental Health Ctr Inc	8093	D	818 896-1161	17073
Hathawy-Sycmres Child Fmly Svc	8322	C	626 395-7100	17997
Volunteers of Amer Los Angeles	8322	D	818 834-9097	18174
Volunteers of Amer Los Angeles	8322	D	818 834-8957	18183
Gonzalez Management Co Inc	8741	D	818 485-0596	20101

PALA, CA - San Diego County

	SIC	EMP	PHONE	ENTRY#
Pala Casino Spa & Resort	7011	A	760 510-5100	10093

PALM DESERT, CA - Riverside County

	SIC	EMP	PHONE	ENTRY#
Platinum Landscape Inc	0781	C	760 200-3673	458
Temalpakh Inc	1542	D	760 770-5778	1042
Dave Williams Plbg & Elec Inc	1711	C	760 296-1397	1417
Cove Electric Inc	1731	C	760 568-9924	1711
United Brothers Concrete Inc	1771	C	760 346-1013	2167
Associated Desert Shoppers Inc (DH)	2741	D	760 346-1729	2553
Gary Cardiff Enterprises Inc	4119	D	760 568-1403	3265
Entravsion Communications Corp	4833	D	760 836-0466	4428
Southern California Gas Co	4924	D	714 262-0091	4733
Coachlla Vly Wtr Dst Pub Fclti (PA)	4941	C	760 398-2651	4776
Coachlla Vly Wtr Dst Pub Fclti	4941	C	760 398-2651	4777
Connecticut Ctr Plastic Surg	5995	D	760 779-9595	7568
Morgan Stnley Smith Barney LLC	6022	C	760 568-3500	7698
Webb Del California Corp (DH)	6552	B	760 772-5300	9280
Ashford Trs Seven LLC	7011	D	760 776-0050	9618
Destination Residences LLC	7011	D	760 346-4647	9740
Host Hotels & Resorts LP	7011	D	760 341-2211	9868
Marriott Vacation Club Intl	7011	D	760 674-2927	10008
Palm Desert Hospitality LLC	7011	B	760 568-1600	10095
Premier Residential Svcs LLC	7299	D	760 773-4081	10571
Universal Services America LP	7381	A	760 200-2865	13065
Califrnia Clnic Plstic Surgery	7389	D	760 346-0611	13223
Resort Parking Services Inc	7521	D	760 328-4041	13627
Friends of Cultural Center Inc	7922	D	760 346-6505	14039
Desert Willow Golf Resort	7992	D	760 346-7060	14256
Desert Willow Golf Resort Inc	7992	D	760 346-0015	14257
Palm Dsert Rcrtl Fclities Corp	7992	D	760 346-0015	14280
Quarry At La Quinta Inc (PA)	7992	D	760 777-1100	14283
Bighorn Golf Club Charities	7997	D	760 773-2468	14345
Lakes Country Club Assn Inc (PA)	7997	C	760 568-4321	14394
Mountain Vista Golf Course At	7999	D	760 200-2200	14548
Eisenhower Medical Center	8011	D	760 836-0232	14733
Mariner Health Care Inc	8051	C	760 776-7700	15568
Watermark Rtrment Cmmnties Inc	8051	D	760 346-5420	15728
Visiting Angels	8082	C	800 365-4189	16962
Rai Care Ctrs Sthern Cal II LL	8092	C	760 346-7588	16996
Able Health Group LLC	8099	D	760 610-2093	17164
Desert ARC	8322	B	760 346-1611	17952
Living Desert	8422	C	760 346-5694	18689
Leighton Group Inc	8621	C	760 776-4192	18750
Palm Desert Greens Association	8641	D	760 346-8005	18892
Sun City Palm Dsert Cmnty Assn (PA)	8641	C	760 200-2100	18912
Firstsrvice Rsidential Cal LLC	8741	D	760 834-2480	20088
Hands Working Virtually Inc	8741	D	760 459-8138	20108

PALM SPRINGS, CA - Riverside County

	SIC	EMP	PHONE	ENTRY#
S S W Mechanical Cnstr Inc	1711	C	760 327-1481	1552
Western Pacific Roofing Corp	1761	C	661 273-1336	2091
Carefusion 207 Inc	3841	B	760 778-7200	3050
American Medical Response Inc	4119	C	760 883-5000	3232
First Student Inc	4151	B	760 320-4659	3338
Desert Water Agency Fing Corp	4941	D	760 323-4971	4784
Palm Springs Disposal Services	4953	D	760 327-1351	4917

Employee Codes: A=Over 500 employees, B=251-500
C=101-250, D=51-100, E=20-50, F=10-19, G=1-9

PALM SPRINGS CA

	SIC	EMP	PHONE	ENTRY#
Smart & Final Stores LLC	5141	D	760 322-8639	6329
Lowes Home Centers LLC	5211	C	760 866-1901	7053
Loandepotcom LLC	6162	A	760 797-6000	7998
Agua Clnte Band Chilla Indians	7011	B	800 854-1279	9600
Colony Palms Hotel LLC	7011	D	760 969-1800	9711
Diamond Resorts LLC	7011	D	760 866-1800	9742
Hyatt Hotels Management Corp	7011	D	760 322-9000	9900
Kittridge Hotels & Resorts LLC	7011	D	760 325-9676	9949
Margartvlle Rsort Orlndo Rsort	7011	C	760 327-8311	10001
Parker Palm Springs LLC	7011	D	760 770-5000	10107
R P S Resort Corp	7011	B	760 327-8311	10135
Rbd Hotel Palm Springs LLC	7011	D	760 322-9000	10141
Remington Hotel Corporation	7011	D	760 322-6000	10148
Riviera Palm Sprng A Trbute PR	7011	C	760 327-8311	10166
Robray Hotel Partnership LLP	7011	C	760 325-4372	10168
Smoke Tree Inc	7011	C	760 327-1221	10250
Spa Resort Casino	7011	A	760 883-1034	10258
Spa Resort Casino (PA)	7011	D	888 999-1995	10259
Sydell Palm Springs LLC	7011	D	760 323-1711	10299
Walters Family Partnership	7011	C	760 320-6868	10352
Worldmark Club	7011	D	760 416-4428	10381
OLinn Security Incorporated	7381	C	760 320-5303	13010
Alamo Rental (us) Inc	7514	D	760 778-6271	13578
Metropolitan Theatres Corp	7832	D	760 323-3221	14003
Mount San Jcnto Winter Pk Corp	7999	D	760 325-1449	14547
Desert Medical Group Inc (PA)	8011	C	760 320-8814	14726
Califrnia Nrsing Rhbltition Ctr	8051	D	760 325-2937	15363
Ensign Palm I LLC	8051	D	760 323-2638	15456
Desert Regional Med Ctr Inc (HQ)	8062	A	760 323-6511	16038
Desert Regional Med Ctr Inc	8062	D	760 416-4613	16039
Eisenhower Medical Center	8062	C	760 325-6621	16067
Desert Aids Project (PA)	8322	D	760 323-2118	17951
Palm Springs Art Museum Inc	8412	D	760 322-4800	18665
Agua Clnte Band Chilla Indians (PA)	8699	A	760 699-6800	19033
Mariner Health Care Inc	8741	C	760 327-8541	20145
Kings Garden LLC	8742	C	760 275-4969	20424
Smg Holdings LLC	8742	D	760 325-6611	20555

PALMDALE, CA - Los Angeles County

	SIC	EMP	PHONE	ENTRY#
Csi Electrical Contractors Inc	1731	B	661 723-0869	1713
Aero Bending Company	3444	D	661 948-2363	2743
Battle-Tested Strategies LLC	4215	D	661 802-6509	3607
Palmdale Water District	4941	D	661 947-4111	4818
Waste Management Cal Inc	4953	C	661 947-7197	4956
Passport To Learning Inc	5047	D	661 538-9200	5440
Smart & Final Stores Inc	5141	B	661 722-6210	6310
Lowes Home Centers LLC	5211	D	661 267-9888	7070
Golden Empire Mortgage Inc	6162	B	661 949-3388	7971
Thi Holdings (delaware) Inc	6411	B	661 266-7423	8671
Delta Scientific Corporation (PA)	7382	C	661 575-1100	13105
Xi Enterprise Inc	7991	D	661 266-3200	14244
Rancho Vista Development Co	7992	D	661 272-9082	14284
Antelope Vly Cntry CLB Imprv	7997	D	661 947-3142	14325
Rockin Jump Holdings LLC	7999	B	661 233-9907	14555
Garrison Family Med Group Inc	8011	D	661 947-7100	14760
Sierra Prmry Care Med Group A	8011	D	661 273-0100	15061
Tarzana Treatment Centers Inc	8093	D	818 654-3815	17137
Child Care Resource Center Inc	8322	C	661 723-3246	17877
People Creating Success Inc	8322	D	661 225-9700	18082
Kinkisharyo International	8748	C	661 265-1647	20792

PALO ALTO, CA - Santa Clara County

	SIC	EMP	PHONE	ENTRY#
Pete Moffat Construction	1521	D	650 656-9720	709
Vance Brown Inc (PA)	1541	D	650 849-9900	854
Dlight Design Inc	1711	A	415 872-6136	1422
Bridgebio Pharma Inc (PA)	2834	C	650 391-9740	2582
Kodiak Sciences Inc (PA)	2834	D	650 281-0850	2595
Orphan Medical Inc	2834	D	650 496-3777	2601
Danisco US Inc (HQ)	2835	C	650 846-7500	2612
HP Inc (PA)	3571	A	650 857-1501	2806
Indigo America Inc	3571	A	650 857-1501	2807
Varian Medical Systems Inc (DH)	3845	A	650 493-4000	3079
Navan Inc (PA)	4724	C	888 505-8747	3941
Joguru Inc	4725	D	855 526-4332	3964
Skype Inc	4813	D	650 493-7900	4339
Maxar Space LLC (HQ)	4899	D	650 852-4000	4543
Xerox Corporation	5044	D	650 813-7138	5261
Business Objects Inc	5045	A	650 849-4000	5285
Convrgd Data Tech Inc	5045	C	650 461-4488	5287
Dazz Inc	5045	D	800 956-8019	5295
Fintech Open Source Foundation	5045	B	650 665-9773	5305
Spin Technology Inc	5045	D	888 883-2993	5353
Nest Labs Inc	5065	D	855 469-6378	5680

	SIC	EMP	PHONE	ENTRY#
Scilex Inc (HQ)	5122	D	650 516-4310	6144
Dinahs Garden Hotel Inc	5812	D	650 493-2844	7473
Stanford Federal Credit Union (PA)	6061	D	650 725-1000	7807
Merrill Lynch Prce Fnner Smith	6211	C	650 842-2440	8109
Point Digital Finance Inc	6211	C	888 764-6823	8162
Assured Insurance Tech Inc	6411	C	650 753-1070	8497
Next Insurance Inc	6411	C	855 222-5919	8625
Bpr Properties Berkeley LLC	6512	D	650 424-1400	8703
Instrumental Global Hq	6512	D	650 681-9361	8727
Oak Creek Apartments	6513	C	650 327-1600	8848
Deleon Realty Inc	6531	C	650 543-8500	8977
Marcus Millichap Corp RE Svcs (HQ)	6531	D	650 391-1700	9094
Broadrach Cpitl Prtners Fund I	6722	A	650 331-2500	9362
Highland Capital Partners LLC	6799	C	650 687-3800	9519
Norwest Venture Partners VI LP	6799	D	650 289-2243	9544
4290 El Camino Properties LP	7011	C	650 857-0787	9591
Comfort Inn Palo Alto	7011	D	650 493-3142	9718
M10 Dev LLC	7011	D	650 565-8100	9994
Pacific Hotel Dev Ventr LP	7011	C	650 347-8260	10080
Pacific Hotel Management LLC	7011	D	650 328-2800	10084
Beauty Bazar Inc	7231	C	650 326-8522	10492
Palo Alto Hlls Golf Cntry CLB	7299	D	650 948-1800	10568
U P C Inc	7299	C	650 462-2010	10579
Thunder Industries	7311	D	415 228-0861	10680
Total Quality Maintenance Inc	7349	C	650 846-4700	10974
Aisera Inc	7371	C	650 667-4308	11391
Alfresco Software Americas Inc	7371	C	888 317-3395	11395
Anvilogic Inc	7371	D	650 665-7707	11409
Autonomic LLC (PA)	7371	D	650 823-1806	11438
Balboa Intrmdiate Holdings LLC (PA)	7371	A	650 846-1000	11449
Bionic Stork Inc	7371	C	650 600-1494	11456
Docker Inc (PA)	7371	B	415 941-0376	11548
Essential Products Inc	7371	C	650 300-0000	11579
Hypergrid Inc	7371	D	650 316-5524	11651
Infoworksio Inc	7371	C	408 899-4687	11663
Instabug Inc	7371	D	650 422-9555	11669
Intapp Us Inc (HQ)	7371	D	650 852-0400	11671
Konsus Inc	7371	C	415 659-9852	11696
Leena Ai Inc	7371	D	332 232-9740	11705
Luminary Cloud Inc	7371	D	650 279-9579	11720
Machine Zone Inc	7371	D	650 320-1678	11722
Machinify Inc	7371	D	650 313-2932	11723
Making Sense Inc	7371	D	210 364-0050	11728
Mattermost Inc (PA)	7371	C	650 667-8512	11737
Mercari Inc	7371	B	855 464-7482	11744
Modular Inc	7371	D	408 508-4539	11755
Moomoo Technologies Inc	7371	A	650 798-5700	11758
Mudflap Inc	7371	D	888 885-3835	11761
Revinate LLC	7371	C	415 671-4703	11879
Robert Bosch Healthcare Systems Inc	7371	C	650 690-9100	11886
Safe Securities Inc (PA)	7371	C	650 398-3669	11893
Salt Security Inc	7371	D	650 254-6580	11896
Sambanova Systems Inc (PA)	7371	B	650 263-1153	11897
Signalwire Inc	7371	D	650 382-0000	11915
Tangible Play Inc (HQ)	7371	C	650 667-1693	11966
Tightdb Inc	7371	C	415 766-2020	11980
Touchpint Rest Innovations Inc	7371	C	800 992-9540	11983
Unravel Data Systems Inc	7371	D	650 741-3442	12005
Woven By Toyota US Inc	7371	B	808 221-7117	12050
Adaptive Insights LLC (HQ)	7372	C	650 528-7500	12075
Adara Inc (PA)	7372	D	408 876-6360	12076
Applovin Corporation (PA)	7372	C	800 839-9646	12095
Ariba Inc (DH)	7372	C	650 849-4000	12101
Boomerang Commerce Inc (PA)	7372	C	602 459-2578	12123
Cxapp Inc	7372	C	650 575-4456	12153
D-Wave Quantum Inc	7372	C	604 630-1428	12156
Duda Mobile Inc	7372	D	855 790-0003	12169
Jacada Inc	7372	D	770 352-1300	12247
Lastline Inc (PA)	7372	C	877 671-3239	12255
Salesforce	7372	D	650 327-0110	12342
Sap Labs LLC (DH)	7372	B	650 849-4000	12345
Vmware Inc (PA)	7372	A	650 427-5000	12393
Xcelmobility Inc	7372	D	650 320-1728	12404
My Ally Inc	7373	D	650 387-9118	12497
Branch Metrics Inc (PA)	7374	B	650 209-6461	12554
Everypath Inc	7374	D	408 562-8000	12572
Rubrik Inc (PA)	7374	A	650 300-5862	12619
Declara Inc	7379	D	877 216-0604	12775
Gemini Solutions LLC	7379	C	650 329-8194	12797
Smartek21 LLC	7379	B	650 617-3221	12879
Global Risk Solutions Inc	7381	D	888 981-9484	12978
Armis Federal LLC	7382	B	888 452-4011	13098
Deserve Inc	7389	C	800 418-7353	13265

GEOGRAPHIC SECTION

PASADENA CA

	SIC	EMP	PHONE	ENTRY#
Chattopadhyay Runi MD	8011	D	650 853-2946	14678
Packard Childrens Hlth Aliance	8011	D	650 497-8000	14947
Palo Alto Medical Foundation	8011	A	650 321-4121	14949
Stanford Health Care	8011	C	650 723-5281	15100
Sutter Bay Medical Foundation (HQ)	8011	A	650 321-4121	15110
Veterans Health Administration	8011	A	650 493-5000	15188
Gentle Dental	8021	C	650 341-8008	15227
Covenant Care California LLC	8051	D	415 327-0511	15400
Channing House	8059	D	650 327-0950	15829
Stanford Health Care	8062	A	650 723-5171	16486
Stanford Health Care	8062	A	650 497-8953	16488
Stanford Health Care	8062	B	650 723-8561	16490
Stanford Health Care	8062	B	650 736-7844	16491
Stanford Health Care	8062	B	650 213-8360	16492
Stanford Health Care	8062	C	650 723-4000	16498
Lucile Slter Pckard Chld Hosp (HQ)	8069	A	650 497-8000	16686
Guardant Health Inc (PA)	8071	B	855 698-8887	16724
Nuevacare LLC	8082	D	650 396-3596	16901
Thekey LLC	8082	D	650 462-6900	16950
Baker & McKenzie LLP	8111	D	650 856-2400	17375
Cooley LLP (PA)	8111	B	650 843-5000	17413
Covington & Burling LLP	8111	D	650 632-4700	17422
Gibson Dunn & Crutcher LLP	8111	D	650 849-5300	17467
King & Spalding LLP	8111	D	650 422-6700	17519
Kirkland & Ellis LLP	8111	D	650 859-7000	17521
LLP Mayer Brown	8111	D	650 331-2000	17553
Morrison & Foerster LLP	8111	B	650 813-5600	17579
Pillsbury Wnthrop Shaw Pttman	8111	D	650 233-4500	17612
Sidley Austin LLP	8111	C	650 565-7000	17654
Skadden Arps Slate Mgher Flom	8111	D	650 470-4500	17656
Vinson & Elkins LLP	8111	D	650 617-8400	17672
White & Case LLP	8111	D	650 213-0300	17678
Wilson Snsini Gdrich Rsati Pro (PA)	8111	A	650 493-9300	17681
Emerson Collective LLC (PA)	8299	D	650 422-2152	17809
Family & Children Services	8322	D	650 326-6576	17973
Oshman Family Jewish Cmnty Ctr	8322	D	650 223-8700	18074
Challenger Schools	8351	D	650 213-8245	18279
Childrens Crative Lrng Ctr Inc	8351	B	650 473-1100	18291
Stanford Health Care	8621	D	650 498-5032	18762
Gordon Betty Moore Foundation	8641	D	650 213-3000	18867
Legion Technologies Inc	8641	C	408 605-2603	18878
Startx	8699	D	408 230-3300	19108
Bridgebio Services Inc	8731	D	650 438-1302	19666
Cellanome Inc	8731	D	510 736-0922	19669
Epri International Inc (HQ)	8731	D	650 855-2000	19689
Palo Alto Research Center Inc	8731	C	650 812-4000	19755
Gator Bio Inc	8732	D	650 800-7651	19809
Knowledge Networks Inc	8732	A	650 289-2000	19829
Suning Cmmerce R D Ctr USA Inc	8732	D	650 834-9800	19851
Electric Power RES Inst Inc (PA)	8733	A	650 855-2000	19880
Palo Alto Vterans Inst For RES	8733	C	650 858-3970	19902
Intellectual Ventures LLC	8741	B	650 941-1330	20118
Veterans Health Administration	8741	C	650 493-5000	20244
Wurl Inc	8741	D	662 649-8825	20255
End To End Analytics LLC	8742	D	650 331-9659	20356
Harris Mycfo Inc	8742	D	480 348-7725	20401
Strateos Inc (PA)	8742	D	650 763-8432	20570
Vulcan Cyber Inc	8742	D	415 429-4311	20607
Gordon E Btty I More Foundation	8748	D	650 213-3000	20767
Symphony Technology Group LLC (DH)	8748	A	650 935-9500	20858

PALOS VERDES ESTATES, CA - Los Angeles County

	SIC	EMP	PHONE	ENTRY#
Palos Verdes Golf Club	5813	D	310 375-2759	7521
Grosvenor Inv MGT US Inc	6411	D	310 265-0297	8578
Rolling Hills Country Club	7997	D	424 903-0000	14431
Sqa Services Inc	8742	B	800 333-6180	20562

PALOS VERDES PENINSU, CA - Los Angeles County

	SIC	EMP	PHONE	ENTRY#
County of Los Angeles	8062	C	310 222-2401	16024

PANORAMA CITY, CA - Los Angeles County

	SIC	EMP	PHONE	ENTRY#
Crestview Landscape Inc	0781	D	818 962-7771	425
Import Collection (PA)	5199	D	818 782-3060	6917
Southern Cal Prmnnte Med Group	6324	B	800 272-3500	8362
American Protection Group Inc (PA)	7381	C	818 279-2433	12928
Kaiser Foundation Hospitals	8011	A	818 375-4023	14794
Kaiser Foundation Hospitals	8011	A	818 375-2000	14810
Ensign Group Inc	8051	D	818 893-6385	15452
Deanco Healthcare LLC	8062	A	818 787-2222	16037

PARADISE, CA - Butte County

	SIC	EMP	PHONE	ENTRY#
Pacific Gas and Electric Co	4911	D	530 327-7633	4638
Sunbrdge Prdise Rhblttion Ctr	8051	A	530 872-3200	15687
Feather River Hospital	8062	A	530 877-9361	16089

PARAMOUNT, CA - Los Angeles County

	SIC	EMP	PHONE	ENTRY#
Drillmec Inc	1382	D	281 885-0777	599
South Coast Piering Inc	1542	D	800 922-2488	1031
Reliable Energy Management Inc	1711	D	562 984-5511	1547
Advanced Industrial Svcs Inc	1721	D	562 940-8305	1602
MB Herzog Electric Inc	1731	C	562 531-2002	1772
Golden State Engineering Inc	3549	C	562 634-3125	2784
Mv Transportation Inc	4111	D	562 259-9911	3180
City of Downey	4151	D	562 529-5465	3323
Durham School Services L P	4151	D	562 408-1206	3326
Cnet Express	4212	C	949 357-5475	3384
Contractors Cargo Company (PA)	4213	C	310 609-1957	3457
Calmet Inc (PA)	4953	C	323 721-8120	4875
Staub Metals LLC	5051	D	562 602-2200	5519
Transtar Metals Corp	5051	B	562 630-1400	5528
Aylesva Inc	5139	C	562 688-0592	6228
Home Depot USA Inc	5211	C	562 272-8055	6989
Continental Exch Solutions Inc	6099	D	562 790-8532	7844
CCC Property Holdings LLC	6719	C	310 609-1957	9306
Braun Linen Service (PA)	7213	C	909 623-2678	10432
Modern Dev Co A Ltd Partnr	7389	D	949 646-6400	13379

PARLIER, CA - Fresno County

	SIC	EMP	PHONE	ENTRY#
ONeill Beverages Co LLC	0172	C	559 638-3544	81
Custom Produce Sales (HQ)	5148	C	559 254-5800	6529
University Cal Rvrside Almni A	8733	D	559 646-6500	19928

PASADENA, CA - Los Angeles County

	SIC	EMP	PHONE	ENTRY#
Exeter Packers Inc	0174	C	626 993-6245	98
Boswell Properties Inc	0722	B	626 583-3000	247
C W Driver LLC (PA)	1542	D	626 351-8800	887
Dpr Construction A Gen Partnr	1542	C	626 463-1265	909
Acco Engineered Systems Inc	1711	A	818 244-6571	1334
Atk Space Systems LLC	3812	D	626 351-0205	3002
Gmto Corporation	3827	D	626 204-0500	3036
Hemodialysis Inc	3841	D	626 792-0548	3052
Call-The-Car	4119	D	855 282-6968	3245
Fresgo LLC	4212	D	626 389-3500	3393
United Couriers Inc (DH)	4512	C	213 383-3611	3848
Spokeo Inc	4813	C	877 913-3088	4341
Multicultural Rdo Brdcstg Inc	4832	D	626 844-8882	4397
American Multimedia TV USA	4833	C	626 466-1038	4411
Blue Chip Stamps Inc	5051	A	626 585-6700	5479
Curiosity Ink Media LLC	5085	C	561 287-5776	5897
Deliverr Inc	5141	B	213 534-8686	6249
Mhh Holdings Inc	5149	C	626 744-9370	6646
Idealab (HQ)	5511	D	626 356-3654	7235
Symes Cadillac Inc	5511	D	626 689-4386	7308
Dine Brands Global Inc (PA)	5812	B	818 240-6055	7474
CIT Bank NA (HQ)	6021	C	626 859-5400	7612
Northern Trust of California (inc)	6021	A		7635
Community Bank	6022	B	626 577-1700	7675
East West Bancorp Inc (PA)	6022	A	626 768-6000	7678
East West Bank (HQ)	6022	A	626 768-6000	7679
First Foundation Inc	6029	C	626 993-1300	7732
Onewest Bank Group LLC	6035	A	626 535-4870	7744
Firefighters First Credit Un (PA)	6061	C	323 254-1700	7768
First Financial Federal Cr Un	6061	C	800 537-8491	7770
Wescom Central Credit Union (PA)	6062	B	888 493-7266	7834
Law School Financial Inc	6111	C	626 243-1800	7866
Merrill Lynch Prce Fnner Smith	6211	C	800 637-7455	8132
Guardian Life Insur Co Amer	6311	D	626 792-1935	8234
Southern Cal Prmnnte Med Group (HQ)	6324	D	626 405-5704	8369
Los Angles Cnty Emplyees Rtrme (PA)	6371	C	626 564-6000	8463
B&C Liquidating Corp (HQ)	6411	C	626 799-7000	8506
Bitco Cnstr Insur Agcy Inc	6411	D	626 683-5200	8513
Southern California Permanente	6411	A	626 405-5722	8661
Tm Claims Service Inc	6411	C	626 568-7800	8672
United Agencies Inc (PA)	6411	D	818 952-8818	8678
Collins & Collins	6512	C	626 243-1100	8711
Invitation Homes Inc	6531	D	805 372-2900	9054
Solariant Capital LLC	6719	C	626 544-0279	9337
Western Asset Core Plus Bond P	6722	C	626 844-9400	9393
Western Assets Management Co	6726	D	626 844-9400	9410
Ironwrker Employees Benefit Corp	6733	C	626 792-7337	9429
Operating Engineers Funds Inc (PA)	6733	C	866 400-5200	9440
Western Asset Mrtg Capitl Corp	6798	A	626 844-9400	9480
Are/Cal-Sd Region No 62 LLC	6799	D	626 578-0777	9488
Idealab Holdings LLC (PA)	6799	A	626 585-6900	9520
Sabal Capital Partners LLC	6799	C	949 255-1007	9558
Langham Hotels Pacific Corp	7011	C	617 451-1900	9965

Employee Codes: A=Over 500 employees, B=251-500
C=101-250, D=51-100, E=20-50, F=10-19, G=1-9

PASADENA CA

Name	SIC	EMP	PHONE	ENTRY#
Pacific Huntington Hotel Corp	7011	A	626 568-3900	10086
Pasadena Hotel Dev Ventr LP	7011	D	626 449-4000	10108
Dy-Dee Service Pasadena Inc	7219	D	626 792-6183	10485
Hair Perfect International	7231	D	626 304-9286	10497
Ayzenberg Group Inc	7311	D	626 584-4070	10589
One & All Inc (HQ)	7311	C		10658
Tetra Tech Executive Svcs Inc	7361	C	626 470-2400	11248
Bluebeam Inc (PA)	7371	C	626 788-4100	11466
Netease Information Tech Corp	7371	D	919 579-3051	11768
Qxv Software LLC	7371	D	626 219-0522	11860
Snapcomms Inc	7371	C	805 715-0300	11929
Everbridge Inc (PA)	7372	C	818 230-9700	12184
Evolution Robotics Inc	7372	C	626 993-3000	12186
Guidance Software Inc (HQ)	7372	C	626 229-9191	12215
Intellectyx Inc	7372	D	720 256-7540	12235
Gemalto Cogent Inc (HQ)	7373	D	626 325-9600	12459
Greensoft Technology Inc	7374	C	323 254-5961	12577
Near Intelligence Inc	7374	B	628 889-7680	12601
Zoominfo Technologies LLC	7375	A	360 783-6924	12690
Tpusa - Fhcs Inc (DH)	7376	C	213 873-5100	12699
Cloud Creations Inc	7379	D	800 951-7651	12759
Inter-Con Security Systems Inc (PA)	7381	A	626 535-2200	12989
Casecentral Inc (DH)	7389	D	415 989-2300	13228
Pasadena Center Operating Co	7389	C	626 795-9311	13420
Scratch Financial Inc	7389	D	855 727-2395	13468
Parking Concepts Inc	7521	D	626 577-8963	13616
Annandale Golf Club	7997	D	626 796-6125	14324
Rose Bowl Aquatics Center	7997	D	626 564-0330	14432
Arroyo Seco Medical Group (PA)	8011	D	626 795-7556	14616
Huntington Medical Foundation	8011	D	626 795-4210	14776
Kaiser Foundation Hospitals	8011	C	626 440-5639	14828
Kaiser Prmnnte Schl Anesthesia	8011	C	626 564-3016	14857
Southern CA Gastroenterology	8011	B	818 425-9761	15070
Tao of Wllness Snta Mnica A PR	8049	D	626 397-1000	15309
Accredited Nursing Services	8051	C	626 573-1234	15316
Highland Hlthcare Cmllia Grdns	8051	D	626 798-6777	15515
Pasadena Hospital Assn Ltd	8051	B	626 397-3322	15621
Pasadena Madows Nursing Ctr LP	8051	D	626 796-1103	15622
Brighton Convalescent Center	8059	D	626 798-9124	15823
Park Marino Convalescent Ctr	8059	D	626 463-4105	15888
Two Palms Nursing Center Inc	8059	C	626 796-1103	15905
Community Hlth Alance Pasadena (PA)	8062	D	626 398-6300	16008
Huntington Medical Foundation	8062	C	626 792-3141	16138
Kaiser Foundation Hospitals	8062	B	626 440-5659	16186
Pasadena Hospital Assn Ltd (PA)	8062	A	626 397-5000	16319
Vincent-Hayley Enterprises Inc	8062	D	626 398-8182	16621
Aurora Behavioral Health Care	8063	D	818 515-4735	16637
Aurora Las Encinas LLC	8063	C	626 795-9901	16639
Gooden Center	8069	D	626 356-0078	16683
Shriners Hspitals For Children	8069	B	626 389-9300	16696
Lotus Clinical Research LLC	8071	D	626 381-9830	16734
Confido LLC	8082	A	310 361-8558	16845
Grandcare Health Services LLC (PA)	8082	D	866 554-2447	16866
Huntington Care LLC	8082	C	877 405-6990	16873
Pacific Clnics Psdena Calworks	8093	C	626 419-3228	17105
County of Los Angeles	8099	D	626 229-3825	17213
Legacy Healthcare Center LLC	8099	D	626 798-0558	17268
Polytechnic School	8211	B	626 792-2147	17740
County of Los Angeles	8322	D	626 356-5281	17913
County of Los Angeles	8322	D	626 356-5281	17927
Foothill Family Service	8322	D	626 795-6907	17984
Hillsides	8322	B	323 254-2274	18002
Optima Family Services Inc	8322	D	323 300-6066	18071
Asian Rehabilitation Svc Inc (PA)	8331	D	562 632-1141	18208
Pacific Clinics Head Start	8351	C	626 254-5000	18341
Hathawy-Sycmres Child Fmly Svc (PA)	8361	D	626 395-7100	18447
Monte Vista Grove Homes	8361	D	626 796-8155	18489
Rosemary Childrens Services (PA)	8361	D	626 844-3033	18514
DVeal Corporation	8399	C	626 296-8900	18585
Kidspce A Prticipatory Museum	8412	D	626 449-9144	18653
Norton Smon Mseum Art At Psden	8412	D	626 449-6840	18662
Southern Cal Ibw-Neca Hlth Tr	8631	D	323 221-5861	18795
Shriners International	8641	D	626 389-9300	18907
Valley Hunt Club	8641	D	626 793-7134	18921
Automobile Club Southern Cal	8699	D	626 795-0601	19051
Pasadena Humane Society	8699	D	626 792-7151	19096
Jacobs Atcs Fema A Joint Ventr	8711	D	571 218-1115	19274
Jacobs Engineering Company	8711	A	626 449-2171	19276
Jacobs Engineering Group Inc	8711	D	626 578-3500	19279
Jacobs Engineering Inc (DH)	8711	A	626 578-3500	19280
Jacobs International Ltd Inc	8711	B	626 578-3500	19282
Maxar Space Robotics LLC	8711	D	626 296-1373	19318
Pacifica Services Inc	8711	D	626 405-0131	19348
Parsons Engrg Science Inc (DH)	8711	B	626 440-2000	19351
Parsons Intl Cayman Islands	8711	A	626 440-6000	19353
Parsons Service Corporation	8711	D	626 440-2000	19354
Parsons Wtr Infrastructure Inc	8711	D	626 440-7000	19355
Ptsi Managed Services Inc	8711	D	626 440-3118	19366
Stantec Consulting Svcs Inc	8711	D	626 796-9141	19396
Tetra Tech Inc (PA)	8711	C	626 351-4664	19409
Tetra Tech Nus Inc	8711	C	412 921-7090	19413
Ttg Engineers	8711	B	626 463-2800	19421
Stantec Architecture Inc	8712	D	626 796-9141	19507
Cachet Financial Services	8721	D	626 578-9400	19545
Kbkg Inc	8721	C	626 449-4225	19592
Krost (PA)	8721	C	626 449-4225	19596
Aerospace Corporation	8733	D	626 873-7700	19860
California Institute Tech	8733	A	818 354-9154	19872
Carnegie Institution Wash	8733	D	626 577-1122	19874
Doheny Eye Institute (PA)	8733	D	323 342-7120	19879
Tmt Intrntonal Observatory LLC	8733	D	626 395-1651	19921
Parsons Constructors Inc	8741	A	626 440-2000	20173
Dowling Advisory Group	8742	D	626 319-1369	20348
Ameriko Inc (PA)	8744	D	626 795-7988	20647
Land Design Consultants Inc	8748	D	626 578-7000	20797
Msla Management LLC	8748	A	626 824-6020	20807

PASO ROBLES, CA - San Luis Obispo County

Name	SIC	EMP	PHONE	ENTRY#
J & L Vineyards	0172	D	559 268-1627	75
City of Paso Robles	1611	D	805 237-3999	1089
Boneso Brothers Cnstr Inc	1711	D	805 227-4450	1383
Worldwind Services LLC	1731	A	661 822-4877	1877
Mge Underground Inc	1794	B	805 238-3510	2223
Joslyn Sunbank Company LLC	3678	B	805 238-2840	2938
Applied Technologies Assoc Inc (HQ)	3829	C	805 239-9100	3042
Michael Dusi Trucking Inc	4213	D	805 237-9499	3516
Aviation Consultants Inc	4581	D	805 596-0212	3878
Cco Holdings LLC	4841	C	805 440-1002	4486
Smart & Final Stores Inc	5141	B	805 237-0323	6301
Hope Family Wines	5182	B	805 238-6979	6799
Lowes Home Centers LLC	5211	B	805 602-9051	7039
Paq Inc	5541	B	805 227-1660	7389
Heritage Oaks Bancorp	6022	B	805 369-5200	7693
Heritage Oaks Bank	6022	B	805 239-5200	7694
Emeritus Corporation	6513	C	805 239-1313	8806
Ayres - Paso Robles LP	7011	C	714 850-0409	9624
Volt Management Corp	7363	D	805 237-0882	11349
Iqms LLC (DH)	7372	C	805 227-1122	12246
Ravine Waterpark LLC	7996	C	805 237-8500	14311
Carbon Health Technologies Inc	8011	C	805 226-4222	14652
County of Los Angeles	8322	C	805 237-3110	17932
Marsh Consulting Group	8748	D	239 433-5500	20803

PATTERSON, CA - Stanislaus County

Name	SIC	EMP	PHONE	ENTRY#
Cartel Transport LLC	4212	C	209 892-3880	3379
Longs Drug Stores Cal LLC	4225	A	209 895-7839	3726
California Northern RR Co	4731	D	530 406-8981	3991
Traina Dried Fruit Inc	5149	C	209 892-5472	6682
Traina Dried Fruit Inc (PA)	5149	C	209 892-5472	6683
Golden Bear Physical Therapy	8049	D	209 895-4206	15284

PATTON, CA - San Bernardino County

Name	SIC	EMP	PHONE	ENTRY#
Califrnia Dept State Hospitals	8063	A	909 425-7000	16644

PAUMA VALLEY, CA - San Diego County

Name	SIC	EMP	PHONE	ENTRY#
T - Y Nursery Inc	5193	C	760 742-2151	6876
Pauma Band of Mission Indians	7011	B	760 742-2177	10109
New Pvcc Inc	7997	D	760 742-1230	14414

PEBBLE BEACH, CA - Monterey County

Name	SIC	EMP	PHONE	ENTRY#
I Cypress Company (PA)	7011	C	831 647-7500	9903
Lone Cypress Company LLC	7011	D	831 625-8563	9983
Pebble Bch Rsort DBA Lone Cypr	7011	C	831 624-3811	10110
Pebble Beach Co A Ltd Partnr	7011	B	800 877-0597	10112
Tap Room At Lodge	7011	C	831 624-3811	10305
Pebble Beach Co A Ltd Partnr	7539	B	831 624-0348	13682
Lone Cypress Company LLC (PA)	7992	C	831 647-7500	14270
Lone Cypress Company LLC	7997	D	831 625-8507	14396
Monterey Peninsula Country CLB	7997	C	831 373-1556	14410

PENN VALLEY, CA - Nevada County

Name	SIC	EMP	PHONE	ENTRY#
Lake Wildwood Association	8641	C	530 432-1152	18877

PENRYN, CA - Placer County

Name	SIC	EMP	PHONE	ENTRY#
Sinclair Concrete	1771	D	916 663-0303	2158

GEOGRAPHIC SECTION

PLAYA DEL REY CA

	SIC	EMP	PHONE	ENTRY#

PERRIS, CA - Riverside County

	SIC	EMP	PHONE	ENTRY#
Parkco Building Company	1542	D	714 444-1441	983
Silver Creek Industries LLC	1542	C	951 943-5393	1028
Mamco Inc (PA)	1611	C	951 776-9300	1132
HB Parkco Construction Inc (PA)	1771	B	714 567-4752	2126
Integrity Rebar Placers	1791	C	951 696-6843	2183
Jeff Carpenter Inc	1794	C	951 657-5115	2219
Aoc LLC	2295	D	951 657-5161	2447
R-Cold Inc	3585	D	951 436-5476	2844
National Retail Trnsp Inc	4213	D	951 243-6110	3517
Lowes Home Centers LLC	4225	C	951 443-2500	3727
Eastern Municipal Water Dst (PA)	4941	B	951 928-3777	4789
Eastern Municipal Water Dst	4941	C	951 657-7469	4790
CR&r Incorporated	4953	D	951 634-8079	4882
Eldorado Stone LLC	5032	A	951 601-3838	5202
Global Plastics Inc	5093	C	951 657-5466	6008
Soco Group Inc	5172	D	951 657-2350	6740
Village Nurseries Whl LLC	5193	B	951 657-3940	6878
Iherb LLC (PA)	5499	A	951 616-3600	7161
White House Sanitation Inc	7699	D	951 943-1550	13810
Big Lgue Dreams Consulting LLC	7941	C	619 846-8855	14128
Dropzone Waterpark	7999	C	951 210-1600	14514
Oak Grove Inst Foundation Inc	8322	C	951 238-6022	18069
Pacific Hydrotech Corporation	8711	C	951 943-8803	19347

PESCADERO, CA - San Mateo County

	SIC	EMP	PHONE	ENTRY#
Silver Terrace Nurseries Inc	0181	D	650 879-2110	155
King-Reynolds Ventures LLC	7389	D	650 879-2136	13337
Joie De Vivre Hospitality LLC	8741	D	650 879-1100	20126

PETALUMA, CA - Sonoma County

	SIC	EMP	PHONE	ENTRY#
Reichardt Duck Farm Inc	0259	D	707 762-6314	230
Jensen Corporate Holdings Inc	0782	C	707 527-6187	502
Midstate Construction Corp	1521	D	707 762-3200	702
North Bay Construction Inc	1611	D	707 283-0093	1146
Incom Mechanical Inc	1711	D	707 586-0511	1461
Simply Solar	1711	D	707 285-7037	1562
Syserco Inc	1711	D	707 664-8443	1581
Spg Solar Inc	1731	D	707 781-1000	1847
Petalumaidence Opco LLC	2084	C	707 763-4109	2391
Kval Inc	3553	C	707 762-4363	2786
Pure Luxury Limousine Service	4119	C	800 626-5466	3290
Shift Network	4899	D	415 223-7560	4549
Pacific Gas and Electric Co	4911	C	707 765-5118	4622
Daymen US Inc	5043	C	707 827-4053	5237
Braden Prtners LP A Cal Ltd PR (HQ)	5047	D	415 893-1518	5406
Labcon North America	5047	C	707 766-2163	5429
Cyan Inc	5065	C	707 735-2300	5644
Niles Audio Corporation	5065	C	760 710-0992	5681
Sunrise Farms LLC	5144	C	707 778-6450	6451
Clover-Stornetta Farms LLC (PA)	5149	C	707 769-3282	6614
Morris Distributing	5181	D	707 769-7294	6778
Ontrac Logistics Inc	5941	C	707 773-1564	7543
Wcf Select Insurance Company	6311	C	415 899-2000	8252
Allianz Reinsurance Amer Inc	6321	B	415 899-2000	8257
Allianz Globl Risks US Insur	6331	B	415 899-3758	8374
Sonoma Hotel Partners LP	7011	D	707 283-2888	10254
Optio Solutions LLC	7322	B	800 360-2827	10746
Universal Bldg Svcs & Sup Co	7349	C	707 781-7434	10979
Kaiser Foundation Hospitals	8011	B	707 765-3900	14832
Permanente Medical Group Inc	8011	A	707 765-3900	14989
Petaluma Health Center Inc	8011	B	707 559-7500	14992
Srm Alliance Hospital Services (PA)	8062	B	707 778-1111	16452
Leisure Care LLC	8361	C	707 769-3300	18468
Stantec Architecture Inc	8712	C	707 765-1660	19509
Point Reyes Bird Observatory	8733	D	707 781-2555	19904
Legacy Marketing Group (PA)	8742	C	707 778-8638	20435
Sonoma Technology Inc	8748	D	707 665-9900	20851

PICO RIVERA, CA - Los Angeles County

	SIC	EMP	PHONE	ENTRY#
Genesis Foods Corporation	2064	D	323 890-5890	2374
GPde Slva Spces Incrporation (PA)	2099	D	562 407-2643	2435
Bay Cities Container Corp	2653	D	562 948-3751	2512
Endpak Packaging Inc	2674	D	562 801-0281	2532
Feit Electric Company Inc (PA)	3645	C	562 463-2852	2872
Pacific Logistics Corp (PA)	4731	C	562 478-4700	4069
United Pacific Waste	4953	D	562 699-7600	4947
Unisource Solutions Inc	5021	C	562 654-3500	5106
Aurora World Inc	5092	C	562 205-1222	5985
Three Sons Inc	5147	D	562 801-4100	6506
Bakemark USA LLC (PA)	5149	C	562 949-1054	6607
Lowes Home Centers LLC	5211	C	562 942-9909	7065
Noble Rents Inc	7353	D	855 767-4424	11003
Showroom Interiors LLC	7359	C	323 348-1551	11054
Sectran Security Incorporated (PA)	7381	C	562 948-1446	13033
Los Angeles Unified School Dst	7389	C	562 654-9007	13358
Krikorian Premiere Theatre LLC	7832	D	562 205-3456	14002
Mariner Health Care Inc	8051	D	562 942-7019	15561
Rivera Sanatarium Inc	8051	D	562 949-2591	15640
Riviera Nursing & Conva	8051	D	562 806-2576	15643
Altamed Health Services Corp	8099	D	562 949-8717	17173
Bms Healthcare Inc	8099	D	562 942-7019	17193
Public Hlth Fndation Entps Inc	8099	D	562 801-2323	17304

PINE GROVE, CA - Amador County

	SIC	EMP	PHONE	ENTRY#
Volcano Communications Company (PA)	4813	D	209 296-7502	4356

PINECREST, CA - Tuolumne County

	SIC	EMP	PHONE	ENTRY#
Dodge Ridge Corporation	7011	B	209 536-5300	9758
Dodge Ridge Mtn Resort LLC	7011	C	209 965-3474	9759

PINOLE, CA - Contra Costa County

	SIC	EMP	PHONE	ENTRY#
Califrnia Atism Foundation Inc	8399	C	510 724-1751	18568

PIONEER, CA - Amador County

	SIC	EMP	PHONE	ENTRY#
Pacific Gas and Electric Co	4911	C	209 295-2651	4657

PIRU, CA - Ventura County

	SIC	EMP	PHONE	ENTRY#
La Verne Nursery Inc	0181	D	805 521-0111	136

PISMO BEACH, CA - San Luis Obispo County

	SIC	EMP	PHONE	ENTRY#
Pacific Gas and Electric Co	4911	C	805 546-5267	4652
Pismo Coast Village Inc	7011	D	805 773-1811	10122
Tic Hotels Inc	7011	D	805 773-4671	10311
Vpb Operating Co LLC	7011	D	805 773-1011	10346

PITTSBURG, CA - Contra Costa County

	SIC	EMP	PHONE	ENTRY#
Performance Mechanical Inc (HQ)	1541	A	925 432-4080	839
Redwood Painting Co Inc	1721	C	925 432-4500	1638
Pacific Gas and Electric Co	4911	D	925 757-2000	4618
Ravig Inc	5045	D	925 526-1234	5340
Viking Industrial Corporation	5051	C	925 427-2518	5530
Rfid Corporation	7213	C	925 473-9978	10455
CC Co Health Cntr Information	8011	C	925 431-2300	14661
La Clinica De La Raza Inc	8011	C	925 431-1250	14869
SSC Pittsburg Operating Co LP	8059	B	925 427-4444	15899
Lincoln Child Center Inc	8361	C	925 521-1270	18472
McCampbell Analytical Inc	8734	D	925 252-9262	19986

PIXLEY, CA - Tulare County

	SIC	EMP	PHONE	ENTRY#
California Dairies Inc	5143	C	559 752-5200	6432
CT Commodities Inc	6221	D	559 757-3996	8180

PLACENTIA, CA - Orange County

	SIC	EMP	PHONE	ENTRY#
Mddr Inc	1711	C	714 792-1993	1498
Elljay Acoustics Inc	1742	D	714 961-1173	1926
GD Heil Inc	1795	C	714 687-9100	2236
Linda Yorba Water District (PA)	4941	D	714 701-3000	4801
Hardy Window Company (PA)	5031	C	714 996-1807	5163
Facility Solutions Group Inc	5063	C	714 993-3966	5557
Bejac Corporation (PA)	5084	C	714 528-6224	5820
Sunrise Growers Inc	5148	C	714 706-6090	6587
Alta Vista Country Club LLC	7997	D	714 524-1591	14320
Interface Rehab Inc	8049	A	714 646-8300	15293
Tenet Healthsystem Medical Inc	8069	B	714 993-2000	16699
Roman Cthlic Diocese of Orange	8211	C	714 528-1794	17745

PLACERVILLE, CA - El Dorado County

	SIC	EMP	PHONE	ENTRY#
Doug Veerkamp General Engineering Inc (PA)	1611	C	530 626-0825	1097
Pacific Gas and Electric Co	4911	C	530 621-7237	4630
El Dorado Irrigation District	4941	B	530 622-4513	4791
Advanced Gases and Eqp Inc	5999	D	530 344-0771	7569
Lyon Realty	6519	C	530 295-4444	8887
National 9 Motels Inc	7011	D	530 622-3884	10039
Shingle Sprng Trbal Gming Auth	7011	A	530 677-7000	10230
El Dorado County Health Dept	8011	C	530 621-6100	14736
Gold Country Health Center Inc (PA)	8051	C	530 621-1100	15498
Marshall Medical Center (PA)	8062	A	530 622-1441	16249
Northern California Inalliance	8322	D	530 344-1244	18066
Summitview Child & Family Svcs	8322	D	530 644-2412	18147
Mother Lode Rhbltion Entps In	8361	C	530 622-4848	18491

PLAYA DEL REY, CA - Los Angeles County

	SIC	EMP	PHONE	ENTRY#
Chipton-Ross Inc	3721	D	310 414-7800	2981
Los Angeles Dept Wtr & Pwr	4939	A	310 524-8500	4759
Cronos USA Client Services LLC	6719	D	323 843-2741	9309

Employee Codes: A=Over 500 employees, B=251-500
C=101-250, D=51-100, E=20-50, F=10-19, G=1-9

PLAYA DEL REY CA

	SIC	EMP	PHONE	ENTRY#
Parking Concepts Inc.	7521	D	310 322-5008	13624
You ME and Sciences Inc.	7929	D	310 406-7350	14113

PLAYA VISTA, CA - Los Angeles County

	SIC	EMP	PHONE	ENTRY#
Cpl Holdings LLC	5331	C	310 348-6800	7136
Lmb Opco LLC	6163	B	310 348-6800	8047
Tcg Capital Management LP	6799	C	310 633-2900	9572
Canvas Worldwide LLC	7313	C	424 303-4300	10708
Commercial RE Exch Inc	7371	C	888 273-0423	11506
Chownow Inc	7372	D	888 707-2469	12134
Ordermark Inc.	7374	C	833 673-3762	12603
Yahoo Cv LLC	7374	D	408 349-3300	12644
Lowermybills Inc.	7375	D	310 348-6800	12676
Lee Burkhart Liu Inc.	8712	D	310 829-2249	19485
Buyerzonecom LLC	8741	D	888 393-5000	20049

PLEASANT GROVE, CA - Sutter County

	SIC	EMP	PHONE	ENTRY#
Withrow Cattle	0241	D	916 780-0364	223
Holt of California (HQ)	5082	C	916 991-8200	5791
Sysco Sacramento Inc.	5141	B	916 275-2714	6402

PLEASANT HILL, CA - Contra Costa County

	SIC	EMP	PHONE	ENTRY#
500 Startups Management Co LLC	6799	C	650 743-4738	9481
Diablo Vly College Foundation (PA)	7389	B	925 685-1230	13267
Contra Costa Country Club	7997	D	925 798-7135	14362
Helios Healthcare LLC	8051	C	925 935-6630	15513
Pleasant Hillidence Opco LLC	8051	C	925 935-5222	15628
Anka Behavioral Health Incorporated	8093	A	925 825-4700	17004
Choice In Aging (PA)	8093	D	925 682-6330	17027
Firm McNamara Law	8111	D	925 939-5330	17457
Mc Namara Ddge Ney Batt Sltter (PA)	8111	D	925 939-5330	17564
Contra Costa Cnty Off Educatn (PA)	8211	D	925 942-3388	17707
Carlton Senior Living Inc.	8361	C	925 935-1001	18385
Maze & Assoc Accounting Corp.	8721	D	925 930-0902	19610
The Source Group Inc	8748	D	925 944-2856	20865

PLEASANTON, CA - Alameda County

	SIC	EMP	PHONE	ENTRY#
Brightview Landscape Dev Inc	0781	C	925 463-0700	396
Brightview Landscape Svcs Inc	0781	C	925 924-8900	415
Landcare USA LLC	0782	C	925 462-2193	512
Signature Homes Inc.	1521	D	925 463-1122	724
Hensel Phelps Construction Co.	1542	C	408 452-1800	935
Dresser/Areia Construction	1623	C	800 392-9891	1207
Dillingham Construction NA	1629	A	925 249-8850	1295
Aegis Fire Systems LLC	1711	D	925 417-5550	1338
Blocka Construction Inc.	1711	C	510 657-3686	1380
Can-AM Plumbing Inc.	1711	C	925 846-1833	1393
On-Time AC & Htg LLC (HQ)	1711	D	925 598-1911	1518
Pmn Design Electric Inc.	1731	C	925 846-0650	1807
Nolo	2731	C	510 549-1976	2549
RMC Pacific Materials LLC (PA)	3241	C		2697
Teichert Inc (PA)	3273	C	916 484-3011	2714
Omron Robotics Safety Tech Inc (HQ)	3535	C	925 245-3400	2775
Cooper Bussmann LLC	3629	C	925 924-8500	2869
Black Tie Transportation LLC	4119	C	925 847-0747	3241
Fashion Apparel Service Trnsp	4225	C	866 835-1112	3703
Blackrock Logistics Inc (PA)	4731	D	925 523-3878	3989
Gtt Communications (mp) Inc (DH)	4813	C	415 687-3870	4292
Megapath Inc	4813	A	877 611-6342	4313
Thunderhead One Inc.	5045	D	877 838-8945	5361
AOC Technologies Inc.	5051	B	925 875-0808	5474
Hitachi High-Tech America Inc.	5065	D	925 218-2800	5658
Rn Chidakashi Technologies Inc.	5092	C	415 687-6145	5995
Unisource Packaging Inc.	5113	C	925 227-6000	6091
Acosta Inc.	5141	D	925 600-3500	6236
McLane Foodservice Dist Inc.	5142	D	252 985-7200	6423
Ata Retail Services LLC	5199	A	925 621-4700	6889
Hendrick Automotive Group	5511	D	925 463-4700	7232
Wells Fargo Bank National Assn	6021	D	925 463-1983	7641
1st United Credit Union (PA)	6061	D	800 649-0193	7750
Blackhawk Network Inc (DH)	6099	A	925 226-9990	7841
Blackhawk Network Holdings Inc (HQ)	6099	B	925 226-9990	7842
E-Loan Inc (DH)	6163	A	925 847-6200	8039
Merrill Lynch Prce Fnner Smith.	6211	D	925 227-6600	8123
Kaiser Fundation Hlth Plan Inc.	6324	D	510 271-5800	8336
State Compensation Insur Fund	6331	C	888 782-8338	8419
Insurance Company of West.	6411	D	925 474-2800	8591
S&J Stadtler Inc.	6531	B	925 847-8900	9173
American Property Management	7011	C	925 463-8000	9605
Trevi Partners A Calif LP (PA)	7011	C	925 225-4000	10322
ABM Elctrcal Ltg Solutions Inc.	7349	D	408 399-3030	10846
Cjs Model Home Maint Inc.	7349	D	925 485-3280	10875
Excel Building Services LLC	7349	A	925 474-1080	10894
Solid Personnel Inc.	7361	D	510 370-3550	11232
Sfn Group Inc.	7363	A	925 847-8500	11335
314e Corporation (PA)	7371	C	510 371-6736	11366
Bayone Solutions	7371	C	408 930-1600	11450
Dotsolved Systems Inc.	7371	C	925 218-6903	11552
Evidentio Inc (HQ)	7371	D	855 933-1337	11586
Flexon Technologies Inc.	7371	C	925 398-8280	11602
Maxplore Technologies Inc.	7371	D	925 621-1400	11739
Micro Focus LLC	7371	C	925 784-3242	11746
Sandbox Vr Mission Valley LLC	7371	C	323 207-0840	11901
Servicemax Inc (HQ)	7371	C	800 756-4960	11910
Tryfacta Inc.	7371	B	408 419-9200	11995
Vagaro Inc.	7371	C	800 919-0157	12010
Workday Inc (PA)	7371	A	925 951-9000	12046
Zantaz Inc.	7371	B	925 598-3000	12058
Ice Mortgage Technology Inc (HQ)	7372	B	855 224-8572	12227
Medallia Inc (HQ)	7372	C	650 321-3000	12267
Steelwedge Software Inc.	7372	C	925 460-1700	12363
Veeva Systems Inc (PA)	7372	B	925 452-6500	12389
Brillius Technologies Inc.	7373	C	510 379-9027	12427
Celestix Networks Inc.	7373	C	510 668-0700	12432
Trapeze Networks Inc.	7373	C	925 474-2200	12536
Redica Systems Inc.	7374	D	844 332-3320	12614
Proctoru Inc.	7375	B	205 870-8122	12682
Akshaya Inc (PA)	7379	C	925 914-7395	12726
Bodhtree Solutions Inc.	7379	C	844 409-0510	12744
NeutonAI Inc.	7379	C	925 399-6400	12845
Springml Inc.	7379	C	916 316-1566	12881
Iraje Inc.	7382	C	925 400-6558	13126
Accurate Firestop Inc.	7389	C	925 701-8600	13176
Simplicontract Tech Inc.	7389	D	403 833-5556	13476
Ruby Hill Golf Club LLC	7992	D	925 417-5840	14285
Castlewood Country Club	7997	C	925 846-2871	14357
Cs-Pleasanton LLC	7997	A	925 463-2822	14366
Alameda County AG Fair Assn.	7999	D	925 426-7600	14488
Lifetime Tennis Inc.	7999	D	925 931-3449	14540
Mission Peak Orthopedics	8011	D	510 797-3933	14904
Ghc of Pleasanton LLC	8051	D	925 462-2400	15496
Kaiser Foundation Hospitals	8062	B	925 598-2799	16168
Kaiser Foundation Hospitals	8062	A	925 847-5000	16183
Stanford Health Care	8062	A	925 847-3000	16495
Stanford Hlth Care Tri-Valley	8069	D	925 416-3562	16698
Spring Bioscience Corp	8071	A	925 474-8463	16755
Unchained Labs (PA)	8071	C	925 587-9800	16757
Axis Community Health Inc.	8093	D	925 462-1755	17009
David Howard	8093	D	925 426-0979	17050
Kaiser	8099	D	925 924-6930	17260
Laborers Fnds Admnstrtive Offi (PA)	8631	D	707 864-2800	18786
Young MNS Chrstn Assn of E Bay	8641	D	925 475-6100	18980
Mackay Smps Cvil Engineers Inc (PA)	8711	D	925 416-1790	19312
Shums Coda Associates Inc.	8711	D	925 463-0651	19387
Zoho Corporation	8711	B	925 924-9500	19447
Dahlin Group Inc (PA)	8712	C	925 251-7200	19462
Martin ATI-AC Inc (PA)	8712	C	925 648-8800	19494
Capincrouse LLP	8721	D	925 201-1187	19548
10x Genomics Inc (PA)	8731	C	925 401-7300	19642
Roche Molecular Systems Inc (DH)	8731	B	925 730-8000	19764
Roche Nimblegen Inc.	8731	C	608 316-3890	19765
Simbol Inc.	8731	D	925 226-7400	19771
Bon Appetit Management Co.	8741	C	925 730-3653	20039
Clorox Services Company	8741	C	925 368-6000	20059
Stanford Hlth Care Tri-Valley (DH)	8741	B	925 847-3000	20217
Devcool Inc.	8742	D	408 372-4313	20344
Harbor Industries Inc.	8742	C	925 461-1366	20400
Smartzip Analytics Inc.	8742	D	855 661-1064	20554
Zoho Corporation	8742	B	925 924-9500	20627
2dream Inc.	8748	D	650 943-2366	20669
City of Pleasanton	9224	D	925 454-2341	20933

PLS VRDS PNSL, CA - Los Angeles County

	SIC	EMP	PHONE	ENTRY#
West Shores Realty Inc.	6531	C	310 541-8000	9212
Episcopal Communities & Servic.	8051	D	310 544-2204	15464

PLYMOUTH, CA - Amador County

	SIC	EMP	PHONE	ENTRY#
Sierra Sunrise Vineyard Inc.	2084	D	209 245-6942	2393

POINT RICHMOND, CA - Contra Costa County

	SIC	EMP	PHONE	ENTRY#
Hartmann Studios Inc.	7389	C	510 232-5030	13309

POLLOCK PINES, CA - El Dorado County

	SIC	EMP	PHONE	ENTRY#
Intell Detection Systems Inc.	5999	D	530 644-1904	7585

GEOGRAPHIC SECTION

QUINCY CA

	SIC	EMP	PHONE	ENTRY#

POMONA, CA - Los Angeles County

Centrescapes Inc	0782	D	909 392-3303	481
Ultimate Removal Inc	1521	C	909 524-0800	734
Henkels & McCoy Inc	1623	B	909 517-3011	1214
Spiniello Companies	1623	C	909 629-1000	1267
t McGee Electric Inc	1731	D	909 591-6461	1860
Frank S Smith Masonry Inc	1741	D	909 468-0525	1882
Spectra Company	1741	D	909 599-0760	1893
Commercial Door Company Inc	1751	D	714 529-2179	1994
Howard Roofing Company Inc	1761	D	909 622-5598	2069
Trussworks International Inc	3441	D	714 630-2772	2740
Valley Tool and Machine Co Inc	3599	D	909 595-2205	2856
Southern Cal Rgional Rail Auth	4111	C	213 808-7043	3216
Covenant Transport Inc	4213	A	909 469-0130	3458
W Why W Enterprises Inc	4214	D	626 969-4292	3604
C & B Delivery Service	4225	C	909 623-4708	3679
Kkw Trucking Inc (PA)	4225	A	909 869-1200	3721
Warehouse Specialists LLC	4225	D	909 596-2566	3781
Southern California Edison Co	4911	A	909 274-1925	4684
Southern California Edison Co	4911	A	909 469-0251	4687
Ferguson Fire Fabrication Inc (DH)	5074	D	909 517-3085	5748
Ol Old Company	5084	D	800 492-6864	5849
Inter Valley Pool Supply Inc	5091	D	626 969-5657	5978
Smart & Final Stores LLC	5141	D	909 622-3321	6354
NW Packaging LLC (PA)	5199	D	909 706-3627	6932
PHD Marketing Inc	5199	D	909 620-1000	6935
Continental Exch Solutions Inc	6099	D	909 622-0500	7849
Lereta LLC (PA)	6211	B	626 543-1765	8099
Yamamoto of Orient Inc (HQ)	6512	C	909 594-7356	8785
Murcor Inc	6531	C	909 623-4001	9107
Starwood Htels Rsrts Wrldwide	7011	C	909 622-2220	10275
Merchants Building Maint Co	7349	A	909 622-8260	10928
Global Rental Co Inc	7353	C	909 469-5160	10997
Maxim Healthcare Services Inc	7363	D	626 962-6453	11310
J&E Private Security Corp	7381	D	909 594-1111	12992
County of Los Angeles	7992	C	909 231-0549	14253
Fairplex Enterprises Inc	7999	D	909 623-3111	14520
Los Angeles County Fair Assn (PA)	7999	D	909 623-3111	14543
Western Univ Hlth Sciences	8011	D	909 865-2565	15205
Inland Valley Partners LLC	8049	C	909 623-7100	15288
Casa Clina Hosp Ctrs For Hlthc (HQ)	8062	B	909 596-7733	15967
Pomona Valley Hospital Med Ctr (PA)	8062	A	909 865-9500	16331
Landmark Medical Services Inc	8063	D	909 593-2585	16654
Immunalysis Corporation	8071	D	909 482-0840	16727
Latara Enterprise Inc (PA)	8071	D	909 623-9301	16732
Tri-City Mental Health Auth (PA)	8093	D	909 623-6131	17145
American National Red Cross	8322	C	909 859-7006	17831
Casa Colina Inc (PA)	8322	A	909 596-7733	17863
County of Los Angeles	8322	D	909 469-4500	17921
San Gbrl/Pmona Vlleys Dvlpmnta	8322	B	909 620-7722	18115
Walden House Inc	8361	C	626 258-0300	18545
Pomona Community Health Center	8621	D	909 630-7927	18757
Mesa Associates Inc	8711	D	909 979-6609	19320
Circle Wood Services Inc	8741	D	909 784-0733	20056

PORT HUENEME, CA - Ventura County

AV Fenix Llc	0191	D	805 279-3457	167
Brusco Tug & Barge Inc	4492	C	805 986-1600	3821
NAVY UNITED STATES DEPARTMENT	7699	C	805 989-1328	13786
Advantedge Technology Inc	8711	D	805 488-0405	19128

PORTER RANCH, CA - Los Angeles County

New America Funding LLC	6153	D	818 235-0640	7899
Cyberpolicy Inc	6411	C	877 626-9991	8540
Kaiser Foundation Hospitals	8062	D	833 574-2273	16179
American Technical Svcs Inc	8711	D	951 372-9664	19140

PORTERVILLE, CA - Tulare County

Exeter Packers Inc	0723	C	559 784-8820	266
Cco Holdings LLC	4841	C	559 560-5323	4477
Cco Holdings LLC	4841	C	559 202-1001	4482
E M Tharp Inc (PA)	5012	D	559 782-5800	5007
Home Depot USA Inc	5211	D	559 782-4611	6990
Lowes Home Centers LLC	5211	D	559 306-5000	7105
Bank of Sierra (HQ)	6022	C	559 782-4300	7657
Eagle Mountain Casino	7011	C	559 788-6220	9770
Sierra View Dst Hosp Leag Inc (PA)	8011	B	559 784-1110	15062
Califrnia Dept Dvlpmental Svcs	8051	A	559 782-2222	15362
Hacienda Care Center Inc	8051	D	559 784-7375	15504
Valley Careidence Opco LLC	8051	D	559 784-8371	15715
Wescordon Incorporated	8051	D	559 784-8371	15729
Sierra View Local Hospital Dst	8062	C	559 781-7877	16427
Porterville Dialysis Center	8092	C	559 781-5551	16990
Tule River Indian Hlth Ctr Inc	8093	D	559 784-2316	17147
Clemmie Gill Schl of Scnce Cns	8351	C	559 782-0883	18294
Tule River Alcoholism Program	8361	D	559 781-8797	18534
Tule River Economic Dev	8748	D	559 781-4271	20868

PORTOLA, CA - Plumas County

Eastern Plmas Hlth Care Fndtio (PA)	8099	C	530 832-4277	17231
R Joy Inc	8711	D	530 832-5760	19370

PORTOLA VALLEY, CA - San Mateo County

Azumo LLC	7371	C	415 610-7002	11443
Mach49 LLC	7699	D	415 939-1943	13781
Northern California Presbyteri	8361	C	650 851-1501	18496

POTTER VALLEY, CA - Mendocino County

Pacific Gas and Electric Co	4911	D	707 743-1197	4600

POWAY, CA - San Diego County

Benchmark Landscape Svcs Inc	0781	C	858 513-7190	390
Richmond Engineering Co Inc	0782	C	800 589-7058	534
Pacific Mfg & Design LLC (PA)	1541	D	813 784-9958	838
Kiewit Corporation	1542	D	858 208-4285	951
Eagle Paving Company Inc	1611	D	858 486-6400	1101
Harper Federal Cnstr LLC	1611	D	619 543-1296	1118
BCM Customer Service	1711	D	858 679-5757	1374
Western Fire Protection Inc (PA)	1711	D	858 513-4949	1598
Climatec LLC	1731	D	858 391-7000	1699
Electronic Control Systems LLC	1731	D	858 513-1911	1727
Gould Electric Inc	1731	D	858 486-1727	1738
Morrow-Meadows Corporation	1731	B	858 974-3650	1783
D and D Concrete Cnstr Inc	1771	D	858 748-5011	2113
Demcon Concrete Contrs Inc	1771	D	858 748-5090	2114
Quality Reinforcing Inc	1791	D	858 748-8400	2195
B Young Enterprises Inc	2434	D	858 748-0935	2479
Hpi Liquidations Inc	2653	C	858 391-7302	2518
Liberty Diversified Intl Inc	2653	C	858 391-7302	2519
Rugged Systems Inc	3571	D	858 391-1006	2812
Corovan Corporation (PA)	4214	C	858 762-8100	3581
Corovan Moving & Storage Co (HQ)	4214	D	858 748-1100	3582
Home Depot USA Inc	4225	C	858 859-4143	3717
Corodata Records MGT Inc	4226	D	858 748-1100	3789
Phonecom Inc	4813	D	973 577-6380	4330
IMS Electronics Recycling Inc	4953	C	858 679-1555	4899
Bay City Equipment Inds Inc	5063	D	619 938-8200	5542
Decision Sciences Intl Corp	5065	D	858 571-1900	5645
Time Motion Tools Inc	5072	C	858 679-0303	5736
Wassco	5084	D	858 679-0444	5882
Maintex Inc	5087	D	858 513-8286	5945
Chef Works Inc (PA)	5136	C	858 643-5600	6170
Moteng Inc	5136	C	858 715-2500	6181
Smart Stores Operations LLC	5141	C	858 748-0101	6390
Sysco San Diego Inc	5141	B	858 513-7300	6403
Perry Ford of Poway LLC	5511	D	858 748-1400	7278
Poway Toyota Scion Inc	5511	C	858 486-2900	7281
Southern Cal Disc Tire Co Inc	5531	C	858 486-3600	7367
Geico General Insurance Co	6411	A	858 848-8200	8574
Eappraiseit LLC (PA)	6531	D	800 281-6200	8991
First Amrcn Appraisal Svcs Inc (DH)	6541	D	619 938-7078	9234
Champion Investment Corp	7011	D	917 712-7807	9694
Williams Scotsman Inc	7319	C	619 710-8468	10733
Digirad Imaging Solutions Inc	7352	C	800 947-6134	10990
Hubb Systems LLC	7373	C	510 865-9100	12465
Califrnia Crtive Solutions Inc (PA)	7379	C	458 208-4131	12748
Body Beautiful Car Wash Inc	7542	C	858 748-4400	13686
Pkl Services Inc	7699	D	858 679-1755	13792
Maderas Golf Club	7992	D	858 451-8100	14272
Floaties Swim School LLC	7999	B	877 277-7946	14525
United Studios Self Def Inc	7999	C	858 486-8773	14580
Pomerado Operations LLC	8051	D	858 487-6242	15632
Palomar Health	8062	A	760 739-3000	16309
Palomar Health	8062	A	858 613-4000	16310
Palomar Health Medical Group (HQ)	8062	C	858 675-3100	16311
Palomar Medical Center	8062	B	858 613-4000	16313
Liberty Residential Svcs Inc	8082	D	858 500-0852	16889
Lorber Greenfield & Polito LLP (PA)	8111	D	858 486-6757	17557
Community Food Connection	8322	D	858 751-4613	17892
Community Dev Inst Head Start	8351	B	858 668-2985	18301
ISE Corporation	8731	D	858 413-1720	19715
T G T Enterprises Inc	8742	C	858 413-0300	20576

QUINCY, CA - Plumas County

Sierra Pacific Industries	2421	C	530 283-2820	2476
Feather River Disposal Inc	4212	B	530 283-2065	3389

QUINCY CA

GEOGRAPHIC SECTION

Company	SIC	EMP	PHONE	ENTRY#
Plumas Hospital District (PA)	8062	C	530 283-2121	16330
Sierra Cscade Fmly Opprtnities (PA)	8351	D	530 283-1242	18352

RAMONA, CA - San Diego County

Company	SIC	EMP	PHONE	ENTRY#
Demler Brothers LLC	0252	D	760 789-2457	224
Pro Traffic Services Inc	1711	D	760 906-6961	1534
Triton Logistics Corporation	4731	D	619 822-8832	4113
Spe Go Holdings Inc	7992	D	858 638-0672	14290
San Diego Country Estates Assn	8641	C	760 789-3788	18904

RANCHO CASCADES, CA - Los Angeles County

Company	SIC	EMP	PHONE	ENTRY#
Tutor Perini Corporation (PA)	1542	C	818 362-8391	1047
Tutor-Saliba Corporation (HQ)	1542	D	818 362-8391	1048
Becho Inc	1611	D	818 362-8391	1081
Desert Mechanical Inc	1711	A	702 873-7333	1421
Fisk Electric Company	1731	C	818 884-1166	1736
A A Gonzalez Inc	1742	D	818 367-2242	1898
Janco Corporation	3679	C	818 361-3366	2943
Spears Manufacturing Co (PA)	5083	C	818 364-1611	5812

RANCHO CORDOVA, CA - Sacramento County

Company	SIC	EMP	PHONE	ENTRY#
Els Investments	0781	C	916 388-0308	429
Landcare USA LLC	0782	D	916 635-0936	509
Teichert Inc	1442	D	916 351-0123	644
Judson Enterprises Inc (PA)	1522	B	916 596-6721	762
Central Striping Service Inc	1611	C	916 635-5175	1087
C C Myers Inc	1622	C	916 635-9370	1179
Russell Mechanical Inc	1711	C	916 635-2522	1551
Alessandro Electric Inc	1731	C	916 283-6966	1659
Bergelectric Corp	1731	C	916 636-1880	1681
North State Elec Contrs Inc	1731	C	916 572-0571	1790
D7 Roofing Services Inc	1761	D	916 447-2175	2055
Ron Nurss Inc	1771	C	916 631-9761	2154
Urata & Sons Concrete Inc	1771	C	916 638-5364	2168
Urata & Sons Concrete LLC	1771	C	916 638-5364	2169
Hmi Industrial Contractors Inc	1796	C	916 386-2586	2248
Pacific Coast Building Products Inc (PA)	3275	C	916 631-6500	2715
JL Haley Enterprises Inc	3599	C	916 631-6375	2854
Vander-Bend Manufacturing Inc	3599	C	916 631-6375	2857
Usko Express Inc	4222	D	916 515-8065	3667
Verizon Bus Netwrk Svcs LLC	4812	C	916 779-5600	4239
Atlas Disposal Industries LLC	4953	D	916 455-2800	4861
Automotive Importing Manufacturing Inc (PA)	5013	B	916 985-8505	5026
Sierra PCF HM & Comfort Inc	5075	C	916 638-0543	5771
Tri Tool Inc (HQ)	5084	C	916 288-6100	5875
McKesson Corporation	5122	D	916 636-8700	6127
Sffi Company Inc (PA)	5148	D	323 586-0000	6579
Simply Fresh Fruit Inc	5148	D	323 586-0000	6581
Lowes Home Centers LLC	5211	C	916 267-2850	7102
Southern Cal Disc Tire Co Inc	5531	D	916 638-2388	7358
E-Filliate Inc	5961	D	916 858-1000	7560
Educational Credit MGT Corp	6111	D	800 367-1590	7864
Wells Fargo Coml Dist Fin LLC	6153	D	916 636-2020	7912
Franklin Tmpleton Inv Svcs LLC (DH)	6211	A	916 463-1500	8085
Blue Shield of CA	6324	D	916 841-0584	8285
Health Net Federal Svcs LLC (DH)	6324	A	916 935-5000	8300
Health Net Pharmaceutical Svcs	6324	D	800 977-7532	8302
Vision Service Plan (PA)	6324	D	916 851-5000	8372
Aspire General Insurance Co	6411	D	877 789-4742	8496
Orba Insurance Services Inc	6411	D	916 858-1222	8632
Franklin Tmpleton Inv Svcs LLC	6722	B	650 312-4053	9371
Presidio Hotel Group LLC	7011	D	916 631-7500	10127
Corelogic Inc	7323	D	916 431-2146	10758
Bissell Brothers Janitorial	7349	D	916 635-1852	10863
Infor Public Sector Inc (DH)	7372	D	916 921-0883	12230
California Department Tech	7379	D	916 464-3747	12746
Enterprise Ntwrking Sltons Inc	7379	C		12786
ABI Document Support Svcs LLC	7389	D	909 793-0613	13171
Pacific Coast Companies Inc	7389	C	916 631-6500	13414
River City Auto Recovery Inc	7389	D	916 851-1100	13450
Woodland Memorial Hospital	7389	C	916 851-2100	13556
JJR Enterprises Inc (HQ)	7629	D	916 363-2666	13741
Permanente Medical Group Inc	8011	B	916 631-3000	14990
Center For Social Dynamics LLC	8049	D	916 382-4447	15273
A B C D Associates	8051	C	916 363-4843	15315
Dignity Health	8062	C	916 379-2996	16044
Dignity Health Med Foundation (DH)	8062	C	916 851-2000	16056
Kaiser Foundation Hospitals	8062	B	916 631-3088	16178
Mercy Healthcare Sacramento	8062	A	916 379-2871	16259
Accentcare HM Hlth Scrmnto Inc	8082	A	916 852-5888	16788
Turning Point Cmnty Programs (PA)	8093	D	916 364-8395	17148
Califrnia Dept Child Spport Sv (DH)	8322	D	916 464-5000	17858
Califrnia Fire Rscue Trning Au	8331	C	916 475-1660	18216
Child Action Inc (PA)	8351	C	916 369-0191	18281
Capital Engineering Cons Inc (PA)	8711	D	916 851-3500	19171
Consor North America Inc	8711	D	916 368-9181	19181
Dewberry Engineers Inc	8711	D	916 363-4210	19198
Falcon Technologies Inc	8711	D	916 638-1221	19223
Power Constructors Inc	8711	D	916 858-8601	19361
LLP Moss Adams	8721	D	916 503-8100	19599
CBA Site Services Inc	8748	D	925 754-7633	20721
Lyle Company	8748	D	916 266-7000	20801
TRC Solutions	8748	D	916 962-7001	20866

RANCHO CUCAMONGA, CA - San Bernardino County

Company	SIC	EMP	PHONE	ENTRY#
Schoolsfirst Federal Credit Un	0291	D	800 462-8328	238
Merchants Landscape Services	0781	D	909 981-1022	444
American De Rosa Lamparts LLC	1541	D	800 777-4440	804
Ledesma & Meyer Cnstr Co Inc	1542	D	909 297-1100	958
Penwal Industries Inc	1542	D	909 466-1555	988
WE Oneil Construction Co Cal	1542	C	909 466-5300	1053
Laird Construction Co Inc	1611	D	909 989-5595	1128
Precision Pipeline LLC	1623	B	909 229-6858	1250
Calvin Dubois	1711	D	909 222-6662	1392
General Coatings Corporation	1721	D	909 204-4150	1615
Professnal Elec Cnstr Svcs Inc	1731	C	909 373-4100	1812
Superior Elec Mech & Plbg Inc	1731	B	909 357-9400	1858
TRL Systems Incorporated	1731	D	909 390-8392	1866
La Rocque Better Roofs Inc	1761	D	909 476-2699	2071
Yellow Jacket Drlg Svcs LLC	1781	C	909 989-8563	2174
Jones/Covey Group Incorporated	1799	D	888 972-7581	2289
Reyes Coca-Cola Bottling LLC	2086	B	909 980-3121	2409
Doubleco Incorporated	3452	D	909 481-0799	2749
Rafco-Brickform LLC (PA)	3545	D	909 484-3399	2782
First Transit Inc	4111	D	909 948-3474	3130
Priority One Med Trnspt Inc (PA)	4119	D	909 948-4400	3287
Durham School Services L P	4151	C	909 899-1809	3329
Fox Transportation Inc (PA)	4212	D	909 291-4646	3390
New Legend Inc	4213	C	855 210-2300	3520
Honeyville Inc	4221	D	909 980-9500	3650
Distribution Alternatives Inc	4225	D	909 746-5600	3698
Home Depot USA Inc	4225	D	909 483-8115	3716
Msblous LLC	4225	D	909 929-9689	3733
NRG California South LP	4911	D	909 899-7241	4592
Cucamonga Valley Water Dst	4941	D	909 987-2591	4783
Falken Tire Holdings Inc	5014	D	800 723-2553	5069
Sumitomo Rubber North Amer Inc (HQ)	5014	C	909 466-1116	5073
Casabella Holdings LLC	5021	D	845 348-0012	5082
Bradshaw International Inc (PA)	5023	B	909 476-3884	5112
General Micro Systems Inc (PA)	5045	D	909 980-4863	5308
Yuneec USA Inc	5065	D	855 284-8888	5719
California Box II	5113	D	909 944-9202	6075
L & R Distributors Inc	5131	B	909 980-3807	6156
Cerenzia Foods Inc	5141	D	909 989-4000	6245
Nongshim America Inc (HQ)	5141	C	909 481-3698	6272
Frito-Lay North America Inc	5145	B	909 941-6214	6461
Shining Ocean Inc	5146	C	253 826-3700	6481
Evolution Fresh Inc	5148	C	800 794-9986	6537
Newco Distributors Inc	5191	D	909 291-2240	6829
Home Depot USA Inc	5211	D	909 948-9200	7028
Lowes Home Centers LLC	5211	D	909 476-9697	7032
M & G Jewelers Inc	5944	D	909 989-2929	7551
Arrowhead Central Credit Union (PA)	6061	B	866 212-4333	7755
CU Cooperative Systems Inc (PA)	6062	B	909 948-2500	7824
Thrive Mortgage LLC	6162	D	909 527-3736	8024
ML Mortgage Corp	6163	D	909 652-0780	8048
Carrington Mortgage Svcs LLC	6211	C	909 226-7963	8072
Agent Franchise LLC	6321	C	949 930-5025	8256
Inland Empire Health Plan (PA)	6321	A	909 890-2000	8266
Lereta LLC	6512	C	626 332-1942	8732
National Community Renaissance	6513	C	909 948-7579	8846
Allmark Inc (PA)	6531	C	909 989-7556	8898
Firstsrvice Rsidential Cal Inc (DH)	6531	D	909 981-4131	9016
Mainstreet Realtors	6531	D	909 373-3821	9090
Rexford Industrial LLC	6531	D	909 987-2174	9166
National Cmnty Renaissance Cal	6552	C	619 223-9222	9265
National Cmnty Renaissance Cal (PA)	6552	D	909 483-2444	9266
Oakwood Corporate Housing Inc	7021	C	909 922-8272	10395
Collection Technology Inc	7322	D	800 743-4284	10739
Butler America Holdings Inc	7361	D	909 417-3660	11099
Career Strategies Tmpry Inc	7361	C	909 230-4504	11104
Novatime Technology Inc (DH)	7361	D	909 895-8100	11185
All Starz Stffing Cnslting Inc	7363	D	909 870-9559	11270
Network Intgrtion Partners Inc	7373	D	909 919-2800	12500
Diplomatic Security Svcs LLC	7381	D	909 463-8409	12965
Nationwide Guard Services Inc	7381	B	909 608-1112	13007

GEOGRAPHIC SECTION

REDDING CA

	SIC	EMP	PHONE	ENTRY#
Harrison Iyke	7382	D	909 463-8409	13123
Formerra LLC	7389	D	888 502-0951	13293
Par Western Line Contrs LLC	7389	A	760 737-0925	13417
Starco Group Inc (PA)	7389	D	909 989-9898	13486
Red Hill Country Club	7997	D	909 982-1358	14427
Grove Diagnstc Imaging Ctr Inc	8011	B	909 982-8638	14768
Professional Assessment &	8049	D	909 980-1000	15300
Knd Development 55 LLC	8062	C	909 581-6400	16206
Perris Valley Cmnty Hosp LLC	8062	C	909 581-6400	16322
Branlyn Prominence Inc (PA)	8082	D	909 476-9030	16826
Blomberg Bnson Grrett Inc A La	8111	D	909 945-5000	17388
Universal Technical Inst Inc	8249	C	909 484-1929	17798
Horrigan Enterprises Inc	8322	C	909 481-9663	18006
In-Roads Creative Programs	8322	B	909 989-9944	18012
Vocational Imprv Program Inc (PA)	8331	D	909 483-5924	18256
Monte Vista Child Care Ctr Inc	8351	C	909 476-6780	18335
CDM Constructors Inc	8711	D	909 579-3500	19177
Eide Bailly LLP	8721	B	909 466-4410	19569
Gentex Corporation	8731	C	909 481-7667	19703
Accent Computer Solutions LLC	8748	D	909 825-2772	20673

RANCHO DOMINGUEZ, CA - Los Angeles County

	SIC	EMP	PHONE	ENTRY#
Bi Nutraceuticals Inc	2087	C	310 669-2100	2415
Ethos Seafood Group LLC	2092	D	312 858-3474	2420
Santa Monica Seafood Company (PA)	2092	D	310 886-7900	2423
Heavy Load Transfer LLC	4212	D	310 816-0260	3403
Nippon Ex Nec Lgstics Amer Inc	4212	D	310 604-6100	3416
Unis LLC	4225	D	310 747-7388	3774
Kw International Inc	4226	D	213 703-6914	3794
Kw International Inc	4731	D	310 747-1380	4047
Iap West Inc	5013	D	310 667-9720	5045
CDS Moving Equipment Inc (PA)	5084	D	310 631-1100	5825
Neway Packaging Corp (PA)	5113	D	602 454-9000	6080
Afc Distribution Corp	5141	C	310 604-3630	6238
Union Sup Cmsy Solutions Inc	5141	B	785 357-5005	6408

RANCHO MIRAGE, CA - Riverside County

	SIC	EMP	PHONE	ENTRY#
Cellco Partnership	4812	D	760 568-5542	4201
Agua Clnte Band Chilla Indians	7011	A	760 321-2000	9599
Hst Lessee Mission Hills LP	7011	D	760 328-5955	9878
Ksl Rancho Mirage Operating Co Inc	7011	B	760 568-2727	9951
Omni Hotels Corporation	7011	B	760 568-2727	10065
Ritz-Carlton Hotel Company LLC	7011	B	760 321-8282	10164
Richman Management Corporation	7381	B	760 832-8520	13028
Country Villa Service Corp	7389	C	760 340-0053	13246
Df One Operator LLC	7389	D	310 961-9739	13266
Mission Hills Country Club Inc	7997	C	760 324-9400	14407
Springs Club Inc	7997	D	760 328-0254	14464
Thunderbird Country Club	7997	D	760 328-2161	14472
Desert Crdlgy Cons Med Group I	8011	C	760 346-0642	14725
Desert Orthpd Ctr A Med Group (PA)	8011	D	760 568-2684	14727
Eisenhower Medical Center (PA)	8062	A	760 340-3911	16068
Eisenhower Medical Center	8071	D	760 773-1364	16717
Eisenhower Medical Center	8082	C	760 773-1888	16857
Betty Ford Center (HQ)	8093	C	760 773-4100	17014
Dual Diagnosis Trtmnt Ctr Inc	8099	D	949 324-4531	17229
Palm Valley School	8211	D	760 328-0861	17739
Country Vlla Rncho Mrage Hlthc	8322	D	760 340-0053	17902
Mission Hills Senior Living	8361	D	760 770-7737	18488
Morningside Community Assn	8641	C	760 328-3323	18884
Ameritac Inc (PA)	8744	D	925 989-2942	20649

RANCHO MISSION VIEJO, CA - Orange County

	SIC	EMP	PHONE	ENTRY#
NRG Health & Fitness LLC	7991	D	310 570-5436	14221

RANCHO MURIETA, CA - Sacramento County

	SIC	EMP	PHONE	ENTRY#
Buena Vista Cnstr Group Inc	1521	D	916 354-9832	664
Rancho Murieta Country Club	7997	D	916 354-2400	14425

RANCHO PALOS VERDES, CA - Los Angeles County

	SIC	EMP	PHONE	ENTRY#
Smart & Final Stores LLC	5141	D	310 832-4179	6388
Long Point Development LLC	7011	A	310 265-2800	9985
Masergy Cloud Cmmnications Inc	7389	D	310 921-7000	13364
Estates At Trump Nat Golf CLB	7992	D	310 265-5000	14261
Bay Clubs Company LLC	7997	B	310 541-2582	14336
Salvation Army (HQ)	8322	C	562 264-3600	18106

RANCHO SANTA FE, CA - San Diego County

	SIC	EMP	PHONE	ENTRY#
First National Bank	6021	B	858 756-3023	7626
Pacific Western Bank	6021	B	858 756-3023	7636
Merrill Lynch Prce Fnner Smith	6211	D	800 403-8796	8120
Archipelago Development Inc	6552	D	858 699-6272	9245
Groves Capital Inc	6799	C	619 519-4453	9515
Huntington Hotel Company	7011	D	858 756-1131	9880
Rancho Vlncia Rsort Prtners LL	7011	B	858 756-1123	10139
Del Mar Country Club Inc	7997	D	858 759-5500	14367
Fairbanks Ranch Cntry CLB Inc	7997	C	858 259-8811	14375
Rancho Santa Fe Association	7997	D	858 756-1182	14426

RANCHO SANTA MARGARI, CA - Orange County

	SIC	EMP	PHONE	ENTRY#
Lowes Home Centers LLC	5211	D	949 589-5005	7033
Group Rossignol Usa Inc	5941	D	949 452-9050	7542
Foundation 9 Entertainment Inc (PA)	7372	C	949 698-1500	12197
Jipc Management Inc	8741	A	949 916-2000	20123

RCHO STA MARG, CA - Orange County

	SIC	EMP	PHONE	ENTRY#
Park West Landscape Maint Inc (PA)	0782	B	949 546-8300	528
Tracy Ryder Landscape Inc	0782	D	949 858-7017	540
Barr Engineering Inc	1711	D	562 944-1722	1371
Santa Margarita Water District	4941	C	949 459-6400	4834
Virtium LLC	5045	D	949 888-2444	5369
Felt Racing LLC	5941	D	949 452-9050	7541
Kisco Senior Living LLC	6513	D	949 888-2250	8838
Melissa Data Corporation (PA)	7371	D	949 858-3000	11740
Fakouri Electrical Engrg Inc	7378	D	949 888-2400	12707
Green-N-Clean Ex Car Wash Inc	7542	D	949 749-4977	13693
Capital Invstmnts Vntures Corp (PA)	8621	C	949 858-0647	18743
Padi Americas Inc	8621	C	949 858-7234	18756
Savice Inc	8641	D	949 888-2444	18906
Expitrans Inc	8742	D	949 650-4600	20368
Gmu Geotechnical Inc	8999	D	949 888-6513	20889

RED BLUFF, CA - Tehama County

	SIC	EMP	PHONE	ENTRY#
Outback Contractors Inc	1611	C	530 528-2225	1150
Cedar Creek Corporation	1623	C	530 364-2143	1203
John Wheeler Logging Inc	2411	C	530 527-2993	2474
Walmart Inc	4225	A	530 529-0916	3779
Concessionaires Urban Park (PA)	7999	B	530 529-1512	14507
Concessionaires Urban Park	7999	D	530 529-1513	14509
Northern Vly Indian Hlth Inc	8021	D	530 529-2567	15242
St Elizabeth Community Hosp (DH)	8062	C	530 529-7760	16455
Restpadd Health Corp	8099	D	530 727-9390	17314
Rolling Hills Clinic	8099	D	530 690-2334	17317

REDDING, CA - Shasta County

	SIC	EMP	PHONE	ENTRY#
Maximus Tree Works LLC	0783	D	480 822-8050	557
JF Shea Construction Inc	1521	D	530 246-4292	683
Muse Concrete Contractors Inc	1611	D	530 226-5151	1142
Bill Sharp Electrical Contr	1731	D	530 338-1735	1683
Redding Aero Enterprises Inc	4111	D	530 224-2300	3191
American Med Rspnse Inland Emp	4119	A	530 241-2686	3229
Redding Lumber Transport Inc	4214	D	530 241-8193	3592
California Oregon Broadcasting (HQ)	4833	D	530 243-7777	4414
Cco Holdings LLC	4841	C	530 646-4026	4479
Cco Holdings LLC	4841	C	864 679-1745	4488
Maas Energy Works LLC	4911	C	530 710-8545	4585
Pacific Gas and Electric Co	4911	A	530 365-7672	4634
Gulfside Supply Inc	5033	C	530 241-1615	5221
Peterson Machinery Co	5082	A	530 243-5410	5797
Lassen Canyon Nursery Inc (PA)	5141	C	530 223-1075	6260
Shasta-Siskiyou Transport	5171	D	530 241-1167	6718
Harbor Distributing LLC	5181	D	530 691-5811	6767
Lowes Home Centers LLC	5211	D	530 351-0181	7094
North Valley Bancorp	6022	B	530 226-2900	7700
North Valley Bank	6022	C	530 226-2920	7701
Change Lending LLC	6162	D	530 282-1166	7946
Merrill Lynch Prce Fnner Smith	6211	D	530 223-3005	8106
California Physicians Service	6324	D	530 351-6115	8287
Bridge Bay Resort & Marina	7011	D	530 275-3021	9659
Kaidan Hospitality LP	7011	D	530 221-8700	9933
Larkspur Group LLC	7011	C	530 223-9344	9966
Redding Rancheria (PA)	7011	D	530 225-8979	10144
Redding Rnchria Ecnmic Dev Cor	7011	B	530 243-3377	10145
Sheraton Rdding Ht At Sndial B	7011	D	530 364-2800	10228
Win River Hotel Corporation	7011	A	530 226-5111	10370
Cleanrite Inc	7217	D	530 246-4886	10471
Pre-Employcom Inc	7361	D	800 300-1821	11202
Sfn Group Inc	7363	A	530 222-3434	11334
Altexsoft Inc	7379	C	877 777-9097	12730
Enterprise Rnt--car Scrmnto LL	7514	C	530 223-0700	13585
Walsh Group Inc	7991	D	530 221-4405	14241
Yanaco Inc	7996	C	530 246-9550	14317
Big Lgue Dreams Consulting LLC	7997	D	530 223-1177	14344
Riverview Golf and Country CLB	7997	D	530 224-2254	14430
MD Imaging Inc A Prof Med Corp	8011	D	530 243-1249	14889
Redding Pathologists Lab (PA)	8011	C	530 225-8000	15012

Employee Codes: A=Over 500 employees, B=251-500
C=101-250, D=51-100, E=20-50, F=10-19, G=1-9

REDDING CA

GEOGRAPHIC SECTION

	SIC	EMP	PHONE	ENTRY#
Crestwood Behavioral Hlth Inc	8051	C	530 221-0976	15414
Ku Kyoung	8051	C	510 582-2765	15533
Ocadian Care Centers LLC	8051	A	530 246-9000	15605
Windsor Redding Care Ctr LLC	8051	D	530 246-0600	15741
Mercy HM Svcs A Cal Ltd Partnr **(DH)**	8062	A	530 225-6000	16260
Mercy Surgery Center LP	8062	D	530 225-7400	16269
Northern Cal Rhblttion Hosp LL	8062	D	530 246-9000	16287
Patients Hospital	8062	D	530 225-8700	16320
Prime Hlthcare Svcs - Shsta LL	8062	A	530 244-5400	16343
Vibra Healthcare LLC	8062	C	530 246-9000	16618
Dunamis Center Inc	8093	D	530 338-0087	17057
Vitalant Research Institute	8099	C	530 221-0600	17350
County of Shasta	8322	D	530 246-9622	17941
Far Nrthern Crdnting Cncil On **(PA)**	8322	D	530 222-4791	17981
Northern Vly Cthlic Scial Svc	8322	C	530 241-0552	18067
Shascade Community Svcs Inc	8322	D	530 247-8324	18130
Shascade Community Svcs Inc	8322	D	530 243-1653	18131
Veterans of Foreign Wars of US	8641	D	530 241-9168	18926
Pace Engineering Inc	8711	D	530 244-0202	19345
Northstar Senior Living Inc	8741	A	530 242-8300	20164
City of Redding **(PA)**	9111	A	530 225-4079	20914

REDLANDS, CA - San Bernardino County

	SIC	EMP	PHONE	ENTRY#
Larry Jacinto Farming Inc	0762	D	909 794-2276	377
Westcor Construction of Cal	1521	D	909 796-8900	741
Russell Hobbs Inc	1541	D	909 792-8257	841
Robert Clapper Cnstr Svcs Inc	1542	D	909 829-3688	1009
Larry Jacinto Construction Inc	1611	D	909 794-2151	1129
Ach Mechanical Contractors Inc	1711	D	909 307-2850	1335
Plumbing Systems West Inc	1711	D	909 794-3823	1531
Pro-Craft Construction Inc	1711	D	909 790-5222	1535
Enerpath Services Inc	1731	D	909 335-1699	1730
Faith Electric LLC	1731	C	909 767-2682	1733
Mobiz It Inc	1731	D	909 453-6700	1779
Advanced Chemical Trnspt Inc	4212	C	951 790-7989	3365
CJ Logistics America LLC	4213	D	909 363-4354	3454
Ashley Furniture Inds LLC	4225	B	909 825-4900	3676
Lamps Plus Inc	4225	D	909 801-5333	3723
Maersk Whsng Dist Svcs USA LLC	4731	C	801 301-1732	4054
Socalgas	4924	D	909 307-7022	4726
Southern California Gas Co	4924	B	909 335-7802	4734
Spectra Premium (usa) Corp	5013	C	951 653-0640	5062
Environmental Systems Research Inst **(PA)**	5045	A	909 793-2853	5300
Hydro Tek Systems Inc	5087	D	909 799-9222	5943
P & R Paper Supply Co Inc **(HQ)**	5113	D	909 389-1807	6088
Haralambos Beverage Co	5181	C	562 347-4300	6764
Home Depot USA Inc	5211	C	909 748-0505	6978
Lowes Home Centers LLC	5211	D	909 307-8883	7083
Dick Dewese Chevrolet Inc	5511	D	909 793-2681	7195
Ken Grody Redlands LLC	5511	D	909 793-3211	7245
Akh Company Inc	5531	D	909 748-5016	7339
Mountain West Financial Inc **(PA)**	6162	B	909 793-1500	8004
Lois Lauer Realty **(PA)**	6531	D	909 748-7000	9076
ABI Attorneys Service Inc **(PA)**	7334	D	909 793-0613	10781
Redlands Ford Inc	7532	D	909 793-3211	13647
Advanced Innovative Tech Corp	7538	D	417 831-9444	13654
Chp	7822	D	909 213-3788	13962
Harkins Theatres Inc	7832	D	909 793-7993	13998
Redlands Country Club	7997	D	909 793-2661	14428
Beaver Medical Clinic Inc **(PA)**	8011	D	909 793-3311	14629
Kaiser Foundation Hospitals	8011	C	888 750-0036	14805
Ash Holdings LLC	8051	D	909 793-2609	15334
Humangood Norcal	8059	C	909 793-1233	15861
Loma Linda University Med Ctr	8062	D	909 558-4000	16222
Loma Linda University Med Ctr	8062	D	909 558-9275	16228
Redlands Community Hospital **(PA)**	8062	D	909 335-5500	16359
Interntional Un Oper Engineers	8631	A	909 307-8700	18783
YMCA of East Valley **(PA)**	8641	C	909 798-9622	18933
Epic Management LP **(PA)**	8741	D	909 799-1818	20083
RHS Corp	8741	A	909 335-5500	20195
Bon Appetit Management Co	8742	D	909 748-8970	20299

REDONDO BEACH, CA - Los Angeles County

	SIC	EMP	PHONE	ENTRY#
Fire Safe Systems Inc	1711	D	310 542-0585	1438
Northrop Grmmn Spce & Mssn Sys	3714	B	310 812-4321	2975
Northrop Grumman Systems Corp	3721	B	310 812-1089	2982
Dsd Trucking Inc	4581	D	310 338-3395	3891
Mapcargo Global Logistics **(PA)**	4731	D	310 297-8300	4057
Stevens Global Logistics Inc **(PA)**	4731	A	800 229-7284	4100
Scat Enterprises Inc	5013	C	310 370-5501	5059
Brownstone Companies Inc	5065	A	310 297-3600	5636
Smart & Final Stores Inc	5141	C	323 497-8528	6307
Smart & Final Stores LLC	5141	D	310 540-6157	6348
Bicara Ltd	5147	B	310 316-6222	6489
HMC Assets LLC	6331	C	310 535-9293	8386
Main Street Management LLC **(PA)**	6531	D	310 640-3100	9089
Greenhedge Escrow	6541	C	310 640-3040	9235
Wedgewood Inc **(PA)**	6799	D	310 640-3070	9578
Portofino Hotel Partners LP	7011	C	310 379-8481	10124
K & P Janitorial Services	7349	D	310 540-8878	10914
Cputer Inc	7379	D	844 394-1538	12769
Gsg Protective Services CA Inc	7381	C	310 371-5300	12980
Gable House Inc	7933	D	310 378-2265	14115
Optumcare Management LLC	8011	D	310 316-0811	14942
Nurturing Tots Inc	8351	D	818 996-1602	18338
Beach Cities Health District	8399	C	310 374-3426	18566
Westwind Engineering Inc	8711	C	310 831-3454	19439
NBC Consulting Inc	8742	D	310 798-5000	20484

REDWOOD CITY, CA - San Mateo County

	SIC	EMP	PHONE	ENTRY#
Sears Home Imprv Pdts Inc	1521	C	650 645-9974	716
Dpr Construction Inc **(PA)**	1542	A	650 474-1450	906
Dpr Construction A Gen Partnr **(HQ)**	1542	A	650 474-1450	911
S J Amoroso Cnstr Co LLC **(PA)**	1542	B	650 654-1900	1016
WL Butler Inc	1542	D	650 361-1270	1064
Granite Rock Co	1611	D	650 869-3370	1114
Barnard Bessac Joint Venture	1629	D	650 212-8957	1287
Obsidian Security Inc	1731	D	949 520-2866	1793
Sound Inpatient Physicians Inc	1731	C	650 257-3470	1841
Codexis Inc **(PA)**	2819	C	650 421-8100	2573
Adverum Biotechnologies Inc **(PA)**	2836	C	650 656-9323	2616
Granite Rock Co	2951	D	650 482-3800	2649
Oracle America Inc **(HQ)**	3571	A	650 506-7000	2809
Nvent Thermal LLC **(DH)**	3822	B	650 474-7414	3014
Seer Inc **(PA)**	3826	C	650 453-0000	3033
Menlo Worldwide Forwarding Inc	4513	A	650 596-9600	3858
Slashsupport Inc	4813	C	650 385-2000	4340
Together Labs Inc	4813	C	650 231-4688	4351
Silicon Valley Clean Water	4952	C	650 591-7121	4851
ABC Bus Inc	5012	D	650 368-3364	5000
Cyara Solutions Corp	5045	C	650 549-8522	5290
I2c Inc	5045	B	650 593-5400	5313
Core & Main Inc	5099	C	650 366-3833	6037
Piercey North Inc	5511	C	408 240-1400	7279
Putnam Motors Inc	5511	C	650 381-3152	7283
Towne Motor Company	5511	C	650 366-5744	7315
Southern Cal Disc Tire Co Inc	5531	C	650 366-4003	7370
San Mateo Credit Union	6061	D	650 363-1725	7798
Provident Credit Union **(PA)**	6062	D	650 508-0300	7831
Bluevine Capital Inc	6163	B	888 216-9619	8030
Permanente Medical Group Inc	6324	A	650 598-2852	8354
Kaspick & Co LLC **(DH)**	6411	D	650 585-4100	8599
Chapel of Chimes	6553	D	650 349-4411	9283
Equinix Inc **(PA)**	6798	C	650 598-6000	9466
Shiva Enterprises Inc	7011	C	650 366-2000	10231
Aricent Inc	7371	C	650 632-4310	11422
Aricent US Inc	7371	C	650 632-4310	11423
Azumio Inc **(PA)**	7371	D	719 310-3774	11442
Delphix Corp **(PA)**	7371	A	650 494-1645	11537
Eacom Inc	7371	D	650 628-1500	11560
Epic Creations Inc	7371	C	650 918-7327	11572
Findem Inc	7371	C	925 212-7277	11600
Glu Mobile Inc **(HQ)**	7371	D	415 800-6100	11627
Isheriff Inc	7371	C	650 412-4300	11682
Lmi Inc **(PA)**	7371	D	650 453-8305	11713
Marklogic Corporation **(HQ)**	7371	C	650 655-2300	11736
Minio Inc	7371	D	833 696-6342	11751
Moloco Inc **(PA)**	7371	A	858 531-6550	11756
Oc Acquisition LLC **(HQ)**	7371	C	650 506-7000	11791
Paracel Inc	7371	C	858 309-4733	11813
Peopleai Inc	7371	D	888 997-3675	11820
Perfect World Entrmt Inc	7371	C	650 590-7700	11821
Pubmatic Inc **(PA)**	7371	B	650 331-3485	11851
Reltio Inc **(PA)**	7371	B	855 360-3282	11872
Satmetrix Systems Inc	7371	C	650 227-8300	11903
Steppechange LLC	7371	D	415 279-7638	11947
Sumo Logic Inc **(PA)**	7371	A	650 810-8700	11955
Synack Inc **(PA)**	7371	C	855 796-2251	11959
True North America Inc	7371	D	877 525-8783	11992
Workspan	7371	D	650 223-4243	12048
Actiance Inc	7372	C	650 631-6300	12072
Agiloft Inc **(PA)**	7372	B	650 459-5637	12081
Alation Inc **(PA)**	7372	C	650 779-4440	12086
Box Inc **(PA)**	7372	A	877 729-4269	12124
C3AI INC **(PA)**	7372	A	650 503-2200	12127
Cyara Inc **(PA)**	7372	C	650 549-8522	12154

GEOGRAPHIC SECTION

RIDGECREST CA

	SIC	EMP	PHONE	ENTRY#
Electronic Arts Inc (PA)	7372	B	650 628-1500	12179
Gearbox Pubg San Francisco Inc	7372	D	650 590-7700	12203
Informatica Holdco Inc	7372	A	650 385-5000	12231
Informatica Inc	7372	A	650 385-5000	12232
Informatica LLC (DH)	7372	B	650 385-5000	12233
Invoice2go LLC (DH)	7372	C	650 300-5180	12244
Material Security Inc	7372	D	408 649-9882	12262
Nreach Online Services Inc	7372	B	425 301-9168	12293
Oracle Usa Inc	7372	A	650 506-7000	12309
Paxata Inc	7372	D	650 542-7897	12315
Planful Inc (HQ)	7372	C	650 249-7100	12319
Poshmark Inc (HQ)	7372	A	650 262-4771	12325
Simpplr Inc (PA)	7372	C	650 396-2646	12350
Smarsh Inc	7372	C	650 631-6300	12353
Trion Worlds Inc	7372	B	650 631-9800	12385
Workboard Inc (PA)	7372	C	650 294-4480	12403
Zuora Inc (PA)	7372	B	800 425-1281	12410
Inflection Risk Solutions LLC	7374	C	650 618-9910	12582
Split Software Inc (PA)	7374	C	650 399-0005	12629
Digital Insight Corporation (HQ)	7375	C	818 879-1010	12658
Zyme Solutions Inc (PA)	7375	D	650 585-2258	12691
Flipboard Inc (PA)	7379	C	650 323-6547	12792
Itco Solutions Inc	7379	B	650 367-0514	12819
Oracle Systems Corporation (HQ)	7379	A	650 506-7000	12850
Sizmek Dsp Inc (PA)	7379	C	650 595-1300	12878
Anomali Incorporated	7382	C	844 484-7328	13095
Redwood Support Group Inc	7382	D	650 815-8933	13140
Shutterfly LLC (HQ)	7384	C	650 610-5200	13162
Assured Relocation Inc	7389	C	888 670-9700	13199
Equilar Inc	7389	C	877 441-6090	13280
Trilliant Networks Inc (PA)	7389	D	650 204-5050	13518
Century Theatres Inc	7833	C	866 322-4547	14014
Bay Clubs Company LLC	7991	B	650 593-1112	14179
Baysport Inc	8011	C	650 593-2800	14628
Kaiser Foundation Hospitals	8011	A	650 299-2000	14820
Permanente Medical Group Inc	8011	A	650 299-2000	14973
Permanente Medical Group Inc	8011	A	650 299-2015	14974
Sequoia Health Services (DH)	8062	B	650 369-5811	16411
Sequoia Health Services	8062	A	650 367-5544	16412
Genomic Health Inc (HQ)	8071	A	650 556-9300	16723
Stanford Health Care	8099	A	650 723-5256	17329
Fish & Richardson PC	8111	C	650 839-5070	17458
Gunderson Dttmer Stugh Vllnuve (PA)	8111	C	650 321-2400	17488
Weil Gotshal & Manges LLP	8111	C	650 802-3000	17675
Leland Stanford Junior Univ	8221	A	650 935-5365	17763
Abilitypath	8322	C	650 259-8500	17820
Abilitypath Housing (PA)	8322	D	650 494-0550	17821
Breakthrough Behavioral Inc	8322	C	888 282-2522	17855
Kainos HM Trning Ctr For Dvlpm	8322	C	650 361-1355	18032
Wider Circle Inc	8361	D	650 924-2491	18550
Care 2	8699	D	650 622-0860	19075
Bkf Engineers (PA)	8711	C	650 482-6300	19155
Des Architects Engineers Inc	8712	C	650 364-6453	19465
Yougov America Inc	8713	B	650 462-8000	19528
Seiler LLP (PA)	8721	C	650 365-4646	19629
Karius Inc	8731	C	866 452-7487	19718
Kartos Therapeutics Inc	8731	D	650 542-0130	19719
Verve Group Inc	8732	C	760 536-8350	19856
Aviso Inc	8742	C	650 567-5470	20286
Kyo Autism Therapy Inc	8742	C	877 264-6747	20429
Motorola Good Technology Group	8742	D	408 327-6000	20476
Mythic Inc	8742	D	734 707-7339	20481
Xdbs Corporation	8742	D	415 513-0068	20618
Inflectioncom Inc	8748	C	650 618-9910	20778
Zeno Group Inc	8999	D	650 801-7950	20909

REDWOOD VALLEY, CA - Mendocino County

	SIC	EMP	PHONE	ENTRY#
Consoldted Tribal Hlth Prj Inc	8093	D	707 485-5115	17034

REEDLEY, CA - Fresno County

	SIC	EMP	PHONE	ENTRY#
Gerawan Farming LLC	0175	C	559 638-9281	106
Ito Packing Co Inc	0723	C	559 638-2531	280
Walter L Jones Family Ltd	0723	C	559 591-1515	313
Youngstown Grape Distrs Inc	0723	C	559 638-2271	320
Cal Packing and Storage LP	4222	D	559 638-2929	3653
Moonlight Packing Corporation	4783	A	559 638-7799	4133
Moonlight Packing Corporation	5142	D	559 638-7799	6424
Moonlight Packing Corporation (PA)	5148	D	559 638-7799	6563
Pacific Housing Group LLC	5271	D	559 651-1133	7127
Trinity Packing Company Inc	7389	B	559 433-3785	13519
Trinity Packing Company Inc (PA)	7389	B	559 743-3913	13520
Sierra View Homes	8051	C	559 637-2256	15666
Reedley Community Hospital	8062	D	559 638-8155	16361
Sierra Kings District Hospital	8062	B	559 638-8155	16426
Gar Bennett LLC (PA)	8741	C	559 638-6311	20097

RESEDA, CA - Los Angeles County

	SIC	EMP	PHONE	ENTRY#
Valley Management Associates (PA)	5812	D	818 881-6801	7515
Eisenberg Vlg of The Los Angle	8051	D	818 774-3372	15429
Los Angles Jewish HM For Aging (PA)	8051	B	818 774-3000	15554
Los Angles Jewish HM For Aging	8051	B	818 774-3000	15555
Longwood Management Corp	8062	C	818 881-7414	16238
Child Development Institute	8322	B	818 888-4559	17879
County of Los Angeles	8322	A	818 708-4500	17911
Advanced Bioservices LLC (PA)	8741	D	818 342-0100	20011
Chase Group Llc	8742	B	818 708-3533	20314

RIALTO, CA - San Bernardino County

	SIC	EMP	PHONE	ENTRY#
Sierra Lathing Company Inc	1742	C	909 421-0211	1963
Radial South LP	4225	B	610 491-7000	3748
Hazmat Tsdf Inc (PA)	4953	D	909 873-4411	4898
Jeld-Wen Inc	5031	C	909 879-8700	5171
Ricoh Electronics Inc	5044	D	714 566-2500	5254
Distribution Alternatives Inc	5122	D	909 770-8900	6105
Lane Winpak Inc (HQ)	5199	D	909 386-1762	6923
Walmart Inc	5311	A	909 820-9912	7135
Burlingame Industries Inc (PA)	7033	D	909 355-7000	10414
Mercy Air Tri-County LLC	7623	C	909 829-1051	13727

RICHGROVE, CA - Tulare County

	SIC	EMP	PHONE	ENTRY#
Vincent B Zaninovich Sons Inc	0172	A	661 720-9031	88
Famous Vineyards LLC	5148	D	661 392-5000	6539
Sun Pacific Marketing Coop Inc	5148	B	559 784-6845	6583
T & R Bangis Argriculture Svcs	7361	A	661 725-1948	11241

RICHMOND, CA - Contra Costa County

	SIC	EMP	PHONE	ENTRY#
Siteworks Landscape Inc	0781	D	510 843-0409	464
Gardeners Guild Inc	0782	C	415 457-0400	491
Alten Construction Inc	1521	D	510 234-4200	653
C Overaa & Co (PA)	1542	C	510 234-0926	885
Oliver & Company Inc	1542	D	510 412-9090	980
Manson Construction Co	1629	D	510 232-6319	1310
Bay City Mechanical Inc (PA)	1711	D	510 233-7000	1372
Sunpower Corporation Systems (DH)	1711	D	510 260-8200	1576
Champion Scaffold Services Inc	1799	D	510 788-4731	2265
First Student Inc	4151	C	510 237-6677	3336
United Parcel Service Inc	4215	B	510 262-2338	3632
Shm Mbyh LLC	4493	D	510 236-1013	3825
MBA Polymers Inc	4953	D	510 231-9031	4911
Palecek Imports Inc (PA)	5021	C	510 236-7730	5099
My True Image Mfg Inc	5047	D	510 970-7990	5433
Dahl-Beck Electric Co	5063	D	510 237-2325	5552
Sims Group USA Corporation (DH)	5093	D	510 412-5300	6017
Oakland Paper & Supply Incorporated (PA)	5113	C	510 307-4242	6082
Advanced Lubrication Spc Inc	5172	C	215 244-2114	6721
T F Louderback Inc	5181	C	510 965-6120	6784
Breakthru Beverage Cal LLC	5182	D	510 236-2233	6788
Monterey Pine Apartments	6513	C	510 215-1926	8845
Spr Op Co Inc	6719	C	510 232-5030	9338
Pacific Hotel Management LLC	7011	C	510 262-0700	10083
Rubicon Programs Incorporated (PA)	7349	D	510 235-1516	10956
Universal Bldg Svcs & Sup Co (PA)	7349	D	510 527-1078	10980
Qrs Corporation (PA)	7371	D	510 215-5000	11855
Richmond Sanitary Service Inc (HQ)	7699	D	510 262-7100	13795
Century Theatres Inc	7833	B	510 758-9626	14015
California Dept of Pub Hlth	8011	B	510 231-7408	14643
Kaiser Foundation Hospitals	8011	A	510 307-1500	14808
Permanente Medical Group Inc	8011	A	510 231-5406	14975
Young MNS Chrstn Assn of E Bay	8641	B	510 412-5640	18965
Young MNS Chrstn Assn of E Bay	8641	C	510 223-7070	18972
Young MNS Chrstn Assn of E Bay	8641	A	510 222-9622	18977
Young MNS Chrstn Assn of E Bay	8641		510 412-5647	18978
Young MNS Chrstn Assn of E Bay	8641	B	510 222-9622	18979
Young MNS Chrstn Assn of E Bay	8641	C	510 262-6588	18986

RICHVALE, CA - Butte County

	SIC	EMP	PHONE	ENTRY#
Wehah-Lundberg Inc	2044	C	530 882-4551	2363

RIDGECREST, CA - Kern County

	SIC	EMP	PHONE	ENTRY#
Directv Group Holdings LLC	4841	C	760 375-8300	4500
Southern California Edison Co	4911	C	760 375-1821	4694
Home Depot USA Inc	5211	C	760 375-4614	6996
Desert Area Resources Training (PA)	5932	D	760 375-9787	7532
Altaone Federal Credit Union (PA)	6061	C	760 371-7000	7752
New Directions Tech Inc (PA)	7373	D	760 384-2444	12501
Ridgecrest Regional Hospital (PA)	8062	B	760 446-3551	16363

RIDGECREST CA

GEOGRAPHIC SECTION

	SIC	EMP	PHONE	ENTRY#
Community Action Partnr Kern	8399	D	760 371-1469	18576
DCS Corporation	8711	D	760 384-5600	19194
Crl Technologies Inc	8731	D	760 495-3000	19673

RIO LINDA, CA - Sacramento County

	SIC	EMP	PHONE	ENTRY#
Longo Construction	1521	D	916 397-5869	697
Marques Gen Engrg Inc A Cal Co	8711	B	916 923-3434	19315

RIO VISTA, CA - Solano County

	SIC	EMP	PHONE	ENTRY#
Paul Graham Drilling & Svc Co	1381	C	707 374-5123	595
Trilogy At Rio Vista Mstr Assn	1521	D	707 374-6871	730
California Vegetable Spc Inc	5148	D	707 374-2111	6521

RIPON, CA - San Joaquin County

	SIC	EMP	PHONE	ENTRY#
Norco Ranch Inc (DH)	0291	B	951 737-6735	236
Apple Freight Inc	4213	D	510 423-4000	3442
Nulaid Foods Inc (PA)	5144	D	209 599-2121	6447
Fishers Nursery	5193	D	209 599-3412	6858
Bethany HM Soc San Jquin Cnty	8051	C	209 599-7670	15357
Demand Gen Inc	8621	D	415 373-2450	18748

RIVERBANK, CA - Stanislaus County

	SIC	EMP	PHONE	ENTRY#
Save Mart Supermarkets Disc	5411	D	209 863-1480	7150
Econtactlive Inc	7389	D	209 548-4300	13277

RIVERDALE, CA - Fresno County

	SIC	EMP	PHONE	ENTRY#
Linda Terra Farms (PA)	0213	C	559 867-3473	212
Maddox Dairy LLC	0241	D	559 866-5308	219
Maddox Dairy A Ltd Partnership (PA)	0241	D	559 867-3545	220

RIVERSIDE, CA - Riverside County

	SIC	EMP	PHONE	ENTRY#
A-G Sod Farms Inc	0181	D	951 687-7581	119
Corona - Cllege Hts Ornge Lmon	0723	B	951 359-6451	262
Azteca Landscape	0781	D	951 369-9210	388
Brightview Landscape Svcs Inc	0781	D	951 684-2730	399
Brightview Landscape Svcs Inc	0781	D	714 939-6600	409
Brightview Tree Care Svcs Inc	0781	D	951 684-2730	418
FS Commercial Landscape Inc (PA)	0781	D	951 360-7070	432
Liberty Landscaping Inc (PA)	0782	C	951 683-2999	517
County of Riverside	1521	D	951 955-4800	668
MGB Construction Inc	1521	C	951 342-0303	701
Silverado Framing & Cnstr	1521	D	951 352-1100	725
Van Daele Homes Inc	1522	D	951 354-2121	782
Van Daele Development Corp	1531	C	951 354-6800	799
Hal Hays Construction Inc (PA)	1541	C	951 788-0703	823
J D Diffenbaugh Inc	1542	D	951 351-6865	942
Bens Asphalt & Maint Co Inc	1611	D	951 248-1103	1082
National Paving Company Inc	1611	D	951 369-1332	1145
Riverside Construction Company Inc	1611	C	951 682-8308	1156
Rsvc Company	1611	C	951 684-6578	1159
Skanska USA Cvil W Cal Dst Inc (DH)	1611	A	951 684-5360	1164
Hci LLC (HQ)	1623	B	951 520-4200	1213
Herman Weissker Inc (HQ)	1623	C	951 826-8800	1215
Kana Pipeline Inc	1623	C	714 986-1400	1226
Skanska USA Cvil W Rcky Mtn Ds (DH)	1629	D	970 565-8000	1319
20/20 Plumbing & Heating Inc (PA)	1711	D	951 396-2020	1327
Dynamic Plumbing Systems Inc	1711	B	951 343-1200	1423
Lozano Plumbing Services Inc	1711	C	951 683-4840	1490
M & M Plumbing Inc	1711	D	951 354-5388	1494
New Power Inc	1711	D	800 980-9825	1509
Ppc Enterprises Inc	1711	D	951 354-5402	1532
Solcius LLC	1711	D	951 772-0030	1568
J M V B Inc	1721	D	714 288-9797	1623
West Coast Interiors Inc	1721	A	951 778-3592	1645
Champion Electric Inc	1731	D	951 276-9619	1695
Elite Electric	1731	D	951 681-5811	1728
J Ginger Masonry LP (PA)	1741	B	951 688-5050	1885
Masonry Group Nevada Inc	1741	D	951 509-5300	1890
West Coast Drywall & Co Inc	1742	B	951 778-3592	1972
Craftsman Lath and Plaster Inc	1751	D	951 685-9922	1996
Roy E Whitehead Inc	1751	D	951 682-1490	2016
Hy-Tech Tile Inc	1752	D	951 788-0550	2035
Pacific Strucframe LLC	1761	D	951 405-8536	2075
Bedrock Company	1771	D	951 273-1931	2098
Century West Concrete Inc	1771	B	951 712-4065	2108
Inland Cc Inc	1771	C	909 355-1318	2128
Z-Best Concrete Inc	1771	D	951 774-1870	2171
Allied Steel Co Inc	1791	D	951 241-7000	2176
Fencecorp (HQ)	1799	C	951 686-3170	2277
Fenceworks Inc (PA)	1799	D	951 788-5620	2278
PSG Fencing Corporation	1799	D	951 275-9252	2308
West Coast Countertops Inc	1799	D	951 719-3670	2332
American Bottling Company	2086	D	951 341-7500	2398
Heritage Container Inc	2653	D	951 360-1900	2514
Plz Corp	2844	D	951 683-2912	2631
Polymer Logistics Inc	3089	D	951 567-2900	2678
Pacific Consolidated Inds LLC	3569	D	951 479-0860	2801
Riverside Transit Agency (PA)	4111	B	951 565-5000	3192
American Med Rspnse Amblnce Sv (DH)	4119	D	303 495-1217	3228
American Med Rspnse Inland Emp (HQ)	4119	D	951 782-5200	3231
High Performance Logistics LLC	4212	D	702 300-4880	3405
Neal Trucking Inc	4212	D	951 685-5048	3415
Top Priority Couriers Inc (PA)	4215	D	951 781-1000	3630
Powered By Fulfillment Inc	4222	D	626 825-9841	3656
Walmart Inc	4225	C	951 320-5722	3778
Empire Med Transportations LLC	4731	D	877 473-6029	4013
20/20 Mobile Corp	4812	D	909 587-2973	4180
Your Wireless Retailer Inc	4812	D	310 293-3706	4245
City of Riverside	4941	D	951 826-5312	4774
Jurupa Community Services Dst	4941	D	951 685-7073	4798
Arakelian Enterprises Inc	4953	C	951 342-3300	4858
Recycler Core Company Inc	4953	D	951 276-1687	4930
MSRS INC	5023	D	310 952-9000	5125
Novo Distribution LLC	5031	D	951 742-5273	5175
Crest Steel Corporation	5051	D	951 727-2600	5486
Harbor Pipe and Steel Inc	5051	C	951 369-3990	5496
Steel Unlimited Inc	5051	D	909 873-1222	5520
Everpac	5082	D	951 774-3274	5787
Johnson Machinery Co (PA)	5082	D	951 686-4560	5794
McLane Foodservice Inc	5141	C	951 867-3555	6266
Smart & Final Stores LLC	5141	D	951 341-8230	6347
Smart & Final Stores LLC	5141	D	951 352-5715	6377
Sysco Riverside Inc	5141	B	951 601-5300	6401
Airgas Specialty Products Inc	5169	D	951 353-2390	6704
Premier Fuel Distributors Inc	5172	D	760 423-3610	6735
B & B Nurseries Inc	5193	C	951 352-8383	6850
Boise Cascade Company	5211	D	951 343-3000	6958
Dixieline Lumber Company LLC	5211	A	951 224-8491	6959
Home Depot USA Inc	5211	D	951 358-1370	6966
Lowes Home Centers LLC	5211	D	951 509-5500	7043
David A Campbell Corporation	5511	C	951 785-4444	7191
Pearson Ford Co (PA)	5511	D	877 743-0421	7276
Raceway Ford Inc	5511	D	951 571-9300	7285
Toyota of Riverside Inc	5511	C	951 687-1622	7317
Walters Auto Sales and Svc Inc	5511	C	888 316-4097	7329
Fairprice Enterprises Inc	5713	D	951 684-8578	7430
City National Bank	6021	D	951 276-8800	7618
Pacific Premier Bancorp Inc	6022	B	951 274-2400	7705
Populus Financial Group Inc	6099	D	951 509-3506	7859
Secure Choice Lending	6159	D	951 733-8925	7923
Morgan Stnley Smith Barney LLC	6211	C	951 682-1181	8146
Southern Cal Prmnnte Med Group	6324	D	866 984-7483	8363
State Compensation Insur Fund	6331	C	888 782-8338	8418
Farmers Insurance	6411	C	951 681-1068	8560
Insurance Inc Southern Cal	6411	D	951 300-9333	8592
Encore Senior Living III LLC	6513	D	951 360-1616	8808
Professional Cmnty MGT Cal Inc	6531	D	951 359-2840	9140
Realty One Group Inc	6531	D	951 565-8105	9156
Remn Inc	6531	D	951 697-8135	9163
Westcoe Realtors Inc	6531	D	951 784-2500	9214
Historic Mission Inn Corp	7011	B	951 784-0300	9857
Pinnacle Rvrside Hspitality LP	7011	C	951 784-8000	10121
A-Check America LLC (HQ)	7323	C	951 750-1501	10755
Your Way Fumigation Inc	7342	D	951 699-9116	10844
ServiceMaster By Best Pros Inc	7349	D	951 515-9051	10965
Kimco Staffing Services Inc	7361	A	951 686-3800	11161
Officeworks Inc	7361	D	951 784-2534	11191
Volt Management Corp	7363	D	951 789-8133	11351
Stromasys Inc	7372	D	919 239-8450	12366
Allied Digital Services LLC	7376	C	310 431-2361	12692
Barrys Security Services Inc (PA)	7381	D	951 789-7575	12939
313 Acquisition LLC	7382	A	801 234-6374	13081
ADT LLC	7382	C	951 782-6900	13092
Corporate Alnce Strategies Inc	7382	C	877 777-7487	13104
Canyon Springs Pkwy Qsr LLC	7389	D	951 413-6081	13225
New America Funding LLC	7389	D	951 637-2300	13392
Rgis LLC	7389	D	951 369-7131	13446
Hamblins Bdy Pnt Frame Sp Inc	7538	D	951 689-8440	13663
Fleetwood Motor Homes-Califinc	7699	C	951 274-2000	13770
Peggs Company Inc (PA)	7699	D	253 584-9548	13791
Adventist Media Center Inc (PA)	7922	C	805 955-7777	14025
Canyon Crest Country Club Inc	7997	D	951 274-7900	14355
Victoria Club	7997	D	951 683-5323	14476
County of Riverside	8011	C	951 955-0840	14716
Kaiser Foundation Hospitals	8011	D	951 353-3790	14789
Kaiser Foundation Hospitals	8011	D	951 352-0292	14826

GEOGRAPHIC SECTION — ROSEVILLE CA

Company	SIC	EMP	PHONE	ENTRY#
Kaiser Foundation Hospitals	8011	A	951 353-2000	14840
Onrad Inc	8011	D	800 848-5876	14938
Riverside Medical Clinic Inc	8011	D	951 683-6370	15019
Riverside Medical Clinic Inc	8011	D	951 360-5250	15020
Riverside Medical Clinic Inc	8011	D	951 782-3614	15021
Riverside Medical Clinic Inc	8011	D	951 683-6370	15022
Riverside Medical Clinic Inc	8011	D	951 683-6370	15024
Riverside Medical Clinic Inc (PA)	8011	D	951 683-6370	15024
Riverside Medical Clinic Inc	8011	D	951 782-3615	15025
Riverside Medical Clinic Inc	8011	D	951 782-3684	15026
Riverside Medical Clinic Inc	8011	D	951 782-3846	15027
Interdent Service Corporation	8021	D	951 682-1720	15229
Air Force Village West Inc	8051	B	951 697-2000	15319
Community Care On Palm Rvrside	8051	D	951 686-9001	15380
Mt Rubidouxidence Opco LLC	8051	C	951 681-2200	15593
Rhf Plymouth Tower	8051	D	951 248-0456	15637
Riverside Care Inc	8051	D	951 683-7111	15641
Riverside Equities LLC	8051	B	951 688-2222	15642
Sunrise Senior Living LLC	8051	D	951 686-6075	15691
Villa Convalescent Hosp Inc	8051	D	951 689-5788	15722
Orange Treeidence Opco LLC	8052	B	951 785-6060	15782
Magnolia Rhblttion Nursing Ctr	8059	C	951 688-4321	15874
Windsor Cypress Grdns Hlthcare	8059	A	951 688-3643	15912
Orangtree Cnvalescent Hosp Inc	8062	C	951 785-6060	16298
Parkview Cmnty Hosp Med Ctr	8062	A	951 354-7404	16318
Riverside Cmnty Hlth Systems (DH)	8062	A	951 788-3000	16364
Riverside Univ Hlth Sys Fndtio (PA)	8062	B	951 358-5000	16365
Interim Healthcare Inc	8082	C	951 684-6111	16878
CRC Health Group Inc	8093	D	951 784-8010	17049
County of Riverside	8111	C	951 955-6000	17419
Carolyn E Wylie Ctr For Chldre	8322	D	951 683-5193	17860
County of Riverside	8322	D	951 955-4900	17935
County of Riverside	8322	D	800 510-2020	17936
County of Riverside	8331	D	951 955-3434	18225
FSA Arlanza Child Dev Ctr	8351	D	951 353-0129	18317
Keystone NPS LLC	8399	C	951 785-0504	18603
County of Riverside	8641	C	951 683-7691	18845
Automobile Club Southern Cal	8699	D	951 684-4250	19056
Albert A Webb Associates (PA)	8711	C	951 686-1070	19134
Construction Tstg & Engrg Inc	8711	B	951 571-4081	19183
Hunsaker & Assoc Irvine Inc	8711	B	951 352-7200	19261
Sitesol	8711	D	562 746-5884	19389
University Cal Riverside	8732	C	951 827-4801	19854
Babcock Laboratories Inc	8734	D	951 653-3351	19952
Inland Cnties Regional Ctr Inc	8741	B	951 826-2600	20113
Team Group LLC	8741	D	951 688-8593	20227
City of Riverside	8742	B	951 826-5485	20318
Muth Machine Works	8742	D	951 685-1521	20478
Riverside Cnty Flood Ctrl Wtr	8999	D	951 955-1200	20900
Westview Services Inc	8999	D	951 343-2356	20908
County of Riverside	9222	D	951 955-5659	20932
County of Riverside	9431	D	951 248-0014	20939
California Dept Social Svcs	9441	D	951 782-4200	20941
County of Riverside	9441	C	951 358-5000	20943

RLLNG HLS EST, CA - Los Angeles County

Company	SIC	EMP	PHONE	ENTRY#
Spalding Srgcal Ctr Bvrly Hlls	8011	D	949 863-0022	15096

ROBBINS, CA - Sutter County

Company	SIC	EMP	PHONE	ENTRY#
Valley Truck and Tractor Inc	5083	D	530 738-4421	5815

ROCKLIN, CA - Placer County

Company	SIC	EMP	PHONE	ENTRY#
Brightview Landscape Svcs Inc	0781	D	916 415-1004	403
Quality Telecom Cons Inc (PA)	1623	D	916 315-0500	1254
W M Lyles Co	1623	C	916 375-1833	1279
Infinity Energy Cnstr Inc	1711	D	888 839-2937	1463
JR Perce Plbg Inc Sacramento	1711	C	916 434-9554	1474
SMA Solar Technology Amer LLC	1711	C	916 625-0870	1564
Sonoran Roofing Inc	1761	D	916 624-1080	2085
Amazing Facts Inc	2731	C	916 434-3880	2548
Bmi Inc	3433	D	530 749-0808	2735
United Natural Foods West Inc (HQ)	4225	B	916 625-4100	3775
Educational Media Foundation (PA)	4832	C	916 251-1600	4377
Trane US Inc	5075	D	916 577-1100	5774
Golden Eagle Distributing Corp	5084	D	916 645-6600	5837
Orora Packaging Solutions	5113	D	916 645-8100	6086
Bi Warehousing Inc (PA)	5531	D	916 624-0654	7344
Bi Warehousing Inc	5531	C	916 624-0654	7345
Pottery World Inc	5999	D	916 624-8080	7590
First Technology Federal Cr Un	6061	D	855 855-8805	7773
Builders Trdsmens Insur Svcs I	6411	D	916 772-9200	8514
Financial Pacific Insurance Co	6411	D	916 630-5000	8567
SE Scher Corporation	7361	A	916 632-1363	11226
Oracle Corporation	7372	B	916 315-3500	12307
Global Blue Dvbe Inc	7376	D	916 632-2583	12695
Road Safety Inc	7389	C	916 543-4600	13451
Jkf Auto Service Inc	7542	D	916 315-0555	13695
Purple Language Services Co	7812	C	916 435-8216	13883
Strikes Unlimited Inc	7933	D	916 626-3600	14122
University California Davis	8011	A	916 295-5700	15159
Horizon West Healthcare Inc (HQ)	8051	D	916 624-6230	15517
Westgate Gardens Care Ctr Inc	8051	C	916 624-6230	15731
American Hlthcare ADM Svcs Inc	8099	B	916 773-7227	17177
Oasis Materials Company LLC	8711	C	858 842-1338	19338
Marksys LLC	8742	C	916 745-4883	20453
Marksys Holdings LLC	8742	C	916 745-4883	20454
Pacific Secured Equities Inc	8742	B	916 677-2500	20499

RODEO, CA - Contra Costa County

Company	SIC	EMP	PHONE	ENTRY#
Eagle Ambulance	4119	D	800 304-6985	3252
Young MNS Chrstn Assn of E Bay	8641	C	510 412-5644	18964

ROHNERT PARK, CA - Sonoma County

Company	SIC	EMP	PHONE	ENTRY#
OHagins Inc	1711	D	707 303-3660	1515
North Bay Rhblitation Svcs Inc (PA)	2399	C	707 585-1991	2472
World Centric	2679	D	707 241-9190	2534
Lemo USA Inc	5065	D	707 206-3700	5669
Pace Supply Corp (PA)	5074	B	707 755-2499	5758
Solarnet LLC	5074	D	707 992-3100	5760
Soligent Leasing LLC	5074	C	707 992-3100	5761
Sonata Solar LLC	5074	C	707 992-3100	5762
Inoxpa Usa Inc	5084	B	707 585-3900	5841
Chick-Fil-A Inc	5812	D	707 585-7462	7465
Kaiser Foundation Hospitals	6324	C	707 206-3000	8325
State Compensation Insur Fund	6331	C	888 782-8338	8421
Kisco Senior Living LLC	6513	D	707 585-1800	8840
Federted Indans Grton Rncheria	7011	A	707 588-7100	9795
Inn Hampton & Suites	7011	D	707 586-8700	9909
Park US Lessee Holdings LLC	7011	C	707 887-7838	10106
Red Condor Inc	7371	D	707 569-7419	11868
Graton Resort & Casino	7999	C	707 588-7100	14531
St Joseph Hlth Nthrn Cal LLC	8093	B	707 584-0672	17132
Artizen Inc	8742	C	707 595-5998	20281

ROLLING HILLS, CA - Los Angeles County

Company	SIC	EMP	PHONE	ENTRY#
Trams Inc (DH)	7373	D	310 641-8726	12534

ROMOLAND, CA - Riverside County

Company	SIC	EMP	PHONE	ENTRY#
Southern California Edison Co	4911	D	800 336-2822	4706
Southern California Gas Co	4924	C	213 244-1200	4736

ROSEMEAD, CA - Los Angeles County

Company	SIC	EMP	PHONE	ENTRY#
Irish Communication Company (DH)	1623	D	626 288-6170	1219
Irish Construction (HQ)	1623	C	626 288-8530	1221
Chinese Overseas Mktg Svc Corp (PA)	2741	C	626 280-8588	2554
Durham School Services L P	4151	A	626 573-3769	3333
Cco Holdings LLC	4841	C	626 500-1214	4478
Edison International (PA)	4911	A	626 302-2222	4574
Edison Mission Energy (PA)	4911	C	626 302-5778	4575
Edison Mssion Midwest Holdings	4911	A	626 302-2222	4576
Southern California Edison Co	4911	B	626 302-1212	4702
Southern California Edison Co (HQ)	4911	A	626 302-1212	4703
Panda Systems Inc	5812	C	626 799-9898	7501
Sunshine Inn A Cal Ltd Partnr	7011	D	323 722-8800	10285
Travelodge Hotels Inc	7011	C	800 257-2297	10319
Success Healthcare 1 LLC	8011	A	626 288-1160	15103
Uplift Family Services	8011	C	626 287-2988	15169
Ensign Group Inc	8051	D	626 607-2400	15455
Longwood Management Corp	8051	C	626 280-2293	15551
Longwood Management Corp	8051	C	626 280-4820	15552
Bhc Alhambra Hospital Inc	8099	B	626 286-1191	17187
Maryvale	8361	C	626 280-6510	18479
County of Los Angeles	8399	D	626 291-2200	18582

ROSEVILLE, CA - Placer County

Company	SIC	EMP	PHONE	ENTRY#
Ltc Construction Inc (HQ)	0781	D	916 246-9987	441
Clark & Sullivan Builders Inc	1542	C	916 338-7707	895
Clark & Sullivan Constrs Inc	1542	C	916 338-7707	896
Flint Builders Inc	1542	D	916 757-1000	919
Reeve-Knight Construction Inc	1542	D	916 786-5112	1006
Rudolph and Sletten Inc	1542	C	916 781-8001	1014
Sierra Traffic Markings Inc	1611	D	916 784-0430	1163
Teichert Inc	1611	D	916 645-4800	1172
Nor-Cal Pipeline Services	1623	D	916 442-5400	1242
Envirnmntal Htg A Slutions Inc	1711	D	916 990-2952	1430
Intech Mechanical Company Inc	1711	D	916 797-4900	1466
Intech Mechanical Company LLC	1711	C	916 797-4900	1467

ROSEVILLE CA

	SIC	EMP	PHONE	ENTRY#
Rountree Plumbing and Htg Inc	1711	D	650 298-0300	1550
Lancaster Burns Cnstr Inc	1742	C	916 624-8404	1942
Production Framing Systems Inc (PA)	1751	C	916 978-2888	2012
Dwayne Nash Industries Inc	1761	C	916 253-1900	2060
Pasco Scientific (PA)	3826	C	916 786-3800	3031
Mv Transportation Inc	4111	C	916 788-3000	3170
Pride Industries (PA)	4226	C	916 788-2100	3796
Cal Consoldated Communications	4813	B	916 786-6141	4259
Clearcaptions LLC	4813	B	866 868-8695	4265
Lumen Tech Gvrnment Sltons Inc	4813	A	916 781-7772	4309
Amazing Facts International	4832	D	916 434-3880	4372
Audacy Inc	4832	C	916 766-5000	4373
Northern California Power Agcy (PA)	4911	D	916 781-3636	4591
Vexillum Inc	4911	C	916 218-3815	4717
Home Depot USA Inc	5211	D	916 787-0201	6968
Lowes Home Centers LLC	5211	D	916 771-7111	7054
Ford Future Inc	5511	C	916 786-3673	7208
John L Sullivan Chevrolet Inc	5511	C	916 742-7663	7242
RPM Luxury Auto Sales Inc	5511	C	916 783-9111	7292
Westrup-Sadler Inc	5511	D	916 783-2077	7334
Rabobank National Association	6022	A		7712
Topmark Funding LLC	6153	D	866 627-6644	7911
Nations First Capital LLC	6159	D	855 396-3600	7922
American Pacific Mortgage Corp (PA)	6162	C	916 960-1325	7929
Goodleap LLC (PA)	6162	C	916 290-9999	7974
Guaranteed Rate Inc	6162	C	916 501-3919	7977
Universal American Mrtg Co Cal	6162	A	916 773-2722	8026
Charles Schwab Corporation	6211	D	916 789-2120	8078
Merrill Lynch Prce Fnner Smith	6211	D	916 984-3200	8118
Mother Lode Holding Co	6361	D	916 624-8141	8449
Old Rpblic Title Info Concepts	6361	B	916 781-4100	8454
Claims Management Inc	6411	D	916 631-1250	8527
Interwest Insurance Svcs LLC	6411	D	916 784-1008	8593
Networked Insurance Agents LLC	6411	C	800 682-8476	8621
Waterhouse Management Corp	6515	D	916 772-4918	8882
Dick James & Associates Inc	6531	C	916 332-7430	8982
Lyon Realty	6531	C	916 784-1500	9081
Lyon Realty	6531	C	916 787-7700	9083
Nick Sadek Sothebys Intl Rlty	6531	D	916 257-3229	9109
USA Multifamily Management Inc	6531	C	916 773-6060	9206
Inn Ventures Inc	7011	D	916 773-7171	9910
California Sun Inc	7299	D	916 789-1034	10532
Advanced Integrated Pest Management	7342	C	916 786-2404	10827
Wright Celebrations Inc	7359	D	916 773-2133	11065
Abso	7361	C	800 943-2589	11071
Calabria Group Inc (PA)	7361	C	916 773-3900	11101
Flexcare LLC	7361	A	866 564-3589	11139
Maxim Healthcare Services Inc	7363	C	916 771-7444	11305
Volt Management Corp	7363	D	916 923-0454	11360
Global Touchpoints Inc	7371	D	916 878-5954	11624
Iptor Supply Chain Systems USA (DH)	7371	C	916 542-2820	11678
10up Inc (PA)	7373	D	888 571-7130	12412
Revenue Solutions Inc	7374	B	916 780-8741	12616
Cokeva Inc	7378	C	916 462-6001	12705
Esl Technologies Inc	7378	B	916 677-4500	12706
Teleplan Service Solutions Inc	7378	C	916 677-4500	12712
Directapps Inc (PA)	7379	C	916 787-2200	12779
Quest Media & Supplies Inc (PA)	7379	C	916 338-7070	12865
Denios Rsvlle Frmrs Mkt Actn I	7389	C	916 782-2704	13262
Wise Buys Liquidators Inc	7389	C	916 773-3998	13555
Life Time Inc	7991	C	916 472-2000	14214
Sun City Rsvlle Cmnty Assn Inc (PA)	7992	C	916 774-3880	14292
Sierra View Country Club	7997	C	916 782-3741	14453
Spare-Time Inc	7997	C	916 782-2600	14461
Roseville Golfland Ltd Partnr	7999	D	916 784-1273	14556
Kaiser Foundation Hospitals	8011	D	916 784-4000	14834
Mercy San Juan Medical Center	8011	C	916 773-1188	14898
Permanente Medical Group Inc	8011	A	916 784-4000	14981
Sutter Health	8011	C	916 783-8114	15111
Sutter Valley Med Foundation	8011	C	916 865-1140	15118
Clearchoice MGT Svcs LLC	8021	C	916 742-6055	15221
Crocus Holdings LLC	8051	D	916 782-1238	15418
Horizon West Healthcare Inc	8059	D	916 786-3173	15857
Adventist Hlth Systm/West Corp (PA)	8062	B	844 574-5686	15922
Kaiser Foundation Hospitals	8062	C	916 746-3937	16150
Kaiser Foundation Hospitals	8062	A	916 784-4000	16188
Mercy Medical Group	8062	D	916 536-2500	16267
South Coast Medical Center (PA)	8062	A	916 781-2000	16436
Sutter Health	8062	C	916 797-4725	16519
Sutter Health	8062	A	916 797-4700	16539
Sutter Roseville Medical Ctr	8062	A	916 781-1000	16556
Sutter Rsvlle Med Ctr Fndation	8062	B	916 781-1000	16557
Unilab Corporation	8071	A	916 781-3031	16762

	SIC	EMP	PHONE	ENTRY#
Abcsp LLC	8082	C	855 470-2273	16784
Altus Health Inc	8082	D	916 781-6500	16804
Barbee Elc	8082	D	916 884-1983	16814
Coleman Chavez & Assoc LLP	8111	D	916 787-2310	17407
Alta Cal Regional Ctr Inc	8322	C	916 786-8110	17829
Wellness Together	8322	C	877 412-8031	18191
Eskaton Properties Inc	8361	C	916 334-0810	18426
Westmont Living Inc	8361	C	916 786-3277	18547
Califrnia Rur Indian Hlth Bd I	8399	D	916 437-0104	18569
Merchant Valley Corporation	8611	C	916 786-7227	18714
Hospitality Bennett Group LLC	8621	C	916 750-5150	18749
Willdan Engineering	8711	C	916 924-7000	19441
Cliftonlarsonallen LLP	8721	B	916 784-7800	19551
Eisneramper LLP	8721	C	916 563-7790	19571
Med-Data Incorporated	8721	D	916 771-1362	19611
Matrix Absence Management Inc	8741	C	916 773-5737	20148
Sutter Valley Med Foundation	8741	C	916 865-1140	20222
Varis LLC	8742	C	916 294-0860	20601

ROSS, CA - Marin County

	SIC	EMP	PHONE	ENTRY#
Cedars of Marin (PA)	8211	D	415 454-5310	17700

ROWLAND HEIGHTS, CA - Los Angeles County

	SIC	EMP	PHONE	ENTRY#
Hanson Distributing Company	5531	D	626 839-4026	7351
Moonrider LLC	7011	D	318 828-1375	10027
Emanate Health	8011	C	626 912-5282	14737

ROYAL OAKS, CA - Santa Cruz County

	SIC	EMP	PHONE	ENTRY#
Gino Rinaldi Inc	1743	D	831 761-0195	1983

RUNNING SPRINGS, CA - San Bernardino County

	SIC	EMP	PHONE	ENTRY#
Pali Camp	7032	C	909 867-5743	10410
Snow Valley Mtn Resort LLC	7032	D	909 867-2751	10412

RUTHERFORD, CA - Napa County

	SIC	EMP	PHONE	ENTRY#
Terre Du Soleil Ltd	7011	B	707 963-1211	10308

SACRAMENTO, CA - Sacramento County

	SIC	EMP	PHONE	ENTRY#
Natura Holdings LLC	0139	D	916 209-0038	15
Matsudas By Green Acres LLC	0181	C	916 673-9290	138
Brightview Landscape Dev Inc	0781	C	916 386-4875	397
Brightview Landscape Svcs Inc	0781	C	916 381-2800	412
Coast Lm Inc	0781	C	800 578-8810	423
Frank Carson Ldscp & Maint Inc	0781	C	916 856-5400	431
Dominguez Landscape Svcs Inc	0782	C	916 381-8855	486
Procida Landscape Inc	0782	C	916 387-5296	531
Sungarden Company Inc	0782	D	916 379-9088	538
Teichert Inc	1442	C	916 386-6900	645
Golden Coast Cnstr Restoration	1521	D	916 955-7461	679
North Wind Cnstr Svcs LLC	1521	D	916 333-3015	705
XI Construction Corporation	1521	D	916 282-2900	743
Hurley Construction Inc	1522	D	916 446-7599	759
Advanced Restoration Inc	1542	D	916 888-9816	860
Alston Construction Co Inc (PA)	1542	C	916 340-2400	863
Dpr Construction A Gen Partnr	1542	C	916 568-3434	908
Halstead Partnership	1542	D	916 830-8000	926
John F Otto Inc	1542	C	916 441-6870	948
Kitchell Corporation	1542	C	916 648-9700	952
Swinerton Builders Hc	1542	C	916 383-4825	1036
Turner Construction Company	1542	D	916 444-4421	1046
Unger Construction Co	1542	C	916 325-5500	1050
Whiting-Turner Contracting Co	1542	C	916 355-1355	1063
A-1 Advantage Asphalt Inc	1611	D	916 388-2020	1069
Martin Brothers Cnstr LLC (PA)	1611	D	916 386-1600	1135
Myers & Sons Construction LP (HQ)	1611	D	916 283-9950	1144
Irish Communication Company	1623	C	916 383-9000	1220
Myers & Sons Construction LLC	1623	C	916 283-9950	1241
Auburn Constructors LLC	1629	D	916 924-0344	1286
Patricks Construction Clean-Up	1629	D	916 452-5495	1313
Air Systems Svc & Cnstr LLC	1711	D	916 368-0336	1341
Airco Mechanical Inc (PA)	1711	C	916 381-4523	1343
Blue Oak Energy LLC	1711	D	530 747-2026	1382
Clarke & Rush Mechanical Inc	1711	D	916 306-5835	1399
Innovative Maintenance Solutions Inc	1711	C	916 568-1400	1465
Iron Mechanical Inc (PA)	1711	D	916 341-3530	1469
Lawson Mechanical Contractors (PA)	1711	D	916 381-5000	1482
Luppen and Hawley Inc	1711	C	916 456-7831	1493
Pro-Tech Fire Prtction Systems	1711	C	916 388-0255	1536
Refrigeration Solutions LLC	1711	D	916 281-2000	1546
Barnum & Celillo Electric Inc (PA)	1731	C	916 646-4661	1673
H & D Electric	1731	B	916 332-0794	1741
Mark III Construction Inc (PA)	1731	C	916 381-8080	1769
May-Han Electric Inc	1731	D	916 929-0150	1771

GEOGRAPHIC SECTION

SACRAMENTO CA

	SIC	EMP	PHONE	ENTRY#
Republic Electric Inc	1731	C	916 294-0140	1816
Republic Electric West Inc	1731	D	916 294-0140	1817
Rex Moore Group Inc	1731	B	916 372-1300	1818
Rex More Elec Cntrs Engners In (PA)	1731	B	916 372-1300	1819
Schetter Electric Inc (PA)	1731	D	916 446-2521	1832
Schetter Electric LLC	1731	D	916 446-2521	1834
Valley Communications Inc (PA)	1731	D	916 349-7300	1867
Vasko Electric Inc	1731	D	916 568-7700	1869
Vellutini Corporation	1731	C	916 226-2100	1871
John Jackson Masonry	1741	D	916 381-8021	1886
Kleary Masonry Inc	1741	C	916 869-6835	1887
Alcal Specialty Contg Inc	1742	D	916 929-3100	1900
New West Partitions	1742	C	916 456-8365	1948
Fischer Tile and Marble Inc	1743	C	916 452-1426	1982
National Crmic Tile Stone Corp	1743	D	916 776-8715	1986
Shermn-Lehr Cstm Tile Wrks Inc	1743	D	916 386-0417	1987
Capitol Builders Hardware Inc (HQ)	1751	C	916 451-2821	1991
Creative Design Interiors Inc (PA)	1752	D	916 641-1121	2030
Simas Floor Co Inc (PA)	1752	C	916 452-4933	2039
Zimmerman Roofing Inc	1761	D	916 454-3667	2093
Rescue Concrete Inc	1771	C	916 852-2400	2151
Lupton Excavation Inc	1794	D	916 387-1104	2221
Dave Gross Enterprises Inc	1799	D	916 388-2000	2272
Fencecorp Inc	1799	D	916 388-0887	2276
Nmi Industrial Holdings Inc	1799	D	916 635-7030	2301
Parc Specialty Contractors	1799	D	916 992-5405	2304
Skyline Scaffold Inc	1799	D	916 391-8929	2316
Seven Up Btlg Co San Francisco	2086	C	916 929-7777	2412
McClatchy Newspapers Inc (DH)	2711	A	916 321-1855	2539
Washoe Equipment Inc	3645	A	916 395-4700	2873
Siemens Industry Inc	3822	C	916 681-3000	3015
All Weather Inc	3829	B	916 928-1000	3040
Califrnia High Speed Rail Auth	4011	D	916 324-1541	3115
Mv Transportation Inc	4111	B	916 854-2638	3181
Sacramento Regional Trnst Dist (PA)	4111	A	916 726-2877	3193
Medstar LLC	4119	D	916 669-0550	3279
Paratransit Incorporated (PA)	4119	D	916 429-2009	3285
Universal Limousine & Trnsp Co	4119	D	916 361-5466	3302
Amador Stage Lines Inc	4142	D	916 444-7880	3315
Elk Grove Unified School Dst	4151	C	916 686-7733	3335
B & G Delivery System Inc	4212	C	916 921-4401	3371
Hendrickson Truck Lines Inc	4213	C	916 387-9614	3488
Hendrickson Trucking Inc	4213	B	916 387-9614	3489
Masuta National Inc	4213	C	916 520-0904	3511
Matheson Fast Freight Inc	4213	B	209 342-0184	3512
Rcg Logistics LLC	4213	D	916 999-1234	3530
Saia Inc	4213	C	916 483-8331	3538
Xpo Logistics Freight Inc	4213	D	916 399-8291	3571
On Trac	4215	D	916 921-6016	3622
Baco Realty Corporation	4225	D	916 974-9898	3677
C&S Wholesale Grocers Inc	4225	B	916 383-5275	3680
Cv Logistics Inc	4225	C		3693
County of Sacramento	4581	B	916 874-0912	3889
Gat - Arln Ground Support Inc	4581	B	916 923-2349	3895
Accent Hospitality Group LLC	4725	C	415 286-2867	3957
Kls Air Express Inc	4731	D		4043
Khaira Logistics Inc	4789	D	916 308-4740	4164
Cellco Partnership	4812	D	916 838-9525	4189
Verizon Bus Netwrk Svcs LLC	4812	C	916 569-5999	4240
Adelante Media Group LLC	4832	D	801 908-8777	4370
Entercom Media Corp	4832	D	916 923-6800	4383
Channel 40 Inc	4833	C	916 454-4422	4420
Hearst Stations Inc	4833	C	916 446-3333	4438
Kvie Inc (PA)	4833	D	916 929-5843	4450
Kxtv Inc	4833	C	916 441-2345	4451
Sefnco Communications Inc	4899	D	925 271-2943	4548
Pacific Gas and Electric Co	4911	C	916 275-2763	4601
Pacific Gas and Electric Co	4911	B	916 923-7007	4613
Sacramento Municpl Utility Dst (PA)	4911	A	916 452-3211	4663
Sacramento Municpl Utility Dst	4911	A	916 452-3211	4664
Sacramento Municpl Utility Dst	4911	D	916 732-5155	4665
Sacramento Municpl Utility Dst	4911	A	916 732-5616	4666
Siemens Energy Inc	4911	D	916 391-2993	4678
Sacramnto Subn Wtr Dst Fing Co	4941	D	916 972-7171	4821
City of Sacramento	4953	C	916 808-4949	4878
Sacramnto Rgnal Cnty Snttion D (PA)	4959	C	916 876-6000	4983
Adesa Corporation LLC	5012	D	916 388-8899	5001
B T Mancini Co Inc	5023	C	916 381-3660	5111
Milgard Manufacturing LLC	5031	D	916 387-0700	5173
Oregon PCF Bldg Pdts Calif Inc	5031	D	916 381-8051	5178
Royal Plywood Company LLC	5031	D	916 426-3292	5184
Jensen Enterprises Inc	5039	D	916 992-8301	5227
Tracpatch Health Inc	5047	D	916 355-7123	5456
Granite Electrical Supply Inc	5063	D	916 648-3900	5558
Graybar Electric Company Inc	5063	D	916 561-1900	5560
Independent Electric Sup Inc	5063	D	916 924-4848	5566
Asomeo Envmtl Rstrtion Indust	5082	D	530 434-6869	5782
Case Power and Equipment	5082	C	916 649-0096	5785
Capitol Barricade Inc (PA)	5084	D	916 451-5176	5824
Vantage Elevation LLC	5084	D	916 426-2347	5881
Eriks North America Inc	5085	D	916 366-9340	5901
Valley Rubber & Gasket Company Inc	5085	D	916 369-8885	5934
Chem Quip Inc	5091	D	800 821-1678	5974
Pick Pull Auto Dismantling Inc	5093	D	916 689-1446	6013
Burgett Incorporated (PA)	5099	D	916 567-9999	6031
Amerisourcebergen Drug Corp	5122	C	916 830-4500	6095
Pacific Sfood - Sacramento LLC	5142	C	916 419-5500	6425
General Prod A Cal Ltd Partnr (PA)	5148	C	916 441-6431	6551
Core-Mark International Inc	5149	D	509 535-9768	6620
Java City (HQ)	5149	D	916 565-5500	6637
Shamrock Foods Company	5149	B	602 819-1654	6666
Starwest Botanicals LLC (PA)	5149	D	916 638-8100	6671
Trinity Fresh Distribution Llc	5149	D	916 714-7368	6685
Sacramento Intl Jet Ctr Inc	5172	D	916 428-8292	6737
Markstein Bev Co Sacramento	5181	C	916 920-3911	6772
Saccani Distributing Company	5181	D	916 441-0213	6781
Village Nurseries Whl LLC	5193	B	916 993-2292	6877
Calvey Incorporated	5199	D	916 681-4800	6895
Huhtamaki Inc	5199	C	916 688-4938	6916
Home Depot USA Inc	5211	C	916 726-0620	6962
Home Depot USA Inc	5211	C	916 381-3181	6973
Penney Opco LLC	5311	C	916 564-0315	7129
Trifecta Nutrition Inc	5499	D	530 564-8388	7163
Gordon Turner Motors	5511	C	916 488-2400	7222
Mel Rapton Inc	5511	C	916 514-4050	7257
Niello Imports II Inc	5511	C	916 480-2800	7267
Wesley B Lasher Inv Corp (PA)	5511	D	916 290-8500	7333
Southern Cal Disc Tire Co Inc	5531	D	916 427-1961	7369
Southern Tire Mart LLC	5531	D	916 447-4220	7377
MILES TREASTER & ASSOCIATES	5712	D	916 373-1800	7424
Arden Hills Country Club Inc	5812	D	916 482-6111	7457
Cucina Holdings Inc (DH)	5812	B	916 565-5500	7471
Timberlake Corporation	5999	D	916 423-2198	7595
Rcb Corporation (PA)	6022	D	916 567-2600	7713
River City Bank (HQ)	6022	D	916 567-2600	7714
Bank of Sacramento	6035	D	916 648-2100	7742
Schools Financial Credit Union (PA)	6061	C	916 569-5400	7801
Golden 1 Credit Union	6062	D	916 732-2900	7825
Golden 1 Credit Union (PA)	6062	B	916 732-2900	7826
Sacramento Credit Union (PA)	6062	D	916 444-6070	7832
Merrill Lynch Prce Fnner Smith	6211	D	916 648-6200	8121
Massmutual Pacific	6311	C	916 437-1713	8240
Western Health Advantage	6321	D	916 567-1950	8273
Delta Dental of California	6324	D	916 853-7373	8296
Dentists Insurance Company (HQ)	6324	D	916 443-4567	8297
Kaiser Foundation Hospitals	6324	A	916 688-2000	8321
Kaiser Foundation Hospitals	6324	C	916 973-5000	8329
Allied Insurance	6331	B	916 924-4000	8376
State Compensation Insur Fund	6331	C	888 782-8338	8411
State Compensation Insur Fund	6331	C	916 924-5100	8415
Califrnia Pub Emplyees Rtrment (DH)	6371	A	916 795-3000	8458
Public Employees Retirement	6371	A	916 795-3400	8466
Benetech Inc (PA)	6411	D	916 484-6811	8510
Bickmore and Associates Inc (DH)	6411	D	916 244-1100	8512
Geico General Insurance Co	6411	B	916 923-5050	8573
Interwest Insurance Svcs LLC (PA)	6411	C	916 488-3100	8594
Sacramnto Hsing Rdvlpment Agcy	6411	B	916 440-1376	8650
Santos Legacy Builders LLC	6411	D	916 439-2777	8652
Sedgwick Claims MGT Svcs Inc	6411	C	916 568-7394	8654
Broadway Sacramento	6512	C	916 446-5880	8704
Eskaton	6512	C	916 395-1722	8719
John Stewart Company	6513	D	415 345-4400	8837
Best Sac Homes Grp At Big Blck	6531	D	916 891-2641	8912
Cbre Inc	6531	D	916 446-6800	8926
Ethan Conrad Properties Inc (PA)	6531	D	916 779-1000	8995
Fusion Growth Partners Inc	6531	D	916 448-3174	9020
John Stewart Company	6531	C	916 561-0323	9059
Lyon Realty	6531	D	916 481-3840	9082
Lyon Realty (PA)	6531	D	916 574-8800	9086
Opendoor Labs Inc	6531	C	888 352-7075	9114
Sacramnto Hsing Rdvlpment Agcy	6531	C	916 440-1399	9174
William L Lyon & Assoc Inc	6531	B	916 447-7878	9219
Pw Fund B LP	6722	D	916 379-3852	9388
Atrium Finance I LP	7011	A	916 446-0100	9620
Capitol Regency LLC	7011	B	916 443-1234	9678
Cy Sac Operator LLC	7011	D	916 455-6800	9738

SACRAMENTO CA   GEOGRAPHIC SECTION

Company	SIC	EMP	PHONE	ENTRY#
G B Commercial LLC	7011	D	916 263-9000	9805
Pacifica Hosts Inc	7011	C	619 296-9000	10090
Recp/Wndsor Scramento Ventr LP	7011	D	916 455-6800	10142
Sacramento 49er Travel Plaza	7011	C	916 927-4774	10187
Welcome Group Inc	7011	C	916 920-5300	10356
Ameripride Services Inc	7213	C	916 689-1111	10431
Mission Linen Supply	7213	C	916 423-3179	10442
Coit Services Inc	7217	D	916 731-7006	10472
Mering Holdings (PA)	7311	D	916 441-0571	10647
Runyon Saltzman Inc	7311	D	916 446-9900	10672
Valassis Direct Mail Inc	7331	D	916 923-2398	10780
Cleanrite Inc	7342	C	916 381-1321	10834
City of Sacramento	7349	B	916 808-4044	10873
Crown Building Maintenance Co	7349	B	916 920-9556	10881
Crown Building Maintenance Co	7349	B	415 546-6534	10885
Spencer Building Maintenance	7349	B	916 922-1900	10971
United Building Maint Inc	7349	C	916 772-8101	10978
Apria Healthcare LLC	7352	C	530 677-2713	10989
Carter Aston Inc	7361	C	916 431-3922	11110
Northwest Stffing Rsources Inc	7361	A	916 960-2668	11184
Valley Health Care Systems Inc	7361	C	916 505-4112	11252
Epn Enterprises Inc	7363	D	888 788-5424	11285
Maxim Healthcare Services Inc	7363	D	916 614-9539	11302
Weave Inc (PA)	7363	C	916 448-2321	11362
Abacus Service Corporation	7371	C	916 288-8948	11373
Dealertrack Clltral MGT Svcs I	7371	C	916 368-5300	11534
Redtail Technology Inc	7371	C	800 206-5030	11870
Rhombus Systems Inc	7371	C	877 746-6797	11880
Zennify LLC	7371	D	208 739-2118	12061
Lpa Insurance Agency Inc	7372	C	916 286-7850	12258
Meditab Software Inc	7372	D	510 201-0130	12268
Delegata Corporation	7373	D	916 609-5400	12446
Experian Health Inc	7373	C	415 716-6633	12454
System Integrators Inc	7373	C	916 830-2400	12531
Trinity Technology Group Inc	7373	D	916 779-0201	12537
Research America Inc	7374	C	916 443-4722	12615
County of Sacramento	7376	B	916 874-7752	12694
Ntt Glbal Data Ctrs Amrcas Inc (DH)	7376	B	916 286-3000	12698
California Department Tech (DH)	7379	C	916 319-9223	12747
Cgi Technologies Solutions Inc	7379	C	916 830-1100	12755
Lexisnexis Examen Inc	7379	C	916 921-4300	12827
Pcg Consulting Solutions LLC	7379	C	916 565-8090	12854
Performance Tech Partners LLC	7379	C	800 787-4143	12857
Iunlimited Incorporated	7381	C	916 218-6198	12990
Lead Star Security Inc	7381	D	916 971-6218	12997
Paladin Prtction Spcalists Inc	7381	C	916 331-3175	13018
Probe Information Services Inc	7381	C	916 676-1826	13023
Wade Casey	7381	D	916 395-9996	13074
Administrative Systems Inc	7389	D	916 563-1121	13178
City of Sacramento	7389	C	916 808-5291	13235
Gordon and Schwenkmeyer Inc	7389	C	916 569-1740	13307
Signet Testing Labs Inc	7389	D	916 374-0754	13474
Southwest Dealer Services Inc	7389	C	925 753-0696	13482
Tele-Direct Communications Inc	7389	C	916 348-2170	13506
U-Haul Business Consultants	7513	C	916 331-7601	13568
Enterprise Rnt--car Scrmnto LL	7514	C	916 576-3164	13582
Eugene Harris	7514	C	916 776-3393	13586
Ray Gaskin Service	7532	C	916 682-5155	13646
PDQ Automatic Transm Parts Inc	7537	C	916 681-7701	13653
Pleasanton Truck & Eqp RPS Inc	7538	C	916 387-5288	13670
Inland Business Machines Inc (DH)	7699	D	916 928-0770	13776
Regal Cinemas Inc	7832	D	916 419-0205	14007
Century Theatres Inc	7833	B	916 332-2622	14020
Century Theatres Inc	7833	C	916 363-6572	14022
Broadway Sacramento (PA)	7922	D	916 446-5880	14030
Sacramento Theatre Company	7922	D	916 446-7501	14061
Sacramento Theatrical Ltg Ltd	7922	D	916 447-3258	14062
Pinsetters Inc	7933	D	916 488-7545	14121
Kings Arena Ltd Partnership	7941	D	916 928-0000	14144
Sacramnto Rpub Fotball CLB LLC	7941	D	916 307-6100	14155
Spare-Time Inc	7991	C	916 649-0909	14233
Spare-Time Inc	7991	C	916 488-8100	14234
Morton Golf Management LLC	7992	D	916 481-4653	14278
Del Paso Country Club	7997	C	916 489-3681	14368
Capitol Casino	7999	C	916 446-0700	14503
Associated Fmly Physicians Inc	8011	D	916 689-4111	14619
Cares Community Health	8011	C	916 443-3299	14659
Central Ansthsia Svc Exch Med	8011	D	916 481-6800	14665
Permanente Medical Group Inc	8011	B	916 486-5686	14976
Permanente Medical Group Inc	8011	A	916 688-2055	14991
Sacramnto Bhvral Hlthcare Hosp	8011	C	916 437-6410	15031
Sacramnto Ntiv Amercn Hlth Ctr	8011	C	916 341-0575	15032
Sutter Health	8011	D	916 929-3593	15112
Sutter Hlth Scrmnto Sierra Reg	8011	B	916 386-3000	15113
University California Davis	8011	D	916 734-8514	15156
University California Davis	8011	D	916 734-3588	15158
University California Davis	8011	D	916 442-1011	15160
University California Davis	8011	C	916 734-2846	15161
Wellspace Womens Health Center	8011	D	916 313-8462	15201
Willow Springs LLC	8011	A	916 288-0300	15210
Landmark Healthcare Svcs Inc (DH)	8041	C	800 638-4557	15262
Community Psychiatry MGT LLC (PA)	8049	D	855 501-1004	15278
Sutter Valley Med Foundation	8049	D	916 924-7764	15308
Asbury Pk Nrsing Rhblttion Ctr	8051	C	916 649-2000	15333
Cathedral Pioneer Church Homes (PA)	8051	D	916 442-4906	15367
Covenant Care California LLC	8051	D	916 391-6011	15398
Mariner Health Care Inc	8051	D	916 481-5500	15562
Merakey USA	8051	C	916 923-9823	15584
Oleander Holdings LLC	8051	D	916 331-4590	15610
Sacramento Operating Co LP	8051	C	916 422-4825	15648
Saint Claires Nursing Ctr LLC	8051	C	916 392-4440	15650
Advanced HM Hlth & Hospice Inc	8052	C	916 978-0744	15745
RES-Care Inc	8052	C	916 567-1244	15789
Stratgies To Empwer People Inc (PA)	8052	D	916 679-1555	15797
Crestwood Behavioral Hlth Inc	8059	C	916 452-1431	15838
Hank Fisher Properties Inc	8059	C	916 921-1970	15853
Davis Uc Medical Center	8062	C	916 734-2011	16036
Dignity Health	8062	C	916 423-5940	16051
Kaiser Foundation Hospitals	8062	C	916 558-6520	16163
Kaiser Foundation Hospitals	8062	A	916 973-5000	16171
Kaiser Foundation Hospitals	8062	C	916 525-6300	16190
Mercy Medical Group	8062	D	916 681-6000	16264
Mercy Medical Group (DH)	8062	D	916 733-3333	16268
Shriners Hspitals For Children	8062	B	916 453-2050	16425
Sutter Health	8062	D	916 733-9588	16521
Sutter Health	8062	C	916 566-4819	16525
Sutter Health	8062	C	707 864-4660	16530
Sutter Health (PA)	8062	A	916 733-8800	16534
Sutter Hlth Rhabilitation Svcs	8062	D	916 733-3040	16540
Sutter Hlth Scrmnto Sierra Reg	8062	C	916 733-7080	16543
Sutter Hlth Scrmnto Sierra Reg (HQ)	8062	D	916 733-8800	16544
Sutter Hlth Scrmnto Sierra Reg	8062	B	916 454-2222	16546
Sutter Hlth Scrmnto Sierra Reg	8062	B	916 446-3100	16547
Sutter Hlth Scrmnto Sierra Reg	8062	C	916 924-7666	16548
Sutter Hlth Scrmnto Sierra Reg	8062	A	916 733-3095	16550
Sutter Medical Center	8062	D	916 887-0000	16553
Sutter Valley Hospitals (HQ)	8062	B	916 733-8800	16560
University California Davis	8062	D	916 734-3141	16598
University California Davis	8062	C	916 734-2011	16599
University California Davis	8062	D	916 734-5113	16600
Willow Springs LLC	8062	A	916 489-3336	16630
Psychnp Consultants Inc	8069	D	800 205-6107	16691
Radiological Associates of Sacramen	8071	A	916 646-8300	16746
Unilab Corporation	8071	A	916 733-3330	16759
Unilab Corporation	8071	A	916 927-9900	16761
Dura-Metrics Inc (PA)	8072	D	707 546-5138	16771
Advanced Home Health Inc	8082	D	916 978-0744	16796
Blossom Ridge HM Hlth Agcy LLC	8082	D	800 991-6147	16823
Califrnia Prson Hlthcare Rcvrs	8082	D	916 691-6721	16832
Coram Healthcare Corp Nevada	8082	D	916 857-7000	16847
Interim Healthcare Inc	8082	C	916 486-8181	16877
Oakland Hospice Inc	8082	D	916 779-0811	16903
Greater Sacramento Sur	8093	D	916 929-7229	17067
HealthSouth Corporation	8093	D	916 929-9431	17070
Kaiser Foundation Hospitals	8093	B	916 482-1132	17081
Medmark Trtmnt Ctrs - Scrmnto	8093	D	916 391-4293	17087
River Oak Center For Children (PA)	8093	C	916 609-5100	17121
Sierra Hlth Wellness Group LLC	8093	C	530 854-4119	17126
Sutter Health	8093	C	916 220-1927	17135
Cenpatico Behavioral Hlth LLC	8099	D	877 858-3855	17201
Center To Prmote Hlthcare Acce	8099	C	916 563-4004	17202
Easter Seal Soc Superior Cal (PA)	8099	C	916 485-6711	17230
Ehealthwirecom Inc	8099	C	916 924-8092	17233
Health Lf Orgnization Inc Halo	8099	D	916 428-3788	17246
Permanente Medical Group Inc	8099	B	916 973-5175	17297
Angelo Kilday & Kilduff	8111	C	916 564-6100	17365
Downey Brand LLP (PA)	8111	C	916 444-1000	17441
Greenberg Traurig LLP	8111	C	916 442-1111	17485
Kronick Mskvitz Tdmann Grard A (PA)	8111	C	916 321-4500	17531
Matheny Sars Linkert Jaime LLP	8111	D	916 978-3434	17563
Nationwide Legal LLC	8111	D	916 443-4400	17587
Orrick Hrringtn Sut Foundtn	8111	C	916 329-7928	17595
Pillsbury Wnthrop Shaw Pttman	8111	C	916 329-4700	17610
Scott A Porter Prof Corp	8111	D	916 929-1481	17634
Seyfarth Shaw LLP	8111	C	916 448-0159	17640
Wilke Fleury Hoffelt Gould & Birney	8111	D	916 441-2430	17679

GEOGRAPHIC SECTION

SAN ANDREAS CA

	SIC	EMP	PHONE	ENTRY#
Community College Foundation (PA)	8299	D	916 418-5100	17807
University Enterprises Inc.	8299	A	916 278-7001	17818
Childrens Recvg Hm Sacramento	8322	D	916 482-2370	17885
Develop Disabilities Svc Org.	8322	D	916 973-1951	17953
Heartland Child & Family Svcs.	8322	D	916 922-9868	18000
La Familia Counseling Ctr Inc.	8322	C	916 452-3601	18037
Northern California Inalliance (PA)	8322	D	916 381-1300	18065
Sacramento Area Emerg Housing	8322	D	916 455-2160	18102
Sacramnto Chnese Cmnty Svc Ctr.	8322	C	916 442-4228	18103
Sierra Forever Families.	8322	D	916 368-5114	18133
Stanford Youth Solutions (PA)	8322	D	916 344-0199	18143
Tlcs Inc.	8322	C	916 441-0123	18151
Volunters Amer Nthrn Cal Nthrn	8322	D	916 488-0171	18186
Sacramento Job Corp.	8331	D	916 391-1016	18244
Sacramnto Emplyment Trning AGC	8331	C	916 263-3800	18245
Sacramnto Emplyment Trning AGC (PA)	8331	C	916 263-3800	18246
Appleridge Assisted Living Inc.	8361	C	916 451-1212	18373
Carlton Senior Living Inc.	8361	D	916 971-4800	18386
Eskaton Properties Inc.	8361	D	916 441-1015	18424
Eskaton Properties Inc.	8361	C	916 393-2550	18428
Lbn Leisure Care LLC	8361	D	916 604-3780	18466
Sacramento Childrens Home (PA)	8361	D	916 452-3981	18518
California Chamber Commerce (PA)	8611	D	916 444-6670	18701
Califrnia Rdvlpment Assn Fndti.	8611	D	916 449-6229	18703
Electric & Gas Industries Association (PA)	8611	D	916 609-5300	18708
California Dental Association (PA)	8621	C	916 443-0505	18736
California Health Benefit Exch.	8621	D	916 228-8210	18737
California Medical Association (PA)	8621	D	916 444-5532	18738
Califrnia Assn Hsptals Hlth Sy (PA)	8621	D	916 443-7401	18742
Califrnia State Employees Assn (PA)	8631	D	916 444-8134	18778
Interntional Un Oper Engineers (PA)	8631	D	916 444-6880	18781
Each One Teach One Foundation.	8641	D	916 428-5627	18853
Girl Scouts Heart Central Cal.	8641	C	916 452-9181	18861
Rose Fmly Crtive Empwrment Ctr.	8641	D	916 376-7916	18903
Sutter Club.	8641	D	916 442-0456	18913
Califrnia Yuth Soccer Assn Inc.	8699	D	925 426-5437	19074
Crocker Art Museum Association	8699	D	916 808-7000	19079
Sacramnto Soc For The Prvntion.	8699	D	916 383-7387	19100
Kratos Unmnned Arial Systems I (HQ)	8711	C	916 431-7977	19302
Nv5 Inc (DH)	8711	D	916 641-9100	19336
Stantec Consulting Svcs Inc.	8711	D	916 924-8844	19395
Wood Rodgers Inc (PA)	8711	C	916 341-7760	19444
Cgl Companies LLC.	8712	D	916 678-7890	19460
Lionakis (PA)	8712	C	916 558-1901	19486
Lpas Inc.	8712	D	916 443-0335	19488
Stantec Architecture Inc.	8712	A	916 442-3230	19508
Gilbert Associates Inc.	8721	D	916 646-6464	19580
Macias Gini & OConnell LLP (PA)	8721	D	310 277-3373	19608
Orca Biosystems Inc.	8731	D	916 822-4235	19753
Vacuum Process Engineering Inc.	8731	D	916 925-6100	19794
California Cmplte CNT Cnsus.	8733	D	916 852-2020	19869
California Dept Wtr Resources.	8733	D	916 574-1423	19870
Jackson Laboratory.	8733	D	800 422-6423	19890
Western States Info Netwrk Inc.	8733	D	916 263-1188	19938
Integrted Pain MGT Med Group I.	8741	D	916 333-5800	20117
Vanir Construction MGT Inc (PA)	8741	D	916 444-3700	20241
Capitol Services Inc.	8742	C	916 443-0657	20307
Cooperative Personnel Services (PA)	8742	C	916 263-3600	20328
Excel Managed Care Disa.	8742	C	916 944-7185	20366
Fni International Inc.	8742	D	916 643-1400	20383
Modsquad Inc (PA)	8742	C	916 913-4465	20474
Sutter Physician Services (HQ)	8742	A	916 854-6600	20573
League of California Cities (PA)	8743	D	916 658-8200	20637
Reach Adult Development Inc.	8748	D	916 203-6246	20838
Sacramento Housing Dev Corp (PA)	8748	D	916 440-1333	20843
Sacramnto Mtro A Qulty MGT Dst.	8748	D	916 874-4800	20844
Spectrum Services Group Inc.	8748	D	916 760-7913	20855
Westervelt Company.	8748	D	916 646-3644	20879
Ygrene Energy Fund Inc.	8748	B	916 444-9700	20880
Kaiser Foundation Hospitals.	9224	A	916 974-6211	20935
Formosa Together.	9532	B	916 661-8835	20947

SAINT HELENA, CA - Napa County

	SIC	EMP	PHONE	ENTRY#
Jack Neal & Son Inc.	0172	C	707 963-7303	76
C Mondavi & Family (PA)	2084	D	707 967-2200	2378
Sutter Home Winery Inc (PA)	2084	C	707 963-3104	2395
Meadowood Assoc A Ltd Partnr (PA)	5812	D	707 963-3646	7495
Silverado Orchards LLC (PA)	6513	D	707 963-1461	8861
St Helena Hospital (HQ)	8062	A	707 963-3611	16457

SALIDA, CA - Stanislaus County

	SIC	EMP	PHONE	ENTRY#
Western Drywall Inc.	1742	D	209 543-9361	1973
Flory Industries (PA)	3523	D	209 545-1167	2769

	SIC	EMP	PHONE	ENTRY#
Silliker Inc.	8734	D	209 549-7508	20001

SALINAS, CA - Monterey County

	SIC	EMP	PHONE	ENTRY#
American Farms LLC.	0139	D	831 424-1815	10
DArrigo Bros Co California.	0161	B	831 455-2913	28
Fresh Leaf Farms LLC.	0161	C	831 796-3760	30
Henry Hibino Farms LLC.	0161	D	831 757-3081	34
Tanimura Antle Fresh Foods Inc (PA)	0161	D	831 455-2950	44
Norcal Harvesting LLC (PA)	0171	D	831 443-4999	57
Scheid Vineyards Inc (PA)	0172	D	831 455-9990	86
Csn Winddown Inc.	0181	D	831 444-0523	121
Matsui Nursery Inc (PA)	0181	D	831 422-6433	139
Growers Transplanting Inc (HQ)	0182	D	831 449-3440	161
Red Blossom Sales Inc.	0191	B	831 751-9169	196
Hilltown Packing Co Inc.	0723	B	831 784-1931	279
Jlg Harvesting Inc.	0723	B	831 422-7871	282
Newstar Fresh Foods LLC.	0723	A	831 758-7800	292
Taylor Fresh Foods (PA)	0723	C	831 676-9023	310
Vals Plumbing and Heating Inc.	1711	D	831 424-1633	1590
Organicgirl LLC.	2099	A	831 758-7800	2439
Rm Esop Inc.	2653	C	831 789-8300	2524
Valley Fabrication Inc.	3523	D	831 757-5151	2772
Monterey-Salinas Transit Corp.	4131	D	831 754-2804	3308
SMD Logistics Inc.	4731	C	831 758-5300	4096
Mann Packing Co Inc.	4783	D	831 796-2670	4131
Win Telecom Global Corporation.	4822	D	408 477-5672	4368
Hearst Stations Inc.	4833	C	831 758-8888	4439
Pacific Gas and Electric Co.	4911	D	800 684-4648	4627
BFI Waste Systems N Amer Inc.	4953	D	831 775-3850	4866
Quinn Company.	5082	D	831 758-8461	5799
Rjms Corporation.	5084	C	831 757-1091	5867
Smart & Final Stores LLC.	5141	D	831 754-1068	6359
BlazerWilkinsonGee LLC.	5148	B	831 455-3700	6516
Church Brothers LLC (PA)	5148	D	831 796-1000	6526
Newstar Fresh Foods LLC (PA)	5148	C	888 782-7220	6566
River Ranch Fresh Foods LLC (PA)	5148	B	831 758-1390	6576
Sunberry Growers LLC.	5148	A	805 922-9888	6585
Sturdy Oil Company.	5172	D	831 970-9897	6741
Valley Pacific Petro Svcs Inc.	5172	D	209 461-3635	6743
Altman Specialty Plants LLC.	5193	A	831 758-4850	6847
B2b Industrial Products LLC.	5199	C	630 396-6300	6891
Empire West Solutions LLC.	5199	C	831 783-1649	6903
Goodwill Central Coast (PA)	5932	B	831 423-8611	7534
Goodwill Central Coast.	5932	D	831 755-8668	7535
Continental Exch Solutions Inc.	6099	D	562 345-2156	7850
Mission Linen Supply.	7213	D	831 423-1630	10440
Mission Linen Supply.	7213	D	831 424-1707	10443
Mission Linen Supply.	7218	D	831 424-1753	10479
A Oseguera Company Inc.	7361	B	831 443-4155	11070
Bc Labor Contractors.	7361	C	831 751-6000	11094
Employnet Inc.	7361	A	831 233-9999	11129
Growers Company Inc.	7361	D	831 424-3850	11147
Interim Inc.	7363	D	831 758-9457	11294
Volt Management Corp.	7363	D	831 975-4374	11350
ASset Private Security Inc.	7381	D	831 809-9779	12934
J Waters Inc.	7381	D	866 424-1946	12991
Corral De Tierra Country Club.	7997	D	831 484-1325	14364
Salinas Golf and Cntry CLB Inc.	7997	D	831 449-6617	14435
Central Cast Crdlgy A Med Corp.	8011	C	831 758-2100	14672
Salinas Valley Medical Clinic.	8011	D	831 424-7389	15034
Emeritus Corporation.	8051	C	831 443-6467	15434
Windsor Cnvlscent Rhbltion CT.	8051	D	831 424-0687	15740
Salinasidence Opco LLC.	8052	D	831 424-8072	15793
Communty Hsptal of The Mntrey.	8062	D	831 596-8986	16018
County of Monterey.	8062	C	831 755-4201	16028
Natividad Medical Center.	8062	A	831 755-4111	16279
Salinas Valley Health (PA)	8062	A	831 757-4333	16373
Unilab Corporation.	8071	A	831 424-3858	16765
Central Coast Vna Hospice Inc.	8082	C	831 758-8243	16837
Sutter Vsting Nrse Assn Hspice.	8082	C	831 455-8901	16943
Community Action Prtnr San Lui.	8351	C	831 751-9779	18296
County of Monterey.	8699	D	831 755-3856	19078
Baronhr LLC.	8742	D	831 272-7980	20290
Geographic Solutions Inc.	8742	B	831 757-4400	20393
Interim Inc.	8999	D	831 754-3838	20893

SAN ANDREAS, CA - Calaveras County

	SIC	EMP	PHONE	ENTRY#
K W Emerson Inc.	1623	D	209 754-3839	1225
Calaveras County Water Dst.	4941	D	209 754-3543	4766
Avalon Care Ctr - San Andreas.	8051	D	209 754-3823	15344
Mark Twain Medical Center (DH)	8062	C	209 754-3521	16248

Employee Codes: A=Over 500 employees, B=251-500
C=101-250, D=51-100, E=20-50, F=10-19, G=1-9

2024 Directory of California
WholeSalers and Service Companies

© Mergent Inc. 1-800-342-5647

SAN ANSELMO CA

	SIC	EMP	PHONE	ENTRY#

SAN ANSELMO, CA - Marin County
Garcia and Associates	8748	C	415 458-5803	20757

SAN ARDO, CA - Monterey County
PSC Industrial Outsourcing LP	4212	C	831 627-2595	3419

SAN BERNARDINO, CA - San Bernardino County
	SIC	EMP	PHONE	ENTRY#
Lucky Farms Inc	0161	D	909 799-6688	36
Original Mowbrays Tree Svc Inc (PA)	0783	C	909 383-7009	558
Matich Corporation (PA)	1611	D	909 382-7400	1136
Metricom Networks	1623	D	480 522-0700	1236
Caston Inc	1742	C	909 381-1619	1919
Innocor West LLC	3069	B	909 307-3737	2657
Optivus Proton Therapy Inc	3829	D	909 799-8300	3043
Omnitrans (PA)	4111	C	909 379-7100	3184
San Bernardino Cnty Trnsp Auth	4111	D	909 884-8276	3194
Air Methods	4119	C	909 382-0045	3226
Amazoncom Inc	4225	D	626 260-6954	3674
Penney Opco LLC	4225	D	972 431-2618	3743
World Class Distribution Inc	4225	C	909 574-4140	3786
United Parcel Service Inc	4512	C	800 742-5877	3849
Aviation & Defense Inc	4581	C	909 382-3487	3877
CJ Logistics America LLC	4731	C	540 377-2302	3998
Gxo Logistics Supply Chain Inc	4731	D	909 838-5631	4029
Gxo Logistics Supply Chain Inc	4731	D	909 253-5356	4030
HAM Brokerage	4731	C	909 659-5392	4031
Loma Linda University Med Ctr	4731	D	909 558-4000	4051
Gunderson Rail Services LLC	4789	C	909 478-0541	4158
Meridian Rail Acquisition	4789	C	909 478-0541	4167
Sprint Communications Co LP	4813	D	909 382-6030	4345
San Brnrdino Cmnty College Dst	4832	C	909 384-4444	4402
Southern California Gas Co	4924	C	909 335-7941	4741
Burrtec Waste Industries Inc	4953	C	909 889-1969	4871
Metropolitan Automotive Warehouse	5013	A	909 885-2886	5049
H and H Drug Stores Inc	5047	D	909 890-9700	5422
CMC Rebar West	5051	C	909 713-1130	5483
S&E Gourmet Cuts Inc	5145	C	909 370-0155	6464
Gate City Beverage Distrs (PA)	5181	B	909 799-0281	6763
L & L Nursery Supply Inc (HQ)	5191	C	909 591-0461	6827
Harbill Inc	5511	D	909 883-8833	7230
Ocelot Engineering Inc	5571	C	800 841-2960	7398
Inland Empire Health Plan	6324	A	866 228-4347	8304
Woodman Realty Inc	6531	C	909 425-5324	9222
S B H Hotel Corporation	7011	A	909 889-0133	10184
San Bernardino Hilton (HQ)	7011	C	909 889-0133	10193
Job Options Incorporated	7219	A	909 890-4612	10486
Scdrg Inc	7311	D	818 874-3050	10674
Avalon Building Maint Inc	7349	B	714 693-2407	10859
Barrett Business Services Inc	7361	A	909 890-3633	11090
Nursefinders LLC	7361	C	909 890-2286	11188
Maxim Healthcare Services Inc	7363	D	951 684-4148	11308
United Guard Security Inc	7381	C	909 402-0754	13061
ADT LLC	7382	C	951 824-7205	13089
Jenco Productions Inc (PA)	7389	D	909 381-9453	13332
Inland Empire 66ers Bsbal CLB	7941	C	909 888-9922	14143
Evergreen Alliance Golf Ltd LP	7997	D	909 886-0669	14374
San Brnrdino Cnty Rgonal Parks	7999	D	909 387-2583	14558
Sb Waterman Holdings Inc (PA)	8011	C	909 883-8611	15051
Boyd Dental Corporation	8021	C	909 890-0421	15218
Michael P Byko DDS A Prof Corp (PA)	8021	D	909 888-7817	15240
Robert Ballard Rehab Hospital (HQ)	8049	D	909 473-1200	15305
Del Rosa Villa Inc	8051	D	909 885-3261	15423
Far West Inc	8051	D	909 884-4781	15475
Waterman Convalescent Hosp Inc (PA)	8051	C	909 882-1215	15727
Del Rosa Villaidence Opco LLC	8052	B	909 885-3261	15753
Watermanidence Opco LLC	8052	B	909 882-1215	15804
Marna Health Services Inc	8059	D	909 882-2965	15877
San Bernardino Care Company	8059	C	909 884-4781	15893
United Medical Management Inc	8059	D	909 886-5291	15907
Community Hosp San Bernardino (DH)	8062	B	909 887-6333	16010
St Bernardine Med Ctr Aux Inc	8062	B	909 881-4320	16453
St Bernardine Medical Center	8062	D	909 883-8711	16454
Maxim Healthcare Services Inc	8082	B	760 243-3377	16895
Vnacare	8082	D	909 384-0737	16970
Vnacare (PA)	8082	D	909 624-3574	16971
Institute For Bhvoral Hlth Inc	8093	B	909 289-1041	17076
Victor Cmnty Support Svcs Inc	8093	D	909 890-5930	17157
Bio-Medics Inc	8099	C	909 883-9501	17188
Blood Bnk San Brnrdino Rvrside (HQ)	8099	C	909 885-6503	17190
Inland Bhavioral Hlth Svcs Inc (PA)	8099	D	909 881-6146	17255
San Brnrdino Cy Unified Schl Ds	8099	D	909 881-8000	17318
California City San Bernardino (PA)	8111	B	909 384-7272	17397
Lewis Brsbois Bsgard Smith LLP	8111	D	909 387-1130	17548
Inland Cnties Regional Ctr Inc (PA)	8322	C	909 890-3000	18015
San Brnrdino Cnty Prbtion Offc	8322	B	909 887-2544	18110
Think Together	8351	B	909 723-1400	18359
Omnitrans	8361	C	909 383-1680	18501
Victor Treatment Centers Inc	8361	D	951 436-5200	18538
Community Action Prtnr San Brn	8399	D	909 723-1500	18578
YMCA of East Valley	8641	D	909 881-9622	18935
Allen Engineering Contractor Inc	8711	C	909 478-5500	19136
Northrop Grmmn Spce & Mssn Sys	8731	D	909 382-6800	19746
Mentor Mdia USA Sup Chain MGT	8741	D	909 930-0800	20150
Amtex Supply Holdings Inc	8742	C	909 985-8918	20275
Gibson Overseas Inc	8748	C	323 832-8900	20763

SAN BRUNO, CA - San Mateo County
	SIC	EMP	PHONE	ENTRY#
Alba Wheels Up Intl LLC	4731	D	650 952-0815	3983
Lowes Home Centers LLC	5211	C	650 616-7800	7052
Police Credit Union of Cal (PA)	6061	D	415 242-2142	7792
Artichoke Joes	7999	B	650 589-8812	14493
Permanente Medical Group Inc	8011	A	650 742-2100	14963
Center For Social Dynamics LLC	8049	D	650 243-9849	15276
San Brunoidence Opco LLC	8062	D	650 583-7768	16377
Lash Group LLC	8399	C	800 788-9637	18605

SAN CARLOS, CA - San Mateo County
	SIC	EMP	PHONE	ENTRY#
Peninsula Custom Homes Inc	1521	D	650 574-0241	708
Mp Nexlevel California Inc	1623	B	650 486-1359	1239
Level 5 Drywall Inc	1742	D	650 486-1657	1943
D & J Tile Company Inc	1743	D	650 632-4000	1978
Peninsula Crrdor Jint Pwers Bd	4111	C	650 508-6200	3189
San Mateo County Transit Dst (PA)	4111	C	650 508-6200	3203
San Mateo County Transit Dst	4173	C	650 508-6412	3358
Lifestreet Corporation	5199	D	650 508-2220	6925
E La Carte Inc	5734	D	650 468-0680	7442
Oportun Financial Corporation (PA)	6141	A	650 810-8823	7883
Lawyers Title Insurance Corp	6361	C	650 445-6300	8445
Peninsula Parking Inc	7299	D	650 596-5728	10569
Bynder	7371	D	415 227-4886	11480
Pivot Health Technologies Inc	7371	D	650 216-9680	11829
Check Point Software Tech Inc (HQ)	7372	C	650 628-2000	12133
Revjet Corporation	7372	D	650 508-2215	12337
Hello Digit LLC	7389	D	415 260-2684	13311
Starvista	8322	C	650 591-9623	18144
Alkahest Inc	8731	D	650 801-0474	19651
Helix Holdings I LLC	8731	D	415 805-3360	19705
Nautilus Biotechnology Inc	8731	D	206 333-2001	19742
Transiris Corporation	8742	D	650 303-3495	20590

SAN CLEMENTE, CA - Orange County
	SIC	EMP	PHONE	ENTRY#
Consolidated Contg Svcs Inc	1542	D	949 498-7500	900
Bemus Landscape Inc	1629	B	714 557-7910	1289
Millennium Reinforcing Inc	1791	C	949 361-9730	2191
Dana Innovations (PA)	3651	C	949 492-7777	2878
Rosen & Rosen Industries Inc	3949	D	949 361-9238	3094
Casa Logistics LLC	4789	D	949 636-3391	4148
San Diego Gas & Electric Co	4931	C	949 361-8090	4753
Buyefficient LLC	5046	C	949 382-3129	5375
Cameron Health Inc	5047	D	949 940-4400	5407
Pacific Medical Group Inc	5047	D	949 493-1030	5438
Stance Inc (PA)	5137	C	949 391-9030	6222
Sambazon Inc (PA)	5148	D	877 726-2296	6577
Grain To Green Inc	5153	C	760 845-6107	6692
Lowes Home Centers LLC	5211	D	949 369-4644	7041
Evr Lending Inc	6531	D	949 492-4868	8997
Luxre Realty Inc	6531	D	949 498-3702	9080
Matsushita International Corp (PA)	6799	D	949 498-1000	9531
Life Time Inc	7991	D	949 492-1515	14213
Heritage Golf Group LLC	7992	D	949 369-6226	14266
Bella Collina San Clemente	7997	D	949 498-6604	14341
Pacific Golf & Country Club	7997	D	949 498-6604	14421
Monarch Healthcare A Medical	8011	C	949 489-1960	14910
Orange Coast Wns Med Group Inc	8011	D	949 829-5522	14943
Dual Diagnosis Trtmnt Ctr Inc (PA)	8093	C	949 276-5553	17056
Automobile Club Southern Cal	8699	D	949 489-5572	19059
Garwood Laboratories Inc	8734	D	562 949-2727	19980
Evolution Hospitality LLC (HQ)	8741	D	949 325-1350	20084
Leaf Communications LLC	8748	D	949 388-0192	20798

SAN DIEGO, CA - San Diego County
	SIC	EMP	PHONE	ENTRY#
VCA Animal Hospitals Inc	0742	D	858 560-8006	347
Veterinary Practice Assoc Inc	0742	C	949 833-9020	350
Veterinary Specialty Hosp	0742	C	858 875-7500	351
Brightview Landscape Dev Inc	0781	B	858 458-9900	395
Brightview Landscape Svcs Inc	0781	C	858 458-1900	404

GEOGRAPHIC SECTION

SAN DIEGO CA

	SIC	EMP	PHONE	ENTRY#
Shoreline Land Care Inc (PA)	0781	D	858 560-8555	463
Heaviland Enterprises Inc	0782	C	858 412-1576	496
Landcare USA LLC	0782	C	858 453-1755	510
Namvars Inc	0782	D	858 792-5461	524
New Way Landscape & Tree Svcs	0782	C	858 505-8300	525
Aptim Federal Services LLC	1521	A	619 239-1690	656
JR Construction Inc	1521	C	858 505-4760	687
Largo Concrete Inc	1521	C	619 356-2142	695
Fairfield Development Inc (PA)	1522	C	858 457-2123	756
Wermers Multi-Family Corp	1522	C	858 535-1475	784
Amaya Curiel Corporation	1541	A	619 661-1230	803
CMC Rebar West	1541	C	858 737-7700	813
Isec Incorporated	1541	C	858 279-9085	826
Kevcon Inc	1541	D	760 432-0307	829
Ledcor CMI Inc	1541	D	602 595-3017	831
T B Penick & Sons Inc	1541	C	858 558-1800	848
Austin Commercial LP	1542	C	619 446-5637	867
Balfour Beatty Cnstr LLC	1542	C	858 635-7400	869
Barnhart Inc	1542	B	858 635-7400	870
Bycor General Contractors Inc	1542	C	858 587-1901	884
C W Driver Incorporated	1542	C	619 696-5100	886
Dpr Construction A Gen Partnr	1542	C	858 646-0757	910
Harvey Inc	1542	C	858 769-4000	930
Pacific Building Group (PA)	1542	D	858 552-0600	982
PCL Construction Services Inc	1542	C	858 657-3400	986
Rancho Santa Fe Technology Inc (PA)	1542	C	858 565-7224	1001
Solpac Inc	1542	C	619 296-6247	1030
Swinerton Builders	1542	D	858 622-4040	1035
Triton Structural Concrete Inc	1542	C	858 866-2450	1044
Webcor Construction LP	1542	C	619 798-3891	1055
West Pacific Services Inc	1542	C	888 401-0188	1060
City of San Diego	1611	C	619 527-7482	1090
Ies Commercial Inc	1611	C	858 210-4900	1120
Cameron Intrstate Pipeline LLC	1623	D	619 696-3110	1201
Sempra LNG International LLC	1623	D	661 399-2077	1261
Vadnais Trenchless Svcs Inc	1623	C	858 550-1460	1274
A & D Fire Protection Inc	1711	D	619 258-7697	1330
A O Reed & Co LLC	1711	B	858 565-4131	1331
Alpha Mechanical Inc	1711	C	858 278-3500	1349
Alpha Mechanical Heating & Air Cond	1711	C	858 279-1300	1351
Apex Mechanical Systems Inc	1711	D	858 536-8700	1361
ASI Hastings Inc	1711	C	619 590-9300	1364
Atlas Mechanical Inc (PA)	1711	D	858 554-0700	1367
Bill Howe Plumbing Inc	1711	D	800 245-5469	1378
Cosco Fire Protection Inc	1711	D	858 444-2000	1409
Greater San Diego AC Co Inc	1711	C	619 469-7818	1452
Jackson & Blanc	1711	C	858 831-7900	1472
National Air Inc	1711	C	619 299-2500	1507
Pacific Rim Mech Contrs Inc (PA)	1711	B	858 974-6500	1523
Pan-Pacific Mechanical LLC	1711	B	858 764-2464	1526
Schmidt Fire Protection Co Inc	1711	D	858 279-6122	1555
Sherwood Mechanical Inc	1711	D	858 679-3000	1560
General Coatings Corporation (PA)	1721	C	858 587-1277	1617
4liberty Inc	1731	D	619 400-1000	1648
Allied Universal	1731	C	619 444-0219	1661
Communction Wirg Spcalists Inc	1731	C	858 278-4545	1703
Fishel Company	1731	C	858 658-0830	1735
Helix Electric Inc (PA)	1731	C	858 535-0505	1746
Wirtz Quality Installations	1741	D	858 569-3816	1897
Best Interiors Inc	1742	C	858 715-3760	1909
Pacific Building Group	1742	D	858 552-0600	1952
J W Floor Covering Inc (PA)	1752	C	858 536-8565	2038
A Preman Roofing Inc	1761	D	619 276-1700	2041
Ben F Smith Inc	1771	C	858 271-4320	2099
Cement Cutting Inc	1771	D	619 296-9592	2107
Coffman Specialties Inc (PA)	1771	C	858 536-3100	2109
American Scaffold Inc (PA)	1796	D	619 231-4898	2245
Herzog Contracting Corp	1799	D	619 849-6990	2283
My Office Inc	1799	D	858 549-6700	2299
Proform Interior Cnstr Inc	1799	D	619 881-0041	2307
Yyk Enterprises Operations LLC (PA)	1799	C	619 474-6229	2336
Natural Balance Pet Foods Inc	2048	D	800 829-4493	2364
Reyes Coca-Cola Bottling LLC	2086	B	619 266-6300	2410
Creative Design Industries	2321	C	619 710-2525	2450
Terry Town Corporation	2384	D	619 421-5354	2467
Montbleau & Associates Inc (PA)	2521	C	619 263-5550	2496
San Diego Union-Tribune LLC (PA)	2711	A	619 299-3131	2542
Elitra Pharmaceuticals	2834	D	858 410-3030	2585
Mirati Therapeutics Inc (PA)	2834	A	858 332-3410	2598
Polypeptide Labs San Diego LLC	2834	D	858 408-0808	2602
Prometheus Laboratories Inc	2834	B	858 824-0895	2603
Rayzebio Inc	2834	D	619 937-2754	2606
Travere Therapeutics Inc (PA)	2834	C	888 969-7879	2610
Cidara Therapeutics Inc (PA)	2836	D	858 752-6170	2620
Frazee Industries Inc	2851	A	858 626-3600	2635
Cibus Inc	2879	C	858 450-0008	2640
Saint-Gobain Solar Gard LLC (DH)	3081	D	866 300-2674	2661
MI Technologies Inc	3089	A	619 710-2637	2674
Nishiba Industries Corporation	3089	D	619 661-8866	2676
Price Industries Inc	3312	D	858 673-4451	2720
Continuous Computing Corp	3571	C	858 882-8800	2803
Kontron America Incorporated	3571	D	800 822-7522	2808
Teradata Operations Inc (HQ)	3571	D	937 242-4030	2814
C Enterprises Inc	3577	D	760 599-5111	2827
Mitek Systems Inc (PA)	3577	C	619 269-6800	2833
Voyetra Turtle Beach Inc (DH)	3577	D	914 345-2255	2840
Thermocraft	3585	D	619 813-2985	2845
Aemi Holdings LLC	3613	D	858 481-0210	2860
Crydom Inc (DH)	3625	D	619 210-1590	2864
S R C Devices Inccustomer	3625	B	866 772-8668	2868
Clear Blue Energy Corp	3648	D	858 451-1549	2875
Sony Electronics Inc (DH)	3651	A	858 942-2400	2881
Qualcomm Incorporated (PA)	3663	A	858 587-1121	2897
Johnson Cntrls Fire Prtction L	3669	D	858 633-9100	2902
Daylight Solutions Inc (DH)	3674	C	858 432-7500	2916
Kyocera International Inc (HQ)	3674	D	858 492-1456	2925
Qualcomm Technologies Inc (HQ)	3674	B	858 587-1121	2932
Cubic Defense Applications Inc	3699	C	858 505-2870	2956
Achates Power Inc	3714	D	858 535-9920	2970
Kratos Def & SEC Solutions Inc (PA)	3761	C	858 812-7300	2998
Cubic Corporation (HQ)	3812	A	858 277-6780	3003
Northrop Grumman Systems Corp	3812	A	410 765-5589	3006
Northrop Grumman Systems Corp	3812	B	858 592-4518	3007
Northrop Grumman Systems Corp	3812	C	858 618-4349	3008
D & K Engineering (PA)	3824	C	858 451-8999	3021
Bae Systems Info Elctrnic Syst	3825	A	858 592-5000	3024
Bae Systems National Security Solutions Inc	3825	A	858 592-5000	3025
L3harris Interstate Elec Corp	3825	D	858 592-9500	3027
Accriva Dgnostics Holdings Inc (DH)	3841	B	858 404-8203	3046
Resmed Inc (PA)	3841	A	858 836-5000	3059
Carefusion Corporation (HQ)	3845	B	858 617-2000	3074
Orca Arms LLC	3949	D	858 586-0503	3093
Signtech Electrical Advg Inc	3993	C	619 527-6100	3101
San Diego Metro Trnst Sys	4111	A	619 231-1466	3195
San Diego Transit Corporation (PA)	4111	A	619 238-0100	3196
San Diego Trolley Inc	4111	B	619 595-4933	3197
Americare Ambulance	4119	C	760 739-9723	3235
Care Medical Trnsp Inc	4119	C	858 653-4520	3246
Ace Relocation Systems Inc (PA)	4212	D	858 677-5500	3364
J D L Motor Express	4212	D	619 232-6136	3407
American Freightways LP	4213	D	866 326-5902	3441
Complete Logistics Company	4213	D	619 661-9610	3455
Xpo Logistics Freight Inc	4213	D	858 569-8921	3566
Covan World-Wide Moving Inc	4214	D	858 558-0439	3583
United Parcel Service Inc	4215	A	909 279-5111	3640
Casas International Brkg Inc (PA)	4225	D	619 661-6162	3682
MCR Printing and Packg Corp	4225	C	619 488-3012	3730
San Diego Gas & Electric Co	4225	D	858 547-2086	3751
Hornblower Yachts LLC	4489	D	619 686-8700	3808
San Diego Unified Port Dst (PA)	4491	C	619 686-6200	3817
Shelter Pointe LLC	4493	C	619 221-8000	3824
San Dego Cnty Rgnal Arprt Auth (PA)	4581	C	619 400-2400	3909
San Dego Cnty Rgnal Arprt Auth	4581	D	619 400-2404	3910
Lbf Travel Inc	4724	B	858 429-7599	3939
Seat Planners LLC	4724	D	619 237-9434	3950
Expeditors Intl Wash Inc	4731	D	619 710-1900	4016
Golden Hour Data Systems Inc	4731	C	858 768-2500	4026
Innovel Solutions Inc	4731	A	619 497-1123	4039
Miramar Transportation Inc	4731	D	858 693-0071	4059
Chandler Packaging A Transpak Company	4783	D	858 292-5674	4126
Mek Enterprises Inc	4783	D	619 527-0957	4132
Petco Animal Supplies Inc (DH)	4783	B	858 453-7845	4134
Accord Logistics Llc	4789	D	281 687-1181	4141
Nerys Logistics Inc	4789	C	619 616-2124	4169
Secure Transportation Co Inc	4789	D	858 790-3958	4174
Cricket Communications LLC (DH)	4812	D		4211
Cubic Secure Communications I	4812	B	858 505-2000	4212
New Cingular Wireless Svcs Inc	4812	D	619 238-3638	4219
Trellisware Technologies Inc (HQ)	4812	C	858 753-1600	4238
Castle Access Inc	4813	D	858 836-0200	4262
Digitalmojo Inc	4813	D	800 413-5916	4268
Fortitude Technology Inc	4813	D	858 974-5080	4274
Mp3com Inc	4813	D	858 623-7000	4316
Nuera Communications Inc (DH)	4813	D	858 625-2400	4322
Paychex Benefit Tech Inc	4813	C	800 322-7292	4328
Sydata Inc	4813	C	760 444-4368	4346

Employee Codes: A=Over 500 employees, B=251-500
C=101-250, D=51-100, E=20-50, F=10-19, G=1-9

2024 Directory of California
WholeSalers and Service Companies

© Mergent Inc. 1-800-342-5647

SAN DIEGO CA — GEOGRAPHIC SECTION

Company	SIC	EMP	PHONE	ENTRY#
Telisimo International Corp.	4813	B	619 325-1593	4349
Kifm Smooth Jazz 981 Inc.	4832	C	619 297-3698	4389
Local Media San Diego LLC	4832	D	858 888-7000	4395
Univision Radio Inc	4832	D	619 744-4370	4408
Bay City Television Inc (PA)	4833	D	858 279-6666	4412
EW Scripps Company	4833	C	619 237-1010	4430
Herring Networks Inc.	4833	C	858 270-6900	4440
McKinnon Publishing Company	4833	A	858 571-5151	4453
Station Venture Operations LP	4833	D	619 231-3939	4463
Cox Communications Cal LLC	4841	B	619 262-1122	4494
Spectrum MGT Holdg Co LLC	4841	D	858 695-3220	4521
Spectrum MGT Holdg Co LLC	4841	D	619 684-6106	4522
Siege Media LLC	4899	D	858 751-4439	4551
Edf Renewables Inc (PA)	4911	C	858 521-3300	4572
San Diego Gas & Electric Co.	4911	B	858 654-6377	4668
San Diego Gas & Electric Co.	4911	C	858 613-3216	4669
San Diego Gas & Electric Co.	4911	D	858 654-1289	4670
San Diego Gas & Electric Co.	4911	C	619 699-1018	4673
San Diego Gas & Electric Co.	4911	C	858 541-5920	4674
Sempra Energy	4911	A	619 696-2000	4675
Sempra Energy Global Entps.	4911	A	619 696-2000	4676
Sempra Energy International	4911	A	619 696-2000	4677
Solv Energy LLC (HQ)	4911	C	858 251-4888	4680
Twin Oaks Power LP (HQ)	4911	D	619 696-2034	4715
Calpine Energy Solutions LLC (DH)	4931	C	877 273-6772	4748
San Diego Gas & Electric Co (DH)	4931	B	619 696-2000	4751
San Diego Gas & Electric Co.	4931	D	866 616-5565	4752
Sempra (PA)	4932	A	619 696-2000	4756
San Diego County Water Auth (PA)	4941	D	858 522-6600	4822
California Marine Cleaning Inc (PA)	4953	C	619 231-8788	4872
IMS Recycling Services Inc (PA)	4953	D	619 231-2521	4900
Sullivan International Group Inc.	4959	C	619 260-1432	4984
Rain Bird Corporation.	4971	D	619 661-4493	4994
Adesa Corporation	5012	D	619 661-5565	5002
Miramar Ford Truck Sales Inc	5012	D	619 272-5340	5016
Meridian Rack & Pinion Inc.	5013	D	888 875-0026	5048
BKM Officeworks LLC (PA)	5021	D	858 569-4700	5079
Goforth & Marti (PA)	5021	D	800 686-6583	5089
Parron-Hall Corporation	5021	D	858 268-1212	5100
Mirama Enterprises Inc.	5023	D	858 587-8866	5124
R W Smith & Co (HQ)	5023	D	858 530-1800	5132
Expo Industries Inc.	5031	D	858 565-3110	5155
Atlas Construction Supply Inc (PA)	5032	D	858 277-2100	5195
Mr Copy Inc (DH)	5044	D	858 573-6300	5251
San Diego Cash Register Co Inc	5044	D	858 790-7327	5255
Baker & Taylor Holdings LLC	5045	A	858 457-2500	5279
Broadway Typewriter Co Inc	5045	D	800 998-9199	5284
Eset LLC (HQ)	5045	C	619 876-5400	5302
Mediatek USA Inc.	5045	C	858 731-9200	5329
PC Specialists Inc (DH)	5045	C	858 566-1900	5333
Southland Technology Inc.	5045	D	858 694-0932	5352
Jetro Holdings LLC.	5046	B	858 564-0466	5381
Jones Signs Co Inc.	5046	D	858 569-1400	5383
R W Smith & Co.	5046	D	858 530-1800	5387
Better Night LLC.	5047	D	619 299-6299	5403
Binding Site Inc (HQ)	5047	D	858 453-9177	5404
Biosite Inc.	5047	C	510 683-9063	5405
Nexcoil Incorporated.	5051	D	619 671-9247	5502
Anixter Inc.	5063	D	800 854-2088	5537
Beacon Electric Supply.	5063	D	858 279-9770	5543
Cableconn Industries Inc.	5063	D	858 571-7111	5544
Graybar Electric Company Inc.	5063	D	858 578-8606	5561
Dragon Trade Intl Corp.	5064	D	619 816-6062	5601
Philips North America LLC	5064	D	858 677-6390	5610
Bear Communications Inc.	5065	D	619 263-2159	5628
Motorola Mobility LLC.	5065	D	858 455-1500	5678
Performance Designed Pdts LLC (PA)	5065	D	800 331-3844	5688
Presidio Components LLC	5065	D	858 578-9390	5689
Steren Electronics Intl LLC (PA)	5065	D	800 266-3333	5701
Eurodrip USA Inc.	5083	D	559 674-2670	5808
Waxies Enterprises LLC (DH)	5087	C	800 995-4466	5952
Kettenburg Marine Corporation.	5088	C	619 224-8211	5960
Irisys Inc.	5122	D	858 623-1520	6114
Specialty Textile Services LLC	5131	C	619 476-8750	6162
Mad Engine Global LLC	5137	B	858 558-5270	6206
Piveg Inc.	5141	C	858 436-3070	6278
Smart & Final Stores Inc.	5141	B	619 291-1842	6306
Smart & Final Stores Inc.	5141	B	858 578-7343	6314
Smart & Final Stores LLC.	5141	D	619 239-3377	6341
Smart & Final Stores LLC.	5141	D	858 286-0688	6369
Smart & Final Stores LLC.	5141	D	858 541-2090	6370
Canteen Vending - San Diego	5145	A	619 527-1900	6457
Catalina Offshore Products Inc.	5146	D	619 297-9797	6467
Jensen Meat Company Inc.	5147	D	619 754-6400	6496
Jetro Cash and Carry Entps LLC	5147	D	619 233-0200	6497
Mpci Holdings Inc.	5147	D	619 294-2222	6499
Coast Citrus Distributors (PA)	5148	D	619 661-7950	6527
Lenore John & Co (PA)	5149	C	619 232-6136	6644
Perfect Bar LLC.	5149	C	866 628-8548	6657
Chembridge Corporation (PA)	5169	B	858 451-7400	6707
Jankovich Company LLC.	5172	D	619 232-4939	6731
Crest Beverage LLC.	5181	C	858 452-2300	6757
Montesquieu Corp.	5182	D	877 705-5669	6802
Ahern Agribusiness Inc.	5191	D	619 661-9450	6821
Zoological Society San Diego.	5191	D	619 718-3000	6839
Baker & Taylor LLC.	5192	C	858 457-2500	6840
White Digital Media Inc.	5192	D	760 827-7800	6845
Bella Terra Nursery Inc.	5193	D	619 585-1118	6852
Tcp Global Corporation.	5198	D	858 909-2110	6884
Pro Specialties Group Inc.	5199	D	858 541-1100	6938
Schroff Inc.	5199	A	858 740-2400	6947
Home Depot USA Inc.	5211	D	619 263-1533	6991
Lowes Home Centers LLC	5211	C	619 584-5500	7034
Courtesy Chevrolet Center.	5511	D	619 297-4321	7187
Europa Auto Imports Inc.	5511	C	858 569-6900	7203
Mossy Automotive Group Inc (PA)	5511	D	858 581-4000	7261
Mossy Ford Inc.	5511	C	858 273-7500	7262
Mossy Nissan Inc.	5511	D	858 565-6608	7263
San Diego V Inc (PA).	5511	D	888 308-2260	7293
Southern Cal Disc Tire Co Inc.	5531	C	858 278-0661	7375
La Mesa R V Center Inc (PA)	5561	C	858 874-8000	7395
South Sun Products Inc.	5632	D	858 694-0910	7405
Cintas Corporation No 3.	5699	C	619 239-1001	7414
Gosecure Inc (PA).	5734	C	301 442-3432	7445
Citrus Restaurant LLC.	5812	C	858 277-8888	7468
Jack In Box Inc (PA).	5812	A	858 571-2121	7489
Qdoba Restaurant Corporation (HQ)	5812	C	858 766-4900	7505
Red Robin International Inc.	5812	B	858 202-1651	7506
Sharp Healthcare (PA).	5912	A	858 499-4000	7527
Sharp Healthcare Aco LLC.	5912	D	619 688-3543	7528
Ssd Management LLC.	5947	D	619 291-2900	7558
Greatcall Inc.	5999	A	800 733-6632	7581
Jam Fire Protection Inc.	5999	D	858 495-2335	7586
Petco Health & Wellness Co Inc.	5999	D	858 453-7845	7588
United Access LLC.	5999	D	623 879-0800	7596
Wells Fargo Investments LLC.	6021	D	619 702-6949	7646
California Bank & Trust.	6022	A	801 844-7637	7666
Enterprise Bank & Trust.	6022	C	858 432-7000	7680
Seacoast Cmmerce Banc Holdings.	6022	C	858 432-7000	7716
Commercial Fin Lsg Bnk Crdiff.	6029	D	888 234-0166	7730
Mission Federal Credit Union.	6061	C	858 531-5106	7782
Mission Federal Credit Union (PA)	6061	C	858 546-2184	7783
Mission Federal Services LLC (PA)	6061	C	858 524-2850	7784
San Diego County Credit Union	6061	C	877 732-2848	7796
United Svcs Amer Federal Cr Un (PA)	6061	C	858 831-8100	7814
California Coast Credit Union (PA)	6062	D	858 495-1600	7820
North Island Financial Credit Union	6062	B	619 656-6525	7829
Encore Capital Group Inc (PA)	6153	A	877 445-4581	7893
Midland Credit Management Inc.	6153	A	877 240-2377	7896
National Funding Inc (PA).	6153	C	888 733-2383	7898
Reliant Services Group LLC.	6153	C	877 850-0998	7904
Retirement Fnding Solutions Inc.	6153	D	802 238-4216	7905
Investbank Corp.	6159	D	858 225-7825	7920
American Internet Mortgage Inc.	6162	D	888 411-4246	7928
Amnet Mortgage LLC.	6162	A	858 909-1200	7932
Berkshire Hthway HM Svcs Cal P.	6162	C	619 302-8082	7936
Blufi Lending Corporation.	6162	C		7938
Goal Financial LLC.	6162	D	619 684-7600	7968
Guaranteed Rate Inc.	6162	C	760 310-6008	7978
Guild Holdings Company (PA)	6162	B	858 560-6330	7979
Integrity Mortgage Group.	6162	D	858 225-5000	7984
Iserve Residential Lending LLC.	6162	D	858 486-4169	7985
Lendsure Mortgage Corp.	6162	C	888 707-7811	7988
Change Lending LLC.	6163	D	858 500-3060	8032
Charles Schwab Corporation.	6211	D	800 435-4000	8079
First Allied Securities Inc (HQ)	6211	D	619 702-9600	8083
Lpl Financial Holdings Inc (PA)	6211	B	800 877-7210	8100
Merrill Lynch Prce Fnner Smith.	6211	C	619 699-3700	8114
Merrill Lynch Prce Fnner Smith.	6211	D	858 673-6700	8136
Merrill Lynch Prce Fnner Smith.	6211	D	858 677-1300	8141
Morgan Stnley Smith Barney LLC.	6211	C	619 238-1226	8155
Plaza Home Mortgage Inc.	6211	C	858 346-1208	8161
UBS Americas Inc.	6211	C	619 557-2400	8170
Brandes Inv Partners Inc (PA)	6282	C	858 755-0239	8191
C2 Financial Corporation.	6282	C	858 220-2112	8194
Independent Fincl Group Inc.	6282	D	858 436-3180	8204

GEOGRAPHIC SECTION

SAN DIEGO CA

Company	SIC	EMP	PHONE	ENTRY#
American Spclty Hlth Group Inc	6324	B	858 754-2000	8279
Blue Shield Cal Lf Hlth Insur	6324	A	619 686-4200	8284
Sharp Health Plan	6324	B	858 499-8300	8361
Southern Cal Prmnnte Med Group	6324	B	858 974-1000	8368
Arrowhead Gen Insur Agcy Inc (HQ)	6331	C	619 881-8600	8377
Golden Eagle Insurance Corp (DH)	6331	C	619 744-6000	8384
Icw Group Holdings Inc (PA)	6331	C	858 350-2400	8387
Insurance Company of West	6331	D	858 350-2400	8388
Mercury Insurance Company	6331	A	858 694-4100	8397
State Compensation Insur Fund	6331	C	888 782-8338	8412
Stewart Title California Inc (DH)	6361	C	619 692-1600	8455
AIG Direct Insurance Svcs Inc	6411	B	858 309-3000	8481
American Spclty Hlth Plans Cal	6411	B	619 297-8100	8487
Anchor General Insur Agcy Inc	6411	C	858 527-3600	8490
Atlas General Insur Svcs LLC	6411	C	858 529-6700	8500
Barney & Barney Inc	6411	C	800 321-4696	8507
Cbiz Life Insur Solutions Inc	6411	C	858 444-3100	8523
Customzed Svcs Admnstrtors Inc	6411	C	858 810-2004	8539
Cypress Pnt-Rrowhead Gen Insur	6411	C	619 681-0560	8541
Epstein White Rtrment Income S	6411	D	858 564-8036	8555
GS Levine Insurance Svcs Inc	6411	D	858 481-8692	8579
Insurance Company of West (HQ)	6411	D	858 350-2400	8590
John Hancock Life Insur Co USA	6411	C	858 292-1667	8598
Marsh & McLennan Agency LLC	6411	C	858 457-3414	8606
Preferred Employers Insur Co	6411	D	619 688-3900	8643
Premier Dealer Services Inc	6411	D	858 810-1700	8644
Qualitas Insurance Company	6411	D	619 876-4355	8645
Quality Claims Management Corp	6411	D	619 450-8600	8646
Wateridge Insurance Svcs Inc	6411	D	858 452-2200	8683
C & D Wax Inc	6512	C	858 292-5954	8705
Icw Valencia LLC	6512	C	858 350-2600	8725
Realty Income Corporation (PA)	6512	D	858 284-5000	8754
San Diego Theatres Inc	6512	C	619 615-4007	8755
Barker Management Incorporated	6513	D	619 236-8130	8791
Ffrt Residential LLC	6513	C	858 457-2123	8812
HG Fenton Company	6513	C	619 400-0120	8817
Nomad Temporary Housing Inc (PA)	6513	D	619 313-4300	8847
Pacifica Senior Living MGT LLC	6513	D	619 296-9000	8852
Wamc Company Inc	6513	D	858 454-2753	8869
Willmark Cmmnties Univ Vlg Inc (PA)	6513	D	858 271-0582	8874
HG Fenton Property Company (PA)	6519	C	619 400-0120	8885
Cbre Inc	6531	C	858 546-4600	8927
Conam Management Corporation (PA)	6531	C	858 614-7200	8951
Cushman & Wakefield Cal Inc	6531	A	858 452-6500	8958
Daymark Realty Advisors Inc	6531	B	714 975-2999	8975
Dorothy Sarkozy	6531	C	858 259-0555	8987
Hanken Cono Assad & Co Inc	6531	C	619 575-3100	9036
Loan Signing System LLC	6531	D	619 878-3431	9075
Phase Ten Strategic Corp	6531	C	619 298-1445	9132
RA Snyder Properties Inc (PA)	6531	C	619 297-0274	9148
Rexford Industrial LLC	6531	D	858 536-8914	9165
Roman Cthlic Bshp of San Diego	6531	C	619 264-3127	9171
SHe Manages Properties Inc (PA)	6531	C	619 291-6300	9178
Southern Cal Pipe Trades ADM	6531	D	619 224-3125	9182
Strategic Property Management	6531	D	619 295-2211	9188
Terra Vista Management Inc	6531	B	858 581-4200	9193
Wilmark Management Svcs Inc (PA)	6531	D	858 271-0583	9221
Corinthian Title Company Inc	6541	D	619 299-4800	9227
Colrich Communities Inc	6552	D	858 350-7672	9249
Bridge Group Hh Inc	6719	C	858 455-5000	9305
DMS Ue Acqisition Holdings Inc	6719	D	800 466-4178	9310
Mlim Holdings LLC	6719	A	619 299-3131	9322
McMillin Management Svcs LP (HQ)	6722	D	619 477-4117	9379
Bridgewest Ventures LLC (PA)	6726	A	858 529-6600	9398
Charles Schwab Corporation	6726	A	800 435-4000	9400
Guild Mortgage Company LLC (HQ)	6733	C	800 365-4441	9427
Kaiser Foundation Hospitals	6733	A	619 528-5888	9430
Quality Loan Service Corp	6733	B	619 645-7711	9446
Trust Will	6733	D	415 246-4503	9448
Qualcomm International Inc (HQ)	6794	A	858 587-1121	9454
Biomed Realty Trust Inc (PA)	6798	B	858 207-2513	9462
Excel Trust Inc	6798	D	858 613-1800	9467
Pacifica Companies LLC (PA)	6798	C	619 296-9000	9475
7th & C Investments LLC	6799	C	619 233-7327	9482
McMillin Companies LLC (PA)	6799	D	619 477-4117	9532
Medimpact Holdings Inc (PA)	6799	A	858 566-2727	9533
Tapetech Tool Company	6799	C	858 268-0656	9571
Westcore Delta Venture LLC	6799	C	858 625-4100	9579
1835 Columbia Street LP	7011	D	619 564-3993	9587
8110 Aero Holding LLC	7011	C	858 277-8888	9596
American Prprty-Mnagement Corp	7011	A	619 232-3121	9606
Atlas Hotels Inc	7011	A	619 291-2232	9619
Bartell Hotels	7011	D	619 291-6700	9632
Best Rest Management Inc	7011	D	619 543-1130	9643
Bh Partnership LP (PA)	7011	B	858 539-7635	9648
Bhr Operations LLC	7011	C	619 232-3861	9650
Boykin Mgt Co Ltd Lblty Co	7011	D	619 299-6633	9655
Braemar Partnership	7011	B	858 488-1081	9657
C N L Hotel Del Partners LP	7011	D	619 522-8299	9671
Chase Suite Hotel	7011	D	858 314-7910	9695
Cy Gaslamp LLC	7011	D	619 544-1004	9737
Diamondrock San Dego Tnant LLC	7011	D	619 239-4500	9743
Gentry Associates LLC	7011	D	619 291-0999	9809
Grand Del Mar Resort LP	7011	A	858 314-2000	9813
Greenwood Holdings LLC	7011	D	619 299-6633	9821
Gringteam Inc	7011	D	858 485-4145	9822
Gringteam Inc	7011	B	619 297-5466	9824
Hampstead Lafayette Hotel LLC	7011	C	619 296-2101	9831
Handlery Hotels Inc	7011	C	415 781-4550	9833
Harbor View Hotel Ventures LLC	7011	D	619 239-6800	9836
Hilton Dbltree San Dego Rgnal	7011	D	619 270-2600	9850
Historical Properties Inc (PA)	7011	D	619 230-8417	9858
Hotel Circle Property LLC	7011	B	619 291-7131	9870
Hst Lessee Boston LLC	7011	D	619 692-2255	9877
Hyatt Corporation	7011	C	858 453-0018	9895
Hyatt Corporation	7011	D	619 232-1234	9897
Hyatt Corporation	7011	D	619 849-1234	9898
Lfs Development LLC	7011	D	619 501-5400	9973
Lho Mssion Bay Rsie Lessee Inc	7011	B	619 276-4010	9976
M4dev LLC	7011	D	619 696-6300	9995
Manchester Grand Resorts LP	7011	D	619 232-1234	9999
Mbp Land LLC	7011	A	619 291-5720	10011
Mhf Mv Operating VI LLC	7011	D	619 481-5881	10018
Narven Enterprises Inc	7011	D	619 239-2261	10038
Noiro West LLC	7011	D	619 819-6620	10050
Oak Valley Hotel LLC	7011	D	619 297-1101	10053
Old Town Fmly Hospitality Corp	7011	D	619 246-8010	10062
Pan Pcfic Htels Rsrts Amer Inc	7011	C	619 239-4500	10096
Paradise Lessee Inc	7011	B	858 274-4630	10099
Pinnacle Hotels Usa Inc	7011	D	858 974-8201	10120
Reh Company	7011	C	619 238-1818	10146
Residence Inn By Marriott Inc	7011	D	858 740-2200	10155
Resortcomm International	7011	D	619 683-2470	10158
Rgc Gaslamp LLC	7011	D	619 738-7000	10159
Royal Hospitality Inc	7011	D	858 278-0800	10177
Rp Scs Wsd Hotel LLC	7011	D	619 398-3020	10178
RPC Old Town Jffrson Owner LLC	7011	D	619 725-4221	10180
San Diego Farah Partners LP	7011	D	619 239-2261	10194
San Diego Hotel Company LLC	7011	C	619 696-0234	10195
San Diego Lessee LLC	7011	B	619 297-5466	10196
San Diego Mission Bay Resorts	7011	D	619 677-1161	10197
San Diego Sheraton Corporation	7011	C	619 291-6400	10198
Sandm San Dego Mrriott Del Mar	7011	A	858 523-1700	10205
SD Hotel Circle LLC	7011	D	619 881-6800	10212
Select Hotels Group LLC	7011	D	858 597-0500	10220
Sheraton Ht San Dego Mssion VI	7011	C	619 321-4602	10226
Souldriver Lessee Inc	7011	D	619 819-9500	10255
Starwood Inc	7011	C	888 559-1749	10269
Starwood Htels Rsrts Wrldwide	7011	C	619 239-2200	10274
Sunstone Hotel Properties Inc	7011	D	858 277-1199	10290
Sunstone Top Gun Lessee Inc	7011	C	949 330-4000	10291
Swvp Del Mar Hotel LLC	7011	D	858 481-5900	10294
T-12 Three LLC	7011	B	619 702-3000	10301
The Lodge At Torrey Pines Partnership L P	7011	B		10309
Tic Hotels Inc	7011	D	619 238-7577	10312
Torrey Suites LP	7011	D	858 720-9500	10315
US Grant Hotel Ventures LLC	7011	D	619 744-2007	10336
Westgroup San Diego Associates	7011	C	858 274-4630	10363
Win Time Ltd (PA)	7011	C	858 695-2300	10371
Ws Mmv Hotel LLC	7011	D	619 962-3800	10382
Ww San Diego Harbor Island LLC	7011	C	619 291-6700	10383
Bonded Inc (PA)	7217	D	858 576-8400	10469
Colt Services Inc	7217	D	858 271-9910	10473
Star Laundry Services Inc	7219	D	619 572-1009	10488
Sport Clips Inc	7231	A	858 273-9993	10507
Beyond Finance LLC	7299	A	800 282-7186	10530
Empyr Incorporated	7299	D	888 664-5669	10544
Instant Checkmate LLC	7299	C	800 222-8985	10553
Intelicare Direct Llc	7299	D	858 299-3636	10554
Intelius LLC	7299	C	888 245-1655	10555
Pacific Event Productions Inc (PA)	7299	C	858 458-9908	10567
Visage Imaging Inc	7299	D	858 345-4410	10583
Control Group Media Co LLC	7311	D	858 242-1350	10600
Homes Media Solutions LLC	7311	D	888 510-8795	10624
Ignite Visibility LLC	7311	D	619 752-1955	10629
Mindgrve Holdings Inc	7311	C	619 757-1325	10649

Employee Codes: A=Over 500 employees, B=251-500
C=101-250, D=51-100, E=20-50, F=10-19, G=1-9

SAN DIEGO CA

GEOGRAPHIC SECTION

Company	SIC	EMP	PHONE	ENTRY#
Rescue Agency Pub Benefit LLC (PA)	7311	D	619 231-7555	10670
Stn Digital LLC	7311	D	619 292-8683	10676
Ue Authority Co	7311	D	800 466-4178	10683
Vitrorobertson LLC	7311	D	619 234-0408	10688
Corelogic Credco LLC	7323	B	619 938-7028	10760
American Legal Copy - Oc LLC	7334	D	415 777-4449	10782
Knox Attorney Service Inc (PA)	7334	C	619 233-9700	10789
Mirum Inc	7336	C	619 237-5552	10814
Thinkbasic Inc	7336	C	858 755-6922	10819
Aquaclean Janitorial	7349	D	858 537-9090	10857
Crown Building Maintenance Co	7349	B	858 560-5785	10884
GMI Building Services Inc	7349	C	858 279-6262	10904
Kbm Fclity Sltons Holdings LLC	7349	B	858 467-0202	10915
Life Cycle Engineering Inc	7349	C	619 785-5990	10919
Merchants Building Maint Co	7349	B	858 455-0163	10927
Pe Facility Solutions LLC (PA)	7349	D	858 467-0202	10939
Pegasus Building Svcs Co Inc	7349	C	858 444-2290	10941
Priority Building Services LLC	7349	B	858 695-1326	10945
Professional Maint Systems Inc	7349	A	619 276-1150	10948
Protec Association Services (PA)	7349	C	858 569-1080	10951
Rhino Building Services Inc	7349	C	858 455-1440	10954
Servi-Tek Inc	7349	B	858 638-7735	10963
RAC & Associates	7352	D	858 694-5800	10991
Hawthorne Machinery Co (PA)	7353	D	858 674-7000	10999
Hawthorne Rent-It Service (HQ)	7353	C	858 674-7000	11000
Advanced Test Equipment Corp	7359	D	858 558-6500	11012
P J J Enterprises Inc	7359	D	619 232-6136	11048
Raphaels Party Rentals Inc (PA)	7359	C	858 444-1692	11052
Access Nurses Inc	7361	D	858 458-4400	11072
Advanced Med Prsonnel Svcs Inc	7361	D	386 756-4395	11078
Amn Healthcare Inc	7361	D	800 282-0300	11081
Barrett Business Services Inc	7361	A	858 314-1100	11089
Delta-T Group Inc	7361	C	619 543-0556	11123
Eplica Corporate Services Inc	7361	A	619 282-1400	11132
Garich Inc (PA)	7361	B	858 453-1331	11141
Innovative Placements Inc	7361	C	800 322-9796	11156
Integrated Associates Inc	7361	C	858 412-6189	11158
MHS Customer Services Inc	7361	D	858 695-2151	11178
Nursechoice	7361	D	866 557-6050	11186
Nursefinders LLC (HQ)	7361	C	858 314-7427	11189
Personal Energy Finance Inc	7361	D	877 858-3855	11200
Pioneer Healthcare Svcs LLC	7361	B	800 683-1209	11201
Preferred Hlthcare Rgistry Inc	7361	C	800 787-6787	11204
R&D Consulting Group Inc	7361	C	415 697-2585	11211
SE Scher Corporation	7361	A	858 546-8300	11227
Teg Staffing Inc	7361	A	800 918-1678	11244
Vish Consulting Services Inc	7361	D	916 800-3762	11253
Wmbe Payrolling Inc	7361	C	858 810-3000	11258
Workway Inc	7361	C	619 278-0012	11260
Aya Healthcare Inc (PA)	7363	B	858 458-4410	11273
Eplica Inc (PA)	7363	C	619 260-2000	11284
June Group LLC	7363	D	858 450-4290	11296
Mek Industries Inc	7363	C	858 610-9601	11311
Merritt Hawkins & Assoc LLC (HQ)	7363	C	858 792-0711	11313
Rx Pro Health LLC	7363	A	858 369-4050	11326
San Diego Pro Staffing	7363	D	858 731-3116	11328
Sfn Group Inc	7363	A	858 458-9200	11330
Vanpike Inc (PA)	7363	D	858 453-1331	11346
Vaya Workforce Solutions LLC	7363	C	866 687-7390	11348
Volt Management Corp	7363	D	858 576-3140	11357
Abacus Data Systems Inc (PA)	7371	C	858 452-4280	11371
Adaptamed LLC	7371	C	877 478-7773	11379
Adler Dev LLC	7371	D	707 229-3162	11381
Bakbone Software Inc (HQ)	7371	D	858 450-9009	11447
Brain Corporation	7371	D	858 689-7600	11472
Cognitive Medical Systems Inc (PA)	7371	D	858 509-4949	11501
Colsa Corporation	7371	D	619 553-0031	11504
Component Controlcom Inc	7371	D	619 696-5400	11508
Computer Proc Unlimited Inc	7371	C	858 530-0875	11510
Cordial Experience Inc	7371	D	619 793-9787	11515
Corelation Inc	7371	C	619 876-5074	11516
Cubic Trnsp Systems Inc (DH)	7371	A	858 268-3100	11526
Daybreak Game Company LLC	7371	B	858 239-0500	11531
Einstein Industries Inc	7371	C	858 459-1182	11567
Evernote Corporation (PA)	7371	B	650 216-7700	11583
G2 Software Systems Inc	7371	C	619 222-8025	11611
H & R Accounts Inc	7371	D	619 819-8844	11636
ID Analytics LLC	7371	C	858 312-6200	11655
Innovasystems Intl LLC	7371	C	619 955-5890	11666
Inseego Corp (PA)	7371	D	858 812-3400	11667
Isaac Fair Corporation	7371	D	858 369-8000	11680
Mango Technologies Inc (PA)	7371	A	888 625-4258	11729
Mir3 Inc	7371	D	858 724-1200	11752
Mitchell International Inc (PA)	7371	C	858 368-7000	11753
Neubloc LLC (PA)	7371	D	858 674-8701	11769
Nucleushealth LLC	7371	B	858 251-3400	11788
Perspectium Corp	7371	D	858 530-8093	11824
Petdesk	7371		202 431-3045	11825
Platform Science Inc	7371	C	844 475-8724	11834
Primero Systems Incorporated	7371	D	866 426-0779	11844
Psyonix LLC	7371	D	619 622-8772	11850
Reapplications Inc	7371	C	619 230-0209	11866
Reciprocal Labs Corp	7371	D	608 251-0470	11867
Rmd Group LLC	7371	D	619 955-5750	11884
San Diego Home Seller Inc	7371	D	619 909-6345	11900
Smartdrive Systems Inc (PA)	7371	B	858 225-5550	11925
Symitar Systems Inc	7371	C	619 542-6700	11958
Tapestry Solutions Inc (HQ)	7371	B	858 503-1990	11968
Verseio Inc	7371	D	888 373-9942	12020
Appfolio Inc	7372	D	866 648-1536	12091
Ascender Software Inc	7372	C	877 561-7501	12102
Chatmeter Inc	7372	D	619 300-1050	12132
Classy Inc	7372	C	619 961-1892	12138
Intuit Inc	7372	C	858 780-2846	12241
Intuit Inc	7372	B	858 215-8000	12242
Musicmatch Inc	7372	C	858 485-4300	12278
New Bi US Gaming LLC	7372	D	858 592-2472	12286
Solv Energy LLC	7372	B	858 622-4040	12358
Teradata Corporation (PA)	7372	A	866 548-8348	12376
Wme Bi LLC	7372	D	877 592-2472	12400
Wordsmart Corporation	7372	D		12402
Automation Holdco Inc	7373	D	858 967-8650	12423
Caci Enterprise Solutions LLC	7373	B	619 881-6000	12428
Captiva Software Corporation (DH)	7373	D	858 320-1000	12430
Clinicomp International Inc (PA)	7373	D	858 546-8202	12434
Cubic Corporation	7373	A	858 277-6780	12442
Inseego North America LLC (HQ)	7373	D	541 685-9045	12469
Koam Engineering Systems Inc	7373	C	858 292-0922	12475
Merge Healthcare Solutions Inc	7373	D	858 625-3344	12487
Miro Technologies Inc	7373	D	858 677-2100	12490
Miva Inc	7373	C	858 490-2570	12492
Mobisystems Inc	7373	D	858 350-0315	12494
Nurlogic Design Inc (DH)	7373	D	858 455-7570	12505
Science Applications Intl Corp	7373	A	858 826-3061	12523
Tusimple Holdings Inc (PA)	7373	B	619 916-3144	12538
Ultisat Inc	7373	A	240 243-5107	12540
Amazon Processing LLC	7374	C	858 565-1135	12549
Emerald Connect LLC (HQ)	7374	D	800 233-2834	12568
Fico	7374	A	858 369-8000	12573
San Diego Data Processing Corporation Inc	7374	A	858 581-9600	12621
Spoutable LLC	7374	C	609 743-7491	12630
Tealium Inc (PA)	7374	A	858 779-1344	12634
Relationedge LLC	7375	C	858 451-4665	12683
Autovitals Inc	7379	D	866 949-2848	12735
Cgi Federal Inc	7379	D	619 260-0602	12754
Closingcorp Inc	7379	D	858 551-1500	12758
Defensesweb Technologies Inc	7379	D	858 272-8505	12776
General Dynamics Info Tech Inc	7379	D	619 881-8989	12798
Positioning Universal Inc	7379	D	619 639-0235	12858
Science Applications Intl Corp	7379	D	703 676-4300	12873
Sentek Consulting Inc	7379	C	619 543-9550	12875
Strata Information Group Inc	7379	D	619 296-0170	12884
Tactical Engrg & Analis Inc (PA)	7379	D	858 573-9869	12889
ATI Systems International Inc	7381	A	858 715-8484	12935
Elite Show Services Inc	7381	A	619 574-1589	12969
Guard Management Inc	7381	C	858 279-8282	12981
Locator Services Inc	7381	C	619 229-6100	12998
Staff Pro Inc	7381	A	619 544-1774	13051
Brightcloud Inc	7382	B	858 652-4803	13100
Johnson Cntrls SEC Sltions LLC	7382	D	561 988-3600	13127
Kratos Public Safety & Security Solutions Inc	7382	D	858 812-7300	13130
Securitas Technology Corp	7382	D	858 812-7349	13143
Symons Fire Protection Inc	7382	C	619 588-6364	13149
1111 6th Ave LLC	7389	D	312 283-3683	13164
Affinity Auto Programs Inc	7389	B	858 643-9324	13180
Alorica Customer Care Inc	7389	D	619 298-7103	13184
Cetera Financial Group Inc (PA)	7389	C	866 489-3100	13230
County of San Diego	7389	C	858 694-2960	13248
Dividend Finance	7389	D	858 880-7710	13271
Fraser Yachts Florida Inc	7389	D	619 225-0588	13295
Interior Specialists Inc	7389	B	909 983-5386	13327
Mabie Marketing Group Inc	7389	C	858 279-5585	13360
Mood Media North America LLC	7389	D	858 362-2323	13382
Phone Ware Inc	7389	B	858 530-8550	13425
Puff Global Inc	7389	D	619 520-3499	13439
Quidel Cardiovascular Inc	7389	D	858 552-1100	13441

GEOGRAPHIC SECTION

SAN DIEGO CA

Company	SIC	EMP	PHONE	ENTRY#
Rgn-San Diego I LLC	7389	C	619 344-2500	13448
San Dego Cnvntion Ctr Corp Inc (PA)	7389	B	619 782-4388	13459
Sherpa Clinical Packaging LLC	7389	C	858 997-1493	13472
Shinwoo P&C Usa Inc (HQ)	7389	B	619 407-7164	13473
Staccato Communications Inc	7389	D	858 812-1000	13483
Strategic Operations Inc	7389	C	858 244-0559	13487
Tecma Group LLC	7389	A	619 918-7371	13504
Truepic Inc	7389	D	619 848-3632	13521
UPS Store Inc (HQ)	7389	D	858 455-8800	13535
Vastek Inc	7389	C	925 948-5701	13538
Vintage Design LLC	7389	D	858 695-9544	13542
Visual Pak San Diego LLC	7389	C	847 689-1000	13546
Washington Inventory Service	7389	A	858 565-8111	13550
Midway Rent A Car Inc	7514	D	619 238-9600	13592
Modern Parking Inc	7521	D	619 233-0412	13613
Greenwlds Atbody Frmeworks Inc	7532	D	619 477-2600	13637
San Diego Saturn Retailers Inc	7532	D	858 373-3001	13648
City Chevrolet of San Diego	7538	C	619 276-6171	13659
Edf Renewables Services Inc (HQ)	7539	D	858 521-3575	13681
Allied Gardens Towing Inc (PA)	7549	D	619 563-4060	13706
Sunbelt Towing Inc (PA)	7549	D	619 297-8697	13720
Schroff	7629	C	858 740-2400	13743
Chromalloy San Diego Corp	7699	C	858 877-2800	13766
Fresh Water Systems Inc	7699	D	619 933-8275	13771
Propulsion Controls Engrg (PA)	7699	D	619 235-0961	13793
Upwind Blade Solutions Inc	7699	D	866 927-3142	13808
Zef Scientific Inc (PA)	7699	D	781 791-5799	13813
Edwards Theatres Circuit Inc	7832	C	858 635-7716	13993
Old Globe Theatre	7922	B	619 234-5623	14050
San Dego Repertory Theatre Inc	7922	D	619 231-3586	14063
San Diego Opera Association	7922	C	619 232-5911	14064
San Diego Opera Association	7922	C	619 232-5911	14065
Hob Entertainment LLC	7929	D	619 299-2583	14085
Inmotion Entrmt Group LLC	7929	C	904 332-0459	14089
San Diego Symphony Orchstra Ass	7929	C	619 235-0800	14102
San Diego Symphony Foundation	7929	C	619 235-0800	14103
California Sportservice Inc	7941	B	619 795-5000	14131
City of San Diego	7941	B	619 795-5000	14133
Padres LP	7941	A	619 795-5000	14153
Socal Sportsnet LLC	7941	C	619 795-5000	14161
Rancho La Puerta Inc	7991	D	858 764-5500	14225
Salvation Army Ray & Joan	7991	B	619 287-5762	14230
TW Holdings Inc	7991	A	858 217-8750	14239
Seaworld Parks & Entrmt LLC	7996	D	619 226-3910	14314
Bay Clubs Company LLC	7997	B	858 509-9933	14334
San Diego State University	7997	C	619 594-4263	14437
Santaluz Club Inc	7997	C	858 759-3120	14444
The San Diego Yacht Club	7997	C	619 221-8400	14470
Westgroup Kona Kai LLC	7997	D	619 221-8000	14483
Fit Athletic Club	7999	D	858 592-2440	14524
Marine Corps Community Svcs	7999	B	858 577-1061	14544
Rancho Bernardo Golf Club	7999	D	858 487-1134	14552
San Diego Gulls Hockey CLB LLC	7999	C	619 359-4700	14559
Volume Services Inc	7999	B	619 525-5800	14584
Amn Healthcare Inc (HQ)	8011	B	858 792-0711	14611
Belville Enterprises Inc	8011	B	858 652-6960	14632
California Schools Veba	8011	D	888 276-0250	14645
Cardionet Inc	8011	D	619 243-7500	14656
Childrens Spclsts of San Diego (PA)	8011	B	858 576-1700	14683
Curology Inc	8011	C	617 959-2480	14721
Department of Public Health	8011	B	619 338-2493	14724
Family Hlth Ctrs San Diego Inc	8011	B	619 515-2526	14745
Family Hlth Ctrs San Diego Inc	8011	B	619 515-2435	14746
Family Hlth Ctrs San Diego Inc	8011	B	619 515-2400	14747
Family Hlth Ctrs San Diego Inc	8011	B	619 515-2444	14749
Igo Medical Group A Med Corp (PA)	8011	D	858 455-7520	14779
Imaging Hlthcare Spcalists LLC	8011	C	619 229-2299	14780
La Maestra Family Clinic Inc (PA)	8011	C	619 584-1612	14871
MainStay Medical Limited	8011	D	619 261-9144	14885
NAVY UNITED STATES DEPARTMENT	8011	B	858 577-9849	14916
Operation Samahan Inc	8011	C	619 477-4451	14939
Pediatric Nrology Therapeutics	8011	D	858 304-6440	14954
Perlman Clinic	8011	D	858 554-1212	14956
Psychtric Ctrs At San Dego Inc (HQ)	8011	D	619 528-4600	15004
Rady Childrens Specialists	8011	D	858 966-8197	15010
San Dego Pthlgsts Med Group In	8011	D	619 297-4012	15037
San Dego Spt Mdcine Fmly Hlth	8011	D	619 229-3909	15038
San Diego Family Care	8011	D	858 279-9676	15039
San Diego Family Care (PA)	8011	D	858 279-0925	15040
San Diego Family Care	8011	D	619 563-0250	15041
Sharp Healthcare	8011	D	858 621-4090	15056
Sharp RES-Stealy Med Group Inc	8011	C	619 221-9547	15058
Sleep Data Services LLC	8011	D	619 299-6299	15063
Southern Cal Prmnnte Med Group	8011	B	619 528-5000	15076
Southern Cal Prmnnte Med Group	8011	C	619 516-6000	15086
Stallergenes Greer	8011	D	858 292-1060	15099
Ucsd Neuroscience Center	8011	D	619 287-7661	15137
University Cal San Diego	8011	D	619 294-3746	15146
Family Hlth Ctrs San Diego Inc	8021	B	619 515-2300	15226
Jose C Castillo DDS Inc	8021	D	619 295-2288	15231
Lance Rygg Dental Corp	8021	C	858 492-9300	15233
Artemis Inst For Clncal RES LL	8031	D	858 278-3647	15255
Chirotech Inc	8041	C	619 528-0040	15261
Locums Unlimited LLC	8049	A	619 550-3763	15295
Accredited Nursing Services	8051	D	619 265-1234	15317
Emeritus Corporation	8051	C	858 292-8044	15437
Five Star Senior Living Inc	8051	D	858 673-6300	15480
Icare Private Duty Inc	8051	D	858 634-1012	15520
La Jolla Skilled Inc	8051	D	858 625-8700	15534
Mission Hills Health Care Inc	8051	D	619 297-4086	15587
Point Loma Convalescent Hosp	8051	D	619 224-4141	15630
Point Loma Rhblitation Ctr LLC	8051	D	619 308-3200	15631
Bernardo Hts Healthcare Inc	8059	C	858 673-0101	15818
Crestwood Behavioral Hlth Inc	8059	C	619 481-6790	15839
San Dego Ctr For Chldren Fndti (PA)	8059	D	858 277-9550	15894
Alvarado Hospital LLC (DH)	8062	C	619 287-3270	15939
Alvarado Hospital Med Ctr Inc	8062	A	619 287-3270	15940
Kaiser Foundation Hospitals	8062	C	619 528-2583	16165
Kaiser Foundation Hospitals	8062	C	858 573-1504	16169
Kaiser Foundation Hospitals	8062	D	619 641-4663	16172
NAVY UNITED STATES DEPARTMENT	8062	A	619 532-6400	16280
Palomar Health	8062	B	858 675-5218	16307
Rady Childrens Hosp & Hlth Ctr (PA)	8062	A	858 576-1700	16356
Rady Chld Hospital-San Diego (HQ)	8062	A	858 576-1700	16357
Scripps Clinic	8062	C	858 794-1250	16397
Scripps Health	8062	C	619 294-8111	16399
Scripps Health	8062	B	858 271-9770	16400
Scripps Health (PA)	8062	A	800 727-4777	16403
Scripps Health	8062	C	619 294-8111	16405
Scripps Mercy Hospital	8062	D	619 294-8111	16408
Sharp Chula Vista Medical Ctr	8062	D	858 499-5150	16415
Sharp Healthcare	8062	C	858 939-5434	16417
Sharp Healthcare Aco LLC	8062	D	619 398-2988	16419
Sharp Healthcare Aco LLC	8062	C	619 446-1575	16420
Sharp Healthcare Aco LLC	8062	A	858 627-5152	16421
Sharp Mary Birch H	8062	B	858 939-3400	16422
Sharp Memorial Hospital (HQ)	8062	A	858 939-3636	16423
University Cal San Diego	8062	A	619 543-6654	16590
University Cal San Diego	8062	C	619 543-6170	16592
University Cal San Diego	8062	D	619 471-9393	16593
Vibra Healthcare LLC	8062	C	619 260-8300	16619
Aurora - San Diego LLC (DH)	8063	D	858 487-3200	16636
County of San Diego	8063	B	619 692-8200	16649
Sharp Memorial Hospital	8063	D	858 278-4110	16657
Sharp McDonald Center	8069	A	858 637-6920	16693
Biora Therapeutics Inc (PA)	8071	D	855 293-2639	16707
Decipher Corp	8071	D	888 975-4540	16715
DR Systems Inc	8071	C	858 625-3344	16716
Epic Sciences Inc	8071	D	858 356-6610	16718
Miracor Diagnostics Inc (PA)	8071	D	858 455-7127	16735
Precision Toxicology	8071	C	800 635-6901	16742
Sequenom Ctr For Mlclar Mdcine	8071	B	858 202-9051	16752
A Circle of Care LLC	8082	D	858 798-5005	16781
ABC Home Health Care Llc	8082	C	858 455-5000	16783
Accentcare Inc	8082	B	858 576-7410	16786
Accredited Nursing Services	8082	D	818 986-1234	16791
All Valley Home Hlth Care Inc	8082	D	619 276-8001	16803
Bridge Home Health LLC	8082	D	858 277-5200	16827
Buena Vista MGT Svcs LLC	8082	C	619 450-4300	16829
Faith Jones & Associates Inc (PA)	8082	D	619 297-9601	16862
Firstat Nursing Services Inc	8082	C	619 220-7600	16864
Integrity Hlthcare Sltions Inc	8082	D	760 432-9811	16875
Interim Hlthcare San Diego LLC	8082	B	858 576-9501	16879
Liberty Healthcare Cal Inc	8082	D	610 668-8800	16888
Maxim Healthcare Services Inc	8082	B	619 299-9350	16893
Mission HM Hlth San Diego LLC	8082	D	619 757-2700	16896
Mission Hspice Svcs San Dego L	8082	D	619 814-4020	16897
Mitre Corporation	8082	D	858 459-9701	16898
San Diego Hospice & Palliative Care	8082	A	619 688-1600	16923
Sharp Healthcare Aco LLC	8082	D	858 541-4850	16926
Rai Care Ctrs Sthern Cal II LL	8092	C	619 229-1070	16994
Center For Atism RES Evltion S	8093	C	858 444-8823	17020
Centro De Salud De La Comuni (PA)	8093	B	619 428-4463	17024
Choices	8093	D	619 692-8200	17028
Family Hlth Ctrs San Diego Inc (PA)	8093	D	619 515-2303	17063
Mental Health Systems Inc (PA)	8093	D	858 573-2600	17089

Employee Codes: A=Over 500 employees, B=251-500
C=101-250, D=51-100, E=20-50, F=10-19, G=1-9

SAN DIEGO CA — GEOGRAPHIC SECTION

Company	SIC	EMP	PHONE	ENTRY#
National Med Assn Cmprhnsive H	8093	D	619 231-9300	17099
Planned Prnthood of PCF Sthwes (PA)	8093	D	619 881-4500	17110
Planned Prnthood of PCF Sthwes	8093	D	619 881-4652	17112
Apreva Corporation	8099	D	619 450-4414	17178
Aya Locums Services Inc	8099	A	866 687-7390	17182
Califrnia Frnsic Med Group Inc	8099	D	858 694-4690	17198
Coast Care Partners	8099	D	619 354-2544	17207
Cortica Healthcare Inc	8099	B	858 304-6440	17211
Examone World Wide Inc	8099	D	619 299-3926	17237
Kelly Thomas MD Ucsd Hlth Care	8099	C	619 543-2885	17264
Molina Healthcare Inc	8099	D	858 614-1580	17276
San Diego Blood Bank (PA)	8099	C	619 400-8132	17319
Synergy Orthpd Specialists Inc	8099	D	858 450-7118	17339
Vital Health Sciences Inc	8099	D	619 675-5521	17346
Aldridge Pite LLP	8111	B	858 750-7700	17360
County of San Diego	8111	D	619 446-2900	17420
County of San Diego	8111	D	619 531-4040	17421
Duckor Mtzger Wynne A Prof Law	8111	D	619 209-3000	17444
Federal Dfenders San Diego Inc (PA)	8111	D	619 234-8467	17452
Fish & Richardson PC	8111	C	858 678-5070	17459
Gordon Rees Scully Mansukhani	8111	D	619 696-6700	17478
Higgs Fletcher & Mack Llp	8111	C	619 236-1551	17493
Jones Day Limited Partnership	8111	D	858 314-1200	17507
Kimball Tirey & St John LLP (PA)	8111	D	619 234-1690	17518
Knobbe Martens Olson Bear LLP	8111	D	858 707-4000	17528
Latham & Watkins LLP	8111	B	858 523-5400	17535
Lewis Brsbois Bsgard Smith LLP	8111	D	619 233-1006	17545
Mintz Levin Cohn Ferris GL	8111	D	858 314-1500	17571
Morrison & Foerster LLP	8111	B	858 720-5100	17578
Paul Hastings LLP	8111	D	858 458-3000	17604
Petti Kohn Ingrassia & L PR Co	8111	D	310 649-5772	17607
Procopio Cory Hargreaves & Savitch LLP (PA)	8111	C	619 238-1900	17619
Robbins Geller Rudman Dowd LLP (PA)	8111	B	619 231-1058	17625
Robinson Calcagnie Inc	8111	D	619 338-4060	17626
Sdcda	8111	C	619 459-9632	17635
Seltzer Cplan McMhon Vtek A La (PA)	8111	C	619 685-3003	17638
Sheppard Mllin Rchter Hmpton L	8111	D	619 338-6500	17645
Sheppard Mllin Rchter Hmpton L	8111	D	858 720-8900	17647
Solomon Ward Sdnwurm Smith LLP	8111	D	619 231-0303	17659
Thorsnes Bartolotta & McGuire	8111	D	619 236-9363	17667
Tyson & Mendes	8111	D	858 459-1476	17671
Wingert Grbing Brbker Jstkie L	8111	D	619 232-8151	17682
Withers Bergman LLP	8111	B	203 974-0412	17684
San Diego Cmnty College Dst	8211	C	619 388-4850	17746
San Diego State University	8221	D	619 594-1515	17767
San Diego Cmnty College Dst	8222	D	619 388-3453	17786
San Diego Cmnty College Dst	8222	A	619 388-2600	17787
San Diego Elec Training Tr	8249	D	858 569-6633	17796
Vista Hill Foundation	8299	D	619 281-5511	17819
American Red Cross San Dg-Mpri (PA)	8322	D	858 309-1200	17834
Autism Otrach Southern Cal LLC	8322	D	619 795-9925	17841
Aya Living Inc	8322	C	619 446-6469	17844
Behavral Hlthcare Slutions Inc	8322	C	858 573-2600	17849
County of San Diego	8322	A	619 515-8202	17937
Deaf Cmnty Svcs San Diego Inc	8322	D	619 398-2441	17950
G&L Penasquitos Inc	8322	A	858 538-0802	17992
Neighborhood House Association (PA)	8322	B	858 715-2642	18059
Neighborhood House Association	8322	D	619 263-7761	18060
New Alternatives Incorporated	8322	A	619 863-5855	18061
Project Concern International (PA)	8322	C	858 279-9690	18087
San Dg-Mprial Cnties Dvlpmntal (PA)	8322	C	858 576-2996	18111
Social Advctes For Yuth San De	8322	C	619 283-9624	18135
Toward Maximum Independence (PA)	8322	C	858 467-0600	18153
Turning Point For God	8322	D	619 258-3600	18158
Vista Hill Foundation	8322	D	619 266-0166	18171
Options For All Inc	8331	B	858 565-9870	18239
Children of Rainbow Inc (PA)	8351	D	619 615-0652	18287
Harmonium Inc (PA)	8351	C	858 684-3080	18319
Kare Klub	8351	C	858 538-5437	18322
Navy Exchange Service Command	8351	D	619 556-7466	18337
Atria Management Company LLC	8361	C	619 326-0190	18375
Casa De Las Campanas Inc (PA)	8361	B	858 451-9152	18388
Collwood Ter Stellar Care Inc	8361	D	619 287-2920	18397
County of San Diego	8361	D	619 338-2558	18404
Independent Options Inc	8361	D	858 598-5260	18459
St Pauls Episcopal Home Inc	8361	D	619 239-2097	18525
St Pauls Episcopal Home Inc	8361	D	619 239-8687	18527
Working Alternatives Inc	8361	D	714 898-6400	18551
ARC of San Diego (PA)	8399	C	619 685-1175	18557
Automted Rgnal Jstice Info Sys	8399	D	619 533-4201	18564
San Diego Rescue Mission Inc (PA)	8399	D	619 819-1880	18621
Sharp Healthcare Foundation	8399	C	858 499-4800	18622
Museum Cntmprary Art San Diego (PA)	8412	D	858 454-3541	18659
New Childrens Museum	8412	D	619 233-8792	18661
Reuben H Fleet Science Center	8412	C	619 238-1233	18666
San Dego Soc of Ntural History	8412	C	619 232-3821	18668
San Diego Air & Space Museum	8412	D	619 234-8291	18669
San Diego Museum of Art	8412	D	619 696-1909	18670
Zoological Society San Diego	8422	C	619 744-3325	18695
Zoological Society San Diego	8422	C	619 231-1515	18697
Zoological Society San Diego (PA)	8422	A	619 231-1515	18698
Electra Owners Assoc	8611	C	619 236-3310	18707
San Diego Assn Governments (PA)	8611	C	619 699-1900	18720
Medimpact Hlthcare Systems Inc (HQ)	8621	C	858 566-2727	18752
Sharp Community Medical Group	8621	C	858 499-4525	18761
Tsia	8621	D	858 674-5491	18767
Interntional Un Oper Engineers	8631	A	619 295-3186	18782
Armed Services YMCA of USA	8641	C	619 751-5755	18813
Girl Scuts San Dg-Mprial Cncil (PA)	8641	D	619 610-0751	18864
Mission Bay Youth Wtr Spt Camp	8641	D	858 539-2003	18883
Urban Corps San Diego County	8641	C	619 235-6884	18920
Veterans Med RES Fndtion San D	8641	C	858 642-3080	18922
Vietnam Veterans of San Diego (PA)	8641	D	619 497-0142	18927
YMCA of San Diego County	8641	D	858 496-9622	18937
YMCA of San Diego County (PA)	8641	B	858 292-9622	18939
YMCA of San Diego County	8641	D	619 428-1168	18940
YMCA of San Diego County	8641	D	619 280-9622	18943
YMCA of San Diego County	8641	D	619 281-8313	18945
YMCA of San Diego County	8641	D	619 226-8888	18946
YMCA of San Diego County	8641	D	619 264-0144	18947
YMCA of San Diego County	8641	D	619 521-3055	18948
YMCA of San Diego County	8641	B	619 298-3576	18950
Kennedy Team Inc	8651	D	619 921-5582	19010
Congrgtion Beth Israel San Deg	8661	D	858 535-1111	19016
San Dego Chrstn Foundation Inc	8661	D	858 273-1306	19026
Affinity Development Group Inc	8699	C	858 643-9324	19032
Assocted Stdnts San Dego State (PA)	8699	A	619 594-0234	19035
Assocted Stdnts San Dego State	8699	C	619 594-5200	19036
Automobile Club Southern Cal	8699	C	858 483-4960	19039
Automobile Club Southern Cal	8699	D	619 233-1000	19044
Automobile Club Southern Cal	8699	C	858 486-0786	19061
San Diego Humane Soc & Spca	8699	D	619 299-7012	19101
Ata Engineering Inc (PA)	8711	D	858 480-2000	19147
Atkins North America Inc	8711	D	858 874-1810	19148
Ausgar Technologies Inc	8711	C	855 428-7427	19149
Bae Systems Maritime Engineering &	8711	B	619 238-1000	19151
Bit Medtech LLC	8711	D	858 613-1200	19154
DMS Facility Services LLC	8711	A	858 560-4191	19203
Encore Semi Inc	8711	D	858 225-4993	19213
Engineering Partners Inc	8711	D	858 824-1761	19215
Enginring Sftwr Sys Sltons Inc (PA)	8711	D	619 338-0380	19216
Epsilon Systems Sltons Mssion	8711	D	619 702-1700	19218
Epsilon Systems Solutions Inc (PA)	8711	D	619 702-1700	19219
Forward Slope Incorporated	8711	D	619 299-4400	19230
Geocon Incorporated	8711	D	858 558-6900	19239
Glenn A Rick Engrg & Dev Co (PA)	8711	D	619 291-0708	19243
Highbury Defense Group	8711	D	619 316-7979	19250
Hntb Corporation	8711	D	619 684-6586	19253
Indus Technology Inc	8711	C	619 299-2555	19265
Ingenium Technologies Corp	8711	D	858 227-4422	19268
Kleinfelder Inc (HQ)	8711	D	619 831-4600	19294
Kleinfelder Associates	8711	D	619 831-4600	19296
Kleinfelder Group Inc (PA)	8711	D	619 831-4600	19297
Kratos Tech Trning Sltions Inc (HQ)	8711	D	858 812-7300	19301
Naval Facilities Engineer Comm	8711	D	619 532-1158	19333
Nv5 Inc	8711	C	858 385-0500	19337
P2s Inc	8711	D	562 497-2999	19344
Parsons Government Svcs Inc	8711	B	619 685-0085	19352
Photon Research Associates Inc	8711	C	858 455-9741	19360
Quartus Engineering Inc (PA)	8711	C	858 875-6000	19368
Sabre Systems Inc	8711	D	619 528-2226	19380
San Diego Composites Inc	8711	D	858 751-0450	19381
San Diego Services LLC	8711	C	858 654-0102	19382
SC Wright Construction Inc	8711	B	619 698-6909	19383
Serco Inc	8711	D	858 569-8979	19385
Strategic Command US	8711	D	858 603-8901	19400
Tri Star Engineering Inc	8711	D	619 710-8038	19419
VT Milcom Inc	8711	D	619 424-9024	19433
Architectural Mtls USA Inc	8712	D	888 219-2126	19452
Austin Veum Rbbins Prtners Inc (PA)	8712	D	619 231-1960	19453
Carrier Johnson (PA)	8712	D	619 236-9462	19458
Delawie	8712	D	619 299-6690	19464
Gkk Corporation	8712	D	619 398-0215	19470
NTD Architects	8712	D	858 565-4440	19499
Baker Tilly Us LLP	8721	B	858 597-4100	19536
Considine Cnsdine An Accntncy	8721	C	619 231-1977	19555

GEOGRAPHIC SECTION

SAN DIMAS CA

	SIC	EMP	PHONE	ENTRY#
Deloitte & Touche LLP	8721	A	619 232-6500	19560
Gatto Pope Walwick LLP	8721	D	619 282-7366	19578
Innovtive Emplyee Slutions Inc (PA)	8721	D	858 715-5100	19590
LLP Moss Adams	8721	D	858 627-1400	19605
Optima Office Inc	8721	D	858 361-0481	19619
Pro Back Office LLC	8721	D	858 622-1681	19624
Signature Analytics LLC	8721	D	888 284-3842	19631
Tgg Accounting	8721	D	760 697-1033	19634
Acea Biosciences Inc	8731	D	858 724-0928	19644
Agouron Pharmaceuticals Inc	8731	C	858 455-3200	19648
Alimentiv US Inc	8731	C	858 356-5665	19650
Allele Bio & Pharmaceuticals	8731	C	858 410-0299	19652
Archimdes Tech Group Hldngs LL	8731	D	858 642-9170	19657
Arcturus Therapeutics Inc	8731	C	858 900-2660	19658
Biolegend Inc (HQ)	8731	C	858 455-9588	19663
Cibus Global Ltd	8731	C	858 450-0008	19672
Dermtech Operations Inc	8731	B	866 450-4223	19679
Ebioscience Inc	8731	D	858 642-2058	19685
Ferring Research Institute Inc	8731	D	858 657-1400	19693
General Atomics	8731	D	858 455-4141	19699
General Atomics	8731	D	858 676-7100	19700
General Atomics	8731	D	858 455-4000	19701
Genomics Inst of Nvrtis RES FN	8731	D	858 812-1805	19702
Halozyme Inc	8731	C	858 794-8889	19704
Hii Fleet Support Group LLC	8731	B	858 522-6319	19707
Inova Diagnostics Inc (HQ)	8731	B	858 586-9900	19710
Leidos Inc	8731	C	703 676-4300	19725
Leidos Inc	8731	C	858 826-6000	19727
Leidos Inc	8731	C	858 826-9416	19728
Leidos Engrg & Sciences LLC	8731	D	619 542-3130	19729
Maravai Lf Scnces Holdings LLC (HQ)	8731	C	650 697-3600	19733
Mesa Biotech Inc	8731	D	858 800-4929	19737
NAVY UNITED STATES DEPARTMENT	8731	D	619 524-6727	19744
Novartis Inst For Fnctnal Gnmi	8731	A	858 812-1500	19747
Pharmron San Dego Lab Svcs LLC	8731	D	858 560-9000	19759
Sequenom Inc (HQ)	8731	D	858 202-9000	19769
Shoreline Biosciences Inc	8731	D	619 890-0383	19770
Spreadtrum Cmmncations USA Inc	8731	D	858 546-0895	19773
Tanvex Biopharma Usa Inc (PA)	8731	C	858 210-4100	19780
Tnk Therapeutics Inc (HQ)	8731	C	858 210-3700	19786
Trilink Biotechnologies LLC	8731	C	800 863-6801	19787
Truvian Sciences Inc	8731	C	858 251-3646	19788
Turning Point Therapeutics Inc	8731	D	858 926-5251	19789
CIC Research Inc	8732	D	858 637-4000	19805
General Atomics (HQ)	8732	A	858 455-2810	19810
Luth Research Inc (PA)	8732	B	619 234-5884	19830
Quintiles Pacific Incorporated	8732	B	858 552-3400	19845
Soleil Communications LLC	8732	C	619 624-2888	19848
Trendsource Inc	8732	D	619 718-7467	19853
Verance Corporation	8732	D	858 202-2800	19855
Biosplice Therapeutics Inc	8733	D	858 926-2900	19866
Healthpoint Capital LLC (PA)	8733	C	212 935-7780	19883
Institute For Defense Analyses	8733	C	858 622-5439	19887
Mitre Corporation	8733	D	619 758-7818	19897
Nanocomposix LLC	8733	D	858 565-4227	19899
Regulus Therapeutics Inc	8733	D	858 202-6300	19907
Takeda Dev Ctr Americas Inc (HQ)	8733	C	858 622-8528	19917
University Cal San Diego	8733	D	858 622-1771	19929
Whittier Inst For Diabetes	8733	D	877 944-8843	19939
Atlas Engineering West Inc (DH)	8734	C	619 280-4321	19951
Catalent San Diego Inc	8734	C	858 805-6383	19954
Intertek USA Inc	8734	D	858 558-2599	19984
Millennium Health LLC	8734	B	877 451-3534	19989
Phamatech Incorporated	8734	C	888 635-5840	19994
Xcom Labs Inc	8734	C	858 987-9266	20006
Activcare Living Inc (PA)	8741	C	858 565-4424	20009
Allegis Residential Svcs Inc	8741	D	858 430-5700	20015
Asset Management Tr Svcs LLC	8741	D	858 457-2202	20027
Azul Hospitality Group Inc	8741	D	619 223-4200	20031
Gafcon Inc (PA)	8741	D	858 875-0010	20096
Hotel Managers Group Llc	8741	B	858 673-1534	20111
JC Resorts LLC	8741	B	760 944-1936	20120
JC Resorts LLC	8741	D	858 675-8500	20121
Ka Management II Inc	8741	D	858 404-6080	20131
Premier Hlthcare Solutions Inc	8741	D	858 569-8629	20178
Scripps Clinic Med Group Inc	8741	D	858 554-9000	20203
Solpac Construction Inc	8741	D	619 296-6247	20211
Southern California Physica	8741	D	858 824-7000	20213
Suna Solutions Inc	8741	D	888 223-4788	20219
Sunroad Asset Management Inc	8741	C	858 362-8500	20221
T3w Business Solutions Inc	8741	D	619 298-0888	20224
Whiskey Girl	8741	C	619 236-1616	20253
AA Blocks LLC	8742	D	858 523-8231	20258
Accenture Federal Services LLC	8742	A	619 574-2400	20259
Artemis Consulting LLC	8742	D	619 573-6328	20280
Asset Mktg Systems Insur Svcs	8742	D	888 303-8755	20283
Co-Production Intl Inc	8742	A	619 429-4344	20320
Covario Inc	8742	D	858 397-1500	20332
Eastern Goldfields Inc	8742	C	619 497-2555	20350
Ecg Management Consultant	8742	C	206 689-2200	20351
Fairway Technologies LLC (PA)	8742	D	858 454-4471	20373
First Allied Holdings Inc	8742	D	800 499-5489	20378
Gcorp Consulting	8742	D	619 587-3160	20392
HP Capital LLC	8742	D	858 753-8486	20405
Independent Fincl Group LLC	8742	D	858 436-3180	20410
Leadcrunch Inc	8742	D	888 708-6649	20433
Lotus Workforce LLC	8742	A	480 264-0773	20441
Lpl Holdings Inc (HQ)	8742	D	858 450-9606	20442
Mapp Digital Us LLC	8742	B	619 342-4340	20448
Marcus Evans Inc	8742	D	858 679-1275	20449
Medical Management Cons Inc	8742	A	858 587-0609	20462
Mindlance Inc	8742	A	858 433-9298	20472
One Heart Worldwide	8742	D	415 379-4762	20494
Power Digital Marketing Inc (PA)	8742	B	619 501-1211	20511
Raindrop Agency Inc	8742	D	661 724-6237	20522
Sendlane Inc	8742	D	301 520-3812	20541
Swinerton Renewable Energy	8742	D	858 622-4040	20574
Trace3 LLC	8742	D	858 345-2650	20589
Upstrem Inc	8742	D	858 229-2979	20600
Vistage International Inc (PA)	8742	D	858 523-6800	20605
Havas Formula LLC	8743	D	619 234-0345	20634
Chugach Government Svcs Inc	8744	B	858 578-0276	20652
Techflow Inc (PA)	8744	D	858 412-8000	20665
Aecom Usa Inc	8748	C	858 947-7144	20679
Alliant Insurance Services Inc	8748	D	619 238-1828	20685
Aptim Corp	8748	B	619 239-1690	20693
Astrya Global Inc	8748	D	888 808-3138	20694
BE Smith Inc	8748	B	913 341-9116	20701
Bmv Direct II LP	8748	D	858 485-9840	20708
Cask Nx LLC	8748	C	858 232-8900	20719
Center For Sustainable Energy	8748	D	858 244-1177	20724
Environmental Science Assoc	8748	D	858 638-0900	20746
Garrad Hassan America Inc (DH)	8748	D	858 836-3370	20758
Geocon Consultants Inc (PA)	8748	D	858 558-6900	20760
Haley & Aldrich Inc	8748	D	619 280-9210	20769
Humano LLC	8748	D	844 448-6266	20772
Icf Jones & Stokes Inc	8748	C	858 578-8964	20774
Johnson Johnson Innovation LLC	8748	D	858 242-1504	20786
Multifamily Utility Co Inc	8748	D	858 442-7873	20808
Ninyo More Gtchncal Envmtl Scn (PA)	8748	D	858 576-1000	20816
Project Design Consultants LLC	8748	D	619 235-6471	20832
Recon Environmental Inc (PA)	8748	D	619 308-9333	20839
Sanyo North America Corp	8748	B	619 661-1134	20847
Source 44 LLC	8748	D	877 916-6337	20852
Tangoe-PI Inc	8748	C		20862
Team Risk MGT Strategies LLC	8748	A	877 767-8728	20863
Veterans EZ Info Inc	8748	C	866 839-1329	20873
Overseas Service Corporation	8999	D	858 408-0751	20898
County of San Diego	9199	D	858 505-6100	20924
San Diego Unified Port Dst	9221	C	619 686-6585	20930

SAN DIMAS, CA - Los Angeles County

	SIC	EMP	PHONE	ENTRY#
Walton Construction Inc	1522	D	909 267-7777	783
Pacific W Space Cmmnctions Inc	1623	D	909 592-4321	1248
Pacific Systems Interiors Inc	1742	C	310 436-6820	1953
Hagen-Renaker Inc (PA)	3269	D	909 599-2341	2699
Wavestream Corporation (HQ)	3679	D	909 599-9080	2947
Medic-1 Ambulance Service Inc	4119	D	909 592-8840	3276
Southern California Edison Co	4911	C	909 592-3757	4696
Southern California Gas Co	4924	B	909 305-8297	4743
American States Water Company (PA)	4941	A	909 394-3600	4764
Golden State Water Company (HQ)	4941	D	909 394-3600	4794
Custom Cooler Inc (HQ)	5078	D	909 592-1111	5777
Smart & Final Stores Inc	5141	B	909 592-2190	6289
Edgebanding Services Inc (PA)	5162	D	909 599-2336	6698
Christian Community Credit Un (PA)	6062	D	626 915-7551	7822
Southern Cal Prmnnte Med Group	6324	C	909 394-2505	8366
San Dimas Retirement Center (PA)	6513	D	909 599-8441	8859
Second Image National LLC (PA)	7334	D	800 229-7477	10794
Industrial Janitor Service	7349	D	818 782-5658	10910
Signature Select Personnel LLC	7361	B	626 940-3351	11229
Webmetro	7372	D	909 599-8885	12395
Automatic Data Processing Inc	7374	C	800 225-5237	12552
Bolide Technology Group Inc	7382	D	909 305-8889	13099
Financial Svc Ctrs Coop Inc	7389	D	909 753-1213	13287
National Hot Rod Association (PA)	7948	C	626 914-4761	14165

Employee Codes: A=Over 500 employees, B=251-500
C=101-250, D=51-100, E=20-50, F=10-19, G=1-9

SAN DIMAS CA   GEOGRAPHIC SECTION

	SIC	EMP	PHONE	ENTRY#
Raging Waters Group Inc	7996	A	909 802-2200	14310
Toan D Nguyen DDS Inc	8021	D	909 599-3398	15251
Emeritus Corporation	8051	C	909 394-0304	15436
Kaiser Foundation Hospitals	8062	C	909 394-2530	16164
Prime Hlthcare Svcs - San Dmas	8062	B	909 599-6811	16341
Positive Behavior Steps Corp	8093	C	626 940-5180	17113
Qtc Management Inc (DH)	8099	D	800 682-9701	17308
Qtc Mdcal Group Inc A Med Corp	8099	A	800 260-1515	17309
Legal Solutions Holdings Inc	8111	C	800 244-3495	17543
Med-Legal LLC	8111	C	626 653-5160	17566
County of Los Angeles	8322	D	909 599-2391	17929
Prime Health Care	8351	C	909 394-2727	18350
McKinley Childrens Center Inc (PA)	8361	D	909 599-1227	18482
Alliance Health Care Unions (PA)	8631	D	909 599-8622	18770
Brault	8721	C	626 447-0296	19541
Ego Inc	8721	C	626 447-0296	19568

SAN FERNANDO, CA - Los Angeles County

Scenario Cockram USA Inc	1521	C	407 613-2949	714
Bernards Builders Inc	1522	B	818 898-1521	747
Brightview Landscape Dev Inc	1711	D	818 838-4700	1384
La Solar Group Inc	1711	D	818 373-0077	1481
American Bottling Company	2086	D	818 898-1471	2400
Mv Transportation Inc	4111	C	323 666-0856	3163
First Student Inc	4151	B	818 896-0333	3343
Frontier California Inc	4813	B	818 365-0542	4277
Jme Inc (PA)	5063	D	201 896-8600	5570
World-Wide Foods	5141	D	818 887-1338	6415
American Fruits & Flavors LLC	7299	B	818 899-9574	10528
Universal Mail Delivery Svc (PA)	7331	D	818 365-3144	10779
Industrial Stitchtech Inc	7389	C	818 361-6319	13322
Northeast Valley Health Corp (PA)	8322	D	818 898-1388	18063
Child Care Resource Center Inc	8351	C	818 837-0097	18282
All State Association Inc	8611	C	877 425-2558	18699
Bernards Inc	8741	D	818 898-1521	20037
Cockram Construction Inc	8742	B	818 650-0999	20321

SAN FRANCISCO, CA - San Francisco County

Pax Labs Inc	0139	D	415 829-2336	16
Vh 10 Vh LP	0742	D	415 554-3000	353
Hart Howerton Ltd (PA)	0781	D	415 439-2200	435
Colombia Energy Resources Inc	1241	C		576
Lennar Homes California Inc (DH)	1521	D	949 349-8000	696
Macarthur Trnst Cmnty Prtners	1521	D	415 989-1111	698
SC Builders Inc	1521	D	415 757-0405	713
Suffolk Construction Co Inc	1521	B	415 848-0500	726
Untitled Labs Inc	1521	D	415 858-7078	735
CP Employer Inc (PA)	1522	C	415 273-2900	752
CP Multifamily Cnstr Cal Inc	1522	C	415 273-2900	753
Nibbi Bros Associates Inc	1522	C	415 863-1820	766
Project Frog Inc	1522	D	415 814-8500	769
Herrero Builders Incorporated (PA)	1541	C	415 824-7675	825
Boldt Company	1542	D	415 762-8300	874
Build Group Inc (PA)	1542	D	415 367-9399	881
Cahill Contractors Inc (PA)	1542	D	415 986-0600	888
Cahill Contractors LLC	1542	D	415 986-0600	889
Clune Construction Company LP	1542	D	415 395-7245	898
Hathaway Dinwiddie Cnstr Co	1542	B	415 986-2718	932
Hathaway Dinwiddie Cnstr Group (PA)	1542	D	415 986-2718	933
Mission Constructors Inc	1542	D	415 282-8453	971
Nibbi Bros Inc	1542	C	415 863-1820	978
Plant Construction Company LP	1542	A	415 285-0500	992
RMR Construction Company	1542	C	415 647-0884	1008
Swinerton Incorporated (PA)	1542	D	415 421-2980	1037
Webcor Construction LP (DH)	1542	D	415 978-1000	1059
Ranger Pipelines Incorporated	1623	C	415 822-3700	1255
RE La Mesa LLC	1629	D	415 675-1500	1315
Anderson Rowe & Buckley Inc	1711	C	415 282-1625	1358
Ayoob & Peery Plumbing Co Inc	1711	D	415 550-0975	1370
Daggett Solar Power 3 LLC	1711	C	415 627-1600	1416
Forefront Power LLC	1711	D	415 800-1604	1439
Sunrun Delphi Manager 2016 LLC	1711	D	415 536-6704	1578
CBF Inc	1731	C	415 495-3085	1693
Cupertino Electric Inc	1731	A	415 970-3400	1718
Decker Electric Co Inc Electrical C (PA)	1731	D	415 552-1622	1720
McKee and Company Electric	1731	D	415 724-2738	1774
McMillan Electric	1731	B	415 826-5100	1775
Metropolitan Elec Cnstr Inc	1731	D	415 642-3000	1777
Paganini Electric Corporation	1731	C	415 575-3900	1799
Skywalker Sound	1731	D	415 662-1000	1839
Spanio Inc	1731	C	415 598-8578	1844
Very Good Security Inc	1731	C	844 847-0232	1872
Young Electric Co	1731	C	415 648-3355	1879

	SIC	EMP	PHONE	ENTRY#
RFJ Corporation	1742	D	415 824-6890	1959
Lawson Roofing Co Inc	1761	D	415 285-1661	2072
Berkel & Company Contrs Inc	1771	D	415 495-3627	2100
Progress Glass Co Inc (PA)	1793	C	415 824-7040	2203
Aetna International Inc (DH)	1799	D	415 575-0912	2253
Malcolm Drilling Company Inc (PA)	1799	D	415 901-4400	2295
Rainbow Wtrproofing Restoration	1799	C	415 641-1578	2311
Infoworld Media Group Inc (DH)	2721	D	415 243-4344	2545
Viz Media LLC	2721	D	415 546-7073	2546
Wired Ventures Inc	2721	C	415 276-8400	2547
Kinnate Biopharma Inc (PA)	2834	D	858 299-4699	2594
H2o Plus LLC (PA)	2844	D	800 242-2284	2628
Associated Materials Inc	3089	A	415 788-5111	2670
American Industrial Partners LP	3559	A	415 788-7354	2788
Dolby Laboratories Inc (PA)	3651	A	415 558-0200	2879
Isolation Network Inc (PA)	3651	D	818 212-2600	2880
Chevron Energy Solutions LP	3822	B	415 894-4188	3013
Invuity Inc	3841	C	415 665-2100	3055
Mahana Therapeutics Inc (PA)	3841	D	650 483-4720	3057
Bart	4111	D	510 421-3768	3123
Metropolitan Trnsp Comm (PA)	4111	C	415 778-6700	3162
Mv Transportation Inc	4111	B	415 206-7386	3178
Sfo Airporter Inc	4111	C	415 495-3909	3212
Supershuttle International Inc	4111	C	415 558-8500	3221
Bauers Intelligent Trnsp Inc (PA)	4119	C	415 263-4020	3239
Carrentalscom Inc	4119	C	866 468-9473	3247
Cruise LLC (HQ)	4119	C	415 335-4097	3250
Dav-El Reservations System Inc	4119	C	415 206-7950	3251
Lyft Inc (PA)	4119	B	844 250-2773	3274
Voyage Auto Inc	4119	D	917 588-1249	3304
First Student Inc	4151	C	415 647-9012	3341
Western Messenger Service Inc	4212	C	415 487-4229	3438
United Parcel Service Inc	4215	A	415 252-4564	3638
Blue and Gold Fleet	4489	D	415 705-8200	3805
Cross Link Inc	4492	D	415 495-3191	3822

SAN FRANCISCO, CA - San Mateo County

American Airlines Inc	4512	D	650 877-6000	3829
Skywest Airlines Inc	4512	D	650 827-7000	3844

SAN FRANCISCO, CA - San Francisco County

Dhl Express (usa) Inc	4513	D	415 826-7338	3852
Boutique Air Inc (PA)	4522	D	415 449-0505	3864

SAN FRANCISCO, CA - San Mateo County

Alliance Ground Intl LLC	4581	B	650 821-0855	3874
Certified Aviation Svcs LLC	4581	D	650 588-8665	3881

SAN FRANCISCO, CA - San Francisco County

Pacific Aviation Corporation	4581	A	650 821-1190	3902

SAN FRANCISCO, CA - San Mateo County

Primeflight Aviation Svcs Inc	4581	C	650 877-1560	3907
Swissport Usa Inc	4581	D	650 821-6220	3916

SAN FRANCISCO, CA - San Francisco County

Hipcamp Inc (PA)	4724	C	242 377-8982	3932
Hornblower Group Inc (PA)	4724	B	415 635-2210	3933
Hornblower Yachts LLC (PA)	4724	C	415 424-4309	3934
Onelink Corporation	4724	D	415 293-8277	3944
Snapcommerce Inc (PA)	4724	C	917 704-4588	3952
Alcatraz Cruises LLC	4725	D	415 981-7625	3958
Fritz Companies Inc	4731	A	650 635-2693	4022
Sourceblue LLC	4731	C	510 267-8100	4098
Golden Gate Brdge Hwy Trnsp Ds (PA)	4785	C	415 921-5858	4138
Postmates Inc (HQ)	4789	D	800 882-6106	4171
Credo Mobile Inc	4812	D	415 369-2000	4210
Lets Talkcom Inc	4812	D	415 357-7600	4217
Pacific Bell Telephone Company	4812	D	415 978-0881	4224
Brafton Incorporated	4813	D	617 206-3040	4257
Decentral TV Corporation	4813	C	415 480-6800	4267
Formagrid Inc	4813	B	415 200-2040	4273
Hotwire Inc	4813	C	415 343-8400	4294
Indiegogo Inc	4813	C	866 641-4646	4298
Ingenio Inc	4813	C	415 248-4000	4300
Justanswer LLC	4813	C	800 785-2305	4301
Kijiji Classifieds LLC	4813	D	408 376-4952	4303
Launch Media Inc (HQ)	4813	C	310 593-6152	4305
Listencom Inc	4813	D	415 934-2000	4306
Mobitv Inc (PA)	4813	D	510 981-1303	4315
Nexxen Group LLC (PA)	4813	D	425 279-1222	4321
Pacific Bell Telephone Company (HQ)	4813	A	415 542-9000	4325
Pacnet Services Usa Inc	4813	C	415 287-2500	4326

GEOGRAPHIC SECTION

SAN FRANCISCO CA

Company	SIC	EMP	PHONE	ENTRY#
Ustream Inc	4813	D	415 489-9400	4353
Webpass Inc	4813	D	415 233-4100	4358
Disney Streaming Services LLC	4832	C	818 560-1000	4376
Entercom Media Corp	4832	C	415 765-4097	4381
San Francisco Radio Assets LLC (DH)	4832	C	415 216-1300	4403
Tunein Inc	4832	C	650 319-7100	4407
ABC Cable Networks Group	4833	C	415 954-7911	4409
CBS Broadcasting Inc	4833	D	415 765-0928	4416
Chronicle Broadcasting Co	4833	B	415 561-8000	4421
Comcast Sprtsnet Bay Area Hldn	4833	C	415 896-2557	4423
Kqed Inc (PA)	4833	B	415 864-2000	4446
Young Brdcstg of San Francisco	4833	D	415 441-4444	4471
Activision Blizzard Media LLC	4899	D	206 890-4996	4528
Kramer Media LLC	4899	D	415 439-4601	4541
Transon Media LLC	4899	D	415 621-9830	4556
Txtmequickcom	4899	C	703 596-8989	4557
Cypress Creek Renewables LLC	4911	D	415 306-5300	4569
Edward W Scott Electric Co Inc	4911	C	415 206-7120	4577
Leemah Electronics Inc	4911	C	415 394-1288	4583
Natural Gas Corp California	4911	B	415 973-7000	4590
Pacific Energy Fuels Company	4911	A	415 973-8200	4599
Pacific Gas and Electric Co	4911	B	415 695-3513	4607
Steelrver Infrstrcture Fund N (HQ)	4924	C	415 291-2200	4747
Azulworks Inc	4941	D	415 558-1507	4765
Recology Inc (PA)	4953	D	415 875-1000	4924
Sunset Scavenger Company	4953	B	415 330-1300	4942
Zocalo	5021	D	415 293-1600	5109
Discount Builders Supply	5031	D	415 285-2800	5153
International Bus Mchs Corp	5044	C	415 545-4747	5248
Abnormal Security Corporation (PA)	5045	B	415 690-7347	5264
Alloy Technologies Inc (PA)	5045	D	415 990-5140	5267
Insideview Technologies Inc	5045	C	415 728-9309	5316
Juniper Square Inc	5045	B	415 841-2722	5319
Qventus Inc	5045	C	585 690-9638	5338
Rapid Robotics Inc	5045	D	972 741-2627	5339
Riverbed Technology LLC (HQ)	5045	C	415 247-8800	5343
Sega of America Inc	5045	C	415 701-6000	5347
Switchfly LLC (PA)	5045	C	415 541-9100	5358
Wrangler Topco LLC	5045	A	415 439-1400	5371
AES Heavy Equipment Rental Inc	5046	D	817 615-1044	5374
Trimark Erf Inc (PA)	5046	D	415 626-5611	5390
Independent Electric Sup Inc	5063	D	415 734-4700	5568
Purcell-Murray Company Inc (PA)	5064	C	415 468-6620	5611
Aliphcom	5065	B	415 230-7600	5624
Sol Republic Inc	5065	D	877 400-0310	5700
Wildenradt-Mcmurray Inc	5072	D	510 835-5500	5738
Mma Renewable Ventures LLC	5074	D	415 229-8817	5756
Otis Elevator Company	5084	C	415 546-0880	5855
Capcom Entertainment Inc	5092	D	650 350-6500	5987
Capcom U S A Inc (HQ)	5092	C	650 350-6500	5988
Super7 Retail Inc	5092	D	415 374-7190	5999
Bliss World LLC	5094	D	415 217-7047	6019
Bossa Nova Robotics Inc (HQ)	5099	D	415 234-5136	6029
Minted LLC (PA)	5112	C	415 399-1100	6067
Benefit Cosmetics LLC (DH)	5122	D	415 781-8153	6098
McKesson Property Company Inc	5122	C	415 983-8300	6129
Sak Brand Group	5137	C	415 486-1200	6218
Thirdlove Inc	5137	C	415 692-0089	6225
Lukes Local Inc	5141	C	415 742-4207	6262
RDM Express Inc	5141	D	415 642-4916	6280
Simco Foods Inc	5141	D	415 982-5872	6286
Smart & Final Stores LLC	5141	B	415 751-9951	6322
California Shellfish Co Inc	5146	C	707 542-9490	6466
Earls Organic Produce	5148	D	415 824-7419	6536
Bay Bread LLC	5149	D	415 440-0356	6609
Natural Balance Pet Foods Inc	5149	D	415 247-3020	6652
Grove Collaborative Inc	5169	C	800 231-8527	6709
Wilbur-Ellis Company LLC (DH)	5191	B	415 772-4000	6838
Baggu Corporation	5199	D	800 605-0759	6892
Mission Pets LLC	5199	D	415 904-9914	6930
Lowes Home Centers LLC	5211	C	415 486-8611	7037
German Motors Corporation	5511	C	415 590-3773	7220
Tinyco Inc	5734	C	415 644-8101	7450
Events Management Inc	5812	B	415 487-9114	7478
Mosser Vctrian Ht Arts Mus Inc	5812	C	415 777-1200	7497
Portco Inc	5812	D	415 771-5200	7504
Ten 15 Inc	5813	D	415 431-1200	7523
Goodwill of the San Francisco (PA)	5932	B	415 575-2101	7540
American Conservatory Theater (PA)	5999	D	415 749-2228	7571
Babycenter LLC (DH)	5999	C	415 537-0900	7572
Wilbur-Ellis Holdings II Inc (HQ)	5999	D	415 772-4000	7601
Banc America Lsg & Capitl LLC (DH)	6021	C	415 765-7349	7604
Citibank FSB (HQ)	6021	B	415 627-6000	7613
Citibank FSB	6021	C	415 649-6971	7615
Merrill Lynch Prce Fnner Smith	6021	D	415 676-2500	7630
Unionbancal Mortgage Corp	6021	D	415 705-7350	7638
Wells Fargo & Company (PA)	6021	A	866 249-3302	7639
Wells Fargo Bank National Assn (HQ)	6021	C	605 575-6900	7643
Wfc Holdings LLC (HQ)	6021	C	415 396-7392	7649
Bank of Orient Foundation (HQ)	6022	D	415 338-0668	7656
Bmo Bank NA	6022	C	415 765-4886	7661
First Repub Securities Co LLC	6022	C	877 348-5576	7686
First Republic Trust Company	6022	C	415 392-1400	7687
Wells Fargo Financing Corporation	6022	A	415 222-4292	7723
Standard Chartered Bank	6029	D	877 308-2182	7738
Redwood Credit Union	6061	D	415 861-7928	7794
San Francisco Federal Cr Un (PA)	6061	C	415 775-5377	7797
Fuji Bank Ltd	6081	D	415 362-4740	7835
Paribas Asset Management Inc	6082	C	415 772-1300	7836
Airbnb Payments Inc	6099	D	415 861-2325	7839
Continental Exch Solutions Inc	6099	D	415 824-4280	7847
Finastra Merchant Services Inc (PA)	6099	D	415 277-9900	7855
Okcoin USA Inc	6099	D	415 991-2033	7858
Xoom Corporation	6099	C	415 777-4800	7862
Federal Hm Ln Bnk San Frncisco (PA)	6111	D	415 616-1000	7865
Lendingclub Corporation (PA)	6141	B	415 632-5600	7876
Affirm Inc (HQ)	6153	C	415 984-0490	7888
Affirm Holdings Inc (PA)	6153	A	415 984-0490	7889
Bankamerica Financial Inc	6153	D	415 622-3521	7892
Atel 14 LLC	6159	D	415 989-8800	7915
Atel Capital Group (PA)	6159	D	800 543-2835	7916
Trinity Capital Corporation	6159	C	415 956-5174	7924
Blend Insurance Agency Inc	6162	C	650 550-4810	7937
Chase Manhattan Mortgage Corp	6162	C	858 605-3300	7949
Parkside Lending LLC	6162	C	415 771-3700	8008
Real Estate Equity Exchange	6162	D	415 992-4200	8014
Conventus Lending LLC	6163	D	415 923-8069	8037
Earnest Operations LLC	6163	D	888 601-2801	8040
Figure Lending LLC	6163	B	888 819-6388	8042
Guarantee Mortgage Corporation	6163	C	415 441-5050	8043
Lendingclub Asset MGT LLC	6163	D	415 632-5600	8045
Prosper Marketplace Inc (PA)	6163	C	415 593-5400	8053
Bbam US LP	6211	B	415 267-1600	8066
Btig LLC (PA)	6211	D	415 248-2200	8068
Canaccord Genuity LLC	6211	C	415 229-7171	8069
Casey Securities Inc (PA)	6211	D	415 544-5030	8073
Conifer Securities LLC	6211	D	415 677-1500	8081
Emmett A Larkin Company Inc (PA)	6211	D	415 986-2332	8082
Forex Capital Markets LLC	6211	C	415 343-4874	8084
Fremont Group Management LLC	6211	D	415 284-8500	8086
Global Invstments Aricor Group	6211	B	415 735-9191	8087
Goldman Sachs & Co LLC	6211	D	415 393-7500	8089
Jmp Group LLC (HQ)	6211	D	415 835-8900	8096
Merrill Lynch Prce Fnner Smith	6211	C	415 955-3700	8113
Morgan Stnley Smith Barney LLC	6211	C	415 984-6500	8148
North Pt Mrgers Acqsitions Inc	6211	D	415 358-3500	8158
Schwab Prvate Clent Inv Advsor	6211	A	415 667-0820	8165
Svb Securities LLC	6211	C	800 778-1164	8167
Thomas Weisel Partners LLC (DH)	6211	B	415 364-2500	8168
Vector Capital Management LP (PA)	6211	D	415 293-5000	8172
W R Hambrecht Co Inc (PA)	6211	D	415 551-8600	8174
Wells Fargo Prime Services LLC	6211	D	415 848-0269	8177
Artisan Partners Ltd Partnr	6221	B	415 283-2444	8179
Nyse Arca Inc	6231	C	415 393-4000	8181
Allspring Funds Distr LLC	6282	D	415 396-8000	8185
Callan LLC (PA)	6282	C	415 974-5060	8195
Forward Management LLC	6282	D	415 869-6300	8199
Highmark Capital MGT Inc	6282	D	800 582-4734	8202
Jordan Park Group LLC	6282	D	415 417-3000	8205
McMorgan & Company LLC (HQ)	6282	D	415 788-9300	8207
National Financial Svcs LLC	6282	A	415 912-2805	8210
Pantheon Ventures (us) LP	6282	C	415 249-6200	8213
Tarrant Capital Ip LLC (PA)	6282	A	415 743-1500	8222
The Rromeo Corporation	6282	C	415 781-3300	8224
Wetherby Asset Management LLC	6282	D	415 399-9159	8228
Alterra Spcalty Insur Svcs Ltd	6311	C	415 490-4615	8231
Transamerica Corporation	6311	D	415 392-9742	8248
Transamerica Finance Corp (DH)	6311	C	415 983-4000	8249
Advise Health Holdings LLC	6321	C	415 723-1723	8255
Anthem Insurance Companies Inc	6324	D	415 617-1700	8281
Delta Dental of California (PA)	6324	B	415 972-8300	8295
On Lok Senior Health Services (PA)	6324	A	415 292-8888	8347
Hartford Casualty Insurance Co	6331	C	415 836-4800	8385
Metromile Operating Company (DH)	6331	D	888 244-1702	8400
Republic Indemnity Co Amer	6331	D	415 981-3200	8403
State Compensation Insur Fund (PA)	6331	D	888 782-8338	8407

Employee Codes: A=Over 500 employees, B=251-500
C=101-250, D=51-100, E=20-50, F=10-19, G=1-9

SAN FRANCISCO CA

GEOGRAPHIC SECTION

	SIC	EMP	PHONE	ENTRY#
Swiss RE Solutions Holdg Corp	6331	D	415 834-2200	8422
Rreef Management Company	6371	C	415 781-3300	8467
Federal Deposit Insurance Corp	6399	C	415 546-0160	8472
American Cmmrcal Clims Admnstr	6411	C	415 782-3933	8485
AON Consulting & Insur Svcs	6411	C	415 486-7500	8491
At-Bay Specialty Insurance Co	6411	C	888 338-9522	8498
Berkshire Hathaway Homestates (HQ)	6411	C	415 433-1650	8511
Cal Insurance and Assoc Inc	6411	D	415 661-6500	8517
Collectivehealth Inc (PA)	6411	C	844 265-3288	8529
CRC Insurance Services Inc	6411	C	415 986-5050	8534
Edgewood Partners Insur Ctr (PA)	6411	C	415 365-8000	8551
Esurance Insurance Svcs Inc (HQ)	6411	D	415 875-4500	8556
Flexport Inc (PA)	6411	C	415 231-5252	8570
Grosvenor Inv MGT US Inc	6411	D	415 773-0275	8577
New York Life RE Investors	6411	D	415 402-4117	8622
Norcal Insurance Company (HQ)	6411	B	415 735-2000	8627
Oak River Insurance Company	6411	C	800 661-6029	8630
Pathpoint Inc	6411	D	914 500-7154	8636
Pennbrook Insurance Service	6411	D	415 820-2200	8638
Selectqote Auto HM Insur Svcs	6411	A	415 977-1300	8656
Symphony Risk Sltons Insur Svc	6411	C	415 957-0600	8667
Woodruff-Sawyer & Co (PA)	6411	C	415 391-2141	8693
Coinlist	6512	D	408 230-4375	8710
Mmi Realty Services Inc	6512	D	415 288-6888	8737
Parthenon-Ey	6512	D	617 478-2550	8743
Pier 39 Limited Partnership (PA)	6512	D	415 705-5500	8744
Shorenstein Properties LLC (PA)	6512	C	415 772-7000	8760
Skywalker Properties Ltd LLC	6512	D	415 746-5296	8761
4th & Folsom Associates LP	6513	B	415 417-3086	8787
Presidio Gate Apartments	6513	C	415 567-1050	8855
Trulia Inc	6513	A	415 648-4358	8866
Fremont Realty Capital LP	6519	D	415 284-8665	8884
Maximus Real Estate Partners	6519	D	415 584-4832	8888
Pacific Ygnacio Corporation	6519	C	925 939-3275	8890
American Marketing Systems Inc	6531	D	800 747-7784	8900
Bridge Housing Corporation (PA)	6531	D	415 989-1111	8916
Citiscape Prprty MGT Group LLC	6531	D	415 401-2000	8934
Colliers International	6531	D	415 788-3100	8947
Cushman & Wakefield Inc	6531	D	415 781-8100	8956
Cushman & Wakefield Cal Inc (DH)	6531	C	408 275-6730	8957
Cushman & Wakefield Cal Inc	6531	A	415 828-1923	8972
Digital Realty	6531	C	415 738-6500	8984
Gic Real Estate Inc (DH)	6531	D	415 229-1800	9022
Grosvenor Properties Ltd	6531	B	415 421-1899	9030
Inside Real Estate	6531	D	415 525-4913	9049
Insignia/Esg Ht Partners Inc	6531	B	415 772-0123	9051
Internet Escrow Services Inc	6531	D	888 511-8600	9052
John Stewart Company (PA)	6531	D	415 345-4400	9061
Laramar Group LLC	6531	C	415 292-1800	9071
Meridian Management Group	6531	C	415 434-9700	9097
Pacific Union Co	6531	D	415 474-6600	9120
Pacific Union RE Group (DH)	6531	D	415 929-7100	9122
Parkmerced Management Corp	6531	D	415 405-4600	9128
Personal	6531	D	321 219-9161	9131
Sfii Fos Hldngs 1333 Brdway LL	6531	D	925 771-8198	9176
Side Inc	6531	C	415 525-4913	9179
Tenderloin Housing Clinic Inc (PA)	6531	D	415 771-9850	9192
Zephyr Realestate	6531	D	415 552-9500	9226
Boston Properties Ltd Partnr	6552	D	415 772-0700	9246
Edaw Inc (HQ)	6552	C	415 955-2800	9251
Better Place Forests	6553	D	888 958-7674	9281
Social Finance Inc (HQ)	6712	C	415 930-4467	9295
Bpaz Holdings 18 LLC	6719	D	972 354-6250	9303
Bpaz Holdings 6 LLC	6719	D	415 295-8080	9304
Condor Trading LP	6719	A	415 248-2200	9308
Ggc Administration LLC	6719	A	415 983-2700	9315
Project Fortress Parent LLC	6719	A	415 599-1100	9328
Tradeshift Holdings Inc (PA)	6719	D	800 381-3585	9343
Blackrock Funds III	6722	C	415 597-2000	9359
Blackrock Global Investors	6722	A	415 670-2000	9360
Blackrock Instnl Tr Nat Assn (HQ)	6722	A	415 597-2000	9361
Charles Schwab Family of Funds	6722	B	415 627-7000	9365
Dodge & Cox	6722	C	415 981-1710	9367
Farallon Capital Partners LP (PA)	6722	D	415 421-2132	9368
Hall Capital Partners LLC (PA)	6722	D	415 288-0544	9374
Mellon Global Oprtnty Fund LLC	6722	D	415 546-6056	9380
Rs Investment Management LP	6722	C	415 591-2700	9389
Millennium Management LLC	6726	A	415 844-4048	9403
Community Partners Intl	6732	C	510 225-9676	9412
Rpx Corporation (HQ)	6794	D	866 779-7641	9456
Bre Properties Inc	6798	A	415 445-6530	9463
Kiavi Inc (PA)	6798	B	844 415-4663	9471
Prologis Inc (PA)	6798	B	415 394-9000	9477
Prologis LP (HQ)	6798	B	415 394-9000	9478
ABS Capital Partners III LP	6799	B	415 617-2800	9483
Alpine Invstors Cnfrnce Call H	6799	D	415 392-9100	9486
Arabella Philanthropic	6799	C	415 677-9700	9487
Bain Capitl Ventr Partners LLC	6799	C	415 213-2400	9491
Broadreach Capitl Partners LLC	6799	A	415 354-4640	9494
Citadel Entp Americas LLC	6799	C	415 354-7200	9500
Cppib America Inc (DH)	6799	D	646 564-4900	9503
First Round Capital LLC	6799	C	415 646-0072	9508
Francisco Partners MGT LP (PA)	6799	C	415 418-2900	9509
Golden Gate Private Equity Inc (PA)	6799	D	415 983-2706	9512
Gryphon Investors Inc (PA)	6799	C	415 217-7400	9516
Kingfish Group Inc	6799	D	650 980-0200	9525
M & H Realty Partners LP	6799	D	415 693-9900	9528
Nightdragon Acquisition Corp (PA)	6799	D	510 306-7780	9541
Parthenon Capital LLC	6799	A	415 913-3900	9549
Qatalyst Partners LP	6799	D	415 844-7700	9553
Saints Management LLC (PA)	6799	A	415 773-2080	9559
Serent Capital LLC	6799	C	415 343-1050	9561
Sfiii Lake LLC	6799	D	415 395-9701	9562
Starwood Capital Group LLC	6799	C	415 247-1220	9565
Swander Pace Capital LLC (PA)	6799	A	415 477-8500	9569
Swift Real Estate Partners LLC	6799	D	415 395-9701	9570
Accor Services US LLC (HQ)	7011	A	415 772-5000	9598
Best Western Hotel Tomo	7011	C	415 921-4000	9644
Bhr Operations LLC	7011	C	415 771-9000	9649
Bre/Japantown Owner LLC	7011	D	415 922-3200	9658
Broadmoor Hotel (PA)	7011	D	415 776-7034	9662
Broadmoor Hotel	7011	D	415 673-2511	9664
Canterbury Hotel Corp	7011	D	415 345-3200	9677
Cb-1 Hotel	7011	D	415 633-3838	9686
Cdc San Francisco LLC	7011	D	415 616-6512	9688
Chesapeake Lodging Trust	7011	C	415 296-2900	9697
Chsp Trs Fisherman Wharf LLC	7011	B	415 563-1234	9698
Columbia Hospitality Inc	7011	D	415 362-8878	9712
Comfort California Inc	7011	C	415 928-5000	9716
Dtrs St Francis LLC	7011	D	415 397-7000	9768
Equinox Hotel Management Inc	7011	D	415 668-6887	9785
First Orleans Hotel Assoc LP	7011	C	415 397-5572	9797
Florence Villa Hotel	7011	C	415 397-7700	9799
Four Seasons Hotel Inc	7011	D	415 633-3441	9802
Galleria Park Associates LLC	7011	B	415 781-3060	9806
Geary Darling Lessee Inc	7011	C	415 292-0100	9808
Handlery Hotels Inc	7011	C	415 781-7800	9832
Hilton San Francisco Fincl Dst	7011	D	415 433-6600	9855
Hmb Investors LLC	7011	B	415 474-5400	9860
Hotel Nikko San Francisco Inc	7011	B	415 394-1111	9874
Hotel Whitcomb	7011	D	415 626-8000	9875
Hyatt Corporation	7011	B	415 848-6050	9885
Hyatt Corporation	7011	A	415 788-1234	9886

SAN FRANCISCO, CA - San Mateo County

	SIC	EMP	PHONE	ENTRY#
Hyatt Corporation	7011	C	650 452-1234	9888

SAN FRANCISCO, CA - San Francisco County

	SIC	EMP	PHONE	ENTRY#
Hyatt Corporation	7011	A	415 788-1234	9892
Ihms (sf) LLC	7011	C	415 781-5555	9907
Intercntnntal Htels San Frncsc	7011	D	770 604-5000	9911
Intercntnntal Htels San Frncsc	7011	C	415 616-6500	9912
Jame Hotel Corporation	7011	D	415 885-2500	9918
Joie De Vivre Hospitality LLC	7011	C	415 278-3700	9922
Joie De Vivre Hospitality LLC	7011	C	415 567-8467	9923
Joie De Vivre Hospitality LLC	7011	D	415 441-2700	9925
Joie De Vivre Hospitality LLC	7011	D	415 921-5520	9926
Joie De Vivre Hospitality LLC	7011	D	415 776-1380	9927
Joie De Vivre Hospitality LLC	7011	C	415 775-1755	9929
Kimpton Hotel & Rest Group LLC	7011	B	415 885-2500	9939
Kimpton Hotel & Rest Group LLC (HQ)	7011	D	415 397-5572	9941
Kimpton Hotel & Rest Group LLC	7011	C	415 561-1100	9942
Kimpton Hotel & Rest Group LLC	7011	C	415 392-8800	9943
Kimpton Hotel & Rest Group LLC	7011	C	415 561-1111	9944
Kimpton Hotel & Rest Group LLC	7011	C	415 292-0100	9945
Kssf Enterprises Ltd	7011	C	415 817-7840	9953
L-O Soma Hotel Inc	7011	A	415 974-6400	9959
Mason Street Opco LLC	7011	A	415 772-5000	10009
Mile Post Properties LLC	7011	D	415 673-4711	10020
Morgans Hotel Group MGT LLC	7011	B	415 775-4700	10031
Mosser Companies Inc	7011	D	415 284-9000	10032
Nob Hill Properties Inc	7011	B	415 474-5400	10047
One Nob Hill Associates LLC	7011	D	415 392-3434	10068
Paradigm Hotels Group LLC	7011	D	415 534-6500	10097
Parc 55 Lessee LLC	7011	D	415 392-8000	10100
Park Hotels & Resorts Inc	7011	D	415 771-1400	10103

GEOGRAPHIC SECTION

SAN FRANCISCO CA

	SIC	EMP	PHONE	ENTRY#
Personality Hotels Inc.	7011	C	415 885-0200	10115
PHF Ruby LLC	7011	C	415 885-4700	10117
Pine & Powell Partners LLC	7011	D	415 989-3500	10119
Post St Rnssnce Prtners A Cal	7011	B	415 563-0303	10126
Renaissance Hotel Operating Co	7011	B	415 989-3500	10151
Reneson Hotels Inc	7011	C	415 621-7001	10154
Ritz-Carlton Hotel Company LLC	7011	B	415 773-6168	10163
Rp/Kinetic Parc 55 Owner LLC	7011	C	415 392-8000	10179
Salt Lake Hotel Associates LP (PA)	7011	C	415 397-5572	10192
San Francisco Hotel Group LLC	7011	D	415 276-9888	10199
SF Marriott Marquis	7011	C	415 896-1600	10222
Sfd Partners LLC	7011	C	415 392-7755	10223
Six Continents Hotels Inc	7011	C	415 626-6103	10245
Six Continents Hotels Inc	7011	D	415 771-9000	10246
Sonesta Intl Hotels Corp	7011	B	415 929-2393	10252
Southbourne Inc	7011	C	415 781-5555	10257
Starwood Htels Rsrts Wrldwide	7011	B	415 397-7000	10271
Starwood Htels Rsrts Wrldwide	7011	C	415 512-1111	10273
Tides Center	7011	C	415 359-9401	10313
Van Ness Hotel Inc	7011	D	415 673-4711	10342
Warwick California Corporation	7011	D	415 992-3809	10353
Yhb San Francisco LLC	7011	D	415 421-7500	10388
Club Quarters MGT Co LLC	7041	D	415 392-7400	10419
Styleseat Inc	7231	D	415 638-6658	10508
Everest Wtrprfing Rstrtion Inc	7299	D	415 282-9800	10545
Homebound Technologies Inc	7299	B	415 854-3296	10551
Jasper Hall LLC	7299	D	415 872-5745	10556
Jn Projects Inc	7299	D	415 766-0273	10558
Myhealthteams Inc	7299	D	415 860-7878	10563
Soiree Valet Parking Service	7299	D	415 284-9700	10577
Tiny Pictures Inc	7299	D	415 513-5998	10578
Visa Inc	7299	D	415 805-4000	10582
BBDO Worldwide Inc	7311	C	415 808-6200	10590
Bernard Hodes Group Inc	7311	B	212 999-9000	10591
Brightroll Inc	7311	B	415 677-9222	10594
DDB Worldwide	7311	C	415 732-3600	10604
Digitas Inc	7311	D	617 867-1000	10609
Doremus & Company	7311	D	415 273-7800	10611
Eleven Inc	7311	C	415 707-1111	10612
Giant Creative Strategy Llc	7311	C	415 655-5200	10615
Godfrey Dadich Partners LLC	7311	D	415 217-2800	10619
Goodby Slverstein Partners Inc	7311	C	415 392-0669	10620
Hvsf Transition LLC	7311	C	415 477-1999	10626
Kane & Finkel LLC	7311	D	415 777-4990	10635
Kinesso LLC	7311	C	415 262-5900	10638
McCann-Erickson Corporation (HQ)	7311	C	415 348-5600	10645
Mypointscom LLC (HQ)	7311	C	415 615-1100	10655
Rapp Worldwide California Inc	7311	C	415 248-7983	10667
Sizmek Dsp Inc	7311	C	415 757-2300	10675
Swirl Inc	7311	C	415 276-8300	10678
Venables/Bell & Partners LLC	7311	C	415 288-3300	10687
Vungle Inc (PA)	7311	D	415 800-1400	10689
Yume Inc (HQ)	7311	B	650 591-9400	10694
Volta Charging LLC	7312	D	415 735-5169	10697
Appsflyer Ltd	7313	D	415 636-9430	10701
David Wood and Associates Inc	7313	C	415 296-8050	10709
Tm Holdco LLC (PA)	7313	C		10721
CBS Interactive Inc (HQ)	7319	A	415 344-2000	10727
Checkout Holding Corp	7319	A	415 788-5111	10728
Business Services Network Corp	7331	D	415 282-8161	10768
Bps Reprographics Services	7334	C	415 495-8700	10785
Destination Moon LP	7336	D	415 675-7777	10805
Ideo LP (PA)	7336	C	415 615-5000	10811
Kixeye	7336	D	415 400-8280	10812
Landor Associates Intl Ltd (HQ)	7336	C	415 365-1700	10813
Young & Rubicam LLC	7336	C	415 365-1700	10823
Crane Acquisition Inc	7342	A	415 922-1666	10836
American Bldg Maint Co-West (HQ)	7349	C	415 733-4000	10855
Billing Svcs Plus DBA Apex Jnt	7349	C	415 604-3515	10862
Cappstone Inc	7349	C	415 821-6757	10872
Crown Building Maintenance Co	7349	B	303 680-3713	10883
Green Living Planet LLC	7349	C	415 715-4718	10905
Lewis & Taylor LLC	7349	D	415 781-3496	10918
Little Giant Bldg Maint Inc (PA)	7349	D	415 508-0282	10920
Recology King County Inc	7349	C	415 348-9700	10953
Sheedy Drayage Co (PA)	7353	D	415 648-7171	11007
Ba Leasing & Capital Corp (DH)	7359	C	415 765-1804	11021
Macqurie Arcft Lsg Svcs US Inc	7359	D	415 829-6600	11040
United Terminal Leasing LLC	7359	B	510 302-3900	11061
80 Twenty LLC	7361	D	415 592-7773	11069
Alois LLC	7361	C	215 297-4492	11080
Bluecrew LLC	7361	D	510 684-7362	11095
Career Group Inc	7361	C	415 781-8188	11103

	SIC	EMP	PHONE	ENTRY#
Cvpartners Inc (HQ)	7361	C	415 543-8600	11119
Glassdoor Inc (HQ)	7361	D	415 275-7411	11143
Granite Solutions Groupe Inc (PA)	7361	C	415 963-3999	11146
Modus LLC	7361	C	415 989-1102	11179
Sage Group	7361	D	415 512-8200	11224
Stat Nursing Services Inc (PA)	7361	C	415 673-9791	11240
Ursus It Staffing and Services	7361	C	877 668-7787	11251
Wonolo Inc	7361	C	415 766-7692	11259
Advantage Workforce Svcs LLC	7363	C	415 212-6464	11269
Felton Institute (PA)	7363	C	415 474-7310	11286
Taos Mountain LLC	7363	D	888 826-7686	11341
Advent Software Inc (HQ)	7371	C	415 543-7696	11384
Airbyte Inc	7371	D	415 307-4864	11390
Akkodis Inc	7371	C	415 896-5566	11392
Amber Holdings Inc	7371	A	415 765-6500	11402
Amplitude Inc (PA)	7371	D	650 988-5131	11404
Angaza Design Inc (PA)	7371	D	415 993-5595	11405
Animoto LLC	7371	D	415 987-3139	11406
Anyscale Inc	7371	D	650 248-8086	11410
Appdynamics LLC (HQ)	7371	B	408 526-4000	11413
Appsflyer Inc	7371	C	408 367-9938	11417
Arctouch LLC	7371	C	415 944-2000	11419
Aria Systems Inc (PA)	7371	C	415 852-7250	11421
Automotivemastermind Inc	7371	D	646 679-3441	11436
Birst Inc	7371	B	415 766-4800	11458
Bitalign Inc	7371	D	415 395-9525	11460
Boku Inc (PA)	7371	C	415 375-3160	11468
Bolt	7371	D	650 804-0633	11469
Brience Inc (DH)	7371	D	415 974-5300	11474
Brighterion Inc	7371	D	415 986-5600	11475
Bynd LLC	7371	C	415 944-2293	11479
Callfire Inc	7371	D	213 221-2289	11481
Captivateiq Inc	7371	D	650 930-0619	11482
Carbonfive Incorporated	7371	D	415 546-0500	11483
Casetext Inc	7371	C	317 407-0790	11484
Castle Global Inc	7371	C	401 523-9531	11485
Chipper Cash Inc	7371	C	844 386-3753	11488
Cleo Labs Inc	7371	C	415 234-3437	11494
Codesignal Inc	7371	C	669 200-9704	11499
Codility US Inc	7371	C	415 568-5055	11500
Commure Inc (PA)	7371	C	888 994-2443	11507
Concord Worldwide Inc	7371	D	415 689-5488	11512
Convex Labs Inc	7371	D	408 692-0852	11514
Coveo Software Corp	7371	D	800 635-5476	11520
Craft Machine Inc (PA)	7371	D	650 862-9580	11521
Daily Co	7371	C	855 660-1224	11527
Datavant Inc (PA)	7371	C	415 520-1171	11530
Deepgram Inc	7371	D	415 302-7624	11535
Delinea Inc (HQ)	7371	C	669 444-5200	11536
Directly Inc	7371	D	650 714-7334	11542
Discord Inc	7371	C	650 389-2453	11543
Domino Data Lab Inc (PA)	7371	C	415 570-2425	11550
Doximity Inc (PA)	7371	A	650 549-4330	11553
Duetto Research Inc	7371	C	415 968-9389	11556
Efront Financial Solutions Inc	7371	D	415 653-3239	11562
Ellation LLC (DH)	7371	C	415 796-3560	11569
Etch Mobile Inc	7371	D	512 299-3514	11581
Exigen (usa) Inc (PA)	7371	B	415 402-2600	11588
Expanse LLC	7371	C	415 590-0129	11589
Fastly Inc (PA)	7371	B	844 432-7859	11593
Fictiv Inc	7371	C	415 580-2509	11597
Figma Inc (PA)	7371	D	888 236-4310	11598
Fluxx Labs Inc	7371	D	415 851-2453	11603
Forgerock Inc (PA)	7371	C	415 599-1100	11605
Functional Software Inc (PA)	7371	D	415 823-8009	11609
Gem Software Inc	7371	C	650 924-1622	11615
Gigster Inc	7371	C	941 888-4447	11619
Gingerio Inc	7371	D	408 455-0574	11620
Gorgias Inc	7371	C	917 859-5689	11630
Gree International Inc	7371	C	415 409-5200	11631
Gree International Entrnmt Inc	7371	C	415 409-5200	11632
Hashicorp Inc (PA)	7371	A	415 301-3250	11639
Horizon 3 Ai Inc	7371	D	304 677-4102	11646
Htec Group Inc (PA)	7371	A	213 785-7824	11647
Hustle Inc	7371	C	415 851-4878	11649
Influxdata Inc	7371	C	415 295-1901	11659
Innovaccer Inc (PA)	7371	B	510 327-8900	11665
Intercom Inc	7371	B	831 920-7088	11676
Jiff Inc (DH)	7371	C	415 829-1400	11685
Jotform Inc	7371	D	347 624-5569	11686
Jumpshot Inc (PA)	7371	D	415 212-9250	11688
Kabam Inc (HQ)	7371	A	604 256-0054	11690
Kallidus Inc	7371	D	877 554-2176	11691

Employee Codes: A=Over 500 employees, B=251-500
C=101-250, D=51-100, E=20-49, F=10-19, G=1-9

2024 Directory of California
WholeSalers and Service Companies

© Mergent Inc. 1-800-342-5647

1489

SAN FRANCISCO CA — GEOGRAPHIC SECTION

Company	SIC	EMP	PHONE	ENTRY#
Leadiq Inc.	7371	D	888 653-2347	11704
Lever Inc.	7371	D	415 458-2731	11706
Lightbend Inc.	7371	D	877 989-7372	11707
Lightyear Corporation.	7371	D	415 605-9050	11708
Linden Research Inc.	7371	D	415 243-9000	11711
Livefyre Inc.	7371	C	415 800-0900	11712
Lucidlink Corp.	7371	D	650 517-0855	11718
Magic Labs Inc.	7371	D	707 653-5739	11724
Marigold.	7371	A	888 533-8098	11732
Meraki Inc.	7371	C	415 632-5800	11743
Middesk Inc.	7371	D	408 306-2663	11747
Mightyhive Inc (HQ)	7371	D	888 727-9742	11748
Motion Math Inc.	7371	A	415 590-2961	11759
Mozilla Foundation (PA)	7371	B	650 903-0800	11760
Navagis Inc (PA)	7371	D	800 819-7872	11764
Ncircle Network Security Inc.	7371	D	415 625-5900	11765
Neutron Holdings Inc (PA)	7371	A	888 546-3345	11772
Niantic Inc (PA)	7371	D	415 570-8871	11777
Nimble Robotics Inc.	7371	D	267 864-6879	11778
Ninthdecimal Inc (PA)	7371	C	415 264-1849	11779
Nisum Technologies Inc.	7371	A	714 619-7989	11780
Nitro Software Inc (HQ)	7371	C	415 632-4894	11782
Noodle Analytics Inc.	7371	D	415 412-2139	11784
Nuna Incorporated.	7371	D	415 942-5200	11789
Onfleet Inc.	7371	D	650 283-7547	11795
Openai Inc (PA)	7371	C	650 387-6701	11798
Oracle Corporation.	7371	D	415 541-9462	11800
Pantheon Systems Inc (PA)	7371	D	855 927-9387	11812
Parafin Inc.	7371	D	646 919-0669	11815
Parallel Domain Inc.	7371	D	585 943-8571	11816
Patreon Inc (PA)	7371	C	415 967-2735	11818
Pencil and Pixel Inc.	7371	D	510 422-5036	11819
Pivotal Software Inc (HQ)	7371	C	415 777-4868	11830
Pixlee Turnto Inc.	7371	C	718 753-5307	11831
Planetscale Inc.	7371	D	415 706-2184	11833
Postman Inc (PA)	7371	D	415 796-6470	11841
Primary Diagnostics Inc.	7371	C	619 356-3701	11843
Pulsora Inc.	7371	C	650 575-5255	11854
Quadriga Inc.	7371	D	650 270-6326	11856
R Software Inc (PA)	7371	D	650 575-7633	11861
Reflektive Inc (DH)	7371	C	203 886-9240	11871
Remix Software Inc.	7371	D	415 900-4332	11874
Riskoptics Inc.	7371	C	415 851-8667	11883
Roo Veterinary Inc.	7371	D	917 805-5220	11887
Sano Intelligence Inc.	7371	C	408 483-6518	11902
Sift Science Inc (PA)	7371	C	415 882-7709	11914
Silicon Valley Commerce LLC.	7371	D	888 507-8266	11916
Sisu Data Inc.	7371	D	415 795-8250	11917
Skillz Inc (PA)	7371	A	415 762-0511	11918
Sliderule Labs Inc (PA)	7371	C	646 748-0378	11922
Smartrecruiters Inc (PA)	7371	B	415 659-9130	11926
Snackpass LLC.	7371	D	203 684-5156	11927
Solana Labs Inc.	7371	D	628 629-3265	11932
Starship Technologies Inc.	7371	C	844 445-5333	11943
Streamlabs LLC.	7371	D	415 990-9187	11951
Styra Inc.	7371	D	650 980-4280	11953
Sysdig Inc (PA)	7371	C	415 872-9473	11963
Task Help LLC.	7371	D	833 229-0726	11969
Taulia LLC (HQ)	7371	C	415 376-8280	11970
Thismoment Inc.	7371	D	415 200-4730	11975
Thunkable Inc.	7371	C	415 200-3736	11978
Trove Information Tech Inc (PA)	7371	C	610 945-6533	11990
Truework.	7371	C	833 878-3967	11993
Trussworks Inc.	7371	D	415 891-0828	11994
Twilio Segment.	7371	D	415 603-6900	11997
Ubisoft Holdings Inc.	7371	C	415 547-4000	11999
Unity Software Inc (PA)	7371	B	415 539-3162	12004
Vida Health Inc.	7371	D	415 989-1017	12021
Vim Inc.	7371	C	910 727-1834	12023
Vrp Consulting Inc.	7371	A	415 225-6466	12032
Wideorbit LLC (PA)	7371	D	415 675-6700	12041
Wisetack Inc.	7371	D	415 918-2380	12043
Woocommerce Inc.	7371	B	650 388-0901	12044
Workforcelogic.	7371	D	707 939-4300	12047
Workstream Technologies Inc.	7371	D	415 767-1006	12049
Zappos Ip Inc.	7371	A	702 943-7725	12059
Zazmic Inc (PA)	7371	C	415 728-1621	12060
Zenput Inc.	7371	D	800 537-0227	12062
Zignal Labs Inc.	7371	D	415 683-7871	12065
Afresh Technologies Inc.	7372	C	415 651-5068	12078
Airbase Inc.	7372	B	415 625-6222	12084
Aktana Inc (PA)	7372	B	888 707-3125	12085
Appetize Technologies Inc.	7372	C	877 559-4225	12090
Area 1 Security Inc.	7372	D	650 924-1637	12100
Atob Asset Vehicle I LLC.	7372	D	703 663-0658	12103
Augmedix Inc (PA)	7372	A	888 669-4885	12104
Aurora Innovation Inc.	7372	B	646 725-4999	12105
Autodesk Inc (PA)	7372	B	415 507-5000	12106
Autodesk Inc.	7372	D	415 356-0700	12107
Beats Music LLC.	7372	D	415 590-5104	12112
Blueshift Labs Inc.	7372	C	844 258-3735	12122
Climate Corporation (DH)	7372	D	415 363-0500	12140
Cloudflare Inc (PA)	7372	A	888 993-5273	12141
Docusign Inc (PA)	7372	B	415 489-4940	12162
Doubledutch Inc (DH)	7372	D	800 748-9024	12164
Driver Inc.	7372	D	415 999-4960	12167
Dropbox Inc (PA)	7372	D	415 857-6800	12168
Eis Group Inc.	7372	C	415 402-2622	12178
Etech-360 Inc (PA)	7372	A	714 900-3486	12183
Firstup Inc (PA)	7372	B	844 975-2533	12189
Fitstar Inc.	7372	A	415 409-8348	12190
Forgerock Us Inc (HQ)	7372	D	415 599-1100	12193
Fortezza Iridium Holdings Inc.	7372	D	415 765-6500	12195
Frontapp Inc.	7372	D	415 680-3048	12199
Gainsight Inc (PA)	7372	B	888 623-8562	12200
Groove Labs Inc.	7372	D	650 999-0200	12214
Gusto Inc (PA)	7372	C	800 936-0383	12217
Hearsay Systems Inc (PA)	7372	C	888 399-2280	12219
Heavyai Inc.	7372	D	415 997-2814	12221
Hitachi Energy USA Inc.	7372	D	415 527-2850	12223
Hvr Software Usa Inc.	7372	D	415 489-3427	12226
Labelbox Inc.	7372	C	415 294-0791	12254
Medrio Inc (PA)	7372	D	415 963-3700	12269
Mursion Inc.	7372	C	415 746-9631	12277
New Relic Inc (PA)	7372	A	650 777-7600	12287
Nextroll Inc (PA)	7372	A	415 236-3956	12290
Ngrok Inc.	7372	D	415 323-4184	12291
Nursefly Inc.	7372	D	760 641-5940	12296
Okta Inc (PA)	7372	A	888 722-7871	12299
On24 Inc (PA)	7372	B	415 369-8000	12300
Onelogin Inc (DH)	7372	C	415 645-6830	12301
Opentv Inc.	7372	B	415 962-5000	12304
Outreach Corporation.	7372	B	888 938-7356	12310
Pagerduty Inc (PA)	7372	A	844 800-3889	12311
Plangrid Inc (HQ)	7372	D	800 646-0796	12320
Popout Inc (PA)	7372	D	415 691-7447	12324
Replicant Solutions Inc.	7372	C	415 854-3296	12334
Retail Zipline Inc (PA)	7372	D	510 390-4904	12336
Salesforce Inc (PA)	7372	A	415 901-7000	12343
Salesforceorg LLC.	7372	A	415 901-7000	12344
Sight Machine Inc.	7372	D	888 461-5739	12348
Sitecore Usa Inc (DH)	7372	C	415 380-0600	12351
Slack Technologies Inc (HQ)	7372	C	970 299-4848	12352
Splunk Inc (PA)	7372	C	415 848-8400	12360
Stackla Inc.	7372	C	415 789-3304	12361
Standard Cognition Corp (PA)	7372	C	415 324-4156	12362
Stryder Corp (PA)	7372	C	415 981-8400	12367
Thousandeyes LLC (HQ)	7372	D	415 513-4526	12379
Verana Health Inc.	7372	C	888 774-0077	12390
Vindicia Inc.	7372	C	650 264-4700	12392
Yourpeople Inc.	7372	A	888 249-3263	12406
Zendesk Inc (HQ)	7372	C	415 418-7506	12408
Zinio Systems Inc.	7372	D	415 494-2700	12409
Aizon LLC.	7373	C	312 285-4605	12416
Ashton-Tate LLC.	7373	C	415 639-5873	12419
Cnet Networks Inc.	7373	A	415 344-2000	12435
Conduent State Lcal Sltons Inc.	7373	A	415 486-2409	12438
Dealpath Inc.	7373	D	415 876-8441	12444
Francisco Partners GP III LP (HQ)	7373	D	415 418-2900	12457
Grammarly Inc (PA)	7373	C	888 318-6146	12461
Hasura Inc.	7373	C	415 861-9195	12463
Humane Inc.	7373	C	415 891-1900	12466
Lambdatest Inc.	7373	C	866 430-7087	12477
Lookout Inc (PA)	7373	C	650 241-2358	12481
Lucidworks Inc (PA)	7373	C	415 329-6515	12483
Mozilla Corp.	7373	C	650 903-0800	12496
Noyo Technologies Inc.	7373	D	347 721-2816	12503
Oto Analytics Inc.	7373	B	310 683-0000	12508
Safelyyou Inc.	7373	D	713 822-6924	12520
Samsara Inc (PA)	7373	A	415 985-2400	12521
Soul Machines Inc.	7373	D	649 283-0863	12528
Zelar Soft LLC.	7373	C	510 262-2801	12545
6 Sense Insights Inc (PA)	7374	D	415 212-9225	12546
Castlight Health Inc (HQ)	7374	D	415 829-1400	12555
Jaspersoft Corporation.	7374	C	415 348-2300	12584
Leanplum Inc.	7374	C	844 532-6758	12587

GEOGRAPHIC SECTION

SAN FRANCISCO CA

Company	SIC	EMP	PHONE	ENTRY#
Liveramp Holdings Inc (PA)	7374	B	888 987-6764	12589
Maplebear Inc (PA)	7374	C	888 246-7822	12592
Marin Software Incorporated (PA)	7374	B	415 399-2580	12593
Merchant Services Inc (PA)	7374	B	817 725-0900	12594
People Data Labs Inc	7374	D	415 568-8415	12606
Pinterest Inc (PA)	7374	B	415 762-7100	12607
Planet Labs Inc (HQ)	7374	B	415 829-3313	12608
R/GA Media Group Inc	7374	D	415 624-2000	12611
Shipt	7374	A	408 592-1029	12624
Shoppingcom Inc	7374	C	650 616-6500	12625
Skael Inc	7374	D	415 653-9433	12626
Sweetrush Inc	7374	C	415 647-1956	12632
Talkwalker Inc	7374	C	415 805-7240	12633
Trulia Inc (HQ)	7374	B	415 648-4358	12638
Webflow Inc (PA)	7374	B	916 607-8280	12642
Aerial Topco LP	7375	A	415 983-2700	12650
Ancestrycom LLC	7375	B	415 795-6000	12651
Betterdoctor Inc	7375	C	844 668-2543	12653
Changeorg (PA)	7375	C	415 817-1840	12654
Facebook Park Tower	7375	A	949 725-8637	12663
Internet Archive	7375	C	415 561-6767	12668
Logik Systems Inc (HQ)	7375	D	844 363-3347	12674
Nextdoorcom Inc (PA)	7375	D	415 236-0000	12679
Plaid Inc (PA)	7375	D	415 799-1354	12681
X Corp	7375	A	415 222-9670	12688
Yelp Inc (PA)	7375	D	415 908-3801	12689
Allcloud USA LLC	7379	D	510 717-3785	12728
Anaplan Inc (PA)	7379	B	415 742-8199	12731
Asana Inc (PA)	7379	A	415 525-3888	12733
Be School Inc	7379	C	650 576-5263	12740
Beyondid Inc	7379	D	415 878-6210	12742
Capgemini America Inc	7379	D	415 796-6777	12749
Computacenter US Inc (HQ)	7379	A	714 861-2200	12764
Datagrail	7379	D	650 781-3680	12774
Elation Health Inc (PA)	7379	D	415 213-5164	12784
Eventbrite Inc (PA)	7379	B	415 692-7779	12790
Future State	7379	C	925 956-4200	12793
Hackerone Inc (PA)	7379	C	415 891-0777	12801
Homestar Systems Inc	7379	C	415 323-4008	12803
Incode Technologies Inc (PA)	7379	C	650 446-3444	12807
Liquid Thinking Inc	7379	D	415 869-3300	12828
Littlethings Inc	7379	D	917 364-9277	12829
Meraki LLC (HQ)	7379	A	415 632-5800	12836
Ncc Group Inc (HQ)	7379	D	415 268-9300	12844
Primitive Logic Inc	7379	C	415 391-8080	12862
Redfish Labs Inc	7379	C	415 935-4249	12868
Toptal LLC	7379	B	888 604-3188	12897
Yammer Inc	7379	C	415 796-7400	12911
A1 Protective Services Inc	7381	D	415 467-7200	12914
Corporate Security Service Inc	7381	C	415 626-9271	12952
Cypress Private Security LP (DH)	7381	D	866 345-1277	12960
Firstcall	7381	D	415 781-4300	12972
Marina Security Services Inc	7381	B	415 773-2300	13000
Universal Protection Svc LP (HQ)	7381	D	866 877-1965	13063
WSB & Associates Inc	7381	C	415 864-3510	13079
Nozomi Networks Inc (HQ)	7382	D	800 314-6114	13135
Proguard Security Services Inc	7382	D	415 672-0786	13139
Business Wire Inc (HQ)	7383	C	415 986-4422	13156
Giga Omni Media Inc	7383	D	415 974-6355	13157
Ad Art Inc (PA)	7389	D	415 869-6460	13177
Airbnb Inc (PA)	7389	A	415 510-4027	13182
Ample Inc (PA)	7389	D	617 504-3557	13191
Atel Corporation	7389	D	415 989-8800	13200
Augmedix Operating Corporation	7389	D	855 720-2929	13201
Back of House Inc	7389	D	415 550-8626	13206
Black Knight Infoserv LLC	7389	C	415 989-9800	13215
Brex Inc (PA)	7389	A	844 725-9569	13218
Checkr Inc (PA)	7389	D	844 824-3257	13231
Clearxchange LLC	7389	D	415 813-4801	13237
Credit Karma Inc	7389	A	415 510-5059	13253
Current Tv LLC	7389	C	415 995-8328	13254
Decimal Inc	7389	D	855 980-6612	13259
Figure Technologies Inc	7389	B	888 819-6388	13286
Forma LLC	7389	D	415 477-0700	13292
Forusall Inc	7389	D	844 401-2253	13294
Hh Global Limited	7389	D	847 984-2448	13314
Landor & Fitch LLC (HQ)	7389	D	415 365-1700	13347
Loyal3 Holdings Inc	7389	D	415 981-0700	13359
Migo Money Inc	7389	D	415 906-4040	13376
Nirvana Tech Inc	7389	D	617 800-6650	13398
Opentable Inc (HQ)	7389	C	415 344-4200	13408
Precision Ideo Inc	7389	B	650 688-3400	13428
Program Plg Professionals Inc	7389	C	415 692-5870	13433
Regus Equity Business Ctrs LLC	7389	D	415 293-8000	13444
Rgn-San Francisco IV LLC	7389	D	415 882-6300	13449
San Francisco Foundation	7389	D	415 733-8500	13461
San Francisco Travel Assn	7389	D	415 974-6900	13462
Smg Holdings LLC	7389	D	415 974-4040	13478
Talentburst Inc	7389	D	415 813-4011	13499
Translations LLC	7389	D	415 373-7396	13515
Treasury Prime Inc	7389	D	415 439-0241	13517
Uber Technologies Inc (PA)	7389	A	415 612-8582	13523
Alamo Rental (us) Inc	7514	D	415 693-0191	13577
Turo Inc	7514	C	866 735-2901	13594
Imperial Parking (us) LLC	7521	A	415 495-3909	13606
Parking Concepts Inc	7521	D	415 553-6883	13619
San Francisco Parking Inc	7521	A	415 495-3909	13628
Arcline Elvtion Svcs Hldngs LL	7699	A	860 805-2025	13765
Clean Power Finance Inc	7699	C		13767
United California Glass & Door	7699	D	415 824-8500	13807
Cybernet Entertainment LLC	7812	C	415 865-0230	13835
Lucasfilm Ltd LLC (DH)	7812	A	415 623-1000	13862
New Paradigm Productions Inc (PA)	7812	D	415 924-8000	13869
Century Theatres Inc	7833	C	415 776-2388	14017
Century Theatres Inc	7833	B	415 661-2539	14021
Figureplant LLC	7922	D	503 289-2070	14038
Playwrights Foundation Inc	7922	D	415 626-2176	14055
San Francisco Ballet Assn	7922	C	415 865-2000	14066
San Francisco Opera Assn	7922	A	415 861-4008	14067
San Francisco Symphony (PA)	7929	B	415 552-8000	14104
Ubicom Inc	7929	D	415 547-4000	14110
Yanka Industries Inc	7929	B	855 981-8208	14112
City View At Metreon	7941	C	415 369-6142	14134
Golden State Warriors LLC	7941	B	415 388-0100	14141
San Francisco Baseball Associates LLC (PA)	7941	A	415 972-2000	14156
Bay Clubs Company LLC (HQ)	7991	D	415 781-1874	14175
Club One Inc	7991	A	415 477-3000	14188
Crunch LLC	7991	D	415 543-1110	14192
Crunch LLC	7991	D	415 495-1939	14193
Equinox Holdings Inc	7991	D	415 243-0492	14197
Equinox-76th Street Inc	7991	C	415 398-0747	14201
Western Athletic Clubs Inc	7991	B	415 781-1874	14242
Bay Club America Inc	7997	C	415 781-1874	14328
Bay Clubs Company LLC	7997	B	415 362-7800	14335
Metropolitan Club	7997	D	415 673-0600	14406
Olympic Club	7997	D	415 676-1412	14419
South Park Commons LLC	7997	D	978 815-7723	14456
St Francis Yacht Club	7997	C	415 563-6363	14465
House of Air LLC (PA)	7999	D	415 345-9675	14535
Lime	7999	C	650 762-9697	14541
San Francisco Zoological Soc	7999	C	415 753-7080	14560
Self-Help For Elderly	7999	D	415 677-7581	14564
Senor Sisig	7999	D	415 608-5048	14565
Tonal Systems Inc	7999	C	855 698-6625	14575
Volume Services Inc	7999	B	415 972-1500	14582
1life Healthcare Inc (HQ)	8011	D	415 814-0927	14591
Brown & Toland Medical Group	8011	C	415 923-3015	14639
Brown & Toland Medical Group	8011	D	415 752-8038	14640
Devron H Char MD	8011	D	415 522-0700	14729
Gastroenterology Division	8011	C	415 206-8823	14761
Kaiser Foundation Hospitals	8011	D	415 833-2616	14800
Kaiser Foundation Hospitals	8011	A	415 833-2000	14803
Kaiser Foundation Hospitals	8011	D	415 833-2200	14804
Kaiser Foundation Hospitals	8011	C	415 833-3450	14835
Kaiser Foundation Hospitals	8011	A	415 833-2000	14842
Mission Neighborhood Hlth Ctr (PA)	8011	D	415 552-3870	14903
North East Medical Services (PA)	8011	D	415 391-9686	14926
On Lok Inc	8011	D	415 292-8888	14936
One Medical Group Inc (HQ)	8011	D	415 578-3100	14937
Pacific Hmtlogy Oncology Assoc	8011	D	415 923-3012	14945
Permanente Medical Group Inc	8011	A	415 833-2000	14965
Permanente Medical Group Inc	8011	A	415 833-2000	14983
Plushcare Inc	8011	D	415 231-5333	14996
Sutter Bay Hospitals	8011	D	415 600-2632	15135
U C San Francisco Gynecology	8011	C	415 885-7788	15135
Ucsf Medical Center	8011	C	415 353-9229	15140
University Cal San Francisco	8011	C	415 989-5339	15147
University Cal San Francisco	8011	C	415 353-2383	15148
University Cal San Francisco	8011	C	415 353-7900	15149
University Cal San Francisco	8011	C	415 353-1915	15150
University Cal San Francisco	8011	C	415 353-7576	15151
University Cal San Francisco	8011	D	415 476-9575	15152
Veterans Health Administration	8011	A	415 750-2009	15189
University Cal San Francisco	8021	D	415 476-5608	15253
Teachorg Which Will Do Bus In	8031	D	650 575-5277	15259
San Francisco Sport and Spine	8049	C	415 861-1856	15306

Employee Codes: A=Over 500 employees, B=251-500
C=101-250, D=51-100, E=20-50, F=10-19, G=1-9

2024 Directory of California
WholeSalers and Service Companies

© Mergent Inc. 1-800-342-5647

SAN FRANCISCO CA — GEOGRAPHIC SECTION

Company	SIC	EMP	PHONE	ENTRY#
Hebrew Home For Aged Disabled	8051	A	415 334-2500	15511
Northern California Presbyteri	8051	C	415 922-9700	15598
Scott St Snior Hsing Cmplex In	8051	C	415 345-5083	15656
Ucsf Btty Irene Moore Wns Hosp (HQ)	8051	D	415 476-1000	15709
Big Health Inc	8052	C	707 653-5570	15747
Golden Gateidence Opco LLC	8052	C	415 922-5085	15758
San Franciscoidence Opco LLC	8059	D	415 584-3294	15895
Catholic Healthcare West	8062	A	415 668-1000	15968
Chinese Hospital Association (PA)	8062	B	415 982-2400	16000
City & County San Francisco	8062	A	415 206-8000	16002
Dignity Health (HQ)	8062	C	415 438-5500	16049
Dignity Health	8062	A	415 668-1000	16054
Kaiser Foundation Hospitals	8062	D	415 833-4393	16180
Saint Francis Memorial Hosp (DH)	8062	A	415 353-6000	16369
Sollis Health La PC A Med Corp	8062	D	415 233-9901	16433
St Lukes Health Care Center	8062	C	415 647-8600	16479
St Lukes Hospital	8062	A	415 600-3959	16480
St Marys Med Ctr Foundation	8062	C	415 668-1000	16484
St Marys Medical Center Inc	8062	A	415 668-1000	16485
Sutter Bay Hospitals (HQ)	8062	C	415 600-6000	16507
Sutter Bay Hospitals	8062	C	415 600-2403	16509
Sutter Health	8062	D	415 600-7034	16520
Sutter Health	8062	C	415 600-1020	16524
Sutter Health	8062	D	415 600-4280	16527
Sutter Health	8062	C	415 600-6000	16533
Sutter Health	8062	C	415 600-6000	16536
Sutter Health	8062	C	415 600-6000	16537
University Cal San Francisco	8062	C	415 476-7000	16594
University Cal San Francisco	8062	C	415 476-1611	16595
University Cal San Francisco	8062	C	415 567-6600	16596
University Cal San Francisco	8062	D	415 206-8812	16597
University Cal San Francisco	8063	C	415 206-8430	16660
University Cal San Francisco	8069	D	415 502-8516	16700
Invitae Corporation (PA)	8071	A	415 374-7782	16728
Advisory Board Company	8082	C	415 671-7750	16797
Asian American Home Care Inc	8082	C	415 434-0138	16809
Charolais Care V Inc	8082	D	415 921-5038	16839
Kinsa Inc	8082	D	347 405-4315	16885
Omada Health Inc	8082	B	888 987-8337	16904
Patient Home Monitoring Inc	8082	C	415 693-9690	16909
Sutter Vsting Nrse Assn Hspice	8082	C	415 600-6200	16940
Vivian Health Inc	8082	D	415 851-1168	16967
Vynca Inc	8082	D	650 427-0573	16972
Baker Places Inc	8093	D	415 503-3137	17010
Jcyc	8093	D	415 921-5537	17078
Mental Hlth Assn San Francisco	8093	D	415 421-2926	17091
Mhm Services Inc	8093	C	415 416-6992	17097
Modern Life Inc (PA)	8093	D	617 980-9633	17098
Octave Health Group Inc	8093	C	415 360-3833	17102
Richmond Area Mlt-Services Inc	8093	D	415 579-3021	17118
Richmond Area Mlt-Services Inc (PA)	8093	D	415 800-0699	17119
University Cal San Francisco	8093	D	415 597-8047	17152
Curology Inc (PA)	8099	D	858 859-1188	17217
Dssv Inc	8099	B	415 216-8495	17228
Evolent Health Inc	8099	B	571 389-6000	17236
Health Link	8099	D	415 664-5500	17247
Hinge Health Inc (PA)	8099	A	855 902-7777	17252
Included Health Inc (PA)	8099	C	800 929-0926	17253
Memora Health Inc	8099	C	415 874-9390	17275
Rally Health Inc	8099	C	408 821-5414	17310
Tenderloin Housing Clinic Inc	8099	C	415 771-2427	17340
Tms Health Solutions	8099	C	844 867-8444	17341
Vitalant Research Institute (PA)	8099	C	415 923-5771	17348
Andatha International Inc	8111	C		17364
Arnold & Porter PC	8111	B	415 434-1600	17367
Baker & McKenzie LLP	8111	C	415 576-3000	17373
Bartko Znkel Bnzel Mller A Pro	8111	D	415 956-1900	17381
Berry Appleman & Leiden LLP (PA)	8111	C	628 215-2800	17385
Carroll Burdick Mc Donough LLP (PA)	8111	C	415 989-5900	17400
Coblentz Patch Duffy Bass LLP (PA)	8111	D	510 655-4598	17406
Cooley LLP	8111	C	415 693-2000	17412
Cooper White & Cooper LLP (PA)	8111	C	415 433-1900	17414
Covington & Burling LLP	8111	C	415 591-6000	17423
Cox Wtton Grffin Hnsen Plos LL	8111	C	415 438-4600	17426
Dannis Wlver Klley A Prof Corp (PA)	8111	D	415 543-4111	17430
Davis Wright Tremaine LLP	8111	D	415 276-6500	17432
Dechert LLP	8111	D	415 262-4500	17436
Duane Morris LLP	8111	D	415 957-3000	17443
Epstein Becker & Green PC	8111	D	415 398-3500	17448
Essey LLC	8111	B	212 490-7400	17450
Fenwick & West LLP	8111	C	415 875-2300	17456
Fox Rothschild LLP	8111	D	415 539-3336	17462
Gibson Dunn & Crutcher LLP	8111	D	415 393-8200	17471
Gordon Rees Scully Mansukhani (PA)	8111	B	415 986-5900	17479
Graham & James LLP	8111	A	415 954-0200	17480
Greenberg Traurig LLP	8111	D	415 655-1300	17482
Greene Rdvsky Maloney Share LP	8111	D	415 981-1400	17487
Hanson Bridgett LLP (PA)	8111	B	415 543-2055	17490
Hassard Bonnington LLP (PA)	8111	D	415 288-9800	17492
Hunton Andrews Kurth LLP	8111	D	415 975-3700	17498
Justice Dvrsity Ctr of The Bar	8111	D	415 575-3130	17509
K&L Gates LLP	8111	D	415 882-8200	17510
Keker Van Nest & Peters LLP	8111	D	415 391-5400	17516
Kilpatrick Twnsend Stckton LLP	8111	D	415 576-0200	17517
King & Spalding LLP	8111	D	415 318-1200	17520
Kirkland & Ellis LLP	8111	C	415 439-1400	17524
Latham & Watkins LLP	8111	C	415 391-0600	17539
Lewis Brsbois Bsgard Smith LLP	8111	C	415 362-2580	17547
Lieff Cbrser Hmann Brnstein LL (PA)	8111	C	415 788-0245	17549
Littler Mendelson PC (PA)	8111	B	415 433-1940	17551
Lubin Olson & Niewiadomski LLP	8111	D	415 981-0550	17559
Morgan Lewis & Bockius LLP	8111	A	415 442-1000	17574
Morrison & Foerster LLP (PA)	8111	B	415 268-7000	17577
Nossaman LLP	8111	D	415 398-3600	17590
Orrick Hrrington Sutcliffe LLP (PA)	8111	A	415 773-5700	17596
Paragon Legal Group LLC	8111	C	415 738-7870	17600
Paul Hastings LLP	8111	C	415 856-7000	17605
Pillsbury Winthrop Shaw	8111	D	415 983-1000	17608
Pillsbury Winthrop Shaw	8111	B	415 983-1075	17609
Reed Smith LLP	8111	C	415 543-8700	17623
Scale LLP	8111	D	415 735-5933	17633
Sedgwick LLP	8111	A	415 781-7900	17636
Severson & Werson A Prof Corp (PA)	8111	C	415 398-3344	17639
Seyfarth Shaw LLP	8111	D	415 397-2823	17643
Shartsis Friese LLP	8111	C	415 421-6500	17644
Sheppard Mllin Rchter Hmpton L	8111	D	415 434-9100	17648
Shook Hardy & Bacon LLP	8111	C	415 544-1900	17651
Sideman & Bancroft LLP	8111	D	415 392-1960	17653
Steele Cis LLC	8111	B	415 692-5000	17661
Winston & Strawn LLP	8111	D	415 591-1000	17683
California School of Mech Arts	8211	D	415 333-4021	17697
Jewish Cmnty Ctr San Francisco (PA)	8211	C	415 292-1200	17719
Presidio Hill School	8211	D	415 213-8600	17741
San Francisco Unified Schl Dst (PA)	8211	C	415 241-6000	17747
American Cllege of Trdtnal Chn (PA)	8221	D	415 282-0316	17760
San Francisco Art Institute Inc	8221	C	415 771-7020	17768
University Cal San Francisco	8221	D	415 476-2695	17770
University Cal San Francisco	8221	D	415 353-2757	17771
University Cal San Francisco	8221	D	415 885-7257	17772
University Cal San Francisco	8221	C	415 476-3016	17773
University Cal San Francisco	8221	D	415 353-7700	17774
University Cal San Francisco	8221	D	415 353-7300	17775
University Cal San Francisco	8221	D	415 885-3668	17776
University Cal San Francisco	8221	D	415 885-7495	17777
University Cal San Francisco	8221	D	415 885-3610	17778
University Cal San Francisco	8221	D	415 476-3061	17779
University Cal San Francisco	8221	D	415 353-2961	17780
University Cal San Francisco	8221	D	415 885-7478	17781
Arden Wood Inc	8249	D	415 681-5500	17793
Ayusa International	8299	C	888 552-9872	17802
San Frncsco Cnservatory of Mus (PA)	8299	C	415 864-7326	17815
The Roman Catholic Archbishop of Sa	8299	C	415 614-5500	17817
Baker Places Inc	8322	D	415 387-2275	17845
Childrens Cncil San Francisco (PA)	8322	D	415 343-3378	17882
Compass Family Services	8322	D	415 644-0504	17896
Compass Family Services	8322	D	415 644-0504	17897
Golden Gate Regional Ctr Inc (PA)	8322	C	415 546-9222	17993
Hamilton Families	8322	D	415 409-2100	17996
Homebridge Inc	8322	B	415 255-2079	18004
Institute On Aging	8322	C	415 600-2690	18016
Institute On Aging (PA)	8322	D	415 750-4101	18017
Jewish Family and Chld Svcs (PA)	8322	D	415 449-1200	18025
Larkin Street Youth Services	8322	D	415 567-1020	18039
Pomeroy Rcrtion Rhbltation Ctr (PA)	8322	C	415 665-4100	18084
Project Open Hand	8322	C	415 292-3400	18088
Raphael Hse San Francisco Inc	8322	D	415 345-7200	18092
Sage Project Inc	8322	D	415 905-5050	18104
Salesforcecom/Foundation	8322	C	800 667-6389	18105
San Francisco Aids Foundation (PA)	8322	D	415 487-3000	18112
San Francisco Food Bank	8322	D	415 282-1900	18113
San Frncsco Prtclar Cncil of T	8322	D	415 255-3525	18114
Self-Help For Elderly	8322	D	415 391-3843	18121
Self-Help For Elderly (PA)	8322	D	415 677-7600	18122
Self-Help For Elderly	8322	D	415 677-7556	18123
Urban Alchemy	8322	D	415 757-0896	18165
ARC San Francisco (PA)	8331	D	415 255-7200	18207

GEOGRAPHIC SECTION

SAN FRANCISCO CA

	SIC	EMP	PHONE	ENTRY#
Mission Economic Dev Agcy	8331	D	415 282-3334	18236
Toolworks Inc (PA)	8331	D	415 733-0990	18253
Compass Family Services	8351	D	415 644-0504	18302
Christian Church Homes	8361	C	415 814-2670	18394
Delancey Street Foundation (PA)	8361	B	415 957-9800	18415
Edgewood Ctr For Chldren Fmlie (PA)	8361	C	415 681-3211	18420
Front Porch Communities & Svcs	8361	D	415 776-0500	18438
Little Ssters of The Poor Okla	8361	D	415 751-6510	18474
Masonic Homes of California (PA)	8361	B	415 776-7000	18480
San Frncsco Ldies Prtction Rli	8361	C	415 931-3136	18519
Super Home Inc	8361	D	844 997-8737	18529
University Cal San Frncsco Fnd	8361	D	415 775-2111	18535
Walden House Inc	8361	C	415 554-1131	18544
Walden House Inc	8361	C	415 554-1480	18546
Department Hmlssness Spprtive	8399	C	628 652-7700	18584
Expensifyorg	8399	C	971 365-3939	18587
Habitat For Hmnity Grter San F	8399	D	415 625-1000	18591
Japanese Cmnty Youth Council (PA)	8399	D	415 202-7905	18599
Jewish Cmnty Fdrtion of San Fr (PA)	8399	D	415 777-0411	18600
Kipp Foundation	8399	C	415 399-1556	18604
Northern Cal Inst For RES Edca	8399	B	415 750-6954	18613
Poll Everywhere Inc	8399	D	800 388-2039	18618
Tides Inc (PA)	8399	D	415 561-6400	18630
Asian Art Mseum Fndtion San Fr	8412	D	415 581-3500	18638
Childrens Creativity Museum	8412	D	415 820-3320	18643
City & County San Francisco	8412	D	415 581-3500	18644
Corportion of Fine Arts Mseums	8412	C	415 750-3600	18645
Corportion of Fine Arts Mseums	8412	C	415 750-3600	18646
Corportion of Fine Arts Mseums	8412	C	415 750-3600	18647
Corportion of Fine Arts Mseums	8412	C	415 750-3600	18648
Corportion of Fine Arts Mseums (PA)	8412	C	415 750-3600	18649
Exploratorium	8412	B	415 528-4462	18652
San Francisco Museum Modrn Art (PA)	8412	B	415 357-4035	18671
The Origin Project Inc	8412	D	415 601-2409	18680
Walt Disney Family Museum	8412	C	415 345-6800	18682
Bayorg	8422	D	415 623-5300	18684
California Academy Sciences (PA)	8422	A	415 379-8000	18685
Contentful Inc	8611	D	415 248-7801	18705
American Acdemy Ophthlmlogy In (PA)	8621	C	415 561-8500	18729
Bar Asscation of San Francisco (PA)	8621	D	415 982-1600	18733
Bvoh LLC	8621	D	415 738-0901	18734
San Francisco Health Authority (PA)	8621	D	415 615-4407	18760
State Bar of California (PA)	8621	B	415 538-2000	18764
Califrnia Dept Indus Relations	8631	D	415 703-5133	18776
UA Local 38 Pension Tr Fund	8631	D	415 626-2000	18800
Bohemian Club (PA)	8641	D	415 885-2440	18818
Cloud Native Cmpt Foundation	8641	C	415 723-9709	18843
Earthjustice (PA)	8641	D	415 217-2000	18854
Ehdd	8641	D	415 285-9193	18855
Envirnment Ntral Resources Div	8641	A	415 744-6491	18857
Foundtion For Stdnts Rsing ABO	8641	D	415 333-4222	18859
Golden Gate Nat Prks Cnsrvancy	8641	C	415 933-6760	18865
Ideoorg	8641	D	415 426-7080	18870
Jamestown Community Center Inc	8641	D	415 647-4709	18871
Nature Conservancy	8641	D	415 777-0487	18885
Olympic Club (PA)	8641	C	415 345-5100	18887
Techsoup Global (PA)	8641	C	800 659-3579	18915
The Linux Foundation (PA)	8641	C	415 723-9709	18916
Young MNS Chrstn Assn San Frnc	8641	D	415 447-9622	18992
Young MNS Chrstn Assn San Frnc	8641	D	415 957-9622	18995
Young MNS Chrstn Assn San Frnc	8641	D	415 885-0460	18996
Young MNS Chrstn Assn San Frnc	8641	C	415 586-6900	18998
Fuse Corps	8699	D	855 687-9905	19084
Haas Jr Evelyn & Walter Fund	8699	D	415 856-1400	19086
Henry J Kaiser Fmly Foundation (PA)	8699	D	650 854-9400	19087
Open Philanthropy Project	8699	D	415 429-0423	19095
San Francisco Spca	8699	D	415 554-3000	19102
San Frncsco Soc For The Prvnti (PA)	8699	C	415 554-3000	19103
Uc Hastings Foundation	8699	C	415 565-4704	19114
United States Enrgy Foundation	8699	D	415 561-6700	19115
Wikimedia Foundation Inc	8699	B	415 839-6885	19120
Arup North America Limited (DH)	8711	C	415 957-9445	19145
Bkf/Fli	8711	D	415 930-7900	19157
Bridge Design LLC	8711	D	415 487-7100	19159
Buro Happold Consulting Engine	8711	C	310 945-4808	19165
Carbon Lighthouse Inc	8711	C	415 787-3550	19173
Consor Pmcm Inc	8711	D	415 596-5399	19182
Degenkolb Engineers (PA)	8711	D	415 392-6952	19195
Jacobs Project Management Co	8711	D	949 224-7908	19283
Kennedy/Jenks Consultants Inc (PA)	8711	D	415 243-2150	19293
Kpff Inc	8711	D	415 989-1004	19300
Lopezgarcia Group Inc (DH)	8711	C	415 796-8100	19308
Pae Consulting Engineers Inc	8711	D	503 226-2921	19349

	SIC	EMP	PHONE	ENTRY#
Stantec Architecture Inc	8711	A	415 882-9500	19394
T Y Lin International (HQ)	8711	D	415 291-3700	19404
Teecom	8711	C	510 337-2800	19406
Tetra Tech Em Inc	8711	D	415 265-3715	19412
TYlin Intl Group Ltd (PA)	8711	C	415 291-3700	19422
URS Holdings Inc (DH)	8711	B	415 774-2700	19429
Bar Architects	8712	D	415 293-5700	19454
Forge Architecture	8712	D	415 434-0320	19467
Gensler Asscts/Ntrnational Ltd (HQ)	8712	D	415 433-3700	19469
Gould Evans P C	8712	D	415 503-1411	19472
Hellmuth Obata & Kassabaum Inc (DH)	8712	D	415 243-0555	19475
Huntsman Architectural Group (PA)	8712	D	415 394-1212	19479
Interior Architects Inc (PA)	8712	D	415 434-3305	19480
M Arthur Gensler Jr Assoc Inc (PA)	8712	B	415 433-3700	19489
Myles Stevens Architecture	8712	D	415 397-6500	19497
Perkins + Will Inc	8712	C	415 856-3000	19500
Skidmore Owings & Merrill LLP	8712	C	415 981-1555	19504
Smithgroup Inc	8712	C	313 442-8351	19505
URS Global Holdings Inc	8712	B	415 774-2700	19516
Woods Bagot Architects PC	8712	C	415 277-3000	19521
Burr Pilger Mayer Inc (PA)	8721	C	415 421-5757	19543
Cfgi LLC	8721	C	415 670-9041	19550
Collabrus Inc	8721	C	415 288-1826	19553
Deloitte & Touche LLP	8721	B	415 783-4000	19564
Deloitte Tax LLP	8721	B	415 783-4000	19566
Eisneramper LLP	8721	D	415 974-6000	19570
Hood & Strong LLP (PA)	8721	D	415 781-0793	19586
LLP Moss Adams	8721	C	415 956-1500	19601
Nigro Krlin Sgal Fldstein Blno	8721	C	415 463-1300	19616
Novogradac & Company LLP (PA)	8721	C	415 356-8000	19617
Recurly Inc (PA)	8721	D	844 732-8759	19627
Withumsmith+brown PC	8721	D	415 434-3744	19640
Catalyst Bio Inc	8731	B	650 871-0761	19668
Environmental Science Assoc (PA)	8731	D	415 896-5900	19687
Howard Hughes Medical Inst	8731	D	415 476-9668	19708
Metabiota Inc	8731	D	415 398-4712	19738
Nurix Therapeutics Inc (PA)	8731	D	415 660-5320	19749
Vir Biotechnology Inc (PA)	8731	C	415 906-4324	19796
Bloomberg LP	8732	C	415 283-4872	19801
Glass Lewis & Co LLC (HQ)	8732	C	415 678-4110	19812
Inner Circle Labs LLC	8732	D	415 684-9400	19822
Iqvia Inc	8732	D	415 692-9898	19826
National Opinion Research Ctr	8732	C	415 315-2000	19833
Nielsen Mobile LLC (DH)	8732	C	917 435-9301	19836
Orange Silicon Valley LLC	8732	D	415 284-9765	19839
Otr Global Holdings II Inc	8732	C	415 675-7660	19840
Asia Foundation (PA)	8733	D	415 982-4640	19863
Chan Zuckerberg Biohub Inc	8733	C	628 200-3246	19876
Element Science Inc	8733	D	415 872-6500	19881
The J David Gladstone Institutes	8733	B	415 734-2000	19919
United Sttes Dept Enrgy Lvrmor	8733	A	415 648-3878	19926
University Cal San Francisco	8733	D	628 206-2400	19930
University Cal San Francisco	8733	D	415 476-9323	19931
Wested (PA)	8733	C	415 565-3000	19937
Arceo Labs Inc (PA)	8734	C	332 203-4971	19950
Found Health Inc	8734	C	415 854-3296	19978
Fuzzy Pet Health Inc	8734	D	415 692-1875	19979
Active Wellness LLC	8741	A	415 741-3300	20010
Alliant Insurance Services Inc	8741	D	415 403-1400	20016
Anglepoint Group Inc (PA)	8741	C	855 512-6453	20023
Bechtel Capital MGT Corp	8741	D	415 768-1234	20033
Cornerstone Hotel Management (DH)	8741	C	415 397-5572	20062
Dewolf Realty Co Inc	8741	D	415 221-2032	20078
Jewish Senior Living Group	8741	D	415 334-2500	20122
Joie De Vivre Hospitality LLC	8741	C	415 346-2880	20124
Joie De Vivre Hospitality LLC	8741	D	415 986-2000	20125
Meritage Group LP	8741	A	415 399-5330	20151
Pacific Park Management	8741	D	415 440-4840	20170
Persona Identities Inc (PA)	8741	C	415 355-4050	20175
Ps24 Inc	8741	D	415 834-5105	20189
San Frncsco Cmnty Clnic Cnsrti	8741	C	415 355-2222	20199
Sodexo Management Inc	8741	A	925 325-9657	20209
Standish Management LLC	8741	C	925 300-3277	20216
United Behavioral Health (HQ)	8741	C	415 547-1403	20237
Viva Soma Lessee Inc	8741	A	415 974-6400	20246
Accenture LLP	8742	C	415 537-5000	20260
Adivo Associates LLC	8742	D	415 992-1449	20261
Aki Technologies	8742	D	415 624-3253	20265
Akqa Inc (HQ)	8742	B	415 645-9400	20266
Ampush Media Inc	8742	D	415 638-9663	20273
Archetype Consulting Inc	8742	D	888 644-8445	20279
Aspireiq Inc	8742	D	415 445-3567	20282
Bain & Company Inc	8742	C	415 627-1000	20288

Employee Codes: A=Over 500 employees, B=251-500
C=101-250, D=51-100, E=20-50, F=10-19, G=1-9

2024 Directory of California
WholeSalers and Service Companies

© Mergent Inc. 1-800-342-5647
1493

SAN FRANCISCO CA

	SIC	EMP	PHONE	ENTRY#
Betterup Inc (PA)	8742	C	415 862-0708	20295
Bite Communications LLC (HQ)	8742	D	415 365-0222	20296
Brandwatch LLC	8742	C	415 429-5800	20301
Cal Golden Healthcare LLC	8742	D	415 567-2967	20306
Celerity Consulting Group LLC (PA)	8742	D	415 986-8850	20312
Cience Technologies Inc	8742	D	949 424-2906	20315
Code For America Labs Inc	8742	D	415 816-1286	20323
Continuumglobal Inc	8742	A	415 685-3301	20327
Deloitte Consulting LLP	8742	C	510 251-4400	20340
Digitalthink Inc (DH)	8742	C	415 625-4000	20346
Double Forte	8742	D	415 863-4900	20347
Ethos Event Collective LLC	8742	D	415 762-9773	20364
Ey-Parthenon	8742	C	415 486-3600	20371
Firewood Marketing Inc	8742	C	415 872-5132	20377
Five Stars Loyalty Inc	8742	C	860 578-2770	20382
Frederick Labs LLC	8742	C	646 738-8303	20387
H&H Catering LP	8742	D	408 354-1964	20398
Inkling Systems Inc	8742	D	415 975-4420	20413
Jumpstart Digital Mktg Inc (DH)	8742	C	415 844-6336	20423
Kinsale Holdings Inc (PA)	8742	C	415 400-2600	20425
Linqia Inc	8742	C	415 913-7179	20438
Liveramp Inc (HQ)	8742	A	866 352-3267	20439
Manifold LLC	8742	D	415 978-9500	20447
Marketbridge Corp	8742	D	240 752-1800	20450
Marketerhire LLC	8742	C	312 870-0008	20451
Mars & Co Consulting LLC	8742	C	415 288-6970	20455
McKinsey & Company Inc	8742	B	415 981-0250	20459
Metric Theory LLC	8742	D	415 659-8600	20467
Pulsepoint Inc	8742	C	415 937-8208	20516
PWC STRategy& (us) LLC	8742	C	415 498-5000	20517
Slalom LLC	8742	B	415 593-3450	20552
Sterling Consulting Group LLC	8742	D	415 248-7900	20567
University of California	8742	C	415 353-2057	20599
Zillow Inc	8742	D	877 215-8423	20623
Access Public Relations LLC	8743	D	415 904-7070	20628
Atomic Public Relations (HQ)	8743	D	415 402-0230	20629
Igel Technology Corporation	8743	C	845 589-5900	20635
Ketchum Incorporated	8743	C	415 984-6100	20636
Outcast Agency LLC	8743	C	415 392-8282	20640
R/GA Media Group Inc	8743	C	415 913-7531	20642
Radiumone Inc	8743	C	415 418-2840	20643
Young & Rubicam LLC	8743	C	650 287-4000	20644
Enginrng/Rmdtion Rsrces Group	8744	C	415 395-9974	20653
Bay Area Air Quality (PA)	8748	A	415 749-4900	20699
Bay Area Air Quality MGT Dst	8748	B	415 749-4900	20700
Bishop Fox Inc	8748	C	480 621-8967	20707
Connor Consulting Corp (PA)	8748	C	415 678-5002	20732
Detecon Inc	8748	B	415 549-6999	20738
Eco Bay Services Inc	8748	C	415 643-7777	20740
Francsco Prtners III Cayman LP	8748	C	415 418-2900	20750
Fti Consulting Inc	8748	D	415 283-4200	20753
Fuse Project LLC	8748	D	415 908-1492	20755
GI Partners LLC (PA)	8748	A	415 688-4800	20762
Jones It Consulting LLC	8748	C	415 578-7111	20787
Keystone Strategy LLC	8748	D	877 419-2623	20791
Kruze Consulting Inc	8748	C	415 601-6967	20795
Multiplier	8748	C	415 421-3774	20809
Popularmedia Inc	8748	C	415 928-5880	20830
Qualia Labs Inc	8748	C	440 477-5625	20835
Quorum One LLC	8748	C	760 786-7861	20836
Stok LLC	8748	C	415 265-2366	20856
Surefox North America Inc	8748	C	650 665-1852	20857
VSC Sports Inc	8748	D	415 820-3525	20877
Golden Gate Nat Prks Cnsrvancy (PA)	8999	C	415 561-3000	20891
Klingstubbins Inc	8999	D	415 356-2040	20894
Presidio Trust	8999	C	415 561-5300	20899
Zoe Holding Company Inc	8999	C	415 421-4900	20910

SAN GABRIEL, CA - Los Angeles County

	SIC	EMP	PHONE	ENTRY#
Inveserve Corporation	6531	D	626 458-3435	9053
Park Cleaners Inc (PA)	7213	D	626 281-5942	10454
Informtion Rfrral Fdrtion of L	7299	D	626 350-1841	10552
San Gabriel Country Club	7997	D	626 287-9671	14438
San Gbriel Ambltory Srgery Ctr	8011	C	626 300-5300	15043
Country Villa Service Corp	8059	C	626 285-2165	15832
Longwood Management Corp	8059	D	626 289-3763	15872
Ahmc Healthcare Inc (PA)	8062	D	626 943-7526	15931
San Gabriel Valley Medical Ctr	8062	A	626 289-5454	16378
Ahmc Healthcare Inc	8099	C	626 284-3452	17166
Providnce Facey Med Foundation	8099	D	626 576-0800	17302
Clairbourn School	8211	D	626 286-3108	17704

SAN JACINTO, CA - Riverside County

	SIC	EMP	PHONE	ENTRY#
Agri-Empire	5148	C	951 654-7311	6512
Soboba Band Luiseno Indians	7389	A	951 665-1000	13479
Borrego Cmnty Hlth Foundation	8011	C	951 487-8506	14635
Riversd-San Brnrdino Cnty Indi	8011	C	951 654-0803	15018

SAN JOAQUIN, CA - Fresno County

	SIC	EMP	PHONE	ENTRY#
Standard Cattle LLC	0751	D	559 693-1977	356

SAN JOSE, CA - Santa Clara County

	SIC	EMP	PHONE	ENTRY#
Brightview Landscape Svcs Inc	0781	C	408 453-5904	411
Heavenly Construction Inc	0781	D	408 723-4954	437
Petalon Landscape MGT Inc	0781	D	408 453-3998	456
Blossom Valley Cnstr Inc	0782	C	408 993-0766	476
Jensen Corp Landscape Contr	0782	C	408 446-4881	501
Landcare USA LLC	0782	D	408 727-4099	513
Bill Brown Construction Co	1521	D	408 297-3738	660
Casa Acquisition Corp	1521	C	400 207-9499	665
De Mattei Construction Inc	1521	D	408 295-7516	671
MAI Construction Inc	1521	D	408 434-9880	699
Mike Rovner Construction Inc	1521	C	408 453-6070	703
Tupaz Homes LLC	1521	D	408 377-1622	731
Ucp Inc	1521	C	408 207-9499	732
Gilbane Building Company	1522	D	858 658-6700	758
Greenbriar Homes Communities	1531	D	510 497-8200	791
Blach Construction Company (PA)	1541	C	408 244-7100	808
Dpr Construction A Gen Partnr	1542	C	408 370-2322	907
Draeger Construction Inc	1542	A		912
Webcor Construction LP	1542	C	408 277-0311	1054
Lewis and Tibbitts Inc	1623	C	408 925-0220	1230
Schwager Davis Inc	1629	D	408 281-9300	1316
Air Systems Inc	1711	B	408 280-1666	1340
Aqualine Piping Inc	1711	C	408 745-7100	1362
Axis Mechanical Inc	1711	C	408 573-7400	1369
California United Mech Inc (PA)	1711	B	408 232-9000	1391
Critchfield Mechanical Inc (PA)	1711	C	408 437-7000	1414
Icom Mechanical Inc	1711	C	408 292-4968	1460
J & J Air Conditioning Inc	1711	D	408 920-0662	1470
Lefco Inc	1711	C	408 729-4800	1484
Monster Mep Inc	1711	D	408 727-8362	1502
O C McDonald Co Inc	1711	C	408 295-2182	1514
Silicon Valley Mechanical Inc	1711	C	408 943-0380	1561
W L Hickey Sons Inc	1711	C	408 736-4938	1593
Schaper Construction Inc	1721	C	408 437-0337	1641
C H Reynolds Electric Inc (PA)	1731	B	408 436-9280	1689
Cupertino Electric Inc (PA)	1731	C	408 808-8000	1717
Ics Integrated Comm Systems	1731	D	408 491-6000	1753
Netronix Integration Inc (HQ)	1731	D	800 600-3939	1788
New Age Electric Inc	1731	D	408 279-8787	1789
Phase 3 Communications Inc (PA)	1731	D	408 946-9011	1804
Prime Electric Inc	1731	A	925 961-1600	1811
Rosendin Electric Inc (PA)	1731	A	408 286-2800	1825
Rosendin Electric Inc	1731	A	408 321-2200	1827
Sprig Electric Co (HQ)	1731	C	408 298-3134	1848
Synchronoss Technologies Inc	1731	B	800 575-7606	1859
Therma Holdings LLC (PA)	1731	C	408 347-3400	1863
C R S Drywall Inc	1742	D	408 998-4360	1914
California Drywall Co (PA)	1742	C	408 292-7500	1916
DH Smith Company Inc	1742	C	408 532-7617	1924
Eric Stark Interiors Inc	1742	D	408 441-6136	1927
Magnum Drywall Inc	1742	C	510 979-0420	1944
MGM Drywall Inc	1742	C	408 292-4085	1946
S & S Drywall Inc (PA)	1742	C	408 294-4393	1962
Della Maggiore Tile Inc	1743	D	408 286-3991	1979
All Fab Prcsion Sheetmetal Inc	1761	D	408 279-1099	2043
Mass Precision Inc	1761	D	408 786-0378	2074
Topbuild Services Group Corp	1799	A	408 882-0411	2322
Olivera Egg Ranch LLC	2015	D	408 258-8074	2345
Imerys Talc America Inc (DH)	3295	B		2718
Mac Cal Company	3444	C	408 441-1435	2744
Super Micro Computer Inc (PA)	3571	A	408 503-8000	2813
Netapp Inc (PA)	3572	A	408 822-6000	2817
Aruba Networks Inc (HQ)	3577	B	408 941-4300	2824
Brocade Cmmnctions Systems LLC (DH)	3577	A	408 333-8000	2826
Cisco Systems Inc (PA)	3577	A	408 526-4000	2828
Synaptics Incorporated (PA)	3577	B	408 904-1100	2838
Haig Precision Mfg Corp	3599	D	408 374-4920	2853
Microsemi Frequency Time Corp (DH)	3625	C	480 792-7200	2866
Infinera Corporation (PA)	3661	B	408 572-5200	2885
Jetstream Communications Inc	3661	D	408 361-7000	2887
Netgear Inc (PA)	3661	C	408 907-8000	2888
Lockheed Martin Corporation	3663	D	408 473-3000	2893
Xilinx Inc (HQ)	3672	A	408 559-7778	2911

GEOGRAPHIC SECTION

SAN JOSE CA

Company	SIC	EMP	PHONE	ENTRY#
Altera Corporation (HQ)	3674	B	408 544-7000	2912
Aptina LLC	3674	A	408 660-2699	2913
Chrontel Inc (PA)	3674	C	408 383-9328	2914
Dsp Group Inc (HQ)	3674	D	408 986-4300	2918
Microsemi Soc Corp (DH)	3674	C	408 643-6000	2928
Pure Wafer Inc	3674	C	408 945-8112	2930
Qualcomm Atheros Inc (HQ)	3674	A	408 773-5200	2931
Rambus Inc (PA)	3674	B	408 462-8000	2933
Tessera Technologies Inc (DH)	3674	C	408 321-6000	2934
Wafer Reclaim Services LLC	3674	C	408 945-8112	2936
Ghangor Cloud Inc	3699	D	408 713-3303	2958
Britelab Inc	3824	D	650 961-0671	3020
A D A C Laboratories (inc)	3829	A	408 321-9100	3039
Venus Concept Inc	3841	D	408 489-4925	3061
Santa Clara Valley Trnsp Auth (PA)	4111	A	408 321-2300	3206
Santa Clara Valley Trnsp Auth	4111	C	408 321-5559	3207
Sfo Airporter Inc (PA)	4111	D	650 246-2734	3211
Transitamerica Services Inc	4111	D	408 961-4350	3223
Vta	4111	D	408 546-7777	3224
Rm Executive Transportation	4119	C	650 260-1240	3291
Transdev Services Inc	4119	C	408 282-4706	3300
Royal Coach Tours (PA)	4142	C	408 279-4801	3320
First Student Inc	4151	C	408 971-3466	3342
Doudell Trucking Company (PA)	4213	D	408 263-7300	3467
Fedex Freight West Inc	4213	A	775 356-7600	3476
Xpo Logistics Freight Inc	4213	C	408 435-3876	3568
Legacy Transportation Svcs Inc (PA)	4214	C	408 294-9800	3589
United Parcel Service Inc	4215	C	408 291-2942	3637
Storagepro Inc	4225	D	408 560-0511	3759
Atlantic Aviation Fbo Inc	4581	D	408 297-7552	3875
City of San Jose	4581	C	408 392-3600	3883
City of San Jose	4581	C	650 965-4156	3884
Norman Y Mnt-San Jose Intl Arp	4581	C	408 392-3600	3901
Classic Vacations LLC	4725	C	408 287-4550	3962
Advantage Logistics Inc	4731	C	408 943-6300	3977
Yamato Enterprises Inc	4731	D	408 677-3554	4122
Innovated Packaging Co Inc	4783	D	510 745-8180	4129
Deliverimates LLC	4789	D	857 445-7736	4150
Aeris Communications Inc (PA)	4813	C	408 557-1900	4252
Gogrid LLC	4813	C	415 869-7444	4289
Kijiji Classifieds LLC	4813	D	669 213-9255	4302
Kijiji Classifieds LLC (HQ)	4813	D	408 376-4952	4304
Vta Telephone Information	4813	B	408 321-7127	4357
Roku Inc (PA)	4841	C	408 556-9040	4519
Calix Inc (PA)	4899	A	408 514-3000	4530
Cambium Networks Inc	4899	C	847 640-3809	4532
Itron Networked Solutions Inc (HQ)	4899	B	669 770-4000	4540
California Water Service Co (HQ)	4941	D	408 367-8200	4767
California Water Service Group (PA)	4941	C	408 367-8200	4768
San Jose Water Company (HQ)	4941	C	408 288-5314	4827
San Jose Water Company	4941	C	408 298-0364	4828
Santa Clara Vly Wtr Dst Pub Fc (PA)	4941	C	408 265-2600	4829
Santa Clara Vly Wtr Dst Pub Fc	4941	C	408 630-2560	4830
SJW Group (PA)	4941	B	408 279-7800	4835
California Waste Solutions Inc (PA)	4953	D	408 292-0830	4874
Waste Connections Cal Inc (DH)	4953	C	408 282-4400	4952
County of Santa Clara	4959	B	408 573-2400	4976
Butler-Johnson Corporation	5023	C	800 776-2167	5113
Galleher LLC	5023	D	408 850-1990	5119
Aura Hardwood Lumber Inc	5031	D	800 411-2872	5148
County Building Materials Inc	5031	D	408 274-4920	5152
Expert Dry Wall Systems Inc	5031	D	408 271-5044	5154
Hardwoods Specialty Pdts US LP	5031	D	408 275-1995	5162
Archlynk LLC (PA)	5045	C	408 214-3140	5274
MA Laboratories Inc (PA)	5045	B	408 941-0808	5326
Quanta Cloud Tech USA LLC	5045	A	510 270-6111	5337
Sk Hynix America Inc (HQ)	5045	D	408 232-8000	5349
Solid State Stor Tech USA Corp	5045	D	510 687-1800	5351
Super Talent Technology Corp	5045	A	408 957-8133	5357
Trend Micro Incorporated	5045	D	408 257-1500	5363
Geneo United LLC	5047	D	224 548-5854	5415
ABB Enterprise Software Inc	5049	B	408 770-8968	5463
Chester C Lehmann Co Inc (PA)	5063	D	408 293-5818	5546
Zspace Inc	5063	D	408 498-4050	5598
Advantest America Corporation (holding Co)	5065	B	408 456-3600	5621
Avago Technologies US Inc (HQ)	5065	B	800 433-8778	5626
Exponential Tech Group Inc	5065	D	408 414-1450	5650
Lg Display America Inc (HQ)	5065	D	408 350-0190	5670
Nuvoton Technology Corp Amer	5065	D	408 544-1718	5685
Parade Technologies Inc	5065	D	408 329-5540	5687
Rfmw Ltd	5065	D	408 414-1450	5696
Samsung Semiconductor Inc (DH)	5065	C	408 544-4000	5698
Sumitomo Elc DVC Innvtons USA	5065	D	408 232-9500	5702
Winbond Electronics Corp Amer	5065	D	408 943-6666	5716
United Green Mark Inc	5083	D	408 295-3376	5814
Valin Corporation (PA)	5084	D	408 730-9850	5878
Cse Holdings Inc	5087	C	408 436-1907	5937
Captain Kirk Services Inc	5099	D	408 320-0230	6033
Supplyworks	5099	D	408 954-1234	6055
Lee Bros Foodservices Inc (PA)	5141	D	408 275-0700	6261
Marquez Brothers Intl Inc (PA)	5141	C	408 960-2700	6264
Smart & Final Stores Inc	5141	D	408 251-0109	6298
Smart & Final Stores LLC	5141	D	408 517-8803	6344
Race Street Partners Inc (PA)	5144	D	408 294-6161	6448
Galli Produce Company	5148	D	408 436-6100	6550
Specialty Baking Inc	5149	D	408 298-6950	6670
Coast Oil Company LLC	5172	D	408 252-7720	6725
Easy Fuel Inc	5172	D	408 280-5235	6727
ME Fox & Company Inc	5181	C	408 435-8510	6776
Pacific Groservice Inc	5194	B	408 727-4826	6881
Cloudradiant Corp	5199	A	408 256-1527	6898
Home Depot USA Inc	5211	C	408 978-1099	6975
Lowes Home Centers LLC	5211	D	408 518-4165	7042
Halrec Inc	5511	D	408 984-1234	7228
Mission Vly Ford Trck Sls Inc	5511	D	408 933-2300	7259
Southern Cal Disc Tire Co Inc	5531	D	408 436-8274	7374
Sutters Place Inc (PA)	5812	D	408 451-8888	7511
Delave Inc (PA)	5994	D	408 293-7200	7567
Avidbank Holdings Inc	6022	C	408 200-7390	7654
Bridge Bank National Association	6022	D	408 423-8500	7663
Heritage Bank of Commerce (HQ)	6022	C	408 947-6900	7692
Western Alliance Bank	6022	D	408 423-8500	7725
Patent and Trademark Office US	6029	B	831 332-7127	7734
Standard Chartered Bank	6029	C	408 629-3219	7737
Commonwealth Central Credit Un (PA)	6061	D	408 531-3100	7760
Excite Credit Union (PA)	6061	C	800 232-8669	7764
First Technology Federal Cr Un (PA)	6061	D	855 855-8805	7772
Keypoint Credit Union (PA)	6061	C	408 731-4100	7777
Meriwest Credit Union (PA)	6061	C	408 363-3200	7781
Technology Credit Union (PA)	6061	C	408 451-9111	7810
Loan Factory Inc	6141	D	408 646-6662	7877
New America Funding LLC	6153	D	408 429-2085	7900
Citigroup Global Markets Inc	6211	D	408 947-2200	8080
Merrill Lynch Pierce Fenner	6211	D	408 260-6001	8103
Merrill Lynch Prce Fnner Smith	6211	C	408 283-3000	8119
Morgan Stnley Smith Barney LLC	6211	C	408 346-0105	8153
Bam Advisor Services LLC	6282	D	800 366-7266	8188
Kaiser Foundation Hospitals	6324	D	408 972-6560	8309
Kaiser Foundation Hospitals	6324	C	408 972-3376	8330
Valley Health Plan	6324	A	408 885-4760	8371
Chicago Title Company	6361	C	408 292-4212	8436
Chelbay Schuler & Chelbay (PA)	6371	D	408 288-4400	8460
Melita-Mcdonald Insur Svcs Inc	6411	D	408 882-0800	8611
Johnson Service Group Inc	6512	A	408 728-9510	8729
Irvine APT Communities LP	6513	C	408 943-1595	8832
Westlake Development Group LLC	6513	D	408 251-2746	8872
Mobilehome Communities America	6515	D	408 298-3230	8880
Coldwell Banker RE LLC	6531	D	408 723-3300	8939
Cushman & Wakefield Cal Inc	6531	B	408 572-4134	8961
Cushman & Wakefield Cal Inc	6531	B	408 436-5500	8964
Cushman & Wakefield Cal Inc	6531	C	415 397-1700	8971
Insignia/Esg Ht Partners Inc	6531	B	408 288-2900	9050
Onerent Inc	6531	D	408 675-5490	9113
Steelwave LLC	6552	A	408 564-7678	9277
Nxs Holding Corp	6719	C	408 791-3300	9325
Netapp Capital Solutions Inc	6726	D	408 822-6000	9404
Tivo Corporation (HQ)	6794	D	408 519-9100	9458
Granite Rick Co	6799	C	831 768-2000	9514
Avr San Jose Downtown Ht LLC	7011	D	408 924-0900	9623
Garden City Inc	7011	A	408 244-3333	9807
Hayes Mansion Conference Ctr	7011	D	408 226-3200	9842
Marriott Hotel Services Inc	7011	B	408 280-1300	10002
San Jose Fairmont Lessee LLC	7011	B	408 998-1900	10200
San Jose Lessee LLC	7011	D	408 453-4000	10201
Santana Row Hotel Partners LP	7011	D	408 551-0010	10210
Stay Cal San Jose LLC	7011	C	408 275-2147	10277
West Hotel Partners LP	7011	C	408 947-4450	10361
West San Crlos Ht Partners LLC	7011	D	408 990-0400	10362
Buena Vista Business Svcs LP (PA)	7231	D	908 452-9002	10495
Ocbang Inc	7299	D	650 625-7908	10564
Firsthive Tech Corporation	7311	D	408 368-3424	10613
H&H Resolution LLC	7322	D	408 362-2293	10743
Far Western Graphics Inc	7334	D	408 481-9777	10788
Harding Mktg Cmmunications Inc (PA)	7336	D	408 345-4545	10810
Agurto Corporation	7342	C	408 564-6196	10828
Homeguard Incorporated (PA)	7342	D	855 331-1900	10837

Employee Codes: A=Over 500 employees, B=251-500
C=101-250, D=51-100, E=20-49, F=10-19, G=1-9

SAN JOSE CA — GEOGRAPHIC SECTION

Company	SIC	EMP	PHONE	ENTRY#
Natural Orange Inc.	7342	D	408 963-6868	10838
Rentokil North America Inc.	7342	D	408 293-6032	10840
Brilliant General Maint Inc (PA)	7349	D	408 287-6708	10865
C&W Facility Services Inc.	7349	A	408 600-4169	10869
Customized Performance Inc.	7349	C	408 437-1720	10887
Facility Masters Inc (PA)	7349	C	408 436-9090	10895
Flagship Airport Services Inc (HQ)	7349	C	408 977-0155	10896
Flagship Facility Services Inc (HQ)	7349	B	408 977-0155	10898
Flagship Facility Services Inc (HQ)	7349	C	408 977-0155	10899
Fluor Facility & Plant Svcs.	7349	C	408 256-1333	10901
Janpro Inc.	7349	C	408 293-7679	10913
Moreno & Associates Inc.	7349	D	408 924-0353	10933
Property Maintenance Company (PA)	7349	C	408 297-7849	10950
San Jose Unified School Dst.	7349	D	408 535-6200	10957
Santa Clara Valley Corporation.	7349	D	408 947-1100	10958
Significant Cleaning Svcs LLC	7349	C	408 559-5959	10967
Universal Bldg Svcs & Sup Co.	7349	D	408 995-5111	10982
United Site Services Cal Inc.	7359	C	408 295-2263	11059
40 Hrs Inc.	7361	A	408 414-0158	11067
Crowdstaffing.	7361	D	844 467-2300	11116
Josephines Prof Staffing Inc (PA)	7361	C	408 943-0111	11159
Pds Defense Inc.	7361	D	408 916-4848	11197
Peak Technical Services Inc.	7361	B	855 650-7325	11199
Randstad Professionals Us LLC	7361	D	408 573-1111	11215
Slingshot Connections LLC.	7361	D	408 247-8233	11231
Staffing Solutions Inc.	7361	D	408 980-9000	11237
Talent Space Inc.	7361	D	408 330-1900	11242
Goodwill of Silicon Valley (PA)	7363	D	408 998-5774	11288
SE Scher Corporation.	7363	A	408 844-0772	11329
Sfn Group Inc.	7363	A	408 526-0115	11333
Sfn Group Inc.	7363	A	408 452-4845	11336
22nd Century Technologies Inc.	7371	B	866 537-9191	11365
4d Inc.	7371	C	408 557-4600	11369
Aidash Inc (PA)	7371	C	408 703-1099	11389
Akkodis Inc.	7371	B	408 441-7144	11393
Arrcus Inc.	7371	D	408 884-1965	11425
Automation Anywhere Inc (PA)	7371	B	888 484-3535	11435
Balbix Inc.	7371	D	866 936-3180	11448
Bea Systems Inc (HQ)	7371	A	650 506-7000	11451
Behaviosec Inc.	7371	B	833 248-6732	11452
Beta Soft Systems Inc.	7371	C	408 766-0000	11454
Bristlecone Incorporated.	7371	A	650 386-4000	11476
Cohesity Inc (PA)	7371	B	855 926-4374	11503
Econosoft Inc.	7371	D	408 442-3663	11561
Einfochips Inc (HQ)	7371	D	408 496-1882	11566
Fcs Software Solutions Limited.	7371	D	408 324-1203	11594
Financialforcecom Inc (PA)	7371	A	866 743-2220	11599
Forescout Technologies Inc (PA)	7371	A	408 213-3191	11604
Glassbeam Inc.	7371	D	408 740-4600	11622
Icann Inc.	7371	D	408 432-8818	11654
Inspira Inc.	7371	C	408 247-9500	11668
International Bus Mchs Corp.	7371	A	408 463-2000	11677
Iscs Inc.	7371	C	408 362-3000	11681
Ixsystems Inc (PA)	7371	C	408 943-4100	11684
Lambda Inc.	7371	C	650 741-0738	11701
Loglogic Inc.	7371	C	408 215-5900	11716
Magma Design Automation Inc (HQ)	7371	B	408 565-7500	11725
Magma Design Automation Inc.	7371	D	408 432-7288	11726
Mavenir International Holdings Inc.	7371	D	408 855-2900	11738
Minerva Networks Inc (PA)	7371	D	800 806-9594	11750
One Convergence Inc.	7371	D	669 292-5251	11794
Panasas Inc (PA)	7371	D	408 215-6800	11810
Pernixdata Inc.	7371	D	408 724-8413	11822
Playphone Inc.	7371	D	408 261-6200	11837
Polaris Networks Incorporated.	7371	D	408 625-7273	11838
Pulse Secure LLC (DH)	7371	D	408 372-9600	11852
Ready Price LLC.	7371	A	408 357-0931	11864
Resonate I Inc (PA)	7371	D	408 545-5500	11877
Retailnext Inc (PA)	7371	C	408 884-2162	11878
Roadster Inc.	7371	A	833 568-5968	11885
Securiti Inc (PA)	7371	C	408 401-1160	11908
Skybox Security Inc (PA)	7371	D	408 441-8060	11919
Skylite Networks.	7371	D	408 934-9349	11920
SLI Systems Inc.	7371	D	408 255-2487	11921
Sperasoft Inc.	7371	B	408 715-6615	11939
Threatmetrix Inc (DH)	7371	C	408 200-5700	11977
V2solutions Inc.	7371	D	408 981-3075	12009
Vcomply Technologies Inc.	7371	D	650 319-8842	12013
Weride Corp.	7371	C	408 645-7118	12038
Whi Solutions Inc (HQ)	7371	D	914 697-9301	12039
Xgrid Inc.	7371	C	408 242-7937	12053
Zoom Video Communications Inc (PA)	7371	A	888 799-9666	12068
Zscaler Inc (PA)	7371	A	408 533-0288	12069
Adobe Inc (PA)	7372	A	408 536-6000	12077
Aptiv Digital LLC.	7372	D	818 295-6789	12096
Bill Holdings Inc (PA)	7372	B	650 621-7700	12115
Billcom LLC (HQ)	7372	C	650 353-3301	12116
Cadence Design Systems Inc (PA)	7372	A	408 943-1234	12129
Cato Networks Inc.	7372	D	646 975-9243	12131
Ciphercloud Inc (HQ)	7372	C	408 687-4350	12136
Cisco Systems LLC (HQ)	7372	B	650 989-6500	12137
Demandwhiz LLC.	7372	D	408 600-2720	12161
Former Nt Corp.	7372	D	330 702-3070	12194
Golinks Enterprises Inc.	7372	C	562 715-4848	12208
Hpe Enterprises LLC (HQ)	7372	C	650 857-5817	12225
Kranem Corporation.	7372	C	650 319-6743	12253
McAfee LLC (DH)	7372	C	888 847-8766	12264
McAfee Corp (HQ)	7372	C	866 622-3911	12265
Metricstream Inc (PA)	7372	C	650 620-2955	12271
Montavista Software LLC (DH)	7372	D	408 572-8000	12274
Numerical Technologies Inc.	7372	C	408 919-1910	12295
Nutanix Inc (PA)	7372	A	408 216-8360	12297
Plx Technology Inc (DH)	7372	C		12322
Signifyd Inc.	7372	B	866 220-1415	12349
Smartlogic Semaphore Inc.	7372	C	408 213-9500	12354
Sony Biotechnology Inc.	7372	D	800 275-5963	12359
Stellar Cyber Inc.	7372	D	408 548-0860	12364
Trackonomy Systems Inc (PA)	7372	B	833 872-2566	12382
Yuja Inc.	7372	C	888 257-2278	12407
Activevideo Networks LLC (DH)	7373	D	408 931-9200	12414
Cadent Inc.	7373	C	408 470-1000	12429
Cast Iron Systems Inc.	7373	D	914 499-1900	12431
Diligente Technologies LLC.	7373	B	510 304-0852	12448
Force10 Networks Global Inc.	7373	A	800 289-3355	12456
Ictv.	7373	D	408 931-9200	12467
Korea Trade and Inv Prom Agcy.	7373	C	408 432-5000	12476
Mobica US Inc.	7373	A	650 450-6654	12493
Northrop Grumman Space & Mission Sy.	7373	A	703 280-2900	12502
Ubiquiti Networks Inc.	7373	C	408 942-3085	12539
Cyber Infrastructure Inc.	7374	D	408 364-6849	12561
Maintenancenet LLC.	7374	A	408 526-4000	12590
Rackspace Hosting Inc.	7374	B	201 792-1918	12613
Truelite Trace Inc.	7374	D	833 663-5338	12637
Corventis Inc.	7375	C	408 790-9300	12655
Jeppesen Dataplan Inc.	7375	A	408 961-2825	12669
A10 Networks Inc (PA)	7379	A	408 325-8668	12717
Acer America Corporation (DH)	7379	A	408 533-7700	12720
Biarca Inc (PA)	7379	D	408 564-4465	12743
Idea Solutions Inc.	7379	A	408 436-3800	12804
Infostride Inc.	7379	D	415 360-1700	12811
Kenna Security Inc.	7379	C	855 474-7546	12823
Mezmo Inc.	7379	C	408 471-9997	12838
Mips Tech LLC.	7379	D	408 530-5000	12839
Nagarro Inc (PA)	7379	C	408 436-6170	12842
Simility LLC.	7379	D	650 351-7592	12876
Systech Integrators Inc.	7379	C	408 441-2700	12888
Tech Mahindra Cerium Systems.	7379	D	408 623-0787	12893
Thales Esecurity Inc (HQ)	7379	D	408 433-6000	12895
Wazuh Inc (PA)	7379	C	844 349-2984	12906
Xcommerce Inc (HQ)	7379	D	310 954-8012	12909
Creative Security Company Inc.	7381	B	408 295-2600	12957
Cypress Security LLC.	7381	D	408 217-6063	12962
Orion Security Patrol Inc.	7381	B	408 287-4411	13013
Security Indust Spcialists Inc.	7381	A	408 247-0100	13037
Silicon Vly SEC & Patrol Inc (PA)	7381	C	408 267-1539	13046
Universal Services America LP.	7381	A	408 993-1965	13067
Yosh Enterprises Inc (PA)	7381	C	408 287-4411	13080
First Alarm SEC & Patrol Inc (PA)	7382	C	408 866-1111	13119
Pacific West Security Inc.	7382	D	801 748-1034	13136
Bad Boys Bail Bonds Inc (PA)	7389	D	408 298-3333	13207
Cisco Systems Capital Corp (HQ)	7389	C	610 386-5870	13232
Cisco Webex LLC (HQ)	7389	D	408 526-4000	13233
Paypal Inc (HQ)	7389	B	877 981-2163	13422
Paypal Holdings Inc (PA)	7389	A	408 967-1000	13423
Proplus Design Solutions Inc (PA)	7389	C	408 459-6128	13436
Santa Clara County of.	7389	C	408 793-6410	13464
Team San Jose.	7389	A	408 295-9600	13502
Classic Parking Inc.	7521	C	408 278-1444	13604
Caliber Bodyworks Texas Inc.	7532	D	408 972-0300	13634
Aligntech.	7538	D	714 605-7114	13655
Lark Avenue Car Wash.	7542	D	408 371-2565	13697
Nsg Technology Inc.	7629	B	408 547-8770	13742
Kettmann Machining Inc.	7699	C	408 727-5538	13777
Century Theatres Inc.	7832	C	408 226-2251	13983
Imax Corporation.	7832	D	408 294-8324	13999
Aramark Spt & Entrmt Group LLC.	7929	D	408 999-5735	14077

GEOGRAPHIC SECTION

SAN JUAN CAPISTRANO CA

	SIC	EMP	PHONE	ENTRY#
Earthquakes Soccer LLC	7941	D	408 556-7700	14135
San Jose Sharks LLC **(PA)**	7941	C	408 999-6810	14158
Sharks Sports & Entrmt LLC	7941	A	408 287-7070	14160
Almaden Valley Athletic Club	7991	D	408 445-4900	14171
City of San Jose	7992	D	408 441-4653	14252
Traditions Golf LLC	7992	D	408 323-5200	14294
Festival Fun Parks LLC	7996	C	408 238-9900	14303
Almaden Golf & Country Club	7997	D	408 323-4812	14319
San Jose Country Club	7997	D	408 258-4901	14440
Silver Creek Vly Cntry CLB Inc	7997	D	408 239-5775	14454
Villages Golf and Country Club	7997	D	408 274-4400	14477
San Jose Arena Management LLC	7999	D	408 279-6000	14561
Santa Clara Cnty Frgrnds MGT C	7999	D	408 494-3100	14563
Winchester Mystery House LLC	7999	D	408 247-2101	14586
Chme Inc	8011	D	650 931-8713	14685
County of Santa Clara	8011	A	408 885-5000	14719
Foothill Health Center Inc	8011	C	408 729-4290	14752
Gardner Family Hlth Netwrk Inc	8011	C	408 254-5197	14757
Indian Hlth Ctr Snta Clara Vly	8011	C	408 445-3400	14782
Kaiser Foundation Hospitals	8011	A	408 972-7000	14817
Kaiser Foundation Hospitals	8011	C	408 972-3000	14852
OConnor Hospital	8011	C	408 947-2804	14931
Permanente Medical Group Inc	8011	B	408 972-6883	14966
Santa Clara Valley Medical Ctr	8011	A	408 885-6300	15046
Santa Clara Valley Medical Ctr	8011	A	408 792-5586	15047
Clearchoice MGT Svcs LLC	8021	D	408 288-7710	15222
A Is For Apple Inc	8049	C	877 991-0009	15267
American-Way Services Corp	8051	C	408 223-8912	15325
Aquinas Corporation	8051	C	408 248-7100	15330
Mariner Health Care Inc	8051	C	408 298-3950	15565
Mariner Health Care Inc	8051	D	408 377-9275	15576
Ocadian Care Centers LLC	8051	B	408 295-2665	15608
SSC San Jose Operating Co LP	8051	A	408 249-0344	15680
Crestwood Behavioral Hlth Inc	8059	C	408 275-1067	15837
Institute On Aging	8059	C	510 536-3377	15863
County of Santa Clara	8062	D	408 885-7470	16030
Good Samaritan Hospital LP **(DH)**	8062	A	408 559-2011	16110
Kaiser Foundation Hospitals	8062	D	408 363-4801	16157
Kaiser Foundation Hospitals	8062	C	408 972-6010	16166
Kaiser Foundation Hospitals	8062	C	408 972-6087	16185
Maternal Cnnctons El Cmino Hos	8062	D	650 988-8287	16251
OConnor Hospital	8062	C	408 947-2929	16291
OConnor Hospital **(HQ)**	8062	A	408 947-2500	16292
San Jose Healthcare System LP	8062	D	408 259-5000	16383
Stanford Health Care	8062	A	408 426-4900	16494
Verity Health System Cal Inc	8062	A	408 947-2500	16617
Asian Amercn Recovery Svcs Inc	8069	C	408 271-3900	16662
Bay Area Clinical Assoc PC	8069	D	408 996-7950	16666
El Camino Hospital	8069	C	650 988-4825	16680
Unilab Corporation	8071	A	408 927-8331	16764
Asian American Home Care Inc	8082	C	408 283-5100	16810
Kaiser Foundation Hospitals	8082	C	408 361-2100	16882
Maxim Healthcare Services Inc	8082	C	408 914-7478	16891
Prohealth Home Care Inc **(PA)**	8082	D	408 451-9055	16914
Satellite Healthcare Inc **(PA)**	8092	D	650 404-3600	16998
Behavior Frontiers LLC	8093	C	310 856-0800	17011
Ed Supports LLC	8093	D	201 478-8711	17059
Planned Prnthood Mar Monte Inc	8093	C	408 287-7532	17109
Santa Clara County of	8099	C	408 362-9817	17321
Santa Clara Valley Medical Ctr	8099	A	408 885-5730	17322
Hopkins & Carley A Law Corp **(PA)**	8111	D	408 286-9800	17496
Christian Milpitas School **(PA)**	8211	D	408 945-6530	17702
Metropolitan Education Dst **(PA)**	8211	D	408 723-6464	17728
Catholic Chrties Snta Clara CN	8322	C	408 282-8600	17867
Catholic Chrties Snta Clara CN **(PA)**	8322	D	408 468-0100	17868
County of Santa Clara	8322	B	408 299-5437	17940
Downtown Streets Inc	8322	D	650 462-1795	17958
Health Trust	8322	D	408 513-8700	17999
Jay Nolan Community Svcs Inc	8322	C	408 293-5002	18023
Outreach & Escort Inc **(PA)**	8322	D	408 678-8585	18075
San Andreas Regional Center **(PA)**	8322	C	408 374-9960	18109
Tupaz Day Care Services Inc	8322	D	408 377-1622	18156
Unity Care Group	8322	D	408 971-9822	18162
Center For Employment Training **(PA)**	8331	D	408 287-7924	18217
San Jose Conservation Corps	8331	D	408 283-7171	18247
Work2future Foundation	8331	C	408 216-6202	18264
Work2future Foundation	8331	C	408 794-1234	18265
Challenger Schools	8351	C	408 723-0111	18278
Childrens Crative Lrng Ctr Inc	8351	B	408 978-1500	18288
Kidango Inc	8351	D	408 258-9129	18323
Kidango Inc	8351	D	408 353-0473	18325
Kids Haven	8351	C	408 274-8766	18327
Sjb Child Development Centers **(PA)**	8351	D	408 538-0200	18353

	SIC	EMP	PHONE	ENTRY#
Advent Group Ministries Inc	8361	D	408 281-0708	18367
Carlton Senior Living Inc	8361	C	408 972-1400	18384
Lincoln Glen Manor LLC	8361	C	408 267-1492	18473
Asian Amrcans For Cmnty Invlvm **(PA)**	8399	C	408 975-2730	18560
Supportlogic Inc **(PA)**	8399	D	408 471-4710	18629
San Jose Chld Discovery Museum	8412	D	408 298-5437	18672
San Jose Museum of Art Assn	8412	D	408 271-6840	18673
Tech Interactive **(PA)**	8412	C	408 795-6116	18677
Tech Interactive	8412	D	408 795-6168	18678
City of San Jose	8422	D	408 794-6400	18686
Cws Utility Services Corp	8611	D	408 367-8200	18706
Calif Schl Employees Assoc Rtre	8631	C	408 473-1000	18773
California Schl Employees Assn **(PA)**	8631	C	408 473-1000	18774
Seiu Local 521	8631	C	650 801-3500	18791
Young MNS Chrstn Assn Slcon Vl	8641	D	650 493-9622	19000
Young MNS Chrstn Assn Slcon Vl	8641	C	408 298-1717	19001
Young MNS Chrstn Assn Slcon Vl	8641	C	408 226-9622	19003
Young MNS Chrstn Assn Slcon Vl	8641	C	408 729-4223	19004
YWCA Golden Gate Silicon Vly	8641	D	408 295-4011	19009
Acer Cloud Technology Inc	8711	A	408 830-9809	19126
Acronics Systems Inc	8711	C	408 432-0888	19127
Alfa Tech Cnslting Engners Inc **(PA)**	8711	C	408 487-1200	19135
Applied Innovation Group Inc	8711	C	408 452-5716	19141
Biggs Cardosa Associates Inc **(PA)**	8711	C	408 296-5515	19152
Carter & Burgess Inc	8711	C	408 428-2010	19176
Engeo Incorporated	8711	C	408 574-4900	19214
Gener8 LLC **(PA)**	8711	D	650 940-9898	19238
Hntb Corporation	8711	C	408 451-7300	19255
Jacobs Engineering Group Inc	8711	D	408 436-4936	19278
Kaga Fei America Inc **(DH)**	8711	D		19292
Malema	8711		408 970-3419	19313
Qlm Inc	8711	C	408 265-0904	19367
Radius Product Development Inc	8711	B	408 361-6000	19371
Semiconductor Tooling Services LLC	8711	D	408 776-6646	19384
URS Group Inc	8711	D	408 297-9585	19427
Watlow Electric Mfg Co	8711	D	408 776-6646	19436
Abbott Strngham Lynch A Prof A	8721	C	408 377-8700	19529
Armanino LLP	8721	B	408 200-6400	19532
Bpm LLP	8721	C	408 961-6300	19540
County of Santa Clara	8721	C	408 885-7200	19557
County of Santa Clara	8721	C	408 885-7354	19558
Deloitte & Touche LLP	8721	B	408 704-4000	19561
Deloitte Tax LLP	8721	D	408 704-4000	19567
Ernst & Young LLP	8721	C	408 947-5500	19575
Pricewaterhousecoopers LLP	8721	A	408 817-3700	19623
RSM US LLP	8721	A	408 572-4440	19628
Ariosa Diagnostics Inc	8731	A	408 229-7500	19660
International Bus Mchs Corp	8731	B	408 927-1080	19712
Lab-Gistics LLC	8731	C	650 309-2627	19723
Labcyte Inc	8731	D	408 747-2000	19724
Solopower Inc	8731	C	503 388-3710	19772
Virident Systems Inc	8731	C	408 573-5000	19797
Global Industry Analysts Inc	8732	C	408 528-9966	19813
Complete Genomics Inc **(HQ)**	8733	C	408 648-2560	19878
United Sttes Dept Enrgy Lvrmor	8733	A	408 267-1413	19927
Semiconductor Technologies Inc	8734	B	408 240-7000	19999
Related Management Corporation	8741	D	408 272-0356	20192
Deloitte Consulting LLP	8742	C	212 492-4000	20341
Ek Health Services Inc **(PA)**	8742	C	408 973-0888	20354
Latentview Analytics Corp	8742	D	408 493-6653	20431
Q Analysts LLC **(PA)**	8742	D	408 907-8500	20519
Tsmc North America **(HQ)**	8742	B	408 382-8000	20596
Global Infotech Corporation	8748	D	408 567-0600	20764
Mackin Consultancy LLC	8748	C	828 755-4073	20802
Peopleshores Pbc	8748	D	408 431-4686	20828
San Jose Redevelopment Agency	8748	D	408 535-8500	20845
County of Santa Clara	9512	D	408 224-7476	20946

SAN JUAN BAUTISTA, CA - San Benito County

	SIC	EMP	PHONE	ENTRY#
Speedling Incorporated	0181	D	813 645-3221	156
Earthbound Farm LLC **(PA)**	0723	A	831 623-7880	263
Willis Construction Co Inc	3272	C	831 623-2900	2709

SAN JUAN CAPISTRANO, CA - Orange County

	SIC	EMP	PHONE	ENTRY#
Devil Mountain Whl Nurs LLC	0181	D	949 496-9356	123
Brightview Landscape Svcs Inc	0781	D	714 546-7843	401
Fluidmaster Inc **(PA)**	3089	C	949 728-2000	2672
Quest Diagnostics Nichols Inst **(HQ)**	3826	A	949 728-4000	3032
Solag Incorporated	4953	A	949 728-1206	4937
Mission Volkswagen	5511	C	949 493-4511	7260
Freedom Properties-Hemet LLC	6512	C	949 489-0430	8721
Rancho Mission Viejo LLC	6531	D	949 240-3363	9150
Marriott International Inc	7011	D	949 503-5700	10005

Employee Codes: A=Over 500 employees, B=251-500
C=101-250, D=51-100, E=20-50, F=10-19, G=1-9

SAN JUAN CAPISTRANO CA

	SIC	EMP	PHONE	ENTRY#
Diamond Peo LLC	7361	C	714 728-5186	11124
Medusind Solutions Inc (PA)	7389	D	949 240-8895	13368
Southern Cal Prmnnte Med Group	8011	C	949 234-2139	15085
Congaree Health Holdings LLC	8051	D	949 487-9500	15387
Diamond Vly Hlth Holdings LLC	8051	D	949 487-9500	15425
Endura Healthcare Inc	8051	C	949 487-9500	15448
Ensign Services Inc	8051	C	949 487-9500	15458
Ensign Southland LLC	8051	C	949 487-9500	15460
Grand Avenue Hlth Holdings LLC	8051	D	949 487-9500	15502
Summit Trail Hlth Holdings LLC	8051	D	949 487-9500	15685
Clarient Inc	8071	C	949 445-7300	16711
Nichols Inst Reference Labs (DH)	8071	A	949 728-4000	16738
Infospan	8742	A	949 260-9990	20412

SAN LEANDRO, CA - Alameda County

	SIC	EMP	PHONE	ENTRY#
Tree Sculpture Group	0782	D	510 562-4000	541
Eric F Anderson Incorporated	1542	D	510 430-8404	915
Silman Venture Corporation (PA)	1542	C	510 347-4800	1027
Acco Engineered Systems Inc	1711	C	510 346-4300	1333
Fidelity Home Energy Inc	1711	C	858 220-7784	1437
Aa/Acme Locksmiths Inc	1731	C	510 483-6584	1651
Brayer Electric Company (PA)	1731	D	800 581-2544	1686
H A Bowen Electric Inc	1731	C	510 483-0500	1742
St Francis Electric Inc	1731	D	510 639-0639	1850
St Francis Electric LLC	1731	C	510 639-0639	1851
TRM Corporation (PA)	1743	D	510 895-2700	1988
Roofing Constructors Inc	1761	C	415 648-6472	2082
State Roofing Systems Inc	1761	D	510 317-1477	2086
Johnson Western Gunite Company	1771	D	510 568-8112	2130
Penhall Company	1771	D	510 357-8810	2146
Bluewater Envmtl Svcs Inc	1795	D	510 346-8800	2230
Bigge Crane and Rigging Co (PA)	1796	C	510 638-8100	2246
Hub Parking Technology USA Inc	1799	D	510 483-7275	2285
Karcher Environmental Inc	1799	D	510 297-0180	2290
Kp LLC (PA)	2752	C	510 346-0729	2561
Peggy S Lane Inc	3088	D	510 483-1202	2669
Ariat International Inc (PA)	3199	A	510 477-7000	2687
A-Para Transit Corp	4111	C	510 562-5500	3119
Mv Transportation Inc	4111	A	510 351-1603	3164
American Medical Response Inc	4119	C	415 794-9204	3233
Royal Ambulance Inc	4119	C	877 995-6161	3292
Frank Ghiglione Inc	4212	D	510 483-2063	3392
Estes Express Lines	4213	C	510 635-0165	3472
Unity Courier Service Inc	4215	C	510 568-8890	3647
UPS Expedited Mail Svcs Inc	4215	B	510 297-4600	3648
UPS Expedited Mail Svcs Inc	4215	B	510 297-5029	3649
Travis Flight Service Inc	4581	D	707 437-4900	3919
Alameda County Industries LLC	4953	C	510 357-7282	4855
Koffler Elec Mech Apprtus Repr	5063	D	510 567-0630	5572
Peterson Holding Company (PA)	5082	D	510 357-6200	5796
Buckeye Fire Equipment Company	5084	B	510 483-1815	5823
Cummins West Inc	5084	B	510 351-6101	5828
Nan Fang Dist Group Inc	5084	D	510 297-5382	5847
Tk Elevator Corporation	5084	C	510 476-1900	5873
Alco Iron & Metal Co (PA)	5093	C	510 562-1107	6004
True Wrld Fods San Frncsco LLC	5146	D	510 352-8140	6488
Webers Quality Meats Inc	5147	D	510 635-9892	6508
Bay Cities Produce Inc	5148	C	510 346-4943	6514
American Bottling Company	5149	D	510 346-3777	6599
Shaw Bakers LLC	5149	B	650 273-1440	6668
Crossroad Services Inc	5199	B	714 728-3915	6899
Rof Ferrari Lending 1 LLC	5411	C	510 351-5520	7148
Ghirardelli Chocolate Company (DH)	5441	B	510 483-6970	7158
Nicholas K Corporation	5511	C	510 352-2000	7265
Concreteworks Studio Inc	5712	D	510 534-7141	7420
Living Spaces Furniture LLC	5712	D	510 351-6783	7421
Floor & Decor Outlets Amer Inc	5713	D	510 394-9976	7431
Friant & Associates LLC (PA)	5932	D	510 535-5113	7533
Vivio Health Inc	6324	D	925 365-6600	8373
Farmers Insurance Exchange	6411	D	510 895-6000	8563
Propel Inc	6513	D	510 733-1700	8856
Vasona Management Inc	6513	D	510 352-8728	8867
Osisoft LLC (DH)	7371	B	510 297-5800	11804
East Bay Innovations	7389	D	510 618-1580	13275
Bae Systems Srra Dtroit Desl A (HQ)	7538	D	510 635-8991	13657
Applied Fusion LLC	7699	D	510 351-8314	13764
Kone Inc	7699	D	510 351-5141	13778
Kaiser Foundation Hospitals	8011	C	510 454-1000	14815
Permanente Medical Group Inc	8011	A	510 454-1000	14977
All Saintsidence Opco LLC	8051	B	510 481-3200	15322
San Leandro Hlth Care Ctr Inc	8051	D	510 357-4015	15652
Sutter Vsting Nrse Assn Hspice	8051	C	510 618-5277	15701
Marymount Villa LLC	8052	D	510 895-5007	15772
Maubertidence Opco LLC	8052	C	510 481-3200	15773
Sutter Health	8052	D	510 618-5200	15798
14766 Wash Ave Operations LLC	8059	D	510 352-2211	15807
Sanhyd Inc	8059	D	510 483-6200	15896
County of Alameda	8062	B	510 895-4200	16021
Kindred Healthcare Oper LLC	8062	B	510 357-8300	16205
San Leandro Hospital LP	8062	B	510 357-6500	16385
Washington Center LLC	8062	D	510 352-2211	16623
Bestliving Care LLC	8082	D	510 862-3508	16820
RES-Care Inc	8082	D	510 357-4222	16919
Sutter Vsting Nrse Assn Hspice	8082	C	510 895-4403	16941
Subacute Trtmnt For Adlscent R (PA)	8093	D	510 352-9200	17133
Davis Street Community Center (PA)	8322	D	510 347-4620	17949
Regional Center of E Bay Inc (PA)	8322	D	510 618-6100	18096
Cuberg Inc	8731	C	510 725-4200	19674
L3 Applied Technologies Inc	8731	D	510 577-7100	19722
Contemporary Services Corp	8742	A	650 524-8889	20326
McIntyre	8742	D	510 614-5890	20458

SAN LORENZO, CA - Alameda County

	SIC	EMP	PHONE	ENTRY#
Aidells Sausage Company Inc	2013	A	510 614-5450	2341
Oakland Pallet Company Inc (PA)	5031	C	510 278-1291	5177

SAN LUIS OBISPO, CA - San Luis Obispo County

	SIC	EMP	PHONE	ENTRY#
Mainstream Energy Corporation	1711	B	805 528-9705	1495
Rec Solar Commercial Corp	1711	C	844 732-7652	1545
Specialty Construction Inc	1731	C	805 543-1706	1845
R H Strasbaugh (PA)	3541	D	805 541-6424	2781
Zoo Med Laboratories Inc	3999	C	805 542-9988	3114
First Transit Inc	4111	D	805 544-2730	3138
San Luis Obispo Rgnal Trnst Aut	4111	D	805 781-4465	3202
San Luis Ambulance Service Inc	4119	C	805 543-2626	3294
Meathead Movers Inc (PA)	4213	D	805 544-6328	3515
American West Worldwide Ex Inc (PA)	4214	D	800 788-4534	3579
Eschat	4812	D	805 541-5044	4216
Ksby Communications LLC	4833	C	805 541-6666	4447
Pacific Gas and Electric Co	4911	C	805 545-4562	4619
Integrated Health Concepts Inc	5122	D	866 239-3784	6113
Amk Foodservices Inc	5141	C	805 544-7600	6239
All About Produce Company	5148	D	805 543-9000	6513
Berry Man Inc	5148	D	805 543-9000	6515
Madonna Inn Inc	5461	D	805 543-3000	7159
Apple Farm Collections-Slo Inc (PA)	5812	B	805 544-2040	7456
Gaigaew Inc	5812	D	805 545-5996	7483
Goodwill Central Coast	5932	C	805 544-0542	7536
Mission Community Bancorp	6021	C	805 782-5000	7632
Sesloc Federal Credit Union (PA)	6061	C	805 543-1816	7804
Guaranteed Rate Inc	6162	C	805 550-6933	7976
Merrill Lynch Prce Fnner Smith	6211	D	805 596-2222	8142
Morris Grritano Insur Agcy Inc	6411	D	805 543-6887	8616
Harvest Management Sub LLC	6513	A	805 543-0187	8816
King Ventures	6552	C	805 544-4444	9256
Sycamore Mineral Spring Resort	7011	D	805 595-7302	10296
Travelodge Downtown	7011	D	805 543-6443	10318
USA Staffing Inc	7363	D	805 269-2677	11344
Dzkicorp Inc	7371	D	805 464-0573	11558
Land Gorilla LLC	7371	D	805 242-5847	11702
Dozuki	7372	D	805 464-0573	12165
Lockheed Martin Unmanned	7373	D	805 503-4340	12480
Mindbody Inc (PA)	7374	C	877 755-4279	12599
San Luis Obispo Golf Cntry CLB	7997	D	805 543-3400	14441
Bayshore Healthcare Inc	8051	C	805 544-5100	15351
Compass Health Inc	8051	C	805 543-0210	15381
County of San Luis Obispo	8062	D	805 781-4753	16029
French Hospital Medical Center (DH)	8062	B	805 543-5353	16095
Sierra Vista Hospital Inc (HQ)	8062	A	805 546-7600	16428
Community Action Prtnr San Lui	8093	D	805 544-2478	17031
Transitions - Mental Hlth Assn	8093	D	805 540-6500	17144
Booth Mitchel & Strange LLP	8111	D	805 400-0703	17391
Associated Students Inc (PA)	8322	D	805 756-1281	17840
Community Action Partnership	8322	D	805 541-4122	17889
Life Steps Foundation Inc	8322	D	805 549-0150	18043
Lumina Alliance	8322	D	805 781-6400	18048
Tri-Cnties Assn For Dvlpmntlly	8322	C	805 543-2833	18155
United Crbral Plsy Assn San Lu	8322	D	805 543-2039	18161
Community Action Prtnr San Lui (PA)	8351	D	805 544-4355	18297
Community Action Prtnr San Lui	8351	C	805 541-2272	18298
Family Care Network Inc (PA)	8351	D	805 503-6240	18314
State Bar of California	8621	D	805 544-7551	18765
San Luis Obispo County YMCA	8641	D	805 544-7225	18905
Automobile Club Southern Cal	8699	D	805 543-6454	19040
AME Unmanned Air Systems Inc	8711	D	805 541-4448	19137
Ashley & Vance Engineering Inc	8711	D	805 545-0010	19146

GEOGRAPHIC SECTION

SAN MATEO CA

	SIC	EMP	PHONE	ENTRY#
Trust Automation Inc.	8711	D	805 544-0761	19420
Rrm Design Group (PA)	8712	D	805 439-0442	19503
Cannon Corporation (PA)	8713	D	805 544-7407	19523
Aviation Consultants Inc (PA)	8741	D	805 782-9722	20028
Entegris Inc.	8741	D	805 541-9299	20082
Postalio Inc.	8742	D	408 616-9284	20510
Rincon Consultants Inc.	8748	C	805 547-0900	20842

SAN MARCOS, CA - San Diego County

	SIC	EMP	PHONE	ENTRY#
San Diego Farms LLC	0191	C	760 736-4072	197
Hollandia Dairy Inc (PA)	0241	C	760 744-3222	217
Shasta Landscaping Inc.	0781	D	760 744-6551	462
Doose Landscape Incorporated	0782	D	760 591-4500	487
Rentokil North America Inc.	0782	D	858 689-9161	532
20/20 Plumbing & Heating Inc.	1711	D	760 535-3101	1328
Csi Electrical Contractors Inc.	1731	B	760 227-0577	1714
Sol Nova Electric LLC	1731	C	833 765-6682	1840
Southern Contracting Company	1731	C	760 744-0760	1843
M Bar C Construction Inc.	1791	D	760 744-4131	2187
Fish House Foods Inc.	2092	B	760 597-1270	2421
Winchster Intrcnnect CM CA Inc.	3357	C	800 848-4257	2726
Hughes Circuits Inc (PA)	3672	D	760 744-0300	2907
Spinergy Inc.	3751	D	760 496-2121	2996
Vallecitos Water District Financing (HQ)	4941	D	760 744-0460	4843
Hunter Industries Incorporated (PA)	4971	C	760 744-5240	4989
Sumitomo Elc Intrcnnect Pdts I	5063	D	760 761-0600	5595
La Provence Inc.	5149	C	760 736-3299	6642
Southern Cal Disc Tire Co Inc.	5531	C	760 744-3526	7363
Bestop Baja LLC	5571	C	760 560-2252	7396
Osf International Inc.	5812	D	760 471-0155	7500
Severson Group LLC	5812	C	760 550-9976	7508
Centurion Group Inc (PA)	6211	C	760 471-8536	8074
Americare Hlth Retirement Inc.	6512	C	760 744-4484	8701
Chateau Lk San Mrcos Hmwners A	6513	C	760 471-0083	8799
Whv Resort Group Inc (HQ)	6531	C	760 652-4913	9218
Golden Door Properties LLC	7011	C	760 744-5777	9810
Whv Resort Properties Inc.	7011	D	760 481-7739	10369
Corkys Pest Control Inc.	7342	D	760 432-8801	10835
Diamond Environmental Svcs LP	7359	C	760 744-7191	11028
Blast Motion Inc.	7371	D	760 803-2724	11463
Rgis LLC	7389	C	760 736-9241	13447
Control Air Enterprises LLC	7623	B	760 744-2727	13726
North County Health Prj Inc (PA)	8011	C	760 736-6755	14923
Rancho Physical Therapy Inc.	8049	C	760 752-1011	15303
Plum Healthcare Group LLC	8051	C	760 471-0388	15629
Casa De Amparo (PA)	8361	D	760 754-5500	18387
ARC of San Diego	8399	B	760 740-6800	18559
Primary Care Assod Med Group I (PA)	8741	C	760 471-7505	20180
Chicexecs	8743	D	760 484-2116	20633
Olympus Building Services Inc.	8744	A	760 750-4629	20660
Kros-Wise	8748	C	619 607-2899	20794

SAN MARINO, CA - Los Angeles County

	SIC	EMP	PHONE	ENTRY#
Huntington Lib Art Cllctons BT	8231	B	626 405-2100	17791

SAN MARTIN, CA - Santa Clara County

	SIC	EMP	PHONE	ENTRY#
Hanson Drywall Inc.	1742	D	831 297-4581	1933
Cordevalle Golf Club LLC	7997	A	408 695-4500	14363

SAN MATEO, CA - San Mateo County

	SIC	EMP	PHONE	ENTRY#
Belectric Inc.	1629	D	510 896-3940	1288
Tesla Energy Operations Inc (HQ)	1711	A	888 765-2489	1583
Beigene Usa Inc.	2834	B	877 828-5568	2580
Cala Health Inc.	3845	D	415 890-3961	3073
Gopro Inc (PA)	3861	B	650 332-7600	3084
Kotobuki-Ya Inc.	4111	D	650 344-7955	3145
Total Airport Services LLC	4581	C	650 358-0144	3918
Pacific Bell Telephone Company	4812	A	650 572-6807	4222
Rakuten Usa Inc.	4813	D	650 383-1328	4335
Intelpeer Cloud Cmmnctions LLC (PA)	4899	C	650 525-9200	4538
Tile Inc (HQ)	5065	D	650 274-0676	5712
Smart & Final Stores LLC	5141	D	650 345-1335	6343
Commercial Fueling Network	5172	C	800 899-2236	6726
San Mateo Credit Union	6061	C	650 363-1725	7799
Upstart Network Inc.	6141	C	650 204-1000	7887
Merrill Lynch Prce Fnner Smith	6211	C	650 579-3050	8137
Franklin Resources (PA)	6282	B	650 312-2000	8200
California Casualty Mgt Co (HQ)	6331	C	650 574-4000	8380
Califrnia Cslty Indemnity Exch (PA)	6331	C	650 574-4000	8381
Camico Mutual Insurance Co (PA)	6351	D	800 652-1772	8428
Abd Insurance & Fncl Svcs Inc (PA)	6411	D	650 488-8565	8476
Amwins Connect Insur Svcs LLC (PA)	6411	D	650 348-4131	8488
Sequoia Bnefits Insur Svcs LLC (PA)	6411	D	650 369-0200	8660
David D Bohannon Organization (PA)	6512	D	650 345-8222	8714
Westlake Development Group LLC (PA)	6512	D	650 579-1010	8783
Essex Portfolio LP (HQ)	6513	B	650 655-7800	8809
Essex Property Trust Inc (PA)	6513	B	650 655-7800	8810
Auctioncom LLC	6531	C	949 609-5376	8907
Glenborough LLC (PA)	6531	C	650 343-9300	9024
Prometheus RE Group Inc (PA)	6531	C	650 931-3400	9146
Westlake Realty Group Inc (PA)	6531	C	650 579-1010	9217
Steelwave Inc (PA)	6552	C	650 571-2200	9275
Milestone Holdco Inc.	6719	A	650 376-2300	9321
Franklin Advisers Inc.	6722	A	650 312-2000	9369
Franklin Templeton Svcs LLC	6722	A	650 312-3000	9370
Franklin Tmpleton Inv Svcs LLC	6722	C	650 312-2100	9372
Forge Trust Co.	6733	D	650 591-3335	9426
Sunstone Partners LLC	6799	D	650 289-4400	9567
Sunstone Partners MGT LLC	6799	D	650 289-4400	9568
Atrium Plaza LLC	7011	D	650 653-6000	9621
Island Hospitality MGT LLC	7011	D	650 574-4700	9915
Freedom Financial Network LLC (PA)	7299	C	650 393-6619	10546
Isearch Media LLC	7311	D	415 358-0882	10634
City of San Mateo	7349	D	650 522-7300	10874
Barrett Business Services Inc.	7361	A	650 653-7588	11091
Maxim Healthcare Services Inc.	7363	D	410 910-1500	11306
Actuate Corporation (HQ)	7371	D	650 645-3000	11378
Alinor Holdings Inc.	7371	D	650 393-4865	11396
Brain Technologies Inc.	7371	B	650 918-2245	11473
Demandtec LLC	7371	B	914 499-1900	11538
Evidation Health Inc.	7371	C	650 389-2494	11585
Feedzai Inc.	7371	B	650 649-9486	11595
Genium Inc.	7371	C	415 935-3593	11617
Getfeedback Inc.	7371	D	888 684-8821	11618
Honor Technology Inc (PA)	7371	D	512 762-2195	11645
Humanapi Inc.	7371	D	650 542-9800	11648
Imperva Inc (HQ)	7371	D	650 345-9000	11657
Jupiter Intelligence Inc.	7371	D	650 477-2117	11689
Logigear Corporation (PA)	7371	A	650 572-1400	11715
Lohika Systems Inc.	7371	C	216 904-9751	11717
Manticore Games Inc (PA)	7371	D	650 257-8177	11730
Marketo Inc (HQ)	7371	B	650 376-2303	11735
N Model Inc (PA)	7371	B	650 610-4600	11762
Relyance Inc.	7371	D	866 735-9623	11873
Super Evil Mega Corp (PA)	7371	D	650 696-0608	11956
Synarc Inc (DH)	7371	C	415 817-8900	11960
Turing Video	7371	D	877 730-8222	11996
Virtunet LLC	7371	D	650 847-8633	12024
Wise Commerce Inc.	7371	C	855 469-4737	12042
Coupa Software Incorporated (HQ)	7372	C	650 931-3200	12150
Freshworks Inc (PA)	7372	C	650 513-0514	12198
Gazillion Inc.	7372	B	650 393-6500	12201
Guidewire Software Inc (PA)	7372	C	650 357-9100	12216
Netsuite Inc (DH)	7372	A	650 627-1000	12285
Onesignal Inc (PA)	7372	C	408 506-0701	12302
Roblox Corporation (PA)	7372	C	888 858-2569	12339
Snaplogic Inc (PA)	7372	C	888 494-1570	12355
Successfactors Inc (DH)	7372	D		12368
Aryaka Networks Inc (PA)	7373	B	888 692-7925	12418
Lattice Engines Inc (DH)	7373	C	877 460-0010	12478
D E M Enterprises Inc.	7374	D	650 641-6200	12564
Keynote LLC	7374	B	650 376-3033	12585
Zynga Inc (HQ)	7374	C	855 449-9642	12647
Backblaze Inc.	7375	C	650 352-3738	12652
Neeva Inc.	7375	D	408 220-9086	12678
Accellion Inc.	7379	C	650 485-4300	12718
Treering Corporation	7379	D	650 385-8733	12898
Zinier Inc.	7379	C	787 504-4826	12912
Arkose Labs Holdings Inc (PA)	7382	C	415 917-8701	13097
Verkada Inc (PA)	7382	A	650 514-2500	13153
5 Palms LLC	7389	C	650 457-0539	13166
All About Parking	7521	D	650 508-8886	13601
Vyond	7812	D	888 360-9639	13912
Sony Interactive Entrmt LLC	7929	C	650 655-8000	14105
Peninsula Golf & Country Club	7997	D	650 638-2200	14423
A B C Pediatrics	8011	C	650 579-6500	14592
County of San Mateo	8011	A	650 208-3480	14717
County of San Mateo	8011	C	650 573-2662	14718
Permanente Medical Group Inc	8011	A	650 358-7000	14988
Elder Care Alliance San Mateo	8051	C	650 212-4400	15432
Mission Hospice & HM Care Inc.	8052	C	650 554-1000	15774
Sutter Health	8062	D	650 262-4262	16535
Sutter Care & Home	8082	D	650 685-2800	16938
Meru Health Holding Inc.	8093	D	760 841-8040	17092
St Matthews Episcopal Day Schl	8211	C	650 342-5436	17752
Bay Area Senior Services Inc.	8322	C	650 579-5500	17848

Employee Codes: A=Over 500 employees, B=251-500
C=101-250, D=51-100, E=20-50, F=10-19, G=1-9

2024 Directory of California
WholeSalers and Service Companies

© Mergent Inc. 1-800-342-5647
1499

SAN MATEO CA

GEOGRAPHIC SECTION

	SIC	EMP	PHONE	ENTRY#
Brightline Inc	8322	C	650 769-5810	17856
Center For Lrng Atism Spport S	8322	B	800 538-8365	17871
Peninsula Family Service (PA)	8351	D	650 403-4300	18343
Womens Rcvery Assn San Mteo CN	8621	C	650 348-6603	18769
Silicon Vly Cmnty Foundation	8641	C	650 458-2660	18910
Young MNS Chrstn Assn San Frnc	8641	C	650 286-9622	18993
Anita Borg Inst For Women Tech	8699	D	650 236-4756	19034
Delta Project Management Inc	8711	D	415 590-3202	19196
Helix Opco LLC	8731	C	415 805-3360	19706
Konica Minolta Laboratory USA Inc	8731	D	650 522-9619	19721
Inclin Inc (PA)	8732	D	650 961-3422	19820
Archives Management Corp (PA)	8741	C	650 544-2200	20025
Topia Mobility Inc (PA)	8742	D	415 666-2130	20585
Goalbook	8748	D	650 207-9388	20765

SAN PABLO, CA - Contra Costa County

	SIC	EMP	PHONE	ENTRY#
Lytton Rancheria	7011	A	510 215-7888	9992
Mariner Health Care Inc	8051	B	510 232-5945	15567
Vale Operating Company LP	8051	A	510 232-5945	15714
Doctors Medical Center LLC	8062	A	510 970-5000	16060
West Contra Costa Healthcare District	8082	A	510 970-5102	16975
Stand For Fmlies Free Volence	8322	D	510 964-7109	18141
Promab Biotechnologies Inc	8731	C	510 860-4615	19761

SAN PEDRO, CA - Los Angeles County

	SIC	EMP	PHONE	ENTRY#
State Fish Co Inc	2092	C	310 547-9530	2424
Larson Al Boat Shop	3731	D	310 514-4100	2994
Polar Tankers Inc	4424	C	310 519-8260	3800
Catalina Channel Express Inc (HQ)	4489	C	310 519-7971	3806
So Cal Ship Services	4489	D	310 519-8411	3809
Marine Terminals Corporation	4491	B	310 519-2300	3812
Port of Los Angeles	4491	B	310 732-3508	3815
Yusen Terminals LLC (DH)	4491	B	310 548-8000	3820
APM Terminals Pacific LLC	4731	B	310 221-4000	3986
Crowley Marine Services Inc	4731	B	310 732-6500	4001
Toll Global Fwdg Scs USA Inc	4731	C	732 750-9000	4108
Contessa Liquidating Co Inc	5142	C		6417
Qualy Pak Specialty Foods Inc	5146	C	310 541-3023	6478
Tri-Marine Fish Company LLC	5146	C	310 547-1144	6486
Select Home Warranty Ca Inc	6351	B	732 835-0110	8434
Meristar San Pedro Hilton LLC	7011	D	310 514-3344	10013
Spf Capital Real Estate LLC	7011	D	310 519-8200	10261
Fenix Marine Services Ltd (DH)	7359	C	310 548-8877	11032
Advent Resources Inc	7371	D	310 241-1500	11383
Patrol Black Knight Inc	7381	D	213 985-6499	13019
Little Ssters of The Poor Los	8051	D	310 548-0625	15546
San Pedro Convalescent HM Inc	8051	D	310 832-6431	15653
Seacrest Convalescent Hosp Inc	8051	D	310 833-3526	15658
San Pedro Peninsula Hospital	8062	A	310 832-3311	16386
Healthview Inc (PA)	8361	C	310 638-4113	18449
City of Los Angeles	9621	A	310 732-3734	20948

SAN RAFAEL, CA - Marin County

	SIC	EMP	PHONE	ENTRY#
Guide Dogs For Blind Inc (PA)	0752	C	415 499-4000	362
San Rafael Rock Quarry Inc (HQ)	1429	D	415 459-7740	635
Redhorse Constructors Inc	1542	D	415 492-2020	1005
Dutra Dredging Company (HQ)	1629	D	415 721-2131	1297
Dutra Group (PA)	1629	D	415 258-6876	1298
Allied Heating & Air Conditioning Co Inc	1711	D	415 459-5232	1348
GAF Energy LLC	1711	D	510 330-6870	1448
Jerry Thompson & Sons Pntg Inc	1721	D	415 454-1500	1625
Urban Painting Inc	1721	D	415 485-1130	1643
Idex Global Services Inc	1731	C	415 482-4242	1754
Ghilotti Bros Inc	1794	B	415 454-7011	2217
Maggiora and Ghilotti Inc	1794	C	415 459-8640	2222
First Student Inc	4151	C	415 455-9098	3337
Travel Wizard LLC	4724	D	415 446-5252	3955
Pasha Group (PA)	4731	B	415 927-6400	4073
Golden Gate Bridge High	4785	A	415 457-3110	4140
Marin Clean Energy	4911	D	415 464-6028	4586
Pacific Gas and Electric Co	4911	D	800 743-5000	4620
Marin Sanitary Service (PA)	4953	D	415 456-2601	4909
Marin Sanitary Service	4953	C	415 485-5646	4910
Jacksons Hardware Inc	5072	D	415 870-4083	5730
Cellmark Pulp & Paper Inc	5099	D	415 927-1700	6035
Mighty Leaf Tea	5149	D	415 491-2650	6647
Quaker Pet Group Inc	5199	D	415 721-7400	6941
Home Depot USA Inc	5211	D	415 458-8675	7027
Westamerica Bancorporation (PA)	6022	D	707 863-6000	7724
Managed Health Network (DH)	6324	B	415 460-8168	8345
Eah Elena Gardens LP	6513	C	415 295-8840	8803
Smith Rnch Hmes Hmeowners Assn	6513	D	415 492-4900	8862
Eah Inc (PA)	6514	D	415 258-1800	8877

	SIC	EMP	PHONE	ENTRY#
R C Roberts & Co (PA)	6515	C	415 456-8600	8881
Hotel McInnis Marin	7011	D	415 499-9222	9873
Interctive Med Specialists Inc	7363	D	415 472-4204	11293
Layline Automation	7371	D	415 758-0044	11703
Fair Isaac International Corp (HQ)	7372	A	415 446-6000	12188
Petroleum Sales Inc (PA)	7542	C	415 256-1600	13701
Century Theatres Inc	7832	A	415 448-8400	13984
Lucas Digital Ltd (DH)	7922	B	415 258-2000	14044
Kaiser Foundation Hospitals	8011	A	415 444-2000	14807
Permanente Medical Group Inc	8011	A	415 444-2000	14978
Cbem LLC Corporate Office	8049	D	415 454-3700	15272
Ghc of San Rafael LLC	8051	D	415 499-1000	15497
Mariner Health Care Inc	8051	C	415 479-3610	15575
Marinidence Opco LLC	8051	C	415 479-3450	15578
Ocadian Care Centers LLC	8051	B	415 499-1000	15607
Promedica Health System Inc	8052	C	415 472-2637	15785
Rafael Convalescent Hospital	8059	D	415 479-3450	15890
Kaiser Permanent	8062	C	415 492-6311	16195
Community Action Marin	8093	C	415 459-6330	17030
Muir Wood LLC	8099	D	310 903-1155	17279
Canal Alliance	8111	C	415 485-3074	17398
Marin County Office Education (PA)	8211	B	415 472-4110	17726
Miller Creek School District	8211	C	415 472-3776	17729
Bernard Osher Mrin Jwish Cmnty	8322	C	415 444-8000	17851
Casa Allegra Community Svcs	8322	C	415 499-1116	17861
Family Svc Agcy of Marin Cnty (PA)	8322	C	415 491-5700	17978
Integrated Community Services	8322	C	415 455-8481	18018
Jewish Family and Chld Svcs	8322	B	415 449-3862	18026
Lifehouse Inc (PA)	8322	C	415 472-2373	18044
Mhn Government Services LLC	8322	D	916 294-4941	18055
Vivalon	8322	C	415 454-0964	18172
Villa Marin Homeowners Assn	8641	C	415 499-8711	18928
Young MNS Chrstn Assn San Frnc	8641	C	415 492-9622	18991
Bacr	8699	B	415 444-5580	19069
Gilardi & Co LLC	8741	C	415 798-5900	20099
Enterprise Events Group Inc	8742	C	415 499-4444	20361
Kyo Autism Therapy LLC	8742	C	877 264-6747	20430
Pedersen Media Group Inc	8743	D	415 512-9800	20641
Golden Gate Nat Prks Cnsrvancy	8999	D	415 785-4787	20890

SAN RAMON, CA - Contra Costa County

	SIC	EMP	PHONE	ENTRY#
Bishop Ranch Veterinary Center	0742	D	925 743-9300	330
KB Home South Bay Inc	1522	D	925 983-2500	763
Tri Pointe Homes Inc	1522	C	925 804-2220	780
Legacy Mech & Enrgy Svcs Inc	1711	D	925 820-6938	1485
Chevron Corporation (PA)	2911	A	925 326-2189	2646
Chevron Global Energy Inc (HQ)	2911	D	925 842-1000	2647
Overland Storage Inc (HQ)	3572	B	408 283-4700	2818
J B Hunt Transport Inc	4213	C	866 759-1127	3496
Baco Realty Corporation	4225	D	925 275-0100	3678
AT&T Corp	4812	C	925 823-6949	4182
Enpower Management Corp	4911	D	925 244-1100	4578
Pacific Gas and Electric Co	4911	C	650 513-0700	4617
App Orchid Inc	5045	C	833 277-6724	5272
Endoscopic Technologies Inc	5047	C	925 866-7111	5413
Japonesque LLC	5122	C	925 866-6670	6115
Chevron Shipping Company LLC	5541	D	925 842-1000	7386
Chevron Stations Inc	5541	C	925 328-0292	7388
Texaco Inc (HQ)	5541	A	925 842-1000	7391
Cmg Financial Services	6162	A	925 983-3073	7951
Mason McDuffie Mortgage Corp (PA)	6162	C	925 242-4400	8000
Cmg Mortgage Inc (PA)	6163	B	619 554-1327	8036
Benefitstreet Inc	6411	D	925 831-0800	8509
Edgewood Partners Insur Ctr	6411	C	925 244-7700	8548
Edgewood Partners Insur Ctr	6411	C	925 244-7700	8550
Old Republic HM Protection Inc	6411	B	925 866-1500	8631
Sunset Development Company (PA)	6512	C	925 277-1700	8767
Homegaincom Inc	6531	D	925 983-2852	9040
Realty One Group BMC Assoc	6531	D	925 230-0700	9157
Brookfeld Bay Area Hldings LLC	6552	D	925 743-8000	9247
Ets-Esc Holdings LLC	6719	B	925 314-7100	9311
Courtyard By Marriott	7011	D	925 866-2900	9722
Hyatt Corporation	7011	B	925 743-1882	9894
Pac-12 Enteprises LLC	7313	C	415 580-4200	10717
Netpace Inc	7361	C	925 543-7760	11181
Plus Group Inc	7363	C	925 831-8551	11320
AMP Technologies LLC	7371	C	877 442-2824	11403
Good Technology Corporation (HQ)	7371	C	408 352-9102	11629
Lumin Digital LLC	7371	D	727 561-2227	11719
Spruce Technology Inc	7371	C	925 415-8160	11941
Accela Inc (PA)	7372	C	925 659-3200	12071
Blackberry Corporation (HQ)	7372	D	972 650-6126	12118
Cylance Inc (DH)	7372	D	949 375-3380	12155

GEOGRAPHIC SECTION

SANTA ANA CA

Company	SIC	EMP	PHONE	ENTRY#
Five9 Inc (PA)	7372	A	925 201-2000	12191
GE Digital LLC	7372	B	925 242-6200	12202
Reputationcom Inc (PA)	7372	B	800 888-0924	12335
Apttus Corporation (PA)	7373	A	650 445-7700	12417
Ecifm Solutions Inc	7373	C	925 830-1925	12450
Wavestrong Inc	7373	D	844 299-8264	12543
Grid Dynamics Intl LLC (HQ)	7379	C	650 523-5000	12800
Enterprise Rent-A-Car Co of San Fra (DH)	7514	D	925 464-5100	13579
Clubsport San Ramon LLC (PA)	7991	C	925 735-1182	14190
Bridges At Gale Ranch LLC	7992	D	925 735-4253	14246
Hill Physicians Med Group Inc (PA)	8011	B	800 445-5747	14773
Reproductive Science Center	8011	C	925 867-1800	15016
Adarsh Kaur DDS Inc	8021	C	530 892-1218	15215
San Ramon Regional Med Ctr LLC	8062	A	925 275-9200	16387
Castro Valley Health Inc	8082	C	510 690-1930	16835
Cvh Care	8082	C	650 393-5657	16854
Atlas Lift Tech Inc	8099	C	415 283-1804	17181
Berkeley Emrgncy Med Group Inc	8099	D	925 962-1067	17186
Donor Network West (PA)	8099	C	925 480-3100	17225
Skillsets Online Corporation	8331	C	925 964-0531	18249
Surplus Line Association Cal	8611	C	415 434-4900	18725
Carlson Barbee & Gibson Inc	8711	D	925 866-0322	19174
Armanino LLP	8721	C	925 790-2600	19533
Primed MGT Consulting Svcs Inc	8741	B	925 327-6710	20182
Energy Experts International	8742	D	925 242-0446	20358
Expressworks International LLC (PA)	8742	D	925 244-0900	20369
Atlas Technical Cons LLC	8748	B	925 314-7100	20695
Buxton Consulting	8748	C	925 467-0700	20712
Trident Consulting	8999	D	925 352-3885	20903

SAN SIMEON, CA - San Luis Obispo County

Company	SIC	EMP	PHONE	ENTRY#
Cavalier Inn Inc	7011	D	805 927-4688	9685

SANGER, CA - Fresno County

Company	SIC	EMP	PHONE	ENTRY#
Blue Diamond Growers	0723	D	559 251-4044	257
Cal Custom Tile	1743	D	559 875-1460	1975
Cobblestone Fruit	2033	C	559 524-1005	2352
D & D Cahill Inc	7389	D	559 708-7601	13255

SANTA ANA, CA - Orange County

Company	SIC	EMP	PHONE	ENTRY#
Bill & Daves Ldscp Maint Inc	0781	C	714 850-0213	392
Brightview Landscape Svcs Inc	0781	B	714 546-7843	407
Mission Ldscp Companies Inc	0781	C	714 545-9962	445
Nieves Landscape Inc	0781	C	714 835-7332	451
Southwest Landscape Inc	0781	D	714 545-1084	465
Landcare USA LLC	0782	D	949 559-7771	507
Mpl Enterprises Inc	0782	D	714 545-1717	523
John M Frank Construction Inc	1542	D	714 210-3600	949
McCarthy Bldg Companies Inc	1542	D	949 851-8383	967
Moorefield Construction Inc (PA)	1542	D	714 972-0700	972
Macro-Z-Technology Company (PA)	1611	D	714 664-1130	1131
Systems Paving Inc (PA)	1611	D	949 263-8301	1169
Oc 405 Partners Joint Venture	1622	D	858 251-2200	1187
Sukut Construction LLC	1623	D	714 540-5351	1269
Orange County Services Inc	1711	D	714 541-9753	1520
Pacific Rim Mech Contrs Inc	1711	C	714 285-2600	1522
Sterling Plumbing Inc	1711	D	714 641-5480	1571
Gps Painting Wallcovering Inc	1721	C	714 730-8904	1621
Sun Electric LP	1731	D	714 210-3744	1855
Prime Tech Cabinets Inc	1751	C	949 757-4900	2011
Trimco Finish Inc	1751	C	714 708-0300	2022
Tecta America Southern Cal Inc	1761	D	714 973-6233	2088
Reed Thomas Company Inc	1794	D	714 558-7691	2224
Sukut Construction Inc	1794	C	714 540-5351	2226
The Sweet Life Enterprises Inc	2041	C	949 261-7400	2360
Heritage Paper Co (HQ)	2653	D	714 540-9737	2515
McDonald Packaging Inc	2653	C		2521
2100 Freedom Inc (HQ)	2711	C	714 796-7000	2535
Freedom Communications Inc	2711	A	714 796-7000	2537
Robinson Pharma Inc	2834	C	714 241-0235	2608
Yokohama Corp North America (HQ)	3011	C	540 389-5426	2653
CD Video Manufacturing Inc	3695	D	714 265-0770	2952
Undersea Systems Intl Inc	3699	D	714 754-7848	2964
Impco Technologies Inc (HQ)	3714	D	714 656-1200	2974
Thi Inc	3841	D	714 444-4643	3060
Certified Trnsp Svcs Inc	4142	D	714 835-8676	3316
Durham School Services L P	4173	B	714 542-8989	3355
RPM Transportation Inc (DH)	4213	D	714 388-3500	3534
Southwest Airlines Co	4512	D	949 252-5200	3846
Aviation Consultants Inc	4581	D	949 201-2550	3879
Transit Air Cargo Inc	4731	C	714 571-0393	4110
K Wave 1079	4832	D	714 918-6207	4388
Lbi Media Holdings Inc	4832	B	714 554-5000	4392
Petes Road Service Inc	5014	D	714 545-5818	5072
Yokohama Tire Corporation (DH)	5014	C	714 870-3800	5076
Contractors Flrg Svc Cal Inc	5023	C	714 556-6100	5114
Foundation Building Mtrls Inc (HQ)	5031	C	714 380-3127	5157
Duplo USA Corporation (PA)	5044	D	949 752-8222	5245
Regal Technology Partners Inc	5045	D	714 835-1162	5341
Main Electric Supply Co LLC (PA)	5063	D	949 833-3052	5577
Ace Wireless & Trading Inc	5065	B	949 748-5700	5618
Hirsch Electronics LLC	5065	C	949 250-8888	5657
Rbc Transport Dynamics Corp	5085	C	203 267-7001	5921
Aftco Mfg Co Inc	5091	D	949 660-8757	5972
Vantage Custom Classics Inc	5136	C	714 755-1133	6193
Smart & Final Stores Inc	5141	B	714 549-2362	6294
Ingardia Bros Produce Inc	5148	C	949 645-1365	6559
Coastal Cocktails Inc (PA)	5149	D	949 250-8951	6615
Goglanian Bakeries Inc (HQ)	5149	B	714 338-1145	6631
Celmol Inc	5199	C	714 259-1000	6896
Home Depot USA Inc	5211	D	714 259-1030	6969
Home Depot USA Inc	5211	C	714 966-8551	7010
Crevier Classics LLC	5511	B	714 835-3171	7189
Toms Truck Center Inc	5511	C	714 835-1978	7314
Waxies Enterprises LLC	5999	D	714 545-8441	7600
Banc California National Assn (HQ)	6021	D	877 770-2262	7605
Banc of California Inc (PA)	6021	C	855 361-2262	7606
Orange Countys Credit Union (PA)	6061	D	714 755-5900	7788
Schoolsfirst Federal Credit Un (PA)	6061	B	714 258-4000	7802
Deutsche Bank National Tr Co	6091	D	714 247-6054	7837
Continental Currency Svcs Inc (PA)	6099	D	714 667-6699	7843
Home Mrtg Aliance Corp Hmac (PA)	6162	B	800 900-7040	7980
Homexpress Mortgage Corp	6162	C	714 944-3022	7982
Jmac Lending Inc	6162	D	949 345-1508	7986
Lenox Financial Mortgage Corp	6162	C	949 428-5100	7990
Turnkey Foundation Inc	6162	D	949 557-6203	8025
Tarbell Financial Corporation (PA)	6163	C	714 972-0988	8060
Admar Corporation	6324	C	714 953-9600	8274
Pacifcare Hlth Plan Admnstrtor (DH)	6324	B	714 825-5200	8350
State Compensation Insur Fund	6331	C	714 565-5000	8409
First American Financial Corp (PA)	6361	A	714 250-3000	8440
First American Mortgage Svcs	6361	D	714 250-4210	8441
First American Title Insur Co (HQ)	6361	B	800 854-3643	8443
Amwins Connect Insur Svcs LLC	6399	D	714 460-5153	8471
First Amrcn Prprty Insur Cslty	6411	C	949 477-7500	8569
H & H Agency Inc (PA)	6411	C	949 260-8840	8580
Seneca Family of Agencies	6411	B	714 881-8600	8657
Sureco Hlth Lf Insur Agcy Inc	6411	D	949 333-0263	8666
Domino Realty Management Co	6513	D	714 556-0466	8802
Argent Management LLC (PA)	6531	A	949 777-4000	8902
Argent Management LLC	6531	D	949 777-4070	8903
F M Tarbell Co (HQ)	6531	C	714 972-0988	9001
First American Data Co LLC	6531	D	714 250-6594	9005
Grubb & Ellis Company	6531	A	714 667-8252	9031
Grubb & Ellis Management Services Inc	6531	A	412 201-8200	9032
Satellite Management Co (PA)	6531	C	714 558-2411	9175
First American Title Company	6541	A	714 250-3109	9233
Property Insight LLC	6541	C	877 747-2537	9238
Skeffington Enterprises Inc	6719	D	714 540-1700	9336
2100 Trust LLC (PA)	6733	C	877 469-7344	9419
Chen & Huang Partners LP	7011	D	714 557-8700	9696
Jhc Investment Inc	7011	D	714 751-2400	9919
S W K Properties LLC	7011	C	714 481-6300	10185
Windsor Capital Group Inc	7011	C	714 241-3800	10375
Cintas Sales Corporation	7213	D	714 957-2852	10433
Optima Tax Relief LLC	7291	D	714 361-4636	10524
Debtmerica LLC	7299	D	714 389-4200	10540
Pps Parking Inc	7299	A	949 223-8707	10570
Dgwb Inc	7311	D	714 881-2300	10607
Precision Effect Inc	7311	D	800 634-5315	10663
Experian Corporation	7323	D	714 830-7000	10761
Financial Statement Svcs Inc (PA)	7331	C	714 436-3326	10772
Advanced Clnroom McRclean Corp	7349	D	714 751-1152	10849
Landmark Services Inc	7349	D	714 240-7913	10916
Merchants Building Maint Co	7349	B	714 973-9272	10926
Universal Services America LP	7349	A	714 923-3700	10983
County of Orange	7353	D	714 647-1552	10996
Executive Personnel Services	7361	B	714 310-9506	11135
L&T Staffing Inc (PA)	7361	C	714 558-1821	11168
Pds Defense Inc	7361	C	214 647-9600	11198
Cognizant Trztto Sftwr Group I	7373	C	714 481-0396	12436
Black Knight Infoserv LLC	7374	C	904 854-5100	12553
Compushare Inc	7374	C	714 427-1000	12559
Verys LLC	7379	C	949 423-3295	12904
Community Patrol Inc	7381	D	657 247-4744	12946
Guardsmark LLC (DH)	7381	D	714 619-9700	12985

Employee Codes: A=Over 500 employees, B=251-500
C=101-250, D=51-100, E=20-50, F=10-19, G=1-9

SANTA ANA CA

	SIC	EMP	PHONE	ENTRY#
Shield Security Inc (DH)	7381	B	714 210-1501	13041
Universal Prtction SEC Systems (DH)	7381	D	714 923-3700	13064
Dekra-Lite Industries Inc	7389	D	714 436-0705	13260
Fntech	7389	D	714 429-7833	13290
Fresh Grill LLC	7389	C	714 444-2126	13297
Orange Coast Title Company (PA)	7389	D	714 558-2836	13409
Partners Capital Group Inc (PA)	7389	D	949 916-3900	13419
Trans-Pak Incorporated	7389	C	310 618-6937	13514
Parking Concepts Inc	7521	D	714 543-5725	13617
Brake Depot Systems Inc	7538	B	714 623-9030	13658
Collectors Universe Inc (PA)	7699	C	949 567-1234	13768
La Boxing Franchise Corp	7991	B	714 668-0911	14211
Santa Ana Country Club	7997	D	714 556-3000	14442
Altamed Health Services Corp	8011	D	714 426-5400	14605
Carbon Health Technologies Inc	8011	D	714 710-3030	14654
Kaiser Foundation Hospitals	8011	D	714 830-6500	14818
Kaiser Foundation Hospitals	8011	D	714 967-4700	14847
South Coast Global Med Ctr Inc	8011	D	714 754-5454	15069
Southern Cal Prmnnte Med Group	8011	D	714 967-4760	15093
St Jseph Heritg Med Group LLC (PA)	8011	C	714 633-1011	15098
University California Irvine	8011	B	714 480-2443	15164
Chromium Dental II LLC	8021	C	949 733-3111	15220
Lucero Dental Clinic	8021	D	714 557-0201	15236
Intergro Rehab Service	8049	D	714 901-4200	15294
Sunrise Senior Living LLC	8051	D	714 544-5959	15697
Town Cntry Mnor of Chrstn Mssn	8051	C	714 547-7581	15706
County of Orange	8052	D	714 834-6021	15752
Orange Cnty Ryale Cnvlscent Ho (PA)	8059	B	714 546-6450	15886
Health Resources Corp	8062	B	714 754-5454	16122
Orange Cnty Globl Med Ctr Aux (DH)	8062	C	714 835-3555	16295
Orange Cnty Globl Med Ctr Inc	8062	D	714 953-3500	16296
Southern Cal Spcialty Care Inc	8062	C	714 564-7800	16442
Ctsh LLC	8082	D	949 916-6705	16853
Visiting Nrse Assn of Inland C (PA)	8082	A	951 413-1200	16963
Child Guidance Center Inc	8093	C	714 953-4455	17026
CRC Health Corporate	8093	A	714 542-3581	17046
Reimagine Network (PA)	8093	C	714 633-7400	17117
Rio	8093	C	714 633-7400	17120
Altamed Health Services Corp	8099	D	714 919-0280	17169
Optumcare Management LLC	8099	D	714 964-6229	17288
Optumcare Management LLC	8099	D	714 835-8501	17290
Hart Knle Pntecost A Prof Corp	8111	D	714 432-8700	17491
Moore Law Group A Prof Corp	8111	D	714 431-2000	17573
Wolf Firm A Law Corporation	8111	D	949 720-9200	17686
Family Asssment Cnsling Edcat	8322	D	714 447-9024	17975
Orangewood Foundation	8322	D	714 619-0200	18073
Priority Ctr Ending The Gnrtna	8322	D	714 543-4333	18086
United Crbral Plsy Assn Ornge	8322	D	949 333-6400	18160
Volunteers of Amer Los Angeles	8322	D	714 426-9834	18179
City of Santa Ana	8331	D	714 647-6545	18221
Success Strategies Inst Inc	8331	D	949 721-6808	18252
Calvary Church Santa Ana Inc	8351	D	714 973-4800	18274
Orange County Head Start Inc (PA)	8351	D	714 241-8920	18340
Olive Crest (PA)	8361	B	714 543-5437	18500
Charles W Bowers Museum Corp	8412	D	714 567-3600	18642
Discovery Scnce Ctr Ornge Cnty	8412	C	866 552-2823	18650
Mercy House Living Centers	8611	C	714 836-7188	18715
Orange County Health Care Agcy	8621	D	714 568-5683	18755
Serve People Inc	8699	D	714 352-2911	19104
Aerospace Engineering Corp LLC	8711	D	714 641-5884	19131
Air Liquide Electronics US LP	8711	A	713 624-8000	19133
Concept Technology Inc	8711	B	949 851-6550	19180
Embee Processing LLC	8711	D	714 546-9842	19212
Hntb Corporation	8711	D	714 460-1600	19256
Hntb Gerwick Water Solutions	8711	C	714 460-1600	19258
Michael Baker International Inc (DH)	8711	B	949 472-3505	19321
Psomas	8713	C	714 751-7373	19525
Dhs Consulting LLC	8741	C	714 276-1135	20080
Medical Network Inc	8741	D	949 863-0022	20149
Pipeline Group LLC	8741	C	949 296-8375	20177
Prospect Medical Group Inc (HQ)	8741	B	714 796-5900	20186
Wolf & Raven LLC	8741	D	800 431-6471	20254
Alan B Whitson Company Inc	8742	A	949 955-1200	20267
Ferry International LLC	8742	D	888 866-3377	20375
Kvc Group LLC	8742	D	855 438-0377	20428
Solutions Inc	8742	C	949 899-0448	20559
Chambers Group Inc (PA)	8748	D	949 261-5414	20726
Irvine Technology Corporation	8748	C	714 445-2624	20782
Profit Recovery Partners LLC	8748	D	949 851-2777	20831
Data Trace Info Svcs LLC (HQ)	8999	D	714 250-6700	20884
Califrnia Dept Indus Relations	9199	D	714 558-4121	20921
Regional Ctr Orange Cnty Inc (PA)	9431	B	714 796-5100	20940

SANTA BARBARA, CA - Santa Barbara County

	SIC	EMP	PHONE	ENTRY#
Brightview Golf Maint Inc	0781	C	805 968-6400	393
Dennis Allen Associates (PA)	1521	D	805 884-8777	672
Granite Construction Company	1611	D	805 964-9951	1112
One Call Plumber Santa Barbara	1711	D	805 364-6337	1519
Specialty Team Plastering Inc	1742	C	805 966-3858	1964
JM Roofing Company Inc	1761	D	805 966-3696	2070
Graphiq LLC	2741	C	805 335-2433	2555
Motion Engineering Inc (DH)	3577	D	805 696-1200	2834
Santa Barbara Metro Trnst Dst (PA)	4111	D	805 963-3364	3205
Santa Barbara City of	4725	D	805 962-6464	3967
Santa Barbara Adventure Co	4725	D	805 884-9283	3968
Landmark Distribution LLC	4789	D	805 965-3058	4165
Smith Broadcasting Group Inc	4833	B	805 882-3933	4462
Marborg Industries (PA)	4953	C	805 963-1852	4907
Curvature LLC (DH)	5045	B	800 230-6638	5289
Mentor Worldwide LLC	5047	B	805 681-6000	5432
Jordanos Inc (PA)	5181	C	805 964-0611	6769
Volkswagen of Van Nuys Inc	5511	D	323 873-3311	7325
Sansum Clinic	5912	D	805 681-7500	7526
Merrill Lynch Prce Fnner Smith	6211	D	805 695-7028	8116
Merrill Lynch Prce Fnner Smith	6211	C	805 963-0333	8124
Morgan Stnley Smith Barney LLC	6211	C	805 963-3381	8154
Mercer Global Securities LLC	6282	D	805 565-1681	8208
Santa Brbara San Luis Obspo RG	6321	C	800 421-2560	8270
Chicago Title Insurance Co (HQ)	6361	C	805 565-6900	8438
Western Penn AAA Insur Agcy	6411	D	805 682-5811	8686
Nevins/Adams Properties Inc (PA)	6512	C	805 963-2884	8738
University Business Ctr Assoc	6512	D	601 354-3555	8774
Coldwell Banker Premier Prpts	6531	D	805 565-2200	8938
Pitts & Bachmann Realtors Inc	6531	D	805 969-5005	9134
Pitts & Bachmann Realtors Inc	6531	D	805 963-1391	9135
Miramar Acquisition Co LLC	6799	C	805 900-8338	9534
Vantagepoint Management Inc (PA)	6799	D	650 866-3100	9577
1260 Bb Property LLC	7011	B	805 969-2261	9585
Bcra Resort Services Inc	7011	C	805 571-3176	9635
El Encanto Inc	7011	D	805 845-5800	9777
Encina Pepper Tree Joint Ventr (PA)	7011	D	805 687-5511	9782
Encina Pepper Tree Joint Ventr	7011	D	805 682-7277	9783
Fess Prker-Red Lion Gen Partnr	7011	C	805 564-4333	9796
H D G Associates	7011	C	805 963-0744	9830
Interstate Hotels Resorts Inc	7011	D	805 966-2285	9913
Marriott Intl Hotels Inc	7011	D	805 975-0660	10007
Morgans Hotel Group MGT LLC	7011	C	805 969-2203	10029
Paradise Hotel Inc	7011	D	805 687-6444	10098
Ritz-Carlton Hotel Company LLC	7011	A	805 968-0100	10162
San Ysidro Bb Property LLC	7011	C	805 368-6788	10203
El Capitan Canyon LLC	7033	D	805 685-3887	10417
Mission Linen Supply	7213	D	805 963-0414	10448
Mission Linen Supply	7213	C	805 962-7687	10449
Signature Parking LLC	7299	D	805 969-7275	10575
Perceptioneering Inc	7311	D	805 962-4550	10660
Fastclick Inc	7319	A	805 689-9839	10730
Town & Cntry Event Rentals Inc	7359	B	805 770-5729	11057
Butler International Inc (PA)	7361	B	805 882-2200	11100
Eastern Staffing LLC	7361	B	805 882-2200	11127
Partners Prsnnel - MGT Svcs LL	7361	A	805 689-8191	11195
Select Temporaries LLC (DH)	7361	B	805 882-2200	11228
Butler Service Group Inc (HQ)	7363	D	201 891-5312	11276
Volt Management Corp	7363	D	805 560-8658	11358
Bitwarden Inc	7371	D	904 664-9194	11462
Shiphawk	7371	D	805 335-2432	11913
Trackr Inc	7371	D	855 981-1690	11984
Yardi Systems Inc (PA)	7371	B	805 699-2040	12054
Appfolio Inc (PA)	7372	B	805 364-6093	12092
Green Hills Software LLC (HQ)	7372	C	805 965-6044	12211
Qad Inc (HQ)	7372	D	805 566-6000	12330
Logicmonitor Inc (PA)	7375	C	805 394-8632	12673
US Data Management LLC (PA)	7379	D	888 231-0816	12903
Continental Exch Solutions Inc	7389	D	805 965-0663	13245
Bay Clubs Company LLC	7997	B	805 965-0999	14330
Bay Clubs Company LLC	7997	B	805 563-8700	14332
Birnam Wood Golf Club (PA)	7997	D	805 969-2223	14346
La Cumbre Country Club	7997	D	805 687-2421	14387
Montecito Country Club Inc	7997	D	805 969-0800	14409
Anesthsia Med Group Snta Brbar	8011	D	805 682-7751	14613
Cancer Center of Santa Barbara	8011	D	805 898-2182	14650
Sansum Clinic (PA)	8011	D	805 681-7700	15044
Compass Health Inc	8051	C	805 687-6651	15386
Covenant Care California LLC	8051	D	805 964-4871	15404
Covenant Rtirement Communities	8051	D	805 687-0701	15410
Montecito Retirement Assn	8051	B	805 969-8011	15590
Powers Park Healthcare Inc	8051	D	805 687-6651	15633

GEOGRAPHIC SECTION

SANTA CLARA CA

	SIC	EMP	PHONE	ENTRY#
Hillside House	8052	D	805 687-0788	15761
Front Porch Communities & Svcs	8059	C	805 687-0793	15845
Goleta Valley Cottage Hosp Aux	8062	B	805 681-6468	16109
Santa Barbara Cottage Hospital	8062	B	805 569-7367	16388
Santa Brbara Cttage Hosp Fndti	8062	B	805 569-7224	16389
Santa Brbara Cttage Hosp Fndti (HQ)	8062	C	805 682-7111	16391
Visiting Nurse & Hospice	8082	C	805 965-5555	16965
Visiting Nurse & Hospice Care (PA)	8082	C	805 965-5555	16966
Santa Brbara Artfl Kdney Ctr L	8092	D	805 682-9942	16997
Price Postel and Parma LLP	8111	D	805 962-0011	17616
Laguna Blanca School (PA)	8211	C	805 687-2461	17720
Santa Brbara Cmnty College Dst	8222	B	805 683-4191	17788
Music Academy of West	8299	D	805 969-4726	17812
Family Svc Agcy Snta Brbara CN	8322	D	805 965-1001	17979
People Creating Success Inc	8322	D	805 692-5290	18083
Tri-Cnties Assn For Dvlpmntlly (PA)	8322	C	805 962-7881	18154
Cliff View Terrace Inc	8361	D	805 682-7443	18395
Covenant Living West	8361	D	805 687-0701	18408
Santa Barbara Museum of Art (PA)	8412	D	805 963-4364	18674
Santa Brbara Mseum Ntral Hstor	8412	D	805 682-4711	18675
Santa Brbara Zlgcal Foundation	8422	C	805 962-1673	18694
African Women Rising	8641	C	415 278-1784	18810
Channel Islnds Yung MNS Chrstn	8641	D	805 963-8775	18834
Channel Islnds Yung MNS Chrstn	8641	D	805 687-7727	18837
Channel Islnds Yung MNS Chrstn	8641	D	805 969-3288	18838
Automobile Club Southern Cal	8699	C	805 682-5811	19038
Lash Construction Inc	8711	D	805 963-3553	19304
MNS Engineers Inc (PA)	8711	D	805 692-6921	19324
Penfield & Smith Engineers Inc	8711	D	805 963-9532	19357
Nasif Hicks Harris & Co LLP	8721	D	805 966-1521	19614
Dupont Displays Inc	8731	C	805 562-5400	19684
Ontraport Inc	8741	D	805 568-1424	20166
Smith Broadcasting Group Inc (PA)	8741	C	805 965-0400	20207
Pensinmark Rtirement Group LLC	8742	C	805 456-6260	20503
Riviera Data Corp	8742	D	805 456-7082	20528
Tecolote Research Inc	8742	C	805 964-6963	20580
Tempest Telecom Solutions LLC (HQ)	8748	D	805 879-4800	20864

SANTA CLARA, CA - Santa Clara County

	SIC	EMP	PHONE	ENTRY#
Build Group Inc	1542	D	408 986-8711	882
Hathaway Dinwiddie Cnstr Co	1542	D	415 986-2718	931
L & S Hallmark Construction Inc	1542	C	408 727-4422	956
McCarthy Bldg Companies Inc	1542	B	408 908-7005	963
San Jose Construction Co Inc	1542	D	408 986-8711	1018
Michels Pacific Energy Inc	1623	D	920 924-8725	1237
Anderson PCF Engrg Cnstr Inc	1629	D	408 970-9900	1285
Envirnmntal Systems Inc Nthrn (PA)	1711	D	408 980-1711	1431
Ray L Hellwig Mechanical Co Inc	1711	D	408 727-5080	1542
Ray L Hellwig Plumbing & Heating Inc	1711	B	408 727-5612	1543
Thermal Mechanical	1711	D	408 988-8744	1584
Elcor Electric Inc	1731	C	408 986-1320	1724
Redwood Electric Group Inc (PA)	1731	A	707 451-7348	1815
J & J Acoustics Inc	1742	C	408 275-9255	1937
Waterproofing Associates Inc	1761	D	650 937-1299	2090
Dolan Concrete Construction	1771	D	408 869-3250	2115
Joseph J Albanese Inc	1771	A	408 727-5700	2131
Robert A Bothman Inc (PA)	1771	D	408 279-2277	2153
Royal Glass Company Inc	1793	D	408 969-0444	2204
Burdick Painting	1799	D	408 567-1330	2261
United Marble & Granite Inc	1799	D	408 347-3300	2325
Valley Waterproofing Inc	1799	D	408 985-7701	2327
Compass Innovations Inc	3081	C	408 418-3985	2660
Violin Memory Inc (PA)	3572	C	650 396-1500	2820
Arista Networks Inc (PA)	3577	B	408 547-5500	2823
Gigamon Inc (HQ)	3577	C	408 831-4000	2830
Palo Alto Networks Inc (PA)	3577	B	408 753-4000	2835
Greenliant Systems Inc	3674	C	408 217-7400	2920
Intel Corporation (HQ)	3674	A	408 765-8080	2923
Miasole Hi-Tech Corp (DH)	3674	C	408 919-5700	2927
Natron Energy Inc	3691	D	408 498-5828	2949
Agilent Technologies Inc (PA)	3826	A	800 227-9770	3028
Abbott Laboratories	3841	D	408 845-3000	3045
Mission Trail Wste Systems Inc	4212	D	408 727-5365	3413
Tq Logistics Inc	4213	D	408 565-0188	3554
Three Way Inc	4214	C	408 748-6902	3598
UPS Freight	4789	D	408 727-0703	4177
2wire Inc (DH)	4813	C	408 235-5500	4247
Asiainfo-Linkage Inc	4813	A	408 970-9788	4253
Envivio Inc	4813	C	650 243-2700	4270
Ericsson Inc	4813	A	408 750-5000	4271
Futurewei Technologies Inc	4813	D	469 277-5700	4285
Gaia Interactive Inc	4813	C		4287
Synaptics Incorporated	4813	D	408 454-5100	4347
Intel Media Inc	4841	B	408 765-0063	4511
Vertical Communication (HQ)	4899	D	408 969-9600	4558
City of Santa Clara	4911	D	408 615-2300	4565
City of Santa Clara	4911	D	408 615-2046	4566
Bay Counties Waste Svcs Inc	4953	D	408 565-9900	4863
Fast Pro Inc	5013	D	408 566-0200	5038
One Workplace L Ferrari LLC (PA)	5021	C	669 800-2500	5098
Yubico Inc	5044	B	408 774-4064	5263
Advanced Micro Devices Inc (PA)	5045	A	408 749-4000	5266
Bizcom Electronics Inc (HQ)	5045	D	408 262-7877	5281
Bramasol Inc	5045	D	408 831-0046	5283
Cybercsi Inc	5045	D	408 727-2900	5291
Leandata Inc	5045	C	669 600-5676	5323
Litmus Automation Inc (PA)	5045	D	765 418-7405	5325
Savvion Inc	5045	D	408 330-3400	5346
Wyse Technology LLC (DH)	5045	C	800 438-9973	5372
Alpha Innotech Corp	5047	C	408 510-5500	5396
Mpower Electronics Inc	5063	D	408 320-1266	5581
Advantest America Inc	5065	B	408 988-7700	5622
California Eastern Labs Inc (PA)	5065	D	408 919-2500	5639
Globalfoundries Americas Inc	5065	C	408 462-3900	5653
Renesas Electronics America Inc	5065	A	408 588-6000	5695
Hitachi America Ltd (HQ)	5084	D	914 332-5800	5839
Golden N-Life Diamite Intl Inc (PA)	5122	D	510 651-0405	6110
Smart & Final Stores LLC	5141	D	408 296-3293	6342
Air Products and Chemicals Inc	5169	D	408 988-6263	6703
C B Tool & Supply Inc	5251	D	916 568-7514	7115
Frontier Ford (PA)	5511	C	408 241-1800	7216
Pivot Interiors Inc (PA)	5712	C	408 432-5600	7425
Family Christian Stores LLC	5942	D	616 554-8700	7546
San Jose Bluprt Svc & Sup Co	5999	D	408 295-5770	7593
Svb Financial Group (PA)	6022	A	408 654-7400	7718
Ehealth Inc (PA)	6411	C	650 584-2700	8552
Ehealthinsurance Services Inc (HQ)	6411	D	650 584-2700	8553
Acco Management Company	6531	D	408 241-3000	8895
Move Inc (HQ)	6531	B	408 558-7100	9104
Move Sales Inc (DH)	6531	D	805 557-2300	9105
Tensilica Inc (PA)	6794	D	408 986-8000	9457
Msr Hotels & Resorts Inc	6799	C	408 496-6400	9537
Hyatt Regency Santa Clara	7011	D	408 200-1234	9902
Ontario Airport Hotel Corp	7011	C	408 562-6709	10069
Santa Clara Travelodge	7011	D	408 984-3364	10206
Sierra Lodgings Inc	7011	D	408 748-9800	10234
Stanford Hotels Corporation	7011	D	408 330-0001	10267
Brandvia Alliance Inc (HQ)	7311	D	408 955-0500	10593
Flair Building Services	7349	D	408 987-4040	10900
Impec Group Inc (PA)	7349	D	408 330-9350	10909
Advance Staffing Inc	7361	B	408 205-6154	11077
Legacy Personnel Inc	7361	B	877 850-5132	11171
Spec Personnel LLC	7361	D	408 727-8000	11235
Upwork Inc (PA)	7361	C	650 316-7500	11250
Coast Personnel Services Inc (PA)	7363	A	408 653-2100	11282
Iconma LLC	7363	C	888 451-2519	11292
6wind Usa Inc	7371	D	408 816-1366	11370
Access Systems Americas Inc	7371	D	408 400-3000	11376
Alpha Net Consulting Llc (PA)	7371	C	408 550-5686	11398
Cignex Holding Corp	7371	C	408 327-9900	11489
Cloudera Inc (HQ)	7371	D	650 362-0488	11496
Clumio Inc	7371	D	603 321-2495	11497
Couchbase Inc (PA)	7371	C	650 417-7500	11518
Datastax Inc (PA)	7371	B	650 389-6000	11529
Eitacies Inc	7371	D	805 500-4366	11568
Everyone Counts Inc	7371	D		11584
Evolveware Inc	7371	D	408 748-8301	11587
Globallogic Inc (HQ)	7371	C	408 273-8900	11625
Gridiron Systems Inc	7371	C	201 502-0512	11633
Hcl America Solutions Inc	7371	A	408 733-0480	11640
Hitachi Vantara LLC (HQ)	7371	C	858 225-2095	11642
Infoblox Inc (HQ)	7371	B	408 986-4000	11660
Netbase Solutions Inc (PA)	7371	C	650 810-2100	11767
Ntt Cloud Infrastructure Inc (HQ)	7371	D	408 567-2000	11787
Persistent Systems Inc (HQ)	7371	D	408 216-7010	11823
Propel Software Solutions	7371	D	408 755-3780	11848
Quid LLC (PA)	7371	C	415 813-5300	11859
Ramy Infotech Inc	7371	C	408 317-9256	11863
Ryzlink Corp	7371	D	510 296-5433	11890
Solix Technologies Inc (PA)	7371	D	408 654-6405	11933
Strivr Labs Inc	7371	C	650 656-9987	11952
Tao Digital Solutions Inc	7371	C	408 391-0930	11967
Tavant Technologies Inc (PA)	7371	C	408 519-5400	11971
Ushur Inc (PA)	7371	C	408 744-6802	12007
Valgenesis Inc (PA)	7371	D	510 445-0505	12011
Veritas Technologies LLC (DH)	7371	C	866 837-4827	12016

Employee Codes: A=Over 500 employees, B=251-500
C=101-250, D=51-100, E=20-50, F=10-19, G=1-9

2024 Directory of California
WholeSalers and Service Companies

© Mergent Inc. 1-800-342-5647

SANTA CLARA CA

GEOGRAPHIC SECTION

	SIC	EMP	PHONE	ENTRY#
Veritas US Inc	7371	C	650 933-1000	12018
Versa Networks Inc **(PA)**	7371	C	408 385-7660	12019
Wanclouds Inc	7371	D	408 663-6753	12034
Whiterabbitai Inc	7371	D	408 215-8876	12040
Yvaai Inc	7371	D	650 704-5503	12057
Big Switch Networks LLC	7372	D	650 322-6510	12113
Ca Inc	7372	C	800 225-5224	12128
Eightfold Ai Inc **(PA)**	7372	C	650 265-7380	12177
Espressive Inc	7372	D	408 753-8766	12182
Forward Networks Inc	7372	D	844 393-6389	12196
Ginsberg Holdco Inc	7372	B	408 831-4000	12205
Hortonworks Inc **(DH)**	7372	A	408 916-4121	12224
Kno Inc	7372	D	408 844-8120	12252
Malwarebytes Inc **(PA)**	7372	A	408 852-4336	12260
McAfee Finance 2 LLC	7372	A	888 847-8766	12266
Mojo Networks Inc **(HQ)**	7372	D	650 961-1111	12273
Net Optics Inc	7372	D	408 737-7777	12282
Netskope Inc **(PA)**	7372	A	800 979-6988	12283
Nominum Inc	7372	C	650 381-6000	12292
Onvantage Inc	7372	D	408 562-3388	12303
Oracle America Inc	7372	C	408 276-3331	12305
Pdf Solutions Inc **(PA)**	7372	C	408 280-7900	12317
Plusai Inc	7372	D	408 508-4758	12321
Pure Storage Inc **(PA)**	7372	B	800 379-7873	12329
Solidcore Systems Inc **(DH)**	7372	D	408 387-8400	12357
Atac **(PA)**	7373	D	408 736-2822	12421
Data Domain LLC	7373	A	408 980-4800	12443
O2 Micro Inc	7373	C	408 987-5920	12506
Soft Machines Inc	7373	D	408 969-0215	12524
Synapse Design Automation Inc **(DH)**	7373	C	408 850-9527	12530
Hewlett Packard Enterprise Co	7374	A	408 914-2390	12578
Hcl America Inc **(DH)**	7376	C	408 733-0480	12696
Tusa Inc **(PA)**	7378	C	888 848-3749	12713
BT Ins Inc	7379	A	408 330-2700	12745
Capiot Software Inc	7379	C	408 216-7010	12750
Cloudinary Inc	7379	B	650 772-1833	12760
Incedo Inc	7379	C	408 531-6040	12806
Innova Solutions Inc	7379	A	408 889-2020	12812
Intellipro Group Inc **(PA)**	7379	B	408 200-9891	12815
Luminous Computing Inc	7379	D	650 275-5950	12831
Norland Group Inc	7379	C	408 855-8255	12846
Tata America Intl Corp	7379	C	408 569-5845	12891
Truu Inc	7379	D	888 498-0107	12899
United SEC Specialists Inc	7381	C	408 878-5120	13062
Innovative Silicon Inc	7389	C	408 572-8700	13325
Maria Aleen Villarin Balce Inc	7389	D	408 320-2684	13362
Santa Clara Convention Center	7389	D	408 748-7000	13465
Yahoo Inc	7389	D	408 248-3589	13558
Simco Electronics **(PA)**	7629	D	408 734-9750	13745
Yes Videocom Inc	7812	D	408 907-7600	13921
Forty Niners Football Co LLC	7941	D	408 562-4949	14137
San Francisco Forty Niners **(PA)**	7941	C	408 562-4949	14157
Bay Clubs Company LLC	7991	B	408 738-2582	14176
Cedar Fair LP	7996	C	408 988-1776	14300
Sutter Bay Medical Foundation	8011	D	650 812-3751	15108
Golden Optical Corporation	8042	D	408 246-4500	15263
Center For Social Dynamics LLC	8049	D	408 320-2590	15275
Covenant Care California LLC	8051	D	408 248-3736	15401
TLC of Bay Area Inc	8051	D	408 988-7667	15704
Community Home Partners LLC	8052	D	408 985-5252	15750
Kaiser Foundation Hospitals	8062	D	408 235-4005	16170
Kaiser Foundation Hospitals	8062	A	408 851-1000	16192
Cardiodx Inc	8071	C	650 475-2788	16709
Direct Flow Medical Inc	8099	C	707 576-0420	17222
West Vlly-Mssion Cmnty Cllege	8222	B	408 988-2200	17790
Pacific Autism Ctr For Educatn	8299	C	408 245-3400	17814
Nourish Inc	8322	D	917 572-6691	18068
Sourcewise	8322	D	408 350-3200	18136
Young MNS Chrstn Assn Slcon Vl **(PA)**	8641	D	408 351-6400	18999
DSP Concepts Inc **(PA)**	8711	C	408 747-5200	19205
Macaulay Brown Inc	8711	A	937 426-3421	19311
Six3 Advanced Systems Inc	8711	C	408 878-4920	19390
Fujifilm Dimatix Inc	8731	D	408 565-0670	19695
Symyx Technologies Inc	8731	B	408 764-2000	19776
Accion Labs Us Inc	8734	A	408 970-9809	19943
Eag Holdings LLC	8734	D	408 530-3500	19966
Eurofins Eag Engrg Science LLC **(DH)**	8734	D	408 588-0050	19971
Evans Analytical Group LLC	8734	D	408 454-4600	19976
SE Laboratories Inc	8734	D	408 727-3286	19998
Bon Appetit Management Co	8741	C	408 554-2728	20040
Bon Appetit Management Co	8741	C	408 554-5771	20043
Matrix Absence Management Inc	8741	D	408 330-0754	20147
San Jose Earthquakes MGT LLC	8741	C	408 556-7700	20201
Tilton Pacific Cnstr Inc	8741	D	408 551-0492	20229
Eva Automation Inc	8742	B	650 513-6875	20365
Roche Molecular Systems Inc	8742	C	408 217-5400	20531
Beyondsoft Consulting Inc	8748	C	408 806-0715	20704
Cavisson Systems Inc	8748	B	800 701-6125	20720
Enterprise Solutions Inc	8748	C	408 727-3627	20743
Fungible Inc	8748	C	669 292-5522	20754
Futurewei Technologies Inc **(HQ)**	8748	C	469 277-5700	20756
One Diversified LLC	8748	D	408 969-1972	20821
Qmetry Inc	8748	C	408 727-1101	20834
Agora Lab Inc	8999	D	408 879-5885	20883

SANTA CLARITA, CA - Los Angeles County

	SIC	EMP	PHONE	ENTRY#
Delphic Enterprises Inc	0742	D	661 254-2000	334
Emerald Landscape Services Inc	0782	D	714 844-2200	488
Gothic Landscaping Inc **(PA)**	0782	D	661 678-1400	493
California Resources Prod Corp **(HQ)**	1311	C	661 869-8000	583
Califrnia Rsrces Elk Hills LLC	1382	B	661 412-0000	596
Califrnia Rsurces Long Bch Inc	1382	D	888 848-4754	597
Sheldon Mechanical Corporation	1711	C	661 286-1361	1559
Tri-Signal Integration Inc **(PA)**	1731	C	818 566-8558	1864
Clear View Windows & Doors Inc	1751	D	661 257-5050	1992
Curtiss-Wrght Cntrls Elctrnic **(DH)**	3625	C	661 702-1494	2865
Santa Barbara Trnsp Corp	4131	D	661 259-7285	3309
Funnelcloudsales	4215	D	661 284-6032	3612
Princess Cruise Lines Ltd **(HQ)**	4481	A	661 753-0000	3804
Princess Cruise Lines Ltd	4724	A	661 753-2197	3948
Princess Cruise Lines Ltd	4725	A	661 753-0000	3966
Cellco Partnership	4812	D	661 296-7585	4196
CBS Studios Inc	4833	B	661 964-6020	4419
Santa Clarita Valley Wtr Agcy	4941	C	661 259-2737	4832
Santa Clrita Vly Wtr Agcy Fing	4941	C	661 259-2737	4833
Marathon Industries Inc	5012	C	661 286-1520	5015
White Cap Supply Group Inc	5039	A	661 294-7737	5233
Paul Mitchell John Systems **(PA)**	5122	D	800 793-8790	6137
Allied Company Holdings Inc	5181	C	661 510-6533	6750
Home Depot USA Inc	5211	C	661 252-7800	7023
Lowes Home Centers LLC	5211	D	661 678-4430	7108
RE/Max of Valencia Inc **(PA)**	6531	C	661 255-2650	9153
Jt Resources Inc	7361	C	661 367-6827	11160
Partnership Staffing Svcs Inc	7361	A	661 542-7074	11196
Canon Recruiting Group LLC	7363	B	661 252-7400	11277
Valtron Technologies Inc	7378	D	805 257-0333	12714
Cottrell Paul Enterprises LLC **(PA)**	7381	C	661 212-2357	12953
Wrights Supply Inc	7694	C	661 254-8400	13759
Kaiser Foundation Hospitals	8011	D	661 222-2323	14839
Providnce Facey Med Foundation	8011	D	661 513-2100	15002
Southern Cal Prmnnte Med Group	8011	C	661 222-2150	15090
Southern Cal Prmnnte Med Group	8062	B	661 290-3100	16439
Providnce Facey Med Foundation	8099	C	661 250-5225	17301
Child & Family Center	8322	C	661 259-9439	17874
Santa Clrita Vly Cmmttee On AG	8322	D	661 259-9444	18117
Los Angeles Residential Comm F	8361	C	661 296-8636	18477
Curtiss-Wrght Cntrls Elctrnic	8711	C	661 257-4430	19191
Santa Clrita Hlth Care Assn In **(PA)**	8741	D	661 253-8000	20202

SANTA CRUZ, CA - Santa Cruz County

	SIC	EMP	PHONE	ENTRY#
Jacobs Farm/Del Cabo Inc	0191	D	831 421-9171	185
Green Valley Corporation	1542	D	831 475-7100	924
Acco Engineered Systems Inc	1711	C	831 423-9522	1332
Geo H Wilson Inc	1711	D	831 423-9522	1451
ONeill Wetsuits LLC **(PA)**	3069	D	831 475-7500	2658
First Transit Inc	4111	C	831 460-9911	3133
Santa Cruz Metro Trnst Dst	4111	D	831 429-5455	3208
Santa Cruz Metro Trnst Dst	4111	D	831 469-1954	3209
American Med Rspnse Inland Emp	4119	A	831 423-7030	3230
Granite Rock Co	5032	D	831 471-3440	5205
Jane Technologies Inc	5045	D	617 259-2466	5318
Rope Partner Inc	5085	C	831 460-9448	5922
Performance Food Group Inc	5141	C	831 462-4400	6277
Stagnaro Bros Seafood Inc	5146	D	831 423-1188	6485
Reyes Holdings LLC	5181	C	831 761-6400	6780
First American Title Insur Co	6361	C	831 426-6500	8442
Dominican Oaks Corporation	6513	D	831 462-6257	8801
Canyon View Capital Inc	6798	D	831 480-6335	9464
Chaminade Ltd	7011	C	831 475-5600	9693
Santa Cruz Seaside Company	7011	A	831 427-3400	10207
Affiliate Traction	7319	C	831 464-1441	10725
Supplyshift **(PA)**	7372	D	831 824-4326	12370
National Security Industries	7381	B	831 425-2052	13006
Santa Cruz Warriors	7941	D	831 466-3200	14159
Crossfit LLC	7991	C	619 540-5017	14191
Santa Cruz Seaside Company **(PA)**	7996	B	831 423-5590	14312

GEOGRAPHIC SECTION

SANTA MARIA CA

	SIC	EMP	PHONE	ENTRY#
Palo Alto Med Fndtion STA Cruz	8011	D	831 458-5670	14948
Santa Cruz Medical Foundation (HQ)	8011	D	831 458-5537	15048
Santa Cruz Medical Foundation	8011	A	831 477-2325	15049
Mariner Health Care Inc	8051	D	831 475-6323	15572
Front St Inc	8052	C	831 420-0120	15757
Dominican Hospital Foundation (DH)	8062	C	831 462-7700	16061
Santa Cruz Medical Foundation	8062	A	831 477-2375	16393
Sutter Bay Hospitals	8062	D	831 423-4111	16511
Sutter Health	8062	D	831 458-6310	16523
Sutter Mtrnty/Srgry Ctr-Snt Cr	8062	D	831 477-2200	16554
Janus of Santa Cruz	8069	D	831 462-1060	16684
Visiting Nrse Assn of Snta Cru (DH)	8082	D	831 477-2600	16964
Housing Matters	8322	D	831 458-6020	18007
Dominican Hospital Foundation	8361	C	831 457-7057	18417
Regent Assisted Living Inc	8361	C	831 459-8400	18511
Ccof Foundation	8641	D	831 423-2263	18831
Friends Santa Cruz State Parks	8641	D	831 429-1840	18860
Smartrevenuecom Inc	8732	B	203 733-9156	19847
F2 Consulting (PA)	8742	D	415 844-0641	20372
Murj Inc	8748	D	831 588-4462	20810

SANTA FE SPRINGS, CA - Los Angeles County

	SIC	EMP	PHONE	ENTRY#
CMC Rebar West	1541	D	714 692-7082	811
Holbrook Construction Inc	1542	D	714 523-1150	938
Griffith Company	1611	D	562 929-1128	1117
Kiewit Infrastructure West Co	1611	C	562 946-1816	1127
S E Pipe Line Construction Co	1623	D	562 868-9771	1258
Valverde Construction Inc	1623	D	562 906-1826	1275
Key Air Cnditioning Contrs Inc	1711	D	562 941-2233	1477
Csi Electrical Contractors Inc (HQ)	1731	C	562 946-0700	1715
Johnson-Peltier	1731	D	562 944-3408	1760
Leed Electric Inc	1731	D	562 270-9500	1766
RGA Electric Inc	1731	D	562 941-6380	1821
Masonry Concepts Inc	1741	D	562 802-3700	1889
Bligh Roof Co	1761	D	562 944-9753	2047
Rebar Engineering Inc	1791	C	562 946-2461	2197
Northstar Contg Group Inc	1795	D	714 639-7600	2241
Crown Fence Co	1799	D	562 864-5177	2269
Shoring Engineers	1799	D	562 944-9331	2315
Apffels Coffee Inc	2095	D	562 309-0400	2425
Reliable Container Corporation	2653	B	562 861-6226	2523
Seal Methods Inc (PA)	2672	D	562 944-0291	2529
Vomela Specialty Company	2752	C	562 944-3853	2567
Superior Printing Inc	2759	D	888 590-7998	2570
Vantage Associates Inc	3089	D	562 968-1400	2683
Process Fab Inc	3599	C	562 921-1979	2855
V&H Performance LLC	3751	D	562 921-7461	2997
Rohrback Cosasco Systems Inc (DH)	3823	D	562 949-0123	3019
Altro Usa Inc	3996	D	562 944-8292	3104
Gale/Triangle Inc (PA)	4212	D	562 741-1300	3394
General Lgstics Systems US Inc	4212	C	562 577-6037	3398
Savage Services Corporation	4212	D	562 400-2044	3422
Trail Lines Inc	4212	D	562 758-6980	3426
Contract Transportation Sys Co	4213	D	562 696-3262	3456
Van King & Storage Inc	4213	D	562 921-0555	3561
Xpo Logistics Freight Inc	4213	D	562 946-8331	3576
FN Logistics Llc	4214	A	213 625-5900	3586
Great Amrcn Logistics Dist Inc	4214	D	562 229-3601	3588
Van Torrance & Storage Company (PA)	4214	D		3602
Weber Distribution LLC (PA)	4222	D	855 469-3237	3668
Southern California Edison Co	4911	B	562 903-3191	4697
Ralco Holdings Inc (DH)	5013	C	949 440-5500	5054
Vgp Holdings LLC	5013	B	562 906-6200	5066
Lakin Tire West Incorporated (PA)	5014	C	562 802-2752	5071
Janus Et Cie (PA)	5021	C	310 601-2958	5093
New Tangram LLC	5021	C	562 365-5000	5095
Galleher LLC (PA)	5023	C	562 944-8885	5118
Tri-West Ltd (PA)	5023	C	562 692-9166	5140
Ugm Citatah Inc (PA)	5032	C	562 921-9549	5211
Coast Aluminum Inc (PA)	5051	C	562 946-6061	5484
Fry Steel Company	5051	C	562 802-2721	5492
Kloeckner Metals Corporation	5051	D	562 906-2020	5501
Reliance Steel & Aluminum Co	5051	D	562 944-3322	5516
The E Jordan Brookes Co Inc	5051	D	562 968-2100	5524
Tmx Aerospace	5051	C	562 215-4410	5526
Nelson & Associates Inc	5063	D	562 921-4423	5583
Swann Communications USA Inc	5065	D	562 777-2551	5704
Talley Inc (PA)	5065	C	562 906-8000	5706
Great Western Sales Inc	5074	D	310 323-7900	5751
Larsen Supply Co (PA)	5074	D	562 698-0731	5754
Ellison Technologies Inc	5084	D	562 949-8311	5832
Material Handling Supply Inc (HQ)	5084	D	562 921-7715	5844
Maxon Lift Corp (PA)	5084	C	562 464-0099	5845
Raymond Handling Solutions Inc (DH)	5084	C	562 944-8067	5863
Rebas Inc	5084	C	562 941-4155	5864
Lord & Sons Inc	5085	D	562 529-2500	5908
McMaster-Carr Supply Company	5085	B	562 692-5911	5911
Millennia Stainless Inc	5085	D	562 946-3545	5913
Southern California Valve Inc	5085	D	562 404-2246	5927
United States Luggage Co LLC	5099	D	562 293-4400	6057
Kelly Spicers Inc (HQ)	5111	C	562 698-1199	6060
Georgia-Pacific LLC	5113	B	562 861-6226	6078
McKesson Corporation	5122	C	562 463-2100	6126
Steven Label Corporation (PA)	5131	C	562 698-9971	6163
Mias Fashion Mfg Co Inc	5137	B	562 906-1060	6208
Wismettac Asian Foods Inc (HQ)	5141	C	562 802-1900	6414
LA Specialty Produce Co (PA)	5148	B	562 741-2200	6560
Access Business Group LLC	5169	B	808 422-9482	6700
Brenntag Pacific Inc (DH)	5169	D	562 903-9626	6706
Triangle Distributing Co	5181	B	562 699-3424	6785
Target Specialty Products Inc	5191	D	562 865-9541	6835
Pactiv LLC	5199	D	562 693-1451	6934
Premiere Packaging Inds Inc	5199	D	562 799-9200	6937
Royal Imex Inc	5199	D	562 777-9787	6944
Westrux International Inc (PA)	5511	D	562 404-1020	7335
Global Trade Alliance Inc	5531	C	562 944-6422	7349
Freestyle Sales Co Ltd Partnr	5946	D	323 660-3460	7553
Riviera Finance of Texas Inc	6153	D	562 777-1300	7906
Tydg Enterprises Inc	6719	D	562 903-9030	9345
Rentokil North America Inc	7342	D	562 802-2238	10843
Crossing Guard Company	7381	A	310 202-8284	12959
Cypress Private Security LP	7381	D	562 222-4197	12961
Johnson Controls	7382	C	562 405-3817	13128
Haringa Inc (PA)	7389	D	800 499-9991	13308
Lauren Andrew Surfaces Inc	7389	D	562 921-9549	13351
Newport Diversified Inc	7389	C	562 921-4359	13396
Pro-Tech Design & Mfg Inc (PA)	7389	D	562 207-1680	13430
El Monte Rents Inc (HQ)	7519	C	562 404-9300	13598
Valvoline Instant Oil Chnge Fr	7549	D	562 906-6200	13721
Think Together	7991	B	562 236-3835	14237
B & E Convalescent Center Inc (PA)	8059	D	562 923-9449	15815
Crescent Healthcare Inc (DH)	8082	C	714 520-6300	16852
County of Los Angeles	8322	D	562 903-5000	17909
Peoples Care Inc	8351	C	562 320-0174	18344
Ninos Latino Unidos FSA	8361	D	562 801-5454	18493
California Lab Sciences LLC	8734	C	562 758-6900	19953
Westpac Labs Inc	8734	B	562 906-5227	20005
Fujitec America Inc	8741	C	310 464-8270	20095
Matt Construction Corporation (PA)	8742	C	562 903-2277	20456
Greater Los Angles Cnty Vctor	8748	C	562 944-7976	20768

SANTA MARIA, CA - Santa Barbara County

	SIC	EMP	PHONE	ENTRY#
Teixeira Farms Desert Inc	0161	D	805 928-3801	45
Darensberries LLC	0171	C	805 937-8000	50
Freshway Farms LLC	0171	C	805 349-7170	54
J&G Berry Farms LLC	0171	C	831 750-9408	55
Red Blossom Farms Inc	0171	D	805 686-4747	59
Red Blossom Sales Inc	0171	A	805 349-9404	60
Reiter Affl Companies LLC	0171	C	805 925-8577	61
Glad-A-Way Gardens Inc	0181	C	805 938-0569	128
Plantel Nurseries Inc	0181	B	805 934-4300	147
Blackjack Frms De La Csta Cntl	0191	C	805 347-1333	168
Rancho Laguna Farms LLC	0191	C	805 925-7805	195
New Hope Harvesting LLC	0722	D	805 478-4469	251
Pacific Petroleum California Inc	1389	B	805 925-1947	625
Smith McHncl-Lctrical-Plumbing	1541	D	805 621-5000	843
Curation Foods Inc (HQ)	2099	D	800 454-1355	2433
Atlas Copco Mafi-Trench Co LLC (DH)	3564	C	805 928-5757	2795
Certified Frt Logistics Inc (PA)	4213	C	800 592-5906	3453
Frontier California Inc	4813	B	805 925-0000	4284
Valley Garbage Rubbish Co Inc	4953	C	805 614-1131	4949
Hardy Diagnostics Inc (PA)	5047	B	805 346-2766	5423
Quinn Company	5082	D	805 925-8611	5802
Foothill Packing Inc	5141	B	805 925-7755	6254
Central Coast Distributing LLC	5181	D	805 922-2108	6755
Smith Packing Inc	5199	C	805 348-1817	6949
Coasthills Credit Union (PA)	6062	D	805 733-7600	7823
Automobile Club Southern Cal	6411	D	805 922-5731	8503
Mission Linen Supply	7213	A	805 922-3579	10452
Ramco Enterprises LP	7361	B	805 922-9888	11213
Cali Beach Bears LLC	7389	D	805 361-0260	13220
Santa Brbara Cnty Pub Hlth Dep	8011	D	805 739-8718	15045
Country Oaks Care Center Inc	8051	D	805 922-6657	15391
Genesis Healthcare LLC	8051	A	805 922-3558	15493
Dignity Health	8062	B	805 739-3000	16042
Marian Community Clinic	8062	D	805 739-3867	16244

Employee Codes: A=Over 500 employees, B=251-500
C=101-250, D=51-100, E=20-50, F=10-19, G=1-9

SANTA MARIA CA

Company	SIC	EMP	PHONE	ENTRY#
Marian Medical Center	8062	A	805 739-3000	16245
Santa Brbara Cttage Hosp Fndti	8062	B	805 346-7135	16390
Life Steps Foundation Inc	8322	D	805 349-9810	18041
Work Inc	8322	D	805 739-0451	18196
Vtc Enterprises (PA)	8331	D	805 928-5000	18258
Ensign Group Inc	8361	C	805 925-8713	18421
Nursecore Management Svcs LLC	8361	A	805 938-7660	18497
American Management Svcs W LLC	8741	C	805 352-1921	20021
Peoples Self-Help Housing Corp	8748	D	805 349-9341	20827

SANTA MONICA, CA - Los Angeles County

Company	SIC	EMP	PHONE	ENTRY#
Morley Builders Inc (PA)	1541	C	310 399-1600	835
Taslimi Construction Co	1542	D	310 447-3000	1038
Morley Construction Company (HQ)	1771	C	310 399-1600	2138
Executive Network Entps Inc	4119	A	310 457-8822	3256
Santa Monica City of	4131	B	310 458-1975	3310
Casestack LLC (HQ)	4225	D	310 473-8885	3683
Atlantic Aviation Holding Corp	4581	D	310 396-6770	3876
Verizon Services Corp	4812	B	310 315-1100	4243
Connexity Inc (DH)	4813	C	310 571-1235	4266
Hulu LLC (HQ)	4813	C	310 571-4700	4296
Pandora Media LLC	4832	C	424 653-6803	4399
Entravsion Communications Corp (PA)	4833	C	310 447-3870	4429
SF Broadcasting Wisconsin Inc	4833	C	310 586-2410	4461
Game Show Network Music LLC (DH)	4841	C	310 255-6800	4509
Time Warner Companies Inc	4841	A	310 315-4437	4525
Religion of Sports Hq	4899	D	214 557-1766	4547
Cypress Creek Holdings LLC	4911	D	310 581-6299	4568
Inspire Energy Holdings LLC	4911	C	866 403-2620	4581
Solarreserve Inc	4911	D	310 315-2200	4679
K-Micro Inc	5045	D	310 442-3200	5320
Trey Arch LLC	5045	B	310 581-4700	5365
TV Guide Entrmt Group LLC	5064	D	310 360-1441	5616
Glamour Industries Co	5087	D	213 687-8600	5939
Spilo Worldwide Inc	5087	B	213 687-8600	5948
Genius Products Inc	5099	C	310 453-1222	6043
Guthy-Renker LLC	5099	D	310 581-6250	6045
Johnny Was LLC	5137	D	310 656-0600	6201
Converse Inc	5139	C	310 451-0314	6231
Ford of Santa Monica Inc	5511	D	310 451-1588	7209
Volkswagen Santa Monica Inc (PA)	5511	C	310 829-1888	7326
Hallmark Labs LLC	5947	C	424 210-3600	7556
CIT Bank NA	6021	D	310 399-9262	7611
Wells Fargo Capital Fin LLC (DH)	6159	D	310 453-7300	7925
Merrill Lynch Prce Fnner Smith	6211	D	310 477-3400	8112
Mercury Insurance Company	6331	B	310 451-4943	8394
Gumbiner Savett Inc	6512	D	310 828-9798	8723
Watt Properties Inc (PA)	6512	D	310 314-2430	8776
Irvine APT Communities LP	6513	C	310 255-1221	8830
William Warren Properties Inc	6513	D	310 454-1500	8873
Carmel Partners LLC	6722	D	916 479-5286	9363
Clearlake Capital Group LP (PA)	6722	B	310 400-8800	9366
Guggenheim Prtners Inv MGT LLC	6722	D	310 576-1270	9373
Wilshire 2015 Fund	6722	D	310 451-3051	9394
Wilshire Income Opportunities	6722	D	310 451-3051	9395
Macerich Company (PA)	6798	D	310 394-6000	9473
Full Stack Finance	6799	D	800 941-0356	9510
Inventure Capital Corporation (PA)	6799	A	213 262-6903	9523
Tennenbaum Capitl Partners LLC (HQ)	6799	D	310 566-1000	9573
By The Blue Sea LLC	7011	B	310 458-0030	9670
C W Hotels Ltd	7011	C	310 395-9700	9672
Dtrs Santa Monica LLC	7011	D	310 458-6700	9767
Edward Thomas Hospitality Corp	7011	B	310 458-0030	9773
Et Whitehall Seascape LLC	7011	C	310 581-5533	9787
M&C Hotel Interests Inc	7011	D	310 399-9344	9993
Ocean Avenue LLC	7011	B	310 576-7777	10056
Roscoe Real Estate Ltd Partnr	7011	D	310 260-7500	10173
Santa Monica Hotel Owner LLC	7011	C	310 395-3332	10208
Santa Monica Proper Jv LLC	7011	D	310 620-9990	10209
Second Street Corporation	7011	C	310 394-5454	10218
Windsor Capital Group Inc	7011	C	310 566-1100	10376
Ad Populum LLC (PA)	7311	D	619 818-7644	10585
Adconion Media Inc (PA)	7311	D	310 382-5521	10586
Advertise Purple	7311	D	424 272-7400	10587
Movers and Shakers LLC	7311	D	310 893-7051	10651
Ogilvy Group LLC	7311	D	310 280-2200	10657
Postaer Rubin and Associates	7311	C	312 644-3636	10662
Rubin Postaer and Associates (PA)	7311	C	310 394-4000	10671
Beachbody Company Inc (PA)	7313	C	310 883-9000	10705
Edmundscom Inc (HQ)	7313	A	310 309-6300	10710
Kargo Global Inc	7313	C	212 979-9000	10713
Dronebase Inc (PA)	7335	D	310 684-3076	10796
Platinum Clg Indianapolis LLC	7349	B	310 584-8000	10943
First Call Staffing Inc	7361	D	310 264-9914	11138
Bird Rides Inc	7371	D	866 205-2442	11457
Fair Financial Corp (PA)	7371	D	800 584-5000	11591
Kixie Online Inc	7371	D	424 800-3330	11694
Playhaven LLC	7371	C	310 308-9668	11836
School-Link Technologies Inc	7371	D	310 434-2700	11904
Snap Inc (PA)	7371	A	310 399-3339	11928
Activision Blizzard Inc (HQ)	7372	B	310 255-2000	12073
Amber Holding Inc	7372	D	603 324-3000	12089
Clearlake Capital Partners	7372	A	310 400-8800	12139
Cornerstone Ondemand Inc (HQ)	7372	D	310 752-0200	12149
Delart Technology Services LLC	7373	D	949 229-2786	12445
Epochcom LLC	7374	C	310 664-5700	12571
Flyr Inc (PA)	7374	D	415 841-3597	12574
Goodrx Holdings Inc (PA)	7374	B	855 268-2822	12576
Leaf Group Ltd (HQ)	7374	C	310 394-6400	12586
Society6 LLC	7374	D	310 394-6400	12627
Edmunds Holding Company (PA)	7375	A	310 309-6300	12661
Tigerconnect Inc (PA)	7379	D	310 401-1820	12896
Advanstar Communications Inc (DH)	7389	C	310 857-7500	13179
Hct Packaging Inc (PA)	7389	C	310 260-7680	13310
Hirsch/Bedner Intl Inc (PA)	7389	D	310 829-9087	13316
Universal Mus Investments Inc (PA)	7389	D	888 583-7176	13530
Universal Music Group Inc (HQ)	7389	D	310 865-0770	13531
Wells Fargo Capital Finance Inc	7389	C	310 453-7300	13553
M2 Automotive	7532	A	310 399-3887	13641
Artisan Entertainment Inc	7812	D	310 449-9200	13819
Blind Decker Productions Inc	7812	D	310 264-4247	13822
Focus Features LLC (DH)	7812	D		13850
Jerry Bruckheimer Inc	7812	D	310 664-6260	13858
Lions Gate Films Inc	7812	C	310 449-9200	13861
Luma Pictures Inc	7812	C	310 888-8738	13863
SPS West LLC	7812	D	818 845-8050	13897
Bad Robot Productions Inc	7822	D	310 664-3456	13961
Lionsgate Productions Inc	7822	B	310 255-3937	13966
Sonar Entertainment Inc (PA)	7822	D	424 230-7140	13967
Innovtive Artsts Tlent Ltrary (PA)	7922	D	310 656-0400	14040
Tennis Channel Inc (HQ)	7922	D	310 392-1920	14070
Illumination Entertainment	7929	C	626 298-1879	14088
Red Bull North America Inc (HQ)	7929	D	310 460-5356	14100
Boxunion Santa Monica LLC (PA)	7991	C	310 882-5508	14182
Santa Monica Amusements LLC	7996	B	310 451-9641	14313
Bay Clubs Company LLC	7997	B	310 829-4995	14337
Beach Club	7997	D	310 395-3254	14338
Jonathan Club	7997	D	310 393-9245	14385
Medical Imging Ctr Sthern Cal	8011	D	310 829-9788	14891
Saint Jhns Hlth Ctr Foundation	8011	D	310 315-6111	15033
Ucla Snta Mnica Gstrenterology	8011	D	310 582-6240	15136
Venice Family Clinic	8011	D	310 392-8636	15179
Manske Dental Corporation	8021	D	213 907-4027	15238
Ocean Park Optometry	8042	D	310 452-1039	15264
American Retirement Corp	8051	C	310 399-3227	15324
Asmb LLC	8051	D	949 347-7100	15335
Coastal Health Care Inc	8051	D	310 828-5596	15376
Berkeley E Convalescent Hosp	8059	C	310 829-5377	15817
Golden State Health Ctrs Inc	8059	C	310 451-9706	15852
Providence St Johns Hlth Ctr	8062	B	971 268-7643	16351
Saint Johns Health Center Foundation (DH)	8062	A	310 829-5511	16370
Ucla Healthcare	8062	D	310 319-4560	16586
Clare Matrix (PA)	8069	D	310 314-6200	16673
Step Up On Second Street Inc (PA)	8082	D	310 394-6889	16936
Regents of The University Cal	8099	D	310 267-9308	17312
Sensei Wellness Holdings Inc	8099	D	602 499-9862	17324
Bryan Cave Lighton Paisner LLP	8111	D	310 576-2100	17393
County of Los Angeles	8322	D	310 266-3711	17922
People Concern	8322	C	310 883-1222	18080
People Concern	8322	C	310 450-0650	18081
Vista Del Mar Child Fmly Svcs	8361	C	310 836-1223	18543
Mens Apparel Guild In Cal Inc	8611	D	310 857-7500	18713
Boys Grls CLB Snta Monica Inc	8641	D	310 361-8500	18824
Elizabeth Glser Pdtric Aids FN	8641	B	310 593-0047	18856
Milken Family Foundation	8641	D	310 570-4800	18882
Pacific Neuroscience Inst LLC	8641	D	310 829-8271	18891
Los Angeles Intl Ch Chrst	8661	C	213 351-2300	19023
Automobile Club Southern Cal	8699	C	310 453-1909	19063
California Semiconductor Tech	8711	C	310 579-2939	19170
Bjarke Ingels Group Nyc LLC	8712	C	347 549-4141	19456
Kite Pharma Inc (HQ)	8731	D	310 824-9999	19720
Smartmatic USA Corp	8733	D	424 581-6604	19913
The Rand Corporation (PA)	8733	A	310 393-0411	19920
911 Health Inc	8734	D	310 560-8509	19942
Global-Dining Inc California	8741	D	310 576-9922	20100
Provident Financial Management	8741	D	310 282-0477	20188

GEOGRAPHIC SECTION

SARATOGA CA

	SIC	EMP	PHONE	ENTRY#
Cloud9 Esports Inc	8742	D	424 256-8391	20319
Mgid Inc	8742	D	424 322-8059	20470
Stardust Studios Inc	8742	D	310 399-6047	20565
Wilshire Advisors LLC (PA)	8742	C	310 451-3051	20614
Ziprecruiter Inc	8742	A	877 252-1062	20626
Capital Oversight Inc (PA)	8748	D	310 453-8000	20717
Ocean Park Community Center	8748	C	310 828-6717	20819

SANTA PAULA, CA - Ventura County

	SIC	EMP	PHONE	ENTRY#
Saticoy Lemon Association (PA)	0723	D	805 654-6500	302
Oil Well Service Company	1389	D	805 525-2103	624
Keller North America Inc	1799	C	805 933-1331	2291
Calavo Growers Inc (PA)	2099	D	805 525-1245	2431
Weber Orthopedic LP (PA)	3842	D	800 221-5465	3064
Pavement Coatings Co	4953	C	805 647-0693	4918
Aurora Casting & Engrg Inc	5051	D	805 933-2761	5477
Troop Real Estate Inc	6531	C	805 921-0030	9202
United Site Services Cal Inc	7359	D	805 933-2793	11060
Ventura County Medical Center	8011	C	805 933-8600	15182
Tissue-Grown Corporation	8731	D	805 525-1975	19785
Ventura County Medical Center	8742	D	805 677-5184	20602

SANTA ROSA, CA - Sonoma County

	SIC	EMP	PHONE	ENTRY#
Balletto Ranch Inc (PA)	0161	C	707 568-2455	20
Balletto Ranch Inc	0172	C	707 568-2455	69
Canine Cmpnons For Indpendence (PA)	0752	D	707 577-1700	359
Landesign Cnstr & Maint Inc	0782	D	707 578-2657	514
Murphy-True Inc	1542	D	707 576-7337	973
Wright Contracting LLC	1542	D	707 528-1172	1066
Argonaut Constructors Inc	1623	C	707 542-4862	1193
Ghilotti Construction Co Inc (PA)	1629	C	707 585-1221	1304
Famand Inc	1711	D	707 255-9295	1435
Jackson Family Wines Inc (PA)	2084	D	707 544-4000	2387
Mildara Blass Inc	2084	B	707 836-5000	2389
Keysight Technologies Inc (PA)	3823	A	800 829-4444	3017
Mv Transportation Inc	4111	C	707 546-1999	3182
Sonoma County Airport Ex Inc	4111	B	707 837-8700	3215
West County Trnsp Agcy	4111	C	707 206-9988	3225
Atech Warehousing & Dist Inc (PA)	4213	D	707 526-1910	3444
Ss Skikos Incorporated	4214	D	707 575-3000	3597
J Kenneth Forester	4522	E	201 288-5040	3865
Kaiserair Inc	4581	D	707 528-7400	3896
Sonoma Cnty Scuritization Corp	4581	D	707 565-2241	3911
Atech Logistics Inc	4731	C	707 526-1910	3987
New Cingular Wireless Svcs Inc	4812	D	707 535-0891	4220
Pacific Gas and Electric Co	4911	D	707 579-6337	4616
Pacific Gas and Electric Co	4911	B	800 756-7243	4624
Pacific Gas and Electric Co	4911	D	707 577-7283	4636
Sonoma County Water Agency (PA)	4941	C	707 526-5370	4836
Recology Sonoma Marin	4953	B	707 586-8261	4927
Myers Restaurant Supply LLC	5046	C	707 570-1200	5386
CPI International	5049	C	707 521-6327	5465
City Electric Supply	5063	C	707 523-4600	5547
La Tortilla Factory Inc (PA)	5149	B	707 586-4000	6643
Redwood Coast Petroleum Inc	5172	D	707 546-0766	6736
Regal III LLC	5182	C	707 836-2100	6804
Freeman Motors Inc	5511	C	707 542-1791	7213
Hansel - Prestige Inc	5511	B	707 578-4717	7229
Goodwill Inds of Rdwood Empire (PA)	5932	D	707 523-0550	7538
Wells Fargo Center For Arts	6021	D	707 527-7006	7644
Big Poppy Holdings Inc	6022	C	707 636-9020	7659
Exchange Bank (PA)	6036	C	707 524-3000	7748
Redwood Credit Union (PA)	6061	C	707 545-4000	7793
American Agcredit Flca (PA)	6159	D	707 545-1200	7913
Chase Manhattan Mortgage Corp	6162	C	707 525-5060	7948
Provident Funding Assoc LP	6162	D	707 568-2420	8013
Change Lending LLC	6163	D	707 596-5111	8033
Merrill Lynch Prce Fnner Smith	6211	D	707 575-8475	8128
Wells Fargo Investments LLC	6211	D	707 521-1232	8176
State Compensation Insur Fund	6331	B	888 782-8338	8414
First American Home Warranty	6541	D	707 596-5151	9232
Meda Cypress Ridge LP	6552	C	707 526-9782	9263
Bavarian Lion Company Cal (PA)	7011	D	707 545-8530	9633
Vintners Inn	7011	C	707 575-7350	10345
Optima Building Services Inc	7349	D	707 586-6640	10938
Tekberry Inc	7361	B	707 313-5345	11245
Volt Management Corp	7361	D	707 547-1660	11254
Visiquate Inc	7371	C	707 546-4377	12026
Probusiness Holdings Inc	7374	D	845 354-5372	12609
Armourous	7381	D	707 387-4400	12933
First Alarm SEC & Patrol Inc	7381	B	707 584-1110	12970
Icon Design and Display Inc	7389	D	707 284-3400	13320
Korvalabs Inc	7389	C	888 702-9042	13341
Venture Design Services Inc	7389	D	707 524-8368	13539
Santa Rosa City of	7538	D	707 543-3882	13675
North American Cinemas Inc	7832	C	707 571-1412	14004
North American Cinemas Inc	7832	C	707 539-6773	14005
Luther Burbank Mem Foundation	7922	D	707 546-3600	14045
Fountaingrove Golf & Athc CLB	7992	D	707 701-3050	14262
Oakmont Golf Club Inc	7992	D	707 538-2454	14279
Mayacama Golf Club LLC	7997	D	707 569-2900	14402
Redwood Empire Ice Oprtons LLC (PA)	7999	D	707 546-7147	14553
Eye Care Institute	8011	D	707 546-9800	14743
Kaiser Foundation Hospitals	8011	A	707 393-4000	14797
Mark E Jacobson M D	8011	D	707 571-4022	14887
Permanente Medical Group Inc	8011	A	707 393-4000	14964
Sonoma Cnty Indian Hlth Prj In (PA)	8011	C	707 521-4545	15064
Sutter Med Group of Rdwods Inc	8011	C	707 546-2788	15114
Interdent Service Corporation	8021	D	707 528-7000	15230
Ensign Group Inc	8051	C	707 525-1250	15454
Santa Rosaidence Opco LLC	8051	C	707 546-0471	15655
Emeritus Corporation	8052	C	707 324-7087	15756
Santa Rosa Surgery Center LP	8062	C	707 575-5831	16394
St Joseph Hlth Nthrn Cal LLC	8062	C	707 547-2221	16458
St Joseph Hlth Nthrn Cal LLC	8062	B	707 542-4704	16459
St Joseph Hlth Nthrn Cal LLC	8062	B	707 921-4717	16461
St Joseph Hlth Nthrn Cal LLC (PA)	8062	C	949 381-4000	16462
Redwood Rgnal Med Group DRG LL (PA)	8071	D	707 525-4080	16748
Redwood Toxicology Lab Inc	8071	C	707 577-7958	16749
Centerwell Health Services Inc	8082	D	707 545-7114	16836
Sisters of St Joseph Orange	8082	A	747 206-9124	16928
St Joseph Home Care Network (DH)	8082	D	714 712-9500	16933
Aurora Bhvral Hlthcare - STA R	8093	D	707 800-7700	17007
Drug Abuse Alternatives Center	8093	D	707 571-2233	17055
Mhm Services Inc	8093	C	707 623-9080	17096
Blood Bank of Redwoods (PA)	8099	D	707 545-1222	17189
Lanahan & Reilley LLP (PA)	8111	C	415 856-4700	17534
Sonoma County Office Education	8111	D	707 524-2690	17660
Sonoma Country Day School	8211	D	707 284-3200	17750
California Parenting Institute	8299	D	707 585-6108	17804
California Human Dev Corp (PA)	8331	C	707 523-1155	18214
Community Child Care Cncil Sno (PA)	8351	C	707 544-3077	18300
Front Porch Communities & Svcs	8361	D	707 538-8400	18437
Victor Treatment Centers Inc	8361	C	707 360-1509	18539
Community Action Prtnr Snoma C	8399	D	707 544-0120	18559
Anova Edcatn Behavioral Cnsltn	8621	D	707 527-0183	18730
Deposition Sciences Inc	8731	D	707 573-6700	19678
Catalyst Group LLC	8742	D	707 527-8551	20310
Dema Consulting & MGT LLC	8742	D	707 757-5010	20342
Inquiring Systems Inc	8742	D	707 939-3900	20414
New America Funding LLC	8742	D	707 392-4254	20487

SANTA YNEZ, CA - Santa Barbara County

	SIC	EMP	PHONE	ENTRY#
Channel Islnds Yung MNS Chrstn	8641	D	805 686-2037	18840

SANTEE, CA - San Diego County

	SIC	EMP	PHONE	ENTRY#
T C Construction Company Inc	1623	C	619 448-4560	1270
Chula Vista Electric Co	1731	D	619 420-4500	1697
Towne Drywall Inc	1742	D	619 334-3750	1970
Challenger Sheet Metal Inc	1761	D	619 596-8040	2050
Tower Glass Inc	1793	D	619 596-6199	2207
CCM Enterprises (PA)	2541	D	619 562-2605	2501
European Wholesale Counter	2541	D	619 562-0565	2503
Terra Nova Technologies Inc	3535	D	619 596-7400	2777
Padre Dam Municipal Water Dst (PA)	4941	D	619 258-4617	4816
Padre Dam Municipal Water Dst	4941	D	619 258-4662	4817
Smart & Final Stores LLC	5141	B	619 449-2396	6287
Lowes Home Centers LLC	5211	C	619 212-4100	7082
JMS Interiors Inc	7389	D	619 749-5098	13333
County of San Diego	8051	D	619 956-2800	15396
Santee Senior Retirement Com	8322	D	619 955-0901	18118
Scantibodies Laboratory Inc (PA)	8734	C	619 258-9300	19997
Cgp Maintenance Cnstr Svcs Inc	8741	D	858 454-7326	20054

SARATOGA, CA - Santa Clara County

	SIC	EMP	PHONE	ENTRY#
Distinctive Corporation	7389	D	408 568-5598	13270
Saratoga Country Club Inc	7997	D	408 253-0340	14445
Our Lady Fatima Villa Inc	8051	D	408 741-2950	15614
Progressive Sub-Acute Care	8062	D	408 378-8875	16345
Precious Enterprises Inc	8351	D	408 265-2226	18348
Odd Fellows Home California	8361	B	408 741-7100	18499
Montalvo Association	8422	D	408 961-5800	18691
Young MNS Chrstn Assn Slcon Vl	8699	C	408 370-1877	19122
Stage 4 Solutions Incorporated	8742	D	408 868-9739	20564

	SIC	EMP	PHONE	ENTRY#
SAUGUS, CA - Los Angeles County				
Admiral Refrigeration Inc.	1711	D	661 505-7913	1337
SAUSALITO, CA - Marin County				
Swa Group (PA)	0781	D	415 332-5100	468
Yardzen Co.	0781	D	415 729-0115	471
Paul Ryan Associates	1521	D	415 861-3085	707
Alta Mira Recovery Ctrs LLC	5812	D	415 332-1350	7455
Steelrver Infrstrcture Prtners (PA)	6719	C	415 512-1515	9340
Casa Madrona Hotel and Spa LLC	7011	A	415 332-0502	9683
Butler Shine Stern Prtners LLC	7311	C	415 331-6049	10595
Ubics Inc	7371	C	415 289-1400	11998
Waggl Inc (PA)	7372	C	415 399-9949	12394
Zhoug Hong	8322	D	415 647-7742	18201
Young MNS Chrstn Assn San Frnc	8641	C	415 331-9622	18997
Ro Rocket Design Inc	8712	C	415 289-0830	19502
Wested	8733	D	415 289-2300	19936
SCOTTS VALLEY, CA - Santa Cruz County				
Bfp Fire Protection Inc	1711	D	831 461-1100	1377
Intrado Interactive Svcs Corp	4822	D	888 527-5225	4365
Reliance Communications LLC	4822	D	408 827-4726	4367
Morgan Stnley Smith Barney LLC	6211	D	831 440-5200	8147
Pacific Sthwest Cnfrnce of Eva	6512	D	831 335-9133	8742
John Stewart Company	6531	D	831 438-5725	9060
Ert Operating Company	7371	A	412 390-3000	11578
Hospice of Santa Cruz County (PA)	8082	D	831 430-3000	16871
Pearl Automation Inc	8711	D	831 316-5207	19356
Ava The Rabbit Haven Inc	8748	D	831 600-7479	20696
SEAL BEACH, CA - Orange County				
Samedan Oil Corporation	1382	B	661 319-5038	604
P2f Holdings	5199	D	562 296-1055	6933
Merrill Lynch Prce Fnner Smith	6211	D	562 493-1300	8135
First Team RE - Orange Cnty	6531	B	562 596-9911	9011
Olson Company LLC (PA)	6552	D	562 596-4770	9268
Olson Urban Housing LLC	6552	D	562 596-4770	9269
Talent & Acquisition LLC	7371	C	888 970-9575	11965
Tenet Healthsystem Medical Inc	8011	C	562 493-9581	15124
Action Hlth Care Prsnnel Svcs	8082	C	562 799-5523	16793
Premier Healthcare Svcs LLC (DH)	8082	C	626 204-7930	16912
Country Villa Service Corp	8322	C	562 598-2477	17900
Sisters of St Joseph Orange	8661	A	562 430-4638	19028
Fisheries Resource Vlntr Corps	8742	C	562 596-9261	20381
SEASIDE, CA - Monterey County				
Seaside Hospitality LP	7011	C	831 394-5335	10216
Bsl Golf Corp	7992	C	831 899-7271	14247
Professional Health Care Inc	8361	D	831 899-2644	18506
SEBASTOPOL, CA - Sonoma County				
General Hydroponics Inc	2875	D	707 824-9376	2639
Tbc Shared Services LLC	5531	A	707 829-9864	7378
Precision Dermatology Inc	8011	D	415 202-1540	14997
County of Sonoma	8062	C	707 823-8511	16031
Sonoma West Medical Center	8062	C	707 823-8511	16435
North Bay Fire	9224	D	707 823-1084	20936
SELMA, CA - Fresno County				
Circle K Ranch LP (PA)	0175	D	559 834-1571	104
Pacific Gas and Electric Co	4911	D	559 891-2143	4629
Fresno Valves & Castings Inc (PA)	4971	D	559 834-2511	4988
Poindexter Nut Company Inc	5145	B	559 834-1555	6463
Bethel Lutheran Home Inc	8059	D	559 896-4900	15819
Hanford Community Hospital	8062	B	559 891-1000	16118
SEQ NATL PK, CA - Tulare County				
DNC Parks & Resorts At Sequoia	7011	C	559 565-4070	9754
DNC Prks Rsorts At Sequoia Inc	7011	C	559 565-4070	9756
SHAFTER, CA - Kern County				
Garlic Company	0139	C	661 393-4212	12
Wonderful Orchards LLC (HQ)	0173	C	661 399-4456	95
Grimmway Enterprises Inc	0191	C	661 399-0844	180
Grimmway Enterprises Inc	0723	B	661 393-3320	272
Wonderful Company LLC	0723	A	661 399-4456	318
Cummings Vacuum Service Inc	1389	C	661 746-1786	612
Oil Well Service Company	1389	D	661 746-4809	622
Tryad Service Corporation	1389	D	661 391-1524	631
CJ Logistics America LLC	4225	D	847 390-6800	3687
Jti Elctrcal Instrmntation LLC	4911	D	661 393-5535	4582
Standard Industries Inc	5033	D	661 387-1110	5225
Bps Supply Group (PA)	5051	D	661 589-9141	5480
Farm Pump & Irrigation Co Inc (PA)	5084	D	661 589-6901	5834
Varner Family Ltd Partnership (PA)	6733	D	661 399-1163	9450
SHELL BEACH, CA - San Luis Obispo County				
Dolphin Bay Ht & Residence Inc	7011	D	805 773-4300	9761
La Bonne Vie Inc	7991	D	805 773-5003	14210
SHERMAN OAKS, CA - Los Angeles County				
Best Friends Animal Hospital	0742	D	818 766-2140	329
Ram Plumbing	1711	D	800 487-5812	1540
Coastal Tile Inc	1743	D	818 988-6134	1977
Xsolla (usa) Inc (PA)	4813	A	818 435-6613	4359
Vubiquity Holdings Inc (DH)	4841	C	818 526-5000	4527
Sggh LLC	5063	A	805 435-1255	5590
Jarrow Formulas Inc (PA)	5122	D	310 204-6936	6116
Neurobrands LLC	5149	C	310 393-6444	6654
Center Automotive Inc	5511	D	818 907-9995	7180
Miller Automotive Group Inc (HQ)	5511	B	818 787-8400	7258
Psychic Eye Book Shops Inc (PA)	5942	D	818 906-8263	7549
Homebridge Financial Svcs Inc	6163	A	818 981-0606	8044
Royal Specialty Undwrt Inc	6331	C	818 922-6700	8406
Beverly and Company Inc	6531	C	323 422-3253	8913
Moss & Company Inc (PA)	6531	C	310 453-0911	9102
Moss Management Services Inc	6531	C	818 990-5999	9103
Prospect Mortgage LLC	6719	A		9330
Burbank Partners LLC	7011	C	818 263-8704	9666
Serviz Inc	7299	D	818 381-4826	10574
Adactive Media Ca Inc	7313	D	818 465-7500	10699
Waldberg Inc	7313	D	818 843-0004	10723
Caine & Weiner Company Inc (PA)	7322	C	818 226-6000	10737
Branded Entrmt Netwrk Inc (PA)	7335	C	310 342-1500	10795
Ben Group Inc	7371	B	310 342-1500	11453
Reel Security California Inc	7381	D	818 928-4737	13027
Alternative Ira Services LLC	7389	D	877 936-7175	13188
Lendingusa LLC	7389	D	800 994-6177	13352
Mega Appraisers Inc	7389	A	818 246-7370	13369
Prager University Foundation	7812	D	833 772-4378	13882
Premiere Radio Network Inc (DH)	7922	C	818 377-5300	14057
Mpc Productions LLC	7929	D	310 418-8115	14097
Lucky Strike Entertainment LLC	7933	D	248 374-3420	14118
Big3 Basketball LLC	7941	D	213 417-2013	14130
Prime Hlthcare Svcs - Shrman O	8062	B	818 981-7111	16342
Sherman Oaks Health System	8062	D	818 981-7111	16424
Dynamic Home Care Service Inc (PA)	8082	D	818 981-4446	16856
Help Group West (PA)	8093	D	818 781-0360	17072
Working With Autism Inc	8093	D	818 501-4240	17162
Star of Ca LLC	8099	D	818 986-7827	17332
Law Offices Michael Burgis PC	8111	D	818 994-9870	17542
Tharpe & Howell (PA)	8111	D	818 205-9955	17666
SHINGLE SPRINGS, CA - El Dorado County				
Calnet Inc	4813	D	530 672-1078	4261
SIERRA MADRE, CA - Los Angeles County				
Deasy Penner Podley	6531	C	626 408-1280	8976
Kensington Sierra Madre LP	8361	D	626 355-5700	18463
SIGNAL HILL, CA - Los Angeles County				
Fenderscape Incorporated	0782	C	562 988-2228	490
Oil Well Service Company (PA)	1389	C	562 612-0600	623
Jmh Engineering and Cnstr	1521	C	562 317-1700	686
2h Construction Inc	1542	D	562 424-5567	858
Har-Bro LLC (HQ)	1542	D	562 528-8000	928
Gregg Drilling LLC	1781	C	562 427-6899	2172
Lovco Construction Inc	1794	D	562 595-1601	2220
Gregg Drilling & Testing Inc (PA)	1799	C	562 427-6899	2282
Ancon Marine Inc	4212	C	562 326-5900	3367
Edco Disposal Corporation (PA)	4953	C	619 287-7555	4890
Nsv International Corp	5013	D	562 438-3836	5052
Viking Office Products Inc (DH)	5112	B	562 490-1000	6071
Boulevard Automotive Group (PA)	5511	D	562 492-1000	7176
MD Care Inc	6321	D	562 344-3400	8268
First American Team Realty Inc (PA)	6531	C	562 427-7765	9006
Accountble Hlth Cre IPA A Prof	8099	C	562 435-3333	17165
SIMI VALLEY, CA - Ventura County				
Specialized Ldscp MGT Svcs Inc	0781	D	805 520-7590	466
Cobalt Construction Company	1522	D	805 577-6222	749
Suttles Plumbing & Mech Corp	1711	D	818 718-9779	1580
B & M Contractors Inc	1771	D	805 581-5480	2096
Qualitylogic Inc	3577	D	208 424-1905	2836
Meggitt Safety Systems Inc (DH)	3699	C	805 584-4100	2960
Waste Management Cal Inc	4953	C	805 522-7023	4958

GEOGRAPHIC SECTION

SOUTH LAKE TAHOE CA

	SIC	EMP	PHONE	ENTRY#
Shopper Inc.	5046	B	805 527-6700	5388
Electromed Inc.	5047	B	805 523-7500	5412
Quad-C Jh Holdings Inc.	5047	C	800 966-6662	5446
Foreign Trade Corporation.	5065	C	805 823-8400	5651
Howmet Globl Fstning Systems I (HQ).	5085	C	805 426-2270	5904
Andwin Corporation (PA).	5113	D	818 999-2828	6073
Smart & Final Stores Inc.	5141	D	805 520-6035	6319
Smart & Final Stores LLC.	5141	D	805 582-9231	6380
Lowes Home Centers LLC.	5211	D	805 426-2780	7089
Lumber City Corp.	5251	D	805 522-0533	7123
Ford of Simi Valley Inc.	5511	D	805 583-0333	7210
Am-Pac Tire Dist Inc (DH).	5531	D		7341
Coast To Coast Cmpt Pdts Inc.	5734	D	805 244-9500	7441
First & La Realty Corp (PA).	6531	D	805 581-0021	9003
Troop Real Estate Inc (PA).	6531	D	805 581-3200	9201
Wsm Investments LLC.	6794	C	818 332-4600	9460
Holiday Inn Express.	7011	C	805 584-6006	9861
Simi West Inc.	7011	C	760 346-5502	10240
Pico Rents Inc.	7359	D	310 275-9431	11050
Anjana Software Solutions Inc.	7371	D	805 583-0121	11407
Bestitcom Inc (PA).	7379	D	602 667-5613	12741
Edgeworth Integration LLC.	7382	D	805 915-0211	13110
American Vision Windows Inc.	7699	C	805 582-1833	13762
Young MNS Chrstn Assn Sthast V.	7999	C	805 583-5338	14590
Setarehshenas Dental Corp.	8021	C	805 583-5700	15250
Providnce Facey Med Foundation.	8031	D	805 206-2000	15257
Simi Vly Hosp & Hlth Care Svcs.	8062	A	805 955-6000	16429
Simi Vly Hosp & Hlth Care Svcs (HQ).	8062	A	805 955-6000	16430
Good Shepherd Lutheran HM of W.	8361	C	805 526-2482	18441
Ronald Rgan Prsdntial Fndtion.	8412	D	805 522-2977	18667
Computerized Mgt Svcs Inc.	8721	D	805 522-5940	19554
Chase Group Llc.	8732	B	805 522-9155	19804
Weapon X Security Inc.	8999	D	818 818-9950	20906

SKYFOREST, CA - San Bernardino County

	SIC	EMP	PHONE	ENTRY#
Spsv Entertainment LLC.	7929	D	909 744-9373	14106

SMITH RIVER, CA - Del Norte County

	SIC	EMP	PHONE	ENTRY#
Smith River Lucky 7 Casino.	7011	D	707 487-7777	10249

SNELLING, CA - Merced County

	SIC	EMP	PHONE	ENTRY#
JS Homen Trucking Inc.	4212	D	209 723-9559	3409

SODA SPRINGS, CA - Nevada County

	SIC	EMP	PHONE	ENTRY#
Boreal Ridge Corporation.	7011	C	530 426-1012	9654
Royal Gorge Nordic Ski Resort (PA).	7011	C	530 426-3871	10176

SOLANA BEACH, CA - San Diego County

	SIC	EMP	PHONE	ENTRY#
Spectrum Cnstr Group Inc.	1541	D	949 299-1400	844
Simon Golub & Sons Inc (DH).	5094	D		6026
Southern Cal Disc Tire Co Inc.	5531	C	858 481-6387	7366
Pacifica Hosts Inc.	7011	C	858 792-8200	10092
Srg Holdings LLC (HQ).	7359	A	858 792-9300	11055
Lumiradx Inc.	7371	C	951 201-9384	11721
Trovata Inc (PA).	7371	D	312 914-8106	11989
Onehealth Solutions Inc.	7379	D	858 947-6333	12849
Simulstat Incorporated.	7379	D	858 546-4337	12877
Acacia Pharma Inc.	7389	D	317 941-9576	13174
Alamo Rental (us) Inc.	7514	D	858 792-2522	13576

SOLEDAD, CA - Monterey County

	SIC	EMP	PHONE	ENTRY#
Braga Fresh Family Farms Inc (PA).	0191	D	831 675-2154	169
El Camino Labor LLC.	0761	D	831 809-9537	364
Soledad Cmnty Hlth Care Dst FN.	8051	D	831 678-2462	15676
Community Action Prtnr San Lui.	8351	D	831 678-1584	18299

SOLVANG, CA - Santa Barbara County

	SIC	EMP	PHONE	ENTRY#
Holzheus El Rancho Market Inc.	5411	D	805 688-4300	7144
Alisal Properties (PA).	7032	C	805 688-6411	10397
Solvang Lutheran Home Inc.	8051	D	805 688-3263	15677
Cottage Health.	8062	B	805 688-6432	16020
Santa Ynez Vly Cttage Hosp Inc.	8062	B	805 688-6431	16396

SOMIS, CA - Ventura County

	SIC	EMP	PHONE	ENTRY#
Saticoy Country Club.	7997	D	805 647-1153	14446

SONOMA, CA - Sonoma County

	SIC	EMP	PHONE	ENTRY#
Peterson Mechanical Inc.	1711	D	707 938-8481	1528
Retail Realm Distribution Inc (PA).	5141	D	707 996-5400	6282
Diageo North America Inc.	5182	C	707 939-6200	6795
South Bay Wine Group LLC.	5182	D	310 465-0551	6806
Vintage Senior Management Inc.	6513	A	707 595-0009	8868
Four Sisters Inns.	7011	D	707 939-1340	9803
LAuberge De Sonoma LLC.	7011	C	707 938-2929	9969
Sonoma Hotel Operator Inc.	7011	C	707 938-9000	10253
After-Party2 Inc.	7359	D	408 457-1187	11014
Speedway Sonoma LLC.	7948	D	707 938-8448	14167
Ensign Sonoma LLC.	8051	C	707 938-8406	15459
Emeritus Corporation.	8052	C	707 996-7101	15755
Sonomaidence Opco LLC.	8052	D	707 938-1096	15796
Sonoma Valley Health Care Dst (PA).	8062	B	707 935-5000	16434
Bookheaded Learning LLC.	8351	D	707 996-3427	18271

SONORA, CA - Tuolumne County

	SIC	EMP	PHONE	ENTRY#
Diestel Turkey Ranch (PA).	0253	C	209 532-4950	227
Tuolumne Utilities District.	4941	D	209 532-5536	4842
Leavitt United Insur Svcs Inc.	6411	D	209 532-6951	8602
Front Porch Inc (PA).	7371	D	209 288-5500	11607
Sierra Intrnal Mdcine Med Grou.	8011	D	209 536-3738	15059
Sonora Community Hospital.	8011	C	209 536-5012	15065
Avalon Care Ctr - Sonora LLC.	8051	C	209 533-2500	15345
Adventist Health Sonora (HQ).	8062	A	209 532-5000	15918
Kingsview Corp.	8093	C	209 533-6245	17084
Sierra Mountain Cnstr Inc.	8322	D	209 928-1900	18134
Amador Tlmne Cmnty Action Agcy.	8399	D	209 533-1397	18555

SOQUEL, CA - Santa Cruz County

	SIC	EMP	PHONE	ENTRY#
Bay Photo Inc.	7221	C	831 475-6090	10489
Unfold Agency Inc.	7311	D	818 679-4837	10684

SOULSBYVILLE, CA - Tuolumne County

	SIC	EMP	PHONE	ENTRY#
Milestone Rtrment Cmmnties LLC.	8361	D	209 533-4822	18487

SOUTH EL MONTE, CA - Los Angeles County

	SIC	EMP	PHONE	ENTRY#
Bali Construction Inc.	1623	D	626 442-8003	1196
American Wrecking Inc.	1795	D	626 350-8303	2229
Fresh Air Envmtl Svcs Inc.	1799	D	323 913-1965	2279
Promotnal Design Concepts Inc.	3069	D	626 579-4454	2659
Amro Fabricating Corporation (PA).	3728	D	626 579-2200	2989
California Med Response Inc.	4119	D	562 968-1818	3243
Leader Industries Inc.	4119	C	626 575-0880	3271
Integrated Parcel Network.	4215	B	714 278-6100	3616
Pactrack Inc.	4731	D	213 201-5856	4070
Gama Contracting Services Inc.	5082	C	626 442-7200	5788
Ted Levine Drum Co (PA).	7699	D	626 579-1084	13805
Ahmc Healthcare Inc.	8062	D	626 579-7777	15932
Lincoln Trning Ctr Rhbltion W.	8331	D	626 442-0621	18233

SOUTH GATE, CA - Los Angeles County

	SIC	EMP	PHONE	ENTRY#
World Oil Corp.	1311	C	562 928-0100	587
Herbert Malarkey Roofing Co.	1761	D	562 806-8000	2068
Interior Rmoval Specialist Inc.	1795	C	323 357-6900	2237
Saputo Cheese USA Inc.	2022	B	562 862-7686	2347
Sunopta Grains and Foods Inc.	2041	D	323 774-6000	2359
Metal Supply LLC.	3441	D	562 634-9940	2738
Cimc Intermodal Equipment LLC (HQ).	3715	D	562 904-8600	2978
California Transport Enterprises Inc.	4212	D		3377
Pan Pacific Petroleum Co Inc (PA).	4213	D	562 928-0100	3525
Samuel J Piazza & Son Inc (PA).	4214	C	323 357-1999	3594
Sprint Corporation.	4812	C	323 357-0797	4236
Pcs Mobile Solutions LLC.	4813	C	323 567-2490	4329
Privilege International Inc.	5021	C	323 585-0777	5104
Firma Plastic Co Inc.	5093	C	323 567-7767	6007
Berkshire Hthway HM Svcs CA Rp.	6531	D	562 307-5636	8911
Century 21 A Better Svc Rlty.	6531	D	562 806-1000	8930
5 Star Job Source.	7361	D	562 788-7391	11068
Koos Manufacturing Inc.	7389	A	323 249-1000	13340
Meribear Productions Inc.	7389	D	310 204-5353	13371
Altamed Health Services Corp.	8099	C	323 562-6700	17170
County of Los Angeles.	8099	D	562 861-0316	17214
Dickson Testing Co Inc (DH).	8734	D	562 862-8378	19965

SOUTH LAKE TAHOE, CA - El Dorado County

	SIC	EMP	PHONE	ENTRY#
South Tahoe Public Utility Dst.	4952	C	530 544-6474	4852
South Tahoe Refuse Co.	4953	D	530 541-5105	4939
Cha-Dor Realty LLC.	5251	C	530 544-2237	7116
Tahoe Ssons Rsort Time Intrval.	6531	C	530 541-6700	9189
Grclt Condominium Inc.	7011	D	530 542-8400	9818
Roppong-Thoe LP A Cal Ltd Prtn.	7011	C	530 544-5400	10171
Stateline Travelodge Inc.	7011	D	530 544-6000	10276
Tahoe Beach & Ski Club.	7011	D	530 541-6220	10304
Steven P Abelow MD.	8011	D	530 544-8033	15102
Barton Memorial Hospital.	8062	A	530 543-5581	15958
Healthcare Barton System (PA).	8062	A	530 541-3420	16123

SOUTH PASADENA CA

GEOGRAPHIC SECTION

	SIC	EMP	PHONE	ENTRY#

SOUTH PASADENA, CA - Los Angeles County

	SIC	EMP	PHONE	ENTRY#
Citadel Panda Express Inc	5812	D	626 799-9898	7467
Equity Smart Home Loans Inc	6162	D	626 864-8774	7961
Stratus Real Estate Inc	6163	D	626 441-5549	8058
Tokio Marine Highland Insurance Ser (DH)	6411	D	626 463-6486	8673
Cccc Growth Fund LLC	6799	D	626 441-8770	9497
Drivenbi LLC	7371	D	626 795-2088	11555
Stargate Films Inc	7812	D	626 403-8403	13898
City of Hope	8011	C	626 396-2900	14687

SOUTH SAN FRANCISCO, CA - San Mateo County

	SIC	EMP	PHONE	ENTRY#
Jacobs Farm/Del Cabo Inc	0191	C	650 827-1133	186
Plenty Unlimited Inc (PA)	0191	D	650 735-3737	194
Dome Construction Corporation (PA)	1542	C	650 416-5600	905
JMB Construction Inc	1542	D	650 267-5300	947
Frank M Booth Inc	1711	D	650 871-8292	1441
Alvah Contractors Inc	1731	B	650 741-6785	1662
Hoem & Associates Inc	1752	C	650 871-5194	2033
Quality Systems Instlltons Ltd	1799	D	650 875-9000	2309
Cytokinetics Incorporated (PA)	2834	C	650 624-3000	2584
Five Prime Therapeutics Inc	2834	C	415 365-5600	2586
Global Blood Therapeutics Inc	2834	D	650 741-7700	2587
Intermune Inc (DH)	2834	C	415 466-4383	2590
Kezar Life Sciences Inc (PA)	2834	D	650 822-5600	2593
Rapt Therapeutics Inc	2834	D	650 489-9000	2605
Rigel Pharmaceuticals Inc (PA)	2834	C	650 624-1100	2607
Allogene Therapeutics Inc (PA)	2836	C	650 457-2700	2617
Senti Biosciences Inc (PA)	2836	D	650 382-3281	2622
Vox Network Solutions Inc	3661	D	650 989-1000	2890
Standard Biotools Inc (PA)	3826	B	650 266-6000	3034
Toshiba America Mri Inc	3845	C	650 737-6686	3078
San Mateo County Transit Dst	4111	B	650 588-4860	3204
Supershuttle International Inc	4111	D	650 246-2786	3220
Supershuttle International Inc	4119	D	650 246-2704	3297
Mad Dog Express Inc (PA)	4212	D	650 588-1900	3411
University Cal San Francisco	4225	D	510 987-0700	3777
ABM Aviation Inc	4581	D	650 872-5400	3870
Aeroground Inc (DH)	4581	A	650 266-6965	3871
Trux Transport	4581	D	650 244-0200	3920
LBC Holdings USA Corporation (PA)	4724	C	650 873-0750	3938
Rxo Cstoms Clrnce Slutions LLC	4731	D	650 589-8150	4088
Race Telecommunications LLC (PA)	4813	D	650 246-8900	4334
ABS-Cbn International (DH)	4841	C	800 527-2820	4472
South San Frncsco Scvenger Inc	4953	D	650 589-4020	4938
Cenket Inc	5013	D		5032
Ssf Imported Auto Parts LLC (DH)	5013	D	800 203-9287	5063
Peking Handicraft Inc (PA)	5023	C	650 871-3788	5131
AES Heavy Equipment Rental Inc	5046	D	817 615-1044	5373
Tosoh Bioscience Inc	5047	D	650 615-4970	5455
Steven Engineering Inc (HQ)	5063	C	650 588-9200	5594
Monster (PA)	5099	B	415 840-2000	6046
Italfoods Inc	5141	D	650 877-0724	6259
Lehar Sales Co	5144	D	510 465-3255	6446
Antonelli & Sons Fish & Poultry	5146	D	650 952-7413	6465
Vegiworks Inc	5148	D	415 643-8686	6592
Ashbury Market Inc	5149	D	650 952-8889	6603
Dbi Beverage San Francisco	5181	C	415 643-9900	6759
Nomis Solutions Inc (PA)	5734	D	650 588-9800	7447
First National Bank of Northern California	6021	C	650 583-8450	7627
FNB Bancorp	6022	C	650 588-6800	7688
Tri Counties Bank	6029	C	650 583-8450	7741
Permanente Medical Group Inc	6324	B	650 827-6500	8353
Gateway Portfolio Holdings LLC	6798	D	626 578-0777	9468
Djont/Cmb Ssf Leasing LLC	7011	D	650 589-3400	9750
Grosvenor Properties Ltd	7011	D	650 873-3200	9828
Larkspur Hsptality Dev MGT LLC	7011	D	650 827-1515	9967
Larkspur Hsptality Dev MGT LLC	7011	D	650 872-1515	9968
Summit Hotel Trs 115 LLC	7011	D	650 424-3700	10281
American Etc Inc	7211	B	650 873-5353	10422
Medical Linen Service Inc	7213	D	650 873-1221	10437
Inter-City Cleaners LLC	7216	C	650 875-9200	10467
Peninou French Ldry & Clrs Inc (PA)	7219	D	800 392-2532	10487
Harry McCune Sound Service Inc (PA)	7359	C	650 873-1111	11036
Leadstack Inc	7361	D	628 200-3063	11170
Aechelon Technology Inc (PA)	7371	C	415 255-0120	11385
Zipline International Inc	7371	C	508 340-3291	12066
Education Elements Inc	7372	D	650 440-7860	12173
Digitalist USA Ltd	7373	A	949 278-1354	12447
Stripe Heavy Industries Inc (HQ)	7373	C	877 887-7815	12529
23andme Inc (HQ)	7375	A	650 961-7152	12648
Stripe Inc (PA)	7389	D	888 963-8955	13489
Pribuss Engineering Inc	7623	D	650 588-0447	13729
Califrnia Golf CLB San Frncsco	7997	D	650 588-9021	14353
Kaiser Foundation Hospitals	8011	A	650 742-2000	14837
Myriad Womens Health Inc	8071	B	888 268-6795	16737
Veracyte Inc (PA)	8071	D	650 243-6300	16768
Aegis Senior Communities LLC	8082	C	650 952-6100	16801
Alpha Health Inc	8099	C	970 209-1462	17168
California Cryobank Inc	8099	B	650 635-1420	17195
Pathways Home Health	8099	D	650 634-0133	17293
San Mateo Health Commission	8099	C	650 616-0050	17320
Peninsula Family Service	8322	D	650 952-6848	18078
Crown Energy Services Inc	8711	C	415 546-6534	19190
Fluor Enterprises Inc	8711	D	925 307-1200	19228
Genentech Inc	8721	A	650 225-1000	19579
Ambys Medicines Inc	8731	D	408 373-4030	19655
Calico Life Sciences LLC	8731	B	650 754-6200	19667
Culture Biosciences Inc	8731	D	919 622-5123	19675
Dice Therapeutics Inc	8731	D	650 566-1402	19680
Emerald Cloud Lab Inc	8731	D	650 257-7554	19686
Genentech Inc	8731	A	650 225-1000	19698
Insitro Inc	8731	C	650 730-7074	19711
Janssen Alzheimer Immunothera	8731	D	650 794-2500	19717
Ls9 Inc	8731	C	650 243-5400	19730
Lyell Immunopharma Inc	8731	C	650 383-5381	19731
Portola Pharmaceuticals Inc (DH)	8731	C	650 246-7300	19760
Twist Bioscience Corporation (PA)	8731	B	800 719-0671	19790
Abbvie Stemcentrx LLC	8733	C	415 298-9242	19859
Genentech Inc (DH)	8733	A	650 225-1000	19882
Bon Appetit Management Co	8741	C	650 467-3767	20044
Zipline International Inc	8742	C	408 475-8625	20625

SPRING VALLEY, CA - San Diego County

	SIC	EMP	PHONE	ENTRY#
Treebeard Landscape Inc	0781	D	619 697-8302	470
Commercial Indus Roofg Co Inc	1761	D	619 465-3737	2053
Casper Company	1771	C	619 589-6001	2105
West Coast Iron Inc	1796	D	619 464-8456	2252
J&M Keystone Inc	1799	C	619 466-9876	2286
Burns and Sons Trucking Inc	4212	D	619 460-5394	3374
Otay Water District	4941	C	619 670-2222	4815
Rossin Steel Inc	5051	D	619 656-9200	5517
Smart & Final Stores Inc	5141	B	619 668-9039	6303
Metabase Inc	7374	D	415 767-0490	12598
Kaizen Syndicate LLC	7379	D	858 309-2028	12822
Encompass Fmly Physcans Med Gr	8011	D	619 660-6212	14739
Family Hlth Ctrs San Diego Inc	8011	B	619 515-2555	14748
David Toma DDS Inc	8021	D	858 583-6147	15224
B-Spring Valley LLC	8051	D	619 797-3991	15346
Mt Miquel Covenant Village	8051	D	619 479-4790	15592
365 Home Care	8082	D	310 908-5179	16780
Covenant Living West	8361	D	619 931-1114	18407
D A V Industries	8641	D	619 337-9244	18850

STANFORD, CA - Santa Clara County

	SIC	EMP	PHONE	ENTRY#
Hoover Institution	7389	C	650 723-1754	13318
Stanford Law Schl Off Fncl Aid	7389	C	650 723-9247	13484
Essence Healthcare Cal Inc	8062	A	650 723-4000	16088
Leland Stanford Junior Univ	8062	A	650 723-4000	16213
Stanford Health Care	8062	A	650 736-6661	16487
Stanford Health Care	8062	A	650 723-4000	16489
Stanford Health Care	8062	A	650 723-4000	16493
Stanford Health Care (HQ)	8062	A	650 723-4000	16497
Stanford Health Care	8099	D	650 723-4841	17330
Leland Stanford Junior Univ (PA)	8221	A	650 723-2300	17762
Leland Stanford Junior Univ	8221	C	650 721-2726	17764
Stanford Univ Med Ctr Aux	8322	C	650 723-6636	18142
Palo Alto Community Child Care	8351	C	650 855-9828	18342
Associated Students Stanford (PA)	8641	D	650 723-4331	18814
Leland Stanford Junior Univ	8641	C	650 723-2021	18879
Stanford Univ Frman Spgli Inst	8733	C	650 723-8681	19916

STANTON, CA - Orange County

	SIC	EMP	PHONE	ENTRY#
Denver D Darling Inc	1541	D	714 761-8299	816
USS Cal Builders Inc	1542	C	714 828-4882	1051
All Metals Processing of San Diego Inc	3471	C	714 828-8238	2757
All Mtals Proc Orange Cnty LLC	3471	C	714 828-8238	2758
Haulaway Storage Cntrs Inc	4225	B	800 826-9040	3714
Modern Alloys Inc	5039	D	714 893-0551	5230
Paramount Home Care Inc	8082	D	714 994-1250	16908
California Friends Homes	8361	B	714 530-9100	18383

STEVENSON RANCH, CA - Los Angeles County

	SIC	EMP	PHONE	ENTRY#
Site Helpers LLC	8742	D	877 217-5395	20548

STOCKTON, CA - San Joaquin County

	SIC	EMP	PHONE	ENTRY#
Farmington Fresh Sales LLC	0175	C	209 983-9700	105

GEOGRAPHIC SECTION

STUDIO CITY CA

	SIC	EMP	PHONE	ENTRY#
Unilever United States Inc.	0191	B	209 466-9580	204
Pearl Crop Inc (PA)	0723	D	209 808-7575	299
West Coast Arborists Inc.	0782	C	408 855-8660	548
Rudolph and Sletten Inc.	1542	C	209 941-1040	1013
Midstate Barrier Inc.	1611	D	209 944-9565	1139
Teichert Inc.	1611	B	209 983-2300	1170
Comfort Air Inc.	1711	D	209 466-4601	1402
Sahargun Plumbing Inc.	1711	D	209 474-2611	1553
Vivint Solar Developer LLC	1711	D	209 942-2040	1592
Bockmon & Woody Elc Co Inc	1731	C	209 464-4878	1685
Collins Electrical Company Inc (PA)	1731	D	209 466-3691	1701
Con J Franke Electric Inc.	1731	D	209 462-0717	1706
Hammer Head Security Inc.	1731	C	209 227-6566	1744
Pacific Metro Electric Inc.	1731	D	209 939-3222	1797
Kenyon Construction Inc.	1742	D	209 462-4060	1941
Guy Yocom Construction Inc.	1771	C	951 284-3456	2124
Mid State Steel Erection (PA)	1791	D	209 464-9497	2190
Strocal Inc.	1791	B	209 948-4646	2201
Cozad Trailer Sales LLC	3715	D	209 931-3000	2979
Mv Transportation Inc.	4111	C	209 547-7879	3166
San Joaquin Regional Trnst Dst	4111	C	209 948-5566	3201
First Student Inc.	4151	C	209 466-7737	3339
Gillies Trucking Inc.	4212	D	209 948-6268	3399
John Aguilar & Company Inc.	4212	C	209 546-0171	3408
California Bulk Inc.	4213	C	209 983-1069	3451
Fuel Delivery Services Inc.	4213	D	209 751-2185	3480
Gillson Trucking Inc.	4213	C	925 400-9094	3482
GLS US Freight Inc (PA)	4213	D	209 823-2168	3483
J B Hunt Transport Inc.	4213	C	209 235-1371	3494
Reeve Trucking Company Inc (PA)	4213	D	209 948-4061	3531
Reliance Intermodal Inc.	4213	D	209 946-0200	3532
Scan-Vino LLC	4213	C	209 931-3570	3542
Williams Tank Lines (PA)	4213	C	209 944-5613	3564
Xpo Logistics Freight Inc.	4213	D	209 983-8285	3567
Allen Distribution (PA)	4225	C	717 258-3040	3673
Nautilus Intl Holdg Corp.	4225	B	209 465-5713	3735
World Class Distribution Inc.	4225	D	909 574-4140	3784
Stockton Port District.	4491	D	209 946-0246	3818
Cellco Partnership.	4812	D	209 474-9071	4204
Pac-West Telecomm Inc.	4813	C	877 626-4325	4324
Pacific Gas and Electric Co	4911	B	209 942-1787	4606
Pacific Gas and Electric Co	4911	C	209 932-6550	4610
Pacific Gas and Electric Co	4911	D	209 942-5142	4621
Pacific Gas and Electric Co	4911	A	209 942-1523	4639
Ecs Refining Inc.	4953	C	209 774-5000	4888
Interstate Truck Center LLC (PA)	5012	D	209 944-5821	5013
Conti Materials Service LLC	5031	D	209 467-0626	5151
Golden State Lumber Inc.	5031	D	209 234-7700	5159
International Window Corp.	5031	D	562 928-6411	5168
USG Interiors LLC	5031	B	209 466-4636	5192
Burlingame Industries Inc.	5033	C	209 464-9001	5220
H and H Drug Stores Inc.	5047	C	209 931-5200	5421
Pacific Steel Group.	5051	B	707 297-8922	5507
PDM Steel Service Centers Inc (HQ)	5051	D	209 943-0555	5508
Holt of California.	5082	C	209 466-6000	5793
Delta Rubber Co Inc.	5085	D	209 948-0511	5899
Valley Wholesale Drug Co LLC	5122	D	209 466-0131	6150
Dorfman Milano Company (HQ)	5136	C	209 982-1400	6172
Coastal Pacific Fd Distrs Inc (PA)	5141	C	909 947-2066	6246
Highland Wholesale Foods Inc.	5141	D	209 933-0580	6257
Martin-Brower Company LLC	5141	B	209 466-2980	6265
Smart & Final Stores LLC	5141	C	209 952-1030	6323
Southwest Traders Incorporated	5141	D	209 462-1607	6392
Sygma Network Inc.	5141	C	209 932-5300	6398
Yosemite Foods Inc.	5147	D	209 990-5400	6509
Fresh Innovations Cal LLC	5148	D	209 983-9700	6543
Morada Produce Company LP	5148	A	209 546-0426	6564
Boboli International LLC	5149	D	209 473-3507	6611
Iris Usa Inc.	5149	D	209 982-9100	6634
Super Store Industries	5149	B	209 858-3365	6675
US Foods Inc.	5149	C	209 948-0793	6690
Valley Pacific Petro Svcs Inc (PA)	5172	D	209 948-9412	6744
Van De Pol Enterprises Inc (PA)	5172	C	209 465-3421	6746
Home Depot USA Inc.	5211	C	209 474-8285	6972
Lowes Home Centers LLC	5211	D	209 956-7200	7061
Penney Opco LLC.	5311	C	209 951-1110	7132
Berberian Bros Inc.	5511	D	209 944-5514	7171
Big Valley Ford Inc.	5511	C	209 870-4400	7172
Chase Chevrolet Co Inc.	5511	C	209 475-6600	7183
Cintas Corporation No 3.	5699	C	209 922-0500	7416
Goodwill Inds San Jquin Vly FN (PA)	5932	D	209 466-2311	7539
Bank of Stockton (HQ)	6022	C	209 929-1600	7658
Loandepot Inc.	6162	B	209 323-7900	7991
Loandepot Inc.	6162	B	209 229-4120	7995
Merrill Lynch Prce Fnner Smith.	6211	D	209 472-3500	8127
Old Republic Title Company.	6361	D	209 951-9460	8451
Old Republic Title Holdg Inc.	6361	D	209 956-7663	8452
Wm Michael Stemler Inc (PA)	6411	C	209 948-8483	8689
OConner Woods A California.	6513	C	209 956-3400	8849
OConnor Woods Housing Corp.	6513	C	209 956-3400	8850
Grupe Company (PA)	6531	D	209 473-6000	9033
Lee & Associates Central Vly.	6531	D	209 983-1111	9073
Grupe Commercial Company.	6552	C	209 473-6000	9254
Rodolo Inc.	6719	D		9331
Castlehill Properties Inc.	7011	D	209 472-9700	9684
Alsha Academy.	7021	D	310 908-1962	10390
Wtmg Inc.	7349	D	209 888-6600	10987
Adecco Employment Services.	7363	D	209 474-0443	11266
Volt Management Corp.	7363	D	209 952-5627	11361
Allied Universal Topco LLC	7381	A	209 472-0455	12924
First Alarm SEC & Patrol Inc.	7382	B	209 473-1110	13117
Canepas Car Wash.	7542	D	209 951-9772	13689
Covey Auto Express Inc (PA)	7549	D	253 826-0461	13712
In Shape Management Company.	7991	B	209 472-2231	14208
Brookside Country Club.	7997	D	209 956-6200	14351
Stockton Golf and Country Club.	7997	D	209 466-4313	14467
Kings Card Club.	7999	C	209 267-4567	14538
Permanente Medical Group Inc	8011	A	209 476-3737	14982
Permanente Medical Group.	8011	A	209 476-2000	14985
St Josephs Surgery Center LP.	8011	D	209 467-6316	15097
Beaver Dam Health Care Center.	8051	D	707 546-0471	15354
Covenant Care California LLC	8051	C	209 477-5252	15399
Crestwood Behavioral Hlth Inc.	8051	D	209 478-5291	15417
Five Star Qulty Care-CA II LLC	8051	C	209 466-2066	15479
Genesis Healthcare LLC	8051	B	209 478-6488	15492
Hospice of San Joaquin	8051	D	209 957-3888	15518
RES-Care Inc.	8052	D	209 473-1202	15788
Stockton Edson Healthcare Corp.	8059	D	209 948-8762	15901
Dameron Hospital Association (HQ)	8062	A	209 944-5550	16035
Dignity Health.	8062	C	209 467-6353	16045
Kaiser Foundation Hospitals.	8062	A	209 476-3101	16191
Lodi Regional Hlth Systems Inc.	8062	B	209 948-0808	16221
St Josephs Behavioral Hlth Ctr (DH)	8062	D	209 462-2826	16475
St Josephs Med Ctr Stockton	8062	A	209 943-2000	16476
St Josephs Medical Center Inc.	8062	C	209 943-2000	16477
Kaiser Foundation Hospitals.	8071	B	209 476-3646	16729
Pacific Coast Services Inc.	8082	D	209 956-2532	16906
Welbe Health LLC	8082	C	209 800-0621	16973
Community Medical Centers Inc (PA)	8093	D	209 373-2800	17032
County of San Joaquin.	8093	D	209 468-8750	17041
Victor Cmnty Support Svcs Inc.	8093	C	209 465-1080	17158
Delta Blood Bank LLC (HQ)	8099	D	800 244-6794	17221
Freeman D Aiuto Prof Law Corp.	8111	D	209 474-1818	17463
Linden Unified School District.	8211	D	209 946-0707	17721
Central Vly Training Ctr Inc.	8322	D	209 951-1504	17873
County of San Joaquin.	8322	D	209 468-2601	17938
El Concilio California (PA)	8322	C	209 644-2600	17966
Friends Outside.	8322	D	209 955-0701	17990
San Joaquin Cnty Aging & Commu.	8322	D	209 468-9455	18116
Valley-Mntain Regional Ctr Inc (PA)	8322	C	209 473-0951	18167
Womens Ctr - Youth & Fmly Svcs (PA)	8322	D	209 941-2611	18195
Brookside Christian School Inc (PA)	8351	D	209 954-7650	18272
Christian Brookside Schools.	8351	D	209 954-7656	18293
Creative Child Care Inc.	8351	B	209 462-2282	18303
Head Start Child Development Council Inc.	8351	A		18320
Childrens Home of Stockton.	8361	C	209 466-0853	18393
Communication Svc For Deaf Inc.	8399	D	209 475-5000	18574
Mexican Heritg Ctr Gallery Inc.	8412	D	209 969-9306	18657
United Cerebral Palsy Assoc (PA)	8621	C	209 956-0290	18768
City of Stockton.	8641	C	209 937-8453	18842
Electronic Medical Management (PA)	8721	D	209 473-6555	19572
LLP Moss Adams.	8721	D	209 955-6100	19600
County of San Joaquin.	8742	C	209 472-7127	20331
Smg.	8744	B	209 937-7433	20663
Acrt Pacific LLC	8748	B	330 945-7500	20674
Synergy Companies.	8748	C	800 439-9610	20859
County of San Joaquin.	9111	D	209 468-3090	20916

STRATFORD, CA - Kings County

	SIC	EMP	PHONE	ENTRY#
Stone Land Company (PA)	0131	D	559 947-3185	5

STUDIO CITY, CA - Los Angeles County

	SIC	EMP	PHONE	ENTRY#
Fort Hill Construction (PA)	1521	D	323 656-7425	677
CBS Broadcasting Inc.	4833	C	818 655-8500	4417
Hallmark Media US LLC (DH)	4833	D	818 755-2400	4437
Crown Media Holdings Inc (HQ)	4841	D	888 390-7474	4495

Employee Codes: A=Over 500 employees, B=251-500
C=101-250, D=51-100, E=20-50, F=10-19, G=1-9

STUDIO CITY CA

	SIC	EMP	PHONE	ENTRY#
Motion Pcture Indust Pnsion HI	6371	C	818 769-0007	8464
Backbone Capital Advisors LLC	6799	C	818 769-8016	9490
Sportsmens Lodge Hotel LLC	7011	D	818 769-4700	10262
CBS Studios Inc	7812	C	818 655-5160	13827
Columbia Pictures Inds Inc	7812	D	818 655-5820	13829
High Technology Video Inc	7812		323 969-8822	13854
Radford Studio Center LLC	7922	B	818 655-5000	14059
Yoga Shelter LLC	7999	D	818 691-3000	14587
Longwood Management Corp	8059	C	818 980-8200	15871
American Private Duty Inc	8082	D	818 386-6358	16806
Art Drctors Gild Itse Lcal 876	8631	C	818 762-9995	18772
Coding School	8641	D	424 339-3977	18844

SUISUN CITY, CA - Solano County

	SIC	EMP	PHONE	ENTRY#
Shimmick Construction Co Inc	1629	C	707 419-5434	1317
E B Stone & Son Inc	5191	D	707 426-2500	6823
UNItogether Inc	8699	D	707 208-7602	19116

SUN VALLEY, CA - Los Angeles County

	SIC	EMP	PHONE	ENTRY#
Rawlings Mechanical Corp (PA)	1711	D	323 875-2040	1541
Ceramic Tile Art Inc	1743	D	818 767-9088	1976
Pacific Pavingstone Inc	1771	C	818 244-4000	2142
Columbia Showcase & Cab Co Inc	2541	C	818 765-9710	2502
Marfred Industries	2653	B		2520
PMC Leaders In Chemicals Inc (HQ)	3086	C	818 896-1101	2665
Rico Corporation (HQ)	3931	C	818 394-2700	3087
Los Angles Cnty Mtro Trnsp Aut	4111	A	213 922-6215	3158
Firstmed Ambulance Svcs Inc	4119	D	818 982-8333	3263
Arakelian Enterprises Inc	4212	C	818 768-2644	3369
Waste Management Recycling	4212	D	818 767-6180	3434
Ontrac Logistics Inc	4215	D	818 504-9043	3624
Los Angeles Dept Wtr & Pwr	4941	A	213 367-1342	4804
Araco Enterprises LLC	4953	B	818 767-0675	4856
BFI Waste Systems N Amer Inc	4953	D	323 321-1722	4867
Recology Los Angeles	4953	B	818 767-0675	4926
USA Waste of California Inc	4953	D	818 252-3112	4948
Waste Management Cal Inc (HQ)	4953	C	877 836-6526	4953
PRI Medical Technologies Inc	5047	C	818 394-2800	5444
REM Optical Company Inc	5049	C	818 504-3950	5468
Norman Industrial Mtls Inc (PA)	5051	C	818 729-3333	5503
Beacon Roofing Supply Inc	5085	D	818 768-4661	5893
Lowrys Inc	5085	D	818 768-4661	5909
Aadlen Bros Auto Wrecking Inc (PA)	5093	D	323 875-1400	6002
PMC Capital Partners LLC	6799	A	818 896-1101	9550
Sugar Foods Corporation	7389	C	818 768-7900	13490
Wet (PA)	7389	C	818 769-6200	13554
Hawker Pacific Aerospace	7699	B	818 765-6201	13773
LA Hydro-Jet Rooter Svc Inc	7699	D	818 768-4225	13779
Rose Brand Wipers Inc	7922	D	818 505-6290	14060
Serra Community Med Clinic Inc	8011	C	818 768-3000	15054
Pacifica of Valley Corporation	8062	A	818 767-3310	16304
Pine Grove Hospital Corp	8063	C	818 348-0500	16656
Mountain View Child Care Inc	8351	C	818 252-5863	18336

SUNLAND, CA - Los Angeles County

	SIC	EMP	PHONE	ENTRY#
Brightview Tree Company	0811	D	818 951-5500	566
Patriot Brokerage Inc	4731	D	910 227-4142	4074
EAM Enterprises Inc	6531	D	818 951-6464	8989
Arcadia Convalescent Hosp Inc	8051	D	818 352-4438	15332
Shadow Hlls Cnvlscent Hosp Inc	8051	D	818 352-4438	15661
Valley Village	8052	D	818 446-0366	15800
New Vista Health Services	8059	D	818 352-1421	15881
Tierra Del Sol Foundation (PA)	8361	D	818 352-1419	18532

SUNNYVALE, CA - Santa Clara County

	SIC	EMP	PHONE	ENTRY#
Siliconsage Construction Inc	1522	C	408 916-3205	777
Gordon Prill Inc	1542	D	408 745-7164	922
Level 10 Construction LP (PA)	1542	C	408 747-5000	959
Comtel Systems Technology Inc	1731	D	408 543-5600	1705
Adiana Inc	2834	B	650 421-2900	2578
Yasheng Group	2879	A	650 363-8345	2641
Fujitsu Management Services of America Inc	3577	C	408 746-6000	2829
Juniper Networks Inc (PA)	3577	B	408 745-2000	2832
Clover Network Inc	3578	D	650 210-7888	2841
Aruba Networks Inc	3663	A	408 227-4500	2892
Nokia Inc	3663	A	408 530-7600	2896
Umc Group (usa)	3674	D	408 523-7800	2935
Meggitt (orange County) Inc	3812	D	408 739-3533	3005
Pareto Networks Inc	4813	B	877 727-8020	4327
Sendmail Inc	4813	C	510 594-5400	4337
Plaxo Inc	4841	D	408 900-8701	4518
Drobo Inc	5045	D	408 454-4200	5296
Matterport Operating LLC (HQ)	5045	C	650 641-2241	5328
Lge Electrical Sales Inc	5063	C	408 992-4145	5573
Idec Corporation (HQ)	5065	D	408 747-0550	5662
Xp Power LLC (DH)	5065	D	408 732-7777	5718
Specialty A/C Products Inc (PA)	5075	D	408 481-3611	5773
Otis Elevator Company	5084	C	408 727-1231	5852
Interfocus Inc (PA)	5137	D	844 972-8728	6200
Polyvore Inc	5199	D	650 968-1195	6936
Lowes Home Centers LLC	5211	C	408 470-1680	7093
Larry Hopkins Inc	5511	C	408 720-1888	7250
Star One Credit Union (PA)	6061	C	408 543-5202	7808
Coadna Holdings Inc	6719	C	408 736-1100	9307
Life Science Angels Inc	6799	D	408 541-1152	9527
Executive Inn Inc	7011	C	408 245-5330	9791
Island Hospitality MGT LLC	7011	C	408 720-8893	9916
K3 Dev LLC	7011	C	408 733-7950	9931
K3 Dev LLC	7011	C	408 733-7950	9932
Msr Hotels & Resorts Inc	7011	C	408 745-6000	10034
Silicon Valley Inns Inc	7011	C	408 734-3742	10238
US Interactive Delaware	7311	C	408 863-7500	10686
Body Fit Plus Inc	7361	C	925 226-7744	11096
West Valley Engineering Inc (PA)	7363	A	408 735-1420	11363
Armorblox Inc	7371	B	831 428-2124	11424
Clari Inc (PA)	7371	A	650 265-2111	11492
Evergent Technologies Inc	7371	B	877 897-1240	11582
Future Dial Incorporated (PA)	7371	D	408 245-8880	11610
Illumio Inc (PA)	7371	B	669 800-5000	11656
Innopath Software Inc	7371	C	408 962-9200	11664
Maplelabs Inc	7371	C	408 743-4414	11731
Merit International Inc	7371	C	833 463-7487	11745
Outright Inc	7371	D	918 926-6578	11806
Pingcap (us) Inc	7371	C	650 382-9973	11828
Prevedere Inc	7371	D	888 686-7746	11842
PSI Systems Inc	7371	C	650 321-2640	11849
Real-Time Innovations Inc (PA)	7371	D	408 990-7400	11865
Sonatus Inc	7371	C	650 488-8500	11935
Yugabytedb Inc (PA)	7371	B	408 663-6632	12056
Arcaris Inc (PA)	7372	C	415 854-3801	12097
Arctic Wolf Networks Inc	7372	C	888 272-8429	12099
Azul Systems Inc (PA)	7372	C	650 230-6500	12109
Cloudshield Technologies LLC	7372	C	408 331-6640	12142
Egain Corporation (PA)	7372	B	408 636-4500	12175
Entco LLC	7372	A	312 580-9100	12181
Good Technology Software Inc	7372	C	408 212-7500	12209
Intermdia Cloud Cmmnctions Inc	7372	C	650 641-4000	12237
Ipolipo Inc	7372	C	408 916-5290	12245
Kloudgin Inc	7372	C	877 256-8303	12250
Kloudspot Inc	7372	C	800 709-2211	12251
Matterport Inc (PA)	7372	C	650 641-2241	12263
Synopsys Inc (PA)	7372	B	650 584-5000	12372
Aarki Inc (PA)	7373	C	408 382-1180	12413
Cerebras Systems Inc	7373	C	650 933-4980	12433
Fujitsu North America Inc (HQ)	7373	C	408 746-6000	12458
Juniper Networks Inc	7373	A	408 745-2000	12472
Juniper Networks (us) Inc (HQ)	7373	D	408 745-2000	12474
Nuage Networks	7373	D	415 439-9420	12504
Packeteer Inc	7373	B	408 220-2200	12509
PFU America Inc (HQ)	7373	B	800 626-4686	12510
Qsolv Inc	7373	C	408 429-0918	12513
Glint Inc	7374	D	650 817-7240	12575
Inko Industrial Corporation	7374	D	408 830-1040	12583
Ooma Inc (PA)	7374	D	650 566-6600	12602
Proofpoint Inc (HQ)	7374	C	408 517-4710	12610
Yahoo Cv LLC (HQ)	7374	D	408 349-3300	12643
Linkedin Corporation (HQ)	7375	B	650 687-3600	12672
Apstra Inc (HQ)	7379	D	650 307-3245	12732
Baidu USA LLC	7379	C	669 224-6400	12738
Centerbeam Inc	7379	C		12752
Headstrong Corporation	7379	C	408 732-8700	12802
Xoriant Corporation (PA)	7379	C	408 743-4400	12910
Zultys Inc	7379	D	408 328-0450	12913
Cashedge Inc	7389	D	408 541-3900	13229
Uplift Inc	7389	C	408 396-3374	13534
Price-Simms Inc (PA)	7538	C	408 245-6640	13671
Pacific Coast Sales & Service Inc (PA)	7623	D	408 481-3600	13728
California Skin Institute	8011	D	408 736-0441	14646
Carbon Health Technologies Inc	8011	C	650 318-3384	14653
Healthtap Inc	8011	C	650 268-9806	14770
Sutter Bay Medical Foundation	8011	C	408 730-4321	15107
Sutter Bay Medical Foundation	8011	D	650 934-7956	15109
Helios Healthcare LLC	8051	B	408 739-2383	15512
Sunnyvale Healthcare Center	8051	D	408 245-8070	15689
Sunrise Senior Living LLC	8051	D	408 749-8600	15695
Pts Diagnostics California Inc	8071	C	877 870-5610	16745

GEOGRAPHIC SECTION

THERMAL CA

	SIC	EMP	PHONE	ENTRY#
South Pninsula Hebrew Day Schl	8211	D	408 738-3060	17751
Fremont Un High Schols Fndtion	8399	A	408 522-2200	18588
Synopsys Foundation	8699	D	650 584-5000	19109
Fujitsu Research America Inc (PA)	8731	D	800 385-4878	19696
National Opinion Research Ctr	8732	C	415 315-3800	19834
Eurofins Eag Mtls Science LLC (DH)	8734	C	408 454-4600	19972
Joie De Vivre Hospitality LLC	8741	D	408 738-0500	20127
Drawbridge Inc	8742	D	650 513-2323	20349
Edelman Financial Engines LLC (HQ)	8742	C	408 498-6000	20352
Lta Research & Exploration LLC (PA)	8742	D	408 396-0577	20443
Myers-Briggs Company (PA)	8742	D	650 969-8901	20480
Northbound LLC	8742	C	408 333-9780	20488
Symphony Comm Svcs LLC (PA)	8742	D	650 733-6660	20575
Stormgeo (DH)	8999	C	408 731-8600	20902
Verizon Media Inc	8999	A	310 907-3016	20905

SUNOL, CA - Alameda County

Brightview Tree Company	0811	D	925 862-2485	568

SUSANVILLE, CA - Lassen County

Sierra-Cascade Nursery Inc (PA)	0181	B	530 254-6867	154
Diamond Mountain Casino	7011	C	530 252-1100	9741
Northeastern Rur Hlth Clinics (PA)	8011	D	530 251-5000	14928
CF Susanville LLC	8051	D	530 257-5341	15372
Banner Lssen Med Ctr Fndtion I	8062	C	530 252-2000	15957

SUTTER CREEK, CA - Amador County

Resource Connection of Amador	8322	D	209 223-7685	18098

SYLMAR, CA - Los Angeles County

Tutor-Saliba Perini	1542	A	818 362-8391	1049
Frontier-Kemper Constructors Inc (HQ)	1629	D	818 362-2062	1303
Superior Gunite (HQ)	1771	D	818 896-9199	2163
Anthony Inc	3231	C	818 365-9451	2691
Carroll Fulmer Logistics Corp	4731	B	626 435-9940	3995
Oak Springs Nursery Inc	4971	D	818 367-5832	4992
Pearson Dental Supplies Inc (PA)	5047	D	818 362-2600	5441
Advanced Mnlythic Ceramics Inc	5065	D	818 364-9800	5619
American Nuts LLC	5145	C	818 364-8855	6453
Allied Company Holdings Inc (PA)	5181	C	818 493-6400	6749
Home Depot USA Inc	5211	C	818 365-7662	7022
Sigue Corporation (PA)	7389	D	818 837-5939	13475
Schindler Elevator Corporation	7699	C	818 336-3000	13798
Star Waggons LLC	7819	D	818 367-5946	13950
Olive View-Ucla Medical Center (PA)	8011	D	818 364-1555	14934
County of Los Angeles	8361	D	818 364-2011	18403

TAFT, CA - Kern County

Taft Production Company	1241	D	661 765-7194	578
Jerry Melton & Sons Cnstr Inc	1389	D	661 765-5546	614
General Production Svc Cal Inc	1623	C	661 765-5330	1211
Watkins Construction Co Inc	1623	C	661 763-5395	1280
Mashburn Trnsp Svcs Inc	4213	C	661 763-5724	3510
Cellco Partnership	4812	C	661 765-5397	4197

TAHOE CITY, CA - Placer County

Granlibakken Management Co Ltd	7011	D	800 543-3221	9817
Pepper Tree Inn	7011	D	530 583-3711	10114

TAHOE VISTA, CA - Placer County

Liberty Utlties Clpeco Elc LLC	4911	D	800 782-2506	4584

TARZANA, CA - Los Angeles County

Sinanian Development Inc	1542	D	818 996-9666	1029
Shapp International Trdg Inc	5031	C	818 348-3000	5187
Airey Enterprises LLC	5088	C	818 530-3362	5954
JMJ Enterprises Inc	5812	D	818 343-5151	7490
Attorney Recovery Systems Inc (PA)	7322	D	818 774-1420	10736
Braemar Country Club Inc	7997	A	323 873-6880	14349
El Caballero Country Club	7997	D	818 654-3000	14371
AMI-Hti Trzana Encino Jint Vnt	8062	D	818 881-0800	15943
Amisub of California Inc (DH)	8062	A	818 881-0800	15944
Providence Tarzana Medical Ctr	8062	A	818 881-0800	16352
Tarzana Treatment Centers Inc (PA)	8093	C	818 996-1051	17141
Wasserman Comden & Casselman (PA)	8111	D	323 872-0995	17674
Temple Jdea of W San Frnndo Vl	8351	D	818 758-3800	18357
Avantgarde Senior Living	8361	C	818 881-0055	18379

TECATE, CA - San Diego County

Temarry Recycling Inc	4953	D	619 270-9453	4945
Benchpro Inc	5021	C	619 478-9400	5078

TEHACHAPI, CA - Kern County

World Wind Electrical Svcs Inc	1731	B	661 822-4877	1876
Chemtool Incorporated	2992	C	661 823-7190	2652
Pjbs Holdings Inc (PA)	4953	D	661 822-5273	4920
Selecta Products Inc (PA)	5063	D	661 823-7050	5589
LLC Woodward West	7032	D	661 822-7900	10407
Truxtun Radiology Med Group LP	8011	D	661 822-6619	15129
Adventist Health Med Tehachapi (PA)	8062	C	661 750-4848	15917
Bear Valley Springs Assn	8641	C	661 821-5537	18816

TEMECULA, CA - Riverside County

Hines Growers Inc	0181	A	800 554-4065	130
Sierra Pacific Farms Inc (PA)	0762	D	951 699-9980	380
Irriscape Construction Inc	0782	D	951 694-6936	499
Murrieta Development Company Inc	1623	C	951 719-1680	1240
Solex Contracting Inc	1623	C	951 308-1706	1265
W M Lyles Co	1623	C	951 296-2354	1278
Freedom Forever LLC (PA)	1711	D	888 557-6431	1443
Freedom Solar Services	1711	C	888 557-6431	1445
Solar Spectrum LLC	1711	B	844 777-6527	1567
Medley Communications Inc (PA)	1731	C	951 245-5200	1776
Leonard Roofing Inc	1761	D	951 506-3811	2073
Falkner Winery Inc	2084	C	951 676-6741	2384
Wilson Creek Wnery Vnyards Inc	2084	C	951 699-9463	2397
Milgard Manufacturing LLC	3089	B	480 763-6000	2675
Phs / Mwa	4581	C	951 695-1008	3904
Adcom Express Inc	4731	D	626 606-5160	3975
Kaydan Logistics LLC	4789	C	951 961-9000	4163
Sprint Communications Co LP	4812	C	951 303-8501	4228
Rancho California Water Dst (PA)	4941	C	951 296-6900	4820
Bbk Performance Inc	5013	D	951 296-1771	5029
Evertek Computer Corporation	5045	C	951 252-8700	5303
Genica Corporation	5045	B	855 433-5747	5310
FFF Enterprises Inc (PA)	5122	B	951 296-2500	6108
Southwest Traders Incorporated (PA)	5141	C	951 699-7800	6393
Gifting Group LLC	5199	D	951 296-0310	6911
Lowes Home Centers LLC	5211	C	951 296-1618	7071
DCH Acura of Temecula	5511	D	877 847-9532	7192
Rancho Ford Inc	5511	C	951 699-1302	7286
Cal Mutual Inc	6162	D	888 700-4650	7941
Charles Schwab Corporation	6211	C	800 435-4000	8076
Sft Realty Galway Downs LLC	6531	D	951 232-1880	9177
Pechanga Development Corp	7011	A	951 695-4655	10113
Temecula Hhg Hotel Dev LP	7011	C	951 331-3622	10307
Windsor Capital Group Inc	7011	A	951 676-5656	10374
Maxim Healthcare Services Inc	7363	C	951 694-0100	11307
Raintree Systems Inc	7371	C	951 252-9400	11862
Saalex Corp	7371	C	951 543-9259	11891
Applied Statistics & MGT Inc	7372	D	951 699-4600	12094
Richman Management Corporation	7381	B	909 296-6189	13029
Identity Intlligence Group LLC	7382	C	626 522-7993	13125
Incircle LLC	7389	A	800 843-7477	13321
Edwards Theatres Circuit Inc	7832	C	951 296-0144	13995
McMillin Communities Inc	7992	A	951 506-3303	14274
James Rebecca Prouty Entps Inc	8082	D	951 292-9777	16880
Temecula Vly Unified Schl Dst	8211	D	951 302-5140	17753
Westview Services Inc	8331	C	951 699-0047	18261
Ameresco Solar LLC	8711	B	888 967-6527	19139
Oreq Corporation	8741	D	951 296-5076	20167
Telus Health (us) Ltd Inc	8742	D	888 577-3784	20582
Hqe Systems Inc	8748	D	800 967-3036	20771

TEMESCAL VALLEY, CA - Riverside County

Glen Ivy Hot Springs (PA)	7299	D	951 277-3529	10548

TEMPLE CITY, CA - Los Angeles County

Sears Home Imprv Pdts Inc	1521	C	626 988-9134	719
Santa Anita Cnvlscent Hosp Rtr	8051	C	626 579-0310	15654
Exquisite Dental Technology	8071	D	626 237-0107	16720

TEMPLETON, CA - San Luis Obispo County

Mesa Vineyard Management Inc (PA)	0762	D	805 434-4100	378
Pacific Gas and Electric Co	4911	D	805 434-4418	4659
T and B Boots Inc	5661	D	805 434-9904	7411
Twin Cities Community Hosp Inc	8011	B	805 434-3500	15134
Compass Health Inc	8051	C	805 434-3035	15385

TERRA BELLA, CA - Tulare County

Sierra Frest Pdts Holdings Inc	0831	C	559 535-4893	571
Sierra Forest Products	5031	C	559 535-4893	5188

THERMAL, CA - Riverside County

Nissho of California Inc	0175	B	760 727-9719	110

THERMAL CA

GEOGRAPHIC SECTION

	SIC	EMP	PHONE	ENTRY#
Red Earth Casino	7011	C	760 395-1200	10143

THOUSAND OAKS, CA - Ventura County

	SIC	EMP	PHONE	ENTRY#
Oltmans Construction Co	1541	B	805 495-9553	836
General Pavement Management Inc	1771	D	805 933-0909	2119
Cal-State Steel Corporation	1791	C	310 632-2772	2181
Natren Inc	2099	D	805 371-4737	2438
Atara Biotherapeutics Inc (PA)	2836	A	650 278-8930	2619
Baxalta US Inc	3841	B	805 498-8664	3049
Mv Transportation Inc	4111	C	805 557-7372	3171
Full Scale Logistics LLC	4789	C	805 279-6799	4156
Red Pocket Inc	4812	D	888 993-3888	4225
Southern California Edison Co	4911	D	818 999-1880	4685
Calleguas Mncpl Wtr Dst Pub Fc	4941	B	805 526-9323	4769
Tecom Industries Incorporated	5065	C	805 267-0100	5710
Easton Diamond Sports LLC	5091	D	800 632-7866	5977
Penney Opco LLC	5311	C	805 497-6811	7131
Countrywide Home Loans Inc (HQ)	6162	A		7953
Pennymac Broker Direct	6162	D	614 288-5126	8009
Ormond Beach LP	6512	D	805 496-4948	8741
Gemmm Corporation (PA)	6531	C	805 496-0555	9021
American Recovery Service Inc (DH)	7322	C	805 379-8500	10734
Staff Assistance Inc	7361	B	805 371-9980	11236
A P R Inc	7363	C	805 379-3400	11265
Sensata Technologies Inc	7379	D	805 716-0322	12874
Carmike Cinemas LLC	7832	D	805 494-4702	13980
Bay Clubs Company LLC	7997	B	310 643-6878	14331
Sherwood Country Club	7997	C	805 496-3036	14452
Los Robles Regional Med Ctr	8011	B	805 494-0880	14882
Rolling Oaks Radiology Inc	8011	D	805 778-1513	15030
Five Star Qulty Care-CA II LLC (DH)	8051	D	805 492-2444	15478
Los Robles Regional Med Ctr (DH)	8062	A	805 497-2727	16240
Thousand Oaks Surgical Hosp LP	8062	D	805 777-7750	16574
Staff Assistance Inc (PA)	8082	B	818 894-7879	16935
La Ventana Treatment Programs	8093	D	805 644-5745	17085
Star of Ca LLC	8099	D	805 379-1401	17331
Westlake Oaks Healthcare LLC	8099	D	805 494-1233	17353
Rowi Usa Inc	8322	D	805 356-3372	18100
Young MNS Chrstn Assn Sthast V	8641	D	805 523-7613	19006
Automobile Club Southern Cal	8699	D	805 497-0911	19041
Charles River Laboratories Inc	8731	B	877 274-8371	19671
Teledyne Scentific Imaging LLC (HQ)	8731	C	805 373-4545	19783
Briotix	8742	D	805 864-2711	20303

THOUSAND PALMS, CA - Riverside County

	SIC	EMP	PHONE	ENTRY#
San Val Corp (PA)	0781	B	760 346-3999	460
Jacobsson Engrg Cnstr Inc	1611	C	760 345-8700	1122
10x Hvac of Ca LLC	1711	D	760 343-7488	1326
Harrison Enterprises Inc	1711	D	760 343-7488	1455
Kincaid Industries Inc	1711	D	760 343-5457	1478
Sunline Transit Agency (PA)	4111	C	760 343-3456	3219
Gulf- California Broadcast Co	4833	D	760 773-0342	4436
Readylink Inc	7361	D	760 343-7000	11217
Readylink Healthcare	7361	D	760 343-7000	11218

THREE RIVERS, CA - Tulare County

	SIC	EMP	PHONE	ENTRY#
Roman Catholic Bishp of Fresno	7032	D	559 561-4499	10411

TIPTON, CA - Tulare County

	SIC	EMP	PHONE	ENTRY#
Calftech Corporation	0212	D	559 752-2302	210
Bosman Dairy LLC	0241	C	559 752-7018	214

TOLUCA LAKE, CA - Los Angeles County

	SIC	EMP	PHONE	ENTRY#
Tre Venezie Inc	5812	D	818 985-4669	7514

TORRANCE, CA - Los Angeles County

	SIC	EMP	PHONE	ENTRY#
Dicaperl Corporation (DH)	1499	D	610 667-6640	647
Taisei Construction Corporation	1541	C	714 886-1530	849
ACS Communications Inc	1731	D	310 767-2145	1656
Vector Resources Inc (PA)	1731	C	310 436-1000	1870
Naturalife Eco Vite Labs	2023	D	310 370-1563	2348
Asiana Cuisine Enterprises Inc	2099	A	310 327-2223	2430
Doug Mockett & Company Inc	2511	D	310 318-2491	2487
Bbm Fairway Inc (PA)	2721	C		2544
Nyx Los Angeles Inc	2844	C	323 869-9420	2629
Totex Manufacturing Inc	3089	D	310 326-2028	2682
Storm Industries Inc (PA)	3523	D	310 534-5232	2771
Moog Inc	3625	B	310 533-1178	2867
Navcom Technology Inc (HQ)	3663	D	310 381-2000	2895
Ace Clearwater Enterprises Inc (PA)	3728	C	310 323-2140	2986
Ryans Express Trnsp Svcs Inc (PA)	4119	C	310 219-2960	3293
Fashion Logistics Inc	4225	C	424 201-4100	3704
Express Imaging Services Inc	4226	D	888 846-8804	3791
Jtb Americas Ltd (HQ)	4724	D	310 406-3121	3937
Air Express Intl USA Inc	4731	D	310 297-4401	3980
Binex Line Corp (PA)	4731	D	310 416-8600	3988
Capable Transport Inc	4731	D	310 697-0198	3992
Ceva Logistics LLC	4731	B	310 223-6500	3996
Dcw Dcw Inc	4731	D	310 324-3147	4002
Expeditors Intl Wash Inc	4731	B	310 343-6200	4015
Fns Inc (PA)	4731	D	661 615-2300	4021
Hitachi Transport System (america) Ltd	4731	B	310 787-3420	4034
Kuehne + Nagel Inc	4731	C	310 641-5500	4045
Nippon Express	4731	C	310 782-3000	4065
Nippon Express USA Inc	4731	D	310 527-4237	4066
Panalpina Inc	4731	C	310 819-4060	4071
Salson Logistics Inc	4731	C	973 986-0200	4091
American Honda Motor Co Inc (HQ)	5012	A	310 783-2000	5004
Virco Inc (HQ)	5021	C	310 533-0474	5107
Kubota Industrial Equipment	5046	C	817 756-1171	5385
Convaid Products LLC	5047	D	310 618-0111	5410
Sakura Finetek USA Inc (HQ)	5047	C	310 972-7800	5448
Shimadzu Precision Instrs Inc	5047	C	310 217-8855	5450
Oriental Motor USA Corporation (DH)	5063	D	310 715-3300	5586
Fujitsu Ten Corp of America	5064	C	310 327-2151	5605
I C Class Components Corp (PA)	5065	C	310 539-5500	5661
Quinstar Technology Inc	5065	C	310 320-1111	5691
Seville Classics Inc (PA)	5072	C	310 533-3800	5734
Howmet Globl Fstning Systems I	5085	C	310 784-0700	5906
Pacific Echo Inc	5085	D	310 539-1822	5917
Sweis Inc (PA)	5087	C	310 375-0558	5949
Citizen Watch Company of America Inc (HQ)	5094	C	800 321-1023	6021
Pentel of America Ltd (HQ)	5112	C	310 320-3831	6069
Murad LLC	5122	C	310 726-3300	6132
Topwin Corporation (PA)	5136	C	310 325-2255	6189
Smart & Final Stores LLC	5141	D	310 328-3023	6368
Calbee America Incorporated	5145	D	310 370-2500	6456
Lowes Home Centers LLC	5211	C	310 787-1469	7072
Martin Chevrolet	5511	D	323 772-6494	7256
Southbay European Inc	5511	D	310 939-7300	7302
American Business Bank	6022	D	310 808-1200	7652
Unify Fncl Cr Un Prof Corp (PA)	6061	D	877 254-9328	7813
Happy Money Inc	6099	B	949 430-0630	7856
American Honda Finance Corp (DH)	6141	C	310 972-2239	7869
Keenan & Associates (HQ)	6411	B	310 212-3344	8601
Alpine Village	6512	D	310 327-4384	8700
Hunt Enterprises Inc	6531	D	310 325-1496	9044
Remax Exec King Harbor	6531	D	310 378-9889	9161
AME-Gyu Co Ltd	6719	A	310 214-9572	9298
Navitas Semiconductor Corp (PA)	6799	C	901 685-2865	9539
Ctc Group Inc (DH)	7011	C	310 540-0500	9731
Kintetsu Enterprises Co Amer (HQ)	7011	C	310 782-9300	9946
Long Beach Golden Sails Inc	7011	D	562 596-1631	9984
Msr Hotels & Resorts Inc	7011	C	310 543-4566	10033
V Todays Inc	7011	C	310 781-9100	10338
Xld Group LLC	7011	C	310 316-3636	10386
Wash Mltfmily Ldry Systems LLC (PA)	7215	C	800 421-6897	10465
Saatchi & Saatchi N Amer LLC	7311	C	310 437-2500	10673
Lomita Logistics LLC	7331	D	310 784-8485	10773
Flagship Airport Services Inc	7349	D	310 328-8221	10897
Bright Event Rentals LLC (PA)	7359	C	310 202-0011	11022
Choura Events	7359	D	310 320-6200	11024
Classic/Prime Inc	7359	D	310 328-5060	11026
Act 1 Group Inc (PA)	7361	C	310 750-3400	11075
Prime One Inc	7361	D	310 378-1944	11206
Platinum Empire Group Inc	7363	D	310 821-5888	11318
Volt Management Corp	7363	D	310 316-8523	11353
Good Sports Plus Ltd	7371	B	310 671-4400	11628
BQE Software Inc	7372	D	310 602-4020	12126
Nc4 Soltra LLC	7372	D	408 489-5579	12281
Luxury Presence Inc	7373	C	310 955-1077	12484
CCH Incorporated	7374	A	310 800-9800	12556
Delta Computer Consulting	7379	C	310 541-9440	12777
US Security Associates Inc	7381	B	714 352-0773	13069
Contemporary Services Corp	7382	C	310 320-8418	13102
Bankcard Services (PA)	7389	D	213 365-1122	13209
Credit Card Services Inc (PA)	7389	D	213 365-1122	13251
Docmagic Inc	7389	D	800 649-1362	13272
Ezcaretech Usa Inc	7389	B	424 558-3191	13283
Pioneer Theatres Inc	7389	D	310 532-8183	13426
Singer Vehicle Design LLC (PA)	7549	C	213 592-2728	13719
Clearchoice MGT Svcs LLC	8021	D	424 337-1178	15223
Louis F Mascola DDS	8021	C	310 986-2930	15235
Occupational Therapy	8049	D	310 323-6887	15297
Del AMO Grdns Cnvlscent Hosp S	8051	D	310 378-4233	15421
Fh & Hf-Torrance I LLC	8051	D	310 320-4130	15476

GEOGRAPHIC SECTION

TURLOCK CA

	SIC	EMP	PHONE	ENTRY#
Genesis Healthcare LLC	8051	B	310 370-3594	15491
Geri-Care Inc	8051	D	310 320-0961	15495
Mariner Health Care Inc	8051	C	310 371-4628	15560
Torrance Care Center West Inc	8051	C	310 370-4561	15705
Geri-Care II Inc	8059	C	310 328-0812	15848
Cedars-Sinai Medical Center	8062	A	310 967-1900	15982
Little Company Mary Hospital	8062	A	310 540-7676	16215
Little Company of Mary Health Services	8062	A	310 540-7676	16216
Torrance Health Assn Inc (PA)	8062	A	310 325-9110	16575
Torrance Memorial Medical Ctr	8062	B	310 784-6316	16576
Torrance Memorial Medical Ctr	8062	B	310 784-3740	16578
Torrance Memorial Medical Ctr (HQ)	8062	A	310 325-9110	16579
Gky Dental Arts Inc (PA)	8072	D	310 214-8007	16772
Premier Infsion Hlthcare Svcs	8082	D	310 328-3897	16913
Harbor-Ucla Med Foundation Inc	8092	B	310 533-0413	16986
Clear Recovery Center	8093	D	310 318-2122	17029
Del AMO Hospital Inc	8093	B	310 530-1151	17051
Pediatric Therapy Network	8093	C	310 328-0276	17107
365 Hlthcare Staffing Svcs Inc	8099	D	310 436-3650	17163
Collinson Law A Prof Corp	8111	C	424 212-7777	17408
Compex Legal Services Inc (PA)	8111	C	310 782-1801	17410
Der Kinder Garden Preschool	8351	D	213 318-3838	18305
Dream Home Care Inc	8361	D	562 595-9021	18418
Harbor Dvlpmntal Dsblties Fndt	8399	D	310 540-1711	18593
Orthalliance Inc	8399	A	310 792-1300	18615
Special Service For Groups Inc	8399	C	310 323-6887	18628
21515 Hawthorne Owner LLC	8641	D	310 406-3730	18808
Public Hlth Fndation Entps Inc	8641	C	310 320-5215	18898
Young MNS Chrstn Assn Mtro Los	8641	D	310 325-5885	18957
Automobile Club Southern Cal	8699	C	310 325-3111	19042
Divergent Technologies Inc	8711	C	424 542-2158	19200
Friction Materials LLC	8711	C	248 362-3600	19231
International Energy Services USA Inc	8711	C	310 257-8222	19271
Sonic Industries Inc	8711	C	310 532-8382	19391
Hotta Liesenberg Saito LLP	8721	D	424 246-2000	19587
Garrett Motion Inc	8731	C	310 512-5424	19697
Honda R&D Americas LLC	8732	A	310 781-5500	19818
Lundquist Institute For Biomedical	8733	A	877 452-2674	19894
Als Group Usa Corp	8734	D	310 214-0043	19946
Daicel America Holdings Inc	8741	B	480 798-6737	20074
Harbor-Ucla Med Foundation Inc (PA)	8741	D	310 222-5015	20109
Proactive Risk Management Inc	8741	D	213 840-8856	20184
Dcw Services LLC	8742	D	310 324-3147	20339
Pathology Inc	8742	B	310 769-0561	20502
Amplus Group	8748	D	424 316-5913	20688
Midnight Sun Enterprises Inc	8748	D	310 532-2427	20804
City of Torrance	9111	D	310 781-7150	20915

TRABUCO CANYON, CA - Orange County

	SIC	EMP	PHONE	ENTRY#
Seeds of Change Inc	5191	C	310 764-7700	6832
Total Recon Solutions Inc	8742	D	949 584-8417	20587

TRACY, CA - San Joaquin County

	SIC	EMP	PHONE	ENTRY#
Triple E Produce LP	0161	C	209 835-5123	46
Arnaudo Bros Transport Inc (PA)	0191	D	209 835-0406	166
Teichert Inc	1442	D	209 832-4150	640
American Engrg Contrs Inc	1731	D	209 229-1591	1663
United States Cold Storage Inc	4222	D	209 835-2653	3666
APL Logistics Americas Ltd	4225	D	209 836-0302	3675
CJ Logistics America LLC	4225	C	209 362-2232	3686
Home Depot USA Inc	4225	C	209 855-7000	3719
Pacific Gas and Electric Co	4911	D	559 263-5438	4650
South San Jquin Cnty Fire Auth	4941	D	209 831-6702	4837
Tracy Dlta Solid Waste Mgt Inc	4953	D	209 835-0601	4946
Smart & Final Stores LLC	5141	D	323 219-6352	6351
Unified Grocers Inc	5141	C	209 832-6200	6407
Lucky Stores II LLC	5411	D	209 830-1977	7145
Tracy Auto LP	5511	D	209 834-1111	7318
Chevron Stations Inc	5541	C	209 830-0370	7387
Cultura Technologies Inc	7379	D	209 923-6278	12773
Courtesy Security Inc	7381	D	888 572-5545	12954
Trine Integrated Services Inc	7381	D	209 521-1590	13056
Pacific Medical Inc (PA)	7389	D	800 726-9180	13416
Tracy Sutter Community Hosp	8062	D	209 835-1500	16580
Autism Treatment Solutions LLC	8093	A	209 910-5038	17008
Califrnia Dept Indus Relations	8631	D	209 830-7200	18777
Akvarr Inc	8748	C	240 370-4182	20682
Controller Consulting Svcs Inc	8748	C	408 221-2492	20733

TRAVER, CA - Tulare County

	SIC	EMP	PHONE	ENTRY#
Maf Industries Inc (HQ)	3565	D	559 897-2905	2798
Foster Poultry Farms	5191	D	559 457-6509	6825

TRINIDAD, CA - Humboldt County

	SIC	EMP	PHONE	ENTRY#
Cher-Ae Heights Indian Cmnty	7999	C	707 677-3611	14505

TRONA, CA - San Bernardino County

	SIC	EMP	PHONE	ENTRY#
Trona Railway Company	4011	A	760 372-2312	3117

TRUCKEE, CA - Nevada County

	SIC	EMP	PHONE	ENTRY#
Teichert Inc	1442	D	530 587-3811	639
Truckee Dnner Pub Utility Dst F	4911	D	530 587-3896	4713
Tahoe Truckee Disposal Co Inc	4953	D	530 583-7825	4943
Western Nevada Supply Co	5074	D	530 582-5009	5764
Trimont Land Company (DH)	6531	B	530 562-1010	9198
Lahontan LLC	6552	D	530 550-2990	9257
Bhr Trs Tahoe LLC	7011	C	530 562-3045	9651
Joyable Inc	7371	A	914 552-6753	11687
Vibrant Planet Pbc	7389	D	530 208-9839	13540
Lahontan Golf Club	7997	D	530 550-2400	14392
Truckee Dnner Rcreation Pk Dst	7999	D	530 582-7720	14578
Tahoe Forest Hospital District	8062	C	530 582-3277	16566
Tahoe Forest Hospital District (PA)	8062	B	530 587-6011	16567
Martis Camp Club	8322	B	530 550-6000	18051

TUJUNGA, CA - Los Angeles County

	SIC	EMP	PHONE	ENTRY#
Smart & Final Stores LLC	5141	D	818 352-9399	6386
Volunteers of Amer Los Angeles	8322	C	818 352-5974	18178
Crescenta-Canada YMCA	8641	C	818 352-3255	18849

TULARE, CA - Tulare County

	SIC	EMP	PHONE	ENTRY#
Dan Freitas Electric Inc	1731	D	559 686-9572	1719
Valmetal Tulare Inc	3523	D	559 685-0340	2773
Knight Transportation Inc	4212	D	559 685-9838	3410
Kings County Truck Lines (HQ)	4213	C	559 686-2857	3499
Lowes Home Centers LLC	5211	D	559 366-5000	7096
Morris Levin and Son	5251	C	559 686-8665	7124
Tulare Lodging Associates LLC	7011	D	559 686-4700	10328
Altura Centers For Health	8011	C	559 686-9097	14609
Moyles Health Care Inc	8059	A	559 686-1601	15879
Adventist Health Tulare	8062	B	559 688-0821	15919
Tulare Local Health Care Dst	8062	A	559 685-3462	16582
Sundale Fndtion For Stdnts Cmn	8351	D	559 688-3419	18356

TUOLUMNE, CA - Tuolumne County

	SIC	EMP	PHONE	ENTRY#
Black Oak Casino	7999	D	209 928-9300	14499
Tuolumne M-Wuk Indian Hlth Ctr	8011	D	209 928-5400	15133

TURLOCK, CA - Stanislaus County

	SIC	EMP	PHONE	ENTRY#
Valley Milk LLC	0241	D	209 410-6701	222
Gemperle Enterprises	0252	D	209 667-2651	226
Humphrey Plumbing Inc	1711	D	209 634-4626	1459
PJs Lumber Inc	1791	D	209 850-9444	2193
Super Store Industries	2024	D	209 668-2100	2350
Superherb Farms	2099	C	209 633-3600	2443
Northern Rfrigerated Trnsp Inc (PA)	4213	C	209 664-3800	3521
Poppy State Express Inc	4213	D	209 664-3950	3528
Ruan	4213	C	209 634-4928	3535
Ruan Transport Corporation	4213	D	209 599-5000	3536
United States Cold Storage Inc	4222	D	209 668-1636	3663
Freshpoint Central Cal Inc	4783	C	209 216-0200	4128
Cco Holdings LLC	4841	C	209 585-1001	4476
Turlock Irrgtion Dst Employees (PA)	4911	D	209 883-8222	4714
Independent Electric Sup Inc	5063	D	209 667-2659	5567
Tdr Development Inc	5083	D	209 667-6455	5813
Central Valley Cheese Inc	5143	D	209 664-1080	6433
Evergreen Packaging LLC	5199	C	209 664-3426	6906
Lowes Home Centers LLC	5211	D	209 656-3020	7099
Bonander Auto Truck & Trlr Inc (PA)	5511	D	209 632-8871	7175
Garton Tractor Inc (PA)	5999	D	209 632-3931	7580
USA Seller Co	5999	A	209 656-7085	7597
Yosemite Farm Credit Aca (PA)	6111	D	209 667-2366	7868
Winton-Ireland Insur Agcy Inc (PA)	6411	D	209 667-0995	8688
Turlock Hospitality LLC	7011	D	209 250-1501	10329
Crimetek Security Inc	7381	C	209 668-6208	12958
Funtopia Inc	7999	C	510 246-3098	14527
Covenant Care California LLC	8051	D	209 632-3821	15405
Mark One Corporation	8059	C	209 667-2484	15875
Covenant Living West	8062	D	209 667-5600	16034
EMC Health Inc (DH)	8062	A	209 667-4200	16080
County of Stanislaus	8093	D	209 664-8044	17043
Christian Turlock Schools (PA)	8211	D	209 632-2337	17703
Diocese Stockton Eductl Off	8211	C	209 634-3575	17708
Covenant Living West	8361	D	209 632-9976	18409
Creative Alternatives	8361	D	209 668-9361	18410
Millerick Engineering Inc	8711	D	209 664-9111	19322

Employee Codes: A=Over 500 employees, B=251-500
C=101-250, D=51-100, E=20-50, F=10-19, G=1-9

2024 Directory of California
WholeSalers and Service Companies

TURLOCK CA

GEOGRAPHIC SECTION

	SIC	EMP	PHONE	ENTRY#
Sodexo Management Inc.	8741	A	209 667-3634	20210

TUSTIN, CA - Orange County

	SIC	EMP	PHONE	ENTRY#
Superior Sod I LP	0181	C	909 923-5068	158
R Ranch Market	0291	C	714 573-1182	237
Veternary Srgcal Spclsts A VTR	0742	D	949 936-0055	352
Tricon American Homes LLC	1521	C	844 874-2661	729
US Best Repair Service Inc	1521	C	888 750-2378	736
Healthcare Design & Cnstr LLC	1542	D	714 245-0144	934
Bergelectric Corp	1731	B	949 250-7005	1682
Briggs Electric Inc (PA)	1731	D	714 544-2500	1687
Largo Concrete Inc (PA)	1771	D	714 731-3600	2135
Woodbridge Glass Inc	1793	C	714 838-4444	2210
Design West Technologies Inc	3089	D	714 731-0201	2671
Shade Structures Inc	3444	D	714 427-6980	2745
Add-On Cmpt Peripherals LLC	3572	D	949 546-8200	2815
Add-On Cmpt Peripherals Inc	3577	C	949 546-8200	2822
Millenworks	3711	B	714 426-5500	2967
Coherent Aerospace & Def Inc	3827	D	714 247-7100	3035
Lightworks Optics Inc	3827	D	714 247-7100	3038
Stanley G Alexander Inc (PA)	4213	C	714 731-1658	3545
Schick Moving & Storage Co (PA)	4214	D	714 731-5500	3595
Cellco Partnership	4812	D	714 258-8870	4203
AB Cellular Holding LLC	4813	A	562 468-6846	4249
Trinity Brdcstg Netwrk Inc	4833	C	714 665-3619	4465
Lsf9 Cypress LP (PA)	5039	B	714 380-3127	5228
Lsf9 Cypress Parent 2 LLC	5039	A	714 380-3127	5229
Syspro Impact Software Inc	5045	C	714 437-1000	5360
Canon Medical Systems USA Inc (DH)	5047	B	714 730-5000	5408
Mobile Line Communications Corporation	5065	D		5677
Pphm Inc	5122	D	714 508-6100	6139
M & S Trading Inc	5136	D	714 241-7190	6180
Ansar Gallery Inc	5141	C	949 220-0000	6240
Republic Nat Distrg Co LLC (PA)	5182	C	714 368-4615	6805
Youngs Market Company LLC (HQ)	5182	B	800 317-6150	6814
Logomark Inc	5199	C	714 675-6100	6926
Lowes Home Centers LLC	5211	D	714 913-2663	7103
Nissan of Tustin	5511	C	714 669-8282	7268
Provenza Floors Inc (PA)	5713	D	949 788-0900	7433
Diamond Goldenwest Corporation (PA)	5944	C	714 542-9000	7550
Schoolsfirst Federal Credit Un	6061	A	480 777-5995	7803
New American Funding LLC (PA)	6141	A	949 430-7029	7881
Southern Cal Prmnnte Med Group	6324	C	714 734-4500	8365
Wood Gutmann Bogart Insur Brkg	6411	D	714 505-7000	8691
Wood Gutmann Bogart Insur Brks	6411	C	714 505-7000	8692
Irvine APT Communities LP	6513	B	714 505-7181	8835
First Team RE - Orange Cnty	6531	C	714 544-5456	9015
Crestmont Capital LLC	6799	D	949 537-3882	9504
Maverick Hospitality Inc	7011	D	714 730-7717	10010
Crown Building Maintenance Co	7349	B	714 434-9494	10882
B2 Services Llc	7361	D	714 363-3481	11087
Professnal Rgistry Netwrk Corp	7361	D	714 832-5776	11207
Pts Advance	7361	C	949 268-4000	11209
Xbp Inc	7371	D	888 895-7116	12052
A P R Consulting Inc	7379	A	714 544-3696	12716
Rjn Investigations Inc	7381	D	951 686-7638	13030
Autocrib Inc	7389	C	714 274-0400	13202
Coastal Intl Holdings LLC	7389	B	714 635-1200	13239
Caliber Bodyworks Texas Inc	7532	C	714 665-3905	13633
Sterling Collision LLC (PA)	7532	C	714 259-1111	13649
Allied Lube Inc	7538	D	949 651-8814	13656
Alta Hospitals System LLC	8062	A	714 619-7700	15938
Foothill Regional Medical Ctr	8062	C	310 943-4500	16090
Health Investment Corporation	8062	A	714 669-2085	16121
Kaiser Foundation Hospitals	8062	D	951 353-4000	16153
Pacific Health Corporation	8062	A	714 838-9600	16303
Core Holdings Inc	8082	C	714 969-2342	16848
Roman Cthlic Diocese of Orange	8211	D	714 544-1533	17744
Tustin Unified School District	8211	D	714 542-4271	17754
Salvation Army	8322	N	714 832-7100	18107
Eurofins Epk Blt Envmt Tstg L (DH)	8734	D	330 497-9350	19974
Crown Golf Properties LP	8742	C	714 730-1611	20336

TWENTYNINE PALMS, CA - San Bernardino County

	SIC	EMP	PHONE	ENTRY#
HI Pro Inc	4213	C	760 367-7734	3491
Mark Clemons	4213	C	760 361-1531	3509
NAVY UNITED STATES DEPARTMENT	8099	D	760 830-2124	17281

TWIN BRIDGES, CA - El Dorado County

	SIC	EMP	PHONE	ENTRY#
Sierra At Taho Ski Resorts	7011	C	530 659-7519	10233

UKIAH, CA - Mendocino County

	SIC	EMP	PHONE	ENTRY#
City of Ukiah	1623	C	707 467-2818	1204
City of Ukiah	4941	C	707 463-6233	4775
Waste MGT Collectn Recycl Inc	4953	D	707 462-0210	4965
Mendocino Forest Pdts Co LLC	5031	D	707 468-1431	5172
Home Depot USA Inc	5211	D	707 462-3009	7003
Savings Bank Mendocino County (PA)	6022	D	707 462-6613	7715
Redwood Health Club (PA)	7991	D	707 468-0441	14226
Mendocino Cmnty Hlth Clnic Inc (PA)	8011	D	707 468-1010	14895
Ensign Pleasanton LLC	8051	C	707 462-8864	15457
Ukiah Adventist Hospital (HQ)	8062	B	707 462-3111	16588
Sequoia Senior Solutions Inc	8082	D	707 621-9235	16925
Redwood Community Services Inc	8322	C	707 472-2922	18095

UNION CITY, CA - Alameda County

	SIC	EMP	PHONE	ENTRY#
La Terra Fina Usa LLC	1541	D	510 404-5888	830
Best Contracting Services Inc	1761	D	510 886-7240	2044
Mv Transportation Inc	4111	C	510 441-0698	3168
Rxo Freight Forwarding Inc	4731	A	630 795-1300	4090
UPS Worldwide Logistics Inc	4731	C	510 476-4000	4115
Union Sanitary District	4952	C	510 477-7500	4853
Reliance Steel & Aluminum Co	5051	C	510 476-4400	5513
Graybar Electric Company Inc	5063	D	925 557-3000	5562
Dynapower Company LLC	5084	C	802 860-7200	5830
Mercado Latino Inc	5141	D	510 475-5500	6269
SSC Inc (HQ)	5146	D	510 477-0008	6484
Daylight Foods Inc	5148	D	510 931-4207	6533
Sugar Foods Corporation	5149	D	510 441-0311	6672
Southern Glzers Wine Sprits LL	5182	B	510 477-5500	6807
Emerald Packaging Inc	5199	C	510 429-5700	6902
Manufactured Packaging Pdts	5199	D	510 487-1211	6927
Lowes Home Centers LLC	5211	D	510 476-0600	7051
Southern Cal Disc Tire Co Inc	5531	C	510 429-1977	7357
Permanente Medical Group Inc	6324	A	510 675-4010	8356
Gcm Holding Corporation	6719	B	510 475-0404	9314
Lotus Hotels - Union City LLC	7011	B	510 475-0600	9986
1st Class Laundry	7218	C	510 487-8297	10475
Ucertify LLC	7299	D	800 796-3062	10580
Ultimo Software Solutions Inc	7371	C	408 943-1490	12001
EMR Cpr LLC	7373	B	408 471-6804	12453
Rentex Incorporated	7377	D	833 737-6839	12700
AAA Restaurant Fire Ctrl Inc	7389	D	510 786-9555	13169
Touchofmodern Inc	7389	C	888 868-1232	13512
Kaiser Prmanente Un Cy Landing	8011	D	408 235-4005	14856
Child Family & Cmnty Svcs Inc	8351	C	510 796-9512	18286
Masonic Homes of California	8361	B	510 441-3700	18481
Western Allied Mechanical Inc	8711	C	650 326-0750	19438
Navis Corporation (PA)	8748	D	510 267-5000	20811

UNIVERSAL CITY, CA - Los Angeles County

	SIC	EMP	PHONE	ENTRY#
Sprint Communications Co LP	4813	C	818 755-7100	4344
Nbcuniversal Media LLC	4832	A	818 777-1000	4398
NBC Subsidiary (knbc-Tv) LLC	4833	D	818 684-5746	4454
Universal Stdios Licensing LLC	6794	C	818 695-1273	9459
Hilton Los Angles Universal Cy	7011	C	818 506-2500	9854
Lh Universal Operating LLC	7011	B	818 980-1212	9975
Shen Zhen New World II LLC	7011	D	818 980-1212	10225
Sun Hill Properties Inc	7011	B	818 506-2500	10282
Universal Mus Group Dist Corp	7389	D	818 508-9550	13529
Amblin Partners	7812	D	818 733-9665	13817
Creative Park Productions LLC	7812	C	818 622-3702	13833
NBC Universal Inc	7812	A		13868
Universal City Studios Lllp	7812	A	818 622-8477	13906
Universal Pctres HM Entrmt LLC (DH)	7812	D	818 777-1000	13907
Gramercy Productions LLC	7822	D	818 777-1677	13964
NBC Studios Inc	7922	A	818 777-1000	14048

UPLAND, CA - San Bernardino County

	SIC	EMP	PHONE	ENTRY#
V C A Central Animal Hospital	0742	D	909 981-2855	344
California Skateparks	0781	C	909 949-1601	421
California Ldscp & Design Inc	0782	C	909 949-1601	480
Lewis Companies (PA)	1531	C	909 985-0971	796
Paat & Kimmel Development Inc	1542	D	909 315-8074	981
Mladen Buntich Cnstr Co Inc	1623	D	909 920-9977	1238
Vci Construction LLC (HQ)	1623	D	909 946-0905	1276
Largo Concrete Inc	1771	B	909 981-7844	2133
Holliday Trucking Inc (PA)	3273	D	909 982-1553	2710
Walton Electric Corporation	3669	C	909 981-5051	2903
Motogistics Logistics Inc	4789	D	626 975-6470	4168
Dependble Break Rm Sltions Inc	5046	D	909 982-5933	5376
Camstar International Inc	5072	D	909 931-2540	5724
Lowes Home Centers LLC	5211	D	909 982-4795	7050
Park Place Ford LLC	5511	D	909 946-5555	7275
Hamilton Brwart Insur Agcy LLC	6411	D	909 920-3250	8581
Diamond Ridge Corporation	6531	C	909 949-0605	8981

GEOGRAPHIC SECTION
VALLEY CENTER CA

Name	SIC	EMP	PHONE	ENTRY#
Employnet Inc.	7361	A	909 458-0961	11130
Sapphire Softech Solutions LLC	7379	D	888 357-5222	12872
Master Lightning SEC Solutions.	7381		626 337-2915	13001
Shield Security Inc.	7381	B	909 920-1173	13044
San Antnio Ambltory Srgcal Ctr	8011	D	909 579-1500	15036
Inland Empire Therapy Provider **(PA)**	8049	D	909 985-7905	15287
Sela Healthcare Inc **(PA)**	8051	C	909 985-1981	15659
Upland Community Care Inc.	8051	D	909 985-1903	15712
San Antonio Regional Hospital **(PA)**	8062	A	909 985-2811	16374
Inland Vly DRG Alchol Rcvery S **(PA)**	8093	D	909 932-1069	17075
Families Chice HM Care Svcs In	8322	D	909 303-9377	17972
Reach Out West End.	8399	D	909 982-8641	18620
Upland Highlanders High Ptsa.	8641	D	909 949-7880	18919
Victoria Place Community Assn.	8699	D	909 981-4131	19118
Garrett J Gentry Gen Engrg Inc.	8711	D	909 693-3391	19236
Bms Parent Inc **(PA)**	8721	D	909 981-2341	19538
Lewis Management Corp.	8741	C	909 985-0971	20139
Lexxiom Inc.	8741	B	909 581-7313	20140
Utility Line MGT Svcs Inc.	8741	D	909 920-0812	20240
Bni Enterprises Inc.	8743	A	909 305-1818	20630
B & L Consulting LLC.	8748	D	682 238-6994	20698

UPPER LAKE, CA - Lake County

Name	SIC	EMP	PHONE	ENTRY#
Running Creek Casino.	7011	C	707 275-9209	10183

VACAVILLE, CA - Solano County

Name	SIC	EMP	PHONE	ENTRY#
Mariani Packing Co Inc **(PA)**	0723	B	707 452-2800	287
Blue Mountain Cnstr Svcs Inc.	1711	C	800 889-2085	1381
Allied Framers Inc.	1751	C	707 452-7050	1990
North Bay Distribution Inc **(PA)**	4225	D	707 452-9984	3740
Kuic Inc.	4832	C	707 446-0200	4391
Pacific Gas and Electric Co.	4911	D	707 452-1983	4651
County of Solano.	4941	C	707 451-6090	4782
Solano Irrigation District.	4971	D	707 448-6847	4995
Transpac Inc.	5023	D	707 452-0600	5139
Lowes Home Centers LLC.	5211	D	707 455-4400	7047
Continental Pacific Bank.	6022	D	707 448-1200	7676
Travis Credit Union **(PA)**	6061	B	707 449-4000	7812
State Compensation Insur Fund.	6331	C	415 565-1222	8408
Premium Outlet Partners LP.	6512	C	707 448-3661	8749
Vacaville Healthcare Inc.	7363	D	707 449-8000	11345
Triumph Protection Group Inc.	7381	B	800 224-0286	13057
Brenden Theatre Corporation.	7832	D	707 469-0180	13978
Sutter Regional Med Foundation.	8011	A	707 454-5800	15117
Vacavlle Cnvalescent Rehab Ctr.	8059	D	707 449-8000	15908
Westlake Development Group LLC.	8059	D	707 447-7496	15911
Kaiser Foundation Hospitals.	8062	A	707 624-4000	16149
Northbay Healthcare Group	8062	B	707 446-4000	16286
Thriving Seniors LLC.	8082	D	707 317-1740	16952
Consolidated Networks Corp.	8621	D	707 422-0791	18745
Interntnl Brthd Elc Wkr Lcal **(PA)**	8631	D	707 452-2700	18784

VALENCIA, CA - Los Angeles County

Name	SIC	EMP	PHONE	ENTRY#
Oakridge Landscape Inc **(PA)**	0721	D	661 295-7228	242
Gothic Landscaping Inc.	0781	C	661 257-5085	434
Landscape Development Inc **(PA)**	0782	B	661 295-1970	516
California Strl Concepts Inc.	1542	D	661 257-6903	890
Summer Systems Inc.	1542	D	661 257-4419	1034
Awhap Acquisition Corp.	1711	C	888 611-4328	1368
AAA Elctrcal Cmmunications Inc **(PA)**	1731	C	800 892-4784	1652
Sound River Corporation.	1731	D	661 705-3700	1842
Weslar Inc.	1751	D	661 702-1362	2026
JT Wimsatt Contg Co Inc **(PA)**	1771	B	661 775-8090	2132
Precision Dynamics Corporation **(HQ)**	2672	C	818 897-1111	2528
King Bros Enterprises LLC.	3088	C	661 257-3262	2668
Sdi Industries Inc **(DH)**	3535	C	818 890-6002	2776
Iwerks Entertainment Inc.	3699	D	661 678-1800	2959
Boston Scntfic Nrmdlation Corp **(HQ)**	3842	A	661 949-4310	3063
Bioness Inc.	3845	C	661 362-4850	3072
Central States Logistics Inc.	4212	C	661 295-7222	3381
Dawson Delivery LLC.	4212	D	505 385-1074	3385
D C Shower Doors Inc.	4213	C	661 257-1177	3463
Advantage Media Services Inc.	4225	C	661 705-7588	3671
Advantage Media Services Inc **(PA)**	4783	D	661 775-0611	4124
Nexus Is Inc.	4899	B	704 694-7290	4545
Southern California Edison Co.	4911	A	661 607-0207	4689
Southern California Gas Co.	4924	C	800 427-2200	4745
Whi Solutions Inc.	5045	D	661 257-2120	5370
Avita Medical Americas LLC.	5047	B	661 367-9170	5401
Klm Laboratories Inc.	5047	C	661 295-2600	5428
Shield-Denver Health Care Ctr **(HQ)**	5047	D	661 294-4200	5449
Cicoil LLC.	5065	D	661 295-1295	5641
Hypercel Corporation.	5065	D	661 310-1000	5660
Novacap LLC.	5065	B	661 295-5920	5684
Malys of California Inc.	5087	B	661 295-8317	5946
Falcon Aerospace Holdings LLC.	5088	A	661 775-7200	5957
Regent Aerospace Corporation **(PA)**	5088	C	661 257-3000	5967
Wesco Aircraft Hardware Corp.	5088	D	661 775-7200	5971
Cardinal Health Inc.	5122	D	661 295-6100	6100
N Qiagen Amercn Holdings Inc **(HQ)**	5122	C	800 426-8157	6133
Smart & Final Stores LLC.	5141	D	661 775-1416	6381
Sunkist Growers Inc **(PA)**	5148	C	661 290-8900	6586
Bluemark Inc.	5199	C	323 230-0770	6893
Magic Acquisition Corp.	5511	B	661 382-4700	7255
Dharma Ventures Group Inc **(PA)**	5999	B	661 294-4200	7577
Merrill Lynch Prce Fnner Smith.	6211	D	661 802-0764	8107
Mercury Insurance Company.	6331	A	661 291-6470	8398
Farmers Insurance.	6411	C	661 257-0844	8559
Global Building Services Inc **(PA)**	7349	D	800 675-6643	10903
Worldbridge Partners.	7361	C	661 775-9999	11262
Maxim Healthcare Services Inc.	7363	B	661 964-6350	11300
Sage Staffing Consultants Inc **(PA)**	7363	C	661 254-4026	11327
Krg Technologies Inc **(PA)**	7371	B	661 257-9967	11698
Infogen Labs Inc.	7379	C	323 816-4813	12809
Fpk Security Inc.	7381	B	661 702-9091	12973
ADT LLC.	7382	C	818 373-6200	13091
Hrd Aero Systems Inc **(PA)**	7699	C	661 295-0670	13774
Russell-Warner Inc.	7699	C	661 295-9200	13796
Sunvair Aerospace Group Inc **(PA)**	7699	D	661 294-3777	13801
Magic Mountain LLC.	7922	A	661 255-4100	14046
Heritage Golf Group LLC.	7992	C	661 254-4401	14267
Six Flags Magic Mountain Inc.	7996	A	661 255-4100	14315
US Healthworks Inc **(DH)**	8011	A	661 678-2300	15172
Henry Mayo Newhall Mem Hosp **(PA)**	8062	A	661 253-8000	16126
Henry Mayo Nwhall Mem Hlth Fnd.	8062	A	661 253-8000	16127
Specialty Laboratories Inc **(DH)**	8071	A	661 799-6543	16753
Volunteers of Amer Los Angeles.	8322	D	661 290-2894	18177
Curtiss-Wrght Cntrls Intgrted **(DH)**	8711	A	661 257-4430	19192
Aspen.	8741	D	661 476-5138	20026
Fdsi Logistics LLC.	8742	D	818 971-3300	20374
Scorpion Design LLC **(PA)**	8742	A	661 702-0100	20539
Geologics Corporation.	8748	C	661 259-5767	20761
Engeo Incorporated.	8999	D	661 257-4004	20885

VALLEJO, CA - Solano County

Name	SIC	EMP	PHONE	ENTRY#
A Plus Tree LLC.	0783	C	707 644-1672	551
Timec Acquisitions Inc **(DH)**	1629	A	707 642-2222	1321
Jeffco Painting & Coating Inc.	1721	D	707 562-1900	1624
Steiny and Company Inc.	1731	C	707 552-6900	1853
M F Maher Inc.	1771	D	707 552-2774	2136
Meyer Corporation US **(HQ)**	3469	D	707 551-2800	2752
Medic Ambulance Service Inc **(PA)**	4119	C	707 644-1761	3275
Michaels Trnsp Svc Inc.	4141	D	707 674-6013	3312
Smart & Final Stores LLC.	5141	D	707 644-4281	6332
Kaiser Foundation Hospitals.	6324	B	707 645-2720	8313
Kaiser Foundation Hospitals.	6324	C	707 651-1000	8315
Califrnia Mrtime Acdemy Fndtio.	6732	C	707 654-1000	9411
Sfn Group Inc.	7363	A	707 551-2719	11337
Century Theatres Inc.	7832	C	707 648-3456	13981
Marine World Foundation.	7996	B	707 644-4000	14307
Park Management Corp.	7996	C	707 644-6722	14309
Greater Vallejo Recreation Dst.	7999	D	707 648-4600	14532
La Clinica De La Raza Inc.	8011	C	707 556-8100	14865
Permanente Medical Group Inc.	8011	A	707 765-3930	14960
Emeritus Corporation.	8051	C	707 552-3336	15439
Empres Financial Services LLC.	8051	A	707 643-2793	15446
Evergreen At Springs Road LLC.	8051	D	360 892-6628	15471
Kaiser Foundation Hospitals.	8062	A	707 651-1000	16184
Sutter Hlth Scrmnto Sierra Reg.	8062	B	707 554-4444	16549
Sutter Solano Med Ctr Guild **(HQ)**	8062	A	707 554-4444	16558
Sutter Solano Medical Center.	8062	A	707 554-4444	16559
Mhm Services Inc.	8093	C	707 652-2688	17093
Center For Social Dynamics LLC.	8322	D	707 553-1784	17872
Sutter Regional Med Foundation.	8641	D	707 551-3616	18914
Roman Cathlic Bishp Sacramento.	8661	D	707 556-9317	19025
Vallejo Flood & Wastewater Dst.	8748	D	707 644-8949	20869
Vallejo Flood Wstwter Dst Fing.	8748	D	707 644-8949	20870

VALLEY CENTER, CA - San Diego County

Name	SIC	EMP	PHONE	ENTRY#
Mercy Medical Trnsp Inc.	4119	C	760 739-8026	3281
Valley Ctr Mncpl Wtr Dst Fclti.	4941	D	760 735-4500	4844
Valley Center Municpl Wtr Dst.	4952	D	760 735-4500	4854
Hcal LLC.	7011	B	760 751-3100	9844
San Psqual Band Mssion Indians.	7011	C	760 291-5500	10202
Survival Systems Intl Inc **(PA)**	7699	D	760 749-6800	13802
Caesars Entrtnment Oprting Inc.	7999	A	760 751-3100	14501

Employee Codes: A=Over 500 employees, B=251-500
C=101-250, D=51-100, E=20-50, F=10-19, G=1-9

VALLEY CENTER CA

GEOGRAPHIC SECTION

	SIC	EMP	PHONE	ENTRY#
Indian Health Council Inc **(PA)**	8011	D	760 749-1410	14781
San Psqual Band Mssion Indians **(PA)**	9131	D	760 749-3200	20919

VALLEY SPRINGS, CA - Calaveras County

East Bay Mncpl Utlity Dst Wstw	4941	C	209 772-8204	4786

VALLEY VILLAGE, CA - Los Angeles County

Douglas Steel Supply Inc **(PA)**	5051	D	323 587-7676	5488
Afm & Sg-Ftra Intllctual Prprt	7389	D	818 255-7980	13181
Zeus Networks LLC	7929	D	323 910-4420	14114
Healthy Medical Solutions Inc	8099	D	818 974-1980	17250
Adat ARI El	8211	C	818 766-4992	17693

VAN NUYS, CA - Los Angeles County

Parkwood Landscape Maint Inc	0782	D	818 988-9677	529
Energy Enterprises USA Inc **(PA)**	1711	D	424 339-0005	1429
Climatec LLC	1731	C	818 855-8528	1700
Dfs Flooring Inc **(PA)**	1752	D	818 374-5200	2031
Eberhard	1761	C	818 782-4604	2061
Mp Aero LLC	1799	D	818 901-9828	2298
Leigh Jerry California Inc **(PA)**	2361	B	818 909-6200	2465
Danmer Inc	2431	C	516 670-5125	2477
Digital Room Holdings Inc **(HQ)**	2759	D	310 575-4440	2568
Consolidated Fabricators Corp **(PA)**	3443	C	800 635-8335	2742
Edo Communications and Countermeasu	3812	D	818 464-2475	3004
Keolis Transit America Inc	4111	D	818 616-5254	3143
Mv Transportation Inc	4111	B	818 374-9145	3177
American Prof Ambulance Corp	4119	C	818 996-2200	3234
Catered Fit Corp	4212	C	855 400-2348	3380
United Parcel Service Inc	4215	B	404 828-6000	3639
Moulton Logistics Management	4225	C	818 997-1800	3732
Pegasus Elite Aviation Inc	4522	C	818 742-6666	3867
Clay Lacy Aviation Inc **(PA)**	4581	C	818 989-2900	3885
Broadview Networks Inc	4813	D	818 939-0015	4258
Apu Inc **(PA)**	5013	D	661 948-2880	5022
E & S International Entps Inc **(PA)**	5064	C	818 887-0700	5602
American Industrial Source Inc	5085	C	800 661-0622	5889
Grht Inc	5199	D	323 873-6593	6914
Home Depot USA Inc	5211	D	818 780-5448	6964
Keyes Motors Inc **(PA)**	5511	D	818 782-0122	7246
Keylex Inc **(PA)**	5511	D	818 379-4000	7247
Cinema Secrets Inc	5999	D	818 846-0579	7574
Napoleon Perdis Cosmetics Inc	5999	D	323 817-3611	7587
Los Angeles Police Credit Un **(PA)**	6062	D	818 787-6520	7828
Century-National Insurance Co **(DH)**	6411	B	818 760-0880	8524
Dewitt Stern Group Inc	6411	C	818 933-2700	8544
Momentous Insurance Brkg Inc	6411	D	818 933-2700	8613
All Valley Washer Service Inc	7215	D	818 787-1100	10460
Icon Media Direct Inc **(PA)**	7311	D	818 995-6400	10627
Lees Maintenance Service Inc	7349	B	818 988-6644	10917
L A Party Rents Inc	7359	C	818 989-4300	11039
Microlease Inc **(DH)**	7359	D	866 520-0200	11043
Town & Cntry Event Rentals Inc **(PA)**	7359	B	818 908-4211	11056
Nafees Memon	7381	D	818 997-1666	13004
Anheuser-Busch LLC	7389	B	805 381-4700	13194
Modern Parking Inc	7521	C	818 783-3143	13610
Pride Collision Centers Inc **(HQ)**	7532	C	818 909-0660	13645
Harpo Productions Inc	7812	C	312 633-1000	13852
Fusefx LLC	7819	B	818 237-5052	13938
Nep Bexel Inc **(HQ)**	7819	C	818 565-4399	13943
Weststar Cinemas Inc	7832	D	818 779-0323	14008
Southern Cal Orthpd Inst LP **(PA)**	8011	C	818 901-6600	15073
Valley Presbyterian Hospital	8062	A	818 782-6600	16614
Alta Hllywood Cmnty Hosp Van N	8063	D	818 787-1511	16635
Csa Silicon Valley LLC	8071	D	818 922-2416	16713
Primex Clinical Labs Inc **(PA)**	8071	D		16743
Americare Home Health Inc	8082	D	818 881-0005	16807
Greater Valley Medical Group	8093	C	818 781-7097	17069
County of Los Angeles	8111	D	818 374-2406	17417
County of Los Angeles	8322	D	818 374-2000	17923
Strength United	8322	D	818 787-9700	18146
Apprentice Jrnymen Trning Tr F	8331	C	310 604-0892	18204
Foothill Child Dev Svcs Inc	8351	D	818 353-3772	18316
Onegeneration	8351	D	818 708-6625	18339
Southland Rgnal Assn Rltors In **(PA)**	8611	D	818 786-2110	18723
Young MNS Chrstn Assn Mtro Los	8641	D	818 989-3800	18958
Interviewing Service Amer LLC **(PA)**	8732	C	818 989-1044	19824
Consumer Safety Analytics LLC	8734	D	818 922-2416	19960
Sylmark Inc **(PA)**	8741	D	818 217-2000	20223
Ganz USA LLC	8742	C	818 901-0077	20390

VANDENBERG AFB, CA - Santa Barbara County

Sumaria Systems LLC	8711	D	805 606-4973	19401
Henry Call Inc	8744	C	805 734-2762	20654
Indyne Inc	8744	B	805 606-7225	20655

VENICE, CA - Los Angeles County

Pacific Structures Sc Inc **(PA)**	1771	C	415 970-5434	2144
Los Angles Cnty Mtro Trnsp Aut	4111	A	310 392-8636	3151
Load Delivered Logistics LLC	4213	C	310 822-0215	3507
Southern California Gas Co	4924	B	310 823-7945	4740
Trg Inc	6531	D	310 396-6750	9197
Proper Hospitality LLC	7011	C	310 277-5221	10129
DDB Wrldwide Cmmnctons Group L	7311	D	310 907-1500	10605
Dynasty Marketplace Inc	7371	B	804 837-0119	11557
Sameday Technologies Inc	7371	C	310 697-8126	11898
First Team Security Inc	7381	D	310 709-4921	12971
Parking Concepts Inc	7521	C	310 821-1081	13622
Power Studios Inc	7812	C	310 314-2800	13881
Venice Fmly Clinic Foundation **(PA)**	8011	C	310 664-7703	15180
St Joseph Center	8322	C	310 396-6468	18139
Magiclinks Inc	8742	D	626 808-2215	20445
Gateb Consulting Inc	8748	D	310 526-8323	20759

VENTURA, CA - Ventura County

Saticoy Lemon Association	0174	D	805 654-6500	101
Brightview Landscape Svcs Inc	0781	C	805 642-9300	413
American Landscape MGT Inc	0782	C	805 647-5077	473
West Coast Arborists Inc	0783	C	805 671-5092	561
Nabors Well Services Co	1389	C	805 648-2731	617
A M Ortega Construction Inc	1521	C	951 360-1352	650
Ais Construction Company	1542	C	805 928-9467	861
Oilfield Electric Company	1731	C	805 648-3131	1795
Taft Electric Company **(PA)**	1731	C	805 642-0121	1861
Tidwell Excav Acquisition Inc	1794	D	805 647-4707	2227
G W Surfaces **(PA)**	1799	C	805 642-5004	2280
Streamline Dsign Slkscreen Inc **(PA)**	2329	C	805 884-1025	2456
Cco Holdings LLC	4841	C	805 232-5887	4489
E J Harrison & Sons Inc	4953	C	805 647-1414	4884
Parts Authority LLC	5013	C	805 676-3410	5053
ALI Roofg Mtls Long Bch Inc	5033	C	805 656-4259	5217
Peter Brasseler Holdings LLC	5047	C	805 650-5209	5442
High Tech Pet Products	5065	C	805 644-1797	5656
Smart & Final Stores Inc	5141	B	805 647-4276	6312
Smart & Final Stores LLC	5141	C	805 643-6556	6346
Del Mar Seafoods Inc	5146	C	805 850-0421	6469
Lowes Home Centers LLC	5211	C	805 675-8800	7075
Gregory Consulting Inc **(PA)**	5511	C	805 642-0111	7224
R E Barber-Ford	5511	C	805 656-4259	7284
Southern Cal Disc Tire Co Inc	5531	D	805 639-0166	7364
Ventura County Credit Union **(PA)**	6061	D	805 477-4000	7818
E&S Financial Group Inc	6162	C	805 644-1621	7956
Fin-West Group	6162	D	805 658-7435	7963
Triad Properties	6512	C	805 648-5008	8771
Rgc Services Inc **(PA)**	6531	D	805 644-1242	9167
Harbor Island Hotel Group LP	7011	D	805 650-7770	9835
Ventura Hsptality Partners LLC	7011	C	805 648-2100	10343
Giddyup Group Inc	7311	D	800 828-2785	10617
MCM Harvesters Inc	7361	C	805 659-6833	11176
Trade Desk Inc **(PA)**	7371	B	805 585-3434	11985
Arcoro Holdings Corp	7372	C	818 222-1836	12098
Boyd and Associates **(PA)**	7381	C	818 752-1888	12941
Ost Trucks and Cranes Inc	7389	D	805 643-9963	13413
Penske Corporation	7513	C	805 983-3788	13563
Weststar Cinemas Inc	7832	D	805 658-6544	14010
Century Theatres Inc	7833	B	805 641-6555	14016
Ventura Cnty Obstet Gynclgic M	8011	C	805 643-8695	15181
Ventura County Medical Center	8011	C	805 652-6201	15183
Ventura County Medical Center	8049	C	805 652-6729	15311
Coastal View Hlthcare Ctr LLC	8051	D	805 642-4101	15377
Victoria Care Center	8051	C	805 642-1736	15718
Victoria Vntura Healthcare LLC	8051	B	805 642-1736	15720
Community Mem Hosp San Bnvntur	8062	D	805 652-5072	16015
Community Memorial Health Sys **(PA)**	8062	A	805 652-5011	16016
Aegis Senior Communities LLC	8082	C	805 650-1114	16800
Califrnia Frnsic Med Group Inc	8099	C	805 654-3343	17199
Star of Ca LLC **(HQ)**	8099	C	805 644-7827	17333
Vitalant	8099	D	805 641-1603	17347
Catholic Chrties Snta Clara CN	8322	D	805 643-4694	17869
County of Ventura	8322	C	805 654-2561	17942
Channel Islnds Yung MNS Chrstn	8641	D	805 484-0423	18839
C D Lyon Construction Inc **(PA)**	8711	D	805 650-0173	19166
Oasis Systems LLC	8711	C	805 644-2191	19339
Willdan Engineering	8711	D	805 653-6597	19442
County of Ventura	8721	D	805 654-3152	19559
Livingston Mem Vna Hlth Corp	8741	B	805 642-0239	20143

GEOGRAPHIC SECTION

VISALIA CA

	SIC	EMP	PHONE	ENTRY#
Ventura Medical Management LLC	8741	B	805 477-6220	20243
County of Ventura	9111	D	805 652-6100	20917

VERNON, CA - Los Angeles County

	SIC	EMP	PHONE	ENTRY#
Edna H Pagel Inc	1541	D	323 234-2200	817
Square H Brands Inc	1541	D	323 267-4600	845
West Coast Distribution Inc	1541	D	323 588-6508	857
J & J Snack Foods Corp Cal (HQ)	2052	C	323 581-0171	2371
American Bottling Company	2086	C	323 268-7779	2402
Pacific American Fish Co Inc (PA)	2091	C	323 319-1551	2417
Sas Textiles Inc	2259	C	323 277-5555	2446
New Chef Fashion Inc	2311	D	323 581-0300	2449
National Corset Supply House (PA)	2341	D	323 261-0265	2464
A Rudin Inc (PA)	2512	C	323 589-5547	2488
Southland Box Company	2653	C	323 583-2231	2526
Continental Vitamin Co Inc	2834	D	323 581-0176	2583
Sewing Collection Inc	3053	D	323 264-2223	2655
Starco Enterprises Inc (PA)	3559	D	323 266-7111	2791
Westgate Mfg Inc	3699	D	323 826-9490	2965
C R Laurence Co Inc (HQ)	3714	B	323 588-1281	2972
UPD INC	3942	D	323 588-8811	3089
Los Angeles Junction Rlwy Co	4011	C	323 277-2004	3116
California Transit Inc	4111	D	323 234-8750	3125
Saia Motor Freight Line LLC	4213	D	323 277-2880	3541
Vernon Central Warehouse Inc	4214	C	323 234-2200	3603
Preferred Frzr Svcs - Lbf LLC	4222	D	323 263-8811	3657
Generational Properties Inc	4225	B	323 583-3163	3710
United Parcel Service Inc	4513	C	323 260-8957	3859
R Planet Earth LLC	4953	C	213 320-0601	4922
Reliance Steel & Aluminum Co	5051	C	323 583-6415	5515
Omniteam Inc	5078	C	562 923-9660	5780
City Fibers Inc (PA)	5093	C	323 583-1013	6006
Rggd Inc (PA)	5099	D	323 581-6617	6049
Jordana Cosmetics LLC	5122	C	310 730-4400	6118
Morgan Fabrics Corporation (PA)	5131	D	323 583-9981	6158
Unicolors Inc	5131	C	323 307-9878	6164
Karen Kane Inc (PA)	5137	C	323 588-0000	6202
Nydj Apparel LLC	5137	C	323 581-9040	6212
O & K Inc (PA)	5137	C	323 846-5700	6213
Same Swim LLC	5137	C	323 582-2588	6219
Tarrant Apparel Group	5137	D	323 780-8250	6224
Palisades Ranch Inc	5141	B	323 581-6161	6275
Contessa Premium Foods Inc	5142	C	310 832-8000	6418
Golden West Trading Inc	5142	D	323 581-3663	6421
West Pico Foods Inc	5142	D	323 586-9050	6428
Rogers Poultry Co (PA)	5144	D	323 585-0802	6449
H & N Foods International Inc (HQ)	5146	C	323 586-9300	6470
Red Chamber Co (PA)	5146	D	323 234-9000	6479
HV Randall Foods LLC	5147	C	323 261-6565	6495
Rancho Foods Inc	5147	C	323 585-0503	6501
Rite-Way Meat Packers Inc	5147	D	323 826-2144	6502
Sydney & Anne Bloom Farms Inc	5147	A	323 261-6565	6505
Wayne Provision Co Inc (PA)	5147	D	323 277-5888	6507
Farmers Link Inc	5148	D	213 623-5242	6540
Gourmet Specialties Inc	5148	D	323 587-1734	6555
Natures Produce	5148	C	323 235-4343	6565
V & L Produce Inc	5148	C	323 589-3125	6588
World Variety Produce Inc	5148	B	800 588-0151	6598
Completely Fresh Foods Inc	5149	C	323 722-9136	6617
Core-Mark International Inc	5149	C	323 583-6531	6619
Soofer Co Inc	5149	D	323 234-6666	6669
Tadin Inc	5149	D	213 406-8880	6677
Tama Trading Company	5149	D	213 748-8262	6678
TL Montgomery & Associates Inc	5149	D	323 583-1645	6680
BTG S CORP (PA)	5199	D	323 582-4444	6894
Revoltion Cnsmr Sltions CA LLC (DH)	5199	D	323 980-0918	6943
Shims Bargain Inc (PA)	5199	D	323 881-0099	6948
Atv Canter LLC (PA)	5531	D	562 977-8565	7342
Good Fellas Industries Inc	5719	D	323 924-9495	7438
Kelly Toys Holdings LLC	6719	C	323 923-1300	9319
Ameriprise Services Inc	7213	C	323 587-3941	10430
Paradigm Industries Inc	7389	D	310 965-1900	13418
Rose & Shore Inc	7389	B	323 826-2144	13453
Los Angeles Regional Food Bank	8322	C	323 234-3030	18046

VICTORVILLE, CA - San Bernardino County

	SIC	EMP	PHONE	ENTRY#
Baja Fresh Supermarket	0291	B	760 843-7730	232
Cwp Cabinets Inc	1751	C	760 246-4530	1997
A-Team Delivers LLC	4212	D	858 254-8401	3363
Hartwick & Hand Inc (PA)	4212	D	760 245-1666	3402
TT Trucking Services LLC	4212	D	323 790-3408	3428
Landforce Corporation	4213	C	760 843-7839	3502
Valley Bulk Inc	4213	D	760 843-0574	3560
Comav LLC	4581	C	760 523-5100	3886
Comav Technical Services LLC	4581	C	760 530-2400	3887
Robertsons Ready Mix Ltd	5032	D	702 798-0568	5209
Pacific Aerospace Resources & Techn	5088	D		5964
Centerline Wood Products	5099	D	760 246-4530	6036
Premier Food Services Inc	5141	B	760 843-8000	6279
Home Depot USA Inc	5211	C	760 955-2999	7018
Lowes Home Centers LLC	5211	D	760 949-9565	7035
Sunland Ford Inc	5511	D	760 241-7751	7306
Vahi Toyota Inc (PA)	5511	C	760 241-6484	7321
Coldwell Banker Home Source	6531	D	760 684-8100	8937
Victorvlle Trsure Holdings LLC	7011	D	760 245-6565	10344
American Prtctive Svcs Invstgt	7381	C	626 705-8600	12929
Victorville Speedwash Inc	7542	D	760 388-0112	13704
Victorville Speedwash Inc	7542	D	760 388-0113	13705
Desert Valley Med Group Inc (PA)	8011	B	760 241-8000	14728
Kaiser Foundation Hospitals	8011	D	888 750-0036	14811
Encore Senior Living III LLC	8051	D	760 243-2271	15447
Knolls Convalescent Hosp Inc (PA)	8051	C	760 245-5361	15530
Knolls West Enterprise	8051	C	760 245-0107	15531
Spring Valley Post Acute Inc	8051	C	760 245-6477	15678
Desert Valley Hospital Inc (DH)	8062	C	760 241-8000	16040
Branlyn Prominence Inc	8082	C	760 843-5655	16825
Peoples Care Inc	8082	C	760 962-1900	16911
Jamboor Medical Corporation	8092	D	760 241-8063	16989
Victor Cmnty Support Svcs Inc	8093	C	760 987-8225	17153
Victor Cmnty Support Svcs Inc	8093	C	760 245-4695	17156
Heritage Medical Group	8099	B	760 956-1286	17251
Family Assistance Program	8322	D	760 843-0701	17974
Think Together	8699	B	760 269-1230	19112

VIEW PARK, CA - Los Angeles County

	SIC	EMP	PHONE	ENTRY#
Hathawy-Sycmres Child Fmly Svc	8322	C	323 733-0322	17998

VILLA PARK, CA - Orange County

	SIC	EMP	PHONE	ENTRY#
Tropical Plaza Nursery Inc	0782	D	714 998-4100	542

VINA, CA - Tehama County

	SIC	EMP	PHONE	ENTRY#
Andersen & Sons Shelling Inc	0723	D	530 839-2236	254

VISALIA, CA - Tulare County

	SIC	EMP	PHONE	ENTRY#
L E Cooke Co	0181	C	559 732-9146	135
Scalia Farms	0191	D	559 651-2711	198
Toor Farming LLC	0191	D	559 500-1331	201
Kreger Inc	0761	A	559 884-2585	366
Original Mowbrays Tree Svc Inc	0783	D	559 798-0530	559
American Incorporated (PA)	1542	D	559 651-1776	864
R & L Brosamer Inc	1542	B	559 739-8215	998
R Lang Company	3442	D	559 651-0701	2741
Orange Belt Stages (PA)	4142	D	559 733-4408	3319
Santa Barbara Trnsp Corp	4151	C	559 738-5780	3350
Indian River Transport Co	4213	C	209 664-0456	3492
Sierra Agricultural Trnsp Inc	4213	C	559 738-5448	3544
General Lgstics Systems US Inc	4215	C	559 651-1850	3614
Pappas Telecasting of The Midlands LP	4833	B	559 733-7800	4456
Mlb Advanced Media LP	4841	A	559 625-0480	4513
Hanson Distributing Company	5013	D	559 802-1198	5043
Veterinary Service Inc	5047	D	559 651-1633	5458
Smart & Final Stores LLC	5141	D	559 625-9044	6352
Hydrite Chemical Co	5169	D	559 651-3450	6712
Sequoia Beverage Company LP	5181	C	559 651-2444	6782
Graphic Packaging Intl LLC	5199	C	559 651-3535	6913
Lowes Home Centers LLC	5211	D	559 624-4300	7073
Penney Opco LLC	5311	D	559 732-4171	7128
Guardian Safety and Supply LLC	5999	D	559 651-0919	7582
Valley Business Bank	6022	D	559 622-9000	7721
Valley Commerce Bancorp	6022	D	559 622-9000	7722
Country Club Mortgage Inc	6162	D	559 636-3333	7952
Merrill Lynch Prce Fnner Smith	6211	D	559 741-9033	8122
Arthur J Gallagher & Co	6411	D	559 733-1181	8494
Caliente Creek Prtners A Cal L (PA)	6531	D	559 651-1000	8920
Hyde & Company Inc	6531	D	559 741-3636	9045
Jordan - Link & Company (PA)	6531	D	559 733-9696	9063
Allen Development Partners LLC (PA)	6552	D	559 732-5425	9244
Thyme Holdings LLC	6719	D	559 733-0901	9342
Welcome Group Management LLC	7011	D	310 378-6666	10357
Mission Linen Supply	7211	D	559 625-5423	10424
Central Valley Presort Inc	7331	D	559 906-2003	10769
ABM Janitorial Services Inc	7349	D	559 651-1612	10847
Tim Hofer Inc	7349	D	559 732-6676	10973
Valley Agricultural Sftwr Inc	7371	B	559 686-9496	12012
Matson Alarm Co Inc	7382	D	559 438-8000	13133
Todd Plumbing Inc	7699	C	559 651-5820	13806

Employee Codes: A=Over 500 employees, B=251-500
C=101-250, D=51-100, E=20-50, F=10-19, G=1-9

VISALIA CA

GEOGRAPHIC SECTION

	SIC	EMP	PHONE	ENTRY#
Visalia Country Club	7997	D	559 734-3733	14480
Visalia Medical Clinic Inc (PA)	8011	B	559 733-5222	15195
Far West Inc	8051	C	559 627-1241	15474
PCI Care Venture I	8051	D	559 735-0828	15625
Quail Park Retirement Vlg LLC	8052	D	559 624-3500	15786
Far West Inc	8059	D	559 733-0901	15844
Kaweah Delta Health Care Dst	8062	C	559 624-4800	16198
Kaweah Dlta Hlth Care Dst Gild (PA)	8062	A	559 624-2000	16200
Kaweah Dlta Hlth Care Dst Gild	8063	C	559 624-3300	16652
Central Vly Regional Ctr Inc	8093	C	559 738-2200	17022
Kaweah Dlta Hlth Care Dst Gild	8099	C	559 624-3100	17263
Turning Point Central Cal Inc	8322	D	559 627-1490	18157
Community Services and Employment T	8331	D	559 757-3539	18223
Pro-Youth	8641	B	559 374-2030	18896

VISTA, CA - San Diego County

	SIC	EMP	PHONE	ENTRY#
Color Spot Holdings Inc (PA)	0181	A	760 695-1430	120
Plug Connection Inc	0181	D	760 631-0992	148
I Pwlc Inc	0781	D	760 630-0231	440
Nissho of California Inc (PA)	0781	C	760 727-9719	452
Pac West Land Care Inc	0781	C	760 630-0231	453
Habitat Rstration Sciences Inc (PA)	0782	D	760 479-4210	495
Heaviland Enterprises Inc (PA)	0782	D	760 598-7065	497
Burtech Pipeline Incorporated	1623	D	760 634-2822	1199
Orion Construction Corporation	1623	D	760 597-9660	1247
Industrial Coml Systems Inc	1711	C	760 300-4094	1462
Neal Electric Corp (HQ)	1731	D	858 513-2525	1787
Excel Mdular Scaffold Lsg Corp	1799	A	760 598-0050	2273
Zodiac Pool Systems LLC	1799	D	760 599-9600	2337
Earthlite LLC (DH)	2514	D	760 599-1112	2490
American Peptide Company Inc	2836	D	408 733-7604	2618
Applied Membranes Inc	3589	C	760 727-3711	2847
Flux Power Holdings Inc (PA)	3691	C	877 505-3589	2948
Amron International Inc (PA)	3949	C	760 208-6500	3091
Directed LLC	4731	C	800 876-0800	4008
Patriot Logistics Services LLC	4789	C	443 994-9660	4170
Tempo Communications Inc (PA)	4813	C	800 642-2155	4350
Vista Irrigation District	4971	D	760 597-3100	4997
Winners Only Inc	5021	C	760 599-0300	5108
Jeld-Wen Inc	5031	B	760 597-4201	5170
H20 Innovation USA Holding Inc	5074	D	760 639-4400	5752
Swarco McCain Inc (DH)	5084	C	760 727-8100	5871
D & D Saw Works Inc	5085	C		5898
Apical Industries Inc	5088	C	760 724-5300	5955
Smart & Final Stores Inc	5141	B	760 732-1480	6300
Hay House Inc (PA)	5192	D	760 431-7695	6843
Altman Specialty Plants LLC (PA)	5193	A	800 348-4881	6848
Bandy Ranch Floral Corp	5193	B	805 757-9905	6851
Gringo Ventures LLC	5193	C	760 477-7999	6860
Ponto Nursery	5193	C	760 724-6003	6872
Spectrum Equipment LLC	5193	D	760 599-8849	6873
Jon Renau Collection Inc	5199	C	760 598-0067	6919
Lee-Mar Aquarium & Pet Sups	5199	C	760 727-1300	6924
Lowes Home Centers LLC	5211	C	760 631-6255	7063
County Ford North Inc (PA)	5511	C	760 945-9900	7186
Living Spaces Furniture LLC	5712	C	760 945-6805	7422
Inception Homes Inc	6531	D	760 726-4302	9048
Professional Cmnty MGT Cal Inc	6531	D	760 918-8040	9143
Meeting Services Inc	7359	D	858 348-0100	11041
Epitec Inc	7371	A	760 650-2515	11573
Off Duty Officers Inc	7381	A	888 408-5900	13009
All-Pro Bail Bonds Inc	7389	D	760 512-1969	13183
Krikorian Premiere Theatre LLC	7832	D	760 945-7469	14001
Spa Havens LP	7991	C	760 945-2055	14232
Vista Valley Country Club	7997	D	760 758-2800	14481
Kaiser Foundation Hospitals	8011	D	619 528-5000	14798
Vista Community Clinic (PA)	8031	B	760 631-5000	15260
Vista Woods Health Assoc LLC	8051	D	760 630-2273	15726
Rancho Vista Health Center	8052	C	760 941-1480	15787
Care Choice Health Systems Inc	8059	D	760 798-4508	15828
Life Care Centers America Inc	8059	D	760 724-8222	15865
Exagen Diagnostics Inc	8071	D	505 272-7966	16719
Planned Prnthood of PCF Sthwes	8093	D	619 881-4500	17111
Grifols Bio Supplies Inc	8099	C	760 651-6042	17242
Alpha Project For Homeless	8322	D	760 630-9922	17826
Community Interface Services	8322	D	760 729-3866	17893
Vista Care Group LLC (PA)	8322	D	760 295-3900	18170
HMS Construction Inc (PA)	8711	D	760 727-9808	19252
Leidos Inc	8731	C	858 826-9090	19726
Plug Connection LLC	8742	D	760 631-0992	20508

WALNUT, CA - Los Angeles County

	SIC	EMP	PHONE	ENTRY#
JF Shea Construction Inc (HQ)	1521	C	909 594-9500	685
Shea Homes At Montage LLC	1521	C	909 594-9500	721
Shea Homes Vantis LLC	1522	D	909 594-9500	776
M & R Joint Venture Electrical	1731	C	909 598-7700	1768
United Riggers & Erectors Inc (PA)	1796	D	909 978-0400	2251
Unis Transportation LLC	4212	D	626 271-9800	3430
Bulk Transportation (PA)	4213	D	909 594-2855	3449
General Electric Company	4225	D	909 869-7404	3709
Lava Scs LLC	4225	D	909 437-7881	3724
Tropicana Manufacturing Co Inc	4225	D	909 444-1025	3771
Straight Forwarding Inc	4731	D	909 594-3400	4102
Unis LLC (PA)	4731	C	909 839-2600	4114
Tae Sook Chung	5023	D	909 598-6255	5136
Adesso Inc	5045	C	909 839-2929	5265
Servers Direct LLC	5045	C	800 576-7931	5348
Lina Gale (usa) Inc (PA)	5122	D	909 595-8898	6122
Sysco Los Angeles Inc	5141	A	909 595-9595	6400
Shea La Quinta LLC	6512	D	909 594-9500	8758
Guesty Inc (PA)	7011	D	415 244-0277	9829
Ahg Inc	7291	B	703 596-0111	10518
Gremlin Inc	7372	D	408 214-9885	12212
Ronsin Ltgtion Spport Svcs Inc (PA)	7389	D	909 594-5995	13452
Los Angles Ryal Vsta Golf Crse	7997	D	909 595-7441	14400
Emeritus Corporation	8051	C	909 595-5030	15443
Pregel America Inc	8351	D	909 598-8980	18349
Autism Intervention Profession	8399	D	909 245-9979	18563
Shogun Labs Inc (PA)	8734	C	317 676-2719	20000
Vistancia Marketing LLC	8742	D	909 594-9500	20606

WALNUT CREEK, CA - Contra Costa County

	SIC	EMP	PHONE	ENTRY#
Tony Lrssas Anmal Rscue Fndtio	0742	D	925 256-1273	343
David L Gates & Associates Inc	0781	D	925 736-8176	426
Tnhc Realty and Cnstr Inc	1521	D	925 244-0700	728
Build Group Inc	1542	D	415 367-9399	883
Wencon Development Inc	1711	D	925 478-8269	1595
Falcon Crtical Care Trnspt LLC	4119	D	510 223-1171	3260
Waste MGT Collectn Recycl Inc	4212	D	925 935-8900	3435
Verizon Bus Netwrk Svcs LLC	4813	D	925 934-3030	4355
LN Curtis and Sons (PA)	5087	D	510 839-5111	5944
Del Monte Foods Inc (HQ)	5149	C	925 949-2772	6624
Excel Garden Products	5191	C	925 948-4000	6824
Walnut Creek Associates 2 Inc	5511	C	925 934-0530	7327
Nordstrom Inc	5651	C	925 930-7959	7408
Wells Frgo Bnk NA As Trstee Fo	6021	D	925 765-6316	7648
Mechanics Bank (DH)	6022	D	800 797-6324	7696
Pacific Coast Bankers Bank	6022	D	415 399-1900	7703
Mortgage Solutions Fcs Inc	6162	D	925 954-8364	8003
Merrill Lynch Prce Fnner Smith	6211	D	925 945-4800	8130
C2 Financial Corporation	6282	C	925 938-1300	8192
Provident Lf Accident Insur Co	6311	D	925 944-4700	8246
Western National Life Insur Co	6311	C	925 946-5100	8253
Kaiser Foundation Hospitals	6324	D	925 926-3000	8320
Compwest Insurance Company	6331	C	415 593-5100	8382
XI Specialty Insurance Company	6351	B	925 942-6142	8435
Csaa Insurance Exchange (PA)	6411	D	925 279-2300	8536
Csaa Insurance Services Inc (HQ)	6411	C	925 279-3153	8537
Heffernan Insurance Brokers	6411	B	925 934-8500	8585
Relation Insurance Inc (PA)	6411	D	925 937-5858	8648
Standard Insurance Company	6411	D	925 947-3950	8662
Travelers Property Cslty Corp	6411	C	925 945-4000	8675
Barcelon Associates MGT Corp	6531	D	925 627-7000	8909
Cushman & Wakefield Cal Inc	6531	B	925 935-0770	8967
Diablo Realty	6531	C	925 933-9300	8980
Golden Rain Foundation (PA)	6531	D	925 988-7700	9025
A F Evans Development Inc	6552	B	510 267-4612	9242
Spectra Services Acquisition L	6799	B	510 734-8394	9564
J M D Enterprises (PA)	7231	D	925 935-4780	10500
One Planet Ops Inc (PA)	7311	C	925 983-2800	10659
Bay Area Techworkers (PA)	7361	D	925 359-2200	11093
Career Strategies Tmpry Inc	7361	C	925 296-9600	11106
Career Strategies Tmpry Inc	7361	C	925 296-9600	11108
Harvest Technical Service Inc	7361	C	925 937-4874	11148
Kugga Inc	7371	D	925 639-0721	11700
Paracosma Inc	7371	D	650 924-9896	11814
Spectrum Labs Inc	7371	D	415 295-2752	11938
Exadel Inc	7372	A	925 363-9510	12187
Mackevision LLC	7373	C	248 656-6566	12485
Computer Sciences Corporation	7376	D	702 558-8092	12693
Deplabs Inc	7379	D	415 456-5600	12778
A3 Smart Home LP	7381	C	800 669-7779	12915
First Alarm SEC & Patrol Inc	7382	B	925 295-5245	13118
Safe & Sound Security	7382	C	925 942-0795	13142
A F Evans Company Inc	7389	D	925 937-1700	13167
Derivative Path Inc	7389	D	415 992-8200	13263

GEOGRAPHIC SECTION
WEST HOLLYWOOD CA

	SIC	EMP	PHONE	ENTRY#
Derouen Enterprises LLC	7389	D	925 360-5743	13264
Tactical Telesolutions Inc	7389	C	415 788-8808	13498
Yapstone Inc (PA)	7389	D	866 289-5977	13559
Parking Concepts Inc	7521	D	925 944-1964	13618
Amerit Fleet Solutions Inc (HQ)	7549	D	877 512-6374	13709
Broadway By Bay	7922	C	650 579-5565	14029
Bay Area Srgcal Spclsts Inc A	8011	C	925 350-4044	14624
Bay Imaging Cons Med Group Inc (PA)	8011	C	925 296-7150	14625
Bay Medical Management LLC	8011	C	925 296-7150	14626
Kaiser Foundation Hospitals	8011	C	925 295-4145	14801
Kaiser Foundation Hospitals	8011	A	925 295-4000	14821
Medical Anesthesia Cons LLC	8011	C	925 287-1505	14890
Muir Orthopedic Specialists	8011	C	925 939-8585	14913
Permanente Medical Group Inc	8011	A	925 906-2000	14979
Ucsf Benioff Childrens Hosp	8011	D	925 979-4000	15138
Womens Cancer Center	8011	C	925 627-3440	15212
John Muir Health (HQ)	8062	A	925 947-4449	16143
John Muir Health	8062	A	925 939-3000	16144
John Muir Physician Network (PA)	8062	A	925 296-9700	16145
Kaiser Foundation Hospitals	8062	C	925 906-2380	16156
Kaiser Foundation Hospitals	8062	B	925 906-2000	16182
Bass Medical Group	8071	C	925 690-5056	16705
Abraham Rest Home	8082	D	925 287-8382	16785
Kimco Staffing Services Inc	8099	A	925 945-1444	17265
Archer Norris A Professional Law Corporation	8111	C	925 930-6000	17366
Berding & Weil LLP (PA)	8111	D	925 838-2090	17383
Miller Starr Rglia A Prof Law (PA)	8111	D	925 935-9400	17570
Covia Affordable Communities	8322	C	925 956-7100	17945
Atria Management Company LLC	8361	C	925 787-6149	18377
Golden Rain Foundation	8641	B	925 988-7800	18866
Redwood Forest Foundation Inc	8641	D	510 459-1131	18902
California State Automobile Associa (HQ)	8699	A	925 287-7600	19073
Brosamer & Wall Inc	8711	C	925 932-7900	19161
Brown and Caldwell (PA)	8711	C	925 937-9010	19162
Carollo Engineers Inc (PA)	8711	D	925 932-1710	19175
Erm-West Inc (DH)	8711	B	925 946-0455	19220
Fehr & Peers (PA)	8711	D	925 977-3200	19224
Fugro William Lettis Assoc Inc (DH)	8711	D	925 256-6070	19233
Mka International Inc	8711	C	925 934-3235	19323
Stantec Consulting Svcs Inc	8711	D	925 627-4500	19397
Blackstone Development Inc	8712	C	925 718-3126	19457
Thomas Wirig Doll & Co Cpas	8721	D	925 939-2500	19635
Integrated Pain Managemen	8741	C	925 691-9806	20116
Kelleyamerit Holdings Inc (PA)	8741	D	877 512-6374	20133
Firstcall	8742	D	415 781-4300	20380
Invision Communications Inc (PA)	8742	D	925 944-1211	20417
Amerit Fleet Solutions Inc	8744	C	877 512-6374	20648
Axiom Global Technologies Inc	8748	D	925 393-5800	20697
Kcctech LLC	8748	C	628 400-2420	20790

WASCO, CA - Kern County

	SIC	EMP	PHONE	ENTRY#
Supreme Almonds California Inc	0173	D	661 746-6475	94
Bethlehem Construction Inc	1541	D	661 758-1001	807
Sunpower Corporation Systems	1711	D	661 758-2501	1575
Hec Asset Management Inc	5046	D	661 587-2250	5379
South Valley Almond Co LLC	5159	C	661 391-9000	6697
Adventist Health Delano	6733	D	661 758-4184	9420
Community Support Options Inc	8322	C	661 758-5331	17895

WATSONVILLE, CA - Santa Cruz County

	SIC	EMP	PHONE	ENTRY#
Reiter Affl Companies LLC	0171	C	831 786-4244	62
Reiter Affl Companies LLC	0171	C	831 761-1424	63
Lakeside Organic Gardens LLC (PA)	0191	B	831 722-6266	189
Granite Rock Co (PA)	1442	D	831 768-2000	637
Granite Cnstr Northeast Inc	1611	B	831 724-1011	1108
Granite Construction Company (HQ)	1611	B	831 724-1011	1109
Granite Construction Inc (PA)	1622	B	831 724-1011	1183
Santa Cruz Metro Trnst Dst	4111	D	831 426-6080	3210
Waste MGT Collectn Recycl Inc	4953	C	831 768-9505	4964
Granite Rock Co	5032	D	831 724-3847	5206
Sv Labs Corporation (PA)	5122	D	831 722-9526	6146
Superior Foods Inc	5141	D	831 728-3691	6396
Driscolls Inc (PA)	5148	D	831 424-0506	6534
Driscolls Inc	5148	D	800 871-3333	6535
Field Fresh Farms LLC	5148	D	831 722-1422	6541
Watsonville Coast Produce Inc	5148	D	831 722-3851	6594
Afc-Bpi Inc	5191	B	541 441-2847	6819
Camflor Inc	5193	C	831 726-1330	6855
E & B Marine Inc (HQ)	5551	D	831 728-2700	7393
Ameri-Kleen	7349	C	831 722-8888	10852
Ramco Enterprises LP	7361	B	831 722-3370	11212
Spa Fitness Center Inc	7991	D	831 722-3895	14231
Salud Para La Gente	8011	C	831 728-0222	15035
Halsen Healthcare LLC	8062	A	831 724-4741	16116
Hospice of Santa Cruz County	8082	D	831 430-3000	16872
Community Bridges	8322	D	831 724-2024	17891
Encompass Community Services	8322	D	831 724-3885	17968
Central Coast YMCA	8641	C	831 728-9622	18833
Granite Power Inc	8741	B	831 724-1011	20102

WEAVERVILLE, CA - Trinity County

	SIC	EMP	PHONE	ENTRY#
United Parcel Service Inc	4215	C	530 623-3938	3631
Trinity River Lumber Company (PA)	5031	D	530 623-5561	5191
Mountain Cmmnties Hlth Care Ds (PA)	8062	D	530 623-5541	16276

WEED, CA - Siskiyou County

	SIC	EMP	PHONE	ENTRY#
Roseburg Forest Products Co	5031	D	530 938-2721	5183

WEST COVINA, CA - Los Angeles County

	SIC	EMP	PHONE	ENTRY#
Sears Home Imprv Pdts Inc	1521	C	626 671-1892	715
Turn Around Communications Inc	1623	D	626 443-2400	1272
Harris & Ruth Painting Contg (PA)	1721	D	626 960-4004	1622
Penney Opco LLC	5311	C	626 960-3711	7133
Allen/Clark Cadillac	5511	D	626 966-7441	7168
P A Motorcars LLC	5511	A	877 433-3517	7273
Pmb Motorcars LLC	5511	A	626 384-3600	7280
Kaiser Foundation Hospitals	6324	D	866 319-4269	8317
Kaiser Foundation Hospitals	6324	D	626 856-3045	8326
Southern Cal Prmnnte Med Group	6324	B	626 960-4844	8364
RM Galicia Inc	7322	D	626 813-6200	10751
RSI Leasing LLC	7359	D	626 966-6129	11053
Os4labor LLC	7361	C	626 838-6745	11192
Volt Management Corp	7363	D	626 931-1437	11355
Lfp Ecommerce LLC	7389	D	314 428-5069	13353
Penske Motor Group LLC	7513	B	626 859-1200	13564
Big Lgue Dreams Consulting LLC	7941	C	626 839-1100	14129
South Hills Country Club	7997	D	626 339-1231	14455
West Covina Medical Clinic Inc (PA)	8011	C	626 960-8614	15203
Citrus Vly Hlth Partners Inc	8062	A	626 962-4011	16001
Doctors Hospital W Covina Inc	8062	A	626 338-8481	16058
Emanate Health Medical Center (PA)	8062	A	626 962-4011	16074
Emanate Health Medical Center	8062	B	626 963-8411	16076
Southern Cal Specialty Care Inc	8062	D	626 339-5451	16443
A Plus Home Health Specialists	8082	D	626 918-9905	16782
Assisted Home Recovery Inc	8082	D	626 915-5595	16811
East Valley Cmnty Hlth Ctr Inc (PA)	8093	C	626 919-3402	17058
Volunteers of Amer Los Angeles	8322	C	626 337-9878	18176
Westview Services Inc	8331	D	626 962-0956	18259
Regent Assisted Living Inc	8361	D	626 332-3344	18510
Hsa & Associates Inc	8711	D	626 521-9931	19260

WEST HILLS, CA - Los Angeles County

	SIC	EMP	PHONE	ENTRY#
Mamba Logistics Inc	4212	D	661 234-8050	3412
Lowes Home Centers LLC	5211	C	818 610-1960	7049
911 Restoration Entps Inc	7349	B	832 887-2582	10845
Citiguard Inc	7381	B	800 613-5903	12944
Inpatient Consultants Ala Inc	8011	D	888 447-2362	14785
Holman Family Counseling Inc (PA)	8049	D	818 704-1444	15285
Leisure Care Inc	8052	C	818 713-0900	15770
West Valleyidence Opco LLC	8052	C	818 348-8422	15806
Unilab Corporation (HQ)	8071	B	818 737-6000	16763
Dlh Davinci LLC	8072	C	818 703-5100	16770
Tobin Lucks A Prof Corp (PA)	8111	D	818 226-3400	17668
One Lambda Inc (HQ)	8731	D	747 494-1000	19752

WEST HOLLYWOOD, CA - Los Angeles County

	SIC	EMP	PHONE	ENTRY#
Lm Veterinary Enterprises Inc	0742	D	310 659-5287	335
Dreamteam Logistics LLC	4789	D	818 300-7785	4152
CBS Films Inc	4833	D		4418
Hwood Group	5021	D	310 859-1011	5091
J Robert Scott Inc (PA)	5131	C		6155
Seafood Family Partners LP	5146	C	310 761-1500	6480
Velaro Incorporated	5734	D	800 983-5276	7451
Startengine Crowdfunding Inc	6153	D	800 317-2200	7910
Auto Club Enterprises	6321	B	310 914-8500	8259
Carlyle Group Inc (PA)	6531	D	310 550-8656	8922
Oppenheim Group Inc	6531	D	310 927-7048	9115
Rsg Group USA Inc	6719	A	214 574-4653	9333
Le Montrose Hotel	7011	C	310 855-1115	9972
Mondrian Holdings LLC	7011	B	323 848-6004	10022
Ols Hotels & Resorts LLC	7011	A	310 855-1115	10064
Valadon Hotel LLC	7011	D	310 854-1111	10340
West Hollywood Edition	7011	D	310 795-7103	10360
One Events Inc	7299	D	310 498-5471	10566
Dailey & Associates	7311	D	323 490-3847	10601
Suissa Miller Advertising LLC	7311	D	310 392-9666	10677

Employee Codes: A=Over 500 employees, B=251-500
C=101-250, D=51-100, E=20-50, F=10-19, G=1-9

WEST HOLLYWOOD CA

GEOGRAPHIC SECTION

	SIC	EMP	PHONE	ENTRY#
Liveuniverse Inc.	7313	D	310 492-2200	10714
Lumicity LLC.	7361	D	213 262-2064	11173
Grindr LLC.	7371	C	310 776-6680	11634
Kinsta Inc.	7371	C	310 736-9306	11693
Neonroots LLC.	7371	C	310 907-9210	11766
Replicated Inc.	7371	D	424 672-6624	11875
Watt Inc.	7371	D	310 896-8197	12036
Tegra118 Wealth Solutions Inc (HQ)	7374	C	888 800-0188	12636
Executive Car Leasing Company (PA)	7515	D	800 800-3932	13596
Annapurna Pictures LLC.	7819	D	310 385-7701	13925
Biscuit Filmworks LLC.	7922	D	323 856-9200	14028
Tri Star Spt Entrmt Group Inc.	7929	D	615 309-0969	14107
Rsg Group North America LP.	7991	C	714 609-0572	14229
Kids Empire USA LLC.	7999	D	424 527-1039	14536
Ticketmaster Entertainment LLC.	7999	A	800 653-8000	14571
Cedars-Sinai Medical Center.	8062	B	310 855-7701	15971
Cedars-Sinai Medical Center.	8062	C	310 423-5468	15972
Cedars-Sinai Medical Center.	8062	C	310 423-5841	15976
Cedars-Sinai Medical Center.	8062	C	310 423-5147	15977
Cedars-Sinai Medical Center.	8062	C	310 423-9310	15978
Cedars-Sinai Medical Center.	8062	C	310 423-8780	15984
Cedars-Snai Imging Med Group A.	8062	C	310 423-8000	15985
White Rabbit Partners Inc.	8361	C	310 975-1450	18549
Automobile Club Southern Cal.	8699	D	323 525-0018	19068
Cpe Hr Inc.	8742	D	310 270-9800	20333
Operam Inc.	8742	D	855 673-7261	20497
Promote Media LP.	8742	D	323 433-7950	20514
Zero Gravity Consulting LLC.	8748	A	310 989-7989	20882

WEST SACRAMENTO, CA - Yolo County

	SIC	EMP	PHONE	ENTRY#
Farm Fresh To You LLC (PA)	0191	C	916 303-7145	178
Brown Construction Inc.	1542	D	916 374-8616	880
Cirks Construction Inc.	1542	D	916 362-5460	894
Vss International Inc (HQ)	1611	D	916 373-1500	1176
AEP Span Inc.	1761	D	916 372-0933	2042
Blazona Concrete Cnstr Inc.	1771	D	916 375-8337	2102
Tk Elevator Corporation.	1796	D	916 376-8700	2250
Walton Engineering Inc.	1799	D	916 372-1888	2328
Valley Rlction Stor Nthrn Cal.	4214	D	916 375-0001	3600
United Parcel Service Inc.	4215	B	916 373-4076	3633
Devine & Son Trucking Co Inc (PA)	4449	C	559 486-7440	3803
Sacramento Television Stns Inc (HQ)	4833	C	916 374-1452	4460
Pacific Gas and Electric Co.	4911	B	916 375-5005	4609
Clark - Pacific Corporation (PA)	5032	B	916 371-0305	5200
Perryman Mechanical Inc.	5039	C	916 371-8888	5231
Agiliti Inc.	5047	C	952 465-9993	5395
ASC Profiles LLC (DH)	5051	C	916 376-2800	5476
Holt of California.	5082	C	916 373-4100	5792
Tonys Fine Foods (HQ)	5143	B	916 374-4000	6443
Nor-Cal Produce Inc.	5148	C	916 373-0830	6567
Artisan Bakers.	5149	D	707 939-1765	6602
Kag West LLC.	5172	D	916 371-4581	6732
Capital Beverage Company (PA)	5181	C	916 371-8164	6754
Harbor Distributing LLC.	5181	B	916 373-5700	6766
Nor-Cal Beverage Co Inc (PA)	5181	D	916 372-0600	6779
Riverview Intl Trcks LLC (PA)	5511	D	916 372-8541	7289
Goodyear Coml Tire & Svc Ctrs.	5531	B	479 788-6400	7350
Ramos Oil Co Inc (PA)	5541	D	916 371-2570	7390
Califrnia State Tchers Rtrment (DH)	6371	B	858 258-5077	8459
Ahtna Facility Services Inc.	7349	C	916 375-0199	10850
Marathon Staffing Solutions.	7361	D	978 649-6230	11175
All Phase Security Inc.	7381	D	916 919-3859	12921
ABM Security Services Inc.	7382	D	916 614-9571	13083
Unity Courier Service Inc.	7389	D	916 246-0390	13527
River Bend Holdings LLC.	8051	C	916 371-1890	15639
Sutter Hlth Scrmnto Sierra Reg.	8062	B	916 373-3400	16545
DCI Donor Services Inc.	8099	D	877 401-2546	17219
DCI Donor Services Inc.	8099	D	916 567-1600	17220
Rural Cmnty Assistance Corp (PA)	8322	D	916 447-2854	18101
Creative Living Options Inc.	8361	C	916 372-2102	18411
California School Boards Assn.	8621	D	800 266-3382	18740
Califrnia Crrctnal Pace Ofcer (PA)	8631	C	916 372-6060	18775
Seiu Local 2015.	8631	C	213 985-0419	18790
Wallace-Kuhl Investments LLC (PA)	8711	C	916 372-1434	19435
Cgi Technologies Solutions Inc.	8731	C	916 281-3200	19670
Core-Mark International Inc.	8742	D	916 374-8677	20329
Redstone Print & Mail Inc.	8742	D	916 318-6350	20526

WESTLAKE VILLAGE, CA - Ventura County

	SIC	EMP	PHONE	ENTRY#
Dole Holding Company LLC.	0179	A	818 879-6600	115
National Veterinary Assoc Inc (HQ)	0742	D	805 777-7722	339
Sperber Ldscp Companies LLC (PA)	0781	C	818 437-1029	467
The Ryland Group Inc.	1531	A	805 367-3800	797
Castle & Cooke Investments Inc.	1542	C	310 208-3636	891
Dennis M McCoy & Sons Inc.	1611	D	818 874-3872	1094
Security Paving Company Inc (PA)	1611	D	818 362-9200	1160
Sdg Enterprises.	1711	D	805 777-7978	1556
Pleasant Holidays LLC (HQ)	4724	B	818 991-3390	3947
Frontier California Inc.	4813	B	805 372-6000	4279
Hendrie Radio Inc.	4832	D	818 259-8175	4385
Southern California Edison Co.	4911	C	805 496-3406	4683
AP Global Inc.	5065	D	818 707-3167	5625
Hec Inc.	5065	B	818 879-7414	5655
Baxter Healthcare Corporation.	5122	C	805 372-3000	6096
Smart & Final Stores Inc.	5141	C	818 889-8253	6311
Country Floral Supply Inc (PA)	5193	D	805 520-8026	6856
Mamolos Cntntl Bailey Bakeries.	5461	C	805 496-0045	7160
Bana Home Loan Servicing.	6021	A	213 345-7975	7603
Amerihome Inc.	6162	A	888 469-0810	7930
Anchor Loans LP.	6162	C	310 395-0010	7933
Dignified Home Loans LLC.	6162	D	818 421-7753	7955
Pennymac Financial Svcs Inc (PA)	6162	B	818 224-7442	8010
Pnmac Holdings Inc (HQ)	6162	B	818 224-7442	8011
Amerihome Mortgage Company LLC.	6211	A	888 469-0810	8065
Merrill Lynch Prce Fnner Smith.	6211	C	805 381-2600	8138
Kramer-Wilson Company Inc (PA)	6331	C	818 760-0880	8389
Chivaroli & Assoc Inc.	6411	D	208 338-6640	8525
Pacific Compensation Insur Co.	6411	C	818 575-8500	8633
Cushman & Wakefield Cal Inc.	6531	B	805 418-5811	8959
Troop Real Estate Inc.	6531	C	805 402-3028	9200
Fidelity Nat Title Insur Co NY.	6541	A	805 370-1400	9230
Pmt Crdit Risk Trnsf Tr 2015-1.	6733	D	818 224-7028	9441
Pmt Crdit Risk Trnsf Tr 2015-2.	6733	C	818 224-7442	9442
Pmt Crdit Risk Trnsf Tr 2019-2.	6733	D	818 224-7028	9443
Pmt Crdit Risk Trnsf Tr 2020-1.	6733	D	818 224-7028	9444
Pnmac Gmsr Issuer Trust.	6733	A	818 746-2271	9445
Burton Way Htels Ltd A Cal Ltd.	7011	C	818 575-3000	9668
Sky Court USA Inc.	7011	C	805 497-9991	10247
Swvp Westlake LLC.	7011	C	805 557-1234	10295
Westlake Properties Inc.	7011	C	818 889-0230	10365
C&W Facility Services Inc.	7349	C	805 267-7123	10868
Microfinancial Incorporated.	7359	C	805 367-8900	11042
Digital Insight Corporation.	7375	D	818 879-1010	12657
Lantz Security Systems Inc.	7381	C	805 496-5775	12994
Securitas SEC Svcs USA Inc.	7381	B	818 706-6800	13035
Bankcard USA Merchant Srvc.	7389	B	818 597-7000	13210
Rvl Packaging Inc.	7389	C	818 735-5000	13455
Thousand Oaks Prtg & Spc Inc.	7389	C	818 706-8330	13509
Weststar Cinemas Inc.	7832	C	805 379-8966	14009
Equinox-76th Street Inc.	7991	C	805 367-3925	14199
North Ranch Country Club.	7997	C	818 889-3531	14416
Coastal Rdtion Onclogy Med Gro.	8011	D	805 494-4483	14693
Los Robles Regional Med Ctr.	8011	B	805 370-4531	14883
Symbion Inc.	8011	C	805 413-7920	15120
Select Home Care.	8082	C	805 777-3855	16924
Feld Care Therapy Inc.	8093	D	818 926-9057	17064
Comprhnsive Indus Dsblity MGT.	8099	C	866 301-6568	17208
JD Power and Associates Inc.	8732	C	805 418-8000	19828
Truog-Ryding Company Inc.	8742	D	805 371-9222	20595
Ninjio Llc.	8748	D	805 864-1992	20815

WESTMINSTER, CA - Orange County

	SIC	EMP	PHONE	ENTRY#
Emerald Acquisition LLC.	1611	C	714 891-8752	1103
Inlog Inc.	4731	D	949 212-3867	4037
Southern California Edison Co.	4911	A	714 895-0420	4690
Southern California Edison Co.	4911	C	714 895-0163	4693
Southern California Edison Co.	4911	C	714 895-0119	4699
Honda World Westminster.	5511	C	714 890-8900	7234
Lbs Financial Credit Union (PA)	6062	C	562 598-9007	7827
All-In Prdctons Csino Rntals L.	7359	D	866 875-8628	11018
New CAM Commerce Solutions LLC.	7371	C	714 338-0200	11773
Staff Pro Inc (PA)	7382	A	714 230-7200	13148
Extended Care Hosp Westminster.	8051	D	714 891-2769	15473
University California Irvine.	8062	C	714 775-3066	16604
Abrazar Inc.	8322	C	714 893-3581	17822
County of Orange.	8322	C	714 896-7188	17934
Westview Services Inc.	8331	D	714 418-2090	18260
360 Health Plan Inc.	8741	C	800 446-8888	20007

WHEATLAND, CA - Yuba County

	SIC	EMP	PHONE	ENTRY#
Enterprise Development Auth.	7011	A	833 337-3473	9784
Hard Rock Cafe Intl Inc.	7011	A	530 633-6938	9837
Northern California Inalliance.	8322	D	530 633-9695	18064

WHITTIER, CA - Los Angeles County

	SIC	EMP	PHONE	ENTRY#
Oltmans Construction Co (PA)	1541	D	562 948-4242	837

GEOGRAPHIC SECTION

WOODLAND HILLS CA

	SIC	EMP	PHONE	ENTRY#
California Department Trnsp	1611	D	562 692-0823	1085
County of Los Angeles	4151	C	562 945-2581	3324
Sprint Communications Co LP	4812	D	562 943-8907	4227
Southern California Gas Co	4924	D	562 803-3341	4739
Sanittion Dstrcts Los Angles C	4953	A	562 908-4288	4935
Los Angles Cnty Snttion Dstrct (PA)	4959	A	562 699-7411	4981
Indio Products Inc (PA)	5049	C	323 720-1188	5466
Equipment Depot Inc	5084	C	562 949-1000	5833
Southern California Material Handling Inc	5084	C	562 949-1006	5869
Grand Supercenter Inc	5141	D	562 318-3451	6256
Smart & Final Stores	5141	B	562 907-7037	6315
Gourmet India Food Company LLC	5149	C	562 698-9763	6632
Khw Enterprises Inc	5199	D	562 236-8440	6921
Home Depot USA Inc	5211	C	562 789-4121	7009
Cintas Corporation No 3	5699	D	562 692-8741	7415
Kaiser Foundation Hospitals	6324	C	866 340-5974	8322
Katella Properties	6512	D	562 704-8695	8730
Rose Hills Company (DH)	6553	A	562 699-0921	9292
Rose Hills Holdings Corp (HQ)	6553	B	562 699-0921	9293
Pronto Janitorial Svcs Inc	7349	C	562 273-5997	10949
Los Angeles Truck Centers LLC (PA)	7538	C	562 447-1200	13666
Friendly Hlls Cntry CLB Fndtio	7997	C	562 698-0331	14377
Bright Health Physicians (PA)	8011	C	562 947-8478	14638
Ensign Group Inc	8051	C	562 947-7817	15453
Ensign Whittier East LLC	8051	C	562 947-7817	15461
Orchard - Post Acute Care Ctr	8051	D	562 693-7701	15613
Ahmc Whittier Hosp Med Ctr LP	8062	A	562 945-3561	15934
Longwood Management Corp	8062	D	562 693-5240	16237
Pih Health Inc (PA)	8062	A	562 698-0811	16323
Pih Health Whittier Hospital (HQ)	8062	A	562 698-0811	16327
Whittier Hospital Med Ctr Inc	8062	C	562 945-3561	16628
Barlow Respiratory Hospital	8069	A	562 698-0811	16665
Interhealth Services Inc (HQ)	8082	C	562 698-0811	16876
Whittier Union High Schl Dist	8211	C	562 693-8826	17759
County of Los Angeles	8322	D	562 908-3119	17917
Inclusion Services LLC	8322	C	562 945-2000	18014
Plaza De La Raza Child Develop	8351	C	562 695-1070	18347
Mercedes Diaz Homes Inc	8361	D	562 945-4576	18484
Capc Inc	8399	D	562 693-8826	18570
Automobile Club Southern Cal	8699	D	562 698-3721	19055
Mdh Network Inc	8742	C	562 945-4576	20460

WILDOMAR, CA - Riverside County

	SIC	EMP	PHONE	ENTRY#
Diverscape Inc	0782	D	951 245-1686	485
KB Home Grater Los Angeles Inc	1521	C	951 691-5300	693
Sunpro Solar Inc	1711	D	951 678-7733	1577
Fcp Inc (PA)	3448	D	951 678-4571	2747
General Lgstics Systems US Inc	4212	C	951 677-3972	3397
Sprint Communications Co LP	4812	D	951 461-9786	4231
Inland Vly Rgional Med Ctr Inc	8062	B	951 677-1111	16139
Kaiser Foundation Hospitals	8062	C	951 353-2000	16173

WILLIAMS, CA - Colusa County

	SIC	EMP	PHONE	ENTRY#
Vann Brothers	0161	C	530 473-2607	48
Vann Family LLC	0175	C	530 473-3317	114
ACC-Gwg LLC	8748	D	530 473-2827	20672

WILLITS, CA - Mendocino County

	SIC	EMP	PHONE	ENTRY#
Sherwood Valley Rancheria	7011	D	707 459-7330	10229
Mendocino Cmnty Hlth Clnic Inc	8011	C	707 456-9600	14896
Ensign Willits LLC	8051	C	707 459-5592	15463
Willits Hospital Inc	8062	B	707 459-6801	16629
Western Health Resources	8742	C	707 459-1818	20612

WILLOWS, CA - Glenn County

	SIC	EMP	PHONE	ENTRY#
Pacific Gas and Electric Co	4911	C	530 229-4164	4623
Kumar Hotels Inc (PA)	7011	C	530 934-8900	9955
Glenn Medical Center Inc	8062	C	530 934-4681	16106

WILMINGTON, CA - Los Angeles County

	SIC	EMP	PHONE	ENTRY#
Cfwf Inc	2092	C	310 221-6280	2419
Air Liquide Electronics US LP	2813	A	310 549-7079	2571
Potential Industries Inc (PA)	4953	C	310 549-5901	4921
Konoike-E Street Inc	5078	D	310 233-7300	5779
Icpk Corporation	5141	D	310 830-8020	6258
Tesoro Refining & Mktg Co LLC	5172	C	877 837-6762	6742
Acx Intermodal Inc	5191	C	310 241-6229	6818
Stratus Real Estate Inc	6163	D	310 549-7028	8059
Harbor Industrial Svcs Corp	7353	C	310 522-1193	10998
Marine Technical Services Inc	7389	D	310 549-8030	13363
Public Hlth Fndation Entps Inc	8099	C	310 518-2835	17306
South Bay Ctr For Counseling	8322	D	310 414-2090	18137
Volunteers of Amer Los Angeles	8322	C	310 830-3404	18184

	SIC	EMP	PHONE	ENTRY#
Harbor Area Gang Altrntves Prg	8399	D	310 519-7233	18592
Advanced Cleanup Tech Inc	8744	B	310 763-1423	20646

WINDSOR, CA - Sonoma County

	SIC	EMP	PHONE	ENTRY#
Shook & Waller Cnstr Inc	1751	D	707 578-3933	2017
Selex Inc	1799	D	707 836-8836	2314
Sonoma Tilemakers Inc	4225	D	707 837-8177	3754
Home Depot USA Inc	5211	D	707 836-0377	6977
Big Poppy Holdings Inc	6022	C	707 836-1588	7660
Encore Events Rentals Inc	7359	D	707 431-3500	11030
Cali Calmecac Language Academy	8641	D	707 837-7747	18827

WINNETKA, CA - Los Angeles County

	SIC	EMP	PHONE	ENTRY#
Valley Village (PA)	8322	D	818 587-9450	18166

WINTERHAVEN, CA - Imperial County

	SIC	EMP	PHONE	ENTRY#
Quechan Indian Tribe	7999	C	760 572-2413	14551

WINTON, CA - Merced County

	SIC	EMP	PHONE	ENTRY#
Cederlind Farms LP	0172	D	209 606-8586	70
Central Valley Oprtnty Ctr Inc (PA)	8331	D	209 357-0062	18218

WOODBRIDGE, CA - San Joaquin County

	SIC	EMP	PHONE	ENTRY#
City Rise LLC	7389	D	209 334-2703	13236
The Woodbridge Golf Cntry CLB	7997	D	209 369-2371	14471

WOODLAND, CA - Yolo County

	SIC	EMP	PHONE	ENTRY#
Muller Ranch LLC	0111	D	530 662-0105	1
Broward Builders Inc	1542	D	530 666-5635	879
McCarthy Bldg Companies Inc	1542	A	530 665-4774	969
Butterfield Electric Inc	1731	C	530 666-2116	1688
Nugget Market Inc	4225	D	530 662-5479	3741
Target Corporation	4225	D	530 666-3705	3764
County of Yolo	4731	C	530 661-0816	4000
County of Yolo	4953	D	530 666-8729	4880
Waste MGT Collectn Recycl Inc	4953	C	530 662-8748	4962
Core & Main Inc	5099	B	530 662-7700	6038
Sunfoods LLC (HQ)	5141	D	530 661-1923	6395
Liberty Packing Company LLC (PA)	5148	D	209 826-7100	6562
Pioneer Hi-Bred Intl Inc	5191	D	530 666-1084	6830
Voloagri Inc	5191	C	805 547-9391	6837
Nau Country Insurance Company	6411	C	530 662-7466	8619
Sunrise Hospitality Inc	7011	D	916 419-4440	10283
The Morning Star Company (PA)	7363	D	530 666-6600	11342
Interpac Technologies Inc	7389	D	530 662-6363	13328
Communications & Pwr Inds LLC	7629	D	530 662-7553	13737
CPI Econco Division	7629	D	530 662-7553	13738
Woodside Electronics Corp	7699	D	530 666-9190	13812
Communicare Health Centers	8011	C	530 753-3498	14697
United Health Systems Inc	8051	C	530 662-9161	15711
St Johns Retirement Village	8059	D	530 662-9674	15900
Sutter Hlth Scrmnto Sierra Reg	8062	D	530 406-5616	16551
Woodland Healthcare (DH)	8062	B	530 662-3961	16631
Woodland Healthcare	8062	D	530 669-5680	16632
Woodland Healthcare	8062	D	530 668-2600	16634
Northern Vly Indian Hlth Inc	8063	D	530 661-4400	16655
Fresenius Med Care Wdlnd Cal L	8092	D	530 668-4503	16984
Alta Cal Regional Ctr Inc	8322	C	530 663-3391	17828
Child Development Incorporated	8351	B	530 666-4822	18284
Itc Srvice Group Acqsition LLC	8748	D	530 717-0485	20783

WOODLAND HILLS, CA - Los Angeles County

	SIC	EMP	PHONE	ENTRY#
VCA Animal Hospitals Inc	0742	D	818 883-8387	346
Boething Treeland Farms Inc (PA)	0811	D	818 883-1222	564
Blh Construction Company	1522	C	818 905-3837	748
Environmental Construction Inc	1542	D	818 449-8920	914
Sierra Pacific Constrs Inc	1542	D	747 888-5000	1026
WM Klorman Construction Corp	1542	D	818 591-5969	1065
Memeged Tevuot Shemesh (PA)	1711	C	866 575-1211	1499
Coolish Holdings LLC	2051	D	818 575-7280	2366
Weider Health and Fitness	2087	B	818 884-6800	2416
IDS Inc	4724	D	866 297-5757	3936
Mpulse Mobile Inc (PA)	4813	D	888 678-5735	4318
United Ribbon Company Inc	5044	D	818 716-1515	5260
Conquistador International LLC	5122	D	424 249-9304	6103
E Management Services LLC	5122	D	818 835-9525	6106
Reseda Dodge Sales Inc	5511	D	805 581-9090	7287
Assocted Fgn Exch Holdings Inc (HQ)	6099	D	818 386-2702	7840
Input 1 LLC	6153	C	818 340-0030	7895
Interlink Securities Inc	6211	D	818 992-6700	8095
Merrill Lynch Prce Fnner Smith	6211	D	818 340-9500	8104
Morgan Stnley Smith Barney LLC	6211	D	818 715-1800	8150
Beating Wall Street Inc (PA)	6282	C	818 332-9696	8189

WOODLAND HILLS CA

GEOGRAPHIC SECTION

	SIC	EMP	PHONE	ENTRY#
John Alden Life Insurance Co.	6311	C	818 595-7600	8236
Truck Underwriters Association	6311	A	323 932-3200	8251
21st Century Lf & Hlth Co Inc (PA)	6321	C	818 887-4436	8254
Lifecare Assurance Company	6321	C	818 887-4436	8267
Blue Cross of California (HQ)	6324	C	805 557-6050	8282
California Physicians Service	6324	C	818 598-8000	8289
Health Net LLC (HQ)	6324	C	818 676-6000	8298
Health Net Inc	6324	A	818 676-6000	8301
Managed Dental Care	6324	C	818 598-6599	8342
Mid-Century Insurance Company	6331	C	323 932-7116	8401
State Compensation Insur Fund	6331	A	818 888-4750	8417
Zenith Insurance Company (DH)	6331	B	818 713-1000	8426
21st Century Life Insurance Co (DH)	6411	A	877 310-5687	8475
Amwins Insurance Brkg Cal LLC (HQ)	6411	D	818 772-1774	8489
Farmers Group Inc (HQ)	6411	A	323 932-3200	8557
Farmers Insurance	6411	B	818 876-3400	8558
Farmers Insurance Exchange (DH)	6411	A	888 327-6335	8565
Fire Insurance Exchange (PA)	6411	A	323 932-3200	8568
Grosslight Insurance Inc	6411	D	310 473-9611	8576
Howards Mbs Inc	6411	D	202 570-4074	8586
Markel Corp	6411	B	818 595-0600	8605
Westwood Insurance Agency LLC (HQ)	6411	D	818 990-9715	8687
Cirrus Asset Management Inc (PA)	6531	D	818 222-4840	8933
Greystar Management Svcs LP	6531	C	818 596-2180	9028
AIG Capital Services Inc	6726	D	800 445-7862	9397
Jmg Investments Inc	6799	C	818 519-0670	9524
HEI Hospitality LLC	7011	C	818 887-4800	9845
Hilton Woodland Hills & Towers	7011	D	818 595-1000	9856
Conduit Lngage Specialists Inc	7299	D	859 299-3178	10538
Kern Organization Inc	7311	D	818 703-8775	10637
Reachlocal Inc (DH)	7311	C	818 274-0260	10669
United Online Advg Netwrk Inc	7311	D	818 287-3000	10685
Panavision Inc (PA)	7359	A	818 316-1000	11049
Career Strategies Tmpry Inc	7361	C	818 883-0440	11105
Mediscan Diagnostic Svcs LLC	7361	C	818 758-4224	11177
Corptax LLC	7371	C	818 316-2400	11517
Emids Tech Private Ltd Corp	7371	C	805 304-5986	11571
Intelex Systems Inc	7371	D	818 992-2969	11672
Mindspark Inc	7371	D	310 396-9292	11749
Blackline Inc (PA)	7372	C	818 223-9008	12119
Intuit Inc	7372	C	818 436-7800	12239
Thq Inc	7372	A	818 591-1310	12380
Netapp Inc	7373	C	818 227-5025	12499
Adcom Interactive Media Inc	7379	D	800 296-7104	12722
Pro-Tek Consulting (PA)	7379	C	805 807-5571	12863
Mventix Inc (PA)	7389	D	818 337-3747	13387
Network Telephone Services Inc (PA)	7389	D	800 742-5687	13391
Scherzer International Corp (PA)	7389	D	818 227-2770	13467
Sync Brokerage Inc	7389	D	818 770-3663	13497
Dark Burn Creative LLC	7812	D	818 471-4948	13836
Film Roman Llc	7812	C	818 748-4000	13849
Southern Cal Prmnnte Med Group	8011	C	818 592-3038	15089
Verity Medical Foundation (PA)	8011	D	408 278-3000	15186
Kaiser Foundation Hospitals	8062	A	818 719-2000	16152
Kaiser Foundation Hospitals	8062	A	818 592-3100	16177
Motion Picture and TV Fund (PA)	8062	A	818 876-1777	16275
Accredited Fms Inc	8082	A	818 435-4200	16790
Barry & Taffy Inc	8082	A	818 986-1234	16815
Berger Inc	8082	A	818 986-1234	16818
Dunn & Berger Inc	8082	A	818 986-1234	16855
Infinite Home Health Inc	8082	D	818 888-7772	16874
Destinations For Teens	8093	D	818 737-2221	17052
Prober & Raphael A Law Corp	8111	D	818 227-0100	17618
Los Angeles Unified School Dst	8211	C	818 346-3540	17724
Wise & Healthy Aging	8322	D	818 876-1402	18193
Benefitvision Inc	8331	D	818 348-3100	18211
Tutor Time Learning Ctrs LLC	8351	C	818 710-1677	18363
Pacific Lodge Youth Svcs Inc	8361	C	818 347-1577	18502
Automobile Club Southern Cal	8699	D	818 883-2660	19053
Kellogg Andlson Accntancy Corp (PA)	8721	D	818 971-5100	19593

	SIC	EMP	PHONE	ENTRY#
LLP Moss Adams	8721	C	310 477-0450	19603
Physicians Choice LLC	8721	D	818 340-9988	19622
Goetzman Group Inc	8742	D	818 595-1112	20395
8020 Consulting LLC	8748	D	818 523-3201	20671
Allied Industries Inc (PA)	8748	C	800 605-5323	20686

WOODSIDE, CA - San Mateo County

	SIC	EMP	PHONE	ENTRY#
Ecullet Inc	4953	D	650 493-7300	4889
Fisher Investments Inc	6282	C	888 823-9566	8198
Skywood Events Corporation	7299	D	650 851-1606	10576
Katch Entertainment LLC	7929	D	650 380-0607	14091

WRIGHTWOOD, CA - San Bernardino County

	SIC	EMP	PHONE	ENTRY#
MHRP Resort Inc	7011	D	760 249-5808	10019

YORBA LINDA, CA - Orange County

	SIC	EMP	PHONE	ENTRY#
Mesa Contracting Corporation	1611	C		1138
Srd Engineering Inc	1623	D	714 630-2480	1268
Romac Supply Co Inc	3613	D	323 721-5810	2861
Metropltan Wtr Dst of Sthern C	4941	D	714 577-5031	4810
Vident	5047	D	714 221-6700	5459
Precision Fluorescent West Inc (DH)	5063	D	352 692-5900	5587
Nasser Company Inc (PA)	5141	D	714 279-2100	6271
Enterprise Security Inc (PA)	7382	D	714 630-9100	13113
Nobel Biocare Usa LLC	8072	B	714 282-4800	16775
Rgbx Inc	8351	D	714 524-1350	18351

YOSEMITE NTPK, CA - Mariposa County

	SIC	EMP	PHONE	ENTRY#
DNC Prks Rsrts At Yosemite Inc	7011	A	209 372-1001	9757

YOUNTVILLE, CA - Napa County

	SIC	EMP	PHONE	ENTRY#
Domaine Chandon Inc (DH)	2084	D	707 944-8844	2379

YREKA, CA - Siskiyou County

	SIC	EMP	PHONE	ENTRY#
Siskiyou Hospital Inc	8062	A	530 842-4121	16431

YUBA CITY, CA - Sutter County

	SIC	EMP	PHONE	ENTRY#
Sierra Gold Nurseries Inc	0181	D	530 674-1145	153
Bianchi Ag Services Inc	0762	D	530 923-7675	372
A & E Arborists Tree Care Inc	0783	B	530 790-5312	550
Hilbers Inc	1542	D	530 673-2947	936
R4k3 LLC	1799	D	425 462-0375	2310
New Legend Inc	4213	B	530 674-3100	3519
Direct Parcel Inc	4215	D	303 381-4099	3610
Western AG Incorporated	4789	D	530 713-7901	4178
Lowes Home Centers LLC	5211	D	530 844-5000	7098
Wheeler Auto Group Inc	5531	D	530 673-3765	7382
Sierra Central Credit Union (PA)	6061	D	530 671-3009	7805
Citifinancial Credit Company	6141	D	530 671-7970	7873
Virga Investment Property	6512	C	530 755-4409	8775
Express Personnel Services	7361	D	530 671-9202	11136
Sutter North Med Foundation (PA)	8011	C	530 741-1300	15115
Ampla Health (PA)	8021	C	530 674-4261	15216
United Com-Serve	8051	C	530 790-3000	15710
Sutter N Med Group A Prof Corp (PA)	8062	D	530 749-3661	16555
County of Sutter	8093	D	530 822-7250	17044
Alta Cal Regional Ctr Inc	8322	C	530 674-3070	17827
City of Yuba City	8331	C	530 822-4601	18222
E Center	8351	C	530 634-1200	18310
Yuba Cy Unified Schl Dst Fing C	8399	A	530 822-7601	18634

YUCAIPA, CA - San Bernardino County

	SIC	EMP	PHONE	ENTRY#
M C C Equipment Rentals Inc	1623	D	909 795-9300	1233
Google International LLC (DH)	4813	D	650 253-0000	4291
Calimesa Operations LLC	8051	C	909 795-2421	15364
Cedar Operations LLC	8051	C	909 790-2273	15369
Veterans of Foreign Wars of US	8641	D	909 797-1898	18924

YUCCA VALLEY, CA - San Bernardino County

	SIC	EMP	PHONE	ENTRY#
Psychrom Inc	7389	D	760 366-9811	13437
Eisenhower Medical Center	8011	D	760 228-9900	14734